GALE DIRECTORY OF PUBLICATIONS AND BROADCAST MEDIA

ISBN 1048-7972

133rd Edition

Published annually since 1869

GALE DIRECTORY OF PUBLICATIONS AND BROADCAST MEDIA

(Formerly ***Ayer Directory of Publications***)

An annual Guide to Publications and Broadcasting Stations
Including Newspapers, Magazines, Journals, Radio Stations,
Television stations, And Cable Systems

Volume I

Alabama-New Hampshire

Entries 1-18752

Kristen B.Mallegg, Editor

GALE GROUP

Detroit
San Francisco
London
Boston
Woodbridge, CT

Kristin B. Mallegg, *Editor*
Amy L. Rance, *Assistant Editor*
Dawn Conzett DesJardins, Carolyn A. Fischer, Louise Gagné, John Krol, Kevin McCoy, Erin Nagel, Annette Novallo, Michael Paré, and Jeff Sumner, *Contributors*

Kathleen Lopez Nolan, *Managing Editor*

Theresa A. Rocklin, *Manager, Technical Support Services*
Venus Little, *Programmer/Analyst*

Mary Beth Trimper, *Production Director*
Evi Seoud, *Assistant Production Manager*
Dorothy Maki, *Manufacturing Manager*
Nekita McKee, *Buyer*

Carmela Adams, Nikkita Bankston, Katrina Coach, Arlene Kevonian, Frances Monroe, and Elizabeth Pilette, *Data Entry Associates*

Barbara Yarrow, *Graphic Services Manager*
Christine O'Bryan, *Desktop Publisher*

ISBN 0-7876-2397-0 (complete set with Update)
ISBN 0-7876-2398-9 (Volume 1)
ISBN 0-7876-2399-7 (Volume 2)
ISBN 0-7876-2400-4 (Volume 3)
ISBN 0-7876-3751-3 (Volume 4)
ISSN 1048-7972

Contents

Volume 1

Alabama - New Hampshire

Volume 2

New Jersey - Wyoming * Canada

Volume 3

Indexes and Tables

Volume 4

Regional Market Index and Maps

Introduction

The *Gale Directory of Publications and Broadcast Media*, (*GDPBM*) has been the definitive media source since its inception in 1869. Formerly the *Ayer Directory of Publications*, and now in its 133rd edition, *GDPBM* has grown with U.S. and Canadian media, and increased its scope to include the communication technologies of the twentieth century. *GDPBM* now covers almost 38,000 newspapers, magazines, journals, and other periodicals, as well as radio, television, and cable stations and systems. Organized to help users find facts fast, *GDPBM* covers the whole media picture--ad rates, circulation statistics, local programming, names of key personnel, and other useful, accurate information.

Highlights of this Edition

- *Over 1600 new entries*, with an emphasis on Broadcast entries.
- *E-mail information has been augmented.*
- *Syndicate information has been added to the Master Index.*

Features

◆ Geographic arrangement provides easy access to listings. Only *GDPBM* presents print and broadcast entries in one geographic sort, then alphabetically within state, province, or territory; city; and media category (Print or Broadcast).

◆ Descriptive and statistical data are included for most cities, as well as states, provinces, and territories.

◆ Volume 3 contains four unique tables of industry statistics that provide specific media market numbers and segments indispensable to research. Each year the editors of *GDPBM* provide these numbers in a custom format to the U.S. Bureau of the Census for inclusion in the prestigious *Statistical Abstract of the United States*.

Scope and Preparation of *GDPBM*

The following categories of publications are excluded from the *Gale Directory of Publications and Broadcast Media's* coverage of the U.S. and Canadian print and broadcast arenas:

- newsletters
- directories

Information provided in *GDPBM* is obtained primarily from questionnaire responses. Some clarification and verification of data is obtained through telephone calls. Other published sources are used to verify some information, such as the audited circulation data in publication listings.

Listings identified as defunct are removed from the main body of entries and listed in the Master Name and Keyword Index as "*Ceased*." The same basic procedure is followed for listings that cannot be located either through direct mail or subsequent attempts at telephone follow-up; these entries are listed in the Master Index as "*Unable to locate*." Efforts to clarify the status of such nonrespondents are ongoing.

Arrangement

GDPBM comprises four volumes:

- Volume 1 includes entries from Alabama to New Hampshire.
- Volume 2 encompasses listings from New Jersey to Wyoming and Canada.
- Volume 3 contains industry activity and statistics, the broadcast and cable networks, the news and feature syndicates, and the 21 indexes.
- Volume 4 contains maps for all areas covered and the regional market index.

Please refer to the Sample Entries and Index Notes sections following this Introduction for more details on specific content and use of the *Directory's* listings and indexes.

Free *Update* Issued Between *GDPBM* Editions

Approximately midway between main editions of *GDPBM*, an *Update* is sent free to all subscribers. It provides timely coverage of newspapers, magazines, journals, radio stations, television stations, and cable systems not included in the current edition of the *Directory*.

Acknowledgments

The editors are grateful to the many media professionals who generously responded to our requests for updated information, provided additional data by telephone or fax, and helped in the shaping of this edition with their comments and suggestions throughout the year. A special thanks to Hilary Weber for her contributions.

Available in Electronic Formats

Diskette/Magnetic Tape. *Gale Directory of Publications and Broadcast Media* is available for licensing on magnetic tape or diskette in a fielded format. The database is available for internal data processing and nonpublishing purposes only. For more information, call 800-877-GALE.

Online. *Gale Directory of Publications and Broadcast Media* (along with *Directories in Print* and *Newsletters in Print*) is accessible as File 469: *Gale Database of Publications and Broadcast Media* through the Dialog Corporation's DIALOG service. For more information, contact The Dialog Corporation, 11000 Regency Parkway, Ste. 400, Cary, NC 27511, phone (919)462-8600 or toll-free 800-3-DIALOG.

GaleNet. *GDPBM* (along with *Directories in Print* and *Newsletters in Print*) is available as the *Gale Database of Publications and Broadcast Media* on a subscription basis through GaleNet, Gale's online information resource that features an easy-to-use end-user interface, powerful search capabilities, and ease of access through the World-Wide Web. For more information, call 800-877-GALE. *GDPBM* is also accessible as part of *Gale's Ready Reference Shelf* on GaleNet.

CD-ROM. *GDPBM* is available on CD-ROM as part of *Gale's Ready Reference Shelf* CD-ROM.

Comments and Suggestions Welcome

We invite comments and suggestions for improvement and ask the users of this book to send us possible sources of additional listings. Please contact:

Kristin B. Mallegg, Editor
Gale Directory of Publications and Broadcast Media
Gale Group
27500 Drake Road
Farmington Hills, MI 48331-3535
800-877-GALE

Sample Entries

The samples that follow are fabricated entries in which each numbered section designates information that might appear in a listing. The numbered items are explained in the descriptive paragraphs following each sample.

SAMPLE PUBLICATION LISTING

① **222** ② **American Computer Review**
③ Jane Doe Publishing Company, Inc.
④ 199 E. 49th St. ⑤ Phone: (518)555-9277
PO Box 724866 ⑥ Fax: (518)555-9288
Salem, NY 10528-5555
⑦ Free: 800-555-5432
⑧ Publication E-mail: acr@jdpci.com
⑨ Publisher E-mail: jdpci@jdpci.com
⑩ Magazine for users of Super Software Plus products. ⑪ **Subtitle:** The Programmer's Friend. ⑫ **Founded:** June 1979. ⑬ **Freq:** Monthly (combined issue July/Aug.). ⑭ **Print Method:** Offset. ⑮ **Trim Size:** 8/12 x 11. ⑯ **Cols./Page:** 3. ⑰ **Col. Width:** 24 nonpareils. ⑱ **Col. Depth:** 294 agate lines. ⑲ **Key Personnel:** Ian Smith, Editor, phone (518)555-1201, fax (518)555-1202, ismith@jdpci.com; James Newman, Publisher; Steve Jones Jr., Advertising Mgr. ⑳ **ISSN:** 5555-6226. ㉑ **Subscription Rates:** $25; $30 Canada; $2.50 single issue.
㉒ **Remarks:** Color advertising not accepted. ㉓ **Online:** Lexis-Nexis **URL:** http://www.acrmagazine.com. ㉔ **Alternate Format(s):** Braille; CD-ROM; Microform. ㉕ **Formerly:** Computer Software Review (Dec. 13, 1986).
㉖ **Feature Editors:** Ann Walker, *Consumer Affairs, Editorials,* phone (518)555-2306, fax (518)555-2307, aw@jdpci.com.
㉗ **Additional Contact Information: Advertising:** 123 Main St., New York, NY 10016, (201)555-1900, fax: (201)555-1908.
㉘ **Ad Rates:** BW: $850 ㉙ **Circulation:** 25,000
PCI: $.75

① **Symbol/Entry Number.** Each publication entry number is preceded by a symbol (a magazine or newspaper) representing the publishing industry. Entries are numbered sequentially. Entry numbers, rather than page numbers, are used in the index to refer to listings.

② **Publication Title.** Publication names are listed *as they appear on the masthead or title page*, as provided by respondents.

③ **Publishing Company.** The name of the commercial publishing organization, association, or academic institution, as provided by respondents.

④ **Address.** Full mailing address information is provided wherever possible. This may include: street address; post office box; city; state or province; and ZIP or postal code. ZIP plus-four numbers are provided when known.

⑤ **Phone.** Phone numbers listed in this section are usually the respondent's switchboard number.

⑥ **Fax.** Facsimile numbers are listed when provided.

⑦ **Free.** Toll-free numbers are listed when provided.

⑧ **Publication E-mail.** Electronic mail addresses for the publication are included as provided by the listee.

⑨ **Publisher E-mail:** Electronic mail addresses for the publishing company are included as provided by the listee.

⑩ **Description.** Includes the type of publication (i.e., newspaper, magazine) as well as a brief statement of purpose, intended audience, or other relevant remarks.

⑪ **Subtitle.** Included as provided by the listee.

⑫ **Founded.** Date the periodical was first published.

⑬ **Frequency.** Indicates how often the publication is issued--daily, weekly, monthly, quarterly, etc. Explanatory remarks sometimes accompany this information (e.g., for weekly titles, the day of issuance; for collegiate titles, whether publication is limited to the academic year; whether certain issues are combined.)

⑭ **Print Method.** Though offset is most common, other methods are listed as provided.

⑮ **Trim Size.** Presented in inches unless otherwise noted.

⑯ **Number of Columns Per Page.** Usually one figure, but some publications list two or more, indicating a variation in style.

⑰ **Column Width.** Column sizes are given exactly as supplied, whether measure in inches, picas (6 picas to an inch), nonpareils (each 6 points, 72 points to an inch), or agate lines (14 to an inch).

⑱ **Column Depth.** Column sizes are given exactly as supplied, whether measure in inches, picas (6 picas to an inch), nonpareils (each 6 points, 72 points to an inch), or agate lines (14 to an inch).

⑲ **Key Personnel.** Presents the names and titles of contacts at each publication. May include phone, fax, and e-mail addresses if different than those for the publication and company.

⑳ **International Standard Serial Number (ISSN).** Included when provided. Occasionally, United States Publications Serial (USPS) numbers are reported rather than ISSNs.

㉑ **Subscription Rates.** Unless otherwise stated, prices shown in this section are the individual annual subscription rate. Other rates are listed when known, including multiyear rates, prices outside the United States, discount rates, library/institution rates, and single copy prices.

㉒ **Remarks.** Information listed in this section further explains the Ad Rates.

㉓ **Online.** If a publication is accessible online via computer, that information is listed here. If the publication is available online but the details of the URL (universal resource locator) or vendor are not known, the notation '**Available Online.**' will be listed.

㉔ **Alternate Format(s).** Lists additional mediums in which a publication may be available (other than online), including CD-ROM and microform.

㉕ **Variant Name(s).** Lists former or variant names of the publication, including the year the change took place, when known.

㉖ **Feature Editors.** Lists the names and beats of any feature editors employed by the publication.

㉗ **Additional Contact Information.** Includes mailing, advertising, news, and subscription addresses and phone numbers when different from the editorial/publisher address and phone numbers.

㉘ **Ad Rates.** Respondents may provide non-contract (open) rates in any of six categories:

GLR = general line rate
BW = one-time black & white page rate
4C = one-time four-color page rate
SAU = standard advertising unit rate
CNU = Canadian newspaper advertising unit rate
PCI = per column inch rate

Occasionally, explanatory information about other types of advertising appears in the Remarks section of the entry.

㉙ **Circulation.** Figures represent various circulation numbers; the figures are accompanied by a symbol (except for sworn and estimated figures). Following are explanations of the eight circulation classifications used by *GDPBM*, the corresponding symbols, if any, are listed at the bottom of each right hand page. All circulation figures *except* publisher's reports and estimated figures appear in boldface type.

These audit bureaus are independent, nonprofit organizations (with the exception of VAC, which is for-profit) that verify circulation rates. Interested users may contact the association for more information.

ABC: Audit Bureau of Circulations, 900 N. Meacham Rd., Schaumburg, IL 60173; (847)605-0909
CAC: Certified Audit of Circulations, Inc., 155 Willowbrook Blvd., 4th Fl., Wayne, NJ 07470-7036; (201)785-3000
CCAB: Canadian Circulations Audit Board, 188 Eglinton Ave. E, Ste. 304, Toronto, ON Canada M4P 2X7; (416)487-2418
VAC: Verified Audit Circulation, 319 Miller Ave., Mill Valley, CA 90292; (415)383-3623
Post Office Statement: These figures were verified from a U.S. Post Office form.
Publisher's Statement: These figures were accompanied by the signature of the editor, publisher, or other officer.
Sworn Statement: These figures, which appear in **boldface** without a symbol, were accompanied by the notarized signature of the editor, publisher, or other officer of the publication.
Estimated Figures: These figures, which are shown in lightface without a symbol, are the unverified report of the listee.

The footer on every odd-numbered page contains a key to circulation and entry type symbols, as well as advertising abbreviations.

SAMPLE BROADCAST LISTING

① **111** ② **WCAF-AM - 1530**
③ 199 E. 49th St.
PO Box 724866
Salem, NY 10528-5555
④ Phone: (518)555-9277
⑤ Fax: (518)555-9288
⑥ Free: 800-555-5432
⑦ **E-mail:** wcaf@wcaf.com
⑧ **Format:** Classical. ⑨ **Simulcasts:** WCAF-FM. ⑩ **Network(s):** Westwood One Radio; ABC. ⑪ **Owner:** Affici Communications, Inc., at above address. ⑫ **Founded:** 1996. ⑬ **Formerly:** WCAH-AM (1992). ⑭ **Operating Hours:** Continuous; 90% local, 10% network. ⑮ **ADI:** Elmira, NY. ⑯ **Key Personnel:** James Smith, General Mgr., phone (518)555-1002, fax (518)555-1010, jsmith@wcaf.com; Don White, Program Dir. ⑰ **Cities Served:** Salem, NY. ⑱ **Postal Areas Served:** 10528; 10529. ⑲ **Local Programs:** Who's Beethoven? Clement Goebel, Contact, (518)555-1301, fax (518)555-1320. ⑳ **Wattage:** 5000. ㉑ **Ad Rates:** Underwriting available. $10-15 for 30 seconds; $30-35 for 60 seconds. Combined advertising rates available with WCAF-FM. ㉒ **Additional Contact Information:** Mailing address: PO Box 555, Elmira, NY, 10529.
㉓ **URL:** http://www.wcaf.com.

① **Entry Number.** Each broadcast or cable entry is preceded by a symbol (a microphone) representing the broadcasting industry. Entries are numbered sequentially. Entry numbers (rather than page numbers) are used in the index to refer to listings.

② **Call Letters and Frequency/Channel** or **Cable Company Name**.

③ **Address.** Location and studio addresses appear as supplied by the respondent. If provided, alternate addresses are listed in the Additional Contact Information section of the entries (see ㉒ below).

④ **Phone.** Telephone numbers are listed as provided.

⑤ **Fax.** Facsimile numbers are listed when provided.

⑥ **Free.** Toll-free numbers are listed when provided.

⑦ **E-mail.** Electronic mail addresses are included as provided by the listee.

⑧ **Format.** For television station entries, this subheading indicates whether the station is commercial or public. Radio station entries contain industry-defined (and, in some cases, station-defined) formats as indicated by the listee.

⑨ **Simulcasts.** Lists stations that provide simulcasting.

⑩ **Network(s).** Notes national and regional networks with which a station is affiliated. The term 'independent' is used if indicated by the listee.

⑪ **Owner.** Lists the name of an individual or company, supplemented by the address and telephone number, when provided by the listee. If the address is the same as that of the station or company, the notation 'at above address' is used, referring to the station or cable company address.

⑫ **Founded.** In most cases, the year the station/company began operating, regardless of changes in call letters/names and ownership.

⑬ **Variant Name(s).** For radio and television stations, former call letters and the years in which they were changes are presented as provided by the listee. Former cable company names and the years in which they were changed are also noted when available.

⑭ **Operating Hours.** Lists on-air hours and often includes percentages of network and local programming.

⑮ **ADI (Area of Dominant Influence).** The Area of Dominant Influence is a standard market region defined by the Arbitron Ratings Company for U.S. television stations. Some respondents also list radio stations as having ADIs.

⑯ **Key Personnel.** Presents the names and titles of contacts at each station or cable company.

⑰ **Cities Served.** This heading is primarily found in cable system entries and provides information on channels and the number of subscribers.

⑱ **Postal Areas Served.** This heading is primarily found in cable system entries and provides information on the postal (zip) codes served by the system.

⑲ **Local Programs.** Lists names, air times, and contact personnel of locally-produced television and radio shows.

⑳ **Wattage.** Applicable to radio stations, the wattage may differ for day and night in the case of AM stations. Occasionally a station's ERP (effective radiated power) is given in addition to, or instead of, actual licensed wattage.

㉑ **Ad Rates.** Includes rates for 10, 15, 30, and 60 seconds as provided by respondents. Some stations price advertisement spots "per unit" regardless of length; these units vary.

㉒ **Additional Contact Information.** Includes mailing, advertising, news, and studio addresses and phone numbers when different from the station, owner, or company address and phone numbers.

㉓ **Online.** If a radio station or cable company is accessible online via computer, that information is listed here. If the station or company is available online but the details of the URL (universal resource locator) or vendor are not known, the notation '**Available Online.**' will be listed.

Entry information appearing in the Sample Entries portion of this directory has been fabricated. The entries named here do not, to the best of our knowledge, exist.

Index Notes

Volume 3 of the *Gale Directory of Publications and Broadcast Media* features a publishers index, referring to main section listings by entry number. It also includes an index to subject terms, multiple subject indexes, and a master name and keyword index. These indexes refer to main section listings by entry number and geographic location. Volume 4 features a regional market index divided by publication or broadcast type. This index also refers back to main section listings by entry number.

Publishers Index

This is an alphabetical listing of more than 11,000 publishers, whose publications are listed in *GDPBM*. Entries in this index include publisher name, address, phone and fax numbers, and periodicals published. Multiple addresses for publishers are listed geographically by state.

Index to Subject Terms

This is a consolidated alphabetical listing of the nearly 1,000 subject terms appearing in the Subject Indexes. Terms listed in this index are followed by page numbers in the appropriate subject index. Multiple page number citations indicate repeated uses of the terms. Additionally, "see" and "see also" references are provided.

Subject Indexes

Seventeen indexes in *GDPBM* group listings by broad type or subject. These indexes have been regrouped under eight major categories with bleed tabs to facilitate use. Citations are presented in one of two arrangements:

- ◆ geographically, by states and provinces
- ◆ by subject, and within subject, geographically

Major categories are noted in the Table of Contents. Subcategories, shown as subheadings in the indexes, are listed alphabetically in the Index to Subject Terms.

Citations in the indexes refer to entry number, and for publications, provide circulation figures. (Circulation symbols are explained in footnotes on odd-numbered pages.) Additionally, the Daily Newspapers Index provides complete address and telephone information, and the College Publications Index includes the names of issuing colleges and universities.

Master Name and Keyword Index

The Master Index is a comprehensive listing of all entries, both print and broadcast, included in *GDPBM*. Citations in this index are interfiled alphabetically throughout regardless of media type.

Publication citations include the following:
- titles
- keywords within titles
- titles of cessations
- former titles
- foreign-language titles
- alternate titles

Broadcast media citations include the following:
- station call letters
- cable company names
- former call letters
- former cable company names
- radio, television, and cable company cessations

Indexing is word-by-word rather than letter-by-letter. Thus, "New York" is listed before "News." Current listings in the Index include geographic information and entry number. Former names, whether publication or broadcast, include only the number of the entry in which they are mentioned.

INDEXING SAMPLE

(1) Administration in Mental Health (2) (New York, NY) 575

(1) Allied Cable Systems (2) (Lancaster, NH) 476

(3) Mental Health; Administration in (New York, NY) .... (4) 575

(5) Metro Tattler (Chicago, IL) *Ceased*

(6) Administration in Mental and Physical Health 575*

(7) WMDC-TV (Detroit, MI) *Unable to Locate*

(1) The full name (i.e. publication title, station call letters, or cable company name) of each entry is cited as it appears in the main body.

(2) Citations include in parentheses the city and state (or province and country for Canadian entries) in which the entry is located.

(3) Publications are also indexed by subject keywords and other important words within titles.

(4) References are to entry numbers rather than page numbers.

(5) Notices of cessations are included.

(6) Former names and call letters indicated by an * and do not include a geographic designation.

(7) Notices are included in cases where the editors have not been able to verify the location or continued existance of a publication, broadcast station, or cable company.

Regional Market Index

New to this edition. Volume 4 of the *Gale Directory of Publications and Broadcast Media*, (*GDPBM*) features a regional market index, referring to main section entries by entry number. This index is divided into five sections:

- Newspaper Index
- Periodical Index
- Cable Index
- Radio Index
- Television Index

Each section is arrranged geographically by region and then sorted by circulation, number of subscribing households, or Area of Dominant Influence (ADI).

Abbreviations, Symbols, and Codes

Miscellaneous Abbreviations

& .... And
4C .... One-Time Four Color Page Rate

ABC .... Audit Bureau of Circulations
Acad. .... Academy
Act. .... Acting
Adm. .... Administrative, Administration
Admin. .... Administrator
AFB .... Air Force Base
AM .... Amplitude Modulation
Amer. .... American
APO .... Army Post Office
Apt. .... Apartment
Assn. .... Association
Assoc. .... Associate
Asst. .... Assistant
Ave. .... Avenue

Bldg. .... Building
Blvd. .... Boulevard
boul. .... boulevard
BPA .... Business Publications Audit of Circulations
BTA .... Best Time Available
BW .... One-time Black & White Page Rate

C .... Central
CAC .... Certified Audit of Circulations
CCAB .... Canadian Circulations Audit Board
CEO .... Chief Executive Officer
Chm. .... Chairman
Chwm. .... Chairwoman
CNU .... Canadian Newspaper Advertising Unit Rate
c/o .... Care of
Col. .... Column
Coll. .... College
Comm. .... Committee
Co. .... Company
COO .... Chief Operating Officer
Coord. .... Coordinator
Corp. .... Corporation
Coun. .... Council
CP .... case postale
Ct. .... Court

Dept. .... Department
Dir. .... Director
Div. .... Division
Dr. .... Doctor, Drive

E. .... East
EC .... East Central
ENE .... East Northeast
ERP .... Effective Radiated Power
ESE .... East Southeast
Eve. .... Evening
Exec. .... Executive
Expy. .... Expressway

Fed. .... Federation
Fl. .... Floor
FM .... Frequency Modulation
FPO .... Fleet Post Office
Fri. .... Friday
Fwy. .... Freeway

Gen. .... General
GLR .... General Line Rate

Hd. .... Head
Hwy. .... Highway

Inc. .... Incorporated
Info. .... Information
Inst. .... Institute
Intl. .... International
ISSN .... International Standard Serial Number

Jr. .... Junior

Libn. .... Librarian
Ln. .... Lane
Ltd. .... Limited

Mgr. .... Manager
mi. .... miles
Mktg. .... Marketing
Mng. .... Managing
Mon. .... Monday
Morn. .... Morning

N. .... North
NAS .... Naval Air Station
Natl. .... National
NC .... North Central
NE .... Northeast
NNE .... North Northeast
NNW .... North Northwest
No. .... Number
NW .... Northwest

Orgn. .... Organization

PCI .... Per Column Inch Rate
Pkwy. .... Parkway
Pl. .... Place
PO .... Post Office
Pres. .... President
Prof. .... Professor

Rd. .... Road
RFD .... Rural Free Delivery
Rm. .... Room
ROS .... Run of Schedule
RR .... Rural Route
Rte. .... Route

S. .... South
Sat. .... Saturday
SAU .... Standard Advertising Unit Rate
SC .... South Central
SE .... Southeast
Sec. .... Secretary
Soc. .... Society
Sq. .... Square
Sr. .... Senior
SSE .... South Southeast
SSW .... South Southwest
St. .... Saint, Street
Sta. .... Station
Ste. .... Sainte, Suite
Sun. .... Sunday
Supt. .... Superintendent
SW .... Southwest

Terr. .... Terrace
Thurs. .... Thursday
Tpke. .... Turnpike
Treas. .... Treasurer
Tues. .... Tuesday

Univ. .... University
USPS .... United States Publications Serial

VAC .... Verified Audit Circulation
VP .... Vice President

W. .... West
WC .... West Central
Wed. .... Wednesday
WNW .... West Northwest
WSW .... West Southwest

x/month .... Times per Month
x/week .... Times per Week
x/year .... Times per Year

U.S. State and Territory Postal Codes

AK .... Alaska
AL .... Alabama
AR .... Arkansas
AZ .... Arizona
CA .... California
CO .... Colorado
CT .... Connecticut
DC .... District of Columbia
DE .... Delaware
FL .... Florida
GA .... Georgia
HI .... Hawaii
IA .... Iowa
ID .... Idaho
IL .... Illinois
IN .... Indiana
KS .... Kansas
KY .... Kentucky
LA .... Louisiana
MA .... Massachusetts
MD .... Maryland
ME .... Maine
MI .... Michigan
MN .... Minnesota
MO .... Missouri
MS .... Mississippi
MT .... Montana
NC .... North Carolina
ND .... North Dakota
NE .... Nebraska
NH .... New Hampshire
NJ .... New Jersey
NM .... New Mexico
NV .... Nevada
NY .... New York
OH .... Ohio
OK .... Oklahoma
OR .... Oregon
PA .... Pennsylvania
PR .... Puerto Rico
RI .... Rhode Island
SC .... South Carolina
SD .... South Dakota
TN .... Tennessee
TX .... Texas
UT .... Utah
VA .... Virginia
VT .... Vermont
WA .... Washington
WI .... Wisconsin
WV .... West Virginia
WY .... Wyoming

Canadian Province and Territory Postal Codes

AB	Alberta	NT	Northwest Territories
BC	British Columbia	ON	Ontario
MB	Manitoba	PE	Prince Edward Island
NB	New Brunswick	PQ	Quebec
NF	Newfoundland	SK	Saskatchewan
NS	Nova Scotia	YT	Yukon Territory

ALABAMA

State Capital, MONTGOMERY

Alabama is bounded on the north by Tennessee, east by Georgia and Florida, south by Florida and the Gulf of Mexico, and west by Mississippi. Its extreme length, north to south, is 336 miles; its breadth varies from 150 to 200 miles. The total land area is 50,750 square miles. The Allegheny range enters the state at the northeast and extends toward the center, finally losing itself in mere foothills; then follows a tract of rolling prairies interspersed with pine barrens and rich alluvial bottom lands. These bottom lands include the black belt region, one of the greatest cattle producing districts in the world. From this region to the Florida border and the Gulf the land is gently undulating and is covered with forests. The mountain districts and the valley of the Tennessee are covered with fine forests of hardwood timber. The mineral region occupies the northeastern part, while the northwest is a good agricultural and stock raising country. The climate is temperate and fairly uniform. The Weather Bureau at Mobile gives the temperature (annual average) at 67.5; highest on record, 107; lowest on record, -5. Total annual precipitation is 63.96 inches. Much of the state's foreign commerce passes through Mobile. The largest institution of higher education in the state is the University of Alabama, located at Birmingham.

POPULATION: 4,136,000 (1992). Rank among the states, 22nd.

AGRICULTURE: Number of farms: 46,000 (1992). Farm acreage: 10,000,000 (1992). Cash receipts from farm marketings: crops, $759,000,000 (1991); livestock and products, $2,219,000,000 (1991).

FISHERIES: Total catch: 22,000,000 lbs. (1991), $37,000,000 value. Principal fish: shrimp, red snapper, catfish and bullheads, oysters, mussel shells.

FORESTS: Total forest land: 1,280,000 acres (1991). Principal woods: southern yellow pine, oak, red gum, yellow poplar, black and tupelo gum, hickory, cottonwood, aspen, sycamore, beech, elm, ash, maple.

MINERALS: Value of production: $540,000,000 (1991). Principal minerals: lime, cement, stone. Value of petroleum production: $355,000,000 (1991).

MANUFACTURES: Value added by manufacture: $21,056,000,000 (1991). Leading industry groups: primary metal industries, chemicals and allied products, textile mill products.

LIST OF COUNTIES

Total number of counties 67

County, Location on Map, and County Seat	Pop.
Autauga (C), Prattville	34,222
Baldwin (SW), Bay Minette	98,280
Barbour (SE), Clayton	25,417
Bibb (C), Centreville	16,576
Blount (N), Oneonta	39,248
Bullock (SE), Union Springs	11,042
Butler (S), Greenville	21,892
Calhoun (NE), Anniston	116,034
Chambers (E), Lafayette	36,876
Cherokee (NE), Centre	19,543
Chilton (C), Clanton	32,458
Choctaw (SW), Butler	16,018
Clarke (SW), Grove Hill	27,240
Clay (E), Ashland	13,152
Cleburne (NE), Heflin	12,730
Coffee (SE), Elba	40,240
Colbert (NW), Tuscumbia	51,666
Conecuh (S), Evergreen	14,054
Coosa (C), Rockford	36,478
Covington (S), Andalusia	36,478
Crenshaw (S), Luverne	13,635
Cullman (N), Cullman	67,613
Dale (SE), Ozark	49,633
Dallas (S), Selma	48,130
DeKalb (NE), Fort Payne	54,651
Elmore (C), Wetumpka	49,210
Escambia (S), Brewton	35,518
Etowah (NE), Gadsden	99,840
Fayette (NW), Fayette	17,962
Franklin (NW), Russellville	27,814
Geneva (SE), Geneva	23,647
Greene (W), Eutaw	10,153
Hale (W), Greensboro	15,498
Henry (SE), Abbeville	15,374
Houston (SE), Dothan	81,331
Jackson (NE), Scottsboro	47,796
Jefferson (C), Birmingham	651,525
Lamar (NW), Vernon	15,715
Lauderdale (NW), Florence	79,661
Lawrence (N), Moulton	31,513
Lee (E), Opelika	87,146
Limestone (N), Athens	54,135
Lowndes (S), Hayneville	12,658
Macon (E), Tuskegee	24,928
Madison (N), Huntsville	238,912
Marengo (W), Linden	23,084
Marion (NW), Hamilton	29,830
Marshall (N), Guntersville	70,832
Mobile (SW), Mobile	378,643
Monroe (S), Monroeville	23,968
Montgomery (S), Montgomery	209,085
Morgan (N), Decatur	100,043
Perry (C), Marion	12,759
Pickens (W), Carrollton	20,699
Pike (SE), Troy	27,595
Randolph (E), Wedowee	19,881
Russell (E), Phenix City	46,860
St. Clair (N), Ashville and Pell City	50,009
Shelby (C), Columbiana	99,358
Sumter (W), Livingston	16,174
Talladega (C), Talladega	74,107
Tallapoosa (E), Dadeville	38,826
Tuscaloosa (W), Tuscaloosa	150,522
Walker (N), Jasper	67,670
Washington (SW), Chatom	16,694
Wilcox (SW), Camden	13,568
Winston (N), Double Springs	22,053

STATISTICS

Newspapers

Period of Issue	
Daily	20
Evening Daily	15
Morning Daily	12
Daily with Sunday edition	23
Semiweekly	12
Weekly	81
Biweekly	3
Semimonthly	2
Monthly	6
Free or partly free	10
Shopper	2
Total Newspapers	133

Periodicals

Period of Issue	
Weekly	2
Semimonthly	1
Monthly	20

Bimonthly 8
Quarterly 29
Total Periodicals 92

Total number of publications 225

Radio Stations

AM Stations 118
FM Stations 109

Total Radio Stations 227

TV Stations

Total TV Stations 37

Cable Stations

Total Cable Systems 29

Total number of broadcast listings 293

ABBEVILLE†, pop. 3,155.

SE AL. Herry Co. 28 mi. NE of Dothan. Saw, veneer mills; sheet factory. Agriculture. Cotton, corn, peanuts.

1 The Abbeville Herald
PO Box 609 Phone: (334)585-2331
Abbeville, AL 36310 Fax: (334)585-6835

Newspaper with a Democratic orientation. **Founded:** 1912. **Freq:** Weekly (Thurs.). **Print Method:** Offset. **Cols./Page:** 6. **Col. Width:** 26 nonpareils. **Col. Depth:** 294 agate lines. **ISSN:** 0006-3754. **Subscription Rates:** $140.40 in area. **Remarks:** Accepts advertising. **URL:** http://www.collegian.psu.edu.
Ad Rates: BW: $2,176.55 **Circ:** 2,080
4C: $2,446.55
SAU: $16.87
PCI: $16.87

ALABASTER

C. AL. Shelby Co. 20 mi. SE of Birmingham. Shelby Co. (C). 20 m SE of Birmingham.

2 WGTT-AM - 1500
PO Box 584 Phone: (205)664-1515
Alabaster, AL 35007 Fax: (205)664-1547

Format: Religious. **Networks:** USA Radio. **Owner:** WGTT, Inc., at above address. **Founded:** 1981. **Formerly:** WQMS-AM (1983). **Operating Hours:** Sunrise-sunset. **ADI:** Birmingham (Gadsden), AL. **Key Personnel:** John Sides, President; Dave Robinson, Operations Dir. **Wattage:** 1000. **Ad Rates:** $5-9 for 30 seconds; $8-12 for 60 seconds.

ALBERTVILLE, pop. 12,039.

N. AL. Marshall Co. 21 mi. NW of Gadsen. Manufactures cottonseed products, woven fabrics, lumber, electric heaters, mobile homes, aluminum awnings. Hatcheries. Hardwood timber. Agriculture. Poultry, cotton, corn.

3 The Sand Mountain Reporter
3760 US Hwy 431 Phone: (256)878-1311
PO Box 190 Fax: (256)878-2104
Albertville, AL 35950
Community newspaper. **Founded:** 1955. **Freq:** 3/week. **Print Method:** Offset. **Trim Size:** 14 x 22 3/4. **Cols./Page:** 6. **Col. Width:** 2 1/16 inches. **Col. Depth:** 21 1/2 inches. **Key Personnel:** Avis Holderfield, Editor; Mike Hudgins, Publisher; Debra Hedgepath, Advertising Mgr. **Subscription Rates:** $25 individuals; $45 out of area.
Ad Rates: SAU: $8.75 **Circ:** ‡11,500

4 WAVU-AM - 630
PO Box 190 Phone: (205)878-8575
Albertville, AL 35950 Fax: (205)878-1051

Format: Southern Gospel. **Owner:** Sand Mountain Broadcasting Service, Inc., at above address. **Founded:** 1948. **Operating Hours:** Continuous. **Key Personnel:** Warren Penney, General Mgr.; Allen Taylor, News Dir.; Jim Carter, Program Dir.; Pat Courington, Jr., President; Barry Calloway, Operations Mgr. **Wattage:** 1000 day; 28 night. **Ad Rates:** $7.20 for 30 seconds; $9 for 60 seconds.

5 WQSB-FM - 105.1
PO Box 190 Phone: (205)878-8575
Albertville, AL 35950 Fax: (205)878-1051
Free: (800)233-1051

Format: Contemporary Country. **Networks:** Independent. **Owner:** Sand Mountain Broadcasting Service, Inc., at above address. **Founded:** 1949. **Operating Hours:** Continuous; 100% local. **Key Personnel:** Pat Courington, Jr., President; Warren Penney, General Mgr.; Ted McCreless, Sales Mgr.; Allen Taylor, News Dir.; Barry Galloway, Program Dir.; Walt Howard, Chief Engineer. **Wattage:** 100,000. **Ad Rates:** $40 for 30 seconds; $48 for 60 seconds.

ALEXANDER CITY, pop. 13,807.

E. AL. Tallapoosa Co. 13 mi. NW of Dadeville. Residential.

6 Alexander City Outlook
Alexander City Outlook Inc.
548 Cherokee Rd. Phone: (205)234-4281
PO Box 999 Fax: (205)234-6550
Alexander City, AL 35010-0999
General newspaper. **Founded:** 1892. **Freq:** Tues. - Sun. (morn.). **Print Method:** Offset. **Cols./Page:** 6. **Col. Width:** 25 nonpareils. **Col. Depth:** 301 agate lines. **Key Personnel:** Bruce Wallace, Publisher; Ryan Carter, Circulation Mgr.; Kathy Hollis, Advertising Mgr. **Subscription Rates:** $9.50 individuals monthly.
Ad Rates: SAU: $6.50 **Circ:** (Not Reported)

7 The Dadeville Record
Tallapoosa Publishers
PO Box 999 Phone: (205)234-4281
Alexander City, AL 35010-0999 Fax: (205)234-6550

Newspaper. **Founded:** 1898. **Freq:** Weekly (Thurs.). **Print Method:** Offset. **Cols./Page:** 6. **Col. Width:** 25 nonpareils. **Col. Depth:** 301 agate lines. **Key Personnel:** Lon Williams, Publisher. **Subscription Rates:** $10 individuals. **Remarks:** Accepts advertising.
Ad Rates: BW: $451.50 **Circ:** 1,988
4C: $691.50
SAU: $3.50

8 Charter Communications, L.P.
1232 Cherokee Rd. Phone: (205)234-3456
PO Box 687 Fax: (205)329-0716
Alexander City, AL 35010

Owner: Charter Communications, L.P., 12444 Powerscourt Dr., Ste. 550, St. Louis, MO 63131-3660, (314)965-0555. **Founded:** July 1964. **Formerly:** Alexander City Cablevision, Inc./McDonald Group (Apr. 1994). **Key Personnel:** Ronda Blythe, Office Mgr.; Mac McKenzie, Chief Technician; Tom Early, General Mgr. **Cities Served:** Alexander City, Camp Hill, Goodwater, Jackson's Gap, New Site, Rockford, AL; Portions of Coosa, Tallapoosa, Talladega, and Clay counties.: subscribing households 12,500; 47 channels; 1 community access channel; 21 hours per week community access programming.

9 WDLK-AM - 1450
PO Box 909 Phone: (205)825-4221
Alexander City, AL 35011 Fax: (205)825-4270

Format: Country. **Networks:** Alabama Radio (ALANET). **Owner:** Dale Broadcasting Inc., at above address. **Operating Hours:** 5 a.m.-10 p.m.; 5% network, 95% local. **Key Personnel:** Marie Hoffman, Manager; Mike McNeill, Contact; Tim Lassiter, News Dir.; Hank Humphery, Sports Dir. **Wattage:** 1000. **Ad Rates:** $2-2.50 for 15 seconds; $2.95-3.60 for 30 seconds; $3.50-4.85 for 60 seconds.

10 WRFS-AM - 1050
PO Box 1640 12 Phone: (404)596-5100
Columbus, GA 31994 Fax: (404)596-5115
Free: (800)445-4106
E-mail: wayout@mindspring.com

Format: Middle-of-the-Road (MOR). **Networks:** ABC. **Owner:** Solar Broadcasting Co. Inc., at above address, (706)596-5100, Fax: (706)596-5115. **Founded:** 1947. **Formerly:** WXTH-AM (1992); WTLM-AM (1994). **Operating Hours:** Sunrise-sunset. **ADI:** Birmingham (Gadsden), AL. **Key Personnel:** Jim Powell, Pres./Gen. Mgr. **Wattage:** 1000. **Ad Rates:** $10-15 for 30 seconds. Combined advertising rates available with WOAK, WSTH.

WZLM-FM - See Dadeville

ANDALUSIA†, pop. 10,415.

S. AL. Covington Co. 85 mi. S. of Montgomery. Manufactures textiles, cardboard boxes, polypropolene fibers, caskets. Processes pecans, peanuts. Pine timber. Agriculture. Cattle, soybeans, cotton.

11 The Andalusia Star News
209 Dunson St. Phone: (334)222-2402
PO Drawer 430 Fax: (334)222-6597
Andalusia, AL 36420-0430
General newspaper. **Founded:** 1917. **Freq:** Tues.-Sat. (morn.). **Print Method:** Offset. **Cols./Page:** 6. **Col. Width:** 24 nonpareils. **Col. Depth:** 301 agate lines. **Key Personnel:** Stephen Weeks, Editor; William Beckner, Publisher; Kemi Simmons, Advertising Mgr. **ISSN:** 0746-2115. **Subscription Rates:** $36 individuals. **Remarks:** Accepts advertising.
Ad Rates: PCI: $5.53 **Circ:** (Not Reported)

12 TV Cable Co. of Andalusia Inc.
213 Dunston St. Phone: (334)222-6464
Andalusia, AL 36420 Fax: (334)222-7226

Key Personnel: Ivan Bishop, Vice President. **Cities Served:** Andalusia, AL.

13 WAAO-FM - 103.7
PO Box 987 Phone: (334)222-1166
Andalusia, AL 36420-0987 Fax: (334)222-1167

Format: News; Sports; Agricultural. **Founded:** 1987. **Operating Hours:** Continuous. **Key Personnel:** Lee Williams, Manager; Jamey Williams, Program Mgr.; Wayne Caylor, Music Dir. **Wattage:** 3000. **Ad Rates:** $6-9 for 30 seconds; $9-15 for 60 seconds.

ANNISTON†, pop. 29,523.

NE AL. Calhoun Co. 60 mi. NE of Birmingham. Manufacturing.

14 The Anniston Star
PO Box 189 Phone: (256)236-1551
Anniston, AL 36202 Fax: (256)231-0027
Publication E-mail: news@annistonstar.com

Newspaper with a Democratic orientation. **Founded:** 1883. **Freq:** Daily. **Print Method:** Offset. **Cols./Page:** 6. **Col. Width:** 25 nonpareils. **Col. Depth:** 301 agate lines. **Key Personnel:** P.A. Sanguinetti, President, phone (256)235-9202, tti@annistonstar.com; Ken Warren, Director, phone (256)935-9200, kwarren@annistonstar.com; Ed Fowler, V-P Operations, phone (256)235-9232, efowler@annistonstar.com. **USPS:** 026-440. **Subscription Rates:** $120 individuals. **Remarks:** Accepts advertising. **Alt. Formats:** Microform.
Ad Rates: GLR: $.94 **Circ:** Mon.-Sat. ★**27,416**
BW: $2,315.55 Sun. ★**29,554**
4C: $2,735.55
SAU: $17.95
PCI: $17.95

15 Through the Gears Trucking Magazine
J. B. Scott Publishing
PO Box 2685 Phone: (256)835-4901
Anniston, AL 36202 Fax: (256)835-4905
Free: (800)240-2130
Publisher E-mail: jbscottpub.@aol.com

Trucking magazine. **Founded:** July 1995. **Freq:** Monthly. **Trim Size:** 5 1/2 X 8 1/2. **Key Personnel:** Eric Larson, Contributing Editor; Jeff Borrelli, Advertising Mgr.; Tammy Borrelli, Business Mgr. **Subscription Rates:** Free. **Remarks:** Accepts advertising.
Ad Rates: 4C: $2,195 **Circ:** 125,000

16 Cable One
620 Noble St. Phone: (205)236-7034
Anniston, AL 36201 Fax: (205)236-4475

Founded: 1960. **Formerly:** Anniston NewChannels; Time Warner Cable. **Key Personnel:** Terry L. Womack, General Mgr.; Becky Woods, Ad Sales. **Cities Served:** Alexandria, Anniston, Fort McClellan, Jacksonville, Munford, Ohatchee, Oxford, Weaver, AL; Saks, Bynum, Blue Mountain, Eastaboga: subscribing households 36,000; 69 channels; 1 community access channel.

17 WANA-AM - 1490
PO Box 609 Phone: (205)237-1627
Anniston, AL 36202 Fax: (205)237-1628

Format: Religious. **Networks:** Alabama Radio (ALANET); USA Radio. **Owner:** Joe Burney, at above address, (205)237-4613. **Founded:** 1954. **Operating Hours:** 5 a.m.-11 p.m.; 5% network, 95% local. **ADI:** Anniston, AL. **Key Personnel:** Joe Burney, Contact. **Wattage:** 1000. **Ad Rates:** $7 for 30 seconds; $8 for 60 seconds.

18 WDNG-AM - 1450
PO Box 1450 Phone: (205)236-8291
Anniston, AL 36202 Fax: (205)236-2892

Format: Adult Contemporary. **Networks:** ABC. **Founded:** 1957. **ADI:** Anniston, AL. **Key Personnel:** J.J. Dark, Contact; Ralph Burgess, General Sales Mgr. **Wattage:** 1000.

19 WGRW-FM -
404 Sequoya Dr. Phone: (256)820-3711
Anniston, AL 36206 Fax: (256)237-1102

Format: Religious; Talk. **Networks:** Moody Broadcasting. **Owner:** Word Works, Inc., at above address. **Founded:** 1996. **Operating Hours:** Continuous. **Wattage:** 3000. **Ad Rates:** Noncommercial.

20 WHMA-AM - 1390
PO Box 278 Phone: (205)237-8741
Anniston, AL 36202 Fax: (205)231-9414
E-mail: jjames@alabamaloo.com

Format: Sports; Talk. **Owner:** Susquehanna Radio Corp., at above address, Fax: (800)876-1436, Free: (800)367-8261. **Founded:** 1938. **Operating Hours:** 5 a.m.-midnight; 20% network, 80% local. **ADI:** Birmingham (Gadsden), AL. **Key Personnel:** Tom Williams, General Mgr., twilliams@internettport.net; Stewart Young, News Dir.; Shannon Smith, Office Mgr., ssmith@internettport.net; Tom Headrick, Operations Mgr., cowboy@internettport.net. **Wattage:** 5000 day; 1000 night. **Ad Rates:** Advertising accepted; rates available upon request. **URL:** http://www.alabama100.com.

21 WHMA-FM - 100.5
Williamson Commerce Center, 8th Fl. Phone: (205)237-8741
801 Noble St. Fax: (205)231-9414
Anniston, AL 36201
Free: (800)264-0902

Format: Country; Hot Country. **Networks:** NBC. **Owner:** Sapphire Broadcasting, at above address. **Founded:** 1947. **Operating Hours:** Continuous. **ADI:** Birmingham (Gadsden), AL. **Key Personnel:** Shannon Smith, Office Mgr.; Stewart Young, News Dir.; Tom Williams, General Mgr.; Tom Headrick, Operations Mgr.; Larry James, Sales Mgr. **Wattage:** 100,000. **Ad Rates:** Advertising accepted; rates available upon request.

22 WJSU-TV - 40
1330 Noble St. Phone: (205)237-8651
PO Box 40, Radio Bldg. Fax: (205)236-7336
Anniston, AL 36202

Format: Commercial TV. **Networks:** CBS. **Founded:** 1969. **Operating Hours:** 5:30 a.m.-2 a.m. weekdays; 6 a.m.-1 a.m. Sat.; 7 a.m.-1 a.m. Sun. **ADI:** Anniston, AL. **Key Personnel:** Betty Johnson, Controller/Business Manager; Jon Mangum, News Dir.; Phil Cox, VP/General Manager; Boyce Holt, General Sales Mgr.; Lisa Bedford, Program Dir.; Kathy Bridges, Traffic Mgr.; Mark Norman, Production & Promotions Mgr. **Local Programs:** *Midday Today* noon; *News* 5 p.m., 6 p.m, 10 p.m. **Wattage:** 720.

ARAB, pop. 5,967.

N. AL. Marshall Co. 60 mi. NE of Birmingham. Manufactures textiles, electronic components, plastics, chemicals. Nursery. Agriculture. Poultry, corn, cotton.

23 The Arab Tribune
Reed Publish Supply
South Brindlee Mountain Pkwy. Phone: (205)586-3188
Box 605 Fax: (205)586-3190
Arab, AL 35016
Newspaper. **Founded:** 1981. **Freq:** Weekly (Wed.). **Print Method:** Offset. **Cols./Page:** 6. **Col. Width:** 24 nonpareils. **Col. Depth:** 301 agate lines. **Subscription Rates:** $8 individuals. **Remarks:** Accepts advertising.
Ad Rates: SAU: $4.25 **Circ:** ‡6,980

24 WRAB-AM - 1380
329 S. Main St. Phone: (256)586-4123
PO Box 625 Fax: (256)586-4124
Arab, AL 35016-0625

Format: Country; Religious. **Networks:** ABC. **Owner:** Arab Broadcasting, Inc., at above address. **Founded:** 1962. **Operating Hours:** Sunrise-sunset; 5 % network, 95% local. **Key Personnel:** Kerry Rich, Pres./Gen. Mgr.; Tim Maze, Program/Music Dir.; Linda Whitehorn, Office Mgr.; Ronald Anderson, Asst. Mgr./News Dir. **Local Programs:** *Gospel Show*, Tim Maze, Program/Music Dir.; *Helping Hand*, Ronald Anderson, Asst. Mgr./News Dir.; *Morning Show*, Ronald Anderson, Asst. Mgr./News Dir. **Wattage:** 1000. **Ad Rates:** $2.40-3 for 15 seconds; $2.75-3.00 for 15 seconds; $3.70-5 for 30 seconds; $4.25-4.85 for 30 seconds; $4.80-6.25 for 60 seconds; $5.45-5.95 for 60 seconds.

ASHLAND†, pop. 1,921.

C. AL. Clay co. 26 mi. S. of Anniston. Cotton ginning.

25 WASZ-FM - 95.5
PO Box 395 Phone: (205)354-4600
Ashland, AL 36251 Fax: (205)354-7224

Format: Country; Gospel. **Networks:** Alabama Radio (ALANET); ABC; Satellite Music Network. **Owner:** Perry Communications, Inc., PO Box 343, Wedowee, AL 36278, (205)357-2333. **Founded:** 1984. **Operating Hours:** Continuous. **ADI:** Birmingham (Gadsden), AL. **Key Personnel:** Robert A. Perry, President; Al Haynes, General Mgr.; Jon Pace, News Dir.; Michelle Rose, Traffic Mgr. **Wattage:** 6,000. **Ad Rates:** $4.80-7.60 for 30 seconds; $6.90-9.60 for 60 seconds.

26 WZZX-AM - 780
PO Box 395 Phone: (205)354-4600
Ashland, AL 36251 Fax: (205)354-7224

Format: Country; Gospel; Talk. **Networks:** Alabama Radio (ALANET); Satellite Music Network. **Owner:** Robert A. Perry, PO Box 343, Wedowee, AL 36278, (205)357-2333. **Founded:** 1967. **Formerly:** WANL-AM (1985). **Operating Hours:** Sunrise-sunset. **ADI:** Birmingham (Gadsden), AL. **Key Personnel:** Robert A. Perry, President; Al Haynes, General Mgr. **Wattage:** 5000. **Ad Rates:** $3 for 30 seconds; $6.50 for 60 seconds.

ATHENS†, pop. 14,558.

N. AL. Limestone Co. 13 mi. N. of Decatur. Athens State College. Nuclear industry. Cotton gins, grist and saw mills. Pine, oak timber. Agriculture. Cotton, hay, corn, dairying.

27 Athens News Courier
410 W. Green St. Phone: (256)232-2720
PO Box 670 Fax: (256)233-7753
Athens, AL 35611-2518
Free: (800)844-5480

General newspaper. **Founded:** 1880. **Freq:** Tues-Fri. (morn); Sun (morn). **Print Method:** Offset. **Cols./Page:** 6. **Col. Width:** 25 nonpareils. **Col. Depth:** 301 agate lines. **Key Personnel:** Sonny Turner, Editor; Ben Sheroan, Publisher, blspaper@hotmail.com; Randall Wynn, Circulation Mgr.; Tony Riley, Advertising Mgr. **USPS:** 035-640. **Subscription Rates:** $50 /year. **Remarks:** Accepts advertising.
Ad Rates: SAU: $7 **Circ:** Tues.-Fri. ★7,363
PCI: $6 Sun. ★8,305

28 WKAC-AM - 1080
PO Box 1083 Phone: (205)232-6827
Athens, AL 35611
E-mail: wkac@companet.net

Format: Oldies. **Networks:** CNN Radio. **Founded:** 1965. **Operating Hours:** Sunrise-sunset; 7% network, 93% local. **ADI:** Huntsville-Decatur-Florence, AL. **Key Personnel:** Keith A. Casey, General Mgr.; Kirk Harvey, Program Dir.; Joyce Casey, Traffic Mgr. **Wattage:** 5000. **Ad Rates:** $4-7 for 30 seconds; $6-9 for 60 seconds. **URL:** http://www.wkac1080.com.

29 WPZM-FM - 93.3
PO Box 389 Phone: (205)430-0110
Athens, AL 35611 Fax: (205)232-6842

Format: Country. **Networks:** Independent. **Owner:** Fortune Media Communications, at above address. **Founded:** 1970. **Formerly:** WKQD-FM (1983); WHUK-FM (1995). **Operating Hours:** Continuous; 100% local. **ADI:** Huntsville-Decatur-Florence, AL. **Key Personnel:** Bill Dunnauant, President; Mary Dunnauant, Vice President; Keith Parker, Sales Mgr.; Tim Mercer, Program Dir. **Wattage:** 100,000. **Ad Rates:** $40 for 30 seconds; $75 for 60 seconds. **URL:** http://www.possum.com.

30 WVNN-AM - 770
PO Box 389 Phone: (205)232-3911
Athens, AL 35611 Fax: (205)232-6842

Format: Talk; News. **Networks:** ABC. **Founded:** 1948. **Formerly:** WJMW-AM (1988). **Operating Hours:** Continuous; 10% network, 90% local. **ADI:** Huntsville-Decatur-Florence, AL. **Key Personnel:** Bill Dunnavant, General Mgr.; Peter Thiele, Contact; Bill West, Sales Mgr. **Local Programs:** *Dave Stone*; *Rush Limbaugh*. **Wattage:** 10,000. **URL:** http://wvnn.com.

31 WZYP-FM - 104.3
1717 Hwy. 72 E. Phone: (205)233-1414
PO Box 389 Fax: (205)232-6842
Athens, AL 35611-0389

Format: Top 40. **Networks:** ABC. **Founded:** 1958. **Formerly:** WJOF-FM (1978). **Operating Hours:** Continuous; 100% local. **ADI:** Huntsville-Decatur-Florence, AL. **Key Personnel:** Bill Dunnavant, General Mgr.; Bill West, Program Dir.; Peter Thiefe, News Dir.; Bill West, Sales Mgr. **Local Programs:** *Ace and T.J.*. **Wattage:** 100,000. **URL:** http://www.wzyp.net.

ATMORE, pop. 9,500.

SW AL. Escambia Co. 40 mi. NE of Mobile. Lumber milling, cotton ginning, and bottling. Agriculture. Corn, cotton, strawberries.

32 Atmore Advance
Boone Newspapers, Inc.
PO Drawer 28 Phone: (205)368-2123
Atmore, AL 36504 Fax: (205)368-2124

Local newspaper. **Founded:** 1927. **Freq:** Semiweekly. **Print Method:** Offset. **Cols./Page:** 6. **Col. Width:** 12.5 picas. **Col. Depth:** 21 1/2 inches. **Key Personnel:** Ryan Carter, Editor and Publisher. **Subscription Rates:** $40 individuals; $50 out of state. **Remarks:** Accepts advertising.
Ad Rates: BW: $619.20 **Circ:** 4,213
4C: $859.20
SAU: $8.60
PCI: $4.05

33 WASG-AM - 550
1318 S. Main St. Phone: (205)368-2511
Atmore, AL 36502-2899 Fax: (205)368-4227

Format: Country; Agricultural; News; Talk. **Networks:** Talknet; ABC. **Owner:** PCI Communications, Inc., at above address. **Founded:** 1981. **Operating Hours:** Continuous; 50% network; 50% local. **ADI:** Mobile, AL-Pensacola, FL. **Key Personnel:** Rick Dean, Program Dir.; Nathan Martin, General Mgr.; Fred Stephens, Sales Mgr. **Wattage:** 5000. **Ad Rates:** $12.50-20 for 30 seconds; $20-25 for 60 seconds.

34 WPHG-AM - 1620
PO Box 10 Phone: (334)368-9495
Atmore, AL 36502 Fax: (334)368-2713
E-mail: lavirn@frontier.gulf.net

Format: Gospel. **Networks:** USA Radio. **Founded:** 1949. **Formerly:** WATM-AM; WSKR-AM; WIZD-AM; WGYJ-AM. **Operating Hours:** Continuous. **Key Personnel:** John K. Mathis, Pres./Gen. Mgr. **Wattage:** 10,000.

35 WPHG-FM - 90.9
PO Box 10 Phone: (334)867-9090
Atmore, AL 36502 Fax: (334)368-2713
E-mail: wphg@usa.net

Format: Religious. **Owner:** Marranatha Ministries Foundation Inc., at above address. **Founded:** 1998. **Operating Hours:** Continuous. **Key Personnel:** John Mathis, Pres./General Mgr. **Wattage:** 45,000. **Ad Rates:** Noncommercial.

36 WYDH-FM - 105.9
1210 S. Main St. Phone: (205)368-2511
Atmore, AL 36502 Fax: (205)368-4227

Format: Adult Contemporary. **Networks:** ABC; AP. **Owner:** P.C.I. Communications, at above address. **Founded:** 1991. **Operating Hours:** Continuous; 90% network; 10% local. **Key Personnel:** William Reynolds, Sales Mgr.; Rick Dean, Contact; Lisa Larrabee, Office Mgr. **Wattage:** 6000. **Ad Rates:** $6-12.50 for 30 seconds; $8-15 for 60 seconds.

AUBURN, pop. 28,471.

E. AL. Lee Co. 52 mi. NE of Montgomery. Auburn University. Manufactures door locks, wood products, power transmitting gears, laboratory furniture, pollution monitoring devices, greenhouses, signs, wire products, asphalt, drill bits, cutting tools. Agriculture. Livestock. Cotton.

37 The Auburn Bulletin-Eagle
Auburn Bulletin
PO Box 3240 Phone: (334)821-7150
Auburn, AL 36830 Fax: (334)887-0037

Local newspaper. **Founded:** 1936. **Freq:** Semiweekly (Wed. and Sat.). **Print Method:** Letterpress and offset. **Cols./Page:** 6. **Col. Width:** 2 inches. **Col. Depth:** 21 1/2 inches. **Key Personnel:** Bill White, Editor; Alan Davis, Advertising Mgr. **Subscription Rates:** $26 individuals. **Remarks:** Accepts advertising.
Ad Rates: BW: $1,290 **Circ:** Paid 3,200
4C: $1,600 Free 7,000

38 Auburn Magazine
Auburn University Alumni Association
317 S. College St. Phone: (334)844-2586
Auburn University Fax: (334)844-3716
Auburn, AL 36849-5150
Publication E-mail: aubmag@alumni.auburn.edu

Magazine (tabloid) for college alumni. **Founded:** Jan. 1946. **Freq:** Quarterly. **Print Method:** Offset. **Trim Size:** 8 1/2 x 11. **Cols./Page:** 4. **Col. Width:** 29 nonpareils. **Col. Depth:** 189 agate lines. **Key Personnel:** Mike Jernigan, Editor, phone (334)844-1163, fax (334)844-1477. **ISSN:** 1077-8640. **Subscription Rates:** $35 individuals. **Remarks:** Accepts advertising. **Formerly:** The Auburn Alumnews (1994).
Ad Rates: BW: $1,250 **Circ:** ‡45,000
4C: $1,750

39 The Auburn Plainsman
Auburn University
B-100 Foy Union Bldg. Phone: (334)844-4130
Auburn, AL 36849 Fax: (334)844-9114

Collegiate newspaper. **Subtitle:** The Auburn Plainsman. **Founded:** 1894. **Freq:** Weekly (Thurs.). **Print Method:** Offset. **Trim Size:** 13 x 21. **Cols./Page:** 6. **Col. Width:** 26 nonpareils. **Col. Depth:** 294 agate lines. **Key Personnel:** Chad Barwick, Editor, phone (334)844-9021; Shane Harris, Business Mgr., phone (334)844-9102; Jan Waters, General Mgr. **Subscription Rates:** $20 individuals per year; $7 Quarterly. **Remarks:** Accepts advertising.
Ad Rates: GLR: $7 **Circ:** 19,500
BW: $567
4C: $895.50
SAU: $6.75
PCI: $6.75

40 The Coleopterists Bulletin
Coleopterists Society
Auburn University Phone: (334)844-2565
Department of Entomology Fax: (334)844-5005
Auburn, AL 36849-5413
Magazine on the biology, taxonomy, and evolution of beetles. **Subtitle:** An international journal devoted to the study of beetles. **Founded:** 1947. **Freq:** Quarterly. **Print Method:** Offset. **Trim Size:** 6 x 9. **Cols./Page:** 1. **Col. Width:** 52 nonpareils. **Col. Depth:** 101 agate lines. **Key Personnel:** Dr. Wayne E. Clark, Editor, wclark@acesag.auburn.edu; Terry Seeno, Treasurer, tseeno@ns.net. **ISSN:** 0010-065X. **Subscription Rates:** $50 individuals; $30 members. **Remarks:** Advertising not accepted.
Circ: ‡850

41 Highlights of Agricultural Research
Alabama Agricultural Experiment Station
Auburn University Phone: (334)844-4877
2 Comer Hall Fax: (334)844-5892
Auburn, AL 36849
Scientific agricultural magazine. **Founded:** June 1954. **Freq:** Quarterly. **Print Method:** Offset. **Trim Size:** 8 1/2 x 11. **Cols./Page:** 3. **Col. Width:** 28 nonpareils. **Col. Depth:** 130 agate lines. **Key Personnel:** J.R. Roberson, Editor; T.R. Rodriguez, Designer. **Remarks:** Advertising not accepted.
Circ: Non-paid ‡12,000

42 Journal of the Alabama Academy of Science
10 Cary Hall Phone: (334)844-9262
Auburn University Fax: (334)844-4065
Auburn, AL 36830
Science journal. **Founded:** 1924. **Freq:** Quarterly. **Print Method:** Offset. Accepts mats. **Trim Size:** 6 x 9. **Cols./Page:** 1. **Col. Width:** 54 nonpareils. **Col. Depth:** 105 agate lines. **Key Personnel:** Dr. James T. Bradley, Editor, bradljt@mail.auburn.edu. **ISSN:** 0002-4112. **Subscription Rates:** $25 individuals. **Remarks:** Advertising not accepted.
Circ: ‡1,200

43 National Forum (Auburn)
Honor Society of Phi Kappa Phi
129 Quad Center Phone: (334)844-5200
Mell St. Fax: (334)844-5994
Auburn, AL 36849-5306
Journal of the Honor Society of Phi Kappa Phi covering education. **Founded:** 1915. **Freq:** Quarterly. **Key Personnel:** James P. Kaetz, Editor, kaetzjp@mail.auburn.edu; Mary Wood Littleton, Assoc. Editor; Stephanie Johns Bond, Assoc. Editor. **ISSN:** 0162-1831. **Subscription Rates:** $25 individuals. **Remarks:** Advertising not accepted. **Online:** Electric Library (Infonautics).
Circ: Paid 120,000

44 Noise Control Engineer Journal
Institute of Noise Control Engineering
212 Ross Hall Phone: (205)844-3306
Dept. of Mechanical Engineering Fax: (205)844-3307
Auburn, AL 36849-3541
Refereed journal containing technical articles for professionals concerned with noise reduction in industry, buildings, transportation, products, and communities. **Founded:** 1973. **Freq:** Bimonthly. **Print Method:** Offset. **Trim Size:** 8 1/2 x 11. **Cols./Page:** 3 and 2. **Col. Width:** 13.6 and 21 picas. **Col. Depth:** 135 agate lines. **Key Personnel:** Malcolm J. Crocker, Editor; Rebecca Haack, Advertising Mgr. **ISSN:** 0736-2501. **Subscription Rates:** $60 individuals. **Remarks:** Accepts advertising. **Formerly:** Noise Control Engineering Journal.
Ad Rates: BW: $1,275 **Circ:** Paid ‡2,000
4C: $1,825 Controlled ‡100

45 Professional Educator
Auburn University
3084 Haley Ctr. Phone: (334)844-5793
Auburn, AL 36849-5218 Fax: (334)844-5785

Trade journal covering issues in teacher education and professional development of teachers. **Founded:** 1976. **Freq:** Semiannual. **Cols./Page:** 2. **Col. Width:** 8 centimeters. **Col. Depth:** 20.2 centimeters. **Key Personnel:** Rhonda Porter, Editor, porterc@mail.auburn.edu; Donald Preslar, Associate Editor; Jeffrey Gorrell, Editor-in-Chief. **ISSN:** 0196-786X. **Subscription Rates:** $20; $35 two years; $10 single issue. **Remarks:** Advertising not accepted. **URL:** http://www.auburn.edu/academic/education/tpi/proedmp.htm.
Circ: Combined 200

46 Southern Humanities Review
Auburn University
9088 Haley Center Phone: (334)844-9088
Auburn, AL 36849 Fax: (334)844-9027
Publication E-mail: shrengl@mail.auburn.edu

Scholarly journal covering poetry, fiction and essays. **Founded:** 1967. **Freq:** Quarterly. **Trim Size:** 6 x 9. **Key Personnel:** Dan R. Latimer, Editor; Virginia M. Kouidis, Editor; Karen Beckwith, Editorial Asst. **ISSN:** 0038-4168. **Subscription Rates:** $15 individuals; $27 two years; $20 out of country; $36 out of country two-year; $5 single issue; $7 out of country single copy. **Alt. Formats:** Microform, University Microfilm International.
Circ: Combined 700

47 WANI-AM - 1400
PO Box 950 Phone: (334)826-2929
Auburn, AL 36831-0950 Fax: (334)826-9151

Format: Talk; News; Sports. **Networks:** Westwood One Radio. **Owner:** at above address. **Founded:** 1940. **Formerly:** WJHO-AM. **Operating Hours:** Continuous; 75% network, 25% local. **ADI:** Columbus, GA (Opelika, AL). **Key Personnel:** Red Bramblett, General Mgr. **Local Programs:** *Daily Planner* 6 a.m.-8 a.m., Jerry Katz. **Wattage:** 1000. **Ad Rates:** $8-14 for 30 seconds; $10-14 for 60 seconds. Combined advertising rates available with WJHO-AM.

48 WAUD-AM - 1230
2514 S. College St. Phone: (334)887-3401
Auburn, AL 36830 Fax: (334)826-9599

Format: Sports; Easy Listening; News. **Networks:** ABC; Alabama Radio (ALANET). **Owner:** Tiger Communications, at above address. **Founded:** 1947. **Operating Hours:** Continuous. **ADI:** Columbus, GA (Opelika, AL). **Key Personnel:** Bob Sanders, Contact. **Wattage:** 1,000. **Ad Rates:** $5.15-6 for 15 seconds; $6.50-9.25 for 30 seconds; $8.25-12 for 60 seconds. Combined advertising rates available with WTGT "Tiger 95.9".

49 WEGL-FM - 91.1
116 Foy Union Phone: (334)844-4057
Auburn University Fax: (334)844-4118
Auburn, AL 36849
E-mail: wegl@mail.auburn.edu

Format: Album-Oriented Rock (AOR); Alternative/New Music/Progressive. **Networks:** CNN Radio. **Founded:** 1971. **Operating Hours:** Continuous; 1% network, 99% local. **Key Personnel:** Paige Brennan, Station Mgr.; Miller Paraison, Program Dir.; Dan Ratanasit, Music Dir.; Age Roth, Sports and News Dir.; Rick Potter, Promotions Dir.; Lucas Alexander, Grants Dir.; Chris Phorrough, Production Dir. **Wattage:** 3000. **Ad Rates:** Noncommercial. **URL:** http://www.wegl.org.

BAY MINETTE†, pop. 7,455.

SW AL. Baldwin Co. 23 mi. NE of Mobile. Manufactures corrugated boxes, dental equipment, aluminum wire, lumber, furniture. Pine timber. Agriculture. Soybeans, hay, cattle.

50 Baldwin Times
Gulf Coast Newspapers
PO BOX 519 Phone: (334)937-2511
Bay Minette, AL 36507 Fax: (334)937-1637

Community newspaper. **Founded:** 1890. **Freq:** Weekly. **Print Method:** Offset. **Cols./Page:** 6. **Col. Width:** 18 nonpareils. **Col. Depth:** 294 agate lines. **Key Personnel:** Dan Rutledge, Editor; Mike Mueck, Publisher. **Subscription Rates:** $17.12 individuals. **Remarks:** Accepts advertising.
Ad Rates: GLR: $.23 **Circ:** ‡4,800

51 WBCA-AM - 1110
720 S. White Ave. Phone: (334)937-5596
PO Box 426 Fax: (334)937-5597
Bay Minette, AL 36507

Format: Eclectic; News. **Networks:** ABC; Mutual Broadcasting System. **Founded:** 1956. **Operating Hours:** 13 hours Daily; 10% network, 90% local. **Key Personnel:** Gordon Earls, Contact; Keith Hammond, Program Dir.; Ted Allen, Sales Mgr. **Wattage:** 10,000. **Ad Rates:** $4.50-7.50 for 30 seconds; $6-9 for 60 seconds.

BESSEMER, pop. 31,729.

SW AL. Jefferson Co. Just SW of Birmingham. Manufactures steel and steel products. Bottling works, meat-packing plant.

52 The Western Star
Trib Publications
1709 3rd Ave. N. Phone: (205)424-7827
Bessemer, AL 35020 Fax: (205)424-8118

Weekly newspaper and legal paper. **Founded:** 1984. **Freq:** Weekly (Wed.). **Print Method:** Offset. **Cols./Page:** 6. **Col. Width:** 2 1/16 inches. **Col. Depth:** 21 1/2 inches. **Key Personnel:** Cathy O'Berry, Editor and Publisher. **Subscription Rates:** $21 individuals; $26 out of state; $.50 single issue. **Formerly:** Bessemer Advertiser.
Ad Rates: GLR: $7.30 **Circ:** ⊕**10,000**
BW: $7.30
4C: $50

53 WSMQ-AM - 1450
3300 Jaybird Rd. Phone: (205)428-0146
Bessemer, AL 35020

Format: Sports; Talk. **Networks:** CNN Radio. **Owner:** Bessemer Radio, Inc., at above address. **Founded:** 1950. **Formerly:** WBCO-AM; WYAM-AM; WENN-AM. **Operating Hours:** Continuous. **Key Personnel:** Betty Landau, Contact. **Wattage:** 1000. **Ad Rates:** $4-25 for 30 seconds; $8-50 for 60 seconds.

BIRMINGHAM†, pop. 284,413.

C. AL. Jefferson Co. 90 mi. NW of Montgomery. Jefferson Co. (C). 90 m NW of Montgomery. Univ. of Alabama, Samford Univ., Birmingham Southern; Miles College.Coal mines. Limestone quarries. Telecommunications industry. Manufacturing. Major transportation distribution center. Retail, wholesale trade center. Medical center. Financial center.

54 Alabama Wildlife
PO Box 190032 Phone: (205)941-1768
Birmingham, AL 35219 Fax: (205)945-5627
Publication E-mail: awf@mindspring.com
Publisher E-mail: alabamawf@mindspring.com

Magazine covering environmental issues, conservation, sportsmen's issues, and land management in Alabama for members. **Founded:** 1987. **Freq:** Quarterly. **Key Personnel:** Tim Gothard, Editor; April Lupardus, Managing Editor. **Subscription Rates:** Free to qualified subscribers; $2.50 single issue. **Remarks:** Accepts advertising. **Former name:** Alabama Outdoors.
Ad Rates: BW: $650 **Circ:** Controlled 7,500
4C: $750

55 The Apostle
The Episcopal Diocese of Alabama
521 N. 20th St. Phone: (205)715-2060
Birmingham, AL 35203-2682 Fax: (205)715-2066
Publication E-mail: apostledit@aol.com

Newspaper (tabloid) for members of the Episcopal diocese of Alabama. **Founded:** Feb. 1892. **Freq:** Monthly (not published June and July). **Print Method:** Offset. **Trim Size:** 11 1/2 x 13 1/2. **Cols./Page:** 4. **Col. Width:** 2 1/2 inches. **Col. Depth:** 13 1/2 inches. **Key Personnel:** Norma E. McKittrick, Editor, phone (205)979-2680. **ISSN:** 1041-3316. **Subscription Rates:** Free; $5 (mail). **Remarks:** Advertising not accepted. **URL:** http://www.brasenhill.com/alabiocese. **Formerly:** The Alabama Churchman; The Apostle; The Alabama Apostle.
Circ: Non-paid ‡13,000

56 Arthritis Care and Research
University of Alabama at Birmingham Station, MEB 615
1813 6th Ave. S. Phone: (205)934-2799
Birmingham, AL 35294
Subtitle: The Official Journal of the Association of Rheumatology Health Professionals. **Founded:** 1988. **Freq:** Quarterly. **Print Method:** Offset. **Trim Size:** 8 1/4 x 11. **Cols./Page:** 2. **Col. Width:** 3 1/4 inches. **Col. Depth:** 10 inches. **Key Personnel:** Ruth E. Martin, R.N., Executive Director. **ISSN:** 0893-7524. **Subscription Rates:** $55 individuals; $110 institutions. **Remarks:** Accepts advertising.
Ad Rates: BW: $570 **Circ:** ‡1,575
4C: $850

57 Associated Plumbing Heating & Cooling
PO Box 36972 Phone: (205)987-5100
Birmingham, AL 35236-6972 Fax: (205)733-1006

Trade and technical magazine for plumbing, heating, and cooling contractors. **Subtitle:** Alabama Contractor. **Founded:** 1940. **Freq:** Annual. **Trim Size:** 8 1/2 x 11. **Cols./Page:** 2. **Col. Width:** 4 inches. **Col. Depth:** 8 inches. **Key Personnel:** Bob Moscia, Contact. **Subscription Rates:** Free. **Remarks:** Accepts advertising.
Ad Rates: BW: $350 **Circ:** Non-paid ‡2,000

58 Aura Literary/Arts Review
University of Alabama at Birmingham
University Ctr. Phone: (205)934-3354
Box 76 Fax: (205)934-8050
Birmingham, AL 35294-1150
Publication E-mail: aura@larry.huc.vab.edu

Literary and arts magazine. **Founded:** 1974. **Freq:** Semiannual. **Print Method:** Offset. **Trim Size:** 6 x 9. **Key Personnel:** Daniel Williams, Editor, phone (205)934-3216. **ISSN:** 0889-7433. **Subscription Rates:** $12 individuals; $6 per issue. **Remarks:** Advertising not accepted.
Circ: Non-paid ‡500

59 The Birmingham News
PO Box 2553 Phone: (205)325-2444
Birmingham, AL 35202 Fax: (205)325-2283
Free: (800)283-4144
Publication E-mail: 70550.3405@compuserve.com

General newspaper. **Founded:** 1888. **Freq:** Daily (morn.). **Print Method:** Offset. **Cols./Page:** 6. **Col. Width:** 25 nonpareils. **Col. Depth:** 21 3/4 inches. **Key Personnel:** Victor H. Hanson II, Publisher, phone (205)325-2411; Victor H. Hanson III, General Mgr., phone (205)325-3126; Thomas V. Scarritt, Editor, phone (205)325-2205, fax (205)325-3278; Carol F. Nunnelley, Managing Editor, phone (205)325-2111, fax (205)325-2283. **Subscription Rates:** $142.80 individuals. **Remarks:** Accepts advertising. **Feature Editors:** Tom Arenberg, *Sports*, phone (205)325-2433, fax (205)325-2425; Betsy Butgereit, *Lifestyle*, phone (205)325-2282, fax (205)325-2494; Kenneth Carter, *Sunday*, phone (205)325-3419, fax (205)325-2283; Alec Harvey, *Lifestyle*, phone (205)325-2100, fax (205)325-2494; Randy Henderson, *City*, phone (205)325-2444, fax (205)325-2283; Wayne Hester, *Metro*, phone (205)325-2478, fax (205)325-2283; Glenn Stephens, *State*, phone (205)325-2482, fax (205)325-2283; Jerry Underwood, *Financial/Business*, phone (205)325-3250, fax (205)325-2283.
Ad Rates: BW: $14,047.02 **Circ:** Mon.-Fri. ★**148,835**
4C: $15,847.02 Sun. ★**186,663**
PCI: $107.64

60 Birmingham Poetry Review
University of Alabama
Birmingham, AL 35294 Phone: (205)934-4250

Literary journal covering poetry. **Founded:** 1988. **Freq:** Semiannual. **Key Personnel:** Robert Collins, Editor; Randy Blythe, Editor. **ISSN:** 1047-2258. **Subscription Rates:** $4 individuals; $7 two years; $2 single issue. **Remarks:** Advertising not accepted.
Circ: Paid 700

61 Birmingham Post-Herald
Birmingham Post Co.
2200 4th Ave. N. Phone: (205)325-2344
Birmingham, AL 35203 Fax: (205)325-2410
Publication E-mail: mailbox@postherald.com
Publisher E-mail: postherald@aol.com

Daily newspaper. **Founded:** 1921. **Freq:** Mon.-Sat. (morn.) effective 8/5/96-afternoon. **Print Method:** Offset. **Cols./Page:** 6. **Col. Width:** 12 3/5 picas. **Col. Depth:** 21 3/4 inches. **Key Personnel:** Jim Willis, Editor/President, phone (205)325-2215, jwillis@postherald.com; Don Kausler, phone (205)325-2127, dkausler@scripps.com. **Subscription Rates:** $54 individuals. **Remarks:** Accepts advertising. **URL:** http://www.postherald.com. **Feature Editors:** Steve Bell, *Metro*, phone (205)325-2344; Chet Fussman, *Sports*, phone (205)325-2127; Karl Seitz, *Editorials*, phone (205)325-2411, kseitz@postherald.com.
Ad Rates: GLR: $3.65 **Circ:** Mon.-Fri. ★**21,250**
BW: $1,990.13
4C: $3,385.13
PCI: $18.36

62 Birmingham World
407 15th St. N. Phone: (205)251-6523
PO Box 2285 Fax: (205)328-6729
Birmingham, AL 35203-1877
Black community newspaper. **Founded:** Apr. 1930. **Freq:** Weekly. **Print Method:** Offset. **Cols./Page:** 6. **Col. Width:** 2 4/5 inches. **Col. Depth:** 21 1/2 inches. **Key Personnel:** Joe N. Dickson, Editor and Publisher. **Subscription Rates:** $26 individuals. **Remarks:** Accepts advertising.
Ad Rates: BW: $1,575 **Circ:** Paid ‡12,600
4C: $2,455
SAU: $12.60

63 Business Alabama Monthly
PMT Publishing Co., Inc.
529 Beacon Pkwy. W., Ste. 110 Phone: (334)473-6269
Birmingham, AL 35209 Fax: (334)479-8822

Magazine for owners, managers, and presidents of companies covering issues and people in business in Alabama. **Founded:** Jan. 1986. **Freq:** Monthly. **Print Method:** Offset. **Trim Size:** 8 1/8 x 11. **Cols./Page:** 3. **Col. Width:** 25 1/2 nonpareils. **Col. Depth:** 140 agate lines. **Key Personnel:** Chris McFadyen, Editor; T.J. Potts, Publisher; Tim Young, Advertising Mgr., phone (205)941-1425, fax (205)941-1494; Jane Potts, Circulation Mgr. **ISSN:** 0886-3024. **Subscription Rates:** $24. **Remarks:** Accepts advertising. **Formerly:** Business Alabama.
Ad Rates: BW: $1,783 **Circ:** Paid 10,000
4C: $2,511 Controlled 8,000

64 Civitan Magazine
Civitan International
1 Civitan Place Phone: (205)591-8910
PO Box 130744 Fax: (205)592-6307
Birmingham, AL 35213-0744
Publication E-mail: civitan@civitan.org
Publisher E-mail: civitan@civitan.org

Magazine covering civic club activities and interests. **Founded:** 1920. **Freq:** Bimonthly. **Print Method:** Offset. **Trim Size:** 8 1/2 x 11. **Cols./Page:** 4. **Col. Width:** 10 picas. **Col. Depth:** 57 picas. **Key Personnel:** Dorothy Wellborn, Editor. **ISSN:** 0914-5785. **Subscription Rates:** $2 members; $6 nonmembers. **Remarks:** Accepts advertising.
Ad Rates: BW: $1,000 **Circ:** ‡36,000
4C: $2,000
PCI: $75

65 Construction Monthly
3132 Valley Park Dr. Phone: (205)969-5314
Birmingham, AL 35243 Fax: (205)969-0088
Free: (800)999-5314

Trade publication featuring articles for buyers of construction equipment, trucks, and related products. **Founded:** July 1995. **Freq:** Monthly. **Print Method:** Web offset. **Trim Size:** 8 1/8 x 10 7/8. **Cols./Page:** 3. **Col. Width:** 2 3/8 inches. **Col. Depth:** 9 7/8 inches. **Key Personnel:** Steve Harrell, Managing Editor, sharrell@wwisp.com; Chuck Adams, VP, Sales/Mktg., cadams@wwisp.com; Steve Harrell, Circulation Mgr. **Subscription Rates:** $14 individuals; $8 associations; $2 single issue. **Remarks:** Accepts advertising. **URL:** http://www.constmonthly.com.
Ad Rates: BW: $4,350 **Circ:** Paid 4,000
4C: $5,455 Controlled 30,000

66 Convene
Professional Convention Management Association
100 Vestavia Parkway, Ste. 220 Phone: (205)978-4917
Birmingham, AL 35216-3743 Fax: (205)822-3891

Magazine for suppliers of association meetings and conventions and association meeting managers and CEOs. **Subtitle:** Official Journal of Professional Convention Management. **Founded:** Mar. 1986. **Freq:** 11/year. **Print Method:** Web offset. **Trim Size:** 8 1/8 x 10 7/8. **Cols./Page:** 3. **Col. Width:** 2 1/8 inches. **Col. Depth:** 9 inches. **Key Personnel:** Peter Shure, Editor, phone (914)693-6246, fax (914)693-7005, pshure@pcma.org; Roy B. Evans, Jr., Publisher, phone (205)978-4900, fax (205)822-3891, revans@pcma.org; Carla Krause, Managing Editor, phone (205)978-4917, fax (205)822-3891, ckrause@pcma.org. **Subscription Rates:** $50. **Remarks:** Accepts advertising.
Ad Rates: BW: $4,765 **Circ:** Paid ‡4,000
4C: $7,435 Controlled ‡35,010

67 COOKING LIGHT
Southern Progress
2100 Lakeshore Dr. Phone: (205)877-6000
Birmingham, AL 35209-6721 Fax: (205)877-6600
Free: (888)737-3529
Publication E-mail: cookinglight@timeinc.com

Magazine for people who enjoy an active lifestyle and who see good nutrition as a key to good health. **Subtitle:** The Magazine of Food and Fitness. **Founded:** Mar. 1987. **Freq:** 10/year. **Print Method:** Offset. **Trim Size:** 8 x 10 7/8. **Cols./Page:** 3. **Key Personnel:** Doug Crichton, Editor, phone (205)877-6099; Chris Allen, Publisher, phone (212)878-6500, fax (212)878-6680. **ISSN:** 0886-4446. **Subscription Rates:** $20; $2.95 single issue. **Remarks:** Accepts advertising. **Available Online. URL:** http://www.cookinglight.com.
Ad Rates: BW: $37,620 **Circ:** Paid ★**1425,1070**
4C: $48,900

68 The Daily Herald
CNHI
3800 Colonnade Pkwy., Ste. 450
Birmingham, AL 35243

Community newspaper. **Founded:** 1874. **Freq:** Mon.-Sat. **Print Method:** Offset. **Cols./Page:** 6. **Col. Width:** 24 nonpareils. **Col. Depth:** 301 agate lines. **Key Personnel:** Jim Rainey, General Mgr./Executive Editor; Charles Martin, Publisher; Colleen Mitchell, Advertising Dir. **Subscription Rates:** $25 individuals; $35 other countries. **Remarks:** Accepts advertising. **Formerly:** The Henry Herald.
Ad Rates: BW: $715.95 **Circ:** ‡7,000
4C: $1,115.95
SAU: $6.50
PCI: $5.55

69 Dimension
Woman's Missionary Union
PO Box 830010 Phone: (205)991-8100
Hwy 280, 100 Missionary Ridge Fax: (205)991-4990
Birmingham, AL 35243-5235
Free: (800)968-7301
Publisher E-mail: 70420.55@compuserve.com

Administrative magazine for general officers and directors of the Woman's Missionary Union. **Freq:** Quarterly. **Key Personnel:** Joe Smith, Design Editor; Stephanie Key, Copy Editor. **ISSN:** 0162-6825. **Subscription Rates:** $12.95; $3.25 single issue. **Remarks:** Advertising not accepted.
Circ: (Not Reported)

70 The Jewish Star
PO Box 130603 Phone: (205)956-3929
Birmingham, AL 35213 Fax: (205)967-1417
Free: (888)261-STAR

Jewish/Christian interest newspaper. **Founded:** Sept. 1976. **Freq:** Monthly. **Print Method:** Offset. **Cols./Page:** 6. **Col. Width:** 21 nonpareils. **Col. Depth:** 13 inches. **Key Personnel:** Margie Rudolph, Editor and Publisher; Marvin Rudolph, Publisher. **Subscription Rates:** $10 individuals; $15 two years. **Remarks:** Accepts advertising.
Ad Rates: BW: $600 **Circ:** ‡8,000
4C: $850

71 Kaleidoscope
University of Alabama at Birmingham
University Ctr. Phone: (205)934-3354
Box 76 Fax: (205)934-8050
Birmingham, AL 35294-1150
Publication E-mail: kscope@larry.huc.uab.edu

Collegiate newspaper (broadsheet). **Founded:** 1967. **Freq:** Weekly. **Print Method:** Offset. **Trim Size:** 13 x 21 1/2. **Cols./Page:** 6. **Col. Width:** 2 inches. **Col. Depth:** 21 1/2 inches. **Key Personnel:** Yin Yeap, Business Mgr., yinyeap@uab.edu; Paul Isom, Advisor, paalisom@uab.edu. **Subscription Rates:** $25 individuals. **Remarks:** Accepts advertising. **Available Online. URL:** http://www.thewantads.com/kscope/kscope.htm.
Ad Rates: GLR: $3 **Circ:** Paid 300
BW: $750 Free 8,000
4C: $300
SAU: $6
PCI: $11

72 McCall's Needlework
Primedia Special Interest Publication
405 Riverhills Business Park Phone: (205)995-8860
Birmingham, AL 35242 Fax: (205)995-8428

Magazine emphasizing needlework techniques: knitting, crochet, needlepoint, quilting, and cross-stitch. **Founded:** 1913. **Freq:** Bimonthly. **Print Method:** Offset. **Trim Size:** 7 7/8 x 10 1/2. **Cols./Page:** 3. **Key Personnel:** Judith Carter, Editor; Phyllis Hoffman, Editor-in-Chief; Kip Dubois, Advertising Mgr. **ISSN:** 0024-8924. **Subscription Rates:** $16.95; $3.95 single issue. **Remarks:** Accepts advertising. **Formerly:** McCall's Needlework and Crafts; McCall's Embroidery.
Circ: Non-paid 500

73 Moberly Monitor-Index & Democrat
Community Newspaper Holdings, Inc.
3800 Colonnade Pkwy., Ste. 450 Phone: (205)298-7100
Birmingham, AL 35243 Fax: (205)298-7101
Publication E-mail: moberlymonitor@missvalley.com

General newspaper. **Subtitle:** Daily Newspaper. **Founded:** 1869. **Freq:** Daily (eve.), Sunday (morn.). **Print Method:** Offset. **Trim Size:** 14 x 23. **Cols./Page:** 6. **Col. Width:** 2 1/16 inches. **Col. Depth:** 21 1/2 inches. **Key Personnel:** Ruth Carr, Editor, phone (660)263-4123, fax (660)263-3626; Bob Cunningham, Publisher, phone (660)263-4123, fax (660)263-3626; Judy Orton, Advertising Mgr., phone (660)263-4123, fax (660)263-3626. **Subscription Rates:** $78 individuals carrier; $84 out of area; $90 out of state. **Remarks:** Accepts advertising.
Ad Rates: BW: $816.57 **Circ:** Mon.-Fri. 6,395
4C: $1,079.57 Sun. 6,700
SAU: $10.61
PCI: $10.61

74 Phoenix Magazine
University of Alabama at Birmingham
University Ctr. Phone: (205)934-3354
Box 76 Fax: (205)934-8050
Birmingham, AL 35294-1150
College feature magazine. **Founded:** Nov. 1984. **Freq:** 2/year. **Print Method:** Offset. **Trim Size:** 8 1/2 x 11 in. **Cols./Page:** 3. **Key Personnel:** Paul Isom, Advisor, paulisom@uab.edu. **Subscription Rates:** Free. **Remarks:** Accepts advertising. **Alt. Formats:** CD-ROM.
Ad Rates: BW: $260 **Circ:** Non-paid ‡2,500
4C: $560

75 Progressive Farmer
Southern Progress
PO Box 2581
Birmingham, AL 35202

Agricultural magazine, published in 18 editions, for farmers and ranchers. **Founded:** 1886. **Freq:** Monthly. **Print Method:** Offset. **Trim Size:** 8 x 10 7/8. **Cols./Page:** 3. **Col. Width:** 2 1/4 inches. **Col. Depth:** 140 agate lines. **Key Personnel:** Jack Odle, Editor, jodle@progressivefarmer.com; Ed Dickinson, Publisher; Vicki A. Denmark, General Mgr. **ISSN:** 0033-0760.

Subscription Rates: $16 individuals; $2.95 single issue. **Remarks:** Advertising not accepted for alcoholic beverages. **URL:** http://www.progressivefarmer.com.
Ad Rates: BW: $35,460 **Circ:** Combined ★**628,929**
4C: $49,940

76 Pure Heart Magazine
PO Box 11130 Phone: (205)815-2179
Birmingham, AL 35202 Free: (888)591-4133
Publication E-mail: phsingles@aol.com

Consumer magazine for Christian singles. **Subtitle:** A Publication for Christian Singles. **Founded:** Sept. 1996. **Freq:** Quarterly. **Trim Size:** 8 1/2 x 11. **Cols./Page:** 2. **Key Personnel:** Nicol King, Publisher, nbham@aol.com. **Subscription Rates:** $8 individuals; $2 single issue. **Remarks:** Accepts advertising. **Online:** AmericaOnline. **URL:** http://www.switchboard.pureheart.com; http://pureheartmagazine.com.
Ad Rates: BW: $300 **Circ:** (Not Reported)
4C: $400

77 Research Update
University of Alabama at Birmingham (UAB)
Spain Rehabiliation Center Phone: (205)934-3283
RRTC Training Office, Rm. 529
1717 6th Ave. S.
Birmingham, AL 35233-7330
Publication E-mail: lindsey@sun.rehabm.uab.edu

Newsletter reporting on current research related to spinal cord injury. **Freq:** Annual. **Subscription Rates:** Free. **Remarks:** Advertising not accepted. **URL:** http://www.spinalcord.uab.edu. **Alt. Formats:** Fax on demand.
Circ: Non-paid 3,000

78 The Samford Crimson
Samford University
The Samford Crimson Phone: (205)871-2998
PO Box 292269
Birmingham, AL 35229
Collegiate newspaper. **Founded:** 1915. **Freq:** Weekly. **Print Method:** Offset. **Trim Size:** 11 1/2 x 17 1/2. **Cols./Page:** 5. **Col. Width:** 30 nonpareils. **Col. Depth:** 224 agate lines. **Key Personnel:** Dennis Jones, Advisor; Heather Gibson, Editor; Heather Strehlow, Managing Editor. **Subscription Rates:** $30 individuals. **Remarks:** Accepts advertising.
Ad Rates: BW: $475 **Circ:** Non-paid ‡5,000
PCI: $5.95

79 The Sampson Independent
Community Newspaper Holdings, Inc.
3800 Colonnade Pkwy., Ste. 450 Phone: (205)298-7100
Birmingham, AL 35243 Fax: (205)298-7101

General newspaper. **Founded:** 1924. **Freq:** Tuesday - Sunday. **Print Method:** 14 x 22 1/2. Offset. **Cols./Page:** 6. **Col. Width:** 24 nonpareils. **Col. Depth:** 301 agate lines. **Key Personnel:** Debby Chiarella, Editor. **Subscription Rates:** $84. **Remarks:** Accepts advertising.
Ad Rates: SAU: $6.10 **Circ:** Combined 17,500

80 Southern Accents
Southern Progress
2100 Lakeshore Dr. Phone: (205)877-6000
Birmingham, AL 35209-6721 Fax: (205)877-6600
Free: (888)737-3529

Consumer magazine. **Subtitle:** The Magazine of Fine Southern Interiors and Gardens. **Founded:** 1977. **Freq:** Monthly 6/year. **Print Method:** Offset. **Trim Size:** 8 3/8 x 10 7/8. **Cols./Page:** 3 and 2. **Col. Width:** 28 and 42 nonpareils. **Col. Depth:** 133 agate lines. **Key Personnel:** Mark Mayfield, Editor; Bill Carey, Publisher. **ISSN:** 0149-516X. **Subscription Rates:** $28 individuals; $5 single issue. **Remarks:** Accepts advertising.
Ad Rates: BW: $17,320 **Circ:** Paid ★**377,276**
4C: $23,630

81 Southern Building
Southern Building Code Congress International, Inc.
900 Montclair Rd. Phone: (205)591-1853
Birmingham, AL 35213-1206 Fax: (205)591-0775
Publication E-mail: magnews@shcci.org
Publisher E-mail: info@sbcci.org

Magazine covering building codes, construction, and engineering. **Founded:** 1943. **Freq:** Bimonthly. **Print Method:** Offset. **Trim Size:** 8 1/2 x 11. **Cols./Page:** 3 and 2. **Col. Width:** 26 and 41 nonparells. **Col. Depth:** 140 agate lines. **Key Personnel:** Karla P. Higgs, Manager, khiggs@sbcci.org. **Subscription Rates:** $25 individuals. **Remarks:** Accepts advertising.
Ad Rates: BW: $800 **Circ:** ‡15,900
4C: $2,000

82 Southern Living
Southern Progress
2100 Lakeshore Dr. Phone: (205)877-6000
Birmingham, AL 35209-6721 Fax: (205)877-6600
Free: (888)737-3529

Magazine featuring food, homes, garden, travel, and features edited for southern tastes. **Subtitle:** Lifestyle Magazine of the Changing South. **Founded:** Feb. 1966. **Freq:** Monthly. **Print Method:** Offset. **Trim Size:** 8 x 10 7/8. **Cols./Page:** 3. **Col. Width:** 31 nonpareils. **Col. Depth:** 140 agate lines. **Key Personnel:** John A. Floyd, Jr., Editor; Michael Carlton, Exec. Editor; Eleanor Griffin, Exec. Editor; Kaye Mabry Adams, Exec. Editor; Scott Sheppard, Group Publisher; Kevin Lynch, Publisher; Greg Keyes, VP, Marketing; Rich Smyth, Advertising Dir. **ISSN:** 0038-4305. **Subscription Rates:** $28.96 subscription; $4.95 single issue. **Remarks:** Accepts advertising.
Ad Rates: BW: $64,310 **Circ:** Paid ★**2,518,732**
4C: $89,850

83 Southern Living Vacations
Southern Progress
2100 Lakeshore Dr. Phone: (205)877-6000
Birmingham, AL 35209-6721 Fax: (205)877-6600
Free: (888)737-3529

Themed guides covering travel in the South. **Subtitle:** Family Vacations, Texas Vacations, Summer Vacations, Weekend Vacations. **Founded:** Feb. 1987. **Freq:** Quarterly 3/year. **Print Method:** Offset. **Trim Size:** 8 x 10 7/8. **Cols./Page:** 3. **Col. Width:** 2 1/4 inches. **Col. Depth:** 10 inches. **Key Personnel:** Karen Lingo, Editor. **ISSN:** 0891-8023. **Subscription Rates:** $3.99. **Remarks:** Accepts advertising. **Formerly**: Travel South (1993); Southern Living Travel Guides (1995); Southern Travel.
Ad Rates: BW: $10,580 **Circ:** ‡200,000
4C: $14,330

84 Southern Medical Journal
Southern Medical Association
35 Lakeshore Dr. Phone: (205)945-1840
PO Box 190088 Fax: (205)945-1548
Birmingham, AL 35219-0088
Free: (800)423-4992
Publication E-mail: smj@sma.org

Multispecialty medical journal. **Subtitle:** A Multispecialty Publication of the Southern Medical Association. **Founded:** 1908. **Freq:** Monthly. **Print Method:** Offset. **Trim Size:** 8 1/8 x 10 7/8. **Cols./Page:** 2. **Col. Width:** 20 picas. **Col. Depth:** 56 picas. **Key Personnel:** J. Graham Smith, Jr. MD, Editor; Jessica Scott, Advertising Mgr. **ISSN:** 0038-4348. **Subscription Rates:** $55 individuals. **Remarks:** Accepts advertising. **Online:** Health Gate Data Corp. **URL:** http://www.sma.org/smj. **Alt. Formats:** CD-ROM, Ebsco; Microform.
Ad Rates: BW: $2,508 **Circ:** ‡25,000
4C: $4,383

85 The Southern Shofar
Lawrence Brook
Box 130052 Phone: (205)595-9255
Birmingham, AL 35213 Fax: (205)595-9256
Publication E-mail: soshofar@aol.com

Jewish community newspaper. **Founded:** Dec. 1990. **Freq:** Monthly. **Print Method:** Web offset. **Trim Size:** 10 7/8 x 13 3/4. **Cols./Page:** 5. **Col. Width:** 2 inches. **Col. Depth:** 13 inches. **Key Personnel:** Lawrence Brook, Editor and Publisher; Bob Glina, Advertising. **ISSN:** 1082-3484. **Subscription Rates:** $14 individuals; $24 two years. **Remarks:** Accepts advertising. **URL:** http://www.bham.net/shofar.
Ad Rates: BW: $535 **Circ:** Combined 2,600
PCI: $9.10

86 U.S. Piper
U.S. Pipe and Foundry Co.
PO Box 10406 Phone: (205)254-7162
Birmingham, AL 35202-0406 Fax: (205)254-7165
Publication E-mail: marketing@uspipe.com
Publisher E-mail: marketing@uspipe.com

Trade magazine covering the water and waster water industry. **Founded:** 1928. **Freq:** Semiannual. **Trim Size:** 8 1/2 x 11. **Key Personnel:** George J. Bogs, Sales Promotion Mgr. **Subscription Rates:** Free to qualified subscribers. **Remarks:** Advertising not accepted. **URL:** http://www.uspipe.com.
Circ: Non-paid 8,500

87 The Voice
Communications Voice
898 Arkadelphia Rd. Phone: (205)226-7972
Birmingham, AL 35204 Fax: (205)226-7941
Free: (888)448-6423

United Methodist magazine. **Subtitle:** Serving North Alabama Conference. **Founded:** 1881. **Freq:** Monthly. **Print Method:** Offset. **Trim Size:** 8 1/2 x 11. **Cols./Page:** 3. **Col. Width:** 2 1/4 inches. **Col. Depth:** 10 inches. **Key Personnel:** Ron Council, Director, phone (205)226-7973, rcouncil@umcna.bsc.edu; Harper Cossar, Editor, Dclifton@umcna.bsc.edu. **USPS:** 680-570. **Subscription Rates:** $15 individuals; $1.50 single issue. **Remarks:** Accepts advertising. **Available Online. URL:** http://www.umcna.bsc.edu. **Formerly**: United Methodist Christian Advocate.
Ad Rates: BW: $645 **Circ:** Paid 6700
PCI: $25

88 Weight Watchers Magazine
Southern Progress
2100 Lakeshore Dr. Phone: (205)877-6000
Birmingham, AL 35209-6721 Fax: (205)877-6600
Free: (888)737-3529

Magazine promoting self-esteem through healthy eating, fitness and weight-control. Reports on health, nutrition, fitness, food, healthful recipes, fashion and beauty. **Founded:** Feb. 1968. **Freq:** 9/year. **Print Method:** Offset. **Trim Size:** 8 x 10 7/8. **Cols./Page:** 3. **Col. Width:** 2 1/4 inches. **Col. Depth:** 140 agate lines. **Key Personnel:** Kate Greer, Editor, phone (205)877-5730, kate_greer@spc.com; Jeff Ward, Publisher, phone (205)877-6489, fax (205)877-6469. **ISSN:** 0043-2180. **Subscription Rates:** $18 individuals; $2.95 single issue. **Remarks:** Accepts advertising. **URL:** http://www.mag@mindspring.com.
Ad Rates: BW: $29,240 **Circ:** Paid ★**1,143,045**
4C: $38,000

89 Wheels of Time
American Truck Historical Society
PO Box 531168 Phone: (205)870-0566
Birmingham, AL 35253-1168 Fax: (205)870-3069
Publisher E-mail: aths@mindspring.com

Magazine dedicated to news about the collection and preservation of trucks, the trucking industry, and pioneers of the industry. **Founded:** Oct. 1980. **Freq:** Semimonthly. **Print Method:** Offset. **Trim Size:** 8 1/2 x 11. **Cols./Page:** 2. **Col. Width:** 3 5/8 inches. **Col. Depth:** 9 1/2 inches. **Key Personnel:** Shirley Sponholtz, Editor; Larry L. Scheef, Managing Dir. **ISSN:** 0738-565X. **Subscription Rates:** $25 individuals; $35 other countries; $3.50 single issue. **Remarks:** Advertising accepted; rates available upon request. **URL:** http://www.aths.org.
Circ: 21,500

90 Masada Corp.
3900 Montclair Rd., Ste. 301 Phone: (205)871-3470
Birmingham, AL 35213 Fax: (205)871-3574
Free: (800)767-3470

Founded: 1978. **Key Personnel:** Daryl Harms, Contact; Terry Johnson, President; Joe Gibbs, Contact. **Cities Served:** subscribing households 62,139; 60 channels; 6 community access channels.

91 McDonald Investments
1 Office Park Circle, Ste. 300 Phone: (205)879-0456
Birmingham, AL 35223 Fax: (205)879-0479

Key Personnel: William W. McDonald, President. **Cities Served:** Birmingham, AL.

92 Time Warner Cable—Birmingham Division
6429 1st Ave. S. Phone: (205)290-1300
Birmingham, AL 35212 Fax: (205)599-5657

Founded: 1976. **Formerly**: Birmingham Bessemer Cable Communications. **Key Personnel:** Mike Hugunin, President; Terri Weber, Contact; Tim Stout, Program Mgr.; Bill Day, Contact; Rod Clark, Contact. **Cities Served:** subscribing households 78,000; 72 channels; 1 community access channel; 56 hours per week community access programming.

93 WABM-TV - 68
517 Beacon Pkwy. W. Phone: (205)943-2168
Birmingham, AL 35209 Fax: (205)290-2114

Format: Commercial TV. **Networks:** United Paramount Network. **Owner:** Glencairn Broadcasting, at above address. **Founded:** 1980. **Formerly**: WCAJ-TV. **Operating Hours:** Continuous; 50% network, 50% local. **ADI:** Birmingham (Gadsden), AL. **Key Personnel:** Stephen Mann, General Mgr.; David Inman, Business Mgr.; John Batson, Chief Engineer; Margaret King, Traffic Mgr. **Local Programs:** *Children's Explorers Club.*

94 WAGG-AM - 1320
424 16th St. N. Phone: (205)254-1820
Birmingham, AL 35203-1929 Fax: (205)254-1833

Format: Religious. **Networks:** Independent. **Founded:** 1950. **Operating Hours:** Sunrise-sunset. **ADI:** Birmingham (Gadsden), AL. **Key Personnel:** Kirkwood Balton, General Mgr. **Wattage:** 5000.

95 WAPI-AM - 1070
244 Goodwin Crest Dr., Ste. 300 Phone: (205)942-1004
Birmingham, AL 35205 Fax: (205)942-8959

Format: News; Talk. **Networks:** CNN Radio. **Founded:** 1922. **Operating Hours:** Continuous. **ADI:** Birmingham (Gadsden), AL. **Key Personnel:** Ben McWhorter, General Sales Mgr.; Davis Hawkins, General Mgr.; Frank Giarding, Chief Engineer; Kelly Cruise, Promotions Dir.; Lisa Hollyfield, News Dir.; Brent E. Seale, Program Dir. **Wattage:** 50,000. **Ad Rates:** $10-60 per unit. **URL:** http://www.quicklink.net/wapi/.

96 WATV-AM - 900
3025 Ensley Ave. Phone: (205)780-2014
Box 39054
Birmingham, AL 35208

Format: Full Service. **Networks:** ABC. **Founded:** 1946. **Operating Hours:** Continuous; 10% network, 90% local. **ADI:** Birmingham (Gadsden), AL. **Key Personnel:** Erskine R. Faush, Contact; Shelley Stewart, Contact; Ron January, Music Dir. **Wattage:** 1000. **Ad Rates:** $22-33 for 30 seconds; $28-52 for 60 seconds.

97 WBFR-FM - 89.5
244 Goodwin Crest Dr., Ste. 118 Phone: (205)942-3530
Birmingham, AL 35209-3711

Format: Religious; Eclectic. **Networks:** Family Stations Radio. **Owner:** Family Stations, Inc., 290 Hegenberger Rd., Oakland, CA 94621, (415)568-6200. **Founded:** 1989. **Operating Hours:** Continuous. **ADI:** Birmingham (Gadsden), AL. **Key Personnel:** Bill Sadlier, Contact; David Pope, Operations Mgr. **Wattage:** 100. **Ad Rates:** Noncommercial.

98 WBHK-FM - 98.7
2301 1st Ave. N., Ste. 102 Phone: (205)322-2987
Birmingham, AL 35203 Fax: (205)324-6327

Format: Urban Contemporary. **Networks:** ABC. **Owner:** Cox Radio, Inc., at above address. **Formerly:** WLBI-FM. **Operating Hours:** Continuous. **ADI:** Birmingham (Gadsden), AL. **Key Personnel:** Mike Abrams, Program Dir., mike.abrams@cox.com; Regina Waller, News Dir., regina.waller@cox.com; Paul Bankston, Dir. of Sales, phone (205)326-2545, paul.bankston@cox.com. **Local Programs:** *Talk Back*, Oliver Brower; *Streets of the South*, Regina Waller. **Wattage:** 10,000.

99 WBIQ-TV - 10
2112 11th Ave. S., Ste. 400 Phone: (205)328-8756
Birmingham, AL 35205 Fax: (205)251-2192
E-mail: w.wood@aptu.org

Format: Public TV. **Networks:** Public Broadcasting Service (PBS). **Owner:** Alabama Educational Television Commission, at above address. **Founded:** 1955. **Operating Hours:** Continuous. **ADI:** Birmingham (Gadsden), AL. **Key Personnel:** Henry Bonner, Program Dir.; Judy Stone, Exec. Dir., jstone@aptv.org; Joanna Cleary, News Dir.; Windell Wood, Dir. of Eng.; Phil Hutcheson, Deputy Director, CFO. **Local Programs:** *For the Record*. **Wattage:** 316,000 visual; 31,600 aural. **Ad Rates:** Noncommercial. **URL:** http://www.aptv.org.

100 WBMG-TV - 42
2075 Golden Crest Dr. Phone: (205)322-4200
Birmingham, AL 35209 Fax: (205)320-2713

Format: Commercial TV. **Networks:** CBS. **Founded:** 1965. **Operating Hours:** 5:30-4:59 a.m. weekdays; 6:30-3 a.m. Saturday and Sunday. **ADI:** Birmingham (Gadsden), AL. **Key Personnel:** Hoyle Broome, General Mgr.

101 WBRC-TV - 6
Atop Red Mountain Phone: (205)322-6666
Box 6 Fax: (205)583-4386
Birmingham, AL 35201
Free: (800)624-WBRC
E-mail: wbrctv@traveller.com

Format: Commercial TV. **Networks:** Fox. **Founded:** July 1, 1949. **Operating Hours:** Continuous. **ADI:** Birmingham (Gadsden), AL. **Key Personnel:** Deborah Wilson, VP/Sales; Stan Knott, Vice Pres./Gen. Mgr.; Jerry Thorn, VP of Engineering; Joanna Bellanger, Programming Coord. **Local Programs:** *News*. **Wattage:** 100 KW. **Ad Rates:** Advertising accepted; rates available upon request. **URL:** http://www.wbrc.com.

102 WCIQ-TV - 7
2112 11th Ave. South, Ste 400 Phone: (205)328-8756
Birmingham, AL 35205-2884 Fax: (205)251-2192
Free: (800)239-5233
E-mail: w.wood@apto.org

Format: Public TV. **Simulcasts:** WBIQ-TV. **Networks:** Public Broadcasting Service (PBS). **Founded:** Jan. 1953. **Operating Hours:** 7 a.m.-11 p.m. daily. **ADI:** Birmingham (Gadsden), AL. **Key Personnel:** Henry Bonner, Program Dir.; Judy Stone, Exec. Dir.; Windell Wood, Dir. of Eng.; Phil Hutcheson, Deputy Director, CFO. **Wattage:** 316,000 visual; 31,600 aural. **Ad Rates:** Noncommercial. **URL:** http://www.aptv.org.

WDIQ-TV - See Dozier

103 WDJC-FM - 93.7
Box 59621 Phone: (205)879-3324
Birmingham, AL 35259-9621

Format: Religious. **Owner:** Donald C. Crawford, PO Box 3003, Blue Bell, PA 19422-3003. **Founded:** 1968. **Operating Hours:** Continuous; 100% local. **ADI:** Birmingham (Gadsden), AL. **Key Personnel:** Larry Adcock, Sales Mgr.; Rachel H. Miller, Program Dir. **Wattage:** 100,000.

WEIQ-TV - See Mobile

104 WENN-FM - 107.7
424 16th St. N. Phone: (205)254-1820
PO Box 697 Fax: (205)254-1833
Birmingham, AL 35203-0697

Format: Urban Contemporary. **Networks:** Independent. **Founded:** 1969. **Operating Hours:** Continuous. **ADI:** Birmingham (Gadsden), AL. **Key Personnel:** Kirkwood Balton, General Mgr. **Wattage:** 100,000.

105 WERC-AM - 960
530 Beacon Pkwy. W., Ste. 600 Phone: (205)942-9600
Birmingham, AL 35209 Fax: (205)985-2933

Format: News; Talk. **Networks:** ABC. **Founded:** 1925. **Operating Hours:** Continuous. **ADI:** Birmingham (Gadsden), AL. **Key Personnel:** Bill Thomas, President; John Jenkins, V.P./Programming Mgr., jjenkins@mindspring.com. **Local Programs:** *The Fineline (Current Events)*, Dee Fine; *John Ed Show (Humor)*, John Byrd; *Paul Finebaum (Sports)*, Pat Smith. **Wattage:** 5000. **URL:** http://www.werc960am.com.

WFIQ-TV - See Florence

106 WGIB-FM - 91.9
1137 10th Pl. Phone: (205)323-1516
Birmingham, AL 35205 Fax: (205)323-2747

Format: Religious. **Founded:** 1983. **Operating Hours:** Continuous. **ADI:** Birmingham (Gadsden), AL. **Key Personnel:** Steve Kluth, Contact; Michael C. Scott. **Wattage:** 1,000. **Ad Rates:** Noncommercial.

WGIQ-TV - See Louisville

107 WHIQ-TV - 25
212 11th Ave. S., Ste. 400 Phone: (205)328-8756
Birmingham, AL 35205-2884 Fax: (205)251-2192
Free: (800)239-5233
E-mail: w.wood@aptu.org

Format: Public TV. **Simulcasts:** WBIQ-TV. **Networks:** Public Broadcasting Service (PBS). **Founded:** Oct. 1965. **Operating Hours:** 7 a.m.-11 p.m. daily. **ADI:** Huntsville-Decatur-Florence, AL. **Key Personnel:** Henry Bonner, Program Dir.; Judy Stone, Exec. Dir.; Windell Wood, Dir. of Eng.; Phil Hutcheson, Deputy Director, CFO. **Local Programs:** *For the Record*, Johanna Cleary. **Wattage:** 1,225,000 visual; 122,500 aural. **URL:** http://www.aptv.org.

WIIQ-TV - See Demopolis

108 WJLD-AM - 1400
1449 Spaulding Ishkooda Rd. Phone: (205)942-1776
Birmingham, AL 35211 Fax: (205)942-4814
E-mail: wjld@juno.com

Format: Blues; Gospel; Talk. **Networks:** ABC; Mutual Broadcasting System; American Urban Radio. **Owner:** Richardson Broadcasting Corp., at above address. **Founded:** 1942. **Operating Hours:** Continuous; 10% network, 90% local. **ADI:** Birmingham (Gadsden), AL. **Key Personnel:** Gary Richardson, Contact; Curtis Bell, Music Dir.; Bob Friedman, Sales Mgr. **Local Programs:** *Blues and the Oldies Party*, Curtis Bell; *Curtis Evening Drive*, Curtis Bell; *Morning Talk-The Talk of the Morning*, Gary Richardson. **Wattage:** 1000. **Ad Rates:** $10-29 for 30 seconds; $14-35 for 60 seconds.

109 WJOX-AM - 690
244 Goodwin Crest Dr., Ste. 300 Phone: (205)942-6690
Birmingham, AL 35209 Fax: (205)942-8959
E-mail: wjox@quicklink.net

Format: Sports. **Founded:** 1947. **Formerly:** WVOK-AM (1991). **Operating Hours:** Continuous. **ADI:** Birmingham (Gadsden), AL. **Key Personnel:** Davis Hawkins, General Mgr.; Brent E. Seale, Program Dir. **Local Programs:** *Sports Jamboree*, Lee Davis, 205917-1935; *Sports Talk 690*, Lee Davis, (205)917-1935. **Wattage:** 50,000. **Ad Rates:** $50-125 per unit.

110 WJSR-FM - 91.1
2601 Carson Rd. Phone: (205)856-7702
Birmingham, AL 35215-3098 Fax: (205)853-0340
E-mail: wjsr911fm@hotmail.com

Format: Adult Contemporary. **Owner:** Jefferson State Community College, at above address, (205)853-1200. **Founded:** 1977. **Operating Hours:** 7:30 a.m.-10 p.m. **ADI:** Birmingham (Gadsden), AL. **Key Personnel:** Ray Edwards, Contact, phone (205)856-6095. **Wattage:** 100. **Ad Rates:** Noncommercial. **URL:** http://www.jscc.cc.al.us/wjsr.htm.

111 WLJR-FM - 88.5
2200 Briarwood Way Phone: (205)978-2278
Birmingham, AL 35243 Fax: (205)824-8419

Format: Contemporary Christian. **Networks:** Moody Broadcasting. **Owner:** Briarwood Presbyterian Church, at above address. **Operating Hours:** Continuous. **Key Personnel:** James Hulgan, Manager, jhulgan@briarwood.org; Tom Arledge, Engineer, tarledge@briarwood.org. **Wattage:** 200. **Ad Rates:** Noncommercial.

112 WLPH-AM - 1480
PO Box 100067 Phone: (205)956-5470
Birmingham, AL 35210 Fax: (205)956-5471

Format: Religious. **Networks:** Independent. **Founded:** 1960. **Formerly:** WIXI-AM (1964). **Operating Hours:** Sunrise-sunset. **ADI:** Birmingham (Gadsden), AL. **Key Personnel:** Carol Hatcher, General Mgr.; Frankie Haonir, Program Dir.; Alice Kennedy, Traffic Dir.; Mike Croce, Assistant Product; Tom Coledge, Chief Engineer. **Wattage:** 5000. **Ad Rates:** $5-10 for 30 seconds; $5.25-12 for 60 seconds.

113 WMJJ-FM - 96.5
530 Beacon Hwy. W., Ste. 600 Phone: (205)942-9600
Birmingham, AL 35209 Fax: (205)942-2536

Format: Adult Contemporary. **Founded:** 1982. **Operating Hours:** Continuous. **ADI:** Birmingham (Gadsden), AL. **Key Personnel:** Bill Thomas, President/CEO; John Jenkins, V.P./Product, jjenkins@mindspring.com. **Local Programs:** *Rob & Shannon Show*, Shannon Stevens. **Wattage:** 100,000. **URL:** http://www.magic96fm.com.

114 WTTO-TV - 21
651 Beacon Parkway W., Ste. 105 Phone: (205)943-2168
P.O. Box 832100 Fax: (205)290-2114
Birmingham, AL 35209

Format: Commercial TV. **Networks:** Warner Brothers Studios. **Owner:** H R Broadcasting Corp. of Birmingham, Inc., 3456 N. Maple Dr., Beverly Hills, CA 90210, (213)281-2600. **Founded:** 1982. **ADI:** Birmingham (Gadsden), AL. **Key Personnel:** Stephen Mann, Contact; Lucrecia Rubio, Program Dir.; Karen Cole, Contact; Sandy Stewart, Contact; John Batson, Contact; Phillip Shiver, Chief Engineer; Margaret King, Contact; Mark Jerald, Contact. **Ad Rates:** Advertising accepted; rates available upon request.

115 WVSU-FM - 91.1
800 Lakeshore Dr. Phone: (205)870-2877
Birmingham, AL 35229 Fax: (205)870-2586

Format: Jazz. **Networks:** Independent. **Owner:** Samford University, at above address, (205)870-2763. **Operating Hours:** 18 hours daily; 100% local. **ADI:** Birmingham (Gadsden), AL. **Key Personnel:** Pete Williams, Station Mgr.; David Stenhouse, PSA/Production Dir.; Ryan Morgan, News Dir.; Mike Murphy, Assistant Manager/Alternative Music Dir. **Wattage:** 125.

116 WVTM-TV - 13
1732 Valley View Dr Phone: (205)933-1313
Birmingham, AL 35209 Fax: (205)933-7516

Format: Commercial TV. **Networks:** NBC. **Formerly:** WAPI-TV. **Operating Hours:** Continuous. **ADI:** Birmingham (Gadsden), AL. **Key Personnel:** Gary Stokes, General Mgr.; Connie Howard, News Dir.; Mark Beckwith, General Sales Mgr.; Greg Miller, Dir. of Station Operations.

117 WYSF-FM - 94.5
244 Goodwin Crest Dr., Ste. 300 Phone: (205)945-4646
Birmingham, AL 35209-3714 Fax: (205)945-3999

Format: Adult Contemporary. **Networks:** ABC. **Owner:** Dick Broadcasting, at above address. **Founded:** 1947. **Formerly:** WAPI-FM (1994); WMXQ-FM. **Operating Hours:** Continuous. **ADI:** Birmingham (Gadsden), AL. **Key Personnel:** Davis Hawkins, General Mgr., phone (205)945-4646; Jeff Tyson, Program Dir.; Kelly Cruise, Promotions Dir.; Valerie Vining, Music Dir.; Steve Harrison, General Sales Mgr.; Steve Atkins,

Production Dir.; Lisa Holifield, News Dir. **Wattage:** 100,000. **Ad Rates:** $35-200 per unit. **URL:** http://www.softrock94.

118 WZZK-AM - 610
530 Beacon Pkwy. W., No. 300 Phone: (205)961-1100
Birmingham, AL 35209-3175 Fax: (205)916-1150

Format: Contemporary Country. **Simulcasts:** WZZK-FM. **Founded:** 1927. **Operating Hours:** Continuous. **ADI:** Birmingham (Gadsden), AL. **Key Personnel:** Jerdan Bullard, General Mgr.; John Henley, General Sales Mgr.; Jim Tice, Program Dir.; Despina Vodantis, Promotions Mgr.; Melanie Berry, News Dir. **Wattage:** 5000 day; 1000 night. **Ad Rates:** $40-325 per unit.

119 WZZK-FM - 104.7
530 Beacon Pkwy. W., No. 300 Phone: (205)942-7800
Birmingham, AL 35209-3175 Fax: (205)916-1151

Format: Contemporary Country. **Simulcasts:** WZZK-AM. **Founded:** 1948. **Operating Hours:** Continuous. **ADI:** Birmingham (Gadsden), AL. **Key Personnel:** Richard Ferguson, Contact; John Henley, General Sales Mgr.; Jerdan Bullard, General Mgr.; Jim Tice, Program Dir.; Despina Vodantis, Promotions Mgr.; Melanie Berry, News Dir. **Wattage:** 100,000. **Ad Rates:** $40-325 per unit.

BOAZ

NE AL. Marshall Co. 15 mi. NW of Gadsden.

120 WBSA-AM - 1300
1525 Wills Rd. Phone: (205)593-4264
Boaz, AL 35957 Fax: (205)543-4265

Format: Gospel; Southern Gospel. **Networks:** Independent. **Owner:** Watkins Broadcasting Co., Inc, 1525 Wills Rd., Boaz, AL 35957, Fax: (205)593-4265. **Founded:** 1959. **Formerly:** WAVC-AM (1961). **Operating Hours:** 6 a.m.-10 p.m.; 100% local. **Key Personnel:** Roger Watkins, Station Manager/General Manager. **Wattage:** 1000. **Ad Rates:** $5.00-7.00 for 30 seconds; $6.00-7.75 for 60 seconds.

BREWTON†, pop. 6,680.

S. AL. Escambia Co. 60 mi. N. of Pensacola, FL. Manufactures paper, textiles, lumber. Iron works. Timber. Agriculture. Cotton, livestock.

121 The Brewton Standard & The Plus
Brewton Newspapers, Inc.
PO Box 887 Phone: (205)867-4876
Brewton, AL 36427 Fax: (205)867-4877

Community newspaper. **Founded:** 1885. **Freq:** Semiweekly Wed. and Mon. **Print Method:** Offset. **Cols./Page:** 6. **Col. Width:** 12 picas. **Col. Depth:** 301 agate lines. **Key Personnel:** George R. Turner, Editor and Publisher. **Subscription Rates:** $35 individuals; $45 out of state. **Remarks:** Accepts advertising.
Ad Rates: BW: $954.60 **Circ:** ‡4,100
4C: $1154.66
SAU: $8.30
PCI: $8.30

122 WEBJ-AM - 1240
301 Downing St. Phone: (334)867-5717
Brewton, AL 36426 Fax: (334)867-5718

Format: Oldies. **Networks:** Independent. **Founded:** 1947. **Operating Hours:** 6 a.m.-8 p.m.; 5 a.m. - 12 midnight. **Key Personnel:** Dennis Dunaway, Gen. Manager; Candy Smith, Music Dir. **Local Programs:** *Brewton Today*, Gene Cashman; *Farm Agent*, Gene Cashman; *Veteran's Affairs*, Gene Cashman. **Wattage:** 1000. **Ad Rates:** $4 for 30 seconds; $5 for 60 seconds.

BRIDGEPORT

NE AL. Jackson Co. 30 mi. NE of Huntsville.

123 WBTS-AM - 1480
PO Box U Phone: (205)495-2274
Bridgeport, AL 35740-0080 Fax: (205)495-2274

Format: Religious; News; Sports. **Networks:** Christian Broadcasting (CBN); Sun Radio. **Owner:** Bridgeport Broadcasting Co., at above address. **Founded:** 1961. **Operating Hours:** Sunrise-sunset. **Key Personnel:** Roy C. McCloud, Sales/Station Mgr. **Wattage:** 1000. **Ad Rates:** $1.75 for 15 seconds; $2.25 for 30 seconds; $3 for 60 seconds.

BUTLER†, pop. 1,882.

SW AL. Choctaw Co. 35 mi. SE of Meridian, MS. Manufactures textiles, lumber. Pulpwood and timber.

124 Choctaw Advocate
PO Box 475 Phone: (205)459-2858
Butler, AL 36904-2934 Fax: (205)459-3000

Community newspaper. **Founded:** June 11, 1890. **Freq:** Weekly (Thurs.). **Print Method:** Offset. **Trim Size:** 13 x 21. **Cols./Page:** 6. **Col. Width:** 25 nonpareils. **Col. Depth:** 301 agate lines. **Key Personnel:** Tommy J. Campbell, Editor and Publisher. **USPS:** 106-200. **Subscription Rates:** $26 individuals. **Remarks:** Accepts advertising.
Ad Rates: BW: $441 **Circ:** ‡4,400
PCI: $4

125 WPRN-FM - 107.7
PO Box 566 Phone: (205)459-3222
Butler, AL 36904 Fax: (205)459-4140

Format: Country; Southern Gospel. **Networks:** Alabama Radio (ALANET); ABC. **Owner:** Butler Broadcasting Corp., at above address. **Founded:** 1959. **Formerly:** WPRN-AM. **Operating Hours:** Sunrise-sunset. **Key Personnel:** Darryl Jackson, Contact; George Vice, Sales Mgr.; Lisa Downey, Traffic Mgr.; Steve O'Conner, Operations Mgr./Program Dir. **Wattage:** 5000. **Ad Rates:** Advertising accepted; rates available upon request. Combined advertising rates available with WKZB-FM.

CALERA

C. AL. Shelby Co. 20 mi. SE of Birmingham.

126 WBYE-AM - 1370
PO Box 1727 Phone: (205)668-1370
Calera, AL 35040

Format: Country; Gospel; Sports. **Networks:** Alabama Radio (ALANET). **Owner:** Benjamin H. Franklin, at above address. **Founded:** 1958. **Operating Hours:** 12 hours daily; 10% network, 90% local. **Key Personnel:** Benjamin H. Franklin, Contact; Elizabeth Franklin, Contact. **Local Programs:** *Good Country Music*; *Midday Gospel Favorites*; *Sports Page*. **Wattage:** 1000. **Ad Rates:** $5 for 30 seconds; $10 for 60 seconds; $25-60 per unit.

CAMDEN†, pop. 1,742.

C. AL. Wilcox Co.

127 Wilcox Progressive Era
Progressive Era
PO Box 100 Phone: (334)682-4422
Camden, AL 36726 Fax: (334)682-5163

Local newspaper. **Freq:** Weekly. **Key Personnel:** Hollis Curl, Editor and Publisher.

128 WCOX-AM - 1450
Box 820 Phone: (205)682-9048
Camden, AL 36726 Fax: (205)682-4726

Format: Gospel; Religious; Talk. **Operating Hours:** 5 a.m.-7 p.m. **Key Personnel:** Leroy T. Griffith, General Mgr.; William Pompey, President; Paul Johnson, Contact. **Wattage:** 1000.

129 WCOX-FM - 102.3
Box 820 Phone: (205)682-9048
Camden, AL 36726 Fax: (205)682-4726

Format: Gospel; Religious; Talk. **Founded:** 1989. **Operating Hours:** 5 a.m.-midnight. **Key Personnel:** Leroy T. Griffith, General Mgr.; William Pompey, President; Paul Johnson, Contact. **Wattage:** 6000.

CARROLLTON†, pop. 923.

C. AL. Pickens Co. 30 mi. W. of Tuscaloosa. Lumber milling and cotton ginning.

130 Pickens County Herald
PO Box 390 Phone: (205)367-2217
Carrollton, AL 35447 Fax: (205)367-2217

Community newspaper. **Founded:** 1848. **Freq:** Weekly. **Cols./Page:** 6. **Col. Width:** 2 1/16 inches. **Col. Depth:** 21 1/2 inches. **Key Personnel:** Doug Sanders, Jr., Editor and Publisher. **Subscription Rates:** $20 in county; $30 out of country. **Remarks:** Accepts advertising.
Ad Rates: SAU: $4.93 **Circ:** Paid ‡4,500
PCI: $4.30

131 WCKO-FM - 94.1
Hwy. 17 S. Phone: (205)367-8136
Carrollton, AL 35447 Fax: (205)367-8689

Format: Oldies. **Networks:** AP. **Owner:** FirstStar Broadcasting Inc., at above address. **Founded:** 1970. **Formerly:** WAQT-FM (1991). **Operating Hours:** Continuous. **Key Personnel:** Bill Fancher, General Mgr. **Wattage:** 100,000. **Ad Rates:** $7.50-14 for 30 seconds; $10-22 for 60 seconds.

132 WRAG-AM - 590
Hwy. 17 S. Phone: (205)367-8136
PO Box 71 Fax: (205)367-8689
Carrollton, AL 35447-0071

Format: Gospel; Southern Gospel; Urban Contemporary. **Networks:** Alabama Radio (ALANET). **Owner:** FirstStar Broadcasting Systems Inc., at above address. **Founded:** 1951. **Operating Hours:** 6 a.m.-sunset. **Key Personnel:** Mike Hall, Contact. **Wattage:** 1000. **Ad Rates:** $3.30-5.60 for 30 seconds; $4.40-7.45 for 60 seconds.

CENTRE†, pop. 2,351.

NE AL. Cherokee Co. 20 mi. S. of Fort Payne.

133 Cherokee County Herald
News Publishing Co.
107 W. 1st Ave. Phone: (205)927-5236
Centre, AL 35960 Fax: (205)927-4853

Newspaper with a Democratic orientation. **Founded:** 1939. **Freq:** Weekly (Wed.). **Print Method:** Offset. **Trim Size:** 13 x 21 1/4. **Cols./Page:** 6. **Col. Width:** 12 picas. **Col. Depth:** 295 agate lines. **Key Personnel:** Paul W. Dale, Editor, phone (205)927-5037; B.H. Mooney III, Publisher. **USPS:** 102-380. **Subscription Rates:** $14 individuals; $22 out of area. **Remarks:** Accepts advertising.
Ad Rates: GLR: $6.80 **Circ:** Paid 5,000
BW: $867
PCI: $6.80

134 WAGC-AM - 1560
PO Box 602 Phone: (205)927-5353
Centre, AL 35960 Fax: (205)927-4722

Format: Country. **Networks:** USA Radio. **Owner:** Bill Shedd, at above address. **Founded:** 1962. **Operating Hours:** 6 a.m.-sunset; 100% local. **Key Personnel:** Bill Shedd, Pres./Owner; Tony Michael, Office Mgr.; Bill Shedd, General Mgr. **Wattage:** 1000. **Ad Rates:** $4.25-6.50 for 30 seconds; $6.00-8.00 for 60 seconds.

135 WEIS-AM - 990
PO Box 297 Phone: (256)927-5152
Centre, AL 35960 Fax: (256)927-6503
Free: (888)454-5002
E-mail: jbaker@peop.tdsnet.com

Format: Country; Southern Gospel. **Networks:** Alabama Radio (ALANET); ABC. **Owner:** Baker Enterprises, Inc., at above address. **Founded:** 1961. **Operating Hours:** Continuous; 5% network, 95% local. **Key Personnel:** Jerry Baker, Co-Owner/Sports Dir., jbaker@peop.tdsnet.com; Shelia Richardson. **Wattage:** 1000. **Ad Rates:** $5.00-8.25 for 30 seconds; $5.50-10.00 for 60 seconds.

CENTREVILLE†, pop. 2,504.

C. AL. Bibb Co. 34 mi. SE of Tuscaloosa. Lumber, grist mills; cotton gin. Manufactures wooden toys, pulpwood. Timber. Agriculture. Cotton, corn.

136 Centreville Press
Bibb Publications
119 Court Square W. Phone: (205)926-9769
PO Box 127 Fax: (205)926-9760
Centreville, AL 35042-0127
Community newspaper. **Founded:** Oct. 29, 1879. **Freq:** Weekly (Wed.). **Print Method:** Offset. Accepts mats. **Cols./Page:** 6. **Col. Width:** 24 nonpareils. **Col. Depth:** 301 agate lines. **Key Personnel:** Judy Farnetti, General Mgr.; Tammy Ingram, Advertising Mgr. **Subscription Rates:** $19.44 individuals. **Remarks:** Accepts advertising.
Ad Rates: GLR: $.28 **Circ:** 4,200
BW: $490.20
SAU: $4.25
PCI: $4

CHATOM†, pop. 1,122.

SW AL. Washington Co. 55 mi. N. of Mobile. Naval stores. Cotton-gins. Oil wells. Pine timber. Agriculture. Cotton, corn, poultry.

137 Washington County News
Washington County Publications, Inc.
305 Jordan St. Phone: (334)847-2599
PO Box 510 Fax: (334)847-3847
Chatom, AL 36518
Newspaper. **Founded:** 1892. **Freq:** Weekly (Wed.). **Print Method:** Offset. **Trim Size:** 14 x 23. **Cols./Page:** 6. **Col. Width:** 2 1/16 inches. **Col. Depth:** 21.5 picas. **Key Personnel:** Jim Specht, Publisher. **Subscription Rates:** $19.26

individuals plus tax; $23.76. **Remarks:** Accepts advertising. **Formerly**: Call-News Dispatch.
Ad Rates: BW: $795 **Circ:** ‡4,000
4C: $9.10 5,000
PCI: $5

CITRONELLE

138 WHXT-FM - 102.1
21615 Odom Rd. Phone: (334)886-5454
PO Box 127 Fax: (334)380-9029
Citronelle, AL 36522

Format: Country. **Owner:** Lyn Communication of Mobile County Inc., at above address. **Founded:** 1989. **Formerly**: WKQR-FM (1992). **Operating Hours:** 6 a.m. - 10 p.m. **Key Personnel:** Tom Wilson, General Mgr.; Melisa Young, Office Mgr. **Local Programs:** *Sunday in the Heart of Country*, Larry Sutton; *Weekday Morning Gospel*, Melissa Young. **Wattage:** 25,000. **Ad Rates:** $5 for 30 seconds; $6 for 60 seconds.

CLANTON†, pop. 5,832.

C. AL. Chitton Co. 40 mi. NW of Montgomery. Residential.

139 Chilton County News
PO Box 189 Phone: (205)755-0110
Clanton, AL 35046 Fax: (205)755-6227

Community newspaper. **Founded:** 1922. **Freq:** Weekly (Thurs.). **Print Method:** Offset. **Trim Size:** 11 x 14. **Cols./Page:** 5. **Col. Width:** 2 1/16 inches. **Col. Depth:** 13 inches. **Key Personnel:** Bob Tucker, Editor and Publisher. **ISSN:** 0888-451X. **Subscription Rates:** $17.50 individuals; $22.50 out of state. **Remarks:** Accepts advertising.
Ad Rates: GLR: $.31 **Circ:** Paid 2,000
BW: $282.10
SAU: $4.06
PCI: $4.34

140 The Clanton Advertiser
Selma Times Journal
PO Box 1379 Phone: (205)755-5747
Clanton, AL 35045 Fax: (205)755-5857

Community newspaper. **Founded:** 1890. **Freq:** Semiweekly (Wed. and Fri.). **Print Method:** Offset. **Cols./Page:** 6. **Col. Width:** 26 nonpareils. **Col. Depth:** 301 agate lines. **Key Personnel:** Michael R. Kelley, Editor and Publisher; Dan Cook, Advertising Dir.; David McElroy, General Mgr. **Subscription Rates:** $23 individuals; $30 out of state. **Remarks:** Accepts advertising. **Formerly**: Independent Advertiser (1990).
Ad Rates: PCI: $5.81 **Circ:** Paid ‡4,000
Free ‡8,500

141 WEZZ-FM - 97.7
PO Box 1820 Phone: (205)755-0980
Clanton, AL 35046 Fax: (205)280-0980

Format: Country; Contemporary Country. **Networks:** ABC; Alabama Radio (ALANET). **Owner:** James Dennis, at above address, (205)755-0966, Fax: (205)280-0980. **Founded:** 1953. **Formerly**: WKLF-FM. **Operating Hours:** 5 a.m.-10 p.m.; 5% network, 95% local. **Key Personnel:** James Dennis, Manager. **Local Programs:** *Chilton County High Football*, James Dennis, (205)755-0980, Fax (205)280-0980. **Wattage:** 3000. **Ad Rates:** $5-9 for 30 seconds; $7-11 for 60 seconds.

142 WKLF-AM - 980
PO Box 1820 Phone: (205)755-0980
Clanton, AL 35046 Fax: (205)280-0980

Format: Religious. **Networks:** Alabama Radio (ALANET). **Founded:** 1947. **Operating Hours:** 6 a.m.-sunset; 5% network, 95% local. **Key Personnel:** James Dennis, Manager. **Local Programs:** *Americas Favorites*, Jack Dennis, (205)755-0980; *Singing the Gospel with Billy Lawrence*, Jack Dennis, (205)755-0980; *Sunday Morning Gospel*, Jack Dennis, (205)755-0980. **Wattage:** 1000. **Ad Rates:** $5-9 for 30 seconds; $7-11 for 60 seconds.

CLAYTON†, pop. 1,589.

SE AL. Barbour Co. 50 mi. Se of Montgomery. Residental.

143 The Clayton Record
PO Box 69 Phone: (334)775-3254
Clayton, AL 36016 Fax: (334)775-8554

Local newspaper. **Founded:** 1870. **Freq:** Weekly (Thurs.). **Print Method:** Offset. **Cols./Page:** 6. **Col. Width:** 24 nonpareils. **Col. Depth:** 294 agate lines. **Key Personnel:** Rebecca Beasley, Editor and Publisher, rbeasley@zebra.net. **USPS:** 116-960. **Subscription Rates:** $18 individuals; $20 out of state. **Remarks:** Accepts advertising.
Ad Rates: GLR: $5.25 **Circ:** ‡2,500
BW: $300
SAU: $5.25
PCI: $4.50

COLUMBIANA†, pop. 2,655.

C. AL. Shelby Co. 30 mi. SE of Birmingham. Wire, foundry, textile mills. Timber. Diversified farming.

144 Shelby County Reporter
Shelby County Newspapers Inc.
PO Box 947 Phone: (205)669-3131
Columbiana, AL 35051 Fax: (205)669-4217

Community newspaper. **Founded:** 1843. **Freq:** Weekly (Wed.). **Print Method:** Offset. **Cols./Page:** 6. **Col. Width:** 22 nonpareils. **Col. Depth:** 280 agate lines. **Key Personnel:** Kim N. Price, Publisher. **USPS:** 492-480. **Subscription Rates:** $27 individuals. **Remarks:** Accepts advertising.
Ad Rates: 4C: $1,200 **Circ:** Paid 9,588
PCI: $12.50

CULLMAN†, pop. 13,084.

N. AL. Cullman Co. 34 mi. S. of Decatur. Manufactures lumber, cotton oil products, chrome trim, files, air conditioning compressors, missile components, truck wheels, cigars, boxes, textiles, fertilizer, headings, staves. Hatcheries. Pine, oak timber. Agriculture. Cotton, poultry.

145 Broiler Industry
Watt Publishing Co.
PO Box 947 Phone: (205)734-6800
Cullman, AL 35056 Fax: (205)739-6945

Magazine focusing on production, processing, and marketing in the North American broiler meat industry. **Founded:** 1938. **Freq:** Monthly. **Print Method:** Offset. **Trim Size:** 8 x 10 3/4. **Cols./Page:** 3. **Col. Width:** 27 nonpareils. **Col. Depth:** 140 agate lines. **Key Personnel:** Gary Thornton, Editor; Charles Olentine, Jr., Publisher; John Todd, Advertising Mgr. **Subscription Rates:** $54 individuals; $8 single issue. **Remarks:** Accepts advertising.
Ad Rates: BW: $3,040 **Circ:** Combined 15,152
4C: $3,690

146 The Cullman Times
Cullman Times
300 4th Ave. SE Phone: (205)734-2131
Cullman, AL 35055 Fax: (205)734-7310
Free: (800)844-5369

General newspaper. **Founded:** 1901. **Freq:** Tues.-Fri. (morn.); Sun. (morn.). **Print Method:** Offset. **Cols./Page:** 8. **Col. Width:** 25 nonpareils. **Col. Depth:** 301 agate lines. **Key Personnel:** Robert Bryan, Editor and Publisher; Bill McCartney, Advertising Mgr.; Sam Mazzara, Circulation Mgr. **Subscription Rates:** $40 individuals. **Remarks:** Accepts advertising.
Ad Rates: SAU: $6.75 **Circ:** Mon.-Sat. ★**10,631**
Sun. ★**11,749**

147 The Cullman Tribune
Blalock Publishing
219 2nd Ave. SE Phone: (205)739-1351
Cullman, AL 35055 Fax: (205)739-4422

Local newspaper. **Founded:** 1874. **Freq:** Weekly (Thurs.). **Print Method:** Offset. **Trim Size:** 13 x 21. **Cols./Page:** 6. **Col. Width:** 23 nonpareils. **Col. Depth:** 224 agate lines. **Key Personnel:** Delton Blalock, Editor and Publisher; Barbara Blalock, Publisher; Nina Hurst, Advertising Mgr.; Deanna Chapman, Acct./Circulation Mgr.; Kim Creel, Exec. Asst. **Subscription Rates:** $20 individuals; $25 out of area; $0.50 single issue. **Remarks:** Accepts advertising.
Ad Rates: PCI: $6 **Circ:** ‡15,000

148 Poultry Digest
Watt Publishing Co.
PO Box 947 Phone: (205)734-6800
Cullman, AL 35056 Fax: (205)739-6945

Magazine serving those involved with production in the poultry, broiler, turkey, and egg industries. **Founded:** 1939. **Freq:** Monthly. **Print Method:** Web offset. **Trim Size:** 8 x 10 3/4. **Cols./Page:** 3. **Col. Width:** 27 nonpareils. **Col. Depth:** 140 agate lines. **Key Personnel:** Charles E. Perry, Editor; Dr. Charles Olentine, Jr., Editor; Mirdza Kalnins, Advertising Mgr. **ISSN:** 0032-5716. **Subscription Rates:** $48 individuals. **Remarks:** Accepts advertising.
Ad Rates: BW: $3,150 **Circ:** Combined 18,702
4C: $4,345

149 Century Cullman Corp.
256 US Hwy. 278 E. Phone: (205)739-4451
PO Box 1225 Fax: (205)734-8463
Cullman, AL 35055
Free: (800)462-4976

Owner: Century Communications Corp., 50 Locust Ave., PO Box 1225, New Canaan, CT 06840, (203)972-2000. **Cities Served:** Blountsville, Cullman, Hanceville, Warrior, AL: subscribing households 12,000; 34 channels; 1 community access channel; 10 hours per week community access programming.

150 WFMH-AM - 1460
1707 Warnke Rd. NW Phone: (256)734-3271
Cullman, AL 35055 Fax: (256)734-3622
E-mail: 101fm@linkfast.net

Format: Southern Gospel; Gospel. **Owner:** Eddins Braodcasting Co. Inc., at above address. **Founded:** 1950. **Operating Hours:** Continuous. **ADI:** Birmingham (Gadsden), AL. **Key Personnel:** Mary Evelyn Jones, General Mgr. **Wattage:** 5000. **Ad Rates:** $7.50 for 30 seconds; $10.50 for 60 seconds. Combined advertising rates available with WFMH-FM, WXXR-AM.

151 WFMH-FM - 95.51
1707 Warnke Rd. NW Phone: (256)734-3271
Cullman, AL 35055-2231 Fax: (256)734-3622
E-mail: 101fm@linkfast.netet

Format: Country. **Networks:** ABC. **Founded:** 1949. **Formerly**: WXXR-FM (1998). **Operating Hours:** Continuous. **ADI:** Birmingham (Gadsden), AL. **Key Personnel:** Mary Evelyn Jones, General Mgr., fax (256)734-2707. **Local Programs:** *Afternoon, Driving You Home*, Carol Lynn; *Morning Show (Barry and Terry)*. **Wattage:** 6. **Ad Rates:** $10 for 30 seconds; $15 for 60 seconds. Combined advertising rates available with WFMH-AM, WXXR-AM, & WXXR-FM.

152 WKUL-FM - 92.1
PO Box 803 Phone: (205)734-0183
Cullman, AL 35056 Fax: (205)739-2999

Format: Contemporary Country; Talk; Country. **Networks:** ABC. **Founded:** 1967. **Formerly**: WKLN-FM. **Operating Hours:** 5 a.m.-midnight. **Key Personnel:** Ron Mosley, General Mgr. **Wattage:** 6,000. **Ad Rates:** $16 for 30 seconds; $28 for 60 seconds.

153 WXXR-AM - 1340
1708 Brantley Ave. NW Phone: (205)734-3171
PO Drawer 968 Fax: (205)734-8085
Cullman, AL 35056-0968

Format: Oldies. **Networks:** Unistar. **Owner:** Larry Baker, 2039 Sandy Ave., Cullman, AL 35055, (205)734-8600, Fax: (205)734-8600. **Founded:** 1946. **Formerly**: WKUL-AM. **Operating Hours:** 6 a.m.-midnight; 90% network, 10% local. **ADI:** Birmingham (Gadsden), AL. **Key Personnel:** Larry Baker, Operations Dir.; Dennis Borwick, General Mgr.; Bill Lewis, PR/Agency Marketing Consultant. **Wattage:** 1000. **Ad Rates:** $5.40-8.80 for 30 seconds; $6.80-11.20 for 60 seconds.

DADEVILLE†, pop. 3,263.

E. AL. Tallapoosa Co. 48 mi. NW of Columbus, GA. Resort area. Lumber, textile mills; cotton gins. Timber. Agriculture.

154 WELL-FM - 88.7
PO Box 284 Phone: (205)825-6426
Dadeville, AL 36853 Fax: (205)825-6626
Free: (800)938-4887
E-mail: radiofil@lakemartin.net

Format: Southern Gospel. **Networks:** USA Radio. **Owner:** Winds of Change, Inc., at above address. **Founded:** 1990. **Formerly**: WDVI-FM (1997). **Operating Hours:** Continuous. **Key Personnel:** Donald Bailey, President; Philip L. Williams, General Mgr. **Wattage:** 100,000. **Ad Rates:** Underwriting available.

155 WZLM-FM - 97.3
PO Box 909 Phone: (205)825-4221
Alexander City, AL 35010 Fax: (205)825-4270

Format: Adult Contemporary. **Networks:** ABC. **Founded:** 1989. **Wattage:** 3000.

DAUPHIN ISLAND

156 Gulf of Mexico Science
Dauphin Island Sea Lab
Box 369-370 Phone: (334)861-2141
Dauphin Island, AL 36528
Technical, trade magazine covering marine science in the Gulf of Mexico. **Key Personnel:** William Schroeder, Editor. **ISSN:**

1087-688X. **Subscription Rates:** $4 single issue. **Formerly**: Northeast Gulf Science; Journal of Marine Science.

DECATUR†, pop. 42,002.

N. AL. Morgan Co. On Tennessee River, 22 mi. SW of Huntsville. Manufactures cotton and cottonseed products, automobile parts, chemicals, tile,bridge steel, sheet metal, copper tubing, leather soles and belting, paper, air conditioners, refrigerators, boxes, baskets, gasoline tanks, fertilizer. Shipyard; meat packing, poultry processing plants, bottling works.

157 Decatur Daily
Tennessee Valley Printing
PO Box 2213
Decatur, AL 35609-2213

Newspaper with a Democratic orientation. **Founded:** 1912. **Freq:** Daily (eve.), Sat. and Sun. (morn.). **Print Method:** Offset. **Cols./Page:** 6. **Col. Width:** 25 nonpareils. **Col. Depth:** 301 agate lines. **Key Personnel:** Tom Wright, Exec.; Doug Mendenhall, Managing Editor; Henry Burt, Advertising Mgr.; Bobby English, Circulation Mgr. **Subscription Rates:** $108 individuals. **Remarks:** Accepts advertising.
Ad Rates: SAU: $11.86 **Circ:** Mon.-Fri. 27,050
Sun. 29,161
Sat. 28,163

158 WAJF-AM - 1490
1301 Central Pkwy. SW Phone: (205)340-1490
Decatur, AL 35601-4817 Fax: (205)351-1234

Format: Urban Contemporary. **Owner:** WAJF Inc., at above address. **Founded:** 1953. **Operating Hours:** Continuous. **ADI:** Huntsville-Decatur-Florence, AL. **Key Personnel:** Gene Newman, Manager. **Wattage:** 1000. **Ad Rates:** $20 for 60 seconds. $10 for 60 seconds. Combined advertising rates available with WHRT-AM, WJAR-AM, and WYAM-FM.

159 WAVD-AM - 1400
1209 N. Danville Rd. SW Phone: (205)353-1400
Decatur, AL 35601 Fax: (205)353-0363

Format: Talk; News; Sports. **Owner:** R & B Communications, Inc., at above address. **Founded:** 1935. **Formerly**: WMSL-AM (1985). **Operating Hours:** Continuous. **ADI:** Huntsville-Decatur-Florence, AL. **Key Personnel:** Terry Arnold, Contact, tarnold@wavd.com; Brian Black, Contact. **Local Programs:** *The Right Side* 4:00 pm - 6:00 pm Monday-Friday, Terry Arnold, General Mgr., (256)353-1400; *Let's Talk Books* Wed. & Sat., 6:00 pm and 10:00 am & pm; *The Money Game*, Dave Ramsey; *The Morning Mix*; *Duke & The Doctor*, *Doug Rye's Home Remedies*; *Alabama Outdoors*, Pat Dye. **Wattage:** 1000. **Ad Rates:** $5-7.50 for 30 seconds; $7.50-10 for 60 seconds.

160 WDRM-FM - 102.1
PO Box 789 Phone: (205)353-1750
Decatur, AL 35602 Fax: (205)355-8013
E-mail: comments@wdrm.com

Format: Country. **Networks:** Independent. **Founded:** 1951. **Operating Hours:** Continuous. **ADI:** Huntsville-Decatur-Florence, AL. **Key Personnel:** Mark Goodwin, General Sales Mgr. **Wattage:** 100,000. **Ad Rates:** $355 per unit. **URL:** http://wdrm.com.

161 WHOS-AM - 800
401 14th St. SE Phone: (205)353-1750
PO Box 789 Fax: (205)355-8013
Decatur, AL 35602
E-mail: comments@wdrm.com

Format: News. **Networks:** Independent. **Founded:** 1948. **Operating Hours:** Continuous. **ADI:** Huntsville-Decatur-Florence, AL. **Key Personnel:** Mark Goodwin, General Sales Mgr. **Wattage:** 1,000. **URL:** http://wdrm.com.

162 WJRA-AM - 1310
Rte. 2, Box 71 Phone: (256)353-4060
Decatur, AL 35603-9732 Fax: (256)353-2450
E-mail: wjra1310@aol.com

Format: Gospel; Religious. **Networks:** Independent. **Owner:** Alvin Abercrombie, 1431 Hwy. 31 N., Hartselle, AL 35640, (205)351-1081. **Founded:** 1986. **Operating Hours:** 6 a.m.-6 p.m.; 100% local. **ADI:** Huntsville-Decatur-Florence, AL. **Key Personnel:** Ray Mosley, General Mgr.; Rob Lawler, Program Mgr. **Wattage:** 1000. **Ad Rates:** $10 for 60 seconds. $10 for 60 seconds. Combined advertising rates available with WAJF-AM, WHRT-AM, and WYAM-FM.

163 WYAM-AM - 890
1301 Central Parkway S.W. Phone: (205)355-4567
Decatur, AL 35601 Fax: (205)351-1234

Format: Country. **Networks:** Satellite Music Network. **Owner:** Gene Newman, at above address. **Founded:** 1956. **Formerly**: WHRT-AM. **Operating Hours:** Daytime. **ADI:** Huntsville-Decatur-Florence, AL. **Key Personnel:** Gene Newman, Manager. **Wattage:** 2500. **Ad Rates:** $20 for 60 seconds. $5 for 60 seconds. Combined advertising rates available with WAJF-AM, WJRA-AM, and WYAM-FM.

DEMOPOLIS, pop. 7,700.

NW AL. Marengo Co. 48 mi. W. of Selma. Cotton, cattle, dairy farms, soybeans.

164 The Demopolis Times
Boone Newspapers, Inc.
315 E. Jefferson Phone: (205)289-4017
PO Box 860 Fax: (205)289-4019
Demopolis, AL 36732-0860
Community newspaper. **Founded:** 1905. **Freq:** Semiweekly (Wed. and Sun.). **Print Method:** Offset. **Cols./Page:** 6. **Col. Width:** 2 inches. **Col. Depth:** 21.5 inches. **Key Personnel:** Jerry Turner, Publisher; Evelyn Ferrell, Advertising Mgr. **USPS:** 153-520. **Subscription Rates:** $23 individuals. **Remarks:** Accepts advertising.
Ad Rates: BW: $645 **Circ:** ‡2,750
4C: $925
PCI: $5

165 WIIQ-TV - 41
c/o WBIQ-TV Phone: (205)328-8756
2112 11th Ave. S., Ste. 400 Fax: (205)251-2192
Birmingham, AL 35205
Free: (800)239-5233
E-mail: wwood@apto.org

Format: Public TV. **Simulcasts:** WBIQ-TV Birmingham, AL. **Networks:** Public Broadcasting Service (PBS). **Owner:** Alabama Public Television, at above address. **Founded:** Sept. 13, 1971. **Operating Hours:** 7 a.m.-11 p.m. daily. **ADI:** Montgomery-Selma, AL. **Key Personnel:** Henry Bonner, Program Dir.; Joanna Cleary, News Dir.; Judy Stone, Exec. Dir.; Windell Wood, Dir. of Eng.; Phil Hutcheson, Deputy Director CPO. **Local Programs:** *For the Record*. **Wattage:** 1,968,000 visual; 196,800 aural. **Ad Rates:** Noncommercial. **URL:** http://www.aptv.org.

166 WVFG-FM - 107.5
1502 E. Highway 80 Phone: (334)628-2888
Demopolis, AL 36732 Fax: (334)628-6800
E-mail: chazjr@hotmail.com

Format: Blues. **Owner:** Charles E. Jones, Jr., at above address. **Founded:** Jan. 1994. **Operating Hours:** Continuous. **Wattage:** 6000. **Ad Rates:** $9.50 for 30 seconds; $14.50 for 60 seconds.

167 WXAL-AM - 1400
1028 Hwy. 80 East Phone: (205)289-1400
Demopolis, AL 36732 Fax: (205)289-2156

Format: Talk; Religious. **Simulcasts:** WZNJ-FM. **Networks:** USA Radio. **Founded:** 1947. **Operating Hours:** 60% network, 40% local. **Key Personnel:** Bill Jones, General Mgr. **Wattage:** 1000. **Ad Rates:** $3.09-8.26 for 30 seconds; $4.28-9.26 for 60 seconds.

168 WZNJ-FM - 106.5
1028 Hwy. 80 East Phone: (334)289-1400
Demopolis, AL 36732 Fax: (334)289-2156

Format: Oldies. **Simulcasts:** WXAL-AM. **Networks:** Westwood One Radio; USA Radio. **Founded:** 1975. **Formerly**: WNAN-FM (1984). **Operating Hours:** Continuous; 80% network, 20% local. **Key Personnel:** Bill Jones, General Mgr., phone (334)289-1400, fax (334)289-2156. **Wattage:** 25,000 Watts. **Ad Rates:** $6.50-11.00 for 30 seconds; $4.28-12.70 for 60 seconds.

DIXONS MILLS

169 WMBV-FM - 91.9
10564 Marengo County Rd. 30 Phone: (334)992-2925
PO Box 91.9 FM Fax: (334)992-2637
Dixons Mills, AL 36736
Free: (888)624-7234
E-mail: wmbv@moody.edu

Format: Religious. **Networks:** Moody Broadcasting. **Founded:** 1988. **Operating Hours:** Continuous. **Key Personnel:** Robbie Moore, General Mgr.; Alan Kilgore, Chief Engineer; Bill Ralph, Production Mgr. **Local Programs:** *Morning Light* 6:00 am - 8:00 am Monday-Friday, Bill Ralph, Mailing contact, (334)992-2425. **Wattage:** 62,000. **Ad Rates:** Noncommercial.

DORA, pop. 2,327.

N. AL. Walker Co. 22 mi. NW of Birmingham. Cotton fabric mill. Coal mining, steel, iron milling. Agriculture. Cotton, corn, hay, poultry.

170 The Community News
PO Box 880 Phone: (205)648-3231
Dora, AL 35062 Fax: (205)648-3246

Community newspaper. **Freq:** Weekly (Wed.). **Cols./Page:** 6. **Col. Width:** 10 picas. **Col. Depth:** 21 1/2 inches. **Key Personnel:** Liz S. Carey, Editor and Publisher. **Subscription Rates:** $9 individuals; $12.50; $17.50 out of state. **Remarks:** Accepts advertising.
Ad Rates: GLR: $3.82 **Circ:** 2,000
4C: $45
SAU: $4

171 WPYK-AM - 1010
PO Box 460 Phone: (205)648-3242
Dora, AL 35062

Format: Talk; Classical; Country; Religious. **Networks:** USA Radio. **Owner:** Paul T. Johnson, at above address. **Founded:** 1981. **Operating Hours:** Sunrise-sunset; 100%. **ADI:** Birmingham (Gadsden), AL. **Key Personnel:** Bill Purdue, Program Mgr.; Paul Johnson, Owner; Clay Barnes, Manager. **Local Programs:** *Shop Talk*, Sherry Dilbeck, (205)648-6670. **Wattage:** 5000. **Ad Rates:** $10-14 per unit.

DOTHAN†, pop. 48,750.

SE AL. Houston Co. 110 mi. SE of Montgomery. Manufactures magnetic tapes, electric motors, peanut oil, latex products, furniture, pajamas, cigars, charcoal briquettes. Agriculture. Soybeans, peanuts.

172 The Dothan Eagle
Eagle
227 N. Oates St. Phone: (334)792-3141
PO Box 1968 Fax: (334)712-7979
Dothan, AL 36302
General newspaper. **Founded:** 1902. **Freq:** Daily and Sunday (morn.). **Print Method:** Offset. **Cols./Page:** 6. **Col. Width:** 24 nonpareils. **Col. Depth:** 301 agate lines. **Key Personnel:** Ronnie Agnew, Managing Editor; Steve McPhail, Publisher, phone (334)712-7924, fax (334)712-7992; Rick Martin, Advertising Mgr., phone (334)794-8818, fax (334)793-2040; Roger Underwood, Circulation Mgr., phone (334)712-790, fax (334)712-7975. **Subscription Rates:** $73.20 individuals. **Remarks:** Accepts advertising.
Ad Rates: SAU: $11.22 **Circ:** Mon.-Sat. **★34,846**
Sun. **★37,379**

173 The Dothan Progress
PO Box 1927 Phone: (334)793-9586
Dothan, AL 36302 Fax: (334)712-7975

Community newspaper. **Founded:** Feb. 1, 1971. **Freq:** Weekly (Thurs.). **Print Method:** Offset. **Cols./Page:** 6. **Col. Width:** 2 1/16 inches. **Col. Depth:** 21 1/2 inches. **Key Personnel:** Elaine Brackin, Managing Editor, phone (334)712-7987. **Subscription Rates:** Free distribution. **Remarks:** Accepts advertising.
Ad Rates: GLR: $10.92 **Circ:** Paid 361
BW: $1,408.68 Free 24,860
4C: $1,758.68
SAU: $10.92

174 The Headland Observer
The Dothan Progress
PO Box 1927 Phone: (334)793-9586
Dothan, AL 36302 Fax: (334)712-7975

Local newspaper. **Founded:** 1966. **Freq:** Weekly (Thurs.). **Print Method:** Offset. **Cols./Page:** 6. **Col. Width:** 2 1/16 inches. **Col. Depth:** 21 1/2 inches. **Key Personnel:** Terry Grimes, Editor; Mike Mullins, Publisher; Betty Gamble, Advertising Mgr. **Subscription Rates:** $9 In County; $11 Out of County. **Remarks:** Accepts advertising.
Ad Rates: GLR: $.22 **Circ:** Paid ‡1,683
BW: $393.45 Free ‡67
4C: $633.45
PCI: $3.05

175 Time Warner
104 S. Woodburn Phone: (334)793-1752
Dothan, AL 36305 Fax: (334)793-5667

Formerly: Wometco Cable TV of Alabama; Cablevision Industries. **Key Personnel:** Alan Levy, General Mgr. **Cities Served:** 60 channels.

176 WDHN-TV - 18
Hwy. 52 E. Phone: (334)793-1818
PO Box 6237 Fax: (205)793-2623
Dothan, AL 36302

Format: Commercial TV. **Networks:** ABC. **Founded:** 1970. **Operating Hours:** 5:30 a.m.-midnight; 70% network, 30%

local. **ADI:** Dothan, AL. **Key Personnel:** Aubrey Wood, General Mgr.; Ken Curtis, News Dir. **Ad Rates:** $35-800 per unit.

177 WDJR-FM - 96.9
PO Box 9663 Phone: (334)712-9233
Dothan, AL 36304 Fax: (334)712-0374
Free: (800)264-0969
E-mail: wdjrfm@aol.com

Format: Country. **Founded:** 1948. **Formerly:** WLHQ-FM. **Operating Hours:** Continuous. **ADI:** Dothan, AL. **Key Personnel:** Tom Nebel, General Mgr., tom@wdjr.com; Jerry Broadway, Program Dir., jerry@wdjr.com; Teena Saffold, Business Mgr. **Local Programs:** *The Breakfast Bunch*, Jerry Broadway, Program Dir., (334)712-9233, Fax (334)712-0374. **Wattage:** 100,000. **Ad Rates:** Combined advertising rates available with WBCD-FM.

178 WESP-FM - 102.5
256 Honeysuckle Rd., Ste. 12 Phone: (334)671-1025
Dothan, AL 36301 Fax: (334)794-6155
Free: (888)593-1025
E-mail: thearrow@alanet.com

Format: Classic Rock. **Owner:** Signal Enterprises, at above address. **Founded:** 1989. **Operating Hours:** Continuous. **ADI:** Dothan, AL. **Key Personnel:** Janie Bush, General Mgr.; Ryan Kelly, Public Service Dir.; Andrea Boutwell, News Dir.; Amy Galletly, Office Mgr.; Lora Scott, Operations Mgr./Music Dir. **Local Programs:** *Friday Night Special*; *Southern Fried Saturday Nights*; *Wake Up Show*. **Wattage:** 25,000. **Ad Rates:** $6-23 for 30 seconds; $8-27 for 60 seconds. **URL:** http://www.thearrow1025.com.

179 WGTF-FM - 89.5
107 Wanda Ct. Phone: (334)794-4770
Dothan, AL 36303-2963 Fax: (334)794-4770
E-mail: wgtf@aol.com

Format: Religious. **Networks:** Bible Broadcasting. **Owner:** Dothan Community Educational Radio, Inc., at above address, Dothan, AL 36303. **Founded:** 1988. **Operating Hours:** Continuous. **ADI:** Dothan, AL. **Key Personnel:** Jim Cannavan, General Mgr. **Wattage:** 19,000.

180 WTVY-FM - 95.5
PO Box 2088 Phone: (334)792-0047
Dothan, AL 36302-2088 Fax: (334)712-9346

Format: Agricultural; Country; Contemporary Country. **Owner:** Charles Woods, at above address. **Founded:** 1969. **Operating Hours:** Continuous. **ADI:** Dothan, AL. **Key Personnel:** Bobby Price, General Sales Mgr.; Jerome Jackson, Program & Music Dir. **Local Programs:** *Morning Show*, Shannon O'Neal. **Wattage:** 100,000. **Ad Rates:** $20-135 for 30 seconds; $30-145 for 60 seconds. **URL:** http://www.WTVYFM.COM.

181 WTVY-TV - 4
285 N. Foster Phone: (334)792-3195
P.O. Box 1089 Fax: (334)793-3947
Dothan, AL 36302
E-mail: wtvy@wtvy.com

Format: Commercial TV. **Networks:** CBS. **Owner:** Benedek Broadcasting Corp., 100 Park Ave., Rockford, IL 61101, (815)987-5350, Fax: (815)987-5335. **Founded:** 1955. **Operating Hours:** Continuous; 80% network, 20% local. **ADI:** Dothan, AL. **Key Personnel:** Dale Stafford, Sales Mgr., phone (334)712-7448, fax (334)793-3947, dstafford@wtvy.com; Jeff Raker, News Dir., phone (334)712-7431, fax (334)712-7452, raker@wtvy.com; Reggie Mitchell, Traffic/Prog. Dir., phone (334)712-7416, fax (334)793-3947; Pat Dalbey, General Mgr., fax (334)712-7401, pat@wtvy.com. **Local Programs:** *Gene Ragan Farm Show* 12 noon Monday-Friday; *Morning Talk* 9 a.m. - 10 a.m. Monday-Friday; *WTVY This Morning* 6 a.m.- 7 a.m. Monday-Friday. **Ad Rates:** $40-600 per unit. **URL:** http://www.wtvy.com.

182 WVOB-FM - 91.3
Box 1944 Phone: (334)793-3189
Dothan, AL 36302 Fax: (334)793-4344
E-mail: bethanybc@ala.net

Format: Religious; Educational. **Networks:** USA Radio. **Founded:** 1988. **Operating Hours:** Continuous. **ADI:** Dothan, AL. **Key Personnel:** H.D. Shuemake, General Mgr.; Steve A. Shuemake, Station Mgr.; Keith D. Brady, Operations Dir. **Wattage:** 2500. **Ad Rates:** Noncommercial.

DOZIER

SC AL. Crenshaw Co. 50 mi. S. of Montgomery.

183 WDIQ-TV - 2
c/o WBIQ-TV Phone: (205)328-8756
2112 11th Ave. S., Ste. 400 Fax: (205)251-2192
Birmingham, AL 35205
E-mail: w.wood@aptu.org

Format: Public TV. **Simulcasts:** WBIQ-TV. **Networks:** Public Broadcasting Service (PBS). **Owner:** Alabama Public Television, at above address. **Founded:** Aug. 8, 1956. **Operating Hours:** 7 a.m.-11 p.m. daily. **ADI:** Montgomery-Selma, AL. **Key Personnel:** Henry Bonner, Program Dir.; Joanna Cleary, News Dir.; Judy Stone, Exec. Dir.; Windell Wood, Dir. of Eng.; Phil Hutcheson, Deputy Director, CFO. **Wattage:** 100,000 visual; 10,000 aural. **Ad Rates:** Noncommercial. **URL:** http://www.aptv.org.

ELBA†, pop. 4,355.

SE AL. Coffee Co. 40 mi. NW of Dothan. Manufactures truck trailers, fork lifts, textiles, lumber. Meat packing plant. Pine, oak timber. Diversified farming. Broilers, peanuts, livestock.

184 The Elba Clipper
PO Drawer A Phone: (334)897-2823
Elba, AL 36323 Fax: (334)897-3434

Newspaper. **Founded:** 1897. **Freq:** Weekly (Thurs.). **Print Method:** Offset. **Cols./Page:** 6. **Col. Width:** 21 1/2 nonpareils. **Col. Depth:** 294 agate lines. **Key Personnel:** John Ferrin Cox, Publisher. **Subscription Rates:** $15 individuals; $17 out of area; $18 out of state.
Ad Rates: GLR: $.28 **Circ:** 3,200
BW: $549.54
4C: $774.54
SAU: $3.88

185 WELB-AM - 1350
1800 Neil Granthum Dr. Phone: (205)897-2216
Elba, AL 36323 Fax: (205)897-3694

Format: Oldies. **Owner:** Elba Radio Co., at above address. **Founded:** 1958. **Key Personnel:** William D. Holderfield, Contact; Michael Holderfield, Chief Engineer. **Wattage:** 1000.

186 WZTZ-FM - 101.1
1800 Neil Granthum Dr. Phone: (205)897-2216
Elba, AL 36323 Fax: (205)897-3694

Format: Contemporary Country. **Owner:** Elba Radio Co., at above address. **Founded:** 1986. **Key Personnel:** Jerome Jackson, Contact. **Wattage:** 640.

ENTERPRISE†, pop. 18,033.

SE AL. Coffee Co. 80 mi. S. of Montgomery. Manufactures weather and satellite radars, portable runway planking, flatbed trailers, forklifts, castings, door hinges, textiles. Poultry. Peanuts. Dairy farming.

187 Daleville Sun Courier
QST Publications, Inc.
PO Box 311546 Phone: (334)598-3891
Enterprise, AL 36331-1546 Fax: (334)393-2987

Local newspaper. **Founded:** 1986. **Freq:** Weekly (Wed.). **Print Method:** Offset. **Trim Size:** 14 x 22 3/4. **Cols./Page:** 6. **Col. Width:** 25.5 nonpareils. **Col. Depth:** 301 agate lines. **Key Personnel:** Kay Kirkland, Managing Editor; Howard Quattlebaum, Publisher; Russell Quattlebaum, Advertising Mgr. **Subscription Rates:** Free; $28.50 (mail). **Remarks:** Accepts advertising.
Ad Rates: BW: $909.45 **Circ:** Free 5,960
4C: $1,349.45 Paid 67
SAU: $14
PCI: $7.05

188 Enterprise Ledger
PO Box 311130 Phone: (334)347-9533
Enterprise, AL 36331 Fax: (334)347-0825

General newspaper. **Founded:** 1898. **Freq:** Daily (eve.), Sunday (morn.). **Print Method:** Offset. **Cols./Page:** 6. **Col. Width:** 24 nonpareils. **Col. Depth:** 301 agate lines. **Key Personnel:** Amelia Morrison Hall, Managing Editor; Tommy Gilmore, Advertising Dir.; Shane Blevins, Circulation Dir. **Subscription Rates:** $50 individuals. **Remarks:** Accepts advertising.
Ad Rates: SAU: $9.45 **Circ:** (Not Reported)

189 The Southeast Sun
QST Publications, Inc.
905 Rucker Blvd. Phone: (334)393-2969
PO Box 1536 Fax: (334)393-2987
Enterprise, AL 36331
Local newspaper. **Founded:** May 1982. **Freq:** Weekly (Wed.). **Print Method:** Offset. **Trim Size:** 14 x 22 3/4. **Cols./Page:** 6. **Col. Width:** 25 1/2 nonpareils. **Col. Depth:** 301 agate lines. **Key Personnel:** Howard Quattlebaum, Publisher; Russell Quattlebaum, Advertising Mgr. **Subscription Rates:** $28.50 by mail. **Remarks:** Combined advertising rates available with Daleville Sun Courier.
Ad Rates: BW: $1019.10 **Circ:** Free 12,905
4C: $1,349.10 Paid 66
SAU: $2.13
PCI: $7.90

190 WKMX-FM - 106.7
100 N. Main Phone: (334)347-2278
Enterprise, AL 36330 Fax: (334)393-2141

Format: Adult Contemporary. **Networks:** Independent. **Founded:** 1974. **Operating Hours:** Continuous. **ADI:** Dothan, AL. **Key Personnel:** Wallace Miller, President; Al Miller, Chief Engineer; Fred Grase, Sales Mgr.; Angela DeLoney, Contact, phone (334)793-2274, fax (334)793-4171; Terry Duffie, Exec. V.P./General Mgr. **Wattage:** 100,000. **Ad Rates:** Advertising accepted; rates available upon request.

EUFAULA†, pop. 12,097.

SE AL. Barbour Co. On Chattahoochee River, 45 mi. S. of Columbus, GA. Manufactures cotton cloth and yarn, fishing lures, depth finders, textiles, cottonseed oil, shoes, carpet yarn, lumber, doors, paper, soft drinks, bricks. Pine timber. Agriculture. Cotton, peanuts, cattle.

191 The Cuthbert Times & News Record
The Eufaula Tribune Corp.
PO Box 628 Phone: (205)687-3229
Eufaula, AL 36072-0628
Newspaper. **Founded:** 1866. **Freq:** Weekly (Thurs.). **Print Method:** Offset. **Cols./Page:** 6. **Col. Width:** 26 nonpareils. **Col. Depth:** 129 agate lines. **Key Personnel:** Joel P. Smith, Publisher. **Subscription Rates:** $10.95 individuals. **Remarks:** Accepts advertising.
Ad Rates: GLR: $.35 **Circ:** ‡2,100
BW: $384.42
4C: $704.42
SAU: $2.98

192 The Eufaula Tribune
Tribune Publishing Co.
514 E. Barbour St. Phone: (205)687-3507
PO Box 628 Fax: (205)687-3229
Eufaula, AL 36072
Community newspaper. **Founded:** 1929. **Freq:** Semiweekly (Wed. and Sun.). **Print Method:** Offset. **Cols./Page:** 6. **Col. Width:** 26 nonpareils. **Col. Depth:** 301 agate lines. **Key Personnel:** Joel P. Smith, Editor and Publisher, phone (334)687-3506, fax (334)687-3229. **Subscription Rates:** $26.50 local; $34.95 in state; $44.95 out of state. **Remarks:** Accepts advertising.
Ad Rates: GLR: $.32 **Circ:** 6,350
SAU: $4.27
PCI: $5.05

193 WULA-AM - 1240
Hwy. 431 S. Phone: (205)687-2067
Eufaula, AL 36027

Format: News; Talk. **Networks:** People's Network. **Owner:** McGowan Mediallc, at above address, (334)687-2066, Fax: (334)687-2067. **Founded:** 1948. **Operating Hours:** Continuous; 95% network, 5% local. **ADI:** Dothan, AL. **Key Personnel:** B. Smith, News Dir.; Steve McGowan, President; Russell Baty, Operations Mgr. **Ad Rates:** $4-25 per unit.

194 WULA-FM - 92.7
Hwy. 431 S. Phone: (205)687-2067
Eufaula, AL 36027

Format: Adult Contemporary. **Networks:** Jones Satellite. **Owner:** McGowan Mediallc, at above address, (334)687-2066, Fax: (334)687-2067. **Founded:** 1973. **Formerly:** WKQK-FM. **Operating Hours:** Continuous; 95% network, 5% local. **ADI:** Dothan, AL. **Key Personnel:** B. Smith, News Dir.; Steve McGowan, President; Russell Baty, Operations Mgr. **Wattage:** 6000. **Ad Rates:** $4-25 per unit.

EUTAW†, pop. 2,464.

W. AL. Greene Co. 30 mi. SW of Tuscaloosa. Lumber mills; cotton gin; cattle market. Timber. Agriculture. Cotton, potatoes.

195 Greene County Democrat
Greene County Newspaper Co.
214 Boligee St. Phone: (205)372-3373
PO Box 598 Fax: (205)372-2243
Eutaw, AL 35462
Black community newspaper. **Founded:** 1890. **Freq:** Weekly (Wed.). **Print Method:** Offset. **Cols./Page:** 6. **Col. Width:** 21 nonpareils. **Col. Depth:** 294 agate lines. **Key Personnel:** John Zippert, Publisher; Carol Zippert, Publisher; Laddi Jones, Advertising Mgr. **ISSN:** 0889-518X. **Subscription Rates:** $16

individuals; $20 out of area; $25 out of state. **Remarks:** Accepts advertising.
Ad Rates: BW: $1,210 **Circ:** ‡3,500
SAU: $6.00
PCI: $10.00

EVERGREEN†, pop. 4,171.

S. AL. Conecuh Co. 86 mi. N. of Pensacola, FL. Manufactures lumber, bus bodies, wood products, textiles. Cotton gins. Timber. Agriculture. Cotton, peanuts, strawberries.

196 KDKO-AM - 1510
PO Box 350 Phone: (334)578-3693
Evergreen, AL 36401 Fax: (334)578-5399

Format: Urban Contemporary; Religious. **Networks:** CNN Radio. **Owner:** Peoples Wireless Inc., at above address, (303)295-1225, Fax: (303)295-1521. **Founded:** 1957. **Operating Hours:** Continuous. **Key Personnel:** Jim Walker, Owner/Gen. Mgr. **Local Programs:** *Dr. Daddios Blues Show*; *Inner City Vision*; *Thierry Smith's Sports Rap*. **Wattage:** 10,000 day; 1300 night. **Ad Rates:** $40-85 per unit.

197 WPGG-FM - 93.3
PO Box 350 Phone: (334)578-3693
Evergreen, AL 36401 Fax: (334)578-5399

Format: Country. **Networks:** CNN Radio. **Founded:** 1982. **Formerly:** WEGN-FM (1987). **Operating Hours:** Continuous; 100% local. **Key Personnel:** Luther Upton, General Mgr. & Program Dir. **Wattage:** 100,000. **Ad Rates:** $8 for 30 seconds; $12 for 60 seconds.

FAIRHOPE, pop. 7,286.

SW AL. Baldwin Co. 15 mi. SE of Mobile. Residential.

198 WABF-AM - 1220
460 S. Section St., Box 1220 Phone: (334)928-2384
PO Drawer 1220 Fax: (205)928-9229
Fairhope, AL 36533-1220

Format: Big Band/Nostalgia; Jazz. **Networks:** Mutual Broadcasting System; Alabama Radio (ALANET). **Owner:** Jubilee Broadcasting Co., Inc., at above address. **Founded:** 1961. **Operating Hours:** 6 am-6pm weekdays; 7 am-6 pm Sun.; 20% network, 80% local. **ADI:** Mobile, AL-Pensacola, FL. **Key Personnel:** John Ward Hinds, Jr., President/Gen. Mgr.; Robbie Jones, Office Mgr.; Charles Strozier, Chief Engineer. **Wattage:** 1000. **Ad Rates:** $3.50 for 10 seconds; $4.60-6 for 30 seconds; $5.60-7 for 60 seconds.

FAYETTE†, pop. 5,287.

C. AL. Fayette Co. 35 mi. NNW of Tuscaloosa.

199 Cattle Today
Cattle Today, Inc.
204 Temple Ave. S. Phone: (205)932-8000
Fayette, AL 35555 Fax: (205)932-8000

Newspaper (tabloid) serving purebred and commercial cattle producers in the southeastern states. **Founded:** July 1, 1987. **Freq:** Semimonthly. **Key Personnel:** Belinda Hood, Editor. **Subscription Rates:** $10.
Circ: ‡15,000

200 Mid-South Horse Review
Color Printing
422 Columbus St. E. Phone: (205)932-6793
Fayette, AL 35555
Magazine covering horses. **Founded:** Apr. 1992. **Freq:** Monthly. **Print Method:** Offset. **Cols./Page:** 4. **Col. Width:** 2 3/8 inches. **Col. Depth:** 13 inches. **Key Personnel:** Don L. Dowdle, Editor and Publisher; Anne Fordyce, Editor. **Subscription Rates:** $15. **Remarks:** Accepts advertising.
Ad Rates: BW: $395 **Circ:** Free 12,500
4C: $575

201 West Alabama TV Cable Co.
Box 660 Phone: (205)932-4700
Fayette, AL 35555 Fax: (205)932-3585

Key Personnel: Tommy Norwood, Business Mgr.; Charles Gann, Asst. Mgr. **Cities Served:** Belk, Brilliant, Detroit, Fayette, Hamilton, Winfield, AL: subscribing households 6,775; 53 channels.

202 WLDX-AM - 990
733 Columbus St. E. Phone: (205)932-3318
PO Box 189 Fax: (205)932-3318
Fayette, AL 35555

Format: Contemporary Country. **Networks:** ABC; Alabama Radio (ALANET). **Owner:** Sis Sound of Fayette, Inc., at above address. **Founded:** 1949. **Formerly:** WWWF-AM (1987). **Operating Hours:** 5:30 a.m.-11 p.m.; 12% network, 88% local. **ADI:** Birmingham (Gadsden), AL. **Key Personnel:** Chuck Jones, Program Dir.; Eloise Thomley, Contact; Joe Jackson, Music Dir.; Carolyn Stough, Contact; Lana Bynum, Office Mgr. **Wattage:** 1000. **Ad Rates:** $4.25 for 15 seconds; $5.25 for 30 seconds; $6.25 for 60 seconds.

203 WTXT-FM - 98.1
PO Box 1109 Phone: (205)333-9800
Northport, AL 35476 Fax: (205)333-8834

Format: Contemporary Country. **Networks:** ABC. **Owner:** Tuscaloosa Broadcasting Co., at above address. **Founded:** 1977. **Formerly:** WHKW-FM. **Operating Hours:** Continuous. **Key Personnel:** Bill Dunnavant, President; Bo Chambers, General Mgr.; Russ L. Williams, Program Dir. **Wattage:** 100,000.

FLOMATON, pop. 1,882.

SW AL. Escambia Co. 40 mi. N. of Pensacola, FL. Residential.

204 Tri-City Ledger
PO Drawer F Phone: (334)296-3491
Flomaton, AL 36441 Fax: (334)296-0010

Newspaper. **Founded:** 1971. **Freq:** Weekly (Thurs.). **Print Method:** Offset. **Cols./Page:** 6. **Col. Width:** 26 nonpareils. **Col. Depth:** 301 agate lines. **Key Personnel:** Joe Thomas, Editor and Publisher. **Subscription Rates:** $25 individuals; $30 FL & AL; $35 outside of FL & AL. **Remarks:** Accepts advertising. **Feature Editors:** Anne Tyree, *Lifestyle*.
Ad Rates: GLR: $.27 **Circ:** ‡5,300
BW: $490.20
4C: $715.20

FLORALA, pop. 2,701.

SE AL. Covington Co. On Florida border. Sawmills.

205 WKWL-AM - 1230
427 South Sixth Street Phone: (334)858-6162
PO Box 159 Fax: (334)858-6132
Florala, AL 36442-0159
Free: (888)354-WKWL
E-mail: wkwl1230am@aol.com

Format: Religious; Country. **Networks:** USA Radio. **Founded:** 1979. **Operating Hours:** 6 a.m-6 p.m. Mon-Fri.; 7:00 a.m-5:00 p.m. Sat & Sun. **Key Personnel:** Tom Fleetwood, Gen. Mgr./Program dir.; Lisa Martin, Operations Mgr. **Wattage:** 1000. **Ad Rates:** $5.50 for 30 seconds; $6.25 for 60 seconds.

FLORENCE†, pop. 37,029.

NW AL. Lauderdale Co. On Tennessee River, directly across the river from Sheffield. University of North Alabama. Manufactures chemicals, aluminum, corrugated containers, concrete blocks, pipe, chloride, caustic soda, fertilizer, nitrate, phosphate, boats. Machine shops, stove foundry; agriculture.

206 The Flor-Ala
University of North Alabama
Box 5300 Phone: (205)765-4364
Florence, AL 35632-0001 Fax: (205)765-4659

Collegiate newspaper. **Founded:** Dec. 3, 1931. **Freq:** Weekly (Thurs.) (during the academic year). **Print Method:** Offset. **Cols./Page:** 6. **Col. Width:** 12 picas. **Col. Depth:** 13.5 picas. **Key Personnel:** Tyler Greer, Exec. Editor, phone (205)765-4364, fax (205)765-4275, tgreer@unaalpha.una.edu; Amy Bridges, Business Mgr., phone (204)765-4427, fax (204)765-4275, abridges@unaalpha.una.edu. **Subscription Rates:** $20 individuals. **Remarks:** Accepts advertising.
Ad Rates: GLR: $.32 **Circ:** Paid 300
BW: $630 Non-paid 4,200
PCI: $5

207 Journal of Legal Economics
University of North Alabama
PO Box 5077 Phone: (256)765-4144
Florence, AL 35632-0001 Fax: (256)765-4170
Publication E-mail: leglecon@unanov.una.edu

Journal for economists and attorneys. **Founded:** Mar. 1991. **Freq:** 3/year. **Trim Size:** 6 3/4 x 9 3/4. **Cols./Page:** 1. **Key Personnel:** Michael W. Butler, Editor; Christine Heaton, Editor; Michael W. Butler, Editor. **ISSN:** 1054-3023. **Remarks:** Accepts advertising.
Ad Rates: PCI: $250 **Circ:** Paid 400
Controlled 35

208 Shoals News Leader
PO Box 427 Phone: (205)766-5542
Florence, AL 35631 Fax: (205)760-1117

Black community newspaper. **Founded:** 1980. **Freq:** Weekly. **Key Personnel:** William R. Liner, Editor and Publisher.
Circ: 10,000

209 Times Daily
219 W. Tennessee Phone: (205)766-3434
Florence, AL 35630 Fax: (205)740-4717
Publication E-mail: timesdly@timesdaily.com

General newspaper. **Founded:** 1869. **Freq:** Daily and Sunday (morn.). **Print Method:** Offset. **Cols./Page:** 6. **Col. Width:** 25 nonpareils. **Col. Depth:** 301 agate lines. **Key Personnel:** Kathy Silverberg, Editor; Gary Thatcher, Managing Editor; Frank Helderman, Publisher; Tim Thompson, Advertising Mgr.; Aileen Hood, Circulation Mgr. **Subscription Rates:** $135 individuals. **Remarks:** Accepts advertising. **Online:** CompuServe Information Service; OCLC; Ovid Technologies; LEXIS-NEXIS; Westlaw. **URL:** http://www.dbmsmag.com; http://www.macalstr.edu/; http://www.timesdaily.com. **Alt. Formats:** CD-ROM.
Ad Rates: GLR: $2.50 **Circ:** Mon.-Sat. ★**33,249**
SAU: $19.35 Sun. ★**36,072**

210 WBCF-AM - 1240
525 E. Tennessee St. Phone: (205)764-8170
Box 1316
Florence, AL 35631-1316

Format: News; Talk; Big Band/Nostalgia. **Networks:** UPI; Sun Radio; Westwood One Radio. **Owner:** Benny Carle Broadcasting, Inc., at above address. **Founded:** 1943. **Formerly:** WOWL-AM (1977). **Operating Hours:** Continuous; 80% network, 20% local. **ADI:** Huntsville-Decatur-Florence, AL. **Key Personnel:** Benjy Carle, Contact; Pat Costa, Contact; Alan Counts, Music Dir. **Wattage:** 1000. **Ad Rates:** $20-25 for 30 seconds; $30-35 for 60 seconds.

211 WBHL-FM - 91.3
PO Box 3086 Phone: (205)760-9191
3625 Helton Dr. Fax: (205)760-0981
Florence, AL 35630
Free: (800)982-4807

Format: Easy Listening; Oldies; Jazz. **Networks:** USA Radio. **Founded:** 1988. **Operating Hours:** 5 a.m.-midnight. **ADI:** Huntsville-Decatur-Florence, AL. **Key Personnel:** Jim Lancaster, Sales Mgr.; Johnny Behel, Operations Mgr.; Sarah Shirley, Program Dir.; Jim Lancaster, General Mgr. **Wattage:** 30,000. **Ad Rates:** Noncommercial.

212 WFIQ-TV - 36
c/o WBIQ-TV Phone: (205)328-8756
2112 11th Ave. S., Ste. 400 Fax: (205)251-2192
Birmingham, AL 35205
E-mail: w.wood@aptu.org

Format: Public TV. **Simulcasts:** WBIQ-TV. **Networks:** Public Broadcasting Service (PBS). **Founded:** Aug. 16, 1967. **Operating Hours:** 7 a.m.-11 p.m. daily. **ADI:** Huntsville-Decatur-Florence, AL. **Key Personnel:** Henry Bonner, Program Dir.; Joanna Cleary, News Dir.; Judy Stone, Exec. Dir.; Windell Wood, Dir. of Eng.; Phil Hutcheson, Deputy Director, CFO. **Wattage:** 851,000 visual; 85,100 aural. **Ad Rates:** Noncommercial. **URL:** http://www.aptv.org.

213 WOWL-TV - 15
840 Cypress Mill Rd. Phone: (205)767-1515
Florence, AL 35630 Fax: (205)764-7750

Format: Commercial TV. **Networks:** NBC. **Founded:** 1957. **Operating Hours:** 6 a.m.-1 a.m.; 80% network, 20% local. **ADI:** Huntsville-Decatur-Florence, AL. **Key Personnel:** Thomas Shannon, General Mgr.; Verbon Jones, General Sales Mgr.; Carol Strength, Business Mgr.; Debbie Summers, Traffic Mgr.; Tim Rovere, Chief Engineer; David Yancey, Programming/Operations Manager; David Hale, Promotion/Community Affairs Manager. **Ad Rates:** $50-175 for 30 seconds. **URL:** http://www.wowl.com.

214 WQLT-FM - 107.3
624 Sam Phillips St.
PO Box 932
Florence, AL 35631
E-mail: walt@hiwaay.net

Format: Adult Contemporary. **Networks:** ABC; Unistar. **Owner:** Big River Broadcasting Group, at above address. **Founded:** 1967. **Operating Hours:** Continuous; 100% local. **ADI:** Huntsville-Decatur-Florence, AL. **Key Personnel:** Charlie Ross, Program Mgr., cross@wqlt.com; Bill Thomas, General Mgr., bthomas@bigriverbroadcasting.com; Nick Martin, Sales Mgr., nmartin@bigriverbroadcasting.com. **Wattage:** 100,000. **Ad Rates:** $22-50 for 30 seconds. Combined advertising rates available with WXFL-FM, WSBM-AM. **URL:** http://www.bigriverbroadcasting.com.

215 WSBM-AM - 1340
624 Sam Phillips St. Phone: (205)764-8121
PO Box 932 Fax: (205)764-1869
Florence, AL 35631

Format: Urban Contemporary. **Networks:** ABC. **Owner:** Big River Broadcasting, at above address, Fax: (205)764-8169. **Founded:** 1946. **Formerly**: WJOI-AM (1973). **Operating Hours:** Continuous; 12% network, 88% local. **ADI:** Huntsville-Decatur-Florence, AL. **Key Personnel:** Tim Turner, Program Dir.; Bill Thomas, General Mgr.; Nick Martin, Sales Mgr. **Wattage:** 1000. **Ad Rates:** $10-22 for 30 seconds. Combined advertising rates available with WQLT, WXFL.

216 WXFL-FM - 96.1
624 Sam Phillips St. Phone: (256)764-8121
Florence, AL 35630 Fax: (256)764-8169

Format: Contemporary Country. **Networks:** ABC. **Owner:** Big River Broadcasting Corp., at above address. **Founded:** July 1, 1996. **Operating Hours:** Continuous. **ADI:** Huntsville-Decatur-Florence, AL. **Key Personnel:** Bill Thomas, General Mgr.; Nick Martin, General Sales Mgr.; Gary Murdock, Program Dir.; Greg Pace, Chief Engineer. **Wattage:** 6000. **Ad Rates:** $25 per unit. **URL:** http://www.wqlt.com.

FOLEY, pop. 3,368.

SC AL. Baldwin Co. 30 mi. SE of Mobile. Fertilizer factory. Potatoes.

217 Riviera Utilities Cable TV
413 E. Laurel Ave. Phone: (334)943-5001
PO Box 2050 Fax: (334)943-5275
Foley, AL 36536

Founded: 1982. **Key Personnel:** H. Sewell St. John, General Mgr. **Cities Served:** subscribing households 6,478; 34 channels.

218 WHEP-AM - 1310
PO Box 1747 Phone: (334)943-7131
Foley, AL 36536 Fax: (334)943-5866

Format: News; Sports; Talk. **Networks:** Mutual Broadcasting System; Alabama Radio (ALANET). **Owner:** Stewart Broadcasting Co., Inc., at above address. **Founded:** 1953. **Operating Hours:** 6 a.m.-6 p.m.; 10% network, 90% local. **ADI:** Mobile, AL-Pensacola, FL. **Key Personnel:** Jim Stewart, President; Clark Stewart, General Mgr. **Wattage:** 1000. **Ad Rates:** $6.50-7 for 30 seconds; $6.75-7.15 for 60 seconds.

FORT MC CLELLAN

219 Military Police
U.S. Army Military Police School
Fort Mc Clellan, AL 36205-5030

Professional magazine covering Military Police functions worldwide. **Freq:** Semiannual. **Key Personnel:** Kay Mundy, Editor. **Subscription Rates:** $5 individuals; $4.75 single issue. **Remarks:** Advertising not accepted. **URL:** http://www.mcclellan.army.mil/usamps. **Formerly**: Military Police Journal.
Circ: Controlled 8,300

FORT PAYNE†, pop. 11,485.

NE AL. DeKalb Co. 32 mi. N. of Gadsden. Manufactures office furniture, steel fabricators. Pine timber. Agriculture. Poultry.

220 Times-Journal
Fort Payne Newspapers, Inc.
PO Box 680349 Phone: (256)845-2550
Fort Payne, AL 35968-1604 Fax: (256)845-7459
Free: (800)348-4637

Community newspaper. **Founded:** 1878. **Freq:** Daily (morn.) Tues.-Sat. **Print Method:** Offset. **Cols./Page:** 6. **Col. Width:** 26 nonpareils. **Col. Depth:** 301 agate lines. **Key Personnel:** Ben Shurett, Publisher; Gloria Jackson, Advertising Mgr. **Subscription Rates:** $66 individuals; $72 by mail; $84 out of state; $54 Senior citizens; $78 individuals in adjacent counties. **Remarks:** Accepts advertising. **Formerly**: Northeast Alabamian Shopping News (1989).
Ad Rates: BW: $1,161 **Circ:** Combined 6,700
4C: $1,351
PCI: $9

221 The Times-Journal Midweek
Fort Payne Newspapers, Inc.
PO Box 680349 Phone: (256)845-2550
Fort Payne, AL 35968-1604 Fax: (256)845-7459
Free: (800)348-4637

Community newspaper. **Founded:** 1980. **Freq:** Weekly (Thurs.). **Print Method:** Offset. **Cols./Page:** 6. **Col. Width:** 26 nonpareils. **Col. Depth:** 301 agate lines. **Key Personnel:** Ben Shurett, Editor and Publisher; Gloria Jackson, Advertising Mgr. **Subscription Rates:** Free. **Remarks:** Accepts advertising.
Ad Rates: GLR: $.57 **Circ:** ‡7,100
BW: $877.20
4C: $1,170.20
SAU: $6.80
PCI: $5.90

222 WZOB-AM - 1250
PO Box 748 Phone: (205)845-2810
Fort Payne, AL 35967

Format: Country. **Networks:** CNN Radio; Alabama Radio (ALANET). **Owner:** Central Broadcasting Co., at above address. **Founded:** 1950. **Operating Hours:** 6 a.m.-midnight. **Key Personnel:** Peggy H. Kirby, President; Gloria Vogel, Operations Mgr. **Wattage:** 5000.

GADSDEN†, pop. 47,565.

NE AL. Etowah Co. On Coosa River, 60 mi. NE of Birmingham. Tourist attraction, Noccalula Falls. Hub of trade and healthcare for NE Alabama. Steel mill. High tech engineering, tooling, fabrication and manufacturing. Tire manufacturing.

223 Gadsden Times
The Gadsden Times, Inc.
401 Locust St. Phone: (205)549-2000
PO Box 188 Fax: (205)549-2105
Gadsden, AL 35901-3737
General newspaper. **Founded:** 1867. **Freq:** Daily (eve.), Sat. and Sun. (morn.). **Print Method:** Offset. **Cols./Page:** 6. **Col. Width:** 2 1/16 inches. **Col. Depth:** 21 1/2 inches. **Key Personnel:** Rusty Starr, Editor; Frank Helderman, Jr., Publisher. **Remarks:** Accepts advertising.
Ad Rates: BW: $2,322 **Circ:** Mon.-Sat. ★**26,133**
4C: $2,822 Sun. ★**28,155**
SAU: $18

224 WAAX-AM - 570
6510 Whorton Bend Rd. Phone: (256)543-9229
Gadsden, AL 35901 Fax: (256)543-3279

Format: Talk; News. **Networks:** ABC; Unistar. **Owner:** Southern Star Communications, Inc., 1500 NW 49th St., Ste. 605, Fort Lauderdale, FL 33309, (954)202-5848, (954)202-5848. **Founded:** 1947. **Operating Hours:** Continuous; 30% network, 70% local. **ADI:** Birmingham (Gadsden), AL. **Key Personnel:** Bill Thomas, General Mgr., bthomas@mindspring.com; Dave Fitz, News Dir. **Wattage:** 5000.

225 WGAD-AM - 1350
823 Forrest Ave. Phone: (205)546-1611
P.O. Box 1350 Fax: (205)547-9062
Gadsden, AL 35902
E-mail: wgad@cybertyme.com

Format: News; Sports; Talk. **Networks:** NBC. **Owner:** Ed Carrell, 109 Merit, Gadsden, AL 35901, (205)547-2378. **Founded:** 1947. **Operating Hours:** 5 a.m.-midnight; 80% network, 20% local. **ADI:** Birmingham (Gadsden), AL. **Key Personnel:** Ed Carrell, General Mgr.; Archie Wade, News Dir.; David Burgess, Chief Engineer; Randy Frawley, P.D. **Local Programs:** *Songs of Inspiration* 6 a.m. - 11 a.m. Sunday, Archie Wade. **Wattage:** 5000. **Ad Rates:** $8-14 for 30 seconds; $10-18 for 60 seconds. **URL:** http://www.wgad.com.

226 WJBY-AM - 930
2725 Rainbow Dr. Phone: (205)442-1222
Gadsden, AL 35901 Fax: (205)442-1229

Format: Religious. **Networks:** USA Radio; Alabama Radio (ALANET). **Owner:** Hinton Mitchem and Brian Pitts, Hwy.431, Albertsville, Albertville, AL 35950, (205)878-4660, (205)878-1000. **Founded:** 1926. **Operating Hours:** 5:30 a.m.-10 p.m. **ADI:** Birmingham (Gadsden), AL. **Key Personnel:** Mike Hooks, Program/Music Director; Rick Hester, Sports Dir.; Hinton Mitchem, President. **Wattage:** 5000. **Ad Rates:** $4 for 10 seconds; $8-14 for 30 seconds; $10-16 for 60 seconds.

227 WNAL-TV - 44
510 Chestnut St. Phone: (205)547-4444
Gadsden, AL 35901 Fax: (205)547-1789

Format: Commercial TV. **Networks:** CBS. **Owner:** Paxson Communications, at above address. **Founded:** Apr. 12, 1986. **Operating Hours:** Continuous. **ADI:** Birmingham (Gadsden), AL. **Key Personnel:** Debra White, Business Mgr.; Jim Moss, Sales/General Mgr. **Local Programs:** *Archie Phillips Show*; *The Local News.* **Wattage:** 1,800,000. **Ad Rates:** $35-500 per unit.

228 WQEN-FM - 103.7
6510 Whorton Bend Rd. Phone: (256)543-9229
Gadsden, AL 35901 Fax: (256)543-3279

Networks: Unistar; ABC. **Owner:** Southern Star Communications, Inc., at above address, (954)202-5848, Fax: (954)202-5848. **Founded:** 1976. **Operating Hours:** Continuous. **ADI:** Birmingham (Gadsden), AL. **Key Personnel:** Bill Thomas, General Mgr., bthomas@mindspring.com. **Wattage:** 100,000. **URL:** http://www.WQEN.ORG.

229 WSGN-FM - 91.5
PO Box 227 Phone: (205)549-8439
Gadsden, AL 35902-0227 Fax: (205)549-8404

Format: Jazz; Educational; Classical; Classic Rock; Information. **Networks:** National Public Radio (NPR); Public Radio International (PRI). **Owner:** Gadsden State Community College, at above address. **Founded:** 1975. **Formerly**: WEXP (1985). **Operating Hours:** Continuous. **ADI:** Birmingham (Gadsden), AL. **Key Personnel:** Neil D. Mullin, General Mgr.; A. Faye Brewer, Program Dir. **Wattage:** 6300. **Ad Rates:** Advertising not accepted.

230 WTJP-TV - 60
313 Rosedale Ave. Phone: (256)546-8860
Gadsden, AL 35901-5361 Fax: (256)543-8623

Format: Religious; Public Radio. **Owner:** All American TV, Inc., 3000 W. MacArthur Blvd., Ste. 530, Santa Ana, CA 92704, (714)957-9689, Fax: (714)957-9699. **Operating Hours:** Continuous; 97% network, 3% local. **ADI:** Birmingham (Gadsden), AL. **Key Personnel:** Gary Hodges, Station Mgr.; Curtiss Kemp, Chief Engineer; JoAnn Hodges, Contact. **Ad Rates:** Noncommercial.

GENEVA†, pop. 4,866.

SE AL. Geneva Co. On Choctawhatchee River, 33 mi. SW of Dothan. Manufactures textiles, aluminum registers, cotton goods, veneer. Timber. Agriculture. Soybeans, peanuts, corn, cattle, hogs, cotton.

231 Geneva County Reaper
Geneva Publications Inc.
PO Box 160 Phone: (334)684-2287
Geneva, AL 36340 Fax: (334)684-3099

Newspaper. **Founded:** 1899. **Freq:** Weekly (Wed.). **Print Method:** Offset. **Cols./Page:** 6. **Col. Width:** 2 1/16 inches. **Col. Depth:** 21 1/2 inches. **Key Personnel:** Jim Specht, Editor and Publisher. **USPS:** 577-760. **Subscription Rates:** $16 individuals; $24 out of state; $0.50 single issue.
Ad Rates: BW: $838.50 **Circ:** 3,300
SAU: $6.50

232 Hartford News-Herald
Geneva Publications Inc.
PO Box 160 Phone: (334)684-2287
Geneva, AL 36340 Fax: (334)684-3099

Community newspaper. **Founded:** 1899. **Freq:** Weekly (Wed.). **Cols./Page:** 6. **Col. Width:** 12 1/2 picas. **Col. Depth:** 21 1/2 inches. **Key Personnel:** Jim Specht, Publisher. **Subscription Rates:** $16 individuals; $24 out of state; $0.50 single issue.
Ad Rates: BW: $838.50 **Circ:** 1,400
SAU: $6.50

233 Ledger
Geneva Publications Inc.
PO Box 160 Phone: (334)684-2287
Geneva, AL 36340 Fax: (334)684-3099

Local newspaper. **Founded:** 1899. **Freq:** Weekly (Wed.). **Print Method:** Offset. Uses mats. **Cols./Page:** 6. **Col. Width:** 12 1/2 picas. **Col. Depth:** 21 1/2 inches. **Key Personnel:** Jim Specht, Editor and Publisher. **USPS:** 609-080. **Subscription Rates:** $16 individuals; $24 out of state; $0.50 single issue.
Ad Rates: BW: $838.50 **Circ:** Paid 1100
SAU: $6.50 Free 35

234 WGEA-AM - 1150
PO Box 339 Phone: (205)684-7079
Geneva, AL 36340 Fax: (205)684-0329

Format: Country; Talk; Southern Gospel. **Networks:** USA Radio; Precision Racing. **Owner:** Shelley Broadcasting Co., at above address. **Founded:** 1953. **Operating Hours:** 6 a.m.-5 p.m. **Key Personnel:** Doc Parker, General Mgr.; Kitty Parker, Sales Mgr. **Wattage:** 1000. **Ad Rates:** $3 for 30 seconds; $4 for 60 seconds.

GEORGIANA†, pop. 1,993.

S. AL. Butler Co. 60 mi. SW of Montgomery. Manufactures plywood, gloves, uniforms. Pine timber. Agriculture. Cotton, corn, peanuts, tobacco, cattle, hogs.

235 The Butler County News
Andalusia Star
PO Box 620 Phone: (334)376-2325
Georgiana, AL 36033 Fax: (334)376-9302

Newspaper with a Democratic orientation. **Founded:** 1911. **Freq:** Weekly (Thurs.). **Print Method:** Offset. **Cols./Page:** 6. **Col. Width:** 25 nonpareils. **Col. Depth:** 301 agate lines. **Key Personnel:** R.W. Pride, Jr., Editor and Publisher. **Subscription Rates:** $12.72 individuals. **Remarks:** Accepts advertising.
Ad Rates: GLR: $.12 **Circ:** 2,200

GREENSBORO†, pop. 3,371.

W. AL. Hale Co. 38 mi. S. of Tuscaloosa. Small industry. Cotton gin. Catfish production. Timber. Agriculture. Cotton, dairying, hay, cattle.

236 The Greensboro Watchman
1005 Market St. Phone: (334)624-8323
PO Drawer 550
Greensboro, AL 36744
Community newspaper. **Founded:** 1876. **Freq:** Weekly (Thurs.). **Print Method:** Offset. **Trim Size:** 14 x 22 1/2. **Cols./Page:** 6. **Col. Width:** 2 1/16 inches. **Col. Depth:** 21 1/2 inches. **Key Personnel:** Edward E. Lowry, Jr., Publisher. **USPS:** 228-960. **Subscription Rates:** $18.50; $20.50 out of country; $26.50 out of state. **Remarks:** Accepts advertising.
Ad Rates: GLR: $.45 .35 **Circ:** 3,050
BW: $812.70
SAU: $6.30
PCI: $6.30

GREENVILLE†, pop. 7,807.

S. AL. Butler Co. 44 mi. SW of Montgomery. Manufactures textiles, fertilizer, automobile seat belts, gloves, store fixtures, generators, air conditioners, electrical connectors, heavy logging equipments, plywood. Lumber, feed mills; cotton gins. Pecan shelling. Timber. Agriculture. Cotton, strawberries.

237 WGYV-AM - 1380
PO Box 585 Phone: (334)382-5444
Greenville, AL 36037-0585 Fax: (334)382-5444
E-mail: sisterry@alaweb.com

Format: Oldies; News; Talk. **Networks:** Alabama Radio (ALANET). **Owner:** Golden Broadcasting, at above address. **Founded:** 1948. **Operating Hours:** 6 a.m.-6 p.m. **Key Personnel:** Terry Golden, General Mgr. **Wattage:** 1000. **Ad Rates:** $3.15-4.85 for 30 seconds; $3.95-6.05 for 60 seconds.

238 WKXN-FM - 95.9
PO Box 369 Phone: (334)382-6555
Greenville, AL 36037 Fax: (334)382-6555

Format: Urban Contemporary. **Networks:** Alabama Radio (ALANET); American Urban Radio. **Owner:** Autaugaville Radio, Inc., at above address. **Founded:** 1977. **Operating Hours:** Continuous. **Key Personnel:** Roscoe Miller, Contact; Mike Morris, News Dir.; Beth Golden, Office Mgr. **Wattage:** 4000. **Ad Rates:** $8-13.50 for 30 seconds; $8-15 for 60 seconds.

WLVN-AM - See Luverne

239 WQZX-FM - 94.3
205 W. Commerce Phone: (334)382-6633
Greenville, AL 36037-2217 Fax: (334)382-6634

Format: Country; Sports. **Networks:** NBC; AP. **Owner:** Haynes Broadcasting Inc., at above address. **Founded:** 1985. **Operating Hours:** 5 a.m.-11 p.m.; 1% network, 99% local. **Key Personnel:** Robert Haynes, Contact; Kyle Haynes, Station Mgr. **Wattage:** 3000. **Ad Rates:** $5.10-7.40 for 30 seconds; $6.90-9.45 for 60 seconds.

GROVE HILL†.

SW AL. Clarke Co. 50 mi. N. of Mobile.

240 Clarke County Democrat
PO Box 39 Phone: (334)275-3375
Grove Hill, AL 36451-0039 Fax: (334)275-3060
Publication E-mail: ccd@dixienet.com

Community newspaper. **Founded:** Jan. 1856. **Freq:** Weekly. **Print Method:** Offset. **Cols./Page:** 6. **Col. Width:** 12 nonpareils. **Col. Depth:** 21 1/2 inches. **Key Personnel:** James A. Cox, Editor and Publisher. **Subscription Rates:** $13.91. **Remarks:** Accepts advertising.
Ad Rates: BW: $645 **Circ:** ‡5,000
PCI: $3.80

241 Vista Communications, Ltd.
PO Box 879 Phone: (334)275-3118
Grove Hill, AL 36451-0879 Fax: (334)275-3120

Owner: Vista Communications, Ltd. Partnership I, 40 Nagog Park, Acton, MA 01720, (508)635-9488. **Founded:** 1988. **Cities Served:** Fulton, Orrville, Thomaston, Pine Hill, Grove Hill, and Uniontown, Alabama.

GUIN

NW AL. Marion Co. 50 mi. NW of Birmingham.

242 Tri-County Cable
Box 886 Phone: (205)468-3601
Guin, AL 35563 Fax: (205)468-2200

Founded: 1965. **Key Personnel:** Jim Sloan, General Mgr. **Cities Served:** Lamar County: subscribing households 3,400; 29 channels.

GULF SHORES

243 Crossties
Covey Communications Corp.
PO Box 2267 Phone: (334)968-5300
Gulf Shores, AL 36547 Fax: (334)968-4532

Trade magazine for users and producers of treated wood crossties. **Freq:** Bimonthly. **Print Method:** Sheetfed offset. **Trim Size:** 8 1/2 x 11. **Cols./Page:** 3. **Col. Width:** 2 3/8 inches. **Key Personnel:** Kristin McIntosh, Exec. Editor; Abby Farris, Asst. Editor. **ISSN:** 0097-4536. **Subscription Rates:** $35 individuals. **Remarks:** Accepts advertising. **Former name:** Crosstie Bulletin.
Ad Rates: BW: $985 **Circ:** Controlled ‡3,000
4C: $1,485

244 Islander
Gulf Coast Newspaper
PO Box 1128 Phone: (334)947-7712
1278 Cove Rd. Fax: (334)947-7652
Gulf Shores, AL 36547
Community newspaper. **Freq:** Weekly. **Key Personnel:** Francis Coleman, Editor.

245 WCSN-FM - 105.7
PO Box 1919 Phone: (334)967-1057
Gulf Shores, AL 36547 Fax: (334)967-1050
E-mail: sunny105@gulftel.com

Format: Adult Contemporary. **Owner:** Purchase, Inc., at above address. **Founded:** July 8, 1996. **Operating Hours:** Continuous. **Key Personnel:** Lee Hagan, President; Damon Collins, General Mgr.; Ron Wain Scott, Program Dir. **Wattage:** 5000. **Ad Rates:** $10 for 30 seconds; $12 for 60 seconds. **URL:** http://www.sunny105.com.

GUNTERSVILLE†, pop. 7,041.

N. AL. Marshall Co. On southern point of Tennessee River, 35 mi. SE of Huntsville. Recreation and tourist center. Manufactures high tech components, disposable clothing.

246 The Advertiser-Gleam
PO Box 190 Phone: (205)582-3232
Guntersville, AL 35976 Fax: (205)582-3231
Free: (800)239-5319

Community newspaper. **Founded:** Oct. 1, 1880. **Freq:** Semiweekly (Wed. and Sat.). **Print Method:** Offset. **Trim Size:** 6 x 21 1/2. **Cols./Page:** 6. **Col. Width:** 24 nonpareils. **Col. Depth:** 301 agate lines. **Key Personnel:** Sam Harvey, Editor; John Harvey, Advertising Mgr. **Subscription Rates:** $19 individuals; $34 out of country. **Remarks:** Accepts advertising.
Ad Rates: 4C: $300 **Circ:** Wed. ★11,327
SAU: $6.90 Sat. ★11,327
PCI: $5.60

247 WGSV-AM - 1270
PO Box 220 Phone: (205)582-8131
Guntersville, AL 35976

Format: Adult Contemporary. **Networks:** ABC. **Owner:** Guntersville Broadcasting Co., at above address. **Founded:** 1950. **Key Personnel:** Lavell Jackson, President; Kerry Jackson, Operations Mgr. **Wattage:** 1000.

248 WTWX-FM - 95.9
PO Box 220 Phone: (205)582-8131
Guntersville, AL 35976 Fax: (205)582-4347

Format: Country. **Networks:** ABC. **Owner:** Guntersville Broadcasting Co., at above address. **Founded:** 1969. **Wattage:** 3000.

HALEYVILLE, pop. 5,306.

N. AL. Winston Co. 40 mi. S. of Florence. Cotton, lumber and grist mills. Manufactures textiles, furniture, mobile homes, truck trailers. Timber. Hatcheries. Agriculture. Cotton, cattle.

249 Northwest Alabamian
PO Box 430 Phone: (205)486-9461
Haleyville, AL 35565 Fax: (205)486-4849

Community newspaper. **Founded:** 1944. **Freq:** Semiweekly (Wed. and Sat.). **Print Method:** Offset. **Trim Size:** 13 3/4 x 22 1/2. **Cols./Page:** 6. **Col. Width:** 25 nonpareils. **Col. Depth:** 301 agate lines. **Key Personnel:** Horace Moore, Publisher; Melica Allen, Managing Editor; Buford Thompson, Advertising Manager; Roger Carden, Sales Representative; Lolita Hayes, Sales Representative. **Subscription Rates:** $23 individuals. **Remarks:** Advertising accepted; rates available upon request.
Circ: ‡7,200

250 The Times-Record
Northwest Alabamian
PO Box 430 Phone: (205)486-9461
Haleyville, AL 35565 Fax: (205)486-4849

Local newspaper. **Founded:** Aug. 24, 1977. **Freq:** Weekly (Wed.). **Print Method:** Offset. **Trim Size:** 13 x 21. **Cols./Page:** 6. **Col. Width:** 2 1/16 inches. **Col. Depth:** 21 inches. **Key Personnel:** David T. Poynor, Jr., Editor and Publisher; Michael James, Associate Editor; Mrs. Bobbie Cross, Advertising Mgr. **USPS:** 390-130. **Subscription Rates:** $12 individuals; $18 out of area. **Remarks:** Accepts advertising.
Ad Rates: GLR: $.32 **Circ:** Paid ‡4,600
BW: $504 Free ‡9,196
PCI: $4.50

251 WJBB-AM - 1230
PO Drawer 370 Phone: (205)486-2277
Haleyville, AL 35565-0370 Fax: (205)486-3905

Format: News; Southern Gospel. **Networks:** Mutual Broadcasting System. **Owner:** Haleyville Broadcasting Co., Inc., at above address. **Founded:** 1949. **Operating Hours:** 5 a.m.-midnight; 10% network, 90% local. **ADI:** Birmingham (Gadsden), AL. **Key Personnel:** John L. Slatton, President/Sales and General Manager; Bryan Walker, Program Dir.; Terry Slatton, Vice President/Sports Director; Elizabeth Gentle, News Dir. **Wattage:** 1000. **Ad Rates:** $5.45-6.15 for 30 seconds; $7.75-8.75 for 60 seconds.

252 WJBB-FM - 92.7
PO Box 370 Phone: (205)486-2277
Haleyville, AL 35565 Fax: (205)486-3905

Format: Country. **Networks:** Mutual Broadcasting System. **Owner:** Haleyville Broadcasting Co., Inc., at above address. **Founded:** 1979. **Operating Hours:** 5 a.m.-midnight; 5% network, 95% local. **Key Personnel:** John L. Slatton, President; Tracy Kinkead, Program Dir.; Danny Gotton, News Dir. **Wattage:** 4000. **Ad Rates:** $5.25-6 for 30 seconds; $7.25-8.50 for 60 seconds.

HAMILTON†, pop. 4,792.

NW AL. Marion Co. 4 mi. S. of Weston. Residential.

253 The Journal-Record
Mid-South Newspapers, Inc.
PO Drawer 1477 Phone: (205)921-3104
Hamilton, AL 35570-1477 Fax: (205)921-3105

General interest newspaper. **Founded:** 1971. **Freq:** Semiweekly (Wed. and Sat.). **Print Method:** Offset. **Cols./Page:** 6. **Col. Width:** 12 picas. **Col. Depth:** 21.5 picas. **Key Personnel:** Les Walters, Managing Editor; Horace Moore, Publisher, phone (205)486-9461; Rena Watson, Sales Representitive; Vicky Massey, Sales Representitive, phone (205)487-3278. **Subscription Rates:** $27; $29.50 out of area; $39 out of state; $22 senior citizens in county.
Ad Rates: BW: $657.90 **Circ:** 8,500
PCI: $5.10

254 WERH-AM - 970
PO Box 1119 Phone: (205)921-3481
Hamilton, AL 35570 Fax: (205)921-7187

Format: Country. **Owner:** Kate F. Fite, at above address. **Founded:** 1950. **Operating Hours:** Sunrise-sunset. **Key Personnel:** Kate F. Fite, Contact; James B. Fowler, General Mgr.; Geraldine Miller, Office Mgr. **Wattage:** 5000. **Ad Rates:** Advertising accepted; rates available upon request. Combined advertising rates available with WERH-FM.

HANCEVILLE

Cullman Co. (NC). 40 m SW of Huntsville.

255 The Hanceville Herald
Hanceville Herald
PO Box 880 Phone: (205)352-4775
Hanceville, AL 35077
Community newspaper. **Founded:** 1977. **Freq:** Weekly (Wed.). **Print Method:** Offset. **Cols./Page:** 8. **Col. Width:** 10 1/2 picas. **Col. Depth:** 21 1/2 inches. **Key Personnel:** Jennifer Grantham, Publisher. **Subscription Rates:** $8. $.25 single issue. **Remarks:** Accepts advertising.
Ad Rates: PCI: $2.70 **Circ:** 1,600

256 WRJL-AM - 1170
PO Box 290 Phone: (205)352-9556
Hanceville, AL 35077-0290 Fax: (205)352-9787

Format: Gospel; Southern Gospel. **Networks:** USA Radio. **Founded:** 1986. **Formerly:** WHZI-AM (1990). **Operating Hours:** Sunrise-sunset; 100% local. **Key Personnel:** Rolland French, Contact; Jo French, Contact. **Wattage:** 460.

HARTSELLE, pop. 8,858.

N. AL. Morgan Co. 12 mi. S. of Decatur. Manufactures air conditioner compressors, insulated electrical wire, electronics components, wood products, textiles, doors, metal cable reels, seat cushions. Timber. Agriculture. Cotton, soybeans, cattle, poultry.

257 Hartselle Enquirer
Hartselle Newspapers, LLC
407 W. Chestnut St. Phone: (334)773-6566
PO Box 929 Fax: (334)773-1953
Hartselle, AL 35640
Community newspaper. **Founded:** May 20, 1932. **Freq:** Weekly (Thurs.). **Print Method:** Offset. **Trim Size:** 13 1/2 x 21 1/2. **Cols./Page:** 6. **Col. Width:** 12 picas. **Col. Depth:** 21.5 picas. **Key Personnel:** C.P. Knight, Editor; Steven W. Smith, Publisher. **USPS:** 236-380. **Subscription Rates:** $16 individuals; $24 out of area. **Remarks:** Accepts advertising.
Ad Rates: GLR: $.30 **Circ:** Paid 7,650
BW: $554.70 Free 7,980
PCI: $5.65

258 Hartselle Shopping Guide
Hartselle Newspapers, LLC
407 W. Chestnut St. Phone: (334)773-6566
PO Box 929 Fax: (334)773-1953
Hartselle, AL 35640
Shopper. **Founded:** 1982. **Freq:** Weekly. **Print Method:** Offset. **Cols./Page:** 6. **Col. Width:** 12 picas. **Col. Depth:** 21 1/2 inches. **Key Personnel:** C.P. Knight, Editor; Steve Smith, Publisher. **Subscription Rates:** $16; $22 out of area; $24 out of state. **Remarks:** Accepts advertising.
Ad Rates: GLR: $6 **Circ:** Paid ‡7,019
BW: $716 Free ‡7,980
4C: $853
SAU: $6.50
PCI: $7.40

HEFLIN†, pop. 3,014.

NE AL. Cleburne Co. 15 mi. E. of Anniston. Manufactures business forms, chenille, mica products, textiles. Saw and planning mills. Cotton gins. Yellow pine timber. Agriculture. Poultry, cotton, corn, hay.

259 The Cleburne News
Consolidated Publishing
938 Ross St. Phone: (205)463-2872
PO Box 67 Fax: (205)463-7127
Heflin, AL 36264
Free: (800)408-2872

Community newspaper. **Founded:** 1907. **Freq:** Weekly (Thurs.). **Print Method:** Offset. **Cols./Page:** 6. **Col. Width:** 21 nonpareils. **Col. Depth:** 290 agate lines. **Key Personnel:** Mickey Bragg, Publisher; Patricia Surrett, Editor. **Subscription Rates:** $18; $24 Out of County. **Remarks:** Accepts advertising.
Ad Rates: SAU: $3 **Circ:** Paid ‡3,500

HOOVER

260 TCI Cablevision of Alabama, Inc.
Box 360268 Phone: (205)822-8731
Hoover, AL 35216 Fax: (205)823-0353

Founded: 1967. **Cities Served:** Jefferson County, Shelby County, Bluff Park, Forest Brook, Green Valley, Homewood, Riverchase, Rocky Ridge, Shades Mountain, and Vestavia Hills, AL.

HUNTSVILLE†, pop. 142,513.

N. AL. Madison Co. 85 mi. N. of Birmingham. Madison Co. (N). 85 m N of Birmingham. Manufactures cotton goods, compact audio discs, sheet metal products, flags, missiles, polyvinyl chloride film, ballistic missile fuel, electronic components, cottonseed oil, veneer, stoves, electric heaters, wire staples, farm implements, abrasives, toys, telephone instruments, auto tires, airplane glass, air handling equipment, modular buildings, hardware, space metals, aircraft instruments, perfumes, machine tools & parts, plastics, fiberglass bathroom fixtures, refrigeration equipment, electric generating units. Timber. Agriculture.

261 The Cumberland Flag
General Assembly Cumberland Presbyterian Church in America
226 Church St. Phone: (205)536-7481
Huntsville, AL 35801 Fax: (205)536-7482

Presbyterian magazine. **Founded:** 1915. **Freq:** Monthly. **Print Method:** Letterpress and offset. **Trim Size:** 8 1/2 x 11. **Cols./Page:** 3. **Col. Width:** 30 nonpareils. **Col. Depth:** 126 agate lines. **Key Personnel:** Robert S. Wood, Editor. **USPS:** 139-980. **Subscription Rates:** $6 individuals. **Remarks:** Advertising not accepted.
Circ: Paid ‡600
Non-paid ‡25

262 The Exponent
The University of Alabama in Huntsville
704 B South Loop Rd. Phone: (205)864-2429
Huntsville, AL 35805 Fax: (205)890-6090
Publication E-mail: ocasiog@iquiest.com

Collegiate magazine. **Founded:** 1966. **Freq:** Weekly. **Print Method:** Offset. **Cols./Page:** 4. **Col. Width:** 2 1/4 inches. **Col. Depth:** 15 inches. **Key Personnel:** Alicia Tyson, Business Mgr. **Subscription Rates:** $10 individuals. **Remarks:** Accepts advertising.
Ad Rates: SAU: $3.50 **Circ:** Non-paid ‡4,500
PCI: $5.40

263 The Huntsville Times
PO Box 1487, West Sta. Phone: (205)532-4000
Huntsville, AL 35807-0487 Fax: (205)532-4420
Free: (800)240-8463

General newspaper. **Founded:** Mar. 23, 1910. **Freq:** Daily (eve.), Sunday (morn.). **Print Method:** Offset. **Trim Size:** 13 1/2 x 21 1/4. **Cols./Page:** 6. **Col. Width:** 12 picas. **Col. Depth:** 21 inches. **Key Personnel:** Bob Ward, Editor; William C. Green, Jr., Publisher; William Cooper Green III, General Mgr.; Chris Welch, Sports Dir. **USPS:** 254-640. **Subscription Rates:** $118.20 individuals; $126 out of area; $144 out of state. **Remarks:** Accepts advertising. **Feature Editors:** John Anderson, *Political*, phone (205)532-4293; Martin Burkey, *Aviation, Environmental*, phone (205)532-4418; Don Cox, *Garden/Home*, phone (205)532-4443; Joe Duncan, *News*, phone (205)532-4402; John Ehinger, *Editorials*, phone (205)532-4218; Mickey Ellis, *Food*, phone (205)532-4403; Ray Garner, *Financial/Business*, phone (205)532-4424; Guy Hollis, *State*; Melinda Joiner, *Family*, phone (205)532-4404; Mike Kaylor, *Entertainment*, phone (205)532-4406; Ann Marie Martin, *Drama*, phone (205)532-4412; Ann Marie Martin, *Book*, phone (205)532-4407; John Pruett, *Sports*, phone (205)532-4430; Lee Roop, *City*, phone (205)532-4423; Yvonne White, *Religion*, phone (205)532-4419.
Ad Rates: BW: $4,207 **Circ:** Mon.-Fri. ★**60,243**
4C: $4,682.14 Sat. ★**62,763**
SAU: $33.39 Sun. ★**79,915**

264 Peace Progress
International Association of Educators for World Peace (IAEWP)
PO Box 3282, Mastin Lake Sta. Phone: (256)534-5501
Huntsville, AL 35810-0282 Fax: (256)536-1018
Publication E-mail: mercieca@hiwaay.net

Professional journal covering peace education, environmental protection, and human rights issues. **Subtitle:** IAEWP Journal of Education. **Founded:** 1974. **Freq:** Semiannual. **Key Personnel:** Dr. Charles Mercieca, Editor; Dr. Surya N. Prasad, Assoc. Editor; Hyok K. Shim, Circulation Mgr. **Subscription Rates:** $30 individuals; $15 single issue. **Remarks:** Accepts advertising.
Circ: (Not Reported)

265 Poem
Huntsville Literary Magazine
University of Alabama in Huntsville Phone: (256)890-6320
English Dept.
c/o N. F. Dillard, Editor
Huntsville, AL 35899
Scholarly magazine of poetry. **Founded:** 1967. **Freq:** Semiannual. **Key Personnel:** N. F. Dillard, Editor. **Subscription Rates:** Included in membership; $15 libraries OOA.
Circ: 400

266 Sew Beautiful
Martha Pullen Co., Inc.
518 Madison St. Phone: (256)533-9586
Huntsville, AL 35801-4205 Fax: (256)533-9630

Magazine of heirloom and heirloom related sewing featuring techniques, articles, designs, and pictorials. **Subtitle:** A Magazine of Smocking & Heirloom Sewing. **Founded:** 1987. **Freq:** 6/year. **Print Method:** Web offset. **Trim Size:** 8 1/8 x 10 7/8. **Cols./Page:** 3. **Col. Width:** 2.25 picas. **Col. Depth:** 9 7/8 inches. **Key Personnel:** Kathy Brower, Editorial Dir.; Martha Pullen, Publisher; Leighann Simmons, Art and Production Dir. **ISSN:** 1063-9160. **Subscription Rates:** $25.95. **Remarks:** Accepts advertising.
Ad Rates: BW: $1,300 **Circ:** ‡80,000
4C: $1,525

267 Speakin' Out News
1300 Meridian St. Phone: (205)551-1020
PO Box 2826 Fax: (205)551-0607
Huntsville, AL 35804
Publisher E-mail: info@speakinoutnews.com

Black community newspaper. **Subtitle:** Speakin' Out News. **Founded:** 1980. **Freq:** Weekly (Wed.). **Print Method:** Offset. **Trim Size:** 10 1/4 x 16. **Cols./Page:** 6. **Col. Width:** 1 1/2 inches. **Col. Depth:** 16 inches. **Key Personnel:** William Smothers, Editor and Publisher, editor@speakinoutnews.com. **Subscription Rates:** $20. **Remarks:** Accepts advertising. **Available Online. URL:** http://www.speakinoutnews.com.
Ad Rates: GLR: $1.08 **Circ:** ‡24,000
BW: $1,440
4C: $1,790
SAU: $15
PCI: $17.25

268 UAH (The University of Alabama in Huntsville) Magazine
The University of Alabama in Huntsville
118 Alumni House Phone: (205)890-6414
Huntsville, AL 35899 Fax: (205)890-6462

Alumni and university interest magazine. **Founded:** 1988. **Freq:** Quarterly. **Print Method:** Offset. **Trim Size:** 81/2 x 11. **Cols./Page:** 3. **Key Personnel:** Phillip Gentry, Editor. **Subscription Rates:** $25 five years. **Remarks:** Advertising not accepted.
Circ: ‡19,000

269 Comcast Cablevision
2047 Max Luther Dr. Phone: (205)859-7800
Huntsville, AL 35810 Fax: (205)852-5599
Free: (800)327-1270

Founded: 1954. **Key Personnel:** Jim Pickens, Contact. **Cities Served:** subscribing households 45,000; 65 channels.

270 WAAY-TV - 31
1000 Montesano Blvd. Phone: (205)533-3131
Huntsville, AL 35801 Fax: (205)533-6616

Format: Commercial TV. **Networks:** ABC. **Operating Hours:** Continuous. **ADI:** Huntsville-Decatur-Florence, AL. **Key Personnel:** M.D. Smith, Contact.

271 WAFF-TV - 48
1414 N. Memorial Pkwy. Phone: (205)533-4848
Huntsville, AL 35810 Fax: (205)533-1337

Format: Commercial TV. **Networks:** NBC. **Founded:** 1954. **Formerly:** WYUR-TV. **Operating Hours:** 5:30 a.m.-1 a.m. **ADI:** Huntsville-Decatur-Florence, AL. **Key Personnel:** Mark Pimentel, General Mgr.

272 WAFN-FM - 92.7
PO Box 4184 Phone: (256)586-9300
Huntsville, AL 35815 Fax: (256)586-9301
Free: (800)867-9270
E-mail: funradio@mindspring.com

Format: Oldies. **Networks:** Mutual Broadcasting System. **Founded:** 1979. **Formerly:** WCRQ-FM (1998). **Operating Hours:** Continuous. **ADI:** Huntsville-Decatur-Florence, AL. **Key Personnel:** Susan McKenney, Sales Mgr.; Michael St. John, General Mgr. **Local Programs:** *The Fun House* 6:00 am - 9:00 am Monday-Friday, Michael St. John, General Mgr. **Wattage:** 3KW. **Ad Rates:** $6-30 per unit.

273 WAHR-FM - 99.1
2714 Lawrence Ave. Phone: (205)536-1568
Huntsville, AL 35801 Fax: (205)536-4416

Format: Adult Contemporary; Soft Rock. **Networks:** NBC. **Owner:** WAHR Inc., 2312 S. Pkwy., Huntsville, AL 35801. **Founded:** 1959. **Operating Hours:** Continuous. **ADI:** Huntsville-Decatur-Florence, AL. **Key Personnel:** Arnold Hornbuckle, President; Freida Jordan, General Mgr., phone (205)534-1666, fax (205)534-1667; Tom Panucci, Sales Mgr.; John Malone, Program Dir.; Bonny O'Brien, News Dir.; Chuck

Miller, Technical Dir.; Mark Hunter, Production Dir.; Abby Kay, Music Dir.; Shellie Erskine, Traffic Dir., phone (205)534-1666, fax (205)534-1667. **Wattage:** 100,000. **Ad Rates:** $35-125 for 30 seconds.

274 WDJL-AM - 1000
6420 Springfield Rd. Phone: (205)852-1223
Huntsville, AL 35806 Fax: (205)852-1900

Format: Urban Contemporary; Gospel. **Networks:** Independent. **Owner:** 5th Ave. Broadcasting, at above address, (256)852-1223, Fax: (256)852-1900. **Founded:** 1968. **Formerly:** WVOV-AM (1980); WTAK-AM (1994). **Operating Hours:** Sunrise-sunset; 100% local. **ADI:** Huntsville-Decatur-Florence, AL. **Key Personnel:** Keith Sharp, Owner; Walter Peavy, Station Mgr.; Tammy Gilliam, Traffic. **Wattage:** 10,000. **Ad Rates:** $10 for 30 seconds.

275 WEUP-AM - 1600
PO Box 11398 Phone: (205)837-9387
Huntsville, AL 35814 Fax: (205)837-9404

Format: Urban Contemporary. **Networks:** American Urban Radio. **Founded:** 1958. **Operating Hours:** Continuous. **ADI:** Huntsville-Decatur-Florence, AL. **Key Personnel:** Virginia Caples, Contact; Hundley Batts, Sr., Contact; Dee Handley, Station Mgr.; Shirley Pride, Traffic Mgr.; Steve Murry, Contact. **Wattage:** 5000 day; 500 night. **Ad Rates:** $18-56 for 30 seconds; $22-70 for 60 seconds.

276 WHNT-TV - 19
200 Holmes Ave. Phone: (205)533-1919
Huntsville, AL 35801 Fax: (205)536-9468
Free: (800)533-8819

Format: Commercial TV. **Networks:** CBS. **Founded:** 1963. **ADI:** Huntsville-Decatur-Florence, AL. **Key Personnel:** Robert Browning, Contact.

277 WLRH-FM - 89.3
University of Alabama-Huntsville Phone: (205)895-9574
S. Loop Rd. Fax: (205)830-4577
Huntsville, AL 35899

Format: Classical; Jazz; News; Public Radio. **Networks:** National Public Radio (NPR). **Owner:** Alabama ETV Commission, at above address. **Founded:** 1976. **Operating Hours:** Continuous. **ADI:** Huntsville-Decatur-Florence, AL. **Key Personnel:** George Dickerson, Station Mgr.; Wayne Blackwell, Program Dir.; Jeff Stratton, News Dir.; Arlene Yedid, Development Director; Cheryl Carlson, Development Assistant; David Brown, Music Dir.; Kenneth Gurley, Music Dir.; Judy Watters, Fine Arts Director. **Wattage:** 100,000. **Ad Rates:** Noncommercial.

278 WNDA-FM - 95.1
2407 9th Ave. SW Phone: (205)534-2433
Huntsville, AL 35805-4198 Fax: (205)533-6265
E-mail: wnda@juno.com

Format: Contemporary Christian. **Networks:** Sun Radio. **Owner:** Wells Broadcasting Co. Inc., at above address. **Founded:** 1971. **Operating Hours:** Continuous; 10% network, 90% local. **ADI:** Huntsville-Decatur-Florence, AL. **Key Personnel:** Fred E. Wells, Station Mgr.; Mike Wilson, Program Mgr./Music Dir. **Wattage:** 50,000. **Ad Rates:** $16 for 30 seconds; $20 for 60 seconds.

279 WOCG-FM - 90.1
Oakwood Rd. NW Phone: (205)726-7418
Huntsville, AL 35896 Fax: (205)726-7417
E-mail: wocg@traveller.com

Format: Religious. **Networks:** USA Radio. **Owner:** Oakwood College, at above address, (205)726-7000. **Founded:** 1979. **Operating Hours:** Continuous; 20% network, 80% local. **ADI:** Huntsville-Decatur-Florence, AL. **Key Personnel:** Victoria L. Miller, General Mgr.; Jody Jones Stennis, Program Dir. **Local Programs:** *Connections*, Jody Jones Stennis. **Wattage:** 25,000. **Ad Rates:** Noncommercial.

280 WRSA-FM - 96.9
PO Box 4144 Phone: (205)498-2634
Huntsville, AL 35802 Fax: (205)498-2791
E-mail: wrsa@mindspring.com

Format: Easy Listening. **Networks:** CBS. **Owner:** NCA, Inc., 287 Tel. Tower Rd., Laceys Spring, AL 35754, (205)498-5259. **Founded:** 1965. **Operating Hours:** Continuous. **ADI:** Huntsville-Decatur-Florence, AL. **Key Personnel:** Paul Nielsen, General Mgr. **Wattage:** 100,000. **Ad Rates:** $75-110 for 30 seconds; $95-140 for 60 seconds.

281 WTKI-AM - 1450
2305 Holmes Ave. NW Phone: (205)533-1450
Huntsville, AL 35816-4017 Fax: (205)536-4349
Free: (800)985-6633

Format: Talk; Sports. **Networks:** ABC; Business Radio. **Owner:** WTKI McDaniel & McDaniel Media, at above address. **Founded:** 1946. **Formerly:** WFIX-AM (1992). **Operating Hours:** Continuous. **ADI:** Huntsville-Decatur-Florence, AL. **Key Personnel:** Fred Holland, General Mgr.; N.H. Shearer, Operations Dir.; Mike Sweeney, News Dir.; Butch Menefer, Station Mgr. **Local Programs:** *Good Morning Huntsville*, Fred Holland; *Sportsnite*, N.H. Shearer. **Wattage:** 1000. **Ad Rates:** $6-28 for 30 seconds; $8-32 for 60 seconds. **URL:** http://www.wtki1450.com.

282 WZDX-TV - 54
PO Box 3889 Phone: (205)533-5454
Huntsville, AL 35810 Fax: (205)533-5315

Format: Commercial TV. **Networks:** Fox. **Founded:** 1985. **ADI:** Huntsville-Decatur-Florence, AL. **Key Personnel:** Milton Grant, General Mgr.

JACKSON, pop. 6,073.

SW AL. Clarke Co. On Tombigbee River, 63 mi. N. of Mobile. Manufactures tricot cloth, textiles, fine printing papers. Lumber, oil, pulpwood, grist mills; cotton gin. Pine timber. Agriculture. Cotton, corn, sweet potatoes.

283 North Jackson Progress
PO Drawer 625 Phone: (256)437-2395
Stevenson, AL 35772 Fax: (256)437-2592

Community newspaper. **Freq:** Semiweekly (Mon. and Thurs.). **Cols./Page:** 6. **Col. Width:** 2 inches. **Col. Depth:** 21 1/2 inches. **Key Personnel:** Larry Glass, Publisher. **Subscription Rates:** $17 local; $14 Senior citizens; $23 out of area. **Remarks:** Accepts advertising.
Ad Rates: PCI: $5.90 **Circ:** 3,500

284 The South Alabamian
PO Box 68 Phone: (205)246-4494
Jackson, AL 36545 Fax: (334)246-7486

Community newspaper. **Subtitle:** The South Alabamian. **Founded:** 1887. **Freq:** Weekly (Thurs.). **Print Method:** Offset. **Cols./Page:** 6. **Col. Width:** 12 inches. **Col. Depth:** 21 inches. **Key Personnel:** Michael M. Breedlove, Publisher; Linda Breedlove, Publisher. **USPS:** 501-840. **Subscription Rates:** $18 individuals; $24 out of area.
Ad Rates: GLR: $5 **Circ:** ‡4,900
BW: $441
SAU: $4
PCI: $4.75

285 WHOD-AM - 1230
4428 Hwy. 43 N. Phone: (334)246-4431
PO Box 518 Fax: (334)246-1980
Jackson, AL 36545-0518

Format: News; Talk; Sports. **Networks:** ABC. **Founded:** 1950. **Operating Hours:** Continuous. **ADI:** Mobile, AL-Pensacola, FL. **Key Personnel:** Dave Hedrick, Manager; Bob Summer, Program Dir. **Wattage:** 1000. **Ad Rates:** $5 for 30 seconds; $7 for 60 seconds.

286 WHOD-FM - 94.5
4428 Hwy. 43 N. Phone: (334)246-4431
PO Box 518 Fax: (334)246-1980
Jackson, AL 36545-0518
Free: (800)462-0945

Format: Adult Contemporary. **Networks:** ABC. **Owner:** Hewett Broadcast Group, at above address. **Founded:** 1967. **Operating Hours:** Continuous. **ADI:** Mobile, AL-Pensacola, FL. **Key Personnel:** Dave Hedrick, Manager; Bob Summer, Program Dir. **Wattage:** 50,000. **Ad Rates:** $7 for 30 seconds; $9 for 60 seconds.

JACKSONVILLE, pop. 7,715.

NE AL. Calhoun Co. 11 mi. N. of Anniston. Jacksonville State University. Residential.

287 The Jacksonville News
Consolidating Publishing
203 Pelham Rd. S. Phone: (256)435-5021
Jacksonville, AL 36265 Fax: (256)435-1028
Publisher E-mail: news@jaxnews.com

Community newspaper. **Founded:** 1936. **Freq:** Weekly (Wed.). **Print Method:** Offset. **Trim Size:** 13 3/4 x 23 3/4. **Cols./Page:** 6. **Col. Width:** 24 nonpareils. **Col. Depth:** 301 agate lines. **Key Personnel:** Phillip A. Sanguinetti, Editor and Publisher. **USPS:** 272-480. **Subscription Rates:** $18 individuals; $28 out of country. **Remarks:** Accepts advertising.
Ad Rates: GLR: $7.25 **Circ:** Combined ‡3,300
BW: $729.17
4C: $984.17
PCI: $7.25

288 WLJS-FM - 91.9
Jacksonville State University Phone: (205)782-5571
Jacksonville, AL 36265 Fax: (205)782-5593

Format: Alternative/New Music/Progressive; Jazz; Classic Rock. **Networks:** National Public Radio (NPR). **Owner:** Board of Trustees of Jacksonville State University, 700 Pelham Rd. North, Jacksonville, AL 36265. **Founded:** 1975. **Operating Hours:** Continuous; 75% local, 25% NPR. **ADI:** Anniston, AL. **Key Personnel:** Joe Langston, General Mgr.; Hose Hosier, Program Dir. **Local Programs:** *The CrossRoads*, Tim Spivy, (205)782-5593; *Exit 185*, Richard Howell, (205)782-5593; *The Process*, Keith Tasker, (205)782-5593. **Wattage:** 3000. **Ad Rates:** Noncommercial.

JASPER†, pop. 11,894.

N. AL. Walker Co. 35 mi. NW of Birmingham. Manufactures lumber, textiles, golf bags. Poultry, poultry processing. Coal mines; timber. Agriculture. Cattle.

289 Daily Mountain Eagle
1301 Viking Dr. Phone: (205)221-2840
PO Box 1469 Fax: (205)221-2421
Jasper, AL 35501
Newspaper with a Democratic orientation. **Founded:** 1872. **Freq:** Daily (eve.), Sunday (morn.). **Print Method:** Offset. **Cols./Page:** 6. **Col. Width:** 25 nonpareils. **Col. Depth:** 308 agate lines. **Key Personnel:** Douglas Pearson, Editor and Publisher; Steve Cox, Managing Editor; John Walker, Advertising Mgr.; Amos Bleich, Circulation Mgr. **Subscription Rates:** $43.20 individuals. **Remarks:** Accepts advertising.
Ad Rates: SAU: $6.30 **Circ:** Mon.-Fri. ★**12,068**
Sun. ★**12,675**

290 WARF-AM - 1240
1499 N. Airport Rd. Phone: (205)221-2222
Jasper, AL 35504 Fax: (205)384-6069

Format: Contemporary Country. **Owner:** Houston L. Pearce, at above address. **Founded:** 1957. **Operating Hours:** Continuous. **Key Personnel:** Fred M. Erwin, General Mgr. **Wattage:** 1000.

291 WFFN-FM - 95.3
1499 N. Airport Rd. Phone: (205)221-2222
Jasper, AL 35504 Fax: (205)384-6069

Format: Contemporary Country. **Owner:** Houston L. Pearce, at above address. **Founded:** 1987. **Operating Hours:** Continuous. **Key Personnel:** Fred M. Erwin, General Mgr. **Wattage:** 3000.

292 WZPQ-AM - 1360
9th Ave. Phone: (205)384-3461
PO Box 622 Fax: (205)384-3462
Jasper, AL 35501

Format: Talk. **Networks:** ABC; Alabama Radio (ALANET). **Owner:** SIS Sound Inc., at above address. **Founded:** 1946. **Formerly:** WWWB-AM (1988). **Operating Hours:** 6 a.m.-10 p.m. **Key Personnel:** W.A. Grant, Jr., President; Joe Cooke, General Mgr. **Wattage:** 1000.

LAFAYETTE

293 Lafayette Sun
The Lafayette Sun
PO Box 378 Phone: (334)864-8885
Lafayette, AL 36862 Fax: (334)864-8310

Community newspaper. **Founded:** 1880. **Freq:** Weekly (Wed.). **Print Method:** Offset. **Cols./Page:** 6. **Col. Width:** 2 inches. **Col. Depth:** 21 1/2 inches. **Key Personnel:** Michael Hand, Publisher. **Subscription Rates:** $14.50 individuals; $0.25 single issue. **Remarks:** Accepts advertising.
Ad Rates: BW: $580.50 **Circ:** 2,800
4C: $730.50
SAU: $9.50
PCI: $4.50

LANETT, pop. 6,897.

E. AL. Chambers Co. 75 mi. NE of Montgomery. Manufactures textiles, textile machinery, cleaning and polishing preparations. Agriculture. Corn, grain, peaches.

294 Valley Times News
220 N. 12th St. Phone: (334)644-1101
Lanett, AL 36863 Fax: (334)644-5587
Publication E-mail: vt-n@wp_ lag.mindspring.com

General newspaper. **Founded:** 1890. **Freq:** Daily (eve.). **Print**

Method: Offset. **Key Personnel:** Nell Walls, Editor and Publisher. **Remarks:** Accepts advertising.
Ad Rates: GLR: $.65 **Circ:** Paid ‡9,500
BW: $754.65 Free ‡40
4C: $984.65
SAU: $5.85
PCI: $6.50

LEEDS, pop. 8,638.

C. AL. Jefferson, Saint Clair, and Shelby Co. 11 mi e. of Birmingham. Residential.

295 The Leeds News
Bryan Publications
720 Parkway Dr. SE Phone: (205)699-2214
Leeds, AL 35094 Fax: (205)699-3157

Community newspaper. **Founded:** 1939. **Freq:** Weekly (Thurs.). **Print Method:** Offset. **Cols./Page:** 6. **Col. Width:** 26 nonpareils. **Col. Depth:** 301 agate lines. **Key Personnel:** Robert Bryan, Publisher; Stephen Adams, Advertising Mgr.; Lionel Green, Editor. **USPS:** 308-980. **Subscription Rates:** $18 individuals; $16.20 senior citizens; $25 out of area; $0.50 single issue. **Remarks:** Accepts advertising.
Ad Rates: GLR: $11.05 **Circ:** Combined 2,998
SAU: $4.05
PCI: $5.85

LINDEN†, pop. 2,773.

W. AL. Marengo Co. 50 mi. W. of Selma. Saw and paper mills. Pine and hardwood timber. Agriculture. Cotton, hay, soybeans.

296 The Democrat-Reporter
PO Box 480040 Phone: (334)295-5224
Linden, AL 36748
Newspaper. **Founded:** Oct. 31, 1879. **Freq:** Weekly (Thurs.). **Print Method:** Offset. **Trim Size:** 14 x 22 3/4. **Cols./Page:** 6. **Col. Width:** 12 picas. **Col. Depth:** 21 1/2 inches. **Key Personnel:** Goodloe Sutton, Editor and Publisher. **USPS:** 153-380. **Subscription Rates:** $25 individuals; $30 out of county; $35 out of state. **Remarks:** Accepts advertising.
Ad Rates: GLR: $.328 **Circ:** ‡7,125
BW: $710.79
4C: $1,000
SAU: $5.51

LINEVILLE, pop. 2,257.

E. AL. Clay Co. 25 mi. SE of Anniston. Lumber, saw and grist mills. Cotton gins. Bottling works. Timber. Agriculture. Cotton, corn, hay.

297 The Clay Times Journal
60132 Hwy 49 Phone: (205)396-5760
PO Box 97 Fax: (205)396-5760
Lineville, AL 36266
Community newspaper. **Founded:** 1990. **Freq:** Weekly (Thurs.). **Print Method:** Web. **Cols./Page:** 6. **Col. Width:** 24 nonpareils. **Col. Depth:** 297 agate lines. **Key Personnel:** C. David Proctor, Editor and Publisher. **ISSN:** 1082-293. **Subscription Rates:** $18 individuals; $24 out of area. **Remarks:** Accepts advertising. **Formerly:** The Lineville Tribune. **Merged with:** The Ashland Progress.
Ad Rates: GLR: $5.75 **Circ:** 3,700
BW: $645
4C: $985
PCI: $5

LIVINGSTON

298 Alabama Counseling Association Journal
Alabama Counseling Association
St. 36, UWA Phone: (205)652-3578
Livingston, AL 35470 Fax: (205)652-3522
Publication E-mail: livelwol@uwamail.westal.edu; elw@univ.westal.edu

Professional journal covering mental health and counseling issues. **Founded:** 1967. **Freq:** Semiannual. **Key Personnel:** Michael LeBeau, Editor, phone (205)665-6262, fax (205)665-6255, lebeaum@um.montevallo.edu. **Subscription Rates:** $18 individuals. **Remarks:** Advertising not accepted.
Circ: (Not Reported)

299 Sumter County Record-Journal
PO Drawer B Phone: (205)652-6100
Livingston, AL 35470 Fax: (205)652-4466

Community newspaper. **Founded:** 1864. **Freq:** Weekly (Thurs.). **Print Method:** Offset. **Cols./Page:** 6. **Col. Width:** 2 inches. **Col. Depth:** 21 1/2 inches. **Key Personnel:** Tommy McGraw, Publisher. **USPS:** 579-740. **Subscription Rates:** $14 individuals; $22 out of state. **Remarks:** Accepts advertising. **Available Online. Formed by the merger of:** Sumter County Record; Sumter County Journal. **Formerly:** Home Record.
Ad Rates: BW: $599.85 **Circ:** 4,000
4C: $999.85
SAU: $4.65
PCI: $4.65

LOUISVILLE

SE AL. Barbour Co. 50 mi. SE of Montgomery.

300 WGIQ-TV - 43
c/o WBIQ-TV Phone: (205)328-8756
2112 11th Ave. S., Ste. 400 Fax: (205)251-2192
Birmingham, AL 35205
E-mail: w.wood@apt.org

Format: Public TV. **Simulcasts:** WBIQ-TV. **Networks:** Public Broadcasting Service (PBS). **Owner:** Alabama Public Television, at above address. **Founded:** Sept. 9, 1968. **Operating Hours:** 7 a.m.-11 p.m. daily. **ADI:** Columbus, GA (Opelika, AL). **Key Personnel:** Henry Bonner, Program Dir.; Joanna Cleary, News Dir.; Judy Stone, Exec. Dir.; Windell Wood, Dir. of Eng.; Phil Hutcheson, Deputy Director, CFO. **Wattage:** 5,000,000 visual; 500,000 aural. **Ad Rates:** Noncommercial. **URL:** http://www.aptv.org.

LUVERNE†, pop. 2,639.

S. AL. Crenshaw Co. 45 mi. S. of Montgomery. Cotton gins and warehouses; bottling works; lumber, grist mills. Timber. Agriculture. Cotton, peanuts, corn.

301 Luverne TV Cable Service
514 Forest Ave. Phone: (334)335-5059
Luverne, AL 36049

Founded: 1967. **Key Personnel:** Marsha Baines. **Cities Served:** Brantley, Crenshaw County, Glenwood, Luverne, Rutledge, AL: subscribing households 1,550; 47 channels; 1 community access channel; 5 hours per week community access programming.

302 WLVN-AM - 1080
415 N. College St. Phone: (205)382-8048
Greenville, AL 36037 Fax: (205)382-2940

Format: Country. **Founded:** 1970. **Operating Hours:** Sunrise-sunset. **Key Personnel:** Joan Reynolds, Contact. **Wattage:** 500. **Ad Rates:** $7-12.50 for 30 seconds; $8.75-15.60 for 60 seconds.

MADISON, pop. 4,057.

N. AL. Madison Co. 5 mi. W. of Huntsville. Residential.

303 Madison County Record
PO Box 175 Phone: (205)772-8666
Madison, AL 35758 Fax: (205)461-6397

Community newspaper. **Founded:** 1968. **Freq:** Weekly (Thurs.). **Print Method:** Offset. Accepts mats. **Cols./Page:** 6. **Col. Width:** 25 nonpareils. **Col. Depth:** 301 agate lines. **Key Personnel:** Richard A. Haston, Editor and Publisher. **ISSN:** 0889-4205. **Subscription Rates:** $15 individuals; $21.50 out of area. **Remarks:** Accepts advertising.
Ad Rates: BW: $967.50 **Circ:** Paid ‡4,000
4C: $1,099.15 Free ‡8,500
SAU: $7.50

MARION†, pop. 4,467.

C. AL. Perry Co. 28 mi. NW of Selma. Judson College (women). Marion Military Institute (men). Cotton gins, lumber, grist mills. Pine timber. Agriculture. Cotton, corn, cattle, poultry.

304 Marion Military Institute Alumni Bulletin
Marion Military Institute
PO Box 420 Phone: (334)683-2530
Marion, AL 36756 Fax: (334)683-2380

Subtitle: A Publication for Alumni, Parents, & Friends. **Founded:** 1904. **Freq:** Quarterly. **Print Method:** Offset. **Trim Size:** 8 x 11. **Cols./Page:** 3. **Col. Depth:** 140 agate lines. **Key Personnel:** Col. Ed. M. Bradford, Editor. **USPS:** 700-900. **Subscription Rates:** Free to qualified subscribers. **Remarks:** Advertising not accepted.
Circ: Controlled ‡10,000

305 Marion Times-Standard
PO Box 418 Phone: (334)683-6318
Marion, AL 36756 Fax: (334)683-4616

Community newspaper. **Freq:** Weekly (Thurs.). **Cols./Page:** 6. **Col. Width:** 12 2/5 picas. **Col. Depth:** 21 1/2 inches. **Key Personnel:** Dave Davis, Publisher.
Circ: 2,400

306 WAJO-AM - 1310
PO Box 930 Phone: (205)683-6168
Marion, AL 36756 Fax: (205)683-9926

Format: Urban Contemporary. **Founded:** 1984. **Formerly:** WJAM-AM. **Operating Hours:** Sunrise-sunset. **Key Personnel:** Elijah Rollins III, Contact; Quentin Rollins, Contact; Bill Bryant, Contact; Glenn King, Contact. **Wattage:** 5000. **Ad Rates:** $5 for 30 seconds; $8 for 60 seconds.

MAXWELL AFB

307 Civil Air Patrol News
Civil Air Patrol, Inc.
105 South Hansell St.
Maxwell AFB, AL 36112-6332
Publication E-mail: cap-news-editor@cap.af.mil

Newspaper (tabloid) covering search and rescue activities, aviation, cadet programs, and aerospace education. **Founded:** Nov. 1968. **Freq:** Monthly. **Print Method:** Offset. **Trim Size:** 11 x 15. **Cols./Page:** 5. **Col. Width:** 22 nonpareils. **Col. Depth:** 196 agate lines. **Key Personnel:** James F. Tynan, Editor. **ISSN:** 0009-7810. **Subscription Rates:** $5 individuals. **Remarks:** Accepts advertising. **URL:** http://www.cap.af.mil.
Ad Rates: BW: $1860 **Circ:** ‡60,000
PCI: $35

MC CALLA

308 Twin County Cable TV, Inc.
Box 483 Phone: (205)477-6210
Mc Calla, AL 35111

Founded: 1988. **Cities Served:** Jefferson and Tuscaloosa Counties, Abernant, Bucksville, and Million Dollar Lake, AL.

MOBILE†, pop. 200,452.

SW AL. Mobile Co. On Mobile River, 157 mi. NE of New Orleans, LA. Important seaport. Shipbuilding and repair center. Commerce in cotton, lumber, coal, aluminum, tobacco, naval stores, citrus fruit, pitch pine, pecans, vegetables, cattle, hog raising. Principal manufacturing: chemicals, lumber, paper, textiles, ships, barges, roofing materials, petroleum products, natural gas, drugs, dyewood extracts, heating and plumbing materials, oxygen and acetylene, soft drinks, rayon. Seafood canning. Fish, shrimp, oyster fisheries. Resort.

309 The Catholic Week
356 Government St. Phone: (205)432-3529
PO Box 349 Fax: (205)434-1547
Mobile, AL 36601
Roman Catholic (tabloid) publication. **Subtitle:** Official Weekly Publication of the Archdiocese of Mobile. **Founded:** Dec. 13, 1934. **Freq:** Weekly (Fri.). **Print Method:** Offset. **Trim Size:** 11 1/2 x 15. **Cols./Page:** 5. **Col. Width:** 26 nonpareils. **Col. Depth:** 196 agate lines. **Key Personnel:** Mary Ann Stevens, Advertising Mgr., phone (334)434-1543; Larry Wahl, Editor. **Subscription Rates:** $12 inside diocese; $17 outside diocese; $30 other countries. **Remarks:** Accepts advertising.
Ad Rates: GLR: $.60 **Circ:** Paid 15,750
BW: $705.60 Non-paid 400
4C: $1,000
PCI: $10.10

310 Christian Conquest Magazine
Charles Simpson Ministries
PO Box Z Phone: (334)633-7900
Mobile, AL 36616 Fax: (334)639-0489
Free: (888)811-2276
Publisher E-mail: csmresources@zebra.net

Christian teaching to equip readers for action. **Founded:** 1969. **Freq:** Quarterly. **Print Method:** Offset. **Trim Size:** 8 1/2 x 10 7/8. **Cols./Page:** 3. **Col. Width:** 28 nonpareils. **Col. Depth:** 133 agate lines. **Key Personnel:** Charles Simpson, Editor-in-Chief; Stephen Simpson, Editor; Candace Dyess, Production Mgr. **ISSN:** 0892-9300. **Subscription Rates:** $2.95 single issue By Contribution. **Remarks:** Advertising not accepted. **Formerly:** New Wine.
Circ: Non-paid ‡10,000

311 College Student Journal
Project Innovation of Mobile
Spring Hill Sta. Phone: (334)343-1878
PO Box 8508 Fax: (334)343-1878
Mobile, AL 36689-0508
Education periodical. **Founded:** 1966. **Freq:** Quarterly. **Print Method:** Offset. **Trim Size:** 5 x 8. **Cols./Page:** 2. **Col. Width:** 30 nonpareils. **Col. Depth:** 110 agate lines. **Key Personnel:** George Uhlig, Ph.D., Editor and Publisher. **ISSN:** 0146-3934.

Subscription Rates: $24 individuals; $30 institutions; $40 other countries. **Remarks:** Advertising not accepted.
Circ: ‡800

312 College & Undergraduate Libraries
The Haworth Press, Inc.
Library Director, Spring Hill College Phone: (334)380-3871
4000 Dauphin St. Fax: (334)460-2086
Mobile, AL 36608
Publisher E-mail: getinfo@haworthpressinc.com

Journal designed to assist librarians at small academic libraries and large undergraduate libraries. **Founded:** 1994. **Freq:** Biennial. **Trim Size:** 6x8 1/2. **Key Personnel:** Alice Harrison Bahr, PhD, Editor, bahr@azalea.shc.edu. **ISSN:** 1069-1316. **Subscription Rates:** $28; $38 industry; $60 libraries. **Remarks:** Accepts advertising.
Ad Rates: BW: $300 **Circ:** 227

313 Elevator World
Elevator World, Inc.
356 Morgan Ave. Phone: (334)479-4514
Mobile, AL 36606 Fax: (334)479-7043
Free: (800)730-5093
Publication E-mail: editorial@elevator-world.com
Publisher E-mail: sales@elevatorworld.com

Magazine for the elevator industry. **Subtitle:** International Publication for the Short Range Vertical Transportation Industry. **Founded:** 1953. **Freq:** Monthly. **Print Method:** Offset. **Trim Size:** 8 1/2 x 11. **Cols./Page:** 3. **Col. Width:** 35 nonpareils. **Col. Depth:** 136 agate lines. **Key Personnel:** Stacie Hyman, Managing Editor; Ricia S. Hendrick, President & Publisher; Linda A. Williams, Vice Pres. & Dir. of Administration; Patricia Cartee, Vice Pres. & Director Commercial Oper.; Val Banks, Director of Production; Robert Caporale, Editor; Iris Weiss, Mktg. Mgr. **ISSN:** 0013-6158. **Subscription Rates:** $67 individuals; $110 other countries. **URL:** http://www.elevator-world.com.
Ad Rates: BW: $1,540 **Circ:** Paid ‡6,200
4C: $2,340 Non-paid ‡162

314 Gulf Coast Historical Review
University of South Alabama
Humanities 344 Phone: (334)460-6210
Mobile, AL 36688 Fax: (334)460-7650

Scholarly journal covering history of the Gulf Coast and the Southern U.S. **Founded:** 1985. **Freq:** Semiannual. **Trim Size:** 9 x 6. **Key Personnel:** Michael Thomason, Managing Editor, phone (334)434-3800, mthomaso@jaguarl.usoutgak,edy. **ISSN:** 0892-9025. **Subscription Rates:** $20 individuals; $8 single issue. **Remarks:** Advertising not accepted.
Circ: Combined 1,150

315 Journal of Instructional Psychology
PO Box 8826, Spring Hill Sta. Phone: (334)343-1878
Mobile, AL 36689-0826 Fax: (334)343-1878

Professional journal aimed at those interested in instructional and educational management. Bilingual and multicultural aspects are treated as well as technology and education. **Founded:** 1974. **Freq:** Quarterly. **Print Method:** Offset. **Trim Size:** 5 x 8. **Key Personnel:** Dr. George E. Uhlig, Editor and Publisher; Mary Ann Robinson, Assoc. Editor; Margaret Mika, Assoc. Editor. **ISSN:** 0094-1956. **Subscription Rates:** $24 individuals; $40 two years; $60 three years; $54 two years institutions; $75 institutions three years; $30 one year; $30 institutions. **Remarks:** Advertising not accepted.
Circ: ‡450

316 Mobile Beacon
2311 Costarides St. Phone: (334)479-0629
PO Box 1407
Mobile, AL 36633
Black community newspaper. **Founded:** 1943. **Freq:** Weekly (Sat.). **Print Method:** Offset. **Cols./Page:** 6. **Col. Width:** 2 1/8 inches. **Col. Depth:** 21 inches. **Key Personnel:** Cleretta T. Blackmon, Editor; Lancie M. Thomas, Publisher. **Subscription Rates:** $19 individuals. **Remarks:** Accepts advertising.
Ad Rates: BW: $912.24 **Circ:** ‡4,952
4C: $305
PCI: $8.11

317 The Mobile Press
304 Government St. Phone: (334)433-1551
PO Box 2488 Fax: (334)434-8662
Mobile, AL 36630
Free: (800)239-1659

General newspaper. Combined weekend edition with the Mobile Register as The Mobile Press Register. **Founded:** 1929. **Freq:** Daily (eve.), Sat. and Sun. (morn.). **Print Method:** Letterpress. **Cols./Page:** 6. **Col. Width:** 2 1/16 inches. **Col. Depth:** 20 1/4 inches. **Key Personnel:** Thomas A. Taylor, Editor; W.J. Hearin, Publisher; John W. Winter, Advertising Mgr.
Circ: Mon.-Fri. 9,471

318 The Mobile Register
The Mobile Press
304 Government St. Phone: (334)433-1551
PO Box 2488 Fax: (334)434-8662
Mobile, AL 36630
Free: (800)239-1659
Publication E-mail: register@bibbs.com

General newspaper. Combined weekend edition with the Mobile Press as the The Mobile Press Register. **Founded:** 1813. **Freq:** Mon.-Sun. (morn.). **Print Method:** Letterpress. **Cols./Page:** 6. **Col. Width:** 2 1/16 inches. **Col. Depth:** 20 1/4 inches. **Key Personnel:** Stan Tiner, Editor; Howard Bronson, Publisher; John W. Winter, Advertising Mgr. **Remarks:** Accepts advertising. **URL:** http://www.mobileregister.com. **Feature Editors:** Robert Buchanan, *Saturday*; Roy C. McAuley, *Photo*; Vivian Cannon, *Religion*; Charles Croft, *Rural Development*; Kathy Dean, *Education*; Kathy Ferchaud, *Environmental*; Pat Goodrich, *Fashion*; Sylivia Hart, *Medical*; David Helms, *Entertainment, Lifestyle, Movie*; David Holloway, *City, News, Political*; Janice Hume, *Family, Food, Living, Society, Women's*; Kathy Jumper, *Aviation, Financial/Business, Real Estate*; Mary Lee Conwell, *Music, Radio, TV*; Steve Mitchell, *Metro*; Ralph Poore, *Editorials*; John Sellers, *Features*; Kim Shugart, *Sports*; Gordon Tatum, *Book, Drama, Garden/Home, Sunday, Travel*.
Ad Rates: BW: $6,075 **Circ:** Mon.-Fri. ★**95,776**
4C: $6,660 Sat. ★**92,207**
PCI: $50 Sun. ★**113,655**

319 National Inner City
National Inner City Enterprises, Inc. (NICE)
1318 Polaris Dr. Phone: (334)602-0210
PO Box 1545
Mobile, AL 36633-1545
African-American community-oriented newspaper. **Founded:** Jan. 1977. **Freq:** Weekly (Thurs.). **Print Method:** Offset. **Trim Size:** 13 x 21.5. **Cols./Page:** 6. **Col. Width:** 2 inches. **Col. Depth:** 21 1/2 inches. **Key Personnel:** Charles W. Porter, Editor and Publisher. **Subscription Rates:** $25 individuals. **Alt. Formats:** Diskette. **Formerly:** Inner City News.
Ad Rates: BW: $2,289.46 **Circ:** ‡8,000
4C: $3,160
SAU: $17.74
PCI: $17.74

320 Negative Capability
Negative Capability Press
62 Ridgelawn Dr. E. Phone: (334)343-6163
Mobile, AL 36608-6116 Fax: (334)344-8478
Publication E-mail: negcap@datasync.com
Publisher E-mail: negcap@datasync.com

Literary review. **Founded:** 1981. **Freq:** 1/year. **Trim Size:** 5 1/2 x 8 1/2. **Key Personnel:** Sue Walker, Editor; Ron Walker, Advertising Mgr. **ISSN:** 0227-5166. **Subscription Rates:** $15; $20 other countries. $5 single issue. $12. **Remarks:** Accepts advertising.
Ad Rates: BW: $50 **Circ:** ‡1,000
4C: $150

321 The New Times
New Times of Mobile
PO Box 40536 Phone: (205)432-0356
Mobile, AL 36640-0536 Fax: (205)432-8320

Black community newspaper. **Founded:** 1981. **Freq:** Biweekly. **Print Method:** Offset. **Cols./Page:** 6. **Col. Width:** 26 nonpareils. **Col. Depth:** 294 agate lines. **Key Personnel:** Vivian Davis Figures, Editor/Administration. **Subscription Rates:** $11 individuals. **Remarks:** Accepts advertising.
Ad Rates: BW: $1,260 **Circ:** Paid ‡5,000
4C: $2,060 Free ‡150
SAU: $10

322 Reading Improvement
Project Innovation of Mobile
Spring Hill Sta. Phone: (334)343-1878
PO Box 8508 Fax: (334)343-1878
Mobile, AL 36689-0508
Magazine for teachers of reading and language arts. **Founded:** 1963. **Freq:** Quarterly. **Print Method:** Offset. **Trim Size:** 8 1/2 x 11. **Cols./Page:** 2. **Col. Width:** 30 nonpareils. **Col. Depth:** 112 agate lines. **Key Personnel:** Phil Feldman, Ed.D., Editor and Publisher, pfeldman@jaguar1.usouthal.edu. **ISSN:** 0034-0510. **Subscription Rates:** $27 individuals; $33 institutions; $43 other countries. **Remarks:** Advertising not accepted.
Circ: ‡2,500

323 The Springhillian
Spring Hill College
4000 Dauphin St. Phone: (334)380-3850
Mobile, AL 36608 Fax: (334)460-2185
Publication E-mail: pmcgraw@shc.edu

Collegiate newspaper. **Founded:** 1923. **Freq:** Weekly. **Print Method:** Offset. **Cols./Page:** 5. **Col. Width:** 2 inches. **Col. Depth:** 14.5 inches. **Key Personnel:** J.P. McGraw, Faculty Advisor, phone (334)380-3845, pmcgraw@shc.edu. **Subscription Rates:** $10 individuals. **Remarks:** Accepts advertising. **URL:** http://azalea.shc.edu/.
Ad Rates: BW: $350 **Circ:** Free ‡2,000
4C: $530
PCI: $5

324 The Vanguard
University of South Alabama
University Board of Publications Phone: (334)460-6442
PO Drawer U-25100 Fax: (334)414-8293
Mobile, AL 36688
Collegiate weekly newspaper. **Founded:** 1964. **Freq:** Weekly. **Print Method:** Offset. **Trim Size:** 13 x 21. **Cols./Page:** 6. **Col. Width:** 2 1/16 inches. **Col. Depth:** 21 inches. **Key Personnel:** Sean Dunlap, Student Publications Mgr., phone (334)460-6897, sdunlap@jaguar/.usouthal.edu.htm. **Subscription Rates:** $30 individuals. **Remarks:** Accepts advertising. **URL:** http://www.usouthal/edu/usa/vanguard/index.html. **Alt. Formats:** Microform.
Ad Rates: BW: $693 **Circ:** Free ‡8,000
4C: $1,013
SAU: $5.50
PCI: $5.50

325 Enstar Cable of Mobile County
6700-A Moffat Rd Phone: (205)649-4900
Mobile, AL 36618 Fax: (205)649-3150

Founded: 1984. **Cities Served:** Mobile County, Mobile, and Prichard, AL.

326 WABB-AM - 1480
1551 Springhill Ave. Phone: (334)432-5572
PO Box 2148 Fax: (334)438-4044
Mobile, AL 36652
E-mail: vinsell@aol.com

Format: Sports; Information; Sports; Information; News; Talk. **Networks:** ABC; NBC; CBS. **Owner:** The Dittman Corp., at above address. **Founded:** 1948. **Operating Hours:** Continuous; 75% network, 25% local. **ADI:** Mobile, AL-Pensacola, FL. **Key Personnel:** Bernard Dittman, Contact; Kathy Richardson, Program Dir. **Local Programs:** *The Bay Today*, David Underhill, (334)432-5572, Fax (334)438-4044; *The Investors' Edge*, Joseph McCarron, (334)478-7818, Fax (334)478-7854. **Wattage:** 5000. **Ad Rates:** $6-20 for 30 seconds; $8-25 for 60 seconds. $6-$20 for 30 seconds; $8-$25 for 60 seconds. Combined advertising rates available with WABB-FM.

327 WABB-FM - 97.5
1551 Springhill Ave. Phone: (334)432-5572
PO Box 2148 Fax: (334)438-4044
Mobile, AL 36652
Free: (800)678-97FM

Format: Contemporary Hit Radio (CHR). **Networks:** ABC. **Owner:** The Dittman Corp., at above address. **Founded:** 1973. **Operating Hours:** Continuous; 10% network, 90% local. **ADI:** Mobile, AL-Pensacola, FL. **Key Personnel:** Bernard Dittman, Contact; Darrin Stone, Program Dir. **Wattage:** 100,000. **Ad Rates:** $24-70 for 30 seconds; $29-88 for 60 seconds. $24-$70 for 30 seconds; $29-$88 for 60 seconds. Combined advertising rates available with WABB-FM.

328 WALA-TV - 10
210 Government St. Phone: (205)434-1050
Mobile, AL 36602 Fax: (205)434-1110

Format: Commercial TV. **Networks:** Fox. **Founded:** 1953. **Operating Hours:** Continuous; 25% network, 75% local. **ADI:** Mobile, AL-Pensacola, FL. **Key Personnel:** Joe Cook, General Mgr.; Scott Wilson, General Sales Mgr.; Bebe Francis, Local Sales Mgr.; Larry Pate, Contact. **Ad Rates:** $10-3000 per unit.

329 WBHY-AM - 840
PO Box 1328 Phone: (334)473-8488
Mobile, AL 36633-1328 Fax: (334)473-8854

Format: Religious. **Owner:** Goforth Media, Inc., at above address. **Founded:** 1943. **Operating Hours:** Sunrise-sunset. **ADI:** Mobile, AL-Pensacola, FL. **Key Personnel:** Wilbur Goforth, Pres./Gen. Mgr., wgoforth@goforth.org; Stephen Goforth, V.P. Programming. **Wattage:** 10,000. **URL:** http://www.goforth.org.

330 WBHY-FM - 88.5
PO Box 1328 Phone: (334)473-8488
Mobile, AL 36633-1328

Format: Religious. **Owner:** Goforth Media Inc., at above address. **Founded:** 1991. **Formerly:** WAYF-FM (1991). **Operating Hours:** Continuous. **ADI:** Mobile, AL-Pensacola, FL. **Key Personnel:** Wilbur Goforth, Pres./General Mgr., wgoforth@goforhth.org. **Wattage:** 33,000. **Ad Rates:** Noncommercial. **URL:** http://www.goforth.org.

331 WBLX-FM - 92.9
1204 Dauphin St. Phone: (334)432-7609
Mobile, AL 36604 Fax: (334)432-2054

Format: Urban Contemporary. **Networks:** ABC. **Owner:** April Broadcasting, 280 Hwy. 35, Red Bank, NJ 07701, (732)758-8900. **Founded:** 1973. **Operating Hours:** Continuous. **ADI:** Mobile, AL-Pensacola, FL. **Key Personnel:** Niecy Davis, Program Dir.; Ed Papie, General Mgr.; Candace Minnefield, General Sales Mgr.; Darlene Eaton, Business Mgr.; Michelle Ritter, Advertising Dir. **Wattage:** 100,000.

332 WDLT-AM - 660
1204 Dauphin St. Phone: (334)432-1660
Mobile, AL 36604 Fax: (334)432-2054

Format: Top 40; Adult Contemporary. **Owner:** April Broadcasting, 280 Hwy. 35, Middletown, NJ 07748, (732)758-8900. **Founded:** 1965. **Formerly**: WHOZ-AM; WBLX-AM. **Operating Hours:** Continuous. **ADI:** Mobile, AL-Pensacola, FL. **Key Personnel:** Ed Papie, General Mgr.; Candace Minnefield, General Sales Mgr.; Mark Dylan, Program Dir. **Local Programs:** *American Alarm Clock*; *Radio AAHS*; *StoryTime Theater*. **Wattage:** 10,000 day; 850 night. **Ad Rates:** $25 for 30 seconds; $50 for 60 seconds. **URL:** http://ww.radio-aahs.com.

333 WDLT-FM - 98.3
PO Box 180426 Phone: (334)380-9098
Mobile, AL 36618-0426 Fax: (334)380-9029

Format: Urban Contemporary. **Networks:** ABC. **Owner:** April Broadcasting, 280 Hwy. 35, Red Bank, AL 07701. **Founded:** 1992. **Formerly**: WJQY-FM (1983). **Operating Hours:** Continuous. **ADI:** Mobile, AL-Pensacola, FL. **Key Personnel:** Ed Papie, General Mgr.; Mark Dylan, Program Dir.; Candace Minnefield, General Sales Mgr. **Wattage:** 50,000. **Ad Rates:** $20 for 30 seconds; $30 for 60 seconds.

334 WEIQ-TV - 42
c/o WBIQ-TV Phone: (205)328-8756
2112 11th Ave. S., Ste. 400 Fax: (205)251-2192
Birmingham, AL 35205
E-mail: w.wood@aptu.org

Format: Public TV. **Simulcasts:** WBIQ-TV Birmingham, AL. **Networks:** Public Broadcasting Service (PBS). **Founded:** Nov. 6, 1964. **Operating Hours:** Continuous (sign off for maintenance Sunday 11 p.m.-Monday 4 a.m.). **ADI:** Mobile, AL-Pensacola, FL. **Key Personnel:** Henry Bonner, Program Dir.; Joanna Cleary, News Dir.; Judy Stone, Exec. Dir.; Windell Wood, Dir. of Eng.; Phil Hutcheson, Deputy Director, CFO. **Wattage:** 1170 Vis 117.0 Aur. **Ad Rates:** Noncommercial. **URL:** http://www.aptv.org.

335 WGOK-AM - 900
Box 1425 Phone: (334)432-8661
Mobile, AL 36633-1425 Fax: (334)432-1921

Format: Urban Contemporary. **Networks:** Southern Broadcasting. **Founded:** 1958. **Operating Hours:** Continuous. **ADI:** Mobile, AL-Pensacola, FL. **Key Personnel:** Irene Wehe, General Mgr.; Charles Merritt, Jr., Program Dir.; Terry Roberds, Station Mgr.; Dickie Roberds, President. **Wattage:** 1000.

336 WHIL-FM - 91.3
PO Box 8509 Phone: (334)380-4685
Mobile, AL 36689-0509 Fax: (334)460-2189
Free: (800)239-9445
E-mail: whil@whil.org

Format: Public Radio; Classical. **Networks:** Public Radio International (PRI); National Public Radio (NPR). **Founded:** 1979. **Operating Hours:** 5 a.m.-midnight. **ADI:** Mobile, AL-Pensacola, FL. **Key Personnel:** Jeff Stoll, General Mgr., stoll@whil.org; Rhoda Baldwin, Development Dir., phone (334)380-4687, baldwin@whil.org; Charles Smoke, Program Dir., phone (334)380-4695, smoke@whil.org. **Wattage:** 100,000. **Ad Rates:** Noncommercial; underwriting available. **URL:** http://www.whil.org.

337 WKRG-TV - 5
555 Broadcast Dr. Phone: (334)479-5555
Mobile, AL 36606 Fax: (334)473-8130
E-mail: tv5@wkrg.com

Format: Commercial TV. **Networks:** CBS. **Owner:** D.H. Long, at above address. **Founded:** 1955. **Operating Hours:** Continuous. **ADI:** Mobile, AL-Pensacola, FL. **Key Personnel:** D.H. Long, Contact.

338 WKSJ-AM - 1270
PO Box 161489 Phone: (334)344-9900
Mobile, AL 36616-2489 Fax: (334)344-3525

Format: Country. **Networks:** Alabama Radio (ALANET). **Founded:** 1966. **Operating Hours:** Continuous. **ADI:** Mobile, AL-Pensacola, FL. **Key Personnel:** Wayne Gardner, General Mgr.; Scott Johnson, Program Dir.; Bill Roth, General Sales Mgr. **Wattage:** 5000.

339 WKSJ-FM - 94.9
PO Box 161489 Phone: (334)344-9900
Mobile, AL 36616-2489 Fax: (334)344-3525

Format: Contemporary Country. **Networks:** ABC. **Owner:** Capitol Broadcasting Corp., PO Box 160706, Mobile, AL 36616-1706, (205)343-1000. **Founded:** 1970. **Operating Hours:** Continuous; 1% network, 99% local. **ADI:** Mobile, AL-Pensacola, FL. **Key Personnel:** Wayne Gardner, General Mgr.; Bill Roth, General Sales Mgr.; Jeff Funk, Music Dir.; Michael P. Sloan, News Dir.; Scott Johnson, Program Dir.; Jim Koblas, Sports Dir. **Wattage:** 100,000.

340 WLPR-AM - 960
PO Box 1328 Phone: (334)473-8488
Mobile, AL 36633-1328 Fax: (334)473-8854
E-mail: wgoforth@goforth.org

Format: Contemporary Christian. **Founded:** 1964. **Formerly**: WGRR-AM (1989). **Operating Hours:** Continuous; 98% network, 2% local. **ADI:** Mobile, AL-Pensacola, FL. **Key Personnel:** Wilbur Goforth, President, wgoforth.org. **Wattage:** 5000. **URL:** http://www.goforth.org; http://www.goforthmedia.net.

341 WMPV-TV - 21
754 Saint Michael St. Phone: (205)633-2100
Mobile, AL 36602-1306 Fax: (205)633-2174

Format: Religious. **Owner:** Sonlight Broadcasting Systems, Inc., at above address. **Founded:** 1989. **Operating Hours:** Continuous; 100% network. **ADI:** Mobile, AL-Pensacola, FL. **Key Personnel:** Stuart J. Roth, Gen. Counsel/CEO; Stephen B. Box, CFO. **Ad Rates:** $55 for 30 seconds; $77 for 60 seconds.

342 WMXC-FM - 99.9
555 Broadcast Dr. Phone: (334)450-0100
PO Box 160587 Fax: (334)479-3418
Mobile, AL 36606

Format: Adult Contemporary. **Networks:** Independent. **Owner:** WKRG-TV, Inc., at above address, Free: (800)527-8643. **Founded:** 1947. **Formerly**: WKRG-FM (1994); WKRD-FM (1994). **Operating Hours:** Continuous; 100% local. **ADI:** Mobile, AL-Pensacola, FL. **Key Personnel:** Kenneth S. Johnson, Jr., General Mgr.; Renee Kirby, Sales Mgr.; Bill Black, Program Dir.; Greg Gordon, Program Dir. **Wattage:** 100,000. **Ad Rates:** Advertising accepted; rates available upon request.

343 WNTM-AM - 710
PO Box 160587 Phone: (334)479-5555
Mobile, AL 36616 Fax: (334)479-3418
E-mail: wntm@capitolweb.com

Format: News; Talk. **Networks:** CBS; Mutual Broadcasting System. **Owner:** Ken Johnson, 555 Broadcast Dr., Mobile, AL 36606, (334)450-0100, Fax: (334)479-3418. **Founded:** 1946. **Formerly**: WKRG-AM. **Operating Hours:** Continuous. **ADI:** Mobile, AL-Pensacola, FL. **Key Personnel:** Rick Brown, Sales Mgr.; Mike Malone, Program Dir.; Lee Shirvanian, Sports Dir.; Rennie Brabner, News Dir.; Ken Johnson, President; Jim Camp, General Mgr. **Local Programs:** *Ask the Expert*, Dick Scott, (205)450-0100; *Ken Allen*, Ken Allen, (205)450-0100; *Mike Malone Show*, Mike Malone, (205)450-0100. **Wattage:** 1000. **Ad Rates:** Advertising accepted; rates available upon request. **URL:** http://www.capitolweb.com.

344 WPMI-TV - 15
661 Azalea Rd. Phone: (205)602-1500
Mobile, AL 36609 Fax: (205)602-1515

Format: Commercial TV. **Networks:** NBC. **Founded:** 1982. **Operating Hours:** Continuous Mon.-Sat.; 5 a.m.-midnight Sun. **ADI:** Mobile, AL-Pensacola, FL. **Key Personnel:** Betty Gurley, Public Affairs Dir.; Pam Seals, Business Mgr.; Sharon Moloney, General Mgr.; Mary Clark, General Sales Mgr.; Perry Dawson, Production Mgr.; Jean Sranley, Promotions Mgr.; Joe Raia, News Dir. **URL:** http://www.wpmi.com.

MONROEVILLE†, pop. 5,674.

S. AL. Monroe Co. 65 mi. SW of Selma. Manufactures pulp, plywood, furniture, precast cement panels, textiles, aluminum doors and windows. Cotton gins. Timber. Agriculture. Cotton, corn, potatoes. Beef cattle.

345 The Monroe Journal
Bolton Newspapers, Inc.
126 Hines St. Phone: (334)575-3282
PO Box 826 Fax: (334)575-3284
Monroeville, AL 36461-0826
Free: (800)239-1985
Publication E-mail: monjour@monroeville.gulf.net

Newspaper. **Founded:** 1866. **Freq:** Weekly (Thurs.). **Print Method:** Offset. **Trim Size:** 13 3/4 x 22 3/4. **Cols./Page:** 6. **Col. Width:** 24 nonpareils. **Col. Depth:** 294 agate lines. **Key Personnel:** Marilyn Handley, Editor; Bo Bolton, Advertising Mgr./Publisher. **ISSN:** 0884-8750. **Subscription Rates:** $23 individuals; $30. **Remarks:** Accepts advertising. **URL:** http://www.monroeville.gulf.net/emall/monjour/. **Alt. Formats:** Microform.
Ad Rates: BW: $685 **Circ:** ‡6,700
SAU: $6.85

346 WMFC-AM - 1360
820 Pineville Rd. Phone: (334)575-3281
PO Box 645 Fax: (334)575-3280
Monroeville, AL 36461-0645

Format: Country. **Networks:** ABC. **Owner:** Monroe Board Company, Inc., at above address. **Founded:** 1952. **Operating Hours:** 6 a.m.-Sunset. **Key Personnel:** David Stewart, Sales Mgr.; David Stewart, General Mgr.; Carol Casey, Music, Programming Office Asst. **Wattage:** 1000. **Ad Rates:** $3.89-7.65 for 30 seconds; $6.76-11.47 for 60 seconds.

347 WMFC-FM - 99.3
820 Pineville Rd. Phone: (334)575-3281
PO Box 645 Fax: (334)575-3280
Monroeville, AL 36461-0645

Format: Country. **Networks:** ABC. **Owner:** Monroe Broadcasting Co., Inc., at above address. **Founded:** 1965. **Operating Hours:** 5am-midnight Mon-Fri; 6am-midnight; Sat-Sun. **ADI:** Mobile, AL-Pensacola, FL. **Key Personnel:** David Stewart, General Mgr.; David Stewart, Sales Mgr.; Carol Casey, Music, Programming, Office Asst. **Wattage:** 30,000. **Ad Rates:** $3.89-7.65 for 30 seconds; $6.76-11.47 for 60 seconds. Combined advertising rates available with WMFC-AM.

MONTEVALLO, pop. 3,965.

C. AL. Shelby Co. 30 mi. S. of Birmingham. Residential.

348 The Alabamian
University of Montevallo Phone: (205)665-2222
PO Box 6222 Fax: (205)665-6232
Montevallo, AL 35115

Collegiate newspaper. **Founded:** 1922. **Freq:** Biweekly. **Print Method:** Offset. **Cols./Page:** 6. **Col. Width:** 24 nonpareils. **Col. Depth:** 294 agate lines. **Key Personnel:** Lean Haney, Editor; April Brush, Business Mgr. **Subscription Rates:** $20. **Remarks:** Accepts advertising.
Ad Rates: BW: $360 **Circ:** Paid 40
4C: $600 Non-paid 2,500
SAU: $2.80

MONTGOMERY†, pop. 178,157.

S. AL. Montgomery Co. On Alabama River, 90 mi. SE of Birmingham. The State Capital. Maxwell Air Force Base. Alabama State University, Faulkner University, Huntingdon College, U.S.A.F Air University. Auburn University at Montgomery, Troy State University. Large livestock and meat packing market; regional distribution center. Manufactures lumber, glass products, furniture, canned foods, fertilizer, textiles, syrup, chemicals, plumbing, heating and air conditioning supplies, cottonseed oil, soft drinks, plastic products, electronics, automotive products.

349 Airpower Journal
Maxwell Air Force Base Phone: (334)953-5322
401 Chennault Cir. Fax: (334)953-5811
Montgomery, AL 36112-6428
Publication E-mail: editor@max1.au.af.mil/air-chronicles.html

Professional military journal covering the development, fielding, and application of air combat power. **Founded:** 1947. **Freq:** Quarterly. **Print Method:** Offset. **Trim Size:** 7 5/8 x 9 3/4. **Cols./Page:** 2. **Col. Width:** 17 picas. **Col. Depth:** 48 picas. **Key Personnel:** Lt. Col. James W. Spencer, Editor. **ISSN:** 0897-0823. **Subscription Rates:** $15 individuals; $18 other countries. **Remarks:** Advertising not accepted. **URL:** http://www.cdsar.af.mil/air-chronicles.html. **Formerly**: Air University Review (1987).
Circ: Paid ‡1,200
Controlled ‡20,000

350 Alabama Arts
State Council on the Arts
201 Monroe St. Phone: (334)242-4076
Montgomery, AL 36104 Fax: (334)240-3269

Magazine covering the arts and artists in Alabama. **Founded:** 1969. **Freq:** Quarterly. **Trim Size:** 8 1/2 x 11. **Key Personnel:** Sharon Heflin, Contact, sharon@arts.al.us. **Subscription Rates:** Free. **Remarks:** Advertising not accepted.
Circ: (Not Reported)

351 The Alabama Cattleman
Alabama Cattleman's Association
201 S. Bainbridge St. Phone: (205)265-1867
PO Box 2499 Fax: (334)834-5326
Montgomery, AL 36102-2499
Publisher E-mail: patca@bellsouth.net

Magazine focusing on cattle breeding. **Founded:** 1958. **Freq:** Monthly. **Print Method:** Offset. **Trim Size:** 8 1/2 X 11. **Cols./Page:** 3. **Col. Width:** 28 nonpareils. **Col. Depth:** 133 agate lines. **Key Personnel:** William E. Powell, Editor. **Subscription Rates:** $30 ACA Members. **Remarks:** Accepts advertising.
Ad Rates: BW: $725 **Circ:** 17,000
4C: $1,175

352 Alabama Farmer
Rural Press USA
7701 Six Forks Rd., Ste. 132 Phone: (919)676-3276
Raleigh, NC 27624 Fax: (919)676-9803
Publication E-mail: farmnews@aol.com

Agricultural newspaper. **Founded:** 1985. **Freq:** Monthly. **Print Method:** Offset. **Trim Size:** 13 1/4 x 10 1/2. **Cols./Page:** 4. **Col. Width:** 2 1/4 inches. **Col. Depth:** 12 7/8 inches. **Key Personnel:** Jeff Tennant, Editor-in-Chief; Donald S. Holland, Advertising Mgr.; Mike Coan, Circulation Mgr.; Pam Golden, Contributing Editor. **Subscription Rates:** Free. **Remarks:** Accepts advertising.
Ad Rates: BW: $1,105 **Circ:** Free ‡12,000
4C: $1,605
PCI: $14

353 Alabama Forests
Alabama Forestry Association
555 Alabama St. Phone: (334)265-8733
Montgomery, AL 36104-4395 Fax: (334)262-1258
Publisher E-mail: alforest@mindspring.com

Magazine devoted to forest management and wood products. **Founded:** Aug. 1958. **Freq:** Quarterly. **Print Method:** Offset. **Trim Size:** 8 1/2 x 11. **Cols./Page:** 3. **Col. Width:** 26 nonpareils. **Col. Depth:** 126 agate lines. **Key Personnel:** Rei Boyce, Editor. **ISSN:** 0275-6625. **Subscription Rates:** $30 individuals. **Remarks:** Accepts advertising.
Circ: ‡3,500

354 The Alabama Librarian
Alabama Library Association
400 S. Union St., No. 255 Phone: (334)262-5210
Montgomery, AL 36104 Fax: (334)262-5255
Publisher E-mail: alala@mindspring.com

Professional magazine (tabloid) for librarians. **Founded:** 1949. **Freq:** Quarterly. **Print Method:** Offset. Desk top. **Trim Size:** 8 1/2 x 11. **Cols./Page:** 3. **Col. Width:** 2 1/4 inches. **Col. Depth:** 10 inches. **Key Personnel:** Rachel Parker, Editor; Missy Mathis, Advertising Mgr./Exec. Dir. **ISSN:** 0002-4295. **Subscription Rates:** $25 U.S.; $55 other countries. **Remarks:** Accepts advertising.
Ad Rates: BW: $210 **Circ:** ‡1,600

355 Alabama Medicine
Medical Association of Alabama
19 S. Jackson St. Phone: (334)263-6441
PO Box 1900 Fax: (205)269-5200
Montgomery, AL 36102-1900
Medical journal. **Freq:** Monthly. **Print Method:** Offset. **Trim Size:** 8 1/4 x 11. **Cols./Page:** 2. **Col. Width:** 3.25 picas. **Col. Depth:** 57 picas. **Key Personnel:** Bill McDonald, Editor; Rhonda Myers, Advertising Mgr. **ISSN:** 0738-4947. **Subscription Rates:** $30 individuals. **Remarks:** Accepts advertising. **Formerly**: Journal of the Medical Association of the State of Alabama.
Ad Rates: BW: $220 **Circ:** Paid ‡5,200
4C: $625 Non-paid ‡100

356 Alabama Municipal Journal
Alabama League of Municipalities
PO Box 1270 Phone: (334)262-2566
Montgomery, AL 36102 Fax: (334)263-0200

Magazine covering municipal government activities. **Founded:** 1943. **Freq:** Monthly. **Print Method:** Offset. **Trim Size:** 8 1/2 x 11. **Cols./Page:** 3. **Col. Width:** 14 picas. **Col. Depth:** 57 picas. **Key Personnel:** Carrie Banks, Media Director/Editor, carrieb@alalm.org. **ISSN:** 0002-4309. **Subscription Rates:** $12 individuals; $1 single issue. **Remarks:** Accepts advertising. **URL:** http://www.alalm.org.
Ad Rates: BW: $348 **Circ:** Paid ‡200
4C: $1,044 Controlled ‡4,300

357 Alfa News
ALFA/Alabama Farmers Federation
PO Box 11000 Phone: (334)288-3900
Montgomery, AL 36191-0001 Fax: (334)284-3957

Fitness magazine with articles on diet and exercise. **Founded:** 1924. **Freq:** Quarterly. **Trim Size:** 8 1/4 x 10 3/4. **Cols./Page:** 3. **Col. Width:** 33 nonpareils. **Col. Depth:** 154 agate lines. **Key Personnel:** Mark A. Morrison, Editor; Ronnie McKinney, Advertising Mgr., phone (334)263-6050, fax (334)263-5933. **Subscription Rates:** $1 nonmembers. **Remarks:** Accepts advertising. **Formerly**: Alabama Farm Bureau News (June 1987).
Ad Rates: GLR: $6 **Circ:** ‡280,000
BW: $1,780
4C: $2,280
PCI: $85

358 Bassmaster Magazine
B.A.S.S. Inc.
5845 Carmichael Rd. Phone: (334)272-9530
Montgomery, AL 36117-2329 Fax: (334)279-7148
Publication E-mail: bmadv@mindspring.com
Publisher E-mail: bassinc@mindspring.com

Magazine covering boating and freshwater bass fishing. **Subtitle:** Published for B.A.S.S. Members. **Founded:** 1968. **Freq:** 10/year. **Print Method:** Offset. Uses mats. **Trim Size:** 7 7/8 x 10 1/2. **Cols./Page:** 3. **Col. Width:** 28 nonpareils. **Col. Depth:** 138 agate lines. **Key Personnel:** Dave Precht, Editor; Helen Sevier, Publisher; Ken Woodard, Advertising Dir.; JoAnna Pitts, Asst. to the Editor. **ISSN:** 0199-3291. **Subscription Rates:** $20 individuals; $3.95 single issue. **Remarks:** Accepts advertising. **URL:** http://www.bassmaster.com.
Ad Rates: BW: $21,170 **Circ:** Paid ★**594,430**
4C: $30,975
PCI: $1,060

359 Developing Alabama
Alabama Development Office
401 Adams Ave. Phone: (334)242-0400
Montgomery, AL 36130 Fax: (334)242-2414
Free: (800)248-0033
Publisher E-mail: aidinfo@www.ado.sate.al.us

Industrial development in Alabama. **Founded:** 1970. **Freq:** Quarterly. **Print Method:** Offset. **Trim Size:** 8 1/2 x 11. **Cols./Page:** 3. **Col. Width:** 28 nonpareils. **Col. Depth:** 140 agate lines. **Key Personnel:** Gerri Miller, Editor, phone (334)242-0476, millerg@www.ado.state.al.us. **Remarks:** Advertising not accepted. **URL:** http://www.ado.state.al.us. **Formerly**: Alabama Development News.
Circ: (Not Reported)

360 Fishing Tackle Retailer
B.A.S.S. Inc.
5776 Carmichael Parkway Phone: (334)272-9530
Montgomery, AL 36117 Fax: (334)279-7148
Publisher E-mail: bassinc@mindspring.com

Magazine for the fishing tackle industry. **Founded:** Aug. 1980. **Freq:** Monthly. **Print Method:** Offset. **Trim Size:** 8 1/8 x 10 7/8. **Cols./Page:** 3. **Col. Width:** 13 picas. **Col. Depth:** 10 inches. **Key Personnel:** Dave Ellison, Editor; Deborah Johnson, Managing Editor; Clem Dippel, Publisher. **ISSN:** 8750-1287. **Subscription Rates:** Free to qualified subscribers. **Remarks:** Accepts advertising.
Ad Rates: BW: $2,728 **Circ:** Controlled ‡22,884
4C: $4,330
PCI: $139

361 Guns&Gear
B.A.S.S. Inc.
PO Box 17900 Phone: (334)272-9530
Montgomery, AL 36141
Publication E-mail: gunsgear@mindspring.com
Publisher E-mail: bassinc@mindspring.com

Hunting and shooting related news and product reviews. **Subtitle:** The Newsmonthly and Equipment Guide for Hunters and Shooters. **Founded:** 1998. **Freq:** 12/year. **Print Method:** Web offset. **Trim Size:** 10 3/4 x 14 3/4. **Cols./Page:** 5. **Key Personnel:** Colin Moore, Editor; Helen Sevier, Publisher; Mike Swain, Adv./Sales Mgr.; Celeste McCaleb, Promotions Coord.; Stephen Mitchell, Adv. Director. **ISSN:** 1521-0138. **Subscription Rates:** $24 individuals; $3.95 single issue. **Remarks:** Accepts advertising. **Formerly**: Southern Outdoors.
Ad Rates: BW: $8,355 **Circ:** Paid 125,000
4C: $10,465

362 The Montgomery Advertiser
MultiMedia Inc.
200 Washington Ave. Phone: (334)262-1611
PO Box 1000 Fax: (334)261-1591
Montgomery, AL 36101-1000
General newspaper. **Founded:** 1828. **Freq:** Mon.-Sun. (morn.). **Print Method:** Offset. **Cols./Page:** 6. **Col. Width:** 2 1/16 inches. **Col. Depth:** 21 inches. **Key Personnel:** William B. Brown, Executive Editor; Richard H. Amberg, Jr., Publisher; Bob Long, Advertising Mgr.; Dave Stillwell, Circulation Mgr.
Circ: Mon.-Sat. ★**55,258**
Sun. ★**70,295**

363 Montgomery Independent
1812 W. Fifth St. Phone: (334)265-7323
Montgomery, AL 36106-1516 Fax: (334)265-7320
Publisher E-mail: independent1@mindspring.com

Community newspaper (tabloid). **Founded:** 1964. **Freq:** Weekly (Thurs.). **Print Method:** Offset. **Trim Size:** 11 1/2 x 17 1/2. **Cols./Page:** 5. **Col. Width:** 2 inches. **Col. Depth:** 16 inches. **Key Personnel:** Robert Martin, Editor and Publisher. **USPS:** 361-180. **Subscription Rates:** $24 individuals; $26 out of area. **Remarks:** Accepts advertising. **URL:** http://www.montgomery-al.com/indy.
Ad Rates: BW: $500 **Circ:** Paid ‡4,700
4C: $700 Free ‡2,300
SAU: $8.82
PCI: $7.50

364 Neighbors
ALFA/Alabama Farmers Federation
PO Box 11000 Phone: (334)288-3900
Montgomery, AL 36191-0001 Fax: (334)284-3957

Magazine covering agriculture, gardening, and rural lifestyles. **Founded:** 1975. **Freq:** Monthly. **Print Method:** Offset. **Trim Size:** 8 1/4 x 10 3/4. **Cols./Page:** 3. **Col. Width:** 27 nonpareils. **Col. Depth:** 140 agate lines. **Key Personnel:** Mark Morrison, Editor; Ronnie McKinney, Advertising Mgr., phone (334)263-6050, fax (334)263-5933. **ISSN:** 0162-2274. **Subscription Rates:** $21 individuals included in membership dues. **Remarks:** Accepts advertising.
Ad Rates: BW: $1,650 **Circ:** Paid 101,159
4C: $2,150
PCI: $85

365 Outdoor Alabama
Alabama Dept. of Conservation and Natural Resources
64 N. Union St. Phone: (334)242-3151
Montgomery, AL 36130-1901 Fax: (334)242-1880
Free: (800)262-3151

State Department of Conservation magazine covering wildlife, state parks, marine resources, marine police and state lands. **Founded:** 1929. **Freq:** 5/year. **Print Method:** Offset. **Trim Size:** 8 3/8 x 10 7/8. **Cols./Page:** 3. **Col. Width:** 28 nonpareils. **Col. Depth:** 133 agate lines. **Key Personnel:** Dan Brothers, Editor, phone (334)242-3130, dbrothers@dcnr.state.al.us. **ISSN:** 0002-4171. **Subscription Rates:** $8 individuals. **Remarks:** Advertising not accepted. **Formerly**: Alabama Conservation.
Circ: ‡12,000

366 Panel World
Hatton-Brown Publishers
PO Box 2268 Phone: (334)834-1170
Montgomery, AL 36102 Fax: (334)834-4525
Free: (800)669-5613
Publisher E-mail: httnbrwn@aol.com

Business magazine serving the worldwide veneer, plywood, and panel board industry. **Founded:** 1960. **Freq:** Bimonthly. **Print Method:** Offset. **Trim Size:** 8 1/8 x 10 7/8. **Cols./Page:** 3. **Col. Width:** 2 1/4 inches. **Col. Depth:** 10 inches. **Key Personnel:** David E. Knight, Publisher; David H. Ramsey, Publisher; John Hibbard, Advertising Mgr.; Dianne Sullivan, General Mgr. **ISSN:** 0889-731X. **Subscription Rates:** $28; Free to qualified subscribers. **Remarks:** Accepts advertising. **Formerly**: Plywood & Panel World (1990).
Ad Rates: BW: $1,975 **Circ:** Controlled ‡12,402
4C: $2,920
PCI: $55

367 Paper Industry
PO Box 5675 Free: (888)224-6611
Montgomery, AL 36103-5675
Tabloid magazine describing new products, processes and services and their application in the North America pulp and paper industries. **Subtitle:** North America's New Product News Leader. **Founded:** 1984. **Freq:** Bimonthly. **Print Method:** Offset. **Trim Size:** 11 x 14 1/2. **Cols./Page:** 4 and 3. **Col. Width:** 36 and 28 nonpareils. **Col. Depth:** 210 agate lines. **Key Personnel:** Peter N. Williamson, Editor; Tim Shaddick, Publisher. **Subscription Rates:** $12 Free to qualified subscribers. **Remarks:** Accepts advertising.
Ad Rates: BW: $2,490 **Circ:** Controlled 17,120
4C: $3,485
PCI: $65

368 Power Equipment Trade
Hatton-Brown Publishers
PO Box 2268 Phone: (334)834-1170
Montgomery, AL 36102 Fax: (334)834-4525
Free: (800)669-5613
Publisher E-mail: httnbrwn@aol.com

Magazine covering outdoor power equipment trade for servicing power equipment dealers. **Subtitle:** First Choice of Power Equipment Professionals. **Founded:** Aug. 1952. **Freq:** 11/year (July/Aug. issues combined). **Print Method:** Offset. **Trim Size:** 8 1/8 x 10 7/8. **Cols./Page:** 3. **Col. Width:** 2 1/4 inches.

Col. Depth: 10 inches. **Key Personnel:** Dianne Sullivan, General Mgr.; D.K. Knight, Publisher; Dave Ramsey, Publisher/Advertising Mgr.; Rich Donnell, Editorial Mgr.; Rhonda Thomas, Circulation Mgr. **ISSN:** 0009-093X. **Subscription Rates:** $40; Free to qualified subscribers. **Remarks:** Accepts advertising. **Formerly:** Chain Saw Age (1989); Chain Saw Age/Power Equipment Trade (1992).
Ad Rates: BW: $1890 **Circ:** Controlled 24,480
4C: $2725
PCI: $33

369 Southern Business & Economic Journal
Auburn University at Montgomery
PO Box 244023
Montgomery, AL 36124-4023

Trade journal covering business and busines research. **Founded:** 1977. **Freq:** Quarterly. **Trim Size:** 6 x 9. **Cols./Page:** 1. **Key Personnel:** Joy L. Clark, Editor; Steven T. Jones, Editor. **ISSN:** 0743-779X. **Subscription Rates:** $25 individuals; $30 libraries; $10 single issue. **Remarks:** Advertising not accepted.
Circ: Combined 950

370 Southern Loggin' Times
Hatton-Brown Publishers
PO Box 2268 Phone: (334)834-1170
Montgomery, AL 36102 Fax: (334)834-4525
Free: (800)669-5613
Publication E-mail: httnbrwn@aol.com
Publisher E-mail: httnbrwn@aol.com

Magazine serving the Southern U.S. logging industry. **Subtitle:** The Southern Logger's Best Friend. **Founded:** 1972. **Freq:** Monthly. **Print Method:** Offset. **Trim Size:** 10 1/4 x 13 3/4. **Cols./Page:** 4. **Col. Width:** 2 1/4 inches. **Col. Depth:** 13 inches. **Key Personnel:** D.K. Knight, Publisher; David H. Ramsey, Pub. and Ad. Dir.; Rhonda Thomas, Circulation Dir.; Dianne Sullivan, General Mgr.; Rich Donnell, Editorial Mgr. **ISSN:** 0744-2106. **Subscription Rates:** $40; Free to qualified subscribers. **Remarks:** Accepts advertising.
Ad Rates: BW: $1,855 **Circ:** Controlled 13,419
4C: $2,800
PCI: $45

371 Timber Harvesting
Hatton-Brown Publishers
P.O.Box 2268 Phone: (334)834-1170
Montgomery, AL 36102 Fax: (334)834-4525
Free: (800)669-5613
Publisher E-mail: httnbrwn@aol.com

National magazine for the U.S. logging industry. **Subtitle:** America's Only National Logging Magazine. **Founded:** 1953. **Freq:** 10/year. **Print Method:** Offset. **Trim Size:** 8 1/8 x 10 7/8. **Cols./Page:** 3. **Col. Width:** 2 1/4 inches. **Col. Depth:** 10 inches. **Key Personnel:** D.K. Knight, Publisher; David H. Ramsey, Publisher/Advertising Dir.; Rich Donnell, Editorial Dir.; Dianne Sullivan, General Mgr.; Rhonda Thomas, Circulation Mgr. **ISSN:** 0160-6433. **Subscription Rates:** Free to qualified subscribers; $40.
Ad Rates: BW: $3535 **Circ:** Controlled 17,679
4C: $4480
PCI: $65

372 Timber Processing
Hatton-Brown Publishers
PO Box 2268 Phone: (334)834-1170
Montgomery, AL 36102 Fax: (334)834-4525
Free: (800)669-5613
Publisher E-mail: httnbrwn@aol.com

North American lumber and wood products industries magazine. **Founded:** 1976. **Freq:** 10Xyearly, Jan/Feb & Jul/Aug issues combined. **Print Method:** Offset. **Trim Size:** 8 1/8 x 10 7/8. **Cols./Page:** 3. **Col. Width:** 2 1/4 inches. **Col. Depth:** 10 inches. **Key Personnel:** David E. Knight, Publisher; David H. Ramsey, Publisher/Advertising Mgr.; Rich Donnell, EDitorial Mgr.; Dianne Sullivan, General Mgr.; Rhonda Thomas, Circulation Dir. **ISSN:** 0885-906X. **Subscription Rates:** $40; Free to qualified subscribers. **Remarks:** Accepts advertising. **Formerly:** Timber Processing Industry (1986).
Ad Rates: BW: $2080 **Circ:** Controlled 19,382
4C: $3025
PCI: $60

373 WAIQ-TV - 26
1255 Madison Ave. Phone: (334)264-9900
Montgomery, AL 36107 Fax: (334)264-7045
Free: (800)239-5239
E-mail: ftr@aptv.org

Format: Public TV. **Simulcasts:** WBIQ-TV. **Networks:** Public Broadcasting Service (PBS). **Founded:** 1955. **Operating Hours:** 7 a.m.-11 p.m. weekdays; 7a.m-11 p.m. Sat.; 7 a.m.-11 p.m. Sun. **ADI:** Montgomery-Selma, AL. **Key Personnel:** Henry Bonner, Program Dir.; Johanna Cleary, News Dir.

374 WAKA-TV - 8
3020 East Blvd. Phone: (334)279-8787
Montgomery, AL 36116 Fax: (334)272-6444
Free: (800)467-0424

Format: Commercial TV. **Networks:** CBS. **Owner:** Cy Bahakel, at above address, (334)271-8888, Fax: (334)272-6444. **Founded:** 1960. **Formerly:** WSLA-TV. **Operating Hours:** Continuous. **ADI:** Montgomery-Selma, AL. **Key Personnel:** David Price, Contact; George Singleton, General Mgr.; Mark Smith, Station Mgr.; Bob Brunner, News Dir. **Wattage:** 316KW ERP. **URL:** http://www.waka.com.

375 WBAM-FM - 98.9
4101 A Wall St. Phone: (334)213-0598
Montgomery, AL 36106 Fax: (334)279-9563

Format: Adult Contemporary; Top 40. **Networks:** Unistar. **Owner:** Deep South Broadcasting Co., at above address. **Founded:** 1978. **Formerly:** WFMI-FM (1978). **Operating Hours:** Continuous; 100% local. **ADI:** Montgomery-Selma, AL. **Key Personnel:** Robert G. Brennan, General Mgr.; Tom Jones, Chief Engineer; Trish Carpenter, Program Dir.; Neal Smith, Contact. **Wattage:** 100,000.

376 WCOV-TV - 20
1 WCOV Ave. Phone: (334)288-7020
Montgomery, AL 36111-2099 Fax: (334)288-5414
E-mail: wcovtv20@mont.mindspring.com

Format: Commercial TV. **Networks:** Fox. **Owner:** David Woods, at above address. **Founded:** 1953. **Operating Hours:** Continuous. **ADI:** Montgomery-Selma, AL. **Key Personnel:** Mary Sledge, Traffic Mgr.; David Woods, Owner/Pres.; John Greenwood, General Mgr.; Phil Witt, Chief Engineer; Amy Drone, Business Mgr.; Dennis Christine, General Sales Mgr.; Glenn Rolston, Nat'l Sales Mgr.; Chris Razavi, Promotions Mgr.; Sandi Owen, Creative Services. **Wattage:** 2,667,000. **Ad Rates:** $15-2000 per unit. **URL:** http://www.wcov.com.

377 WHHY-AM - 1440
3435 Norman Bridge Rd. Phone: (205)264-2288
PO Box 250210 Fax: (205)834-9102
Montgomery, AL 36105

Format: Contemporary Hit Radio (CHR). **Simulcasts:** WHHY-FM. **Networks:** ABC. **Founded:** 1930. **Operating Hours:** Continuous; 5% network, 95% local. **Key Personnel:** Robert Robinson, CEO; Robert Naftel, Program Dir.; Bob Barnes, News Dir.; Bob Robinson, Jr., Sales Mgr. **Wattage:** 100. **Ad Rates:** $20-55 for 30 seconds; $30-65 for 60 seconds.

378 WHHY-FM - 101.9
3435 Norman Bridge Rd. Phone: (205)264-2288
PO Box 250210 Fax: (205)834-9102
Montgomery, AL 36105

Format: Top 40. **Simulcasts:** WHHY-AM. **Founded:** 1962. **Operating Hours:** 100% local. **ADI:** Montgomery-Selma, AL. **Key Personnel:** Ron Walton, General Mgr.; Jimmy Bradley, Sales Mgr.; Scott Hamilton, Operations Mgr.; Bob Barnes, News Dir.; Mary Brazell, Business Mgr. **Wattage:** 100,000. **Ad Rates:** $20-55 for 30 seconds; $30-65 for 60 seconds.

379 WHOA-TV - 32
3251 Harrison Rd. Phone: (334)270-3200
Montgomery, AL 36109 Fax: (334)271-6348

Format: Commercial TV. **Networks:** ABC. **Owner:** Media General, at above address. **Founded:** 1964. **Formerly:** WKAB-TV (1989). **Operating Hours:** 6 a.m.-1 a.m. **ADI:** Montgomery-Selma, AL. **Key Personnel:** Mike Brooks, General Mgr.; Tom Stahl, General Sales Mgr.; Dale Spigner, Controller; James McKenzie, News Dir.; Dan Metzger, Chief Engineer. **Wattage:** 4.6 MW.

380 WLBF-FM - 89.1
PO Box 210789 Phone: (334)271-8900
381 Mendel Pkwy. E. Fax: (334)260-8962
Montgomery, AL 36121
Free: (800)239-8900

Format: Religious. **Networks:** Moody Broadcasting; USA Radio. **Owner:** Faith Broadcasting, Inc, at above address. **Founded:** 1984. **Operating Hours:** Continuous; 90% network. **Key Personnel:** Jon Bulkey, General Mgr.; Bob Crittenden, Music Dir. **Wattage:** 100,000. **Ad Rates:** Noncommercial.

381 WLWI-FM - 92.3
PO Box 4999 Phone: (334)240-9274
Montgomery, AL 36103-4999 Fax: (334)240-9219

Format: Country. **Networks:** Mutual Broadcasting System. **Owner:** Colonial Broadcasting, at above address. **Founded:** 1978. **Operating Hours:** Continuous. **Key Personnel:** Christy Patrick, General Mgr., patrick@wlw1; Al Mason, PD; Joy Smithson, General Sales Mgr. **Wattage:** 100,000. **Ad Rates:** Combined advertising rates available with WMXS. **URL:** http://www.colonialbroadcasting.com.

382 WMCF-TV - 45
300 Mendel Parkway, West Phone: (334)277-4545
Montgomery, AL 36117-5406 Fax: (334)277-6635

Format: Religious. **Networks:** Independent. **Owner:** Sonlight Broadcasting Systems, Inc., at above address, (334)272-0045. **Formerly:** WMPV-TV. **Operating Hours:** 24hrs. **ADI:** Montgomery-Selma, AL. **Key Personnel:** Willie Fears, Station Mgr. **Local Programs:** *Deeper Life* 7:30 p.m. Friday. **Ad Rates:** $40 for 30 seconds; $56 for 60 seconds.

383 WMGY-AM - 800
2305 Upper Weumpka Rd. Phone: (334)834-3710
Montgomery, AL 36107-1345 Fax: (334)834-3711

Format: Religious; Sports. **Networks:** USA Radio. **Owner:** George H. Buck Jr., 1206 Decatur St., New Orleans, LA. **Founded:** 1946. **Operating Hours:** Continuous; 50% local, 50% network. **Key Personnel:** June N. Phelps, Vice President; George H. Buck, Jr., President/Owner; Dane Harris, P.D. and General Mgr. **Wattage:** 1000. **Ad Rates:** $2.50-5 for 30 seconds; $3.50-7.50 for 60 seconds.

384 WMSP-AM - 740
PO Box 4999 Phone: (334)240-9274
Montgomery, AL 36103 Fax: (334)240-9219
Free: (800)239-9544
E-mail: sportsline@sportsradio740.com

Format: Sports. **Networks:** NBC; ESPN Radio; Westwood One Radio. **Founded:** 1953. **Formerly:** WBAM-AM; WLWI-AM. **Operating Hours:** Continuous. **Key Personnel:** Christy Patrick, General Mgr., patrick@wlwl; Michael Butler, Program Dir. **Local Programs:** *The Morning Line*, Richard Bradley; *Sportsline*, John Longshore, Station Mgr. **Wattage:** 50,000 day; 183 night. **Ad Rates:** $10-30 for 30 seconds; $15-35 for 60 seconds.

385 WSFA-TV - 12
PO Box 251200 Phone: (334)288-1212
Montgomery, AL 36125-1200 Fax: (334)613-8302
E-mail: webmaster@wsfa.com

Format: Commercial TV. **Networks:** NBC. **Founded:** 1954. **Operating Hours:** Continuous. **ADI:** Montgomery-Selma, AL. **Key Personnel:** Harold Culver, General Mgr.; Steve Watkins, Business Mgr.; Hoyt Andres, General Sales Mgr.; Tina Joly, News Dir. **Wattage:** 316,000. **URL:** http://www.wsfa.com.

386 WVAS-FM - 90.7
915 S. Jackson St. Phone: (334)229-4287
Montgomery, AL 36101-0271 Fax: (334)269-4995
Free: (800)631-2893
E-mail: wvas@asunet.alasu.edu

Format: Jazz. **Networks:** National Public Radio (NPR). **Founded:** 1984. **Operating Hours:** 19 hrs. Daily; 5% network, 95% local. Continuous Fri-Sat. **ADI:** Montgomery-Selma, AL. **Key Personnel:** John F. Knight, Jr., General Mgr., phone (334)229-4286, fax (334)265-0914; Steve Myers, Program Mgr., phone (334)229-5072, smyers@asunet.alasu.edu. **Wattage:** 80,000. **Ad Rates:** Noncommercial.

MOODY

387 WURL-AM - 760
2999 Radio Park Dr. Phone: (205)699-9875
Moody, AL 35004 Fax: (205)640-4379

Format: Gospel. **Networks:** Independent. **Founded:** 1984. **Operating Hours:** Sunrise-sunset. **Key Personnel:** Bill Davison, Gen. Mgr./Program/Music Dir.; Don Kiser, Station Mgr. **Wattage:** 1000. **Ad Rates:** $3.50-5.90 for 30 seconds; $4.70-7.10 for 60 seconds.

MOULTON†, pop. 3,197.

N. AL. Lawrence Co. 20 mi. SW of Decatur. Manufactures textiles, paper. Cotton gins, metal fabrication, sawmill. Timber. Agriculture. Cotton, corn, hay.

388 The Moulton Advertiser
Slaton Newspapers, Inc.
PO Box 517 Phone: (205)974-1114
Moulton, AL 35650 Fax: (205)974-3097

Newspaper. **Founded:** 1828. **Freq:** Weekly (Thurs.). **Print Method:** Offset. **Cols./Page:** 6. **Col. Width:** 28 nonpareils. **Col. Depth:** 301 agate lines. **Key Personnel:** Luke Slaton, Editor and Publisher. **Subscription Rates:** $21 individuals. **Remarks:** Accepts advertising. **Formerly:** Advertiser.
Ad Rates: BW: $540.51 **Circ:** 5,500
PCI: $5.68

389 WHIY-AM - 1190
13471 Court St. Phone: (205)974-0681
PO Box 307 Fax: (205)905-0103
Moulton, AL 35650

Format: Country. **Simulcasts:** WXKI-FM. **Networks:** USA Radio. **Owner:** Moulton BRD Co., Inc., at above address, Moulton, AL. **Founded:** 1963. **Formerly**: WLCB-AM (1971). **Operating Hours:** 7am-3:30pm. **ADI:** Huntsville-Decatur-Florence, AL. **Key Personnel:** Ray Wallace, General and Sales Manager; Ted Wallace, Program Dir. **Local Programs:** *Hot Trax*, Jeff Towry, (205)974-0681, Fax (205)905-0103. **Wattage:** 2500. **Ad Rates:** $7-9.10 for 30 seconds; $11.25-14.50 for 60 seconds. Combined advertising rates available with WXKI-FM.

MUSCLE SHOALS

390 WLAY-FM - 105.5
620 E. 2nd St. Phone: (205)383-2525
Muscle Shoals, AL 35661 Fax: (205)381-1450

Format: Country. **Networks:** Mutual Broadcasting System. **Owner:** D.Mitchell Self Broadcasting, at above address. **Founded:** 1964. **Operating Hours:** Continuous. **ADI:** Huntsville-Decatur-Florence, AL. **Key Personnel:** John L. Slatton, President; Mark Allen, Station Mgr.; Dave Morrow, Contact. **Wattage:** 6000 KW. **Ad Rates:** $36 per unit. **URL:** http://www.wlay.com.

391 WQPR-FM - 88.7
Box 870370 Phone: (205)348-6644
Tuscaloosa, AL 35487-0370 Fax: (205)348-6648
Free: (800)654-4262

Format: Public Radio; News; Jazz; Classical. **Networks:** National Public Radio (NPR); American Public Radio (APR). **Owner:** University of Alabama, at above address. **Founded:** 1987. **Operating Hours:** Continuous. **Key Personnel:** Roger Duvall, Dir., phone (205)348-8024, rduvall@sa.va.edu; Kathy Henalee, Director of Development; Faye Colbern, Business Mgr. **Wattage:** 100,000. **Ad Rates:** Noncommercial. **URL:** http://www.apr.org.

392 WSHK-FM - 97.7
PO Box 9797 Phone: (205)389-9700
Muscle Shoals, AL 35662 Fax: (205)389-9702

Format: Country. **Networks:** Independent. **Owner:** J. Michael Self Broadcasting, Inc., at above address. **Founded:** 1986. **Formerly**: WZMX-FM (1990). **Operating Hours:** Continuous; 100% local. **ADI:** Huntsville-Decatur-Florence, AL. **Key Personnel:** Kevin Self, General Mgr. **Wattage:** 6000.

NEW HOPE

NC AL. Madison Co. 20 mi. SE of Huntsville.

393 New Hope Telephone Cooperative Inc.
Box 452 Phone: (205)723-4211
New Hope, AL 35760 Fax: (205)723-2800

Founded: 1963. **Key Personnel:** Tom Butler, General Mgr.; Virginia Mann, Contact. **Cities Served:** New Hope, Owens Cross Road, and Grant, AL.

NORTHPORT

394 Charter Communications
Box 778 Phone: (205)339-7972
Northport, AL 35476 Fax: (205)339-0178
Free: (800)239-5609

Founded: May 1995. **Formerly**: CableSouth, Inc.; West Alabama Cable TV. **Key Personnel:** Tom Early, General Mgr.; Kristie Maddox, Office Mgr.; Derrick Harris, Chief Tech.; Steve Dowdle, Accounts Payable & Warehouse. **Cities Served:** Northport, AL; Tuscaloosa, AL; Moundville, AL; Coker, AL.: subscribing households 8,500; 43 channels; 1 community access channel; 168 hours per week community access programming.

395 WNPT-FM - 102.9
5200 Flatwoods Rd. Phone: (205)758-3311
Northport, AL 35473 Fax: (205)330-5605

Format: Blues; Gospel; Urban Contemporary. **Owner:** Willis Broadcasting Coporation, at above address. **Founded:** 1990. **Operating Hours:** Continuous. **Key Personnel:** Wilene Prewitt, Station Mgr.; Bruce Browne, Music Dir.; John E. Owens, Jr., Gospel Music Dir. **Wattage:** 50,000. **Ad Rates:** $8-12 for 30 seconds; $14-18 for 60 seconds. $8-$12 for 30 seconds; $10-$15 for 60 seconds. Combined advertising rates available with WNPT-FM: $12-$18 for 30 seconds; $14-$.

WTXT-FM - See Fayette

ONEONTA†, pop. 4,824.

N. AL. Blount Co. 36 mi. NE of Birmingham. Manufactures aluminum utensils, plastic tubing, textiles, lime, cement. Lumber, coal. Agriculture. Cotton, hay, truck crops, soybeans, beef, cattle, dairying.

396 The Blount Countian
The Southern Democrat, Inc.
PO Box 310 Phone: (205)625-3231
Oneonta, AL 35121 Fax: (205)625-3239
Publication E-mail: countian@nacell.net

County newspaper. **Founded:** 1894. **Freq:** Weekly (Wed.). **Print Method:** Offset. **Cols./Page:** 6. **Col. Width:** 2 1/16 inches. **Col. Depth:** 21 1/2 inches. **Key Personnel:** Molly Howard Ryan, Editor and Publisher. **Subscription Rates:** $12; $15 other counties; $20 out of state. **Remarks:** Advertising not accepted for alcoholic beverages. **Formerly**: The Southern Democrat (1991).
Ad Rates: GLR: $5 **Circ:** 6,500
BW: $645
SAU: $4.75

397 The Blount County Shopping Guide
Arab Tribune
PO Box 310 Phone: (205)625-3231
Oneonta, AL 35121 Fax: (205)625-3239

Shopper. **Freq:** Weekly (Wed.). **Print Method:** Offset. **Trim Size:** 13 3/4 x 22 3/4. **Cols./Page:** 6. **Col. Width:** 25 nonpareils. **Col. Depth:** 301 agate lines. **Key Personnel:** Molly Howard Ryan, Editor and Publisher. **Remarks:** Accepts advertising. **Formerly**: The Southerner (1991).
Ad Rates: SAU: $5.25 **Circ:** Free ‡7,300

398 Oneonta Telephone Co.
PO Box 1500
Oneonta, AL 35121-0017

Key Personnel: Brian Corr, General Mgr. **Cities Served:** subscribing households 2,200; 36 channels.

399 WCRL-AM - 1570
908 2nd Ave. E. Phone: (205)625-3333
PO Box 490 Fax: (205)625-5433
Oneonta, AL 35121

Format: Oldies. **Networks:** Jones Satellite; Alabama Radio (ALANET). **Owner:** Blount Country Broadcasting, at above address. **Founded:** 1952. **Operating Hours:** Sunrise-11 p.m.; 90% network, 10% local. **Key Personnel:** L.D. Bentley, News Dir.; Danny Bentley, Contact. **Wattage:** 2500 day. **Ad Rates:** $3-7 for 30 seconds; $4-8 for 60 seconds. $3-$7 for 30 seconds; $4-$8 for 60 seconds. Combined advertising rates available with WKLD-FM.

400 WKLD-FM - 97.7
908 2nd Ave. E. Phone: (205)625-3333
PO Box 490 Fax: (205)625-5433
Oneonta, AL 35121

Format: Country. **Networks:** Satellite Music Network. **Owner:** Blount County Broadcasting System, at above address. **Founded:** 1967. **Operating Hours:** Continuous; 60% network, 40% local. **Key Personnel:** L.D. Bentley, News Dir.; Danny Bentley, Contact. **Wattage:** 4000. **Ad Rates:** $4-8 for 30 seconds; $6-10 for 60 seconds. $3-$7 for 30 seconds; $4-$8 for 60 seconds. Combined advertising rates available with WCRL-AM.

OPELIKA†, pop. 21,896.

E. AL. Lee Co. 26 mi. NW of Columbus, GA. Manufactures cotton goods, magnetic tape, auto tires, plastics, lumber, fertilizer, athletic equipment, bakery and dairy products. Pine timber. Agriculture. Dairying.

401 Opelika-Auburn News
3505 Pepperell Pkwy. Phone: (205)749-6271
PO Box 2208 Fax: (205)749-1228
Opelika, AL 36801
General newspaper. **Founded:** 1904. **Freq:** Daily and Sunday (morn.). **Print Method:** Offset. **Cols./Page:** 6. **Col. Width:** 25 nonpareils. **Col. Depth:** 303 agate lines. **Key Personnel:** Steve F. McPhaul, Publisher; Phillip Lucas, Managing Editor; Jack Nolan, Advertising Dir.; Tim Maxwell, Plant Mgr.; Dina Lidestri, Composing Foreman; Earl Mitchell, Circulation Mgr. **ISSN:** 1044-7539. **Subscription Rates:** $101.75 individuals. **Remarks:** Accepts advertising. Monday-Friday: BW: $1,700; 4C: $310; PCI: $12.92; Sunday: PCI: $13.98.
Circ: Mon.-Fri. ★13,992
Sun. ★14,249

402 WSWS-TV - 66
PO Box 870 Phone: (334)749-5766
Opelika, AL 36803-0870 Fax: (334)749-5583

Format: Religious. **Owner:** Pappas Telecasting Companies, PO Box 6922, Clearwater, FL 34618, (813)535-5622. **Founded:** 1984. **Operating Hours:** 6 a.m.-midnight. **ADI:** Columbus, GA (Opelika, AL). **Key Personnel:** Jack Moffit, General Mgr.; Walter Dix, Station & General Sales Mgr.; Linda Daniels, Local Sales Mgr.; Jeremy Campbell, Traffic Mgr./Satellite Coordinator; Connie Dawson, Head of Research.

403 WZMG-AM - 910
915 Saugahatchee Lake Rd. Phone: (334)745-4656
PO Box 2329 Fax: (334)749-1520
Opelika, AL 36803

Format: Urban Contemporary; Gospel. **Networks:** ABC. **Owner:** Fuller Broadcasting Co, Inc., at above address. **Founded:** 1968. **Formerly**: WAOA-AM (1985). **Operating Hours:** Continuous. **ADI:** Columbus, GA (Opelika, AL). **Key Personnel:** Gary Fuller, President/Gen. Mgr.; Richard La Grand, Sales Mgr.; Russell Baty, News/Sports Dir.; Yvonne Batts, Program Dir. **Local Programs:** *Lee County Report*, Russell Baty; *Morning Show*, Russell Baty. **Wattage:** 1000. **Ad Rates:** $9.20-10.90 for 30 seconds; $11.45-13.65 for 60 seconds.

OPP, pop. 7,204.

S. AL. Covington Co. 75 mi. S. of MOntgomery. Manufactures textiles, lumber. Agriculture. Hogs, cotton, peanuts.

404 The Opp News
PO Box 409 Phone: (334)493-3595
Opp, AL 36467 Fax: (334)493-4901

Local newspaper. **Founded:** 1901. **Freq:** Weekly (Thurs.). **Print Method:** Offset. **Cols./Page:** 6. **Col. Width:** 21 nonpareils. **Col. Depth:** 308 agate lines. **Key Personnel:** Tracey Nelson, Editor; Randy Pebworth, Publisher; Pam Messick, Advertising Mgr. **Subscription Rates:** $22 individuals; $14 Six Months. **Remarks:** Accepts advertising.
Ad Rates: BW: $459.90 **Circ:** (Not Reported)
4C: $759.90
SAU: $3.40
PCI: $4

405 Opp Cablevision
Box 311 Phone: (334)493-4571
Opp, AL 36467 Fax: (334)493-6666

Owner: Opp Utilities, at above address. **Key Personnel:** Mike Russell, Contact; Charles McGowan, General Mgr. **Cities Served:** Opp and Kinston, AL.

406 WAMI-AM - 860
Box 169 Phone: (334)493-3588
Opp, AL 36467-0169 Fax: (334)493-4182

Format: Country. **Simulcasts:** WAMI-FM. **Networks:** Alabama Radio (ALANET); ABC. **Owner:** Opp Broadcasting Co., Inc., at above address. **Founded:** 1952. **Operating Hours:** 5 a.m.-midnight; 100% local. **Key Personnel:** William P. Smith, Contact; Amy Ladwig, News Dir.; Mike Glisson, Music Dir. **Wattage:** 1000. **Ad Rates:** $3-6 for 30 seconds; $4-10 for 60 seconds.

407 WAMI-FM - 102.3
Box 169 Phone: (334)493-3588
Opp, AL 36467 Fax: (334)493-4182

Format: Country. **Simulcasts:** WAMI-AM. **Networks:** ABC. **Owner:** Opp Broadcasting Co., Inc., at above address. **Founded:** 1974. **Operating Hours:** Continuous; 100% local. **Key Personnel:** Bill Smith, General Mgr.; Chris Michael, Contact; Mike Glisson, Music Dir. **Wattage:** 3400. **Ad Rates:** $5-7 for 30 seconds; $8-10 for 60 seconds.

408 WOPP-AM - 1290
1101 Cameron Rd. Phone: (334)493-4545
Opp, AL 36467 Fax: (334)493-4546
Free: (800)239-3323
E-mail: wopp@wopp.com

Format: Country. **Networks:** Standard Broadcast News; ABC. **Founded:** 1980. **Operating Hours:** Continuous. **Key Personnel:** Robert H. Boothe, Jr., General Mgr.; Cris Anderson, Program Dir.; Ruth Boothe, Station Mgr.; Ronnie L. Boothe, Chief Engineer; Tara Rhoads, Music Dir. **Wattage:** 2500. **Ad Rates:** $5 for 30 seconds; $9 for 60 seconds. **URL:** http://www.wopp.com.

OXFORD, pop. 8,939.

NE AL. Calhoun Co. 5 mi. S. of Anniston. Manufactures machinery, prefabricated buildings, cordage, feed, cleaning preparations. Hatcheries. Agriculture. Cotton, dairying, poultry.

409 WOXR-AM - 1580
PO Box 3770 Phone: (205)835-1580
Oxford, AL 36203 Fax: (205)831-1500

Format: Country. **Owner:** Joe Woodard, at above address. **Founded:** 1986. **Formerly:** WEYY-FM. **Operating Hours:** 6 a.m.-10 p.m.; 100% local. **ADI:** Anniston, AL. **Key Personnel:** Joe Woodard, Owner; Julie Daniels, Public Affairs Dir.; Chris Wright, Program Dir.; Harry Mabry, Sales Mgr. **Wattage:** 2500. **Ad Rates:** $6-9 for 30 seconds; $8-11 for 60 seconds. Combined advertising rates available with WVOK-FM.

410 WTBJ-FM - 91
1500 Airport Rd. Phone: (256)831-3333
Oxford, AL 36203 Fax: (256)831-5895
E-mail: cog@nti.net

Format: Contemporary Christian; Religious. **Founded:** May 1994. **Operating Hours:** Continuous. **Key Personnel:** Dr. C. O. Grinstead, General Mgr.; Jerry Johnston, Program Mgr. **Ad Rates:** Noncommercial.

411 WVOK-FM - 97.9
PO Box 3770 Phone: (256)835-1580
Oxford, AL 36203 Fax: (256)831-1500
E-mail: k98@nti.net

Format: Adult Contemporary. **Owner:** Woodward Broadcasting Co., Inc., at above address. **Founded:** Feb. 19, 1990. **Former name:** WKFN-FM (1992). **Operating Hours:** Continuous. **Key Personnel:** George Salmon, General Mgr.; Bill Giddens, Sales Mgr.; Chris Wright, Program Dir. **Wattage:** 3000. **Ad Rates:** $16-20 for 30 seconds; $20-26 for 60 seconds. **URL:** http://www.nti.net/k98.

OZARK†.

SE AL. Dale Co. 30 mi. N. of Florida.

412 The Southern Star
PO Box 1729 Phone: (334)774-2715
Ozark, AL 36361 Fax: (334)774-9619

Community newspaper. **Freq:** Weekly (Wed.). **Cols./Page:** 6. **Col. Width:** 12 1/2 picas. **Col. Depth:** 21 1/2 inches. **Key Personnel:** Joseph H. Adams, Publisher. **Subscription Rates:** $19.44; $21.60 out of area; $25 out of state. **Remarks:** Accepts advertising.
Ad Rates: 4C: $100 **Circ:** 5,000
PCI: $5

413 WDFX-TV - 34
318 El Palacia Plaza Phone: (334)774-8000
Ozark, AL 36360 Fax: (334)774-1118
E-mail: wdfx@ala.net

Format: Commercial TV. **Networks:** Fox. **Owner:** Woods Television Co., L.L.C., at above address. **Former name:** WDAU-TV. **Operating Hours:** Continuous. **ADI:** Dothan, AL. **Key Personnel:** Renee Rutledge, Promotions Dir./Operations Mgr.; Leisl Strength, Traffic Mgr.; David Woods, General Mgr. **Wattage:** 1,100,000. **URL:** http://www.wdfx.com.

414 WOAB-FM - 104.9
Enterprise Hwy. Phone: (334)774-5600
PO Box 911
Ozark, AL 36361

Format: Country. **Networks:** Independent. **Founded:** 1967. **Operating Hours:** 100% local. **Key Personnel:** Howard Parrish, Jr., General Mgr. **Wattage:** 3500. **Ad Rates:** $4.90 for 30 seconds; $6.90 for 60 seconds.

415 WOZK-AM - 900
Enterprise Hwy. Phone: (334)774-5600
PO Box 911
Ozark, AL 36361

Format: Middle-of-the-Road (MOR); Easy Listening; Oldies. **Networks:** Independent. **Founded:** 1953. **Operating Hours:** 17 hrs. Daily; 100% local. **Key Personnel:** Howard Parrish, Jr., General Mgr. **Wattage:** 1000. **Ad Rates:** $4.90 for 30 seconds; $6.90 for 60 seconds.

416 WRJM-FM - 93.7
409 E. Broad St. Phone: (334)774-7673
Ozark, AL 36360 Fax: (205)774-7979
Free: (800)848-0937

Format: Soft Rock; Adult Contemporary. **Owner:** Stage Door Corp., at above address. **Founded:** 1969. **Operating Hours:** Continuous. **Key Personnel:** Jack Mizell, General Mgr.; Susannahye Hodges, Operations Mgr.; Vince Hodges, Sales Mgr.; Susannah Mizell, Operations Mgr. **Wattage:** 100,000. **Ad Rates:** $18 for 30 seconds; $24 for 60 seconds.

PELL CITY†, pop. 6,616.

N. AL. Saint Clair Co. On Coosa River, 32 mi. NE of Birmingham. Manufactures cotton goods, lumber, barrel heads, plastic pipe. Timber. Agriculture. Cotton, corn.

St. Clair News-Aegis - See St. Clair

417 WFHK-AM - 1430
22 Cogswell Ave. Phone: (205)338-1430
Pell City, AL 35125-2438 Fax: (205)338-2238

Format: Country. **Networks:** ABC; Alabama Radio (ALANET). **Owner:** St. Clair Broadcasting System, Inc., at above address. **Founded:** 1956. **Operating Hours:** 6 a.m.-6 p.m.; 5% network, 95% local. **Key Personnel:** Doug Williamson, Contact. **Wattage:** 5000. **Ad Rates:** $4.70 for 30 seconds; $7.35 for 60 seconds. Combined advertising rates available with WSSY-FM.

PHENIX CITY†, pop. 26,928.

E. AL. Lee and Russell Co. 5 mi. N. of Brickyard. Residential.

418 The Phenix Citizen
Chicken Dinner News
PO Box 1267 Phone: (205)298-0679
Phenix City, AL 36868 Fax: (205)298-0690

Local newspaper. **Founded:** 1954. **Freq:** Weekly (Thurs.). **Print Method:** Offset. **Cols./Page:** 6. **Col. Width:** 26 nonpareils. **Col. Depth:** 301 agate lines. **Key Personnel:** Mike Venable, Publisher; Jill Tigner, Publisher. **USPS:** 429-680. **Subscription Rates:** $15 individuals; $17.50 out of area; $25 out of state. **Remarks:** Accepts advertising.
Ad Rates: BW: $535.50 **Circ:** ‡5,000
4C: $655.50
PCI: $4.25

419 Phenix City CATV
PO Box 130 Phone: (334)298-7000
Phenix City, AL 36868 Fax: (334)298-0833

Owner: Roy M. Greene, at above address. **Founded:** 1964. **Key Personnel:** Lynne Frakes, General Mgr.; Roy Greene, Contact. **Cities Served:** Crawford, Fort Mitchell, Hatchechubee, Hurtsboro, Phenix City, Salem, Seale, Smiths, AL: subscribing households 17,000; 67 channels; 1 community access channel; 80 hours per week community access programming.

420 WFRC-FM - 90.5
1010 7th Pl. Phone: (205)291-0399
Phenix City, AL 36867 Free: (800)543-1495

Format: Religious. **Networks:** Family Stations Radio. **Owner:** Family Stations Inc., 290 Hegenberger Rd., Oakland, CA 94621, (415)568-6200. **Founded:** 1985. **Operating Hours:** Continuous; 85% network, 15% local. **Key Personnel:** Sandra Salewski, Contact; Harold Camping, President. **Wattage:** 8500 ERP.

PIEDMONT, pop. 5,544.

NE AL. Calhoun Co. 75 mi. NE of Birmingham. Cotton yarn, lumber mills; cotton gins. Iron mines; mineral springs. Dairy, poultry, fruit, grain farms.

421 The Journal Independent
115 N. Center Ave. Phone: (205)447-2837
Piedmont, AL 36272 Fax: (205)447-2837

Community newspaper. **Founded:** 1907. **Freq:** Weekly (Wed.). **Print Method:** Offset. **Cols./Page:** 6. **Col. Width:** 26 nonpareils. **Col. Depth:** 21 1/2 inches. **Key Personnel:** Lane Weatherbee, Editor and Publisher; Carol Weatherbee, Advertising Mgr. **USPS:** 432-080. **Subscription Rates:** $16.05 individuals. **Remarks:** Accepts advertising. **Alt. Formats:** Mailing labels; Mailing labels.
Ad Rates: GLR: $2.50 **Circ:** ‡3,450
BW: $607.59
4C: $4.50
PCI: $5.04

422 TCI Cablevision of Alabama
109 Seaboard Ave. Phone: (205)447-7871
Piedmont, AL 36272 Fax: (205)447-8630

Key Personnel: Earl Hines, Contact; Barry Kerr, Contact; Darrel Currier, Contact; Cindy Smith, Office Mgr. **Cities Served:** Piedmont and Centre, AL; Cherokee, CO. 36 channels.

PINSON

423 Journal of Religion in Disability and Rehabilitation
The Haworth Press, Inc.
6473 Pine Tree Ln. Phone: (205)681-1457
Pinson, AL 35126
Publication E-mail: getinfo@haworth.com
Publisher E-mail: getinfo@haworthpressinc.com

Journal for religious professionals on the developments in the field of disability and rehabilitation. **Founded:** 1994. **Freq:** Quarterly. **Trim Size:** 6x8 1/2. **Key Personnel:** William A. Blair and Dana Y. Davidson, Editor; Bill Cohen, Publisher. **ISSN:** 1059-9258. **Subscription Rates:** $36 individuals; $48 Industry; $105 libraries 30% more for Canada,40% more for other countries. **Remarks:** Accepts advertising.
Ad Rates: BW: $300 **Circ:** Paid 335

PRATTVILLE†, pop. 18,647.

C. AL. Autauga Co. 12 mi. NW of Montgomery. Manufactures cotton gin machinery, textiles, cotton, paper, rope, boxes, brake shoes, webbing. Timber. Agriculture.

424 The Prattville Progress
Montgomery Advertiser Corp.
PO Drawer C Phone: (334)365-6739
Prattville, AL 36067 Fax: (334)365-1400

Newspaper. **Founded:** Oct. 29, 1886. **Freq:** Biweekly. **Print Method:** Offset. **Cols./Page:** 6. **Col. Width:** 24 nonpareils. **Col. Depth:** 294 agate lines. **Key Personnel:** Brighman Broch, Editor; Lamar Smitherman, Publisher; Chris Caver, Advertising Mgr. **Subscription Rates:** $32 individuals; $40 out of area. **Remarks:** Accepts advertising.
Ad Rates: GLR: $.56 **Circ:** ‡5,800
PCI: $7.84

RAINSVILLE, pop. 3,907.

NE AL. DeKalb Co. 30 mi. N. of Gadsden. State College at Rainsville. Manufactures textiles, furniture, feed. Agriculture. Cotton, poultry.

425 The Weekly Post
PO Box 849 Phone: (256)638-4027
Rainsville, AL 35986-0849 Fax: (256)638-2329

Newspaper. **Founded:** July 1980. **Freq:** Weekly (Thurs.). **Print Method:** Offset. **Trim Size:** 13 x 21 1/2. **Cols./Page:** 6. **Col. Width:** 2 1/8 inches. **Col. Depth:** 21 1/2 inches. **Key Personnel:** Carey Baker, Publisher; Keith Mooney, Advertising Mgr. **USPS:** 567-110. **Subscription Rates:** Free; $5.50 by mail; $6.50 Out of County; $7.50 out of state. **Remarks:** Accepts advertising. **Merged with:** The Tri-City Times.
Ad Rates: GLR: $.30 **Circ:** Paid ‡2,250
BW: $516 Free ‡200
4C: $776
PCI: $4

426 WVSM-AM - 1500
368 McCurdy Ave N Phone: (205)638-2137
PO Box 339
Rainsville, AL 35986

Format: Southern Gospel. **Networks:** USA Radio. **Owner:** Sand Mountain Advertising Co., Inc., at above address. **Founded:** 1967. **Operating Hours:** Sunrise-sunset; 100% local. **Key Personnel:** Mark Huber, Contact; Kayron Guffey, Contact; Annie Ruth Huber, Sales Mgr. **Wattage:** 1000. **Ad Rates:** $4 for 10 seconds; $6.25-7.25 for 30 seconds; $7.25-8.25 for 60 seconds. **URL:** http://www.rainsville.com/wusm.

RED BAY, pop. 3,232.

NW AL. Franklin Co. 38 mi. SW of Florence. Recreation areas. Feed mills. Manufactures mobile and motor homes, textiles. Lumber. Agriculture. Cotton, grain, soybeans, livestock, poultry.

427 The Red Bay News
120 4th Ave., SE Phone: (205)356-2148
PO Box 1339 Fax: (205)356-2787
Red Bay, AL 35582-1339
Community newspaper. **Founded:** 1963. **Freq:** Weekly (Wed.). **Print Method:** Offset. **Cols./Page:** 6. **Col. Width:** 24 nonpareils. **Col. Depth:** 301 agate lines. **Key Personnel:** Susan Harp, Editor and Publisher. **Subscription Rates:** $13 individuals. **Remarks:** Accepts advertising.
Ad Rates: SAU: $3.99 **Circ:** 5,300

428 WRMG-AM - 1430
PO Box 656 Phone: (205)356-4458
Red Bay, AL 35582-0656

Format: Country; Religious. **Networks:** Alabama News. **Own-**

er: Redmont Broadcasting Corp., at above address. **Founded:** 1968. **Operating Hours:** Daylight. **Key Personnel:** Keith Ledbetter, Station Mgr. **Wattage:** 1000. **Ad Rates:** $4 for 30 seconds; $5.50 for 60 seconds.

ROANOKE, pop. 5,896.

E. AL. Randolph Co. 25 mi. NW of La Grange, GA. Manufactures art supplies, doors, industrial fabrics, textile yarns, metal furniture, textiles, lumber. Pine, hardwood timber. Agriculture. Apples, corn, poultry, cattle.

429 The Randolph Leader
Randolph Publishers, Inc.
524 Main St. Phone: (334)863-2819
PO Box 1267 Fax: (334)863-4006
Roanoke, AL 36274
Local newspaper. **Founded:** 1892. **Freq:** Weekly (Wed.). **Print Method:** Offset. **Cols./Page:** 6. **Col. Width:** 26 nonpareils. **Col. Depth:** 301 agate lines. **Key Personnel:** John W. Stevenson, Editor and Publisher; Peggy Seabolt, Advertising Mgr. **USPS:** 467-240. **Subscription Rates:** Free; $18 by mail; $24 out of area. **Remarks:** Accepts advertising.
Ad Rates: GLR: $.27 **Circ:** Paid ‡6,200
SAU: $4 Free ‡100
PCI: $4.75

430 Better Vision Cable Co.
Box 863 Phone: (334)863-8112
Roanoke, AL 36274 Fax: (334)863-2027

Owner: James Cable Partners, L.P., 710 N. Woodward Ave., Ste 180, Bloomfield Hills, MI 48304, (810)647-1080. **Founded:** 1968. **Key Personnel:** Jim Sloan, Contact. **Cities Served:** subscribing households 5,700; 36 channels.

431 WELR-AM - 1360
705 Main Phone: (334)863-4139
PO Box 709 Fax: (334)863-2540
Roanoke, AL 36274

Format: News; Talk. **Networks:** ABC. **Founded:** 1950. **Operating Hours:** 5 a.m.-6 p.m.; 2% network, 98% local. **Key Personnel:** Jim Vice, Contact; Kay C. Vice, Operations Mgr. **Wattage:** 1000. **Ad Rates:** $6 for 30 seconds; $11 for 60 seconds.

432 WELR-FM - 102.3
705 N. Main St. Phone: (334)863-4139
Roanoke, AL 36274 Fax: (334)863-2540

Format: Contemporary Country. **Networks:** ABC. **Owner:** Jim Vice, PO Box 709, Roanoke, AL. **Founded:** 1964. **Operating Hours:** Continuous. **Key Personnel:** Jim Vice, Manager; Kay Vice, Operations Mgr. **Wattage:** 25,000. **Ad Rates:** $10 for 30 seconds; $16 for 60 seconds.

ROBERTSDALE, pop. 2,306.

SW AL. Baldwin Co. 20 mi. SE of Mobile. Residential.

433 Fairhope Courier
Gulf Coast Newspapers
PO Box 509 Phone: (334)947-7712
Robertsdale, AL 36567 Fax: (334)947-2062
Publication E-mail: courier@gulftel.com

Community newspaper. **Founded:** 1894. **Freq:** Semiweekly (Wed. and Sat.). **Print Method:** Offset. **Cols./Page:** 6. **Col. Width:** 25 nonpareils. **Col. Depth:** 294 agate lines. **Key Personnel:** Sheila Propp, Editor, phone (334)928-2321, fax (334)928-9963; Dennis Thomas, Publisher; Milly Stephens, Advertising Rep. **Subscription Rates:** $30 individuals; $32.50 out of state; $25.75 senior citizens; $28.50 out of state senior citizens. **Remarks:** Accepts advertising. **URL:** http://www.courier@gulftel.com. **Formerly**: Eastern Shore Courier.
Ad Rates: SAU: $2.63 **Circ:** ‡4,400

434 The Independent
Gulf Coast Newspapers
PO Box 509 Phone: (334)947-2511
Robertsdale, AL 36567 Fax: (334)947-7652
Publication E-mail: indy96@gulftel.com

Local newspaper. **Founded:** June 30, 1976. **Freq:** Weekly (Thurs.). **Print Method:** Offset. **Trim Size:** 13 x 20. **Cols./Page:** 6. **Col. Width:** 24 nonpareils. **Col. Depth:** 21 1/2 inches. **Key Personnel:** Tammy Leytham, Exec. Ed.; Jeniece Hooper, Advertising Mgr. **Subscription Rates:** $23 individuals; $13.50 senior citizens. **Remarks:** Accepts advertising.
Ad Rates: GLR: $1,064.25 **Circ:** 4,500
BW: $741.75
4C: $1,121.75
SAU: $8.25
CNU: $7.25
PCI: $1,444.25

435 WHBR-TV - 33
22080 County Rd. 64 Phone: (334)960-1191
Robertsdale, AL 36567 Fax: (334)960-1192
Free: (800)533-9427
E-mail: whbrtv@aol.com

Format: Religious. **Networks:** Christian Television. **Owner:** Christian Television Corp. of Pensacola/Mobile Inc., at above address, (813)535-5622, Fax: (813)531-2497. **Founded:** 1986. **Operating Hours:** 24Hrs a day. **ADI:** Mobile, AL-Pensacola, FL. **Key Personnel:** Don Price, President; Don MacAllister, Vice President; David Mayo, General Mgr.; Cardin A. Hesselton, Sales Dir.; Dave Miniard, Chief Engineer. **Wattage:** 3 million. **Ad Rates:** $232-561 per unit.

436 WXWY-AM - 1000
PO Box 578 Phone: (334)947-2346
Robertsdale, AL 36567 Fax: (334)947-2347
Free: (800)500-8834

Format: Southern Gospel; Religious. **Networks:** Moody Broadcasting. **Owner:** JTL Broadcasting Co., at above address. **Founded:** 1985. **Operating Hours:** Sunrise-sunset; 10% network, 90% local. **Key Personnel:** James T. Lee, General Mgr. **Wattage:** 1000. **Ad Rates:** $3.50-5.50 for 30 seconds; $4.50-6.50 for 60 seconds.

ROGERSVILLE

437 East Lauderdale News
PO Box 179 Phone: (205)247-5565
Rogersville, AL 35652 Fax: (205)247-1902

Community newspaper. **Founded:** 1966. **Freq:** Weekly (Thurs.). **Print Method:** Offset. **Cols./Page:** 8. **Col. Width:** 10.5 picas. **Col. Depth:** 21 1/2 inches. **Key Personnel:** James B. Cox, Publisher; Phyllis D. Cox, Publisher. **USPS:** 787-940. **Subscription Rates:** $15; $20 out of state.
Ad Rates: PCI: $5.50 **Circ:** ‡4,400

RUSSELLVILLE†, pop. 8,195.

NW AL. Franklin Co. 20 mi. S. of Florence. Manufactures textiles, artificial flowers. Aluminum reduction plants. Stone quarries. Agriculture. Cotton, corn, hay.

438 Franklin County Times
Franklin County Times Inc.
142 Hwy., 43 Bypass Phone: (205)332-1881
PO Box 1088 Fax: (205)332-1883
Russellville, AL 35653
Newspaper. **Founded:** 1879. **Freq:** Semiweekly (Wed. and Sun.). **Print Method:** Offset. **Cols./Page:** 6. **Col. Width:** 26 nonpareils. **Col. Depth:** 301 agate lines. **Key Personnel:** Rick Cameron, Editor and Publisher; Diane Hall, Advertising Representative; Jim Head, Advertising Representative. **Subscription Rates:** $39.96 individuals.
Ad Rates: GLR: $1.25 **Circ:** Paid ‡4,000
BW: $1386.75 Free ‡8,500
4C: $1611.75
SAU: $10.75
PCI: $9.35

439 WKAX-AM - 1500
113 Washington Ave. Phone: (205)332-6104
Russellville, AL 35653

Format: Gospel; Southern Gospel. **Founded:** 1974. **Operating Hours:** Sunrise-sunset; 75% network, 25% local. **ADI:** Huntsville-Decatur-Florence, AL. **Key Personnel:** Ron Underwood, General Mgr.; Al Gray, Music Dir.; Pat Underwood, Operations Mgr. **Wattage:** 1000. **Ad Rates:** $3.50 for 60 seconds.

ST. CLAIR

440 St. Clair News-Aegis
PO Box 748 Phone: (205)884-2310
Pell City, AL 35125 Fax: (205)884-2312

Community newspaper. **Subtitle:** St. Clair News-Aegis. **Founded:** 1873. **Freq:** Weekly (Thurs.). **Print Method:** Offset. **Cols./Page:** 8. **Col. Width:** 22 nonpareils. **Col. Depth:** 301 agate lines. **Key Personnel:** Gary Hanner, Editor/Ad. Mgr.; Ed Darling, Publisher. **Subscription Rates:** $18 individuals; $25 out of area. **Remarks:** Accepts advertising.
Ad Rates: GLR: $.20 **Circ:** Paid 5,167
BW: $735.30
4C: $860.30
PCI: $5.70

SAMSON

441 Samson Ledger
105 Main St. Phone: (205)898-2491
PO Box 66
Samson, AL 36477
County newspaper. **Founded:** 1958. **Freq:** Weekly. **Print Method:** Offset. **Trim Size:** 12 1/4 x 21 1/2. **Cols./Page:** 6. **Col. Width:** 2 inches. **Col. Depth:** 21 1/2 inches. **Key Personnel:** Jackie Hudson, Editor; Jim Specht, Publisher, phone (205)684-2280. **Subscription Rates:** Free; $17.12 by mail; $18.02 out of state. **Remarks:** Accepts advertising.
Ad Rates: BW: $677.25 **Circ:** Paid ‡5,700
PCI: $5.25 Free ‡9,400

SCOTTSBORO

442 The Daily Sentinel
Scottsboro Newspapers, Inc.
701 Veterans Dr. Phone: (205)259-1020
Scottsboro, AL 35768-2132 Fax: (205)259-2709

General newspaper. **Founded:** 1889. **Freq:** Tues.-Fri. (morn.); Sun. (morn.). **Print Method:** Offset. **Cols./Page:** 6. **Col. Width:** 25 nonpareils. **Col. Depth:** 301 agate lines. **Key Personnel:** Byron Woodfin, Managing Editor; Billy J. Cornwell, Jr., Editor and Publisher; Terri Kirby, Advertising Mgr.; Helen Wilmon, Circulation Mgr. **Subscription Rates:** $34 individuals. **Remarks:** Accepts advertising.
Ad Rates: SAU: $5.10 **Circ:** (Not Reported)

443 Jackson County Chronicles
Jackson County, Alabama Historical Association
435 Barbee Ln. Phone: (256)259-5286
Scottsboro, AL 35769-3745
Journal covering local history. **Founded:** Jan. 1976. **Freq:** Quarterly. **Trim Size:** 8 1/2 x 11. **Key Personnel:** Ann B. Chambless, Editor, abc@HiWAAY.net. **Subscription Rates:** $10 individuals; $3.50 single issue. **Remarks:** Advertising not accepted.
Circ: Paid 400

444 Falcon Cable TV
PO Box 988 Phone: (205)574-4115
Scottsboro, AL 35768 Fax: (205)259-0152

Key Personnel: M.C. Grigsby, General Mgr. **Cities Served:** Hollywood, Gurley, Paint Rock, Rainsville, Fyffe, Shiloh, Powell, Section, Dutton, Cedar Bluff, and Scottsboro.

445 WKEA-FM - 98.3
John T. Reid Pkwy. Phone: (205)259-2341
Rte. 4 Fax: (205)574-2156
PO Box 966
Scottsboro, AL 35768-0966
Free: (800)388-9802

Format: Contemporary Country. **Networks:** ABC. **Founded:** 1966. **Formerly**: WCNA-FM (1981). **Operating Hours:** Continuous; 5% network, 95% local. **ADI:** Huntsville-Decatur-Florence, AL. **Key Personnel:** Ronald H. Livengood, Contact. **Wattage:** 6000 ERP. **Ad Rates:** $6.75 for 30 seconds; $13.70 for 60 seconds.

446 WMXN-AM - 1400
PO Box 966
Scottsboro, AL 35768

Format: Adult Contemporary. **Networks:** Westwood One Radio. **Owner:** Fort Payne Broadcasting Co., Inc., at above address, (256)259-2341, Fax: (256)574-2156, Free: (800)388-9802. **Founded:** 1941. **Formerly**: WFPA-AM. **Operating Hours:** Continuous; 95% network, 5% local. **ADI:** Huntsville-Decatur-Florence, AL. **Key Personnel:** Ron Livergood, General Mgr.; Campbell Smith, News Dir.; Roger Allen, Program Dir.; Leroy Stancell, Sports Dir. **Wattage:** 1000. **Ad Rates:** $5.95 for 30 seconds; $8 for 60 seconds. Combined advertising rates available with WMXN-FM.

447 WWIC-AM - 1050
815 W. Willow St. Phone: (256)259-1050
PO Box 759 Fax: (256)574-6397
Scottsboro, AL 35768
E-mail: wwic@websun.com

Format: Country. **Networks:** Mutual Broadcasting System. **Owner:** WWIC, at above address. **Founded:** 1949. **Formerly**: WCRI-AM (1982). **Operating Hours:** Continuous; 5% network, 95% local. **ADI:** Chattanooga (Cleveland), TN. **Key Personnel:** Greg Bell, Station/Product. **Wattage:** 1000. **Ad Rates:** $2.40-2.95 for 15 seconds; $4.60-5.97 for 30 seconds; $6.24-7.62 for 60 seconds.

448 WZCT-AM - 1330
East Willow St. Phone: (205)259-1313
PO Drawer A Fax: (205)218-3013
Scottsboro, AL 35768

Format: Southern Gospel. **Networks:** USA Radio; Alabama Radio (ALANET). **Owner:** Bonner-Carlile Enterprises, 2002 East Willow, Scottsboro, AL 35768. **Founded:** 1952. **Formerly:** WROS-AM (1978). **Operating Hours:** Continuous. **ADI:** Huntsville-Decatur-Florence, AL. **Key Personnel:** Rob Carlile, General Mgr., phone (205)574-1330, fax (205)218-3013; Ann Kennamen, Sales Mgr., phone (205)574-1330, fax (205)218-3013. **Local Programs:** *Community Update*, Ken Bonner; *Wildcat Sports*, Ken Bonner. **Wattage:** 5000. **Ad Rates:** $6.15 for 30 seconds; $8.25 for 60 seconds.

SELMA

449 The Selma Times-Journal
Selma Newspapers, Inc.
1018 Water Ave. Phone: (334)875-2110
PO Box 611 Fax: (205)875-5896
Selma, AL 36701
General newspaper. **Founded:** 1827. **Freq:** Daily and Sunday (morn.). **Print Method:** Offset. **Cols./Page:** 6. **Col. Width:** 25 nonpareils. **Col. Depth:** 301 agate lines. **Key Personnel:** K.A. Turner, Managing Editor, katurner@zebra.net; E. Wilson Koeppel, Publisher, ewkoeppel@zebra.net; Marcia A. Jowers, Advertising Mgr. **Subscription Rates:** $110 individuals. **Remarks:** Accepts advertising.
Ad Rates: SAU: $7 **Circ:** Paid 10,000

450 WDXX-FM - 100.1
505 Lauderdale St. Phone: (334)875-3350
PO Box 1055 Fax: (334)875-4254
Selma, AL 36701

Format: Contemporary Country. **Networks:** Independent. **Owner:** Broad South Communications, at above address. **Founded:** 1970. **Formerly:** WTUN-FM (1989). **Operating Hours:** Continuous; 100% local. **ADI:** Montgomery-Selma, AL. **Key Personnel:** James M. Reynolds, President. **Wattage:** 50,000. **Ad Rates:** $15-35 for 30 seconds; $17-40 for 60 seconds.

451 WHBB-AM - 1490
505 Lauderdale St. Phone: (334)875-3350
PO Box 1055 Fax: (334)875-4254
Selma, AL 36701

Format: News; Talk. **Networks:** ABC. **Owner:** Broadsouth Communications, Inc., at above address. **Founded:** 1935. **Operating Hours:** Continuous. **ADI:** Montgomery-Selma, AL. **Key Personnel:** James M. Reynolds, President; Ellis Stewart, General Mgr. **Wattage:** 1000. **Ad Rates:** $12-25 for 30 seconds; $14-28 for 60 seconds. $3-$13 for 30 seconds; $4-$16 for 60 seconds. Combined advertising rates available with WDXX-FM.

452 WMRK-AM - 1340
273 Persimmon Tree Rd. Phone: (205)875-9360
Selma, AL 36701 Fax: (205)875-1340

Format: Easy Listening. **Networks:** Mutual Broadcasting System. **Owner:** Alexander Broadcasting Co. Inc., at above address. **Founded:** 1946. **Operating Hours:** Continuous. **Key Personnel:** Scott Alexander, General Mgr. **Wattage:** 1000.

SHEFFIELD

453 Journal of Muscle Shoals History
Tennessee Valley Historical Society
105 Terrace St.
Sheffield, AL 35660

Journal of Alabama history. **Founded:** 1974. **Freq:** Irregular. **Trim Size:** 7 x 8 1/2. **Cols./Page:** 1. **Key Personnel:** Richard C. Sheridan, Contact. **ISSN:** 0094-8039. **Remarks:** Advertising not accepted.
Circ: Paid 1,000

454 WBTG-AM - 1290
1605 Gospel Rd. Phone: (205)383-1290
PO Box 518 Fax: (205)381-6801
Sheffield, AL 35660-0518

Format: Religious. **Networks:** Sun Radio; USA Radio. **Owner:** Slatton & Associates Broadcasters Inc., at above address. **Founded:** 1977. **Formerly:** WHCM-AM (1987); WSHF-AM. **Operating Hours:** 6 a.m.-7 p.m.; 85% network, 15% local. **Key Personnel:** Paul Slatton, Contact; Randy Hafner, Program Dir.; Johnny Lee, Production Mgr.; Brian Mercer, Music Dir. **Wattage:** 1000. **Ad Rates:** $4.50-12 for 30 seconds. $4.50-$12 for 30 seconds; $6-$16.50. Combined advertising rates available with WBTG-FM.

455 WBTG-FM - 106.3
1605 Gospel Rd. Phone: (205)381-6800
PO Box 518 Fax: (205)381-6801
Sheffield, AL 35660-0518

Format: Gospel. **Networks:** USA Radio. **Owner:** Slatton & Associates Broadcasters Inc., at above address. **Founded:** 1969. **Formerly:** WRCK-FM (1977). **Operating Hours:** Continuous; 10% network, 90% local. **Key Personnel:** Paul Slatton, Gen. Mgr./Natl. Sales Mgr.; Lincoln Hughes, News Dir.; Randy Hafner, Program Dir.; Terry Edgil, Music Dir.; Harry Underwood, Local Sales Mgr.; Brenda Richardson, Office Mgr. **Wattage:** 25,000. **Ad Rates:** $6-16 for 30 seconds; $8-22 for 60 seconds. $6-$16 for 30 seconds; $8-$22 for 60 seconds. Combined advertising rates available with WBTG-AM.

SPANISH FORT

456 WMMV-FM - 105.5
PO Box 901
Spanish Fort, AL 36527-0901

Format: Urban Contemporary. **Networks:** CBS; American Urban Radio. **Owner:** Faulkner-Phillips Media Inc., at above address. **Founded:** Jan. 1, 1958. **Formerly:** WLPR-FM (1988). **Operating Hours:** 24 hrs. **Key Personnel:** W.H. Phillips, General Mgr.; Sonny Love, Contact; Gwin Chesnutt, Sales Mgr.; Bill Lamb, Station Mgr. **Wattage:** 3000. **Ad Rates:** $15-50 for 30 seconds; $18-60 for 60 seconds.

STEVENSON

North Jackson Progress - See Jackson

SULLIGENT, pop. 2,130.

NW AL. Lamar Co. 82 mi. NW of Birmingham. Timber, metal working industry. Textile plants. Oil, natural gas.

457 Lamar Leader
PO Box 988 Phone: (205)698-8148
Sulligent, AL 35586 Fax: (205)698-8146
Free: (800)269-0234

Community newspaper. **Founded:** Nov. 15, 1973. **Freq:** Weekly (Wed.). **Print Method:** Offset. **Trim Size:** 13 x 21 1/2. **Cols./Page:** 6. **Col. Width:** 12 1/2 picas. **Col. Depth:** 129 picas. **Key Personnel:** Don Dollar, Editor and Publisher; Rebecca Cox, Advertising Mgr. **USPS:** 002-510. **Subscription Rates:** $14 individuals; $17 other countries; $20 out of state. **Remarks:** Accepts advertising.
Ad Rates: GLR: $3 **Circ:** ‡3,500
BW: $370
4C: $135
SAU: $4
PCI: $3.25

SUMITON

458 WRSM-AM - 1540
PO Drawer 100 Phone: (205)648-3241
Sumiton, AL 35148

Format: Country; Religious; Bluegrass. **Networks:** NBC. **Owner:** T. Herb Steadman, at above address. **Founded:** 1978. **Operating Hours:** Sunrise-sunset. **Key Personnel:** Sara Steadman, Contact. **Wattage:** 1000.

SYLACAUGA

EC AL. Talladega Co. 40 mi. SE of Birmingham.

459 WAWV-FM - 98.3
P.O. Box 629 Phone: (205)245-3281
Sylacauga, AL 35150 Fax: (256)245-4355
E-mail: wyea@rocketmail.com

Format: Adult Contemporary. **Networks:** ABC. **Owner:** Coosa Valley Broadcasting, Inc., at above address, (256)249-4263, Fax: (256)245-4355. **Founded:** 1959. **Formerly:** WMLS-FM (1986); Alabama Broacasting Co., Inc. **Operating Hours:** 24 hours. **ADI:** Birmingham (Gadsden), AL. **Wattage:** 5,000. **Ad Rates:** $5.75-8.50 for 30 seconds; $6.50-9 for 60 seconds.

460 WFEB-AM - 1340
1209 Millerville Hwy. Phone: (256)245-3281
PO Box 358 Fax: (256)245-3050
Sylacauga, AL 35150

Format: News; Talk; Sports. **Networks:** Mutual Broadcasting System. **Owner:** Alabama Broadcasting Co., Inc., at above address. **Founded:** 1945. **Operating Hours:** 6 a.m.-10 p.m.; 7% network, 93% local. **ADI:** Birmingham (Gadsden), AL. **Key Personnel:** Bruce C. Carr, General Mgr. **Wattage:** 1000. **Ad Rates:** $8.65 for 30 seconds; $10.45 for 60 seconds.

TALLADEGA†, pop. 19,128.

Talladega Co. 24 mi. SW of Anniston. Talladega College (Black); State Schools for the Deaf and Blind. Federal Correctional Institute. Manufactures cotton yarn, textiles, bags, soil pipe fittings, plywood, textile machine parts, sawmill machinery, insecticides, lumber. Timber. Agriculture. Cotton, corn, soybeans, hay, cattle.

461 The Daily Home
Consolidated Publishing Co., Inc.
4 Sylacauga Hwy. Phone: (205)362-1000
PO Box 977 Fax: (205)249-4315
Talladega, AL 35160
General newspaper. **Founded:** 1867. **Freq:** Mon.-Sat. (morn.). **Print Method:** Offset. **Trim Size:** 13 3/4 x 22 3/4. **Cols./Page:** 6. **Col. Width:** 25 nonpareils. **Col. Depth:** 21 1/2 inches. **Key Personnel:** Bill Keller, Editor and Publisher; Stanley Allison, Advertising Mgr.; Charles Osborne, Circulation Mgr. **USPS:** 143-180. **Subscription Rates:** $90 individuals. **Remarks:** Accepts advertising.
Ad Rates: BW: $1,060.33 **Circ:** Paid 9,736
4C: $1,235.38 Free 75
PCI: $8.22

462 WEYY-FM - 92.7
PO Drawer 329 Phone: (205)362-8890
Talladega, AL 35160 Fax: (205)362-3440

Format: Country. **Networks:** ABC. **Owner:** Jacobs Broadcast Group, Inc., at above address, (205)362-9041. **Founded:** 1972. **Formerly:** WHTB-FM (1984). **Operating Hours:** Continuous; 10% network, 90% local. **Key Personnel:** Jim Jacobs, President; Laura Jacobs, Contact; Richard Yates, Sales Mgr.; Tom Kelley, Operations Mgr. **Wattage:** 400. **Ad Rates:** $5.30-8.40 for 30 seconds; $7.05-11.10 for 60 seconds.

TALLASSEE

EC AL. Elmore Co. 25 mi. NE of Montgomery.

463 Tribune
301 Gilmer Phone: (334)283-6568
PO Drawer 780730 Fax: (334)283-6569
Tallassee, AL 36078-0730
Community newspaper. **Founded:** 1899. **Freq:** Weekly (Thurs.). **Print Method:** Offset. **Cols./Page:** 6. **Col. Width:** 12 1/5 picas. **Col. Depth:** 21 1/2 inches. **Key Personnel:** Jack Venable, Editor and Publisher; Jane Parker, Circulation Mgr. **Subscription Rates:** $20; $26 out of area.
Ad Rates: PCI: $5.00 **Circ:** 4,200

464 WACQ-AM - 1130
320 Barnett Blvd. Phone: (334)283-6888
Tallassee, AL 36078-1506 Fax: (334)283-2152
Free: (800)923-4699

Format: Adult Contemporary. **Networks:** Alabama Radio (ALANET); USA Radio. **Owner:** Tuskegee Communications Co. Inc., at above address. **Founded:** 1979. **Formerly:** WSFU-AM (1985). **Operating Hours:** Sunrise-sunset; 15% network, 85% local. **ADI:** Montgomery-Selma, AL. **Key Personnel:** Fred Randall Hughey, Contact; Debra Hughey, Contact; Reid Spann, Program Dir.; Windle Jayream, Music Dir. **Wattage:** 1000. **Ad Rates:** $5 for 30 seconds; $7.50 for 60 seconds.

465 WACQ-FM - 99.9
320 Barnett Blvd. Phone: (205)283-6888
Tallassee, AL 36078-1506

Format: Adult Contemporary. **Networks:** Alabama Radio (ALANET); USA Radio. **Owner:** Tuskegee Communication Co. Inc., at above address. **Operating Hours:** Continuous. **ADI:** Montgomery-Selma, AL. **Key Personnel:** Fred Randall Hughey, Contact; Debra Hughey, Contact; Reid Spann, Program Dir.; Windle Jayrean, Music Dir. **Wattage:** 6000. **Ad Rates:** $10 for 30 seconds; $15 for 60 seconds.

466 WTLS-AM - 1300
1702 Gilmer Phone: (334)283-6566
Box 129 Fax: (334)283-6565
Tallassee, AL 36078

Format: Talk; News; Eclectic; Sports. **Networks:** Alabama Radio (ALANET). **Founded:** 1954. **Operating Hours:** 15% network, 20% local. **Key Personnel:** Betty S. Butler, Contact; Cathy Butler, Traffic Dir. **Wattage:** 1000.

THOMASVILLE, pop. 4,387.

SW AL. Clarke Co. 55 mi. SW of Selma. Saw, planing, stave,

and paper mills.; Cotton gins; machine shop. Textile factory. Pine and hardwood timber. Agriculture. Cotton, corn, peanuts.

467 The Thomasville Times
PO Box 367
Thomasville, AL 36784

Newspaper. **Founded:** 1921. **Freq:** Weekly (Thurs.). **Print Method:** Offset. **Trim Size:** 13 x 21 1/2. **Cols./Page:** 6. **Col. Width:** 12.5 picas. **Key Personnel:** Tonya P. Joyce, Advertising Rep.; Jim Cox, Publisher; Mike Breedlove, Publisher. **USPS:** 628-060. **Subscription Rates:** $16.00 individuals; $22.00 out of area.
Ad Rates: BW: $439 **Circ:** Paid 6,130
4C: $699
SAU: $15
PCI: $5

468 WJDB-AM - 630
2211 Hwy. 43 S. Phone: (334)636-4438
PO Box 219 Fax: (334)636-4439
Thomasville, AL 36784
Free: (800)245-9532

Format: Southern Gospel. **Networks:** CBS. **Owner:** Griffin Broadcasting Corp., at above address. **Founded:** 1956. **Operating Hours:** 6 a.m.-sunset; 100% network. **Key Personnel:** Ivey Griffin, President. **Wattage:** 1000. **Ad Rates:** $5.00 for 30 seconds; $7.00 for 60 seconds.

469 WJDB-FM - 95.5
PO Box 219 Phone: (334)636-4438
Thomasville, AL 36784 Fax: (334)636-4439
Free: (800)245-WJDB

Format: Country. **Networks:** CBS. **Owner:** Griffin Broadcasting Corp., at above address. **Founded:** 1972. **Operating Hours:** Continuous. **Key Personnel:** Ivey Griffin, President; Gary Downs, Sports Dir.; George Rivers, P.D.; Karen Hill, News Dir. **Local Programs:** *WJDB News*, George Riveus. **Wattage:** 25,000. **Ad Rates:** $5.00-7.00 for 30 seconds.

TROY†, pop. 12,587.

SE AL. Pike Co. 43 mi. SE of Montgomery. Troy State University. Manufactures truck bodies, latex products, plastic containers, textiles, wood products, circuit boards. Pecan shelling plants. Timber. Agriculture. Cotton, peanuts, pecans.

470 Messenger
Troy Publishing Corp.
918 S. Brundidge St. Phone: (334)566-4270
PO Box 727 Fax: (334)566-4281
Troy, AL 36081
Publication E-mail: dlnews@p-c-net.net

Indiana. **Founded:** 1866. **Freq:** Tues.-Fri. (morn.); Sun. (morn.). **Print Method:** Offset. **Cols./Page:** 6. **Col. Width:** 25 nonpareils. **Col. Depth:** 21 1/2 inches. **Key Personnel:** Rick Reynolds, Publisher; Chris Day, Editor; Stephanie Middlebrooks, Circulation Mgr.; Deedie Carter, Circulation and Advertising Mgr. **Subscription Rates:** $72 individuals. **Remarks:** Accepts advertising.
Ad Rates: SAU: $5.88 **Circ:** Paid 4,000
Non-paid 14,000

471 Tropolitan
Troy State University
Wallace Hall Phone: (334)670-3327
Troy State University Fax: (205)670-3435
Troy, AL 36082
Collegiate newspaper (tabloid). **Freq:** Weekly (Thurs.) (during the academic year). **Print Method:** Offset. **Trim Size:** 10 x 12 3/4. **Cols./Page:** 4. **Col. Width:** 28 nonpareils. **Col. Depth:** 181 agate lines. **Key Personnel:** Kristy Galbiaith, Editor; Rhonda Salter, Business Mgr. **Subscription Rates:** Free; $20 by mail. **Remarks:** Accepts advertising.
Ad Rates: BW: $182 **Circ:** Free 4,000
SAU: $3.00

472 WRWA-FM - 88.7
Troy State University Phone: (334)670-3268
Wallace Hall Fax: (334)670-3934
Troy, AL 36081
Free: (800)800-6616
E-mail: wtsu@trojan.troyst.edu

Format: New Age; Classical; Public Radio. **Networks:** National Public Radio (NPR); American Public Radio (APR). **Owner:** Southeastern Public Radio Network, at above address. **Founded:** 1985. **Operating Hours:** 6 a.m.-midnight. **Key Personnel:** Russell Wells, Program Mgr.; Judy Davis, Operations Mgr.; Carolyn Hutcheson, Development Mgr. **Wattage:** 50,000. **Ad Rates:** Noncommercial. **URL:** http://www.trojan.troyst.edu/wtsu.

473 WTBF-AM & FM - 970
67 W. Court Sq. Phone: (334)566-0300
Troy, AL 36081-2611 Fax: (334)566-5689
Free: (888)970-8769
E-mail: wtbf@p-c-net.net

Format: Contemporary Country. **Networks:** Mutual Broadcasting System; Alabama Radio (ALANET); ABC. **Owner:** Troy Broadcasting Corp., at above address. **Founded:** 1947. **Formerly:** WTBF-AM (1947). **Operating Hours:** Continuous. **Key Personnel:** Joe Gilchrist, Chief Engineer; Jim Roling, General Mgr.; Doc Kirby, Program and Music Dir.; Buddy Johnson, Sales Mgr. **Local Programs:** *Gospel Music Time* 6 a.m.-8:30 a.m. Sunday, Mac Seay; *Morning Show* 5:30 am - 9:00 am Monday-Saturday, Jim Roling; *Live Adlib 60's*; *The Sports Page* Continuous Monday-Friday. **Wattage:** 5000. **Ad Rates:** $6.50 for 15 seconds; $11 for 30 seconds; $15 for 30 seconds; $18 for 60 seconds; $22.50 for 60 seconds. WTBF-FM.

474 WTBF-FM - 94.7
67 Court Sq. Phone: (334)566-0300
Troy, AL 36081 Fax: (334)566-5689
E-mail: wtbf@p-c-net

Format: Oldies. **Networks:** ABC. **Owner:** Troy Broadcasting Corp., at above address. **Founded:** Nov. 1997. **Operating Hours:** Continuous. **Key Personnel:** Jim Roling, General Mgr.; Joe Gilchrist, Chief Engineer; Dave Kirby, Program Dir.; Dim Peltzer, Traffic. **Wattage:** 25,000.

475 WTJB-FM - 91.7
University Ave. Phone: (334)670-3268
Troy, AL 36082 Fax: (334)670-3934
Free: (800)800-6616
E-mail: wtsu@trojan.troyst.edu

Format: Public Radio; Jazz; News; Classical. **Networks:** National Public Radio (NPR); American Public Radio (APR). **Founded:** 1984. **Operating Hours:** 18 hrs. Daily; 75% network, 25% local. **Key Personnel:** Judy Davis, Contact; James Clower, Contact. **Wattage:** 3000. **Ad Rates:** Noncommercial. **URL:** http://www.trogst.edu/wtsu.

476 WTSU-FM - 89.9
University Ave. Phone: (334)670-3268
Troy, AL 36082 Fax: (334)670-3934
Free: (800)800-6616
E-mail: wtsu@trojan.troyst.edu

Format: Jazz; News; Classical; Public Radio. **Simulcasts:** WRWA-FM, WTJB-FM. **Networks:** National Public Radio (NPR); American Public Radio (APR). **Founded:** 1977. **Operating Hours:** 18 hrs. Daily; 75% network, 25% local. **Key Personnel:** Judy Davis, Contact; James Clouder, Contact; Russell Wells, Contact. **Wattage:** 100,000. **Ad Rates:** Noncommercial. **URL:** http://www.trojan.troyst.edu/wtsu.

TUSCALOOSA†, pop. 75,143.

W. AL. Tuscaloosa Co. On Black Warrior River, 56 mi. SW of Birmingham. Manufactures chemicals, paper, lumber, cast iron pipe, veneer, fertilizer, feeds, cottonseed products, auto and truck tires and tubes. Meat packing plants, oil refinery.

477 Accounting Historians Journal
Academy of Accounting Historians
c/o William D. Samson Phone: (205)348-2903
Culverhouse School of Accounting Fax: (205)348-8453
University of Alabama
Tuscaloosa, AL 35401
Professional journal for accounting historians. **Freq:** Semiannual. **Key Personnel:** Dick Fleischman, Journal Editor; Elliot Slocum, Notebook Editor. **Subscription Rates:** $40 individuals; $50 institutions.

478 Alabama Alumni Magazine
University of Alabama
PO Box 861928 Phone: (205)348-5963
Tuscaloosa, AL 35486-0017 Fax: (205)348-5958

University alumni magazine. **Founded:** 1917. **Freq:** Bimonthly. **Print Method:** Offset. **Trim Size:** 8 1/4 x 10 3/4. **Cols./Page:** 3. **Col. Width:** 28 nonpareils. **Col. Depth:** 134 agate lines. **Key Personnel:** Pat Whetstone, Publisher; Linda Southern, Advertising Mgr., lsouthern@alumni.ua.edu; Pamela T. Burt, Editor, pburt@alumni.ua.edu. **USPS:** 011-040. **Remarks:** Accepts advertising.
Ad Rates: BW: $1,000 **Circ:** Non-paid 34,000
4C: $1,500

479 Alabama Economic Outlook
Center for Business and Economic Research
University of Alabama Phone: (205)348-6191
Box 870221 Fax: (205)348-2952
Tuscaloosa, AL 35487-0221
Publisher E-mail: uacber@cba.ua.edu

Trade magazine covering economic conditions in the nation and Alabama. **Founded:** 1980. **Freq:** Annual. **Remarks:** Advertising not accepted.
Circ: (Not Reported)

480 Alabama Heritage
University of Alabama Phone: (205)348-7467
Box 870342 Fax: (205)348-7473
Tuscaloosa, AL 35487-0342
Historical magazine for the general public. Covers cultural heritage of Alabama and the South. **Founded:** 1986. **Freq:** Quarterly. **Print Method:** Offset. **Trim Size:** 8 1/2 x 11. **Cols./Page:** 3. **Key Personnel:** Suzanne R. Wolfe, Editor; Sara Martin, Director. **ISSN:** 0887-493X. **Subscription Rates:** $16.95 individuals; $28.95 two years; $38.95 Three Years. **Remarks:** Accepts advertising.
Ad Rates: BW: $600 **Circ:** ‡15,000
4C: $850
PCI: $50

481 American Journal of Tax Policy
American College of Tax Counsel
Box 870382 Phone: (205)348-7372
Tuscaloosa, AL 35487-0382 Fax: (205)348-3917

Scholarly journal covering tax policy. **Founded:** 1982. **Freq:** Semiannual. **Key Personnel:** James D. Bryce, Editor, jbryce@law.ua.edu. **ISSN:** 0739-7569. **Subscription Rates:** $22 individuals; $11 single issue. **Remarks:** Advertising not accepted. **Online:** LEXIS-NEXIS; Westlaw.
Circ: Combined 1,100

482 Black Warrior Review
University of Alabama
PO Box 862936 Phone: (205)348-4518
Tuscaloosa, AL 35486-0027 Fax: (205)348-8036

Literary magazine. **Founded:** 1974. **Freq:** Semiannual. **Trim Size:** 6 x 9. **Key Personnel:** Laura Didyk, Editor; T.J. Beitelman, Managing Editor. **ISSN:** 0193-6301. **Subscription Rates:** $14 individuals; $8 single issue. **Remarks:** Accepts advertising. **URL:** http://www.sa.ua.edu/osm/bwr.
Circ: Paid 2,000

483 Dreams and Nightmares
1300 Kicker Rd. Phone: (205)553-2284
Tuscaloosa, AL 35404-3954
Publisher E-mail: dragontea@earthlink.net

Journal covering science fiction, fantasy, and horror. **Founded:** Jan. 1986. **Freq:** Semiannual. **Print Method:** Photocopy. **Trim Size:** 8 1/2 x 5 1/2. **Key Personnel:** David Kopaska-Merkel, Editor and Publisher. **ISSN:** 0897-0238. **Subscription Rates:** $12 6 issues. **Remarks:** Accepts advertising. **URL:** http://home.earthlink.net/~dragontea/index.html.
Circ: Combined 200

484 Equipment World
Randall Publishing Co.
Box 2029 Phone: (205)349-2990
Tuscaloosa, AL 35403 Fax: (205)349-4174
Free: (800)633-5953

Magazine providing construction equipment information including application, purchase, maintenance, and replacement. **Founded:** 1989. **Freq:** Monthly. **Print Method:** Offset. **Trim Size:** 8 1/2 x 11. **Cols./Page:** 6. **Col. Width:** 18 nonpareils. **Col. Depth:** 210 agate lines. **Key Personnel:** Marcia Gruver, Editor, mgruverm@randallpub.com; Jim Longton, Assoc. Publisher, jlongton@randallpub.com. **Subscription Rates:** $99 individuals. **URL:** http://www.equipmentworld.com.
Ad Rates: BW: $9900 **Circ:** Controlled ‡90,649
4C: $2359

485 Journal for Research in Music Education
Music Educators National Conference
University of Alabama Phone: (205)348-6054
School of Music Fax: (205)348-1675
Box 870366
Tuscaloosa, AL 35487
Publication E-mail: hprice@bana.ua.edu
Publisher E-mail: mbmenc@vais.net

Scholarly publication. **Founded:** 1953. **Freq:** Quarterly. **Print Method:** Offset. **Trim Size:** 6 x 9. **Cols./Page:** 1. **Col. Width:** 4 1/2 inches. **Key Personnel:** Dr. Harry E. Price, Editor, phone (205)348-1431, fax (205)348-1675, hprice@bama.ua.edu; Ella Wilcox, Managing Editor. **ISSN:** 0022-4292. **Subscription Rates:** $28 individuals; $41 institutions and libraries. **Remarks:** Advertising not accepted.
Circ: Paid ‡3,500
Controlled ‡19

486 National Genealogical Society Quarterly
National Genealogical Society
Dept of History Phone: (205)752-4031
Univ. of Alabama Fax: (205)752-5979
Box 870212
Tuscaloosa, AL 35487-0212
Publisher E-mail: ngs@ngsgenealogy.org

Genealogy journal. **Subtitle:** A Journal for Today's Family Historian. **Founded:** 1912. **Freq:** Quarterly. **Print Method:** Web press. **Trim Size:** 7 x 10 INS, trim. **Cols./Page:** 1. **Col. Width:** 60 nonpareils. **Col. Depth:** 112 agate lines. **Key Personnel:** Elizabeth Shown Mills, Editor, eshown@msn.com; Gary B. Mills, Coeditor. **ISSN:** 0027-934X. **Subscription Rates:** $40 institutions and libraries; $40 individuals and libraries. **Alt. Formats:** CD-ROM; Microform.
Ad Rates: BW: $325 **Circ:** ‡17,500

487 Overdrive
Overdrive Magazine, Inc.
PO Box 3187 Phone: (205)349-2990
Tuscaloosa, AL 35403 Fax: (205)349-3765
Free: (800)633-5953
Publication E-mail: editors@overdriveonline.com

Business/lifestyle publication for owner-operators. **Subtitle:** The Magazine for the American Trucker. **Founded:** 1961. **Freq:** Monthly. **Print Method:** Offset. **Trim Size:** 8 1/8 x 10 7/8. **Cols./Page:** 3. **Col. Width:** 2 1/4 inches. **Col. Depth:** 10 inches. **Key Personnel:** Linda Longton, Editorial Dir., fax (205)750-8070, longton@overdriveonline.com. **ISSN:** 0030-7394. **Subscription Rates:** $24.97 for 12 issues; $3.95 single copy. **Remarks:** Accepts advertising. **URL:** http://www.overdriveonline.com.
Ad Rates: BW: $9,990 **Circ:** Paid 6,138
4C: $12,440 Controlled 141,969
PCI: $246

488 The Tuscaloosa News
6th St. & 20th Ave. Phone: (205)345-0505
PO Box 20587 Fax: (205)349-0845
Tuscaloosa, AL 35401
General newspaper. **Founded:** 1818. **Freq:** Daily (eve.), Sat. and Sun. (morn.). **Print Method:** Offset. **Cols./Page:** 6. **Col. Width:** 25 nonpareils. **Col. Depth:** 301 agate lines. **Key Personnel:** Donald A. Brown, Editor; Charles H. Land, Publisher. **USPS:** 644-320. **Subscription Rates:** $135 individuals. **Remarks:** Accepts advertising. Monday-Saturday: GLR: $1.84; BW: $2,843.16; 4C: $3,238.16; SAU: $25.70; PCI: $25.70; Sunday: GLR: $1.91; SAU: $26.70; PCI: $26.70.
Circ: Mon.-Sat. ★37,445
Sun. ★39,151

489 Comcast Cablevision of Tuscaloosa
700 Parkview Center Phone: (205)345-0424
Tuscaloosa, AL 35402 Fax: (205)345-8223

Founded: 1957. **Key Personnel:** Scott Randall, General Mgr.; Kathy Falk, Marketing/Customer Service Manager; Danny Brasher, Plant Manager. **Cities Served:** Northport, Tuscaloosa County, AL: subscribing households 35,000; 45 channels; 1 community access channel.

490 WACT-AM - 1420
3900 11th Ave. Phone: (205)349-3200
PO Box 020126 Fax: (205)752-9269
Tuscaloosa, AL 35402-0126

Format: Gospel; Southern Gospel. **Networks:** USA Radio. **Founded:** 1958. **Operating Hours:** Continuous. **Key Personnel:** Lynn Woods, General Mgr.; Loni Moore, Sales Mgr.; Roy Gregg, Program Dir. **Local Programs:** *Hotline*, Rick Cobb, Mailing contact, (205)349-3200; *Mornings with Jack Hamm*, Jack Hamm, (205)349-3200. **Wattage:** 5000. **Ad Rates:** $8-18 for 30 seconds; $10-24 for 60 seconds.

491 WCFT-TV - 33
4000 37th St. E. Phone: (205)553-1333
Tuscaloosa, AL 35405 Fax: (205)556-4814

Format: Commercial TV. **Networks:** CBS. **Owner:** Federal Broadcasting Co., 1533 N. Woodward Ave., Ste. 240, Bloomfield Hills, MI 48304. **Founded:** 1965. **Operating Hours:** 6 a.m.-1:30 a.m.; 80% network, 20% local. **ADI:** Tuscaloosa, AL. **Key Personnel:** W. Tommy Ray, General Mgr.; Kip Tyner, News Dir.; Orzell Spencer, Program Dir.; Christina Perez, Promotions Mgr.; David Lamb, Sports Dir.; Ron Quarles, Sales Mgr.; Rob Martin, Contact. **Ad Rates:** $30-350 per unit.

492 WFFX-FM - 95.7
Box 2000 Phone: (205)758-5523
Tuscaloosa, AL 35403-2000 Fax: (205)752-9696

Format: Adult Contemporary. **Networks:** CNN Radio. **Founded:** 1952. **Formerly:** WUOA-FM. **Operating Hours:** Continuous. **ADI:** Tuscaloosa, AL. **Key Personnel:** Warren Kirk, General Mgr.; Keith LaCoste, Sales Mgr. **Wattage:** 100,000. **Ad Rates:** $20 for 30 seconds; $25 for 60 seconds.

WQPR-FM - See Muscle Shoals

493 WRTR-FM - 105.5
3900 11th Ave. Phone: (205)349-3200
PO Box 20126 Fax: (205)752-9269
Tuscaloosa, AL 35402-0126

Format: Classic Rock. **Founded:** 1966. **Formerly:** WACT-FM. **Operating Hours:** Continuous. **ADI:** Tuscaloosa, AL. **Key Personnel:** Mark Bass, General Mgr.; Lori Moore, Sales Mgr.; Bill Flanagan. **Local Programs:** *Positive Country*, Rick Cobb, Mailing contact; *Saturday Morning Memories*, Mike Robinson, Mailing contact. **Wattage:** 6000. **Ad Rates:** $16-28 for 30 seconds; $18-30 for 60 seconds.

494 WSPZ-AM - 1150
PO Box 20618 Phone: (205)339-3700
Tuscaloosa, AL 35402 Fax: (205)339-3704

Format: Sports. **Networks:** ESPN Radio. **Founded:** 1936. **Operating Hours:** Continuous. **ADI:** Tuscaloosa, AL. **Key Personnel:** Walter B. Grant, President; Rick L. Jones, VP/Gen. Mgr.; Matt Jones, Program Dir. **Local Programs:** *The Front Row* 7a.m.-9a.m., Lee Tracey; *Ridin' The Ping* 4p.m.-6p.m., Matt Jones. **Wattage:** 5000 day; 1000 night.

495 WTBC-AM - 1230
Box 2000 Phone: (205)758-5523
Tuscaloosa, AL 35403-2000 Fax: (205)752-9696
Free: (800)518-1977
E-mail: wtbc@dbtech.net

Format: News; Talk; Sports. **Networks:** ABC; CNN Radio; USA Radio. **Founded:** 1946. **Formerly:** WTNW-AM (1997); James L. Kirk II. **Operating Hours:** Continuous. **ADI:** Tuscaloosa, AL. **Key Personnel:** Johnny Price, General Mgr.; Johnny Price, Sales Mgr. **Wattage:** 1000. **Ad Rates:** $8 for 30 seconds; $10 for 60 seconds. **URL:** http://www.wtbc1230.com.

496 WTSK-AM - 790
142 Skyland Blvd. Phone: (205)345-7200
Tuscaloosa, AL 35405-4015 Fax: (205)349-1715

Format: Blues. **Networks:** American Urban Radio. **Founded:** 1958. **Operating Hours:** Continuous. **Key Personnel:** Houston Pearce, General Mgr. **Wattage:** 3000.

497 WTUG-FM - 92.9
142 Skyland Blvd. Phone: (205)345-7200
Tuscaloosa, AL 35405-4015 Fax: (205)349-1715

Format: Urban Contemporary. **Networks:** American Urban Radio. **Founded:** 1979. **Operating Hours:** Continuous. **Key Personnel:** Houston Pearce, General Mgr. **Wattage:** 100,000.

498 WUAL-FM - 91.5
PO Box 870370 Phone: (205)348-6644
Ste. 297, Phifer Hall Fax: (205)348-6648
Tuscaloosa, AL 35487-0370
Free: (800)654-4262

Format: Public Radio; News; Jazz; Classical. **Networks:** National Public Radio (NPR); American Public Radio (APR). **Founded:** 1982. **Operating Hours:** Continuous. **Key Personnel:** Sam Hendren, Contact, shendren@sa.va.edu; Melanie Peeples, Business Mgr., mpeeples@sa.va.edu; Roger Duvall, Station Mgr., rduvall@sa.va.com. **Wattage:** 100,000. **Ad Rates:** Noncommercial.

499 WVUA-FM - 90.7
University of Alabama Phone: (205)348-6461
PO Box 870152 Fax: (205)348-0375
Tuscaloosa, AL 35487-0152
E-mail: wvuamusicdept@hotmail.com

Format: Alternative/New Music/Progressive. **Founded:** 1972. **Operating Hours:** Continuous. **Key Personnel:** Dr. Loy Singleton, General Mgr., phone (205)348-7182; Geoff Calhoun, Station Mgr., totheteeth@gotmail.com. **Wattage:** 150. **Ad Rates:** Advertising accepted; rates available upon request.

500 WWPG-AM - 1280
PO Box 70427 Phone: (205)345-4787
Tuscaloosa, AL 35401 Fax: (205)345-4790

Format: Talk; Gospel. **Simulcasts:** WSLY-FM. **Networks:** ABC. **Owner:** W.A.N.R., Inc., at above address. **Founded:** 1951. **Formerly:** WNPT-AM; WWPJ-AM. **Operating Hours:** Continuous; 10% network, 90% local. **Key Personnel:** Jim Lawson, General Mgr.; Mildred Porter, Operations Mgr. **Wattage:** 5000. **Ad Rates:** $10 for 30 seconds; $15 for 60 seconds.

501 WZBQ-FM - 94.1
PO Box 20618 Phone: (205)339-3700
Tuscaloosa, AL 35402 Fax: (205)339-3704
E-mail: wzbq94@dbtech.net

Format: Contemporary Hit Radio (CHR). **Founded:** 1962. **Formerly:** WWWB-FM (1992); WCKO-FM (1994). **Operating Hours:** Continuous. **ADI:** Tuscaloosa, AL. **Key Personnel:** Rick L. Jones, VP/Gen. Mgr.; Lori Moore, Local Sales Mgr.; Walter B. Grant, President; Teddy S. Katz, Natl. Sales Mgr. **Local Programs:** *Louie Linguini* 6 - Midnight; *Steve & D.C.* 5-10 a.m.; *Steve Russell Show* 2-6 p.m., Steve Russell. **Wattage:** 100,000. **URL:** http://www.wzbq.com.

TUSCUMBIA†.

NW AL. Colbert Co. 10 mi. NE of Montgomery.

502 WZZA-AM - 1410
1570 Woodmont Dr. Phone: (205)381-1862
Tuscumbia, AL 35674

Format: Blues; Talk; News; Gospel. **Networks:** American Urban Radio. **Owner:** Bob Carl Bailey, 1570 Woodmont Dr., Tuscumbia, AL 35674, (205)381-6006. **Founded:** 1978. **Operating Hours:** Continuous; 10% network, 90% local. **ADI:** Huntsville-Decatur-Florence, AL. **Key Personnel:** Bob Carl Bailey, President/Gen. Mgr. **Wattage:** 500. **Ad Rates:** $3-6 for 10 seconds; $6-10.50 for 30 seconds; $8-12.50 for 60 seconds.

TUSKEGEE†, pop. 12,716.

E. AL. Macon Co. 40 mi. E. of Montgomery. Tuskegee University.

503 Campus Digest
Tuskegee University
Tuskegee, AL 36083 Phone: (205)727-8263

Black collegiate newspaper. **Founded:** 1931. **Freq:** Semi-monthly. **Print Method:** Offset. **Cols./Page:** 5. **Col. Width:** 20 nonpareils. **Col. Depth:** 196 agate lines. **Key Personnel:** Derrick T. Darteh, Editor. **Remarks:** Accepts classified advertising.
Circ: Non-paid 2,000

504 The Tuskegee News
Tuskegee Newspapers, Inc.
120 Eastside St
Tuskegee, AL 36083

Local newspaper serving the communities of Macon county. **Subtitle:** Macon County's Newspaper Since 1895. **Founded:** Apr. 1865. **Freq:** Weekly. **Print Method:** Offset. **Cols./Page:** 6. **Col. Width:** 2 inches. **Col. Depth:** 21 1/2 inches. **Key Personnel:** Paul Davis, Publisher; Mike Smelley. **Subscription Rates:** $19 individuals; $24 out of area; $26 out of state. **Remarks:** Accepts advertising.
Ad Rates: GLR: $.35 **Circ:** Paid 4,800
BW: $625.65
4C: $802.61
SAU: $5.76
PCI: $4.85

505 Sammons Communications of Alabama
204C S. Elm St. Phone: (205)727-4484
Tuskegee, AL 36083 Fax: (205)727-4554

Owner: Sammons Communications Inc., 3010 LBJ Freeway, Ste. 800, Dallas, TX 75234, (214)484-8888. **Founded:** Sept. 1972. **Formerly:** Tuskegee Cablevision (1981); Bece Cable Inc. (1985). **Key Personnel:** Cynthia Walford, General Mgr.; Randy Phillips, Chief Engineer; Alton Rye, Operations Mgr.; Mark Weber, President. **Cities Served:** Tuskegee, AL: subscribing households 3000; 35 channels; 1 community access channel; 24 hours per week community access programming.

506 WBIL-AM - 580
PO Box 869 Phone: (205)727-2100
Tuskegee, AL 36083 Fax: (205)724-9169

Format: Blues. **Founded:** 1975. **Operating Hours:** Continuous. **Key Personnel:** Nettie Echols, General Mgr.; Akilak Graham, Office Mgr., phone (334)724-9169; Costee McNair, Program Dir. **Wattage:** 500.

UNION SPRINGS

507 Union Springs Herald
PO Box 600 Phone: (334)738-2360
Union Springs, AL 36089 Fax: (334)738-2342

Community newspaper. **Freq:** Weekly (Wed.). **Cols./Page:** 6. **Col. Width:** 12 1/5 picas. **Col. Depth:** 21 1/2 inches. **Key Personnel:** Thomas May, Publisher.
Circ: 2,900

508 Com-Link Inc.
1500 E. Connecuh Ave. Fax: (334)738-5555
Box 272 Free: (800)722-2805
Union Springs, AL 36089

Owner: Com-Link Inc., at above address, (800)722-2805, (334)738-5555, Free: (800)722-2805. **Founded:** Apr. 7, 1989. **Key Personnel:** Larry C. Grogan, Exec. VP; Lynn Rotton, Technician; Van Hasson, Engineer. **Cities Served:** Autaugaville, AL: subscribing households 105; 21 channels.

509 Pagosa Vision Inc.
Box 272 Phone: (970)387-5504
Union Springs, AL 36089 Fax: (334)738-5555
Free: (800)222-1332

Owner: Com-Link Inc., at above address, (334)738-2204. **Founded:** Dec. 8, 1986. **Formerly:** San Juan Cable (Dec. 8, 1986). **Key Personnel:** Larry C. Grogan, Exec. VP; Lynn Rotton, Technician; Van Hasson, Engineer. **Cities Served:** Silverton and Rio Grande counties.: subscribing households 107; 28 channels.

VALLEY HEAD

NE AL. DeKalb Co. 20 mi. NE of Ft. Payne.

510 WQRX-AM - 870
870 Jeff Cook Dr. Phone: (205)635-6284
PO Box 309 Fax: (205)845-0872
Valley Head, AL 35989-0309

Format: Adult Contemporary; News. **Networks:** USA Radio. **Owner:** Jeff Cook, at above address. **Founded:** 1986. **Formerly:** WZRX-AM. **Operating Hours:** Sunrise-sunset. **Key Personnel:** Joyce Hamilton, General Mgr.; Johnny Allen, Sales Mgr.; Debbie Allen, Traffic Mgr.; Tim Dobson, Chief Engineer; Karen Cook, Program Dir. **Wattage:** 10,000.

VERNON†, pop. 2,609.

NW AL. Lamar Co. 27 mi. NE of Columbus, MS. Cotton gins. Textile factories, timber products. Agriculture. Cotton, corn, potatoes.

511 The Lamar Democrat
PO Box 587 Phone: (205)695-7029
Vernon, AL 35592 Fax: (205)695-9501

Newspaper with a Democratic orientation. **Founded:** Oct. 1, 1896. **Freq:** Weekly (Wed.). **Print Method:** Offset. **Trim Size:** 13 x 21. **Cols./Page:** 6. **Col. Width:** 12 picas. **Col. Depth:** 21 inches. **Key Personnel:** Howard L. Reeves, Editor; H. Rex Rainwater, Publisher; Tammy Bardon, Advertising Mgr. **USPS:** 303-480. **Subscription Rates:** $12.50 individuals; $15 out of area; $20 out of state. **Remarks:** Accepts advertising.
Ad Rates: GLR: $5 **Circ:** ‡3,300
BW: $400
4C: $500
SAU: $5
PCI: $5

512 WJEC-FM - 106.5
PO Box 630 Phone: (205)695-9191
Vernon, AL 35592 Fax: (205)695-9131

Format: Southern Gospel. **Networks:** USA Radio. **Owner:** Lamar County Broadcasting Co., Inc., at above address. **Founded:** 1991. **Operating Hours:** Continuous. **Key Personnel:** Patricia Davis, General Mgr.; Curt Smith, Station Mgr.; Jerry Oakes, Sales Mgr.; Randy Wright, Music Dir.; R. William Davis, Owner. **Wattage:** 6,000. **Ad Rates:** Advertising accepted; rates available upon request.

513 WVSA-AM - 1380
PO Box 630 Phone: (205)695-9191
Vernon, AL 35592 Fax: (205)695-9131

Format: Country; Gospel. **Owner:** Lamar City Broadcasting Co., Inc., at above address. **Founded:** 1966. **Operating Hours:** 12 hours Daily. **Key Personnel:** Randy Wright, Music Dir.; Patricia Davis, General Mgr.; Curt Smith, Station Mgr.; Jerry Oakes, Sales Mgr. **Wattage:** 5,000. **Ad Rates:** Advertising accepted; rates available upon request.

WETUMPKA†, pop. 4,341.

C. AL. Elmore Co. On Coosa River, 13 mi. NE of Montgomery. Recreation, tourism. Textile, lumber and grist mills; cotton gins. Agriculture. Cotton, corn, oats. Beef and dairy products.

514 The Wetumpka Herald
The Wetumpka Herald, Inc.
300 Green St. Phone: (334)567-7811
PO Box 99 Fax: (334)567-3284
Wetumpka, AL 36092-0029
Publication E-mail: wetumpkaherald@mindspring.com

Local newspaper. **Founded:** 1898. **Freq:** Weekly (Thurs.). **Print Method:** Offset. **Trim Size:** 14 x 22 3/4. **Cols./Page:** 6. **Col. Width:** 24 nonpareils. **Col. Depth:** 301 agate lines. **Key Personnel:** Ellen T. Williams, Publisher; Gerald Williams, Editor. **USPS:** 681-260. **Subscription Rates:** $18 individuals; $22 out of area; $26 out of state. **Remarks:** Color advertising accepted; rates available upon request.
Ad Rates: BW: $715.95 **Circ:** ‡4,400
4C: $250
PCI: $5.55

515 WAPZ-AM - 1250
2821 US Hwy 231 Phone: (205)567-2251
Wetumpka, AL 36092 Fax: (205)567-7971

Format: Gospel; Blues. **Networks:** American Urban Radio. **Founded:** 1954. **Operating Hours:** Continuous. **Key Personnel:** Robert Henderson, General Mgr. **Wattage:** 5000. **Ad Rates:** $15 for 30 seconds; $18 for 60 seconds.

YORK, pop. 3,392.

W. AL. Sumter Co. 28 mi. NE of Meridian, MS. Lumber mills; cotton ginning. Pine, hickory timber. Agriculture. Cotton, beans, potatoes.

516 WSLY-FM - 104.9
11474 U.S. Hwy. 11 Phone: (205)392-5234
York, AL 36925 Fax: (205)392-5234

Format: Blues; Urban Contemporary. **Owner:** William B. Grant, at above address. **Founded:** 1976. **Operating Hours:** Continuous. **ADI:** Meridian, MS. **Key Personnel:** William B. Grant, Contact; Tim Craddock, Contact. **Wattage:** 50,000. **Ad Rates:** $6 for 30 seconds; $10 for 60 seconds.

517 WYLS-AM - 670
11474 U.S. Hwy. 11 Phone: (205)392-5234
York, AL 36925 Fax: (205)392-5234

Format: Middle-of-the-Road (MOR); Big Band/Nostalgia. **Networks:** NBC; Alabama Radio (ALANET); Mississippi. **Owner:** William B. Grant, at above address. **Founded:** 1970. **Operating Hours:** 7 A.M. - 4:45 P.M. **ADI:** Tuscaloosa, AL. **Key Personnel:** William B. Grant, Contact; Tim Craddock, Contact. **Wattage:** 4800. **Ad Rates:** $6 for 30 seconds; $10 for 60 seconds.

ALASKA

State Capital, JUNEAU

Alaska is bounded on the north by the Arctic Ocean, east by the Yukon Territory and British Columbia, Canada, south by the Pacific Ocean, and west by Bering Sea and Strait and the Arctic Ocean. Including the Aleutian Islands, it has a total land area of 570,374 square miles; rank in area, first. Its greatest length from north to south is 1,420 miles; its breadth over 800 miles. The northern half is low with great morasses along the streams, and is populates only by a few Indians. The southern half is mountainous and along the southeast coast are some of the highest peaks in North America. Near the center is Mt. McKinley (20,320 feet), highest elevation on the entire continent. The southwesterly section comprises the peninsula of Alaska and the Aleutian Islands. This district is mountainous and actively volcanic. The coast from the southern boundary to Cape Spencer is lined with a chain of islands between which and the mainland are salt water channels navigable for the largest cruiseships. The Yukon River has a length of 2,300 miles, of which 1,765 miles are in Alaska and 1,200 miles are navigable. In the interior temperatures range from zero to 80 degrees. The northerly province bordering the polar sea is the only one in which arctic conditions prevail. The Weather Bureau at Juneau gives the temperatures (annual average) as 40.6; highest on record is 100; lowest on record -80. Total annual precipitation is 54.31 inches.

POPULATION: 587,000 (1992). Rank among the states, 48th.

AGRICULTURE: Number of farms: 1000 (1992). Farm acreage: 1,000,000 (1992). Cash receipts from farm marketings: crops, $20,000,000 (1991); livestock and products, $6,000,000 (1991).

FISHERIES: Total catch: 5,145,000,000 lbs. (1991), $1,216,000,000 value. Principal fish: salmon, crab, shrimp, herring.

FORESTS: Total forest land: 24,345,000 acres (1991).

MINERALS: Value of production: $494,000,000 (1991). Principal minerals: zinc, lead, and silver. Value of petroleum production: $7,659,000,000 (1991).

MANUFACTURES: Value added by manufacture: $1,291,000,000 (1991).

LIST OF CENSUS DIVISIONS

Total number of census divisions 23

Aleutians East Borough	2,464
Aleutians West Census Area	9,478
Anchorage Borough	226,338
Bethel Census Area	13,656
Bristol Bay Census Area	1,410
Dillingham Census Area	4,012
Fairbanks North Star Borough	77,720
Haines Borough	2,117
Juneau Borough	26,751
Kenai Peninsula Borough	40,802
Ketchikan Gateway Borough	13,828
Kodiak Island Borough	13,309
Lake and Peninsula Borough	1,668
Matanuska-Susitna Borough	39,683
Nome Census Area	8,288
North Slope Borough	5,979
Northwest Arctic Borough	6,113
Prince of Wales-Outer Ketchikan Census Area	6,278
Sitka Borough	8,588
Skagway-Yakutat-Angoon Census Area	4,385
Southeast Fairbanks Census Area	5,913
Valdez-Cordova Census Area	9,952
Wade Hampton Census Area	5,791
Wrangell-Petersburg Census Area	7,042
Yukon-Koyukuk Census Area	8,478

STATISTICS

Newspapers

Period of Issue	
Daily	6
Evening Daily	2
Morning Daily	3
Daily with Sunday edition	3
Semiweekly	1
Weekly	20
Biweekly	3
Semimonthly	1
Monthly	3
Bimonthly	1
Free or partly free	3
Shopper	1
Total Newspapers	35

Periodicals

Period of Issue	
Biweekly	1
Monthly	1
Quarterly	2
Bimonthly	1
Weekly	1
Total Periodicals	12

Total number of publications 47

Radio Stations

AM Stations	32
FM Stations	41
Total Radio Stations	73

TV Stations

Total TV Stations 12

Cable Stations

Total Cable Systems 11

Total number of broadcast listings 96

ANCHORAGE, pop. 173,017.

Anchorage Census Div. (S). Situated on a broad plain at the head of Cook Inlet in Southcentral Alaska. Tourism. Wholesale retail trade. Oil.

518 Alaska Business Monthly
Alaska Business Publishing Co., Inc.
PO Box 241288 Phone: (907)276-4373
Anchorage, AK 99524-1288 Fax: (907)279-2900
Free: (800)770-4373
Publication E-mail: editor@akbizmag.com
Publisher E-mail: info@akbizmag.com

Magazine featuring news, analysis, and profiles related to business in Alaska. **Founded:** 1985. **Freq:** Monthly. **Print Method:** Offset. **Trim Size:** 8 1/4 x 10 7/8. **Cols./Page:** 3. **Col. Width:** 27 nonpareils. **Col. Depth:** 140 agate lines. **Key Personnel:** Debbie Cutler, Editor; Vern C. McCorkle, Publisher. **ISSN:** 8756-4092. **Subscription Rates:** $21.95 individuals; $3 single issue. **Remarks:** Accepts advertising. **URL:** http://www.akbizmag.com/.
Ad Rates: BW: $1,560 **Circ:** Paid ‡3,000
4C: $3,179 Non-paid ‡7,000

519 Alaska Commercial Fisherman
Lindauer Newspapers
3709 Spenard Rd., Ste. 200
Anchorage, AK 99501

Magazine for commercial fishermen. **Founded:** 1989. **Freq:** Biweekly. **Print Method:** Offset. **Cols./Page:** 4. **Col. Width:** 27 nonpareils. **Col. Depth:** 210 agate lines. **Key Personnel:** Jacqueline Lindauer, Editor; John Lindauer, Advertising Mgr. **Subscription Rates:** $25. **Remarks:** Accepts advertising.
Ad Rates: BW: $990 **Circ:** ‡19,317
4C: $1,385
PCI: $14

520 Alaska Geographic
Alaska Geographic Society
PO Box 93370 Phone: (907)562-0164
Anchorage, AK 99509 Fax: (907)562-0479
Publisher E-mail: akgeo@aol.com

Trade magazine covering Alaska and Northern U.S. **Founded:** 1968. **Freq:** Quarterly. **Trim Size:** 10 3/8 x 8 3/8. **Key Personnel:** Penny Rennick, Editor; Kathy Doogan, Production Dir.; Jill Brubaker, Marketing Dir. **ISSN:** 0361-1353. **Subscription Rates:** $49 individuals. **Remarks:** Advertising not accepted.
Circ: (Not Reported)

521 Alaska History
Alaska Historical Society
PO Box 100299 Phone: (907)276-1596
Anchorage, AK 99510-0299 Fax: (907)276-1596
Publisher E-mail: ahs@alaska.net

Journal covering original research on Alaskan and northern U.S. history. **Founded:** 1984. **Freq:** Semiannual. **Trim Size:** 6 x 9. **Key Personnel:** James H. Ducker, Editor. **ISSN:** 0890-6149. **Subscription Rates:** $12 individuals; $6 single issue.
Circ: Paid 500

522 Alaska People Magazine
PO Box 190648 Phone: (907)277-3675
Anchorage, AK 99519 Fax: (907)277-3857
Publication E-mail: akpeople@alaskana.com

Lifestyle magazine featuring information of interest to the Alaskan community. **Founded:** Mar. 1994. **Freq:** Quarterly. **Print Method:** Offset. **Trim Size:** 8 1/4 x 10 3/4. **Key Personnel:** Jim Rosen, Publisher, jimrosen@webtv.net; Diana Giffer, Editor. **Subscription Rates:** $19.95 five issues; $29.95 ten issues. **Remarks:** Accepts advertising. **URL:** http://www.alaskana.com/akpeople.
Ad Rates: BW: $1,500 **Circ:** Paid 2,000
4C: $2,100 Controlled 8,000

523 Aleutians East Borough Advocate
Lindauer Newspapers
3709 Spenard Rd., Ste. 200
Anchorage, AK 99501

Community newspaper (tabloid). **Founded:** 1987. **Freq:** Weekly. **Print Method:** Offset. **Cols./Page:** 4. **Col. Width:** 27 nonpareils. **Col. Depth:** 210 agate lines. **Key Personnel:** Jeanette Somers, Editor; Jacqueline Lindauer, Publisher. **Subscription Rates:** $30. **Remarks:** Accepts advertising.
Ad Rates: BW: $560 **Circ:** ‡1,600
4C: $965
PCI: $12

524 Anchorage Daily News
1001 Northway Dr. Phone: (907)257-4200
PO Box 149001 Fax: (907)258-2157
Anchorage, AK 99514-9001
Publication E-mail: newsroom@pop.adn.com

General newspaper. **Founded:** 1946. **Freq:** Mon.-Sun. (morn.). **Print Method:** Offset. **Cols./Page:** 6. **Col. Width:** 24 nonpareils. **Col. Depth:** 298 agate lines. **Key Personnel:** Mike Dunham, Art Editor; Fuller Cowell, Publisher; Ken Carter, Production Dir.; Pat Dougherty, Acting Editor; Bill White, Business Editor; Gene Gilbert, TV Editor; David Hulen, City Editor; Michael Carey, Editorial Page Editor. **ISSN:** 0194-8670. **Subscription Rates:** $135 individuals. **Remarks:** Accepts advertising. **Online:** Dialog (The Dialog Corporation); DataTimes Corporation; LEXIS-NEXIS; Dow Jones. **URL:** http://www.adn.com. **Alt. Formats:** Microform. **Feature Editors:** George Bryson, *Metro*.
Ad Rates: GLR: $4.82 **Circ:** Mon.-Sat. ★**71,011**
BW: $4,202 Fri. ★**80,777**
4C: $4,504.50 Sun. ★**89,644**
PCI: $45

The Arctic Sounder - See Kotzebue

525 Borough Post
Lindauer Newspapers
3709 Spenard Rd., Ste. 200
Anchorage, AK 99501

Community newspaper (tabloid). **Founded:** 1988. **Freq:** Weekly. **Print Method:** Offset. **Cols./Page:** 4. **Col. Width:** 27 nonpareils. **Col. Depth:** 210 agate lines. **Key Personnel:** Barry Bialick, Editor; Nick Coltman, Advertising Mgr. **Subscription Rates:** $45. **Remarks:** Accepts advertising.
Ad Rates: BW: $560 **Circ:** ‡2,600
4C: $955
PCI: $12

526 GreatLander Bush Mailer
3110 Spenard Rd. Phone: (907)274-0611
Anchorage, AK 99503 Fax: (907)272-2105
Publication E-mail: api@micronet.net

Shopper. **Founded:** 1985. **Freq:** Monthly. **Print Method:** Offset. **Trim Size:** 11 1/2 x 14. **Cols./Page:** 4. **Col. Width:** 24 nonpareils. **Col. Depth:** 171 agate lines. **Key Personnel:** Charles Rhodes, Publisher. **Remarks:** Accepts advertising.
Ad Rates: BW: $700 **Circ:** Free 36,343
4C: $1,200
SAU: $10
PCI: $32

527 Journal of Energy Finance and Development
JAI Press, Inc.
School of Business Phone: (907)786-4153
University of Alaska, Anchorage Fax: (907)786-4119
Anchorage, AK 99508-8244
Publication E-mail: afmme@uaa.alaska.edu

Covers financial and developmental aspects in the energy industry. **Founded:** 1996. **Freq:** Semiannual. **Trim Size:** 7 x 10. **Key Personnel:** Musa Essayyad, Editor. **ISSN:** 1085-7443. **Subscription Rates:** $70 individuals; $125 institutions. **Remarks:** Accepts advertising.
Circ: (Not Reported)

528 Senior Voice
Older Persons Action Group, Inc.
325 E. 3rd Ave., Ste. 300 Phone: (907)277-0787
Anchorage, AK 99501 Fax: (907)278-6724

News/features for Alaska's seniors. **Subtitle:** Official Publication of Older Persons Action Group. **Founded:** 1978. **Freq:** Monthly. **Print Method:** Offset. **Trim Size:** Tab 16. **Cols./Page:** 5. **Col. Width:** 22 nonpareils. **Col. Depth:** 224 agate lines. **Key Personnel:** Kaylene Johnson, Managing Editor; Linda G. Faro, Advertising Mgr. **ISSN:** 0741-2894. **Subscription Rates:** $15 In Alaska for those over 55; $20 In Alaska for those under 55; $25 Outside Alaska. **Remarks:** Advertising not accepted for hearing aides.
Ad Rates: BW: $598.40 **Circ:** Combined ‡6,000
4C: $823

The Seward Phoenix LOG - See Seward

529 Sourdough Sentinel
Bypass Publishing
Public Affairs Office Phone: (907)552-2493
Elmendorf AFB, AK 99506 Fax: (907)552-5111
Publication E-mail: sourdough@3wgpapo.topcover.af.mil

Newspaper serving Elmendorf Air Force Base. **Founded:** 1942. **Freq:** Weekly. **Print Method:** Offset. **Trim Size:** 11 x 17. **Cols./Page:** 4. **Col. Width:** 11.5 picas. **Col. Depth:** 15 inches. **Key Personnel:** Barry Bialik, Publisher; John Asselin, Editor. **Subscription Rates:** Free. **Remarks:** Accepts advertising.
Ad Rates: SAU: $13.70 **Circ:** Free 7,500

530 Tundra Times
Eskimo, Indian, Aleut Publishing Co.
PO Box 92247 Phone: (907)349-2512
Anchorage, AK 99509-2247 Fax: (907)349-0335
Free: (800)764-2512
Publication E-mail: tundratimes@tribalnet.org

Statewide Native American newspaper. **Founded:** 1962. **Freq:** Biweekly (Wed.). **Print Method:** Offset. **Trim Size:** 11 x 17. **Cols./Page:** 4. **Col. Width:** 14 picas. **Col. Depth:** 210 agate lines. **Key Personnel:** Jeff Richardson, Editor; Toni Kahklen-Jones, Publisher. **Subscription Rates:** $30 individuals; $55 other countries. **Remarks:** Accepts advertising.
Ad Rates: GLR: $3 **Circ:** Paid 2,800
BW: $900 Free 200
PCI: $15

Valdez Pioneer - See Valdez

531 KADX-FM - 94.7
1255 Post St., Ste. 1011 Phone: (415)441-3377
San Francisco, CA 94109

Format: Talk. **Networks:** Westwood One Radio; ABC. **Owner:** American Radio Brokers Inc., 9200 Lake Otis Pkwy., Anchorage, AK 99507, (907)344-5625, Fax: (907)344-5728. **Founded:** Nov. 1, 1998. **Operating Hours:** Continuous. **ADI:** Anchorage, AK. **Key Personnel:** Chester Coleman, General Mgr./Program Dir., phone (415)441-3377; Susan Richards, Product Mgr.; Julie Zucchini, Music Dir.; Remington Noble, News Dir. **Wattage:** 50,000. **Ad Rates:** $22 for 15 seconds; $24 for 30 seconds; $25 for 60 seconds.

532 KATB-FM - 89.3
6401 E. Northern Lights Blvd.
Anchorage, AK 99504

Format: Religious. **Networks:** Moody Broadcasting; International Broadcasting. **Founded:** 1985. **Operating Hours:** Continuous. **ADI:** Anchorage, AK. **Key Personnel:** Michael D. Murray, General Mgr.; Allan Woosley, Program Dir. **Wattage:** 4900. **Ad Rates:** Noncommercial.

533 KAXX-AM - 1020
1255 Post St., Ste. 1011 Phone: (415)441-3377
San Francisco, CA 94109

Format: Sports. **Networks:** Westwood One Radio; CBS. **Owner:** American Radio Brokers, Inc., 9200 Lake Otis Pkwy., Anchorage, AK 99507, (907)344-5625, Fax: (907)344-5728. **Founded:** May 27, 1997. **Former name:** KFFR-AM (1994). **Operating Hours:** Continuous. **ADI:** Anchorage, AK. **Key Personnel:** Chester Coleman, General Mgr./Program Dir., phone (415)441-3377; Susan Richards, Product Mgr.; Julie Zucchlnl, Music Dir.; Remington Noble, News Dir. **Wattage:** 10,000. **Ad Rates:** $20 for 15 seconds; $24 for 30 seconds; $25 for 60 seconds.

534 KBRJ-FM - 104.1
11259 Tower Rd. Phone: (907)344-2200
Anchorage, AK 99515 Fax: (907)349-3299

Format: Hot Country. **Networks:** AP. **Owner:** Alaska Broadcast Communications, at above address. **Founded:** 1976. **Formerly:** KKLV-FM (1992). **Operating Hours:** Continuous. **ADI:** Anchorage, AK. **Key Personnel:** John Ruby, General Mgr. **Wattage:** 55,000. **Ad Rates:** $15-37 for 30 seconds; $18-41 for 60 seconds.

535 KBYR-AM - 700
1007 W. 32nd Ave. Phone: (907)273-3171
Anchorage, AK 99503 Fax: (907)273-3189
E-mail: knik@pobox.alaska.net

Format: News; Talk; Sports. **Networks:** CBS. **Owner:** NTV Inc., at above address, (907)273-3100. **Operating Hours:** Continuous; 85% network, 15% local. **ADI:** Anchorage, AK. **Key Personnel:** Hank Hove, President; Bob Dehn, Gen. Mgr./Gen. Sales Mgr./PD; Bob Dehn, Operations Mgr. **Wattage:** 10,000. **Ad Rates:** $10-15 for 60 seconds.

536 KDMD-TV - 33
6407 Brayton Dr., Ste. K Phone: (907)349-5899
Anchorage, AK 99507-2488 Fax: (907)344-7817

Format: Commercial TV. **Networks:** Home Shopping Club. **Founded:** 1989. **Operating Hours:** Continuous. **ADI:** Anchorage, AK. **Key Personnel:** Cheri Howland, General Mgr.

537 KENI-AM - 550
800 E. Diamond Blu., Ste.3-320 Phone: (907)522-1515
Anchorage, AK 99515 Fax: (907)349-6801

Format: Talk; News. **Networks:** ABC; NBC; Mutual Broadcasting System. **Owner:** TCT Communications, Inc., at above address. **Founded:** 1948. **Operating Hours:** Continuous; 75% network, 25% local. **ADI:** Anchorage, AK. **Key Personnel:** Andrew Lohman, General Mgr.; Wayne Maloney, Operations Dir./News Dir.; Pete Armstrong, General Sales Mgr. **Wattage:** 5000. **Ad Rates:** $21-51 per unit.

538 KFQD-AM - 750
9200 Lake Otis Pkwy. Phone: (907)344-9622
Anchorage, AK 99507 Fax: (907)349-7326
E-mail: kfqd@ corcom.com

Format: News. **Networks:** AP; ABC. **Owner:** Pioneer Broadcasting Co., Inc., at above address, Fax: (907)344-0742. **Founded:** 1924. **Operating Hours:** Continuous. **ADI:** Anchorage, AK. **Key Personnel:** Scott K. Smith, General Mgr.; Greg Wilkinson, Program Dir. **Wattage:** 50,000. **Ad Rates:** $18-30 per unit. Combined advertising rates available with KWHL-FM. **URL:** http://www.kfqd.com.

539 KGOT-FM - 101.3
500 L St., No. 200 Phone: (907)272-5945
Anchorage, AK 99501-5909 Fax: (907)272-5055
E-mail: kgot@alaskanet.com

Format: Contemporary Hit Radio (CHR). **Founded:** 1967. **Operating Hours:** Continuous. **ADI:** Anchorage, AK. **Key Personnel:** Gary Donovan, General Mgr.; Paul Walker, PD; Van Kraft, Engineer; Sezy Gerow, Promotions; Prudy Erickson, Sales Mgr.; Mark Murphy, Operations Mgr. **Wattage:** 26,000. **Ad Rates:** $43-48 per unit. **URL:** http://www.alaskanet.com/kgot.

540 KHAR-AM - 590
11259 Tower Rd. Phone: (907)344-2200
Anchorage, AK 99515 Fax: (907)349-3299

Format: Big Band/Nostalgia. **Networks:** NBC. **Owner:** Alaska Broadcast Communications, at above address. **Founded:** 1961. **Operating Hours:** Continuous. **ADI:** Anchorage, AK. **Key Personnel:** John Ruby, General Mgr. **Wattage:** 5000. **Ad Rates:** $10-25 for 30 seconds; $13-28 for 60 seconds.

541 KIMO-TV - 13
2700 E. Tudor Rd. Phone: (907)561-1313
Anchorage, AK 99507 Fax: (907)561-1377
E-mail: newslinkak@anc.ak.net

Format: Commercial TV. **Networks:** ABC. **Founded:** 1967. **Operating Hours:** 24 hrs. **ADI:** Anchorage, AK. **Key Personnel:** Mark Chassman, General Mgr., phone (907)762-8820, fax (907)561-1377, mchassman@aksuperstation.com. **URL:** http://www.aksupersite.com.

542 KLEF-FM - 98.1
3601 C St., Ste. 290 Phone: (907)561-5556
Anchorage, AK 99503 Fax: (907)562-4219
E-mail: classical198@klef.rom

Format: Classical. **Networks:** Concert Music Network (CMN). **Owner:** Chinook Concert Broadcasters Inc., at above address. **Founded:** 1988. **Operating Hours:** 5 a.m.-midnight. **ADI:** Alaska. **Key Personnel:** Rick Goodfellow, General Mgr.; Janice Ingram, Operations Mgr.; Jan Sands, Sales Mgr. **Local Programs:** *Kaladi Brothers Morning Show*, Rick Goodfellow; *Sacred Concert*, Jon Sharpe; *Saturday Night at the Opera*, Peter Brown. **Wattage:** 25,000. **Ad Rates:** $19-30 for 30 seconds; $25-35 for 60 seconds.

543 KMXS-FM - 103.1
9200 Lake Otis Parkway Phone: (907)522-5103
Anchorage, AK 99507 Fax: (907)349-7326
E-mail: mix@kmxs.com

Format: Adult Contemporary. **Owner:** Pioneer Broadcasting Co., at above address. **Founded:** 1995. **Operating Hours:** Continuous. **ADI:** Anchorage, AK. **Key Personnel:** Scott K. Smith, General Mgr.; Roxi Lennox, Program Mgr., roxilennox@aol.com. **Local Programs:** *80's at Eight*; *New at Nine*. **Wattage:** 27,000. **Ad Rates:** $30-60 per unit.

544 KNIK-FM - 105.3
1007 W. 32nd Ave. Phone: (907)273-3171
Anchorage, AK 99503 Fax: (907)273-3189
E-mail: knik@poboxalaska.net

Format: Jazz. **Owner:** NTV Inc., at above address, (907)273-3100. **Founded:** 1960. **Operating Hours:** Continuous; 100% local. **ADI:** Anchorage, AK. **Key Personnel:** Hank Hove, President; Bob Dehn, Gen. Mgr./GSM/PD. **Wattage:** 25,000. **Ad Rates:** $14-21 for 60 seconds.

545 KRUA-FM - 88.1
3211 Providence Dr. Phone: (907)786-6800
Anchorage, AK 99508 Fax: (907)786-6806
E-mail: aykrua@uaa.alaska.edu

Format: Alternative/New Music/Progressive. **Founded:** 1987. **Formerly:** KMPS-FM. **Operating Hours:** 7 a.m.-1 a.m. **ADI:** Anchorage, AK. **Key Personnel:** Margaret Knowles, Station Mgr.; Tuesday Carr, Program Dir.; Jeremy Linden, Production Mgr.; Stephen Barnett, News Dir.; Tony Hardt, Sports Dir. **Local Programs:** *Native American Music*, Marvin Parent; *Righteous Babes*, Michele Wellck; *Trip II Utopia*, Jeremy Linden. **Wattage:** 160. **Ad Rates:** Noncommercial. **URL:** http://www.netcasting.krua.

546 KSKA-FM - 91.1
3877 University Dr. Phone: (907)561-1161
Anchorage, AK 99508 Fax: (907)273-9435
E-mail: news@kakm.pbs.org

Format: Public Radio; Eclectic; News. **Networks:** National Public Radio (NPR); Alaska Public Radio. **Founded:** 1975. **Operating Hours:** Continuous; 57% network, 43% local. **ADI:** Anchorage, AK. **Key Personnel:** Susan Reed, General Mgr.; Bede Trantina, Program Dir.; Robert Howk, News Dir. **Wattage:** 100,000. **Ad Rates:** Noncommercial. **URL:** www.alaska.net/~kakm1.

547 KTBY-TV - 4
1840 S. Bragaw St., Ste. 101 Phone: (907)274-0404
Anchorage, AK 99508 Fax: (907)264-5180

Format: Commercial TV. **Networks:** Fox. **Founded:** 1983. **Operating Hours:** Continuous. **ADI:** Anchorage, AK. **Key Personnel:** Sean M. Bradley, Contact, phone (907)2740404, fax (907)2645180. **Local Programs:** *Fox 4 Kids Club*, Chris Munroe. **Wattage:** 40,000 watts.

548 KTVA-TV - 11
1007 W. 32nd Ave. Phone: (907)273-3100
Anchorage, AK 99503 Fax: (907)273-3189
E-mail: news//@alaska.net

Format: Commercial TV. **Networks:** CBS. **Owner:** Northern Television Inc., at above address. **Founded:** 1953. **Operating Hours:** Continuous; 75% network, 25% local. **ADI:** Anchorage, AK. **Key Personnel:** Robert Gottstein, CEO/President, phone (907)257-5601, fax (907)257-5620, rgottstein@ktva.com; Jerry Beaver, Vice President, phone (907)273-3101, jbever@ktva.com; Lauren Maxwell, News Dir., phone (907)273-3113, fax (907)273-3188, lmaxwell@ktva.com; Ron Blair, Promotions Dir., phone (907)273-3106, rblair@ktva.com; Norma Goodman, Asst. VP/Public Affairs Dir., phone (907)273-3102, ngoodman@ktva.com. **Local Programs:** *Norma Goodman Show* 9 a.m. Monday-Friday, Norma Goodman. **Wattage:** 50,000 ERP. **Ad Rates:** $20-550 for 30 seconds; $40-1,100 for 60 seconds.

549 KWHL-FM - 106.5
9200 Lake Otis Pkwy. Phone: (907)344-9622
Anchorage, AK 99507 Fax: (907)349-7326
E-mail: kwhl@corcom.com

Format: Album-Oriented Rock (AOR). **Owner:** Pioneer Broadcasting Co., Inc., at above address. **Founded:** 1982. **Operating Hours:** Continuous. **ADI:** Anchorage, AK. **Key Personnel:** Scott K. Smith, General Mgr.; JJ Michaels, Program Dir. **Wattage:** 100,000. **Ad Rates:** $25-75 per unit. Combined advertising rates available with KFQD-AM.

550 KYAK-AM - 650
500 L St., Ste. 200 Phone: (907)272-5945
Anchorage, AK 99501 Fax: (907)272-5055

Format: Educational. **Networks:** Christian Broadcasting (CBN). **Founded:** 1967. **Operating Hours:** Continuous; 100% local. **ADI:** Anchorage, AK. **Key Personnel:** Gary Donovan, Contact; Prudy Erickson, Sales Mgr.; Mark Murphy, Operations Mgr.; Sezy Gerow, Promotions Dir.; April Aahs, Program Dir. **Wattage:** 50,000. **Ad Rates:** $8-16 for 30 seconds.

551 KYES-TV - 5
3700 Woodland Dr. Ste. 600 Phone: (907)248-5937
Anchorage, AK 99517 Fax: (907)243-0709
E-mail: fireweed@alaska.net

Format: Commercial TV. **Networks:** United Paramount Network. **Founded:** 1989. **Operating Hours:** 6 a.m.-2 p.m. **ADI:** Anchorage, AK. **Key Personnel:** Carol Schatz, General Mgr., phone (907)2438610; Jeremy Lansman, President, phone (907)2485959. **Wattage:** 100,000. **Ad Rates:** Advertising accepted; rates available upon request.

552 KYMG-FM - 98.9
500 L St., Ste. 200 Phone: (907)272-5945
Anchorage, AK 99501 Fax: (907)272-5055

Format: Adult Contemporary. **Networks:** Independent. **Owner:** Pacific Star Broadcasting, Inc., at above address. **Founded:** 1989. **Operating Hours:** Continuous; 100% local. **ADI:** Anchorage, AK. **Key Personnel:** Gary Donovan, General Mgr.; Devan Mitchell, P.D.; Van Craft, Chief Engineer; Sezy Gerow, Promotions; Prudy Erickson, Sales Mgr.; Mark Murphy, Operations Mgr.; Phil Kirn, Production Dir. **Wattage:** 100,000. **Ad Rates:** $25-50 for 30 seconds; $25-50 for 60 seconds.

553 Prime Cable of Alaska, Inc.
5151 Fairbanks St. Phone: (907)786-9260
Anchorage, AK 99503 Fax: (907)786-9270

Founded: 1980. **Cities Served:** Anchorage, Bethel, and Kenai Peninsula counties, Bethel, Chugiak, Eagle River, Elmendorf AFB, Fort Richardson, Kenai, Kenai Peninsula, Ridgeway, and Soldotna, AK.

BARROW

North Slope Borough. (C). 60 m NE of Wainwright.

554 KBRW-AM - 680
1695 Okpik St. Phone: (907)852-6811
PO Box 109 Fax: (907)852-2274
Barrow, AK 99723
E-mail: kbrw@barrow.org

Format: Public Radio; Eclectic; Educational. **Networks:** Public Radio International (PRI); National Public Radio (NPR); Alaska Public Radio. **Owner:** Silakkuagvik Communications, Inc., at above address. **Founded:** 1975. **Operating Hours:** Continuous. 33% network 67% local. **Key Personnel:** Don Rinker, General Mgr., don@kbrw.org; Steve Hamlin, Program Dir./Asst. General Mgr., steve@kbrw.org; Isaac Tuckfield, Operations Dir.; Charles Lakaytis, Engineer; David Dean, Production Asst.; Sherie Wallace, Administrative Asst. **Wattage:** 10,000. **Ad Rates:** Noncommercial.

555 KBRW-FM - 91.9
1695 Okpik St. Phone: (907)852-6811
PO Box 109 Fax: (907)852-2274
Barrow, AK 99723

Format: Public Radio; Eclectic; Educational. **Networks:** National Public Radio (NPR); Alaska Radio Network. **Owner:** Silakkuagvik Communications, Inc., at above address. **Founded:** 1975. **Operating Hours:** Continuous, 33% network, 67% local. **Key Personnel:** Don Rinker, General Mgr., don@kbrw.org; Steve Hamlin, Program Dir./Asst. Gen. Mgr., steve@kbrw.org; Isaac Tuckfield, Operations Dir. **Local Programs:** *62 News*. **Wattage:** 10,000. **Ad Rates:** Noncommercial.

BETHEL, pop. 3,576.

Bethel Census Div. (SW). 5 m W of Kwenthluk. Residential.

556 Tundra Drums
PO Box 868 Phone: (907)543-3500
Bethel, AK 99559 Fax: (907)543-3312

Community newspaper. **Subtitle:** The Beat of the Yukon-Kuskokwim Delta. **Founded:** Apr. 1, 1974. **Freq:** Weekly (Thurs.). **Print Method:** Offset. **Trim Size:** 9 3/4 x 15 1/2. **Cols./Page:** 5. **Col. Width:** 22 nonpareils. **Col. Depth:** 217 agate lines. **Key Personnel:** Patty Sullivan, Editor; Javier Marguez, Reporter. **Subscription Rates:** $45 third class mail; $90 first class mail. **Remarks:** Accepts advertising.
Ad Rates: GLR: $2.68 **Circ:** ‡6,800
BW: $656.25
4C: $1,106.25
SAU: $8.75
PCI: $13.65

557 KYKD-FM - 100.1
PO Box 2428 Phone: (907)543-5953
Bethel, AK 99559-0820 Fax: (907)543-5952

Format: Easy Listening; Religious. **Networks:** USA Radio. **Founded:** 1983. **Operating Hours:** 6a.m.- 12a.m. **ADI:** Bethel, AK. **Key Personnel:** Bob Eldridge, General Mgr.; Kelvin Schubert, Station Mgr.; Carl Cutforth, Chief Engineer. **Wattage:** 7.9 Khz. **Ad Rates:** $5-10 for 30 seconds; $7.50-15 for 60 seconds.

558 KYUK-AM - 640
640 Radio St. Phone: (907)543-3131
Pouch 468 Fax: (907)543-3130
Bethel, AK 99559
Free: (800)478-3640

Format: Eclectic; Adult Contemporary; Country; Oldies; Blues; Talk; News; Sports; Jazz; Classical. **Networks:** National Public Radio (NPR); Alaska Public Radio; Public Radio International (PRI). **Owner:** Bethel Broadcasting Inc., at above address, (907)543-3130. **Founded:** 1971. **Operating Hours:** 6 a.m.-midnight. **ADI:** Bethel, AK. **Key Personnel:** Joe Seibert, General Mgr., phone (907)543-3131, fax (907)543-3130, joe_ seibert@ddc-alaska.org; Kate Hamilton, Program Dir., kate_ hamilton@ddc-alaska.org. **Wattage:** 10,000. **Ad Rates:** Underwriting available.

559 KYUK-TV - 4
Pouch 468 Phone: (907)543-3131
Bethel, AK 99559 Fax: (907)543-3130
Free: (800)478-3654

Format: Public TV. **Networks:** Public Broadcasting Service (PBS). **Owner:** Bethel Broadcasting, Inc., at above address. **Founded:** 1973. **Operating Hours:** 9 a.m. - midnight. **ADI:** Bethel, AK. **Key Personnel:** John A. McDonald, General Mgr.; Michael Martz, Production Mgr.; Ronda McBride, News Dir.; Allen Auxier, Program Dir. **Local Programs:** *Contact Ronda McBride.* **Wattage:** 5000. **Ad Rates:** Advertising accepted; rates available upon request.

CORDOVA, pop. 1,879.

Valdez-Cordova Census Div. (S). On Gulf of Alaska, 140 m SE of Anchorage. Ferry connections. Crab, clam, herring, black cod, halibut, salmon canneries. Fisheries. Coal mining. Oil drilling in vicinity. Cold storage plants. Spruce, hemlock, timber.

560 The Cordova Times
Alaska Newspapers, Inc.
PO Box 200 Phone: (907)424-7181
Cordova, AK 99574-0200 Fax: (907)424-5799

Community newspaper. **Founded:** 1914. **Freq:** Weekly (Thurs.). **Print Method:** Offset. **Cols./Page:** 5. **Col. Width:** 22 nonpareils. **Col. Depth:** 224 agate lines. **Key Personnel:** Don P. Adams, Editor; Mimi Macavinta, Advertising Mgr. **Subscription Rates:** $30 individuals. **Remarks:** Accepts advertising.
Ad Rates: GLR: $.37 **Circ:** ‡1,800
PCI: $6

561 KLAM-AM - 1450
PO Box 60 Phone: (907)424-3796
Cordova, AK 99574 Fax: (907)424-3737

Format: Eclectic; News. **Networks:** ABC. **Owner:** RISOC, Inc., Box 60, Cordova, AK 99574-0060. **Founded:** 1950. **Operating Hours:** Continuous. **Key Personnel:** J.R. Lewis, President/GM. **Local Programs:** *Cordova Live Talk Show*, J.R. Lewis; *Cordova Live Trivia*, J.R. Lewis; *Swap Shop*, J.R. Lewis. **Wattage:** 250. **Ad Rates:** $6.50-12 for 30 seconds; $7.50-15 for 60 seconds.

DELTA JUNCTION, pop. 942.

Fairbanks Census Div. (C). 100 m SE of Fairbanks. Residential

562 Delta Wind
TriDelta, Inc.
PO Box 986 Phone: (907)895-5115
Delta Junction, AK 99737 Fax: (907)895-4950

Community newspaper. **Founded:** 1992. **Freq:** Biweekly. **Print Method:** Offset. **Trim Size:** 11 1/4 x 17 1/2. **Cols./Page:** 4. **Col. Width:** 14 picas. **Col. Depth:** 16 1/4 inches. **Key Personnel:** Loretta Schooley, Managing Editor. **Subscription Rates:** $22.10. **Remarks:** Accepts advertising. **Formerly**: The Delta Paper (1992).
Ad Rates: BW: $390 **Circ:** Paid ‡950
4C: $840 Free ‡125
PCI: $6

DILLINGHAM

On the Alaskan Peninsula.

563 The Bristol BayTimes
Alaska Newspapers, Inc.
PO Box 1770 Phone: (907)842-5572
Dillingham, AK 99576 Fax: (907)842-5562
Publication E-mail: aknewspr@alaska.net
Publisher E-mail: mail@organsociety.org

Community newspaper. **Founded:** 1965. **Freq:** Weekly. **Print Method:** Web offset. **Cols./Page:** 5. **Col. Width:** 2 1/2 inches. **Col. Depth:** 15 1/2 inches. **Key Personnel:** Christopher Casati, Editor; John Woodbury, Managing Editor. **USPS:** 010-399. **Subscription Rates:** $45 individuals. **Remarks:** Accepts advertising. **URL:** http://alaska.net/~aknewspr.
Ad Rates: GLR: $1.50 **Circ:** Controlled ⊕**2,076**
BW: $1,115.22
4C: $1,515.22
PCI: $14.39

564 KDLG-AM - 670
Box 670 Phone: (907)842-5281
Dillingham, AK 99576 Fax: (907)842-5645
E-mail: rsoal@aurora.alaska.edu

Format: Public Radio; Full Service. **Networks:** Alaska Radio Network; Public Radio International (PRI); AP; National Public Radio (NPR). **Owner:** Dillingham City Schools, at above address. **Founded:** 1975. **Operating Hours:** 18 hrs. Daily; 10% network, 90% local. **Key Personnel:** Rob Carpenter, Manager, kdlg@dcsd.k12.ak.us; Gary Richardson, Program Dir., gary@dcsd.k12.ak.us; Alexi Rubenstein, News Dir., alexi@dcsd.k12.ak.us; Rob Carpenter, Engineer. **Wattage:** 10,000. **Ad Rates:** Noncommercial; underwriting available.

DUTCH HARBOR

565 The Dutch Harbor Fisherman
Alaska Newspapers, Inc.
PO Box 920472 Phone: (907)581-2092
Dutch Harbor, AK 99692 Fax: (907)581-2090
Publication E-mail: aknewspr@alaska.net
Publisher E-mail: mail@organsociety.org

Community newspaper. **Founded:** 1992. **Freq:** Weekly. **Print Method:** Web offset. **Cols./Page:** 5. **Col. Width:** 2 1/2 inches. **Col. Depth:** 15 1/2 inches. **Key Personnel:** Christopher Casati, Publisher; John Woodbury, Editor; Brandy Johnson, Dir. of Sales/Mrktg. **USPS:** 015-185. **Subscription Rates:** $45 individuals. **Remarks:** Accepts advertising. **URL:** http://alaska.net/~aknewspr.
Ad Rates: GLR: $1.50 **Circ:** Paid ⊕**1,002**
BW: $1,115.22 Controlled 1,046
4C: $1,515.22
PCI: $14.39

EAGLE RIVER, pop. 2,437.

Anchorage Census Div. (S). 20 m S of Palmer. Gateway to Chugach State Park. Service businesses, construction and land development.

566 Alaska Star
Star Publishing Co.
16941 N. Eagle River Loop Rd. Phone: (907)694-2719
Eagle River, AK 99577 Fax: (907)694-1545
Publication E-mail: akstar@micronet.net

Community newspaper. **Founded:** Jan. 14, 1971. **Freq:** Weekly (Thurs.). **Print Method:** Offset. **Trim Size:** 11 x 17. **Cols./Page:** 5. **Col. Width:** 23 nonpareils. **Col. Depth:** 224 agate lines. **Key Personnel:** Lee B. Jordan, Editor and Publisher. **USPS:** 939-280. **Subscription Rates:** $25 individuals /year. **Remarks:** Accepts advertising. **Formerly**: Chugiak-Eagle River Alaska Star.
Ad Rates: BW: $1170 **Circ:** Paid ‡7,380
4C: $1,620 Free ‡1,200
PCI: $14.80

ELMENDORF AFB

Sourdough Sentinel - See Anchorage

FAIRBANKS†, pop. 22,645.

Fairbanks North Star Census Div. 300 m NE OF Anchorage. University of Alaska. Terminus Alaska Highway and Alaska Railroad. Distribution and Supply Center for Interior and Northern Alaska, including North Slope, petroleum development and pipeline distribution system. Diversified mining.

567 Agroborealis
University of Alaska Fairbanks
PO Box 757200 Phone: (907)474-5042
Fairbanks, AK 99775 Fax: (907)474-6184
Publisher E-mail: fynrpub@uaf.edu

Trade magazine covering agriculture, forestry research, and natural resources management and education. **Freq:** Semiannual. **Trim Size:** 8 1/2 x 11. **ISSN:** 0002-1822. **Subscription Rates:** Free. **Remarks:** Advertising not accepted. **URL:** http://bonanza.lter.uaf.edu/~salrm/station/AFES.html.
Circ: Non-paid 3,500

568 Fairbanks Daily News-Miner
200 N. Cushman Phone: (907)456-6661
Box 70710 Fax: (907)452-5054
Fairbanks, AK 99707-0710
Publication E-mail: mail@newsminer.com
Publisher E-mail: newsroom@newsminer.com

General newspaper. **Founded:** 1904. **Freq:** Daily (morn.). **Print Method:** Offset. **Trim Size:** 12 1/2 x 22 3/4. **Cols./Page:** 6. **Col. Width:** 11.2 nonpareils. **Col. Depth:** 294 agate lines. **Key Personnel:** Kelly Bostian, Managing Editor, phone (907)459-7585, fax (907)452-7917, editor@newsminer.com; Paul Massey, Publisher, phone (907)459-7512, fax (907)451-9060, pmassey@newsminer.com; Marilyn Romano, Advertising Dir., phone (907)459-7525, fax (907)451-8962, mromano@newsminer.com. **ISSN:** 8750-5495. **Subscription Rates:** $156. **Remarks:** Accepts advertising. **URL:** http://www.newsminer.com.
Ad Rates: GLR: $1.43 **Circ:** Mon.-Sat. ★**17,095**
BW: $2,392.74 Sun. ★**22,613**
4C: $2,892.74
SAU: $18.99
PCI: $22.96

569 Northland News
Fairbanks Daily News-Miner
200 N. Cushman St. Phone: (907)459-7504
Fairbanks, AK 99701 Fax: (907)452-7917
Publisher E-mail: newsroom@newsminer.com

Newspaper on Alaska. **Founded:** 1983. **Freq:** Monthly. **Print Method:** Offset. **Cols./Page:** 5. **Col. Width:** 12.2 picas. **Col. Depth:** 12.5 inches. **Key Personnel:** Marmian Grimes, Editor, phone (907)459-7504. **Subscription Rates:** Free. **Remarks:** Accepts advertising.
Ad Rates: GLR: $1.45 **Circ:** Non-paid ‡18,000
BW: $1,034.38
4C: $565
PCI: $16.55

570 Sun Star
University of Alaska
Wood Center Phone: (907)474-7540
Publications Board Fax: (907)474-5508
Fairbanks, AK 99775
Publication E-mail: fystar@auron.alask.edu

Collegiate newspaper. **Subtitle:** University of Alaska Fairbanks. **Founded:** 1981. **Freq:** Weekly (Tues.). **Print Method:** Offset. **Trim Size:** 11 x 17. **Cols./Page:** 4. **Col. Width:** 2 7/16 inches. **Col. Depth:** 204 agate lines. **Key Personnel:** Mariam Denton, Editor; Erica East, Administrative Assistant; Tracy Regan, Editor. **Subscription Rates:** $20 by mail. **Remarks:** Accepts advertising. **Formerly**: Polar Star.
Ad Rates: BW: $435 **Circ:** Free ‡4,000
4C: $935
PCI: $8

571 GCI
505 Old Steve Hwy. Phone: (907)452-7191
Fairbanks, AK 99701 Fax: (907)456-3163

Owner: GCI Cable, at above address. **Founded:** 1979. **Formerly**: ACN; Alaskan Cable Network. **Key Personnel:** Mike Baker, Regional Mgr.; Janice Lunney, Business Mgr. **Cities Served:** Eielson, Fairbanks, Fort Greely, Fort Wainwright, North Pole, North Star Bourough, AK: subscribing households 10,000; 51 channels; 1 community access channel.

572 KATN-TV - 2
516 2nd Ave. Phone: (907)452-2125
Suite 400 Fax: (907)456-8225
Fairbanks, AK 99701

Format: Commercial TV. **Networks:** ABC. **Owner:** Smith Broadcast Group, Inc., at above address, (907)561-1313, Fax: (907)561-1377. **Founded:** 1955. **Formerly**: KFAR-TV (1980). **Operating Hours:** Continuous. 90% network, 10% local. **ADI:** Fairbanks (North Pole), AK. **Key Personnel:** Bob Underwood, General Mgr.; Tracy Helm, News Dir.; Victoria Dockery, Office Mgr. **Wattage:** 10,000. **Ad Rates:** Advertising accepted; rates available upon request.

573 KCBF-AM - 820
3528 International St. Phone: (907)452-5121
Fairbanks, AK 99701-7382 Fax: (907)452-5120
E-mail: kcbf@polarnet.com

Format: Oldies; Talk. **Networks:** CBS. **Owner:** Northern Television, Inc., at above address. **Founded:** 1948. **Formerly**: KFRB-AM. **Operating Hours:** Continuous. **ADI:** Fairbanks (North Pole), AK. **Key Personnel:** Bill Holzheimer, Station Mgr./Sales, holzheimer@kxtr.com. **Wattage:** 10,000. **Ad Rates:** $4-20 for 30 seconds; $6-35 for 60 seconds. Combined advertising rates available with KXLZ-FM. **URL:** http://www.kcbf.com.

574 KFAR-AM - 660
1060 Aspen St. Phone: (907)451-5910
Fairbanks, AK 99709-5501 Fax: (907)451-5999
E-mail: kfar@polarnet.com

Format: Talk; News; Public Radio. **Networks:** ABC; NBC; Mutual Broadcasting System. **Owner:** Borealis Broadcasting, Inc., at above address. **Founded:** 1939. **Operating Hours:** Continuous; 63% network, 37% local. **ADI:** Fairbanks (North Pole), AK. **Key Personnel:** Terry Walley, Contact; Wanda Osborne, Contact; Bev Meyers, Traffic Mgr. **Local Programs:** *Problem Corner* 10:00 am -12:00 pm Monday-Friday, David Arlan, Producer; *Problem Corner*, David Arlen. **Wattage:** 10,000. **Ad Rates:** $6-21.50 for 30 seconds. Combined advertising rates available with KWLF-FM, KUWL-FM.

575 KIAK-AM - 970
PO Box 73410 Phone: (907)457-1921
Fairbanks, AK 99701 Fax: (907)457-2128

Format: Contemporary Country. **ADI:** Fairbanks (North Pole), AK. **Key Personnel:** Peter Van Nort, General Mgr. **Wattage:** 5000.

576 KIAK-FM - 102.5
PO Box 73410 Phone: (907)457-1921
Fairbanks, AK 99701

Format: Country. **Founded:** 1972. **Formerly**: KQRZ-FM (1990). **Operating Hours:** Continuous. **ADI:** Fairbanks (North Pole), AK. **Key Personnel:** Peter Van Nort, General Mgr. **Wattage:** 26,500.

577 KSUA-FM - 91.5
307 Constitution Hall Phone: (907)474-7054
University of Alaska, Fairbanks Fax: (907)474-7054
Fairbanks, AK 99775
E-mail: fyksua@aurora.alaska.edu

Format: Alternative/New Music/Progressive. **Networks:** Pacifica. **Owner:** University of Alaska, at above address, Fax: (907)474-6314. **Founded:** 1984. **Operating Hours:** Continuous 100% local. **ADI:** Fairbanks (North Pole), AK. **Key Personnel:** Leigh A. Patton, Chief Oper./General Mgr.; Brandon Wilks, Program Dir., phone (907)474-7054, fax (907)474-6314, fsbw2@avrora.alaska.edu; Anthony Snow, Chief Engineer; Matthew Layral, Broadcast Engineer, phone (907)474-7054, fax (907)474-6314, fsmal@avrora.alaska.edu. **Local Programs:** *The Asylum*, Kurt Kriebbhal, (907)455-8536; *Captain Midnight*, Matt Lynch; *Speak Up & Speak Out*, Dr. Nag Rao. **Wattage:** 3000. **Ad Rates:** $3-10 per unit. **URL:** http://www.vaf.edu/ksva.

578 KTNL-TV - 13
Business Office Phone: (907)457-3670
158 Berkeley Fax: (907)457-3672
Fairbanks, AK 99708-1309
E-mail: wrights@alaska.net.com

Format: Commercial TV. **Networks:** CBS. **Owner:** Wright Home, Inc., at above address. **Founded:** 1966. **Formerly**: KIFW-TV (1983). **Operating Hours:** 2 a.m.-12:35 A.M. **ADI:** Sitka, AK. **Key Personnel:** Bill Wright, President, phone (907)452-5124, fax (907)457-3672, bwright@ktuf.com; Cindy Wright, V.P. & Prog. PSA Promo Dir. **Wattage:** 1000. **Ad Rates:** $25 for 30 seconds; $50 for 60 seconds.

579 KTVF-TV - 11
3528 International Way Phone: (907)452-5121
Fairbanks, AK 99701 Fax: (907)452-5120

Format: Commercial TV. **Networks:** NBC. **Owner:** Northern Television, Inc., PO Box 102200, Anchorage, AK 99510, (907)562-3456. **Founded:** 1954. **Operating Hours:** 6 a.m.-2:45 a.m. **ADI:** Fairbanks (North Pole), AK. **Key Personnel:** Hank Hove, President; Sally Crawford, Contact; Melissa Lewis, Program Dir.; Chuck Hinde, News Dir.; Meg Gaydosik, Station Mgr. **Ad Rates:** $20-400 per unit.

580 KUAC-FM - 89.9
University of Alaska Phone: (907)474-7491
PO Box 775620 Fax: (907)474-5064
Fairbanks, AK 99775-5620

Format: Public Radio; News; Classical; Jazz. **Networks:** National Public Radio (NPR); Alaska Public Radio; Public Radio International (PRI). **Founded:** 1962. **Operating Hours:** 40% network, 60% local. **ADI:** Fairbanks (North Pole), AK. **Key Personnel:** Jerry Brigham, General Mgr., ffjcb@aurora.alaska.edu; Scott Diseth, Program Dir., phone (907)474-5097, fnsscl@aurora.alaska.edu. **Wattage:** 10,500. **Ad Rates:** Noncommercial.

581 KUAC-TV - 9
University of Alaska Phone: (907)474-7491
PO Box 775620 Fax: (907)474-5064
Fairbanks, AK 99775-5620
E-mail: fykuacm@aurora.alaska.edu

Format: Public TV. **Networks:** Public Broadcasting Service (PBS). **Founded:** 1971. **Operating Hours:** 6 a.m.-midnight weekdays; 8 a.m.-midnight Saturday and Sunday. **ADI:** Fairbanks (North Pole), AK. **Key Personnel:** Suhtling Wong, Production Mgr.; Jerry Brigham, General Mgr.; Scott Rosengren, Program Coordinator. **Local Programs:** *Reel Magic* 8 p.m. Saturday. **Wattage:** 47 kw ERP. **URL:** http://www.kuac.alaska.edu/kuac.

582 KWLF-FM - 98.1
1060 Aspen St. Phone: (907)451-5910
Fairbanks, AK 99709-5501 Fax: (907)451-5999
E-mail: kwlf@akradio.com; Combined advertising rates available with KFAR-AM, KUWL-FM

Format: Contemporary Hit Radio (CHR); Adult Contemporary. **Networks:** ABC. **Owner:** Borealis Broadcasting, Inc., at above address. **Founded:** 1987. **Operating Hours:** Continuous; 67% network, 33% local. **ADI:** Fairbanks (North Pole), AK. **Key Personnel:** Terry Walley, General Mgr.; Wanda Osborne, Contact; Maria Anderson, Traffic Mgr.; Rocky Barnette, Program Dir. **Local Programs:** *Glenner in the Morning* 6:00 am - 10:00 am Monday-Friday, Glen Anderson, Producer. **Wattage:** 10,000 (25,000 ERP). **Ad Rates:** $6-23.50 for 30 seconds.

583 KXLR-FM - 95.9
3528 International Way Phone: (907)452-5121
Fairbanks, AK 99701 Fax: (907)452-5120

Format: Classic Rock. **Networks:** Satellite Music Network. **Owner:** Northern Television Inc., at above address. **Founded:** 1990. **Formerly**: KINQ-FM. **Operating Hours:** Continuous. **ADI:** Fairbanks (North Pole), AK. **Key Personnel:** Bill Holzheimer, Station Mgr./Sales, holzheimers@kxlr.com; Tim Palmer, Operations Mgr. **Wattage:** 25,000. **Ad Rates:** Combined advertising rates available with KCBF-AM.

FORT RICHARDSON

584 Alaska Post
Public Affairs Office Phone: (907)384-2072
600 Richardson Dr., No. 5900 Fax: (907)384-2060
Fort Richardson, AK 99505-5900
Army newspaper. **Founded:** Nov. 4, 1994. **Freq:** Weekly. **Print Method:** Offset. **Trim Size:** 11 1/4 x 17. **Cols./Page:** 3. **Col. Width:** 7 1/4 inches. **Col. Depth:** 16 INS inches. **Key Personnel:** Patricia A. Douglas, Editor; Nelson Mumma, Managing Editor. **Subscription Rates:** Free. **Remarks:** Accepts advertising. **Formerly**: Arctic Star.
Ad Rates: BW: $1,120 **Circ:** Controlled 10,000
4C: $450
PCI: $12

GALENA

585 KIYU-AM - 910
Box 165 Phone: (907)656-1488
Galena, AK 99741 Fax: (907)656-1734
E-mail: kiyu@artic.net

Format: Public Radio; Eclectic. **Networks:** Alaska Public Radio. **Owner:** Big River Public Broadcasting Corp., at above address. **Founded:** 1986. **Operating Hours:** Continuous 50% network, 50% local. **Key Personnel:** Robert C. Sommer, General Mgr. **Wattage:** 5000. **Ad Rates:** Noncommercial.

GLENNALLEN

586 KCAM-AM - 790
Box 249 Phone: (907)822-3434
Glennallen, AK 99588 Fax: (907)822-3761
E-mail: kcam@alaska.net

Format: Country; Religious. **Networks:** SkyLight Satellite; Ambassador Inspirational Radio; Moody Broadcasting; USA Radio. **Owner:** Northern Light Network, PO Box 369, Glennallen, AK 99588, (907)822-3291, Fax: (907)822-3290. **Founded:** 1964. **Operating Hours:** Continuous; 80% network, 20% local. **Key Personnel:** George Reichman, Sales, sales@pobox.alaska.net; Scott Yahr, Station Mgr., manager@pobox.alaska.net; Doug Mather, Music Dir.; Scott Hill, News & Program Dir., engineer@pobox.alaska.net. **Wattage:** 5000. **Ad Rates:** $6-14 for 30 seconds; $10.50-18.50 for 60 seconds. **URL:** http://www.alaska.net/˜kcam.

HAINES, pop. 993.

Haines Census Div. (SE). 75 m NW of Juneau. Tourism center. Outdoor recreation, state park camping facilities. Chilkat Indian dancers. State preserve for world's largest gathering of bald eagles. Sport and commercial fishing.

587 Chilkat Valley News
Main St. Phone: (907)766-2688
Box 630
Haines, AK 99827
Community newspaper. **Founded:** 1966. **Freq:** Weekly (Thurs.). **Print Method:** Offset. **Cols./Page:** 5. **Col. Width:** 11 picas. **Col. Depth:** 15 inches. **Key Personnel:** Bonnie Hedrick, Editor and Publisher. **ISSN:** 8750-3336. **Subscription Rates:** $42 in Alaska; $48 to lower 48/Hawaii. **Remarks:** Accepts advertising.
Ad Rates: GLR: $1.25 **Circ:** ‡1,300
BW: $490
PCI: $7

588 ECC, Inc.
Box 1229 Phone: (907)766-2337
Haines, AK 99827 Fax: (907)766-2345
E-mail: pglackin@yahoo.com

Owner: Patty Glackin, at above address. **Founded:** 1967. **Formerly**: Lynn Canal Cablevision; Skagway Network Television; E.D. AND D., Inc. **Key Personnel:** Patty Glackin, Owner; Larry Glackin, Owner. **Cities Served:** Haines, Skagway, AK: subscribing households 130; 29 channels; 1 community access channel.

589 Haines Cable TV
Box 454 Phone: (907)766-2137
Haines, AK 99827 Fax: (907)766-2382
E-mail: pglackin@yahoo.com

Founded: 1964. **Formerly**: Lynn Canal Cablevision; Skyway Network TV. **Key Personnel:** Patty Glackin, Owner. **Cities Served:** Haines, Skagway, AK: subscribing households 380; 29 channels; 1 community access channel; 168 hours per week community access programming.

590 KHNS-FM - 102.3
PO Box 1109 Phone: (907)766-2020
Haines, AK 99827 Fax: (907)766-2022

Format: Public Radio; Eclectic. **Networks:** National Public Radio (NPR); American Public Radio (APR). **Founded:** 1980. **Operating Hours:** 6 a.m.-midnight. **Key Personnel:** Mike Sica, General Mgr.; Joanne Waterman, Program Dir. **Local Programs:** *Evening Report*, Steve Williams; *Midday Report*, Steve Williams. **Wattage:** 3000. **Ad Rates:** Noncommercial.

591 Skagway Cable TV
Box 454 Phone: (907)983-2205
Haines, AK 99827 Fax: (907)766-2382

Owner: E.D. & D. Inc., at above address, (907)766-2337, Fax: (907)766-2345. **Founded:** Apr. 1979. **Key Personnel:** Patty Glackin, President, plackin@yahoo.com. **Cities Served:** Skagway, AK: subscribing households 100; 23 channels; 1 community access channel; 168 hours per week community access programming.

HOMER, pop. 2,209.

Kenai Peninsula Census Div. (SC) 115 m SW of Anchorage. Recreational area. Sport fishing. Manufactures boats. Canning.

592 The Homer News
3482 Landings St. Phone: (907)235-7767
Homer, AK 99603 Fax: (907)235-4199
Publication E-mail: hnews@alaska.net
Publisher E-mail: hnews@alaska.net

Community newspaper. **Founded:** 1964. **Freq:** Weekly (Thurs.). **Print Method:** Offset. **Trim Size:** 10 x 16. **Cols./Page:** 6. **Col. Width:** 19 nonpareils. **Col. Depth:** 210 agate lines. **Key Personnel:** Mark Turner, Editor and Publisher; Jane Alberts, Advertising Dir.; Joel Gay, Managing Editor. **Subscription Rates:** $35 individuals; $38 out of county; $48 out of state. **Remarks:** Accepts advertising. **URL:** http://www.homealaska.com.
Ad Rates: GLR: $.40 **Circ:** Paid ★3,707
BW: $840
4C: $1,140
PCI: $8.75

593 KBBI-AM - 890
3913 Kachemak Way Phone: (907)235-7721
Homer, AK 99603 Fax: (907)235-2357
Free: (800)478-5224
E-mail: kbbi@alaska.net

Format: Public Radio; Full Service. **Simulcasts:** partial @ KDLL-FM in Kena. **Networks:** National Public Radio (NPR); Alaska Public Radio; American Public Radio (APR). **Owner:** Kachemak Bay Broadcasting, Inc., at above address. **Founded:** 1979. **Operating Hours:** Continuous; 60% network, 40% local. **Key Personnel:** David Hammock, Program Dir./General Mgr., kbbigm@alaska.net; Dave Webster, News Dir., kbbinews@alaska.net; Kathy Steberl, Program Dir.; Anne Marie Moylan, Development Director, kbbiffund@xyz.net; Sara Woltjen, Office Mgr., kbbiadmn@alaska.net; Tricia King, Operations Assistant. **Local Programs:** *Coffee Table*, Joe Gallagher; *Differant Drums*, Tricia King. **Wattage:** 10,000. **Ad Rates:** Noncommercial.

594 KGTL-AM - 620
66140 Diamond Ridge Rd. Phone: (907)235-6000
PO Box 109 Fax: (907)235-6683
Homer, AK 99603

Format: Adult Contemporary. **Networks:** Independent. **Owner:** Peninsula Communications, Inc., at above address. **Founded:** 1981. **Formerly**: KCNL-AM (1982). **Operating Hours:** 5 a.m.-midnight; 100% local. **Key Personnel:** David F. Becker, Contact; Terry Coval, Sales Mgr.; Dave Webb, Contact; Tim White, Operations Mgr. **Local Programs:** *Flea Market*, Tim White; *Newscan*, Tim White; *Songs of Praise*, Dave Becker. **Wattage:** 5000. **Ad Rates:** $6-13 for 30 seconds; $9-18 for 60 seconds. Combined advertising rates available with KWVV-FM, KPEN-FM, KXBA-FM.

595 KPEN-FM - 101.7
66140 Diamond Ridge Rd. Phone: (907)235-6000
PO Box 109
Homer, AK 99603

Format: Country. **Networks:** Independent. **Owner:** Peninsula Communications, Inc., at above address. **Founded:** 1984. **Formerly:** KENY-FM (1986). **Operating Hours:** Continuous; 100% local. **Key Personnel:** David F. Becker, Contact; Terry Coval, Sales Mgr.; Dave Webb, Contact; Tim White, Operations Mgr. **Local Programs:** *Flea Market*, Tim White; *Newscan*, Tim White; *Songs of Praise*, Dave Becker. **Wattage:** 25,000. **Ad Rates:** $9-13 for 30 seconds; $13-18 for 60 seconds. Combined advertising rates available with KWVV-FM, KXBA-FM, KGTL-AM.

596 KWVV-FM - 105
PO Box 109 Phone: (907)235-6000
Homer, AK 99603 Fax: (907)235-6683

Format: Adult Contemporary. **Owner:** Peninsula Communications, Inc., at above address. **Founded:** Sept. 1979. **Operating Hours:** Continuous. **Key Personnel:** Tim White, News Dir./Operations Mgr.; David Becker, General Mgr./Program Dir.; Dave Webb, Production Dir. **Local Programs:** *Straight Talk*, Tim White; *Songs of Praise*, Dave Becker. **Wattage:** 100,000. **Ad Rates:** $12-18 per unit.

HOONAH

Skagway-Yakutat-Angoon Co. (SE). 50 m SW of Juneau.

597 Hoonah Community Television
Box 510 Phone: (907)945-3649
Hoonah, AK 99829 Fax: (907)945-3549

Key Personnel: Jeanne Hill, General Mgr. **Cities Served:** Hoonah, AK.

JUNEAU, pop. 19,528.

Juneau Census Div. (SE) 175 m N of Wrangell. State Capital. Residential.

598 Alaska Fishery Research Bulletin
Alaska Department of Fish and Game
Box 25526 Phone: (907)465-4210
Juneau, AK 99802-5526 Fax: (907)465-2604

Technical, scientific journal covering fishery science. **Founded:** 1961. **Freq:** Semiannual. **Print Method:** Offset. **Trim Size:** 8 1/2 x 11. **Cols./Page:** 2. **Col. Width:** 3 1/4 inches. **Col. Depth:** 8 3/4 inches. **Key Personnel:** Robert L. Wilbur, Editor, bobw@fishgame.state.ak.us. **Remarks:** Advertising not accepted. **URL:** http://www.state.ak.us/adfg/geninfo/pubs/afrb/afrbhome.htm. **Former name:** Fishery Research Bulletin, Informational Leaflet.
Circ: Controlled 750

599 Inside Passage
419 6th St. Phone: (907)586-2237
Juneau, AK 99801 Fax: (907)463-3237
Publication E-mail: junodio@ptialaska.net

Official newspaper of the Catholic Diocese of Juneau. **Founded:** 1970. **Freq:** Biweekly. **Print Method:** Offset. **Trim Size:** 11 1/2 x 14. **Cols./Page:** 5. **Col. Width:** 1 15/16 inches. **Col. Depth:** 12 inches. **Key Personnel:** Louise Miller, Editor. **USPS:** 877-080. **Subscription Rates:** $35. **Remarks:** Advertising not accepted.
Circ: Paid 2,267

600 Juneau Empire
Morris Communications Corp.
3100 Channel Dr. Phone: (907)586-3740
Juneau, AK 99801-7814 Fax: (907)586-9097
Publisher E-mail: 73711.1232@compuserve.com

General newspaper. **Founded:** 1912. **Freq:** Daily (eve.). **Print Method:** Offset. **Cols./Page:** 6. **Col. Width:** 2 1/32 inches. **Col. Depth:** 294 agate lines. **Key Personnel:** Carl Sampson, Managing Editor; Jeffrey A. Wilson, Publisher; Robin Herdman-Paul, Advertising Mgr.; F.B. Howard, Circulation Mgr. **Subscription Rates:** $120 individuals.
Ad Rates: BW: $1,586.34 **Circ:** Paid 7,066
4C: $2,141.34 Free 190
PCI: $12.59

601 UAS Explorations
c/o Art Petersen, Editor Phone: (907)465-6418
11120 Glacier Hwy. Fax: (907)465-6406
Juneau, AK 99801-8671
Publisher E-mail: jfamp@uas.alaska.edu

Literary journal covering poetry and fiction. **Founded:** 1981. **Freq:** Annual. **Print Method:** Offset. **Trim Size:** 5 1/2 x 8 1/2. **Key Personnel:** Prof. Art Petersen, Editor. **ISSN:** 1081-325X. **Subscription Rates:** $6; $5 multi-year subscription.
Circ: 650

602 Alaskan Cable Network Inc.
Ste. 1, 3161 Channel Dr. Phone: (907)586-3320
Juneau, AK 99801 Fax: (907)463-3080

Owner: GCI Cable/Juneau, at above address. **Founded:** 1966. **Formerly:** Cooke Cablevision. **Key Personnel:** Dean D. Bardenheuer, Contact, dbardenheur@gci.com; Terry Dunlap, Contact, tdunlap@gci.com; Lea J. Ike, Contact, like@gci.com; Dollie Jewell, Office Mgr., djewell@gci.com. **Cities Served:** Douglas, Juneau County, AK: subscribing households 8,500; 60 channels; 3 community access channels.

603 GCI
3161 Channel Dr., Ste. 1 Phone: (907)586-3320
Juneau, AK 99801 Fax: (907)463-3080
Free: (800)800-4800

Founded: 1970. **Formerly:** Cooke Cablevision; Alaskan Cable Network. **Key Personnel:** Dean Bardenheuer, Contact. **Cities Served:** Juneau, Douglas, Alaska: subscribing households 8,000; 65 channels; 3 hours per week community access programming.

604 KINY-AM - 800
1107 W. 8th St., No. 2 Phone: (907)586-1800
Juneau, AK 99801 Fax: (907)586-3266
E-mail: kiny@ptialaska.net

Format: Adult Contemporary; Full Service. **Networks:** ABC. **Owner:** Alaska-Juneau Communications, Inc., at above address, (907)586-2430, Fax: (907)586-3266. **Founded:** 1935. **Operating Hours:** Continuous. **ADI:** Juneau, AK. **Key Personnel:** Dennis W. Egan, Contact, phone (907)586-2430; Kelly Peres, Operations Mgr., phone (907)586-1063; Guy James, Program Dir.; Dan King, Sales Mgr., phone (907)586-4466. **Wattage:** 10,000. **Ad Rates:** $16-33 for 30 seconds; $29-50 for 60 seconds. **URL:** http://www.juneau.com.

605 KJNO-AM - 630
3161 Channel Dr., Ste. 2 Phone: (907)586-3630
Juneau, AK 99801 Fax: (907)463-3685
E-mail: kjno@micronet.net

Format: Talk; Sports. **Networks:** CBS. **Owner:** Alaska Broadcast Communications, Inc., at above address. **Founded:** 1952. **Operating Hours:** 5 a.m.-midnight Sun.-Thurs.; continuous Fri.-Sat. **ADI:** Juneau, AK. **Key Personnel:** Steven L. Rhyner, General Mgr.; Terry Jones, General Sales Mgr.; Justin McDonald, Program Dir. **Wattage:** 5000 day; 1000 night. **Ad Rates:** $20-30 for 30 seconds; $24-35 for 60 seconds. Combined advertising rates available with KTKU-FM.

606 KJUD-TV - 8
175 S. Franklin St. Phone: (907)586-3145
Juneau, AK 99801 Fax: (907)463-3041
E-mail: news8@ptialaska.net

Format: Commercial TV. **Networks:** ABC. **Owner:** Smith Board Group of Alaska, L.P., 2700 E. Tudor Rd., Anchorage, AK 99507, (901)561-1313. **Operating Hours:** 4 a.m. - 4 a.m.; 90% network, 10% local. **ADI:** Juneau, AK. **Key Personnel:** Joe Holbert, Station Mgr.; Dave Geesin, Program Dir.; Charles Fedullo, News Producer. **Ad Rates:** Advertising accepted; rates available upon request.

607 KSUP-FM - 106.3
1107 W. 8th St., No. 2 Phone: (907)586-1063
Juneau, AK 99801 Fax: (907)586-3266
E-mail: ksup@ptialaska.net

Format: Album-Oriented Rock (AOR); Adult Album Alternative. **Networks:** ABC; Westwood One Radio. **Owner:** Alaska-Juneau Communications, Inc., at above address. **Founded:** 1984. **Operating Hours:** Continuous. **ADI:** Juneau, AK. **Key Personnel:** Dennis W. Egan, General Mgr.; Dan King, Sales Mgr.; Kelly Peres, Contact; Ron Davis, Music Dir. **Wattage:** 10,000. **Ad Rates:** $16-33 for 30 seconds; $29-50 for 60 seconds. Combined advertising rates available with KINY-AM. **URL:** http://www.ptialaska.net/~ksup.

608 KTKU-FM - 105.1
3161 Channel Dr., Ste. 2 Phone: (907)586-3630
Juneau, AK 99801 Fax: (907)463-3685
E-mail: ktku@ptialaska.net

Format: Hot Country. **Founded:** 1984. **Operating Hours:** Continuous. **ADI:** Juneau, AK. **Key Personnel:** Steve Rhyner, General Mgr.; Shelly Kincaid, Program Dir.; Terry Jones, General Sales Mgr. **Local Programs:** *Greatland Radio News*, Pete Carran. **Wattage:** 3840. **Ad Rates:** $20-30 for 30 seconds; $24-35 for 60 seconds. Combined advertising rates available with KUNO-AM.

609 KTOO-FM - 104.3
360 Egan Dr Phone: (907)586-1670
Juneau, AK 99801-1748 Fax: (907)586-3612
Free: (800)478-3636
E-mail: ktoo@juneau.com

Format: Public Radio; News; Classical; Jazz. **Networks:** National Public Radio (NPR); American Public Radio (APR); Alaska Public Radio. **Owner:** Capital Community Broadcasting, at above address, Fax: (907)586-2561. **Founded:** 1974. **Operating Hours:** Continuous; 35% network, 65% local. **ADI:** Juneau, AK. **Key Personnel:** Bill Legere, Contact; Jamie Waste, Contact; Jeff Brown, Program Dir. **Wattage:** 1200.

610 KTOO-TV - 3
360 Egan Dr. Phone: (907)586-1670
Juneau, AK 99801-1748 Fax: (907)586-3612
Free: (800)478-3636
E-mail: ktoo@juneau.com

Format: Public TV. **Networks:** Public Broadcasting Service (PBS). **Owner:** Capital Community Broadcasting, Inc., at above address. **Founded:** 1978. **Operating Hours:** 16 hrs. Daily. **ADI:** Juneau, AK. **Key Personnel:** Bill Legere, Contact; Paul Zavinsky, Program Dir.; Jim Mahan, Production Mgr. **URL:** http://www.juneau.com/ktoo/.

KENAI, pop. 4,324.

Kenai Peninsula Census Div. (SC). 53 m SW of Anchorage. Residential.

611 Dispatch
Box 3009 Phone: (907)283-7551
Kenai, AK 99611 Fax: (907)283-8144

Newspaper. **Founded:** 1971. **Freq:** Weekly (Wed.). **Print Method:** Offset. **Cols./Page:** 6. **Col. Width:** 2 3/4 inches. **Col. Depth:** 21 inches. **Key Personnel:** Stan Pitlo, Publisher; Michelle Glaves, Advertising Dir., glaves@pobox.alaska.net. **Subscription Rates:** $50 individuals. **Remarks:** Accepts advertising. **Formerly:** Advisor.
Ad Rates: BW: $1,091.16 **Circ:** Non-paid 8,500
4C: $1,361.16
PCI: $8.66

612 Peninsula Clarion
Southeastern Newspapers, Inc.
PO Box 3009 Phone: (907)283-7551
Kenai, AK 99611 Fax: (907)283-3299

General newspaper. **Founded:** 1974. **Freq:** Daily (morn.). **Print Method:** Offset. **Trim Size:** 13 x 21 1/2. **Cols./Page:** 6. **Col. Width:** 19 nonpareils. **Col. Depth:** 210 agate lines. **Key Personnel:** Stan Pitlo, General Mgr.; Lori Evans, Editor; Michelle Glaves, Advertising Dir.; Tom Janz, Circulation Mgr. **Remarks:** Accepts advertising. **Alt. Formats:** CD-ROM.
Ad Rates: PCI: $111.40 **Circ:** Paid ⊕**6,500**

613 KDLL-FM - 91.9
Box 2111 Phone: (907)283-8433
Kenai, AK 99611 Fax: (907)283-9798
E-mail: kbbi@alaska.net

Format: Full Service. **Networks:** National Public Radio (NPR); Public Radio International (PRI); American Public Radio (APR). **Owner:** Pickle Hill Broadcasting Inc., at above address. **Founded:** 1977. **Operating Hours:** 24 hours Daily. **Key Personnel:** Bill Hatch, President, phone (907)283-5221, hatch@alaska.net. **Wattage:** 5000. **Ad Rates:** Noncommercial.

614 KWHQ-FM - 100.1
40960 K-Beach Rd. Phone: (907)283-9430
Kenai, AK 99611 Fax: (907)283-9177
E-mail: radio92@ptialaska.net

Format: Contemporary Country. **Networks:** ABC. **Owner:** KSRM, Inc., at above address. **Founded:** 1976. **Formerly:** KQOK-FM. **Operating Hours:** Continuous. **Key Personnel:** John C. Davis, General Mgr.; Tom Farrell, Operations Mgr.; Jim Heim, News Dir. **Wattage:** 3000. **Ad Rates:** $14-30 for 30 seconds; $26-60 for 60 seconds. Combined advertising rates available with KSRM-AM, KSLD-AM, KKIS-FM.

KETCHIKAN, pop. 7,198.

Ketchikan Census Div. (SE). 237 m SE of Juneau. Ferry connections. Soft drink factory; pulp and saw mills; salmon canning and freezing and packing plants. Important shipping center. Commercial fisheries. Uranium, molybdenum mine. Logging camps.

615 Ketchikan Daily News
Pioneer Printing Co., Inc.
501 Dock St. Phone: (907)225-3157
PO Box 7900 Fax: (907)225-1096
Ketchikan, AK 99901
Publication E-mail: kdnkjmw@ptialska.net

General newspaper. **Founded:** 1934. **Freq:** Mon.-Sat. (morn.). **Print Method:** Offset. **Cols./Page:** 6. **Col. Width:** 27 nonpareils. **Col. Depth:** 294 agate lines. **Key Personnel:** Belinda Chase, Editor; Lew W. Williams III, Publisher; Tena Williams, Publisher; Lew Williams III, Advertising Mgr. **USPS:** 293-940. **Subscription Rates:** $122 individuals; $169 by mail. **Remarks:** Accepts advertising.
Ad Rates: GLR: $.686 **Circ:** ‡5,823
BW: $1,682.10
4C: $1,920.10
PCI: $13.25

616 KGTW-FM - 106.7
526 Stedman St. Phone: (907)225-2193
Ketchikan, AK 99901 Fax: (907)225-0444
E-mail: ktknkgtw@ktn.net

Format: Country. **Networks:** ABC. **Owner:** Alaska Broadcast Communication Inc., at above address, (907)586-3630, Free: (888)225-9300. **Founded:** 1987. **Operating Hours:** Continuous. **ADI:** Ketchikan, AK. **Key Personnel:** Kent Colby, Gen. Mrg./Sales Dir.; Nicole A. Bonham, PSA/News Dir.; Geoff Brandt, Sales; Mareen Summerlin, Office Mgr./Traffic; Ken Eckland, Engineer; John Ruby, Sales. **Wattage:** 5000. **Ad Rates:** $21-32 for 30 seconds; $24-36 for 60 seconds. $21-$32 for 30 seconds; $24-$36 for 60 seconds. Combined advertising rates available with KTKN-AM.

617 KRBD-FM - 105.9
123 Stedman Phone: (907)225-9655
Ketchikan, AK 99901 Fax: (907)247-0808
E-mail: krbd@ptialaska.net

Format: Eclectic; Public Radio. **Networks:** National Public Radio (NPR); Alaska Public Radio; Public Radio International (PRI). **Founded:** 1976. **Operating Hours:** Continuous. **ADI:** Ketchikan, AK. **Key Personnel:** Marty West, General Mgr.; David Kiffer, Program Dir.; Tim Barry, News Dir. **Wattage:** 15,000. **Ad Rates:** Noncommercial.

618 KTKN-AM - 930
526 Stedman St. Phone: (907)225-2193
Ketchikan, AK 99901 Fax: (907)225-0444
Free: (888)225-9300
E-mail: ktknkgtw@ktn.net

Format: Adult Contemporary; Soft Rock; News; Sports. **Networks:** ABC. **Owner:** Alaska Broadcasters, Inc., at above address. **Founded:** 1942. **Operating Hours:** Continuous. **ADI:** Ketchikan, AK. **Key Personnel:** Kent L. Colby, General Mgr., klcolby@aol.com; Lance Colby, Sales; Nicole A. Bonham, PSA/News Dir.; Geoff Brandt, Sales; Maureen Summerlin, Office/Traffic Mgr. **Local Programs:** *First City Forum*, Rick Krueger, Mailing contact. **Wattage:** Day 5000; night 1000. **Ad Rates:** $21-32 for 30 seconds; $24-36 for 60 seconds. $21-$32 for 30 seconds; $24-$36 for 60 seconds. Combined advertising rates available with KGTW-FM.

KING COVE

Aleutian Island Co. (SW). 700 m SW of Anchorage.

619 Mt. Dutton Cable Corp.
Box 38 Phone: (907)497-2346
King Cove, AK 99612 Fax: (907)497-2444

Key Personnel: Connie Newton, President; Della Trumble, Office Mgr. **Cities Served:** subscribing households 125; 12 channels.

KODIAK, pop. 4,756.

Kodiak Island Census Div. (S). On Gulf of Alaska, 250 m SW of Anchorage. Boat connections. U.S. Coast Guard Base. Salmon, herring, tanner crab & shrimp canneries. Fisheries. Spruce timber. Stock farms.

620 KJJZ-FM - 101.1
1227 Mill Bay Rd. Phone: (907)486-5159
PO Box 708 Fax: (907)486-3044
Kodiak, AK 99615

Format: Adult Contemporary. **Networks:** ABC. **Owner:** Cobb Communications, 1777 Forest Park Dr., Anchorage, AK 99517, (907)272-7461. **Founded:** 1985. **Operating Hours:** 6 a.m.-midnight; 10% network, 90% local. **Key Personnel:** Phil Nevitt, Contact; Nancy Brown, Contact; Diane Bahe, Office Mgr.; Frank Townsend, General Mgr.; Jack Emmerson, Operations Mgr.; John Valentin, Program Dir.; David Headley, Contact; Peggy Rauwolf, Contact. **Wattage:** 1000. **Ad Rates:** $7-28 for 30 seconds; $10-32 for 60 seconds.

621 KMXT-FM - 100.1
620 Egan Way Phone: (907)486-3181
Kodiak, AK 99615 Fax: (907)486-2733
E-mail: kmxt@ptialaska.net

Format: Public Radio; Full Service. **Networks:** Alaska Public Radio; National Public Radio (NPR); Public Radio International (PRI). **Owner:** Kodiak Public Broadcasting Corp., at above address. **Founded:** 1976. **Operating Hours:** Continuous. **Key Personnel:** Dave Perkins, General Mgr.; Mike Wall, Program Dir.; Doug Letch, News Dir. **Local Programs:** *Alaska Fisheries Report*; *My Green Earth*. **Wattage:** 3000 ERP. **Ad Rates:** Noncommercial. **URL:** http://www.ptialaska.net/~kmxt/.

622 Kodiak Cablevision
2011 Mill Bay Rd. Phone: (907)486-3334
Kodiak, AK 99615 Fax: (907)486-5160

Owner: GCI Cable, Inc., 2550 Denali St., Anchorage, AK 99503, (907)822-0252, Fax: (907)828-0226. **Founded:** 1982. **Key Personnel:** Judy Drennen, System Mgr., jdrennen@gci.com. **Cities Served:** Kodiak, AK: subscribing households 2,900; 54 channels; 2 community access channels; 37 hours per week community access programming.

623 KVOK-AM - 560
1227 Mill Bay Rd. Phone: (907)486-5159
PO Box 708 Fax: (907)486-3044
Kodiak, AK 99615

Format: Adult Contemporary. **Networks:** ABC. **Owner:** Cobb Communications, 1777 Forest Park Dr., Anchorage, AK 99517, (907)272-7461. **Founded:** 1974. **Operating Hours:** 6 a.m.-midnight; 10% network, 90% local. **Key Personnel:** Phil Nevitt, Contact; Nancy Brown, Contact; Diane Bahe, Office Mgr.; Frank Townsend, General Mgr.; Jack Emmerson, Operations Mgr.; John Valentine, Program Dir.; David Headley, Contact; Peggy Rauwolf, Contact. **Wattage:** 3100. **Ad Rates:** $7-28 for 30 seconds; $10-32 for 60 seconds.

KOTZEBUE

Northwest Artic Borough Co. (NW). 200 m NE of Nome.

624 The Arctic Sounder
Alaska Newspapers, Inc.
336 E 5th Ave. Phone: (907)272-9830
Anchorage, AK 99501 Fax: (907)272-9512
Free: (800)770-9830
Publication E-mail: aknewspr@alaska.net
Publisher E-mail: mail@organsociety.org

Community newspaper serving the Arctic Alaska communities of Kotzebue, Barrow and the North Slope Borough. **Founded:** Apr. 2, 1986. **Freq:** Weekly. **Print Method:** Web press. **Key Personnel:** Chris Casati, Publisher; R. A. Dillon, Managing Editor, phone (907)442-2716, fax (907)442-2654; John Woodbury, Editor. **USPS:** 002-382. **Subscription Rates:** $45. **Remarks:** Accepts advertising.
Ad Rates: PCI: $14.39 **Circ:** Paid ⊕2,231

625 KOTZ-AM - 720
Box 78 Phone: (907)442-3435
Kotzebue, AK 99752-0078 Fax: (907)442-2292
E-mail: kotzam@eagle.ptialaska.net

Format: Public Radio; News; Eclectic. **Networks:** American Public Radio (APR); Alaska Radio Network; AP. **Owner:** Kotzubue Broadcasting Inc., at above address, (907)442-3434. **Founded:** 1973. **Operating Hours:** 6 p.m.-midnight; 20% network, 80% local. **Key Personnel:** Pierre Lonewolf, General Mgr., kotzgm@eagle.ptialaska.net; Dean Tongen, Program Dir., kotzpgm@eagle.ptialaska.net; Bill Murray, News Dir., phone (907)442-6397, fax (907)442-2292, kotznews@eagle.ptialaska.net. **Local Programs:** *Morning Line*, Al Sonders; *News* 5:30 p.m., Bill Murray; *Request Show*, Wes Goodwin. **Wattage:** 10,000. **Ad Rates:** Underwriting available.

MCGRATH

626 KSKO-AM - 870
Box 70 Phone: (907)524-3001
McGrath, AK 99627 Fax: (907)524-3436
E-mail: ksko870@ aol.com

Format: News; Public Radio; Contemporary Hit Radio (CHR); Album-Oriented Rock (AOR); Country; Soft Rock. **Networks:** Public Radio International (PRI). **Owner:** Kuskokwim Public Broadcasting Corp., at above address, (907)524-3002. **Founded:** 1981. **Operating Hours:** Continuous. **Key Personnel:** Amie Hind, General Mgr.; Scott Stevens, News Dir.; Anita Cruise, Program Dir.; Ab Ross, Chief Engineer. **Wattage:** 10,000. **Ad Rates:** Noncommercial.

NAKNEK

627 KAKN-FM - 100.9
PO Box 214 Phone: (907)246-7492
Naknek, AK 99633 Fax: (907)246-7462

Format: Religious; Easy Listening. **Networks:** AP. **Owner:** Lutheran Mission Societies, Inc., at above address. **Founded:** 1985. **Operating Hours:** 6 a.m.-midnight; Continuous June and July. **Key Personnel:** Dan Carlson, General Mgr. **Wattage:** 3000. **Ad Rates:** $4.50-11 for 30 seconds; $6.50-16 for 60 seconds.

NENANA

628 KIAM-AM - 630
Box 474 Phone: (907)832-5426
Nenana, AK 99760 Fax: (907)832-5450

Format: Religious. **Founded:** 1985. **Operating Hours:** 6 a.m.-12 p.m. **Key Personnel:** Robert C. Eldridge, Contact; Harvey Clothier, Receptionist; Myrna Clothier, Receptionist; Kelvin Schubert, Contact. **Wattage:** 10,000 DAY 3,100 NIGHT. **Ad Rates:** $8-10 for 30 seconds; $14-17.50 for 60 seconds. Combined advertising rates available with KYKD.

NOME, pop. 2,301.

Nome Census Div. (NW) On Norton Sound, 500 m W of Fairbanks. Tourism. Winter sports. Recreation center. Boat and air connections. Gold mines. Commercial fisheries.

629 Bering Strait Record
Alaska Newspapers, Inc.
PO Box 1290 Phone: (907)443-6397
Nome, AK 99762 Fax: (907)443-5600
Publication E-mail: aknewspr@alaska.net
Publisher E-mail: mail@organsociety.org

Community newspaper. **Founded:** 1996. **Freq:** Weekly. **Print Method:** Web offset. **Cols./Page:** 5. **Col. Width:** 2 1/2 inches. **Col. Depth:** 15 1/2 inches. **Key Personnel:** Christopher Casati, Publisher; John Woodbury, Editor-in-Chief; Mark Gillespie, Managing Editor. **USPS:** 015-186. **Subscription Rates:** $29 individuals. **Remarks:** Accepts advertising. **URL:** http://alaska.net/~aknewspr.
Ad Rates: GLR: $1.50 **Circ:** Controlled ⊕1,508
BW: $1,115.22
4C: $1,515.22
PCI: $14.39

630 KICY-AM - 850
Box 820 Phone: (907)443-2213
Nome, AK 99762 Fax: (907)443-2344
E-mail: kicy@nook.net

Format: Southern Gospel; Religious. **Networks:** ABC; Sun Radio; Moody Broadcasting; USA Radio. **Owner:** at above address. **Founded:** 1960. **Operating Hours:** 5:30 a.m.-12:30 a.m. 10% network, 90% local. **Wattage:** 50,000. **Ad Rates:** $7-13 for 30 seconds; $10-17 for 60 seconds. $7-$13 for 30 seconds; $10-$17 for 60 seconds. Combined advertising rates available with KICY-FM.

631 KICY-FM - 100.3
Box 820 Phone: (907)443-2213
Nome, AK 99762 Fax: (907)443-2344
Free: (800)478-5429
E-mail: kicy@nook.net

Format: Adult Contemporary; Contemporary Christian. **Networks:** Independent. **Owner:** at above address. **Founded:** 1977. **Operating Hours:** 5:20 a.m.-midnight; 100% local. **Key Personnel:** David Oseland, General Mgr. **Wattage:** 83. **Ad Rates:** $7-13 for 30 seconds; $10-17 for 60 seconds. $7-$13 for 30 seconds; $10-$17 for 60 seconds. Combined advertising rates available with KICY-AM.

632 KNOM-AM - 780
270 E 3rd Ave. Phone: (907)443-5221
PO Box 988 Fax: (907)443-5757
Nome, AK 99762
E-mail: busch@knom.org

Format: Educational. **Networks:** AP; Alaska Public Radio. **Owner:** Catholic Bishop Of Northern, 1316 Peger Rd., Fairbanks, AK 99709. **Founded:** 1971. **Operating Hours:** Continuous; 15% network, 85% local. **Key Personnel:** Tom Busch, General Mgr., tbusch@knom.org; Ric Schmidt, Program Dir., rschmidt@knom.org; Paul Korchin, News Dir., news@knom.org. **Wattage:** 25,000. **Ad Rates:** Noncommercial. **URL:** http://www.knom.org.

633 KNOM-FM - 96.1
PO Box 988 Phone: (907)443-5221
Nome, AK 99762 Fax: (907)443-5757
E-mail: busch@knom.org

Format: Educational; Religious. **Networks:** AP; Alaska Public Radio. **Owner:** Catholic Bishop of Northern Alaska, at above address. **Founded:** July 14, 1971. **Operating Hours:** Continuous. **Key Personnel:** Tom Busch, General Mgr., busch@knom.org; Ric Schmidt, Program Dir., rschmidt@knom.org. **Ad Rates:** Noncommercial. **URL:** http://www.knom.org.

PALMER

Matanuska-Susitna Borough Co. (SC). 20 m NE of Anchorage.

634 Home Education Magazine
PO Box 1587 Phone: (907)746-1336
Palmer, AK 99645 Fax: (907)746-1335
Free: (800)236-3278
Publication E-mail: homeedmag@aol.com
Publisher E-mail: homeedmag@aol.com

Magazine on home schooling. **Founded:** Dec. 1983. **Freq:** Bimonthly. **Print Method:** Web offset. **Trim Size:** 8 1/2 x 11. **Cols./Page:** 3. **Col. Width:** 26 nonpareils. **Col. Depth:** 140 agate lines. **Key Personnel:** Helen E. Hegener, Editor, hem-editor@home-ed-magazine.com; Mark J. Hegener, Publisher, hem@home-ed-magazine.com. **ISSN:** 0888-4633. **Subscription Rates:** $24 individuals; $48 two years. **Online:** America Online. **URL:** http://www.home-ed-magazine.com.
Ad Rates: BW: $925 **Circ:** Paid ‡12,700
4C: $1,200 Non-paid ‡12,400
PCI: $20

PETERSBURG, pop. 2,821.

Wrangell-Petersburg Census Div. (SE). 140 m S of Juneau. Boat connections. Fish packing plants; seafood canneries; saw, pulp mills. Commercial fisheries. Spruce timber.

635 Petersburg Pilot
Pilot Publishing Inc.
PO Box 930 Phone: (907)722-9393
Petersburg, AK 99833 Fax: (907)772-4871
Publisher E-mail: psqpub@mitkof.net

Local newspaper serving Mitkof Island and surrounding area. **Founded:** Feb. 8, 1974. **Freq:** Weekly (Thurs.). **Print Method:** Offset. **Trim Size:** 11 3/8 x 16. **Cols./Page:** 5. **Col. Width:** 22 nonpareils. **Col. Depth:** 196 agate lines. **Key Personnel:** Ronald J. Loesch, Publisher. **ISSN:** 0535-7000. **Subscription Rates:** $40 individuals; $52 Alaska; $62 out of state; $96 first class. **Remarks:** Accepts advertising.
Ad Rates: GLR: $2.50 **Circ:** ‡1,800
BW: $680
4C: $1230
PCI: $8.50

636 KFSK-FM - 100.9
PO Box 149 Phone: (907)772-3808
Petersburg, AK 99833 Fax: (907)772-9296

Format: News; Soft Rock. **Founded:** 1977. **Key Personnel:** Matt Holmes, General Mgr.; Deb Boettcher, Program Dir. **Wattage:** 2000.

637 KRSA-AM - 580
PO Box 650 Phone: (907)772-3891
Petersburg, AK 99833 Fax: (907)772-4538
Free: (800)478-0580
E-mail: krsa@cris.com

Format: Full Service. **Networks:** AP; SkyLight Satellite. **Owner:** Northern Light Network, Box 369, Glennallen, AK 99588, (907)822-3291, Fax: (907)822-3290. **Founded:** 1982. **Operating Hours:** Continuous; 50% network, 50% local. **Key Personnel:** Andrew Mazzella, General Mgr.; John Mosher, Traffic Mgr.; Dan Zachary, Chief Engineer & Operator. **Wattage:** 5000. **Ad Rates:** $10-16 for 30 seconds; $16-18 for 60 seconds.

ST. PAUL ISLAND

638 KUHB-FM - 91.9
Pribilof School District Phone: (907)546-2254
St. Paul Island, AK 99660

Format: Country; Album-Oriented Rock (AOR). **Founded:** 1985. **Wattage:** 3000.

SAND POINT

639 KSDP-AM - 830
PO Box 328 Phone: (907)383-5737
Sand Point, AK 99661 Fax: (907)383-5271
Free: (888)260-5737
E-mail: ksdpak@arctic.net

Networks: American Public Radio (APR); National Public Radio (NPR). **Owner:** Aleutian Peninsula Broadcasting, Inc., at above address, (907)383-5373. **Founded:** 1983. **Operating Hours:** Continuous. **Key Personnel:** Roger Daniels, General Mgr. **Wattage:** 1000. **Ad Rates:** Noncommercial; underwriting available.

SEWARD

640 The Alaskan Viewpoint
HCR 64, Box 453 Phone: (907)288-3168
Seward, AK 99664
True stories on lives of Alaskan women. **Founded:** 1986. **Freq:** Semiannual. **Trim Size:** 8 1/2 x 11. **Cols./Page:** 6. **Col. Width:** 1 9/16 inches. **Col. Depth:** 13 7/8 inches. **Key Personnel:** Lory B. Leary, Editor and Publisher. **Subscription Rates:** $7 single issue. **Remarks:** Advertising not accepted for alcohol, drugs, tobacco, or color ads.
Ad Rates: BW: $300 **Circ:** (Not Reported)

641 The Seward Phoenix LOG
Alaska Newspapers, Inc.
336 E 5th Ave. Phone: (907)272-9830
Anchorage, AK 99501 Fax: (907)272-9512
Free: (800)770-9830
Publisher E-mail: mail@organsociety.org

Local newspaper. **Founded:** Oct. 6, 1966. **Freq:** Weekly (Thurs.). **Print Method:** Offset. **Cols./Page:** 5. **Col. Width:** 1 13/16 inches. **Col. Depth:** 15 inches. **Key Personnel:** Chris Casati, Editor; John Woodbury, Editor; Colleen Kelly, Managing Editor, phone (907)224-8070, fax (907)224-3157. **USPS:** 610-520. **Subscription Rates:** $45 individuals. **Remarks:** Accepts advertising.
Ad Rates: BW: $543.75 **Circ:** Paid 1,905
PCI: $14.39 Free 31

SITKA

642 The Daily Sitka Sentinel
112 Barracks Phone: (907)747-3219
Sitka, AK 99835 Fax: (907)747-8898
Publisher E-mail: sitkanews@hotmail.com

General newspaper. **Founded:** 1940. **Freq:** Daily (eve.). **Print Method:** Offset. **Cols./Page:** 6. **Col. Width:** 26 nonpareils. **Col. Depth:** 294 agate lines. **Key Personnel:** Thad Poulson, Editor and Publisher, thadp@ptialaska.; Sandy Poulson, Editor; Cathy Bagley, Advertising Mgr. **USPS:** 146-160. **Subscription Rates:** $80 individuals.
Ad Rates: GLR: $.57 **Circ:** ‡3,335
BW: $800
4C: $577
PCI: $8.45

643 KCAW-FM - 104.7
2B Lincoln St. Phone: (907)747-5877
Sitka, AK 99835 Fax: (907)747-5877
E-mail: kcaw@pti.alaska.net

Format: Public Radio. **Networks:** National Public Radio (NPR); American Public Radio (APR). **Founded:** 1982. **Operating Hours:** Continuous. **ADI:** Sitka, AK. **Key Personnel:** Barnaby Dow, General Mgr.; Ken Fate, Program Dir.; Lisa Nurnberger, News Dir. **Wattage:** 5000. **Ad Rates:** Noncommercial.

644 KIFW-AM - 1230
Box 299 Phone: (907)747-6626
Sitka, AK 99835 Fax: (907)747-8455
E-mail: kifw@ptialaska.net

Format: Full Service. **Networks:** ABC. **Owner:** Alaska Broadcasting Co. Inc., 3161 Channel Dr., Juneau, AK 99801, (907)586-3630, Fax: (907)463-3685. **Founded:** 1949. **Operating Hours:** Continuous; 90% network, 10% local. **ADI:** Sitka, AK. **Key Personnel:** Bobbi Rusk, Station Mgr.; Sherrie Fullmer, Office Mgr. **Local Programs:** *Problem Corner*, John J. Detemple. **Wattage:** 1000. **Ad Rates:** $12-25 for 30 seconds; $19-40 for 60 seconds. $7-$19 for 30 seconds; $13-$30 for 60 seconds. Combined advertising rates available with KSBZ-FM.

645 KSBZ-FM - 103.1
Box 299 Phone: (907)747-6626
Sitka, AK 99835 Fax: (907)747-8455

Format: Country. **Networks:** Unistar. **Owner:** Alaska Broadcasting Co, Inc, 3161 Channel Dr., Juneau, AK 99801, (907)586-3630. **Founded:** 1990. **Operating Hours:** Continuous. **ADI:** Sitka, AK. **Key Personnel:** Bobbi Rusk, Station Mgr.; Sherrie Fullmer, Traffic Mgr. **Local Programs:** *Problem Corner*, Kitty Kainulainen. **Wattage:** 3000.

SKAGWAY

646 The Skagway News
264 Broadway Phone: (907)983-2354
PO Box 1898 Fax: (907)983-2356
Skagway, AK 99840-0498
Publication E-mail: skagnews@ptialaska.net

Community newspaper. **Founded:** 1978. **Freq:** Semimonthly. **Print Method:** Offset. **Trim Size:** 10 1/8 x 13 1/2. **Cols./Page:** 5. **Col. Width:** 28 nonpareils. **Col. Depth:** 196 agate lines. **Key Personnel:** William J. Brady, Publisher; Dimitra Laurakas, Editor. **ISSN:** 0745-872X. **Subscription Rates:** $20 individuals; $30 out of area. **Remarks:** Accepts advertising.
Ad Rates: BW: $371.25 **Circ:** ‡950
4C: $900
PCI: $8

SOLDOTNA

647 KSRM-AM - 920
Mile 16 1/2 K-Beach Rd. Phone: (907)283-9430
HC-2, Box 852 Fax: (907)283-9177
Soldotna, AK 99669
E-mail: ksrm@ptialaska.net

Format: Talk; Adult Contemporary; News. **Networks:** ABC. **Owner:** KSRM Inc., at above address. **Founded:** 1967. **Operating Hours:** Continuous; 70% network, 30% local. **Key Personnel:** Jim Helm, News Dir.; Steve Holloway, Sports Dir.; Tom Farrell, Promotions Dir.; John C. Davis, General Mgr. **Local Programs:** *Sound-Off*, Jim Helm, Mailing contact, (907)283-9430, Fax (907)283-9177. **Wattage:** 5000. **Ad Rates:** $18 for 30 seconds; $34 for 60 seconds. Combined advertising rates available with KWHQ-FM, KKIS-FM, KSLD-AM.

TALKEETNA

648 KTNA-FM - 88.5
PO Box 300 Phone: (907)733-1700
Talkeetna, AK 99676
E-mail: ktna@matnet.com

Format: Eclectic. **Owner:** Talkeetna Community Radio, Inc., at above address. **Operating Hours:** Continuous. **Key Personnel:** Julianne McGuinness, Station Mgr.; Diane Ziegner, Fundraising Dir.; Sarah Birdsall, News Dir.; Jim Kloss, Technical Operations. **Wattage:** 1,000. **Ad Rates:** Underwriting available. **URL:** http://www.ktna.org.

THORNE BAY

649 Island News
Island Printing
PO Box 19430 Phone: (907)828-3377
Thorne Bay, AK 99919 Fax: (907)828-3351
Publication E-mail: islnews@thornebay.net

Community newspaper (tabloid) serving 23 communities on and around Prince of Wales Island. **Founded:** Dec. 4, 1981. **Freq:** Weekly (Mon.). **Print Method:** Web offset. **Trim Size:** 9 3/4 x 14 1/8. **Cols./Page:** 4. **Col. Width:** 2.25 inches. **Col. Depth:** 14.25 inches. **Key Personnel:** William MacCannell, Editor; Colleen MacCannell, Publisher. **Subscription Rates:** $55 individuals; $55 out of state. **Remarks:** Accepts advertising.
Ad Rates: BW: $406 **Circ:** Paid ‡1700
4C: $781 Free ‡100
PCI: $7

TOK

650 Mukluk News
PO Box 90 Phone: (907)883-2571
Tok, AK 99780 Fax: (907)883-2571
Publication E-mail: mukluk@polarnet.com

Community newspaper. **Founded:** 1976. **Freq:** Bimonthly. **Print Method:** Offset. **Trim Size:** 10 x 16. **Cols./Page:** 3. **Col. Width:** 3 1/4 inches. **Col. Depth:** 15 3/4 inches. **Key Personnel:** Beth Jacobs, Editor. **Subscription Rates:** $20. **Remarks:** Accepts advertising.
Ad Rates: BW: $240 **Circ:** Paid 700
PCI: $5

UNALASKA

651 KIAL-AM - 1450
Box 181 Phone: (907)581-1888
Unalaska, AK 99685 Fax: (907)581-1634
E-mail: ucb@ansi.net

Format: Public Radio; Jazz; Ethnic; Top 40; Country. **Networks:** National Public Radio (NPR); Alaska Public Radio. **Founded:** 1984. **Operating Hours:** 5:30 a.m.-1 or 2 a.m.;

60% network, 40% local. **Key Personnel:** Roger Leff, General Mgr. **Wattage:** 10,000. **Ad Rates:** Noncommercial.

VALDEZ, pop. 3,079.

Valdez-Cordova Census Div. (SC). 150 m S of Seward. Tourism. Main economy of the community is oil industry. Fisheries. Foreign Trade Zone.

652 Valdez Pioneer
Lindauer Newspapers
3709 Spenard Rd., Ste. 200
Anchorage, AK 99501

Local newspaper (tabloid). **Founded:** 1989. **Freq:** Weekly. **Print Method:** Offset. **Cols./Page:** 4. **Col. Width:** 27 nonpareils. **Col. Depth:** 210 agate lines. **Key Personnel:** Pat Lynn, Editor; John Lindauer, Advertising Mgr. **Subscription Rates:** $40. **Remarks:** Accepts advertising.
Ad Rates: BW: $560 **Circ:** ‡2,200
4C: $955
SAU: $12

653 KCHU-AM - 770
PO Box 467 Phone: (907)835-4665
Valdez, AK 99686 Fax: (907)835-2847
E-mail: kchu@alaska.net

Format: Public Radio; Eclectic. **Networks:** National Public Radio (NPR); Public Radio International (PRI); American Public Radio (APR). **Owner:** Terminal Radio, Inc., at above address. **Founded:** 1986. **Operating Hours:** 24 hrs.; 75% network, 25% local. **Key Personnel:** Ken Smith, General Mgr.; Lisa West, Prog. Dir/Operations Mgr.; Dan Bross, News Dir. **Wattage:** 10,000. **Ad Rates:** Noncommercial.

654 KCHU-FM - 88.1
128 Pioneer Dr. Phone: (907)835-4665
PO Box 467 Fax: (907)835-2847
Valdez, AK 99686

Format: Eclectic. **Networks:** National Public Radio (NPR). **Owner:** Terminal Radio, Inc., at above address. **Founded:** 1984. **Operating Hours:** 5 a.m.-midnight. **Key Personnel:** Shanna Simmons, General Mgr.; David Perkins, Program Dir.; Greg Williams, News Dir. **Wattage:** 10,000. **Ad Rates:** Noncommercial.

655 KVAK-AM - 1230
PO Box 367 Phone: (907)835-5825
Valdez, AK 99686 Fax: (907)835-5158

Format: Adult Contemporary. **Networks:** ABC. **Founded:** 1981. **Operating Hours:** Continuous; 90% network. **ADI:** Alaska. **Key Personnel:** Laurie L. Prax, General Mgr. **Wattage:** 1000. **Ad Rates:** $7-8 for 30 seconds.

WASILLA, pop. 1,559.

Matanuska - Susitna Census Div. (CS). 5 m W of Palmer. Residential

656 Frontiersman
Wick Communications, Inc.
5751 E. Mayflower Ct. Phone: (907)376-5225
Wasilla, AK 99654-8334 Fax: (907)352-2277
Publisher E-mail: printadv@alaska.net

Community newspaper. **Founded:** 1947. **Freq:** Semiweekly (Wed. and Fri.). **Print Method:** Offset. **Cols./Page:** 6. **Col. Width:** 21 1/2 nonpareils. **Col. Depth:** 301 agate lines. **Key Personnel:** Paul Stewart, Managing Editor; Kari Sleight, Publisher; Jerry Gamb, Advertising Mgr. **ISSN:** 8750-1740. **Subscription Rates:** $29 individuals; $44 out of area; $48 out of state. **Remarks:** Accepts advertising.
Ad Rates: BW: $1,354.50 **Circ:** Fri. 6,671
4C: $1,684.50
PCI: $17.50

657 Valley Sun
Wick Communications, Inc.
5751 E. Mayflower Ct. Phone: (907)376-5225
Wasilla, AK 99654-8334 Fax: (907)352-2277
Publisher E-mail: printadv@alaska.net

Shopper serving the Matanuska-Susitna Borough. **Founded:** 1973. **Freq:** Weekly (Wed.). **Print Method:** Offset. **Cols./Page:** 5. **Col. Width:** 16 nonpareils. **Col. Depth:** 16 agate lines. **Key Personnel:** Paul Stuart, Managing Editor; Kari Sleight, Publisher. **Subscription Rates:** Free; $32 institutions; $48.75 out of borough; $53 out of state. **Remarks:** Combined advertising rates available with Frontiersman.
Ad Rates: GLR: $.85 **Circ:** Paid 42
BW: $984 Free 9,750
4C: $1,314
PCI: $17.50

658 KMBQ-FM - 99.7
PO Box 87-1526 Phone: (907)373-0222
Wasilla, AK 99687 Fax: (907)376-1575

Format: Adult Contemporary. **Networks:** NBC. **Owner:** KMBQ Corporation, at above address. **Founded:** 1985. **Formerly:** KNBZ-FM (1990). **Operating Hours:** Continuous. **ADI:** Anchorage, AK. **Key Personnel:** Garry Buell, President. **Wattage:** 51,000. **Ad Rates:** $16.50-22.50 for 30 seconds; $18-28 for 60 seconds.

659 Rogers Cablesystems of Alaska
Box 873107 Phone: (907)373-2288
Wasilla, AK 99687-3107 Fax: (907)376-8888
E-mail: rogers@catv.com

Owner: Kevin Sheridan, at above address. **Formerly:** Northern Sights; Matanuska Valley Cablevision. **Key Personnel:** Kevin Sheridan, General Mgr.; Don Smith, Chief Technician; Chris Brogdon, Office Mgr. **Cities Served:** Palmer, Wasilla, AK: subscribing households 5,600; 43 channels; 1 community access channel; 168 hours per week community access programming.

WRANGELL, pop. 2,184.

Wrangell-Petersburg Census Div. (SE). Seaport on Wrangell Island, at mouth of Stikine River, 175 m S of Juneau. Boat connections. Saw mills; fish canneries. Commercial fisheries. Logging. Mineral exploration. Tourism.

660 Wrangell Sentinel
Jade River Publishing
PO Box 798 Phone: (907)874-2301
Wrangell, AK 99929 Fax: (907)874-2303

Community newspaper. **Founded:** Nov. 20, 1902. **Freq:** Weekly (Thurs.). **Print Method:** Offset. **Cols./Page:** 5. **Col. Width:** 11 picas. **Col. Depth:** 14 1/2 inches. **Key Personnel:** Seanne Gillen Saunders, Publisher; Joellen Stephens, Editor. **USPS:** 626-480. **Subscription Rates:** $30 individuals; $34 out of area. **Alt. Formats:** CD-ROM, Mac.
Ad Rates: GLR: $6.50 **Circ:** Paid ‡1,475
BW: $471.25 Free ‡25
4C: $971.25
SAU: $8.09
CNU: $8.40
PCI: $6.50

661 KSTK-FM - 101.7
202 St. Michaels St. Phone: (907)874-2345
PO Box 1141 Fax: (907)874-3293
Wrangell, AK 99929
Free: (800)874-KSTK
E-mail: kstkfm@seapac.net

Format: Full Service; Public Radio. **Networks:** Alaska Public Radio; AP; Public Radio International (PRI); National Public Radio (NPR). **Owner:** Wrangell Radio Group, at above address. **Founded:** 1977. **Operating Hours:** Continuous; 15% network, 85% local. **Key Personnel:** Peter Helgeson, News Dir.; Tis Peterman, Station Mgr.; Dawn Hutchinson, Program Dir.; Dixie Hutchinson, Reporter. **Local Programs:** *Aunty Judy*, Judy Sarber, Mailing contact, (907)874-2345; *S.E. Basketball Report*, John Morse, Mailing contact, (907)874-2345; *Zimovia Straits*, Tis Peterman, (907)874-2345. **Wattage:** 3000. **Ad Rates:** $11.80 for 20 seconds. **URL:** seapac.net/kstkfm.

YAKUTAT

662 KJFP-FM - 103.9
PO Box 388 Phone: (907)784-3421
Yakutat, AK 99689

Format: Eclectic. **Founded:** 1980. **Key Personnel:** Cheryl Eames, General Mgr. **Wattage:** 10.

ARIZONA

State Capital, PHOENIX

Arizona is bounded on the north by Utah and Nevada, south by Mexico, east by New Mexico, and west by California and Nevada. Its length, north to south, is 390 miles, its breadth about 300 miles. The total land area is 113,642 square miles, its rank in area, sixth. The Colorado River flows through the northern part of the state, and forms nearly all the western boundary. Its Grand Canyon is one of the scenic wonders of the world. The state is generally picturesque and in addition to the Grand Canyon has other outstanding items of interest as the Petrified Forest, Natural Bridge, Indian pueblos, ruins of cliff dwellers, and the great Roosevelt Dam, which supplies irrigating waters for the richest agricultural district, the Salt River Valley. Hoover Dam in the Black Canyon harnesses the Colorado and is the greatest dam in the world. Extending from Grand Canyon to the Mogollan Mountains are large forests of pine. In the center of the state is a richly mineralized belt. Hot springs are found in the southwest, and the arid, semi-tropical southeast affords relief to sufferers from pulmonary complaints. At Flagstaff is located the Lowell Observatory. The University of Arizona is at Tucson. The Weather Bureau at Phoenix gives the temperature (annual average) as 72.6; highest on record, 118; lowest on record, 16. Total annual precipitation is 7.66 inches.

POPULATION: 3,832,000 (1992). Rank among the states, 23rd.

AGRICULTURE: Number of farms: 8,000 (1992). Farm acreage: 36,000,000 (1992). Cash receipts from farm marketings: crops, $1,104,000,000 (1991); livestock and products: $786,000,000 (1991).

FORESTS: Total forest land: 11,880,000 acres. Principal woods: ponderosa pine, douglas fir, white fir.

MINERALS: Value of production: $2,829,000,000 (1991). Principal minerals: bromine, stone, and sand and gravel.

MANUFACTURES: Value added by manufacture: $11,551,000,000 (1991). Leading industry groups: primary metal industries, electrical machinery.

LIST OF COUNTIES

Total number of counties 15

County , Location on Map, and County Seat	Pop.
Apache (NE), Saint Johns	61,591
Cochise (SE), Bisbee	97,624
Coconino (N), Flagstaff	96,591
Gila (C), Globe	40,216
Graham (SE), Safford	26,554
Greenlee (SE), Clifton	8,008
La Paz	13,844
Maricopa (C), Phoenix	2,122,101
Mohave (NW), Kingman	93,497
Navajo (NE), Holbrook	77,658
Pima (S), Tucson	666,880
Pinal (S), Florence	116,379
Santa Cruz (S), Nogales	29,676
Yavapai (C), Prescott	107,714
Yuma (SW), Yuma	106,895

STATISTICS

Newspapers

Period of Issue	
Daily	22
Evening Daily	12
Morning Daily	8
Daily with Sunday edition	11
Semiweekly	8
Weekly	50
Biweekly	3
Semimonthly	3
Monthly	7
Free or partly free	9
Shopper	5
Total Newspapers	96

Periodicals

Period of Issue	
Weekly	1
Biweekly	1
Semimonthly	4
Monthly	31
Bimonthly	23
Quarterly	29
Variant	1
Total Periodicals	111

Total number of publications 207

Radio Stations

AM Stations	59
FM Stations	63
Total Radio Stations	122

TV Stations

Total TV Stations 22

Cable Stations

Total Cable Systems 17

Total number of broadcast listings 161

AJO, pop. 5,978.

Pima Co. (S). 110 m SW of Phoenix. Winter resort. Copper, gold, silver, lead mines.

663 Ajo Copper News
10 Pajaro Phone: (520)387-7688
PO Box 39 Fax: (520)387-7505
Ajo, AZ 85321
Publication E-mail: cunews@tabletoptelephone.com
Publisher E-mail: cunews@ajo.net

Community newspaper. **Founded:** 1916. **Freq:** Weekly (Wed.). **Print Method:** Offset. **Cols./Page:** 5. **Col. Width:** 24 nonpareils. **Key Personnel:** Gabrielle David, Editor; Hollister David, Publisher. **USPS:** 010-660. **Subscription Rates:** $25 individuals. **Remarks:** Accepts advertising.
Ad Rates: BW: $195 **Circ:** ‡1,955
PCI: $3.25

APACHE JUNCTION, pop. 9,935.

Pinal Co. (S). 30 m SE of Phoenix. Residential.

664 Apache Junction Independent
Independent Newspapers, Inc.
201 W. Apache Trail, No. 708
Apache Junction, AZ 85220
Publication E-mail: ajeditor@yahoo.com
Publisher E-mail: suncityind@aol.com

Community newspaper. **Founded:** 1959. **Freq:** Weekly (Tues.). **Print Method:** Offset. **Trim Size:** 13 x 21. **Cols./Page:** 6. **Col. Width:** 2 1/16 inches. **Col. Depth:** 21 1/2 inches. **Key Personnel:** Kris Baxter, Editor, phone (602)671-0016; Lisa Howell, Major Accounts Exec. **Subscription Rates:** Free. **Remarks:** Accepts advertising.
Ad Rates: BW: $1,571.22 **Circ:** Free 13,854
SAU: $16.10 Paid 1,323

665 East Mesa Independent
Independent Newspapers, Inc.
201 W. Apache Trail, No. 708
Apache Junction, AZ 85220
Publisher E-mail: suncityind@aol.com

Community newspaper. **Founded:** 1963. **Freq:** Weekly (Wed.). **Print Method:** Offset. **Trim Size:** 13 x 21. **Cols./Page:** 6. **Col. Width:** 2 1/16 inches. **Col. Depth:** 21 1/2 inches. **Key Personnel:** Richard Dyer, Editor; Lisa Howell, Major Accounts Exec. **Subscription Rates:** Free; $14 by mail. **Remarks:** Accepts advertising. **Formerly:** Mesa Independent (June 1988).
Ad Rates: BW: $1,986.60 **Circ:** Combined 28,193
SAU: $20.72

BENSON, pop. 4,190.

Cochise Co. (SE). 40 m SE of Tucson. Tourism. Manufactures explosives. Mining. Stock, poultry, dairy farms.

666 Arizona Range News
Drawer 1000 Phone: (520)586-3382
Benson, AZ 85602 Fax: (520)586-2387
Publication E-mail: arn@theriver.com

Community newspaper. **Founded:** 1884. **Freq:** Weekly (Wed.). **Print Method:** Offset. **Trim Size:** broadsheet. **Cols./Page:** 6. **Col. Width:** 19 nonpareils. **Col. Depth:** 294 agate lines. **Key Personnel:** Jim Tiffin, Managing Editor. **USPS:** 030-860. **Subscription Rates:** $22 individuals; $26 out of area; $28 out of state.
Ad Rates: GLR: $615 **Circ:** 3,200
SAU: $6.45
PCI: $6.45

667 Review
Wick Communication
PO Drawer 1000 Phone: (602)586-3382
Benson, AZ 85602 Fax: (602)586-3382

General newspaper. **Founded:** 1898. **Freq:** Daily and Sunday (morn.). **Print Method:** Offset. **Cols./Page:** 8. **Col. Width:** 25 nonpareils. **Col. Depth:** 301 agate lines. **Key Personnel:** Walt Wick, Publisher. **Subscription Rates:** $52.08 individuals. **Remarks:** Accepts advertising.
Ad Rates: SAU: $8.15 **Circ:** (Not Reported)

668 San Pedro Valley News-Sun
Wick Communication
200 S. Ocotillo Phone: (520)586-3382
Drawer 1000 Fax: (520)586-2382
Benson, AZ 85602
Publication E-mail: spvns@theriver.com

Newspaper. **Founded:** 1892. **Freq:** Weekly (Wed.). **Print Method:** Offset. **Trim Size:** broadsheet. **Cols./Page:** 6. **Col. Width:** 21 nonpareils. **Col. Depth:** 294 agate lines. **Key Personnel:** Jim Tiffin, Managing Editor. **USPS:** 480-680. **Subscription Rates:** $22 individuals; $26 out of area. **Remarks:** Accepts advertising.
Ad Rates: SAU: $5.55 **Circ:** 2,800
PCI: $5.85

BISBEE†, pop. 7,154.

Cochise Co. (SE). 85 m SE of Tucson. Retirement community. Historic old mining camp. Tourism. Live theater and concerts. Agriculture. Cattle.

669 The Bisbee Observer
7 Bisbee Rd., No. L Phone: (520)432-7254
Bisbee, AZ 85603-1140 Fax: (520)432-4192
Publication E-mail: bisbeeobserver@theriver.com
Publisher E-mail: bisbeeobserver@theriver.com

Community newspaper. **Founded:** Apr. 1985. **Freq:** Weekly. **Print Method:** Offset. **Cols./Page:** 5. **Col. Width:** 1 19/20 inches. **Col. Depth:** 13 inches. **Key Personnel:** Richard Senti, Editor; Laura Swan, Advertising Mgr.; Paul Lewis, Circulation Mgr.; Nancy Weaver, Editor. **ISSN:** 0895-2450. **Subscription Rates:** $24 individuals; $.50 single issue. **Remarks:** Accepts advertising. **URL:** http://www.theriver.com. **Former name:** The Ketchum Co./Bisbee Observer.
Ad Rates: GLR: $.10 **Circ:** Controlled ‡1,700
BW: $6.69
4C: $165
PCI: $6.69

670 Pay Dirt Magazine
Copper Queen Publishing Co., Inc.
Drawer 48 Phone: (520)432-2244
Bisbee, AZ 85603 Fax: (520)432-2247
Publication E-mail: paydirt@theriver.com
Publisher E-mail: paydirt@therwer.com

Magazine bringing mining developments, government mining policies, environmental issues, and mining heritage to the U.S. and around the world. **Founded:** 1938. **Freq:** Monthly. **Print Method:** Offset. **Trim Size:** 8 1/2 x 10 7/8. **Cols./Page:** 3. **Col. Width:** 15 picas. **Col. Depth:** 10 inches. **Key Personnel:** Bruce Rubin, Editor. **ISSN:** 0886-0912. **Subscription Rates:** $30 individuals; $3 single issue. **Formerly:** Southwestern Pay Dirt.
Ad Rates: GLR: $1.36 **Circ:** ‡6,512
BW: $570
4C: $930
PCI: $19

671 Post-Newsweek Cable
99 Bisbee Rd. Phone: (520)432-4807
Bisbee, AZ 85603 Fax: (520)432-7981

Owner: Post-Newsweek Cable, 2621 E. Camelback Rd., Ste. 150, Phoenix, AZ 85016, (602)468-1177. **Founded:** 1952. **Key Personnel:** Don Olander, General Mgr. **Cities Served:** subscribing households 3,000; 36 channels.

BUCKEYE, pop. 3,434.

Maricopa Co. (SC). 31 m W of Phoenix. Agriculture. Cotton, alfalfa, grain. Cattle.

672 Buckeye Valley News
PO Box 217 Phone: (602)386-4426
Buckeye, AZ 85326 Fax: (602)386-4427

Newspaper. **Founded:** 1925. **Freq:** Weekly (Thurs.). **Print Method:** Offset. **Cols./Page:** 5. **Col. Width:** 10.5 picas. **Col. Depth:** 210 agate lines. **Key Personnel:** Sharon Butler, Editor and Publisher; Rhoda Sylvester, Advertising Dir. **Subscription Rates:** $15.95 individuals. **Remarks:** Accepts advertising.
Ad Rates: GLR: $.23 **Circ:** 2,600
4C: $65
CNU: $5
PCI: $4.50

BULLHEAD CITY, pop. 10,350.

Mohave Co. (W). Fishing, boating, recreation area.

673 Mohave Valley Daily News
2435 Miracle Mile Phone: (602)763-2505
PO Box 21209 Fax: (602)763-7820
Bullhead City, AZ 86442
Free: (800)571-3835

Newspaper covering Mohave County. **Founded:** 1964. **Freq:** 6/week. **Print Method:** Offset. **Cols./Page:** 6. **Col. Width:** 12 picas. **Col. Depth:** 21 inches. **Key Personnel:** Chuck Rathson, Publisher; Darrylls Purcell, Managing Editor. **ISSN:** 1061-8569. **Subscription Rates:** $78.50 individuals; $148 by mail. **Remarks:** Accepts advertising. **Alt. Formats:** CD-ROM, Multi Ad Creator. **Formerly:** Mohave Valley News.
Ad Rates: BW: $2,003.40 **Circ:** Paid 9,000
4C: $2,363.40
PCI: $18.25

674 Cablevision of Bullhead City
937 Marina Blvd. Phone: (602)758-4844
Bullhead City, AZ 86442 Fax: (520)758-8691
E-mail: npgbhc@catz.com

Founded: 1974. **Formerly:** Dimension Cable; Time Warner Cable; American Cable. **Key Personnel:** Maggie Gold, Manager, phone (520)758-6641, fax (520)758-8691; Janine Arvizu, Office Mgr., phone (520)758-6641, fax (520)758-8691, janine@ctaz.com; John Williams, Operations Mgr., jwbhc@ctaz.com. **Cities Served:** Bullhead City, Mohave County, AZ: subscribing households 12,000; 70 channels; 1 community access channel; 168 hours per week community access programming.

675 KFLG-AM - 1000
1343 Hancock Rd. Phone: (602)763-2100
Bullhead City, AZ 86442 Fax: (602)763-3957

Format: Contemporary Country. **Simulcasts:** KFLG-FM. **Networks:** ABC. **Owner:** Continental Bradcasting Inc., at above address. **Founded:** 1976. **Formerly:** KRHS-AM (1991). **Operating Hours:** Sunrise-sunset. **Key Personnel:** Cal Hall, General Mgr.; Dave Peshaeu, President. **Wattage:** 1000. **Ad Rates:** $12-14 for 15 seconds; $14-20 for 30 seconds; $16-22 for 60 seconds.

CAMP VERDE, pop. 1,100.

Yavapai Co. (NE). 35 m E of Prescott on Verde River. Cattle raising and farming.

676 The Journal
PO Box 2048 Phone: (520)567-3341
Camp Verde, AZ 86322 Fax: (520)567-2373

Local newspaper. **Subtitle:** Voice of Camp Verde and the Lower Verde Valley. **Founded:** Feb. 1981. **Freq:** Weekly. **Print Method:** Offset. **Cols./Page:** 6. **Col. Width:** 12.60 picas. **Col. Depth:** 21 inches. **Key Personnel:** Robert B. Larson, Publisher. **USPS:** 664-770. **Subscription Rates:** $19 individuals. **Remarks:** Combined advertising rates available with Journal Extra and Sedona Red Rock News.
Ad Rates: BW: $957.60 **Circ:** Combined 2,245
4C: $1,247.60
SAU: $7.60

CASA GRANDE, pop. 14,971.

Pinal Co. (S). 45 m SE of Phoenix. Manufactures textiles, furniture, mobile homes, shotgun shell components. Copper mines. Health resort. Agriculture. Cotton, alfalfa, grain, cattle.

677 Casa Grande Dispatch
Casa Grande Valley Newspapers, Inc.
PO Box 15002 Phone: (520)836-7461
Casa Grande, AZ 85230-5002 Fax: (520)836-0343
Free: (800)821-1746

General newspaper. **Founded:** 1912. **Freq:** Daily (eve.) and Sat. (morn.). **Print Method:** Offset. **Cols./Page:** 6. **Col. Width:** 26 nonpareils. **Col. Depth:** 301 agate lines. **Key Personnel:** Jim Fickess, Managing Editor; Dono van M. Kramer, Sr., Publisher; Kara K. Bugbee, Advertising Mgr. **Subscription Rates:** $78 individuals; $89 Out of County. **Remarks:** Combined advertising rates available with Tri Valley.
Ad Rates: BW: $1,051.80 **Circ:** Mon.-Sat. ★**8,285**
4C: $1,351.80
SAU: $18.58
PCI: $8.20

Eloy Enterprise - See Eloy

678 Wampum Saver
Kramer Publications
PO Box 15002 Phone: (520)836-7461
Casa Grande, AZ 85222 Fax: (520)836-0343

Shopper. **Print Method:** Offset. **Cols./Page:** 6. **Col. Width:** 26 nonpareils. **Col. Depth:** 301 agate lines. **Key Personnel:** Dono van M. Kramer, Sr., Publisher.

CAVE CREEK, pop. 1,200.

Maricopa Co (C). 3 m N of Carefree. Residential.

679 Foothills Sentinel
Desert Foothills Newspapers, Inc.
PO Box 1569 Phone: (602)488-3436
Cave Creek, AZ 85327 Fax: (602)488-4779
Publisher E-mail: foothillsnewspapers@mcimail.com

Regional newspaper. **Subtitle:** Desert Winds. **Founded:** Oct. 1956. **Freq:** Weekly (Wed.). **Print Method:** Offset. **Trim Size:** Broad sheet. **Cols./Page:** 6. **Col. Width:** 20 nonpareils. **Col. Depth:** 294 agate lines. **Key Personnel:** Cheryl Lopez, Publisher. **ISSN:** 8750-3016. **Subscription Rates:** $22.50 individuals. **Remarks:** Accepts advertising. **Online:** Western Newspapers Inc. **Formerly**: Black Mountain News.
Ad Rates: GLR: $12.35 **Circ:** Paid 3,071
BW: $1,593.15 Non-paid 14,000
4C: $2,043.15
PCI: $12.35

CHANDLER, pop. 29,673.

Maricopa Co. (SC). 22 m SE of Phoenix. Winter resort. Manufactures fertilizer, electronics. Cotton gins. Agriculture. Citrus fruits.

680 Chandler Independent
Independent Newspapers, Inc.
325 E. Elliot, No. 21 Phone: (602)497-0048
Chandler, AZ 85225 Fax: (602)926-1019
Publisher E-mail: suncityind@aol.com

Community newspaper. **Founded:** Feb. 5, 1986. **Freq:** Weekly (Wed.). **Print Method:** Offset. **Trim Size:** 13 x 21. **Cols./Page:** 6. **Col. Width:** 2 1/16 inches. **Col. Depth:** 21 1/2 inches. **Key Personnel:** John Wolfe, General Mgr. **Subscription Rates:** Free; $14 by mail. **Remarks:** Accepts advertising.
Ad Rates: BW: $1,462.86 **Circ:** Combined 21,382
SAU: $11.34
PCI: $16.52

CLAYPOOL

681 KIKO-FM - 106.1
4501 Broadway Phone: (602)425-4471
Miami, AZ 85539 Fax: (602)425-9393
E-mail: kikoradio@aol.com

Format: Adult Contemporary. **Networks:** Westwood One Radio. **Owner:** Willard Shoecraft, Rt. 1, Box 25, Globe, AZ 85501, (520)425-3051. **Founded:** 1991. **Operating Hours:** Continuous. **Key Personnel:** Willard Shoecraft, Owner/Gen. Mgr.; Ted Thayer, News Dir. **Wattage:** 6000. **Ad Rates:** $8-10 for 30 seconds; $10-12 for 60 seconds.

CLIFTON†, pop. 4,245.

Greenlee Co. (SE) 169 m NE of Tucson. Residential.

682 The Copper Era
1 Ward's Canyon Phone: (520)865-3162
PO Box 1357 Fax: (520)428-3110
Clifton, AZ 85533
Publication E-mail: eacourier@aepnet.com

Community newspaper. **Founded:** 1889. **Freq:** Weekly (Wed.). **Print Method:** Offset. **Cols./Page:** 6. **Col. Width:** 2 inches. **Col. Depth:** 21 1/2 inches. **Key Personnel:** Jim Hornbeck, Editor and Publisher, phone (520)428-2560, eapublisher@aepnet.com; Hal T. Ward, News Editor. **Subscription Rates:** $17 individuals; $22.50 out of area; $30 out of state. **Remarks:** Accepts advertising.
Ad Rates: GLR: $.49 **Circ:** ‡2,450
BW: $728.85
4C: $245
PCI: $6.85

COLORADO CITY

683 KCCA-FM - 107.1
PO Box 711
Colorado City, AZ 86021

Format: Easy Listening. **Owner:** Uzona Broadcasting Co., at above address. **Founded:** Dec. 23, 1992. **Operating Hours:** Continuous. **Key Personnel:** Terri Barlow, Asst. Mgr.; Arden Barlow, Music Dir. **Wattage:** 6000. **Ad Rates:** $9 for 30 seconds; $18 for 60 seconds.

COOLIDGE, pop. 6,851.

Pinal Co. (S). 65 m SE of Phoenix. Tourism. Casa Grande Ruins National Monument. Cotton gin. Diversified farming. Cotton, alfalfa, vegetables.

684 Coolidge Examiner
Kramer Publications
PO Box 129 Phone: (602)723-5441
Coolidge, AZ 85228 Fax: (602)723-7899

Newspaper. **Founded:** 1930. **Freq:** Weekly (Wed.). **Print Method:** Offset. **Cols./Page:** 6. **Col. Width:** 26 nonpareils. **Col. Depth:** 301 agate lines. **Key Personnel:** Donovan M. Kramer, Jr., Publisher; R. E. Tuley, Advertising Mgr.; Thomas R. Martinez, Editor, tmart19@aol.com; Anne Holliday-Abbott, Editor. **Subscription Rates:** $21 individuals in county; $25 individuals in state; $32 out of state. **Remarks:** Accepts advertising.
Ad Rates: PCI: $5.87 **Circ:** ‡2,364

COTTONWOOD, pop. 4,550.

Yavapai Co. (C). 30 m NE of Prescott. Cement plant. Electronic assembly. Construction materials. Mining.

685 Verde Independent/Bugle
Western Newspapers, Inc.
116 S. Main St. Phone: (520)634-2241
Cottonwood, AZ 86326 Fax: (520)634-2312
Free: (800)647-9565
Publication E-mail: verdevalleynews@mcimail.com

Community newspaper (printed in 2 zoned editions). **Founded:** 1947. **Freq:** Semiweekly (Wed. and Fri.). **Print Method:** Offset. **Cols./Page:** 6. **Col. Width:** 2 1/8 inches. **Col. Depth:** 21 1/2 inches. **Key Personnel:** Dick Larson, Publisher. **Subscription Rates:** $42. **Remarks:** Accepts advertising. **Available Online. URL:** http://www.sedonaverdevalley.com.
Ad Rates: GLR: $.67 **Circ:** Combined ❑4,930
BW: $1,222.92
4C: $1,594.92
PCI: $9.48

686 Cable One
144 S. Main St. Phone: (602)634-9677
Cottonwood, AZ 86326

Owner: Post-Newsweek Cable, at above address. **Founded:** 1959. **Formerly**: Cablecom; Post-Newsweek Cable. **Key Personnel:** Scott Flake. **Cities Served:** subscribing households 3,000; 47 channels. **URL:** http://www.cableone.net.

687 KVRD-FM - 105.7
PO Box 187 Phone: (602)634-2286
Cottonwood, AZ 86326 Fax: (602)634-0583
Free: (800)473-KVRD

Format: Hot Country. **Owner:** Richard Dehnert, at above address. **Founded:** 1991. **Operating Hours:** Continuous. **Key Personnel:** W. Grant Haffley, President; Mark Bachman, Program Dir.; Jackie Bessler, Business Mgr.; David Kesser, Operations Mgr.; Gary Hershey, Sales Mgr. **Local Programs:** *Mark in the Morning.* **Wattage:** 50,000. **Ad Rates:** Combined advertising rates available with KVRD-AM.

688 KYBC-AM - 1600
PO Box 187 Phone: (520)634-2286
Cottonwood, AZ 86326 Free: (800)473-KVRD

Format: Adult Contemporary. **Networks:** Westwood One Radio. **Owner:** W. Grant Hafley, at above address. **Founded:** 1964. **Formerly**: KVRD-AM; KVIO-AM. **Operating Hours:** Continuous. **Key Personnel:** W. Grant Haffley, President & General Mgr.; Paul David, News Dir.; Carol Spencer, Program Dir.; Jackie Bessler, Business Mgr.; David Kessel, Operations Mgr.; Gary Hershey, Sales Mgr. **Wattage:** 1000. **Ad Rates:** $5-14 for 30 seconds. $5-$14 for 30 seconds. Combined advertising rates available with KVRD-FM.

DOUGLAS, pop. 13,058.

Cochise Co. (SE). 105 m SE of Tucson. Tourism. Art gallery. Parks. Recreation center. Industrial park. Garment, electronic manufactures. Food processing firms. Food packing industry. Copper smelter. Agriculture and ranching.

689 The Argus
Cochise College
Hwy. 80 W Phone: (602)364-0323
Douglas, AZ 85607 Fax: (602)364-0320

Collegiate newspaper. **Subtitle:** The voice of Cochise College. **Founded:** 1982. **Freq:** Semimonthly. **Print Method:** Offset. **Trim Size:** 13 x 21. **Cols./Page:** 6. **Col. Width:** 27 nonpareils. **Col. Depth:** 140 agate lines. **Subscription Rates:** Free. **Remarks:** Accepts advertising. **Formerly**: Heliograph, Arrow, Messenger; The Apache.
Ad Rates: BW: $150 **Circ:** Controlled 3,000

690 The Daily Dispatch
Daily Dispatch
530 11th St. Phone: (520)364-3424
PO Drawer H Fax: (520)364-6750
Douglas, AZ 85608
Publication E-mail: dispatch@primenet.com

Local newspaper. **Founded:** 1902. **Freq:** Daily (eve.). **Print Method:** Offset. **Cols./Page:** 6. **Col. Depth:** 21 inches. **Key Personnel:** Sharilyn Cox, Editor and Publisher; Sue Hays, Advertising Mgr. **Subscription Rates:** $102 individuals. **Remarks:** Accepts advertising. **URL:** http://www.wicknet.com.
Ad Rates: GLR: $.34 **Circ:** ‡2,582
BW: $793.80
PCI: $6.30

691 The Mirage
Cochise College
Hwy. 80 W Phone: (602)364-0323
Douglas, AZ 85607 Fax: (602)364-0320

Literary arts magazine. **Founded:** 1974. **Freq:** 1/year. **Trim Size:** 6 x 9. **Cols./Page:** 1. **Col. Width:** 5 1/2 inches. **Col. Depth:** 8 1/2 inches. **Subscription Rates:** Free. **Remarks:** Accepts advertising.
Ad Rates: BW: $150 **Circ:** Non-paid 2,000

692 KAPR-AM - 930
3434 N. Washington Ave. Phone: (520)364-4495
Douglas, AZ 85607 Fax: (520)364-5277

Format: Hispanic. **Owner:** Pyramid Broadcasting, Inc., at above address. **Founded:** 1958. **Operating Hours:** Continuous; 95% network, 5% local. **ADI:** Tucson, AZ. **Key Personnel:** Sharilyn Cox, General Mgr. **Local Programs:** *Sal Ocano Show*, Sal Ocano, (602)364-4467, Fax (602)364-5277. **Wattage:** 2500. **Ad Rates:** $4 for 30 seconds; $5 for 60 seconds.

693 KDAP-AM - 1450
2031 N. G Ave. Phone: (602)364-3484
PO Box 1179
Douglas, AZ 85608

Format: Ethnic; Hispanic. **Owner:** KDAP, Inc., at above address. **Founded:** 1946. **Operating Hours:** 5:30 a.m.-midnight. **Key Personnel:** Howard Henderson, General Mgr.; Luis Aguilar, Program Dir. **Wattage:** 1000. **Ad Rates:** $5.85-8.90 for 30 seconds; $8.15-12.45 for 60 seconds.

694 KEAL-FM - 95.3
3434 North Washington Ave Phone: (520)364-4495
Douglas, AZ 85607 Fax: (520)364-5277

Format: Classic Rock. **Networks:** Westwood One Radio. **Owner:** Pryamid Broadcasting, Inc., at above address. **Founded:** 1979. **Formerly**: KKRK-FM. **Operating Hours:** Continuous 95% network, 5% local. **ADI:** Tucson, AZ. **Key Personnel:** Sharilyn Cox, General Mgr. **Wattage:** 3000. **Ad Rates:** Advertising accepted; rates available upon request.

ELOY, pop. 6,240.

Pinal Co. (S). 50 m NW of Tucson. Light industrial. Agribusiness. Agriculture. Wheat, alfalfa, cotton.

695 Eloy Enterprise
Casa Grande Valley Newspapers, Inc.
PO Box 15002 Phone: (520)836-7461
Casa Grande, AZ 85230-5002 Fax: (520)836-0343
Free: (800)821-1746

Newspaper. **Founded:** 1947. **Freq:** Weekly (Thurs.). **Print Method:** Offset. **Cols./Page:** 6. **Col. Width:** 26 nonpareils. **Col. Depth:** 301 agate lines. **Key Personnel:** Joe Meahl, Editor; Dono van M. Kramer, Jr., Publisher; Kara K. Bugbee, Advertising Mgr. **Subscription Rates:** $15 In County; $19 Out of County. **Remarks:** Accepts advertising.
Ad Rates: PCI: $4.40 **Circ:** ‡1,154

FLAGSTAFF†, pop. 34,641.

Coconino Co. (N). 90 m SE OF Grand Canyon. Northern Arizona University. Resort. National parks and monuments. Lumber mill.

696 American Indian Quarterly
University of Nebraska Press
Department of History
Northern Arizona University
Flagstaff, AZ 86011
Publication E-mail: aiquarterly@nau.edu

An interdisciplinary journal featuring anthropology, history, literature, religion and the arts of Native America. **Subtitle:** Journal of American Indian Studies. **Founded:** 1982. **Freq:** Quarterly. **Print Method:** Offset. **Trim Size:** 6 x 9. **Cols./Page:** 1. **Col. Width:** 56 nonpareils. **Col. Depth:** 100 agate lines. **Key Personnel:** Devon A. Mihesuah, Editor, phone

(520)523-6219, fax (520)523-1277, devon.mihesuah@nau.edu. **ISSN:** 0095-182X. **Subscription Rates:** $25 individuals; $45 institutions. **Remarks:** Accepts advertising. **Alt. Formats:** Microform.
Circ: 900

697 Arizona Daily Sun
Pulitzer
417 W. Santa Fe Ave. Phone: (520)774-4545
PO Box 1849 Fax: (520)773-1934
Flagstaff, AZ 86001
Publication E-mail: dailysun@azaccess.com

General newspaper. **Freq:** Daily (eve.), Sat. and Sun. (morn.). **Print Method:** Offset. **Cols./Page:** 6. **Col. Width:** 24 nonpareils. **Col. Depth:** 301 agate lines. **Key Personnel:** Don Rowley, Publisher, fax (520)556-2265; Theresa Givens, Advertising Mgr., phone (535)556-2279; Randy Wilson, Managing Editor, phone (520)556-2254, fax (520)774-4790. **ISSN:** 1054-9536. **Subscription Rates:** $123 individuals; $264 out of state. **Remarks:** Accepts advertising. Monday-Saturday: GLR: $12.94; BW: $1,438.40; 4C: $1,665.65; PCI: $12.94; Sunday: GLR: $14.20; BW: $1,580.41; 4C: $1,807.66; PCI: $12.94. **Feature Editors:** J. Leon Keith, *Art, Entertainment*, phone (520)556-2255, flare@azaccess.com.
Circ: Mon.-Sat. 12,382
Sun. 14,863

698 Canyon Shopper
Western Newspapers, Inc.
2608 N. Steves Blvd. Phone: (520)526-3115
Flagstaff, AZ 86004 Fax: (520)527-0217
Publication E-mail: media@flagstaff.az.us

Newspaper. **Subtitle:** Navajo - Hopi Observer. **Freq:** Weekly. **Cols./Page:** 6. **Col. Width:** 2 1/16 inches. **Col. Depth:** 21 1/2 inches. **Key Personnel:** Doug Wells, Publisher; Jo Adams, General Mgr. **Subscription Rates:** $45 individuals. **Remarks:** Accepts advertising. **URL:** http://www.flagguide.com/media.
Ad Rates: PCI: $13.73 **Circ:** Free ‡27,000

699 Journal of the Flagstaff Institute
The Flagstaff Institute
PO Box 986 Phone: (520)779-0052
Flagstaff, AZ 86002 Fax: (520)774-8589
Publisher E-mail: instflag@aol.com

Trade journal covering trade between advanced and developing countries for banks, universities, and export traders. **Founded:** Feb. 1977. **Freq:** Semiannual. **Trim Size:** 6 1/2 x 9 1/4. **Cols./Page:** 1. **Key Personnel:** Richard L. Bolin, Editor. **ISSN:** 0146-1958. **Subscription Rates:** $150 institutions; $50 individuals and nonprofit organizations; $40 single issue. **Remarks:** Advertising not accepted.
Circ: Combined 150

700 Navajo-Hopi Observer
Western Newspapers, Inc.
2608 N. Steves Blvd. Phone: (520)526-3115
Flagstaff, AZ 86004 Fax: (520)527-0217
Publication E-mail: observer@infomagic.com

Native-American reservation newspaper. **Founded:** 1981. **Freq:** Weekly (Wed.). **Cols./Page:** 6. **Col. Width:** 2 inches. **Key Personnel:** Doug Wells, Publisher; Tanya Lee, Editor; Jo Adams, General Mgr. **Subscription Rates:** $35 individuals; $45 out of area. **Remarks:** Accepts advertising.
Ad Rates: PCI: $10.28 **Circ:** (Not Reported)

701 KFLX-FM - 105.1
112 E. Route 66, Ste. 105 Phone: (520)779-1177
Flagstaff, AZ 86001 Fax: (520)774-5149
E-mail: radio@infomagic.com

Format: Adult Album Alternative. **Networks:** NBC. **Owner:** Red Rock Communications, Ltd., at above address. **Founded:** Feb. 1995. **Operating Hours:** 8 a.m.-5 p.m. **Key Personnel:** Greg Roberts, Operations Mgr. **Wattage:** 50,000.

702 KNAU-FM - 88.7
Box 5764 Phone: (520)523-5628
Flagstaff, AZ 86011-5764 Fax: (520)523-7647
Free: (800)523-KNAU
E-mail: knau@nau.edu

Format: Public Radio; Classical; News; Information. **Networks:** National Public Radio (NPR); AP. **Owner:** Northern Arizona University, at above address. **Founded:** 1972. **Formerly:** KAXR-FM (1972). **Operating Hours:** Continuous. **ADI:** Flagstaff, AZ. **Key Personnel:** John Stark, Station Mgr.; Erik Nycklemoe, Program Dir.; Valerie Kahler, Music Dir.; Dave Riek, Operations Mgr.; Julie Pastrick, Underwriting Mgr. **Wattage:** 100,000. **Ad Rates:** $20-30 per unit. **URL:** http://www.knau.org.

703 KNAZ-TV - 2
PO Box 3360 Phone: (602)526-2232
Flagstaff, AZ 86003 Fax: (602)526-8110

Format: Commercial TV. **Networks:** NBC. **Owner:** Grand Canyon Television Co., Inc., at above address. **Founded:** 1969. **Formerly:** KOAI-TV. **Operating Hours:** Continuous. **ADI:** Flagstaff, AZ. **Key Personnel:** Dan Robbins, Contact; Nick Matesi, Contact; Michele Madril, Contact; Stan Koplowitz, General Sales Mgr. **Local Programs:** *In Our Schools*, Kim Lodge, Contact; *Indian Country USA*, Don Decker, Contact. **Wattage:** 100,000. **Ad Rates:** $25-200 for 30 seconds.

704 KSED-FM - 107.5
112 E. Rte. 66, Ste. 105 Phone: (520)779-1177
Flagstaff, AZ 86001 Fax: (520)774-5147
E-mail: radio@infomagic.com

Format: Country. **Networks:** NBC. **Owner:** Red Rock Communications, Ltd., at above address. **Operating Hours:** 8 a.m.-5 p.m. **Key Personnel:** Greg Roberts, Operations Dir.; Charee Tillotson, Traffic Dir.

705 KVNA-AM - 600
2690 Huntington Dr. Phone: (520)526-2700
Flagstaff, AZ 86004 Fax: (602)774-5852

Format: Talk; Sports; News. **Networks:** ABC. **Owner:** The Parklane Group, at above address, Fax: (520)774-5852. **Founded:** 1958. **Operating Hours:** Continuous; 90% Syndicated 10% Local. **ADI:** Flagstaff, AZ. **Key Personnel:** Max O'brien, Program Dir.; Sage Barrett, News Dir.; Len Jarvela, General Mgr. **Local Programs:** *El Hispano De Hoy*, Jose Rivera; *The Locker Room*, Mark Asher; *Northern Arizona Exposure*, Sage Barrett. **Wattage:** 1,000. **Ad Rates:** $25 for 30 seconds. KVNA-FM.

706 KVNA-FM - 97.5
2690 Huntington Dr. Phone: (602)526-2700
Flagstaff, AZ 86004 Fax: (602)774-5852

Format: Adult Contemporary. **Networks:** NBC; Satellite Music Network. **Owner:** The Park Lane Group, at above address. **Founded:** 1958. **Formerly:** KENR-FM (1987). **Operating Hours:** Continuous; 100% Local. **ADI:** Flagstaff, AZ. **Key Personnel:** Sandy Gamblin, General Mgr.; Gary Toms, Operations Mgr. **Wattage:** 100,000. **Ad Rates:** $25 for 30 seconds. $22 for 30 seconds; Combined advertising rates available with KVNA-AM.

FLORENCE†, pop. 3,391.

Pinal Co. (S). On Gila River, 68 m N of Tucson. Health resort. Copper mines. Agriculture. Cotton, wheat, alfalfa.

707 Florence Reminder & Blade-Tribune
Kramer Publications
PO Box 910 Phone: (520)868-5897
Florence, AZ 85232
Newspaper. **Founded:** 1881. **Freq:** Weekly (Thurs.). **Print Method:** Offset. **Cols./Page:** 6. **Col. Width:** 26 nonpareils. **Col. Depth:** 301 agate lines. **Key Personnel:** Donovan M. Kramer, Jr., Publisher; Kara K. Cooper, Advertising Mgr.; Mark Cowling, Editor. **Subscription Rates:** $21 individuals; $35 other countries; $45 out of state. **Remarks:** Accepts advertising.
Ad Rates: SAU: $5.35 **Circ:** ‡1,700

FORT HUACHUCA

708 Commander
Intelligence Center and Fort Huachuca
ATZS-CLM Phone: (602)538-1015
Fort Huachuca, AZ 85613-6000 Fax: (602)533-6308

Military journal. **Founded:** 1974. **Freq:** Quarterly. **Print Method:** Offset. **Trim Size:** 8 1/2 x 11. **Cols./Page:** 3. **Col. Width:** 2 1/16 inches. **Col. Depth:** 9 inches. **Key Personnel:** Deborah A. English, Editor; M C Govern, Associate Editor. **ISSN:** 0026-4028. **Subscription Rates:** $7.5 individuals; $9.40 Other Countries; $3 single issue; $3.75 single issue Other Countries. **Remarks:** Advertising not accepted. **Formerly:** Military Intelligence Professional Bulletin.
Circ: Paid ‡900
Controlled ‡4,500

FOUNTAIN HILLS, pop. 2,000.

Maricopa Co. (C). 12 m E of Scottsdale. Residential.

709 American Amateur Journalist
American Amateur Press Association
PO Box 18117 Phone: (602)837-7074
Fountain Hills, AZ 85269
Membership magazine of the American Amateur Press Association (AAPA). **Founded:** Jan. 1937. **Freq:** Bimonthly. **Print Method:** Offset. **Trim Size:** 5 1/2 x 8 1/2. **Key Personnel:** Mike O'Connor, Editor, mikeoc3941@aol.com. **ISSN:** 1046-0470. **Subscription Rates:** $15 members. **Remarks:** Advertising not accepted.
Circ: Paid 300

Illinois Insurance Broker - See Springfield, Illinois

710 The Times of Fountain Hills
Western State Publisher
PO Box 17869 Phone: (602)837-1925
Fountain Hills, AZ 85269 Fax: (602)837-1951

Local newspaper. **Founded:** 1974. **Freq:** Weekly (Wed.). **Print Method:** Offset. **Cols./Page:** 6. **Col. Width:** 26 nonpareils. **Col. Depth:** 294 agate lines. **Key Personnel:** L. Alan Cruikshank, Publisher; Michael Scharnow, Editor, mscharnow@aol.com. **ISSN:** 0607-5000. **Subscription Rates:** $25 individuals. **Remarks:** Accepts advertising. **URL:** http://www.f.h.times˜goodnet.com.
Ad Rates: BW: $768.60 **Circ:** 5200
4C: $1,055.60
SAU: $6.10

GLENDALE, pop. 96,988.

Maricopa Co. (SC). 9 m NW of Phoenix. Manufactures avionics, instrumentations, cable connections, precision machined parts, building materials, packaging materials. Food processing. Plastic extrusions.

711 The Glendale Star
Pueblo Publishers, Inc.
7122 N. 59th Ave. Phone: (602)842-6000
Glendale, AZ 85301 Fax: (602)842-6017

Community newspaper. **Founded:** 1978. **Freq:** Weekly (Thurs.). **Print Method:** Offset. **Trim Size:** 11x17. **Cols./Page:** 6. **Col. Width:** 9.5 picas. **Col. Depth:** 16 picas. **Key Personnel:** Carolyn Dryer, Editor, cdryer@startimes.com; William V. Toops, Publisher, w.toops@star-times.com. **USPS:** 998-340. **Subscription Rates:** $20 individuals; $25 out of area.
Ad Rates: BW: $692 **Circ:** ‡10,000
4C: $1,067
SAU: $8.65
PCI: $6

Peoria Times - See Peoria

712 Southwest Computer Monthly
5208 W. Calavar Rd. Phone: (602)978-4842
Glendale, AZ 85306 Fax: (602)978-4842
Free: (800)TOOM-WEB
Publication E-mail: swcm@sprynet.com

Magazine containing software and product information, industry news, listings of local bulletin boards, and feature articles, as well as other computer-related information. **Subtitle:** Arizona's Monthly Computer Connection. **Founded:** Oct. 1994. **Freq:** Monthly. **Print Method:** newsprint. **Trim Size:** 8 1/8 x 10 7/8. **Cols./Page:** 3. **Col. Width:** 2.33 inches. **Key Personnel:** Anthony J. Ardito, Publisher. **ISSN:** 1081-1109. **Subscription Rates:** $21 U.S.; $40 other countries; $3 single issue. **URL:** http://www.tccmweb.com/swcm/. **Formerly:** Tri-City Computing Magazine.
Ad Rates: BW: $650 **Circ:** Paid 18,000
4C: $875 Non-paid 32,000

713 Tallyho
Pueblo Publishers, Inc.
7122 N. 59th Ave. Phone: (602)842-6000
Glendale, AZ 85301 Fax: (602)842-6017

Newspaper for personnel of Luke Air Force Base. **Founded:** 1950. **Freq:** Weekly (Fri.). **Print Method:** Offset. **Trim Size:** 11x17. **Cols./Page:** 6. **Col. Width:** 95 picas. **Col. Depth:** 16 inches. **Key Personnel:** William E. Toops, Advertising Mgr., w.toops@star-times.com. **Subscription Rates:** Free.
Ad Rates: BW: $740 **Circ:** Free ‡11,500
4C: $1,115
SAU: $9.25
PCI: $7.70

GLOBE†, pop. 6,708.

Gilla Co. (C). 94 m E of Phoenix. Copper. Cattle raising.

714 Arizona Silver Belt
American Publishing Co.
298 N. Pine St. Phone: (520)425-7121
PO Box 31 Fax: (520)425-7001
Globe, AZ 85502
Community newspaper. **Founded:** 1878. **Freq:** Semiweekly (Thurs. and Mon.). **Print Method:** Offset. **Cols./Page:** 6. **Col. Width:** 21 nonpareils. **Col. Depth:** 294 agate lines. **Key Personnel:** Douglas Knight, Publisher. **Subscription Rates:**

$21 individuals; $24 Out of County. **Remarks:** Accepts advertising.
Ad Rates: BW: $722.40 **Circ:** ‡7,336
4C: $992.40
SAU: $5.60

715 Copper Country News
270 S. Sutherland St. Phone: (520)425-0355
Globe, AZ 85501 Fax: (520)425-6535

Community newspaper. **Founded:** Sept. 1985. **Freq:** Weekly. **Cols./Page:** 5. **Col. Width:** 11 picas. **Col. Depth:** 16 inches. **Key Personnel:** Pat Burke, Advertising Mgr.; Stoney Burke, Advertising Mgr., dburke@gila.net. **Subscription Rates:** Free; $39 by mail. **Remarks:** Accepts advertising. **URL:** http://www.ccn.pair.com.
Ad Rates: PCI: $5.75 **Circ:** Controlled ‡8,300

716 Cable One
727 Paxton Ave. Phone: (602)425-3161
PO Box 69 Fax: (602)425-5404
Globe, AZ 85501

Owner: Cable One, 4742 N. 24th St., Ste. 270, Phoenix, AZ 85016. **Founded:** 1953. **Formerly:** Post-Newsweek Cable. **Key Personnel:** Ingo Radicke, General Mgr., ingo@gila.net; Joanne Harvey, Office Mgr.; Dennis Fraze, Chief Engineer. **Cities Served:** subscribing households 5700; 42 channels; 1 community access channel.

717 KJAA-AM - 1240
1240 S. Saguaro Dr. Phone: (520)425-8185
PO Box 1161 Fax: (520)425-6741
Globe, AZ 85502

Format: News; Sports; Hispanic; Ethnic; Talk. **Networks:** CBS. **Owner:** Gila Co. Broadcasting Co., Inc., at above address. **Founded:** 1971. **Formerly:** KSML-AM (1986). **Operating Hours:** 4am-11pm. **Key Personnel:** Patricia Pearsall, Station Mgr.; J.E. Thayer, Chief Engineer; John Rau, News Dir. **Local Programs:** *Local News*, John Rau; *Open House*, Pat Pearsall; *Sports Talk*, John Rau. **Wattage:** 1000. **Ad Rates:** $10 for 30 seconds; $12 for 60 seconds.

GREEN VALLEY, pop. 6500.

Pima Co. (S). 23 m S of Tucson. Residential.

718 Green Valley News & Sun
PO Box 567 Phone: (520)625-5511
Green Valley, AZ 85622 Fax: (520)625-1603
Publication E-mail: greenvalley@earthlink.net

Community newspaper serving the Santa Cruz Valley and Green Valley area. **Founded:** 1964. **Freq:** Semiweekly (Wed. and Fri.). **Print Method:** Offset. **Cols./Page:** 6. **Col. Width:** 25 nonpareils. **Col. Depth:** 294 agate lines. **Key Personnel:** Frank H. Newell, Publisher, phone (520)625-5511, fax (520)625-8046, greenvalley@earthlink.net; Tom Henry, Asst. to the Publisher; Kathy Engle, Editor, fax (520)625-1603; Kara Campbell, Advertising Dir., fax (520)625-8046. **Subscription Rates:** $47 individuals 1 year carrier; $65 1 year mail. **Remarks:** Accepts advertising.
Ad Rates: BW: $1,580.25 **Circ:** 11,500
4C: $420
SAU: $12.25

719 gsdReview
German Shepherd Dog Club of America
1902C N. Abrego Dr. Phone: (520)625-9528
Green Valley, AZ 85614 Fax: (520)625-4789
Publication E-mail: gsreview@azstarnet.com

Magazine covering all areas of interest to breeders and owners of German Shepherd dogs. **Subtitle:** Official Magazine of The German Shepherd Dog Club of America. **Founded:** 1922. **Freq:** Monthly. **Print Method:** Offset. **Trim Size:** 8 1/2 x 11. **Col. Depth:** 57 picas. **Key Personnel:** Gail Sprock, Editor. **ISSN:** 0046-5852. **Subscription Rates:** $53 individuals; $8 single issue. **Remarks:** Accepts advertising. **Former name:** German Shepherd Dog Review.
Ad Rates: BW: $225 **Circ:** ‡4,000
4C: $450

720 KGVY-AM - 1080
PO Box 767 Phone: (520)399-1000
Green Valley, AZ 85622 Fax: (520)399-9300

Format: Big Band/Nostalgia; Full Service. **Networks:** Independent. **Owner:** Green Valley Broadcasting, Inc., PO Box 767, Green Valley, AZ 85622. **Founded:** 1981. **Formerly:** Crystal Sets, Inc. **Operating Hours:** 6 a.m.-sunset; 5% network, 95% local. **ADI:** Tucson, AZ. **Key Personnel:** Bonnie Crystall, General Mgr.; Larry Nelson, President; Tim McKay, Program Dir.; Dick Hall, News Dir. **Local Programs:** *Around the Cracker Barrel*, Joe Crystall, Mailing contact; *Crystall Gazing*, Joe Crystall. **Wattage:** 1000. **Ad Rates:** $28 per unit. for 30 seconds 25 times per week-$32 for 60 seconds one time.

HOLBROOK†, pop. 5,785.

Navajo Co. (NE). 90 m SE of Flagstaff. Trading and tourist center. Petrified Forest. National Park and Painted Desert. Lakes. Navajo Hopi, and Apache Reservations. Ponderosa pine timber. Coal fired electric generating. Agriculture. Cattle, sheep, pigs, poultry, dairying.

721 Holbrook Tribune-News
Navajo County Publisher
PO Box 670 Phone: (520)524-6203
Holbrook, AZ 86025-0670 Fax: (520)524-3541
Publication E-mail: holbrooktribune@cybertrails.com

Newspaper. **Founded:** 1909. **Freq:** Semiweekly (Wed. and Fri.). **Print Method:** Offset. **Cols./Page:** 6. **Col. Width:** 24 nonpareils. **Col. Depth:** 294 agate lines. **Key Personnel:** Paul Barger, Editor and Publisher. **USPS:** 247-160. **Subscription Rates:** $24 individuals; $26 out of area. **Remarks:** Accepts advertising.
Ad Rates: GLR: $.45 **Circ:** Paid ‡3,700
BW: $793.80 Free ‡2,600
4C: $1,048.80
PCI: $6.30

722 KDJI-AM - 1270
250 N. Broadcast Ln. Phone: (520)524-3994
PO Box 430 Fax: (520)524-3561
Holbrook, AZ 86025
E-mail: z92@cybertrails.com

Format: Oldies; News; Sports. **Networks:** Mutual Broadcasting System; Jones Satellite. **Owner:** Navajo Broadcasting Co. Inc., at above address. **Founded:** 1959. **Operating Hours:** Continuous; 20% network, 80% local. **Key Personnel:** Roy Roberts, Contact; Denise Scorse, News Dir.; Keith Gardener, Contact. **Wattage:** 5000. **Ad Rates:** $6.80-8.40 for 30 seconds; $8-9.90 for 60 seconds. Combined advertising rates available with KZUA-FM.

723 KZUA-FM - 92.1
250 N. Broadcast Ln. Phone: (520)524-3994
PO Box 430 Fax: (520)524-3561
Holbrook, AZ 86025
E-mail: z92@cybertrails.com

Format: Contemporary Country. **Networks:** CNN Radio; Westwood One Radio. **Owner:** Navajo Broadcasting Co., at above address. **Founded:** 1993. **Operating Hours:** Continuous; 40% network, 60% local. **Key Personnel:** Roy Roberts, General Mgr.; Rich Jones, Sales Mgr., phone (520)5370-0448, fax (520)537-3379; Vickie Gentri, Music Dir. **Wattage:** 100,000. **Ad Rates:** $12 for 30 seconds; $15 for 60 seconds. Combined advertising rates available with KDJI-AM.

HUALAPAI

724 The Searcher Combined with The Faithist Journal
Kosmon Publishing, Inc.
PO Box 4670
Hualapai, AZ 86412-4670

Consumer magazine covering inspirational and New Age issues. **Founded:** 1969. **Freq:** Bimonthly. **Print Method:** Photo/Electronic. **Trim Size:** 5 x 8. **Key Personnel:** K. Kares, Editor, phone (520)692-7973. **Subscription Rates:** $25 individuals; $35 out of country. **Remarks:** Advertising not accepted. **Formerly:** The Faithist Journal.
Circ: (Not Reported)

KEARNY, pop. 2,646.

Pinal Co. (S). 80 m SE of Phoenix. Retirement community. Copper. Cattle.

725 Copper Basin News
Copper Area Publishing
PO Box 579 Phone: (520)363-5554
Kearny, AZ 85237 Fax: (520)363-9663

Community newspaper. **Founded:** 1958. **Freq:** Weekly (Wed.). **Print Method:** Offset. **Cols./Page:** 6. **Col. Width:** 12 nonpareils. **Col. Depth:** 290 agate lines. **Key Personnel:** Gayle Carnes, Editor. **Subscription Rates:** $25.50 individuals. **Remarks:** Accepts advertising.
Ad Rates: GLR: $0.28 **Circ:** ‡2,600
SAU: $4.75

726 Cablevision
PO Box 567 Phone: (602)363-5525
Kearny, AZ 85237 Fax: (602)363-5191
Free: (800)626-0297

Owner: Cablevision of Texas, Box 310, Lockney, TX 79241, (806)652-3328. **Formerly:** Empire Cable TV. **Key Personnel:** Skeeter Cope, General Mgr.; Don Howe, Chief, phone (Tec)hnician; Brenda Arandas, Office Mgr. **Cities Served:** subscribing households 5,000; 1 community access channel.

KINGMAN†, pop. 9,257.

Mohave Co. (NW). 100 m NW of Prescott. Industrial park. Gold, silver, lead, zinc, copper, feldspar mines. Cattle raising.

727 Kingman Daily Miner
Western Newspapers, Inc.
3015 Stockton Hill Rd. Phone: (602)753-6397
Kingman, AZ 86402 Fax: (602)753-5661

General newspaper. **Founded:** Aug. 1882. **Freq:** Daily (eve.), Sunday (morn.). **Print Method:** Offset. **Cols./Page:** 6. **Col. Width:** 25 nonpareils. **Col. Depth:** 294 agate lines. **Key Personnel:** Brian Johnson, Editor; Kit K. Atwell, Publisher; Mike Alexieff, Advertising Mgr. **Subscription Rates:** $66 individuals. **Remarks:** Accepts advertising. **Formerly:** Mohave Daily Miner.
Ad Rates: GLR: $.49 **Circ:** Mon.-Fri. 7,718
BW: $887.52 Sun. 8,069
4C: $1,232.46
SAU: $6.88

728 The Prospector
Western Newspapers, Inc.
3015 Stockton Hill Rd. Phone: (602)753-6397
Kingman, AZ 86402 Fax: (602)753-5661

Newspaper. **Freq:** Weekly. **Key Personnel:** Kit Atwell, Publisher. **Subscription Rates:** $6; $10. by Mail.
Circ: Free 9,749

729 KAAA-AM - 1230
2534 Hualapai Mountain Rd. Phone: (520)753-2537
Kingman, AZ 86401 Fax: (520)753-1551

Format: News; Talk. **Networks:** ABC. **Owner:** Regent Communications Inc., 50 E. Rivercenter Blvd. 180, Covington, KY 41011, (606)292-0030, Fax: (606)292-0352. **Founded:** 1949. **Formerly:** The Park Lane Group. **Operating Hours:** Continuous; 10% network, 10% local, 80% satellite. **ADI:** Phoenix (Kingman, Prescott), AZ. **Key Personnel:** Cal Hall, Manager, calhall@ctaz.com; Bill Larsen, Program Dir.; Jim Cross, News Dir. **Local Programs:** *Kingman Today*, Steve Johnson. **Wattage:** 1000. **Ad Rates:** Advertising accepted; rates available upon request.

730 KGMN-FM - 99.9
812 E. Beale St. Phone: (520)753-9100
Kingman, AZ 86401 Fax: (520)753-1978
Free: (800)996-5466

Format: Country. **Networks:** USA Radio. **Owner:** Joe Hart, at above address. **Founded:** 1984. **Operating Hours:** Continuous. **ADI:** Phoenix (Kingman, Prescott), AZ. **Key Personnel:** Ken Campbell, Contact; Rhonda Hart, Contact. **Wattage:** 5000. **Ad Rates:** $13 for 30 seconds; $15 for 60 seconds.

731 KZZZ-FM - 94.7
2534 Hualapai Mountain Rd. Phone: (602)753-2537
Kingman, AZ 86401 Fax: (602)753-1551
E-mail: sunny94.7@kingman.com

Format: Adult Contemporary; News. **Owner:** Regent Communications Inc., 50 E. Rivercenter Blvd. 180, Covington, KY 41011. **Founded:** 1974. **Formerly:** The Park Lane Group. **Operating Hours:** Continuous; 100% local. **ADI:** Phoenix (Kingman, Prescott), AZ. **Key Personnel:** Cal Hall, Manager, calhall@ctaz.com; Bill Larsen, Program Dir. **Wattage:** 100,000 ERP. **Ad Rates:** Advertising accepted; rates available upon request.

LAKE HAVASU CITY, pop. 15,737.

Mohave Valley Co. (NW). 185 m E of Phoenix. London bridge. Chain saw & boat plants.

732 River Extra
River City Newspapers
2225 W. Acoma Blvd. Phone: (520)855-2197
Lake Havasu City, AZ 86403 Fax: (520)855-2637

Newspaper. **Freq:** Semiweekly (Wed. and Sun.). **Print Method:** offset. **Cols./Page:** 6. **Col. Width:** 2 1/16 inches. **Col. Depth:** 21 inches. **Key Personnel:** Mike Quinn, Publisher;

Steve Stevens, Advertising Dir. **Remarks:** Accepts advertising.
Ad Rates: BW: $441 **Circ:** Free 6,400
4C: $691
SAU: $3.50

733 Today's News - Herald
River City Newspapers
2225 W. Acoma Blvd. Phone: (520)855-2197
Lake Havasu City, AZ 86403 Fax: (520)855-2637
Publication E-mail: news@havasunews.com

Daily newspaper. **Freq:** Daily except Monday & Saturday. **Print Method:** offset. **Cols./Page:** 6. **Col. Width:** 2 1/16 inches. **Col. Depth:** 21 inches. **Key Personnel:** Mike Quinn, Editor and Publisher; Stan Usinowicz, Managing Editor; Steve Stevens, Advertising Dir. **ISSN:** 1084-9009. **Subscription Rates:** $62 individuals. **Remarks:** Accepts advertising.
Ad Rates: BW: $2024.74 **Circ:** Tues.-Fri. 9,475
SAU: $15.99 Sun. 11,645
PCI: $13.99

734 White Sheet-The Lake Havasu City Advertiser
Associated Desert Shoppers, Inc.
73-400 Hwy. 111 Phone: (760)346-1729
Palm Desert, CA 92260 Fax: (760)346-7350
Free: (800)678-4237

Shopper. **Subtitle:** White Sheet. **Founded:** 1965. **Freq:** Weekly (Tues.). **Print Method:** Web. **Trim Size:** 11 x 12 1/2. **Cols./Page:** 6. **Col. Width:** 9 1/2 picas. **Col. Depth:** 11 1/2 inches. **Key Personnel:** Hal Paradis, Publisher, phone (760)346-1729, fax (760)346-7350; John Schneider, Sales Mgr., phone (520)855-7871520, fax (520)855-8193. **Subscription Rates:** $163.80 out of area.
Ad Rates: BW: $365.00 **Circ:** Free ‡14,000
4C: $650.00

735 Cablevision of Lake Havasu City
730 N. Acoma Phone: (520)855-7815
Lake Havasu City, AZ 86403 Fax: (520)855-1979

Founded: 1991. **Formerly:** London Bridge Cablevision. **Key Personnel:** Donna Baker, General Mgr., dbaker@npgcable.com. **Cities Served:** Desert Hills, Lake Havasu City, AZ; subscribing households 13200; 61 channels.

736 KBBC-FM - 101.1
1642 McCulloch Blvd. N., No. 193 Phone: (602)855-4098
Lake Havasu City, AZ 86403-0961 Fax: (602)855-5395

Format: Top 40; Contemporary Hit Radio (CHR). **Owner:** London Bridge Broadcasting, Inc., at above address. **Operating Hours:** Continuous. **Key Personnel:** Lee Shoblom, Gen. Mgr.; Terry Watt, Vice President; Doreen Ridenour, Office Mgr. **Wattage:** 100,000. **Ad Rates:** $9.50 for 30 seconds; $11.25 for 60 seconds.

737 KFWJ-AM - 980
1642 McCulloch Blvd. N., No. 193 Phone: (602)855-4098
Lake Havasu City, AZ 86403-0961 Fax: (602)855-5395

Format: Oldies. **Networks:** Unistar. **Owner:** London Bridge Broadcasting, Inc., at above address. **Founded:** 1970. **Operating Hours:** Continuous. **Key Personnel:** Lee Shoblom, General Mgr.; Terry Watt, Vice President; Doreen Ridenour, Office Mgr. **Wattage:** 1000. **Ad Rates:** $6.50-9.50 for 30 seconds; $8.50-11.25 for 60 seconds. $6.50-$9.50 for 30 seconds; $8.50-$11.25 for 60 seconds. Combined advertising rates available with KBBC-FM.

738 KNLB-FM - 91.1
510 N. Acoma Blvd. Phone: (520)855-9110
Lake Havasu City, AZ 86403 Fax: (520)453-2588
Free: (800)721-9313
E-mail: info@knlb.com

Format: Religious. **Networks:** USA Radio; International Broadcasting. **Owner:** Advance Ministries, 510 N. Acoma Blvd., Lake Havasu City, AZ 86403. **Founded:** 1983. **Operating Hours:** Continuous; 40% network, 60% local. **Key Personnel:** Richard D. Tatham, General Mgr.; Faron Eckelbarger, Station Mgr./Chief Engineer, faron@knlb.com. **Wattage:** 1000. **Ad Rates:** Noncommercial.

739 KZUL-FM - 105.1
1845 McCulloch Blvd., Ste. A-14 Phone: (520)855-1051
PO Box 1866 Fax: (520)855-7996
Lake Havasu City, AZ 86405-1866
Free: (800)582-ROCK

Format: Adult Contemporary. **Networks:** Unistar. **Owner:** Mad Dog Wireless, Inc., 839 Landon Dr., Bullhead City, AZ 86430, (602)763-7565. **Founded:** 1986. **Operating Hours:** Continuous; 70% network, 30% local. **Key Personnel:** Steven Greeley, General Mgr.; Steven Reno, Program Dir.; Brian Caulkins, News Dir.; Chuck Denney, General Sales Mgr. **Wattage:** 286. **Ad Rates:** $11-16 for 30 seconds; $16.50-24 for 60 seconds.

LITCHFIELD PARK

740 West Valley View
200 W. Wisconsin Blvd. Phone: (602)535-8439
Litchfield Park, AZ 85340-4636 Fax: (602)935-2103

Community newspaper. **Founded:** Apr. 1986. **Freq:** Weekly. **Print Method:** Web offset. **Cols./Page:** 6. **Col. Width:** 9 picas. **Col. Depth:** 16 inches. **Key Personnel:** E. Freireich, Publisher; John Conway, Editor; Stephanie Hillebrand, Advertising Dir. **Subscription Rates:** $32 individuals. **Remarks:** Accepts advertising.
Ad Rates: BW: $997 **Circ:** Controlled 29,094
4C: $1,497
SAU: $18

MESA, pop. 152,453.

Maricopa Co. (SC). 16 m SE of Phoenix. Culture and art centers. Museums. Fishing and hunting. Manufactures integrated circuits, heavy equipment, propellant, rocket motors, electronic interconnectors, helicopters, steel doors & frames, metal corrals and horse trailer, plastic counter tops; frozen food. Agriculture.

741 Arizona Hunter & Angler
Allstar Bass Fishing Tournaments, Inc.
PO Box 859 Phone: (602)890-2547
Mesa, AZ 85211
Magazine on fishing and hunting in Arizona. **Founded:** 1984. **Freq:** Monthly. **Print Method:** Offset. **Trim Size:** 8 3/8 x 10 7/8. **Cols./Page:** 3. **Col. Width:** 2 1/4 inches. **Col. Depth:** 9 3/4 inches. **Key Personnel:** Tom Stiles, Editor and Publisher; Harry Morgan, Editor; Tony Messenger, Editor; John Ellis, Advertising Mgr. **ISSN:** 0888-840X. **Subscription Rates:** $19; $23 out of area. **Remarks:** Accepts advertising. **Formerly:** Arizona Hunter (July 1985).
Ad Rates: BW: $1480 **Circ:** Paid ‡44,850
4C: $2040 Non-paid ‡280

742 Autograph Times
1125 W. Baseline Rd., No. 2-153 Phone: (602)777-8552
Mesa, AZ 85210-9501 Fax: (602)777-0844
Free: (877)860-0349
Publication E-mail: marlanpub@aol.com
Publisher E-mail: autotimes@aol.com

Newsmagazine directed toward autograph collectors. Covers autographs of people from all fields – sports, celebrities, politics, etc. **Subtitle:** The International Newsmagazine for Autograph Collectors. **Founded:** Feb. 1994. **Freq:** Monthly. **Print Method:** Offset. **Trim Size:** 8 1/4 x 10. **Cols./Page:** 4. **Col. Width:** 2 3/8 inches. **Col. Depth:** 10 inches. **Key Personnel:** Marty Marsh, Publisher; Barbara Bigham, Editor; Ardith Wilson, Editor; Alan LeVan, Circulation Mgr. **Subscription Rates:** $24 individuals; $36 two years. **Remarks:** Accepts advertising.
Ad Rates: BW: $295 **Circ:** Paid 4,600
4C: $450 Non-paid 1,800

743 Journal of Nursing Jocularity
Box 40416 Phone: (602)835-6165
Mesa, AZ 85274 Fax: (602)835-6922
Publication E-mail: candace@jocularity.com

Trade magazine covering humor for nurses and other health care professionals. **Founded:** 1991. **Freq:** Quarterly. **Print Method:** Web offset. **Trim Size:** 8 3/8 x 10 7/8. **Key Personnel:** Doug Fletcher, RN, Publisher; Fran London, MS, RN, Editor. **Subscription Rates:** $17.95 individuals. **Remarks:** Accepts advertising.
Ad Rates: GLR: $5 **Circ:** Paid 17,000
BW: $1,000
4C: $1,250

744 Mesa Legend
Mesa Community College
1833 W. Southern Ave. Phone: (602)461-7330
Mesa, AZ 85202 Fax: (602)461-7334
Publication E-mail: legend@eu.maricopa.edu

Collegiate newspaper. **Founded:** 1965. **Freq:** Biweekly. **Print Method:** Offset. **Trim Size:** 21.5 x 13. **Cols./Page:** 6. **Col. Width:** 12 picas. **Col. Depth:** 20 inches. **Subscription Rates:** Free. **Remarks:** Accepts advertising. **Available Online.**
Ad Rates: GLR: $6.20 **Circ:** Free ‡15,000
BW: $500
4C: $600
SAU: $10.00
PCI: $10

745 New Thought
International New Thought Alliance
5003 E. Broadway Rd. Phone: (602)830-2461
Mesa, AZ 85206 Fax: (602)830-2561

Magazine focusing on spiritual enlightenment. **Founded:** 1914. **Freq:** Quarterly. **Print Method:** Offset. **Trim Size:** 8 1/2 x 11. **Cols./Page:** 3. **Col. Width:** 28 nonpareils. **Col. Depth:** 130 agate lines. **Key Personnel:** Mimi Ronnie, Managing Editor. **ISSN:** 0146-7832. **Subscription Rates:** $12 individuals. **Remarks:** Accepts advertising.
Ad Rates: BW: $608.50 **Circ:** ‡3,000
PCI: $26

746 The Tribune
Thomson Newspapers
120 W. 1st Ave. Phone: (602)898-6500
Mesa, AZ 85210 Fax: (602)898-6463

General newspaper. **Founded:** 1890. **Freq:** Mon.-Sun. (morn.). **Print Method:** Offset. **Trim Size:** 13 3/4 x 22. **Cols./Page:** 6. **Col. Width:** 21 nonpareils. **Col. Depth:** 294 agate lines. **Key Personnel:** Alan Geere, Editor, phone (602)898-6305; Karen Wittmer, COO/Publisher, phone (602)898-6504; Mike Romero, VP of Circulation, phone (602)898-6560; Jim Ripley, Managing Editor. **ISSN:** 0888-0271. **Subscription Rates:** $96 individuals. **Remarks:** Accepts advertising. **URL:** http://www.tribaz.com. **Formerly:** Mesa Tribune. **Feature Editors:** Liz Merritt, *Features*, phone (602)898-6572; Bob Schuster, *Editorials*, phone (602)898-6507.
Ad Rates: GLR: $2.57 **Circ:** Mon.-Sat. 109,786
BW: $4,533.48 Sun. 110,679
4C: $5,504.73
SAU: $36.70
PCI: $61.66

747 Cable America Corp.
350 E. 10th Dr. Phone: (602)461-0715
Mesa, AZ 85210 Fax: (602)644-1338
Free: (800)327-4375
E-mail: info@cableamerica.com

Owner: Cable America Corp., at above address. **Founded:** 1989. **Key Personnel:** Jerry Blount, Western Regional Manager, phone (602)892-9222. **Cities Served:** subscribing households 20,000; 79 channels. **URL:** http://www.cableamerica.com.

748 Eagle West, L. L. C.
9333 E. Apache, No. 3C Phone: (800)558-5564
Mesa, AZ 85207 Fax: (602)380-5877

Owner: at above address, (602)380-5855, Fax: (602)380-5877. **Founded:** 1998. **Formerly:** Mission Cable Co. **Key Personnel:** Al Williams, General Mgr. **Cities Served:** Alpine, Bagdad, Black Canyon City, Casa Grande, Christopher Creek, Coucho, Eagar, East Mesa, Florence Gardens, Kohl's Ranch, Springerville, St. Johns, Tonto Village, Williams, Yarnell, AZ; Glenwood, Reserve, NM: subscribing households 12,000; 39 channels; 2 community access channels; 16 hours per week community access programming.

749 KBAQ-FM - 89.5
1435 S. Dobson Rd. Phone: (602)833-1122
Mesa, AZ 85202 Fax: (602)835-5925
E-mail: kbaq@rio.maricopa.edu

Format: Classical. **Networks:** National Public Radio (NPR). **Owner:** Maricopa County Community College District, at above address. **Founded:** Apr. 1993. **Operating Hours:** Continuous. **ADI:** Phoenix (Kingman, Prescott), AZ. **Key Personnel:** Carl E. Williams, General Mgr., matthusen@rio.maricopa.edu; Scott Williams, Program Dir., williamss@rio.maricopa.edu; Mario Ramos, Development Dir., ramos@rio.maricopa.edu. **Wattage:** 12,500. **Ad Rates:** Noncommercial.

750 KDKB-FM - 93.3
1167 W. Javelina Phone: (602)897-9300
Mesa, AZ 85210 Fax: (602)491-8482

Format: Album-Oriented Rock (AOR). **Networks:** Independent. **Founded:** 1968. **Operating Hours:** Continuous. **Key Personnel:** Chuck Artigue, General Mgr. **Wattage:** 100,000.

751 KJZZ-FM - 91.5
1435 S. Dobson Rd. Phone: (602)834-5627
Mesa, AZ 85202 Fax: (602)835-5925

Format: Public Radio; Jazz; News. **Networks:** National Public Radio (NPR). **Owner:** Maricopa County Community College District, 2411 W. 14th St., Tempe, AZ 85282. **Founded:** 1951. **Formerly:** KMCR-FM (1985). **Operating Hours:** Continuous; 60% network, 40% local. **Key Personnel:** Carl Matthusen, General Mgr., matthusen@rio.maricopa.edu; Scott Williams, Program Dir., williams_s@rio.maricopa.edu; Mario Ramoson, Development Dir., phone (602)517-4915, fax (602)517-1779, ramos@rio.maricopa.edu; Mark Moran, News Dir., phone (602)969-5614, moran@rio.maricopa.edu; Bill Shedd, Operations Dir., shedd@rio.maricopa.edu; Bob Glazar, Dir. of Corp. Services, phone (602)517-4915, glazar@rio.maricopa.edu; Yolanda Soliz, Office Mgr., soliz@rio.maricopa.edu. **Wattage:** 100,000. **URL:** http://www.kjzz.org.

752 KXAM-AM - 1310
6900 E. Camelback, Ste. 540 Phone: (602)423-1310
Scottsdale, AZ 85251 Fax: (602)423-3867
E-mail: kxam@phnx.uswest.net

Format: Talk. **Networks:** ABC; Westwood One Radio. **Owner:** Embee Broadcasting Inc., at above address. **Founded:** 1946. **Operating Hours:** Continuous. **ADI:** Phoenix (Kingman, Prescott), AZ. **Key Personnel:** Mike Knox, General Mgr.; Matt Gerson, Vice Pres., News/Entertainment. **Local Programs:** *Health Remedies/Dr. Radio*, Michael Reagan, (602)451-0168; *Matt Gerson Shows*, Bill Ledbetter, (602)423-1310, Fax (602)423-3867; *Sam Steiger Show*, Maryann Watkins, (602)833-1111, Fax (602)969-2895. **Wattage:** 5000. **Ad Rates:** $40 for 60 seconds.

753 KZZP-FM - 104.7
Box 5159 Phone: (602)964-4000
Mesa, AZ 85211-5159 Fax: (602)898-8583
E-mail: kzzp@netzone.com

Format: Adult Contemporary. **Networks:** American Public Radio (APR). **Owner:** Jacor Communications, 50 E. Rivercenter Blvd., Covington, KY 41011. **Founded:** 1976. **Formerly:** KZZP-AM (1992); KVRY-FM. **Operating Hours:** Continuous. **ADI:** Phoenix (Kingman, Prescott), AZ. **Key Personnel:** Dave Pugh, General Mgr., phone (602)279-5577, fax (602)230-2781; Susan Karis-Madigan, General Sales Mgr. **Local Programs:** *Chronicles*, Gordon Nobriga. **Wattage:** 100,000. **Ad Rates:** Advertising accepted; rates available upon request. **URL:** www.kzzp.com.

MIAMI

754 KIKO-AM - 1340
4501 Broadway Phone: (520)425-4471
Miami, AZ 85539 Fax: (520)425-9393
E-mail: kikoradio@aol.com

Format: Oldies; News; Sports. **Networks:** ABC. **Owner:** Willard Shoecraft, Rt. 1, Box 25, Globe, AZ 85501, (520)425-3051. **Founded:** 1958. **Operating Hours:** Continuous. **ADI:** Phoenix (Kingman, Prescott), AZ. **Key Personnel:** Willard Shoecraft, Owner/Mgr.; Ted Thayer, News Dir.; Steve Cullen, Sports Dir.; Norm Seeley, Program Mgr. **Local Programs:** *The BIG Show*, John Libynski; *Open Line*, Willard Shoecraft; *Trading Post*, Willard Shoecraft. **Wattage:** 1000. **Ad Rates:** $8-10 for 30 seconds; $10-12 for 60 seconds.

KIKO-FM - See Claypool

755 KQSS-FM - 98.3
PO Box 292 Phone: (520)425-7186
Miami, AZ 85539 Fax: (520)425-7982

Format: Contemporary Country. **Owner:** Bill Taylor, Box 292, Miami, AZ 85539. **Founded:** 1987. **Operating Hours:** Continuous; 100% local. **Key Personnel:** Bill Taylor, Contact. **Wattage:** 3000.

NOGALES†, pop. 15,683.

Santa Cruz Co. (S). 65 m S of Tucson. Port of entry on Mexican border with important export and import trade. Ships winter vegetables. Copper, silver, lead mines. Cattle farms.

756 Herald
87 N. Grand Phone: (602)287-3622
Nogales, AZ 85621
General newspaper. **Founded:** 1914. **Freq:** Daily (eve.). **Print Method:** Letterpress. Uses mats. **Cols./Page:** 9. **Col. Width:** 22 nonpareils. **Col. Depth:** 294 agate lines. **Key Personnel:** Alvin Sisk, Editor and Publisher. **Subscription Rates:** $17.85 individuals. **Remarks:** Accepts advertising.
Ad Rates: PCI: $4.50 **Circ:** (Not Reported)

757 Nogales International
268 W. ViewPoint Dr.
Nogales, AZ 85621

Community newpaper. **Founded:** 1925. **Freq:** Biweekly Tuesday-Friday. **Print Method:** Offset. **Cols./Page:** 6. **Col. Width:** 12.3 picas. **Col. Depth:** 21.5 inches. **Key Personnel:** Don Henson, Editor and Publisher. **Subscription Rates:** $32 individuals; $36 out of area. **Remarks:** Accepts advertising.
Ad Rates: GLR: $0.30 **Circ:** 5,000
BW: $977.18
4C: $1,277.18
SAU: $7.50
PCI: $7.50

758 Mediacom Az, LLc
PO Box 400 Phone: (520)287-3123
Nogales, AZ 85628-0400 Fax: (520)287-4010
E-mail: mediacom@dakotacom.net

Founded: 1996. **Key Personnel:** Dwight J. Ogden, General Mgr. **Cities Served:** Ajo, Amado, Arivaca Jct., Nogales, Rio Rico, AZ: subscribing households 8,500; 62 channels; 1 community access channel; 24 hours per week community access programming.

ORO VALLEY

759 KVOI-AM - 690
3222 S. Richey Blvd. Phone: (602)790-2440
Tucson, AZ 85713-5453 Fax: (602)790-2937

Format: Religious. **Founded:** 1953. **Operating Hours:** Sunrise-sunset. **ADI:** Tucson, AZ. **Key Personnel:** Doug Martin, General Mgr.; Galen Waterson, Program Dir. **Wattage:** 250,000.

PAGE, pop. 4,907.

Coconino Co. (N). On Lake Powell, 139 m N of Flagstaff. National recreation area. Glen Canyon, Lake Powell, Rainbow Bridge. Navajo generating station.

760 Cable One
155 5th Ave. Phone: (520)645-2132
PO Box 666
Page, AZ 86040

Owner: Post Newseek Cable, 4742 N. 24th St., Ste 270, Phoenix, AZ 85016, (602)468-1177. **Founded:** 1960. **Formerly:** Post Newsweek Cable (1998). **Key Personnel:** H. R. Chlarson, General Mgr. **Cities Served:** subscribing households 2000; 54 channels.

761 KPGE-AM - 1340
91 N. 7th Ave. Phone: (602)645-8181
PO Box 1030 Fax: (602)645-3347
Page, AZ 86040

Format: Oldies. **Networks:** Jones Satellite; ABC. **Owner:** Lake Powell Communications, Inc., at above address. **Founded:** 1962. **Operating Hours:** Continuous. **Key Personnel:** J.D. Brown, General Mgr.; Lance Newman, Contact; Eli Joseph, News Dir. **Local Programs:** *Floor it at Four*, Beth Russler; *Mike in the Morning*, Mike Phillips; *Outdoors with Bubba*, Jerry Puckett. **Wattage:** 1000. **Ad Rates:** Advertising accepted; rates available upon request.

762 KXAZ-FM - 93.3
91 N. 7th Ave. Phone: (602)645-8181
PO Box 1030 Fax: (602)645-3347
Page, AZ 86040

Format: Adult Contemporary. **Networks:** ABC; Jones Satellite. **Owner:** Lake Powell Communications, INC., at above address. **Founded:** 1983. **Operating Hours:** Continuous. **Key Personnel:** J.D. Brown, General Mgr.; Lance Newman, Contact; Eli Joseph, News Dir. **Wattage:** 12,000. **Ad Rates:** Advertising accepted; rates available upon request.

PARADISE VALLEY

763 Paradise Valley Independent
Independent Newspapers, Inc.
10220 W. Bell Rd., Ste. 116 Phone: (602)972-6101
Sun City, AZ 85351 Fax: (602)948-0496
Publication E-mail: pvi_ depnt@aol.com
Publisher E-mail: suncityind@aol.com

Community newspaper. **Founded:** 1982. **Freq:** Weekly. **Print Method:** Offset. **Trim Size:** 13 x 21. **Cols./Page:** 6. **Col. Width:** 2 1/16 inches. **Col. Depth:** 21 1/2 inches. **Key Personnel:** Anne Rymer, Editor; Lisa Howell, Advertising Mgr. **Subscription Rates:** Free; $14 (mail). **Remarks:** Accepts advertising.
Ad Rates: BW: $1,571.22 **Circ:** Combined 19,546
SAU: $15.96

PARKER, pop. 2,542.

Yumba Co. (SW). 135 m W of Phoenix. Residential.

764 Arizona West
Hale Communications, Inc.
1212 4th St. Phone: (602)669-6464
Parker, AZ 85344 Fax: (602)669-6464

Magazine covering travel and the Old West. **Founded:** 1988. **Freq:** Bimonthly. **Print Method:** Offset. **Trim Size:** 5 1/2 x 8 1/2. **Cols./Page:** 2. **Key Personnel:** Gerald Hale, Publisher. **Subscription Rates:** $5. **Remarks:** Accepts advertising. **Formerly:** Arizona Coast (1992).
Ad Rates: BW: $325 **Circ:** Non-paid 15,000
4C: $409

765 Parker Pioneer
Wick Communications Co.
1001-12th St. Phone: (602)669-2275
PO Box N Fax: (602)669-9624
Parker, AZ 85344
Community newspaper. **Founded:** 1954. **Freq:** Weekly (Wed.). **Print Method:** Offset. **Cols./Page:** 6. **Col. Width:** 26 nonpareils. **Col. Depth:** 294 agate lines. **Key Personnel:** Jon Fishman, Publisher; John Schneider, Operations Dir.; John F. Moeur, Editor; Joan M. Travis, News Dir. **USPS:** 422-120. **Subscription Rates:** $16 individuals. **Remarks:** Accepts advertising.
Ad Rates: BW: $749.70 **Circ:** 5,149
4C: $210
SAU: $6.30
PCI: $6.30

766 White Sheet-The Parker Advertiser
Associated Desert Shoppers, Inc.
73-400 Hwy. 111 Phone: (760)346-1729
Palm Desert, CA 92260 Fax: (760)346-7350
Free: (800)678-4237

Shopper. **Subtitle:** White Sheet. **Founded:** 1965. **Freq:** Weekly (Tues.). **Print Method:** Web. **Trim Size:** 11 1/2 x 14. **Cols./Page:** 4. **Col. Width:** 9 1/2 picas. **Col. Depth:** 11 1/2 inches. **Key Personnel:** Hal Paradis, Publisher, phone (760)346-1729, fax (760)346-7350; John Schneider, Sales Mgr., phone (520)855-7876, fax (520)855-8183. **Subscription Rates:** $163.80 out of area. **Merged with:** The Parker/Blythe Advertiser.
Ad Rates: BW: $365.00 **Circ:** Free ‡12,500
4C: $650.00

767 KLPZ-AM - 1380
816 6th St. Phone: (520)669-9274
Parker, AZ 85344 Fax: (520)669-9300
Free: (800)448-1380
E-mail: pennied@redrivernet.com

Format: Contemporary Country; News; Talk. **Networks:** ABC; Satellite Network News. **Owner:** The Scofield Broadcasting Co., Inc., at above address. **Founded:** 1974. **Formerly:** KZUL (1983). **Operating Hours:** Continuous. **Key Personnel:** Charles L. Scofield, President; Pennie Dickinson, General Sales Mgr., phone (520)669-9274, fax (520)669-9300, pennied@redrivernet.com. **Wattage:** 2500. **Ad Rates:** $10.50 for 30 seconds; $14 for 60 seconds.

768 KWFH-FM - 90.1
401 15th St. Phone: (520)669-5683
Parker, AZ 85344 Fax: (520)669-5683

Format: Religious. **Networks:** Moody Broadcasting. **Founded:** 1984. **Operating Hours:** Continuous. **Key Personnel:** Louie Marsh, Program Dir.; Gary Covert, Operations Mgr. **Local Programs:** *River of Life*, Louie Marsh, (520)669-5683, Fax (520)669-5683; *Sonrise Show*, Gary Covert, (520)669-5683, Fax (520)669-5683; *2-Xtremes*, Louie Marsh, (520)669-5683, Fax (520)669-5683. **Wattage:** 460. **Ad Rates:** Noncommercial.

PAYSON, pop. 5,100.

Gila Co. (NC). 70 m NE of Phoenix. Tourism, cattle, and lumber.

769 Payson Roundup and Advisor
Payson Roundup Newspaper
PO Box 2520 Phone: (520)474-5251
Payson, AZ 85547 Fax: (520)474-1893
Publication E-mail: tproundup@aol.com

Community newspaper. **Founded:** July 1, 1937. **Freq:** Semiweekly Tues. and Fri. **Print Method:** Offset. **Trim Size:** 13 1/2 x 23. **Cols./Page:** 6. **Col. Width:** 12.5 picas. **Col. Depth:** 301 agate lines. **Key Personnel:** Brian Beck, Editor; Richard Haddad, Publisher. **Subscription Rates:** $32 individuals; $44 other countries. **Remarks:** Accepts advertising. **URL:** http://paysonroundup.com.
Ad Rates: BW: $1,077.15 **Circ:** Paid 7,200
4C: $1,079.85
SAU: $8.35
PCI: $8.35

770 KBZG-FM - 104.3
200 W. Frontier Ste. P Phone: (602)994-9100
P.O. Box 2579 Fax: (602)423-8770
Payson, AZ 85547-2579
Free: (800)254-7510

Format: Oldies. **Simulcasts:** KBZR-FM. **Owner:** Jay Brentlinger, 7434 E. Stetson Dr., Ste. 255, Scottsdale, AZ 85251.

Founded: 1988. **Formerly:** KKJJ-FM (1987); KRIM-FM (1998). **Operating Hours:** Continuous. **ADI:** Phoenix (Kingman, Prescott), AZ. **Key Personnel:** Jim Seemiller, General Mgr.; Brian Beazer, Program Dir.; Sherilyn McLain, Promotions Dir.; Greg Smith, Sales Mgr. **Wattage:** 100,000. **Ad Rates:** Advertising accepted; rates available upon request.

771 KMOG-AM - 1420
HCR Box 44-A Phone: (602)474-5214
Payson, AZ 85541 Fax: (602)474-0236
E-mail: kmog@cybertrails.com

Format: Country. **Networks:** ABC. **Owner:** Mike Farrell, at above address. **Founded:** 1983. **Operating Hours:** 24 hours; 15% network, 85% local. **Key Personnel:** Blaine Kimball, General Mgr.; Tina Myers, Program Dir.; Blaine Kimball, Sales Mgr. **Wattage:** 2500. **Ad Rates:** $7-14 for 30 seconds; $9-16 for 60 seconds.

PEORIA

772 Peoria Times
Pueblo Publishers, Inc.
7122 N. 59th Ave. Phone: (602)842-6000
Glendale, AZ 85301 Fax: (602)842-6017

Community newspaper. **Founded:** 1952. **Freq:** Weekly (Fri.). **Print Method:** Offset. **Trim Size:** 11x17. **Cols./Page:** 6. **Col. Width:** 9 1/2 inches. **Col. Depth:** 16 inches. **Key Personnel:** Carolyn Dryer, Editor, c.dryer@star-times.com; William V. Toops, Publisher, w.toops@star-times.com; Darlene M. Toops, Publisher, d.toops@star-times.com. **USPS:** 427-760. **Subscription Rates:** $20 individuals; $25 out of area.
Ad Rates: BW: $576 **Circ:** ‡6,200
4C: $951
SAU: $7.20
PCI: $5

773 Sun Life Magazine
Sun Life Co.
9192 W. Cactus, Ste. C Phone: (602)878-2210
Peoria, AZ 85381
Community magazine reflecting the lifestyle and activities of residents of the retirement communties in the N.W. Valley of Phoenix area. **Founded:** Sept. 1984. **Freq:** Monthly (except July). **Print Method:** Offset. **Trim Size:** 8 1/4 x 10 3/4. **Cols./Page:** 2 and 3. **Col. Width:** 20.5 and 13.5 picas. **Col. Depth:** 9 3/4 inches. **Key Personnel:** Kathy H. Wilson, Editor; Jerry A. Svendsen, Publisher; Bob Budorick, Advertising Mgr. **Remarks:** Accepts advertising. **Formerly:** Sun Cities Life (1989).
Ad Rates: BW: $1,615 **Circ:** Free 40,000
4C: $1,990

PHOENIX†, pop. 764,911.

Maricopa Co. (C). The State Capital, 107 m NW of Tucson. Arizona State University. Trade and Business center of the State. Winter resort. Private and ranch schools. American Graduate School for International Management is located in NW Phoenix. Manufactures aircraft and aircraft parts, electronic equipment, steel castings, flour, boxes and crates, agricultural chemicals, aluminum products, radios, mobile homes, air conditioning machinery, steel fabrications, creamery products, beer, liquor, saddles and leather goods, men's and women's apparel, Indian and Mexican novelties, textile goods. Meat packing plants; citrus juices, pickle and olive canneries; sugar refinery; lettuce, cantaloupe, vegetable packing and shipping; cotton products.

774 AFA Watchbird
American Federation of Aviculture
3118 W. Thomas Rd., No. 713 Phone: (602)484-0931
PO Box 56218 Fax: (602)484-0109
Phoenix, AZ 85079-6218
Publication E-mail: stat@wizard.net

Magazine on bird conservation and captive breeding, care and maintenance. **Founded:** 1974. **Freq:** Bimonthly. **Print Method:** Offset. **Trim Size:** 8 1/2 x 11. **Cols./Page:** 3. **Col. Width:** 27 nonpareils. **Col. Depth:** 140 agate lines. **Key Personnel:** Dale Thompson, Editor; Sharon Rosenblatt, Promotions. **ISSN:** 0199-543X. **Subscription Rates:** $30 individuals; $5 single issue. **Remarks:** Accepts advertising.
Ad Rates: BW: $495 **Circ:** Paid 10,000
4C: $795 Non-paid 100

775 Agave
Desert Botanical Garden
1201 N. Galvin Pkwy. Phone: (602)941-1225
Phoenix, AZ 85008 Fax: (602)754-8124

Trade magazine covering botany. **Subtitle:** Quarterly Magazine of the Desert Botanical Garden. **Founded:** 1983. **Freq:** Irregular. **ISSN:** 0735-8652. **Remarks:** Advertising not accepted.
Circ: Paid 2,000

776 Ahwatukee Foothills News
Ahwautkee Foothills News
10631 S. 51st St., Ste. 1 Phone: (602)496-0665
Phoenix, AZ 85044 Fax: (602)893-1684
Publisher E-mail: afn@netzone.com

Community newspaper. **Founded:** 1977. **Freq:** Semiweekly (Wed. and Sat.). **Print Method:** Offset. **Trim Size:** 10 x 15 7/8. **Cols./Page:** 6. **Col. Width:** 1 1/2 inches. **Subscription Rates:** $100 individuals; Free to qualified subscribers. **Remarks:** Accepts advertising. **URL:** http://www.ahwatakee.com. **Alt. Formats:** CD-ROM. **Formerly:** Ahwatakee Weekly News.
Ad Rates: GLR: $15 **Circ:** Controlled 52,000
BW: $1,152
4C: $1,302
PCI: $15

777 America West Airlines Magazine
Skyword Marketing Inc.
4636 E. Elwood St. Phone: (602)997-7200
Suite 5 Fax: (602)997-9875
Phoenix, AZ 85040-1963
Inflight magazine for America West. **Founded:** Mar. 1986. **Freq:** Monthly. **Print Method:** W eb offset. **Trim Size:** 8 x 10 7/8. **Cols./Page:** 3. **Key Personnel:** Michael Derr, Editor; Mark Cipriani, Advertising/Traffic Asst. **ISSN:** 1073-0745. **Subscription Rates:** $29. $3 single issue. **Remarks:** Accepts advertising.
Ad Rates: BW: $6,900 **Circ:** Controlled 130,000
4C: $8,380

778 The Apis
CITA International (USA)
3464 W. Earll Dr., Ste. E Phone: (602)447-0480
Phoenix, AZ 85017 Fax: (602)447-0305

Journal discussing animal health, veterinary products, Ag chemical, lawn and garden, and livestock and poultry. **Founded:** 1989. **Freq:** Quarterly. **Trim Size:** 8 1/2 x 12. **Cols./Page:** 2. **Col. Width:** 7 inches. **Col. Depth:** 10 inches. **Key Personnel:** D.R. Gorloff, Ph.D., Editor-in-Chief; R. Romano, Ph.D., Editor-in-Chief. **ISSN:** 0887-7386. **Subscription Rates:** $275; $495 two years; $290, Europe; $522 two years, Europe; $295 other countries; $531 two years, other countries. $80 single issue. **Remarks:** Accepts advertising.
Ad Rates: BW: $425 **Circ:** ‡2,000
4C: $725

779 Arizona Archaeologist
Arizona Archaeological Society, Inc.
Box 9665
Phoenix, AZ 85068

Professional magazine covering Southwest US archaeology. **Founded:** 1966. **Freq:** Annual. **Trim Size:** 8 x 11. **Key Personnel:** Alan Ferg, Publication Chairor. **Remarks:** Advertising not accepted.
Circ: Controlled 780

780 Arizona Beverage Analyst
Bell Publications
2403 Champa St. Phone: (303)296-1600
Denver, CO 80205-2621 Fax: (303)295-2159

Trade magazine for the liquor, beer, and wine industries. **Founded:** 1936. **Freq:** Monthly. **Print Method:** Offset. **Trim Size:** 8 3/8 x 10 7/8. **Cols./Page:** 3. **Col. Width:** 28 nonpareils. **Col. Depth:** 120 agate lines. **Key Personnel:** Lawrence Bell, Publisher; Sherry Smith, Arizona Editor. **USPS:** 462-150. **Subscription Rates:** $15 individuals. **Remarks:** Accepts advertising.
Ad Rates: BW: $570 **Circ:** Paid ‡135
4C: $1,120 Controlled ‡4,417

781 Arizona Business Gazette
Phoenix Newspapers, Inc.
200 E. Van Buren St. Phone: (602)271-8632
PO Box 85004 Fax: (602)271-8004
Phoenix, AZ 85004-2227
Business and legal newspaper. **Founded:** Sept. 30, 1880. **Freq:** Weekly (Thurs.). **Print Method:** Offset. **Trim Size:** 14 x 22 1/2. **Cols./Page:** 5. **Col. Width:** 2 1/8 inches. **Col. Depth:** 182 agate lines. **Key Personnel:** Stephanie H. Pressly, General Mgr. **ISSN:** 0273-6950. **Subscription Rates:** $30 individuals. **Remarks:** Accepts advertising. **Online:** DataTimes Corporation; LEXIS-NEXIS; Dialog (The Dialog Corporation); CompuServe Information Service.
Ad Rates: BW: $1,657.50 **Circ:** Paid 10,208
4C: $1,957.50 Free 5,744
PCI: $29

782 Arizona Capitol Times
PO Box 2260 Phone: (602)258-7026
Phoenix, AZ 85002 Fax: (602)258-2504

Newspaper covering government, politics, business, and legislation in Arizona. **Founded:** 1946. **Freq:** Weekly. **Print Method:** Web offset. **Trim Size:** 11 1/4 x 13 3/4. **Cols./Page:** 4. **Col. Width:** 2 3/8 inches. **Col. Depth:** 12 1/4 inches. **Key Personnel:** Ned Creighton, Managing Editor; Dave Hurlbert, Advertising Mgr.; Brenda Abraham, Advertising Mgr.; Mary Davis, Circulation Mgr. **Subscription Rates:** $48 individuals; $58 out of state. **Remarks:** Accepts advertising. **Former name:** Arizona Legislative Review.
Ad Rates: BW: $1,156 **Circ:** Combined 5,000
PCI: $23.60

783 Arizona Farm Bureau News
Arizona Farm Bureau Federation
3401 E. Elwood St. Phone: (602)470-0088
Phoenix, AZ 85040-1625 Fax: (602)470-0178

Magazine for the agricultural industry. Specializes in issue specificand regulatory news. **Founded:** 1940. **Freq:** Semimonthly. **Print Method:** Offset. **Trim Size:** 11 x 17. **Cols./Page:** 4. **Col. Width:** 22 nonpareils. **Col. Depth:** 205 agate lines. **Key Personnel:** Mike G. Shirra, Contact, mshirra@azfb.com. **ISSN:** 0274-7014. **Subscription Rates:** $25 individuals. **Remarks:** Advertising not accepted for insurance and workman's compensation.
Ad Rates: BW: $685 **Circ:** ‡4,300
4C: $1,285

784 Arizona Grocer
Arizona Grocers Publishing Co., Inc.
120 E. Pierce St. Phone: (602)252-9761
Phoenix, AZ 85004 Fax: (602)252-9021

Retail grocers magazine. **Subtitle:** The Official Publication of the Arizona Food Marketing Alliance. **Founded:** 1944. **Freq:** Monthly. **Print Method:** Offset. **Trim Size:** 8 1/2 x 11. **Cols./Page:** 3. **Col. Width:** 28 nonpareils. **Col. Depth:** 140 agate lines. **Key Personnel:** Richard V. Jennings, Publisher; Debra A. Roth, Editor. **Subscription Rates:** $50 individuals. **Remarks:** Accepts advertising.
Ad Rates: BW: $500 **Circ:** ‡2,100
4C: $1,080

785 Arizona Highways
2039 W. Lewis Ave.
Phoenix, AZ 85009

Travel magazine covering regional history, natural science, folklore, and natural history. **Founded:** Apr. 1925. **Freq:** Monthly. **Print Method:** Offset. **Trim Size:** 9 x 12. **Cols./Page:** 2. **Col. Width:** 42 nonpareils. **Col. Depth:** 140 agate lines. **Key Personnel:** Robert J. Early, Editor; Rebecca Mong, Managing Editor; Nina LaFrance, Publisher. **ISSN:** 0004-1521. **Subscription Rates:** $19 individuals; $2.99 out of area SNG. **Remarks:** Advertising not accepted. **URL:** http://www.arizhwys.com/.
Circ: ‡442,536

786 Arizona Informant
1746 E. Madison, No. 2 Phone: (602)257-9300
Phoenix, AZ 85034 Fax: (602)257-0547

Black community newspaper. **Founded:** 1958. **Freq:** Weekly (Wed.). **Print Method:** Web offset. **Trim Size:** 9 3/4 x 16. **Cols./Page:** 6. **Col. Width:** 20 nonpareils. **Col. Depth:** 116 agate lines. **Key Personnel:** Charles R. Campbell, Editor and Publisher; Cloves C. Campbell, Sr., Publisher; Cloves C. Campbell, Jr., Advertising Mgr.; Roland Campbell, Mgr. of Sales & Promotions. **USPS:** 051-770. **Subscription Rates:** $18.75 individuals; $25 out of area. **Remarks:** Accepts advertising.
Ad Rates: GLR: $1.71 **Circ:** ‡1,800
BW: $1,152
4C: $1,702
PCI: $18

787 Arizona Medicine
Arizona Medical Association, Inc.
810 W Bethany Home Rd. Phone: (602)246-8901
Phoenix, AZ 85013 Fax: (602)242-6283
Publication E-mail: azmedicine@armadoz.com

Medical journal. **Founded:** 1945. **Freq:** Bimonthly. **Trim Size:** 8 1/2 X 11. **Cols./Page:** 5. **Key Personnel:** Abby Perry, Editorial Content; Marian Paulson, Advertising, fax (602)246-1161. **Subscription Rates:** $100. **Remarks:** Accepts advertising.
Circ: Controlled 4,300

788 Arizona Parenting from A to Z
PO Box 63922 Phone: (602)348-2772
Phoenix, AZ 85082-3922 Fax: (602)948-3488
Publication E-mail: azparent@aol.com

Newspaper. **Founded:** Aug. 1, 1989. **Freq:** Monthly. **Trim Size:** 10 1/2 x 13. **Cols./Page:** 4. **Col. Width:** 2 3/8 inches. **Col. Depth:** 12 inches. **Key Personnel:** Greg Stiles, Editor. **Subscription Rates:** $18 individuals. **Remarks:** Accepts advertising.
Ad Rates: BW: $1,725 **Circ:** Free 60,000
4C: $2,275 Paid 700

789 The Arizona Republic
Phoenix Newspapers, Inc.
200 E. Van Buren St. Phone: (602)271-8632
PO Box 85004 Fax: (602)271-8004
Phoenix, AZ 85004-2227

General newspaper. **Founded:** May 1803. **Freq:** Mon.-Sun. (morn.). **Print Method:** Letterpress and offset. **Cols./Page:** 6. **Col. Width:** 25 nonpareils. **Col. Depth:** 301 agate lines. **Key Personnel:** John Oppedahl, Managing Editor; H. Kenneth Clouse, Advertising Dir.; Conrad Kloh, Dir. of Sales/Marketing; Louis A. Weil III, Publisher. **Subscription Rates:** $158.60 individuals. **Remarks:** Accepts advertising. **Online:** Data-Times Corporation; LEXIS-NEXIS; Dialog (The Dialog Corporation); CompuServe Information Service. **URL:** http://www.a3central.com. **Alt. Formats:** CD-ROM. **Feature Editors:** David Cannella, *Medical*, phone (602)271-8106; Sal Caputo, *Music*, phone (602)271-8096; Amy Carlile, *Entertainment, Family, Fashion, Society, Women's*, phone (602)238-4440; Joe Coleman, *Photo*, phone (602)271-8980; Jeff Dozbaba, *Sports*, phone (602)271-8255; Bob Fenster, *Movie*, phone (602)271-8825; Howard Finberg, *Features, Sunday*, phone (602)271-8248; Greg Joseph, *TV & Radio*, phone (602)271-8974; Dave Michaels, *Living, Religion, Travel*, phone (602)271-8123; Patricia Myers, *Food*, phone (602)271-8624; Don Nicoson, *Financial/Business, Real Estate, Rural Development*, phone (602)271-8667; Thomas Ropp, *Garden/Home*, phone (602)271-8820; Maureen West, *News*, phone (602)271-8221.
Ad Rates: PCI: $164.90 **Circ:** Mon.-Fri. 449,996
Sat. 519,044

790 Arizoo
Arizona Zoological Society
455 N. Galvin Pkwy. Phone: (602)273-1341
Phoenix, AZ 85008-3431 Fax: (602)273-7078

Magazine reporting on people, animals, and events at the Phoenix Zoo. **Subtitle:** The Magazine of the Phoenix Zoo. **Founded:** Apr. 1961. **Freq:** Quarterly. **Print Method:** Offset. **Trim Size:** 8 1/2 x 11. **Cols./Page:** 3. **Col. Width:** 14 picas. **Col. Depth:** 9 5/8 inches. **Key Personnel:** Dick George. **Subscription Rates:** Free Members; $9 nonmembers; $10.50 other countries. **Remarks:** Advertising not accepted.
Circ: Paid ‡34,000
Non-paid ‡2,000

791 Beauty Inc.
Beauty and Barber Supply Institute Inc.
11811 N. Tatum Blvd., Ste. 1085 Phone: (602)604-1800
Fax: (602)404-8900
Phoenix, AZ 85028
Free: (800)468-2274

Trade magazine for professional salon industry distributors and manufacturers. **Founded:** May 1994. **Freq:** Bimonthly. **Print Method:** Web offset. **Trim Size:** 8 1/2 x 10 7/8. **Cols./Page:** 3. **Col. Width:** 2 5/16 inches. **Col. Depth:** 9 5/8 inches. **Key Personnel:** Denise M. Rucci, Editor-in-Chief, denise@bbsi.org; Brian T. Condit, Art Dir., brian@bbsi.org. **ISSN:** 1078-1781. **Subscription Rates:** Free to qualified subscribers. **Remarks:** Accepts advertising.
Ad Rates: BW: $1,425 **Circ:** Combined ⊕**6,767**
4C: $2,025

792 Bus Ride
Friendship Publications, Inc.
7250 N. 16th St., Ste. 406 Phone: (602)944-8414
Phoenix, AZ 85020 Fax: (602)944-8334
Publisher E-mail: friend@busride.com

Magazine for managers of bus,motorcoach and transit operations. **Founded:** 1965. **Freq:** 10/year. **Print Method:** Offset. **Trim Size:** 8 1/4 x 11. **Cols./Page:** 2 and 3. **Col. Depth:** 133 agate lines. **Key Personnel:** Bruce Sankey, Editor and Publisher. **ISSN:** 0192-8902. **Subscription Rates:** Free to qualified subscribers; $35 individuals; $4.50 single issue. **Remarks:** Accepts advertising. **URL:** http//www.busride.com/frend/.
Ad Rates: GLR: $7.50 **Circ:** Paid ‡7,200
BW: $1420 Non-paid ‡6,500
4C: $2180

793 CAMBIO!
LM Ortiz & Associates, Inc.
PO Box 33904 Phone: (602)395-9111
Phoenix, AZ 85067 Fax: (602)253-6896

Magazine addressing special issues of the Hispanic community. **Subtitle:** Offical Publication for Alma de la Gente Fiestas Patrias. **Founded:** Sept. 1988. **Freq:** Biweekly. **Print Method:** Offset. **Trim Size:** 7 x 9 7/8. **Cols./Page:** 3. **Col. Width:** 2 1/4 inches. **Col. Depth:** 9 7/8 inches. **Key Personnel:** Luis Ortiz, Editor and Publisher; Elvira Ortiz, Editor. **Subscription Rates:** $18. **Remarks:** Accepts advertising.
Ad Rates: BW: $650 **Circ:** Non-paid 25,000
4C: $950
PCI: $50

794 Cat World International
PO Box 35635 Phone: (602)995-1822
Phoenix, AZ 85069 Fax: (602)995-1822

Magazine for people who breed and show registered mixed breed and pedigreed cats. **Subtitle:** Serving the Interests of the Show Cat, in the ring and in the home, since 1973. **Founded:** 1973. **Freq:** Bimonthly. **Print Method:** Litho. **Trim Size:** 8 1/2 x 11. **Cols./Page:** 2 and 3. **Col. Width:** 2 1/2 and 3 inches. **Col. Depth:** 10 inches. **Key Personnel:** Tom Corn, Publisher, tom.corn@iotp.com. **Subscription Rates:** $23.00 individuals; $25.00 other countries. **Remarks:** Accepts advertising. **Formerly:** Daphne Negus' Cat World (1984); Cat World.
Circ: Paid 8,000
Non-paid 100

795 The Catholic Sun
Roman Catholic Diocese of Phoenix
400 E. Monroe Phone: (602)257-5565
PO Box 13549 Fax: (602)258-6404
Phoenix, AZ 85002-3549
Publication E-mail: cdcasserly@aol.com; a2cathsun@aol.com

Religious newspaper providing news, information, and commentary about the Catholic church and the Catholic Diocese of Phoenix, Arizona. **Founded:** Apr. 4, 1985. **Freq:** Semimonthly. **Print Method:** Offset. **Trim Size:** 11 x 13 3/4. **Cols./Page:** 5. **Col. Width:** 11 1/2 picas. **Col. Depth:** 180 agate lines. **Key Personnel:** Christopher Gunty, Assoc. Publisher, phone (602)257-5564, cguntysun@aol.com; Bishop Thomas J. O'Brien, Publisher, phone (602)257-5567; Lynn R. Wurth, Advertising Mgr., phone (602)257-5567, lwurth@cathdioc.org. **USPS:** 741-630. **Subscription Rates:** $10. **Remarks:** Accepts advertising. **URL:** http://www.catholicsun.org.
Ad Rates: GLR: $3 **Circ:** Paid 96,377
BW: $2,275 Free 200
4C: $2,675
PCI: $35

796 Computer Literature Index
Applied Computer Research
PO Box 82266 Phone: (602)216-9100
Phoenix, AZ 85071-2266 Fax: (602)216-9200
Free: (800)234-2227
Publisher E-mail: 72603.2553@compuserve.com

Magazine serving as a bibliography of computer-related publications; categorized into 360 classifications. **Founded:** 1971. **Freq:** Quarterly. **Print Method:** Offset. **Trim Size:** 8 1/2 x 11. **Cols./Page:** 2. **Col. Width:** 42 nonpareils. **Col. Depth:** 140 agate lines. **Key Personnel:** Phillip C. Howard, Publisher. **ISSN:** 0270-4846. **Subscription Rates:** $245 individuals; $275 other countries. **Remarks:** Advertising not accepted. **URL:** http://www.acrhq.com.
Circ: Controlled 500

797 Current Index to Journals in Education
Oryx Press
PO Box 33889 Phone: (602)265-2651
Phoenix, AZ 85067-3889 Fax: (602)265-6250
Publisher E-mail: info@oryxpress.com

Journal covering the periodical literature of education. Indexes an average of 1,600 journal articles per month from approximately 980 publications. **Founded:** 1969. **Freq:** Monthly. **Trim Size:** 8 1/2 x 11. **Cols./Page:** 3. **Col. Width:** 2 inches. **Col. Depth:** 10 inches. **Key Personnel:** Phyllis Steckler, President. **ISSN:** 0011-3565. **Subscription Rates:** $245. **Remarks:** Advertising not accepted. **Available Online.**
Circ: (Not Reported)

798 Daily Racing Form
2231 E. Camel Back Rd., Ste. 100 Phone: (602)468-6500
Fax: (602)468-6507
Phoenix, AZ 85016
Racing peridicals. **Founded:** 1894. **Freq:** Daily. **Print Method:** Offset. **Cols./Page:** 6. **Col. Width:** 25 nonpareils. **Col. Depth:** 297 agate lines. **Key Personnel:** George Bernet, Editor; William H. Williams, Publisher; Diane Morgenthaler, Advertising Dir. **Remarks:** Accepts advertising.
Ad Rates: BW: $1,606.50 **Circ:** Mon.-Thurs. 19,260
4C: $19,927.80 Fri. 25,960
Sat. 34,412
Sun. 26,722

799 Daily Racing Form (Midwest Edition)
Daily Racing Form
2231 E. Camel Back Rd., Ste. 100 Phone: (602)468-6500
Fax: (602)468-6507
Phoenix, AZ 85016
Publication E-mail: drf.com

Regional horse racing newspaper. **Founded:** 1894. **Freq:** Mon.-Sun. (morn.). **Print Method:** Offset. **Trim Size:** 9 11/16 x 13 3/4. **Cols./Page:** 4. **Col. Width:** 30 nonpareils. **Col. Depth:** 13 inches. **Key Personnel:** Bill Dow, phone (602)468-6565; Steve Martin, phone (609)443-7926, fax (609)448-1860. **ISSN:** 1053-5411. **Subscription Rates:** $76.50 individuals. **Remarks:** Accepts advertising.
Ad Rates: GLR: $12.33 **Circ:** Mon. 6,139
BW: $678.15 Tues. 4,856
PCI: $12.33 Mon.-Fri. 17,503
Sat. 29,322
Sun. 21,983

800 Exhibitor Times
Virgo Publishing, Inc.
3300 N. Central Ave., Ste. 2500 Phone: (602)990-1101
Phoenix, AZ 85012 Fax: (602)990-0819

Magazine dedicated to corporate exhibit managers responsible for company tradeshow participation. **Founded:** July 1993. **Freq:** Monthly. **Print Method:** Web offset. **Key Personnel:** Valerie A.M. Demetros, Editor; Troy Bix, Publisher; Cassy Turner, Circulation Mgr.; Lisa Kolich, Advertising Mgr. **Subscription Rates:** $55. **Remarks:** Accepts advertising.
Ad Rates: BW: $2,400 **Circ:** Combined 13,623
4C: $3,300

801 For Formulation Chemists Only
CITA International (USA)
3464 W. Earll Dr., Ste. E Phone: (602)447-0480
Phoenix, AZ 85017 Fax: (602)447-0305

Journal covering chemical industrial technology for technicians in the chemical specialty and consumer product industries. **Founded:** 1991. **Freq:** Annual 3/year. **Trim Size:** 7 x 10. **Cols./Page:** 2. **Key Personnel:** E. Morsy, Editor; R. Porte, Advertising Mgr. **ISSN:** 0887-736X. **Subscription Rates:** $285 North America; $300 Europe; $305 other countries. $170 single issue. **Remarks:** Advertising accepted; rates available upon request.
Circ: 2,000

802 Jewish News of Greater Phoenix
Phoenix Jewish News, Inc.
1625 E. Northern Ave. Phone: (602)870-9470
Ste. 106 Fax: (602)870-0426
Phoenix, AZ 85020
Publication E-mail: jngphx@aol.com

Jewish community newspaper (tabloid). **Founded:** Jan. 15, 1948. **Freq:** Weekly. **Print Method:** Offset. **Trim Size:** 11 x 13 3/4. **Cols./Page:** 5. **Col. Width:** 22 nonpareils. **Col. Depth:** 175 agate lines. **Key Personnel:** Florence Newmark Eckstein, Editor and Publisher, eckstein@jewishaz.com. **ISSN:** 0747-444X. **Subscription Rates:** $46 individuals. **Remarks:** Accepts advertising. **Available Online. URL:** http://www.jewishaz.com. **Formerly:** Greater Phoenix Jewish News.
Ad Rates: BW: $1,813 **Circ:** ‡6,500
4C: $2,338
PCI: $29

803 Loud
Loud Magazine
PO Box 56425
Phoenix, AZ 85079

Magazine featuring reviews of records, videos, and concerts of heavy metal bands. **Freq:** Bimonthly. **Key Personnel:** Joe Lopez, Editor. **Subscription Rates:** $15. $2.95 single issue.

804 The Mini-Storage Messenger
MiniCo, Inc.
2531 W. Dunlap, No. 201 Phone: (602)870-1711
Phoenix, AZ 85021 Fax: (602)861-1094
Free: (800)824-6864
Publication E-mail: messenger@minico.com
Publisher E-mail: publishing@minico.com

Magazine for the mini-storage trade. **Founded:** 1979. **Freq:** Monthly. **Print Method:** Offset. **Trim Size:** 8 1/2 x 11. **Cols./Page:** 3. **Col. Width:** 14 picas. **Col. Depth:** 59 picas. **Key Personnel:** Hardy Good, Publisher; Pamela Balin, Advertising Mgr.; Bill Marks, Dir. of Publishing. **ISSN:** 0273-5822. **Subscription Rates:** $59.95 individuals; $5.95 single issue. **Remarks:** Accepts advertising. **URL:** http://www.minico.com.
Ad Rates: BW: $1,300 **Circ:** Paid 4,500
4C: $1,750 Non-paid 500

805 New Times
New Time
1201 E. Jefferson Phone: (602)271-0040
PO Box 2510 Fax: (602)340-8806
Phoenix, AZ 85002
Publication E-mail: phoenixnewtimes.com

Weekly newspaper serving as a comprehensive news, arts, entertainment and resta urant guide for Phoenix. **Founded:** 1970. **Freq:** Weekly (Thurs.). **Print Method:** Offset. **Trim Size:** 10 x 12 7/8. **Cols./Page:** 8. **Col. Width:** 6.5 picas. **Col. Depth:** 77 picas. **Key Personnel:** Jeremy Voas, Editor; Joe Larkin, Advertising Dir., phone (602)258-1073, fax (602)495-9954, joe_larkin@newtimes.com; Michele Laven, Publisher.

ISSN: 0279-3962. **Subscription Rates:** $30 individuals. **URL:** http://www.phoenixnewtimes.com.
Ad Rates: BW: $4,173 **Circ:** Non-paid 130,902
4C: $1,200
PCI: $43

806 Paraplegia News
Paralyzed Veterans of America
2111 E. Highland Ave., Ste. 180 Phone: (602)224-0500
Phoenix, AZ 85016-4732 Fax: (602)224-0507
Free: (888)888-2201
Publication E-mail: pvapub@aol.com

Magazine spotlighting independent living for paraplegics and quadriplegics. **Founded:** 1946. **Freq:** Monthly. **Print Method:** Web offset. **Trim Size:** 8 1/8 x 10 7/8. **ISSN:** 0031-1766. **Subscription Rates:** $23 individuals. **Remarks:** Accepts advertising.
Ad Rates: BW: $1,677 **Circ:** 28,000
4C: $2,527

807 PC AI
Knowledge Technology, Inc.
PO Box 30130 Phone: (602)971-1869
Phoenix, AZ 85046 Fax: (602)971-2321
Publication E-mail: info@pcai.com

Geared toward practical application of intelligent technology, covers developments in expert systems, neural networks, fuzzy logic, object-oriented development, languages and all other areas of artificial intelligence. **Subtitle:** Where Intelligent Technology Meets the Real World. **Founded:** 1987. **Freq:** Bimonthly. **Print Method:** Web offset. **Trim Size:** 8 3/8 x 10 7/8. **Cols./Page:** 3. **Col. Width:** 2 1/4 inches. **Key Personnel:** Terry Hengl, Publisher, terry@pcai.com; Elizabeth Olsen, Managing Editor, liz@pcai.com; Robin Okun, Vice Pres. of Marketing, robin@pcai.com. **ISSN:** 0894-0711. **Subscription Rates:** $32 individuals 1 year. **Remarks:** Accepts advertising 0. **URL:** http://www.pcai.com/pcai/. **Alt. Formats:** CD-ROM.
Ad Rates: BW: $1,650 **Circ:** Combined 20,000
4C: $2,340

808 Phoenix Magazine
MAC America Communications, Inc.
5555 N. 7th Ave., No. B200 Phone: (602)207-3750
Phoenix, AZ 85013-1755 Fax: (602)207-3777

Magazine with local interest news, features, and style. **Founded:** 1966. **Freq:** Monthly. **Print Method:** Web Offset. **Trim Size:** 8 3/8 x 10 7/8. **Cols./Page:** 3. **Col. Width:** 13 picas. **Col. Depth:** 58 picas. **Key Personnel:** Beth Deveny, Editor, beth_deveny@azfamily.com; Diane Craig, Advertising Dir., fax (602)207-3789, diane_craig@azfamily.com; Win Holden, Editor-in-Chief/Publisher, win_holden@azfamily.com. **Subscription Rates:** $18 individuals; $2.95 single issue. **Remarks:** Accepts advertising. **Formerly:** Phoenix Metro Magazine (1991).
Ad Rates: GLR: $35 **Circ:** Paid ★**52,487**
BW: $3,725
4C: $5,495
PCI: $145

809 Southwest Contractor
McGraw-Hill, Inc.
3110 N. Central, Ste. 155 Phone: (602)631-3068
Phoenix, AZ 85012 Fax: (602)631-3073
Free: (800)580-3406

Regional trade magazine for the contracting industries including highway, municipal, utility, heavy construction, and mining. **Founded:** Aug. 1938. **Freq:** Monthly. **Print Method:** Offset. **Trim Size:** 8 1/2 x 11. **Cols./Page:** 2 and 3. **Col. Width:** 21 and 14 picas. **Col. Depth:** 10 inches. **Key Personnel:** Danielle Beaugureau, Editor. **ISSN:** 1064-6914. **Subscription Rates:** $40 individuals. **Remarks:** Accepts advertising. **Absorbed:** Southwest Builder (1989). **Formerly:** Contractor Engineer.
Ad Rates: BW: $920 **Circ:** Combined 6,000
4C: $1,415

810 Sports 'n Spokes
Paralyzed Veterans of America
2111 E. Highland Ave., Ste. 180 Phone: (602)224-0500
Phoenix, AZ 85016-4732 Fax: (602)224-0507
Free: (888)888-2201
Publication E-mail: snsmagaz@aol.com

Magazine covering wheelchair sports and recreation news. **Founded:** May 1975. **Freq:** Bimonthly 8/year Jan, Mar, May, June, July, Sept, Nov and Dec. **Print Method:** Web. **Trim Size:** 8 1/8 x 10 7/8. **Cols./Page:** 3. **Col. Width:** 14 picas. **Col. Depth:** 9 5/8 inches. **Key Personnel:** Cliff Crase, Editor; Sherri Shea, Advertising Mgr. **ISSN:** 0161-6706. **Subscription Rates:** $21 individuals; $27 other countries. **Remarks:** Accepts advertising.
Ad Rates: BW: $1072 **Circ:** ‡14,000
4C: $1,795
PCI: $45

811 Swim Fashion Quarterly
Virgo Publishing, Inc.
3300 N. Central Ave., Ste. 2500 Phone: (602)990-1101
Phoenix, AZ 85012 Fax: (602)990-0819
Publication E-mail: sfqmag@vpico.com

Magazine on merchandising and trends in the swimwear industry. For retailers and buyers. **Founded:** 1988. **Freq:** Quarterly. **Print Method:** Web offset. **Trim Size:** 8 1/8 x 10 7/8. **Cols./Page:** 3. **Col. Width:** 13.6 picas. **Col. Depth:** 58 picas. **Key Personnel:** Teresa Nevil, Editor; Gary Abeyta, Publisher. **Subscription Rates:** $20. $5 single issue. **Remarks:** Accepts advertising.
Ad Rates: BW: $1,765 **Circ:** (Not Reported)
4C: $2,465

812 Team Licensing Business Magazine
Virgo Publishing, Inc.
3300 N. Central Ave., Ste. 2500 Phone: (602)990-1101
Phoenix, AZ 85012 Fax: (602)990-0819

Subtitle: The Professional Journal for Retailers of Team Licensed Products. **Founded:** 1989. **Freq:** Monthly. **Print Method:** Web offset. **Trim Size:** 8 3/8 x 10 7/8. **Cols./Page:** 3. **Key Personnel:** Alisa Klemm, Editor; Michael A. Nichols, Publisher. **Subscription Rates:** $40; $105 other countries. **Remarks:** Accepts advertising.
Ad Rates: BW: $3,745 **Circ:** Controlled ‡25,000
4C: $5,195

813 CableAmerica Corp.
2720 E. Camelback Rd., Ste. 200 Phone: (602)957-2500
Phoenix, AZ 85016-4317 Fax: (602)957-2555
E-mail: cableamerica.com

Founded: 1971. **Key Personnel:** William G. Jackson, President; Christopher A. Dyrek, Vice President; William H. Lewis, Contact. **Cities Served:** Huntsville, AL; Coolidge, Florence, Mesa, Queen Creek, Wickenburg, AZ; St. Robert, MO; Placitas, NM; Sacramento County, CA; St. Louis County and Republic, MO.: subscribing households 72,000; 72 channels; 2 community access channels; 40 hours per week community access programming.

814 Cox Communications
PO Box 78142 Phone: (602)866-0072
Phoenix, AZ 85023 Fax: (602)863-3532

Founded: 1982. **Formerly:** Republic Cable Partners (1990); Dimension Cable Services. **Key Personnel:** Gregg Holmes, Contact. **Cities Served:** Buckeye, Carefree, Casa Grande, Chandler, Fountain Hills, Glendale, Goodyear, Guadalupe, Litchfield Park, Mesa, Paradise Valley, Peoria, Phoenix, Rio Verde, Scottsdale, Surprise, Tempe, Youngtown, AZ; Maricopa County, AZ: subscribing households 605,791; 80 channels. **URL:** http://www.phx.cox.com.

815 Indevideo Co. Inc.
Box 56339 Phone: (602)248-8333
Phoenix, AZ 85079 Fax: (602)248-0690
Free: (800)234-8333

Owner: Indevideo Co., Inc., at above address. **Founded:** 1972. **Key Personnel:** David Rolan, Owner; Al H. Williams, General Mgr. **Cities Served:** Keams Canyon, Shonto, Tuba City, AZ: subscribing households 2000; 18 channels; 1 community access channel; 28 hours per week community access programming.

816 Insight Communications
21200 N. Black Canyon Hwy. Phone: (602)780-2222
Phoenix, AZ 85027 Fax: (602)582-9649

Owner: Insight Communications Co., 126 E. 56th St., New York, NY 10022, (212)371-2266, Fax: (212)935-2575. **Founded:** 1981. **Formerly:** Premiere Cable (1988); Insight Cablevision; Masada. **Key Personnel:** David Servies, General Mgr.; Doug Brown, Operations Mgr.; Cindy Largay, Sales Mgr. **Cities Served:** Avondale, El Mirage, Gilbert, Phoenix (northwest), Tolleson, AZ: subscribing households 30,349; 53 channels; 1 community access channel; 4 hours per week community access programming.

817 KASA-AM - 1540
1445 W. Baseline Rd. Phone: (602)276-4241
Phoenix, AZ 85041 Fax: (602)276-8119

Format: Religious. **Networks:** Independent. **Owner:** Ostrander-Wilson Stations, 114 Lakeside Ave., Seattle, WA 98122, (206)324-2000. **Founded:** 1966. **Operating Hours:** Daylight hours; 100% local. **ADI:** Phoenix (Kingman, Prescott), AZ. **Key Personnel:** Donna R. Phelps, Contact; Tom Bogner, Contact. **Wattage:** 10,000. **Ad Rates:** $6-8 for 30 seconds; $8-12 for 60 seconds.

818 KDDX-TV - 51
11 W. Medlock Dr.
Phoenix, AZ 85027

Format: Commercial TV. **Owner:** America 51, L. P., at above address. **Founded:** 1985. **Former name:** KAJW-TV. **ADI:** Phoenix (Kingman, Prescott), AZ. **Key Personnel:** Hector G. Salvatierra, General Mgr., phone (602)957-1354.

819 KEDJ-FM - 106.3
4745 N 7th St No. 410 Phone: (602)266-1360
Phoenix, AZ 85014 Fax: (602)263-4820

Format: Alternative/New Music/Progressive. **Networks:** CBS. **Owner:** New Century Arizona, at above address, Fax: (602)263-4844. **Founded:** 1975. **Formerly:** KWAO-FM (1992); KMZK-FM; KONC-FM. **Operating Hours:** Continuous; 100% local. **ADI:** Phoenix (Kingman, Prescott), AZ. **Key Personnel:** Bob Case, General Mgr./Vice Pres.; Michael Mallace, Dir. of Sales. **Local Programs:** *Edge Factor (Sat Nite mix-show)*; *Triple Exposure (Local Music)*. **Wattage:** 6,000. **Ad Rates:** Advertising accepted; rates available upon request. **URL:** http://www.kedj.com.

820 KESZ-FM - 99,9
5555 N. 7th Ave. Phone: (602)207-9999
Phoenix, AZ 85013 Fax: (602)207-3177
E-mail: kez@azfamily.com

Format: Adult Contemporary. **Owner:** Mac America Communications, Inc., at above address. **Former name:** KTWC-FM. **Operating Hours:** Continuous. **Key Personnel:** Michael Owens, General Mgr.; Mike Del Rosso, Program Dir.; Patty Graham, Local Sales Mgr. **Wattage:** 100,000. **URL:** http://www.azfamily.com.

821 KFLR-FM - 90.3
702 E. Thunderbird Rd. Phone: (602)978-0903
Phoenix, AZ 85022-5310 Fax: (602)548-8089
Free: (800)776-1080
E-mail: kflr@flc.org

Format: Religious. **Networks:** Moody Broadcasting. **Owner:** Family Life Broadcasting System, Box 35300, Tucson, AZ 85740, (520)742-6976. **Founded:** 1985. **Operating Hours:** Continuous; 25% network, 75% local. **ADI:** Phoenix (Kingman, Prescott), AZ. **Key Personnel:** Alan Cook, Manager; Fred Morse, Asst. Mgr.; Bruce Thurman, News Dir.; Jim Nelson, Chief Engineer; Bruce Thurman, Community Relations. **Local Programs:** *Midday*, Fred Morse; *On Line*, Jan Tanner; *Sunrise Sounds*, Alan Cook. **Wattage:** 50.000. **Ad Rates:** Noncommercial.

822 KFNN-AM - 1510
4800 N. Central Ave. Phone: (602)241-1510
Phoenix, AZ 85012-1722 Fax: (602)241-1540
Free: (800)293-KFNN
E-mail: kfnnradio@juno.com

Format: Talk; News. **Networks:** Business Radio. **Owner:** CRC Broadcasting, at above address. **Founded:** 1962. **Formerly:** KJAA-AM (1988). **Operating Hours:** 24 hrs. **ADI:** Phoenix (Kingman, Prescott), AZ. **Key Personnel:** Ron Cohen, General Mgr.; Forrest Spencer, Operations Mgr.; Ken Hong, Sales Mgr.; Carolyn Vasos, Traffic Mgr.; Sinclair Noe, News Dir. **Local Programs:** *Business Day Arizona*, Mike Ross, Mailing contact; *Financial Review*, Sinclair Noe, Mailing contact; *Kenn Morning News Block*, Mike Ross, Mailing contact. **Wattage:** 22,000.

823 KFYI-AM - 910
631 N. 1st Ave. Phone: (602)258-6161
Phoenix, AZ 85003-1415 Fax: (602)817-1199

Format: News; Talk. **Networks:** CBS. **Founded:** 1940. **Formerly:** KJJJ-AM (1985). **Operating Hours:** Continuous. **ADI:** Phoenix (Kingman, Prescott), AZ. **Key Personnel:** Ed Walsh, Program Dir. **Wattage:** 5000.

824 KGME-AM - 1360
4745 N 7 Ste. 410 Phone: (602)266-1360
Phoenix, AZ 85014 Fax: (602)263-4820

Format: Sports. **Networks:** Mutual Broadcasting System; ESPN Radio; ABC. **Owner:** Resource Media, at above address. **Founded:** 1946. **Formerly:** KLFF-AM. **Operating Hours:** Continuous. **ADI:** Phoenix (Kingman, Prescott), AZ. **Key Personnel:** Bob Case, General Mgr.; Wendy Irumroy, Controller; Craig Boston, Sales Mgr. **Wattage:** 50,000 Day; 1,000 night.

825 KHEP-AM - 1280
100 W. Clarendon Ave., No. 720 Phone: (602)234-1280
Phoenix, AZ 85013-3528 Fax: (602)234-1586
Free: (888)247-1280
E-mail: khep@primenet.com

Format: News; Talk. **Networks:** NBC. **Owner:** Christian

Communications, Inc., at above address. **Founded:** 1957. **Operating Hours:** Continuous; 80% network, 20% local. **ADI:** Phoenix (Kingman, Prescott), AZ. **Key Personnel:** Tom Brown, General Mgr., tgbrown@msn.com; Jim Hanemaayer, General Sales Mgr. **Wattage:** 2500. **Ad Rates:** $16 for 30 seconds; $28 for 60 seconds.

826 KHTC-FM - 96.9
645 E. Missouri Ave., No. 360 Phone: (602)279-5577
Phoenix, AZ 85012-1369 Fax: (602)230-2781

Founded: 1964. **Formerly:** KMEO-FM (1992); KPSN-FM. **ADI:** Phoenix (Kingman, Prescott), AZ. **Key Personnel:** Buz Powers, General Mgr.; Tom Watson, Program Dir.; Mike Shields, General Sales Mgr. **Wattage:** 100,000.

827 KIDR-AM - 740
3030 N. Central Ave., Ste. 1110
Phoenix, AZ 85012
E-mail: matt@kids.com

Format: Public Radio; Educational; Information. **Networks:** Children's Radio. **Founded:** 1992. **Formerly:** KMEO-AM (1992). **Operating Hours:** Continuous. **ADI:** Phoenix (Kingman, Prescott), AZ. **Key Personnel:** Matt Miller, Program Dir., phone (602)234-8998, fax (602)234-8993, natt@kids.com. **Wattage:** 1000 day; 250 night. **Ad Rates:** $30 per unit. **URL:** http://www.kidr.com.

828 KISO-AM - 1230
840 N. Central Ave. Phone: (602)258-8181
Phoenix, AZ 85004 Fax: (602)420-9916

Format: Urban Contemporary. **Networks:** Independent. **Owner:** Colfax Communications, at above address, Fax: (602)440-6500. **Founded:** 1949. **Formerly:** KPMX-AM (1991); KAMJ-AM; KISP-AM. **Operating Hours:** Continuous. **ADI:** Phoenix (Kingman, Prescott), AZ. **Key Personnel:** Jerry Davis, Program Dir.; Terry Hardin, General Mgr.; Autrey Jones, Sales Mgr. **Wattage:** 1000.

829 KKFR-FM - 92.3
631 N. 1st Ave. Phone: (602)258-6161
Phoenix, AZ 85003-1514 Fax: (602)817-1199

Format: Contemporary Hit Radio (CHR). **Networks:** CBS. **Founded:** 1979. **Operating Hours:** Continuous. **ADI:** Phoenix (Kingman, Prescott), AZ. **Key Personnel:** Ron Parker, Program Dir. **Wattage:** 100,000.

830 KKLT-FM - 98.7
5300 N. Central Ave. Phone: (602)274-6200
Phoenix, AZ 85012-1410 Fax: (602)266-3858

Format: Adult Contemporary. **Networks:** Independent. **Founded:** 1960. **Operating Hours:** Continuous. **ADI:** Phoenix (Kingman, Prescott), AZ. **Key Personnel:** Christopher Gallu, General Mgr.; Brad Walso, Program Dir.; Jack Nietzel, Marketing Dir. **Wattage:** 115,000 ERP.

831 KNXV-TV - 15
4625 S. 33rd Pl. Phone: (602)243-4151
Phoenix, AZ 85040 Fax: (602)304-3000
Free: (800)803-3277
E-mail: news15@primenet.com

Format: Commercial TV. **Networks:** ABC. **Owner:** Scripps Howard Broadcasting, 312 Walnut St., 28th Fl., Cincinnati, OH 45202, (513)977-3000. **Founded:** 1979. **Operating Hours:** Continuous. **ADI:** Phoenix (Kingman, Prescott), AZ. **Key Personnel:** Bradley R. Nilsen, Vice Pres./General Mgr.; Michael Kronley, Station Mgr.; Michael Barich, General Sales Mgr.; Mary Flynn, Business Mgr.; Jeff Harrelson, Program Mgr.; Jeff Klotzman, News Dir.; Paul Hallowell, Production Mgr.; Don Thomas, Engineering Mgr.; Colleen Herman, Public Affairs Mgr. **Ad Rates:** $30-14,000 per unit.

832 KOOL-FM - 94.5
4745 N. 7th St., No. 210 Phone: (602)956-9696
Phoenix, AZ 85014 Fax: (602)285-1450

Format: Oldies. **Founded:** 1956. **Operating Hours:** Continuous. **ADI:** Phoenix (Kingman, Prescott), AZ. **Key Personnel:** Dave Siebert, General Mgr.; Tom Peake, Operations Dir.; Louis Valdivia, Contact; Kerry O'Connor, Promotions Dir.; Tom Peake, Program Dir. **Wattage:** 100,000.

833 KOY-AM - 550
840 N. Central Ave. Phone: (602)258-8181
Phoenix, AZ 85004 Fax: (602)420-9916

Format: Big Band/Nostalgia. **Networks:** CNN Radio; Unistar. **Owner:** Chancellor Broadcasting, at above address, Fax: (602)440-6500. **Founded:** 1921. **Operating Hours:** Continuous. **ADI:** Phoenix (Kingman, Prescott), AZ. **Key Personnel:** Terry Hardin, General Mgr.; Jerry Davis, Program Dir.; Dean Moomey, Sales Mgr.; Roger Heinrich, News Dir. **Wattage:** 5000 day; 1000 night.

834 KPAZ-TV - 21
3551 E. McDowell Phone: (602)273-1477
Phoenix, AZ 85008 Fax: (602)267-9427

Format: Commercial TV. **Operating Hours:** Continuous. **ADI:** Phoenix (Kingman, Prescott), AZ. **Key Personnel:** Billie Watts, Station Mgr.

835 KPHO-TV - 5
4016 N. Black Canyon Phone: (602)264-1000
Phoenix, AZ 85017 Fax: (602)263-8818

Format: Commercial TV. **Networks:** Independent; CBS. **Owner:** Meredith Corp., 1716 Locust St, Des Moines, IA 50309. **Founded:** 1949. **Operating Hours:** Continuous. **ADI:** Phoenix (Kingman, Prescott), AZ. **Key Personnel:** Patrick North, VP/GM.

836 KPHX-AM - 1480
824 E. Washington St. Phone: (602)257-1351
Phoenix, AZ 85034 Fax: (602)256-0741

Format: Hispanic; Adult Contemporary; News; Eclectic; Sports; Top 40; Religious. **Networks:** UPI. **Founded:** 1958. **Operating Hours:** Continuous. **ADI:** Phoenix (Kingman, Prescott), AZ. **Key Personnel:** Freddy Morales, General Mgr. **Wattage:** 5000.

837 KPNX-TV - 12
1101 N. Central Ave. Phone: (602)257-1212
PO Box 711 Fax: (602)258-8186
Phoenix, AZ 85004
E-mail: tv12news@aol.com

Format: Commercial TV. **Networks:** NBC. **Owner:** Gannett Co., Inc., 1000 Wilson Blvd., Arlington, VA 22234. **Founded:** 1953. **Formerly:** KTYL-TV (1954). **Operating Hours:** Continuous; 60% network, 40% local. **ADI:** Phoenix (Kingman, Prescott), AZ. **Key Personnel:** C.E. "Pep" Cooney, President; Winnie Stolper, VP, Prog. Oper.; Collen Brown, Pres./Gen. Mgr.; Jeff Burnton, General Sales Mgr.; David Pennington, Local Sales Mgr.; Sherrie Freitag, National Sales Mgr.; Donna Voit, VP, Prom. Mktg.; Lucia Madrid, VP, Community Affairs; Chuck Deen, VP, Chief Engineer; Joan Barrett, News Dir. **Ad Rates:** Advertising accepted; rates available upon request.

838 KPXQ-AM - 960
2425 E. Camelback, No. 570 Phone: (602)955-9600
Phoenix, AZ 85016 Fax: (602)955-7860

Format: Talk. **Founded:** 1947. **Formerly:** KOOL-AM (1996); KARL-AM. **Operating Hours:** Continuous. **ADI:** Phoenix (Kingman, Prescott), AZ. **Key Personnel:** Michael Hamilton, General Mgr.; Paul Creasman, Program Dir.; Renee Larsen, Sales Mgr. **Wattage:** 5000.

839 KRDS-AM - 1190
8611 N. Black Canyon Hwy. 206 Phone: (602)995-9555
Fax: (602)995-3390
Phoenix, AZ 85021-4188

Format: Religious. **Networks:** USA Radio. **Owner:** Paul Toberty, 1748 W. Katella, Orange, CA 92667. **Founded:** 1979. **Operating Hours:** Continuous; 10% network, 90% local. **ADI:** Phoenix (Kingman, Prescott), AZ. **Key Personnel:** Timothy Watson, Station Mgr.; Mary Beth Senachal, Sales Mgr. **Wattage:** 5000. **Ad Rates:** $13.20-25.50 for 30 seconds; $16.50-32 for 60 seconds.

840 KRDS-FM - 105.3
8611 N. Black Canyon Hwy., Ste. 206 Phone: (602)995-9555
Fax: (602)995-3390
Phoenix, AZ 85021-4188

Format: Contemporary Christian. **Networks:** Independent. **Owner:** Interstate Broadcasting Systems of Arizona, at above address. **Founded:** 1983. **Formerly:** KCIW-FM (1983). **Operating Hours:** Continuous. **ADI:** Phoenix (Kingman, Prescott), AZ. **Key Personnel:** Timothy Watson, Station Mgr.; Mary Beth Senechal, Sales Mgr. **Wattage:** 50,000. **Ad Rates:** $28-50 for 60 seconds.

841 KSAZ-TV - 10
511 W. Adams St. Phone: (602)257-1234
Phoenix, AZ 85003 Fax: (602)262-0177

Format: Commercial TV. **Networks:** Fox. **Founded:** 1953. **Formerly:** KOOL-TV; KTSP-TV. **Operating Hours:** Continuous. **ADI:** Phoenix (Kingman, Prescott), AZ. **Key Personnel:** Daniel J. Berkery, President/General Manager; Tim Ermish, Vice President; Bill Berra, Vice President; Karen Donner, Vic President of Business; Jim Girodo, Vice-Predident of Creative Services; Cassandra Larsen, Comm. Service Director; John Dolive, Broadcast Operations/Engineer.

842 KSUN-AM - 1400
714 N. 3rd St. Phone: (602)252-0030
Phoenix, AZ 85004-2018 Fax: (602)252-4211

Format: Adult Contemporary; Hispanic. **Networks:** Independent. **Owner:** Radio Fiesta Inc., at above address. **Founded:** 1986. **Operating Hours:** Continuous. **ADI:** Phoenix (Kingman, Prescott), AZ. **Key Personnel:** Pedro Morquez, President; Gloria Cauazos, Contact; Mario Gonzalez, Contact. **Wattage:** 1000. **Ad Rates:** $15-45 for 30 seconds; $25-60 for 60 seconds.

843 KTAR-AM - 620
5300 N. Central Ave. Phone: (602)274-6200
Phoenix, AZ 85012-1410 Fax: (602)266-3858

Format: News; Talk; Sports. **Networks:** ABC; AP. **Founded:** 1922. **Operating Hours:** Continuous. **ADI:** Phoenix (Kingman, Prescott), AZ. **Key Personnel:** Christopher Gallu, General Mgr.; Jack Nietzel, Contact; Gail Schmeling, Business Mgr. **Local Programs:** *Bill Heywood Az Morning News* 5:00 am - 9:00 am Monday-Friday, David Moskowitz, Producer, Fax (602)265-9941; *Pat McMahon Show* 9:00 am - 12:00 noon Monday-Friday, Rosemary Scarfo; *Preston Westmouland Show* 1:00 pm - 3:00 pm Monday-Friday, Rosemary Scarfo, Producer. **Wattage:** 5000 day; 1000 night.

844 KTVK-TV - 3
5555 N. 7th Ave. Phone: (602)207-3333
Phoenix, AZ 85013 Fax: (602)207-3377

Format: Commercial TV. **Owner:** Delbert Lewis, at above address. **Founded:** 1955. **Operating Hours:** Continuous. **ADI:** Phoenix (Kingman, Prescott), AZ. **Key Personnel:** Bill Miller, Vice President, phone (602)207-3307; Sue Schwartz, Vice President, phone (602)207-3305; Laurie Ficarra, Sales Mgr., phone (602)207-3392; Joe Canty, Sales Mgr., phone (602)207-3390; Phil Alvidrez, Vice President, phone (602)207-3455; Dennis O'Neill, News Dir., phone (602)207-3453; Randy Mossburg, Program Dir., phone (602)207-3543; Richard Holland, Director, phone (602)207-3423; Marlene Klotz-Collins, Vice President, phone (602)207-3331; Bill Lawrence, Vice President of Engineering, phone (602)207-3355; Jim Cole, Chief Engineer, phone (602)207-3369; Jim Tuton, Vice Pres. Finance, phone (602)207-3319; Wendy Pryslak, Business Mgr., phone (602)207-3329; Jeanette Nichols, Traffic Manager, phone (602)207-3338; Christy McKendry, Director, phone (602)207-3315. **Ad Rates:** Combined advertising rates available with KASW-TV.

845 KTVW-TV - 33
3019 E. Southern Ave. Phone: (602)243-3333
Phoenix, AZ 85040 Fax: (602)276-8658

Format: Commercial TV; Ethnic. **Networks:** Univision. **Founded:** Sept. 1979. **Operating Hours:** Continuous;. **ADI:** Phoenix (Kingman, Prescott), AZ. **Key Personnel:** Ruben R. Luera, General Mgr.; Tom Kioski, Production Mgr.; Virginia Luna, Program Dir. **Local Programs:** *Noticias 33*; *TeleDia*.

846 KUTP-TV - 45
4630 S. 33rd St. Phone: (602)268-4500
Phoenix, AZ 85040 Fax: (602)276-4082

Format: Commercial TV. **Networks:** Independent. **Owner:** United Television Inc., 132 S. Rodeo Dr., 4th Fl., Beverly Hills, CA 90212-2425, Fax: (310)281-4844. **Founded:** 1985. **Operating Hours:** Continuous; 100% local. **ADI:** Phoenix (Kingman, Prescott), AZ. **Key Personnel:** Bob Furlong, General Mgr.; Michael Durand, General Sales Mgr.; Mitch Nye, Local Sales Manager; Curtis Pap, National Sales Manager; Tom Foy, Chief Engineer; Seth Parker, Program Dir.; Alice Lafond, Traffic Mgr.; Cheryl Strong, PSA Director; Don Mitchell, Business Mgr.

847 KVVA-AM - 860
1641 E. Osborne Rd., Ste. 8 Phone: (602)266-2005
PO Box 390 Fax: (602)279-2921
Phoenix, AZ 85001-0390

Format: Hispanic. **Networks:** Independent. **Owner:** Betacom Inc., at above address. **Founded:** 1949. **Formerly:** KIFN-AM (1981). **Operating Hours:** Continuous; 100% local. **ADI:** Phoenix (Kingman, Prescott), AZ. **Key Personnel:** Richard Torres, General Sales Mgr.; Luis Trujillo, Program Dir.; Bob Feinman, General Mgr. **Wattage:** 1000.

848 KVVA-FM - 107.1
1641 E. Osborn Rd. Phone: (602)266-2005
PO Box 390 Fax: (602)279-2921
Phoenix, AZ 85001-0390

Format: Hispanic; Adult Contemporary. **Owner:** Z-Spanish Radio Network, 1436 Auburn Blvd., Sacramento, CA 95815, (916)646-4000, Fax: (916)676-8267. **Founded:** 1983. **Formerly:** KSTM-FM (1987). **Operating Hours:** Continuous; 100% local. **ADI:** Phoenix (Kingman, Prescott), AZ. **Key Personnel:** Manny Simo, General Sales Mgr.; Gilberto Romo,

Program Dir.; Ricardo Torres, General Mgr. **Wattage:** 25,000. **Ad Rates:** Advertising accepted; rates available upon request.

849 KWCY-FM - 103.5
5555 N. 7th Ave., No. A-100
Phoenix, AZ 85013

Format: Contemporary Country. **Owner:** Mac American Communications, Inc., at above address. **Founded:** Aug. 1997. **Former name:** KOAZ-FM (1997). **Operating Hours:** Continuous. **ADI:** Phoenix (Kingman, Prescott), AZ. **Key Personnel:** Michael Owens, General Mgr., phone (602)966-6236. **Wattage:** 100,000.

850 KYOT-FM - 95.5
840 N. Central Ave. Phone: (602)258-8181
Phoenix, AZ 85004 Fax: (602)420-9916

Format: Jazz. **Networks:** Independent. **Owner:** Colfax Communications, at above address, Fax: (602)440-9916. **Founded:** 1963. **Formerly:** KOY-FM. **Operating Hours:** Continuous. **ADI:** Phoenix (Kingman, Prescott), AZ. **Key Personnel:** Terry Hardin, General Mgr.; Brad Gould, Sales Mgr.; Nick Francis, Program Dir. **Wattage:** 96,000.

851 KZON-FM - 101.5
840 N. Central Ave. Phone: (602)258-8181
Phoenix, AZ 85004 Fax: (602)420-9916

Format: Alternative/New Music/Progressive. **Networks:** Independent. **Owner:** Colfax Communications, at above address. **Founded:** 1964. **Formerly:** KAMJ-FM (1992); KMXX-FM. **Operating Hours:** Continuous. **ADI:** Phoenix (Kingman, Prescott), AZ. **Key Personnel:** Terry Hardin, General Mgr.; Bill Pugh, Promotions Dir.; Dave Griffin, General Sales Mgr. **Wattage:** 100,000.

852 Post-Newsweek Cable
4742 N. 24th St., Ste. 270 Phone: (602)468-1177
Phoenix, AZ 85016 Fax: (602)468-9216

Founded: 1981. **Cities Served:** subscribing households 500,000.

PRESCOTT†, pop. 20,055.

Yavapai Co. (C). 90 m NW of Phoenix. Tourism. Prescott National Forest.

853 Chino Valley Review
Western Newspapers, Inc.
PO Box 312 Phone: (602)445-6020
Prescott, AZ 86302 Fax: (602)445-4756

Newspaper. **Freq:** Weekly. **Key Personnel:** John Harrell, Circulation Dir. **Subscription Rates:** $13.
Circ: Free 2,678
Paid 341

854 Dick Tracy Adventures
Bruce Hamilton Publishing, Inc.
212 S. Montezuma Phone: (520)776-1300
Prescott, AZ 86303 Fax: (520)445-7536

Magazine featuring Tracy strips in black and white. **Founded:** 1983. **Freq:** Monthly. **Trim Size:** 6 5/8 x 10 1/8. **Key Personnel:** Bruce Hamilton, Publisher. **Subscription Rates:** $1.95 single issue. **Remarks:** Accepts advertising.
Circ: (Not Reported)

855 Dread of Night
Bruce Hamilton Publishing, Inc.
212 S. Montezuma Phone: (520)776-1300
Prescott, AZ 86303 Fax: (520)445-7536

Magazine featuring horror stories. **Freq:** Semimonthly. **Key Personnel:** Bruce Hamilton, Publisher; Leonard Clark, Editor. **Subscription Rates:** $19.50. $3.95 single issue.

856 Grave Tales
Bruce Hamilton Publishing, Inc.
212 S. Montezuma Phone: (520)776-1300
Prescott, AZ 86303 Fax: (520)445-7536

Magazine featuring tales of horror. **Freq:** Semimonthly. **Key Personnel:** Bruce Hamilton, Editor and Publisher. **Subscription Rates:** $19.50. $3.95 single issue.

857 Handloader
Wolfe Publishing Co.
6471 Airpark Dr. Phone: (520)445-7810
Prescott, AZ 86301 Fax: (520)778-5124
Free: (800)899-7810
Publisher E-mail: circ@futureone.com

Magazine covering ammunition handloading. **Subtitle:** The Journal of Ammunition Reloading. **Founded:** 1966. **Freq:** Bimonthly. **Print Method:** Web. **Trim Size:** 8 1/8 x 10 7/8. **Cols./Page:** 3. **Col. Width:** 27 nonpareils. **Col. Depth:** 140 agate lines. **Key Personnel:** Dave Scovill, Editor; Mark Harris, Publisher; Don Polacek, Advertising Mgr. **ISSN:** 0017-7393. **Subscription Rates:** $22 individuals. **Remarks:** Accepts advertising. **URL:** http://www.alloutdoors.com; http://www.stokesworld.com.
Ad Rates: BW: $1,674 **Circ:** ‡100,000
4C: $2,703
PCI: $66

858 Maggots
Bruce Hamilton Publishing, Inc.
212 S. Montezuma Phone: (520)776-1300
Prescott, AZ 86303 Fax: (520)445-7536

Magazine features black and white horror comic book stories. **Freq:** Semimonthly. **Key Personnel:** Bruce Hamilton, Editor and Publisher. **Subscription Rates:** $19.95. $3.95 single issue.

859 The Prescott Courier
The Daily Courier
147 N. Cortez Phone: (602)445-3333
Prescott, AZ 86301
General newspaper. **Founded:** 1882. **Freq:** Daily (eve.), Sunday (morn.). **Print Method:** Offset. **Trim Size:** 13 3/4 x 22 5/8. **Cols./Page:** 6. **Col. Width:** 26 nonpareils. **Col. Depth:** 21 1/2 inches. **Key Personnel:** Jim Garner, Editor; Karen Despain, Managing Editor; Pam Carpenter, Advertising Dir.; R. D. Gilliland, Publisher. **Subscription Rates:** $11.34 individuals Per month. **Remarks:** Accepts advertising.
Ad Rates: BW: $1,184.22 **Circ:** Mon.-Fri. 17,647
4C: $1,544.22 Sun. 19,500
SAU: $9.18

860 Prescott Valley Tribune
Western Newspapers, Inc.
PO Box 312 Phone: (520)445-6020
Prescott, AZ 86302 Fax: (520)445-4756

Newspaper. **Freq:** Weekly. **Key Personnel:** John Harrell, Circulation Dir. **Subscription Rates:** $13.
Circ: Free 8,196
Paid 202

861 Rifle
Wolfe Publishing Co.
6471 Airpark Dr. Phone: (520)445-7810
Prescott, AZ 86301 Fax: (520)778-5124
Free: (800)899-7810
Publisher E-mail: circ@futureone.com

Covers all types of rifles-centerfires, rimfires, air rifles and muzzle loaders. **Subtitle:** The Sporting Firearms Journal. **Founded:** 1968. **Freq:** Bimonthly. **Print Method:** Offset. **Trim Size:** 8 1/8 x 10 7/8. **Cols./Page:** 3. **Col. Width:** 27 nonpareils. **Col. Depth:** 140 agate lines. **Key Personnel:** Dave Scovill, Editor; Mark Harris, Publisher; Don Polacek, Advertising Mgr. **ISSN:** 0162-3583. **Subscription Rates:** $19 individuals. **Remarks:** Accepts advertising. **URL:** http://www.alloutdoors.com; http://www.stokesworld.com.
Ad Rates: BW: $1,674 **Circ:** ‡95,000
4C: $2,703

862 KGCB-FM - 90.9
3231 Tower Dr. Phone: (520)776-0909
Prescott, AZ 86305 Fax: (520)776-1736
Free: (800)720-0909
E-mail: kgcb@primenet.com

Format: Religious; Adult Contemporary. **Owner:** Grand Canyon Broadcasters, Inc., at above address. **Founded:** 1994. **Operating Hours:** Continuous. **ADI:** Phoenix (Kingman, Prescott), AZ. **Key Personnel:** Tom Brown, General Mgr., phone (602)234-1280, tgbrown@msn.com; Carole Stensrud, Station Mgr., kgcbcs@primenet.com; Julie Peterson, Program Dir., kgcb@primenet.com; Sam Bigler, Operations, kgcb@primenet.com. **Wattage:** 58,000. **Ad Rates:** Underwriting available.

863 KNOT-AM - 1450
116 S. Alto St. Phone: (602)445-6880
PO Box 151 Fax: (602)445-6852
Prescott, AZ 86302
E-mail: knot@mwaz.com

Format: Big Band/Nostalgia. **Networks:** ABC. **Owner:** William F. Payne, at above address, (520)445-6880, Fax: (520)445-6852. **Founded:** 1957. **Operating Hours:** 90% network; 10% local. **ADI:** Phoenix (Kingman, Prescott), AZ. **Key Personnel:** William F. Payne, Pres./Gen. Mgr.; Traci Thomas, Program Dir.; Doreen Conti, News Dir.; Tricia Williams, Traffic Mgr.; Bill Kafka, Chief Engineer; Paul Hunt, Music Dir. **Local Programs:** *Health Talk*, Debra Senn; *In Focus*, Doreen Conti. **Wattage:** 1000. **Ad Rates:** $8.50-16 for 30 seconds; $12.75-24 for 60 seconds.

864 KNOT-FM - 99.1
116 S. Alto St. Phone: (602)445-6880
PO Box 151 Fax: (602)445-4090
Prescott, AZ 86302
E-mail: knot@mwaz.com

Format: Country. **Networks:** ABC. **Owner:** William F. Payne, at above address, Fax: (520)445-6852. **Founded:** 1977. **Operating Hours:** 10% network; 90% local. **ADI:** Phoenix (Kingman, Prescott), AZ. **Key Personnel:** William F. Payne, Pres./Gen. Mgr.; Traci Thomas, Program Dir.; Doreen Conti, News Dir.; Tricia Williams, Office/Traffic Mgr.; Bill Kafka, Chief Engineer; Paul Hurt, Music Dir. **Local Programs:** *CD Concert*, Mark Vulcz. **Wattage:** 6000. **Ad Rates:** $8.50-16 for 30 seconds; $12.75-24 for 60 seconds.

865 KPPV-FM - 106.7
Box 26523 Phone: (520)775-5277
Prescott, AZ 86312 Fax: (520)775-4188
Free: (800)264-5449
E-mail: hello.kppv.com

Format: Adult Contemporary. **Networks:** AP. **Founded:** 1985. **Formerly:** KIHX (Oct. 31, 1994). **Operating Hours:** Continuous; 10% network; 90% local. **ADI:** Phoenix (Kingman, Prescott), AZ. **Key Personnel:** Sanford Cohen, President. **Wattage:** 50,000 ERP. **Ad Rates:** $14-26 per unit.

866 KUSK-TV - 7
3211 Tower Rd. Phone: (520)778-6770
Prescott, AZ 86305 Fax: (520)445-5210
E-mail: team@kusk.com

Format: Commercial TV. **Networks:** Independent. **Owner:** KUSK, Inc, at above address. **Founded:** 1982. **Operating Hours:** Continuous. **ADI:** Phoenix (Kingman, Prescott), AZ. **Key Personnel:** Richard C. Howe, Contact, rich@kusk.com; Patricia Gray, Contact, pat@kusk.com; Arnold Corella, Production Mgr. **Wattage:** 8,700. **Ad Rates:** $20-150 per unit. **URL:** http://www.kusk.com.

867 KYCA-AM - 1490
600 6th St., Box 1631 Phone: (602)445-1700
PO Box 86302
Prescott, AZ 86301

Format: News; Sports; Talk. **Networks:** CBS; Mutual Broadcasting System; Wall Street Journal Radio. **Owner:** Southwest Broadcasting Co., at above address. **Founded:** 1940. **Operating Hours:** 5:45 a.m.-midnight. **ADI:** Phoenix (Kingman, Prescott), AZ. **Key Personnel:** Lou Silverstein, General Mgr.; Julie Peters, Sales Mgr. **Wattage:** 1000.

PRESCOTT VALLEY

Yavapai Co.

868 Trail Blazer Horseback Trail Riding
4284 Gelding Dr. Phone: (520)772-9233
Prescott Valley, AZ 86314
Publisher E-mail: tblazer@northlink

Magazine for horseback trail riding on a competition or recreational level. **Founded:** 1978. **Freq:** Bimonthly. **Print Method:** Sheet fed. **Trim Size:** 8 1/2 x 11. **Cols./Page:** 3. **Key Personnel:** Susan Gibson, Editor and Publisher, phone (541)318-5505. **ISSN:** 5274-8274. **Subscription Rates:** $22 individuals; $3.95 single issue. **Remarks:** Accepts advertising. **Available Online. URL:** http://www.horsetrails.com. **Formerly:** Trail Blazer Competition Horseback Riding.
Ad Rates: BW: $1200 **Circ:** Paid 13,000
4C: $1600 Non-paid 4,000

869 KQNA-AM - 1130
PO Box 26523 Phone: (520)775-5277
Prescott Valley, AZ 86312 Fax: (520)775-4188
Free: (800)264-5449
E-mail: sanford@kpbu.com

Format: Talk; Sports; News. **Networks:** CNN Radio; AP. **Owner:** Prescott Valley Broadcasting Co., Inc., at above address. **Founded:** June 26, 1986. **Operating Hours:** Sunrise-sunset. **ADI:** Phoenix (Kingman, Prescott), AZ. **Wattage:** 1000. **URL:** http://www.kqna.com.

QUARTZSITE

LaPaz Co. (SW). 60 m NE of Yuma.

870 KBUX-FM - 94.3
16031 Camel Dr. Phone: (520)927-5111
PO Box 1
Quartzsite, AZ 85346

Format: Country; Easy Listening; Oldies. **Networks:** Independent. **Owner:** Buck Burdette, at above address. **Founded:** 1988. **Operating Hours:** Continuous; 100% local. **Key Personnel:** Buck Burdette, Contact; Maude Burdette, Sales Mgr.

Wattage: 205 ERP. **Ad Rates:** $3-7.50 for 30 seconds; $5-10 for 60 seconds.

SAFFORD†, pop. 7,010.

Graham Co. (SE). 85 m NE of Tucson. Copper.Stock, poultry, grain farms. Cotton, cattle.

871 Eastern Arizona Courier
Wick Publishing
301 E. Hwy. 70 Phone: (520)428-2560
PO Box N Fax: (520)428-5396
Safford, AZ 85548
Publication E-mail: eacourier@aepnet.com

Local newspaper. **Founded:** 1967. **Freq:** Weekly (Wed.). **Print Method:** Offset. **Cols./Page:** 6. **Col. Width:** 26 nonpareils. **Col. Depth:** 294 agate lines. **Key Personnel:** Lawrence L. Blaskey, Managing Editor; Jim Hornbeck, Editor and Publisher. **Subscription Rates:** $22 individuals. **Remarks:** Accepts advertising. **Feature Editors:** Toni Williams, *Lifestyle.*
Ad Rates: GLR: $.56 **Circ:** 8,742
BW: $1,057.80
4C: $1,302.80
SAU: $8.20

872 KATO-AM - 1230
Drawer L Phone: (520)428-1230
Safford, AZ 85548 Fax: (520)428-1311

Format: News; Talk; Sports. **Networks:** ABC. **Founded:** 1961. **Operating Hours:** 5 a.m.-midnight; 75% network, 25% local. **Key Personnel:** Jerri Matoza, General Mgr., jmatoza@eaznet.com. **Local Programs:** *Tom Armshaw* 7 a.m.-9 a.m., Tom Armshaw. **Wattage:** 1000. **Ad Rates:** $10 for 30 seconds; $15 for 60 seconds. Combined advertising rates available with KXKQ/KWRQ.

873 KCUZ-AM - 1490
301-B E. Highway 70 Phone: (520)428-0916
PO Box 1330 Fax: (520)428-7797
Safford, AZ 85548
E-mail: kfmm@eaznet.com

Format: Country; Sports; News. **Simulcasts:** KFMM. **Networks:** Satellite Music Network; Mutual Broadcasting System. **Founded:** 1969. **Operating Hours:** Continuous; 95% network, 5% local. **Key Personnel:** Mike Hallford, General Mgr.; Steve Reno, Program Dir.; Camden Smith, Sales Mgr. **Wattage:** 1000. **Ad Rates:** $4.50-10.50 for 30 seconds; $6.75-15.50 for 60 seconds. **URL:** http://www.eaznet.com/˜kfmm.

874 KFMM-FM - 99.1
PO Box 1330 Phone: (520)428-0916
Safford, AZ 85548 Fax: (520)428-7797
Free: (888)591-9910
E-mail: kfmm@eaznet.com

Format: Country; Religious; Sports; News. **Networks:** Satellite Music Network; Mutual Broadcasting System. **Founded:** 1977. **Operating Hours:** Continuous; 95% network, 5% local. **Key Personnel:** Mike Hallford, General Mgr.; Steve Reno, Program Dir.; Mike Hallford, Sales Mgr. **Local Programs:** *Eastern Arizona College Sports Broadcasts*; *Gila Outdoor Report*; *Local News from the Real Country News Room.* **Wattage:** 50,000. **Ad Rates:** $4.50-10.50 for for 30 seconds; $6.75-15.50 for 60 seconds. **URL:** http://www.eaznet.com˜kfmm.

875 KXKQ-FM - 94.1
Drawer L Phone: (520)428-4994
Safford, AZ 85546 Fax: (520)428-6818
Free: (800)566-4994

Format: Contemporary Country. **Networks:** Jones Satellite. **Founded:** 1979. **Operating Hours:** Continuous. **ADI:** Tucson, AZ. **Key Personnel:** Reed Richins, Operations Dir./Engineer, rrich@eaznet.com; Jerri Lynn Matoza, General Mgr., phone (520)428-1230, fax (520)428-1311, jmatoza@eaznet.com. **Local Programs:** *Reed Richins* 6 a.m.-9 a.m., Reed Richins. **Wattage:** 100,000. **Ad Rates:** $10-15 per unit. Combined advertising rates available with KATO-AM/KWRQ.

SAN MANUEL, pop. 4,332.

Pinal Co. (SE).

876 San Manuel Miner
PO Box 60 Phone: (520)385-2266
San Manuel, AZ 85631 Fax: (520)385-4666

Community newspaper. **Founded:** Dec. 17, 1953. **Freq:** Weekly. **Print Method:** Offset. **Trim Size:** 14 x 22. **Cols./Page:** 6. **Col. Width:** 12 picas. **Col. Depth:** 290.5 picas. **Key Personnel:** Gayles Carnes, Editor; James Carnes, Publisher. **Subscription Rates:** $21.50 individuals; $25.50 out of area. **Remarks:** Accepts advertising.
Ad Rates: GLR: $.29 **Circ:** 3,200
BW: $504
4C: $500
SAU: $5.10

SCOTTSDALE, pop. 88,364.

Maricopa Co. (C). 13 m NE of Phoenix. Tourism. Electronic and ceramic plants. Regional trade. Stock.

877 American Indian Art Magazine
American Indian Art, Inc.
7314 E. Osborn Dr. Phone: (602)994-5445
Scottsdale, AZ 85251 Fax: (602)945-9533

Journal covering all areas of Native American art. **Founded:** Nov. 1975. **Freq:** Quarterly. **Print Method:** Offset. **Trim Size:** 8 1/2 x 11. **Cols./Page:** 2. **Col. Width:** 20 picas. **Col. Depth:** 9.5 picas. **Key Personnel:** Roánne P. Goldfein, Editor; Mary G. Hamilton, Publisher; Ronda Rawlings, Advertising Mgr. **Subscription Rates:** $6 single issue. **Remarks:** Accepts advertising.
Ad Rates: BW: $1,060 **Circ:** Paid ‡16,000
4C: $1,510

878 Arizona Trends
Dandick Co.
PO Box 8508 Phone: (602)948-1799
Scottsdale, AZ 85252 Fax: (602)994-9284

Community lifestyle newspaper. **Founded:** Nov. 1982. **Freq:** Monthly. **Print Method:** Web. **Cols./Page:** 4. **Col. Width:** 14 picas. **Col. Depth:** 12 3/4 inches. **Key Personnel:** Penny Johnson, Editor; Suzanne Eder, Advertising; Renee Cohen, Advertising. **ISSN:** 0742-034X. **Subscription Rates:** $18 individuals; Free to qualified subscribers. **Remarks:** Accepts advertising.
Ad Rates: BW: $1,620 **Circ:** Controlled 32,000
4C: $1,920

879 Document Management
Pinnacle Peak Publishing Ltd.
8711 E. Pinnacle Peak Rd., No. 249 Phone: (602)585-5580
Fax: (602)585-7417
Scottsdale, AZ 85255
Publication E-mail: docmanage@aol.com

Magazine on productive use of document management. **Subtitle:** The Magazine on Information Assets for Top 1000 Company Decision Makers. **Founded:** Sept. 1991. **Freq:** Bimonthly. **Print Method:** 4-C Webb offset. **Trim Size:** 8 3/8 x 10 7/8. **Cols./Page:** 3. **Col. Width:** 2 1/4 inches. **Col. Depth:** 9 1/2 inches. **Key Personnel:** Richard N. Stover, Editor and Publisher; Carolyn Sherris, Circulation Mgr., phone (602)975-2880, fax (602)975-2879. **ISSN:** 1071-8567. **Subscription Rates:** $30 U.S.; $45 Canada and Mexico; $70 other countries. **Remarks:** Accepts advertising. **Available Online. URL:** http://www.docmanage.com. **Formerly:** Document Management and Windows Imaging.
Ad Rates: BW: $3,679 **Circ:** Controlled ⊕45,000
4C: $4,929

880 Frank Lloyd Wright Quarterly
Wright Foundation
Taliesin West Phone: (602)860-2700
Cactus Rd. & 114th St. Fax: (602)451-8989
Scottsdale, AZ 85261-4430
Publisher E-mail: fllwfdn@franklloydwright.org

Scholarly magazine covering the life and work of architect Frank Lloyd Wright. **Founded:** 1990. **Freq:** Quarterly. **Print Method:** Offset. **Trim Size:** 8 1/2 x 11. **Cols./Page:** 3. **Key Personnel:** Suzette Lucas, Editorial Dir. **Subscription Rates:** Included in membership; $40 individuals; $20 institutions; $5 single issue. **Remarks:** Advertising not accepted.
Circ: Controlled 10,000

881 The Lucid Stone
PO Box 940
Scottsdale, AZ 85252-0940

Literary and poetry journal. **Founded:** Feb. 1994. **Freq:** Quarterly. **Print Method:** Offset. **Trim Size:** 7 x 8 1/2. **Cols./Page:** 1. **Key Personnel:** Pauline Mounsey, Contact, paulinem@aztec.asu.edu. **ISSN:** 1079-896X. **Subscription Rates:** $16 individuals; $24 out of country; $6 single issue. **Remarks:** Advertising not accepted.
Circ: Paid 125

882 National Horseman
The National Horseman
16101 N. 82nd St., Ste. 10 Phone: (602)922-5202
Scottsdale, AZ 85260 Fax: (602)922-5212

Magazine featuring horse breeding, training, and showing. **Founded:** 1865. **Freq:** Monthly 2 extra issues in July & August. **Print Method:** Offset. **Trim Size:** 8 1/2 x 11. **Cols./Page:** 3. **Col. Width:** 28 nonpareils. **Col. Depth:** 134 agate lines. **Key Personnel:** Karen Owens, Publisher. **ISSN:** 0027-9455. **Subscription Rates:** $48 individuals; $76 two years; $98 three years; $5.95 single issue plus $3 shipping. **Remarks:** Advertising accepted; rates available upon request.
Circ: Paid 3,500
Non-paid 1,000

883 Scottsdale Progress Tribune
Thomson Newspapers
7525 E. Camelback Rd. Phone: (602)898-6500
PO Box 1150 Fax: (602)970-2360
Scottsdale, AZ 85252-1150
Community newspaper. **Founded:** 1949. **Freq:** Daily (morn.). **Print Method:** Offset. **Cols./Page:** 6. **Col. Width:** 26 nonpareils. **Col. Depth:** 294 agate lines. **Key Personnel:** Karen Wittmer, Publisher; Hal Dekeyser, Editor. **Subscription Rates:** $20 individuals. **Remarks:** Accepts advertising. **Alt. Formats:** Microform. **Formerly:** Scottsdale Progress (1993); Scottsdale Tribune (Dec. 1996); Scottsdale Daily Progress.
Ad Rates: GLR: $1.05 **Circ:** Mon.-Sat. 18,387
BW: $2,124.36 Sun. 18,429
4C: $2,761.36
PCI: $16.86

KXAM-AM - See Mesa

SEDONA, pop. 6,500.

Coconino Co. (C) 102 m N. of Phoenix. Residential.

884 Sedona Red Rock News
PO Box 619 Phone: (520)282-7795
Sedona, AZ 86339 Fax: (520)282-6011

Local newspaper. **Founded:** Oct. 1963. **Freq:** Semiweekly (Wed. and Fri.). **Print Method:** Offset. **Cols./Page:** 6. **Col. Width:** 2 1/10 inches. **Col. Depth:** 21 inches. **Key Personnel:** Robert B. Larson, Publisher, bob1@redrocknews.com; Thomas L. Brossart, Managing Editor, tomb@redrocknews.com. **USPS:** 458-460. **Subscription Rates:** $36 individuals. **Remarks:** Accepts advertising. **Formerly:** Red Rock News (Jan. 1988).
Ad Rates: GLR: $10.60 **Circ:** Paid ❑6,827
BW: $1,335.60 Free ❑85
4C: $1,625.60
SAU: $10.60
PCI: $10.60

885 Swimming Technique
Sports Publications, Inc.
PO Box 2025 Phone: (520)282-4799
Sedona, AZ 86339-2205 Fax: (520)282-4697
Publication E-mail: swimworld@aol.com

Magazine on the coaching and administration of swimming. **Subtitle:** The Journal for Swim Coaches Everywhere. **Founded:** 1967. **Freq:** Quarterly. **Print Method:** Sheetfed Offset. **Trim Size:** 8 3/8 x 10 7/8. **Cols./Page:** 2 and 3. **Col. Width:** 40 and 26 nonpareils. **Col. Depth:** 140 agate lines. **Key Personnel:** Phillip Whitten, Editor-in-Chief; Richard Deal, Publisher; Brent Rutemiller, Advertising Dir., phone (310)607-9956, fax (310)607-9963; Bob Ingram, Senior Editor; Jonty Skinner, Technical Editor. **ISSN:** 0039-7415. **Subscription Rates:** $13 individuals; $2.76 single issue. **Remarks:** Accepts advertising.
Ad Rates: BW: $860 **Circ:** ‡8,133
4C: $1,550

886 Swimming World and Junior Swimmer
Sports Publications, Inc.
PO Box 2025 Phone: (520)282-4779
Sedona, AZ 86339-2025 Fax: (520)282-4697
Publication E-mail: swimworld@aol.com; swiminfo.com

Magazine on competitive swimming, diving and water polo. **Founded:** 1960. **Freq:** Monthly. **Print Method:** Offset. **Trim Size:** 8 1/4 x 10 3/4. **Cols./Page:** 2 and 3. **Col. Width:** 42 and 26 nonpareils. **Col. Depth:** 140 agate lines. **Key Personnel:** Bob Ingram, Senior Editor; Richard Deal, Publisher; Toni Blake, Ad.Rep., spiblake@aol.com; Phillip Whitten, Editor-in-Chief; Brent Rutemiller, Ad. Rep. **ISSN:** 0039-7431. **Subscription Rates:** $29.95 individuals; $2.95 single issue. **Remarks:** Accepts advertising. **URL:** http://www.swiminfo.com.
Ad Rates: BW: $1,875 **Circ:** ‡33,000
4C: $2,730

887 KAZM-AM - 780
PO Box 1525 Phone: (520)282-4154
Sedona, AZ 86339 Fax: (520)282-2230

Format: Talk; News; Sports; Contemporary Hit Radio (CHR). **Networks:** Independent. **Owner:** Tabback Broadcasting Co., at above address. **Founded:** 1974. **Operating Hours:** Continuous; 100% local. **ADI:** Phoenix (Kingman, Prescott), AZ. **Key Personnel:** Joseph Tabback, Owner; Terry Tabback, Music Dir.; Brad Miller, Program Dir.; Tom Tabback, General Mgr.

Local Programs: *Dynamic Duo*, Tom Tabback, (520)282-4154, Fax (520)282-2230; *Dynamic Duo*, Tom Tabback, (520)282-4154. **Wattage:** 5000 day; 250 night. **Ad Rates:** $26-33 for 30 seconds; $35-41 for 60 seconds.

888 Sedona Cablevision
65 Coffee Pot Dr. Phone: (520)282-7711
Sedona, AZ 86336 Fax: (520)282-6336

Formerly: Time Warner Cable. **Key Personnel:** Larry Douglas, General Mgr.; Bess Driver, Business Mgr.; Joe Scrum, Chief Engineer. **Cities Served:** Sedona, Village of Oak Creek, AZ: subscribing households 5,671; 41 channels; 2 community access channels; 168 hours per week community access programming.

SHOW LOW, pop. 4,298.

Navajo Co. (NE). 45 m S of Holbrook. Lumber mill. Timber. Agriculture. Cattle.

889 KVWM-AM - 970
PO Box 970 Phone: (520)537-2345
Show Low, AZ 85901 Fax: (520)537-3991

Format: Adult Contemporary. **Owner:** Dorothy L. Woodworth, PO Box 970, Show Low, AZ 85901. **Founded:** 1957. **Operating Hours:** 6 a.m. to 10 p.m. **Key Personnel:** Gary Woodworth, General Mgr., phone (520)537-2345, fax (520)537-3991; Michael Woodworth, Sales Mgr., phone (520)537-2345, fax (520)537-3991. **Wattage:** 5,000. **Ad Rates:** Advertising accepted; rates available upon request.

890 KVWM-FM - 93.5
PO Box 970 Phone: (520)537-2345
Show Low, AZ 85901 Fax: (520)537-3991

Format: Adult Contemporary. **Founded:** 1964. **Operating Hours:** 6 a.m. - 10 p.m. **Key Personnel:** Gary S. Woodworth, General Mgr.; Michael Woodworth, Sales Mgr./Chief Engineer. **Local Programs:** *Local/Regional News*, Gary S. Woodworth. **Wattage:** 25,000.

SIERRA VISTA, pop. 25,968.

Cochise Co. (SE). 70 m SE of Tucson. Tourism. Electronic devices manufactured. Ranching.

891 The Huachuca Scout
Five Star Publishing
PO Box 1119 Phone: (520)458-3340
Sierra Vista, AZ 85636 Fax: (520)458-9338
Publisher E-mail: fivestr@cziz.com

Community military newspaper for Ft. Huachuca. **Founded:** 1954. **Freq:** Weekly (Thurs.). **Print Method:** Offset. **Trim Size:** 10 1/4 x 13. **Cols./Page:** 6. **Col. Width:** 13 inches. **Col. Depth:** 240 agate lines. **Key Personnel:** Mark Evans, Sales Mgr. **USPS:** 684-730. **Subscription Rates:** Free; $30 Postage and Handling Fee. **Remarks:** Accepts advertising.
Ad Rates: BW: $620.10 **Circ:** 13,500
4C: $500
PCI: $7.95

892 The Mountain View News
Five Star Publishing
PO Box 1119 Phone: (520)458-3340
Sierra Vista, AZ 85636 Fax: (520)458-9338
Publisher E-mail: fivestr@cziz.com

Community newspaper/Shopping guide. **Founded:** 1975. **Freq:** Weekly (Fri.). **Print Method:** Offset. **Trim Size:** 10 1/4 x 16. **Cols./Page:** 6. **Col. Width:** 20 nonpareils. **Col. Depth:** 224 agate lines. **Key Personnel:** Barry Bishop, Publisher; Mark Evans, Advertising Mgr. **Subscription Rates:** $24 individuals. **Remarks:** Accepts advertising. **Formerly:** The News Paper.
Ad Rates: GLR: $8.18 **Circ:** Free ‡22,000
BW: $667
4C: $1,050
PCI: $6.95

893 Sierra Vista Herald
102 Fab Ave. Phone: (520)458-9440
Sierra Vista, AZ 85635 Fax: (520)459-0120
Publication E-mail: svhads@c2i2.com
Publisher E-mail: svhnews@c2i2.com

General newspaper. **Founded:** 1955. **Freq:** Daily (eve.), Sunday (morn.) Mon.-Fri. (eve.), Sunday (morn.). **Print Method:** Offset. **Cols./Page:** 6. **Col. Width:** 2 1/16 inches. **Col. Depth:** 21 1/2 inches. **Key Personnel:** John Moeur, Managing Editor; Walter M. Wick, Publisher; Robert J. Wick, Publisher; Philip Vega, General Mgr.; Dennis Benth, Advertising Mgr. **Subscription Rates:** $105.60 individuals.
Ad Rates: 4C: $190.00 **Circ:** Mon.-Fri. ❑**10,876**
SAU: $9.75 Tues. ❑**8,080**
PCI: $9.75 Sun. ❑**12,458**

894 KNXN-AM - 1470
680 Avenida del Sol Phone: (602)459-1470
Sierra Vista, AZ 85635 Fax: (602)459-5418
E-mail: mix1470@theriver.com

Format: Full Service; News; Talk. **Networks:** NBC; Sun Radio; Southern Farm. **Owner:** Blue Horizon Broadcasting, at above address. **Founded:** 1980. **Formerly:** KSVA-AM; KMFI-AM. **Operating Hours:** 24 hrs.; 100% network. **Key Personnel:** William Yarbrough, Owner; Alix Orton, Station Mgr. **Wattage:** 2500. **Ad Rates:** $5-7 for 30 seconds; $8-11 for 60 seconds.

895 KTAN-AM - 1420
PO Box 2770 Phone: (520)458-4313
Sierra Vista, AZ 85636-2770 Fax: (520)458-4317
E-mail: ktan@c2i2.com

Format: News; Talk; Sports. **Networks:** AP. **Owner:** DB Broadcasting, Inc., at above address. **Founded:** 1958. **Formerly:** KTAN-AM; KLTW-AM. **Operating Hours:** Continuous; 90% network, 10% local. **ADI:** Tucson, AZ. **Key Personnel:** Paul Orlando, General Mgr./Sales Mgr. **Local Programs:** *Radio Buena*, Oscar Flures; *Slim Harper Show*, Slim Harper; *Spectrum*, Darryl Wilson. **Wattage:** 1500. **Ad Rates:** Advertising accepted; rates available upon request. Combined advertising rates available with KZMK, KWCD.

896 KWCD-FM - 92.3
PO Box 2770 Phone: (602)458-4313
Sierra Vista, AZ 85636-2770 Fax: (602)458-4317
E-mail: kwcd@c2i2.com

Format: Contemporary Country. **Networks:** Jones Satellite. **Owner:** DB Broadcasting, LLC., at above address. **Founded:** 1983. **Formerly:** KZMK-FM (1993). **Operating Hours:** Continuous. **Key Personnel:** Paul Orlando, General and Sales Mgr. **Wattage:** 3000. **Ad Rates:** Combined advertising rates available with KZMK, KTAN.

897 KWRB-FM - 90.9
PO Box 1086 Phone: (520)452-8022
Sierra Vista, AZ 85636 Fax: (520)452-0927
E-mail: kwrb909@juno.com

Format: Educational. **Networks:** Moody Broadcasting. **Owner:** World Radio Network, Inc., PO Box 3333, McAllen, TX 78502. **Operating Hours:** Continuous. **Key Personnel:** Brayton Back, General Mgr.; Robert Rice, Chief Engineer. **Local Programs:** *Word For Today*, James Hoston; *Pastor's Corner*, Brayton Back; *Strength For Today*, Pat Laszovich. **Ad Rates:** Noncommercial.

898 KZMK-FM - 100.9
PO Box 2770 Phone: (520)458-4313
Sierra Vista, AZ 85636 Fax: (520)458-4317
E-mail: k101@212.com

Format: Adult Contemporary. **Networks:** ABC. **Founded:** 1973. **Formerly:** KTAZ-FM (1990); KFFN-FM (Sept. 1993). **Operating Hours:** Continuous. **Key Personnel:** Paul Orlando, General Mgr./Sales Mgr. **Wattage:** 3000. **Ad Rates:** Advertising accepted; rates available upon request. Combined advertising rates available with KWCD-FM, KTAN-AM.

SOLOMON

899 Wild West News
PO Box 216 Phone: (520)428-0098
Solomon, AZ 85551
Publisher E-mail: wildwn@wildwestnews.com

Community newspaper. **Founded:** Jan. 1990. **Freq:** Biweekly. **Print Method:** Web offset. **Cols./Page:** 4. **Col. Width:** 2.47 inches. **Col. Depth:** 15 1/2 inches. **Key Personnel:** Chuck Rosa III, Contact. **ISSN:** 1808-8035. **Subscription Rates:** $25 individuals; $30 out of state; $.50 single issue. **Remarks:** Accepts advertising. **Online:** EazNet. **URL:** http://www.wildwestnews.com.
Ad Rates: BW: $200 **Circ:** Paid 3,300
PCI: $3.75

SPRINGERVILLE

900 KQAZ-FM - 101.7
1367 E. Main Phone: (520)333-2080
PO Box 1069 Fax: (520)333-2081
Springerville, AZ 85938

Format: Adult Contemporary. **Networks:** Jones Satellite; CNN Radio. **Founded:** 1984. **Operating Hours:** 24 hrs.; 85% network, 15% local. **Key Personnel:** Ted Barbone, Pres./General Manager; Pam Schoolcraft, Station Mgr. **Wattage:** 3000. **Ad Rates:** $9 for 30 seconds; $11 for 60 seconds.

901 KRVZ-AM - 1400
1367 E. Main Phone: (520)333-2080
P.O. Box 1069 Fax: (520)333-2081
Springerville, AZ 85938

Format: Country. **Networks:** Jones Satellite; CNN Radio. **Owner:** Double "Z" Enterprises, Inc., at above address. **Founded:** 1982. **Operating Hours:** 24 hrs.; 85% network, 15% local. **Key Personnel:** Ted Barbone, President/General Manager; Pam Schoolcraft, Station Mgr. **Wattage:** 1000. **Ad Rates:** $9 for 30 seconds; $11 for 60 seconds.

SUN CITY, pop. 58,000.

Maricopa Co. (C). 3 m W of Peoria. Retirement Community.

902 Daily News-Sun
News-Sun, Inc.
10102 Santa Fe Dr. Phone: (602)977-8351
PO Box 1779 Fax: (602)876-3698
Sun City, AZ 85372
General newspaper. **Founded:** 1957. **Freq:** Daily (eve.) and Sat. (morn.). **Print Method:** Offset. **Cols./Page:** 6. **Col. Width:** 12 picas. **Col. Depth:** 21 1/2 inches. **Key Personnel:** Maryanne Leyshon, Editor; Jim Kehole, Advertising Dir.; Don Leyshon, Operations Dir.; Sam Gett, Publisher. **Subscription Rates:** $92 individuals. **Remarks:** Accepts advertising.
Ad Rates: BW: $1,598.31 **Circ:** Mon.-Sat. 20,516
4C: $1,968.31
PCI: $12.39

Paradise Valley Independent - See Paradise Valley

903 Sun City Independent
Independent Newspapers, Inc.
10327 W. Coggins Dr. Fax: (602)974-6004
Sun City, AZ 85351
Publisher E-mail: suncityind@aol.com

Community newspaper. **Founded:** 1960. **Freq:** Weekly (Wed.). **Print Method:** Offset. **Trim Size:** 13 x 21. **Cols./Page:** 6. **Col. Width:** 2 1/16 inches. **Col. Depth:** 21 1/2 inches. **Key Personnel:** Bret McKeand, Editor and Publisher; Bill Siewert, Advertising Mgr.; Jeanne Cummings, Major Accounts Exec. **Subscription Rates:** Free; $14 by mail. **Remarks:** Accepts advertising.
Ad Rates: BW: $2,131.08 **Circ:** Combined 23,373
SAU: $17.36

SUPERIOR, pop. 4,600.

Pinal Co. (SC). 50 m SE of Phoenix.

904 Superior Sun
467 Main St. Phone: (520)689-2436
Superior, AZ 85273 Fax: (520)363-9663

Community newspaper. **Founded:** 1924. **Freq:** Weekly (Wed.). **Print Method:** Offset. **Cols./Page:** 6. **Col. Width:** 12 nonpareils. **Col. Depth:** 294 agate lines. **Key Personnel:** Gayle Carnes, Editor; James Carnes, Publisher. **Subscription Rates:** $25.50 individuals; $30.50 out of area.
Ad Rates: PCI: $4.80 **Circ:** ‡1,300

TEMPE, pop. 106,743.

Maricopa Co. (SC). 10 m SE of Phoenix. Arizona State University. Electronic plants; semi conductor plants; garment factories. Diversified farming. Alfalfa, wheat, cotton, citrus fruit.

905 Arizona Pennysaver
Arizona Pennysaver, L.L.C.
250 W. 1st St. Phone: (602)968-5700
Tempe, AZ 85282 Fax: (602)968-8694
Publication E-mail: psaver@aol.com

Shopper, published in 32 zoned editions. **Founded:** 1973. **Freq:** Weekly (Wed.). **Print Method:** Offset. **Trim Size:** 11 x 11 1/2. **Cols./Page:** 4. **Col. Width:** 14.5 picas. **Col. Depth:** 11 inches. **Key Personnel:** Steve Ferber, Publisher, successm@aol.com; Ed Marks, Publisher. **Subscription Rates:** Free. **Remarks:** Accepts advertising.
Ad Rates: PCI: $11.65 **Circ:** Free 604,000

906 Bilingual Review/Revista Bilingue
Bilingual Review/Press
Hispanic Research Center Phone: (602)965-3867
Arizona State University Fax: (602)965-8309
PO Box 872702
Tempe, AZ 85287-2702
Publisher E-mail: kvhbrp@asu.edu

Scholarly journal covering literature, poetry and reviews in Spanish and English. **Founded:** 1974. **Freq:** Triennial. **Key Personnel:** Karen VanHooft, Managing Editor, kvhbrp@asu.edu; Barbara Firoozye, Assoc. Editor; Karen Akins, Marketing. **ISSN:** 0094-5366. **Subscription Rates:** $19

individuals; $30 institutions; $7 single issue. **Remarks:** Accepts advertising.
Circ: (Not Reported)

907 The Condor
Cooper Ornithological Society
Zoology Dept. Phone: (602)965-9483
Arizona State University Fax: (602)965-3209
Tempe, AZ 85287-1501
Major ornithological journal with international circulation. **Subtitle:** A Journal of Avian Biology. **Founded:** 1898. **Freq:** Quarterly. **Print Method:** Offset. **Trim Size:** 7 3/4 x 10. **Cols./Page:** 2. **Col. Width:** 34 nonpareils. **Col. Depth:** 81 agate lines. **Key Personnel:** Glenn E. Walsberg, Editor and Administration. **ISSN:** 0010-5422. **Subscription Rates:** $30 individuals. **Remarks:** Accepts advertising.
Ad Rates: BW: $325 **Circ:** ‡3,300

908 Ecological Monographs
Ecological Society of America
Center for Environmental Studies Phone: (602)965-3000
Arizona State University
Tempe, AZ 85287-3211
Journal promoting ecological research and the development of the utilities which may be served by ecological principles. **Founded:** 1931. **Freq:** Quarterly. **Print Method:** Offset. **Cols./Page:** 2. **Col. Width:** 36 nonpareils. **Col. Depth:** 108 agate lines. **Key Personnel:** Lee N. Miller, Editor. **ISSN:** 0012-9615. **Subscription Rates:** $32 individuals; $45 institutions.
Circ: 4,200

909 Education and Training in Mental Retardation and Developmental Disabilities
Council for Exceptional Children
Arizona State University Phone: (602)965-1449
Special Education Program Fax: (602)965-0223
Tempe, AZ 85287-2011
Journal covering theory and research in eductation of individuals with mental retardation and/or developmental disabilities. **Founded:** 1966. **Freq:** Quarterly. **Trim Size:** 10 x 7. **Cols./Page:** 2. **Col. Width:** 15 inches. **Key Personnel:** Stanley H. Zucker, Editor. **ISSN:** 0013-1237. **Subscription Rates:** $30 individuals; $34 other countries; $75 institutions; $79.50 institutions, other countries. **Remarks:** Accepts advertising. **Formerly:** Education and Training of the Mentally Retarded (Dec. 1986).
Ad Rates: BW: $500 **Circ:** ‡8,500

910 General Music Today
Music Educators National Conference
Arizona State University
School of Music
Tempe, AZ 85287
Publisher E-mail: mbmenc@vais.net

Professional journal covering general music from early childhood through high school for teachers. **Freq:** 3/year. **Key Personnel:** Dr. Sandra Stauffer, Contact. **Remarks:** Advertising not accepted.
Circ: (Not Reported)

911 German Studies Review
German Studies Association
Box 973204
Tempe, AZ 85287-3204

Scholarly journal covering research in German history, literature, politics, and related fields. **Founded:** Feb. 1978. **Freq:** Quarterly. **Key Personnel:** Gerald R. Kleinfeld, Ph.D., Editor, kleinfeld@asu.edu. **Subscription Rates:** $30 individuals; $15 single issue. **Remarks:** Accepts advertising.
Ad Rates: BW: $125 **Circ:** Combined 2,050

912 International Journal of Aging and Human Development
Baywood Publishing Co., Inc.
Dr. Robert Kastenbaum Phone: (602)965-6650
Box 871205 Fax: (602)965-4291
Arizona State University
Tempe, AZ 85287-1205
Publisher E-mail: baywood@baywood.com

Adult development and aging featuring original research theory, critial reviews. **Founded:** 1970. **Freq:** 8/year. **Print Method:** Offset. **Trim Size:** 6 x 9. **Cols./Page:** 1. **Col. Width:** 4 1/2 inches. **Col. Depth:** 7 1/2 inches. **Key Personnel:** Robert J. Kastenbaum, Editor; Stuart Cohen, Publisher; Lorna Roher, Contact; S. Edwards, Circulation Mgr.; Jon Henrdicks, Ph.D, Associate. **ISSN:** 0091-4150. **Subscription Rates:** $54 Canada 2 volume group: 8 issues ANN; $174 institutions; $174 Industry, U.S. & Canada; $183 Industry, other countries; $72 other countries. **Remarks:** Advertising not accepted.
Circ: (Not Reported)

913 International Journal of Purchasing & Materials Management
National Association of Purchasing Management
2055 E. Centennial Circle Phone: (602)752-6276
PO Box 22160 Fax: (602)752-7890
Tempe, AZ 85285-2160
Free: (800)888-6276

Academic journal covering purchasing and supply management. **Founded:** 1965. **Freq:** Quarterly. **Print Method:** Offset. **Trim Size:** 8 1/2 x 11. **Cols./Page:** 2. **Col. Width:** 41 nonpareils. **Col. Depth:** 115 agate lines. **Key Personnel:** Phil Carter, D.B.A., Editor, pcarter@napm.org; Liz O'Neall, Business Mgr., loneall@napm.org; Tracy Motlok, Production Editor, tmotlok@napm.org. **ISSN:** 0094-8594. **Subscription Rates:** $49 domestic; $59 international. **Remarks:** Advertising not accepted. **URL:** www.napm.org. **Formerly:** Journal of Purchasing & Materials Management.
Circ: ‡3,000

914 Java Magazine
119 E. 7th St., Ste. 2 Phone: (602)966-6352
Tempe, AZ 85281 Fax: (602)967-0168
Publication E-mail: javamag@aol.com

Consumer magazine covering alternative arts and culture. **Subtitle:** Art . Ideas . Tast . Phx Culture. **Founded:** June 1994. **Freq:** Monthly. **Print Method:** Web offset. **Trim Size:** 10 x 10 3/4. **Key Personnel:** Robert Sintinery, EDC; Jim Nissen, Art Dir. **Subscription Rates:** $24 individuals. **Remarks:** Accepts advertising.
Ad Rates: BW: $690 **Circ:** Controlled 27,000
4C: $1,175

915 Journal of High Technology Management Research
Elseiver
Dept. of Management Phone: (602)965-3220
Arizona State University
Tempe, AZ 85287
Publication E-mail: 102062.2525@compuserve.com; virginia.gallegos@asu.edu
Publisher E-mail: fcentres@gpu.stv.ualberta.ca

Scholarly journal. **Founded:** 1990. **Freq:** Semiannual. **Key Personnel:** Luis R. Gomez, Editor, phone (606)965-8221, fax (602)965-8314, luis.gomez-mejia@isu.edu; Michael Lawless, Editor. **ISSN:** 1047-8310. **Subscription Rates:** $80 individuals; $180 institutions. **Remarks:** Advertising not accepted.
Circ: (Not Reported)

916 Journal of Quality Management
Elsevier Science Inc.
Dept. of Management Phone: (602)965-6445
Arizona State University Fax: (602)965-8314
Tempe, AZ 85287-4006
Publisher E-mail: usinfo@elsevier.com

Scholarly journal emphasizing management in quality organizational environments. **Subtitle:** Journal of Management Related Research, Theory Development, and Applications. **Founded:** 1996. **Freq:** Semiannual. **Trim Size:** 10 x 6 3/4. **Key Personnel:** Robert L. Cardy, Editor, robert.cardy@asu.edu. **ISSN:** 1084-8568. **Subscription Rates:** $95 individuals; $195 institutions; $215 institutions in Canada; $235 institutions other countries. **Remarks:** Advertising not accepted.
Circ: (Not Reported)

917 Jurimetrics
American Bar Association
College of Law Phone: (602)727-6523
Arizona State University Fax: (602)965-2427
PO Box 877906
Tempe, AZ 85287-7906
Publication E-mail: jurimetrics@adv.edu; jurimetrics@asu.edu

Legal journal. **Subtitle:** The Journal of Law, Science and Technology. **Founded:** 1959. **Freq:** Quarterly. **Print Method:** Offset. **Trim Size:** 6 x 9. **Cols./Page:** 1. **Col. Width:** 26 picas. **Col. Depth:** 43.5 picas. **Key Personnel:** Gail K. Geer, Managing Editor, phone (602)727-6523, fax (602)965-2427, gail.geer@asu.edu. **ISSN:** 0022-6793. **Subscription Rates:** $34 individuals; $38 other countries; $11 single issue; $12 single issue other countries. **Remarks:** Advertising not accepted. **Online:** Westlaw; LEXIS-NEXIS. **URL:** http://www.law.asu.edu/jurimetrics. **Formerly:** Jurimetrics Journal.
Circ: 5,800

918 KAET Magazine
Arizona State University
PO Box 871405 Phone: (602)965-3506
Tempe, AZ 85287-1405 Fax: (602)965-1000
Publication E-mail: kaet@asu.edu

Program guide. **Subtitle:** Channel Eight's Program Guide. **Founded:** 1975. **Freq:** Monthly except July. **Print Method:** Web offset. **Trim Size:** 5 3/8 x 8 1/4. **Cols./Page:** 2. **Col. Width:** 7 3/8 inches. **Col. Depth:** 2 1/8 inches. **Key Personnel:** Sondra Mesnik, Editor, sondra.mesnik@asu.edu. **ISSN:** 1045-5744. **Subscription Rates:** Free to qualified subscribers. **Remarks:** Accepts advertising.
Ad Rates: BW: $1,350 **Circ:** Controlled ‡55,000
4C: $2,100

919 OMEGA-Journal of Death and Dying
Baywood Publishing Co., Inc.
Dr. Robert Kastenbaum Phone: (602)965-6650
Box 871205 Fax: (602)965-4291
Arizona State University
Tempe, AZ 85287-1205
Publisher E-mail: baywood@baywood.com

Journal provides a psychological study of dying, death, bereavement, suicide, and other lethal behaviors. **Founded:** 1969. **Freq:** 8/year. **Print Method:** Offset. **Trim Size:** 6 x 9. **Cols./Page:** 1. **Col. Width:** 4 1/2 inches. **Col. Depth:** 7 1/2 inches. **Key Personnel:** Robert J. Kastenbaum, Ph.D., Editor, rkastenassistantimap2.asu.edu; Stuart Cohen, Publisher; Lorna Roher, Advertising Mgr.; S. Edwards, Circulation Mgr.; Kenneth J. Doka. **ISSN:** 0030-2228. **Subscription Rates:** $54 U.S. and Canada 2 volumes, 8 issues ANN; $174 institutions; $174 Industry; $183.70 Industry, other countries. **Remarks:** Advertising not accepted.
Circ: (Not Reported)

920 Pool Dust
PO Box 419
Tempe, AZ 85280-0419

Magazine covering skateboarding and music. **Founded:** Dec. 1989. **Freq:** Irregular. **Print Method:** Offset. **Trim Size:** 8 x 10 1/2. **Key Personnel:** Chris Lundry, Editor, lundry@asu.edu. **Subscription Rates:** $2 single issue. **Remarks:** Accepts advertising.
Ad Rates: BW: $100 **Circ:** Non-paid ‡5,000

921 Professional Speaker
National Speakers Association
1500 S. Priest Dr. Phone: (602)968-2552
Tempe, AZ 85281 Fax: (602)968-0911
Publication E-mail: cecile@nsaspeaker.org
Publisher E-mail: information@nsaspeaker.org

Trade magazine covering news and events in the speaking industry. **Freq:** Monthly. **Trim Size:** 8 1/2 X 11. **Key Personnel:** M. Cecile Blaine, Editor; Bill Van Nimwegen, Graphics Designer. **ISSN:** 1076-9838. **Subscription Rates:** $49 individuals; $5.50 single issue. **Remarks:** Accepts advertising. **URL:** http://www.nsaspeaker.org.
Ad Rates: BW: $860 **Circ:** Controlled ⊕4,200
4C: $1,350

922 Psychology of Women Quarterly
Cambridge University Press
Arizona State University Phone: (602)965-0380
Tempe, AZ 85287-1109 Fax: (602)965-8544
Publication E-mail: journals_ marketing@cup.org

Psychology journal. **Founded:** 1976. **Freq:** Quarterly. **Print Method:** Offset. **Trim Size:** 6 x 9. **Cols./Page:** 1. **Key Personnel:** Judith Worell, Editor; Michelle Alumkal, Advertising Mgr. **ISSN:** 0361-6843. **Subscription Rates:** $118 institutions; $44 individuals; $30 single issue. **Remarks:** Accepts advertising.
Ad Rates: BW: $550 **Circ:** Paid ‡4437
4C: $1950 Non-paid ‡75

923 Purchasing Today
NAPM
PO Box 22160 Phone: (602)752-6276
Tempe, AZ 85285-2160 Fax: (602)752-7890
Free: (800)888-6276

Trade magazine for purchasing and supply managers. **Founded:** Oct. 1, 1990. **Freq:** Monthly. **Print Method:** Web offset. **Trim Size:** 8 3/8 x 10 7/8. **Cols./Page:** 3. **Col. Width:** 13 1/2 picas. **Col. Depth:** 57 picas. **Key Personnel:** Julie Murphree, Editor, jmurphree@napm.org; Liz O'Neall, Mgr. Communication, lloneell@napm.org; Jolene Gully, Advertising Mgr., jgully@napm.org. **ISSN:** 1086-5853. **Subscription Rates:** $24 university and public libraries. **Remarks:** Accepts advertising. **URL:** napm.org. **Formerly:** NAPM Insights.
Ad Rates: BW: $3,400 **Circ:** Paid ⊕42,000
4C: $4,425 Non-paid ⊕1,800

924 Stage of the Art
American Alliance for Theater & Education
Theatre Department Phone: (602)965-6064
Arizona State University Fax: (602)965-5351
Tempe, AZ 85287-2002
Publisher E-mail: aateinfo@asuvm.inre.asu.edu

Magazine for theatre artists and educators serving young people. **Freq:** Quarterly. **Key Personnel:** Lorenzo Garcia, Editor. **ISSN:** 1080-7268. **Subscription Rates:** $28 individu-

als; $40 out of country; $7.50 single issue. **Remarks:** Accepts advertising.
Circ: (Not Reported)

925 State Press
Arizona State University
PO Box 871405 Phone: (602)965-3506
Tempe, AZ 85287-1405 Fax: (602)965-1000
Publication E-mail: idjxe@asuvm.inre.asu.edu; krw2714@imat2.asu.edu

Collegiate newspaper (tabloid) published by the students of Arizona State University. **Founded:** 1890. **Freq:** Daily (morn.). **Print Method:** Offset. **Trim Size:** 10 5/16 x 16. **Cols./Page:** 6. **Col. Width:** 19 nonpareils. **Col. Depth:** 224 agate lines. **Key Personnel:** Brian Anderson, Editor; Jackie Eldridge, Advertising Mgr.; Bruce Itule, Advisor. **Subscription Rates:** $73 individuals; $143 by mail 1st class. **Remarks:** Accepts advertising. **URL:** http://news.vpsa.asu.edu. **Alt. Formats:** Braille.
Ad Rates: BW: $993.60 **Circ:** Free ‡18,000
4C: $1,443.60
PCI: $10.35

926 SWEAT Magazine
SWEAT Marketing
736 E. Loyala Dr. Fax: (602)968-3555
Tempe, AZ 85282
Publication E-mail: westwoman@aol.com
Publisher E-mail: sweatmag@is.netcom.com

Tabloid magazine format. Arizona's premiere sports, wellness, fitness and outdoor publication. **Founded:** Dec. 1991. **Freq:** Monthly. **Trim Size:** 10 3/4 x 13 1/4. **Cols./Page:** 4. **Col. Width:** 2 5/16 inches. **Key Personnel:** Susan Berliner, Publisher; Joan Westlake, Editor, fax (602)968-3555. **Subscription Rates:** $15. **Remarks:** Accepts advertising. **URL:** http://www.sweatmagazine.com.
Ad Rates: BW: $1,258 **Circ:** Free 40,000
4C: $1,708 Paid 100

927 Tempe Daily News Tribune
Thomson Newspapers
51 W. 3rd St., Ste. 106 Phone: (602)898-5682
Tempe, AZ 85281 Fax: (602)968-8030

General newspaper. **Founded:** 1887. **Freq:** Mon.-Sun. (morn.). **Print Method:** Offset. **Trim Size:** 13 3/4 x 22. **Cols./Page:** 6. **Col. Width:** 2 1/4 inches. **Col. Depth:** 21 inches. **Key Personnel:** Jeff Bruce, Editor. **Subscription Rates:** $96 individuals. **Remarks:** Accepts advertising.
Ad Rates: GLR: $2.57 **Circ:** Mon.-Sat. 10,193
BW: $4,533.48 Sun. 10,276
4C: $5,504.73
PCI: $36.70

928 VMEbus Systems
2618 S Shannon Dr. Phone: (602)967-5581
Tempe, AZ 85282 Fax: (602)968-3446
Publication E-mail: micrology@aol.com

Magazine covering VMEbus computer technology. **Subtitle:** The Magazine for Engineers by Engineers. **Founded:** Aug. 1985. **Freq:** Bimonthly. **Print Method:** Web Press. **Trim Size:** 8 x 10 7/8. **Cols./Page:** 2 and 3. **Col. Width:** 3 5/16 and 2 1/8 inches. **Col. Depth:** 20 and 20 inches. **Key Personnel:** John Black, Editor-in-Chief; Wayne Kristoff, Production Dir., phone (602)837-3756, fax (602)837-3768; Mike Hopper, Dir. of Sales and Marketing, phone (313)774-8180, fax (313)774-8182; Karen Layman, Business Mgr., phone (313)774-8180, fax (313)774-8182; Pat Hopper, Advertising/Sales Manager. **ISSN:** 0884-1357. **Subscription Rates:** Free to qualified subscribers; $24 U.S. and Canada; $80 outside U.S. and Canada. **Remarks:** Accepts advertising. **URL:** http://www.primenet.com/~magpub; http://www.vmebus-system.com. **Feature Editors:** Bev Black, *News*; Russ Brock, *Consumer Affairs*, phone (602)967-5581, fax (602)968-3446.
Ad Rates: BW: $3,680 **Circ:** Controlled ‡18,000
4C: $4,555

929 Youth Theatre Journal
American Alliance for Theater & Education
Theatre Department Phone: (602)965-6064
Arizona State University Fax: (602)965-5351
Tempe, AZ 85287-2002
Publisher E-mail: aateinfo@asuvm.inre.asu.edu

Research journal covering theatre and education. **Freq:** Annual. **Key Personnel:** Jeanne Klein, Editor. **ISSN:** 0892-9092. **Subscription Rates:** $25 individuals; $35 out of country. **Remarks:** Accepts advertising.
Circ: (Not Reported)

930 KAET-TV - 8
Arizona State University Phone: (602)965-3506
Tempe, AZ 85287-1405 Fax: (602)965-1000
E-mail: kaet@asu.edu

Format: Public TV. **Networks:** Public Broadcasting Service (PBS). **Owner:** Arizona State University Board of Regents, at above address. **Founded:** 1961. **Operating Hours:** Continuous. **ADI:** Phoenix (Kingman, Prescott), AZ. **Key Personnel:** Charles R. Allen, General Mgr.; Beth Versure, Station Mgr.; Joe Manning, Engineering Mgr.; Carl Eidsvaag, Marketing Mgr.; Ray Murdock, Business Mgr.; Joe Campbell, Program Mgr. **Ad Rates:** Noncommercial.

931 KCWW-AM - 1580
Box 3174 Phone: (602)966-6236
600 E. Gilbert Dr. Fax: (602)921-6301
Tempe, AZ 85281
E-mail: kcww.aol.com

Format: Country. **Networks:** ABC. **Owner:** Owens Broadcasting Co. L.L.C., 3223 Sillect, Bakersfield, CA 93308, (805)326-1011. **Founded:** 1967. **Formerly**: KTUF-AM (1973). **Operating Hours:** Continuous. **ADI:** Phoenix (Kingman, Prescott), AZ. **Key Personnel:** Michael Owens, General Mgr.; Larry Daniels, General Program Manager; Bob Podolsky, General Sales Mgr.; Dave Nicholson, Program Dir.; Buddy Owens, Music Dir. **Wattage:** 50,000.

932 KNIX-FM - 102.5
600 Gilbert Dr. Phone: (602)966-6236
PO Box 3174 Fax: (602)966-7435
Tempe, AZ 85280

Format: Country. **Networks:** Independent. **Owner:** Owens Broadcasting, LLC., 3223 Sillect, Bakersfield, CA 93308, (805)326-1011, Fax: (805)328-7503. **Founded:** 1968. **Operating Hours:** Continuous. **Key Personnel:** Michael Owens, General Mgr., fax (602)941-6301; Larry Daniels, Gen. Program Manager; Bob Podolsky, General Sales Mgr.; Buddy Owens, Music Dir.; Deborah J. Leason, Administrative Assistant. **Local Programs:** *Inside Arizona Country*, Mary Ganir; *KNIX Country Countdown*, George King; *When Country Was Cool*, Richard Lee. **Wattage:** 100,000.

933 KUKQ-AM - 1060
1900 W. Carmen Phone: (602)838-0400
Tempe, AZ 85283 Fax: (602)820-8469

Format: Alternative/New Music/Progressive. **Networks:** Independent. **Founded:** 1960. **Operating Hours:** Continuous. **Key Personnel:** Chuck Artigue, General Mgr.; Dana Beaudin, General Sales Mgr. **Wattage:** 5000 day; 500 night.

934 KUPD-FM - 97.9
1900 W. Carmen Phone: (602)838-0400
Tempe, AZ 85283 Fax: (602)820-8469

Format: Album-Oriented Rock (AOR). **Networks:** Independent. **Founded:** 1960. **Operating Hours:** Continuous. **Key Personnel:** Chuck Artigue, General Mgr.; Dana Beaudin, General Sales Mgr. **Wattage:** 100,000. **Ad Rates:** Advertising accepted; rates available upon request.

THATCHER, pop. 3,374.

Graham Co. (SE). 120 m NE of Tucson. Eastern Arizona College. Agriculture. Stock, poultry, grain farm, cotton & cattle.

935 The Gila Monster
Eastern Arizona College
Thatcher, AZ 85552-0769 Phone: (520)428-8321
Fax: (520)428-8462
Publication E-mail: dugan@eac.cc.az.us

Collegiate newspaper. **Founded:** 1921. **Freq:** Monthly 8/year. **Print Method:** Offset. **Trim Size:** 11 1/2 x 14. **Cols./Page:** 5. **Col. Width:** 25 nonpareils. **Col. Depth:** 175 agate lines. **Key Personnel:** Published by the students of Eastern Arizona College. **Subscription Rates:** Free. **Remarks:** Advertising not accepted. **URL:** http://www.eac.cc.az.us.
Circ: Free 1,000

TOMBSTONE, pop. 1,632.

Cochise Co. (SE). 65 m SE of Tucson. Registered national historic landmark. Resort. Silver mining. Agriculture. Cattle.

936 The Tombstone Epitaph
Tombstone Epitaph Corp.
Box 1880 Phone: (602)457-2211
Tombstone, AZ 85638
Journal featuring articles by contemporary historians and archival material concerning 19th century western history. **Founded:** 1880. **Freq:** Monthly. **Print Method:** Letterpress and offset. **Cols./Page:** 4. **Col. Width:** 28 nonpareils. **Col. Depth:** 219 agate lines. **Key Personnel:** Dean Prichard, Editor. **ISSN:** 0890-068X. **Subscription Rates:** $15 individuals; $20 other countries; $18; $25 outside U.S. **Remarks:** Accepts advertising. **Formerly**: The National Tombstone Epitaph (1992).
Ad Rates: BW: $350 **Circ:** ‡8,500
PCI: $25

TUBA CITY

937 KGHR-FM - 91.5
PO Box 160 Phone: (520)283-6271
Tuba City, AZ 86045 Fax: (520)283-6604

Format: Ethnic. **Owner:** Tuba City High School Board, Inc., at above address. **Founded:** 1986. **Operating Hours:** 7 a.m.-4 p.m. **Key Personnel:** Elaine Wilson, General Mgr.; Darrin Elmer, Radio Announcer. **Wattage:** 100. **Ad Rates:** $25 per unit.

938 KTBA-AM - 1050
Cemetery Rd. Phone: (520)283-5776
PO Box 1050 Fax: (520)371-5588
Tuba City, AZ 86045

Format: Religious. **Networks:** Moody Broadcasting. **Owner:** Western Indian Ministries, Inc., P.O. Drawer F, Window Rock, AZ 86515. **Founded:** 1980. **Operating Hours:** Continuous. **Key Personnel:** Jim Maiorand, General Mgr.; Lavor Thomas, Program Dir.; John Mexicano, Contact. **Wattage:** 5000. **Ad Rates:** $5-6 for 30 seconds; $7-8 for 60 seconds.

TUCSON†, pop. 330,537.

Pima Co. (S). 125 m SE of Phoenix. University of Arizona, State School for Deaf and Blind, Pima Community College, private schools. Health and winter resort. Manufactures aerospace weapons, air conditioners, airplane instruments, electronics, ammunition, bricks, clay, cement, dairy products, dental tools, filters, optics, paint, plastics, women's wear. Poultry processing, meat packing plants. Copper, silver, gold mines. Agriculture. Cotton, cattle, grain, pecans.

939 The Arizona Daily Star
Star Publishing Co.
4850 S. Park Ave. Phone: (520)573-4400
Tucson, AZ 85726-6807
General newspaper. **Founded:** Mar. 1, 1877. **Freq:** Mon.-Sun. (morn.). **Print Method:** Offset. **Trim Size:** 13 3/4 x 23. **Cols./Page:** 6. **Col. Width:** 25 nonpareils. **Col. Depth:** 301 agate lines. **Key Personnel:** Michael Pulitzer, Publisher; Stephen Auslander, Editor; Bobbie Jo Buel, Managing Editor; Elaine Raines, Librarian, phone (602)573-4130. **Subscription Rates:** $140.40 individuals. **Remarks:** Accepts advertising. **Online:** DataTimes Corporation. **Feature Editors:** B. J. Bartlett, *Sports*, phone (602)573-4150; John Bolton, *Financial/Business*, phone (602)573-4177; Jane Erikson, *Medical*, phone (602)573-4118; Jim Kiser, *Editorials*, phone (602)573-4235; Debbie Kornmiller, *City*, phone (602)573-4127; Joe McDermott, *News*, phone (602)573-4173; Ann-Eve Petersen, *News*, phone (602)573-4101; James Reel, *Music*, phone (602)573-4128; Linda Salazar, *Photo*, phone (602)573-4155; Tom Turner, *Food*, *Travel*, phone (602)573-4124.
Ad Rates: GLR: $4.79 **Circ:** Mon.-Sat. 102,960
BW: $8,385 Sun. 187,003
4C: $9,495
SAU: $67
PCI: $67

940 Arizona Daily Wildcat
University of Arizona
Student Union Bldg., Rm. 4 Phone: (520)621-1714
Tucson, AZ 85721 Fax: (520)621-3094
Publication E-mail: wceditor@ccit.arizona.edu; wcads@ccit.arizona.edu

Collegiate newspaper (tabloid). **Founded:** 1914. **Freq:** Daily (during academic year); summer 1/wk (Wed.). **Print Method:** Offset. **Trim Size:** 9 13/16 x 16. **Cols./Page:** 6. **Col. Width:** 18 nonpareils. **Col. Depth:** 224 agate lines. **Key Personnel:** Zack Thomas, Editor, phone (520)621-3551; Jeannette Brauchli, Advertising Mgr.; Mark Woodhams, Director, phone (520)621-3408. **Subscription Rates:** $90 individuals. **Remarks:** Accepts advertising. **Available Online. URL:** http://wildcat.arizona.edu.
Ad Rates: PCI: $9.55 **Circ:** Free ‡20,000

941 Arizona Jewish Post
Jewish Federation of Southern Arizona
3812 E. River Rd. Phone: (520)529-1500
Tucson, AZ 85718-6635 Fax: (520)577-0734
Publication E-mail: 6809162@mcimail.com

Jewish interest newspaper. **Founded:** Sept. 24, 1946. **Freq:** Semimonthly. **Print Method:** Offset. **Cols./Page:** 6. **Col. Depth:** 13 inches. **Key Personnel:** Sandra R. Heiman, Editor; Jerry Rosen, Advertising Mgr.; Phyllis Braun, Asst. Editor. **Subscription Rates:** $20 individuals. **Formerly**: Arizona Post.
Ad Rates: 4C: $70 **Circ:** 8,200
PCI: $16.25

942 Arizona Quarterly
University of Arizona Main Library, 541-B
Tucson, AZ 85721
Phone: (602)621-6396
Fax: (520)621-7397
Publication E-mail: azq@u.arizona.edu

Scholarly journal on American literature, culture, and theory. **Founded:** 1945. **Freq:** Quarterly. **Print Method:** Offset. **Trim Size:** 6 x 9. **Cols./Page:** 1. **Col. Width:** 54 nonpareils. **Col. Depth:** 81 agate lines. **Key Personnel:** Edgar A. Dryden, Editor. **ISSN:** 0004-1610. **Subscription Rates:** $12 individuals; $16 institutions. **Remarks:** Accepts advertising. **Alt. Formats:** Microform.
Ad Rates: BW: $150 **Circ:** Paid ‡350
Non-paid ‡300

943 Astrophysical Journal Supplement Series
The Astrophysical Journal
Kitt Peak National Observatory
Box 26732
Tucson, AZ 85726-6732
Phone: (520)318-8214
Fax: (520)318-8183
Publication E-mail: apj@noao.edu

Astronomical research journal. **Founded:** 1954. **Freq:** Monthly. **Print Method:** Offset. **Trim Size:** 8 1/2 x 11 1/2 in. **Cols./Page:** 2. **Col. Width:** 3 1/2 inches. **Col. Depth:** 9 1/4 inches. **Key Personnel:** Dr. Helmut A. Abt, Editor-in-Chief, phone (520)318-8215. **Subscription Rates:** $220 institutions, other countries and students; $45 individuals. **Remarks:** Advertising not accepted. **Available Online.**
Circ: Paid ‡1,800

944 Auditing
American Accounting Association
c/o William L. Felix, Jr., Editor
University of Arizona
College of Business
Dept. of Accounting
Tucson, AZ 85721-0108
Phone: (520)621-2443
Fax: (520)621-3742
Publication E-mail: wfelix@bpa.arizona.edu
Publisher E-mail: aaahq@packnet.net

Trade journal covering the practice and theory of auditing for accounting professionals. **Subtitle:** A Journal of Practice & Theory. **Founded:** 1981. **Freq:** Semiannual. **Trim Size:** 7 x 10. **Cols./Page:** 2. **Col. Width:** 16 picas. **Col. Depth:** 49 picas. **Key Personnel:** William L. Felix, Jr., Editor, wfelix@bpa.arizona.edu; James DeLa, AAA Publications Coord., aaajimd@aol.com; Lynn Zook, Advertising Coord. **ISSN:** 0278-0380. **Subscription Rates:** $25 individuals. **URL:** http://AAA-edu.org.
Circ: Paid 2,400

945 Aztec Press
Pima County Community College
2202 W. Anklam Rd.
Tucson, AZ 85709-0001
Phone: (520)260-6800
Fax: (520)260-6834
Publication E-mail: aztec_ press@west.pima.edu

Collegiate newspaper. **Founded:** 1973. **Freq:** Weekly (Wed.). **Print Method:** Offset. **Trim Size:** 10 1/4 x 13. **Cols./Page:** 5. **Col. Width:** 24 nonpareils. **Col. Depth:** 224 agate lines. **Key Personnel:** John O'Keefe, Advisor; Diane Kreinbring, Business Mgr.; Andrew Cutting, Operations Mgr. **Subscription Rates:** Free; $15 by mail. **Available Online. URL:** http://west.pima.edu/˜aztec_ press. **Formerly**: Aztec News; Campus News.
Ad Rates: GLR: $1.50 **Circ:** Free ‡7,000
PCI: $8

946 Catholic Vision
PO Box 31
Tucson, AZ 85702
Phone: (520)792-3410
Fax: (520)792-1179
Publication E-mail: cathuis@azstarnet.com
Publisher E-mail: cathvis@azstarnet.com

Official newspaper of the Diocese of Tucson. **Founded:** 1986. **Freq:** Monthly. **Print Method:** web press. **Trim Size:** 11 1/2 x 14. **Key Personnel:** Kate Harrison, Editor, fax (520)792-1179; Bishop Manuel D. Moreno, Publisher. **Subscription Rates:** Free. **URL:** http://www.azstarnet.com/˜rccdot/news.html. **Formerly**: Catholic Today.
Ad Rates: 4C: $400 **Circ:** (Not Reported)
PCI: $520

947 College & Career Guide News for College Students
Corporate Marketing & Publishing Inc.
PO Box 12217
Tucson, AZ 85732
Phone: (520)790-4044
College and career news source for high school teens and college bound individuals. **Founded:** Oct. 1994. **Freq:** Quarterly. **Print Method:** Offset. **Trim Size:** 13 x 14. **Cols./Page:** 5. **Col. Width:** 2 1/2 inches. **Col. Depth:** 12 inches. **Key Personnel:** Patrick McGuire, Editorial Manager. **Remarks:** Accepts advertising. **Alt. Formats:** CD-ROM. **Formerly**: College & Career Guide News for High School Teens.
Ad Rates: BW: $1,360 **Circ:** (Not Reported)
4C: $1,855

948 Collegiate Baseball Newspaper
Collegiate Baseball Newspaper, Inc.
2515 N. Stone Ave.
Tucson, AZ 85705
Phone: (520)623-4530
Fax: (520)624-5501
Publication E-mail: cbn@azstarnet.com

Amateur baseball magazine. **Founded:** Jan. 1958. **Freq:** 14/year. **Print Method:** Offset. **Cols./Page:** 5. **Col. Width:** 23 nonpareils. **Col. Depth:** 194 agate lines. **Key Personnel:** Louis Pavlovich, Jr., Editor; Louis F. Pavlovich, Publisher; Diane Pavlovich, Advertising Mgr. **ISSN:** 0530-9751. **Subscription Rates:** $22 individuals; $2.50 single issue. **Remarks:** Advertising not accepted for alcohol and tobacco. **URL:** http://www.baseballnews.com.
Ad Rates: BW: $1,380 **Circ:** ‡8,000
4C: $1,920
PCI: $23

949 Contact! (Tucson)
Aeronautics Education Enterprises
2900 E. Weymouth
Tucson, AZ 85716-1249
Phone: (520)881-2232
Fax: (520)795-6776
Publication E-mail: contact!@flash.net

Trade journal covering experimental aircrafts and power plants. **Subtitle:** Experimental Aircraft and PowerPlant News forum for Designers and Builders. **Founded:** 1991. **Freq:** Bimonthly. **Print Method:** Offset. **Trim Size:** 8 1/2 x 11. **Cols./Page:** 2. **Col. Width:** 3 65/100 inches. **Col. Depth:** 9 1/2 inches. **Key Personnel:** Michael C. Myal, Contact. **Subscription Rates:** $20 individuals; $27 Canada; $29 other countries; $4 single issue; $38 out of country Airmail. **Remarks:** Advertising not accepted.
Circ: Combined 1,290

950 Cryptozoology
International Society of Cryptozoology (ISC)
PO Box 43070
Tucson, AZ 85733
Phone: (520)884-8369
Fax: (520)884-8369
Publisher E-mail: iscz@azstarnet.com

Scholarly journal covering cryptozoology. **Subtitle:** Interdisciplinary Journal of the International Society of Cryptozoology. **Founded:** 1982. **Freq:** Annual. **Trim Size:** 6 x 9. **Cols./Page:** 1. **Col. Width:** 4 3/4 inches. **Col. Depth:** 7 inches. **Key Personnel:** J. Richard Greenwell, Editor. **ISSN:** 0736-7023. **Subscription Rates:** $42 individuals; $22 single issue. **Remarks:** Accepts advertising.
Ad Rates: BW: $480 **Circ:** Paid 900

951 The Daily Territorial
Territorial Newspapers
3280 E. Hemisphere Lp., Ste. 174
PO Box 27087
Tucson, AZ 85726-7087
Phone: (520)294-4040
Fax: (520)294-1200
Publication E-mail: itbnews@aol.com

Newspaper featuring business and legal news. **Founded:** 1930. **Freq:** Daily (morn.). **Print Method:** Offset. **Cols./Page:** 4. **Col. Width:** 2 3/8 inches. **Col. Depth:** 14 inches. **Key Personnel:** Stephen Jewett, Publisher; Rod Smith, Editor; Loretta Olguin, Legal Adv.Mgr. **ISSN:** 0743-8397. **Subscription Rates:** $100 individuals. **Remarks:** Accepts advertising.
Ad Rates: GLR: $.39 **Circ:** Paid 892
BW: $390 Free 100
4C: $840
PCI: $7.50

952 Desert Plants
2120 E. Allen Rd.
Tucson, AZ 85719
Phone: (520)318-7046
Fax: (520)621-1296
Publisher E-mail: mnorem@ag.arizona.edu

Professional journal covering plants in arid and semi-arid environments. **Founded:** 1979. **Freq:** Semiannual. **Cols./Page:** 2. **Key Personnel:** Margaret Norem, Editor, mnorem@ag.arizona.edu. **ISSN:** 0734-3434. **Subscription Rates:** $20 individuals; $5 single issue; $25 out of country; $50 institutions. **Remarks:** Advertising not accepted.
Circ: Combined 1,000

953 Entertainment Magazine
Southwest Alternatives Institute, Inc.
PO Box 3355
Tucson, AZ 85722
Phone: (520)623-3733
Publication E-mail: emol@emol.org
Publisher E-mail: gale@emol.org

Entertainment, tourism and dining guide for Arizona. **Founded:** 1977. **Freq:** Weekly. **Key Personnel:** Robert E. Zucker, Publisher. **ISSN:** 0742-9568. **Remarks:** Accepts advertising. **Available Online. URL:** http://www.emol.org/emol/.
Ad Rates: BW: $299 **Circ:** Non-paid 24,000
4C: $649
PCI: $9.21

954 Environment and Behavior
Sage Publications Inc.
Dept. Of Psychology
University of Arizona
Tucson, AZ 85721
Phone: (520)621-7430
Fax: (520)621-9306
Publisher E-mail: info@sagepub.com

Journal studying the effects of environment, geography, and architecture on human behavior. **Founded:** 1969. **Freq:** Bimonthly. **Print Method:** Offset. **Trim Size:** 5 1/2 x 8 1/2. **Cols./Page:** 1. **Col. Width:** 50 nonpareils. **Col. Depth:** 100 agate lines. **Key Personnel:** Robert Bechtel, Editor, bechtel@u.arizona.edu; Lisa Cuevas, Circulation Mgr. **ISSN:** 0013-9165. **Subscription Rates:** $79 individuals; $280 institutions; $15 single issue; $49 single issue industry. **Remarks:** Accepts advertising.
Ad Rates: BW: $250 **Circ:** Paid ‡1,600
Non-paid ‡152

955 Handball
U.S. Handball Association
2333 N. Tucson Blvd.
Tucson, AZ 85716-2726
Phone: (520)795-0434
Fax: (520)795-0465
Free: (800)345-2048
Publication E-mail: handball@ushandball.org
Publisher E-mail: handball@ushandball.org

Trade magazine featuring handball instruction, national events and results. **Subtitle:** Official Voice of the U.S. Handball Association. **Founded:** 1951. **Freq:** Bimonthly. **Print Method:** Offset. **Trim Size:** 8 1/8 x 10 3/8. **Cols./Page:** 3. **Col. Width:** 27 nonpareils. **Col. Depth:** 140 agate lines. **Key Personnel:** Bob Hickman, Publisher; Vern Roberts, Executive Dir.; Mark Carpenter, Development Coordinator. **ISSN:** 0046-6778. **Subscription Rates:** $30 individuals; $45 other countries. **Remarks:** Accepts advertising. **URL:** http://www.ushandball.org. **Formerly**: Ace Magazine.
Ad Rates: BW: $855 **Circ:** ‡10,000
4C: $1,140
PCI: $450

956 Inside Tucson Business
Territorial Newspapers
3280 E. Hemisphere Lp., Ste. 174
PO Box 27087
Tucson, AZ 85726-7087
Phone: (520)294-4040
Fax: (520)294-1200
Publication E-mail: itbnews@aol.com

Newspaper featuring business news. **Founded:** 1990. **Freq:** Weekly (Mon.). **Print Method:** Offset. **Cols./Page:** 4. **Col. Width:** 2 1/2 inches. **Col. Depth:** 12 1/2 inches. **Key Personnel:** Stephen Jewett, Publisher; Rod Smith, Editor; David Stoler, Advertising Mgr.; Michael McFate, Circulation Mgr. **ISSN:** 1069-5184. **Subscription Rates:** $35 individuals; $45 out of area. **Remarks:** Accepts advertising. **Online:** Info Plus.
Ad Rates: BW: $1552 **Circ:** Paid 2,000
4C: $2002 Non-paid 6,000
PCI: $29.85

957 Journal of Arizona History
Arizona Historical Society
949 E. 2nd St.
Tucson, AZ 85719
Phone: (520)628-5774
Fax: (602)628-5695

Journal covering the history of the Southwestern U.S., northern Mexico, and Arizona, particularly. **Founded:** 1960. **Freq:** Quarterly. **Key Personnel:** Bruce J. Dinges, Editor. **Subscription Rates:** $40 individuals; $10 single issue. **Remarks:** Advertising not accepted.
Circ: Controlled 3,050

958 Journal of the Southwest
University of Arizona
1052 N. Highland Ave.
Tucson, AZ 85721
Phone: (520)621-2484
Fax: (520)621-9922

Scholarly journal covering natural and human history, literature, folklore, politics, and anthropology of the Southwest U.S. **Founded:** 1959. **Freq:** Quarterly. **Key Personnel:** Joseph C. Wilder, Editor. **ISSN:** 0894-8410. **Subscription Rates:** $18 individuals; $24 institutions; $6 single issue. **Remarks:** Accepts advertising. **Online:** Information Access Co. **Former name**: Arizona and tbe West (1987).
Ad Rates: BW: $100 **Circ:** (Not Reported)

959 Kiva
Arizona Archaeological and Historical Society
Arizona State Museum
University of Arizona
Tucson, AZ 85721
Phone: (602)621-3656
Southwestern anthropology journal. **Subtitle:** The Quarterly Journal of the Arizona Archaeological and Historical Society. **Founded:** 1935. **Freq:** Quarterly. **Print Method:** Offset. **Trim Size:** 6 x 9. **Cols./Page:** 1. **Col. Width:** 27 picas. **Col. Depth:** 42 picas. **Key Personnel:** Tobi Taylor, Editor; Dale S. Brenneman, Asst. Editor. **ISSN:** 0023-1940. **Subscription**

Rates: $40; $30 students. **Remarks:** Accepts advertising. **Former name:** The Kiva.
Ad Rates: BW: $100 **Circ:** Paid ‡1,200
Non-paid ‡25

960 Light of Consciousness
Truth Consciousness at Desert Ashram
3403 W. Sweetwater Dr. Phone: (520)743-8821
Tucson, AZ 85745-9301 Fax: (520)743-3394

Consumer magazine on spirituality. **Subtitle:** A Journal of Spiritual Awakening. **Founded:** 1988. **Freq:** 3/year. **Print Method:** Offset. **Trim Size:** 8 1/2 x 10 7/8. **Cols./Page:** 2. **Key Personnel:** Sita Stuhlmiller, Editor; Marianne Martin, Asst. Editor. **ISSN:** 1040-7448. **Subscription Rates:** $13 /year; $24 two years; $4.50 single issue.
Ad Rates: BW: $500 **Circ:** Paid 7,600

961 The Match!
The Match
PO Box 3488
Tucson, AZ 85722

Political commentary magazine. **Subtitle:** An Anarchist Journal. **Founded:** 1969. **Freq:** Periodic. **Print Method:** Offset. **Trim Size:** 6 1/2 x 9. **Cols./Page:** 2. **Col. Width:** 16.5 picas. **Col. Depth:** 8 1/4 inches. **Key Personnel:** Fred Woodworth, Editor and Publisher. **Subscription Rates:** $10. $2.50 single issue. **Remarks:** Advertising not accepted.
Circ: 1,750

962 Oxidation of Metals
Plenum Publishing Corp.
4715 Fort Lowell Rd. Phone: (520)322-2979
Tucson, AZ 85712
Publication E-mail: journalsdept@plenum.com
Publisher E-mail: info@plenum.com

Journal focusing on gas and solid reactions. **Founded:** 1967. **Freq:** Monthly. **Print Method:** Offset. **Trim Size:** 6 x 9. **Cols./Page:** 1. **Col. Width:** 54 nonpareils. **Col. Depth:** 103 agate lines. **Key Personnel:** D.L. Douglass, Editor. **ISSN:** 0030-770X. **Subscription Rates:** $645; $755 other countries. **Remarks:** Accepts advertising. **Online:** CatchWord.
Ad Rates: BW: $275 **Circ:** (Not Reported)

963 Paleoclimates
International Publisher Direct
The University of Arizona Phone: (520)621-4595
Gould-Simpson Bldg. Fax: (520)621-2672
Tucson, AZ 85721
Publisher E-mail: info@gbhap.com

Journal focusing on the interdisciplinary subject area of paleoclimatology, specifically the study of past climate change. Includes articles on all aspects of the climate and environment of the Quaternary and earlier times. **Subtitle:** Data and Modelling. **Founded:** 1995. **Freq:** Quarterly. **Key Personnel:** Paul J. Valdes, Editor; Judith Totman Parrish, Editor, parrish@geo.arizona.edu. **ISSN:** 1063-7176. **Subscription Rates:** $70.

964 Perspectives in Mexican American Studies
Mexican American Studies & Research Center (MASRC)
Economics Bldg., Rm. 208 Phone: (520)626-8103
Tucson, AZ 85721-0023 Fax: (520)621-7966
Publisher E-mail: masrc@u.arizona.edu

Scholarly journal covering Mexican American issues. **Founded:** 1989. **Freq:** Annual. **Trim Size:** 6 x 9. **Cols./Page:** 1. **Key Personnel:** Juan Garcia, Editor. **ISSN:** 0889-8448. **Remarks:** Advertising not accepted.
Circ: Paid 500

965 Political Research Quarterly
University of Utah
Univ. of Arizona Phone: (520)621-1347
Dept. of Political Science Fax: (520)621-5051
315 Social Sciences
Tucson, AZ 85721
Publication E-mail: prq@arizona.edu

Political science journal. **Founded:** 1948. **Freq:** Quarterly. **Print Method:** Offset. **Trim Size:** 6 x 9. **Cols./Page:** 1. **Col. Width:** 59 nonpareils. **Col. Depth:** 116 agate lines. **Key Personnel:** Lyn Ragsdale, Editor, ragsdale@u.arizona.edu; William J. Dixon, Editor, dixon@u.arizona.edu; Susan M. Alson, Managing Editor, smolson@poli-sci.utah.edu. **ISSN:** 1065-9129. **Subscription Rates:** $30; $32.50 Canada/Mexico; $34 other countries; $11 students; $13.50 Canadian/Mexican students; $15 other countries students; $50 Industry; $52.50 Canadian/Mexican Industry; $54 other countries Industry. **Remarks:** Color advertising not accepted. **Alt. Formats:** Microfiche. **Formerly:** Western Political Quarterly.
Ad Rates: BW: $100 **Circ:** ‡2,200

966 Quest
Muscular Dystrophy Association, Inc.
3300 E. Sunrise Dr. Phone: (520)529-2000
Tucson, AZ 85718 Fax: (520)529-5300
Free: (800)572-1717
Publisher E-mail: publications@mdausa.org

Magazine focusing on issues important to people who have muscular dystrophy and other neuromuscular diseases. **Freq:** Bimonthly. **ISSN:** 1087-1578. **Subscription Rates:** Free for MDA registrants; $12 per year. **Online:** Compuserve Go MDA. **URL:** http://www.mdausa.org.
Ad Rates: BW: $2,330 **Circ:** Non-paid 110,000
4C: $2,750
CNU: $2,600
PCI: $90

967 Restoration
International Society for Vehicle Preservation
PO Box 50046 Phone: (520)622-2201
Tucson, AZ 85703
Publisher E-mail: isvp@aztexcorp.com

Technical magazine covering the how-to of vehicle resoration. **Subtitle:** Restoration Magazine; Restoration News Bulletin. **Founded:** Sept. 1983. **Freq:** Semiannual. **Print Method:** Offset. **Trim Size:** 8 1/2 x 11. **Cols./Page:** 3 and 2. **Col. Width:** 14 and 22 picas. **Col. Depth:** 60 picas. **Key Personnel:** Walter Haessner, Editor and Publisher; Elaine C. Jordan, Advertising Mgr. **ISSN:** 0736-5934. **Subscription Rates:** $20 members; $3 single issue. **URL:** http://www.aztexcomp.com/root/isvp.html; http://www.aztexcorp.com.
Ad Rates: BW: $295 **Circ:** Paid ‡1,500
4C: $795 Controlled ‡3,500

968 Safari Magazine
Safari Club Intl.
4800 W. Gates Pass Rd. Phone: (520)620-1220
Tucson, AZ 85745 Fax: (520)622-1205
Publication E-mail: editorsci@earthlink.net

Official publication of Safari Club International. **Subtitle:** The Journal of Big Game Hunting. **Founded:** 1971. **Freq:** Bimonthly. **Print Method:** Web offset. **Trim Size:** 8 3/8 x 10 7/8. **Cols./Page:** 3. **Col. Width:** 26 nonpareils. **Col. Depth:** 140 agate lines. **Key Personnel:** William R. Quimby, Director; Eric Hubbell, Advertising Mgr. **ISSN:** 0199-5316. **Subscription Rates:** $55 members To Members; $4 single issue; $5 back issue. **Remarks:** Accepts advertising.
Ad Rates: BW: $1,540 **Circ:** Controlled ‡39,000
4C: $2,564

969 Serb World U.S.A.
Serb World U.S.A., Inc.
415 E. Mabel St. Phone: (602)624-4887
Tucson, AZ 85705
Magazine covering Serbian-American history and culture, including recipes, customs, family stories, legends, and book reviews. **Founded:** 1979. **Freq:** Bimonthly. **Print Method:** Offset. **Trim Size:** 8 1/2 x 11. **Cols./Page:** 3. **Col. Width:** 41 nonpareils. **Col. Depth:** 140 agate lines. **Key Personnel:** Mary Nicklanovich Hart, Editor; Philip D. Hart, Production & Advertising. **ISSN:** 8756-5579. **Subscription Rates:** $21 individuals; $3.50 single issue; $5 back issues. **Remarks:** Accepts advertising.
Ad Rates: BW: $155 **Circ:** ‡3,800

970 Social Psychology Quarterly
University of Arizona
Department of Sociology Phone: (520)621-3531
Tucson, AZ 85721 Fax: (520)621-9875
Publication E-mail: spq@u.arizona.edu
Publisher E-mail: edwards@asanet.org

Journal on society's impact on the individual and on individual interaction in small groups and communities. **Founded:** 1937. **Freq:** Quarterly. **Print Method:** Offset. **Trim Size:** 6 3/4 x 9 7/8. **Cols./Page:** 2. **Col. Width:** 27 nonpareils. **Col. Depth:** 112 agate lines. **Key Personnel:** Linda D. Molm, Co-Editor, phone (520)626-6499, fax (520)621-9875, molml@u.arizona.edu; Lynn Smith-Lovin, Co-Editor, phone (520)626-6499, fax (520)621-9875, smithlov@u.arizona.edu. **ISSN:** 0190-2725. **Subscription Rates:** $25 members; $50 nonmembers; $95 institutions. **Remarks:** Accepts advertising. **Formerly:** Sociometry; Social Psychology.
Ad Rates: BW: $200 **Circ:** ‡3,250

971 Spirit & Life
Benedictine Sisters of Perpetual Adoration
800 N. Country Club Rd. Phone: (520)325-6401
Tucson, AZ 85716-4583
Publisher E-mail: benpubotr@theriver.com

Spiritual growth magazine for Christians. **Founded:** 1905. **Freq:** Bimonthly. **Print Method:** Offset. **Trim Size:** 6 x 9. **Cols./Page:** 1. **Key Personnel:** Sr. Lenora Black, OSB, Editor, fax (520)321-4358. **ISSN:** 0038-7592. **Subscription Rates:** $10 individuals; $12 other countries. **Remarks:** Advertising not accepted. **Alt. Formats:** Microform. **Formerly:** Tabernacle & Purgatory.
Circ: ‡3,200

972 Survey of Anesthesiology
Lippincott Williams & Wilkins
8301 East Canyon Side Rd.
Tucson, AZ 85715

Medical journal. **Founded:** 1957. **Freq:** Bimonthly. **Print Method:** Offset. **Trim Size:** 8 1/8 x 10 7/8. **Cols./Page:** 2. **Col. Width:** 32 nonpareils. **Col. Depth:** 119 agate lines. **Key Personnel:** Burnell R. Brown Jr., MD, Contact; Gary Walchli, Advertising Dir.; Carol Stockton, Representative. **Subscription Rates:** $73 individuals; $95 other countries. **Remarks:** Accepts advertising.
Ad Rates: BW: $500 **Circ:** Paid ‡3,048
4C: $1,150 Non-paid ‡142

973 Tucson Citizen
4850 S. Park Ave. Phone: (520)573-4561
Tucson, AZ 85714 Fax: (520)573-4569
Free: (800)695-4492

General newspaper. **Founded:** 1870. **Freq:** Daily (eve.). **Print Method:** Offset. **Trim Size:** 13 5/8 x 22 3/4. **Cols./Page:** 6. **Col. Width:** 24 nonpareils. **Col. Depth:** 301 agate lines. **Key Personnel:** C. Donald Hatfield, Editor and Publisher. **Subscription Rates:** $182 individuals. **Remarks:** Accepts advertising. **Available Online. Alt. Formats:** Microform.
Ad Rates: BW: $7,436.85 **Circ:** Mon.-Sat. ★**41,118**
4C: $8,434.85
SAU: $57.65

974 Tucson Comic News
PO Box 510 Phone: (520)320-5105
Tucson, AZ 85702-0510 Fax: (520)320-5105
Publication E-mail: comicnews@earthlink.net

Cartoon and features newspaper. **Founded:** Sept. 1993. **Freq:** Monthly. **Print Method:** Web. **Key Personnel:** Mark Zepezauer, Contact. **Subscription Rates:** $10 individuals; Free single copy. **Remarks:** Accepts advertising. **URL:** http://tucson.com/ComicNews.
Ad Rates: BW: $200 **Circ:** Paid 12,000

975 Tucson Lifestyle Magazine
Citizen Publishing Co.
7000 E. Tanque Verde Phone: (602)721-2929
Tucson, AZ 85715 Fax: (602)721-8665
Publication E-mail: tucsonlife@aol.com

Tucson lifestyle magazine. **Founded:** 1982. **Freq:** Monthly. **Print Method:** Offset. **Trim Size:** 8 1/8 x 10 3/4. **Cols./Page:** 3. **Col. Width:** 120 picas. **Col. Depth:** 58.5 picas. **Key Personnel:** Steve Rosenberg, Publisher; Fran Katz, Advertising Mgr.; Sue Giles, Editor-in-Chief; Ralph Obert, Production Mgr. **ISSN:** 1062-2861. **Subscription Rates:** $18 individuals; $18 out of area; $2.95 single issue. **Remarks:** Accepts advertising.
Ad Rates: BW: $2,211 **Circ:** Paid ‡4,000
4C: $3,325 Controlled ‡28,000

976 Tucson Shopper
Shopper's Guide, Inc.
1861 W. Grant Rd. Phone: (602)622-0101
Tucson, AZ 85745 Fax: (602)622-9651
Publication E-mail: shopperads@aol.com

Shopping guide zoned in 26 community editions. **Founded:** 1978. **Freq:** Weekly (Wed.). **Subscription Rates:** Free.
Circ: Free ‡293,400

977 Tucson Teen
Southwest Alternatives Institute, Inc.
PO Box 3355 Phone: (520)623-3733
Tucson, AZ 85722
Publication E-mail: emol@emol.org; teenonline@emol.org
Publisher E-mail: gale@emol.org

Periodical for and by youth. **Subtitle:** Teens-Online. **Founded:** 1977. **Freq:** Monthly. **Print Method:** electronic. **Key Personnel:** Robert E. Zucker, Publisher. **ISSN:** 1044-954X. **Subscription Rates:** $15. **URL:** http://emol.org/emol/tucsonteen/. **Formerly:** Youth Awareness Press; Youth Alternatives Press.
Ad Rates: 4C: $699 **Circ:** Non-paid 15,000
PCI: $9.21

978 Tucson Weekly
The Tucson Weekly Inc.
PO Box 2429 Phone: (520)792-3630
Tucson, AZ 85701-2941 Fax: (520)792-2096
Publication E-mail: tucsonweekly@desert.net

Tucson metropolitan newspaper (tabloid) covering news and arts. **Founded:** Feb. 22, 1984. **Freq:** Weekly. **Print Method:** Offset. **Trim Size:** 10 x 13 3/4. **Cols./Page:** 8. **Col. Width:** 6.5 picas. **Col. Depth:** 182 agate lines. **Key Personnel:** Douglas

Biggers, Editor and Publisher, dbiggers@tucsonweekly.com; John Hankinson, Sales Dir., johnh@tucsonweekly.com. **ISSN:** 0742-0692. **Subscription Rates:** Free; $40 by 3rd class mail. **Remarks:** Accepts advertising. **URL:** http://www.tucsonweekly.com.
Ad Rates: BW: $2,211 **Circ:** Free 45,848
4C: $2,711 Paid 52

979 Water Conditioning & Purification
Publicom, Inc.
2800 E. Fort Lowell Rd. Phone: (520)323-6144
Tucson, AZ 85716 Fax: (520)323-7412
Publisher E-mail: publicom@azstarnet.com

Magazine on Domestic and commercial water conditioning and purification. **Founded:** 1959. **Freq:** Monthly. **Print Method:** Web offset. **Trim Size:** 8 1/4 x 10 7/8. **Cols./Page:** 3. **Col. Width:** 26 nonpareils. **Col. Depth:** 140 agate lines. **Key Personnel:** Kurt Peterson, Publisher; C. David Mogollon, Managing Editor; Patricia Steiner, Assoc. Publisher; Sharon M. Peterson, Owner. **ISSN:** 0746-4029. **Subscription Rates:** $45 U.S. and Canada; $95 other countries. **Remarks:** Accepts advertising. **URL:** http://www.wcp.net.
Ad Rates: BW: $2,375 **Circ:** Paid 1,071
4C: $3,255 Controlled 19,824

980 Working Moms & Dads Magazine
Corporate Marketing & Publishing Inc.
PO Box 12217 Phone: (520)790-4044
Tucson, AZ 85732
Contains national and local news on parenting, childcare, education, and work issues. **Founded:** 1988. **Freq:** Monthly. **Print Method:** Offset. **Trim Size:** 13 x 14. **Cols./Page:** 5. **Col. Width:** 2 1/2 inches. **Col. Depth:** 12 inches. **Key Personnel:** Roberta McGuire, Editor. **Remarks:** Accepts advertising. **Alt. Formats:** CD-ROM.
Ad Rates: BW: $1,360 **Circ:** (Not Reported)
4C: $1,855

981 KCEE-AM - 940
3202 North Oracle Rd. Phone: (520)618-2100
Tucson, AZ 85705 Fax: (520)618-2135
E-mail: cool-fm@theriver.com

Format: Big Band/Nostalgia. **Networks:** Westwood One Radio; NBC. **Owner:** Capstar Broadcasting, Inc., 150 E. 58th St., New York, NY 10155, Free: (800)450-7827. **Formerly:** Broadcasting, Inc. **Operating Hours:** Continuous. **ADI:** Tucson, AZ. **Key Personnel:** Debbie Wagner, General Sales Mgr., phone (520)618-2139, fax (520)618-2190, dwagner@capstarbroadcasting.com; Todd Lawley, phone (520)618-2157, fax (520)618-2122, tlawley@capstarbroadcasting.com; Joan Lee, News Dir., phone (520)618-2120, fax (520)618-2200; Toni Nichols, Business Mgr., phone (520)618-2141, fax (520)618-2165, tnichols@capstarbroadcasting.com; Jack Landreth, Operations Mgr., phone (520)618-2172, fax (520)618-2170, jlandreth@capstarbroadcasting.com. **Wattage:** 1250. **Ad Rates:** $50-160 per unit.

982 KCUB-AM - 1290
575 W. Roger Rd. Phone: (602)887-1000
Tucson, AZ 85705 Fax: (602)887-6397

Format: Country. **Networks:** Independent. **Founded:** 1929. **Operating Hours:** Continuous; 100% local. **ADI:** Tucson, AZ. **Key Personnel:** Jamie Slone, General Mgr.; Jeff Martin, News Dir.; Herb Crowe, PD. **Wattage:** 1000.

983 KFFN-AM - 1490
3438 N. Country Club Phone: (602)795-1490
Tucson, AZ 85716 Fax: (602)327-2260

Format: Sports; Talk. **Networks:** CBS. **Owner:** Journal Broadcast Group, Inc., at above address, (414)967-5219, Fax: (414)967-5400. **Founded:** 1957. **Formerly:** KKND-AM (1996). **Operating Hours:** Continuous. **ADI:** Tucson, AZ. **Key Personnel:** Allan Hammerel, Operations Mgr.; Jim Bednarck, Program Dir. **Wattage:** 1000. **Ad Rates:** Advertising accepted; rates available upon request.

984 KFLT-AM - 830
7355 N. Orade, No. 102 Phone: (520)797-3700
PO Box 36868 Fax: (520)797-3375
Tucson, AZ 85740
E-mail: kflt@flc.org

Format: Talk; News; Middle-of-the-Road (MOR); Religious. **Networks:** USA Radio; Moody Broadcasting. **Owner:** Family Life Radio, at above address, (602)742-6976. **Founded:** 1977. **Formerly:** KOPO-AM. **Operating Hours:** Continuous; 10% network, 90% local. **ADI:** Tucson, AZ. **Key Personnel:** Lee Escobed, Manager; Dave Ficere, Program Dir.; Carl Jackson, Community Relations. **Wattage:** 50,000 day; 1000 night. **Ad Rates:** Noncommercial.

985 KGUN-TV - 9
PO Box 17990 Phone: (602)722-5486
Tucson, AZ 85731-7990 Fax: (602)290-7738
E-mail: kgun9@aol.com

Format: Commercial TV. **Networks:** ABC. **Owner:** Lee Enterprises, Inc., 400 Putnam Bldg., 215 N. Main St., Davenport, IA 52801-1924, (319)383-2100, Fax: (319)323-9609. **Founded:** 1956. **Operating Hours:** 24Hrs. **ADI:** Tucson, AZ. **Key Personnel:** Karen Lee Rice, General Mgr.; Forrest Carr, News Dir., phone (602)290-7710, fax (602)733-7050; Karen Rice, Program; Vickie Duprey, Business Mgr., phone (602)290-7605, fax (602)733-7031; Randy Foulds, Audience Development, phone (602)290-7617, fax (602)733-7058; Martin Glos, Chief Engineer, phone (602)290-7652, fax (602)733-7045; Gregg Moss, Production Mgr., phone (602)290-7660, fax (602)733-7065; Carmen Thomas, HR, phone (602)290-7640, fax (602)733-7025. **Ad Rates:** $20-2,000 per unit.

986 KHRR-FM - 101.7
2919 E. Broadway Phone: (602)322-6888
Tucson, AZ 85716 Fax: (602)881-7926

Format: Hispanic. **Networks:** Telemundo. **Founded:** 1990. **Formerly:** KGMS-FM (1994). **Operating Hours:** Continuous. **ADI:** Tucson, AZ. **Key Personnel:** Laury Browning, Dir. of Arizona Broadcasting; Lupita Celaya, Program Dir.; Peter Padilla, General Mgr.; Peter Padilla, General Mgr. **Local Programs:** *En Vivo*, Pablo Sierra, Mailing contact, (602)322-6888 x21; *Encuentro Con Tucson*, Jill Casey, Mailing contact, (602)322-6888 x41; *Telenoticias*, Abelardo Oquita, Mailing contact, (602)322-6888 x27. **Wattage:** 250. **Ad Rates:** Advertising accepted; rates available upon request.

987 KHRR-TV - 40
2919 E. Broadway Phone: (602)322-6888
Tucson, AZ 85716 Fax: (602)881-7926

Format: Hispanic. **Networks:** Telemundo. **Founded:** 1989. **Formerly:** KHR-TV (1989). **Operating Hours:** Continuous. **ADI:** Tucson, AZ. **Key Personnel:** Laury. Browning, Dir. of Arizona Broadcasting; Pablo Sierra, Production Dir.; Bob Amorosi, Chief Engineer; Lupita Celeya, Program Dir.; Peter Padilla, General Mgr. **Local Programs:** *Caliente y Mas.* **Wattage:** 1,534,000. **Ad Rates:** Advertising accepted; rates available upon request.

988 KIIM-FM - 99.5
575 W. Roger Rd. Phone: (602)887-1000
Tucson, AZ 85705 Fax: (602)887-6397

Format: Contemporary Country. **Networks:** Independent. **Owner:** Slone Broadcasting, at above address, (520)887-1000, (520)887-6397. **Founded:** 1983. **Formerly:** KNDE-FM. **Operating Hours:** Continuous. **ADI:** Tucson, AZ. **Key Personnel:** Jamie Slone, General Mgr.; Herb Crowe, PD; Jeff Martin, News Dir. **Wattage:** 100,000.

989 KLPX-FM - 96.1
1920 W. Copper Dr. Phone: (520)622-6711
Tucson, AZ 85745 Fax: (520)624-3226
E-mail: 96@klpx.com

Format: Album-Oriented Rock (AOR). **Founded:** 1979. **Operating Hours:** Continuous. **ADI:** Tucson, AZ. **Key Personnel:** Jim Cooley, General Mgr.; Larry Miles, Program Dir., fax (520)623-6261, lars@klpx.com. **Wattage:** 100,000. **Ad Rates:** Advertising accepted; rates available upon request. Combined advertising rates available with KFMA-FM, KTKI-AM, KTKT-AM. **URL:** http://www.monoxide.com.

990 KMSB-TV - 11
1855 N. 6th Ave. Phone: (520)770-1123
Tucson, AZ 85705 Fax: (520)629-7185

Format: Commercial TV. **Networks:** Fox. **Owner:** A.H. Belo, at above address. **Founded:** 1967. **Formerly:** KZAZ-TV (1985). **Operating Hours:** 6 a.m.-2 a.m. **ADI:** Tucson, AZ. **Key Personnel:** Diane Frisch, Contact; Harry West, Contact.

991 KMXZ-FM - 94.9
3438 N. Country Club Phone: (520)795-1490
Tucson, AZ 85716 Fax: (520)327-2260
E-mail: themix@theriver.com

Format: Adult Contemporary. **Owner:** Journal Broadcast Group, Inc., at above address, Fax: (520)967-5400. **Founded:** 1973. **Formerly:** KKLD-FM (1989). **Operating Hours:** Continuous; 100% local. **ADI:** Tucson, AZ. **Key Personnel:** Bobby Rich, Program Dir. **Wattage:** 100,000. **Ad Rates:** Advertising accepted; rates available upon request.

992 KNST-AM - 790
3202 N. Oracle Rd. Phone: (520)618-2100
Tucson, AZ 85710 Fax: (520)618-2135

Format: Talk; Sports; News. **Networks:** ABC; Westwood One Radio; ESPN Radio. **Owner:** Capstar Broadcasting, at above address, (512)340-7800, Fax: (512)340-7890, Free: (800)450-7827. **Founded:** 1981. **Formerly:** KHOS-AM; KMGX-AM. **Operating Hours:** Continuous. **ADI:** Tucson, AZ. **Key Personnel:** Jack Landreth, News Dir., jlandreth@capstarbroadcasting.com; Jack Landreth, Operations Mgr., phone (520)618-2172, fax (520)618-2170, jlandreth@capstarbroadcasting.com; Brian Jeffries, Sports Dir., phone (512)618-2115, fax (512)618-2135; Terry Daniels, Promotions Dir., phone (512)618-2128, fax (512)618-2170; Debbie Wagner, General Mgr., phone (510)618-2139, fax (520)618-2170, dwagner@capstarbroadcasting.com; Todd Lawley, phone (520)618-2157, fax (520)618-2122, tlawley@capstarbroadcasting.com. **Local Programs:** *Week in Review*, Mary Beal, (520)323-9400, Fax (520)327-9384. **Wattage:** 5000 day; 500 night. **Ad Rates:** Advertising accepted; rates available upon request. **URL:** http://www.knst.com. **Additional Contact Info: Advertising:** 2100 N. Silverbell Rd., Tucson, AZ 85745, (602)623-7556, fax: (602)628-2122.

993 KOHT-FM - 98.3
889 W. El Puente Ln. Phone: (520)623-6429
Tucson, AZ 85713 Fax: (520)622-2680

Format: Ethnic. **Owner:** Cactus Broadcasting Ltd., at above address, (602)623-6429. **Founded:** 1985. **Formerly:** KOPO-FM (1985); KXMG-FM (1992). **Operating Hours:** Continuous; 100% local. **ADI:** Tucson, AZ. **Key Personnel:** Allan Herman, General Mgr.; Art Labor, Program Dir. **Local Programs:** *Oldies Show*, James Rivas. **Wattage:** 3000. **Ad Rates:** $45-50 for 30 seconds; $50-65 for 60 seconds.

994 KOLD-TV - 13
7831 N. Business Park Dr. Phone: (520)744-1313
Tucson, AZ 85743 Fax: (520)744-5233

Format: Commercial TV. **Networks:** CBS. **Operating Hours:** 24 hrs. **ADI:** Tucson, AZ. **Key Personnel:** Jeff Sales, VP/GM; Ann Staff, Business Mgr.; Kevin Branigan, General Sales Mgr.; Carolyn Kane, News Dir.

995 KQTL-AM - 1210
PO Box 1511 Phone: (602)628-1200
Tucson, AZ 85702-1511 Fax: (602)326-4927

Format: Ethnic; Hispanic. **Networks:** Independent. **Owner:** Cima Broadcasting, L.L.C., at above address. **Founded:** 1985. **Operating Hours:** Continuous. **ADI:** Tucson, AZ. **Key Personnel:** Raul B. Gamez, CEO; Ernesto V. Portillo, Natl./Reg. Sales; Bertha Gallego, Operations Mgr.; Frank Fregoso, Chief Engineer; Amparo Maldonado, News Dir. **Wattage:** 10,000 day; 1000 night.

996 KRQQ-FM - 93.7
3202 North Oracle Rd. Phone: (520)618-2100
Tucson, AZ 85705 Fax: (520)618-2170

Format: Contemporary Hit Radio (CHR). **Networks:** Independent. **Founded:** 1971. **Operating Hours:** Continuous; 100% local. **ADI:** Tucson, AZ. **Key Personnel:** Debbie Wagner, Contact, dwagner@capstar croadcasting.com; Tim Richards, Regional Program Dir., phone (520)618-2174, fax (520)618-2170, ttrichards@aol.com; Randy Williams, Music Dir., phone (520)618-2179, fax (520)618-2170; Lisa Wadors, Promotions Dir., phone (520)618-1226, fax (520)618-2170; Todd Lawley, Dir. of Sales, phone (520)618-2157, fax (520)618-2122, tlawley@capstarbroadcasting.com; Betsy Bruce, News Dir., phone (520)618-2187, fax (520)618-2170; Toni Nichols, Business Mgr., phone (520)618-2141, fax (520)618-2165, tnichols@capstarbroadcasting.com. **Wattage:** 100,000. **Ad Rates:** Advertising accepted; rates available upon request.

997 KSJM-FM - 97.5
2761 N. Country Club Phone: (520)326-8788
Tucson, AZ 85716 Fax: (520)325-3057

Owner: Maloney Broadcasting, at above address. **Founded:** 1992. **Formerly:** KRKN-FM; KCDI-FM. **Operating Hours:** Continuous. **ADI:** Tucson, AZ. **Key Personnel:** Tom Hassey, Vice President, thassey@prodigy.com; Rick Verdugo, General Mgr. **Wattage:** 3000. **Ad Rates:** $35 per unit.

998 KTKT-AM - 990
1920 W. Copper Phone: (520)622-6711
Tucson, AZ 85745 Fax: (520)624-3226

Format: News. **Networks:** CNN Radio. **Founded:** 1949. **Operating Hours:** Continuous. **ADI:** Tucson, AZ. **Key Personnel:** Jim Cooley, General Mgr. **Wattage:** 10,000 day; 1000 night.

999 KTTU-TV - 18
1855 N. 6th Ave. Phone: (520)624-0180
Tucson, AZ 85705 Fax: (520)629-7185

Networks: United Paramount Network. **Founded:** Dec. 1984. **Formerly:** KDTU-TV (1989). **Operating Hours:** Continuous. **ADI:** Tucson, AZ.

1000 KTUC-AM - 1400
2761 N. Country Club Rd., Ste. 201 Phone: (602)326-8788
Tucson, AZ 85716-2271 Fax: (602)326-9655

Format: News; Talk; Sports. **Networks:** CBS; NBC. **Owner:** KTUC, Inc., at above address. **Founded:** 1926. **Operating Hours:** Continuous. **ADI:** Tucson, AZ. **Key Personnel:** Tom Hassey, President, thassey@prodigy.com; Laurie Haines, Vice Pres., Sales and Operations. **Wattage:** 1000.

1001 KUAS-TV - 27
c/o KUAT-TV Fax: (602)621-9105
University of Arizona
Tucson, AZ 85721
E-mail: serres@kuat.pbs.org

Format: Public TV. **Simulcasts:** KUAT-TV Tucson, AZ. **Networks:** Public Broadcasting Service (PBS). **Operating Hours:** 6 a.m. - midnight. **ADI:** Tucson, AZ. **Key Personnel:** Don Burgess, General Mgr., phone (520)6215828, fax (520)6213360. **URL:** http://www.arizona.edu/~kuat.

1002 KUAT-AM - 1550
University of Arizona Phone: (520)621-7548
Tucson, AZ 85721 Fax: (520)621-3360
Free: (800)521-5828

Format: Public Radio; Jazz; News; Eclectic; Ethnic; Hispanic. **Simulcasts:** KUAZ-FM. **Networks:** National Public Radio (NPR); Public Radio International (PRI). **Owner:** University of Arizona Board of Regents, at above address. **Founded:** 1968. **Operating Hours:** Sunrise-sunset; 50% network, 50% local. **ADI:** Tucson, AZ. **Key Personnel:** Edward Kupperstein, Station Mgr., phone (602)621-5805; David Ross, Chief Engineer; Ronald Stewart, Technical Services Dir., phone (602)621-7365; Jeff Rice, Chief Engineer, phone (602)621-7362; Thomas Machamer, Public Affairs/News Dir., phone (602)621-1569; Steve Hahn, Music Coord., phone (602)621-7355; Ed Kesterson, Program Mgr., phone (602)621-1904; Manuel Arcadia, Spanish Language Program Dir., phone (602)621-1565. **Wattage:** 50,000. **Ad Rates:** Noncommercial.

1003 KUAT-TV - 6
University of Arizona Phone: (520)621-5828
Tucson, AZ 85721 Fax: (520)621-9105

Format: Public TV. **Networks:** Public Broadcasting Service (PBS). **Founded:** 1959. **Operating Hours:** 17 hours daily; 97.5% network, 2.5% local. **ADI:** Tucson, AZ. **Key Personnel:** Don Burgess, General Mgr.; Michael Serres, Promotions Dir.; Hector Gonzales, Contact; Carol Bribach, Contact.

1004 KUAZ-FM - 89.1
University of Arizona Phone: (520)621-7548
Modern Lang., Rm. 222 Fax: (520)621-3360
Tucson, AZ 85721

Format: News; Jazz; Public Radio. **Simulcasts:** KUAT-AM. **Networks:** National Public Radio (NPR); AP; Public Radio International (PRI). **Owner:** Board of Regents, at above address. **Founded:** 1992. **Operating Hours:** 5 a.m.-midnight. **ADI:** Tucson, AZ. **Key Personnel:** Edward Kupperstein, Station Mgr., phone (520)621-5828; Lyle Kesterson, Program Mgr., phone (520)621-1904; Jeff Rice, News Dir., phone (520)621-1569. **Wattage:** 3000. **Ad Rates:** Noncommercial.

1005 KVOA-TV - 4
Box 5188 Phone: (520)792-2270
Tucson, AZ 85703 Fax: (520)620-1309

Format: Commercial TV. **Networks:** NBC. **Operating Hours:** Continuous Sun. - Fri.; 5:30a.m. - 12:30a.m. Sat. **ADI:** Tucson, AZ. **Key Personnel:** Jon F. Ruby, Contact.

KVOI-AM - See Oro Valley

1006 KWFM-FM - 92.9
3202 North Oracle Rd. Phone: (520)618-2100
Tucson, AZ 85705 Fax: (520)618-2200
E-mail: cool-fm@theriver.com

Format: Oldies. **Networks:** CBS. **Operating Hours:** Continuous. **ADI:** Tucson, AZ. **Key Personnel:** Debbie Wagner, Contact, phone (520)618-2139, fax (520)618-2190; Rich Robbin, Program Dir., phone (520)618-2149, fax (520)618-2200; Alan Michaels, Assoc. Program Director, phone (520)618-2134, fax (520)618-2200; Lori Ruboyianes, Promotions Dir., phone (520)618-2150, fax (520)618-2170; Todd Lawley, Dir. of Sales, phone (520)618-2157, fax (520)618-2122, tlawley@capstarbroadcasting.com; John Lee, News Dir., phone (520)618-2120, fax (520)618-2200; Toni Nichols, Business Mgr., phone (520)618-2120, fax (520)618-2165, tnichols@capstarbroadcasting.com. **Wattage:** 100,000. **Ad Rates:** Advertising accepted; rates available upon request. **URL:** http://www.theriver.com/cool-fm.

1007 KXCI-FM - 91.3
220 S. 4th Ave. Phone: (520)623-1000
Tucson, AZ 85701-2104 Fax: (520)882-5820

Format: Full Service. **Founded:** 1983. **Operating Hours:** Continuous; 10% network, 90% local. **ADI:** Tucson, AZ. **Key Personnel:** Russell Lowes, Business Mgr.; Mike Landwehr, Program Dir.; Michael Hyatt, Underwriting Dir.; Jenny Smeltzer, Membership Dir. **Wattage:** 50,000 ERP. **Ad Rates:** Noncommercial.

1008 KXEW-AM - 1600
889 W. El Puente Ln. Phone: (520)623-6429
Tucson, AZ 85713 Fax: (520)622-2680

Format: Tejano. **Owner:** Cactus Broadcasting Ltd., at above address. **Founded:** 1963. **Operating Hours:** Continuous; 4% network, 96% local. **ADI:** Tucson, AZ. **Key Personnel:** Allan Herman, General Mgr.; Hector Youtsey, Program Dir.; Richard Korzoch, Sales Mgr.; Diane Shafer, Office Mgr. **Wattage:** 1000. **Ad Rates:** $45-50 for 30 seconds; $50-65 for 60 seconds.

1009 TCI of Tucson
1440 E. 15th St. Phone: (520)629-8410
Tucson, AZ 85719-6495 Fax: (520)624-5918

Founded: 1982. **Formerly:** Tucson Cablevision. **Key Personnel:** Ken Watts, General Mgr. **Cities Served:** Davis-Monthan AFB, Foothills, Green Valley, Pataginia, Santos Thomas, South Tucson, AZ: 64 channels; 12 community access channels.

WHITERIVER

1010 KNNB-FM - 88.1
Hwy. 73, Skill Center Rd. Phone: (520)338-5229
Box 310 Fax: (520)338-1744
Whiteriver, AZ 85941

Format: Eclectic; Ethnic. **Owner:** White Mountain Apache Tribe, PO Box 700, Whiteriver, AZ 85941, (520)338-4346. **Founded:** 1982. **Operating Hours:** 18 hours daily. **Key Personnel:** Wayne C. Cody, General Mgr.; Kandi Lee, Program & Music Dir.; McCoy Aday, Producer; Udell Opah, Technician; Vangie Natan, Secretary. **Local Programs:** *Education & You*, Kandi Lee, Mailing contact; *Healthy Nations Program*; *To Your Health*, Dr. Hamstra, Mailing contact. **Wattage:** 630. **Ad Rates:** Noncommercial; underwriting available.

WICKENBURG, pop. 3,535.

Maricopa Co. (SC). 52 m NW of Phoenix. Winter resort. Gold, silver, lead mines. Cattle.

1011 The Wickenburg Sun
Brehm Communications, Inc.
180 N. Washington Phone: (520)684-7218
Wickenburg, AZ 85390-1298 Fax: (520)684-3185

Community newspaper. **Founded:** 1888. **Freq:** Weekly (Wed.). **Print Method:** Offset. **Cols./Page:** 6. **Col. Width:** 12.3 picas. **Col. Depth:** 21 1/2 inches. **Key Personnel:** Phil Swift, Editor; Kevin Cloe, Publisher. **Subscription Rates:** $14 individuals; $15 out of area; $16 out of state. **Remarks:** Accepts advertising.
Ad Rates: BW: $419.25 **Circ:** ‡3,749
4C: $969.25
PCI: $3.30

1012 KBSZ-AM - 1250
801 W. Wickenburg Way Phone: (602)684-7804
Wickenburg, AZ 85390 Fax: (602)684-7805

Format: Oldies. **Owner:** Circle S Broadcasting Co., Inc., at above address. **Founded:** 1968. **Formerly:** KCIW-AM (1989); KTIM-AM (1995). **Operating Hours:** Continuous. **Key Personnel:** Harold R. Shumway, General Mgr.; Sharon Shumway, Operations Mgr.; Mike Shumway, Sales Mgr. **Local Programs:** *New Book News*, Sharon Shumway, Producer, (520)684-7804, Fax (602)254-6644. **Wattage:** 1000 day; 202 night.

1013 KSWG-FM - 94.1
801 W. Wickenburg Way Phone: (602)254-6644
Wickenburg, AZ 85390 Fax: (602)684-7805
E-mail: info@kswg.com

Format: Country. **Networks:** Westwood One Radio. **Owner:** Circle S Broadcasting Co, Inc, at above address, Fax: (520)684-7804. **Founded:** 1992. **Formerly:** KMEO-FM; KBSZ-FM. **Operating Hours:** Continuous. **Key Personnel:** Mike Shumway, Sales Mgr.; Sharon Shumway, Operations Mgr.; Harold Shumway, Program Dir./Gen. Mgr. **Local Programs:** *New Book News*, Sharon Shumway, Producer. **Wattage:** 25,000. **Ad Rates:** $50-70 per unit. **URL:** http://www.kswg.com.

WILLIAMS, pop. 2,266.

Coconino Co. (N). 33 m W of Flagstaff. Tourist resort. Gateway to the Grand Canyon. Lumber mill. Pine timber. Livestock.

1014 Route 66 Magazine
326 W. Rte. 66 Phone: (520)635-4322
Williams, AZ 86046 Fax: (520)635-4470
Publication E-mail: info@route66magazine.com

Travel publication. **Founded:** Dec. 1993. **Freq:** Quarterly. **Print Method:** Web offset. **Trim Size:** 8 3/8 x 10 7/8. **Cols./Page:** 3. **Col. Width:** 2 1/4 inches. **Key Personnel:** Paul Taylor, Publisher; Sandi Taylor, Publisher. **Subscription Rates:** $14 individuals; $3.95 single issue. **Remarks:** Accepts advertising.
Circ: Paid 5,000
Non-paid 35,000

1015 Williams-Grand Canyon News
Central Printing Facility
118 S. 3rd St. Phone: (520)635-4426
PO Box 667 Fax: (520)635-4887
Williams, AZ 86046
Free: (800)408-4726
Publication E-mail: wmgcnews@primenet.com

Community newspaper. **Founded:** Sept. 1889. **Freq:** Weekly (Wed.). **Print Method:** Offset. **Cols./Page:** 6. **Col. Width:** 27 nonpareils. **Col. Depth:** 21 1/2 inches. **Key Personnel:** Cliff Larimer, Editor; Doug Wells, Publisher; Joyce Fuller McNally, Advertising Dir.; Darren Fitzgerald, Circulation Mgr. **USPS:** 684-640. **Subscription Rates:** $24.50 individuals; $29.50 out of state. **Remarks:** Accepts advertising. **URL:** http://www.grandcanyontourguide.com. **Feature Editors:** Doug Cook, *Sports*.
Ad Rates: GLR: $.58 **Circ:** ‡5,000
BW: $1,032
4C: $1,287
SAU: $8
PCI: $8

WINDOW ROCK, pop. 1,500.

Apache Co. (NE). 100 m NE of Winslow. Agriculture. Cattle, sheep, grains.

1016 The Navajo Times
The Navajo Nation
PO Box 310 Phone: (520)871-6641
Window Rock, AZ 86515-0310 Fax: (520)871-6409

Weekly newspaper for the Navajo people and Native Americans. **Subtitle:** Native American Newspaper. **Founded:** 1959. **Freq:** Weekly (Thurs.). **Print Method:** Offset. **Trim Size:** 13 x 21. **Cols./Page:** 6. **Col. Width:** 12 1/2 picas. **Col. Depth:** 21 inches. **Key Personnel:** Tom Arviso, Jr., Editor. **USPS:** 375-040. **Subscription Rates:** $45 individuals. **Remarks:** Accepts advertising. **Formerly:** Navajo Times Today.
Ad Rates: GLR: $.80 **Circ:** 17,800
BW: $1,134
4C: $1,534
SAU: $9
PCI: $9

1017 KHAC-AM - 880
PO Box 9090 Phone: (520)371-5587
Window Rock, AZ 86515-5003 Fax: (520)371-5588
E-mail: tpruitt106@aol.com

Format: Religious. **Networks:** Moody Broadcasting. **Owner:** Western Indian Ministries, Inc., at above address. **Founded:** 1967. **Operating Hours:** Sunrise-sunset; 20% network, 80% local. **Key Personnel:** Laurence Harper, Contact; Lenore Brown, Announcer; Larry Harper, Dir. of Broadcasting; Jerry Wagner, Traffic Mgr. **Local Programs:** *How to Manage Your Money* 9:25 am Monday-Friday, Larry Burkett, Mailing contact; *Insight for Living* 8:00 am Monday-Friday, Charles Swindoll, Mailing contact; *Focus on the Family* 9:30 am Monday-Friday, James Dobson, Mailing contact; *Grace to You* 10:00 am Monday-Friday, John MacArthur, Mailing contact; *Turning Point* 11:00 am Monday-Friday, David Jeremiah, Mailing contact; *Renewing Your Mind* 11:28 am Monday-Friday, R. C. Sproul, Mailing contact; *Gateway to Joy* 7:34 am Monday-Friday, Elizabeth Elliott, Mailing contact; *Breakpoint* 12:01 pm Monday-Friday, Chuck Colson, Mailing contact; *In Touch* 8:30 am Monday-Friday, Charles Stanley, Mailing contact. **Wattage:** 10,000 day; 430 night. **Ad Rates:** $4.75-10 for 30 seconds; $5-11.50 for 60 seconds.

1018 KTNN-AM - 660
PO Box 2569 Phone: (520)871-2582
Window Rock, AZ 86515 Fax: (520)871-3479

Format: Contemporary Country; Ethnic. **Networks:** NBC; Interstate Radio; Alaska Public Radio. **Owner:** Navajo Nation, PO Box 9000, Window Rock, AZ 86515, (602)871-4941.

Founded: 1986. **Operating Hours:** Continuous; 8% network, 92% local. **Key Personnel:** Tazbah McCallah, General Mgr.; Roy Tracy, Program Dir.; Selena Manychildren, News Dir.; Lori Lee, Production Dir.; Roy Lynn Tracy, Music Dir. **Wattage:** 50,000. **Ad Rates:** $10-12 for 15 seconds; $10-20 for 30 seconds; $12-24 for 60 seconds.

WINSLOW, pop. 7,921.

Navajo Co. (NE). 55 m SE of Flagstaff. Indian Reservation. Sawmills. Manufactures women's and children's garments. Sheep, cattle.

1019 The Winslow Mail
Northern Arizona Newspapers, Inc.
208 W. 1st St. Phone: (520)289-2467
Box AW Fax: (520)289-4151
Winslow, AZ 86047
Newspaper. **Founded:** 1894. **Freq:** Weekly (Wed.). **Print Method:** Offset. **Cols./Page:** 6. **Col. Width:** 24 nonpareils. **Col. Depth:** 21 inches. **Key Personnel:** Doug Wells, Publisher, phone (520)635-4426, fax (520)635-4887; Jo Adams, General Mgr., phone (520)526-3115, fax (520)526-3881; Dick Schwalje, Advertising/Office Mgr., phone (520)289-2467, fax (520)289-4151; Tom Schutes, News Editor, phone (520)289-2467, fax (520)289-4151. **USPS:** 686-960. **Subscription Rates:** $24 individuals; $30 out of area; $38 out of state. **Remarks:** Accepts advertising.
Ad Rates: 4C: $910.20 **Circ:** Wed. ‡5,360
PCI: $6.30 Fri. ‡1,700

1020 KINO-AM - 1230
Drawer K Phone: (520)289-3364
Winslow, AZ 86047 Fax: (520)289-3366

Format: Country; News; Sports. **Networks:** CBS; ESPN Radio. **Owner:** Sunflower Communications, Inc., at above address. **Founded:** 1962. **Operating Hours:** 6 a.m.-10 p.m. **Key Personnel:** Steve Adams, Sales Mgr.; Loy Engelhardt, Contact; Jeff Budka, Music Dir. **Local Programs:** *Coaches Corner*, Loy Engelhardt; *Koffee Klatch*, Loy Engelhardt. **Wattage:** 1000. **Ad Rates:** $4-5.50 for 30 seconds; $5.25-7.75 for 60 seconds.

YUMA†, pop. 42,433.

Yuma Co. (SW). On Colorado River 180 m SW of Phoenix on Calif./Mexico border. Tourism. Resort. Modest manufacturing complex. Predominately agricultural.

1021 The Sun Visitor
Thomson Newspapers
2055 S. Arizona Ave. Phone: (520)783-3333
Yuma, AZ 85365 Fax: (520)782-7369

Community newspaper for visitors covering community events. **Founded:** Sept. 1996. **Freq:** Weekly. **Key Personnel:** Pam M. Smith, Editor; Samuel J. Pepper, Publisher. **Subscription Rates:** Free. **Remarks:** Accepts advertising. **Former name:** Valley Foothills News.
Circ: Controlled 22,000

1022 The Western Voice
Arizona Western College
PO Box 929 Phone: (602)726-1000
Yuma, AZ 85369
Collegiate. **Founded:** 1989. **Freq:** Monthly. **Print Method:** Offset. **Cols./Page:** 5. **Col. Width:** 22 nonpareils. **Col. Depth:** 210 agate lines. **Remarks:** Accepts advertising. **Formerly:** Western Press.
Ad Rates: SAU: $3 **Circ:** Free 1,000

1023 The Yuma Daily Sun
2055 Arizona Ave. Phone: (520)783-3333
PO Box 271 Fax: (520)343-1009
Yuma, AZ 85364
Publication E-mail: yumasun@primenet.com

General newspaper. **Founded:** 1872. **Freq:** Daily (eve.), Sat. and Sun. (morn.). **Print Method:** Offset. **Cols./Page:** 6. **Col. Width:** 24 nonpareils. **Col. Depth:** 126 agate lines. **Key Personnel:** Terry Ross, Editor; Sam Pepper, Publisher. **Subscription Rates:** $147 individuals. **Remarks:** Accepts advertising. **URL:** http://www.yumasun.com.
Ad Rates: SAU: $11.84 **Circ:** Mon.-Sat. ★**15,664**
Sun. ★**19,134**

1024 KAWC-FM - 88.9
Arizona Western College Phone: (520)344-7690
Campus Fax: (520)344-7740
Business Administration Bldg.
Box 929
Yuma, AZ 85366-0929
E-mail: aw_ preciado@awc.c.c.az.us

Format: Classical; Jazz; News. **Networks:** National Public Radio (NPR). **Founded:** 1992. **Operating Hours:** 6 a.m.-9 p.m. **ADI:** El Centro, CA-Yuma, AZ. **Key Personnel:** Frank Preciado, Contact. **Wattage:** 3000. **Ad Rates:** Noncommercial.

1025 KBLU-AM - 560
755 W. 28th St. Phone: (520)344-4980
Yuma, AZ 85364 Fax: (520)344-4983

Format: Oldies. **Networks:** CNN Radio; Westwood One Radio. **Owner:** Commonwealth Board of AZ., L.L.C., 2550 5th Ave, 11th Fl., San Diego, CA 92103, (619)236-9599, Fax: (619)233-6517. **Founded:** 1940. **Formerly:** KYUM-AM (1970). **Operating Hours:** Continuous. **ADI:** El Centro, CA-Yuma, AZ. **Key Personnel:** Sheila Booth, General Sales Mgr.; Keith Lewis, General Mgr.; Richard Nix, Chief Engineer. **Wattage:** 1000. **Ad Rates:** $4-$22 for 30 seconds; $7-$28 for 60 seconds. Combined advertising rates available with KTTI-FM.

1026 KCFY-FM - 88.1
PO Box 1669 Phone: (520)341-9730
Yuma, AZ 85366 Fax: (520)341-9099
E-mail: kcfy88@yahoo.com

Format: Contemporary Christian. **Networks:** USA Radio. **Owner:** The Voice of International Christian Evangelism, Inc., at above address. **Founded:** 1992. **Operating Hours:** Continuous. **ADI:** El Centro, CA-Yuma, AZ. **Key Personnel:** Greg S. Myers, General Mgr., radiomania@yahoo.com; Don Durham, Program Dir.; Mickie Francher, Office Mgr.; Angel Milner, Promotions Dir. **Wattage:** 3,000. **Ad Rates:** Noncommercial; underwriting available. **URL:** http://www.freeyellow.com/members/kcfy88/index.html.

1027 KJOK-AM - 1400
949 S. Ave. B Phone: (520)782-4321
Yuma, AZ 85364 Fax: (520)343-1710
E-mail: z93radio@juno.com

Format: Full Service; News; Sports; Talk; Oldies. **Networks:** ABC. **Owner:** MonsterMedia, LLC, at above address. **Founded:** 1950. **Formerly:** KVOY-AM (1985); KEZC-AM (1996). **Operating Hours:** Continuous. **Key Personnel:** Keith Lewis, Owner/Gen. Mgr., monsterdude2@juno.com; Kim Johnson, News Dir., newsman1400@juno.com; John Schofield, Program Dir., littlejohn.z@juno.com. **Local Programs:** *Talk of Yuma* 8:00 am - 10:00 am Monday-Friday, John Phillips, Mailing contact. **Wattage:** 1000. **Ad Rates:** $18-22 per unit. $35-43 per unit. KLJZ-FM.

1028 KLJZ-FM - 93.1
949 S. Ave. B Phone: (520)782-4321
Yuma, AZ 85364 Fax: (520)343-1710
E-mail: z93radio@juno.com

Networks: ABC. **Owner:** MonsterMedia, LLC, at above address. **Founded:** 1970. **Formerly:** KJOK-FM (1996). **Operating Hours:** Continuous. **Key Personnel:** Keith Lewis, Owner/Gen. Manager, monsterdude@juno.com; Kim Johnson, News Dir., newsman1400@juno.com; John Schofield, Program Dir., littlejohn@juno.com. **Wattage:** 100,000. **Ad Rates:** $23.00-27.00 per unit. Combined advertising rates available with KJOK: $36-$44.

1029 KSWT-TV - 13
1301 S. 3rd Ave. Phone: (520)782-5113
Yuma, AZ 85364 Fax: (520)782-0320
Free: (800)313-3013

Format: Commercial TV. **Networks:** CBS; Telemundo. **Owner:** KB Media Inc., at above address. **Founded:** 1963. **Formerly:** KSWT-TV. **Operating Hours:** Continuous. **ADI:** El Centro, CA-Yuma, AZ. **Key Personnel:** Chris Willis, News Dir.; John Radeck, President.

1030 KYMA-TV - 11
1385 S. Pacific Ave. Phone: (520)782-1111
PO Box 550 Fax: (520)782-5401
Yuma, AZ 85366
Free: (800)944-6101
E-mail: kyma@msn.com

Format: Commercial TV. **Networks:** NBC. **Owner:** SunBelt Broadcasting, 1500 Foremaster Ln., Las Vegas, NV 89101, (702)342-3333. **Founded:** 1988. **Operating Hours:** Daily; 65% network, 35% local. **ADI:** El Centro, CA-Yuma, AZ. **Key Personnel:** Paul Heebink, Contact, pheebink@kyma.com; David Miller, Sales Mgr., fax (520)343-1813, dmiller@kyma-tv.com; Gail Chango, Program Mgr., gchango@kyma.com; Sergio Bustamante, Production Mgr., sbustamante@kyma.com; George Mills, News Dir., phone (520)782-4944, fax (520)782-5529, gmills@kyma.com. **Local Programs:** *First News 11* 5:30 am, 12 pm, 5 pm, 6 pm 10 Monday-Friday, George Mills, News Dir., (520)782-4944, Fax (520)782-5229. **Ad Rates:** Advertising accepted; rates available upon request. **URL:** http://www.kyma.com.

ARKANSAS

State Capital, LITTLE ROCK

Arkansas is bounded on the north by Missouri, east by Missouri, Tennessee, and Mississippi, south by Louisiana, southwest by Texas, and west by Oklahoma. Its greatest length, north to south, is 240 miles; its breadth varies from 170 to 250 miles. The total land area is 52,075 square miles. Nearly the entire state lies in the drainage bason of the lower Mississippi, which flows along most of its eastern border. In the eastern and southeastern portion are the cotton and timber belts. Every sort of tree that grows in the temperate zone abounds. The valley of the Arkansas is unsurpassed as a cotton producing region. In the west are the Ozark Mountains and fruit and mineral-bearing lands. Near the center of the state are the famous Hot Springs and other mineral spring resorts, attractive to tourists and invalids. In the south are the largest of the state's oil fields. The University of Arkansas is located at Fayetteville. The summer season is long, the winters usually short and mild. The Weather Bureau at Little Rock gives the temperature (annual average) as 61.8; highest on record, 110; lowest on record, -12. Total annual precipitation is 50.86 inches.

POPULATION: 2,399,000 (1992). Rank among the states, 33rd.

AGRICULTURE: Number of farms: 46,000 (1992). Farm acreage: 16,000,000 (1992). Cash receipts from farm marketings: crops, $1,631,000,000 (1991); livestock and products, $2,680,000,000.

FORESTS: Total forest land: 3,490,000 acres (1991). Principal woods: southern yellow pine, oak, red and sap gum, cypress, cottonwood and aspen, black and tupelo gum, elm, hickory, sycamore, beech, maple, ash.

MINERALS: Value of production: $303,000,000 (1991). Principal minerals: bromine, stone, and sand and gravel. Value of petroleum production: $186,000,000 (1991).

MANUFACTURES: Value added by manufacture: $12,826,000,000 (1991). Leading industry groups: food and related products, lumber and products (except furniture), paper and allied products.

LIST OF COUNTIES

Total number of counties 75

County, Location on Map, and County Seat	Pop.
Arkansas (E), De Witt and Stuttgart	21,653
Ashely (SE), Hamburg	24,319
Baxter (N), Mountain Home	31,186
Benton (NW), Bentonville	97,499
Boone (NW), Harrison	28,297
Bradley (S), Warren	11,793
Calhoun (S), Hampton	5,826
Carroll (NW), Berryvilla and Eureka Springs	18,654
Chicot (SE), Lake Village	15,713
Clark (SW), Arkadelphia	21,437
Clay (NE), Corning and Piggott	18,107
Cleburne (NC), Heber Springs	19,411
Cleveland (S), Rison	7,781
Columbia (SE), Magnolia	25,691
Conway (C), Morrilton	19,151
Craighead (NE), Jonesboro and Lake City	68,956
Crawford (NW), Van Buren	42,493
Crittenden (E), Marion	49,939
Cross (E), Wynne	19,225
Dallas (S), Fordyce	9,614
Desha (SE), Arkansas City	9,614
Drew (SE), Monticello	17,369
Faulkner (C), Conway	60,006
Franklin (NW), Charleston and Ozark	14,897
Fulton (N), Salem	10,037
Garland (WC), Hot Springs National Park	73,397
Grant (C), Sheridan	13,948
Greene (NE), Paragould	31,804
Hempstead (SW), Hope	21,621
Hot Springs (SWC), Malvern	26,115
Howard (SW), Nashville	13,569
Independence (N), Batesville	31,192
Izard (N), Melbourne	11,364
Jackson (NE), Newport	18,944
Jefferson (SEC), Pine Bluff	85,487
Johnson (NW), Clarksville	18,221
Lafayette (SW), Lewisville	9,643
Lawrence (NE), Walnut Ridge	17,457
Lee (E), Marianna	13,053
Lincoln (SE), Star City	13,690
Little River (SW), Ashdown	13,996
Logan (W), Booneville and Paris	20,557
Lonoke (C), Lonoke	39,268
Madison (NW), Huntsville	11,618
Marion (N), Yellville	12,001
Miller (SW), Texarkana	38,467
Mississippi (NE), Blytheville and Osceola	57,525
Monroe (E), Clarendon	11,333
Montgomery (W), Mount Ida	7,841
Nevada (SW), Prescott	10,101
Newton (NW), Jasper	7,666
Ouachita (S), Camden	30,574
Perry (C), Perryville	7,969
Phillips (E), Helena	28,838
Pike (SW), Murfreesboro	10,086
Poinsett (NE), Harrisburg	24,664
Polk (W), Mena	17,347
Pope (NW), Russelville	45,883
Prairie (C), Des Arc and De Valls Bluff	9,518
Pulaski (C), Little Rock	349,660
Randolph (NE), Pocahontas	16,558
St. Francis (E), Forrest City	28,497
Saline (C), Benton	64,183
Scott (W), Waldron	10,205
Searcy (W), Marshall	7,841
Sebastian (W), Fort Smith and Greenwood	99,590
Sevier (SW), De Queen	13,637
Sharp (N), Evening Shade and Hardy	14,109
Stone (N), Mountain View	9,775
Union (S), El Dorado	46,719
Van Buren (NWC), Clinton	14,008
Washington (NW), Fayetteville	113,409
White (NEC), Searcy	54,676
Woodruff (NEC), Augusta	9,520
Yell (W), Danville and Daranelle	17,759

STATISTICS

Newspapers

Period of Issue	
Daily	26
Evening Daily	12
Morning Daily	9
Daily with Sunday edition	14
Semiweekly	5
Weekly	86
Monthly	2
Triweekly	1
Free or partly free	4
Shopper	6
Total Newspapers	122

Periodicals

Period of Issue	
Weekly	3
Semimonthly	1
Bimonthly	2
Monthly	10
Quarterly	13
Total Periodicals	38

Total number of publications 273

Radio Stations

AM Stations 64
FM Stations 94
Total Radio Stations 158

TV Stations

Total TV Stations 16

Cable Stations

Total Cable Systems 23

Total number of broadcast listings 197

ARKADELPHIA†, pop. 10,005.

SW AR. Clark Co. On Ouachita River, 36 mi. S. of Hot Springs. Henderson State University. Ouachita Baptist University. Manufactures lumber, bearings, boats, roofing materials, rebuilt brake shoes, hotel-motel furniture. Saw mills. Timber. Diversified farming.

1031 Daily Siftings Herald
Donrey Media Group
205 S. 26th St. Phone: (501)246-5525
PO Box 10 Fax: (501)246-6556
Arkadelphia, AR 71923
General newspaper. **Freq:** Daily (eve.). **Print Method:** Offset. **Key Personnel:** Judith Collis, Publisher. **Subscription Rates:** $60 annually; $66 motor route. **Remarks:** Accepts advertising.
Ad Rates: SAU: $4.52 **Circ:** Paid ‡3,100
PCI: $6.69 Non-paid ‡125

1032 AETN - 2,6,9,13,19
350 S. Donaghey Phone: (501)682-2386
Conway, AR 72032 Fax: (501)682-4122
Free: (800)662-2386
E-mail: info@aetn.org

Format: Public TV. **Networks:** Public Broadcasting Service (PBS). **Owner:** Arkansas Educational Television Commission, at above address. **Founded:** 1976. **Formerly:** KETG. **Operating Hours:** 6 a.m.-11:30 p.m. weekdays; 7 a.m.-11:30 p.m. Saturday and Sunday. **ADI:** Little Rock, AR. **Key Personnel:** Susan Howarth, Exec. Dir.; Allen Weatherly, Deputy Dir.; Kathy Atkinson, Program Dir.; Ron Johnson, Communications Dir.; Carole Adornetto, Production Dir.; Gary Schultz, Engineering Dir.; Kathleen Stafford, Operations Dir.; Jane Havens, Traffic Mgr. **Local Programs:** *Arkansas Outdoors*; *Arkansas Week*; *Good Times Picture Show*. **Ad Rates:** Noncommercial. **URL:** http://www.aetn.com.

1033 KDEL-FM - 100.9
PO Box 40 Phone: (870)246-4561
Arkadelphia, AR 71923 Fax: (870)246-4562

Format: Adult Contemporary. **Networks:** Independent. **Owner:** Graham Broadcasting Inc., at above address. **Founded:** 1974. **Operating Hours:** Continuous. **Key Personnel:** Eddie Graham, Manager; Jerry Westmoreland, News/Sports Dir.; Steve Thomas, Music Dir. **Wattage:** 3000. **Ad Rates:** $4.50 for 30 seconds; $5.50 for 60 seconds. $4.00 for 30 seconds; $5.00 for 60 seconds. Combined advertising rates available with KVRC-AM.

1034 KVRC-AM - 1240
PO Box 40 Phone: (870)246-4561
Arkadelphia, AR 71923 Fax: (870)246-4562

Format: Contemporary Country. **Networks:** Arkansas Radio. **Owner:** Graham Broadcasting, at above address. **Founded:** 1948. **Operating Hours:** 5 a.m.-11 p.m.; 12% network, 88% local. **Key Personnel:** Eddie Graham, Program Dir.; Jerry Westmoreland, News Dir.; Frank Rippeto, Music Dir. **Wattage:** 1000. **Ad Rates:** $4.50 for 30 seconds; $5.50 for 60 seconds. $4.00 for 30 seconds; $5.00 for 60 seconds. Combined advertising rates available with KDEL-FM.

1035 TCA Cable TV of Arkadelphia
2505 Pine St. Phone: (870)246-7611
Box 709
Arkadelphia, AR 71923

Owner: T.C.A., 3015 SSE Loop 323, Tyler, TX 75701, (903)595-3701. **Key Personnel:** Mark Badgwell, Contact, phone (501)332-6254; Alan Wardlaw, Contact. **Cities Served:** subscribing households 4278; 36 channels; 1 community access channel; 2 hours per week community access programming.

ASHDOWN†, pop. 4,218.

SW AR. Little River Co. 20 mi. NW of Texarkana, near Lake Millwood. Manufactures lumber, trailers, lingerie, paper. Sawmills. Timber. Agriculture. Cotton, corn, oats, soybeans. Cattle.

1036 Little River News
45 E. Commence Phone: (870)898-3462
PO Box 608 Fax: (870)898-6213
Ashdown, AR 71822
Newspaper with Democratic orientation. **Founded:** 1898. **Freq:** Weekly (Thurs.). **Print Method:** Offset. **Cols./Page:** 7. **Col. Width:** 26 nonpareils. **Col. Depth:** 294 agate lines. **Key Personnel:** James W. Williamson, Publisher. **Subscription Rates:** $20 individuals. **Remarks:** Accepts advertising.
Ad Rates: BW: $882 **Circ:** 4,100
PCI: $6

1037 KARQ-FM - 92.1
PO Box 705 Phone: (501)898-3624
Ashdown, AR 71822 Fax: (501)898-6435

Format: Country. **Networks:** Jones Satellite. **Founded:** 1984. **Operating Hours:** Continuous; 90% network, 10% local. **Key Personnel:** Loren Hinton, Jr., Manager; Steve Pearce, Production Dir.; Jay Bunyard, General Mgr. **Wattage:** 3000. **Ad Rates:** $3.75-7.25 for 30 seconds; $6-9.50 for 60 seconds.

ATKINS, pop. 3,002.

NWC AR. Pope Co. 50 mi. NW of Little Rock. Lumber mill. Manufactures aluminum containers. Pickle plant. Oak, gum, cypress timber. Diversified farming. Cucumbers, peppers, spinach, tomatoes, cotton, rice, wheat & soybeans.

1038 Chronicle
The Atkins Chronicle
PO Box 188 Phone: (501)641-7161
Atkins, AR 72823 Fax: (501)641-1604
Publication E-mail: chronicl@cswnet.com

Newspaper with Democratic orientation. **Subtitle:** The Heart of the Arkansas River Valley. **Founded:** 1894. **Freq:** Weekly (Wed.). **Print Method:** Offset. **Cols./Page:** 6. **Col. Width:** 12.5 picas. **Col. Depth:** 294 agate lines. **Key Personnel:** Van A. Tyson, Publisher, vtyson@cswnet.com; Ginnie Tyson, Publisher; Gail Murdoch, Managing Editor; Mark Murdoch, Photo Editor; Brooka Hamilton, Circulation Mgr.; Bill Spinks, Sports Editor. **USPS:** 035-740. **Subscription Rates:** $20 in county; $25 out of area; $30 out of state. **Remarks:** Accepts advertising. **URL:** http://cswnet.com/~chronicl.
Ad Rates: GLR: $.13 **Circ:** 2,700
BW: $400
4C: $600
SAU: $5.10
PCI: $4.00

BALD KNOB, pop. 2,500.

NE AR. White Co. 55 mi. NE of Little Rock.

1039 Bald Knob Banner
PO Box 1480 Phone: (501)724-0398
Bald Knob, AR 72010-1480 Fax: (501)724-6362
Free: (888)515-3255
Publisher E-mail: wcrecord@ipa.net

Community newspaper. **Founded:** 1905. **Freq:** Weekly (Wed.). **Print Method:** Offset. **Trim Size:** 13 x 21. **Cols./Page:** 6. **Col. Width:** 2 1/16 inches. **Col. Depth:** 21 inches. **Key Personnel:** Barth Grayson, Editor and Publisher. **Subscription Rates:** $19.95 out of area for senior citizens; $25 for regular. **Remarks:** Combined advertising rates available with White County Record.
Ad Rates: GLR: $6 **Circ:** ‡3,500
BW: $400
4C: $500
PCI: $4

BARLING

KOLX-FM - See Fort Smith

BATESVILLE†, pop. 8,263.

N. AR. Independence Co. On White River, 80 mi. NE of Little Rock. Arkansas College. Manufactures white lime, marble and silica, rubber, lumber, staves, shoes, dairy products. Cotton ginning and compressing; saw mills; bottling works. Manganese, white and black marble, limestone, silica quarries; hardwood, pine timber. Diversified farming. Corn, hay, livestock, poultry.

1040 Batesville Guard
Batesville Guard-Record Co., Inc.
258 W. Main St. Phone: (501)793-2383
Box 2036 Fax: (501)793-9268
Batesville, AR 72501
Publication E-mail: batguard@intellinet.com

General newspaper. **Founded:** 1876. **Freq:** Daily (eve.). **Print Method:** Offset. **Cols./Page:** 6. **Col. Width:** 12 picas. **Col. Depth:** 21 inches. **Key Personnel:** Debbie Miller, Editor; Dr. O. E. Jones, Publisher; Mike Smith, Advertising Mgr. **USPS:** 045-220. **Subscription Rates:** $46 individuals; $50 out of state. **Remarks:** Accepts advertising.
Ad Rates: SAU: $8.61 **Circ:** Paid 8,973
PCI: $8.61 Non-paid ⊕**121**

1041 Mid-America Folklore
Mid-America Folklore Society
c/o Lyon College
Batesville, AR 72501

Consumer magazine covering academic articles on folklore. **Founded:** 1972. **ISSN:** 0275-6013. **Subscription Rates:** $10 individuals. **Remarks:** Advertising not accepted. **Former name:** Mid-South Folklore.
Circ: Paid 200

1042 Independence County Cable TV Inc.
Box 3799 Phone: (501)793-4174
Batesville, AR 72501 Fax: (501)793-7439
Free: (800)364-0834

Cities Served: Northern Arkansas.

1043 KAAB-AM - 1130
PO Box 2276 Phone: (501)793-4196
Batesville, AR 72503 Fax: (501)793-5222

Format: Religious. **Owner:** W.R.D. Entertainment, Inc., at above address. **Founded:** 1980. **Operating Hours:** Continuous; 5% network, 95% local. **Key Personnel:** Bob Connell, Contact; Pam Connell, Program Dir. **Wattage:** 1000. **Ad Rates:** $4.50-5 for 30 seconds; $5.50-6 for 60 seconds.

1044 KBTA-AM - 1340
PO Box 2077 Phone: (501)793-3861
Batesville, AR 72503-2077 Fax: (501)793-4437

Format: Oldies. **Networks:** AP. **Owner:** W.R.D Entertainment, Inc., at above address. **Founded:** 1950. **Operating Hours:** 6.00 a.m.-midnight; 100% local. **Key Personnel:** Preston Grace, Jr., President. **Wattage:** 1000. **Ad Rates:** $4-7 for 30 seconds; $5-8 for 60 seconds.

1045 KZLE-FM - 93.1
PO Box 2077 Phone: (501)793-3861
Batesville, AR 72503-2077 Fax: (501)793-4437

Format: Adult Contemporary. **Networks:** AP. **Owner:** W.R.D. Entertainment, Inc., at above address. **Founded:** 1982. **Operating Hours:** Continuous; 100% local. **ADI:** Little Rock, AR. **Key Personnel:** Preston Grace, Jr., President; Gary Bridgman, General Mgr.; Bob Connell, Operations Mgr.; Chad Whiteaker, Program Director; Rob Grace, Managing Director. **Local Programs:** *Mark & Lisa Show*, Chad Whiteaker. **Wattage:** 100,000. **Ad Rates:** $8.50-12.50 for 30 seconds; $11.50-15 for 60 seconds.

BEEBE, pop. 2,805.

SW AR. White Co. 27 mi. NE of Little Rock. Agriculture and sawmills.

1046 Beebe News
PO Box 0 Phone: (501)882-5414
Beebe, AR 72012 Fax: (501)882-3576
Publication E-mail: tbn@tpa.net

Community newspaper. **Founded:** 1948. **Freq:** Weekly (Wed.). **Print Method:** Offset. **Cols./Page:** 6. **Col. Width:** 2 1/16 inches. **Col. Depth:** 21 1/2 inches. **Key Personnel:** Lee McLane, Publisher. **USPS:** 047-880. **Subscription Rates:** $20 individuals; $35 out of state. **Remarks:** Accepts advertising. **URL:** http://www.biz.ipa.net/tbnews.
Ad Rates: SAU: $8.00 **Circ:** ‡2,500

BELLA VISTA, pop. 2,589.

NC AR. Benton Co. 4 mi. N. of Bentonville in the Ozarks. Mineral springs.

1047 The Weekly Vista
Community Publishers, Inc.
313 Town Center W. Phone: (501)855-3724
Bella Vista, AR 72714 Fax: (501)855-6992

Community newspaper. **Founded:** 1965. **Freq:** Weekly (Wed.). **Print Method:** Offset. **Cols./Page:** 5. **Col. Width:** 2 inches. **Col. Depth:** 15 3/4 inches. **Key Personnel:** Mark L. Elwood, Gen. Mgr./Managing Ed., marke@nwanews.com. **USPS:** 067-130. **Subscription Rates:** $25 individuals in county; $28 out of area. **Remarks:** Accepts advertising. **URL:** http://nwanews.com/vista. **Feature Editors:** Sally Carroll, *Lifestyle*, *Regional*, dscarroll@juno.com.
Ad Rates: GLR: $.80 **Circ:** Paid ‡5,000
BW: $661.60
4C: $940
PCI: $8.27

BENTON†, pop. 17,437.

C. AR. Saline Co. 23 mi. SW of Little Rock. Aluminum ore mines. Manufactures furniture, pulpwood, lumber. Agriculture. Poultry, beef. Dairy farming.

1048 KAKI-FM - 107.1
202 E. Cross Phone: (501)778-8257
Benton, AR 72015

Format: Big Band/Nostalgia. **Networks:** Unistar; CNN Radio. **Owner:** Bridges Broadcasting Service, at above address. **Founded:** 1979. **Operating Hours:** 6 a.m.-midnight. **Key Personnel:** Randall T. Bridges, General Mgr. **Wattage:** 2500 ERP. **Ad Rates:** $12 for 30 seconds; $15 for 60 seconds.

BENTONVILLE†, pop. 8,756.

NW AR. Benton Co. 79 mi. N. of Fort Smith. Resort. Manufactures plastics, lumber, injection molds, electronic controls, textile items, canned fruits and vegetables, cabinets, cheese, butter, evaporated fruits, clothing. Monument plants. Ships poultry. Hardwood timber. Agriculture. Poultry, apples, grapes.

1049 Benton County Daily Record
104 SW A St. Phone: (501)271-3700
PO Box 1049 Fax: (501)273-7777
Bentonville, AR 72712
General newspaper. **Founded:** 1886. **Freq:** Daily (morn.). **Print Method:** Offset. **Cols./Page:** 6. **Col. Width:** 26 nonpareils. **Col. Depth:** 301 agate lines. **Key Personnel:** Mike Brown, Editor and Publisher. **USPS:** 050-560. **Subscription Rates:** $64.80 individuals. **Remarks:** Accepts advertising. **URL:** http://www.n.wanews.com. **Formerly**: Benton County Daily Democrat.
Ad Rates: BW: $1,336 **Circ:** Paid 10,240
4C: $1,501 Free ‡26,600
PCI: $9.70

1050 The Herald-Leader
Community Publishers, Inc.
PO Box 1049 Phone: (501)271-3700
Bentonville, AR 72712 Fax: (501)273-7777

Community newspaper. **Founded:** 1892. **Freq:** Semiweekly (Sunday and Wed.). **Print Method:** Offset. **Cols./Page:** 6. **Col. Width:** 24 nonpareils. **Col. Depth:** 301 agate lines. **Key Personnel:** Mark Kelly, Managing Editor; Mike Brown, Publisher. **USPS:** 001-729. **Subscription Rates:** $19 individuals; $32 out of area. **Remarks:** Accepts advertising. **URL:** http:// nwanews.com/leader.html; http://www.pcinew:com/pci. **Formerly**: The Herald-Democrat (1992).
Ad Rates: GLR: $.25 **Circ:** Paid 4,358
BW: $677.25 Non-paid 60
4C: $882.25
SAU: $5.25

1051 Neighbor Shopper
Community Publishers, Inc.
PO Box 1049 Phone: (501)271-3700
Bentonville, AR 72712 Fax: (501)273-7777

Shopper. **Founded:** 1969. **Freq:** Weekly. **Print Method:** Offset. **Trim Size:** 13 1/2 x 11 1/2. **Cols./Page:** 6. **Col. Width:** 2 1/16 inches. **Col. Depth:** 21 1/2 inches. **Key Personnel:** Mike Brown, Publisher. **Subscription Rates:** Free. **URL:** http://www.nwanews.com//leader.html. **Formerly**: Ozark Neighbor; Shopper News.
Ad Rates: BW: $657.90 **Circ:** Free 12,059
4C: $852.90
PCI: $5.10

1052 KESE-AM - 1190
1101 S. Walton Blvd. Phone: (501)273-9039
Bentonville, AR 72712-6238 Fax: (501)273-9030
Free: (800)273-9030

Format: News. **Owner:** JEM Broadcasting Co. Inc., at above address. **Founded:** 1979. **Operating Hours:** 6 a.m.-sunset; 80% network, 20% local. **Key Personnel:** Elvis Moody, General Mgr.; Gary Borchert, Program Dir. **Wattage:** 2500.

1053 KJEM-FM - 93.3
1101 S. Walton Blvd Phone: (501)273-9039
Bentonville, AR 72712-6238 Fax: (501)273-9030

Format: Middle-of-the-Road (MOR). **Networks:** ABC. **Founded:** 1986. **Formerly**: KHHC-FM (1988). **Operating Hours:** Continuous. **Key Personnel:** Elvis Moody, General Mgr. **Local Programs:** *The Breakfast Club*, Gary Borchert. **Wattage:** 100,000.

1054 TCA Cable TV
Box 489 Phone: (501)273-5644
Bentonville, AR 72712 Fax: (501)273-0829

Key Personnel: Dennis Yocum, Manager. **Cities Served:** subscribing households 8,500; 35 channels; 1 community access channel.

BERRYVILLE†, pop. 2,271.

NW AR. Carroll Co. 80 mi. SE of Joplin, MO. Lumber mill; corrugated box factory; electronic components plant. Timber. Dairy, fruit, truck farms. Poultry processing.

1055 Berryville Star Progress
PO Box 232 Phone: (870)423-6636
Berryville, AR 72616-0232 Fax: (870)423-6640
Publication E-mail: cctynews@ccswnet.com

Local newspaper. **Founded:** 1872. **Freq:** Weekly (Thurs.). **Print Method:** Offset. **Cols./Page:** 6. **Col. Width:** 26 nonpareils. **Col. Depth:** 301 agate lines. **Key Personnel:** Ken O'Toole, Editor; Cynthia Chappell, Publisher; Lance Holman, Advertising Mgr. **Subscription Rates:** $21.50 individuals local; $26 out of area; $31 out of state. **Remarks:** Accepts advertising.
Ad Rates: SAU: $6.25 **Circ:** ‡3,850

1056 KTHS-AM - 1480
PO Box 191 Phone: (501)423-2147
Berryville, AR 72616 Fax: (501)423-2146

Format: Country; Religious. **Networks:** ABC. **Founded:** 1958. **Operating Hours:** 6 am-8:30 pm; network five-minute newscasts; remainder local. **ADI:** Springfield, MO. **Key Personnel:** Jim Earls, General Mgr.; Carroll Autry, Sales Mgr. **Wattage:** 5000. **Ad Rates:** $9.42 for 30 seconds; $13.57 for 60 seconds.

1057 KTHS-FM - 107.1
PO Box 191 Phone: (501)423-2147
Berryville, AR 72616 Fax: (501)423-2146

Format: Country; Sports. **Networks:** ABC. **Founded:** 1974. **Formerly**: KSCC-FM (1991). **Operating Hours:** Continuous; five minute network newscasts, remainder local. **ADI:** Springfield, MO. **Key Personnel:** Tom Earls, General Mgr.; Jim Earls, Program Dir.; Jerry Blackston, News Dir.; Carroll Autry, Sales Mgr. **Wattage:** 18,000. **Ad Rates:** $9.42-11.18 for 30 seconds; $13.53-16.47 for 60 seconds.

BLYTHEVILLE, pop. 24,314.

NE AR. Mississippi Co. 70 mi. N. of Memphis, TN. Mississippi County Community College.Manufactures industrial valves, electric tools, automotive emission controls, flexible duct systems, metal work, cable assemblies, canned goods, agrichemicals and fertilizers, battery chargers Agriculture. Soybeans, cotton, milo, wheat rice.

1058 Blytheville Courier News
Village News, Inc.
PO Box 1108 Phone: (870)763-4461
Blytheville, AR 72316-1108 Fax: (870)763-6874

Newspaper. **Founded:** 1903. **Freq:** Daily and Sunday. **Key Personnel:** David Tennyson, Publisher. **Subscription Rates:** $87 individuals.
Circ: Mon.-Fri. 4,348
Wed. 11,737

1059 Courier News
Blytheville Courier News
PO Box 1108 Phone: (501)763-4461
Blytheville, AR 72316 Fax: (501)763-6874

General newspaper. **Founded:** 1894. **Freq:** Daily (eve.), Sunday (morn.). **Print Method:** Offset. **Cols./Page:** 6. **Col. Width:** 2 1/4 inches. **Col. Depth:** 21 1/2 inches. **Key Personnel:** Webb Laseter III, Editor; C.F. McClugham, Publisher. **ISSN:** 0746-9527. **Subscription Rates:** $90.60 individuals; $57 out of area. **Remarks:** Accepts advertising.
Ad Rates: BW: $961.05 **Circ:** Mon.-Fri. 4,308
PCI: $7.45

1060 Village News
Tennyson Publishing
PO Box 13 Phone: (501)763-4461
Blytheville, AR 72315 Fax: (501)763-6874

Community newspaper. **Founded:** 1976. **Freq:** Semiweekly (Wed. and Sun.). **Print Method:** Offset. **Cols./Page:** 6. **Col. Width:** 2 1/16 inches. **Col. Depth:** 21 inches. **Key Personnel:** Sandra Tennyson, Editor; Max Andrews, Advertising Mgr.; David Tennyson, Publisher; Herb Smith, Advertising Mgr.; Annabell Walker, Office Mgr.; Susie Robinson, Production Mgr. **Subscription Rates:** Free in area; $30 individuals. **Remarks:** Accepts advertising.
Ad Rates: BW: $464.94 **Circ:** Free 9,348
4C: $864.94
SAU: $3.99

1061 Blytheville TV Cable Co.
Box 127 Phone: (501)763-6688
Blytheville, AR 72316 Fax: (501)763-8459

Owner: Harold Sudbury, 121 S. 2nd St., Blytheville, AR 72316, (501)762-2093, Fax: (501)763-8459. **Founded:** 1968. **Key Personnel:** Tom Hill, General Mgr., phone (501)263-6688, fax (501)763-8459. **Cities Served:** Blytheville, Dell, AR: subscribing households 6,400; 43 channels; 1 community access channel; 168 hours per week community access programming.

1062 KHLS-FM - 96.3
125 S. 2nd Phone: (501)762-2093
PO Box 989 Fax: (501)763-8459
Blytheville, AR 72316-0989

Format: Country. **Networks:** ABC; Progressive Farmer. **Founded:** 1948. **Operating Hours:** Continuous. **Key Personnel:** Harold Sudbury, President; Ed White, Station and Sales Mgr.; Keith Cole, Music and Public Service Dir.; Randy Meyers, News and Sports Dir. **Wattage:** 100,000. **Ad Rates:** $6.20-7.15 for 15 seconds; $7.60-14.30 for 30 seconds; $9.85-19 for 60 seconds.

1063 KLCN-AM - 910
Box 989 Phone: (501)762-2093
Blytheville, AR 72316 Fax: (501)763-8459
Free: (800)737-0096

Format: News. **Founded:** 1922. **Operating Hours:** Continuous. **Key Personnel:** Harold Sudbury, President; Ed White, Station and Sales Mgr.; Randy Meyers, News and Sports Dir. **Wattage:** 5000. **Ad Rates:** Advertising accepted; rates available upon request.

BOONEVILLE†, pop. 3,718.

SW AR. Logan Co. 34 mi. SE of Fort Smith. Sawmills, natural gas; tuberculosis sanatorium.

1064 Booneville Democrat
Donrey Media Group
PO Box 208 Phone: (501)675-4455
Booneville, AR 72927 Fax: (501)675-5457

Community newspaper. **Freq:** Weekly (Wed.). **Key Personnel:** Donna S. Martin, Editor; Donald Reynolds, Publisher; Cary M. Garner, Advertising Mgr. **Remarks:** Advertising accepted; rates available upon request.
Circ: (Not Reported)

BRINKLEY, pop. 4,909.

E. AR. Monroe Co. 67 mi. E. of Little Rock. Manufactures men's shirts, electric motors, lumber, cooperage. Hardwood timber. Diversified farming. Cotton, soybeans, rice.

1065 KBRI-AM - 1570
Hwy. 70 W. Phone: (501)734-1570
PO Box 111
Brinkley, AR 72021

Format: Adult Contemporary; News; Religious; Agricultural. **Networks:** Independent. **Founded:** 1959. **Operating Hours:** 6 a.m.-10 p.m.; 10% network, 90% local. **Key Personnel:** J.R. Rodgers, Contact. **Wattage:** 250 day; 43.9 night. **Ad Rates:** $6.00 for 30 seconds; $7.00 for 60 seconds.

1066 KQMC-FM - 102.3
Hwy. 70 W. Phone: (501)734-1570
PO Box 111
Brinkley, AR 72021

Format: Country; News; Agricultural. **Networks:** Independent. **Owner:** Bobby Caldwell, at above address. **Founded:** 1969. **Formerly**: KBRI-FM (1984). **Operating Hours:** 6 a.m.-10 p.m.; 10% network, 90% local. **Key Personnel:** J.R. Rodgers, Contact. **Wattage:** 3000. **Ad Rates:** $6.00 for 30 seconds; $7.00 for 60 seconds.

CABOT, pop. 4,806.

C. AR. Lonoke Co. 20 mi. NE of Little Rock. Manufactures furniture, net hoops, wearing apparel, military caps, satellite antenna dishes, mobile homes. Agriculture. Dairying. Soybeans, Corn, potatoes, strawberries. Poultry.

1067 Cabot Star-Herald
Magie Enterprises, Inc.
903 S. Pine St. Phone: (501)843-3534
PO Box 1058 Fax: (501)843-6447
Cabot, AR 72023
Publisher E-mail: arknews@aristotle.net

Community newspaper. **Founded:** 1922. **Freq:** Weekly (Wed.). **Print Method:** Offset. **Cols./Page:** 6. **Col. Width:** 2 1/8 inches. **Col. Depth:** 21 inches. **Key Personnel:** Mark Magie, Publisher/General Mgr.; Susie Magie, Advertising Mgr. **USPS:** 082-320. **Subscription Rates:** $19 individuals.
Ad Rates: GLR: $.43 **Circ:** Paid 6,250
BW: $1,008 Free 250
4C: $1,258
PCI: $8

Jacksonville Patriot - See Jacksonville

1068 Lonoke Democrat
Magie Enterprises, Inc.
903 S. Pine St. Phone: (501)843-3534
PO Box 1058 Fax: (501)843-6447
Cabot, AR 72023
Publisher E-mail: arknews@aristotle.net

Community newspaper. **Founded:** 1871. **Freq:** Weekly (Wed.). **Print Method:** Offset. **Cols./Page:** 6. **Col. Width:** 26 nonpareils. **Col. Depth:** 294 agate lines. **Key Personnel:** F. Cone Magie, Publisher; Mark Magie, General Mgr. **USPS:** 153-040. **Subscription Rates:** $14 individuals; $17 out of area; $28 Out of State. **Remarks:** Accepts advertising.
Ad Rates: GLR: $.47 **Circ:** Paid 2,600
BW: $588 Free 100
SAU: $4

1069 Friendship Cable
Box 1030 Phone: (501)495-7111
Cabot, AR 72023 Fax: (501)843-5255

Founded: 1973. **Absorbed:** Douglas Communications Mid-South (1996). **Formerly:** Premier Cable (1990). **Key Personnel:** Todd Sanders, Contact. **Cities Served:** subscribing households 1,800; 24 channels.

CAMDEN†, pop. 15,356.

S. AR. Ouachita Co. On Ouachita River at head of navigation, 30 mi. N. of El Dorado. Manufactures paper, paper bags, disposable diapers, roofing materials, industrials ceramics, rubber adhesives, defense systems. lumber, monuments, fertilizer. Pine, hardwood timber. Hatcheries. Agriculture. Poultry, cotton, corn.

1070 Camden News
Walter Hussman
PO Box 798 Phone: (501)836-8192
Camden, AR 71701 Fax: (501)837-1414

Community newspaper. **Founded:** 1949. **Freq:** Weekly (Thurs.). **Print Method:** Offset. **Cols./Page:** 6. **Col. Width:** 26 nonpareils. **Col. Depth:** 301 agate lines. **Key Personnel:** Margie L. Wagnon, Editor; W.E. Hussman, Publisher. **Subscription Rates:** $12 individuals. **Remarks:** Accepts advertising. **Formerly:** Stephens Star.
Ad Rates: SAU: $2.27 **Circ:** 350

1071 Cam-Tel Co.
113 Madison Ave. Phone: (870)836-8111
Box 835 Fax: (870)836-2109
Camden, AR 71701

Founded: 1963. **Formerly:** Cam-Telco. **Key Personnel:** Paul Morbeck, Contact, phone (501)378-3529, fax (501)376-8594; Charles Launius, Contact, phone (870)836-8111, fax (870)836-2109. **Cities Served:** 3 community access channels.

1072 KAMD-AM - 910
113 Madison Phone: (501)836-5091
Camden, AR 71701 Fax: (501)836-8196

Format: Country; Religious. **Networks:** Mutual Broadcasting System. **Owner:** Camden Radio Inc., at above address. **Founded:** 1946. **Operating Hours:** 5 a.m.-11 p.m.; 5% network, 95% local. **ADI:** Little Rock, AR. **Key Personnel:** Bill Snearly, General Mgr.; Greg Arnold, Program Dir.; Greg Arnold, Music Dir. **Wattage:** 5000. **Ad Rates:** $4.50-6.50 for 30 seconds; $6.50-8.50 for 60 seconds.

1073 KAMD-FM - 97.1
113 W. Washington St., Ste. A Phone: (501)836-5091
Camden, AR 71701-3955 Fax: (501)836-8196

Format: Contemporary Country. **Networks:** Mutual Broadcasting System. **Owner:** Camden Radio Inc., at above address, (501)836-8197. **Founded:** 1968. **Operating Hours:** 5 a.m.-11 p.m.; 5% network, 95% local. **ADI:** Little Rock, AR. **Key Personnel:** Freda Carter, General Mgr.; Greg Arnold, Contact. **Wattage:** 39,000. **Ad Rates:** $4.50-6.50 for 30 seconds; $6.50-8.50 for 60 seconds.

1074 KCAC-FM - 89.5
327 Stewart St. S. W. Phone: (870)836-5289
Camden, AR 71701 Fax: (870)836-9369
E-mail: kcac89@mail.cei.net

Format: Alternative/New Music/Progressive. **Owner:** Camden Fairview School District, at above address. **Operating Hours:** Continuous. **Key Personnel:** Steve Taylor, General Mgr., phone (870)836-9367; Paul Fesh, Production Specialist; Bonnie Burt, Program Specialist, bburt@ccc.scsc.k12.ar.us. **Local Programs:** *Bedtime Stories*, Steve Taylor. **Wattage:** 250. **URL:** http://www.cei.net/kcac89.

1075 KCXY-FM - 95.3
PO Box 956 Phone: (870)836-9567
Camden, AR 71701 Fax: (870)836-9500
E-mail: y95@y95.net

Format: Contemporary Country. **Networks:** ABC. **Owner:** Gary D. Terrell, at above address. **Founded:** 1987. **Formerly:** KCEZ-FM (1987). **Operating Hours:** Continuous; 90% local, 10% network. **ADI:** Little Rock, AR. **Key Personnel:** Gary D. Terrell, Pres./Gen. Mgr./Engineer, gary@v95.net; Bob Parks, Sales Mgr.; Craig T. Dale, Program Dir. **Wattage:** 100,000. **Ad Rates:** $14.11-18.23 for 30 seconds; $19.41-25.88 for 60 seconds. **URL:** http://www.y95.net.

CARLISLE, pop. 2,567.

C. AR. Lonoke Co. 35 mi. E. of Little Rock. Rice and sawmills; cotton ginning; cheese factory. Hardwood timber. Agriculture. Rice, oats, cotton.

1076 Carlisle Independent
Magie Enterprises, Inc.
PO Box 47 Phone: (501)552-3111
Carlisle, AR 72024
Publisher E-mail: arknews@aristotle.net

Community newspaper. **Founded:** 1895. **Freq:** Weekly (Wed.). **Print Method:** Offset. **Cols./Page:** 6. **Col. Width:** 21 nonpareils. **Col. Depth:** 294 agate lines. **Key Personnel:** F. Cone Magie, Publisher; Mark Magie, General Mgr.; Rose Mary Buffalo, Editor. **USPS:** 090-800. **Subscription Rates:** $14 individuals; $17 out of area; $28 out of state. **Remarks:** Accepts advertising.
Ad Rates: GLR: $.21 **Circ:** Paid 1,515
BW: $441 Free 109
SAU: $3

CAVE CITY

1077 KZIG-FM - 89.9
PO Box 190 Phone: (501)283-5331
Cave City, AR 72521 Fax: (501)283-6887

Format: Religious; Educational. **Networks:** USA Radio. **Owner:** Cave City Board of Education, PO Box 600, Cave City, AR 72521, (501)283-5391, Fax: (501)283-6887. **Founded:** 1981. **Operating Hours:** 6 a.m.-9 p.m. **Key Personnel:** Becky Sisk, Manager, bsisk@cavecity.nesc.k12.ar.us; Dave Fisher, News Dir.; Becky Sisk, Music Dir. **Wattage:** 3500. **Ad Rates:** Noncommercial.

CHARLESTON†, pop. 1,748.

SW AR. Franklin Co.

1078 Charleston Express
PO Box 39 Phone: (501)965-7368
Charleston, AR 72933 Fax: (501)965-7206

Community newspaper. **Freq:** Weekly (Wed.). **Print Method:** Offset. **Cols./Page:** 6. **Col. Width:** 13 inches. **Col. Depth:** 21 1/2 inches. **Key Personnel:** Dolores A. James, Editor/Administration; Bill Hagerman, Publisher. **Subscription Rates:** $17 individuals; $21 out of area. **Remarks:** Accepts advertising.
Ad Rates: BW: $416.67 **Circ:** Paid 2,250
4C: $666.67 Free 25
SAU: $3.53

CHEROKEE VILLAGE

1079 Villager Journal
PO Box 480 Phone: (870)257-2417
Cherokee Village, AR 72525 Fax: (870)257-5487
Free: (800)897-2417
Publication E-mail: roundhouse@centuryinter.net

Local newspaper. **Founded:** 1955. **Freq:** Weekly. **Print Method:** Offset. **Trim Size:** 11 5/16 x 17 7/16. **Cols./Page:** 5. **Col. Width:** 2 1/16 inches. **Col. Depth:** 16 inches. **Key Personnel:** David Cox, Editor and Publisher; Heidi Cox, General Mgr.; Carl Lotz, Advertising Mgr.; Fran Lotz, Office Mgr. **ISSN:** 0899-7780. **Subscription Rates:** $20 in county; $29 out of county. **Remarks:** Accepts advertising. **URL:** http://www.villageronline.com. **Formerly:** The Cherokee Villager.
Ad Rates: BW: $500 **Circ:** Paid 3,373
4C: $650
PCI: $6.50

1080 KFCM-FM - 100.9
PO Box 909 Phone: (870)856-3249
Cherokee Village, AR 72525 Fax: (870)856-4408

Format: Middle-of-the-Road (MOR). **Networks:** Satellite Music Network; ABC. **Owner:** KFCM, Inc., at above address. **Operating Hours:** Continuous. **ADI:** Jonesboro, AR. **Key Personnel:** Ruth Bragg, Sales Mgr.; Hazel Barker, Traffic Mgr.; Justin Sisk, Operations Mgr. **Local Programs:** *Morning Meeting* 9:00 am - 11:00 am, John Power. **Ad Rates:** $6.50-8 for 30 seconds; $13-16 for 60 seconds.

CLARENDON†, pop. 2,361.

E. AR. Monroe Co. 75 mi. E. of Little Rock. Residential.

1081 Monroe County Sun
PO Box 315 Phone: (501)734-1056
Clarendon, AR 72029 Fax: (870)734-1494

Newspaper. **Founded:** 1874. **Freq:** Weekly (Thurs.). **Print Method:** Offset. **Cols./Page:** 6. **Col. Width:** 26 nonpareils. **Col. Depth:** 294 agate lines. **Key Personnel:** Thomas Tocanes; Catherine Tocanes. **Subscription Rates:** $18 individuals.
Ad Rates: BW: $510 **Circ:** 1,600
4C: $720
SAU: $4.40

CLARKSVILLE†, pop. 5,237.

NW AR. Johnson Co. 60 mi. E. of Fort Smith. College of the Ozarks. Lumber and stave mills. Brick, shoes, power tools, stainless steel tubing plants. Gas wells; coal mines; pine, oak timber. Poultry and sweet potato processing. Dairy, poultry, stock farms. Peaches.

1082 Johnson County Graphic
PO Box 289 Phone: (501)754-2005
Clarksville, AR 72830 Fax: (501)754-2098
Publication E-mail: graphic@cswnet.com

Community newspaper. **Founded:** 1877. **Freq:** Weekly (Wed.). **Print Method:** Offset. **Trim Size:** 13 1/8 x 21 1/2. **Cols./Page:** 6. **Col. Width:** 25 nonpareils. **Col. Depth:** 301 agate lines. **Key Personnel:** Robert L. Fisher, Publisher; Margaret Wylie, Editor; Ron Wylie, General Mgr., rwylie@cswnet.com. **USPS:** 276-380. **Subscription Rates:** $30 individuals. **Remarks:** Accepts advertising. **URL:** http://www.cswnet.com/~graphic.
Ad Rates: GLR: $.68 **Circ:** ‡8,200
BW: $1,225.50
4C: $1,350.50
SAU: $9.50
PCI: $9.50

1083 KLYR-AM - 1360
PO Box 188 Phone: (501)754-3092
Clarksville, AR 72830-0188

Format: Country. **Networks:** Independent. **Founded:** 1957. **Operating Hours:** 6 a.m.-10 p.m. **Key Personnel:** Randall Forrester, Contact; Jay Davis, General Mgr.; Myron Been, Music Dir. **Wattage:** 500 day; 98 nights. **Ad Rates:** $3.53-8.09 for 30 seconds; $5.31-12.14 for 60 seconds.

CLINTON†, pop. 1,284.

NWC AR. Van Buren Co. 70 mi. N. of Little Rock. Manufactures electrical cord. Diversified farming. Poultry processing; beef and dairy cattle, hay.

1084 Van Buren County Democrat
114 South Court St. Phone: (501)745-5175
PO Box 119 Fax: (501)745-8865
Clinton, AR 72031-0119
Community newspaper. **Founded:** May 8, 1909. **Freq:** Weekly (Wed.). **Print Method:** Offset. **Cols./Page:** 6. **Col. Width:** 2.4 inches. **Col. Depth:** 21 inches. **Key Personnel:** Roger Smith, Editor and Publisher. **USPS:** 656-540. **Subscription Rates:** $17 individuals; $567 local; $693 national. **Remarks:** Accepts advertising.
Ad Rates: SAU: $5.50 **Circ:** Non-paid ‡4,500

CONWAY†, pop. 20,375.

C. AR. Faulkner Co. 32 mi. NW of Little Rock. Hendrix College; University of Central Arkansas. Manufactures shoes, school & office furniture, bus bodies, refrigerated cabinets, folding boxes, automotive testing equipment, dance floors, machine tools, vending machines. Dairy, stock, poultry farms.

1085 Log Cabin Democrat
1058 Front St. Phone: (501)327-6621
Conway, AR 72032 Fax: (501)327-6787
Free: (800)678-4523
Publication E-mail: letters@thecabin.net

General newspaper. **Founded:** 1879. **Freq:** Daily (eve.), Sunday (morn.). **Print Method:** Offset. **Trim Size:** 22 3/4. **Cols./Page:** 6. **Col. Width:** 12 picas. **Col. Depth:** 21 1/2 inches. **Key Personnel:** Mike Hengel, Publisher, phone (501)505-1211, mhengel@thecabin.net; Donna Spears, Advertising Dir., phone (501)505-1225, fax (501)505-1284, dspears@thecabin.net. **USPS:** 142-780. **Subscription Rates:** $94. **Remarks:** Accepts advertising. Monday-Friday: GLR:

$.72; BW: $980.40; PCI: $7.60; Sunday: GLR: $.72; BW: $1,077.15; PCI: $8.35. **URL:** http://www.thecabin.net.
Circ: Mon.-Fri. 10,004
Sun. 11,019

AETN - See Arkadelphia

1086 Conway Corp.
1307 Prairie St. Phone: (501)450-6000
Box 99 Fax: (501)450-6099
Conway, AR 72032-5344

Founded: 1980. **Key Personnel:** Richie Arnold, CEO, phone (501)450-6020; Bret Carroll, CFO, phone (501)450-6030; Linda Johnson, Communications Coordinator, phone (501)450-6025, ljohnson@conwaycorp.net; Earnest Hicks, Telecommunications, phone (501)450-6055; Roger Mills, COO, phone (501)450-6050. **Cities Served:** Conway, AR: subscribing households 15,684; 62 channels; 1 community access channel. **URL:** http://www.conwaycorp.com.

KAFT-TV - See Fayetteville

1087 KCON-AM - 1230
PO Box U-5145 Phone: (501)450-3326
201 Ponaghey Ave. Fax: (501)450-5874
Conway, AR 72035

Format: Adult Contemporary; News; Sports. **Networks:** Arkansas Radio. **Owner:** KCON Broadcasting Co., Inc., at above address. **Founded:** 1950. **Operating Hours:** Continuous. **Key Personnel:** Monty Rowell, General Mgr., montyr@mail.uca.edu. **Wattage:** 1000. **Ad Rates:** $2.50 for 30 seconds; $3 for 60 seconds.

KEMV-TV - See Mountain View

1088 KETS-TV - 2
350 S. Donaghey Phone: (501)682-2386
Conway, AR 72032 Fax: (501)682-4122
Free: (800)662-2386

Format: Public TV. **Networks:** Public Broadcasting Service (PBS). **Owner:** Arkansas Educational Television Commission, at above address. **Founded:** 1966. **Operating Hours:** Continuous. **ADI:** Little Rock, AR. **Key Personnel:** Kathy Atkinson, Program Dir.; Susan Howarth, Exec.Dir.; Carole Adornetto, Production Dir.; Ron Johnson, Communications Dir.; Allen Weatherly, Deputy Dir.; Jane Havens, Traffic Mgr.; Gary Schultz, Engineering Dir.; Kathleen Stafford, Operations Dir. **Local Programs:** *Arkansas Outdoors*; *Arkansas Week*; *Good Times Picture Show*. **Ad Rates:** Noncommercial. **URL:** http://www.aetn.com.

1089 KFCA-AM - 1330
PO Box 1266 Phone: (501)327-6611
Conway, AR 72032 Fax: (501)327-7920

Format: Sports; News; Information. **Owner:** Creative Media, Inc., at above address. **Operating Hours:** Continuous. **Key Personnel:** Mike Harrison, General Mgr. **Wattage:** 500 day, 64 night.

1090 KHDX-FM - 93.1
Hendrix College Phone: (501)450-1339
Washington & Independence Fax: (501)450-1200
Conway, AR 72032

Format: Alternative/New Music/Progressive. **Owner:** Hendrix College, at above address. **Founded:** 1973. **Operating Hours:** Noon-Midnight; 100% local. **Key Personnel:** Jenny Daniels, Station Mgr.; Laurie Winstead, Program Dir.; Lee Razer, Music Dir. **Wattage:** 10. **Ad Rates:** Noncommercial.

KTEJ-TV - See Jonesboro

1091 KTOD-FM - 92.7
PO Box 1266 Phone: (501)327-6611
Conway, AR 72032 Fax: (501)327-7920

Format: Contemporary Country; Country. **Networks:** AP. **Owner:** Creative Media, Inc., at above address. **Founded:** 1989. **Operating Hours:** Continuous. **Key Personnel:** Diane Vinson, Pres./Gen. Mgr.; David Paul, Program Dir. **Wattage:** 3000. **Ad Rates:** $8.50-11.50 for 30 seconds; $12.50-15 for 60 seconds.

CORNING

1092 Clay County Courier
PO Box 128, Hwy. 67 N. Phone: (501)857-3531
Corning, AR 72422 Fax: (501)857-5204

Community newspaper. **Freq:** Weekly (Wed.). **Cols./Page:** 8. **Col. Width:** 12 1/2 picas. **Col. Depth:** 21 1/2 inches. **Key Personnel:** Jan Rockwell, Publisher.
Circ: 3,400

1093 KCCB-AM - 1260
W. 2nd St. Phone: (501)857-6646
PO Box 398
Corning, AR 72422

Format: Country. **Networks:** Arkansas Radio. **Owner:** Clay County Broadcasting Co., at above address, Fax: (501)857-6795. **Founded:** 1959. **Operating Hours:** Sunrise-sunset. **Key Personnel:** Jim Adkins, Owner; Tina Privett, Sales Mgr.; Bruce Roach, Program Dir.; Claudia Schoeder, Science and Women's Issues. **Local Programs:** *Corning Community Events*, Tina Privett; *Corning High School Football, Basketball, and Baseball*, Bruce Roach; *The Twelve Days of Christmas*, Bruce Roach. **Wattage:** 1000.

CROSSETT, pop. 6,706.

SE AR. Ashley Co. 15 mi. S. of Hamburg. Residential

1094 Ashley News Observer
Ashley County Publishing Co., Inc.
PO Box 798 Phone: (501)364-5186
Crossett, AR 71635 Fax: (501)364-2116

General newspaper. **Founded:** 1906. **Freq:** Weekly. **Print Method:** Offset. **Cols./Page:** 6. **Col. Width:** 2 1/16 inches. **Col. Depth:** 21 1/2 inches. **Key Personnel:** Steve Sanders, Editor; Larry Johnson, Publisher. **Subscription Rates:** $26 individuals; $42 out of county. **Remarks:** Accepts advertising. **Alt. Formats:** CD-ROM.
Ad Rates: GLR: $0.45 **Circ:** 4,950
BW: $823.02
4C: $1,223.02
SAU: $6.82
PCI: $6.82

1095 KAGH-AM - 800
Hwy. 82 E., Box 697 Phone: (870)364-2181
Crossett, AR 71635 Fax: (870)364-2183

Format: Contemporary Country. **Networks:** Arkansas Radio; Mutual Broadcasting System; Westwood One Radio. **Owner:** Barry Medlin, at above address, (870)364-2182. **Founded:** 1951. **Operating Hours:** Continuous. **Key Personnel:** Barry Medlin, Contact. **Wattage:** 240. **Ad Rates:** $2.05-5.85 for 15 seconds; $3.05-7.30 for 30 seconds; $4.45-10.35 for 60 seconds.

1096 KAGH-FM - 104.9
Hwy. 82 E., Box 697 Phone: (870)364-2181
Crossett, AR 71635 Fax: (870)364-2183

Format: Contemporary Country. **Networks:** Arkansas Radio; Mutual Broadcasting System; Westwood One Radio. **Owner:** Barry Medlin, at above address, (870)364-2182. **Founded:** 1967. **Operating Hours:** Continuous. **Key Personnel:** Barry Medlin, Contact. **Wattage:** 6000 ERP. **Ad Rates:** $2.05-5.85 for 15 seconds; $3.05-7.30 for 30 seconds; $4.45-10.35 for 60 seconds.

1097 KWLT-FM - 102.7
PO Box 697 Phone: (870)364-2182
Crossett, AR 71635 Fax: (870)364-2183
E-mail: medbone@cei.net

Format: Oldies. **Networks:** ABC. **Owner:** South Ark Broadcasting, Inc., at above address. **Founded:** May 1995. **Operating Hours:** Continuous. **Key Personnel:** Russ Miller, Chief Engineer; Charlie Pack, News Dir.; JoAnn Johnson, Traffic. **Wattage:** 25,000. **Ad Rates:** $8 for 15 seconds; $11 for 30 seconds; $14 for 60 seconds.

DANVILLE†.

NC AR. Yell Co.

1098 Yell County Record
Courier
PO Box 189 Phone: (501)495-2354
Danville, AR 72833 Fax: (501)495-3501

Community newspaper. **Founded:** Jan. 1899. **Freq:** Weekly (Wed.). **Print Method:** offset. **Cols./Page:** 6. **Col. Width:** 12 picas. **Col. Depth:** 21 1/2 inches. **Key Personnel:** David Fisher, Publisher, dfisher@cswnet.com. **Subscription Rates:** $14 individuals. **Remarks:** Accepts advertising.
Ad Rates: BW: $780.45 **Circ:** 4,700
PCI: $6.05

DARDANELLE†, pop. 3,621.

NW AR. Yell Co. 15 mi. S. of Russellville. Residential.

1099 Post Dispatch
Russellville Newspapers
107 Harrison St. Phone: (501)229-2250
PO Box 270 Fax: (501)229-1159
Dardanelle, AR 72834-0270
Community newspaper. **Founded:** 1854. **Freq:** Weekly (Wed.). **Print Method:** Offset. **Cols./Page:** 6. **Col. Width:** 26 nonpareils. **Col. Depth:** 301 agate lines. **Key Personnel:** Sharon A. Grindstaff, Editor. **USPS:** 148-400. **Subscription Rates:** $14 individuals; $22 out of area. **Remarks:** Accepts advertising.
Ad Rates: GLR: $.21 **Circ:** Paid ‡2,462
BW: $457.95 Free ‡96
4C: $632.95
SAU: $3.55
PCI: $3.75

DE QUEEN†, pop. 4,594.

SW AR. Sevier Co. 45 mi. NW of Texarkana. Timber and pole treating plant. Poultry processing, broiler chickens, beef cattle. Pine, oak, gum, timber.

1100 De Queen Bee
De Queen Bee Co.
404 De Queen Ave. Phone: (501)642-2111
PO Box 1000 Fax: (501)642-3138
De Queen, AR 71832
Publisher E-mail: dqbee@ipa.net'

Newspaper with a Democratic orientation. **Founded:** 1897. **Freq:** Weekly (Thurs.). **Print Method:** Offset. **Cols./Page:** 7. **Col. Width:** 25 nonpareils. **Col. Depth:** 294 agate lines. **Key Personnel:** Billy Ray McKelvy, Editor; Ray Kimball, Publisher; Gail Mitchell, Advertising Mgr. **Subscription Rates:** $20 individuals.
Ad Rates: BW: $992.25 **Circ:** ‡1,677
PCI: $6.75

1101 De Queen Daily Citizen
404 De Queen Ave. Phone: (501)642-2111
PO Box 1000 Fax: (501)642-3138
De Queen, AR 71832
Publisher E-mail: dqbee@ipa.net

Newspaper with a Democratic orientation. **Founded:** 1933. **Freq:** Daily (eve.). **Print Method:** Offset. **Cols./Page:** 7. **Col. Width:** 25 nonpareils. **Col. Depth:** 294 agate lines. **Key Personnel:** Billy Ray McKelvy, Editor; Ray Kimball, Publisher; Gail Mitchell, Advertising Mgr. **Subscription Rates:** $84 individuals.
Ad Rates: BW: $992.25 **Circ:** ‡2,601
PCI: $6.75

1102 KDQN-AM - 1390
Box 311 Phone: (501)642-2446
De Queen, AR 71832 Fax: (501)642-2442

Format: Hispanic. **Owner:** Bunyard Broadcasting, Inc., at above address, (504)642-2446, Fax: (504)642-2442. **Founded:** 1956. **Operating Hours:** Daytime. **Key Personnel:** Jay Bunyard, President; Steve Cole, Sales Mgr.; Gerald Nix, Music Dir. **Wattage:** 500. **Ad Rates:** $6 for 30 seconds; $12 for 60 seconds.

1103 KDQN-FM - 93.1
Box 311 Phone: (501)642-2446
De Queen, AR 71832 Fax: (501)642-2442

Format: Country; Contemporary Country. **Owner:** Jay Bunyard, at above address. **Founded:** 1978. **Operating Hours:** Continuous. **Key Personnel:** Jay Bunyard, Contact; Steve Cole, Sales Mgr.; Gerald Nix, Music Dir.; Bonita Smith, Traffic Dir. **Wattage:** 50,000. **Ad Rates:** $6 for 30 seconds; $12 for 60 seconds.

DE WITT†, pop. 3,660.

C. AR. Arkansas Co. 40 mi. E. of Pine Bluff. Rice mills, cotton gins, shipping.

1104 De Witt Era-Enterprise
326 Court Sq. Phone: (870)946-3241
PO Box 431 Fax: (870)946-1888
De Witt, AR 72042
Community newspaper. **Founded:** 1882. **Freq:** Weekly (Thurs.). **Print Method:** Offset. **Cols./Page:** 6. **Col. Width:** 13 picas. **Col. Depth:** 21 inches. **Key Personnel:** C.F. Scott, Publisher. **Subscription Rates:** $14 individuals; $18 out of country. **Remarks:** Accepts advertising.
Ad Rates: PCI: $4.50 **Circ:** 3,300

DECATUR, pop. 847.

W. AR. Benton Co. 18 mi. W. of Rogers in the Ozarks.

1105 Decatur Herald
Community Publishers, Inc.
POB 7 Phone: (501)524-5144
Decatur, AR 72722
Community newspaper. **Freq:** Weekly (Wed.). **Print Method:** Offset. **Cols./Page:** 6. **Col. Width:** 12 1/2 picas. **Col. Depth:** 294 agate lines. **Key Personnel:** Bev Saunders, Editor; Mike Brown, Publisher. **Subscription Rates:** $16 individuals; $22 out of area. **Remarks:** Accepts advertising.
Ad Rates: BW: $670.80 **Circ:** Combined 509
4C: $865.80
SAU: $5.20

DUMAS, pop. 6,091.

SE AR. Desha Co. 42 mi. SE of Pine Bluff. Manufactures lumber, handles, furniture, automotive and marine electrical harnesses, steel building fabrication, refrigeration units, concrete blocks, garments. Cotton ginning; sawmills. Hardwood, cypress timber. Agriculture. Cotton, soybeans, fish, rice, milo, corn. Cattle, hogs.

1106 Dumas Clarion
Clarion Publishing Co.
136 E. Waterman St. Phone: (870)382-4925
PO Box 220 Fax: (870)382-6421
Dumas, AR 71639
Local newspaper. **Founded:** 1898. **Freq:** Weekly (Wed.). **Print Method:** Offset. **Cols./Page:** 6. **Col. Width:** 22 nonpareils. **Col. Depth:** 301 agate lines. **Key Personnel:** Terry G. Hawkins, Editor and Publisher, thawkins@seark.net. **Subscription Rates:** $18 individuals; $21 out of area; $28 out of state; $16.50 students in state; $20 students out of state. **Remarks:** Accepts advertising.
Ad Rates: GLR: $.29 **Circ:** ‡3,800
BW: $645
4C: $200
SAU: $5.50

1107 KDDA-AM - 1560
Hwy. 54 W., Box 720 Phone: (501)382-5606
Dumas, AR 71639 Fax: (501)382-6369

Format: Country; News. **Networks:** Unistar; ABC; Arkansas Radio. **Owner:** Alan W. Eastham, Craig L. Eastham, at above address. **Founded:** 1966. **Operating Hours:** Sunrise-sunset. **Key Personnel:** Alan W. Eastham, President; Craig L. Eastham, General Mgr. **Wattage:** 500. **Ad Rates:** $6-7.50 for 30 seconds; $7-8.50 for 60 seconds.

1108 KXFE-FM - 107.1
Hwy. 54 W., Box 720 Phone: (501)382-5606
Dumas, AR 71639 Fax: (501)382-6369

Format: Country; Sports. **Networks:** ABC; Arkansas Radio. **Owner:** Alan W. Eastham, Craig L. Eastham, at above address. **Founded:** 1980. **Formerly:** KDDA-FM (1991). **Operating Hours:** 5 a.m.-10 p.m. **Key Personnel:** Alan W. Eastham, President; Craig L. Eastham, General Mgr. **Wattage:** 3000 ERP. **Ad Rates:** $6-7.50 for 30 seconds; $7-8.50 for 60 seconds.

EL DORADO, pop. 26,685.

S. AR. Union Co. 85 mi. E. of Texarkana. Manufactures refined petroleum, petro-chemical products, asphalt and foundry products, lighting fixtures, wood fabricators, oil well equipment, lumber, fertilizer, tool and diecasting, industrial rubber products. Saw mill; nursery. Gas and oil wells; pine and hardwood timber. Livestock, poultry.

1109 El Dorado News-Times
111 N. Madison Phone: (870)862-6611
PO Box 912 Fax: (870)862-5226
El Dorado, AR 71731-0912
General newspaper. **Founded:** 1888. **Freq:** Mon.-Sun. (morn.). **Print Method:** Offset. **Trim Size:** 13 3/4 x 22 1/2. **Cols./Page:** 6. **Col. Width:** 13 inches. **Col. Depth:** 21 1/2 inches. **Key Personnel:** Walter E. Hussman, Jr., Publisher; Tim Lewallen, General Mgr.; Karen Williams, Advertising Dir., fax (870)862-9482; George Arnold, Managing Editor, fax (870)862-9482; Gus Looney, Production Forman. **Subscription Rates:** $105 individuals; $0.50 single issue. **Remarks:** Accepts advertising. **URL:** http://www.eldoradonews.com.
Ad Rates: GLR: $0.86 **Circ:** Mon.-Sat. ★**10,340**
BW: $1,560.90
4C: $1,810.90
PCI: $12.00

1110 El Dorado Cablevision
1127 N. Madison Phone: (501)862-1306
El Dorado, AR 71730 Fax: (501)862-7080

Founded: 1964. **Cities Served:** Union County and Old Union, AR.

1111 KELD-AM - 1400
2525 Northwest Ave. Phone: (501)862-1400
El Dorado, AR 71730 Fax: (501)863-4555

Format: News; Talk. **Networks:** USA Radio; Independent Broadcasting. **Owner:** Noalmark Broadcasting Corp, at above address, (501)862-7777. **Founded:** 1935. **Operating Hours:** Continuous. **ADI:** Little Rock, AR. **Key Personnel:** Don Travis, News Dir.; Leann Arndt, General Mgr. **Local Programs:** *El Dorado Information*, Don Travis; *Open Mike*, Don Travis. **Wattage:** 1000. **Ad Rates:** $7 for 30 seconds; $14 for 60 seconds.

1112 KIXB-FM - 103.3
2525 Northwest Ave. Phone: (501)864-0103
El Dorado, AR 71730 Fax: (501)863-4555
E-mail: totalradio@kix.com

Format: Country. **Founded:** 1963. **Formerly:** KELD-FM; KEZU-FM; KAYZ-FM. **Operating Hours:** Continuous. **ADI:** Monroe, LA-El Dorado, AR. **Key Personnel:** Leanne L. Arndt, General Mgr.; Don Travis, News Dir.; J.B. Billingsly, Operations Mgr. **Wattage:** 100,000. **Ad Rates:** $30 for 30 seconds; $35 for 60 seconds.

1113 KLBQ-FM - 99.3
1904 W. Hillsboro Phone: (501)863-5121
El Dorado, AR 71730 Fax: (501)863-6221
E-mail: klbq@infogo.com

Format: Adult Contemporary; Top 40. **Networks:** ABC. **Owner:** Eldorado Broadcasting Co., at above address. **Founded:** 1963. **Operating Hours:** Continuous. **ADI:** Monroe, LA-El Dorado, AR. **Key Personnel:** Rosh Partridge, Contact; Rick Finch, Sales Mgr.; Brandt Heisner, Contact; Kevin Davis, Program Dir. **Wattage:** 3000 ERP.

ENGLAND, pop. 3,081.

C. AR. Lonoke Co. 20 mi. S. of Lonoke. Residential.

1114 The England Democrat
PO Drawer 250 Phone: (501)842-3111
England, AR 72046 Fax: (501)842-3081

Newspaper with a Democratic orientation. **Founded:** 1934. **Freq:** Weekly (Wed.). **Print Method:** Offset. **Cols./Page:** 7. **Col. Width:** 21 nonpareils. **Col. Depth:** 294 agate lines. **Key Personnel:** Jerry M. Jackson, Publisher. **Subscription Rates:** $22 individuals. **Remarks:** Accepts advertising.
Ad Rates: GLR: $.23 **Circ:** ‡1,426
SAU: $3.22
PCI: $3.22

EUDORA

1115 Eudora Enterprise
PO Box 552 Phone: (501)265-2071
Lake Village, AR 71653 Fax: (501)265-2807

Community newspaper. **Freq:** Weekly (Wed.). **Print Method:** Offset. **Cols./Page:** 6. **Col. Width:** 12 1/2 picas. **Col. Depth:** 21 1/2 inches. **Key Personnel:** Steven Russell, Publisher. **USPS:** 179-420. **Subscription Rates:** $17; $25 other countries. **Remarks:** Color advertising not accepted.
Ad Rates: BW: $483.75 **Circ:** ‡800
SAU: $3.75
PCI: $4.48

EUREKA SPRINGS†, pop. 1,989.

NW AR. Carroll Co. 80 mi. NE of Fort Smith. Manufactures lumber. Saw mills. Tourism, health resort; mineral springs. Oak, pine timber. Agriculture. Corn, wheat, poultry, livestock.

1116 Lucidity
Bearhouse Publishing
398 Mundell Rd. Phone: (501)253-9351
Eureka Springs, AR 72631
Publisher E-mail: tbadger@ipa.net

Poetry journal. **Subtitle:** Quarterly Journal of Verse. **Founded:** 1985. **Freq:** Quarterly. **Print Method:** photocopy. **Trim Size:** 5 1/2 x 8 1/2. **Cols./Page:** 1. **Col. Width:** 4 1/4 inches. **Col. Depth:** 40 agate lines. **Key Personnel:** Ted O. Badger, Publisher, tbadger@ipa.net. **ISSN:** 0897-6481. **Subscription Rates:** $11 individuals; $2.75 single issue. **Remarks:** Advertising not accepted. **URL:** http://www.ipa./~tbadger.
Circ: Paid ‡230
Non-paid ‡75

1117 Search
Owl Press
PO Box 614
Eureka Springs, AR 72632-0614

Journal on parapsychology and paranormal studies. **Founded:** 1953. **Freq:** Quarterly. **Print Method:** Sheetfed offset. **Trim Size:** 8 3/8 x 10 3/4. **Cols./Page:** 3. **Col. Width:** 27 nonpareils. **Col. Depth:** 138 agate lines. **Key Personnel:** Judith M. Statezny, Publisher. **ISSN:** 0037-0290. **Subscription Rates:** $14; $22 two years. **Remarks:** Accepts advertising.
Ad Rates: BW: $240 **Circ:** Paid ‡1,000
4C: $320 Non-paid ‡2,000

FAIRFIELD BAY

Van Buren and Cleburne Co's.

1118 KFFB-FM - 106.1
Box 1050 Phone: (501)884-6812
Fairfield Bay, AR 72088 Fax: (501)884-6814
Free: (800)356-5106
E-mail: kffb@artelco.com

Format: Adult Contemporary. **Networks:** ABC; Arkansas Radio. **Founded:** 1985. **Operating Hours:** Continuous. **ADI:** Little Rock, AR. **Key Personnel:** Bob Connell, General Mgr. **Local Programs:** *The Morning Show*, Dan P. Meadows. **Wattage:** 50,000. **Ad Rates:** Advertising accepted; rates available upon request.

FAYETTEVILLE†, pop. 36,604.

NW AR. Washington Co. 60 mi. NE of Fort Smith. University of Arkansas. Manufactures tools, clothing, business forms, steel towers, electronic organs, wheels, pipe fittings, electrical components. Poultry processing; bottling works; hatchery. Resort. Hardwood timber. Poultry, fruit, dairy, stock farms.

1119 Arkansas Business & Economic Review
Bureau of Business and Economic Research
University of Arkansas Phone: (501)575-4151
College of Business Fax: (501)575-7687
Administration
Fayetteville, AR 72701
Publisher E-mail: bberinfo@cavern.uark.edu

Journal on business and economics. **Founded:** 1933. **Freq:** Quarterly. **Print Method:** Offset. **Trim Size:** 6 x 9. **Cols./Page:** 2. **Key Personnel:** Craig T. Schulman, Editor, schulma@comp.uark.edu. **Subscription Rates:** Free to qualified subscribers. **Remarks:** Advertising not accepted.
Circ: Controlled 4,000

1120 Arkansas Historical Quarterly
Arkansas Historical Association
University of Arkansas Phone: (501)575-5884
History Dept., 416 Old Main Fax: (501)575-2642
Fayetteville, AR 72701
Historical magazine. **Founded:** Mar. 1942. **Freq:** Quarterly. **Print Method:** Offset. **Trim Size:** 6 x 9. **Cols./Page:** 1. **Col. Width:** 48 nonpareils. **Col. Depth:** 91 agate lines. **Key Personnel:** Jeannie M. Whayne, Editor, jwhayne@comp.uark.edu; Gretchen Gearhart, Assistant Editor, gearhart@compuark.edu; Patrick Williams, Assoc. Editor, pgwillia@comp.uark.edu; Rhonda Hukill, Business Mgr., rhondak@comp.uark.edu. **ISSN:** 0004-1823. **Subscription Rates:** $16 individuals; $24 other countries; $4.50 single issue. **Remarks:** Accepts advertising.
Ad Rates: BW: $100 **Circ:** ‡1,600

1121 Arkansas Law Review
William S. Hein & Co., Inc.
University of Arkansas Phone: (501)575-5610
School of Law Fax: (501)575-3320
Waterman Hall
Fayetteville, AR 72701
Publication E-mail: lreview1@law.uark.edu
Publisher E-mail: wsheinco@class.org

Law journal. **Founded:** 1947. **Freq:** Quarterly. **Key Personnel:** Eva Madison, Editor-in-Chief; Shane Raley, Managing Editor. **ISSN:** 0004-1831. **Subscription Rates:** $15 individuals; $17.50 out of country; $7.50 single issue. **Remarks:** Advertising not accepted.
Circ: (Not Reported)

1122 The Arkansas Traveler
University of Arkansas Phone: (501)575-3406
119 Kimpel Hall Fax: (501)575-3306
Fayetteville, AR 72701
Publication E-mail: traveler@comp.uark.edu

Student newspaper of the University of Arkansas. **Founded:** 1901. **Freq:** Triweekly Mon., Wed., Fri. **Print Method:** Web offset. **Trim Size:** 13 x 21. **Cols./Page:** 6. **Col. Width:** 2.065 inches. **Col. Depth:** 21 inches. **Key Personnel:** Steve Wilkes, Dir. of Student Publications, phone (501)575-3887, swilkes@comp.uark.edu; Tammy Williams, Editor; Kim Brown, Advertising Mgr., phone (501)575-3839, kimbrown@comp.uark.edu. **Subscription Rates:** Free; $40 by

mail. **Remarks:** Accepts advertising. **URL:** http://www.uark.edu/campus-resources/travinfo.
Ad Rates: BW: $725 **Circ:** Non-paid ‡7,500
4C: $900
PCI: $7

1123 Flashback
Washington County Historical Society, Inc.
118 E. Dickson St. Phone: (501)521-2970
Fayetteville, AR 72701-5612
Magazine covering local history. **Founded:** 1951. **Freq:** Quarterly. **Key Personnel:** Don E. Schaefer, Editor. **ISSN:** 0428-5573. **Subscription Rates:** $15 members individual; $25 members family; $4 single issue. **Remarks:** Advertising not accepted.
Circ: Non-paid 850

1124 Journal of Disability Policy Studies
University of Arkansas
Dept. of Rehabilitation Phone: (501)575-3656
346 N. West Ave. Fax: (501)575-3253
Fayetteville, AR 72701
Journal addressing a wide range of topics pertaining to disability policy. **Founded:** 1990. **Freq:** Semiannual. **Key Personnel:** Kay Schriner, Ph.D., Editor, phone (501)575-3656, fax (501)575-3253, kays@comp.uark.edu. **ISSN:** 1044-2073. **Subscription Rates:** $24 individuals; $29 out of country. **Remarks:** Advertising accepted; rates available upon request.
Circ: Paid 500

1125 Journal of Education Finance
ASBO International
c/o Dr. Mary F. Hughes Phone: (501)575-7019
University of Arkansas
217 Graduate Education Bldg.
Fayetteville, AR 72701
Publisher E-mail: asboi@aol.com

Journal covering research on the funding of public schools. **Freq:** Quarterly. **Trim Size:** 6 3/4 x 10. **Cols./Page:** 1. **Col. Width:** 4 1/2 inches. **Col. Depth:** 8 inches. **Key Personnel:** Dr. Mary F. Hughes, Editor; Barbara Cook, Production Mgr. **ISSN:** 0098-0495. **Subscription Rates:** $40 individuals; $60 libraries; $15 single issue. **Remarks:** Advertising not accepted. **URL:** http://www.uark.edu/misc/elfc/jef/home.html.
Circ: Paid ⊕1,200

1126 Northwest Arkansas Times
PO Box 1607 Fax: (501)442-1714
Fayetteville, AR 72702 Free: (800)498-1991
Publication E-mail: email@nwarktimes.com

General newspaper. **Subtitle:** Fayetteville's Hometown Newspaper, proudly serving Washington County. **Founded:** 1860. **Freq:** Mon.-Sun. (morn.). **Print Method:** Letterpress and offset. **Cols./Page:** 6. **Col. Width:** 25 nonpareils. **Col. Depth:** 301 agate lines. **Key Personnel:** Jeff Jeffus, Publisher, fax (501)442-5477, publisher@nwarktimes.com; Mike Masterson, Exec. Editor, fax (501)442-1714, editor@nwarktimes.com; Nanci Batson, Advertising Mgr. and Mktg. Mgr.; Hector Cueva; Ritta Martin Basu, fax (501)442-1714, mamed@newarktimes.com. **Subscription Rates:** $60 individuals. **Remarks:** Accepts advertising. **Available Online. URL:** http://www.nwarktimes.com.
Ad Rates: PCI: $11.87 **Circ:** Sun. 14,320
Mon.-Sat. 13,524

1127 Philosophical Topics
University of Arkansas Press
201 Ozark Ave. Phone: (501)575-3246
Fayetteville, AR 72701 Fax: (501)575-6044
Free: (800)626-0090
Publisher E-mail: uaprinfo@cavern.uark.edu

Journal covering topics in philosophy. **Freq:** Semiannual. **Key Personnel:** Christopher Hill, Editor. **Subscription Rates:** $25 individuals. **Remarks:** Accepts advertising.
Circ: (Not Reported)

1128 Rehabilitation Education
University of Arkansas Phone: (501)575-3658
West Ave. Annex Fax: (501)575-3253
Fayetteville, AR 72701
Scholarly journal. **Founded:** 1987. **Freq:** Quarterly. **Trim Size:** 6 1/2 x 9 1/2. **Cols./Page:** 1. **Key Personnel:** Dr. Brian Bolton, Co-Editor; Dr. Dan Cook, Co-Editor, dcoook@comp.uark.edu. **ISSN:** 0889-7018. **Subscription Rates:** $90 individuals. **Remarks:** Accepts advertising.
Ad Rates: BW: $250 **Circ:** Paid ‡700
Non-paid ‡50

1129 KAFT-TV - 13
350 S. Donaghey Phone: (501)682-2386
Conway, AR 72032 Fax: (501)682-4122
Free: (800)662-2386

Format: Public TV. **Networks:** Public Broadcasting Service (PBS). **Owner:** Arkansas Educational Television Commission, at above address. **Founded:** 1976. **Operating Hours:** 6 a.m.-11:30 p.m. weekdays; 7 a.m.-11:30 p.m. Saturday and Sunday. **ADI:** Fort Smith, AR. **Key Personnel:** Susan Howarth, Exec.Dir.; Allen Weatherly, Deputy Dir.; Kathy Atkinson, Program Dir.; Ron Johnson, Communications Dir.; Carole Adornetto, Production Dir.; Gary Schultz, Engineering Dir.; Kathleen Stafford, Operations Dir.; Jane Havens, Traffic Mgr. **Local Programs:** *Arkansas Outdoors*; *Arkansas Week*; *Good Times Picture Show*. **Wattage:** transmitter for the Arkansas Educational Television Network. **Ad Rates:** Noncommercial. **URL:** http://www.aetn.com.

1130 KFAY-AM - 1030
PO Box 878 Phone: (501)442-9859
Fayetteville, AR 72702-0878 Fax: (501)521-0751
Free: (800)621-0751

Format: News; Sports; Talk. **Networks:** AP. **Owner:** Demaree Media, Inc., at above address, (501)521-9792. **Operating Hours:** Continuous; 50% network, 50% local. **Key Personnel:** Scott Smith, Program Dir., phone (501)521-5566, ssmith@fm98.com; Brett Kincaid, News Dir./Program Dir., phone (501)521-5566. **Local Programs:** *A.M. Talk with Tim Brooker*; *Public Opinion Hotline*; *Sports Rap with Chuck Barrott*. **Wattage:** 10,000. **Ad Rates:** $8-22 per unit.

1131 KHOG-TV - 29
15 N. Church St. Phone: (501)521-1010
Fayetteville, AR 72701 Fax: (501)521-9124
Free: (800)364-0290
E-mail: tv4029@aol.com

Format: Commercial TV. **Networks:** ABC. **Founded:** 1977. **Formerly:** KTVP-TV (1987). **Operating Hours:** 6 a.m.-1 a.m.; 90% network, 10% local. **ADI:** Fort Smith, AR. **Key Personnel:** Brent Hensley, General Mgr.; Don Young, Sales Mgr.; Ed Taylor, News Dir.; Tim Bass, Program Mgr.; Craig Cannon, News Dir.; Robbie Lewis, Contact; Sonny Hildebrand, Sales Mgr.

1132 KKEG-FM - 92.1
PO Box 878 Phone: (501)521-5566
Fayetteville, AR 72702 Fax: (501)521-0751

Format: News; Sports; Album-Oriented Rock (AOR); Classic Rock. **Networks:** AP. **Owner:** Demaree Media, Inc., at above address, (501)521-9792. **Operating Hours:** Continuous; 1% network, 99% local. **ADI:** Fort Smith, AR. **Key Personnel:** Ginger Mackenzie, Program Dir.; Debbi Hyer, Contact. **Wattage:** 3000. **Ad Rates:** $10-25 per unit.

1133 KKIX-FM - 103.9
PO Box 104 Phone: (501)521-0104
Fayetteville, AR 72702 Fax: (501)444-8600

Format: Country. **Networks:** Independent. **Owner:** Noalmark Broadcasting Corp., at above address. **Founded:** 1983. **Formerly:** KNWA-FM (1983). **Operating Hours:** Continuous; 100% local. **ADI:** Fort Smith, AR. **Key Personnel:** Doug Whitman, General Mgr.; Jeff Wood, General Sales Mgr. **Wattage:** 100,000. **Ad Rates:** $125 for 60 seconds.

1134 KOFC-AM - 1250
2553 N. College, Box 550 Phone: (501)443-2900
Fayetteville, AR 72703-3311 Fax: (501)443-2978
E-mail: kofc@ipa.net

Format: Talk; Southern Gospel; Contemporary Christian. **Networks:** USA Radio; Ambassador Inspirational Radio; Voice of Christian Youth America. **Founded:** 1987. **Operating Hours:** Daily; 6 a.m.-10 p.m. **Key Personnel:** Jeff Clardy, Program Dir.; Terry Evans, Sales Mgr.; Robert Johnson, General Mgr. **Wattage:** 1000. **Ad Rates:** $3-9 for 30 seconds; $5-11 for 60 seconds.

1135 KOLZ-FM - 98.3
PO Box 878 Phone: (501)443-0098
Fayetteville, AR 72702 Fax: (501)521-0751

Format: Oldies. **Networks:** Unistar. **Owner:** Pat Demery, at above address. **Founded:** 1983. **Formerly:** KBCV-FM (1992). **Operating Hours:** Continuous; 80% network, 20% local. **Key Personnel:** Brett Hash, General Mgr.; Marsha Johnson, Station Mgr.; Steve Johns, Sales Mgr.; Dennis Shew, Program Dir. **Wattage:** 3000. **Ad Rates:** $7-12 for 30 seconds.

1136 KUAF-FM - 91.3
747 W. Dickson St., No. 2 Phone: (501)575-2556
Fayetteville, AR 72701-5023 Fax: (501)575-8440

Format: Public Radio; News; Classical. **Networks:** National Public Radio (NPR). **Founded:** 1973. **Operating Hours:** Continuous; 45% network, 55% local. **Key Personnel:** Rick Stockdell, General Mgr., phone (501)575-6573; P.J. Robowski, Music Dir., phone (501)575-6574; Kyle Kellams, News Dir., phone (501)575-2556. **Wattage:** 60,000. **Ad Rates:** Noncommercial; underwriting available. $22.00-27.00 per unit.

1137 KZRA-AM - 1590
70 North East St., Ste. 100 Phone: (501)521-5128
Fayetteville, AR 72701 Fax: (501)521-4968

Format: Hispanic. **Owner:** Hochman Communications, Inc., at above address. **Operating Hours:** Continuous. **Key Personnel:** George Hochman, Contact. **Wattage:** 2,500. **Ad Rates:** $15 for 30 seconds; $20 for 60 seconds.

1138 TCA Cable-TV
3390 N. Futrall Dr. Phone: (501)751-2000
Fayetteville, AR 72703 Fax: (501)521-3825

Founded: 1953. **Formerly:** Warner Cable Communications, Inc. **Key Personnel:** Dennis Yocum, General Mgr., phone (501)717-3736, fax (501)756-1081, dryyool@tca-cable.com. **Cities Served:** subscribing households 20,500; 60 channels; 3 community access channels; 54 hours per week community access programming.

FORDYCE†, pop. 5,175.

S. AR. Dallas Co. 48 mi. SW of Pine Bluff. Manufactures picture frames, garments, folders & filing systems, telephone, electrical cable, wire, plywood, lumber, caskets, furniture, cross ties. Hardwood, pine timber & pulpwood. Poultry, livestock, truck crops, fruit.

1139 News-Advocate
Fordyce Publishing Co.
304 Spring St. Phone: (501)352-3144
PO Box 559 Fax: (501)352-8091
Fordyce, AR 71742
Publication E-mail: newsadvo@ipa.net

Community newspaper. **Founded:** 1884. **Freq:** Weekly (Wed.). **Print Method:** Offset. **Cols./Page:** 6. **Col. Width:** 26 nonpareils. **Col. Depth:** 294 agate lines. **Key Personnel:** W.R. Whitehead, Jr., Editor and Publisher. **USPS:** 204-380. **Subscription Rates:** $16 individuals.
Ad Rates: SAU: $5.80 **Circ:** ‡3,286
PCI: $5.20

1140 KBJT-AM - 1570
303 N. Spring St. Phone: (501)352-7137
Fordyce, AR 71742-3317 Fax: (501)352-7139

Format: News; Talk; Gospel. **Owner:** Gary Coates, at above address. **Founded:** 1959. **Operating Hours:** 16 hours daily; 90% network, 10% local. **Key Personnel:** Saxon Coates, News Dir.; Carna Coates, Contact. **Wattage:** 1000. **Ad Rates:** $3.54-6 for 30 seconds; $5.96-8 for 60 seconds.

1141 KQEW-FM - 102.3
303 Spring St. Phone: (501)352-7137
Fordyce, AR 71742 Fax: (501)352-7139

Format: News; Country. **Networks:** Independent. **Owner:** Gary Coates, at above address. **Founded:** 1982. **Operating Hours:** 19 hours daily; 100% local. **Key Personnel:** Wade Totty, News Dir.; Carna Coates, Contact. **Wattage:** 3000. **Ad Rates:** $3.54-6.00 for 30 seconds; $5.96-8.00 for 60 seconds. Combined advertising rates available with KBJT-AM.

FORREST CITY†, pop. 13,803.

E. AR. Saint Francis Co. 9 mi. SW of Palestine. Residential.

1142 Home with Homeland
HWH News & Printing
PO Box 454 Phone: (870)630-6450
Forrest City, AR 72336 Fax: (870)630-9072

A Black-owned, Black-interest community newspaper focusing on Arkansas and surrounding areas. **Subtitle:** At Home Reporting Your News. **Founded:** Oct. 1, 1991. **Freq:** Monthly. **Trim Size:** 8 1/2 x 11. **Key Personnel:** Henerine Hunter, Editor. **Subscription Rates:** $15. **Remarks:** Accepts advertising. **Alt. Formats:** Mailing labels. **Former name:** Homeland (May 1, 1998).
Ad Rates: BW: $696 **Circ:** 15,000

1143 Times Herald
222 N. Izard St. Phone: (870)633-3130
PO Box 1699 Fax: (870)633-0599
Forrest City, AR 72336
Publisher E-mail: fctimes@ipa.net

General newspaper. **Founded:** 1871. **Freq:** Daily (eve.). **Print Method:** Offset. **Cols./Page:** 6. **Col. Width:** 2 1/16 inches. **Col. Depth:** 21 inches. **Key Personnel:** Tamara Johnson, Editor; Weston Lewey, Publisher; Jim Wirski, Advertising Mgr. **Subscription Rates:** $48.50 individuals. **Remarks:** Accepts advertising. **URL:** http://www.thnews.com.
Ad Rates: SAU: $8.96 **Circ:** Paid 4,800

1144 East Arkansas Video, Inc.
521 N. Washington Phone: (501)633-8932
Forrest City, AR 72335

Founded: 1970. **Key Personnel:** Harold L. Kinnel, General Mgr. **Cities Served:** subscribing households 11,000; 35 channels; 8 community access channels.

1145 KBFC-FM - 93.5
501 E. Broadway, Box 707 Phone: (501)633-1252
Forrest City, AR 72335 Fax: (501)633-9500

Format: Country. **Owner:** Forrest City Broadcasting Co., at above address. **Founded:** 1960. **Operating Hours:** 6 a.m.-10 p.m. **Key Personnel:** William Fogg, General Mgr. **Wattage:** 25,000 ERP. **Ad Rates:** $5.25-10 for 30 seconds; $8.50-13 for 60 seconds.

FORT SMITH†, pop. 71,384.

W. AR. Sebastian Co. On Arkansas River, 134 mi. SE of Tulsa, Okla. Livestock, feed and food processors. Furniture, glass, bottles, bricks, chimneys, mattresses, cottonseed oil, lumber, kitchen cabinets, handles, tents, caskets, auto bodies, refrigerators, air conditioners, paper cups, concrete pipe and concrete blocks, iron and sheet metal, optical goods, paper boxes, scissors, coal briquettes, heavy trailers, rubber products, clothing, electrical appliances manufactured. Coal mines; hardwood timber.

1146 Fort Smith Historical Society Journal
Fort Smith Historical Society, Inc.
2121 Wolfe Ln. Phone: (501)783-1237
Fort Smith, AR 72901-6243 Fax: (501)782-0649

Journal covering local history and genealogy. **Founded:** Sept. 1997. **Freq:** Semiannual April and Sept. **Trim Size:** 8 1/2 x 11. **Cols./Page:** 2. **Col. Width:** 3 1/4 inches. **Col. Depth:** 9 1/2 inches. **Key Personnel:** Amelia Martin, Editor, artmartin@ipa.net. **ISSN:** 0736-4261. **Subscription Rates:** $15 individuals; $7.50 single issue. **Remarks:** Advertising not accepted.
Circ: Paid 450

1147 Kilgore News Herald
Donrey Media Group
PO Box 17017 Phone: (501)785-7810
Fort Smith, AR 72917-7017 Fax: (501)785-9467

General newspaper. **Founded:** 1931. **Freq:** Daily (eve.), Sunday (morn.). **Print Method:** Offset. **Cols./Page:** 6. **Col. Width:** 26 nonpareils. **Col. Depth:** 301 agate lines. **Key Personnel:** Chip Souza, Publisher, phone (903)984-2593, fax (903)984-7462, csouza@kilgore.net; Greg Collins, Managing Ed., phone (903)984-2593, fax (903)984-7462; Don Alexander, Advertising Mgr., phone (903)984-2593. **USPS:** 294-700. **Subscription Rates:** $66; $84; $96. **Remarks:** Accepts advertising.
Ad Rates: GLR: $.43 **Circ:** Mon.-Fri. ‡3,737
BW: $754.65 Sun. ‡4,316
4C: $999.65
PCI: $6.60

1148 Orchid Isle Television
Donrey Media Group
PO Box 17017 Phone: (501)785-7810
Fort Smith, AR 72917-7017 Fax: (501)785-9467

Television features magazine. **Founded:** 1967. **Freq:** Weekly (Sun.). **Print Method:** Offset. **Cols./Page:** 6. **Col. Width:** 20 nonpareils. **Col. Depth:** 196 agate lines. **Key Personnel:** Maxine Hughes, Editor; Donald W. Reynolds, Publisher. **Remarks:** Accepts advertising.
Ad Rates: GLR: $.55 **Circ:** 22,000

1149 Southwest Times Record
Donrey Media Group
920 Rogers Ave. Phone: (501)785-7700
Fort Smith, AR 72901 Fax: (501)784-0413
Free: (888)274-4049

General newspaper. **Founded:** 1882. **Freq:** Mon.-Sun. (morn.). **Print Method:** Offset. **Cols./Page:** 6. **Col. Width:** 25 nonpareils. **Col. Depth:** 301 agate lines. **Key Personnel:** Jack Moseley, Editor, phone (501)785-7743; Gene Kincy, Publisher, phone (501)785-7702; Debbie Foliert, Advertising Mgr. **Subscription Rates:** $54 individuals. **Remarks:** Accepts advertising.
Ad Rates: SAU: $18.20 **Circ:** Mon.-Sat. ★41,224
Sun. ★44,273

1150 Gans TV Cable Co.
5203 E. Hwy. 45 Phone: (501)648-1966
Fort Smith, AR 72901

Founded: Mar. 1988. **Key Personnel:** Ron Bartel, Mgr. Technician. **Cities Served:** Wagoner county: subscribing households 810; 28 channels.

1151 KAYR-AM - 1060
PO Box 5084 Phone: (501)474-3422
Fort Smith, AR 72913 Fax: (501)474-2649

Format: Southern Gospel. **Networks:** Independent. **Owner:** LKR Communications, at above address. **Founded:** 1979. **Operating Hours:** 6 a.m.-6 p.m. **ADI:** Fort Smith, AR. **Key Personnel:** Larry Ruth, General Mgr. **Wattage:** 500. **Ad Rates:** $6-8 for 30 seconds; $8-12 for 60 seconds.

1152 KBBQ-FM - 100.7
323 N. Greenwood Phone: (501)783-5379
PO Box 303 72902 Fax: (501)785-2638
Fort Smith, AR 72901

Format: Oldies. **Networks:** ABC; Arkansas Radio. **Owner:** Gordon Brown, at above address. **Founded:** 1978. **Formerly:** KFPW-FM. **Operating Hours:** 5 a.m.-midnight. **ADI:** Fort Smith, AR. **Key Personnel:** Gordon Brown, Contact; Margie Cole, Contact; Brad Cason, News Dir.; Jack Riley, Contact. **Local Programs:** *Larry's Call-in Express*, Larry Yothee, (501)783-5379. **Wattage:** 50,000. **Ad Rates:** $4-6 for 15 seconds; $9-14 for 30 seconds; $16-20 for 60 seconds. $4-$6 for 15 seconds; $9-$11 for 30 seconds; $12-$14 for 60 seconds. Combined advertising rates available with KFPW-AM.

1153 KEZU-FM - 104.7
9001 Rogers Ave., Ste. 105 Phone: (501)452-0105
Fort Smith, AR 72903 Fax: (501)484-7808
E-mail: zebra@ipa.net

Format: Adult Contemporary. **Networks:** ABC. **Founded:** 1990. **Formerly:** KBSS-FM. **Operating Hours:** Continuous. **ADI:** Fort Smith, AR. **Key Personnel:** Larry Tate, General Mgr.; Mike Ichnoiowski, Sales Mgr.; Larry McKay, Program Dir. **Wattage:** 50,000.

1154 KFDF-AM - 1580
PO Box 573 Phone: (501)288-0040
Fort Smith, AR 72902-0573 Fax: (501)785-4484

Format: Sports; Talk. **Simulcasts:** Sportsrap 4p.m.-6p.m. M-F. **Networks:** ESPN Radio. **Owner:** Pharis Broadcasting, Inc., at above address, (501)785-4600, Fax: (501)785-4844. **Founded:** 1959. **Operating Hours:** Continuous. **ADI:** Fort Smith, AR. **Key Personnel:** Marty Houston, Station Mgr.; Tim Johns, Sales Mgr. **Wattage:** 1000. **Ad Rates:** $3 for 30 seconds; $6 for 60 seconds.

1155 KFPW-AM - 1230
323 N. Greenwood Phone: (501)783-5379
PO Box 303 72902 Fax: (501)785-2638
Fort Smith, AR 72901

Format: Easy Listening. **Networks:** ABC; Arkansas Radio. **Owner:** Gordon Brown, at above address. **Founded:** 1930. **Operating Hours:** 6 a.m.-midnight; 98% network, 2% local. **ADI:** Fort Smith, AR. **Key Personnel:** Gordon Brown, Contact; Margie Cole, Contact; Brad Cason, News Dir.; Jack Riley, Contact. **Local Programs:** *Contar de mi Tierra* 7 p.m. - 12 a.m. Sunday, Rudy Hernandez, Mailing contact; *Let's Talk Sports* 6 p.m. - 7 p.m. Monday, Margie Cole, Mailing contact. **Wattage:** 1000. **Ad Rates:** $3-5 for 15 seconds; $7-9 for 30 seconds; $10-12 for 60 seconds. $3-$5 for 15 seconds; $7-$9 for 30 seconds; $10-$12 for 60 seconds. Combined advertising rates available with KBBQ-FM.

1156 KFSA-AM - 950
601 N. Greenwood Phone: (501)782-9125
PO Box 488 Fax: (501)782-9127
Fort Smith, AR 72901

Format: News; Southern Gospel. **Networks:** ABC. **Founded:** 1947. **Operating Hours:** Continuous. **ADI:** Fort Smith, AR. **Key Personnel:** Fred H. Baker, President; Gary Keifer, General Mgr.; Jerry Lynch, General Sales Mgr.; David Burdue, Program Dir. **Local Programs:** *Coffee with Bruce*, F.H. Baker; *People, Places and Polly*, F.H. Baker. **Wattage:** 1000 day; 500 night. **Ad Rates:** $5-10 for 30 seconds; $8-15 for 60 seconds.

1157 KFSM-TV - 5
PO Box 369 Phone: (501)783-3131
Fort Smith, AR 72902

Format: Commercial TV. **Networks:** CBS. **Owner:** New York Times Company, 229 W. 43rd St., New York, NY 10036. **Operating Hours:** 6 a.m.-1 a.m. **ADI:** Fort Smith, AR. **Key Personnel:** Tim Morrisey, General Mgr.; Gene Graham, Vice Pres; Mark Howell, VP/Controller.

1158 KHBS-TV - 40
2415 North Albert Pike Phone: (501)783-4040
Fort Smith, AR 72904-5698 Fax: (501)783-0550

Format: Commercial TV. **Networks:** ABC. **Operating Hours:** Continuous Sun.-Thurs.; 6:30 a.m.-1:40 a.m. Sat. **ADI:** Fort Smith, AR. **Key Personnel:** Jeff Rosser, General Mgr.; Tim Bass, Program Coordinator. **Ad Rates:** $40-600 for 30 seconds; $75-1100 for 60 seconds. **URL:** http://www.khbs-khog.com.

1159 KLSZ-FM - 102.7
PO Box 3471 Phone: (501)474-3422
Fort Smith, AR 72913 Fax: (501)474-2649
Free: (888)800-1073

Format: Classic Rock. **Networks:** Westwood One Radio. **Owner:** Elkhead Broadcasting, LLC, at above address. **Founded:** 1983. **Formerly:** KXXI-FM. **Operating Hours:** Continuous. **ADI:** Fort Smith, AR. **Key Personnel:** John Friend, Gen. Mgr./Sales Mgr.; Scott Stevens, Program Dir.; Dana Brooks, Traffic Dir. **Wattage:** 25,000. **Ad Rates:** $16-35 for 30 seconds; $22-50 for 60 seconds.

1160 KMAG-FM - 99.1
423 Garrison Ave. Phone: (501)782-8888
Fort Smith, AR 72901-1931 Fax: (501)785-5946

Format: Country. **Operating Hours:** Continuous. **ADI:** Fort Smith, AR. **Key Personnel:** Paul Swint, General Mgr.; Mark Scott, Program Dir. **Wattage:** 100,000. **Ad Rates:** $36-85 for 30 seconds; $50-120 for 60 seconds. Combined advertising rates available with KZBB-FM, KWHN-AM.

1161 KOLX-FM - 94.5
1912 Church St. Phone: (501)452-0569
Barling, AR 72923-2305 Fax: (501)452-0569

Format: Religious; Talk. **Networks:** USA Radio. **Founded:** 1987. **Operating Hours:** Continuous. **ADI:** Fort Smith, AR. **Key Personnel:** Anthony Caton, General Mgr. **Wattage:** 50,000. **Ad Rates:** $6 for 30 seconds; $9 for 60 seconds.

1162 KPBI-AM - 1510
PO Box 573 Phone: (501)785-4600
Fort Smith, AR 72902 Fax: (501)785-4844

Format: Sports; Talk. **Owner:** Pharis Broadcasting, at above address. **Founded:** 1982. **Formerly:** KACJ-AM; KZKZ-AM. **Operating Hours:** Sunrise-sunset. **ADI:** Fort Smith, AR. **Key Personnel:** Don Jones, General Mgr.; Tim Johns, Sales Mgr. **Wattage:** 1000. **Ad Rates:** $3 for 30 seconds; $6 for 60 seconds.

1163 KPOM-TV - 24
4624 Kelley Hwy. Phone: (501)785-2400
PO Box 4610,72914 Fax: (501)785-3169
Fort Smith, AR 72904
E-mail: mailbox@nbc24-51.com

Format: Commercial TV. **Networks:** NBC. **Founded:** 1978. **Formerly:** KLMN-TV. **Operating Hours:** 6 a.m. **ADI:** Fort Smith, AR. **Key Personnel:** Verlene Tadlock, Program Coord., vtadlock@nbc24-51.com; David Needham, General Mgr., dneedham@nbc24-51.com; Steve House, Operations Mgr., shouse@nbc24-51.com; Jennifer Irwin, Promotions Mgr., jirwin@nbc24-51.com; Brian Schleicher, Business Mgr., brians@nbc24-51.com. **Local Programs:** *The Polly Show* 9:30 am - 10:00 am Sunday, Polly Crews, Public Affairs. **Ad Rates:** Advertising accepted; rates available upon request. **URL:** http://www.nbc24-51.com.

1164 KTCS-AM - 1410
Box 180188 Phone: (501)646-6151
Fort Smith, AR 72918-0188 Fax: (501)646-3509

Format: Contemporary Country. **Simulcasts:** KTCS-FM. **Networks:** Independent. **Owner:** Big Chief Broadcasting, at above address. **Founded:** 1961. **Operating Hours:** Continuous. **ADI:** Fort Smith, AR. **Key Personnel:** Lee Young, General Mgr.; Mark Harper, Operations Mgr. **Wattage:** 1000. **Ad Rates:** $10 for 30 seconds; $15 for 60 seconds. Combined advertising rates available with KTCS-FM: $25-$48 for 30 seconds; $34-$65 for 60 seconds.

1165 KTCS-FM - 99.9
Box 180188 Phone: (501)646-6151
Fort Smith, AR 72918-0188 Fax: (501)646-3509

Format: Hot Country. **Simulcasts:** KTCS-AM. **Networks:** Independent. **Owner:** Big Chief Broadcasting, at above address. **Founded:** 1964. **Operating Hours:** Continuous. **ADI:** Fort Smith, AR. **Key Personnel:** Lee Young, General Mgr.; Mark Harper, Operations Mgr. **Wattage:** 100,000. **Ad Rates:** Combined advertising rates available with KTCS-AM: $25-$48 for 30 seconds; $34-$65 for 60 seconds.

1166 KWHN-AM - 1320
423 Garrison Ave. Phone: (501)782-8888
Fort Smith, AR 72901-1931 Fax: (501)785-5946

Format: News; Talk; Sports. **Networks:** ABC. **Founded:** 1947. **Operating Hours:** Continuous; 25% network, 75% other. **ADI:** Fort Smith, AR. **Key Personnel:** Paul Swint, General Mgr.; Gary Elmore, Program Dir. **Wattage:** 5000. **Ad**

Rates: $10-25 for 30 seconds; $15-60 for 60 seconds. KMAG-FM, KZBB-FM.

1167 KZKZ-FM - 106.3
PO Box 6210 Phone: (501)646-6700
Fort Smith, AR 72906 Fax: (501)646-1373
Free: (800)583-7960

Format: Contemporary Christian. **Networks:** USA Radio. **Owner:** PO Box 6210, Fort Smith, AR 72906. **Founded:** 1993. **Formerly:** KAJJ-FM. **Operating Hours:** Continuous; 100% local. **ADI:** Fort Smith, AR. **Key Personnel:** Jerry Lynch, General Mgr., jlynch2505@aol.com; Dave Burdue, Program Dir. **Local Programs:** *Exciting E.T.*, Don Hutchings, (501)782-9181; *Word of Faith*, Bob Whiteley, (501)782-1442; *Word of Life*, Robert Jones, (501)785-4585. **Wattage:** 6000. **Ad Rates:** $11 for 30 seconds; $18 for 60 seconds.

1168 TCA Cable TV
314 S. 17th Phone: (501)782-8941
Fort Smith, AR 72901-3898 Fax: (501)783-7892

Owner: TCA Cable Management, 3015 SSE Loop 323, Tyler, TX 75701, (903)595-3701, Fax: (903)595-1929. **Founded:** 1961. **Formerly:** Ft. Smith CableTV; Rogers Cablesystem; Communications Svc. Inc.; TCI of Ark. **Key Personnel:** James Anderson, General Mgr.; Michael Rogers, Marketing Dir.; Linda Savage, Business Mgr.; Paul Zander, Operations Mgr. **Cities Served:** Alma, Barling, Ft. Smith, Greenwood, Van Buren, AR; Muldrow, Roland, OK: subscribing households 38,000; 55 channels; 3 community access channels; 4 hours per week community access programming.

GLENWOOD, pop. 1,389.

SW AR. Pike Co. 81 mi. SW of Little Rock. Residential.

1169 KWXE-FM - 104.5
PO Box 740 Phone: (501)356-2151
Glenwood, AR 71943 Fax: (501)356-4684
E-mail: kwxe@ipa.net

Format: Country. **Simulcasts:** KWXI-AM. **Networks:** CBS. **Owner:** PGR Communications, Inc., at above address. **Founded:** 1991. **Operating Hours:** Continuous. **Key Personnel:** Larry Morphew, General Mgr.; Kim Morphew, Sales Mgr.; Doug Dumont, Operations Mgr. **Wattage:** 3,000. **Ad Rates:** $5.88 for 30 seconds; $8.82 for 60 seconds. Combined advertising rates available with KYXK-FM.

1170 KWXI-AM - 670
PO Box 740 Phone: (501)356-2151
Glenwood, AR 71943 Fax: (501)356-4684
E-mail: kwxe@ipa.net

Format: Country. **Networks:** CBS. **Owner:** PGR Communications, Inc., at above address. **Founded:** 1980. **Operating Hours:** Continuous. **ADI:** Little Rock, AR. **Key Personnel:** Larry Morphew, General Mgr.; Kim Morphew, Sales Mgr.; Doug Dumont, Operations Mgr. **Local Programs:** *Ask Your Neighbor*, Tom Nichols; *Morning Report*, Doug Dumont; *Swap Shop*, Doug Dumont. **Wattage:** 5,000. **Ad Rates:** $5.88 for 30 seconds; $8.82 for 60 seconds.

GREENWOOD†, pop. 3,317.

W. AR. Sebastian Co. 15 mi. S. of Fort Smith. Residential

1171 Greenwood Democrat
PO Box 398 Phone: (501)996-4494
Greenwood, AR 72936-0398 Fax: (501)996-4122

Community newspaper. **Founded:** 1882. **Freq:** Weekly (Wed.). **Print Method:** Offset. **Cols./Page:** 6. **Col. Width:** 26 nonpareils. **Col. Depth:** 301 agate lines. **Key Personnel:** Donna Forst, Editor; Cindy Wells, Publisher. **Subscription Rates:** $17.95 individuals; $24.95 institutions; $27.95 out of state.
Ad Rates: BW: $527.61 / 4C: $787.61 / PCI: $4.09 — **Circ:** Paid 2,494 / Non-paid 50

GURDON, pop. 2,707.

SW AR. Clark Co. 65 mi. NE of Texarkana. Lumber mills. Plywood plant. Pine timber. Agriculture. Cattle, poultry.

1172 The Gurdon Times
PO Box 250
Gurdon, AR 71743-0250

Community newspaper. **Founded:** 1880. **Freq:** Weekly (Thurs.). **Print Method:** Offset. **Trim Size:** 13 3/4 x 22 3/4. **Cols./Page:** 6. **Col. Width:** 2 1/16 inches. **Col. Depth:** 21 1/2 inches. **Key Personnel:** Clay Franklin, Editor and Publisher. **USPS:** 232-180. **Subscription Rates:** $10 individuals; $12.50 Out of County. **Remarks:** Accepts advertising.
Ad Rates: BW: $409.50 / SAU: $3.25 — **Circ:** ‡2,132

HAMBURG†, pop. 3,394.

SE AR. Ashley Co. 15 mi. NE of Crossett. Lakes. Manufactures die & moulding, apparel, shirts.

1173 Ashley County Ledger
Ashley Publishing Co., Inc.
PO Box 471 Phone: (501)853-2424
Hamburg, AR 71646 Fax: (501)853-8203

Newspaper. **Founded:** 1969. **Freq:** Weekly (Wed.). **Print Method:** Offset. **Cols./Page:** 6. **Col. Width:** 2 1/16 inches. **Col. Depth:** 21 1/2 inches. **Key Personnel:** David Moyers, Editor and Publisher; Jan Roberts, Advertising Mgr. **Subscription Rates:** $22 individuals; $26 Out of County. **Remarks:** Accepts advertising.
Ad Rates: GLR: $4.25 — **Circ:** ‡3,000

HAMPTON, pop. 1,627.

SE AR. Calhoun Co. 8 mi. NW of Harrell. Residential.

1174 South Arkansas Accent
PO Box 766 Phone: (501)798-2236
Hampton, AR 71744 Fax: (501)798-2005

Newspaper with a local orientation. **Founded:** 1899. **Freq:** Weekly (Wed.). **Print Method:** Offset. **Cols./Page:** 6. **Col. Width:** 24 nonpareils. **Col. Depth:** 294 agate lines. **Key Personnel:** Ovid Goode, Editor and Publisher. **USPS:** 992-940. **Subscription Rates:** $11.50 individuals; $15.00 out of area; $18 out of state. **Remarks:** Accepts advertising.
Ad Rates: GLR: $0.23 / BW: $378 / SAU: $3 — **Circ:** ‡1,600

HARRISBURG†, pop. 1,921.

NE AR. Poinsett Co. 23 mi. S. of Jonesboro. Rice mills; cotton ginning. Hardwood timber. Agriculture. Cotton, rice, soybeans, dairy products.

1175 The Modern News
PO Box 400 Phone: (501)578-2121
Harrisburg, AR 72432 Fax: (501)578-9415

Newspaper with a Democratic orientation. **Founded:** Nov. 1888. **Freq:** Weekly (Thurs.). **Print Method:** Offset. **Trim Size:** 13 7/8 x 22 1/2. **Cols./Page:** 6. **Col. Width:** 2 1/16 inches. **Col. Depth:** 21 inches. **Key Personnel:** Charles D. Nix, Editor; Mrs. L.D. Freeman, Publisher. **USPS:** 357-680. **Subscription Rates:** $18.20 individuals; $20.80 out of area.
Ad Rates: SAU: $4 / PCI: $4.25 — **Circ:** Paid 2,500 / Free 30

HARRISON, pop. 9,567.

NW AR. Boone Co. 30 mi. SE of Berryville. Residential.

1176 Boone County Headlight
Times Publishing Co.
111 W. Rush Ave. Phone: (501)741-2325
PO Box 40 Fax: (501)741-5632
Harrison, AR 72602
Community newspaper. **Freq:** Weekly (Wed.). **Print Method:** Offset. **Cols./Page:** 6. **Col. Width:** 12 picas. **Col. Depth:** 129 inches. **Key Personnel:** J.E. Dunlap, Jr., Publisher. **Subscription Rates:** $21. $.25 single issue.
Circ: 1,700

1177 KCWD-FM - 96.7
600 S. Pine St., Box 850 Phone: (501)741-1402
Harrison, AR 72601 Fax: (501)741-9702

Format: Country. **Networks:** ABC. **Owner:** Harrison Radio Station, Inc., at above address. **Founded:** 1982. **Operating Hours:** Continuous. **Key Personnel:** Tom Arnold, General Mgr.; Patrick Kelly, General Sales Mgr.; Glenn Rowe, Contact. **Wattage:** 3,000 ERP.

HARTFORD, pop. 613.

W. AR. Sebastian Co. 13 mi. S. of Greenwood. Coal mining. Diversified farming.

1178 The Gamecock
Marburger Publishing Co., Inc.
PO Box 158 Phone: (501)639-2324
Hartford, AR 72938-0158
Magazine on game fowl. **Founded:** May 1935. **Freq:** 11/year. **Print Method:** Offset. **Trim Size:** 6 3/4 x 9 1/2. **Cols./Page:** 2. **Col. Width:** 32 nonpareils. **Col. Depth:** 119 agate lines. **Key Personnel:** J.C. Griffiths, Editor. **ISSN:** 0016-4313. **Subscription Rates:** $25 individuals; $40 other countries. **Remarks:** Accepts advertising.
Ad Rates: BW: $250 / 4C: $400 / PCI: $27 — **Circ:** 14,300

HAZEN, pop. 1,636.

EC AR. Prairie Co. 40 mi. E. of Little Rock. Manufactures men's shirts. Agriculture. Rice, soybeans, cotton.

1179 The DeValls Bluff Times
Herald Publishing
N. Front St. Phone: (870)255-4538
PO Box 370 Fax: (870)255-4539
Hazen, AR 72064
Publication E-mail: herald_ @aristotle.net

Local newspaper. **Founded:** 1954. **Freq:** Weekly (Wed.). **Print Method:** Offset. **Cols./Page:** 6. **Col. Width:** 21 nonpareils. **Col. Depth:** 294 agate lines. **Key Personnel:** Betty L. Woods, President; Bill Rutherford, Exec. Editor; Bill Bradow, Managing Editor. **USPS:** 150-380. **Subscription Rates:** $15 individuals; $20 out of country; $25 out of state. **Remarks:** Accepts advertising.
Ad Rates: GLR: $.25 / PCI: $2.75 — **Circ:** Paid 486 / Free 14

1180 Grand Prairie Herald
Herald Publishing
N. Front St. Phone: (870)255-4538
PO Box 370 Fax: (870)255-4539
Hazen, AR 72064
Publication E-mail: herald_ @aristotle.net

Newspaper with a Democratic orientation. **Founded:** 1901. **Freq:** Weekly (Thurs.). **Print Method:** Offset. **Cols./Page:** 6. **Col. Width:** 2 inches. **Col. Depth:** 21 inches. **Key Personnel:** Betty L. Woods, Publisher; Bill Rutherford, Executive Editor; Bill Bradow, Managing Editor. **USPS:** 225-680. **Subscription Rates:** $15 individuals; $20 Out of County; $25 out of state. **Remarks:** Accepts advertising.
Ad Rates: GLR: $.25 / BW: $370.44 / PCI: $3.25 — **Circ:** Paid 1,650 / Free 50

HEBER SPRINGS†, pop. 4,589.

NC AR. Cleburne Co. 62 mi. N. of Little Rock. Resort, mineral springs. Manufactures lumber, gloves, circular saws, weed eaters, bendable hose, concrete handling products, men's shirts. Stone quarries. Dairy, stock, poultry and cattle.

1181 Sun Times
Liberty Group Publishing
107 N. 4th St. Phone: (501)362-2425
PO Box 669 Fax: (501)362-5877
Heber Springs, AR 72543
Publication E-mail: suntimes@ipa.net

Community newspaper. **Founded:** 1888. **Freq:** Semiweekly (Wed. and Fri.). **Print Method:** Offset. **Cols./Page:** 6. **Col. Depth:** 21 inches. **Key Personnel:** Randy Kemp, Editor; Susanne Reed, Publisher. **ISSN:** 1050-5106. **Subscription Rates:** $29.75 individuals; $39 out of area. **Remarks:** Accepts advertising. **URL:** http://www.thesuntimes.com. **Formed by the merger of:** Cleburne County Times; Heber Springs Arkansas Sun.
Ad Rates: GLR: $4 / BW: $617.40 / 4C: $732.40 / SAU: $6.10 / PCI: $7.19 — **Circ:** Wed. 4,685 / Fri. 4,810

1182 KAWW-AM - 1370
422 W. Main St. Phone: (501)362-5863
PO Box 324 Fax: (501)362-5864
Heber Springs, AR 72543

Format: Southern Gospel. **Networks:** Arkansas Radio. **Founded:** 1967. **Operating Hours:** 6 a.m.-2 hours post sunset. **Key Personnel:** Charles E. Howell, General Mgr.; Karol Berry, Contact; Louis Short, News Dir.; Clay Marshall, Public Service Dir.; Connie Owens, Traffic Dir. **Local Programs:** *Contemporary Gospel with Karol Berry*; *Good Time Gospel Show with Karol Berry.* **Wattage:** 1000. **Ad Rates:** $5 for 30 seconds; $9 for 60 seconds.

1183 KAWW-FM - 100.7
422 W. Main St. Phone: (501)362-5863
PO Box 909 Fax: (501)362-5864
Heber Springs, AR 72543
Free: (888)206-0101
E-mail: kaww101@intellinet.com

Format: Oldies. **Networks:** Arkansas Radio. **Founded:** 1972.

Operating Hours: Continuous. **Key Personnel:** Charles E. Howell, General Mgr.; Clay Marshal, Program Dir.; Louis Short, News Dir.; Clay Marshal, Public Service Dir.; Connie Owens, Traffic Dir. **Local Programs:** *Evenings with the Northern Hillbilly.* **Wattage:** 50,000. **Ad Rates:** $8 for 30 seconds; $12 for 60 seconds.

HELENA†, pop. 9,598.

E. AR. Phillips Co. On Mississippi River, 90 mi. SW of Memphis, TN. Port of entry. Manufactures cottonseed oil, bean oil, chemicals, lumber, swim pools, soybean products, luggage, men's clothing, farm implements, barges; fertilizer. Cotton ginning and compressing; cannery; sawmills. Ships cotton, lumber. Crude oils. Timber. Agriculture. Rice, wheat, soybeans.

1184 The Daily World
American Publishing
417 York St. Phone: (501)338-9181
PO Box 340 Fax: (501)338-9184
Helena, AR 72342
Newspaper with a Democratic orientation. **Founded:** Dec. 5, 1871. **Freq:** Daily and Sunday (eve.). **Print Method:** Offset. **Trim Size:** 13 x 21 1/2. **Cols./Page:** 6. **Col. Width:** 25 nonpareils. **Col. Depth:** 294 agate lines. **Key Personnel:** Robert Shearon, Editor; Derwood A. Brett, Publisher. **Subscription Rates:** $39.90 individuals. **Remarks:** Accepts advertising. **Formerly:** The Helena-West Helena Daily World.
Ad Rates: SAU: $4.65 **Circ:** (Not Reported)

1185 Phillips County Historical Review
623 Pecan St. Phone: (870)338-3271
Helena, AR 72342
Periodical covering local history. **Key Personnel:** Ivey S. Gladin, Editor. **Subscription Rates:** $10 individuals; $5 single issue. **Former name:** Phillips County Historical Quarterly.

1186 KFFA-AM - 1360
Box 430 Phone: (501)338-8331
Helena, AR 72342 Fax: (501)338-8332

Format: Talk; Information; Blues; Sports; Music of Your Life. **Networks:** Agrinet Farm Radio; AP; St. Louis Cardinals; UPI. **Founded:** 1941. **Operating Hours:** 24 hrs. **Key Personnel:** J. M. Howe, Contact; Dennis Littleton, Operations Mgr.; Lorie Smith, Music Dir. **Local Programs:** *King Biscuit Time* 5 days, Sonny Payne. **Wattage:** 1000. **Ad Rates:** $9.50-28.3 per unit. Combined advertising rates available with KFFA-FM. **URL:** http://www.kingbiscuit.com.

1187 KFFA-FM - 103.1
PO Box 430 Phone: (870)338-8331
Helena, AR 72342 Fax: (870)338-8332

Format: Country; News; Agricultural. **Owner:** Delta Broadcasting, Inc., at above address, (870)338-8361, Fax: (870)338-8332. **Founded:** 1971. **Formerly:** KCRI-FM (1994). **Operating Hours:** Continuous. **ADI:** Memphis, TN. **Key Personnel:** Jim Howe, General Sales Mgr.; Dennis Littleton, Operations Mgr. **Wattage:** 13,000 ERP. **Ad Rates:** $10.25 for 30 seconds; $14.45 for 60 seconds. Combined advertising rates available with KFFA-AM. **URL:** http://www.kingbiscuit.com.

HOPE, pop. 10,290.

SW AR. Hempstead Co. 34 mi. NE of Texarkana. Lumber; insecticide, floor sweep, electronic speaker factories; brickworks; hatcheries, egg processing plants. Hard and softwood timber. Diversified farming. Poultry, livestock.

1188 Hope Star
Star Publishing Co., Inc.
PO Box 648 Phone: (501)777-8841
Hope, AR 71802 Fax: (501)777-3311
Free: (888)840-8841
Publication E-mail: hopestar@ipa.net

General newspaper. **Founded:** 1899. **Freq:** Daily. **Print Method:** Offset. **Cols./Page:** 6. **Col. Width:** 25 nonpareils. **Col. Depth:** 301 agate lines. **Key Personnel:** Pat Harris, Editor; Ronnie Cupstid, Publisher; Richard Haycox, Advertising Mgr. **Subscription Rates:** $62 individuals; $70 out of area. **Remarks:** Accepts advertising.
Ad Rates: GLR: $85 **Circ:** 5,068
4C: $260
SAU: $6.90

1189 KHPA-FM - 104.9
500 W. Ave. D Phone: (501)777-8868
PO Box 424 Fax: (501)777-8888
Hope, AR 71801-0424

Format: Contemporary Country. **Networks:** Independent. **Owner:** Newport Broadcasting, PO Box 989, Blytheville, AR 72316, (501)762-2093. **Founded:** 1976. **Operating Hours:** 6 a.m.-midnight. **Key Personnel:** Danny Ingram, Contact; Mark Hobson, Program Dir.; Larry Rhodes, Contact. **Wattage:** 3000.

1190 KTPA-AM - 1370
Washington Rd. Phone: (501)887-2638
PO Box 424 Fax: (501)778-8888
Hope, AR 71801

Format: Country. **Networks:** Arkansas Radio. **Owner:** Newport Broadcasting, PO Box 989, Blytheville, AR 72315, (501)762-2093. **Founded:** 1959. **Operating Hours:** 6 a.m.-6 p.m.; 5% network, 95% local. **Key Personnel:** David Paul, Contact; Larry Rhodes, News Dir.; Danny Ingram, Manager. **Wattage:** 1000. **Ad Rates:** $2.50-4.30 for 15 seconds; $3.30-5.50 for 30 seconds; $4.30-6.50 for 60 seconds.

1191 KXAR-AM - 1490
PO Box 320 Phone: (501)777-3601
Hope, AR 71801-0320 Fax: (501)777-3535

Format: Talk; Country. **Networks:** ABC; Arkansas Radio. **Owner:** KdB, Inc., 2806 Country Club Ln., Hope, AR 71801, (870)722-2299, Fax: (870)722-5927. **Founded:** 1988. **Operating Hours:** Continuous; 30% network, 70% local. **Key Personnel:** Bill Hoglund, President; Scott Neal, Operations Mgr.; Patti Bryant, Office Mgr.; Jodi Neal, Sales. **Wattage:** 3,000. **Ad Rates:** Advertising accepted; rates available upon request.

1192 KXAR-FM - 101.7
PO Box 320 Phone: (501)777-3601
Hope, AR 71801-0320 Fax: (501)777-3535

Format: Urban Contemporary. **Networks:** American Urban Radio. **Owner:** KdB, Inc., 2806 Country Club Ln., Hope, AR 71801, (870)722-2299, Fax: (870)722-5927. **Founded:** 1988. **Operating Hours:** Continuous; 5% network, 95% local. **Key Personnel:** Bill Hoglund, President; Scott Neal, Operations Mgr.; W.A. "Big Daddy" Griffin, Program Dir.; Patti Bryant, Office Mgr.; Jodi Neal, Sales. **Wattage:** 50,000. **Ad Rates:** Advertising accepted; rates available upon request.

HOT SPRINGS†, pop. 35,166.

WC AR. Garland Co. 47 mi. SW of Little Rock. Manufactures lumber, aluminum, bottled mineral water, ladies' shoes, rubber bands, mail handling equipment, hydraulic cylinders auto fabricast parts; cables. Vanadium oxide mill. Aluminum storm doors and windows. Pine timber.

1193 Arkansas Family Historian
Arkansas Genealogical Society, Inc.
1411 Shady Grove Rd. Phone: (501)262-4513
PO Box 908 Fax: (501)262-4513
Hot Springs, AR 71902-0908
Journal covering genealogy and history in Arkansas. **Founded:** 1962. **Freq:** Quarterly. **ISSN:** 0571-0472. **Subscription Rates:** $20 individuals. **Remarks:** Advertising not accepted.
Circ: Paid 1,000

1194 The Sentinel-Record
PO Box 580 Phone: (501)623-7711
Hot Springs, AR 71902 Fax: (501)623-2984
Publication E-mail: hotsr@direclynx.com

General newspaper. **Founded:** 1877. **Freq:** Mon.-Sun. (morn.). **Print Method:** Offset. **Cols./Page:** 6. **Col. Width:** 26 nonpareils. **Col. Depth:** 301 agate lines. **Key Personnel:** Melinda Gassaway, Editor, hotsr@direclynx.com; W.E. Hussman, Jr., Publisher; Floyd Emerson, Advertising Dir.; Wallace Ballentine, General Mgr. **USPS:** 490-720. **Subscription Rates:** $142.50 individuals. **Remarks:** Accepts advertising.
Ad Rates: GLR: $1.73 **Circ:** Mon.-Sat. ★**17,432**
BW: $2,193.30 Sun. ★**19,607**
4C: $2,543
PCI: $17

1195 KLAZ-FM - 105.9
PO Box 1739 Phone: (501)525-4600
Hot Springs, AR 71902-1739 Fax: (501)525-4344

Format: Contemporary Hit Radio (CHR). **Networks:** Independent. **Owner:** Noalmark Broadcasting Corp., 202 W. 19th St., El Dorado, AR 71730, (501)862-7777. **Founded:** 1971. **Formerly:** KACQ-FM (1985). **Operating Hours:** Continuous; 100% local. **ADI:** Little Rock, AR. **Key Personnel:** Jeff Wood, Contact; J. Randal Harvey, Program Dir.; Jack Ihrie, News Dir. **Wattage:** 100,000. **Ad Rates:** $8.50 for 30 seconds; $19.75 for 60 seconds.

1196 KLXQ-FM - 96.7
125 Coporate Ter. Phone: (501)525-9700
Hot Springs, AR 71913 Fax: (501)525-9739

Format: Classic Rock. **Networks:** Westwood One Radio. **Owner:** Kellstrom Broadcasting, Inc., at above address. **Founded:** Feb. 1992. **Operating Hours:** Continuous. **Key Personnel:** Jim Kellstrom, Pres./General Mgr.; Todd Woerpel, General Sales Mgr.; Dennis Little, Program Dir. **Wattage:** 6,000. **Ad Rates:** $8 for 30 seconds; $12 for 60 seconds.

1197 KQUS-FM - 97.5
125 Corporate Terrace Phone: (501)525-9700
Hot Springs, AR 71913 Fax: (501)501-9739

Format: Country. **Networks:** ABC. **Owner:** Demaree Media, Inc., at above address. **Founded:** 1969. **Operating Hours:** Continuous. **ADI:** Little Rock, AR. **Key Personnel:** Jim Kellstrom, General Mgr.; Todd Woerpel, General Sales Mgr.; Mario Garcia, Music and Program Dir. **Wattage:** 100,000. **Ad Rates:** $15-28 for 30 seconds; $18-40 for 60 seconds.

1198 KSBC-FM - 90.1
600 Garland Phone: (501)624-4455
Hot Springs, AR 71913 Fax: (501)624-7870

Format: Religious. **Networks:** Moody Broadcasting. **Owner:** Central Arkansas Christian Broadcasting, Inc., at above address. **Founded:** 1984. **Operating Hours:** Continuous; 95% network. **Key Personnel:** Rick Armstrong, Manager. **Wattage:** 5000.

1199 KXOW-AM - 1420
PO Box 1739 Phone: (501)525-1301
Hot Springs, AR 71902-1739 Fax: (501)525-4344

Format: Easy Listening. **Networks:** Mutual Broadcasting System. **Owner:** Noalmark Broadcasting Corp., 202 W. 19th St., El Dorado, AR 71730, (501)862-7777. **Founded:** 1966. **Formerly:** KIXT-AM (1992). **Operating Hours:** Continuous; 10% network, 90% local. **ADI:** Little Rock, AR. **Key Personnel:** Jeff Wood, Contact; J. Randal Harvey, Program Dir.; Jack Ihrie, News Dir. **Wattage:** 5000. **Ad Rates:** $4.25 for 30 seconds; $10.75 for 60 seconds.

1200 KZNG-AM - 1340
125 Corporate Terrace Phone: (501)525-9700
Hot Springs, AR 71913 Fax: (501)525-9739

Format: Talk; News. **Networks:** ABC. **Owner:** Demaree Media Inc., at above address. **Founded:** 1953. **Operating Hours:** Continuous. **ADI:** Little Rock, AR. **Key Personnel:** Jim Kellstrom, General Mgr.; Todd Woerpel, General Sales Mgr.; Tom Duke, Program Dir. **Wattage:** 1000. **Ad Rates:** $5-18 for 30 seconds; $8-25 for 60 seconds.

1201 Resort TV Cable Co., Inc.
410 Airport Rd., Ste. H Phone: (501)624-5781
Box 2770 Fax: (501)624-0502
Hot Springs, AR 71914

Founded: 1970. **Key Personnel:** Harvey Oxner, General Mgr.; Wanda Ritter, Office Mgr.; Mike Allbright, Contact. **Cities Served:** Hot Springs, Mt. Pine, AR; Garland County: subscribing households 22,595; 1 community access channel; 168 hours per week community access programming.

HOT SPRINGS VILLAGE

1202 La Villa News
American Publishing Co.
121 Desoto Center Dr. Phone: (501)922-1900
Hot Springs Village, AR 71909 Fax: (501)922-0958
Free: (800)833-4050

Community newspaper (broadsheet) catering to retirees. **Founded:** 1970. **Freq:** Semiweekly. **Print Method:** Web. **Trim Size:** 14 x 23. **Cols./Page:** 6. **Col. Width:** 12.2 picas. **Col. Depth:** 21 1/2 inches. **Key Personnel:** Randal Hunhoff, Publisher/Contact. **Subscription Rates:** $20 individuals; $25 out of area.
Ad Rates: GLR: $6 **Circ:** Paid 4,310
BW: $600 Free ‡400
4C: $750
SAU: $5
PCI: $6

HUNTSVILLE†, pop. 1,394.

SC AR. Madison Co.

1203 Madison County Record
PO Drawer A Phone: (501)738-2141
Huntsville, AR 72740 Fax: (501)738-1250

Community newspaper. **Founded:** May 29, 1879. **Freq:** Weekly (Thurs.). **Print Method:** Offset. **Cols./Page:** 6. **Col. Width:** 2 1/4 inches. **Key Personnel:** Carol Whittemore, Editor; Alta Saubus, Publisher; Randy Bohannan, Advertising Mgr. **Subscription Rates:** $12 individuals; $15 Out of County. **Remarks:** Color advertising not accepted.
Ad Rates: SAU: $3.10 **Circ:** 4,700

1204 Huntsville TV Cable Inc.
Box 627 Phone: (501)738-6828
Huntsville, AR 72740 Free: (800)364-0834

Key Personnel: Gene Barnett, General Mgr. **Cities Served:** Huntsville and Alpena, AR.

IMBODEN

1205 The Ozark Journal
PO Box 598 Phone: (870)869-2220
Imboden, AR 72434
Community newspaper. **Founded:** 1915. **Freq:** Weekly (Thurs.). **Print Method:** Offset. **Cols./Page:** 6. **Col. Width:** 2 inches. **Col. Depth:** 21 1/2 inches. **Key Personnel:** Karen Glass, Editor; Bob Glass, Jr., Publisher. **Subscription Rates:** $10 individuals; $14 out of area. **Remarks:** Accepts advertising.
Ad Rates: SAU: $3 **Circ:** ‡1800
PCI: $3.50

JACKSONVILLE†, pop. 27,589.

C. AR. Pulaski Co. 9 mi. N of Galloway. Residential.

1206 Jacksonville Patriot
Magie Enterprises, Inc.
903 S. Pine St. Phone: (501)843-3534
PO Box 1058 Fax: (501)843-6447
Cabot, AR 72023
Publisher E-mail: arknews@aristotle.net

Community newspaper. **Founded:** 1958. **Freq:** Daily. **Print Method:** Offset. **Cols./Page:** 6. **Col. Width:** 12 picas. **Col. Depth:** 294 agate lines. **Key Personnel:** Jon Parham, Editor; Susie Magie, Advertising Mgr.; Mark Magie, General Mgr. **ISSN:** 0891-5601. **Subscription Rates:** $36 individuals. **Remarks:** Accepts advertising. **Formerly:** Jacksonville News (1992).
Ad Rates: GLR: $.46 **Circ:** Paid ‡2,000
BW: $825.50 Non-paid ‡131
4C: $1,075.50
SAU: $6.50
PCI: $6.50

JASPER, pop. 519.

NW AR. Newton Co. 100 mi. NW of Little Rock. Residential.

1207 Newton County Times
Box 453 Phone: (870)446-2645
Jasper, AR 72641 Fax: (870)446-6286

Local newspaper. **Founded:** 1908. **Freq:** Weekly (Wed.). **Print Method:** Offset. **Cols./Page:** 6. **Col. Width:** 24 nonpareils. **Col. Depth:** 301 agate lines. **Key Personnel:** Ruth Wilson, Editor, rwilson@yournet.com; Jane Christenson, Publisher; Rebecca Raulston, Advertising Mgr. **Subscription Rates:** $17.95 individuals; $0.35 single issue.
Ad Rates: BW: $670 **Circ:** ‡3,000
4C: $735
PCI: $5.20

JONESBORO†, pop. 31,530.

NE AR. Craighead Co. 70 mi. NW of Memphis. Arkansas State University. Manufactures lift equipment, tool boxes, agriculture machinery, aluminum castings, drapery hardware, medical testing equipment, truck transmissions, tennis balls, conveyor equipment, electric motors, shoes, lumber products, brakes; rice milling; beverage bottling. Agriculture. Rice, wheat, cotton, soybeans.

1208 The Jonesboro Sun
PO Box 1249 Phone: (501)935-5525
Jonesboro, AR 72403 Fax: (501)935-1674
Free: (800)237-5341

Newspaper with a Democratic orientation. **Founded:** 1903. **Freq:** Mon.-Sun. (morn.). **Print Method:** Offset. **Cols./Page:** 6. **Col. Width:** 24 nonpareils. **Col. Depth:** 294 agate lines. **Key Personnel:** John Troutt, Jr., Editor and Publisher; Jerry P. Donohue, Advertising Mgr. **Subscription Rates:** $98 individuals. **Remarks:** Accepts advertising.
Ad Rates: GLR: $1.20 **Circ:** Mon.-Sat. ★**28,248**
BW: $2,160.75 Sun. ★**31,206**
4C: $2,635.75
PCI: $16.75

1209 U.S. Gospel News
603 W. Matthews Phone: (870)802-0414
Jonesboro, AR 72401 Fax: (870)932-6397
Publication E-mail: usgospelnews@insolwwb.net

Religious magazine. **Founded:** 1988. **Freq:** Monthly. **Trim Size:** 11 x 13 1/16. **Key Personnel:** Paul R. Boden, Editor and Publisher; Donna K. Rogers, Sales Mgr. **Subscription Rates:** $20. **Remarks:** Accepts advertising. **Formerly:** Mid-South Gospel News (1991).
Ad Rates: BW: $500 **Circ:** Paid 50,000
4C: $700 Non-paid 20,000

1210 KAIT-TV - 8
Box 790 Phone: (501)931-8888
Jonesboro, AR 72403 Fax: (501)931-1371
E-mail: gm@kait8.com

Format: Commercial TV. **Networks:** ABC. **Owner:** Cosmos Broadcasting Co., P.O. Box 789, Greenville, SC 29602, (864)609-4370, Fax: (864)609-4420. **Founded:** 1963. **Operating Hours:** 5:30 a.m.-12:30 a.m.; 60% network, 40% local. **ADI:** Jonesboro, AR. **Key Personnel:** Harvey Cox,Jr, News Dir., news8@kait8.com; Clyde Anderson, V.P. & General Mgr.; Artie Bedard, Business Mgr., main@kait8.com; Toni Inboden, Program Dir., main@kait8.com. **Ad Rates:** $25-850 per unit. **URL:** http://www.kait8.com.

1211 KDEZ-FM - 100.5
1720 S. Caraway Rd., Ste. 2010 Phone: (501)933-8800
Jonesboro, AR 72401 Fax: (501)933-0403

Format: Classic Rock. **Founded:** 1988. **Operating Hours:** Continuous; 100 % Local. **ADI:** Jonesboro, AR. **Key Personnel:** Danny Barton, General Mgr.; Brett Hall, Contact; Bill Pressly, VP/GM; Kevin Neathery, Sales Mgr.; Trey Stafford, Vice President. **Wattage:** 5000. **Ad Rates:** $10-24 for 30 seconds; $12-28 for 60 seconds.

1212 KFIN-FM - 107.9
Drawer 1737 Phone: (870)932-1079
403 W. Parker Rd. Fax: (870)932-0892
Jonesboro, AR 72403
E-mail: heartland@insolwwb.net

Format: Contemporary Country. **Networks:** CNN Radio. **Owner:** Duke Broadcasting Corp., 407 W. Parker Rd, Jonesboro, AR 72401. **Founded:** 1974. **Operating Hours:** Continuous; 3% network, 97% local. **ADI:** Memphis, TN. **Key Personnel:** Clyde Bass, Station Mgr.; Christy Ellison, National Sales Mgr.; James Guthrie, Farm Dir.; Dave Ashcraft, Program Dir.; Larry A. Duke, CEO. **Local Programs:** *Open Mic*, Terry Bill. **Wattage:** 100,000. **Ad Rates:** $30-45 for 30 seconds; $38-57 for 60 seconds.

1213 KIYS-FM - 101.9
PO Box 1757 Phone: (501)935-5598
Jonesboro, AR 72403-1757 Fax: (501)935-5620

Format: Adult Contemporary; Contemporary Hit Radio (CHR). **Founded:** 1947. **Formerly:** KBTM-FM (1982); KJBR-FM (1993). **Operating Hours:** Continuous. **ADI:** Jonesboro, AR. **Key Personnel:** Clyde Bass, V.P. of Broadcasting, phone (870)932-8400, fax (870)932-3814; Terry Bowden, Sales Mgr.; Chad Davidson, Program Dir., chaddavidson@yahoo.com; Christy L. Ellison, National Sales Manager, phone (870)932-8400, fax (870)932-3814, heartland@insolwwb.net. **Wattage:** 100,000. **Ad Rates:** $34-49 for 30 seconds; $50-70 for 60 seconds. Combined advertising rates available with KFIN-FM, KBTM-AM.

1214 KNEA-AM - 970
603 W. Matthews Phone: (501)932-8381
Jonesboro, AR 72401-3453 Fax: (501)932-6397

Format: Gospel; Top 40. **Networks:** Arkansas Radio; Ambassador Inspirational Radio. **Owner:** Paul R. Boden, 520 S. McClure, Jonesboro, AR 72401, (501)932-7072, Fax: (501)932-6397. **Founded:** 1950. **Operating Hours:** 6 a.m.-10 p.m.; 20% network, 80% local. **ADI:** Jonesboro, AR. **Key Personnel:** Paul R. Boden, General Mgr.; Donna K. Rogers, Sales Mgr.; Joni Jumper, Office Mgr.; Shane Hubbard, Sports Dir.; Mia Boden, Traffic Mgr. **Local Programs:** *KNEA Top 20 Countdown*, Bryan Benson, (501)972-9797, Fax (501)932-6397; *Local Sports Football, Basketball, Baseball*, Shane Hubbard, (501)972-9797, Fax (501)932-6397; *Swap Shop*, Bryan Benson, (501)972-9797, Fax (501)932-6397. **Wattage:** 1000. **Ad Rates:** $6-8 for 30 seconds; $12 for 60 seconds.

1215 KOCY-FM - 105.3
1309 Twin Oaks Ave. Phone: (870)933-0044
Jonesboro, AR 72401 Fax: (870)933-9652
Free: (888)410-5336

Format: Adult Contemporary. **Networks:** Ambassador Inspirational Radio. **Owner:** Mindy R. Worlow, at above address. **Founded:** Jan. 1, 1996. **Former name:** KHOX-FM (1996). **Operating Hours:** Continuous. **Wattage:** 25,000. **Ad Rates:** $10 for 30 seconds; $15 for 60 seconds. **URL:** http://www.kozyfm.com.

1216 KOZY-FM - 105.3
PO Box 540 Phone: (870)933-0044
Jonesboro, AR 72403 Fax: (870)933-9652
Free: (888)410-5336

Format: Sports. **Founded:** 1996. **Operating Hours:** Continuous; 10% network, 90% local. **Key Personnel:** Mindy Worlow, General Mgr.; Farrell Gates, Operations Mgr.; Steve Stigall, Music Dir.; Barry Sellers, Sales Mgr. **Local Programs:** *Open House Party*. **Wattage:** 25,000. **Ad Rates:** $10 for 30 seconds; $15 for 60 seconds. Combined advertising rates available with KNEA0AM, KJBR-FM, KKEY-FM. **URL:** http://www.kozyfm.com.

1217 KTEJ-TV - 19
350 S. Donaghey Phone: (501)682-2386
Conway, AR 72032 Fax: (501)682-4122

Format: Public TV. **Networks:** Public Broadcasting Service (PBS). **Owner:** Arkansas Educational Television Commission, at above address. **Founded:** 1976. **Operating Hours:** 6 a.m.-11:30 p.m. weekdays; 7 a.m.-11:30 p.m. Saturday and Sunday. **ADI:** Jonesboro, AR. **Key Personnel:** Gary Schultz, Engineering Dir.; Ron Johnson, Communications Dir.; Jane Havens, Traffic Mgr.; Susan Howarth, Exec.Dir.; Allen Weatherly, Deputy Dir.; Kathy Atkinson, Program Dir.; Carole Adornetto, Production Dir.; Kathleen Stafford, Operations Dir. **Local Programs:** *Arkansas Outdoors*; *Arkansas Week*; *Good Times Picture Show*. **Wattage:** transmitter for the Arkansas Educational Television Network. **URL:** http://www.aetn.com; http://www.aetn.org.

1218 TCA Cable TV
1520 Caraway Rd. Phone: (870)935-3615
Box 19127 Fax: (870)935-8141
Jonesboro, AR 72401

Owner: TCA Management, PO Box 130489, Tyler, TX 75713-0489, (903)595-3701. **Formerly:** Walnut Ridge Cablevision (1992); TCI Cablevision. **Key Personnel:** Gary Bowman, General Mgr. **Cities Served:** Bay, Jonesboro, AR.

LAKE VILLAGE

1219 Chicot County Spectator
105 N. Court St. Phone: (870)265-2071
PO Box 552 Fax: (870)265-2807
Lake Village, AR 71653
Publication E-mail: arccs@ipa.net

Community newspaper. **Freq:** Weekly (Wed.). **Print Method:** Offset. **Cols./Page:** 6. **Col. Width:** 12 3/10 picas. **Col. Depth:** 21 1/2 inches. **Key Personnel:** Lynette Sills, Publisher. **USPS:** 104-260. **Subscription Rates:** $17; $25 out of county. **Remarks:** Accepts advertising.
Ad Rates: BW: $483.75 **Circ:** ‡2,000
4C: $583.75
SAU: $3.75
PCI: $4.48

Eudora Enterprise - See Eudora

LEWISVILLE†, pop. 1,476.

SE AR. Lafayette Co. 33 mi. E. of Texarkana. Sawmills. Pine timber. Agriculture. Cotton, corn, potatoes.

1220 Lafayette County Democrat
107 Spruce Phone: (501)921-5711
PO Box 507 Fax: (501)921-5712
Lewisville, AR 71845
Publication E-mail: arklacon@infogo.com

Newspaper with Report orientation. **Founded:** 1905. **Freq:** Weekly (Thurs.). **Print Method:** Offset. **Cols./Page:** 6. **Col. Width:** 20 nonpareils. **Col. Depth:** 210 agate lines. **Key Personnel:** Liz Lamkin, Editor; George Wanstrath, Publisher; Sue Terry, Operations Mgr. **Subscription Rates:** $21 individuals; $26 out of area. **Alt. Formats:** CD-ROM.
Ad Rates: GLR: $0.29 **Circ:** 2,900
BW: $322.50
SAU: $4.95

LINCOLN, pop. 1,422.

NW AR. Washington Co. 17 mi. SW of Fayetteville. Manufactures steel poultry buildings. Hatchery. Agriculture. Strawberries, cattle, apples.

1221 Lincoln Leader
PO Box 520 Phone: (501)824-3263
Lincoln, AR 72744
Community newspaper. **Founded:** June 19, 1937. **Freq:** Weekly (Thurs.). **Print Method:** Offset. **Cols./Page:** 6. **Col. Width:** 2 1/16 inches. **Col. Depth:** 129 agate lines. **Key Personnel:** Boyce Druis, Editor and Publisher; Scott F. Davis, Advertising Mgr. **Subscription Rates:** $10.50 individuals; $12.50 out of area; $16.50 out of state. **Remarks:** Accepts advertising.
Ad Rates: SAU: $3.65 **Circ:** Paid ‡1,700
Free ‡100

LITTLE ROCK†, pop. 158,461.

C. AR. Pulaski Co. In the center of the state on the Arkansas River. The State Capital. University of Arkansas School of Medicine, Nursing, Pharmacy; University of Arkansas Graduate School of Technology; University of Arkansas at Little Rock; several colleges; many state institutions. Retail and wholesale trading center. Manufactures chemicals, furniture, cottonseed products, clothing, building and plumbing supplies, lumber, paper boxes, paint, pumps, valves, plastic piping, fertilizer, light bulbs, watches, radio and television cabinets, electrical equipment, cameras, teletypes, innertubes and related rubber products. Steel foundry; packing houses. Crushed stone, bauxite mines.

1222 Aging Arkansas
Arkansas Aging Foundation, Inc.
706 S. Pulaski St. Phone: (501)376-6083
Little Rock, AR 72201 Fax: (501)376-6084

Newspaper covering senior citizen interests. **Founded:** Jan. 1988. **Freq:** Monthly. **Print Method:** Offset. **Trim Size:** 10 1/4 x 16. **Cols./Page:** 3. **Col. Width:** 3 1/4 inches. **Col. Depth:** 16 inches. **Key Personnel:** Anne Howard Wasson, Editor and Publisher. **Subscription Rates:** $7 individuals. **Remarks:** Accepts advertising. **Alt. Formats:** Large-print.
Ad Rates: PCI: $20 **Circ:** Controlled 38,000

1223 AMCA Trucking Report
Arkansas Motor Carriers Association
501 Woodlane St., Ste. 107 Phone: (501)372-3462
Little Rock, AR 72201 Fax: (501)376-1810
Publication E-mail: lane.kidd@cwixmail.com

Trade magazine containing articles for executives and management personnel of the trucking industry. **Freq:** Bimonthly. **Print Method:** Offset - color. **Trim Size:** 8 3/8 x 10 7/8. **Cols./Page:** 3. **Key Personnel:** Wendi Sharp, Vice President. **Remarks:** Accepts advertising.. **Formerly**: The Arkansas Motor Carrier (1992).
Circ: 1300

1224 American Fern Journal
American Fern Society, Inc.
Dept. of Biology Phone: (501)569-3270
2801 S. University Ave. Fax: (501)569-8020
University of Arkansas
Little Rock, AR 72204
Magazine on ferns and allied plants. **Founded:** 1910. **Freq:** Quarterly. **Print Method:** Offset. **Trim Size:** 7 x 10. **Cols./Page:** 1. **Col. Width:** 5 inches. **Col. Depth:** 7 3/4 inches. **Key Personnel:** James H. Peck, Editor; Carol Peck, Advertising Mgr. **ISSN:** 0002-8444. **Subscription Rates:** $15 individuals; $20 institutions, Canada. **Remarks:** Accepts advertising.
Ad Rates: BW: $80 **Circ:** ‡1,200

1225 Arkansas Banker
Arkansas Bankers Association
The Carvill Building Phone: (501)376-3741
1220 W. 3rd St. Fax: (501)376-9243
Little Rock, AR 72201
The official monthly publication of The Arkansas Bankers Association. **Founded:** 1917. **Freq:** Monthly. **Print Method:** Offset. **Trim Size:** 9 3/8 x 12 1/2. **Cols./Page:** 4. **Col. Width:** 27 nonpareils. **Col. Depth:** 156 agate lines. **Key Personnel:** Tres Williams, Editor-in-Chief, twilliam@arkansas.net; Jason A. Lee, Communications Coordinator. **ISSN:** 0004-1726. **Subscription Rates:** $19.95 individuals; $2.95 single issue; $15.95 other. **Remarks:** Accepts advertising. **URL:** http://www.arkbankers.org.
Ad Rates: BW: $539.90 **Circ:** ‡2,000
4C: $920.90
PCI: $17.85

1226 Arkansas Business
Arkansas Business Publishing Group
201 E. Markham Phone: (501)372-1443
PO Box 3686 Fax: (501)375-0933
Little Rock, AR 72203
Publication E-mail: abnews@abnews.com

Business magazine on the Arkansas business community, covering people and recent news events statewide. **Founded:** Mar. 19, 1984. **Freq:** Weekly. **Print Method:** Offset. **Trim Size:** 11 x 13 3/4. **Cols./Page:** 4. **Col. Width:** 14 picas. **Col. Depth:** 74 picas. **Key Personnel:** Jeff Hankins, Editor and Publisher; Sheila Palmer, Assoc. Publisher; Kristin Wade, Sales Mgr. **USPS:** 730-650. **Subscription Rates:** $48.95 individuals. **Remarks:** Accepts advertising. **URL:** http://www.abnews.com. **Alt. Formats:** Mailing labels.
Ad Rates: BW: $1,828 **Circ:** Paid 6,500
4C: $2,230 Controlled 2,000

1227 Arkansas Catholic
2500 N. Tyler Phone: (501)664-0340
PO Box 7239 Fax: (501)661-9075
Little Rock, AR 72217-7417
Catholic newspaper of the Diocese of Little Rock. **Founded:** 1911. **Freq:** Weekly (Sat.). **Print Method:** Offset. **Trim Size:** 10.25 x 14. **Cols./Page:** 4. **Col. Width:** 28 nonpareils. **Col. Depth:** 182 agate lines. **Key Personnel:** Fr. Francis I. Malone, Managing Editor; Malea Walters, Editor; Most Rev. Andrew J. McDonald, Publisher; Ron M. Hall, Advertising Mgr. **USPS:** 853-320. **Subscription Rates:** $15 individuals. **Remarks:** Advertising not accepted for political endorsements. **Formerly**: The Guardian (1985).
Ad Rates: GLR: $1 **Circ:** ‡7,000
BW: $616
PCI: $14

1228 Arkansas Cattle Business
Arkansas Cattlemen's Association
310 Executive Ct. Phone: (501)224-2114
Little Rock, AR 72205 Fax: (501)224-5377

Beef cattle business magazine, featuring a different breed each month. **Founded:** 1965. **Freq:** Monthly. **Print Method:** Offset/Web. **Trim Size:** 8 1/2 x 11. **Cols./Page:** 3. **Col. Width:** 27 nonpareils. **Col. Depth:** 140 agate lines. **Key Personnel:** Jodi Shull, Production Mgr.; Carol Ann Johnson, Advertising Dir.; Sandi Walker, Advertising Dir. **Subscription Rates:** $20 individuals. **Remarks:** Accepts advertising.
Ad Rates: BW: $600 **Circ:** Paid 13,000
4C: $910 Controlled 1,000
PCI: $27

1229 Arkansas Democrat-Gazette
Arkansas Democrat-Gazette, Inc.
Capitol Ave. & Scott St. Phone: (501)378-3400
PO Box 2221 Fax: (501)372-3908
Little Rock, AR 72203
General newspaper. **Founded:** Nov. 20, 1819. **Freq:** Mon.-Sun. (morn.). **Print Method:** Offset. **Trim Size:** 13 2/3 x 22. **Cols./Page:** 6. **Col. Width:** 12 3/5 nonpareils. **Col. Depth:** 301 agate lines. **Key Personnel:** Griffin Smith, Jr., Exec. Editor, phone (501)399-3610; W.E. Hussman, Jr., Publisher, phone (501)378-3402; Dick Browning, National Advertising, phone (501)378-3447, dbrowning@ardemgaz.com; David Bailey, Managing Editor, phone (501)378-3594; Phyllis Brandon, High Profile Ed., phone (501)378-3574; John Mobbs, Advertising Dir., phone (501)378-3437; Ron Beach, Classified Advertising Mgr. **ISSN:** 1060-4332. **Subscription Rates:** $216 individuals. **Remarks:** Advertising accepted; rates available upon request. Monday-Saturday: BW: $15,222; 4C: $16,472; SAU: $118; PCI: $118; Sunday: BW: $22,575; 4C: $23,825; SAU: $175; PCI: $175. **URL:** http://www.ardemgaz.com. **Formerly**: Arkansas Democrat (1992). **Feature Editors:** Barry Arthur, *Photo*, phone (501)378-3484; Paul Greenberg, *Editorials*, phone (501)378-3482; Wally Hall, *Sports*, phone (501)399-3612; Jack Schnedle, *Features*, phone (501)399-3677; Irene Wassell, *Food*, phone (501)378-3497.
Circ: Mon.-Sat. 173,934
Sun. 283,376

1230 Arkansas Educator
Arkansas Education Association
1500 W. 4th St. Phone: (501)375-4611
Little Rock, AR 72201-1064 Fax: (501)375-4620

Educational magazine. **Founded:** 1924. **Freq:** Monthly 8/year. **Print Method:** Offset. **Cols./Page:** 4. **Col. Width:** 28 nonpareils. **Col. Depth:** 224 agate lines. **Key Personnel:** Cara A. Elmore, Editor. **Subscription Rates:** $4 individuals. **Remarks:** Accepts advertising.
Ad Rates: BW: $800 **Circ:** ‡18,268

1231 Arkansas Living
Arkansas Writers' Project, Inc.
PO Box 34010 Phone: (501)375-2985
Little Rock, AR 72203-4010 Fax: (501)375-3523

Consumer magazine covering lifestyle in Arkansas. **Founded:** Sept. 1996. **Freq:** Monthly. **Print Method:** Web offset. **Trim Size:** 10 1/16 x 12 5/16. **Cols./Page:** 4. **Col. Width:** 2 1/3 inches. **Col. Depth:** 12 5/16 inches. **Key Personnel:** Karen Willett, Editor, karen@arktimes.com. **Subscription Rates:** $26 individuals. **Remarks:** Accepts advertising. **Former name**: Arkansas Homes.
Ad Rates: BW: $2,430 **Circ:** Controlled 36,000
4C: $2,915

1232 Arkansas Pharmacist
Arkansas Pharmacist's Association, Inc.
417 S Victory
Little Rock, AR 72201-2923

Professional journal for pharmacists. **Freq:** Bimonthly. **Key Personnel:** Barbara McMillan, Circulation Mgr. **Remarks:** Advertising accepted; rates available upon request.
Circ: (Not Reported)

1233 Arkansas Register
Office of the Secretary of State
State Capitol Phone: (501)682-3527
Little Rock, AR 72201-1094 Fax: (501)682-3548

Professional magazine. **Founded:** July 1977. **Freq:** Monthly. **Cols./Page:** 2. **Key Personnel:** Jon Davidson, jedavidson@sosmail.st.ar.us. **Subscription Rates:** $40 individuals; $3.50 single issue. **Remarks:** Advertising not accepted. **URL:** http://www.sosweb.state.ar.us.
Circ: Combined 200

1234 Arkansas Times
PO Box 34010 Phone: (501)375-2985
Little Rock, AR 72203 Fax: (501)375-3623
Publication E-mail: arktimes@arktimes.com
Publisher E-mail: arktimes@arktimes.com

Newspaper aimed at informing and educating readers about life in Arkansas; including articles on people, places, history, environment, politics, and current events. **Subtitle:** Arkanasas Weekly Newspaper of Politics & Culture. **Founded:** Sept. 1974. **Freq:** Weekly. **Print Method:** Cold press. **Trim Size:** 11 x 13 3/4. **Cols./Page:** 4. **Col. Width:** 14 picas. **Col. Depth:** 74 picas. **Key Personnel:** Max Brantley, Editor; Alan Leveritt, Publisher. **Subscription Rates:** $26 individuals.
Ad Rates: BW: $2,250 **Circ:** Non-paid 30,000
4C: $2,700 Paid 6,000

1235 Arkansas Wildlife
Arkansas Game & Fish Commission
2 Natural Resources Dr. Phone: (501)223-6300
Little Rock, AR 72205 Fax: (501)223-6447
Free: (800)364-GAME
Publication E-mail: kbsutton@agfc.state.ar.us

Wildlife, hunting, fishing, and environment magazine. **Founded:** 1967. **Freq:** Quarterly calendar. **Print Method:** Offset. **Trim Size:** 8 1/4 x 10 7/8. **Key Personnel:** Keith Sutton, Editor, kbsutton@agfc.state.ar.us; Jim Spencer, Asst. Editor. **ISSN:** 0004-1807. **Subscription Rates:** $8 individuals; $2.95 single issue. **Remarks:** Advertising not accepted. **Formerly**: Arkansas Game and Fish Magazine (1992).
Circ: Paid 20,000

1236 The Baptist Challenge
PO Box 25848 Phone: (501)868-7703
Little Rock, AR 72221-5848 Fax: (501)868-7622
Free: (800)594-4876

Religious magazine. **Subtitle:** A Voice of Independent Baptists. **Founded:** 1961. **Freq:** Monthly. **Print Method:** Offset. **Trim Size:** 8 1/2 x 11. **Cols./Page:** 4. **Col. Width:** 28 nonpareils. **Col. Depth:** 140 agate lines. **Key Personnel:** M.L. Moser, Jr., Editor and Publisher. **USPS:** 547-400. **Subscription Rates:** Free. **Remarks:** Accepts advertising.
Ad Rates: BW: $250 **Circ:** Free ‡6,000
PCI: $8

1237 Baptist Trumpet
Baptist Missionary Association of Arkansas
10712 Interstate 30 Phone: (501)565-4601
PO Box 192208 Fax: (501)565-NEWS
Little Rock, AR 72219-2208
Baptist tabloid. **Founded:** Sept. 25, 1940. **Freq:** Weekly (Wed.). **Print Method:** Offset. **Trim Size:** 11 1/2 x 14. **Cols./Page:** 5. **Col. Width:** 11 picas. **Key Personnel:** David Tidwell, Editor. **ISSN:** 0888-9074. **Subscription Rates:** $15 individuals; $13.34 Church Plan. **Remarks:** Advertising not accepted for promotion of books, films, or material not in agreement with the Association's Doctrinal Statement.
Ad Rates: GLR: $.28 **Circ:** ‡13,400
BW: $180
PCI: $5

1238 Construction News
10825 Financial Centre Pkwy., Phone: (501)227-8551
Ste. 131 Fax: (501)227-6856
Little Rock, AR 72211-3555
Free: (800)766-2611

Construction industry magazine. **Founded:** 1934. **Freq:** Semimonthly. **Print Method:** Offset. **Trim Size:** 7 7/8 x 10 7/8. **Cols./Page:** 3. **Col. Width:** 26 nonpareils. **Col. Depth:** 140 agate lines. **Key Personnel:** Brian Welch, Editor; Mary A. Nichol, Publisher. **ISSN:** 0160-5607. **Subscription Rates:** $65 individuals; $3 single issue.
Ad Rates: BW: $1,552 **Circ:** Paid 168
4C: $2,165 Controlled 6,279
PCI: $36

1239 Farm Bureau Press
Arkansas Farm Bureau Federation
Box 31 Phone: (501)228-1307
Little Rock, AR 72203-0031 Fax: (501)228-1557

Association newspaper covering farm issues in Arkansas and nationally. **Subtitle:** Official Publication of Arkansas Farm Bureau Federation. **Founded:** 1936. **Freq:** 6/year (Feb., Apr., June, Aug., Oct., Dec.). **Print Method:** Offset. **Cols./Page:** 4. **Col. Width:** 2 1/4 inches. **Col. Depth:** 12 1/2 inches. **Key Personnel:** A. Audie Ayer, Editor; James M. Kester, Advertising Mgr., phone (501)228-1274. **Subscription Rates:** includ-

ed in membership fee.; $12 nonmembers. **Remarks:** Accepts advertising. **Alt. Formats:** Mailing labels.
Ad Rates: BW: $3,010 **Circ:** ‡205,000
4C: $3,635
PCI: $98

1240 The Journal of the Arkansas Medical Society
Arkansas Medical Society
PO Box 55088 Phone: (501)224-8967
Little Rock, AR 72215 Fax: (501)224-6489
Publisher E-mail: ams@arkmed.org

Medical journal. **Founded:** 1890. **Freq:** Monthly. **Print Method:** Offset. **Trim Size:** 8 1/4 x 10 7/8. **Cols./Page:** 2. **Col. Width:** 34 nonpareils. **Col. Depth:** 126 agate lines. **Key Personnel:** Tina Wade, Managing Editor. **ISSN:** 0004-1858. **Subscription Rates:** $30 individuals; $40 other countries Other Countries; $3 single issue. **Remarks:** Accepts advertising.
Ad Rates: BW: $360 **Circ:** Paid ‡3,000
4C: $810 Non-paid ‡1,200

1241 Journal of Registry Management
National Cancer Registrars Association
4301 W Markham, Slot 629 Phone: (501)686-8803
Little Rock, AR 72205 Fax: (501)686-6479
Publication E-mail: amp-info@applmeapro.com

Contains articles, research papers, and opinion papers on topics related to management of health registries, and the collection, management and use of cancer, trauma, AIDS, and other health registry data. **Founded:** June 1995. **Freq:** Quarterly. **Print Method:** Offset. **Trim Size:** 8.5 x 11. **Cols./Page:** 3. **Col. Width:** 2.375 inches. **Col. Depth:** 6.25 inches. **Key Personnel:** Deborah O. Erwin, PhD, Editor, erwindeborahо@exchange.uams.edu; Beth Panther, Advertising Mgr., bpanther@applmeapro.com. **Subscription Rates:** $40 individuals; $12 single issue; $15 single issue, out of country. **Remarks:** Accepts advertising. **Formerly:** The Abstract (1995).
Ad Rates: BW: $225 **Circ:** Non-paid 2,600

1242 Rural Arkansas
Arkansas Electric Cooperative, Inc.
8000 Scott Hamilton Dr. Phone: (501)570-2200
PO Box 510 Fax: (501)570-2205
Little Rock, AR 72203-0510
Magazine for cooperative members and consumers. **Founded:** 1946. **Freq:** Monthly. **Key Personnel:** Ouida H. Cox, Editor and Publisher. **ISSN:** 0048-878X. **Subscription Rates:** $2 individuals.
Circ: Paid 294,313

1243 Southeastern College Art Conference Review
c/o Floyd Martin Phone: (501)569-3182
University of Arkansas, Little Rock Fax: (501)569-8775
Art Dept.
2801 S. University Ave.
Little Rock, AR 72204-1099
Professional and scholarly journal covering visual arts. **Founded:** 1966. **Freq:** Annual. **Key Personnel:** Floyd Martin, Editor, phone (501)569-3182, fwmarbin@valr.edu; Anne W. Thomas, Admin., SECAC, phone (914)929-0547, fax (919)933-1777. **Subscription Rates:** $30 single issue. **Remarks:** Advertising not accepted.
Circ: (Not Reported)

1244 Comcast Cablevision
801 Scott St. Phone: (501)376-5700
Little Rock, AR 72201 Fax: (501)375-1042

Founded: 1980. **Formerly:** Riverside Cable TV. **Key Personnel:** Gordon Tullock, President; Allan H. Meltzer, Vice President. **Cities Served:** Pulaski and Saline Counties, Bryant, and Cammack Village, AR.

1245 KAAY-AM - 1090
7123 I-30, Ste. 1 Phone: (501)661-1090
Little Rock, AR 72209 Fax: (501)562-9188

Format: Religious. **Networks:** USA Radio. **Formerly:** Beasley Broadcasting of Arkansas. **Operating Hours:** Continuous. **ADI:** Little Rock, AR. **Key Personnel:** Neal Gladner, General Mgr.; Gena Wilfong, Business Mgr.; Paul Massey, General Sales Mgr.; Gary Bruce, Operations Mgr.; Scott Taylor, Music & Public Service Director. **Wattage:** 50,000. **Ad Rates:** $4.50-8 for 30 seconds; $9-14 for 60 seconds.

1246 KABF-FM - 88.3
1501 Arch St. Phone: (501)372-6119
Little Rock, AR 72202
E-mail: kabf@igc.apc.org

Format: Full Service; Eclectic. **Owner:** Arkansas Broadcasting Foundation/KABF, at above address. **Founded:** 1983. **Operating Hours:** Continuous. **ADI:** Little Rock, AR. **Key Personnel:** Valerie Coffin, Station Mgr.; John Cain, Program Dir.; Dimitri Ferrell, Public Affairs; Cody Ausler, Pledge Drive Coordinator. **Local Programs:** *Ozark Mt. Hop*, Janice Brewer; *The People Speak*, Jerry Bradley. **Wattage:** 100,000. **Ad Rates:** Noncommercial. $10-15 for 30 seconds.

1247 KARK-TV - 4
PO Box 748 Phone: (501)376-4444
Little Rock, AR 72203 Fax: (501)376-1852

Format: Commercial TV. **Networks:** NBC. **Founded:** 1954. **Operating Hours:** Continuous. **ADI:** Little Rock, AR. **Key Personnel:** Troy Thompson, Production Mgr.; Bill Addington, Chief Engineer; Dean Hinson, President & General Mgr.; Bob Denman, Sales Mgr.; Al Sandubrae, News Dir.; Joe Welch, Business Mgr.; Michael Whitt, Marketing Mgr.

1248 KARN-AM - 920
4021 W. 8th St. Phone: (501)661-7500
PO Box 251920 Fax: (501)661-7620
Little Rock, AR 72225
Free: (800)264-7500

Format: Talk; News. **Simulcasts:** KARN-FM; KKRN-FM. **Networks:** CBS. **Owner:** Citadel Communications Corp., at above address. **Founded:** 1928. **Formerly:** KGJF-AM (1958). **Operating Hours:** Continuous; 40% network, 60% local. **ADI:** Little Rock, AR. **Key Personnel:** Neal Gladner, VP/General Mgr.; Chuck Martin, News Dir.; Greg Foster, Program Dir. **Wattage:** 5000. **Ad Rates:** Advertising accepted; rates available upon request.

1249 KASN-TV - 38
11711 W. Markham St. Phone: (501)225-0038
Little Rock, AR 72211 Fax: (501)225-0428

Format: Commercial TV. **Networks:** Independent. **Founded:** 1986. **Formerly:** KJTM-TV (1988). **Operating Hours:** 6 a.m.-2 a.m. **ADI:** Little Rock, AR. **Key Personnel:** Miquel Copello, Station Mgr.; Bob Dunn, Sales Mgr. **Ad Rates:** $15-250 per unit.

1250 KATV-TV - 7
PO Box 77 Phone: (501)372-7777
Little Rock, AR 72203 Fax: (501)324-7852

Format: Commercial TV. **Networks:** ABC. **Founded:** 1953. **Operating Hours:** 4:30 a.m.-1:30 a.m. **ADI:** Little Rock, AR. **Key Personnel:** Dale Nicholson, Contact.

1251 KBBL-AM - 1350
1300 S. Main, No. 102
PO Box 164100
Little Rock, AR 72202

Format: Religious. **Networks:** Christian Broadcasting (CBN). **Founded:** 1980. **Formerly:** KBOT-AM; KYXZ-AM. **Operating Hours:** Continuous. **ADI:** Little Rock, AR. **Key Personnel:** Phil Hall, President; Nicole Beam, Program Dir. **Wattage:** 2500. **Ad Rates:** $15 per unit.

1252 KIPR-FM - 92.3
415 N. McKinley, Ste. 920 Phone: (501)663-0092
Little Rock, AR 72205 Fax: (501)664-9201

Format: Urban Contemporary. **Networks:** ABC. **Operating Hours:** Continuous. **ADI:** Little Rock, AR. **Key Personnel:** Gordon Heiges, General Mgr.; Joe Booker, Program Dir.; Mark Dillon, Music Dir.; Joe Rook, Sales Mgr. **Wattage:** 100,000.

1253 KITA-AM - 1440
723 W. 14th St. Phone: (501)375-1440
Little Rock, AR 72202-3721 Fax: (501)375-0947

Format: Talk; Ethnic; Religious. **Networks:** USA Radio. **Owner:** KITA, Inc., at above address. **Founded:** 1957. **Formerly:** KOKY-AM. **Operating Hours:** Continuous. **ADI:** Little Rock, AR. **Key Personnel:** Gary Vaile, General Mgr.; Johnny Jackson, Program Dir.; Ulysses Robinson, Music Dir.; Kenneth Robinson, Program Mgr. **Wattage:** 5000 day, 250 night. **Ad Rates:** $10 for 30 seconds; $13 for 60 seconds.

1254 KKPT-FM - 94.1
2400 Cottondale Ln. Phone: (501)664-9410
Little Rock, AR 72202 Fax: (501)664-5871

Format: Classic Rock. **Networks:** Independent. **Owner:** Signal Media of Arkansas, at above address. **Founded:** 1960. **Formerly:** KLPQ-FM (1985); KHLT-FM. **Operating Hours:** Continuous; 100% local. **ADI:** Little Rock, AR. **Key Personnel:** Glen Buercklin, Production Dir.; Randi McCall, Traffic Dir.; Philip R. Jonsson, President; Ron Collar, General Mgr.; Eric Brown, News Dir. **Wattage:** 100,000. **Ad Rates:** $45-65 for 60 seconds.

1255 KLRE-FM - 90.5
2801 S. University Ave. Phone: (501)569-8485
Little Rock, AR 72204 Fax: (501)569-8488
E-mail: klre@ualr.edu

Format: Classical. **Networks:** National Public Radio (NPR). **Owner:** Little Rock School District, at above address. **Operating Hours:** Continuous. **Key Personnel:** Ben Fry, Station Mgr.; Taylor Lewis, Program Dir.; Avis Moore, Business Mgr.; Steve Barham, Underwriting and Marketing Coor. **Wattage:** 40,000. **Ad Rates:** Underwriting available.

1256 KLRT-TV - 16
11711 W. Markham Phone: (501)225-0016
Little Rock, AR 72211 Fax: (501)225-0428

Format: Commercial TV. **Networks:** Fox. **Founded:** 1983. **Operating Hours:** 6 a.m.-1:30 a.m. **ADI:** Little Rock, AR. **Key Personnel:** Bob Dunn, Contact, bdunn@klrt.com; Chuck Spohn, Contact, cspohn@klrt.com. **Wattage:** 5,000,000. **Ad Rates:** $20-950 per unit. **URL:** http://www.klrt.com.

1257 KSSN-FM - 95.7
8114 Cantrell Rd. Phone: (501)227-9696
Little Rock, AR 72207 Fax: (501)228-9547

Format: Contemporary Country. **Owner:** Triathlon Broadcasting Co., at above address. **Founded:** 1965. **Formerly:** KMYO-FM (1976). **Operating Hours:** Continuous; 100% local. **ADI:** Little Rock, AR. **Key Personnel:** Gordon Barnes, Farm Dir.; Richard D. Booth, General Mgr.; Bill Dotson, Program Dir.; Bill Dotson, Music Dir.; John Signaiga, Sales Mgr.; Trudy Smith, Bus. Mgr. **Wattage:** 100,000. **Ad Rates:** $50-200 for 60 seconds. Combined advertising rates available with KDDK-FM. **URL:** www.kssn.com.

1258 KTHV-TV - 11
720 Izard St. Phone: (501)376-1111
PO Box 269 Fax: (501)376-3719
Little Rock, AR 72203
E-mail: brawlins@kthvpo.gannett.com

Format: Commercial TV. **Networks:** CBS. **Founded:** 1955. **Operating Hours:** Sunday-Thurs Continuous; Friday & Saturday 4:30a.m.-1:30a.m. **ADI:** Little Rock, AR. **Key Personnel:** Susan Newkink, Vice President. **Wattage:** 316kw.

1259 KUAR-FM - 89.1
2801 S. University Ave. Phone: (501)569-8485
Little Rock, AR 72204 Fax: (501)569-8488

Format: News; Information. **Networks:** National Public Radio (NPR). **Owner:** Board of Trustees of the University of Arkansas, at above address. **Operating Hours:** Continuous. **ADI:** Little Rock, AR. **Key Personnel:** Ben Fry, Station Mgr.; Taylor Lewis, Program Dir.; Avis Moore, Business Mgr.; Steve Barham, Underwriting Marketing Coord. **Wattage:** 100,000. **Ad Rates:** Noncommercial. **URL:** http://www.ualr.edu/~kuar.

1260 KVTN-TV - 25
PO Box 22007 Phone: (501)223-2525
Little Rock, AR 72221 Fax: (501)221-3837

Format: Religious. **Owner:** Agape Church Inc., 701 Napa Valley Dr., Little Rock, AR 72211, (501)225-0612. **Founded:** 1988. **Operating Hours:** Continuous. **ADI:** Little Rock, AR. **Key Personnel:** Jim Grant, General Mgr., jgrant@aristotle.net; Kim Worden, Program/Sales/Promotion Dir.; David Osburn, Production Mgr.; Randy Wright, Chief Engineer. **Local Programs:** *Arkansas Alive*, Darin Drennan; *In His Presence*, Darin Drennan; *Kids Like You*, Cathie Dorsch. **Ad Rates:** $40 for 30 seconds; $60 for 60 seconds.

1261 KYFX-FM - 99.5
13910 Cooper Orbit Cove Phone: (501)666-9499
Little Rock, AR 72210 Fax: (501)666-9699

Format: Jazz; Urban Contemporary. **Networks:** CNN Radio; ABC. **Owner:** Nameloc Inc., 610 Plaza West Bldg., Little Rock, AR 72205. **Operating Hours:** Continuous. **Key Personnel:** Loretta Lever, General Mgr.; Carolyn Cooper, Operations Mgr.; Pamela King, Sales Mgr.; Rick Vaughn, Program Mgr. **Wattage:** 6,000. **Ad Rates:** Advertising accepted; rates available upon request.

1262 WEHCO Video Inc.
Box 2221 Phone: (501)378-3529
Little Rock, AR 72203 Fax: (501)376-8594

Key Personnel: Jim Willbanks, General Mgr. **Cities Served:** Operates systems in Arkansas, Mississippi, Oklahoma, and Texas.

MAGNOLIA†, pop. 11,909.

SW AR. Columbia Co. 50 mi. SE of Texarkana. Southern Arkansas University. Manufactures fabric dams, bromine, aluminum extrusion, steel, plastic pipe, rubber coated fabric.

Oil and natural gas. Pine, oak, gum timber. Agriculture. Cotton, corn, hogs.

1263 Banner-News
Banner-News Publishing Co.
134 S. Washington Phone: (870)234-5130
Box 100 Fax: (870)234-2551
Magnolia, AR 71753
General newspaper. **Founded:** 1878. **Freq:** Daily (eve.). **Print Method:** Offset. **Cols./Page:** 6. **Col. Width:** 24 nonpareils. **Col. Depth:** 303 agate lines. **Key Personnel:** Mike McNeill, Editor; W.E. Hussman, Jr., Publisher; Betty Chatham, General Mgr. **Subscription Rates:** $42 individuals. **Remarks:** Accepts advertising.
Ad Rates: SAU: $5.37 **Circ:** (Not Reported)

1264 KVMA-AM - 630
Box 430 Phone: (870)234-5862
Magnolia, AR 71753 Fax: (870)234-5865

Format: Country. **Networks:** ABC; Arkansas Radio. **Owner:** Magnolia Broadcasting Co., Inc., at above address. **Founded:** 1948. **Operating Hours:** 6 a.m.-sunset; 5% network, 95% local. **Key Personnel:** Rachel Gore, News Dir.; Ken Sibley, Music Dir.; Dan Gregory, Sales Mgr.; Ken Siblay, Manager. **Wattage:** 1000. **Ad Rates:** $2.75-3.50 for 15 seconds; $3.50-6.50 for 30 seconds; $6-12 for 60 seconds.

1265 KVMA-FM - 107.9
Box 430 Phone: (501)234-5862
Magnolia, AR 71753 Fax: (501)234-5865

Format: Adult Contemporary. **Networks:** Arkansas Radio. **Founded:** 1973. **Operating Hours:** Continuous. **Key Personnel:** Ken Sibley, President; Dan Gregory, Vice President. **Wattage:** 100,000. **Ad Rates:** $3.50-6.50 for 30 seconds; $6-12 for 60 seconds.

1266 KZHE-FM - 100.5
909 E. Main Phone: (501)234-7790
Magnolia, AR 71753-2912 Fax: (501)234-7791

Format: Country. **Owner:** A-1 Communications, at above address. **Founded:** 1981. **Formerly:** KQIT-FM (1981). **Operating Hours:** Continuous. **Key Personnel:** Troy Alphin, President; Dave Sehon, General Mgr.; Gwenna McClellan, Sales Mgr. **Wattage:** 50,000. **Ad Rates:** $1.75-3.40 for 15 seconds; $.75-6 for 30 seconds; $1.15-7 for 60 seconds.

MALVERN†, pop. 10,163.

SWC AR. Hot Spring Co. 20 mi. SE of Hot Spring. Manufactures brick, aluminum, telephone and electrical cable, lumber, building board, plastic utility pipe, brass fittings, aluminum and fiberglass boats, window frames, portable buildings, camper trailers, egg cartons. Mining barite. Poultry, livestock, timber.

1267 Malvern Daily Record
American Publishing Co.
219 Locust St. Phone: (501)337-7523
PO Box 70 Fax: (501)337-1226
Malvern, AR 72104-3721
Newspaper. **Founded:** Oct. 7, 1916. **Freq:** Daily (eve.). **Print Method:** Offset. **Trim Size:** 13 x 21 1/2. **Cols./Page:** 6. **Col. Width:** 2 1/16 inches. **Col. Depth:** 21 1/2 inches. **Key Personnel:** Cleo Beard, Editor; Ron Causey, Publisher; Richard Folds, Advertising Mgr. **USPS:** 326-860. **Subscription Rates:** $78 individuals; $84 out of area. **Remarks:** Accepts advertising.
Ad Rates: SAU: $7.80 **Circ:** Paid ‡5,300
Free ‡8,000

1268 KBOK-AM - 1310
1402 Hwy. 270 W. Phone: (501)332-6981
Malvern, AR 72104 Fax: (501)332-6984
E-mail: sgray@alpha-net.net

Format: News; Country. **Owner:** Malvern Entertainment Corp., at above address. **Founded:** 1951. **Former name:** KDAS-AM (1955). **Operating Hours:** Sunrise-sunset. **ADI:** Little Rock, AR. **Key Personnel:** Scott Gray, General Mgr. **Wattage:** 1000. **Ad Rates:** $4.71-5.88 per unit.

1269 KBOK-FM - 93.3
1402 Hwy 270 W. Phone: (501)332-6981
Malvern, AR 72104 Fax: (501)332-6984
E-mail: kbok@hotmail.com

Format: Hot Country. **Networks:** Jones Satellite. **Owner:** Malvern Entertainment Corporation, at above address. **Founded:** 1989. **Operating Hours:** Continuous. **Key Personnel:** Scott A. Gray, Pres./Gen. Mgr., sgray@mail.alpha-net.net; Janet L. Gray, Sales. **Local Programs:** *Hometown Reporter*, *Open-line*; *Swap and Shop*. **Wattage:** 5800 ERP. **Ad Rates:** $12.60-15.40 for 30 seconds; $14-17.50 for 60 seconds. KBOK-AM & KISI-AM.

1270 KISI-FM - 101.5
1402 Highway 270 W. Phone: (501)332-6981
Malvern, AR 72104 Fax: (501)332-6984
E-mail: sgray@alph-net.net

Format: Oldies. **Owner:** Malvern Entertainment Corp., at above address. **Founded:** Apr. 1991. **Operating Hours:** Continuous. **ADI:** Little Rock, AR. **Key Personnel:** Scott Gray, General Mgr. **Wattage:** 6000. **Ad Rates:** Advertising accepted; rates available upon request.

MAMMOTH SPRING

1271 KAMS-FM - 95.1
PO Box 193 Phone: (417)264-7211
Mammoth Spring, AR 72554 Fax: (417)264-7212
Free: (800)72995FM
E-mail: kamsfm@evergreen.com; kamsfm@enet.net

Format: Country; Contemporary Country; News; Sports. **Networks:** ABC. **Owner:** Shawn Marhefka, PO Box 1007, West Plains, MO 65775, (417)256-4949, (417)264-7063, Fax: (417)264-7012, Free: (800)729-95FM. **Founded:** 1955. **Operating Hours:** Continuous. **ADI:** Springfield, MO. **Key Personnel:** Bob Eckman, Station Mgr.; Lynn Hobbs, Asst.Manager/ Accounting; Liz McCoy, News; Chris Atkins, Program Dir.; Mark Martin, Operations Mgr.; Sarah Wiggs, Traffic Mgr.; Mike Robertson, PSA Dir.; Mike Crase, Promotional Director. **Wattage:** 100,000. **Ad Rates:** $11.20 for 30 seconds; $16.50 for 60 seconds. $3.35-$5.15 for 15 seconds; $5.20-$8.05 for 30 seconds; $6.95-$10.30 for 60 seconds. Combined advertising rates available with.

MANILA, pop. 2,553.

NE AR. Mississippi Co. 20 mi. W. of Blytheville. Residential.

1272 Northeast Arkansas Town Crier
PO Box 1326 Phone: (501)561-4634
Manila, AR 72442-1326 Fax: (501)561-3602

Local newspaper. **Founded:** 1971. **Freq:** Weekly (Tues.). **Print Method:** Offset. **Cols./Page:** 6. **Col. Width:** 24 nonpareils. **Col. Depth:** 294 agate lines. **Key Personnel:** Ron Kemp, Publisher. **Subscription Rates:** $20 individuals; $25 out of area; $30 out of state. **Remarks:** Accepts advertising.
Ad Rates: BW: $378 **Circ:** Paid 3,000
4C: $718 Free 4,400
SAU: $4.50
PCI: $4.50

MARIANNA†, pop. 6,220.

E. AR. Lee Co. 56 mi. SW of Memphis, TN. Manufactures lumber, auto seat frames, ladies' lingerie, sawmill; cotton ginning. Timber. Agriculture. Cotton, rice, soybeans, peaches. Livestock.

1273 Courier-Index
Box 569 Phone: (501)295-2521
Marianna, AR 72360-0569 Fax: (501)295-9662

Newspaper with a Democratic orientation. **Subtitle:** Lee County's Only Newspaper. **Founded:** 1875. **Freq:** Weekly (Thurs.). **Print Method:** Offset. **Cols./Page:** 6. **Col. Width:** 24 nonpareils. **Col. Depth:** 294 agate lines. **Key Personnel:** Robert Shearon, Managing Editor; Bonner McCollum, Publisher. **Subscription Rates:** $16.50 individuals; $24 Out of County; $35 out of state. **Remarks:** Accepts advertising.
Ad Rates: GLR: $.24 **Circ:** ‡2,350
BW: $617.40
SAU: $4.90

MARKED TREE

NE AR. Poinsett Co. 20 mi. E. of Harrisburg.

1274 Tri-City Tribune
PO Box 490 Phone: (870)358-2993
Marked Tree, AR 72365 Fax: (870)358-4538

Community newspaper. **Founded:** 1902. **Freq:** Weekly (Thurs.). **Print Method:** Offset. **Trim Size:** 17 x 22. **Cols./Page:** 6. **Col. Width:** 12 1/2 picas. **Col. Depth:** 21 inches. **Key Personnel:** John Boxley, Publisher. **Subscription Rates:** $24; $27 out of area. **Remarks:** Accepts advertising. **Formed by the merger of:** Marked Tree Tribune (1989); News Record (1989).
Ad Rates: SAU: $3.95 **Circ:** ‡2,500

MARSHALL†, pop. 1,595.

N. AR. Searcy Co. 90 mi. N. of Little Rock. Recreation area in Ozark Mountains. Buffalo National River. Hardwood timber. Agriculture. Vegetables. Dairy products.

1275 Mountain Wave
103 E. Main Phone: (870)448-3321
PO Box 220 Fax: (870)448-5659
Marshall, AR 72650
Community newspaper. **Founded:** 1890. **Freq:** Weekly (Thurs.). **Print Method:** Offset. **Cols./Page:** 6. **Col. Width:** 26 nonpareils. **Col. Depth:** 301 agate lines. **Key Personnel:** Shayla Adams, Circulation/Advertising Mgr. **Subscription Rates:** $18 individuals; $20 out of area; $24 out of state. **Remarks:** Accepts advertising.
Ad Rates: GLR: $4 **Circ:** ‡4,450
BW: $756
4C: $1,116
SAU: $6
PCI: $6

1276 KCGS-AM - 960
260 Battle St. Phone: (870)448-5567
Marshall, AR 72650 Fax: (870)448-5384
E-mail: kcgs960@yahoo.com

Format: Talk; News; Religious; Southern Gospel. **Networks:** Independent; USA Radio. **Founded:** 1975. **Operating Hours:** 6 a.m.-sunset; 100% local. **Key Personnel:** Roy C. Ragland, President; Gail Ragland, Office Mgr.; John Richmond, Music. **Local Programs:** *Swap Shop* 9:00 am - 10:30 am Monday-Friday, Roy Ragland. **Wattage:** 5000. **Ad Rates:** $2.50-3.50 for 15 seconds; $5-7.50 for 30 seconds; $7-10 for 60 seconds.

1277 Treece TV Cable
PO Box 167 Phone: (870)448-2550
Marshall, AR 72650

Owner: Mrs. Jack Treece, 400 Bellview Dr., Heber Springs, AR 72543, (501)362-2363. **Founded:** 1952. **Cities Served:** subscribing households 560; 18 channels.

MCCRORY, pop. 1,942.

C. AR. Woodruff Co. Shoes, cotton gin.

1278 McCrory Monitor-Leader-Advocate
Gladys Price Press
PO Box 898 Phone: (870)731-2263
McCrory, AR 72101 Fax: (870)731-5899
Publication E-mail: wcm@ipa.net

Local newspaper. **Subtitle:** The Monitor. **Founded:** 1990. **Freq:** Weekly. **Print Method:** Offset. **Cols./Page:** 6. **Col. Width:** 2 1/4 inches. **Col. Depth:** 21 1/2 inches. **Key Personnel:** Bill Riddle, Editor; Paula Davis, Publisher; Maryln Moody, Advertising Mgr. **USPS:** 006-506. **Subscription Rates:** $18 individuals; $22 out of area; $25 out of state. **Remarks:** Accepts advertising. **Formerly:** McCrory Leader; McCrory Monitor; Augusta Advocate.
Ad Rates: GLR: $.10 **Circ:** ‡1,800
SAU: $5
CNU: $6
PCI: $4

MCGEHEE, pop. 5,671.

SE AR. Desha Co. 45 mi. NW of Greenville, MS. Cotton ginning; logging; paper & rice mills; glove factory. Agriculture. Cotton, corn, rice, hay.

1279 Times-News
McGehee Publishing Co.
PO Box 290 Phone: (501)222-3922
McGehee, AR 71654 Fax: (501)222-3726
Publication E-mail: m.d.times@infogo.com

Newspaper with a Democratic orientation. **Founded:** 1924. **Freq:** Weekly (Wed.). **Print Method:** Offset. **Cols./Page:** 6. **Col. Width:** 26 nonpareils. **Col. Depth:** 301 agate lines. **Key Personnel:** James P. White, Jr., Publisher; Arlene White, Accounting. **Subscription Rates:** $24 individuals.
Ad Rates: PCI: $5.35 **Circ:** ‡3,400

1280 KVSA-AM - 1220
PO Box 110 Phone: (501)222-4200
McGehee, AR 71654-0110 Fax: (501)538-3389

Format: Full Service. **Owner:** Southeast Arkansas Broadcasters, Inc., at above address, (501)538-5200. **Founded:** 1953. **Operating Hours:** 6 a.m.-7 p.m.; 100% local. **Key Personnel:** Abbott F. Kinney, Contact. **Wattage:** 1,000. **Ad Rates:** $3.35-4.20 for 30 seconds; $4.25-5.25 for 60 seconds.

MELBOURNE

1281 The Times
PO Box 308 Phone: (501)368-4421
Melbourne, AR 72556 Fax: (501)368-4721

Community newspaper. **Freq:** Weekly (Wed.). **Cols./Page:** 6. **Col. Width:** 12 1/2 picas. **Col. Depth:** 21 1/2 inches. **Key**

Personnel: P.M. Dutton, Publisher. **Formerly:** Melbourne Times-Progress (1992).
Circ: 1,200

MENA†, pop. 5,154.

W. AR. Polk Co. 65 mi S. of Fort Smith. Manufactures jeans, furniture rubber and plastic products, electric motors. Sawmills. Timber. Agriculture. Corn, potatoes, berries, poultry, dairy products. Cattle.

1282 The Mena Star
Mena Star Co., Inc.
501-507 Mena St. Phone: (501)394-1900
PO Box 1307 Fax: (501)394-1908
Mena, AR 71953
Free: (800)446-5158
Publication E-mail: jcorbett@cswnet.com

General newspaper. **Founded:** 1896. **Freq:** 5/wk. (Tues.-Sat.). **Print Method:** Offset. **Cols./Page:** 6. **Col. Width:** 2 1/16 inches. **Col. Depth:** 21 1/2 inches. **Key Personnel:** Perry Quinn, Editor and Publisher; Jess Cogburn, Advertising Mgr. **ISSN:** 0747-1513. **Subscription Rates:** $48 individuals. **Remarks:** Accepts advertising.
Ad Rates: BW: $722.40 **Circ:** Paid 2,958
SAU: $5.60 Free 80
PCI: $5.60

1283 KENA-AM - 1450
1600 S. Reine St. Phone: (501)394-1450
PO Box 1450 Free: (800)844-5362
Mena, AR 71953

Format: News; Sports; Contemporary Country; Religious; Gospel. **Simulcasts:** KENA-FM. **Networks:** ABC; Arkansas Radio. **Owner:** Ouachita Broadcasting, Inc., at above address. **Founded:** 1950. **Formerly:** Quachita Communications, Inc. **Operating Hours:** 5 a.m.-12 a.m.; 15% network, 85% local. **Key Personnel:** Dwight Douglas, News Dir.; Jay Bunyard, Owner; Bevona Williams, Contact. **Wattage:** 1000. **Ad Rates:** $3.50-4.50 for 15 seconds; $5.50-7 for 30 seconds; $7.50-9 for 60 seconds.

1284 KENA-FM - 102.1
1600 S. Reine St. Phone: (501)394-1450
PO Box 1450 Fax: (501)394-1459
Mena, AR 71953
Free: (800)844-5362

Format: News; Sports; Contemporary Country. **Networks:** ABC. **Owner:** Duachita Broadcasting, Inc., at above address. **Founded:** 1969. **Formerly:** KSKR-FM; KUOL-FM. **Operating Hours:** 5 a.m.-12 p.m.; 15% network, 85% local. **Key Personnel:** Dwight Douglas, News Dir.; Bevona Williams, Contact; Jay Bunyard, Owner. **Wattage:** 25,000. **Ad Rates:** $3.50-4.50 for 15 seconds; $5.50-7 for 30 seconds; $7.50-9 for 60 seconds.

MONTICELLO†, pop. 8,259.

SE AR. Drew Co. 50 mi. SE of Pine Bluff. University of Arkansas. Manufactures boats, paper and plastic bags, Rugs, yarn mills. Bottling works. Timber. Tomatoes, soybeans.

1285 Advance-Monticellonian
Tom White
314 N. Main St. Phone: (501)367-5325
PO Box 486 Fax: (501)367-6612
Monticello, AR 71655
Publication E-mail: advance@ipa.net

Community newspaper. **Founded:** 1870. **Freq:** Weekly (Wed.). **Print Method:** Offset. **Cols./Page:** 6. **Col. Width:** 29 nonpareils. **Col. Depth:** 305 agate lines. **Key Personnel:** Betty Evans, Editor; Tom White, Publisher; Janey Honeycutt, Advertising Mgr. **Subscription Rates:** $26; $34; $.50 single issue. **Remarks:** Accepts advertising.
Ad Rates: GLR: $.34 **Circ:** ‡5,850
SAU: $5.50

1286 Drew County Shopper's Guide
Tom White
314 N. Main St. Phone: (501)367-5325
PO Box 486 Fax: (501)367-6612
Monticello, AR 71655
Publication E-mail: advance@ipa.net

Shopping guide. **Founded:** 1975. **Freq:** Weekly. **Print Method:** Web offset. **Cols./Page:** 6. **Col. Width:** 2 1/8 inches. **Subscription Rates:** Free. **Remarks:** Accepts advertising.
Ad Rates: SAU: $5.50 **Circ:** 9,200
PCI: $4.35

1287 Community Communications Co.
425 N. Phone: (501)367-7300
Box 558 Fax: (501)367-9770
Monticello, AR 71655

Key Personnel: Paul Gardner, General Mgr. **Cities Served:** Arkansas City, Eudora, Monticello, Warren, AR.

1288 KGPO-FM - 99.9
PO Box 308 Phone: (870)367-8525
Monticello, AR 71655 Fax: (870)367-8527
Free: (888)261-8525

Format: Adult Contemporary. **Networks:** Westwood One Radio. **Owner:** P. Q. Gardner, 539 W. Gaines, Monticello, AR 71655. **Operating Hours:** Continuous. **Key Personnel:** Bonnie Ellis, General Mgr.; Jason Camden, Station Mgr., phone (870)367-6999; Becky Tucker, Marketing Rep.; Charles Gardner, Sales Exec. **Wattage:** 25,000.

1289 KHBM-AM - 1430
Box 446 Phone: (870)367-6854
Monticello, AR 71657-0446 Fax: (870)367-9564
E-mail: khbn@seark.com

Format: Religious. **Networks:** AP; Arkansas Radio; ABC. **Owner:** Midway Broadcasting Co., at above address. **Founded:** 1955. **Operating Hours:** Continuous; 99% local, 1% other. **Key Personnel:** Truman Hamilton, Sales/Gen. Mgr.; Mary Hamilton, Traffic Dir. **Wattage:** 1000. **Ad Rates:** Advertising accepted; rates available upon request.

1290 KHBM-FM - 93.5
Box 446 Phone: (501)367-6854
Monticello, AR 71657 Fax: (501)367-9564
E-mail: khbm@seark.net

Format: Adult Contemporary. **Networks:** AP; Arkansas Radio; ABC. **Owner:** Midway Broadcasting Co., at above address. **Founded:** 1955. **Operating Hours:** Continuous; 1% network, 99% local. **Key Personnel:** Truman Hamilton, Sales/Gen. Mgr.; Mary Hamilton, Traffic Dir. **Wattage:** 6,000. **Ad Rates:** Advertising accepted; rates available upon request. Combined advertising rates available with KYSA-FM.

1291 KXSA-FM - 103.1
PO Box 446 Phone: (870)367-8528
Monticello, AR 71657 Fax: (870)367-9564
E-mail: khbm@seark.net

Format: Country. **Owner:** Midway Broadcasting Company, at above address. **Founded:** 1983. **Formerly:** KAKA-FM (1988). **Operating Hours:** Continuous. **Key Personnel:** Truman Hamilton, Contact; Ed Davis, Contact. **Wattage:** 6000. **Ad Rates:** $6-10 for 30 seconds; $9-13 for 60 seconds. Combined advertising rates available with KHBM-AM/FM.

MOUNT IDA†, pop. 1,026.

W. AR. Montgomery Co. 85 mi. W. of Little Rock. Residential.

1292 Montgomery County News
Graves Publishing Co.
PO Box 195 Phone: (501)867-2821
Mount Ida, AR 71957 Fax: (501)356-4400

Local newspaper. **Founded:** 1951. **Freq:** Weekly (Thurs.). **Print Method:** Offset. **Cols./Page:** 5. **Col. Width:** 11 picas. **Col. Depth:** 180 agate lines. **Key Personnel:** Mike McCoy, Editor. **Remarks:** Accepts advertising.
Ad Rates: GLR: $.23 **Circ:** ‡1,950
PCI: $3.21

MOUNTAIN HOME†, pop. 7,447.

N. AR. Baxter Co. 18 mi. N. of Buffalo City. Residential

1293 The Baxter Bulletin
PO Drawer A Phone: (870)425-3133
Mountain Home, AR 72653 Fax: (870)425-5091
Publication E-mail: bulletin@mtnhome.com

General newspaper. **Founded:** 1901. **Freq:** Mon.-Sat. (morn.). **Print Method:** Offset. **Trim Size:** 13 3/4 x 22 3/4. **Cols./Page:** 6. **Col. Width:** 24 nonpareils. **Col. Depth:** 294 agate lines. **Key Personnel:** Bob Qualls, Editor; Betty Barker Smith, Publisher; Eddie Majeste, Advertising Dir. **ISSN:** 0745-7707. **Subscription Rates:** $68.64 individuals; $93.90 out of area. **Remarks:** Accepts advertising.
Ad Rates: BW: $976.50 **Circ:** Mon.-Sat. ★**10,817**
4C: $1,171.50
SAU: $7.75
PCI: $7.75

1294 The Daily News
North Arkansas Newspapers, Inc.
PO Box 1087
Mountain Home, AR 72653
Publication E-mail: thedaily@interhome.com

Community newspaper. **Founded:** Sept. 1985. **Freq:** Mon.-Sat. (morn.). **Print Method:** Offset. **Trim Size:** 13 3/4 x 22 3/4. **Cols./Page:** 6. **Col. Width:** 2 1/6 inches. **Col. Depth:** 21 1/2 inches. **Key Personnel:** Joe Dobson, Editor; Chuck Pullins, Publisher. **USPS:** 753-970. **Subscription Rates:** $35; $55. **Remarks:** Accepts advertising. **Formerly:** The North Arkansas View.
Ad Rates: BW: $903 **Circ:** ‡25
4C: $203.50
PCI: $7

1295 KCMH-FM - 91.5
126 S. Church St. Phone: (870)425-2525
Mountain Home, AR 72653-3828 Fax: (870)424-2626

Format: Religious; Educational. **Networks:** Moody Broadcasting; Ambassador Inspirational Radio; USA Radio. **Founded:** 1988. **Operating Hours:** Continuous; 100% network. **Key Personnel:** Carl Albright, President; Penny Neal, Office Mgr. **Wattage:** 400. **Ad Rates:** Noncommercial.

1296 KKTZ-FM - 107.5
2352 Highway 62 E. Phone: (870)492-6022
Mountain Home, AR 72653-6847 Fax: (870)424-2137

Format: Adult Contemporary. **Networks:** ABC. **Founded:** 1985. **Operating Hours:** Continuous. **ADI:** Springfield, MO. **Key Personnel:** Stewart Brunner, Gen./Sales Mgr.; Ray Miller, Program Dir.; Mark Matlock, News Dir. **Wattage:** 100,000. **Ad Rates:** Advertising accepted; rates available upon request.

1297 KPFM-FM - 105.5
2352 Highway 62 E. Phone: (870)492-6022
Mountain Home, AR 72653-6847 Fax: (501)424-2137

Format: Country; Contemporary Country. **Networks:** ABC. **Founded:** 1984. **Formerly:** KGHI-FM (1985). **Operating Hours:** Continuous. **Key Personnel:** Stewart Brunner, Contact; Roger Lowery, Program Dir.; Ben McDade, News Dir. **Wattage:** 50,000. **Ad Rates:** Advertising accepted; rates available upon request.

1298 KTLO-AM - 1240
620 Hwy. 5 N. Phone: (870)425-3101
PO Box C Fax: (870)424-4314
Mountain Home, AR 72653
E-mail: ktlo@mtnhome.com

Format: Country. **Networks:** ABC. **Owner:** KTLO Limited Partnership, at above address. **Founded:** 1953. **Operating Hours:** Continuous; 50% network, 50% local. **ADI:** Springfield, MO. **Key Personnel:** Bob Knight, General Mgr.; Danny Ward, Sales Mgr.; Jim Bodenhammer, News Dir.; Brad Haworth, Music Dir.; Sue Knight, Traffic and Office Mgr. **Wattage:** 1000. **Ad Rates:** $6.50-8 for 30 seconds; $11.50-15.50 for 60 seconds. $4.50-$7 for 30 seconds; $7-$11 for 60 seconds. Combined advertising rates available with KTLO-FM.

1299 KTLO-FM - 97.9
PO Box C Phone: (870)425-3101
Mountain Home, AR 72653 Fax: (870)424-4314
E-mail: ktlo@mtnhome.com

Format: Middle-of-the-Road (MOR). **Networks:** ABC. **Owner:** KTLO Limited Partnership/KTLO-FM, at above address. **Founded:** 1970. **Operating Hours:** Continuous; 60% network, 40% local. **ADI:** Springfield, MO. **Key Personnel:** Bob Knight, General Mgr.; Danny Ward, Sales Mgr.; Jim Bodenhammer, News Dir.; Brad Haworth, Music Dir.; Sue Knight, Traffic and Office Mgr. **Wattage:** 50,000. **Ad Rates:** $8-11 for 30 seconds; $13-17 for 60 seconds. $7-$10 for 30 seconds; $12-$17 for 60 seconds. Combined advertising rates available with KTLO-AM.

MOUNTAIN VIEW†.

NC AR. Stone Co. 30 mi. NW of Independence.

1300 Stone County Leader
Stone County Publishing Co.
PO Box 509 Phone: (501)269-3841
Mountain View, AR 72560-0509 Fax: (501)269-2171

Local newspaper. **Founded:** 1951. **Freq:** Weekly (Wed.). **Print Method:** Offset. **Cols./Page:** 6. **Col. Width:** 12 picas. **Col. Depth:** 21 inches. **Key Personnel:** Lori Freeze, Editor; James R. Fraser, Publisher. **USPS:** 009-255. **Subscription Rates:** $16; $26 other countries. **Remarks:** Accepts advertising.
Ad Rates: SAU: $4.45 **Circ:** ‡4,339

1301 KEMV-TV - 6
350 S. Donaghey Phone: (501)682-2386
Conway, AR 72032 Fax: (501)682-4122
Free: (800)662-2386

Format: Public TV. **Networks:** Public Broadcasting Service (PBS). **Owner:** Arkansas Educational Television Commission, at above address. **Founded:** 1980. **Operating Hours:** 6 a.m.-11:30 p.m. weekdays; 7 a.m.-11:30 p.m. Saturday and Sunday. **ADI:** Little Rock, AR. **Key Personnel:** Susan Howarth, Exec. Dir.; Allen Weatherly, Deputy Dir.; Kathy Atkinson, Program Dir.; Ron Johnson, Communications Dir.; Carole Adornetto, Production Dir.; Gary Schultz, Engineering Dir.; Kathleen Stafford, Operations Dir.; Jane Havens, Traffic Mgr. **Local Programs:** *Arkansas Outdoors*; *Arkansas Week*; *Good Times Picture Show*. **Ad Rates:** Noncommercial. **URL:** http://www.aetn.com.

MURFREESBORO

1302 Murfreesboro Diamond
Graves Publishing Co.
PO Box 297 Phone: (501)845-2010
Nashville, AR 71852 Fax: (501)845-5091

Community newspaper (tabloid). **Founded:** Aug. 1975. **Freq:** Weekly (Wed.). **Print Method:** Offset. **Cols./Page:** 5. **Col. Width:** 2 inches. **Col. Depth:** 13 inches. **Key Personnel:** Jim Welch, Editor. **Subscription Rates:** $15. **Remarks:** Accepts advertising.
Ad Rates: PCI: $2.92 **Circ:** ‡1,800

NASHVILLE, pop. 4,554.

SW AR. Howard Co. 39 mi. NE of Texarkana. Manufactures cement products, gypsum wallboard, chainsaws, baskets, garments, Sawmills; cutlery plants. Major poultry area. Cattle. peaches.

Murfreesboro Diamond - See Murfreesboro

1303 KBHC-AM - 1260
1513 S. 4th St. Phone: (501)845-3601
Nashville, AR 71852 Fax: (501)845-3680

Format: Country; Religious. **Networks:** Arkansas Radio. **Owner:** Pete Gathright, at above address. **Founded:** 1959. **Operating Hours:** Sunrise-sunset. **Key Personnel:** Pete Gathright, Contact; Ann Gathright, Contact; Rick Castleberry, Contact; Brent Pinkerton, News Dir. **Wattage:** 500. **Ad Rates:** $3-4.12 for 30 seconds; $3.50-5 for 60 seconds.

1304 KMTB-FM - 99.5
1513 4th St. Phone: (870)845-3601
Nashville, AR 71852 Fax: (870)845-3680
E-mail: pag@iosa.com

Format: Country. **Owner:** PAG Broadcasting, Inc., at above address. **Operating Hours:** Continuous. **Key Personnel:** Ann Gathright, President; Pete Gathright, Sec.; Rick Castleberry, Operations Mgr. **Wattage:** 20,500.

1305 KNAS-FM - 105.5
1513 S. 4th St. Phone: (501)845-3601
Nashville, AR 71852 Fax: (501)845-3680

Format: Oldies. **Networks:** Arkansas Radio. **Owner:** Pete Gathright, at above address. **Founded:** 1977. **Operating Hours:** Continuous. **Key Personnel:** Pete Gathright, Contact; Ann Gathright, Contact; Rick Castleberry, Contact; Brent Pinkerton, News Dir. **Wattage:** 3000 ERP. **Ad Rates:** $3-4.12 for 30 seconds; $4.12-5.88 for 60 seconds.

NORTH LITTLE ROCK, pop. 64,419.

C. AR. Pulaski Co. On Arkansas River, opposite Little Rock. Manufactures chemicals, coke, fertilizer, excelsior, furniture, baking powder, concrete products. Soybeans, cottonseed. Pulp mill; stock yards; poultry processing plant.

1306 City & Town
Arkansas Muncipal League
PO Box 38 Phone: (501)374-3484
North Little Rock, AR 72115-0038 Fax: (501)374-0541
Publication E-mail: jkw@arml.org

Municipal urban magazine. **Founded:** 1947. **Freq:** Monthly. **Print Method:** Offset. **Trim Size:** 7 1/2 x 10. **Cols./Page:** 2 and 3. **Col. Width:** 26 and 40 nonpareils. **Col. Depth:** 140 agate lines. **Key Personnel:** John Woodruff, Editor, jwoodruff@arml.org. **ISSN:** 0193-8371. **Subscription Rates:** $15 individuals. **Remarks:** Accepts advertising.
Ad Rates: BW: $375 **Circ:** ‡7,000
4C: $555

1307 The Times
KDC Communications, Inc.
PO Box 428 Phone: (501)758-2571
North Little Rock, AR 72115 Fax: (501)758-2597
Publication E-mail: thetimes@cel.net
Publisher E-mail: thetimes@lr.cleaf.com

Suburban newspaper serving North Pulaski County. **Founded:** 1898. **Freq:** Weekly (Thurs.). **Print Method:** Offset. **Trim Size:** 13 1/2 x 21 1/2. **Cols./Page:** 6. **Col. Width:** 2 inches. **Col. Depth:** 129 inches. **Key Personnel:** Kitty Chism, Editor; David Chism, Publisher. **USPS:** 617-620. **Subscription Rates:** $16.50 individuals; $0.50 single issue. **Remarks:** Accepts advertising.
Ad Rates: GLR: $0.69 **Circ:** ‡9,253
BW: $1515.75
4C: $1915.75
SAU: $11.75
PCI: $11.75

1308 KLRG-AM - 1150
1403 Main St. Phone: (501)376-1063
North Little Rock, AR 72114-4128 Fax: (501)376-7627

Format: Gospel; Urban Contemporary. **Networks:** Mutual Broadcasting System. **Founded:** 1946. **Formerly:** KEZQ-AM (1990). **Operating Hours:** Continuous. **Key Personnel:** Robin May, General Mgr., fax (501)374-6381, robinmay7@hotmail.com; Darryl White, Program Dir. **Wattage:** 5000 day; 1000 night. **Ad Rates:** $12-31 for 30 seconds; $14-37 for 60 seconds. **URL:** http://www.klrg.com.

1309 KMTL-AM - 760
2808 E. Kiehl Ave. Phone: (501)835-1554
PO Box 6460
North Little Rock, AR 72120-3244

Format: Gospel. **Founded:** 1983. **Operating Hours:** Sunrise-sunset. **Wattage:** 10,000.

1310 KMZX-FM - 106.3
1403 Main St.
North Little Rock, AR 72114-4128

Format: Urban Contemporary; Adult Contemporary. **Networks:** Mutual Broadcasting System. **Founded:** 1982. **Formerly:** KWTD-FM (1990). **Operating Hours:** Continuous. **Key Personnel:** Kenn Flemmons, General Mgr.; Neal Scoggins, Program Dir. **Wattage:** 3000. **Ad Rates:** $12-31 for 30 seconds; $14-37 for 60 seconds.

1311 KQAR-FM - 100.3
314 Main St. Phone: (501)372-7740
North Little Rock, AR 72114 Fax: (501)372-7787

Format: Top 40. **Owner:** Clear Channel Broadcasting, Inc., 200 Concord Plaza, Ste. 600, San Antonio, TX 78216, (210)822-2828. **Formerly:** KDDK-FM; KEZQ-FM. **Operating Hours:** Continuous. **ADI:** Little Rock, AR. **Key Personnel:** Richard D. Booth, V. P. Marketing/General Mgr.; Gary Robinson, Program Mgr.; Cathleen Cavender, Traffic Dir.; Trudy Smith, Business Mgr., phone (501)227-9696; Susan Cochran, Promotions Dir. **Local Programs:** *Hometown Countdown*, Gary Robinson; *Tanner in the Morning*, Rob Tanner; *The Afternoon Hoo-Ha*, Jason Addams. **Wattage:** 81,000. **Ad Rates:** $8-23 per unit.

1312 Storer Cable Communications
4609 Camp Robinson Rd. Phone: (501)758-3490
Box 838 Fax: (501)375-1042
North Little Rock, AR 72118

Founded: 1973. **Cities Served:** Pulaski County, Jacksonville, and Sherwood, AR.

OSCEOLA†, pop. 8,510.

EC AR. Mississippi Co. On Mississippi River, 16 mi. S. of Blytheville. Feed, cottonseed, oil and alphafa.

1313 Osceola Times
Rust Communications
112 N. Poplar Phone: (501)563-2615
Osceola, AR 72370-2665 Fax: (501)563-2616

Community newspaper. **Founded:** 1870. **Freq:** Weekly (Wed.). **Print Method:** King Press. **Cols./Page:** 6. **Col. Width:** 2 inches. **Col. Depth:** 21 inches. **Key Personnel:** David Cooke, Publisher. **Subscription Rates:** $12; $15 out of area. **Remarks:** Accepts advertising.
Ad Rates: PCI: $3.25 **Circ:** 6,500

1314 KOSE-AM - 860
509 S. Walnut Phone: (501)563-2641
PO Box 249
Osceola, AR 72370

Format: Oldies. **Networks:** ABC; Arkansas Radio. **Owner:** Pollack Broadcasting Co., at above address. **Founded:** 1949. **Operating Hours:** 17 hours daily; 100% local. **Key Personnel:** Bob Abel, Contact; Jamie Williams, Traffic Dir.; Bob Abel, News Dir.; Craig Koon, Contact; Ed White, Station Mgr.; Chris Webster, Operations Dir.; Ed White, Program Dir./Sales Mgr. **Wattage:** 1000. **Ad Rates:** $8-10.50 for 30 seconds; $10-13 for 60 seconds.

OZARK

1315 Ozark Spectator
Ozark Spectator Corp.
207 W. Main Phone: (501)667-2136
Ozark, AR 72949 Fax: (501)667-4365

Community newspaper. **Founded:** Aug. 1911. **Freq:** Weekly (Wed.). **Cols./Page:** 6. **Col. Width:** 12 1/2 picas. **Col. Depth:** 21 1/2 inches. **Key Personnel:** Bob Bevil, Publisher. **Subscription Rates:** $14; $18 out of area; $20 out of state. **Remarks:** Advertising accepted; rates available upon request.
Circ: 5,600

1316 KDYN-AM - 1540
Box 1086 Phone: (501)667-4567
Ozark, AR 72949 Fax: (501)667-5214

Format: Contemporary Country. **Networks:** ABC; Arkansas Radio. **Owner:** Ozark Communications Inc., at above address. **Founded:** 10, 1985. **Formerly:** KZRK-AM. **Operating Hours:** Sunrise-sunset. **Key Personnel:** Marc Dietz, Gen./Sales Mgr.; Shae Dietz, Office Mgr. **Wattage:** 500. **Ad Rates:** $3.50-7 for 30 seconds; $5.10-10 for 60 seconds.

PARAGOULD†, pop. 15,214.

NE AR. Greene Co. 69 mi. NW of Memphis, TN. Manufactures electric motors. shock absorbers, sprockets and gears, gas grills, shirts, burial vaults, trailers. Cotton ginning; bottling works. Soybeans, cotton, corn, hay. Cattle, hogs. Milk, dairy products.

1317 KDRS-AM - 1490
Box 117 Phone: (870)236-7627
Paragould, AR 72451 Fax: (870)239-4583

Format: Contemporary Christian. **Networks:** NBC; Arkansas Radio; Progressive Farmer. **Owner:** Paragould Radio Broadcasting, LLC., at above address. **Founded:** 1947. **Operating Hours:** 6 a.m.- midnight. **Key Personnel:** Monte Lyons, General Mgr.; Juli Page, Operations Mgr.; Peggy Richardson, Sales Mgr.; Karen Lenderman, Traffic Mgr.; David White, Program Dir. **Wattage:** 1000. **Ad Rates:** $3-5 for 30 seconds; $5-7 for 60 seconds. $2.50-$3.93 for 30 seconds; $4-$5.33 for 60 seconds. Combined advertising rates available with KLQZ-FM: $5-$7.86 for 30 seconds.

1318 KLQZ-FM - 107.1
PO Box 117 Phone: (870)236-4583
Paragould, AR 72451 Fax: (870)239-4583

Format: Classic Rock. **Networks:** NBC; Arkansas Radio. **Owner:** Paragould Radio Broadcasting, LLC, at above address. **Founded:** 1984. **Operating Hours:** Continuous. **Key Personnel:** Monte Lyons, General Mgr.; Juli Page, Program Dir.; Peggy Richardson, Sales Mgr.; Karen Lenderman, Traffic Mgr. **Wattage:** 3000. **Ad Rates:** $4-8 for 30 seconds; $6-10 for 60 seconds.

PARIS

1319 Paris Express
PO Box 551 Phone: (501)963-2901
Paris, AR 72855 Fax: (501)963-3062

Community newspaper. **Freq:** Weekly (Wed.). **Print Method:** Offset. **Cols./Page:** 6. **Col. Width:** 12 picas. **Col. Depth:** 21 1/2 inches. **Key Personnel:** Vickey Wiggins, Publisher. **Subscription Rates:** $.50. **Remarks:** Advertising accepted; rates available upon request.
Circ: 3,800

1320 KERX-FM - 95.3
24 S. Express St. Phone: (501)963-8362
Paris, AR 72855 Fax: (501)963-8461
Free: (877)953-9953

Format: Classic Rock. **Owner:** Pearson Broadcasting Group, at above address, (417)335-2261, Fax: (417)335-2377. **Founded:** 1959. **Formerly:** KCCL-FM (Feb. 18, 1994). **Operating Hours:** Continuous. **Key Personnel:** Max Pearson, President; Doug Raines, General Mgr.; Carol Patterson,

Station Mgr. **Wattage:** 50,000. **Ad Rates:** $17-7.50 for 30 seconds.

PEA RIDGE, pop. 1,488.

NW AR. Benton Co. 30 mi. N. of Fayetteville. Resort, water recreation. Vegetable preparation. Agriculture. Poultry, cattle.

1321 The Times of Northeast Benton County
PO Box 25 Phone: (501)451-1196
Pea Ridge, AR 72751
Community newspaper. **Founded:** 1966. **Freq:** Weekly (Wed.). **Print Method:** Offset. **Cols./Page:** 6. **Col. Width:** 24 nonpareils. **Col. Depth:** 297 agate lines. **Key Personnel:** Mike Freeman, Editor and Publisher. **Subscription Rates:** $12 individuals; $18 out of area. **Remarks:** Accepts advertising.
Ad Rates: GLR: $.19 **Circ:** ‡1,690
BW: $318.75
PCI: $3.25

PIGGOTT†, pop. 3,762.

NE AR. Clay Co. 40 mi. NW of Blytheville. Manufactures church furniture, electric transformers, picture frames, electrical components, lamps and shades. Cotton ginning; sawmill. Oak, gum, hickory timber. Ships hogs. Dairy, poultry farms. Cotton, soybeans, rice, corn, wheat, grain, milo.

1322 The Piggott Times
Delta Publishing Co.
209 Main St. Phone: (870)598-2201
PO Box 59 Fax: (870)598-5189
Piggott, AR 72454-0059
Community newspaper. **Founded:** May 25, 1967. **Freq:** Weekly (Wed.). **Print Method:** Offset. **Trim Size:** 6 x 21. **Cols./Page:** 6. **Col. Width:** 26 nonpareils. **Col. Depth:** 182 agate lines. **Key Personnel:** Ronald E. Kemp, Editor, rkemp@cswnet.com; Nancy Kemp, Office Mgr. and Editor, njkemp@cswnet.com. **USPS:** 848-240. **Subscription Rates:** $20 individuals; $25 out of area; $30 out of state. **Remarks:** Color advertising not accepted. **URL:** http://www.townnews.com/ar/nearnews.
Ad Rates: GLR: $.25 **Circ:** Paid 3,100
BW: $567
SAU: $4
PCI: $4.75

PINE BLUFF†, pop. 56,576.

SEC AR. Jefferson Co. 45 mi. SE of Little Rock, on Arkansas River. University of Arkansas at Pine Bluff. Pine Bluff Convention Center. Manufactures lumber, agricultural machinery, wood products, cotton pickers, electric transformers, pillow cases, bed sheets, furniture, paper bags, & cartons, chemicals, aluminum & steel casting, archery equipment, newsprint, jumbo barges, towboats. Cotton market and livestock; cotton oil mills; cotton compresses and warehouses; stockyards. Pine, gum, oak timber. Agriculture. Cattle, hogs, cotton, rice, soybeans.

1323 Pine Bluff Commercial
Donrey Media Group
300 Beech St. Phone: (501)534-3400
Pine Bluff, AR 71601 Fax: (501)543-1455

General newspaper. **Founded:** 1881. **Freq:** Mon.-Sun. (morn.). **Print Method:** Letterpress. **Cols./Page:** 6. **Col. Depth:** 293 agate lines. **Key Personnel:** Jane Ramus, Editor; Donald W. Reynolds, Publisher; Nancy Donaldson, Advertising Mgr. **Subscription Rates:** $78 individuals. **Remarks:** Accepts advertising.
Ad Rates: GLR: $.49 **Circ:** Mon.-Sat. 19,052
BW: $1,542.24 Sun. 19,976
4C: $1,842.24
SAU: $12.24

White Hall Journal - See White Hall

1324 KCAT-AM - 1340
PO Box 8808 Phone: (501)534-5001
Pine Bluff, AR 71611-8808

Format: Urban Contemporary; Religious. **Networks:** American Urban Radio. **Owner:** J.B. Scanlon, at above address. **Founded:** 1963. **Operating Hours:** Continuous; 10% network, 90% local. **Key Personnel:** J.B. Scanlon, Contact. **Wattage:** 1000. **Ad Rates:** $12-16 for 30 seconds; $15-20 for 60 seconds.

POCAHONTAS†, pop. 5,995.

NE AR. Randolph Co. On Black River, 35 mi. NW of Jonesboro. Manufactures handles, tool chests, shoes, electronic component parts, heavy trailers, pickup campers. Timber. Dairy, poultry, grain and hog farms.

1325 Pocahontas Star Herald
Rockwell Publishing Co.
109 N. VanBibber Phone: (501)892-4451
PO Box 608 Fax: (501)892-4453
Pocahontas, AR 72455
Newspaper with a Democratic orientation. **Founded:** 1880. **Freq:** Weekly (Thurs.). **Print Method:** Offset. **Cols./Page:** 6. **Col. Width:** 12 picas. **Col. Depth:** 21 1/2 inches. **Key Personnel:** J.V. Rockwell, Publisher; Anita Murphy, General Mgr. **Subscription Rates:** $20 individuals; $30 out of area. **Remarks:** Accepts advertising.
Ad Rates: GLR: $4.34 **Circ:** ‡6,100
BW: $403.77
4C: $175
SAU: $3.90

1326 Randco Trading Post
Rockwell Publishing Co.
109 N. VanBibber Phone: (501)892-4451
PO Box 608 Fax: (501)892-4453
Pocahontas, AR 72455
Shopper. **Freq:** Weekly. **Cols./Page:** 6. **Col. Width:** 1 15/16 inches. **Col. Depth:** 21 1/2 inches. **Key Personnel:** Anita Murphy, General Mgr.
Ad Rates: GLR: $5.10 **Circ:** Free ‡8,000

1327 KPOC-AM - 1420
No. 1 Radio Dr. Phone: (870)892-5234
Pocahontas, AR 72455 Fax: (870)892-5235

Format: Adult Contemporary. **Networks:** ABC. **Owner:** Timothy Scott, PO Box 508, Pocahontas, AR 72455. **Founded:** 1950. **Operating Hours:** 6 a.m.-6 p.m.; 10% network, 90% local. **ADI:** Jonesboro, AR. **Key Personnel:** Timothy Scott, Contact; Lloyd Lewallen, Music Dir. **Wattage:** 1000. **Ad Rates:** $8.50-10.75 per unit.

1328 KPOC-FM - 103.9
No. 1 Radio Dr. Phone: (870)892-5234
Pocahontas, AR 72455 Fax: (870)892-5235

Format: Adult Contemporary. **Networks:** ABC. **Owner:** Timothy Scott, PO Box 508, Pocahontas, AR 72455. **Founded:** 1969. **Formerly:** KCYN (1992). **Operating Hours:** 5 a.m.-10 p.m.; 10% network, 90% local. **ADI:** Jonesboro, AR. **Key Personnel:** Timothy Scott, Vice Pres./Gen. Mgr.; Lloyd Lewallen, Music Dir. **Wattage:** 6,000. **Ad Rates:** $8.50-10.75 per unit.

PRAIRIE GROVE, pop. 1,708.

Washington Co. 10 mi. SW of Fayetteville. Residential.

1329 Prairie Grove Enterprise
The Cherokee Group
107 N. Mock Phone: (501)846-2191
PO Box 650 Fax: (501)824-5540
Prairie Grove, AR 72753
Publisher E-mail: pgnews@aol.com

Community newspaper. **Founded:** June 12, 1936. **Freq:** Weekly (Thurs.). **Print Method:** Offset. **Cols./Page:** 6. **Col. Width:** 2 1/16 inches. **Col. Depth:** 294 agate lines. **Key Personnel:** Scott F. Davis, Mktg. Dir., phone (501)824-3263, fax (501)824-5540, sfd53@aol.com; Boyce R. Davis, Editor and Publisher, phone (501)846-2191. **Subscription Rates:** $15 individuals; $20 out of county. **Remarks:** Accepts advertising.
Ad Rates: GLR: $.64 **Circ:** Paid ‡2,200
BW: $531.48 Free ‡100
SAU: $4.12
PCI: $4.12

1330 KDAB-FM - 94.9
PO Box 949 Phone: (501)846-3653
Prairie Grove, AR 72753 Fax: (501)846-3296

Format: Gospel. **Networks:** USA Radio. **Owner:** Joe Hart, at above address, (501)846-0949. **Founded:** 1990. **Operating Hours:** Continuous. **Key Personnel:** Joe Hart, Contact; Cheryl Hart, Contact. **Wattage:** 50,000. **Ad Rates:** $5 for 30 seconds.

PRESCOTT†, pop. 4,103.

SW AR. Nevada Co. 48 mi. NE of Texarkana. Lumber, cottonseed oil mills. Pine timber. Agriculture. Cotton, corn.

1331 Nevada County Picayune
Nevada County
PO Box 60 Phone: (501)887-2002
Prescott, AR 71857 Fax: (501)887-2949

Community newspaper. **Founded:** 1878. **Freq:** Weekly (Thurs.). **Print Method:** Offset. **Cols./Page:** 6. **Col. Width:** 26 nonpareils. **Col. Depth:** 301 agate lines. **Key Personnel:** John Ragsdale, Publisher. **Subscription Rates:** $12.50 individuals; $20 out of area; $25 out of state. **Remarks:** Accepts advertising.
Ad Rates: BW: $580.50 **Circ:** 2,800
PCI: $4.50

RECTOR

1332 Clay County Democrat
Delta Publishing Co.
PO Box 366 Phone: (870)595-3611
Rector, AR 72461 Fax: (870)595-3611

Community newspaper. **Freq:** Weekly (Wed.). **Print Method:** Offset. **Trim Size:** 6 x 21. **Cols./Page:** 6. **Col. Width:** 12 1/2 picas. **Col. Depth:** 21 inches. **Key Personnel:** Ron Kemp, Contact, phone (870)598-2201, fax (870)598-5189, rkemp@cswnet.com. **USPS:** 116-620. **Subscription Rates:** $20; $25 out of county; $30 out of state. **Remarks:** Accepts advertising.
Ad Rates: BW: $756 **Circ:** 2,000
4C: $841
SAU: $4.50

RISON†.

SC AR. Cleveland Co. 20 mi. S. of Pine Bluff.

1333 Cleveland County Herald
Cleveland Herald
PO Box 325 Phone: (501)325-6412
Rison, AR 71665 Fax: (501)325-6127

Community newspaper. **Founded:** 1888. **Freq:** Weekly (Wed.). **Print Method:** Offset. **Trim Size:** Quarter. **Cols./Page:** 6. **Col. Width:** 12 picas. **Col. Depth:** 21 inches. **Key Personnel:** Stan M. Sadler, Publisher. **USPS:** 117-660. **Subscription Rates:** $15; $18 out of area; $21 out of state. **Remarks:** Accepts advertising.
Ad Rates: PCI: $3.50 **Circ:** 2,800

ROGERS, pop. 17,429.

NW AR. Benton Co. 75 mi. N. of Fort Smith. Lake and mountain resort. Manufactures electric motors, air guns, vinegar, brooder equipment, corrugated paper products, plastic bags. Hatchery, poultry processing, meat packing, and rabbit processing. Beef, dairy, cattle; turkey, chicken raising. Grape, apple growing.

1334 Backtracker
Northwest Arkansas Genealogical Society
Box 796 Phone: (501)273-3890
Rogers, AR 72757-0796
Genealogical journal of Northwest Arkansas. **Founded:** 1972. **Freq:** Quarterly. **Print Method:** Offset. **Trim Size:** 8 1/2 x 11. **Key Personnel:** George Crabtree, Editor. **ISSN:** 0094-6915. **Subscription Rates:** $12.50 individuals; $3.50 single issue. **Remarks:** Advertising not accepted.
Circ: Combined 295

1335 The Morning News of Northwest Arkansas
Donrey Media Group
313 S. 2nd St. Phone: (501)636-4411
PO Box 718 Fax: (501)636-6270
Rogers, AR 72757
General newspaper. **Founded:** 1907. **Freq:** Daily and Sunday (morn.). **Print Method:** Offset. **Cols./Page:** 6. **Col. Width:** 25 nonpareils. **Col. Depth:** 301 agate lines. **Key Personnel:** Rusty Turner, Editor. **Subscription Rates:** $72 individuals. **Remarks:** Accepts advertising. **URL:** http://www.mornews.com. **Formerly:** Northwest Arkansas Morning News.
Ad Rates: BW: $1,264.20 **Circ:** Mon.-Sat. 35,035
4C: $1,689.20 Sun. 36,443
SAU: $10.50
PCI: $10.45

1336 Rogers Hometown News
Community Publishers, Inc.
1400 W. Walnut, No. 123 Phone: (501)621-6397
Rogers, AR 72756 Fax: (501)621-6399

Community newspaper. **Founded:** 1994. **Freq:** Weekly (Wed.). **Print Method:** Offset. **Trim Size:** 11 1/2 x 13 1/2. **Cols./Page:** 6. **Col. Width:** 2 1/16 inches. **Col. Depth:** 21 1/2 inches. **Key Personnel:** Jeff Thacker, General Mgr. **Subscription Rates:** $22 individuals. **Remarks:** Accepts advertising. **Available Online. URL:** http://www.nwanews.com//leader.html.
Ad Rates: GLR: $6.51 **Circ:** Non-paid 19,250
BW: $839.79 Paid 3,000
4C: $1,094.79

1337 Donrey Cablevision
1401 S. 8th St. Phone: (501)636-3400
Box 190 Fax: (501)631-1858
Rogers, AR 72756

Owner: Donrey Media Group Inc., 3600 Wheeler Ave., PO Box 17017, Fort Smith, AR 72917, (501)785-7810, Fax: (501)785-9430. **Founded:** 1957. **Formerly:** Rogers Cable TV (1984). **Key Personnel:** Mike Wyatt, General Mgr. **Cities Served:** Little Flock, Rogers, AR; Benton county: subscribing households 10,400; 38 channels.

1338 KAMO-AM - 1390
4001 W. Walnut Phone: (501)636-4611
Rogers, AR 72756 Fax: (501)631-6902

Format: Eclectic; News; Talk. **Networks:** ABC. **Founded:** 1954. **Operating Hours:** Continuous. **Key Personnel:** Glen Scheer, Program Dir.; Steve Johns, Station Mgr.; George Hochman, General Mgr. **Wattage:** 1000. **Ad Rates:** $8 for 30 seconds; $10 for 60 seconds.

1339 KAMO-FM - 94.3
4001 W. Walnut Phone: (501)636-4611
Rogers, AR 72756-1842 Fax: (501)631-6902
Free: (800)751-8800

Format: Country. **Simulcasts:** KAMO-AM. **Networks:** ABC. **Founded:** 1971. **Operating Hours:** Continuous. **Key Personnel:** Troy Walker, Program Dir.; Cathy Bass, Sales Mgr. **Wattage:** 28,000.

1340 KURM-AM - 790
212 N. 2nd Phone: (501)636-7979
Rogers, AR 72756-6645 Fax: (501)631-9711
Free: (800)767-7979

Format: News; Talk. **Networks:** CBS. **Founded:** 1979. **Operating Hours:** 5 a.m.-midnight. **Key Personnel:** Steve Womack, General Mgr.; Kermit Womack, Contact. **Wattage:** 5000. **Ad Rates:** $5-7 for 30 seconds; $6.50-10 for 60 seconds.

1341 Southern Cablecom
PO Box 669 Phone: (501)631-1650
Rogers, AR 72757 Fax: (501)631-7831

Founded: 1981. **Key Personnel:** Pat Adams, General Mgr. **Cities Served:** subscribing households 2,600; 27 channels.

1342 West Ark Cable TV
PO Box 2106 Phone: (501)631-1650
Rogers, AR 72757-2106 Fax: (501)632-7831

Founded: 1974. **Cities Served:** Bloomer Community; subscribing households 799; 18 channels.

RUSSELLVILLE†, pop. 14,000.

NW AR. Pope Co. 75 mi. NW of Little Rock. Arkansas Tech University. Manufactures furniture, shoes, frozen foods, inner tubes, corrugated boxes, concrete forms, chlorine extraction cells, metal products; rendering plant. Timber. Diversified farming. Feed producers hatcheries.

1343 Arka Tech
Arkansas Tech University
Bryan Hall, Rm. 102 Phone: (501)968-0390
Russellville, AR 72801-2222 Fax: (501)890-8074

Collegiate newspaper. **Founded:** 1923. **Freq:** Weekly (Tues.). **Print Method:** Offset. **Cols./Page:** 5. **Col. Width:** 11 picas. **Col. Depth:** 13 inches. **Key Personnel:** Tommy Mumert, Advisor, nbtm@atuvm.atu.edu. **Subscription Rates:** $12 individuals.
Ad Rates: PCI: $3 **Circ:** Free ‡2,500

1344 Nebo
Arkansas Tech University
Russellville, AR 72801 Phone: (870)968-0256
Publication E-mail: gnebo@atuvm.atu.edu

Student publication covering poetry and prose. **Subtitle:** A Literary Journal. **Founded:** 1981. **Freq:** Semiannual. **Key Personnel:** Karyn Trahan, Editor; Vickie Lee, Asst. Editor. **Subscription Rates:** $10 individuals; $6 single issue. **Remarks:** Advertising not accepted.
Circ: (Not Reported)

1345 KCJC-FM - 100.9
205 Amy Lyn Pl. Phone: (501)968-6816
PO Box 2350 Fax: (501)968-2946
Russellville, AR 72801-2204

Format: Country. **Networks:** ABC. **Founded:** 1985. **Formerly:** KAIO-FM (1990). **Operating Hours:** Continuous. **Key Personnel:** Dewey Johnson, President; Jim Kelley, Station Mgr.; Mitchell Johnson, Contact. **Wattage:** 6000. **Ad Rates:** $15 for 30 seconds; $20 for 60 seconds.

1346 KMTC-FM - 91.1
PO Box 570 Phone: (501)967-7400
Russellville, AR 72811-0570

Format: Contemporary Christian. **Networks:** USA Radio. **Owner:** Russellville Educational Broadcast Foundation, at above address. **Founded:** 1987. **Operating Hours:** 6 a.m.-midnight; 2% network, 98% local. **Key Personnel:** Debbie Feemster, General Mgr. **Local Programs:** *Jesus Is Alive*, Tom Underhill, Mailing contact, (501)968-7965; *Rockin' Rodney's Pick of the Week*, Debbie Feemster, Mailing contact, (501)967-7400; *Anthony B's Top Ten at 10:10*, Tod Rye, Mailing contact, (501)967-4700. **Wattage:** 360. **Ad Rates:** $4-6 for 30 seconds; $5-9 for 60 seconds.

1347 KXRJ-FM - 91.9
Arkansas Tech University Phone: (501)968-0641
Hwy. 7 N. Fax: (501)964-0504
Russellville, AR 72801
E-mail: sjjg@atuvm.atu.edu

Format: Jazz; Album-Oriented Rock (AOR); Classical; News. **Founded:** 1989. **Operating Hours:** Daily, noon-midnight; 100% local. **Key Personnel:** John A. Gale, Contact; George Cotton, Engineer, phone (501)968-0347. **Wattage:** 100. **Ad Rates:** Noncommercial.

SALEM†.

NC AR. Fulton Co. 30 mi. NW of Ash Flat.

1348 The News
Area Wide Media
PO Box 248 Phone: (870)895-3207
Salem, AR 72576 Fax: (870)895-4277
Free: (800)995-3209

Community newspaper. **Freq:** Weekly (Thurs.). **Cols./Page:** 6. **Col. Width:** 12 picas. **Col. Depth:** 21 inches. **Key Personnel:** Janie Flynn, General Mgr.; Angelia Roberts, Editor; Carolyn Clarke, Advertising Dir. **USPS:** 477-627. **Subscription Rates:** $20 individuals; $25 out of area. **Formerly:** Salem News (1990); Salem Headlight.
Ad Rates: BW: $756 **Circ:** 3,550
SAU: $6.50
PCI: $5

1349 KSAR-FM - 95.9
PO Box 458 Phone: (870)895-2665
Salem, AR 72576 Fax: (870)895-4088

Format: Country; News. **Networks:** Satellite Music Network; ABC. **Owner:** Bragg Broadcasting Corp., at above address. **Operating Hours:** Continuous. **ADI:** Springfield, MO. **Key Personnel:** Hazel Barker, Traffic Dir.; Justin Sisk, Operations Mgr. **Local Programs:** *Hometown News* 7:05 am - 12:05 pm, Justin Sisk; *Tradio*, John Power. **Ad Rates:** $6.50-8 for 30 seconds; $13-16 for 60 seconds.

SEARCY†, pop. 13,612.

NEC AR. White Co. 50 mi. NE of Little Rock. Harding University. Manufactures refrigeration and aircraft components, printer's and industrial rollers, hydraulic valves, washing machines, leather goods. Food and egg processing. Pine, oak timber. Cattle, livestock.

1350 The Daily Citizen
Paxton Media Group
3000 E. Race Ave. Phone: (501)268-8621
Searcy, AR 72143 Fax: (501)268-6277
Free: (800)400-3142
Publication E-mail: citizen@cswnet.com

General newspaper. **Founded:** 1854. **Freq:** Daily (morn.) (Tues.-Sun.). **Print Method:** Offset. **Cols./Page:** 6. **Col. Width:** 25 nonpareils. **Col. Depth:** 258 agate lines. **Key Personnel:** Tommy Jackson, Editor; David Mosesso, Publisher; Nick Coltharp, Advertising Mgr. **Subscription Rates:** $87 individuals. **Remarks:** Advertising not accepted for abortion, adoption services and alcoholic beverages. **Formerly:** The Searcy Citizen.
Ad Rates: GLR: $.65 **Circ:** ‡7,251
BW: $1,173.90 Sun. ‡7,833
4C: $1,443.90
SAU: $9.10
PCI: $9.52

1351 Merchant Shopper
705 N. Marion St. Phone: (501)268-0700
PO Box 368 Fax: (501)268-9410
Searcy, AR 72143
Shopper. **Founded:** 1980. **Freq:** Weekly (Wed.). **Print Method:** Offset. **Trim Size:** 13 x 21 1/2. **Cols./Page:** 8. **Col. Width:** 26 nonpareils. **Col. Depth:** 301 agate lines. **Key Personnel:** David Mosesso, Publisher; Greg Dollins, Sales Mgr. **Remarks:** Advertising not accepted for abortion services and alcoholic beverages.
Ad Rates: BW: $1,006.20 **Circ:** Free ‡27,600
4C: $1,665
PCI: $6.60

1352 KAPZ-AM - 710
PO Box 1488 Phone: (501)268-0596
Searcy, AR 72143-1488 Fax: (501)268-3838

Format: Contemporary Country. **Simulcasts:** KKSY-FM. **Networks:** ABC; Arkansas Radio. **Owner:** John Paul Capps, at above address. **Founded:** 1984. **Operating Hours:** 6 a.m.-sunset; 15% network, 85% local. **Key Personnel:** John Paul Capps, Contact; Ron Price, News Dir.; Gary Cook, Music Dir.; Elizabeth Capps, Promotions Mgr. **Wattage:** 250. **Ad Rates:** $5-8 for 30 seconds; $7-12 for 60 seconds.

1353 KKSY-FM - 107.1
PO Box 1488 Phone: (501)268-0596
Searcy, AR 72143-1488 Fax: (501)268-3838

Format: Contemporary Country. **Simulcasts:** KAPZ-AM. **Networks:** ABC; Arkansas Radio. **Owner:** John Paul Capps, at above address. **Founded:** 1984. **Operating Hours:** 5 a.m.-midnight; 15% network, 85% local. **Key Personnel:** John Paul Capps, Contact; Ron Price, News Dir.; Gary Cook, Music Dir.; Elizabeth Capps, Promotions Mgr. **Wattage:** 3000. **Ad Rates:** $5-8 for 30 seconds; $7-12 for 60 seconds.

SHERIDAN

1354 Sheridan Headlight
Sheridan Headlights
PO Box 539 Phone: (501)942-2142
Sheridan, AR 72150 Fax: (501)942-8823

Community newspaper. **Founded:** 1881. **Freq:** Weekly (Wed.). **Cols./Page:** 6. **Col. Width:** 12 1/2 picas. **Col. Depth:** 21 1/2 inches. **Key Personnel:** Melody A. Moorehouse, Publisher. **Subscription Rates:** $13; $15 in county; $21 out of county; $28 out of state. **Remarks:** Accepts advertising.
Ad Rates: SAU: $5.20 **Circ:** ‡4,050
PCI: $4.26

SILOAM SPRINGS, pop. 7,940.

NW AR. Benton Co. 60 mi. N. of Fort Smith. John Brown University. Manufactures gates, rubber, telephone cables, cutting tools, motors, plastic pipes. Diversified farming. Fruit, poultry, livestock.

1355 KLRC-FM - 101.1
John Brown University Phone: (501)524-7101
2000 W. University Fax: (501)524-7451
Siloam Springs, AR 72761
E-mail: klrc@acc.jbu.edu

Format: Religious. **Networks:** USA Radio. **Owner:** John Brown University, at above address. **Founded:** 1984. **Operating Hours:** Continuous; 40% network, 60% local. **Key Personnel:** Rick Sparks, Manager, phone (501)524-7110, rsparks@acc.jbu.edu; Sean Sawatzky, Program Dir., phone (501)524-7227, seans@acc.jbu.edu; Jane Clayberg, phone (501)524-7395. **Wattage:** 6000. **Ad Rates:** Noncommercial. **URL:** http://www.klrc.com.

1356 KUOA-AM - 1290
GND, 2000 West University Phone: (501)524-3154
Siloam Springs, AR 72761 Fax: (501)524-6335
E-mail: Kuoa1290@tcac.net

Format: Country. **Networks:** CNN Radio; Jones Satellite. **Founded:** 1923. **Operating Hours:** Sunrise-sunset. **ADI:** Fort Smith, AR. **Key Personnel:** Ken Flory, General and Sales Mgr.; Kathy Harp, Traffic Mgr.; Kip Casper, Program Dir.; Mike Davis, Sports Dir.; Elizabeth Granderson, News Dir. **Wattage:** 5000. **Ad Rates:** $5-6 for 15 seconds; $7-9 for 30 seconds; $10-12 for 60 seconds.

SMACKOVER, pop. 2,453.

SC AR. Union Co. 18 mi. NW of El Dorado. Residential.

1357 Smackover Journal
PO Box 147 Phone: (870)725-3131
Smackover, AR 71762
Local newspaper. **Founded:** 1922. **Freq:** Weekly (Thurs.). **Print Method:** Offset. **Cols./Page:** 6. **Col. Width:** 26 nonpareils. **Col. Depth:** 301 agate lines. **Key Personnel:** Donna Faulkner, Editor; Walter Hussman, Jr., Publisher. **Subscription Rates:** $14.00 individuals; $17.50 out of area.
Ad Rates: GLR: $1.60 **Circ:** 1,200
SAU: $4.22
PCI: $3.82

STAR CITY†, pop. 2,066.

SE AR. Lincoln Co. 27 mi. SE of Pine Bluff. Cotton ginning; sawmills. Agriculture. Tomatoes, cotton, corn, peaches, soybeans, rice, fish. Cattle, swine. Timber. State Park Game and Fish Com. Lake.

1358 Lincoln Ledger
Lincoln County Publishing Co., Inc.
216 W. Bradley — Phone: (501)628-4161
Star City, AR 71667 — Fax: (501)628-3802

General newspaper. **Founded:** 1876. **Freq:** Weekly (Wed.). **Print Method:** Offset. **Trim Size:** 8 1/2 x 11. **Cols./Page:** 6. **Col. Width:** 2 inches. **Col. Depth:** 21 inches. **Key Personnel:** Joe Vance Mason, Editor and Publisher. **ISSN:** 0807-9367. **Subscription Rates:** $9 individuals; $12 out of area; $15 out of state. **Available Online.**
Ad Rates: GLR: $.15 — **Circ:** Paid ‡2,225
BW: $378 — Free ‡75
4C: $627.60
PCI: $3

STATE UNIVERSITY

1359 Arkansas Review
Arkansas State University — Phone: (870)972-3043
Department of English & Philosophy — Fax: (870)972-2795
Box 1890
State University, AR 72467
Publisher E-mail: delta@toltec.nstate.edu

Regional studies review. **Subtitle:** A Journal of Delta Studies. **Founded:** 1996. **Freq:** 3/year. **Print Method:** Offset. **Trim Size:** 8 1/2 x 11. **Cols./Page:** 2. **Col. Width:** 3 inches. **Col. Depth:** 9 inches. **Key Personnel:** William M. Clements, Editor. **ISSN:** 0022-8745. **Subscription Rates:** $20 individuals; $7.50 single issue. **Remarks:** Advertising not accepted. **Formerly**: Kansas Quarterly; Kansas Quarterly/Arkansas Review.
Circ: Paid 900

1360 The Herald of Arkansas State University
Arkansas State University
Box 1930 — Phone: (501)972-3075
State University, AR 72467 — Fax: (501)972-3828

Collegiate newspaper. **Founded:** 1920. **Freq:** Semiweekly (Tues. and Fri.). **Print Method:** Offset. **Key Personnel:** Jennifer Winningham, Ad Coordinator. **Subscription Rates:** Free. **Remarks:** Accepts advertising.
Ad Rates: GLR: $.218 — **Circ:** ‡8,000
BW: $567
PCI: $4.50

1361 Southwestern Mass Communication Journal
Southwest Education Council for Journalism and Mass Communication
Arkansas University — Phone: (870)972-3075
PO Box 1930 — Fax: (870)972-3856
State University, AR 72467
Publication E-mail: osa@kiowa.astate.edu

Trade journal covering journalism and mass communication. **Founded:** 1985. **Freq:** Semiannual. **Print Method:** Offset. **Trim Size:** 6 x 9. **Key Personnel:** Gil Fowler, Business Mgr., gfowler@kiowa.astate.edu. **Subscription Rates:** $25 individuals; $15 single issue. **Remarks:** Accepts advertising.
Ad Rates: BW: $150 — **Circ:** Paid 500

1362 KASU-FM - 91.9
104 Cooley Dr. — Phone: (870)972-2200
Arkansas State University — Fax: (870)972-2997
Box 2160
State University, AR 72467
Free: (800)643-8269
E-mail: kasu@kiowa.astate.edu

Format: Classical; Jazz; News; Folk; Agricultural; New Age; Blues. **Networks:** National Public Radio (NPR); AP; Public Radio International (PRI). **Owner:** Arkansas State University, at above address. **Founded:** 1957. **Operating Hours:** Continuous; 30% network, 70% local. **ADI:** Jonesboro, AR. **Key Personnel:** Richard Carvell, Dir. of Broadcasting, rcarvell@kiowa.astate.edu; Greg Chance, News Dir.; Keith Merritt, Development Dir., kmerritt@kiowa.astate.edu; Terri Pratt, Promotions Dir., tpratt@kiowa.astate.edu; Mark Smith, Program Host, msmith@kiswa.astate.edu; Marty Scarbrough, Program Dir., mscarbro@kiowa.astate.edu; Robert A. Franklin, Station Mgr., rfrankli@kiowa.astate.edu; June Taylor, Operations/Engineering, jtaylor@kiowa.astate.edu. **Wattage:** 100,000. **Ad Rates:** Noncommercial.

STUTTGART†, pop. 10,941.

E. AR. Arkansas Co. 50 mi. SE of Little Rock. Rice mills. Soybean plant. Hardwood lumber mill. Oak, Gum timber. Agriculture; rice, soybeans, and oats.

1363 The Stuttgart Daily Leader
American Publishing
111 W. 6th St. — Phone: (501)673-8533
PO Box 531 — Fax: (501)673-3671
Stuttgart, AR 72160
General newspaper. **Founded:** 1885. **Freq:** Daily (eve.). **Print Method:** Offset. **Cols./Page:** 6. **Col. Width:** 25 nonpareils. **Col. Depth:** 301 agate lines. **Key Personnel:** Bill Park, Publisher; Renee Hunter, Manager. **USPS:** 143-170. **Subscription Rates:** $48 individuals. **Remarks:** Accepts advertising.
Ad Rates: SAU: $7.59 — **Circ:** Paid 3,600
PCI: $7.59 — Non-paid 6,000

1364 KWAK-AM - 1240
PO Box 907 — Phone: (501)673-1595
Stuttgart, AR 72160-0907 — Fax: (501)673-8445

Format: News; Contemporary Country. **Networks:** ABC. **Founded:** May 1, 1948. **Operating Hours:** 6 a.m.-10 p.m.; 5% network, 95% local. **Key Personnel:** Scott Siler, Sales Mgr.; Jay Toddy, Contact. **Wattage:** 1000. **Ad Rates:** $12 for 30 seconds; $17 for 60 seconds. Combined advertising rates available with KWAK-FM.

1365 KWAK-FM - 105.5
PO Box 907 — Phone: (501)673-1595
Stuttgart, AR 72160-0907 — Fax: (501)673-8445

Format: Oldies. **Networks:** ABC. **Founded:** 1987. **Formerly**: KXDX-FM. **Operating Hours:** 5 a.m.-midnight; 5% network, 95% local. **Key Personnel:** Scott Siler, Sales Mgr.; Jay Toddy, News/Sports Dir. **Wattage:** 3000. **Ad Rates:** $12 for 30 seconds; $17 for 60 seconds. KWAK-AM.

TEXARKANA†, pop. 21,459.

SW AR. Miller Co. 157 mi. S. of Little Rock. Lumber. Cotton seed oil. Cotton ginning and Compressing. Creosoted Poles. Clay, sulphur. Sheet metal products, ammunition, crossarms, medicine, caskets, lead manufactured. Timber, Agriculture. Cattle.

1366 KKYR-AM - 790
2324 Arkansas Blvd. — Phone: (501)772-3771
Texarkana, AR 75502-2016 — Fax: (501)772-0364

Format: Contemporary Country. **Owner:** Broadcasters Unlimited Inc., 3810 Brookside Dr., Tyler, TX 75701, (214)581-0606. **Founded:** 1989. **Formerly**: KOSY-AM (1989). **Operating Hours:** Continuous; 100% local. **Key Personnel:** Craig D. Reininger, General Mgr.; Gary Lawrence, Program Dir.; Rebecca Mullens, News Dir.; Melvin C. Jones, Sr., Contact. **Wattage:** 1000.

1367 KKYR-FM - 102.5
2324 Arkansas Blvd. — Phone: (501)772-3771
Texarkana, AR 75502-2016 — Fax: (501)772-0364

Format: Contemporary Country. **Owner:** Gulfstar Communications, Inc., 600 Congress Ave., Austin, TX 78701, (512)320-7222, Fax: (512)322-7222. **Founded:** 1989. **Formerly**: KOSY-FM (1989). **Operating Hours:** Continuous; 100% local. **Key Personnel:** Bob Gipson, General Mgr.; Gary Lawrence, Program Dir.; John Williams, News Dir.; Demetrica Dayries, Personnel Dir. **Wattage:** 100,000.

1368 KLLI-FM - 95.9
2324 Arkansas Blvd. — Phone: (903)832-5536
Texarkana, AR 71854-2016 — Fax: (903)838-7941

Format: Country. **Owner:** John T. Mitchell, at above address. **Founded:** 1985. **Operating Hours:** Continuous. **ADI:** Shreveport, LA-Texarkana, TX. **Key Personnel:** Bob Gipson, General Mgr.; Rob Ryan, Program Dir.; Chuck Zach, News Dir.; Jay James, Operations Mgr.; Phil O'Brian, Production Dir. **Wattage:** 25,000. **Ad Rates:** $18 for 30 seconds; $23 for 60 seconds.

TRUMANN, pop. 5,938.

NE AR. Poinsett Co. 16 mi. S. of Jonesboro. Lumber. Cotton gin. Manufacturing plant. Warehouse. Oak, gum timber. Agriculture. Cotton, corn, hay.

1369 Trumann Democrat
200 Hwy. 463 S. — Phone: (501)483-6317
Trumann, AR 72472 — Fax: (501)483-6031

Community newspaper. **Founded:** 1923. **Freq:** Weekly (Wed.). **Print Method:** Offset. **Trim Size:** 13 x 21 1/2. **Cols./Page:** 6. **Col. Width:** 2 1/16 inches. **Col. Depth:** 21 1/2 inches. **Key Personnel:** Toney Bussy, Managing Editor; Charles Nix, Publisher. **USPS:** 642-640. **Subscription Rates:** $16 individuals; $19 out of area; $0.50 single issue. **Remarks:** Accepts advertising.
Ad Rates: GLR: $3 — **Circ:** ‡2,500
BW: $327.60
PCI: $4.25

WALDRON†.

WC AR. Scott Co. 40 mi. NW of Montgomery. Scott Co. (WC). 40 m NW of Montgomery.

1370 Waldron News
PO Box 745 — Phone: (501)637-4161
Waldron, AR 72958 — Fax: (501)637-4162
Free: (800)647-4161
Publication E-mail: mbackus461@aol.com

Community newspaper. **Founded:** 1965. **Freq:** Weekly (Wed.). **Print Method:** Offset. **Cols./Page:** 6. **Col. Width:** 2 inches. **Col. Depth:** 21 1/2 inches. **Key Personnel:** Marty Backus, Editor and Publisher. **USPS:** 049-045. **Subscription Rates:** $15; $26 out of state. **Remarks:** Accepts advertising.
Ad Rates: BW: $315 — **Circ:** 2,250
SAU: $5.20
PCI: $4.15

1371 The Waldron News - Bulletin
Waldron News
PO Box 745 — Phone: (501)637-4161
Waldron, AR 72958 — Fax: (501)637-4162
Free: (800)647-4161

Community newspaper. **Freq:** Weekly. **Print Method:** Web offset. **Cols./Page:** 6. **Col. Width:** 2 1/16 inches. **Col. Depth:** 22 inches. **Key Personnel:** Marty Backus, Publisher. **Subscription Rates:** $15. **Remarks:** Advertising accepted; rates available upon request.
Circ: Paid ⊕1,600
Non-paid ⊕5,400

WALNUT RIDGE†, pop. 4,152.

NE AR. Lawrence Co. 20 mi W. of Jonesboro. Southern Baptist College. Vacuum cleaner, auto parts, power tools, striking tool, shoe, dress and shoe-last factories. Timber. Agriculture. Rice, wheat, milo, soybeans.

1372 Times Dispatch
The Times Dispatch
225 W. Main St. — Phone: (501)886-2464
Box 389 — Fax: (501)886-9369
Walnut Ridge, AR 72476-0389
Newspaper with a Democratic orientation. **Founded:** 1910. **Freq:** Weekly (Wed.). **Print Method:** Offset. **Cols./Page:** 6. **Col. Width:** 26 nonpareils. **Col. Depth:** 294 agate lines. **Key Personnel:** John Bland, Editor; John A. Bland, Publisher. **Subscription Rates:** $30 by mail. **Remarks:** Accepts advertising.
Ad Rates: BW: $5.67 — **Circ:** Paid ‡6,000
SAU: $2.34 — Free ‡39

1373 KRLW-AM - 1320
Box 30 — Phone: (501)886-6666
Walnut Ridge, AR 72476 — Fax: (501)886-5719

Format: Oldies. **Simulcasts:** KRLW-FM. **Networks:** USA Radio; Arkansas Radio. **Founded:** 1951. **Operating Hours:** Continuous. **ADI:** Jonesboro, AR. **Key Personnel:** David Coker, General Mgr. **Local Programs:** *Tradio*, Aaron Sims. **Wattage:** 1000. **Ad Rates:** $8 for 30 seconds; $12 for 60 seconds. Combined advertising rates available with KRLW-FM.

1374 KRLW-FM - 106.3
Box 30 — Phone: (501)886-6666
Walnut Ridge, AR 72476 — Fax: (501)886-5719

Format: Oldies; Country. **Simulcasts:** yes KRLW-AM. **Networks:** Arkansas Radio; USA Radio. **Operating Hours:** Continuous. **ADI:** Jonesboro, AR. **Key Personnel:** David Coker, General Mgr. **Local Programs:** *Tradio.* **Wattage:** 3 kw. **Ad Rates:** $8 for 30 seconds; $12 for 60 seconds.

WARREN

1375 Shoppers Guide Weekly
Warren Eagle Democrat
200 W. Cypress St. — Phone: (870)226-5831
Warren, AR 71671 — Fax: (870)226-6601

Shopping guide. **Founded:** 1975. **Freq:** Weekly. **Print Method:** Offset. **Cols./Page:** 6. **Col. Width:** 2 1/8 inches. **Col. Depth:** 21 inches. **Key Personnel:** Danny Cook, Publisher. **Subscription Rates:** Free. **Remarks:** Accepts advertising.
Ad Rates: GLR: $.35 — **Circ:** Free 6,500
BW: $617.40
PCI: $5.90

📖 **1376 Warren Eagle Democrat**
200 W. Cypress St. Phone: (870)226-5831
Warren, AR 71671 Fax: (870)226-6601

Community newspaper. **Founded:** 1885. **Freq:** Weekly (Wed.). **Print Method:** Offset. **Cols./Page:** 6. **Col. Width:** 12 1/2 picas. **Col. Depth:** 21 inches. **Key Personnel:** Danny Cook, Publisher. **Subscription Rates:** $15; $23; $30. **Remarks:** Accepts advertising.
Ad Rates: GLR: $.43 **Circ:** 4,700
BW: $680
4C: $5.50
SAU: $5.90
PCI: $5

🎙 **1377 KWRF-AM - 860**
1255 N. Myrtle St. Phone: (870)226-2653
Warren, AR 71671 Fax: (870)226-3039

Format: Country; Full Service. **Networks:** Arkansas Radio. **Owner:** Pines Broadcasting, Inc., at above address. **Founded:** 1953. **Operating Hours:** Continuous. **Key Personnel:** Jimmy Sledge, General Mgr. **Wattage:** 250. **Ad Rates:** $7.25 for 30 seconds; $9 for 60 seconds.

🎙 **1378 KWRF-FM - 105.5**
1255 N. Myrtle St. Phone: (870)226-2653
Warren, AR 71671 Fax: (870)226-3039

Format: Country. **Networks:** Arkansas Radio; Satellite Music Network. **Owner:** Pines Broadcasting, Inc., at above address. **Founded:** 1953. **Operating Hours:** Continuous. **Key Personnel:** Jimmy Sledge, General Mgr. **Wattage:** 3,000. **Ad Rates:** $7.25 for 30 seconds; $9 for 60 seconds.

WEST FORK, pop. 1,526.

NW AR. Washington Co. 11 mi. S. of Fayetteville. University of Arkansas. Agriculture. Poultry and cattle.

📖 **1379 Washington County Observer**
Cherokee Communications Group
PO Box 377 Phone: (501)839-2771
West Fork, AR 72774 Fax: (501)824-5440

Multi-community newspaper. **Subtitle:** Voice of the Boston Mountains. **Founded:** 1972. **Freq:** Weekly (Thurs.). **Print Method:** Offset. **Cols./Page:** 6. **Col. Width:** 26 nonpareils. **Col. Depth:** 294 agate lines. **Key Personnel:** Parker Rushing, Editor and Publisher. **Subscription Rates:** $12.95 individuals; $17.50 out of area. **Remarks:** Color advertising accepted; rates available upon request.
Ad Rates: GLR: $.25 **Circ:** ‡3,000
BW: $371.52
4C: $611.52
SAU: $4

WEST HELENA

🎙 **1380 KCLT-FM - 104.9**
307 Hwy 49B Phone: (501)572-9506
Box 2870 Fax: (501)572-1845
West Helena, AR 72390

Format: Urban Contemporary. **Networks:** Southern Broadcasting; American Urban Radio. **Founded:** 1984. **Operating Hours:** Continuous. **Wattage:** 3000.

WEST MEMPHIS, pop. 28,138.

E. AR. Crittenden Co. Two bridges to Memphis, TN. Manufactures flakeboard, box, bleach, gypsum, and concrete slab. Oil refinery and terminal. Cotton seed oil compressing. Agricultural equipment. Agriculture. Cotton, soybeans, rice.

🎙 **1381 KSUD-AM - 730**
102 N. 5th St. Phone: (870)735-6622
West Memphis, AR 72301 Fax: (870)735-6646

Format: Contemporary Christian; Talk; Sports. **Owner:** Pollack Broadcasting Co., at above address. **Founded:** 1961. **Operating Hours:** Continuous. **ADI:** Memphis, TN. **Key Personnel:** Frank Hammond, Contact; Scott Blakely, Program Dir.; Lyn Sperling, Traffic Mgr. **Wattage:** 250. **Ad Rates:** $20 for 30 seconds; $25 for 60 seconds.

WHITE HALL

📖 **1382 White Hall Journal**
Forest Communicators, Inc.
PO Box 1166 Phone: (501)247-4700
Pine Bluff, AR 71613-1166 Fax: (501)247-4755
Publication E-mail: wjournal@eark.net

Community newspaper. **Founded:** 1982. **Freq:** Weekly (Wed.). **Print Method:** Offset. **Cols./Page:** 6. **Col. Width:** 12.5 picas. **Col. Depth:** 21.5 picas. **Key Personnel:** Frank Lightfoot, Publisher. **USPS:** 715-310. **Subscription Rates:** $18 individuals. **Remarks:** Accepts advertising.
Ad Rates: BW: $549.36 **Circ:** ‡2,350
SAU: $6

WYNNE†, pop. 7,805.

E. AR. Cross Co. 45 mi. W. of Memphis, TN. Manufactures copper tubing and air conditioning components, men's slacks, shoes, horse trailers, building equipment. Cotton ginning; farm machinery, rice drier. Fruit shipped. Agriculture. Peaches, cotton, cucumbers, rice, soybeans.

📖 **1383 East Arkansas News Leader**
Wynne Progress, Inc.
702 N. Falls Blvd. Phone: (870)238-2375
PO Box 308 Fax: (870)238-4655
Wynne, AR 72396
Free Newspaper. **Founded:** 1971. **Freq:** Weekly (Wed.). **Print Method:** Offset. **Cols./Page:** 6. **Col. Width:** 26 nonpareils. **Col. Depth:** 294 agate lines. **Key Personnel:** Todd Wilson, Editor; David M. Boger, Publisher; Brandon Boger, Advertising Mgr. **Remarks:** Advertising not accepted for tobacco products. **Formerly**: Shoppers News.
Ad Rates: GLR: $9 **Circ:** 22,531
BW: $1,134
4C: $1,484
PCI: $8

📖 **1384 Wynne Progress**
Wynne Progress, Inc.
702 N. Falls Blvd. Phone: (870)238-2375
PO Box 308 Fax: (870)238-4655
Wynne, AR 72396
Publication E-mail: editor@earknewsleader.com

Community newspaper. **Founded:** 1898. **Freq:** Weekly (Fri.). **Print Method:** Offset. **Cols./Page:** 6. **Col. Width:** 26 nonpareils. **Col. Depth:** 294 agate lines. **Key Personnel:** Tod Wilson, Editor; David M. Boger, Publisher; Brandon Boger, Advertising Mgr. **Subscription Rates:** $26 individuals; $33 out of area; $42 out of state. **Remarks:** Advertising not accepted for tobacco products.
Ad Rates: BW: $1,071 **Circ:** ‡3,500
4C: $1,421
PCI: $8.50

🎙 **1385 KWYN-AM - 1400**
Hwy. 64 W. Phone: (501)238-8141
Wynne, AR 72396 Fax: (501)238-5997

Format: Country; Talk; Information. **Networks:** NBC. **Owner:** East Arkansas Broadcasters, PO Box 789, Wynne, AR 72396. **Founded:** 1956. **Operating Hours:** 5:00 a.m.-midnight; 5% network, 95% local. **ADI:** Memphis, TN. **Key Personnel:** Bobby Caldwell, Contact; Steve Chapman, Contact; Lindell Staggs, Contact. **Wattage:** 1000. **Ad Rates:** $16 for 30 seconds; $20 for 60 seconds.

🎙 **1386 KWYN-FM - 92.5**
2758 Hwy. 64 Phone: (501)238-8141
Wynne, AR 72396 Fax: (501)238-5997

Format: Country. **Owner:** East Arkansas Broadcasters, PO Box 789, Wynne, AR 72396. **Founded:** 1969. **Operating Hours:** 5:00 a.m.-midnight; 100% local. **ADI:** Memphis, TN. **Key Personnel:** Bobby Caldwell, Contact; Steve Chapman, Contact; Lindell Staggs, Contact. **Wattage:** 35,000. **Ad Rates:** $16 for 30 seconds; $20 for 60 seconds.

YELLVILLE†, pop. 1,044.

N. AR. Marion Co. On White River and Bull Shoals Lake, 100 mi. SE of Springfield, MO. Manufactures furniture, building blocks. Saw and stave, mills . Zinc and lead mines. Pine, oak and cedar timber. Dairy, poultry and stock farms. Corn, hay, wheat.

📖 **1387 Mountain Echo**
North Arkansas Newspapers, Inc.
PO Box 528 Phone: (501)449-4257
Yellville, AR 72687 Fax: (501)449-6605

Local newspaper. **Founded:** 1886. **Freq:** Weekly (Thurs.). **Print Method:** Offset. **Cols./Page:** 6. **Col. Width:** 2 1/16 inches. **Col. Depth:** 21 1/2 inches. **Key Personnel:** Ray Dean Davis, Editor; John McDougal, Publisher; Andrea Berlin, Advertising Mgr. **Subscription Rates:** $17 individuals; $24 out of area; $27 out of state. **Remarks:** Accepts advertising.
Ad Rates: BW: $774 **Circ:** ‡2,300
4C: $959
PCI: $6

🎙 **1388 KCTT-FM - 101.7**
Box 100 Phone: (501)449-4002
Yellville, AR 72687 Fax: (501)449-4001

Format: Country. **Owner:** A & J Broadcasting, at above address. **Founded:** 1983. **Operating Hours:** Continuous. **Key Personnel:** Glen Adams, General Mgr.; Linda Duren, Music Dir. **Wattage:** 3000. **Ad Rates:** $4-6 for 30 seconds; $7-10 for 60 seconds.

CALIFORNIA

State Capital, SACRAMENTO

California is bounded on the north by Oregon, east by Nevada and Arizona, south by Mexico, and west by the Pacific Ocean. Its length is approximately 770 miles; its breadth 230 miles; land area, 155,973 square miles; rank, in area, third. The state has a coast line of 1,000 miles indented by many bays, among them Humboldt, San Francisco (of Golden Gate fame), and San Diego. Crossing these waterways are the San Francisco-Oakland Bay Bridge and the Golden Gate Bridge, both of which have attracted wide attention as feats of engineering. Two mountain ranges traverse the state, the Sierra Nevada in the east and the Coast Range in the west. Between them lie the beautiful and fertile Sacramento and San Joaqin Valleys. Peaks of the Coast Range rise to 8,000 feet; in the Sierras altitudes exceed 10,000 feet. Mt. Whitney is 14,495 feet above sea level and the highest point in the United States outside Alaska. Only 84 miles from it, in the same county, is the lowest point in the entire Western Hemisphere, Death Valley, a depression that is 282 feet below sea level. The northern part of the state is an elevated mountain region, noted for timber, mineral, and fruits. The central and southern portions, except in the mountainous districts, have soils of unexcelled fertility. The southwestern part is valuable for minerals, contains some fertile valleys and also arid, barren deserts. Like the topography, the climate is extremely varied, ranging from the temperatures in the snowcapped mountains to those of the tropics. And its rainfall varies from over 100 inches in the wet season in the north to about two inches in the desert regions. The Weather Bureau at Los Angeles gives the temperature (annual average) as 63.0; highest on record, 115; lowest on record, 17. Total annual precipitation is 12.01 inches. There are large forests in the state, especially on the North Coast Range. In several of the national parks, among them celebrated Yosemite, are to be seen the giant Sequoias. The University of California, one of the largest universities in the country, consists of nine campuses located in Berkeley, Davis, Irvine, Los Angeles, Riverside, San Diego, San Francisco, Santa Barbara, and Santa Cruz. Two other noted universities are Stanford at Palo Alto and University of Southern California at Los Angeles. Lick Observatory is located at Mt. Hamilton. Near San Diego is the Palomar Mountain Observatory.

POPULATION: 30,867,000 (1992). Rank among the states, 1st.

AGRICULTURE: Number of farms: 85,000 (1992). Farm acreage: 30,000,000 (1992). Cash receipts from farm marketings: crops, $12,615,000,000 (1991); livestock and products, $5,272,000,000 (1991).

FISHERIES: Total catch: 348,000,000 lbs. (1991), $140,000,000 value. Principal fish: tuna, salmon, mackerel, flounder.

FORESTS: Total forest land: 24,401,000 acres (1991). Principal woods: ponderosa pine, douglas fir, redwood, white fir, sugar pine, incense cedar, sitko spruce, port orford cedar, alder, hemlock, lodgepole pine, oak.

MINERALS: Value of production: $2,532,000,000 (1991). Principal minerals: sand and gravel, cement, boron. Value of petroleum production: $4,358,000,000 (1991).

MANUFACTURES: Value added by manufacture: $144,908,000,000 (1991). Leading industry groups: transportation equipment, food and related products, electrical machinery, other machinery.

LIST OF COUNTIES

Total number of counties 58

County, Location on Map, and County Seat	Pop.
Alameda (W), Oakland	1,276,702
Alpine (E), Markleeville	1,113
Amador (EC), Jackson	30,039
Butte (N), Oroville	182,120
Calaveras (C), San Andreas	31,998
Colusa (N), Colusa	16,275
Contra Costa (W), Martinez	803,732
Del Norte (NW), Crescent City	23,460
El Dorado (EC), Placerville	125,995
Fresno (C), Fresno	667,490
Glenn (NWC), Willows	24,798
Humboldt (NW), Eureka	119,118
Imperial (SE), El Centro	109,303
Inyo (SE), Independence	18,281
Kern (S), Bakersfield	543,981
Kings (SW), Hanford	101,469
Lake (N), Lakeport	50,631
Lassen (NE), Susanville	27,598
Los Angeles (S), Los Angeles	8,863,052
Madera (SC), Madera	88,090
Marin (W), San Rafael	230,096
Mariposa (C), Mariposa	14,302
Mendocino (NW), Ukiah	80,345
Merced (C), Merced	178,403
Modoc (NE), Alturas	9,678
Mono (E), Bridgeport	9,956
Monterey (W), Salinas	355,660
Napa (W), Napa	110,765
Nevada (NE), Nevada City	78,510
Orange (S), Santa Ana	2,410,668
Placer (NE), Auburn	172,796
Plumas (NE), Quincy	19,739
Riverside (SE), Riverside	1,170,413
Sacramento (NC), Sacramento	1,041,219
San Benito (W), Hollister	36,697
San Bernardino (SE), San Bernardino	1,418,380
San Diego (S), San Diego	2,498,016
San Francisco (W), San Francisco	723,959
San Joaquin (S), Stockton	480,628
San Luis Obispo (SW), San Luis Obispo	217,162
San Mateo (W), Redwood City	649,623
Santa Barbara (SW), Santa Barbara	369,608
Santa Clara (W), San Jose	1,497,577
Santa Cruz (W), Santa Cruz	229,734
Shasta (N), Redding	147,036
Sierra (NE), Downieville	3,318
Siskiyou (N), Yreka	43,531
Solano (NWC), Fairfield	339,471
Sonoma (NE), Santa Rosa	388,222
Stanislaus (C), Modesto	370,522
Sutter (C), Yuba City	64,415
Tehama (N), Red Bluff	49,625
Trinity (NW), Weaverville	13,063
Tulare (SC), Visalia	311,921
Tuolumne (EC), Sonora	48,456
Ventura (SW), Ventura	669,016
Yolo (C), Woodland	141,210
Yuba (NS), Marysville	58,228

STATISTICS

Newspapers

Period of Issue	
Daily	119
Evening Daily	46
Morning Daily	55
Daily with Sunday edition	59
Triweekly	1
Semiweekly	65
Weekly	427
Biweekly	10
Semimonthly	8

Monthly 52
Bimonthly 7
Free or partly free 148
Shopper 51
Total Newspapers 740

Periodicals

Period of Issue
Daily 2
Weekly 32
Biweekly 10
Semimonthly 12
Monthly 399
Bimonthly 217
Quarterly 382
Variant 3
Free or partly free 2

Total Periodicals 1337

Total number of publications 2,077

Radio Stations

AM Stations 207
FM Stations 322
Total Radio Stations 529

TV Stations

Total TV Stations 88

Cable Stations

Total Cable Systems 101

Total number of broadcast listings 718

ACTON

1389 The Vanguard News
PO Box 69 Phone: (818)866-5224
Acton, CA 93510 Fax: (818)886-1026
Publisher E-mail: acton@wgn.net

Community newspaper. **Founded:** Jan. 1, 1980. **Freq:** Weekly. **Trim Size:** 11 x 17. **URL:** http://www.vanguardnews.com.
Circ: Non-paid 1,000

AGOURA, pop. 380.

S. CA. Los Angeles Co. 10 mi.W. of Calabasas. Residential.

1390 Diehard Game Fan
Game Fan
5137 Clareton Dr., No. 210 Phone: (818)706-3260
Agoura, CA 91301 Fax: (818)706-1367

Consumer magazine covering video games. **Founded:** Oct. 1992. **Freq:** Monthly. **Trim Size:** 8 1/8 x 10 7/8. **Key Personnel:** Jay Puryear, Editor and Publisher, jpuryearmetropolitanropolismedia.com. **Subscription Rates:** $24.99 individuals. **Remarks:** Accepts advertising. **URL:** http://www.gamefan.com.
Ad Rates: BW: $5,700 **Circ:** Combined 200,500
4C: $8,500

AGOURA HILLS, pop. 11,399.

Los Angeles Co.

1391 Acorn
Baker Communications, Inc.
30423 Conwood St., Ste. 223 Phone: (818)706-0266
Agoura Hills, CA 91301 Fax: (805)379-1864

Local newspaper. **Founded:** 1983. **Freq:** Weekly (Wed.). **Print Method:** Offset. **Cols./Page:** 6. **Col. Width:** 18 nonpareils. **Col. Depth:** 224 agate lines. **Key Personnel:** Steve Holt, Editor; James E. Rule, Publisher. **Remarks:** Accepts advertising.
Ad Rates: GLR: $1.97 **Circ:** Paid ‡200
BW: $1,354.56 Free ‡26,600
PCI: $14.11

1392 American Rodder
Paisano Publications, Inc.
PO Box 3075 Phone: (818)889-8740
Agoura Hills, CA 91376-3075 Fax: (818)889-4726

Magazine for mature hot-rod and custom-car enthusiasts. **Founded:** Aug. 1988. **Freq:** Monthly. **Trim Size:** 8 x 10 7/8. **Cols./Page:** 3. **Col. Width:** 2 1/4 inches. **Col. Depth:** 10 inches. **Key Personnel:** Joe Kress, Editor; Joe Teresi, Publisher; Lizette Hotinger, Advertising Mgr. **ISSN:** 1041-3138. **Subscription Rates:** $29.95. $3.50 single issue. **Remarks:** Accepts advertising.
Ad Rates: BW: $1,408 **Circ:** Paid ★**32,324**
4C: $1,920

1393 Biker
Paisano Publications, Inc.
PO Box 3075 Phone: (818)889-8740
Agoura Hills, CA 91376-3075 Fax: (818)889-4726

Motorcycle lifestyle magazine. **Founded:** Mar. 12, 1987. **Freq:** Monthly. **Print Method:** Offset. **Trim Size:** 8 x 10 7/8. **Cols./Page:** 3. **Col. Width:** 2 1/4 inches. **Col. Depth:** 10 inches. **Key Personnel:** Joe Teresi, Publisher; Greg Andes, Advertising Mgr.; Dean Shawer, Editor. **ISSN:** 1058-7926. **Subscription Rates:** $34.50. $3.50 single issue. **Remarks:** Accepts advertising. **Formerly:** Biker Lifestyle.
Ad Rates: BW: $2,525 **Circ:** Paid 48,033
4C: $2,910
PCI: $64

1394 In the Wind
Paisano Publications, Inc.
PO Box 3000 Phone: (818)889-8740
Agoura Hills, CA 91376-3000 Fax: (818)889-1252

Motorcycle lifestyle magazine. **Subtitle:** If It's Out There, It's In Here. **Founded:** June 1978. **Freq:** Bimonthly. **Print Method:** Offset. **Trim Size:** 8 x 10 7/8. **Cols./Page:** 3. **Col. Depth:** 10 inches. **Key Personnel:** Kim Peterson, Editor; Joe Teresi, Publisher; Lizette Hotinger, Advertising Mgr. **ISSN:** 1059-759X. **Subscription Rates:** $24.95 individuals; $4.99 single issue. **Remarks:** Accepts advertising. **URL:** http://www.easyriders.com.
Ad Rates: BW: $2,500 **Circ:** Paid 78,859
4C: $3,000

1395 Tattoo
Paisano Publications, Inc.
PO Box 3075 Phone: (818)889-8740
Agoura Hills, CA 91376-3075 Fax: (818)889-4726

Magazine for tattoo enthusiasts. **Subtitle:** The Magazine of Dermagraphics. **Founded:** July 7, 1988. **Freq:** Monthly. **Print Method:** Offset. **Trim Size:** 8 x 10 7/8. **Cols./Page:** 3. **Col. Width:** 2 1/4 inches. **Col. Depth:** 10 inches. **Key Personnel:** Billy Tinney, Editor; Joe Teresi, Publisher; Greg Andes, Advertising Mgr., fax (818)889-5214. **ISSN:** 1041-3146. **Subscription Rates:** $33. $3.95 single issue. **Remarks:** Accepts advertising.
Ad Rates: BW: $5,180 **Circ:** Paid ★**111,550**
4C: $7,508
PCI: $64

1396 You! Magazine
Veritas Communications
29963 Mulholland Hwy. Phone: (818)991-1813
Agoura Hills, CA 91301-3009 Fax: (818)991-2024
Free: (800)359-0177
Publication E-mail: youmag@earthlink.net

Catholic youth magazine. **Subtitle:** The Alternative Youth Magazine. **Founded:** 1987. **Freq:** Monthly. **Trim Size:** 10 1/4 x 16 1/2. **Key Personnel:** Paul Lauer, Editor and Publisher; Michelle Michon, Circulation Dir./Office Mgr. **ISSN:** 1064-8682. **Subscription Rates:** $19.95 individuals; $29.95 other countries. **Remarks:** Accepts advertising. **URL:** http://www.youmagazine.com. **Formerly:** Veritas.
Ad Rates: BW: $1,498 **Circ:** Paid 30,000
4C: $2,496

ALAMEDA, pop. 63,852.

W. CA. Alameda Co. An island in San Francisco Bay, 12 mi. E. of San Francisco. U.S. Navel Air Base. Recreation. Manufactures pumps, diesel engines, boxes. Military aircraft engine repair. Marine related products. High tech hardware and software products, biogenetics.

1397 Alameda County Observer
Observer Newspapers
Box 817
San Leandro, CA 94577

Community newspaper. **Founded:** May 22, 1972. **Freq:** Weekly (Fri.). **Print Method:** Offset. **Cols./Page:** 6. **Key Personnel:** Ad Fried, Managing Editor; Michael Robert, Publisher; R.A. Burrell, Advertising Mgr. **Subscription Rates:** $25 individuals. **Remarks:** Accepts advertising.
Ad Rates: BW: $3,000 **Circ:** ‡30,000
4C: $3,600
SAU: $40
PCI: $35

1398 The Alameda Times-Star
Alameda Newspaper Group
1516 Oak St. Phone: (510)523-1200
Alameda, CA 94501 Fax: (510)748-0437

Daily Newspaper. **Founded:** 1881. **Freq:** Mon.-Sat. (morn.). **Print Method:** Offset. **Cols./Page:** 6. **Col. Width:** 26 nonpareils. **Col. Depth:** 301 agate lines. **Key Personnel:** Tom Tuttle, Editor; J. Allen Meath, Publisher; Sharon Kinkade, Advertising Mgr.; Bob Oristaglio, General Mgr. **Remarks:** Accepts advertising.
Ad Rates: PCI: $86.85 **Circ:** Wed. 21,780
Sun. 21,780

1399 Bay and Delta Yachtsman
Recreation Publications, Inc.
2033 Clement Ave., No. 100 Phone: (510)865-7500
Alameda, CA 94501 Fax: (510)865-0186
Publication E-mail: customer.service@yachtsforsale.com

Magazine for boating and yachting enthusiasts. **Founded:** 1965. **Freq:** Monthly. **Print Method:** Offset. **Trim Size:** 9 3/4 x 13. **Cols./Page:** 5. **Col. Width:** 21 nonpareils. **Col. Depth:** 182 agate lines. **Key Personnel:** Don Abbott, Publisher, don.abbott@yachtsforsale.com. **ISSN:** 0191-4731. **Subscription Rates:** $17.60 new subscribers. **Remarks:** Accepts advertising.
Ad Rates: BW: $1,450 **Circ:** ‡30,000
4C: $1,800

ALBANY, pop. 15,650.

NW CA. Alameda Co. N. of Oakland on San Francisco Bay. Residential.

1400 Yellow Silk
Verygraphics
PO Box 6374 Phone: (510)644-4188
Albany, CA 94706-0374
Erotic literary magazine featuring fiction, poetry, essays, reviews, and fine arts. **Subtitle:** Journal of Erotic Arts. **Founded:** 1981. **Freq:** Annual. **Print Method:** Sheetfed. **Trim Size:** 6 x 9. **Cols./Page:** 1. **Key Personnel:** Lily Pond, Editor and Publisher. **ISSN:** 0736-9212. **Subscription Rates:** $15. **Remarks:** Accepts advertising.
Ad Rates: BW: $1,057.00 **Circ:** (Not Reported)

ALHAMBRA

1401 Alhambra Post Advocate
Wave Community Newspapers
819 W. Whitter Blvd. Phone: (213)727-1117
Montebello, CA 90640-3623 Fax: (213)727-9515

Newspaper. **Founded:** 1917. **Freq:** Semiweekly Thurs. and Sat. **Print Method:** Offset. **Cols./Page:** 6. **Col. Width:** 26 nonpareils. **Col. Depth:** 301 agate lines. **Key Personnel:** Arthur J. Aguilar, Exec. Editor/Publisher, phone (213)290-3000, fax (213)291-0219. **Subscription Rates:** Free local; $125 yr/mailed.
Circ: Paid 701
Free 24,210

1402 Charter Communications
2215 Mission Rd. Phone: (818)300-6100
Alhambra, CA 91802 Fax: (818)300-6108

Owner: Charter Communications, 12444 Powerscourt Dr., Ste. 160, St. Louis, MO 63131, (314)965-0555. **Founded:** 1981. **Formerly:** Cencom Cable Television; Falcon. **Key Personnel:** Kevin Maguire, Manager, phone (818)300-6100. **Cities Served:** Duarte: subscribing households 116,804; 65 channels; 3 community access channels.

ALISO VIEJO

1403 Alternative Therapies in Health and Medicine
InnoVision Communications
101 Columbia Ave. Phone: (949)448-7370
Aliso Viejo, CA 92656 Fax: (949)362-2049
Free: (800)899-1712
Publication E-mail: alttherapy@aol.com

Professional medical journal covering alternative health care. **Founded:** Mar. 1995. **Freq:** Bimonthly. **Print Method:** Web offset. **Trim Size:** 8 3/4 x 10 3/4. **Key Personnel:** Bonnie T. Hornigan, Publisher; Larry Dossey, M.D., Exec. Editor; Bob Vrooman, Advertising Mgr. **ISSN:** 1078-6791. **Subscription Rates:** $59 individuals; $10 single issue. **Remarks:** Accepts advertising.
Circ: Paid 14,000

1404 American Journal of Critical Care
American Association of Critical-Care Nurses (AACN)
101 Columbia Phone: (949)362-2000
Aliso Viejo, CA 92656 Fax: (949)362-2049
Free: (800)809-2273
Publication E-mail: ajcc@aol.com
Publisher E-mail: aacninfo@aacn.org

Professional journal covering nursing. **Subtitle:** An Official Publication of A.A.C.N. **Founded:** Jan. 1992. **Freq:** Bimonthly. **Trim Size:** 8 1/8 x 10 7/8. **Key Personnel:** Michelle Hopkins, Managing Editor, michelle.hopkins@aacn.org; Bob Vrooman, Advertising Dir., bob.vrooman@aacn.org. **Subscription Rates:** $48 individuals; $8 single issue. **Remarks:** Accepts advertising.
Ad Rates: GLR: $32 **Circ:** Combined 80,000
BW: $3,365
4C: $7,750

1405 Computing News & Reviews
Thurman Marketing Services, Inc.
92 Argonaut, No. 275 Phone: (949)581-3993
Aliso Viejo, CA 92656 Fax: (949)581-3399
Publication E-mail: editor@newsrev.com
Publisher E-mail: compnews@newsrev.com

Trade magazine covering computing. **Subtitle:** The Managers' Publication for Database Trends. **Founded:** 1987. **Freq:** Monthly. **Print Method:** Web offset. **Trim Size:** 10 5/8 x 13. **Cols./Page:** 4. **Col. Width:** 2 3/8 inches. **Col. Depth:** 11 inches. **ISSN:** 1089-019x. **Subscription Rates:** Free to qualified subscribers. **Remarks:** Accepts advertising.
Ad Rates: BW: $3,000 **Circ:** Controlled 30,000
4C: $4,200

1406 Critical Care Nurse
101 Columbia Phone: (949)362-2000
Aliso Viejo, CA 92656 Fax: (949)362-2049
Free: (800)899-1712
Publication E-mail: ccn@aol.com

Nursing journal. **Founded:** Nov. 1980. **Freq:** Bimonthly. **Print Method:** Web offset. **Trim Size:** 8 1/8 x 10 7/8. **Cols./Page:** 3. **Col. Width:** 12 1/2 picas. **Col. Depth:** 140 agate lines. **Key Personnel:** JoAnn Alspach, R.N.,, Editor; Bonnie J. Horrigan, Director, bonnie.horrigan@aacn.org; Michael Villaire, Manag-

ing Editor, michael.villaire@aacn.org. **ISSN:** 0279-5442. **Subscription Rates:** $30; $8 single issue. **Remarks:** Accepts advertising.
Ad Rates: GLR: $32 **Circ:** ‡96,000
BW: $4,985
4C: $6,530

ALPINE, pop. 6,476.

S. CA. San Diego Co. 30 mi. E. of San Diego. Established as a stage stop in 1760. Light industry. Small ranches.

1407 Alpine Sun
2144 Alpine Blvd. Phone: (619)445-3288
PO Box 1089 Fax: (619)445-6776
Alpine, CA 91903
Community newspaper. **Founded:** 1952. **Freq:** Weekly (Thurs.). **Print Method:** Offset. Uses mats. **Trim Size:** 10 x 13. **Cols./Page:** 5. **Col. Width:** 11.5 picas. **Col. Depth:** 65 picas. **Key Personnel:** Jay Harn, Editor, jayharn@flash.net. **ISSN:** 8750-8257. **Subscription Rates:** $18 individuals; $24 out of area. **Remarks:** Accepts advertising. **URL:** http://alpine-sun.com.
Ad Rates: BW: $275 **Circ:** Paid ‡2,200
4C: $750
PCI: $6

ALTADENA, pop. 39,400.

S. CA. Los Angeles Co. 4 mi. N. of Pasadena. Space age research center. Residential.

1408 Skeptic
Skeptic Magazine
PO Box 338 Phone: (626)794-3119
Altadena, CA 91001 Fax: (626)794-1301
Publication E-mail: skepticmag@aol.com

Magazine promoting scientific method, critical thinking and the skepticism of the paranormal and superstition. **Subtitle:** Extraordinary claims, revolutionary ideas, and the promotion of science. **Founded:** May 1992. **Freq:** Quarterly. **Trim Size:** 8 3/8 x 10 7/8. **Cols./Page:** 3. **Key Personnel:** Michael Shermer, PhD, Editor. **ISSN:** 1063-9330. **Subscription Rates:** $30 annual. **Remarks:** Advertising accepted; rates available upon request. **Online:** Information Access; UMI; EBSCO. **URL:** http://www.skeptic.com.
Circ: Controlled 40,000

ALTURAS†, pop. 3,025.

NE CA. Modoc Co. 3 mi. E. of Cederville. Residential.

1409 Modoc County Record
Box 531 Phone: (913)233-2632
Alturas, CA 96101 Fax: (916)233-5113
Publisher E-mail: record1@modocrecord.com

Newspaper. **Founded:** 1892. **Freq:** Weekly (Thurs.). **Print Method:** Offset. **Cols./Page:** 6. **Col. Width:** 26 nonpareils. **Col. Depth:** 294 agate lines. **Key Personnel:** Richard R. Holloway, Publisher; Jane S. Holloway, Publisher. **Subscription Rates:** $25 out of state. **Remarks:** Accepts advertising.
Ad Rates: BW: $504 **Circ:** 4,500
4C: $400
SAU: $3.35
PCI: $4

1410 KCNO-FM - 94.5
Hwy. 395 N. Phone: (916)233-3570
PO Box 580 Fax: (916)233-5570
Alturas, CA 96101-0570

Format: Country. **Owner:** KCNO, Inc., at above address. **Founded:** 1988. **Formerly:** KYAX-FM. **Operating Hours:** 6 a.m.-10 p.m.; 90% sat., 10% local. **Key Personnel:** W.H. Hansen, Station Mgr.; Carol Irwin, Program Dir. **Wattage:** 100,000. **Ad Rates:** $14-16 for 30 seconds; $16-18 for 60 seconds.

1411 KK7J-AM - 570
PO Box 580 Phone: (916)233-3570
Alturas, CA 96101-0580 Fax: (916)233-5570

Format: Talk. **Networks:** USA Radio; Jones Satellite. **Owner:** KCNO, Inc., at above address. **Founded:** 1951. **Formerly:** KCNO-AM. **Operating Hours:** 6 a.m.-10 p.m., 50% network, 50% local. **Key Personnel:** Carol Irwin, Contact; Dan Frey, Contact; W.H. Hansen, Station Mgr.; Carol Irwin, Program Dir. **Wattage:** 5,000. **Ad Rates:** Advertising accepted; rates available upon request.

ANAHEIM, pop. 221,847.

S. CA. Orange Co. 26 mi. SE of Los Angeles. Home of Disneyland. Seaside and mountain resort. Manufactures aircraft parts, surface to air missile launchers. Mobile homes. Electronic computer components, electric motors, auto batteries, citrus fruit packing plants. Agriculture. Strawberries.

1412 Anaheim Hills News
The Orange County Register
1771 S. Lewis Phone: (714)634-1567
Anaheim, CA 92825 Fax: (714)704-3714

Community newspaper. **Founded:** 1964. **Freq:** Weekly (Wed.). **Print Method:** Offset. **Cols./Page:** 7. **Col. Width:** 1 1/4 inches. **Col. Depth:** 14 inches. **Key Personnel:** David Threshie, Publisher; Frank Mickadeit, Editor; Gus Santoyo, City Editor. **Remarks:** Accepts advertising. **Formerly:** Anaheim Hills Highlander.
Ad Rates: PCI: $9.68 **Circ:** Paid 25
Free 10,200

1413 The Automotive Booster of California
KAL Publications, Inc.
559 S. Harbor Blvd., Ste. A Phone: (714)563-9300
Anaheim, CA 92805 Fax: (714)563-9310

Trade magazine for members of Automotive Booster Clubs, automotive distributors, automotive parts jobbers, and others. **Founded:** 1929. **Freq:** Monthly. **Print Method:** Web offset. **Trim Size:** 8 1/2 x 11. **Cols./Page:** 3. **Col. Width:** 14 picas. **Col. Depth:** 10 inches. **Key Personnel:** Kathy Laderman, Editor, kathy@kalpub.com; James Pen, Advertising Mgr., jmpenn@kalpub.com. **USPS:** 908-240. **Subscription Rates:** $6 individuals. **Remarks:** Accepts advertising. **URL:** http://www.kalpub.com.
Ad Rates: BW: $600 **Circ:** Non-paid ‡4,700
4C: $1,100
PCI: $30

1414 O & A Marketing News
KAL Publications, Inc.
559 S. Harbor Blvd., Ste. A Phone: (714)563-9300
Anaheim, CA 92805 Fax: (714)563-9310

News magazine (tabloid) targeting people engaged in the marketing, distribution, merchandising, installation, and servicing of gasoline, fuels, oil, tires, batteries, accessories, and automotive aftermarket products for service stations, convenience stores and carwashes in the thirteen Pacific Western states. **Founded:** Jan. 1966. **Freq:** 7/year. **Print Method:** Webb. **Trim Size:** 11 1/2 x 17. **Cols./Page:** 4. **Col. Width:** 14 picas. **Col. Depth:** 16 inches. **Key Personnel:** Kathy Laderman, Editor and Publisher, kathy@kalpub.com; Jim Penn, Advertising Mgr., jpenn@kalpub.com. **ISSN:** 0192-009X. **Subscription Rates:** $20 individuals. **Remarks:** Accepts advertising. **URL:** http://www.kalpub.com.
Ad Rates: BW: $2,200 **Circ:** Paid ‡4,522
4C: $3,200 Free ‡2,732
SAU: $50
PCI: $55

1415 Orange County Living
Affluent Target Marketing
1219 N Tustin Ave. Phone: (714)632-9810
Anaheim, CA 92807 Fax: (714)632-3435
Free: (800)662-5577

Consumer magazine covering home improvement for an affluent audience. **Founded:** Jan. 1979. **Freq:** Bimonthly. **Print Method:** Web offset. **Trim Size:** 8 1/8 x 10 7/8. **Key Personnel:** Morris Miller, Contact. **Subscription Rates:** Free to qualified subscribers. **Remarks:** Accepts advertising.
Ad Rates: BW: $2,450 **Circ:** Non-paid 1,600,000
4C: $3,425

Pacific News Group - See Los Angeles

1416 KEZY-FM - 95.9
1190 E. Ball Rd. Phone: (714)774-9600
Anaheim, CA 92805-5919 Fax: (714)774-1631
E-mail: kezyradio@aol.com

Format: Contemporary Hit Radio (CHR). **Networks:** ABC. **Owner:** RP Radio, 350 Park Ave., 16th Fl., New York, NY 10022, (212)980-7110, Fax: (212)753-2805. **Founded:** 1961. **Operating Hours:** Continuous. **Key Personnel:** Miles Sexton, General Mgr.; Dave Weiss, Promotions Dir.; Mark Moceri, Chief Engineer; Dawn McKahan, General Sales Mgr.; Eleanor Jorge, Business Mgr. **Wattage:** 7000.

1417 KIKF-FM - 94.3
1045 S. East St. Phone: (714)502-9494
Anaheim, CA 92805 Fax: (714)502-9400

Format: Country. **Networks:** AP. **Owner:** N. Art Astor., at above address. **Founded:** 1961. **Formerly:** KGGK-FM (1967). **Operating Hours:** Continuous; 1% network, 99% local. **ADI:** Los Angeles (Corona & San Bernardino), CA. **Key Personnel:** Art Astor, General Mgr.; Bill Martinez, National Sales Mgr.; Frank Cisco, Program Dir. **Wattage:** 3000. **Ad Rates:** $50-100 for 30 seconds; $80-150 for 60 seconds. **URL:** http://www.kikf.com.

1418 KORG-AM - 1190
1190 E. Ball Rd. Phone: (714)776-1190
Anaheim, CA 92805-5919 Fax: (714)774-1631

Format: Talk. **Owner:** RP Radio, 350 Park Ave., 16th Fl., New York, NY 10022, (212)980-7110, Fax: (212)753-2805. **Founded:** 1959. **Formerly:** KEZY-AM (1985); KPZE-AM (1989). **Operating Hours:** Continuous. **ADI:** Los Angeles (Corona & San Bernardino), CA. **Key Personnel:** Miles Sexton, General Mgr.; Chris Adams, Station Mgr.; Mark Moceri, Chief Engineer; Eleanor Jorge, Business Mgr. **Wattage:** 11,000. **Ad Rates:** $400-600 per unit.

1419 Multivision Cable TV
3041 E. Miraloma Ave. Phone: (714)632-9222
Anaheim, CA 92806 Fax: (714)630-4353

Founded: 1986. **Formerly:** ML Media Cable TV (1992). **Key Personnel:** Donald Granger, Vice Pres./Gen. Mgr.; Rick Cable, Advertising/Mktg. Mgr.; Arthur Maulsby, Program Mgr. **Cities Served:** subscribing households 66,000; 60 channels; 2 community access channels; 40 hours per week community access programming.

ANDERSON, pop. 7,381.

N. CA. Shasta Co. 10 mi. SE of Redding. Sawmills, veneer, machine shops, paper mills, logging. Diversified farming.

1420 The Valley Post
North Valley Newspapers, Inc.
2680 Gateway Dr. Phone: (916)365-2797
PO Box 1148 Fax: (916)365-2829
Anderson, CA 96007
Community newspaper. **Founded:** 1886. **Freq:** Weekly (Tues.). **Print Method:** Offset. **Cols./Page:** 6. **Col. Width:** 12.3 picas. **Col. Depth:** 21 inches. **Key Personnel:** Doug Hirsch, Publisher. **USPS:** 894-890. **Subscription Rates:** Free; $14 by mail; $17 out of area (by mail); $9 Senior Citizens in Shasta. **Remarks:** Accepts advertising.
Ad Rates: BW: $900 **Circ:** Paid ‡3,500
PCI: $8.50 Free ‡10,000

ANGWIN

Napa Co.

1421 KNDL-FM - 89.9
PO Box 89 Phone: (707)965-7141
Angwin, CA 94508 Fax: (707)965-7147
Free: (800)321-5237
E-mail: kcds@puc.edu

Format: Religious. **Networks:** Moody Broadcasting; Ambassador Inspirational Radio; USA Radio. **Owner:** Howell Mtn. Broadcasting, at above address. **Founded:** 1983. **Formerly:** KANG-FM (1981); KCDS-FM (1998); KPRN-FM. **Operating Hours:** Continuous; 5% network; 95% local. **Key Personnel:** David Shantz, General Mgr. **Wattage:** 50,000. **Ad Rates:** Noncommercial.

ANTIOCH, pop. 45,559.

W. CA. Contra Costa Co. On San Joaquin River, 50 mi. NE of San Francisco. Manufactures fibreboard, chemicals, glass containers. Fruit, vegetable canneries. Diversified farming. Asparagus, almonds, grapes.

Brentwood News - See Brentwood

1422 The Ledger Dispatch
Contra Costa Newspapers, Inc.
PO Box 2299 Phone: (510)935-2525
Antioch, CA 94531 Fax: (510)754-9483

General newspaper. **Founded:** 1870. **Freq:** Daily and Sunday (eve.). **Print Method:** Offset. **Cols./Page:** 8. **Col. Width:** 22 nonpareils. **Col. Depth:** 301 agate lines. **Key Personnel:** George Riggs, Publisher, phone (510)945-4754, fax (510)945-4767; Gloria Thomas, General Mgr., phone (510)779-7102, fax (510)754-9483; Bob Goll, Managing Editor, phone (510)779-7181, fax (510)706-2305. **Subscription Rates:** $8.25 per month; $10.50 per month by mail. **Remarks:** Accepts advertising. **Formerly:** Daily Ledger; Post Dispatch.
Ad Rates: BW: $1,845.99 **Circ:** Mon.-Sat. 20,933
4C: $2,105.99 Sun. 21,903
PCI: $14.31

APTOS

W. CA. Santa Cruz Co. 20 mi. E. of Santa Cruz. Residential.

1423 International California Mining Journal
PO Box 2260 Phone: (408)662-2899
Aptos, CA 95001 Fax: (408)662-3014
Publication E-mail: camining@aol.com

Mining trade magazine covering prospecting and mining throughout the world. **Founded:** Sept. 1933. **Freq:** Monthly. **Print Method:** Offset. Uses mats. **Trim Size:** 8 1/2 x 11. **Cols./Page:** 3. **Col. Width:** 28 nonpareils. **Col. Depth:** 133 agate lines. **Key Personnel:** Kenneth L. Harn, Editor and Publisher; Diane Craig, Advertising Mgr.; Silvia Pardo, Circulation Mgr. **ISSN:** 0008-1299. **Subscription Rates:** $22.95 individuals; $3.00 single issue; $35.95 other countries. **Remarks:** Accepts advertising. **Formerly:** California Mining Journal.
Ad Rates: BW: $426.80 **Circ:** ‡10,000
4C: $641.30
PCI: $21.90

ARCADIA, pop. 45,994.

S. CA. Los Angeles Co. 15 mi. NE of Los Angeles. Manufactures sash and doors, plastics, boats, airplane tools. Nurseries. Hatcheries. Ranches. Orange and walnut groves.

1424 California Thoroughbred
California Thoroughbred Breeders Association
201 Colorado Pl. Phone: (626)445-7800
PO Box 60018 Fax: (626)574-0852
Arcadia, CA 91066-6018
Magazine about horse breeding and racing. **Founded:** 1941. **Freq:** Monthly. **Print Method:** Offset. **Trim Size:** 8 1/2 x 11. **Cols./Page:** 3. **Col. Width:** 2 1/8 inches. **Col. Depth:** 12 3/4 inches. **Key Personnel:** Doug Burge, Editor; Michael Compton, Managing Editor; Jean Kuennen, Advertising Mgr. **ISSN:** 0049-3821. **Subscription Rates:** Free to Members; $45 nonmembers. **Remarks:** Accepts advertising. **Formerly:** The Thoroughbred of California.
Ad Rates: BW: $490 **Circ:** 5,500
4C: $980
PCI: $41

1425 Electrical News
PO Box 660760 Phone: (626)446-8652
Arcadia, CA 91066-0760 Fax: (626)447-6047
Free: (800)782-5493
Publication E-mail: editor@electricalnews.com
Publisher E-mail: editor@electricalnews.com; sales@electricalnews.com

Trade magazine serving the electrical building and maintenance industry in the western states. Audience includes wholesale distributors, contractors, and plant engineers. **Founded:** 1984. **Freq:** Monthly. **Print Method:** Offset. **Trim Size:** 10 x 16. **Cols./Page:** 5. **Col. Width:** 1 13/16 inches. **Col. Depth:** 16 inches. **Key Personnel:** Basil E. Mellon, Publisher; Jennifer Vargas, Office Mgr., jennifer@electricalnews.com. **Subscription Rates:** Free to qualified subscribers; $20 individuals. **Remarks:** Accepts advertising. **URL:** http://www.electricalnews.com.
Ad Rates: BW: $1,862 **Circ:** Paid ‡1,100
4C: $2,202 Free ‡18,900

ARCATA, pop. 12,338.

NW CA. Humboldt Co. On Humboldt Bay and Pacific Ocean, 8 mi. NE of Eureka. Humboldt State University. Tourism. Lumbering. Light industry. Mobile homes. Trucking. Construction, machine shops. Timber. Agriculture.

1426 The Lumberjack Newspaper
Humboldt State University
Nelson Hall East 6 Phone: (707)826-3259
Arcata, CA 95521 Fax: (707)826-5921
Publication E-mail: thejack@axe.humboldt.edu

Collegiate newspaper (tabloid). **Founded:** 1929. **Freq:** Weekly (Wed.). **Print Method:** Offset. **Trim Size:** 5 x 12 1/2. **Cols./Page:** 5. **Col. Width:** 11.5 picas. **Col. Depth:** 12 1/2 inches. **Key Personnel:** Pam Yagotin, Advertising Mgr., pyl7001@axe.humbold.edu; Howard L. Seemann, Advisor. **Subscription Rates:** Free; $14 by mail. **Remarks:** Accepts advertising. **URL:** http://www.lumberjack.humbolt.edu.
Ad Rates: GLR: $5 **Circ:** Free ‡6,500
BW: $491.25
4C: $340
PCI: $7.86

1427 KHSU-FM - 90.5
Humboldt State University
Arcata, CA 95521 Phone: (707)826-4807 Fax: (707)826-6082
E-mail: khsu@axe.humboldt.edu

Format: Public Radio. **Networks:** Public Radio International (PRI); National Public Radio (NPR). **Owner:** Humboldt State University, at above address. **Founded:** 1960. **Formerly:** KHSC-FM (1974). **Operating Hours:** Continuous. **Key Personnel:** Kathleen Heil, General Mgr.; Terry Green, Assistant Mgr./Chief Engineer. **Local Programs:** *The KHSU Homepage*, Lynn Evans; *Tuesday Night Talk*, Lynn Evans. **Wattage:** 9,000. **Ad Rates:** Noncommercial.

AROMAS

1428 The Rottweiler Quarterly
GRQ Publications
PO Box 900 Phone: (408)728-8461
Aromas, CA 95004 Fax: (408)728-4708

Magazine covering the training, breeding, health, and showing of rottweilers. **Founded:** 1987. **Freq:** Quarterly. **Print Method:** Sheet-fed offset. **Trim Size:** 8 1/4 x 10 3/4. **Cols./Page:** 3. **Col. Width:** 2 1/4 inches. **Col. Depth:** 9 3/4 inches. **Key Personnel:** Robin Stark, Editor, phone (408)848-1313; Tomi Edmiston, Publisher. **ISSN:** 1040-8037. **Subscription Rates:** $40/yr; $55 other countries; $13 single issue. **Remarks:** Accepts advertising.
Ad Rates: BW: $175 **Circ:** 3,850
4C: $400 Non-paid 250

ARROYO GRANDE, pop. 11,290.

SW CA. San Luis Obispo Co. 90 mi. NW of Santa Barbara. Trade center. Ships vegetables. Tourism. Agriculture. Beans, peas, artichokes, celery, walnuts.

1429 Five Cities Times Press Recorder
South County Publishing Co., Inc.
PO Box 460 Phone: (805)489-4206
Arroyo Grande, CA 93421 Fax: (805)473-0571

Local newspaper. **Founded:** 1887. **Freq:** 3/week. **Print Method:** Offset. **Cols./Page:** 6. **Col. Width:** 24 nonpareils. **Col. Depth:** 294 agate lines. **Key Personnel:** Richard E. Blankenburg, Publisher; Dick Blankenburg, Advertising Mgr. **Subscription Rates:** $42. **Remarks:** Accepts advertising.
Ad Rates: GLR: $5.05 **Circ:** ‡10,885
BW: $1,102.95
4C: $1,382.95
SAU: $9.95
PCI: $9.95

1430 Five Cities Times Press Shopper's News
South County Publishing Co., Inc.
PO Box 460 Phone: (805)489-4206
Arroyo Grande, CA 93421 Fax: (805)473-0571

Shopper. **Founded:** 1887. **Freq:** Weekly. **Print Method:** Offset. **Cols./Page:** 6. **Col. Width:** 24 nonpareils. **Col. Depth:** 301 agate lines. **Key Personnel:** Richard Blankenburg, Publisher. **Subscription Rates:** Free. **Remarks:** Accepts advertising.
Ad Rates: GLR: $5.05 **Circ:** Free ‡8,575
BW: $1,102.95
4C: $1,382.95
SAU: $9.95
PCI: $9.95

1431 KWBR-FM - 95.3
1303 Grand Ave., Ste. 229 Phone: (805)473-2778
Arroyo Grande, CA 93420 Fax: (805)473-2438

Format: Album-Oriented Rock (AOR). **Owner:** Winsome Media, LLC, at above address. **Founded:** 1974. **Formerly:** KPGA-FM (1989). **Operating Hours:** Continuous. **Key Personnel:** Bruce W. Howard, General Mgr.; Joe Alvino, Program Dir.; Dean Kattari, Music Dir.; Branden Howard, Operations Mgr.; Warren Flaschen, General Sales Mgr. **Wattage:** 4280. **Ad Rates:** $15-35 for 30 seconds; $15-35 for 60 seconds.

ATASCADERO, pop. 15,930.

SW CA. San Luis Obispo Co. 19 mi. N. of San Luis Obispo. Residential. Meat plant. Agriculture. Grain.

1432 Atascadero News
PO Box 6068 Phone: (805)466-2585
Atascadero, CA 93423 Fax: (805)466-2714

Community newspaper. **Key Personnel:** Lon Allan, Editor; Jeff McMahon, News Dir.; Jud Porter, Publisher; Jim Porter, Publisher. **Subscription Rates:** $18 individuals. **Remarks:** Accepts advertising.
Ad Rates: BW: $642.60 **Circ:** ‡6,450
PCI: $6.50

1433 KIQO-FM - 104.5
14350 Morningside Dr., Box 6028 Phone: (805)466-6511 Fax: (805)466-5362
Atascadero, CA 93423
E-mail: oldies@fix.net

Format: Oldies. **Networks:** Satellite Music Network. **Owner:** Garry & Virginia Brill, at above address. **Founded:** 1979. **Operating Hours:** Continuous. **Key Personnel:** Garry Brill, Manager; Dell McCulley, Sales Mgr.; Seth Blackburn, Operations Mgr. **Wattage:** 5600 ERP. **Ad Rates:** Combined advertising rates available with KWEZ-FM.

ATWATER, pop. 17,530.

C. CA. Merced Co. 8 mi. NW of Merced. Military air museum. Cannery. Fruit, dairy, truck farms. Sweet potatoes, watermelons, peaches, almonds.

1434 KTFM-AM - 1580
514 E Bellevue Rd. Phone: (209)722-1520
Atwater, CA 95301 Fax: (209)358-9793

Format: Hispanic. **Founded:** 1956. **Formerly:** KLOQ-AM. **Operating Hours:** Daytime; 100% local. **Key Personnel:** Maria Emma Herrera, Office Mgr.; Eduardo E. Rodriguez, Program Dir.; Javier Fuentes, Sales; Dolores Aguirre, Sales. **Wattage:** 1000.

1435 KVRQ-FM - 92.5
514 E. Bellevue Rd. Phone: (209)358-9723
Atwater, CA 95301 Fax: (209)358-9793

Format: Classic Rock. **Owner:** Clarke Broadcasting Corp., at above address. **Founded:** Nov. 16, 1995. **Operating Hours:** Continuous. **Key Personnel:** Steve Wrath, General Mgr.; Todd Martin, Program Dir.; Bob Romanko, Sales Mgr.; Donna Williams, Traffic Mgr. **Wattage:** 4000. **Ad Rates:** $12-21 for 30 seconds; $15-25 for 60 seconds.

AUBURN†, pop. 7,540.

NE CA. Placer Co. 35 mi. NE of Sacramento. Mountain resort. Gold mines. Fruits, poultry products shipped. Saw, planing mills; nursery. Fruit, stock, poultry farms.

1436 Auburn Journal
1030 High St. Phone: (530)885-5656
PO Box 5910 Fax: (530)887-1231
Auburn, CA 95603-4707
Publication E-mail: ajournal@foothill.net

General newspaper. **Founded:** 1872. **Freq:** Daily and Sunday (morn.). **Print Method:** Offset. **Cols./Page:** 6. **Col. Width:** 12 picas. **Col. Depth:** 294 agate lines. **Key Personnel:** Deric Rothe, Editor; Martin Cody, Publisher; Susan Pryce, Advertising Dir., fax (530)885-4902. **USPS:** 036-860. **Subscription Rates:** $96.53 individuals. **Remarks:** Accepts advertising.
Ad Rates: BW: $1,828 **Circ:** Mon.-Fri. ★**12,699**
4C: $2,128 Sun. ★**13,653**
SAU: $14.51

1437 Bromeliad Society Journal
Bromeliad Society, Inc.
720 Millertown Rd. Phone: (530)885-0201
Auburn, CA 95603 Fax: (530)885-0201
Publication E-mail: blackburn@neworld.net

Publications on botany and gardening. **Founded:** 1951. **Freq:** Bimonthly. **Print Method:** Offset. **Trim Size:** 6 x 9. **Key Personnel:** Chet Blackburn, Editor, phone (530)885-0201, fax (530)885-0201, blackburn@neworld.net. **ISSN:** 0090-8738. **Subscription Rates:** $25 individuals; $4.50 single issue. **Remarks:** Accepts advertising.
Ad Rates: BW: $125 **Circ:** Combined 1700

1438 FPC/Fire Protection Contractor
Haden B. Brumbeloe and Associates, Inc.
12972 Earhart Ave., Ste 302 Phone: (530)823-0706
Auburn, CA 95602 Fax: (530)823-6937
Publication E-mail: editorial@fpcmag.com
Publisher E-mail: fpcmag@foothill.net

Trade magazine for fire sprinkler industry professionals. **Founded:** Mar. 1978. **Freq:** Monthly. **Print Method:** Offset. **Trim Size:** 8 1/2 x 11. **Key Personnel:** Brant Brumbeloe, Editor. **ISSN:** 1043-2485. **Subscription Rates:** $65 individuals. **Remarks:** Accepts advertising.
Ad Rates: BW: $1,047 **Circ:** Controlled 2,300
4C: $1,469

1439 Sentinel
PO Box 9148 Phone: (530)823-3986
Auburn, CA 95604 Fax: (530)823-0209
Publisher E-mail: ssierra@ns.net

Community newspaper. **Founded:** 1989. **Freq:** Weekly. **Print Method:** Web offset. **Cols./Page:** 6. **Col. Width:** 2 1/16 inches. **Col. Depth:** 21 inches. **Key Personnel:** Laurie Penn, Editor; Richard Kerr, Advertising Mgr.; Grace Mandel, Production Mgr. **Subscription Rates:** $25 individuals. **Remarks:** Accepts advertising.
Ad Rates: BW: $1,200 **Circ:** Controlled 10,000
4C: $1,800
SAU: $10.75
PCI: $10.75

1440 Shotgun Sports
Shotgun Sports, Inc.
PO Box 6810 Phone: (916)889-2220
Auburn, CA 95604 Fax: (916)889-9106
Free: (800)676-8920
Publication E-mail: shotsports@aol.com; shotgunsports@mcocnoxies.org; shotgun_sports@macnexus.org

Magazine for clay target shooting and hunting. **Subtitle:** America's Leading Shotgun Magazine. **Founded:** 1979. **Freq:** 11/year. **Print Method:** Offset. **Trim Size:** 8 x 10 7/8. **Cols./Page:** 3. **Col. Width:** 27 nonpareils. **Col. Depth:** 140 agate lines. **Key Personnel:** Frank Kodl, Editor and Publisher. **ISSN:** 0774-3773. **Subscription Rates:** $28 individuals; $3.50 single issue. **Remarks:** Accepts advertising. **URL:** http://www.shotgun_ sports.com.
Ad Rates: BW: $3,820 **Circ:** ‡108,000
4C: $5,330

1441 West Art
PO Box 6868 Phone: (530)885-0969
Auburn, CA 95604
Professional and amateur art magazine. **Founded:** 1962. **Freq:** Semimonthly. **Print Method:** Offset. **Cols./Page:** 4. **Col. Width:** 30 nonpareils. **Col. Depth:** 196 agate lines. **Key Personnel:** Martha Garcia, Editor; Bud Pisarek, Publisher. **ISSN:** 0738-0402. **Subscription Rates:** $15 individuals. **Remarks:** Accepts advertising. **Alt. Formats:** Microform.
Ad Rates: BW: $420 **Circ:** ‡4,000
PCI: $7

1442 KAHI-AM - 950
1230 High St., Ste. 120 Phone: (530)885-5636
Auburn, CA 95603 Fax: (530)885-0166

Format: Talk; Sports; News. **Networks:** AP. **Owner:** KAHI CORP, at above address. **Founded:** 1957. **Operating Hours:** Continuous; 60% network, 40% local. **Key Personnel:** Craig Conlee, Operations Mgr.; Jim Ruffalo, Contact. **Wattage:** 5000. **Ad Rates:** $15 for 30 seconds; $17-18 for 60 seconds.

AVALON, pop. 2,022.

S. CA. Los Angeles Co. 50 mi. S. of Los Angeles. Resort.

1443 The Catalina Islander
PO Box 428 Phone: (310)510-0500
Avalon, CA 90704 Fax: (310)510-2882

Community newspaper. **Founded:** 1914. **Freq:** Weekly (Fri.). **Print Method:** Web press. **Cols./Page:** 5. **Col. Width:** 2 inches. **Col. Depth:** 16 inches. **Key Personnel:** Sherri Walker, Editor and Publisher. **Subscription Rates:** $28 individuals; $30 Off the island. **Remarks:** Accepts advertising.
Ad Rates: BW: $680 **Circ:** Paid ‡4,000
4C: $1,040 Free ‡2,000
PCI: $8.50

1444 Catalina Cable TV Co.
Box 2143 Phone: (310)510-0255
Avalon, CA 90704 Fax: (310)510-2565

Founded: 1985. **Key Personnel:** Mitzi Seibert, Mgr. **Cities Served:** Avalon, CA: subscribing households 1,123; 60 channels; 1 community access channel; 50 hours per week community access programming.

AZUSA, pop. 29,380.

S. CA. Los Angeles Co. 3 mi. E. of Duarte. Residential.

1445 Clause
Azusa Pacific University
Box 9521, Unit 5504 Phone: (626)815-6000
Azusa, CA 91702-7000 Fax: (626)812-3017
Publication E-mail: clause@apu.edu

College newspaper. **Freq:** Weekly. **Cols./Page:** 4. **Col. Width:** 2 1/2 inches. **Col. Depth:** 16 inches. **Key Personnel:** Andrew Delander, Editor; Reagan Tucker, Advertising Mgr. **Subscription Rates:** $15 semester. **Remarks:** Accepts advertising. **URL:** http://www.apu.edu/~clause.
Ad Rates: GLR: $5 **Circ:** Non-paid 2,300
BW: $464
PCI: $7.75

1446 Journal of Psychology and Christianity
Christian Association for Psychological Studies
Azusa Pacific University Phone: (626)815-6000
Dept. of Psychology Fax: (626)812-3072
Azusa, CA 91702-7000
Publisher E-mail: capsintl@compuvision.net

Journal on topics relating Christianity with psychological and pastoral professions. **Founded:** 1982. **Freq:** Quarterly. **Print Method:** Offset. **Trim Size:** 6 x 9. **Cols./Page:** 1. **Col. Width:** 54 nonpareils. **Col. Depth:** 100 agate lines. **Key Personnel:** Peter C. Hill, Ph.D., Editor, phone (412)458-2004, fax (412)458-2003, phill@gcc.edu; Brian E. Eck, Ph.D., Managing Editor, beck@apu.edu. **ISSN:** 0733-4273. **Subscription Rates:** Free to members; $50 libraries. **Remarks:** Color advertising not accepted. **Alt. Formats:** Braille; Microform.
Ad Rates: BW: $425 **Circ:** Paid ‡2,300
Non-paid ‡200

BAKERSFIELD†, pop. 105,611.

S. CA. Kern Co. 109 mi. N. of Los Angeles. Oil wells and refineries. Borax, tungsten mines. Manufactures oil well tools, pumps, steel castings & riveted pipe, cottonseed oil, furniture, textile bags, Meat packing plant; bottling works. Ships citrus fruits, grapes, melons, cotton, cottonseed, potatoes, alfalfa, wheat.

1447 Amelia
329 E St. Phone: (661)323-4064
Bakersfield, CA 93304 Fax: (661)323-5326
Publisher E-mail: amelia@lightspeed.net

Literary magazine containing fiction, poetry, drama, belles lettres, essays, reviews, cartoons, illustrations, and photography. **Founded:** Apr. 1984. **Freq:** Quarterly. **Print Method:** Offset. **Trim Size:** 5 1/2 x 8 1/2. **Cols./Page:** 1. **Col. Width:** 54 nonpareils. **Col. Depth:** 105 agate lines. **Key Personnel:** Frederick A. Raborg, Jr., Editor and Publisher; Eileen M. Raborg, Advertising Mgr. **ISSN:** 0743-2755. **Subscription Rates:** $30 individuals; $9.95 single issue; $44 out of country; $15 single issue out of country.
Ad Rates: BW: $450 **Circ:** Paid ‡1,750
PCI: $50 Non-paid ‡250

1448 The Bakersfield Californian
PO Box BIN 440 Phone: (805)395-7500
Bakersfield, CA 93302 Fax: (805)395-7519
Free: (800)404-4949

General newspaper. **Founded:** 1866. **Freq:** Mon.-Sun. (morn.). **Print Method:** Offset. **Cols./Page:** 6. **Col. Width:** 25 nonpareils. **Col. Depth:** 294 agate lines. **Key Personnel:** Virgina Moorhouse, Publisher/Chairman of the Board, phone (661)395-7200, fax (661)395-7280, vmoorhouse@bakersfield.com; Richard Beene, Pres./CEO, phone (661)395-7284, fax (661)395-7280, rbeene@bakersfield.com; Fred Fedesco, VP of Circ. and Operations, phone (661)395-5730, fax (661)392-5727, ffedesco@bakersfield.com; Daniel Lacey, VP/Chief Financial Officer, phone (661)395-7202, fax (661)395-7339, dlacey@bakersfield.com; John Wells, VP of Ad. Sales and Mktg., phone (661)395-7227, fax (661)395-7561, jwells@bakersfield.com; Mike Jenner, VP of Interactive Media/Exec. Ed., phone (661)395-7387, fax (661)395-7519, mjenner@bakersfield.com; Linda Wienandt, Managing Ed., phone (661)395-7225, lwienandt@bakersfield.com; Logan Molen, Asst. Managing Ed./Days, phone (661)395-7373, lmolen@bakersfield.com; Tim Heinrichs, Asst. Managing Ed./Nights, phone (661)395-7365, theinrichs@bakersfield.com; Glenn Hammett, Graphics Ed., phone (661)395-7467, ghammett@bakersfield.com; John Furtak, Wire/Copy Desk Supervisor., phone (661)395-7383, jfurtak@bakersfield.com; Dianne Hardisty, Editorial Page Ed., phone (661)395-7414, fax (661)395-7380. **Subscription Rates:** $312.12 individuals in Kern County; $348.36 individuals out of county; $386.88 out of state. **Remarks:** Accepts advertising. **URL:** http://www.bakersfield.com/. **Feature Editors:** Lois Henry, *Metro*, phone (661)395-7413, lhenry@bakersfield.com; Tony Lacava, *Financial/Business*, phone (661)395-7418, tlavaca@bakersfield.com; John Millman, *Sports*, phone (661)395-7737, fax (661)395-7323, jmillman@bakersfield.com; Robert Price, *Features*, phone (661)395-7434, rprice@bakersfield.com.
Ad Rates: GLR: $3 **Circ:** Mon.-Sat. ★72,754
BW: $7,552.44 Sun. ★87.471
4C: $8,672.44
PCI: $59.94

1449 Bakersfield News Observer
1219 20th St. Phone: (805)324-9466
Bakersfield, CA 93301 Fax: (805)324-9472
Free: (800)482-6156

Black community newspaper. **Freq:** Weekly (Wed.). **Print Method:** offset. **Trim Size:** 12 x 21 1/2. **Key Personnel:** Ellen Cleek, Managing Editor, phone (805)324-9466, fax (805)324-9472; Joseph L. Coley, Publisher. **Remarks:** Accepts advertising.
Ad Rates: GLR: $1.10 **Circ:** (Not Reported)
BW: $260.00
4C: $750.00
PCI: $13

1450 Bakersfield's Shopper
Hamilton Diversified Services, Inc.
5725 Canberra Ave.
Bakersfield, CA 93307-6611

Newspaper. **Freq:** Weekly.
Circ: Free 103,560

1451 Cicada
Amelia
329 E St. Phone: (661)323-4064
Bakersfield, CA 93304 Fax: (661)323-5326
Publisher E-mail: amelia@lightspeed.net

Literary magazine featuring haiku and Japanese-oriented fiction. **Founded:** 1984. **Freq:** Quarterly. **Print Method:** Offset. **Trim Size:** 5 1/2 x 8 1/2. **Cols./Page:** 1. **Col. Width:** 4 1/2 inches. **Col. Depth:** 7 1/2 inches. **Key Personnel:** Frederick A. Raborg, Jr., Editor. **ISSN:** 0891-2386. **Subscription Rates:** $24 out of country; $6 single issue. **Remarks:** Accepts advertising.
Ad Rates: BW: $100 **Circ:** Paid 750
PCI: $10 Non-paid 100

1452 El Mexicalo
931 Niles St. Phone: (805)323-9334
Bakersfield, CA 93305-4535 Fax: (805)323-6951

Community newspaper (English and Spanish). **Founded:** 1980. **Freq:** Weekly (Thurs.). **Cols./Page:** 6. **Col. Width:** 2 1/16 inches. **Col. Depth:** 21 inches. **Key Personnel:** Tony Manzano, Jr., Editor; Esther H. Manzano, Publisher; Erlinda H. Manzano, Advertising Mgr. **Subscription Rates:** $36 individuals. **Remarks:** Accepts advertising.
Ad Rates: GLR: $1.11 **Circ:** Paid ‡9,676
PCI: $15 Free ‡5,563

1453 El Popular
El Popular Newspaper Group of California, Inc.
1206 California Ave. Phone: (805)398-1000
Bakersfield, CA 93304 Fax: (805)325-1351
Publisher E-mail: elpoplr@lightspeed.net

Community newspaper (Hispanic) with three separate editions, serving Bakersfield, Fresno, and Sacramento. **Founded:** 1983. **Freq:** Weekly. **Print Method:** Offset. **Cols./Page:** 6. **Col. Width:** 2 inches. **Col. Depth:** 21 inches. **Key Personnel:** Raul Camacho, Sr., Editor and Publisher; George Camachu, General Mgr. **Subscription Rates:** $30.
Ad Rates: SAU: $36 **Circ:** 25,000

1454 Historic Kern
Kern County Historical Society
PO Box 141 Phone: (805)322-4962
Bakersfield, CA 93302
Journal covering local history. **Founded:** 1930. **Freq:** Quarterly. **Key Personnel:** Curtis Darling, Editor. **ISSN:** 0018-2397. **Subscription Rates:** $3.50 individuals; $10 members; $1 single issue. **Remarks:** Advertising not accepted.
Circ: Controlled 450

1455 Horseless Carriage Gazette
Horseless Carriage Club of America
3311 Faorhaven Dr. Phone: (714)538-HCCA
Bakersfield, CA 93308 Fax: (714)538-5764

Auto hobby magazine covering automobiles produced prior to 1916. **Founded:** 1937. **Freq:** Bimonthly. **Print Method:** Offset. **Trim Size:** 8 1/2 x 11. **Cols./Page:** 3. **Col. Width:** 14 picas. **Col. Depth:** 59 picas. **Key Personnel:** John C. Meyer III, Editor, phone (818)703-7421. **ISSN:** 0018-5213. **Subscription Rates:** $35 individuals. **Remarks:** Accepts advertising.
Ad Rates: BW: $495 **Circ:** 5,500

1456 SPSM&H
Amelia
329 E St. Phone: (661)323-4064
Bakersfield, CA 93304 Fax: (661)323-5326
Publisher E-mail: amelia@lightspeed.net

Literary magazine presenting sonnets and romantic fiction. **Founded:** 1984. **Freq:** Quarterly. **Print Method:** Offset. **Trim Size:** 5 1/2 x 8 1/2. **Cols./Page:** 1. **Col. Width:** 4 1/2 inches. **Col. Depth:** 7 1/2 inches. **Key Personnel:** Frederick A. Raborg, Jr., Editor. **ISSN:** 0891-2378. **Subscription Rates:** $20 individuals; $6 single issue; $24 out of country; $8.50 out of country single issue. **Remarks:** Accepts advertising.
Ad Rates: BW: $100 **Circ:** Paid 600
PCI: $10 Non-paid 100

1457 Wasco Tribune
Reed Print Inc.
5409 Aldrin Court Phone: (805)758-3063
Bakersfield, CA 93313 Fax: (805)746-5571

Local newspaper. **Founded:** Aug. 4, 1982. **Freq:** Weekly. **Print Method:** Offset. **Cols./Page:** 6. **Col. Width:** 21 nonpareils. **Col. Depth:** 294 agate lines. **Key Personnel:** Levi Pagsuberon, Editor; Donald Reed, Publisher; Jerry Watts,

Advertising Mgr. **Subscription Rates:** $17 individuals; $19 Out of county; $22 out of state. **Remarks:** Accepts advertising.
Ad Rates: BW: $667.80 **Circ:** Controlled 5,600
SAU: $5.55
PCI: $6.60

1458 Cox Cable Bakersfield
820 22nd St. Phone: (805)327-0821
Bakersfield, CA 93301 Fax: (805)327-7921

Founded: 1965. **Key Personnel:** Jill Campbell, Gen Mgr. & V. Pres. **Cities Served:** Bakersfield, CA: subscribing households 22,600; 54 channels.

1459 KAXL-FM - 88.3
110 S. Montclair, Ste. 205 Phone: (805)832-2800
Bakersfield, CA 93309

Format: Religious. **Networks:** SkyLight Satellite. **Owner:** Skyride Unlimited, at above address. **Founded:** May 1994. **Operating Hours:** Continuous. **Key Personnel:** Judy Kurtz, Public Relations, kaxl@kaxl.com; Mark Heffernan, Announcer; Martin Garza, Music Dir.; Terri Blankenship, Station Mgr. **Wattage:** 10,000. **URL:** http://www.kaxl.com.

1460 KBAK-TV - 29
1901 Westwind Phone: (805)327-7955
Bakersfield, CA 93301 Fax: (805)327-5603

Format: Commercial TV. **Networks:** CBS. **Owner:** Westwind Communications, PO Box 2929, Bakersfield, CA 93303. **Founded:** 1953. **Operating Hours:** Continuous weekdays; 6 a.m.-2 a.m. Saturday and Sunday. **ADI:** Bakersfield, CA. **Key Personnel:** Wayne W. Lansche, General Mgr.; Nancy Clarke, Program Dir.; Sandy Edwards, Local Sales Mgr.; Phil Dunton, Chief Engineer; Janice Curliss, Traffic Mgr.; Eric Rosenfeld, Production Mgr. **Wattage:** 1,700,000.

1461 KCHJ-AM - 1010
5200 Standard St. Phone: (805)725-2121
Bakersfield, CA 93308 Fax: (805)721-1010
Free: (800)699-1490

Format: Hispanic. **Networks:** Independent. **Owner:** KCHJ Inc., at above address, (805)327-9711. **Founded:** 1949. **Operating Hours:** Continuous. **ADI:** Bakersfield, CA. **Wattage:** 5000 day; 1000 night.

1462 KCWR-FM - 107.1
3223 Sillect Ave. Phone: (805)326-1011
Bakersfield, CA 93308 Fax: (805)328-7503

Format: Country. **Owner:** Buck Ownes Productions Co., Inc., at above address. **Operating Hours:** Continuous. **Key Personnel:** Buck Owens, President; Mel Owens, Jr., CEO/General Mgr.

1463 KERI-AM - 1180
110 S. Montclair Phone: (805)832-3100
Ste. 205 Fax: (805)832-3164
Bakersfield, CA 93309
E-mail: keri@keri.com

Format: Religious; Talk. **Networks:** USA Radio; International Broadcasting; Moody Broadcasting. **Owner:** KWSO, Inc., at above address. **Founded:** 1950. **Formerly**: KWSO-AM (1984). **Operating Hours:** Continuous; 75% network, 25% local. **ADI:** Bakersfield, CA. **Key Personnel:** Don Bevilacqua, Owner; Terri Blankenship, Contact. **Wattage:** 50,000 day; 10,000 night. **Ad Rates:** $7.50-15 for 30 seconds; $9.50-18.75 for 60 seconds.

1464 KERN-AM - 1410
Box 2700 Phone: (805)328-1410
Bakersfield, CA 93303 Fax: (805)328-0190
Free: (800)640-KERN
E-mail: kernradio@lightspeednet.com

Format: Talk; News. **Networks:** Independent. **Founded:** 1932. **Operating Hours:** Continuous. **ADI:** Bakersfield, CA. **Key Personnel:** Roger Fessler, General Mgr.; Jonathan L. Zimney, Operations Dir., jzimney@aol.com. **Wattage:** 1000.

1465 KERO-TV - 23
321 21st St. Phone: (805)637-2323
Bakersfield, CA 93301 Fax: (805)324-3852
E-mail: kero99a@prodigy-com

Format: Commercial TV. **Networks:** ABC. **Owner:** McGraw-Hill, Inc., 1221 Avenue of the Americas, New York, NY 10020, (212)512-2000. **Founded:** 1953. **Operating Hours:** 20 hours. Daily; 62% network, 38% local. **ADI:** Bakersfield, CA. **Key Personnel:** Don Lundy, General Mgr.; Barry Zoeller, News Dir.; Roger Perez, Promotions Mgr.; Mike Knotek, General Sales Mgr. **Wattage:** 1,750,000.

1466 KGEO-AM - 1230
1400 Sastun Dr. No. 134 Phone: (805)631-1230
Box 260 Fax: (805)327-0786
Bakersfield, CA 93309

Format: News; Talk. **Networks:** NBC. **Founded:** 1946. **Formerly**: KGEE-AM (1979); KGAM-AM (1988). **Operating Hours:** Continuous. **ADI:** Bakersfield, CA. **Key Personnel:** Rogers Brandon, General Mgr.; Bill Curtis, Operations Mgr.; Rich Watson, Sales Mgr. **Wattage:** 1000.

1467 KGET-TV - 17
2831 Eye St. Phone: (805)327-7511
Bakersfield, CA 93301 Fax: (805)327-1994

Format: Commercial TV. **Networks:** NBC. **Operating Hours:** Continuous. **ADI:** Bakersfield, CA. **Key Personnel:** Ray Watson, General Mgr.; Shirley Sanford, Program Dir.; Tom Randour, General Sales Mgr.; Jack Bowe, News Dir.

1468 KGFM-FM - 101.5
1400 Easton Dr., Ste.144 Phone: (805)631-1410
PO Box 2700 Fax: (805)326-6388
Bakersfield, CA 93303-2700

Format: Soft Rock. **Networks:** Independent. **Founded:** 1964. **Formerly**: KGEE-FM (1968). **Operating Hours:** Continuous; 100% local. **ADI:** Bakersfield, CA. **Key Personnel:** Roger Fessler, General Mgr.; Chris Edwards, Operations Mgr., phone (805)635-1700, cedwards@lightspeed.net; Rich Watson, Sales Mgr. **Local Programs:** *Love Songs and Dedications*, Rex Howard. **Wattage:** 4800. **Ad Rates:** Combined advertising rates available with KERN-AM, KERN-FM, KGEO, KBID, KLYD-FM.

1469 KHIS-AM - 800
1100 Mohawk St., Ste. 280 Phone: (805)322-9929
Bakersfield, CA 93309-7416 Fax: (805)322-9239
E-mail: rickn@lightspeed.net

Format: Religious. **Networks:** Independent. **Founded:** 1959. **Operating Hours:** 5 a.m.-midnight. **ADI:** Bakersfield, CA. **Key Personnel:** Davis Nathan, General Mgr.; Rick Neuwirth, Operations/Sales/Prog. Mgr., rickn@lightspeed.net. **Wattage:** 1000 day; 440 night. **Ad Rates:** $15 for 60 seconds.

1470 KHIS-FM - 96.5
521 H St. Phone: (805)327-0631
Bakersfield, CA 93304 Fax: (805)327-0633

Format: Religious. **Networks:** Independent. **Founded:** 1963. **Operating Hours:** 5 a.m.-1 a.m. Mon.-Fri.; 5 a.m.-midnight Saturday and Sunday. **ADI:** Bakersfield, CA. **Key Personnel:** Scott Williams, Station Mgr. **Wattage:** 50,000. **Ad Rates:** $5-10 for 30 seconds; $8-12 for 60 seconds.

1471 KIWI-FM - 92.1
5200 Standard St. Phone: (805)325-5494
Bakersfield, CA 93308 Fax: (805)327-0797

Format: Hispanic. **Networks:** Independent. **Owner:** KMAP Inc., at above address, (805)327-9711. **Founded:** 1986. **Operating Hours:** Continuous; 100% local. **ADI:** Bakersfield, CA. **Key Personnel:** Edwards R. Hopple, President; Mike Allen, General Mgr.; Lydia Vernon, Natl. Sales Mgr. **Wattage:** 6000. **Ad Rates:** $40-50 for 60 seconds.

1472 KKXX-FM - 105.3
1100 Mohawk St., Ste. 280 Phone: (661)322-9929
Bakersfield, CA 93309-7416 Fax: (661)322-7239
E-mail: x965@lightspeed.net

Format: Contemporary Hit Radio (CHR). **Networks:** Independent. **Founded:** 1963. **Formerly:** Lithosphere Broadcasting Lp. **Operating Hours:** Continuous. **ADI:** Bakersfield, CA. **Key Personnel:** Davis Nathan, General Mgr., davisn@lightspeed.net; Patti Amenta, General Sales Mgr., patriciah@lightspeed.net; Sherry Sherrer, Local Sales Mgr., sherris@lightspeed.net; Chris Squires, Dir. of Bakersfield Programming, csquires@lightspeed.net; Carol Cummings, Office Mgr.; Debra Rivera, Traffic Dir.; Craig marshall, Music Dir., phone (661)323-KKXX, craigm@lightspeed.net. **Wattage:** 50 KW. **URL:** http://www.x965.com.

1473 KLLY-FM - 95.3
3651 Pegasus Phone: (805)393-1900
Bakersfield, CA 93308 Fax: (805)393-1915
E-mail: klly@klly.com

Format: Adult Contemporary. **Founded:** 1985. **Operating Hours:** Continuous; 100% local. **ADI:** Bakersfield, CA. **Key Personnel:** Randy Warwick, General Mgr.; Mark McKay, Program Dir.; Woody Chaves, News Dir.; Diana Armstrong, Office Mgr. **Wattage:** 12,500. **Ad Rates:** $30-45 for 60 seconds.

1474 KNZR-AM - 1560
PO Box 80658 Phone: (805)393-1900
Bakersfield, CA 93380 Fax: (805)393-1915

Format: Talk; News. **Networks:** CBS. **Owner:** Buckley Broadcasting, at above address. **Founded:** 1935. **Formerly**: KPMC-AM (1992). **Operating Hours:** Continuous. **ADI:** Bakersfield, CA. **Key Personnel:** Woody Chaves, News Dir.; Randy Warwick, General Mgr.; Chris Townshend, Program Dir. **Wattage:** 25,000. **Ad Rates:** $26 for 60 seconds.

1475 KSUV-FM - 102.9
3701 Pegasus Dr., Ste. 102 Phone: (805)393-0103
Bakersfield, CA 93308-6842 Fax: (805)393-0286

Format: Adult Contemporary; Hispanic; Ethnic. **Founded:** 1988. **Formerly**: KXEM-FM. **Operating Hours:** Continuous. **ADI:** Bakersfield, CA. **Key Personnel:** Richard Keating Keating, General Mgr.; Carmando Cuellar, Program Dir.; Bruce Moreno, General Sales Mgr. **Wattage:** 20,500. **Ad Rates:** Advertising accepted; rates available upon request.

1476 KUVI-TV - 45
3223 Sillect Ave. Phone: (805)328-7545
Bakersfield, CA 93308 Fax: (805)328-7576

Format: Commercial TV. **Networks:** United Paramount Network. **Owner:** Buck Owens Prod. Inc., at above address, Bakersfield, CA 93388. **Founded:** 1988. **Formerly**: KDOB-TV, KUZZ-TV. **Operating Hours:** Continuous; 100% local. **ADI:** Bakersfield, CA. **Key Personnel:** Theresa Ford, Station Mgr., fax (805)328-7549, tford4@aol.com; Rich Ross, General Sales Mgr., rross4@aol.com; Teresa Ford, Program/Operations Mgr. **Wattage:** 5,000,000.

1477 KUZZ-AM - 550
3223 Sillect Ave. Phone: (805)326-1011
Bakersfield, CA 93308 Fax: (805)328-9535

Format: Country. **Simulcasts:** KUZZ-FM. **Owner:** Buck Owens Production Co., Inc., at above address, Fax: (805)328-7535. **Founded:** 1958. **Formerly**: KCWR-AM. **Operating Hours:** Continuous. **ADI:** Bakersfield, CA. **Key Personnel:** Buck Owens, President; Mel Owens, Jr., General Mgr.; Evan Birdwell, Program Mgr.; Julie Randolph, Local Sales Manager; Harvey Campbell, National Sales Manager. **Wattage:** 5000.

1478 KUZZ-FM - 107.9
3223 Sillect Ave. Phone: (805)326-1011
Bakersfield, CA 93308

Format: Contemporary Country. **Simulcasts:** KUZZ-AM. **Owner:** Buck Owens Production Co., Inc., at above address, Fax: (805)328-7535. **Founded:** 1968. **Formerly:** KKXX-FM. **Operating Hours:** Continuous. **ADI:** Bakersfield, CA. **Key Personnel:** Buck Owens, President; Mel Owens, Jr., CEO and General Mgr.; Evan Bridwell, Program Dir.; Julie Randolph, Local Sales Manager; Harvey Campbell, National Sales Manager. **Wattage:** 5800 ERP.

1479 KWAC-AM - 1490
5200 Standard St. Phone: (805)327-9711
Bakersfield, CA 93308 Fax: (805)327-0797

Format: Hispanic. **Owner:** KMAP, Inc., at above address. **Founded:** 1946. **Formerly**: KMAP-AM (1960). **Operating Hours:** Continuous; 2% network, 98% local. **ADI:** Bakersfield, CA. **Key Personnel:** Edwards R. Hopple, President; Mike Allen, General Mgr.; Lydia Vernon, Natl. Sales Mgr.; Loca Trevino, Program Dir. **Wattage:** 1000. **Ad Rates:** $21-30 for 30 seconds; $26-34 for 60 seconds.

1480 Time Warner Cable
3600 N. Sillect Ave. Phone: (805)327-8655
Bakersfield, CA 93308 Fax: (805)327-3721

Founded: 1966. **Formerly**: Warner Cable. **Cities Served:** subscribing households 83,000; 90 channels.

BALBOA

1481 California Philanthropy Report
California Philanthropic Sector
PO Box 4098 Phone: (714)675-7175
Balboa, CA 92661
Journal on philanthropy. **Freq:** Quarterly. **Key Personnel:** Chris Stuart, Editor. **ISSN:** 1065-7282. **Subscription Rates:** $68. **Remarks:** Advertising accepted; rates available upon request.
Circ: (Not Reported)

BANNING, pop. 14,020.

SE CA. Riverside Co. 22 mi. NW of Palm Springs. Resort. Industrial park. Electronic components, shirts, cabinets and trailers manufactured. Fruit farms. Apricots, peaches. Livestock.

1482 The Record-Gazette
Record, Inc.
218 N. Murray St. Phone: (909)849-4586
PO Box 727 Fax: (909)849-2437
Banning, CA 92220-0005
Newspaper. **Founded:** 1908. **Freq:** Mon.-Fri. **Print Method:** Offset. **Cols./Page:** 6. **Col. Width:** 25 nonpareils. **Col. Depth:** 294 agate lines. **Key Personnel:** Charlie Ferrell, Editor and Publisher. **Subscription Rates:** Free; $63 by mail. **Remarks:** Accepts advertising.
Ad Rates: GLR: $10.55 **Circ:** Paid 2,962
BW: $10.08 Free 15,500
SAU: $8.50
PCI: $10.08

1483 The Record-Gazette TMC
Record, Inc.
218 N. Murray St. Phone: (909)849-4586
PO Box 727 Fax: (909)849-2437
Banning, CA 92220-0005
Shopper. **Founded:** 1957. **Freq:** Weekly (Wed.). **Print Method:** Offset. **Cols./Page:** 6. **Col. Width:** 22 nonpareils. **Col. Depth:** 294 agate lines. **Key Personnel:** Charles R. Freeman, Publisher. **Subscription Rates:** $63. **Remarks:** Accepts advertising. **Formerly**: Record-Gazette Pass Area This Week (1989); This Week.
Ad Rates: BW: $1,096.50 **Circ:** Free 17,600

BARSTOW, pop. 17,690.

SE CA. San Bernardino Co. 55 mi. NE of San Bernardino. Silver, borax, salt, barium mines. Agriculture. Alfalfa, cotton, melons, poultry.

1484 Barstow Log
Aerotech
Public Affairs Office MCLB Phone: (760)577-6430
PO Box 110100 Fax: (760)577-6350
Barstow, CA 92311-5001
Publication E-mail: bokholtw@bam.usmc.mil; aerosale@netport.com
Publisher E-mail: aerotech@netport.com

Military base publication for Marine Corps Logistics Base, Barstow. **Founded:** Nov. 1996. **Freq:** Weekly. **Print Method:** Offset. **Trim Size:** 11 1/2 x 13 3/4. **Cols./Page:** 5. **Col. Width:** 1.875 inches. **Col. Depth:** 13 inches. **Key Personnel:** Paul Kinison, Publisher. **Subscription Rates:** Free to qualified subscribers. **Remarks:** Accepts advertising. **Formerly**: MCLB today!.
Ad Rates: PCI: $5.50 **Circ:** Non-paid 3,500

1485 Desert Dispatch
130 Coolwater Ln. Phone: (619)256-2257
Barstow, CA 92311-3222 Fax: (619)256-0685

General newspaper. **Founded:** 1917. **Freq:** Mon.-Sat. (eve.). **Print Method:** Offset. **Cols./Page:** 8. **Col. Width:** 21 nonpareils. **Col. Depth:** 301 agate lines. **Key Personnel:** Kenneth O. Light, Publisher. **Subscription Rates:** $72 individuals. **Remarks:** Accepts advertising.
Ad Rates: PCI: $7.56 **Circ:** Mon.-Sat. ★5,529

1486 KDUC-FM - 94.3
PO Box 250 Phone: (619)256-2121
Barstow, CA 92311 Fax: (619)256-5090
Free: (800)852-7850
E-mail: kduc943@aol.com

Format: Oldies. **Simulcasts:** KDUQ FM. **Networks:** Westwood One Radio; Satellite Music Network. **Owner:** Tele-Media Broadcasting LLC, at above address. **Founded:** 1986. **Formerly:** KPRD-FM; First American Communications Corp. **Operating Hours:** Continuous; 100% local. **ADI:** Los Angeles (Corona & San Bernardino), CA. **Key Personnel:** Tom Shealy, General Mgr.; John Simmons, General Sales Mgr.; Richard Korzuch, Station Mgr. **Local Programs:** *Casey's Top 40*, Casey Kasem; *Chamber Roundtable*, Michael Garcia, (619)256-2121, Fax (619)256-5090; *Hot Mix*, Michael Garcia; *Sunday Night Killer Oldies Show with Art Laboe*, Art Labde. **Wattage:** 25,000. **Ad Rates:** $11-15 for 30 seconds; $15-20 for 60 seconds. Combined advertising rates available with KSZL-AM. **URL:** http://www.highdesert.com/kduc.

1487 KDUQ-FM - 105.5
PO Box 250
Barstow, CA 92312

Format: Adult Contemporary. **Networks:** ABC; Westwood One Radio; Jones Satellite. **Owner:** First American Communications Corp., at above address. **Operating Hours:** Continuous. **Key Personnel:** Tom Shealy, General Mgr.; John Simmons, General Sales Mgr.; Kenn Price, Business Mgr.; Mike Garcia, Program Dir. **Wattage:** 25,000. **Ad Rates:** Advertising accepted; rates available upon request.

1488 KSZL-AM - 1230
PO Box 250 Phone: (760)256-2121
Barstow, CA 92311 Fax: (760)256-5090
Free: (800)852-7850
E-mail: kduc943@aol.com

Format: Talk; Ethnic. **Networks:** ABC; Westwood One Radio; EFM. **Owner:** Tele-Media Broadcasting, LLC, at above address, Free: (800)944-5382. **Founded:** 1986. **Formerly**: KWTC-AM; First American Communications Corp. **Operating Hours:** Continuous; 90% network, 10% local. **ADI:** Los Angeles (Corona & San Bernardino), CA. **Key Personnel:** Tom Shealy, General Mgr.; John Simmons, General Sales Mgr.; Michael Garcia, Program Dir. **Local Programs:** *Chamber Roundtable*, Michael Garcia; *Las Horas Alegres (Spanish Music)* 7 a.m.-12 p.m. Saturday. **Wattage:** 1000. **Ad Rates:** $8-12 for 30 seconds; $12-15 for 60 seconds. Combined advertising rates available with KDUC-FM, KDUQ-FM. **URL:** http://www.highdesert.com/kduc.

BAYSIDE

1489 Borderlands
Borderland Sciences Research Foundation
PO Box 220 Phone: (707)825-7733
Bayside, CA 95524 Fax: (707)825-7779
Free: (888)825-2773
Publisher E-mail: info@borderlands.com; bsrf@asis.com

Journal for scholars and researchers "on the frontiers of science and awareness.". **Subtitle:** a Quarterly Journal of Borderland Research. **Founded:** Feb. 1945. **Freq:** Quarterly. **Print Method:** Web offset. **Trim Size:** 8 1/2 x 11. **Cols./Page:** 2. **Key Personnel:** Michael Theroux, Editor and Publisher, editor@borderlands.com; Patrick Armstrong, Business Mgr. **ISSN:** 0897-0394. **Subscription Rates:** $25 individuals. **Remarks:** Advertising accepted; rates available upon request. **URL:** http://www.borderlands.com. **Formerly**: Journal of Borderland Research (1992).
Circ: Paid ‡1,100
Non-paid ‡100

BELL, pop. 25,450.

S. CA. Los Angeles Co. 6 mi. S. of Los Angeles. Residential. Manufactures steel and ornamental iron products, paint, auto parts, airplane engines, cabinets.

1490 Bell/Maywood/Cudahy Industrial Post
Wave Community Newspapers
819 W. Whitter Blvd. Phone: (213)727-1117
Montebello, CA 90640-3623 Fax: (213)727-9515

Newspaper. **Founded:** 1917. **Freq:** Semiweekly (Wed. and Sat.). **Print Method:** Offset. **Cols./Page:** 6. **Col. Width:** 26 nonpareils. **Col. Depth:** 301 agate lines. **Key Personnel:** Arthur J. Aquilar, Exec.Editor/Publisher. **Subscription Rates:** $125 by mail /yr.; Free local. **Remarks:** Advertising accepted; rates available upon request.
Circ: Paid 134
Free 21,662

BELL GARDENS

1491 Bell Gardens Review
Wave Community Newspapers
819 W. Whitter Blvd. Phone: (213)727-1117
Montebello, CA 90640-3623 Fax: (213)727-9515

Community newspaper. **Founded:** 1917. **Freq:** Semiweekly (Wed. and Sat.). **Print Method:** Offset. **Cols./Page:** 6. **Col. Width:** 26 nonpareils. **Col. Depth:** 301 agate lines. **Key Personnel:** Arthur Aguilar, Exec. Editor/Publisher. **Subscription Rates:** Free; $125 by mail. **Remarks:** Advertising accepted; rates available upon request.
Circ: Paid 70

BELLFLOWER, pop. 53,441.

S. CA. Los Angeles Co. 8 mi. N. of Long Beach. Residential.

1492 American Fire Journal
9072 E. Artesia Blvd., Ste. 7 Phone: (562)866-1664
Bellflower, CA 90706-6299 Fax: (562)867-6434
Publisher E-mail: afjm@access1.net

Magazine about fire protection. **Founded:** 1949. **Freq:** Monthly. **Print Method:** Offset. **Trim Size:** 8 1/2 x 11. **Cols./Page:** 4 and 3. **Col. Width:** 28 and 55 nonpareils. **Col. Depth:** 140 agate lines. **Key Personnel:** Carol Carlsen Brooks, Editor; John Ackerman, Publisher; Bruce Davis, Advertising. **ISSN:** 0739-3709. **Subscription Rates:** $22.95 individuals; $42 institutions; $3.50 single issue. **Formerly**: Western Fire Journal.
Ad Rates: BW: $980 **Circ:** ‡5,800
4C: $1,755

BELVEDERE, pop. 2,401.

W. CA. Marin Co. 5 mi. N of Saulsalito. Residential.

1493 E.L.A. Brooklyn-Belvedere Comet
Eastern Group Publications Inc.
2500 S. Atlantic Blvd., No. A Phone: (213)263-5743
Los Angeles, CA 90040-2004 Fax: (213)263-9169

Hispanic community newspaper (English and Spanish). **Founded:** 1950. **Freq:** Weekly (Thurs.). **Print Method:** Offset. **Trim Size:** 13 x 21 1/2. **Cols./Page:** 6. **Col. Width:** 2 1/16 inches. **Col. Depth:** 294 agate lines. **Key Personnel:** Dolores Sanchez, Publisher; John Sanchez, Advertising Mgr. **Subscription Rates:** $92.50 individuals. **Remarks:** Accepts advertising.
Ad Rates: GLR: $28 **Circ:** Paid ‡26
BW: $3,150 Free ‡5,300
4C: $4,281
SAU: $28
PCI: $28

BEN LOMOND

1494 AGAIN Magazine
Conciliar Press
PO Box 76 Phone: (831)336-5118
Ben Lomond, CA 95005-0076 Fax: (831)336-8882
Free: (800)967-7377
Publisher E-mail: marketing@conciliarpress.com

Journal featuring articles on Orthodox Christianity. **Subtitle:** A Call for the People of God to Return to Their Roots in Historic Christianity Once... Again. **Founded:** Jan. 1977. **Freq:** Quarterly. **Trim Size:** 8 1/2 x 11. **Cols./Page:** 3. **Col. Width:** 14 picas. **Col. Depth:** 9 inches. **Key Personnel:** Weldon M. Hardenbrook, Editor, phone (408)3362228; Raymond L. Zell, Managing Editor; Peter E. Gillquist, Publisher. **ISSN:** 0885-9795. **Subscription Rates:** $14.50; $16.50 other countries. **Remarks:** Advertising not accepted. **URL:** http://www.conciliarpress.com.
Circ: Paid 5,000
Free 50

BENICIA, pop. 15,376.

W. CA. Solano Co. 30 mi. NE of San Francisco, on Strait of Carquinez. Boat connections. Dredges manufactured. Agriculture.

1495 Benicia Herald
Gibson Publications, Inc.
820 1st St. Phone: (707)745-0733
Benicia, CA 94510-3216 Fax: (707)557-6380

Daily newspaper. **Founded:** 1898. **Freq:** Daily. **Print Method:** Offset. **Trim Size:** 12 1/2 x 21 1/2. **Cols./Page:** 6. **Col. Width:** 2 inches. **Col. Depth:** 21 1/2 inches. **Key Personnel:** John R. Moses, Editor. **Remarks:** Accepts advertising.
Ad Rates: BW: $630 **Circ:** Free ❑6,128
4C: $240 Paid ❑4,891
SAU: $5
PCI: $6.95

1496 etc magazine
B B & B Publishing
1036 1st St. Phone: (707)746-8368
Benicia, CA 94510 Fax: (707)746-6102

Consumer lifestyle magazine covering the San Francisco North Bay. **Founded:** June 1995. **Freq:** Bimonthly. **Print Method:** Web. **Trim Size:** 7 1/4 x 10. **Key Personnel:** Deanna Brady, Contact. **Subscription Rates:** Free to qualified subscribers. **Remarks:** Accepts advertising.
Ad Rates: BW: $600 **Circ:** Non-paid 17,000

BERKELEY, pop. 103,328.

W. CA. Alameda Co. On San Francisco Bay, adjoining Oakland. Boat connections. University of California at Berkeley and several religious colleges, private schools. Manufactures gasoline engines, castings, steel tanks, structural aluminum, computer software, pumps, carbon dioxide, dry ice, silicate of soda.

1497 Agricultural History
University of California Press/Journals
2120 Berkeley Way Phone: (510)643-7154
Berkeley, CA 94720-0001 Fax: (510)642-9917
Publisher E-mail: journal@ucop.edu

Journal covering agricultural history. **Founded:** 1927. **Freq:** Quarterly. **Print Method:** Offset. **Trim Size:** 6 x9. **Cols./Page:** 1. **Col. Width:** 52 nonpareils. **Col. Depth:** 100 agate lines. **Key Personnel:** R. Douglas Hurt, Editor. **ISSN:** 0002-1482.

Subscription Rates: $34 individuals; $82 institutions; $20 students and retired.
Ad Rates: GLR: $133 **Circ:** ‡1,200
BW: $275

1498 American Journal of Comparative Law
School of Law (Boalt Hall) Phone: (510)643-6115
University of California Fax: (510)643-2698
Berkeley, CA 94720-7200
Law journal covering other countries, private, and international law. **Founded:** 1952. **Freq:** Quarterly. **Cols./Page:** 1. **Col. Width:** 54 nonpareils. **Col. Depth:** 101 agate lines. **Key Personnel:** Richard Buxbaum, Editor; Nancy Reiko Kato, Managing Editor. **Subscription Rates:** $30 individuals. **Remarks:** Advertising not accepted. **Online:** Westlaw; LEXIS-NEXIS.
Circ: 2,000

1499 Asian American and Pacific Islands Law Journal
University of California-Berkeley
Boalt Hall School of Law Phone: (510)643-9643
589 Simon Tower Fax: (510)643-6171
Berkeley, CA 94720-1900
Journal focusing on legal issues of concern to Asian Americans. **Cols./Page:** 2. **Key Personnel:** Theresa Han, Editor-in-Chief; Gary Braun, Editor. **Remarks:** Accepts advertising.
Circ: (Not Reported)

1500 Asian Law Journal
University of California-Berkeley
Boalt Hall School of Law Phone: (510)643-9643
589 Simon Tower Fax: (510)643-6171
Berkeley, CA 94720-1900
Publication E-mail: alj@rocketmail.com

Journal focusing on legal issues of concern to Asian Americans. **Founded:** May 1994. **Freq:** Annual. **Print Method:** Perfect bound. **Key Personnel:** Sheila Swaroop. **ISSN:** 1078-439X. **Subscription Rates:** $20 individuals; $20 single issue; $30 international rate. **Remarks:** Accepts advertising. **Online:** Westlaw. **URL:** http://www.law.berkeley.edu/~alj.
Ad Rates: BW: $250 **Circ:** Paid 200

1501 Bad Subjects
University of California
322 Wheeler Hall
Berkeley, CA 94720
Publication E-mail: bad@uclink.berkeley.edu

Journal that focuses on broadening the views on leftist and progressive work. **Subtitle:** Political Education for Everyday Life. **Founded:** Sept. 1992. **Freq:** 6/year. **Key Personnel:** Annalee Newitz, Co-Director, phone (510)486-0366, fax (510)642-8738. **Subscription Rates:** Free. **Remarks:** Advertising not accepted. **Available Online. URL:** http://eng.hss.cmu.edu/bs.
Circ: (Not Reported)

1502 Bay Sports Review
PO Box 4520 Phone: (925)934-7647
Berkeley, CA 94704 Fax: (925)934-7650
Publication E-mail: baysport@aol.com

Journal of sports-related articles and fan commentary for the San Francisco Bay Area. **Subtitle:** A Journal of Uncensored Fan Commentary. **Founded:** July 1991. **Freq:** Bimonthly. **Print Method:** Web. **Trim Size:** 13 x 10. **Cols./Page:** 3. **Col. Width:** 2 1/2 inches. **Col. Depth:** 10 inches. **Key Personnel:** Christopher Weills, Publisher; Paul Matson, Editor; Tom Stern, Editor. **ISSN:** 1067-0548. **Subscription Rates:** $26 for 12 issues. **Remarks:** Accepts advertising. **URL:** http://www.baysportsreview.com.
Ad Rates: BW: $1600.00 **Circ:** Paid 1,000
4C: $1900 Non-paid 49,000

1503 Berkeley Journal of Employment and Labor Law
University of California Press/Journals
2120 Berkeley Way Phone: (510)643-7154
Berkeley, CA 94720-0001 Fax: (510)642-9917
Publisher E-mail: journal@ucop.edu

Professional journal covering employment and labor law.

1504 Berkeley Journal of International Law
University of California Press/Journals
University of California Phone: (510)642-9759
126 Bualt Hall Fax: (510)643-6197
Berkeley, CA 94720
Publication E-mail: itbl@violet.berkeley.edu
Publisher E-mail: journal@ucop.edu

Journal covering international law. **Freq:** Semiannual. **Key Personnel:** Marge Dean, Advertising & Circulation Mgr. **Subscription Rates:** $45 individuals; $23 single issue. **Remarks:** Accepts advertising.
Ad Rates: BW: $275 **Circ:** (Not Reported)

1505 Berkeley Technology Law Journal
University of California Press/Journals
University of California, Berkeley Phone: (510)643-6454
587 Simon Hall Fax: (510)643-6816
Berkeley, CA 94720
Publisher E-mail: journal@ucop.edu

Journal covering technology and law. **Freq:** Semiannual. **Key Personnel:** Marge Dean, Advertising & Circulation Mgr. **Subscription Rates:** $50 individuals; $27 single issue. **Remarks:** Accepts advertising. **URL:** btlj@www.law.berkeley.edu; http://www.law.berkeley.edu/journal/btlj.
Ad Rates: BW: $275 **Circ:** (Not Reported)

1506 Berkeley Tri City Post
The Alameda Publishing Corp./Oakland Post
PO Box 1350 Phone: (510)763-1120
Oakland, CA 94604-1350 Fax: (510)763-9670

Black community newspaper. **Founded:** 1963. **Freq:** Semiweekly (Wed. and Sun.). **Print Method:** Offset. **Cols./Page:** 6. **Col. Width:** 1 1/16 inches. **Col. Depth:** 21 1/2 inches. **Key Personnel:** Gail Berkley, Editor; Thomas Berkley, Publisher; Donald V. Welcher, Advertising Mgr. **Subscription Rates:** $42 individuals. **Remarks:** Accepts advertising.
Ad Rates: BW: $5,641.17 **Circ:** Free ‡20,000

1507 Berkeley Women's Law Journal
University of California Press/Journals
University of California Phone: (510)642-6263
491 Simon Hall
Berkeley, CA 94720
Publication E-mail: bwlj@violet.berkeley.edu
Publisher E-mail: journal@ucop.edu

Journal covering women and law. **Freq:** Annual. **Key Personnel:** Marge Dean, Advertising & Circulation Mgr. **Subscription Rates:** $18 individuals; $40 institutions; $9 students. **Remarks:** Accepts advertising.
Ad Rates: BW: $275 **Circ:** (Not Reported)

1508 California Business Law Reporter
Continuing Education of the Bar (CEB)
2300 Shattuck Ave. Phone: (510)642-3974
Berkeley, CA 94704 Fax: (510)642-3788
Free: (800)232-3444

Legal recent developments in business law. **Founded:** Jan. 1980. **Freq:** 6/year. **Print Method:** Offset. **Cols./Page:** 2. **Col. Width:** 21 picas. **Col. Depth:** 55 picas. **Key Personnel:** Hale Kronenberg, Editor. **ISSN:** 0199-669X. **Subscription Rates:** $175 individuals. **Alt. Formats:** CD-ROM.

1509 California Engineer
California Engineer Publishing Co.
University of California, Berkeley Phone: (510)642-8679
221 Bechtel Engineering Ctr.
Berkeley, CA 94720-0001
Collegiate engineering journal serving the students, faculty, and staff of the University of California Engineering Colleges at Berkeley, Los Angeles, Davis, Irvine, San Diego, and Santa Barbara. **Founded:** 1922. **Freq:** Quarterly (during academic year). **Print Method:** Offset. **Trim Size:** 8 1/2 x 11. **Cols./Page:** 3. **Col. Width:** 15 picas. **Col. Depth:** 9 inches. **ISSN:** 0008-1027. **Subscription Rates:** $5 individuals. **Remarks:** Accepts advertising.
Ad Rates: BW: $500 **Circ:** Controlled ‡10,000

1510 California Law Review
University of California Press/Journals
2120 Berkeley Way Phone: (510)643-7154
Berkeley, CA 94720-0001 Fax: (510)642-9917
Publisher E-mail: journal@ucop.edu

Legal journal. **Founded:** 1912. **Freq:** 6/year (during the academic year). **Print Method:** Offset. **Trim Size:** 5 1/2 x 8. **Cols./Page:** 1. **Col. Width:** 57 nonpareils. **Col. Depth:** 105 agate lines. **ISSN:** 0008-1221. **Subscription Rates:** $40 individuals; $9 out of country surface postage; $11 single issue. **Remarks:** Accepts advertising.
Ad Rates: BW: $275 **Circ:** ‡1,500

1511 California Management Review (CMR)
University of California, Berkeley
S549 Haas School of Business, Phone: (510)642-7159
No. 1900 Fax: (510)642-1318
Berkeley, CA 94720-1900
Publication E-mail: cmr@haas.berkeley.edu

Magazine covering research and creative thought in business and public policy, corporate strategy and organization, and the international economy. **Founded:** 1958. **Freq:** Quarterly. **Print Method:** Offset. **Trim Size:** 7 x 10. **Cols./Page:** 1. **Col. Width:** 56 nonpareils. **Col. Depth:** 112 agate lines. **Key Personnel:** David Vogel, Editor. **ISSN:** 0008-1256. **Subscription Rates:** $65 individuals; $105 individuals /two years; $135 individuals /three years; $90 institutions; $145 institutions /two years; $190 institutions /three years; $105 other countries; $175 other countries /two years; $235 other countries /three years. **Remarks:** Color advertising not accepted. **Alt. Formats:** Microform.
Ad Rates: BW: $350 **Circ:** ‡5,500

1512 California Monthly
California Alumni Association
Alumni House Phone: (510)642-5781
Berkeley, CA 94720-7520 Fax: (510)642-6252
Free: (800)225-2586

University alumni magazine. **Founded:** Jan. 1923. **Freq:** 6/year. **Print Method:** Web offset. **Trim Size:** 8 1/2 x 11. **Cols./Page:** 4. **Col. Width:** 32 nonpareils. **Col. Depth:** 194 agate lines. **Key Personnel:** Russell Schoch, Editor, phone (510)642-5782, russ@alumni.berkeley.edu; William Rodarmor, Managing Editor, phone (510)642-0760, rodarmor@alumni.berkeley.edu; Lora Dinga, Advertising Mgr., phone (415)898-6400. **ISSN:** 0008-1302. **Subscription Rates:** $40 individuals. **Remarks:** Accepts advertising. **URL:** http://www.alumni.berkeley.edu.
Ad Rates: GLR: $12 **Circ:** Paid ‡80,000
BW: $2,570 Non-paid ‡7,000
4C: $3,870

1513 Cambridge Quarterly of Healthcare Ethics
Cambridge University Press
University Hall
University of California, Berkeley
Berkeley, CA 94720

Journal focusing on the challenges of biology, medicine and healthcare and those individuals on ethics committees. **Subtitle:** The International Journal for Healthcare Ethics and Ethics Committees. **Freq:** Quarterly. **Key Personnel:** David Thomasma, Editor; Thomasine Kushner, Editor; Steve Heilig, Editor. **ISSN:** 0963-1801. **Subscription Rates:** $94 institutions; $47 individuals. **Remarks:** Advertising accepted; rates available upon request. **Also known as:** CQ.
Circ: (Not Reported)

1514 Carmelite Digest
Discalced Carmelites
2542 Hilgard Ave. Phone: (510)549-3918
Berkeley, CA 94709-1105 Fax: (510)549-3964
Publication E-mail: elijah@vdn.com

Journal providing historical, biographical, and liturgical commentary, with emphasis on contributions to the church by Ste. Theresa of Avila and other Carmelite Saints. **Founded:** 1986. **Freq:** Quarterly. **Trim Size:** 5 1/2 x 8 1/2. **Cols./Page:** 1. **Col. Width:** 4 inches. **Col. Depth:** 7 inches. **Key Personnel:** Rev. David Centner, O.C.D., Editor. **ISSN:** 0887-123X. **Subscription Rates:** $15; $19 other countries. **Remarks:** Accepts advertising.
Ad Rates: BW: $300 **Circ:** ‡2,014

1515 The Cherotic (r)Evolutionary
Inter-Relations
PO Box 11445 Phone: (510)526-7858
Berkeley, CA 94712 Fax: (510)524-2053

"'Zine about 'the edge' for and by people on the edge." Includes erotic and transgressive fiction, poetry, and art. **Founded:** Apr. 1991. **Freq:** Irregular. **Trim Size:** 8 1/2 x 11. **Key Personnel:** Frank Moore, Editor and Publisher, fmoore@eroplay.com; Linda Mac, Editor and Publisher, lindamac@eroplay.com; Michael LaBash, Art Editor, phone (510)524-2053, mlabash@babylabash.com; Alexi Malenky, Circulation Mgr., phone (510)652-9764, coralhei@eroplay.com. **ISSN:** 1083-8872. **Subscription Rates:** $5 single issue. **Remarks:** Accepts advertising. **URL:** http://www.eroplay.com.
Circ: 500

1516 Computer Currents
Computer Currents Publishing, Inc.
1250 Ninth St. Phone: (510)527-0333
Berkeley, CA 94710 Fax: (510)527-4106
Free: (800)365-7773
Publication E-mail: cceditorial@compcurr.com; ccgenmail@compcurr.com; mail@compcurr.com

Magazine for business microcomputer users. **Subtitle:** National Business Computer Magazine. **Founded:** 1983. **Freq:** Biweekly. **Print Method:** Heatset. **Trim Size:** 10 1/8 x 12 1/4. **Cols./Page:** 4. **Col. Width:** 13 1/2 picas. **Col. Depth:** 12 inches. **Key Personnel:** Robert Luhn, Editor-in-Chief; Stan Politi, Publisher. **ISSN:** 8756-0046. **Subscription Rates:** $29.95 individuals. **URL:** http://www.currents.net.
Ad Rates: BW: $2,850 **Circ:** Paid 1,000
4C: $3,600 Non-paid 670,000

1517 Connexions
People's Translation Service
PO Box 14431 Phone: (510)549-3505
Berkeley, CA 94701-5431
Collectively-run magazine featuring news and interviews otherwise unattainable in the English-language press. **Subti-**

tle: An International Women's Quarterly. **Founded:** May 1981. **Freq:** Quarterly. **Print Method:** Offset. **Trim Size:** 8 1/2 x 11. **Cols./Page:** 3. **Col. Width:** 2 1/2 inches. **Key Personnel:** Donna Scism. **ISSN:** 0886-7062. **Subscription Rates:** $15 individuals; $24 institutions. **Remarks:** Accepts advertising.
Ad Rates: BW: $600 **Circ:** Paid ‡1,000
Non-paid ‡150

1518 Contemporary Drug Problems
Federal Legal Publications, Inc.
2000 Hearst Ave. Phone: (415)642-5208
Berkeley, CA 94709 Fax: (415)642-7175

Policy, social science, legal, historical, and international studies of alcohol and drug problems. **Founded:** 1972. **Freq:** Quarterly. **Print Method:** Offset. Uses mats. **Cols./Page:** 1. **Col. Width:** 60 nonpareils. **Col. Depth:** 112 agate lines. **Key Personnel:** Robin Room, Editor; Martin Greenberg, Publisher. **ISSN:** 0091-4509. **Subscription Rates:** $45.
Circ: ‡2,000

1519 Coracle
1516 Euclid Ave. Phone: (510)849-2540
Berkeley, CA 94708
Literary journal covering poetry and fiction. **Founded:** 1994. **Freq:** Semiannual. **Trim Size:** 8 x 10. **Key Personnel:** Jane Hall, Editor. **Subscription Rates:** $12 individuals; $8 single issue. **Remarks:** Advertising not accepted.
Circ: Paid 50

1520 The Daily Californian
Independent Berkeley Student Publishing Co. Inc.
600 Eshleman Hall Phone: (510)548-8300
University of California Berkeley Fax: (510)849-2803
Berkeley, CA 94720
Publication E-mail: dailycal@ocf.berkeley.edu; dailycal@dailycal.org

Tabloid newspaper covering both the University of California and the city of Berkeley. **Subtitle:** Berkeley's Independent Daily: Established 1871. **Founded:** 1871. **Freq:** Daily (morn.). **Print Method:** Offset. **Trim Size:** 10 1/4 x 16. **Cols./Page:** 5. **Col. Width:** 11.5 picas. **Col. Depth:** 96 picas. **Key Personnel:** Hubert Brucker, General Mgr. **ISSN:** 1050-2300. **Subscription Rates:** $95 individuals. **Remarks:** Accepts advertising. **URL:** http://server.berkeley.edu/dailycal/; http://www.dailycal.org.
Ad Rates: GLR: $7 **Circ:** Paid 200
BW: $1,172 Free 23,000
4C: $1,772
CNU: $17
PCI: $17

1521 Design Book Review
1418 Spring Way Phone: (510)486-1956
Berkeley, CA 94708 Fax: (510)644-3930
Publication E-mail: dbreview@ix.netcom.com

Magazine reviewing architecture and design publications; including interviews, essays, and design criticism in the fields of architecture, landscape architecture, urbanism, and design. **Founded:** 1983. **Freq:** Quarterly. **Print Method:** Offset. **Trim Size:** 8 3/16 x 11. **Cols./Page:** 2. **Col. Width:** 36 picas. **Col. Depth:** 9 inches. **Key Personnel:** Richard Ingersoll, Editor; Cathy Lang Ho, Managing Editor; Elizabeth Snowden, Publisher; John Parman, Publisher. **ISSN:** 0737-5344. **Subscription Rates:** $34 individuals; $30 students and retirees; $98 institutions. **Remarks:** Accepts advertising.
Ad Rates: BW: $990 **Circ:** ‡7,000
4C: $1,590

1522 Early China
Institute of East Asian Studies
2223 Fulton St., 6th Fl. Phone: (510)643-6325
Berkeley, CA 94720-2318 Fax: (510)643-7062
Publisher E-mail: easia@uclink.berkeley.edu

Scholarly journal covering prehistoric China history. **Founded:** 1978. **Freq:** Annual. **Trim Size:** 6 x 9. **Cols./Page:** 1. **Col. Width:** 26 picas. **Key Personnel:** Prof. Donald Harper, Editor. **Subscription Rates:** $30 individuals. **Remarks:** Advertising not accepted.
Circ: Controlled 350

1523 Ecology Law Quarterly
University of California Press/Journals
University of California Phone: (510)642-0457
493 Simon Hall Fax: (510)643-9042
Berkeley, CA 94720
Publisher E-mail: journal@ucop.edu

Journal covering ecology and law. **Freq:** Quarterly. **Key Personnel:** Marge Dean, Advertising & Circulation Mgr. **Subscription Rates:** $30 individuals; $50 institutions; $22 students; $8 single issue; $14 single issue institutions; $6 single issue students. **Remarks:** Accepts advertising.
Ad Rates: BW: $275 **Circ:** (Not Reported)

1524 Ecology Terrain
Ecology Center
2530 San Pablo Ave. Phone: (415)548-2220
Berkeley, CA 94702
Trade magazine covering environmental issues. **Subtitle:** Northern California's Environmental Magazine. **Founded:** 1969. **Freq:** Quarterly. **Key Personnel:** Laird Townsend, Editor. **Subscription Rates:** $15 individuals. **Remarks:** Accepts advertising.
Ad Rates: BW: $5 **Circ:** Paid 2,000

1525 Estate Planning and California Probate Reporter
California Continuing Education of the Bar
2300 Shattuck Ave. Phone: (510)642-2040
Berkeley, CA 94704 Fax: (510)642-3788
Free: (800)232-3444

Trade magazine concentrating on recent legislation and court decisions affecting estates, trusts, and related taxation in California. **Founded:** Oct. 1980. **Freq:** Bimonthly. **Print Method:** Offset/Electronic. **Trim Size:** 8 1/2 x 11. **Cols./Page:** 2. **Col. Width:** 21 picas. **Col. Depth:** 55 picas. **Key Personnel:** Jeffrey A. Dennis-Strathmeyer, Staff Editor, strathj@ceb.ucop.edu. **ISSN:** 0273-7027. **Subscription Rates:** $125 individuals. **Remarks:** Advertising not accepted. **Alt. Formats:** CD-ROM.
Circ: (Not Reported)

1526 Express
Express Publishing
PO Box 3198 Phone: (510)540-7400
Berkeley, CA 94703 Fax: (510)540-7700

Alternative community newspaper. **Founded:** Oct. 20, 1978. **Freq:** Weekly (Fri.). **Print Method:** Offset. **Trim Size:** 11 1/2 x 17. **Cols./Page:** 5. **Col. Width:** 11.5 picas. **Col. Depth:** 16 inches. **Key Personnel:** John Raeside, Editor, jraeside@eastbayexpress.com. **Subscription Rates:** Free; $25 by mail. **Remarks:** Accepts advertising.
Ad Rates: BW: $1,679 **Circ:** Free ‡65,000
4C: $2,554
PCI: $25.85

1527 Film Quarterly
University of California Press/Journals
2120 Berkeley Way Phone: (510)643-7154
Berkeley, CA 94720-0001 Fax: (510)642-9917
Publisher E-mail: journal@ucop.edu

Critical journal covering the art of cinema. **Founded:** 1945. **Freq:** Quarterly. **Print Method:** Offset. **Trim Size:** 8 1/2 x 11. **Cols./Page:** 2. **Col. Width:** 39 nonpareils. **Col. Depth:** 125 agate lines. **Key Personnel:** Ann Martin, Editor, phone (510)601-9010, fax (510)601-9036, ann.martin@ucop.edu. **ISSN:** 0015-1386. **Subscription Rates:** $25 individuals; $63 institutions. **Remarks:** Accepts advertising.
Ad Rates: GLR: $155 **Circ:** ‡1,500
BW: $390

1528 Five Fingers Review
Five Fingers Press
PO Box 12955 Phone: (510)632-5769
Berkeley, CA 94712-3955
Literary magazine covering fiction, poetry, and essays. **Founded:** 1984. **Freq:** Irregular. **Print Method:** Offset. **Trim Size:** 6 x 9. **Cols./Page:** 1. **Key Personnel:** Jaime Robles, General Editor, jrobles@best.com; Renata Ewing, Managing Editor; Sari Broner, Editor; Linda Norton, Editor. **Subscription Rates:** $10 single issue. **Remarks:** Accepts advertising.
Circ: Paid 1,000

1529 Folio
Pacifica Foundation
1929 Martin Luther King Jr. X-Way Phone: (510)848-6767
Fax: (510)848-3812
Berkeley, CA 94704
Radio guide (tabloid) for noncommercial radio stations. **Subtitle:** Program guide for KPFA-FM. **Founded:** 1949. **Freq:** Bimonthly. **Print Method:** Offset. **Cols./Page:** 4. **Col. Width:** 27 nonpareils. **Col. Depth:** 140 agate lines. **Key Personnel:** Ralph Steiner, Editor; Marci Lockwood, Publisher; Ralph Steiner, Advertising Mgr. **USPS:** 937-360. **Subscription Rates:** $60 individuals. **Remarks:** Accepts advertising. **URL:** http://www.kpfa.org.
Ad Rates: BW: $480 **Circ:** ‡21,000
PCI: $15

1530 The Four Seasons
Regional Parks Botanic Garden
Tilden Regional Park Phone: (510)841-8732
Berkeley, CA 94708-2396 Fax: (510)848-6025
Publisher E-mail: bgarden@ebparks.org

Professional journal covering natural history, biology, ecology, conservation, botany, and horticulture, with an emphasis on California's native plants. **Subtitle:** Journal of the Regional Parks Botanic Garden. **Founded:** Sept. 8, 1964. **Freq:** Annual. **Print Method:** Offset. **Trim Size:** 6 1/2 x 9 1/2. **Cols./Page:** 1. **Col. Width:** 4 1/2 inches. **Col. Depth:** 7 1/10 inches. **Key Personnel:** Stephen W. Edwards, Editor; Gregory Whipple, Asst. Editor/Circulation Mgr. **ISSN:** 0532-3215. **Subscription Rates:** $4 single issue. **Remarks:** Advertising not accepted.
Circ: Combined 431

1531 Gesar
2425 Hillside Ave. Fax: (510)845-7540
Berkeley, CA 94704
Magazine offering articles on Buddhism in the West, including Buddhist philosophy, psychology, and meditation practice. Includes relaxation practices and translations from Tibetan sources. **Founded:** 1973. **Freq:** Periodic. **Print Method:** Offset. **Trim Size:** 7 x 9 1/4. **Cols./Page:** 2. **Col. Width:** 33 nonpareils. **Col. Depth:** 108 agate lines. **Key Personnel:** Leslie Bradburn, Editor/Administration, phone (510)548-7539; Dharma Mudralanaya, Publisher, dharma-publishing@tdl.com. **ISSN:** 0738-2294. **Subscription Rates:** $12 individuals; $15 other countries; $3.50 single issue. **Remarks:** Accepts advertising.
Ad Rates: BW: $250 **Circ:** ‡3,000

1532 Health Marketing Quarterly
The Haworth Press, Inc.
PO Box 8566 Phone: (510)524-6144
Berkeley, CA 94707
Publisher E-mail: getinfo@haworthpressinc.com

Journal for marketing health and human services. **Founded:** 1983. **Freq:** Quarterly. **Key Personnel:** William J. Winston, Editor; Bill Cohen, Publisher. **ISSN:** 0735-9683. **Subscription Rates:** $45; $95 Industry; $200 libraries. **Remarks:** Accepts advertising. **Formerly:** Health Medical Care Services Review.
Ad Rates: BW: $300 **Circ:** (Not Reported)

1533 Hip Magazine
1563 Solano Ave., No. 137 Phone: (510)848-9650
Berkeley, CA 94707 Fax: (510)848-9639
Publisher E-mail: folks@hipmag.org

Educational magazine for deaf and hearing impaired children ages 8-14 years. **Founded:** Oct. 1994. **Freq:** Bimonthly. **Print Method:** Sheetfed offset. **Trim Size:** 11 x 17. **Key Personnel:** Robin Gladstone, Publisher; Ellen Dolich, Publisher. **ISSN:** 1090-5707. **Subscription Rates:** $16.95 individuals. **Remarks:** Accepts advertising.
Circ: Paid 8,000

1534 Home Energy
Energy Auditor and Retrofitter, Inc.
2124 Kitteredge St., No. 95
Berkeley, CA 94704
Publication E-mail: homeenergy@anl.gov

Trade magazine covering residential energy conservation issues. **Founded:** Oct. 1994. **Freq:** Bimonthly. **Print Method:** Web offset. **Key Personnel:** Colleen Turrell, Managing Editor, cturrell@dante.lbl.gov; Louis Rasky, Advertising & Marketing Mgr., larhem@dante.lbl.gov; Rebecca Anaya, Circulation Mgr., raahem@dante.lbl.gov. **ISSN:** 0896-9442. **Subscription Rates:** $49 individuals; $54 Canada; $59 other countries; $8.50 single issue. **Remarks:** Accepts advertising. **URL:** http://www.homeenergy.org.
Ad Rates: BW: $675 **Circ:** Combined ‡4,091
4C: $1,290

1535 Index to Foreign Legal Periodicals
University of California Press/Journals
2120 Berkeley Way Phone: (510)643-7154
Berkeley, CA 94720-0001 Fax: (510)642-9917
Publisher E-mail: journal@ucop.edu

Magazine covering legal periodicals published worldwide. **Founded:** 1960. **Freq:** Quarterly. **Trim Size:** 6 x 9. **Key Personnel:** T.H. Reynolds, Editor; R.K. Durkin, Managing Editor. **ISSN:** 0019-400X. **Subscription Rates:** $605 individuals. **Remarks:** Advertising not accepted.
Circ: 600

1536 Journal of Chinese Linguistics
Project on Linguistic Analysis
2222 Piedmont Ave. Phone: (510)642-5937
Berkeley, CA 94720 Fax: (510)841-7205
Publication E-mail: jcl@socrates.berkeley.edu

Journal covering Chinese linguistics. **Founded:** 1973. **Freq:** Semiannual. **Trim Size:** 5 1/2 x 8 1/2. **Cols./Page:** 1. **Col. Width:** 4 1/4 inches. **Col. Depth:** 6 1/2 inches. **Key Personnel:** Prof. William Wang. **ISSN:** 0091-3723. **Subscription Rates:** $25 individuals; $35 institutions. **Remarks:** Advertising not accepted.
Circ: (Not Reported)

1537 Journal of Customer Service in Marketing and Management
The Haworth Press, Inc.
PO Box 8566 Phone: (510)524-6144
Berkeley, CA 94707 Fax: (510)524-6144
Publisher E-mail: getinfo@haworthpressinc.com

Journal on marketing. **Founded:** 1994. **Freq:** Quarterly. **Trim Size:** 6 x 8 1/2. **Key Personnel:** William J. Winston, Editor; Bill Cohen, Publisher. **ISSN:** 1069-2533. **Subscription Rates:** $40 individuals 30% more for Canada; 40% more for other countries; $60 institutions 30% more for Canada; 40% more for other countries; $125 libraries 30% more for Canada; 40% more for other countries. **Remarks:** Accepts advertising.
Ad Rates: BW: $300 **Circ:** Paid 148

1538 Journal of Hospital Marketing
The Haworth Press, Inc.
PO Box 8566 Phone: (510)524-6144
Berkeley, CA 94707 Free: (800)342-9678
Publisher E-mail: getinfo@haworthpressinc.com

Journal on marketing hospital services. **Founded:** 1987. **Freq:** Biannual. **Trim Size:** 6x8 1/2. **Key Personnel:** William J. Winston, Editor; Bill Cohen, Publisher. **ISSN:** 0883-7570. **Subscription Rates:** $45 individuals 30% more for Canada; 40% more for other countries; $95 institutions 30% more for Canada; 40% more for other countries; $200 libraries 30% more for Canada; 40% more for other countries. **Remarks:** Accepts advertising.
Ad Rates: BW: $300 **Circ:** Controlled ‡250

1539 Journal of Professional Services Marketing
The Haworth Press, Inc.
PO Box 8566 Phone: (510)524-6144
Berkeley, CA 94707
Publisher E-mail: getinfo@haworthpressinc.com

Journal on services marketing. **Founded:** 1985. **Freq:** Biannual. **Trim Size:** 6x8 1/2. **Key Personnel:** William Winston, PHD, Editor; Bill Cohen, Publisher. **ISSN:** 0748-4623. **Subscription Rates:** $48 individuals 30% more for Canada; 40% more for other countries; $90 institutions 30% more for Caanda; 40% more for other countries; $225 libraries 30% more for Canada; 40% more for other countries. **Remarks:** Accepts advertising.
Ad Rates: BW: $300 **Circ:** Controlled ‡453

1540 Journal of Retailing
Elseiver
Dept. of Marketing
University of California
Berkeley, CA 94720
Publication E-mail: 102062-2525@compuserve.com
Publisher E-mail: fcentres@gpu.stv.ualberta.ca

Journal focusing on retailing, marketing, and general business. **Founded:** 1923. **Freq:** Quarterly. **Print Method:** offset. **Trim Size:** 6 7/8 x 10. **Cols./Page:** 1. **Col. Width:** 50 nonpareils. **Col. Depth:** 104 agate lines. **Key Personnel:** Louis P. Bucklin, Editor, phone (510)642-4782, fax (510)642-4700. **ISSN:** 0022-4359. **Subscription Rates:** $180 institutions; $200 institutions, other countries; $220 institutions, other countries airmail; $80 individuals; $100 other countries; $120 other countries airmail; $47.50 single issue; $52.50 single issue other couuntries; $57.50 single issue other countries airmail. **Remarks:** Accepts advertising.
Ad Rates: BW: $300 **Circ:** Paid 2,500

1541 Jump Cut
Jump Cut Associates
Box 865 Phone: (202)544-2798
Berkeley, CA 94701 Fax: (202)544-5076

Journal covering film, video, and media criticism. **Subtitle:** A Review of Contemporary Media. **Founded:** 1974. **Freq:** Annual. **Print Method:** Web offset. **Trim Size:** 8 1/4 x 10 3/4. **Key Personnel:** John Hess, Editor, jhess@iqc.apc.org; Chuck Kleinhaus, Editor; Julia Lesage, Editor. **ISSN:** 0146-5546. **Subscription Rates:** $20 individuals; $24 out of country; $10 single issue U.S.; $12 single issue out of country. **Remarks:** Accepts advertising. **URL:** http://www.tcf.ua.edu/jumpcut.
Ad Rates: BW: $250 **Circ:** Paid 3,000

1542 Linguistics of the Tibeto-Burma Area
University of California at Berkeley
1203 Dwinelle Hall Phone: (510)643-9910
Berkeley, CA 94720-2652 Fax: (510)643-9911

Scholarly journal covering the languages of the Southeast Asian linguistic area. **Founded:** 1974. **Freq:** Semiannual. **Key Personnel:** James A. Matisoff, Editor. **Subscription Rates:** $28 individuals; $15 single issue. **Remarks:** Advertising not accepted. **URL:** http://www.linguistics.berkeley.edu/ltba.
Circ: (Not Reported)

1543 Marion Zimmer Bradley's Fantasy Magazine
PO Box 249 Phone: (510)644-9222
Berkeley, CA 94701
Publisher E-mail: mzbfm@well.com

Consumer magazine covering fantasy short stories. **Founded:** 1988. **Freq:** Quarterly. **Key Personnel:** Marion Z. Bradley, Editor. **ISSN:** 0897-9286. **Subscription Rates:** $20 individuals; $27 Canada; $44 other countries; $5.95 single issue. **Remarks:** Accepts advertising.
Circ: Paid 5,000

1544 Mountain Research and Development
University of California Press/Journals
2120 Berkeley Way Phone: (510)643-7154
Berkeley, CA 94720-0001 Fax: (510)642-9917
Publisher E-mail: journal@ucop.edu

Journal concerned with the balance between mountain environments, development, and the well being of mountain people. **Freq:** Quarterly. **Print Method:** Offset. **Trim Size:** 8 1/2 x 11. **Key Personnel:** Jack D. Ives, Editor; Rebecca R. Simon, Journals Manager. **ISSN:** 0276-4741. **Subscription Rates:** $42 individuals; $24 students and retirees; $112 institutions and industry; $11 single issue; $24 single issue institutions.
Ad Rates: BW: $275 **Circ:** 900

1545 Music Perception
University of California Press/Journals
2120 Berkeley Way Phone: (510)643-7154
Berkeley, CA 94720-0001 Fax: (510)642-9917
Publisher E-mail: journal@ucop.edu

Music magazine. **Founded:** 1984. **Freq:** Quarterly. **Print Method:** Offset. **Trim Size:** 7 x 10. **Cols./Page:** 1. **Col. Width:** 56 nonpareils. **Col. Depth:** 105 agate lines. **Key Personnel:** Jamshed J. Bharucha, Editor. **ISSN:** 0730-7829. **Subscription Rates:** $135 institutions; $52 individuals.
Ad Rates: GLR: $155 **Circ:** ‡1,450
BW: $275

1546 Mystery Readers Journal
Mystery Readers International
Box 8116 Phone: (510)339-2800
Berkeley, CA 94707-8116 Fax: (510)339-8309
Publisher E-mail: whodunit@murderonthemenu.com

Journal covering mystery reviews. **Founded:** 1985. **Freq:** Quarterly. **Print Method:** Offset. **Trim Size:** 7 x 8. **Cols./Page:** 2. **Key Personnel:** Janet A. Rudolph, Editor. **ISSN:** 1043-3473. **Subscription Rates:** $24 individuals; $7 single issue. **Remarks:** Advertising not accepted. **URL:** http://www.murderonthemenu.com/mystery.
Circ: Controlled 2,000

1547 New Directions for Higher Education
Jossey-Bass Inc., Publishers
2807 Shasta Rd. Phone: (510)848-7918
Berkeley, CA 94708
Publisher E-mail: webperson@jbp.com

Journal covering major issues and administrative problems confronting institutions of higher education. **Founded:** 1973. **Freq:** Quarterly. **Print Method:** Sheetfed offset. **Trim Size:** 6 x 9. **Cols./Page:** 1. **Col. Width:** 27 picas. **Col. Depth:** 45 picas. **Key Personnel:** Martin Kramer, Editor. **ISSN:** 0271-0560. **Subscription Rates:** $47 individuals; $62 institutions. **Remarks:** Advertising not accepted.
Circ: Paid 1,927
Non-paid 63

1548 New Oxford Review
New Oxford Review, Inc.
1069 Kains Ave. Phone: (510)526-5374
Berkeley, CA 94706 Fax: (510)526-3492

Religious magazine. **Founded:** Feb. 1977. **Freq:** Monthly (combined issue July/August). **Print Method:** Offset. **Trim Size:** 8 1/2 x 11. **Cols./Page:** 2 and 3. **Col. Width:** 26 and 41 nonpareils. **Col. Depth:** 133 agate lines. **Key Personnel:** Dale Vree, Editor. **ISSN:** 0149-4244. **Subscription Rates:** $19 individuals; $3.50 single issue. **Remarks:** Accepts advertising.
Ad Rates: BW: $640 **Circ:** ‡16,364

1549 News from Native California
Heyday Books
PO Box 9145 Phone: (510)549-3564
Berkeley, CA 94709 Fax: (510)549-1889
Publication E-mail: nnc@heydaybooks.com
Publisher E-mail: heyday@heydaybooks.com

Magazine featuring material relating to California Indians, past and present. **Subtitle:** An Inside View of the California Indian World. **Founded:** 1987. **Freq:** Quarterly. **Print Method:** Offset. **Trim Size:** 8 1/2 x 11. **Cols./Page:** 3. **Col. Width:** 14 picas. **Col. Depth:** 57 picas. **Key Personnel:** Jeannine Gendar, Managing Editor; Malcolm Margolin, Publisher. **ISSN:** 1040-5437. **Subscription Rates:** $19 individuals; $4.95 single issue. **Remarks:** Accepts advertising.
Ad Rates: BW: $390 **Circ:** Paid 5,000
Controlled 500

1550 Nineteenth-Century Literature
University of California Press/Journals
2120 Berkeley Way Phone: (510)643-7154
Berkeley, CA 94720-0001 Fax: (510)642-9917
Publisher E-mail: journal@ucop.edu

Journal on literature. **Founded:** 1945. **Freq:** Quarterly. **Print Method:** Offset. **Trim Size:** 6 x 9. **Cols./Page:** 1. **Col. Width:** 52 nonpareils. **Col. Depth:** 100 agate lines. **Key Personnel:** Joseph Bristow, Editor; Thomas Wortham, Editor. **ISSN:** 0891-9356. **Subscription Rates:** $32 individuals; $62 institutions; $19 students; $13 single issue; $36 other countries for surface mail; $62 other countries for airmail; $19 single issue other countries. **URL:** http://library.berkeley.edu:8080/ucalpress/journals.
Ad Rates: GLR: $133 **Circ:** ‡2,500
BW: $275

1551 19th-Century Music
University of California Press/Journals
2120 Berkeley Way Phone: (510)643-7154
Berkeley, CA 94720-0001 Fax: (510)642-9917
Publisher E-mail: journal@ucop.edu

Scholarly journal covering music. **Key Personnel:** Chris Acosta, Managing Editor; Rebecca Simon, Journal Director. **Subscription Rates:** $35 individuals; $89 institutions. **Remarks:** Accepts advertising.
Circ: (Not Reported)

1552 Pacific Historical Review
University of California Press/Journals
2120 Berkeley Way Phone: (510)643-7154
Berkeley, CA 94720-0001 Fax: (510)642-9917
Publisher E-mail: journal@ucop.edu

Journal covering the history of American expansionism to the Pacific. **Founded:** 1932. **Freq:** Quarterly. **Print Method:** Offset. **Trim Size:** 6 x 9. **Cols./Page:** 1. **Col. Width:** 52 nonpareils. **Col. Depth:** 100 agate lines. **Key Personnel:** David Johnson, Editor; Carl Abbott, Editor. **ISSN:** 0030-8684. **Subscription Rates:** $28 individuals; $19 students; $24 other countries; $69 institutions; $58 institutions, other countries; $16 students, other countries; $9 single issue; $16 single issue institutions. **Remarks:** Accepts advertising. **URL:** http://library.berkeley.edu:8080/ucalpress/journals.
Ad Rates: GLR: $133 **Circ:** ‡1,700
BW: $275

1553 PaleoBios
University of California at Berkeley
Berkeley, CA 94720 Phone: (510)642-1821
Fax: (510)642-1822
Publication E-mail: pbios@ucmp1.berkeley.edu

Scientific journal covering paleontology and paleobiology. **Founded:** 1967. **Freq:** Irregular. **Cols./Page:** 2. **Key Personnel:** Diane Erwin, Editor, phone (510)642-3921, derwin@ucmp1.berkeley.edu; Amy Lesen, Asst. Editor. **ISSN:** 0031-0298. **Subscription Rates:** $20 single issue. **Remarks:** Advertising not accepted. **URL:** http://www.ucmp1.berkeley.edu/museum/PBSI.html.
Circ: (Not Reported)

1554 Parents' Press
1454 6th St. Phone: (510)524-1602
Berkeley, CA 94710-1431 Fax: (510)524-0912
Publication E-mail: parentsprs@aol.com
Publisher E-mail: parentspks@aol.com

Local consumer magazine covering parenting. **Subtitle:** The Monthly Newspaper for Bay Area Parents. **Founded:** June 1980. **Freq:** Monthly. **Print Method:** Offset web. **Trim Size:** 10 x 16. **Key Personnel:** Dixie Jordan, Editor. **ISSN:** 0889-8863. **Subscription Rates:** $15 individuals. **Remarks:** Accepts advertising.
Ad Rates: BW: $1,845 **Circ:** Combined 75,000
4C: $2,445

1555 Poetry Flash
Poetry Flash Inc.
1450 4th St., Ste. 4 Phone: (510)525-5476
Berkeley, CA 94710-1336 Fax: (510)525-6752

Literary magazine (tabloid) containing reviews, interviews and essays on poetry and literary topics. **Subtitle:** A Poetry Review & Literary Calendar for the West. **Founded:** Nov. 1972. **Freq:** 6/year. **Print Method:** Web offset. **Trim Size:** 11 1/2 x 15. **Cols./Page:** 3. **Col. Width:** 3 1/8 inches. **Col. Depth:** 13 3/4 inches. **Key Personnel:** Joyce Jenkins, Editor and Publisher; Richard Silberg, Assoc. Editor. **ISSN:** 0737-4747. **Subscription Rates:** Free at certain literary bookstores

and art centers; $16 individuals; $16 institutions; $30 other countries. **Remarks:** Color advertising not accepted.
Ad Rates: BW: $580 **Circ:** Paid ‡3,000
PCI: $14.50 Controlled ‡23,000

1556 Psychic Reader
Deja Vu Publishing
2210 Harold Way Phone: (510)644-1600
Berkeley, CA 94704-1425 Fax: (510)644-1686
Publisher E-mail: dejavu@dnai.com

New Age and spiritual newspaper. **Founded:** 1975. **Freq:** Monthly. **Key Personnel:** Kirstin Miller, Editor; Pat King, Advertising Mgr. **Subscription Rates:** $13.50 individuals; $25 two years. **Remarks:** Advertising accepted; rates available upon request.
Circ: (Not Reported)

1557 The Public Historian
University of California Press/Journals
2120 Berkeley Way Phone: (510)643-7154
Berkeley, CA 94720-0001 Fax: (510)642-9917
Publisher E-mail: journal@ucop.edu

Journal covering public history and policy. **Freq:** Quarterly. **Print Method:** Offset. **Trim Size:** 6 x 9. **Key Personnel:** Shelley Bookspan, Editor, phone (805)893-3667; Rebecca R. Simon, Journals Dir.; Lindsey Reed, Managing Editor. **ISSN:** 0272-3433. **Subscription Rates:** $47; $79 institutions; $21 students retired.
Ad Rates: GLR: $133 **Circ:** 1,500
BW: $275

1558 The REAL Girls Papers
The Real Girls Papers
PO Box 13947 Phone: (510)433-2830
Berkeley, CA 94712-4947
Publication E-mail: rgirls@aol.com

Magazine written by and about girls ages 13-20 which focuses on activities, activism, and awareness. **Subtitle:** The Magazine for Girls with Better Things to do Than Their Hair. **Founded:** Mar. 1995. **Freq:** Monthly. **Print Method:** Offset. **Trim Size:** 8 1/2 x 11. **Cols./Page:** 4. **Col. Width:** 2 inches. **Key Personnel:** Susan M. Brooks, Publisher, phone (510)528-9453. **ISSN:** 1090-8560. **Subscription Rates:** $12 for six months; $24. **Remarks:** Accepts advertising. **Formerly:** REAL Girls Magazine.
Ad Rates: BW: $380 **Circ:** (Not Reported)
PCI: $15

1559 Real Property Law Reporter
Continuing Education of the Bar (CEB)
2300 Shattuck Ave. Phone: (510)642-3974
Berkeley, CA 94704 Fax: (510)642-3788
Free: (800)232-3444

Legal publication on real property law developments in California. **Founded:** 1977. **Freq:** 8/year. **Print Method:** Offset/Electronic. **Trim Size:** 8 1/2 x 11. **Cols./Page:** 3. **Col. Width:** 21 picas. **Col. Depth:** 55 picas. **ISSN:** 0898-1698. **Subscription Rates:** $175 individuals. **Remarks:** Advertising not accepted. **URL:** http://ceb.ucop.edu. **Alt. Formats:** CD-ROM.
Circ: (Not Reported)

1560 Representations
University of California Press/Journals
2120 Berkeley Way Phone: (510)643-7154
Berkeley, CA 94720-0001 Fax: (510)642-9917
Publisher E-mail: journal@ucop.edu

Journal featuring literary and art criticisms and cultural studies. **Founded:** 1982. **Freq:** Quarterly. **Print Method:** Offset. **Trim Size:** 7 x 10. **Cols./Page:** 1. **Col. Width:** 56 nonpareils. **Col. Depth:** 105 agate lines. **Key Personnel:** Jean Day, Managing Editor. **ISSN:** 0734-6018. **Subscription Rates:** $38 individuals; $8.95 single issue or retired; $102 institutions; $25 students. **URL:** http://library.berkeley.edu:8080/ucalpress/journals.
Ad Rates: GLR: $133 **Circ:** ‡2,800
BW: $325

1561 Revista de Critica Literaria
Latinoamericana Editores
5319 Dwinelle Hall Phone: (510)883-9443
University of California Fax: (510)883-9443
Berkeley, CA 94720
Publisher E-mail: acorpol@socrates.berkeley.edu

Scholarly journal covering Latin American literature in Spanish and Portuguese. **Founded:** 1975. **Freq:** Semiannual. **Key Personnel:** Raul Bueno, Director; Cristina Soto, Manager. **ISSN:** 0252-8843. **Subscription Rates:** $35 individuals; $60 institutions; $18 single issue. **Remarks:** Accepts advertising.
Circ: (Not Reported)

1562 Rhetorica
University of California Press/Journals
2120 Berkeley Way Phone: (510)643-7154
Berkeley, CA 94720-0001 Fax: (510)642-9917
Publisher E-mail: journal@ucop.edu

Journal covering the theory and practice of rhetoric in all aspects. **Freq:** Quarterly. **Print Method:** Offset. **Trim Size:** 6 x 9. **Key Personnel:** Peter Mack, Editor; Rebecca R. Simon, Journal Dir. **ISSN:** 0734-8584. **Subscription Rates:** $44 individuals; $88 institutions; $18 single issue students, retired.
Ad Rates: BW: $275 **Circ:** 1,000

1563 Romance Philology
University of California Press/Journals
2120 Berkeley Way Phone: (510)643-7154
Berkeley, CA 94720-0001 Fax: (510)642-9917
Publisher E-mail: journal@ucop.edu

Journal. **Founded:** 1947. **Freq:** Quarterly. **Print Method:** Offset. **Trim Size:** 6 x 9. **Cols./Page:** 1. **Col. Width:** 56 nonpareils. **Col. Depth:** 105 agate lines. **Key Personnel:** Peter Mack, Editor. **ISSN:** 0035-8002. **Subscription Rates:** $44 individuals; $106 institutions; $24 students; $12 single issue. **Remarks:** Accepts advertising. **URL:** http://library.berkeley.edu:8080/ucalpress/journals.
Ad Rates: BW: $275 **Circ:** ‡1050

1564 SCP Journal
2606 Dwight Way Phone: (510)540-0300
Berkeley, CA 94704 Fax: (510)540-1107

Magazine covering spiritual phenomena and cultural trends such as near-death experiences, deep ecology, Gaia, witchcraft, and UFOs. Analyzes spiritual trends from a Christian perspective. **Subtitle:** Spritual Counterfeits Journal/Newsletter. **Founded:** 1973. **Freq:** Quarterly. **Trim Size:** 8 1/2 x 11. **Key Personnel:** Tal Brooke, President/Editor; Brooks Alexander, Research Director; John Moore, Associate Editor; Edward Schnerder, Business Mgr. **Subscription Rates:** $25 individuals; $35 out of country. **Remarks:** Advertising not accepted. **URL:** http://www.scp-inc.org.
Circ: Paid 15,000

1565 Sinister Wisdom
PO Box 3252 Phone: (510)532-5222
Berkeley, CA 94703-0252
Lesbian literary journal. **Subtitle:** A Journal for the Lesbian Imagination in the Arts and Politics. **Founded:** 1976. **Freq:** Quarterly. **Print Method:** Offset. **Trim Size:** 5 1/2 x 8 1/2. **Cols./Page:** 1. **Col. Width:** 24 picas. **Col. Depth:** 100 agate lines. **Key Personnel:** Margo Mercedes Rivera, Editor. **ISSN:** 0196-1853. **Subscription Rates:** $20 individuals; $25 other countries; $33 institutions; $10 Hardship; Free To women in prison or mental institutions. **Remarks:** Color advertising not accepted. **Available Online.**
Ad Rates: BW: $200 **Circ:** Paid ‡3,000
Non-paid ‡500

1566 Soccer America
Berling Communications, Inc.
1235 10th St. Phone: (510)528-5000
Berkeley, CA 94710 Fax: (510)528-5177
Publisher E-mail: john@socceramerica.com

Soccer magazine (tabloid) for players and fans. Publishes news, scores, statistics, Personality Profiles, camp/tournament listings. **Subtitle:** The National Weekly of U.S. Soccer. **Founded:** Apr. 8, 1971. **Freq:** Weekly. **Print Method:** Offset. **Trim Size:** 10 1/4 x 13 3/4. **Cols./Page:** 5. **Col. Width:** 22 nonpareils. **Col. Depth:** 176 agate lines. **Key Personnel:** Lynn Berling-Manuel, Publisher; John Hooper, Mkts. Dir., phone (510)559-2218, john@socceramer.com; Paul Kennedy, Managing Editor, paul@socceramer.com. **ISSN:** 0163-4070. **Subscription Rates:** $94 individuals; $3.75 single issue. **Remarks:** Accepts advertising. **URL:** http://www.socceramerica.com/sa; http://www.socceramerica.com.
Ad Rates: BW: $2,785 **Circ:** Paid ‡35,000
4C: $3,738
PCI: $65

1567 Social Problems
University of California Press/Journals
2120 Berkeley Way Phone: (510)643-7154
Berkeley, CA 94720-0001 Fax: (510)642-9917
Publication E-mail: journal@garnet.berkeley.edu
Publisher E-mail: journal@ucop.edu

Journal addressing social issues. **Founded:** 1952. **Freq:** Quarterly. **Trim Size:** 7 x 10. **Key Personnel:** Joel Best, Editor. **ISSN:** 0037-7791. **Subscription Rates:** $97 nonmembers; $24 single issue. **URL:** http://www.library.berkeley.edu.
Ad Rates: GLR: $133 **Circ:** 2,700
BW: $275

1568 The Threepenny Review
PO Box 9131 Phone: (510)849-4545
Berkeley, CA 94709 Fax: (510)849-4551

Liberal left-wing literary arts magazine. **Founded:** 1980. **Freq:** Quarterly. **Print Method:** Offset. **Trim Size:** 10 x 15. **Cols./Page:** 4. **Col. Width:** 27 nonpareils. **Col. Depth:** 203 agate lines. **Key Personnel:** Wendy Lesser, Editor and Publisher. **ISSN:** 0275-1410. **Subscription Rates:** $20 individuals. **Remarks:** Accepts advertising.
Ad Rates: BW: $900 **Circ:** Paid ‡8,000
PCI: $30 Non-paid ‡2,000

1569 Tradeswomen
Tradeswomen, Inc.
PO Box 2622 Phone: (510)433-1378
Berkeley, CA 94702
Magazine written by and for women in blue-collar non-traditional jobs. **Subtitle:** A Quarterly Magazine for Women in Blue-Collar Work. **Founded:** Jan. 1981. **Freq:** Quarterly. **Print Method:** Offset. **Trim Size:** 8 1/4 x 10 7/8. **Cols./Page:** 2 and 3. **Col. Width:** 2 and 3 inches. **Col. Depth:** 10 inches. **Key Personnel:** Molly Martin, Editor. **ISSN:** 0739-344X. **Subscription Rates:** $35 individuals; $3.50 single issue; $50 institutions. **Remarks:** Accepts advertising.
Ad Rates: GLR: $100 **Circ:** Paid ‡1,700
BW: $400 Non-paid ‡300

1570 Yoga Journal
California Yoga Teachers Association
2054 University Ave., Suite 600 Phone: (510)841-9200
Berkeley, CA 94704 Fax: (510)644-3101
Free: (800)IDO-YOGA
Publication E-mail: yoga@sirius.com

Magazine devoted to holistic living and yoga. **Subtitle:** For Health and Conscious Living. **Founded:** 1975. **Freq:** Bimonthly. **Print Method:** Web offset. **Trim Size:** 8 x 10 1/2. **Cols./Page:** 3. **Col. Width:** 2 1/4 inches. **Col. Depth:** 9 3/8 inches. **Key Personnel:** Rick Fields, Editor; John Abbott, Interim Pub.; Deena Brown, Advertising Dir. **ISSN:** 0191-0965. **Subscription Rates:** $19.97 individuals. **URL:** http://www.yogajournal.com.
Ad Rates: BW: $2,340 **Circ:** ‡100,000
4C: $3,120
PCI: $140

1571 KALX-FM - 90.7
26 Barrows Hall, No. 5650 Phone: (510)642-1111
Berkeley, CA 94720-5650

Format: News; Eclectic; Alternative/New Music/Progressive; Sports. **Founded:** 1967. **Operating Hours:** Continuous. **Key Personnel:** Sandra Wasson, General Mgr.; Lawrence Kay, Music Dir.; Peter Fiske, News Dir.; Matt Foley, Sports Dir.; Peter Crimmins, Public Affairs Dir. **Local Programs:** *Calliope*, Dennis Cook; *Straight Jacket*, Tom Mannarelli; *Women in the Arts*, W. La Guzza. **Wattage:** 500. **Ad Rates:** Noncommercial. **URL:** http://www.oms1.berkeley.edu/kalx.

1572 KPFA-FM - 94.1
1929 Martin Luther King Jr. Way Phone: (510)848-6767
Berkeley, CA 94704 Fax: (510)848-3812
Free: (800)439-5732
E-mail: kpfa@well.com

Format: Full Service; Eclectic. **Networks:** Pacifica. **Owner:** Pacifica Foundation, at above address. **Founded:** 1949. **Operating Hours:** Continuous; 2% network, 98% local. **Key Personnel:** Phil Osegueda, Asst. Manager, grateph-il@aol.com; Nicole Sawaya, General Mgr., gmnicole@aol.com; Aileen Alfandary, News Dir.; Mark Mericle, News Dir.; Carrie Core, Public Affairs; Chuy Varela, Contact; Phillip Maldari, Contact; Kris Welch, Contact; Asata Iman, Apprenticeship Program; Amina Hassan, Development Director. **Wattage:** 59,000. **Ad Rates:** Noncommercial.

BEVERLY HILLS, pop. 32,367.

S. CA. Los Angeles Co. Surrounded by city of Los Angeles. Manufactures cameras, aircraft parts, recording instruments, building materials, tools, food, clothing, plastics, heating equipment, petroleum products. Residential.

1573 The Beverly Hills Courier
8840 W. Olympic Blvd. Phone: (213)278-1322
Beverly Hills, CA 90211 Fax: (213)271-5118
Publication E-mail: bhcourier@aol.com

Local Community newspaper (tabloid). **Founded:** July 22, 1965. **Freq:** Weekly (Fri.). **Print Method:** Offset. **Trim Size:** 11 x 14. **Cols./Page:** 5. **Col. Width:** 12 picas. **Col. Depth:** 14 inches. **Key Personnel:** March J. Schwartz, Editor and Publisher, phone (310)278-1322, fax (310)271-5118. **Sub-**

scription Rates: $75 by mail; $45 by mail. **Remarks:** Accepts advertising.
Ad Rates: GLR: $34 **Circ:** Paid ‡2,930
BW: $2,100 Free ‡46,000
4C: $4,200
SAU: $30
PCI: $30

1574 Beverly Hills Independent
Copley Los Angeles Newspapers, Inc.
7776 Ivanhoe Ave.
La Jolla, CA 92037

Newspaper. **Founded:** 1967. **Freq:** Weekly (Wed.). **Print Method:** Offset. **Cols./Page:** 6. **Col. Width:** 26 nonpareils. **Col. Depth:** 301 agate lines. **Key Personnel:** Bertram Winrow, Publisher. **Subscription Rates:** $24 individuals. **Remarks:** Accepts advertising.
Ad Rates: GLR: $.65 **Circ:** Free 18,400

1575 Chic Magazine
L.F.P., Inc.
8484 Wilshire Blvd., Ste. 900 Phone: (323)651-5400
Beverly Hills, CA 90211 Fax: (323)651-2741
Publisher E-mail: hustler@lfp.com

Men's magazine. **Founded:** 1976. **Freq:** Monthly. **Print Method:** Offset. **Trim Size:** 8 1/2 x 11. **Col. Width:** 27 nonpareils. **Col. Depth:** 140 agate lines. **Key Personnel:** Allen MacDonell, Director; Larry Flynt, Publisher; Allen Maine, Advertising Dir., phone (213)651-7907, fax (213)657-0651; Lisa Jenio, Editor. **ISSN:** 0194-648X. **Subscription Rates:** $39.95 individuals; $5.99 single issue. **Remarks:** Advertising accepted; rates available upon request. **URL:** http://www.hustler.com.
Circ: Paid 50,000
Non-paid 100

1576 Computer Technology Review
West World Productions
420 N. Camden Dr. Phone: (310)276-9500
Beverly Hills, CA 90210 Fax: (310)246-1405

Computer tabloid. **Founded:** 1981. **Freq:** Monthly. **Print Method:** Web offset. **Trim Size:** 10 x 14 3/8. **Cols./Page:** 5 and 3. **Col. Width:** 11 and 15 nonpareils. **Col. Depth:** 80 and 60 agate lines. **Key Personnel:** Yuri R. Spiro, Publisher; Carol L. Stagg, Assoc. Pub.; George McNamara, Editorial Dir.; Mitzie Dobson, Production Mgr. **Subscription Rates:** $80 individuals; $100 other countries. **Remarks:** Accepts advertising.
Ad Rates: BW: $14,450 **Circ:** Controlled 72,552
4C: $10,525

1577 The Ethiopian Mirror
PO Box 6881 Phone: (323)939-3059
Beverly Hills, CA 90212 Fax: (323)939-2636
Publication E-mail: ethimirror@aol.com

A Monthly Publication Featuring News, Interviews, Arts & Entertainment. **Founded:** Sept. 1988. **Freq:** Monthly. **Trim Size:** 11 x 15. **Cols./Page:** 4. **Key Personnel:** Tesfaye Davino, Publisher. **Subscription Rates:** $24 individuals; $2 single issue. **Remarks:** Accepts advertising. **Alt. Formats:** Large-print.
Ad Rates: BW: $400 **Circ:** Paid 11,000
4C: $450 Non-paid 15,000

1578 Hustler Busty Beauties
L.F.P., Inc.
8484 Wilshire Blvd., Ste. 900 Phone: (323)651-5400
Beverly Hills, CA 90211 Fax: (323)651-2741
Publication E-mail: busty@lfp.com
Publisher E-mail: hustler@lfp.com

Adult magazine. **Subtitle:** North America's Breast Magazine. **Founded:** Oct. 1988. **Freq:** 13/year. **Print Method:** Offset. **Trim Size:** 8 1/4 x 10 7/8. **Cols./Page:** 3. **Col. Width:** 14 picas. **Col. Depth:** 58 1/2 picas. **Key Personnel:** N. Morgen Hagen, Editor; Larry Flynt, Publisher; Allen Maine, Advertising Dir., phone (213)951-7907, fax (213)651-5400. **ISSN:** 1058-6798. **Subscription Rates:** $39.95; $69.95 two years. $6.99 single issue. **Remarks:** Accepts advertising.
Ad Rates: BW: $1,250 **Circ:** ‡205,000
4C: $1,750

1579 Hustler Magazine
L.F.P., Inc.
8484 Wilshire Blvd., Ste. 900 Phone: (323)651-5400
Beverly Hills, CA 90211 Fax: (323)651-2741
Publisher E-mail: hustler@lfp.com

Men's entertainment magazine. **Founded:** July 1974. **Freq:** Monthly. **Print Method:** Offset. **Trim Size:** 8 1/2 x 11. **Cols./Page:** 3. **Col. Width:** 28 nonpareils. **Col. Depth:** 140 agate lines. **Key Personnel:** Allan MacDonell, Editor, amacdonell@lfp.com; Larry Flynt, Publisher; Allen Maine, Advertising Dir., phone (323)951-7907, fax (323)651-0651, amaine@lfp.com. **ISSN:** 0149-4635. **Subscription Rates:** $39.95 individuals; $6.99 single issue. **Remarks:** Advertising accepted; rates available upon request. **URL:** http://www.hustler.com.
Circ: 1,066,537

1580 Inside Film Magazine
8421 Wilshire Blvd. Phone: (213)852-0434
Beverly Hills, CA 90211-3205
Publication E-mail: editor@insidefilm.com

Magazine covering the film industry. **Founded:** 1979. **Freq:** Bimonthly. **Print Method:** Sheetfed offset. **Trim Size:** 8 3/8 x 10 7/8. **Cols./Page:** 3. **Subscription Rates:** $16; $4. **Remarks:** Advertising not accepted. **URL:** http://www.insidefilm.com. **Formerly:** American Premiere.
Circ: (Not Reported)

1581 Interrace Magazine
Heritage Publishing Group
PO Box 17479 Phone: (310)358-2932
Beverly Hills, CA 90209 Fax: (310)479-5353
Publication E-mail: intrace@aol.com

Magazine for interracial couples, families, and people, and transracial adoptive families. **Founded:** 1989. **Freq:** Quarterly. **Print Method:** Web offset. **Trim Size:** 8 1/8 x 10 7/8. **Key Personnel:** Candy Mills, Publisher. **ISSN:** 1047-5370. **Subscription Rates:** $20 individuals; $4.50 single issue. **Remarks:** Accepts advertising.
Ad Rates: BW: $400 **Circ:** Paid 15,000
4C: $600
PCI: $50

1582 PC Portables Magazine
L.F.P., Inc.
8484 Wilshire Blvd., Ste. 900 Phone: (323)651-5400
Beverly Hills, CA 90211 Fax: (323)651-2741
Publisher E-mail: hustler@lfp.com

Consumer magazine focusing on portable computers, their software, and applications. **Founded:** 1989. **Freq:** Monthly. **Print Method:** Web offset. **Trim Size:** 8 x 10 7/8. **Cols./Page:** 3. **Key Personnel:** Mark A. Kellner, Editor-in-Chief, mkellner@lfp.com; Michelle Anderson, Advertising Dir., manderson@lfp.com. **ISSN:** 1043-1314. **Remarks:** Accepts advertising. **URL:** http://www.pcportablesmag.com. **Formerly:** PC Laptop Computers Magazine.
Ad Rates: BW: $2,500 **Circ:** Paid 70,000
4C: $3,150

1583 Raising Black Children
Heritage Publishing Group
PO Box 17479 Phone: (310)358-2932
Beverly Hills, CA 90209 Fax: (310)479-5353
Publication E-mail: blachild@aol.com

Magazine covering parenting issues relating to African-American and interracial children from birth through their teens. **Subtitle:** The African American Parenting 'zine. **Founded:** 1995. **Freq:** Bimonthly. **Print Method:** Web offset. **Trim Size:** 8 1/8 x 10 7/8. **Key Personnel:** Candy Mills, Editor and Publisher. **ISSN:** 1083-7485. **Subscription Rates:** $12.95 individuals; $2.50 single issue. **Remarks:** Accepts advertising. **Formerly:** Black Child Magazine.
Ad Rates: PCI: $85 **Circ:** Paid 30,000

1584 RIP
L.F.P., Inc.
8484 Wilshire Blvd., Ste. 900 Phone: (323)651-5400
Beverly Hills, CA 90211 Fax: (323)651-2741
Publisher E-mail: hustler@lfp.com

Music magazine. **Founded:** Dec. 1986. **Freq:** Monthly. **Trim Size:** 8 1/2 x 11. **Cols./Page:** 3. **Col. Width:** 13 1/2 picas. **Col. Depth:** 60 1/2 inches. **Key Personnel:** Greg Kennerson, Editor; Michael Mathieson, Advertising. **ISSN:** 0889-5791. **Subscription Rates:** $1.92 single issue. **Remarks:** Accepts advertising. **Available Online.**
Ad Rates: BW: $2,565 **Circ:** Paid 120,000
4C: $3,420 Non-paid 120,000

1585 SuperCycle
L.F.P., Inc.
8484 Wilshire Blvd., Ste. 900 Phone: (323)651-5400
Beverly Hills, CA 90211 Fax: (323)651-2741
Publisher E-mail: hustler@lfp.com

Magazine containing cartoons, humor, and fiction; covering custom, antique, and performance motorcycles for adult enthusiasts. **Founded:** 1987. **Freq:** Monthly. **Print Method:** Web offset. **Trim Size:** 8 x 10 7/8. **Cols./Page:** 3. **Key Personnel:** Paula Thornton, Editor. **Subscription Rates:** $21.25. $2.95 single issue.

BIG BEAR LAKE

SE CA. San Bernardino Co. 25 mi. NE of San Bernardino. Mountain resort. Fishing, skiing center.

1586 Big Bear Life & the Grizzly
The Grizzly
PO Box 1789 Phone: (714)866-3456
Big Bear Lake, CA 92315 Fax: (714)866-2302

General newspaper. **Founded:** 1941. **Freq:** Semiweekly (Wed. and Sat.). **Print Method:** Offset. **Cols./Page:** 6. **Col. Width:** 26 nonpareils. **Col. Depth:** 301 agate lines. **Key Personnel:** John Emig, Editor; Jerry M. Wright, Publisher. **ISSN:** 1073-6867. **Subscription Rates:** $21 individuals; $30 out of county; $39 out of state. **Remarks:** Accepts advertising.
Ad Rates: GLR: $12.60 **Circ:** ‡11,000
BW: $1,625
4C: $1,885
SAU: $12

1587 Falcon Cablevision
41490 Big Bear Blvd. Phone: (909)866-3416
Box 1771 Fax: (909)866-9519
Big Bear Lake, CA 92315

Founded: 1952. **Cities Served:** San Bernardino County, Big Bear City, Boulder Bay, Fawnskin, and Moonridge, CA.

BISHOP, pop. 3,333.

SE CA. Inyo Co. 265 mi. N. of Los Angeles. Gateway high sierra ski, mountain resort. Ancient bristlecone pines. Old west museums. Dairy, livestock grazing, poultry, grain farms.

1588 Inyo Register
Register Review Publishing Co.
450 E. Line St. Phone: (760)873-3535
Bishop, CA 93514 Fax: (760)873-3591
Free: (800)293-3535

Newspaper. **Founded:** 1870. **Freq:** 3/week. **Print Method:** Offset. **Cols./Page:** 8. **Col. Width:** 18 nonpareils. **Col. Depth:** 294 agate lines. **Key Personnel:** Jay Byrne, Publisher; Barbara Laughon, Editor. **Subscription Rates:** $56 individuals. **Remarks:** Accepts advertising.
Ad Rates: GLR: $.675 **Circ:** 7,590
BW: $1194
4C: $1494
PCI: $6.64

1589 KBOV-AM - 1230
S. Hwy. 395 Phone: (760)873-6324
Bishop, CA 93514 Fax: (760)872-2639
E-mail: kibskbou@qnet.com

Format: Oldies. **Networks:** ABC. **Owner:** Great Country Broadcasting, Inc., PO Box 757, Bishop, CA 93515. **Founded:** 1953. **Formerly:** KIBS-AM (1985). **Operating Hours:** 24 hrs.; 90% network, 10% local. **Key Personnel:** John Dailey, President. **Local Programs:** *Dodger Baseball*, Jeff Marsell, Mailing contact, (760)873-6324. **Wattage:** 1000. **Ad Rates:** $9-10.40 for 30 seconds; $13-15 for 60 seconds. Combined advertising rates available with KIBS-FM.

1590 KIBS-FM - 100.7
S. Hwy. 395 Phone: (760)873-6324
Bishop, CA 93514 Fax: (760)872-2639
E-mail: kibskbov@qnet.com

Format: Country. **Networks:** Jones Satellite; ABC. **Owner:** Great Country Broadcasting, Inc., PO Box 757, Bishop, CA 93515. **Founded:** 1974. **Formerly:** KIOQ-FM (1985). **Operating Hours:** Continuous; 33% network, 67% local. **Key Personnel:** John Dailey, President. **Wattage:** 50,000 ERP. **Ad Rates:** $10 for 30 seconds; $12 for 60 seconds. $13 for 30 seconds; $16 for 60 seconds. Combined advertising rates available with KBOV-AM.

BLYTHE, pop. 6,805.

SE CA. Riverside Co. 169 mi. W. of Phoenix, AZ. Hunting and fishing. cotton gins; feed mills; seed plants. Stock, truck farms. Cotton, alfalfa, lettuce, cantaloupes. Citrus fruits.

1591 Palo Verde Valley Times
231 N. Spring St. Phone: (760)922-3181
PO Box 1159 Fax: (760)922-3184
Blythe, CA 92226
Publication E-mail: paloverdenews@mcimail.com

Newspaper. **Founded:** 1925. **Freq:** Semiweekly (Wed. and Fri.). **Print Method:** Offset. **Trim Size:** 6 x 21 1/2. **Cols./Page:** 6. **Col. Width:** 25 nonpareils. **Col. Depth:** 294 agate lines. **Key Personnel:** Robin Mauser, Publisher; Ivam Murray, Editor. **USPS:** 419-240. **Subscription Rates:** $58 individuals. **Remarks:** Accepts advertising.
Ad Rates: GLR: $.43 **Circ:** ‡4,200
4C: $1,494.54
SAU: $8.04
PCI: $9.84

1592 Spirit to Spirit
PO Box 1107, Dept. GR Free: (888)922-0835
Blythe, CA 92226-1107
Consumer magazine covering poetry and short fiction on metaphysical subjects. **Founded:** 1990. **Freq:** 3/year. **Trim Size:** 5 x 8. **Key Personnel:** Marjorie E. Navarro, Managing Editor; Richard Navarro, Exec. Editor/Art Dir. **Subscription Rates:** $20 individuals; $7 single issue. **Remarks:** Advertising not accepted. **Formerly:** Merlana's Magickal Messages.
Circ: (Not Reported)

1593 White Sheet-The Blythe Advertiser
Associated Desert Shoppers, Inc.
73-400 Hwy. 111 Phone: (760)346-1729
Palm Desert, CA 92260 Fax: (760)346-7350
Free: (800)678-4237

Shopper. **Founded:** 1965. **Freq:** Weekly (Tues.). **Print Method:** Web. **Trim Size:** 11 x 12 1/2. **Cols./Page:** 6. **Col. Width:** 9 1/2 picas. **Col. Depth:** 11 3/4 inches. **Key Personnel:** Hal Paradis, Publisher; John Schneider, Sales Mgr. **Subscription Rates:** $163.80 out of area. **Merged with:** The Blythe Advertiser.
Ad Rates: BW: $331 **Circ:** Free ‡7,400
4C: $650
PCI: $4.50

1594 KJMB-FM - 100.3
681 N. 4th St. Phone: (760)922-7143
Blythe, CA 92225 Fax: (760)922-2844

Format: Adult Contemporary. **Owner:** Blythe Radio Inc., at above address. **Founded:** 1975. **Operating Hours:** Continuous. **Key Personnel:** Jim Mayson, President; Jim Morris, General Mgr. **Wattage:** 36,400. **Ad Rates:** $16 for 30 seconds; $22 for 60 seconds.

BODEGA BAY

1595 The Bodega Bay Navigator
1580 Eastshore Rd., Ste. H Phone: (707)875-3574
PO Box 969 Fax: (707)875-3875
Bodega Bay, CA 94923
Publication E-mail: stargaze@monitor.net

Community newspaper covering southwestern Sonoma County and northwestern Marin County, CA. Covers local news and current events, weather, and stories. **Founded:** 1984. **Freq:** Weekly. **Print Method:** Web offset. **Trim Size:** 11.25 x 17. **Key Personnel:** Joel Hack, Editor and Publisher. **Subscription Rates:** $18 local; $32 outside of Sonoma county; $40 outside of California. **URL:** http://www.bodegabay.com/features/navigator.
Ad Rates: BW: $600 **Circ:** Paid 1,400
PCI: $7.50 Non-paid 400

BOLINAS

1596 Coastal Post
PO Box 31 Phone: (415)868-1600
Bolinas, CA 94924-0031 Fax: (415)868-0502
Publication E-mail: editor@coastalpost.com

Environmental and political newspaper. **Founded:** Sept. 1975. **Freq:** Monthly. **Col. Width:** 1 1/2 inches. **Col. Depth:** 15 1/2 inches. **Key Personnel:** Don Deans, Editor and Publisher, editor@coastalpost.com. **Subscription Rates:** $24 individuals. **Remarks:** Accepts advertising.
Ad Rates: PCI: $12 **Circ:** Combined 14,500

BOONVILLE, pop. 750.

NW CA. Mendocino Co. On Pacific Ocean, 50 mi. NW of Santa Rosa. Sawmill. Wineries. Orchards, vineyards, sheep, cattle.

1597 The Anderson Valley Advertiser
12451 Anderson Valley Way Phone: (707)895-3016
Boonville, CA 95415 Fax: (707)895-3355

Socialist rural newspaper. **Founded:** Sept. 1954. **Freq:** Weekly (Wed.). **Print Method:** Offset. **Cols./Page:** 8. **Col. Width:** 19 nonpareils. **Col. Depth:** 308 agate lines. **Key Personnel:** Bruce Anderson, Editor and Publisher. **Subscription Rates:** $38 individuals. **Remarks:** Accepts advertising.
Ad Rates: GLR: $.95 **Circ:** 4,000
PCI: $2.95

BORREGO SPRINGS, pop. 1,900.

S. CA. San Diego Co. 90 mi. NE of San Diego. Resort. State Park.

1598 Borrego Sun
707 Christmas Circle Phone: (760)767-5338
PO Box 249 Fax: (760)767-4971
Borrego Springs, CA 92004-0249
Community newspaper (tabloid). **Founded:** Mar. 1949. **Freq:** Semimonthly (every other Thursday). **Print Method:** Offset. **Trim Size:** 10 x 12 3/4. **Cols./Page:** 4. **Col. Width:** 14 picas. **Col. Depth:** 12 3/4 inches. **Key Personnel:** David C. Copley, Publisher; Kay Colby-Levie, Advertising Mgr.; Judy Meier, Editor/General Mgr. **USPS:** 061-260. **Subscription Rates:** $15 individuals; $28 two years. **Remarks:** Accepts advertising.
Ad Rates: BW: $505 **Circ:** ‡4,200
4C: $765
PCI: $11

1599 Tele-Cable Service Corp.
Box 336 Phone: (619)767-5607
Borrego Springs, CA 92004 Fax: (619)767-3609

Owner: Tele-Cable Service Corp., at above address. **Key Personnel:** Arthur C. Barnett, General Mgr. **Cities Served:** Borrego Springs, CA.

BRAWLEY

1600 KKSC-AM - 1300
120 S. Plaza Phone: (619)344-1300
PO Box 238 Fax: (619)344-1763
Brawley, CA 92227

Networks: ESPN Radio. **Owner:** Stodelle Broadcasting Corp., at above address. **Founded:** 1946. **Formerly:** KROP-AM. **Operating Hours:** Continuous. **ADI:** El Centro, CA-Yuma, AZ. **Key Personnel:** Tony Dee, Manager; Tony Dee, Program Dir.; Steve Stodelle, Owner/Pres./Gen. Mgr.; Bill Stewart, Production Dir. **Wattage:** 1000 day; 500 night. **Ad Rates:** $12.50-16 for 30 seconds; $15-20 for 60 seconds. $12.50-$16 for 30 seconds; $15-$20 for 60 seconds. Combined advertising rates available with KSIQ-FM.

1601 KMXX-FM - 99.3
626 Main St. Phone: (760)352-2277
El Centro, CA 92243-2920 Fax: (760)352-1430

Format: Hispanic. **Founded:** 1980. **Operating Hours:** Continuous. **ADI:** El Centro, CA-Yuma, AZ. **Key Personnel:** Cal Mandel, General Mgr. **Wattage:** 6000.

1602 KSIQ-FM - 96.1
120 S. Plaza Phone: (760)344-1300
PO Box 238 Fax: (760)344-1763
Brawley, CA 92227

Format: Contemporary Hit Radio (CHR); News; Eclectic. **Owner:** Stodelle Broadcasting Corp., at above address. **Founded:** 1981. **Operating Hours:** Continuous. **ADI:** El Centro, CA-Yuma, AZ. **Key Personnel:** Tony Dee, Program Dir.; Steve Stodelle, Owner; Tony Dee, Manager; Tony Driskill, News Dir.; Bill Stewart, Production Dir. **Wattage:** 50,000 H. **Ad Rates:** $12.50-16 for 30 seconds; $15-20 for 60 seconds. $12.50-$16 for 30 seconds; $15-$20 for 60 seconds.

BREA, pop. 28,000.

S. CA. Orange Co. 12 mi. S. of Anaheim. Residential.

1603 The Original Pennysaver
The Pennysaver
2830 Orbiter St. Phone: (714)996-8900
Brea, CA 92622 Fax: (714)993-4711

Shopper. **Founded:** 1962. **Freq:** Weekly (Wed.). **Print Method:** Offset. **Trim Size:** 7 x 9 1/2. **Cols./Page:** 2. **Col. Width:** 21 nonpareils. **Col. Depth:** 130 agate lines. **Key Personnel:** Harry Buckel, Editor and Publisher; Peter Gorman, Exec. V.P.; R. Steve Morris, V.P. Sales and Mktg.; Ken Fricka, Contact. **Remarks:** Accepts advertising. **URL:** http://www.thepennysaver.com.
Circ: Free ‡4,710,500

1604 Century Communications
185 E. Alder St. Phone: (714)529-4918
Box 547 Fax: (714)529-1960
Brea, CA 92621

Founded: 1970. **Formerly:** Century Cable of California. **Cities Served:** Los Angeles and Orange Counties, La Habra, and La Habra Heights, CA.

BRENTWOOD, pop. 4,434.

E. CA. Contra Costa Co. 38 mi. E. of San Francisco. Diversified agriculture.

1605 Brentwood News
Contra Costa Newspapers, Inc.
1650 Cavallo Rd. Phone: (925)757-2525
Antioch, CA 94509 Fax: (925)754-9483

Community newspaper. **Founded:** 1903. **Freq:** Semiweekly (Tues. and Fri.). **Print Method:** Offset. **Key Personnel:** Katharine Ball, Asst. City Editor, phone (925)779-7113, fax (925)634-1149. **Subscription Rates:** $36.87 individuals. **Remarks:** Advertising accepted; rates available upon request. **Additional Contact Info: Mailing Address:** PO Box 517, Brentwood, CA 94513.
Circ: 3,728

1606 Brentwood-Westwood Press
Copley Los Angeles Newspapers, Inc.
7776 Ivanhoe Ave.
La Jolla, CA 92037

Newspaper. **Founded:** 1927. **Freq:** Weekly (Thurs.). **Print Method:** Offset. **Cols./Page:** 6. **Col. Width:** 26 nonpareils. **Col. Depth:** 301 agate lines. **Key Personnel:** Bill Beebe, Editor; Bertram Winrow, Publisher; Mark Walter, Advertising Mgr. **Subscription Rates:** $24 individuals. **Remarks:** Accepts advertising.
Ad Rates: GLR: $.71 **Circ:** Free 20,300

1607 The Value News
PO Box 1060 Phone: (925)634-6393
Brentwood, CA 94513
Shopper. **Freq:** Weekly (Tues.). **Subscription Rates:** Free.
Circ: Non-paid 20,721

BRISBANE

1608 Next Generation
Imagine Publishing Inc.
150 N Hill Dr.
Brisbane, CA 94005

Consumer magazine covering computers and games.

1609 KTSF-TV - 26
100 Valley Dr. Phone: (415)468-2626
Brisbane, CA 94005 Fax: (415)467-7559

Format: Commercial TV. **Networks:** Independent. **Owner:** Lincoln Broadcasting Co., at above address. **Founded:** 1976. **Operating Hours:** Continuous; 100% local. **ADI:** San Francisco-Oakland-San Jose. **Key Personnel:** Brian Holton, General Mgr.; Rose Shirinian, News Dir. **Local Programs:** *Cantonese Evening News* 8-9 p.m.; rebroadcast midnight; *Mandarin News* 7:30-8 p.m. **Wattage:** 2.5 million watts ERP.

BUENA PARK

1610 Hang Gliding
U.S. Hang Gliding Association, Inc.
6950 Aragon Cir., Ste. 6 Phone: (714)994-3050
Buena Park, CA 90620 Fax: (714)994-3050

Magazine on hang gliding flight. **Founded:** 1971. **Freq:** Monthly. **Print Method:** Offset. **Trim Size:** 8 1/2 x 11. **Cols./Page:** 3. **Col. Width:** 28 nonpareils. **Col. Depth:** 140 agate lines. **Key Personnel:** Gil Dodgen, Editor; Jeff Elgart, Advertising and Marketing Mgr. **USPS:** 017-970. **Subscription Rates:** $35 individuals; $3.95 single issue. **Remarks:** Accepts advertising.
Ad Rates: GLR: $.50 **Circ:** Paid ‡9,500
BW: $615 Non-paid ‡212
4C: $900
PCI: $25

BURBANK, pop. 84,625.

S. CA. Los Angeles Co. 10 mi. N. of Los Angeles. Manufactures airplanes, aircraft equipment and instruments, motion picture films and sound equipment, electronics equipment, plastics.

1611 Action Pursuit Games
C.F.W. Enterprises, Inc.
4201 Vanowen Pl. Phone: (818)845-2656
Burbank, CA 91505-1139 Fax: (818)845-7761

Games magazine featuring paintball sports. **Subtitle:** World's Leading Magazine of Paintball Sports. **Founded:** 1987. **Freq:** Monthly. **Key Personnel:** Dan Reeves, Editor. **ISSN:** 0893-9489. **Subscription Rates:** $3.95 single issue; $27 /year. **Remarks:** Accepts advertising.
Ad Rates: BW: $1,704 **Circ:** (Not Reported)
4C: $2,124

1612 Beverage Bulletin
California Beverage Publications
PO Box 4110 Phone: (213)930-4831
Burbank, CA 91503-4110 Fax: (213)930-4835
Publication E-mail: dbolton@primenet.com

Newspaper (tabloid) covering the beverage and food industry in California. **Founded:** Jan. 1936. **Freq:** Monthly. **Print Method:** Offset. **Trim Size:** 11 x 15. **Cols./Page:** 5. **Col. Width:** 22 nonpareils. **Col. Depth:** 14 agate lines. **Key Personnel:** Michael Lynn, Editor; Max J. Kerstein, Publisher. **ISSN:** 0192-1835. **Subscription Rates:** $24 individuals. **Remarks:** Accepts advertising.
Ad Rates: BW: $3,201 **Circ:** Controlled ‡13,136
4C: $4,176
PCI: $50

1613 Burbank Leader
California Community News Corp.
220 N. Glenoaks Blvd. Phone: (818)843-8700
Ste. B Fax: (818)954-9439
Burbank, CA 91502
General newspaper. **Freq:** Semiweekly (Wed. and Sat.). **Print Method:** Offset. **Cols./Page:** 6. **Col. Width:** 12.5 inches. **Col. Depth:** 20.5 inches. **Key Personnel:** Judee Kendall, Publisher. **Subscription Rates:** $48. **Formerly**: Burbank Daily Review.
Ad Rates: GLR: $5.25 **Circ:** Wed. ❑**25,110**
BW: $3,024 Sat. ❑**32,263**
4C: $3,474
PCI: $24

1614 California Bowling News
2606 W. Burbank Blvd. Phone: (818)849-4664
Burbank, CA 91505-2303 Fax: (818)845-6321

Sports magazine (tabloid) for bowling enthusiasts. **Founded:** Sept. 11, 1940. **Freq:** Weekly (Thurs.). **Print Method:** Offset. **Trim Size:** 10 x 16. **Cols./Page:** 6. **Col. Width:** 9 1/2 picas. **Col. Depth:** 16 inches. **Key Personnel:** Carol Mancini, Editor and Publisher; Charles Kinstler, Editor and Publisher; Lillian Oak, Advertising Mgr. **ISSN:** 0008-0918. **Subscription Rates:** $35 individuals. **Remarks:** Accepts advertising.
Ad Rates: BW: $265 **Circ:** ‡14,000
PCI: $5

1615 California Broker
McGee Publishers
217 E. Alameda Ave., Ste. 301 Phone: (818)848-2957
Burbank, CA 91502-1500 Fax: (818)843-3489

Magazine providing financial planning information for life and health insurance brokers. **Founded:** 1982. **Freq:** Monthly. **Print Method:** Offset. **Trim Size:** 8 3/8 x 10 7/8. **Cols./Page:** 3. **Col. Width:** 28 nonpareils. **Col. Depth:** 140 agate lines. **Key Personnel:** Richard Madden, Publisher; Scott Halversen, VP Marketing, phone (818)848-5992. **ISSN:** 0883-6159. **Subscription Rates:** $42 individuals. **Remarks:** Accepts advertising.
Ad Rates: GLR: $10 **Circ:** ‡25,000
BW: $3,371
4C: $4,256
PCI: $80

1616 Entertainment Today
Best Publishing, Inc.
801 S. Main St., Ste. L Phone: (818)566-4030
Burbank, CA 91506 Fax: (818)566-4295
Publication E-mail: enttoday@artnet.net

Entertainment newspaper covering film, music, arts, video, theater, multimedia, and dining. **Founded:** 1967. **Freq:** Weekly (Fri.). **Print Method:** Web offset. **Trim Size:** 11 3/8 x 14. **Cols./Page:** 5. **Col. Width:** 22 nonpareils. **Col. Depth:** 196 agate lines. **Key Personnel:** John Salazar, Publisher, phone (808)841-4030. **Subscription Rates:** $115 individuals; $250 other countries. **Remarks:** Accepts advertising. **URL:** http://www.ent-today.com.
Ad Rates: BW: $1,820 **Circ:** ‡215,000
4C: $2,500

1617 Environmental Testing and Analysis
The Target Group
1907 W. Burbank Blvd., 2nd Fl. Phone: (818)842-4777
Burbank, CA 91506-1316 Fax: (818)842-0578

Trade journal covering methods, regulation, technology, management, and markets. **Founded:** 1989. **Freq:** Bimonthly. **Print Method:** Offset. **Trim Size:** 8 x 10 3/4. **Subscription Rates:** Free to qualified subscribers.

1618 Inside Tae Kwon Do
C.F.W. Enterprises, Inc.
4201 Vanowen Pl. Phone: (818)845-2656
Burbank, CA 91505-1139 Fax: (818)845-7761

Magazine focusing on the Korean martial arts. **Founded:** Feb. 1993. **Freq:** Bimonthly. **Print Method:** Web offset. **Cols./Page:** 3. **Key Personnel:** John Corcoran, Editor. **ISSN:** 1065-4682. **Subscription Rates:** $3 single issue. **Remarks:** Accepts advertising.
Ad Rates: BW: $700 **Circ:** Paid ⊕**33,965**
Non-paid ⊕**39,375**

1619 L.A. Parent
PO Box 3204 Phone: (818)846-0400
Burbank, CA 91504 Fax: (818)841-4300

Magazine for parents. **Founded:** 1979. **Freq:** Monthly. **Print Method:** Offset. **Trim Size:** 9 1/2 x 12 1/4. **Cols./Page:** 4. **Col. Width:** 15 picas. **Key Personnel:** Christine Elston, Editor, fax (818)841-4380; Kay Mount, General Mgr., fax (818)841-4380. **Subscription Rates:** $12.
Ad Rates: BW: $4,270 **Circ:** Free ❑**109,155**
4C: $5,170 Paid ❑**326**

1620 Paintball Magazine
C.F.W. Enterprises, Inc.
4201 Vanowen Pl. Phone: (818)845-2656
Burbank, CA 91505-1139 Fax: (818)845-7761

Sports magazine featuring articles on pre-game preparations and equipment. The magazine also answers questions about paintball. **Freq:** Monthly. **Key Personnel:** Jessica Sparks, Editor; Curtis Wong, Publisher. **Subscription Rates:** $19.95. $3 single issue.

1621 Parenting
PO Box 3204 Phone: (818)846-0400
Burbank, CA 91504 Fax: (818)841-4300

Newspaper. **Subtitle:** The Magazine for Southern California Families. **Founded:** 1985. **Freq:** Monthly. **Print Method:** Offset. **Trim Size:** 9 1/2 x 12 1/4. **Key Personnel:** Christine Elston, Editor, fax (818)841-4380; Kay Mount, General Mgr., fax (818)841-4380. **Subscription Rates:** $14 individuals. **Remarks:** Accepts advertising. **Available Online. URL:** http://family.com.
Ad Rates: BW: $3,350 **Circ:** Free ❑**79,414**
4C: $2,150 Paid ❑**108**

1622 Preview Theater Magazine
Hogan Communications
150 E. Olive Ave., Ste. 208 Phone: (818)848-4876
Burbank, CA 91502 Fax: (818)848-4995

Movie, home video, and music magazine for college students. **Founded:** 1986. **Freq:** 6/year (September-November, February-April). **Print Method:** Offset. **Trim Size:** 8 x 10 1/2. **Cols./Page:** 3. **Key Personnel:** Michael P. Hogan, Publisher. **Subscription Rates:** $6.50. **Remarks:** Accepts advertising.
Ad Rates: BW: $7,400 **Circ:** ‡250,000
4C: $8,000

1623 San Diego Parent
PO Box 3204 Phone: (818)846-0400
Burbank, CA 91504 Fax: (818)841-4300

Newspaper. **Subtitle:** Magazine for Southern California Families. **Founded:** 1986. **Freq:** Monthly. **Print Method:** Offset. **Trim Size:** 9 1/2 x 12 1/4. **Key Personnel:** Christine Elston, Editor; Kay Mount, General Mgr. **Remarks:** Accepts advertising.
Ad Rates: BW: $3,350 **Circ:** Free ❑**79,036**
4C: $2,150 Paid ❑**61**

1624 The Tolucan Times
10215 Riverside Dr. Phone: (818)762-2171
Toluca Lake, CA 91602 Fax: (818)980-1900

Community newspaper. **Founded:** 1958. **Freq:** Weekly (Wed.). **Print Method:** Offset. **Trim Size:** 11 x 15. **Cols./Page:** 5. **Col. Width:** 2 inches. **Col. Depth:** 14 inches. **Key Personnel:** Jackie Girard, Managing Editor; Mardi Rustam, Publisher. **Subscription Rates:** $40 individuals. **Remarks:** Accepts advertising. **Formerly**: Tolucan.
Ad Rates: GLR: $4 **Circ:** 25,000
BW: $910
4C: $1,500
SAU: $12.50
PCI: $13

1625 KIIS-AM - 1150
3400 Riverside Dr., Ste.800 Phone: (818)845-1027
Burbank, CA 91505 Fax: (818)556-5447

Format: Top 40. **Simulcasts:** KIIS-FM. **Networks:** Independent. **Founded:** 1927. **Operating Hours:** Continuous. **Key Personnel:** Marc Kaye, Contact. **Wattage:** 5000.

1626 KIIS-FM - 102.7
3400 Riverside Dr. Phone: (818)845-1027
Burbank, CA 91505

Format: Top 40. **Simulcasts:** KXTA-AM, XTRA-AM. **Networks:** Independent. **Founded:** 1948. **Operating Hours:** Continuous. **Key Personnel:** Roy Laughlin, Station Mgr., roy@kiism.com; Dan Kieley, Program Dir.; Charlie Rahilly, General Sales Mgr. **Wattage:** 8000.

1627 KNBC-TV - 4
3000 W. Alameda Ave. Phone: (818)840-4444
Burbank, CA 91523 Fax: (818)840-4271

Format: Commercial TV. **Networks:** NBC. **Operating Hours:** Continuous. **ADI:** Los Angeles (Corona & San Bernardino), CA. **Key Personnel:** L. Reed Manville, Contact.

1628 KPWR-FM - 105.9
2600 W. Olive Ave., Ste. 850 Phone: (818)953-4200
Burbank, CA 91505-4549 Fax: (818)848-0961

Format: Contemporary Hit Radio (CHR). **Networks:** Independent. **Founded:** 1986. **Formerly**: KMGG-FM. **Operating Hours:** Continuous. **Key Personnel:** Doyle L. Rose, Contact. **Wattage:** 72,000. **Ad Rates:** Noncommercial.

1629 KROQ-FM - 106.7
Box 10670 Phone: (818)567-1067
Burbank, CA 91510 Fax: (818)841-5903

Format: Album-Oriented Rock (AOR); Alternative/New Music/Progressive. **Networks:** Independent. **Founded:** 1974. **Operating Hours:** Continuous. **Key Personnel:** Trip Reeb, General Mgr.; Kevin Weatherly, Program Dir.; Jan Kopic, Sales Mgr.; Stacie Seifrit, Promotions Dir.; Boyd Britton, News Dir.; Scott Mason, Operations Mgr. **Wattage:** 5600.

1630 KYSR-FM - 98.7
3500 W. Olive Ave., Ste. 250 Phone: (818)955-7000
Burbank, CA 91505 Fax: (818)953-7759

Format: Adult Contemporary; Contemporary Hit Radio (CHR). **Owner:** Chancellor Media Corp., 99 Revere Pkwy., Medford, MA 02155, (781)393-7715, Fax: (781)391-8367. **Founded:** 1954. **Formerly**: KJOI-FM (1990). **Operating Hours:** Continuous. **Key Personnel:** Traci Cox, Contact, phone (818)953-7582; Ken Christensen, VP/General Manager, phone (818)955-7000, fax (818)953-7759; Paul O'Malley, General Sales Mgr., fax (818)955-7050; Lisa Teagardner, National Sales Mgr., fax (818)955-7050; Robert Lyles, Dir. of Marketing, fax (818)955-6436; Angela Perelli, Program Dir., fax (818)955-6436; Lisa Foxx, Director of Public Affairs, fax (818)955-6436; Bruce James, Traffic Mgr., fax (818)955-6433. **Wattage:** 75,000. **Ad Rates:** Advertising accepted; rates available upon request.

BURLINGAME, pop. 26,173.

W. OA. San Mateo Co. 15 mi. S. of San Francisco. Residential. Independent retail. Light industry.

1631 California Educator
California Teachers Association
1705 Murchison Dr. Phone: (415)697-1400
PO Box 921 Fax: (415)697-0786
Burlingame, CA 94010
California Teachers Association tabloid covering political and professional issues. **Founded:** 1962. **Freq:** 9/year. **Print Method:** Web offset. **Trim Size:** 12 x 18. **Cols./Page:** 4. **Col. Width:** 27 nonpareils. **Col. Depth:** 102 agate lines. **Key Personnel:** Trudy Willis, Editor, phone (916)443-3354, fax (916)443-3055; Greg Smith, Advertising Mgr. **ISSN:** 0896-7326. **Subscription Rates:** Included in membership; $10 nonmembers. **Remarks:** Color advertising accepted; rates available upon request. **Formerly**: CTA/NEA Action (Sept. 1987); CTA Action.
Ad Rates: BW: $3,709 **Circ:** ‡269,942

Hillsborough/Burlingame Boutique and Villager - See Hillsborough

Millbrae Sun - See Millbrae

1632 Pacific Cable TV
401 California Dr. Phone: (415)340-8141
Burlingame, CA 94010

Owner: Post-Newsweek Cable Inc., 4742 24th St., Ste. 270, Phoenix, AZ 85016, (602)468-1177. **Founded:** 1981. **Key Personnel:** Susan Adams, General Mgr.; Victoria Spicer, Asst. Mgr.; Clay Keleher, Chief Engineer; John Pitoniak, Customer Service Mgr. **Cities Served:** Burlingame, Burlingame Hills, CA: subscribing households 7,937; 53 channels; 1 community access channel; 5 hours per week community access programming.

BURNEY, pop. 2,190.

N. CA. Shasta Co. 51 mi. NE of Redding. Tourism. Resort. Saw pulp, veneer mills. Agriculture. Cattle, grain.

1633 Intermountain News
PO Box 1030 Phone: (530)335-4533
Burney, CA 96013-1030 Fax: (530)335-5335
Publication E-mail: editor@im-news.com

Local newspaper. **Founded:** Mar. 1958. **Freq:** Weekly (Wed.). **Print Method:** Offset. **Cols./Page:** 6. **Col. Width:** 2 1/8 inches. **Col. Depth:** 21 inches. **Key Personnel:** Craig Harrington, Publisher. **Subscription Rates:** $30 individuals; $35 out of area. **Remarks:** Accepts advertising.
Ad Rates: BW: $669.38 **Circ:** ‡3,254
4C: $879
PCI: $7.23

1634 KAVA-AM - 1450
37185 Park Ave. Phone: (916)335-4515
Burney, CA 96013-4208

Format: News; Sports; Country. **Networks:** ABC. **Owner:** Tom Collins, 235 Fremont Ave., Los Altos, CA 94022, (415)547-4388. **Founded:** 1967. **Operating Hours:** 5 a.m.-midnight; 5% network, 95% local. **Key Personnel:** Mark W. Collins, Contact; Kelly Ray Tuss, Contact; Bert Jonas, Contact. **Wattage:** 1000. **Ad Rates:** $3-6 for 30 seconds; $5-8 for 60 seconds.

1635 KIBC-FM - 90.5
20410 Marquette St. Phone: (530)335-5422
Burney, CA 96013
E-mail: kibcfm@norcalis.net

Format: Religious; Educational. **Owner:** Burney Educational Broadcasting Foundation, at above address. **Founded:** 1985. **Operating Hours:** Continuous. **Key Personnel:** Wayne B. Hennessey, Jr., President, phone (530)335-2859. **Wattage:** 3000.

CALEXICO, pop. 14,412.

S. CA. Imperial Co. 95 mi. SE of San Diego. Ships fruit and vegetables for eastern markets. Cotton gins; cottonseed oil mill; sheet metal works. Diversified farming. Lettuce, cantaloupes, alfalfa, flax.

1636 Calexico Chronicle
PO Box 72 Phone: (619)357-3214
Calexico, CA 92231 Fax: (619)359-3811

Newspaper. **Founded:** Aug. 4, 1904. **Freq:** Weekly (Thurs.). **Print Method:** Offset. **Cols./Page:** 6. **Col. Width:** 9.5 picas. **Col. Depth:** 182 agate lines. **Key Personnel:** Hildy Carrillo-Rivera, Editor; Lupe T. Acuna, Publisher. **Subscription Rates:** $20 by mail. **Remarks:** Accepts advertising.
Ad Rates: GLR: $.22 **Circ:** Paid 1,926
BW: $600 Free 1,000

1637 KICO-AM - 1490
PO Box 232 Phone: (619)357-5055
Calexico, CA 92231-0232 Fax: (619)357-4168

Format: Hispanic. **Owner:** Calmex Broadcasting Co., at above address, CA, (619)357-1490. **Founded:** 1946. **Operating Hours:** Continuous. **Key Personnel:** Rogelio Gamez, Office Mgr., phone (619)357-5055; Noe Diaz, Program Dir., phone (619)357-5055; Paul E Raine, National Sales Mgr; Doug Hanson, General Mgr., phone (619)357-5055, fax (619)357-4168. **Wattage:** 1000. **Ad Rates:** $10 for 30 seconds; $15 for 60 seconds.

1638 KQVO-FM - 97.7
PO Box 232 Phone: (619)357-5055
Calexico, CA 92231-0232 Fax: (619)357-4168

Format: Adult Contemporary; Hispanic. **Owner:** CAL-MEX Broadcasting Co., Inc., at above address, CA. **Founded:** 1984. **Operating Hours:** Continuous. **Key Personnel:** Doug Hanson, General Mgr.; Paul Raine, Sales Mgr.; Rogelio Gamez, Office Mgr.; Noe Diaz, Program Dir. **Local Programs:** *Desfile De Exitos*, Jesus Hernandez, Mailing contact; *Guitarras De America*, Rufino De La Cruz; *La Hora De Javien Solis*, David Hernandez, Mailing contact. **Wattage:** 6000. **Ad Rates:** $16-23 for 30 seconds; $20-28 for 60 seconds. Combined advertising rates available with KICO-AM.

CALIFORNIA CITY, pop. 2,743.

S. CA. Kern Co. 12 mi. SE of Boron. Residential.

1639 The Mojave Desert News
MOCAL News Corp.
8046 California City Blvd. Phone: (760)373-4812
California City, CA 93505 Fax: (760)373-2941
Free: (800)541-4460
Publication E-mail: mdn@ccis.com

Local newspaper. **Founded:** 1938. **Freq:** Weekly (Thurs.). **Print Method:** off site. **Cols./Page:** 6. **Col. Width:** 12 picas. **Col. Depth:** 21.5 inches. **Key Personnel:** Connie Baker, Editor. **Subscription Rates:** $20 individuals. **Remarks:** Accepts advertising. **Formerly:** The Enterprise.
Ad Rates: GLR: $1.20 **Circ:** Paid ‡5,800
BW: $945 Free ‡200
SAU: $7.50

CALISTOGA, pop. 3,879.

W. CA. Napa Co. 16 mi. NE of Santa Rosa. Resort. Hot mineral springs. Mud baths. bottling works, wineries. Agriculture. Grapes.

1640 The Weekly Calistogan
PO Box 385 Phone: (707)942-6242
Calistoga, CA 94515 Fax: (707)942-4617
Publication E-mail: calnews@netwiz.net

Newspaper with liberal orientation. **Founded:** 1877. **Freq:** Weekly (Thurs.). **Print Method:** Offset. **Cols./Page:** 6. **Col. Width:** 25 nonpareils. **Col. Depth:** 301 agate lines. **Key Personnel:** Scott Jorgeson, Editor. **USPS:** 672-180. **Subscription Rates:** $23 individuals. **Remarks:** Accepts advertising. **URL:** http://www.sonic.net/~johnfr/calistogan. **Formerly:** Independent Calistogan; Calistoga Calistogian.
Ad Rates: GLR: $2.40 **Circ:** ‡3,000
BW: $913.50
PCI: $7.83

CAMARILLO, pop. 37,732.

SW CA. Ventura Co. 15 mi. E. of Ventura. Fruit and nuts shipped. Nurseries. Agriculture. Beans, oranges, lemons, walnuts.

1641 The Camarillo Star
Ventura County Star
2245 Ventura Blvd. Phone: (805)987-5001
Camarillo, CA 93010 Fax: (805)482-8631

General newspaper. **Founded:** 1926. **Freq:** Mon.-Sun. (morn.). **Print Method:** Offset. **Cols./Page:** 6. **Col. Width:** 2 1/16 inches. **Col. Depth:** 21 1/2 inches. **Key Personnel:** Mike Craft, Managing Editor; Hank Crockett, Publisher. **Remarks:** Accepts advertising. **Formerly:** The Camarillo Daily News.
Ad Rates: SAU: $9.90 **Circ:** Mon.-Fri. 10,878
Sun. 11,286

1642 Powerlifting USA Magazine
Powerlifting USA
PO Box 467 Phone: (805)482-2378
Camarillo, CA 93011-0467 Fax: (805)987-4275
Free: (800)448-7693

Magazine covering the sport of powerlifting. **Founded:** 1977. **Freq:** Monthly. **Print Method:** Web offset. **Trim Size:** 8 1/2 x 10 7/8. **Cols./Page:** 4. **Col. Width:** 20 nonpareils. **Col. Depth:** 140 agate lines. **Key Personnel:** Michael Robert Lambert, Editor and Publisher. **ISSN:** 0199-2536. **Subscription Rates:** $31.95 individuals; $3.50 single issue. **Remarks:** Accepts advertising.
Ad Rates: BW: $768 **Circ:** Paid ‡18,700
4C: $1043 Non-paid ‡99

1643 KADY-TV - 63
950 Flynn Rd. Phone: (805)388-0081
Camarillo, CA 93012 Fax: (805)388-9693
E-mail: kadytz@aol.com

Format: Commercial TV. **Networks:** United Paramount Network. **Owner:** Biltmore Broadcasting LLC, at above address. **Founded:** 1985. **Formerly:** KTIE-TV (1987); Riklis Broadcasting. **Operating Hours:** Continuous. **ADI:** Santa Barbara-Santa Maria-San Luis Obispo,CA. **Key Personnel:** Brian E. Cobb, President/CEO; Jeanette Kuszlyk, Business Mgr.; Stan Martin, Production Mgr.; Guadalupe Paniagua, Master Control Mgr.; Denise LeRette, Promotion/Public Affairs Mgr.; Joel B. Day, C.O.O./General Mgr.; John Dobel, Internet Mgr., http://www.kadynet.com; Judy Dykeman, Traffic/Program Mgr.; Georgette Gramanz, Accounting Mgr.; Alan Nichols, Chief Engineer. **Ad Rates:** $30-400 for 30 seconds. **URL:** http://www.kadynet.com.

1644 KEYQ-AM - 980
2310 Ponderosa Dr., No. 28 Phone: (805)482-4797
Camarillo, CA 93010 Fax: (805)388-5202

Format: Hispanic; Religious. **Simulcasts:** KMRO. **Networks:** Independent. **Owner:** The Association for Communication Education, Inc., at above address. **Founded:** 1957. **Formerly:** KEAP-AM (1990). **Operating Hours:** 6 a.m.-midnight. **Wattage:** 500. **Ad Rates:** Noncommercial.

1645 KGZO-FM - 90.9
2310 Ponderosa Dr., Ste. 28 Phone: (805)792-9071
Camarillo, CA 93010 Fax: (805)388-5202

Format: Ethnic; Religious. **Owner:** The Association for Community Education, Inc., at above address. **Founded:** 1996. **Operating Hours:** Continuous. **ADI:** Bakersfield, CA. **Key Personnel:** Pepe Caballero, Operations Dir.; Mary Guthrie, General Mgr. **Ad Rates:** Noncommercial.

1646 KMRO-FM - 90.3
2310 Ponderosa Dr. Phone: (805)482-4797
Camarillo, CA 93010 Fax: (805)388-5202

Format: Ethnic; Religious. **Owner:** The Association for Community Education, Inc., at above address. **Founded:** 1987. **Operating Hours:** Continuous. **ADI:** Bakersfield, CA. **Key Personnel:** Peter Caballero, Operations Dir.; Mary Guthrie, General Mgr. **Wattage:** 4430. **Ad Rates:** Noncommercial.

CAMBRIA, pop. 1,716.

SW CA. San Luis Obispo Co. On Pacific Ocean, halfway between Los Angeles and San Francisco. Resort. Hearst-San Simeon State Park.

1647 Arabian Horse World
1316 Tamson Dr., Ste. 101 Phone: (805)927-6511
Cambria, CA 93428 Fax: (805)927-6522
Free: (800)955-9423

Magazine covering Arabian horse-breeding news and information for owners, breeders, and admirers. **Founded:** May 1960. **Freq:** Monthly. **Print Method:** Offset. **Trim Size:** 8 3/8 x 10 7/8. **Key Personnel:** Denise Hearst, Publisher; Wendy Flynn, Adv. Mgr. **ISSN:** 0003-7494. **Subscription Rates:** $40.00 individuals; $5 single issue; $65 out of country; $5 single issue. **Remarks:** Accepts advertising. **Online:** Odyssey Online.
Ad Rates: BW: $400 **Circ:** 12,000
4C: $650

1648 The Cambrian
PO Box 67 Phone: (805)927-8652
Cambria, CA 93428-0067
Community newspaper. **Founded:** 1931. **Freq:** Weekly (Thurs.). **Print Method:** Offset. **Cols./Page:** 6. **Col. Width:** 11.2 picas. **Col. Depth:** 21 1/2 inches. **Key Personnel:** Bill Morem, Managing Editor, phone (805)927-8895; Nancy Carr, Business Mgr. **Subscription Rates:** $23 individuals; $32 out of area; $.50 single issue. **Remarks:** Accepts advertising.
Ad Rates: GLR: $1 **Circ:** 4,100
PCI: $8.14

1649 KOTR-FM - 94.9
840 Sheffield St. Phone: (805)927-5021
Cambria, CA 93428-2804 Fax: (805)927-0235

Format: Adult Album Alternative. **Owner:** Central Coast Community Broadcasting, Inc., at above address. **Founded:** 1984. **Operating Hours:** Continuous; 100% local. **ADI:** Santa Barbara-Santa Maria-San Luis Obispo,CA. **Key Personnel:** Bruce W. Howard, Pres./Gen. Mgr.; Drew Ross, Program Dir.; Dean Kattari, Music Dir. **Wattage:** 25,000. **Ad Rates:** $15 for 30 seconds; $20 for 60 seconds. **URL:** http://www.kotrfm.com.

CAMP PENDLETON

1650 Flight Jacket
South Orange County News
PO Box 3629 Phone: (714)768-3631
Mission Viejo, CA 92690 Fax: (714)454-7354

Community newspaper (El Toro and Tustin Marine Corps bases). **Founded:** 1945. **Freq:** Weekly (Fri.). **Print Method:** Offset. **Cols./Page:** 5. **Col. Depth:** 13 inches. **Key Personnel:** Capt. Betsy Sweatt, Editor; Douglas E. Hanes, Publisher; Peggy Blevens, Advertising Mgr. **Subscription Rates:** Free. **Remarks:** Accepts advertising.
Ad Rates: PCI: $32.17 **Circ:** Free ‡13,000

1651 The Scout
PO Box 555019 Phone: (760)725-9376
Camp Pendleton, CA 92055-5019 Fax: (760)385-0053
Military newspaper. **Founded:** 1945. **Freq:** Weekly. **Cols./Page:** 6. **Key Personnel:** Judy Jones, Editor, jonesjpennsylvaniadleton.usmc.mil. **Subscription Rates:** $20 individuals. **Remarks:** Accepts advertising.
Ad Rates: GLR: $19.50 **Circ:** (Not Reported)
BW: $25,500

CAMPBELL, pop. 27,067.

W. CA. Santa Clara Co. 5 mi. SW of San Jose. Residential.

1652 Campbell Express
Hanchett Publishing
334 E. Campbell Ave. Phone: (408)374-9700
Campbell, CA 95008 Fax: (408)374-0813

Independent newspaper (tabloid). **Founded:** Jan. 1, 1954. **Freq:** Weekly (Wed.). **Print Method:** Offset. **Trim Size:** 11 x

17. **Cols./Page:** 6. **Col. Width:** 1 3/4 inches. **Col. Depth:** 16 inches. **Key Personnel:** Wilton von Gease, Editor; Glenna von Gease, Publisher. **Subscription Rates:** $5 individuals; $10 out of state. **Remarks:** Accepts advertising. **Formerly:** Cambrian News (May 1, 1987).
Ad Rates: GLR: $.20 **Circ:** ‡1,562
BW: $268
PCI: $2.80

CANOGA PARK

S. CA. Los Angeles Co. Suburb of Los Angeles. Aerospace, rocket engines for space shuttle. Residential.

1653 Affordable Aircraft
Challenge Publications, Inc.
7950 Deering Ave. Phone: (818)887-0550
Canoga Park, CA 91304-5063 Fax: (818)884-1343
Publisher E-mail: mail@challengeweb.com

Magazine profiling airplanes pilots can fly without licenses. **Founded:** 1991. **Freq:** Quarterly. **Key Personnel:** Norm Goyer, Editor; Edwin A. Schenpf, Publisher. **Subscription Rates:** $5.95 single issue.

1654 Air Combat
Challenge Publications, Inc.
7950 Deering Ave. Phone: (818)887-0550
Canoga Park, CA 91304-5063 Fax: (818)884-1343
Publisher E-mail: mail@challengeweb.com

Consumer magazine covering military fighter jets and bombers. **Founded:** 1973. **Freq:** Bimonthly. **Cols./Page:** 3. **Key Personnel:** Michael O'Leary, Editor; Michael Astamendi, Advertising Mgr.; Susan Duprey, Circulation Mgr. **ISSN:** 0044-6955. **Subscription Rates:** $16.95 individuals; $4.50 single issue. **Remarks:** Accepts advertising.
Circ: Controlled ⊕**35,484**

1655 Aviation Art
Challenge Publications, Inc.
7950 Deering Ave. Phone: (818)887-0550
Canoga Park, CA 91304-5063 Fax: (818)884-1343
Publisher E-mail: mail@challengeweb.com

Guide to aviation artists, galleries, and distributors. **Founded:** 1991. **Freq:** Quarterly. **Key Personnel:** Michael O'Leary, Editor; Edwin A. Schepf, Publisher. **Subscription Rates:** $23.95. $5.95 single issue.

1656 Battle of Britain
Challenge Publications, Inc.
7950 Deering Ave. Phone: (818)887-0550
Canoga Park, CA 91304-5063 Fax: (818)884-1343
Publisher E-mail: mail@challengeweb.com

Magazine commemorating the Battle of Britain. **Founded:** 1991. **Freq:** Quarterly. **Key Personnel:** Michael O'Leary, Editor; Edwin Schnepf, Publisher. **Subscription Rates:** $5.95 single issue.

1657 Central California Jewish Heritage
Heritage Publishing Co.
7334 Topanga Canyon Blvd., Ste. 110 Phone: (818)999-9921
Fax: (818)999-6715
Canoga Park, CA 91303-3345
Publisher E-mail: heritagepub@earthlink.net

Tabloid serving Jewish life in Central California. **Founded:** 1959. **Freq:** Monthly. **Print Method:** Offset. **Cols./Page:** 6. **Col. Width:** 19 nonpareils. **Col. Depth:** 210 agate lines. **Key Personnel:** Dan Brin, Editor; Herb Brin, Publisher. **Subscription Rates:** $15 individuals. **Remarks:** Accepts advertising.
Circ: (Not Reported)

1658 Future War
Challenge Publications, Inc.
7950 Deering Ave. Phone: (818)887-0550
Canoga Park, CA 91304-5063 Fax: (818)884-1343
Publisher E-mail: mail@challengeweb.com

Magazine highlighting the Army, Navy, and Air Force roles in the Gulf War. **Founded:** 1991. **Freq:** Quarterly. **Key Personnel:** Joe Poyer, Editor; Edwin Schnepf, Publisher. **Subscription Rates:** $5.95 single issue.

1659 Heritage Southwest Jewish Press
Heritage Publishing Co.
7334 Topanga Canyon Blvd., Ste. 110 Phone: (818)999-9921
Fax: (818)999-6715
Canoga Park, CA 91303-3345
Publisher E-mail: heritagepub@earthlink.net

Newspaper serving local Jewish communities. **Founded:** 1914. **Freq:** Weekly. **Print Method:** Offset. **Cols./Page:** 6. **Col. Width:** 18 nonpareils. **Col. Depth:** 196 agate lines. **Key Personnel:** Herb Brin, Publisher. **Subscription Rates:** Free; $30 by mail. **Remarks:** Accepts advertising.
Ad Rates: BW: $1,563 **Circ:** Free ‡13,500
PCI: $23

1660 Junior Baseball Magazine
2D Publishing
PO Box 9099 Phone: (818)710-1234
Canoga Park, CA 91309 Fax: (818)710-1877
Publication E-mail: editor@juniorbaseball.com; publisher@juniorbaseball.com

Magazine for youth baseball players, parents, coaches. **Subtitle:** America's Youth Baseball Magazine. **Founded:** Aug. 1996. **Freq:** Bimonthly. **Print Method:** Web offset. **Trim Size:** 8 1/4 x 10 7/8. **Key Personnel:** Dave Destler, Publisher; Dayna Destler, Customer Service. **Subscription Rates:** $17.70 individuals; $2.95 single issue. **Remarks:** Accepts advertising. **Formerly:** Junior League Baseball.
Ad Rates: BW: $3,900 **Circ:** Paid 60,000
4C: $5,100

1661 Mountain Biking
Challenge Publications, Inc.
7950 Deering Ave. Phone: (818)887-0550
Canoga Park, CA 91304-5063 Fax: (818)884-1343
Publisher E-mail: mail@challengeweb.com

Sports magazine featuring mountain bike riding and racing. **Freq:** Monthly. **Trim Size:** 7 3/4 x 10 7/8. **Cols./Page:** 3. **Key Personnel:** Chris Hatounian, SP, Editor; Ed Schnepf, Publisher. **Subscription Rates:** $3.50. **Remarks:** Advertising accepted; rates available upon request. **Formerly:** Sport Cycling Freewheelin.
Circ: (Not Reported)

1662 Navy Seals
Challenge Publications, Inc.
7950 Deering Ave. Phone: (818)887-0550
Canoga Park, CA 91304-5063 Fax: (818)884-1343
Publisher E-mail: mail@challengeweb.com

Magazine reporting on the activities of the Navy Seals. **Founded:** 1991. **Freq:** Quarterly. **Key Personnel:** Edwin Schnepf, Editor and Publisher. **Subscription Rates:** $3.95 single issue.

1663 Rod Action
Challenge Publications, Inc.
7950 Deering Ave. Phone: (818)887-0550
Canoga Park, CA 91304-5063 Fax: (818)884-1343
Publisher E-mail: mail@challengeweb.com

Magazine covering street rods and customized automobiles. **Founded:** 1971. **Freq:** Monthly. **Key Personnel:** Rex Reese, Editor; Edwin A. Schnepf, Publisher. **Subscription Rates:** $21.95 individuals; $3.99 single issue. **Remarks:** Accepts advertising. **Formerly:** Street Rod Action (Oct. 1996); Rod Action & Street Machines.
Ad Rates: BW: $1170 **Circ:** (Not Reported)
4C: $1655

1664 Sea Classics
Challenge Publications, Inc.
7950 Deering Ave. Phone: (818)887-0550
Canoga Park, CA 91304-5063 Fax: (818)884-1343
Publisher E-mail: mail@challengeweb.com

Consumer magazine covering current and historical maritime and naval events. **Founded:** 1968. **Freq:** Monthly. **Key Personnel:** Ed Schnepf, Editor; Belinda Henderson, Advertising Mgr.; Susan Duprey, Circulation Mgr. **ISSN:** 0048-9867. **Subscription Rates:** $29.95 individuals; $4.50 single issue. **Remarks:** Accepts advertising.
Circ: Paid ⊕**57,346**

CANYON COUNTRY

1665 KBET-AM - 1220
27565 Sierra Hwy. Phone: (805)298-1220
Canyon Country, CA 91351-0220 Fax: (805)252-2679

Format: Adult Contemporary. **Networks:** CNN Radio; Westwood One Radio. **Founded:** 1989. **Operating Hours:** Continuous. **ADI:** Los Angeles (Corona & San Bernardino), CA. **Key Personnel:** A.J. Morgan, News Dir.; Carl Goldman, General Mgr.; Chip Ehrhardt, Sales Mgr. **Wattage:** 1000.

1666 Time Warner Cable
18356 Soledad Canyon Rd. Phone: (805)252-2318
Canyon Country, CA 91351 Fax: (805)251-6181

Founded: 1963. **Formerly:** Western CATV Inc. **Cities Served:** Los Angeles County, Newhall, Santa Clarita, and Saugus, CA.

CAPISTRANO BEACH, pop. 4,149.

S. CA. Orange Co. 30 mi. S. of Santa Ana. Residential.

1667 Gun World
Gallant/Charger Publications, Inc.
34249 Camino Capistrano Phone: (714)493-2101
Capistrano Beach, CA 92624 Fax: (714)240-8680
Free: (800)767-1017

Magazine for gun enthusiasts. **Founded:** 1960. **Freq:** 7/year. **Print Method:** Offset. **Trim Size:** 8 x 10 3/4. **Cols./Page:** 3. **Col. Width:** 2 1/4 inches. **Col. Depth:** 10 inches. **Key Personnel:** Jack Lewis, Editor and Publisher; Jack Mitchell, Advertising Mgr. **ISSN:** 0017-5641. **Subscription Rates:** $18 individuals; $23 other countries; $2.95 single issue. **Remarks:** Accepts advertising.
Ad Rates: BW: $1560 **Circ:** Paid ‡115,000
4C: $2470 Non-paid ‡485
PCI: $53

CARDIFF-BY-THE-SEA

1668 Journal of Unconventional History
Box 459 Phone: (619)459-5748
Cardiff-by-the-Sea, CA 92007 Fax: (619)459-0936

Journal of unconventional history. **Founded:** 1989. **Freq:** Triennial. **Cols./Page:** 1. **Key Personnel:** Dr. Aline Hornaday, Editor, ahornaday@ucsd.edu; Dr. Ann Elwood, Editor, phone (760)944-2936, aelwood@coyote.csusm.edu. **ISSN:** 1085-4851. **Subscription Rates:** $20 individuals; $22.50 institutions; $7.50 single issue. **Remarks:** Accepts advertising.
Ad Rates: BW: $75 **Circ:** Combined 400

CARLSBAD, pop. 35,490.

S. CA. San Diego Co. 35 mi. N. of San Diego. Resort. Tourism. Industrial parks. Electronics, computers, silicon chips. Agriculture. Fruit, vegetables, flowers.

1669 Carlsbad Sun
West Coast Community Newspapers
2841 Loker Ave. E. Phone: (619)431-4850
Carlsbad, CA 92008 Fax: (619)431-4888

Community newspaper. **Founded:** 1925. **Freq:** Weekly (Thurs.). **Print Method:** Offset. **Trim Size:** 13 3/4 x 21 3/4. **Cols./Page:** 6. **Col. Width:** 12.3 picas. **Col. Depth:** 297 agate lines. **Key Personnel:** Donna Medeiros, Publisher. **Subscription Rates:** Free; $50 individuals. **Remarks:** Accepts advertising. **URL:** http://www.thinklocal.com. **Formerly:** Carlsbad Journal.
Ad Rates: PCI: $7 **Circ:** Free ‡70,000

Del Mar Sun - See Del Mar

1670 Digital Systems Report
Computer Economics, Inc.
5841 Edison Pl. Phone: (760)438-8100
Carlsbad, CA 92008-6519 Fax: (760)431-1126
Free: (800)326-8100
Publication E-mail: info@compecon.cm
Publisher E-mail: info@compecan.com

Software journal for Digital professionals. **Subtitle:** For Digital Software professionals. **Founded:** 1979. **Freq:** Quarterly. **Print Method:** Web offset. **Trim Size:** 8 1/2 x 11. **Cols./Page:** 2. **Col. Width:** 42 nonpareils. **Col. Depth:** 137 agate lines. **Key Personnel:** Bruno Bassi, Publisher; Anne Zalatan, Group Publisher; Mark McManus, Executive Editor. **ISSN:** 1086-9638. **Subscription Rates:** $95 individuals; $30 single issue. **Remarks:** Advertising not accepted. **Formerly:** VAX Professional; Digital Systems Journal; The Software Journal for VMS.
Circ: (Not Reported)

1671 Fire-Rescue Magazine
Jems Communications
PO Box 2789 Phone: (760)431-9797
Carlsbad, CA 92018-2789 Fax: (760)930-9567
Free: (800)266-5367

Magazine addressing the needs of emergency response personnel, including techniques for extrication, treatment, and transport on all terrain. **Founded:** Mar. 1997. **Freq:** Monthly. **Print Method:** Offset. **Trim Size:** 7 7/8 x 10 7/8. **Cols./Page:** 3. **Col. Width:** 13 picas. **Col. Depth:** 9 1/2 inches. **Key Personnel:** Larry Stevens, Editor, phone (702)423-7675, fax (702)423-7579, larry.stevens@jems.com; James O. Page, Publisher; Veronica Brisley, Advertising Dir. **Subscription Rates:** $25.95 individuals. **Remarks:** Accepts advertising. **URL:** http://www.jems.com. **Alt. Formats:** Microform. **Formed by the merger of:** Firefighter's News; Rescue Magazine.
Ad Rates: BW: $2,020 **Circ:** Paid ‡50,000
4C: $2,695 Non-paid ‡39,000
PCI: $70

1672 Gems & Gemology
Gemological Institute of America
5345 Armada Dr. Phone: (760)603-4000
Carlsbad, CA 92008 Fax: (760)603-4070
Free: (800)421-7250
Publication E-mail: akeller@gia.edu
Publisher E-mail: gia.edu

Gemology and mineralogy magazine featuring articles on gemstone identification, localities, synthetics, simulants, treatments, and antique jewelry. **Founded:** 1934. **Freq:** Quarterly. **Print Method:** Offset. **Trim Size:** 8 1/2 x 11. **Cols./Page:** 2. **Col. Width:** 19 picas. **Col. Depth:** 52 picas. **Key Personnel:** Alice S. Keller, Editor, phone (760)603-4504, fax (760)603-4595, akeller@gia.edu; Brendan Laurs, Sr. Editor, phone (760)603-4503. **ISSN:** 0016-626X. **Subscription Rates:** $64.95 individuals; $75 other countries; $11 single issue; $16 single issue elsewhere. **Remarks:** Advertising not accepted. **URL:** http://www.gia.giaonline.edu.
Circ: 10,000

1673 JEMS
Jems Communications
PO Box 2789 Phone: (760)431-9797
Carlsbad, CA 92018-2789 Fax: (760)930-9567
Free: (800)266-5367

Subtitle: Journal of Emergency Medical Services. **Founded:** Mar. 1980. **Freq:** Monthly. **Print Method:** Offset. **Trim Size:** 8 3/8 x 10 7/8. **Cols./Page:** 3 and 2. **Col. Width:** 13 and 20 picas. **Col. Depth:** 140 agate lines. **Key Personnel:** A.J. Heightman, Contact, phone (760)804-6689, aj.heightman@jems.com; Lisa Dionne, Managing Editor; James O. Page, Publisher, james.page@jems.com. **ISSN:** 0197-2510. **Subscription Rates:** $24.97 individuals. **Remarks:** Accepts advertising. **URL:** http://www.jems.com. **Alt. Formats:** Microform.
Ad Rates: GLR: $1.75 **Circ:** Paid 32,000
BW: $2,565 Controlled 8,000
4C: $3,265
PCI: $75

1674 Mexico Events & Destinations
Travel Mexico Magazine Group
PO Box 188037 Phone: (619)433-0090
Carlsbad, CA 92009-0801 Fax: (619)433-0197

Magazine focusing on travel in Mexico. **Founded:** 1992. **Freq:** Quarterly. **Print Method:** Web offset. **Trim Size:** 8 3/8 x 10 7/8. **Cols./Page:** 3. **Col. Width:** 2 5/16 inches. **Col. Depth:** 10 inches. **Key Personnel:** Kirk Waisler, Publisher; Jim Sullivan, Advertising Dir. **ISSN:** 1048-5139. **Subscription Rates:** $11 individuals; $3.50 single issue. **Remarks:** Accepts advertising.
Ad Rates: BW: $4,200 **Circ:** Paid 30,000
4C: $5,600 Controlled 70,000

Rancho Santa Fe Sun - See Rancho Santa Fe

1675 The Record
Horses Magazine
21 Greenview Ter. Phone: (619)931-9958
Carlsbad, CA 92009 Fax: (619)931-0650
Free: (800)254-6773

Worldwide jumping and dressage horse competition. **Founded:** 1961. **Freq:** Quarterly. **Print Method:** Offset. **Trim Size:** 8 1/2 x 11. **Key Personnel:** John Quirk, Publisher; Terry Reim, Managing Editor; Rick Sudler, Advertising Dir. **ISSN:** 0046-7936. **Subscription Rates:** $19.95 individuals; $7.50 single issue. **Remarks:** Accepts advertising. **Alt. Formats:** CD-ROM. **Formerly:** Horses Magazine.
Ad Rates: BW: $390 **Circ:** Paid ‡350
4C: $595 Non-paid ‡2,300
PCI: $6.00

1676 West Coast Community Newspaper
West Coast Community Newspapers
2841 Loker Ave. E. Phone: (619)431-4850
Carlsbad, CA 92008 Fax: (619)431-4888
Publication E-mail: suneditor@wccnews.com.

Community newspaper. **Print Method:** Offset. **Trim Size:** 13 3/4 x 21 3/4. **Cols./Page:** 6. **Col. Width:** 12 picas. **Col. Depth:** 297 agate lines. **Key Personnel:** D. Medeiros, Publisher. **Remarks:** Accepts advertising. **URL:** http://www.thinklocal.com.
Circ: (Not Reported)

1677 Daniels Cablevision
5720 El Camino Real Phone: (760)438-7741
Carlsbad, CA 92008 Fax: (760)438-8461

Founded: 1977. **Key Personnel:** Joni Odum, General Mgr.; Valarie Brown, Local Programming; Phil Urbina, Contact; Sue Otto, Marketing; John McGuiness, Sales Mgr. **Cities Served:** Carlsbad, Del Mar, Enantas, Encinetas, Fallbrook, Lake San Marcos, Vista, CA: subscribing households 59,000; 57 channels; 1 community access channel; 25 hours per week community access programming.

1678 KCEO-AM - 1000
550 Laguna Dr. Phone: (760)729-1000
Carlsbad, CA 92008 Fax: (760)434-2367

Format: Talk; News. **Networks:** Mutual Broadcasting System. **Founded:** 1967. **Formerly:** KVSD-AM (1990). **Operating Hours:** Continuous. **ADI:** San Diego, CA. **Key Personnel:** John Van Zante, Program Dir.; Art Astor, General Mgr. **Local Programs:** *Market Talk*, Mike Green, Mailing contact, (619)551-9449, Fax (619)729-7067; *Money in the Morning*, Sara Chamberlin, Mailing contact, (619)746-5371, Fax (619)729-7067; *Nature of Health*, Don Bodenbach, Mailing contact, (619)752-7447, Fax (619)729-7067. **Wattage:** 2500. **Ad Rates:** Advertising accepted; rates available upon request. Combined advertising rates available with KFSD, KSPA.

1679 KSPA-AM - 1450
550 Laguna Dr. Phone: (760)745-8511
Carlsbad, CA 92008 Fax: (760)745-5828
E-mail: kfsdkspa@pacbell.net

Format: Adult Contemporary. **Owner:** Astor Broadcast Group, at above address, (760)729-1000, Fax: (760)434-2367. **Founded:** 1958. **Formerly:** KOWN-AM (1987). **Operating Hours:** Continuous; 100% local. **ADI:** San Diego, CA. **Key Personnel:** Art Astor, President, phone (714)502-9494, fax (714)502-9400; Bob Royster, Engineering; Sandra Jennings, Station Mgr.; Melissa Eyler, Traffic Mgr.; John VanZante, Operations Mgr. **Local Programs:** *The Golden Page of Music* Noon - 1 p.m., Rod Page; *The Lyons Den* 6 a.m. - 12 noon, Tom Lyons. **Wattage:** 1000. **Ad Rates:** Combined advertising rates available with KECD-FM, KCED-AM.

CARMEL, pop. 4,707.

W. CA. Monterey Co. On Pacific Ocean, 4 mi. SW of Monterey. Exclusive residential community.

1680 Carmel Pine Cone
Carmel Communications
PO Box G-1 Phone: (408)624-0162
Carmel, CA 93921 Fax: (408)624-8463
Publication E-mail: mail@carmelpinecone.com

Community newspaper. **Founded:** 1915. **Freq:** Weekly (Fri.). **Print Method:** Offset. **Cols./Page:** 6. **Col. Width:** 21 nonpareils. **Col. Depth:** 224 agate lines. **Key Personnel:** Paul Miller, Publisher. **Subscription Rates:** Free; $95 individuals 3rd class. **Remarks:** Accepts advertising.
Ad Rates: GLR: $19.10 **Circ:** Paid ‡25,000
PCI: $13.20

1681 Community Spirit Magazine (Carmel)
Community Spirit Publications
Box 4628 Phone: (408)625-1557
Carmel, CA 93921 Fax: (408)625-3424
Publisher E-mail: mediamanagement@mcimail.com

Trade magazine covering environmental, technology and travel issues. **Founded:** 1979. **Freq:** Weekly. **Print Method:** Web offset. **Trim Size:** 8 1/2 x 11 1/2. **Key Personnel:** Susan Hawthorne, Editor; Sharon Ewing, Advertising. **Subscription Rates:** $28 individuals; $4 single issue. **Remarks:** Accepts advertising.
Circ: Combined 125,000

1682 Guest Life Monterey Bay
Pacific/Guest Life Inc.
PO Box 7540 Phone: (408)375-5711
Carmel, CA 93921-7540 Fax: (408)626-5744

General interest magazine serving local areas. **Founded:** 1985. **Freq:** Semimonthly. **Trim Size:** 8 3/8 x 10 7/8. **Key Personnel:** Sharon Bates, Publisher. **ISSN:** 1047-3610. **Subscription Rates:** $12.95. $2.95 single issue. **Remarks:** Accepts advertising. **URL:** http://www.guestlife.com. **Formerly:** Pacific, The Monterey Bay; Monterey Bay.
Ad Rates: BW: $2,400 **Circ:** Paid 500
4C: $3,200 Controlled 20,000

1683 Key Magazine/Carmel and Monterey Peninsula
Tri-County Publications
PO Box 223859 Phone: (408)624-3411
Carmel, CA 93922 Fax: (408)625-0767

Tourist magazine for the peninsula area. **Founded:** Apr. 1, 1969. **Freq:** Monthly. **Print Method:** Offset. **Trim Size:** 5 1/2 x 8 1/2. **Cols./Page:** 2. **Col. Width:** 14 picas. **Col. Depth:** 7 3/4 inches. **Key Personnel:** Dane Riggenbach, Publisher. **Subscription Rates:** $20 individuals; $2 single issue. **Remarks:** Accepts advertising.
Ad Rates: BW: $800 **Circ:** Non-paid ‡39,000
4C: $1,100

1684 KRML-AM - 1410
PO Box 22440 Phone: (408)624-6431
Carmel, CA 93922 Fax: (408)625-5598

Format: Jazz. **Simulcasts:** KLON-FM. **Networks:** Independent. **Founded:** 1957. **Operating Hours:** Continuous. **ADI:** Salinas-Monterey, CA. **Key Personnel:** Gilbert Wisdom, Co-Owner; Alan P. Schultz, Co-Owner/Gen. Mgr. **Local Programs:** *Concord Jazz Program*, Alan Schultz; *Morning Brew*, Michael Coleman. **Wattage:** 2500. **Ad Rates:** $20-30 for 30 seconds; $50 for 60 seconds.

CARMICHAEL

NC CA. Sacramento Co. 80 mi. NE of San Francisco.

1685 Carmichael Times
PO Box 88 Phone: (916)483-0946
Carmichael, CA 95609-0088 Fax: (916)483-1902

Community newspaper. **Founded:** 1981. **Freq:** Weekly. **Print Method:** Web offset. **Trim Size:** 10 x 16. **Cols./Page:** 5. **Col. Width:** 1 7/8 inches. **Key Personnel:** Shirley Turner, Editor and Publisher; Paul O'Brien, Publisher. **Subscription Rates:** $39 individuals. **Remarks:** Accepts advertising.
Ad Rates: GLR: $1 **Circ:** (Not Reported)
BW: $830.40
PCI: $17

1686 KFIA-AM - 710
5705 Marconi Ave. Phone: (916)485-7710
Carmichael, CA 95608 Fax: (916)485-1446
E-mail: kfia@calweb.com

Format: Contemporary Christian. **Founded:** 1979. **Operating Hours:** Continuous. **ADI:** Sacramento-Stockton, CA. **Key Personnel:** Joe Cruz, General Mgr.; Dennis Goode, Program Mgr. **Local Programs:** *Best of Health*, Steve Gauer; *Homefront*, Steve Gauer; *More that is Money*, Steve Gauer. **Wattage:** 25,000. **Ad Rates:** $18-25 for 30 seconds; $28-40 for 60 seconds.

CARPINTERIA, pop. 10,835.

SW CA. Santa Barbara Co. On Pacific Ocean, 12 mi. S. of Santa Barbara. Tourism. Light manufacturing. Agriculture.

1687 California Grower
Rincon Information Management
PO Box 370 Phone: (805)684-6581
Carpinteria, CA 93014 Fax: (805)684-1535
Publication E-mail: cgeditor@west.net

Magazine focusing on growing and marketing techniques for citrus, avocado, apple stonefruit, grapes, trees and vines. **Founded:** Oct. 1977. **Freq:** 11/year. **Print Method:** Offset. **Trim Size:** 8 3/8 x 10 7/8. **Cols./Page:** 3. **Col. Width:** 13.5 picas. **Col. Depth:** 9 3/4 inches. **Key Personnel:** Willard Thompson, Publisher, phone (805)684-6581; John Larralde, Publisher; Christine Jutzi, Editor; Jo Thompson, Circulation. **ISSN:** 0888-1715. **Subscription Rates:** $22 individuals; $33 two years. **Remarks:** Accepts advertising.
Ad Rates: BW: $1,870 **Circ:** Paid ‡3,000
4C: $2,750 Controlled ‡7,000
PCI: $0.62

1688 Coastal View
4856 Carpinteria Ave. Phone: (805)684-4428
Carpinteria, CA 93013 Fax: (805)684-4650
Publisher E-mail: cvnews@west.net

Community newspaper. **Founded:** Oct. 23, 1994. **Freq:** Weekly. **Print Method:** Web offset. **Trim Size:** 11 x 17. **Cols./Page:** 4. **Col. Width:** 2 1/2 inches. **Col. Depth:** 16 inches. **Key Personnel:** Michael VanStry, Publisher. **Subscription Rates:** $42 individuals; Free to qualified subscribers. **Remarks:** Accepts advertising. **URL:** http://www.coastalview.com.
Ad Rates: GLR: $1 **Circ:** Non-paid 6,000
BW: $544 Paid 177
4C: $619
PCI: $9.50

1689 Freebies
Freebies Publishing Co.
1135 Eugenia Pl Phone: (805)566-1225
Carpinteria, CA 93014 Fax: (805)566-1407
Publication E-mail: freebies@aol.com; freebies@earthlink.net

Consumer publication containing information on free product samples. **Subtitle:** The Magazine With Something for Nothing. **Founded:** 1977. **Freq:** 5/year. **Print Method:** Web offset. **Trim Size:** 8 1/2 x 11. **Cols./Page:** 3. **Col. Width:** 2 1/4 inches. **Col. Depth:** 9 1/4 inches. **Key Personnel:** Abel Magana, Editor; Harry Short, Publisher. **ISSN:** 0148-2092.

Subscription Rates: $8.95 individuals. **Remarks:** Accepts advertising.
Ad Rates: BW: $4,000 **Circ:** Paid ⊕**356,815**
4C: $6,000 Non-paid ⊕**1,825**
PCI: $255

CARSON

1690 Trailer Boats Magazine
Poole Publications, Inc.
20700 Belshaw Ave. Phone: (310)537-6322
PO Box 5427 Fax: (310)537-8735
Carson, CA 90749-5427
Publication E-mail: tbmeditors@aol.com

Magazine for owners and prospective buyers of trailerable boats under 30 feet. **Subtitle:** America's Only Trailerboating Magazine. **Founded:** 1971. **Freq:** 11/year. **Print Method:** Offset. **Trim Size:** 8 x 10 7/8. **Cols./Page:** 3. **Col. Width:** 27 nonpareils. **Col. Depth:** 140 agate lines. **Key Personnel:** Ralph Poole, President; Wiley Poole, Publisher. **ISSN:** 0300-6557. **Subscription Rates:** $3.95 single issue; $19.97 individuals. **Remarks:** Accepts advertising.
Ad Rates: BW: $5,150 **Circ:** Paid ★**80,173**
4C: $7,995

CARUTHERS, pop. 8,280.

C. CA. Fresno Co. 15 mi. N. of Fresno. Residential.

Twin City Times-Riverdale Press - See Riverdale

CASTRO VALLEY

1691 Airliners
World Transport Press, Inc.
PO Box 20189 Phone: (510)732-2747
Castro Valley, CA 94546 Fax: (510)732-2699
Publication E-mail: airliners@nidlink.com
Publisher E-mail: airliners@bellsouth.net

Magazine for airliner professionals. Includes news, air transport trends, travel adventures, nostalgia, humor, and photography. **Subtitle:** The World's Airline Magazine. **Founded:** 1988. **Freq:** Bimonthly. **Trim Size:** 8 1/2 x 11. **Cols./Page:** 3. **Col. Width:** 2 1/4 inches. **Key Personnel:** Nicholas A. Veronico, Editor, phone (510)732-2747, aleditor@aol.com. **ISSN:** 0896-6575. **Subscription Rates:** $4.50 cover price; $23.95 yearly subscription. **Remarks:** Accepts advertising. **URL:** http://www.airliners.viaweb.com.
Ad Rates: GLR: $14 **Circ:** ‡35,000
BW: $1,180
4C: $1,780

CATHEDRAL CITY

Riverside Co.

1692 The Desert Post
Desert Sun Community Newspaper Group
82-632B Hwy. 11 Phone: (619)775-4200
Indio, CA 92201 Fax: (619)342-7128

Newspaper. **Founded:** 1979. **Freq:** Weekly (Wed.). **Print Method:** Offset. **Cols./Page:** 8. **Col. Width:** 18 nonpareils. **Col. Depth:** 294 agate lines. **Key Personnel:** Robert Cidkey, Publisher; Walter Hennig, General Mgr.; Ken Stagg, Operations Mgr.; Dick Gazi, Executive Editor; Joan Bioko, Editor. **Subscription Rates:** $12 individuals. **Remarks:** Accepts advertising. **Formerly:** Cathedral City Post (1992).
Ad Rates: BW: $1,180.35 **Circ:** ‡5,125
4C: $1,535.35
SAU: $9.15
PCI: $6.85

1693 Truck Fleet Management
Adams Business Media
68-860 Perez Rd.
Cathedral City, CA 92234

Truck fleet equipment management. **Founded:** 1923. **Freq:** Monthly. **Print Method:** Offset. **Trim Size:** 8 1/4 x 10 7/8. **Cols./Page:** 3. **Col. Depth:** 140 picas. **Key Personnel:** Seth Skydel, Editor; Dennis O'Connor, Publisher. **Subscription Rates:** $35 individuals. **Remarks:** Accepts advertising. **Formerly:** Diesel Equipment Superintendent.
Ad Rates: BW: $4,120 **Circ:** Paid 383
4C: $1,450 Non-paid 25,058

1694 KWXY-FM - 98.5
68700 Dinah Shore Dr. Phone: (619)328-1104
Cathedral City, CA 92236 Fax: (619)328-7814

Format: Easy Listening. **Networks:** Independent. **Founded:** 1969. **Operating Hours:** Continuous. **Key Personnel:** Fred Barton, News Dir.; Larry Collins, Operations Mgr.; Jim Keye, Sales Mgr. **Local Programs:** *V.J.s Corner*, V.J. Hume. **Wattage:** 50,000. **Ad Rates:** $18-30 for 30 seconds; $40-24 for 60 seconds. Combined advertising rates available with KWXY-AM. **URL:** http://www.kwxy.com.

CEDARVILLE

1695 Floating Island
Floating Island Publications
PO Box 296 Phone: (530)279-2337
Cedarville, CA 96104
Consumer journal covering poetry, fiction, and art. **Founded:** 1976. **Freq:** Irregular. **Print Method:** Offset. **Trim Size:** 8 1/2 x 11. **Key Personnel:** Michael Sykes, Editor. **Subscription Rates:** $15 single issue. **Remarks:** Advertising not accepted.
Circ: (Not Reported)

CERES, pop. 13,281.

C. CA. Stanislaus Co. 4 mi. S. of Modesto. Residential. Industrial. Diversified farming.

1696 The Ceres Courier
2940 4th St. Phone: (209)537-5032
PO Box 7 Fax: (209)537-0543
Ceres, CA 95307
Community newspaper. **Founded:** 1910. **Freq:** Semiweekly (Wed. and Fri.). **Print Method:** Offset. **Cols./Page:** 6. **Col. Width:** 18 nonpareils. **Col. Depth:** 294 agate lines. **Key Personnel:** Darell Phillips, Publisher; Jeff Benziger, Editor. **Subscription Rates:** $24 individuals.
Ad Rates: GLR: $.42 **Circ:** Free 17,000
BW: $185
PCI: $5.88

1697 KADV-FM - 90.5
2031 Academy Pl. Phone: (209)537-1201
Ceres, CA 95307 Fax: (209)537-1945
E-mail: kadv@inreach.com

Format: Religious. **Networks:** Sun Radio. **Founded:** 1988. **Operating Hours:** Continuous; 100% local. **Key Personnel:** Gaylord Boyer, General Mgr.; John P. Geli, Station Mgr. **Wattage:** 1500. **Ad Rates:** Noncommercial. **URL:** http://www.tagnet.org/kadv.

CERRITOS

1698 Apollo Cablevision Inc.
13100 Alondra Blvd., Ste. 104 Fax: (310)926-8017
Cerritos, CA 90703

Founded: Nov. 1995. **Key Personnel:** Don Bache, Systems Mgr. **Cities Served:** Cerritos, CA: subscribing households 7,900; 81 channels; 2 community access channels.

CHATSWORTH

1699 The National Notary
National Notary Association
9350 DeSoto Ave. Phone: (818)739-4000
PO Box 2402 Fax: (818)700-0920
Chatsworth, CA 91313-2402
Free: (800)876-6827
Publication E-mail: nna@nationalnotany.org
Publisher E-mail: natlnotary@aol.com

Legal trade magazine. **Founded:** 1957. **Freq:** Bimonthly. **Print Method:** Offset. **Cols./Page:** 3 and 2. **Col. Width:** 28 and 42 nonpareils. **Col. Depth:** 138 agate lines. **Key Personnel:** Charles N. Faerber, Editor, phone (818)739-4015; Deborah M. Thaw, Publisher, phone (818)739-4015. **ISSN:** 0894-7872. **Subscription Rates:** $34 members includes magazine & bulletin. **Remarks:** Accepts advertising.
Ad Rates: BW: $1,400 **Circ:** ‡153,000
4C: $1,700

CHESTER, pop. 3,504.

NE CA. Plumas Co. 70 mi. E. of Red Bluff. Residential. Tourism. Forest products.

1700 Chester Progressive
Feather Publishing
PO Box 557 Phone: (530)258-3115
Chester, CA 96020 Fax: (530)258-2365
Publisher E-mail: featherpub@aol.com

Community newspaper. **Founded:** 1946. **Freq:** Weekly (Wed.). **Print Method:** Offset. **Cols./Page:** 6. **Col. Width:** 11.5 picas. **Col. Depth:** 301 agate lines. **Key Personnel:** Robert Mann, Editor; Michael Taborski, Publisher. **ISSN:** 0010-2880. **Subscription Rates:** $25 individuals. **Remarks:** Accepts advertising. **Online:** America Online, Inc. **URL:** http://plumasnews.com.
Ad Rates: BW: $612.75 **Circ:** 2,390
4C: $762.75
SAU: $4.75
PCI: $4.75

CHICO, pop. 26,601.

N. CA. Butte Co. 90 mi. N. of Sacramento. California State University At Chico. Manufactures aluminum, lumber, canned goods, pruning saws, foundry, concrete products, beverages. Fruit drying and packing, almond & walnut hulling and processing plants; Agriculture.

1701 Chico Enterprise-Record
Donrey Media Group
400 E. Park Ave. Phone: (916)891-1234
Chico, CA 95928 Fax: (916)342-3617

General newspaper. **Founded:** 1853. **Freq:** Daily and Sunday (morn.). **Print Method:** Offset. **Cols./Page:** 6. **Col. Width:** 25 nonpareils. **Col. Depth:** 294 agate lines. **Key Personnel:** Jack Winning, Editor; Milt Moore, Advertising Dir.; Jim Dimmitt, Publisher. **Subscription Rates:** $78. **Remarks:** Accepts advertising. **Absorbed:** Oroville Mercury-Register.
Ad Rates: BW: $3,652.74 **Circ:** Mon.-Sat. 33,674
4C: $4,012.74 Sun. 28,161
SAU: $18.16
PCI: $28.99

1702 Chico News & Review
Chico Community Publishing, Inc.
353 E. 2nd St. Phone: (916)894-2300
Chico, CA 95928 Fax: (916)894-0143

Community newspaper (tabloid). **Founded:** Aug. 1977. **Freq:** Weekly (Thurs.). **Print Method:** Offset. Uses mats. **Cols./Page:** 5. **Col. Width:** 2 1/16 inches. **Col. Depth:** 13 1/8 inches. **Key Personnel:** Joe Martin, Editor; Jeff von Kaenel, Publisher; Kathy Barrett, Advertising Mgr. **Subscription Rates:** $25 individuals. **URL:** http://www.talkingpersonals.com. **Alt. Formats:** Microform.
Ad Rates: GLR: $1.86 **Circ:** Free ❑**38,245**
BW: $1,237 Paid ❑**60**
4C: $1,567
PCI: $18.40

1703 The Orion
California State University
Dept. of Journalism, No. 600 Phone: (530)898-4237
Chico, CA 95929-0600 Fax: (530)898-4799
Publication E-mail: orion@macgate.csuchico.edu

College newspaper. **Founded:** Mar. 16, 1975. **Freq:** Weekly (Wed.). **Print Method:** Offset. **Trim Size:** 13 1/3 x 21. **Cols./Page:** 6. **Col. Width:** 12 1/2 picas. **Col. Depth:** 126 picas. **Key Personnel:** Dave Waddell, Adviser, phone (916)898-4782, fax (916)898-4839, dwaddell@oavax.csuchico.edu. **Subscription Rates:** $25 individuals. **Remarks:** Accepts advertising. **Available Online. URL:** http://orion.csuchico.edu.
Ad Rates: BW: $730.80 **Circ:** ‡10,000
4C: $1,030
SAU: $9.50
PCI: $7.99

1704 Videomaker
Videomaker, Inc.
920 Main St. Phone: (530)891-8410
PO Box 4591 Fax: (530)891-8443
Chico, CA 95927
Free: (800)284-3226
Publisher E-mail: editor@videomaker.com

Videomaker covers camcorders, video editing, desktop video and audio production for video. It is focused soley on the making of videos. Articles survey and review the latest equipment, teach production techniques explain the technology. The numerous "how to" articles provide a thorough education in video production. Columns explore audio concerns, desktop video, video business skills, the work of interesting videomakers, Q & A, tools and tips and the latest products. There is a buyer's guide to a relevant product type in every issue. Videomaker gives awards annually to manufactures of innovative products and prizes to winners of its videomakerscompetition. It is edited for anyone from video novices to entrepreneurial professions. **Subtitle:** Camcorders, Computers, Tools & Techniques for Creating Video. **Founded:** 1986. **Freq:** Monthly. **Print Method:** Offset. **Trim Size:** 7 7/8 x 10 1/12. **Cols./Page:** 2 and 3. **Col. Width:** 26 and 40 nonpareils. **Col. Depth:** 124 agate lines. **Key Personnel:** Stephen Muratore, Exec. Editor, editor@videomaker.com; Matthew York, Editor and Publisher, editor@videomaker.com; Kelly Schulman, Assoc. Publisher, kschulman@videomaker.com. **ISSN:** 0889-4973. **Subscription**

Rates: $22.50 individuals; $3.95 single issue. **URL:** http://www.videomaker.com.
Ad Rates: BW: $4,190 **Circ:** Paid ★**68,237**
4C: $5,218 Non-paid ★**6,519**
PCI: $200

1705 KCPM-TV - 24
180 E. 4th St. Phone: (916)893-2424
Chico, CA 95928 Fax: (916)893-1033

Format: Commercial TV. **Networks:** NBC. **Owner:** Gocom Corporation, 7621 Little Ave., Ste. 506, Charlotte, NC 28226, (704)341-0944, Fax: (704)345-0945. **Founded:** 1985. **Operating Hours:** 8:30 a.m. - 5:30 p.m. **ADI:** Chico-Redding, CA. **Key Personnel:** Matt James, General Mgr., phone (530)893-2424, fax (916)893-1033. **URL:** http://www.kcpm.com.

1706 KFMF-FM - 93.9
1459 Humboldt Rd., Ste. D Phone: (916)899-3600
Chico, CA 95928 Fax: (916)343-0243

Format: Album-Oriented Rock (AOR). **Simulcasts:** KALF-FM, KPPL-FM. **Networks:** Independent. **Owner:** The Park Lane Group, 750 Menlo Ave., Ste. 340, Menlo Park, CA 94025, (415)324-6464. **Founded:** 1974. **Operating Hours:** Continuous; 100% local. **ADI:** Chico-Redding, CA. **Key Personnel:** Dick Stein, Vice Pres./Gen. Mgr.; Marty Griffin, Program Dir. **Wattage:** 25,000. **Ad Rates:** $65 for 60 seconds.

1707 KHSL-FM - 103.5
2654 Cramer Ln. Phone: (530)345-0021
Chico, CA 95928 Fax: (530)893-2121

Format: Country; Contemporary Country. **Owner:** McCoy Broadcasting, at above address. **Founded:** 1983. **Formerly:** KRIJ-FM; KCHH-FM. **Operating Hours:** Continuous. **ADI:** Chico-Redding, CA. **Key Personnel:** Dave Brower, General Mgr., dwb@sunset.net; Clark Michael, Program Dir., clarkm@sunset.net; Peggy Mead, General Sales Mgr., peggy@sunset.net; Dan Butner, Chief Engineer, danb@sunset.net. **Wattage:** 1,650.

1708 KHSL-TV - 12
3460 Silverbell Rd. Phone: (530)342-0141
Chico, CA 95973-0388 Fax: (530)342-4905
E-mail: khsltv@maxinet.com

Format: Commercial TV. **Networks:** CBS. **Owner:** Catamount Broadcasting of Chico Redding Inc., 715 58th St., Kenosha, WI 53141. **Founded:** 1953. **Formerly:** United Communications Corp. **Operating Hours:** 6 a.m.-2 a.m.; 50% network, 50% local. **ADI:** Chico-Redding, CA. **Key Personnel:** Ivan Seredni, Contact, accts@khsltv.com; Ray Tucker, General Sales Mgr., rtucker@khsltv.com; Dino Corbin, General Mgr., dcorbin@khsltv.com; Bruce Lang, News Dir., phone (530)342-2405, khslnews@khsltv.com; Ivan Seredni, Business Mgr., accts@khsltv.com. **Wattage:** 316 kw Visual, 3.68 kw Aural. **Ad Rates:** $45-650 per unit. **URL:** http://www.khsltv.com.

1709 KMXI-FM - 95.1
2654 Cramer Ln. Phone: (916)345-0021
Chico, CA 95928-8838 Fax: (916)345-1060
E-mail: clarkm@sunset.net

Format: Adult Contemporary. **Founded:** 1972. **Formerly:** KPAY-FM (Apr. 1, 1994). **Operating Hours:** Continuous. **ADI:** Chico-Redding, CA. **Key Personnel:** Dave Brower, General Mgr.; Clark Michael, Program Mgr.; Peggy Mead, Sales Mgr.; Dan Butner, Chief Engineer; Veronica Carter, News Dir. **Wattage:** 8700. **Ad Rates:** Advertising accepted; rates available upon request. **URL:** http://www.kmxi.com.

1710 KPAY-AM - 1060
2654 Cramer Ln. Phone: (916)345-0021
Chico, CA 95928-8838 Fax: (916)345-1060
E-mail: tonyk@sunset.net

Format: News; Talk. **Networks:** Mutual Broadcasting System; CBS; EFM. **Founded:** 1949. **Operating Hours:** Continuous. **ADI:** Chico-Redding, CA. **Key Personnel:** Dave Brower, V.P./Gen. Mgr.; Clark Michael, Program Mgr.; Peggy Mead, Sales Mgr.; Dan Butner, Chief Engineer; Veronica Carter, News Dir. **Local Programs:** *Computer Blues*, Dennis Corkery, (916)345-0021; *Kpay Collectables*, John Humphries, (916)894-4822; *Kpay Live-Line*, John Humphries, (916)894-4822. **Wattage:** 10,000. **Ad Rates:** Advertising accepted; rates available upon request. **URL:** http://www.kpay.com.

1711 KPPL-FM - 107.5
1459 Humboldt Rd., Ste. D Phone: (916)899-3600
Chico, CA 95928 Fax: (916)343-0243

Format: Soft Rock. **Owner:** The Park Lane Group, 750 Menlo Ave., Ste. 340, Menlo Park, CA 94025, (415)324-8464. **Founded:** 1987. **Formerly:** KTMX-FM (1994). **Operating Hours:** Continuous; 100% local. **ADI:** Chico-Redding, CA. **Key Personnel:** Dick Stein, Vice President. **Local Programs:** *Chronicles*, Dan Barnett; *Peopleview*, Dan Barnett. **Wattage:** 30,000. **Ad Rates:** $50 for 60 seconds.

1712 KZAP-FM - 96.7
407 W. 9th St. Phone: (530)893-1200
Chico, CA 95928 Fax: (530)895-3740

Format: Classic Rock. **Owner:** Paradise Broadcasting, Inc., at above address. **Founded:** 1977. **Formerly:** KNVR-FM. **Operating Hours:** Continuous. **ADI:** Chico-Redding, CA. **Key Personnel:** Robb Cheal, V. P./General Mgr. **Ad Rates:** $10-14 per unit. **URL:** http://www.kzap.com.

1713 KZFR-FM - 90.1
PO Box 3173 Phone: (530)895-0788
Chico, CA 95927 Fax: (530)895-0775

Format: Educational. **Owner:** Golden Valley Community Broadcasters, at above address. **Operating Hours:** 6 a.m.-12 a.m. **ADI:** Chico-Redding, CA. **Key Personnel:** Dirk Wohlau, President; Lars Larson, Vice President; Beth Carr, Office Mgr. **Wattage:** 5,000. **Ad Rates:** Advertising accepted; rates available upon request. **URL:** http://www.kzfr.org.

CHINO, pop. 40,165.

SW CA. San Bernardino Co. 37 mi. E. of Los Angeles. Manufactures computer components, lumber, bricks. Diversified farming. Poultry, and horses, Dairying.

1714 Chino Champion
Champion Newspapers
13179 9th St. Phone: (909)628-5501
Chino, CA 91710 Fax: (909)590-1217

Community newspaper. **Founded:** 1887. **Freq:** Weekly (Thurs.). **Print Method:** Offset. **Trim Size:** 13 3/4 x 22 1/4. **Cols./Page:** 6. **Col. Width:** 12 1/3 picas. **Col. Depth:** 21 inches. **Key Personnel:** Allen P. McCombs, Editor and Publisher; Bruce M. Wood, General Mgr.; Bruce M. Wood, General Mgr. **USPS:** 106-000. **Subscription Rates:** $10; $25 mailed; $.50 single issue. **Remarks:** Accepts advertising. **Absorbed:** Champion (Aug. 4, 1994). **Formerly:** Chino Valley News.
Ad Rates: GLR: $1.555 **Circ:** Combined 34,406
BW: $1,842.12
4C: $2,172.12
SAU: $21.77
PCI: $21.77

1715 Chino Hills Champion
Champion Newspapers
13179 9th St. Phone: (909)628-5501
Chino, CA 91710 Fax: (909)590-1217

Community newspaper. **Founded:** July 6, 1887. **Freq:** Weekly (Thurs.). **Print Method:** Offset. **Trim Size:** 13 3/4 x 21 1/2. **Cols./Page:** 6. **Col. Width:** 2 1/16 inches. **Col. Depth:** 21 inches. **Key Personnel:** Rina Miller, Editor; Allen P. McCombs, Publisher; Steve Arthur, General Mgr. **Subscription Rates:** Free; $27.50 (mail). **Remarks:** Accepts advertising.
Ad Rates: GLR: $1.45 **Circ:** Combined 35,000
BW: $2,557.80
4C: $2,947.80
SAU: $20.30
PCI: $20.30

1716 Chino Valley News
Champion Newspapers
PO Box 607
Chino, CA 91708-0607

Community newspaper. **Founded:** 1887. **Freq:** Weekly (Thurs.). **Print Method:** Offset. **Trim Size:** 13 3/4 x 22 1/4. **Cols./Page:** 6. **Col. Width:** 12 1/3 picas. **Col. Depth:** 21 inches. **Key Personnel:** Allen P. McCombs, Editor and Publisher; Rina Miller, Editor; Steve Arthur, General Mgr. **USPS:** 106-000. **Subscription Rates:** $10; $25 by mail.
Ad Rates: GLR: $1.45 **Circ:** 35,000
BW: $2,557.70
4C: $2,947.80
SAU: $20.30
PCI: $20.30

South Ontario News - See Ontario

1717 Century Communications
5944 Sycamore Ct. Phone: (909)591-9571
Chino, CA 91708 Fax: (909)590-1390

Founded: 1983. **Formerly:** Chino Valley Cable Television Co. **Key Personnel:** Melinda Bitney, General Mgr. **Cities Served:** subscribing households 24,000; 62 channels; 12 community access channels.

CHOWCHILLA, pop. 5,122.

SC CA. Madera Co. 38 mi. N. of Fresno. Manufactures cottonseed oil, steel buildings, Compressed wood, chemicals, fertilizer, alfalfa pellets, creamery products. Agriculture. Cotton, almonds, seed crops, dairying, grain.

1718 Northland Cable
405 Trinity Ave. Phone: (209)665-5748
Chowchilla, CA 93610 Fax: (209)665-7014
Free: (800)726-3212
E-mail: north.chow@thegrid.net

Founded: 1982. **Key Personnel:** Alice Weaver, System Mgr.; Joe Roan, Customer Service Tech. **Cities Served:** subscribing households 1,800; 50 channels; 1 community access channel.

CHULA VISTA, pop. 83,927.

S. CA. San Diego Co. 6 mi. SE of San Diego. Manufactures cabinets, aircraft and motor vehicle parts, chemicals, electric motors, machinery, metal, concrete products.

1719 California Weekly
News Baja, Inc.
296 H St., 2nd Fl. Phone: (619)425-2132
Nes Plaza Bldg.
Chula Vista, CA 91910
Newspaper. **Freq:** Weekly. **Key Personnel:** Oscar Bonilla Valdez, General Mgr. **Subscription Rates:** $18.
Circ: Free 48,298
Paid 2,623

1720 Education
Project Innovation
1362 Santa Cruz Ct. Phone: (619)421-9377
Chula Vista, CA 91910-7114
Education magazine. **Founded:** 1880. **Freq:** Quarterly. **Print Method:** Letterpress. **Trim Size:** 7 x 10. **Cols./Page:** 2. **Col. Width:** 30 nonpareils. **Col. Depth:** 110 agate lines. **Key Personnel:** Russell Cassel, Editor, rcassel5@aol.com. **ISSN:** 0013-1172. **Subscription Rates:** $24 individuals; $38 two years; $54 Three/years; $30 institutions; $48 institutions Two/years; $69 institutions Three/years; $8 other countries. **Remarks:** Advertising not accepted. **URL:** http://www.rcassel.com. **Alt. Formats:** CD-ROM, EBSCO; Microform.
Circ: ‡3,500

1721 The Healthkeepers Journal
Holistic Publications
880 Canarios Ct. Ste. 210 Phone: (619)482-8533
Chula Vista, CA 91910 Fax: (619)482-0938

Magazine covering health and nutrition. **Founded:** 1980. **Freq:** Monthly - Bimonthly. **Print Method:** Offset. **Trim Size:** 8 1/2 x 10 1/2. **Cols./Page:** 3. **Col. Width:** 12 1/2 picas. **Col. Depth:** 9 1/2 inches. **Key Personnel:** Dr. Kurt W. Donsbach, Editor and Publisher. **ISSN:** 8750-2370. **Subscription Rates:** $15. $2 single issue. **Remarks:** Advertising not accepted. **Formerly:** The Al-Don Report; The Nutrition & Dietary Consultant.
Circ: Paid 38,732
Non-paid 4,035

1722 Star-News
279 3rd Ave. Phone: (619)427-3000
Chula Vista, CA 91910 Fax: (619)426-6346
Publication E-mail: starnews@wccnews
Publisher E-mail: starnew@wccnews

Community newspaper (tabloid). **Founded:** 1881. **Freq:** Weekly (Sat.). **Print Method:** Offset. **Cols./Page:** 6. **Col. Width:** 9 picas. **Col. Depth:** 16 inches. **Key Personnel:** Joe Guerin, Editor. **Subscription Rates:** $25 individuals. **Remarks:** Accepts advertising.
Ad Rates: GLR: $5.40 **Circ:** Mon.-Fri. ★**40,575**
BW: $1,320 Mon.-Sat. ★**42,264**
4C: $1,590 Sun. ★**40,857**
SAU: $19.95
PCI: $17.60

1723 KSWB-TV - 69
1696 Frontage Rd. Phone: (619)575-6955
Chula Vista, CA 91911 Fax: (619)423-5889

Format: Commercial TV. **Networks:** Warner Brothers Studios. **Owner:** Tribune Broadcasting Co., 1696 Frontage Rd., Chula Vista, CA 91911-3999. **Founded:** 1984. **Formerly:** KTTY-TV. **Operating Hours:** Continuous. **ADI:** San Diego, CA. **Key Personnel:** Lise Markham, Vice Pres. & General Mgr.; Dan Mitrovich, Controller; John Weigand, Chief Engineer; Kelly Mackin, General Sales Mgr.; Sandy Lapacz, Traffic Mgr.; Will Givens, Dir. of Creative Services; Sandi Banister, Promotions Dir.; Sam Bickel, Dir. of Programming. **Wattage:** 4500 kw. **Ad Rates:** Advertising accepted; rates available upon request.

1724 XEWT-TV - 12
637 Third Ave., Ste. B Phone: (619)585-9398
Chula Vista, CA 91915 Fax: (619)585-9463
E-mail: energy@slctnet.com

Format: Commercial TV; Hispanic. **Founded:** 1960. **Operating Hours:** Continuous. **ADI:** San Diego, CA. **Key Personnel:** Ricardo Azcarraga, General Mgr.; P. Alvarez, General Sales Mgr.; Fernando Del Monte, News Mgr.; Salvador Hernandez, Chief Engineer; Juan Urias, Operations Mgr.; Ninfa Romero, Production Mgr. **Local Programs:** *Dos Norteno*; *En Exclusiva*; *Kid's Club*; *Movie Club*; *Notivisa Buenos Dias* 7 a.m. **Wattage:** 325,000. **Ad Rates:** $95 for 10 seconds; $125 for 30 seconds; $350 for 60 seconds. **URL:** http://www.televisa.com.

1725 XHKY-FM - 99.3
1229 3rd Ave., Ste. C Phone: (619)585-9090
Chula Vista, CA 91911 Fax: (619)426-3690

Format: Hispanic. **Founded:** 1975. **Operating Hours:** Continuous. **ADI:** San Diego, CA. **Key Personnel:** Victor Diaz, General Mgr. **Wattage:** 30,000. **Ad Rates:** $75-165 for 30 seconds; $100-220 for 60 seconds.

1726 XHTZ-FM - 90.3
1229 3rd Ave., Ste. C Phone: (619)585-9090
Chula Vista, CA 91911 Fax: (619)426-3690

Format: Contemporary Hit Radio (CHR). **Founded:** 1971. **Operating Hours:** Continuous. **ADI:** San Diego, CA. **Key Personnel:** Victor Diaz, General Mgr.; Ranoaz Phillips, General Sales Mgr.; Rodger Seelent, Sales Mgr.; Lisa Vazquez, Program Dir. **Wattage:** 100,000.

1727 XLTN-FM - 104.5
1229 3rd Ave., Ste. C Phone: (619)585-9090
Chula Vista, CA 91911 Fax: (619)426-3690

Format: Hispanic; Adult Contemporary. **Founded:** 1969. **Operating Hours:** Continuous. **ADI:** San Diego, CA. **Key Personnel:** Victor Diaz, General Mgr. **Wattage:** 60,000. **Ad Rates:** $75-165 for 30 seconds; $100-220 for 60 seconds.

CITRUS HEIGHTS

NC CA. Sacramento Co. 13 mi. SW of Sacramento. Residential.

1728 The Computer Journal
PO Box 3900 Phone: (916)722-4970
Citrus Heights, CA 95611-3900 Fax: (916)722-7480
Free: (800)424-8825
Publication E-mail: tcj@psyber.com

Journal featuring programming and user support applications for collectible computers. **Subtitle:** "TCJ - For Having Fun With Any Computer". **Founded:** 1982. **Freq:** Bimonthly. **Print Method:** Offset. **Trim Size:** 8 1/2 x 11. **Key Personnel:** David Baldwin, Editor and Publisher. **ISSN:** 0748-9331. **Subscription Rates:** $24 individuals; $44 two years; $32 institutions, Canada and Mexico; $34 other countries.
Ad Rates: BW: $120 **Circ:** ‡1,500

CITY OF INDUSTRY

1729 TCI Cablevision of California Inc. Arcadia
15255 Salt Lake Ave. Phone: (818)574-7171
City of Industry, CA 91745-1130 Fax: (818)574-7333

Owner: Tele-Communications Inc., 5619 DTC Pkwy., Englewood, CO 80111, (303)267-5500, Fax: (303)779-1228. **Key Personnel:** Gary Stone, Operations Mgr.; Juan Castro, Chief Engineer; Keith Cooper, Public Affairs Mgr.; Danielle Guzman, Customer Service Mgr. **Cities Served:** Arcadia, Sierra Madre, CA: subscribing households 13,750; 64 channels; 1 community access channel; 35 hours per week community access programming.

1730 TCI Cablevision of Los Angeles County
15255 Salt Lake Ave. Phone: (818)333-4265
City of Industry, CA 91745 Fax: (818)855-3385

Formerly: United Artist Cable (1994); United Cable TV. **Key Personnel:** Danielle Guzman, Customer Service Mgr., phone (818)855-3356; John Few, Operations Mgr., phone (818)855-3372. **Cities Served:** Arcadia, Baldwin Park, Hacienda Heights, Pico Rivera, South Whittier, CA: subscribing households 50,000; 68 channels; 1 community access channel; 24 hours per week community access programming.

CLAREMONT, pop. 30,950.

S. CA. Los Angeles Co. 35 mi. E. of Los Angeles. Pomona College. Claremont College. Retirement Center. Rancho Santa Ana Botanical Gardens. Air cleaners, scientific instruments.

1731 Aliso
Rancho Santa Ana Botanic Garden
1500 N. College Ave. Phone: (909)625-8767
Claremont, CA 91711 Fax: (909)626-3489
Publication E-mail: richard.benjamin@cgu.edu

Trade magazine covering systematics and evolutionary botany. **Subtitle:** A Journal of Taxonomic and Evolutionary Botany. **Founded:** Apr. 1948. **Freq:** Semiannual. **Trim Size:** 8 x 11. **Cols./Page:** 2. **Col. Width:** 3 3/8 inches. **Key Personnel:** Dr. Richard K. Benjamin, Editor-in-Chief, richard.benjamin@cgu.edu; Janet R. Taylor, Managing Editor, janet.taylor@cgu.edu. **ISSN:** 0065-6275. **Subscription Rates:** $40 individuals; $45 out of country; $20 single issue; $23 single issue outside USA. **Remarks:** Advertising not accepted. **Formerly**: El Aliso.
Circ: Combined 300

1732 Claremont Courier
PO Box 820 Phone: (909)621-4761
Claremont, CA 91711-0820 Fax: (909)621-4072

Newspaper. **Founded:** 1908. **Freq:** Semiweekly (Wed. and Sat.). **Print Method:** Offset. **Trim Size:** 11 x 15. **Cols./Page:** 6. **Col. Width:** 19 nonpareils. **Col. Depth:** 196 agate lines. **Key Personnel:** Martin Weinberger, Publisher. **USPS:** 115-180. **Subscription Rates:** $32.5 individuals. **Remarks:** Accepts advertising.
Ad Rates: GLR: $.52 **Circ:** ⊕6,035
BW: $638.40
4C: $838.40
PCI: $7.60

1733 Collage
The Claremont Colleges
175 E. 8th St. Phone: (909)607-3646
Claremont, CA 91711 Fax: (909)607-7825

Collegiate newspaper. **Founded:** 1966. **Freq:** 21/year (during academic year). **Print Method:** Offset. Uses mats. **Cols./Page:** 4. **Col. Width:** 14 picas. **Col. Depth:** 15 inches. **Key Personnel:** Katinka Soto, Advertising Mgr. **Subscription Rates:** $25 individuals. **Remarks:** Accepts advertising. **URL:** http://www.claremont.edu/or4/collage. **Formerly**: Claremont Collegian.
Ad Rates: GLR: $12.44 **Circ:** Controlled 8,500
BW: $746.40
4C: $200
PCI: $12.44

1734 Women's Studies
Gordon and Breach Publishers
Department of English Phone: (909)607-2974
Claremont Graduate University
McManus Hall, 170 E. 10th St.
Claremont, CA 91711
Publication E-mail: womnstudj@cgu.edu
Publisher E-mail: info@g6hap.com

Scholarly, interdisciplinary journal covering women's studies. **Subtitle:** An Interdisciplinary Journal. **Founded:** 1972. **Freq:** Bimonthly. **Trim Size:** 6 x 9. **Cols./Page:** 1. **Col. Width:** 4 1/4 inches. **Col. Depth:** 6 1/2 inches. **Key Personnel:** Wendy Martin, Editor; Lisa Colletta, Assoc. Editor; Janet Rathert, Assoc. Editor. **ISSN:** 0049-7878. **Subscription Rates:** $118 individuals. **Remarks:** Advertising accepted; rates available upon request.
Circ: Paid 500

1735 KSPC-FM - 88.7
340 N. College Ave. Phone: (909)621-8157
Thatcher Music Bldg. Fax: (909)607-1259
Claremont, CA 91711
E-mail: kspc@pomona.claremont.edu

Format: Alternative/New Music/Progressive. **Networks:** Independent. **Owner:** Pomona College Board of Trustees, at above address. **Founded:** 1956. **Operating Hours:** 8 a.m.-3 a.m.; 100% local. **Key Personnel:** Erica Tyron, Dir. of College Radio; Scot Oxholm, Program Dir.; Adam Graham-Silverman, General Mgr.; Richard Carperton, Music Dir.; Dan Finley, Music Dir. **Local Programs:** *Between The Lines (Inverviews with Authors)*, Joe Wakelee Lynch, (909)621-8157, Fax (909)607-1259; *Public Affairs Show*, Junor Francis, (909)621-8157, Fax (909)607-1259. **Wattage:** 3000 ERP. **Ad Rates:** Noncommercial.

CLEARLAKE, pop. 13,275.

N. CA. Lake Co. 45 mi. N. of Santa Rosa. Lake Resorts. Machine shops. Vineyards. Agriculture. Walnuts, pears, cattle.

1736 Clear Lake Observer-American
Lake County Publishing
PO Box 6200 Phone: (707)994-6444
Clearlake, CA 95422 Fax: (707)994-5335

Community newspaper. **Founded:** 1935. **Freq:** Semiweekly. **Print Method:** Offset. **Cols./Page:** 6. **Col. Width:** 23 nonpareils. **Col. Depth:** 280 agate lines. **Key Personnel:** Mark Bredt, Editor; Judi Pollace, Publisher, phone (707)263-5636, fax (707)263-0600; Melissa Fulton, Advertising Dir., phone (707)263-5636, fax (707)263-0600; Sharon Lewis, Office Mgr. **USPS:** 117-140. **Subscription Rates:** $21.94 individuals; $42.86 out of area. **Remarks:** Accepts advertising.
Ad Rates: GLR: $.46 **Circ:** ‡3,363

CLIPPER MILLS, pop. 170.

N. CA. Butte Co. 17 mi SW of Downieville. Residential. Tourism. Timber.

1737 Rabbit Creek Journal
PO Box 309 Phone: (530)675-2270
Clipper Mills, CA 95930 Fax: (530)675-0415
Publisher E-mail: daysnews@rcj.net

Community newspaper. **Founded:** Jan. 1, 1978. **Freq:** Weekly (Thurs.). **Print Method:** Offset. **Cols./Page:** 5. **Col. Width:** 26 nonpareils. **Col. Depth:** 301 agate lines. **Key Personnel:** Gretchen H. Fowler, Publisher; Bruce Livingston, P.R./Advertising; Chris Gillespie, Editor; Betty Livingston, Managing Editor. **Subscription Rates:** $24 individuals; $.50 single issue. **Remarks:** Accepts advertising.
Ad Rates: BW: $373.75 **Circ:** ‡2,000
4C: $673.75
PCI: $5.75

CLOVERDALE, pop. 3,989.

NW CA. Sonoma Co. 35 mi. NW of Santa Rosa. Residential.

1738 Cloverdale Reveille
207 N. Cloverdale Blvd. Phone: (707)894-3339
PO Box 157 Fax: (707)894-3343
Cloverdale, CA 95425-3318
Publication E-mail: reveille@thegrid.net

Local newspaper. **Founded:** 1879. **Freq:** Weekly (Wed.). **Print Method:** Offset. **Cols./Page:** 6. **Col. Width:** 24 nonpareils. **Col. Depth:** 294 agate lines. **Key Personnel:** Bonny J. Hanchett, Editor and Publisher, reveille@thegrid.net. **Subscription Rates:** $22.50 individuals. **Remarks:** Accepts advertising. **URL:** http://www.thegrid.net/reiville. **Feature Editors:** Roberta Lyons, *Environmental.*
Ad Rates: BW: $126 **Circ:** Paid ‡2,400
SAU: $4.75
PCI: $4.75

CLOVIS, pop. 33,021.

C. CA. Fresno Co. 4 mi. NE of Fresno. Fruit packing and concrete plants. Granite quarries; timber. Diversified farming. Dairy products, grapes.

1739 The Clovis Independent
420 Bullard, No. 105 Phone: (559)298-8081
Clovis, CA 93612 Fax: (559)298-0459

Community newspaper. **Founded:** Mar. 3, 1905. **Freq:** Weekly (Fri.). **Print Method:** Offset. **Trim Size:** 14 x 22 3/4. **Cols./Page:** 6. **Col. Width:** 21 inches. **Col. Depth:** 301 agate lines. **Key Personnel:** Patti J. Lippert, Editor, phone (559)324-5406. **USPS:** 119-060. **Subscription Rates:** $21 individuals; $15 Senior Citizens. **Remarks:** Accepts advertising.
Ad Rates: BW: $1,799.28 **Circ:** Paid ‡5,500
4C: $2,034.28 Free ‡18,500
PCI: $14.28

1740 KAIL-TV - 53
1590 Alluvial Ave. Phone: (209)299-9753
Clovis, CA 93612 Fax: (209)299-1523

Format: Commercial TV. **Networks:** United Paramount Network. **Owner:** A.J. Williams, at above address. **Founded:** 1965. **Operating Hours:** 24hrs. **ADI:** Fresno-Visalia (Hanford), CA. **Key Personnel:** Robert Jenkins, Program and Promotions Mgr.; Charles Williams, Sales Mgr. **Local Programs:** *Community Close Up* 6:30 a.m. Sunday. **Wattage:** 2.8 million.

COACHELLA

1741 KCLB-AM - 970
1694 6th St. Phone: (619)398-2171
Coachella, CA 92236-1716 Fax: (619)398-2739

Format: Hispanic. **Networks:** UPI. **Owner:** Coachella Valley Broadcasting, at above address. **Founded:** 1954. **Formerly:** KVIM-AM (1990). **Operating Hours:** Continuous. **Key Personnel:** Gene Abraham, Station Mgr.; Ramiro Islas, Contact; Alfonso Garfias, News Dir.; Susan Gorges, General Mgr. **Wattage:** 5000. **Ad Rates:** Advertising accepted; rates available upon request.

1742 KCLB-FM - 93.7
1694 6th St. Phone: (619)398-2171
Coachella, CA 92236-1716 Fax: (619)398-2739

Format: Album-Oriented Rock (AOR). **Owner:** Coachella Valley Broadcasting, at above address. **Founded:** 1960. **Formerly**: KCHV-FM (1992); KELB-FM. **Operating Hours:** Continuous. **Key Personnel:** Susan Gorges, General Mgr.; Gene Abraham, Contact; Bob Cady, Program Dir.; Doug Ray, Program Dir. **Wattage:** 50,000. **Ad Rates:** Advertising accepted; rates available upon request.

COALINGA, pop. 6,593.

C. CA. Fresno Co. 67 mi. SW of Fresno. Oil well supplies; machinery, iron works, creamery products, asbestos fibre, concrete pipes manufactured. Oil wells; quicksilver mines. Agriculture. Livestock, grain, melons, dairying.

1743 Coalinga Record
Central CA Weeklies, Inc.
227 Coalinga Plaza Phone: (209)935-2906
PO Box 496 Fax: (209)935-5257
Coalinga, CA 93210
Newspaper. **Founded:** 1904. **Freq:** Weekly (Wed.). **Print Method:** Offset. **Cols./Page:** 4. **Col. Width:** 12 picas. **Col. Depth:** 21 1/2 inches. **Key Personnel:** Bill Howell, Editor. **Subscription Rates:** $13 individuals. **Remarks:** Accepts advertising. **Absorbed**: Coalinga Courier (1990).
Ad Rates: PCI: $6.62 **Circ:** ‡7,500

1744 Coalinga CATV
100 1st St. Phone: (209)935-1674
Coalinga, CA 93210 Fax: (209)935-9040
Free: (800)962-1387

Owner: McVay Communications Inc., at above address. **Founded:** 1979. **Key Personnel:** Judy Price, Contact. **Cities Served:** Coalinga, CA: subscribing households 2,900; 43 channels; 1 community access channel; 2 hours per week community access programming.

1745 Huron CATV
100 1st St. Phone: (209)935-1674
Coalinga, CA 93210 Fax: (209)935-9040
Free: (800)962-1387

Owner: McVay Communications Inc., at above address. **Founded:** 1981. **Key Personnel:** Judy Price, Contact. **Cities Served:** subscribing households 300; 20 channels.

COLEVILLE

NE CA. Mono Co. 60 mi. S. of Lake Tahoe.

1746 HFU TV
26 HFU Circle Phone: (530)495-2224
Coleville, CA 96107 Fax: (530)495-2500

Owner: David Charlton, at above address. **Founded:** 1979. **Key Personnel:** Chuck Evans, Manager. **Cities Served:** Coleville, Walker, CA; Holbrook Junction, Topaz Lake, Topaz Ranch Estates, NV: subscribing households 880; 17 channels.

COLFAX, pop. 981.

NE CA. Placer Co. 45 mi. NE of Sacramento. Residential. Lake & river sports. Timber. Gold mining.

1747 Colfax Record
Auburn Journal
25 W. Church Phone: (916)346-2232
PO Box 755 Fax: (916)346-2700
Colfax, CA 95713
Community newspaper. **Founded:** 1908. **Freq:** Weekly (Tues.). **Print Method:** Offset. **Cols./Page:** 6. **Col. Width:** 2 1/16 inches. **Col. Depth:** 21 1/2 inches. **Key Personnel:** Jill Fallbeck, Publisher. **Subscription Rates:** $11 individuals; $15 Out of County. **Remarks:** Accepts advertising.
Ad Rates: GLR: $.63 **Circ:** 1,830
SAU: $5

Coverstory - See Foothill

COLTON, pop. 27,419.

SE CA. San Bernardino Co. 3 mi. SW of San Bernardino. Manufactures cement, lime, animal feeds, concrete pipe, evaporative air coolers, china & porcelain bathroom fixtures, meat packing plant.

1748 Colton Courier
Inland Empire Community Newspapers
PO Box 6247 Phone: (909)381-9898
San Bernardino, CA 92412-6247 Fax: (909)384-0406
Publisher E-mail: iecn@gte.net
Newspaper. **Founded:** 1877. **Freq:** Weekly (Thurs.). **Print Method:** Offset. **Cols./Page:** 4. **Col. Width:** 2.375 inches. **Col. Depth:** 15 inches. **Key Personnel:** Gloria Marcias Harrison, Publisher; Bill Harrison, Publisher. **Subscription Rates:** $50 out of state. **Remarks:** Accepts advertising.
Ad Rates: GLR: $1 **Circ:** Free ‡16,000
BW: $1,512 Paid ‡1,000
4C: $2,162
PCI: $12

1749 KOOJ-FM - 92.7
900 E. Washington, Ste. 315 Phone: (909)825-9525
Colton, CA 92324 Fax: (909)825-0441

Format: Country. **Founded:** 1959. **Formerly**: KCAK-FM (1975). **Operating Hours:** Continuous. **ADI:** Los Angeles (Corona & San Bernardino), CA. **Key Personnel:** Tom Hoyt, General Mgr.; Lee Logan, Operations Mgr.; Robin Diamond, Promotions/Marketing Mgr.; Richard Lee, News Dir. **Local Programs:** *Brooke Daniels Nightime*, Brooke Daniels; *Doug Wilson Afternoons*, Doug Wilson; *Gary Wilson Morning Show*, Gary Wilson. **Wattage:** 6,000. **Ad Rates:** Advertising accepted; rates available upon request.

COMPTON, pop. 81,286.

S. CA. Los Angeles Co. 6 mi. S. of Los Angeles. Manufactures aircraft parts, oil well supplies, steel castings, furniture. Mobile homes. Nurseries. Oil Wells. Truck, dairy, poultry farms.

1750 Carson Bulletin
Rapid Publishing
349 W. Compton Phone: (213)774-0018
PO Box 4248
Compton, CA 90224
Black community newspaper. **Freq:** Weekly (Wed.). **Cols./Page:** 6. **Col. Width:** 12 1/2 picas. **Col. Depth:** 21 1/2 inches. **Key Personnel:** O. Ray Watkins, Publisher. **Remarks:** Accepts advertising.
Ad Rates: SAU: $10.65 **Circ:** Paid 8,000
Free 9,000

1751 Compton Bulletin
Rapid Publishing
349 W. Compton Phone: (213)774-0018
PO Box 4248
Compton, CA 90224
Black community newspaper. **Freq:** Weekly (Wed.). **Cols./Page:** 6. **Col. Width:** 12 1/2 picas. **Col. Depth:** 21 1/2 inches. **Key Personnel:** O. Ray Watkins, Publisher. **Remarks:** Accepts advertising.
Ad Rates: SAU: $10.65 **Circ:** Paid 12,000
Free 10,000

1752 Compton/Carson Wave
Wave Community Newspapers, Inc.
2621 W. 54th St. Phone: (213)290-3000
Los Angeles, CA 90043 Fax: (213)291-0219

Black community newspaper sold in combination with the Central News/Journal/Star Wave and Lynwood Press. **Freq:** Biweekly Wednesday & Saturday. **Print Method:** Offset. **Trim Size:** 13 3/4 x 21 1/2. **Cols./Page:** 6. **Col. Width:** 5 nonpareils. **Col. Depth:** 21 1/2 inches. **Key Personnel:** C.Z. Wilson, President. **Subscription Rates:** Free; $125 by mail. **Remarks:** Advertising accepted; rates available upon request.
Circ: Non-paid 40,365

1753 Compton Metropolitan Gazette
First-Line Publishers/L.A. Metro Group
14621 Titus St., Ste. 228 Phone: (818)782-8695
Van Nuys, CA 91402 Fax: (818)782-2924

Black community newspaper serving Compton and Carson. **Founded:** 1966. **Freq:** Weekly (Thurs.). **Print Method:** Offset. **Trim Size:** 13 x 21 1/2. **Cols./Page:** 6. **Col. Width:** 2 inches. **Key Personnel:** Hillary Hamm, Publisher; Hillard Hamm, Editor. **Subscription Rates:** Free; $25. **Remarks:** Accepts advertising.
Ad Rates: PCI: $32 **Circ:** Free 60,000

Inglewood Tribune - See Inglewood

Lynwood Journal - See Lynwood

Wilmington Beacon - See Wilmington

CONCORD, pop. 103,251.

W. CA. Contra Costa Co. 25 mi. E. of Oakland. Oil refineries; cement plant; winery; electronic parts manufactured. Fruit, grain.

1754 California Farmer
Farm Progress Companies
1410 Danzig Plaza, No. 250 Phone: (510)687-1662
Concord, CA 94520 Fax: (510)687-4945

Publication for Californias diversified farmers and ranchers. **Founded:** 1854. **Freq:** 15/year. **Trim Size:** 8 x 10 3/4. **Cols./Page:** 3. **Col. Width:** 2 1/8 inches. **Col. Depth:** 10 inches. **Key Personnel:** Len Richardson, Editor. **Subscription Rates:** $17.95 individuals; $43.85 out of area for 3 yrs.; $45 other countries for 1 yr. **Remarks:** Accepts advertising.
Ad Rates: GLR: $140 **Circ:** Paid 14,116
BW: $3,350 Non-paid 23,673
4C: $4,690
PCI: $140

1755 CMEA News
California Music Education Association
3924 Cottonwood Dr. Phone: (925)685-3237
Concord, CA 94519 Fax: (510)687-5246
Publisher E-mail: cmea@calmusiced.com

Journal on music education. **Founded:** 1947. **Freq:** Quarterly. **Print Method:** Offset. **Trim Size:** 8 1/2 x 11. **Cols./Page:** 3. **Col. Width:** 27 nonpareils. **Col. Depth:** 140 agate lines. **Key Personnel:** Jerri Burke, Editor. **ISSN:** 0007-8638. **Subscription Rates:** $12 individuals; $3 single issue. **Remarks:** Accepts advertising.
Ad Rates: BW: $299 **Circ:** Paid ‡3,250

1756 ETC
International Society for General Semantics
Box 728 Phone: (925)798-0311
Concord, CA 94522 Fax: (925)798-0312
Publication E-mail: internetisgs@a.crl.com

Scholarly journal covering language, behavior, and education. **Founded:** 1943. **Freq:** Quarterly. **Trim Size:** 6 x 9. **Subscription Rates:** $35 individuals; $9 single issue.

1757 Tole World
EGW Publishing Co.
1041 Shary Cir. Phone: (925)671-9852
Concord, CA 94518 Fax: (925)671-0692

Magazine for tole and decorative painting hobbyists. **Subtitle:** Creative Designs for Decorative Painting. **Founded:** 1977. **Freq:** Bimonthly. **Print Method:** Offset. **Trim Size:** 8 1/8 x 10 7/8. **Cols./Page:** 3. **Col. Width:** 28 nonpareils. **Col. Depth:** 133 agate lines. **Key Personnel:** Judy Swager, Editor, jswager@egw.com; D'Ann Giordano, Advertising Mgr., rwilson@egw.com. **ISSN:** 0199-4514. **Subscription Rates:** $19.95 individuals; $4.95 single issue. **Remarks:** Accepts advertising.
Ad Rates: BW: $1,500 **Circ:** ‡90,000
4C: $2,250
PCI: $90

1758 Veggie Life
EGW Publishing Co.
1041 Shary Cir. Phone: (925)671-9852
Concord, CA 94518 Fax: (925)671-0692
Publication E-mail: veggieed@aol.com

Consumer magazine covering health, nutrition, and vegetarian cooking. **Subtitle:** Growing Green, Cooking Lean, Feeling Good. **Founded:** 1993. **Freq:** Semimonthly. **Print Method:** Web offset. **Trim Size:** 8 x 10 1/2. **Cols./Page:** 3. **Key Personnel:** Sharon Barela, Editor; Robert Marshall, Advertising Mgr.; Lea Reiter, Advertising Mgr. **ISSN:** 1065-2728. **Subscription Rates:** $23.70 individuals; $3.95 single issue. **Remarks:** Accepts advertising.
Ad Rates: BW: $5,148 **Circ:** Paid 250,000
4C: $6,435

1759 Weekend Woodcrafts
EGW Publishing Co.
1041 Shary Cir. Phone: (925)671-9852
Concord, CA 94518 Fax: (925)671-0692

Consumer magazine covering craft and woodworking projects. **Founded:** 1992. **Freq:** Bimonthly. **Print Method:** Web offset. **Trim Size:** 8 x 10 1/2. **Cols./Page:** 3. **Key Personnel:** Robert Joseph, Editor, rjoseph@egw.com; Rickie Wilson, Advertising Mgr., rwilson@egw.com; Robert Lenart, Advertising Mgr. **ISSN:** 1058-9821. **Subscription Rates:** $29.70 individuals; $5.99 single issue. **Remarks:** Accepts advertising. **URL:** http://www.weekendwoodcrafts.com.
Ad Rates: BW: $1,000 **Circ:** Paid 33,000
4C: $1,300

1760 Wood Strokes & Woodcrafts
EGW Publishing Co.
1041 Shary Cir. Phone: (925)671-9852
Concord, CA 94518 Fax: (925)671-0692

Consumer magazine covering wood crafts. **Founded:** 1992. **Freq:** Semimonthly. **Print Method:** Heatset web. **Key Personnel:** Sandra Wagner, Editor. **ISSN:** 1069-6962. **Subscrip-

tion Rates: $29.70 individuals; $4.95 single issue. **Remarks:** Accepts advertising. **URL:** http://www.woodstrokes.com.
Ad Rates: BW: $3,860 **Circ:** Paid 120,000
4C: $3,718

1761 Concord Cable TV
2450 Whitman Rd. Phone: (510)685-2330
Concord, CA 94518 Fax: (510)686-1257

Founded: 1967. **Cities Served:** Contra Costa County and Clayton, CA.

1762 KTNC-TV - 42
5101 Port Chicago Hwy. Phone: (510)686-4242
Concord, CA 94520 Fax: (510)825-4242

Format: Commercial TV. **Networks:** Independent. **Owner:** Pappas Telecasting, at above address. **Founded:** 1983. **Operating Hours:** Continuous. **ADI:** San Francisco-Oakland-San Jose. **Key Personnel:** Gary Johnson, Production Mgr. **Local Programs:** *Accent on Health* 4:30 p.m. Wednesday, Lila Schoch; *Coast to Coast* 10-11 a.m.; 2-3 p.m. Monday-Friday, Liz Farkas; *Informed Viewer* 4 p.m. Saturday, Bud Swanson.

1763 KVHS-FM - 90.5
1101 Alberta Way Phone: (925)682-5847
Concord, CA 94521 Fax: (925)609-5847
E-mail: music@kvhs.com

Format: Alternative/New Music/Progressive. **Networks:** Independent. **Owner:** Clayton Valley High School, at above address. **Founded:** 1969. **Operating Hours:** 6 a.m.-10 p.m.; 100% local. **Key Personnel:** Melissa Wilson, General Mgr., phone (923)682-8000 Ext. 3121, wilson143@aol.com; Nassim Bakhtiari, Operations Mgr., info@kvhs.com; Stephen Jester, Programming Manager, music@kvhs.com. **Wattage:** 410. **Ad Rates:** Noncommercial. **URL:** http://www.kvhs.com.

1764 KZWC-AM - 990
1430 Willow Pass Rd., Ste. 200 Phone: (510)825-9000
Concord, CA 94520-5287 Fax: (510)825-9393
Free: (800)921-9292

Format: Adult Contemporary. **Owner:** Z-Spanish Network, at above address. **Founded:** 1949. **Formerly:** KKIS-AM. **Operating Hours:** Continuous. **Key Personnel:** Picar Gariv, General Mgr.; Salvador Campos, Program Dir.; Jorge Leyton, News Dir. **Wattage:** 3000. **Ad Rates:** $60-70 for 60 seconds.

1765 KZWC-FM - 92.1
1430 Willow Pass Rd., Ste. 200 Phone: (510)825-9000
Concord, CA 94520-3288 Fax: (510)825-9393
Free: (800)921-9292

Format: Hispanic. **Founded:** Nov. 1, 1993. **Formerly:** KDFM-FM; KINQ-FM; KKIS-FM. **Operating Hours:** Continuous. **Key Personnel:** Pilar Garcia, VP/Gen. Mgr.; Manuel Salazar, General Sales Mgr.; Jorge Leyton, Contact. **Wattage:** 3000. **Ad Rates:** $50 for 30 seconds; $60 for 60 seconds.

COPPEROPOLIS

1766 Copperopolis Herald
PO Box 220 Phone: (209)887-3112
Copperopolis, CA 95228 Fax: (209)887-3111

Community newspaper. **Founded:** Feb. 19, 1998. **Freq:** Weekly. **Print Method:** Offset web. **Cols./Page:** 8. **Col. Width:** 1 1/2 inches. **Col. Depth:** 22 inches. **Key Personnel:** Brian Reilly, Contact. **Subscription Rates:** $25 individuals; $.50 single issue. **Remarks:** Accepts advertising.
Ad Rates: BW: $800 **Circ:** Non-paid 1,000

1767 The Linden Herald
PO Box 220
Copperopolis, CA 95228

Community newspaper. **Founded:** 1959. **Freq:** Weekly (Thurs.). **Print Method:** Offset. **Cols./Page:** 8. **Col. Width:** 22 inches. **Col. Depth:** 13 & 22 inches. **Key Personnel:** Brian Reilly, Editor and Publisher. **USPS:** 587-180. **Subscription Rates:** $25 individuals. **Remarks:** Color advertising accepted; rates available upon request.
Ad Rates: GLR: $5 **Circ:** Paid ‡1,200
BW: $784
SAU: $8
PCI: $5.50

CORCORAN, pop. 6,454.

SC CA. Kings Co. 45 mi. S. of Fresno. Flour, feed, cottonseed oil mills; cotton gins. Agriculture. Dairying. Cotton, grain, beef cattle.

1768 The Corcoran Journal
PO Box 487 Phone: (209)992-3115
Corcoran, CA 93212 Fax: (209)992-5543
Publication E-mail: lama@lightspeed.net

Community newspaper. **Founded:** Sept. 1908. **Freq:** Weekly (Thurs.). **Print Method:** Offset. **Trim Size:** 13 x 21 1/2. **Cols./Page:** 6. **Col. Width:** 19 nonpareils. **Col. Depth:** 301 agate lines. **Key Personnel:** Jeanette Todd, Editor and Publisher. **Subscription Rates:** $23 individuals; $27 Out of County; $30 out of state. **Remarks:** Accepts advertising. **Feature Editors:** Tina Botill, *Society*.
Ad Rates: GLR: $1 **Circ:** Paid 2,500
BW: $548 Free 26
SAU: $4

CORNING, pop. 4,745.

N. CA. Tehama Co. 47 mi. S. of Redding. Extensive olive packing and shipping; wood products, furniture factories: fruit dehydrating plant. Agriculture. Olives, walnuts, almonds, grain, fruits. Cattle. Dairying.

1769 Corning Observer
Morris Newspaper Corp.
710 5th St. Phone: (916)824-5464
Corning, CA 96021 Fax: (916)824-4804

General newspaper. **Founded:** 1887. **Freq:** Triweekly. **Print Method:** Offset. **Cols./Page:** 6. **Col. Width:** 26 nonpareils. **Col. Depth:** 301 agate lines. **Key Personnel:** Mike Griffin, Editor. **USPS:** 132-940. **Subscription Rates:** $48 individuals. **Remarks:** Accepts advertising.
Ad Rates: SAU: $4.76 **Circ:** ‡2,350
PCI: $3.61

CORONA, pop. 37,791.

SE CA. Riverside Co. 15 mi. SE of Riverside. Citrus fruit packed. Fiberglass insulation, plywood paneling, furniture, mattresses, die castings manufactured. Fruit, dairy farms.

1770 Autograph Collector
Odyssey Publications, Inc.
510-A South Corona Mall Phone: (909)734-9636
Corona, CA 91719 Fax: (909)371-7139
Free: (800)395-1359

Magazine for museums, manuscript libraries, and worldwide collectors of autographs, signed photos, first day covers, and documents of historical significance. **Founded:** 1986. **Freq:** Monthly 10/year. **Print Method:** Offset. **Trim Size:** 8 3/8 x 10 7/8. **Cols./Page:** 3. **Col. Width:** 2 1/4 inches. **Col. Depth:** 10 inches. **Key Personnel:** Kevin Sherman, Editor; Darrell Talber, Publisher. **Subscription Rates:** $38 individuals U.S.; $62 single issue. **Remarks:** Accepts advertising. **URL:** http://www.odysseygroup.com.
Ad Rates: BW: $370 **Circ:** Paid 3,000
4C: $600 Non-paid 15,000

Corona-Norco Independent - See Norco

1771 The Western Dairyman
HFW Communications, Inc.
PO Box 819 Phone: (909)735-2730
Corona, CA 91718 Fax: (909)735-2460
Free: (800)735-7100
Publication E-mail: westdairy2@aol.com

Magazine for commercial milk producers in the Western U.S. **Founded:** 1922. **Freq:** Monthly. **Print Method:** Web offset. **Trim Size:** 8 x 10 7/8. **Cols./Page:** 3. **Col. Width:** 13 picas. **Col. Depth:** 10 inches. **Key Personnel:** Dennis J. Halladay, Editor; Stanley E Bird, Publisher. **ISSN:** 0011-572X. **Subscription Rates:** $35. **Remarks:** Accepts advertising. **Formerly:** The Dairyman.
Ad Rates: BW: $2,620 **Circ:** ‡17,500
4C: $3,515
PCI: $160

1772 KWRM-AM - 1370
210 Radio Rd. Phone: (909)737-1370
PO Box 100 Fax: (909)735-9572
Corona, CA 91718

Format: Hispanic. **Founded:** 1948. **Operating Hours:** Continuous. **ADI:** Los Angeles (Corona & San Bernardino), CA. **Key Personnel:** Dee Galiffa, General Mgr. **Wattage:** 5000 day; 2500 night. **Ad Rates:** $40 for 60 seconds.

CORONA DEL MAR

1773 News for Kids
D.M. Publishing, Inc.
400 Heliotrope Ave.
Corona Del Mar, CA 92625-2921

News magazine for kids 7 to 12 years of age. **Freq:** Monthly. **Key Personnel:** Fran Mulvania, Editor and Publisher. **Subscription Rates:** $18.95. $2.95 single issue.

CORONADO, pop. 16,859.

S. CA. San Diego Co. On San Diego Bay, 1 mi. SW of San Diego. Resort.

1774 Coronado Journal
1224 10th St., Ste. 104 Phone: (619)435-3141
Coronado, CA 92118 Fax: (619)435-3051
Publication E-mail: coronadojournal@wccnews.com

Community newspaper. **Founded:** 1912. **Freq:** Weekly (Fri.). **Print Method:** Offset. **Trim Size:** 11 1/8 x 13 5/8. **Cols./Page:** 6. **Col. Width:** 24 nonpareils. **Col. Depth:** 298 agate lines. **Key Personnel:** Heather McCluskey, Editor; Linda Rosas, Advertising Mgr. **Subscription Rates:** $20 individuals. **Remarks:** Accepts advertising.
Ad Rates: GLR: $1.65 **Circ:** 11,500
BW: $645
4C: $1,990
SAU: $12.75

CORTE MADERA, pop. 8,074.

W. CA. Marin Co. 12 mi. NW of San Francisco. Residential.

1775 The Crafts Fair Guide
Crafts Fair Guide
PO Box 688 Phone: (415)924-3259
Corte Madera, CA 94976-0688 Fax: (415)924-3259
Free: (800)871-2341

Magazine reviewing West Coast craft fairs, providing information about a show's environment, weather, attendance, fees, promoters' names and addresses, and old and new dates. **Founded:** 1974. **Freq:** Quarterly. **Print Method:** Offset. **Trim Size:** 8 1/2 x 11. **Cols./Page:** 2. **Col. Width:** 2 1/2 inches. **Col. Depth:** 10 inches. **Key Personnel:** Lee Spiegel, Editor and Publisher, leecfg@pacbell.net; Dianne Spiegel, Editor. **ISSN:** 0273-7957. **Subscription Rates:** $45 individuals; $16 single issue.
Ad Rates: BW: $300 **Circ:** 4,250
PCI: $12

1776 Journal of Social Behavior and Personality
Select Press
PO Box 37 Phone: (415)924-1612
Corte Madera, CA 94976-0037
Journal covering psychology, speech, business, and sociology. **Founded:** 1986. **Freq:** Quarterly. **Print Method:** Offset. **Trim Size:** 5 1/2 x 8 1/2. **Cols./Page:** 1. **Col. Width:** 4 inches. **Col. Depth:** 7 inches. **Key Personnel:** Dr. Rick Crandall, Ph.D., Editor. **ISSN:** 0886-1641. **Subscription Rates:** $70 institutions; $30 individuals; $15 single issue.
Ad Rates: BW: $300 **Circ:** Paid ‡600

1777 Marin Scope
Marin Scope Community Newspapers, Inc.
PO Box 1806 Phone: (415)332-3778
Corte Madera, CA 94925 Fax: (415)332-8714

Community newspaper serving Sausalito, CA. **Founded:** Apr. 1971. **Freq:** Weekly (Tues.). **Print Method:** Web offset. **Trim Size:** 13 x 21. **Key Personnel:** Billie Anderson, Editor; Paul Anderson, Publisher. **Subscription Rates:** $20. **Remarks:** Accepts advertising.
Ad Rates: SAU: $16.10 **Circ:** Combined ‡2,000
PCI: $7.60

1778 Ross Valley Reporter
Marin Scope Community Newspapers, Inc.
PO Box 1806 Phone: (415)332-3778
Corte Madera, CA 94925 Fax: (415)332-8714

Local community newspaper. **Founded:** 1967. **Freq:** Weekly (Wed.). **Print Method:** Offset. **Trim Size:** 13 x 21. **Cols./Page:** 8. **Col. Width:** 8.5 picas. **Col. Depth:** 21 inches. **Key Personnel:** Cinda Becker, Editor; Billie Anderson, Managing Editor; Paul Anderson, Publisher. **Subscription Rates:** $20 individuals.
Ad Rates: 4C: $400 **Circ:** ‡11,500
PCI: $12.75

1779 Twin Cities Times
Marin Scope Community Newspapers, Inc.
PO Box 1806   Phone: (415)332-3778
Corte Madera, CA 94925   Fax: (415)332-8714

Community newspaper serving Corte Madera, Larkspur, and Greenbrae. **Freq:** Weekly (Wed.). **Print Method:** Web offset. **Trim Size:** 13 x 21. **Cols./Page:** 8. **Col. Width:** 8.5 picas. **Col. Depth:** 21 inches. **Key Personnel:** Billie Anderson, Editor; Paul Anderson, Publisher. **Subscription Rates:** $21.45.
Ad Rates: 4C: $400   **Circ:** Combined ‡5,500
PCI: $12

1780 KKHI-FM - 100.7
770 Tamalpais Dr., Ste. 208   Phone: (415)924-1292
Corte Madera, CA 94925   Fax: (415)924-1291

Format: Classical. **Networks:** Independent. **Owner:** Mt. Wilson FM Broadcasters, Inc., at above address. **Founded:** 1963. **Formerly**: KTIM-FM (1987); KTID-FM. **Operating Hours:** Continuous. **Key Personnel:** Andi Polisky, General Mgr. **Wattage:** 6000.

COSTA MESA, pop. 82,291.

S. CA. Orange Co. 8 mi. S. of Santa Ana. Orange Coast College. Southern California College. University of California. Manufactures boats, electronic and airplane parts, plastics, fiberglass fabrications.

1781 Ability Magazine
1001 W. 17th St.   Phone: (714)854-8700
Costa Mesa, CA 92627   Fax: (714)548-5966
Publication E-mail: ability@pacbell.net

Lifestyle magazine featuring celebrity interviews about health and diabetes, new technologies, and general human interest. **Subtitle:** An Informative Resource on Disability Issues. **Founded:** 1991. **Freq:** Bimonthly. **Print Method:** Web heat-set. **Trim Size:** 8 x 10 7/8. **Cols./Page:** 3. **Key Personnel:** Fred Bailey, Editor; Chet Cooper, Advertising Mgr. **ISSN:** 1062-5321. **Subscription Rates:** $29.70. **Remarks:** Accepts advertising. **URL:** http://www.abilitymagazine.com.
Ad Rates: BW: $5,190   **Circ:** ‡165,000
4C: $7,990

1782 Avenues
Automobile of S. California
3333 Fairview Rd., A327   Phone: (714)885-2376
Costa Mesa, CA 92626   Fax: (714)885-2335

Magazine for members of the Automobile Club of Southern California. **Founded:** 1934. **Freq:** Bimonthly. **Print Method:** Web Offset. **Trim Size:** 8x10 1/2. **Cols./Page:** 3. **Col. Width:** 2.1 inches. **Col. Depth:** 8.25 inches. **Key Personnel:** Gail Harrington, Editor-in-Chief; Marc Titel, Publisher; Bob Bradley, Dir. of Advertising; Mike Bonk, Circulation Mgr., phone (213)741-3472, fax (213)741-3303. **ISSN:** 1073-1903. **Subscription Rates:** $3 individuals; $.75 single issue; $2 institutions; $4 other countries. **Remarks:** Accepts advertising. **Formerly:** Auto Club News.
Ad Rates: BW: $32,360   **Circ:** Paid 2,738,634
4C: $40,990

1783 Cycle News
CN Publishing
PO Box 5084   Phone: (310)427-7433
Costa Mesa, CA 92628-5084   Fax: (310)427-6685
Publication E-mail: editor@cyclenews.com

Newspaper (tabloid) for motorcycle enthusiasts. **Subtitle:** America's Weekly Motorcycle Newspaper. **Founded:** 1963. **Freq:** Weekly. **Print Method:** Offset. **Trim Size:** 11 x 14 1/2. **Cols./Page:** 4. **Col. Width:** 27 nonpareils. **Col. Depth:** 193 agate lines. **Key Personnel:** Paul Carruthers, Editor; Michael D. Klinger, Publisher. **Subscription Rates:** $50 individuals. **Remarks:** Accepts advertising. **URL:** http://www.cyclenews.com.
Ad Rates: BW: $4,810   **Circ:** Paid 35,496
4C: $6,010   Free 1,247
PCI: $58

1784 Daily Pilot
330 W. Bay St.   Phone: (714)642-4321
Costa Mesa, CA 92627   Fax: (714)631-5902

Community newspaper. **Founded:** 1907. **Freq:** Daily. **Print Method:** Offset. **Cols./Page:** 6. **Col. Width:** 2 1/16 inches. **Col. Depth:** 21 1/2 inches. **Key Personnel:** Bill Lobdell, Editor.
Circ: 40,000

1785 Dune Buggies & Hot VWs
2950 Airway, Ste. A7   Phone: (714)979-2560
PO Box 2260   Fax: (714)979-3998
Costa Mesa, CA 92626
Magazine offering VW automotive news for the consumer. **Founded:** 1967. **Freq:** Monthly. **Print Method:** Offset. **Trim Size:** 8 x 10 7/8. **Cols./Page:** 3. **Col. Width:** 27 nonpareils. **Col. Depth:** 140 agate lines. **Key Personnel:** Judy Wright, Publisher; Bruce Simurda, Editor; Linda Dill, Advertising Mgr. **ISSN:** 0012-7132. **Subscription Rates:** $21.97 individuals; $3.50 single issue. **Remarks:** Accepts advertising.
Ad Rates: BW: $1,925   **Circ:** ‡92,000
4C: $2,785

1786 New Homes Magazine
MDM Publications
3151 Airway Ave., Ste. C-3
Costa Mesa, CA 92626

New real estate magazine. **Subtitle:** And Map Guide To New Home Communities. **Founded:** 1967. **Freq:** Bimonthly. **Print Method:** Offset. **Trim Size:** 8 1/4 x 10 3/4. **Cols./Page:** 3 and 2. **Col. Width:** 27 and 42 nonpareils. **Col. Depth:** 137 agate lines. **Key Personnel:** Daniel B. Ciauri, Publisher. **Subscription Rates:** $30 individuals; Free single issues. **Remarks:** Accepts advertising.
Ad Rates: BW: $2,600   **Circ:** Non-paid ‡100,000
4C: $2,950

Newport Beach/Costa Mesa Daily Pilot - See Newport Beach

1787 Off Duty
Off Duty Enterprises
3505 Cadillac Ave., Ste. 0-105   Phone: (714)549-7172
Costa Mesa, CA 92626-1434   Fax: (714)549-4222
Publication E-mail: odutyedit@aol.com; wbrdmr@aol.com

Leisuretime magazine for U.S. military personnel and their families stationed in the United States, Europe and the Pacific. **Subtitle:** The Military Leisur Time Magazine. **Founded:** 1980. **Freq:** 8/year. **Print Method:** Offset. **Trim Size:** 8 x 10 3/4. **Cols./Page:** and 3. **Key Personnel:** Gary Burch, Executive Editor; Walter B. Rios, Publisher; Dagmar Rios, Publisher; Chuck Emerson, Advertising Mgr. **Subscription Rates:** Free. **Remarks:** Accepts advertising.
Ad Rates: BW: $11,760   **Circ:** Non-paid 507,000
4C: $14,700

1788 Off Duty Europe
Off Duty Enterprises
3505 Cadillac Ave., Ste. 0-105   Phone: (714)549-7172
Costa Mesa, CA 92626-1434   Fax: (714)549-4222

Leisuretime magazine for U.S. military personnel and their families stationed in Europe. **Founded:** Sept. 1970. **Freq:** Monthly. **Print Method:** Offset. **Trim Size:** 8 x 10 3/4. **Cols./Page:** 4 and 3. **Col. Width:** 24 and 30 nonpareils. **Col. Depth:** 140 agate lines. **Key Personnel:** Jim Shaw, Editor; Walter B. Rios, Publisher; Chuck Emerson, European General Manager. **Subscription Rates:** Free to qualified subscribers; $10 individuals. **Remarks:** Accepts advertising.
Ad Rates: BW: $4,170   **Circ:** Controlled ‡50,000
4C: $5,000

1789 Off Duty Pacific
Off Duty Enterprises
3505 Cadillac Ave., Ste. 0-105   Phone: (714)549-7172
Costa Mesa, CA 92626-1434   Fax: (714)549-4222

Leisuretime magazine for U.S. military personnel and their families stationed in the Pacific. **Founded:** 1971. **Freq:** 8/year. **Print Method:** Offset. **Trim Size:** 8 x 10 3/4. **Cols./Page:** 4 and 3. **Col. Width:** 24 and 30 nonpareils. **Col. Depth:** 140 agate lines. **Key Personnel:** Jim Shaw, Editor, jsofduty@aol.com; Walter B. Rios, Publisher; Robert Bonds, Advertising Mgr. **Remarks:** Accepts advertising.
Ad Rates: BW: $4,700   **Circ:** Non-paid 61,000
4C: $5,640

1790 Personal Watercraft Illustrated
Cycle News Inc.
PO Box 5084   Phone: (310)427-7433
Costa Mesa, CA 92628-5084   Fax: (310)427-6685

Personal watercraft magazine. **Founded:** June 1987. **Freq:** Monthly. **Trim Size:** 8 1/8 x 10 3/4. **Cols./Page:** 3. **Col. Width:** 27 nonpareils. **Col. Depth:** 120 agate lines. **Key Personnel:** Paul Carruthers, Editor, editor@watercraft.com; Mike Klinger, Publisher; Tom Gonter, Advertising Mgr.; Mark Thome, Mktg. and Promotions Dir. **Subscription Rates:** $21 individuals. **URL:** http://www.watercraft.com; http://www.cyclenews.com.
Ad Rates: BW: $2,070   **Circ:** Paid ‡66,510
4C: $3,220   Non-paid ‡2,009

1791 PTI Journal
PTI Partnership
1666 Newport Blvd., Ste. 141   Phone: (714)752-1292
Costa Mesa, CA 92627   Fax: (714)752-9533
Publication E-mail: publish@pti-journal.com

Magazine covering innovative transportation, new technology and private sector involvement in the provision of public transportation services. **Subtitle:** Journal of Public Transportation Innovation. **Founded:** Mar. 1987. **Freq:** 2/year. **Print Method:** Offset. **Trim Size:** 8 1/4 x 10 7/8. **Cols./Page:** 3. **Col. Width:** 2.3 inches. **Col. Depth:** 8.5 inches. **Key Personnel:** Steven Rooney, Publisher. **Subscription Rates:** Free to qualified subscribers; $38. **Remarks:** Accepts advertising. **URL:** http://www.pti-journal.com.
Ad Rates: BW: $1,764   **Circ:** Paid ‡1,000
4C: $2,514   Controlled ‡20,000

1792 The Source
2900 Bristol St., Ste. J101
Costa Mesa, CA 92626

Trade journal serving retailers, rent-to-own, rent-to-rent dealers and suppliers. **Subtitle:** Retail-Rent to Own-Services. **Founded:** 1987. **Freq:** Monthly. **Trim Size:** 8 1/4 x 10 7/8. **Cols./Page:** 3. **Col. Width:** 2 1/4 inches. **Col. Depth:** 9 3/4 inches. **Key Personnel:** Marie Nay, CEO, phone (714)546-9501. **ISSN:** 1051-7057. **Subscription Rates:** $36. **Formerly**: Rental Dealer News.
Ad Rates: 4C: $2,400   **Circ:** ‡22,000

1793 Westways
Automobile of S. California
3333 Fairview Rd., A327   Phone: (714)885-2376
Costa Mesa, CA 92626   Fax: (714)885-2335

Magazine covering regional, domestic and international travel, recreation, and events. **Founded:** 1909. **Freq:** Monthly. **Print Method:** Web Offset. **Trim Size:** 8x10 1/2. **Cols./Page:** 3. **Col. Width:** 27 nonpareils. **Col. Depth:** 137 agate lines. **Key Personnel:** Susan LaTempa, Editor-in-Chief, phone (714)885-2406; John Dinkel, Publisher, phone (714)885-2401; Bob Bradley, Dir. of Advertising, phone (714)885-2403; Richard Stayton, Managing Editor, phone (714)885-2359. **Subscription Rates:** $14.95 individuals yearly; $2.95 single issue. **Remarks:** Accepts advertising.
Ad Rates: BW: $5,170   **Circ:** Paid 193,192
4C: $6,580

1794 Workforce
ACC Communications Inc.
245 Fischer Ave., B-2   Phone: (714)751-1883
Costa Mesa, CA 92626   Fax: (714)751-4106
Publication E-mail: mailroom@workforcemag.com

A Business magazine for human resources management leaders. **Subtitle:** Real Human Resource, Real Impact. **Founded:** May 1922. **Freq:** Monthly. **Print Method:** Offset. **Trim Size:** 8 3/8 x 10 7/8. **Cols./Page:** 3. **Col. Width:** 27 nonpareils. **Col. Depth:** 140 agate lines. **Key Personnel:** Allan Halcrow, Publisher, halcrow@workforcemag.com; Margaret Magnus, Pres./CEO. **ISSN:** 1092-8332. **Subscription Rates:** $59 individuals; $8 single issue. **Remarks:** Accepts advertising. **Online:** EBSCO. **URL:** http://www.workforceonline.com. **Alt. Formats:** Microform. **Formerly:** Personnel Journal.
Ad Rates: BW: $3,539   **Circ:** ‡32,000
4C: $5,498

1795 KBRT-AM - 740
3183 Airway Ave., No. D   Phone: (714)754-4450
Costa Mesa, CA 92626   Fax: (714)754-0735
Free: (800)227-ADDS

Format: Religious; Talk. **Networks:** Independent. **Founded:** 1952. **Operating Hours:** Sunrise-sunset. **Key Personnel:** Edward Personius, Station Mgr. **Local Programs:** *Cross Talk*, Kim Iverson, (714)754-4450, Fax (714)754-0735; *Jane Chastain Show*, Kit Kushin, (714)754-4450, Fax (714)754-0735. **Wattage:** 10,000.

1796 XBACH-AM - 540
1500 Cotner Ave.   Phone: (310)478-5540
PO Box 250028   Fax: (310)478-4189
Los Angeles, CA 90025

Format: News. **Networks:** Independent. **Owner:** Mt. Wilson FM Broadcasters Inc., at above address. **Founded:** 1990. **Formerly:** KJQI-AM. **Operating Hours:** Continuous. **ADI:** Los Angeles (Corona & San Bernardino), CA. **Key Personnel:** Saul Levine, President. **Wattage:** 25,000.

COVINA, pop. 33,751.

S. CA. Los Angeles Co. 9 mi. W. of Pomona. Citrus fruit packing and cold storage plants; steel fabricating. Spray products, ladders manufactured. Agriculture. Oranges, lemons, walnuts.

1797 SAMPE Journal
Society for the Advancement of Material & Process Engineering
1161 Parkview Drive   Phone: (626)331-0616
Covina, CA 91724-3748   Fax: (626)332-8929
Free: (800)562-7360
Publication E-mail: sampeibo@aol.com

Publisher E-mail: sampeibo@aol.com

Magazine covering materials and process engineering. **Founded:** 1962. **Freq:** Bimonthly. **Print Method:** Offset. **Trim Size:** 8 1/8 x 10 7/8. **Cols./Page:** 3. **Col. Width:** 27 nonpareils. **Col. Depth:** 140 agate lines. **Key Personnel:** Daun E. White, Exec. Dir., DaunWhite@aol.com. **ISSN:** 0091-1062. **Subscription Rates:** $65 individuals. **Remarks:** Accepts advertising.
Ad Rates: BW: $1,590 4C: $2,655 **Circ:** Paid ‡5,000

1798 San Gabriel Valley Business Journal
Southwest Business Publishing Co.
1274 E. Center Court Dr., No. 207
Covina, CA 91724
Phone: (626)858-3351
Fax: (626)339-6783
Publication E-mail: swpub@aol.com

Professional journal for the business community in eastern Los Angeles County. **Founded:** Oct. 1993. **Freq:** Monthly. **Print Method:** Web. **Trim Size:** 10 3/4 x 14. **Cols./Page:** 4. **Col. Width:** 2 1/4 inches. **Col. Depth:** 13 inches. **Key Personnel:** Richard Lawrence, Publisher, richswbiz@aol.com; Ewin Grace, Editor; Julie Lawrence, Circulation Mgr.; Ken Hanson, President. **Subscription Rates:** $29 individuals. **Remarks:** Accepts advertising.
Ad Rates: BW: $1,680 4C: $2,080 **Circ:** Controlled 10,000

CRESCENT CITY†, pop. 3,099.

NW CA. Del Norte Co. On Pacific Ocean, 70 mi. N. of Eureka. Redwood National Park. Resort. Light Industry. Lumber, wooden novelties manufactured. Creamery. Redwood timber; fisheries. Dairy farms.

1799 The Kerf
College of the Redwoods
883 W. Washington Blvd.
Crescent City, CA 95531
Phone: (707)464-7457
Fax: (707)464-6867

Journal containing poetry focusing on the environment and humanity. **Founded:** May 1995. **Freq:** Annual. **Print Method:** Offset. **Trim Size:** 5 x 8 1/2. **Key Personnel:** Ken Letko, Editor. **Subscription Rates:** $5 single issue. **Remarks:** Advertising not accepted.
Circ: Non-paid 275

1800 The Triplicate
PO Box 277
Crescent City, CA 95531-0277
Phone: (707)464-2141
Fax: (707)464-5102

Community newspaper. **Founded:** 1879. **Freq:** 5/wk (Tues.-Sat.). **Print Method:** Offset. **Cols./Page:** 6. **Col. Width:** 12 3/5 picas. **Col. Depth:** 21 inches. **Key Personnel:** Geoffrey T. White, Publisher. **Subscription Rates:** $54 individuals; $69 out of area. **Remarks:** Accepts advertising. **Formerly**: Del Norte Triplicate.
Ad Rates: GLR: $.46 BW: $895.22 4C: $1,015.22 SAU: $6.47 **Circ:** Tues.-Fri. ★**4,972** Sat. ★**5,879**

1801 KPOD-AM - 1240
825 Mason Mall
PO Box 1915
Crescent City, CA 95531
Free: (800)232-5763
Phone: (707)464-3183
Fax: (707)464-6703

Format: Country. **Simulcasts:** KPOD-FM. **Networks:** ABC. **Owner:** Pati R. Stamps, at above address. **Founded:** 1958. **Operating Hours:** Continuous; 15% network, 85% local. **Key Personnel:** William E. Stamps, Sr., General Mgr.; Pati R. Stamps, Contact; Ken Olson, News Dir.; Bill Stamps, Music Dir.; Teresa Throop, Station Mgr.; Kim Osborne, Director. **Wattage:** 1000. **Ad Rates:** $7.00-7.50 for 30 seconds.

1802 KPOD-FM - 97.9
825 Mason Mall
PO Box 1915
Crescent City, CA 95531
Free: (800)232-5763
Phone: (707)464-3183
Fax: (707)465-6703

Format: Country. **Simulcasts:** KPOD-AM. **Networks:** ABC. **Founded:** 1989. **Operating Hours:** Continuous; 15% network, 85% local. **ADI:** Eureka, CA. **Key Personnel:** William E. Stamps, Sr., General Mgr.; Pati R. Stamps, Contact; Ken Olson, News Dir.; Bill Stamps, Music Dir.; Teresa Throop, Station Mgr.; Kim Osborne, Director. **Wattage:** 6000. **Ad Rates:** $7.00-7.50 for 30 seconds; $9.50-11.50 for 60 seconds.

CULVER CITY, pop. 38,139.

S. CA. Los Angeles Co. 7 mi. SE of Santa Monica. Motion picture studios. Aircraft, textiles, plastics, machine tools, electronics, draperies, auto batteries, rubber products, industrial alcohol, shoes manufactured. Truck farms.

1803 Culver City/Ladera Independent
Copley Los Angeles Newspapers, Inc.
7776 Ivanhoe Ave.
La Jolla, CA 92037

Newspaper. **Founded:** 1931. **Freq:** Weekly (Wed.). **Print Method:** Offset. **Cols./Page:** 6. **Col. Width:** 25 nonpareils. **Col. Depth:** 301 agate lines. **Key Personnel:** Bertram Winrow, Publisher. **Subscription Rates:** $24 individuals. **Remarks:** Accepts advertising.
Ad Rates: GLR: $.65 **Circ:** Free 30,100

1804 Culver City News
Coast Media Newspaper
4043 Irving Pl.
Culver City, CA 90232-2809
Phone: (310)839-5271
Fax: (310)839-9372

Community newspaper. **Founded:** 1923. **Freq:** Semiweekly (Thurs. and Sat.). **Print Method:** Offset. **Cols./Page:** 6. **Col. Width:** 18 nonpareils. **Col. Depth:** 301 agate lines. **Key Personnel:** Richard Bronner, Publisher; Bob Payson, Publisher. **Subscription Rates:** $36 individuals. **Remarks:** Accepts advertising.
Ad Rates: BW: $1,382.88 4C: $2,082.88 **Circ:** Free 14,926

1805 Culver City Star
Wave Community Newspapers, Inc.
2621 W. 54th St.
Los Angeles, CA 90043
Phone: (213)290-3000
Fax: (213)291-0219

Black community newspaper sold in combination with the Westchester. **Founded:** 1980. **Freq:** Biweekly Wednesday and Saturday. **Print Method:** Offset. **Cols./Page:** 6. **Col. Width:** 5 nonpareils. **Col. Depth:** 21 1/2 inches. **Key Personnel:** C.Z. Wilson, President, fax (213)292-8289. **Subscription Rates:** Free; $125 by mail. **Remarks:** Advertising accepted; rates available upon request. **Formerly**: Culver City/Westchester Wave (1992).
Circ: Non-paid 29,109

1806 Hawthorne Community News/Lawndale Tribune
Coast Media Newspaper
4043 Irving Pl.
Culver City, CA 90232-2809
Phone: (310)839-5271
Fax: (310)839-9372

Community newspaper. **Founded:** 1925. **Freq:** Semiweekly (Thurs. and Sat.). **Print Method:** Offset. **Cols./Page:** 6. **Col. Width:** 18 nonpareils. **Col. Depth:** 301 agate lines. **Key Personnel:** Richard Bronner, Publisher; Bob Payson, Publisher. **Subscription Rates:** $36 individuals. **Remarks:** Accepts advertising.
Ad Rates: BW: $1,382.88 4C: $2,082.88 **Circ:** Free 19,898

Inglewood News Lennox Citizen - See Inglewood

1807 KEY Magazine
Falcon Publications
8432 Steller Dr.
Culver City, CA 90232

Consumer magazine covering travel and tourist information for Los Angeles. **Subtitle:** This Week in Los Angeles and Southern California. **Founded:** 1920. **Freq:** Weekly. **Key Personnel:** George Falcon, Editor and Publisher. **Remarks:** Accepts advertising.
Ad Rates: BW: $892 **Circ:** Combined 19,500

1808 Library Mosaics
Yenor, Inc.
Box 5171
Culver City, CA 90231
Phone: (310)645-4998
Magazine for and about library/media support staff. **Subtitle:** The Magazine for Support Staff. **Founded:** 1989. **Freq:** Bimonthly. **Key Personnel:** Raymond G. Roney, Publisher, rroney@librarymosaics.com. **ISSN:** 1054-9676. **Subscription Rates:** $21 individuals; $46 other countries; $3.50 single issue; $32 Canada.
Ad Rates: BW: $135 **Circ:** 5,000

1809 Turning the Tide
People Against Racist Terror (PART)
PO Box 1055
Culver City, CA 90232
Phone: (310)288-5003
Publisher E-mail: part2001@usa.net

Magazine detailing antiracist, antisexist, and anti-imperialist beliefs and information. **Subtitle:** Journal of Anti-Racist Activism, Research & Education. **Founded:** 1987. **Freq:** Quarterly. **Print Method:** Web press. **Trim Size:** 8 x 10 3/4. **Cols./Page:** 2. **Col. Width:** 3 1/4 inches. **Col. Depth:** 9 inches. **Key Personnel:** Michael Novick, Editor. **ISSN:** 1082-6491. **Subscription Rates:** $15 individuals; $4 single issue; $25 institutions; $25 other countries. **Remarks:** Accepts display advertising. **URL:** http://www.igc.apc.org/prisons; gopher.igc.apc.org, 3, 14.
Circ: Paid ‡750 Non-paid ‡7,250

1810 KTWV-FM - 94.7
8944 Lindblade St.
Culver City, CA 90232
Phone: (310)840-7100
Fax: (310)815-1129
E-mail: wave@ktwv.groupw.wec.com

Format: Jazz. **Networks:** Independent. **Founded:** 1961. **Formerly**: KMET-FM (1987). **Operating Hours:** Continuous. **Key Personnel:** Tim Pohlman, General Mgr. **Local Programs:** *Points of Light*, Tina Arana, (213)769-0878; *World Music Hour*, Talaya Trigueros, (213)769-0821. **Wattage:** 58,000.

CUPERTINO, pop. 25,770.

W. CA. Santa Clara Co. 10 mi. W. of San Jose. Residential. Winery. Electronic products manufactured.

1811 Bottomfish
De Anza College
21250 Stevens Creek Blvd.
Cupertino, CA 95014
Phone: (408)864-5626
Fax: (408)864-8603

Literary journal. **Founded:** 1976. **Freq:** Annual. **Print Method:** Offset. **Key Personnel:** David Denny, Editor. **ISSN:** 1086-9042. **Subscription Rates:** $5 single issue. **Remarks:** Advertising not accepted. **URL:** http://laws.atc.fhda.edu/documents/bottomfish/bottomfish.htm.
Circ: (Not Reported)

1812 La Voz
De Anza College
21250 Stevens Creek Blvd.
Cupertino, CA 95014
Phone: (408)864-5626
Fax: (408)864-8603

Collegiate newspaper broadsheet. **Subtitle:** The Voice of De Anza. **Founded:** 1967. **Freq:** Weekly (Tues.). **Print Method:** Offset. **Trim Size:** 12 x 28. **Cols./Page:** 6. **Col. Width:** 24 nonpareils. **Col. Depth:** 224 agate lines. **Key Personnel:** Nelson Ching, Editor-in-Chief, phone (408)864-5626, fax (408)864-5533, lavoz_ editor@hotmail.com; Beth Grobman Burruss, Advisor, phone (408)864-8588, fax (408)864-5533, grobman@fhda.edu. **Subscription Rates:** $7 individuals. **Remarks:** Accepts advertising.
Ad Rates: BW: $600 PCI: $5 **Circ:** Free ‡3,000

1813 Natural Language Engineering
Cambridge University Press
Apple Research Laboratories, Apple Computer, Inc.
One Infinite Loop, MS: 301-3S
Cupertino, CA 95014
Phone: (408)974-1048
Fax: (408)974-8414
Publication E-mail: journals.marketing@cup.org

Journal focusing on computerized language processing. **Founded:** Mar. 1995. **Freq:** Quarterly. **Cols./Page:** 1. **Col. Width:** 5 inches. **Col. Depth:** 8.5 inches. **Key Personnel:** Branimir Boguraev, Editor, bkb@apple.com; Roberto Garigliano, Editor; John I. Tait, Editor. **ISSN:** 1351-3249. **Subscription Rates:** $118 institutions; $59 individuals; $31 single issue. **Remarks:** Accepts advertising.
Ad Rates: BW: $400 4C: $1450 **Circ:** Paid ‡245 Non-paid ‡59

1814 KKUP-FM - 91.5
PO Box 820
Cupertino, CA 95015
Phone: (408)260-2999

Format: Eclectic. **Networks:** Independent. **Founded:** 1972. **Operating Hours:** Continuous; 100% local. **Key Personnel:** Jim Maley, Program Dir.; Ron Butler, Music Dir. **Wattage:** 200. **Ad Rates:** Noncommercial. **URL:** http://www.deepideas.com/kkup.

CYPRESS

1815 MediaOne
5595 Corporate Dr.
Cypress, CA 90630
Phone: (714)816-0569
Fax: (714)821-0249
E-mail: lsmilkstein@mediaone.com

Founded: 1985. **Formerly**: Copley/Colony Cablevision (1995). **Key Personnel:** Laura Smilkstein, Program Dir.; Michael Marks, Head End Mgr., phone (714)816-0570. **Cities Served:** Cypress, LaPalma, Lakewood, CA: subscribing households 25,000; 83 channels; 5 community access channels; 12 hours per week community access programming.

DALY CITY, pop. 78,519.

W. CA. San Mateo Co. 5 mi. N. of San Francisco. Residential.

1816 Daly City Record
North County Publications
1080 S. Amphlett Blvd. Phone: (650)348-4321
PO Box 5400 Fax: (650)348-4446
San Mateo, CA 94402-1860
Newspaper. **Founded:** 1903. **Freq:** Semiweekly (Wed. and Sat.). **Print Method:** Offset. **Trim Size:** 13 x 21 1/2. **Cols./Page:** 6. **Col. Width:** 26 nonpareils. **Col. Depth:** 301 agate lines. **Key Personnel:** Will Thomas, Editor; John Hart Clinton, Jr., Publisher; Larry Boline, Advertising Mgr. **Subscription Rates:** Free. **Remarks:** Accepts advertising.
Ad Rates: BW: $1,606.05 **Circ:** Paid 1,070
4C: $1,906.05 Free 23,180
SAU: $12.45

1817 Pro Tooner
PO Box 2270 Phone: (650)755-4827
Daly City, CA 94017-2270 Fax: (650)994-4131
Publisher E-mail: protooner@earthlink.net

Magazine for the professional cartoonist and gagwriter. **Founded:** Mar. 1995. **Freq:** Monthly. **Print Method:** Offset. **Trim Size:** 8 1/2 x 11. **Cols./Page:** 2. **Col. Width:** 3 1/2 inches. **Col. Depth:** 9 inches. **Key Personnel:** Joyce Miller, Editor. **ISSN:** 1087-9013. **Subscription Rates:** $50 individuals; $55 other countries; $5 single issue. **Remarks:** Accepts advertising.
Ad Rates: BW: $20 **Circ:** Paid 625

DANA POINT, pop. 4,745.

S. CA. Orange Co. 40 mi. SE of Long Beach. Residential. Tourism. Boat harbor. Manufactures surf boards. Nurseries.

1818 Dana Point News
South Orange County News
PO Box 3629 Phone: (714)768-3631
Mission Viejo, CA 92690 Fax: (714)454-7354

Community newspaper. **Founded:** 1965. **Freq:** Weekly (Thurs.). **Print Method:** Offset. **Cols./Page:** 5. **Col. Width:** 12 1/16 inches. **Col. Depth:** 13 inches. **Key Personnel:** Sherrie Good, Editor; Mike Weaver, Publisher; Pat Norton, Advertising Mgr. **Subscription Rates:** $12 individuals. **Remarks:** Color advertising accepted; rates available upon request. **Formerly:** Dana Point/Laguna Niguel News (1989).
Ad Rates: PCI: $32.17 **Circ:** Paid 7,783
Controlled 3,605

1819 POWDER
PO Box 1028 Phone: (714)496-5922
Dana Point, CA 92629 Fax: (714)496-7849
Free: (800)289-8983
Publication E-mail: powdermag@aol.com

Magazine for ski enthusiasts (advanced and intermediate). **Subtitle:** The Skier's Magazine. **Founded:** 1971. **Freq:** 7/year. **Print Method:** Offset. **Trim Size:** 8 1/8 x 10 3/4. **Cols./Page:** 3. **Col. Width:** 27 nonpareils. **Col. Depth:** 140 agate lines. **Key Personnel:** Steve Casimiro, Managing Editor; Brent Diamond, Publisher; Ben Warrer, Advertising Dir. **ISSN:** 0145-4471. **Subscription Rates:** $12.95 individuals; $21.95 other countries; $3.99 single issue; $4.59 Canada. **Remarks:** Accepts advertising.
Ad Rates: BW: $7,935 **Circ:** ‡112,000
4C: $11,015

1820 SURFER Magazine
Surfer Publications, Inc.
Box 1028 Phone: (714)496-5922
Dana Point, CA 92629 Fax: (714)496-7849

Magazine about the sport of surfing. **Founded:** 1960. **Freq:** Monthly. **Print Method:** Offset. **Trim Size:** 8 1/8 x 10 1/2. **Cols./Page:** 3. **Col. Width:** 30 nonpareils. **Col. Depth:** 144 agate lines. **Key Personnel:** Steve Hawk, Editor; Doug Palladini, Publisher; Laurie Smith, Advertising Coordinator. **ISSN:** 0039-6036. **Subscription Rates:** $20.95 individuals; $29.95 other countries; $3.99 single issue. **Remarks:** Accepts advertising. **URL:** http://www.surfermag.com.
Ad Rates: BW: $7,353 **Circ:** Paid 170,430
4C: $10,935

1821 Coast Cable
33574 Seawind Ct.
Dana Point, CA 92629-1834

Owner: Coast Cable Partners, at above address. **Founded:** 1986. **Key Personnel:** Floyd (Bob) Loew, General Mgr. **Cities Served:** 42 channels; 1 community access channel.

DANVILLE, pop. 35,000.

W. CA. Contra Costa Co. 15 mi. E. of Oakland. Residential. Parks, rolling hills. Unique shops.

1822 San Ramon Valley Times
Contra Costa Newspapers, Inc.
524 Hartz Ave. Phone: (510)837-4267
PO Box 68 Fax: (510)837-4334
Danville, CA 94526
General newspaper. **Founded:** 1945. **Freq:** Daily (morn.). **Print Method:** Offset. **Cols./Page:** 8. **Col. Width:** 19 nonpareils. **Col. Depth:** 294 agate lines. **Key Personnel:** Paula Mabry, Editor; Dean S. Lesher, Publisher. **Remarks:** Accepts advertising. **Formerly:** Valley Pioneer (Sept. 1, 1988).
Ad Rates: GLR: $.26 **Circ:** ‡15,000

DAVIS, pop. 36,640.

C. CA. Yolo Co. 14 mi. W. of Sacramento. University of California at Davis. Manufactures almond hullers, farm equipment, Agriculture. Sugar beets, grain, tomatoes.

1823 American Journal of Clinical Nutrition
American Society for Clinical Nutrition
University of California Phone: (530)752-8363
3247 Meyer Hall Fax: (530)752-8371
One Shields Ave.
Davis, CA 95616-8790
Publication E-mail: ajcn@ucdavis.edu; journal@ascn.faseb.edu

Journal of basic and clinical studies relevant to human nutrition. **Subtitle:** Official Publication of The American Society for Clinical Nutrition, Inc. **Founded:** 1952. **Freq:** Monthly. **Print Method:** Offset. **Trim Size:** 8 1/8 x 11. **Cols./Page:** 2. **Col. Width:** 32 nonpareils. **Col. Depth:** 119 agate lines. **Key Personnel:** Charles H. Halsted, Editor-in-Chief. **ISSN:** 0002-9165. **Subscription Rates:** $60 members; $120 nonmembers; $190 institutions; $50 students. **Remarks:** Accepts advertising. **URL:** http://www.ajcn.org. **Alt. Formats:** Microform.
Ad Rates: BW: $1,270 **Circ:** ‡7,934
4C: $2,365

1824 The California Aggie
University of California, Davis
25 Lower Freeborn Hall Phone: (916)752-0208
Davis, CA 95616 Fax: (916)752-0355
Publication E-mail: aggie@ucdavis.edu

Collegiate newspaper. **Founded:** Sept. 29, 1915. **Freq:** Daily (morn.). **Print Method:** Offset. **Cols./Page:** 6. **Col. Width:** 2 1/16 inches. **Col. Depth:** 21 inches. **Key Personnel:** Matthias Gafni, Editor-in-Chief; Demian Warner, Business Mgr.; Paul Wellman, Advertising Mgr.; Katie Reece, Art Dir., Adv. **Subscription Rates:** Free; $35 individuals per year. **Remarks:** Accepts advertising. **URL:** http://www.ucdavis.edu.
Ad Rates: GLR: $1 **Circ:** Free ‡13,000
BW: $1,001.70
4C: $1,186.70
PCI: $7.95

1825 California Water Resources Center Contribution
Water Resources Center
Centers for Water & Wildland Resources
University of California
1 Shields Ave.
Davis, CA 95616

Formal publication of water resources research. **Founded:** 1977. **Freq:** Irregular. **Key Personnel:** Jeff Woled, Editor/Publications Mgr., jlwoled@ucdavis.edu. **Subscription Rates:** Free. **Remarks:** Advertising not accepted. **URL:** http://www-cwwr.ucdavis.edu.
Circ: Non-paid 450

1826 Clinical Reviews in Allergy & Immunology
Humana Press, Inc.
c/o M.E. Gershwin Phone: (916)752-2884
University of California, Davis Fax: (916)752-4669
Div. of Rheumatology/Allergy
Davis, CA 95616
Publisher E-mail: humana@humanapr.com

Professional journal for allergists and clinical immunologists. **Freq:** Quarterly. **Trim Size:** 7 x 10. **Key Personnel:** M. E. Gershwin, Editor. **ISSN:** 1080-0549. **Subscription Rates:** $100 individuals; $40 single issue. **Remarks:** Accepts advertising.
Circ: (Not Reported)

1827 Davis Enterprise
McNaughton Newspapers
PO Box 1470 Phone: (916)756-0800
Davis, CA 95617 Fax: (916)756-6707
Publication E-mail: editor@davis.com

General newspaper. **Founded:** 1897. **Freq:** Daily (eve.), Sunday (morn.). **Print Method:** Offset. **Cols./Page:** 6. **Col. Width:** 25 nonpareils. **Col. Depth:** 294 agate lines. **Key Personnel:** Debbie Davis, Editor; Burt McNaughton, Publisher; Erin Rose Handy, Retail Ad Mgr.; Kim Yarris, Nationals Ad Mgr.; David DeLeon, Advertising Mgr. **Subscription Rates:** $88.00 individuals; $.50 single issue. **Remarks:** Accepts advertising. **URL:** http://www.davisenterprise.com.
Ad Rates: BW: $1,625.40 **Circ:** Mon.-Fri. ★10,047
4C: $1,925.40 Sun. ★10,298
SAU: $12.60

1828 KDVS-FM - 90.3
University of California Phone: (916)752-0728
14 Lower Freeborn Hall Fax: (916)752-8548
Davis, CA 95616

Format: News; Eclectic. **Networks:** Independent. **Owner:** Regents of the University of California, at above address. **Founded:** 1964. **Formerly:** KCD-FM (1967). **Operating Hours:** Continuous; 100% local. **Key Personnel:** Paul Wilbur, General Mgr., phone (530)752-0728, fax (530)752-8548. **Wattage:** 5000. **Ad Rates:** Noncommercial; underwriting available. **URL:** http://www.kdvs.org.

1829 TCI Cablevision of Davis
1605 2nd St. Phone: (916)757-2220
Davis, CA 95616 Fax: (916)757-2853

Founded: 1984. **Formerly:** Davis Community Cable Co-Op (1988). **Key Personnel:** Dean Darlin, General Mgr.; Jay Baur, Technical Operations. **Cities Served:** subscribing households 7,274; 62 channels; 1 community access channel.

DEL MAR, pop. 5,017.

W. CA. San Diego Co. 20 mi. N. of San Diego. Residential.

1830 Del Mar Sun
West Coast Community Newspapers
2841 Loker Ave. E. Phone: (619)431-4850
Carlsbad, CA 92008 Fax: (619)431-4888

Community newspaper. **Founded:** 1960. **Freq:** Weekly (Thurs.). **Print Method:** Offset. **Trim Size:** 13 3/4 x 21 3/4. **Cols./Page:** 6. **Col. Width:** 12 picas. **Col. Depth:** 297 agate lines. **Key Personnel:** Dennis Lhota, Editor; Bill Lyke, Jr., Publisher. **Subscription Rates:** $15 individuals; $35 Out of County. **Remarks:** Accepts advertising. **Formerly:** Del Mar Surfcomber (1992).
Ad Rates: 4C: $1,215 **Circ:** Paid 1,741
PCI: $7.06 Free 204

DELANO, pop. 16,491.

S. CA. Kern Co. 32 mi. NW of Bakersfield. Vegetables, fruit shipped. Wineries; cotton gin; concrete pipe factory. Diversified farming. Grapes, potatoes, cotton.

1831 Delano Record
Reed Print, Inc. Community Newspapers
1231 Jefferson St. Phone: (805)725-0600
Delano, CA 93215 Fax: (805)725-4373

Community newspaper. **Founded:** 1908. **Freq:** Weekly (Thurs.). **Print Method:** Offset. **Cols./Page:** 6. **Col. Width:** 12 picas. **Col. Depth:** 21 inches. **Key Personnel:** Donald L. Reed, Publisher; Franklin W. Reed, Publisher. **USPS:** 151-760. **Subscription Rates:** $21 Kern and Tulare Counties; $24 out of Kern and Tulare Counties; $26 out of area. **Remarks:** Accepts advertising.
Ad Rates: BW: $661.50 **Circ:** ‡4,650
4C: $886
PCI: $5.80

1832 Market Shopper
Reed Print, Inc. Community Newspapers
1231 Jefferson St. Phone: (805)725-0600
Delano, CA 93215 Fax: (805)725-4373

Shopper. **Founded:** 1950. **Freq:** Weekly. **Print Method:** Offset. **Cols./Page:** 6. **Col. Width:** 12 picas. **Col. Depth:** 21 inches. **Key Personnel:** C. Bob Schettler, Editor; Donald L. Reed, Publisher, phone (805)834-0496; Franklin W. Reed, Publisher. **Subscription Rates:** Free.
Ad Rates: PCI: $2.65 **Circ:** Free ‡11,350

1833 KDNO-FM - 98.5
1305 Glenwood Phone: (805)725-2345
Delano, CA 93215 Fax: (805)725-2609

Format: Religious. **Networks:** Independent. **Founded:** Nov. 1, 1968. **Operating Hours:** Continuous; 80% network, 20% local. **Key Personnel:** Richard Palmquist, Contact. **Wattage:** 50,000. **Ad Rates:** $8 for 30 seconds; $16 for 60 seconds. **URL:** http://www.audionet.com.

DELHI

1834 The SDC Magazine
Studebaker Drivers Club, Inc.
13150 El Captain Way Phone: (209)634-7544
Delhi, CA 95315 Fax: (209)634-2163
Publication E-mail: fox@earthlink.net
Publisher E-mail: studepubs@aol.com

Magazine of the Studebaker Drivers Club. **Subtitle:** Turning Wheels. **Founded:** Sept. 1972. **Freq:** Monthly. **Print Method:** Offset. **Trim Size:** 11 x 8 1/2. **Cols./Page:** 4. **Col. Width:** 2.4 inches. **Col. Depth:** 7.3 inches. **Key Personnel:** Linda Fox, Editor, llfox@earthlink.net; Laurence Swanson, Publisher. **USPS:** 928-820. **Subscription Rates:** $27.50 individuals. **Remarks:** Accepts advertising.
Ad Rates: BW: $275 **Circ:** Paid ‡12,800
PCI: $17 Non-paid ‡50

DELTA

1835 Elk Grove-Laguna Neighbors
Neighbors Publishing
8690 Elk Grove Blvd., Ste. 6 Phone: (916)685-3000
Elk Grove, CA 95624 Fax: (916)685-1890
Publication E-mail: jhoward@sacbee.com

Community newspaper. **Founded:** 1989. **Freq:** Semiweekly (Thurs. and Sun.). **Key Personnel:** Julie Howard, Editor, jhoward@sacbee.com. **Subscription Rates:** $84 individuals. **Remarks:** Accepts advertising. **Formerly:** Elk Grove Neighbors.
Circ: Controlled 45,000

DENAIR, pop. 1,128.

C. CA. Stanislaus Co. 13 mi. SE of Modesto. Farming.

1836 Denair Dispatch
Mid-Valley Publications
6950 Gerard St. Phone: (209)358-5311
Winton, CA 95388 Fax: (209)358-7108

Community newspaper. **Founded:** 1925. **Freq:** Weekly. **Print Method:** Offset. **Trim Size:** 14 x 21. **Cols./Page:** 6. **Subscription Rates:** $19; $23 out of area.
Ad Rates: GLR: $7.95 **Circ:** ‡3,300
SAU: $10.95
PCI: $7.95

DESERT CENTER

SW CA. Riverside Co. 140 mi. W. of Santa Ana. Riverside Co. (SW). 140 m W of Santa Ana.

1837 American Pacific Co.
Box 246 Phone: (760)227-3245
Desert Center, CA 92239 Fax: (760)227-3245
E-mail: stevej8460@aol.com

Founded: 1964. **Key Personnel:** Stephen H. Jones, General Mgr., stevej8460@aol.com. **Cities Served:** Desert Center, CA: subscribing households 42; 18 channels; 1 community access channel.

DESERT HOT SPRINGS, pop. 5,941.

SE CA. Riverside Co. 10 mi. N. of Palm Springs. Health resort. Retirement Community.

1838 Desert Sentinel
Desert Sun Publishing
PO Box 338 Phone: (619)329-1411
Desert Hot Springs, CA 92240 Fax: (619)329-3860

Community newspaper. **Founded:** 1941. **Freq:** Weekly (Wed.). **Print Method:** Offset. **Trim Size:** 13 3/4 x 23 1/2. **Cols./Page:** 6. **Col. Width:** 18 nonpareils. **Col. Depth:** 294 agate lines. **Key Personnel:** John Waters, Jr., Editor; Linda Munsey, General Mgr. **USPS:** 154-980. **Subscription Rates:** $19.40 individuals; $28.55 out of area. **Remarks:** Accepts advertising.
Ad Rates: BW: $1486.80 **Circ:** ‡3,000
4C: $1846.80
PCI: $11.80

1839 Desert Hot Springs Cablevision
11855 Palm Dr. Phone: (760)329-6436
Desert Hot Springs, CA 92240 Fax: (760)329-0792

Owner: Daniels & Associates, at above address, (760)329-6310. **Founded:** 1967. **Key Personnel:** Joni Odum, President/General Manager; Tim Lapis, Operations Mgr.; Rhonda Stilen, Office Mgr. **Cities Served:** Desert Hot Springs, CA; Riverside County: subscribing households 10,000; 78 channels; 1 community access channel; 8 hours per week community access programming.

DIAMOND SPRINGS

1840 MediaOne
6517 F Commerce Way Phone: (916)622-7022
Diamond Springs, CA 95619 Fax: (916)622-2075

Owner: US West, Inc., 188 Inverness Dr. W, Englewood, CO 80112. **Founded:** 1972. **Formerly:** King Videocable Co. (1998). **Key Personnel:** Bill Erickson, Operations Mgr.; Pat Odenthal, Tech. Mgr., podenthal@mediaone.com; Tamzin L. Johnson, Marketing Specialist. **Cities Served:** subscribing households 18,604; 36 channels; 1 community access channel.

DINUBA, pop. 9,907.

NW CA. Tulare Co. 25 mi. SE of Fresno. Irrigated region.

1841 Dinuba Sentinel
Sentinel Printing and Publishing
145 South L Phone: (209)591-4632
PO Box 247 Fax: (209)591-1322
Dinuba, CA 93618
Community newspaper. **Founded:** 1909. **Freq:** Weekly (Thurs.). **Print Method:** Offset. **Trim Size:** 14 x 21 1/2. **Cols./Page:** 6. **Col. Width:** 2 1/16 inches. **Col. Depth:** 21 inches. **Key Personnel:** Bob Raison, Editor and Publisher, bobra@theworks.com. **ISSN:** 0745-6654. **Subscription Rates:** $16 individuals; $19 out of country; $20 out of state. **Remarks:** Accepts advertising.
Ad Rates: BW: $730.80 **Circ:** Paid 3,693
4C: $1,200 Free 9
SAU: $5.80

1842 The Sentinel-Advertiser
Sentinel Printing and Publishing
145 South L Phone: (209)591-4632
PO Box 247 Fax: (209)591-1322
Dinuba, CA 93618
Free shopper. **Freq:** Weekly (Wed.). **Cols./Page:** 6. **Col. Width:** 2 1/16 inches. **Col. Depth:** 21 inches. **Key Personnel:** Bob Raison, Editor and Publisher. **Subscription Rates:** Free. **Remarks:** Accepts advertising.
Ad Rates: BW: $730.80 **Circ:** Free 16,041
4C: $1,200
SAU: $4.20

1843 KJOI-FM - 98.9
597 N. Alta Ave. Phone: (209)591-1130
Dinuba, CA 93618-3202 Fax: (209)591-5250

Format: Adult Contemporary. **Networks:** Independent. **Founded:** 1975. **Formerly:** KOJY-FM. **Operating Hours:** Continuous. **Key Personnel:** Scott Moseley, General Mgr. **Wattage:** 19,000.

1844 KRDU-AM - 1130
597 N. Alta Ave. Phone: (209)591-1130
Dinuba, CA 93618 Fax: (209)591-5250

Format: Religious. **Networks:** Independent. **Owner:** Radio Dinuba Company, at above address. **Founded:** 1946. **Operating Hours:** Continuous. **ADI:** Fresno-Visalia (Hanford), CA. **Key Personnel:** Jim Tuck, Operations Dir.; Ken Adams, News and Public Affairs Director. **Wattage:** 5000. **Ad Rates:** $15 for 60 seconds.

DIXON, pop. 7,541.

NWC CA. Solano Co. 25 mi. SW of Sacramento. Meat packing, alfalfa dehydrators, wool processing plants; feed mill. Diversified farming. Sheep.

1845 The Dixon Tribune
Gibson Publications
145 E. A St. Phone: (707)678-5594
Dixon, CA 95620 Fax: (707)678-5404

General newspaper. **Founded:** 1874. **Freq:** 3/week. **Print Method:** Offset. **Cols./Page:** 6. **Col. Width:** 2 inches. **Col. Depth:** 21 inches. **Key Personnel:** David Payne, Publisher; Sarah Villec, Advertising Mgr.; Earl Parker, Editor. **USPS:** 158-880. **Subscription Rates:** $30 individuals. **Remarks:** Accepts advertising.
Ad Rates: GLR: $.32 **Circ:** Paid ‡4,400
BW: $768.60 Free ‡1,000
4C: $1,018.60
PCI: $6.10

DORRIS, pop. 836.

N. CA. Siskiyou Co. 22 mi. S. of Klamath Falls, OR. Lumber mills. Fir, cedar, pine timber. Agriculture. Potatoes, alfalfa. Grain.

1846 Butte Valley Star
111 W. 3rd St. Phone: (916)397-2601
PO Box 708
Dorris, CA 96023
Community newspaper. **Founded:** 1926. **Freq:** Weekly (Wed.). **Print Method:** Offset. **Cols./Page:** 6. **Col. Width:** 24 nonpareils. **Col. Depth:** 21 1/2 inches. **Key Personnel:** Beth Carleton, Publisher; Carol McKay, Publisher. **Subscription Rates:** $13.50 individuals. **Remarks:** Accepts advertising.
Ad Rates: GLR: $.16 **Circ:** ‡3,000
BW: $434.70
PCI: $3.95

DOWNEY, pop. 82,602.

S. CA. Los Angeles Co. 12 mi. SE of Los Angeles. Manufactures asbestos, textiles, aerospace products, farm machinery, cement pipe, soap, chemicals, carpeting, plastics, food, wire, rubber products, furniture, industrial castings and blowers, brass fittings, mobile homes. Nurseries.

1847 Downey Herald American
Wave Community Newspapers
819 W. Whitter Blvd. Phone: (213)727-1117
Montebello, CA 90640-3623 Fax: (213)727-9515

Newspaper. **Founded:** 1903. **Freq:** Semiweekly Thurs. and Sat. **Print Method:** Offset. Uses mats. **Cols./Page:** 6. **Col. Width:** 26 nonpareils. **Col. Depth:** 301 agate lines. **Key Personnel:** Arthur J. Aguilar, Exec. Editor/Publisher. **Subscription Rates:** $80 individuals.
Circ: Paid 291
Free 25,500

1848 ECA Magazine
Engineering Contractors Association
8310 Florence Ave. Phone: (310)861-0929
Downey, CA 90240 Fax: (310)923-6179

Magazine for the construction engineering field. **Founded:** 1965. **Freq:** Monthly. **Print Method:** Offset. **Trim Size:** 8 1/2 x 11. **Cols./Page:** 3 and 2. **Col. Width:** 28 and 40 nonpareils. **Col. Depth:** 140 agate lines. **Key Personnel:** John Simpson, Editor. **USPS:** 089-631. **Subscription Rates:** Free; $10 by mail; $1 single issue. **Remarks:** Accepts advertising.
Ad Rates: BW: $291 **Circ:** Non-paid ‡1,800
4C: $566

1849 The Sabbath Watchman
Seventh-Day Adventist Church Reform Movement
10238 Bellman Ave.
Downey, CA 90241

Magazine for the SDA Church Reform Movement, American Union and the International Missionary Society covering religious doctrines. **Founded:** 1926. **Freq:** 6/year. **Print Method:** Offset. **Trim Size:** 8 3/8 x 11. **Cols./Page:** 3. **Col. Width:** 14 picas. **Col. Depth:** 58.5 picas. **Key Personnel:** Branko Cholich, Managing Editor; Evelyn Holmstroem, Senior Editor, phone (510)886-0940. **ISSN:** 0098-9517. **Subscription Rates:** $12 U.S.; $15 other countries. **Remarks:** Advertising not accepted.
Circ: ‡750

DOWNIEVILLE†, pop. 500.

NE CA. Sierra Co. 80 mi. NE of Sacramento. Gold mining. Saw mill. Agriculture.

1850 The Mountain Messenger
Mountain Messenger
Drawer A Phone: (916)289-3262
Downieville, CA 95936-0395 Fax: (916)289-3262

Community newspaper. **Subtitle:** California's Oldest Weekly Newspaper. **Founded:** 1853. **Freq:** Weekly. **Print Method:** Offset. **Cols./Page:** 6. **Col. Width:** 11.5 picas. **Col. Depth:** 293 agate lines. **Key Personnel:** Donald S. Russell, Editor and Publisher. **USPS:** 366-440. **Subscription Rates:** $17 individuals; $21 Out of county. **Formerly:** Independent Messenger (1989).
Ad Rates: GLR: $5 **Circ:** Paid ‡3,000
BW: $600
4C: $1,000
PCI: $5

1851 Downieville TV
PO Box 393 Phone: (530)289-3619
Downieville, CA 95936

Owner: Downieville Television Corporation, at above address. **Founded:** May 1954. **Key Personnel:** Thomas Vilas, Chairman, phone (530)289-3582; Rae Kalustian, Sec./Treas. **Cities Served:** Downieville, CA: subscribing households 200; 12 channels; 1 community access channel; 168 hours per week community access programming.

EAST LOS ANGELES

1852 East Los Angeles Commerce Tribune
Wave Community Newspapers
819 W. Whitter Blvd. Phone: (213)727-1117
Montebello, CA 90640-3623 Fax: (213)727-9515

Newspaper. **Founded:** 1930. **Freq:** Semiweekly (Wed. and Sat.). **Print Method:** Offset. **Cols./Page:** 6. **Col. Width:** 26 nonpareils. **Col. Depth:** 301 agate lines. **Key Personnel:** Arthur J. Aguilar, Exec. Editor/Publisher, phone (213)290-3000, fax (213)292-8289. **Subscription Rates:** $80 individuals. **Remarks:** Advertising accepted; rates available upon request. **Formerly:** East Los Angeles Commerce.
Circ: Paid 1,325
Free 17,349

EDWARDS

1853 Desert Wings
Aerotech
AFFTC/PAI Phone: (805)277-2345
Edwards, CA 93524-1225
Publication E-mail: wings@sc.edw
Publisher E-mail: aerotech@netport.com

Military and family interest newspaper distributed to Air Force families, government employees and contractor personnel. **Founded:** 1948. **Freq:** Weekly (Fri.). **Print Method:** Offset. **Trim Size:** 11 1/2 x 13 3/4. **Cols./Page:** 5. **Col. Width:** 1 7/8 inches. **Col. Depth:** 13 inches. **Key Personnel:** Paul Kinison, Publisher. **Subscription Rates:** Free.
Ad Rates: PCI: $11.55 **Circ:** Non-paid 9,650

EL CAJON, pop. 73,892.

S. CA. San Diego Co. 15 mi. NE of San Diego. Light industry. Citrus truck, poultry farms. Recreation.

1854 Christian Times
KompuKeen Publishing Inc.
PO Box 2606 Phone: (619)660-5500
El Cajon, CA 92021 Fax: (619)660-5505
Publication E-mail: chtimes@cts.com

Publication featuring local, state, and national news fron a christian perspective. **Founded:** 1983. **Freq:** Monthly. **Print Method:** Web. **Trim Size:** 11 x 17 Tabloid. **Cols./Page:** 5. **Col. Width:** 1 7/8 inches. **Col. Depth:** 16 inches. **Key Personnel:** Theresa L. Keener, Editor; Lamar H. Keener, Publisher. **Subscription Rates:** $19.95. **Remarks:** Accepts advertising. **Formerly:** Southern California Christian Times.
Ad Rates: GLR: $114 **Circ:** Combined 130,000
BW: $4,701
4C: $6,501

1855 The Daily Californian
1000 Pioneer Way Phone: (619)442-4404
PO Box 1565 Fax: (619)447-5419
El Cajon, CA 92022
General newspaper. **Founded:** 1892. **Freq:** Daily except Monday and Saturday. **Print Method:** Offset. **Trim Size:** 13 x 21 1/2. **Cols./Page:** 6. **Key Personnel:** Della Elliott, Editor; Tom Schmitt, Publisher; Larry Nash, Advertising Dir. **Subscription Rates:** $78 individuals. **Remarks:** Accepts advertising.
Ad Rates: BW: $2,011.82 **Circ:** Paid ❑**8,645**
4C: $2,476.53
PCI: $13.75

1856 Get Up & Go! Magazine
Age Wave Communications
500 Felsen St., Ste. 101
El Cajon, CA 92020
Publication E-mail: npti@retirehouse.com

Niche publication (50-plus). **Founded:** 1982. **Freq:** Monthly. **Print Method:** Web offset. **Trim Size:** 10 x 13. **Cols./Page:** 4. **Col. Width:** 13 picas. **Col. Depth:** 12 inches. **Key Personnel:** Laura Impastato, Editor, phone (619)593-2910, fax (619)442-4043; Terri Teahune, Publisher. **Subscription Rates:** $28 individuals. **Remarks:** Accepts advertising. **Former name:** Northwest Prime Time Journal; Senior World Newsmagazine; Senior Highlights. **Feature Editors:** Alice McCracken, *Science, Sports*, phone (619)593-2910; Holly Tani, *Entertainment*, phone (619)593-2916; Genie Thompson, *Financial/Business*, phone (619)593-2912.
Ad Rates: BW: $2,434 **Circ:** Combined 165,000
4C: $3,109

Senior World Newsmagazine - See San Diego

1857 The Summit
Grossmont College
8800 Grossmont College Dr. Phone: (619)644-7271
El Cajon, CA 92020 Fax: (619)644-7914

Collegiate newspaper. **Founded:** 1963. **Freq:** Weekly (Thurs.). **Print Method:** Offset. **Cols./Page:** 5. **Col. Width:** 1 7/8 inches. **Col. Depth:** 14 inches. **Key Personnel:** Michael Grant, Advisor. **Remarks:** Accepts advertising. **Formerly:** The G.
Ad Rates: GLR: $5 **Circ:** Free ‡3,600
BW: $320
PCI: $5

1858 Unarius Light
Unarius Educational Foundation
145 S. Magnolia Ave. Phone: (619)444-7062
El Cajon, CA 92020-4522 Fax: (619)444-9637
Free: (800)475-7062
Publisher E-mail: uriel@unarius.org

Journal covering philosophy and spirituality. **Subtitle:** A Journal of Logic & Reason. **Freq:** Quarterly. **Key Personnel:** Celeste Appel, Editor; Dr. Charles L. Spiegel, Editor-in-Chief. **ISSN:** 1069-9465. **Subscription Rates:** $30 individuals. **Remarks:** Advertising not accepted.
Circ: Combined 1,500

EL CENTRO†, pop. 23,996.

S. CA. Imperial Co. 120 mi. E. of San Diego. Mines. Agriculture.

1859 Imperial Valley Press
Associated Desert Newspapers, Inc.
POB 2770 Phone: (619)337-3425
El Centro, CA 92244 Fax: (619)353-3003

General newspaper. **Founded:** 1901. **Freq:** Daily (eve.), Sunday (morn.). **Print Method:** Offset. **Trim Size:** 13 3/4 x 27 1/2. **Cols./Page:** 6. **Col. Width:** 21.5 nonpareils. **Col. Depth:** 301 agate lines. **Key Personnel:** E. Mayor Maloney, Jr., Editor and Publisher; William A. Gay, General Mgr. **USPS:** 260-060. **Subscription Rates:** $151 by mail. **Remarks:** Accepts advertising.
Ad Rates: GLR: $14.50 **Circ:** Mon.-Fri. ★**15,169**
BW: $1,962.09 Sun. ★**15,905**
4C: $2,272.09
SAU: $14.49
PCI: $15.21

1860 Valley Shopper-The El Centro Advertiser
Associated Desert Shoppers, Inc.
73-400 Hwy. 111 Phone: (760)346-1729
Palm Desert, CA 92260 Fax: (760)346-7350
Free: (800)678-4237

Shopper. **Subtitle:** Valley Shopper/White Sheet. **Founded:** Dec. 12, 1979. **Freq:** Weekly (Wed.). **Print Method:** Web. **Trim Size:** 11 x 12 1/2. **Cols./Page:** 6. **Col. Width:** 9 1/2 picas. **Col. Depth:** 11 1/2 inches. **Key Personnel:** Hal J. Paradis, Publisher, phone (760)346-1729, fax (760)346-7350; Rey Verdugo, Sales Mgr., phone (760)353-8400, fax (760)352-0936. **Subscription Rates:** Free. **Remarks:** Accepts advertising.
Ad Rates: BW: $365 **Circ:** Paid ‡19,525
4C: $650
PCI: $4.50

1861 KAMP-AM - 1430
Box 1018 Phone: (760)352-2277
El Centro, CA 92244 Fax: (760)352-1430

Founded: 1958. **Operating Hours:** 24 hrs. **ADI:** El Centro, CA-Yuma, AZ. **Key Personnel:** Cal Mandel, General Mgr. **Wattage:** 1000.

1862 KECY-TV - 9
646 Main St. Phone: (619)353-9990
El Centro, CA 92243 Fax: (619)352-5471

Format: Commercial TV. **Networks:** CBS. **Owner:** Pacific Media Corp., at above address. **Founded:** 1968. **Operating Hours:** Continuous; 80% network, 20% local. **ADI:** El Centro, CA-Yuma, AZ. **Key Personnel:** Pete Sieler, General Mgr.; Gloria Flores, Contact; Mickey Dale, News Dir.

1863 KGBA-FM - 100.1
605 State St. Phone: (760)352-9860
El Centro, CA 92243 Fax: (760)352-1883
E-mail: kgba100@juno.com

Format: Adult Contemporary; Religious. **Networks:** Ambassador Inspirational Radio; Family Stations Radio; Sun Radio; CRN International. **Owner:** The Voice, Inc., 605 State Street, El Centro, CA 92243. **Founded:** 1983. **Operating Hours:** 5:30 am-6 pm (English) 6 pm-5:30 am (Spanish); 30% local. **ADI:** El Centro, CA-Yuma, AZ. **Key Personnel:** Bob Seager, Station Mgr., kgba100@hotmail.com; Denine Key, Program Dir.; Mike Leonard, Financial Development Mgr. **Wattage:** 3000. **Ad Rates:** $7.50-15 for 30 seconds.

KMXX-FM - See Brawley

1864 KXO-AM - 1230
420 Main St. Phone: (619)352-1230
El Centro, CA 92243

Format: Oldies; News; Sports; Agricultural. **Networks:** CBS. **Owner:** Gene P. Brister, at above address. **Founded:** 1927. **Operating Hours:** Continuous. **ADI:** El Centro, CA-Yuma, AZ. **Key Personnel:** Gene P. Brister, Pres./Gen. Mgr.; Carroll Buckley, Vice Pres./Sales Mgr./News Dir. **Wattage:** 1000. **Ad Rates:** $15-18 for 30 seconds; $17-20 for 60 seconds. KXO-FM.

1865 KXO-FM - 107.5
420 Main St. Phone: (619)352-1230
El Centro, CA 92243

Format: Adult Contemporary. **Owner:** Gene Brister/Carroll Buckley, at above address. **Founded:** 1976. **Operating Hours:** Continuous. **ADI:** El Centro, CA-Yuma, AZ. **Key Personnel:** Gene Brister, Contact; Carroll Buckley, Contact. **Wattage:** 25,500. **Ad Rates:** $15-18 for 30 seconds; $17-20 for 60 seconds. $14.00-$17.00 for 30 seconds; $16.00-$20.00 for 60 seconds. Combined advertising rates available with KXO-AM.

1866 KXO-FM - 107.5
420 Main St. Phone: (760)352-1230
El Centro, CA 92243

Format: Adult Contemporary. **Networks:** CBS. **Owner:** KXO, Inc., at above address. **Founded:** July 1, 1975. **Operating Hours:** Continuous. **Key Personnel:** Gene P. Brister, Pres./General Mgr.; J. Carroll Buckley, VP/Production Dir. **Wattage:** 25,500. **Ad Rates:** $19-24 for 30 seconds; $21-26 for 60 seconds.

EL CERRITO

1867 Grand Times
Grand Times Publishing
403 Village Dr.
El Cerrito, CA 94530-3355
Publisher E-mail: mags@grandtimes.com

Consumer Internet magazine for senior citizens. **Founded:** 1995. **Freq:** Weekly. **Remarks:** Accepts advertising. **URL:** http://www.grandtimes.com.
Circ: (Not Reported)

EL DORADO

1868 El Dorado Gazette/Georgetown Gazette and Town Crier
2775 Miners Flat Phone: (530)333-4481
PO Box 49 Fax: (530)333-0152
Georgetown, CA 95634-0156
Community newspaper. **Founded:** Apr. 9, 1880. **Freq:** Weekly (Thurs.). **Print Method:** Offset. **Trim Size:** 11 1/2 x 12 5/8. **Cols./Page:** 6. **Col. Width:** 9 picas. **Col. Depth:** 78 picas. **Key Personnel:** Mark Lantz, Editor and Publisher. **USPS:** 005-478. **Subscription Rates:** $15 individuals; $25 out of area. **Remarks:** Accepts advertising.
Ad Rates: BW: $420.00 **Circ:** ‡1,500
SAU: $8
PCI: $5.50

EL DORADO HILLS

1869 Reference and User Services Quarterly
American Library Association (ALA)
5000 Windplay Dr., Ste. 4 Phone: (916)939-9620
El Dorado Hills, CA 95762 Fax: (916)939-9626
Publication E-mail: rusa@ala.org

Magazine focusing on library reference and adult services. **Founded:** 1960. **Freq:** Quarterly. **Print Method:** Offset. **Trim Size:** 8 3/8 x 10 7/8. **Cols./Page:** 2. **Key Personnel:** Gail Schlachter, Editor. **ISSN:** 0033-7072. **Subscription Rates:** $30 members of RUSA; $50 nonmembers; $60 other countries; $15 single issue. **Remarks:** Color advertising not accepted. **Alt. Formats:** Microfilm. **Formerly:** RQ.
Ad Rates: BW: $630 **Circ:** ‡7,645

EL GRANADA

1870 Coastside Cable TV Inc.
525 Obispo Rd. Phone: (650)726-9049
PO Box 190 Fax: (650)726-9091
El Granada, CA 94018
E-mail: cable@half-moon.net

Key Personnel: Anthony J. Iacopi, General Mgr. **Cities Served:** El Granada, Half Moon Bay, La Honda, Loma Mar, Montara, Moss Beach, Pescadero, CA: subscribing households 7,526; 52 channels; 1 community access channel. **URL:** http://www.half-moon.net.

EL SEGUNDO, pop. 13,752.

S. CA. Los Angeles Co. 13 mi. NW of Los Angeles. Residential.

1871 Astro News
Aerotech
SMC/PAI Phone: (310)363-1221
2430 E. El Segundo Blvd., Ste. 4049
El Segundo, CA 90245-4687
Publication E-mail: astronews2@losangeles.af.mil
Publisher E-mail: aerotech@netport.com

Military and family interest newspaper. **Freq:** Biweekly. **Print Method:** Offset. **Trim Size:** 11 1/2 x 17. **Cols./Page:** 5. **Col. Width:** 2 3/8 inches. **Col. Depth:** 16 inches. **Key Personnel:** Paul Kinison, Publisher. **Subscription Rates:** Free to qualified subscribers. **Remarks:** Accepts advertising.
Circ: Non-paid 5,500

1872 El Segundo Herald
El Segundo Herald, Inc.
PO Box 188 Phone: (213)322-1830
El Segundo, CA 90245-0188 Fax: (310)322-2787

Community newspaper. **Founded:** 1911. **Freq:** Weekly (Thurs.). **Print Method:** Offset. **Cols./Page:** 4. **Col. Width:** 29 nonpareils. **Col. Depth:** 224 agate lines. **Key Personnel:** Linda Collins, Editor; Ben Pitcher, Publisher; Lloyd Lind, Advertising Mgr.; Sally Randall, Advertising Mgr. **Subscription Rates:** Free; $25 individuals. **Remarks:** Accepts advertising.
Ad Rates: BW: $640 **Circ:** Paid ‡266
SAU: $12 Free ‡15,000

EL SOBRANTE

1873 American Window Cleaner Magazine
27 Oak Creek Rd. Phone: (510)222-7080
El Sobrante, CA 94803 Fax: (510)223-7080
Publication E-mail: awcmag@aol.com

Designed to make professional window cleaners work faster, safer and more profitably. **Subtitle:** Voice of the Professional Window Cleaner. **Founded:** 1986. **Freq:** Bimonthly. **Print Method:** Web offset & Sheetfed. **Trim Size:** 8 3/8 x 10 3/4. **Cols./Page:** 3. **Col. Width:** 2 1/4 inches. **Col. Depth:** 9 1/2 inches. **Key Personnel:** Richard Fabry, Publisher. **ISSN:** 1047-9090. **Subscription Rates:** $35; $40 Canada; $60 other countries. $6 single issue. **Remarks:** Accepts advertising. **Available Online. URL:** http://www.awcmag.com.
Ad Rates: BW: $980 **Circ:** Paid 1,100
4C: $1,290 Controlled 7,900

1874 Portuguese Journal
5404 Valley View Rd. Phone: (510)237-0888
El Sobrante, CA 94803-3447 Fax: (510)237-3790
Free: (800)309-0233
Publication E-mail: portjornal@aol.com

Statewide newspaper (Portuguese and English). **Founded:** 1888. **Freq:** Weekly (Thurs.). **Print Method:** Offset. **Cols./Page:** 5. **Col. Width:** 24 nonpareils. **Col. Depth:** 224 agate lines. **Key Personnel:** Albert C. Pacciorini, Publisher; Maria Leal, Editor. **ISSN:** 8756-2200. **Subscription Rates:** $35 individuals; $50 out of state/Canada; $80 out of country. **Remarks:** Accepts advertising. **Foreign language name:** Jornal Portugues.
Ad Rates: BW: $800 **Circ:** ‡9,000
PCI: $10

EL TORO, pop. 8,654.

S. CA. Orange Co. 15 mi. N. of Santa Ana. Residential.

1875 Public Enema
Publik Enema
25686 Nugget
El Toro, CA 92630

AntiConsumer magazine covering alternative views and social issues. **Subtitle:** Fine Literature for Your. **Founded:** 1992. **Freq:** Irregular. **Trim Size:** 7 x 8 1/2. **Cols./Page:** 1. **Col. Width:** 7 inches. **Subscription Rates:** $1 single issue. **Remarks:** Advertising not accepted.
Circ: Non-paid 250

ELK GROVE, pop. 11,300.

NC CA. Sacramento Co. 6 mi. SE of Sacramento. Wineries. Light industry. Chemicals. Feed mill. Fruit, dairy, grain farms. Grapes, hops, Ladino clover.

1876 Delphi Informant
Informant Communications Group
10519 E. Stockton Blvd., Ste. 100 Phone: (916)686-6610
Fax: (916)686-8497
Elk Grove, CA 95624-9703
Publication E-mail: circulation@informant.com

Technical magazine covering development in Borland Delphi. **Subtitle:** The Complete Monthly Guide to Delphi. **Founded:** Apr. 1995. **Freq:** Monthly. **Print Method:** Web offset. **Trim Size:** 8 x 10 3/4. **Cols./Page:** 2. **Col. Width:** 3 3/8 inches. **ISSN:** 1080-0662. **Subscription Rates:** $49.95. **Remarks:** Accepts advertising. **URL:** http://www.informant.com. **Alt. Formats:** CD-ROM.
Ad Rates: BW: $1320 **Circ:** Paid ‡22,500
4C: $1620 Non-paid ‡500

Elk Grove-Laguna Neighbors - See Delta

1877 The Fish Sniffer
Northern California Angler Publications
PO Box 994 Phone: (916)685-2245
Elk Grove, CA 95759-0994 Fax: (916)685-1498
Free: (800)748-6599
Publication E-mail: sniffer@softcom.net

Tabloid covering recreational fishing in northern California and Nevada. **Founded:** Apr. 16, 1982. **Freq:** Biweekly (Fri.). **Print Method:** Web offset. **Trim Size:** 10 x 14 1/2. **Cols./Page:** 4. **Col. Width:** 14 picas. **Key Personnel:** Harold A. Bonslett, Editor and Publisher; Paul J. Kneeland, Advertising Mgr. **ISSN:** 0747-3397. **Subscription Rates:** $40 individuals; $2.25 single issue. **Remarks:** Accepts advertising.
Ad Rates: BW: $1,448 **Circ:** Paid ‡20,500
4C: $2,172 Controlled ‡1,150
PCI: $19.55

1878 Oracle Informant
Informant Communications Group
10519 E. Stockton Blvd., Ste. 100 Phone: (916)686-6610
Fax: (916)686-8497
Elk Grove, CA 95624-9703
Publication E-mail: mkoulouris@informant.com

Technical magazine covering database programming and client/server development with Oracle tools. **Subtitle:** The Independent Monthly Guide to Oracle Development. **Founded:** Jan. 1996. **Freq:** Monthly. **Print Method:** Web offset. **Trim Size:** 8 x 10 3/4. **Cols./Page:** 2. **Col. Width:** 3 3/8 inches. **ISSN:** 1080-0654. **Subscription Rates:** $49.95 individuals. **Remarks:** Accepts advertising. **URL:** http://www.informant.com. **Alt. Formats:** CD-ROM.
Ad Rates: BW: $1,150 **Circ:** Paid 10,000
4C: $1,545 Non-paid 5,000

EMERYVILLE, pop. 3,763.

W. CA. Alameda Co. 4 mi. N. of Oakland. Residential.

1879 Electronic Musician
Intertec Publishing
6400 Hollis St., Ste. 12 Phone: (510)653-3307
Emeryville, CA 94608 Fax: (510)653-5142

Magazine on music and home or personal recording industry technology. **Founded:** 1985. **Freq:** Monthly. **Print Method:** Offset. **Trim Size:** 8 x 10 1/8. **Cols./Page:** 3. **Col. Width:** 27 nonpareils. **Col. Depth:** 140 agate lines. **Key Personnel:** John Pledger, Publisher; Steve Oppenheimer, Editor; Christen Pocock, Promotions Dir. **Subscription Rates:** $27.95 individuals. **Remarks:** Accepts advertising. **URL:** http://www.emusician.com.
Circ: Paid 45,908
Non-paid 16,142

1880 Mix
Intertec Publishing
6400 Hollis St., Ste. 12 Phone: (510)653-3307
Emeryville, CA 94608 Fax: (510)653-5142

Magazine focusing on audio and video music production in the recording industry. **Subtitle:** Professional Recording, Sound and Music Production. **Founded:** 1977. **Freq:** Monthly. **Print Method:** Offset. **Trim Size:** 8 x 10 1/8. **Cols./Page:** 3. **Col. Width:** 27 nonpareils. **Col. Depth:** 140 agate lines. **Key Personnel:** George Peterson, Editor; Jeffrey Turner, Publisher. **Subscription Rates:** $37.95 individuals. **Remarks:** Accepts advertising. **URL:** http//www.mixonline.com.
Ad Rates: BW: $4,045 **Circ:** Paid 16,931
4C: $5,595 Controlled 53,671

1881 The Monthly
Klaber Publishing Corp.
1301 59th St. Phone: (510)658-9811
Emeryville, CA 94608 Fax: (510)658-9902
Publication E-mail: themonthly@aol.com

General interest magazine emphasizing food, health, science, the environment, entertainment, personal essays, interviews, investigative features, and local h istory. **Founded:** Oct. 1970. **Freq:** Monthly. **Print Method:** Offset. **Trim Size:** 10 7/8 x 14 5/8. **Cols./Page:** 5. **Col. Width:** 11 picas. **Col. Depth:** 13 3/4 picas. **Key Personnel:** Tim Devaney, Editor; Karen Klaber, Publisher. **Subscription Rates:** $10 individuals; $1.50 single issue. **Remarks:** Accepts advertising. **Formerly:** The Berkeley Monthly.
Ad Rates: GLR: $6 **Circ:** Controlled ‡77,000
BW: $2,660 Paid ‡500
4C: $3,410
PCI: $58

1882 Sybase Magazine
Sybase Inc.
6475 Christie Ave. Phone: (510)596-3500
Emeryville, CA 94608-1050 Fax: (510)658-9441
Free: (800)879-2273

Magazine on client/server technology. **Founded:** 1994. **Freq:** Quarterly. **Key Personnel:** Stewart Schuster, Editor.
Circ: Controlled 52,000

ENCINO

S. CA. Los Angeles Co. 20 mi. NW of Los Angeles. Nursery. Residential.

1883 Journal of Acoustic Emission
Acoustic Emission Group
16350 Ventura Blvd., No. 106 Fax: (818)990-1686
Encino, CA 91436
International technical publication on technology and science of acoustic emission. **Founded:** Jan. 1982. **Freq:** Quarterly. **Trim Size:** 8-1/2 x 11. **Cols./Page:** 2. **Key Personnel:** K. Ono, Contact, ono@ucla.edu. **ISSN:** 0730-0050. **Subscription Rates:** $96 individuals; $25 single issue. **Remarks:** Advertising not accepted.
Circ: Paid 200

ENGLEWOOD

1884 TCI of California
5619 DTC Peskwey Phone: (408)918-3200
Englewood, CA 80111-3000 Fax: (408)292-7280
E-mail: bucek.stefan@tci.com

Owner: Tele-Communications, Inc., at above address, (303)267-5500. **Founded:** 1968. **Formerly:** Gill Cable (1968); Heritage Communications, Inc. **Key Personnel:** Dave Walton, General Mgr., walton.dave@tci.com; Curt Christenson, Technical Mgr., christenson.curt@tcl.com. **Cities Served:** Campbell, San Jose, Santa Clara West County, CA: subscribing households 196,000; 107 channels; 1 community access channel; 35 hours per week community access programming.

ESCALON, pop. 3,127.

C. CA. San Joaquin Co. 21 mi. SE of Stockton. Wineries. Alfalfa dehydrating plant, walnut huller, metal, factories. Fruit shipped, Agriculture. Grapes, peaches, fruit. Dairy.

1885 Escalon Times
Live Oak Publishing
1537 2nd St. Phone: (209)838-7043
PO Box 98
Escalon, CA 95320
Newspaper. **Founded:** 1925. **Freq:** Weekly (Wed.). **Print Method:** Offset. **Col. Width:** 2 1/16 inches. **Col. Depth:** 294 agate lines. **Key Personnel:** Stanley L. Cook, Publisher; Marge Jackson, Editor. **Subscription Rates:** $25 individuals. **Remarks:** Accepts advertising.
Ad Rates: BW: $1,260 **Circ:** 4,700
PCI: $10

ESCONDIDO, pop. 62,480.

S. CA. San Diego Co. 30 mi. N. of San Diego. Manufactures clothing, aircraft tools, chemicals, electronic components. Wineries, fruit, meat, egg packing plants. Diversified farming. Avocados, citrus fruit, poultry.

1886 Escondido News-Reporter
Metropolitan News Co.
210 S. Spring St. Phone: (213)628-4384
Los Angeles, CA 90012 Fax: (213)687-3886

Community newspaper. **Founded:** 1986. **Freq:** 3/week. **Print Method:** Offset. **Cols./Page:** 4. **Col. Width:** 15 picas. **Col. Depth:** 15 1/2 inches. **Key Personnel:** Roger Grace, Editor. **Remarks:** Accepts advertising.
Ad Rates: PCI: $6 **Circ:** Paid 200
Non-paid 1,000

1887 Hands on Guide
Christel Luther
1835 S. Centre City Pkwy., Ste. A434 Phone: (760)747-8206
Fax: (760)747-8206
Escondido, CA 92025-6544
Publication E-mail: hog92025@aol.com

Newspaper covering arts and craft shows, festivals, fairs, boutiques, farmers markets, and more in California and eleven other western states. **Founded:** Apr. 1988. **Freq:** 10 times a year. **Trim Size:** 11 x 17. **Cols./Page:** 4. **Col. Width:** 2 1/2 inches. **Col. Depth:** 16 inches. **ISSN:** 0897-5345. **Subscription Rates:** $30 individuals; $6 single issue.
Ad Rates: PCI: $3 **Circ:** Paid 1,300
Non-paid 700

1888 Hidden Valley Journal
Escondido Genealogical Society
1750 W. Citracado Pkwy., Spc. 47 Fax: (760)741-4030
Escondido, CA 92029-4127
Magazine covering local and family history and genealogy. **Founded:** 1978. **Freq:** Annual. **Trim Size:** 8 1/2 x 11. **Cols./Page:** 2. **Key Personnel:** Sandy Sneider, Editor. **ISSN:** 0741-4773. **Subscription Rates:** $10 single issue. **Remarks:** Accepts advertising.
Circ: (Not Reported)

1889 Inn Room Visitors Magazine
PO Box 3395
Escondido, CA 92033

Visitor magazine covering restaurants, shopping, entertainment, and television listing placed in hotel-motel rooms for travelers. **Founded:** 1977. **Freq:** Monthly. **Print Method:** Offset. **Trim Size:** 8 x 10 7/8. **Cols./Page:** 3. **Col. Width:** 32 nonpareils. **Col. Depth:** 140 agate lines. **Key Personnel:** Donna J. Abate, Editor; Arnold Jerry Barash, Jr., Publisher; Suzanne Wilkinson, Advertising Dir. **Remarks:** Accepts advertising.
Ad Rates: BW: $4,915 **Circ:** Paid 60,000
4C: $6,250 Controlled 24,000

1890 North County Times
207 E. Pennsylvania Ave. Phone: (619)745-6611
Escondido, CA 92025 Fax: (619)745-8809

Newspaper for Inland North County, CA. **Founded:** 1886. **Freq:** Daily. **Key Personnel:** Richard K. Peterson, Editor; Richard High, President; Scott Putnicki, Advertising Dir. **Remarks:** Accepts advertising. **Formerly:** Escondido Times-Advocate. **Merged with:** Oceanside Blade-Citizen.
Circ: Mon.-Sat. ★91,180
Sun. ★93,193

1891 Vivarium (Escondido)
Vivarium Publishing Group
PO Box 300067 Phone: (760)747-4948
Escondido, CA 92030-0067 Fax: (760)747-5224

Trade magazine covering the keeping and breeding of reptiles and amphibians. **Founded:** 1987. **Freq:** Bimonthly. **Print Method:** Web Press. **Trim Size:** 10 5/8 x 8 3/8. **Key Personnel:** David Schultz. **Subscription Rates:** $28 individuals; $53 two years; $36 out of country; $69 two years out of country; $6.95 single issue; $10 single issue Canada. **Remarks:** Accepts advertising. **URL:** http://www.thevivarium.com.
Ad Rates: BW: $557 **Circ:** Paid ⊕20,500
4C: $1190

EUREKA†, pop. 24,153.

NW CA. Humboldt Co. On Humboldt Bay, 2 mi. from Pacific Ocean, 285 mi. N. of San Francisco. Boat Connections. Manufactures lumber, plywood, paper pulp, woolen goods, wine. Halibut, salmon, crab, cod fisheries. Redwood timber. Dairy, truck, stock farms.

1892 Times-Standard
PO Box 3580 Phone: (707)441-0500
Eureka, CA 95502 Fax: (707)441-0565
Free: (800)564-5630

General newspaper. **Subtitle:** A Division of Garden State Newspapers. **Founded:** 1854. **Freq:** Daily (eve.), Sat. and Sun. (morn.). **Print Method:** Offset. **Cols./Page:** 6. **Col. Width:** 12.25 picas. **Col. Depth:** 301 agate lines. **Key Personnel:** Rex Wilson, Managing Editor; Stephan J. Sosinski, Publisher; Gary Siegel, Advertising Dir.; Lynn Johnson, Controller. **Subscription Rates:** $13.50 month by mail; $11 month local. **Remarks:** Accepts advertising.
Ad Rates: GLR: $1.42 **Circ:** Mon.-Sat. ★20,749
BW: $1,568.70 Sun. ★22,886
4C: $240
SAU: $19.94
PCI: $19.94

1893 Tri-City Weekly
V & P Publishing Co., Inc.
PO Box 134 Phone: (707)443-5672
Eureka, CA 95502 Fax: (707)443-5022

Shopper. **Founded:** 1977. **Freq:** Weekly (Tues.). **Print Method:** Web Offset. **Trim Size:** 11 1/2 x 17. **Cols./Page:** 7. **Col. Width:** 1 5/16 inches. **Col. Depth:** 16 inches. **Key Personnel:** Ronald E. Pileggi, Editor and Publisher; David Lippman, Advertising Mgr. **Subscription Rates:** $52 individuals. **Remarks:** Accepts advertising.
Ad Rates: PCI: $10.55 **Circ:** Combined 47,500

1894 Tri-City Weekly (Del Norte Edition)
V & P Publishing Co., Inc.
PO Box 134 Phone: (707)443-5672
Eureka, CA 95502 Fax: (707)443-5022

Shopping guide serving Curry, Del Norte and Humboldt Counties, CA. **Freq:** Monthly. **Key Personnel:** Ronald Pileggi, Publisher. **Subscription Rates:** Free. **Remarks:** Advertising accepted; rates available upon request.
Circ: Non-paid ❑33,335

1895 Tri-City Weekly (Southern Edition)
V & P Publishing Co., Inc.
PO Box 134 Phone: (707)443-5672
Eureka, CA 95502 Fax: (707)443-5022

Shopping guide serving Humboldt and Trinity Counties, CA. **Freq:** Weekly. **Key Personnel:** Ronald Pileggi, Publisher. **Subscription Rates:** $1 single issue. **Remarks:** Accepts advertising.
Circ: Combined ❑13,438

1896 KATA-AM - 1340
5640 S. Broadway St. Phone: (707)822-7223
Eureka, CA 95503-6905 Fax: (707)822-7226

Format: Oldies. **Networks:** Satellite Music Network. **Founded:** 1956. **Operating Hours:** Continuous. **Key Personnel:** Mark Lovell, General Mgr.; Dave Roble, Program Mgr.; Freddie Burns, News/Sports Dir.; Pete Meyer, Production Mgr.; Peggy Hernandez, Office Mgr.; Laurie Tate, Traffic Mgr. **Local Programs:** *Local News*; *Local Sports Report*; *San Francisco Giants/San Jose Sharks*. **Wattage:** 1000. **Ad Rates:** $18 for 30 seconds; $25 for 60 seconds.

1897 KEET-TV - 13
7246 Humboldt Hill Rd. Phone: (707)445-0813
Eureka, CA 95503

Format: Public TV. **Networks:** Public Broadcasting Service (PBS). **Owner:** Redwood Empire Public Television, Inc., at above address. **Founded:** 1962. **Operating Hours:** Continuous; 75% network, 25% local. **ADI:** Eureka, CA. **Key Personnel:** Amanda Schleef, Public Information; Karen Barnes, Program Dir.; St. Clair Adams, General Mgr.; Joel M. Householter, Dir. of Engineering. **Ad Rates:** Noncommercial. **URL:** http://www.keet.org.

1898 KEKA-FM - 101.5
1101 Marsh Rd. Phone: (707)442-5744
Eureka, CA 95501-1574

Format: Contemporary Country. **Networks:** ABC. **Founded:** 1984. **Operating Hours:** Continuous. **ADI:** El Centro, CA-Yuma, AZ. **Key Personnel:** Hugo Papstein, Contact; Brian Papstein, Manager; Mark Householter, Contact; Barbara Papstein, Office Mgr. **Wattage:** 100,000 ERP.

1899 KFMI-FM - 96.3
5640 Broadway St. Phone: (707)822-7223
Eureka, CA 95503-6905 Fax: (707)822-7226
E-mail: kfmi@power963.com; kfmi@wcinet.net

Format: Adult Contemporary. **Networks:** Independent. **Founded:** 1968. **Operating Hours:** Continuous. **Key Personnel:** Mark Lovell, Gen. Mgr./Owner; Dave Roble, Program Dir.; Freddie Burns, News Dir.; Pete Meyer, Production Mgr.; Laura Tate, Traffic Coord.; Peggy Hernandez, Office Mgr. **Wattage:** 30,000. **Ad Rates:** $26.40-36 for 60 seconds. Combined advertising rates available with KATA-AM.

1900 KGOE-AM - 1480
5640 S. Broadway Phone: (707)443-1621
Eureka, CA 95501 Fax: (707)443-6848

Networks: ABC; Jones Satellite. **Owner:** North Country Communications, at above address, (707)263-6113, Fax: (707)262-1645. **Founded:** 1933. **Formerly:** KRED-AM; KTMA-AM. **Operating Hours:** Continuous. **ADI:** Eureka, CA. **Key Personnel:** William Groody, President; Kathy Murphy, General Sales Mgr., phone (707)442-2000, fax (707)443-6848; Dennis Edgmon, Operations Mgr., phone (707)442-2000, fax (707)443-6848. **Local Programs:** *Redwood Sports Talk*. **Wattage:** 5000 day; 1000 night.

1901 KIEM-TV - 3
5650 S. Broadway Phone: (707)443-3123
Eureka, CA 95503 Fax: (707)442-6084

Format: Commercial TV. **Networks:** NBC. **Owner:** Pollack/Belz Broadcasting Co., L.L.C., at above address. **Founded:** 1953. **Operating Hours:** Continuous; 60% network, 40% local. **ADI:** Eureka, CA. **Key Personnel:** Hank Ingham, General Sales Mgr.; Mark Demsky, Sports Dir.; Phil Wright, Operations Mgr.; Thomas J. Spain, Contact. **Wattage:** 100,000.

1902 KINS-AM - 980
1101 Marsh Rd. Phone: (707)442-5744
Eureka, CA 95501 Fax: (707)444-3899

Format: Talk; News; Sports. **Networks:** CBS; ABC; Talknet. **Founded:** 1958. **Operating Hours:** Continuous. **ADI:** El Centro, CA-Yuma, AZ. **Key Personnel:** Hugo Papstein, Contact; Brian Papstein, Manager; Mark Householder, Contact; Barbara Papstein, Office Mgr. **Wattage:** 5000.

1903 KRED-FM - 92.3
5640 S. Broadway Phone: (707)443-1621
Eureka, CA 95501 Fax: (707)443-6848

Format: Country. **Networks:** Jones Satellite. **Owner:** KRED Radio Inc., at above address. **Founded:** 1979. **Operating Hours:** Continuous. **ADI:** Eureka, CA. **Key Personnel:** William. Groody, President; Jim Dowd, General Mgr.; Kathy Murphy, Sales Mgr. **Local Programs:** *Rollin Trehearne*. **Wattage:** 25,000 ERP.

1904 KVIQ-TV - 6
1800 Broadway Phone: (707)443-3061
Eureka, CA 95501 Fax: (707)443-4435
Free: (800)310-4246

Format: Commercial TV. **Networks:** CBS. **Operating Hours:** Continuous. **ADI:** Eureka, CA. **Key Personnel:** Jeanne Buheit, General Mgr.; Terri Jensen, Program Dir. **Local Programs:** *Action News 6* 5:00 pm, 6:00 pm, 11:00 pm.

1905 KXGO-FM - 93.1
603 F St. Phone: (707)445-8104
Eureka, CA 95501 Fax: (707)445-3906
E-mail: kxgo@razorlogic.com

Format: Classic Rock. **Networks:** ABC. **Owner:** Miller Broadcasting, at above address. **Founded:** 1970. **Operating Hours:** Continuous; 20% network, 80% local. **ADI:** Eureka, CA. **Key Personnel:** Pattison J. Christensen, Contact. **Local Programs:** *The Blues Review* 7 p.m. - 11 p.m. Sunday; *Mind Over Metal* 10 p.m. - 1 a.m. Friday; *Plant X - 90's Alternative Rock* 10 p.m. - 1 a.m. Thursday; *Seventh Day* 10 a.m. - 4 p.m. Sunday. **Wattage:** 100,000. **Ad Rates:** $10-30 for 30 seconds.

EXETER, pop. 5,619.

SC CA. Tulane Co. 50 mi. SE of Fresno. Fruit packed and shipped. Diversified farming. Oranges, grapes, peaches.

1906 The Exeter Sun
Mineral King Publishing
120 N. E St. Phone: (209)592-3171
PO Box 7 Fax: (209)592-4308
Exeter, CA 93221
Publication E-mail: exetrsun@lightspeed.net

Community newspaper. **Founded:** 1901. **Freq:** Weekly (Wed.). **Print Method:** Offset. Uses mats. **Trim Size:** 13 1/8 x 21. **Cols./Page:** 6. **Col. Width:** 25 nonpareils. **Col. Depth:** 294 agate lines. **Key Personnel:** Katie Byrne, General Mgr.; David Adalian, Editor; David William, Advertising Dir. **Subscription Rates:** $7 individuals. **Remarks:** Accepts advertising. **Absorbed:** Famersville Herald.
Ad Rates: SAU: $5.00 **Circ:** ‡3,099
PCI: $9.78

FAIRFAX

1907 Horizon Cable TV, Inc.
Box 937 Phone: (415)883-9251
Fairfax, CA 94978 Fax: (415)382-0814
E-mail: xber05a@prodigy.com

Founded: 1987. **Key Personnel:** Kevin Daniel, President; Susan Daniel, Vice Pres./Gen. Mgr. **Cities Served:** Dillon Beach, Inverness, Novato, Olema, Pt. Keyes, Stinson Beach, CA: subscribing households 2300; 36 channels; 1 community access channel.

FAIRFIELD†, pop. 58,099.

NWC CA. Solano Co. 45 mi. SW of San Francisco. Residential. Wineries. Explosives, Canvas products, can manufacturing. Ranching.

1908 Daily Republic
1250 Texas St. Phone: (707)425-4646
PO Box 47 Fax: (707)425-5924
Fairfield, CA 94533-0747
Publication E-mail: drnews@dailyrepublic.com

General newspaper. **Founded:** 1855. **Freq:** Mon.-Sun. (morn.). **Print Method:** Offset. **Cols./Page:** 6. **Col. Width:** 2 1/16 inches. **Col. Depth:** 21 1/2 inches. **Key Personnel:** Bill James, Editor, phone (707)427-6983; Foy S. McNaughton, Publisher, phone (707)427-6962, fmcnaughton@aol.com. **ISSN:** 0746-5858. **Subscription Rates:** $115.80 individuals. **Remarks:** Accepts advertising. **URL:** http://www.dailyrepublic.com.
Ad Rates: GLR: $1.27 **Circ:** Mon.-Sat. 19,289
BW: $2,289.75 Sun. 21,265
4C: $2,679.75
PCI: $17.75

1909 Single Again Magazine
Scholl & Associates
PO Box 3528 Phone: (707)425-3381
Fairfield, CA 94533 Fax: (707)434-1262
Free: (800)836-9180

Magazine for single men and women who are divorced, separated, or widowed. **Founded:** 1977. **Freq:** Bimonthly. **Print Method:** Offset. **Trim Size:** 7 x 10. **Cols./Page:** 3. **Col. Width:** 2 1/4 inches. **Col. Depth:** 10 inches. **Key Personnel:** Paul V. Scholl, Publisher; Steven Marschke, Exec. Editor; Donalee Hill, Managing Editor; Nancy Ohr, Advertising Dir. **Subscription Rates:** $15 individuals. **Remarks:** Accepts advertising.
Ad Rates: BW: $423 **Circ:** Paid 10,000
4C: $892

1910 ML Media Cable TV (Multi-Vision)
2250 Boynton Ave. Phone: (707)422-4622
Fairfield, CA 94533

Key Personnel: Fran Parkey, General Mgr. **Cities Served:** subscribing households 25,000; 41 channels; 1 community access channel.

FALL RIVER MILLS, pop. 600.

N. CA. Shasta Co. 10 mi. N. of Burmey. Residential.

1911 Mountain Echo
Mountain Echo, Inc.
PO Box 224 Phone: (916)336-6262
Fall River Mills, CA 96028 Fax: (916)336-6262
Publication E-mail: mtecho@shasta.org
Publisher E-mail: mtecha@shasta.com

Community newspaper. **Founded:** Oct. 3, 1977. **Freq:** Weekly (Tues.). **Print Method:** Offset. **Cols./Page:** 6. **Col. Width:** 24 nonpareils. **Col. Depth:** 298 agate lines. **Key Personnel:** Walt Caldwell, Editor and Publisher. **USPS:** 052-610. **Subscription Rates:** $18 Shasta, Lassen, and Modoc—senior; $14 outside Shasta, Lassen, or Modoc—senior; $16 Shasta, Lassen, or Modoc—non-senior; $22 outside of Shasta, Lassen, or Modoc—non-senior; $26 out of state. **Remarks:** Accepts advertising. **URL:** http://www.intermountainet.com/mtecho.
Ad Rates: BW: $677.25 **Circ:** Paid ‡2,554
SAU: $6.50 Free ‡444
PCI: $6

FALLBROOK, pop. 9,000.

S. CA. San Diego Co. 45 mi. N. of San Diego. Citrus fruit packed. Diversified farming. Avocadoes, lemons, strawberries.

1912 Enterprise
North County Times
PO Box 2800 Phone: (619)728-5511
Fallbrook, CA 92088 Fax: (619)723-4967

Newspaper. **Freq:** Weekly (Thurs.). **Print Method:** Offset. **Cols./Page:** 6. **Col. Width:** 21 nonpareils. **Col. Depth:** 294 agate lines. **Key Personnel:** Betty Johnston, Editor; G.L. Don Taylor, Publisher. **Remarks:** Accepts advertising. **Formerly:** Extraprize (1996).
Ad Rates: BW: $821.52 **Circ:** Free ‡6,950
4C: $1,181.52
SAU: $1.54

1913 KBAX-FM - 107.1
1588 S Mission Rd., No. 200 Phone: (619)731-5229
Fallbrook, CA 92028-7112

Format: Gospel. **Networks:** AP. **Founded:** 1977. **Formerly:** KAVO-FM (1991); KMLQ-FM. **Operating Hours:** Continuous. **Key Personnel:** Linda Johnson-Hayes, General Mgr.; Bob Gorley, Program Dir.; Claudia Moonier, Contact. **Wattage:** 3000. **Ad Rates:** $22-40 for 30 seconds; $28-45 for 60 seconds.

FELTON, pop. 5,000.

W. CA. Santa Cruz Co. 10 mi. N. of Santa Cruz. Residential.

1914 Scotts Valley Banner
Melmac Media, Inc.
PO Box V-1 Phone: (831)335-5321
Felton, CA 95018 Fax: (831)438-4141
Publication E-mail: info@pressbanner.com

Newspaper. **Founded:** 1974. **Freq:** Weekly (Wed.). **Print Method:** Offset. **Cols./Page:** 6. **Col. Width:** 26 nonpareils. **Col. Depth:** 294 agate lines. **Key Personnel:** Kingsley Gerlach, Publisher, kgerlach@pressbanner.com; Garth Merrill, Editor, gmerrill@pressbanner.com. **Subscription Rates:** $17.50 individuals. **Remarks:** Accepts advertising. **URL:** http://www.pressbanner.com.
Ad Rates: GLR: $9.90 **Circ:** Paid ‡700
BW: $1,2470 Free ‡4,300
4C: $1,522
CNU: $9.90
PCI: $9.90

1915 The Valley Press
Melmac Media, Inc.
5901 Hwy 9 Phone: (831)335-5321
Felton, CA 95018 Fax: (831)438-4141
Publication E-mail: info@pressbanner.com

Community newspaper. **Founded:** 1960. **Freq:** Weekly (Wed.). **Print Method:** Offset. **Cols./Page:** 6. **Col. Width:** 24 nonpareils. **Col. Depth:** 294 agate lines. **Key Personnel:** Kingsley Gerlach, Publisher, kgerlach@pressbanner.com; Garth Merrill, Editor, gmerrill@pressbanner.com. **USPS:** 906-620. **Subscription Rates:** $20 In County; $27 Out of County. **Remarks:** Accepts advertising. **URL:** http://www.pressbanner.com.
Ad Rates: GLR: $9.90 **Circ:** ‡4,600
BW: $1,247
4C: $1,522
CNU: $9.90
PCI: $9.90

FERNDALE, pop. 1,367.

NW CA. Humboldt Co. 20 mi. S. of Eureka. Residential. Art galleries. Dairy products manufactured. Dairy, stock, mushroom farms. Potatoes.

1916 The Ferndale Enterprise
Ferndale Enterprise, Inc.
PO Box 1066 Phone: (707)786-4611
Ferndale, CA 95536 Fax: (707)786-4311
Publication E-mail: entr1878@humboldt1.com

Newspaper. **Founded:** 1878. **Freq:** Weekly (Thurs.). **Print Method:** Offset. **Cols./Page:** 6. **Col. Width:** 2 inches. **Col. Depth:** 280 agate lines. **Key Personnel:** Caroline Titus, Editor-in-Chief; Peter Hannaford, Publisher. **Subscription Rates:** $20; $25 out of area; $35 out of state. **Remarks:** Accepts advertising.
Ad Rates: SAU: $10.50 **Circ:** 1,350
PCI: $5.95

FILLMORE, pop. 9,602.

SW CA. Ventura Co. 24 mi. E. of Ventura. Ships citrus fruit, oil. Oil wells. Agriculture. Oranges, lemons, walnuts.

1917 The Fillmore Herald
Sentinel Media Inc.
PO Box 727 Phone: (805)524-0153
Fillmore, CA 93016
Newspaper serving Fillmore and Piru in northeastern Ventura County. **Founded:** 1907. **Freq:** Weekly (Thurs.). **Print Method:** Offset. **Cols./Page:** 6. **Col. Width:** 2 inches. **Col. Depth:** 21 inches. **Key Personnel:** Doug Huff, Editor and Publisher. **USPS:** 190-400. **Subscription Rates:** $15.29 individuals; $21.95 out of state. **Remarks:** Accepts advertising.
Ad Rates: GLR: $.33 **Circ:** ‡3,000
BW: $582.12
4C: $862.12
SAU: $5
PCI: $5

FIRESTONE PARK

1918 Firestone Park News/Southeast News Press
Herald Dispatch
4053 Marlton Ave. Phone: (213)291-9486
Los Angeles, CA 90008 Fax: (213)291-2123

Newspaper serving the black community of L.A. **Founded:** 1924. **Freq:** Weekly (Thurs.). **Print Method:** Offset. **Trim Size:** 13 x 21 1/2. **Cols./Page:** 6. **Col. Width:** 29 nonpareils. **Col. Depth:** 294 agate lines. **Key Personnel:** Lela Ward Oliver, Editor; John H. Holoman, Publisher; Eric L. Holoman, Advertising Mgr. **ISSN:** 8550-2038. **Subscription Rates:** $20 individuals; $40 National. **Remarks:** Accepts advertising.
Ad Rates: GLR: $.75 **Circ:** Paid ‡18,000
BW: $1,764 Free ‡6,000
4C: $2,764
SAU: $14
PCI: $14

FOLSOM, pop. 11,003.

NC CA. Sacramento Co. 22 mi. NE of Sacramento. Recreation. Stock farms.

1919 Folsom Telegraph
Brehm Communications, Inc.
555 Oakdale St. Phone: (916)985-2581
Folsom, CA 95630 Fax: (916)985-0720

Community newspaper. **Founded:** 1856. **Freq:** Weekly (Wed.). **Print Method:** Offset. **Cols./Page:** 6. **Col. Width:** 2 1/16 inches. **Col. Depth:** 21 1/2 inches. **Key Personnel:** Patty McAlpin, Community Ed.; Dave Johnson, Sports Ed.; Dave Reese, Publisher. **Subscription Rates:** $20 individuals. **Remarks:** Accepts advertising.
Ad Rates: GLR: $2.50 **Circ:** Paid 8,000
BW: $7,820
4C: $1018.20
SAU: $8.85

1920 KCMT-FM - 98.9
PO Box 189 Phone: (916)283-1370
Folsom, CA 95763-0189 Fax: (916)283-2155
E-mail: kcmt@psln.com

Format: Adult Contemporary; Classical. **Networks:** CNN Radio. **Owner:** John Samuels, at above address. **Founded:** 1989. **Formerly:** KCFM-FM (1989). **Operating Hours:** Continuous. **Key Personnel:** John Samuels, Owner; Laurie Wann, General Mgr., phone (916)257-5600. **Local Programs:** *Breakfast Club*, Craig Allen; *Jett Set*, Janet Jett. **Wattage:** 25,000. **Ad Rates:** $8-9 for 30 seconds; $9.75-11 for 60 seconds. $8-$9 for 30 seconds; $9.75-$11 for 60 seconds. Combined advertising rates available with KPCO-AM.

1921 KPCO-AM - 1370
PO Box 189 Phone: (916)283-1370
Folsom, CA 95763-0189 Fax: (916)283-2155

Format: News; Talk. **Networks:** ABC. **Owner:** John Samuels, at above address. **Founded:** 1963. **Operating Hours:** Continuous. **Key Personnel:** John Samuels, General Mgr. **Wattage:** 5000. **Ad Rates:** $8-9 for 30 seconds; $9.75-11 for 60 seconds. $8-$9 for 30 seconds; $9.75-$11 for 60 seconds. Combined advertising rates available with KCMT-FM.

FONTANA, pop. 37,109.

SE CA. San Bernardino Co. 10 mi. W. of San Bernardino. Manufacturing steel, ceramics, clothing, electronic products, explosives. Poultry.

1922 Fontana Herald-News
Fontana Herald Publishing
PO Box 549 Phone: (909)822-2231
Fontana, CA 92335 Fax: (909)355-9358

General newspaper. **Founded:** 1923. **Freq:** Weekly. **Print Method:** Offset. **Cols./Page:** 6. **Col. Width:** 25 nonpareils. **Col. Depth:** 301 agate lines. **Key Personnel:** Pat Lehman, Advertising Dir. **Subscription Rates:** $19 individuals. **Remarks:** Accepts advertising. **Formerly:** Herald News.
Ad Rates: GLR: $2.28 **Circ:** Paid 3,500
BW: $1,053.36 Free 7,000
4C: $1,263.36
SAU: $8.36

FOOTHILL

1923 Coverstory
Gold Country Media
PO Box 755 Phone: (530)346-2232
Colfax, CA 95713 Fax: (530)346-2700

Shopper. **Founded:** 1904. **Freq:** Weekly (Wed.). **Print Method:** Offset. **Cols./Page:** 6. **Col. Width:** 2 1/16 inches. **Col. Depth:** 21 inches. **Key Personnel:** Jim Fallbeck, Publisher. **Remarks:** Accepts advertising.
Ad Rates: GLR: $.78 **Circ:** Paid 1500
4C: $300 4200
SAU: $7.86

FOOTHILL RANCH

1924 Jet Sports
Sports, Inc.
27142 Burbank Phone: (949)598-5860
Foothill Ranch, CA 92610-2503 Fax: (949)598-5872

Membership magazine for personal watercraft owners. **Subtitle:** Official Publication of the International Jet Sports Boating Association. **Founded:** 1982. **Freq:** 9/year. **Print Method:** Web offset. **Trim Size:** 9 1/4 x 12. **Cols./Page:** 3. **Col. Width:** 16 picas. **Col. Depth:** 62 picas. **Key Personnel:** Kirk Holland, Dir. of Communications; Rick Lake, Advertising Mgr. **Subscription Rates:** $25. **Remarks:** Accepts advertising. **Formerly:** Jet Skier Magazine (1991).
Ad Rates: BW: $1,620 **Circ:** Paid ★40,504
4C: $2,665

1925 SportsCar
Sports, Inc.
27142 Burbank Phone: (949)598-5860
Foothill Ranch, CA 92610-2503 Fax: (949)598-5872

Official magazine of the Sports Car Club of America. **Founded:** 1944. **Freq:** Monthly. **Print Method:** Offset. **Trim Size:** 8 3/8 x 10 7/8. **Cols./Page:** 3. **Key Personnel:** R.A. McCormack, Editor; Joanna Glass, Publisher; Richard James, Sr. Editor; Paul Pfanner, President/Executive Publisher; Celia Shambaugh, Advertising Mgr. **ISSN:** 0300-6387. **Subscription Rates:** $35.40. $2.95 single issue. **Remarks:** Accepts advertising.
Ad Rates: BW: $2,045 **Circ:** Paid ★39,315
4C: $2,870

FORESTVILLE

1926 Epiphany Journal
Epiphany Press
PO Box 336 Fax: (707)887-9023
Forestville, CA 95436
Christian magazine for traditional Orthodox, Episcopalians and Catholics and those seeking traditional values. **Subtitle:** A Journal of Faith and Insight. **Founded:** 1979. **Freq:** Quarterly. **Print Method:** Offset. **Trim Size:** 8 x 10 3/4. **Cols./Page:** 2. **Col. Width:** 3 inches. **Col. Depth:** 8 1/4 inches. **Key Personnel:** Fr. Philip Tolbert, Editor; Monk Nikodim, Business Mgr., phone (707)887-9740, fax (707)887-9023. **ISSN:** 0273-6969. **Subscription Rates:** $22.50; $28.50 outside U.S. **Remarks:** Advertising not accepted. **Formerly:** Epiphany.
Circ: Paid 700
Controlled 125

FORT BRAGG, pop. 5,019.

NW CA. Mendocino Co. On Pacific Ocean, 165 mi. N. of San Francisco. Year round resort. Manufactures lumber. Nurseries. Fisheries. Redwood, pine, fir timber.

1927 Fort Bragg Advocate-News
Donrey Media Group
PO Box 1188 Phone: (707)964-5642
Fort Bragg, CA 95437 Fax: (707)964-0424
Publication E-mail: advocatenews@mcn.org

Community newspaper. **Founded:** 1889. **Freq:** Semiweekly (Tues. and Thurs.). **Print Method:** Offset. **Cols./Page:** 6. **Col. Width:** 78.6 picas. **Col. Depth:** 129 picas. **Key Personnel:** Katherine Lee, Editor; Sharon Brewer, Publisher, sbrewer@mcn.org. **Subscription Rates:** $22 individuals in county; $30 out of county. **Remarks:** Accepts advertising.
Ad Rates: GLR: $6.40 **Circ:** Thurs. ⊕5,164
BW: $825.60
4C: $350
PCI: $7

1928 KOZT-FM - 95.3
110 S. Franklin St. Phone: (707)964-7277
Fort Bragg, CA 95437-4202 Fax: (707)964-9536
E-mail: thecoast@kozt.com

Format: Adult Album Alternative; Album-Oriented Rock (AOR); Classic Rock. **Networks:** Independent. **Owner:** California Radio Partners, at above address, Fort Bragg, CA 95437. **Founded:** 1981. **Operating Hours:** Continuous; 100% local. **Key Personnel:** Tom Yates, Contact; Vicky Watts, General Sales Mgr. **Local Programs:** *Breakfast with the Beatles* 8:00 am - 10:00 am Sunday, Tom Yates; *Local Licks* 9:00 pm Wednesday, Tom Yates. **Wattage:** 25,000.

1929 KSAY-FM - 98.5
684-C S. Main St. Phone: (707)964-KSAY
PO Box 2269 Fax: (707)964-2722
Fort Bragg, CA 95437
E-mail: ksay@inreach.com

Format: Adult Contemporary; News. **Networks:** Westwood One Radio; CNN Radio. **Owner:** Wade Axell, at above address. **Founded:** 1988. **Operating Hours:** 24 hours. **ADI:** San Francisco-Oakland-San Jose. **Key Personnel:** Wade Axell, Contact. **Local Programs:** *Good News Guys*; *Spanish Show*. **Wattage:** 3700. **Ad Rates:** $9 for 30 seconds; $9 for 60 seconds. **URL:** http://www.mcn.org/ksay/b.

FORT IRWIN

1930 Tiefort Telegraph
Aerotech
Public Affairs Office Phone: (760)380-3303
PO Box 105067 Fax: (760)380-3080
National Training Center
Fort Irwin, CA 92310
Publisher E-mail: aerotech@netport.com

Newspaper for military and military family interests. **Founded:** 1980. **Freq:** Weekly. **Print Method:** Offset. **Trim Size:** 11 1/2 x 13 3/4. **Cols./Page:** 5. **Col. Width:** 1.875 inches. **Col. Depth:** 13 inches. **Key Personnel:** Paul Kinison, Publisher; Donna McIntyre, Command Information Officer. **Subscription Rates:** Free to qualified subscribers. **Remarks:** Accepts advertising.
Ad Rates: PCI: $7.95 **Circ:** Non-paid 6,500

FORT JONES

NC CA. Siskiyou Co. 10 mi. S. of Yreka.

1931 Pioneer Press
PO Box 400 Phone: (916)468-5355
Fort Jones, CA 96032 Fax: (916)468-5356

Community newspaper. **Founded:** Nov. 1972. **Freq:** Weekly (Wed.). **Cols./Page:** 6. **Col. Width:** 2 1/8 inches. **Col. Depth:** 21 inches. **Key Personnel:** Gary Morterson, Publisher. **Subscription Rates:** $19; $.5 single issue. **Remarks:** Accepts advertising.
Ad Rates: SAU: $4.22 **Circ:** 2,100
PCI: $5.60

1932 Siskiyou Cablevision Inc.
Box 399 Phone: (530)468-5666
Fort Jones, CA 96032 Fax: (530)468-5523

Owner: Jim Hendricks, at above address, (530)468-2222, Fax: (530)468-5523. **Founded:** 1981. **Key Personnel:** Brenda Kellogg, General Mgr., sisrural@sisqtel.net. **Cities Served:** subscribing households 978; 21 channels; 1 community access channel.

FORTUNA, pop. 7,591.

NC CA. Humboldt Co. 18 mi. S. of Eureka. Residential. Lumber mills; foundry. Nurseries. creameries. Sheep and cattle ranches. Dairy farms.

1933 Humboldt Beacon & Advance
Humboldt Beacon
PO Box 310 Phone: (707)725-6166
Fortuna, CA 95540 Fax: (707)725-4981
Free: (800)632-NEWS
Publication E-mail: beacon@humboldtl.com

Community newspaper for the county of Humboldt. **Founded:** 1902. **Freq:** Weekly (Thurs.). **Print Method:** Offset. **Cols./Page:** 6. **Col. Width:** 12 picas. **Col. Depth:** 21 inches. **Key Personnel:** Patrick O'Dell, Publisher; Jack Hamilton, Editor. **Subscription Rates:** $17.50 individuals; $25 out of area; $30 out of state. **Remarks:** Accepts advertising. **Alt. Formats:** Microform. **Absorbed:** The Redwood Record (Dec. 1995); The Union (Dec. 7, 1995).
Ad Rates: GLR: $8.07 **Circ:** Paid ‡4,750
BW: $1,016.82 Free ‡12,000
4C: $1,416.82
SAU: $6.86

1934 Journal of the American Rhododendron Society
American Rhododendron Society
11 Pinecrest Dr. Phone: (707)725-3043
Fortuna, CA 95540 Fax: (707)725-1217

Journal covering society news and horticultural issues. **Founded:** 1945. **Freq:** Quarterly. **Key Personnel:** Sonja Nelson, Editor; Dee Daneri, Exec. Director. **Subscription Rates:** $28 individuals. **Remarks:** Accepts advertising.
Circ: Controlled 6,000

1935 Satellite TV Week
Fortuna Communications Corp.
180 S. Fortuna Blvd. Phone: (707)725-6951
PO Box 308 Fax: (707)725-4311
Fortuna, CA 95540-0308
Free: (800)345-8876
Publication E-mail: satellit@humboldt1.com

Magazine listing satellite TV programming and industry related news. **Founded:** 1981. **Freq:** Weekly. **Print Method:** Web offset. **Trim Size:** 8 1/4 x 10 3/4. **Cols./Page:** 4. **Col. Width:** 1 3/4 inches. **Key Personnel:** James E. Scott, Editor, fax (707)725-9639, editor@humboldt1.com; Patrick O'Dell, Publisher; George Bryant, Advertising Dir. **ISSN:** 0744-7841. **Subscription Rates:** $59; $2.95 single issue. **Remarks:** Accepts advertising.
Ad Rates: BW: $7,300 **Circ:** Paid 247,272
4C: $9,350 Non-paid 6,174

1936 KQEX-FM - 100.3
1713 Main St. Phone: (707)725-3408
Fortuna, CA 95540 Fax: (707)725-3423

Format: Jazz. **Owner:** North Star Communications, at above address. **Founded:** 1992. **Operating Hours:** Continuous. **ADI:** Eureka, CA. **Key Personnel:** Steve Paulato, Program Dir., ap@kqex.com; Rod Allen, AM/News, rod@kqex.com; Carlos Casarez, News Dir., carlos@kqex.com; Anne Freeman, Specialty Prog. Dir. **Wattage:** 25,000. **Ad Rates:** $12 per unit. **URL:** http://www.kqex.com.

FOSTER CITY

San Mateo Co. 20 mi. S. of San Francisco.

1937 Foster City Islander
1185 Chess Dr., Ste. B Phone: (415)574-5952
Foster City, CA 94404 Fax: (650)574-1096

Community newspaper. **Founded:** Apr. 1973. **Freq:** Weekly (Wed.). **Print Method:** Offset. **Trim Size:** 10 x 16. **Cols./Page:** 5. **Col. Width:** 2 inches. **Col. Depth:** 16 inches. **Key Personnel:** Sam Felser, Editor and Publisher; Marge Felser, Advertising Mgr. **Subscription Rates:** $50 /year - first class. **Remarks:** Accepts advertising.
Ad Rates: GLR: $1.86 **Circ:** Free ‡6,175
BW: $8

1938 MacUser
Ziff-Davis Publishing Co.
950 Tower Ln. Phone: (415)378-5520
Foster City, CA 94404 Fax: (415)341-7242

Magazine for Macintosh computer users. Editorial provides product reviews and analysis. **Founded:** Oct. 1985. **Freq:** Monthly. **Print Method:** Offset. **Trim Size:** 8 x 10 7/8. **Cols./Page:** 3. **Col. Width:** 2 1/4 inches. **Col. Depth:** 10 inches. **Key Personnel:** Jon Zilber, Editor; Janet Ryan Publisher; Jonathan Layne, Publisher. **ISSN:** 0884-0997. **Subscription Rates:** $19.97 individuals; $2.95 single issue. **Remarks:** Accepts advertising. **Online:** CompuServe Information Service.
Ad Rates: BW: $18,995 **Circ:** Paid 528,801
4C: $23,125
PCI: $500

1939 National Motorist
National Automobile Club
1151 E. Hillsdale Blvd. Phone: (650)294-7000
Foster City, CA 94404 Fax: (650)294-7040

Motor and travel magazine covering western U.S. **Subtitle:** Serving the California Motorist and Traveler. **Founded:** 1924. **Freq:** Quarterly. **Print Method:** Offset. **Trim Size:** 8 x 10 3/4. **Cols./Page:** 3. **Col. Width:** 26 nonpareils. **Col. Depth:** 140 agate lines. **Key Personnel:** Jane Offers, Editor. **ISSN:** 0279-3083. **Subscription Rates:** $2 individuals. **Remarks:** Accepts advertising.
Ad Rates: BW: $2,225 **Circ:** ‡64,313
4C: $2,825

1940 PSExtreme
1175 Chess Dr., E Phone: (415)372-0942
Foster City, CA 94404 Fax: (415)372-0753

Gaming publication focusing on the Sony Play Station. **Founded:** Nov. 1995. **Freq:** Monthly. **Key Personnel:** Dave Winding, Publisher; Mark Winding, Advertising Mgr.; Mike Gerrardo, Circulation Mgr. **Subscription Rates:** $19.95 individuals; $4.99 single issue. **Remarks:** Accepts advertising. **Formerly:** Dimension PSX Magazine (Jan. 1996).
Ad Rates: 4C: $3,500 **Circ:** Paid 125,000
Non-paid 250,000

1941 Tundra
248 Beach Park Blvd. Phone: (650)571-9428
Foster City, CA 94404
Literary journal covering short poetry. **Subtitle:** The Journal of Short Poetry. **Founded:** 1989. **Freq:** Triennial. **Print Method:** Offset. **Trim Size:** 6 x 9. **Cols./Page:** 1. **Col. Width:** 4 1/4 inches. **Col. Depth:** 7 1/4 inches. **Key Personnel:** Michael Dylan Welch, Editor and Publisher, WelchM@aol.com. **ISSN:** 1095-6727. **Subscription Rates:** $18 individuals; $7 single issue. **Remarks:** Advertising not accepted. **Former name:** Woodnotes (1998).
Circ: Combined 325

1942 Western Cabled Systems
330 Hatch Dr., Ste. B Phone: (415)571-8041
Foster City, CA 94404 Fax: (415)571-8596

Owner: Balkin Cable Holdings, at above address. **Founded:** 1976. **Key Personnel:** Jeffrey M. Stevens, President; Larry D. Whitney, Operations Mgr. **Cities Served:** Belmont, Daly City, Esparto, Pontola Valley, Redwood City, Richmond, San Leandro, San Mateo, Santa Clara, Sunnyvale, Woodside, CA: subscribing households 12,000.

FOUNTAIN VALLEY, pop. 55,080.

S. CA. Orange Co. 10 mi. NE of Santa Ana. Residential.

1943 Huntington Beach/Fountain Valley Independent
California Community News Corp.
18682 Beach Blvd., Ste. 160 Phone: (714)965-3030
Huntington Beach, CA 92648 Fax: (714)965-7174

Community newspaper. **Founded:** 1966. **Freq:** Weekly. **Print Method:** Offset. **Cols./Page:** 6. **Col. Width:** 2 1/16 inches. **Col. Depth:** 21 1/2 inches. **Key Personnel:** Bill Lobdell, Editor; Dave Garofalo, Publisher. **Subscription Rates:** $14. **Remarks:** Accepts advertising. **URL:** http://www.latimes.com/independence. **Formerly:** Huntington Beach Weekly; Huntington Beach Independent.
Ad Rates: SAU: $23.80 **Circ:** Combined ❑**34,828**

FOWLER, pop. 2,496.

C. CA. Fresno Co. 10 mi. SE of Fresno. Raisins, dried & fresh fruit, nut packing plants; farm implement factory. Agriculture, especially fruit.

1944 The Fowler Ensign
Mid Valley Publication
207 E. Merced St. Phone: (209)834-2535
Fowler, CA 93625 Fax: (209)834-4343

Community newspaper. **Founded:** 1894. **Freq:** Weekly (Thurs.). **Print Method:** Offset. **Trim Size:** 14 x 23. **Cols./Page:** 6. **Col. Width:** 26 nonpareils. **Col. Depth:** 294 agate lines. **Key Personnel:** John Converse, Editor; Fred Hall, Publisher, phone (209)638-2244. **USPS:** 207-460. **Subscription Rates:** $15 individuals in Fresno County; $20 elsewhere in California; $22 out of state. **Remarks:** Accepts advertising.
Ad Rates: BW: $762.30 **Circ:** ‡1,809
4C: $1,395
PCI: $6.05

FRAZIER PARK

SW CA. Kern Co. 30 mi. N. of Ventura. Kern Co. (SW). 30 m N of Ventura.

1945 The Mountain Enterprise
PO Box 610 Phone: (805)245-3794
Frazier Park, CA 93225-0610 Fax: (805)245-5620
Publisher E-mail: mtnmedia@frazmtn.com

Community newspaper. **Subtitle:** Serving the Frazier Mountain Area & I-5 Corridor. **Founded:** 1963. **Freq:** Weekly. **Print Method:** Web offset. **Trim Size:** 10 x 13. **Cols./Page:** 5. **Col. Width:** 1 13/16 inches. **Col. Depth:** 13 inches. **Key Personnel:** Linda Sawyer, Managing Editor; Terry Sawyer, Advertising. **Subscription Rates:** $16 individuals; $.25 single issue. **Remarks:** Accepts advertising. **Alt. Formats:** Microfiche.
Ad Rates: PCI: $3.25 **Circ:** Combined 3,000

1946 Frazier Park Cable TV
PO Box 2169 Phone: (213)722-2990
Frazier Park, CA 93225

Owner: Mountain Cablevision, Inc., at above address. **Founded:** 1966. **Key Personnel:** Robert Weisberg, Contact. **Cities Served:** Frazier Park, Lake of the Woods, Lebec, Pine Mountain, CA: subscribing households 2,600; 21 channels; 2 community access channels.

FREMONT, pop. 131,945.

W. CA. Alameda Co. 17 mi. SE of Oakland. Manufactures automobiles, building materials, fabricated metal, electronics.

1947 The Argus
Alameda Newspaper Group
39737 Paseo Podue Parkway Phone: (510)353-7001
Fremont, CA 94538 Fax: (510)353-7029

General newspaper. **Founded:** 1960. **Freq:** Mon.-Sun. (morn.). **Print Method:** Offset. **Cols./Page:** 6. **Col. Width:** 25 nonpareils. **Col. Depth:** 301 agate lines. **Key Personnel:** Jack Lyness, Editor; Peter Bernahrd, Publisher. **Subscription Rates:** $45 individuals. **Remarks:** Accepts advertising.
Ad Rates: BW: $2,580 **Circ:** Mon.-Sat. 32,568
4C: $2,933 Sun. 31,512
SAU: $20

1948 KFAX-AM - 1100
39138 Fremont Blvd. Phone: (510)713-1100
3rd FL. Fax: (510)505-1448
Fremont, CA 94538

Format: Religious. **Founded:** 1925. **Operating Hours:** Continuous. **ADI:** San Francisco-Oakland-San Jose. **Key Personnel:** Ron Watters, General Mgr.; Craig Roberts, Operations Mgr., opsfax@kfax.com. **Local Programs:** *Life! Line with Craig Roberts* 5 p.m.-7 p.m. Monday-Friday, Neil Gandara, (510)713-1100. **Wattage:** 50,000 clear channel. **URL:** http://www.wfax.com.

1949 KOHL-FM - 89.3
43600 Mission Blvd. Phone: (510)659-6221
Fremont, CA 94539 Fax: (510)659-6001
E-mail: kohl@kohlradio.com

Networks: Independent. **Founded:** 1974. **Operating Hours:** Continuous. **ADI:** San Francisco-Oakland-San Jose. **Key Personnel:** Robert Dochterman, Station Mgr.; Matthew Karl Graf, Contact; Tom Gomez Briseno, Program Dir. **Wattage:** 145. **Ad Rates:** Noncommercial.

FRESNO†, pop. 218,202.

C. CA. Fresno Co. 189 mi. SE of San Francisco. California State University at Fresno. Center of cotton, grapes, dried fruit and sweet wine industry; fresh and dried fruit packing and processing; vegetable oil mills; stock and poultry feed, plastics, olive oil, metal fabrication, machinery, vending machines manufactured.

1950 Agribusiness Fieldman
Western Agricultural Publishing Co., Inc.
4969 E. Clinton Way, No. 119 Phone: (559)252-7000
Fresno, CA 93727-1520 Fax: (559)252-7387

Magazine covering pest control and agricultural chemicals. **Subtitle:** The Newsmagazine for Western Agricultural Pest Control Advisors and Operators. **Founded:** 1971. **Freq:** 9/year. **Print Method:** Offset. **Trim Size:** 8 3/8 x 10 7/8. **Cols./Page:** 3. **Col. Width:** 2 1/8 inches. **Col. Depth:** 10 inches. **Key Personnel:** Marni Katz, Editor; Paul Baltimore, Publisher. **Subscription Rates:** $19.95 individuals. **Remarks:** Accepts advertising.
Ad Rates: BW: $1,416 **Circ:** Controlled ‡8,058
4C: $2,266
PCI: $82

1951 Agricultural Spray Adjuvants
Thomson Publications
PO Box 9335 Phone: (559)435-2163
Fresno, CA 93791 Fax: (559)435-8319

Trade magazine covering agricultural chemicals. **Founded:** 1990. **Key Personnel:** Susan Heflin, Office Mgr. **Subscription Rates:** $24.95 single issue. **Remarks:** Advertising not accepted.
Circ: (Not Reported)

1952 The Business Journal
1315 Van Ness, Ste. 200 Phone: (559)490-3400
Fresno, CA 93721 Fax: (559)490-3532

Journal covering business interests. **Founded:** 1886. **Freq:** Weekly. **Print Method:** Offset. **Cols./Page:** 7. **Col. Width:** 22 nonpareils. **Col. Depth:** 280 agate lines. **Key Personnel:** G.M. Webster, Jr., Publisher, phone (559)490-3421; Reo Carr, Editor, phone (559)490-3522, fax (559)490-3531, editor@thebusinessjournal.com; Betty Wildes, Business Mgr., phone (559)490-3424; Eric McCormick, Sales Mgr., phone (559)490-3423. **Subscription Rates:** $49 individuals. **Remarks:** Accepts advertising. **Formerly:** Fresno Daily Report; Fresno Business Journal.
Ad Rates: BW: $2,199 **Circ:** ‡8,000
4C: $2,649

1953 California Advocate
1715 E St., No. 108 Phone: (209)268-0941
PO Box 11826 Fax: (209)268-0943
Fresno, CA 93706
Black community newspaper. **Founded:** 1967. **Freq:** Weekly. **Cols./Page:** 6. **Col. Width:** 2 inches. **Col. Depth:** 21 inches. **Key Personnel:** Pauline Kimber, Editor; Lesly H. Kimber, Founder. **Remarks:** Accepts advertising.
Ad Rates: PCI: $16.10 **Circ:** 22,500

1954 California-Arizona Texas Cotton
Western Agricultural Publishing Co., Inc.
4969 E. Clinton Way, No. 119 Phone: (559)252-7000
Fresno, CA 93727-1520 Fax: (559)252-7387

Magazine covering the cotton industry in California, Arizona and Texas. **Founded:** 1965. **Freq:** 9/year. **Print Method:** Offset. **Cols./Page:** 3. **Col. Width:** 25 nonpareils. **Col. Depth:** 140 agate lines. **Key Personnel:** Marni Katz, Editor; Paul Baltimore, Publisher. **Subscription Rates:** $15 individuals. **Remarks:** Accepts advertising.
Ad Rates: BW: $2,628 **Circ:** ‡15,000
4C: $3,528

1955 The California Southern Baptist
California Southern Baptist Convention
678 E. Shaw Ave. Phone: (209)229-9533
Fresno, CA 93710-7704 Fax: (209)229-2824
Publication E-mail: 70420.53@compuserve.com

Southern Baptist magazine. **Founded:** 1941. **Freq:** Biweekly. **Print Method:** Offset. **Trim Size:** 8 1/4 x 10 1/2. **Cols./Page:** 3. **Col. Width:** 14 picas. **Col. Depth:** 57 picas. **Key Personnel:** Mark A. Wyatt, Editor. **ISSN:** 0008-1558. **Subscription Rates:** $9.50 individuals. **Remarks:** Advertising not accepted for alcoholic beverages.
Ad Rates: BW: $375.00 **Circ:** ‡11,000
4C: $450.00
PCI: $20

1956 The Central California Catholic Life
1550 N. Fresno Phone: (209)488-7414
Fresno, CA 93703-3788 Fax: (209)488-7435

Newspaper of the Catholic Diocese of Fresno, CA. **Founded:** 1929. **Freq:** 5/year. **Print Method:** Offset. **Cols./Page:** 5. **Col. Width:** 2 inches. **Col. Depth:** 17 inches. **Key Personnel:** Bishop John T. Steinbock, Publisher; William S. Lucido, Editor. **Subscription Rates:** Free. **Remarks:** Accepts advertising. **Formerly:** The Register.
Ad Rates: PCI: $6 **Circ:** Non-paid 20,000

1957 Citrograph
Western Agricultural Publishing Co., Inc.
4969 E. Clinton Way, No. 119 Phone: (559)252-7000
Fresno, CA 93727-1520 Fax: (559)252-7387

Citriculture magazine. **Founded:** 1915. **Freq:** Monthly. **Print Method:** Offset. **Trim Size:** 8 3/8 x 10 7/8. **Cols./Page:** 3. **Col. Width:** 2 1/8 inches. **Col. Depth:** 10 inches. **Key Personnel:** Marni Katz, Editor; Paul Baltimore, Publisher. **Subscription Rates:** $19.95 individuals. **Remarks:** Accepts advertising.
Ad Rates: BW: $1,955 **Circ:** Non-paid 7,658
4C: $2,905
PCI: $82

1958 The Daily Collegian
Associated Students, Inc.
MS 42
Keats Campus Bldg.
Fresno, CA 93740-0042
Publication E-mail: collegian@lennon.csufresno.edu

Collegiate newspaper. **Founded:** 1921. **Freq:** 5/wk (M-F). **Print Method:** Offset. **Cols./Page:** 5. **Col. Width:** 11 1/2 inches. **Col. Depth:** 17 1/2 inches. **Subscription Rates:** $1.50 individuals. **Remarks:** Color advertising not accepted. **URL:** http://www.csufresno.edu/collegian. **Formerly:** The Collegian.
Ad Rates: BW: $460 **Circ:** Free ‡3,500
PCI: $6.40

1959 The Fresno Bee
McClatchy Newspapers, Inc.
3425 N. 1st St., Ste. 201 Phone: (209)441-6111
Fresno, CA 93726-6819 Fax: (209)441-6436

General newspaper. **Founded:** 1922. **Freq:** Mon.-Sun. (morn.). **Print Method:** Flexograph. **Cols./Page:** 6. **Col. Width:** 26 nonpareils. **Col. Depth:** 301 agate lines. **Key Personnel:** Beverly Kees, Exec. Editor; Gary B. Pruitt, Publisher; Ray Steele, Jr., General Mgr.; Alan Truax, Advertising Dir. **Subscription Rates:** $120 individuals; $60 Sunday only. **Remarks:** Accepts advertising. **Online:** Dialog (The Dialog Corporation); DataTimes Corporation. **Feature Editors:** Tom Becker, *Entertainment*, phone (209)441-6281; Jim Boren, *Political*, phone (209)441-6307; Kathleen Burke, *News*, phone (209)441-6486; Wanda Coyle, *Rural Development*, phone (209)441-6272; Madeline Davidson, *Food*, phone (209)441-6297; Thom Halls, *Photo*, phone (209)441-6376; Guy Keeler, *Garden/Home*, phone (209)441-6383; Lanny Larson, *TV & Radio*, phone (209)441-6487; Gail Marshall, *Lifestyle, Society, Women's*, phone (209)441-6321; Sanford Nax, *Real Estate*, phone (209)441-6495; Sam Pollack, *Sports*, phone (209)441-6353; Ken Robison, *Music*, phone (209)441-6279; John Scalzi, *Movie*, phone (209)441-6352; Irwin Speizer, *Financial/Business*, phone (209)441-6329; John Taylor, *Religion*, phone (209)441-6375; Diane Webster, *Features*,

Travel, phone (209)441-6368; Gene Williams, *Metro*, phone (209)441-6446.
Ad Rates: GLR: $4.40 **Circ:** Mon.-Sat. ★**155,931**
BW: $7,391.70 Sun. ★**190,672**
4C: $8,433.70
SAU: $61.50

1960 Global Finance Journal
Elseiver
School of Business
California State Univ. Fresno
Fresno, CA 93740-0007
Publication E-mail: 102062.2525@compuserve.com
Publisher E-mail: fcentres@gpu.stv.ualberta.ca

Journal that presents issues relevant to the international financial scene. **Freq:** Semiannual. **Key Personnel:** Manuchehr Shahrokhi, Editor. **ISSN:** 1044-0283. **Subscription Rates:** $80 individuals; $180 institutions.

1961 Grape Grower Magazine
Western Agricultural Publishing Co., Inc.
4969 E. Clinton Way, No. 119 Phone: (559)252-7000
Fresno, CA 93727-1520 Fax: (559)252-7387

Magazine for grape growers. **Founded:** 1970. **Freq:** Monthly. **Print Method:** Offset. **Trim Size:** 8 1/2 x 11. **Cols./Page:** 3. **Col. Width:** 13 picas. **Key Personnel:** Marni Katz, Editor; Paul Baltimore, Publisher. **ISSN:** 1049-670X. **Subscription Rates:** $19.95. **Remarks:** Accepts advertising. **Formerly**: California and Western States Grape Grower.
Ad Rates: BW: $2,892 **Circ:** Non-paid 11,276
4C: $3,842

1962 Insight
California State University
2225 E. San Ramon Ave. Phone: (209)278-2892
Fresno, CA 93740-0010 Fax: (209)278-4495
Publication E-mail: insight@csufresno.lennon.edu

Collegiate newspaper, published by the Department of Journalism. **Founded:** 1969. **Freq:** Weekly (Wed.). **Print Method:** Offset. **Trim Size:** 13 x 21. **Cols./Page:** 6. **Col. Width:** 28 nonpareils. **Col. Depth:** 294 agate lines. **Remarks:** Color advertising accepted; rates available upon request. **URL:** http://www.csufresno.edu/insight.
Ad Rates: GLR: $.29 **Circ:** Free 5,000
SAU: $4.50

1963 Neighbors
3425 N. First, Ste. 201
Fresno, CA 93726-6819

Community newspaper. **Founded:** Mar. 1988. **Freq:** Weekly. **Key Personnel:** P. J. Lippert, Editor; Barbara Parnell, Advertising Mgr.; Anna Evans, Production Mgr. **Remarks:** Accepts advertising.
Ad Rates: BW: $175 **Circ:** (Not Reported)

1964 Nut Grower
Western Agricultural Publishing Co., Inc.
4969 E. Clinton Way, No. 119 Phone: (559)252-7000
Fresno, CA 93727-1520 Fax: (559)252-7387

Magazine on nut growing. **Subtitle:** The Magazine for Western Tree Nut Producers. **Founded:** 1982. **Freq:** Monthly. **Print Method:** Offset. **Trim Size:** 8 3/8 x 10 7/8. **Cols./Page:** 3. **Col. Width:** 2 1/8 inches. **Col. Depth:** 10 inches. **Key Personnel:** Marni Katz, Editor; Paul Baltimore, Publisher. **ISSN:** 0745-3469. **Subscription Rates:** $19.95 individuals. **Remarks:** Accepts advertising.
Ad Rates: BW: $2,448 **Circ:** 11,993
4C: $3,398
PCI: $82

1965 One to One
Cree Yadio Services
Box 9787 Phone: (559)448-0700
Fresno, CA 93794 Fax: (209)448-0761
Publication E-mail: 76711.1624@compuserve.com; 121@worldnet.att.net

Magazine offering humor, advice, and show prep material for radio personalities. **Subtitle:** The Journal of Creative Broadcasting. **Founded:** 1976. **Freq:** Weekly. **Print Method:** Offset. **Trim Size:** 7 x 8 1/2. **Subscription Rates:** $200 U.S.; $225 Canada; $235 other countries; $150 E-mail only. **Remarks:** Accepts advertising. **Online:** Cree Yadio Services. **Alt. Formats:** Diskette.
Circ: Paid 1,000

1966 One to One II
Cree Yadio Services
Box 9787 Phone: (559)448-0700
Fresno, CA 93794 Fax: (209)448-0761

Magazine containing humor, and show-prep materials for radio personalities. **Founded:** 1978. **Freq:** Monthly. **Print Method:** Offset. **Trim Size:** 8 1/2 x 14. **Key Personnel:** Jay Trachman, Publisher; Linda Richardson, Editor. **Subscription Rates:** $60. **Remarks:** Advertising accepted; rates available upon request.
Circ: Paid 300

1967 Pollstar
4697 W. Jacquelyn Ave. Phone: (559)271-7900
Fresno, CA 93722-6413 Fax: (559)271-7979
Publisher E-mail: info@pollstar.com

Trade magazine covering the international concert business. **Founded:** 1981. **Freq:** Weekly. **Print Method:** Offset. **Trim Size:** 8 1/2 x 11. **Key Personnel:** Jeff Stone, Circulation Mgr. **Subscription Rates:** $315 individuals. **Remarks:** Accepts advertising. **URL:** http://www.pollstar.com.
Ad Rates: BW: $1,299 **Circ:** (Not Reported)
4C: $1,998

1968 Tree Fruit
Western Agricultural Publishing Co., Inc.
4969 E. Clinton Way, No. 119 Phone: (559)252-7000
Fresno, CA 93727-1520 Fax: (559)252-7387

Magazine for people in the tree fruit industry. **Subtitle:** The Magazine for the Western Tree Fruit Industry. **Founded:** 1977. **Freq:** 8/year. **Print Method:** Offset. **Trim Size:** 8 3/8 x 10 7/8. **Key Personnel:** Marni Katz. **Subscription Rates:** $19.95. **Remarks:** Accepts advertising.
Ad Rates: BW: $1,676 **Circ:** Controlled ‡11,008
4C: $2,406

1969 Vegetable
Western Agricultural Publishing Co., Inc.
4969 E. Clinton Way, No. 119 Phone: (559)252-7000
Fresno, CA 93727-1520 Fax: (559)252-7387

Magazine for people in the vegetable industry. **Subtitle:** The Magazine for the Western Vegetable Industry. **Founded:** 1977. **Freq:** 6/year. **Trim Size:** 8 3/8 x 10 7/8. **Key Personnel:** Marni Katz. **Subscription Rates:** $19.95. **Remarks:** Accepts advertising.
Ad Rates: BW: $1,272 **Circ:** Controlled ‡8,371
4C: $2,002

1970 Western Journal of Communication
Western States Communication Association
California State University Phone: (209)278-2565
Fresno, CA 93740-8027 Fax: (209)278-6616
Publication E-mail: conniec@csufresno.edu

Journal on communication for academicians. **Founded:** 1936. **Freq:** Quarterly. **Key Personnel:** Leah Vande Berg, Editor, phone (602)965-4600. **ISSN:** 1057-0314. **Subscription Rates:** $40 libraries. **Remarks:** Advertising accepted; rates available upon request. **Formerly**: Western Journal of Speech Communications (1991).
Circ: 2,600

1971 KEZL-FM - 96.7
4991 E. McKinley, Ste. 124 Phone: (209)251-8614
Fresno, CA 93727-1966 Fax: (209)251-3347

Format: Jazz. **Networks:** Independent. **Owner:** Americom Broadcasting, at above address. **Formerly**: KTED-FM. **Operating Hours:** Continuous. **ADI:** Fresno-Visalia (Hanford), CA. **Key Personnel:** Scott Seidenstricker, VP/General Mgr.; Mike Vasquez, Program Dir. **Wattage:** 25,000. **Ad Rates:** Advertising accepted; rates available upon request.

1972 KFCF-FM - 88.1
PO Box 4364 Phone: (209)233-2221
Fresno, CA 93744 Fax: (209)233-5776

Format: Eclectic. **Networks:** Pacifica. **Owner:** Fresno Free College Foundation, PO Box 4364, Fresno, CA 93744. **Founded:** 1975. **Operating Hours:** Continuous; 85% network, 15% local. **ADI:** Fresno-Visalia (Hanford), CA. **Key Personnel:** Mark Hernandez, Programmer; Randy L. Stover, Chief Engineer; John Tourtillout, Programmer; Rych Withers, Senior Programmer; Kent Stratford, Programmer; Bruce Kennedy, Programmer; Dennis Thompson, Programmer. **Wattage:** 2400. **Ad Rates:** Noncommercial.

1973 KFIG-AM - 1430
336 W. Bedford, Ste. 109 Phone: (209)449-0374
PO Box 4265 Fax: (209)268-2850
Fresno, CA 93744-4265

Format: Hispanic. **Founded:** 1938. **Operating Hours:** Continuous. **ADI:** Fresno-Visalia (Hanford), CA. **Key Personnel:** Antonio Rabago, General Mgr., phone (209)449-0374, fax (209)449-0376; Diane Maze-Ostlund, Station Mgr.; Steve Randall, Operations Mgr. **Wattage:** 5000. **Ad Rates:** $38-45 for 60 seconds.

1974 KFRE-AM - 940
5087 E. McKinley Ave. Phone: (559)453-8879
Fresno, CA 93727-1965 Fax: (209)252-4522

Format: Talk. **Simulcasts:** AG Show. **Networks:** CBS. **Founded:** 1937. **Operating Hours:** 24Hrs. **ADI:** Fresno-Visalia (Hanford), CA. **Key Personnel:** John Carpenter, General Mgr.; Ed Monson, Operations Mgr. **Wattage:** 50,000. **Ad Rates:** Advertising accepted; rates available upon request. MADA. Combined advertising rates available with KMPH-FM. **URL:** http://www.kfre.com.

1975 KFSN-TV - 30
1777 G St. Phone: (209)442-1170
Fresno, CA 93706 Fax: (209)233-5844

Format: Commercial TV. **Networks:** ABC. **Operating Hours:** Continuous. **ADI:** Fresno-Visalia (Hanford), CA. **Key Personnel:** Valari Staab, General Mgr. **URL:** http://www.ABC30.com.

1976 KFSO-FM - 92.9
4991 E. McKinley, Ste. 124 Phone: (209)251-8614
Fresno, CA 93727 Fax: (209)251-3347

Format: Oldies. **Owner:** Americom Broadcasting, 6225 Sunset Blvd., Ste. 1900, Los Angeles, CA 90028. **Founded:** 1974. **Formerly**: KONG-FM (1982). **Operating Hours:** Continuous; 100% local. **ADI:** Fresno-Visalia (Hanford), CA. **Key Personnel:** Scott Seidenstricker, General Mgr.; Mike Bushey, Contact. **Wattage:** 50,000. **Ad Rates:** $45-110 per unit.

1977 KFSR-FM - 90.7
California State University Phone: (209)278-2598
Fresno Fax: (209)278-6985
5201 N. Maple Ave
Fresno, CA 93740

Format: Eclectic; Adult Album Alternative; Jazz; Blues; Hip Hop; Reggae; Soft Rock. **Networks:** Independent. **Owner:** California State University, Fresno, at above address. **Founded:** 1982. **Operating Hours:** Continuous. **ADI:** Fresno-Visalia (Hanford), CA. **Key Personnel:** Kelli Hughes, Program Dir., phone (209)278-6982; Cari Holder, Station Mgr., phone (209)278-2598; Steve Chase, Music Dir., phone (209)278-4500; Justin Girard, News Dir., phone (209)278-6981; John Tyler, Sports Dir., phone (209)278-6981; David Sundberg, Public Affairs Dir., phone (209)278-6981; Marcus Calderon, Promotions Dir., phone (209)278-6982; Greg Tchaparian, Traffic Dir., phone (209)278-6981. **Local Programs:** *Hip Hop*, Davon Salterwhile, (209)278-6981; *Jazz*, Steve Chase, (209)278-4500; *Progressive*, Mark Herring, (209)278-4500. **Wattage:** 2600. **Ad Rates:** $5-20 per unit.

1978 KFTV-TV - 21
3239 W. Ashlan Phone: (209)222-2121
Fresno, CA 93722 Fax: (209)222-0917
Free: (800)733KFTV

Format: Commercial TV. **Networks:** Univision. **Owner:** Univision Communications, Inc., 24 Meadowland Parkway, Secaucus, NJ 07094, (201)348-2841. **Founded:** 1972. **Operating Hours:** 24 hrs. **ADI:** Fresno-Visalia (Hanford), CA. **Key Personnel:** Maria L. Gutierrez, Contact. **Ad Rates:** Advertising accepted; rates available upon request.

1979 KHOT-AM - 1250
PO Box 112 Phone: (209)268-2625
Fresno, CA 93707 Fax: (209)268-2850

Format: Hispanic. **Owner:** KZFO Broadcasting, Inc., at above address. **Founded:** 1956. **Formerly**: KQMD-AM. **Operating Hours:** Continuous. **ADI:** Fresno-Visalia (Hanford), CA. **Key Personnel:** Edward C. Distel, VP/General Mgr.; Dora Del Toro, Business Mgr. **Wattage:** 500. **Ad Rates:** Advertising accepted; rates available upon request.

1980 KJEO-TV - 47
4880 N. 1st St. Phone: (209)222-2411
Fresno, CA 93726 Fax: (209)221-6938

Format: Commercial TV. **Networks:** CBS. **Founded:** 1953. **Operating Hours:** Continuous; 68% network, 32% local. **ADI:** Fresno-Visalia (Hanford), CA. **Key Personnel:** Don Drilling, Vice Pres./General Mgr.; Jeralynn Stout, General Sales Mgr.; Patti Houlihan, Program Dir.; Marc Cotta, News Dir.; Lucy Ruiz, Contact; Jeff Aiello, Promotions Dir.; George Takata, Sports Dir.; Gary Temple, Chief Engineer; Lisa Sims, Traffic Mgr.; Andrew Mastoras, Business Mgr. **Local Programs:** *47 On Your Side* 5:30-8 a.m., Noon, 5, 6 & 11pm.

1981 KJFX-FM - 95.7
1981 N Gateway Blvd., No. 101 Phone: (209)255-8383
Fresno, CA 93727-1605 Fax: (209)453-1313

Format: Classic Rock. **Networks:** Independent. **Founded:** 1970. **Formerly**: KYNO-FM. **Operating Hours:** Continuous. **ADI:** Fresno-Visalia (Hanford), CA. **Key Personnel:** Diana Smart, Program Mgr.; Mary Lou Gunn, General Mgr. **Wattage:** 50,000.

1982 KKTR-AM - 1340
2020 E. McKinley Ave.
Fresno, CA 93703

Format: Talk. **Networks:** Mutual Broadcasting System; CBS; Westwood One Radio; Major Market Radio; USA Radio. **Formerly**: KMAK-AM (1991); KBOS-AM (1993); KKAM-AM. **Operating Hours:** Continuous. **ADI:** Fresno-Visalia (Hanford), CA. **Key Personnel:** Steve Miller, General Mgr.; Rick Hampton, Program Dir., fax (209)266-5267; Charlie Scott; Robert Emler, Sports Dir. **Wattage:** 1000. **Ad Rates:** $25-75 per unit.

1983 KMJ-AM - 580
PO Box 9420 Phone: (209)266-5800
Fresno, CA 93792-9420 Fax: (209)226-3714

Format: Talk; News. **Networks:** NBC. **Owner:** Henry Broadcasting Co., 2277 Jerrold Ave., San Francisco, CA 94124, (415)285-3703. **Founded:** 1925. **Operating Hours:** Continuous; 50% network, 50% local. **ADI:** Fresno-Visalia (Hanford), CA. **Key Personnel:** Al Smith, General Mgr.; Chris Pacheco, Sales Mgr.; Jan Sansom, Office Mgr. **Wattage:** 50,000. **Ad Rates:** Advertising accepted; rates available upon request.

1984 KMPH-FM - 107.5
5089 E. McKinley Ave. Phone: (209)255-5600
Fresno, CA 93727 Fax: (209)255-1060

Format: News. **Networks:** CBS. **Formerly**: KCLQ-FM (1990); KCML-FM. **Operating Hours:** Continuous. **ADI:** Fresno-Visalia (Hanford), CA. **Key Personnel:** John F. Carpenter, Exec. VP/General Mgr. **Wattage:** 50,000. **Ad Rates:** Advertising accepted; rates available upon request.

1985 KMPH-TV - 26
5111 E. McKinley Phone: (209)733-2600
Fresno, CA 93727 Fax: (209)255-0275

Format: Commercial TV. **Networks:** Fox. **Owner:** Harry Pappas, 500 S. Chinowth, Visalia, CA 93277, (209)255-2600. **Founded:** 1971. **Operating Hours:** Continuous. **ADI:** Fresno-Visalia (Hanford), CA. **Key Personnel:** John F. Carpenter, General Mgr.

1986 KMSG-TV - 59
706 W. Herndon Ave. Phone: (209)435-5900
Fresno, CA 93650 Fax: (209)435-1448
Free: (800)698-8859
E-mail: t59@spynet.com

Format: Commercial TV. **Networks:** Telemundo. **Founded:** 1985. **Operating Hours:** Continuous; 85% network, 15% local. **ADI:** Fresno-Visalia (Hanford), CA. **Key Personnel:** Lisa Nilmeir, Station Mgr.; Fran Hernandez, Traffic Mgr.; Gilbert Mosqueda, Contact; Jess Gonzalez, Production Dir.; Diane Dostinich, CEO; Marcella Salazar, Local Sales Mgr. **Local Programs:** *59 Mente*, Juan Carlos Zapata. **Ad Rates:** $30-300 per unit.

1987 KNAX-FM - 97.9
999 N. Van Ness Ave. Phone: (209)441-7600
Fresno, CA 93728-3427 Fax: (209)441-7606

Format: Country; Hot Country. **Networks:** ABC. **Founded:** 1941. **Operating Hours:** Continuous. **ADI:** Fresno-Visalia (Hanford), CA. **Key Personnel:** Al Smith, Mktg. Mgr; Jeff Negrete, General Sales Mgr.; Larry Santiago, Program Dir. **Local Programs:** *Linell's Lunch Bag*; *Moose & Michaels*. **Wattage:** 48,000. **Ad Rates:** Advertising accepted; rates available upon request. Advertising accepted; contact publisher for rates. Combined advertising rates available with KFRE-AM.

1988 KNXT-TV - 49
1550 N. Fresno St. Phone: (209)488-7440
Fresno, CA 93703 Fax: (209)488-7444
E-mail: knxt@pacbell.net

Format: Public TV. **Networks:** Eternal Word TV. **Owner:** Education Corp.-Diocese of Fresno, at above address. **Founded:** 1986. **Operating Hours:** 24 hrs. Daily; 60% network, 40% local. **ADI:** Fresno-Visalia (Hanford), CA. **Key Personnel:** Marvin G. Harrison, General Mgr. **Local Programs:** *Adventurers' Travel Club*, Betty Gerardin. **Wattage:** 2,300,000. **Ad Rates:** Noncommercial.

1989 KOQO-AM - 790
PO Box 9420 Phone: (209)298-7102
Fresno, CA 93792-9420 Fax: (209)298-7812

Format: Hispanic. **Networks:** CBS. **Founded:** 1977. **Operating Hours:** Continuous. **Key Personnel:** Ed Prince, President. **Wattage:** 5000.

1990 KOQO-FM - 101.9
PO Box 9420 Phone: (209)454-7713
Fresno, CA 93792-9420 Fax: (209)454-7721

Format: Hispanic. **Founded:** 1972. **Formerly**: KQPW-FM (1992). **Operating Hours:** Continuous. **ADI:** Fresno-Visalia (Hanford), CA. **Key Personnel:** Ed Prince, President. **Wattage:** 50,000 ERP.

1991 KQEQ-AM - 1210
139 W. Olive Ave. Phone: (209)233-8803
Fresno, CA 93728 Fax: (209)233-8871

Format: Urban Contemporary; Oldies. **Owner:** RAK Communications, Inc., at above address. **Founded:** Mar. 1997. **Formerly**: KRGO (1994). **Operating Hours:** Continuous. **ADI:** Fresno-Visalia (Hanford), CA. **Key Personnel:** Al Perez, General Mgr.; Nancy Talamantes, Business Mgr. **Local Programs:** *Sunday Shout Outs* 6:00 pm - 12:00 am Sunday, Al Perez, (209)2338803. **Wattage:** 375. **Ad Rates:** $15-18 for 30 seconds; $20-25 for 60 seconds. Combined advertising rates available with KXEX.

1992 KSEE-TV - 24
5035 E. McKinley Phone: (209)454-2424
Fresno, CA 93727 Fax: (209)454-2485

Format: Commercial TV. **Networks:** NBC. **Owner:** Granite Broadcasting Corp., 767 3rd Ave., 34th Fl., New York, NY 10017, (212)826-2530, Fax: (212)826-2858. **Founded:** 1953. **Formerly**: KMJ-TV (1980). **Operating Hours:** Continuous.; 75% network, 25% local. **ADI:** Fresno-Visalia (Hanford), CA. **Key Personnel:** John Deushane, General Mgr.; Mark Benscheidt, General Sales Mgr.; Chris Long, News Dir.; Kurt Karlsson, Business Mgr.; George Hillis, Program Mgr.; Shirley Neu Kom, Natl. Sales Mgr.; Ray O'Canto, Local Sales Manager. **Local Programs:** *KSEE 24 Hour News* 5, 6, & 11 p.m. Daily, Eric Hulnick.

1993 KSKS-FM - 93.7
PO Box 9420 Phone: (209)266-5800
Fresno, CA 93792-9420 Fax: (209)266-3714

Format: Country. **Owner:** Henry Broadcasting Co., 2277 Jerrold Ave., San Francisco, CA 94124, (415)285-1133. **Founded:** 1946. **Formerly**: KFYE-FM. **Operating Hours:** Continuous; 100% local. **ADI:** Fresno-Visalia (Hanford), CA. **Key Personnel:** Dave Taylor, Program Dir.; Al Smith, General Mgr.; Karen Franz, Regional Sales Mgr.; Jan Sansom, Office Mgr. **Wattage:** 68,000.

1994 KVPT-TV - 18
1544 Van Ness Ave. Phone: (209)266-1800
Fresno, CA 93721 Fax: (209)650-1880
E-mail: kvpt@cybergate.com

Format: Public TV. **Networks:** Public Broadcasting Service (PBS). **Owner:** Valley Public Television, Inc., at above address. **Founded:** 1977. **Formerly**: KMTF-TV (1990). **Operating Hours:** 5:45 a.m.-midnight. **ADI:** Fresno-Visalia (Hanford), CA. **Key Personnel:** Colin Dougherty, General Mgr./Program Dir. **Local Programs:** *Consumer Line*; *Practical Gardener*. **Ad Rates:** Noncommercial. Combined advertising rates available with KVIE, KIXE. **URL:** http://www.kvpt.org.

1995 KXEX-AM - 1550
139 W. Olive Ave. Phone: (209)233-8803
Fresno, CA 93728 Fax: (209)233-8871

Owner: RAK Communications Inc., at above address. **Founded:** 1962. **Operating Hours:** Continuous. **ADI:** Fresno-Visalia (Hanford), CA. **Key Personnel:** Al Perez, General Mgr.; Nancy Talamantes, Operations Mgr. **Wattage:** 5000 day; 2500 night. **Ad Rates:** $12-15 for 30 seconds; $18-20 for 60 seconds. Combined advertising rates available with KQEQ-AM, KZFO-FM.

1996 KYNO-AM - 1300
1981 N Gateway Blvd., No. 101 Phone: (209)255-8383
Fresno, CA 93727-1605 Fax: (209)453-1313

Format: Talk; Sports. **Founded:** 1947. **Operating Hours:** Continuous;. **ADI:** Fresno-Visalia (Hanford), CA. **Key Personnel:** Dave Case, Contact; Mary Lou Gunn, General Mgr. **Wattage:** 5000. **Ad Rates:** $15-35 per unit.

1997 MediaOne
1945 N. Helm Ave. Phone: (209)253-4050
Fresno, CA 93727 Fax: (209)253-4090

Founded: 1977. **Formerly**: Continental Cablevision. **Key Personnel:** Bob Hargrove, General Mgr.; Marty Murphy, Public Relations Dir.; Randy Reed, Program Mgr. **Cities Served:** Clovis, Madera, CA; Fresno & Madera counties, CA: subscribing households 106,000; 62 channels; 1 community access channel; 20 hours per week community access programming.

FULLERTON, pop. 102,034.

S. CA. Orange Co. 25 mi. SE of Los Angeles. Manufactures canned fruit juices, vegetables, preserves; musical instruments, aircraft parts, missile electronics, fabricated metal, transportation equipment, textiles. Citrus fruits, walnuts packed. Oil wells. Fruit, truck farms. Oranges, lemons.

1998 Closeout News Magazine
Closeout News, Inc.
331 S. State College Blvd. Phone: (714)870-0313
Fullerton, CA 92831 Fax: (714)870-1552
Free: (800)600-7040
Publication E-mail: pilot616@aol.com

Tabloid focusing on surplus and closeout merchandise. **Subtitle:** Voice of the Closeout/Surplus Industry. **Founded:** 1988. **Freq:** Monthly. **Print Method:** Offset. **Trim Size:** 8 3/4 x 12 3/4. **Cols./Page:** 4. **Col. Width:** 2 1/2 inches. **Col. Depth:** 15 1/4 inches. **Key Personnel:** Benadette Archuleta, General Mgr.; Chirstel Chang, Operations Supervisor. **Subscription Rates:** $45 per year/bulk; $55 per year/1st class; $65 per year priority mail. **Remarks:** Accepts advertising. **URL:** http://www.closeoutnews.com.
Ad Rates: 4C: $1,870 **Circ:** Paid ‡84,000
PCI: $75 Controlled ‡14,650

1999 Daily Titan
California State University, Fullerton
213 Humanities Phone: (714)773-2128
Fullerton, CA 92634 Fax: (714)773-2702

Collegiate newspaper. **Founded:** 1961. **Freq:** Tues.-Fri. (during the academic year). **Print Method:** Offset. **Cols./Page:** 6. **Col. Width:** 21 nonpareils. **Col. Depth:** 294 agate lines. **Key Personnel:** Jack McIntyre, Exec. Editor, phone (714)278-5813; Joe Chirco, Business Mgr., phone (714)278-4275, joe_chirco@hotmail.com. **Subscription Rates:** $60 individuals. **Remarks:** Accepts advertising. **URL:** http://www.dailytitan.org.
Ad Rates: GLR: $1.10 **Circ:** Free ‡6,000
BW: $945
4C: $1,395
SAU: $7.50

2000 Theosophical History
California State University, Fullerton
PO Box 6868 Phone: (714)278-3727
Fullerton, CA 92834-6868 Fax: (714)693-0142
Publisher E-mail: jsantucci@fullerton.edu

Scholarly journal covering history of the modern theosophical movement. **Subtitle:** A Quarterly Journal of Research. **Founded:** Jan. 1985. **Freq:** Quarterly. **Print Method:** Offset printing. **Trim Size:** 7 x 8. **Cols./Page:** 2. **Key Personnel:** James Santucci, Editor, jsantucci@fullerton.edu. **ISSN:** 0951-497X. **Subscription Rates:** $6 single issue. **Remarks:** Advertising not accepted.
Circ: Combined 205

2001 Comcast Cablevision
1501 W. Commonwealth Ave. Phone: (714)680-4070
Fullerton, CA 92633 Fax: (714)879-3232

Founded: 1981. **Cities Served:** Orange County, Buena Park, and Placentia, CA.

2002 KBPK-FM - 90.1
321 E. Chapman Ave. Phone: (714)992-7419
Fullerton, CA 92832

Format: Adult Contemporary. **Owner:** Buena Park School District, 6885 Orangethorpe, Buena Park, CA 90620. **Founded:** 1970. **Operating Hours:** 5:00 a.m.-12:00 a.m. **ADI:** Los Angeles (Corona & San Bernardino), CA. **Key Personnel:** Jim Bain, General Mgr.; Ed Berger, News Dir.; Ed Ford, Operations Supervisor, phone (714)992-8203; Randy Routier, Sports Dir. **Local Programs:** *Fullerton College Today*, Ed Berger. **Wattage:** 20. **Ad Rates:** Noncommercial.

2003 KFCR-FM - 93.5
321 E. Chapman Ave. Phone: (714)992-7264
Fullerton, CA 92632

Format: Alternative/New Music/Progressive. **Key Personnel:** Jeff Ryder, Music Dir. **Ad Rates:** Noncommercial.

GALT, pop. 5,514.

NC CA. Sacramento Co. 26 mi. S. of Sacramento. Condensed milk factory. Winery. Seed mill. Dairying. Stock, poultry farms. Grain. Ladino clover.

2004 Elk Grove Citizen
Herburger Publications, Inc.
PO Box 307 Phone: (916)685-5533
Galt, CA 95632 Fax: (209)745-4492

Community newspaper. **Founded:** 1903. **Freq:** Semiweekly (Wed. and Fri.). **Print Method:** Offset. **Trim Size:** 14 x 22 1/2. **Cols./Page:** 6. **Col. Width:** 24 nonpareils. **Col. Depth:** 294 agate lines. **Key Personnel:** Keith Gebers, Editor, phone (916)685-3945, fax (916)676-6675; Dave Herburger, Publish-

er, phone (209)745-1551, dherburger@softcom.net; Dean Davy, Advertising Mgr., phone (209)745-1551, ddavy@softcom.net. **Subscription Rates:** $25.86 individuals; $36.64 out of area. **Remarks:** Accepts advertising.
Ad Rates: 4C: $250 SAU: $8 PCI: $9 **Circ:** Wed. ❑16,480 Fri. ❑7,346

2005 The Galt Herald
Herburger Publications, Inc.
604 N. Lincoln Way Phone: (209)745-1551
PO Box 307 Fax: (209)745-4492
Galt, CA 95632
Community newspaper. **Founded:** 1903. **Freq:** Weekly (Thurs.). **Print Method:** Offset. **Trim Size:** 14 x 22 1/2. **Cols./Page:** 6. **Col. Width:** 12 picas. **Col. Depth:** 21 inches. **Key Personnel:** Mary Drayton, Editor; Roy E. Herburger, Publisher; Dean Davy, Advertising Mgr. **Subscription Rates:** $15 individuals; $29 out of area. **Remarks:** Accepts advertising.
Ad Rates: GLR: $.65 BW: $756 4C: $1,000 SAU: $9.00 **Circ:** Paid ❑4,244 Free ❑5,550

GARDEN GROVE, pop. 123,351.

S. CA. Orange Co. 4 mi. E. of Long Beach. Residential. Citrus fruit, beans packed. Chili and rubber products manufactured. Agriculture. Oranges, walnuts, chili peppers, beans.

2006 Apartment News
Orange County Multi-Housing Service Corp.
12822 Garden Grove Bldvd, No. D Phone: (714)638-8743
Fax: (714)638-9457
Garden Grove, CA 92643
Magazine for apartment managers, owners, and builders. **Founded:** 1961. **Freq:** Monthly. **Print Method:** Offset. **Trim Size:** 8 1/2 x 11. **Cols./Page:** 3. **Col. Width:** 28 nonpareils. **Col. Depth:** 140 agate lines. **Key Personnel:** Erica C. Pierce, Editor, phone (714)638-8743, fax (714)741-9457. **Subscription Rates:** $36 individuals. **Remarks:** Accepts advertising.
Ad Rates: BW: $750 **Circ:** ‡3700

2007 Orange County News
Orange County Publishing
9872 Chapman, Ste. 108 Phone: (714)530-7622
Garden Grove, CA 92841 Fax: (714)530-7142

Community newspaper. **Founded:** 1909. **Freq:** Semiweekly (Wed. and Fri.). **Print Method:** Offset. **Trim Size:** 13 x 21 1/2. **Cols./Page:** 6. **Col. Width:** 2 1/16 inches. **Col. Depth:** 21 1/2 inches. **Key Personnel:** Dave Rogue, Editor; Elberta Kolber, Publisher; Dane Roque, Publisher. **Subscription Rates:** $30 individuals. **Remarks:** Accepts advertising.
Ad Rates: SAU: $11 PCI: $9.38 **Circ:** Paid ‡10,000 Free ‡20,000

2008 Time Warner Communications
7441 Chapman Ave. Phone: (714)895-6886
Garden Grove, CA 92641 Fax: (714)898-1524

Owner: Time Warner, Inc., at above address, Fax: (714)373-1416. **Founded:** 1983. **Formerly:** Paragon Cable; Rogers Cable. **Key Personnel:** Robert V. Moel, General Mgr.; Mike McDonald, VP, Technical Operations; Richard Cozzi, VP, Marketing; Kathy Carr, VP, Customer Operations. **Cities Served:** Fountain Valley, Garden Grove, Huntington Beach, Los Alamitos, Orange, Rossmoor, Stanton, Westminster, CA: subscribing households 130,000; 78 channels; 4 community access channels; 672 hours per week community access programming.

GARDENA, pop. 45,165.

S. CA. Los Angeles Co. 15 mi. S. of Los Angeles. Plastics, trailers, fishing tackle, poultrymen's equipment, drugs, feed, furniture, bricks, soap, glass, aircraft parts, chemicals, oil tools, electronics.

2009 Daily Racing Form (West Coast Edition)
PO Box 47012 Phone: (213)387-5131
Gardena, CA 90247 Fax: (213)480-0472

Regional racing form newspaper. **Founded:** 1894. **Freq:** Mon.-Sun. (morn.). **Print Method:** Offset. **Trim Size:** 9 11/16 x 15. **Cols./Page:** 4. **Col. Depth:** 14 3/4 inches. **Key Personnel:** Wayne Monroe, Editor; Jack L. Farnsworth, Publisher; William Dow, Advertising Mgr. **Subscription Rates:** $84.19 per month. **Remarks:** Accepts advertising. **Formerly:** Daily Racing Form (Pacific Edition) (1992).
Ad Rates: PCI: $12.33 **Circ:** Mon. 21,928 Tues. 3,829 Sat. 35,644 Sun. 32,319

2010 Gardena Valley News
16417 S. Western Ave. Phone: (310)329-6351
PO Box 219 Fax: (310)329-7501
Gardena, CA 90247
Community newspaper. **Founded:** Dec. 8, 1904. **Freq:** Weekly (Thurs.). **Print Method:** Offset. **Trim Size:** 14 x 22 3/4. **Cols./Page:** 6. **Col. Width:** 26 nonpareils. **Col. Depth:** 294 agate lines. **Key Personnel:** Gary Kohatsu, Editor; George D. Algie, Publisher; Dan Gagajena, Advertising Mgr. **Subscription Rates:** $12 individuals. **Remarks:** Accepts advertising.
Ad Rates: GLR: $7.30 BW: $705.60 4C: $1,105.60 PCI: $6 **Circ:** Paid ‡5,700

2011 Latin Beat Magazine
15900 Crenshaw Blvd., Ste. 1-223 Phone: (310)516-6767
Fax: (310)516-9916
Gardena, CA 90249
Consumer magazine covering Latin and world music. **Subtitle:** Latin Beat. **Founded:** Jan. 1991. **Freq:** 10/year. **Trim Size:** 8 1/2 x 11. **Cols./Page:** 2. **Key Personnel:** Rudolph Mangual, Contact; Ivette Mangual, Contact. **Subscription Rates:** $25 individuals; $2.50 single issue. **Remarks:** Accepts advertising.
Ad Rates: BW: $900 4C: $1,500 **Circ:** Combined 50,000

2012 Right of Way
International Right of Way Association
13650 S. Gramercy Pl. Phone: (310)538-0233
Gardena, CA 90249 Fax: (310)538-1471
Publication E-mail: peterhark@aol.com

Trade magazine offering technical articles on right of way management and acquisition, real estate appraisal, and property management. **Founded:** 1954. **Freq:** Bimonthly. **Print Method:** Offset. **Trim Size:** 8 1/2 x 11. **Cols./Page:** 3. **Col. Width:** 28 nonpareils. **Col. Depth:** 133 agate lines. **Key Personnel:** Ken Rose, Editor. **ISSN:** 0035-5275. **Subscription Rates:** $20 individuals. **Remarks:** Accepts advertising.
Ad Rates: BW: $1,000 **Circ:** ‡9,000

GEORGETOWN, pop. 900.

EC CA. El Dorado Co. 40 mi. NE of Sacramento. Tourism. Forestry. Vineyards. Agriculture.

El Dorado Gazette/Georgetown Gazette and Town Crier - See El Dorado

GILROY, pop. 21,641.

W. CA. Santa Clara Co. 29 mi. S. of San Jose. Fruit drying, fruit and vegetable canning; wineries, nurseries. Agriculture.

2013 The Dispatch
6400 Monterey Rd. Phone: (408)842-6400
PO Box 22365 Fax: (408)842-6411
Gilroy, CA 95020-6628
Local newspaper. **Founded:** 1868. **Freq:** Daily (morn.). **Print Method:** Offset. **Trim Size:** 22 1/2 x 13 1/2. **Cols./Page:** 6. **Col. Width:** 26 nonpareils. **Col. Depth:** 301 agate lines. **Key Personnel:** Mark Derry, Editor; Paula Mabry, Publisher; Arlene Hudson, Advertising Dir. **Subscription Rates:** $64.76 individuals. **Remarks:** Accepts advertising.
Ad Rates: GLR: $1.27 BW: $1,238.47 PCI: $9.60 **Circ:** Mon.-Fri. 5,786

2014 Falcon Cable Systems Co.
7630 Eigleberry St. Phone: (408)842-5653
Gilroy, CA 95020

Key Personnel: Bruce Williams, General Mgr.; Filomena Fagundes, Contact; William Kuhne, Contact. **Cities Served:** subscribing households 30,800; 35 channels.

GLENDALE, pop. 139,060.

S. CA. Los Angeles Co. 7 mi. N. of Los Angeles. Manufactures airplanes, aircraft engines, parachutes, lubricating oils, cameras, glass, clay and plastic products, pharmaceuticals, display signs, cleaning compounds, beverages, optical instruments. Dairying.

2015 Administrative Radiology Journal
Glendale Publishing Corp.
934 W. Glenoaks Blvd., Apt. 1 Phone: (818)500-1872
Glendale, CA 91202-2755
Publication E-mail: ar@primenet.com

Monthly Journal of Imaging Administration for Chief Imaging M.D.'s, Imaging Department Managers, Radiation Oncology Directors, and Healthcare Administrators. **Subtitle:** The Journal of Medical Imaging Business, Management & Administration. **Founded:** Aug. 1982. **Freq:** Monthly. **Print Method:** Offset. **Trim Size:** 8 3/8 x 10 7/8. **Cols./Page:** 3. **Col. Width:** 27 nonpareils. **Col. Depth:** 126 agate lines. **Key Personnel:** Rod Durant, Publisher; Adrienne Carey, Managing Editor; Cynthia Stout, Ph.D., Editor-in-Chief; Jasen Morris, Associate, Business Operations. **ISSN:** 0738-6974. **Subscription Rates:** $96 individuals; $126 Canada and Mexico; $196 other countries; $10 single issue. **Remarks:** Accepts advertising. **Available Online.**
Ad Rates: BW: $2,745 4C: $3,695 **Circ:** Paid 12,500

2016 Advance for Administrators in Radiation & Radiation Oncology
Chapman Publication Services
330 Arden Ave., Ste. 210 Phone: (818)241-6866
Glendale, CA 91203 Fax: (818)241-6356

Professional medical magazine for the radiation industry. **Founded:** Dec. 1991. **Freq:** Monthly. **Print Method:** Web offset. **Trim Size:** 8 x 11. **Cols./Page:** 2. **Col. Width:** 2 3/16 inches. **Col. Depth:** 9 inches. **Key Personnel:** Theresa Seltzer, Editor; Judy Thwaites, Advertising Mgr.; Marianne Brinton-Pettit, Circulation Mgr. **ISSN:** 1096-6285. **Subscription Rates:** Free to qualified subscribers. **Remarks:** Accepts advertising.
Ad Rates: BW: $2,427 4C: $3,227 **Circ:** Controlled ‡21,987

2017 California Courier
PO Box 5390 Phone: (818)409-0949
Glendale, CA 91221
Publication E-mail: ccourier@compuserve.com

English language ethnic newspaper covering news and commentary for Armenian-Americans. **Founded:** 1958. **Freq:** Weekly (Thurs.). **Print Method:** Offset. **Trim Size:** 10 x 14. **Cols./Page:** 5. **Col. Width:** 1 7/8 inches. **Col. Depth:** 14 inches. **Key Personnel:** Harut Sassounian, Publisher; Serge L. Samoniantz, Editor. **ISSN:** 0008-0950. **Subscription Rates:** $49 individuals. **Remarks:** Accepts advertising.
Ad Rates: BW: $435 PCI: $8.10 **Circ:** Paid ‡2,800 Free ‡200

2018 Cumulative Index to Nursing & Allied Health Literature (Print Index)
Cinahl Information Systems
1509 Wilson Terr. Phone: (818)409-8005
PO Box 871 Fax: (818)546-5679
Glendale, CA 91209-0871
Free: (800)959-7167
Publication E-mail: cinahl@cinahl.com

Index to nursing and allied health literature. **Subtitle:** The CINAHL Database. **Freq:** Bimonthly. **Print Method:** Offset. **Cols./Page:** 3. **Col. Width:** 27 nonpareils. **Col. Depth:** 130 agate lines. **Key Personnel:** Sarah Marcarian, Editor; June Levy, Managing Dir. **ISSN:** 0146-5554. **Subscription Rates:** $335 individuals. **Remarks:** Advertising accepted; rates available upon request. **Online:** DataStar (The Dialog Corporation); Ovid Technologies, Inc.; OCLC; PaperChase. **URL:** http://www.cinahl.com. **Alt. Formats:** CD-ROM.
Circ: ‡5,200

2019 El Vaquero
Glendale College
1500 N. Verdugo Phone: (818)240-1000
Glendale, CA 91208 Fax: (818)549-9436

Collegiate newspaper. **Founded:** 1927. **Freq:** Weekly (Fri.). **Print Method:** Offset. **Cols./Page:** 5. **Col. Width:** 22 nonpareils. **Col. Depth:** 217 agate lines. **Key Personnel:** Mike Eberts, Advisor. **Remarks:** Accepts advertising.
Ad Rates: PCI: $5.35 **Circ:** Free ‡3,500

2020 Foothill Leader
Glendale News Press
425 West Broadway, Ste. 300 Phone: (818)241-4141
Glendale, CA 91204-1269 Fax: (818)243-5944
Publisher E-mail: gnp@earthlink.net

Community newspaper. **Freq:** Semiweekly (Wed. and Sat.). **Print Method:** Offset. **Key Personnel:** James E. Gressinger, Publisher. **Subscription Rates:** $48.
Circ: Wed. ❑26,284 Sat. ❑31,066

2021 Glendale News Press
425 West Broadway, Ste. 300 Phone: (818)241-4141
Glendale, CA 91204-1269 Fax: (818)243-5944
Publisher E-mail: gnp@earthlink.net

General newspaper. **Founded:** 1905. **Freq:** Mon.-Sat. (morn.). **Print Method:** Offset. **Cols./Page:** 6. **Col. Width:** 12.25 picas. **Col. Depth:** 301 agate lines. **Key Personnel:** Richard Arthur, Senior Managing Editor, phone (818)637-3243, fax (818)241-1975, gnp@earthlink.net; Judee Kendall, Publisher, phone (818)241-4141, fax (818)548-8897; Steve De Sanctd, Special Sections Editor, phone (818)637-3263, fax

(818)243-5944. **Subscription Rates:** $48 individuals. **Remarks:** Accepts advertising.
Ad Rates: GLR: $.82 **Circ:** Mon.-Fri. ❑**9,071**
BW: $1,935 Wed. ❑**20,777**
4C: $2,175 Sat. ❑**24,092**
SAU: $15

2022 KaMai Forum
1108 Vincent Way Phone: (818)956-0551
Glendale, CA 91205 Fax: (818)956-5322
Publisher E-mail: kamaiforum@aol.com

Community newspaper. **Founded:** 1931. **Freq:** 2/mo. (Thursday). **Print Method:** Offset. **Cols./Page:** 5. **Col. Width:** 1 7/8 inches. **Col. Depth:** 15 1/4 inches. **Key Personnel:** Jitsuo Kikunaga, Editor; Hiro E. Hishiki, Editor and Publisher; June Maruya, Advertising Mgr. **ISSN:** 1066-9353. **Subscription Rates:** $22 individuals; $23. **Remarks:** Accepts advertising. **Formerly:** Kashu Mainichi (California Daily News) (1992).
Ad Rates: BW: $1050 **Circ:** ‡12,000
4C: $1550
PCI: $15

2023 Print-Equip News
P-EN Publications, Inc.
POB 5540
Glendale, CA 91221
Publication E-mail: printequip@aol.com

Graphic arts magazine. **Founded:** 1964. **Freq:** Monthly. **Print Method:** Web offset. **Trim Size:** 11 3/8 x 14 7/8. **Cols./Page:** 5. **Col. Width:** 23 nonpareils. **Col. Depth:** 194 agate lines. **Key Personnel:** Richard E. Jutras, Publisher. **USPS:** 995-200. **Subscription Rates:** $24 individuals; $72 other countries. **Remarks:** Accepts advertising.
Ad Rates: BW: $1,775 **Circ:** Controlled 25,258
4C: $2,375

2024 Western Energy
Chapman Publication Services
330 Arden Ave., Ste. 210 Phone: (818)241-6866
Glendale, CA 91203 Fax: (818)241-6356

Magazine covering oil, gas, power, and other energy-related industries. **Founded:** 1991. **Freq:** Quarterly. **Print Method:** Offset. **Trim Size:** 8 1/2 x 11. **Cols./Page:** 3. **Col. Width:** 2 1/8 inches. **Col. Depth:** 10 inches. **Key Personnel:** Robin Kellogg, Editor; Jack Hildreth, Sales Mgr. **ISSN:** 1062-4147. **Remarks:** Accepts advertising.
Ad Rates: BW: $700 **Circ:** Controlled ‡5,276
4C: $1,400

2025 KIEV-AM - 870
5900 San Fernando Rd. Phone: (213)245-2388
Glendale, CA 91202-2797

Format: News; Sports. **Networks:** UPI. **Owner:** Southern California Broadcasting Co. Inc., at above address. **Founded:** 1928. **Operating Hours:** Continuous. **ADI:** Los Angeles (Corona & San Bernardino), CA. **Key Personnel:** Fred S. Beaton, Sales Mgr., fax (818)244-0578; Ronald W. Beaton, Sales Mgr., fax (818)244-0578; George Putnam, News Dir.; Dick Sinclair, Program Dir.; Hal Williams, Chief Engineer. **Local Programs:** *Chef Piero Food and Wine Show*, Lynda Pina, (213)245-2388, Fax (213)245-2388; *Ray Briem Show*, Lynda Pina, (213)245-2388, Fax (213)245-2388; *Talk Back with George Putnam*, Lynda Pina, (213)245-2388, Fax (213)245-5438. **Wattage:** 20,000 day; 3000 night. **Ad Rates:** $38-175 for 30 seconds; $45-225 for 60 seconds.

2026 KKLA-FM - 99.5
701 North Brand Blvd., No. 550 Phone: (818)956-5552
Glendale, CA 91203 Fax: (818)551-1110
Free: (800)499-5552
E-mail: kkla@kkla.com

Format: Religious; Talk. **Simulcasts:** KKLA-AM 1240. **Networks:** Independent. **Founded:** 1985. **Operating Hours:** Continuous. **Key Personnel:** Dave Armstrong, General Mgr. **Local Programs:** *Live From L.A.*, Duane Patterson. **Wattage:** 30,000. **URL:** http://www.kkla@.com.

2027 KLAC-AM - 570
330 N. Brand Blvd. No. No. 800 Phone: (818)246-0939
Glendale, CA 91203 Fax: (818)637-2267

Format: Oldies. **Networks:** AP; Unistar; Westwood One Radio. **Owner:** Chancellor Broadcasting, 2655 N. Central Expy., No. 405, Dallas, TX 75243. **Founded:** 1970. **Operating Hours:** Continuous. **ADI:** Los Angeles (Corona & San Bernardino), CA. **Key Personnel:** Bruce Raven-Stark, General Mgr.; Marcia Davis, General Sales Mgr.; Marida Petitjean, Promotions Mgr.; Marty Miller, Production Mgr. **Local Programs:** *Your Original Hit Favorites*. **Wattage:** 5000. **Ad Rates:** Advertising accepted; rates available upon request.

2028 KLTX-AM - 1390
701 N. Brand Blvd., No. 550 Phone: (818)956-5552
Glendale, CA 91203 Fax: (818)551-1110

Format: Contemporary Christian. **Networks:** Independent. **Owner:** Salem Communications, 4880 Santa Rosa Rd., Ste. 300, Camarillo, CA 93012, (805)987-0400. **Founded:** 1926. **Formerly:** KGER-AM. **Operating Hours:** Continuous. **Key Personnel:** Jason Jeffries, Station Mgr. **Local Programs:** *On the Line*, Bob Noonan; *Speak Out*, Tony Ashlin. **Wattage:** 5000. **Ad Rates:** $35-50 for 30 seconds.

2029 KVEA-TV - 52
1139 Grand Central Ave. Phone: (818)502-5700
Glendale, CA 91201 Fax: (818)502-0029

Format: Commercial TV. **Networks:** Telemundo. **Owner:** Telemundo Group, Miami, at above address, (818)502-5800. **Founded:** 1985. **Operating Hours:** Continuous; 75% network, 25% local. **ADI:** Los Angeles (Corona & San Bernardino), CA. **Key Personnel:** Eduardo G. Dominguez, Station Mgr.; Karen Harmon, Controller. **Local Programs:** *Noticero 52*, Juan Carlos Aviles. **Ad Rates:** $100-1,800 per unit.

2030 Sammons Communications
6246 San Fernando Rd. Phone: (818)246-5581
Box 5104 Fax: (818)242-9553
Glendale, CA 91201

Founded: 1962. **Cities Served:** Los Angeles County, Burbank, La Canada, and La Crescenta, CA.

GLENDORA, pop. 38,654.

S. CA. Los Angeles Co. 12 mi. NW of Pomona. Residential. Light industry.

2031 National Dragster
National Hot Rod Association
2220 E. Alosta, Ste. 101 Phone: (626)963-7695
Glendora, CA 91740 Fax: (626)335-4307
Publisher E-mail: nhra@goracing.com

Magazine. **Subtitle:** Drag Racing's Leading News Weekly. **Founded:** 1960. **Freq:** Weekly (Fri.). **Print Method:** Offset. **Trim Size:** 10 3/4 x 14 1/2. **Cols./Page:** 4. **Col. Width:** 14 picas. **Col. Depth:** 13 3/4 inches. **Key Personnel:** Phil Burgess, Editor; Jeff Morton, Advertising Dir., fax (626)914-9929; Adriane Pierson, Business Mgr., phone (626)914-9929; Cecily Chittick, Production Mgr. **ISSN:** 0466-2199. **Subscription Rates:** Free to qualified subscribers; $3 single issue. **Remarks:** Accepts advertising.
Ad Rates: BW: $2,945 **Circ:** Paid ‡82,666
4C: $3,955 Non-paid ‡2,627

2032 Pacific Coast Nurseryman and Garden Supply Dealer
Cox Publishing Co., Inc.
105 N. Vermont Ave. Phone: (626)914-3916
PO Box 1477 Fax: (626)914-3751
Glendora, CA 91740-1477
Free: (800)577-5225
Publication E-mail: pcnmagazineucnl/36a@prodigy.com

Business management magazine for professionals in the environmental horticulture industry. **Founded:** Jan. 1941. **Freq:** Monthly. **Print Method:** Offset. **Trim Size:** 8 1/2 x 11. **Cols./Page:** 3. **Col. Width:** 28 nonpareils. **Col. Depth:** 140 agate lines. **Key Personnel:** Harold R. Young, Editor and Publisher, hyoungpcn@aol.com. **ISSN:** 0192-7159. **Subscription Rates:** $30 individuals; $40 other countries; $4 single issue. **Remarks:** Accepts advertising. **URL:** http://www.pacificcoastnurseryman.com.
Ad Rates: BW: $1,445 **Circ:** Paid ‡6,840
4C: $2,045 Non-paid ‡3,624

2033 Sharing Ideas News Magazine
Royal Publishing, Inc.
PO Box 398 Phone: (626)335-8069
Glendora, CA 91740 Fax: (626)335-6127
Publication E-mail: call4spkr@aol.com

Magazine for professional speakers, meeting planners, and bureaus. **Subtitle:** News Magazine for Professional Speakers, Meeting Planners, Bureaus, Agents, and Consultants. **Founded:** 1978. **Freq:** Bimonthly. **Print Method:** Offset. **Trim Size:** 8 1/2 x 11. **Cols./Page:** 3. **Col. Width:** 28 nonpareils. **Col. Depth:** 140 agate lines. **Key Personnel:** Dorothy Walters, C.S.P., Editor and Publisher, dottie@walters-intl.com; Michael MacFarlane, Advertising Mgr., michael@walters-intl.com. **ISSN:** 0886-1501. **Subscription Rates:** $95 two years; $10 single issue. **Remarks:** Accepts advertising. **URL:** http://www.walters-intl.com. **Formerly:** Sharing Ideas. **Additional Contact Info: Advertising:** 18825 Hicrest, Glendora, CA 91740.
Ad Rates: BW: $539 **Circ:** Paid ‡5,000
4C: $1,185 Controlled ‡2,000

GOLETA, pop. 70,000.

SW CA. Santa Barbara Co. 7 mi. W. of Santa Barbara. Research development. Manufactures electric measuring instruments, test equipment, electronic components accessories. Avocados, Lemons. Grapes and pickles.

2034 Ancestors West
Santa Barbara County Genealogical Society
Box 1303
Goleta, CA 93116

Journal covering genealogy and local history. **Freq:** Quarterly. **Trim Size:** 8 1/2 x 11. **Cols./Page:** 2. **Key Personnel:** Lesley Fagan, Contact. **ISSN:** 0734-4988. **Subscription Rates:** $15 individuals; $3 single issue. **Remarks:** Advertising not accepted.
Circ: Combined 504

2035 Cox Cable Santa Barbara
22 S. Fairview Ave. Phone: (805)683-7751
Goleta, CA 93117 Fax: (805)964-6069

Founded: 1962. **Cities Served:** Santa Barbara County, Carpinteria, Goleta, Isla Vista, Mission Canyon, and Montecito, CA.

GRASS VALLEY, pop. 6,697.

NE CA. Nevada Co. 50 mi. NE of Sacramento. Tourism. Electronic plants, saw, planing mills, sheet metal works. Fruit shipped. Timber. Agriculture. Pears, apples, plums, dairying.

2036 The Union
11464 Sutton Way Phone: (916)273-9561
Grass Valley, CA 95945 Fax: (916)273-1854

General newspaper. **Founded:** 1864. **Freq:** Mon.-Sat. (eve.). **Print Method:** Offset. **Trim Size:** 13 1/8 x 27 3/4. **Cols./Page:** 6. **Col. Width:** 24 nonpareils. **Col. Depth:** 301 agate lines. **Key Personnel:** John Walker, Publisher; John Seelmeyer, Managing Editor; Matthew Bodourian, Advertising Dir. **Subscription Rates:** $78 individuals. **Remarks:** Accepts advertising. **URL:** http://www.TheUnion.com.
Ad Rates: GLR: $.76 **Circ:** Mon.-Sat. 16,294
BW: $2,515.50
4C: $2,726
SAU: $19.50
PCI: $19.50

2037 KNCO-AM - 830
1255 E. Main St., Ste. A Phone: (530)272-3424
Grass Valley, CA 95945 Fax: (530)272-2872
E-mail: knco@nccn.net

Format: News; Talk. **Networks:** ABC. **Owner:** Nevada County Broadcasters, Inc., at above address. **Founded:** 1978. **Operating Hours:** Continuous; 50% network, 50% local. **ADI:** Sacramento-Stockton, CA. **Key Personnel:** Scott Robertson, Gen. Mgr./Product; Rich Brock, Music Dir. **Local Programs:** *On the Town*, Jim Kerr; *Two Way Radio*, Jim Kerr. **Wattage:** 5000. **Ad Rates:** $15-35 for 30 seconds; $18-40 for 60 seconds.

2038 KNCO-FM - 94.3
1255 E. Main St., Ste. A Phone: (530)272-3424
Grass Valley, CA 95945 Fax: (530)272-2872
Free: (800)578-9494
E-mail: knco@knco.com

Format: Country. **Owner:** Nevada County Broadcasters, Inc., at above address. **Founded:** 1983. **Operating Hours:** Continuous. **ADI:** Sacramento-Stockton, CA. **Key Personnel:** Tom Fitzsimmons, Program Dir.; Lindy Pasus, Sales Mgr.; Rich Brock, Music Dir. **Wattage:** 3000. **Ad Rates:** $11-26 per unit. Combined advertising rates available with KNCO-AM.

GREENFIELD

2039 Greenfield News
South County Newspapers
PO Box 187 Phone: (408)674-5907
Greenfield, CA 93927 Fax: (408)385-4799

Community newspaper. **Founded:** 1936. **Freq:** Weekly (Wed.). **Print Method:** Offset. **Cols./Page:** 6. **Col. Width:** 26 nonpareils. **Col. Depth:** 294 agate lines. **Key Personnel:** John Pekema, Editor; Harry Casey, Publisher; Richard Casey, Advertising Mgr. **Subscription Rates:** $23 individuals within the county; $29 Out of Town. **Remarks:** Accepts advertising.
Ad Rates: SAU: $9.50 **Circ:** ‡1,475

GRIDLEY, pop. 3,982.

N. CA. Butte Co. 70 mi. N. of Sacramento. Cannery, fruit dryer, feed mill. Diversified farming. Poultry, seeds, livestock.

2040 The Gridley Herald
630 Washington St. Phone: (916)846-3661
PO Box 68 Fax: (916)846-4519
Gridley, CA 95948
Newspaper (tabloid) with Report orientation. **Founded:** 1880. **Freq:** Semiweekly (Wed. and Fri.). **Print Method:** Offset. **Trim Size:** 15 x 23. **Cols./Page:** 9. **Col. Width:** 20 nonpareils. **Col. Depth:** 301 agate lines. **Key Personnel:** Lisa VanDe-Hey, Publisher, gherald@manznet.com; John Skaggs, Foreman, gherald@manznet.com. **USPS:** 859-420. **Subscription Rates:** $30 individuals; $34 out of area.
Ad Rates: GLR: $.45 **Circ:** ‡3,400
BW: $761.10
SAU: $6.75

GROVELAND

2041 Sun Country Cable
18634 Main St. Phone: (209)962-6373
Box 435 Fax: (209)962-4923
Groveland, CA 95321

Owner: Sun Country Cable, 7901 Stoneridge Dr, Pleasanton, CA, (510)463-1919. **Founded:** 1987. **Key Personnel:** Greg Holly, Manager; Vickie Kennedy, Office Coordinator. **Cities Served:** Big Oak Flat, Groveland, CA: subscribing households 1700; 31 channels; 1 community access channel.

GUALALA, pop. 600.

C. CA. Mendocino Co. 130 mi. N. of San Francisco. Fort Ross Historical Park. State and county beach parks. Fishing and Lumbering.

2042 Independent Coast Observer
Independent Coast Observer, Inc.
PO Box 1200 Phone: (707)884-3501
Gualala, CA 95445 Fax: (707)884-1710

Community newspaper (tabloid). **Founded:** Apr. 1969. **Freq:** Weekly (Fri.). **Print Method:** Offset. **Cols./Page:** 6. **Col. Width:** 9 1/2 picas. **Col. Depth:** 15 inches. **Key Personnel:** J. Stephen McLaughlin, Editor and Publisher. **USPS:** 881-280. **Subscription Rates:** $32.50 individuals. **Remarks:** Accepts advertising.
Ad Rates: GLR: $7.40 **Circ:** ‡2,900
PCI: $7.40

2043 Wander Cable TV
38951 S. Hwy 1 Phone: (707)785-2319
PO Box 368 Fax: (707)884-4116
Gualala, CA 95445

Formerly: Coast Cable TV. **Key Personnel:** Russ Jarvis, Contact; Gerry Hanneman, Chief Engineer; Poppy Falduto, Office Mgr. **Cities Served:** subscribing households 1,899.

GUERNEVILLE, pop. 900.

NW CA. Sonomo Co. 8 mi. NW of Santa Rosa. Resort. Wineries. Logging camps and contractors. Grapes, prunes and apples.

2044 Tight
Ann Erickson
Box 1591 Phone: (707)865-2737
Guerneville, CA 95446
Literary journal covering experimental poetry, prose, and art. **Founded:** 1990. **Freq:** Quarterly. **Trim Size:** 8 1/2 x 11. **Key Personnel:** Ann Erickson, Editor. **Subscription Rates:** $20 individuals; $5 single issue. **Remarks:** Advertising not accepted.
Circ: Combined 100

HACIENDA HEIGHTS

2045 Clinical Nurse Specialist
Lippincott Williams & Wilkins
17128 Colima Rd., Ste. 544 Phone: (626)964-8465
Hacienda Heights, CA 91745 Fax: (626)913-8667

Nursing journal. **Subtitle:** The Journal For Advanced Nursing Practice. **Founded:** 1987. **Freq:** Bimonthly. **Print Method:** Offset. **Trim Size:** 8 1/8 x 10 7/8. **Key Personnel:** Pauline Beecroft, Ph.D., Contact, pbeec@telis.org. **ISSN:** 0887-6274. **Subscription Rates:** $100 individuals; $142 institutions. **Remarks:** Accepts advertising. **Alt. Formats:** Mailing labels.
Ad Rates: BW: $560 **Circ:** Paid 3,319
4C: $1,355 Non-paid 110

HALF MOON BAY, pop. 7,282.

W. CA. San Mateo Co. 24 mi. SW of San Francisco. Commercial and sport fishing. Floriculture. Fruit, vegetables packed. Nurseries. Resort. Agriculture. Cattle.

Half Moon Bay Review and Pescadero Pebble - See Pescadero

HANFORD†, pop. 20,958.

SC CA. Kings Co. 33 mi. S. of Fresno. Milk condensery, oil refinery, flour, planing mills, canned and dried fruit, meat, poultry, cold storage packing plants; granite works; concrete pipe, tire factories. Oil wells. Agriculture. Dairying, cotton, grain.

2046 The Hanford Sentinel
Sentinel Plus
PO Box 9 Phone: (209)582-0471
Hanford, CA 93232 Fax: (209)502-8631

Community newspaper. **Founded:** 1886. **Freq:** Daily. **Print Method:** Offset. **Cols./Page:** 6. **Col. Width:** 26 nonpareils. **Col. Depth:** 301 agate lines. **Key Personnel:** Neil D. Williams, Publisher; Bob Rankin, Advertising Mgr. **Subscription Rates:** $102 individuals. **Remarks:** Accepts advertising.
Ad Rates: GLR: $1.56 **Circ:** Mon.-Fri. ★13,387
4C: $270 Sun. ★13,336
PCI: $12.48

2047 Sentinel Plus
300 W. 6th St. Phone: (209)582-0471
PO Box 9 Fax: (209)582-8631
Hanford, CA 93230
Shopper. **Founded:** 1924. **Freq:** Weekly (Wed.). **Print Method:** Offset. **Cols./Page:** 6. **Col. Width:** 2 1/16 inches. **Col. Depth:** 301 agate lines. **Key Personnel:** Neil D. Williams, Publisher; Robert Rankin, Advertising Mgr. **Subscription Rates:** Free. **Remarks:** Accepts advertising. **Formerly:** Kings County News (1989).
Ad Rates: 4C: $235 **Circ:** Mon.-Sat. 12,779
PCI: $2.55 Sun. 12,738

2048 KIGS-AM - 620
6165 Hwy. 198 Phone: (209)582-0361
Hanford, CA 93230 Fax: (209)582-3981

Format: Hispanic; Top 40. **Networks:** Independent. **Owner:** Joan Parair, PO Box 1269, Hanford, CA 93231, (209)686-8813. **Founded:** 1948. **Formerly:** KNGS-AM; KCLQ-AM. **Operating Hours:** Continuous; 100% local. **ADI:** Fresno-Visalia (Hanford), CA. **Key Personnel:** Salvador Gardund, Contact; Greg Moya, Contact; Maria Jimenet, Contact; Pedro Miranda, Contact; Anna Alexandre, Contact; Tony Vieira, Contact; Carlos Alexandre, Program Dir.; Maria Gomez, Contact; Moises Ochoa, Contact; Marc Zamora, Contact. **Wattage:** 1000.

HAYWARD, pop. 94,167.

W. CA. Alameda Co. 22 mi. SE of San Francisco. California State University at Hayward. Manufactures truck assembly steel, fabrication, construction equipment machine shops, chemicals and electronics.

2049 American Brewer
Box 510 Phone: (510)538-9500
Hayward, CA 94543-0510 Fax: (510)538-7644
Free: (800)646-2701
Publisher E-mail: ambrew@aol.com

Magazine covering pub and micro brewing equipment, techniques, and ingredients. **Subtitle:** The Business of Microbrewing. **Founded:** 1986. **Freq:** 6/year. **Print Method:** Offset. **Trim Size:** 8 1/2 x 11. **Cols./Page:** 3. **Col. Width:** 2 1/4 inches. **Col. Depth:** 9 1/2 inches. **Key Personnel:** Bill Owens, Publisher. **ISSN:** 0887-7418. **Subscription Rates:** $32 individuals; $5 single issue; $40 out of country. **Remarks:** Accepts advertising. **Available Online. URL:** http://www.ambrew.com.
Ad Rates: BW: $1,100 **Circ:** Paid ‡12,000
4C: $1,500 Non-paid ‡6,000
PCI: $50

2050 The Annals of Applied Probability
Institute of Mathematical Statistics
3401 Investment Blvd., No. 7 Phone: (510)783-8141
Hayward, CA 94545-3819 Fax: (510)783-4131
Publication E-mail: ims@imstat.org
Publisher E-mail: ims@imstat.org

Journal covering the applications of probability. **Founded:** 1991. **Freq:** Quarterly. **Print Method:** Offset. **Trim Size:** 7 x 10. **Cols./Page:** 1. **Col. Width:** 5 inches. **Col. Depth:** 8 inches. **Key Personnel:** Richard R. Durrett, Editor. **ISSN:** 1050-5164. **Subscription Rates:** $100. **Remarks:** Accepts advertising.
Ad Rates: BW: $450 **Circ:** 2,200

2051 The Annals of Probability
Institute of Mathematical Statistics
3401 Investment Blvd., No. 7 Phone: (510)783-8141
Hayward, CA 94545-3819 Fax: (510)783-4131
Publication E-mail: ims@imstat.org
Publisher E-mail: ims@imstat.org

Journal dedicated to publishing the theory of probability and its applications. **Founded:** 1973. **Freq:** Quarterly. **Print Method:** Offset. **Trim Size:** 7 x 10. **Cols./Page:** 1. **Col. Width:** 5 inches. **Col. Depth:** 8 inches. **Key Personnel:** S.R.S. Varadhan, Editor. **ISSN:** 0091-1798. **Subscription Rates:** $150. **Remarks:** Accepts advertising.
Ad Rates: BW: $450 **Circ:** ‡2,700

2052 The Annals of Statistics
Institute of Mathematical Statistics
3401 Investment Blvd., No. 7 Phone: (510)783-8141
Hayward, CA 94545-3819 Fax: (510)783-4131
Publisher E-mail: ims@imstat.org

Journal publishing contributions to the theory of statistics and to its applications. **Founded:** 1973. **Freq:** Bimonthly. **Print Method:** Offset. **Trim Size:** 7 x 10. **Cols./Page:** 1. **Col. Width:** 5 inches. **Col. Depth:** 8 inches. **Key Personnel:** James Berger, Editor; Han Kuensch, Editor. **ISSN:** 0090-5364. **Subscription Rates:** $170. **Remarks:** Accepts advertising.
Ad Rates: BW: $450 **Circ:** ‡4,300

2053 Argus Enterprise
Alameda Newspaper Group
116 W. Wenton Ave. Phone: (510)293-2901
Hayward, CA 94544 Fax: (510)293-2697
Free: (800)743-8742

Newspaper. **Freq:** Weekly.
Circ: Controlled 41,349

2054 The Daily Review
Alameda Newspaper Group
116 W. Winton Ave. Phone: (510)783-6111
PO Box 5050 Fax: (510)293-2341
Hayward, CA 94544
General newspaper. **Founded:** 1891. **Freq:** Mon.-Sun. (morn.). **Print Method:** Offset. **Cols./Page:** 6. **Col. Width:** 22 nonpareils. **Col. Depth:** 298 agate lines. **Key Personnel:** J. Allan Meath, Publisher. **Subscription Rates:** $84 individuals. **Remarks:** Accepts advertising.
Ad Rates: BW: $4,405.35 **Circ:** Mon.-Sat. 43,740
4C: $4,980.35 Sun. 50,518
SAU: $34.15
PCI: $34.15

2055 Hayward & Castro Valley Observer
Observer Newspapers
Box 817
San Leandro, CA 94577

Community newspaper. **Founded:** May 22, 1972. **Freq:** Weekly (Fri.). **Print Method:** Offset. **Cols./Page:** 6. **Col. Width:** 10 picas. **Col. Depth:** 16 inches. **Key Personnel:** Ad Fried, Managing Editor; Michael Robert, Publisher; R.A. Burrell, Advertising Mgr. **Subscription Rates:** $25 individuals. **Remarks:** Advertising not accepted for tobacco products.
Ad Rates: BW: $3,000 **Circ:** ‡30,000
4C: $3,600
SAU: $40
PCI: $35

The Oakland Tribune - See Oakland

2056 Statistical Science
Institute of Mathematical Statistics
3401 Investment Blvd., No. 7 Phone: (510)783-8141
Hayward, CA 94545-3819 Fax: (510)783-4131
Publisher E-mail: ims@imstat.org

Review journal of IMS. **Founded:** 1986. **Freq:** Quarterly. **Print Method:** Offset. **Trim Size:** 8 1/2 x 10. **Cols./Page:** 1. **Col. Width:** 6 1/2 inches. **Col. Depth:** 8 inches. **Key Personnel:** Leon Gleser, Editor. **ISSN:** 0883-4237. **Subscription Rates:** $80. **Remarks:** Accepts advertising.
Ad Rates: BW: $450 **Circ:** Paid 4,700

2057 Voz de Portugal
370 A St. Phone: (510)537-9503
Hayward, CA 94541
Magazine (tabloid, Portuguese). **Subtitle:** Voice of Portugal. **Founded:** 1960. **Freq:** Semimonthly. **Print Method:** Offset. **Cols./Page:** 5. **Col. Width:** 24 nonpareils. **Col. Depth:** 224 agate lines. **Key Personnel:** Lourenco Costa Aguiar, Editor and Publisher. **Subscription Rates:** $10 individuals. **Remarks:** Accepts advertising.
Ad Rates: GLR: $.214 **Circ:** ‡3,200

2058 KCRH-FM - 89.9
25555 Hesperian Blvd. Phone: (510)786-6954
Hayward, CA 94545 Fax: (510)782-9315
E-mail: kcrh@bigfoot.com

Format: Educational. **Networks:** Independent. **Owner:** Chabot-Las Positas Community College District, at above address, (510)786-6600. **Founded:** 1980. **Operating Hours:** 6 a.m.-12 a.m. Mon.-Sun.; 100% local. **Key Personnel:** Rick Strauss, Contact. **Wattage:** 18.

HEALDSBURG, pop. 7,217.

NW CA. Sonoma Co. On Russian River, 65 mi. N. of San Francisco. Wineries. Wood products, machine shops, electronics, ceramics. Agriculture. Prunes, grapes.

2059 The Healdsburg Tribune
Beverly C. Reeves
PO Box 518 Phone: (707)433-4451
Healdsburg, CA 95448 Fax: (707)431-2623

Community newspaper. **Founded:** 1865. **Freq:** Weekly (Wed.). **Print Method:** Offset. **Trim Size:** 13 3/4 x 22 3/4. **Cols./Page:** 6. **Col. Width:** 24 nonpareils. **Col. Depth:** 294 agate lines. **Key Personnel:** Kathryn Roth, Publisher; Cherie Kelsay, Advertising Dir. **Subscription Rates:** $25 individuals; $37.50 other countries; $19.50 Senior Citizens. **Remarks:** Accepts advertising. **Formerly**: The Healdsburg Tribune and Faces & Places.
Ad Rates: BW: $1,669.26 **Circ:** ‡4,100
4C: $1,969.26 Free 3,000
SAU: $12.94

HEMET, pop. 23,211.

SE CA. Riverside Co. 75 mi. SE of Los Angeles. Fruit and vegetable cannery, mobile homes, trailers, aircraft parts, aluminum castings, concrete products manufactured, hatcheries. nurseries. Agriculture. Oranges, apricots, peaches.

2060 Dollarsaver
Save A Dollar, Inc.
340 N. Jacinto St. Phone: (909)658-3117
Hemet, CA 92543 Fax: (909)925-0394

Shopping guide. **Subtitle:** Magazine Size Shopper-One Color Overlay. **Founded:** 1967. **Freq:** Weekly (Wed.). **Print Method:** Offset. **Trim Size:** 8 x 10 1/4. **Cols./Page:** 2. **Col. Width:** 48 nonpareils. **Col. Depth:** 140 agate lines. **Key Personnel:** John Kaiser, Editor; Jane Kaiser, Publisher; Tim Kaiser, Advertising Mgr. **Remarks:** Accepts advertising.
Ad Rates: BW: $410 **Circ:** Free ‡39,000
4C: $460
PCI: $25

HERMOSA BEACH, pop. 18,070.

S. CA. Los Angeles Co. 20 mi. SW of Los Angeles. Manufactures dye and print textiles, clay products, aircraft parts. Summer resort. Oil wells. Residential.

Easy Reader/Redondo Beach Hometown News - See Redondo Beach

HESPERIA, pop. 5,700.

SE CA. San Bernardino Co. 20 mi. N. of San Bernardino. Cement, wooden crates manufactured. Diversified farming.

2061 Hesperia Resorter
Valley Wide Newspaper
16925 Main St. Phone: (619)244-0021
PO Box 400937 Fax: (619)244-6609
Hesperia, CA 92340-0937
Newspaper. **Founded:** 1959. **Freq:** Weekly (Thurs.). **Print Method:** Offset. **Trim Size:** 27 x 1/2. **Cols./Page:** 8. **Col. Width:** 18 nonpareils. **Col. Depth:** 308 agate lines. **Key Personnel:** Jenny Jones, Publisher; Patricia Thomas, General Mgr.; Joyce Bohannan, Editor. **Subscription Rates:** Free; $19 by mail; $21 out of state. **Remarks:** Accepts advertising.
Ad Rates: GLR: $6 **Circ:** Paid ‡2,200
BW: $1,383.75 Free ‡12,000
4C: $1,500
SAU: $10.25

HILLSBOROUGH

2062 Hillsborough/Burlingame Boutique and Villager
Independent News Group
824 Cowan Rd. Phone: (650)692-9406
Burlingame, CA 94010-1205 Fax: (650)692-7587
Publication E-mail: smiedit@aol.com

Community newspaper. **Founded:** 1965. **Freq:** Weekly (Wed.). **Print Method:** Offset. **Cols./Page:** 5. **Col. Width:** 13 inches. **Col. Depth:** 224 agate lines. **Subscription Rates:** $18 individuals. **Remarks:** Accepts advertising.
Ad Rates: PCI: $16.12 **Circ:** ‡17,000

HOLLISTER†, pop. 10,451.

W. CA. San Benito Co. 90 mi. S. of San Francisco. Aero space aircraft. Fruit, tomatoes, canneries and packing houses. Wineries. Beef slaughtering. Fruit, truck, stock farms.

2063 The Free Lance
Central Valley Publishing
PO Box 1417 Phone: (408)637-5566
Hollister, CA 95024-1417 Fax: (408)637-4104
Publisher E-mail: freelance@hollinet.com

General newspaper. **Founded:** 1873. **Freq:** Daily (eve.). **Print Method:** Offset. **Cols./Page:** 6. **Col. Width:** 25 nonpareils. **Col. Depth:** 302 agate lines. **Key Personnel:** Adam Breen, Editor, abreed@freelancenews.com; Michael Eastman, Publisher, meastman@freelancenews.com. **Subscription Rates:** $41 individuals. **Remarks:** Accepts advertising. **URL:** http://www.freelancenews.com.
Ad Rates: SAU: $8.27 **Circ:** Mon.-Fri. 4,500

HOLLYWOOD

S. CA. Los Angeles Co. A residential suburb, NW of and part of Los Angeles. Center of motion picture industry. Pacific coast headquarters of four national radio broadcasting networks. Busy retail commercial center, second only to downtown Los Angeles business district.

2064 The Agencies
Acting World Books
PO Box 3044 Phone: (818)905-1345
Hollywood, CA 90078-3044 Fax: (818)905-1345
Free: (800)210-1197

Magazine covering the Hollywood and New York talent agencies field. **Subtitle:** What The Actor Needs to Know. **Founded:** 1981. **Freq:** Monthly. **Print Method:** Offset. **Trim Size:** 8 1/2 x 11. **Cols./Page:** 1. **Col. Width:** 6 3/4 inches. **Col. Depth:** 10 inches. **Key Personnel:** Lawrence Parke, Editor. **ISSN:** 1069-3890. **Subscription Rates:** $50; $10 single issue. **Remarks:** Advertising accepted; rates available upon request.
Circ: Paid ‡375
Combined 2,000

2065 American Cinematographer
ASC Holding Corp.
1782 N. Orange Dr. Phone: (213)969-4333
Hollywood, CA 90028 Fax: (213)876-4973

Magazine of the American Society of Cinematographers; covering film and video production. **Subtitle:** International Journal of Film and Electronic Production Techniques. **Founded:** 1919. **Freq:** Monthly. **Print Method:** Offset. **Trim Size:** 8 3/8 x 10 7/8. **Cols./Page:** 3. **Col. Width:** 27 nonpareils. **Col. Depth:** 140 agate lines. **Key Personnel:** David Heuring, Editor. **ISSN:** 0002-7928. **Subscription Rates:** $29.95 individuals; $5 single issue.
Ad Rates: BW: $2,680 **Circ:** ‡32,000
4C: $3,675
PCI: $105

2066 Angry Thoreauan
Angry Thoreauan Magazine
PO Box 3478 Phone: (213)488-1572
Hollywood, CA 90078-3478
Consumer magazine covering social and political satire, music, erotica, and alternative views. **Founded:** 1987. **Freq:** Quarterly. **Print Method:** Web offset. **Trim Size:** 8 x 10 5/8. **Key Personnel:** Rev. Randall Tin-ear, Editor. **Subscription Rates:** $15 individuals; $4 single issue. **Remarks:** Accepts advertising. **Former name**: Happy Thrasher.
Ad Rates: BW: $135 **Circ:** (Not Reported)
4C: $200

2067 Ben is Dead
PO Box 3166 Phone: (213)960-7674
Hollywood, CA 90028 Fax: (310)479-2336

Alternative consumer magazine covering social and cultural issues. **Founded:** 1988. **Freq:** Monthly. **Print Method:** Web. **Trim Size:** 8 1/8 x 10 6/8. **Key Personnel:** Darby Romeo, Contact. **Subscription Rates:** $15 individuals; $5 single issue. **Remarks:** Accepts advertising. **URL:** http://www.benisdead.com.
Ad Rates: BW: $550 **Circ:** Controlled 12,000
4C: $900

2068 Cash Box
Cash Box Publishing Co., Inc.
6464 Sunset Blvd.
Ste. 605
Hollywood, CA 90028

Magazine for members of the phonograph record and music industries. **Founded:** 1942. **Freq:** Weekly. **Print Method:** Offset. **Cols./Page:** 4. **Col. Width:** 26 nonpareils. **Col. Depth:** 170 agate lines. **Key Personnel:** George Albert, Publisher. **Subscription Rates:** $180. **Remarks:** Accepts advertising.
Ad Rates: BW: $3,290 **Circ:** (Not Reported)
4C: $3,780

2069 Drama-Logue
Drama-Logue, Inc.
PO Box 38711 Phone: (213)464-5079
Hollywood, CA 90038-0771
Entertainment trade newspaper specializing in casting information for actors, entertainers and technicians, including interviews with major stars and reviews of films and plays. **Founded:** 1969. **Freq:** Weekly (Thurs.). **Print Method:** Offset. **Trim Size:** 10W x 14H. **Cols./Page:** 5. **Col. Width:** 22 nonpareils. **Col. Depth:** 196 agate lines. **Key Personnel:** Faye Bordy, Editor-in-Chief; Bill Bordy, Publisher; Jayne Bordy, Advertising Mgr. **Subscription Rates:** $65 individuals; $3.50 single issue sample issue. **Remarks:** Color advertising not accepted. **Formerly**: The Hollywood Drama-Logue.
Ad Rates: BW: $1,470 **Circ:** Paid ‡17,000
PCI: $29 Non-paid ‡100

2070 The National Record
The Record Publishing Co.
PO Box 116 Phone: (213)461-4196
Hollywood, CA 90028 Fax: (213)461-1738

Educational newsmagazine. **Founded:** 1944. **Freq:** Monthly. **Print Method:** Offset. **Trim Size:** 10 x 13. **Cols./Page:** 5. **Col. Width:** 22 nonpareils. **Col. Depth:** 224 agate lines. **Key Personnel:** Jim Goodson, Editor and Publisher; Sandra Calderon, Advertising Mgr. **Subscription Rates:** $34 individuals. **Remarks:** Accepts advertising.
Ad Rates: BW: $1,700 **Circ:** Paid ‡12,000
PCI: $34 Non-paid ‡41,600

2071 Television International Magazine
Television International Publications Ltd.
PO Box 2430 Phone: (323)462-1099
Hollywood, CA 90028 Fax: (323)462-1099
Publication E-mail: fvi@smartgo.com

Television industry trade magazine. **Founded:** 1956. **Freq:** Bimonthly. **Print Method:** Sheetfed offset. **Trim Size:** 8 1/4 x 10 15/16. **Cols./Page:** 3. **Col. Width:** 10 inches. **Col. Depth:** 60 picas. **Key Personnel:** Josie Cory, Editor and Publisher, josie@smartgo.com. **ISSN:** 8836-4462. **Subscription Rates:** Free to qualified subscribers; $42. **Remarks:** Accepts advertising. **URL:** http://www.smartgo.com. **Formerly**: Telefilm International Magazine.
Ad Rates: BW: $2,495 **Circ:** (Not Reported)
4C: $3,495

2072 KABC-TV - 7
4151 Prospect Ave. Phone: (310)557-7777
Hollywood, CA 90027

Format: Commercial TV. **Networks:** ABC. **Operating Hours:** Continuous. **ADI:** Los Angeles (Corona & San Bernardino), CA. **Key Personnel:** Terry Crofoot, Contact.

2073 KALI-AM - 1430
5723 Melrose Ave. Phone: (213)466-6161
Hollywood, CA 90038-3898 Fax: (213)466-9464
E-mail: gfm75@aol.com

Format: Urban Contemporary; Ethnic. **Networks:** Independent. **Founded:** 1952. **Operating Hours:** Continuous. **ADI:** Los Angeles (Corona & San Bernardino), CA. **Key Personnel:** Gary Mercer, Station Mgr.; Dave Sweeney, Vice President. **Wattage:** 5000. **Ad Rates:** Advertising accepted; rates available upon request.

KKBT-FM - See Los Angeles

2074 KLVE-FM - 107.5
1645 N. Vine, No. 200 Phone: (213)465-3171
Hollywood, CA 90028 Fax: (213)467-5063

Format: Hispanic. **Networks:** Independent. **Founded:** 1959. **Operating Hours:** Continuous. **ADI:** Los Angeles (Corona & San Bernardino), CA. **Key Personnel:** Richard Heftel, President, phone (323)468-5230; Jerry Symon, Vice President, phone (323)468-5255. **Wattage:** 29,500.

2075 KTLA-TV - 5
5800 Sunset Blvd. Phone: (323)460-5500
Hollywood, CA 90028 Fax: (323)460-5952
E-mail: gbrown@tribune.com

Format: Commercial TV. **Founded:** Jan. 22, 1947. **Operating Hours:** Continuous. **ADI:** Los Angeles (Corona & San Bernardino), CA. **Key Personnel:** John Reardon, VP & Gen. Mgr. **Local Programs:** *KTLA Morning News* 7:00 am - 9:00 am Monday-Friday, Marcia Brandwynne, Exec. Prod., Fax (323)460-5404; *News at Ten* 10:00 pm - 11:00 pm, Jeff Wald, News Dir.

2076 KTNQ-AM - 1020
1645 N. Vine, No. 200 Phone: (213)465-3171
Hollywood, CA 90028 Fax: (213)467-5063

Format: Hispanic; News; Talk. **Founded:** 1925. **Operating Hours:** Continuous. **ADI:** Los Angeles (Corona & San Bernardino), CA. **Key Personnel:** Richard Heftel, President, phone (323)468-5230; Jerry Symon, Vice President, phone (323)468-5255. **Wattage:** 50,000.

2077 KWKW-AM - 1330
6290 Sunset Blvd., Ste. 1600 Phone: (213)466-8111
Hollywood, CA 90028 Fax: (213)461-7347

Format: Talk; Hispanic. **Networks:** CBS; Lotus. **Owner:** Howard Kalmenson, at above address. **Founded:** 1942. **Operating Hours:** Continuous. **Key Personnel:** Jim Kalmenson, General Mgr.; John Paley, Vice President, fax (213)461-7347; Mike Addison, General Sales Mgr.; Manolo Molina, LSM; Antonio Gonzalez, Program Dir. **Local Programs:** *El Pueblo Opina*, Robert Anguello; *Naturismo y Salud*, Jaime Cuevas; *Salud; Dinero y Amor*, Elvia Contreras. **Wattage:** Day 5000; night 1000. **Ad Rates:** $51-196 for 30 seconds; $58-245 for 60 seconds.

2078 KWNK-AM - 670
6290 W. Sunset Blvd., 16th Fl. Phone: (818)887-1855
Hollywood, CA 90028-8702 Fax: (818)887-9526

Format: Sports; Talk. **Founded:** 1983. **Operating Hours:** Continuous. **Key Personnel:** M.A. Cabranes, General Mgr.; Bill Cabranes, Contact; Jeff Biggs, Sports Dir. **Wattage:** 5000. **Ad Rates:** $12-60 for 30 seconds; $15-75 for 60 seconds.

HOLTVILLE, pop. 4,399.

S. CA. Imperial Co. 10 mi. E. of El Centro. Geothermal energy project area. Vegetable packing and shipping. Diversified farming. Cattle.

2079 Holtville Tribune
Steve Larson
523 Pine Ave. Phone: (619)356-2995
Holtville, CA 92250-0118 Fax: (619)356-4915

Community newspaper (tabloid). **Founded:** 1905. **Freq:** Weekly (Thurs.). **Print Method:** Offset. **Trim Size:** 11 1/2 x 14. **Cols./Page:** 6. **Col. Width:** 9.5 picas. **Col. Depth:** 13 inches. **Key Personnel:** Steve Larson, Publisher. **ISSN:** 0164-9140. **Subscription Rates:** $18 individuals; $20 out of area California; $29 out of state; $35 other countries. **Remarks:** Accepts advertising.
Ad Rates: GLR: $.178 **Circ:** Paid ‡1,925
BW: $269.10 Free ‡305
4C: $395
SAU: $3.15
PCI: $3.45

Imperial Valley Weekly/Imperial Hometown Review - See Imperial

HOOPA

2080 KIDE-FM - 91.3
Box 1220 Phone: (916)625-4245
Hoopa, CA 95546

Format: Eclectic. **Owner:** Hoopa Valley Telecommunications Corp., at above address. **Founded:** 1980. **Key Personnel:** Joe Orozco, Station Mgr. **Wattage:** 195.

HUGHSON

2081 Hughson Chronicle
Mid-Valley Publications
6950 Gerard St. Phone: (209)358-5311
Winton, CA 95388 Fax: (209)358-7108

Community newspaper. **Founded:** 1925. **Freq:** Weekly. **Print Method:** Offset. **Cols./Page:** 6. **Key Personnel:** Marian White, Editor, phone (209)883-9215; John Derry, Publisher. **Subscription Rates:** $19.
Ad Rates: SAU: $10.95 **Circ:** ‡4,200
PCI: $7.95

HUNTINGTON

2082 Dynamic Chiropractic
21541 Surveyor Cir. Phone: (714)960-6577
Box 6100 Fax: (714)536-1482
Huntington, CA 92646
Publication E-mail: Editorial@DCMedia.com
Publisher E-mail: advertising@dcmedia.com

Magazine for chiropractic professionals. **Subtitle:** Chiropractic News Source. **Founded:** Jan. 1983. **Freq:** Biweekly. **Print Method:** Web offset. **Trim Size:** 10 7/8 x 16 1/8. **Cols./Page:** 4. **Key Personnel:** Donald M. Petersen, Jr., Editor and Publisher, Don@DCMedia.com; Steve Kelly, Managing Editor, editorial@dcmedia.com; Anne Gardner, Advertising Dir., advertising@dcmedia.com. **ISSN:** 1076-9684. **Subscription Rates:** $18 individuals; Free to qualified subscribers. **Remarks:** Accepts advertising. **URL:** http://www.chiroweb.com.
Ad Rates: BW: $2,972 **Circ:** Controlled 72,209
4C: $3,772

HUNTINGTON BEACH, pop. 170,505.

S. CA. Orange Co. 12 mi. SW of Santa Ana. Manufactures oil well equipment. Astronautics space missles, brooms, tile. Oil refineries. Oil wells. Agriculture.

2083 Apartment Management Magazine
Apartment News Publications, Inc.
15502 Graham St. Phone: (714)893-3971
Huntington Beach, CA 92649 Fax: (714)893-6484
Free: (800)931-6666

Trade magazine serving owners, builders, and managers of apartment buildings. **Founded:** Jan. 15, 1959. **Freq:** Monthly. **Print Method:** Offset. **Trim Size:** 8 1/2 x 11. **Cols./Page:** 3. **Col. Width:** 14 picas. **Col. Depth:** 10 inches. **Key Personnel:** Don R Smeallie, Jr., Publisher; Heather Sanchez, Sr., Editor. **Subscription Rates:** $9 individuals; $15 two years; $24 out of area; $43 two years out of area. **Remarks:** Accepts advertising. **Formerly:** Apartment Owner/Builder.
Circ: Paid 5,000
Non-paid 55,000

2084 Economic Inquiry
Western Economic Association Intl.
7400 Center Ave., Ste. 109 Phone: (714)898-3222
Huntington Beach, CA 92647-3039 Fax: (714)891-6715
Publisher E-mail: info@weainternational.org

Journal covering research in all areas of economics. **Founded:** 1962. **Freq:** Quarterly. **Print Method:** Offset. **Trim Size:** 6 7/8 x 10. **Cols./Page:** 2. **Key Personnel:** Wm. S Neilson, Editor, phone (409)845-9952, fax (409)845-8483. **ISSN:** 0095-2583. **Subscription Rates:** $60; $190 libraries; $120 in Europe. single issue. **Remarks:** Accepts advertising.
Ad Rates: BW: $350 **Circ:** Paid 3,300
Non-paid 25

Huntington Beach/Fountain Valley Independent - See Fountain Valley

2085 KOCE Viewers Guide
KOCE-TV Foundation
Box 2476 Phone: (714)895-5623
Huntington Beach, CA 92647-0476 Fax: (714)895-0852
TV magazine for KOCE-TV viewers. **Founded:** Feb. 1, 1974. **Freq:** Monthly. **Print Method:** Offset. **Cols./Page:** 3 and 2. **Col. Width:** 17 and 26 nonpareils. **Col. Depth:** 105 agate lines. **USPS:** 016-203. **Subscription Rates:** $40 member per year. **Remarks:** Accepts advertising. **Available Online.**
Circ: ‡30,000

2086 New Era Magazine
Imperial Printing
22031 Bushard St. Phone: (714)962-1351
Huntington Beach, CA 92646 Fax: (714)962-1354

Magazine for laundry and dry cleaning managers, owners, and operators. **Subtitle:** Laundry and Cleaning Lines. **Founded:** 1959. **Freq:** Monthly. **Print Method:** Offset. **Trim Size:** 8 1/2 x 11. **Cols./Page:** 3. **Col. Width:** 28 nonpareils. **Col. Depth:** 140 agate lines. **Key Personnel:** Judith E. Frye, Publisher. **ISSN:** 1068-7076. **Subscription Rates:** $30 individuals; $5 single issue. **Remarks:** Accepts advertising.
Ad Rates: BW: $2,700 **Circ:** Controlled ‡19,615
4C: $4,050

2087 The Sun Journal
The Sun Newspapers
216 Main St. Phone: (562)430-7555
PO Box 755 Fax: (562)430-3469
Seal Beach, CA 90740-6318
Community newspaper. **Founded:** 1966. **Freq:** Weekly (Thurs.). **Print Method:** Offset. **Cols./Page:** 5. **Col. Width:** 26 nonpareils. **Col. Depth:** 224 agate lines. **Key Personnel:** Melissa Hobbs, Publisher. **Subscription Rates:** Free; $60 by mail. **Remarks:** Accepts advertising. **Formerly:** The Huntington Harbour Journal (1992).
Ad Rates: GLR: $1.58 **Circ:** Free 32,000
BW: $960 Paid 50
4C: $1,300
PCI: $14.10

2088 Turbo & Hi-Tech Performance
Illustrated Graphic Communications
9887 Hamilton Ave. Phone: (714)962-7795
Huntington Beach, CA 92646-8012 Fax: (714)965-2268
Publication E-mail: turbo@turbomagazine.com

Magazine covering automotive performance and engineering. **Founded:** 1985. **Freq:** Monthly. **Print Method:** Offset. Uses mats. **Trim Size:** 8 x 10 7/8. **Cols./Page:** 3. **Col. Width:** 27 nonpareils. **Col. Depth:** 140 agate lines. **Key Personnel:** Kipp E. Kington, Publisher; Debbie Perez, Business Mgr. **ISSN:** 0894-5039. **Subscription Rates:** $28.97 individuals. **Remarks:** Accepts advertising. **URL:** http://www.turbomagazine.com.
Ad Rates: BW: $3,092.00 **Circ:** ‡120,000
4C: $3,892.00

2089 The Western Sun
Golden West College
15744 Golden West St. Phone: (714)895-8786
Huntington Beach, CA 92647 Fax: (714)895-8795

Collegiate newspaper. **Founded:** Oct. 6, 1966. **Freq:** Weekly (Thurs.). **Print Method:** Offset. **Trim Size:** 13 x 21 1/2. **Cols./Page:** 6. **Col. Width:** 24 nonpareils. **Col. Depth:** 301 agate lines. **Key Personnel:** Mary Quinn, Advertising Mgr., phone (714)895-8256, scandiast@aol.com. **Subscription Rates:** Free. **Remarks:** Color advertising accepted; rates available upon request. **Formerly:** Branding Iron (1986).
Ad Rates: GLR: $.71 **Circ:** Free ‡4,500
BW: $756
4C: $1,170
PCI: $6

2090 KOCE-TV - 50
PO Box 2476 Phone: (714)895-5623
Huntington Beach, CA 92647-0476 Fax: (714)895-0852
E-mail: koce@cccd.edu

Format: Public TV. **Networks:** Public Broadcasting Service (PBS). **Owner:** Coast Community College District, at above address. **Founded:** 1972. **Operating Hours:** 5:15 a.m.-12:30 a.m. **ADI:** Los Angeles (Corona & San Bernardino), CA. **Key Personnel:** Mel Rogers, President, fax (714)895-8949, mrogers@cccd.edu; R. Bruce Reed, Station Mgr., breed@cccd.edu; Roberta K. Smith, Program Dir., rksmith@cccd.edu; Ed Miskevich, Producer, edm@cccd.edu. **Local Programs:** *Real Orange* 7:00 pm - 10:30 pm Monday-Friday, Susan Tripp, Fax (714)895-0861; *Marketing Telecourse.* **Wattage:** 5,000,000. **URL:** http://www.koce.org.

HUNTINGTON PARK, pop. 45,932.

Los Angeles Co. S. of Los Angeles.

2091 Huntington Park Bulletin
Wave Community Newspapers
819 W. Whitter Blvd. Phone: (213)727-1117
Montebello, CA 90640-3623 Fax: (213)727-9515

Newspaper. **Founded:** 1904. **Freq:** Semiweekly (Wed. and Sat.). **Print Method:** Offset. **Cols./Page:** 6. **Col. Width:** 26 nonpareils. **Col. Depth:** 301 agate lines. **Key Personnel:** Arthur J. Aguilar, Exec. Editor/Publisher, phone (213)290-3000, fax (213)292-8289. **Subscription Rates:** Free; $125 by mail. **Remarks:** Advertising accepted; rates available upon request.
Circ: Paid 54
Free 12,850

IDYLLWILD, pop. 5,953.

SE CA. Riverside Co. 40 mi. SE of Riverside. Resort Area.

2092 Idyllwild Town Crier
PO Box 157 Phone: (909)659-2145
Idyllwild, CA 92549 Fax: (909)659-2071
Publication E-mail: itc@penet

News tabloid. **Founded:** 1946. **Freq:** Weekly (Thurs.). **Print Method:** Offset. **Cols./Page:** 6. **Col. Width:** 9.5 picas. **Col. Depth:** 182 agate lines. **Key Personnel:** Becky Clark, Editor and Publisher. **Subscription Rates:** $24 individuals; $28. **Remarks:** Accepts advertising. **URL:** http://www/idyllmtn.com/.
Ad Rates: BW: $390 **Circ:** 4,000
PCI: $5.20

IMPERIAL

2093 Imperial Valley Weekly/Imperial Hometown Review
Steve Larson
523 Pine Ave. Phone: (619)356-2995
Holtville, CA 92250-0118 Fax: (619)356-4915

Community newspaper (tabloid) serving Imperial County, CA. **Founded:** 1906. **Freq:** Weekly (Thurs.). **Print Method:** Offset. **Trim Size:** 11 1/2 x 14. **Cols./Page:** 6. **Col. Width:** 9.5 picas. **Col. Depth:** 13 inches. **Key Personnel:** Cesar Soto, Editor; Steve Larson, Publisher. **ISSN:** 0016-9140. **Subscription Rates:** $22 individuals; $26.50 out of area. **Remarks:** Accepts advertising.
Ad Rates: GLR: $1.70 **Circ:** Paid ‡1,785
BW: $327 Free ‡415
4C: $395
SAU: $4.10
PCI: $4.35

INDIO, pop. 21,611.

SW CA. Riverside Co. 125 mi. E. of Los Angeles. Dates, grapefruit, vegetable packing. Truck, fruit farms. grapes, cotton, cattle.

2094 Desert Advertiser
45-140 Towne St. Phone: (619)347-3313
Indio, CA 92202-2564 Fax: (619)342-7128

Shopper. **Founded:** 1965. **Freq:** Weekly (Wed.). **Print Method:** Offset. **Cols./Page:** 6. **Col. Width:** 24 nonpareils. **Col. Depth:** 297 agate lines. **Key Personnel:** Karen Oppenheim, Publisher. **Subscription Rates:** $6 individuals.
Circ: Free 28,000

The Desert Post - See Cathedral City

2095 Desert Rancher
45-140 Towne St., PO Drawer NNN Phone: (619)347-3313
Fax: (619)778-4654
Indio, CA 92202-2564
Agriculture magazine. **Founded:** 1949. **Freq:** Monthly. **Print Method:** Offset. **Cols./Page:** 5. **Col. Width:** 23 nonpareils. **Col. Depth:** 180 agate lines. **Key Personnel:** Karen Oppenheim, Publisher. **Subscription Rates:** $6 individuals.
Circ: Paid 15,532
Non-paid 5,500

Rancho Mirage Post - See Rancho Mirage

INGLEWOOD, pop. 94,245.

S. CA. Los Angeles Co. 10 mi. S. of Los Angeles. Manufactures airplanes. Electronics. Import export, air ground freight.

2096 Inglewood/Hawthorne Wave
Wave Community Newspapers, Inc.
2621 W. 54th St. Phone: (213)290-3000
Los Angeles, CA 90043 Fax: (213)291-0219

Black community newspaper sold in combination with the Culver City/Westchester Star. **Founded:** 1978. **Freq:** Biweekly Wednesday & Saturday. **Print Method:** Offset. **Trim Size:** 13 3/4 x 21 1/2. **Cols./Page:** 6. **Col. Width:** 5 nonpareils. **Col. Depth:** 21 1/2 inches. **Key Personnel:** C.Z. Wilson, President, fax (213)292-8289. **Subscription Rates:** Free; $125 by mail.
Circ: Non-paid 45,453

2097 Inglewood News Lennox Citizen
Coast Media Newspaper
4043 Irving Pl. Phone: (310)839-5271
Culver City, CA 90232-2809 Fax: (310)839-9372

Community newspaper. **Founded:** 1904. **Freq:** Semiweekly (Sat. and Thurs.). **Print Method:** Offset. **Cols./Page:** 6. **Col. Width:** 18 nonpareils. **Col. Depth:** 301 agate lines. **Key Personnel:** Richard Bronner, Publisher; Bob Payson, Publisher. **Subscription Rates:** $36 individuals. **Remarks:** Accepts advertising.
Ad Rates: BW: $1,382.88 **Circ:** Free 13,920
4C: $2,082.88

2098 Inglewood Tribune
Rapid Publishing
349 W. Compton Phone: (213)774-0018
PO Box 4248
Compton, CA 90224
Black community newspaper. **Freq:** Weekly (Wed.). **Cols./Page:** 6. **Col. Width:** 12 1/2 picas. **Col. Depth:** 21 1/2 inches. **Key Personnel:** O. Ray Watkins, Publisher. **Remarks:** Accepts advertising.
Ad Rates: SAU: $10.65 **Circ:** Paid 1,000
Free 9,000

2099 KJLH-FM - 102.3
161 N. La Brea Ave. Phone: (310)330-2200
Inglewood, CA 90301 Fax: (310)330-5555

Format: Urban Contemporary. **Networks:** ABC; American Urban Radio. **Owner:** Taxi Productions Inc., at above address. **Founded:** 1965. **Operating Hours:** Continuous. **ADI:** Los Angeles (Corona & San Bernardino), CA. **Key Personnel:** Karen Slade, VP & General Mgr.; Cheryl Womak, Local Sales Manager; Al Ward, National Sales Manager; Barry Clark, Engineer; Cliff Winston, Program Dir. **Wattage:** 3000.

2100 KTYM-AM - 1460
6803 West Blvd. Phone: (310)672-3700
Inglewood, CA 90302-1895 Fax: (310)673-2259

Format: Ethnic; News; Religious. **Owner:** Trans America Broadcasting Corp., at above address, Fax: (310)672-9696. **Founded:** 1958. **Operating Hours:** Continuous. **Key Personnel:** Gerardo Borrego, General Mgr.; Gary G. Rehers, Sales Mgr.; Ruben Arenas, Jr., News Dir.; Bobby A. Howe, Contact, phone (310)672-0594. **Local Programs:** *Public Affairs Program*, Bobby A. Howe, (213)678-1504. **Wattage:** 5000 day; 500 night. **Ad Rates:** $17-22 for 30 seconds; $25-35 for 60 seconds.

IONE, pop. 2,207.

EC CA. Amador Co. 38 mi. SE of Sacramento. Agriculture. Cattle, truck crops.

2101 Pacific Coast Cable Co.
Box 1018 Phone: (209)274-2660
Ione, CA 95640

Owner: George Laine, at above address. **Key Personnel:** George Laine, General Mgr. **Cities Served:** Ione and Buena Vista, CA.

IRVINE, pop. 62,134.

S. CA. Orange Co. 9 mi. SE of Santa Ana. Manufacturers machinery, electric instruments, test equipment, tools and dies, aircraft parts, industrial chemicals. Truck, fruit farms.

2102 Business Start-Ups
Entrepreneur's Media Inc.
2392 Morse Ave. Phone: (949)261-2325
Irvine, CA 92614 Fax: (714)755-4211
Publication E-mail: bsumag@entrepreneurmag.com

Magazine for Generation X entrepreneurs (age 35 and under). Articles cover hot businesses to start; ideas for running and growing a business; cutting-edge technology; management; motivation and more. **Subtitle:** Smart Ideas for New Businesses. **Founded:** Jan. 1989. **Freq:** Monthly. **Print Method:** Offset. **Trim Size:** 8 x 10 3/4. **Cols./Page:** 3. **Col. Width:** 28 nonpareils. **Col. Depth:** 140 agate lines. **Key Personnel:** Karen Axelton, Managing Editor; Lee Jones, Publisher, phone (212)563-8080, fax (212)563-3852. **ISSN:** 1041-3707. **Subscription Rates:** $14.97 individuals; $2.95 single issue. **Remarks:** Accepts classified advertising. **Available Online. URL:** http://www.entrepreneurmag.com.
Ad Rates: BW: $9,685 **Circ:** Paid ★**250,253**
4C: $11,340

2103 The Ear
Irvine Valley College Phone: (714)451-5341
5500 Irvine Center Dr.
Irvine, CA 92620
Magazine containing poetry, art, and fiction written by residents of Orange County, California. **Founded:** 1983. **Freq:** Annual. **Trim Size:** 5 1/2 x 8 1/2. **Cols./Page:** 1. **Col. Width:** 4 1/2 inches. **Col. Depth:** 6 3/4 inches. **Key Personnel:** Marie Connors, Editor. **ISSN:** 1091-9368. **Subscription Rates:** $5 single issue; Free to students. **Remarks:** Advertising not accepted. **Also known as:** The Elephant Ear.
Circ: (Not Reported)

2104 Entrepreneur Magazine
Entrepreneur's Media Inc.
2392 Morse Ave. Phone: (949)261-2325
Irvine, CA 92614 Fax: (714)755-4211
Publication E-mail: entmag@entrepreneurmag.com

Magazine covering small business management and operation. **Founded:** 1973. **Freq:** Monthly. **Print Method:** Offset. **Trim Size:** 8 x 10 3/4. **Cols./Page:** 3. **Col. Width:** 28 nonpareils. **Col. Depth:** 140 agate lines. **Key Personnel:** Rieva Lesonsky, Editorial Dir. **ISSN:** 0163-3341. **Subscription Rates:** $19.97 individuals; $4 single issue; $4.95 single issue Jan. **Remarks:** Accepts advertising. **URL:** http://www.entrepreneurmag.com.
Ad Rates: BW: $35,150 **Circ:** Paid ★**538,469**
4C: $46,855

2105 Executive Golfer
Pazdur Publishing, Inc.
2171 Campus Dr. Phone: (949)752-6474
Irvine, CA 92612 Fax: (949)752-0398

Magazine providing private country club golfers with information on resorts for meetings, guest policies at private clubs, and golf communities for investment and retirement. Contains instructive articles for executives over 40. **Founded:** May 1972. **Freq:** Bimonthly. **Print Method:** Offset. **Trim Size:** 8 3/8 x 10 7/8. **Cols./Page:** 3. **Col. Width:** 27 nonpareils. **Col. Depth:** 98 agate lines. **Key Personnel:** Edward F. Pazdur, Publisher; Mark Pazdur, Advertising Dir.; Theda Ahern Pazdur, Editor. **Subscription Rates:** Free to qualified subscribers; $9 individuals. **Remarks:** Accepts advertising.
Ad Rates: BW: $8,680 **Circ:** Paid 2,016
4C: $9,980 Controlled 99,778

2106 Frames
Frames Data, Inc.
2 Park Plaza, Ste. 900 Phone: (714)756-2218
Irvine, CA 92714 Fax: (714)756-5322

Technical reference, with pictures & imported and domestic eyeview frames. **Founded:** 1968. **Freq:** Quarterly. **Print Method:** Web. **Trim Size:** 8 1/4 x 10 3/4. **Cols./Page:** 3. **Key Personnel:** Cindi Thomas, Editorial Mgr.; Skip Johnson, Publisher. **Subscription Rates:** $275 individuals.
Ad Rates: BW: $2,700 **Circ:** Paid ★**16,878**
4C: $4,040

2107 Mexican Studies/Estudios Mexicanos
University of California Press/Journals
University of California, Irvine
340 Humanities Office Bldg.
Irvine, CA 92717
Publisher E-mail: journal@ucop.edu

Journal covering Mexican studies. **Freq:** Semiannual. **Key Personnel:** Jaime E. Rodriguez, Editor; Marge Dean, Advertising & Circulation Mgr. **Subscription Rates:** $24 individuals; $58 institutions; $17 students; $14 single issue; $30 single issue institutions. **Remarks:** Accepts advertising.
Ad Rates: BW: $275 **Circ:** (Not Reported)

2108 New University
University of California, Irvine
3100 Gateway Commons Bldg. Phone: (714)824-5011
Irvine, CA 92619 Fax: (714)856-4287
Publication E-mail: newu@uci.edu

Collegiate newspaper featuring campus/community news. **Founded:** 1967. **Freq:** Weekly (Mon.). **Print Method:** Offset. **Trim Size:** 11 x 17. **Cols./Page:** 5. **Col. Width:** 23 nonpareils. **Col. Depth:** 224 agate lines. **Key Personnel:** Susan Gunn, Business Mgr., phone (949)824-2298, fax (949)824-4287, swgunn@uci.edu; Laurie Jane Brown, Advertising Mgr., phone (949)824-4284, fax (949)824-4287, ljbrown@uci.edu. **Subscription Rates:** $38.75 individuals; $1.25 single issue. **Remarks:** Accepts advertising. **Online:** University of California at Irvine.
Ad Rates: PCI: $9.85 **Circ:** Free ‡13,000

2109 Orange County Business Journal
2600 Michelson Blvd., Ste. 170 Phone: (949)833-8373
Irvine, CA 92612 Fax: (949)833-8751

Regional business news journal. **Founded:** 1978. **Freq:** Weekly. **Print Method:** Uses mats offset. **Cols./Page:** 4. **Col. Width:** 29 nonpareils. **Col. Depth:** 195 agate lines. **Key Personnel:** Rick Reiff, Editor, reiff@ocbj.com; Richard Reisman, Publisher, reisman@ocbj.com; Laura Garrett, Advertising Dir., garrett@ocbj.com; Janet Cox, Circulation Director, cox@ocbj.com. **ISSN:** 1051-7480. **Subscription Rates:** $74 individuals; $1.50 single issue. **Remarks:** Accepts advertising.
Ad Rates: BW: $4,695 **Circ:** Paid ★**11,546**
4C: $5,295 Non-paid ★**1,210**

2110 Ostomy Quarterly
United Ostomy Association, Inc.
19772 MacArthur Blvd., Ste. 200 Phone: (714)660-8624
Irvine, CA 92612-2405 Fax: (714)660-9262
Free: (800)826-0826
Publisher E-mail: uoa@deltanet.com

Journal for patients who have had operations to create an artificial passage for bodily elimination. **Founded:** 1963. **Freq:** Quarterly 6/year. **Print Method:** Offset. **Trim Size:** 8 5/8 x 11 3/16. **Cols./Page:** 3. **Col. Width:** 2 3/16 inches. **Col. Depth:** 11 3/16 inches. **Key Personnel:** Tom Kimball, Editor. **ISSN:** 0030-6517. **Subscription Rates:** $25 individuals; $6.50 single issue. **Remarks:** Accepts advertising.
Ad Rates: BW: $1,405 **Circ:** ‡30,000
4C: $3,630

2111 The Psychiatric Times
2801 McGaw Ave. Phone: (714)250-1008
Irvine, CA 92614-5835 Fax: (714)250-0445
Publication E-mail: editor@cmeinc.com

Newspaper (tabloid) serving psychiatrists, other mental health professionals, Neurologists and physicians interested in psychiatric disorders and issues. **Founded:** Jan. 1985. **Freq:** Monthly. **Print Method:** Offset. **Trim Size:** 11 x 14 1/2. **Cols./Page:** 4. **Key Personnel:** John L. Schwartz, M.D., Editor-in-Chief; David J. DeNinno, Publisher; Christine Potvin, Managing Editor. **ISSN:** 0893-2905. **Subscription Rates:** $49 individuals; $120 other countries; $10 single issue. **Remarks:** Accepts advertising. **URL:** http://www.mhsource.com.
Ad Rates: GLR: $12.50 **Circ:** Controlled ‡42,583
BW: $4,875
4C: $61655
PCI: $100

2112 Registered Representative
Intertec Publishing
18818 Teller Ave., Ste. 280 Phone: (949)851-2220
Irvine, CA 92612 Fax: (949)851-1636
Free: (800)621-0720

Magazine providing comprehensive coverage of securities industry trends directly affecting the job performance and productivity of retail stockbrokers. **Subtitle:** The Number One Magazine for Retail Stockbrokers. **Founded:** Sept. 1976. **Freq:** Monthly. **Print Method:** Web offset. **Trim Size:** 8 x 10 7/8. **Cols./Page:** 3. **Col. Width:** 13 1/2 picas. **Col. Depth:** 10 inches. **Key Personnel:** Dan Jamieson, Editor; Rich Santos, Publisher, rich_santos@intertec.com; Tammy Candella, Production Dir. **ISSN:** 0193-1865. **Subscription Rates:** $48 individuals; $57 out of country; $10 single issue. **Remarks:** Accepts advertising. **URL:** http://www.rrmag.com.
Ad Rates: BW: $8,550 **Circ:** Controlled ‡90,000
4C: $11,650
PCI: $180

2113 Sea Magazine
Duncan McIntosh Co., Inc.
17782 Cowan, 2nd Fl. Phone: (949)660-6150
Irvine, CA 92714 Fax: (949)660-6172
Publication E-mail: seamgzh@earthlink.net

Recreational boating magazine printing news and features for power boat enthusiasts in 13 western states. **Subtitle:** America's Western Boating Magazine. **Founded:** Oct. 1908. **Freq:** Monthly. **Print Method:** Offset. **Trim Size:** 8 x 10 7/8. **Cols./Page:** 3 and 4. **Col. Width:** 13 and 9.5 picas. **Col. Depth:** 9 1/2 inches. **Key Personnel:** Duncan McIntosh, Jr., Editor and Publisher; Teresa Ybarra, Publisher; Jeffrey Fleming, Assoc. Editor & Publisher. **ISSN:** 0746-8601. **Subscription Rates:** $16.97 individuals; $2.95 single issue; $26.97 Canada per year; $3.75 single issue, Canada. **Remarks:** Accepts advertising.
Ad Rates: BW: $3,435 **Circ:** Paid 19,759
4C: $5,255 Non-paid 26,166

2114 Waterfront Southern California News
Duncan McIntosh Co., Inc.
17782 Cowan, 2nd Fl. Phone: (949)660-6150
Irvine, CA 92714 Fax: (949)660-6172

Recreational boating Magazine. **Subtitle:** Your Local Boating News. **Founded:** Feb. 1993. **Freq:** Monthly. **Print Method:** Web offset. **Trim Size:** 9 1/2 x 12 1/2. **Cols./Page:** 3. **Col. Width:** 2 3/4 inches. **Col. Depth:** 11 1/2 inches. **Key Personnel:** Duncan McIntosh, Editor and Publisher; Teresa McIntosh, Co-Publisher; Jeffrey Flemming, Associate Editor; Eston Ellis, Senior Editor; Erin Mcniff, Associate Editor. **ISSN:** 0746-8601. **Subscription Rates:** free on stands; $10 home delivery. **Remarks:** Accepts advertising. **Available Online. URL:** http://www.gsn.com/sea.htm.
Ad Rates: BW: $1050 **Circ:** Paid 10,000
4C: $1165 Non-paid 30,000

2115 World Dredging, Mining & Construction
Placer Management Corp.
PO Box 17479 Phone: (949)553-0836
Irvine, CA 92623-7479 Fax: (949)863-9261
Publication E-mail: wdmc@ix.netcom.com
Publisher E-mail: wodcon@juno.com

Trade magazine discussing current issues and technological developments relating to the worldwide dredging and dredge mining industries. **Founded:** June 1, 1965. **Freq:** Monthly. **Print Method:** Offset. **Trim Size:** 8 1/2 x 11. **Cols./Page:** 3. **Col. Width:** 26 nonpareils. **Col. Depth:** 140 agate lines. **Key Personnel:** Bob Lindauer, Ad Sales/Circulation; Mort Richardson, Publisher; Steve Richardson, Editor. **ISSN:** 1045-0343. **Subscription Rates:** $36 individuals; $3 single issue; $84 other countries (airmail). **Remarks:** Accepts advertising. **Formerly:** World Dredging and Marine Construction (1989).
Ad Rates: BW: $1,100 **Circ:** ‡3,400
4C: $1,950
PCI: $50

2116 Cox Communications
2381–2391 Morse Ave. Phone: (714)660-0500
Irvine, CA 92714 Free: (800)426-9266

Owner: Times Mirror, 220 W. 1st St., Los Angeles, CA 90012. **Founded:** 1968. **Formerly:** Times Mirror Cable Television Inc. **Key Personnel:** Larry Wangberg, Contact; James H. Smith III, Contact; Christopher B. Forgy, Contact. **Cities Served:** subscribing households 1,300,000.

2117 KUCI-FM - 88.9
PO Box 4362 Phone: (949)824-6868
Irvine, CA 92716-4362
E-mail: kuci@uci.edu

Format: Eclectic. **Networks:** Independent. **Founded:** 1969. **Operating Hours:** Continuous. **Key Personnel:** Kevin Stockdale, Broadcast Media Coordinator, kmstockd@uci.edu. **Wattage:** 200. **Ad Rates:** Noncommercial. **URL:** http://www.kuci.org.

JACKSON†, pop. 2,331.

EC CA. Amador Co. 40 mi. SE of Sacramento. Creamery, winery, saw, planing mills, bottling works. Gold mines. Marble quarries, clay pits. Sugar pine timber. Truck, stock, poultry farms.

2118 Amador Ledger-Dispatch
PO Box 1328 Phone: (209)223-1767
Jackson, CA 95642 Fax: (209)223-1264
Publication E-mail: ledger@cdepot.net

Community newspaper. **Founded:** 1855. **Freq:** 3/week. **Print Method:** Offset. **Cols./Page:** 6. **Col. Width:** 18 nonpareils. **Col. Depth:** 301 agate lines. **Key Personnel:** Glenn Stifflemire, Publisher, fax (209)223-4245. **Subscription Rates:** $45.05 individuals. **Remarks:** Accepts advertising.
Ad Rates: BW: $835.38 **Circ:** Combined ‡6,874
4C: $1085.38
SAU: $6.63

2119 Calaveras Ledger Dispatch
Central Valley Newspapers, Inc.
PO Box 1328 Phone: (209)736-0921
Jackson, CA 95642 Fax: (209)223-1264
Publication E-mail: ledger@cdepot.net

Community newspaper. **Founded:** 1989. **Freq:** 3/week. **Print Method:** Offset. **Trim Size:** 14 x 21 1/2. **Cols./Page:** 6. **Col. Width:** 2 1/16 inches. **Col. Depth:** 21 inches. **Key Personnel:** Rayce Newman, Editor; Glenn Stifflemire, Advertising Mgr. **Subscription Rates:** $37.50 individuals; $.50 single issue. **Remarks:** Accepts advertising.
Ad Rates: BW: $774.90 **Circ:** Controlled 6,037
4C: $1,024.90
SAU: $6.15
PCI: $6.15

2120 Llamas Magazine
46 Main St. Free: (800)401-5262
Jackson, CA 95642-2322
Magazine for camelid owners and enthusiasts worldwide. **Subtitle:** The International Camelid Journal. **Founded:** 1979. **Freq:** 8/year. **Print Method:** Sheetfed offset. **Trim Size:** 8 1/2 x 11. **Cols./Page:** 3. **Col. Width:** 2 1/4 inches. **Col. Depth:** 9 7/8 inches. **Key Personnel:** Cheryl Dal Porto, Editor. **ISSN:** 0887-9923. **Subscription Rates:** $25. **Remarks:** Accepts advertising. **Formerly:** 3L Llama (1985).
Ad Rates: BW: $561 **Circ:** ‡5,500
4C: $1,067
PCI: $30

2121 KNGT-FM - 94.3
Box 609 Phone: (209)223-0241
Jackson, CA 95642-0609

Format: Adult Contemporary. **Networks:** ABC. **Founded:** 1973. **Operating Hours:** Continuous. **Key Personnel:** Laurence G. Rutter, Contact; Judy Hotchkiss, Sales Mgr.; Jim Guidi, Program Dir. **Wattage:** 230.

JULIAN

SW CA. San Diego Co. 30 mi. SE of Escondido.

2122 Julian News
PO Box 639 Phone: (760)765-2231
Julian, CA 92036-0639 Fax: (760)765-1838

Community newspaper. **Founded:** 1984. **Freq:** Weekly (Wed.). **Cols./Page:** 6. **Col. Width:** 1 7/8 inches. **Col. Depth:** 21 inches. **Key Personnel:** Paul K. Brown, Editor; Kay Howley, Contact. **Subscription Rates:** $30 individuals. **Remarks:** Accepts advertising.
Ad Rates: GLR: $12 **Circ:** Controlled 2,000

2123 Julian Cablevision
Box 1240 Phone: (760)765-1795
Julian, CA 92036 Fax: (760)765-1795

Owner: Monroe Cablevision, 9795 E. Caron St., Scottsdale, AZ 85258, (602)391-1904. **Founded:** 1982. **Key Personnel:** Mary Ann Prue, Office Mgr. **Cities Served:** Julian, CA: subscribing households 700; 41 channels; 1 community access channel.

JUNE LAKE

NE CA. Mono Co. 20 mi. S. of Mono Lake.

2124 Mono County Television Corp.
Box 711 Phone: (619)648-7380
June Lake, CA 93529

Key Personnel: Dan Roberts, Jr., Vice President; Frank Roberts, President; Maria Roberts, Office Mgr. **Cities Served:** subscribing households 640; 18 channels; 1 community access channel.

KENSINGTON

2125 Blue Unicorn
Blue Unicorn, Inc.
22 Avon Rd. Phone: (510)526-8439
Kensington, CA 94707
Poetry Journal. **Subtitle:** A Tri-Quarterly of Poetry. **Founded:** 1977. **Freq:** Tri-quarterly, Feb., June, & Oct. **Key Personnel:** Ruth G. Iodince, Editor; Fred Ostrander, Editor; Martha E. Bosworth, Editor. **ISSN:** 0960-8574. **Subscription Rates:** $14 individuals; $20 out of country; $5 single issue. **Remarks:** Advertising not accepted.
Circ: Combined 475

KERMAN, pop. 4,002.

C. CA. Fresno Co. 15 mi. W. of Fresno. Sugar factory. Alfalfa mill, cotton gins. Agriculture. Sugar beets, grapes, cotton, rice, alfalfa, cattle.

2126 The Kerman News
Kerwest
PO Box 336 Phone: (209)846-6689
Kerman, CA 93630 Fax: (209)846-8045

Community newspaper. **Founded:** 1905. **Freq:** Weekly (Wed.). **Print Method:** Offset. **Cols./Page:** 6. **Col. Width:** 2 1/16 inches. **Col. Depth:** 21 inches. **Key Personnel:** Mark O. Kilen, Editor; Merlyn Wilcox, Advertising Mgr. **Subscription Rates:** $18 individuals. **Remarks:** Accepts advertising.
Ad Rates: GLR: $.59 **Circ:** ‡2,000
BW: $1,036.98
SAU: $8.23

2127 West Side Advance
Key West Inc.
PO Box 336 Phone: (209)846-6689
Kerman, CA 93630 Fax: (209)846-8045

Community newspaper. **Founded:** 1919. **Freq:** Weekly (Wed.). **Print Method:** Offset. **Cols./Page:** 6. **Col. Width:** 2 1/16 inches. **Col. Depth:** 21 inches. **Key Personnel:** Mark O. Kilen, Editor; Merlyn Wilcox, Advertising Mgr. **Subscription Rates:** $18 individuals. **Remarks:** Accepts advertising.
Ad Rates: GLR: $.59 **Circ:** Free ‡10,325
BW: $1,036.98
SAU: $8.23

KING CITY, pop. 5,495.

W. CA. Monterey Co. 48 mi. SE of Salinas. Wax, asbestos products. Garlic onion dehydration. Carrots and tomatoes packed. Agriculture. Cattle, grain, potatoes.

2128 KRKC-AM - 1490
1134 Broadway Phone: (408)385-5421
Box B Fax: (408)385-0635
King City, CA 93930-3317
Free: (800)237-8637

Format: News; Agricultural; Country. **Networks:** CBS. **Owner:** Radio Del Rey, at above address. **Operating Hours:** 5 a.m.-midnight.; 10% network, 90% local. **Key Personnel:** Bill Graff, Operations Dir.; Harold Fuller, News Dir.; Bill Gittler, Contact. **Wattage:** 1000.

2129 KRKC-FM - 102.1
1134 Broadway Phone: (408)385-5421
Box B Fax: (408)385-0635
King City, CA 93930-3317
Free: (800)237-8637
E-mail: krkc@ciaa.com

Format: Soft Rock. **Networks:** CBS. **Owner:** Radio Del Rey, at above address. **Operating Hours:** 5 a.m.-midnight;10% network, 90% local. **Key Personnel:** Bill Graff, Operations Dir.; Alex Rios, News Dir., phone (408)386-5422; Bill Gittler, Owner/Gen. Mgr.; Mike Davis, Program Dir. **Wattage:** 50,000 ERP. **Ad Rates:** Combined advertising rates available with KRKC-AM.

KINGSBURG, pop. 5,115.

C. CA. Fresno Co. 20 mi. SE of Fresno. Cotton gins, cottonseed oil mill, wineries, raisin drying, fruit cannery. Fruit, dairy, poultry farms. Grapes, cotton, peaches.

2130 Recorder
Community Newspapers
1467 Marion St. Phone: (209)897-2993
PO Box 128 Fax: (209)897-4868
Kingsburg, CA 93631
Newspaper. **Founded:** 1904. **Freq:** Weekly (Wed.). **Print Method:** Offset. **Cols./Page:** 6. **Col. Width:** 26 nonpareils. **Col. Depth:** 294 agate lines. **Key Personnel:** Jim Brock, Publisher, phone (209)896-1976, fax (209)896-9160; Joanne Heredia, Advertising Dir., phone (209)896-1976, fax (209)896-9160. **Subscription Rates:** $20 individuals. **Remarks:** Accepts advertising.
Ad Rates: GLR: $13.25 **Circ:** 3,300
4C: $240
SAU: $11

LA CANADA, pop. 20,153.

S. CA. Los Angeles Co. 5 mi. NW of Pasadena. Residential.

2131 La Canada Valley Sun
No. 1 Valley Sun Ln. Phone: (818)790-8774
PO Box 38 Fax: (818)790-5690
La Canada, CA 91012-0038
Local newspaper. **Founded:** Apr. 3, 1946. **Freq:** Weekly (Thurs.). **Print Method:** Offset. **Cols./Page:** 6. **Col. Width:** 19 nonpareils. **Col. Depth:** 224 agate lines. **Key Personnel:** Margaret M. Graf, Managing Editor; Gerald A. Bean, Publisher. **Subscription Rates:** $18 individuals; $24 out of area; $26 out of state. **Remarks:** Accepts advertising.
Ad Rates: GLR: $8.55 **Circ:** ‡5,500
BW: $820.80
4C: $1,235.80

2132 The °not born yesterday' Citizen
Osmon Publications
4805 Alta Canyada Rd. Phone: (818)790-0651
La Canada, CA 91011
Magazine for senior citizens. **Founded:** 1961. **Freq:** Monthly. **Print Method:** Offset. **Trim Size:** 11 1/2 x 13 1/2. **Cols./Page:** 6. **Col. Width:** 9.5 picas. **Col. Depth:** 12 1/2 inches. **Key Personnel:** Oarol Osmon, Editor. **ISSN:** 0748-5727. **Subscription Rates:** $5 individuals. **Remarks:** Accepts advertising. **Formerly:** California Senior Citizen; The Citizen.
Ad Rates: BW: $1,125 **Circ:** Paid ‡47,746
4C: $1,275 Controlled ‡42,286
PCI: $24

LA CRESCENTA

2133 Ward's/Dealer Business
Ward's Communications
3710A Foothill Blvd., Ste. 310 Phone: (818)951-3269
La Crescenta, CA 91214 Fax: (818)951-6669
Publication E-mail: 259-9164@mcimail.com

Business magazine for franchised new car dealers and their management. **Founded:** Oct. 1966. **Freq:** Monthly. **Print Method:** Web offset. **Trim Size:** 8 x 10 3/4. **Cols./Page:** 3. **Col. Width:** 13.5 picas. **Col. Depth:** 10 inches. **Key Personnel:** C. D. Bohon, Editor; Roger K. Powers, Publisher. **ISSN:** 1086-1629. **Subscription Rates:** $36 individuals; $10 single issue. **URL:** http://www.wardsauto.com. **Alt. Formats:** Microfilm. **Formerly:** Auto Age Dealer Business.
Ad Rates: BW: $6,555 **Circ:** Paid 439
4C: $8,815 Controlled 31,500
PCI: $260

LA HABRA, pop. 45,232.

S. CA. Orange Co. 25 mi. E. of Los Angeles. Citrus fruit packing, electronic products manufactured. Agriculture.

2134 Ex-CBI Roundup
Dwight Publishing
Box 2665 Phone: (310)947-2007
La Habra, CA 90632-2665
Military and navy magazine. **Founded:** 1947. **Freq:** Monthly (except August and September). **Print Method:** Offset. **Cols./Page:** 2. **Col. Width:** 30 nonpareils. **Col. Depth:** 110 agate lines. **Key Personnel:** Dwight O. King, Editor and Publisher. **ISSN:** 0014-388X. **Subscription Rates:** $12 individuals. **Remarks:** Accepts advertising.
Ad Rates: BW: $160 **Circ:** ‡6,285

LA HONDA

2135 Schnauzer Shorts
Dan Kiedrowski Co.
P.O. Drawer A Phone: (650)747-0549
La Honda, CA 94020 Fax: (650)747-0549

Trade magazine covering dog breeding and showing. **Founded:** 1960. **Freq:** Bimonthly. **Print Method:** Offset. **Trim Size:** 6 x 9. **Cols./Page:** 1. **Col. Width:** 4 3/4 inches. **Col. Depth:** 7 3/4 inches. **Key Personnel:** Dan Kiedrowski, Editor and Publisher; Denis Shaw, Circulation Mgr. **ISSN:** 0276-1521. **Subscription Rates:** $30 individuals; $6 single issue. **Remarks:** Accepts advertising.
Ad Rates: BW: $120 **Circ:** Combined ⊕**1,000**
4C: $420

2136 Terrier Type
Dan Kiedrowski Co.
P.O. Drawer A Phone: (650)747-0549
La Honda, CA 94020 Fax: (650)747-0549

Trade magazine covering show dogs for breeders, handlers, and owners. **Founded:** 1962. **Freq:** Monthly. **Print Method:** Offset. **Trim Size:** 6 x 9. **Cols./Page:** 1. **Col. Width:** 4 3/4 inches. **Col. Depth:** 7 3/4 inches. **Key Personnel:** Dan Kiedrowski, Publisher; Robert LaRouech, Editor; Denis Shaw, Circulation Mgr. **ISSN:** 0199-6495. **Subscription Rates:** $40 individuals; $6 single issue. **Remarks:** Accepts advertising.
Ad Rates: BW: $120 **Circ:** Combined ‡1,900
4C: $420

LA JOLLA

San Diego Co. On Pacific Ocean, 15 mi. NW of San Diego. University of California at San Diego. Winter and summer resort. Residential.

Beverly Hills Independent - See Beverly Hills

Brentwood-Westwood Press - See Brentwood

2137 The Communication Review
Gordon and Breach Publishers
c/o Robert Horwitz Phone: (619)534-7027
University of California, San Diego Fax: (619)534-7315
Department of Communication
9500 Gilman Dr.
La Jolla, CA 92093
Publication E-mail: rhorwitz@ucsd.edu
Publisher E-mail: info@g6hap.com

Academic journal. **Founded:** 1995. **Freq:** Quarterly. **Trim Size:** 6 x 9. **Cols./Page:** 1. **Key Personnel:** Robert Horwitz, Editor; Daniel Hallin, Assoc. Editor; Michael Schudson, Assoc. Editor; Michael Cole, Assoc. Editor; Romel Hokanson, Managing Editor. **ISSN:** 1071-4421. **Subscription Rates:** $90 individuals. **Remarks:** Advertising accepted; rates available upon request.
Circ: (Not Reported)

Culver City/Ladera Independent - See Culver City

2138 IEEE Antennas & Propogation
IEEE, Inc.
1446 Vista Claridad Phone: (619)459-8305
La Jolla, CA 92037 Fax: (619)459-7140
Publisher E-mail: 71221.621@compuserve.com

Membership magazine covering antennas, propogation, telecommunications, electromagnetics, and computational methods. **Founded:** 1957. **Freq:** Bimonthly. **Print Method:** Web offset. **Trim Size:** 8 1/4 x 10 7/8. **Cols./Page:** 2. **Col. Width:** 3 3/8 inches. **Col. Depth:** 9 7/8 inches. **Key Personnel:** Dr. W. Ross Stone, Editor-in-Chief. **ISSN:** 1045-9243. **Subscription Rates:** Free to qualified subscribers; $210 nonmembers. **Remarks:** Accepts advertising.
Ad Rates: BW: $450 **Circ:** Controlled 10,400
4C: $1,000

2139 Journal of Ultrasound in Medicine
American Institute of Ultrasound in Medicine
JUM Editorial Office
9500 Gilman Dr., Dept. 0990
La Jolla, CA 92093-0990
Publisher E-mail: publications@aium.org

Journal discussing current topics in diagnostic ultrasound. **Subtitle:** Official Journal of the American Institute of Ultrasound in Medicine. **Founded:** 1982. **Freq:** Monthly. **Print Method:** Offset. **Trim Size:** 8 1/4 x 10 7/8. **Cols./Page:** 2. **Col. Width:** 39 nonpareils. **Col. Depth:** 140 agate lines. **Key Personnel:** George R. Leopold, M.D., Editor; Maureen Kalil, Asst. Dir.; Marti Boyer, Sales Mgr. **ISSN:** 0278-4297. **Subscription Rates:** $120 individuals; $165 institutions; $155 out of country; $200 institutions, other countries; $72 students; $93 students, other countries. **Remarks:** Accepts advertising.
Ad Rates: BW: $1,285 **Circ:** Paid **13,000**
4C: $1,390

2140 La Jolla Light
450 Pearl St. Phone: (619)459-4201
PO Box 1927 Fax: (619)459-0977
La Jolla, CA 92037-4901
Local newspaper. **Founded:** 1913. **Freq:** Weekly (Thurs.). **Print Method:** Offset. **Trim Size:** 13 x 21 1/2. **Cols./Page:** 6. **Col. Width:** 2 1/16 inches. **Col. Depth:** 21 1/2 inches. **Key Personnel:** Evan Isreal, Publisher; Carlos Davalos, Editor. **Subscription Rates:** $19.40 individuals. **Remarks:** Accepts advertising. **URL:** http://www.news@flash.net.
Ad Rates: GLR: $3.05 **Circ:** ‡26,000
BW: $2,709
4C: $3,059
PCI: $21

2141 Mathematical Research Letters
International Press of Boston Inc.
c/o M. Salah Baouendi Fax: (619)534-5273
University of Mathematics 0112
University of California, San Diego
La Jolla, CA 92093-0112
Publication E-mail: mrl@ucsd.edu
Publisher E-mail: hugh@descartes.intlpress.com

Academic journal covering announcements in mathematics research. **Founded:** 1993. **Freq:** Bimonthly. **Key Personnel:** M. Salah Baouendi, Managing Editor; Linda P. Rothschild, Managing Editor. **ISSN:** 1073-2780. **Subscription Rates:** $100 individuals; $190 institutions; $33 single issue. **Remarks:** Accepts advertising.
Ad Rates: GLR: $50 **Circ:** Combined 250
BW: $250
4C: $500

2142 New Indicator
9500 Gilman Dr., 323 Student Co-Op Center Phone: (619)534-2016
La Jolla, CA 92093-5003
College newspaper emphasizing progressive views of politics, art, and culture. **Founded:** 1966. **Freq:** 9/year. **Print Method:** Offset. **Trim Size:** 11 x 17. **Cols./Page:** 4. **Col. Width:** 30 nonpareils. **Col. Depth:** 224 agate lines. **Subscription Rates:** $8 individuals. **Remarks:** Accepts advertising.
Ad Rates: BW: $172 **Circ:** Paid ‡100
PCI: $6 Free ‡7,900

2143 Outlook Mail
Copley Los Angeles Newspapers, Inc.
7776 Ivanhoe Ave.
La Jolla, CA 92037

Newspaper. **Founded:** 1982. **Freq:** Weekly (Wed.). **Print Method:** Offset. **Cols./Page:** 6. **Col. Width:** 26 nonpareils. **Col. Depth:** 301 agate lines. **Key Personnel:** Bertram Winrow, Publisher. **Subscription Rates:** $24 individuals. **Remarks:** Accepts advertising.
Ad Rates: GLR: $.65 **Circ:** 37,380

2144 Political Theory
Sage Publications Inc.
Political Theory Phone: (619)534-7081
Dept. of Political Science Fax: (619)534-7130
University of California, San Diego
La Jolla, CA 92093-0521
Publication E-mail: tstrong@weber.ucsd.edu
Publisher E-mail: info@sagepub.com

Political philosophy journal. **Subtitle:** An International Journal of Political Philosophy. **Founded:** 1973. **Freq:** Bimonthly. **Print Method:** Offset. **Trim Size:** 5 1/2 x 8 1/2. **Cols./Page:** 1. **Col. Width:** 50 nonpareils. **Col. Depth:** 100 agate lines. **Key Personnel:** Tracy B. Strong, Editor, tstrong@weber.ucsd.edu; Eric Moran, Sage Pub Com, eric_moran@sagepub.com. **ISSN:** 0090-5917. **Subscription Rates:** $56 individuals; $175 institutions Institutions; $92 two years; $268 two years Institutions; $16 single issue; $36 single issue INS. **Remarks:** Accepts advertising.
Ad Rates: BW: $250 **Circ:** Paid ‡2,350
Non-paid ‡95

2145 Pre-Vue Entertainment Magazine
National Pre-Vue Network Inc.
7825 Fay Ave. Phone: (619)456-5577
La Jolla, CA 92037 Fax: (619)542-0114
Publication E-mail: prevuemag@aol.com

Movie magazine. **Founded:** Jan. 1991. **Freq:** Bimonthly. **Trim Size:** 8 5/16 x 5 5/16. **Cols./Page:** 2. **Subscription Rates:** $10 individuals; $2 single issue. **Remarks:** Accepts advertising.
Ad Rates: BW: $4,000 **Circ:** Paid 2,609
4C: $5,000 Non-paid 200,000

2146 Psychosomatic Medicine
Lippincott Williams & Wilkins
University of California, San Diego Phone: (619)543-5468 Fax: (619)543-5462
Dept. of Psychiatry 0804
9500 Gilman Dr.
La Jolla, CA 92093-0804
Journal on scientific research into psychosomatic processes and relationships. **Founded:** 1938. **Freq:** Bimonthly. **Print Method:** Offset. **Trim Size:** 8 1/8 x 10 7/8. **Key Personnel:** Joel E. Dimsdale, M.D., Editor, jdimsdale@ucsd.edu; Lynn Gibson, Rep., phone (410)528-4281, lgibson@wwilkins.com. **Subscription Rates:** $199 individuals; $239 other countries; $409 institutions; $449 other countries. **Remarks:** Accepts advertising. **URL:** http://www.lww.com. **Alt. Formats:** Mailing labels.
Ad Rates: BW: $620 4C: $1,360 **Circ:** Paid ‡2,193 Non-paid ‡52

2147 UCSD Guardian
University of California at San Diego
Mail Code 0316 UCSD Phone: (619)534-3466
9500 Gilman Dr. Fax: (619)534-7691
La Jolla, CA 92093-0316
Publication E-mail: guardian@ucsd.edu

College newspaper. **Founded:** 1964. **Freq:** Semiweekly (Mon. & Thurs.). **Print Method:** Offset. **Trim Size:** 10 x 16. **Cols./Page:** 5. **Col. Width:** 1 7/8 inches. **Col. Depth:** 16 inches. **Key Personnel:** Ann Barefield, Business Mgr.; Brock Halter, Advertising Mgr.; Terry Lew, Editor-in-Chief. **Subscription Rates:** $70 individuals. **Remarks:** Accepts advertising. **URL:** http://www.ucsd.guardian.edu. **Former name:** Triton Times.
Ad Rates: GLR: $4 BW: $720 4C: $1,120 PCI: $9 **Circ:** Combined 12,000

Venice Marina News - See Venice

2148 Voz Fronteriza
University of California at San Diego
0077, UCSD Phone: (619)534-3616
La Jolla, CA 92093
Student newspaper. **Subtitle:** University of California at San Diego's Chicano Newspaper. **Founded:** 1976. **Freq:** Monthly (during the academic year). **Print Method:** Offset. **Trim Size:** 11 x 17. **Cols./Page:** 5. **Key Personnel:** Gene Chavira, Editor; Adolfo Guzman Lopez, Advertising Mgr. **Remarks:** Advertising accepted; rates available upon request.
Circ: 8,000

West Los Angeles Independent - See Los Angeles

LA MESA, pop. 50,342.

S. CA. San Diego Co. 10 mi. E. of San Diego. Residential. Retirement community.

2149 La Mesa Forum
Forum Publications, Inc.
3434 Grove St. Phone: (619)469-0101
PO Box 127
Lemon Grove, CA 91946-1812
Community newspaper. **Founded:** 1989. **Freq:** Weekly (Thurs.). **Print Method:** Offset. **Trim Size:** 11 x 17. **Cols./Page:** 5. **Col. Width:** 11 1/2 picas. **Col. Depth:** 16 inches. **Key Personnel:** Steve Saint, Editor and Publisher. **Subscription Rates:** $15; $30 other states. **Remarks:** Accepts advertising.
Ad Rates: BW: $400 4C: $720 PCI: $5 **Circ:** ‡4,000

2150 San Diego Jewish Times
Rosenberg Enterprises Inc.
4731 Palm Ave. Phone: (619)463-5575
La Mesa, CA 91941 Fax: (900)370-1190
Publisher E-mail: jewishtimes@msn.com

Newspaper containing information of interest to the Jewish community. **Subtitle:** 4. **Founded:** 1979. **Freq:** Biweekly. **Print Method:** Offset. **Trim Size:** 11 1/2 x 15. **Cols./Page:** 5. **Col. Width:** 2 inches. **Col. Depth:** 14 inches. **Key Personnel:** Carol Rosenberg, Editor; Garry Rosenberg, Advertising Dir./Publisher. **Subscription Rates:** $32 individuals. **Remarks:** Accepts advertising.
Circ: Paid ⊕15,663 Non-paid ⊕510

2151 Union Jack
Union Jack Publishing
PO Box 1823 Phone: (619)466-3129
La Mesa, CA 91944-1823 Free: (800)262-7305
Publication E-mail: 74537.2416@compuserve.com

Newspaper bringing news of Britain to the British community and other interested individuals in the U.S. **Founded:** 1982. **Freq:** Monthly. **Print Method:** Rotary offset. **Trim Size:** 10 1/2 x 17. **Cols./Page:** 5. **Col. Width:** 1 7/8 inches. **Col. Depth:** 15 1/2 inches. **Key Personnel:** Ronald Choularton, Editor and Publisher; Jeff Choularton, Publisher; Mike Sfax, Office Manager. **ISSN:** 1077-3479. **Subscription Rates:** $30 individuals. **Remarks:** Accepts advertising. **URL:** http://sd.znet.com/~unionj.
Ad Rates: GLR: $8 BW: $1,750 4C: $2,350 PCI: $32 **Circ:** Paid 10,500 Free 70,000

LA MIRADA, pop. 40,986.

S. CA. Los Angeles Co. 12 mi. SE of Los Angeles. Biola University. Manufactures plastics, tools, steel, paper products, chemicals, furniture.

2152 The Chimes
Biola University
13800 Biola Ave. Phone: (310)903-4880
La Mirada, CA 90639-0001 Fax: (310)903-4748
Publication E-mail: chimes@peter.biola.edu

Collegiate. **Founded:** 1935. **Freq:** Weekly (Fri.). **Print Method:** Offset. **Cols./Page:** 5. **Col. Width:** 22 nonpareils. **Col. Depth:** 210 agate lines. **Key Personnel:** Jeremy Littau, Editor; James Tweedy, Advertising Dir., james-tweedy@bubbs.biola.edu. **Subscription Rates:** $20 individuals. **Remarks:** Accepts advertising. **URL:** http://chimes.biola.edu/.
Ad Rates: GLR: $.25 BW: $350 PCI: $5.60 **Circ:** Free 2,000

2153 Journal of Psychology and Theology
Marketing Com
Rosemead School of Psychology Phone: (562)903-4727
Biola University Fax: (562)906-4500
13800 Biola Ave.
La Mirada, CA 90639-0001
Publication E-mail: journal@peter.biola.edu; journal_editorial@peter.biola.edu; subscriptions_ @peter.biola.edu; journal_ subscriptions@peter.biola.edu

Theoretical, research, and applied articles on the interrelationships of psychological and theological concepts. Also includes reviews of relevant books. **Subtitle:** An Evangelical Forum for the Integration of Psychology & Theology. **Founded:** 1973. **Freq:** Quarterly. **Print Method:** Offset. **Trim Size:** 6 3/4 x 10. **Cols./Page:** 2. **Col. Width:** 32 nonpareils. **Col. Depth:** 109 agate lines. **Key Personnel:** Patricia L. Pike, Ph.D., Editor; Beverly J. Schlapper, Managing Editor. **ISSN:** 0091-6471. **Subscription Rates:** $38 individuals; $40 by mail; $50 air mail. **Remarks:** Advertising accepted; rates available upon request. **Online:** BRS; Dialog (The Dialog Corporation); UMI. **Alt. Formats:** Microform.
Circ: ‡1,700

LA PUENTE, pop. 30,882.

S. CA. Los Angles Co. 25 mi. E. of Los Angeles. Light industry. Residential.

2154 KGRB-AM - 900
751 Echelon Ave.
La Puente, CA 91744

Format: Big Band/Nostalgia. **Networks:** Independent. **Founded:** 1963. **Operating Hours:** Sunrise-sunset. **Key Personnel:** Robert Burdette, Contact. **Wattage:** 500.

LA VERNE, pop. 23,508.

S. CA. Los Angeles Co. 30 mi. E. of Los Angeles. Residential.

2155 Campus Times
University of La Verne
1950 3rd St. Phone: (909)392-2712
La Verne, CA 91750 Fax: (909)392-2706
Publication E-mail: ctimes@ulv.edu

College newspaper. **Founded:** 1919. **Freq:** Weekly (Fri.). **Print Method:** Offset. **Trim Size:** 11 x 17. **Cols./Page:** 5. **Col. Width:** 10.8 nonpareils. **Col. Depth:** 96 agate lines. **Key Personnel:** Eric Bishop, Editorial Advisor, phone (909)593-3511, bishope@ulv.edu. **URL:** http://www.ulv.edu/~ctimes.
Ad Rates: BW: $350 4C: $700 PCI: $6 **Circ:** Free 2,000

2156 La Verne Magazine
University of La Verne
1950 3rd St. Phone: (909)392-2712
La Verne, CA 91750 Fax: (909)392-2706
Publication E-mail: ctimes@ulv.edu

Community magazine by the students of the University of La Verne. **Founded:** Feb. 1976. **Freq:** Semiannual. **Key Personnel:** Dr. George Keeler, Faculty Advisor. **Subscription Rates:** Free. **Remarks:** Advertising not accepted. **URL:** http://www.ulv.edu/~comms/lvm.htm.
Circ: Combined 2,200

2157 KULV-AM/FM - 550AM/107.9FM
University of La Verne Phone: (909)593-3511
1950 3rd St. Fax: (909)392-2706
La Verne, CA 91750
E-mail: kulv@ulv.edu

Format: Alternative/New Music/Progressive; Adult Contemporary. **Owner:** University of La Verne, at above address. **Founded:** 1976. **Formerly:** KULV-AM. **Operating Hours:** 7 a.m.-10 p.m. Monday-Friday. **Key Personnel:** Mike Laponis, Station Mgr., laponism@ulv.edu; Shane Rodrigues, Operations Mgr., srodrigu@ulv.edu; John Garrison, Program Dir.; Corey Brown, Music Dir.; Erin Sarkisian, Asst. Music Dir.; Kristi Burks, Promotions Dir.; Enrique Gutierrez, Promotions Coordinator; James Cumberland, Public Service Dir.; Sergio Paredes, Public Affairs Dir.; Simon Bouie', Sports Dir. **Local Programs:** *KULV Sports*. **Wattage:** 1. **Ad Rates:** $3-10 for 30 seconds; $2-8 for 60 seconds. **URL:** http://www.ulv.edu/comms/kulv/kulv.htm.

LAFAYETTE, pop. 20,879.

W. CA. Contra Costa Co. 10 mi. NE of Berkeley. Residential.

2158 Contra Costa Sun
Contra Costa Newspapers, Inc.
PO Box 599 Phone: (510)284-4444
Lafayette, CA 94549 Fax: (510)284-1039
Publication E-mail: ccsuned@hotcoco.infi.net

Community newspaper. **Founded:** 1935. **Freq:** Weekly (Wed.). **Print Method:** Offset. **Cols./Page:** 6. **Col. Width:** 22 nonpareils. **Col. Depth:** 301 agate lines. **Key Personnel:** Bev Britton, Managing Editor; George Riggs, Publisher; John Armstrong, Editor-in-Chief. **Subscription Rates:** $30 by mail per year. **Remarks:** Accepts advertising.
Ad Rates: GLR: $.55 **Circ:** Paid 8,000

LAGUNA BEACH, pop. 17,860.

S. CA. Orange Co. On Pacific Ocean, 18 mi. SW of Santa Ana. Summer and winter resort.

2159 Laguna Beach News
South Orange County News
PO Box 3629 Phone: (714)768-3631
Mission Viejo, CA 92690 Fax: (714)454-7354

Community newspaper. **Founded:** 1915. **Freq:** Weekly (Thurs.). **Print Method:** Offset. **Trim Size:** 10 3/4 x 16 3/4. **Cols./Page:** 5. **Col. Width:** 9 picas. **Col. Depth:** 13 inches. **Key Personnel:** Chris Meyer, Editor; Douglas E. Hanes, Publisher; Lynda Benice, Advertising Mgr. **Subscription Rates:** $12 individuals; $25 Out of County. **Remarks:** Accepts advertising. **Formerly:** Laguna News-Post (1990).
Ad Rates: BW: $696 4C: $720 PCI: $32.17 **Circ:** ‡13,223

2160 This is Laguna
Laguna Press
PO Box 1568
Laguna Beach, CA 92652

Magazine profiling Laguna Beach, CA. **Freq:** Bimonthly. **Key Personnel:** Pat Cochran, Editor and Publisher. **Subscription Rates:** $10. $2 single issue.

2161 The Underground Wine Journal
Wine Journal Enterprises Inc.
412 Glenneyre Phone: (626)441-6617
Laguna Beach, CA 92651 Fax: (626)441-6765
Free: (888)946-3576
Publisher E-mail: winejournal@earthlink.net

Trade journal covering wine, food, and travel. **Founded:** 1979. **Freq:** Bimonthly. **Key Personnel:** Christine R. Graham, Editor and Publisher; John Tilson, Assoc. Publisher. **Subscription Rates:** $48 individuals; $8 single issue. **Remarks:** Accepts advertising.
Ad Rates: BW: $1,350 4C: $1,890 **Circ:** Combined 10,000

LAGUNA HILLS, pop. 13,676.

S. CA. Orange Co. 2 mi. S. of El Toro.

📖 **2162 Agency Sales Magazine**
Manufacturers' Agents National Association (MANA)
23016 Mill Creek Rd. Phone: (949)859-4040
PO Box 3467 Fax: (949)855-2973
Laguna Hills, CA 92654
Publication E-mail: mana@manaonline.org
Publisher E-mail: askmana@aol.com

Magazine for manufacturers' agents and manufacturers. Includes tax developments and tips, management aids for manufacturers and agents, legal bulletins, trend-identifying market data, classified ads, and industry trade show calendar. **Founded:** 1947. **Freq:** Monthly. **Print Method:** Offset. **Trim Size:** 8 3/8 x 10 7/8. **Cols./Page:** 3. **Col. Width:** 28 nonpareils. **Col. Depth:** 137 agate lines. **Key Personnel:** Jack Foster, Editor. **ISSN:** 0749-2332. **Subscription Rates:** $49 individuals; $55 Canada; $61.50 other countries. **Remarks:** Accepts advertising.
Ad Rates: GLR: $10.66 **Circ:** ‡18,000
BW: $1,800.81
4C: $2,897.81
PCI: $66

📖 **2163 Bodyshop Expo**
Professional Tool & Equipment News, Inc.
25401 Cabot Rd., Ste. 209 Phone: (949)830-7520
Laguna Hills, CA 92653 Fax: (949)830-7523

Trade magazine for the automobile body and repair shop industry. **Freq:** Bimonthly. **Key Personnel:** Anthony J. Ross, Managing Editor. **Remarks:** Accepts advertising.
Ad Rates: BW: $3,990 **Circ:** Combined ‡61,039
4C: $5,665

📖 **2164 Leisure World News**
South County News
PO Box 3629 Phone: (714)768-3631
Mission Viejo, CA 92691 Fax: (949)454-7354

Newspaper for senior citizens in South Orange County, CA. **Founded:** 1965. **Freq:** Weekly (Thurs.). **Print Method:** Offset. **Cols./Page:** 5. **Col. Width:** 12.2 inches. **Col. Depth:** 13 inches. **Key Personnel:** Chris Meyer, Editor; Douglas E. Hanes, Publisher; Pat Norton, Advertising Mgr. **Subscription Rates:** $11 individuals. **Remarks:** Accepts advertising.
Ad Rates: PCI: $32.17 **Circ:** ‡11,555

📖 **2165 Professional Tool & Equipment News**
Professional Tool & Equipment News, Inc.
25401 Cabot Rd., Ste. 209 Phone: (949)830-7520
Laguna Hills, CA 92653 Fax: (949)830-7523

Magazine for automotive shop owners and technicians. Reports on new tools and equipment. **Founded:** 1990. **Freq:** Bimonthly. **Print Method:** Web offset. **Trim Size:** 7 3/4" x 10 3/4". **Key Personnel:** Tom Carruthers, Editor, phone (708)564-0677, fax (708)564-2708; Rudy Wolf, Publisher; Robert Swenson, Assoc. Publisher, phone (847)981-0007, fax (847)981-0025; Anthony Ross, Managing Editor, anton@pten.com. **ISSN:** 1081-4485. **Subscription Rates:** Free to qualified subscribers. **Remarks:** Accepts advertising. **URL:** http://www.pten.com.
Ad Rates: BW: $7,950 **Circ:** Non-paid ‡110,143
4C: $10,730

📖 **2166 Reeves Journal**
Business News Publishing Co.
23211 S. Pointe Dr., Ste. 101 Phone: (949)830-0881
Laguna Hills, CA 92653-1431 Fax: (949)859-7845
Publication E-mail: reevesjrnl@ao.com

Regional plumbing, heating, and cooling magazine. **Subtitle:** Plumbing, Heating, Cooling. **Founded:** July 1920. **Freq:** Monthly. **Print Method:** Offset. **Trim Size:** 8 1/4 x 11. **Cols./Page:** 3. **Col. Width:** 13 1/2 picas. **Col. Depth:** 140 agate lines. **Key Personnel:** Scott Marshultz, Editor; Mary K. Larson, Publisher; Monica Vasquez, Production Coordinator; Ellyn Fishman, General Mgr. **ISSN:** 0048-7066. **Subscription Rates:** Free to qualified subscribers; $45 individuals. **Remarks:** Accepts advertising. **URL:** http://www.bnp.com/reeves_journal.
Ad Rates: GLR: $10 **Circ:** Controlled ‡13,500
BW: $3,240
4C: $4,780

Senior World Newsmagazine Orange County Edition - See Riverside

🎙 **2167 KEZD-AM - 1580**
502 Avenida Sevilla Apt. D Phone: (707)544-1580
Laguna Hills, CA 92653-3847

Format: Adult Contemporary; Soft Rock; Easy Listening. **Owner:** Owens Communications, at above address. **Founded:** 1991. **Operating Hours:** Continuous. **Key Personnel:** Dale A. Owens, General Mgr. **Wattage:** 700 day; 250 night. **Ad Rates:** $7.50 for 30 seconds; $12.50 for 60 seconds.

LAGUNA NIGUEL, pop. 4,644.

S. CA. Orange Co. 18 mi. SW of Santa Ana.

📖 **2168 Free Lunch**
Free Lunch Arts Alliance
PO Box 7647 Phone: (949)770-2239
Laguna Niguel, CA 92607-7647
Consumer magazine covering poetry and literature. **Subtitle:** A Poetry Miscellany. **Founded:** 1989. **Freq:** Irregular. **Print Method:** Offset. **Trim Size:** 8 1/2 x 5 1/2. **Key Personnel:** Ron Offen, Editor. **ISSN:** 1041-0945. **Subscription Rates:** $12 for 3 issues in U.S.; $15 for 3 issues foreign. **Remarks:** Advertising accepted; rates available upon request.
Circ: Combined ‡1,200

📖 **2169 Laguna Niguel News**
South Orange County News
PO Box 3629 Phone: (714)768-3631
Mission Viejo, CA 92690 Fax: (714)454-7354

Community newspaper. **Founded:** 1965. **Freq:** Weekly (Thurs.). **Print Method:** Offset. **Cols./Page:** 5. **Col. Width:** 12 1/16 inches. **Col. Depth:** 13 inches. **Key Personnel:** Sherrie Good, Editor; Mike Weaver, Publisher; Pat Norton, Advertising Mgr. **Subscription Rates:** Free; $12 by mail. **Remarks:** Accepts advertising. **Formerly:** Dana Point/Laguna Niguel News (1989).
Ad Rates: PCI: $32.17 **Circ:** ‡17,877

LAGUNITAS

📖 **2170 Barnabe Mountain Review**
PO Box 529
Lagunitas, CA 94938

Magazine including works of poetry, fiction, art, photos, interviews, photos, cartoons, reviews, letters, and non-fiction. **Founded:** 1995. **Freq:** Annual. **Trim Size:** 5 1/2 x 8 1/2. **Key Personnel:** Gerald Fleming, Contact. **Subscription Rates:** $10. **Remarks:** Advertising not accepted.
Circ: Paid 500
Non-paid 100

LAKE ARROWHEAD, pop. 400.

SE CA. San Bernardino Co. 10 mi. NE of San Bernardino. Residential. Year-round resort.

📖 **2171 Beverage Record**
PO Box 310 Phone: (909)337-1666
Lake Arrowhead, CA 92352-0310 Fax: (909)337-6986
Publication (tabloid) for the alcoholic beverage trade. **Founded:** Jan. 1, 1935. **Freq:** Monthly. **Print Method:** Offset. **Trim Size:** 11 3/4 x 16. **Cols./Page:** 5. **Col. Width:** 22 nonpareils. **Col. Depth:** 210 agate lines. **Key Personnel:** George L. Anderson, Editor and Publisher. **Subscription Rates:** $10 individuals per year. **Remarks:** Accepts advertising.
Ad Rates: GLR: $.50 **Circ:** Non-paid ‡3,420
BW: $525
4C: $735
PCI: $7

📖 **2172 Crestline Courier-News**
Desert Community Newspaper
PO Box 2410 Phone: (909)336-3555
Lake Arrowhead, CA 92352 Fax: (909)337-5275

Community newspaper. **Founded:** 1946. **Freq:** Weekly (Thurs.). **Print Method:** Offset. **Trim Size:** 13 3/4 x 21 1/2. **Cols./Page:** 6. **Col. Width:** 12 1/3 picas. **Col. Depth:** 20 1/2 inches. **Key Personnel:** Peggy Koolman, Manager; Phil Jaffe, Publisher. **USPS:** 137-780. **Subscription Rates:** $19.80 individuals in county. **Remarks:** Accepts advertising. **URL:** http://www.mountainews.com. **Formerly:** Courier-News (1992).
Ad Rates: BW: $555.96 **Circ:** ‡2,850
4C: $836.28
SAU: $4.52

📖 **2173 Mountain News and Mountaineer**
Brehm Communications, Inc.
Box 2410 Phone: (909)337-6145
Lake Arrowhead, CA 92352-2410 Fax: (909)337-5275
Community newspaper. **Founded:** 1920. **Freq:** Weekly (Thurs.). **Print Method:** Offset. **Cols./Page:** 6. **Col. Width:** 26 nonpareils. **Col. Depth:** 280 agate lines. **Key Personnel:** Bart Ortberg, Editor; Phil Jaffe, Publisher. **Subscription Rates:** $21 individuals. **Remarks:** Accepts advertising.
Ad Rates: BW: $1,315.80 **Circ:** ‡7,500
4C: $1,540.80
SAU: $7.65

📖 **2174 Mountain Shopper**
Brehm Communications, Inc.
Box 2410 Phone: (909)337-6145
Lake Arrowhead, CA 92352-2410 Fax: (909)337-5275
Shopping guide. **Freq:** Weekly. **Print Method:** Offset. **Cols./Page:** 6. **Col. Width:** 26 nonpareils. **Col. Depth:** 280 agate lines. **Key Personnel:** Phil Jaffe, Publisher. **Remarks:** Advertising accepted; rates available upon request.
Circ: (Not Reported)

LAKE ELSINORE

📖 **2175 Lake Elsinore Valley Sun-Tribune**
Press Enterprise
31900 Mission Trl., Ste. 130 Phone: (909)674-1535
Lake Elsinore, CA 92530-4534 Fax: (909)674-0280

Community newspaper covering local events. **Founded:** 1886. **Freq:** Weekly (Fri.). **Print Method:** Offset. **Trim Size:** 13 x 21 1/2. **Cols./Page:** 6. **Key Personnel:** Joe Evans, Editor. **ISSN:** 0745-1350. **Subscription Rates:** Free; $12 (mail); $20 out of area. **Remarks:** Accepts advertising.
Ad Rates: BW: $1,205.82 **Circ:** Paid ‡6,114
4C: $1,462.82 Free ‡4,184
SAU: $9.57

📖 **2176 Roadracing World & Motorcycle Technology**
581 Birch St., Unit C Phone: (909)245-6411
Lake Elsinore, CA 92530 Fax: (909)245-6417

Consumer magazine covering road racing and motor sports worldwide. **Founded:** Oct. 1990. **Freq:** Monthly. **Key Personnel:** John D. Ulrich, Editor. **ISSN:** 1056-4845. **Subscription Rates:** $18 individuals; $40 Canada and Mexico; $50 other countries. **Remarks:** Accepts advertising.
Circ: Controlled ‡20,000

LAKE FOREST

📖 **2177 Aliso Viejo News**
22481 Aspan St.
Lake Forest, CA 92630-1630

Community newspaper. **Freq:** Semiweekly. **Cols./Page:** 5. **Col. Width:** 2 1/16 inches. **Key Personnel:** Lori Dean, contact. **Remarks:** Accepts advertising.
Ad Rates: SAU: $32.17 **Circ:** (Not Reported)

LAKE ISABELLA

SC CA. Kern Co. 40 mi. NE of Bakersfield. Kern Co. (SC). 40 m NE of Bakersfield.

🎙 **2178 KCNQ-FM - 102.5**
PO Box 3434 Phone: (619)379-5636
Lake Isabella, CA 93240-3434 Fax: (619)379-5638
E-mail: kcnq@kernvalles.com

Format: Country. **Networks:** ABC. **Founded:** 1985. **Formerly:** KKRV-FM (1991). **Operating Hours:** Continuous. **ADI:** Bakersfield, CA. **Key Personnel:** Scott Allen, Contact; Scott Allen, General Mgr. **Wattage:** 130. **Ad Rates:** $5.60-12 per unit. Combined advertising rates available with KVLI-FM and KQAB-AM.

🎙 **2179 KQAB-AM - 1140**
3630 Golden Spur Phone: (619)379-5636
PO Box 3434 Fax: (619)379-5638
Lake Isabella, CA 93240
E-mail: kvli@kernvalley.com

Format: Talk. **Networks:** Mutual Broadcasting System; ABC. **Owner:** QAB Media, LLC, at above address. **Founded:** July 15, 1977. **Formerly:** KVLI-AM (1997). **Operating Hours:** Sunrise-sunset. **Key Personnel:** Scott Allen, General Mgr.; Scott Allen, Contact. **Local Programs:** *KVLI Swap Shop*, John Ridenour. **Wattage:** 1000. **Ad Rates:** $8-12 for 15 seconds; $11-15 for 30 seconds; $13-18 for 60 seconds.

🎙 **2180 KVLI-FM - 104.5**
3630 Golden Spur Phone: (619)379-5636
PO Box 3434 Fax: (619)379-5638
Lake Isabella, CA 93240

Format: Oldies. **Owner:** QAB Media, LLC, at above address. **Founded:** Oct. 28, 1992. **Operating Hours:** Continuous. **Key Personnel:** Scott Allen, General Mgr.; Scott Allen, Contact. **Wattage:** 200. **Ad Rates:** $11-15 for 30 seconds; $13-18 for 60 seconds. Combined advertising rates available with KCNQ-FM and KQAB-AM.

LAKEPORT†, pop. 3,675.

N. CA. Lake Co. On Clear Lake, 45 mi. N. of Santa Rosa. Summer resort. Diversified farming. Livestock.

2181 Lake County Record-Bee
Lake County Publishing
PO Box 849 Phone: (707)263-5636
Lakeport, CA 95453 Fax: (707)263-0600

Newspaper with a Republican orientation. **Founded:** 1873. **Freq:** Tues.-Sat. (morn.). **Print Method:** Offset. **Cols./Page:** 6. **Col. Width:** 25 nonpareils. **Col. Depth:** 287 agate lines. **Key Personnel:** Cliff Larimer, Managing Editor; John Lowman, Publisher. **ISSN:** 0746-4304. **Subscription Rates:** $40 individuals. **Remarks:** Accepts advertising.
Ad Rates: SAU: $6.05 **Circ:** Tues.-Fri. 6,614
Sun. 8,387

2182 KNTI-FM - 99.5
75 4th St. Phone: (707)263-1551
Lakeport, CA 95453 Fax: (707)263-0614

Format: Adult Contemporary. **Networks:** Mutual Broadcasting System. **Owner:** Excelsior Comunications, Inc, at above address. **Founded:** 1984. **Operating Hours:** Continuous; 25% network, 75% local. **ADI:** San Francisco-Oakland-San Jose. **Key Personnel:** Kenn Cunningham, General Mgr. **Wattage:** 50,000. **Ad Rates:** $10-15 for 30 seconds; $14-20 for 60 seconds.

2183 KXBX-AM - 1270
PO Box 759 Phone: (707)263-6113
Lakeport, CA 95453-0759 Fax: (707)263-0939

Format: Big Band/Nostalgia. **Networks:** Satellite Music Network. **Owner:** North Country Communications, Inc., PO Box 1329, Lakeport, CA 95453, (707)523-1369. **Founded:** 1966. **Formerly:** KWTR-AM. **Operating Hours:** 6 a.m.-10 p.m.; 80% network, 20% local. **Key Personnel:** Bill Groody, Contact; Gerri Groody, Contact; Rose Pagel, Station Mgr.; Gregg Allen, Operations Mgr. **Wattage:** 500. **Ad Rates:** $8.75 per unit.

LAMONT, pop. 7,007.

S. CA. Kern Co. 10 mi. S. of Bakersfield. Truck, fruit, poultry farms.

2184 Lamont Reporter
Reed Print Publication
Box 548 Phone: (805)845-3704
Lamont, CA 93241 Fax: (805)845-5907

Newspaper. **Founded:** 1949. **Freq:** Weekly (Wed.). **Print Method:** Offset. **Cols./Page:** 6. **Col. Width:** 27 nonpareils. **Col. Depth:** 294 agate lines. **Key Personnel:** Jesse Atondo, Editor; Donald Reed, Publisher, phone (805)834-0496, fax (805)832-0841. **Subscription Rates:** $19 individuals; $21 Out of County; $24 out of state. **Remarks:** Accepts advertising.
Ad Rates: PCI: $5.90 **Circ:** 6,000

LANCASTER

SW CA. Los Angeles Co. 70 mi. NE of Los Angeles.

2185 Aerotech News & Review
Aerotech
456 East Ave. K4, Ste. 8 Phone: (805)945-5634
Lancaster, CA 93535 Fax: (805)723-7757
Publisher E-mail: aerotech@netport.com

Professional journal for the aerospace industry. **Founded:** Feb. 1986. **Freq:** Weekly. **Print Method:** Offset. **Trim Size:** 11 1/2 x 13 3/4. **Cols./Page:** 5. **Col. Width:** 1.875 inches. **Col. Depth:** 13 inches. **Key Personnel:** Paul Kinison, Publisher. **Subscription Rates:** Free to qualified subscribers. **Remarks:** Accepts advertising.
Ad Rates: PCI: $11.55 **Circ:** Non-paid 15,000

2186 Afroasiatic Linguistics
Undena Publications
3064 Holline Ct. Phone: (805)946-2726
Lancaster, CA 93535 Fax: (805)946-2726

Journal covering languages belonging to Afroasiatic family. **Freq:** Irregular.

2187 Assur
Undena Publications
3064 Holline Ct. Phone: (805)946-2726
Lancaster, CA 93535 Fax: (805)946-2726

Journal covering history of Assyria, Assyrian language, and Mesopotamian civilization. **Freq:** Irregular.

2188 Desert Mailer News
123 West Avenue J5 Phone: (805)945-8671
Lancaster, CA 93534 Fax: (805)942-6418

Local newspaper. **Founded:** 1959. **Freq:** Weekly (Tues.). **Print Method:** Offset. **Cols./Page:** 6. **Col. Width:** 14 1/2 picas. **Col. Depth:** 16 inches. **Key Personnel:** Gen Fortis, Editor; Fred Eichenberger, Publisher. **Subscription Rates:** $12 individuals; $15 out of area. **Remarks:** Accepts advertising. **Absorbed:** South Antelope Valley Foothill News (1992).
Ad Rates: SAU: $4.42 **Circ:** Tues. 11,677

2189 Sources from the Ancient Near East
Undena Publications
3064 Holline Ct. Phone: (805)946-2726
Lancaster, CA 93535 Fax: (805)946-2726

Professional journal covering documents in English translation on history, religion, literature, art and archaeology of the Ancient Near East. **Freq:** Irregular. **Remarks:** Advertising not accepted.
Circ: (Not Reported)

2190 Jones Intercable, Inc.
41551 10th St., W. Phone: (805)947-3130
Palmdale, CA 93551 Fax: (805)947-5723
E-mail: brucethompson@jic.com

Founded: 1964. **Key Personnel:** Bruce Thompson, brucethompson@jic.com. **Cities Served:** Lancaster, Palmdale, Quartz Hill, CA; Kern County, Los Angeles County, Elizabeth Lake Green, Leona Valley.: subscribing households 75,000; 70 channels; 2 community access channels; 50 hours per week community access programming.

2191 KAVL-AM - 610
2501 West Ave. I Phone: (805)942-1121
Lancaster, CA 93536 Fax: (805)723-5512
E-mail: lrt@avcn.com

Format: Sports. **Networks:** USA Radio. **Owner:** Antelope Broadcasting Co., at above address. **Founded:** 1950. **Operating Hours:** Continuous. **ADI:** Los Angeles (Corona & San Bernardino), CA. **Key Personnel:** Ivan Ladizinsky, General Mgr.; Larry Thornhill, Program Dir.; Rob Baumgartner, Music Dir.; Henry Schindel, Sales Mgr.; Ron Carter, Owner. **Local Programs:** *Morning Zoo* 6-8 a.m.; *SportsPage* 6-7 p.m. **Wattage:** 5000 daytime; 4000 nighttime.

2192 KAVS-FM - 97.7
2501 West Ave. I Phone: (805)942-1121
Lancaster, CA 93536 Fax: (805)723-5512
E-mail: lvn@avcn.com

Format: Contemporary Hit Radio (CHR); Adult Album Alternative. **Networks:** Independent. **Owner:** Antelope Broadcasting Co., at above address. **Founded:** 1966. **Operating Hours:** Continuous. **ADI:** Los Angeles (Corona & San Bernardino), CA. **Key Personnel:** Ivan Ladizinsky, General Mgr.; Rob Deshay, Program Dir.; Debi Strickland, Business Mgr. **Local Programs:** *Party Out of Bounds* 8 p.m. - midnight Sunday; *Saturday Night Side-Show* 8 p.m. - midnight Saturday. **Wattage:** 3000. **Ad Rates:** $34-50 for 30 seconds; $37-57 for 60 seconds.

LAYTONVILLE

2193 Mendocino County Observer
PO Box 490 Phone: (707)984-6223
Laytonville, CA 95454-0490 Fax: (707)984-8118
Publication E-mail: observer@mcn.org

Community newspaper. **Founded:** 1978. **Freq:** Weekly. **Trim Size:** 13 x 21. **Cols./Page:** 6. **Key Personnel:** Jim Shields, Editor; Susan Shields, Advertising Mgr. **USPS:** 532-670. **Subscription Rates:** $20 individuals; $.50 single issue. **Remarks:** Accepts advertising.
Ad Rates: GLR: $5.50 **Circ:** Controlled 2,000
4C: $400

LE GRAND

2194 KEFR-FM - 89.9
PO Box 52 Phone: (209)389-4659
Le Grand, CA 95333-0052 Fax: (209)389-0215

Format: Religious; Educational. **Founded:** 1985. **Operating Hours:** Continuous; 97% network, 3% local. **Key Personnel:** Larry Milliken, Station Mgr. **Wattage:** 1800. **URL:** http://www.familyradio.com.

LEMON GROVE, pop. 20,780.

S. CA. San Diego Co. 8 mi. E. of San Diego. Residential.

La Mesa Forum - See La Mesa

2195 Lemon Grove Review
Forum Publications, Inc.
3434 Grove St. Phone: (619)469-0101
PO Box 127
Lemon Grove, CA 91946-1812
Community newspaper. **Founded:** 1948. **Freq:** Weekly (Thurs.). **Print Method:** Offset. **Trim Size:** 11 x 17. **Cols./Page:** 5. **Col. Width:** 11 1/2 picas. **Col. Depth:** 16 inches. **Key Personnel:** Peter Kaufman, Editor and Publisher. **Subscription Rates:** $15 individuals; $30 out of state. **Remarks:** Accepts advertising.
Ad Rates: BW: $1,000 **Circ:** ‡2,000
4C: $1,210
PCI: $12.50

Spring Valley Bulletin - See Spring Valley

LEMOORE, pop. 8,832.

SC CA. Kings Co. 32 mi. S. of Fresno. Carpet. Dairy products manufactured, cotton, fruit, grain, poultry, truck farms. Dairying.

2196 The Lemoore Advance
Central CA Weeklies, Inc.
The Lemoore Advance Phone: (209)924-5361
PO Box 547 Fax: (209)924-6220
Lemoore, CA 93245
Newspaper. **Founded:** 1888. **Freq:** Weekly (Thurs.). **Print Method:** Offset. **Trim Size:** 28 x 22 3/4. **Cols./Page:** 6. **Col. Width:** 24 nonpareils. **Col. Depth:** 301 agate lines. **Key Personnel:** Lee Manchester, Editor; Dale Anderson, General Mgr. **USPS:** 309-860. **Subscription Rates:** $18 individuals. **Remarks:** Accepts advertising.
Ad Rates: BW: $1,055.22 **Circ:** ‡10,120
4C: $1,275.22
SAU: $8.18
PCI: $8.18

2197 KJOP-AM - 1240
15279 Hanford Armona Rd. Phone: (209)584-5242
Lemoore, CA 93245 Fax: (209)584-0310

Format: Country; Hispanic. **Founded:** 1981. **Operating Hours:** 4 a.m.-11 p.m. **Key Personnel:** Jesus Larios, General Mgr.; Federico Gomez, Program Dir.; Juan Rodriguez, News Dir.; Joe Hernandez, Sales Mgr.; John Pembroke, Contact. **Wattage:** 250 day; 1000 night. **Ad Rates:** $12-32 for 30 seconds; $16-36 for 60 seconds.

LINCOLN, pop. 4,132.

NE CA. Placer Co. 28 mi. NE of Sacramento. Manufactures formica. Pottery, electronics. Cold storage, grain warehouses. Clay pits. Fruit, grain, dairy & beef farms.

2198 Lincoln News-Messenger
627 5th St. Phone: (916)645-7733
Lincoln, CA 95648-0368 Fax: (916)645-2776
Publication E-mail: newsmessenger@psyber.com

Community newspaper. **Founded:** 1898. **Freq:** Weekly (Thurs.). **Print Method:** Offset. **Trim Size:** 14 x 22. **Cols./Page:** 6. **Col. Width:** 12.5 picas. **Col. Depth:** 21 inches. **Key Personnel:** Ann McCormick, Office Mgr., annlnm@psyber.com; Cathi Krahn, General Mgr., phone (916)624-9713. **USPS:** 386-980. **Subscription Rates:** $17 individuals; $22 out of area. **Remarks:** Accepts advertising.
Ad Rates: GLR: $1.15 **Circ:** ‡3,200
BW: $850
4C: $1,137
SAU: $7
PCI: $7.65

LINDEN, pop. 900.

C. CA. San Joaquin Co. 10 mi. NE of Stockton. Walnut harvesters, church fruniture manufactured. Agriculture. Walnuts, cherries, peaches, livestock.

2199 California Odd Fellow and Rebekah
Linden Publications
19033 E. Main St. Phone: (209)887-3829
PO Box 129 Fax: (209)887-3829
Linden, CA 95236-0129
Official magazine of Odd Fellows and Rebekahs of California. **Founded:** Jan. 1950. **Freq:** Bimonthly. **Print Method:** Offset. **Trim Size:** 8 1/4 x 10 1/2. **Cols./Page:** 4. **Col. Width:** 19 nonpareils. **Col. Depth:** 135 agate lines. **Key Personnel:** Don R. Smith, Editor and Publisher, dons@inreach.com; Darlene Smith, Business Mgr. **USPS:** 084-600. **Subscription Rates:** $4 individuals; $3.50 clubs. **Remarks:** Advertising not accepted.
Circ: ‡11,225

LINDSAY, pop. 6,924.

SC CA. Tulare Co. 60 mi. SE of Fresno. Manufactures telephone cables, mobile homes, cans, canning machinery, irrigation pipes, pumps, olive oil. Fruit, vegetable, olive packing; hatchery. Fruit farms.

2200 The Lindsay Gazette
136 E. Honolulu St. Phone: (209)562-2585
PO Box 308 Fax: (209)562-2214
Lindsay, CA 93247-0308
Community newspaper. **Founded:** 1901. **Freq:** Weekly (Wed.). **Print Method:** Offset. **Cols./Page:** 6. **Col. Width:** 12 nonpareils. **Col. Depth:** 126 agate lines. **Key Personnel:** James A. Runyon, General Mgr.; Jerry Newton, Managing Editor. **Subscription Rates:** $20 in country. **Remarks:** Accepts advertising.
Ad Rates: GLR: $.40 **Circ:** 2,400
SAU: $4.50

LIVERMORE, pop. 48,349.

W. CA. Alameda Co. 33 mi. SE of Oakland. Nuclear weapons, energy research. Wineries. Agriculture.

2201 Tri-Valley Herald
4770 Willow Rd., No. 697 Phone: (510)734-8600
Pleasanton, CA 94588-2762 Fax: (510)416-4850

General newspaper. **Founded:** 1879. **Freq:** Mon.-Sun. (morn.). **Print Method:** Offset. **Cols./Page:** 6. **Col. Width:** 2 1/16 inches. **Col. Depth:** 21 1/2 inches. **Key Personnel:** P. Scott McKibben, Publisher and President; Mary Menard, Advertising Mgr. **Subscription Rates:** $48 individuals. **Remarks:** Accepts advertising. **Formerly:** The Livermore Herald.
Ad Rates: PCI: $27.71 **Circ:** Sun. ★**43,503**
Mon.-Sat. ★**42,930**

LIVINGSTON, pop. 5,326.

C. CA. Merced Co. 25 mi. S. of Modesto. Poultry raising and processing. Produce packing. Agriculture. Grapes, almonds, peaches.

2202 KNTO-FM - 95.9
416 Main St. Phone: (209)394-3344
PO Box 248 Fax: (209)394-8043
Livingston, CA 95334-0248

Format: Middle-of-the-Road (MOR); Hispanic. **Owner:** All American Broadcasting, at above address. **Operating Hours:** Continuous; 5% network, 95% local. **Key Personnel:** R.C. Duckett, Contact; Pablo Estrada, Program Mgr.; Marciano Garci, Music Dir. **Wattage:** 3000. **Ad Rates:** $16-22 for 30 seconds; $19-25 for 60 seconds.

LOCKEFORD, pop. 950.

C. CA. San Joaquin Co. 10 mi. E. of Lodi. Residential.

2203 Lockeford-Clements News
18540 Hwy 88 Phone: (209)727-5776
PO Box 76 Fax: (209)727-3931
Lockeford, CA 95237
Local newspaper (tabloid). **Founded:** 1948. **Freq:** Weekly (Wed.). **Print Method:** Offset. **Cols./Page:** 5. **Col. Width:** 11 picas. **Col. Depth:** 16 inches. **Key Personnel:** Mike Henry, Publisher. **Subscription Rates:** $13.50 individuals; $16.50 out of state. **Remarks:** Accepts advertising.
Ad Rates: GLR: $.25 **Circ:** Paid 2,800
BW: $350 Free 200
PCI: $6.55

LODI, pop. 35,221.

C. CA. San Joaquin Co. 14 mi. N. of Stockton. Extensive fruit packing and shipping. Manufactures canned fruit and vegetables, cereals, cake mixes, wine, olive oil, pumps, concrete pipes, brace aluminum, iron foundries, trailer hitches, juicers. Agriculture. Fruit, poultry, grain.

2204 Lodi News-Merchandiser
PO Box 1360 Phone: (209)369-2761
Lodi, CA 95241 Fax: (209)369-1084
Publication E-mail: lodinews@mail.softcom.net

Shopper. **Freq:** Weekly (Thurs.). **Print Method:** Offset. **Cols./Page:** 6. **Col. Width:** 25 nonpareils. **Col. Depth:** 301 agate lines. **Key Personnel:** Fred Weybret, Editor and Publisher; Dan Battilana, Advertising Mgr. **Subscription Rates:** Free. **Remarks:** Accepts advertising.
Ad Rates: BW: $148.35 **Circ:** Free ‡9,338
4C: $368.35

2205 Lodi News-Sentinel
125 N. Church St. Phone: (209)369-2761
Lodi, CA 95240-2102 Fax: (209)369-1084

General newspaper. **Founded:** July 9, 1881. **Freq:** Mon.-Sat. (morn.). **Print Method:** Offset. **Trim Size:** 14 x 23. **Cols./Page:** 6. **Col. Width:** 12.4 picas. **Col. Depth:** 21 1/2 inches. **Key Personnel:** Fred Weybret, Editor and Publisher; Dan Battilana, Advertising Mgr. **Subscription Rates:** $66 individuals. **Remarks:** Advertising not accepted for pornographic material.
Ad Rates: BW: $1,038.45 **Circ:** Mon.-Sat. ★**17,222**
4C: $1,263.45
SAU: $8.05

LOMA LINDA, pop. 10,694.

SE CA. San Bernardino Co. Residential.

2206 Scope
Loma Linda University
Office of University Relations Phone: (909)558-4526
Loma Linda, CA 92350 Fax: (909)558-4181
Publication E-mail: scope@univ.llu.edu

University alumni magazine. **Founded:** 1933. **Freq:** Quarterly. **Print Method:** Offset. **Trim Size:** 8 1/2 x 11. **Cols./Page:** 3. **Col. Width:** 26 nonpareils. **Col. Depth:** 126 agate lines. **Key Personnel:** W. Agustus Cheatham; Richard Weismeyer, Managing Editor, rweismeyer@univ.llu.edu; Waldena Gaede, Managing Editor, wgaede@univ.llu.edu. **Subscription Rates:** Free. **Remarks:** Advertising not accepted. **URL:** http://www.llu.edu/news/els.
Circ: Free ‡36,000

2207 Today
Loma Linda University
Office of University Relations Phone: (909)558-4526
Loma Linda, CA 92350 Fax: (909)558-4181

Collegiate newspaper. **Founded:** 1969. **Freq:** Semimonthly. **Print Method:** Offset. **Trim Size:** 11 x 15. **Cols./Page:** 5. **Col. Width:** 22 nonpareils. **Col. Depth:** 224 agate lines. **Key Personnel:** W. Agustus Cheatham, Exec. Editor; Richard Weismeyer, Managing Editor, rweismeyer@univ.llu.edu; Waldena Gaede, Managing Editor, wgaede@univ.llu.edu. **Subscription Rates:** Free. **Remarks:** Accepts advertising. **URL:** http://www.llu.edu/news/. **Formerly:** Observer.
Ad Rates: BW: $280.00 **Circ:** Non-paid 4,000
PCI: $4

LOMPOC, pop. 26,267.

SW CA. Santa Barbara Co. 55 mi. NW of Santa Barbara. Insulation, filtration products manufactured. Oil wells. Truck farms. Flower seeds, sugar beets.

2208 Lompoc Record
Los Angeles Newspaper Group
115 N. H St. Phone: (805)737-9027
Lompoc, CA 93436 Fax: (805)735-5118

General newspaper. **Founded:** 1875. **Freq:** Daily (eve.). **Print Method:** Offset. **Trim Size:** 14 x 22. **Cols./Page:** 6. **Col. Width:** 12.3 picas. **Col. Depth:** 301 agate lines. **Key Personnel:** Ron Hoffer, Publisher, phone (805)737-9030, fax (805)736-1744, rhoffer@lompocrecord.com; Dick Bausman, Advertising Mgr., phone (805)737-9026, fax (805)736-5654, advertising@lompocrecord.com. **Subscription Rates:** $75 individuals. **Remarks:** Advertising not accepted for out of state lottery.
Ad Rates: BW: $1,634.43 **Circ:** Mon.-Fri. 7,902
4C: $2,084.43 Sun. 8,038
SAU: $10.60
PCI: $12.67

2209 Space and Missile Times
Ron Hoffer
PO Box 578 Phone: (805)736-2313
Lompoc, CA 93438 Fax: (805)736-5654

Military newspaper for personnel at Vandenberg Air Force Base. **Founded:** 1958. **Freq:** Weekly (Fri.). **Print Method:** Offset. **Trim Size:** 11 3/6 x 13 3/4. **Cols./Page:** 5. **Col. Width:** 13 picas. **Col. Depth:** 224 agate lines. **Key Personnel:** Dick Bausman, Advertising Mgr. **Subscription Rates:** Free To qualified persons. **Remarks:** Advertising not accepted for alcoholic beverages. **Formerly:** Mesa Missilier (1991).
Ad Rates: BW: $766.35 **Circ:** Free ‡8,500
4C: $1,216.35

LONE PINE

NE CA. Inyo Co. 5 mi. S. of Independence.

2210 Lone Pine Television
Box 867 Phone: (760)876-5461
Lone Pine, CA 93545 Fax: (760)876-9101

Founded: 1956. **Key Personnel:** Bruce Branson, General Mgr. **Cities Served:** Lone Pine, CA: subscribing households 616; 32 channels; 1 community access channel; 12 hours per week community access programming.

LONG BEACH, pop. 361,334.

S. CA. Los Angeles Co. On Pacific Ocean, 22 mi. S. of Los Angeles. Long Beach City College; California State University at Long Beach. Summer and winter resort. America's most modern port. U. S. Naval Base and shipyard. Oil and gas wells. Oil production and refining, oil drilling equipment; fisheries, sardines, tuna, mackerel, meat packing plants; soft drink bottlers; shipbuilding and repair; aircraft and aircraft parts; chemicals, technical instruments, machinery, clothing, furnaces and heaters, building and insulation products, glass paper products, plastics manufactured.

2211 Bus Conversions
3431 Cherry Ave. Phone: (562)492-9394
Long Beach, CA 90807 Fax: (562)492-1345
Publisher E-mail: mail@busconversions.com

Magazine about converting buses into motorhomes. **Founded:** Feb. 1992. **Freq:** Monthly. **Print Method:** Web offset. **Trim Size:** 8 1/4 X 10 1/2. **Key Personnel:** John Kadletz, Editor. **ISSN:** 1070-6526. **Subscription Rates:** $45 other countries plus postage; $3.50 single issue; $30 individuals. **Remarks:** Advertising accepted; rates available upon request.
Circ: Paid 10,000

2212 Bus World
MAK Publications
3431 Cherry Ave. Phone: (562)492-9394
Long Beach, CA 90807 Fax: (562)492-1345
Publication E-mail: bus-world.com
Publisher E-mail: mak@busconversions.com

Magazine covering transit and intercity bus systems; provides information on new bus design and technology. **Subtitle:** Magazine of Buses and Bus Systems. **Founded:** 1978. **Freq:** Monthly. **Print Method:** Offset. **Trim Size:** 8 1/4 x 10 7/8. **Cols./Page:** 3. **Col. Width:** 27 nonpareils. **Col. Depth:** 142 agate lines. **Key Personnel:** Michael A. Kadletz, Editor and Publisher, phone (562)492-9394, fax (562)492-1345. **Subscription Rates:** $24 individuals; $3.50 single issue. **Remarks:** Accepts advertising.
Ad Rates: BW: $375 **Circ:** Paid ‡3,800
4C: $825 Non-paid ‡4,000

2213 Daily Forty-Niner
Forty-Niner Advertising
California State University, Long Beach Phone: (562)985-8001
Fax: (562)985-1740
1250 Bellflower Blvd.
SSPA 010-B
Long Beach, CA 90840-4601
Publication E-mail: d49er@csulb.edu

Daily newspaper. **Founded:** 1949. **Freq:** 4/wk (Mon.-Thurs.). **Print Method:** Offset. **Trim Size:** 10 1/4 x 16. **Cols./Page:** 6. **Col. Width:** 1 1/2 inches. **Key Personnel:** William A. Mulligan, Publisher, phone (562)985-4981, fax (562)985-5300, mulligan@csulb.edu; Georganne Sparks, Business Mgr., phone (562)985-2256, fax (562)985-1740, sparks@csulb.edu; Stacey Nail, Advertising Mgr., phone (562)985-5736, fax (562)985-1740, snail@csulb.edu. **Subscription Rates:** $49 individuals. **Remarks:** Accepts advertising. **URL:** http://www.csulb.edu/~d49er.
Ad Rates: GLR: $2 **Circ:** Free ‡10,000
BW: $768
4C: $1,248
SAU: $9
PCI: $12

2214 El Economico
Media News Group, Inc.
604 Pine Ave. Phone: (310)499-1415
Long Beach, CA 90844 Fax: (562)499-1484
Publication E-mail: ptconnect.com/eleconomico
Publisher E-mail: bruno512@ptconnect.infi.net

Spanish newspaper. **Founded:** Apr. 1992. **Freq:** Weekly. **Print Method:** Offset. **Trim Size:** 5 x 12. **Cols./Page:** 5. **Col. Width:** 1 7/8 inches. **Col. Depth:** 13 1/2 inches. **Key Personnel:** Bruno Larosa, General Mgr., phone (562)499-1415, fax (562)499-1484. **Subscription Rates:** Free. **Remarks:** Accepts advertising.
Ad Rates: GLR: $39.46 **Circ:** Free 100,000
BW: $2,367.60
4C: $3,232.60
PCI: $23

2215 The Jazz Review and Collectors Discography
New Century Publishing
2005 Palo Verde Ave., Ste. 158
Long Beach, CA 90815

Magazine reporting on the jazz music industry. **Freq:** Monthly. **Key Personnel:** Ken Borgers, Editor; Gary Wagner, Publisher. **Subscription Rates:** $19.80. $2.75 single issue.

2216 The Jazzologist
New Orleans Jazz Club of California
PO Box 15212 Phone: (562)422-1616
Long Beach, CA 90815 Fax: (562)422-1964

Journal about traditional jazz. **Founded:** 1963. **Freq:** 5/year. **Print Method:** Offset. **Cols./Page:** 2. **Col. Width:** 48 nonpareils. **Col. Depth:** 140 agate lines. **Key Personnel:** Mort Enob, Editor; Bill Bacin, Publisher. **Subscription Rates:** $7.50. **Remarks:** Advertising not accepted.
Circ: ‡4,000

2217 Journal of Electrocardiology
Churchill Livingstone, Inc.
PO Box 90186 Phone: (562)933-2609
Long Beach, CA 90809-0186 Fax: (562)933-2611

Journal covering clinical and experimental studies of the electrical activ ities of the heart. **Subtitle:** Official Journal of the International Society for Computerized Electrocardiology. **Founded:** 1968. **Freq:** Quarterly. **Print Method:** Offset. **Trim Size:** 8 1/4 x 11. **Cols./Page:** 2. **Col. Width:** 19 picas. **Col. Depth:** 54 picas. **Key Personnel:** Ronald H. Selvester, M.D., Editor. **ISSN:** 0022-0736. **Subscription Rates:** $99 individuals; $160 institutions. **Remarks:** Accepts advertising. **Alt. Formats:** Microfiche.
Ad Rates: BW: $655 **Circ:** Paid ‡1,000
4C: $895

2218 Long Beach Express
First-Line Publishers/L.A. Metro Group
14621 Titus St., Ste. 228 Phone: (818)782-8695
Van Nuys, CA 91402 Fax: (818)782-2924

Black community newspaper serving Long Beach. **Founded:** 1966. **Freq:** Weekly (Thurs.). **Print Method:** Offset. **Trim Size:** 13 x 21 1/2. **Cols./Page:** 6. **Col. Width:** 2 inches. **Key Personnel:** Victoria Turner, Publisher; Hillard Hamm, Editor. **Subscription Rates:** Free; $25. **Remarks:** Accepts advertising. **URL:** http://www.xtra99.com.
Ad Rates: PCI: $32 **Circ:** Free 60,000

2219 Pearl
Pearl Editions
3030 E. Second St. Phone: (562)434-4523
Long Beach, CA 90803
Literary magazine covering poetry and fiction. **Founded:** 1974. **Freq:** Triennial. **Print Method:** Offset. **Trim Size:** 5 1/2 x 8 1/2. **Cols./Page:** 1. **Col. Width:** 4 inches. **Col. Depth:** 7 inches. **Key Personnel:** Joan Jobe Smith, Editor; Marilyn Johnson, Editor; Barbara Hauk, Editor. **Subscription Rates:** $15 individuals; $6 single issue. **Remarks:** Accepts advertising.
Circ: Combined 550

2220 Press-Telegram
Knight-Ridder, Inc.
604 Pine Ave. Phone: (310)435-1161
Long Beach, CA 90844 Fax: (310)437-7892
Publication E-mail: ptnews@ptconnect.infi.net

General newspaper. **Subtitle:** Serving Long Beach and 22 Surrounding Communities in L.A./Orange County - Southern California. **Founded:** 1888. **Freq:** Daily. **Print Method:** Letterpress. **Cols./Page:** 6. **Col. Width:** 25 nonpareils. **Col. Depth:** 301 agate lines. **Key Personnel:** Rick Sadowski, Publisher, phone (310)499-1465, fax (310)499-1325; Jim Crutchfield, Executive Editor, phone (310)499-1279, fax (310)437-7892; Rich Archbold, Managing Editor, phone (310)499-1285, fax (310)499-1277; Carolyn Ruszkiewicz, Assistant Mng. Editor, phone (310)499-1293; Hal Wells, Dir. of Photography, phone (310)499-1294; Janice Kowalski, Design Editor, phone (310)499-1368; John Zappe, Webmaster, phone (310)499-1280; Jim McCormack, Senior Editor, phone (310)499-1335. **Subscription Rates:** $116.52 individuals. **Remarks:** Accepts advertising. Monday-Friday: BW: $9,082; 4C: $10,082; PCI: $70.40. **URL:** http://www.ptconnect.com. **Formerly:** Independent Press-Telegram. **Feature Editors:** Larry Allison, *Editorials*, phone (310)499-1244; Jim Buzinski, *Sports*, phone (310)499-1323; Lindsay Chaney, *Financial/Business*; Robin Hinch, *City*; Richard Horrmann, *Entertainment*, phone (310)499-2158; Ron Kitagawa, *News*; Kevin Leung, *News*; Gary North, *City*; Jim Robinson, *City*, phone (310)499-1292; Lane Smith, *Sports*; Iris Yokoi, *City*; Barbara Zumwalt, *City*, phone (310)499-1300.
Circ: Mon.-Fri. ★**105,167**
Sat. ★**99,8380**
Sun. ★**120,496**

2221 Reporter
Pfanstiel Publishers and Printers, Inc.
PO Box 4278 Phone: (310)493-4899
Long Beach, CA 90804 Fax: (310)438-7086

Legal newspaper. **Founded:** 1933. **Freq:** Semiweekly (Tues. and Fri.). **Print Method:** Offset. **Trim Size:** 17 1/2 x 22 1/2. **Cols./Page:** 5. **Col. Width:** 11.5 picas. **Col. Depth:** 280 agate lines. **Key Personnel:** G.B. Pfanstiel, Publisher; Sandy Miller, Editor. **Subscription Rates:** $16.50 individuals. **Remarks:** Accepts advertising.
Ad Rates: PCI: $5.75 **Circ:** ‡650

2222 Viking
Long Beach City College
4901 E. Carson St. Phone: (562)938-4284
Long Beach, CA 90808-1780 Fax: (562)938-4118

Collegiate newspaper. **Founded:** 1927. **Freq:** Weekly (Thurs.). **Print Method:** Offset. **Cols./Page:** 5. **Col. Width:** 24 nonpareils. **Col. Depth:** 196 agate lines. **Key Personnel:** Sharon Filbey, Advertising Mgr. **Subscription Rates:** $5.50 individuals. **Remarks:** Advertising not accepted for family planning and alcohol.
Ad Rates: GLR: $.70 **Circ:** Free 6,000
BW: $480
PCI: $5.50

2223 Western Grower and Shipper
Western Growers Association
4014 Long Beach Blvd., No. 211 Phone: (310)989-5444
Fax: (310)989-5447
Long Beach, CA 90807
Agricultural magazine focusing on fresh vegetables, fruit and nut growing, and shipping. **Founded:** 1929. **Freq:** Monthly. **Print Method:** Offset. **Cols./Page:** 3. **Col. Width:** 27 nonpareils. **Col. Depth:** 140 agate lines. **Key Personnel:** Tim Linden, Editor; Heather Flower, Associate Publisher. **Subscription Rates:** $18 individuals. **Remarks:** Accepts advertising.
Ad Rates: BW: $1,350 **Circ:** Controlled ‡5,535
4C: $2,235

2224 Western Photographer
4150 Long Beach Blvd., 3rd Fl. Phone: (714)535-1166
Long Beach, CA 90807-2650 Fax: (714)535-7546

Amateur photography magazine. **Founded:** 1960. **Freq:** Monthly. **Print Method:** Offset. **Trim Size:** 8 1/4 x 10 1/2. **Cols./Page:** 3. **Col. Width:** 14 picas. **Col. Depth:** 57 picas. **Key Personnel:** S.T. Bear, Editor and Publisher. **ISSN:** 0738-8039. **Subscription Rates:** $26 individuals; $3.50 single issue. **Remarks:** Accepts advertising.
Ad Rates: BW: $400 **Circ:** Paid ‡6,300
4C: $675 Non-paid ‡700
PCI: $20

2225 Cablevision Industries
2931 Redondo Ave. Phone: (310)424-4657
Long Beach, CA 90806 Fax: (310)490-9981

Founded: 1965. **Formerly:** Simmons Cable TV. **Key Personnel:** Frank McNellis, General Mgr.; David Kydd, Program Dir.; John Craig, Contact. **Cities Served:** subscribing households 69,000; 53 channels; 1 community access channel.

2226 KFRN-AM - 1280
105 Linden Ave. Phone: (562)435-0103
Long Beach, CA 90802 Fax: (562)435-0104
E-mail: kfrn@familyradio.com

Format: Religious. **Networks:** Family Stations Radio. **Owner:** Family Stations Inc.,, 290 Hegenberger Rd., Oakland, CA 94621, (510)568-6200, Fax: (510)568-6190. **Founded:** 1977. **Formerly:** KFOX-AM. **Operating Hours:** Continuous. **Key Personnel:** Harold Camping, President, phone (510)568-6190, fax (510)568-6190; Ward Cayot, Operations Mgr., phone (562)435-0103, fax (562)435-0104, kfrn@familyradio.com; Suong Tran, Public Affairs Director, phone (562)435-0103, fax (502)435-0104. **Local Programs:** *Newstalk*, Suong Tran, (310)435-0103, Fax (310)435-0104. **Wattage:** 1000. **Ad Rates:** Noncommercial.

2227 KLON-FM - 88.1
1250 Bellflower Blvd. Phone: (562)985-5566
Long Beach, CA 90840 Fax: (562)597-8453

Format: Jazz; Blues. **Owner:** California State University Long Beach Foundation, at above address. **Founded:** 1951. **Operating Hours:** Continuous. **Key Personnel:** Judy Jankowski, General Mgr.; Mark Roberts, Controller; Ron Thompson, Chief Engineer; Nancy Flordelis, Development Dir. **Wattage:** 8,000. **URL:** http://www.klon.org.

LOOMIS, pop. 1,108.

NE CA. Placer Co. 20 mi. NE of Sacramento. Nurseries. Ships fruit. Agriculture. Pears, plums, peaches.

2228 Loomis News
3651 Taylor Rd. Phone: (916)652-7939
Loomis, CA 95650
Community newspaper. **Founded:** Dec. 20, 1940. **Freq:** Weekly (Thurs.). **Print Method:** Offset. **Cols./Page:** 6. **Col. Width:** 2 inches. **Col. Depth:** 21 inches. **Key Personnel:** Bud Pisarek, Publisher; Martha Garcia, Editor. **Subscription Rates:** $13.50 individuals; $.25 single issue. **Remarks:** Accepts advertising.
Ad Rates: GLR: $1.50 **Circ:** 1,500
BW: $515.34
4C: $700
SAU: $4.09

LOS ALAMITOS, pop. 11,529.

S. CA. Orange Co. 8 mi. E. of Long Beach. Light Manufacturing Lumber.

2229 IEEE Computer Graphics and Applications
IEEE Computer Society
10662 Los Vaqueros Circle Phone: (714)821-8380
Los Alamitos, CA 90720 Fax: (714)821-4010
Publication E-mail: rbaldwin@computer.org
Publisher E-mail: csbooks@computer.org

Magazine addressing the interests and needs of professional designers and users of computer graphics hardware, software, and systems. **Subtitle:** For Computer Graphics Professionals. **Founded:** Jan. 1981. **Freq:** Bimonthly. **Print Method:** Offset. **Trim Size:** 7 7/8 x 10 3/4. **Cols./Page:** 2. **Key Personnel:** Nancy Hays, Editor, n.hays@computer.org; Matt Loeb, Publisher, m.loeb@computer.org; Patricia Garvey, Advertising Mgr., p.garvey@computer.org. **ISSN:** 0272-1716. **Subscription Rates:** $32 members; $320 institutions. **Remarks:** Accepts advertising. **URL:** http://www.computer.org/cga/.
Ad Rates: BW: $2,150 **Circ:** Paid 10,519
4C: $3,250 Non-paid 77

2230 IEEE Design and Test of Computers
IEEE Computer Society
10662 Los Vaqueros Circle Phone: (714)821-8380
Los Alamitos, CA 90720 Fax: (714)821-4010
Publisher E-mail: csbooks@computer.org

Magazine on computer design and testing. **Founded:** 1984. **Freq:** Quarterly. **Print Method:** Offset. **Trim Size:** 8 1/8 x 10 7/8. **Cols./Page:** 2. **Col. Width:** 26 nonpareils. **Col. Depth:** 138 agate lines. **Key Personnel:** Marie English, Editor, menglish@computer.org; Matt Loeb, Publisher, mloeb@computer.org. **Subscription Rates:** $32 CS members. **Remarks:** Accepts advertising. **Available Online. URL:** http://www.computer.org/pubs/dbt/dbt.htm. **Alt. Formats:** CD-ROM, 1995 IEEE Computer Society Publications.
Ad Rates: GLR: $5 **Circ:** Paid 7,423
BW: $382 Non-paid 45
4C: $814
PCI: $96

2231 IEEE Expert
IEEE Computer Society
10662 Los Vaqueros Circle Phone: (714)821-8380
Los Alamitos, CA 90720 Fax: (714)821-4010
Publisher E-mail: csbooks@computer.org

Trade journal covering artificial intelligence, export systems, and intelligent systems. **Subtitle:** Intelligent Systems and Their Applications. **Founded:** 1986. **Freq:** Bimonthly. **Trim Size:** 8 1/8 x 10 7/8. **Cols./Page:** 3. **Col. Width:** 13 picas. **Col. Depth:** 54 picas. **Key Personnel:** Steve Wilcox, Managing Editor; Marilyn Potes, Editor; True Seaborn, Publisher. **ISSN:** 0885-9000. **Subscription Rates:** $20 (members of IEEE Computer Society); $36 (members of other technical societies). $10 single issue. **Remarks:** Accepts advertising. **URL:** http://www.computer.org.
Ad Rates: BW: $2,150 **Circ:** ‡14,127
4C: $3,150
PCI: $5

2232 IEEE Micro
IEEE Computer Society
10662 Los Vaqueros Circle Phone: (714)821-8380
Los Alamitos, CA 90720 Fax: (714)821-4010
Publisher E-mail: csbooks@computer.org

Magazine for engineers, computer scientists, and managers of microcomputer hardware, software, and systems activities. **Founded:** Feb. 1981. **Freq:** Bimonthly. **Print Method:** Offset. **Trim Size:** 8 1/8 x 10 7/8. **Cols./Page:** 2 and 3. **Col. Width:** 42 and 27 nonpareils. **Col. Depth:** 140 agate lines. **Key Personnel:** Marie English, Managing Editor; Matt Loeb, Publisher. **ISSN:** 0272-1732. **Subscription Rates:** $30 CS members. **Remarks:** Accepts advertising. **Available Online. URL:** http://www.computer.org/pubs/micro/micro.htm. **Alt. Formats:** CD-ROM, 1995-96 IEEE Computer Society Publications.
Ad Rates: BW: $2,290 **Circ:** Paid 12,000
4C: $3,390

2233 IEEE Software Magazine
IEEE Computer Society
10662 Los Vaqueros Circle Phone: (714)821-8380
Los Alamitos, CA 90720 Fax: (714)821-4010
Publisher E-mail: csbooks@computer.org

Magazine covering the computer software industry for the community of leading software practitioners. **Subtitle:** Building the Community of Leading Software Practitioners. **Founded:** Jan. 1984. **Freq:** Bimonthly. **Print Method:** Offset. **Trim Size:** 8 1/8 x 10 7/8. **Cols./Page:** 3. **Col. Width:** 26 nonpareils. **Col. Depth:** 138 agate lines. **Key Personnel:** Dale Strok, Managing Editor, phone (714)821-8380, fax (714)821-4010, dstrok@computer.org; Matt Loeb, Publisher; Patricia Garvey, Advertising Mgr. **ISSN:** 0740-7459. **Remarks:** Accepts advertising. **URL:** http://computer.org.
Ad Rates: GLR: $5 BW: $426 4C: $869 PCI: $96 **Circ:** Paid 20,849 Non-paid 93

2234 News-Enterprise
Cavanaugh Publishing
3622 Florista
PO Box 1010
Los Alamitos, CA 90720
Phone: (714)527-8210
Fax: (562)493-2310
Publication E-mail: newsers@aol.com

Community newspaper. **Founded:** 1923. **Freq:** Weekly (Wed.). **Print Method:** Offset. **Cols./Page:** 5. **Col. Width:** 16 inches. **Col. Depth:** 80 inches. **Key Personnel:** T. Pat Cavanaugh, Publisher. **Subscription Rates:** $25 individuals. **Remarks:** Accepts advertising.
Ad Rates: BW: $845 4C: $1,000 SAU: $15 PCI: $15 **Circ:** Paid ‡600 Free ‡30,000

LOS ALTOS, pop. 25,769.

W. CA. Santa Clara Co. 6 mi. SE of Palo Alto. Nurseries. Fruit packed. Residential. Fruit, truck farms.

2235 British Car
Enthusiasts Publications, Ltd.
343 2nd St., Ste. H
Los Altos, CA 94022
Phone: (415)949-9680
Fax: (415)949-9685
Free: (800)520-8292
Publication E-mail: britcarmag@aol.com

Magazine about British sports and luxury cars from classic to contemporary. **Founded:** 1985. **Freq:** Bimonthly. **Print Method:** Web offset. **Trim Size:** 8 1/8 x 10 7/8. **Cols./Page:** 2 and 3. **Col. Width:** 3.5 and 2.25 picas. **Col. Depth:** 10 inches. **Key Personnel:** Gary Anderson, Editor and Publisher. **ISSN:** 1052-0929. **Subscription Rates:** $22.95 individuals; $26 Canada; $35 other countries; $4 single issue; $5 single issue Canada; $7 single issue other countries. **Remarks:** Accepts advertising. **Formerly**: British Car & Bike.
Ad Rates: BW: $1,238 4C: $2,022 PCI: $30 **Circ:** Paid ‡30,000 Non-paid ‡4,500

2236 Integrated System Design
The Verecom Group
5150 EL Camino Real, No. D31
Los Altos, CA 94022
Phone: (415)903-0140
Fax: (415)903-0151
Publication E-mail: asic@asic.com

Trade journal serving the application of specific integrated circuit and electronic design automation markets, and engineers and managers developing system level solutions that incorporate silicon. **Founded:** 1992. **Freq:** Monthly. **Print Method:** Heatset web offset. **Trim Size:** 8 x 10 7/8. **Cols./Page:** 2. **Key Personnel:** James Uhl, Publisher; Jonah McLeod, Editor-in-Chief. **ISSN:** 1080-2797. **Subscription Rates:** $48; $130 other countries; $5 single issue. **Remarks:** Accepts advertising. **URL:** http://www.eedesign.com. **Formed by the merger of**: Design Automation; ASIC Technology and News. **Formerly:** ASIC & EDA.
Ad Rates: BW: $7,380 4C: $8,375 **Circ:** Controlled 55,302

2237 Narrow Gauge and Short Line Gazette
Benchmark Publications, Ltd.
PO Box 26
Los Altos, CA 94023
Phone: (650)941-3823
Fax: (650)941-3845

Magazine for narrow gauge and short line scale model railroad enthusiasts. **Founded:** Mar. 1975. **Freq:** Bimonthly. **Print Method:** Offset. **Trim Size:** 8 3/8 x 10 15/16. **Cols./Page:** 2 and 3. **Col. Width:** 2 1/4 and 2 1/4 inches. **Col. Depth:** 10 and 10 inches. **Key Personnel:** Robert W. Brown, Editor and Publisher. **ISSN:** 0148-2122. **Subscription Rates:** $24 individuals; $34 out of country.
Ad Rates: BW: $382 4C: $814 **Circ:** Paid ‡16,300 Non-paid ‡219

2238 KFJC-FM - 89.7
12345 El Monte Rd.
Los Altos, CA 94022-4504
Phone: (650)949-7260
Fax: (650)948-1085

Format: Full Service. **Networks:** Independent. **Owner:** Foothill College Board of Trustees, at above address. **Founded:** 1959. **Operating Hours:** Continuous; 100% local. **Key Personnel:** Ken Hamilton, Program Dir.; Robert Pelzel, Station Supervisor; Jason Biggs, Music Dir., phone (650)949-7092. **Wattage:** 250. **Ad Rates:** Noncommercial. **URL:** http://www.kfjc.org.

LOS ANGELES†, pop. 2,966,763.

S. CA. Los Angeles Co. A city of 450 square miles on the southern Pacific Coast. Largest city in area in United States, second largest retail center in the nation, largest industrial center west of Chicago and a leading agricultural center. University of Southern California; University of California at Los Angeles, and many other colleges and schools. A diversified economy with a variety of enterprises in agriculture. Manufacturing. Trade fishing, mining, entertaining, constructions, transportation services. Leads in value and added by manufactures of aircraft and aircraft parts, furniture fixtures, ordnance missiles. Other major manufacturing sectors include, electrical equipment, stone, clay, glass, apparel, fabricated metals, rubber, plastics, motion pictures, petroleum, coal, transportation equipment, printing and publishing. Lumber and wood products.

2239 Adam Film World Guide
Knight Publishing Corp.
8060 Melrose Ave.
Los Angeles, CA 90046
Phone: (323)653-8060
Fax: (323)655-9452
Publication E-mail: psi@loop.com

Magazine. **Subtitle:** Adult Video Guide. **Founded:** 1968. **Freq:** Monthly. **Print Method:** Offset. **Trim Size:** 8 x 10 7/8. **Cols./Page:** 3. **Col. Width:** 2 1/4 inches. **Col. Depth:** 10 inches. **Key Personnel:** Jeremy Stone, Editor; Tim Connelly, Advertising Mgr.; Mitchell Neal, Marketing Dir. **Subscription Rates:** $60 individuals; $6.99 single issue; $100 two years. **Remarks:** Accepts advertising. **Formerly**: Adam Film World.
Ad Rates: GLR: $133 BW: $1035 4C: $1,540 PCI: $70 **Circ:** ‡125,000

2240 Adam Magazine
Players International Publications
8060 Melrose Ave.
Los Angeles, CA 90046
Phone: (213)653-8060
Fax: (213)682-2932

Magazine for adult males. **Founded:** 1955. **Freq:** Monthly. **Print Method:** Offset. **Trim Size:** 8 1/4 x 11 1/8. **Cols./Page:** 3. **Col. Width:** 3 1/16 inches. **Col. Depth:** 11 1/8 inches. **Key Personnel:** Jared Rutter, Editor; Tim Connelly, Advertising Mgr. **Subscription Rates:** $45 individuals; $36 institutions; $3.75 single issue.
Ad Rates: BW: $1,600 4C: $2,400 **Circ:** 125,000

2241 The Advocate
Liberation Publications, Inc.
PO Box 4371
Los Angeles, CA 90078-4371
Fax: (213)467-6805
Publication E-mail: newsroom@advocate.com

National gay and lesbian news and lifestyle magazine. **Subtitle:** The National Gay and Lesbian Newsmagazine. **Founded:** Sept. 1967. **Freq:** Biweekly. **Print Method:** Offset. Uses mats. **Trim Size:** 7 7/8 x 10 7/8. **Cols./Page:** 3. **Col. Width:** 2 1/8 inches. **Col. Depth:** 10 1/8 inches. **ISSN:** 0001-8996. **Subscription Rates:** $44 individuals; $74 out of country; $3.95 single issue. **Remarks:** Accepts advertising. **URL:** http://www.advocate.com. **Alt. Formats:** Microform.
Ad Rates: BW: $4,656 4C: $6,501 **Circ:** Paid ★87,707

2242 Adweek Western Edition
BPI Communications, Inc.
5055 Wilshire Blvd., 7th Fl.
Los Angeles, CA 90036
Phone: (323)525-2270
Fax: (323)525-2391

Magazine featuring advertising and marketing news for western states. **Founded:** 1951. **Freq:** Weekly (Mon.). **Print Method:** Offset. **Trim Size:** 8 3/8 x 10 7/8. **Cols./Page:** 3. **Col. Width:** 2 3/8 inches. **Col. Depth:** 10 inches. **Key Personnel:** Charlotte Erwin, Publisher. **Subscription Rates:** $140 individuals; $3.50 single issue. **Remarks:** Accepts advertising. **URL:** http://www.adweek.com.
Ad Rates: BW: $13,520 4C: $19,420 **Circ:** Paid ‡40,441

2243 African Arts
African Studies Center
PO Box 951310
University of California
Los Angeles, CA 90095-1310
Phone: (310)825-1218
Fax: (310)206-3555
Publication E-mail: afriarts@ucla.edu

Journal featuring contemporary and traditional arts of Africa. **Founded:** Nov. 1967. **Freq:** Quarterly. **Print Method:** Offset. **Trim Size:** 8 1/2 x 11. **Cols./Page:** 3. **Col. Width:** 27 nonpareils. **Col. Depth:** 140 agate lines. **Key Personnel:** Donald J. Cosentino, Editor; Doran H. Ross, Advertising Mgr. **ISSN:** 0001-9933. **Subscription Rates:** $42 individuals. **Remarks:** Accepts advertising.
Ad Rates: BW: $1,160 4C: $1,530 **Circ:** 4,000

2244 Al Talib
U.C.L.A.
118 Kerckhoff Hall
308 Westwood Plaza
University of California, Los Angeles
Los Angeles, CA 90024
Phone: (310)825-1004
Fax: (310)206-3165
Publisher E-mail: pacificties@media.ucla.edu

Community magazine for Muslim's. **Subtitle:** The Muslim magazine at UCLA. **Founded:** 1990. **Freq:** Bi-quarterly. **Print Method:** Offset. **Trim Size:** 10 x 16. **Cols./Page:** 5. **Col. Width:** 2 inches. **Col. Depth:** 16 inches. **Key Personnel:** Ahmed Shama, Editor, ashama@ucla.edu; Al Talib, Contact, altalib@media.ucla.edu. **Subscription Rates:** $16 individuals per year. **URL:** http://www.media.asucla.edu.
Ad Rates: BW: $390 **Circ:** Controlled 20,000

2245 Amerasia Journal
UCLA Asian American Studies Center Publications
3230 Campbell Hall
Box 951546
Los Angeles, CA 90095
Phone: (310)825-2974
Fax: (310)206-9844
Journal addressing intercultural interests. **Subtitle:** Asian American Studies. **Founded:** 1971. **Freq:** 3/year. **Trim Size:** 6 x 9. **Cols./Page:** 1. **Col. Width:** 4 1/2 inches. **Col. Depth:** 7 1/2 inches. **Key Personnel:** Russell C. Leong, Editor, rleong@ucla.edu; Glenn Omatsu, Advertising Mgr.; Darryl Mar, Distribution Mgr. **ISSN:** 0044-7471. **Subscription Rates:** $40 institutions; $28 individuals; $49 other countries; $49 Canada. **Remarks:** Accepts advertising. **URL:** http://www.sscnet.ucla.edu/aasc/.
Ad Rates: BW: $160 **Circ:** Paid 1,500 Non-paid 45

2246 American Indian Culture and Research Journal
American Indian Studies Center
3220 Campbell Hall
Box 951548
Los Angeles, CA 90095-1548
Phone: (310)825-7315
Fax: (310)206-7060
Publication E-mail: aiscpubs@ucla.edu
Publisher E-mail: aisc@ucla.edu

Scholarly journal covering Native American studies. **Founded:** 1972. **Freq:** Quarterly. **Trim Size:** 6 x 9. **Key Personnel:** Duane Champagne, Editor. **ISSN:** 0161-6463. **Subscription Rates:** $25 individuals; $60 institutions; $12 single issue. **Remarks:** Accepts advertising.
Ad Rates: BW: $150 **Circ:** Combined 1,200

2247 American Journal of Ophthalmology
Elsevier Science Inc.
Jules Stein Eye Inst.
UCLA
100 Stein Plaza
Los Angeles, CA 90024
Phone: (310)825-8587
Fax: (310)206-3463
Publication E-mail: ajo@ucla.edu
Publisher E-mail: usinfo@elsevier.com

Ophthalmology magazine. **Founded:** 1884. **Freq:** Monthly. **Print Method:** Offset. **Trim Size:** 8 1/8 x 10 7/8. **Cols./Page:** 2. **Col. Width:** 19.25 nonpareils. **Col. Depth:** 56 picas. **Key Personnel:** Bradley R. Straatsma, MD, Editor-in-Chief, straatsma@jsei.ucla.edu; David Dionne, Assoc. Publisher. **ISSN:** 0002-9394. **Subscription Rates:** $79 individuals U.S. and Canada; $283 institutions U.S. and Canada; $154 individuals elsewhere; $358 institutions elsewhere. **Remarks:** Accepts advertising. **Online:** Electronic Ophthalmology Library. **URL:** http://www.ajo.com/; http://www.elsevier.com. **Alt. Formats:** CD-ROM, Electronic Ophthalmology Library.
Ad Rates: BW: $1,340 4C: $2,725 PCI: $110 **Circ:** Paid ★11,468

2248 American Music
University of Illinois Press at Urbana-Champaign
Musicology Department
UCLA Box 951623
Los Angeles, CA 90095-1623
Phone: (310)206-1087
Fax: (310)206-9203
Scholarly journal devoted to American music. **Founded:** 1983. **Freq:** Quarterly. **Print Method:** Offset. **Trim Size:** 6 x 9. **Cols./Page:** 1. **Col. Width:** 52 nonpareils. **Col. Depth:** 101 agate lines. **Key Personnel:** Robert Walser, Editor, walser@humnet.ucla.edu; Carolyn Glassman, Advertising Mgr. **ISSN:** 0734-4392. **Subscription Rates:** $30 individuals; $42 industry; $37 other countries; $49 other countries industry. **Remarks:** Accepts advertising.
Ad Rates: BW: $160 **Circ:** ‡1,704

2249 The American Senior
Publishing and Business Consultants
4427 W. Slauson Ave.
Los Angeles, CA 90043-2717

Magazine covering breakthroughs in health care for seniors. **Founded:** 1991. **Freq:** Quarterly. **Print Method:** Web Offset. **Trim Size:** 8 1/2 x 10 1/4. **Cols./Page:** 3. **Col. Width:** 2 1/2 inches. **Col. Depth:** 9 inches. **Key Personnel:** Atia Napoleon, Editor and Publisher. **ISSN:** 1055-8306. **Subscription Rates:** $26.99; $33.99 Canada; $38.96 other countries. **Remarks:** Accepts advertising.
Ad Rates: BW: $8,290 **Circ:** Paid 120,000
4C: $9,750

2250 Ancient Wisdom for Modern Living
Philosophical Research Society, Inc.
3910 Los Feliz Blvd. Phone: (213)663-2167
Los Angeles, CA 90027 Fax: (213)663-9443
Free: (800)548-4062
Publisher E-mail: info@prs.org

Journal of philosophy, religions, and psychology. **Founded:** 1941. **Freq:** Quarterly. **Print Method:** Offset. **Trim Size:** 8 1/2 x 11. **Cols./Page:** 1. **Col. Width:** 72 nonpareils. **Col. Depth:** 126 agate lines. **Key Personnel:** Daniel Fritz, Publisher. **ISSN:** 0030-8250. **Subscription Rates:** Free. **Remarks:** Advertising not accepted. **Formerly:** P.R.S. Journal (1992); Horizon.
Circ: Free 20,000

2251 Apartment Age Magazine
621 S. Westmoreland Ave. Phone: (213)384-4131
Los Angeles, CA 90005 Fax: (213)382-3970
Publisher E-mail: aagla@aol.com

Magazine for residential rental property owners. **Founded:** 1967. **Freq:** Monthly. **Print Method:** Offset. **Trim Size:** 8 3/8 x 10 5/8. **Cols./Page:** 3. **Col. Width:** 27 nonpareils. **Col. Depth:** 140 agate lines. **Key Personnel:** Kevin B. Postema, Editor; Charles A. Isham, Publisher. **ISSN:** 0192-0030. **Subscription Rates:** Free to qualified subscribers; $48 individuals. **Remarks:** Accepts advertising.
Ad Rates: BW: $426 **Circ:** Paid ‡11,000
4C: $869 Controlled ‡29,000

2252 Apparel News South
Apparel News Group
110 E. 9th St., Ste. A-777 Phone: (213)627-3737
Los Angeles, CA 90079-1777 Fax: (213)627-5707

Clothing industry magazine containing textile information on garments for women and children. **Founded:** 1979. **Freq:** 5/year. **Print Method:** Offset. **Trim Size:** 7 1/8 x 10. **Cols./Page:** 5. **Col. Width:** 22 nonpareils. **Col. Depth:** 210 agate lines. **Key Personnel:** Martin Wernicke, Publisher; Jack Marquette, Marketing Research; Anne Harnegal, Editor-in-Chief. **ISSN:** 0744-6403. **Subscription Rates:** $25 individuals; $5 single issue. **Remarks:** Accepts advertising. **URL:** http://www.apparelnews.net.
Ad Rates: BW: $426 **Circ:** 19,248
4C: $869
PCI: $40

2253 Architectural Digest
Conde Nast Publications, Inc.
6300 Wilshire Blvd. Phone: (213)965-3700
Los Angeles, CA 90048 Fax: (213)937-1458
Publisher E-mail: letters@brides.com

Magazine on interior design, art, and antiques. **Founded:** 1920. **Freq:** Monthly. **Print Method:** Offset. **Cols./Page:** 3. **Col. Width:** 34 nonpareils. **Col. Depth:** 154 agate lines. **Key Personnel:** Thomas P. Losee, Jr., Publisher. **Subscription Rates:** $39.95 individuals; $4.50 single issue. **Remarks:** Accepts advertising.
Ad Rates: BW: $21,750 **Circ:** Paid ★**822,601**
4C: $30,200

2254 Aztlan
UCLA Chicano Studies Research Center Publications
2307 Murphy Hall Phone: (310)825-2642
Los Angeles, CA 90095-1544 Fax: (310)206-1784
Publisher E-mail: aztlan@csrc.ucla.edu

Scholarly journal covering Chicano studies. **Subtitle:** A Journal of Chicano Studies. **Founded:** 1970. **Freq:** Semiannual. **Print Method:** Offset. **Trim Size:** 6 x 9. **Cols./Page:** 1. **Col. Width:** 4 inches. **Col. Depth:** 7 inches. **Key Personnel:** Chon Noriega, Editor; Wendy Belcher, Managing Editor. **ISSN:** 0005-2604. **Subscription Rates:** $25 individuals; $50 institutions; $12.50 single issue. **Remarks:** Accepts advertising. **URL:** http://www.sscnet.ucla.edu/esp.
Circ: Paid ‡600

2255 Baby Huey
The Harvey Entertainment Co.
1999 Avenue of the Stars, No. 2050 Phone: (310)789-1990
Fax: (310)789-1991
Los Angeles, CA 90067
Comic book. **Freq:** Monthly. **Print Method:** Web offset. **Trim Size:** 6 1/8 x 10 1/8. **Key Personnel:** Sid Jacobson, Editor; Ed Shukin, Director; Kevin S. Bricklin, Director. **Subscription Rates:** $1.50 single issue. **URL:** http://www.harvey.com.

2256 Barracuda
Barracuda Magazine
PO Box 291873 Phone: (213)368-6701
Los Angeles, CA 90027
Consumer lifestyle magazine covering automobiles and other men's issues. **Freq:** Quarterly. **Key Personnel:** Jeff Fox, Publisher, jfox@cinenet.net. **Subscription Rates:** $16 individuals; $5 single issue. **URL:** http://www.cinenet.net/~jfox.

2257 The Beat (Los Angeles)
Bongo Productions
PO Box 65856 Phone: (323)257-2328
Los Angeles, CA 90065 Fax: (323)257-2461
Publication E-mail: getthebeat@aol.com

Consumer magazine covering reggae, African, Caribbean, and world music. **Founded:** 1981. **Freq:** Bimonthly. **Print Method:** Offset. **Trim Size:** 8 3/8 x 10 7/8. **Key Personnel:** C.C. Smith, Editor and Publisher; Carol Haile Selassie, Advertising and Circulation. **ISSN:** 1063-5319. **Subscription Rates:** $15 individuals; $20 two years; $3.50 single issue. **Remarks:** Accepts advertising. **Former name:** Reggae Beat; Reggae and African Beat.
Ad Rates: BW: $900 **Circ:** Non-paid 25,000
4C: $1,800

2258 Beirut Times
PO Box 93475 Phone: (323)469-4354
Los Angeles, CA 90093 Fax: (323)469-4988
Free: (888)522-8180
Publication E-mail: info@beiruttimes.com

Covers events, issues, and social needs unique to Arab Americans. **Founded:** 1985. **Freq:** Weekly. **Trim Size:** 12 inches. **Cols./Page:** 5. **Col. Width:** 1.25 inches. **USPS:** 765-440. **Subscription Rates:** $44. **Remarks:** Accepts advertising. **URL:** http://www.beiruttimes.com/. **Alt. Formats:** Microform; Mailing labels.
Ad Rates: PCI: $25 **Circ:** Non-paid 15,000

2259 Beverage Beacon/Ledger
Sam King
6601 S. Hoover St. Phone: (213)778-2522
Los Angeles, CA 90044 Fax: (213)778-2725

Magazine for the liquor trade and businesses, including the Hispanic and African-American markets. **Subtitle:** The Beacon. **Founded:** 1969. **Freq:** Monthly. **Print Method:** Offset. **Trim Size:** 10 x 15. **Cols./Page:** 5. **Col. Width:** 24 nonpareils. **Col. Depth:** 210 agate lines. **Key Personnel:** Sam King, Editor and Publisher. **Subscription Rates:** $12 individuals. **Remarks:** Accepts advertising. **Merged with:** Beverage Beacon; Beverage Ledger.
Ad Rates: GLR: $3.69 **Circ:** Controlled ‡9,000
BW: $2,362.50
4C: $3,262.50

2260 Black Dates
BLK Publishing Company
Box 83912 Phone: (310)410-0808
Los Angeles, CA 90083-0912 Fax: (310)410-9250
Publisher E-mail: newsroom@blk.com

Consumer magazine covering events by and for black lesbians and gays. **Founded:** 1994. **Freq:** Monthly. **Key Personnel:** Alan Bell, Editor. **Subscription Rates:** Free. **Remarks:** Accepts advertising.
Ad Rates: BW: $260 **Circ:** (Not Reported)

2261 Black Lace
BLK Publishing Company
Box 83912 Phone: (310)410-0808
Los Angeles, CA 90083-0912 Fax: (310)410-9250
Publication E-mail: newsroom@blk.com
Publisher E-mail: newsroom@blk.com

Magazine published by and for African-American lesbians. Includes erotica and politically focused articles and analysis. **Founded:** 1991. **Freq:** Quarterly. **Trim Size:** 8 1/8 x 10 7/8. **Key Personnel:** Alycee J. Lane, Editor. **ISSN:** 1049-3298. **Subscription Rates:** $20; $36 other countries; $5.95 single issue. **Remarks:** Accepts advertising. **URL:** http://www.blk.com/blk.
Ad Rates: BW: $300 **Circ:** Paid 9,000
4C: $429 Non-paid 200

2262 Blackfire
BLK Publishing Company
Box 83912 Phone: (310)410-0808
Los Angeles, CA 90083-0912 Fax: (310)410-9250
Publisher E-mail: newsroom@blk.com

Consumer magazine covering black erotica for a gay audience. **Freq:** Bimonthly. **Key Personnel:** Alan Bell, Editor. **ISSN:** 1049-3271. **Subscription Rates:** $30 individuals; $60 two years. **Remarks:** Accepts advertising.
Ad Rates: BW: $1,800 **Circ:** (Not Reported)
4C: $2,574

2263 Blitz
PO Box 48124 Phone: (818)985-8618
Los Angeles, CA 90048-0124
Publication E-mail: blitzmcd@aol.com

Magazine for rock and roll enthusiasts. **Subtitle:** The Rock and Roll Magazine for Thinking People. **Founded:** 1975. **Freq:** Quarterly. **Print Method:** Offset. **Trim Size:** 8 1/2 x 11. **Cols./Page:** 3. **Key Personnel:** Mike McDowell, Editor and Publisher. **ISSN:** 0263-2543. **Subscription Rates:** $15. $2.50 single issue. **Remarks:** Accepts advertising. **Online:** America Online.
Ad Rates: BW: $300 **Circ:** Paid ‡2,000
Controlled ‡500

2264 BLK
BLK Publishing Company
Box 83912 Phone: (310)410-0808
Los Angeles, CA 90083-0912 Fax: (310)410-9250
Publisher E-mail: newsroom@blk.com

Consumer magazine covering lifestyle for gay and lesbian black people. **Founded:** 1988. **Print Method:** Offset. **Trim Size:** 8 1/8 x 10 7/8. **Cols./Page:** 3. **Col. Width:** 2 1/4 inches. **Col. Depth:** 10 inches. **Key Personnel:** Alan Bell, Editor. **ISSN:** 1043-0075. **Subscription Rates:** $2.95 single issue. **Remarks:** Accepts advertising.
Ad Rates: BW: $1,800 **Circ:** (Not Reported)
4C: $2,574

2265 Bon Appetit
Conde Nast Publications, Inc.
6300 Wilshire Blvd. Phone: (213)965-3600
Los Angeles, CA 90048 Fax: (213)937-1206
Publisher E-mail: letters@brides.com

Lifestyle Magazine covering food, travel, and entertaining. **Subtitle:** America's Food and Entertaining Magazine. **Founded:** 1955. **Freq:** 12/year. **Print Method:** Offset. **Trim Size:** 8 x 10 3/4. **Cols./Page:** 3. **Col. Width:** 13 picas. **Key Personnel:** William J. Garry, Editor-in-Chief; Lynn W. Heiler, Publisher; Daniel Lagani, Associate Publisher; Carol Campbell, Advertising Mgr. **Subscription Rates:** $18 individuals; $30 two years; $2.95 single issue. **Remarks:** Accepts advertising. **URL:** http://www.epicurious.com/b-ba/b00-home/ba.html.
Ad Rates: BW: $34,500 **Circ:** Paid ★**1,086,997**
4C: $49,180

2266 Bootstrappin' Entrepreneur Bulletin
6308 W. 89th St., Ste. 306-GDP Phone: (310)568-9861
Los Angeles, CA 90045
Publication E-mail: subscribe@kimberlystansell.com

Bulletin providing tips, ideas, and resources for small businesses. A companion to book Bootstrapper's Success Secrets (Career Press). **Founded:** Jan. 1, 1996. **Freq:** 4/year. **Trim Size:** 8 1/2 x 11. **Key Personnel:** Kimberly Stansell, Editor, kmberlynla@hotmail.com. **Subscription Rates:** Free Send self-addressed, stamped (business-size) envelope. **Remarks:** Accepts advertising.
Circ: (Not Reported)

2267 The Braille Mirror
Braille Institute Press
741 N. Vermont Ave. Phone: (323)663-1111
Los Angeles, CA 90029 Fax: (323)663-0867
Free: (800)BRAILLE
Publisher E-mail: info@brailleinstitute.org

General interest magazine (Braille). **Founded:** 1926. **Freq:** 10/year. **Print Method:** Heidelberg Cylinder Press adapted for zinc braille plates. **Trim Size:** 11 x 11 1/2. **Cols./Page:** 1. **Col. Width:** 9 inches. **Col. Depth:** 10 inches. **Key Personnel:** Douglas Menville, Editor. **Subscription Rates:** Free. **Remarks:** Advertising not accepted. **URL:** http://www.brailleinstitute.org.
Circ: Controlled 2,500

2268 Business Concepts
Publishing and Business Consultants
4427 W. Slauson Ave.
Los Angeles, CA 90043-2717

Magazine featuring money-making ideas and new business opportunities. **Founded:** 1991. **Freq:** Quarterly. **Print Method:** Web offset. **Trim Size:** 8 1/2 x 10 1/4. **Cols./Page:** 3. **Col.**

Width: 2 1/2 inches. **Col. Depth:** 9 inches. **Key Personnel:** Atia Napoleon, Editor and Publisher. **ISSN:** 1055-8217. **Subscription Rates:** $26.99; $33.99 Canada; $38.96 other countries. **Remarks:** Accepts advertising.
Ad Rates: BW: $8,290 **Circ:** Paid 120,000
4C: $9,750

2269 Buzz
Buzz Inc.
11845 W. Olympic Blvd., Ste. 800 Phone: (310)473-2721
Fax: (310)473-2876
Los Angeles, CA 90064
City magazine for and about Los Angeles, focusing on art, politics, culture, and entertainment. **Subtitle:** The Talk of Los Angeles. **Founded:** 1990. **Freq:** Monthly. **Trim Size:** 8 x 10 7/8. **Key Personnel:** Eden Collinsworth, CEO; Scott Kramer, President; Mark Smelzer, Publisher; Marilyn Bethany, Editor-in-Chief; C. Montgomery, Advertising Mgr. **Subscription Rates:** $15 individuals; $3 single issue. **Remarks:** Accepts advertising. **Available Online**. **URL:** http://www.buzzmag.com.
Ad Rates: BW: $11,018 **Circ:** Paid 138,475
4C: $16,950

2270 California Apparel News
Apparel News Group
110 E. 9th St., Ste. A-777 Phone: (213)627-3737
Los Angeles, CA 90079-1777 Fax: (213)627-5707
Publication E-mail: webmaster@apparelnews.net

Weekly newspaper covering the apparel industry and providing information about textiles, trimmings, fashion trends, retailing and business. **Founded:** 1946. **Freq:** Weekly (Fri.). **Print Method:** Web press. **Trim Size:** 10 3/4 x 14 5/8. **Cols./Page:** 5. **Col. Width:** 24 nonpareils. **Col. Depth:** 196 agate lines. **Key Personnel:** Martin Wernicke, Publisher; Jack Marquette, International Marketing; Jerry Sullivan, Exec. Editor. **ISSN:** 0008-0896. **Subscription Rates:** $58 individuals. **Remarks:** Accepts advertising. **URL:** http://www.apparelnews.net.
Ad Rates: BW: $3,300 **Circ:** 15,872
4C: $4,350 Non-paid 6,000
PCI: $60

2271 California Hungarians
207 S. Western Ave., Ste. 201 Phone: (323)463-3473
Los Angeles, CA 90004 Fax: (323)384-7642

Newspaper (tabloid) with an ethnic, political, and cultural orientation (Hungarian). **Founded:** Oct. 6, 1922. **Freq:** Weekly. **Print Method:** Offset. **Trim Size:** 11 x 17. **Cols./Page:** 5. **Col. Width:** 2 inches. **Col. Depth:** 16 inches. **Key Personnel:** Maria Fenyes, Editor and Publisher. **ISSN:** 0744-8600. **Subscription Rates:** $26 individuals; $19 Senior Citizens; $28 Canada; $35 other countries. **Remarks:** Accepts advertising. **Foreign language name**: Californiai Magyarsag.
Ad Rates: GLR: $1.50 **Circ:** ‡7,500
BW: $500
PCI: $10

2272 California Real Estate Journal
Daily Journal Corp.
915 E. 1st St. Phone: (213)229-5300
Los Angeles, CA 90012-4050 Fax: (213)680-3682
Free: (800)652-1700

Commercial real estate newspaper. **Founded:** 1986. **Freq:** Monthly. **Print Method:** Offset. **Trim Size:** 10 x 13 1/2. **Cols./Page:** 4. **Col. Width:** 2 1/2 inches. **Key Personnel:** Roger Vincent, Editor; T. Sumner Robinson, Publisher; Eleanor Johnson, Advertising Dir. **Subscription Rates:** $64. **Remarks:** Accepts advertising. **Formed by the merger of**: Northern California Real Estate Journal; Southern California Real Estate Journal.
Ad Rates: BW: $2,501 **Circ:** Paid ‡2,842
4C: $3,091 Non-paid ‡194

2273 California Real Estate Magazine
California Association of Realtors
525 S. Virgil Ave. Phone: (213)739-8320
Los Angeles, CA 90020-1406 Fax: (213)480-7724

Magazine promoting professionalism and skills of real estate brokers and agents. **Founded:** Jan. 1920. **Freq:** 10/year. **Print Method:** Offset. **Trim Size:** 8 1/4 x 10 3/4. **Cols./Page:** 3. **Col. Width:** 27 nonpareils. **Col. Depth:** 128 agate lines. **Key Personnel:** Stacy Katzin, Advertising Mgr., phone (213)739-8321, stacey-katzin@car.org; Anne Framroze, Communications Mgr. **ISSN:** 0008-1450. **Subscription Rates:** $12 individuals. **Remarks:** Accepts advertising.
Ad Rates: BW: $3,880 **Circ:** Paid 85,000
4C: $5,000 Non-paid 350

2274 California Staats-Zeitung
1201 N. Alvarado Phone: (213)413-5500
PO Box 26308 Fax: (213)413-5469
Los Angeles, CA 90026
Ethnic newspaper (German). **Founded:** 1890. **Freq:** Weekly (Thurs.). **Print Method:** Offset. **Cols./Page:** 7. **Col. Width:** 26 nonpareils. **Col. Depth:** 280 agate lines. **Key Personnel:** Peter Teichmann, Editor and Publisher. **USPS:** 084-920. **Subscription Rates:** $25 individuals; $38 out of state; $0.90 single issue.
Ad Rates: GLR: $.66 **Circ:** 18,700
BW: $2,500
4C: $3,200
PCI: $12

2275 Canine Practice
Veterinary Practice Publishing Co.
PO Box 57900 Phone: (213)385-2222
Los Angeles, CA 90057 Fax: (213)385-8565

Canine medicine and surgery magazine. **Founded:** 1971. **Freq:** Bimonthly. **Print Method:** Offset. **Trim Size:** 8 1/4 x 10 7/8. **Cols./Page:** 2. **Col. Width:** 33 nonpareils. **Col. Depth:** 106 agate lines. **Key Personnel:** J.W. Alexander, D.V.M., Editor; Nancy A. Bull, Publisher. **ISSN:** 1057-6622. **Subscription Rates:** $28 individuals; $35 Canada and Mexico; $45 other countries. **Remarks:** Accepts advertising.
Ad Rates: BW: $1,295 **Circ:** 6,500
4C: $2,120

2276 Car Craft
Petersen Publishing Co., L.L.C.
6420 Wilshire Blvd. Phone: (323)782-2350
Los Angeles, CA 90048-5515 Fax: (323)782-2704

Magazine covering performance cars and drag racing. **Founded:** 1953. **Freq:** Monthly. **Print Method:** Offset. **Trim Size:** 7 7/8 x 10 1/2. **Key Personnel:** Jim McGowan, Editor; Bruce Bakke, Publisher; Peter Clancey, Senior Vice President. **Subscription Rates:** $11.97 individuals; $2.95 single issue. **Remarks:** Accepts advertising.
Ad Rates: BW: $11,830 **Circ:** Paid ★377,647
4C: $20,315
PCI: $651

2277 Casper
The Harvey Entertainment Co.
1999 Avenue of the Stars, No. 2050 Phone: (310)789-1990
Fax: (310)789-1991
Los Angeles, CA 90067
Comic book. **Freq:** Monthly. **Print Method:** Web offset. **Trim Size:** 6 1/8 x 10 1/8. **Key Personnel:** Sid Jacobson, Editor; Ed Shukin, Director; Kevin S. Bricklin, Director. **Subscription Rates:** $1.50 single issue. **URL:** http://www.harvey.com.

2278 Central Star/Journal Wave
Wave Community Newspapers, Inc.
2621 W. 54th St. Phone: (213)290-3000
Los Angeles, CA 90043 Fax: (213)291-0219

Black community newspaper. **Founded:** 1919. **Freq:** Biweekly Wednesday & Saturday. **Print Method:** Offset. **Trim Size:** 13 3/4 x 21 1/2. **Cols./Page:** 6. **Col. Width:** 5 nonpareils. **Col. Depth:** 21 1/2 inches. **Key Personnel:** C.Z. Wilson, President. **Subscription Rates:** $125 by mail; Free. **Remarks:** Advertising accepted; rates available upon request.
Circ: Combined 37,210

Chicago Apparel News - See Chicago, Illinois

2279 Chicano-Latin Law Review
University of California, Los Angeles
School of Law Phone: (310)825-2894
Rm. 2246 Fax: (310)206-6489
405 Hilgard Ave.
Los Angeles, CA 90024-1476
Publication E-mail: clr@lawx.law.ucla.edu

Journal focusing on legal issues of concern to Hispanic Americans. **Founded:** 1972. **Freq:** Semiannual. **Cols./Page:** 1. **Key Personnel:** Carmen Santana, Co-Editor-in-Chief; Salvador Mendoza, Co-Editor-in-Chief. **ISSN:** 1061-8899. **Subscription Rates:** $15 single issue; $19 FOREIGN. **Remarks:** Advertising accepted; rates available upon request. **Online:** WESTLAW.
Circ: 340

2280 City Terrace Comet
Eastern Group Publications Inc.
2500 S. Atlantic Blvd., No. A Phone: (213)263-5743
Los Angeles, CA 90040-2004 Fax: (213)263-9169

Community newspaper (English and Spanish). **Founded:** 1950. **Freq:** Weekly (Thurs.). **Print Method:** Offset. **Trim Size:** 13 x 21 1/2. **Cols./Page:** 6. **Col. Width:** 2 1/16 inches. **Col. Depth:** 294 agate lines. **Key Personnel:** Dolores Sanchez, Publisher; John Sanchez, Advertising Mgr. **Subscription Rates:** $92. **Remarks:** Accepts advertising.
Ad Rates: GLR: $2.50 **Circ:** Paid ‡211
BW: $3,150 Free ‡4,528
4C: $3,570
SAU: $25
PCI: $28

2281 Civic Center NewSource
Metropolitan News Co.
210 S. Spring St. Phone: (213)628-4384
Los Angeles, CA 90012 Fax: (213)687-3886

Community newspaper. **Founded:** 1990. **Freq:** Weekly. **Print Method:** Offset. **Cols./Page:** 4. **Col. Width:** 15 picas. **Col. Depth:** 15 1/2 inches. **Key Personnel:** John Babigian, Publisher. **Remarks:** Accepts advertising. **URL:** http://www.menews.com.
Ad Rates: PCI: $6 **Circ:** Paid 200
Non-paid 7,000

2282 Comitatus
University of California at Los Angeles
302 Royce Hall Phone: (310)825-1537
Los Angeles, CA 90095-1485 Fax: (310)825-0655
Publication E-mail: comitatu@humnet.ucla.edu

Journal containing articles on medieval and renaissance subjects. **Subtitle:** A Journal of Medieval and Renaissance Studies. **Founded:** 1968. **Freq:** Annual. **Trim Size:** 5 1/2 x 8 1/2. **Cols./Page:** 1. **Key Personnel:** Dr. Blair Sullivan, Managing Editor. **ISSN:** 0069-6412. **Subscription Rates:** $15 individuals. **Remarks:** Advertising not accepted.
Circ: Paid 500

2283 The Commentator
Southwestern University
675 S. Westmoreland Phone: (213)738-6873
Los Angeles, CA 90005 Fax: (213)383-1688

Collegiate magazine. **Founded:** 1971. **Freq:** Monthly (during the academic year). **Print Method:** Offset. **Cols./Page:** 4. **Col. Width:** 28 nonpareils. **Col. Depth:** 224 agate lines. **Key Personnel:** Darren Emenstein, Editor-in-Chief; Todd Whiteley, Managing Editor. **Subscription Rates:** $8 Free. **Remarks:** Accepts advertising.
Ad Rates: BW: $450 **Circ:** Non-paid 2,000

Compton/Carson Wave - See Compton

2284 Credit & Finance
Publishing and Business Consultants
4427 W. Slauson Ave.
Los Angeles, CA 90043-2717

Magazine covering personal credit with emphasis on finance. **Founded:** 1991. **Freq:** Quarterly. **Print Method:** Web offset. **Trim Size:** 8 1/2 x 10 1/4. **Cols./Page:** 3. **Col. Width:** 2 1/2 inches. **Col. Depth:** 9 inches. **Key Personnel:** Atia Napoleon, Editor and Publisher. **ISSN:** 1055-8225. **Subscription Rates:** $26.99; $33.99 Canada; $38.96 other countries. **Remarks:** Accepts advertising.
Ad Rates: BW: $8,290 **Circ:** Paid 120,000
4C: $9,750

Culver City Star - See Culver City

2285 Current Employment
Publishing and Business Consultants
4427 W. Slauson Ave.
Los Angeles, CA 90043-2717

Magazine featuring updated information on current government jobs and industry trends. **Founded:** 1991. **Freq:** Quarterly. **Print Method:** Web offset. **Trim Size:** 8 1/2 x 10 1/4. **Cols./Page:** 3. **Col. Width:** 2 1/2 inches. **Col. Depth:** 9 inches. **Key Personnel:** Atia Napoleon, Editor and Publisher. **ISSN:** 1055-8292. **Subscription Rates:** $26.99; $33.99 Canada; $38.96 other countries. **Remarks:** Accepts advertising.
Ad Rates: BW: $8,290 **Circ:** Paid 120,000
4C: $9,750

2286 Daily Bruin
University of California, Los Angeles
118 Kerkhoff Hall Phone: (310)825-9898
308 Westwood Plaza Fax: (310)206-0906
Los Angeles, CA 90024
Publication E-mail: news@media.ucla.edu

Collegiate newspaper (tabloid). **Founded:** 1919. **Freq:** Daily (morn.) (during the academic year). **Print Method:** Offset. Uses mats. **Cols./Page:** 5. **Col. Width:** 11.5 picas. **Col. Depth:** 16 inches. **Key Personnel:** Guy Levy, Business Mgr., phone (310)825-9833, fax (310)206-0538, glevy@media.ucla.edu; Adam Yamaguchi, Editor-in-Chief, phone (310)206-0938, ayamaguchi@media.ucla.edu; Elena Jarvis, Advisor, phone (310)825-2859, ejarvis@media.ucla.edu. **Subscription Rates:** Free; $200 by mail. **Remarks:** Accepts advertising. **URL:** http://www.dailybruin.ucla.edu.
Ad Rates: GLR: $9.70 **Circ:** Free 22,000
BW: $696
4C: $1,056
PCI: $12.30

2287 Daily Commerce
Daily Journal Corp.
915 E. 1st St. Phone: (213)229-5300
Los Angeles, CA 90012-4050 Fax: (213)680-3682
Free: (800)652-1700

Real estate newspaper. **Subtitle:** Serving the Southern California Real Estate Investor. **Founded:** 1917. **Freq:** Daily (eve.). **Print Method:** Offset. **Cols./Page:** 4. **Col. Width:** 2 1/2 inches. **Col. Depth:** 13 1/2 inches. **Key Personnel:** Erik Pedersen, Managing Editor; Nell Fields, Publisher. **ISSN:** 0279-4195. **Subscription Rates:** $165 individuals. **Remarks:** Accepts advertising. **Alt. Formats:** Microfiche.
Ad Rates: BW: $658.80 **Circ:** Free 279
4C: $1,258.80 Paid 2,829
SAU: $12.20

2288 Daily News
21221 Oxnard St. Phone: (818)713-3000
Woodland Hills, CA 91367 Fax: (818)713-0058

General newspaper. **Founded:** 1911. **Freq:** Mon.-Sun. (morn.). **Print Method:** Letterpress and offset. **Cols./Page:** 6. **Col. Width:** 24 nonpareils. **Col. Depth:** 294 agate lines. **Key Personnel:** Robert W. Burdick, Editor; David J. Auger, Publisher; Bob McCroy, Advertising Dir. **Subscription Rates:** $91 individuals. **Remarks:** Accepts advertising. **Online:** Data-Times Corporation; Dialog (The Dialog Corporation); CompuServe Information Service; America Online, Inc. **Feature Editors:** Mark Barnhill, *City*, phone (818)713-3706; Russ Britt, *Aviation*, phone (818)713-3730; Jayne Clark, *Travel*, phone (818)713-3681; Steve Clow, *Features, Lifestyle, Living, Society*, phone (818)713-3699; John Corrigan, *Political*, phone (818)713-3707; Phil Gallo, *Entertainment, Music*, phone (818)713-3684; Natalie Haughton, *Food*, phone (818)713-3692; Sherl Hopkins, *Garden/Home*, phone (818)713-3000; Rebecca Howard, *Fashion*, phone (818)713-3634; Barbara Jones, *Religion*, phone (818)713-3710; Tony Knight, *Environmental*, phone (818)713-3769; Patty Ladd, *TV*, phone (818)713-3690; Bob Lund, *Sunday*, phone (818)713-3717; Diana Lundin, *Medical*, phone (818)713-3679; Craig Mailloux, *Photo*, phone (818)713-3777; Darryl Miller, *Drama*, phone (818)713-3665; Steve O'Sullivan, *Financial/Business, Real Estate*, phone (818)713-3733; Rick Quist, *News*, phone (818)713-3716; Dorothy Reinhold, *Family, Women's*, phone (818)713-3686; Thomas S. Gray, *Editorials*, phone (818)713-3648; Kate Seago, *Book*, phone (818)713-3683; Beth Shuster, *Education*, phone (818)713-3732; Fred Shuster, *Radio*, phone (818)713-3676; Bob Strauss, *Movie*, phone (818)713-3670; Rick Vacek, *Sports*, phone (818)713-3627.
Ad Rates: GLR: $5.61 **Circ:** Mon.-Fri. ‡185,736
BW: $10,269 Sat. ‡173,062
4C: $11,469 Sun. ‡202,614
PCI: $81.50

2289 Daily Trojan
University of Southern California
Student Union 421 Phone: (213)740-5667
University of South California Fax: (213)740-5666
Los Angeles, CA 90089-0895
Publication E-mail: dtrojan@scf.usc.edu

Collegiate newspaper. **Founded:** 1891. **Freq:** Daily (morn.) (during the academic year) Wednesday (during summer months). **Print Method:** Offset. **Trim Size:** 11 x 17. **Cols./Page:** 5. **Col. Width:** 22 nonpareils. **Col. Depth:** 224 agate lines. **Key Personnel:** Elisa Ung, Editor, phone (213)740-8829; Mona Cravens, Publisher, phone (213)740-2707, cravens@mizar.usc.edu. **Subscription Rates:** $75 semester; $140 individuals. **URL:** http://www.usc.edu/dept/DT.
Ad Rates: GLR: $.52 **Circ:** ‡10,000
BW: $636
4C: $1,036
PCI: $8

Dallas Apparel News - See Dallas, Texas

2290 Dirt Rider
Petersen Publishing Co., L.L.C.
6420 Wilshire Blvd. Phone: (323)782-2350
Los Angeles, CA 90048-5515 Fax: (323)782-2704

Off-road motorcycle magazine. **Subtitle:** World's Largest Dirt Bike Publication. **Founded:** 1982. **Freq:** Monthly. **Print Method:** Offset. **Trim Size:** 7 7/8 x 10 1/2. **Key Personnel:** Richard P. Lague, Publisher; Scott Goodwin, Publisher; Peter Clancey, Sr., Marketing Dir. **Subscription Rates:** $11.97 individuals; $2.95 single issue. **Remarks:** Accepts advertising.
Ad Rates: BW: $5,380 **Circ:** Paid ★178,780
4C: $9,065
PCI: $296

2291 The Duckburg Times
The Duckburg News
3010 Wilshire Blvd., Ste. 362 Phone: (213)388-2364
Los Angeles, CA 90010-1146
Magazine devoted to Disney cartoons, films, and related materials. **Founded:** 1977. **Freq:** Periodic. **Print Method:** Offset. **Trim Size:** 7 x 8 1/2. **Cols./Page:** 1. **Col. Width:** 84 nonpareils. **Col. Depth:** 119 agate lines. **Key Personnel:** Dana Gabbard, Editor and Publisher. **ISSN:** 0887-2155.
Circ: ‡1,400

2292 Earth
The Shepherd Media Group
Shepherd Media Group Phone: (562)463-4005
PO Box 226789 Fax: (562)692-5608
Los Angeles, CA 90022-0489
Magazine reporting on engineering construction, equipment, and projects in Los Angeles and Orange counties. **Founded:** 1956. **Freq:** Quarterly. **Print Method:** Offset. **Trim Size:** 8 1/2 x 11. **Cols./Page:** 2 and 3. **Col. Width:** 19 1/2 and 12.5 picas. **Col. Depth:** 9 1/4 and 9 1/4 inches. **Key Personnel:** Pam Pounds, Editor; Paul Hansen, Promotion Coor. **Subscription Rates:** $20; Free to qualified subscribers. **Remarks:** Accepts advertising.
Ad Rates: BW: $925 **Circ:** Controlled ‡6,000
4C: $1,525

2293 Eastside Sun
Eastern Group Publications Inc.
2500 S. Atlantic Blvd., No. A Phone: (213)263-5743
Los Angeles, CA 90040-2004 Fax: (213)263-9169

Hispanic community newspaper (English and Spanish). **Founded:** 1945. **Freq:** Weekly (Thurs.). **Print Method:** Offset. **Trim Size:** 13 x 21. **Cols./Page:** 6. **Col. Width:** 2 1/16 inches. **Col. Depth:** 294 agate lines. **Key Personnel:** Tony Castro, Editor; Dolores Sanchez, Publisher; John Sanchez, Advertising Mgr. **Subscription Rates:** $92 individuals. **Remarks:** Accepts advertising.
Ad Rates: GLR: $2.50 **Circ:** Paid ‡500
BW: $3,150 Free ‡22,000
4C: $3,570
SAU: $28
PCI: $28

2294 The Economic Home Owner
Publishing and Business Consultants
4427 W. Slauson Ave.
Los Angeles, CA 90043-2717

Magazine featuring tips on home maintenance and repair. **Founded:** 1991. **Freq:** Quarterly. **Print Method:** Web offset. **Trim Size:** 8 1/2 x 10 1/4. **Cols./Page:** 3. **Col. Width:** 2 1/2 inches. **Col. Depth:** 9 1/2 inches. **Key Personnel:** Atia Napoleon, Editor and Publisher. **ISSN:** 1055-8284. **Subscription Rates:** $26.99; $33.99 Canada; $39.96 other countries. **Remarks:** Accepts advertising.
Ad Rates: BW: $8,290 **Circ:** Paid 100,000
4C: $9,750

E.L.A. Brooklyn-Belvedere Comet - See Belvedere

2295 Endocrinology
Endocrine Society
8700 Beverly Blvd., Rm B-138 Phone: (310)855-3371
Los Angeles, CA 90048-1865 Fax: (310)657-9656
Publication E-mail: endocrinology@csmc.edu

Medical journal. **Subtitle:** A Publication of the Endocrine Society. **Founded:** 1917. **Freq:** Monthly. **Print Method:** Web offset. **Trim Size:** 8 3/8 x 10 7/8. **Cols./Page:** 2. **Col. Width:** 32 nonpareils. **Col. Depth:** 119 agate lines. **Key Personnel:** Scott Hunt, Exec. Dir., phone (301)941-0200, fax (301)941-0259; Shlomo Melmed, M.D., Editor-in-Chief, phone (301)855-3371, fax (301)657-9656; Lenne P. Miller, Dir of Journal Publications, phone (301)941-0200, fax (301)941-0259. **ISSN:** 0013-7227. **Subscription Rates:** $200 individuals; $275 other countries; $440 industry; $540 industry, other countries; $40 single issue; $45 single issue other countries. **URL:** http://www.endo-society.org.
Ad Rates: BW: $980 **Circ:** Paid ‡4,540
4C: $1,250 Non-paid ‡453

2296 The Episcopal News
The Episcopal Diocese of Los Angeles
840 Echo Park Ave. Phone: (213)482-2040
Los Angeles, CA 90026 Fax: (213)240-7670

Newspaper covering the Episcopal Diocese of Los Angeles, the Episcopal Church in the U.S., the Anglican Communion, and the wider Christian fellowship. **Founded:** 1898. **Freq:** Bimonthly. **Print Method:** Offset. **Trim Size:** 11 x 14. **Cols./Page:** 4. **Col. Width:** 14 picas. **Col. Depth:** 77 picas. **Key Personnel:** Robert Williams, Editor, editor@ladiocese.org. **ISSN:** 0195-0681. **Subscription Rates:** $7. **Remarks:** Color advertising not accepted.
Ad Rates: BW: $1,204.50 **Circ:** ‡30,000
PCI: $24.25

2297 Equine Practice
Veterinary Practice Publishing Co.
PO Box 57900 Phone: (213)385-2222
Los Angeles, CA 90057 Fax: (213)385-8565

Magazine focusing on clinical equine medicine and surgery. **Founded:** 1979. **Freq:** 10/year. **Print Method:** Offset. **Trim Size:** 8 1/4 x 10 7/8. **Cols./Page:** 2. **Col. Width:** 33 nonpareils. **Col. Depth:** 106 agate lines. **Key Personnel:** Charles D. Vail, D.V.M., Editor; Nancy A. Bull, Publisher. **ISSN:** 0162-8941. **Subscription Rates:** $36 individuals; $42 Canada; $50 other countries. **Remarks:** Accepts advertising.
Ad Rates: BW: $1,295 **Circ:** 5,000
4C: $2,120

Escondido News-Reporter - See Escondido

2298 ETCetera
Early Typewriter Collectors Association
PO Box 641824 Phone: (310)477-5229
Los Angeles, CA 90064 Fax: (310)268-8420

Trade journal covering typewriters and other devices relating to the history of business. **Founded:** 1987. **Freq:** Quarterly. **Print Method:** DTP. **Key Personnel:** Darryl Rehr, Editor, dcrehr@earthlink.net. **ISSN:** 1062-9645. **Subscription Rates:** $20 individuals; $25 individuals outside North America. **Remarks:** Accepts advertising. **URL:** http://home.earthlink.net/~dcrehr/etcetera.html.
Circ: Paid 300

2299 Explorer
Los Angeles Southwest College
1600 W. Imperial Hwy. Phone: (213)777-2225
Los Angeles, CA 90047
Collegiate newspaper. **Founded:** 1965. **Freq:** Biweekly. **Cols./Page:** 5. **Col. Width:** 11.06 picas. **Key Personnel:** Javier Medina, Editor; Lee Burger, Managing Editor; Kay Gibbs, Advertising Mgr. **Subscription Rates:** Free. **Remarks:** Accepts advertising.
Ad Rates: BW: $250 **Circ:** (Not Reported)
PCI: $14

2300 Feline Practice
Veterinary Practice Publishing Co.
PO Box 57900 Phone: (213)385-2222
Los Angeles, CA 90057 Fax: (213)385-8565

Journal covering feline medicine and surgery. **Founded:** 1971. **Freq:** Bimonthly. **Key Personnel:** Nancy A. Bull, Publisher. **ISSN:** 1057-6614. **Subscription Rates:** $28; $50 other countries. **Remarks:** Accepts advertising.
Ad Rates: BW: $1,295 **Circ:** 6,500
4C: $2,120

2301 Fem
University of California, Los Angeles
308 Westwood Plaza Phone: (310)825-8500
118 Kerckhoff Hall Fax: (310)206-3165
Los Angeles, CA 90024
Publication E-mail: fem@media.ucla.edu

News magazine for women and feminist students at the University and the surrounding community. **Subtitle:** UCLA's Feminist Newsmagazine. **Founded:** 1973. **Freq:** Biquarterly. **Print Method:** Offset. **Trim Size:** 11 1/2 x 17 5/8. **Cols./Page:** 5. **Col. Width:** 1 7/8 inches. **Key Personnel:** Sarah Yellin, Editor, syellin@media.ucla.edu; Samantha Gianello, sgianello@media.ucla.edu. **Subscription Rates:** $18. **Remarks:** Accepts advertising. **Formerly:** Together - The Feminist Newsletter at UCLA (1992); ASUCLA Together.
Ad Rates: BW: $570 **Circ:** Non-paid ‡10,000
4C: $990
PCI: $7.10

2302 Film Score Monthly
5455 Wilshire Blvd., Ste. 1500 Phone: (323)937-9890
Los Angeles, CA 90036-4201 Fax: (323)937-9277
Publisher E-mail: fsm@filmscoremonthly.com

Consumer magazine covering music in movies and television. **Subtitle:** Music Soundtracks from Motion Pictures and Television. **Founded:** June 1992. **Freq:** Monthly. **Print Method:** Offset. **Trim Size:** 8 3/8 x 10 7/8. **Cols./Page:** 3. **Col. Width:** 2 3/8 inches. **Col. Depth:** 9 3/4 inches. **Key Personnel:** Lukas Kendall, Editor-in-Chief, lukas@filmscoremonthly.com; Jeff Bond, Managing Editor, jbond@filmscoremonthly.com; Tom Brunelle, Advertising Mgr., phone (323)932-5606, fax (323)932-6111, tom@filmmag.com. **ISSN:** 1077-4289. **Subscription Rates:** $36.95 individuals; $50 out of country; $4.95 single issue. **Remarks:** Accepts advertising. **URL:** http://www.filmscoremonthly.com.
Ad Rates: BW: $400 **Circ:** Combined 11,000
4C: $1,000
PCI: $55

Firestone Park News/Southeast News Press - See Firestone Park

2303 First Class Executive Travel
National Association of Business Travel Agents
3255 Wilshire Blvd., Ste. 1514 Phone: (213)382-3335
Los Angeles, CA 90010
Consumer magazine covering business travel, hotels, restaurants, products and destinations. **Founded:** 1970. **Freq:** Bimonthly. **Print Method:** Offset. **Trim Size:** 8 1/2 x 11. **Key**

Personnel: Stuart Faber, Editor. **Subscription Rates:** $64 individuals. **Remarks:** Advertising not accepted.
Circ: (Not Reported)

2304 Flowers
Teleflora
11444 W. Olympic Blvd. Phone: (310)231-9199
Los Angeles, CA 90064 Fax: (310)966-3610
Free: (800)321-2654
Publisher E-mail: flowersand@aol.com

Trade magazine for retail florists. **Founded:** 1934. **Freq:** Monthly. **Print Method:** Offset. **Trim Size:** 8 1/8 x 10 3/4. **Cols./Page:** 2. **Col. Width:** 38 nonpareils. **Key Personnel:** Bruce Wright, Editor-in-Chief, phone (310)966-3543; Richard Salvaggio, Publisher, phone (310)966-3545; Curtis Moore, National Advertising Dir., phone (800)522-0231. **ISSN:** 0199-4751. **Subscription Rates:** $54 individuals. **Remarks:** Accepts advertising.
Ad Rates: BW: $1132 **Circ:** Combined △**30,061**
4C: $2009

2305 Foursquare World Advance
International Church of the Foursquare Gospel
1910 W. Sunset Blvd., Ste. 200 Phone: (213)989-4234
PO Box 26902 Fax: (213)989-4544
Los Angeles, CA 90026-0176
Publication E-mail: comm@foursquare.org

Magazine containing devotional information, teaching, and experiences. **Founded:** 1923. **Freq:** Bimonthly. **Print Method:** Offset. **Trim Size:** 8 1/2 x 11. **Cols./Page:** 3. **Col. Width:** 28 nonpareils. **Col. Depth:** 130 agate lines. **Key Personnel:** Ron Williams, Editor. **ISSN:** 0015-9182. **Subscription Rates:** Free to qualified subscribers. **Remarks:** Advertising not accepted.
Circ: Controlled ‡95,000

2306 FREEDOM Magazine
Church of Scientology International
6331 Hollywood Blvd., Ste. 1200 Phone: (213)960-3500
Los Angeles, CA 90028-6329 Fax: (213)960-3508
Free: (888)576-FREE

Magazine emphasizing social reform, national news and human rights. **Subtitle:** Investigative Reporting in the Public Interest. **Founded:** 1968. **Freq:** Bimonthly. **Print Method:** Offset. **Trim Size:** 9 x 11. **Cols./Page:** 3. **Col. Width:** 2 1/2 inches. **Col. Depth:** 10 inches. **Key Personnel:** Aron Mason, Editor-in-Chief; Tom Whittle, Editor, editor@freedommag.org. **Subscription Rates:** $22.50 individuals; $2.50 single issue. **Remarks:** Accepts advertising. **URL:** http://www.freedommag.org.
Ad Rates: BW: $510 **Circ:** ‡150,000
4C: $924

2307 Freshmen
SL, Inc.
PO Box 4356 Phone: (323)468-1919
Los Angeles, CA 90078-4356 Fax: (323)957-9219
Publication E-mail: info@men-to-men.com
Publisher E-mail: info@men-to-men.com

Magazine featuring gay, male erotica. **Founded:** 1991. **Freq:** Monthly. **Trim Size:** 8 x 10 7/8. **Key Personnel:** Austin Foxxe, Editor-in-Chief, afoxxe@men-to-men.com. **ISSN:** 1060-5266. **Subscription Rates:** $54; $6.95 single issue. **Remarks:** Accepts advertising.
Ad Rates: BW: $2,924 **Circ:** 65,000
4C: $4,431

2308 Genii, The International Conjurers' Magazine
PO Box 36068 Phone: (213)935-2848
Los Angeles, CA 90036 Fax: (213)933-4820
Publication E-mail: thegenii@aol.com

Founded: 1936. **Freq:** Monthly. **Print Method:** Offset. **Trim Size:** 8 1/2 x 11. **Cols./Page:** 3. **Col. Width:** 24 nonpareils. **Col. Depth:** 126 agate lines. **Key Personnel:** Dante Larsen, Editor; William Larsen, Publisher. **ISSN:** 0016-6855. **Subscription Rates:** $30 individuals. **Remarks:** Accepts advertising.
Ad Rates: GLR: $133 **Circ:** Paid 6,700
BW: $382 Controlled 200
4C: $814
PCI: $20

2309 Government Programs
Publishing and Business Consultants
4427 W. Slauson Ave.
Los Angeles, CA 90043-2717

Magazine presenting special government programs covering education, employment, housing, etc. **Founded:** 1991. **Freq:** Quarterly. **Print Method:** Web offset. **Trim Size:** 8 1/2 x 11. **Key Personnel:** Atia Napoleon, Editor and Publisher. **ISSN:** 1055-825X. **Subscription Rates:** $26.99; $33.99 other countries. **Remarks:** Accepts advertising. **Formerly:** Government Subsidized Programs (1992).
Ad Rates: BW: $8,290 **Circ:** Paid 100,000
4C: $9,750

2310 The Griffith Observer
Griffith Observatory
2800 E. Observatory Rd. Phone: (213)664-1181
Los Angeles, CA 90027 Fax: (213)663-4323
Publication E-mail: observer@griffithobs.org
Publisher E-mail: info@griffithobs.org

Magazine covering astronomy and related sciences for the general reader, including monthly sky calendar and monthly star charts. **Founded:** Feb. 1937. **Freq:** Monthly. **Print Method:** Offset. **Trim Size:** 8 1/2 x 6. **Cols./Page:** 2. **Col. Width:** 15 picas. **Col. Depth:** 46 picas. **Key Personnel:** Dr. E.C. Krupp, Editor; John Mosley, Production Editor; Mary Alvarez, Asst. Editor; Teri Gast, Circ. Editor. **ISSN:** 0195-3982. **Subscription Rates:** $18 individuals; $2 single issue. **Remarks:** Accepts advertising.
Ad Rates: BW: $426 **Circ:** Paid 2,400
4C: $869 Controlled 80

2311 The Guild Practitioner
National Lawyers Guild
Box 46205 Phone: (213)653-4510
Los Angeles, CA 90046
Journal of the National Lawyers Guild. **Founded:** 1943. **Freq:** Quarterly. **Trim Size:** 5 1/2 x 8 1/2. **Key Personnel:** Marjorie Cohn, Editor; Cy Gius, Business Mgr. **ISSN:** 0017-5390. **Subscription Rates:** $25 individuals; $40 institutions; $6.50 single issue. **Remarks:** Advertising not accepted.
Circ: Paid 2,300

2312 Guns and Ammo
Petersen Publishing Co., L.L.C.
6420 Wilshire Blvd. Phone: (323)782-2350
Los Angeles, CA 90048-5515 Fax: (323)782-2704

Magazine on firearms for beginners and experts. Features articles on target shooting, defensive techniques, plinking, hunting, law enforcement. **Founded:** 1958. **Freq:** Monthly. **Print Method:** Offset. **Trim Size:** 7 7/8 x 10 1/2. **Key Personnel:** Doug Hamlin, Publisher; Geoff Steer, Publisher; Peter Clancey, Senior Vice President. **Subscription Rates:** $15.95 individuals; $2.95 single issue. **Remarks:** Accepts advertising.
Ad Rates: BW: $382 **Circ:** Paid ★**595,537**
4C: $814
PCI: $804

2313 Ha'Am
210C Kerckhoff Hall Phone: (213)825-6280
Associated Students, U.C.L.A. Fax: (213)206-0906
Los Angeles, CA 90024-1301
News magazine. **Founded:** 1972. **Freq:** 2/trimester. **Subscription Rates:** $16.

2314 Handguns
Petersen Publishing Co., L.L.C.
6420 Wilshire Blvd.
Los Angeles, CA 90048

Gun enthusiast magazine emphasizing coverage on handguns. **Subtitle:** For Sport and Defense. **Founded:** 1987. **Freq:** Monthly. **Print Method:** Web offset. **Trim Size:** 7 7/8 x 10 1/2. **Key Personnel:** Jan Liboruel, Editor; Ken Elliott, Publisher; Thomas J. Siatos, Editor. **ISSN:** 1040-1865. **Subscription Rates:** $17.95; $2.95 single issue. **Remarks:** Accepts advertising.
Ad Rates: BW: $3,450 **Circ:** Paid ★**158,145**
4C: $5,520
PCI: $190

2315 Health Diet & Nutrition
Publishing and Business Consultants
4427 W. Slauson Ave.
Los Angeles, CA 90043-2717

Magazine featuring basic dietary habits, nutritional information and personal health care. **Founded:** 1991. **Freq:** Quarterly. **Print Method:** Web offset. **Trim Size:** 8 1/2 x 10 1/4. **Cols./Page:** 3. **Col. Width:** 2 1/2 inches. **Col. Depth:** 9 inches. **Key Personnel:** Atia Napoleon, Editor and Publisher. **ISSN:** 1055-8241. **Subscription Rates:** $26.99; $33.99 Canada; $38.96 other countries. **Remarks:** Accepts advertising.
Ad Rates: BW: $8,290 **Circ:** Paid 120,000
4C: $9,750

2316 Herald Dispatch
4063 Marlton Ave. Phone: (213)291-9486
PO Box 19027A Fax: (213)291-2123
Los Angeles, CA 90008
Black community newspaper. **Founded:** 1952. **Freq:** Weekly (Thurs.). **Print Method:** Offset. **Trim Size:** 13 x 21 1/2. **Cols./Page:** 6. **Col. Width:** 29 nonpareils. **Col. Depth:** 294 agate lines. **Key Personnel:** Lela Ward Oliver, Editor; John H. Holoman, Publisher. **ISSN:** 8750-2038. **Subscription Rates:** $20 individuals; $40 National. **Remarks:** Accepts advertising.
Ad Rates: GLR: $.85 **Circ:** ‡35,000
BW: $2,016
4C: $3,016
PCI: $16

2317 Heterodoxy
Center for the Study of Popular Culture
PO Box 67398 Phone: (310)843-3699
Los Angeles, CA 90067 Fax: (310)843-3692
Free: (800)752-6562
Publication E-mail: heterodoxy@cspc.org
Publisher E-mail: cspc@cspc.org

Newspaper of conservative political commentary. **Subtitle:** Articles and Animadversions on Political Correctness and Other Follies. **Freq:** Monthly except for July and August. **Trim Size:** 10 7/8 x 17. **Cols./Page:** 3. **Col. Width:** 3 1/8 inches. **Col. Depth:** 15 inches. **Key Personnel:** Peter Collier, Editor, pcollier@cspc.org; David Horowitz, Editor, dhorowitz@cspc.org; Bruce Donaldson, Contact, brdonaldson@cspc.org. **ISSN:** 1069-7268. **Subscription Rates:** $2.50 single issue; $25 individuals. **Remarks:** Accepts advertising. **Feature Editors:** John Ellis, *Book*.
Ad Rates: BW: $1200 **Circ:** Paid 11,000

2318 Hollywood Independent
Los Angeles Independent Newspapers
4201 Wilshire Blvd., Ste. 600 Phone: (323)932-6397
Los Angeles, CA 90010 Fax: (323)932-8250
Publisher E-mail: laingroupamerica online, inc.com

Community newspaper. **Subtitle:** Los Angeles Independent Newspaper Group. **Founded:** 1923. **Freq:** Weekly (Sun.). **Print Method:** Offset. **Trim Size:** 13 1/2 x 22 1/2. **Cols./Page:** 6. **Col. Width:** 2 1/16 inches. **Col. Depth:** 21 inches. **Key Personnel:** Brian Lewis, Editor, fax (323)932-8285; Bruce M. Wood, Publisher, fax (323)932-0884; Michael Manning, Advertising Mgr.; Gwynn Gustafson, Majors. **Subscription Rates:** $80 individuals. **Remarks:** Accepts advertising. **Available Online. URL:** http://www.nminews.com.
Ad Rates: BW: $2,993.76 **Circ:** Controlled 16,880
4C: $3,744
SAU: $23.76

2319 The Hollywood Reporter
5055 Wilshire Blvd., 6th Fl. Phone: (213)525-2000
Los Angeles, CA 90036 Fax: (213)525-2390
Publisher E-mail: thrscoh@hollywoodreporter.com

Film, TV, and entertainment trade newspaper. **Founded:** 1930. **Freq:** Daily (morn.). **Print Method:** Web offset. **Trim Size:** 8 5/8 x 11 1/4. **Cols./Page:** 4. **Col. Width:** 27 nonpareils. **Col. Depth:** 156 agate lines. **Key Personnel:** Bob Dowling, Publisher; Glenn Abel, Executive Editor; Alex Ben Block, Editor; Lynne Segall, Associate Publisher. **ISSN:** 0018-3660. **Subscription Rates:** $199 individuals. **Remarks:** Accepts advertising. **URL:** http://www.hollywoodreporter.com.
Ad Rates: BW: $2,450 **Circ:** Mon.-Fri. 24,584
4C: $4,850 Tues. 36,276

2320 Home Magazine
Hachette Publications
5670 Wilshire Blvd., Ste. 500 Phone: (213)954-0500
Los Angeles, CA 90036 Fax: (213)954-4800

Magazine focusing on home building, remodeling, design, and decorating. **Founded:** 1955. **Freq:** Monthly. **Print Method:** Offset. **Trim Size:** 8 x 10 3/4. **Cols./Page:** 3. **Col. Width:** 26 nonpareils. **Col. Depth:** 140 agate lines. **Key Personnel:** Joseph C. Ruggiero, Editor; William F. Bondlow, Jr., Publisher; George H. Oestreich, Advertising Mgr. **Subscription Rates:** $18. $1.95 single issue.
Circ: 1,043,964

2321 Hospital Podiatrist
American Association of Hospital Podiatrists
3984 S. Figueroa St. Phone: (213)747-7272
Los Angeles, CA 90037 Fax: (310)476-8003

Professional journal of the American Association of Hospital Podiatrists. **Founded:** 1960. **Freq:** Semiannual. **Key Personnel:** Earl L. Cherniak, D.P.M., Contact. **Subscription Rates:** $10 single issue; Free to qualified subscribers. **Remarks:** Advertising not accepted.
Circ: Non-paid 1,000

2322 Hot Rod Magazine
Petersen Publishing Co., L.L.C.
6420 Wilshire Blvd. Phone: (323)782-2350
Los Angeles, CA 90048-5515 Fax: (323)782-2704

Automotive magazine. **Founded:** Jan. 1948. **Freq:** Monthly. **Print Method:** Offset. **Trim Size:** 7 7/8 x 10 1/2. **Key Personnel:** Harry Hibler, Publisher; Ralph V. Panico, Publisher; Peter F. Clancey, Corporate Marketing and Sales. **Sub-**

scription Rates: $12.95 individuals; $2.95 single issue. **Remarks:** Accepts advertising.
Ad Rates: BW: $23,375 **Circ:** Paid ★**788,449**
4C: $39,155
PCI: $1,286

2323 Hot Stuff
The Harvey Entertainment Co.
1999 Avenue of the Stars, No. 2050 Phone: (310)789-1990
Fax: (310)789-1991
Los Angeles, CA 90067
Comic book. **Freq:** Monthly. **Print Method:** Web offset. **Trim Size:** 6 1/8 x 10 1/8. **Key Personnel:** Sid Jacobson, Editor; Ed Shukin, Director; Kevin S. Bricklin, Director. **Subscription Rates:** $1.50 single issue. **Remarks:** Advertising accepted; rates available upon request. **URL:** http://www.harvey.com.
Circ: (Not Reported)

Inglewood/Hawthorne Wave - See Inglewood

2324 Innovation and Ideas
Publishing and Business Consultants
4427 W. Slauson Ave.
Los Angeles, CA 90043-2717

Magazine featuring breakthroughs in science and high technology. **Founded:** 1991. **Freq:** Quarterly. **Print Method:** Web offset. **Trim Size:** 8 1/2 x 10 1/4. **Cols./Page:** 3. **Col. Width:** 2 1/2 inches. **Col. Depth:** 9 inches. **Key Personnel:** Atia Napoleon, Editor and Publisher. **ISSN:** 1059-2091. **Subscription Rates:** $26.99; $33.99 Canada; $38.96 other countries. **Remarks:** Accepts advertising.
Ad Rates: BW: $8,290 **Circ:** Paid ‡120,000
4C: $9,750

2325 International Documentary
International Documentary Association
1551 South Robertson Blvd. Phone: (310)284-8422
Suite 201 Fax: (310)785-9334
Los Angeles, CA 90035-4233
Publication E-mail: idf@netcom.com; idamag@aol.com

Journal promoting non-fiction film and video. **Subtitle:** News and Events of the International Documentary Association. **Founded:** 1984. **Freq:** Monthly. **Trim Size:** 8 1/2 x 11. **Cols./Page:** 3. **Col. Width:** 2 1/4 inches. **Col. Depth:** 9 1/4 inches. **Key Personnel:** Timothy J. Lyons, Editor; Tom White, Asst. Editor; Michael Margolis, Advertising Sales; Nancy Hards, Art Dir. **ISSN:** 0742-533X. **Subscription Rates:** $70 individuals w/membership; $50 institutions; $3.50 single issue. **Remarks:** Accepts advertising.
Ad Rates: GLR: $.75 **Circ:** 5,500
BW: $440
4C: $1,190

2326 International Olympic Lifter
PO Box 65855 Phone: (213)257-8762
Los Angeles, CA 90065 Fax: (213)344-9865
Free: (800)328-8762

Magazine for weightlifters and trainers. **Founded:** 1973. **Freq:** Bimonthly. **Print Method:** Offset. **Trim Size:** 8 1/2 x 11. **Key Personnel:** Bob Hise II, Editor. **Subscription Rates:** $28; $4 single issue. **Remarks:** Accepts advertising.
Ad Rates: BW: $250 **Circ:** Paid 2,000
PCI: $25

2327 Issues in Applied Linguistics
UCLA TESLA/Applied Linguistics
3300 Rolfe Hall Phone: (310)825-4631
PO Box 951531 Fax: (310)206-4118
Los Angeles, CA 90024
Publication E-mail: ial@ucla.edu

Journal concerning issues in applied linguistics. **Founded:** June 1990. **Freq:** Semiannual. **Cols./Page:** 1. **Key Personnel:** Myrna Turner, turner@humnet.ucla.edu; Tanya Stivers, tstivers@ucla.edu. **ISSN:** 1050-4273. **Subscription Rates:** $20 institutions per issue; $15 single issue for individuals. **Remarks:** Advertising accepted; rates available upon request.
Circ: Paid 250
Non-paid 50

2328 The J. Paul Getty Museum Journal
J. Paul Getty Museum
1200 Getty Center Drive, Ste. 1000
Los Angeles, CA 90049-1687

Journal covering objects in the Getty Museum's collections. **Founded:** 1974. **Key Personnel:** John Harris, Editor. **ISSN:** 0362-1979. **Subscription Rates:** $70 individuals. **Remarks:** Advertising not accepted.
Circ: (Not Reported)

2329 Jonathan
Jonathan Club
545 S. Figueroa St. Phone: (213)624-0881
Los Angeles, CA 90071-1704 Fax: (213)488-1425

Club magazine featuring California art, member news, and social activities. **Subtitle:** Official Publication of Jonathan Club. **Founded:** Oct. 1930. **Freq:** Monthly. **Print Method:** Offset. **Trim Size:** 9 x 12. **Cols./Page:** 3. **Col. Width:** 28 nonpareils. **Col. Depth:** 144 agate lines. **Key Personnel:** Edward Rivers, Editor. **USPS:** 276-720. **Subscription Rates:** $24 other countries.
Ad Rates: BW: $691 **Circ:** Controlled ‡3,800
4C: $1,091

2330 Journal of Film and Video
University Film and Video Association
Dept. of Communication Studies Phone: (213)343-4206
California State University-Los Angeles Fax: (213)343-6467
5151 State University Dr.
Los Angeles, CA 90032-8111
Film and video journal. **Founded:** 1949. **Freq:** Quarterly. **Print Method:** Letterpress. **Trim Size:** 6 x 9. **Cols./Page:** 2. **Col. Width:** 28 nonpareils. **Col. Depth:** 102 agate lines. **Key Personnel:** Suzanne Regan, Ph.D., Editor, sregan@calstatela.edu. **ISSN:** 0724-4671. **Subscription Rates:** Included in membership; $35 nonmembers in U.S.; $50 nonmembers other countries. **Remarks:** Accepts advertising. **Formerly:** Journal of the University Film & Video Association (1983).
Ad Rates: BW: $200 **Circ:** 1,200

2331 Journal of Gay and Lesbian Social Services
The Haworth Press, Inc.
School of Health & Human Services Phone: (323)343-4600
5151 State University Dr.
Los Angeles, CA 90032-8160
Publisher E-mail: getinfo@haworthpressinc.com

Journal that aims to promote the well-being of homosexuals and bisexuals in society. **Subtitle:** Issues in Practice, Policy & Research. **Founded:** 1994. **Freq:** Quarterly. **Trim Size:** 6x8 1/2. **Key Personnel:** James J. Kelly, Ph.D, Editor, fax (323)343-5598, jkelly@calstatela.edu; Bill Cohen, Publisher. **ISSN:** 1053-8720. **Subscription Rates:** $38 individuals 30% more for Canada; 40% more for other countries; $48 institutions 30% more for Canada; 40% more for other countries; $60 libraries 30% more for Canada; 40% more for other countries. **Remarks:** Accepts advertising.
Ad Rates: BW: $300 **Circ:** Paid 422

2332 Journal of Health Politics, Policy and Law
Duke University Press
3250 Public Policy Bldg. Phone: (310)794-4260
Box 951656 Fax: (310)206-0337
Los Angeles, CA 90095-1656
Publication E-mail: jhppl@sppsr.ucla.edu

Journal on the initiation, formulation, and implementation of health policy. **Founded:** June 1976. **Freq:** Bimonthly. **Print Method:** Offset. **Trim Size:** 6 x 9. **Cols./Page:** 1. **Col. Width:** 4 1/4 inches. **Col. Depth:** 7 1/4 inches. **Key Personnel:** Mark A. Peterson, Editor, markap@ucla.edu; Steve Cohn, Director, phone (919)687-3606, fax (919)688-3524; Janet Schipporeit, Advertising Mgr., phone (919)687-3636, fax (919)688-3524. **ISSN:** 0361-6878. **Subscription Rates:** $54 individuals; $145 Industry; $27 students. **Remarks:** Accepts advertising. **URL:** http://www.jhppl.org.
Ad Rates: BW: $300 **Circ:** ‡2500

2333 Journal of Intravenous Therapy
PO Box 67159 Phone: (310)475-5141
Los Angeles, CA 90067-0159 Fax: (310)475-5141

Journal covering nursing, pharmacology, and I.V. Therapy. **Founded:** 1978. **Freq:** Bimonthly. **Print Method:** Letterpress and offset. **Cols./Page:** 3. **Col. Width:** 36 nonpareils. **Col. Depth:** 98 agate lines. **Key Personnel:** William J. Kurdi R.N., M.A., Editor and Publisher; Kevin J. Kurdi, Advertising Mgr. **ISSN:** 0194-1658. **Subscription Rates:** $24 individuals; $28 Canada; $36 other countries. **Remarks:** Advertising accepted; rates available upon request.
Circ: ‡1,000

2334 Journal of Management Inquiry
Sage Publications Inc.
University of Southern California Phone: (213)740-0733
School of Business Fax: (310)373-7452
Los Angeles, CA 90089-1421
Publisher E-mail: info@sagepub.com

Journal providing non-traditional research and practice in management and organization. **Founded:** 1992. **Freq:** Quarterly. **Print Method:** Offset. **Trim Size:** 8 1/2 x 11. **Key Personnel:** Thomas G. Cummings, ED, Editor; Cris Anderson, Circulation Mgr.; Cris Anderson, Circulation Mgr. **ISSN:** 1056-4926. **Subscription Rates:** $45; $105 Industry; $15 single issue; $27 single issue Industry. **Remarks:** Accepts advertising.
Ad Rates: BW: $200 **Circ:** Paid 1600
Non-paid 130

2335 Keyboard Companion
Box 24-C-54 Phone: (310)474-8966
Los Angeles, CA 90024 Fax: (310)475-0092
Free: (800)824-5087
Publication E-mail: KCompanion@aol.com
Publisher E-mail: kcompanion@aol.com

Consumer magazine covering early-level piano study. **Founded:** 1990. **Freq:** Quarterly. **Key Personnel:** Richard Chronister, Editor; Marjore Chronister, Circulation Mgr.; Elson Erazo, Advertising Dir. **Subscription Rates:** $17 individuals; $6 single issue. **Remarks:** Accepts advertising.
Ad Rates: BW: $1,150 **Circ:** (Not Reported)
4C: $1,550

2336 Kit Car
Petersen Publishing Co., L.L.C.
6420 Wilshire Blvd. Phone: (323)782-2350
Los Angeles, CA 90048-5515 Fax: (323)782-2704

Magazine on kit cars. **Subtitle:** The Car Builder's Authority. **Founded:** 1980. **Freq:** Bimonthly Web offset. **Trim Size:** 7 3/4 x 10 1/2. **Key Personnel:** Jim Youngs, Editor, phone (323)782-2546, youngsj@petersenpub.com; Aaron Lasky, Publisher, phone (323)782-2732, laskya@petersenpub.com. **ISSN:** 0883-5705. **Subscription Rates:** $9.95; $14.95 other countries. **Remarks:** Accepts advertising. **Formerly:** Speciality Car.
Ad Rates: BW: $2,480 **Circ:** Paid ⊕**60,000**
4C: $3,100

2337 Korea Times
Korean Daily News
141 N. Vermont Ave. Phone: (213)487-5323
Los Angeles, CA 90004 Fax: (213)738-1103

General newspaper (Korean). **Freq:** Mon.-Sat. (eve.). **Key Personnel:** Mr. Byong Yong Min, Editor.

2338 Korean Culture
Korean Cultural Center
5505 Wilshire Blvd. Phone: (323)936-7141
Los Angeles, CA 90036 Fax: (323)936-5712
Publication E-mail: kcc@pdc.net

Magazine about the culture, history, and arts of Korea. **Founded:** 1980. **Freq:** Quarterly. **Print Method:** Offset. **Trim Size:** 8 1/2 x 11. **Cols./Page:** 2. **Col. Width:** 3 1/4 inches. **Col. Depth:** 9 inches. **Key Personnel:** Robert Bushwell, Jr., Editor-in-Chief; Linda Cho, Managing Editor. **ISSN:** 0270-1618. **Subscription Rates:** $12 individuals; $12 institutions, other countries students. **Remarks:** Advertising not accepted.
Circ: Paid 1,500
Non-paid 1,500

2339 Kuumba
BLK Publishing Company
Box 83912 Phone: (310)410-0808
Los Angeles, CA 90083-0912 Fax: (310)410-9250
Publisher E-mail: newsroom@blk.com

Consumer magazine covering poetry celebrating the lives and experiences of black people. **Freq:** Semiannual. **Key Personnel:** Mark Haile, Editor. **ISSN:** 1049-328X. **Subscription Rates:** $7.50 individuals; $14 two years; $4.50 single issue. **Remarks:** Accepts advertising.
Ad Rates: BW: $260 **Circ:** (Not Reported)

2340 La Gente
University of California, Los Angeles
118 Kerkhoff Hall Phone: (310)825-9898
308 Westwood Plaza Fax: (310)206-0906
Los Angeles, CA 90024
Publication E-mail: lagente@media.ucla.edu

A UCLA student publication serving the Native American, Chicano, and Latino communities. **Founded:** Feb. 1, 1971. **Trim Size:** 11 x 17. **Key Personnel:** Sandra Cano, Editor, scano@media.ucla.edu. **Subscription Rates:** $18. **Available Online. URL:** http://www.media.asucla.edu. **Formerly:** La Gente de Aztlan.
Ad Rates: BW: $390 **Circ:** Non-paid 20,000

2341 L.A. Jewish Times
Box 35915 Phone: (213)933-8013
Los Angeles, CA 90035-0915 Fax: (213)933-7867
Publication E-mail: lajtimes@aol.com

Jewish community newspaper. **Founded:** 1897. **Freq:** Weekly. **Key Personnel:** Linda Carter, General Mgr.; Jane Fried, Editor. **Remarks:** Accepts advertising.
Circ: (Not Reported)

2342 La Opinion
Lozano Enterprises
411 W. 5th St. Phone: (213)622-8332
Los Angeles, CA 90013-1028 Fax: (213)896-2151

General newspaper (Spanish). **Founded:** Sept. 16, 1926. **Freq:** Mon.-Sun. (morn.). **Print Method:** Offset. **Cols./Page:** 6. **Col. Width:** 12 picas. **Col. Depth:** 294 agate lines. **Key Personnel:** Monica Lozano, Editor, phone (213)622-8332, fax (213)896-2151; Jose I. Lozano, Publisher. **Subscription Rates:** $226 by mail. **Remarks:** Accepts advertising.
Ad Rates: GLR: $34.96 **Circ:** Mon.-Fri. ★**99,041**
BW: $4510.00 Sat. ★**80,400**
4C: $5429.89 Sun. ★**58,871**

2343 L.A. Weekly
6715 Sunset Blvd. Phone: (213)465-9909
Los Angeles, CA 90028 Fax: (213)465-3220
Free: (800)304-4414
Publication E-mail: webmaster@laweekly.com

Newspaper (tabloid) featuring news, people, entertainment, and the arts. **Founded:** 1978. **Freq:** Weekly (Thurs.). **Print Method:** Offset. **Trim Size:** 10 3/4 x 14 1/2. **Cols./Page:** 4. **Col. Width:** 14 picas. **Col. Depth:** 13 inches. **Key Personnel:** Sue Horton, Editor; Mike Sigman, Publisher; Tom Christie, Arts Editor. **USPS:** 461-370. **Subscription Rates:** Free; $70 individuals (mail). **Remarks:** Accepts advertising. **Online:** America Online, Inc. **URL:** http://www.laweekly.com.
Ad Rates: BW: $6,835 **Circ:** Paid 2,873
4C: $8,234 Free 220,000

2344 LACMA Physician
Los Angeles County Medical Association
PO Box 513465 Phone: (213)683-9900
Los Angeles, CA 90051-1465 Fax: (213)630-1152
Publication E-mail: lpmag@lacmanet.org

Professional magazine for the Los Angeles County medical community. **Subtitle:** Magazine of the Los Angeles County Medical Asssociation. **Founded:** 1871. **Freq:** 12/year. **Print Method:** Offset. **Trim Size:** 8 3/8 x 10 7/8. **Cols./Page:** 4 and 3. **Col. Width:** 1.7 and 2.25 inches. **Col. Depth:** 140 agate lines. **Key Personnel:** Barbara Feiner, Managing Editor, phone (213)630-1123, fax (213)630-1152, bfeiner@lacmanet.org; Charles Murphy, Advertising Coordinator, phone (213)630-1124, fax (213)630-1152, cmurphy@lacmanet.org. **ISSN:** 0162-7163. **Subscription Rates:** $30 individuals. **Remarks:** Accepts classified advertising $70 for classified. **URL:** http://www.lacmanet.org.
Ad Rates: BW: $820 **Circ:** Paid ‡10,154
4C: $1,720 Non-paid ‡651

2345 Let's Live
Franklin Publications
320 N. Larchmont Blvd., 3rd Fl. Phone: (323)469-3901
Box 74908 Fax: (323)469-9597
Los Angeles, CA 90004
Free: (800)225-6473
Publication E-mail: letslive@earthlink.net; letslivelb@aol.com

Publication focuses on natural, holistic health, fitness, sports nutrition, herbs and vitamins/minerals. Articles are mostly written by industry experts. **Subtitle:** America's Foremost Health & Preventive Medicine Magazine. **Founded:** 1933. **Freq:** Monthly. **Print Method:** Offset. **Trim Size:** 8 1/2 x 11. **Cols./Page:** 3. **Col. Width:** 13.5 picas. **Col. Depth:** 61 picas. **Key Personnel:** Beth Salmon, Editor; Paul D. Wolff, Publisher; Laura Barnaby, Managing Editor, nuinsights@asl.com; Laila Bomis, Media Coord. **ISSN:** 0024-1288. **Subscription Rates:** $15.95 individuals; $2.95 single issue. **Remarks:** Accepts advertising.
Ad Rates: BW: $15,083 **Circ:** Combined ‡2,000,000
4C: $20,106

2346 The Library Quarterly
UCLA Graduate School of Education & Information Studies
PO Box 951520 Phone: (310)206-9366
204 GSE&IS Bldg. Fax: (310)206-4460
Los Angeles, CA 90095-1520
Research journal for library and information science scholars, practitioners, teachers, students, and those in related fields. **Subtitle:** A Journal of Investigation in Library and Information Studies. **Founded:** 1931. **Freq:** Quarterly. **Cols./Page:** 1. **Key Personnel:** Dr. John V. Richardson, Advertising Mgr. **ISSN:** 0024-2519. **Subscription Rates:** $35 individuals; $71 institutions; $27 students; $38 other countries; $17.75 single issue. **URL:** http://www.purl.org/net/LQ.
Circ: Paid 1,500

2347 Little Audrey
The Harvey Entertainment Co.
1999 Avenue of the Stars, No. 2050 Phone: (310)789-1990
Fax: (310)789-1991
Los Angeles, CA 90067
Comic book. **Freq:** Monthly. **Print Method:** Web offset. **Trim Size:** 6 1/8 x 10 1/8. **Key Personnel:** Sid Jacobson, Editor; Ed Shukin, Director; Kevin S. Bricklin, Director. **Subscription Rates:** $1.50 single issue. **Remarks:** Advertising accepted; rates available upon request. **URL:** http://www.harvey.com.
Circ: (Not Reported)

2348 Little Lotta
The Harvey Entertainment Co.
1999 Avenue of the Stars, No. 2050 Phone: (310)789-1990
Fax: (310)789-1991
Los Angeles, CA 90067
Comic book. **Freq:** Monthly. **Print Method:** Web offset. **Trim Size:** 6 1/8 x 10 1/8. **Key Personnel:** Sid Jacobson, Editor; Ed Shukin, Director; Kevin S. Bricklin, Director. **Subscription Rates:** $1.50 single issue. **Remarks:** Advertising accepted; rates available upon request. **URL:** http://www.harvey.com.
Circ: (Not Reported)

2349 Los Angeles Bulletin
Metropolitan News Co.
210 S. Spring St. Phone: (213)628-4384
Los Angeles, CA 90012 Fax: (213)687-3886

Daily newspaper. **Founded:** 1991. **Freq:** Daily. **Print Method:** Offset. **Cols./Page:** 4. **Col. Width:** 15 picas. **Col. Depth:** 15 1/2 inches. **Key Personnel:** Roger M. Grace, Editor. **Subscription Rates:** $80. **Remarks:** Accepts advertising.
Ad Rates: PCI: $6 **Circ:** Paid 200
Non-paid 4,000

2350 The Los Angeles Business Journal
5700 Wilshire, No. 170 Phone: (213)549-5225
Los Angeles, CA 90036 Fax: (213)549-5255
Publication E-mail: labjtalk@aol.com

Newspaper (tabloid) covering local business news, business trends, executive profiles, and information for the Los Angeles area executive. **Founded:** 1979. **Freq:** Weekly (Mon.). **Print Method:** Offset. **Trim Size:** 11 3/8 x 15. **Cols./Page:** 4. **Col. Width:** 2 1/4 inches. **Col. Depth:** 13 1/2 inches. **Key Personnel:** Mark Lacter, Editor; Matt Toledo, Publisher. **Subscription Rates:** $79.95 individuals. **Remarks:** Accepts advertising.
Ad Rates: BW: $4,011 **Circ:** Paid ★**20,641**
4C: $4,611

2351 Los Angeles Daily Journal
Daily Journal Corp.
915 E. 1st St. Phone: (213)229-5300
Los Angeles, CA 90012-4050 Fax: (213)680-3682
Free: (800)652-1700

Newspaper for the legal community. **Founded:** 1888. **Freq:** Mon.-Fri. (morn.). **Print Method:** Offset. **Cols./Page:** 6. **Col. Width:** 2 1/4 inches. **Col. Depth:** 20 1/2 inches. **Key Personnel:** Katrina Dewey, Editor; Gerald Salzman, Publisher; Adam Schaffer, Advertising Dir. **ISSN:** 0362-5575. **Subscription Rates:** $495 individuals. **Remarks:** Color advertising not accepted.
Ad Rates: BW: $382 **Circ:** Paid 13,000
4C: $814
PCI: $27

2352 Los Angeles Independent
National Media, Inc.
4201 Wilshire Blvd. Phone: (323)932-6397
Ste. 600 Fax: (323)932-8285
Los Angeles, CA 90010
Publication E-mail: laingroup@aol.com

Community newspaper. **Subtitle:** Los Angeles Independent Newspaper Group. **Founded:** 1927. **Freq:** Weekly. **Print Method:** Offset. **Trim Size:** 13 1/2 x 22 1/2. **Cols./Page:** 6. **Col. Width:** 2 1/16 inches. **Col. Depth:** 21 inches. **Key Personnel:** Brian Lewis, Managing Editor; Stephen Laxineta, President; Bruce M. Wood, Publisher. **Subscription Rates:** $80 individuals. **Remarks:** Accepts advertising. **Available Online. URL:** http://www.laindependent.com. **Formerly:** Los Angeles Independent Newspaper Group.
Ad Rates: BW: $10,471 **Circ:** Wed. 153,510
4C: $11,221 Sat. 36,553
SAU: $83.10

2353 Los Angeles Lawyer
Los Angeles County Bar Association
617 S. Olive St. Phone: (213)896-6503
Los Angeles, CA 90014 Fax: (213)623-4328

Magazine featuring scholarly legal articles. **Subtitle:** The Magazine of the Los Angeles County Bar Assn. **Founded:** 1978. **Freq:** Monthly (July/August issues combined). **Print Method:** Offset. **Trim Size:** 8 3/8 x 10 7/8. **Cols./Page:** 3. **Col. Width:** 2 1/4 inches. **Col. Depth:** 10 inches. **Key Personnel:** Samuel Lipsman, Editor; Linda Lonero, Advertising Mgr. **ISSN:** 0162-2900. **Subscription Rates:** $28 individuals; $3 single issue. **Remarks:** Accepts advertising. **URL:** http://www.lacba.org.
Ad Rates: BW: $2,040 **Circ:** Paid 22,536
4C: $2,940 Non-paid 2,723

2354 Los Angeles Loyolan
Loyola Marymount University
7101 W. 80th St. Phone: (310)338-2700
Los Angeles, CA 90045-2699 Fax: (310)338-1901
Publication E-mail: loyolan@lmumail.lmu.edu

Collegiate newspaper. **Founded:** 1923. **Freq:** Weekly (Wed.). **Print Method:** Uses mats. **Cols./Page:** 5. **Col. Width:** 11 picas. **Col. Depth:** 16 picas. **Subscription Rates:** $30 individuals. **Remarks:** Accepts advertising.
Ad Rates: BW: $570 **Circ:** Free ‡4,000
SAU: $6

2355 Los Angeles Magazine
1888 Century Park E., Ste. 920 Phone: (310)557-7569
Los Angeles, CA 90067 Fax: (310)557-7517

Metropolitan magazine. **Founded:** 1960. **Freq:** Monthly. **Print Method:** Offset. **Cols./Page:** 3. **Col. Width:** 27 nonpareils. **Col. Depth:** 140 agate lines. **Key Personnel:** Lew Harris, Editor; Geoff Miller, Publisher; Katie Marin, Advertising Dir. **USPS:** 653-592. **Subscription Rates:** $19 individuals; $2.50 single issue. **Remarks:** Accepts advertising.
Ad Rates: BW: $426 **Circ:** Paid ★**221,302**
4C: $869

2356 Los Angeles Sentinel
3800 S. Crenshaw Phone: (213)299-3800
PO Box 11456 Fax: (213)299-3896
Los Angeles, CA 90008
Black community newspaper. **Founded:** Jan. 26, 1934. **Freq:** Weekly (Thurs.). **Print Method:** Offset. **Trim Size:** 13 x 22 1/2. **Cols./Page:** 6. **Col. Width:** 26 nonpareils. **Col. Depth:** 294 agate lines. **Key Personnel:** Kenneth R. Thomas, Publisher. **Subscription Rates:** $25 individuals. **Remarks:** Accepts advertising.
Ad Rates: BW: $2,835 **Circ:** 18,664
4C: $3,335
SAU: $22.50
PCI: $22.50

2357 Los Angeles Times
Los Angeles Times, Inc.
Times Mirror Sq. Phone: (213)237-7811
Los Angeles, CA 90053 Fax: (213)237-7386
Free: (800)528-4637

General newspaper. **Founded:** 1881. **Freq:** Mon.-Sun. (morn.). **Print Method:** Offset. **Cols./Page:** 6. **Col. Width:** 24 nonpareils. **Col. Depth:** 301 agate lines. **Key Personnel:** Shelby Coffey III, Managing Editor; Dave Laventhol, Publisher. **Subscription Rates:** $174.32 individuals; $158.40 Mon. -Sat.; $80.64 Sunday only; $504 out of state; $.50 single issue. **Remarks:** Accepts advertising. **Online:** Dow Jones News-Retrieval; CompuServe Information Service; LEXIS-NEXIS; Dialog (The Dialog Corporation); NewsBank, Inc. **Alt. Formats:** CD-ROM. **Feature Editors:** Larry Armstrong, *Photo*, phone (213)237-5000; Richard Barnes, *Real Estate*, phone (213)237-5000; Martin Bernheimer, *Music*, phone (213)237-5000; Sonja Bolle, *Book*, phone (213)237-5000; John Dart, *Religion*, phone (213)237-5000; Maura Dolan, *Environmental*, phone (213)237-5000; Sylvie Drake, *Drama*, phone (213)237-5000; Bill Dwyre, *Sports*, phone (213)237-5000; Larry Gordon, *Education*, phone (213)237-5000; Bob Magnuson, *Financial/Business*, phone (213)237-5000; Janice Mall, *Society*, phone (213)237-5000; Tom Plate, *Editorials*, phone (213)237-5000; Ruth Reichl, *Food*, phone (213)237-5000; Mary Rourke, *Fashion*, phone (213)237-5000; Kelly Scott, *Movie*, phone (213)237-5000; Robert Shogan, *Political*, phone (213)237-5000; Bill Stall, *Political*, phone (213)237-5000; Larry Stammer, *Environmental*, phone (213)237-5000; Sherry Stern, *TV*, phone (213)237-5000; Craig Turner, *City*, phone (213)237-5000; Karen Wada, *Features*, phone (213)237-5000; Leslie Ward, *Travel*, phone (213)237-5000; Elaine Woo, *Education*, phone (213)237-5000.
Ad Rates: 4C: $7,800 **Circ:** Mon.-Fri. ★**1,067,540**
PCI: $565 Sat. ★**991,480**
Sun. ★**1,361,202**

2358 Los Angeles Times Magazine
Los Angeles Times, Inc.
Times Mirror Sq. Phone: (213)237-7811
Los Angeles, CA 90053 Fax: (213)237-7386
Free: (800)528-4637

General interest magazine. **Founded:** Oct. 6, 1985. **Freq:** Weekly (Sun.). **Print Method:** Offset. **Trim Size:** 10 x 12 1/2. **Cols./Page:** 3. **Col. Width:** 1 11/16 inches. **Col. Depth:** 12 inches. **Key Personnel:** Alice Short, Editor, phone (213)237-3408; Mark Willes, Publisher. **Subscription Rates:** Included in Los Angeles. **Remarks:** Accepts advertising. **Available Online.**
Ad Rates: BW: $27,685 **Circ:** Sun. ‡1,531,527
4C: $35,635

Lynwood Press - See Lynwood

2359 Lynx Eye
Scribblefest Literary Group
1880 Hill Dr. Phone: (323)550-8522
Los Angeles, CA 90041
Literary journal. **Founded:** Nov. 1994. **Freq:** Quarterly. **Print Method:** Offset. **Trim Size:** 5 1/2 x 8. **Key Personnel:** Pam McCully, Editor; Kathryn Morrison, Editor. **ISSN:** 1078-1862. **Subscription Rates:** $25 U.S.; $32 other countries; $7.95 single issue. **Remarks:** Accepts advertising.
Ad Rates: BW: $100 **Circ:** Paid 300
Non-paid 200

2360 MEN
SL, Inc.
PO Box 4356 Phone: (323)468-1919
Los Angeles, CA 90078-4356 Fax: (323)957-9219
Publication E-mail: info@men-to-men.com
Publisher E-mail: info@men-to-men.com

Magazine featuring gay, male erotica. **Founded:** 1984. **Freq:** Monthly. **Trim Size:** 8 x 10 7/8. **Key Personnel:** Austin Foxxe, Editor-in-Chief, afoxxe@men-to-men.com. **ISSN:** 0742-4701. **Subscription Rates:** $54; $6.95 single issue. **Remarks:** Accepts advertising. **Formerly:** AdvocateMEN.
Ad Rates: BW: $3,502 **Circ:** 76,000
4C: $5,306

2361 Mercury
The Los Angeles Athletic Club
431 W. 7th St. Phone: (213)675-2211
Los Angeles, CA 90014 Fax: (213)689-1194

Private club magazine. **Founded:** June 1, 1912. **Freq:** Monthly. **Print Method:** Offset. **Cols./Page:** 3. **Col. Width:** 17 nonpareils. **Col. Depth:** 154 agate lines. **Key Personnel:** Vince Mattera, Editor. **ISSN:** 0025-9969. **Subscription Rates:** $11 individuals. **Remarks:** Accepts advertising.
Ad Rates: BW: $382 **Circ:** ‡5,000
4C: $814

2362 Mesa Tribune Wave
Wave Community Newspapers, Inc.
2621 W. 54th St. Phone: (213)290-3000
Los Angeles, CA 90043 Fax: (213)291-0219

Black community newspaper. **Founded:** 1919. **Freq:** Biweekly Wednesday & Saturday. **Print Method:** Offset. **Cols./Page:** 6. **Col. Width:** 5 nonpareils. **Col. Depth:** 21 1/2 inches. **Key Personnel:** C.Z. Wilson, President, phone (213)290-3000, fax (213)292-8289. **Subscription Rates:** $125 individuals. **Remarks:** Accepts advertising.
Ad Rates: PCI: $55.25 **Circ:** 31,609

2363 Metropolitan News-Enterprise
Metropolitan News Co.
210 S. Spring St. Phone: (213)628-4384
Los Angeles, CA 90012 Fax: (213)687-3886

Daily newspaper. **Founded:** 1901. **Freq:** Daily. **Print Method:** Offset. **Cols./Page:** 3. **Col. Width:** 19.5 picas. **Col. Depth:** 15 1/2 inches. **Key Personnel:** Roger M. Grace, Publisher; JoAnn Grace, Publisher. **ISSN:** 0897-2281. **Subscription Rates:** $159. **Remarks:** Accepts advertising.
Ad Rates: PCI: $6 **Circ:** Paid ⊕**1,600**
Non-paid ⊕**40**

2364 Mexican American Sun
Eastern Group Publications Inc.
2500 S. Atlantic Blvd., No. A Phone: (213)263-5743
Los Angeles, CA 90040-2004 Fax: (213)263-9169

Hispanic community newspaper (Spanish and English). **Founded:** 1950. **Freq:** Weekly (Thurs.). **Print Method:** Offset. Uses mats. **Trim Size:** 13 x 21 1/2. **Cols./Page:** 6. **Col. Width:** 2 1/16 inches. **Col. Depth:** 294 agate lines. **Key Personnel:** Rose Soto, Editor; Dolores Sanchez, Publisher; John Sanchez, Advertising Mgr. **Subscription Rates:** $90 individuals. **Remarks:** Accepts advertising.
Ad Rates: GLR: $2.50 **Circ:** Paid ‡112
BW: $3,150 Free ‡13,888
4C: $3,570
SAU: $25
PCI: $25

2365 Model Call
Richard Poirier Model and Talent Agency
3575 Cahuenga Blvd. W., Ste. 254 Phone: (213)969-9990
Fax: (213)850-3382
Los Angeles, CA 90068-1341
Magazine focusing on the professional modeling industry. **Subtitle:** FND 1991. **Freq:** Quarterly. **Print Method:** Offset. **Trim Size:** 8 1/8 x 10 7/8. **Cols./Page:** 3. **Col. Width:** 2 1/4 inches. **Col. Depth:** 10 inches. **Key Personnel:** Richard Poirier, Publisher; Donny Poirier, Advertising Dir. **ISSN:** 1061-4737. **Subscription Rates:** $14. $3.95 single issue. **Remarks:** Accepts advertising.
Ad Rates: BW: $4,410 **Circ:** 20,000
4C: $6,882

Montebello Comet - See Montebello

Monterey Park Comet - See Monterey Park

2366 Motor Trend
Petersen Publishing Co., L.L.C.
6420 Wilshire Blvd. Phone: (323)782-2350
Los Angeles, CA 90048-5515 Fax: (323)782-2704
Publication E-mail: mtletters@aol.com

Consumer automotive publication. **Subtitle:** The World's Automotive Authority. **Founded:** 1949. **Freq:** Monthly. **Print Method:** Offset. **Trim Size:** 7 7/8 x 10 1/2. **Cols./Page:** 3. **Col. Width:** 2 1/8 inches. **Col. Depth:** 9 5/8 inches. **Key Personnel:** Doug Hamlin, Publisher; C. Van Tune, Editor; Lee Kelley, President. **Subscription Rates:** $9.97 per year. **Remarks:** Accepts advertising. **URL:** http://www.motortrend.com.
Ad Rates: BW: $47,500 **Circ:** Paid ★**1,197,118**
4C: $79,800
PCI: $2,613

2367 Motor World
Publishing and Business Consultants
4427 W. Slauson Ave.
Los Angeles, CA 90043-2717

Magazine covering personal car maintenance with information on trends. **Founded:** 1991. **Freq:** Quarterly. **Print Method:** Web offset. **Trim Size:** 8 1/2 x 10 1/4. **Cols./Page:** 3. **Col. Width:** 2 1/2 inches. **Col. Depth:** 9 inches. **Key Personnel:** Atia Napoleon, Editor and Publisher. **ISSN:** 1055-8233. **Subscription Rates:** $26.99; $33.99 Canada; $38.96 other countries. **Remarks:** Accepts advertising. **Formerly:** Car Owners (1992).
Ad Rates: BW: $8,290 **Circ:** Paid 120,000
4C: $9,750

2368 Motorcyclist
Petersen Publishing Co., L.L.C.
6420 Wilshire Blvd. Phone: (323)782-2350
Los Angeles, CA 90048-5515 Fax: (323)782-2704
Publication E-mail: mcmail@petersenpub.com

Motorcycle magazine. Includes road tests, technical competition. **Founded:** 1912. **Freq:** Monthly. **Print Method:** Offset. **Trim Size:** 7 7/8 x 10 1/2. **Key Personnel:** Bob Weber, Publisher, phone (213)782-2801, fax (213)782-2534; Richard Lague, Vice President, phone (213)782-2230, fax (213)782-2483; Peter Clancey, Mkg. Dir. **Subscription Rates:** $19.94 individuals; $3 single issue. **Remarks:** Accepts advertising.
Ad Rates: BW: $11,020 **Circ:** Paid ★**245,926**
4C: $17,850
PCI: $480

2369 Movieline
Movieline, Inc.
1141 S. Beverly Dr. Phone: (310)282-0711
Los Angeles, CA 90035 Fax: (310)282-0859

Film magazine reporting on those who make the movies. **Founded:** Sept. 1989. **Freq:** Monthly. **Trim Size:** 8 1/8 x 10 1/2. **Key Personnel:** Anne Volokh, Publisher. **ISSN:** 1055-0917. **Subscription Rates:** $9.95; $2.99 single issue. **Remarks:** Accepts advertising.
Ad Rates: BW: $10,010 **Circ:** Paid ★**318,716**
4C: $13,691

2370 Mustang & Fords
Petersen Publishing Co., L.L.C.
6420 Wilshire Blvd. Phone: (213)782-2323
Los Angeles, CA 90048 Fax: (213)782-2263

Magazine featuring a variety of Mustang events and other car-related activities across the country. **Founded:** 1980. **Freq:** Bimonthly. **Print Method:** Web offset. **Trim Size:** 7 7/8 x 10 1/2. **Key Personnel:** John Dianna, Publisher; Peter Clancey, Senior V.P.; Jim Smart, Editor; Chris Horn, Assoc. Publisher. **Subscription Rates:** $15.95. $3.25 single issue. **Remarks:** Accepts advertising. **Formerly:** Hot Rod's Mustang (1988); Mustang.
Ad Rates: BW: $2,430 **Circ:** Paid ★**82,648**
4C: $3,890

2371 National Auctions and Sales
Publishing and Business Consultants
4427 W. Slauson Ave.
Los Angeles, CA 90043-2717

Magazine containing specific information on routine government auctions. **Founded:** 1991. **Freq:** Quarterly. **Print Method:** Web offset. **Trim Size:** 8 1/2 x 10 1/4. **Key Personnel:** Andeson Napoleon Atia, Editor and Publisher. **ISSN:** 1055-8268. **Subscription Rates:** $26.99; $33.99 Canada; $38.96 other countries. **Remarks:** Accepts advertising. **Formerly:** Government Auctions Update (1992).
Ad Rates: BW: $8,290 **Circ:** Paid 120,000
4C: $9,750

2372 National Lampoon
J 2 Communications
10850 Wilshire Blvd., Ste. 1000 Phone: (310)474-5252
Los Angeles, CA 90024 Fax: (310)474-1219

Magazine featuring humor and satire. **Founded:** 1970. **Freq:** Quarterly. **Print Method:** Offset. **Trim Size:** 8 x 10 7/8. **Cols./Page:** 3. **Col. Width:** 27 nonpareils. **Col. Depth:** 140 agate lines. **Key Personnel:** Duncan Murray, Publisher. **ISSN:** 0027-9587. **Subscription Rates:** $13.95. $3.95 single issue. **Remarks:** Accepts advertising.
Ad Rates: BW: $1000 **Circ:** ‡231,265
4C: $2000
PCI: $240

2373 New Directions for Community Colleges
Jossey-Bass Inc., Publishers
3051 Moore Hall Phone: (310)825-3931
Box 951521 Fax: (310)206-8095
Los Angeles, CA 90095-1521
Free: (800)832-8256
Publication E-mail: ericcc@ucla.edu
Publisher E-mail: webperson@jbp.com

Journal assisting community colleges in their expanding educational mission. **Founded:** 1973. **Freq:** Quarterly. **Print Method:** Sheetfed offset. **Trim Size:** 6 x 9. **Cols./Page:** 1. **Col. Width:** 27 picas. **Col. Depth:** 45 picas. **Key Personnel:** Arthur M. Cohen, Editor-in-Chief; Florence B. Brawer. **ISSN:** 0194-3081. **Subscription Rates:** $57 individuals; $107 institutions. **Remarks:** Advertising not accepted.
Circ: Paid 827
Non-paid 178

2374 New Directions for Mental Health Services
Jossey-Bass Inc., Publishers
1934 Hospital Place Phone: (213)226-5618
Los Angeles, CA 90033 Fax: (213)226-4268
Publisher E-mail: webperson@jbp.com

Journal containing articles written by mental health specialists. **Founded:** 1979. **Freq:** Quarterly. **Print Method:** Sheetfed offset. **Trim Size:** 6 x 9. **Cols./Page:** 1. **Col. Width:** 27 picas. **Col. Depth:** 45 picas. **Key Personnel:** H. Richard Lamb, Editor, hlamb@hsc.usc.edu. **ISSN:** 0193-9416. **Subscription Rates:** $54 individuals; $75 institutions. **Remarks:** Advertising not accepted.
Circ: Paid 1,303
Non-paid 70

2375 The New Korea
141 S. New Hampshire Ave. Phone: (213)382-9345
Los Angeles, CA 90004-5805 Fax: (213)382-1678

Ethnic magazine (tabloid) (Korean and English). **Founded:** Nov. 22, 1905. **Freq:** Weekly (Thurs.). **Print Method:** Offset. **Cols./Page:** 5. **Col. Width:** 24 nonpareils. **Col. Depth:** 280 agate lines. **Key Personnel:** Woon-Ha Kim, Editor and Publisher; Choong-Ja Kim, Managing Editor and Administration. **USPS:** 380-780. **Subscription Rates:** $54 individuals. **Remarks:** Accepts advertising.
Ad Rates: PCI: $10 **Circ:** Paid ‡3,000
Non-paid ‡100

2376 New Perspectives Quarterly
Blackwell Publishers
Center for the Study of Democracy Phone: (310)474-0011
Fax: (310)474-8061
10951 W. Pico Blvd., 3rd Fl.
Los Angeles, CA 90064
Publication E-mail: npq@pacificnet.net
Publisher E-mail: books@blackwellpub.com

Journal publishing independent thought and criticism by global opinion leaders. Each issue covers one theme. **Subtitle:** A Journal of Social and Political Thought. **Founded:** Oct. 1984. **Freq:** Quarterly. **Print Method:** Web offset. **Trim Size:** 8 1/2 x 11. **Cols./Page:** 2 and 3. **Col. Width:** 30 and 44 nonpareils. **Col. Depth:** 133 agate lines. **Key Personnel:** Nathan Gardels, Editor. **ISSN:** 0893-7850. **Subscription Rates:** $66 individuals; $22.50 single issue. **Remarks:** Advertising not accepted. **Online:** America Online, Inc. **Alt. Formats:** CD-ROM; Microform. **Formerly:** Center Magazine (1989).
Circ: Paid 11,002
Non-paid 559

2377 New Times
The Burnside Group, Inc.
1950 Sawtelle Blvd., No. 200 Phone: (310)477-0403
Los Angeles, CA 90025 Fax: (310)477-8428

Subtitle: The Free Weekly City Magazine. **Founded:** 1978. **Freq:** Weekly. **Print Method:** Offset. **Trim Size:** 10 x 12. **Cols./Page:** 4. **Col. Width:** 12 picas. **Col. Depth:** 11 inches. **Key Personnel:** James Vowell, Editor and Publisher, editor@newtimesla.com. **ISSN:** 1046-2392. **Subscription**

Rates: $49.95 individuals. **Remarks:** Accepts advertising. **Online:** L.A. Online. **Formerly:** Los Angeles Reader.
Ad Rates: GLR: $6.64 BW: $2,399 4C: $3,149 SAU: $73 PCI: $73
Circ: Paid 325 Non-paid 82,925

2378 New York Apparel News
Apparel News Group
110 E. 9th St., Ste. A-777 Phone: (213)627-3737
Los Angeles, CA 90079-1777 Fax: (213)627-5707

Apparel magazine covering textiles and accessories for women and children. **Founded:** 1981. **Freq:** 5/year. **Print Method:** Web press. **Trim Size:** 7 1/8 x 10. **Cols./Page:** 5. **Col. Width:** 24 nonpareils. **Col. Depth:** 186 agate lines. **Key Personnel:** Martin Wernicke, Publisher; Jack Marquette, Marketing Research. **ISSN:** 0279-7844. **Subscription Rates:** $20 individuals; $4 single issue. **Remarks:** Accepts advertising.
Ad Rates: BW: $2450 4C: $3,250 PCI: $40
Circ: 10,049

2379 NOMMO
University of California, Los Angeles
118 Kerkhoff Hall Phone: (310)825-9898
308 Westwood Plaza Fax: (310)206-0906
Los Angeles, CA 90024
A UCLA magazine focusing on African Americans. **Founded:** 1968. **Print Method:** Offset. **Trim Size:** 11 1/2 x 17 5/8. **Col. Width:** 1 7/8 inches. **Col. Depth:** 5 inches. **Key Personnel:** Anika Johnson, ajohnson@media.ucla.edu. **Subscription Rates:** $18. **Remarks:** Advertising accepted; rates available upon request. **Available Online. URL:** http://www.media.asucla.edu.
Circ: Non-paid 10,000

2380 Northeast Sun Commerce Comet
Eastern Group Publications Inc.
2500 S. Atlantic Blvd., No. A Phone: (213)263-5743
Los Angeles, CA 90040-2004 Fax: (213)263-9169

Bilingual community newspaper concentrating on Hispanic issues. **Founded:** Sept. 9, 1986. **Freq:** Weekly (Thurs.). **Print Method:** Offset. **Trim Size:** 6 col. x 21 in. **Cols./Page:** 6. **Col. Width:** 2 1/16 inches. **Col. Depth:** 1 inches. **Key Personnel:** Dolores Sanchez, Editor and Publisher; Jonathan Sanchez, Advertising Mgr. **Subscription Rates:** $95 individuals; Free to qualified subscribers. **Remarks:** Accepts advertising.
Ad Rates: GLR: $2.80 BW: $3,528 PCI: $28
Circ: Controlled ‡92,500

2381 The Occidental
Occidental College
1600 Campus Rd. Phone: (213)259-2896
Box F-40 Fax: (213)341-4982
Los Angeles, CA 90041
Collegiate newspaper. **Founded:** 1904. **Freq:** Weekly (Mon.). **Print Method:** Offset. **Trim Size:** 12 x 16. **Cols./Page:** 5. **Col. Width:** 23 nonpareils. **Col. Depth:** 224 agate lines. **Key Personnel:** Adrienne Carson, Editor-in-Chief; Karen E. Bow, Advisor. **Subscription Rates:** Free; $25 by mail bulk; $50 1st class. **Remarks:** Color advertising not accepted.
Ad Rates: BW: $424.80 SAU: $6.75 PCI: $6.50
Circ: Paid ‡250 Free ‡1,800

2382 Overture
Professional Musicians, Local 47
817 N. Vine St. Phone: (323)462-2159
Los Angeles, CA 90038 Fax: (323)466-1289
Publisher E-mail: benefits@promusic47.org

Union newspaper (tabloid). **Subtitle:** Overture. **Founded:** 1921. **Freq:** Monthly. **Print Method:** Offset. Uses mats. **Cols./Page:** 4. **Col. Width:** 27 nonpareils. **Col. Depth:** 189 agate lines. **Key Personnel:** Serena Kay Williams, Editor, phone (213)993-3160, overture@promusic47.org; Terri Markham, Asst. Editor. **ISSN:** 0030-7556. **Subscription Rates:** included in membership dues. **Remarks:** Accepts advertising.
Ad Rates: BW: $800 PCI: $25
Circ: Paid ‡10,000 Free ‡450

2383 Pacific Journal of Mathematics
University of California at Los Angeles
Los Angeles, CA 90095-1555
Publication E-mail: julie@math.ucla.edu; ip@world.std.com

Research journal in mathematics. **Founded:** 1951. **Freq:** Monthly (except July and August). **Key Personnel:** Sun-Yung Alice Chang, Managing Editor; Bernice Gangale, Subscriptions. **ISSN:** 0030-8730. **Subscription Rates:** $300 individuals. **Remarks:** Advertising not accepted.
Circ: (Not Reported)

2384 Pacific News Group
206 N. Kennebec Dr. Phone: (714)637-5342
Anaheim, CA 92807 Fax: (714)637-4701
Publisher E-mail: pacnewgr@aol.com

Entertainment and travel features syndicate. **Founded:** 1987. **Freq:** Daily and Weekly. **Key Personnel:** Randy Matin, Editor; William Preston, Travel; Candace Chambers, Fashion; Tim Adams, Theatre; C.B. George, Books; Randy Matin, Elec., Interactive Media, Video/Music. **Remarks:** Advertising not accepted. **Formerly:** Pacific Coast Revue; Pacific News & Review.
Circ: Controlled ‡1,000,000

2385 Pacific Ties
U.C.L.A.
118 Kerckhoff Hall Phone: (310)825-1004
308 Westwood Plaza Fax: (310)206-3165
University of California, Los Angeles
Los Angeles, CA 90024
Publisher E-mail: pacificties@media.ucla.edu

Student magazine. **Subtitle:** UCLA's Asian Pacific Islander Newsmagazine. **Founded:** Feb. 1978. **Freq:** Biennial. **Cols./Page:** 4. **Col. Width:** 2 inches. **Col. Depth:** 15.5 inches. **Subscription Rates:** $18. **Remarks:** Advertising accepted; rates available upon request. **URL:** http://www.pacties.media.ucla.edu.
Circ: Controlled ‡5,000

2386 The Paramount Journal
Clarion Publications
Box 531870 Phone: (562)634-1399
Los Angeles, CA 90053-1870
Community newspaper. **Founded:** 1923. **Freq:** Weekly (Thurs.). **Print Method:** Offset. **Cols./Page:** 6. **Col. Width:** 9.5 picas. **Col. Depth:** 16 inches. **Key Personnel:** Don Plunkett, Editor and Publisher. **Subscription Rates:** $20 individuals. **Remarks:** Accepts advertising.
Ad Rates: PCI: $5
Circ: ‡3,000

2387 Park Labrea News and Beverly Press
Park Labrea News & Beverly Press
PO Box 36036 Phone: (323)933-5518
Los Angeles, CA 90036 Fax: (323)933-5812

Community newspaper. **Founded:** 1947. **Freq:** Weekly (Thurs.). **Print Method:** Offset. **Cols./Page:** 5. **Col. Width:** 12 picas. **Col. Depth:** 16 inches. **Key Personnel:** Michael Villalpando, Publisher; Karen Villalpando, Ed./Pub. **Subscription Rates:** $120 by mail. **Remarks:** Accepts advertising.
Ad Rates: GLR: $12 BW: $1,040 4C: $1,440 PCI: $13
Circ: Free ‡12,000

2388 PBC Federal Tax Guide
Publishing and Business Consultants
4427 W. Slauson Ave.
Los Angeles, CA 90043-2717

Magazine covering tax issues that affect individuals, seniors, and businesses. **Founded:** 1991. **Freq:** Quarterly. **Print Method:** Web offset. **Key Personnel:** Atia Napoleon, Editor and Publisher. **ISSN:** 1059-2032. **Subscription Rates:** $26.99; $33.99 other countries. **Remarks:** Accepts advertising.
Ad Rates: BW: $8,290 4C: $9,750
Circ: (Not Reported)

2389 Performing Arts
Performing Arts Network
10350 Santa Monica Blvd. Phone: (310)839-8000
No. 350 Fax: (310)551-1939
Los Angeles, CA 90025
Edited for theatre and concert-goers in greater Los Angeles, San Francisco and San Diego. The publications supply synopses, scenes and, where appropriate, the musical numbers of plays as well as cast biographies and articles dealing with the background of a particular play and historical/analytical program notes for concerts. It also presents articles of a general nature dealing with music, theatre, film and dance, audio and video. Monthly features include columns on travel, fashion and California real estate. **Founded:** May 1967. **Freq:** Monthly. **Print Method:** Offset. **Trim Size:** 8 1/8 x 10 3/4. **Cols./Page:** 3. **Col. Width:** 2 1/4 inches. **Col. Depth:** 10 inches. **Key Personnel:** Dana Kitaj, Editor; Ed Conn, Publisher; Gilman Kroft, President. **ISSN:** 0031-5222. **Subscription Rates:** Free.
Ad Rates: BW: $20,650.00 4C: $30,975.00
Circ: Controlled 300,000 600,000

2390 Petersen's Circle Track
Petersen Publishing Co., L.L.C.
6420 Wilshire Blvd. Phone: (323)782-2350
Los Angeles, CA 90048-5515 Fax: (323)782-2704
Publication E-mail: ctrack@petersenpub.com

Magazine for racing enthusiasts. **Founded:** Oct. 1982. **Freq:** Monthly. **Print Method:** Offset. **Trim Size:** 7 7/8 x 10 1/2. **Key Personnel:** Ralph V. Panico, Publisher; C.J. Baker, Publisher; Steve Zepezauer, Editor. **Subscription Rates:** $17.95 individuals; $3.50 single issue. **Remarks:** Accepts advertising.
Ad Rates: BW: $3,270 4C: $5,995 PCI: $180
Circ: Paid ★**131,355**

2391 Petersen's Custom Classic Trucks
Petersen Publishing Co., L.L.C.
6420 Wilshire Blvd. Phone: (323)782-2350
Los Angeles, CA 90048-5515 Fax: (323)782-2704

Consumer publication covering vintage pickups, panels, and sedan deliveries. **Founded:** 1992. **Freq:** Bimonthly. **Trim Size:** 7 x 10. **Key Personnel:** Bob Carpenter, Editor, phone (213)782-2295, carpentr@petersenpub.com; De Ette Crow, Publisher, phone (213)782-2712, crowd@petersenpub.com; Andrea DeVuono, Ad Sales, phone (213)782-2757, fax (213)782-2746, devuonoa@petersenpub.com; Sheri Arnett, Ad Sales, phone (213)782-2545, fax (213)782-2746, arnetts@petersenpub.com. **ISSN:** 1073-4732. **Subscription Rates:** $3.50 single issue. **Remarks:** Accepts advertising. **Formerly:** Custom and Classic Trucks.
Ad Rates: GLR: $6.79 BW: $1,855 4C: $2,595
Circ: Paid 99,594

2392 Petersen's 4 Wheel & Off Road
Petersen Publishing Co., L.L.C.
6420 Wilshire Blvd. Phone: (323)782-2350
Los Angeles, CA 90048-5515 Fax: (323)782-2704

Automotive magazine. **Founded:** Mar. 1978. **Freq:** Monthly. **Print Method:** Offset. **Trim Size:** 7 7/8 x 10 1/2. **Cols./Page:** 3. **Key Personnel:** John Dianna, Executive Publisher; Jim Ryan, Publisher. **Subscription Rates:** $11.97 individuals; $2.95 single issue. **Remarks:** Accepts advertising.
Ad Rates: BW: $8,365 4C: $14,415 PCI: $460
Circ: Paid ★**369,970**

2393 Petersen's Hunting
Petersen Publishing Co., L.L.C.
6420 Wilshire Blvd. Phone: (323)782-2350
Los Angeles, CA 90048-5515 Fax: (323)782-2704

Sport hunting magazine. **Founded:** 1973. **Freq:** Monthly. **Print Method:** Offset. **Trim Size:** 7 7/8 x 10 1/2. **Key Personnel:** Jeff Young, Publisher; Ken Elliott, Publisher; Peter Clancey, Senior Vice President. **Subscription Rates:** $12.97 individuals; $2.95 single issue. **Remarks:** Accepts advertising.
Ad Rates: BW: $8,645 4C: $14,355
Circ: Paid ★**354,435**

2394 Petersen's Photographic Magazine
Petersen Publishing Co., L.L.C.
6420 Wilshire Blvd. Phone: (323)782-2350
Los Angeles, CA 90048-5515 Fax: (323)782-2704

Photography magazine. **Founded:** May 1972. **Freq:** Monthly. **Print Method:** Offset. **Trim Size:** 7 8/8 x 10 1/2. **Key Personnel:** Jackie Augustine, Publisher. **ISSN:** 0199-4913. **Subscription Rates:** $11.97 individuals; $2.95 single issue. **Remarks:** Accepts advertising.
Ad Rates: BW: $10,030 4C: $17,050 PCI: $552
Circ: Paid ★**208,479**

2395 Pharmaceutical Research
Plenum Publishing Corp.
Dept. of Pharmaceutical Sciences
University of Southern California - Los Angeles
Los Angeles, CA 90089
Publisher E-mail: info@plenum.com

Research journal. **Subtitle:** An Official Journal of the American Association. **Freq:** 12/year. **Print Method:** Offset. **Trim Size:** 8 1/2 x 11. **Key Personnel:** Vincent H.L. Lee, Editor-in-Chief. **ISSN:** 0724-8741. **Subscription Rates:** $525; $615 out of area. **Remarks:** Accepts advertising.
Ad Rates: BW: $995 4C: $2,520
Circ: (Not Reported)

2396 Planetarian
International Planetarium Society
2800 E. Observatory Rd. Phone: (323)664-1181
Los Angeles, CA 90027 Fax: (323)663-4323

Trade journal of the International Planetarium Society. **Founded:** 1972. **Freq:** Quarterly. **Trim Size:** 8 1/2 x 11. **Key Personnel:** John Mosley, Exec. Editor, jmosley@earthlink.net. **ISSN:** 0090-3213. **Subscription Rates:** $50 individuals; $150 other. **Remarks:** Accepts advertising.
Circ: Paid 800

2397 Players
Players International Publications
8060 Melrose Ave. Phone: (213)653-8060
Los Angeles, CA 90046 Fax: (213)682-2932
Publication E-mail: psi@loop.com

Entertainment magazine for the 18-40 year old black American male. **Subtitle:** Something for Everybody. **Founded:** 1973. **Freq:** Monthly. **Print Method:** Web offset. **Trim Size:** 8 x 10 7/8. **Cols./Page:** 3. **Col. Width:** 2 1/4 inches. **Col. Depth:** 10 inches. **Key Personnel:** David Jamison, Editor. **Subscription Rates:** $52 individuals; $95 individuals /2 years; $70 other countries; $131 other countries /2 years; $5.95 single issue. **Online:** AdultNewsStand Players.
Ad Rates: GLR: $133 **Circ:** 50,000
BW: $1,540
4C: $2,420

2398 Pool & Spa News
Leisure Publications
4160 Wilshire Blvd. Phone: (323)964-4800
Los Angeles, CA 90010 Fax: (323)964-4840

Magazine focusing on the swimming pool and spa industries. **Founded:** 1961. **Freq:** Semimonthly. **Print Method:** Web offset. **Trim Size:** 8 1/4 x 10 7/8. **Cols./Page:** 3. **Col. Width:** 27 nonpareils. **Col. Depth:** 140 agate lines. **Key Personnel:** Carolyn Cerbin, Editor; Jules Field, Publisher; Karen Cavallo, Assoc Pub. **Subscription Rates:** $19.97 individuals; $5 single issue. **Remarks:** Accepts advertising.
Ad Rates: BW: $1,745 **Circ:** Paid ★8,086
4C: $2,370 Non-paid ★7,971

2399 Psychological Perspectives
C. G. Jung Institute of Los Angeles
10349 W. Pico Blvd. Phone: (310)556-1193
Los Angeles, CA 90064 Fax: (310)556-2290
Publisher E-mail: junginla@earthlink.net

Journal of Jungian thought featuring articles, interviews, poetry, fiction, and book and film reviews. **Founded:** 1970. **Freq:** Semiannual. **Trim Size:** 6 x 9. **Cols./Page:** 1. **Col. Width:** 4 1/2 inches. **Key Personnel:** Gilda Frantz, Co-Editors in Chief; Anca Colbert, Managing Editor; Margaret Johnson, Co-Editors in Chief. **ISSN:** 0033-2925. **Subscription Rates:** $18 single issue; $32 U.S. /yr; $37 elsewhere. **Remarks:** Accepts advertising. **URL:** http://www.home.earthlink.net/junginla.
Ad Rates: BW: $300 **Circ:** Paid 2,000
Non-paid 2,000

2400 Radio & Records
Radio and Records, Inc.
10100 Santa Monica Blvd., 5th Fl. Phone: (310)553-4330
Fax: (310)203-8727
Los Angeles, CA 90067-4004
Publication E-mail: moreinfo@rronline.com; mailroom@r&ronline.comp
Publisher E-mail: mailroom@rronline.com

Music trade newspaper. **Subtitle:** The Industry's Newspaper. **Founded:** 1973. **Freq:** Weekly. **Print Method:** Web offset. **Trim Size:** 10 1/2 x 14 1/2. **Cols./Page:** 5. **Col. Width:** 22 nonpareils. **Col. Depth:** 186 agate lines. **Key Personnel:** Erica Farber, CEO; Sky Daniels, Vice Pres./Sales; Ron Rodrigues, Managing Editor. **ISSN:** 1076-6502. **Subscription Rates:** $299; $320 Canada; $495 out of country; $6.50 single issue. **Online:** RRONLINE.
Ad Rates: BW: $4,510 **Circ:** Paid 9000
4C: $5,940 Non-paid 500

2401 Rafu Shimpo
Rafushimpo
259 S. Los Angeles St. Phone: (213)629-2231
Los Angeles, CA 90012 Fax: (213)687-0737
Publication E-mail: rafushimpo@aol.com

Community newspaper (English and Japanese). **Founded:** 1903. **Freq:** Daily. **Cols./Page:** 8. **Key Personnel:** John Saito, Editor; Takeshi Ota, Japanese Editor. **Subscription Rates:** $75; $150 Canada; $215 Japan. **Remarks:** Accepts advertising.
Ad Rates: BW: $2,000 **Circ:** Paid 22,000
4C: $3,000
PCI: $13

2402 Rapport
Rapport Publishing Co., Inc.
5265 Fountain Ave. Upper Terrace No. 6 Phone: (213)660-0433
Fax: (213)664-0434
Los Angeles, CA 90029
Free: (800)397-1266

Book and music review magazine. **Subtitle:** West Coast Review of Books, Art, and Entertainment. **Founded:** Oct. 1974. **Freq:** Bimonthly. **Print Method:** Rotary offset. **Trim Size:** 8 1/8 x 10 7/8. **Cols./Page:** 3 and 4. **Col. Width:** 10 and 13.5 picas. **Col. Depth:** 10 inches. **Key Personnel:** D. David Dreis, Editor and Publisher; Lisa Randazzo, Managing Editor; George Tamayo, Assoc. Editor. **ISSN:** 1061-6861. **Subscription Rates:** $11.97 individuals; $3.25 single issue other countries; $2.95 single issue. **Remarks:** Accepts advertising. **Formerly:** West Coast Review of Books.
Ad Rates: BW: $2,250 **Circ:** Paid 50,000
4C: $3,150
PCI: $50

2403 REASON
Reason Foundation
3415 S. Sepulveda Blvd., Ste. 400 Phone: (310)391-2245
Fax: (310)391-4395
Los Angeles, CA 90034
Publication E-mail: letters@reason.com

Magazine for individuals interested in economic, social, and political issues stressing free markets and individual liberties. **Subtitle:** Free minds & free markets. **Founded:** 1968. **Freq:** Monthly (August/September issue combined). **Print Method:** Web offset. **Trim Size:** 8 3/8 x 10 7/8. **Cols./Page:** 10. **Col. Width:** 6.6 picas. **Col. Depth:** 301 agate lines. **Key Personnel:** Virginia I. Postrel, Editor, vpostrel@reason.com; Robert W. Pook, Publisher, publisher@reason.com. **ISSN:** 0048-6906. **Subscription Rates:** $24 individuals. **URL:** http://www.reason.com.
Ad Rates: GLR: $.64 **Circ:** Paid ★47,611
BW: $1,926.40
4C: $2,416.40
PCI: $896

2404 Religious Education
Scholars Press
15600 Mulholland Dr. Phone: (310)476-9777
Los Angeles, CA 90077 Fax: (310)471-1278
Publication E-mail: lande05atsemory.edu
Publisher E-mail: scholars@emory.edu

Journal for religious and education leaders of all faith. **Founded:** 1906. **Freq:** Quarterly. **Print Method:** Letterpress and offset. **Trim Size:** 6 x 9. **Cols./Page:** 1. **Col. Width:** 52 nonpareils. **Col. Depth:** 105 agate lines. **Key Personnel:** Dr. H.A. Alexander, Editor, halexan933@aol.com; Tacy Callies, Managing Editor. **ISSN:** 0034-4087. **Subscription Rates:** $45 individuals. **Remarks:** Accepts advertising.
Ad Rates: BW: $275 **Circ:** Paid ‡2,600
Non-paid ‡200

2405 Richie Rich
The Harvey Entertainment Co.
1999 Avenue of the Stars, No. 2050 Phone: (310)789-1990
Fax: (310)789-1991
Los Angeles, CA 90067
Comic book. **Freq:** Monthly. **Print Method:** Web offset. **Trim Size:** 6 1/8 x 10 1/8. **Key Personnel:** Sid Jacobson, Editor; Ed Shukin, Director; Kevin S. Bricklin, Director. **Subscription Rates:** $1.50 single issue. **Remarks:** Advertising accepted; rates available upon request. **URL:** http://www.harvey.com.
Circ: (Not Reported)

2406 Riverside Bulletin
Metropolitan News Co.
210 S. Spring St. Phone: (213)628-4384
Los Angeles, CA 90012 Fax: (213)687-3886

Community newspaper. **Founded:** 1991. **Freq:** Weekly. **Print Method:** Offset. **Cols./Page:** 4. **Col. Width:** 15 picas. **Col. Depth:** 15 1/2 inches. **Key Personnel:** Roger M. Grace, Editor. **Remarks:** Accepts advertising.
Ad Rates: PCI: $6 **Circ:** Non-paid 1,000

2407 Rod & Custom Magazine
Rod & Custom
6420 Wilshire Blvd. Phone: (323)782-2712
Los Angeles, CA 90048 Fax: (323)782-2223
Publication E-mail: crowd@petersenpub.com

Contemporary street rodding magazine. **Founded:** 1953. **Freq:** Monthly. **Print Method:** Web offset. **Trim Size:** 7 7/8 x 10 1/2. **Cols./Page:** 3. **Col. Width:** 2 1/4 inches. **Col. Depth:** 9 1/2 inches. **Key Personnel:** Marie Crow DeEtte, Publisher, crowd@petersenpub.com. **Subscription Rates:** $15.95. $3.50 single issue. **Remarks:** Accepts advertising.
Ad Rates: BW: $1655 **Circ:** Paid ★136,908
4C: $2315
PCI: $91

2408 Rotary Review
Mazda RX-7 Club
1774 S. Alvira Phone: (323)933-6993
Los Angeles, CA 90035
Magazine for Mazda RX-7 owners. **Subtitle:** Rotary Review. **Founded:** 1978. **Freq:** Quarterly. **Cols./Page:** 2. **Col. Width:** 3 1/2 inches. **Col. Depth:** 10 inches. **Subscription Rates:** $30 individuals; $40 other countries; $5 single issue. **Remarks:** Accepts advertising. **Formerly:** Mazda RX-7 Club (1989).
Ad Rates: BW: $95 **Circ:** 1300

Sacramento Bulletin - See Sacramento

San Bernardino Bulletin - See San Bernardino

San Diego Bulletin - See San Diego

2409 San Diego Jewish Press-Heritage
Heritage
2130 Vermont Ave. Phone: (818)999-9921
Los Angeles, CA 90007
Jewish newspaper. **Subtitle:** Heritage. **Founded:** 1914. **Freq:** Weekly. **Print Method:** Offset. **Cols./Page:** 6. **Col. Width:** 24 nonpareils. **Col. Depth:** 196 agate lines. **Key Personnel:** Dan Brin, Editor; Herb Brin, Publisher; Mark Edelstein, Advertising Mgr. **Subscription Rates:** $20 individuals. **Remarks:** Accepts advertising.
Ad Rates: BW: $850 **Circ:** 15,000
4C: $950
PCI: $15

2410 Science of Mind
United Church of Religious Science
3251 W. 6th St. Phone: (213)388-2181
Los Angeles, CA 90020-5096 Fax: (213)388-1926
Publication E-mail: ed@scienceofmind.com

Religious magazine on metaphysics and self-help. **Founded:** 1927. **Freq:** Monthly. **Print Method:** Offset. **Trim Size:** 5 3/8 x 7 3/4. **Cols./Page:** 2. **Col. Width:** 23 nonpareils. **Col. Depth:** 86 agate lines. **Key Personnel:** Elaine Sane, Editor and Publisher; Jim Shea, Asst. Editor; Randall Friesen, Art Dir.; Debra Clarke, Business Oper. Coord., sombusops@earthlink.net; Constance Conwell, Circulation/Office/Adv. Coord., somcirc@earthlink.net. **ISSN:** 0036-8458. **Subscription Rates:** $19.95 individuals. **Remarks:** Accepts advertising. **Available Online. URL:** http://www.scienceofmind.com. **Alt. Formats:** Audio tape; Braille.
Ad Rates: BW: $1,850 **Circ:** Paid ‡45,000
4C: $2,560 Controlled ‡32,495

2411 Self-Realization
Self-Realization Fellowship, Publishers
3880 San Rafael Avenue
Los Angeles, CA 90065-3298
Publisher E-mail: sales@srfpublishers.org

Magazine promoting the practical application of spiritual principles for 'healing of body, removing mental harmonies by concentration and positive thinking, and freeing the soul from ignorance by yoga meditation.'. **Subtitle:** A Magazine Devoted to Healing of Body, Mind, and Soul. **Founded:** 1925. **Freq:** Quarterly. **Print Method:** Offset. **Trim Size:** 5 1/4 x 7 3/4. **Cols./Page:** 1. **Col. Width:** 49 nonpareils. **Col. Depth:** 87 agate lines. **Key Personnel:** Christopher Bagley, Editor. **ISSN:** 0037-1564. **Subscription Rates:** $6 individuals yearly; $2 single issue; $9 other countries (regular mail); $14 other countries (airmail). **Remarks:** Advertising not accepted.
Circ: 25,000

2412 Si Magazine
Si Magazine Limited Partners
6464 Odin St. Phone: (213)975-9313
Los Angeles, CA 90068 Fax: (213)957-1114
Publication E-mail: simagazine@aol.com

English language lifestyle magazine catering to U.S. Latinos. **Founded:** Sept. 19, 1995. **Freq:** Quarterly. **Print Method:** Web offset. **Trim Size:** 8 7/8 x 10 7/8. **Cols./Page:** 4. **Col. Width:** 2 1/8 and 4 inches. **Col. Depth:** 4 and 10 inches. **Key Personnel:** Joie Davidaw, Editor and Publisher; Eileen Rosaly, Operations Dir. **Subscription Rates:** $8.95; $2.95 single issue. **Remarks:** Accepts advertising. **URL:** http://simagazine.com.
Ad Rates: BW: $3,800 **Circ:** Paid 50,000
4C: $4750

2413 Sinorama/Kuang Hua Hua Pao
Kwang Hwa Publishing Co.
6300 Wilshire Blvd., Ste. 1510A Phone: (213)782-8770
Los Angeles, CA 90048-5217 Fax: (213)782-8761
Publisher E-mail: tecoinfo@soca.com

Bilingual magazine covering Taiwan. **Freq:** Monthly. **ISSN:** 0256-9043. **Subscription Rates:** $32 individuals. **Remarks:** Accepts advertising.
Circ: (Not Reported)

2414 Situations Digest
Publishing and Business Consultants
4427 W. Slauson Ave.
Los Angeles, CA 90043-2717

Magazine covering societal situations. **Founded:** 1991. **Freq:** Quarterly. **Print Method:** Web offset. **Trim Size:** 8 1/2 x 11. **Key Personnel:** Atia Napoleon, Editor and Publisher. **ISSN:** 1059-1958. **Subscription Rates:** $26.99; $33.99 other countries. **Remarks:** Accepts advertising.
Ad Rates: BW: $8,290 **Circ:** (Not Reported)
4C: $9,750

2415 Skin Diver
Petersen Publishing Co., L.L.C.
6420 Wilshire Blvd. Phone: (323)782-2350
Los Angeles, CA 90048-5515 Fax: (323)782-2704

Magazine covers diving, underwater photography, and diving education. **Founded:** 1951. **Freq:** Monthly. **Print Method:** Offset. **Trim Size:** 7 7/8 x 10 1/2. **Key Personnel:** Bill Gleason, Editor and Publisher; Peter Clancey, Senior Vice President. **Subscription Rates:** $12.95 individuals; $3.95 single issue. **Remarks:** Accepts advertising.
Ad Rates: BW: $8,710 **Circ:** Paid ★**217,915**
4C: $13,935
PCI: $479

2416 Soldiers Today
Publishing and Business Consultants
4427 W. Slauson Ave.
Los Angeles, CA 90043-2717

Magazine covering the social aspects of military life. **Founded:** 1991. **Freq:** Quarterly. **Print Method:** Web offset. **Trim Size:** 8 1/2 x 11. **Key Personnel:** Atia Napoleon, Editor and Publisher. **ISSN:** 1059-194X. **Subscription Rates:** $26.99; $33.99 other countries. **Remarks:** Accepts advertising.
Ad Rates: BW: $8,290 **Circ:** (Not Reported)
4C: $9,750

2417 Southern California Anthology
University of Southern California
WPH 404
Los Angeles, CA 90089-4034

Literary journal covering fiction and poetry. **Founded:** 1983. **Freq:** Annual. **Key Personnel:** James Ragan, Editor-in-Chief. **Subscription Rates:** $9.95 single issue. **Remarks:** Advertising not accepted.
Circ: Paid 1,200

2418 Southern California Guide
Westworld Publishing Corp.
11385 Exposition Bldg., No. 102 Phone: (310)391-8255
Los Angeles, CA 90064 Fax: (310)397-7917
Publisher E-mail: socalinfo@aol.com

Magazine including information on restaurants, hotels, special events, attractions, entertainment, art galleries, visitor services, and shopping; contains exclusive restaurant reviews and world-wide travel features (English and Japanese). **Founded:** 1919. **Freq:** Monthly. **Print Method:** Offset. **Trim Size:** 5 3/8 x 8 3/8. **Cols./Page:** 2. **Col. Width:** 14 picas. **Col. Depth:** 7 inches. **Key Personnel:** Valerie Summers, Editor and Publisher, scgvalerie@aol.com; Keith Rockmael, Assoc. Editor. **Subscription Rates:** $20 individuals; $2 single issue. **Remarks:** Accepts advertising.
Ad Rates: GLR: $20 **Circ:** 37,000
BW: $1,135
4C: $1,595

2419 Southern California Law Review
University of Southern California Phone: (213)740-8475
Law Center, Rm. 330 Fax: (213)740-5502
Los Angeles, CA 90089-0071
College law magazine. **Founded:** 1927. **Freq:** Bimonthly 6/year (during academic year). **Print Method:** Offset. **Trim Size:** 17 x 25 cm. **Cols./Page:** 1. **Col. Width:** 55 nonpareils. **Col. Depth:** 105 agate lines. **Key Personnel:** Carlos Matos, Editor-in-Chief. **ISSN:** 0038-3910. **Subscription Rates:** $36 individuals; $45 other countries; $12.50 single issue plus two dollars postage. **Remarks:** Accepts advertising. **Available Online.**
Ad Rates: BW: $140 **Circ:** Paid ‡1,033
Non-paid ‡100

2420 Southern California Quarterly
Historical Society of Southern California
200 East Ave., 43 Phone: (213)222-0546
Los Angeles, CA 90031-1304
Publisher E-mail: hssc@idt.net

Scholarly journal covering local history. **Founded:** 1884. **Freq:** Quarterly. **Key Personnel:** Doyce B. Nunis, Jr., Editor. **Subscription Rates:** Free to qualified subscribers. **Remarks:** Advertising not accepted.
Circ: Paid 1,200

2421 Southern California Senior Life
Senior Media Inc.
6022 W. Pico Blvd., Ste. 7 Phone: (213)933-9228
Los Angeles, CA 90035 Fax: (213)933-9261
Publication E-mail: seniorlife@aol.com

Newspaper (tabloid) for people over the age of fifty. **Subtitle:** Southern California Senior Life. **Founded:** 1983. **Freq:** Monthly. **Print Method:** Web offset. **Trim Size:** 10 x 14. **Cols./Page:** 5. **Col. Width:** 1 7/8 inches. **Col. Depth:** 13 inches. **Key Personnel:** Jerry Beigel, Editor; Estelle Beigel, Publisher. **Subscription Rates:** $20. **Remarks:** Advertising not accepted for tobacco products or pornographic material. **Online:** Senior.com. **URL:** seniorlife.com.
Ad Rates: GLR: $93 **Circ:** Paid ❑**67**
BW: $5,920 Free ❑**217,708**
4C: $6,915
PCI: $93

2422 Southwest News Wave
Wave Community Newspapers, Inc.
2621 W. 54th St. Phone: (213)290-3000
Los Angeles, CA 90043 Fax: (213)291-0219

Black community newspaper. **Founded:** 1919. **Freq:** Semiweekly (Wed. and Sat.). **Print Method:** Offset. **Trim Size:** 13 3/4 x 21 1/2. **Cols./Page:** 6. **Col. Width:** 5 nonpareils. **Col. Depth:** 21 1/2 inches. **Key Personnel:** C.Z. Wilson, Publisher, phone (213)290-3000, fax (213)292-8289. **Subscription Rates:** $125 by mail annually. **Remarks:** Advertising accepted; rates available upon request.
Circ: 38,932

2423 Spectator (Los Angeles)
University of Southern California School of Cinema-TV
University Park Phone: (213)740-3334
Los Angeles, CA 90089-2211 Fax: (213)740-9471

Film and television criticism. **Subtitle:** The University of Southern California Journal of Film and Television Criticism. **Founded:** 1987. **Freq:** 2/year. **Key Personnel:** Sherall Preyer, Circulation Mgr., sherallpreyer@cntv.usc.edu. **ISSN:** 1051-0230. **Subscription Rates:** $10; $6 single issue; $20 Industry; $8 Industry, single issue; $25 other countries; $10 single issue, other countries. **Remarks:** Advertising not accepted.
Circ: (Not Reported)

2424 Sport Truck
Petersen Publishing Co., L.L.C.
6420 Wilshire Blvd. Phone: (323)782-2350
Los Angeles, CA 90048-5515 Fax: (323)782-2704

Magazine covering a range of light-duty trucks, two- and four-wheel drive; with an emphasis on performance. **Founded:** 1988. **Freq:** Monthly. **Print Method:** Web offset. **Trim Size:** 7 7/8 x 10 1/2. **Key Personnel:** Joe Sebergandle, Publisher; Ralph V. Panico, Publisher; Peter Clancey, Vice President; Peter MacGillivray, Editor. **Subscription Rates:** $11.97 individuals; $3.25 single issue. **Remarks:** Accepts advertising.
Ad Rates: BW: $4,135 **Circ:** Paid ★**201,320**
4C: $7,235
PCI: $227

2425 Street Scene
L.A. Free Clinic
6043 Hollywood Blvd. Phone: (323)462-8632
Los Angeles, CA 90028-5459 Fax: (323)462-6731
Publication E-mail: paul.cohen@panasia.com

Newspaper written by and for homeless, runaway, incarcerated and at-risk youth. **Founded:** May 1991. **Freq:** 10 x a yr. **Print Method:** Offset. **Key Personnel:** Paul B. Cohen. **Subscription Rates:** Free. **Remarks:** Advertising not accepted.
Circ: Non-paid 1,000

2426 T'ai Chi
Wayfarer Publications
PO Box 26156 Phone: (323)665-7773
Los Angeles, CA 90026 Fax: (323)665-1627
Publication E-mail: taichi@tai_ chi.com; taichi@taichi.com

A magazine for practitioners of T'ai Chi and related health and fitness disciplines. **Subtitle:** International Magazine of T'ai Chi Ch'uan. **Founded:** Jan. 1977. **Freq:** Bimonthly. **Print Method:** Offset. **Trim Size:** 8 1/2 x 11. **Cols./Page:** 3. **Col. Width:** 2 1/4 inches. **Col. Depth:** 9 3/4 inches. **Key Personnel:** Marvin Smalheiser, Editor and Publisher. **ISSN:** 0730-1049. **Subscription Rates:** $20 individuals; $3.50 single issue U.S.; $5 single issue International; $50 U.S. and other countries International. **URL:** http://www.tai-chi.com.
Ad Rates: BW: $576 **Circ:** (Not Reported)
4C: $1016
PCI: $25

2427 'TEEN
Petersen Publishing Co., L.L.C.
6420 Wilshire Blvd. Phone: (323)782-2350
Los Angeles, CA 90048-5515 Fax: (323)782-2704

Magazine covering beauty, health, fashion, and self-improvement. **Founded:** 1957. **Freq:** Monthly. **Print Method:** Offset. **Trim Size:** 7 7/8 x 10 1/2. **Key Personnel:** Linda Platzner, Executive Publisher, phone (212)886-3600; Launlanne Murphy, Advertising Dir. **ISSN:** 0040-2001. **Subscription Rates:** $19 individuals; $2.95 single issue. **Remarks:** Accepts advertising.
Ad Rates: BW: $42,715 **Circ:** Paid ★**2,077,653**
4C: $69,370
PCI: $859

2428 TenPercent
University of California, Los Angeles
308 Westwood Plaza Phone: (310)825-8500
118 Kerckhoff Hall Fax: (310)206-3165
Los Angeles, CA 90024
Publication E-mail: tenpercent@media.ucla.edu

Lesbian, gay, and bisexual community newspaper. **Subtitle:** UCLA's Lesbian, Gay and Bisexual Magazine. **Founded:** 1979. **Print Method:** Offset. **Trim Size:** 10 x 16. **Cols./Page:** 5. **Col. Width:** 2 inches. **Col. Depth:** 16 inches. **Key Personnel:** Gretchen Greene, Editor; Michael Lopez, Managing Editor. **Subscription Rates:** $18. **Remarks:** Accepts advertising. **Available Online. URL:** http://www.tenpercent.media.asula.ucla.edu.
Ad Rates: BW: $650 **Circ:** 12,000
PCI: $7.10

2429 Theosophy
The Theosophy Co.
245 W. 33rd St. Phone: (213)748-7244
Los Angeles, CA 90007 Fax: (213)748-0634

Magazine devoted to philosophy and science. **Founded:** Nov. 1912. **Freq:** Bimonthly. **Print Method:** Offset. **Trim Size:** 5 1/2 x 8 1/2. **Cols./Page:** 1. **Col. Width:** 48 nonpareils. **Col. Depth:** 100 agate lines. **Key Personnel:** Adella Bivins, Editor. **ISSN:** 0040-5906. **Subscription Rates:** $17 individuals. **Remarks:** Advertising not accepted. **URL:** http://www.theosophycompany.org.
Circ: Paid 800

2430 The Tidings
The Tidings Corp.
3424 Wilshire Blvd., 6th Fl. Phone: (213)637-7360
Los Angeles, CA 90010 Fax: (213)637-6360

Catholic newspaper. **Founded:** 1895. **Freq:** Weekly (Fri.). **Print Method:** Offset. **Cols./Page:** 8. **Col. Width:** 18 nonpareils. **Col. Depth:** 294 agate lines. **Key Personnel:** Tod M. Tamberg, Editor; Archbishop Roger Mahony, Publisher. **ISSN:** 0040-6791. **Subscription Rates:** $15 individuals. **Remarks:** Accepts advertising.
Ad Rates: GLR: $1.56 **Circ:** ‡40,547
BW: $2,757
4C: $3,407
SAU: $21.88
PCI: $21.88

2431 Today's Fireman
Towerhigh Publications, Inc.
PO Box 875108 Phone: (213)432-3806
Los Angeles, CA 90087
Fire service magazine. **Founded:** 1961. **Freq:** Quarterly. **Print Method:** Letterpress and offset. **Cols./Page:** 5. **Col. Width:** 22 nonpareils. **Col. Depth:** 214 agate lines. **Key Personnel:** Jayney Mack, Editor and Publisher. **Subscription Rates:** $9 individuals. **Remarks:** Accepts advertising.
Ad Rates: GLR: $4.10 **Circ:** Paid ‡600
Non-paid ‡15,000

2432 Today's Policeman
Towerhigh Publications, Inc.
PO Box 875108 Phone: (213)432-3806
Los Angeles, CA 90087
Law enforcement magazine. **Founded:** 1961. **Freq:** Quarterly. **Print Method:** Letterpress and offset. **Trim Size:** 10 x 16 1/2. **Cols./Page:** 4. **Col. Width:** 2 1/4 inches. **Col. Depth:** 15 inches. **Key Personnel:** Jayney Mack, Editor and Publisher. **Subscription Rates:** $9 individuals. **Remarks:** Accepts advertising.
Ad Rates: GLR: $4.10 **Circ:** Paid ‡500
Non-paid ‡15,000

2433 Tomorrow's Morning Classroom Edition
Tomorrow's Morning, Inc.
160 N. Thurston Ave. Phone: (310)440-2778
Los Angeles, CA 90049 Fax: (310)476-6406
Publication E-mail: tomorrow@morning.com

Newspaper for elementary school teachers and students. **Subtitle:** Born to Read. **Founded:** Sept. 23, 1996. **Freq:** Biweekly monthly in Sept. and May. **Print Method:** Offset. **Trim Size:** 11 x 17. **Key Personnel:** Adam Linter, Editor and Publisher; Art Stupar, Circulation Mgr.; Phil Brodie, Contact. **ISSN:** 1085-0821. **Subscription Rates:** $16.17 for 9 copies or less; $6.95 for 10 or more copies. **Remarks:** Advertising not accepted. **URL:** http://www.morning.com.
Circ: Paid 10,000

2434 Tozai Times
5810 E. Olympic Blvd. Phone: (213)723-6245
Los Angeles, CA 90022 Fax: (213)722-7865

Newspaper for Japanese communities. **Freq:** Monthly. **Key Personnel:** Joy Yamauchi, Editor.

2435 Tradewinds
Los Angeles Trade Technical College
400 W. Washington Blvd. Phone: (213)744-9046
Los Angeles, CA 90015 Fax: (213)748-7334

Collegiate newspaper. **Founded:** 1927. **Freq:** Monthly. **Print Method:** Offset. **Cols./Page:** 5. **Col. Width:** 2 inches. **Col. Depth:** 17 inches. **Key Personnel:** Theresa Zellers, Advisor, phone (213)744-9372. **Subscription Rates:** Free. **Remarks:** Accepts advertising.
Ad Rates: GLR: $1 **Circ:** Free 2,000
BW: $700
4C: $920
SAU: $14
PCI: $7

2436 Tucumcari Literary Review
Troxey Kemper
3108 W. Bellevue Ave.
Los Angeles, CA 90026

Literary magazine. **Founded:** Sept. 1988. **Trim Size:** 5 1/2 x 8 1/2. **Cols./Page:** 1. **Col. Width:** 4 3/4 inches. **Col. Depth:** 7 3/4 inches. **Key Personnel:** Troxey Kemper, Editor. **Subscription Rates:** $12 individuals; $2 single issue. **Remarks:** Advertising not accepted.
Circ: Controlled 150

2437 20 de Mayo
1824 Sunset Blvd., Ste. 202 Phone: (213)483-8511
Los Angeles, CA 90026 Fax: (213)483-6474
Publication E-mail: may020@aol.com

Newspaper (tabloid, Spanish). **Founded:** 1969. **Freq:** Weekly. **Cols./Page:** 6. **Col. Width:** 1 1/2 inches. **Col. Depth:** 16 inches. **Key Personnel:** Abel Perez, Editor and Publisher; Pedro Cacheiro, Advertising Mgr.; Gina Perez, Public Relations/Circulation Manager. **USPS:** 459-450. **Subscription Rates:** $40. **Remarks:** Accepts advertising.
Ad Rates: PCI: $12.50 **Circ:** 25,000

2438 UCLA Magazine
University of California, Los Angeles
10920 Wilshire Blvd., Ste. 1500 Phone: (310)794-6880
Los Angeles, CA 90024-6517 Fax: (310)794-6883
Publication E-mail: magazine@support.ucla.edu

General interest magazine with articles based on the research and expertise of the UCLA faculty. **Founded:** 1970. **Freq:** Quarterly. **Print Method:** Offset. **Trim Size:** 8 3/8 x 10 3/4. **Key Personnel:** David Greenwald, Editor, phone (310)794-6852, fax (310)794-6883, davidg@support.ucla.edu. **ISSN:** 1075-2749. **Subscription Rates:** $8 individuals; $2 single issue. **Remarks:** Accepts advertising. **URL:** http://www.urelations.ucla.edu/ucomm/pubs/UCLAMag/. **Formerly**: The UCLA Monthly (1989).
Ad Rates: BW: $4450 **Circ:** 100,000
4C: $5950

2439 Ufahamu
University of California at Los Angeles
10244 Bunche Hall Phone: (310)825-6059
405 Hildegard Ave.
Los Angeles, CA 90024
Journal covering multidisciplinary African studies. **Founded:** 1970. **Freq:** Triennial. **Subscription Rates:** $28 individuals; $11 single issue.
Circ: Combined 300

2440 U.S. Immigration
Publishing and Business Consultants
4427 W. Slauson Ave.
Los Angeles, CA 90043-2717

Magazine containing general information on Visas and Green Cards. **Founded:** 1991. **Freq:** Quarterly. **Print Method:** Web offset. **Trim Size:** 8 1/2 x 11. **Key Personnel:** Atia Napoleon, Editor and Publisher. **ISSN:** 1055-8276. **Subscription Rates:** $26.99; $33.99 other countries. **Remarks:** Accepts advertising.
Ad Rates: BW: $8,290 **Circ:** Paid 100,000
4C: $9,750

2441 University Times
California State University
5151 State University Dr. Phone: (213)343-4215
Los Angeles, CA 90032 Fax: (213)343-5337

Collegiate newspaper. **Founded:** 1948. **Freq:** Semiweekly (Mon. and Thurs.) (during the academic year). **Print Method:** Offset. **Cols./Page:** 6. **Col. Width:** 18 nonpareils. **Col. Depth:** 224 agate lines. **Key Personnel:** Prof. George Taylor, Publisher; Irene Anthony, Advertising Mgr. **Remarks:** Accepts advertising.
Ad Rates: GLR: $4.40 **Circ:** Free ‡9,000
BW: $728.64
4C: $480
PCI: $7.59

2442 URB
1680 N. Vine St., Ste 1012 Phone: (323)993-0291
Los Angeles, CA 90028 Fax: (323)466-1207
Free: (800)872-6249
Publisher E-mail: word2urb@aol.com

Consumer magazine covering hip-hop and dance music. **Founded:** 1990. **Freq:** Bimonthly. **ISSN:** 1081-9924. **Subscription Rates:** $15.95. **Remarks:** Accepts advertising.
Ad Rates: 4C: $3,500 **Circ:** Non-paid 50,000

2443 USC Trojan Family
University of Southern California
Office of Public Communications Phone: (213)740-2684
University Park (KAP 246) Fax: (213)740-1746
Los Angeles, CA 90089-2537
Alumni magazine. Includes reviews of faculty publications. **Founded:** 1970. **Freq:** Quarterly. **Print Method:** Offset. **Trim Size:** 10 1/4 x 13 3/8. **Cols./Page:** 3 and 5. **Col. Width:** 16 1/2 and 10 picas. **Col. Depth:** 70 picas. **Key Personnel:** Susan Heitman, Editor. **ISSN:** 8750-7927. **Subscription Rates:** Free to qualified subscribers. **Remarks:** Advertising accepted; rates available upon request. **Formerly**: Trojan Family; University of Southern California Alumni Review.
Circ: Controlled ‡200,000

2444 Variety
Primedia Publishing
5700 Wilshire Blvd., Ste. 120 Phone: (213)857-6600
Los Angeles, CA 90036 Fax: (213)857-0742

Newspaper (tabloid) reporting on theatre, television, radio, music, records, and movies. **Subtitle:** The International Entertainment Weekly. **Founded:** 1905. **Freq:** Weekly (Mon.). **Print Method:** Heatset. **Trim Size:** 10 3/4 x 14 1/2. **Cols./Page:** 5. **Col. Width:** 11 picas. **Col. Depth:** 196 agate lines. **Key Personnel:** Peter Bart, Editor; Gerry Byrne, Vice President. **ISSN:** 0042-2738. **Subscription Rates:** $129. **Remarks:** Accepts advertising.
Ad Rates: BW: $3,200 **Circ:** Mon. 35,004
4C: $5,000
PCI: $75

2445 Variety's on Production
Cahners Business Newspapers
5700 Wilshire Blvd., Ste. 120 Phone: (213)965-4476
Los Angeles, CA 90036 Fax: (213)857-0742

Magazine covering production and post-production in corporate communications, computer graphics, feature films, commercials, television, special venue films, etc. **Founded:** 1992. **Freq:** Monthly. **Print Method:** Full Web. **Trim Size:** 8 1/8 x 10 7/8. **Cols./Page:** 3. **Col. Width:** 2 1/4 inches. **Col. Depth:** 10 inches. **Key Personnel:** Jerry Brandt, Publisher; Greg Solmar, Editor-in-Chief. **ISSN:** 0044-7625. **Subscription Rates:** $52; $87 other countries (surface mail); $107 other countries (airmail); $6 single issue. **Remarks:** Accepts display advertising. **Formerly**: On Production.
Ad Rates: BW: $2149 **Circ:** Paid ‡200
4C: $3387 Controlled ‡28,000

Ventura Bulletin - See Ventura

2446 Verelk
1327 Pleasant Ave. Phone: (213)267-1740
Los Angeles, CA 90033 Fax: (213)261-0522

Official magazine of the Apostolic Exarchate for Armenian Catholics in the U.S.A. (Armenian and English). **Founded:** 1984. **Freq:** Bimonthly. **Key Personnel:** Rev. Basil Ferhatian, Editor.

2447 Veterinary Clinical Nutrition
Veterinary Practice Publishing Co.
PO Box 57900 Phone: (213)385-2222
Los Angeles, CA 90057 Fax: (213)385-8565

Veterinary medicine journal. Official publication of the American Association for Veterinary Clinical Pathology. **Founded:** 1981. **Freq:** Quarterly. **Print Method:** Offset. **Trim Size:** 8 1/2 x 11. **Cols./Page:** 2. **Col. Width:** 33 nonpareils. **Col. Depth:** 106 agate lines. **Key Personnel:** Nancy A. Bull, Publisher. **Subscription Rates:** $50; $75 other countries. **Remarks:** Accepts advertising.
Ad Rates: BW: $648 **Circ:** 1,500
4C: $825

2448 Veterinary Practice Staff
Veterinary Practice Publishing Co.
PO Box 57900 Phone: (213)385-2222
Los Angeles, CA 90057 Fax: (213)385-8565

Professional magazine covering current ideas and new information in veterinary medicine geared to veterinary support staff. **Subtitle:** The Leading Information Source for Animal Health Care Professionals. **Founded:** 1989. **Freq:** Bimonthly. **Trim Size:** 11 x 13 3/4. **Key Personnel:** Steve Senatore, Advertising Dir., phone (212)302-8080, fax (212)302-8289; Scott McElhaney, Publisher, phone (714)855-8822, fax (714)855-3045; Brian Hutchins, Managing Editor, phone (714)855-8822, fax (714)855-3045, bhutchins@fancypubs.com. **ISSN:** 1047-8639. **Subscription Rates:** $28; Free to qualified subscribers.
Circ: 11,000

2449 Vida Nueva
The Tidings Corp.
3424 Wilshire Blvd., 6th Fl. Phone: (213)637-7360
Los Angeles, CA 90010 Fax: (213)637-6360
Publication E-mail: editorial@vida-nueva.com

Neawspaper. **Founded:** Mar. 1991. **Freq:** Semimonthly. **Cols./Page:** 5. **Key Personnel:** Victor Aleman, Editor. **Subscription Rates:** $25. **Remarks:** Accepts advertising.
Ad Rates: BW: $30 **Circ:** Free 90,541
4C: $530 Paid 31

2450 View
The Burnside Group, Inc.
1950 Sawtelle Blvd., No. 200 Phone: (310)477-0403
Los Angeles, CA 90025 Fax: (310)477-8428

Newspaper. **Freq:** Weekly. **Subscription Rates:** $19. **Formerly**: L.A. Village View.
Circ: Free 57,908
Paid 36

2451 Watts Star Review
Herald Dispatch
4053 Marlton Ave.
Los Angeles, CA 90008

Black community newspaper. **Founded:** 1875. **Freq:** Weekly (Thurs.). **Print Method:** Offset. **Cols./Page:** 6. **Col. Width:** 29 nonpareils. **Col. Depth:** 194 agate lines. **Key Personnel:** Lela Ward Oliver, Editor; John H. Holoman, Publisher. **Subscription Rates:** $20 individuals; $40 out of area. **Remarks:** Accepts advertising.
Ad Rates: GLR: $.80 **Circ:** ‡30,000
BW: $1,890
4C: $2,890
PCI: $15

2452 Wendy
The Harvey Entertainment Co.
1999 Avenue of the Stars, No. 2050 Phone: (310)789-1990
Los Angeles, CA 90067 Fax: (310)789-1991
Comic book. **Freq:** Monthly. **Print Method:** Web offset. **Trim Size:** 6 1/8 x 10 1/8. **Key Personnel:** Sid Jacobson, Editor; Ed Shukin, Director; Kevin S. Bricklin, Director. **Subscription Rates:** $1.50 single issue. **Remarks:** Advertising accepted; rates available upon request. **URL:** http://www.harvey.com.
Circ: (Not Reported)

2453 West Los Angeles Independent
Copley Los Angeles Newspapers, Inc.
7776 Ivanhoe Ave.
La Jolla, CA 92037

Newspaper. **Founded:** 1929. **Freq:** Weekly (Wed.). **Print Method:** Offset. **Cols./Page:** 6. **Col. Width:** 26 nonpareils. **Col. Depth:** 301 agate lines. **Key Personnel:** Bertram Winrow, Publisher. **Subscription Rates:** $24 individuals. **Remarks:** Accepts advertising.
Ad Rates: GLR: $.65 **Circ:** Free 29,300

2454 Westchester Star
Wave Community Newspaper
2621 W. 54th St. Phone: (213)290-3000
Los Angeles, CA 90043 Fax: (213)291-0219

Black community newspaper sold in combination with the Culver City Star and the Inglewood/Hawthorne Wave. **Freq:** Biweekly Wednesday and Saturday. **Cols./Page:** 6. **Col. Width:** 5 nonpareils. **Col. Depth:** 21 1/2 inches. **Key Personnel:** C.Z. Wilson, President, fax (213)292-8289. **Subscription Rates:** $125 by mail.
Circ: Non-paid 9,956

2455 Western HVACR News
Palatrom Publishing Co.
4215 Figueroa St. Phone: (213)225-8034
Los Angeles, CA 90065-3011
Publication E-mail: whvacr@aol.com

A monthly western regional trade newspaper (tabloid) for the heating, ventilation, air conditioning, refrigeration, hydronics, sheet metal, solar and allied industries primarily for 13 Pacific and Mountain States in USA. **Founded:** Jan. 1981. **Freq:** Monthly. **Print Method:** Web offset. **Trim Size:** 11 3/8 x 17 3/8. **Cols./Page:** 5. **Col. Width:** 1 7/8 inches. **Col. Depth:** 15 3/4 inches. **Key Personnel:** J. Mascari, Editor; C. Lyons, Marketing MGR; D. Parker, New Products/Literature Editor.

ISSN: 0273-5687. **Subscription Rates:** $12 individuals; $23 two years; $34 three years.
Ad Rates: BW: $2,400 **Circ:** Paid ‡300
4C: $3,600 Non-paid ‡24,000
PCI: $31

2456 Where Los Angeles
Where Magazine
3679 Motor Ave., Ste. 300 Phone: (310)280-2880
Los Angeles, CA 90034 Fax: (310)280-2890
Publication E-mail: wherela@aol.com

Consumer magazine covering travel and tourism in Los Angeles, CA. **Subtitle:** The City Magazine for Visitors. **Freq:** Monthly. **Subscription Rates:** $36 individuals. **Remarks:** Accepts advertising. **URL:** http://www.wherela.com.
Circ: (Not Reported)

2457 Wilshire Independent
The Los Angeles Independent Newspapers
4201 Wilshire Blvd., No. 600 Phone: (323)932-6397
Los Angeles, CA 90010 Fax: (323)932-8250
Publisher E-mail: LAINgroup@aol.com

Community newspaper. **Subtitle:** Los Angeles Independent Newspaper Group. **Founded:** 1964. **Freq:** Weekly. **Print Method:** Offset. **Trim Size:** 13 1/2 x 22 1/2. **Cols./Page:** 6. **Col. Width:** 2 1/16 inches. **Col. Depth:** 21 inches. **Key Personnel:** Brian Lewis, Editor, fax (323)932-8285; Bruce M. Wood, Publisher, fax (323)932-0884; Michael Manning, Advertising Mgr.; Gwynn Gustafson, Majors. **Subscription Rates:** $80 individuals. **Remarks:** Accepts advertising. **Available Online. URL:** http://www.nminews.com.
Ad Rates: BW: $2,993.76 **Circ:** Combined 33,000
4C: $3,744
SAU: $23.76

2458 Woodworkers West
Goldman Communications
PO Box 66751 Phone: (310)216-9265
Los Angeles, CA 90045 Fax: (310)216-9274
Publication E-mail: editor@woodwest.com

Magazine covering woodworking in the Western U.S. **Founded:** Jan. 1988. **Freq:** Bimonthly. **Print Method:** Web offset. **Trim Size:** 8 1/2 x 11. **Cols./Page:** 2. **Col. Width:** 3 1/2 inches. **Col. Depth:** 9 3/4 inches. **Key Personnel:** Ron Goldman, Publisher. **ISSN:** 1080-0042. **Subscription Rates:** $12 individuals; $2.95 single issue. **Remarks:** Accepts advertising. **URL:** http://www.woodwest.com. **Formerly**: Southern California Woodworker.
Ad Rates: BW: $500 **Circ:** Combined 10,000
4C: $600

2459 The World & Science
Publishing and Business Consultants
4427 W. Slauson Ave.
Los Angeles, CA 90043-2717

Magazine featuring aspects of natural science relating to people and their environment. **Founded:** 1991. **Freq:** Quarterly. **Print Method:** Web offset. **Trim Size:** 8 1/2 x 11. **Key Personnel:** Atia Napoleon, Editor and Publisher. **ISSN:** 1059-9131. **Subscription Rates:** $26.99; $33.99 other countries. **Remarks:** Accepts advertising.
Ad Rates: BW: $8,290 **Circ:** (Not Reported)
4C: $9,750

2460 Written By Magazine
Writers Guild America, West
7000 W 3rd St. Phone: (323)782-4522
Los Angeles, CA 90048 Fax: (323)782-4802
Publication E-mail: writtenby@wga.org

Magazine. **Subtitle:** The Magazine of the Writers Guild. **Founded:** Dec. 1996. **Freq:** 11/year. **Print Method:** Web. **Trim Size:** 8.375 x 10.875. **Key Personnel:** Tara E. McCarthy, Acting Editor. **ISSN:** 1092-468X. **Subscription Rates:** $45 Canada and Mexico; $50 other countries; $20 students with copy of valid student I.D.; $5 single issue. **URL:** http://www.wga.org; http://www.wga.org. **Formerly**: The WGAW Journal (1996).
Ad Rates: BW: $2160 **Circ:** 15,000
4C: $3000

2461 Wyvernwood Chronicle
Eastern Group Publications Inc.
2500 S. Atlantic Blvd., No. A Phone: (213)263-5743
Los Angeles, CA 90040-2004 Fax: (213)263-9169

Hispanic community newspaper (English and Spanish). **Founded:** 1950. **Freq:** Weekly (Thurs.). **Print Method:** Offset. **Trim Size:** 13 x 21. **Cols./Page:** 6. **Col. Width:** 2 1/2 inches. **Col. Depth:** 294 agate lines. **Key Personnel:** Dolores Sanchez, Publisher; John Sanchez, Advertising Mgr. **Subscription Rates:** $90 individuals. **Remarks:** Accepts advertising.
Ad Rates: GLR: $2.50 **Circ:** Paid ‡9
BW: $3,150 Free ‡3,691
4C: $3,570
SAU: $25
PCI: $25

2462 Zoo View
Greater Los Angeles Zoo Association
5333 Zoo Dr. Phone: (213)664-1100
Los Angeles, CA 90027 Fax: (213)662-6879

L.A. Zoo Magazine. **Founded:** 1964. **Freq:** Quarterly. **Print Method:** Web offset. **Trim Size:** 8 1/2 x 11. **Key Personnel:** Claire Peeler, Editor. **ISSN:** 0276-3303. **Subscription Rates:** $7. $2 single issue. **Remarks:** Advertising not accepted.
Circ: Paid 48,000
Non-paid 1,000

2463 Buenavision Cable TV
912 N. Eastern Ave. Phone: (213)269-0391
Los Angeles, CA 90063 Fax: (213)269-8257

Key Personnel: Ben Ochoa, General Mgr. **Cities Served:** subscribing households 6,250; 54 channels; 1 community access channel.

2464 ICN - 18
12401 W. Olympic Blvd. Phone: (310)826-4777
Los Angeles, CA 90064 Fax: (310)447-7906

Format: Commercial TV; Ethnic. **Networks:** Independent. **Owner:** Intercontinental Television Group, Inc., at above address. **Founded:** 1990. **Operating Hours:** Continuous. **ADI:** Los Angeles (Corona & San Bernardino), CA. **Key Personnel:** Brad Probek, Dir. of Sales; Cynthia Marchera, Programming; Rosemary Dannon, Executive Vice Pres./General Manager. **Ad Rates:** $90-250 for 15 seconds; $150-400 for 30 seconds; $300-800 for 60 seconds.

2465 KABC-AM - 790
3321 S. La Cienega Blvd. Phone: (310)840-4900
Los Angeles, CA 90016-3114 Fax: (310)840-4977

Format: Talk. **Networks:** ABC. **Founded:** 1929. **Operating Hours:** Continuous. **ADI:** Los Angeles (Corona & San Bernardino), CA. **Key Personnel:** Bill Sommers, General Mgr.; Karen Hoffman, Contact. **Wattage:** 5000. **Ad Rates:** Advertising accepted; rates available upon request.

2466 KACE-FM - 103.9 & 98.3
610 S. Ardmore Ave. Phone: (213)427-1039
Los Angeles, CA 90005 Fax: (213)380-4214
Free: (800)540-1039

Networks: Independent. **Founded:** 1959. **Operating Hours:** Continuous. **ADI:** Los Angeles (Corona & San Bernardino), CA. **Key Personnel:** Howard Neal, General Mgr., phone (213)251-3103, fax (213)380-8364; Kevin Fleming, Program Dir., phone (213)427-7954, fax (213)386-9027; Chuck Rios, Marketing & Promotions Mgr. **Wattage:** 1650.

2467 KBIG-FM - 104.3
7755 Sunset Blvd. Phone: (213)874-7700
Los Angeles, CA 90046 Fax: (213)874-4276
Free: (800)524-4104
E-mail: kbig104@aol.com

Format: Adult Contemporary. **Networks:** Independent. **Owner:** Bonneville International Corp., 55 N 300 West, PO Box 1160, Salt Lake City, UT 84110-1160, (801)575-7500, Fax: (801)575-7548. **Founded:** 1959. **Operating Hours:** Continuous. **ADI:** Los Angeles (Corona & San Bernardino), CA. **Key Personnel:** Linda Whaley, Dir., Human Resources; Dave Verdery, Music Dir.; Dave Ervin, Program Dir.; Steve Oshin, Vice President; Dennis Martin, Chief Engineer; Karen Rike, Vice. Pres. & Bus. Mgr. **Local Programs:** *Carolyn on K-BIG*, Dave Verdery; *Disco Saturday Night*, Dave Verdery; *Friday Night 80's Party*, Dave Verdery. **Wattage:** 105,000. **URL:** http://www.kbig104.com.

KBLA-AM - See Santa Monica

2468 KCAL-TV - 9
5515 Melrose Ave. Phone: (213)467-9999
Los Angeles, CA 90038 Fax: (213)460-6265

Format: Commercial TV. **Networks:** Independent. **Operating Hours:** Continuous. **ADI:** Los Angeles (Corona & San Bernardino), CA. **Key Personnel:** Hugo S. Rossitter, V.P. and General Counsel; Beth Maharrey, V.P. of News.

2469 KCBS-FM - 93.1
6121 Sunset Blvd. Phone: (213)460-3293
Los Angeles, CA 90028 Fax: (213)463-9270
E-mail: vandyked@la.cbs.com

Format: Classic Rock. **Networks:** Westwood One Radio. **Founded:** 1950. **Formerly**: KNX-FM (1992); KKHR-FM; KODJ-FM. **Operating Hours:** Continuous. **ADI:** Los Angeles (Corona & San Bernardino), CA. **Key Personnel:** Dave Van Dyke, General Mgr., phone (213)460-3201, fax (213)463-9270, vandyked@la.cbs.com; Tommy Edwards, Program Dir., phone (213)460-3657; Kim Kelly, Promotions Dir., phone (213)460-3180; Brad West, General Sales Mgr., phone (213)460-3203, fax (213)460-3497; Jackie Herek, Traffic Mgr., phone (213)460-3141; Lon Landis, News Dir., phone (213)460-3192. **Wattage:** 29,000. **URL:** http://www.arrowfm.com.

2470 KCBS-TV - 2
6121 Sunset Blvd. Phone: (323)460-3000
Los Angeles, CA 90028

Format: Commercial TV. **Networks:** CBS. **Owner:** CBS Corporation, 51 W. 52nd St., New York, NY 10019. **Founded:** 1931. **Formerly**: KNXT; Westinghouse/CBS, Inc. **Operating Hours:** Continuous. **ADI:** Los Angeles (Corona & San Bernardino), CA. **Key Personnel:** Larry Perret, News Dir., phone (323)460-3538, fax (323)460-3733; Garen Vandebeek, Creative Services Dir., phone (323)460-3485; Donna Bean, Controller, phone (323)460-3545. **Ad Rates:** Advertising accepted; rates available upon request. **URL:** http://www.channel2000.com.

2471 KCET-TV - 28
4401 Sunset Blvd. Phone: (213)666-6500
Los Angeles, CA 90027 Fax: (213)665-6067

Format: Public TV. **Networks:** Public Broadcasting Service (PBS). **Operating Hours:** 5:15 a.m.-1 a.m. weekdays; 6 a.m.-2 a.m. Saturday and Sunday. **ADI:** Los Angeles (Corona & San Bernardino), CA. **Key Personnel:** Al Jerome, President/CEO; Donald G. Youpa, Exec VP/COO; Gary Ferrell, Senior VP, Finance & CFO; Nancy Rishagen, Senior VP Development & Marketing; Hlen Bendik, Senior VP/General Counsel; Barbara Goen, VP/Public Information; Horace Scott, VP/Engineering & Operations; Peter Rodriquez, VP/Community & Government Relations; Blaine Baggett, VP/Program Development; Valerie Zavala, VP News & Public Affairs. **Local Programs:** *Life & Times*; *The Puzzle Place*; *Storytime*. **URL:** http://www.keet.org.

2472 KCOP-TV - 13
915 N. La Brea Ave. Phone: (213)851-1000
Los Angeles, CA 90038 Fax: (213)851-4187

Format: Commercial TV. **Networks:** Independent; United Paramount Network. **Founded:** 1948. **Operating Hours:** Continuous. **ADI:** Los Angeles (Corona & San Bernardino), CA. **Key Personnel:** Rick Feldman, V.P./Gen. Mgr. **Local Programs:** *L.A. Kids*, Teresa Garay, Exec. Producer, (213)850-2265; *UPN News 13*, Steve Cohon, News Dir., (213)850-2222, Fax (213)850-1265.

KCPB-FM - See Thousand Oaks

KFAC-FM - See Santa Barbara

2473 KFI-AM - 640
610 S. Ardmore Ave. Phone: (213)385-0101
Los Angeles, CA 90005 Fax: (213)385-7076

Format: Talk. **Founded:** 1922. **Operating Hours:** Continuous. **ADI:** Los Angeles (Corona & San Bernardino), CA. **Key Personnel:** Howard Neal, Contact; David G. Hall, Program Dir.; Mark Austin Thomas. **Wattage:** 50,000.

2474 KFSG-FM - 96.3
1910 W. Sunset Blvd., Ste. 480 Phone: (213)483-5374
Los Angeles, CA 90026-3282 Fax: (213)484-8304

Format: Religious. **Owner:** International Foursquare Church, 1910 W.Sunet Blvd, Los Angeles, CA 90026, (213)484-6010, Fax: (213)413-3824. **Founded:** 1949. **Formerly**: KRKD-FM (1970). **Operating Hours:** Continuous. **ADI:** Los Angeles (Corona & San Bernardino), CA. **Key Personnel:** Alan Bowles, General Mgr.; Paul Gulino, Operations Dir.; George Riggs, Chief Engineer; Richard Taylor, Studio Eng.; Margaret Beatty, Music Dir.; Ruby Kashini, Sales Mgr. **Wattage:** 54,000. **Ad Rates:** $27-35 for 30 seconds; $38-48 for 60 seconds.

2475 KFWB-AM - 980
6230 Yucca St. Phone: (213)462-5392
Los Angeles, CA 90028 Fax: (213)871-4670

Format: News. **Networks:** CNN Radio; AP. **Owner:** Group W Westinghouse Broadcasting Co., 888 7th Ave., New York, NY 10106, (212)307-3000, **Founded:** 1925. **Operating Hours:** Continuous; 30% network, 70% local. **ADI:** Los Angeles (Corona & San Bernardino), CA. **Key Personnel:** Roger Nadel, V. Pres./General Mgr.; Greg Tantum, Exec. Editor/Program Dir.; Crys Quimby, News Dir.; Tim Pohlman, General Sales Mgr.; Joeleen Morgan, Marketing and Promotions Mgr.; Rod Van Hook, Sports Dir. **Wattage:** 5000. **Ad Rates:** Advertising accepted; rates available upon request.

2476 KKBT-FM - 92.3
6735 Yucca St. Phone: (213)466-9566
Hollywood, CA 90028 Fax: (213)466-2592

Format: Urban Contemporary. **Owner:** Evergreen Media Corp., 433 E. Las Colinas, Irving, TX 75039, (214)869-9020. **Founded:** 1948. **Formerly:** KFAC-FM (1989). **Operating Hours:** Continuous. **ADI:** Los Angeles (Corona & San Bernardino), CA. **Key Personnel:** Craig Wilbraham, Contact; Sharon Kramer, Contact; Nancy Leichter, General Sales Mgr.; Nancy Giltner, Contact; Blake Mendenhall, General Sales Mgr.; Cliff Winston, Contact. **Wattage:** 43,000.

2477 KKGO-FM - 105.1
1500 Cotner Ave. Phone: (310)478-5540
PO Box 250028 Fax: (310)478-4189
Los Angeles, CA 90025-3303

Format: Jazz; Classical. **Networks:** Independent. **Founded:** 1959. **Operating Hours:** Continuous. **ADI:** Los Angeles (Corona & San Bernardino), CA. **Key Personnel:** Saul Levine, General Mgr. **Wattage:** 18,000.

2478 KKHJ-AM - 930
5724 Hollywood Blvd. Phone: (213)461-9300
Los Angeles, CA 90028 Fax: (213)461-9946

Format: Ethnic; Hispanic; Talk; News. **Owner:** Liberman Broadcasting, Inc., at above address. **Founded:** 1922. **Formerly:** KRTH-AM. **Operating Hours:** Continuous. **ADI:** Los Angeles (Corona & San Bernardino), CA. **Key Personnel:** Lenard Liberman, Contact. **Wattage:** 5000. **Ad Rates:** Combined advertising rates available with KBUE-FM, KWIZ-FM.

2479 KLCS-TV - 58
1061 W. Temple St. Phone: (213)625-6958
Los Angeles, CA 90012 Fax: (213)481-1019

Format: Public TV. **Networks:** Public Broadcasting Service (PBS). **Owner:** Los Angeles Unified School District, 450 Grand Ave., Los Angeles, CA 90012. **Founded:** 1973. **Operating Hours:** 18 hrs. Daily; 10% network, 90% local. **ADI:** Los Angeles (Corona & San Bernardino), CA. **Key Personnel:** Tom Mossman, General Mgr.; John Russell, Chief Engineer; Sabrina Fair Thomas, Contact; Robert V. Greene, Contact; Peggy Toy, Contact. **Wattage:** 2.1 megawatts.

2480 KLOS-FM - 95.5
3321 S. La Cienega Blvd. Phone: (213)840-4800
Los Angeles, CA 90016 Fax: (213)840-4846

Format: Album-Oriented Rock (AOR). **Networks:** ABC. **Owner:** ABC, Inc., at above address. **Founded:** 1957. **Formerly:** KABC-FM. **Operating Hours:** Continuous. **ADI:** Los Angeles (Corona & San Bernardino), CA. **Key Personnel:** Maureen Lesourd, Pres./General Mgr.; John Duncan, Program Dir.; Louis Chelekis, General Sales Mgr.; Leonard Madrid, Local Sales Mgr.; Leon Clark, National Sales Mgr.; Steve Smith, Promotions; Nel Benton, Community Relations; Laurie Howell, News; Charlotte Cox, Research. **Local Programs:** *Morning Show* 6 a.m. - 1 p.m., Mark Show; *Noontime Nuggets* 12 p.m. - 1 p.m., Randy Maranz; *Talk In Transition* 12 a.m. - 6 a.m., Frank Sontag. **Wattage:** 63,100. **Ad Rates:** Advertising accepted; rates available upon request.

2481 KLSX-FM - 97.1
3580 Wilshire Blvd. Phone: (213)383-4222
Los Angeles, CA 90010 Fax: (213)386-3649
E-mail: realradio.com

Format: Full Service. **Networks:** Independent. **Founded:** 1954. **Formerly:** KHTZ-FM. **Operating Hours:** Continuous. **ADI:** Los Angeles (Corona & San Bernardino), CA. **Key Personnel:** Rich Boerner, A.P.D; Jay Clark, Program Dir/Operations Mgr; Bob Moore, General Mgr.; Beki Gomez, Contact; Rich Connor, Promotions Dir. **Local Programs:** *J.D.; Reg Guys Larry & Erik*, Dan Finder, (213)383-4222; *Riki Rachtman.* **Wattage:** 55,000. **Ad Rates:** Advertising accepted; rates available upon request. **URL:** http://realradio.com.

2482 KMEX-TV - 34
6701 Center Dr. W, 15th Fl. Phone: (310)216-3434
Los Angeles, CA 90045 Fax: (310)348-3597

Format: Hispanic. **Networks:** Univision. **Founded:** 1962. **Operating Hours:** Continuous. **ADI:** Los Angeles (Corona & San Bernardino), CA. **Key Personnel:** Augustine Martinez, General Mgr.; Tom Arnost, Station Mgr.; Jairo Marin, News Dir.; Maria Gutierrez, Public Affairs Dir.

2483 KNX-AM - 1070
6121 Sunset Blvd. Phone: (213)460-3000
Los Angeles, CA 90028-6455 Fax: (213)460-3339

Format: News. **Networks:** CBS. **Founded:** 1920. **Operating Hours:** Continuous. **ADI:** Los Angeles (Corona & San Bernardino), CA. **Key Personnel:** George Nicholaw, V. Pres./General Mgr.; Mike Masterson, General Sales Mgr.; Robert Sims, News Dir. **Local Programs:** *Food News Hour.* **Wattage:** 50,000.

2484 KOST-FM - 103.5
610 S. Ardmore Ave. Phone: (213)427-1035
Los Angeles, CA 90005 Fax: (213)385-0281
Free: (800)929-5678

Format: Adult Contemporary. **Owner:** Cox Broadcasting, Inc., at above address. **Founded:** 1957. **Operating Hours:** Continuous. **ADI:** Los Angeles (Corona & San Bernardino), CA. **Key Personnel:** Howard Neal, Contact; Carol Terakawa, General Sales Mgr.; Jhani Kaye, Contact. **Wattage:** 12,500.

KPSC-FM - See Palm Springs

2485 KRLA-AM - 1110
3580 Wilshire Blvd. Phone: (213)383-4222
Los Angeles, CA 90010 Fax: (213)386-3679

Format: Oldies. **Networks:** Independent. **Owner:** CBS Radio, at above address. **Founded:** 1942. **Operating Hours:** Continuous. **ADI:** Los Angeles (Corona & San Bernardino), CA. **Key Personnel:** Bob Moore, General Mgr.; Ricci Filiar, Program Dir.; Ruth Collander, Public Service Director. **Wattage:** 50,000.

2486 KRTH-AM - 930
5901 Venice Blvd. Phone: (213)937-5230
Los Angeles, CA 90034-1708 Fax: (213)936-3427
E-mail: kearth101@aol.com

Format: Oldies. **Networks:** AP. **Founded:** 1922. **Operating Hours:** Continuous. **ADI:** Los Angeles (Corona & San Bernardino), CA. **Key Personnel:** F. Patrick Duffy, Vice Pres./General Mgr.; Mike Phillips, Program Mgr.; Joni Caryl, News Dir.; Peggy Schiavo, Sales Mgr.; Bob Kanner, Chief Engineer; Joji Dominguez, Business Mgr.; Linda Dinwiddie, Traffic Dir.; Diane Morales, Promotions Dir. **Wattage:** 5000.

2487 KRTH-FM - 101.1
5901 Venice Blvd. Phone: (213)937-5230
Los Angeles, CA 90034 Fax: (213)936-3427

Format: Oldies. **Networks:** Westwood One Radio. **Owner:** Infinity Broadcasting Corp., 600 Madison Ave., New York, NY 10022. **Founded:** 1941. **Operating Hours:** Continuous. **ADI:** Los Angeles (Corona & San Bernardino), CA. **Key Personnel:** F. Patrick Duffy, Contact. **Wattage:** 51 KW.

2488 KSCA-FM - 101.9
1645 N. Vine St., Ste. 200 Phone: (213)860-0480
Los Angeles, CA 90028 Fax: (213)468-5337

Founded: 1951. **Formerly:** KEDG-FM; KLIT-FM. **Operating Hours:** Continuous. **ADI:** Los Angeles (Corona & San Bernardino), CA. **Key Personnel:** Bob Sponseller, Contact, phone (213)468-5238, fax (213)468-9337. **Wattage:** 5000.

2489 KSCI-TV - 18
1990 S. Bundy Dr., Ste. 850 Phone: (310)478-1818
Los Angeles, CA 90025 Fax: (310)479-8118
E-mail: kscitv18@compuserve.com

Format: Ethnic. **Networks:** Independent. **Owner:** International Media Group, at above address. **Founded:** 1976. **Operating Hours:** Continuous. **ADI:** Los Angeles (Corona & San Bernardino), CA. **Key Personnel:** Ray Beindorf, Chairman/CEO, rbeindorf@kscitv.com; Jon Yasuda, President/CEO, jyasuda@kscitv.com; Richard Millet, VP/Station Mgr., rmillet@kscitv.com; Anthony Cortese, CFO, acortese@kscitv.com; Bill Welty, Dir., Engineering, bwelty@kscitv.com. **Ad Rates:** Advertising accepted; rates available upon request.

2490 KTTV-TV - 11
1999 S. Bundy Dr. Phone: (310)584-2000
Los Angeles, CA 90025

Format: Commercial TV. **Networks:** Fox. **Owner:** Fox Television Stations, Inc., at above address. **Founded:** 1949. **Operating Hours:** Continuous. **Key Personnel:** Diana L. Vargas, VP/General Mgr., phone (310)584-2000. **Local Programs:** *Good Day LA* 7 - 9a.m. Monday-Friday, Carol Breshears, Assignment Mgr., (310)584-2022.

2491 KTZN-AM - 710
3321 South La Cienega Blvd. Phone: (310)840-2800
Los Angeles, CA 90016

Format: Eclectic. **Networks:** Independent. **Founded:** 1951. **Formerly:** KMPC-AM. **Operating Hours:** Continuous. **ADI:** Los Angeles (Corona & San Bernardino), CA. **Key Personnel:** Maureen Lesourd, President/General Mgr. **Wattage:** 50,000 day; 10,000 night.

2492 KUSC-FM - 91.5
Box 77913 Phone: (213)514-1400
Los Angeles, CA 90007 Fax: (213)747-9400
E-mail: kusc@kusc.org

Format: Public Radio; Classical. **Networks:** National Public Radio (NPR); Public Radio International (PRI). **Owner:** University of Southern California, University Park, Los Angeles, CA 90007, Fax: (213)747-9400. **Founded:** 1946. **Operating Hours:** Continuous. **ADI:** Los Angeles (Corona & San Bernardino), CA. **Key Personnel:** Brenda Pennell, General Mgr., phone (213)514-1450, fax (213)514-1451, bpennell@kusc.org; James Russell, GM/Market Place, phone (213)514-1500, fax (213)514-4506, jrussell@marketplace.org; Sheila Rue, Program Dir., phone (213)514-1430, fax (214)3514-1431, srue@kusc.org. **Local Programs:** *Afternoon Music*, Steve Lama; *Marketplace*, David Brancaccio, (213)743-6555, Fax (213)747-0684; *The Morning Program*, Steve Lama; *Music 'til Midnight*, Jim Svejda. **Wattage:** 17,000. **Ad Rates:** Noncommercial. **URL:** http://www.kusc.org.

2493 KVCA-AM - 670
123 S. Figueroa St. Phone: (213)628-8700
Los Angeles, CA 90012 Fax: (213)628-1216

Format: Hispanic; Talk. **Owner:** Lotus Oxnard Corp., 6920 Sunset Blvd., Los Angeles, CA 90028. **Operating Hours:** Continuous. **Key Personnel:** John Paley, V. P./General Mgr., fax (213)628-8142; Robert Sanchez, Operations Mgr.

2494 KWHY-TV - 22
5545 Sunset Blvd. Phone: (213)466-5441
Los Angeles, CA 90028 Fax: (213)466-3613

Format: Commercial TV. **Networks:** Independent. **Owner:** Harriscope of Los Angeles, Inc., at above address, (310)477-7724, Fax: (310)477-9646. **Founded:** 1963. **Operating Hours:** 6 a.m.-2 a.m. Mon.-Sat.; 6 a.m.-midnight Sun. **ADI:** Los Angeles (Corona & San Bernardino), CA. **Key Personnel:** Burt I. Harris, Sr., Chief Executive Officer, phone (310)477-7724; Burt I. Harris, Jr., President; Martin J. Dugan, General Mgr., phone (213)993-2200, fax (213)993-2428; David Bergen, Operations Mgr., phone (213)993-220, fax (213)469-1283; Olga Aguilar, Operations Mgr., phone (213)993-2200, fax (213)469-1283; David Zulli, Chief Engineer, phone (213)993-2200, fax (213)469-1283; Germain Valdernama, Sales Mgr./Spanish, phone (213)993-2222, fax (213)993-2295; Casandra Moreno, Dir. of Community Affairs, phone (213)993-2200. **Local Programs:** *Inside City Hall* 12:30 p.m. Thursday, Kevin Apper, News Operation Mgr.; *12 Minutes* every hour Monday-Friday, Linda Miller, Sales Mgr.; *You're on the Line* 2 p.m. Monday-Friday, Linda Miller, Sales Mgr. **Ad Rates:** $150-400 for 30 seconds; $300-800 for 60 seconds.

2495 KXLU-FM - 88.9
7900 Loyola Blvd. Phone: (310)338-2866
Los Angeles, CA 90045 Fax: (310)338-5959

Format: Classical; Jazz; Alternative/New Music/Progressive; News; Public Radio; Ethnic. **Founded:** 1957. **Operating Hours:** Continuous. **ADI:** Los Angeles (Corona & San Bernardino), CA. **Key Personnel:** Clarissa Castaneda, General Mgr.; Shamus Halkowich, Program Dir.; Mike Dinoffria, Music Dir.; John Miller, Chief Engineer; Mary O'Malley, News Dir.; Dave McAdam, Production Dir.; Liz Ohanasien, Sales Dir.; Patrick O'Rourke, Sports Dir. **Local Programs:** *Demolisten*, Fred Kiko; *Noyz Pollution*, Peter Taylor; *Psychotechnics*, Damion Romero. **Wattage:** 3000. **Ad Rates:** Noncommercial.

2496 KZLA-FM - 93.9
7755 Sunset Blvd. Phone: (818)246-0939
Los Angeles, CA 90046 Fax: (818)637-2267

Format: Country. **Networks:** AP. **Founded:** 1980. **Formerly:** KPOL-FM. **Operating Hours:** Continuous. **ADI:** Los Angeles (Corona & San Bernardino), CA. **Key Personnel:** Dave Ervin, General Mgr.; Edward Evans, General Sales Mgr.; John Sebastian, Program Dir.; Marida Petitjean, Promotions Mgr.; Phil Jennrich, News Dir. **Local Programs:** *American Country Countdown*; *Boot Scootin' Saturday Night*; *Garabo & Murphy Show.* **Wattage:** 18,500. **Ad Rates:** Advertising accepted; rates available upon request. **URL:** http://www.kzla.net.

2497 MediaOne
2900 Crenshaw Blvd. Phone: (213)730-9444
Los Angeles, CA 90016 Fax: (213)735-7571

Founded: 1988. **Formerly:** American Cablesystems of South Central Los Angeles; Continental Cable (South Central). **Cities Served:** subscribing households 165,000; 80 channels; 4 community access channels; 140 hours per week community access programming.

XBACH-AM - See Costa Mesa

LOS BANOS, pop. 10,341.

C. CA. Merced Co. 60 mi. NW of Fresno. Creamery.

Diversified farming. Dairying, alfalfa, vegetables, cotton, melons.

2498 Los Banos Enterprise
1253 W. I St. Phone: (209)826-3831
Los Banos, CA 93635 Fax: (209)826-2005
Free: (800)491-8848
Publisher E-mail: lbenterprise@cell2000.net

Community newspaper. **Founded:** 1891. **Freq:** Semiweekly (Wed. and Sat.). **Print Method:** Offset. **Cols./Page:** 6. **Col. Width:** 24 nonpareils. **Col. Depth:** 294 agate lines. **Key Personnel:** Rhonda Lowe, Editor and Publisher; Steve Hartsoe, Managing Editor; Suzanne Palazzo, Advertising Mgr.; Martie Lloyd, Business Mgr. **Subscription Rates:** $30.03 individuals; $17.16 for 6 months. **Remarks:** Accepts advertising.
Circ: Paid ‡4,500
Free ‡7,300

2499 KLBS-AM - 1330
401 Pacheco Blvd. Phone: (209)826-0578
Los Banos, CA 93635 Fax: (209)826-1906
E-mail: klb@cell2000.com

Format: Ethnic. **Founded:** 1961. **Operating Hours:** 18 per day; 100% local. **Key Personnel:** Maria DeLourdes, News Dir.; Linda Thomas, Contact; Jose Joao Encarnacao, General Mgr.; Alvaro Aguiar, Program Dir. **Local Programs:** *Dedications*; *Encontro/Talk Show* 5:00 pm - 6:00 pm Monday-Friday, Jose Joao Encarnacao, (209)826-4996. **Wattage:** 5000. **Ad Rates:** $12 for 30 seconds; $15 for 60 seconds.

LOS GATOS, pop. 53,761.

W. CA. Santa Clara Co. 50 mi. S. of San Francisco. Residential. Wineries. Nurseries. Prunes, appricots, peaches.

2500 Bay Area Parent
Bay Area Publishing Group
401 Alberto Way, Ste. A Phone: (408)358-4159
Los Gatos, CA 95032 Fax: (408)356-4903
Free: (800)666-1514

Up-to-the-minute local parenting information for parents who have children aged 0-early teens. **Founded:** 1982. **Freq:** Monthly. **Print Method:** Web offset. **Trim Size:** 10 1/2 x 13 3/4. **Cols./Page:** 4. **Key Personnel:** Lynn Berardo, Editor; Mary Brence Martin, Managing Editor; Sandy Moeckel, Publisher. **Subscription Rates:** Free. **Remarks:** Accepts advertising.
Ad Rates: BW: $2315 **Circ:** Free 71,899
4C: $650 Paid 325

2501 Los Gatos Weekly-Times
Metro Publishing, Inc.
245 Almendra Ave. Phone: (408)354-3110
Los Gatos, CA 95030 Fax: (408)354-3917

Local newspaper. **Founded:** 1881. **Freq:** Weekly (Wed.). **Print Method:** Offset. **Cols./Page:** 5. **Col. Width:** 2 1/6 inches. **Col. Depth:** 13 1/4 inches. **Key Personnel:** Dale Bryant, Editor; Dan Pulerano, Exec. Editor; David Cohen, Publisher; Scott Levander, Advertising Dir. **Subscription Rates:** $26 individuals. **Remarks:** Accepts advertising. **URL:** http://www.virtualvalley.com. **Formerly**: Los Gatos Weekly; Los Gatos Times Observer.
Ad Rates: GLR: $.85 **Circ:** Controlled 19,509
BW: $972
4C: $1,184.82

2502 Valley Parent
Bay Area Publishing Group
401 Alberto Way, Ste. A Phone: (408)358-4159
Los Gatos, CA 95032 Fax: (408)356-4903
Free: (800)666-1514

Magazine for parents in Central Costra County and the Tri-Valley area of Alameda County, California. **Founded:** 1992. **Freq:** Monthly. **Print Method:** Web. **Trim Size:** 10 1/2 x 13 1/2. **Cols./Page:** 4. **Col. Width:** 2 1/4 inches. **Col. Depth:** 11 3/4 inches. **Key Personnel:** Sandy Moeckel, Publisher; Lynn Berardo, Editor-in-Chief; Mary Brence Martin, Managing Editor. **Subscription Rates:** $12 by mail; Free at newsstands, schools, offices, and libraries. **Remarks:** Accepts advertising.
Ad Rates: BW: $1685 **Circ:** Free 54,346
Paid 401

2503 Writing For Our Lives
Running Deer Press
647 N. Santa Cruz Ave., Annex Phone: (408)354-8604
Los Gatos, CA 95030
Consumer magazine covering women, fiction and poetry. **Founded:** 1992. **Freq:** Semiannual. **Print Method:** Offset. **Trim Size:** 5 1/4 x 8 1/4. **Key Personnel:** Janet M. McEwan, Editor and Publisher. **ISSN:** 1062-3434. **Subscription Rates:** $15.50 individuals; $8 single issue. **Remarks:** Advertising not accepted.
Circ: Paid 500

2504 South Bay Cablevision
151 N. Santa Cruz Ave. Phone: (408)356-5773
Los Gatos, CA 95030 Fax: (408)988-3723

Formerly: Hearst; InterMedia Partners. **Key Personnel:** Keith Relph, General Mgr.; Jon Donney, Executive Assistant. **Cities Served:** Los Gatos, Milpitas, Monte Sereno, Mountain View, Newark, Santa Clara, Saratoga, CA: subscribing households 10,500; 72 channels; 1 community access channel; 168 hours per week community access programming.

LOS OSOS

2505 Rapa Nui Journal
Easter Island Foundation
PO Box 6774 Phone: (805)528-6279
Los Osos, CA 93412-6774 Fax: (805)534-9301
Publication E-mail: rapanui@compuserve.com
Publisher E-mail: 74221.2046@compuserve.com

Professional journal covering Easter Island and East Polynesia history, archaeology, and anthropology. **Subtitle:** The Journal of the Easter Island Foundation. **Founded:** 1986. **Freq:** Quarterly. **Print Method:** Offset. **Trim Size:** 8 1/2 x 11. **Cols./Page:** 2. **Col. Width:** 3 1/2 inches. **Col. Depth:** 10 inches. **Key Personnel:** Georgia Lee, Editor; Antoinette Padgett, Asst. Editor. **ISSN:** 1040-1385. **Subscription Rates:** $30 individuals; $40 other countries. **Remarks:** Advertising not accepted.
Circ: 500

LOYALTON, pop. 1,030.

NE CA. Sierra Co. 42 mi. NW of Reno, NV. Recreation. Sawmills. Gold mining. Cattle.

2506 Sierra Booster
PO Box 8 Phone: (916)993-4379
Loyalton, CA 96118 Fax: (916)993-4379

Local newspaper (tabloid). **Subtitle:** Fortnightly Tabloid Newspaper. **Founded:** Oct. 19, 1949. **Freq:** every other Friday. **Print Method:** Offset. **Trim Size:** 11 1/2 x 13. **Cols./Page:** 6. **Col. Width:** 1 5/8 inches. **Col. Depth:** 12 inches. **Key Personnel:** Hal Wright, Editor and Publisher; Allene Wright, Publisher; Jan Buck, Business Mgr. **USPS:** 495-900. **Subscription Rates:** $10 individuals; $17.50 two years. **Remarks:** Accepts advertising.
Ad Rates: BW: $288 **Circ:** Paid ‡2,26
PCI: $4 Free ‡930

LUCERNE VALLEY, pop. 4,210.

SE CA. San Bernardino Co. 30 mi. NE of San Bernardino. Agriculture. Alfalfa, cattle, fowl. Dairying.

2507 The Leader
Hi-Desert Publishing
Box 299 Phone: (760)248-7878
Lucerne Valley, CA 92356 Fax: (760)248-2042

Community newspaper. **Founded:** 1955. **Freq:** Weekly (Wed.). **Print Method:** Offset. **Cols./Page:** 6. **Col. Width:** 12 2/5 nonpareils. **Col. Depth:** 21 1/2 inches. **Key Personnel:** Bill Ewing, General Mgr. **USPS:** 321-700. **Subscription Rates:** $14.50; $20 out of area; $27.50 out of state. **Formerly**: Lucerne Valley Leader (1990).
Ad Rates: SAU: $7.75 **Circ:** Paid ‡1,550
PCI: $7.35 Free ‡50

LYNWOOD, pop. 48,548.

S. CA. Los Angeles Co. Adjacent to Los Angeles. Residential. Manufactures printing presses, chemicals, steel fabricators, scientific instruments. Machine shops.

2508 Lynwood Journal
Rapid Publishing
349 W. Compton Phone: (213)774-0018
PO Box 4248
Compton, CA 90224
Black community newspaper. **Freq:** Weekly (Wed.). **Cols./Page:** 6. **Col. Width:** 12 1/2 picas. **Col. Depth:** 21 1/2 inches. **Key Personnel:** O. Ray Watkins, Publisher. **Remarks:** Accepts advertising.
Ad Rates: SAU: $10.65 **Circ:** (Not Reported)

2509 Lynwood Press
Wave Community Newspapers, Inc.
2621 W. 54th St. Phone: (213)290-3000
Los Angeles, CA 90043 Fax: (213)291-0219

Black community newspaper. **Founded:** 1919. **Freq:** Semiweekly (Thurs. and Sat.). **Print Method:** Offset. **Trim Size:** 13 3/4 x 21 1/2. **Cols./Page:** 6. **Col. Width:** 5 nonpareils. **Col. Depth:** 21 1/2 inches. **Key Personnel:** C.Z. Wilson, President, fax (213)292-8289. **Subscription Rates:** $125 by mail; Free. **Remarks:** Advertising accepted; rates available upon request.
Circ: 12,500

MADERA†, pop. 21,732.

SC CA. Madera Co. 22 mi. NW of Fresno. Manufactures air conditioners, wrought iron, fiber glass insulation, electronics, oil, lumber mills, wineries, sheet metal works, nursery, hatcheries. Granite quarry. Sugar pine timber. Chinchilla farms.

2510 Madera Tribune
Madera Newspapers, Inc.
100 E. 7th St. Phone: (209)674-2424
PO Box 269 Fax: (209)673-6526
Madera, CA 93638
General newspaper. **Founded:** 1892. **Freq:** Daily (eve.) and Sat. (morn.). **Print Method:** Offset. **Trim Size:** 13 1/2 x 21 in. **Cols./Page:** 6. **Col. Width:** 26 nonpareils. **Col. Depth:** 294 agate lines. **Key Personnel:** Robert Adams, Editor; Larry Womack, Publisher, fax (559)674-0178; Terry Earls, General Manager/Administration, fax (559)674-0470. **Subscription Rates:** $80 carrier; $126 by mail.
Ad Rates: GLR: $1.51 **Circ:** Mon.-Sat. 8,585
BW: $801
4C: $918.20
SAU: $7.85
PCI: $7.85

MALIBU, pop. 17,000.

S. CA. Los Angeles Co. Adjacent to Santa Monica. Residential.

2511 The Graphic Weekly
Pepperdine University
24255 Pacific Coast Hwy. Phone: (310)456-4311
Malibu, CA 90263 Fax: (310)456-4411
Publication E-mail: graphic@pepperdine.edu

Collegiate newspaper. **Founded:** 1937. **Freq:** Weekly (Thurs.). **Print Method:** Offset. **Trim Size:** 13 x 21. **Cols./Page:** 6. **Col. Width:** 2 1/16 inches. **Col. Depth:** 21 inches. **Key Personnel:** Dr. Mike Jordan, Advisor. **Subscription Rates:** Free; $12.50 individuals. **Remarks:** Accepts advertising.
Ad Rates: BW: $875 **Circ:** Free ‡3,000
PCI: $8

2512 HomeCare Magazine
Intertec Publishing Corporation
23815 Stuart Ranch Rd. Phone: (310)317-4522
Malibu, CA 90265 Fax: (310)317-9644
Free: (800)543-4116

Magazine serving home medical equipment suppliers, including independent and chain centers specializing in home care, pharmacies or chain drug stores with home care products, and joint-ventured hospital home health care businesses. Contains industry news and new product launches and marketing strategies. **Subtitle:** For Business Leaders in Home Health Care. **Founded:** 1978. **Freq:** Monthly plus annual buyer's guide. **Print Method:** Offset. **Trim Size:** 8 1/4 x 10 7/8. **Cols./Page:** 3. **Col. Width:** 27 nonpareils. **Col. Depth:** 140 agate lines. **Key Personnel:** Susanne Hopkins, Managing Editor, susanne@miramar.com; Sally Matteson, Group Publisher, sally@miramar.com; Roy Felts, Western Sales Mgr., roy@miramar.com; Alison Dermer, Midwest Sales Mgr., alison@miramar.com; Kim McGraw, Eastern Sales Mgr., mcgraw@miramar.com; Joellen Calice, Southeastern Sales Mgr., joellen@miramar.com. **ISSN:** 0882-2700. **Subscription Rates:** $65 individuals; $75 Canada; $150 other countries. **Remarks:** Accepts advertising. **URL:** http://www.homecaremag.com.
Ad Rates: BW: $3,160 **Circ:** Controlled ‡17,069
4C: $4,005

2513 The Malibu Surfside News
PO Box 903 Phone: (310)457-2112
Malibu, CA 90265-0903 Fax: (310)457-9908
Publication E-mail: newsmalibu@aol.com

Regional newspaper. **Subtitle:** Malibu News and Entertainment Voice. **Founded:** 1974. **Freq:** Weekly (Thurs.). **Print Method:** Offset. **Trim Size:** 10 1/2 x 14. **Cols./Page:** 6. **Col. Width:** 18 nonpareils. **Col. Depth:** 224 agate lines. **Key Personnel:** Anne C.S. Soble, Publisher. **ISSN:** 0191-7307. **Subscription Rates:** $19 individuals; $39 out of area; $100 other countries. **Remarks:** Accepts advertising.
Ad Rates: BW: $790 **Circ:** Paid 4,000
4C: $1,260 Free 8,000
SAU: $10
PCI: $9

2514 The Malibu Times
The Malibu Times, Inc.
PO Box 1127 Phone: (310)456-5507
3864 Las Flores Canyon Rd. Fax: (310)456-8986
Malibu, CA 90265
Publication E-mail: malibunews@malibutimes.com

Weekly Community newspaper. **Founded:** May 1946. **Freq:** Weekly (Thurs.). **Print Method:** Web offset. **Trim Size:** 13 x 20.5. **Cols./Page:** 6. **Col. Width:** 2 1/16 inches. **Col. Depth:** 20.5 inches. **Key Personnel:** Arnold G. York, Editor, agyork@malibutimes.com. **USPS:** 935-020. **Subscription Rates:** $45 individuals. **Remarks:** Accepts advertising. **Available Online. URL:** http://www.malibutimes.com.
Ad Rates: BW: $1,643 **Circ:** ‡12,500
PCI: $13.38

2515 Pacific Coast Philology
Pacific Ancient and Modern Language Association
Department of Humanities Phone: (310)456-4435
Pepperdine University
Malibu, CA 90263-4225
Scholarly journal covering ancient and modern languages. **ISSN:** 0078-7469. **Subscription Rates:** $15 individuals. **Remarks:** Advertising not accepted.
Circ: (Not Reported)

2516 Soaring Spirit
Valley of the Sun Publishing Co.
PO Box 38 Phone: (562)488-7880
Malibu, CA 90265 Fax: (562)488-7870

Magazine covering metaphysical New Age philosophy with complete catalog listing of Valley of the Sun products. **Subtitle:** Tools & Teachings to Create Your Own Reality. **Founded:** 1977. **Freq:** Quarterly. **Print Method:** Offset. **Trim Size:** 6 x 10 1/2. **Cols./Page:** 3. **Col. Width:** 10 picas. **Col. Depth:** 9 5/8 inches. **Key Personnel:** Dick Sutphen, Editor. **Subscription Rates:** Free. **Remarks:** Advertising not accepted. **URL:** http://www.sutphenpublishing.com. **Formerly:** Master of Life (1994); Winners (1996).
Circ: Controlled 150,000

2517 Special Events
Miramar Publishing, div. of Miramar Communications Inc.
23815 Stuart Ranch Rd. Phone: (310)317-4522
PO Box 8987 Fax: (310)317-9644
Malibu, CA 90265-8987
Free: (800)543-4116

Magazine providing ideas for putting on special events and showing how specific events were planned and coordinated. **Subtitle:** The National Magazine for Special Events Professionals. **Founded:** 1982. **Freq:** Monthly. **Print Method:** Sheet fed offset. **Trim Size:** 8 1/4 x 10 7/8. **Cols./Page:** 3. **Col. Width:** 13 1/2 picas. **Col. Depth:** 50 picas. **Key Personnel:** Liese Gardner, Editor; Lisa Vested, Publisher. **Subscription Rates:** Free To the trade. **Remarks:** Accepts advertising.
Ad Rates: BW: $2,890 **Circ:** Controlled 21,595
4C: $3,725 Paid 935

2518 Falcon Cablevision
24955 Pacific Coast Hwy., Ste. A102 Phone: (310)456-8888
Malibu, CA 90265 Fax: (310)456-6283

Owner: Falcon Cable TV, 10900 Wilshire Blvd., 15th Fl., Los Angeles, CA 90024, (310)824-9990. **Founded:** 1984. **Key Personnel:** Charles Barrett, Chief Technician; Renee Byrne, Office Mgr. **Cities Served:** Agoura Hills, Calabasas, Los Angeles, Malibu, Thousand Oaks, Topanga, Woodland Hills, CA: subscribing households 14,500; 54 channels; 2 community access channels; 24 hours per week community access programming.

MAMMOTH LAKES, pop. 4,000.

E. CA. Mono Co. 120 mi. S. of Carson City, NV. Mountain and winter sports resort. Manufactures air pumps, cement and archery products.

2519 Mammoth Times
New Times Publishing, Inc.
452 Old Mammoth Rd. Phone: (760)934-3929
PO Box 3929 Fax: (760)934-3951
Mammoth Lakes, CA 93546
Free: (800)782-0300
Publication E-mail: mamtimes@aol.com; mamtimes@qnet.com; news@mammothtimes.com

Weekly community newspaper. **Subtitle:** Eastern Science Times. **Founded:** 1987. **Freq:** Weekly. **Print Method:** Web offset. **Trim Size:** 10 3/4 x 14 1/2. **Cols./Page:** 4. **Col. Width:** 2 1/4 inches. **Col. Depth:** 13 1/4 inches. **Key Personnel:** Wally Hofmann, Editor, phone (760)934-9464, wally@mammothtimes.com. **Subscription Rates:** Free; $40(mail). **Remarks:** Accepts advertising. **Available Online. URL:** http://www.mammothtimes.com.
Ad Rates: GLR: $1 **Circ:** Free 10,163
BW: $462 Paid 1,271
4C: $612
SAU: $8.50
PCI: $12

2520 Review-Herald
Register Review Publishing Co.
PO Box 110 Phone: (760)934-8544
Mammoth Lakes, CA 93546 Fax: (760)934-7385

Local newspaper. **Founded:** 1863. **Freq:** Weekly (Thurs.). **Print Method:** Offset. **Cols./Page:** 6. **Col. Width:** 12 nonpareils. **Col. Depth:** 294 agate lines. **Key Personnel:** Jay Byrne, Publisher; Laurence Steiner, General Mgr.; Jeffrey Munson, Editor. **Subscription Rates:** $32.18 individuals. **Remarks:** Accepts advertising. **Feature Editors:** Joann Ellebracht, *Entertainment*.
Ad Rates: PCI: $5.95 **Circ:** 5,329

2521 KMMT-FM - 106.5
KMMT Bldg., 2nd Fl. Phone: (619)934-2591
94 Laurel Mountain Rd. Fax: (619)934-2429
PO Box 1284
Mammoth Lakes, CA 93546

Format: Classic Rock. **Networks:** Mutual Broadcasting System. **Owner:** Mammoth Mountain FM Associates, Inc., at above address, (619)934-8888. **Founded:** 1973. **Operating Hours:** Continuous. **Key Personnel:** Dave Digerness, President; Nancy Baker, Station Mgr. **Wattage:** 25,000. **Ad Rates:** $12 for 30 seconds; $14 for 60 seconds.

MANHATTAN BEACH, pop. 31,542.

S. CA. Los Angeles Co. 15 mi. SW of Los Angeles. Residential.

2522 Lepidopterists Society Journal
Allen Press
1900 John St.
Manhattan Beach, CA 90266

Professional journal covering the study of insects (butterflies and moths). **Founded:** 1947. **Freq:** Quarterly. **Key Personnel:** Dr. M.D. Bowers, Editor; Ron Leuschner, Publishing Mgr. **ISSN:** 0024-0966. **Subscription Rates:** $35 individuals U.S.; $40 other countries; $50 institutions. **Remarks:** Advertising not accepted.
Circ: Paid 1,700

MANTECA, pop. 24,925.

C. CA. San Joaquin Co. 12 mi. S. of Stockton. Manufactures electronic components. Wineries. Diversified farming.

2523 Manteca Bulletin
Morris Newspaper Publishing
531 E. Yosemite Ave. Phone: (209)239-3531
PO Box 912 Fax: (209)239-1801
Manteca, CA 95336
Newspaper with a Republican orientation. **Founded:** 1908. **Freq:** Mon.-Sun. (morn.). **Print Method:** Offset. **Trim Size:** 13 1/2 x 22 3/4. **Cols./Page:** 8. **Col. Width:** 20 nonpareils. **Col. Depth:** 294 agate lines. **Key Personnel:** Karen Kopecki-Hodges, Editor; Darell Phillips, Publisher. **Subscription Rates:** Free; $72 by mail. **Remarks:** Accepts advertising.
Ad Rates: SAU: $7.90 **Circ:** Mon.-Sat. ★6,946
PCI: $5.56 Sun. ★7,065

MARCH AIR FORCE BASE

2524 The Beacon
The Valley Times
452 AMW Phone: (909)655-4130
March Air Force Base, CA 92518 Fax: (909)655-4113
Newspaper published for personnel of March Air Reserve Base. **Founded:** 1940. **Freq:** Weekly (Fri.). **Print Method:** Offset. **Trim Size:** 11 1/4 x 13 3/4. **Cols./Page:** 5. **Col. Width:** 24 nonpareils. **Col. Depth:** 182 agate lines. **Key Personnel:** Matt Proielti, Editor, phone (909)655-4137, matthew.proelti@riv.afrc.af.mil. **Subscription Rates:** $15 individuals. **Remarks:** Accepts advertising.
Ad Rates: GLR: $7.50 **Circ:** Free 9,100
BW: $485.50
4C: $240
SAU: $8.50

MARINA DEL REY, pop. 11,000.

S. CA. Los Angeles Co. 13 mi. SW of Los Angeles. Residential. Recreation and tourist areas. Small craft harbor.

2525 The Argonaut
The Argonaut Inc.
PO Box 11209 Phone: (310)822-1629
Marina del Rey, CA 90295-7209 Fax: (310)821-8029

Community newspaper. **Founded:** Nov. 25, 1971. **Freq:** Weekly (Thurs.). **Print Method:** Offset. **Cols./Page:** 5. **Col. Width:** 25 nonpareils. **Col. Depth:** 224 agate lines. **Key Personnel:** David Asper Johnson, Editor and Publisher; Joe Pan, Advertising Dir. **Subscription Rates:** $110 individuals first class mail; $85 third class mail. **Remarks:** Accepts advertising.
Ad Rates: BW: $1,872 **Circ:** Paid 21
4C: $2,337 Free 33,104
PCI: $23.40

2526 Candy World Illustrated
Lott Publishing Co.
PO Box 9669 Phone: (310)397-4217
Marina del Rey, CA 90295 Fax: (310)397-4217
Free: (800)359-4554

Confectionery trade magazine. **Founded:** 1968. **Freq:** 3/year. **Print Method:** Offset. **Cols./Page:** 3 and 2. **Col. Width:** 27 and 42 nonpareils. **Col. Depth:** 13 inches. **Key Personnel:** Davis Lott, Publisher. **Subscription Rates:** $12 individuals 3x/yr; $6 single issue. **Remarks:** Accepts advertising.
Ad Rates: BW: $250 **Circ:** Paid ‡500
Non-paid ‡1,500

2527 Cigar Tobacco
Lott Publishing Co.
PO Box 9669 Phone: (310)397-4217
Marina del Rey, CA 90295 Fax: (310)397-4217
Free: (800)359-4554

Trade magazine for merchandisers of tobacco products, sundries, and other new products. **Founded:** Jan. 1968. **Freq:** 3/year. **Print Method:** Offset. **Trim Size:** 11 x 14 1/2. **Cols./Page:** 2 and 3. **Col. Width:** 39 and 60 nonpareils. **Col. Depth:** 13 inches. **Key Personnel:** Davis Lott, Editor and Publisher. **Subscription Rates:** $18 individuals 3x/yr; $6 single issue. **Remarks:** Accepts advertising. **Formerly:** Snack/Sundries/Tobacco World (1988); Tobacco and Sundries World (1989); American Buyer's Review.
Ad Rates: BW: $250 **Circ:** Paid ‡300
PCI: $20 Non-paid ‡1,700

2528 Cracker/Snack World
Lott Publishing Co.
PO Box 9669 Phone: (310)397-4217
Marina del Rey, CA 90295 Fax: (310)397-4217
Free: (800)359-4554

Trade journal for the snacks and deli industries. **Founded:** 1988. **Freq:** Triennial. **Print Method:** Offset. **Trim Size:** 11 x 14 1/2. **Cols./Page:** 2 and 3. **Col. Width:** 39 and 60 nonpareils. **Col. Depth:** 13 inches. **Key Personnel:** Davis Lott, Editor and Publisher. **Subscription Rates:** $12; $6 single issue. **Remarks:** Accepts advertising. **Formerly:** Snacks and Gum Wares (1989); Snacks 'n' Deli World (1991).
Ad Rates: BW: $198 **Circ:** Paid ‡500
PCI: $20 Controlled ‡1,500

2529 HR/PC
DGM Associates
Box 10639 Phone: (310)578-1428
Marina del Rey, CA 90295-6639 Fax: (310)578-1357
Publisher E-mail: dgm@usa.net

Professional magazine covering information technology for human resources management. **Founded:** Oct. 1985. **Freq:** Quarterly. **Key Personnel:** David G. Mahal, Contact. **ISSN:** 0884-9129. **Subscription Rates:** $127 individuals. **Remarks:** Accepts advertising. **URL:** http://www.hrworld.com.
Circ: (Not Reported)

2530 Lott's 3—in—1 Buyer's Guide
Lott Publishing Co.
PO Box 9669 Phone: (310)397-4217
Marina del Rey, CA 90295 Fax: (310)397-4217
Free: (800)359-4554

Features three trade tabliods in one: Tobacco World, Cigar World, and Candy World. **Founded:** 1968. **Freq:** Triennial. **Print Method:** Offset. **Trim Size:** 11 x 14 1/2. **Cols./Page:** 2 and 3. **Col. Width:** 39 and 60 nonpareils. **Col. Depth:** 13 inches. **Key Personnel:** Davis Lott, Editor and Publisher. **Subscription Rates:** $8 individuals 3x/yr; $6 single issue. **Remarks:** Accepts advertising. **Formerly:** Chocolate and Nut World.
Ad Rates: BW: $198 **Circ:** Paid ‡300
PCI: $20 Controlled ‡1,700

2531 Respiratory Therapy Products
CurAnt Communications, Inc.
4676 Admiralty Way, Ste. 202 Phone: (310)306-2206
Marina del Rey, CA 90292 Fax: (310)301-8101
Publication E-mail: rtmag@aol.com

Trade magazine serving as a buyer's guide for the respiratory care practitioner. **Founded:** Dec. 1993. **Freq:** 2/year. **Print Method:** Web offset. **Trim Size:** 8 3/8 x 10 7/8. **Key Personnel:** Michelle Danner, Editor; Tony Ramos, Publisher. **ISSN:** 1068-963X. **Subscription Rates:** Free. **Remarks:** Accepts advertising.
Ad Rates: BW: $2,500 **Circ:** Controlled 30,000
4C: $2,925

2532 Storyette Magazine
Lott Publishing Co.
PO Box 9669 Phone: (310)397-4217
Marina del Rey, CA 90295 Fax: (310)397-4217
Free: (800)359-4554

Magazine of short stories. **Founded:** 1983. **Freq:** Quarterly. **Print Method:** Offset. **Cols./Page:** 1. **Col. Width:** 48 nonpareils. **Col. Depth:** 3 inches. **Key Personnel:** Davis Lott, Editor and Publisher. **Subscription Rates:** $10 individuals. **Remarks:** Accepts advertising.
Ad Rates: BW: $500 **Circ:** Non-paid ‡10,000
PCI: $30

2533 Western Association News
Schneider Publishing Co.
13274 Fiji Way, 4th Fl. Phone: (310)577-3700
Marina del Rey, CA 90292 Fax: (310)577-3715
Publisher E-mail: info@schneiderpublishing.com

Magazine containing management and meeting plan information for association executives and meeting planners. **Subtitle:** The Independent Magazine for Associations. **Founded:** 1976. **Freq:** Monthly. **Print Method:** Offset. **Trim Size:** 8 1/2 x 11. **Cols./Page:** 3. **Col. Width:** 13.5 picas. **Col. Depth:** 10 inches. **Key Personnel:** Timothy Schneider, Editor and Publisher, tim@schneiderpublishing.com; Sandi Kaczmarek, Assoc. Publisher, sandi@schneiderpublishing.com; Ann Shepphird, Managing Editor, ann@schneiderpublishing.com. **ISSN:** 1062-5771. **Subscription Rates:** $48 individuals. **Remarks:** Accepts advertising.
Ad Rates: BW: $2,415 **Circ:** Controlled ‡9,242
4C: $3,450

MARIPOSA†, pop. 8,243.

C. CA. Mariposa Co. 6 mi. N. of Fresno. Tourist. Lumber. Mining. Cattle.

2534 Gazette Mountain Life
Mariposa Gazette
PO Box 38 Phone: (209)966-2500
Mariposa, CA 95338 Fax: (209)966-3384
Publication E-mail: gazette@yosemite.net

Free shopper. **Founded:** 1980. **Freq:** Weekly (Tues.). **Print Method:** Offset. **Trim Size:** 21 1/2. **Cols./Page:** 6. **Col. Width:** 12.5 picas. **Col. Depth:** 21 1/2 inches. **Key Personnel:** R. D. Tucker, Pub./Gen. Mgr. **Remarks:** Accepts advertising. **Formerly:** Poise 'n Oak.
Ad Rates: BW: $820 **Circ:** Paid ‡5,100
4C: $1,160
PCI: $12.75

2535 Mariposa Gazette and Miner
Mariposa Gazette
PO Box 38 Phone: (209)966-2500
Mariposa, CA 95338 Fax: (209)966-3384
Publication E-mail: gazette@yosemite.net

Community newspaper. **Founded:** 1854. **Freq:** Weekly (Thurs.). **Print Method:** Offset. **Cols./Page:** 6. **Col. Width:** 12 1/2 picas. **Col. Depth:** 21 1/2 inches. **Key Personnel:** R. D. Tucker, Pub./Gen. Mgr. **Subscription Rates:** $18.54 individuals; $.50 single issue. **Remarks:** Accepts advertising. **Alt. Formats:** CD-ROM.
Ad Rates: BW: $1,000 **Circ:** Paid ‡5,300
4C: $1,340
PCI: $12.75

2536 The Mariposa Guide
PO Box 2105 Phone: (209)966-3888
Mariposa, CA 95338 Fax: (209)742-6896

Local legally adjudicated paper. **Freq:** Weekly. **Key Personnel:** Jim Heth, Editor and Publisher.

MARTINEZ, pop. 22,582.

W. CA. Contra Costa Co. On Strait of Carquinez, 20 mi. by water NE of San Francisco. Boat connections. Oil refineries. Copper smelter. Wineries. Chemicals, valves.

2537 Martinez News-Gazette
Gibson Publications, Inc.
615 Estudillo St. Phone: (510)228-6400
Martinez, CA 94553 Fax: (707)643-1706

Community newspaper covering local news. **Founded:** 1858. **Freq:** 3/week Tues -Sat. (morn.). **Print Method:** Offset. **Cols./Page:** 6. **Col. Width:** 12 picas. **Col. Depth:** 21 inches. **Key Personnel:** Robert V. Osmond, Editor. **Subscription Rates:** $48 individuals; $84 by mail. **Remarks:** Accepts advertising.
Ad Rates: GLR: $.20 **Circ:** Paid ❑2,856
PCI: $6.80 Free ❑10,344

MARYSVILLE†, pop. 9,898.

NC CA. Yuba Co. On Feather River, 50 mi. N. of Sacramento. Yuba College. Fruit canning and drying; quick freezing plant, logging, welding, boat works. Manufactures fishing tackle, trailers, gunstocks; Fruit, dairying, cattle raising.

2538 Appeal Democrat
Freedom Communications Inc.
1530 Ellis Lake Dr. Phone: (916)741-2345
PO Box 431 Fax: (916)741-1195
Marysville, CA 95901-4269
Free: (800)831-2345

General newspaper. **Founded:** 1860. **Freq:** Daily (eve.) and Sat. (morn.). **Print Method:** Offset. **Cols./Page:** 6. **Col. Width:** 26 nonpareils. **Col. Depth:** 294 agate lines. **Key Personnel:** Milt Carland, Editor; Robert C. Hardie, Publisher; Clau de Lathrop, Sales/Mktg. Dir. **Subscription Rates:** $90 individuals; $114 by mail. **Remarks:** Accepts advertising.
Ad Rates: GLR: $1 **Circ:** Mon.-Sat. ★21,202
BW: $1,770.30 Sun. ★21,761
4C: $2,155.30
PCI: $14.05

2539 CoverStory
Appeal Democrat
1530 Ellis Lake Dr. Phone: (530)741-2345
Marysville, CA 95901 Fax: (530)741-1195
Free: (800)831-2345
Publication E-mail: appeal@syix.com

TMC product. **Founded:** 1982. **Freq:** Weekly (Wed.). **Print Method:** Offset. **Trim Size:** 14 x 22 1/2. **Cols./Page:** 6. **Col. Width:** 26 nonpareils. **Col. Depth:** 294 agate lines. **Key Personnel:** M. Olaf Frandsen, Asst. Publisher, fax (530)741-1061; Robert C. Hardie, Publisher, fax (530)741-1061; David Kugelman, Advertising Mgr. **Remarks:** Accepts advertising. **Formerly:** Metro Shopper.
Ad Rates: BW: $838.50 **Circ:** Free ‡29,000
4C: $1,183.50
PCI: $6.50

2540 KMYC-AM - 1410
Box 631 Phone: (916)742-5555
Marysville, CA 95901-0631 Fax: (916)741-3758

Format: Eclectic. **Founded:** 1947. **Formerly:** KRFD-AM. **Operating Hours:** 6 a.m.-midnight. **Key Personnel:** Jeff Holden, General Mgr. **Wattage:** 5000. **Ad Rates:** Advertising accepted; rates available upon request.

2541 KSXX-FM - 99.9
Box 631 Phone: (916)742-5555
Marysville, CA 95901 Fax: (916)741-3758

Format: Album-Oriented Rock (AOR). **Founded:** 1947. **Formerly:** KRFD-FM. **Operating Hours:** Continuous. **Key Personnel:** Jeff Holder, General Mgr. **Wattage:** 50,000.

MENDOCINO

2542 Mendocino Beacon
PO Box 225 Phone: (707)937-5874
Mendocino, CA 95460 Fax: (707)937-0825
Publication E-mail: mendocinobeacon@mcn.org

Community newspaper. **Founded:** 1877. **Freq:** Weekly (Thurs.). **Print Method:** Offset. **Cols./Page:** 6. **Col. Width:** 78.6 picas. **Col. Depth:** 129 picas. **Key Personnel:** Katherine Lee, Editor, phone (707)964-5642, fax (707)964-0424; Sharon Brewer, Publisher, phone (707)964-5642, fax (707)964-0424. **Subscription Rates:** $22 individuals; $30 out of area. **Remarks:** Accepts advertising.
Ad Rates: GLR: $5.55 **Circ:** Thurs. ⊕2,278
BW: $690.15
4C: $1,040.15
PCI: $5.35

2543 KMFB-FM - 92.7
14200 Prairie Way Phone: (707)964-4653
Mendocino, CA 95460-9720 Fax: (707)964-3299

Format: Oldies; Eclectic. **Networks:** Satellite Radio. **Owner:** Mendocino Broadcasting, Co., at above address. **Founded:** 1966. **Operating Hours:** Continuous; 65% network, 35% local. **ADI:** San Francisco-Oakland-San Jose. **Key Personnel:** Geroge Anderson, General Mgr.; Lindy Peters, Sports Dir.; Fred Colby, News Dir.; Rick O'Shea, Music Dir. **Local Programs:** *B-Side Herself*, Liz Helenchild, (707)964-5307, Fax (707)964-3299; *Lindy Peters Show*, Lindy Peters, (707)964-5307, Fax (707)964-3299; *News with Ed Kowas*, Ed Kowas, (707)964-5307, Fax (707)964-3299. **Wattage:** 3000. **Ad Rates:** $8-12 for 30 seconds; $12-15 for 60 seconds. Combined advertising rates available with KPMO-AM.

MENLO PARK, pop. 25,673.

W. CA. San Mateo Co. 1 mi. NW of Palo Alto. St. Patrick's Seminary (men). Stanford Research Institute. Residential. Electronics manufactured.

2544 AI Magazine
American Association for Artificial Intelligence
445 Burgess Dr. Phone: (650)328-3123
Menlo Park, CA 94025-3496 Fax: (650)321-4457
Publication E-mail: aimagazine@aaai.org
Publisher E-mail: info@aaai.org

Magazine about artificial intelligence. **Founded:** 1980. **Freq:** Quarterly. **Print Method:** Offset. **Trim Size:** 8 3/8 x 10 7/8. **Cols./Page:** 3. **Col. Width:** 13 1/2 picas. **Col. Depth:** 54 picas. **Key Personnel:** David Leake, Editor; David M. Hamilton, Publications Dir.; Carol Hamilton, Exec. Dir. **ISSN:** 0738-4602. **Subscription Rates:** $50 U.S.; $75 other countries. **Remarks:** Accepts advertising. **URL:** http://www.aaai.org/publications/magazine/magazine.html.
Ad Rates: BW: $1,500 **Circ:** 10,000
4C: $2,300

2545 Country Almanac
3525 Alameda de las Pulgas
Menlo Park, CA 94025
Publication E-mail: calmanac@netcom.com

Newspaper. **Subtitle:** Menlo Park's Country Almanac. **Founded:** 1923. **Freq:** Weekly (Wed.). **Print Method:** Offset. **Cols./Page:** 5. **Col. Width:** 11.5 picas. **Col. Depth:** 197 agate lines. **Key Personnel:** Tom Gibboney, Editor and Publisher, phone (415)854-2626 ext. 222; Connie Cotton, Advertising Dir., phone (415)854-2626 ext. 233. **ISSN:** 0192-0111. **Subscription Rates:** $25 individuals; $30 out of area. **Remarks:** Accepts advertising.
Ad Rates: GLR: $0.56 **Circ:** Free ‡17,500
BW: $1,287
4C: $1,617
PCI: $15.85

2546 Gentry Magazine and Northern California Home & Design
18 Media inc.
618 Santa Cruz Ave. Phone: (650)324-1818
Menlo Park, CA 94025 Fax: (650)324-1888
Publication E-mail: editorial@18media.com

Consumer magazine covering San Francisco people, community, and homes. **Founded:** Jan. 1, 1993. **Freq:** Bimonthly 8/year. **Print Method:** Web. **Key Personnel:** Stefanie Lingle, Editor, slingle@18media.com; Dan Oden, Production Mgr., doden@18media.com. **Subscription Rates:** $32 individuals; $4 single issue. **Remarks:** Accepts advertising.
Ad Rates: 4C: $2,995 **Circ:** Non-paid ‡32,500
Non-paid ‡51,500

2547 The Pharos
Alpha Omega Alpha Honor Medical Society
525 Middlefield Rd., Ste. 130 Phone: (415)329-0291
Menlo Park, CA 94025 Fax: (415)329-1618

Scholarly journal featuring non-technical articles on broad aspects of medicine, including history, ethics, medical care, and education. **Founded:** Jan. 1938. **Freq:** Quarterly. **Trim Size:** 8 1/2 x 11. **Cols./Page:** 3. **Col. Width:** 2 1/4 inches. **Col. Depth:** 8 1/4 inches. **Key Personnel:** Edward D. Harris Jr., M.D., Editor, eharris@alphaomegaalpha.org; Helen H. Glaser, M.D., Managing Editor and Associate Editor. **ISSN:** 0031-7179. **Subscription Rates:** Included with membership. **Remarks:** Advertising not accepted. **URL:** http://www.pharos.org.
Circ: Controlled 70,000

2548 Sunset Magazine
Sunset Publishing Corp.
80 Willow Rd. Phone: (415)321-3600
Menlo Park, CA 94025 Fax: (415)321-0551
Free: (800)227-7346

Magazine covering western homes, gardens, food and travel (5 regional editions). **Subtitle:** The Magazine of Western Living. **Founded:** 1898. **Freq:** Monthly. **Print Method:** Letterpress and offset. **Trim Size:** 8 x 10 3/4. **Cols./Page:** 3. **Col. Width:** 27 nonpareils. **Col. Depth:** 140 agate lines. **Key Personnel:** Rosalie Muller-Wright, Editor; Stephen Seabolt,

President; Anthony Glaves, Publisher. **ISSN:** 0039-5404. **Subscription Rates:** $24 individuals; $3.50 single issue. **Remarks:** Accepts advertising. **Online:** CompuServe Information Service. **Alt. Formats:** CD-ROM; CD-ROM.
Ad Rates: BW: $40,400 **Circ:** Paid ★1,458,702
4C: $56,000

MERCED†, pop. 36,499.

C. CA. Merced Co. 55 mi. N. of Fresno. Manufactures pharmaceuticals. Dairy products cannery. Nurseries. Pine timber, diversified farming, alfalfa, peaches sweet potatoes, tomatoes, walnuts, almonds, rice. Cattle.

2549 Merced Sun-Star
U.S. Media, Inc.
3033 N. G St. Phone: (209)722-1511
PO Box 739 Fax: (209)384-2226
Merced, CA 95340
General newspaper. **Founded:** 1869. **Freq:** Mon.-Sat. (morn.). **Print Method:** Offset. **Cols./Page:** 6. **Col. Width:** 26 nonpareils. **Col. Depth:** 294 agate lines. **Key Personnel:** Vern Williams, Managing Editor; Tom Schmitt, Publisher; Jim McClenehan, Advertising Mgr.; Sue Devine, Business Mgr. **Subscription Rates:** $85.80 individuals. **Remarks:** Accepts advertising.
Ad Rates: GLR: $1.42 **Circ:** Mon.-Fri. ★17,105
BW: $2,511.18 Sat. ★19,161
4C: $2,833.18
SAU: $17.46
PCI: $18.08

2550 The Signal
3033 N. G St. Phone: (209)358-6431
Merced, CA 95340 Fax: (209)357-2968
Publication E-mail: atwsignal@cell2000.net

Local newspaper. **Founded:** May 11, 1911. **Freq:** Weekly (Wed.). **Print Method:** Offset. **Trim Size:** 13 x 21 1/2. **Cols./Page:** 6. **Col. Width:** 12 picas. **Col. Depth:** 294 agate lines. **Key Personnel:** David J. Wickenhauser, Editor, phone (209)722-1511; Tom Schmitt, Publisher, phone (209)722-1511, fax (209)384-2221; Sue Devine, Business Mgr., phone (209)722-1511.
Ad Rates: PCI: $9 **Circ:** Free ‡1,500

2551 KABX-FM - 97.5
PO Box 717 Phone: (209)723-2191
Merced, CA 95341 Fax: (209)383-2950

Format: Oldies. **Networks:** Satellite Music Network. **Founded:** 1975. **Formerly:** KMYT-FM (1989). **Operating Hours:** Continuous. **ADI:** Fresno-Visalia (Hanford), CA. **Key Personnel:** Edward Hoyt, General Mgr.; Pat Mullins, Station Mgr.; Jenny West, Program Dir. **Local Programs:** *Morning Show with Dave and Jenny.* **Wattage:** 50,000. **Ad Rates:** Advertising accepted; rates available upon request. KYOS-AM. **Additional Contact Info: Studio:** 1744 G St., Merced, CA 95340.

2552 KAMB-FM - 101.5
90 E. 16th St. Phone: (209)723-1015
Merced, CA 95340 Fax: (209)723-1945
E-mail: kamb@elite.net

Format: Religious; Contemporary Christian. **Networks:** Moody Broadcasting; SkyLight Satellite; Ambassador Inspirational Radio. **Founded:** 1967. **Formerly:** Good News Radio (1994). **Operating Hours:** Continuous. **Key Personnel:** Tim Land, General Mgr., timkamb@elite.net. **Local Programs:** *Conference Highlights*, Mark Murdock, (209)723-1015, Fax (209)723-1945; *Inside Look*, Dave Benton, (209)723-1015, Fax (209)723-1945. **Wattage:** 1,850. **Ad Rates:** Noncommercial. **URL:** http://cwebpages.com/kamb.

2553 KUBB-FM - 96.3
510 W 19th St. Phone: (209)383-7900
PO Box 429 Fax: (209)723-8461
Merced, CA 95341

Format: Country; Agricultural. **Networks:** Westwood One Radio. **Owner:** Buckley Broadcasting, at above address. **Founded:** 1977. **Operating Hours:** Continuous; 25% network, 75% local. **Key Personnel:** Lee Nye, V. Pres./General Mgr., Inyeiamerica online, inc.com; Jon Wailin, Program Dir.; Mike McAdam, Sales Mgr. **Wattage:** 50,000. **URL:** http://www.kubb.com.

2554 KYOS-AM - 1480
PO Box 717 Phone: (209)723-2191
Merced, CA 95341 Fax: (209)383-2950

Format: News; Talk. **Networks:** ABC; Mutual Broadcasting System. **Founded:** 1936. **Operating Hours:** Continuous. **ADI:** Fresno-Visalia (Hanford), CA. **Key Personnel:** Jenny West, PD; Edward Hoyt, General Mgr. **Local Programs:** *The Mid-Day Report* 12noon-1p.m., Michael McGauly; *The Morning Report* 6-9a.m., Michael McGauly. **Wattage:** 5000. **Ad Rates:** Advertising accepted; rates available upon request. $15-30 per unit. Combined advertising rates available with KABX-FM.

MI WUK VILLAGE

2555 Meyerhoff Cable Systems Inc.
Box 340 Phone: (209)586-7622
Mi Wuk Village, CA 95346

Key Personnel: Rich Meyerhoff, General Mgr. **Cities Served:** County of Tolumne, CA.

MIDDLETOWN, pop. 900.

N. CA. Lake Co. 30 mi. NE of Santa Rosa. Summer resort. Quicksilver mine. Agriculture. Barley, pears, walnuts. Livestock. Cattle, quarter horses.

2556 Middletown Times Star
Middletown Times
21168 Calistoga St. Phone: (707)987-3602
PO Box 608 Fax: (707)987-3901
Middletown, CA 95461
Community newspaper (tabloid). **Founded:** 1886. **Freq:** Weekly (Thurs.). **Print Method:** Offset. **Trim Size:** 13 x 21. **Cols./Page:** 6. **Col. Width:** 12 picas. **Col. Depth:** 294 agate lines. **Key Personnel:** Teresa Sanders, Editor and Publisher. **Subscription Rates:** $17 individuals; $20 Out of county. **Remarks:** Accepts advertising. **Formerly:** Times-Star (1992).
Ad Rates: GLR: $0.17 **Circ:** ‡3,000
PCI: $7

MIDWAY CITY

2557 American Cocker Magazine
Premiere Publications
14531 Jefferson St. Phone: (714)893-0053
Midway City, CA 92655 Fax: (714)893-5085

Consumer magazine covering the breeding and exhibiting of Cocker Spaniels. **Founded:** May 1981. **Freq:** Quarterly. **Print Method:** Offset. **Trim Size:** 8 1/4 x 10 3/4. **Cols./Page:** 3. **Col. Width:** 2 1/4 inches. **Col. Depth:** 9 3/4 inches. **Key Personnel:** Michael Allen, Editor. **ISSN:** 0279-358X. **Subscription Rates:** $30 individuals; $8 single issue. **Remarks:** Accepts advertising.
Ad Rates: BW: $155 **Circ:** Controlled 3,980
4C: $550

2558 The Royal Spaniels
Premiere Publications
14531 Jefferson St. Phone: (714)893-0053
Midway City, CA 92655 Fax: (714)893-5085

Consumer magazine covering the breeding and exhibiting of show dogs of the breeds, Cavalier King Charles Spaniels and King Charles Spaniels. **Founded:** 1955. **Freq:** Quarterly. **Print Method:** Offset. **Trim Size:** 8 1/4 x 10 3/4. **Cols./Page:** 3. **Col. Width:** 2 1/4 inches. **Key Personnel:** Michael Allen, Editor. **ISSN:** 1096-0759. **Subscription Rates:** $45 individuals; $13 single issue. **Remarks:** Accepts advertising.
Ad Rates: BW: $145 **Circ:** Combined 3,745
4C: $550

MILL VALLEY, pop. 12,967.

W. CA. Marin Co. On Richardson Bay, 14 mi. N. of San Francisco. Nurseries. Creamery, hardware manufactured. Residential. Dairy, grain farms.

2559 Pacific Sun
21 Corte Madera Ave. Phone: (415)383-4500
Mill Valley, CA 94941 Fax: (415)383-4159
Publication E-mail: letters@mail.pacificsun.com
Publisher E-mail: psun@aol.com

Community newspaper. **Subtitle:** Alternative Newsweekly. **Founded:** 1963. **Freq:** Weekly (Wed.). **Print Method:** Offset. **Trim Size:** 11 3/8 x 15. **Cols./Page:** 4. **Col. Width:** 2 1/4 inches. **Col. Depth:** 13 1/2 inches. **Key Personnel:** Stephen McNamara, Editor and Publisher. **ISSN:** 0048-2641. **Subscription Rates:** Free; $25 out of area. **Remarks:** Accepts advertising.
Ad Rates: GLR: $1.69 **Circ:** Paid 227
BW: $1,360 Free 47,382
4C: $1,860
PCI: $14.96

2560 Vestkusten
237 Ricardo Rd. Phone: (415)381-5149
Mill Valley, CA 94941-2517 Fax: (415)381-9664
Publisher E-mail: vestkust@well.com

Ethnic newspaper (tabloid) (Swedish and English). **Founded:** Oct. 6, 1886. **Freq:** Semimonthly. **Print Method:** Offset. **Trim Size:** 14. **Cols./Page:** 5. **Col. Width:** 2 inches. **Key Personnel:** Bridget Stromberg-Brink, Managing Editor; Lena Sivik, Sales & Marketing. **ISSN:** 1073-6883. **Subscription Rates:** $25 individuals; $50 Sweden; $1.35 single issue. **Remarks:** Color advertising not accepted.
Ad Rates: PCI: $7 **Circ:** Paid ‡1,800
Free ‡400

MILLBRAE, pop. 20,058.

W. CA. San Mateo Co. 16 mi. S. of San Francisco. Light industry. Residential.

2561 Millbrae Sun
Fuchs Publications
824 Cowan Rd. Phone: (415)692-9406
Burlingame, CA 94010-1205 Fax: (415)692-7587

Community newspaper. **Founded:** 1935. **Freq:** Weekly (Wed.). **Print Method:** Offset. **Cols./Page:** 8. **Col. Width:** 21 nonpareils. **Col. Depth:** 294 agate lines. **Key Personnel:** Tim Donohue, Editor; Jerry Fuchs, Publisher; Ellen Fuchs, Publisher. **Subscription Rates:** $12 individuals. **Remarks:** Accepts advertising.
Ad Rates: GLR: $.69 **Circ:** Paid 1,441
BW: $1,661.52 Free 17,824

2562 Pennisula Reporter
Reporter Publications
1791 Vancroft Ave. Phone: (415)931-5778
San Francisco, CA 94124 Fax: (415)931-0214

Local newspaper covering Millbrae. **Founded:** 1923. **Freq:** Semiweekly (Wed. and Sat.). **Print Method:** Offset. **Trim Size:** 13 x 21 1/2. **Cols./Page:** 6. **Col. Width:** 2 1/16 inches. **Col. Depth:** 21.5 picas. **Key Personnel:** Charles E. Belle, Editor, phone (415)391-2030, fax (415)391-2527; John Hart Clinton, Jr., Publisher; Larry Boline, Advertising Mgr. **Subscription Rates:** Free. **Remarks:** Accepts advertising. **Formerly:** Recorder Progress.
Ad Rates: BW: $1,606.05 **Circ:** Paid 27
4C: $1,906.05 Free 7,473
SAU: $12.45

MILPITAS, pop. 37,820.

W. CA. Santa Clara Co. 5 mi. N. of San Jose. Manufactures electric transformers, batteries, industrial water. Auto assembly plant. Agriculture. truck crops.

2563 Milpitas Post
59 Marylinn Dr. Phone: (408)262-2454
Milpitas, CA 95035-4311 Fax: (408)763-9710
Publication E-mail: thepost@cwo.com

Local newspaper. **Founded:** 1955. **Freq:** Weekly (Wed.). **Print Method:** Offset. **Cols./Page:** 5. **Col. Width:** 2 1/16 inches. **Col. Depth:** 13 1/4 inches. **Key Personnel:** Rob Divincenzi, Editor; Mort Levine, Publisher; Deana Melen, Advertising Mgr. **Subscription Rates:** $20 individuals. **Remarks:** Accepts advertising.
Ad Rates: GLR: $1.65 **Circ:** Paid 3,050
BW: $718.15 Free 15,300
4C: $1,000
PCI: $23.10

MISSION VIEJO, pop. 45,000.

S. CA. Orange Co. 4 mi. NE of San Juan Capistrano. Residential.

2564 Aliso Viejo News
South County News
PO Box 3629 Phone: (714)768-3631
Mission Viejo, CA 92691 Fax: (949)454-7354

Community newspaper. **Freq:** Weekly (Wed.). **Key Personnel:** Ray Ellis, Circulation Mgr. **Subscription Rates:** $49.
Circ: Controlled 3,997
Paid 2,100

2565 Barter News
PO Box 3024 Phone: (949)831-0607
Mission Viejo, CA 92690 Fax: (949)831-9378
Publisher E-mail: barter@fea.net

Trade magazine covering bartering information. **Founded:** 1980. **Freq:** Quarterly. **Print Method:** Sheetfed offset. **Trim Size:** 8 1/4 x 10 1/4. **Cols./Page:** 3. **Col. Width:** 2 3/8 inches. **Col. Depth:** 9 1/4 inches. **Key Personnel:** Robert Meyer, Editor and Publisher. **ISSN:** 1092-3608. **Subscription Rates:** $40 individuals; $10 single issue. **Remarks:** Accepts advertising.
Ad Rates: BW: $3,000 **Circ:** Controlled 30,000
4C: $5,000

Capistrano Valley News - See San Juan Capistrano

Dana Point News - See Dana Point

2566 Dogs USA
Fancy Publications
PO Box 6050 Phone: (949)855-8822
Mission Viejo, CA 92690 Fax: (949)855-3045
Free: (800)365-4421

Consumer magazine covering puppies for buyers and owners. **Freq:** Annual. **Key Personnel:** Betty Liddick, Editorial Dir.; Trish Hamm, Circulation Dir. **ISSN:** 0895-5581. **Remarks:** Accepts advertising. **URL:** http://www.animalnetwork.com.
Circ: (Not Reported)

2567 Equine Athlete
Thoroughbred Times Co. Inc.
PO Box 6050 Phone: (949)855-8822
Mission Viejo, CA 92690 Fax: (949)855-3045
Publication E-mail: equineathlete@fancypubs.com

Equine magazine covering sports medicine. **Founded:** 1988. **Freq:** Bimonthly. **Print Method:** Offset. **Trim Size:** 8 1/4 x 10 7/8. **Key Personnel:** Moira Harris, Editor, mharris@fancypubs.com. **ISSN:** 1047-8620. **Subscription Rates:** $19.95 U.S.; $25.20 Canada; $33.95 other countries. **Remarks:** Accepts advertising. **URL:** http://www.equineathlete.com.
Ad Rates: BW: $1,295 **Circ:** 12,000
4C: $2,120

Flight Jacket - See Camp Pendleton

Laguna Beach News - See Laguna Beach

Laguna Niguel News - See Laguna Niguel

2568 Large Animal Practice
Veterinary Practice Publishing
PO Box 6050 Phone: (714)855-8822
Mission Viejo, CA 92690 Fax: (714)855-3045
Free: (800)365-4421

Magazine for food, animal, and equine veterinarians. **Subtitle:** Covering Health & Nutrition. **Founded:** 1945. **Freq:** Bimonthly. **Print Method:** Offset. **Trim Size:** 8 x 10 3/4. **Cols./Page:** 2 and 3. **Col. Width:** 3 3/8 and 2 1/8 inches. **Col. Depth:** 140 and 140 agate lines. **Key Personnel:** Peggy Horkan, Editor, phorkan@fancypubs.com; Norman Ridker, Publisher. **ISSN:** 1092-7603. **Subscription Rates:** $36 individuals; $8 single issue. **Remarks:** Accepts advertising. **Formed by the merger of:** Large Animal Veterinarian; Agri-Practice.
Ad Rates: BW: $3,170 **Circ:** Paid 356
4C: $4,370 Non-paid 15,758

Leisure World News - See Laguna Hills

2569 Medical Industry Information Report
Nicholas Communications, Inc.
26012 Marguerite Pkwy., Ste. 344 Phone: (949)580-0230
Fax: (949)580-0231
Mission Viejo, CA 92692
Publication E-mail: 102367.2521@compuserve.com
Publisher E-mail: nickinfo@ix.netcom.com

Magazine covering information, issues, products, and new techniques within the medical products and pharmaceutical industry. **Subtitle:** Sources, Strategies, and Technologies for Information-based Professionals. **Founded:** Nov. 1, 1995. **Freq:** Bimonthly. **Print Method:** Web offset. **Trim Size:** 8 x 10 7/8. **Key Personnel:** Peggy L. Pargoff, Publisher, ppargoff@ix.netcom.com; Mary Ann Rudnick, Assoc. Editor. **ISSN:** 1084-4392. **Subscription Rates:** Free to qualified subscribers; $48; $75 out of country; $10 for back issues.
Ad Rates: BW: $3,150 **Circ:** Controlled 16,500
4C: $4,000

Rancho Santa Margarita News - See Rancho Santa Fe

2570 Reptiles
Fancy Publications
PO Box 6050 Phone: (949)855-8822
Mission Viejo, CA 92690 Fax: (949)855-3045
Free: (800)365-4421

Consumer magazine covering reptile and amphibian care. **Freq:** Monthly. **Key Personnel:** Phil Samuelson, Editor. **ISSN:** 1068-1965. **Subscription Rates:** $27.97 individuals. **Remarks:** Accepts advertising.
Circ: Paid 62,000

2571 Saddleback Valley News
South Orange County News
PO Box 3629 Phone: (714)768-3631
Mission Viejo, CA 92690 Fax: (714)454-7354

Community newspaper. **Founded:** 1968. **Freq:** Semiweekly (Wed. and Fri.). **Print Method:** Offset. **Cols./Page:** 5. **Col. Width:** 12 1/16 inches. **Col. Depth:** 13 inches. **Key Personnel:** Sherrie Good, Editor; Mike Weaver, Publisher; Pat Norton, Advertising Dir. **Subscription Rates:** $16.25 individuals. **Remarks:** Accepts advertising.
Ad Rates: PCI: $32.17 **Circ:** ‡53,411

San Clemente News - See San Clemente

2572 Thoroughbred Times
Thoroughbred Times Co. Inc.
PO Box 6050 Phone: (949)855-8822
Mission Viejo, CA 92690 Fax: (949)855-3045
Publication E-mail: letters@thoroughbredtimes.com

Subtitle: A Weekly Newsmagazine of Thoroughbred Racing. **Founded:** 1985. **Freq:** Weekly. **Print Method:** Heat set. **Trim Size:** 11 x 14 3/4. **Cols./Page:** 5. **Col. Width:** 1 7/8 inches. **Col. Depth:** 13 3/4 inches. **Key Personnel:** Mark Simon, Editor. **ISSN:** 0887-2244. **Subscription Rates:** $84; $3.95 single issue. **Remarks:** Accepts advertising. **URL:** http://www.thoroughbredtimes.com.
Ad Rates: BW: $2,000 **Circ:** Paid ★22,512
4C: $2,900

2573 The Toastmaster
Toastmasters International, Inc.
PO Box 9052 Phone: (714)858-8255
Mission Viejo, CA 92690 Fax: (714)858-1207
Free: (800)993-7732

Magazine covering leadership, communication and public speaking. **Founded:** 1932. **Freq:** Monthly. **Print Method:** Offset. **Trim Size:** 8 1/4 x 10 7/8. **Cols./Page:** 3. **Col. Width:** 27 nonpareils. **Col. Depth:** 133 agate lines. **Key Personnel:** Suzanne Frey, Editor, sfrey@toastmasters.org. **ISSN:** 0040-8263. **Subscription Rates:** $36 members. **Remarks:** Accepts advertising. **Alt. Formats:** Audio tape.
Ad Rates: BW: $959 **Circ:** 170,000
4C: $1,488.10

2574 KSBR-FM - 88.5
28000 Marquerite Pkwy. Phone: (949)582-5727
Mission Viejo, CA 92692

Format: Jazz; Blues. **Networks:** AP. **Owner:** South Orange County Community College District, at above address. **Founded:** 1979. **Operating Hours:** Continuous; 5% network, 95% local. **Key Personnel:** Terry Wedel, Operations Dir.; Dawn Kamber, News Dir., phone (714)582-4508; Mark Schiffelbein, Chief Engineer, phone (949)582-4882. **Wattage:** 600. **URL:** http://www.saddleback.cc.ca.us/events/ksbr/.

MODESTO†, pop. 106,105.

C. CA. Stanislaus Co. 94 mi. SE of San Francisco. Frozen foods, canning and packing plants. Meat, poultry, dairy products, olive oil, crates, dehydrators, chemicals, wine manufactured. Diversified farming. Peaches, walnuts, almonds.

2575 The Modesto Bee
McClatchy Newspapers, Inc.
1325 H St. Phone: (209)578-2351
Modesto, CA 95354 Fax: (209)578-2207

General newspaper. **Founded:** 1884. **Freq:** Mon.-Sun. (morn.). **Print Method:** Flexography. **Cols./Page:** 6. **Col. Width:** 26 nonpareils. **Col. Depth:** 297 agate lines. **Key Personnel:** Sanders LaMont, Editor-in-Chief; Cheryl Ebright, Advertising Dir.; Judy Sly, Asst. Mng. Editor; Mark Vasche, Managing Editor; Jim Lawrence, Graphics Editor. **Subscription Rates:** $126 individuals. **Remarks:** Accepts advertising. **Available Online. Feature Editors:** Ted Benson, *Photo*; Brian Clark, *Sports*; Dave Hill, *Weekend*; Tom Holliday, *Sports*; Alvie Lindsay, *Financial/Business*; Larry McSwain, *Editorials*; Ed Willhide, *News*.
Ad Rates: GLR: $3.36 **Circ:** Mon.-Sat. ★83,144
BW: $6,447.42 Sun. ★90,435
4C: $7,047.42
PCI: $51.17

2576 KATM-FM - 103.3
1581 Cummins Dr., No. 135 Phone: (209)523-7756
Modesto, CA 95358-6402 Fax: (209)522-2061

Format: Country. **Owner:** Citadel Communications Corp., at above address. **Founded:** 1958. **Formerly:** KBEE-AM (1983). **Operating Hours:** Continuous. **ADI:** Sacramento-Stockton, CA. **Key Personnel:** Bill Betts, V.P./Gen. Mgr.; Ed Hill, Program Dir.; Ryn Stephens, News; Joanne Rea, Business Mgr. **Wattage:** 50,000. **Ad Rates:** Advertising accepted; rates available upon request.

2577 KBEE-AM - 970
1581 Cummins Dr., No. 135 Phone: (209)523-7756
Modesto, CA 95358 Fax: (209)522-2061

Format: Big Band/Nostalgia. **Owner:** Citadel Communicatins Corp., at above address. **Founded:** 1962. **Operating Hours:** Continuous. **ADI:** Sacramento-Stockton, CA. **Key Personnel:** Bill Betts, V.P./Gen. Mgr.; Ryn Stephens, News Dir.; Joanne Rea, Business Mgr. **Wattage:** 1000. **Ad Rates:** Advertising accepted; rates available upon request.

KCIV-FM - See Mount Bullion

2578 KFIV-AM - 1360
Box 1360 Phone: (209)545-5585
Modesto, CA 95353 Fax: (209)545-5587

Format: Talk; News. **Networks:** ABC. **Founded:** 1950. **Formerly:** KASH-AM. **Operating Hours:** Continuous; 80% network, 20% local. **Key Personnel:** Gary L. Halladay, Contact; Thom Reinstein, Operations Dir. **Local Programs:** *Gary Dietrich Show*, Gary Dietrich. **Wattage:** 5000. **Ad Rates:** $35 per unit.

2579 KHOP-FM - 95.1
1581 Cummins Dr., Ste. 135 Phone: (209)572-0104
Modesto, CA 95358-6402 Fax: (209)572-1931

Format: Album-Oriented Rock (AOR). **Owner:** Citadel Communications Corp., at above address. **Founded:** 1949. **Operating Hours:** Continuous. **Key Personnel:** Larry Wilson, President; Bill Betts, General Mgr.; Dave Taylor, Program Dir. **Local Programs:** *Generation U*, Lorene Condron, Mailing contact; *Sproat*, Deana Rica, Mailing contact. **Wattage:** 29,500. **Ad Rates:** Advertising accepted; rates available upon request.

2580 KJAX-AM - 1280
Box 1360 Phone: (209)545-5585
Modesto, CA 95353 Fax: (209)545-5587

Format: News; Sports; Talk. **Networks:** ABC. **Founded:** 1947. **Formerly:** KXOB-AM; KJOY-AM. **Operating Hours:** Continuous. **ADI:** Sacramento-Stockton, CA. **Key Personnel:** Joel Gamble, General Mgr.; A. Wilson, Sales Mgr.; Nadine Livesey, Traffic Mgr.; Theresa Ries, Office Mgr.; Scott Thomas, Program Dir. **Wattage:** 1000. **Ad Rates:** Advertising accepted; rates available upon request.

2581 KJSN-FM - 102.3
3600 Fisk Rd., No. 2B Phone: (209)545-5585
PO Box 3408 Fax: (209)545-5587
Modesto, CA 95356

Format: Adult Contemporary. **Networks:** Independent. **Founded:** 1977. **Formerly:** KFIV-FM (1991). **Operating Hours:** Continuous. **Key Personnel:** Gary Halladay, General Mgr.; Gary Michaels, Program Dir.; Joe Kelly, Music Dir.; Tim St. Martin, News Dir.; Rick Myers, General Sales Mgr. **Wattage:** 6000.

2582 KOSO-FM - 93.1
2121 Lancey Dr., Ste. 1 Phone: (209)551-1306
Modesto, CA 95355-3000 Fax: (209)551-1359

Format: Adult Contemporary. **Networks:** AP. **Founded:** 1966. **Operating Hours:** Continuous. **Key Personnel:** Jim Krebsbach, General Mgr.; Jerri Matoza, General Sales Mgr. **Wattage:** 50,000 ERP. **Ad Rates:** $20-52 for 60 seconds.

2583 KRVR-FM - 105.5
961 N. Emerald Ave., Ste. A Phone: (209)544-1055
Modesto, CA 95351

Format: Jazz. **Owner:** Threshold Communications, at above address. **Founded:** Jan. 1, 1995. **Operating Hours:** Continuous. **Key Personnel:** Jim Bryan, General Mgr.; Doug Wulff, Operations Mgr.; Warren Groeschel, Sales Mgr. **Wattage:** 6000. **Ad Rates:** $28 for 60 seconds. **URL:** http://www.krvr.com.

2584 KTRB-AM - 860
1192 Norwegian Ave. Phone: (209)526-8600
Modesto, CA 95350 Fax: (209)578-3568

Format: Ethnic; Hispanic. **Owner:** Bessie Pappas, at above address. **Founded:** 1933. **Operating Hours:** Continuous. **ADI:** Sacramento-Stockton, CA. **Key Personnel:** Gerald Moore, General Mgr. **Local Programs:** *A Calzon Quitado (The Naked Truth)*, Juan Andres; *El Mundo De Avelar (Avelar's World)*, Prof. Francisco Avelar; *Naturismo y Salud (Nature and Your Health)*, Dr. Jaime Cuevas. **Wattage:** 50,000. **Ad Rates:** $25-100 per unit.

2585 KUVS-TV - 19
2842 Iowa Ave. Phone: (209)578-1900
Modesto, CA 95358 Fax: (209)527-2129

Format: Commercial TV. **Networks:** Univision. **Founded:** 1966. **Formerly:** KCSO-TV. **Operating Hours:** Continuous; 60% network, 40% local. **ADI:** Sacramento-Stockton, CA. **Key Personnel:** Jorge Delgado, General Mgr., phone (916)614-1939, fax (916)614-1902; Lisa Mark, Operations Mgr., phone (916)614-1949, fax (916)614-1907; Chuck Tifft, Chief Engineer.

2586 Post-Newsweek Cable
1639 Princeton Ave. Phone: (209)577-3456
Modesto, CA 95352 Fax: (209)529-6636

Founded: 1969. **Formerly**: CAP Cities; Cablecom. **Key Personnel:** Kenneth Berns, General Mgr.; Richard Lang, Marketing Mgr.; Barbara Etrick, Advertising Sales Mgr.; Michael Monroe, Production Mgr. **Cities Served:** subscribing households 53,000; 78 channels; 40 community access channels; 2 hours per week community access programming.

MOJAVE, pop. 2,800.

S. CA. Kern Co. 58 mi. SE of Bakersfield. Residential. Industry. Mining. Aviation.

2587 Falcon Cable TV
15713 K St. Phone: (805)824-4782
Mojave, CA 93501 Fax: (805)824-4383
Free: (800)347-4565

Owner: Falcon Cable, 10866 Wilshire Blvd., Los Angeles, CA 90024. **Key Personnel:** Neal Niemond, General Mgr. **Cities Served:** Boron, CA.

MONROVIA, pop. 30,531.

S. CA. Los Angeles Co. 17 mi. NE of Los Angeles. Tourism. Manufactures chemicals, electronics, furniture, hardware. Dairy products.

2588 Health Freedom News
National Health Federation
212 W. Foothill Blvd. Phone: (626)357-2181
PO Box 688 Fax: (626)303-0642
Monrovia, CA 91017-0688
Consumer magazine. **Subtitle:** Journal of the National Health Federation. **Founded:** 1955. **Freq:** Monthly (July/Aug issues combined). **Trim Size:** 8 3/8 x 10 7/8. **Cols./Page:** 2. **Key Personnel:** James F. Scheer, Editor. **Subscription Rates:** $36 nonmembers; $48 other countries. **Remarks:** Accepts advertising.
Ad Rates: BW: $800 **Circ:** 15,633
4C: $1,000

2589 Skinned Knuckles
SK Publications
175 May Ave. Phone: (626)358-6255
Monrovia, CA 91016
Consumer magazine covering automobile restoration. **Subtitle:** A Journal of Car Restoration. **Founded:** 1976. **Freq:** Monthly. **Trim Size:** 8 1/2 x 11. **Cols./Page:** 2. **Key Personnel:** Terry Cannon, Editor and Publisher. **ISSN:** 0164-3509. **Subscription Rates:** $18 individuals; $2 single issue. **Remarks:** Accepts advertising.
Circ: Paid 7,500

MONTCLAIR, pop. 22,628.

SE CA. San Bernardino Co. 3 mi. N. of Ontario. Residential.

2590 The Montclarion
Hill Newspapers
6208 LaSalle Ave. Phone: (510)339-8777
Oakland, CA 94611-2804 Fax: (510)339-6101

Newspaper. **Founded:** 1944. **Freq:** Weekly (Tues.). **Print Method:** Offset. **Cols./Page:** 8. **Col. Width:** 20 nonpareils. **Col. Depth:** 301 agate lines. **Key Personnel:** Belinda Taylor, Editor; W.A. Chip, Publisher; Bill Brown, Publisher; Nancy King, Advertising Mgr. **Subscription Rates:** $15 individuals. **Remarks:** Accepts advertising.
Ad Rates: GLR: $.60 **Circ:** Paid 6,099
Free 15,419

MONTEBELLO, pop. 52,929.

S. CA. Los Angeles Co. 3 mi. SE of Los Angeles. Iron and brass foundries, aircraft parts, plastics. Oil wells. Truck farm.

Alhambra Post Advocate - See Alhambra

Bell Gardens Review - See Bell Gardens

Bell/Maywood/Cudahy Industrial Post - See Bell

Downey Herald American - See Downey

2591 Eagle Rock Sentinel
Wave Community Newspapers
819 W. Whitter Blvd. Phone: (213)727-1117
Montebello, CA 90640-3623 Fax: (213)727-9515

Community newspaper. **Freq:** Semiweekly (Wed. and Sat.). **Trim Size:** 6 x 21 1/2. **Cols./Page:** 6. **Col. Depth:** 21 inches. **Key Personnel:** Arthur J. Aguilar, Executive editor/Publisher. **Subscription Rates:** Free; $125 yr/mailed.
Circ: Wed. 8,600
Sat. 8,600

East Los Angeles Commerce Tribune - See East Los Angeles

2592 Eastside Journal
Wave Community Newspapers
819 W. Whitter Blvd. Phone: (213)727-1117
Montebello, CA 90640-3623 Fax: (213)727-9515

Community newspaper. **Freq:** Weekly. **Trim Size:** 6 x 21 1/2. **Cols./Page:** 6. **Col. Depth:** 21 inches. **Key Personnel:** Arthur J. Aguilar, Exec. Editor/Publisher, fax (213)292-8289. **Subscription Rates:** Free local; $125 by mail yearly. **Remarks:** Advertising accepted; rates available upon request.
Circ: Controlled 16,075

2593 El Sereno Star
Wave Community Newspapers
819 W. Whitter Blvd. Phone: (213)727-1117
Montebello, CA 90640-3623 Fax: (213)727-9515

Newspaper. **Founded:** 1949. **Freq:** Semiweekly (Wed. and Sat.). **Print Method:** Letterpress. **Trim Size:** 6 x 21 1/7. **Cols./Page:** 6. **Col. Width:** 22 nonpareils. **Col. Depth:** 21 inches. **Key Personnel:** Arthur Aguilar, Executive editor & Publisher. **Subscription Rates:** Free local; $125 yr/mailed.
Circ: Paid 250
Free 7,400

2594 Highland Park News-Herald and Journal
Urban Newspapers of Los Angeles
819 W. Whitter Blvd. Phone: (213)727-1117
Montebello, CA 90640 Fax: (213)727-9515

Community newspaper. **Freq:** Weekly. **Trim Size:** 6 x 21 1/2. **Cols./Page:** 6. **Col. Depth:** 21 inches. **Key Personnel:** Arthur J. Aguilar, Excutive editor/Publisher. **Subscription Rates:** Free; $15. **Remarks:** Advertising accepted; rates available upon request.
Circ: Wed. 15,250
Sat. 14,850

Huntington Park Bulletin - See Huntington Park

2595 Lincoln Heights Bulletin-News
Wave Community Newspapers
819 W. Whitter Blvd. Phone: (213)727-1117
Montebello, CA 90640-3623 Fax: (213)727-9515

Community newspaper. **Freq:** Semiweekly (Wed. and Sat.). **Trim Size:** 6 x 21 1/2. **Cols./Page:** 6. **Key Personnel:** Arthur J. Aguilar, Exec. Editor/Publisher. **Subscription Rates:** Free; $15. **Remarks:** Advertising accepted; rates available upon request.
Circ: Wed. 9,125
Sat. 9,125

2596 Montebello Comet
Eastern Group Publications Inc.
2500 S. Atlantic Blvd., No. A Phone: (213)263-5743
Los Angeles, CA 90040-2004 Fax: (213)263-9169

Hispanic community newspaper (English and Spanish). **Founded:** 1974. **Freq:** Weekly (Thurs.). **Print Method:** Offset. Uses mats. **Trim Size:** 13 x 21 1/2. **Cols./Page:** 6. **Col. Width:** 2 1/16 inches. **Col. Depth:** 294 agate lines. **Key Personnel:** Dolores Sanchez, Publisher; John Sanchez, Advertising Mgr. **Subscription Rates:** $92 individuals. **Remarks:** Accepts advertising.
Ad Rates: GLR: $1.08 **Circ:** Paid ‡47
BW: $382 Free ‡10,000
4C: $814
SAU: $28
PCI: $28

Monterey Park Progress - See Monterey Park

2597 Mount Washington Star-Review
Wave Community Newspapers
819 W. Whitter Blvd. Phone: (213)727-1117
Montebello, CA 90640-3623 Fax: (213)727-9515

Community newspaper. **Freq:** Semiweekly (Wed. and Sat.). **Trim Size:** 6 x 21 1/2. **Cols./Page:** 6. **Key Personnel:** Arthur J. Aguiler., Exec. Editor/Publisher, fax (213)292-8289. **Subscription Rates:** Free; Local- $125/yr. mailed. **Remarks:** Advertising accepted; rates available upon request.
Circ: Controlled 5,135

2598 News-Herald and Journal
Wave Community Newspapers
819 W. Whitter Blvd. Phone: (213)727-1117
Montebello, CA 90640-3623 Fax: (213)727-9515

Community newspaper. **Founded:** 1905. **Freq:** Semiweekly (Wed. and Sat.). **Print Method:** Letterpress. **Cols./Page:** 6. **Col. Width:** 21 1/2 nonpareils. **Key Personnel:** Arthur J. Aguilar, Exec. Editor/Publisher. **Subscription Rates:** Free; $125 by mail. **Remarks:** Advertising accepted; rates available upon request.
Circ: (Not Reported)

Norwalk Herald American - See Norwalk

Paramount/Bellflower Herald American - See Paramount

Pico Rivera/Santa Fe Springs News - See Pico Rivera

Rosemead/South San Gabriel Progress - See Rosemead

2599 South Gate Press
Wave Community Newspapers
819 W. Whitter Blvd. Phone: (213)727-1117
Montebello, CA 90640-3623 Fax: (213)727-9515

Community Newspaper. **Founded:** 1923. **Freq:** Semiweekly Thurs. and Sat. **Print Method:** Uses mats. Offset. **Trim Size:** 6 x 21 1/2. **Cols./Page:** 6. **Col. Width:** 37 nonpareils. **Col. Depth:** 301 agate lines. **Key Personnel:** Arthur J. Aguilar, Executive editor/Publisher. **Subscription Rates:** Free; $125 yr/mailed.
Circ: Paid 61
Free 24,076

Whittier Independent - See West Whittier

MONTEREY, pop. 27,558.

W. CA. Monterey Co. On Monterey Bay, 125 mi. S. of San Francisco. Resort. Military. Light industry.

2600 Applied Language Learning
Foreign Language Center
AP-AJ, Presidio Phone: (408)242-5638
Monterey, CA 93944-5006 Fax: (408)242-5850
Publication E-mail: woytalk@pom-emh1.army.mil

Professional journal covering information on foreign language instruction and acquisition. **Founded:** 1989. **Freq:** Semiannual. **Trim Size:** 6 x 9. **Cols./Page:** 1. **Col. Width:** 4 3/4 inches. **Col. Depth:** 7 3/4 inches. **Key Personnel:** Dr. Lidia Woytak, Editor. **Subscription Rates:** Free to qualified subscribers. **Remarks:** Advertising not accepted. **URL:** http://lingnet.army.mil.
Circ: Non-paid 4,500

2601 Armed Forces & Society
Transaction Publishers
Department of Systems Management Phone: (831)656-3160
Fax: (831)656-3407
Naval Postgraduate School
Monterey, CA 93943-5000
Publisher E-mail: trans@transactionpub.com

Journal on the military and civil-military relations. Official journal of the Inter-University Seminar on Armed Forces and Society. **Founded:** 1972. **Freq:** Quarterly. **Trim Size:** 6x9. **Cols./Page:** 1. **Col. Width:** 4.25 inches. **Col. Depth:** 7.25 inches. **Key Personnel:** Mark J. Eitelberg, Ph.D., Editor, fax (831)656-3068, meitelberg@nps.navy.mil. **ISSN:** 0095-327X. **Subscription Rates:** $56 individuals; $100 other countries; $112 institutions; $156 other countries institutions; $104 two years individuals; $200 two years institutions. **Remarks:** Accepts advertising.
Ad Rates: BW: $350 **Circ:** 2,000

2602 The Monterey County Herald
Monterey Peninsula Herald Co.
PO Box 271 Phone: (408)372-3311
Monterey, CA 93942 Fax: (408)646-4394
Publication E-mail: mchnewn@montereyherald.com

General newspaper. **Founded:** 1922. **Freq:** Mon.-Sun. (morn.). **Print Method:** Flexography. **Cols./Page:** 6. **Col. Width:** 25 nonpareils. **Col. Depth:** 294 agate lines. **Key Personnel:** Reginald Henry, Editor; Alice Burton, Advertising Mgr.; Christopher S. Dix, General Mgr. **Subscription Rates:** $96 individuals. **Remarks:** Accepts advertising. **Formerly**: The Herald (1992).
Ad Rates: GLR: $4.56 **Circ:** Mon.-Sat. ★**34,197**
BW: $2,961 Sun. ★**38,072**
4C: $3,411
SAU: $23.50

2603 The Observer
485 Church St. Phone: (831)373-2919
PO Box 2079 Fax: (831)373-4510
Monterey, CA 93942
Publication E-mail: obsvr@aol.com

Official newspaper of the Catholic Diocese of Monterey. **Founded:** 1969. **Freq:** Monthly. **Print Method:** Offset. **Trim**

Size: 11 x 14. **Cols./Page:** 4. **Col. Width:** 2 3/8 inches. **Col. Depth:** 13 inches. **Key Personnel:** Rev. Edward J. Kaminski, CSC, Editor; Bishop Sylvester Ryan, Publisher. **Subscription Rates:** $20 individuals. **Remarks:** Accepts advertising.
Ad Rates: BW: $600 **Circ:** ‡15,000
4C: $800
PCI: $12

2604 Spudman Magazine
PO Box 1752
Monterey, CA 93942

Magazine for potato growers and managers involved in packing, shipping, buying, and processing. **Subtitle:** Voice of the Potato Industry. **Founded:** Jan. 1963. **Freq:** 8/year. **Print Method:** Offset. **Trim Size:** 8 1/2 x 11. **Cols./Page:** 3. **Col. Width:** 28 nonpareils. **Col. Depth:** 140 agate lines. **Key Personnel:** Donald Miller, Editor and Publisher; Ernest Kerr, Production Dir.; Dr. Robert Thornton, Technical Review Dir. **ISSN:** 0038-8661. **Subscription Rates:** $1 individuals; $28 other countries. **Formerly:** Supdman.
Ad Rates: BW: $2,453 **Circ:** Paid ‡14,518
4C: $3,767 Non-paid ‡2,874

2605 KBOQ-FM - 95.5
2511 Garden Rd., Ste. C-150 Phone: (831)656-9550
Monterey, CA 93940 Fax: (831)656-9551
E-mail: kbach95.5@aol.com

Format: Classical. **Networks:** Concert Music Network (CMN). **Owner:** J & M Broadcasting, Inc, at above address. **Founded:** 1993. **Operating Hours:** Continuous; 100% local. **ADI:** Salinas-Monterey, CA. **Key Personnel:** Sherrie McCullough, President/Prog. Dir. **Wattage:** 1,700. **Ad Rates:** $25-40 per unit. **URL:** http://www.kbach.com.

2606 KNRY-AM - 1240
651 Cannery Row Phone: (408)373-1234
Monterey, CA 93940 Fax: (408)373-1255
Free: (888)814-6434

Format: Talk; News; Sports. **Networks:** Mutual Broadcasting System; CNN Radio; ESPN Radio; CBS; Westwood One Radio. **Founded:** 1935. **Operating Hours:** Continuous. **ADI:** Salinas-Monterey, CA. **Key Personnel:** Ron Harrison, General Mgr. **Wattage:** 1000. **Ad Rates:** $35 for 30 seconds; $50 for 60 seconds. **URL:** http://www.knrykiezdot.com.

2607 KSMS-TV - 67
67 Garden Ct. Phone: (408)373-6767
Monterey, CA 93940 Fax: (408)373-6700

Format: Commercial TV. **Networks:** Univision. **Founded:** 1986. **Operating Hours:** Continuous. **ADI:** Salinas-Monterey, CA. **Key Personnel:** Carlos Romos, Jr., Contact.

2608 KWAV-FM - 96.9
PO Box 1391 Phone: (408)649-0969
Monterey, CA 93942 Fax: (408)649-3335
E-mail: kwav97fm@aol.com

Format: Adult Contemporary. **Networks:** AP. **Owner:** Richard Buckley, at above address. **Founded:** 1961. **Operating Hours:** Continuous. **ADI:** Salinas-Monterey, CA. **Key Personnel:** Kathy Baker, VP/Gen. Mgr.; Sue Clark, Local Sls. Mgr.; Bernie Moody, Program Dir. **Wattage:** 18,000.

2609 KXDC-FM - 101.7
2511 Garden Rd. C-160 Phone: (408)647-1017
Monterey, CA 93940 Fax: (408)643-1100
E-mail: kxdc@smoothjazz.com

Format: Adult Contemporary. **Networks:** Independent. **Owner:** Elettra Broadcasting, at above address. **Founded:** June 1, 1995. **Formerly:** KWST-FM; KIDD-FM; KAXT-FM. **Operating Hours:** Continuous; 100% local. **ADI:** Salinas-Monterey, CA. **Key Personnel:** Scott O'Brien, Program Dir.; Rebecca Little, Sales Mgr.; Sharon Bonds, Promotions and PSA Dir.; Nancy Normali, Office Mgr.; Ken Dennis, Pres./General Mgr. **Wattage:** 830. **Ad Rates:** $35 per unit. **URL:** http://www.smoothjazz.com.

2610 Monterey Peninsula Cable TV
2455 Henderson Way Phone: (408)649-9100
Box 1711 Fax: (408)649-8680
Monterey, CA 93942

Founded: 1952. **Cities Served:** Monterey County, Carmel-by-the-Sea, Carmel Valley, Del Rey Oaks, Marina, Pacific Grove, Salinas, Sand City, and Seaside, CA.

MONTEREY PARK, pop. 54,338.

S. CA. Los Angeles Co. 2 mi. S. of Alhambra. Residential. Illuminating signs, shoes, electronics, chemicals, hardware, diesel replacement parts manufactured.

2611 Campus News
East Los Angeles College
Journalism Dept. Phone: (213)265-8819
1301 Avenida Cesar Chavez Fax: (213)265-8975
Monterey Park, CA 91754
Community college newspaper. **Founded:** 1945. **Freq:** Weekly (Wed.). **Print Method:** Offset. **Cols./Page:** 6. **Col. Width:** 26 nonpareils. **Col. Depth:** 294 agate lines. **Key Personnel:** Jean Stapleton, Advisor. **Remarks:** Accepts advertising.
Ad Rates: GLR: $.44 **Circ:** Free ‡5,000
SAU: $4.50
PCI: $4.50

2612 Chinese Daily News
Chinese Daily News, Inc.
1588 Corporate Center Dr. Phone: (213)268-4982
Monterey Park, CA 91754 Fax: (213)265-3476

General newspaper (Chinese). **Founded:** 1976. **Freq:** Daily. **Print Method:** Offset web. **Trim Size:** 14 1/2 x 22 1/2. **Key Personnel:** Shih-yaw Chen, Editor, phone (213)268-2600, fax (213)263-9860. **Subscription Rates:** $176; $.50 single issue. **Remarks:** Advertising accepted; rates available upon request. **Formerly:** World Journal.
Circ: ‡85,000

2613 International Daily News
870 Monterey Pass Rd. Phone: (213)265-1317
Monterey Park, CA 91754 Fax: (213)262-1425
Publication E-mail: info@chinesetoday.com

General newspaper (Chinese). **Founded:** 1981. **Freq:** Daily (morn.). **Print Method:** Offset. **Key Personnel:** Simon Y. Chen, Editor; Warren Chang, Editor-in-Chief, ed-warren@chinesetoday.com. **USPS:** 675-590. **Subscription Rates:** $137.48 individuals; $148 out of state. **Remarks:** Accepts advertising. **URL:** http://www.chinesetoday.com. **Alt. Formats:** Microform.
Ad Rates: BW: $750 **Circ:** Paid 23,000
4C: $1,200 Non-paid 1,000
PCI: $4.50

2614 Monterey Park Comet
Eastern Group Publications Inc.
2500 S. Atlantic Blvd., No. A Phone: (213)263-5743
Los Angeles, CA 90040-2004 Fax: (213)263-9169

Newspaper with a Democratic orientation (English and Spanish). **Founded:** 1974. **Freq:** Weekly (Thurs.). **Print Method:** Offset. Uses mats. **Trim Size:** 13 x 21. **Cols./Page:** 6. **Col. Width:** 2 1/16 inches. **Col. Depth:** 294 agate lines. **Key Personnel:** Dolores Sanchez, Publisher; John Sanchez, Advertising Mgr. **Subscription Rates:** $42 individuals; $35 out of state. **Remarks:** Accepts advertising.
Ad Rates: GLR: $1.08 **Circ:** Paid ‡23
BW: $382 Free ‡9,983
4C: $814
SAU: $15.12

2615 Monterey Park Progress
Wave Community Newspapers
819 W. Whitter Blvd. Phone: (213)727-1117
Montebello, CA 90640-3623 Fax: (213)727-9515

Newspaper. **Founded:** 1918. **Freq:** Biweekly Thurs. and Sat. **Print Method:** Offset. **Cols./Page:** 6. **Col. Width:** 26 nonpareils. **Col. Depth:** 301 agate lines. **Key Personnel:** Arthur J. Aguilar, Exec. Editor/Publisher. **Subscription Rates:** $125 by mail /year; Free local. **Remarks:** Advertising accepted; rates available upon request.
Circ: Free 17,788

MOORPARK

2616 Moorpark Star
PO Box 775 Phone: (805)523-7440
Moorpark, CA 93020 Fax: (805)523-7816

Community newspaper. **Founded:** 1976. **Freq:** Daily. **Print Method:** Offset. **Cols./Page:** 6. **Col. Width:** 2 1/8 inches. **Col. Depth:** 21 1/2 inches. **Key Personnel:** Debra W. Ryono, Editor and Publisher. **Subscription Rates:** $.35. **Formerly:** Moorpark News-Mirror.
Ad Rates: BW: $11.50 **Circ:** (Not Reported)

MORAGA, pop. 15,014.

W. CA. Contra Costa Co. 8 mi. SE of Berkeley. Residential.

2617 St. Mary's Collegian
St. Mary's College
PO Box 4407 Phone: (415)376-4111
Moraga, CA 94575
Collegiate newspaper. **Subtitle:** Oldest Fortnightly in the East Bay. **Founded:** 1903. **Freq:** Semimonthly. **Print Method:** Offset. **Trim Size:** 11 x 17. **Cols./Page:** 5. **Col. Width:** 24 nonpareils. **Col. Depth:** 203 agate lines. **Key Personnel:** Timothy Moore, Editor. **Subscription Rates:** $40 individuals. **Remarks:** Accepts advertising.
Ad Rates: GLR: $2.50 **Circ:** 4,500
BW: $340
4C: $600
PCI: $6

2618 KSMC-FM - 89.5
PO Box 3223 Phone: (925)631-4252
St. Mary's College Fax: (925)376-5766
Moraga, CA 94575
E-mail: ksmc895@earthlink.net

Format: Eclectic; Jazz. **Owner:** St. Mary's College, at above address. **Founded:** 1973. **Operating Hours:** Continuous. **Key Personnel:** Edward Tywoniak, Contact; Matt Goswell, General Mgr. **Wattage:** 100. **URL:** http://fermat.stmarys-ca.edu/~ksmc/ksmc.html.

MORENO VALLEY, pop. 18,000.

SE CA. Riverside Co. 8 mi. E. of Riverside. Recreation. Agriculture. Commercial.

2619 The Press-Enterprise
The Valley Times
PO Box 9700 Phone: (909)242-7614
Moreno Valley, CA 92552 Fax: (909)247-1920

Local newspaper. **Founded:** 1878. **Freq:** Mon.-Sun. (morn.). **Print Method:** Offset. **Trim Size:** 21 1/2 x 13 3/4. **Cols./Page:** 6. **Col. Width:** 26 nonpareils. **Col. Depth:** 294 agate lines. **Key Personnel:** Sue Barry, Classified Advertising Sales Manager; Joel Blain, Editor; Jim Maurer, Sales Mgr.; Joe Frederickson, Marketing Dir.; Dave Cornwall, Advertising Dir.; Rich DeAtley, Entertainment Editor; T.E. Foreman, Theater Editor; John Garrett, Sports Editor; Judith Graffam, Editor; Michael Schuerman, Marketing Research Mgr.; Howard Hayes, Jr., Chairman; Robert Hirt, TV Week Editor; Laurie Lucas, Editor; Sally Ann Maas, Assistant Managing Editor Features; Andrew McCue, Business Editor; Marcia McQuern, President; Jim Milbourne, National Advertising Sales Manager; Elaine W. Regus, Education Editor. **Subscription Rates:** $124.80 individuals. **Remarks:** Accepts advertising. **Online:** DataTimes Corporation. **URL:** http://www.pe.net.
Ad Rates: 4C: $8,022 **Circ:** Mon.-Sat. ★**161,612**
PCI: $54.50 Sun. ★**168,222**

2620 Riverside County Agriculture
Riverside County Farm Bureau
21160 Box Springs Rd., Ste. 102 Phone: (714)684-6732
Fax: (714)782-0621
Moreno Valley, CA 92557
Agricultural magazine. **Founded:** 1946. **Freq:** Monthly. **Print Method:** Offset. **Trim Size:** 8 x 10. **Cols./Page:** 3. **Col. Width:** 26 nonpareils. **Col. Depth:** 108 agate lines. **Key Personnel:** Robert E. Perkins, Exec. Mgr. **USPS:** 466-900. **Subscription Rates:** $5 individuals. **Remarks:** Accepts advertising.
Ad Rates: BW: $320 **Circ:** ‡2,500

2621 Valley Times
Donrey Media Group
PO Box 9700 Phone: (909)242-7614
Moreno Valley, CA 92552 Fax: (909)247-1920

General newspaper. **Freq:** Weekly. **Formerly:** Moreno Valley Butterfield Express (1992).
Circ: Mon.-Sat. 41,970
Sun. 43,727

MORGAN HILL, pop. 17,060.

W. CA. Santa Clara Co. 10 mi. SE of San Jose. Canneries, poultry processing, cold storage plants, feed mills. Ranching. Diversified farming. Prunes, grapes, strawberries.

2622 Computer Fair Show Program
National Productions
16175 Monterey Rd. Phone: (408)778-5200
Morgan Hill, CA 95037-5452 Fax: (408)779-1374
Free: (800)800-5600
Publication E-mail: cmplist@aol.com

Periodical listing computer trade shows. **Founded:** 1986. **Freq:** 16/year. **Print Method:** Web offset. **Trim Size:** 8 1/4 x 10 3/4. **Cols./Page:** 3. **Key Personnel:** Kelly Graham, Editor; Brian M. Bowe, Production Dir.; Brian M. Bowe. **Subscription Rates:** Free. **Remarks:** Accepts advertising. **URL:** http://www.lacomputerfair.com. **Formerly:** Computer Marketplace Show Program.
Ad Rates: BW: $100 **Circ:** Non-paid ‡11,000

2623 Morgan Hill Times
Gavilan Publishing
30 E. 3rd St. Phone: (408)779-4106
PO Box 757 Fax: (408)779-3886
Morgan Hill, CA 95038-0757
Free: (800)497-5127

Community newspaper. **Founded:** 1894. **Freq:** Semiweekly (Tues. and Fri.). **Print Method:** Offset. **Cols./Page:** 6. **Col. Width:** 27 nonpareils. **Col. Depth:** 301 agate lines. **Key Personnel:** LeRoy Gorrell, Publisher, phone (408)842-6400, fax (408)842-7105; Cindy Courter, Advertising Mgr., phone (408)842-6400, fax (408)842-7105. **Subscription Rates:** $37.07 individuals. **Remarks:** Accepts advertising. Friday: GLR: $3.96; BW: $2,000.95; 4C: $2,305.95; SAU: $15.55; PCI: $9.15; Tuesday: GLR: $3.96; SAU: $17.95; PCI: $9.15. **Formerly:** Times and San Martin News (1989).
Circ: 4,000

MORONGO BASIN

2624 White Sheet-The Morongo Basin Advertiser
Associated Desert Shoppers, Inc.
73-400 Hwy. 111 Phone: (760)346-1729
Palm Desert, CA 92260 Fax: (760)346-7350
Free: (800)678-4237

Shopper. **Subtitle:** White Sheet. **Founded:** 1965. **Freq:** Weekly (Tues.). **Print Method:** Web. **Trim Size:** 11 x 12 1/2. **Cols./Page:** 6. **Col. Width:** 9 1/2 picas. **Col. Depth:** 11 3/4 inches. **Key Personnel:** Hal Paradis, Publisher; Jim McComb, Sales Mgr. **Subscription Rates:** $163.80 out of area.
Ad Rates: BW: $407 **Circ:** Free ‡9,000
4C: $650
PCI: $4.50

MOUNT BULLION

2625 KCIV-FM - 99.9
1031 15th St., Ste. 1 Phone: (209)524-8999
Modesto, CA 95354 Fax: (209)524-9088
Free: (800)743-5248

Format: Religious. **Networks:** USA Radio. **Owner:** Bott Communications Inc., at above address. **Founded:** 1989. **Operating Hours:** Continuous. **Key Personnel:** Richard Bott, President; Kathleen Reynolds, Operations Mgr. **Wattage:** 1850. **Ad Rates:** $12-21 for 30 seconds; $16-29 for 60 seconds.

MOUNT SHASTA, pop. 2,837.

N. CA. Siskiyou Co. 90 mi. S. of Medford, OR. Sawmill. Pine, fir, cedar timber. Mountain resort. Agriculture.

2626 The Journal of the Order of Buddhist Contemplatives
Order of Buddhist Contemplatives
Shasta Abbey Phone: (916)926-4208
3724 Summit Dr. Fax: (916)926-0428
Mount Shasta, CA 96067-9102
The Journal contains articles on Buddhist meditation and practice written by priests of the Order and lay members of the congregation. **Founded:** 1970. **Freq:** Quarterly. **Print Method:** Offset. **Trim Size:** 5 1/2 x 8 1/2. **Key Personnel:** Rev. Chushin Passmore, Editor. **ISSN:** 0891-1177. **Subscription Rates:** $20 individuals; $5 single issue; $23 other countries. **Remarks:** Advertising not accepted. **Formerly:** Journal of Shasta Abbey.
Circ: Paid 375
Non-paid 175

2627 Mount Shasta Herald, Weed Press, Dunsmuir News
Siskiyou Newspaper
PO Box 127 Phone: (916)926-5214
Mount Shasta, CA 96067 Fax: (916)926-4166

Community newspaper. **Founded:** 1887. **Freq:** Weekly (Wed.). **Print Method:** Offset. **Cols./Page:** 6. **Col. Width:** 25 nonpareils. **Col. Depth:** 301 agate lines. **Key Personnel:** Genny Axtman, Publisher; Orbell & Marge Apperson, Publisher. **Subscription Rates:** $25.50 individuals. **Remarks:** Accepts advertising.
Ad Rates: BW: $928.80 **Circ:** Combined ‡15,075
4C: $1153.80
SAU: $9.93
PCI: $7.20

2628 King Videocable Co.
219 E. Alma St. Phone: (916)926-6128
Box 175 Fax: (916)926-6546
Mount Shasta, CA 96067

Owner: Media One, 550 N. Continental Blvd., Ste. 250, El Segundo, CA 90245, (310)647-3000. **Formerly:** Shasta Cable TV. **Key Personnel:** Vince Reinig, General Mgr. **Cities Served:** Dunsmuir, McCloud, Mt. Shasta, Weed, CA: subscribing households 5,200; 31 channels; 1 community access channel; 6 hours per week community access programming.

MOUNTAIN VIEW, pop. 58,655.

W. CA. Santa Clara Co. 34 mi. S. of San Francisco. Residential. Electronics.

2629 Channel
SEMI
805 E. Middlefield Rd. Phone: (650)940-6960
Mountain View, CA 94043 Fax: (650)940-7916

Trade magazine covering semiconductors and electronics worldwide. **Subtitle:** A Publication of Semiconductor Equipment and Materials International. **Founded:** Aug. 1988. **Freq:** 9/year. **Key Personnel:** Walter Mathews, Editor-in-Chief; Rose Eufinger, Managing Editor, reufinger@mathewsandclark.com; Karen Savala, Publisher, ksavala@semi.org. **Subscription Rates:** Free to qualified subscribers. **Remarks:** Accepts advertising. **URL:** http://www.semi.org.
Circ: Non-paid 11,000

2630 Consulting Rates and Business Practices Annual Survey
Professional and Technical Consultants Association
849-B Independence Ave. Phone: (650)903-8305
Mountain View, CA 94043 Fax: (650)967-0995
Free: (800)747-2822
Publisher E-mail: office@patca.org; info@patca.org

Trade magazine covering business for professional computer and hi-tech consultants. **Founded:** 1981. **Freq:** Semiannual. **Remarks:** Advertising not accepted.
Circ: (Not Reported)

2631 La Red—The Net
Floricanto Press
650 Castro St., Ste. 120-331 Phone: (415)552-1879
Mountain View, CA 94041 Fax: (415)793-2662
Publication E-mail: lared@floricantopress.com
Publisher E-mail: info@floricantopress.com

Hispanic book review journal. **Subtitle:** Hispanic Journal of Commentaries and Reviews. **Founded:** 1979. **Freq:** Semiannual. **Print Method:** Web. **Trim Size:** 8 1/2 x 11. **Cols./Page:** 2. **Col. Width:** 3 1/4 inches. **Col. Depth:** 7 1/2 inches. **Key Personnel:** Roberto Cabello, Editor. **Subscription Rates:** $60 individuals. **Remarks:** Accepts advertising. **URL:** http://www.floricantopress.com/~Lared.
Ad Rates: GLR: $1 **Circ:** Combined 5,000

2632 The People
Socialist Labor Party of America
PO Box 218 Phone: (650)938-8359
Mountain View, CA 94042-0218 Fax: (650)938-8392
Publication E-mail: thepeople@igc.apc.org
Publisher E-mail: socialists@slp.org

News journal with a socialist orientation. **Founded:** Apr. 5, 1891. **Freq:** Monthly. **Print Method:** Offset. **Trim Size:** 11 3/8 x 17 1/2. **Cols./Page:** 4. **Col. Width:** 14 3/4 nonpareils. **Col. Depth:** 230 agate lines. **Key Personnel:** Robert Bills, Editor. **ISSN:** 0199-350X. **Subscription Rates:** $5 individuals. **Remarks:** Advertising not accepted. **URL:** gopher.slp.org.7019; http://www.slp.org. **Alt. Formats:** Microform. **Formerly:** Weekly People (1979).
Circ: 10,900

2633 SCO World Magazine
Venture Publishing, Inc.
480 San Antonio Rd., Ste. 245
Mountain View, CA 94040

Professional magazine covering computers and operating systems. **Founded:** Jan. 1994. **Freq:** Monthly. **Print Method:** Web offset. **Trim Size:** 8 x 10 3/4. **Cols./Page:** 3. **ISSN:** 1075-3265. **Subscription Rates:** $21.95 individuals; $3.95 single issue. **Remarks:** Accepts advertising. **URL:** http://www.scoworld.com.
Ad Rates: BW: $7,200 **Circ:** Controlled 50,000
4C: $9,300

2634 Track & Field News
2570 El Camino Real, Ste. 606 Phone: (650)948-8188
Mountain View, CA 94040 Fax: (650)948-9445
Free: (800)GET-TRAK
Publication E-mail: biz@trackandfieldnews.com

Track and field magazine. **Founded:** 1948. **Freq:** Monthly. **Print Method:** Offset. **Trim Size:** 8 1/2 x 11. **Cols./Page:** 3. **Col. Width:** 28 nonpareils. **Col. Depth:** 152 agate lines. **Key Personnel:** E. Garry Hill, Editor, gh@trackandfieldnews.com; Sieg Lindstrom, Managing Editor, sl@trackandfieldnews.com; Ed Fox, Publisher, ef@trackandfieldnews.com. **ISSN:** 0041-0284. **Subscription Rates:** $38.95 individuals. **Remarks:** Accepts advertising. **URL:** http://www.olympic.nbc.com; http://www.trackandfieldnews.com.
Ad Rates: BW: $2,460 **Circ:** Paid 27,195
4C: $4,055 Non-paid 2,309

MURRIETA

2635 Widescreen Review
26864 Mandelieu Dr. Phone: (909)677-0335
Murrieta, CA 92562 Fax: (909)677-2604

Consumer magazine for home theater enthusiasts with widescreen format laserdiscs and digital video discs, covering laserdisc movie reviews and equipment and technology. **Subtitle:** The Essential Home Theatre Resource. **Founded:** 1992. **Freq:** Bimonthly. **Print Method:** Web offset. **Trim Size:** 8 1/8 x 10 7/8. **Key Personnel:** Gary Reber, Editor and Publisher. **Subscription Rates:** $25 individuals; $5.95 single issue. **Remarks:** Accepts advertising. **URL:** http://www.widescreenreview.com.
Ad Rates: BW: $2,400 **Circ:** (Not Reported)
4C: $3,400

NAPA†, pop. 50,879.

W. CA. Napa Co. On Napa River, 15 mi. E. of Vallejo. Fruit canning and drying. Premier grape growing regions. Manufactures wine. Clothing, dairy products. Quicksilver gold mines. Diversified farming. Grapes, fruits, poultry.

2636 The Napa County Record
David W. Barker
1320 2nd St. Phone: (707)252-8877
PO Box 88 Fax: (707)226-3707
Napa, CA 94559
Publication E-mail: ncrecord@napanet.net

Community newspaper. **Founded:** 1946. **Freq:** Weekly (Thurs.). **Print Method:** Offset. **Cols./Page:** 6. **Col. Width:** 25 nonpareils. **Col. Depth:** 294 agate lines. **Key Personnel:** David W. Barker, Publisher; Melodie Hilton, Editor. **ISSN:** 0744-6942. **Subscription Rates:** $25 individuals. **Remarks:** Accepts advertising.
Ad Rates: BW: $825.22 **Circ:** ‡5,501
PCI: $6.82

2637 The Napa Valley Register
1615 2nd St. Phone: (707)226-3711
PO Box 150 Fax: (707)224-3963
Napa, CA 94559
Publication E-mail: nvrnews@palitzer.net

General newspaper. **Founded:** 1863. **Freq:** Mon.-Sun. (eve.) plus Sat. and Sun. mornings. **Print Method:** Offset. **Trim Size:** 14 x 22 3/4. **Cols./Page:** 6. **Col. Width:** 25 nonpareils. **Col. Depth:** 301 agate lines. **Key Personnel:** Michael Giangreco, Publisher, phone (707)254-3234. **Subscription Rates:** $132 individuals. **Remarks:** Accepts advertising. **Formerly:** The Napa Register.
Ad Rates: BW: $2,251 **Circ:** Mon.-Sat. ★**19,469**
4C: $295 Sun. ★**19,782**
SAU: $12.34
PCI: $19.39

2638 KVON-AM - 1440
1124 Foster Rd. Phone: (707)252-1440
Napa, CA 94558 Fax: (707)226-7544
Free: (888)252-1440

Format: Talk; News; Sports. **Networks:** ABC; NBC; Mutual Broadcasting System. **Owner:** at above address. **Founded:** 1947. **Operating Hours:** Continuous. **ADI:** San Francisco-Oakland-San Jose. **Key Personnel:** Dale Hendry, General Mgr., dalekvyn@aol.com; Barry Martin, Program Dir.; Charlotte Hendry, Office Mgr. **Local Programs:** *Tool Talk* 6:00 am - 8:00 am Saturday, Russ Taft; *Morning Addition Morning Show* 6:00 am - 10:00 am Monday-Friday, Barry Martin; *Wine Authority Radio (food show)* 12:00 noon - 2:00 pm Saturday, Andrew Adams. **Wattage:** 5000. **Ad Rates:** $34-48 for 30 seconds; $42-60 for 60 seconds. Combined advertising rates available with KVYN-FM. **URL:** http://www.kvonkyvn.com.

2639 KVYN-FM - 99.3
1124 Foster Rd. Phone: (707)258-1111
Napa, CA 94558 Fax: (707)226-7544

Format: Adult Contemporary. **Networks:** ABC; Jones Satellite. **Owner:** Moss Entertainment Corp., at above address. **Founded:** 1976. **Operating Hours:** Continuous. **ADI:** San Francisco-Oakland-San Jose. **Key Personnel:** Dale Hendry, General Mgr.; Charlotte Hendry, Office Mgr.; Barry Martin, Program Dir. **Wattage:** 6000. **Ad Rates:** $34-48 for 30 seconds; $42-60 for 60 seconds. Combined advertising rates available with KVON-AM. **URL:** http://www.kvyn.com.

NATIONAL CITY

2640 XHRM-FM - 92.5
2434 Southport Way, Ste. A Phone: (619)336-4900
National City, CA 91950 Fax: (619)336-4925

Format: Alternative/New Music/Progressive. **Owner:** Binational Broadcasting Co. Inc., at above address. **Founded:** 1969. **Operating Hours:** Continuous. **ADI:** San Diego, CA. **Key Personnel:** Luis Kaloyan, President, phone (619)336-4900, fax (619)336-4925, luis@92five.com; Ellen Williams, Chief Fin. Officer, ellen@92five.com; Tim McCarthy, General Mgr., tim@92five.com; Jay Isbell, Marketing and Operations Mgr., jay@92five.com; Chaz Kelly, Music Dir., chaz@92five.com; Mike Halloran, Program Dir., chaz@92five.com. **Wattage:** 100K. **URL:** http://www.92five.com.

NEEDLES, pop. 4,120.

SE CA. San Bernardino Co. On Colorado River, 160 mi. NE of San Bernardino. Mojave indian reservation. Tourism. Power & food packing plants. Agriculture.

2641 KTOX-AM - 1340
PO Box 738 Phone: (619)326-2101
Needles, CA 92363-0738

Format: Talk. **Networks:** CBS; Mutual Broadcasting System; People's Network. **Owner:** Coburn Communications Corp., at above address. **Founded:** 1952. **Formerly:** KSFE-AM (1991). **Operating Hours:** Continuous. **Key Personnel:** Andy Ward, Contact. **Wattage:** 1000. **Ad Rates:** $3-9 for 30 seconds; $4.10-12 for 60 seconds.

NEVADA CITY†, pop. 2,431.

NE CA. Nevada Co. 2 mi. SW of Grass Valley. Residential.

2642 Wild Duck Review
PO Box 388 Phone: (530)478-0134
Nevada City, CA 95959 Fax: (530)265-2304
Free: (888)795-9588
Publication E-mail: casey@wildduckreview.com

Magazine featuring leading literary artists and conservation activists articulating crises in characture, culture and nature. **Subtitle:** Literature, Necessary Mischief and News. **Founded:** 1994. **Freq:** Quarterly. **Print Method:** Offset web. **Trim Size:** 11 1/2 x 13 1/2. **Key Personnel:** Casey Walker, Editor, casey@wildduckreview.com. **Subscription Rates:** $24 individuals; $4 single issue; $32 other countries. **Remarks:** Accepts advertising.
Ad Rates: BW: $800 **Circ:** Paid ‡3,500

NEWBURY PARK

SW CA. Ventura Co. 37 mi. NW of Los Angeles. Manufactures electric measuring instruments, machinery. Motor truck parts, accessories, semiconductors, pumps, plastic and metal products. Agriculture. Citrus fruit, walnuts.

2643 TCI of Ventura County
2323 Teller Rd. Fax: (805)375-3176
Newbury Park, CA 91320 Free: (800)427-3731

Founded: 1963. **Key Personnel:** Dan Deutsch, General Mgr.; Paul Baskin, Dir. of Marketing. **Cities Served:** Agoura, Calabasas, Camarillo, Fillmore, Moorpark, Newbury Park, Ojai, Piru, Santa Paula, Thousand Oaks, Westlake Village, CA: subscribing households 70,000; 115 channels.

NEWHALL, pop. 9,651.

S. CA. Los Angeles Co. 31 mi. NW of Los Angeles. College of the Canyons. Manufactures glassware containers, explosive shells, phonograph records, chemicals. Oil refinery, hatchery. Oil wells. Dairy, stock, grain farms. Hay, alfalfa, vegetables.

2644 Media One
22620 Market St. Phone: (805)259-6909
Newhall, CA 91321 Fax: (805)259-0199

Owner: Colony Communications Inc., 20 Washington Pl., Providence, RI 02903, (401)277-7400, Fax: (401)277-7694. **Formerly:** King Videocable Co. **URL:** http://www.mediaone.com.

NEWMAN, pop. 2,785.

C. CA. Stanislaus Co. 25 mi. SW of Modesto. Manufactures dairy products. Poultry. Dairy, grain farms. Alfalfa, green peppers, cauliflower, tomatoes Spinach.

2645 The Gustine Standard
U.S. Media, Inc.
PO Box 878 Phone: (209)854-3787
Newman, CA 95360 Fax: (209)854-3851

Local newspaper. **Founded:** Nov. 4, 1910. **Freq:** Weekly (Wed.). **Print Method:** Offset. **Cols./Page:** 6. **Col. Width:** 2 inches. **Col. Depth:** 21 inches. **Key Personnel:** Patty Scianni, Managing Editor; Dean Lesher, Publisher; Keith Groniga, Advertising Mgr. **USPS:** 432-340. **Subscription Rates:** $9 individuals; $16 out of area. **Remarks:** Accepts advertising.
Ad Rates: PCI: $6.16 **Circ:** Free 5,300

2646 The West Side Index
Mattos Newspapers, Inc.
1021 Fresno St. Phone: (209)862-2222
PO Box 878 Fax: (209)862-4133
Newman, CA 95360
Community newspaper. **Founded:** 1890. **Freq:** Weekly (Thurs.). **Print Method:** Offset. **Cols./Page:** 6. **Col. Width:** 21 nonpareils. **Col. Depth:** 287 agate lines. **Key Personnel:** William H. Mattos, Publisher. **Subscription Rates:** $20 individuals in county. **Remarks:** Accepts advertising.
Ad Rates: PCI: $3.75 **Circ:** 1,850

NEWPORT BEACH, pop. 63,475.

S. CA. Orange Co. On Pacific Ocean, 12 mi. SW of Santa Ana. Beach resort. Finanical center. Electronics research and development, guidance control systems, boats.

2647 American Journal of Forensic Psychiatry
American College of Forensic Psychiatry
Box 5870 Phone: (949)673-7773
Newport Beach, CA 92662 Fax: (949)673-7710

Professional journal covering interfacing issues of psychiatry and law. **Subtitle:** Interfacing Issues of Psychiatry and Law. **Founded:** 1978. **Freq:** Quarterly. **Print Method:** Offset. **Trim Size:** 7 x 10. **Cols./Page:** 1. **Col. Width:** 63 nonpareils. **Col. Depth:** 124 agate lines. **Key Personnel:** Debra Miller, Editor; Edward Miller, Publisher. **ISSN:** 0163-1942. **Subscription Rates:** $60 individuals. **Remarks:** Accepts advertising. **Alt. Formats:** Microform.
Ad Rates: BW: $250 **Circ:** ‡1,000

2648 American Journal of Forensic Psychology
American College of Forensic Psychiatry
Box 5870 Phone: (949)673-7773
Newport Beach, CA 92662 Fax: (949)673-7710

Professional journal covering psychology as it relates to law. **Subtitle:** Interfacing Issues of Psychology and Law. **Founded:** 1983. **Freq:** Quarterly. **Print Method:** Offset. **Trim Size:** 7 x 10. **Cols./Page:** 1. **Col. Width:** 63 nonpareils. **Col. Depth:** 116 agate lines. **Key Personnel:** Debra Flamm Miller, Editor; Ed Miller, Publisher. **ISSN:** 0733-1290. **Subscription Rates:** $60 individuals. **Remarks:** Accepts advertising. **Alt. Formats:** Microform.
Ad Rates: BW: $250 **Circ:** ‡800

2649 Building Products Digest
Cutler Publishing Inc.
4500 Campus Dr., Ste. 480 Phone: (949)852-1990
Newport Beach, CA 92660 Fax: (949)852-0231
Publication E-mail: dkoenig@ioc.net

Magazine covering lumber yards, home centers, retailers, and wholesalers. **Founded:** Mar. 1982. **Freq:** Monthly. **Print Method:** Offset. **Trim Size:** 8 1/4 x 10 7/8. **Cols./Page:** 3. **Col. Width:** 26 nonpareils. **Col. Depth:** 140 agate lines. **Key Personnel:** David Koenig, Editor; David Cutler, Publisher; Charles Casey, Advertising Mgr. **ISSN:** 0742-5691. **Subscription Rates:** $25 individuals. **Remarks:** Accepts advertising. **URL:** http://www.building-products.com.
Ad Rates: BW: $1,330 **Circ:** Controlled ‡12,750
4C: $2,080
PCI: $45

2650 Cycle World
Hachette Filipacchi Magazines, Inc.
1499 Monrovia Ave. Phone: (714)720-5300
Newport Beach, CA 92663 Fax: (714)631-0651

Magazine on street, dirt, dual-purpose, and all-terrain motorcylces. Covering tests, aftermarket products, parts and accessories, competition, personalities, travel, and nostalgia. **Founded:** Jan. 1962. **Freq:** Monthly. **Print Method:** Offset. **Trim Size:** 7 7/8 x 10 1/2. **Cols./Page:** 3. **Col. Width:** 27 nonpareils. **Col. Depth:** 140 agate lines. **Key Personnel:** David Edwards, Editor, phone (714)720-5369; Larry Little, Vice President, phone (714)720-5337; Paul A. LaBella, Advertising Dir., phone (714)720-5350. **Subscription Rates:** $19.94 individuals; $3.50 single issue. **Online:** America Online, Inc. **Absorbed:** Cycle (1991).
Ad Rates: BW: $16,481 **Circ:** Paid ★316,944
4C: $24,726
PCI: $812

2651 Heavy Duty Trucking
Newport Communications
PO Box W Phone: (714)261-1636
Newport Beach, CA 92658-8910 Fax: (714)261-2904
Free: (800)233-1911
Publication E-mail: aryder@heavytruck.com

Magazine serving large, medium and small fleet managers whose firms operate class 6, 7 and 8 trucks in the U.S. **Subtitle:** The Business Magazine of Trucking. **Founded:** 1922. **Freq:** Monthly. **Print Method:** Offset. **Trim Size:** 7 7/8 x 10 3/4. **Cols./Page:** 3 and 2. **Col. Width:** 26 and 40 nonpareils. **Col. Depth:** 140 agate lines. **Key Personnel:** Doug Condra, Editor; George Jacovides, Publisher. **ISSN:** 0017-9434. **Subscription Rates:** Free to qualified subscribers; $65 Nonqualified. **Remarks:** Accepts advertising. **URL:** http://www.heavytruck.com.
Ad Rates: BW: $9,705 **Circ:** Controlled ‡101,976
4C: $12,390

2652 The Investment Reporter
PO Box 8049-300 Phone: (714)724-0444
Newport Beach, CA 92658
Financial newspaper for stockbrokers, analysts, and fund managers. **Founded:** Sept. 1989. **Freq:** Monthly. **Print Method:** Newsprint. **Trim Size:** Tabloid. **Key Personnel:** John Robbins, Publisher; Peggy Powell, Exec. Editor. **ISSN:** 1062-4678. **Subscription Rates:** $38 individuals; $2.95 single issue. **Remarks:** Accepts advertising. **URL:** http://www.w3otg.com.
Ad Rates: BW: $5,120 **Circ:** Controlled 50,000
4C: $4,096

2653 The Journal of Historical Review
Institute for Historical Review (IHR)
PO Box 2739 Phone: (949)631-1490
Newport Beach, CA 92659 Fax: (949)631-0981
Publisher E-mail: ihr@ihr.org

Journal containing articles and reviews in the tradition of Historical Revisionism. **Founded:** 1980. **Freq:** Bimonthly. **Trim Size:** 8 1/2 x 11. **Cols./Page:** 2. **Key Personnel:** Mark Weber, Editor, weber@ihr.org. **ISSN:** 0195-6752. **Subscription Rates:** $40 individuals annual; $7.50 single issue. **Remarks:** Accepts advertising. **URL:** http://www.ihr.org.
Ad Rates: BW: $500 **Circ:** 2,000

2654 The Merchant Magazine
4500 Campus Dr., Ste. 480 Phone: (949)852-1990
Newport Beach, CA 92660 Fax: (949)852-0231
Publication E-mail: dkoenig@ioc.net
Publisher E-mail: dkoenig@ioc.net

Lumber and building materials magazine for the retailer and wholesaler of lumber & building materials. **Founded:** 1922. **Freq:** Monthly. **Print Method:** Offset. **Trim Size:** 8 1/4 x 10 7/8. **Cols./Page:** 3 and 2. **Col. Width:** 30 and 39 nonpareils. **Col. Depth:** 140 agate lines. **Key Personnel:** David H. Cutler, Editor; Charles Casey, Advertising Mgr. **ISSN:** 0739-9723. **Subscription Rates:** $13 individuals; $3 single issue. **Remarks:** Accepts advertising. **URL:** http://www.building-products.com.
Ad Rates: BW: $1,200 **Circ:** ‡4,011
4C: $1,950 Paid ‡3,000
PCI: $45

2655 NATSO Truckers News
Newport Communications
PO Box W Phone: (714)261-1636
Newport Beach, CA 92658-8910 Fax: (714)261-2904
Free: (800)233-1911

Magazine (tabloid) for professional truck drivers and owner-operators. Official publication of National Association of Truck Stop Operators. **Founded:** 1978. **Freq:** Monthly. **Print Method:** Offset. **Trim Size:** 9 7/8 x 12 1/2. **Cols./Page:** 4. **Col. Width:** 2 1/4 inches. **Col. Depth:** 189 agate lines. **Key Personnel:** Steve Sturgess, Editor, ssturgess@heavytruck.com; Deborah Whistler, Managing Editor. **Subscription Rates:** Free to qualified subscribers; $20 /year. **Remarks:** Combined advertising rates available with Heavy Duty Trucking, Truck and Sales Leasing, and Truckstop World. **URL:** http://www.heavytruck.com.
Ad Rates: BW: $6,135 **Circ:** Non-paid ‡206,000
4C: $8,760

2656 Newport Beach/Costa Mesa Daily Pilot
California Community News Corp.
330 W. Bay St. Phone: (714)642-4321
PO Box 1560 Fax: (714)642-7667
Costa Mesa, CA 92627
General newspaper. **Founded:** 1923. **Freq:** Mon.-Sat. (morn.). **Print Method:** Offset. **Trim Size:** 13 x 21 1/2. **Cols./Page:** 6. **Key Personnel:** Bill Lobdell, Editor; Jim Gressingen, Publisher. **Subscription Rates:** $63 individuals. **Remarks:**

Accepts advertising. **Online:** Los Angeles Times. **Formerly**: Orange Coast Daily Pilot (1992).
Ad Rates: BW: $2264 **Circ:** Free ❑65,520
4C: $275 Paid ❑381
PCI: $35

2657 Newport Beach 714
Baker Communications, Inc.
1901 Westcliff Dr., Ste. 11 Phone: (714)722-1286
Newport Beach, CA 92660 Fax: (714)722-6632

Lifestyle magazine (tabloid) on society, fashion, beauty, interior design, people, social events, and restaurants for residents in and around Newport Beach. **Founded:** June 1984. **Freq:** Monthly. **Print Method:** Offset. **Trim Size:** 11 3/8 x 15. **Cols./Page:** 4. **Key Personnel:** Donna Bunce, Editor, phone (310)275-8850; Seth Baker, Publisher; Poppy Laney, Asst. Ed. **Subscription Rates:** Free; $50 by mail. **Remarks:** Accepts advertising.
Ad Rates: BW: $2,180 **Circ:** Free ‡50,000
4C: $3,460

2658 Orange Coast
3701 Birch St., No. 100 Phone: (949)862-1133
Newport Beach, CA 92660 Fax: (949)862-0133

Consumer magazine for residents and visitors of Orange County, CA. **Subtitle:** The Magazine of Orange County. **Founded:** 1974. **Freq:** Monthly. **Print Method:** Offset. **Trim Size:** 8 3/8 x 10 7/8. **Cols./Page:** 3. **Col. Width:** 13 1/2 picas. **Col. Depth:** 44 picas. **Key Personnel:** Patrick Mott, Editor; Fran Tyler, Circulation Dir.; Linda Goldstein, Advertising Dir.; Judi Lesher, VP of Operations. **ISSN:** 0279-0483. **Subscription Rates:** $19.95; $30 other countries; $2.95 single issue. **Remarks:** Accepts advertising. **URL:** http://www.orangecoast.com.
Ad Rates: BW: $2,970 **Circ:** Paid ★30,385
4C: $3,910

2659 Real Money
4910 Birch St. Fax: (714)752-7214
Newport Beach, CA 92660 Free: (888)300-4004

Consumer financial and lifestyle magazine for an affluent audience. **Founded:** 1995. **Freq:** Quarterly. **Print Method:** Web offset. **Trim Size:** 8 3/8 x 10 7/8. **Cols./Page:** 3. **Key Personnel:** Louis E. Carabini, Editor-in-Chief; William Nelles, Editor; J. Creig Von Gillern, Managing Editor; Judy Kean, Exec. Dir. **Subscription Rates:** $15.80 individuals; $3.95 single issue. **Remarks:** Accepts advertising.
Circ: (Not Reported)

2660 Road & Track
Hachette Filipacchi Magazines, Inc.
1499 Monrovia Ave. Phone: (949)720-5300
Newport Beach, CA 92663 Fax: (949)631-2757

Automotive magazine. **Founded:** June 1947. **Freq:** Monthly. **Print Method:** Offset. **Trim Size:** 7 7/8 x 10 1/2. **Cols./Page:** 3. **Col. Width:** 27 nonpareils. **Col. Depth:** 140 agate lines. **Key Personnel:** Thos L. Bryant, Editor; Brian J. McMahon, Sr. VP and Group Publisher. **ISSN:** 0035-7189. **Subscription Rates:** $21.94 individuals; $3.50 single issue. **Remarks:** Accepts advertising. **Online:** America Online, Inc. **URL:** http://www.roadandtrack.com.
Ad Rates: BW: $39,855 **Circ:** Paid ★758,299
4C: $61,315

2661 Truck Sales & Leasing
Newport Communications
PO Box W Phone: (714)261-1636
Newport Beach, CA 92658-8910 Fax: (714)261-2904
Free: (800)233-1911
Publication E-mail: dkolman@heavytruck.com

Trade journal serving new truck and trailer dealerships, factory branches, rental and leasing companies, equipment dealers, manufacturers, and engine distributors. **Founded:** 1985. **Freq:** Bimonthly. **Trim Size:** 8 x 10 3/4. **Cols./Page:** 3. **Col. Width:** 2 1/4 inches. **Col. Depth:** 9 1/4 inches. **Key Personnel:** Kurt Candra, Managing Editor; Maria Barnett, Production Mgr. **Remarks:** Accepts advertising. **URL:** http://www.heavytruck.com.
Ad Rates: BW: $5,290 **Circ:** Non-paid ‡20,074
4C: $7,650
PCI: $100

2662 Truckers News
Newport Communications
PO Box W Phone: (714)261-1636
Newport Beach, CA 92658-8910 Fax: (714)261-2904
Free: (800)233-1911
Publication E-mail: ssturgess@heavytruck.com

Magazine for patrons of truck stops. **Founded:** 1977. **Freq:** Monthly. **Trim Size:** 9 7/8 x 12 1/2. **Cols./Page:** 4. **Col. Width:** 2 1/4 inches. **Col. Depth:** 11 1/4 inches. **Key Personnel:** Deborah Whistler, Managing Editor; Maria Barnett, Editor; Rick DeMuesy, Advertising Mgr. **Remarks:** Accepts advertising.
Ad Rates: GLR: $120 **Circ:** Non-paid ‡201,343
BW: $6,715
4C: $8,640

2663 Truckstop Travel Plaza
Newport Communications
PO Box W Phone: (714)261-1636
Newport Beach, CA 92658-8910 Fax: (714)261-2904
Free: (800)233-1911

Magazine for managers of truckstops, fuelstops, interstate travel centers, and turnpike plazas. **Subtitle:** The Business Magazine of Truckstops. **Founded:** Aug. 1987. **Freq:** Quarterly. **Print Method:** Offset. **Trim Size:** 8 x 10 3/4. **Cols./Page:** 3. **Col. Width:** 13 picas. **Col. Depth:** 54 picas. **Key Personnel:** Jack Thiessen, Editor, phone (419)882-1145, jthiessen@heavytruck.com; Tom Stanford, Publisher, phone (419)786-3030; Bud Farquhar, Advertising Mgr., phone (203)221-7861, fax (203)226-1440. **ISSN:** 0894-962X. **Subscription Rates:** Free to qualified truckstop profit center managers and purchasing personnel. **Remarks:** Accepts advertising. **URL:** http://www.heavytruck.com. **Formerly**: Truckstop World.
Ad Rates: BW: $3,730 **Circ:** Controlled ‡10,000
4C: $4,875

2664 Viva Petites!
USA Petites
537 Newport Dr. Phone: (714)643-5008
Fashion Island Fax: (714)362-3013
Newport Beach, CA 92660-6937
Fashion magazine for petite women. **Freq:** Monthly. **Subscription Rates:** $18.

2665 Western Outdoors
Western Outdoors Publications
PO Box 2027 Phone: (714)546-4370
Newport Beach, CA 92659-1027 Fax: (714)662-3486
Publication E-mail: woutdoors@aol.com

Fishing and boating magazine. **Subtitle:** The Magazine of Western Sportfishing. **Founded:** 1960. **Freq:** 9/year. **Print Method:** Offset. **Trim Size:** 8 1/8 x 10 7/8. **Cols./Page:** 3. **Col. Width:** 27 nonpareils. **Col. Depth:** 140 agate lines. **Key Personnel:** Jack Brown, Editor; Robert Twilegar, Publisher. **Subscription Rates:** $11.95 individuals; $3.50 single issue. **Remarks:** Accepts advertising.
Ad Rates: BW: $2,787 **Circ:** Paid ★96,028
4C: $4,196

2666 Comcast Cablevision of Newport Beach
901 W. 16th St. Phone: (714)642-7276
Newport Beach, CA 92663 Fax: (714)722-2404

Founded: 1969. **Cities Served:** Orange County, CA.

2667 KBCD-FM - 103.1
2043 Westcliff Dr., Ste. 303 Phone: (714)548-6277
Newport Beach, CA 92660-5511 Fax: (714)548-6856
Free: (800)423-1031
E-mail: groove@grooveradio.com

Format: Adult Contemporary; Contemporary Hit Radio (CHR). **Simulcasts:** KACD-FM (Santa Monica). **Networks:** Independent. **Founded:** 1991. **Absorbed**: KBJZ-FM (1995); KAJZ-FM (1995). **Formerly**: MARS-FM (1991); KSRF-FM; KOCM-FM. **Operating Hours:** Continuous; 100% local. **ADI:** Los Angeles (Corona & San Bernardino), CA. **Key Personnel:** Stephanie Mallon-Hanson, General Sales Mgr., phone (714)548-6277, fax (714)548-2443; Mimi Klein, General Mgr., phone (310)458-1031; Egil Aalvik, Program Dir., phone (310)458-1031. **Wattage:** 2500. **URL:** http://www.grooveradio.com.

NORCO

2668 Animals Exotic and Small
1320 Mountain Ave. Phone: (909)371-4307
Norco, CA 91760-2852 Fax: (909)371-4779
Publisher E-mail: aes01@linkline.com

Trade magazine covering exotic and miniature animals. **Founded:** 1988. **Freq:** Bimonthly. **Print Method:** Web offset. **Cols./Page:** 3. **Key Personnel:** Debbie Hosley, Owner & Editor. **Subscription Rates:** $21 individuals. **Remarks:** Accepts advertising. **URL:** http://animalsexoticandsmall.com. **Former name**: Pygmy Goat Digest.
Circ: (Not Reported)

2669 Corona-Norco Independent
Press Enterprise
823 S. Main St. Phone: (714)737-1234
PO Box 1029 Fax: (714)737-1572
Corona, CA 91720-3421
Weekly newspaper. **Founded:** 1957. **Freq:** Weekly (Fri.). **Print Method:** Offset. **Cols./Page:** 5. **Col. Width:** 2 inches. **Col. Depth:** 13 inches. **Key Personnel:** John Orr, Editor; Joe Hudon, General Mgr., phone (909)301-3500, fax (909)679-2450, jhudon@pe.com. **ISSN:** 0745-3930. **Subscription Rates:** $9 individuals. **Remarks:** Accepts advertising.
Ad Rates: GLR: $.30 **Circ:** Free ‡14,500
BW: $225
4C: $435.75
SAU: $1.75

NORTH HIGHLANDS

2670 Spectrum Newspaper Weekly
Spectrum Newspapers
3628 Madison Ave., Ste. 3 Phone: (916)348-2723
North Highlands, CA 95660 Fax: (916)334-7905

Newspaper serving active senior citizens, 55 and older, in the Sacramento area. **Founded:** 1975. **Freq:** Weekly. **Print Method:** Web offset. **Key Personnel:** Gary Chazen, Editor, phone (916)348-2795; Jim McClenahan, Advertising Dir., phone (916)348-2770. **USPS:** 980-481. **Subscription Rates:** $25 individuals. **Formerly**: Spectrum Newspapers Weekly, Contra Costa/Tri Valley.
Circ: 25,000

NORTH HOLLYWOOD

S. CA. Los Angeles Co. 15 mi. NW of Los Angeles. Manufactures aircraft, motion pictures and equipment, missiles, electronics, television, plastics. Residential.

2671 Emmy
Academy of Television Arts and Sciences
5220 Lankershim Blvd. Phone: (818)754-2800
North Hollywood, CA 91601-3109 Fax: (818)761-2827
Publication E-mail: madonna@emmys.org
Publisher E-mail: academy-info@emmys.org

Magazine covering television industry trends, issues, and profiles. **Subtitle:** The Magazine of the Academy of Television Arts & Sciences. **Founded:** 1979. **Freq:** Bimonthly. **Print Method:** Offset. **Trim Size:** 8 1/2 x 11. **Cols./Page:** 3. **Col. Width:** 13 picas. **Col. Depth:** 52 picas. **Key Personnel:** Hank Rieger, Editor and Publisher, phone (818)754-2861, reiger@emmys.org; John McCarthy, Advertising Mgr., phone (818)706-8066, fax (818)706-8326; Gail Polevoi, Editor. **ISSN:** 0164-3495. **Subscription Rates:** $23 individuals sub. agents; $28 individuals; $30 Canada sub. agents; $42 Canada individuals; $47 other countries sub. agents; $65 other countries individuals. **Remarks:** Accepts advertising.
Ad Rates: BW: $1,850 **Circ:** Paid ‡8,494
4C: $3,265 Non-paid ‡2,186

2672 Fore Magazine
Southern California Golf Association
3740 Cahuenga Blvd. Phone: (818)980-3630
North Hollywood, CA 91604 Fax: (818)980-1808
Publication E-mail: bthomas@scga.org

Southern California Golf Association magazine. **Founded:** 1968. **Freq:** Bimonthly. **Print Method:** Offset. **Trim Size:** 8 1/4 x 10 3/4. **Cols./Page:** 3. **Col. Width:** 27 nonpareils. **Col. Depth:** 140 agate lines. **Key Personnel:** Robert D. Thomas, Editor and Publisher, bthomas@scga.org. **Subscription Rates:** Free With associtton membership; $1 included with SCGA membership. **Remarks:** Accepts advertising.
Ad Rates: BW: $5,405 **Circ:** Paid 141,965
4C: $7,640 Non-paid 3,252

2673 Music Connection Magazine
Music Connection Inc.
4731 Laurel Canyon Blvd. Phone: (818)755-0101
North Hollywood, CA 91607 Fax: (818)755-0102
Publication E-mail: muscon@earthlink.net
Publisher E-mail: muscon@earthlink.net

Consumer trade publication. **Subtitle:** The West Coast Music Trade Magazine. **Founded:** Nov. 1977. **Freq:** Biweekly. **Print Method:** Web. **Trim Size:** 8 3/8 x 11. **Cols./Page:** 4. **Col. Width:** 1 3/14 inches. **Col. Depth:** 10 inches. **Key Personnel:** Mark Wardone, Sr. Editor; E. Eric Bettelli, Publisher; J. Michael Dolan, Publisher. **USPS:** 447-330. **Subscription Rates:** $40 individuals; $2.95 single issue; $65 other countries 1 year; $115 two years other countries; $3.95 other countries single issue; $65 U.S. - 2 yrs. **Remarks:** Accepts advertising. **URL:** http://www.musicconnection.com.
Ad Rates: BW: $1,540 **Circ:** ⊕10,600
4C: $2,180
PCI: $62

2674 Panjandrum Poetry Journal
Panjandrum Press, Inc.
6156 Wilkinson Ave. Phone: (818)506-0202
North Hollywood, CA 91606
Journal covering poetry, prose, and philosophy. **Freq:** Irregular. **Print Method:** Offset. **Trim Size:** 5 x 8. **Key Personnel:**

Dennis Koran, Editor and Publisher. **Subscription Rates:** $6 single issue. **Alt. Formats:** Audio tape; CD-ROM.
Circ: Combined 1,200

2675 Share International
PO Box 971 Phone: (818)785-6300
North Hollywood, CA 91603 Fax: (818)904-9132
Publication E-mail: share@shareintl.org
Publisher E-mail: share@shareintl.org

Magazine reporting on world events and emergence of Maitreya, the World Teacher. **Founded:** Jan. 1982. **Freq:** Monthly. **Print Method:** Offset. **Trim Size:** 8 1/2 x 11. **Cols./Page:** 3. **Col. Width:** 2 3/8 inches. **Col. Depth:** 9 3/8 inches. **Key Personnel:** Benjamin Creme, Editor, phone ( )44-171-267-2881; Peter Liefhebber, Editor. **ISSN:** 0169-1341. **Subscription Rates:** $30 individuals; $32.50 Australia and New Zealand. **Remarks:** Advertising not accepted.
Circ: Paid 5,000
Non-paid 1,000

2676 KPFK-FM - 90.7
3729 Cahuenga Blvd. W. Phone: (818)985-2711
North Hollywood, CA 91604 Fax: (818)763-7526

Format: Eclectic. **Networks:** Pacifica. **Owner:** Pacifica Foundation, 1929 Martin Luther King Jr. Way, Berkeley, CA 94704, (510)843-0130, Fax: (510)845-0289. **Founded:** 1959. **Operating Hours:** Continuous. **Key Personnel:** Mark Schubb, General Mgr.; Kathy Lo, Program Dir.; Sharon Aoki, Development Dir.; Frank Stoltze, News Dir.; Betto Areos, Operations Mgr. **Local Programs:** *Background Briefing (Political & World Affairs Issues)*, Ian Masters; *Radio Nation (Editors & Contributors of the Nations Magazine)*, Mare Cooper; *Up for Air (Morning Magazine)* 7 a.m.-9 a.m., Mareos Frommer. **Wattage:** 112,000. **Ad Rates:** Noncommercial.

NORTHRIDGE

S. CA. Los Angeles Co. 25 mi. N. of Los Angeles. California State University, Northridge. Citrus juices, electronic parts, boats, carbon paper manufactured.

2677 The Daily Sundial
Santa Susana Press
University Library Phone: (818)677-2635
18111 Nordhoff St. Fax: (818)677-2676
Northridge, CA 91330-8326
Publisher E-mail: santa.susana@csun.edu

Key Personnel: Cindy Ventuleth, cindy.ventuleth@csun.edu.

2678 Journal of Drug Education
Baywood Publishing Co., Inc.
Dept. of Health Science Phone: (818)677-2720
C.S.U.N.
18111 Nordhoff St.
Northridge, CA 91330-8285
Publisher E-mail: baywood@baywood.com

Journal on the behavioral consequences of drug use and abuse for education professionals, health professionals, social service and Armed Forces personnel. **Founded:** 1970. **Freq:** Quarterly. **Print Method:** Offset. **Trim Size:** 6 x 9. **Cols./Page:** 1. **Col. Width:** 4 1/2 inches. **Col. Depth:** 7 1/2 inches. **Key Personnel:** Seymour Eiseman, Dr.P.H, Editor; Stuart Cohen, Publisher; Lorna Roher, Advertising Mgr.; S. Edwards, Circulation Mgr. **ISSN:** 0047-2379. **Subscription Rates:** $46.50 U.S. and Canada; $51.75 other countries; $142.50 Industry; $147.75 Industry, other countries. **Remarks:** Advertising not accepted.
Circ: (Not Reported)

2679 KCSN-FM - 88.5
18111 Nordhoff St. Phone: (818)677-3089
Northridge, CA 91330
E-mail: kcsn.request@csn.edu

Format: Public Radio; Classical; Eclectic. **Networks:** AP. **Founded:** 1963. **Operating Hours:** Continuous; 5% network, 95% local. **Key Personnel:** Keith Goldstein, News Dir., phone (818)677-2066, fax (818)677-3069; Mike Worrall, Chief Engineer; Jared Kliger, Program Dir.; Dolly Salazar, Dir. of Development; Rene Engel, General Mgr. **Wattage:** 52 at 652 meters HAAT. **Ad Rates:** Noncommercial. **URL:** http://www.kcsn.org.

NORWALK, pop. 85,232.

S. CA. Los Angeles Co. 10 mi. SE of Anaheim. Residential.

2680 Norwalk Herald American
Wave Community Newspapers
819 W. Whitter Blvd. Phone: (213)727-1117
Montebello, CA 90640-3623 Fax: (213)727-9515

Newspaper. **Founded:** 1892. **Freq:** Semiweekly Thurs. and Sat. **Print Method:** Offset. Uses mats. **Cols./Page:** 6. **Col. Width:** 26 nonpareils. **Col. Depth:** 301 agate lines. **Key Personnel:** Arthur J. Aguilar, Editor and Publisher, fax (213)292-8289. **Subscription Rates:** $125 by mail; Free local.
Circ: Paid 74
Free 24,405

2681 Talon Marks
Cerritos College
11110 Alondra Blvd. Phone: (562)860-2451
Norwalk, CA 90650-6298 Fax: (562)467-5044

Collegiate newspaper. **Founded:** 1956. **Freq:** Biweekly Wednesday. **Print Method:** Offset. **Cols./Page:** 6. **Col. Width:** 25 nonpareils. **Col. Depth:** 294 agate lines. **Key Personnel:** N. Ballard, nballar@cerritos.edu. **Subscription Rates:** $7 local. **Remarks:** Accepts advertising.
Ad Rates: GLR: $6 **Circ:** Free 7,500
SAU: $7
PCI: $8

NOVATO, pop. 43,916.

W. CA. Marin Co. 28 mi. N. of San Francisco. Suburban residential.

2682 Novato Advance
Scripps Marin Publishing Co.
1068 Machin Ave. Phone: (415)892-1516
Novato, CA 94945-2458 Fax: (415)897-0940

Local newspaper. **Founded:** Oct. 1926. **Freq:** Weekly (Wed.). **Print Method:** Offset. **Trim Size:** 14 x 21 1/2. **Cols./Page:** 6. **Col. Width:** 12 picas. **Col. Depth:** 300 agate lines. **Key Personnel:** John Jackson, Editor; John Burns, Publisher, jnburns@unidial.com. **USPS:** 398-840. **Subscription Rates:** $40 individuals. **Remarks:** Accepts advertising.
Ad Rates: BW: $2,070.45 **Circ:** Paid 6,125
4C: $2,186.78 Free 1,155
SAU: $16.05
PCI: $16.05

2683 Woodwork
Ross Periodicals
42 Digital Dr., Ste. 5 Phone: (415)382-0580
Novato, CA 94949 Fax: (415)382-0587

High quality covering all aspects of woodworking. **Subtitle:** A Magazine for All Woodworkers. **Founded:** 1989. **Freq:** Bimonthly. **Print Method:** Web offset. **Trim Size:** 8 3/8 x 10 7/8. **Key Personnel:** John Lavine, Editor; Thomas Toldrian, Publisher. **ISSN:** 1045-3040. **Subscription Rates:** $17.95.
Ad Rates: BW: $2,025 **Circ:** ‡50,000
4C: $2,770

OAKDALE, pop. 8,474.

C. CA. Stanislaus Co. 16 mi. N. of Modesto. Manufactures chocolate, fire trucks. Poultry and egg processing; fruit, vegetable cannery; winery, Diversified farming. Sheep, poultry, dairy, cattle, almonds, peaches.

2684 Oakdale Advertiser
PO Box 278 Phone: (209)847-3021
Oakdale, CA 95361 Fax: (209)847-9750

Shopper. **Freq:** Weekly (Wed.). **Print Method:** Offset. **Cols./Page:** 8. **Col. Width:** 19 nonpareils. **Col. Depth:** 294 agate lines. **Key Personnel:** Stanley L. Cook, Publisher. **Subscription Rates:** $12 individuals.
Circ: Free 4,223

2685 Oakdale Leader
122 S. 3rd Ave. Phone: (209)847-3021
PO Box 278 Fax: (209)847-9750
Oakdale, CA 95361
Community newspaper. **Founded:** 1888. **Freq:** Weekly (Wed.). **Print Method:** Offset. **Trim Size:** 13 1/4 x 21. **Cols./Page:** 8. **Col. Width:** 1 1/2 inches. **Col. Depth:** 21 inches. **Key Personnel:** Steve Breen, Editor; Stan Cook, Publisher; John Burden, Advertising Mgr. **Subscription Rates:** $25 individuals. **Remarks:** Accepts advertising.
Ad Rates: BW: $1,278.48 **Circ:** Paid ‡4,899
4C: $1,618.48 Free ‡5,911
SAU: $12.45
PCI: $9.35

2686 KCBC-AM - 770
10948 Cleveland Ave. Phone: (209)847-7700
Oakdale, CA 95361-0077 Fax: (209)847-1769
Free: (800)593-5222

Format: Talk; News. **Owner:** Crawford Broadcasting Co., PO Box 3003, Blue Bell, PA 19422. **Founded:** 1987. **Formerly:** KPLA-AM (1993). **Operating Hours:** 5 a.m.-12:01 a.m.; 80% network. **ADI:** San Francisco-Oakland-San Jose. **Key Personnel:** Don Crawford, Jr., General Mgr.; Debbie Sill, Office Mgr. **Wattage:** 50,000 day; 1000 night. **Ad Rates:** $15 for 30 seconds; $30 Net for 60 seconds.

OAKHURST, pop. 12,505.

SC CA. Madena Co. 45 mi. NW of Fresno. Residential. Mountain resort.

2687 Sierra Home Advertiser
Central Valley Publishing
PO Box 305 Phone: (209)683-4464
Oakhurst, CA 93644-0305 Fax: (209)683-8102

Shopper. **Founded:** 1978. **Freq:** Weekly (Tues.). **Print Method:** Offset. **Cols./Page:** 6. **Col. Width:** 12 1/2 picas. **Col. Depth:** 21 1/2 inches. **Key Personnel:** Betty E. Linn, Publisher. **Remarks:** Accepts advertising.
Ad Rates: BW: $1,251.30 **Circ:** Free ‡12,500
4C: $1,491.30
SAU: $9.70
PCI: $9.70

2688 Sierra Star
Central Valley Publishing
PO Box 305 Phone: (209)683-4464
Oakhurst, CA 93644-0305 Fax: (209)683-8102

Newspaper. **Founded:** 1958. **Freq:** Weekly (Thurs.). **Print Method:** Offset. **Trim Size:** 13 1/2 x 21 1/2. **Cols./Page:** 6. **Col. Width:** 12 1/2 picas. **Col. Depth:** 21 1/2 inches. **Key Personnel:** Betty E. Linn, Publisher. **Subscription Rates:** $39; $42 other countries. **Remarks:** Accepts advertising.
Ad Rates: GLR: $.51 **Circ:** Paid ‡5,000
BW: $1,251.30
4C: $1,491.30
SAU: $9.70
PCI: $9.70

2689 KAAT-FM - 103.1
PO Box 2020 Phone: (209)683-1031
40356 Oak Parkway Fax: (209)683-5488
Oakhurst, CA 93644
E-mail: mtkaat@sierranet.net

Format: Adult Contemporary; Soft Rock; Big Band/Nostalgia. **Networks:** Jones Satellite. **Founded:** 1982. **Operating Hours:** Continuous; 75% network, 25% local. **ADI:** Fresno-Visalia (Hanford), CA. **Key Personnel:** Larry W. Gamble, Contact; Chris Irvin, Programming V.P.; Bonnie Martucci, Contact. **Local Programs:** *Jazz from the Mountain*, Joe Collins, (209)683-1031, Fax (209)683-5488. **Wattage:** 25,000.

2690 KTNS-AM - 1090
PO Box 2020 Phone: (559)683-1031
Oakhurst, CA 93644 Fax: (559)683-5488
E-mail: mtkaat@sierratel.com

Networks: Jones Satellite. **Founded:** 1988. **Operating Hours:** Sunrise-sunset;. **ADI:** Fresno-Visalia (Hanford), CA. **Key Personnel:** Larry W. Gamble, Contact; Chris Irvin, Programming V.P.; Bonnie Martucci, Contact. **Wattage:** 1,000.

OAKLAND†, pop. 339,288.

W. CA. Alameda Co. On east side of San Francisco Bay, connected by a bridge with San Francisco. Mills College (women). California College of Arts and Crafts. College of Holy Name (women). Coliseum Arena. World's 2nd largest container cargo port. Important seaport. Principally manufactures steel. Iron Paper, tin, building materials, food processing, engines.

2691 Abya Yala News
South and Meso American Indian Rights Center (SAIIC)
PO Box 28703 Phone: (510)834-4263
Oakland, CA 94604 Fax: (510)834-4264
Publisher E-mail: saiic@igc.apc.org

Journal covering indigenous rights and news from Mexico and Central and South America in English and Spanish. **Subtitle:** The Journal of the South and Meso American Indian Rights Center. **Founded:** 1984. **Freq:** Semiannual. **Trim Size:** letter size. **Key Personnel:** Tirso Gonzalez, Editor. **ISSN:** 1071-3182. **Subscription Rates:** $25; $4 single issue; $15. **Remarks:** Accepts advertising. **Alt. Formats:** Large-print. **Formerly:** Eco-Justice and Health.
Circ: (Not Reported)

2692 Affaire de Coeur
Brandywyne Books
3976 Oak Hill Rd. Phone: (510)569-5675
Oakland, CA 94605 Fax: (510)632-8868

Magazine for romantic readers and writers. **Subtitle:** Largest Romance Magazine on the West Coast. **Founded:** 1981. **Freq:** Monthly. **Print Method:** Offset. **Trim Size:** 8 x 10. **Cols./Page:** 3. **Col. Width:** 3 1/2 inches. **Col. Depth:** 8

inches. **Key Personnel:** Louise Snead, Publisher. **ISSN:** 0739-3881. **Subscription Rates:** $35; $5 single issue. **Remarks:** Accepts advertising. **URL:** http://www.sseven.
Ad Rates: BW: $900 **Circ:** Paid 50,000
4C: $1,295 Non-paid 100,000
PCI: $80

2693 Alameda-Contra Medical Association
Alameda-Contra Costa Medical Association
6230 Claremont Ave.
Oakland, CA 94618

Professional journal for Alameda-Contra Medical Association. **Founded:** 1945. **Freq:** Monthly. **Key Personnel:** Dianne Crapo. **Subscription Rates:** Free to qualified subscribers. **Remarks:** Accepts advertising.
Circ: Non-paid 3,000

2694 Alameda County Bar Association Bulletin
Alameda County Bar Association
360 22nd St., Ste. 800 Phone: (510)632-7884
Oakland, CA 94612 Fax: (510)893-3119
Publication E-mail: asanoble@aol.com

Professional magazine covering law. **Founded:** 1960. **Freq:** Monthly (except July and Aug.). **Print Method:** Offset. **Subscription Rates:** Free to qualified subscribers. **Remarks:** Accepts advertising. **URL:** http://www.acbanet.org.
Ad Rates: BW: $800 **Circ:** Controlled 2,800

2695 Almanac
Society for Pacific Coast Native Iris
4333 Oak Hill Rd.
Oakland, CA 94605
Publisher E-mail: irishud@mcn.org

Journal covering hybrid and species Pacific Coast native iris, their care, locations and events. **Founded:** 1978. **Freq:** Semiannual. **Cols./Page:** 2. **Key Personnel:** Lewis Lawyer, Editor/Circulation Mgr. **Subscription Rates:** $4 individuals. **Remarks:** Advertising not accepted.
Circ: Paid 450

2696 American Writer
National Writers Union
National Writers Union/West Phone: (510)839-0110
337 17th St., Ste. 101 Fax: (510)839-6097
Oakland, CA 94612
Publication E-mail: aw@nwu.org
Publisher E-mail: nwu@nwu.org

Journal covering writing and publishing issues for members of the National Writers Union and others. **Subtitle:** The Journal of the National Writers Union/UAW Local 1981. **Founded:** 1986. **Freq:** Quarterly. **Print Method:** Web offset. **Trim Size:** 8 3/8 x 10 7/8. **Key Personnel:** Marcy Rein, Editor. **Subscription Rates:** Included in membership. **Remarks:** Accepts advertising. **URL:** http://www.nwu.org/nwu.
Ad Rates: PCI: $30 **Circ:** Controlled 5,300
Non-paid 3,500

2697 Asian Survey
University of California
6701 San Pablo, Rm. 408 Phone: (510)642-0978
Oakland, CA 94608 Fax: (510)643-9930
Publication E-mail: asiasrvy@socrates.berkeley.edu

Political science journal covering Asia. **Founded:** Mar. 1961. **Freq:** Monthly. **Trim Size:** 6 x 9. **Key Personnel:** Lowell Dittmer, Managing Editor; Leo E. Rose, Emeritus Ed.; Joyce K. Kallgren, Editor; Bonnie Dehler, Asst. Editor; Robert A. Scalapino, Editor Emeritus. **ISSN:** 0004-4687. **Subscription Rates:** $57 individuals; $122 institutions; $32 students. **Remarks:** Accepts advertising.
Ad Rates: BW: $250 **Circ:** ‡3,300

Berkeley Tri City Post - See Berkeley

2698 The Black Scholar
Black World Foundation
PO Box 2869 Phone: (510)547-6633
Oakland, CA 94618 Fax: (510)547-6679
Publication E-mail: blkschlr@aol.com

A journal in which the writings of many of today's finest black thinkers may be viewed. **Subtitle:** Journal of Black Studies and Research. **Founded:** Nov. 1969. **Freq:** Quarterly. **Print Method:** Offset. **Trim Size:** 7 x 10. **Cols./Page:** 2. **Col. Width:** 2 5/8 inches. **Col. Depth:** 8 1/2 inches. **Key Personnel:** Robert Chrisman, Editor and Publisher. **ISSN:** 0006-4246. **Subscription Rates:** $30 individuals; $60 institutions; $75 other countries. **Remarks:** Accepts advertising. **Alt. Formats:** CD-ROM, EBSCO.
Ad Rates: BW: $1,200 **Circ:** Paid 10,000
Non-paid 60,000

2699 Blackjack Forum
RGE Publishing
414 Santa Clara Ave. Phone: (510)465-6452
Oakland, CA 94610 Fax: (510)652-4330

Magazine covering casino blackjack. **Founded:** 1981. **Freq:** Quarterly. **Print Method:** Offset. **Trim Size:** 5 1/2 x 8 1/2. **Cols./Page:** 2. **Col. Width:** 2 inches. **Col. Depth:** 7 1/2 inches. **Key Personnel:** Arnold Snyder, Editor and Publisher; Jesse Hover, Web Master. **Subscription Rates:** $50 individuals; $12.50 single issue. **Remarks:** Accepts advertising. **URL:** http://www.rge21.com.
Ad Rates: BW: $600 **Circ:** Paid 2,500
Non-paid 50

2700 Browbeat Magazine
PO Box 11124 Phone: (510)652-2441
Oakland, CA 94611-2464
Publication E-mail: rizzi@netcom.com

Publication focusing on dissonant music and underground culture. **Founded:** Nov. 1993. **Freq:** Annual. **Print Method:** Offset. **Trim Size:** 8 1/2 x 11. **Cols./Page:** 3. **Col. Width:** 2 1/2 inches. **Key Personnel:** Mike Burma, Contact. **ISSN:** 1075-0371. **Subscription Rates:** $4 single issue. **Remarks:** Accepts advertising.
Ad Rates: BW: $200 **Circ:** Paid 2,000

2701 The Business Picture
Gilman Research Corp.
PO Box 20567 Phone: (510)655-3103
Oakland, CA 94620
Magazine serving as a comprehensive collection of vital economic and financial long term charts. **Founded:** 1988. **Freq:** Quarterly. **Key Personnel:** George Gilman, Editor. **ISSN:** 1064-2471. **Subscription Rates:** $240. **Remarks:** Advertising not accepted.
Circ: (Not Reported)

2702 Cable Yellow Pages
Cable Online
8301 Edgewater Dr. Suite 212
Oakland, CA 94621
Publication E-mail: schnog@cableyellowpages.com

Online Industry Services. **Founded:** 1995. **Freq:** Daily. **Key Personnel:** Gail Colbert, Contact. **Subscription Rates:** Free. **Remarks:** Accepts advertising. **Available Online. URL:** http://www.cable-online.com. **Formerly:** Cable Fax; Cable Online.
Ad Rates: BW: $2,750 **Circ:** (Not Reported)

2703 California Agriculture
111 Franklin St., 6th Floor Phone: (510)987-0044
Agriculture & Natural Resources Fax: (510)465-2659
Oakland, CA 94607-5200
Publication E-mail: calag@ucop.edu

Journal reporting agricultural research at the University of California. **Founded:** Dec. 1946. **Freq:** Bimonthly. **Print Method:** Offset. **Trim Size:** 8 1/2 x 11. **Cols./Page:** 3. **Col. Width:** 2 1/4 inches. **Col. Depth:** 9 1/2 inches. **Key Personnel:** Janet White, Editor, phone (510)987-0045, fax (510)465-2659, janet.white@ucop.edu. **ISSN:** 0008-0845. **Subscription Rates:** Free; $3 back copy; $18 out of country. **Remarks:** Advertising not accepted. **Available Online. URL:** http://www.danr.ucop.edu/calag/.
Circ: Paid 850
Controlled 19,000

2704 California Coast & Ocean
California State Coastal Conservancy
1330 Broadway, Ste. 1100 Phone: (510)286-0934
Oakland, CA 94612-2530 Fax: (510)286-0470
Publisher E-mail: calcoast@igc.org

Journal covering conservation, history, wildlife, and recreation in California. **Founded:** 1985. **Freq:** Quarterly. **Print Method:** Web offset. **Key Personnel:** Rasa Gustaitis, Editor; Dewey Schwartzenburg, Managing Editor, phone (510)286-0515. **ISSN:** 1052-5823. **Subscription Rates:** $18 individuals; $15 teachers; $4.95 single issue. **Remarks:** Advertising not accepted. **URL:** http://www.coastalconservancy.ca.gov. **Former name:** California Waterfront Age (1990).
Circ: Combined 10,000

2705 California Nurse
California Nurses Association
2000 Franklin St., Ste. 300
Oakland, CA 94612-2908
Publication E-mail: knicks@iqc.apc.org
Publisher E-mail: patientwatch@igc.apc.org

Magazine (tabloid) covering the nursing profession. **Founded:** 1904. **Freq:** 10/year. **Print Method:** Web offset. **Trim Size:** 11 1/2 x 14. **Cols./Page:** 4. **Col. Width:** 28 nonpareils. **Col. Depth:** 182 agate lines. **Key Personnel:** Trena Camara, Contact, phone (510)275-2249, fax (510)663-2761. **ISSN:** 0008-1310. **Subscription Rates:** $40 individuals; $50 other countries. **Remarks:** Color advertising not accepted. **URL:** http://www.calnurse.org; http://www.itc.org./CNA.
Ad Rates: GLR: $65 **Circ:** Paid ‡27,000
BW: $1,300 Controlled ‡1,000

2706 CALUnderwriter
California Association of Life Underwriters
70 Washington St., No. 325 Phone: (510)834-2258
Oakland, CA 94607
Publisher E-mail: califalu@aol.com

Magazine containing life and health insurance industry news; official publication of the California Assn. of Life Underwriters. **Founded:** Aug. 1970. **Freq:** Monthly. **Print Method:** Offset. **Trim Size:** 8 1/2 x 11. **Cols./Page:** 3. **Col. Width:** 30 nonpareils. **Col. Depth:** 140 agate lines. **Key Personnel:** Dan Crouch, Editor; Anne Scully, Publisher; Valerie Barbour, Ad Sales, phone (415)388-5495. **ISSN:** 0199-2414. **Subscription Rates:** $5 individuals. **Remarks:** Accepts advertising.
Ad Rates: BW: $1,800 **Circ:** Paid ‡9,000
4C: $2,785 Non-paid ‡230
PCI: $75

2707 The Catholic Voice
3014 Lakeshore Ave. Phone: (510)893-5339
Oakland, CA 94610-3615 Fax: (510)893-4734
Publication E-mail: cathvoice@aol.com

Catholic newspaper. **Founded:** 1963. **Freq:** Biweekly. **Print Method:** Offset. **Cols./Page:** 6. **Col. Width:** 21 nonpareils. **Col. Depth:** 231 agate lines. **Key Personnel:** Monica Clark, Editor; John S. Cummins, Publisher. **Subscription Rates:** $8 individuals; $18 out of area. **Remarks:** Accepts advertising.
Ad Rates: BW: $2,592 **Circ:** Paid 82,500
PCI: $27 Free 500

2708 Construction Market Data, Inc.
80 Swan Way, Suite 130 Phone: (510)636-2480
Oakland, CA 94621 Fax: (510)636-2492
Free: (800)263-6063

Report on general and heavy engineering bid activity for building and construction trade. **Subtitle:** Daily Construction Service. **Founded:** Apr. 1, 1919. **Freq:** Daily. **Print Method:** Offset. **Trim Size:** 8 1/2 x 11. **Cols./Page:** 2. **Col. Width:** 44 nonpareils. **Col. Depth:** 140 agate lines. **Key Personnel:** W.B. Wallace, Publisher; Frank D. Nieto, Editor, frank.nieto@cmdg.com. **ISSN:** 0011-5401. **Subscription Rates:** $1,185 individuals. **Remarks:** Accepts advertising. **URL:** http://www.cmdg.com. **Formerly:** Daily Construction Service.
Ad Rates: BW: $795 **Circ:** Combined ‡3,000

2709 Creation Spirituality Network Magazine
Friends of Creation Spirituality
2141 Broadway Phone: (510)836-4392
Oakland, CA 94612-2309 Fax: (510)835-0564
Free: (800)973-2228
Publication E-mail: csmag@booked.net

Magazine. **Founded:** 1985. **Freq:** Quarterly. **Print Method:** Offset. **Trim Size:** 8 1/8 x 10 3/4. **Cols./Page:** 2. **Key Personnel:** Matthew Fox, Editor-in-Chief; Remi Tremblay, Editor; Rebecca Bier, Editor. **ISSN:** 1053-9891. **Subscription Rates:** $18 individuals; $4.95 single issue. **Remarks:** Accepts advertising. **Available Online. URL:** csnet.org. **Formerly:** Creation; Creation Spirituality Magazine.
Ad Rates: BW: $484 **Circ:** Paid 8,000
4C: $684 Non-paid 100

2710 Diseased Pariah News
Men's Support Center
PO Box 30564
Oakland, CA 94604

Publication focusing on HIV infected gay men. **Freq:** Quarterly. **Subscription Rates:** $10.

2711 EarthLight Magazine
111 Fairmount Ave. Phone: (510)451-4926
Oakland, CA 94611 Fax: (510)451-3505
Publication E-mail: circulation@earthlight.org

Publication on sacred ecology. **Subtitle:** Magazine of Spirituality and Ecology. **Founded:** 1990. **Freq:** Quarterly. **Print Method:** Web offset. **Trim Size:** 8 1/2 x 11. **Cols./Page:** 3. **Col. Width:** 14 picas. **Col. Depth:** 49 picas. **Key Personnel:** K. Lauren de Boer, Editor, klauren@earthlight.org. **ISSN:** 1050-0413. **Subscription Rates:** $20; $5 single issue. **Remarks:** Accepts advertising. **URL:** http://www.earthlight.org.
Ad Rates: BW: $350 **Circ:** Paid 2,500
4C: $600 Non-paid 500
PCI: $15

2712 East Bay Labor Journal
Alameda County Central Labor Council
7992 Capwell Dr. Phone: (510)632-4242
Oakland, CA 94621 Fax: (510)632-3993

Labor journal. **Founded:** 1928. **Freq:** Monthly. **Print Method:** Web offset. **Cols./Page:** 5. **Key Personnel:** Lincoln Smith, Editor. **Subscription Rates:** $5 individuals. **Remarks:** Advertising accepted; rates available upon request.
Circ: Controlled 25,000

2713 El Mundo
The Alameda Publishing Corp./Oakland Post
630-20th St. Phone: (510)287-8200
Oakland, CA 94612
Newspaper with general news, sports, and entertainment (Spanish and English). **Founded:** May 12, 1964. **Freq:** Weekly (Thurs.). **Print Method:** Offset. **Cols./Page:** 6. **Col. Width:** 26 nonpareils. **Col. Depth:** 301 agate lines. **Key Personnel:** William Fonsea, Editor; Thomas Berkley, Publisher; Jose E. Pena, Advertising Mgr. **Subscription Rates:** $42 individuals. **Remarks:** Accepts advertising.
Ad Rates: BW: $3,399.15 **Circ:** Free ‡31,864
4C: $3,649.15
SAU: $26.35

2714 Hip Mama
PO Box 9097 Phone: (510)658-4508
Oakland, CA 94613 Fax: (510)658-4508

Feminist parenting magazine. **Subtitle:** The Parenting Zine. **Founded:** 1993. **Freq:** Quarterly. **Print Method:** Offset. **Trim Size:** 8 1/2 x 11. **Cols./Page:** 2. **Col. Width:** 3 1/2 inches. **Col. Depth:** 7 inches. **Key Personnel:** Ariel Gore, Editor. **ISSN:** 1074-1957. **Subscription Rates:** $15 individuals; $4 single issue. **Remarks:** Accepts advertising.
Ad Rates: BW: $400 **Circ:** Paid 5,000

2715 Impact!
The World Institute on Disability (WID)
510 16th St., Ste. 100 Phone: (510)763-4100
Oakland, CA 94612-1502 Fax: (510)763-4109
Publisher E-mail: wid@wid.org

Magazine reporting on the activities of the World Institute on Disability. **Subtitle:** The World Institute on Disability (WID) Semi-Annual Report. **Founded:** Sept. 1993. **Freq:** Semiannual. **Cols./Page:** 4. **Col. Width:** 2.5 inches. **Col. Depth:** 18 inches. **Key Personnel:** Joan Leon, Editor, phone (510)251-4333. **Subscription Rates:** Free. **Remarks:** Advertising not accepted. **Alt. Formats:** Diskette.
Circ: Non-paid 14,000

2716 Information Services on Latin America (ISLA)
Information Services on Latin America
464 19th St. Phone: (510)835-4692
Oakland, CA 94612 Fax: (510)835-3017

Compilation of newspaper clippings on Latin America. **Founded:** 1970. **Freq:** Monthly. **Trim Size:** 8 1/2 x 11. **Key Personnel:** April Evans, Director. **ISSN:** 0046-8401. **Subscription Rates:** $750; $245 for regional sections. **Remarks:** Advertising not accepted. **Alt. Formats:** Microform.
Circ: Paid ‡220
Non-paid ‡10

2717 The Inter-City Express
Daily Journal Corp.
171 12th St., No. 203 Phone: (510)465-3121
Oakland, CA 94612 Fax: (510)465-1576

Legal and real estate newspaper. **Founded:** 1909. **Freq:** Daily (eve.). **Print Method:** Offset. **Cols./Page:** 4. **Col. Width:** 2 1/2 inches. **Col. Depth:** 13 1/2 inches. **Key Personnel:** Gery Geongherty, Publisher, phone (916)444-2355, liz_smith@dailyjournal.com. **USPS:** 265-620. **Subscription Rates:** $140 individuals. **Remarks:** Accepts advertising.
Ad Rates: BW: $347.20 **Circ:** Paid ‡1,023
PCI: $6.20 Non-paid ‡14

2718 The Journal
Hills Publications, Inc.
5707 Redwood Rd. Phone: (510)339-4040
Oakland, CA 94619 Fax: (510)339-4066

Newspaper. **Freq:** Weekly. **Key Personnel:** Scott Conley, General Mgr. **Subscription Rates:** $80.
Circ: 11,519

2719 Journal of Employee Ownership Law and Finance
National Center for Employee Ownership
1201 Martin Luther King Jr. Way Phone: (510)272-9461
Oakland, CA 94612 Fax: (510)272-9510
Publisher E-mail: nceo@nceo.org

Trade journal covering employee ownership plans and related topics. **Founded:** 1989. **Freq:** Quarterly. **Print Method:** Offset. **Trim Size:** 7 1/2 x 9 1/2. **Cols./Page:** 1. **Col. Width:** 4 3/4 inches. **Col. Depth:** 7 1/2 inches. **Key Personnel:** Scott Rodrick, Editor. **ISSN:** 1046-7491. **Subscription Rates:** $100 individuals; $35 single issue. **Remarks:** Advertising not accepted.
Circ: Combined 550

2720 Left Curve
Left Curve Publications
410 Webster St. Phone: (510)763-7193
Oakland, CA 94607
Publication E-mail: leftcurv@wco.com
Publisher E-mail: leftcurv@wco.com

Left Curve is an artist-produced journal that addresses the problems of cultura l forms emerging from one crises of modernity that strive to be independent from one control of dominent institutions. **Founded:** 1974. **Freq:** Irregular. **Print Method:** Offset. **Trim Size:** 8 1/2 x 11. **Cols./Page:** 2. **Col. Width:** 3 1/2 inches. **Col. Depth:** 9 inches. **Key Personnel:** Csaba Polony, Editor, leftcurv@wco.com; Jack Hirschman, Assoc. Editor; Elizah Escobar, Assoc. Editor; Peter Laska, Assoc. Editor; Susan Schwarzenberg, Assoc. Editor. **ISSN:** 0160-1857. **Subscription Rates:** $30 individuals for 3 issues; $45 institutions. **Remarks:** Accepts advertising. **URL:** http://www.wco.com/~leftcurve; http://www.magmall.com/magazine/81223/leftcurve.htm.
Ad Rates: GLR: $1.50 **Circ:** Paid 1850
BW: $200 2000
PCI: $15

2721 Lifestyle
Alpha General Corp.
421 W. MacArthur Blvd. Phone: (510)420-1381
Oakland, CA 94609 Fax: (510)420-1383

Magazine catering to the singles lifestyle. **Freq:** Semimonthly. **Print Method:** Offset. **Trim Size:** 8 1/2 x 11. **Cols./Page:** 3. **Key Personnel:** Brian Eastman, Editor; Marc Horwitz, Advertising Mgr.; Dave Sawle, Publisher; Gary Gold, Editor. **USPS:** 823-380. **Subscription Rates:** $7; $5 with purchase of personal ad. **Remarks:** Color advertising not accepted.
Ad Rates: BW: $755 **Circ:** Paid ‡3,000
Non-paid ‡90,000

2722 Locus
Locus Press
34 Ridgewood Ln. Phone: (510)339-9196
Oakland, CA 94611 Fax: (510)339-8144
Publication E-mail: locus@locusmag.com
Publisher E-mail: locus@locusmag.com

Trade magazine on science fiction publishing. **Subtitle:** The Newspaper of the Science Fiction Field. **Founded:** Apr. 1968. **Freq:** Monthly. **Print Method:** Offset. **Trim Size:** 8 3/8 x 10 7/8. **Cols./Page:** 3. **Col. Width:** 30 nonpareils. **Col. Depth:** 140 agate lines. **Key Personnel:** Charles N. Brown, Editor-in-Chief/Pub.; Kirstin Gong-Wong, Managing Editor. **ISSN:** 0047-4959. **Subscription Rates:** $43 individuals; $4.95 single issue; $46 institutions. **Remarks:** Accepts advertising. **Alt. Formats:** Microform.
Ad Rates: GLR: $2 **Circ:** ‡10,000
BW: $600
4C: $1,100
PCI: $20

The Montclarion - See Montclair

2723 The Nugget
California Genealogical Society
1611 Telegraph Ave., Suite 200 Phone: (510)663-1358
Oakland, CA 94612-2152 Fax: (510)663-1596
Publisher E-mail: calgensocamerica online, inc.com

Journal covering genealogy. **Freq:** Quarterly. **Trim Size:** 8 1/2 x 11. **Key Personnel:** Marje Kelt. **ISSN:** 1059-9711. **Subscription Rates:** Free to qualified subscribers. **Remarks:** Advertising accepted; rates available upon request.
Circ: 850

2724 Oakland Bay Area Observer
Observer Newspapers
Box 817
San Leandro, CA 94577

Community newspaper. **Founded:** May 22, 1972. **Freq:** Weekly (Fri.). **Print Method:** Offset. **Cols./Page:** 6. **Col. Width:** 10 picas. **Col. Depth:** 16 inches. **Key Personnel:** Ad Fried, Managing Editor; Michael Robert, Publisher; R.A. Burrell, Advertising Mgr. **Subscription Rates:** $25 individuals. **Remarks:** Advertising not accepted for tobacco products.
Ad Rates: BW: $3,000 **Circ:** ‡30,000
4C: $3,600
SAU: $40
PCI: $35

2725 Oakland Post
PO Box 1350 Phone: (510)763-1120
Oakland, CA 94604
Black community newspaper. **Founded:** 1963. **Freq:** Semiweekly (Wed. and Sun.). **Print Method:** Offset. **Cols./Page:** 6. **Col. Width:** 1 1/16 inches. **Col. Depth:** 21 1/2 inches. **Key Personnel:** Gail Berkley, Editor; Thomas Berkley, Publisher; Donald V. Welcher, Advertising Mgr. **Subscription Rates:** $42 individuals. **Remarks:** Accepts advertising.
Ad Rates: GLR: $43.73 **Circ:** Free ‡62,496
BW: $5,641.17

2726 The Oakland Tribune
Alameda Newspaper Group
116 W. Wenton Ave. Phone: (510)293-2901
Hayward, CA 94544 Fax: (510)293-2697
Free: (800)743-8742

General newspaper. **Founded:** 1874. **Freq:** Mon.-Sun. (morn.). **Print Method:** Letterpress. **Cols./Page:** 6. **Col. Width:** 26 nonpareils. **Col. Depth:** 301 agate lines. **Key Personnel:** C. David Burgin, Editor-in-Chief; Tim Graham, Editor; Brian Arnonstam, Managing Editor; Bob Cuddy, Page Editor. **ISSN:** 0745-3841. **Subscription Rates:** $99 individuals. **Remarks:** Accepts advertising. **Online:** DataTimes Corporation. **Feature Editors:** Steve Herendeen, *Sports*; Ron Reisterer, *Photo*; Dave Tong, *Financial/Business*.
Ad Rates: BW: $8,742.33 **Circ:** Mon.-Sat. ★**68,105**
4C: $9,860.33 Sun. ★**64,260**
PCI: $67.77

2727 The Pet Companion
3871 Piedmont Ave., No. 305 Phone: (510)533-7777
Oakland, CA 94611-5351 Fax: (510)533-7571
Publisher E-mail: petcom@earthlink.net

Newspaper covering pet care and ownership. **Subtitle:** Nation's Largest Regional Pet Publication. **Founded:** 1989. **Freq:** Monthly. **Print Method:** Coolset web. **Trim Size:** 11 3/8 x 14. **Cols./Page:** 5. **Col. Width:** 1 7/8 inches. **Col. Depth:** 12 3/4 inches. **Key Personnel:** Grace Neufeld, Editor and Publisher; Branko Romano, Office & Distribution Mgr. **Subscription Rates:** $35 individuals. **Remarks:** Accepts advertising. **Former name:** Pet Gazette.
Ad Rates: GLR: $1.25 **Circ:** Controlled 75,200
BW: $1,800
4C: $2,100
PCI: $25

Piedmont Press - See Piedmont

2728 Radiance
Radiance: The Magazine for Large Women
PO Box 30246 Phone: (510)482-0680
Oakland, CA 94604 Fax: (510)482-0680
Publication E-mail: radmag2@aol.com; publisher@radiancemagazine.com

Magazine encouraging women to feel good about their bodies, whatever their size. Featuring articles on health, media, fashion and politics. A leading resource in the worldwide size acceptance movement. **Subtitle:** The Magazine for Large Women. **Founded:** Oct. 5, 1984. **Freq:** Quarterly. **Print Method:** Web printing. **Trim Size:** 8.375 x 10.875. **Cols./Page:** 3. **Col. Width:** 2 1/4 inches. **Col. Depth:** 10 1/2 inches. **Key Personnel:** Alice Ansfield, Editor and Publisher. **ISSN:** 0889-9495. **Subscription Rates:** $20 individuals; $26 Canada; $34 other countries. **Remarks:** Accepts advertising. **Online:** America Online, Inc. **URL:** http://www.radiancemagazine.com.
Ad Rates: BW: $1,200 **Circ:** Paid ‡15,000
4C: $1,800

Richmond Post - See Richmond

San Francisco Post - See San Francisco

2729 SET Free
Society for the Eradication of Television
Box 10491 Phone: (510)763-8712
Oakland, CA 94610-0491
Publication focusing on the negative aspects of television. **Subtitle:** The Newsletter Against Television. **Founded:** 1980. **Freq:** Quarterly. **Trim Size:** 8 1/2 x 14. **Key Personnel:** Steve Wagner, Dir. **Subscription Rates:** $5. **Remarks:** Advertising not accepted.
Circ: Paid 1,200

2730 TEST Engineering & Management
The Mattingley Publishing Co., Inc.
3756 Grand Ave., Ste. 205 Phone: (510)839-0909
Oakland, CA 94610-1545 Fax: (510)839-2950
Publisher E-mail: testmag@crl.com

Trade publication that covers physical and mechanical testing and environmental simulation; edited for test engineering professionals. **Founded:** Feb. 1959. **Freq:** Bimonthly. **Print Method:** Offset. **Trim Size:** 8 x 10 7/8. **Cols./Page:** 3. **Col. Width:** 26 nonpareils. **Col. Depth:** 140 agate lines. **Key**

Personnel: Eve Mattingley-Hannigan, Editor and Publisher, testmag@mattingley-pub.com. **ISSN:** 0193-4120. **Subscription Rates:** $40 individuals; $55 other countries; $5 single issue. **Remarks:** Accepts advertising.
Ad Rates: BW: $2,950 **Circ:** Non-paid ‡8,772
4C: $3,850
PCI: $90

2731 The Urban Ecologist
Urban Ecology, Inc.
405 14th St., Ste. 900
Oakland, CA 94612-2706

Journal concerning urban ecology. **Freq:** Quarterly. **Subscription Rates:** $35 individuals; $4 single issue. **Remarks:** Advertising not accepted.
Circ: (Not Reported)

2732 The Wise Woman
2441 Cordova St. Phone: (510)536-3174
Oakland, CA 94602
Magazine focusing on feminist issues, Goddess lore, feminist spirituality and Feminist Witchcraft. Contains original research on witch hunts, women's heritage, and women today. **Founded:** 1980. **Freq:** Quarterly. **Print Method:** Offset. **Trim Size:** 8 1/2 x 11. **Key Personnel:** Ann Forfreedom, Publisher. **ISSN:** 0883-119X. **Subscription Rates:** $15 individuals; $27 two years. **Remarks:** Advertising not accepted. **Alt. Formats:** Microfilm.
Circ: (Not Reported)

2733 WorldViews
1515 Webster St. Phone: (510)451-1742
Oakland, CA 94612 Fax: (510)835-9631
Publication E-mail: worldviews@igc.org
Publisher E-mail: worldviews@igc.org

Review of resources from and about the Third World. **Subtitle:** A Quarterly Review of Resources for Education and Action. **Founded:** 1985. **Freq:** Quarterly. **Print Method:** Sheetfed offset. **Trim Size:** 8 1/2 x 11. **Cols./Page:** 3. **Col. Width:** 2 1/2 inches. **Col. Depth:** 10 inches. **Key Personnel:** Tom Fenton, Editor, tfenton@igc.org; Mary Heffron, Book Review Editor. **ISSN:** 1085-7559. **Subscription Rates:** $25 individuals; $45 individuals other countries; $50 institutions U.S. and Canada; $65 institutions other countries. **URL:** http://www.igc.org/worldviews/. **Formerly:** Third World Resources (1996).
Ad Rates: BW: $600 **Circ:** Controlled ‡2,000
PCI: $20

2734 KEAR-FM - 106.9
290 Hegenberger Rd. Phone: (510)568-6200
Family Radio Fax: (510)568-6190
Oakland, CA 94621-1436
Free: (800)543-1495

Format: Religious; Educational. **Networks:** Family Stations Radio. **Founded:** 1959. **Operating Hours:** Continuous; 90% network, 10% local. **ADI:** San Francisco-Oakland-San Jose. **Key Personnel:** Matthew Pearce, Contact, matthew@familyradio.com; Tony Serverdia, Chief Engineer. **Wattage:** 80,000. **Ad Rates:** Noncommercial.

2735 KMKY-AM - 1310
384 Embarcadero W. 3rd Fl. Phone: (510)251-1400
Oakland, CA 94607-3734 Fax: (510)251-2110
E-mail: mouse1310@aol.com

Networks: ABC. **Owner:** Pacific-FM, 2500 Marin St., San Francisco, CA 94124, (415)821-2020, Fax: (415)282-1247. **Founded:** 1922. **Formerly:** KWBR-AM (1959); KDIA-AM (1997). **Operating Hours:** Continuous. **ADI:** San Francisco-Oakland-San Jose. **Key Personnel:** Joan Sommers, General Mgr., fax (510)663-0166, joan.l.sommers@abc.com; Bill Hickey, Chief Engineer, phone (415)954-8116, fax (415)391-2795. **Wattage:** 5000. **Ad Rates:** $80 for 30 seconds; $150 for 60 seconds. **URL:** http://www.disney.com.

2736 KTVU-TV - 2
2 Jack Lyndon Sq. Phone: (510)834-1212
Oakland, CA 94607 Fax: (510)272-9957
Free: (800)678-3375

Format: Commercial TV. **Networks:** Fox; Independent. **Owner:** Cox Enterprises, Inc., PO Box 105357, Atlanta, GA 30348, (404)843-5000. **Founded:** 1958. **Operating Hours:** Continuous; 3% network, 97% local. **ADI:** San Francisco-Oakland-San Jose. **Key Personnel:** Kevin O'Brien, General Mgr., phone (510)874-0239; Fred Zehnder, News Dir., phone (510)451-2610; Sterling Davis, Operations Mgr., phone (510)272-9957; Jeff Block, Station Mgr., phone (510)452-2602; Caroline Chang, Program Mgr.; Steve Poitras, Marketing Dir., phone (510)763-6400; Adina Pasto, Controller, phone (510)874-0190, fax (510)874-0583; Tom Raponi, General Sales Mgr.

2737 TCI Oakland
4215 Foothill Blvd. Phone: (510)534-3364
Oakland, CA 94601 Fax: (510)436-7531

Founded: 1973. **Formerly:** Cable Oakland. **Key Personnel:** Clay Owens, Contact. **Cities Served:** Emeryville, Oakland, Piedmont, CA: subscribing households 72,000; 60 channels; 2 community access channels.

OCCIDENTAL

2738 The Albion Monitor
Monitor Publishing
PO Box 1025 Fax: (707)824-0549
Occidental, CA 95465
Publication E-mail: editor@monitor.net; pub@monitor.net

Presents articles about environmental activism including "non-mainstream" and political issues. Covers both national and international events. **Key Personnel:** Jeff Elliott, Editor. **Subscription Rates:** $9.95 individuals. **Remarks:** Advertising not accepted. **URL:** http://www.monitor.net/monitor/.
Circ: (Not Reported)

OCEANSIDE, pop. 76,698.

S. CA. San Diego Co. On Pacific Ocean, 38 mi. N. of San Diego. Resort. Manufactures Electrical connectors, electronic components, military hardware.

2739 The North County Times
Howard Publications Inc.
PO Box 90 Phone: (714)433-7333
Oceanside, CA 92049-0090
General newspaper. **Founded:** 1892. **Freq:** Daily. **Cols./Page:** 6. **Col. Width:** 13 inches. **Col. Depth:** 21 inches. **Key Personnel:** Kent Davy, Editor; S. Scott Putnicki, Advertising Dir.; Richard High, Publisher. **Subscription Rates:** $127.40 individuals. **Remarks:** Accepts advertising. **Formerly:** The North County Blade-Citizen; The North County Times-Advocate.
Circ: Paid 83,345

2740 Rays from the Rose Cross
Rosicrucian Fellowship
PO Box 713 Phone: (760)757-6600
Oceanside, CA 92049-0713 Fax: (760)721-3806
Publisher E-mail: rosfshp@cts.com

Consumer magazine covering Christianity, spirituality, astrology, vegetarianism, poetry, and reviews. **Founded:** 1915. **Freq:** Bimonthly. **Print Method:** Offset. **ISSN:** 0744-432X. **Subscription Rates:** $20 individuals; $5 single issue. **Remarks:** Advertising not accepted. **URL:** http://www.rosicrucian.com.
Circ: Combined ‡1,000

2741 TransWorld Skateboarding Magazine
TransWorld Media
353 Airport Rd. Phone: (619)722-7777
Oceanside, CA 92054 Fax: (619)722-0653
Publication E-mail: twsnow@twsnet.com

Magazine for skateboarders. **Founded:** 1983. **Freq:** Monthly. **Print Method:** Web offset. **Trim Size:** 8 x 10 7/8. **Key Personnel:** Peggy Cousins, Publisher; Larry Bauma, Publisher. **ISSN:** 0748-7401. **Subscription Rates:** $19.95. $3.50 single issue. **Remarks:** Accepts advertising. **URL:** http://www.twsnow.com.
Ad Rates: BW: $2,710 **Circ:** 100,000
4C: $4,440

2742 TransWorld Snowboarding Magazine
TransWorld Media
353 Airport Rd. Phone: (619)722-7777
Oceanside, CA 92054 Fax: (619)722-0653

Magazine for the snowboarding industry. **Founded:** 1987. **Freq:** Quarterly 7/year. **Print Method:** Web offset. **Trim Size:** 8 1/8 x 10 7/8. **Key Personnel:** Peggy Cousins, Publisher; Larry Bauma, Publisher. **Subscription Rates:** $18.95 individuals; $3.95 single issue; $53.95 out of country; $44.95 Canada. **Remarks:** Accepts advertising.
Ad Rates: BW: $4,855 **Circ:** Paid ‡180,000
4C: $6,799 Non-paid ‡109,000

2743 KKLQ-AM - 1320
2952 Oceanside Blvd. Phone: (619)757-1321
Oceanside, CA 92051 Fax: (619)757-3864

Format: Easy Listening. **Founded:** 1956. **Formerly:** KGMG-AM. **Operating Hours:** Continuous. **Key Personnel:** Steve Jacobs, General Mgr.; Chris Vaccaro, Operations Mgr. **Wattage:** 500. **Ad Rates:** Advertising accepted; rates available upon request.

OJAI, pop. 6,816.

SW CA. Ventura Co. 14 mi. NE of Ventura. Ventura Co. (SW). 14 m NE of Ventura. Mountain resort. Private schools. Fruit packed. Diversified farming.

2744 The Braille Star Theosophist
Theosophical Book Association for the Blind, Inc.
54 Krotona Hill Phone: (805)646-2121
Ojai, CA 93023-3901 Fax: (805)646-2121
Publication E-mail: 75457.633@compuserve.com
Publisher E-mail: tbab@compuserve.com; 75457.633@compuserve.com

Magazine dealing with the Theosophical Book Association for the Blind, Inc. **Freq:** Irregular. **Subscription Rates:** Free. **Remarks:** Advertising not accepted. **Alt. Formats:** Audio tape; Braille.
Circ: Non-paid 5,000

2745 Ojai Valley News
Ojai Valley News, Inc.
PO Box 277 Phone: (805)646-1476
Ojai, CA 93024-0277 Fax: (805)646-4281
Publication E-mail: dewartim@ojaivalleynews.com

Local newspaper. **Founded:** 1891. **Freq:** Semiweekly (Wed. and Fri.). **Print Method:** Offset. **Cols./Page:** 6. **Col. Width:** 18 nonpareils. **Col. Depth:** 294 agate lines. **Key Personnel:** Ren L. Adam, Publisher. **ISSN:** 4059-8000. **Subscription Rates:** $25 individuals. **Remarks:** Accepts advertising. **URL:** http://www.ojaivalleynews.com.
Ad Rates: GLR: $.58 **Circ:** ‡4,940
BW: $1,008
4C: $1,534
SAU: $.58
PCI: $8

2746 Ojai Valley Shopper
Ojai Valley News, Inc.
PO Box 277 Phone: (805)646-1476
Ojai, CA 93024-0277 Fax: (805)646-4281

Community Shopper. **Founded:** 1891. **Freq:** Weekly. **Print Method:** Offset. **Cols./Page:** 6. **Col. Width:** 18 nonpareils. **Col. Depth:** 294 agate lines. **Key Personnel:** Jon Fishman, Publisher. **ISSN:** 4059-8000. **Subscription Rates:** Free.

ONTARIO, pop. 88,820.

SE CA. San Bernardino Co. 30 mi. E. of Los Angeles. Manufactures aircraft and aircraft parts, electrical equipment, tile, steel products, aluminum roofing, missile components. Wineries. Nurseries. Ships citrus fruit. Agriculture. Oranges, lemons, olives, grapes.

2747 Inland Valley Daily Bulletin
Donrey Media Group
2041 E. 4th St. Phone: (909)987-6397
Ontario, CA 91764-2605 Fax: (909)948-3197

General newspaper serving Chino, Chino Hills, Claremont, Diamond Bar, Fontana, La Verne, Montclair, Ontario, Pomona, Rancho Cucamonga, San Dimas, and Upland, CA. **Founded:** 1885. **Freq:** Daily (morn.). **Print Method:** Offset. **Cols./Page:** 6. **Col. Width:** 26 nonpareils. **Col. Depth:** 301 agate lines. **Key Personnel:** Michael R. Ferguson, Publisher. **Subscription Rates:** $91 individuals. **Remarks:** Accepts advertising.
Ad Rates: GLR: $2.95 **Circ:** Mon.-Sat. ★**67,809**
BW: $5,321.25 Sun. ★**73,995**
4C: $6,166.25
PCI: $41.25

2748 Ontario Green Sheet
Associated Desert Shoppers, Inc.
73-400 Hwy. 111 Phone: (760)346-1729
Palm Desert, CA 92260 Fax: (760)346-7350
Free: (800)678-4237

Shopper (tabloid). **Subtitle:** Green Sheet. **Founded:** 1955. **Freq:** Weekly (Wed.). **Print Method:** Web. **Trim Size:** 11 x 12 1/2. **Cols./Page:** 6. **Col. Width:** 9 1/2 picas. **Col. Depth:** 11 3/4 inches. **Key Personnel:** Hal Paradis, Publisher; Chuck Holcomb, Sales Mgr. **Subscription Rates:** $163.80 out of area.
Ad Rates: BW: $564 **Circ:** Free 22,800
4C: $718.30
PCI: $4.50

2749 South Ontario News
Champion Newspapers
13179 9th St. Phone: (909)628-5501
Chino, CA 91710 Fax: (909)590-1217

Community newspaper. **Founded:** Nov. 1978. **Freq:** Weekly (Thurs.). **Print Method:** Offset. **Trim Size:** 13 3/4 x 21 1/2. **Cols./Page:** 6. **Col. Width:** 12 1/3 picas. **Col. Depth:** 20 1/2 inches. **Key Personnel:** Scott Moore, Editor; Allen P.

McCombs, Publisher; Bruce Wood, General Mgr. **Remarks:** Accepts advertising.
Ad Rates: BW: $793.35 **Circ:** Free ‡35,000
4C: $1,093.35
SAU: $6.45

2750 Comcast Cablevision of San Bernardino
1205 DuPont St. Phone: (909)475-5600
Ontario, CA 91761 Fax: (909)988-8432

Founded: 1968. **Cities Served:** San Bernardino County, Bloomington, Fontana, Highland, and Loma Linda, CA.

2751 KHSC-TV - 46
3833 Ebony St. Phone: (909)390-8846
Ontario, CA 91761 Fax: (909)390-8857
Free: (800)695-8353

Format: Commercial TV. **Networks:** Home Shopping Network. **Founded:** 1986. **Formerly:** KIHS-TV. **Operating Hours:** Continuous. **ADI:** Los Angeles (Corona & San Bernardino), CA. **Key Personnel:** Bart Pearce, Station Mgr.; Julio Brito, Chief Engineer; Brian Walek, Traffic & Operations. **Ad Rates:** Advertising accepted; rates available upon request.

ORANGE, pop. 91,788.

S. CA. Orange Co. 35 mi. SE of Los Angeles. Chapman College. Manufactures copper wire, rope, twine, electronic equipment, concrete pipe, steel tanks, plastic hose and bags. Nurseries.

2752 American Survival Guide
V-Vifionary
265 S. Anita Dr. Phone: (714)939-9991
Orange, CA 92868 Fax: (714)939-9909
Publication E-mail: jim4asg@aol.com/scott4asg@aol.com

Monthly magazine for people who prefer an independent lifestyle. **Subtitle:** The Magazine of Self-Reliance. **Founded:** 1979. **Freq:** Monthly. **Print Method:** Web offset. **Trim Size:** 7 7/8 X 10 7/8. **Cols./Page:** 3. **Col. Width:** 2 1/8 inches. **Col. Depth:** 9 7/8 inches. **Key Personnel:** Jim Benson, Editor; Charles Coyne, Assoc. Publisher. **ISSN:** 8756-517X. **Subscription Rates:** $25.97. **Remarks:** Accepts advertising. **Formerly:** Survival Guide (Jan. 1985); Shooters Journal.
Ad Rates: BW: $1,680 **Circ:** Paid ★**52,658**
4C: $2,261

2753 Bow and Arrow Hunting
Y-Visionary Publishing, LP
265 S Anita Dr., Ste. 120 Phone: (714)939-9991
Orange, CA 92868-3310 Fax: (714)939-9901

Magazine for bow hunters and archery enthusiasts. **Founded:** 1963. **Freq:** 7/year. **Print Method:** Offset. **Trim Size:** 10 3/4 x 8. **Cols./Page:** 3. **Col. Width:** 31 nonpareils. **Col. Depth:** 140 agate lines. **Key Personnel:** Bob Torres, Editor, phone (914)989-9991, fax (714)939-9901; Chris Antoniardis, Advertising Mgr. **ISSN:** 0006-8403. **Subscription Rates:** $18 individuals; $3.95 single issue. **Remarks:** Accepts advertising.
Ad Rates: BW: $1,660 **Circ:** Paid ‡98,500
4C: $2,585 Non-paid ‡640
PCI: $70

2754 Diocese of Orange Bulletin
Diocese of Orange
Marywood Center Phone: (714)282-3000
2811 E. Villa Real Dr. Fax: (714)282-3029
Orange, CA 92867-1999
Official newspaper of the Catholic Diocese of Orange. **Founded:** 1976. **Freq:** Monthly. **Trim Size:** 11 x 17. **Cols./Page:** 4. **Col. Width:** 2 1/4 inches. **Col. Depth:** 15 inches. **Key Personnel:** Msgr. Lawrence J. Baird, Editor; Jim Graves, Managing Editor. **Subscription Rates:** Free. **Remarks:** Accepts advertising.
Ad Rates: BW: $850 **Circ:** Free 47,100
PCI: $18.75

2755 Panther
Chapman University
333 N. Glassell St. Phone: (714)997-6870
Orange, CA 92666 Fax: (714)744-7021
Publication E-mail: panther@chapman.edu

Collegiate newspaper. **Founded:** 1923. **Freq:** Weekly (Mon.). **Print Method:** Offset. **Trim Size:** 11 x 14. **Cols./Page:** 5. **Col. Width:** 2 inches. **Col. Depth:** 13 inches. **Key Personnel:** Shay McAffe, Managing Editor. **Subscription Rates:** $20 individuals. **Remarks:** Color advertising not accepted.
Ad Rates: GLR: $1 **Circ:** Non-paid ‡3,500
BW: $480
PCI: $7

2756 KALI-FM - 106.3
1740 W. Katella, Ste. A Phone: (714)633-2020
Orange, CA 92667 Fax: (714)997-0182

Format: Adult Contemporary. **Networks:** Independent. **Owner:** 5723 Melrose Ave., Hollywood, CA 90038. **Founded:** 1975. **Formerly:** KYMS-FM. **Operating Hours:** Continuous. **Key Personnel:** Debbie Toberty, Sales Mgr.; Ken Cooper, Operations Dir.; Paul Toberty, General Mgr. **Wattage:** 3000. **Ad Rates:** $45-70 for 60 seconds.

ORCUTT

2757 KGDP-AM - 660
2225 Dr. Phone: (805)928-7707
Santa Maria, CA 93455 Fax: (805)922-8582

Format: Religious. **Networks:** USA Radio. **Owner:** Radio Representatives Inc., 1416 Hollister Ln., Los Osos, CA 93402. **Founded:** 1987. **Formerly:** KSMI (1990). **Operating Hours:** 5 a.m.-11 p.m., Mon.-Fri.; 6 a.m.-11 p.m., Sat.-Sun. **ADI:** Santa Barbara-Santa Maria-San Luis Obispo,CA. **Key Personnel:** Norwood J. Patterson, President; Sam Jackson, Station Mgr. **Wattage:** 10,000 day; 1000 night. **Ad Rates:** $12-20 for 30 seconds; $15-25 for 60 seconds.

ORINDA, pop. 18,700.

W. CA. Contra Costa Co. 7 mi. NE of Oakland. Residential.

2758 FM Data Monthly
Tradeline, Inc.
115 Orinda Way Phone: (925)254-1744
PO Box 1568 Fax: (925)254-1093
Orinda, CA 94563
Publication E-mail: fmdm@fmdata.com

Trade journal covering planning, architecture, and engineering and management o R&D labs, and other corporate, and institutional facilities. **Founded:** May 1982. **Freq:** Monthly. **Print Method:** Offset. **Trim Size:** 8 1/2 x 11. **Cols./Page:** 4. **Col. Width:** 10 1/2 picas. **Col. Depth:** 65 picas. **Key Personnel:** Steven L. Westfall, Exec. Editor; Lee Ingalls, phone (925)254-6386, fmdm@fmdata.com. **ISSN:** 1096-4436. **Subscription Rates:** $248 individuals; $198.40 organizations; $278 other countries; $222.40 organizations in other countries; $378 two years individuals; $302.40 two years organizations; $428 two years other countries; $342.40 two years organizations in other countries; $15 back issues; sample issue sent free upon request. **Remarks:** Advertising accepted; rates available upon request. **URL:** http://www.fmdata.com. **Formerly:** Facilities Planning News.
Circ: 500

OROVILLE†, pop. 8,683.

N. CA. Butte Co. On Feather River, 75 mi. N. of Sacramento. Olive, fruit, vegetable canning and packing. Olive oil, lumber manufactured. Pine timber. Farming.

2759 The Digger Shopper & News
Great Ad-ventures Publishing, Inc.
2057 Mitchell Ave. Phone: (916)533-2170
PO Box 5006 Fax: (916)533-2181
Oroville, CA 95966
Publication E-mail: digger@cncnet.com

Shopping guide with community news. **Founded:** Aug. 21, 1977. **Freq:** Weekly. **Print Method:** Offset. **Trim Size:** 11 x 13 3/4. **Cols./Page:** 4. **Col. Width:** 2 3/8 picas. **Col. Depth:** 12 3/4 inches. **Key Personnel:** David Miller, Editor and Publisher. **Subscription Rates:** Free; $75 by mail. **Remarks:** Accepts advertising. **Formerly:** The Digger.
Ad Rates: GLR: $0.73 **Circ:** Free ‡22,600
BW: $395
4C: $725
PCI: $8.75

2760 Oroville Shopping News
Mercury Inc.
PO Box 651 Phone: (916)533-3131
Oroville, CA 95965 Fax: (916)533-3127

Shopper. **Founded:** 1957. **Freq:** Weekly (Sat.). **Print Method:** Offset. **Trim Size:** 13 x 21 1/2. **Cols./Page:** 6. **Col. Width:** 2 1/8 inches. **Col. Depth:** 21 1/2 inches. **Key Personnel:** Larry Hashman, Editor; Ronald J. Stewart, Publisher; Lori O'Neill, Advertising Mgr. **Remarks:** Accepts advertising.
Ad Rates: GLR: $1.70 **Circ:** Free 10,200
BW: $537.93
4C: $727.93
PCI: $4.22

2761 KJAZ-AM - 1340
2854-C Olive Hwy. Phone: (916)533-1340
Oroville, CA 95966

Format: Big Band/Nostalgia. **Owner:** at above address, Free: (800)921-9292. **Founded:** 1973. **Formerly:** KAOR-AM (1973); KORV-AM (1996). **Operating Hours:** Continuous; 100% network. **Key Personnel:** Mel Peterson, General Mgr., mel@sierra.net; Juan Villagrana, Sales Rep., phone (916)533-3700, fax (916)533-1349. **Wattage:** 1000. **Ad Rates:** $14 for 30 seconds; $20 for 60 seconds. **URL:** http://www.oroville-ca.com.

OXNARD, pop. 108,195.

SW CA. Ventura Co. 10 mi. SE of Ventura. Manufactures aircraft components, lumber. Seafood, fruit, vegetable canneries, frozen food plants; oil refineries. Nurseries. Agriculture. Citrus fruit, celery, strawberries, tomatoes.

2762 Ironman
Ironman Publishing
1701 Ives Ave. Phone: (805)385-3500
Oxnard, CA 93033 Fax: (805)385-3515
Free: (800)447-0008
Publication E-mail: ironmagagazine@aol.com

Magazine on bodybuilding and fitness. **Subtitle:** Real Bodybuilding Training, Nutrition and Supplementation. **Founded:** 1936. **Freq:** Monthly. **Print Method:** Web offset. **Trim Size:** 7 7/8 x 10 1/2. **Key Personnel:** Steve Holman, Editor, ironchief@aol.com; John Balik, Publisher, ironleader@aol.com. **ISSN:** 0047-1496. **Subscription Rates:** $29.97 individuals; $49.97 out of country; $4.99 single issue. **Remarks:** Accepts advertising. **URL:** http://www.ironmanmagazine.com.
Ad Rates: BW: $3,985 **Circ:** Paid 225,000
4C: $5,020

2763 Ventura County Vida Newspaper
Ventura County News
130 Palm Dr. Phone: (805)483-1008
Oxnard, CA 93030 Fax: (805)483-6233

Community newspaper (Spanish-English). **Founded:** 1983. **Freq:** Weekly (Thurs.). **Print Method:** Offset. **Cols./Page:** 6. **Col. Width:** 2 1/16 inches. **Col. Depth:** 13 inches. **Key Personnel:** Carlos Olea, Editor; Manuel M. Munoz, Publisher. **Subscription Rates:** $124 individuals. **Remarks:** Accepts advertising.
Ad Rates: GLR: $16.75 **Circ:** 35,000
BW: $2,110.50
4C: $2,527.50
SAU: $16.25

2764 KDAR-FM - 98.3
500 Esplanade Dr., Ste. 1500 Phone: (805)656-5327
Oxnard, CA 93030 Fax: (805)656-5330
E-mail: info@kdar.com

Format: Religious; Talk. **Networks:** Sun Radio. **Owner:** Salem Communications Corp., 2310 Ponderosa Dr., Camarrillo, CA 93010, (805)485-8881, Fax: (805)656-5330. **Founded:** 1974. **Operating Hours:** Continuous; 80% network, 20% local. **Key Personnel:** Terri Dawson, General Mgr.; Carl Peetz, Program Dir. **Wattage:** 25,000. **Ad Rates:** $27-31 per unit. **URL:** http://www.kdar.com.

2765 KMLA-FM - 103.7
555 S. A St., Ste. 175 Phone: (805)385-5656
Oxnard, CA 93030 Fax: (805)385-5690

Format: Hispanic. **Owner:** Gold Coast Radio, L. L. C., at above address. **Operating Hours:** Continuous. **Key Personnel:** Yolanda Padilla, Office Mgr.; Guillermo Gonzalez, General and Sales Mgr.; Raul Evangelista, Music Dir.; Gerardo Ceja, Pres./Program Dir. **Local Programs:** *Corridos de alto Range*, Gerardo Ceja; *Las 12 del Recuerdo*, Rosa Rodriguez; *Palenque Musical*, Raul Evangelista. **Wattage:** 3,000.

2766 KOXR-AM - 910
418 W. 3rd St. Phone: (805)487-0444
Oxnard, CA 93030-5710 Fax: (805)487-2117
Free: (800)852-0444

Format: Hispanic. **Founded:** 1955. **Operating Hours:** Continuous. **ADI:** Santa Barbara-Santa Maria-San Luis Obispo,CA. **Key Personnel:** Alberto O. Vera, General Mgr.; Christine Goetz, Business Mgr. **Local Programs:** *Community Interest*, Dr. Mary Barretto, (805)983-1275; *Senora Rebecca (Physic)*; *Un Hora de La Patado (Soccer)*, Ramon Arceo, (805)385-1451. **Wattage:** 5000 day; 1000 night. **Ad Rates:** $35 for 30 seconds; $40 for 60 seconds.

2767 KTRO-AM - 1520
PO Box 2187
Oxnard, CA 93034

Format: Hispanic. **Networks:** Independent. **Owner:** Greater

Pacific Radio Exchange, Inc., at above address. **Founded:** 1958. **Formerly**: KACY-AM (1984). **Operating Hours:** Continuous; 100% local. **ADI:** Santa Barbara-Santa Maria-San Luis Obispo,CA. **Key Personnel:** Alfredo Tristan, News Dir.; Harold A. Frank, President; B.J. Young, Station Mgr.; Alberto Vera, Program Dir.; Armando Ocampo, Music Dir.; Lloyd Maxwel, Promotions Dir.; Martin Ortiz, Production Dir.; Alfredo Tristan, News Dir. **Wattage:** 10,000. **Ad Rates:** $17-38 for 30 seconds; $20-45 for 60 seconds.

PACIFIC GROVE, pop. 15,755.

W. CA. Monterey Co. 20 mi. S. of Santa Cruz. Residential.

2768 KAZU-FM - 90.3
176 Forest Ave. Phone: (408)375-7275
PO Box 210 Fax: (408)375-0235
Pacific Grove, CA 93950-0206
E-mail: mail@kazu.org

Format: Public Radio; Eclectic. **Owner:** Monterey Bay Public Broadcasting Foundation, Inc., at above address. **Founded:** 1977. **Operating Hours:** 6 a.m.-2 a.m. **Key Personnel:** John Minally, General Mgr., jmin@kazu.org; Kathy Mclinich, Bookkeeper; Elinda Hardy, Sta. Producer/ Production Director; Andre Porter, Music Dir.; Dennis O'Brien, Underwriting; Richard McDermott, Special Projects. **Local Programs:** *Morning Becomes Eccentric*, Peter Williams; *My Sisters House*, J.T. Mason; *Rosewood Gales*, Robin Roberts. **Wattage:** 4200. **Ad Rates:** Noncommercial.

PACIFIC PALISADES

S. CA. Los Angeles Co. 4 mi. N. of Santa Monica. Residential suburb. (Pop. incl. in Los Angeles.)

2769 North Shore Shopper
839 Via De La Paz Phone: (213)454-1321
PO Box 725 Fax: (310)454-1078
Pacific Palisades, CA 90272-0725
Publication E-mail: palipost@worldnet.att.net.

Shopper. **Founded:** 1928. **Freq:** Weekly (Thurs.). **Print Method:** Offset. **Cols./Page:** 9. **Col. Width:** 17 nonpareils. **Col. Depth:** 294 agate lines. **Key Personnel:** Tom Small, President; Roberta Donohue, Publisher. **Remarks:** Accepts advertising.
Ad Rates: GLR: $.85 **Circ:** Free 8,500
PCI: $18

2770 Palisadian-Post
839 Via De La Paz Phone: (310)454-1321
Pacific Palisades, CA 90272 Fax: (310)454-1078
Publication E-mail: palipost@aol.com
Publisher E-mail: palipost@aol.com

Local newspaper. **Founded:** 1928. **Freq:** Weekly (Thurs.). **Print Method:** Offset. **Cols./Page:** 6. **Col. Width:** 24 nonpareils. **Col. Depth:** 294 agate lines. **Key Personnel:** Bill Bruns, Managing Editor; Roberta Donohue, Publisher; Eve De Veir, Advertising Mgr. **Subscription Rates:** $29 individuals; $.50 single issue. **Remarks:** Accepts advertising.
Ad Rates: PCI: $18 **Circ:** Paid 4,349
Free 55

PACIFICA, pop. 36,866.

W. CA. San Mateo Co. On Pacific Ocean, 10 mi. S. of San Francisco. Residential. Beach oriented. Recreation.

2771 Pacifica Tribune
59 Aura Vista Phone: (650)359-6666
POBOX 1189 Fax: (650)359-3821
Pacifica, CA 94044
Publisher E-mail: pactrib@hax.com

Newspaper. **Founded:** 1947. **Freq:** Weekly (Wed.). **Print Method:** Offset. **Trim Size:** 6 x 20 1/2. **Cols./Page:** 6. **Col. Depth:** 287 agate lines. **Key Personnel:** Chris Hunter, Editor and Publisher, phone (650)738-4545. **Subscription Rates:** $26 individuals. **Remarks:** Accepts advertising.
Ad Rates: BW: $1,734.30 **Circ:** Wed. ★7,626
SAU: $14.10

2772 The Wave, The Buyer's Guide for the Coastside
Pacifica Tribune
PO Box 1189 Phone: (415)359-6666
Pacifica, CA 94044 Fax: (415)359-3821
Publisher E-mail: pactrib@hax.com

Shopping News. **Founded:** 1955. **Freq:** Weekly. **Print Method:** Offset. **Trim Size:** 6 x 20 1/2. **Cols./Page:** 6. **Col. Width:** 24 nonpareils. **Col. Depth:** 301 agate lines. **Key Personnel:** Chris Hunter, Editor and Publisher, phone (415)738-4545.
Ad Rates: BW: $1,586.70 **Circ:** Free 5,900
4C: $1,986.70 Wed. 7,912
SAU: $12.90

PACOIMA

2773 San Fernando Gazette Express
First-Line Publishers/L.A. Metro Group
14621 Titus St., Ste. 228 Phone: (818)782-8695
Van Nuys, CA 91402 Fax: (818)782-2924

Black community newspaper serving Pacoima, Arleta, and Panorama City. **Founded:** 1966. **Freq:** Weekly (Thurs.). **Print Method:** Offset. **Trim Size:** 13 x 21 1/2. **Cols./Page:** 6. **Col. Width:** 2 inches. **Key Personnel:** Hillard Hamm, Editor. **Subscription Rates:** Free; $25. **Remarks:** Color advertising accepted; rates available upon request.
Ad Rates: BW: $4,128 **Circ:** Free 60,000
PCI: $32

PALM DESERT, pop. 11,801.

SE CA. Riverside Co. 75 mi. SE of Redland. Winter resort.

North San Bernardino Green Sheet - See San Bernardino

Ontario Green Sheet - See Ontario

Redlands Green Sheet - See Redlands

Riverside Green Sheet - See Riverside

2774 Saludos Hispanos
73121 Fred Waring Dr., No. 100 Phone: (619)776-1206
Palm Desert, CA 92260 Fax: (619)776-1214
Free: (800)371-4456

Magazine showcasing successful Hispanic Americans and promoting higher education (English and Spanish). **Founded:** 1984. **Freq:** 6/year. **Trim Size:** 10 1/4 x 13. **Key Personnel:** Mona DeCrinis, Editor. **Remarks:** Accepts advertising. **URL:** http://www.saludos.com.
Ad Rates: BW: $340 **Circ:** 300,000

Valley Shopper-The El Centro Advertiser - See El Centro

2775 Victorville Green Sheet
Associated Desert Shoppers, Inc.
73-400 Hwy. 111 Phone: (760)346-1729
Palm Desert, CA 92260 Fax: (760)346-7350
Free: (800)678-4237

Shopper (tabloid). **Founded:** 1988. **Freq:** Weekly (Thurs.). **Print Method:** Web. **Trim Size:** 11 x 12 1/2. **Cols./Page:** 6. **Col. Width:** 9.5 picas. **Col. Depth:** 11 3/4 inches. **Key Personnel:** Todd Schurz, Publisher; Chuck Holcombe, Editor. **Subscription Rates:** $163.80 out of area; Free to qualified subscribers. **Remarks:** Accepts advertising.
Ad Rates: BW: $564 **Circ:** Free 15,500
PCI: $7.61

West San Bernardino Green Sheet - See San Bernardino

White Sheet-The Blythe Advertiser - See Blythe

2776 White Sheet-The Indio Advertiser
Associated Desert Shoppers, Inc.
73-400 Hwy. 111 Phone: (760)346-1729
Palm Desert, CA 92260 Fax: (760)346-7350
Free: (800)678-4237

Shopper. **Subtitle:** White Sheet. **Founded:** 1965. **Freq:** Weekly (Tues.). **Print Method:** Web. **Trim Size:** 11 x 12 1/2. **Cols./Page:** 6. **Col. Width:** 9 1/2 picas. **Col. Depth:** 11 3/4 inches. **Key Personnel:** Hal Paradis, Publisher; Jim McComb, Sales Mgr. **Subscription Rates:** $163.80 out of area; Free to qualified subscribers.
Ad Rates: BW: $407 **Circ:** Free ‡10,000
4C: $650
PCI: $4.50

White Sheet-The Lake Havasu City Advertiser - See Lake Havasu City, Arizona

White Sheet-The Morongo Basin Advertiser - See Morongo Basin

2777 White Sheet-The Palm Desert Advertiser
Associated Desert Shoppers, Inc.
73-400 Hwy. 111 Phone: (760)346-1729
Palm Desert, CA 92260 Fax: (760)346-7350
Free: (800)678-4237

Shopper. **Founded:** 1965. **Freq:** Weekly (Tues.). **Print Method:** Web. **Trim Size:** 11 x 12 1/2. **Cols./Page:** 6. **Col. Width:** 9 1/2 picas. **Col. Depth:** 11 3/4 inches. **Key Personnel:** Hal J. Paradis, Publisher, phone (760)346-1729, fax (760)346-7350; Lulana Stewart, Sales Mgr. **Remarks:** Accepts advertising.
Ad Rates: BW: $1165 **Circ:** Free ‡30,000
4C: $1550

White Sheet-The Palm Springs Advertiser - See Palm Springs

White Sheet-The Parker Advertiser - See Parker, Arizona

2778 White Sheet-The Tri-State Advertiser
Associated Desert Shoppers, Inc.
73-400 Hwy. 111 Phone: (760)346-1729
Palm Desert, CA 92260 Fax: (760)346-7350
Free: (800)678-4237

Shopper. **Founded:** 1965. **Freq:** Weekly (Tues.). **Print Method:** Web. **Trim Size:** 11 x 12 1/2. **Cols./Page:** 6. **Col. Width:** 9 1/2 picas. **Col. Depth:** 11 1/2 inches. **Key Personnel:** Hal J. Paradis, Publisher, phone (760)346-1729, fax (760)346-7350; John Schneider, Sales Mgr., phone (520)855-7871, fax (520)855-8183. **Subscription Rates:** $163.80 out of area; Free to qualified subscribers. **Remarks:** Accepts advertising.
Ad Rates: BW: $365 **Circ:** Non-paid ‡10,500
4C: $650

2779 KESQ-TV - 42
42650 Melanie Pl. Phone: (760)773-0342
Palm Desert, CA 92211 Fax: (760)773-5107

Format: Commercial TV. **Networks:** ABC. **Owner:** News Press & Gazette Co., PO Box 29, St. Joseph, MO 64502-0029, (816)271-8695. **Founded:** 1968. **Operating Hours:** Continuous. **ADI:** Palm Springs, CA. **Key Personnel:** Bill Evans, Contact; Mark Sucher, Contact; Ken Spaulding, Traffic Mgr.; Shaun Hynes, Promotions Dir.; Rusty Kirkland, General Sales Mgr.; Erin Lacombe, News Dir.; Richard Mechling, Contact; David Gray, Chief Engineer.

2780 KEZN-FM - 103.1
Box 291 Phone: (619)340-9383
Palm Desert, CA 92261 Fax: (619)340-5756

Format: Adult Contemporary. **Founded:** 1977. **Operating Hours:** Continuous. **Key Personnel:** Linda Ward, General Mgr. **Wattage:** 1.9kw. **Ad Rates:** Advertising accepted; rates available upon request.

2781 KMIR-TV - 36
72920 Parkview Dr. Phone: (760)568-3636
Palm Desert, CA 92260 Fax: (760)568-1176
E-mail: kmir@ix.netcom.com

Format: Commercial TV. **Networks:** NBC. **Owner:** Desert Empire Television Corp., at above address. **Founded:** 1968. **Operating Hours:** Continuous; 67% network, 33% local. **ADI:** Palm Springs, CA. **Key Personnel:** John Conte, Pres./Gen. Mgr., fax (760)568-1176; Harry Hein, General Sales Mgr., fax (760)340-5955; Karen Devine, News Dir., fax (760)341-7029. **Wattage:** 10,000. **Ad Rates:** Advertising accepted; rates available upon request.

2782 KNWZ-AM - 1270
PO Box 12700 Phone: (619)346-1270
Palm Desert, CA 92255-2700 Fax: (619)341-6885
Free: (800)376-1270

Format: Talk; News. **Networks:** Westwood One Radio; CNN Radio; NBC. **Founded:** 1965. **Formerly:** KGOR-AM; KGUY-AM. **Operating Hours:** Continuous; 45% network, 55% local. **ADI:** Palm Springs, CA. **Key Personnel:** John Wilks, Vice Pres./Gen. Mgr.; Lou Penrose, Operations and Program Dir., penrose@juno.com. **Wattage:** 5000 directional. **Ad Rates:** $10-18 for 10 seconds; $16-30 for 30 seconds; $20-35 for 60 seconds.

2783 KUNA-AM - 1400
42650 Melanie Pl. Phone: (619)568-6830
Palm Desert, CA 92211-5170 Fax: (619)568-3984

Format: Hispanic; Talk. **Owner:** Pennino Broadcasting, PO Box 13050, Palm Desert, CA 92255. **Founded:** 1959. **Formerly:** KBZT-FM (1993). **Operating Hours:** Continuous. **ADI:** Palm Springs, CA. **Key Personnel:** Mark Wright, Station Mgr.; J.R. Banoczi, Vice President, jbanoczi@ix.netcom.com. **Wattage:** 1,000. **Ad Rates:** $10-20 for 30 seconds; $15-30 for 60 seconds.

2784 KUNA-FM - 96.7
42650 Melanie Pl. Phone: (760)568-6830
Palm Desert, CA 92211-5170 Fax: (760)568-3984

Format: Ethnic; Hispanic. **Owner:** Pennino Broadcasting, PO Box 13050, Palm Desert, CA 92255. **Founded:** 1987. **Formerly:** KBZT-FM (1987). **Operating Hours:** Continuous. **ADI:** Palm Springs, CA. **Key Personnel:** Martin Serna, Station Mgr.; Kathy Banas, National Sales/Promotions Mgr.; Adolpho Iniquez, Operations Mgr. **Wattage:** 650. **Ad Rates:** $10-25 for 30 seconds; $13-30 for 60 seconds.

PALM SPRINGS, pop. 32,271.

SE CA. Riverside Co. 56 mi. E. of Riverside. Desert resort.

2785 Coachella Valley Sun
Desert Sun Publishing Co.
PO Box 27034 Phone: (760)322-8889
Palm Springs, CA 92263 Fax: (760)778-4513
Free: (800)858-0112

Newspaper. **Founded:** 1901. **Freq:** Daily. **Print Method:** Offset. **Cols./Page:** 6. **Col. Width:** 24 nonpareils. **Col. Depth:** 295 agate lines. **Key Personnel:** Robert Dickey, President, phone (760)778-4501, fax (760)778-4654. **Subscription Rates:** $10.99 4 weeks. **Remarks:** Accepts advertising. **URL:** http://www.desertsunonline.com.
Ad Rates: GLR: $2.71 **Circ:** 52,000
BW: $61.75
4C: $795

2786 The Desert Sun
Gannett Co., Inc.
750 N. Gene Autry Tr. Phone: (619)332-8889
PO Box 190 Fax: (619)778-4654
Palm Springs, CA 92263
General newspaper. **Founded:** 1927. **Freq:** Mon.-Sun. (morn.). **Print Method:** Offset. **Trim Size:** 13 x 21. **Cols./Page:** 6. **Col. Width:** 27 nonpareils. **Col. Depth:** 301 agate lines. **Key Personnel:** Joan Behrmann, Editor; Edward Manassah, Publisher; Bob Sweet, Advertising Dir. **Subscription Rates:** $72 individuals. **Remarks:** Accepts advertising.
Ad Rates: BW: $4,016.88 **Circ:** Mon.-Sat. **★44,757**
4C: $4,898.80 Sun. **★47,094**
PCI: $31.88

2787 Palm Springs Life
Milton W. Jones
303 N. Indian Canyon Phone: (760)325-2333
PO Box 2724 Fax: (760)325-7008
Palm Springs, CA 92263-2724
Publication E-mail: desertpubs@aol.com

Lifestyle magazine containing upscale local and social news. **Subtitle:** California's Prestige Magazine. **Founded:** 1946. **Freq:** Monthly. **Print Method:** Offset. **Trim Size:** 8 3/8 x 10 7/8. **Cols./Page:** 3. **Col. Width:** 28 nonpareils. **Col. Depth:** 147 agate lines. **Key Personnel:** Stewart Weiner, Editor; Milton W. Jones, Publisher; William Russom, Design Director. **ISSN:** 0031-0425. **Subscription Rates:** $38 individuals. **Remarks:** Accepts advertising. **URL:** http://www.desert-resorts.com.
Ad Rates: BW: $4,920 **Circ:** Paid **★15,006**
4C: $5,720

2788 Palm Springs Life's Desert Guide
Desert Publication Inc.
303 N. Indian Cyn. Dr. , Phone: (619)325-2333
P.O.Box 2724 Free: (800)775-PALM
Palm Springs, CA 92263
Visitor's guide for the Coachella Valley. **Founded:** 1967. **Freq:** Monthly. **Trim Size:** 8 1/2 x 10 7/8. **Cols./Page:** 3. **Col. Width:** 2 1/4 inches. **Col. Depth:** 9 3/4 inches. **Key Personnel:** Donna Curran, Editor; Milton W. Jones, Publisher. **Remarks:** Accepts advertising.
Ad Rates: BW: $9,610 **Circ:** Non-paid **★68,703**
4C: $10,810

2789 The Public Record
PO Box 2724 Phone: (760)416-9709
Palm Springs, CA 92263-2724 Fax: (760)416-9690

Journal. **Founded:** 1980. **Freq:** Weekly (Fri.). **Print Method:** Offset. **Trim Size:** 11 1/2 x 13 1/2. **Cols./Page:** 3. **Col. Width:** 3 3/8 inches. **Col. Depth:** 12.5 picas. **Key Personnel:** Sharon Apfelbaum, Editor and Publisher. **USPS:** 662-010. **Subscription Rates:** $160. **Remarks:** Accepts advertising.
Ad Rates: BW: $409 **Circ:** Paid ‡420
PCI: $5 Free ‡300

2790 White Sheet-The Palm Springs Advertiser
Associated Desert Shoppers, Inc.
73-400 Hwy. 111 Phone: (760)346-1729
Palm Desert, CA 92260 Fax: (760)346-7350
Free: (800)678-4237

Shopper. **Founded:** 1965. **Freq:** Weekly (Tues.). **Print Method:** Web. **Trim Size:** 11 x 12 1/2. **Cols./Page:** 6. **Col. Width:** 9 1/2 picas. **Col. Depth:** 11 3/4 inches. **Key Personnel:** Hal Paradis, Publisher, phone (760)346-1729, fax (760)346-7350; Jim Donnelly, General Sales Mgr., phone (520)782-3660.
Ad Rates: BW: $365 **Circ:** Free ‡10,000
4C: $650

2791 KCMJ-AM - 1140
490 S. Farrell Dr. Phone: (619)320-6818
Palm Springs, CA 92262 Fax: (619)320-1493
E-mail: kcmjamfm@worldnet.att.net

Format: Oldies; Big Band/Nostalgia. **Owner:** Morris Communication, at above address. **Founded:** 1946. **Formerly:** Westminster Broadcasting Corp. **Operating Hours:** Continuous;. **ADI:** Palm Springs, CA. **Key Personnel:** Gary DeMaroney, Program Dir.; Bruce Johnson, General Mgr. **Wattage:** 10,000. **Ad Rates:** $15 per unit.

2792 KCMJ-FM - 92.7
PO Box 1626 Phone: (619)320-6818
Palm Springs, CA 92263 Fax: (619)320-1493
E-mail: kcmjamfm@worldnet.att.net

Format: Classic Rock; Oldies. **Owner:** Claridge Broadcasting, Inc., at above address. **Founded:** 1942. **Operating Hours:** Continuous. **ADI:** Palm Springs, CA. **Key Personnel:** Barry Gorfine, General Sales Mgr.; Gary DeMaroney, Program Dir.; Bruce Johnson, General Mgr. **Wattage:** 3000. **Ad Rates:** $25 per unit.

2793 KDES-AM - 920
821 N. Palm Canyon Dr. Phone: (619)325-1211
PO Box 2745 Fax: (619)325-8163
Palm Springs, CA 92263
E-mail: kdesradio@aol.com

Format: News. **Networks:** AP. **Owner:** Tourtelot Broadcasting Co., at above address. **Founded:** 1956. **Formerly:** KEDS-AM (1994). **Operating Hours:** Continuous; 100% local. **ADI:** Palm Springs, CA. **Key Personnel:** Danny Fox, Program Dir.; Karla Stone, News Dir.; Joe Tourtalot, Sales Mgr. **Wattage:** 5000; 1000 night. **Ad Rates:** Combined advertising rates available with KDES-FM.

2794 KDES-FM - 104.7
821 N. Palm Canyon Rd. Phone: (760)325-2582
PO Box 2745 Fax: (760)322-3562
Palm Springs, CA 92263-2745
E-mail: kdes1047@aol.com

Format: Oldies. **Owner:** Tourtelot Broadcasting Co., at above address, Palm Springs, CA 92263. **Founded:** 1964. **Operating Hours:** Continuous; 100% local. **ADI:** Palm Springs, CA. **Key Personnel:** Terry Masters, General Mgr.; Mike Keane, Program Dir.; Kirk Gregory, General Sales Mgr. **Wattage:** 42,000. **Ad Rates:** $50 for 30 seconds; $75 for 60 seconds. Combined advertising rates available with KDES-AM; $7-$50 for 30 seconds; $10-$60 for 60 seconds.

2795 KPLM-FM - 106.1
PO Box 1825 Phone: (619)320-4550
Palm Springs, CA 92262-7543 Fax: (619)320-3037

Format: Country. **Networks:** AP. **Owner:** RM Broadcasting LLC, at above address. **Founded:** 1983. **Operating Hours:** Continuous; 1% network, 99% local. **ADI:** Palm Springs, CA. **Key Personnel:** Todd Marker, General Mgr.; Todd Marker, General Sales Mgr.; Al Gordon, Program Dir.; Ford Michaels, News Dir. **Local Programs:** *Access*, Glenda Castelli. **Wattage:** 50,000. **Ad Rates:** $18-40 for 30 seconds; $28-60 for 60 seconds.

2796 KPSC-FM - 88.5
Box 77913 Phone: (213)514-1400
Los Angeles, CA 90007 Fax: (213)747-9400
E-mail: kusc@kusc.org

Format: Classical; Public Radio. **Networks:** AP. **Founded:** 1985. **Operating Hours:** Continuous. **ADI:** Los Angeles (Corona & San Bernardino), CA. **Key Personnel:** Brenda Pennell, General Mgr., phone (213)514-1450, fax (213)514-1451, bpennell@kusc.org; Sheila Rue, Contact, phone (213)514-1430, fax (213)514-1431, srue@kusc.org; James Russell, GM/Market Place Prod., phone (213)514-1500, fax (213)514-1506, jrussell@marketplace.org. **Local Programs:** *Afternoon Music*, Steve Lama; *Marketplace Morning Music*, Steve Lama, VP of Broadcasting & General Mgr.; *Music 'til Midnight*, Steve Lama, VP of Broadcasting & General Mgr. **Wattage:** 3000. **Ad Rates:** Noncommercial. **URL:** http://www.kusc.org.

2797 KPSI-AM - 920
2100 E. Tahquitz Canyon Way Phone: (619)325-2582
Palm Springs, CA 92262 Fax: (619)322-3562
E-mail: kpsi@aol.com

Format: News; Talk. **Simulcasts:** KGAM. **Networks:** ABC. **Founded:** 1954. **Operating Hours:** Continuous; 75% network, 25% local. **ADI:** Palm Springs, CA. **Key Personnel:** Bob Clark, General Mgr.; Mike Keane, Program Dir.; Mike Meenan, News Dir.; Frank Torok, Promotions Dir.; Dengs Arcuri, Producer. **Wattage:** 1000. **Ad Rates:** $9-13 for 15 seconds; $12-16 for 30 seconds; $15-21 for 60 seconds.

2798 KPSI-FM - 100.5
2100 E. Tahquitz Canyon Way Phone: (619)325-2582
Palm Springs, CA 92262 Fax: (619)322-3562
E-mail: kpsi@aol.com

Format: Contemporary Hit Radio (CHR). **Founded:** 1980. **Operating Hours:** Continuous. **ADI:** Palm Springs, CA. **Key Personnel:** Terry Masters, General Mgr.; Mike Meenan, News Dir.; Michael Keane, Program Dir.; Kirk Gregory, General Sales Mgr. **Local Programs:** *News Page with Mike Meenan*, Mike Meenan. **Wattage:** 25,000.

KPSL-AM - See Thousand Palms

2799 KWXY-AM - 1340
68700 Dinah Shore Dr. Phone: (619)328-1104
Palm Springs, CA 92264 Fax: (619)328-7814

Format: Easy Listening. **Networks:** Independent. **Founded:** 1964. **Operating Hours:** Continuous, 100% local. **ADI:** Palm Springs, CA. **Key Personnel:** Bill Hesson, News Dir.; Larry Collins, Operations Mgr.; Jim Keye, Sales Mgr. **Local Programs:** *V.J.s Corner*, V.J. Hume. **Wattage:** 1000. **Ad Rates:** $18 for 30 seconds; $40 for 60 seconds. **URL:** http://www.kwxy.com.

PALMDALE, pop. 12,277.

S. CA. Los Angeles Co. 40 mi. NE of Los Angeles. Air craft manufacturing. Air force flight test center. Rocket lab.

2800 Antelope Valley Press
Antelope Valley Newspapers, Inc.
PO Box 880 Phone: (805)273-2700
Palmdale, CA 93590 Fax: (805)947-4870

General newspaper. **Founded:** 1915. **Freq:** Daily (morn.). **Print Method:** Offset. **Cols./Page:** 6. **Col. Width:** 25 nonpareils. **Col. Depth:** 301 agate lines. **Key Personnel:** William C. Markham, Editor, editor@avpress.com; Linda Rowlee, Retail Advertising Dir.; Cherie Bryant, National Advertising Dir.; Bill Cunningham, Classified Advertising Dir.; Cherie Bryant, Marketing/Promotions Dir.; William Forhan, Controller; Eric Robanske, Circulation Dir.; Wendy Stigge, Personnel Manager. **Subscription Rates:** $104 individuals. **Remarks:** Accepts advertising. **URL:** http://www.avpress.com.
Ad Rates: GLR: $30.40 **Circ:** Mon.-Fri. 45,005
BW: $3,921.60 Sun. 50,788
4C: $4,471.60
SAU: $30.40

Jones Intercable, Inc. - See Lancaster

2801 KAVC-AM - 1340
190 Sierra Ct., B-2 Phone: (805)274-1031
Palmdale, CA 93550 Fax: (805)274-1017

Format: Talk; Contemporary Christian. **Networks:** Independent. **Owner:** Regent Communicatons, Inc., 50 E. River Center Blvd., Ste. 180, Covington, KY 41011, (606)292-0030, Fax: (606)292-0352. **Founded:** 1958. **Formerly:** KVOY-AM (Oct. 1998). **Operating Hours:** Continuous. **Key Personnel:** Bill Hurley, General Mgr., billhurley@ktpi.com. **Wattage:** 1000. **Ad Rates:** $6-85 per unit. Combined advertising rates available with KTPI-FM and KOSS-FM.

2802 KGMX-FM - 106.3
570 E. Ave. Q-9 Phone: (805)947-3107
Palmdale, CA 93550 Fax: (805)272-5688

Format: Adult Contemporary. **Networks:** Westwood One Radio; NBC. **Owner:** High Desert Broadcasting, at above address. **Founded:** 1956. **Operating Hours:** Continuous. **ADI:** Los Angeles (Corona & San Bernardino), CA. **Key Personnel:** Vicki Connor, General Mgr.; Lloyd Heaney, National Sales Mgr.; Craig Morgan, News Dir.; Jeff Ryan, Operations Dir. **Wattage:** 3000. **Ad Rates:** $21 for 30 seconds; $24 for 60 seconds. **URL:** http://www.kmix106.com.

2803 KHJJ-AM - 1470
570 E. Ave. Q-9 Phone: (805)947-3107
Palmdale, CA 93550 Fax: (805)272-5688

Format: News; Talk. **Networks:** NBC; Westwood One Radio; USA Radio. **Owner:** High Desert Broadcasting, at above address. **Founded:** 1970. **Operating Hours:** Continuous. **ADI:** Los Angeles (Corona & San Bernardino), CA. **Key Personnel:** Jeff Ryan, Operations Dir.; Craig Morgan, News Dir.; Vicki Connor, General Mgr.; Lloyd Heaney, Natl. Sales Mgr. **Wattage:** 1000. **Ad Rates:** $21 for 30 seconds; $24 for 60 seconds. **URL:** http://www.kmix106.com.

2804 KTPI-FM - 103.1
190 Sierra Ct., B-2 Phone: (805)274-1031
Palmdale, CA 93550 Fax: (805)274-1017
E-mail: ktpi@ktpi.com

Format: Country. **Networks:** Independent. **Owner:** Regent Communications, Inc., 50 East River Center Blvd. Ste. 180, Covington, KY 41011, (606)292-0030, Fax: (606)292-0352. **Founded:** 1982. **Operating Hours:** Continuous. **Key Personnel:** Bill Hurley, General Mgr., billhurley@ktpi.com. **Wattage:** 6000. **Ad Rates:** $10-75 per unit. Combined advertising rates available with KAVC-AM, and KOSS-FM, available upon request.

2805 KUTY-AM - 1380
570 E. Ave., Q-9 Phone: (805)947-3107
Palmdale, CA 93550 Fax: (805)272-5688

Format: Hispanic. **Networks:** Satellite Music Network. **Founded:** 1981. **Operating Hours:** Continuous. **ADI:** Los Angeles (Corona & San Bernardino), CA. **Key Personnel:** Vicki Connor, General Mgr.; Jeff Ryan, Operations Dir.; Carl Goldman, Vice President; Craig Morgan, News Dir.; Jamie Lee, Public Service Dir. **Wattage:** 5000. **Ad Rates:** $15 for 30 seconds; $20 for 60 seconds. **URL:** http://www.kmix106.com.

PALO ALTO, pop. 55,225.

W. CA. Santa Clara Co. 30 mi. S. of San Francisco. Residential. Stanford University and several private schools. Electronic missile research. Pharmaceuticals. Film processing.

2806 Annual Review of Astronomy and Astrophysics
Annual Reviews, Inc.
4139 El Camino Way Phone: (650)493-4400
PO Box 10139 Fax: (650)424-0910
Palo Alto, CA 94303-0139
Free: (800)523-8635
Publisher E-mail: service@annurev.org

Professional journal covering astronomy and astrophysics. **Founded:** 1963. **Freq:** Annual. **Trim Size:** 00664146. **Key Personnel:** Geoffrey Burbidge, Editor; Allan B. Sandage, Assoc. Editor; Frank H. Shu, Assoc. Editor. **Subscription Rates:** $70 individuals; $75 out of country. **Remarks:** Advertising not accepted. **URL:** http://www.annualreviews.org.
Circ: (Not Reported)

2807 Annual Review of Medicine
Annual Reviews, Inc.
4139 El Camino Way Phone: (650)493-4400
PO Box 10139 Fax: (650)424-0910
Palo Alto, CA 94303-0139
Free: (800)523-8635
Publisher E-mail: service@annurev.org

Professional journal covering medicine and clinical science. **Subtitle:** Selected Topics in the Clinical Sciences. **Founded:** 1950. **Freq:** Annual. **Key Personnel:** C. H. Coggins, Editor; E. William Hancock, Assoc. Editor; Lee J. Levitt, Assoc. Editor. **ISSN:** 0066-4219. **Subscription Rates:** $60 individuals; $65 out of country. **Remarks:** Advertising not accepted. **URL:** http://www.annualreviews.org.
Circ: (Not Reported)

2808 Communication Arts
410 Sherman Ave. Phone: (650)326-6040
PO Box 10300 Fax: (650)326-1648
Palo Alto, CA 94303
Free: (800)258-9111
Publication E-mail: advertising@commands.com; ca@commarts.com

Magazine covering design, advertising, photography, illustration, and multimedia. **Subtitle:** The World's Most Influential Journal on Creativity. **Founded:** Aug. 1959. **Freq:** 8/year. **Print Method:** Web offset. **Trim Size:** 8 5/8 x 10 7/8. **Cols./Page:** 2. **Col. Width:** 41 nonpareils. **Col. Depth:** 140 agate lines. **Key Personnel:** Patrick Coyne, Editor; Michael Krigel, General Mgr. **ISSN:** 0010-3519. **Subscription Rates:** $53 individuals; $8 single issue. **Available Online. URL:** http://www.commarts.com.
Ad Rates: GLR: $175 **Circ:** Paid ★73,246
BW: $6,230
4C: $7,010

2809 Communications Standards Review
757 Greer Rd. Phone: (650)856-9018
Palo Alto, CA 94303-3024 Fax: (650)856-6591

Journal publishing information on TIA and ITU-T Standards Committee Meetings. **Founded:** Jan. 1990. **Freq:** 8-9 times/year. **Print Method:** Copy. **Cols./Page:** 2. **Key Personnel:** Elaine Baskin, Publisher, ebaskin@csrtds.com; Ken Krechmer, Technical Editor, phone (650)856-8836, fax (650)856-6591, krechmer@ix.netcom.com. **ISSN:** 1081-4655. **Subscription Rates:** $695 individuals. **Remarks:** Advertising not accepted. **Available Online. Alt. Formats:** Diskette. **Formerly:** Communications Standards Review-Telecommunications.
Circ: Paid 250
Controlled 30

2810 Communications Standards Summary
Communications Standards Review
757 Greer Rd. Phone: (650)856-9018
Palo Alto, CA 94303-3024 Fax: (650)856-6591

Journal reporting the status of all TIA TR-Committee active standards projects. **Founded:** Feb. 1994. **Freq:** Quarterly. **Print Method:** Copy. **Key Personnel:** Elaine Baskin, Publisher, ebaskin@csrtds.com; Ken Krechmer, Technical Editor, krechmer@ix.netcom.com. **ISSN:** 1075-5721. **Subscription Rates:** $275 individuals. **Remarks:** Advertising not accepted. **Alt. Formats:** Diskette.
Circ: Paid ‡100
Non-paid ‡55

2811 EPRI Journal
EPRI
3412 Hillview Ave. Phone: (650)855-2411
PO Box 10412
Palo Alto, CA 94303
Magazine covering utilities; emphasizing energy technology research and development and related environmental and economic issues globally. **Founded:** Jan. 1976. **Freq:** 6/year. **Print Method:** Offset. **Trim Size:** 9 x 11. **Cols./Page:** 3. **Col. Width:** 27 nonpareils. **Col. Depth:** 140 agate lines. **Key Personnel:** David Dietrich, Editor, ddietric@epri; Jean Smith, Circulation Director. **Subscription Rates:** $32 individuals; $100 other countries. **Remarks:** Advertising not accepted.
Circ: Paid 2,000
Non-paid 17,000

2812 Journal of Oughtred Society
Oughtred Society
2160 Middlefield Rd. Phone: (415)324-1821
Palo Alto, CA 94301
Journal of the history and collection of slide rules. **Founded:** 1991. **Freq:** 2/year. **Print Method:** Photo offset. **Trim Size:** 8 1/2 x 11. **Cols./Page:** 2. **Col. Width:** 4 4/5 inches. **Col. Depth:** 7 1/10 inches. **Key Personnel:** Dr. Robert K. Otnes, Contact, bobotnes@mediacity.com; Dr. Rodger Shepherd, Contact. **ISSN:** 1061-6292. **Subscription Rates:** $25 individuals.
Ad Rates: PCI: $10 **Circ:** Paid 350

2813 Meanderings
SPPGroup, LLC
157 Primrose Way
Palo Alto, CA 94303
Publication E-mail: meanderings-l-request@webcom.com

Magazine dealing with politics, art, and culture from an African-American perspective. **Key Personnel:** Cuda Brown, Editor. **URL:** http://www.webcom.com/sppg/meanderings/.

2814 Palo Alto Weekly
Embarcadero Publishing Co.
703 High St. Phone: (415)326-8210
Palo Alto, CA 94301 Fax: (415)326-3928

Community newspaper. **Founded:** 1979. **Freq:** Semiweekly Wed. and Fri. **Print Method:** Offset. **Cols./Page:** 6. **Col. Width:** 18 nonpareils. **Col. Depth:** 189 agate lines. **Key Personnel:** Paul Gullixson, Editor; William S. Johnson, Publisher; Franklin Elieh, Advertising Mgr. **ISSN:** 0199-1159. **Subscription Rates:** $40. **URL:** http://www.paweekly.com.
Ad Rates: SAU: $36.00 **Circ:** Paid 5,501
Free 41,499

2815 Sleep
American Sleep Disorders Association (ASDA)
Stanford University Sleep Research Ctr. Phone: (415)723-6965
Fax: (415)725-7341
701 Welch Rd., Ste. 2226
Palo Alto, CA 94304
Journal covering findings on sleep and ciradian rhythms. **Founded:** 1978. **Freq:** 10/year. **Print Method:** Offset, sheetfed. **Trim Size:** 8 1/2 x 11. **Cols./Page:** 2. **Col. Width:** 3 5/8 inches. **Col. Depth:** 9 1/8 inches. **Key Personnel:** Christian Guilleminault, MD, Editor; Jennifer L. Miller, Advertising Manager, phone (913)843-1235, fax (913)843-1274. **ISSN:** 0161-8105. **Subscription Rates:** $121; $34 single issue. **Remarks:** Accepts advertising.
Ad Rates: BW: $715 **Circ:** Paid 4,051
4C: $1710

2816 U.S. - Japan Women's Journal
U.S. - Japan Women's Center
926 Bautista Ct. Phone: (415)857-9049
Palo Alto, CA 94303-4046 Fax: (415)494-8160

Publication with English supplement for international exchange on women and gender. **Subtitle:** A Journal for the International Exchange of Gender Studies. **Founded:** 1988. **Freq:** Semiannual. **Trim Size:** 7 1/8 x 10 1/8. **Cols./Page:** 1. **Col. Width:** 5 1/2 inches. **Col. Depth:** 8 1/2 inches. **Key Personnel:** Yoko Kawashima, Editor. **ISSN:** 1059-9770. **Subscription Rates:** $30; $70 institutions. **Remarks:** Accepts advertising.
Ad Rates: BW: $200 **Circ:** (Not Reported)

2817 KZSU-FM - 90.1
Box B Phone: (415)725-4868
Stanford University Fax: (415)725-5865
Palo Alto, CA 94309
E-mail: info@kzsu.stanford.edu

Format: Full Service; Alternative/New Music/Progressive. **Founded:** 1964. **Operating Hours:** Continuous; 100% local. **Key Personnel:** Sean Kennedy, General Mgr.; Mark Lawrence, Chief Engineer; Mike Howes, Program Dir.; Troy Clardy, Sports Dir.; Dave Flemming, Sports Dir.; Darell Tibbles, News Dir.; Chanel Wheeler, Music Dir.; Jimmy Maas, Chief Announcer; Leonard Iniguez, Public Affairs Dir.; Gabriel Bereny, Public Affairs Dir. **Wattage:** 500. **Ad Rates:** Noncommercial.

PALOS VERDES PENINSULA, pop. 61,500.

S. CA. Los Angeles Co. 18 mi. SW of Los Angeles. Residential.

2818 Palos Verdes Peninsula News
PO Box 2609 Phone: (310)377-6877
Palos Verdes Peninsula, CA 90274 Fax: (310)377-4522
Publisher E-mail: pvnews@palosverdes.com

Community newspaper. **Founded:** 1937. **Freq:** Semiweekly (Thurs. and Sat.). **Print Method:** Offset. **Cols./Page:** 6. **Col. Width:** 2 1/16 nonpareils. **Col. Depth:** 294 agate lines. **Key Personnel:** Bruce M. Wood, Publisher; Penny Shapiro, Office Mgr.; Michelle Vargas, Production Supervisor; Michele Fisher, Managing Editor; Chris Boyd, Assistant Editor. **ISSN:** 0419-0300. **Subscription Rates:** $41.41 home delivery; $52.12 local mail. **Remarks:** Accepts advertising minimum size ad is 4 SAU column inches (56 lines). **Alt. Formats:** Microform. **Formerly:** Rolling Hills Herald. **Feature Editors:** Frank Brown, *Society*; Monica Nalcamine, *Education*, phone (FIN); David Thorpe, *Sports*; Tracy Williams, *Education*.
Ad Rates: GLR: $1.73 **Circ:** Thurs. 15,000
BW: $2,583.00 Sat. 6,200
4C: $2,983.00
SAU: $20.50
PCI: $20.50

PARADISE, pop. 22,571.

N. CA. Butte Co. 90 mi. NE of Sacramento. Residential. Grape Juice Cannery, machine shop. Agriculture. Apples, grapes.

2819 Dogtown Territorial Quarterly
6848U Skyway Phone: (530)872-3363
Paradise, CA 95969
Publisher E-mail: cahist@aol.com

Consumer magazine covering California history. **Founded:** Apr. 1990. **Freq:** Quarterly. **Print Method:** Web offset. **Cols./Page:** 2. **Key Personnel:** Bill Anderson, Editor and Publisher, cagust@aol.com. **ISSN:** 1080-7594. **Subscription Rates:** $15 individuals; $4.50 single issue. **Remarks:** Accepts advertising. **URL:** http://www.californiahistory.com.
Ad Rates: BW: $399 **Circ:** Controlled ‡3,000

2820 Genealogical Goldmine
Paradise Genealogical Society, Inc.
PO Box 460 Phone: (530)877-2330
Paradise, CA 95967-0460
Publisher E-mail: pargenso@jps.net

Genealogical journal covering local and general family histories. **Founded:** June 1968. **Freq:** Semiannual. **ISSN:** 0738-3770. **Subscription Rates:** Free to qualified subscribers. **Remarks:** Advertising accepted; rates available upon request.
Circ: Combined 300

2821 The Paradise Post
5399 Clark Rd. Phone: (916)877-4413
PO Drawer 70 Fax: (916)877-5213
Paradise, CA 95967
Publication E-mail: postedit@aol.com

Community newspaper. **Founded:** 1945. **Freq:** 3/week. **Print Method:** Offset. **Trim Size:** 14 x 22 3/4. **Cols./Page:** 6. **Col. Width:** 26 nonpareils. **Col. Depth:** 301 agate lines. **Key Personnel:** Raandy Goldberg, Publisher. **Subscription Rates:** $34 individuals. **Remarks:** Accepts advertising.
Ad Rates: GLR: $.85 **Circ:** Sat. 8,040
BW: $1,529
4C: $1,865

2822 Small Press Review
Dustbooks
PO Box 100 Phone: (916)887-6110
Paradise, CA 95967 Fax: (916)877-0222
Free: (800)477-6110
Publisher E-mail: dustbooks@telis.org

Bi-monthly journal reviews. **Founded:** 1967. **Freq:** Bimonthly. **Print Method:** Web offset. **Trim Size:** 8 x 10. **Cols./Page:** 3. **Col. Width:** 2 1/4 inches. **Col. Depth:** 9 inches. **ISSN:** 0037-7228. **Subscription Rates:** $25 individuals; $31 other countries; $2.50 single issue. **Remarks:** Accepts advertising.
Ad Rates: GLR: $150 **Circ:** Paid 2,800

2823 KKXX-AM - 930
PO Box 2020 Phone: (916)872-5599
Paradise, CA 95967 Fax: (916)877-2545
E-mail: y105@joshuanet.com

Format: Religious. **Networks:** USA Radio; International Broadcasting. **Founded:** 1965. **Formerly:** KEWQ-AM (1972). **Operating Hours:** 6 a.m.-sunset; 20% network, 80% local. **Key Personnel:** Randy Zachary, General Mgr.; Laura Vallance, Operations Mgr.; Thom Vallance, Jr., Program Dir. **Local Programs:** *Christ is the Answer,* Louie Ricci; *The Clavary Road,* Sam Allen; *The Lord Be With You,* Peter Hanson. **Wattage:** 1000. **Ad Rates:** $12 for 30 seconds; $15 for 60 seconds. **URL:** http://y105.joshuanet.com.

PARAMOUNT, pop. 36,407.

S. CA. Los Angeles Co. Adjoins the city of Long Beach. Foundries, machine shops, Oil refinery. Aluminum, aircraft components, hospital equipment, dairy products manufactured.

2824 Paramount/Bellflower Herald American
Wave Community Newspapers
819 W. Whitter Blvd. Phone: (213)727-1117
Montebello, CA 90640-3623 Fax: (213)727-9515

Community Newspaper. **Founded:** 1912. **Freq:** 2/week Thurs. & Sat. **Print Method:** Offset. **Cols./Page:** 6. **Col. Width:** 26 nonpareils. **Col. Depth:** 301 agate lines. **Key Personnel:** Arthur J. Aguilar, Exec. Editor/Publisher. **Subscription Rates:** $80 individuals.
Circ: Paid 24
Free 24,800

PASADENA, pop. 119,374.

S. CA. Los Angeles Co. 12 mi. NE of Los Angeles. California Institute of Technology. Pasadena City College. Art Center and Design. Ambassador College and Foundation. Pacific Oaks College. Residential. Manufactures furniture, aircraft components, aerospace, scientific and precision instruments, chemicals, electronics, pharmaceuticals, plastics, Oil refineries. Nurseries. Citrus fruit packed.

2825 Bovine Gazette
Mad Dog Productions
PO Box 2263
Pasadena, CA 91102

Humor magazine. **Founded:** Dec. 1985. **Freq:** Monthly. **Key Personnel:** S.C. Taylor, Editor. **Subscription Rates:** $5 individuals; $1 single issue. **Remarks:** Accepts advertising.
Circ: (Not Reported)

2826 Boxoffice Magazine
RLD Communications, Inc.
155 S. El Molino Ave., Ste. 100 Phone: (626)396-0250
Pasadena, CA 91101 Fax: (626)396-0248
Publication E-mail: boxoff@earthlink.net
Publisher E-mail: boxoffice@earthlink.net

Trade magazine for the motion picture exhibition industry; including news of film distribution and exhibition, film reviews, and technical articles. **Subtitle:** The Business Magazine of The Global Motion Picture Industry. **Founded:** 1920. **Freq:** Monthly. **Print Method:** Offset. **Trim Size:** 8 1/8 x 10 7/8. **Cols./Page:** 3. **Col. Width:** 27 nonpareils. **Col. Depth:** 140 agate lines. **Key Personnel:** Christine James, Managing Editor; Robert L. Deitmeier, Publisher; Bob Vale, National Advertising Director; Kim Williamson, Editor-in-Chief; Francesca Dinglasan, Assoc. Editor; Linda Andrade, Editorial Asst.; Annlee Ellingson, Asst. Editor. **ISSN:** 0006-8527. **Subscription Rates:** $40 U.S.; $50 Canada and Mexico; $80 other countries. **Remarks:** Accepts advertising. **URL:** http://www.boxoffice.com.
Ad Rates: BW: $2,625 **Circ:** Paid ★6,583
4C: $3,325

2827 The California Tech
The California Institute of Technology
Caltech 1-71 Phone: (626)395-3630
Pasadena, CA 91125 Fax: (626)577-0636

Collegiate newspaper (tabloid). **Founded:** Feb. 1913. **Freq:** Weekly (Fri.). **Print Method:** Offset. **Trim Size:** 11 1/2 x 17 1/2. **Cols./Page:** 5. **Col. Width:** 11 1/2 picas. **Col. Depth:** 16 1/2 inches. **Key Personnel:** Gavin Claypool, National Advertisin Manager. **ISSN:** 0008-1582. **Subscription Rates:** $11 individuals. **Remarks:** Accepts advertising.
Ad Rates: BW: $600 **Circ:** Paid ‡3,400
4C: $1,400 Free ‡100
PCI: $8

2828 The Courier
Pasadena Community College
1570 E. Colorado Blvd. Phone: (818)585-7130
Rm. C220 Fax: (818)585-7912
Pasadena, CA 91106
Collegiate newspaper. **Founded:** 1917. **Freq:** Weekly (Thurs.). **Print Method:** Offset. **Cols./Page:** 6. **Col. Width:** 26 nonpareils. **Col. Depth:** 294 agate lines. **Key Personnel:** Mikki Bolliger, Adviser; Jose Inostrong, Advertising Mgr. **Remarks:** Accepts advertising. **Available Online. URL:** http://www.geocities.com/~pccnewscourier.
Ad Rates: GLR: $1 **Circ:** ‡5,000
BW: $799
PCI: $6.75

2829 Engineering & Science
The California Institute of Technology
Caltech 1-71 Phone: (626)395-3630
Pasadena, CA 91125 Fax: (626)577-0636

Journal on research at California Institute of Technology. **Founded:** 1937. **Freq:** Quarterly. **Print Method:** Offset. **Trim Size:** 8 1/2 x 11. **Cols./Page:** 2. **Col. Width:** 40 nonpareils. **Col. Depth:** 140 agate lines. **Key Personnel:** Jane Dietrich, Editor. **Subscription Rates:** $10 individuals domestic; $20 other countries. **Remarks:** Advertising not accepted.
Circ: Paid 200
Non-paid 15,500

2830 Firsts
The Lucerne Group
1879 E. Orange Blvd.
Pasadena, CA 91104

Magazine for collectors of first editions of modern books. **Subtitle:** Collecting Modern First Editions. **Freq:** Monthly. **Key Personnel:** Brad Munson, Publisher; Robin H. Smiley, Editor. **Subscription Rates:** $35.

2831 Global Prayer Digest
U.S. Center for World Mission
1605 Elizabeth St. Phone: (626)398-2241
Pasadena, CA 91104 Fax: (626)398-2263

Magazine serving as a Christian devotional aid in daily prayer for ethnic groups unreached by the gospel. **Founded:** 1982. **Freq:** Monthly. **Print Method:** 5 3/8 x 8 1/2. **Cols./Page:** 1. **Col. Width:** 3 7/8 inches. **Col. Depth:** 6 1/2 inches. **Key Personnel:** Roberta Winter, Editor-in-Chief, phone (626)794-5544, fax (626)794-6655, roberta.winter@uscwm.org; Elise Christol, Asst. Ed., phone (626)398-2339, elise.christol@uscwm.org; Keith Carey, Managing Editor, keith.carey@uscwm.org; Dan Eddy, Records/Subscription Service Mgr., phone (626)398-2249, fax (626)398-2249, dan.eddy@uscwm.org. **ISSN:** 1045-9731. **Subscription Rates:** $9; $18 other countries surface; $30 other countries air mail; $1 single issue. **Remarks:** Advertising not accepted. **Online:** Brigada. **Formerly:** Daily Prayer Guide.
Circ: ‡10,000

2832 Herald Tribune
Herald Tribune Co., LLC
2793 E. Foothill Blvd. Phone: (626)585-9060
Pasadena, CA 91107-3444 Fax: (626)585-9860
Publisher E-mail: htsales1@aol.com

Newspaper covering local and community news in San Gabriel Valley, California. **Founded:** Oct. 19, 1995. **Freq:** Weekly. **Print Method:** Offset. **Trim Size:** 11 1/2 x 13 1/2. **Cols./Page:** 5. **Col. Width:** 2 1/16 inches. **Col. Depth:** 13 1/2 inches. **Key Personnel:** Alex Suh, CEO; Rob Clyde, Advertising and Marketing; Gary McCarty, Managing Editor, htnews1@aol.com. **USPS:** 480-520. **Subscription Rates:** Free. **Remarks:** Accepts advertising. **URL:** http://www.heraldtribune.com.
Ad Rates: GLR: $5 **Circ:** Non-paid 80,000
BW: $1,430
4C: $1,630
PCI: $22

2833 Iniquities
Iniquities Publications
167 Sierra Bonita Ave.
Pasadena, CA 91106

Magazine covering horror fiction. **Subtitle:** The Magazine of Great Wickedness and Wonders. **Freq:** Quarterly. **Key Personnel:** Buddy Martinez, Editor and Publisher. **Subscription Rates:** $19.95. $4.95 single issue.

2834 Journal of Interdisciplinary Studies
Institute for Interdisciplinary Research
1065 Pine Bluff Dr. Phone: (626)351-0419
Pasadena, CA 91107-1751
Scholarly journal covering the social sciences and humanities. **Subtitle:** An International Journal of Interdisciplinary and Interfaith Dialogue. **Founded:** Sept. 1989. **Freq:** Annual. **Print Method:** Offset. **Trim Size:** 6 x 9. **Cols./Page:** 1. **Key Personnel:** Dr. Oskar Gruenwald, Editor and Publisher, og@isonline.org. **ISSN:** 0890-0132. **Subscription Rates:** $15 individuals; $25 institutions; $10 students. **Remarks:** Accepts advertising. **Online:** Source One Uncover. **Alt. Formats:** CD-ROM, H. W. Wilson Co.
Ad Rates: BW: $250 **Circ:** Non-paid 1,000

2835 Mission Frontiers
U.S. Center for World Mission
1605 Elizabeth St. Phone: (626)398-2241
Pasadena, CA 91104 Fax: (626)398-2263
Publication E-mail: rickwmf@aol.com

Bulletin of the United States Center for World Mission; editorial on evangelical Frontier Christian missions. **Subtitle:** Mission Frontiers. **Founded:** 1978. **Freq:** Bimonthly. **Print Method:** Offset. **Trim Size:** 8 1/2x11. **Cols./Page:** 2 and 3. **Col. Width:** 3 1/2 inches. **Col. Depth:** 9 inches. **Key Personnel:** Ralph D. Winter, Editor. **ISSN:** 0889-9436. **Subscription Rates:** By donation. **Remarks:** Advertising accepted; rates available upon request.
Circ: ‡100,000

2836 Pasadena Gazette
First-Line Publishers/L.A. Metro Group
14621 Titus St., Ste. 228 Phone: (818)782-8695
Van Nuys, CA 91402 Fax: (818)782-2924

Black community newspaper serving Pasadena, Altedena, Monrovia, and Duarte. **Founded:** 1966. **Freq:** Weekly (Thurs.). **Print Method:** Offset. **Trim Size:** 13 x 21 1/2. **Cols./Page:** 6. **Col. Width:** 2 inches. **Key Personnel:** K.R. Hamm, Publisher; Hillard Hamm, Editor. **Subscription Rates:** Free; $25. **Remarks:** Accepts advertising.
Ad Rates: BW: $4,128 **Circ:** Free 60,000
PCI: $32

2837 Pasadena Realtor
Pasadena Board of Realtors
656 N. Los Robles Ave. Phone: (818)795-7076
Pasadena, CA 91101-1098 Fax: (818)795-0345

Real estate trade organization magazine. **Founded:** 1926. **Freq:** Monthly. **Print Method:** Letterpress. **Cols./Page:** 4. **Col. Width:** 24 nonpareils. **Col. Depth:** 140 agate lines. **Key Personnel:** Jacqueline Johnson, Editor. **Subscription Rates:** $1 individuals.
Circ: (Not Reported)

2838 Pasadena Star-News
San Gabriel Newspaper Group
911 E. Colorado Blvd. Phone: (818)578-6300
Pasadena, CA 91109 Fax: (818)578-6460
Publication E-mail: starnews@earthink.net; tribune@earthlink.net
Publisher E-mail: wdailynews@earthlink.net

General newspaper. **Founded:** Apr. 21, 1886. **Freq:** Mon.-Sun. (morn.). **Print Method:** Offset. **Cols./Page:** 6. **Col. Width:** 26 nonpareils. **Col. Depth:** 301 agate lines. **Key Personnel:** Larry Wilson, Exec. Editor; Joe Logan, Publisher. **Subscription Rates:** $104 individuals. **Remarks:** Accepts advertising. **Formerly:** Star-News (1992).
Ad Rates: GLR: $1.80 **Circ:** Mon.-Sat. 40,550
4C: $3,747.90 Sun. 45,528
PCI: $31.50

2839 Pasadena Weekly
50 S. DeLacey Ave., Ste. 200 Phone: (626)584-1500
Pasadena, CA 91105 Fax: (626)795-0149
Publication E-mail: weekly@pasadenaweekly.com

Community newspaper. **Founded:** 1984. **Freq:** Weekly (Fri.). **Print Method:** Offset. **Trim Size:** 10 13/16 x 15 3/4. **Cols./Page:** 5. **Col. Width:** 12 1/2 nonpareils. **Col. Depth:** 221 agate lines. **Key Personnel:** James P. Laris, Publisher; Fred Bankston, Advertising Mgr. **Subscription Rates:** $65 individu-

als. **Remarks:** Accepts advertising. **Online:** LA Online. **URL:** http://www.pasadenaweekly.com.
Ad Rates: GLR: $1.35 **Circ:** Paid 29
BW: $1,150 Free 35,935
4C: $1,850
PCI: $18

2840 The Plain Truth
Plain Truth Ministries
Pasadena, CA 91129 Phone: (626)304-6077
Fax: (626)795-5106
Free: (800)309-4466
Publication E-mail: monte_ wolverton@ptm.org

Religious magazine. **Founded:** 1934. **Freq:** 6/year. **Print Method:** Offset. **Trim Size:** 8 x 10 1/2. **Cols./Page:** 3. **Col. Width:** 25 nonpareils. **Col. Depth:** 133 agate lines. **Key Personnel:** Joseph Trach, President; Greg Albrecht, Editor-in-Chief. **ISSN:** 0032-0420. **Subscription Rates:** $12.95. **Remarks:** Accepts advertising. **URL:** http://www.ptm.org.
Circ: Paid 125,000

2841 Sunrise
Theosophical University Press
PO Box C Phone: (626)798-3378
Pasadena, CA 91109-7107 Fax: (626)798-4749
Publisher E-mail: tupress@aol.com

Scholarly journal covering philosophy, theosophy and scientific themes. **Subtitle:** Theosophic Perspectives. **Founded:** 1951. **Freq:** Bimonthly. **Print Method:** Offset. **Trim Size:** 6 x 9. **Cols./Page:** 1. **Col. Width:** 26 picas. **Col. Depth:** 42 picas. **Key Personnel:** Grace F. Knoche, Editor. **ISSN:** 0562-6048. **Subscription Rates:** $12 individuals; $15 out of country; $2.50 single issue. **Remarks:** Advertising not accepted. **URL:** http://www.theosociety.org/pasadena. **Alt. Formats:** Audio tape.
Circ: (Not Reported)

2842 Falcon Telecable
474 S. Raymond Ave., Ste. 200 Phone: (818)792-7132
Pasadena, CA 91105 Fax: (818)793-5143

Owner: Falcon Telecable, at above address. **Founded:** Sept. 1958. **Formerly:** Midwestern (1984); Comanche Cable (1986); River Communications (1988). **Key Personnel:** George Doss, General Mgr., phone (903)938-8335, fax (903)938-4840; Berry Ray Bingham, Chief Engineer, phone (915)356-2684, fax (915)356-5779. **Cities Served:** Comanche, TX: subscribing households 1166; 31 channels. **URL:** http://www.falconcable.com.

2843 KAZN-AM - 1300
800 Sierra Madre Villa Ave. Phone: (626)351-1300
Pasadena, CA 91107 Fax: (626)351-4204
Free: (800)598-1300
E-mail: kazn@am1300.com

Format: Ethnic. **Founded:** 1989. **Operating Hours:** Continuous. **ADI:** Los Angeles (Corona & San Bernardino), CA. **Key Personnel:** Kevin Chu, President, phone (626)844-0088, fax (626)844-0414; Felix Guo, Program Dir., felix@am1300.com; Nick Gao, News Dir., nick@am1300.com; Jimmy Yaun, Sales/Promotions. **Local Programs:** *Golden Sun*, Felix Guo; *Hello L.A.*, Felix Guo; *L.A.'s Heaven and Earth*, Felix Guo. **Wattage:** 5000 day; 1000 night. **Ad Rates:** $150-200 for 60 seconds. **URL:** http://www.radiochinese.com.

2844 KMAX-FM - 107.1
3350 Electronic Dr., No. 130 Phone: (818)351-0848
Pasadena, CA 91107 Fax: (818)351-6218

Format: Ethnic. **Networks:** Independent. **Founded:** 1960. **Operating Hours:** Continuous. **Key Personnel:** Marv Rubinek, Regional Sales Dir.; Mat Estrada, Operations Dir. **Wattage:** 3000. **Ad Rates:** $15-70 for 30 seconds; $25-95 for 60 seconds.

2845 KPCC-FM - 89.3
1570 E. Colorado Blvd. Phone: (818)585-7000
Pasadena, CA 91106 Fax: (818)585-7916

Format: Big Band/Nostalgia; News; Public Radio. **Networks:** National Public Radio (NPR). **Founded:** 1957. **Operating Hours:** Continuous. **Key Personnel:** Rod Foster, General Mgr.; Larry Mantle, Contact. **Wattage:** 650.

2846 KPPC-AM - 1240
3844 E. Foothill Blvd. Phone: (818)577-1240
Pasadena, CA 91107-2205

Format: Religious. **Networks:** Independent. **Founded:** 1924. **Operating Hours:** Evenings Mon.-Sat.; 6 a.m.-midnight Sun. **Key Personnel:** Mark E. Pompey, Contact. **Wattage:** 250. **Ad Rates:** Advertising accepted; rates available upon request.

PASO ROBLES, pop. 9,133.

SW CA. San Luis Obispo Co. 30 mi. N. of San Luis Obispo. Recreation. Tourism. Light metal fabricating plant, plastic moldings, electronic products manufactured, grain warehouse, nurseries, fruit drying, almonds shipped. Agriculture. Wheat, cattle, almonds, fruits.

2847 Central Coast Times
Paso Robles Newspapers, Inc.
1050 Park St. Phone: (805)237-6060
PO Box 427 Fax: (805)238-6066
Paso Robles, CA 93447-0427
Community newspaper serving the North Coast area of San Luis Obispo County. **Founded:** 1974. **Freq:** Weekly (Thurs.). **Print Method:** Offset. **Trim Size:** 14 x 22 5/8. **Cols./Page:** 6. **Col. Width:** 2 1/16 inches. **Col. Depth:** 21 1/2 inches. **Key Personnel:** Robert O. Vincent, Managing Editor; Ben Reddick, Publisher; R.D. Reddick, General Mgr. **Subscription Rates:** $12 individuals; $15 Out of county; $18.80 out of state. **Remarks:** Accepts advertising.
Ad Rates: BW: $890 **Circ:** Paid ‡237
SAU: $6.90 Free ‡4,100

2848 Country News-Press
1414 Park Phone: (805)237-6060
Paso Robles, CA 93446 Fax: (805)238-6066

Community newspaper with an agricultural emphasis. **Founded:** 1907. **Freq:** Semiweekly (Wed. and Fri.). **Print Method:** Offset. **Trim Size:** 13 x 22. **Cols./Page:** 6. **Col. Width:** 2 1/16 inches. **Col. Depth:** 21 1/2 inches. **Key Personnel:** Greg Haas, Editor; Bob Chute, Publisher/Advertising Mgr., fax (805)237-6079. **Subscription Rates:** $25 individuals; $35 out of state. **Formed by the merger of:** North County Journal; Daily Press.
Ad Rates: SAU: $6.90 **Circ:** Wed. ‡15,000
Fri. ‡5,000

2849 Heritage Village Banner
Paso Robles Newspapers, Inc.
1050 Park St. Phone: (805)237-6060
PO Box 427 Fax: (805)238-6066
Paso Robles, CA 93447-0427
Community newspaper. **Subtitle:** Lake Nacimiento Herald. **Founded:** 1976. **Freq:** Monthly. **Print Method:** Offset. **Trim Size:** 11 1/4 x 14. **Cols./Page:** 5. **Col. Width:** 2 1/16 inches. **Col. Depth:** 13 inches. **Key Personnel:** Pat Woods, Editor; Dick Reddick, General Mgr. **Subscription Rates:** $12; $15 out of county; $18 out of state. **Remarks:** Accepts advertising. **Formerly:** Heritage Ranch Herald.
Ad Rates: BW: $455 **Circ:** Paid ‡217
PCI: $7 Non-paid ‡1,688

2850 Premier Telecard Magazine
BJE Graphics & Publishing, Inc.
PO Box 2297 Phone: (805)227-1024
Paso Robles, CA 93447-2297 Fax: (805)228-2530
Publication E-mail: premier@callamer.com

Phone card publication. **Subtitle:** The Phone Card Network. **Founded:** July 1993. **Freq:** Bimonthly. **Print Method:** Web offset. **Trim Size:** 8 1/2 x 11. **Cols./Page:** 2 and 3. **Col. Width:** 3 1/2 and 2 1/4 inches. **Col. Depth:** 10 and 10 inches. **Key Personnel:** Bill Jordan, Publisher; Carolan Bell, General Mgr. **ISSN:** 1081-4329. **Subscription Rates:** $24.95; $4.95 single issue. **Remarks:** Accepts advertising. **URL:** http://www.callamer.com/premier-tele.com.
Ad Rates: BW: $2100 **Circ:** Paid ‡65,000
4C: $5000 Non-paid ‡30,000
PCI: $166.67

2851 KBAI-AM - 1150
PO Box 1497 Phone: (805)772-8611
Paso Robles, CA 93447

Format: Big Band/Nostalgia. **Networks:** NBC. **Owner:** at above address. **Founded:** 1969. **Operating Hours:** Continuous. **Key Personnel:** Sandra Hertz, Operations; Bill Bordeaux, Chief Engineer. **Wattage:** 5000. **Ad Rates:** $10 for 30 seconds; $12 for 60 seconds. $10 for 30 seconds; $12 for 60 seconds. Combined advertising rates available with KWAV-FM.

2852 KBZX-FM - 103.1
PO Box 1497 Phone: (805)237-6111
Paso Robles, CA 93447 Fax: (805)238-0674
E-mail: breeze@fix.net

Format: Adult Contemporary. **Simulcasts:** KBZK-FM. **Owner:** Sarape Communications, Inc., at above address. **Founded:** 1995. **Formerly:** KNCR-FM. **Operating Hours:** Continuous. **Key Personnel:** Isabelle Drake, Vice Pres./General & Sales Mgr.; Rebecca Davis, Sales Mgr.; Taina Eckland, Traffic; Bill Bordeaux, Chief Engineer. **Wattage:** 1200. **Ad Rates:** Combined advertising rates available with KBZK-FM.

PATTERSON, pop. 3,866.

C. CA. Stanislaus Co. 19 mi. SW of Modesto. Manufactures farm equipment, frozen food; Modular mobile homes. Grain, fruit and vegetable farms.

2853 Patterson Irrigator
26 N. 3rd St. Phone: (209)892-6187
Patterson, CA 95363 Fax: (209)892-3761

Community newspaper. **Founded:** Aug. 31, 1911. **Freq:** Semiweekly. **Print Method:** Offset. **Trim Size:** 15 x 22 3/4. **Cols./Page:** 6. **Col. Width:** 27 nonpareils. **Col. Depth:** 287 agate lines. **Key Personnel:** Ronald Swift, Editor and Publisher; Jerry Musson, Advertising. **ISSN:** 4234-6000. **Subscription Rates:** $22 individuals. **Remarks:** Accepts advertising.
Ad Rates: BW: $567 **Circ:** Paid 2,310
4C: $822
SAU: $5
PCI: $5.50

PAUMA VALLEY

2854 Native Monthly Reader
RedSun Institute
15061 Adams Dr. Phone: (760)742-4416
Pauma Valley, CA 92061 Fax: (760)742-4416
Publication E-mail: nmr@pacbell.net

Newspaper for young adults focusing on Native American issues. **Founded:** 1990. **Freq:** Monthly October-May. **Trim Size:** 11 x 17. **Cols./Page:** 4. **Col. Width:** 2 1/4 inches. **Col. Depth:** 15 inches. **Key Personnel:** Pat Cauerly, Editor. **USPS:** 007-917. **Subscription Rates:** $20 single issue; $75 students 10 per month. **Remarks:** Accepts advertising.
Ad Rates: PCI: $10 **Circ:** Paid 3,000

PEBBLE BEACH

NW CA. Monterey Co. 5 mi. W. of Monterey. Monterey Co. (NW). 5 m W of Monterey.

2855 KSPB-FM - 91.9
PO Box 657 Phone: (408)625-8374
Pebble Beach, CA 93953 Fax: (408)625-5208

Format: Alternative/New Music/Progressive. **Networks:** Public Radio International (PRI); BBC World Service. **Owner:** Board of Trustees, Robert Lewis Stevenson School, at above address, (408)626-5380. **Founded:** 1979. **Operating Hours:** 24 hours. **Key Personnel:** Peter Burchett, Station Mgr.; Kat Ridolfi, Music Dir.; Chris Duke, Sports Dir. **Local Programs:** *The ? Show*, Matt Mink; *The Will Staples Show*, Will Staples; *WWWA Techno Jam*, Sean Langston. **Wattage:** 1000. **Ad Rates:** Noncommercial.

PERRIS, pop. 6,740.

SE CA. Riverside Co. 18 mi. S. of Riverside. Manufactures mobile homes. Steel and wire products, heavy foundry machinery. Gold, silver mine area, granite quarry. Agriculture.

2856 The Perris Progress
240 W. 4th St. Phone: (909)657-2181
PO Box 128 Fax: (909)657-2182
Perris, CA 92572-0128
Community newspaper. **Founded:** 1901. **Freq:** Weekly (Wed.). **Print Method:** Offset. **Cols./Page:** 6. **Col. Width:** 25 nonpareils. **Col. Depth:** 301 agate lines. **Key Personnel:** John Hoban, Owner; Irene Hoban, Owner; Etha Sabel, Editor and Publisher; Steven Sabel, Production Mgr. **USPS:** 428-100. **Subscription Rates:** $7.54 individuals. **Remarks:** Accepts advertising.
Ad Rates: GLR: $.26 **Circ:** Paid ‡5,500
BW: $775.20
4C: $1,079.20
SAU: $6.46
PCI: $3.98

PESCADERO

2857 Half Moon Bay Review and Pescadero Pebble
Half Bay Review
PO Box 68 Phone: (415)726-4424
Half Moon Bay, CA 94019 Fax: (415)726-7054
Publication E-mail: hmbreview@hmbreview.com

Newspaper with Report orientation. **Founded:** 1898. **Freq:** Weekly (Wed.). **Print Method:** Offset. **Cols./Page:** 6. **Col. Width:** 24 nonpareils. **Col. Depth:** 301 agate lines. **Key Personnel:** Debra Godshall, Editor and Publisher, fax (650)726-6025, deb@hmbreview.com; Eric Rice, Editor, erice@hmbreview.com. **Subscription Rates:** $28 in San Mateo

County; $45 out of area. **Remarks:** Color advertising accepted; rates available upon request.
Ad Rates: GLR: $9 **Circ:** ‡7,000
BW: $1,134.00
SAU: $5
PCI: $9

PETALUMA, pop. 33,834.

NW CA. Sonoma Co. 38 mi. N. of San Francisco. Manufactures oil burners, brooder stoves, poultry and stock foods, egg fillers, milk products, soap, fertilizer. Ships baby chicks. Hatcheries. Dairying. Poultry farms.

2858 Petaluma Argus-Courier
Pulitzer Community Newspapers
830 Petaluma Blvd. N. Phone: (707)762-4541
PO Box 1091 Fax: (707)765-1707
Petaluma, CA 94953
General newspaper. **Founded:** 1855. **Freq:** Daily and Sunday (eve.) Tues. and Fri. afternoon. **Print Method:** Offset. **Cols./Page:** 6. **Col. Width:** 12 3/10 picas. **Col. Depth:** 301 agate lines. **Key Personnel:** Chris Samson, Editor; Barry Blansett, Publisher. **Subscription Rates:** $60 annually.
Ad Rates: GLR: $1.15 **Circ:** Combined ❑7,437
BW: $2,091.09
4C: $2,341.09
SAU: $16.21

2859 The Way of St. Francis
Franciscan Friars of California, Inc.
PO Box 656 Phone: (707)763-9189
Petaluma, CA 94953-0656 Fax: (707)763-9189
Publication E-mail: ofmcaway@att.net
Publisher E-mail: ofmcadev@att.net

Magazine presenting Franciscan vision and spirituality applied to today's issues. **Founded:** 1950. **Freq:** Bimonthly. **Print Method:** Offset. **Trim Size:** 5 1/2 x 8 1/2. **Cols./Page:** 1. **Col. Width:** 3.75 inches. **Col. Depth:** Varies inches. **Key Personnel:** Camille Franicevich, Editor-in-Chief. **ISSN:** 0273-8295. **Subscription Rates:** $12 individuals. **Remarks:** Advertising not accepted. **Available Online. URL:** http://www.sbfranciscans.org.
Circ: Controlled 5,000

2860 Wilderness Trails
Trans-Pacific
712 Sartoric Dr.
Petaluma, CA 94954

Magazine for outdoor activists. **Freq:** Quarterly. **Key Personnel:** Palani Velloo, Editor and Publisher. **Subscription Rates:** $12.74. $3.50 single issue.

PHELAN

2861 Mountaineer Progress
PO Box 290130 Phone: (619)868-3245
Phelan, CA 92329 Fax: (619)868-2700

Community newspaper. **Founded:** 1961. **Freq:** Weekly (Thurs.). **Print Method:** Offset. **Cols./Page:** 6. **Col. Width:** 24 nonpareils. **Col. Depth:** 215 agate lines. **Key Personnel:** John Hollis, Managing Editor. **Subscription Rates:** $17 individuals; $28 out of state. **Remarks:** Accepts advertising.
Ad Rates: GLR: $5.25 **Circ:** ‡4,900
BW: $1,283.55
4C: $1433.55
SAU: $9.95
PCI: $9.95

PHILO

2862 KZYX-FM - 90.7
9300 Hwy. 128 Phone: (707)895-2324
PO Box 1 Fax: (707)895-2451
Philo, CA 95466
E-mail: kzyx@pacific.net

Format: Classical; Ethnic; Public Radio; Eclectic. **Networks:** National Public Radio (NPR); Pacifica. **Owner:** Mendocino County Public Broadcasting, Inc., at above address. **Founded:** 1989. **Operating Hours:** 5 a.m.-3 a.m.; 20% network, 80% local. **Key Personnel:** Teresa Simon, Program Dir.; Jack Tyselling, Tech. Operations; Ron O'Brien, Chief Engineer; Annie Esposito, News Dir.; Mary Aigner, Underwriting Rep.; Bruce Longstreet, Station Mgr. **Local Programs:** *KZYX Community News*, Mark Perrin, News Dir.; *Miller Hawkins Show*, Dan Miller; *Radiogram*, Jamie Roberts; *Wonderous World of Music*, Walter Green. **Wattage:** 3400. **Ad Rates:** $11-17 per unit. **URL:** http://www.pacific.net/~kzyx.

PICO RIVERA, pop. 53,459.

S. CA. Los Angeles Co. 10 mi. SE of Los Angeles. Automobile assembly, electronics, plastics, cement, dairy products, drugs, lumber.

2863 Armenian Numismatic Journal
Armenian Numismatic Society
8511 Beverly Park Pl. Phone: (562)695-0380
Pico Rivera, CA 90660-1920 Fax: (562)695-0380
Publisher E-mail: armnumsoc@aol.com

Trade journal covering Armenian coins, bank notes, and medals. **Founded:** 1975. **Trim Size:** 8 1/2 x 11. **Cols./Page:** 1. **Key Personnel:** Y. T. Nercessian, Editor. **ISSN:** 0884-0180. **Subscription Rates:** $30 individuals. **Remarks:** Advertising not accepted.
Circ: Paid 200

2864 Pico Rivera/Santa Fe Springs News
Wave Community Newspapers
819 W. Whitter Blvd. Phone: (213)727-1117
Montebello, CA 90640-3623 Fax: (213)727-9515

Community Newspaper. **Founded:** 1924. **Freq:** Semiweekly (Wed. and Sat.). **Print Method:** Offset. **Cols./Page:** 6. **Col. Width:** 26 nonpareils. **Col. Depth:** 301 agate lines. **Key Personnel:** Arthur J. Aguilar, Exec. Editor/Publisher. **Subscription Rates:** Free local; $125 by mail. **Absorbed:** Santa Fe Springs News.
Circ: Free 19,461

2865 Pulse
Southern California Veterinary Medical Association
8338 Rosemead Blvd. Phone: (562)948-4979
Pico Rivera, CA 90660-5111 Fax: (562)942-2977
Publisher E-mail: scvma@aol.com

Professional magazine covering veterinary medicine. **Founded:** Mar. 1959. **Freq:** Monthly. **Print Method:** Offset. **Trim Size:** 8 1/8 x 10 7/8. **Cols./Page:** 2. **Col. Width:** 27 nonpareils. **Col. Depth:** 105 agate lines. **Key Personnel:** Richard L. Holden, Editor. **Remarks:** Accepts advertising. **URL:** scvma.org.
Ad Rates: BW: $354 **Circ:** Paid ‡1,060
4C: $814 Non-paid ‡78

PIEDMONT, pop. 10,498.

W. CA. Alameda Co. 3 mi. S. of Berkeley. Residential.

2866 Piedmont & Berkeley Observer
Observer Newspapers
Box 817
San Leandro, CA 94577

Community newspaper. **Founded:** May 22, 1972. **Freq:** Weekly (Fri.). **Print Method:** Offset. **Cols./Page:** 6. **Key Personnel:** Ad Fried, Managing Editor; Michael Robert, Publisher; R.A. Burrell, Advertising Mgr. **Subscription Rates:** $25 individuals. **Remarks:** Accepts advertising.
Ad Rates: BW: $3,000 **Circ:** ‡20,000
4C: $3,600
SAU: $40
PCI: $35

2867 Piedmont Press
Press Publications
Box 10151, Grand Lake Sta. Phone: (510)428-2000
Oakland, CA 94610
Community newspaper. **Founded:** 1970. **Freq:** Bimonthly. **Print Method:** Offset. **Cols./Page:** 5. **Col. Width:** 22 nonpareils. **Col. Depth:** 224 agate lines. **Key Personnel:** George Epstein, Editor and Publisher. **Remarks:** Accepts advertising.
Ad Rates: PCI: $18 **Circ:** Paid ‡4
Non-paid ‡26,996

PINE GROVE

Amador Co.

2868 Volcano Vision, Inc.
Box 890 Phone: (209)296-2288
Pine Grove, CA 95665 Fax: (209)296-2230
E-mail: rayc@volcano.net

Founded: 1982. **Key Personnel:** Ray Crabtree, CATV Mgr., phone (209)296-1462. **Cities Served:** Jackson, Kirkwood, Pine Grove, Pioneer, Volcano, West Point, CA: subscribing households 4,000; 50 channels; 2 community access channels; 140 hours per week community access programming.

PINEDALE

2869 KGMC-TV - 43
706 W. Herndon Ave. Phone: (559)435-7000
Pinedale, CA 93650 Fax: (559)435-3201
E-mail: cocolatv@psnw.com

Format: Commercial TV. **Owner:** Gary Cocola, at above address. **Founded:** Sept. 1992. **Operating Hours:** Continuous. **ADI:** Fresno-Visalia (Hanford), CA. **Key Personnel:** Todd Lopes, Vice President. **URL:** http://www.cocolatv.com.

2870 KXVO-TV - 15
706 W. Herndon Ave. Phone: (559)435-7000
Pinedale, CA 93650 Fax: (559)435-3201
E-mail: cocolatv@psnw.com

Format: Commercial TV. **Owner:** Gary Cocola, at above address. **Founded:** Sept. 1992. **Operating Hours:** Continuous. **ADI:** Fresno-Visalia (Hanford), CA. **Key Personnel:** Todd Lopes, Vice President. **URL:** http://www.cocolatv.com.

PINOLE, pop. 14,253.

W. CA. Contra Costa Co. On San Pablo Bay, 15 mi. N. of Oakland. Manufactures chemicals. Agriculture, livestock.

2871 Contra Costa Lawyer
Contra Costa County Bar Association
Office Solutions Phone: (510)758-3868
PO Box 38 Fax: (510)758-3875
Pinole, CA 94564
Professional magazine covering law for members. **Founded:** June 1988. **Freq:** Monthly. **Print Method:** Litho. **Trim Size:** 8 1/2 x 11. **Key Personnel:** Helen L. Peters, Editor, phone (925)820-0204; Nancy Young, Advertising & Circulation Mgr., nyoung2000@aol.com. **ISSN:** 1063-4444. **Subscription Rates:** $25 individuals. **Remarks:** Accepts advertising. **URL:** http://www.cccba.org.
Ad Rates: BW: $400 **Circ:** Combined 1,500
4C: $700

PITTSBURG, pop. 33,034.

W. CA. Contra Costa Co. 44 mi. NE of Oakland. Boat connections. Manufactures steel, chemicals, rubber goods, building materials. Ship repair yard. Salmon, shad fisheries. Grain, stock farms. Wheat, barley, hay.

2872 Experience
Los Medanos College
2700 E. Leland Rd. Phone: (510)439-2181
Pittsburg, CA 94565 Fax: (510)427-1599

Collegiate newspaper. **Founded:** 1974. **Freq:** Weekly (Fri.). **Print Method:** Offset. **Cols./Page:** 6. **Col. Width:** 24 nonpareils. **Col. Depth:** 285 agate lines. **Remarks:** Accepts advertising.
Ad Rates: PCI: $4 **Circ:** Free 2,000

PLACENTIA

2873 All Chevy
McMullen Argus Publishing, Inc.
774 S. Placentia Ave. Phone: (714)939-2400
Placentia, CA 92870 Fax: (714)572-1864

Auto magazine for Chevrolet car enthusiasts. **Subtitle:** The Complete Chevrolet Magazine. **Founded:** 1987. **Freq:** Monthly. **Print Method:** Web offset. **Key Personnel:** Jerry Dexter, Publisher; Dan Sanchez, Editor. **Subscription Rates:** $2.75 single issue. **Remarks:** Accepts advertising.
Ad Rates: BW: $1,025 **Circ:** ‡100,000
4C: $1,895

2874 Classic Trucks
McMullen Argus Publishing, Inc.
774 S. Placentia Ave. Phone: (714)939-2400
Placentia, CA 92870 Fax: (714)572-1864

Magazine of classic American trucks from the 1950's and 1960's. **Freq:** Monthly. **Key Personnel:** Dan Sanchez, Editor. **Subscription Rates:** $3.50 single issue. **Remarks:** Accepts advertising. **URL:** http://www.mcmullenargus.com.
Circ: Paid 57,035

2875 4-Wheel Drive & Sport Utility Magazine
McMullen Argus Publishing, Inc.
774 S. Placentia Ave. Phone: (714)939-2400
Placentia, CA 92870 Fax: (714)572-1864

Magazine for recreational four-wheel drive vehicle enthusiasts. **Subtitle:** The Complete Off-Road Magazine. **Founded:** Aug. 1985. **Freq:** Monthly 9/year. **Print Method:** Web offset. **Trim Size:** 8 x 10 7/8. **Cols./Page:** 3. **Col. Width:** 2 1/4 inches. **Col. Depth:** 10 inches. **Key Personnel:** Phil Howell, Editor; Bill Middaugh, Advertising Dir. **ISSN:** 0898-8964. **Subscription Rates:** $17.98. $2.75 single issue. **Remarks:** Accepts advertising. **Formed by the merger of:** 4WD Sport Utility; 4WD Action.
Ad Rates: BW: $1,555 **Circ:** Paid ★**51,406**
4C: $2,340

2876 Hot Bike
McMullen Argus Publishing, Inc.
774 S. Placentia Ave. Phone: (714)939-2400
Placentia, CA 92870 Fax: (714)572-1864
Publication E-mail: hotbike@mcmullenargus.com

Magazine for motorcyle enthusiasts interested in high performance. **Subtitle:** The Harley-Davidson Enthusiasts' Magazine. **Founded:** 1969. **Freq:** Monthly. **Print Method:** Web offset. **Trim Size:** 8 x 10 7/8. **Cols./Page:** 3. **Col. Width:** 28 nonpareils. **Col. Depth:** 140 agate lines. **Key Personnel:** Howard Kelly, Editor, howard@mcmullenargus.com; Courtney Halowell, Managing Editor, courtneyh@mcmullenargus.com; Mike Reynolds, Assoc. Editor, miker@mcmullenargus.com; Dave Withron, Advertising Mgr. **ISSN:** 8750-3212. **Subscription Rates:** $18.95 individuals; $3.95 single issue. **Remarks:** Accepts advertising. **URL:** http://www.mcmullenargus.com.
Ad Rates: BW: $1,645 **Circ:** Paid ★57,099
4C: $1,750

2877 Kit Car Illustrated
McMullen Argus Publishing, Inc.
774 S. Placentia Ave. Phone: (714)939-2400
Placentia, CA 92870 Fax: (714)572-1864

Magazine for kit car enthusiasts. **Freq:** Bimonthly. **Print Method:** Web offset. **Trim Size:** 8 x 10 7/8. **Cols./Page:** 3. **Key Personnel:** Mike Blake, Editor, phone (714)939-2550, mikeb@mcmullenargus.com; Pat Lester, Advertising Mgr., phone (714)939-2529. **Remarks:** Accepts advertising.
Ad Rates: BW: $1,235 **Circ:** 85,000
4C: $1,860

2878 Knives Illustrated
McMullen Argus Publishing, Inc.
774 S. Placentia Ave. Phone: (714)939-2400
Placentia, CA 92870 Fax: (714)572-1864

Magazine on the development, design, and manufacture of bladed instruments; for people interested in bladed instruments for both everyday use and as collectible works of art. **Subtitle:** The Premier Cutlery Magazine. **Founded:** 1986. **Freq:** Bimonthly. **Trim Size:** 8 1/2 x 11. **Cols./Page:** 3. **Col. Width:** 2 1/4 inches. **Col. Depth:** 10 inches. **Key Personnel:** Bud Lang, Editor; Chris Yee, Publisher; Eric Suter, Advertising Mgr.; Cynthia MacFarlane, Circulation Mgr. **Subscription Rates:** $15. $3.50 single issue. **Remarks:** Accepts advertising.
Ad Rates: BW: $1,195 **Circ:** ‡100,000
4C: $1,795

2879 MiniTruckin'
McMullen Argus Publishing, Inc.
774 S. Placentia Ave. Phone: (714)939-2400
Placentia, CA 92870 Fax: (714)572-1864

Magazine for mini-truck enthusiasts. **Freq:** Quarterly. **Print Method:** Web offset. **Trim Size:** 8 x 10 7/8. **Key Personnel:** Steve Stillwell, Editor; Thomas M. McMullen, Publisher. **Remarks:** Accepts advertising.
Ad Rates: BW: $2,030 **Circ:** ‡325,000
4C: $725

2880 Mustang Illustrated
McMullen Argus Publishing, Inc.
774 S. Placentia Ave. Phone: (714)939-2400
Placentia, CA 92870 Fax: (714)572-1864

Magazine for Mustang and high performance Ford car enthusiasts. **Founded:** 1986. **Freq:** Quarterly. **Print Method:** Web offset. **Trim Size:** 8 1/8 x 10 7/8. **Cols./Page:** 3. **Key Personnel:** Bob McClurg, Editor; Jerry Dexter, Publisher; Arlan Pfohl, Advertising Mgr. **Subscription Rates:** $15.95. $3.50 single issue. **Remarks:** Accepts advertising.
Ad Rates: BW: $1,635 **Circ:** ‡100,000
4C: $2,420

2881 Splash
McMullen Argus Publishing, Inc.
774 S. Placentia Ave. Phone: (714)939-2400
Placentia, CA 92870 Fax: (714)572-1864

Magazine for personal watercraft sports enthusiasts. **Subtitle:** The Complete Watersports Magazine. **Founded:** 1987. **Freq:** 9/year. **Print Method:** Web offset. **Trim Size:** 8 x 10 7/8. **Key Personnel:** Rob Hallstrom, Editor, phone (714)572-6887, fax (714)572-4265; Greg Gill, VP of Advertising. **Remarks:** Accepts advertising.
Ad Rates: BW: $1,875 **Circ:** ‡100,000
4C: $750

2882 Street Cruzin Magazine
McMullen Argus Publishing, Inc.
774 S. Placentia Ave. Phone: (714)939-2400
Placentia, CA 92870 Fax: (714)572-1864

Magazine of cruising cars. **Freq:** Quarterly. **Key Personnel:** Frank Hamilton, Editor; Tom McMullen, Publisher. **Subscription Rates:** $2.95 single issue.

2883 Truckin' Magazine
McMullen Argus Publishing, Inc.
774 S. Placentia Ave. Phone: (714)939-2400
Placentia, CA 92870 Fax: (714)572-1864

Magazine about custom vans, mini trucks, and pickups. **Founded:** June 1975. **Freq:** Monthly. **Print Method:** Web offset. **Trim Size:** 8 x 10 7/8. **Cols./Page:** 3. **Col. Width:** 27 nonpareils. **Col. Depth:** 140 agate lines. **Key Personnel:** Steve Stillwell, Editor; Thomas M. McMullen, Publisher; John Nething, Advertising Mgr. **ISSN:** 0277-5743. **Subscription Rates:** $19.95 individuals; $34.95 two years. **Remarks:** Accepts advertising.
Ad Rates: BW: $2,520 **Circ:** Paid ★170,087
4C: $975

PLACERVILLE†, pop. 6,739.

EC CA. El Dorado Co. 40 mi. NE of Sacramento. Manufactures building lumber poly vinyl pipe, lime products. Fruit packing plant, bottling works. Gold mines; limestone quarries; timber. Agriculture. Pears, apples, grapes, peaches, plums.

2884 Mountain Democrat
PO Box 1088 Phone: (916)622-1255
Placerville, CA 95667 Fax: (916)622-7894
Publication E-mail: mtdemo@calweb.com

Local newspaper. **Founded:** 1851. **Freq:** 4/wk (Mon., Wed., Thurs., Fri.). **Print Method:** Offset. **Cols./Page:** 6. **Col. Width:** 2 1/16 inches. **Col. Depth:** 21 inches. **Key Personnel:** Michael Raffety, Editor; James Webb, Publisher. **Subscription Rates:** $68 individuals; $82 in state; $89.50 out of state. **Remarks:** Accepts advertising. **URL:** http://www.mtdemocrat.com. **Formerly:** Mountain Democrat and Placerville Times.
Ad Rates: BW: $1,581.30 **Circ:** Mon. ★12,790
4C: $1,796.30 Wed. ★12,790
SAU: $13.50 Thurs. ★11,375
PCI: $12.55 Fri. ★12,790

PLATINA, pop. 100.

N. CA. Shasta Co. 10 mi. S. of Omo. Residential.

2885 The Orthodox Word
St. Herman of Alaska Brotherhood
Box 70 Phone: (530)352-4430
Platina, CA 96076 Fax: (530)352-4432
Publisher E-mail: stherman@crl.com

Magazine about the Orthodox Christian spirituality and the monastic tradition. Includes lives and teachings of the holy fathers and recent confessors as well as examinations of current topics. **Founded:** Jan. 1965. **Freq:** Bimonthly. **Print Method:** Offset. **Trim Size:** 6 x 8 1/2. **Cols./Page:** 1. **Col. Width:** 54 nonpareils. **Col. Depth:** 98 agate lines. **Key Personnel:** Abbot Herman Podmoshensky, Editor and Publisher; Father Theodore, Advertising Mgr.; Fr. Damascene, Co-Ed./Pub. **ISSN:** 0030-5839. **Subscription Rates:** $15 individuals; $3 single issue; $18 out of country; $12 students. **Remarks:** Advertising not accepted. **Alt. Formats:** Microform.
Circ: Paid ‡2,790
Controlled ‡400

PLAYA DEL REY

2886 Cancer Victors Journal
International Association of Cancer Victors and Friends
7740 W. Manchester Ave. Phone: (310)822-4193
Ste. 203 Fax: (310)822-4193
Playa del Rey, CA 90293
Publisher E-mail: iacvf@inetworld.net

Association magazine. **Subtitle:** Voice of IACVF. **Founded:** 1963. **Freq:** Quarterly. **Print Method:** Offset or Desk. **Trim Size:** 8 1/2 x 11. **Cols./Page:** 3. **Key Personnel:** Ann Cinquina, Editor; Ann Cinquina, Executive Secretary. **ISSN:** 0891-0766. **Subscription Rates:** $25 membership; $30 family membership. **Remarks:** Accepts advertising. **Formerly:** Cancer News Journal (1990).
Ad Rates: BW: $500 **Circ:** Paid ‡20,000
4C: $1,000

PLEASANT GROVE

2887 Pot-Bellied Pigs
Saman Publications
Box 768 Phone: (916)655-1645
Pleasant Grove, CA 95668 Fax: (916)991-3049

Consumer magazine covering pot-bellied pigs. **Founded:** 1990. **Freq:** Bimonthly. **Key Personnel:** Sally Andresen, Editor. **Subscription Rates:** $30 individuals; $6 single issue. **Remarks:** Accepts advertising.
Ad Rates: BW: $300 **Circ:** (Not Reported)
4C: $750

PLEASANT HILL

2888 BAM Magazine
BAM Media, Inc.
3470 Buskirk Ave. Phone: (925)934-3700
Pleasant Hill, CA 94523-4316 Fax: (925)946-2985
Publisher E-mail: sales@bammedia.com

Regional music magazine. **Subtitle:** California's Music Magazine. **Founded:** 1976. **Freq:** Biweekly. **Print Method:** Offset. **Trim Size:** 10 x 12. **Cols./Page:** 3. **Col. Width:** 21 nonpareils. **Col. Depth:** 189 agate lines. **Key Personnel:** Bill Crandall, Northern California Editor, fax (510)946-9060, editorial@bammedia.com; Kris Smith, Northern California Advt. Mgr., sales@bammedia.com. **ISSN:** 0194-5793. **Subscription Rates:** Free to qualified subscribers; $25 individuals. **Remarks:** Accepts advertising. **URL:** http://www.musicuniverse.com.
Ad Rates: BW: $3,987 **Circ:** Non-paid △119,507
4C: $4,987
PCI: $56

2889 Beverage Industry News
Industry Publications, Inc.
171 Mayhew Way, Ste. 202 Phone: (925)932-4999
Pleasant Hill, CA 94523 Fax: (925)932-4966
Publication E-mail: peck@sso.com

Magazine for the alcoholic beverages retail trade. **Founded:** 1935. **Freq:** Monthly. **Print Method:** Offset. **Trim Size:** 8 3/8 x 10 7/8. **Cols./Page:** 3. **Col. Width:** 27 nonpareils. **Col. Depth:** 140 agate lines. **Key Personnel:** Dave Page, Publisher. **ISSN:** 0271-9894. **Subscription Rates:** $49 individuals. **Remarks:** Accepts advertising. **Formerly:** BIN Merchandiser.
Ad Rates: BW: $1,920 **Circ:** Paid ‡11,250
4C: $4,000 Non-paid ‡5,618

PLEASANTON, pop. 35,160.

W. CA. Alameda Co. 42 mi. SE of San Francisco. Residential. Cheese factories, wineries, Research.

2890 MotoRacing
Kelly Communications
3609 Virgin Islands Ct. Phone: (925)846-7728
Pleasanton, CA 94588-5228 Fax: (925)846-0118
Free: (800)58K-ELLY

Newspaper covering road and off-road automotive racing in the Western U.S. **Founded:** Oct. 1994. **Freq:** Monthly. **Print Method:** Offset litho. **Key Personnel:** John F. Kelly, Jr., Editor and Publisher, 76067.1750@compuserve.com; Patrice J. Kelly, Business Mgr. **ISSN:** 1080-9929. **Subscription Rates:** $18 individuals. **Remarks:** Accepts advertising.
Ad Rates: BW: $760 **Circ:** Combined 2,500
4C: $1,685

2891 North American Pylon
Kelly Communications
PO Box 1203 Free: (800)58-KELLY
Pleasanton, CA 94566
Publication E-mail: 76067.1750@compuserve.com

Newspaper (tabloid) covering solo events, road racing and other motorsports. **Subtitle:** Dedicated to Sports Car Autocrossing. **Founded:** 1990. **Freq:** Monthly. **Print Method:** Offset. **Trim Size:** 11 1/4 x 17 1/2. **Cols./Page:** 4. **Col. Width:** 14 picas. **Col. Depth:** 16 inches. **Key Personnel:** John F. Kelly, Jr., Editor and Publisher; Patricia J. Kelly, Advertising Mgr. **ISSN:** 1053-4881. **Subscription Rates:** $24 U.S.; $27.50 Canada; $2 single issue.
Ad Rates: GLR: $.73 **Circ:** Paid ‡1,300
BW: $528 Free ‡700
4C: $925

2892 Soccer California
California Youth Soccer Association
1249 Quarry Ln., No. 140 Phone: (925)426-5437
Pleasanton, CA 94566-8446 Fax: (925)426-9473
Publisher E-mail: melcysa@aol.com

Sports magazine (tabloid) covering soccer news in northern California. **Freq:** 8/year. **Print Method:** Offset. **Trim Size:** 8 1/2 x 11. **Cols./Page:** 3. **Col. Width:** 2 1/4 inches. **Col. Depth:** 10 inches. **Key Personnel:** Shirley K. Schlueter, Editor. **Subscription Rates:** $12. **Remarks:** Accepts advertising. **URL:** http://www.cysanorth.org.
Ad Rates: BW: $600 **Circ:** ‡15,000

Tri-Valley Herald - See Livermore

2893 Valley Times
Contra Costa Newspapers, Inc.
127 Spring St. Phone: (510)847-2111
PO Box 607 Fax: (510)847-2189
Pleasanton, CA 94566
Daily newspaper. **Founded:** 1971. **Freq:** Mon.-Sun. (morn.). **Print Method:** Offset. **Trim Size:** 13 3/4 x 23. **Cols./Page:** 6.

Col. Width: 25 nonpareils. **Col. Depth:** 301 agate lines. **Key Personnel:** Karen Magnuson, Managing Editor; David Rounds, General Mgr. **Subscription Rates:** $53.50 individuals; $102 out of area. **Remarks:** Accepts advertising. **Former name**: Contra Costa Times. **Feature Editors:** Linda Davis, *Features*; Dave Goll, *Religion*; Kelly Gust, *City*; Jim Ketsdever, *Photo*; Mark Mazzaferro, *City*.
Ad Rates: GLR: $5.80 **Circ:** Mon.-Sat. ★**44,354**
BW: $2,089.80 Sun. ★**46,559**
4C: $2,474.80
SAU: $16.20

2894 KKIQ-FM - 101.7
7901 Stoneridge Dr., No. 525 Phone: (510)455-4500
Pleasanton, CA 94588 Fax: (510)416-1211
E-mail: kkiq1017@aol.com

Format: Adult Contemporary. **Networks:** AP. **Founded:** 1969. **Operating Hours:** Continuous; 100% local. **ADI:** San Francisco-Oakland-San Jose. **Key Personnel:** Jack Chunn, Pres./Gen. Mgr.; Eva Adams, News Dir.; Jim Hampton, Program Dir. **Wattage:** 4500. **Ad Rates:** $80 per unit. **URL:** http://www.kkiq.com.

2895 Viacom Cable
Box 13 Phone: (510)463-0870
Pleasanton, CA 94566 Fax: (510)463-3241

Owner: Viacom International, 1211 Avenue of the Americas, New York, NY 10036. **Key Personnel:** John Goddard, Contact. **Cities Served:** San Ramon, Pittsburg, Napa, Pleasanton, Livermoor, Dublin, Sonoma, San Francisco, Marin, Antioch, Redding, Red Bluff, Oroville, Gridley, Colusa, Petaluma and Castro Valley, CA; Salem, OR; Tacoma, Seattle, Bellevue, Kirkland, King, Snohomish & Everett, WA; Dayton, OH; Nashville, TN.

POINT ARENA

2896 Sagewoman Magazine
Sage Woman: Celebrating The Goddess in Every Woman
PO Box 641 Phone: (707)882-2052
Point Arena, CA 95468 Fax: (707)882-2793
Publication E-mail: info@sagewoman.com

Periodical focusing on women's spirituality. **Subtitle:** Celebrating the Goddess in Every Woman. **Founded:** 1986. **Freq:** Quarterly. **Print Method:** Offset. **Trim Size:** 8 1/2 x 11. **Key Personnel:** Anne Newkirk-Niven, Editor and Publisher. **ISSN:** 1068-1698. **Subscription Rates:** $21 individuals; $6 single issue. **Remarks:** Accepts advertising. **URL:** http://www.sagewoman.com.
Ad Rates: BW: $525 **Circ:** Paid ‡15,000
Non-paid ‡100

POINT REYES STATION, pop. 10,000.

W. CA. Marin Co. On Pacific Ocean, 35 mi. NW of San Francisco. Resort. Commercial fisheries. Dairying.

2897 Point Reyes Light
PO Box 210 Phone: (415)663-8404
Point Reyes Station, CA 94956
Community newspaper. **Founded:** 1948. **Freq:** Weekly (Thurs.). **Print Method:** Offset. **Cols./Page:** 6. **Col. Width:** 19 nonpareils. **Col. Depth:** 200 agate lines. **Key Personnel:** Dave Mitchell, Editor and Publisher; Renee Shannon, Advertising Dir.; Don Schinske, Business Mgr. **Subscription Rates:** $20 individuals. **Remarks:** Accepts advertising. **URL:** http://www.ptreyeslight.com.
Ad Rates: GLR: $.47 **Circ:** ‡4,300

POMONA, pop. 92,742.

S. CA. Los Angeles Co. 30 mi. E. of Los Angeles. Mount San Antonio College. California State Polytechnic University, Pomona. Manufactures tile bricks, fruit processing and citrus packing equipment. Guided missile plant. Fruit packing, oil refinery, paper reclaiming. Fruit, dairy, stock farms. Oranges, lemons, grapefruit.

2898 La Voz
685 W. Mission Blvd. Phone: (909)629-2292
Pomona, CA 91766 Fax: (909)629-7644
Publication E-mail: lavoz1981@earthlinks.net

Community (tabloid) newspaper (English and Spanish). **Subtitle:** La Voz Newspaper Lavoz Publications. **Founded:** 1981. **Print Method:** Web offset. **Trim Size:** 13 x 21. **Cols./Page:** 6. **Col. Width:** 2 1/16 inches. **Col. Depth:** 21 inches. **Key Personnel:** Gustavo Cisneros, Editor; Albert Castro, Publisher. **Subscription Rates:** $35. **Remarks:** Accepts advertising.
Ad Rates: GLR: $1 **Circ:** Paid 200
BW: $1,764 Free 19,800
4C: $75
PCI: $12

2899 The Poly Post
California State Polytechnic University
3801 W. Temple Ave., Bldg. 1-210 Phone: (909)869-3528
Fax: (909)869-3863
Pomona, CA 91768-4007
Collegiate newspaper. **Founded:** 1945. **Freq:** Weekly (Tues. during academic year). **Print Method:** Offset. **Trim Size:** 14 x 22. **Cols./Page:** 6. **Col. Width:** 2 inches. **Col. Depth:** 21 inches. **Key Personnel:** Tim Lynch, Adviser, phone (909)869-3540. **Subscription Rates:** Free to the campus. **Remarks:** Accepts advertising. **Formerly**: The Post.
Ad Rates: GLR: $1 **Circ:** Free ‡6,500
BW: $371
PCI: $7.50

PORT HUENEME, pop. 17,803.

SW CA. Ventura Co. On Pacific Ocean, 60 mi. W. of Los Angeles. Residential. Naval Base.

2900 Seabee Coverall
Aerotech
1000 23rd Ave. Phone: (805)982-4493
Port Hueneme, CA 93043-4301
Publisher E-mail: aerotech@netport.com

Military and family-interest magazine (tabloid) distributed worldwide to Navy bases and government offices. **Founded:** Apr. 20, 1943. **Freq:** Biweekly. **Print Method:** Offset. **Trim Size:** 11 1/2 x 17 1/2. **Cols./Page:** 5. **Col. Width:** 1 7/8 inches. **Col. Depth:** 13 inches. **Key Personnel:** Paul Kinison, Publisher. **Subscription Rates:** Free. **Remarks:** Accepts advertising.
Ad Rates: GLR: $11.25 **Circ:** Non-paid 8,500
PCI: $11.25

PORTERVILLE, pop. 19,707.

SC CA. Tulare Co. 56 mi. N. of Bakersfield. Recreation. Extensive orange and deciduous fruit packing. Electronics, medical instruments, sportswear, paper products. Carpet yarn manufactured. Diversified farming.

2901 Porterville Recorder
Freedom Communications Inc.
115 E. Oak Phone: (209)784-5000
PO Box 151 Fax: (209)784-1689
Porterville, CA 93257
General newspaper. **Founded:** 1908. **Freq:** Mon.-Sat. (eve.). **Print Method:** Offset. **Cols./Page:** 6. **Col. Width:** 24 nonpareils. **Col. Depth:** 21 inches. **Key Personnel:** Rick Elkins, Editor; Jim Lyons, Publisher; Jonell Webb, Advertising Dir. **Subscription Rates:** $90 individuals. **Remarks:** Accepts advertising. **Alt. Formats:** Microform.
Ad Rates: GLR: $.80 **Circ:** Mon.-Sat. ★**10,871**
BW: $1,323
4C: $1,668
PCI: $11.20

2902 KTIP-AM - 1450
1660 N. Newcomb Ave. Phone: (209)784-1450
Porterville, CA 93257 Fax: (209)784-2482
E-mail: ktip1450@aol.com

Format: Talk; News; Sports; Agricultural. **Networks:** NBC; Mutual Broadcasting System; Westwood One Radio; Canadian Broadcasting Corporation (CBC)/Societe Radio-Canada (SRC). **Owner:** Caldwell Broadcasting Co., Inc., at above address. **Founded:** 1947. **Operating Hours:** Continuous; 75% network, 25% local. **ADI:** Fresno-Visalia (Hanford), CA. **Key Personnel:** Douglas Caldwell, President. **Local Programs:** *AM Newswheel*, Trudy Hibler; *Morning Line*, Mike Haskins. **Wattage:** 1000. **Ad Rates:** $9-14 for 30 seconds.

PORTOLA, pop. 1,885.

NE CA. Plumas Co. 40 mi. W. of Reno, NV. Resort. Tourism, recreation. Lumbering. Pine, cedar timber. Dairy, stock farms.

2903 Portola Reporter
Feather Publishing
116 Commercial St. Phone: (916)832-4646
Portola, CA 96122 Fax: (916)832-5319
Publisher E-mail: featherpub@aol.com

Newspaper. **Founded:** June 2, 1927. **Freq:** Weekly (Wed.). **Print Method:** Offset. **Cols./Page:** 6. **Col. Width:** 26 nonpareils. **Col. Depth:** 301 agate lines. **Key Personnel:** David Keller, Editor; Michael Taborski, Publisher. **Subscription Rates:** $25 individuals. **Remarks:** Accepts advertising. **Online:** America Online, Inc.
Ad Rates: BW: $580.50 **Circ:** ‡1,950
4C: $4.50
PCI: $5

2904 Feather River TV Cable Systems
Box 1210 Phone: (916)832-5551
Portola, CA 96122 Fax: (916)832-4465
Free: (800)832-5551

Owner: Sonic Cable TV of Northern California, 1031 Triangle Ct., West Sacramento, CA 95605, (916)372-2221, Fax: (916)372-3865. **Founded:** 1963. **Key Personnel:** Sloan Dayton, Contact; Darrel Housel, Contact. **Cities Served:** Blairsden, Crescent Mills, Graeagle, Greenville, Loyalton, Portola, Quincy, CA: subscribing households 3,650; 36 channels; 1 community access channel.

POWAY, pop. 9,422.

S. CA. San Diego Co. 10 mi. N. of San Diego. San Diego Co. (S). 10 m N of San Diego. Residential.

2905 Corridor News
Pomerado Publishing
PO Box 685 Phone: (619)748-2311
Poway, CA 92064-0685 Fax: (619)748-0413
Publication E-mail: editor@cts.com

Local newspaper. **Founded:** 1971. **Freq:** Weekly (Thurs.). **Print Method:** Offset. **Cols./Page:** 6. **Col. Width:** 25 nonpareils. **Col. Depth:** 294 agate lines. **Key Personnel:** Steve Dreyer, Editor; David W. Calvert, Publisher; Trudy Armstrong, Advertising Dir. **Subscription Rates:** $24 individuals. **Remarks:** Accepts advertising. **Formerly**: Penasquitos News (1995).
Ad Rates: GLR: $.59 **Circ:** Paid ❑**579**
BW: $880 Free ❑**10,726**
4C: $1,150
SAU: $8.31

2906 Poway News Chieftain
Pomerado Publishing
PO Box 685 Phone: (619)748-2311
Poway, CA 92064-0685 Fax: (619)748-0413

Community newspaper. **Founded:** 1955. **Freq:** Weekly (Thurs.). **Print Method:** Offset. **Cols./Page:** 6. **Col. Width:** 25 nonpareils. **Col. Depth:** 294 agate lines. **Key Personnel:** Steve Dreyer, Editor; David W. Calvert, Publisher; Ann Calvert, Advertising Mgr. **USPS:** 440-760. **Subscription Rates:** $24 individuals. **Remarks:** Accepts advertising.
Ad Rates: GLR: $.59 **Circ:** Paid ❑**1.606**
BW: $880 Free ❑**11,847**
4C: $1,150
SAU: $8.31

QUARTZ HILL

2907 Quartz Hill Journal of Theology
43543 51st St. W Phone: (805)722-0891
Quartz Hill, CA 93536 Fax: (805)943-3484
Publication E-mail: info@theology.edu

Religous magazine containing reviews, poetry, and articles. **Founded:** 1993. **Freq:** Quarterly. **Trim Size:** 8-1/2 x 11. **Key Personnel:** R. P. Nettelhorst, Contact, phone (805)948-3438. **ISSN:** 1075-0126. **Subscription Rates:** $20 individuals; $7.50 single issue. **Remarks:** Advertising accepted; rates available upon request. **Available Online**. **URL:** http://www.theology.edu.
Circ: 200

QUINCY†, pop. 6,529.

NE CA. Plumas Co. 25 mi. NW of Portola. Resort. Sawmills, bottling works, lumber mills, machine shop. Fir, pine timber. Dairying. Stock farms.

2908 Feather River Bulletin
Feather Publishing
55 W. Main Phone: (530)283-0800
Quincy, CA 95971 Fax: (530)283-3952
Publication E-mail: plumaspub@aol.com
Publisher E-mail: featherpub@aol.com

Community newspaper. **Founded:** 1866. **Freq:** Weekly (Wed.). **Print Method:** Offset. **Cols./Page:** 6. **Col. Width:** 26 nonpareils. **Col. Depth:** 301 agate lines. **Key Personnel:** Dave Moller, Editor; Michael Taborski, Publisher; Sheri McConnell, Advertising Mgr. **USPS:** 118-550. **Subscription Rates:** $20 individuals. **Remarks:** Accepts advertising. **Online:** America on Line. **URL:** http://www.plumasnews.com.
Ad Rates: BW: $612.75 **Circ:** ‡3,380
SAU: $5
PCI: $4.75

2909 Indian Valley Record
Feather Publishing
55 W. Main Phone: (530)283-0800
Quincy, CA 95971 Fax: (530)283-3952
Publication E-mail: plumaspub@aol.com

Publisher E-mail: featherpub@aol.com

CNP. **Founded:** 1930. **Freq:** Weekly (Wed.). **Print Method:** Offset. **Cols./Page:** 6. **Col. Width:** 11.5 picas. **Col. Depth:** 301 agate lines. **Key Personnel:** Michael C. Taborski, Publisher; Alicia Higbee, Editor. **USPS:** 775-460. **Subscription Rates:** $18.00 individuals; $25.00 out of county; $28.00 out of state; $.50 single issue. **Remarks:** Accepts advertising. **URL:** http://www.plumasnews.com.
Ad Rates: BW: $580.50 **Circ:** 1,205
SAU: $4.75
PCI: $4.25

2910 KNLF-FM - 95.9
440 Lawrence St. Phone: (530)283-4145
PO Box 117 Fax: (530)283-5135
Quincy, CA 95971

Format: Contemporary Christian; Talk; Sports. **Networks:** USA Radio; Ambassador Inspirational Radio. **Owner:** New Life Broadcasting, at above address. **Founded:** 1906. **Operating Hours:** Continuous. **Wattage:** 1000. **Ad Rates:** $5-6 for 30 seconds; $8-10 for 60 seconds.

RAMONA

2911 Ramona Sentinel
Pomerado Publishing
611 Main St. Phone: (619)789-1350
Ramona, CA 92065 Fax: (619)789-4057

Local newspaper. **Founded:** 1886. **Freq:** Weekly (Thurs.). **Print Method:** Offset. **Cols./Page:** 6. **Col. Width:** 25 nonpareils. **Col. Depth:** 294 agate lines. **Key Personnel:** Maureen Robertson, Editor; Julie M. Walker, Publisher; Carol Kinney, Advertising Dir. **ISSN:** 4703-6000. **Subscription Rates:** $21 individuals. **Remarks:** Accepts advertising.
Ad Rates: BW: $1,296.54 **Circ:** Paid 4,806
4C: $1,874.80 Free 135
SAU: $10.29

RANCHO BERNARDO

2912 Rancho Bernardo News Journal
Pomerado Publishing
11650 Iberia Place, Ste. 215 Phone: (619)487-5757
San Diego, CA 92128
Local newspaper. **Founded:** 1971. **Freq:** Weekly (Thurs.). **Print Method:** Offset. **Cols./Page:** 6. **Col. Width:** 25 nonpareils. **Col. Depth:** 294 agate lines. **Key Personnel:** Steve Dreyer, Editor; David W. Calvert, Publisher; Ann Calvert, Advertising Dir. **Subscription Rates:** $24 individuals. **Remarks:** Accepts advertising.
Ad Rates: GLR: $.59 **Circ:** Paid □519
BW: $880 Free □14,175
4C: $1,150
SAU: $8.31

RANCHO CORDOVA

NC CA. Sacramento Co. 5 mi. NE of Mather A.F.B.

2913 Grapevine Independent
3338 Mather Field Rd. Phone: (916)361-1234
Rancho Cordova, CA 95670 Fax: (916)361-0491

Newspaper serving Rancho Cordova and Gold River, California. **Founded:** 1968. **Freq:** Weekly. **Print Method:** Offset. **Cols./Page:** 6. **Col. Width:** 2 1/16 inches. **Col. Depth:** 20 inches. **Key Personnel:** Shelly Blanchard, Editor, phone (916)361-1239; Robert Ling, Publisher. **Subscription Rates:** $24. **Remarks:** Accepts advertising.
Ad Rates: BW: $800 **Circ:** Paid 7,000
PCI: $10.50 Non-paid 4,000

RANCHO CUCAMONGA

2914 Skinner Kinsmen Update
Brandywine Press
Box 2594
Rancho Cucamonga, CA 91729
Publication E-mail: skinner.kinsmen@usa.net

Journal covering genealogy of the Skinner family. **Founded:** Sept. 1984. **Freq:** Quarterly. **Key Personnel:** Gregg Legutki, Editor. **ISSN:** 0985-0202. **Subscription Rates:** $16.50 individuals. **Remarks:** Advertising not accepted. **URL:** http://www.dc.smu.edu/Skinner/SPA/SkinnerFamAssoc.htm.
Circ: Combined 200

2915 KNSE-AM - 1510
8729 E. 9th St. Phone: (909)981-8893
Rancho Cucamonga, CA 91730 Fax: (909)981-2032

Format: Hispanic. **Networks:** Spanish Information Service. **Owner:** Coronado Four-County Broadcasting, Inc., at above address. **Founded:** 1946. **Operating Hours:** Continuous. **ADI:** Los Angeles (Corona & San Bernardino), CA. **Key Personnel:** Fernando Oaxaca, Chairman of the Board; Daniel Balcazar, Sales Mgr.; Malu Hernandez, Vice President; Francisco Sanabra, News Dir. **Wattage:** 10,000 day; 1000 night. **Ad Rates:** $20-36 for 30 seconds; $25-45 for 60 seconds.

RANCHO MIRAGE

2916 GOLF NEWS Magazine
Dan & Joan Poppers
PO Box 1040 Phone: (760)836-3700
Rancho Mirage, CA 92270 Fax: (760)836-3703
Publication E-mail: golfnews@aol.com

Golf magazine covering Southern California. **Subtitle:** Southern California's Premier Golf Magazine. **Founded:** 1984. **Freq:** Monthly. **Print Method:** Web. **Trim Size:** 8 x 10 7/8. **Cols./Page:** 3. **Col. Width:** 2 1/4 inches. **Col. Depth:** 10 1/8 inches. **Key Personnel:** Dan Poppers, Editor and Publisher. **Subscription Rates:** $19.50; $33.60 two years. **Remarks:** Accepts advertising.
Ad Rates: BW: $1,555 **Circ:** Controlled ‡17,050
4C: $2,175

2917 Rancho Mirage Post
Brehm Communications, Inc.
82632-B Hwy. 11 Phone: (619)775-4200
Indio, CA 92201 Fax: (619)342-7128

Indiana. **Subtitle:** Desert Post. **Founded:** 1979. **Freq:** Weekly (Wed.). **Print Method:** Offset. **Cols./Page:** 8. **Col. Width:** 18 nonpareils. **Col. Depth:** 294 agate lines. **Key Personnel:** Joan Boiko, Editor; Robert Dickey, Publisher; Walter Hennig, General Mgr. **Subscription Rates:** $15 individuals. **Remarks:** Accepts advertising.
Ad Rates: BW: $1,180.35 **Circ:** ‡6,000
4C: $1,535.35
SAU: $9.15
PCI: $6.85

RANCHO PALOS VERDES

2918 Friends of French Art
Villa Narcissa
100 Vanderclip Dr. Phone: (310)377-4444
Rancho Palos Verdes, CA 90275 Fax: (310)377-4584
Trade magazine covering art restoration. **Founded:** 1979. **Freq:** Annual. **Key Personnel:** Elin Vanderlip. **Subscription Rates:** Included in membership; $40 single issue. **Remarks:** Advertising not accepted.
Circ: (Not Reported)

RANCHO SANTA FE, pop. 4,014.

WC CA. San Diego Co. 21 mi. N. of San Diego. Citrus fruit, avocado groves; residential.

2919 Rancho Santa Fe Sun
West Coast Community Newspapers
2841 Loker Ave. E. Phone: (619)431-4850
Carlsbad, CA 92008 Fax: (619)431-4888

Community newspaper. **Founded:** 1953. **Freq:** Weekly (Thurs.). **Trim Size:** 13 3/4 x 21 3/4. **Cols./Page:** 6. **Col. Width:** 12 picas. **Col. Depth:** 297 agate lines. **Key Personnel:** Steve Dreyer, Editor; Donna Madeiros, Publisher. **Subscription Rates:** $16.24 individuals. **Remarks:** Accepts advertising. **Formerly:** Rancho Santa Fe Times (1992).
Ad Rates: BW: $300 **Circ:** ‡1,000
PCI: $6

2920 Rancho Santa Margarita News
South Orange County News
PO Box 3629 Phone: (714)768-3631
Mission Viejo, CA 92690 Fax: (714)454-7354

Community newspaper. **Freq:** Semiweekly (Wed. and Fri.). **Print Method:** Offset. **Cols./Page:** 5. **Col. Width:** 12 1/16 inches. **Col. Depth:** 13 inches. **Key Personnel:** Sherrie Good, Editor; Mike Weaver, Publisher; Pat Norton, Advertising Mgr. **Subscription Rates:** Free. **Remarks:** Accepts advertising.
Ad Rates: PCI: $32.17 **Circ:** Free ‡6,177

2921 Silver
PO Box 9690 Phone: (619)756-1054
Rancho Santa Fe, CA 92067 Fax: (619)756-9928
Free: (800)756-1054
Publication E-mail: silver@silvermag.com
Publisher E-mail: silver@silvermag.com

Magazine for collectors of silver with feature articles by noted authorities in the field of silver and silverplate. **Founded:** Jan. 1968. **Freq:** Bimonthly. **Print Method:** Offset. **Trim Size:** 8 1/2 x 11. **Cols./Page:** 2. **Col. Width:** 2 inches. **Col. Depth:** 10 inches. **Key Personnel:** Connie McNally, Editor and Publisher; Bill McNally, Sales Director. **ISSN:** 1074-2107. **Subscription Rates:** $35 individuals; $45 Canada; $50 other countries; $6.50 single issue. **Remarks:** Accepts advertising.
Ad Rates: PCI: $75 **Circ:** ‡5,000

RED BLUFF†, pop. 9,490.

N. CA. Tehama Co. On Sacramento River, 115 mi. N. of Sacramento. Residential. Lumber mills, box factories, pulp plant. Diversified farming. Livestock, fruit, grain.

2922 Daily News
Donrey Media Group
545 Diamond Ave. Phone: (916)527-2151
PO Box 220 Fax: (916)527-3719
Red Bluff, CA 96080
General newspaper. **Founded:** Nov. 1885. **Freq:** Mon.-Sat. (eve.). **Print Method:** Offset. **Cols./Page:** 6. **Col. Width:** 24 nonpareils. **Col. Depth:** 301 agate lines. **Key Personnel:** Bill Goodyear, Editor; Donald W. Reynolds, Founder; Mel Wagner, Publisher; Jean Hanson, Advertising Mgr.; Ken Bohl, Circulation Mgr. **USPS:** 458-200. **Subscription Rates:** $66 individuals. **Remarks:** Accepts advertising.
Ad Rates: BW: $1,193.25 **Circ:** Mon.-Sat. 7,256
4C: $1,378.25
SAU: $9.25

2923 KBLF-AM - 1490
20639 W. Walnut St. Phone: (916)527-1490
Box 1490 Fax: (916)527-3525
Red Bluff, CA 96080-1490

Format: News; Adult Contemporary. **Networks:** ABC. **Owner:** KBLF Inc., at above address. **Founded:** 1946. **Operating Hours:** Continuous. **Key Personnel:** Ernie Hopseker, Manager. **Wattage:** 1000. **Ad Rates:** $4-10 for 30 seconds; $6-12 for 60 seconds.

REDDING†, pop. 41,995.

N. CA. Shasta Co. On Sacramento River, 70 mi. N. of Chico. Mountain resort. Pine timber. Saw, planing mills, box and veneer, machine shops, bottling works, creameries. Diversified farming.

2924 After Five Magazine
PO Box 492905 Phone: (530)335-5360
Redding, CA 96049-2905 Fax: (530)335-5335
Free: (800)637-3540

Lifestyle magazine covering northern California, and southern Oregon. **Subtitle:** The North State Magazine. **Founded:** Oct. 28, 1986. **Freq:** Monthly. **Print Method:** Offset. **Trim Size:** 11 1/4 x 14. **Cols./Page:** 4. **Col. Width:** 2 1/4 inches. **Col. Depth:** 13 inches. **Key Personnel:** Craig Harrington, Publisher. **Subscription Rates:** Free; $20 by mail. **Remarks:** Accepts advertising.
Ad Rates: BW: $720 **Circ:** Non-paid ‡30,122
4C: $980

2925 The Lance
Shasta Community College
11555 N. Old Oregon Trail Phone: (530)225-4744
PO Box 496006 Fax: (530)225-3925
Redding, CA 96049-6006
Publication E-mail: thelance@shastacollege.edu

Collegiate newspaper (tabloid). **Founded:** 1950. **Freq:** Weekly (Thurs.). **Print Method:** Offset. **Cols./Page:** 5. **Col. Width:** 22 nonpareils. **Col. Depth:** 196 agate lines. **Key Personnel:** Judy Crump, Advisor, phone (530)225-4929, jcrump@shastacollege.edu. **Subscription Rates:** Free. **Remarks:** Accepts advertising.
Ad Rates: PCI: $5 **Circ:** Non-paid ‡5,000

2926 Record Searchlight
John P. Scripps Newspapers
1101 Twin View Blvd. Phone: (530)243-2424
Redding, CA 96003 Fax: (530)225-8212
Publication E-mail: recsrch@snowcrest.net

General newspaper. **Founded:** 1852. **Freq:** Daily and Sunday. **Print Method:** Offset. **Cols./Page:** 6. **Col. Width:** 11.5 inches. **Col. Depth:** 21 1/4 inches. **Key Personnel:** Michelle Martin-Streeby, Marketing, phone (530)225-8229, fax (530)225-8212. **USPS:** 458-520. **Subscription Rates:** $15.75 individuals per month. **Remarks:** Accepts advertising. Monday-Saturday: BW: $4,039.20; 4C: $4,244.20; PCI: $31.68; Sunday: BW: $4,553.03; 4C: $4,889.03; PCI: $35.71.
Circ: Mon.-Sat. 35,279
Sun. 38,164

2927 KMCA-AM - 1450
4351 Shannon Pl. Phone: (530)246-1450
Redding, CA 96001
E-mail: kmac1@jett.net

Format: Talk; Sports. **Owner:** M. C. Allen Productions, at above address. **Founded:** 1996. **Operating Hours:** Continuous. **ADI:** Chico-Redding, CA. **Wattage:** 1000. **Ad Rates:** $12.50 per unit. **URL:** http://www.jett.net/˜kmca1.

2928 KNCQ-FM - 97.3
1588 Charles Dr. Phone: (916)244-9700
Redding, CA 96003 Fax: (916)244-9707

Format: Contemporary Country. **Networks:** Independent. **Owner:** McCarthy Wireless Inc., at above address. **Founded:** 1985. **Operating Hours:** Continuous; 100% local. **ADI:** Chico-Redding, CA. **Key Personnel:** Craig McCarthy, President; Beth Healy, General Sales Mgr.; Craig McCarthy, Operations Mgr.; Dave D'Angelo, Production Dir.; Helen Chambers, Contact; Sue Kerr, Office Mgr.; Guy Smith, Chief Engineer. **Wattage:** 100,000. **Ad Rates:** $30-48 for 30 seconds; $40-64 for 60 seconds.

2929 KNNN-FM - 99.3
4352 Caterpillar Rd., Ste. C Phone: (916)243-2222
Redding, CA 96003 Fax: (916)243-2321

Format: Adult Contemporary. **Owner:** Redwood Broadcasting, at above address. **Founded:** 1989. **Formerly:** KCIB-FM. **Operating Hours:** Continuous; 100% local. **ADI:** Chico-Redding, CA. **Key Personnel:** Mel Dolegal, General Mgr.; Scott Fitzgerald, Operations Mgr.; Casey Freeland, Program Dir.; Vince Shadrick, Sales Mgr. **Local Programs:** *Lights Out Redding.* **Wattage:** 5280. **Ad Rates:** $25-95 for 30 seconds; $30-100 for 60 seconds.

2930 KNRO-AM - 600
3360 Alta Mesa Phone: (916)243-2222
Redding, CA 96002 Fax: (916)243-2321

Format: News; Talk; Sports. **Networks:** CNN Radio; NBC. **Founded:** 1936. **Formerly:** KHTE-AM. **Operating Hours:** Continuous. **ADI:** Chico-Redding, CA. **Key Personnel:** Vince Shadrick, Sales Mgr.; Mel Dolezal, General Mgr.; Jim Bremer, Engineer; Scott Fitzgerald, Operations Mgr.; Gary Moore, Program Dir. **Local Programs:** *Newsmakers*, Paul Vietti, (916)-245-0600; *Rap Line*, Jim Bremer, (916)-245-0600; *Talk Back*, Carl Anthony Peel, (916)-245-0600. **Wattage:** 1000.

2931 KQMS-AM - 1400
3360 Alta Mesa Dr. Phone: (916)221-1400
Redding, CA 96002 Fax: (916)221-6653
Free: (800)521-1989

Format: Talk; News. **Networks:** ABC; Mutual Broadcasting System; CBS. **Owner:** Park Lane Group, at above address, CA. **Founded:** 1954. **Operating Hours:** Continuous; 50% network, 50% local. **ADI:** Chico-Redding, CA. **Key Personnel:** Mel Dolegal, General Mgr.; Dean Adraktas, News Dir.; Scott Fitzgerald, Operations Mgr.; Vince Shadrick, Sales Mgr.; Gary Moore, Program Dir. **Wattage:** 1000. **Ad Rates:** Advertising accepted; rates available upon request.

2932 KRCR-TV - 7
755 Auditorium Dr. Phone: (530)243-7777
Redding, CA 96001 Fax: (530)243-0217
Free: (800)222-5727
E-mail: krcrtv@awwwssome.com

Format: Commercial TV. **Networks:** ABC. **Founded:** 1956. **Formerly:** KVIP-TV (1963). **Operating Hours:** 4 a.m.-2 a.m. **ADI:** Chico-Redding, CA. **Key Personnel:** Bob Wise, General Mgr.; Dennis Siewert, General Sales Mgr.; Juanita Ramos, Promotions Dir.; Chuck Williamson, Production Dir.; Cecilia Ilharreguy, Traffic Mgr. **Local Programs:** *News Channel 7: Final Edition*; *News Channel 7: First Edition*; *News Channel 7: Saturday*; *News Channel 7: Sunday*; *News Channel 7: Tonight.* **Wattage:** 115,000 ERP.

2933 KRRX-FM - 106.1
3360 Alta Mesa Phone: (916)243-2222
Redding, CA 96002 Fax: (916)243-2321

Format: Adult Contemporary. **Networks:** USA Radio. **Founded:** 1985. **Formerly:** KARZ-FM (1998). **Operating Hours:** Continuous. **ADI:** Chico-Redding, CA. **Key Personnel:** Mel Dolezal, General Mgr.; Scott Fitzgerald, Operations Mgr.; Vince Shadrick, Sales Mgr.; Casey Freeland, Program Dir. **Wattage:** 100,000.

2934 KSHA-FM - 104.3
3360 Ala Mesa Dr. Phone: (916)221-1400
Redding, CA 96002 Fax: (916)221-6653
Free: (800)521-1989

Format: Soft Rock. **Networks:** ABC; CBS. **Owner:** Park Lane Group, 750 Menlo Ave, Ste. 340, Menlo Park, CA 94025, (916)324-8464, Fax: (916)324-3817. **Founded:** 1981. **Operating Hours:** Continuous; 5% network, 95% local. **ADI:** Chico-Redding, CA. **Key Personnel:** Beth Tappan, Station Mgr.; Jerry McGee, Program Dir.; Dean Adraktas, News Dir. **Wattage:** 100,000 ERP.

2935 KVIP-AM - 540
1139 Hartnell Ave. Phone: (530)222-4455
PO Box 492727 Fax: (530)222-4484
Redding, CA 96049-2727
Free: (800)877-5847

Format: Religious. **Networks:** Moody Broadcasting; USA Radio. **Owner:** Pacific Cascade Communications Corp., at above address. **Founded:** 1970. **Operating Hours:** Continuous; 35% network, 65% local. **ADI:** Chico-Redding, CA. **Key Personnel:** Steve Hafen, General Mgr.; Carolyn McBride, Business Mgr.; David Morrow, Esq., Contact; Ted Hering, Program Dir.; Paul Brown, Chief Engineer. **Local Programs:** *Primer Time*, Dr. Ernie Johnson, Mailing contact, (916)222-4455, Fax (916)222-4484; *Saturday Magazine*, Steve Hafan, Mailing contact, (916)222-4455, Fax (916)222-4484. **Wattage:** 2500. **Ad Rates:** Noncommercial.

2936 KVIP-FM - 98.1
1139 Hartnell Ave. Phone: (530)222-4455
PO Box 492727 Fax: (530)222-4484
Redding, CA 96049-2727
Free: (800)877-5847

Format: Religious. **Networks:** Moody Broadcasting; Sun Radio. **Owner:** Pacific Cascade Communications Corp., at above address. **Founded:** 1975. **Operating Hours:** Continuous; 35% network, 65% local. **ADI:** Chico-Redding, CA. **Key Personnel:** Steve Hafen, General Mgr.; Carolyn McBride, Business Mgr.; David Morrow, Esq., Contact; Ted Hering, Program Dir.; Paul Brown, Chief Engineer. **Local Programs:** *Morning Show*, Lou Hecker, Mailing contact, (916)222-4455, Fax (916)222-4484; *Prayer Time*, Dr. Ernie Johnson, Mailing contact, (916)222-4455, Fax (916)222-4484; *Saturday Magazine*, Steve Hafen, Mailing contact, (916)222-4455, Fax (916)222-4484. **Wattage:** 30,000 ERP. **Ad Rates:** Noncommercial.

REDLANDS, pop. 43,484.

SE CA. San Bernardino Co. 9 mi. SE of San Bernardino. University of Redlands. Extensive orange packing and shipping. Storage batteries, display letters, food, dairy products, plastics electric cars, boxes, recapping equipment manufactured. Nurseries; hatcheries. Fruit farms. Citrus, deciduous fruits, truck crops.

2937 ARC News
Environmental Systems Research Institute
380 New York St. Phone: (909)793-2853
Redlands, CA 92373-8100 Fax: (909)793-5953

Magazine covering geography, maps and mapping, and computers. **Founded:** 1978. **Freq:** Quarterly. **Print Method:** Web offset. **Trim Size:** 11 1/2 x 17. **Cols./Page:** 5. **ISSN:** 1064-6108. **Subscription Rates:** Free. **Remarks:** Accepts advertising.
Ad Rates: BW: $2,650 **Circ:** Non-paid 80,000

2938 Bulldog Weekly
University of Redlands
1200 E. Colton Ave. Phone: (909)335-5137
Redlands, CA 92373 Fax: (909)335-4091

Collegiate newspaper. **Founded:** 1909. **Freq:** Weekly (Thurs.). **Print Method:** Offset. **Trim Size:** 11 x 13 1/2. **Cols./Page:** 4. **Col. Width:** 24 nonpareils. **Col. Depth:** 189 agate lines. **Key Personnel:** Richard Carney, Business Mgr., phone (909)335-5139. **Subscription Rates:** $15 individuals. **Remarks:** Accepts advertising. **URL:** http://www.vor.edu/bulldog/welcome.html. **Alt. Formats:** Mailing labels. **Formerly:** Echo.
Ad Rates: BW: $300 **Circ:** Free ‡2,000
4C: $500
PCI: $5.50

2939 Clinical Gerontologist
The Haworth Press, Inc.
1103 Church St. Phone: (919)793-8288
Redlands, CA 92374
Publisher E-mail: getinfo@haworthpressinc.com

Contains practical information and research on assessment and intervention of mental health needs of aged patients. **Subtitle:** The Journal of Aging and Mental Health. **Founded:** 1982. **Freq:** Quarterly. **Trim Size:** 6x8 1/2. **Key Personnel:** T.L. Brink, Editor, tlbrink@juno.com; Bill Cohen, Publisher. **ISSN:** 1058-8167. **Subscription Rates:** $40 individuals; $90 industry; $150 libraries; $6 single issue. **Remarks:** Advertising accepted; rates available upon request.
Circ: Paid 540

2940 Facts
700 Brookside Ave. Phone: (909)793-3221
PO Box 2240 Fax: (909)793-9588
Redlands, CA 92373
General newspaper. **Founded:** 1890. **Freq:** Daily (eve.). **Print Method:** Offset. **Cols./Page:** 6. **Col. Width:** 24 nonpareils. **Col. Depth:** 301 agate lines. **Key Personnel:** Donald W. Reynolds, Publisher. **Remarks:** Accepts advertising.
Ad Rates: SAU: $46.90 **Circ:** Mon.-Fri. 7,597
Sun. 7,573

2941 Globetrotter
Redlands Daily Facts
PO Box 2240 Phone: (909)382-3012
Redlands, CA 92373-0740 Fax: (909)793-9588

A special interest newspaper published for personnel of Norton Air Force Base. **Founded:** 1950. **Freq:** Weekly (Fri.). **Print Method:** Offset. **Cols./Page:** 6. **Col. Width:** 18 nonpareils. **Col. Depth:** 301 agate lines. **Remarks:** Accepts advertising.
Ad Rates: 4C: $4.38 **Circ:** Free 10,000

2942 Redland's Daily Facts
Donrey Media Group
700 Brookside Ave. Phone: (909)793-3221
Redlands, CA 92373 Fax: (909)793-9588

General interest newspaper. **Founded:** 1891. **Freq:** Daily (eve.), Sunday (morn.). **Print Method:** Offset. **Cols./Page:** 6. **Col. Width:** 12.2 picas. **Col. Depth:** 21 1/2 inches. **Key Personnel:** Carl Baker, Editor; David Berkowitz, Advertising Dir.; Larry Feihenstrom, Circulation Mgr.; Augie J. Chavez, Production Dir. **USPS:** 183-620. **Subscription Rates:** $78 individuals. **Remarks:** Accepts advertising.
Ad Rates: GLR: $1.44 **Circ:** Mon.-Fri. ★**6,667**
BW: $1,575.09 Sun. ★**6,655**
PCI: $12.21

2943 Redlands Green Sheet
Associated Desert Shoppers, Inc.
73-400 Hwy. 111 Phone: (760)346-1729
Palm Desert, CA 92260 Fax: (760)346-7350
Free: (800)678-4237

Shopper (tabloid). **Subtitle:** Green Sheet. **Founded:** 1955. **Freq:** Weekly (Wed.). **Print Method:** Web. **Trim Size:** 11 x 12 1/2. **Cols./Page:** 6. **Col. Width:** 9 1/2 picas. **Col. Depth:** 11 3/4 inches. **Key Personnel:** Hal Purndis, Publisher; Chuck Holcomb, Editor. **Subscription Rates:** $163.80 out of area. **Remarks:** Accepts advertising.
Ad Rates: BW: $564 **Circ:** Free 20,400
PCI: $4.50

2944 San Bernardino County Museum Association Quarterly
San Bernardino County Museum Association
2024 Orange Tree Ln. Phone: (909)798-8570
Redlands, CA 92374
Journal on regional history and natural history. **Founded:** 1956. **Freq:** Quarterly. **Print Method:** Offset. **Trim Size:** 8 1/2 x 11. **Key Personnel:** Jennifer Reynolds, Editor, phone (909)387-2582, jreynold@empirenet.com; jreynold@co.san-bernardino.ca.us. **Subscription Rates:** $60 individuals. **Remarks:** Advertising not accepted. **URL:** http://www.co.san-bernardino.ca.us.
Circ: Paid 2,800
Non-paid 200

2945 KCAL-FM - 96.7
1940 Orangetrtee Ln., Ste. 101 Phone: (909)825-5020
PO Box 3390 Fax: (909)884-5844
Redlands, CA 92373-0997

Format: Album-Oriented Rock (AOR). **Networks:** Independent. **Owner:** Anaheim Broadcasting Corp., 606 Wilshire Blvd., No. 616, Santa Monica, CA 90401, (213)394-1445. **Founded:** 1959. **Operating Hours:** Continuous; 100% local. **Key Personnel:** Tim Sullivan, President; Jeff Parke, General Mgr.; Glenn Watson, Sales Mgr. **Wattage:** 4200. **Ad Rates:** $60-125 per unit.

2946 KRSO-AM - 590
PO Box 3390 Phone: (909)384-9750
Redlands, CA 92373 Fax: (909)884-5844

Format: Middle-of-the-Road (MOR). **Networks:** NBC. **Founded:** 1929. **Formerly:** KFXM-AM. **Operating Hours:** Continuous. **Key Personnel:** Jeff Salgo, Contact; Jan Jefferies, Program Dir.; Vicki Bails, Sales Mgr. **Wattage:** 1000.

2947 KUOR-FM - 89.1
1200 E. Colton Ave. Phone: (909)792-0721
Redlands, CA 92374 Fax: (909)793-2029

Format: Jazz; Adult Contemporary. **Networks:** Independent. **Owner:** University of Redlands, at above address. **Founded:** 1965. **Operating Hours:** Continuous. **Key Personnel:** William Bruns, General Mgr.; Scott Sterl, Business Mgr.; Mitch McClellan, Program/Music Dir. **Local Programs:** *Afternoon Style* 5 a.m. - 9 a.m. Monday-Friday, Brett Malak, Producer; *Sunday Morning* 9:30 a.m. Sunday, Brett Malak, Mailing contact, (909)792-0721, Fax (909)793-2029; *Weekday Smooth Jazz & Vocals* 6 a.m. - 10 a.m. Monday-Friday, Mitch

McClellan, Mailing contact. **Wattage:** 3000 ERP. **Ad Rates:** Noncommercial.

REDONDO BEACH, pop. 57,102.

S. CA. Los Angeles Co. On Pacific Ocean, 19 mi. SW of Los Angeles. Aircraft parts, electronics, missiles, steel, chemicals manufactured; aircraft assembly plant. Residential. Ships cut flowers.

2948 Easy Reader/Redondo Beach Hometown News
832 Hermosa Ave. Phone: (310)372-4611
PO Box 427 Fax: (310)318-6292
Hermosa Beach, CA 90254
Community newspaper. **Founded:** 1970. **Freq:** Weekly (Thurs.). **Print Method:** Offset. **Cols./Page:** 5. **Col. Width:** 24 nonpareils. **Col. Depth:** 175 agate lines. **Key Personnel:** Kevin Cody, Publisher. **Subscription Rates:** $20 individuals. **Remarks:** Accepts advertising. **Online:** LA Online.
Ad Rates: GLR: $1.35 BW: $1,250 4C: $1,850 **Circ:** Combined ❑**61,198**

2949 School Transportation News
William E. Paul, Inc.
700 Torrance Blvd., Ste. C Phone: (310)792-2226
Redondo Beach, CA 90277-3493 Fax: (310)792-2231
Publication E-mail: scholbus@ix.netcom.com
Publisher E-mail: bpaulstn@aol.com

Trade magazine covering pupil transportation. **Founded:** 1991. **Freq:** Monthly. **Print Method:** Web offset. **Key Personnel:** Bill Paul, Editor and Publisher; Peter Cannon, Assoc. Editor; Mark Robinson, Marketing Mgr.; Colette Paul, Vice President. **Remarks:** Accepts advertising. **URL:** http://www.stnonline.com.
Ad Rates: BW: $2,800 **Circ:** Paid ‡2,068 Non-paid ‡16,407

REDWAY

2950 KMUD-FM - 91.1
PO Box 135 Phone: (707)923-2513
1144 Redway Dr. Fax: (707)923-2501
Redway, CA 95560
Free: (800)568-3723
E-mail: kmud@kmud.org

Format: Full Service; Public Radio. **Networks:** Pacifica; Longhorn Radio. **Owner:** Redwood Community Radio, Inc., PO Box 135, Redway, CA 95560. **Founded:** 1986. **Operating Hours:** Continuous; 10% network, 90% local. **Key Personnel:** Simon Frech, General Mgr., simonf@kmud.org; Michael Jacinto, Program Dir., mj@kmud.org; Estelle Fennell, News Dir., news@kmud.org; Mark Sternfield, Underwriting Rep., sterno@kmud.kmud.org. **Wattage:** 200. **URL:** http://www.kmud.org.

2951 Starstream Cable TV
PO Box 767 Phone: (707)923-3106
Redway, CA 95560 Fax: (707)923-3336

Key Personnel: Jack Stock, Contact. **Cities Served:** Hickman Air Force Base, HI.

REDWOOD CITY†, pop. 54,965.

W. CA. San Mateo Co. 26 mi. SE of San Francisco. Financial center. Computer equipment. Ships food products, lumber and petroleum, recording equipment, electronics-components manufactured. Ships cut flowers. Agriculture.

2952 Oracle Magazine
Oracle Corp.
500 Oracle Parkway, Mailstop 5OP10 Phone: (650)506-7000 Fax: (650)633-2424
Redwood City, CA 94065
Oracle Magazine covers database, development, and technology issues of importance to IT professionals. **Founded:** 1987. **Freq:** Bimonthly. **Trim Size:** 8 x 10 7/8. **Key Personnel:** Stuart Gold, Advertising Mgr., phone (650)506-6652, stgold@us.oracle.com; Julie Gibbs, Editor, jgibbs@us.oracle.com. **ISSN:** 1065-3171. **Subscription Rates:** Free to qualified subscribers; $4.95 single copy. **Remarks:** Accepts advertising. **URL:** http://www.oramag.com.
Ad Rates: BW: $9,450 4C: $10,950 **Circ:** Free ‡150,000

2953 Outlook
The California Society of Certified Public Accountants
275 Shoreline Dr. Phone: (415)802-2600
Redwood City, CA 94065 Fax: (415)802-2300

The Professional Publication for California CPAs. **Founded:** 1959. **Freq:** Quarterly. **Print Method:** Offset. **Trim Size:** 8 3/8 x 10 7/8. **Cols./Page:** 3. **Col. Width:** 28 nonpareils. **Col. Depth:** 133 agate lines. **Key Personnel:** David MacFarlane, Editor; James R. Kurtz, Publisher; Bobbi Petrov, Advertising Mgr., phone (415)802-2430, bpetrov@calcpa.org. **ISSN:** 0273-835X. **Subscription Rates:** $30 nonmembers Included in membership dues. **Remarks:** Accepts advertising. **URL:** http://www.calcpa.org.
Ad Rates: BW: $2,200 4C: $3,550 **Circ:** ‡31,000 Controlled ‡500

2954 Redwood City Almanac
PO Box 5347 Phone: (415)364-9500
Redwood City, CA 94063 Fax: (415)364-9502
Publication E-mail: rcalmanac@aol.com

Local newspaper. **Founded:** 1979. **Freq:** Weekly (Wed.). **Print Method:** Offset. **Cols./Page:** 6. **Col. Width:** 19 nonpareils. **Col. Depth:** 224 agate lines. **Key Personnel:** Robert Distefano, Editor and Publisher. **Subscription Rates:** $6 individuals per year; $48 out of area per year. **Remarks:** Accepts advertising.
Ad Rates: GLR: $.40 BW: $500 **Circ:** Paid 4,000

REEDLEY, pop. 11,071.

C. CA. Fresno Co. 25 mi. SE of Fresno. Reedley College. Fruit packing, drying plants, olive oil, wine manufactured. Agriculture. peaches, grapes, plums, nectarines.

2955 Reedley Exponent
Reedley Exponent, Inc.
Box 432 Phone: (209)638-2244
Reedley, CA 93654-0432 Fax: (209)638-5021

Newspaper with a Republican orientation. **Founded:** 1891. **Freq:** Weekly (Thurs.). **Print Method:** Offset. **Cols./Page:** 6. **Col. Width:** 25 nonpareils. **Col. Depth:** 291 agate lines. **Key Personnel:** Budd Brockett, Editor; Paul Wahl, Publisher; Ken Lamarche, Advertising Dir. **Subscription Rates:** $16 individuals; $18 out of area. **Remarks:** Accepts advertising.
Ad Rates: BW: $938.70 4C: $1,238.70 SAU: $9.50 **Circ:** Paid ‡3,650 Free ‡16,400

RESEDA

2956 KOJJ-FM - 100.5
PO Box 370757 Phone: (209)782-1005
Reseda, CA 91337-0757 Fax: (209)782-8497

Format: Hispanic; Adult Contemporary. **Owner:** Tulare Lite Corp., at above address. **Founded:** 1989. **Formerly:** KPOR-FM (1992). **Operating Hours:** Continuous. **Key Personnel:** Jerrold Miller, President; Irene Beristain, Contact. **Wattage:** 3100. **Ad Rates:** $10-14 for 30 seconds; $13-17 for 60 seconds.

RIALTO, pop. 35,615.

SE CA. San Bernardino Co. 7 mi. W. of San Bernardino. Residential. Light industry.

2957 Rialto Record
Inland Empire Community Newspapers
PO Box 6247 Phone: (909)381-9898
San Bernardino, CA 92412-6247 Fax: (909)384-0406
Publisher E-mail: iecn@gte.net

Newspaper. **Founded:** 1911. **Freq:** Weekly (Wed.). **Print Method:** Offset. **Cols./Page:** 5. **Col. Width:** 2.375 inches. **Col. Depth:** 15 inches. **Key Personnel:** Syeda Jafri, Editor; Bill Harrison, Publisher. **Subscription Rates:** $50 out of state. **Remarks:** Accepts advertising. **Formerly:** The Record (1992).
Ad Rates: GLR: $1 BW: $1,512 4C: $2,162 PCI: $12 **Circ:** Free ‡16,000 Paid ‡1,000

RICHMOND

2958 Richmond Post
The Alameda Publishing Corp./Oakland Post
PO Box 1350 Phone: (510)763-1120
Oakland, CA 94604-1350 Fax: (510)763-9670

Black community newspaper. **Founded:** 1963. **Freq:** Semiweekly (Wed. and Sun.). **Print Method:** Offset. **Cols./Page:** 6. **Col. Width:** 2 1/16 inches. **Col. Depth:** 21 1/2 inches. **Key Personnel:** Gail Berkley, Exec. Editor; Thomas Berkley, Publisher. **Subscription Rates:** $42 individuals. **Remarks:** Accepts advertising. **Feature Editors:** Ms. Lupe R. Hernandez, *Art, Entertainment*, phone (510)287-8221.
Ad Rates: GLR: $48.10 BW: $6,204.90 4C: $6,604.90 **Circ:** Free ‡21,900

2959 Bay Cablevision
2900 Technology Ct. Phone: (510)262-1825
Richmond, CA 94806 Fax: (510)262-1838

Key Personnel: Dahlia Moodie, Operations Mgr. **Cities Served:** Berkeley, Richmond, Hercules, El Cerrito, and El Sobrante, CA.

RIDGECREST, pop. 15,929.

S. CA. Kern Co. 125 mi. E. of Bakersfield. Residential. Naval weapons center. Logging. Lumber mill.

2960 Decision Games
PO Box 880 Phone: (760)446-0726
Ridgecrest, CA 93556 Fax: (760)375-3138
Publisher E-mail: decisiongames.com

Consumer magazine covering military history including board game of featured battle. **Founded:** Jan. 1967. **Freq:** Bimonthly. **Trim Size:** 8 1/2 x 11. **Key Personnel:** Joseph Miranda, Editor. **ISSN:** 1040-886X. **Subscription Rates:** $90 individuals; $20 single issue. **Remarks:** Advertising accepted; rates available upon request.
Circ: Paid ⊕**5,200**

2961 News-Review
PO Box 640
Ridgecrest, CA 93556
Publication E-mail: newsruw@ridgecrest.caus

Newspaper serving the communities of Inyokern and Ridgecrest. **Founded:** 1976. **Freq:** Weekly. **Print Method:** Offset. **Trim Size:** 11 x 17. **Cols./Page:** 6. **Col. Width:** 12.5 picas. **Col. Depth:** 21.5 inches. **Key Personnel:** Patricia Farris, Publisher; Patti Cosner, Editor. **ISSN:** 0893-9004. **Subscription Rates:** $24 individuals.
Ad Rates: GLR: $.55 BW: $1,096.50 4C: $1,246.50 PCI: $8.50 **Circ:** Paid 2,006 Free 10,200

2962 KLOA-AM - 1240
731 N. Balsam St. Phone: (619)375-8888
Ridgecrest, CA 93555

Format: Talk; News. **Networks:** CBS. **Founded:** 1956. **Operating Hours:** Continuous; 80% network, 20% local. **Key Personnel:** G. Robert Pinney, News Dir. **Wattage:** 250. **Ad Rates:** $4.50-13 for 30 seconds; $5.50-14 for 60 seconds. $4.50-$13 for 30 seconds; $5.50-$14 for 60 seconds. Combined advertising rates available with KLOA-FM.

2963 KLOA-FM - 104.9
731 N. Balsam St. Phone: (619)375-8888
Ridgecrest, CA 93555

Format: Country. **Networks:** Satellite Music Network. **Founded:** 1982. **Formerly:** KFIO-FM (1988). **Operating Hours:** Continuous; 80% network, 20% local. **Key Personnel:** Richard Smith, General Mgr.; G. Robert Pinney, News Dir.; Toni Heflin, Sales Mgr. **Wattage:** 25,000. **Ad Rates:** $15-26 for 30 seconds; $20-31 for 60 seconds.

2964 KSSI-FM - 102.7
701 C. Inyokern Rd. Phone: (760)446-5774
Ridgecrest, CA 93555
E-mail: kssirock@ndti.net

Format: Album-Oriented Rock (AOR). **Owner:** Sound Enterprises, at above address. **Founded:** Feb. 26, 1996. **Operating Hours:** Continuous. **Key Personnel:** John J. Perrige, Owner/General Mgr. **Wattage:** 3000. **Ad Rates:** $12 for 30 seconds; $15 for 60 seconds.

RIO VISTA, pop. 3,142.

NWC CA. Solano Co. On Sacramento River, 40 mi. S. of Sacramento. Recreation. Waterways. Fruit packing. Natural gas fields, farm machinery manufactured. Agriculture.

2965 River News Herald & Isleton Journal
River News Herald Co.
PO Box 786 Phone: (707)374-6431
Rio Vista, CA 94571 Fax: (707)374-6322

Community newspaper. **Founded:** 1866. **Freq:** Weekly (Wed.). **Print Method:** Offset. **Cols./Page:** 6. **Col. Width:** 20 nonpareils. **Col. Depth:** 301 agate lines. **Key Personnel:** David Payne/Gibson Publications, Publisher, phone (707)643-1706; Irving Shear, Editor. **USPS:** 466-680. **Subscription Rates:** $20.50 individuals; $32 out of area; $32 out of state. **Remarks:** Accepts advertising.
Ad Rates: GLR: $4.25 BW: $6 4C: $250 SAU: $5.50 PCI: $990 **Circ:** ‡60,000

RIPON, pop. 3,509.

C. CA. San Joaquin Co. 10 mi. NW of Modesto. Residential. Wineries. Dairy, fruit, poultry farms. Almonds.

2966 The Ripon Record
130 W. Main St. Phone: (209)599-2194
Ripon, CA 95366 Fax: (209)599-2195

Community newspaper. **Founded:** 1912. **Freq:** Weekly (Wed.). **Print Method:** Offset. Uses mats. **Cols./Page:** 6. **Col. Width:** 25 nonpareils. **Col. Depth:** 294 agate lines. **Key Personnel:** Toni M. Raymus, Managing Editor; Paula J. Cummins, Editor; Antone E. Raymus, Publisher; Evelyn Locarnini, Advertising Mgr. **Subscription Rates:** $12 individuals. **Remarks:** Accepts advertising.
Ad Rates: GLR: $.33 **Circ:** Paid ‡2,600
BW: $356.58
SAU: $3.92

RIVERBANK, pop. 5,695.

C. CA. Stanislaus Co. 9 mi. NE of Modesto. Food processing milk, cheese, can manufacturing. Agriculture.

2967 The Riverbank News
Live Oak Publishing
PO Box 887 Phone: (209)869-2021
Riverbank, CA 95367
Newspaper. **Founded:** 1912. **Freq:** Weekly (Wed.). **Print Method:** Offset. **Cols./Page:** 8. **Col. Width:** 1 1/2 inches. **Col. Depth:** 21 inches. **Key Personnel:** Bill Camp, General Mgr.; Stanley L. Cook, Publisher. **Subscription Rates:** $25. **Remarks:** Accepts advertising.
Ad Rates: BW: $1,034.88 **Circ:** (Not Reported)
4C: $1,374.88
SAU: $9.49
PCI: $7.13

2968 Sonic Cable Television
2946 Stanislaus St. Phone: (209)869-4555
Riverbank, CA 95367 Fax: (209)869-1336

Owner: Sonic Cable TV of Northern California, 1031 W. Triangle Ct., West Sacramento, CA 95605, (916)372-2221. **Key Personnel:** Tom Shears, Contact. **Cities Served:** Riverbank, Escalon, Empire, Waterford, Ripon, Hickman, Hughson, Salida, Livingston and Lathrop, CA: 35 channels.

RIVERDALE

2969 Twin City Times-Riverdale Press
Central CA Weeklies, Inc.
2452 W. Tahoe Fax: (209)864-8923
PO Box 248
Caruthers, CA 93609
Community newspaper. **Founded:** 1976. **Freq:** Weekly (Wed.). **Print Method:** Offset. **Cols./Page:** 8. **Col. Width:** 22 nonpareils. **Col. Depth:** 294 agate lines. **Key Personnel:** Linda Renn, Editor & Pulitzer Publisher. **Subscription Rates:** $18 individuals. **Remarks:** Accepts advertising.
Ad Rates: 4C: $6.95 **Circ:** Paid 176
CNU: $6.95 Free 9,000

RIVERSIDE†, pop. 170,876.

SE CA. Riverside Co. 53 mi. E. of Los Angeles. University of California at Riverside. Riverside City College. Loma Linda University. California Baptist College. Extensive citrus fruit packing, large food distribution center. Manufactures aircraft components, cement, motors, aircraft precision instruments, plant covers, air conditioning equipment, concrete, asbestos pipe. Seed distribution center. Rock quarry. Tourist center.

2970 The Banner
California Baptist College
8432 Magnolia Ave. Phone: (714)689-5771
Riverside, CA 92504-3297 Fax: (714)351-1808

Collegiate newspaper. **Founded:** 1955. **Freq:** Biweekly. **Print Method:** Offset. **Trim Size:** 10 3/4 x 13. **Cols./Page:** 5. **Col. Width:** 10 3/4 picas. **Col. Depth:** 13 inches. **Key Personnel:** Thomas S. Pace, Editor. **Remarks:** Color advertising not accepted.
Ad Rates: BW: $200 **Circ:** Free ‡1,000
PCI: $5

2971 Black Voice News
3585 Main St., No. 201
Riverside, CA 92501
Publication E-mail: blackvoice@eee.org

Newspaper serving African-American communities in what is commonly called the "Inland Empire": Riverside, Moreno Valley, Perris, Banning, Palm Springs, San Bernardino, Ontario, Redlands, and Fontana. **Founded:** 1972. **Freq:** Weekly (Thurs.). **Print Method:** Offset. **Cols./Page:** 6. **Col. Width:** 24 nonpareils. **Col. Depth:** 294 agate lines. **Key Personnel:** Hardy Brown, Publisher. **Subscription Rates:** $35 individuals in California; $45 out of state. **Remarks:** Accepts advertising. **URL:** http://www.eee.org/bus/bvn/.
Ad Rates: BW: $1,638 **Circ:** ‡7,500
4C: $2,288
SAU: $19.50

2972 Breastcare
Smith Durant, Inc.
3870 La Sierra Ave., Ste. 392 Phone: (909)653-0329
Riverside, CA 92505
Publication E-mail: info@breastcaremagazine.com
Publisher E-mail: sdmedia@aol.com

Consumer magazine covering breast cancer awareness. **Subtitle:** The Journal of Awareness, Education & Hope. **Founded:** Jan. 1998. **Freq:** Bimonthly. **Print Method:** Web offset. **Trim Size:** 8 1/8 x 10 7/8. **Key Personnel:** Rod Durant, Publisher; Kemia Thomas, Publishing Operations Dir.; Kristene Smith, CEO. **ISSN:** 1089-3105. **Subscription Rates:** $12 individuals; $2.95 single issue. **Remarks:** Accepts advertising. **URL:** http://www.breastcaremagazine.com.
Ad Rates: BW: $5,390 **Circ:** (Not Reported)
4C: $7,700

2973 Bulletin of the Comediantes
University of California at Riverside
Riverside, CA 92521-0222 Phone: (909)787-5007
Fax: (909)787-2294
Publication E-mail: james.parr@ucr.edu
Publisher E-mail: james.parr@ucr.edu

Scholarly journal covering Spanish drama from 1492 through 1700. **Founded:** 1949. **Freq:** Semiannual. **ISSN:** 0007-5108. **Remarks:** Accepts advertising.
Circ: Paid 500

2974 California Builder & Engineer
California Builder & Engineer, Inc.
7133 Magnolia Ave. Phone: (909)328-1920
Riverside, CA 92504 Fax: (909)328-1928

Magazine on California, Hawaii, Western Nevada, and Western Arizona building and engineering. **Founded:** 1893. **Freq:** Semimonthly. **Print Method:** Offset. **Trim Size:** 8 1/8 x 10 7/8. **Cols./Page:** 3. **Col. Width:** 26 nonpareils. **Col. Depth:** 140 agate lines. **Key Personnel:** David W. Woods, Editor and Publisher; Alan D. Stafford, Associate Editor. **USPS:** 975-580. **Subscription Rates:** $30 individuals; $2 single issue.
Ad Rates: BW: $1,590 **Circ:** Controlled ‡11,281
4C: $2,085
PCI: $35

2975 Central European History
Humanities Press, Inc.
University of California, Riverside Phone: (909)787-6492
Department of History
Riverside, CA 92521
Publisher E-mail: hpmail@humanitiespress.com

Scholarly journal covering the history of German-speaking Central Europe. **Founded:** 1968. **Freq:** Quarterly. **Print Method:** Offset, casebound. **Trim Size:** 6 x 9. **Key Personnel:** Kenneth D. Barkin, Editor, phone (909)787-5401. **ISSN:** 0008-9389. **Subscription Rates:** $42 U.S. individuals; $52 nonmembers USA; $70 institutions USA; $80 institutions non USA. **Remarks:** Accepts advertising.
Ad Rates: BW: $150 **Circ:** (Not Reported)

2976 Cinefex
PO Box 20027 Phone: (909)781-1917
Riverside, CA 92516 Fax: (909)788-1793
Publication E-mail: circulation@cinefex.com

Journal covering motion picture special effects. **Subtitle:** The Journal of Cinematic Illusions. **Founded:** 1980. **Freq:** Quarterly. **Print Method:** Sheetfed offset. **Trim Size:** 9 x 8. **Cols./Page:** 2. **Key Personnel:** Jody Duncan, Editor, editor@cinefex.com; Don Shay, Publisher; Bill Lindsay, Advertising Dir., phone (805)383-0800, fax (805)383-0803, advertising@cinefex.com. **ISSN:** 0198-1056. **Subscription Rates:** $28 /year; $8.50 single issue. **Remarks:** Accepts advertising.
Ad Rates: BW: $1,900 **Circ:** Paid 32,000
4C: $2,750 Non-paid 1,000

2977 First Tuesday
Realty Publications Inc.
1485 Spruce, Ste. H Phone: (909)781-7300
PO Box 20068 Fax: (909)781-4721
Riverside, CA 92507
Magazine for real estate professionals. **Founded:** 1979. **Freq:** Monthly. **Print Method:** Offset. **Trim Size:** 8 1/2 x 10 7/8. **Cols./Page:** 3. **Col. Width:** 26 nonpareils. **Col. Depth:** 117 agate lines. **Key Personnel:** Fred Crane, Editor and Publisher; Pat Radcliffe, Advertising Mgr. **Subscription Rates:** $119 individuals. **Remarks:** Accepts advertising.
Ad Rates: BW: $570 **Circ:** Paid 5,087
Non-paid 90,000

2978 Great Dane Reporter
Tomar Publications
Box 150
Riverside, CA 92502-0150

Consumer magazine covering Great Dane breeding, raising and showing. **Founded:** Sept. 1976. **Freq:** Bimonthly. **Trim Size:** 8 3/8 x 10 7/8. **Key Personnel:** Sally Silva, Editor. **USPS:** 971-580. **Subscription Rates:** $48 individuals; $58 Canada; $68 elsewhere; $10 single issue. **Remarks:** Accepts advertising. **URL:** http://www.gdr.com.
Ad Rates: BW: $165 **Circ:** Combined 2,200
4C: $500

2979 Highlander
University of California, Riverside
Associated Students of the University of California Phone: (909)787-3617
Fax: (909)787-5638
245 Costo Hall
Riverside, CA 92521
Publication E-mail: vivmi@pc.net

Collegiate newspaper. **Founded:** 1954. **Freq:** Weekly (Tues.). **Print Method:** Offset. **Trim Size:** 10 x 15. **Cols./Page:** 5. **Col. Width:** 1 7/8 inches. **Col. Depth:** 84 agate lines. **Key Personnel:** Samita Syed, Editor; Chris Bleyenburg, Business Mgr.; Nicole M. Mukes, Managing Editor. **Subscription Rates:** Free; $45 by mail. **Remarks:** Accepts advertising.
Ad Rates: GLR: $6.70 **Circ:** Free ‡10,000
BW: $864.80
4C: $1,200
PCI: $15

2980 Inland Empire
3769 Tibbetts St., Ste. A Phone: (909)682-3026
Riverside, CA 92506-2606 Fax: (909)682-0246

Magazine on business and lifestyles in Southern California. **Founded:** 1976. **Freq:** Monthly. **Print Method:** Offset. **Trim Size:** 8 1/4 x 11. **Cols./Page:** 3. **Col. Width:** 27 nonpareils. **Col. Depth:** 140 agate lines. **Key Personnel:** Donald D. Lorenzi, Editor and Publisher; Cathy Fife, Managing Editor. **USPS:** 518-650. **Subscription Rates:** $13.95 individuals. **Remarks:** Accepts advertising.
Ad Rates: BW: $1,295 **Circ:** ‡70,000
4C: $1,795

2981 Issues in Education
Elseiver
School of Education
University of California
Riverside, CA 92521-5228
Publication E-mail: 102062.2525@compuserve.com
Publisher E-mail: fcentres@gpu.stv.ualberta.ca

Journal that features coverage of issues in the psychology of education field. **Subtitle:** Contributions from Educational Psychology. **Freq:** Semiannual. **Key Personnel:** Jerry S. Carlson, Editor. **ISSN:** 1080-9724. **Subscription Rates:** $60 individuals; $125 institutions.

2982 Latin American Perspectives
Sage Publications Inc.
Box 5703 Phone: (909)787-5037
Riverside, CA 92517-5703 Fax: (909)787-5685
Publication E-mail: laps@ucrac1.ucr.edu
Publisher E-mail: info@sagepub.com

Journal on capitalism and socialism in Latin America. **Subtitle:** Journal on Capitalism and Socialism in Latin America. **Founded:** 1974. **Freq:** Bimonthly. **Print Method:** Offset. **Trim Size:** 5 1/2 x 8 1/2. **Cols./Page:** 1. **Col. Width:** 50 nonpareils. **Col. Depth:** 100 agate lines. **Key Personnel:** Ronald H. Chilcote, Managing Editor; Sara Miller McCune, Publisher. **ISSN:** 0094-582X. **Subscription Rates:** $54 individuals; $236 institutions; $11 single issue; $41 single issue institutions. **Remarks:** Accepts advertising.
Ad Rates: BW: $250 **Circ:** Paid ‡1,550
Non-paid ‡83

2983 Modern Austrian Literature
International Arthur Schnitzler Research Association
Dept. of Literatures Phone: (909)787-4314
University of California Fax: (909)787-2160
Riverside, CA 92521
Literary journal. **Subtitle:** Journal of the International Arthur Schnitzler Research Association. **Founded:** Nov. 1961. **Freq:** Quarterly. **Print Method:** Letterpress. **Trim Size:** 5 1/4 x 8 1/2. **Cols./Page:** 1. **Col. Width:** 54 nonpareils. **Col. Depth:** 128 agate lines. **Key Personnel:** Donald G. Daviau, Editor, donald.daviau@ucr.edu. **ISSN:** 0026-7503. **Subscription Rates:** $35 individuals; $40 institutions; $7 single issue; $15 special issue. **Remarks:** Accepts advertising. **Alt. Formats:** Microfilm, UMI.
Ad Rates: BW: $100 **Circ:** ‡700

2984 Riverside Green Sheet
Associated Desert Shoppers, Inc.
73-400 Hwy. 111 Phone: (760)346-1729
Palm Desert, CA 92260 Fax: (760)346-7350
Free: (800)678-4237

Shopper (tabloid). **Founded:** 1955. **Freq:** Weekly (Wed.). **Print Method:** Web. **Trim Size:** 11 x 12 1/2. **Cols./Page:** 6. **Col. Width:** 9 1/2 picas. **Col. Depth:** 11 3/4 inches. **Key Personnel:** Hal Paradis, Publisher; Chuck Holcomb, Sales Mgr. **Subscription Rates:** $163.80 out of area.
Ad Rates: BW: $564 **Circ:** Free 13,400
PCI: $4.50

2985 Senior World Newsmagazine Orange County Edition
Kendell Communications, Inc.
26081 Merit Cir., Ste. 101 Phone: (714)898-2893
Laguna Hills, CA 92653-7017 Fax: (714)895-4322

Magazine for mature adults. **Founded:** 1984. **Freq:** Monthly. **Print Method:** Web offset. **Cols./Page:** 5. **Col. Width:** 11.6 picas. **Key Personnel:** Resa Trent, General Mgr.; Laura Impastato, Editor. **Subscription Rates:** $30. $3 single issue. **Remarks:** Accepts advertising.
Ad Rates: BW: $3,809 **Circ:** Paid 36
4C: $4,409 Free 112,044
PCI: $49

2986 Southern California Magazine
3769 Tibbetts St., Ste. A Phone: (909)682-3026
Riverside, CA 92506 Fax: (909)682-0246

Consumer and lifestyle magazine for Southern California. **Founded:** 1991. **Freq:** Semiannual. **Print Method:** Offset. **Trim Size:** 8 1/4 x 11. **Cols./Page:** 3. **Col. Width:** 27 nonpareils. **Col. Depth:** 140 agate lines. **Key Personnel:** Donald D. Lorenzi, Editor and Publisher; Cathy Fife, Managing Editor. **Subscription Rates:** $12.
Ad Rates: BW: $1,895 **Circ:** ‡20,000
4C: $2,595

2987 Women's Imaging
Smith Durant, Inc.
3870 La Sierra Ave., Ste. 392 Phone: (909)653-0329
Riverside, CA 92505
Publication E-mail: WMsImaging@aol.com
Publisher E-mail: sdmedia@aol.com

Women's medical journal for professionals in the medical community. **Subtitle:** The Journal of Women's Diagnostic Medical Imaging. **Founded:** Dec. 1997. **Freq:** Bimonthly. **Print Method:** Web offset. **Trim Size:** 8 1/8 x 10 7/8. **Key Personnel:** Rod Durant, Publisher; S. John Curtis, Editor; Kemia Thomas, Publishing Operations Dir. **ISSN:** 1082-1899. **Subscription Rates:** $42 individuals; $7 single issue. **Remarks:** Accepts advertising. **Formerly:** Mammography Today.
Ad Rates: BW: $3,000 **Circ:** (Not Reported)
4C: $3,845

2988 Charter Communications
6680 View Park Ct. Phone: (909)343-5114
Riverside, CA 92503 Fax: (909)353-1228

Owner: Charter Communications, 12444 Powerscourt Dr., Ste. 550, St. Louis, MO 63131, (314)965-0555. **Founded:** 1988. **Formerly:** Choice TV. **Key Personnel:** Robert Brown, Operations Mgr., phone (909)343-5145; David Murray, Plant Mgr., phone (909)343-5131; Randall Hicks, Marketing Mgr., phone (909)343-5140; Patrice Painter, Ad Sales Mgr., phone (909)343-5151; Rosanna McGeachy, Customer Service Mgr., phone (909)343-5123. **Cities Served:** Home Gardens, Jurupa Hills, Mira Loma, Norco, Riverside West County, Rubidoux, Sunnyslope, CA: subscribing households 48,000; 65 channels; 1 community access channel; 168 hours per week community access programming.

2989 KDIF-AM - 1440
1465-A Spruce St. Phone: (909)784-4210
Riverside, CA 92507 Fax: (909)784-4213

Format: Hispanic. **Owner:** Hispanic Radio Broadcasters, at above address. **Founded:** 1986. **Formerly:** KPRO-AM. **Operating Hours:** Continuous. **ADI:** Los Angeles (Corona & San Bernardino), CA. **Key Personnel:** Gilberto Esquivel, Vice Pres./Gen. Mgr.; Alfonso Camacho, News Dir.; Rudy Bravo, Local Sales Mgr.; Heriberto Ville, Program Dir. **Local Programs:** *Enfasis*, Yolanda Esquivel, (909)784-4210; *Hablando Claeo*, Yolanda Esquivel, (909)784-4210. **Wattage:** 1000.

2990 KGGI-FM - 99.1
2001 Iowa Ave., Ste. 200 Phone: (909)684-1991
Riverside, CA 92507 Fax: (909)274-4949
E-mail: kggifm@earthlink.net

Format: Contemporary Hit Radio (CHR). **Networks:** ABC. **Founded:** Aug. 1979. **Operating Hours:** Continuous; 100% local. **ADI:** Los Angeles (Corona & San Bernardino), CA. **Key Personnel:** Bob Ridzak, VP/General Mgr.; Scott Welsh, General Sales Mgr. **Wattage:** 3100. **Ad Rates:** $150-200 for 60 seconds.

2991 KOLA-FM - 99.9
5005 La Mart Dr., Ste. 100 Phone: (909)793-3554
Riverside, CA 92507

Format: Oldies. **Networks:** ABC. **Owner:** Fred R. Cote, at above address. **Founded:** 1959. **Operating Hours:** Continuous. **Key Personnel:** David Housman, Station Mgr. **Wattage:** 29,500 ERP. **Ad Rates:** $26-34 for 30 seconds; $33-43 for 60 seconds.

2992 KPRO-AM - 1570
7351 Lincoln Ave. Phone: (909)688-1570
Riverside, CA 92504 Fax: (909)698-7009
E-mail: kproval@aol.com

Format: Religious. **Networks:** Mutual Broadcasting System. **Founded:** 1957. **Formerly:** KMAY-AM (1987). **Operating Hours:** Continuous. **Key Personnel:** Ronnie Olenick, General Mgr.; Valorie Stitely, Station Mgr., kproval@aol.com. **Local Programs:** *About Town*, Dee Galiffa, (909)688-1570. **Wattage:** 5000. **Ad Rates:** $15 for 30 seconds; $18 for 60 seconds. **URL:** http://www.bristar.com/kpro.

2993 KSGN-FM - 89.7
11498 Pierce St. Phone: (909)687-5746
Riverside, CA 92505 Fax: (909)785-2288

Format: Religious. **Networks:** UPI. **Founded:** 1958. **Formerly:** KNFP-FM; KSDA-FM; KLLU-FM. **Operating Hours:** Continuous; 5% network, 95% local. **ADI:** Los Angeles (Corona & San Bernardino), CA. **Key Personnel:** Dawn Hibbard, Program Dir., dawnhibbard@aol.com; Bruce Potterton, General Mgr., bpot2@aol.com. **Wattage:** 3000. **Ad Rates:** Noncommercial.

2994 KVAR-AM - 1160
1465 Spruce S. Ste. A
Riverside, CA 92507-2446

Format: Hispanic. **Networks:** Independent. **Founded:** 1979. **Formerly:** KFHM-AM (1992). **Operating Hours:** Continuous; 100% local. **Key Personnel:** Gilberto Esquivel, General Mgr.; Fausto Avalos, Program Dir.; Juan Francisco Cuevas, News Dir.; Yolanda Esquivel, Contact. **Wattage:** 10,000. **Ad Rates:** Advertising accepted; rates available upon request.

ROCKLIN, pop. 7,344.

NE CA. Placer Co. 20 mi. NE of Sacramento. Sawmill, granite stone quarry. Agriculture. Citrus fruits, poultry, livestock.

2995 Placer Herald
Brehm Inc.
5903 Sunset Blvd., Ste. B Phone: (916)624-9713
Rocklin, CA 95677 Fax: (916)624-7469

Community newspaper. **Founded:** 1852. **Freq:** Weekly (Tues.). **Print Method:** Offset. **Trim Size:** 13 x 22. **Cols./Page:** 6. **Col. Width:** 2 1/16 inches. **Col. Depth:** 21 inches. **Key Personnel:** Dave Brumfield, Editor; Cathi Golden, General Mgr. **Subscription Rates:** $12.87 individuals; $21.45 out of state. **Remarks:** Accepts advertising.
Ad Rates: BW: $856.80 **Circ:** Paid 1,000
4C: $156.80 Free 6,500
PCI: $6.80

ROHNERT PARK

NW CA. Sonoma Co. 40 mi. N. of San Francisco.

2996 KRCB-TV - 22
5850 Labath Ave. Phone: (707)585-8522
Rohnert Park, CA 94928 Fax: (707)585-1363
Free: (800)287-2722

Format: Public TV. **Networks:** Public Broadcasting Service (PBS). **Owner:** Rural California Broadcasting Corp., at above address. **Founded:** 1982. **Operating Hours:** 6:30 a.m.-Midnight; 90% network, 10% local. **ADI:** San Francisco-Oakland-San Jose. **Key Personnel:** Nancy Dobbs, President/CEO; Karin Iwata, Program Mgr.; John E. Thompson, Production Mgr. **Ad Rates:** Noncommercial.

2997 KRPQ-FM - 104.9
6640 Redwood Dr., Ste. 202 Phone: (707)584-1058
Rohnert Park, CA 94928 Fax: (707)584-7944

Format: Contemporary Country. **Networks:** Independent. **Founded:** 1986. **Operating Hours:** Continuous; 100% local. **Key Personnel:** Ronald E. Castro, Contact; Neysa Hinton, Sales Mgr. **Wattage:** 3000. **Ad Rates:** $40-55 for 30 seconds; $45-60 for 60 seconds.

2998 KSUN-FM - 91
1801 E. Cotati Ave. Phone: (707)664-2621
Rohnert Park, CA 94928

Format: Alternative/New Music/Progressive. **Key Personnel:** Brigette Chelberg, Music Dir. **Ad Rates:** Noncommercial.

2999 MultiVision Cable TV
595 Martin Ave. Phone: (707)584-4617
Rohnert Park, CA 94928 Fax: (707)585-7547

Owner: MultiVision, 321 Railroad Ave., Greenwich, CT 06830. **Key Personnel:** Dennis Davis, Regional Sales and Marketing Mgr.; Fran Parkey, VPR/Gen. Mgr. **Cities Served:** subscribing households 42,000; 41 channels; 1 community access channel.

ROSAMOND

SW CA. Kern Co. 5 mi. N. of Lancaster.

3000 Acton/Agua Dulce News
Joyce Media, Inc.
PO Box 848 Phone: (805)256-0149
Rosamond, CA 93560 Fax: (805)269-2139
Publisher E-mail: joycemed@pacbell.net

Community newspaper. **Founded:** Nov. 1, 1982. **Freq:** Weekly. **Print Method:** Web offset. **Trim Size:** 11 x 17. **Key Personnel:** Gayle Joyce, Editor; Lynne Sickler, Advertising Mgr. **Subscription Rates:** $49 individuals. **Remarks:** Accepts advertising. **URL:** http://www.joycemediainc.com. **Former name:** Acton News.
Ad Rates: GLR: $14.77 **Circ:** Controlled 4,700

ROSEMEAD, pop. 42,604.

S. CA. Los Angeles Co. 8 mi. E. of Los Angeles. Residential.

3001 American Sports
American Sports Network, Inc.
PO Box 6100 Phone: (626)292-2222
Rosemead, CA 91770 Fax: (626)292-2221

Sports magazine. **Founded:** 1976. **Freq:** Monthly. **Print Method:** Offset. **Trim Size:** 8 x 10. **Cols./Page:** 3. **Col. Width:** 27 nonpareils. **Col. Depth:** 140 agate lines. **Key Personnel:** Sam Sandler, Editor; Louis Zwick, Publisher; Steve Lowenstein, Advertising Mgr. **Subscription Rates:** $54 individuals. **Remarks:** Accepts advertising.
Ad Rates: BW: $4,210 **Circ:** Paid ‡457,136
4C: $7,730 Non-paid ‡3,223

3002 Rosemead/South San Gabriel Progress
Wave Community Newspapers
819 W. Whitter Blvd. Phone: (213)727-1117
Montebello, CA 90640-3623 Fax: (213)727-9515

Newspaper. **Founded:** 1930. **Freq:** Semiweekly Thurs. and Sat. **Print Method:** Uses mats. Offset. **Cols./Page:** 6. **Col. Width:** 26 nonpareils. **Col. Depth:** 301 agate lines. **Key Personnel:** Arthur J. Aguilar, Exec. Editor/Publisher, phone (213)290-3000, fax (213)292-8289. **Subscription Rates:** Free local; $125 yr/mailed.
Circ: Free ‡14,447

ROSEVILLE, pop. 24,347.

NE CA. Placer Co. 18 mi. NE of Sacramento. High tech industries. Railroad marshaling yards. Tile manufacturing. Sand and gravel pits. Agriculture.

3003 Before & After
PageLab, Inc.
1830 Sierra Gardens Dr., Ste. 30 Phone: (916)784-3880
Fax: (916)784-3995
Roseville, CA 95661-2942
Free: (877)cool-stf
Publication E-mail: pagelab@quiknet.com

Trade magazine covering graphic design. **Subtitle:** How to Design Cool Stuff. **Founded:** 1990. **Freq:** Quarterly. **Print Method:** Offset lithograph. **Trim Size:** 8 1/2 x 11. **Key Personnel:** John McWade, Publisher. **ISSN:** 1049-0035. **Subscription Rates:** $36 individuals. **Remarks:** Advertising not accepted.
Circ: Paid ‡33,000

3004 Press-Tribune
Brehm Communications, Inc.
188 Cirby Way Phone: (916)786-6500
Roseville, CA 95678-6420 Fax: (916)783-1183

General newspaper. **Founded:** 1906. **Freq:** Daily (eve.). **Print Method:** Web offset. **Cols./Page:** 6. **Col. Width:** 12.2 picas. **Col. Depth:** 21 1/2 inches. **Key Personnel:** Richard Walker, Editor; Dave Reese, Publisher; Angela Wood, Advertising

Mgr. **Subscription Rates:** $66 individuals; $84 out of area. **Remarks:** Accepts advertising.
Ad Rates: BW: $5.70 **Circ:** Combined 11,081
SAU: $8.55
PCI: $4.80

ROSS

3005 Sports Car International
Ross Periodicals
PO Box 1529 Phone: (415)382-0580
Ross, CA 94957
Magazine featuring articles and graphics for car enthusiasts. **Founded:** Nov. 1985. **Freq:** Bimonthly. **Print Method:** Web offset. **Trim Size:** 9 x 10 7/8. **Cols./Page:** 3. **Col. Width:** 2.5 picas. **Col. Depth:** 9.5 picas. **Key Personnel:** D. Randy Riggs, Editor, phone (415)382-2865; Tom Toldrian, Publisher. **ISSN:** 1042-9662. **Subscription Rates:** $14.99 U.S.; $21 other countries; $28 two years U.S.; $40 two years other countries. **Remarks:** Accepts advertising.
Ad Rates: BW: $2,812 **Circ:** Paid ‡86,630
4C: $4,500 Non-paid ‡1,200

SACRAMENTO†, pop. 275,741.

NC CA. Sacramento Co. 88 mi. NE of San Francisco. The State Capital on Sacramento River. California State University at Sacramento. Dairy products, feeds, meat, poultry packing houses, brick and clay products, rocket engines and guided missiles, mining equipment, lumber boxes manufactured.

3006 Ag Alert
California Farm Bureau Federation
2300 River Plaza Dr. Phone: (916)561-5550
Sacramento, CA 95833 Fax: (916)561-5695
Publisher E-mail: cfbf@cfbf.com

Agricultural magazine (tabloid). **Founded:** Jan. 10, 1974. **Freq:** Weekly. **Print Method:** Offset. **Cols./Page:** 4. **Col. Width:** 2 1/4 inches. **Col. Depth:** 12 3/4 inches. **Key Personnel:** Steve Adler, Editor; James H. Taylor, Advertising Mgr. **Remarks:** Advertising not accepted for alcoholic beverages and tobacco products.
Ad Rates: BW: $5,302 **Circ:** 44,000
4C: $6,452
PCI: $110

3007 Almond Facts
Blue Diamond Growers
PO Box 1768 Phone: (916)446-8353
Sacramento, CA 95812 Fax: (916)325-2880

Magazine on almond growing and marketing. **Founded:** 1922. **Freq:** Bimonthly. **Print Method:** Offset. **Trim Size:** 8 1/2 x 11. **Cols./Page:** 3. **Col. Width:** 27 nonpareils. **Col. Depth:** 140 agate lines. **Key Personnel:** Susan Brauner, Editor; Gray Allen, Managing Editor; Diana Manges, Advertising Coord. **Subscription Rates:** $25 individuals; $40 out of country. **Remarks:** Accepts advertising. **URL:** http://bluediamondgrowers.com.
Ad Rates: BW: $1,363 **Circ:** Controlled 8,000
4C: $1,968

3008 American Journalism
California State University, Sacramento
6000 I St. Phone: (916)278-5323
Sacramento, CA 95819-6070 Fax: (916)278-7216
Publication E-mail: ajha@csus.edu

Journal covering media history. **Founded:** 1983. **Freq:** Quarterly. **Trim Size:** 5 1/2 x 8 1/2. **Key Personnel:** Shirley Biagi, Editor. **Subscription Rates:** $30 individuals; $8.50 single issue. **Remarks:** Accepts advertising.
Circ: Paid 800

3009 Animal Issues
Animal Protection Institute of America
2831 Fruitridge Rd. Phone: (916)731-5521
PO Box 22505 Fax: (916)731-4467
Sacramento, CA 95822
Free: (800)348-7387
Publisher E-mail: onlineapi@aol.com

Magazine concerning animal protection. **Founded:** 1969. **Freq:** Quarterly. **Print Method:** Web offset. **Trim Size:** 8 3/8 x 10 7/8. **Cols./Page:** 3 and 2. **Col. Width:** 13.3 and 20.6 picas. **Col. Depth:** 128 agate lines. **Key Personnel:** Barbara L. Tugaeff, Editor; Gil Lamont, Editor; Alan H. Berger, Editor, ahberger@earthlink.net. **Subscription Rates:** $25 members; $15 libraries. **Remarks:** Advertising not accepted. **URL:** http://www.api4animals.org. **Formerly:** Mainstream (June 30, 1998).
Circ: Paid ‡25,000
Non-paid ‡25,000

3010 Architecture California
AIACC
1303 J St., Ste. 200 Phone: (916)448-9082
Sacramento, CA 95814 Fax: (916)442-5346

Journal covering architecture, design, urban planning, construction and architectural culture in California. **Founded:** 1979. **Freq:** 2/year. **Print Method:** Offset. **Trim Size:** 6 x 9. **Cols./Page:** 3. **Col. Width:** 45 nonpareils. **Col. Depth:** 126 agate lines. **Key Personnel:** Mike Martin, Managing Editor. **ISSN:** 0738-1131. **Subscription Rates:** $24 members; $34 nonmembers; $15 students; $38 Canada; $42 other countries. **Remarks:** Advertising not accepted.
Circ: 10,000

3011 The Business Journal
1401 21st. St. Phone: (916)447-7661
Suite 200 Fax: (916)444-7779
Sacramento, CA 95814-5221
Publisher E-mail: tbj@ns.net

Regional business magazine (tabloid). **Founded:** Dec. 13, 1984. **Freq:** Weekly. **Print Method:** Offset. **Trim Size:** 11 x 14. **Cols./Page:** 4. **Col. Width:** 28 nonpareils. **Col. Depth:** 196 agate lines. **Key Personnel:** Lee Wessman, Editor, fax (916)447-2243, sbjedit@ns.net; Daniel Kennedy, Publisher, publisher@ns.net; Joanna Wessman, Advertising Dir., fax (916)446-3466; Renee Siden, Circulation/Marketing Dir. **ISSN:** 8756-5897. **Subscription Rates:** $65 individuals. **Online:** Dialog (The Dialog Corporation); LEXIS-NEXIS; Dow Jones News-Retrieval; CompuServe Information Service.
Ad Rates: BW: $4,200 **Circ:** Paid ‡13,000
4C: $4,850 Non-paid ‡2,500

3012 California Cattleman
California Cattlemen's Association
1221 H St. Phone: (916)444-0845
Sacramento, CA 95814 Fax: (916)444-2194
Publication E-mail: staff@calcattlemen.org

Magazine covering beef cattle. **Founded:** 1917. **Freq:** 11/year. **Print Method:** Offset. Uses mats. **Trim Size:** 8 1/2 x 11. **Cols./Page:** 3. **Col. Width:** 27 nonpareils. **Col. Depth:** 140 agate lines. **Key Personnel:** Kimberly Bradley, Editor, kbradley@cattlemen.net. **ISSN:** 0008-0942. **Subscription Rates:** $20 individuals. **Remarks:** Accepts advertising.
Ad Rates: BW: $625 **Circ:** Paid ‡3,585
4C: $1,000 Non-paid ‡910

3013 California Community Care News
PO Box 163270 Phone: (916)455-0723
Sacramento, CA 95816-9270
Publisher E-mail: sncnews@aol.com

Magazine covering the community residential care industry for the elderly, mentally ill and developmentally disabled. **Founded:** 1978. **Freq:** Monthly. **Trim Size:** 8 1/2 x 11. **Key Personnel:** Ms. Marty Hampton, Contact. **Subscription Rates:** $45 individuals.
Ad Rates: BW: $700 **Circ:** Paid 5,000
PCI: $20

3014 California Geology Magazine
California Department of Conservation
801 K St. Phone: (916)322-9579
M5 14-33 Fax: (916)327-1853
Sacramento, CA 95814-3532
Earth science magazine. **Founded:** 1948. **Freq:** Bimonthly. **Print Method:** Offset. **Trim Size:** 8 1/2 x 11. **Cols./Page:** 3. **Col. Width:** 13 picas. **Col. Depth:** 140 agate lines. **Key Personnel:** Christy Hunter, Editor. **ISSN:** 0026-4555. **Subscription Rates:** $12 individuals; $2 single issue. **Remarks:** Advertising not accepted.
Circ: 7,000

3015 California Grocer
California Grocers Association
906 G St., Ste. 700 Phone: (916)448-3545
Sacramento, CA 95814-1813 Fax: (916)448-2793

Magazine for the California grocery trade. **Founded:** 1986. **Freq:** 10/year. **Print Method:** Offset. **Trim Size:** 8 1/2 x 11. **Cols./Page:** 3. **Key Personnel:** Dave Heylen, Editor. **Subscription Rates:** $25. **Remarks:** Accepts advertising. **Formerly:** Bulletin (1988).
Ad Rates: BW: $1,500 **Circ:** 700
4C: $2,400

3016 The California Highway Patrolman
California Association of Highway Patrolmen
2030 V St. Phone: (916)452-6751
Sacramento, CA 95818-1730 Fax: (916)457-3398
Publication E-mail: dwolff@chpmagazine.com

Magazine containing news about the California Highway Patrol, historical California, travel, safety, humor and consumer pieces. **Founded:** Mar. 1937. **Freq:** Monthly. **Print Method:** Offset. **Trim Size:** 7 7/8 x 10 1/2. **Cols./Page:** 3. **Col. Width:** 13 picas. **Col. Depth:** 10 inches. **Key Personnel:** Doug Curley, Publisher. **ISSN:** 0008-1140. **Subscription Rates:** $18 individuals; $26 other countries; $2.50 single issue. **Remarks:** Accepts advertising.
Ad Rates: BW: $750 **Circ:** Paid ‡20,000
4C: $1,250 Controlled ‡11,000
PCI: $75

3017 California Journal
Information for Public Affairs, Inc.
2101 K. St. Phone: (916)444-2840
Sacramento, CA 95816 Fax: (916)446-5369

Magazine containing analysis of state government and politics. **Founded:** Jan. 1970. **Freq:** Monthly. **Print Method:** Offset. **Trim Size:** 8 1/2 x 11. **Cols./Page:** 2 and 3. **Col. Width:** 39 and 26 nonpareils. **Col. Depth:** 134 agate lines. **Key Personnel:** A.G. Block, Editor, agb@statenet.com; Mary Foy, Advertising Rep., maryf@statenet.com. **ISSN:** 0008-1205. **Subscription Rates:** $39.95 individuals; $3.95 single issue. **Remarks:** Accepts advertising. **Online:** State Net; LEXIS-NEXIS; Information for Public Affairs, Inc. (IPA).
Ad Rates: BW: $2,400 **Circ:** Paid 13,500
4C: $3,150 Non-paid 225

3018 California Journal of Health-System Pharmacy
California Society of Health-System Pharmacists
725 30th St., Ste. 208 Phone: (916)447-1033
Sacramento, CA 95816-3842 Fax: (916)447-2396
Publisher E-mail: hqcshp@aol.com

Medical journal serving health professionals practicing pharmaceutical care in health-system environments for member of the California Society of Health-System Pharmacists. **Founded:** 1989. **Freq:** Bimonthly (except November and December). **Key Personnel:** Teresa Ann Miller, Pharm., Editor; Priscilla N. Richter, Managing Editor. **ISSN:** 1972-7809. **Subscription Rates:** $75 individuals; $10 single issue. **Remarks:** Accepts advertising.
Ad Rates: BW: $625 **Circ:** (Not Reported)
4C: $1,375

3019 California Manufacturer
California Manufacturers Association
1040 45th St., Ste. 2200 Phone: (916)441-5420
Sacramento, CA 95819 Fax: (916)447-9401
Publication E-mail: jgorell@sna.com

Industrial/political quarterly. **Founded:** 1960. **Freq:** Quarterly. **Print Method:** Offset. **Trim Size:** 8 1/2 x 11. **Cols./Page:** 3. **Col. Width:** 28 nonpareils. **Col. Depth:** 133 agate lines. **Key Personnel:** Douglas Elmets, Editor; Vanessa Sapino, Advertising Dir. **ISSN:** 1042-2331. **Subscription Rates:** $20 Included in membership. **Remarks:** Accepts advertising. **Formerly:** Sacramento Report (Dec. 1987).
Ad Rates: BW: $2,250 **Circ:** ‡10,000
4C: $2,900

3020 California Pharmacist
California Pharmacists Association
1112 I St., Ste. 300 Phone: (916)444-7811
Sacramento, CA 95814 Fax: (916)444-7929
Free: (800)444-3851
Publication E-mail: pubs@cpha.com
Publisher E-mail: cpha@cpha.com

Pharmacy journal. **Founded:** 1954. **Freq:** Quarterly. **Print Method:** Offset. **Trim Size:** 8 1/2 x 11. **Cols./Page:** 2 and 3. **Col. Width:** 26 and 42 nonpareils. **Col. Depth:** 139 agate lines. **Key Personnel:** Carlo Michelotti, Exec. Editor; Jamie Kesweder, Mng. Editor. **ISSN:** 0739-0483. **Subscription Rates:** $25 individuals; $7.50 single issue; $35 out of country. **Remarks:** Accepts advertising.
Ad Rates: BW: $1,000 **Circ:** ‡5,500
4C: $1,790

3021 California Publisher
California Newspaper Publishers Association
1225 8th St. Phone: (916)449-3687
No. 260 Fax: (916)443-6447
Sacramento, CA 95814-4809
Newspaper (tabloid) reports on newspaper publishers and educators. **Founded:** 1920. **Freq:** Bimonthly. **Print Method:** Offset. **Trim Size:** 11 1/4 x 16. **Cols./Page:** 4. **Col. Width:** 14 picas. **Col. Depth:** 17 1/2 inches. **Key Personnel:** David Forester, Editor; David Sams, Advertising Mgr. **ISSN:** 0008-1434. **Subscription Rates:** $15 individuals. **Remarks:** Color advertising accepted; rates available upon request.
Ad Rates: BW: $700 **Circ:** ‡1,300

3022 California State Association of Counties California County
California State Association of Counties
1100 K St., Ste. 101 Phone: (916)327-7529
Sacramento, CA 95814 Fax: (916)492-8873

Journal covering California County programs, officials, and state and federal legislation. **Founded:** 1985. **Freq:** Bimonthly. **Trim Size:** 8 1/2 x 11. **Cols./Page:** 2. **Key Personnel:**

Allison Smith, Editor and Publisher, asmith@counties.org; Marlena DuRon, Advertising Rep. **Subscription Rates:** $25 individuals. **Remarks:** Accepts advertising.
Ad Rates: BW: $1,689 **Circ:** (Not Reported)
4C: $2,389

3023 The California Veteran
Veterans of Foreign Wars of the U.S.
7111 Governors Circle Phone: (916)424-1684
Sacramento, CA 95823 Fax: (916)424-9049

Newspaper (tabloid) for veterans and their families. **Founded:** 1954. **Freq:** Monthly. **Print Method:** Web offset. **Cols./Page:** 4. **Col. Width:** 2 inches. **Col. Depth:** 16 inches. **Key Personnel:** Oren D. Robinson, Editor. **Remarks:** Accepts advertising.
Ad Rates: BW: $2,416 **Circ:** 120,000

3024 California Veterinarian
California Veterinary Medical Association
5231 Madison Ave. Phone: (916)344-4985
Sacramento, CA 95841-3003 Fax: (916)344-6147
Publisher E-mail: cvma@aol.com

Magazine containing general association news and scientific material related to veterinary medicine and business management. **Founded:** Sept. 1947. **Freq:** Bimonthly. **Print Method:** Offset. **Trim Size:** 8 1/2 x 11. **Cols./Page:** 3. **Col. Width:** 27 nonpareils. **Col. Depth:** 133 agate lines. **Key Personnel:** Wendy E. Sharmon, Publications Coord.; Laurie Lynn, Dir. Communications. **ISSN:** 0008-1612. **Subscription Rates:** $35 individuals; $45 Canada and Mexico; $55 other countries. **Remarks:** Accepts advertising.
Ad Rates: BW: $800 **Circ:** Paid ‡4,300
4C: $1,320 Non-paid ‡3,000

3025 Catholic Herald
El Heraldo Catolico
5890 Newman Ct. Phone: (916)452-3691
Sacramento, CA 95819 Fax: (916)452-2945

Catholic newspaper (tabloid). **Founded:** 1908. **Freq:** Biweekly. **Print Method:** Offset. **Trim Size:** 11 x 16 1/2. **Cols./Page:** 6. **Col. Width:** 10 1/4 inches. **Col. Depth:** 15.5 inches. **Key Personnel:** Ricardo Olvera, Editor; Bishop William K. Weigard, Publisher; Tim D. Holden, Business and Marketing Dir., fax (916)733-0680, tdholden2@aol. **ISSN:** 0746-4185. **Subscription Rates:** $15 individuals; $18 other countries. **Remarks:** Accepts advertising.
Ad Rates: GLR: $1.28 **Circ:** Paid 23,500
BW: $624
4C: $824
SAU: $6
PCI: $18

3026 CDA Update
California Dental Association
1201 'K' St. Mall Phone: (916)443-0505
PO Box 13749 Fax: (916)443-2943
Sacramento, CA 95853
News publication for California Dental Association members. **Founded:** 1989. **Freq:** Monthly. **Print Method:** Offset. **Trim Size:** 11 1/2 x 15 1/2. **Cols./Page:** 4. **Col. Width:** 2 1/4 inches. **Col. Depth:** 14 inches. **Key Personnel:** Brian Blomster, Editor, brianb@cda.org; Ingrid Landis, Advertising Mgr. **ISSN:** 1048-3594. **Subscription Rates:** Free CDA members; $12 ADA members; $24 nonmembers. $4 single issue. **Remarks:** Accepts advertising. **URL:** http://www.cda.org/cda.
Ad Rates: BW: $2,055 **Circ:** Paid ‡17,447
4C: $2,825 Non-paid ‡104

3027 Comstock's Magazine
Comstock Carlson California, Inc.
3054 Fite Cir., Ste. 108 Phone: (916)364-1000
Sacramento, CA 95827-1809 Fax: (916)364-0280
Publisher E-mail: jtcomstock@aol.com

Magazine highlighting business and industry trends, community issues, business leaders and their companies, and regional issues. **Subtitle:** The Business of California's Capital Region. **Founded:** June 1989. **Freq:** Monthly. **Print Method:** Sheetfed offset. **Trim Size:** 8 1/8 x 10 7/8. **Cols./Page:** 3. **Col. Width:** 2 1/4 inches. **Col. Depth:** 10 inches. **Key Personnel:** J.T. Long, Managing Editor; Winnie Comstock Carlson, Publisher, fax (916)364-0350; John P. Carlson, VP and Chief Operating Officer. **Subscription Rates:** $30; $3.50 single issue. **Remarks:** Accepts advertising.
Ad Rates: BW: $2,350 **Circ:** Controlled 20,000
4C: $3,525

3028 The Current
American River College
4700 College Oak Dr. Phone: (916)484-8304
Sacramento, CA 95841 Fax: (916)484-8674

Community college newspaper. **Founded:** 1955. **Freq:** Weekly (Mon.). **Print Method:** Offset. **Cols./Page:** 5. **Col. Width:** 22 nonpareils. **Col. Depth:** 210 agate lines. **Key Personnel:** Bruce Patt, Faculty Advisor. **Formerly:** The Beaver.
Ad Rates: GLR: $1.00 **Circ:** (Not Reported)
PCI: $7.00

3029 The Daily Recorder
Daily Journal Corp.
1115 H St. Phone: (916)444-2355
PO Box 1048 Fax: (916)444-0636
Sacramento, CA 95812-1048
Free: (800)652-1700
Publication E-mail: daily_ recorder@dailyjournal.com

Newspaper (tabloid) on law, real estate, and state government. **Subtitle:** Legal/Governmental/R.E. **Founded:** June 27, 1911. **Freq:** Daily (morn.). **Print Method:** Offset. **Trim Size:** 10 x 14. **Cols./Page:** 4. **Col. Width:** 2 3/8 inches. **Col. Depth:** 13 1/2 inches. **Key Personnel:** Brian Taylor, Editor, brian_ taylor@dailyjournal.com; Geny DeVera-Gougherty, Publisher, geny_ gougherty@dailyjournal.com; Dan Gougherty, Sales Mgr., dan_ goughery@dailyjournal.com; Barbara Bennett, Legal Advertising, barbara_ bennett@dailyjournal.com. **ISSN:** 0197-8055. **Subscription Rates:** $246 individuals; $137 students must show proof of current law school registration. **Remarks:** Accepts advertising. **Alt. Formats:** Microfilm.
Ad Rates: BW: $840 **Circ:** ‡1,500
PCI: $15

3030 Education California (EDCAL)
Education California
1517 L St. Phone: (916)444-3216
Sacramento, CA 95814 Fax: (916)444-3245

Newspaper on state and national education issues with focus on school administrators. **Freq:** Weekly. **Print Method:** Web offset. **Trim Size:** 11 x 17. **Cols./Page:** 4. **Col. Width:** 14.6 picas. **Col. Depth:** 16 inches. **Key Personnel:** London Roberts, Editor, phone (916)324-8501, fax (916)444-1085, lroberts@acsa.org. **ISSN:** 0740-0357. **Subscription Rates:** $75. **Remarks:** Accepts advertising.
Ad Rates: BW: $16 **Circ:** Paid ‡15,853
SAU: $25 Controlled ‡1,322
PCI: $25

3031 El Heraldo Catolico
5890 Newman Ct. Phone: (916)452-3691
Sacramento, CA 95819 Fax: (916)452-2945
Publication E-mail: cathoherld@aol.com

Catholic newspaper (Spanish). **Founded:** 1979. **Freq:** Monthly. **Print Method:** Offset. **Trim Size:** 11 x 17. **Cols./Page:** 6. **Col. Width:** 18 nonpareils. **Col. Depth:** 182 agate lines. **Key Personnel:** Ricardo Olvera, Editor, phone (916)452-3691, fax (916)452-2945; Bishop William K. Weigand, Publisher; Susie Aronson, Advertising Mgr., phone (916)733-0684. **Subscription Rates:** $15 individuals; $30 out of country; $.50 single issue. **Remarks:** Accepts advertising.
Ad Rates: GLR: $.91 **Circ:** ‡20,000
PCI: $7.50

3032 El Hispano
Elitispano
928 2nd St. 300 Phone: (916)442-0267
PO Box 2856 Fax: (916)443-2818
Sacramento, CA 95812-2201
Community newspaper (English and Spanish). **Founded:** 1968. **Freq:** Weekly (Wed.). **Print Method:** Web offset. **Cols./Page:** 6. **Col. Width:** 2 inches. **Col. Depth:** 21 inches. **Key Personnel:** Pedro Chavez, Editor and Publisher. **Subscription Rates:** Free; $22 out of area. **Remarks:** Accepts advertising.
Ad Rates: SAU: $11.53 **Circ:** Paid ‡3,250
Free ‡17,000

3033 Fair Dealer
Western Fairs Association
1776 Tribute, No. 210 Phone: (916)927-3100
Sacramento, CA 95815-4410 Fax: (916)927-6397

Trade magazine covering the fair industry. **Freq:** Quarterly. **Print Method:** Web. **Trim Size:** 8 1/2 x 11. **Cols./Page:** 2. **Key Personnel:** Laura C. Trout, Contact, ltrout@fairsnet.org; Connie Lopez, Contact. **Subscription Rates:** $35 individuals; Free to qualified subscribers. **Remarks:** Accepts advertising.
Circ: Controlled 2,200

3034 Geothermal Hotline
Division of Oil, Gas, and Geothermal Resources
801 K St., MS 20-20 Phone: (916)445-9686
Sacramento, CA 95814-3530 Fax: (916)323-0424

Professional journal covering geothermal development in California and the US. **Founded:** 1973. **Freq:** Semiannual. **Trim Size:** 8 1/2 x 11. **Key Personnel:** Susan F. Hodgson, Editor, phone (916)323-2731. **ISSN:** 0735-0503. **Subscription Rates:** Free. **Remarks:** Advertising not accepted.
Circ: (Not Reported)

3035 Gold River News
6231 Center Mall Way Phone: (916)392-5843
Sacramento, CA 95823 Fax: (916)392-5843

Community newspaper. **Founded:** Jan. 1989. **Freq:** Bimonthly. **Print Method:** Web. **Trim Size:** 10 x 16. **Cols./Page:** 5. **Col. Width:** 1 7/8 inches. **Key Personnel:** James E. Jones, Contact. **Subscription Rates:** $16 individuals. **Remarks:** Accepts advertising.
Ad Rates: GLR: $8 **Circ:** Non-paid 4,000
PCI: $6

3036 International Travel News
Martin Publications, Inc.
2120 28th St. Phone: (916)457-3643
Sacramento, CA 95818
Overseas travel magazine. **Founded:** Mar. 1976. **Freq:** Monthly. **Print Method:** Offset. **Trim Size:** 8 1/2 x 11. **Cols./Page:** 3. **Col. Width:** 2 5/16 inches. **Col. Depth:** 10 inches. **Key Personnel:** Armond M. Noble, Publisher; David Tykol, Editor; Helen Noble, Advertising Dir. **USPS:** 115-550. **Subscription Rates:** $18 individuals; $3 single issue. **Remarks:** Advertising not accepted for travel and travel related products outside North America.
Ad Rates: BW: $1,184 **Circ:** 49,000

3037 Journal of the California Dental Association
California Dental Association
1201 'K' St. Mall Phone: (916)443-0505
PO Box 13749 Fax: (916)443-2943
Sacramento, CA 95853
Professional magazine for dentists. **Founded:** July 1973. **Freq:** Monthly. **Print Method:** Half web offset. **Trim Size:** 8 3/8 x 10 7/8. **Cols./Page:** 3. **Col. Width:** 13 1/2 picas. **Col. Depth:** 59 1/2 picas. **Key Personnel:** Jeanne Marie Tokunaga, Managing Editor, phone (916)443-3382, jeannet@cda.org; Ingrid Landis, Advertising Mgr., ingridl@cda.org. **ISSN:** 0746-424X. **Subscription Rates:** $24 ADA members; $60 nonmembers; $6 single issue (10.78 July issue).; $12 members CDA members. **Remarks:** Accepts advertising. **URL:** http://www.cda.org/cda; http://www.cda.org.
Ad Rates: BW: $1,815 **Circ:** Paid ‡18,000
4C: $2,640 Non-paid ‡1,200

3038 LINKS
Community Residential Care Association of California
1924 Alhambra Blvd. Phone: (916)455-0723
PO Box 163270
Sacramento, CA 95816-9270
Publisher E-mail: sncnews@aol.com

Trade publication regarding developmentally challenged. **Founded:** 1970. **Freq:** Monthly. **Print Method:** Letterpress and offset. **Trim Size:** 8 1/2 x 11. **Cols./Page:** 3. **Col. Width:** 22 nonpareils. **Col. Depth:** 140 agate lines. **Key Personnel:** Charles W. Skoien, Jr., Editor and Publisher; Marty Hampton, Asst. **Subscription Rates:** $45 individuals. **Remarks:** Color advertising not accepted.
Ad Rates: BW: $600 **Circ:** Paid 7,000
PCI: $20 Controlled 18,000

3039 Management of the California State Water Project
Department of Water Resources
Box 942836
Sacramento, CA 94236-0001

Trade report covering water delivery in California. **Founded:** 1963. **Freq:** Annual. **Trim Size:** 8 1/2 x 11. **Cols./Page:** 2. **Key Personnel:** Nancy Pate-Rahn. **Remarks:** Advertising not accepted.
Circ: (Not Reported)

3040 McGeorge Law Review
Western Newspaper Publishing Co.
3200 Fifth Ave.
Sacramento, CA 95817

Journal covering legal issues. **Freq:** Quarterly. **Subscription Rates:** $20 individuals. **Remarks:** Advertising not accepted. **Former name:** Pacific Law Journal.
Circ: (Not Reported)

3041 Military
MHR Publishing Corp.
2122 28th St. Phone: (916)457-8990
Sacramento, CA 95818 Free: (800)366-9192

Magazine for American combat veterans. **Subtitle:** The Press of Freedom. **Founded:** June 1984. **Freq:** Monthly. **Print Method:** Web offset. **Trim Size:** 8 1/4 x 10 3/4. **Cols./Page:** 3. **Col. Width:** 14 picas. **Col. Depth:** 10 inches. **Key Personnel:** Lt. Col. Mike Mark, Editor; Armond Noble, Publisher; Helen Noble, Advertising Dir. **ISSN:** 1046-2511. **Subscription Rates:** $15 individuals; $28 two years; $1.50 single issue. **Remarks:** Accepts advertising. **Formerly:** Military History Review.
Ad Rates: BW: $337 **Circ:** ‡17,000
PCI: $18

3042 Mom Guess What Newspaper (MGW)
Mom Guess What Newspaper
1725 L St. Phone: (916)441-6397
Sacramento, CA 95814-4023
Publisher E-mail: info@mgwnew.com

Gay newspaper (tabloid) with political emphasis. **Subtitle:** MGW Newspaper. **Founded:** Oct. 1978. **Freq:** Semimonthly. **Print Method:** Web press. **Trim Size:** 10 x 16. **Cols./Page:** 5. **Col. Width:** 11 picas. **Col. Depth:** 16 inches. **Key Personnel:** Linda Birner, Publisher. **ISSN:** 1093-5908. **Subscription Rates:** $35 individuals. **Remarks:** Accepts advertising. **Available Online. URL:** http://www.mgwnews.com. **Alt. Formats:** Microform.
Ad Rates: BW: $700 **Circ:** Paid ‡21,000
4C: $800 Free ‡700
SAU: $20
PCI: $20

3043 The Pan-Pacific Entomologist
Pacific Coast Entomological Society
c/o California Dept. of Food & Agriculture Phone: (916)654-1211
Fax: (916)654-0555
1220 N St.
Sacramento, CA 95814
Professional journal on entomology. **Founded:** 1924. **Freq:** Quarterly. **Print Method:** Letterpress. **Trim Size:** 7 x 10. **Cols./Page:** 1. **Col. Width:** 48 nonpareils. **Col. Depth:** 95 agate lines. **Key Personnel:** Dr. Robert V. Dowell, Editor, bdowell@cdfa.ca.gov; Vincent F. Lee, Managing Secretary, vlee@calacademy.org. **ISSN:** 0031-0603. **Subscription Rates:** $25 individuals; $40 institutions. **Remarks:** Advertising not accepted.
Circ: ‡850

3044 The Sacramento Bee
2100 Q St. Phone: (916)321-1000
PO Box 15779 Fax: (916)321-1524
Sacramento, CA 95852
Free: (800)876-8700

General newspaper. **Founded:** Feb. 3, 1857. **Print Method:** Mon.-Sun. (morn.). **Trim Size:** 13 1/2 x 22 5/16. **Cols./Page:** 6. **Col. Width:** 25 nonpareils. **Col. Depth:** 294 agate lines. **Key Personnel:** Gregory Favre, Exec. Editor, phone (916)321-1006, fax (916)321-1109, gfavre@sacbee.com; Rick Rodriquez, Managing Editor, phone (916)321-1002, rrodriquez@sacbee.com; Pam Dinsmore, Exec. News Editor, phone (916)321-1024, pdinsmore@sacbee.com; Amy Chance, Capitol Bureau Chief, phone (916)326-5535, achance@sacbee.com; Howard Shintaku, Art/Graphics Dir., phone (916)321-1027, hshintaku@sacbee.com. **Subscription Rates:** $123 individuals. **Remarks:** Accepts advertising. **Online:** Dialog (The Dialog Corporation); DataTimes Corporation; LEXIS-NEXIS; NewsBank, Inc.; CompuServe Information Service. **URL:** http://www.sacbee.com. **Alt. Formats:** CD-ROM. **Feature Editors:** Steve Blust, *Sports*, phone (916)321-1176, fax (916)326-5503, sblust@sacbee.com; Mark Morris, *Photo*, phone (916)321-1166, fax (916)326-5571, mmorris@sacbee.com; Bob Shallit, *Financial/Business*, phone (916)321-1049, fax (916)321-1009, bshallit@sacbee.com; Joyce Terhaar, *City*, phone (916)321-1004, jterhaar@sacbee.com.
Ad Rates: GLR: $6.94 **Circ:** Mon.-Sat. ★**283,589**
BW: $10,538 Sun. ★**344,881**
4C: $12,298
SAU: $97.12

3045 Sacramento Bulletin
Metropolitan News Co.
210 S. Spring St. Phone: (213)628-4384
Los Angeles, CA 90012 Fax: (213)687-3886

Community newspaper. **Founded:** 1991. **Freq:** Weekly. **Print Method:** Offset. **Cols./Page:** 4. **Col. Width:** 15 picas. **Col. Depth:** 15 1/2 inches. **Key Personnel:** Roger M. Grace, Editor. **Remarks:** Accepts advertising.
Ad Rates: PCI: $6 **Circ:** Non-paid 1,000

3046 Sacramento City College Express
Sacramento City College
3835 Freeport Blvd. Phone: (916)558-2561
Sacramento, CA 95822 Fax: (916)558-2282

Community college newspaper. **Founded:** 1922. **Freq:** Weekly (Thurs.). **Print Method:** Offset. **Cols./Page:** 5. **Col. Width:** 28 nonpareils. **Col. Depth:** 195 agate lines. **Key Personnel:** Jan Haag, Advisor. **Subscription Rates:** Free. **Remarks:** Accepts advertising. **Formerly:** Pony Express (1989).
Ad Rates: GLR: $.48 **Circ:** Free 5,000
PCI: $4

3047 The Sacramento Gazette
400 University Ave. Phone: (916)567-9654
Sacramento, CA 95825-6502 Fax: (916)567-9653
Publication E-mail: sacgazette@aol.com

General newspaper. **Subtitle:** Sacramento's Newest Weekly Newspaper. **Founded:** July 12, 1996. **Freq:** Weekly (Fri.). **Print Method:** Web offset. **Trim Size:** 10 13/16 x 13 15/16. **Cols./Page:** 4. **Col. Width:** 28 nonpareils. **Col. Depth:** 182 agate lines. **Key Personnel:** David A. Fong, Editor and Publisher. **ISSN:** 1089-9618. **Subscription Rates:** $49.75 individuals; $44.75 students and educators. **Remarks:** Accepts advertising. **URL:** http://members.aol.com/sacgazette/gazette.html.
Ad Rates: BW: $687.50 **Circ:** Paid 1,480
PCI: $13.75

3048 Sacramento Lawyer
Sacramento County Bar Association
901 H St., Ste. 101 Phone: (916)447-2787
Sacramento, CA 95814 Fax: (916)447-2788

Trade magazine for members covering law. **Founded:** Jan. 1, 1998. **Freq:** Monthly. **Trim Size:** 8 x 11. **Cols./Page:** 3. **Key Personnel:** Mark Shustead, Editor. **USPS:** 981-300. **Subscription Rates:** $6 members; $24 nonmembers. **Remarks:** Accepts advertising. **Former name:** Docket.
Ad Rates: BW: $715 **Circ:** Controlled 3500
4C: $850

3049 Sacramento Magazine
Sacramento Magazines Corp.
4471 D St. Phone: (916)452-6200
Sacramento, CA 95819 Fax: (916)452-6061
Publication E-mail: sacmag.com

Regional interest magazine. **Founded:** 1975. **Freq:** Monthly. **Print Method:** Offset. **Trim Size:** 8 1/8 x 10 7/8. **Cols./Page:** 3. **Col. Width:** 27 nonpareils. **Col. Depth:** 140 agate lines. **Key Personnel:** Krista Minard, Editor; Michael O'Brien, Publisher. **ISSN:** 0191-8796. **Subscription Rates:** $18 individuals; $2.95 single issue. **Remarks:** Accepts advertising. **URL:** http://www.sacmag.com.
Ad Rates: BW: $4,300 **Circ:** △**25,478**
4C: $4,700

3050 Sacramento Medicine
Media Marketing
5380 Elvas Ave. Phone: (916)452-2671
Sacramento, CA 95819 Fax: (916)452-2690

Professional medical journal. **Founded:** 1960. **Freq:** Monthly. **Print Method:** Offset. **Trim Size:** 8 x 11. **Cols./Page:** 3. **Col. Width:** 2 1/4 inches. **Key Personnel:** John Ostrich, M.D., Editor; Chris Albasio, Managing Editor. **USPS:** 753-570. **Subscription Rates:** $24 individuals. **Remarks:** Accepts advertising.
Ad Rates: GLR: $.50 **Circ:** Controlled 1,865
BW: $450
4C: $650
PCI: $25

3051 Sacramento Observer
Observer Newspapers
Box 817
San Leandro, CA 94577

Black community newspaper. **Founded:** 1962. **Freq:** Weekly (Thurs.). **Print Method:** Offset. **Trim Size:** 10 x 15. **Cols./Page:** 5 and 6. **Key Personnel:** Kathryn C. Lee, Managing Editor; Dr. William H. Lee, Publisher. **Subscription Rates:** $20. **Remarks:** Advertising accepted; rates available upon request.
Circ: ‡49,090

3052 Senior Citizens Today
Community Residential Care Association of California
1924 Alhambra Blvd. Phone: (916)455-0723
PO Box 163270
Sacramento, CA 95816-9270
Publisher E-mail: sncnews@aol.com

Magazine for senior citizens. **Founded:** 1970. **Freq:** Bimonthly. **Print Method:** Letterpress and offset. **Trim Size:** 8 1/2 x 11. **Cols./Page:** 3. **Col. Width:** 20 nonpareils. **Col. Depth:** 140 agate lines. **Key Personnel:** Charles W. Skoien, Jr., Editor and Publisher; Marty Hampton, Asst. **Subscription Rates:** $10 individuals. **Remarks:** Color advertising not accepted.
Ad Rates: BW: $600 **Circ:** Combined 25,000
PCI: $20

3053 Theatre Journal
Johns Hopkins University Press
Dept. of Theatre Arts Phone: (916)278-6617
California State Univ.
6000 J St.
Sacramento, CA 95819-6069
Publisher E-mail: jlinfo@jhupress.jhu.edu

Journal covering the theater arts, including social and historical studies, production reviews, and theoretical inquiries illuminating dramatic text and production. **Founded:** 1949. **Freq:** Quarterly. **Print Method:** Offset. **Trim Size:** 6 7/8 x 10. **Cols./Page:** 1. **Col. Width:** 60 nonpareils. **Col. Depth:** 107 agate lines. **Key Personnel:** John Rouse, Editor; Tara Dorai-Berry, Advertising Mgr. **ISSN:** 0192-2882. **Subscription Rates:** $28 individuals; $63 institutions; $8 single issue; $16 single issue, institutions. **Remarks:** Accepts advertising. **Available Online. URL:** http://www.press.jhu.edu/journals/theatre-journal/.
Ad Rates: BW: $385 **Circ:** ‡4,000

3054 Thrust for Educational Leadership
Association of California School Administrators
1517 L St. Phone: (916)444-3216
Sacramento, CA 95814 Fax: (916)444-3245

Practical journal for educators interested in new ways to be effective. **Founded:** 1971. **Freq:** 7/year (during the academic year). **Print Method:** Offset. **Trim Size:** 8 1/2 x 11. **Cols./Page:** 3. **Col. Width:** 2 1/4 inches. **Col. Depth:** 10 inches. **Key Personnel:** Susan Davis, Editor, sdavis@acsa.org. **ISSN:** 1055-2243. **Subscription Rates:** $50 individuals; $8 single issue. **Remarks:** Accepts advertising.
Ad Rates: BW: $1,353 **Circ:** Paid 16,205
4C: $2,153 Non-paid 294

3055 View Camera
Steve Simmons Photography
2774 Harkness St. Phone: (916)441-2557
Sacramento, CA 95818-3060 Fax: (916)441-7407

Consumer magazine of photography. **Freq:** Bimonthly.
Circ: Paid ‡11,819
Controlled ‡225

3056 Western City
League of California Cities
1400 K St. Phone: (916)658-8234
Sacramento, CA 95816 Fax: (916)658-8289
Free: (800)262-1801
Publisher E-mail: wctyinfo@cacities.org

Municipal interest magazine. **Founded:** 1925. **Freq:** Monthly. **Print Method:** Offset. **Trim Size:** 8 1/2 x 11. **Cols./Page:** 3. **Col. Width:** 13.5 picas. **Col. Depth:** 60 picas. **Key Personnel:** Jude Hudson, Editor; Pam Maxwell-Blodgett, Advertising Mgr.; Nancy Van Steinburg, Subscriptions. **Subscription Rates:** $39 individuals; $63 two years. **Remarks:** Accepts advertising. **URL:** http://www.westerncity.com.
Ad Rates: GLR: $18 **Circ:** Paid ‡9,100
BW: $1,830 Controlled ‡300
4C: $3,030

3057 Worldradio
Worldradio, Inc.
2120 28th St. Phone: (916)457-3655
Sacramento, CA 95818 Free: (800)366-9192
Publication E-mail: n6wr@ns.net

Magazine for Amateur Radio operators, including technical articles, international friendship news, and public service information. **Founded:** June 1971. **Freq:** Monthly. **Print Method:** Offset. **Trim Size:** 8 1/4 x 10 3/4. **Cols./Page:** 3. **Col. Width:** 14 picas. **Col. Depth:** 10 inches. **Key Personnel:** Rick McCusker, Editor; Armond M. Noble, Publisher; Helen L. Noble, Advertising Dir. **USPS:** 947-000. **Subscription Rates:** $15; $25 other countries; $2 single issue. **Remarks:** Advertising not accepted for products unrelated to amateur radio. **Alt. Formats:** Audio tape.
Ad Rates: BW: $659 **Circ:** ‡31,500
PCI: $27

3058 KCRA-TV - 3
3 Television Circle Phone: (916)446-3333
Sacramento, CA 95814-0794 Fax: (916)325-3731

Format: Commercial TV. **Networks:** NBC. **Founded:** 1955. **Operating Hours:** Continuous. **ADI:** Sacramento-Stockton, CA. **Key Personnel:** Greg Kelly, General Mgr.; Bill Bauman, News Dir.; Bill Spellman, General Sales Mgr.; Val Nicholas, Dir.

3059 KCTC-AM - 1320
280 Commerce Dr. Phone: (916)441-5282
Sacramento, CA 95815-4212 Fax: (916)446-4142

Format: Middle-of-the-Road (MOR); Sports. **Networks:** Westwood One Radio. **Owner:** American Radio Systems, Inc., at above address. **Founded:** 1945. **Formerly:** KCRA-AM (1978). **Operating Hours:** Continuous; 5% network, 95% local. **ADI:** Sacramento-Stockton, CA. **Key Personnel:** Bryan Jackson, Program Dir.; Jeff Salgo, General Mgr.; Fred Hormell, Sales Mgr. **Wattage:** 5000.

3060 KEBR-AM - 1210
4135 Northgate Blvd., Ste.1 Phone: (916)641-8191
Sacramento, CA 95834 Fax: (916)641-8238

Format: Religious. **Simulcasts:** KEBR-FM. **Networks:** Independent. **Owner:** Family Stations, at above address. **Founded:** 1988. **Operating Hours:** Continuous. **ADI:** Sacramento-Stockton, CA. **Key Personnel:** Peggy Renschler, Station Mgr. **Wattage:** 5000. **Ad Rates:** Noncommercial.

3061 KEBR-FM - 89.3
4135 Northgate Blvd., Ste. 1 Phone: (916)641-8191
Sacramento, CA 95834-1226 Fax: (916)641-8238

Format: Religious. **Networks:** Family Stations Radio. **Owner:** Family Stations, at above address. **Founded:** 1992. **Operating Hours:** Continuous. **Key Personnel:** Peggy Renschler, Station Mgr. **Local Programs:** *Community Issues* 3:00 am Monday-Saturday. **Wattage:** 3100. **Ad Rates:** Noncommercial.

3062 KFBK-AM - 1530
1440 Ethan Way, Ste. 200 Phone: (916)924-3901
Sacramento, CA 95825 Fax: (916)921-5555

Format: News; Talk. **Networks:** ABC; CNN Radio. **Owner:** Chancellor Broadcasting, at above address. **Founded:** 1922. **Operating Hours:** Continuous. **ADI:** Sacramento-Stockton, CA. **Key Personnel:** Rick Eytcheson, Exec. V.P.; Joe Bayliss, General Mgr.; Kevin O'Brien, General Sales Mgr.; Cristi Landes, Exec. Producer, cristalk@aol.com; Paul Hosely, News Dir. **Wattage:** 118,000.

3063 KHTK-AM - 1140
5244 Madison Ave. Phone: (916)338-9200
Sacramento, CA 95841 Fax: (916)338-9202

Format: Talk; Sports. **Networks:** Independent. **Owner:** American Radio Systems, Inc., 116 Huntington Ave., Boston, MA 02116, (617)375-7500, Fax: (617)375-7575. **Founded:** 1926. **Operating Hours:** Continuous. **ADI:** Sacramento-Stockton, CA. **Key Personnel:** Doug Harvill, VP/General Mgr.; Mike Remy, Operations Mgr.; Bob Bartlett, Dir. of Sales; Gordon Pirie, Sales Mgr. **Wattage:** 50,000. **Ad Rates:** Advertising accepted; rates available upon request.

3064 KLOV-FM - 89.3
1425 N. Market Blvd., Ste. 9 Phone: (916)928-1515
Sacramento, CA 95834 Fax: (916)928-0888
Free: (800)525-5683
E-mail: klove@klove.com

Format: Contemporary Christian. **Networks:** Independent. **Owner:** Educational Media Foundation, at above address. **Founded:** 1997. **Former name:** KSKD-FM (1997). **Operating Hours:** Continuous. **Key Personnel:** Richard Jenkins, President; Lloyd Parker, General Mgr.; Ed Lenane, Operations Dir.; Sam Wallington, Engineering Dir. **Wattage:** 1600. **Ad Rates:** Noncommercial. **URL:** http://www.klove.com.

3065 KLOV-FM - 89.3
1425 N. Market Blvd., Ste. 9 Phone: (916)928-1515
Sacramento, CA 95834 Fax: (916)928-0888
Free: (800)525-5683
E-mail: klove@klove.com

Format: Contemporary Christian. **Owner:** Educational Media Foundation, at above address. **Founded:** 1997. **Operating Hours:** Continuous. **Key Personnel:** Richard Jenkins, President; Lloyd Parker, General Mgr.; Ed Lenane, News Dir.; Sam Wallington, Dir., Engineering. **Wattage:** 1600. **Ad Rates:** Noncommercial. **URL:** http://www.klove.com.

3066 KLVA-FM - 105.5
1425 N. Market Blvd., Ste. 9 Phone: (916)928-1515
Sacramento, CA 95834 Fax: (916)928-0888
Free: (800)525-5683
E-mail: klove@klove.com

Format: Contemporary Christian. **Networks:** Independent. **Owner:** Educational Media Foundation, at above address. **Operating Hours:** Continuous. **ADI:** Phoenix (Kingman, Prescott), AZ. **Key Personnel:** Richard Jenkins, President; Lloyd Parker, General Mgr.; Ed Lenane, Operations Dir.; Sam Wallington, Engineering Dir. **Wattage:** 50,000. **Ad Rates:** Noncommercial. **URL:** http://www.klove.com.

3067 KLVB-AM - 730
1425 N. Market Blvd., Ste. 9 Phone: (916)928-1515
Sacramento, CA 95834 Fax: (916)928-0888
Free: (800)525-5683
E-mail: klove@klove.com

Format: Contemporary Christian. **Networks:** Independent. **Owner:** Educational Media Foundation, at above address. **Former name:** KRVC-AM (1997). **Operating Hours:** Continuous. **ADI:** Medford, OR. **Key Personnel:** Richard Jenkins, President; Lloyd Parker, General Mgr.; Ed Lenane, Operations Dir.; Sam Wallington, Engineering Dir. **Wattage:** 1000. **Ad Rates:** Noncommercial. **URL:** http://www.klove.com.

3068 KLVC-FM - 88.3
1425 N. Market Blvd., No. 9 Phone: (916)928-1515
Sacramento, CA 95834 Fax: (916)928-0888
Free: (800)525-5683
E-mail: klove@klove.com

Format: Religious; Contemporary Christian. **Networks:** Independent. **Owner:** Educational Media Foundation, Inc., at above address. **Founded:** 1993. **Formerly:** WKXP-FM. **Operating Hours:** Continuous. **Key Personnel:** Richard Jenkins, President; David Pierce, Program Dir.; Devona Porter, Public Affairs Dir., phone (707)528-9236, fax (707)528-9246; Sam Wallington, Sr. Engineer; Lloyd Parker, General Mgr. **Wattage:** 150,000. **Ad Rates:** Noncommercial. **URL:** http://www.klove.com.

3069 KLVG-FM - 103.7
1425 N. Market Blvd., No. 9 Phone: (916)928-1515
Sacramento, CA 95834 Fax: (916)928-0888
Free: (800)525-5683
E-mail: klove@klove.com

Format: Religious; Contemporary Christian. **Networks:** Independent. **Owner:** Educational Media Foundation, Inc., at above address. **Founded:** 1995. **Formerly:** KWEO-FM. **Operating Hours:** Continuous. **Key Personnel:** Richard Jenkins, President; David Pierce, Program Dir.; Devona Porter, Public Affairs Dir., phone (707)528-9236, fax (707)528-9246; Sam Wallington, Sr. Engineer; Lloyd Parker, General Mgr. **Wattage:** 8,000. **Ad Rates:** Noncommercial. **URL:** http://www.klove.com.

3070 KLVJ-FM - 100.1
1425 N. Market Blvd., Ste. 9 Phone: (916)928-1515
Sacramento, CA 95834 Fax: (916)928-0888
Free: (800)525-5683
E-mail: klove@klove.com

Format: Contemporary Christian. **Networks:** Independent. **Owner:** Educational Media Foundation, at above address. **Former name:** KBBN-FM. **Operating Hours:** Continuous. **ADI:** San Diego, CA. **Key Personnel:** Richard Jenkins, President; Lloyd Parker, General Mgr.; Ed Lenane, Operations Dir.; Sam Wallington, Engineering Dir. **Wattage:** 50. **Ad Rates:** Noncommercial. **URL:** http://www.klove.com.

3071 KLVK-FM - 106.3
1425 N. Market Blvd., No. 9 Phone: (916)928-1515
Sacramento, CA 95834 Fax: (916)928-0888
Free: (800)372-0888
E-mail: klove@klove.com

Format: Religious; Contemporary Christian. **Networks:** Independent. **Owner:** Educational Media Foundation, Inc., at above address, Free: (800)525-5683. **Founded:** 1991. **Formerly:** KLVS-FM (1997); KJET-FM. **Operating Hours:** Continuous. **ADI:** Fresno-Visalia (Hanford), CA. **Key Personnel:** Richard Jenkins, President; David Pierce, Program Dir.; Devona Porter, Public Affairs Dir., phone (707)528-9236, fax (707)528-9236; Sam Wallington, Sr. Engineer; Lloyd Parker, General Mgr. **Wattage:** 3.9 Kw. **Ad Rates:** Noncommercial. **URL:** http://www.klove.com.

3072 KLVN-FM - 100.1
1425 N. Market Blvd., No. 9 Phone: (916)928-1515
Sacramento, CA 95834 Fax: (916)928-0888
Free: (800)525-5683
E-mail: klove@klove.com

Format: Religious; Contemporary Christian. **Networks:** Independent. **Owner:** Educational Media Foundation, Inc., at above address, Free: (800)525-5683. **Founded:** 1991. **Formerly:** KSKD-FM. **Operating Hours:** Continuous. **Key Personnel:** Richard Jenkins, President; David Pierce, Program Dir.; Devona Porter, Public Affairs Dir., phone (707)528-9236, fax (707)528-9246; Sam Wallington, Sr. Engineer; Lloyd Parker, General Mgr. **Wattage:** 48 ERP. **Ad Rates:** Noncommercial. **URL:** http://www.klove.com.

3073 KLVP-AM - 1040
1425 N. Market Blvd., No. 9 Phone: (916)928-1515
Sacramento, CA 95834 Fax: (916)928-0888
Free: (800)372-0888
E-mail: klove@klove.com

Format: Religious; Contemporary Christian. **Networks:** Independent. **Owner:** Educational Media Foundation, Inc., at above address, Free: (800)372-0888. **Founded:** 1990. **Formerly:** KEZF-AM. **Operating Hours:** Continuous. **ADI:** Portland, OR. **Key Personnel:** Richard Jenkins, President; David Pierce, Program Dir.; Devona Porter, Public Affairs Dir.; Sam Wallington, Sr. Engineer; Lloyd Parker, General Mgr. **Wattage:** 2200 daytime, 200 nighttime. **Ad Rates:** Noncommercial. **URL:** http://www.klove.com.

KLVP-AM - See Portland, Oregon

3074 KLVP-FM - 88.7
1425 N. Market Blvd., Ste. 9 Phone: (916)928-1515
Sacramento, CA 95834 Fax: (916)928-0888
Free: (800)525-5683
E-mail: klove@klove.com

Format: Contemporary Christian. **Networks:** Independent. **Owner:** Educational Media Foundation, at above address. **Founded:** 1997. **Operating Hours:** Continuous. **Key Personnel:** Richard Jenkins, President; Lloyd Parker, General Mgr.; Ed Lenane, Operations Dir.; Sam Wallington, Engineering Dir. **Wattage:** 220. **Ad Rates:** Noncommercial. **URL:** http://www.klove.com.

3075 KLVR-FM - 91.9
1425 N. Market Blvd., No. 9 Phone: (916)928-1515
Sacramento, CA 95834 Fax: (916)928-0888
Free: (800)372-0888
E-mail: klove@klove.com

Format: Religious; Contemporary Christian. **Networks:** Independent. **Owner:** Educational Media Foundation, Inc., at above address, Free: (800)525-5683. **Founded:** 1982. **Formerly:** KCLB-FM (1988). **Operating Hours:** Continuous. **Key Personnel:** Richard Jenkins, President; David Pierce, Program Dir.; Sam Wallington, Senior Engineer; Devona Porter, Public Affairs Dir., phone (707)528-9236, fax (707)528-9246; Lloyd Parker, General Mgr. **Wattage:** 210. **Ad Rates:** Noncommercial. **URL:** http://www.klove.com.

3076 KLVU-FM - 107.1
1425 N. Market Blvd., Ste. 9 Phone: (916)928-1515
Sacramento, CA 95834 Fax: (916)928-0888
Free: (800)525-5683
E-mail: klove@klove.com

Format: Contemporary Christian. **Owner:** Educational Media Foundation, at above address. **Former name:** KSKD-FM (1997). **Operating Hours:** Continuous. **Key Personnel:** Richard Jenkins, President; Lloyd Parker, General Mgr.; Ed Lenane, Operations Dir.; Sam Wallington, Engineering Dir. **Wattage:** 9000. **Ad Rates:** Noncommercial. **URL:** http://www.klove.com.

3077 KLVW-FM - 99.1
1425 N. Market Blvd., Ste. 9 Phone: (916)928-1515
Sacramento, CA 95834 Fax: (916)928-0888
Free: (800)525-5683
E-mail: klove@klove.com

Format: Contemporary Christian. **Owner:** Educational Media Foundation, at above address. **Former name:** KKKK-FM (1998). **Operating Hours:** Continuous. **ADI:** Odessa-Midland, TX. **Key Personnel:** Richard Jenkins, President; Lloyd Parker, General Mgr.; Ed Lenane, Operations Dir.; Sam Wallington, Engineering Dir. **Wattage:** 100,000. **Ad Rates:** Noncommercial. **URL:** http://www.klove.com.

3078 KLVY-FM - 91.1
1425 N. Market Blvd., Ste. 9 Phone: (916)928-1515
Sacramento, CA 95834 Fax: (916)928-0888
Free: (800)525-5683
E-mail: klove@klove.com

Format: Contemporary Christian. **Owner:** Educational Media Foundation, at above address. **Founded:** 1998. **Operating Hours:** Continuous. **ADI:** Fresno-Visalia (Hanford), CA. **Key Personnel:** Richard Jenkins, President; Lloyd Parker, General Mgr.; Ed Lenane, Operations Dir.; Sam Wallington, Engineering Dir. **Wattage:** 3400. **Ad Rates:** Noncommercial. **URL:** http://www.klove.com.

3079 KLVY-FM - 91.1
1425 N. Market Blvd., Ste. 9 Phone: (916)928-1515
Sacramento, CA 95834 Fax: (916)928-0888
Free: (800)525-5683
E-mail: klove@klove.com

Format: Contemporary Christian. **Networks:** Independent. **Owner:** Educational Media Foundation, Inc., at above address. **Founded:** 1998. **Operating Hours:** Continuous. **ADI:** Fresno-Visalia (Hanford), CA. **Key Personnel:** Richard Jenkins, President; Lloyd Parker, General Mgr.; Ed Lenane, News Dir.; Sam Wallington, Dir., Engineering. **Wattage:** 3400. **Ad Rates:** Noncommercial. **URL:** http://www.klove.com.

3080 KMAX-TV - 31
500 Media Pl. Phone: (916)925-3100
Sacramento, CA 95815 Fax: (916)920-1078

Format: Commercial TV. **Founded:** 1981. **Formerly:** KMUV-TV (1981); KPWB-TV; KRBK-TV. **Operating Hours:** Continuous; 100% local. **ADI:** Sacramento-Stockton, CA. **Key Personnel:** Cyndi Arjil, Traffic Mgr.; Tom Tucker, Dir. of Sales; Jack Davis, Chief Engineer; Elliott Troshinsky, General Mgr.; Brent Baader, News Dir.; Charles Paige, Promotions/Program Dir. **Ad Rates:** Advertising accepted; rates available upon request.

3081 KNCI-FM - 105.1
1436 Auburn Blvd. Phone: (916)923-9230
PO Box 60408 Fax: (916)923-9202
Sacramento, CA 95815

Format: Country. **Networks:** Independent. **Owner:** EZ Communications, Inc., 10800 Main St., Fairfax, VA 22030. **Founded:** 1960. **Operating Hours:** Continuous. **ADI:** Sacramento-Stockton, CA. **Key Personnel:** Chuck Goldmark, General

Mgr.; Maryanne Ciaraghia, General Sales Mgr. **Wattage:** 50,000. **Ad Rates:** $20-385 per unit.

3082 KRAK-FM - 98.5
5244 Madison Ave. Phone: (916)338-9200
Sacramento, CA 95841 Fax: (916)338-9202

Format: Country. **Owner:** American Radio Systems, Inc., 116 Huntington Ave., Boston, MA 02116, (617)375-7500, Fax: (617)375-7575. **Founded:** 1968. **Formerly:** KZAP-FM (1992). **Operating Hours:** Continuous. **ADI:** Sacramento-Stockton, CA. **Key Personnel:** Doug Harvill, VP/General Mgr.; Mark Evans, Operations Mgr.; Bob Bartlett, Dir. of Sales. **Wattage:** 50,000. **Ad Rates:** Advertising accepted; rates available upon request.

3083 KRXQ-FM - 93.7
5345 Madison, Ste. 100 Phone: (916)334-7777
Sacramento, CA 95841-3109 Fax: (916)339-4292
E-mail: 93rock.com

Format: Album-Oriented Rock (AOR). **Networks:** Independent. **Founded:** 1970. **Operating Hours:** Continuous. **ADI:** Sacramento-Stockton, CA. **Key Personnel:** Mike John, General Mgr.; Judy McNutt, Program Dir.; Tom Schurr, General Mgr.; Curtiss Johnson, Program Dir. **Local Programs:** *Local Licks*, Kylie Brooks, (916)334-7777, Fax (916)339-4293. **Wattage:** 25,000. **Ad Rates:** Advertising accepted; rates available upon request.

3084 KSFM-FM - 102.5
1750 Howe Ave., Ste. 500 Phone: (916)920-1025
Sacramento, CA 95825-3370 Fax: (916)929-5341

Format: Contemporary Hit Radio (CHR). **Networks:** Independent. **Founded:** 1961. **Operating Hours:** Continuous. **ADI:** Sacramento-Stockton, CA. **Key Personnel:** Jerry McKenna, General Mgr.; Bob West, Program Dir. **Wattage:** 50,000.

3085 KSMJ-AM - 1380
1750 Howe Ave., Ste. 500 Phone: (916)920-1025
Sacramento, CA 95825 Fax: (916)929-5341

Format: Oldies. **Networks:** Satellite Music Network. **Founded:** 1952. **Operating Hours:** Continuous. **ADI:** Sacramento-Stockton, CA. **Key Personnel:** Jerry McKenna, General Mgr.; Rus Tracy, Program Dir. **Wattage:** 3000.

3086 KSPX-TV - 29
1029 K St., Ste. 23 Phone: (916)443-2929
Sacramento, CA 95814 Fax: (916)442-6414

Format: Commercial TV. **Networks:** Independent. **Founded:** 1984. **Formerly:** KCMY-TV. **Operating Hours:** Continuous. **ADI:** Sacramento-Stockton, CA. **Key Personnel:** Daniel Briggs, General Mgr., briggsd@calweb.com. **Wattage:** 4750 KW. **Ad Rates:** Advertising accepted; rates available upon request.

3087 KSSU-AM - 1580
California State University Phone: (916)278-5882
c/o ASI Business Office Fax: (916)278-5897
6000 J St.
Sacramento, CA 95819-6011

Format: Alternative/New Music/Progressive. **Founded:** 1991. **Formerly:** KEDG-AM (1992). **Operating Hours:** Continuous. **ADI:** Sacramento-Stockton, CA. **Key Personnel:** David Levine, Program Dir.; Mike Cooper, Music Dir.; Brad Evans, Dev. Dir.; Malcolm Andrews, Promotions Dir. **Wattage:** 2. **Ad Rates:** Noncommercial.

3088 KTXL-TV - 40
4655 Fruitridge Rd. Phone: (916)454-4422
Sacramento, CA 95820 Fax: (916)739-1079

Format: Commercial TV. **Networks:** Fox; Independent. **Founded:** 1968. **Operating Hours:** Continuous. **ADI:** Sacramento-Stockton, CA. **Key Personnel:** Michael A. Fisher, Pres./Gen. Mgr.; Bill Pulliam, General Sales Mgr.; Audrey Farrington, Creative Services Dir.; Michael Burke, News Dir.; Bill Kreutzer, Chief Engineer; Peter Filice, Treas./Controller; Audrey Farrington, Program Mgr.; Rick Corbin, Producer/Dir.; David Sasaki, News Producer; Angella Hughes-Luttrell, News Producer. **Wattage:** 50,000.

3089 KVIE-TV - 6
Box 6 Phone: (916)929-5843
Sacramento, CA 95812-0006 Fax: (916)929-7215
E-mail: member@kvie.org

Format: Public TV. **Networks:** Public Broadcasting Service (PBS). **Founded:** 1959. **Operating Hours:** Continuous. **ADI:** Sacramento-Stockton, CA. **Key Personnel:** David Hosley, President; Jan Tilmon, Exec. Producer; Randy Morgan, CFO; Michael Wall, Engineering. **Wattage:** 100,000. **Ad Rates:** $100-500 for 30 seconds.

3090 KWOD-FM - 106.5
801 K St., 27th Fl. Phone: (916)448-5000
Sacramento, CA 95814 Fax: (916)448-1655

Format: Alternative/New Music/Progressive. **Networks:** CBS. **Founded:** 1977. **Operating Hours:** Continuous. **ADI:** Sacramento-Stockton, CA. **Key Personnel:** Edward Stolz, General Mgr.; Cathy Lage-Woods, Office Mgr.; Andy Spackman, Program Mgr.; Alex Cosper, Program Dir.; Matt Zogaric, Production Dir.; Ronald Givens, Public Affairs Dir. **Wattage:** 50,000. **Ad Rates:** $150-275 for 60 seconds.

3091 KXOA-AM - 1470
280 Commerce Circle Phone: (916)923-6800
Sacramento, CA 95815-4212 Fax: (916)646-3418

Format: Oldies. **Founded:** 1945. **Operating Hours:** Continuous. **ADI:** Sacramento-Stockton, CA. **Key Personnel:** John Geary, General Mgr.; Don Daniels, Operations Mgr. **Wattage:** 5000 day; 1000 night.

3092 KXOA-FM - 107.9
5345 Madison Ave. Phone: (916)334-7777
Sacramento, CA 95841 Fax: (916)334-1092

Networks: Independent. **Founded:** 1945. **Operating Hours:** Continuous. **ADI:** Sacramento-Stockton, CA. **Key Personnel:** John Geary, General Mgr.; Tom Nakashima, Program Dir. **Wattage:** 50,000.

3093 KXPR-FM - 90.9
California State University Phone: (916)480-5900
3416 American River Dr., Ste. B Fax: (916)487-3348
Sacramento, CA 95864-5715
E-mail: npr@csus.edu

Format: Public Radio; News; Classical. **Networks:** National Public Radio (NPR). **Founded:** 1979. **Operating Hours:** Continuous; 20% network, 80% local. **ADI:** Sacramento-Stockton, CA. **Key Personnel:** Jeff Browne, Contact, phone (916)480-5933, jeffbrowne@csus.edu; Mark Jones, Operations Mgr., phone (916)480-5965, jones@csus.edu; Joan Kassis, Director of Finance, phone (916)480-5955, jmkassis@csus.edu; Cynthia Kintigh, Director of Dev., phone (916)480-5926, ckintigh@csus.edu; Michael Lazar, Pres./Gen. Mgr., phone (916)480-5901, mlazar@csus.edu. **Wattage:** 50,000. **Ad Rates:** Noncommercial.

3094 KXTV-TV - 10
Box 10 Phone: (916)441-2345
Sacramento, CA 95812-0010 Fax: (916)321-3384
E-mail: kxtv@kxtv10.com

Format: Commercial TV. **Networks:** ABC. **Owner:** A.H. Belo Corp., 400 S. Record St., Dallas, TX 75202, (214)977-6606, Fax: (214)977-6603. **Operating Hours:** 5:30 a.m.-4 a.m. **ADI:** Sacramento-Stockton, CA. **Key Personnel:** Allan E. Howard, President/General Mgr.; J. Carol Rushton, Controller; Russell Postell, Dir. of Sales, fax (916)441-3054; Gloria Lee, Dir. of Creative Services, fax (916)441-3145; David Duitch, Dir. of News, fax (916)447-6107; Bob Montgomery, Dir. of Programming & Production, fax (916)441-3145; Rod Robinson, Dir. of Engineering, fax (916)321-3275. **URL:** http://www.kxtv10.com.

3095 KYDS-FM - 91.5
4300 El Camino Ave. Phone: (916)971-7453
Sacramento, CA 95821

Format: Contemporary Hit Radio (CHR); Eclectic. **Owner:** San Juan Unified School District, 3738 Walnut Ave., Carmichael, CA 95608, (916)971-7221. **Founded:** 1979. **Operating Hours:** 7 a.m.-5 p.m. **ADI:** Sacramento-Stockton, CA. **Key Personnel:** Steve Ross, Traffic Dir.; Robert Chapman, Sports Dir.; Ed Santillanes, General Mgr.; Kyle Newton, Music Dir.; Mike Cheelister, Station Mgr.; Chris Metcalf, Production Dir.; Kristen Euretig, Promotions Dir. **Wattage:** 414.

3096 KYMX-FM - 96.1
280 Commerce Circle Phone: (916)923-6800
Sacramento, CA 95815 Fax: (916)646-3418

Format: Adult Contemporary. **Founded:** 1947. **Operating Hours:** Continuous. **ADI:** Sacramento-Stockton, CA. **Key Personnel:** Jeff Salgo, General Mgr.; Bryan Jackson, Program Dir.; Fred Hormell, Sales Mgr. **Wattage:** 50,000.

3097 KZCO-FM - 97.7
1436 Auburn Blvd. Phone: (916)646-4000
Sacramento, CA 95815 Fax: (916)648-1688
E-mail: zspanish@calveb.com

Format: Hispanic; Ethnic. **Owner:** KZCO Broadcasting Inc./Z-Spanish Radio Network, Inc., 4058 Flying C Rd., No. 17, Cameron Park, CA 95682, (916)676-5996, Fax: (916)677-9799, Free: (800)9219292. **Founded:** 1996. **Formerly:** KEWE-FM (Apr. 1, 1996). **Operating Hours:** Continuous; 100% network. **ADI:** Chico-Redding, CA. **Key Personnel:** Juan Villagrana, Account Exec. **Wattage:** 25,000. **Ad Rates:** $16 for 30 seconds; $23 for 60 seconds. **URL:** http://www.zspanish.com.

3098 Sacramento Cable
4350 Pell Dr. Phone: (916)927-2225
Sacramento, CA 95838 Fax: (916)923-1706
Free: (800)924-8015

Key Personnel: Kim Rueckert, General Mgr.; Cindy Simonsen, Contact. **Cities Served:** subscribing households 210,000; 60 channels; 6 community access channels.

3099 Wireless Broadcasting Systems of Sacramento, Inc.
1513 Sports Dr., No. 9 Phone: (916)928-1454
Sacramento, CA 95834 Fax: (916)928-0825
E-mail: wbs@cwo.com

Founded: 1988. **Formerly:** Pacific West Cable Television (Mar. 18, 1994). **Key Personnel:** Karen Barko, General Mgr. **Cities Served:** Arden-Arcade, Sacramento, CA; Sacramento County, CA: subscribing households 17,000; 30 channels. **URL:** http://www.wbssac.com.

SAINT HELENA, pop. 4,898.

W. CA. Napa Co. 50 mi. N. of San Francisco. Residential. Wineries. Agriculture.

3100 St. Helena Star
Krsek Publishing, LP
1328 Main St. Phone: (707)963-2731
PO Box 346 Fax: (707)963-8957
Saint Helena, CA 94574
Publication E-mail: starhelena@aol.com

Community newspaper. **Founded:** Sept. 1874. **Freq:** Weekly (Thurs.). **Print Method:** Offset. **Cols./Page:** 6. **Col. Width:** 25 nonpareils. **Col. Depth:** 294 agate lines. **Key Personnel:** Jeremy Hay, Managing Editor; Paul Krsek, Publisher. **Subscription Rates:** $17.50 seniors; $23.50 in county; $26.50 out of country. **Remarks:** Accepts advertising.
Ad Rates: BW: $1,638 **Circ:** ‡12,000
4C: $2,078
SAU: $13
PCI: $13

SALINAS†, pop. 80,479.

W. CA. Monterey Co. 19 mi. E. of Monterey. Hartnell College. Manufactures canned foods, electrical fixtures. Ships lettuce. Diversified farming. Lettuce, sugar beets, artichokes, beans, peas, strawberries.

3101 American Squaredance
661 Middlefield Rd. Phone: (408)443-0761
Salinas, CA 93906 Fax: (408)443-6902
Publication E-mail: amsdmag@dedot.com

Square dancing magazine. **Founded:** 1945. **Freq:** Monthly. **Print Method:** Offset. **Trim Size:** 6 1/4 x 9. **Cols./Page:** 2. **Col. Width:** 28 nonpareils. **Col. Depth:** 111 agate lines. **Key Personnel:** Jon Sanborn, Publisher. **Subscription Rates:** $20. **Remarks:** Accepts advertising.
Ad Rates: BW: $650 **Circ:** ‡18,000

3102 The Californian
Salinas Newspapers, Inc.
123 W. Alisal Phone: (408)754-4260
Salinas, CA 93901 Fax: (408)754-4243
Free: (800)300-6397
Publication E-mail: valleynews@aol.com

General newspaper. **Founded:** 1871. **Freq:** Mon.-Sat. (morn.). **Print Method:** Offset. **Cols./Page:** 6. **Col. Width:** 25 nonpareils. **Col. Depth:** 301 agate lines. **Key Personnel:** Michael A. Chihak, Publisher/President, phone (408)754-4201, fax (408)424-0117; Catharine Hamm, Managing Editor, phone (408)754-4226, fax (408)754-4293. **Subscription Rates:** $108 individuals. **Formerly:** The Salinas Californian.
Circ: Mon.-Sat. ★**19,566**

3103 El Sol
230 Capitol St. Phone: (408)757-8118
PO Box 1610 Fax: (408)757-1006
Salinas, CA 93901-1610
Free: (800)869-0237

Community newspaper (Spanish). **Founded:** 1968. **Freq:** Weekly (Thurs.). **Print Method:** Offset. **Trim Size:** 13 x 21. **Cols./Page:** 6. **Col. Width:** 2 1/16 inches. **Col. Depth:** 21 inches. **Key Personnel:** Oscar S. Parodi, Editor. **ISSN:** 1064-1998. **Subscription Rates:** Free; $50 out of area. **Remarks:** Accepts advertising. **Alt. Formats:** CD-ROM.
Ad Rates: BW: $1,386 **Circ:** Free ‡15,000
4C: $1,676
SAU: $13
PCI: $13

3104 KCBA-TV - 35
1550 Moffett St. Phone: (408)422-3500
Salinas, CA 93905 Fax: (408)754-1120

Format: Commercial TV. **Networks:** Fox. **Founded:** 1981. **Operating Hours:** Continuous. **ADI:** Salinas-Monterey, CA. **Key Personnel:** Mark P. Faylor, VP/General Mgr.; Jeanne Buheit, Program Dir., fax (408)422-6448; Lucy Cerna, National Sales Mgr.; Vickie Dixon, Local Sales Mgr.; Arlo Barbo, Controller/Station Mgr.; Monica Escobedo, Traffic Mgr.; Todd Pinsky, Production Mgr.; Brent Calvin, Promotions Dir.; John Freeman, News Dir.; Adam Perez, Chief Engineer. **Wattage:** 2,328,000. **Ad Rates:** Advertising accepted; rates available upon request. **URL:** http://www.kcba.com.

3105 KCTY-AM - 980
517 S. Main St., Ste. 201 Phone: (408)757-5911
PO Box 1939 Fax: (408)757-9764
Salinas, CA 93901
E-mail: radsuprema@aol.com

Format: Hispanic. **Networks:** Independent. **Owner:** Radio Suprema, Inc., at above address. **Founded:** 1963. **Operating Hours:** Continuous; 100% local. **ADI:** Salinas-Monterey, CA. **Key Personnel:** Rachel Ybarra, Contact; Robert Dahlstrom, Contact; Vicente Romero, Jr., Program Dir.; Jose Valenzuela, Contact. **Wattage:** 1000. **Ad Rates:** $50-80 for 60 seconds. Combined advertising rates available with KRAY-FM, KLXM-FM.

3106 KDON-FM - 102.5
55 Plaza Circle Phone: (408)422-5363
Salinas, CA 93901 Fax: (408)758-1890

Format: Contemporary Hit Radio (CHR). **Networks:** Independent. **Founded:** 1947. **Operating Hours:** Continuous. **ADI:** Salinas-Monterey, CA. **Key Personnel:** Dayton Phillips, General Mgr.; Allyson Trumper, Sales Mgr.; Michael Newman, Program Dir. **Wattage:** 18,500. **Ad Rates:** Advertising accepted; rates available upon request.

3107 KHDC-FM - 90.9
161 Main St., Ste. 1 Phone: (408)757-8039
Salinas, CA 93901 Fax: (408)757-9854

Format: Ethnic; Educational. **Networks:** Independent. **Founded:** 1986. **Formerly**: KUBO-FM. **Operating Hours:** 5 a.m. - 1 a.m. **ADI:** Salinas-Monterey, CA. **Key Personnel:** Bill Valdez, General Mgr.; Klaus Hermann, Contact; Delia Saldivar, News Dir.; Jay Chicano, Contact; Miguel Varela, Contact. **Wattage:** 3000.

3108 KION-TV - 5
PO Box 3560 Phone: (408)784-1702
Salinas, CA 93912-3560 Fax: (408)757-1766

Networks: CBS. **Founded:** 1965. **Formerly**: KMST-TVm KCCN-TV. **Operating Hours:** Continuous. **ADI:** Salinas-Monterey, CA. **Key Personnel:** Jodie Navlyt, General Mgr.; Mark Faylor, Station Mgr.; Jeame Buheit, Program Dir.; Chris Chidlaw, Local Sales Mgr.; John Vera, National Sales Mgr.; Arlo Barbo, Controller; Brent Calvin, Promotions Dir. **URL:** http://www.kiontv.com.

3109 KKMC-AM - 880
8 E. Alisal St., Ste. 501 Phone: (408)424-5562
Salinas, CA 93901 Fax: (408)424-6437

Format: Religious. **Networks:** USA Radio; International Broadcasting; Sun Radio. **Owner:** Monterey County Broadcasters, Inc., at above address. **Founded:** 1982. **Operating Hours:** Continuous. **ADI:** Salinas-Monterey, CA. **Key Personnel:** John N. Dick, General Mgr.; Lorraine Dick, Sales Mgr. **Local Programs:** *Weekly Farm Report*, George Betz, (800)750-6593, Fax (408)722-7708. **Wattage:** 10,000 kw day/1000 night. **Ad Rates:** $12.50 for 30 seconds; $17.50 for 60 seconds.

3110 KOCN-FM - 105.1
PO Box 81380 Phone: (408)375-2242
Salinas, CA 93912-1380 Fax: (408)373-4268
Free: (800)658-8640
E-mail: kocn105.com

Format: Oldies. **Networks:** Westwood One Radio. **Owner:** C.R. Pasquier Properties, Inc., PO Box KOCN, Pacific Grove, CA 93950. **Founded:** 1974. **Operating Hours:** Continuous; 85% network, 15% local. **ADI:** Salinas-Monterey, CA. **Key Personnel:** Roger Pasquier, General Mgr.; David Mans, P.D.; Mark Carbonano, Operations. **Wattage:** 6000. **URL:** http://www.kocn105.com.

3111 KRAY-FM - 103.5
517 S. Main St., Ste. 201 Phone: (408)757-5911
PO Box 1939 Fax: (408)757-9764
Salinas, CA 93902-1939
E-mail: radsuprema@aol.com

Format: Hispanic. **Owner:** Radio Suprema, Inc., at above address. **Founded:** 1976. **Operating Hours:** 24 hours; 100% local. **ADI:** Salinas-Monterey, CA. **Key Personnel:** Robert Dahlstrom, Pres./Gen. Mgr.; Rachel Ybarra, Business Mgr.; Vicente Romero, Jr., Program Dir.; Jose Valenzuela, News Dir. **Local Programs:** *Consejos a la Comunidad*, Vicente Romero, Program Dir.; *Exitometro*, Ernest Verdusco; *Calendario Comunitario*, Vicente Romero, Program Dir. **Wattage:** 6000. **Ad Rates:** $70 for 60 seconds. $50 for 60 seconds. Combined advertising rates available with KCTY-AM.

3112 KSBW-TV - 8
PO Box 81651 Phone: (408)758-8888
Salinas, CA 93912 Fax: (408)424-3750

Format: Commercial TV. **Networks:** NBC. **Owner:** STC Broadcasting, 8202 E. 21st St N. Ste B, Wichita, KS 67206-2906, (316)652-0093. **Founded:** Sept. 11, 1953. **Operating Hours:** Continuous. **ADI:** Salinas-Monterey, CA. **Key Personnel:** Robert E. Rice, President/Gen. Mgr.; Wendy Hillan, General Sales Mgr. **Wattage:** 158,000. **URL:** http://www.KSBW.com.

3113 KTGE-AM - 1570
548 E. Alisal St., Ste. A Phone: (408)757-1910
Salinas, CA 93905-2545 Fax: (408)757-9582

Format: Hispanic. **Networks:** Independent. **Owner:** TGR Broadcasting, at above address. **Founded:** 1987. **Operating Hours:** Continuous. **ADI:** Salinas-Monterey, CA. **Key Personnel:** Hector Villalobos, General Mgr. **Wattage:** 5000.

3114 KTOM-AM - 1380
PO Box 81380 Phone: (408)422-7484
Salinas, CA 93912 Fax: (408)422-5544
Free: (800)660-5866
E-mail: ktom@prodigy.com

Format: Contemporary Country. **Simulcasts:** KTOM-FM. **Networks:** ABC. **Founded:** 1972. **Operating Hours:** Continuous. **ADI:** Salinas-Monterey, CA. **Key Personnel:** KaryAnn Hamilton, Music Dir.; Erik Foxx, Program Dir.; Pam Edwards, News Dir. **Wattage:** 5000. **Ad Rates:** Advertising accepted; rates available upon request. **URL:** http://www.infopoint.com/ktom.

3115 KTOM-FM - 100.7
PO Box 81380 Phone: (408)422-7484
Salinas, CA 93912 Fax: (408)422-5544
Free: (800)660-5866
E-mail: ktom@prodigy.com

Format: Contemporary Country. **Simulcasts:** KTOM-AM. **Networks:** ABC. **Founded:** 1972. **Operating Hours:** Continuous. **ADI:** Salinas-Monterey, CA. **Key Personnel:** Pam Edwards, News Dir.; Erik Foxx, Program Dir.; KaryAnn Hamilton, Music Dir. **Wattage:** 50,000 ERP. **Ad Rates:** Advertising accepted; rates available upon request. **URL:** http://www.infopoint.com/ktom.

SAN ANDREAS, pop. 1,564.

C. CA. Calaveras Co. 40 mi. NE of Stockton. Residental. Gold mines. Agriculture. Cattle, sheep raising.

3116 Calaveras Prospect, Weekly Citizen & Chronicle
Calaveras Publishing Co., Inc.
109 E. St. Charles St. Phone: (209)754-4222
PO Box 605 Fax: (209)736-4137
San Andreas, CA 95249-0605
Community newspaper. **Founded:** June 10, 1881. **Freq:** Weekly (Thurs.). **Print Method:** Offset. **Trim Size:** 7 1/2 x 11 1/2. **Cols./Page:** 6. **Col. Width:** 28 nonpareils. **Col. Depth:** 287 agate lines. **Key Personnel:** John R. Peterson, Editor and Publisher. **USPS:** 082-820. **Subscription Rates:** $10 individuals; $7 Senior citizens and students; $12 out of area. **Remarks:** Accepts advertising. **URL:** http://www.calpubco.com.
Ad Rates: BW: $397 **Circ:** ‡2,260
4C: $772
SAU: $3.75
PCI: $3.15

SAN ANSELMO, pop. 11,927.

W. CA. Marin Co. 20 mi. NW of San Francisco. Manufactures food specialties, automatic weighing machinery, milk products. Nursery.

3117 Acoustic Guitar Magazine
Acoustic Guitar
PO Box 767 Phone: (415)485-6946
San Anselmo, CA 94979-0767 Fax: (415)485-0831
Free: (800)827-6837
Publication E-mail: acguitar@aol.com

Magazine for professional and amateur acoustic guitar enthusiasts offering advice on choosing, maintaining, and playing an acoustic guitar. **Founded:** July 1990. **Freq:** Monthly. **Print Method:** Web offset. **Trim Size:** 8 3/8 x 10 7/8. **Key Personnel:** David A. Lusterman, Publisher; Jeffrey Pepper Rodgers, Editor; Simone Solondz, Managing Editor; Dylan Schorer, Music Editor; Carrie Anderson, Advertising Dir. **ISSN:** 1044-9261. **Subscription Rates:** $29.95 individuals; $44.95 Canada; $59.95 other countries; $4.95 single issue. **Remarks:** Accepts advertising. **URL:** http://www.acguitar.com.
Ad Rates: BW: $2,950 **Circ:** Paid ★53,122
4C: $4,250
PCI: $100

3118 Common Ground
305 San Anselmo Ave. Phone: (415)459-4900
San Anselmo, CA 94960 Fax: (415)459-4974
Free: (800)442-4922
Publication E-mail: comngrnd@ix.netcom.com
Publisher E-mail: comngrnd@ix.netcom.com

Magazine (tabloid) listing over 1000 organizations and individuals offering resources for personal transformation including art, yoga, psychology, psychic arts, spiritual practices, and more in the San Francisco Bay area. **Subtitle:** Resources for Personal Transformation. **Founded:** 1974. **Freq:** Quarterly. **Print Method:** Letterpress and web offset. **Trim Size:** 10 3/4 x 13 1/2. **Cols./Page:** 4. **Col. Width:** 13 picas. **Key Personnel:** Baha Uddin Alpine, Editor and Publisher, phone (415)455-1644. **Subscription Rates:** $13 individuals; $5 single issue. **Remarks:** Accepts advertising. **URL:** http://www.comngrnd.com.
Ad Rates: GLR: $150 **Circ:** Paid ‡2,000
BW: $1,265 Non-paid ‡93,000
4C: $1,875

3119 The Herb Quarterly
Long Mountain Press, Inc.
PO Box 689 Phone: (415)455-9540
San Anselmo, CA 94979-0689 Fax: (415)455-9541
Free: (800)371-4372
Publication E-mail: herbquart@aol.com

Magazine on herb gardening, cooking, crafts, medicinal herbal research, and alternative health care. **Founded:** 1979. **Freq:** Quarterly. **Print Method:** Offset. **Trim Size:** 8 3/8 x 10 7/8. **Cols./Page:** 3. **Col. Width:** 26 nonpareils. **Col. Depth:** 140 agate lines. **Key Personnel:** Jennifer Barrett, Editor, phone (415)621-3590, jbarrett@sirius.com; James Keough, Publisher. **ISSN:** 0163-9900. **Subscription Rates:** $24. $6 single issue. **Remarks:** Accepts advertising.
Ad Rates: GLR: $1.75 **Circ:** Paid ‡50,000
BW: $1,215
4C: $1,575

3120 Piano and Keyboard
PO Box 2626 Phone: (415)458-8672
San Anselmo, CA 94979 Fax: (415)458-2955
Free: (800)233-3690
Publication E-mail: pianokeybd@aol.com

Magazine providing a forum for pianists and piano teachers. **Founded:** Jan. 1, 1952. **Freq:** Bimonthly. **Print Method:** Offset. **Trim Size:** 8 1/8 x 10 7/8. **Cols./Page:** 3. **Col. Depth:** 10 inches. **Key Personnel:** James Keough, Publisher; Marienne Uszler, Editor. **ISSN:** 0031-9554. **Subscription Rates:** $23.95 1yr.; $4.95 single issue. **Remarks:** Accepts advertising. **Formerly:** The Piano Quarterly (1992).
Ad Rates: BW: $1,400 **Circ:** Paid ‡15,000
4C: $2,075 Non-paid ‡150

3121 STRINGS
PO Box 767 Phone: (415)485-6946
San Anselmo, CA 94979-0767 Fax: (415)485-0831
Free: (800)8276837
Publication E-mail: editors.st@stringletter.com; ads.st@stringletter.com; subs.st@stringletter.com

Magazine for musicians of bowed instruments. **Founded:** July 1986. **Freq:** 8/year. **Print Method:** Offset. **Trim Size:** 8 3/8 x 10 7/8. **Cols./Page:** 3. **Col. Width:** 2 1/4 inches. **Col. Depth:** 10 inches. **Key Personnel:** Mary Van Clay, Editor, editors.st@stringletter.com; David A. Lusterman, Publisher; Jeff Jensen, Advertising Mgr.; Jessamyn Reeves-Brown, Assoc. Editor. **ISSN:** 0888-3106. **Subscription Rates:** $32.95 individuals; $4.95 single issue. **Remarks:** Accepts advertising.
Ad Rates: BW: $1,202 **Circ:** ‡15,000
4C: $1,683
PCI: $35

SAN BERNARDINO†, pop. 118,057.

San Bernardino Co. (SE). 60 m E of Los Angeles. San Bernardino Valley College. California State College. Foundry, steel mill, fruit packing. Cement, refrigerator cars, wine, liquor, dairy products, plumbing material, aerospace products manufactured.

Colton Courier - See Colton

3122 El Chicano
Inland Empire Community Newspapers
PO Box 6247 Phone: (909)381-9898
San Bernardino, CA 92412-6247 Fax: (909)384-0406
Publisher E-mail: iecn@gte.net

Newspaper (Spanish and English). **Founded:** 1969. **Freq:** Weekly (Thurs.). **Print Method:** Offset. **Cols./Page:** 4. **Col. Width:** 375 inches. **Col. Depth:** 15 inches. **Key Personnel:** Gloria Marcias Harrison, Publisher; Bill Harrison, Publisher. **Subscription Rates:** $50 out of state. **Remarks:** Accepts advertising.
Ad Rates: GLR: $1 **Circ:** Free ‡16,000
BW: $1,512
4C: $2,162
PCI: $12

3123 North San Bernardino Green Sheet
Associated Desert Shoppers, Inc.
73-400 Hwy. 111 Phone: (760)346-1729
Palm Desert, CA 92260 Fax: (760)346-7350
Free: (800)678-4237

Shopper (tabloid). **Subtitle:** Green Sheet. **Founded:** 1955. **Freq:** Weekly (Wed.). **Print Method:** Web. **Trim Size:** 11 x 12 1/2. **Cols./Page:** 6. **Col. Width:** 9 1/2 picas. **Col. Depth:** 11 3/4 inches. **Key Personnel:** Hal Paradis, Publisher; Chuck Holcomb, Sales Mgr. **Subscription Rates:** $163.80 out of area.
Ad Rates: BW: $564 **Circ:** Free 19,800

3124 Precinct Reporter
1677 W. Baseline St. Phone: (909)889-0597
San Bernardino, CA 92411 Fax: (909)889-1706

Black community newspaper. **Founded:** July 26, 1965. **Freq:** Weekly (Thurs.). **Print Method:** Offset. **Cols./Page:** 6. **Col. Width:** 18 nonpareils. **Col. Depth:** 294 agate lines. **Key Personnel:** Brian Townsend, Publisher. **Subscription Rates:** $20 individuals. **Remarks:** Accepts advertising. **Online:** Softline Information; Ethic News Watch.
Ad Rates: GLR: $1.61 **Circ:** ‡55,000
BW: $2902.50
4C: $750
PCI: $22.50

Rialto Record - See Rialto

3125 The San Bernardino American News
The American News
1583 W. Baseline St. Phone: (909)889-7677
San Bernardino, CA 92411-1756 Fax: (909)889-2882

Black community newspaper. **Founded:** 1969. **Freq:** Weekly (Thurs.). **Print Method:** Offset. **Cols./Page:** 6. **Col. Width:** 26 nonpareils. **Col. Depth:** 294 agate lines. **Key Personnel:** Samuel Martin, Publisher. **Subscription Rates:** $12 individuals. **Remarks:** Accepts advertising.
Ad Rates: GLR: $.70 **Circ:** 5,000
BW: $787.80
PCI: $9.01

3126 San Bernardino Bulletin
Metropolitan News Co.
210 S. Spring St. Phone: (213)628-4384
Los Angeles, CA 90012 Fax: (213)687-3886

Community newspaper. **Founded:** 1991. **Freq:** Weekly. **Print Method:** Offset. **Cols./Page:** 4. **Col. Width:** 15 picas. **Col. Depth:** 15 1/2 inches. **Key Personnel:** Roger M. Grace, Editor. **Remarks:** Accepts advertising.
Ad Rates: PCI: $6 **Circ:** Non-paid 1,000

3127 The San Bernardino County Sun
399 N. D St. Phone: (714)889-9666
San Bernardino, CA 92401-1518 Fax: (714)381-3976
Publication E-mail: sbsun@earthlink.net

General newspaper. **Founded:** 1873. **Freq:** Mon.-Sun. (morn.). **Print Method:** Offset. **Trim Size:** 13 x 21. **Cols./Page:** 6. **Col. Width:** 25 nonpareils. **Col. Depth:** 294 agate lines. **Key Personnel:** O. Ricardo Pimentel, Exec. Editor, fax (919)885-8741; Mark Adkins, Publisher; Jeannine Duvall, Advertising Dir., phone (909)386-3045. **Subscription Rates:** $117 individuals. **Remarks:** Advertising not accepted for guns and tobacco. **Feature Editors:** Ian Cahir, *Entertainment*, phone (714)889-9666; Bill Diepenbrock, *Metro*, phone (714)889-9666; Jill Jess, *News*, phone (714)889-9666; Richard Kimball, *Editorials*, phone (714)889-9666; Gary Miller, *Photo*, phone (714)889-9666; Mike Murphy, *Real Estate*, phone (714)889-9666; Paul Oberjuerge, *Sports*, phone (714)889-9666; Owen Sheeran, *Movie, Music, Travel*, phone (714)889-9666; Jim Steinberg, *Financial/Business*, phone (714)889-9666; John Weeks, *Features*, phone (714)889-9666; Carla Wheeler, *Religion*, phone (714)889-9666.
Ad Rates: GLR: $4.27 **Circ:** Mon.-Sat. ★**77,045**
BW: $6,526.80 Sun. ★**85,160**
SAU: $51.80

3128 West San Bernardino Green Sheet
Associated Desert Shoppers, Inc.
73-400 Hwy. 111 Phone: (760)346-1729
Palm Desert, CA 92260 Fax: (760)346-7350
Free: (800)678-4237

Shopper (tabloid). **Founded:** 1955. **Freq:** Weekly (Thurs.). **Print Method:** Web. **Trim Size:** 11 x 12 1/2. **Cols./Page:** 6. **Col. Width:** 9 1/2 picas. **Col. Depth:** 11 3/4 inches. **Key Personnel:** Hal J. Paradis, Publisher; Chuck Holcomb, Sales Mgr. **Subscription Rates:** $163.80 Free to qualified subscribers. **Remarks:** Combined advertising rates available with other Associated Desert Shoppers.
Ad Rates: BW: $564 **Circ:** Non-paid 18,300

3129 KCKC-AM - 1350
740 W. 4th St. Phone: (909)384-1039
San Bernardino, CA 92410 Fax: (909)888-7302

Format: Country. **Networks:** Westwood One Radio; CNN Radio. **Owner:** Willie Davis, All Pro Broadcasting, at above address. **Founded:** 1947. **Operating Hours:** Continuous. **ADI:** Los Angeles (Corona & San Bernardino), CA. **Key Personnel:** Bill McNulty, General Mgr.; Dwight Arnold, Operations Mgr.; J.W. Bradbury, Program Dir. **Local Programs:** *Ted & Joy in the Morning*, Ray Easley. **Wattage:** 5000 day; 600 night. **Ad Rates:** $40-50 for 30 seconds; $50-75 for 60 seconds. $60-$80 for 30 seconds; $75-$95 for 60 seconds. Combined advertising rates available with KBON-FM.

3130 KCXX-FM - 103.9
740 W. 4th St. Phone: (909)384-1039
No. No. No. No. Fax: (909)888-7302
San Bernardino, CA 92410
E-mail: x1039@local.net

Format: Alternative/New Music/Progressive. **Networks:** Independent. **Founded:** 1978. **Formerly:** KAEV-FM (1992). **Operating Hours:** Continuous; 100% local. **ADI:** Los Angeles (Corona & San Bernardino), CA. **Key Personnel:** Bill McNulty, General Mgr.; Dwight Arnold, Operations Mgr.; Chuck Summers, Program Dir. **Wattage:** 6,000. **Ad Rates:** $75-100 for 30 seconds; $100-125 for 60 seconds. $45-$65 for 30 seconds; $55-$75 for 60 seconds. Combined advertising rates available with KCKC-AM: $80-$120 for 30 seconds; $10.

3131 KKLA-AM - 1240
992 Inlind Center Dr. Phone: (909)885-6555
San Bernardino, CA 92408 Fax: (909)381-9563

Format: Religious; Talk. **Networks:** Independent. **Founded:** 1947. **Formerly:** KLFE-AM. **Operating Hours:** Continuous. **ADI:** Los Angeles (Corona & San Bernardino), CA. **Key Personnel:** Brian Hoerning, Station Mgr.; Shellie Driscoll, Office Mgr. **Wattage:** 1000. **URL:** http://www.kkla.com.

3132 KVCR-FM - 91.9
701 S. Mt. Vernon Ave. Phone: (909)888-6511
San Bernardino, CA 92410 Fax: (909)885-2116
E-mail: hometeam@vcr.pbs.org

Format: Public Radio; Classical; News; Jazz; New Age. **Networks:** National Public Radio (NPR). **Owner:** San Bernardino Community College District, 441 W. 8th St., San Bernardino, CA 92407. **Founded:** 1953. **Operating Hours:** Continuous; 57% network, 43% local. **ADI:** Los Angeles (Corona & San Bernardino), CA. **Key Personnel:** Steve Ward, Program Dir., phone ( )EXT. 1314, steve_ward@kvcr.pbs.org; Robert Ready, Producer "Afternoon Concert", phone ( )EXT. 1316, robert_ready@kvcr.pbs.org; Sonny Love, Producer "Jazz and More", phone ( )EXT. 1317, sonny_love@kvcr.pbs.org; William Eason, Senior Producer, phone ( )EXT.1315; Roger Funk, Chief Engineer, phone ( )EXT. 1614, roger_funk@kvcr.pbs.org; Dave Hinman, Development/Underwriting, phone ( )EXT. 1613, dave_hinman@kvcr.pbs.org; Jim Ness, News Dir., phone (909)369-3900, fax (909)369-8300. **Local Programs:** *The Afternoon Concert*, Robert Ready; *Final Frontier*, William Thorwald; *Jazz & More*, Sonny Love. **Wattage:** 900. **Ad Rates:** Noncommercial.

3133 KVCR-TV - 24
701 S. Mt. Vernon Ave. Phone: (909)888-6511
San Bernardino, CA 92410-2798

Format: Public TV. **Networks:** Public Broadcasting Service (PBS). **Founded:** 1962. **Operating Hours:** 8:30 a.m.-12:00 a.m.; 5:30 a.m. - 1:30 a.m. M-F. **ADI:** Los Angeles (Corona & San Bernardino), CA. **Key Personnel:** Lew Warren, General Mgr.; Al Gondos, Contact; Don Leiffer, Program Dir. **Wattage:** 1300. **Ad Rates:** Noncommercial.

SAN BRUNO, pop. 35,417.

San Mateo Co. (W) 2 m S of South San Francisco. Residential.

3134 San Bruno Herald
North County Publications
1080 S. Amphlett Blvd. Phone: (650)348-4321
PO Box 5400 Fax: (650)348-4446
San Mateo, CA 94402-1860
Newspaper. **Founded:** 1912. **Freq:** Semiweekly (Wed. and Sun.). **Print Method:** Offset. **Cols./Page:** 6. **Col. Width:** 26 nonpareils. **Col. Depth:** 301 agate lines. **Key Personnel:** Will Thomas, Editor; John H. Clinton, Jr., Publisher; Larry Boline, Advertising Mgr. **Subscription Rates:** Free. **Remarks:** Accepts advertising. **URL:** http://www.newschoice.com.
Ad Rates: BW: $1,606.05 **Circ:** 11,495
4C: $906.05
SAU: $12.45

3135 San Bruno Municipal Cable TV
398 El Camino Real Phone: (415)877-8889
San Bruno, CA 94066 Fax: (415)871-5526

Founded: 1971. **Key Personnel:** Dave Thomas, General Mgr. **Cities Served:** subscribing households 12,049; 60 channels.

SAN CARLOS, pop. 24,710.

San Mateo Co. (W). 25 m SE of San Francisco. Residential. Manufactures telescopes, wood products, oil burners, electronic products, gloves, paper cartons, tools. Nurseries.

3136 Golf Today
204 Industrial Way Phone: (650)802-8165
San Carlos, CA 94070 Fax: (650)802-8114
Free: (800)GOLF-PUTT

Subtitle: California, Nevada & Arizona's Golf Magazine. **Founded:** 1983. **Freq:** Monthly. **Print Method:** Web offset. **Trim Size:** 10 x 12. **Cols./Page:** 4. **Col. Width:** 2 1/4 inches. **Col. Depth:** 11 1/2 inches. **Key Personnel:** Bob Koczor, Editor and Publisher. **Subscription Rates:** $22 individuals; $33 two years. **Remarks:** Accepts advertising. **URL:** http://www.golftodaymagazine.com.
Ad Rates: BW: $2,300 **Circ:** Free ‡96,000
4C: $3,100

SAN CLEMENTE, pop. 27,325.

Orange Co. (S). On Pacific Ocean, 32 m SW of Santa Ana. Resort. Residential.

3137 BodyBoarding Magazine
950 Calle Amanecer No. C Phone: (714)492-7873
San Clemente, CA 92673 Fax: (714)498-6485
Publication E-mail: bbdingmag@aol.com
Publisher E-mail: bobyboarding@mcmullenargus.com

Action and personality-oriented magazine featuring bodyboarders and their sport. **Founded:** 1984. **Freq:** 8/year. **Print Method:** Web offset. **Trim Size:** 10 7/8 x 8. **Cols./Page:** 3. **Col. Width:** 13.6 picas. **Col. Depth:** 61 picas. **Key Personnel:** James Lynch, Advertising/Sales Mgr., jamesl@mcmullenargus.com; Nick Long, Editor, nickl@mcmollenargus.com; Bob Mignogna, Publisher, bobmi@mcmullenargus.com; Simon Ramsey, Assoc. Pub., simonr@mcmullenargus.com. **ISSN:** 1047-2223. **Subscription Rates:** $3.95 single issue; $4.95 single issue Canada. **Remarks:** Accepts advertising. **Available Online.**
Ad Rates: BW: $2,389 **Circ:** Paid ‡44,757
4C: $3,419 Controlled ‡3,727

3138 Industrial West
Mitchell Publications
543 Avenida Adobe Phone: (818)442-8321
San Clemente, CA 92672-2414 Fax: (818)443-9124

Trade magazine (tabloid) reporting new technology, products, applications, and corporate moves in the machine tool industry. **Founded:** Jan. 1984. **Freq:** Monthly. **Print Method:** Offset. **Trim Size:** 11 x 17. **Cols./Page:** 6 and 5. **Col. Width:** 9 1/2 and 11 picas. **Col. Depth:** 96 picas. **Key Personnel:** Sid Crown, Editor; Van Mitchell, Publisher. **ISSN:** 0743-3271. **Remarks:** Accepts advertising.
Ad Rates: GLR: $1.50 **Circ:** Controlled ‡24,700
BW: $1,646
4C: $2,171
PCI: $21

3139 Law Enforcement Journal
Law Enforcement Legal Reporter
Box 3699 Phone: (949)361-0446
San Clemente, CA 92674-3699 Fax: (949)361-0481
Free: (800)733-0737

Trade magazine covering California and U.S. Supreme Court decisions affecting law enforcement officers. **Founded:** Oct. 1978. **Freq:** Monthly. **Print Method:** Offset. **Key Personnel:** Elliott E. Alhadeff, Editor. **ISSN:** 0195-0290. **Subscription**

Rates: $29.50 individuals; $2.50 single issue. **Remarks:** Advertising not accepted. **Alt. Formats:** Diskette.
Circ: Controlled 2,053

3140 San Clemente News
South Orange County News
PO Box 3629 Phone: (714)768-3631
Mission Viejo, CA 92690 Fax: (714)454-7354

Community newspaper. **Founded:** 1987. **Freq:** Weekly (Thurs.). **Print Method:** Offset. **Cols./Page:** 5. **Col. Width:** 12.2 inches. **Col. Depth:** 182 agate lines. **Key Personnel:** Chris Meyer, Editor; Douglas E. Hanes, Publisher; Pat Norton, Advertising Mgr. **Subscription Rates:** Free. **Remarks:** Accepts advertising.
Ad Rates: PCI: $32.17 **Circ:** ‡16,322

3141 Sun Post News
Freedom Communications, Inc.
95 Avenida Del Mar
San Clemente, CA 92672

Community newspaper. **Founded:** 1937. **Freq:** Tues., Thurs., Fri. **Print Method:** Offset. **Cols./Page:** 6. **Col. Width:** 18 nonpareils. **Col. Depth:** 301 agate lines. **Key Personnel:** Rommyn Skipper, Editor, phone (714)492-4316, fax (714)492-0401; Stanford Manning, Publisher. **Remarks:** Accepts advertising. **Formerly:** Daily Sun Post.
Ad Rates: BW: $957.18 **Circ:** Mon.-Fri. ‡7,500
PCI: $10.30

3142 Surfing Magazine
McMullen Argus Publishing, Inc.
950 Calle Amanecer, No. C Phone: (714)492-7873
San Clemente, CA 92673 Fax: (714)498-6485
Publication E-mail: surfing@netcom.com

Surfing magazine. **Founded:** 1964. **Freq:** Monthly. **Print Method:** Offset. **Trim Size:** 8 x 10 7/8. **Cols./Page:** 3. **Col. Width:** 26 nonpareils. **Col. Depth:** 140 agate lines. **Key Personnel:** Jamie Brisick, Editor, jamieb@mcmullenargus.com; Robert Mignogna, Publisher, bobmi@mcmullenargus.com; Bob Graff, Sales Mgr.; James Lynch, Advertising Sales Mgr., jamesl@mcmullenargus.com. **ISSN:** 0194-9314. **Subscription Rates:** $21.95 individuals; $3.95 single issue. **Remarks:** Accepts advertising. **Available Online.**
Ad Rates: BW: $5,509 **Circ:** Paid 108,943
4C: $8,079 Non-paid 2,695

3143 Volleyball
McMullen Argus Publishing, Inc.
164 Avendia Granada Phone: (714)366-5910
San Clemente, CA 92672 Fax: (714)366-5975

Magazine about volleyball. **Subtitle:** The Player's Magazine. **Founded:** May 1990. **Freq:** Monthly. **Print Method:** Web offset. **Trim Size:** 8 x 10 3/4. **Key Personnel:** Rick Hazeltine, Editor; Jon Hastings, Publisher, phone (805)541-2294, fax (805)541-2438. **ISSN:** 1058-4668. **Subscription Rates:** $19.95; $2.95 single issue. **Remarks:** Accepts advertising.
Ad Rates: BW: $2,731 **Circ:** Paid ★**52,610**
4C: $4,056

3144 KWVE-FM - 107.9
1644 North El Camino Real Phone: (714)492-9800
San Clemente, CA 92672 Fax: (714)361-0375

Format: Religious. **Founded:** 1971. **Operating Hours:** Continuous. **Key Personnel:** Robert Cadman, Contact, robertcadman@kwve.com. **Wattage:** 50,000. **Ad Rates:** $30 for 30 seconds. **URL:** http://www.kwve.com.

SAN DIEGO†, pop. 772,591.

San Diego Co. (S). On San Diego Bay, 125 m SE of Los Angeles. Splendid harbor with extensive commerce. State College, United States International University. University of San Diego. University of California at San Diego, and many other colleges. Private schools. Army, Navy. Marine Corps and Coast Guard installations and schools. Naval hospital. Tourist resort. Sport and commercial fishing. Manufactures acoustical materials, adhesives, airplane parts, bamboo, dairy, electronic transmission and distribution equipment, electronic computing machines and components, plastic, rubber products, awnings, beverages, paper and clothing, dental specialties, detergents, drugs, chemicals, golf carts, wines, wooden boxes, bricks, brooms, building supplies, caskets, citrus by-products, missilesand missile components, farm and garden equipment, furniture, paint, parachute, processing and packing (meat, fish, fruit and food), plumbing supplies, pumps, tools, dies, uniforms, vending machines. Shipyards and marine ways.

3145 ACE FitnessMatters
American Council on Exercise
Box 910449 Phone: (619)535-8227
San Diego, CA 92191-0449 Fax: (619)535-1778
Publisher E-mail: pubs@acefitness.org

Consumer magazine covering health and fitness news. **Founded:** 1996. **Freq:** Bimonthly. **Print Method:** Sheetfed offset. **Key Personnel:** Mohan Nair, Publications Dir.; Christine Ekeroth, Editor. **ISSN:** 1082-0361. **Subscription Rates:** $25 individuals. **Remarks:** Advertising not accepted.
Circ: Paid 41,000

3146 Adolescence
Libra Publishers, Inc.
3089C Clairemont Dr., Ste. 383 Phone: (619)571-1414
San Diego, CA 92117 Fax: (619)571-1414

Professional journal covering the psychological, physiological, psychiatric, sociological, and educational aspects of the second decade of human life. **Founded:** 1966. **Freq:** Quarterly. **Print Method:** Offset. **Trim Size:** 6 x 9. **Cols./Page:** 1. **Col. Width:** 4 1/2 inches. **Col. Depth:** 7 inches. **Key Personnel:** William Kroll, Editor and Publisher; Betty Beller, Advertising Mgr. **ISSN:** 0001-8449. **Subscription Rates:** $82 individuals; $115 institutions U.S.; $121 institutions foreign; $88 individuals foreign. **Online:** EBSCO. **Alt. Formats:** Microform.
Ad Rates: BW: $300 **Circ:** Paid ‡2,300
Non-paid ‡700

3147 Advances in Applied Mathematics
Academic Press
525 B St., Ste. 1900 Phone: (619)699-6557
San Diego, CA 92101-4495 Fax: (619)699-6305
Free: (800)894-3434
Publisher E-mail: apads@acad.com

Journal publishing original and expository articles on all aspects of applied mathematics. **Founded:** 1980. **Freq:** Quarterly. **Trim Size:** 5 7/8 x 9. **Key Personnel:** Gian-Carlo Rota, Editor; Alison Ward, Advertising Mgr. **ISSN:** 0196-8858. **Subscription Rates:** $150 U.S. and Canada; $189 other countries. **Remarks:** Accepts advertising.
Ad Rates: BW: $675 **Circ:** (Not Reported)
4C: $1,615

3148 Advances in Astronautical Sciences
Univelt Inc.
PO Box 28130 Phone: (760)746-4005
San Diego, CA 92198-0130 Fax: (760)746-3139
Publication E-mail: 76121.1532@compuserve.com
Publisher E-mail: 76121.1532@compuserve.com

Proceedings of the American Astronautical Society. (Irregular serial). **Founded:** 1957. **Freq:** Periodic. **Print Method:** Offset. **Trim Size:** 7 x 9 1/2. **Key Personnel:** Robert H. Jacobs, Publisher. **ISSN:** 0065-3438. **Remarks:** Advertising not accepted. **URL:** http://univelt.staigerland.com.
Circ: 400

3149 Advances in Mathematics
Academic Press
525 B St., Ste. 1900 Phone: (619)699-6557
San Diego, CA 92101-4495 Fax: (619)699-6305
Free: (800)894-3434
Publisher E-mail: apads@acad.com

Journal reporting significant advances in all areas of pure mathematics. **Founded:** 1967. **Freq:** 14/year. **Trim Size:** 6 x 9. **Key Personnel:** Gian-Carlo Rota, Editor; Alison Ward, Advertising Mgr. **ISSN:** 0001-8708. **Subscription Rates:** $756 U.S. and Canada; $906 other countries. **Remarks:** Accepts advertising.
Ad Rates: BW: $675 **Circ:** (Not Reported)
4C: $1,615

3150 Aerostation
Association of Balloon and Airship Constructors
Box 90864 Phone: (619)715-0409
San Diego, CA 92169 Fax: (619)715-0409

Trade journal of the Association of Balloon and Airship Constructors. **Founded:** 1974. **Freq:** Quarterly. **Print Method:** Offset. **Trim Size:** 8 x 11. **Cols./Page:** 2. **Key Personnel:** F. Marc de Piolenc, Publisher, piolene@reporters.net. **Subscription Rates:** $28 individuals. **Remarks:** Advertising not accepted.
Circ: Paid 400

3151 Ahora Now
San Ysidro Publishing & Advertising Co.
675 E. San Ysidro Blvd. Phone: (619)428-1537
San Diego, CA 92173 Fax: (619)428-0871

Newspaper (tabloid) (English and Spanish). **Subtitle:** La Voz de San Diego. **Founded:** 1980. **Freq:** Weekly (Thurs.). **Print Method:** Offset. **Trim Size:** 10 x 16. **Cols./Page:** 5. **Col. Width:** 2 inches. **Col. Depth:** 16 inches. **Key Personnel:** Bertha Alicia Gonzales, Editor, phone (619)428-1537. **Subscription Rates:** $30 (six months). **Formerly:** Ahora Now The Voice of Hispanics & Americans in San Diego.
Ad Rates: BW: $1,152 **Circ:** Paid 100
4C: $1,492 Free 10,000
PCI: $18

3152 American Federation of Musicians
Music Association of San Diego County
1717 Morena Blvd. Phone: (619)276-4324
San Diego, CA 92110 Fax: (619)276-4876

Trade magazine for the music industry. **Subtitle:** Soundpost. **Founded:** 1898. **Print Method:** Offset. **Trim Size:** 8 1/2 x 11. **Key Personnel:** Ed Arias, Editor. **Subscription Rates:** $6 individuals. **Remarks:** Accepts advertising.
Ad Rates: BW: $128 **Circ:** ‡1,200

3153 American Handgunner
Publishers Development Corp.
591 Camino de la Reina, Ste. 200 Phone: (619)297-8520
San Diego, CA 92108 Fax: (619)297-5353
Free: (800)633-8001
Publication E-mail: amergunner@aol.com; 74673.3624@compuserve.com

Magazine for handgun and firearms enthusiasts. **Founded:** Sept. 1976. **Freq:** Bimonthly. **Print Method:** Offset. **Trim Size:** 8 1/2 x 11. **Cols./Page:** 3. **Col. Width:** 27 nonpareils. **Col. Depth:** 140 agate lines. **Key Personnel:** Cameron Hopkins, Editor; George E. Von Rosen, Publisher; Joe McMahon, Advertising Mgr. **ISSN:** 0145-4250. **Subscription Rates:** $16.95 individuals; $2.95 single issue. **Remarks:** Accepts advertising.
Ad Rates: BW: $4,030 **Circ:** (Not Reported)
4C: $6,661

3154 Anaerobe
Academic Press
525 B St., Ste. 1900 Phone: (619)699-6557
San Diego, CA 92101-4495 Fax: (619)699-6305
Free: (800)894-3434
Publisher E-mail: apads@acad.com

Scholarly journal covering research on the biology of anaerobic microorganisms. **Key Personnel:** Larry Barton, Editor-in-Chief. **ISSN:** 1075-9964. **Subscription Rates:** $180 individuals. **URL:** http://www.academicpress.com/anaerobe.

3155 Analytical Biochemistry
Academic Press
525 B St., Ste. 1900 Phone: (619)699-6557
San Diego, CA 92101-4495 Fax: (619)699-6305
Free: (800)894-3434
Publisher E-mail: apads@acad.com

Journal emphasizing methodology in the biological and biochemical sciences. **Founded:** 1960. **Freq:** 18/year. **Print Method:** Offset. **Trim Size:** 8 1/2 x 11. **Cols./Page:** 1. **Key Personnel:** William B. Jakoby, Editor; Alison Ward, Advertising Coordinator. **ISSN:** 0003-2697. **Subscription Rates:** $1,208 U.S. and Canada; $1,434 other countries. **Remarks:** Accepts advertising.
Ad Rates: BW: $800 **Circ:** (Not Reported)
4C: $1,740

3156 Annals of Physics
Academic Press
525 B St., Ste. 1900 Phone: (619)699-6557
San Diego, CA 92101-4495 Fax: (619)699-6305
Free: (800)894-3434
Publisher E-mail: apads@acad.com

Journal publishing original research in basic physics research. **Founded:** 1957. **Freq:** 16/year. **Trim Size:** 6 1/2 x 9 3/8. **Key Personnel:** Herman Feshbach, Editor; Alison Ward, Advertising Mgr. **ISSN:** 0003-4916. **Subscription Rates:** $1,260 U.S. and Canada; $1,462 other countries. **Remarks:** Accepts advertising.
Ad Rates: BW: $800 **Circ:** (Not Reported)
4C: $1,740

3157 Applied and Computational Harmonic Analysis
Academic Press
525 B St., Ste. 1900 Phone: (619)699-6557
San Diego, CA 92101-4495 Fax: (619)699-6305
Free: (800)894-3434
Publisher E-mail: apads@acad.com

Journal publishing information on harmonic analysis and related works, such as phase-space analysis and image compression. **Subtitle:** Time-Frequency and Time-Scale Analysis, Wavelets, Numerical Algorithms, and Applications. **Freq:** Quarterly. **Trim Size:** 8 1/2" x 11". **Key Personnel:** Charles K. Chui, Editor-in-Chief; Ronald R. Coifman, Editor-in-Chief; Ingrid Daubechies, Editor-in-Chief; Alison Ward, Advertising Coordinator. **ISSN:** 1063-5203. **Subscription Rates:** $184 institutions; $184 institutions, Canada; $221 institutions,

other countries; $74 individuals; $74 Canada; $93 other countries. **Remarks:** Accepts advertising.
Ad Rates: BW: $800 **Circ:** (Not Reported)
4C: $1,740

3158 Archives of Biochemistry and Biophysics
Academic Press
525 B St., Ste. 1900 Phone: (619)699-6557
San Diego, CA 92101-4495 Fax: (619)699-6305
Free: (800)894-3434
Publisher E-mail: apads@acad.com

Journal presenting articles in the areas of biochemistry and biophysics. **Founded:** 1943. **Freq:** 18/year. **Print Method:** Offset. **Trim Size:** 8 1/2 x 11. **Key Personnel:** J. Thomas August, Editor; Alison Ward, Advertising Coordinator. **ISSN:** 0003-9861. **Subscription Rates:** $1224 United States and Canada; $1447 other countries. **Remarks:** Accepts advertising. **URL:** http://www.aptnet.com.archivesofbiochemistryandbiophysics.co.
Ad Rates: BW: $800 **Circ:** (Not Reported)
4C: $1,740

3159 Arts & Activities
591 Camino de la Reina, Ste. 200 Phone: (619)297-8520
Fax: (619)297-5352
San Diego, CA 92108
Publication E-mail: apressaa@aol.com

Elementary and high school art education magazine. **Founded:** 1932. **Freq:** Monthly (except July and August). **Print Method:** Offset. **Trim Size:** 8 1/2 x 11. **Cols./Page:** 3. **Col. Width:** 27 nonpareils. **Col. Depth:** 138 agate lines. **Key Personnel:** Maryellen Bridge, Editor; George E. Von Rosen, Publisher; Steve Polite, Advertising Mgr. **ISSN:** 0004-3931. **Subscription Rates:** $24.95 individuals. **Remarks:** Accepts advertising.
Ad Rates: BW: $1,650 **Circ:** Combined 19,557
4C: $2,115

3160 Atomic Data and Nuclear Data Tables
Academic Press
525 B St., Ste. 1900 Phone: (619)699-6557
San Diego, CA 92101-4495 Fax: (619)699-6305
Free: (800)894-3434
Publisher E-mail: apads@acad.com

Journal publishing compilations of experimental and theoretical information in atomic physics, nuclear physics, and related fields. **Founded:** 1973. **Freq:** Bimonthly. **Trim Size:** 8 1/2 x 11. **Key Personnel:** Angela Li-Scholz, Editor; S. Raman, Editor; Wilfried Scholz, Editor; Alison Ward, Advertising Coordinator. **ISSN:** 0092-640X. **Subscription Rates:** $351 U.S. and Canada; $416 other countries. **Remarks:** Accepts advertising.
Ad Rates: BW: $800 **Circ:** (Not Reported)
4C: $1,740

3161 Beach & Bay Press
Mannis Communications, Inc.
4645 Cass St., Ste. 201 Phone: (619)270-3103
PO Box 9550 Fax: (619)270-9325
San Diego, CA 92169
Publication E-mail: sdnws@aol.com

Community newspaper. **Founded:** 1988. **Freq:** Weekly. **Print Method:** Offset. **Trim Size:** 11 x 17. **Cols./Page:** 5. **Col. Width:** 1 15/16 inches. **Col. Depth:** 15 3/4 inches. **Key Personnel:** Julie Mannis, Publisher; David Mannis, Publisher; John Gregory, Editor-in-Chief. **Subscription Rates:** Free. **Remarks:** Combined advertising rates available with Peninsula Beach, La Jolla Village News, Golden Triangle News.
Ad Rates: BW: $1,278 **Circ:** Free 20,000
4C: $1,528 Paid 51
PCI: $17

3162 Biochemical and Biophysical Research Communications
Academic Press
525 B St., Ste. 1900 Phone: (619)699-6557
San Diego, CA 92101-4495 Fax: (619)699-6305
Free: (800)894-3434
Publisher E-mail: apads@acad.com

International scientific journal devoted to the rapid dissemination of timely and significant experimental results in the diverse fields of modern biology, including cell biology. **Founded:** 1959. **Freq:** 36/year. **Print Method:** Offset. **Trim Size:** 6 7/8 x 10. **Key Personnel:** John N. Abelson, Editor; Alison Ward, Advertising Coordinator. **ISSN:** 0006-291X. **Subscription Rates:** $996 United States and Canada; $1222 other countries. **Remarks:** Accepts advertising. **URL:** http://www.biochemicalandbiophysicalresearchcommunications.c.
Ad Rates: BW: $800 **Circ:** (Not Reported)
4C: $1,740

3163 Biochemical and Molecular Medicine
Academic Press
525 B St., Ste. 1900 Phone: (619)699-6557
San Diego, CA 92101-4495 Fax: (619)699-6305
Free: (800)894-3434
Publisher E-mail: apads@acad.com

Journal publishing papers on original research in the fields of biochemistry, physiologic chemistry, and metabolic biology. **Founded:** 1969. **Freq:** Bimonthly. **Trim Size:** 8 1/2 x 11. **Key Personnel:** Edward R. McCabe, Editor; Chandra Mohan, Editor; Alison Ward, Avertising Coordinator. **ISSN:** 0885-4505. **Subscription Rates:** $312 U.S. and Canada; $366 other countries. **Remarks:** Accepts advertising.
Ad Rates: BW: $800 **Circ:** (Not Reported)
4C: $1,740

3164 Biological Control
Academic Press
525 B St., Ste. 1900 Phone: (619)699-6557
San Diego, CA 92101-4495 Fax: (619)699-6305
Free: (800)894-3434
Publisher E-mail: apads@acad.com

Journal containing information on the means of reducing or mitigating pets and pest effects through the use of natural enemies. **Subtitle:** Theory and Application in Pest Management. **Founded:** 1994. **Freq:** Quarterly. **Key Personnel:** Raghavan Charudattan, Editor. **ISSN:** 1049-9644. **Subscription Rates:** $174 individuals; $198 other countries.

3165 Bioorganic Chemistry
Academic Press
525 B St., Ste. 1900 Phone: (619)699-6557
San Diego, CA 92101-4495 Fax: (619)699-6305
Free: (800)894-3434
Publisher E-mail: apads@acad.com

International journal publishing articles on chemical or molecular solutions to biological problems. **Subtitle:** An International Journal. **Founded:** 1971. **Freq:** Quarterly. **Trim Size:** 6 7/8 x 10. **Key Personnel:** Gordon A. Hamilton, Editor; Alison Ward, Advertising Coordinator. **ISSN:** 0045-2068. **Subscription Rates:** $170 United States and Canada; $200 other countries. **Remarks:** Accepts advertising. **URL:** http://www.bioorganicchemistry.com.
Ad Rates: BW: $800 **Circ:** (Not Reported)
4C: $1,740

3166 Blood Cells, Molecules, & Diseases
Academic Press
525 B St., Ste. 1900 Phone: (619)699-6557
San Diego, CA 92101-4495 Fax: (619)699-6305
Free: (800)894-3434
Publisher E-mail: apads@acad.com

Scholarly journal covering hematology, cell biology, immunology and genetics. **Key Personnel:** Ernest Beutler, Editor-in-Chief. **ISSN:** 1079-9796. **Subscription Rates:** $300 U.S. and Canada; $362 elsewhere. **URL:** http://www.academicpress.com/bcmd.

3167 Books
San Diego Union-Tribune
PO Box 191 Phone: (619)293-1531
San Diego, CA 92112 Fax: (619)293-2432
Free: (800)244-6397

Newspaper covering current trends in books. **Founded:** 1977. **Freq:** Weekly. **Print Method:** Offset. **Cols./Page:** 6. **Col. Width:** 2 1/16 inches. **Col. Depth:** 13 inches. **Key Personnel:** Arthur Salm, Books Ed., phone (619)293-1321, fax (619)293-2436, arthur.salm@uniontrib.com; Al Lacranaga, Advertising Mgr. **Remarks:** Advertising accepted; rates available upon request. **Formerly:** Currents in Books (1992).
Circ: ‡422,000

3168 Brain, Behavior, and Immunity
Academic Press
525 B St., Ste. 1900 Phone: (619)699-6557
San Diego, CA 92101-4495 Fax: (619)699-6305
Free: (800)894-3434
Publisher E-mail: apads@acad.com

Journal publishing research data on the interactions between the nervous system and the immune system at the molecular, cellular, and organismic levels. **Founded:** 1987. **Freq:** Quarterly. **Trim Size:** 6 7/8 x 10. **Key Personnel:** Robert Ader, Editor; Nicholas Cohen, Advertising Mgr.; David L. Felton, Editor; Alison Ward, Advertising Coordinator. **ISSN:** 0889-1591. **Subscription Rates:** $160 U.S. and Canada; $182 other countries. **Remarks:** Accepts advertising.
Ad Rates: BW: $800 **Circ:** (Not Reported)
4C: $1,740

3169 Brain and Cognition
Academic Press
525 B St., Ste. 1900 Phone: (619)699-6557
San Diego, CA 92101-4495 Fax: (619)699-6305
Free: (800)894-3434
Publisher E-mail: apads@acad.com

Research in the areas of attention, cognitive processes, consciousness, emotion, hemispheric differences, memory, movement, perception, praxis, sex differences, visual and spatial processes. **Founded:** 1982. **Freq:** 9/year. **Trim Size:** 5 7/8 x 9. **Key Personnel:** Harry A. Whitaker, Editor; Jeffrey L. Cummings, Editor; Alison Ward, Advertising Coordinator. **ISSN:** 0278-2626. **Subscription Rates:** $162 U.S. and Canada; $196 other countries. **Remarks:** Accepts advertising.
Ad Rates: BW: $675 **Circ:** (Not Reported)
4C: $1,615

3170 Brain and Language
Academic Press
525 B St., Ste. 1900 Phone: (619)699-6557
San Diego, CA 92101-4495 Fax: (619)699-6305
Free: (800)894-3434
Publisher E-mail: apads@acad.com

Interdisciplinary journal publishing original research data on human language and other forms of communication as they relate to brain structure and function. **Founded:** 1974. **Freq:** 8/year. **Trim Size:** 5 7/8 x 9. **Key Personnel:** Harry A. Whitaker, Editor; Andre Roch Lecours, Advertising Mgr.; Alison Ward, Editor. **ISSN:** 0093-934X. **Subscription Rates:** $296 U.S. and Canada; $370 other countries. **Remarks:** Accepts advertising.
Ad Rates: BW: $660 **Circ:** (Not Reported)
4C: $1,575

3171 Business Advisor
5675 Ruffin Rd. Phone: (619)278-5600
San Diego, CA 92123 Fax: (619)278-0300
Free: (800)336-6060
Publication E-mail: news@advisor.com

Magazine for developing electronic business applications. **Founded:** Oct. 1983. **Freq:** Monthly. **Print Method:** Offset. **Trim Size:** 8 3/8 x 10 7/8. **Cols./Page:** 3. **Col. Width:** 27 nonpareils. **Col. Depth:** 140 agate lines. **Key Personnel:** John Hawkins, Editor; William T. Ota, Publisher; B.J. Ghiglione, Advertising Mgr.; Tina Bennett, Production Mgr. **ISSN:** 0740-5200. **Subscription Rates:** $39 individuals. **Remarks:** Accepts advertising. **URL:** http://www.advisor.com/. **Alt. Formats:** CD-ROM. **Formerly:** Databased Advisor: Developing Internet, Intranet, and Extranet Database Solutions; Databased Web Advisor.
Ad Rates: BW: $3,450 **Circ:** Paid 36,220
4C: $5,185

3172 Business Opportunities Journal
Business Service Corp.
PO Box 60762 Phone: (619)223-5615
San Diego, CA 92166 Fax: (619)223-1705
Free: (800)854-6570
Publication E-mail: boj@boj.com
Publisher E-mail: boj@boj.com

Newspaper covering business, real estate, and franchises. **Subtitle:** Newspaper covering businesses and franchises for sale. **Founded:** 1969. **Freq:** Monthly. **Print Method:** Offset. **Cols./Page:** 6. **Col. Width:** 19 nonpareils. **Col. Depth:** 196 agate lines. **Key Personnel:** Wayne Wakefield, President. **Subscription Rates:** $30 individuals; $48 two years. **Remarks:** Accepts advertising. **Available Online. URL:** http://www.boj.com.
Ad Rates: BW: $1,775 **Circ:** ‡132,000
4C: $2,155
PCI: $80

3173 California Garden
San Diego Floral Association
2125 Park Blvd. Phone: (619)232-5762
San Diego, CA 92101-4792 Fax: (619)235-1112

Magazine on floriculture and horticulture. **Founded:** 1909. **Freq:** Bimonthly. **Print Method:** Offset. **Trim Size:** 8 1/2 x 11. **Cols./Page:** 2. **Col. Width:** 3 1/2 inches. **Col. Depth:** 9 1/4 inches. **Key Personnel:** Jacqueline Coleman, Editor. **ISSN:** 0008-1116. **Subscription Rates:** $7 individuals; $13 other countries; $1.50 single issue. **Remarks:** Accepts advertising.
Ad Rates: GLR: $2 **Circ:** 2,100
BW: $100
PCI: $20

3174 Cell Biology International
Academic Press
525 B St., Ste. 1900 Phone: (619)699-6557
San Diego, CA 92101-4495 Fax: (619)699-6305
Free: (800)894-3434
Publisher E-mail: apads@acad.com

Scholarly journal covering cell biology for plant and animal scientists. **Key Personnel:** Nancy Lane, Editor-in-Chief. **ISSN:** 0165-6995. **Subscription Rates:** $315 individuals. **URL:** http://www.academicpress.com/cbi.

3175 Cellular Immunology
Academic Press
525 B St., Ste. 1900 Phone: (619)699-6557
San Diego, CA 92101-4495 Fax: (619)699-6305
Free: (800)894-3434
Publisher E-mail: apads@acad.com

International journal publishing original investigations of the immunological activities of cells in experimental or clinical situations. **Subtitle:** An International Journal. **Founded:** 1970. **Freq:** 14/year. **Print Method:** Offset. **Trim Size:** 6 7/8 x 10. **Cols./Page:** 1. **Col. Width:** 5.25 picas. **Col. Depth:** 8.5 picas. **Key Personnel:** H. Sherwood Lawrence, Editor. **ISSN:** 0008-8749. **Subscription Rates:** $983.50 U.S and Canada; $1,194.50 other countries. **Remarks:** Accepts advertising. **URL:** http://www.cellular.immunology.com.
Ad Rates: BW: $850 **Circ:** (Not Reported)
4C: $1,895

3176 Clinical Immunology and Immunopathology
Academic Press
525 B St., Ste. 1900 Phone: (619)699-6557
San Diego, CA 92101-4495 Fax: (619)699-6305
Free: (800)894-3434
Publisher E-mail: apads@acad.com

Journal publishing original research, in the molecular and cellular bases of immunological disease. **Subtitle:** The Molecular and Cellular Basis of Immunological Disease. **Founded:** 1972. **Freq:** Monthly. **Trim Size:** 8 1/2 x 11. **Key Personnel:** Noel R. Rose, Editor; Stanley Cohen, Contact; Alison Ward, Advertising Coordinator. **ISSN:** 0090-1229. **Subscription Rates:** $606 U.S. and Canada; $741 other countries. **Remarks:** Accepts advertising. **URL:** http;//www.clinicalimmunologyandimmunopathology.com.
Ad Rates: BW: $800 **Circ:** (Not Reported)
4C: $1,740

3177 Cognitive Psychology
Academic Press
525 B St., Ste. 1900 Phone: (619)699-6557
San Diego, CA 92101-4495 Fax: (619)699-6305
Free: (800)894-3434
Publisher E-mail: apads@acad.com

Journal publishing research data on studies of memory, language processing, perception, problem-solving, and thinking. **Freq:** 6/year. **Trim Size:** 5 7/8 x 9. **Key Personnel:** Douglas L. Medin, Editor; Alison Ward, Advertising Coordinator. **ISSN:** 0010-0285. **Subscription Rates:** $162.50 U.S. and Canada; $200 other countries. **Remarks:** Accepts advertising.
Ad Rates: BW: $675 **Circ:** (Not Reported)
4C: $1,615

3178 Computer Speech & Language
Academic Press
525 B St., Ste. 1900 Phone: (619)699-6557
San Diego, CA 92101-4495 Fax: (619)699-6305
Free: (800)894-3434
Publisher E-mail: apads@acad.com

Scholarly journal covering speech by humans and machines. **Key Personnel:** S. E. Levinson, Editor; S. Young, Editor. **ISSN:** 0885-2308. **Subscription Rates:** $160 individuals.

3179 Computer Vision and Vision Understanding
Academic Press
525 B St., Ste. 1900 Phone: (619)699-6557
San Diego, CA 92101-4495 Fax: (619)699-6305
Free: (800)894-3434
Publisher E-mail: apads@acad.com

Journal focusing on the computer analysis of pictorial information. **Freq:** Bimonthly. **Trim Size:** 8 1/2 x 11. **Key Personnel:** Linda Shapiro, Editor; Alison Ward, Advertising Coordinator. **Subscription Rates:** $302. **Remarks:** Accepts advertising. **URL:** http://www.aptnet.com.computervisionandvisionunderstanding.c.
Ad Rates: BW: $675 **Circ:** (Not Reported)
4C: $16155

3180 Computers and Biomedical Research
Academic Press
525 B St., Ste. 1900 Phone: (619)699-6557
San Diego, CA 92101-4495 Fax: (619)699-6305
Free: (800)894-3434
Publisher E-mail: apads@acad.com

Journal providing researchers with information on the use of computers in biomedicine. **Founded:** 1969. **Freq:** Bimonthly. **Print Method:** Offset. **Trim Size:** 6 7/8 x 10. **Key Personnel:** Homer R. Warner, Editor; Alison Ward, Advertising Coordinator. **ISSN:** 0010-4809. **Subscription Rates:** $190 U.S. and Canada; $240 other countries. **Remarks:** Accepts advertising. **URL:** http://www.computersandbiomedicalresearch.com.
Ad Rates: BW: $675 **Circ:** (Not Reported)
4C: $1,615

3181 ComputorEdge
The Byte Buyer, Inc.
3655 Ruffin Rd., No. 100 Phone: (619)573-0315
San Diego, CA 92123-1833 Fax: (619)573-0205
Free: (800)573-3247

ComputorEdge is the nation's largest regional computer weekly, with editions in Southern California and Colorado. The magazine provides non-technical, entertaining articles on all aspects of computer hardware and software, including productivity, advice, personal experience and an occasional piece of computer-related fiction. While focusing on novice and intermediate computer users and shoppers, our well-educated readers also include experts. **Founded:** 1983. **Freq:** Weekly. **Trim Size:** 8 1/4 x 10 3/4. **Cols./Page:** 3. **Col. Width:** 2 1/4 inches. **Key Personnel:** John San Filippo, Editor, editor@computoredge.com; Elvira Phipps, Advertising Mgr. **Subscription Rates:** $35 individuals. **Remarks:** Accepts advertising. **URL:** http://www.computoredge.com.
Ad Rates: BW: $1,157 **Circ:** Controlled 250,000

3182 Consciousness and Cognition
Academic Press
525 B St., Ste. 1900 Phone: (619)699-6557
San Diego, CA 92101-4495 Fax: (619)699-6305
Free: (800)894-3434
Publisher E-mail: apads@acad.com

Journal focusing on a natural science approach to consciousness, voluntary control, and self. **Founded:** 1992. **Freq:** Quarterly. **Trim Size:** 6 7/8 x 10. **Key Personnel:** Bernard J. Baars, Editor; William P. Banks, Advertising Mgr.; Alison Ward, Advertising Coordinator. **ISSN:** 1053-8100. **Subscription Rates:** $122. **Remarks:** Accepts advertising.
Ad Rates: BW: $675 **Circ:** (Not Reported)
4C: $1,615

3183 Contemporary Educational Psychology
Academic Press
525 B St., Ste. 1900 Phone: (619)699-6557
San Diego, CA 92101-4495 Fax: (619)699-6305
Free: (800)894-3434
Publisher E-mail: apads@acad.com

Journal of empirical research, theory in the application of psychological methods, and research to problems in education. **Founded:** 1976. **Freq:** Quarterly. **Trim Size:** 5 7/8 x 9. **Key Personnel:** Raymond W. Kullhavy, Editor; Alison Ward, Advertising Mgr. **ISSN:** 0361-476X. **Subscription Rates:** $146 U.S. and Canada; $184 other countries. **Remarks:** Accepts advertising.
Ad Rates: BW: $660 **Circ:** (Not Reported)
4C: $1,575

3184 Continental Newstime
Continental Features/Continental News Service
501 W. Broadway, Ste. 265, Plaza A Phone: (619)492-8696
San Diego, CA 92101
Publisher E-mail: newstime@hotbot.com

Magazine featuring news and commentary on national and world affairs. **Founded:** June 3, 1987. **Freq:** Biweekly. **Print Method:** Offset. **Trim Size:** 8 1/2 x 11. **Cols./Page:** 2 and 3. **Col. Width:** 3 1/2 and 2 inches. **Col. Depth:** 7 3/4 and 10 inches. **Key Personnel:** Gary P. Salamone, Editor-in-Chief. **ISSN:** 1096-1712. **Subscription Rates:** $52 six months. **Remarks:** Accepts advertising.
Ad Rates: BW: $1,400 **Circ:** ‡238,000
PCI: $95.

3185 Cryobiology
Academic Press
525 B St., Ste. 1900 Phone: (619)699-6557
San Diego, CA 92101-4495 Fax: (619)699-6305
Free: (800)894-3434
Publisher E-mail: apads@acad.com

International scientific journal publishing research in the field of low temperature biology and medicine. **Subtitle:** International Journal of Low Temperature Biology and Medicine. **Founded:** 1964. **Freq:** Bimonthly. **Print Method:** Offset. **Trim Size:** 6 7/8 x 10. **Key Personnel:** Arthur W. Rowe, Editor-in-Chief. **ISSN:** 0011-2240. **Subscription Rates:** $176 U.S. and Canada; $212 other countries. **Remarks:** Accepts advertising. **URL:** http://www.cryobiology.com.
Ad Rates: BW: $850 **Circ:** (Not Reported)
4C: $1,895

3186 Cytokine
Academic Press
525 B St., Ste. 1900 Phone: (619)699-6557
San Diego, CA 92101-4495 Fax: (619)699-6305
Free: (800)894-3434
Publisher E-mail: apads@acad.com

Scholarly journal covering molecular biology, biochemistry, immunology and related fields. **Key Personnel:** Gordon W. Duff, Editor; Scott K. Durum, Editor. **ISSN:** 1043-4666. **Subscription Rates:** $370 individuals. **URL:** http://www.academicpress.com/cytokine.

3187 The Daily Aztec
San Diego State University
San Diego, CA 92182-9114 Phone: (619)594-6975
Fax: (619)594-7277
Publication E-mail: daletters@sdsu.edu

College newspaper. **Founded:** 1921. **Freq:** Daily (morn.). **Print Method:** Offset. **Cols./Page:** 5. **Col. Width:** 24 nonpareils. **Col. Depth:** 224 agate lines. **Key Personnel:** Jamie Butow, Editor-in-Chief, butow@mail.sdsu.edu; Kate Nelson, Managing Editor; Melissa Evans, City Editor. **Subscription Rates:** Free; $30 by mail. **Remarks:** Accepts advertising. **URL:** http://www.sdsu.edu/daztec/. **Formerly**: Normal News; Paper Lantern; The Aztec.
Ad Rates: BW: $732 **Circ:** Free 13,000
SAU: $9.15
PCI: $11.25

3188 Developmental Biology
Academic Press
525 B St., Ste. 1900 Phone: (619)699-6557
San Diego, CA 92101-4495 Fax: (619)699-6305
Free: (800)894-3434
Publisher E-mail: apads@acad.com

Journal publishing original research on mechanisms of development, differentiation, growth, regeneration, and tissue repair at the molecular, cellular, and genetic levels (in plants and animals). **Subtitle:** An International Journal Published under the Auspices of the Society for Developmental Biology. **Founded:** 1959. **Freq:** Monthly. **Print Method:** Offset. **Trim Size:** 8 1/2 x 11. **Key Personnel:** Peter J. Bryant, Editor-in-Chief; Alison Ward, Advertising Coord. **ISSN:** 0012-1606. **Subscription Rates:** $1,308 U.S. and Canada; $1,543 other countries. **Remarks:** Accepts advertising.
Ad Rates: BW: $800 **Circ:** (Not Reported)
4C: $1,740

3189 Developmental Review
Academic Press
525 B St., Ste. 1900 Phone: (619)699-6557
San Diego, CA 92101-4495 Fax: (619)699-6305
Free: (800)894-3434
Publisher E-mail: apads@acad.com

Journal reports on issues with important implications for the fields of pediatrics, psychiatry, and education. **Subtitle:** Perspectives in Behavior and Cognition. **Founded:** 1981. **Freq:** Quarterly. **Trim Size:** 5 7/8 x 9. **Key Personnel:** Grover J. Whitehurst, Editor; Alison Ward, Advertising Mgr. **ISSN:** 0273-2297. **Subscription Rates:** $98 U.S. and Canada; $123 other countries. **Remarks:** Accepts advertising.
Ad Rates: BW: $675 **Circ:** (Not Reported)
4C: $1,615

3190 Digital Signal Processing
Academic Press
525 B St., Ste. 1900 Phone: (619)699-6557
San Diego, CA 92101-4495 Fax: (619)699-6305
Free: (800)894-3434
Publisher E-mail: apads@acad.com

Journal containing information on the creativity in the field of signal processing. **Subtitle:** A Review Journal. **Founded:** 1994. **Freq:** Quarterly. **Trim Size:** 8 1/2 x 11. **Key Personnel:** Rao Yarlagadda, Editor. **ISSN:** 1051-2004. **Subscription Rates:** $140 individuals; $140 Canada; $160 other countries. **Remarks:** Accepts advertising.
Ad Rates: BW: $675 **Circ:** (Not Reported)
4C: $1,615

3191 Drug Delivery
Academic Press
525 B St., Ste. 1900 Phone: (619)699-6557
San Diego, CA 92101-4495 Fax: (619)699-6305
Free: (800)894-3434
Publisher E-mail: apads@acad.com

Journal containing information on drug delivery technology at the theoretical as well as the practical level. **Subtitle:** The Journal of Delivery and Targeting of Therapeutic Agents. **Founded:** 1993. **Freq:** Quarterly. **Trim Size:** 8 1/2 x 11. **Key Personnel:** Alfred Stracher, Editor; Alison Ward, Advertising Coordinator. **ISSN:** 1071-7544. **Subscription Rates:** $144

individuals; $144 Canada; $164 other countries. **Remarks:** Accepts advertising.
Ad Rates: BW: $800 **Circ:** (Not Reported)
4C: $1,740

3192 Ecotoxicology and Environmental Safety
Academic Press
525 B St., Ste. 1900 Phone: (619)699-6557
San Diego, CA 92101-4495 Fax: (619)699-6305
Free: (800)894-3434
Publisher E-mail: apads@acad.com

Journal reporting research of the biologic and toxic effects of natural or synthetic chemical pollutants on animal, plant, or microbial ecosystems. **Subtitle:** Official Journal of the International Society of Ecotoxicology and Environmental Safety. **Founded:** 1977. **Freq:** 9 /year. **Trim Size:** 8 1/2 x 11. **Key Personnel:** Frederick Coulston, Editor; Friedhelm Korte, Contact; Alison Ward, Advertising Coordinator. **ISSN:** 0147-6513. **Subscription Rates:** $234 U.S. and Canada; $294 other countries. **Remarks:** Accepts advertising. **URL:** http://www.ecotoncologyandenvironmentalsafety.com.
Ad Rates: BW: $800 **Circ:** (Not Reported)
4C: $1,740

3193 Environmental Research
Academic Press
525 B St., Ste. 1900 Phone: (619)699-6557
San Diego, CA 92101-4495 Fax: (619)699-6305
Free: (800)894-3434
Publisher E-mail: apads@acad.com

Journal covering the toxic effects of environmental agents in humans and animals. **Freq:** 8/year. **Trim Size:** 8 1/2 x 11. **Key Personnel:** Philip J. Landrigan, Editor; Alison Ward, Advertising Coordinator. **Subscription Rates:** $640. **Remarks:** Accepts advertising.
Ad Rates: BW: $800 **Circ:** (Not Reported)
4C: $1,740

3194 Experimental Cell Research
Academic Press
525 B St., Ste. 1900 Phone: (619)699-6557
San Diego, CA 92101-4495 Fax: (619)699-6305
Free: (800)894-3434
Publisher E-mail: apads@acad.com

Journal on cell biology and cancer research featuring experimental studies on the general organization and activity of cells. **Founded:** 1949. **Freq:** Monthly. **Trim Size:** 8 1/2 x 11. **Key Personnel:** Urban Lendahl, Editor-in-Chief; Graham Carpenter, Assoc. Editor; Christen Hood, Assoc. Editor. **ISSN:** 0014-4827. **Subscription Rates:** $2,795 institutions; $330 personal. **Remarks:** Accepts advertising. **Available Online.** **URL:** http://www.academicpress.com/ecr.
Ad Rates: BW: $850 **Circ:** 1,986
4C: $1,045

3195 Experimental Eye Research
Academic Press
525 B St., Ste. 1900 Phone: (619)699-6557
San Diego, CA 92101-4495 Fax: (619)699-6305
Free: (800)894-3434
Publisher E-mail: apads@acad.com

Scholarly journal covering the anatomy, physiology, and biochemistry of the eye, and related fields. **Key Personnel:** J. G. Hollyfield, Editor-in-Chief. **ISSN:** 0014-4835. **Subscription Rates:** $790 individuals. **URL:** http://www.academicpress.com/eer.

3196 Experimental and Molecular Pathology
Academic Press
525 B St., Ste. 1900 Phone: (619)699-6557
San Diego, CA 92101-4495 Fax: (619)699-6305
Free: (800)894-3434
Publisher E-mail: apads@acad.com

Journal presenting articles on disease processes in relation to structural and biochemical alterations in mammalian tissues and fluids, and on the application of new techniques of analytical chemistry, histochemistry, pharmacology, toxicology, and electron microscopy to problems of pathology in man and animals. **Founded:** 1962. **Freq:** Bimonthly. **Trim Size:** 6 7/8 x 10. **Key Personnel:** Frederick Coulston, Editor; Wilbur A. Thomas, Advertising Mgr.; Sean Moore, Managing Editor; Alison Ward, Advertising Coordinator. **ISSN:** 0014-4800. **Subscription Rates:** $368 U.S. and Canada; $441 other countries. **Remarks:** Accepts advertising. **URL:** http://www.experimentalandmolecularpathology.com.
Ad Rates: BW: $800 **Circ:** (Not Reported)
4C: $1,740

3197 Experimental Mycology
Academic Press
525 B St., Ste. 1900 Phone: (619)699-6557
San Diego, CA 92101-4495 Fax: (619)699-6305
Free: (800)894-3434
Publisher E-mail: apads@acad.com

Journal publishing experimental investigations relating structure and function to growth, reproduction, morphogenesis, and differentiation of fungi and their traditional allies. **Subtitle:** An International Journal. **Founded:** 1977. **Freq:** Quarterly. **Trim Size:** 6 7/8 x 10. **Key Personnel:** Robert Brambl; Greta Simpson, Contact; Alison Ward, Advertising Coordinator. **ISSN:** 0147-5975. **Subscription Rates:** $114 U.S. and Canada; $148 other countries. **Remarks:** Accepts advertising.
Ad Rates: BW: $800 **Circ:** (Not Reported)
4C: $1,740

3198 Experimental Neurology
Academic Press
525 B St., Ste. 1900 Phone: (619)699-6557
San Diego, CA 92101-4495 Fax: (619)699-6305
Free: (800)894-3434
Publisher E-mail: apads@acad.com

International journal publishing original research results in neuroscience with emphasis on new findings in neural development, regeneration, plasticity, and transplantation. **Subtitle:** A Journal of Neuroscience Research. **Founded:** 1959. **Freq:** Monthly. **Trim Size:** 8 1/2 x 11. **Key Personnel:** John R. Sladek, Jr., Editor; Alison Ward, Advertising Coordinator. **ISSN:** 0014-4886. **Subscription Rates:** $696 U.S. and Canada; $873 other countries. **Remarks:** Accepts advertising. **URL:** http://www.expermentalneurology.com.
Ad Rates: BW: $800 **Circ:** (Not Reported)
4C: $1,740

3199 Experimental Parasitology
Academic Press
525 B St., Ste. 1900 Phone: (619)699-6557
San Diego, CA 92101-4495 Fax: (619)699-6305
Free: (800)894-3434
Publisher E-mail: apads@acad.com

Journal emphasizing modern approaches to parasitology, including molecular biology and immunology. **Founded:** 1952. **Freq:** 8/year. **Trim Size:** 6 7/8 x 10. **Key Personnel:** Dyann F. Wirth, Editor; Alison Ward, Advertising Mgr. **ISSN:** 0014-4894. **Subscription Rates:** $342 U.S. and Canada; $411 other countries. **Remarks:** Accepts advertising.
Ad Rates: BW: $800 **Circ:** (Not Reported)
4C: $1,740

3200 Explorations in Economic History
Academic Press
525 B St., Ste. 1900 Phone: (619)699-6557
San Diego, CA 92101-4495 Fax: (619)699-6305
Free: (800)894-3434
Publisher E-mail: apads@acad.com

Journal covering the application of economic analysis to history. **Founded:** 1970. **Freq:** Quarterly. **Trim Size:** 6 x 9. **Key Personnel:** Larry Neal, Editor; Alison Ward, Advertising Mgr. **ISSN:** 0014-4983. **Subscription Rates:** $136 U.S. and Canada; $168 other countries. **Remarks:** Accepts advertising.
Ad Rates: BW: $675 **Circ:** (Not Reported)
4C: $1,615

3201 Family Therapy
Libra Publishers, Inc.
3089C Clairemont Dr., Ste. 383 Phone: (619)571-1414
San Diego, CA 92117 Fax: (619)571-1414

Journal covering clinical, family, group, and interactional therapy. **Subtitle:** The Journal of the California Graduate School of Family Psychology. **Founded:** 1972. **Freq:** 3/year. **Print Method:** Offset. **Trim Size:** 6 x 9. **Cols./Page:** 1. **Col. Width:** 4 1/2 inches. **Col. Depth:** 7 inches. **Key Personnel:** Jonathon Kroll, Managing Editor. **ISSN:** 0091-6544. **Subscription Rates:** $77 institutions; $68 individuals.
Ad Rates: BW: $150 **Circ:** Paid ‡1,100
Non-paid ‡50

3202 Finite Fields and Their Applications
Academic Press
525 B St., Ste. 1900 Phone: (619)699-6557
San Diego, CA 92101-4495 Fax: (619)699-6305
Free: (800)894-3434
Publisher E-mail: apads@acad.com

Technical journal covering the finite field theory and applications. **Key Personnel:** Gary L. Mullen, Editor-in-Chief. **ISSN:** 1071-5797. **Subscription Rates:** $200 U.S. and Canada; $232 elsewhere. **URL:** http://www.academicpress.com/ffa.

3203 Food Microbiology
Academic Press
525 B St., Ste. 1900 Phone: (619)699-6557
San Diego, CA 92101-4495 Fax: (619)699-6305
Free: (800)894-3434
Publisher E-mail: apads@acad.com

Journal containing information on the microbiology of foods. **Founded:** 1994. **Freq:** Annual. **Key Personnel:** C. Batt, Editor. **ISSN:** 0740-0020. **Subscription Rates:** $227 individuals.

3204 Frontiers in Neuroendocrinology
Academic Press
525 B St., Ste. 1900 Phone: (619)699-6557
San Diego, CA 92101-4495 Fax: (619)699-6305
Free: (800)894-3434
Publisher E-mail: apads@acad.com

Scholarly journal covering brain-endocrine interactions. **Key Personnel:** William F. Ganong, Editor-in-Chief; Luciano Martini, Editor-in-Chief. **ISSN:** 0091-3022. **Subscription Rates:** $260 U.S. and Canada; $333 elsewhere. **URL:** http://www.academicpress.com/fine.

3205 Fundamental and Applied Toxicology
Academic Press
525 B St., Ste. 1900 Phone: (619)699-6557
San Diego, CA 92101-4495 Fax: (619)699-6305
Free: (800)894-3434
Publisher E-mail: apads@acad.com

Scientific journal on toxicology; contains articles assessing the risk of exposure to toxic agents to human and animal health. **Subtitle:** An Official Journal of the Society of Toxicology. **Founded:** 1981. **Freq:** 8/year. **Print Method:** Sheetfed offset. **Trim Size:** 8 1/2 x 11. **Cols./Page:** 2. **Key Personnel:** Henry A. D'Heck, Editor; Alison Ward, Advertising Coord. **ISSN:** 0272-0590. **Subscription Rates:** $264 U.S. and Canada; $313 other countries. **Remarks:** Accepts advertising. **URL:** http://www.fundamentalandappliedtoxicology.com.
Ad Rates: BW: $800 **Circ:** (Not Reported)
4C: $1,740

3206 Fungal Genetics and Biology
Academic Press
525 B St., Ste. 1900 Phone: (619)699-6557
San Diego, CA 92101-4495 Fax: (619)699-6305
Free: (800)894-3434
Publisher E-mail: apads@acad.com

Scholarly journal covering fungi. **Key Personnel:** John Hamer, Editor-in-Chief. **ISSN:** 0187-1845. **Subscription Rates:** $216 U.S. and Canada; $276 elsewhere. **URL:** http://www.academiopress.com/fgb.

3207 Games and Economic Behavior
Academic Press
525 B St., Ste. 1900 Phone: (619)699-6557
San Diego, CA 92101-4495 Fax: (619)699-6305
Free: (800)894-3434
Publisher E-mail: apads@acad.com

Journal publishing original and survey papers on game-theoretic modeling in the social, biological, and mathematical sciences. **Founded:** 1989. **Freq:** 8 /year. **Trim Size:** 6 x 9. **Key Personnel:** Ehud Kalai, Editor; Alison Ward, Advertising Coordinator. **ISSN:** 0899-8256. **Subscription Rates:** $122 U.S. and Canada; $147 other countries. **Remarks:** Accepts advertising. **URL:** http://www.aptnet.com.gamesandeconomic.behavior.com.
Ad Rates: BW: $675 **Circ:** (Not Reported)
4C: $1,615

3208 General and Comparative Endocrinology
Academic Press
525 B St., Ste. 1900 Phone: (619)699-6557
San Diego, CA 92101-4495 Fax: (619)699-6305
Free: (800)894-3434
Publisher E-mail: apads@acad.com

Journal on endocrinological research. **Subtitle:** Published under the Auspices of the Division of Comparative Endocrinology of the American Society of Zoologists. **Founded:** 1961. **Freq:** Monthly. **Print Method:** Offset. **Trim Size:** 6 7/8 x 10. **Key Personnel:** Frank L. Moore, Editor; Ian W. Henderson, Editor; Alison Ward, Advertising Coordinator. **ISSN:** 0016-6480. **Subscription Rates:** $650 U.S. and Canada; $745 other countries. **Remarks:** Accepts advertising.
Ad Rates: BW: $800 **Circ:** (Not Reported)
4C: $1,740

3209 Genomics
Academic Press
525 B St., Ste. 1900 Phone: (619)699-6557
San Diego, CA 92101-4495 Fax: (619)699-6305
Free: (800)894-3434
Publisher E-mail: apads@acad.com

Founded: 1987. **Freq:** Monthly 18/year. **Trim Size:** 8 1/2 x 11. **Key Personnel:** Victor A. McKusik, Editor; Raju S. Kucherlapati, Advertising Mgr.; Frank H. Ruddle, Editor; Alison Ward, Advertising Coordinator. **Subscription Rates:** $452 U.S. and Canada; $490 other countries. **Remarks:** Accepts advertising.
Ad Rates: BW: $800 **Circ:** (Not Reported)
4C: $1,740

3210 Graphical Models and Image Processing
Academic Press
525 B St., Ste. 1900 Phone: (619)699-6557
San Diego, CA 92101-4495 Fax: (619)699-6305
Free: (800)894-3434
Publisher E-mail: apads@acad.com

To focuses on the synthesis methods and computational methods underlying computer generated or processed imagery. **Founded:** 1983. **Freq:** Bimonthly. **Trim Size:** 8 1/2 x 11. **Key Personnel:** Norman Badler, Editor, phone (215)898-5862, fax (215)573-7453, badler@central.cis.upenn.edu; Ingrid Carlbom, phone (908)582-5501, carlbom@research.bell-labs.com; Alison Ward, Advertising Coordinator. **ISSN:** 1077-3169. **Subscription Rates:** $342.00 U.S. and Canada; $383.00 other countries. **Remarks:** Accepts advertising.
Ad Rates: BW: $675 **Circ:** (Not Reported)
4C: $1,615

3211 Guns Magazine
Publishers Development Corp.
591 Camino de la Reina, Ste. 200 Phone: (619)297-8520
San Diego, CA 92108 Fax: (619)297-5353
Free: (800)633-8001

Magazine on firearms and shooting sports. **Subtitle:** The Finest in the Firearms Field Since 1955. **Founded:** 1954. **Freq:** Monthly. **Print Method:** Offset. **Trim Size:** 8 x 10 7/8. **Cols./Page:** 3. **Col. Width:** 27 nonpareils. **Col. Depth:** 140 agate lines. **Key Personnel:** Scott Farrel, Editor; George E. von Rosen, Publisher; Denny Fallon, Advertising Mgr. **ISSN:** 1044-6257. **Subscription Rates:** $19.95 individuals; $2.95 single issue. **Remarks:** Accepts advertising.
Ad Rates: BW: $3,419 **Circ:** Paid 172,155
4C: $5,472

3212 Gynecologic Oncology
Academic Press
525 B St., Ste. 1900 Phone: (619)699-6557
San Diego, CA 92101-4495 Fax: (619)699-6305
Free: (800)894-3434
Publication E-mail: gyn@acad.com
Publisher E-mail: apads@acad.com

Journal dedicated to publishing clinical and investigative articles concerning tumors of the female reproductive tract. **Subtitle:** The Official Publication of the Society of Gynecologic Oncologists. **Founded:** 1972. **Freq:** Monthly. **Trim Size:** 8 1/2 x 11. **Key Personnel:** Anne Chen, Managing Editor, phone (619)699-6494, fax (619)699-6715, achen@acad.com; Melanie Nowark, Journal Coordinator, phone (619)699-6852, fax (619)699-6280. **ISSN:** 0090-8258. **Subscription Rates:** $995 U.S. and Canada; $1195 other countries. **Remarks:** Advertising accepted; rates available upon request. **URL:** http://www.apnet.com/www/journal/go.htm.
Circ: (Not Reported)

3213 Historia Mathematica
Academic Press
525 B St., Ste. 1900 Phone: (619)699-6557
San Diego, CA 92101-4495 Fax: (619)699-6305
Free: (800)894-3434
Publisher E-mail: apads@acad.com

Journal is concerned with the history of all aspects of the mathematical sciences in all parts of the world and from all historical periods. **Founded:** 1974. **Freq:** Quarterly. **Trim Size:** 6 7/8 x 10. **Key Personnel:** Eberhard Knobloch, Editor; David E. Rowe, Editor; Alison Ward, Advertising Coordinator. **ISSN:** 0315-0860. **Subscription Rates:** $112 U.S. and Canada; $137 other countries. **Remarks:** Accepts advertising.
Ad Rates: BW: $675 **Circ:** (Not Reported)
4C: $1,615

3214 Hormones and Behavior
Academic Press
525 B St., Ste. 1900 Phone: (619)699-6557
San Diego, CA 92101-4495 Fax: (619)699-6305
Free: (800)894-3434
Publisher E-mail: apads@acad.com

Journal covering the evolutionary significance of hormone-behavior and cellular and molecular mechanisms of hormonal actions on tissues relevant to behavior. **Founded:** 1969. **Freq:** Quarterly. **Trim Size:** 6 x 9. **Key Personnel:** Robert Goy, Editor; Richard E. Whalen, Contact; Alison Ward, Advertising Coordinator. **ISSN:** 0018-506X. **Subscription Rates:** $169 U.S. and Canada; $213 other countries. **Remarks:** Accepts advertising.
Ad Rates: BW: $660 **Circ:** (Not Reported)
4C: $1,575

3215 Icarus
Academic Press
525 B St., Ste. 1900 Phone: (619)699-6557
San Diego, CA 92101-4495 Fax: (619)699-6305
Free: (800)894-3434
Publisher E-mail: apads@acad.com

Publication is devoted to original contributions in the field of planetary science. **Subtitle:** An International Journal of Solar System Studies. **Founded:** 1962. **Freq:** Monthly. **Trim Size:** 8 1/2 x 11. **Key Personnel:** Joseph A. Burns, Editor; Alison Ward, Advertising Coordinator. **ISSN:** 0019-1035. **Subscription Rates:** $966 U.S. and Canada; $1,096 other countries. **Remarks:** Accepts advertising.
Ad Rates: BW: $800 **Circ:** (Not Reported)
4C: $1,740

3216 IDEA Personal Trainer
IDEA Inc.
6190 Cornerstone Ct. E, No. 204 Phone: (619)535-8979
San Diego, CA 92121-3773 Fax: (619)535-8234
Free: (800)999-4332
Publisher E-mail: member@ideafit.com

Trade magazine covering business operation and other issues for personal trainers in the health and fitness industry. **Freq:** 10/year. **Print Method:** Web offset. **Trim Size:** 8 1/4 x 11. **Key Personnel:** Peter Davis, Publisher; Patricia Ryan, Editor; Colleen Sharp, New Products Editor. **Subscription Rates:** $95 individuals. **Remarks:** Accepts advertising.
Ad Rates: BW: $1,115 **Circ:** Combined 10,000
4C: $1,795

3217 IDEA Today
IDEA, Inc.
6190 Cornerstone Ct. E, No. 204
San Diego, CA 92121-3773

Trade magazine covering health and fitness research and information for fitness professionals, including instructors, personal trainers, program directors, and club/studio owners. **Freq:** 10/year. **Print Method:** Web offset. **Trim Size:** 8 1/2 x 11. **Key Personnel:** Peter Davis, Publisher; Diane Lofshult, Editor; Therese Hannon, New Products Editor. **Subscription Rates:** $75 individuals. **Remarks:** Accepts advertising.
Ad Rates: BW: $1,778 **Circ:** Paid 23,000
4C: $2,850

3218 ImmunoMethods
Academic Press
525 B St., Ste. 1900 Phone: (619)699-6557
San Diego, CA 92101-4495 Fax: (619)699-6305
Free: (800)894-3434
Publisher E-mail: apads@acad.com

Journal containing information on immunological methods and their applications. **Founded:** 1994. **Freq:** Bimonthly. **Trim Size:** 8 1/2 x 11. **Key Personnel:** John J. Langone, Editor-in-Chief; Alison Ward, Advertising Coordinator. **ISSN:** 1058-6687. **Subscription Rates:** $241 individuals; $241 Canada; $301 other countries. **Remarks:** Accepts advertising.
Ad Rates: BW: $800 **Circ:** (Not Reported)
4C: $1,740

3219 Infant—Toddler Intervention
Singular Publishing Group Inc.
401 W. A St., Ste. 325 Phone: (619)238-6777
San Diego, CA 92101 Fax: (619)238-6789
Free: (800)521-8545
Publisher E-mail: singpub@mail.cerfnet.com

Professional journal covering clinical research, programs, and advocacy issues regarding intervention for early childhood practitioners. **Subtitle:** The Transdisciplinary Journal. **Founded:** 1991. **Freq:** Quarterly. **Print Method:** Offset. **Trim Size:** 7 x 10. **Cols./Page:** 2. **Key Personnel:** Louis M. Rossetti, Ph.D., Editor, phone (920)424-2421, rossetti@uwosh.edu; Angie S. Singh, Advertising/Circulation, asingh@singpub.com. **ISSN:** 1053-5586. **Subscription Rates:** $45 individuals; $90 institutions; $40 single issue. **Remarks:** Advertising accepted; rates available upon request.
Circ: Paid 780

3220 Information and Computation
Academic Press
525 B St., Ste. 1900 Phone: (619)699-6557
San Diego, CA 92101-4495 Fax: (619)699-6305
Free: (800)894-3434
Publisher E-mail: apads@acad.com

Journal publishing original papers on theoretical computer sciences and computational aspects of information theory. **Founded:** 1957. **Freq:** 16/year. **Trim Size:** 8 1/2 x 11. **Key Personnel:** Albert R. Meyer, Editor; Alison Ward, Advertising Coordinator. **ISSN:** 0890-5401. **Subscription Rates:** $552 U.S. and Canada; $687 other countries. **Remarks:** Accepts advertising. **URL:** http://www.aptnet.com.(information&computation).com.
Ad Rates: BW: $675 **Circ:** (Not Reported)
4C: $1,615

3221 The Insurance Journal of the West
Wells Publishing, Inc.
9191 Towne Centre Dr., No. 550 Phone: (619)455-7717
San Diego, CA 92122 Fax: (619)546-1462
Publisher E-mail: ijwest@insurancejrnl.com

Trade journal covering insurance. **Founded:** 1923. **Freq:** Semimonthly. **Key Personnel:** Ellen Coffey, Managing Editor; Dena Kaplan, Assoc. Publisher/Advertising; Alfonso Santana, Production Mgr.; Katie Robley, Circulation Mgr.; Mark Wells, Publisher. **Subscription Rates:** $78 individuals. **Remarks:** Accepts advertising.
Ad Rates: BW: $2,069 **Circ:** Controlled 9,000
4C: $3,058
PCI: $82

3222 International Spectrum
IDBMA, Inc.
10675 Treena St., Ste. 103 Phone: (619)578-3152
San Diego, CA 92131 Fax: (619)271-1032
Free: (800)767-SHOW

News magazine for the computer industry focusing on the PICK/UNIX/DOS-based computer operating environment. **Subtitle:** The Businessperson's Computer Magazine. **Founded:** Mar. 1984. **Freq:** Bimonthly. **Print Method:** Offset. Accepts mats. **Trim Size:** 8 3/8 x 10 7/8. **Cols./Page:** 3. **Col. Width:** 2 1/4 inches. **Col. Depth:** 9 7/8 inches. **Key Personnel:** Nichelle Johnson, Editor; Gus Giobbi, Publisher; Monica Giobbi, Business Mgr. **ISSN:** 1050-9070. **Subscription Rates:** $40 individuals; $7 single issue.
Ad Rates: BW: $1,560 **Circ:** Controlled 22,500
4C: $2,350

3223 Journal of Algebra
Academic Press
525 B St., Ste. 1900 Phone: (619)699-6557
San Diego, CA 92101-4495 Fax: (619)699-6305
Free: (800)894-3434
Publisher E-mail: apads@acad.com

Journal publishing original research in the field of algebra. **Founded:** 1964. **Freq:** 24/year. **Trim Size:** 6 x 9. **Key Personnel:** Walter Feit, Editor; Alison Ward, Advertising Coordinator. **ISSN:** 0021-8693. **Subscription Rates:** $1,085 U.S. and Canada; $1,280 other countries. **Remarks:** Accepts advertising.
Ad Rates: BW: $675 **Circ:** (Not Reported)
4C: $1,615

3224 Journal of Algorithms
Academic Press
525 B St., Ste. 1900 Phone: (619)699-6557
San Diego, CA 92101-4495 Fax: (619)699-6305
Free: (800)894-3434
Publisher E-mail: apads@acad.com

Journal presenting papers on algorithms. **Founded:** 1980. **Freq:** Quarterly. **Trim Size:** 5 7/8 x 9. **Key Personnel:** Donald E. Knuth, Editor; David S. Johnson, Contact; Zvi Galil, Advertising Mgr.; Alison Ward, Editor. **ISSN:** 0196-6774. **Subscription Rates:** $155 U.S. and Canada; $189 other countries. **Remarks:** Accepts advertising.
Ad Rates: BW: $660 **Circ:** (Not Reported)
4C: $1,575

3225 Journal of the American College of Dentists
American College of Dentists
4403 Marlborough Ave. Phone: (619)283-2203
San Diego, CA 92116 Fax: (619)283-2203

Journal reporting on ideas, advances, and opinions in dentistry. **Founded:** 1934. **Freq:** Quarterly. **Print Method:** Offset. **Trim Size:** 8 1/2 x 11. **Cols./Page:** 3. **Key Personnel:** Keith P. Blair, Editor. **ISSN:** 0002-7979. **Subscription Rates:** $30 individuals. **Remarks:** Advertising not accepted.
Circ: Controlled ‡5,000

3226 Journal of Anthropological Archaeology
Academic Press
525 B St., Ste. 1900 Phone: (619)699-6557
San Diego, CA 92101-4495 Fax: (619)699-6305
Free: (800)894-3434
Publisher E-mail: apads@acad.com

Journal covering the development of theory and methodology for the systematic understanding of the organization, operation, and evolution of human societies. **Founded:** 1982. **Freq:** Quarterly. **Trim Size:** 6 7/8 x 10. **Key Personnel:** Robert

Whallon, Ann Ar, Editor; Alison Ward, Advertising Mgr. **ISSN:** 0278-4165. **Subscription Rates:** $84 U.S. and Canada; $108 other countries. **Remarks:** Accepts advertising.
Ad Rates: BW: $675 **Circ:** (Not Reported)
4C: $1,615

3227 Journal of Approximation Theory
Academic Press
525 B St., Ste. 1900 Phone: (619)699-6557
San Diego, CA 92101-4495 Fax: (619)699-6305
Free: (800)894-3434
Publisher E-mail: apads@acad.com

Journal is devoted to new advances in pure and applied approxiamation theory. **Founded:** 1968. **Freq:** Monthly. **Trim Size:** 6 x 9. **Key Personnel:** Paul Nevai, Columb, Editor; Alison Ward, Advertising Coordinator. **ISSN:** 0021-9045. **Subscription Rates:** $486 U.S. and Canada; $570 other countries. **Remarks:** Accepts advertising.
Ad Rates: BW: $675 **Circ:** (Not Reported)
4C: $1,615

3228 Journal of Catalysis
Academic Press
525 B St., Ste. 1900 Phone: (619)699-6557
San Diego, CA 92101-4495 Fax: (619)699-6305
Free: (800)894-3434
Publisher E-mail: apads@acad.com

Journal reporting original research data on heterogeneous and homogeneous catalysis, studies relating catalytic properties with chemical processes at surfaces, studies of the chemistry of surfaces, and engineering studies related to catalysis. **Founded:** 1962. **Freq:** 14/year. **Trim Size:** 8 1/2 x 11. **Key Personnel:** Gary L. Haller, Editor; Frank S. Stone, Advertising Mgr. **ISSN:** 0021-9517. **Subscription Rates:** $1,098 U.S. and Canada; $1,282 other countries. **Remarks:** Accepts advertising. **URL:** http://www.journalofcatalysis.com.
Ad Rates: BW: $850 **Circ:** (Not Reported)
4C: $1,895

3229 Journal of Colloid and Interface Science
Academic Press
525 B St., Ste. 1900 Phone: (619)699-6557
San Diego, CA 92101-4495 Fax: (619)699-6305
Free: (800)894-3434
Publisher E-mail: apads@acad.com

Journal publishing original research data on fundamental principles and their applications in chemistry, physics, engineering, biology, and applied mathematics. **Founded:** 1946. **Freq:** 16/year. **Trim Size:** 8 1/2 x 11. **Key Personnel:** Milton Kerker, Editor; Josip P. Kratohvil, Contact; Alison Ward, Advertising Coordinator. **ISSN:** 1121-9797. **Subscription Rates:** $1,145 U.S. and Canada; $1,335 other countries. **Remarks:** Accepts advertising. **URL:** http://www.aptnet.com.journalofcolloidandinterfacescience.co.
Ad Rates: BW: $800 **Circ:** (Not Reported)
4C: $1,740

3230 Journal of Combinatorial Theory–Series A
Academic Press
525 B St., Ste. 1900 Phone: (619)699-6557
San Diego, CA 92101-4495 Fax: (619)699-6305
Free: (800)894-3434
Publisher E-mail: apads@acad.com

Journal publishing mathematical research on the theoretical and physical aspects of the study of finite and discrete structures in all branches of science. **Founded:** 1971. **Freq:** 8/year. **Trim Size:** 6 x 9. **Key Personnel:** Basil Gordon, Managing Editor; Bruce Rothschild, Contact; Alison Ward, Advertising Coordinator. **ISSN:** 0097-3165. **Subscription Rates:** $468 U.S. and Canada; $570 other countries. **Remarks:** Accepts advertising.
Ad Rates: BW: $675 **Circ:** (Not Reported)
4C: $1,615

3231 Journal of Combinatorial Theory–Series B
Academic Press
525 B St., Ste. 1900 Phone: (619)699-6557
San Diego, CA 92101-4495 Fax: (619)699-6305
Free: (800)894-3434
Publisher E-mail: apads@acad.com

Journal publishing mathematical research on the theoretical and physical aspects of the study of finite and discrete structures in science. **Freq:** Bimonthly. **Trim Size:** 6 x 9. **Key Personnel:** Adrian Bondy, Editor; Alison Ward, Advertising Coordinator. **ISSN:** 0095-8956. **Subscription Rates:** $342 U.S. and Canada; $413 other countries. **Remarks:** Accepts advertising.
Ad Rates: BW: $675 **Circ:** (Not Reported)
4C: $1,615

3232 Journal of Comparative Economics
Academic Press
525 B St., Ste. 1900 Phone: (619)699-6557
San Diego, CA 92101-4495 Fax: (619)699-6305
Free: (800)894-3434
Publisher E-mail: apads@acad.com

Journal devoted to the study and analysis of contemporary, historical, and hypothetical economic systems. **Subtitle:** The Journal of the Association for Comparative Economic Studies. **Founded:** 1977. **Freq:** Quarterly. **Trim Size:** 6 x 9. **Key Personnel:** Josef C. Brada, Editor; Alison Ward, Advertising Coordinator. **ISSN:** 0147-5967. **Subscription Rates:** $176 U.S and Canada; $215 other countries. **Remarks:** Accepts advertising.
Ad Rates: BW: $675 **Circ:** (Not Reported)
4C: $1,615

3233 Journal of Complexity
Academic Press
525 B St., Ste. 1900 Phone: (619)699-6557
San Diego, CA 92101-4495 Fax: (619)699-6305
Free: (800)894-3434
Publisher E-mail: apads@acad.com

Journal original research papers contains substantial mathematical results on complexity. **Founded:** 1985. **Freq:** Quarterly. **Trim Size:** 5 7/8 x 9. **Key Personnel:** Joseph F. Traub, New Yo, Editor; Alison Ward, Advertising Coordinator. **ISSN:** 0885-064X. **Subscription Rates:** $121 U.S. and Canada; $146 other countries. **Remarks:** Accepts advertising.
Ad Rates: BW: $675 **Circ:** (Not Reported)
4C: $1,615

3234 Journal of Computational Physics
Academic Press
525 B St., Ste. 1900 Phone: (619)699-6557
San Diego, CA 92101-4495 Fax: (619)699-6305
Free: (800)894-3434
Publisher E-mail: apads@acad.com

Journal covering the computational aspects of physical problems. **Founded:** 1966. **Freq:** 14/year. **Trim Size:** 8 1/2 x 11. **Key Personnel:** Bernie J. Adler, Advertising Manager; Alison Ward, Advertising Coordinator. **ISSN:** 0021-9991. **Subscription Rates:** $996 U.S. and Canada; $1,202 other countries. **Remarks:** Accepts advertising.
Ad Rates: BW: $675 **Circ:** (Not Reported)
4C: $1,615

3235 Journal of Computer and System Sciences
Academic Press
525 B St., Ste. 1900 Phone: (619)699-6557
San Diego, CA 92101-4495 Fax: (619)699-6305
Free: (800)894-3434
Publisher E-mail: apads@acad.com

Journal focuses on the publication of original research in computer science and system science, with particular attention given to the pertinent mathematical theory and its applications. **Freq:** Bimonthly. **Trim Size:** 8 1/2 x 11. **Key Personnel:** E.K. Blum, Los An, Managing Editor; Alison Ward, Advertising Coordinator. **ISSN:** 0022-0000. **Subscription Rates:** $384 U.S. and Canada; $456 other countries. **Remarks:** Accepts advertising.
Ad Rates: BW: $675 **Circ:** (Not Reported)
4C: $1,615

3236 Journal of Differential Equations
Academic Press
525 B St., Ste. 1900 Phone: (619)699-6557
San Diego, CA 92101-4495 Fax: (619)699-6305
Free: (800)894-3434
Publisher E-mail: apads@acad.com

Journal addressing the theory and application of differential equations. **Founded:** 1965. **Freq:** 18/year. **Trim Size:** 6 x 9. **Key Personnel:** Jack K. Hale, Atlant, Editor; Alison Ward, Advertising Coordinator. **ISSN:** 0022-0396. **Subscription Rates:** $759 U.S. and Canada; $892 other countries. **Remarks:** Accepts advertising.
Ad Rates: BW: $675 **Circ:** (Not Reported)
4C: $1,615

3237 Journal of Economic Theory
Academic Press
525 B St., Ste. 1900 Phone: (619)699-6557
San Diego, CA 92101-4495 Fax: (619)699-6305
Free: (800)894-3434
Publisher E-mail: apads@acad.com

Journal publishing original research on economic theory with an emphasis on the theoretical analysis of economic models. Includes research on related mathematic techniques. **Founded:** 1969. **Freq:** Bimonthly. **Trim Size:** 6 x 9. **Key Personnel:** Karl Shell, Ithaca, Editor; Alison Ward, Advertising Coordinator. **ISSN:** 0022-0531. **Subscription Rates:** $433.50 U.S. and Canada; $516.50 other countries. **Remarks:** Accepts advertising.
Ad Rates: BW: $675 **Circ:** (Not Reported)
4C: $1,615

3238 Journal of Environmental Economics and Management
Academic Press
525 B St., Ste. 1900 Phone: (619)699-6557
San Diego, CA 92101-4495 Fax: (619)699-6305
Free: (800)894-3434
Publisher E-mail: apads@acad.com

Journal publishing theoretical and empirical papers on the relation between economic systems and environmental and natural resources systems. **Founded:** 1975. **Freq:** Bimonthly. **Trim Size:** 6 7/8 x 10. **Key Personnel:** Ronald G. Cummings, Albuqu, Managing Editor; Alison Ward, Advertising Coordinator. **ISSN:** 0095-0696. **Subscription Rates:** $182 U.S. and Canada; $226 other countries. **Remarks:** Accepts advertising.
Ad Rates: BW: $800 **Circ:** (Not Reported)
4C: $1,740

3239 Journal of Environmental Management
Academic Press
525 B St., Ste. 1900 Phone: (619)699-6557
San Diego, CA 92101-4495 Fax: (619)699-6305
Free: (800)894-3434
Publisher E-mail: apads@acad.com

Journal containing information on all aspects of management and use of the environment, both natural and man-made. **Founded:** 1994. **Freq:** Monthly. **Key Personnel:** J.N.R. Jeffers, Editor. **ISSN:** 0301-4797. **Subscription Rates:** $475 individuals. **URL:** http://www.aptnet.com.journalofenvironmetalmanagement.com.

3240 Journal of Environmental Psychology
Academic Press
525 B St., Ste. 1900 Phone: (619)699-6557
San Diego, CA 92101-4495 Fax: (619)699-6305
Free: (800)894-3434
Publisher E-mail: apads@acad.com

Journal containing information on the scientific development and maturation of the study of environmental psychology. **Founded:** 1994. **Freq:** Quarterly. **Key Personnel:** D.V. Canter, Editor. **ISSN:** 0272-4944. **Subscription Rates:** $156 individuals. **URL:** http://www.aptnet.com.journalofenvironmentalpsychology.com.

3241 Journal of Experimental Child Psychology
Academic Press
525 B St., Ste. 1900 Phone: (619)699-6557
San Diego, CA 92101-4495 Fax: (619)699-6305
Free: (800)894-3434
Publisher E-mail: apads@acad.com

Journal covering the psychology of child behavior. **Founded:** 1964. **Freq:** Bimonthly. **Trim Size:** 5 7/8 x 9. **Key Personnel:** Prof. Hayne W. Reese, Contact; Alison Ward, Advertising Coordinator. **ISSN:** 0022-0965. **Subscription Rates:** $274 U.S. and Canada; $333 other countries. **Remarks:** Accepts advertising.
Ad Rates: BW: $675 **Circ:** (Not Reported)
4C: $1,615

3242 Journal of Experimental Social Psychology
Academic Press
525 B St., Ste. 1900 Phone: (619)699-6557
San Diego, CA 92101-4495 Fax: (619)699-6305
Free: (800)894-3434
Publisher E-mail: apads@acad.com

Journal publishing original research and theory on social interaction. **Founded:** 1965. **Freq:** Bimonthly. **Trim Size:** 5 7/8 x 9. **Key Personnel:** Prof. David M. Messick, Contact; Alison Ward, Advertising Coordinator. **ISSN:** 0022-1031. **Subscription Rates:** $155 U.S. and Canada; $196 other countries. **Remarks:** Accepts advertising.
Ad Rates: BW: $675 **Circ:** (Not Reported)
4C: $1,615

3243 Journal of Financial Intermediation
Academic Press
525 B St., Ste. 1900 Phone: (619)699-6557
San Diego, CA 92101-4495 Fax: (619)699-6305
Free: (800)894-3434
Publisher E-mail: apads@acad.com

Publication offering a unifying perspective on the evolution of institutions and the finanioal intermediation process. **Founded:** 1990. **Freq:** Quarterly. **Trim Size:** 5 7/8 x 9. **Key Personnel:** Stuart I. Greenbaum, Managing Editor; Alison Ward, Advertising Coordinator. **Subscription Rates:** $130 U.S. and Canada; $143 other countries. **Remarks:** Accepts advertising.
Ad Rates: BW: $675 **Circ:** (Not Reported)
4C: $1,615

3244 Journal of Food Composition and Analysis
Academic Press
525 B St., Ste. 1900 Phone: (619)699-6557
San Diego, CA 92101-4495 Fax: (619)699-6305
Free: (800)894-3434
Publisher E-mail: apads@acad.com

Journal publishing data on the chemical composition of human foods. **Subtitle:** An official publication of The United Nations University International Network of Food Data Systems. **Founded:** 1987. **Freq:** Quarterly. **Trim Size:** 6 7/8 x 10. **Key Personnel:** Kent K. Stewart, Editor; George H. Beaton, Advertising Mgr.; Ricardo Bressani, Editor; Osman Galal, Editor; William M. Rand, Contact; Kyo den Yasumoto, Editor; Alison Ward, Advertising Coordinator. **ISSN:** 0889-1575. **Subscription Rates:** $96 U.S. and Canada; $112 other countries. **Remarks:** Accepts advertising.
Ad Rates: BW: $800 **Circ:** (Not Reported)
4C: $1,740

3245 Journal of Functional Analysis
Academic Press
525 B St., Ste. 1900 Phone: (619)699-6557
San Diego, CA 92101-4495 Fax: (619)699-6305
Free: (800)894-3434
Publisher E-mail: apads@acad.com

Journal presenting original research papers in all scientific disciplines in which functional analysis plays an important role. **Founded:** May 1967. **Freq:** 16/year. **Trim Size:** 6 x 9. **Cols./Page:** 1. **Key Personnel:** Paul Malliavin, Editor; Ralph S. Phillips, Advertising Mgr.; Irving Segal, Managing Editor; Alison Ward, Advertising Coordinator. **ISSN:** 0022-1236. **Subscription Rates:** $1,012 U.S. and Canada; $1,185 other countries. **Remarks:** Accepts advertising.
Ad Rates: BW: $675 **Circ:** (Not Reported)
4C: $1,615

3246 Journal of Housing Economics
Academic Press
525 B St., Ste. 1900 Phone: (619)699-6557
San Diego, CA 92101-4495 Fax: (619)699-6305
Free: (800)894-3434
Publisher E-mail: apads@acad.com

Journal containing information on economic research related to housing and analytical techniques on housing-related questions. **Founded:** 1993. **Freq:** Quarterly. **Trim Size:** 6 x 9. **Key Personnel:** Henry O. Pollakowski, Editor; Alison Ward, Advertising Coordinator. **ISSN:** 1051-1377. **Subscription Rates:** $110 individuals; $135 Canada; $135 other countries. **Remarks:** Accepts advertising.
Ad Rates: BW: $675 **Circ:** (Not Reported)
4C: $1,615

3247 Journal of Invertebrate Pathology
Academic Press
525 B St., Ste. 1900 Phone: (619)699-6557
San Diego, CA 92101-4495 Fax: (619)699-6305
Free: (800)894-3434
Publisher E-mail: apads@acad.com

Journal publishing research concerned with the nature and study of infectious and noninfectious diseases of invertebrates. **Subtitle:** Published under the auspices of the Society for Invertebrate Pathology. **Founded:** 1959. **Freq:** Bimonthly. **Trim Size:** 8 1/2 x 11. **Key Personnel:** Carol Reinisch, Contact; Katherine Scroop, Advertising Coordinator, kscroop@acad.com. **ISSN:** 0022-2011. **Subscription Rates:** $550 U.S. and Canada; $665 other countries. **Remarks:** Accepts advertising.
Ad Rates: BW: $800 **Circ:** (Not Reported)
4C: $1,740

3248 Journal of Japanese and International Economics
Academic Press
525 B St., Ste. 1900 Phone: (619)699-6557
San Diego, CA 92101-4495 Fax: (619)699-6305
Free: (800)894-3434
Publication E-mail: toniross-smith@acad.com
Publisher E-mail: apads@acad.com

Journal publishing academic analyses of the Japanese economy and its interdependence with other national economies. **Subtitle:** Published in cooperation with the Tokyo Center for Economic Research. **Founded:** 1987. **Freq:** Quarterly. **Trim Size:** 6 x 9. **Key Personnel:** Prof. Masahiko Aoki, Contact; Alison Ward, Advertising Coordinator. **ISSN:** 0889-1583. **Subscription Rates:** $130 U.S. and Canada; $151 other countries. **Remarks:** Accepts advertising.
Ad Rates: BW: $675 **Circ:** (Not Reported)
4C: $1,615

3249 Journal of Magnetic Resonance
Academic Press
525 B St., Ste. 1900 Phone: (619)699-6557
San Diego, CA 92101-4495 Fax: (619)699-6305
Free: (800)894-3434
Publisher E-mail: apads@acad.com

Scholarly journal covering nuclear magnetic resonance and related topics. **Key Personnel:** Stanley J. Opella, Editor. **ISSN:** 1090-7807. **Subscription Rates:** $1,990 U.S. and Canada; $2,308 elsewhere. **URL:** http://www.academicpress.com/jmr.

3250 Journal of Magnetic Resonance - Series A
Academic Press
525 B St., Ste. 1900 Phone: (619)699-6557
San Diego, CA 92101-4495 Fax: (619)699-6305
Free: (800)894-3434
Publisher E-mail: apads@acad.com

Leading source of up-to-date authoritive information on theory, techniques, methods of spectral analysis and interpretation, spectral correlations, and results of magnetic resonance spectroscopy. **Founded:** 1969. **Freq:** Monthly 15/year. **Trim Size:** 8 1/2 x 11. **Key Personnel:** Wallace S. Brey, Jr., Editor; Alison Ward, Advertising Coord. **ISSN:** 1064-1858. **Subscription Rates:** $990 U.S. and Canada; $1,179 other countries. **Remarks:** Accepts advertising. **URL:** http://www.aptnet.com.journalofmagneticresonance-seriesa.com.
Ad Rates: BW: $800 **Circ:** (Not Reported)
4C: $1,740

3251 Journal of Magnetic Resonance - Series B
Academic Press
525 B St., Ste. 1900 Phone: (619)699-6557
San Diego, CA 92101-4495 Fax: (619)699-6305
Free: (800)894-3434
Publisher E-mail: apads@acad.com

Journal containing information on biological or biochemical significance. **Founded:** 1994. **Freq:** 9/year. **Trim Size:** 8 1/2 x 11. **Key Personnel:** Wallace S. Brey, Editor; Alison Ward, Advertising Coordinator. **ISSN:** 1064-1866. **Subscription Rates:** $345 individuals; $345 Canada; $414 other countries. **Remarks:** Accepts advertising.
Ad Rates: BW: $800 **Circ:** (Not Reported)
4C: $1,740

3252 Journal of Marine Science
Academic Press
525 B St., Ste. 1900 Phone: (619)699-6557
San Diego, CA 92101-4495 Fax: (619)699-6305
Free: (800)894-3434
Publisher E-mail: apads@acad.com

Scholarly journal covering marine science. **Key Personnel:** Niels Daan, Editor; J. W. Ramster, Asst. Editor. **ISSN:** 1054-3139. **Subscription Rates:** $320 individuals. **URL:** http://www.academicpress.com/icesjms.

3253 Journal of Mathematical Psychology
Academic Press
525 B St., Ste. 1900 Phone: (619)699-6557
San Diego, CA 92101-4495 Fax: (619)699-6305
Free: (800)894-3434
Publisher E-mail: apads@acad.com

Journal publishing empirical and theoretical papers in mathematical psychology. **Founded:** 1964. **Freq:** Quarterly. **Trim Size:** 8 1/2 x 11. **Key Personnel:** Thomas S. Wallesten, Editor; Alison Ward, Advertising Coordinator. **ISSN:** 0022-2496. **Subscription Rates:** $200 U.S. and Canada; $246 other countries. **Remarks:** Accepts advertising. **URL:** http://www.aptnet.com.journalofmathematical&psychology.com.
Ad Rates: BW: $675 **Circ:** (Not Reported)
4C: $1,615

3254 Journal of Memory and Language
Academic Press
525 B St., Ste. 1900 Phone: (619)699-6557
San Diego, CA 92101-4495 Fax: (619)699-6305
Free: (800)894-3434
Publisher E-mail: apads@acad.com

Journal contributing to the formulation of scientific issues and theories in the areas of language comprehension and production; and human learning and memory. **Founded:** 1985. **Freq:** Bimonthly. **Trim Size:** 6 7/8 x 10. **Key Personnel:** Edward J. Shoben, Contact; Alison Ward, Advertising Coordinator. **ISSN:** 0749-596X. **Subscription Rates:** $155 U.S. and Canada; $188 other countries. **Remarks:** Accepts advertising. **URL:** http://www.aptnet.com.journalofmemoryandlanguage.com.
Ad Rates: BW: $675 **Circ:** (Not Reported)
4C: $1,615

3255 Journal of Molecular Spectroscopy
Academic Press
525 B St., Ste. 1900 Phone: (619)699-6557
San Diego, CA 92101-4495 Fax: (619)699-6305
Free: (800)894-3434
Publisher E-mail: apads@acad.com

Journal publishing experimental and theoretical articles on subjects relevant to molecular spectroscopy and its modern applications. **Founded:** 1957. **Freq:** Monthly. **Trim Size:** 6 7/8 x 10. **Key Personnel:** K. Narahari Rao, Editor; Alison Ward, Advertising Coord. **ISSN:** 0022-2852. **Subscription Rates:** $1,032 U.S. and Canada; $1,196 other countries. **Remarks:** Accepts advertising. **URL:** http://www.aptnet.com.journalofmolecularspectroscopy.com.
Ad Rates: BW: $800 **Circ:** (Not Reported)
4C: $1,740

3256 Journal of Multivariate Analysis
Academic Press
525 B St., Ste. 1900 Phone: (619)699-6557
San Diego, CA 92101-4495 Fax: (619)699-6305
Free: (800)894-3434
Publisher E-mail: apads@acad.com

Journal publishing articles on fundamental theoretical aspects of multivariate analysis. **Founded:** 1971. **Freq:** 8/year. **Trim Size:** 6 x 9. **Key Personnel:** C.R. Rao, Editor; Alison Ward, Advertising Coordinator. **ISSN:** 0047-259X. **Subscription Rates:** $436 U.S. and Canada; $532 other countries. **Remarks:** Accepts advertising.
Ad Rates: BW: $675 **Circ:** (Not Reported)
4C: $1,615

3257 Journal of Network and Computer Applications
Academic Press
525 B St., Ste. 1900 Phone: (619)699-6557
San Diego, CA 92101-4495 Fax: (619)699-6305
Free: (800)894-3434
Publisher E-mail: apads@acad.com

Scholarly journal covering networked computer systems. **Key Personnel:** H. Maurer, Editor-in-Chief. **ISSN:** 1084-8045. **Subscription Rates:** $220 individuals. **URL:** http://www.apnet.com/wwa/ap/jnca.

3258 Journal of Number Theory
Academic Press
525 B St., Ste. 1900 Phone: (619)699-6557
San Diego, CA 92101-4495 Fax: (619)699-6305
Free: (800)894-3434
Publisher E-mail: apads@acad.com

Journal publishing selected research articles on contemporary number thoery and related areas. **Founded:** 1962. **Freq:** Monthly. **Trim Size:** 6 x 9. **Key Personnel:** Hans Zassenhaus, Editor; Alison Ward, Advertising Coordinator. **ISSN:** 0022-314X. **Subscription Rates:** $408 U.S. and Canada; $505 other countries. **Remarks:** Accepts advertising.
Ad Rates: BW: $675 **Circ:** (Not Reported)
4C: $1,615

3259 Journal of Parallel and Distributed Computing
Academic Press
525 B St., Ste. 1900 Phone: (619)699-6557
San Diego, CA 92101-4495 Fax: (619)699-6305
Free: (800)894-3434
Publisher E-mail: apads@acad.com

Journal publishing original research papers and timely review articles on the theory, design, evaluation, and practices of parallel and distributed computing systems. **Founded:** 1984. **Freq:** Monthly 16/year. **Trim Size:** 8 1/2 x 11. **Key Personnel:** Kai Hwang, Contact; Howard Jay Siegel, Editor; Alison Ward, Advertising Coordinator. **ISSN:** 0743-7315. **Subscription Rates:** $295.50 U.S. and Canada; $367.50 other countries. **Remarks:** Accepts advertising.
Ad Rates: BW: $675 **Circ:** (Not Reported)
4C: $1,615

3260 Journal of Rehabilitation Administration
National Rehabilitation Administration Association
PO Box 19891
San Diego, CA 92159
Publication E-mail: libsack@mail.sdsu.edu

Journal of the National Rehabilitation Administration Association. **Founded:** 1976. **Freq:** Quarterly. **Subscription Rates:** $24 individuals; $48 institutions. **Remarks:** Advertising accepted; rates available upon request.
Circ: Paid 2,000

3261 Journal of Research in Personality
Academic Press
525 B St., Ste. 1900 Phone: (619)699-6557
San Diego, CA 92101-4495 Fax: (619)699-6305
Free: (800)894-3434
Publisher E-mail: apads@acad.com

Journal publishing articles on issues in the field of personality study, including the genetic, physiological, motivational, learning, perceptual, cognitive, and social processes of both normal and abnormal personalities in humans and animals. **Founded:** 1965. **Freq:** Quarterly. **Trim Size:** 5 7/8 x 9. **Key Personnel:** William Griffith, Editor; Alison Ward, Advertising Coordinator. **ISSN:** 0092-6566. **Subscription Rates:** $151 U.S. and Canada; $187 other countries. **Remarks:** Accepts advertising.
Ad Rates: BW: $675 **Circ:** (Not Reported)
4C: $1,615

3262 Journal of San Diego History
San Diego Historical Society
PO Box 81825 Phone: (619)232-6203
San Diego, CA 92138 Fax: (619)232-6297

Historical journal. **Freq:** Quarterly. **Trim Size:** 6 5/8 x 10. **Cols./Page:** 1. **Key Personnel:** Richard W. Crawford, Editor, crawford@cfs.com. **ISSN:** 0022-4383. **Subscription Rates:** $40 individuals; $7 single issue. **Remarks:** Accepts advertising.
Ad Rates: BW: $400 **Circ:** Combined 3,200

3263 Journal of Solid State Chemistry
Academic Press
525 B St., Ste. 1900 Phone: (619)699-6557
San Diego, CA 92101-4495 Fax: (619)699-6305
Free: (800)894-3434
Publisher E-mail: apads@acad.com

Journal covering major developments and studies in the field of solid state chemistry. **Founded:** 1969. **Freq:** Monthly. **Trim Size:** 8 1/2 x 11. **Key Personnel:** Prof. J.M. Honig, Editor; Alison Ward, Advertising Coordinator. **ISSN:** 0022-4596. **Subscription Rates:** $834 U.S. and Canada; $1,009 other countries. **Remarks:** Accepts advertising.
Ad Rates: BW: $800 **Circ:** (Not Reported)
4C: $1,740

3264 Journal of Structural Biology
Academic Press
525 B St., Ste. 1900 Phone: (619)699-6557
San Diego, CA 92101-4495 Fax: (619)699-6305
Free: (800)894-3434
Publisher E-mail: apads@acad.com

Journal publishing papers dealing with the structural analysis of biological matter at all levels of organization by means of light, electron microscopy, x-ray diffraction, and nuclear magnetic resonance which yields structural information. **Founded:** 1957. **Freq:** Bimonthly. **Trim Size:** 8 1/2 x 11. **Key Personnel:** Ueli Aebi, Editor; Robert M. Glaser, Advertising Mgr.; Alison Ward, Advertising Coordinator. **ISSN:** 0022-4804. **Subscription Rates:** $364 U.S. and Canada; $450 other countries. **Remarks:** Accepts advertising. **Formerly:** Journal of Ultra Structure; Molecular Structure Research.
Ad Rates: BW: $800 **Circ:** (Not Reported)
4C: $1,740

3265 Journal of Surgical Research
Academic Press
525 B St., Ste. 1900 Phone: (619)699-6557
San Diego, CA 92101-4495 Fax: (619)699-6305
Free: (800)894-3434
Publisher E-mail: apads@acad.com

Journal publishing original articles on clinical and laboratory investigations related to surgical practice and teaching. **Subtitle:** Official Organ of the Association for Academic Surgery. **Founded:** 1967. **Freq:** Monthly. **Trim Size:** 8 1/2 x 11. **Key Personnel:** Christopher K. Zarins, Editor; Mark K. Ferguson, Editor; Ronald V. Maier, Editor; Joel J. Roslyn, Editor; Alison Ward, Advertising Coordinator. **ISSN:** 0022-4804. **Subscription Rates:** $364 U.S. and Canada; $450 other countries. **Remarks:** Accepts advertising.
Ad Rates: BW: $800 **Circ:** (Not Reported)
4C: $1,740

3266 Journal of Urban Economics
Academic Press
525 B St., Ste. 1900 Phone: (619)699-6557
San Diego, CA 92101-4495 Fax: (619)699-6305
Free: (800)894-3434
Publisher E-mail: apads@acad.com

Journal publishing articles that illustrate empirical, theoretical, positive, or normative approaches to urban economics. **Founded:** 1974. **Freq:** Bimonthly. **Trim Size:** 6 x 9. **Key Personnel:** Prof. Edwin S. Mills, Contact; Alison Ward, Advertising Coordinator. **ISSN:** 0094-1190. **Subscription Rates:** $232 U.S. and Canada; $286 other countries. **Remarks:** Accepts advertising.
Ad Rates: BW: $675 **Circ:** (Not Reported)
4C: $1,615

3267 Journal of Visual Communication and Image Representation
Academic Press
525 B St., Ste. 1900 Phone: (619)699-6557
San Diego, CA 92101-4495 Fax: (619)699-6305
Free: (800)894-3434
Publisher E-mail: apads@acad.com

Journal containing information on visual communication and image representation. **Founded:** 1994. **Freq:** Quarterly. **Trim Size:** 8 1/2 x 11. **Key Personnel:** Yehoshua Y. Zeevi, Editor-in-Chief; Alison Ward, Advertising Coordinator. **ISSN:** 1047-3203. **Subscription Rates:** $158 individuals; $158 Canada; $190 other countries. **Remarks:** Accepts advertising.
Ad Rates: BW: $675 **Circ:** (Not Reported)
4C: $1,615

3268 Journal of Vocational Behavior
Academic Press
525 B St., Ste. 1900 Phone: (619)699-6557
San Diego, CA 92101-4495 Fax: (619)699-6305
Free: (800)894-3434
Publisher E-mail: apads@acad.com

Journal publishing empirical and theoretical articles in the areas of vocational behavior and lifelong career development across the life span. **Founded:** 1971. **Freq:** Bimonthly. **Trim Size:** 6 x 9. **Key Personnel:** Howard E. A. Tinsley, Editor; Alison Ward, Advertising Coordinator. **ISSN:** 0001-8791. **Subscription Rates:** $214 U.S. and Canada; $265 other countries. **Remarks:** Accepts advertising.
Ad Rates: BW: $675 **Circ:** (Not Reported)
4C: $1,615

3269 Journal of X-Ray Science and Technology
Academic Press
525 B St., Ste. 1900 Phone: (619)699-6557
San Diego, CA 92101-4495 Fax: (619)699-6305
Free: (800)894-3434
Publisher E-mail: apads@acad.com

Journal covering new developments in the field of x-ray imaging and analysis techniques for scientists and engineers. **Founded:** 1989. **Freq:** Quarterly. **Trim Size:** 6 7/8 x 10. **Key Personnel:** Prof. Larry Knight, Contact; Alison Ward, Advertising Coordinator. **ISSN:** 0895-3996. **Subscription Rates:** $104 U.S. and Canada; $116 other countries. **Remarks:** Accepts advertising.
Ad Rates: BW: $800 **Circ:** (Not Reported)
4C: $1,740

3270 La Jolla Village News
San Diego Community Newspaper Group
PO Box 9550 Phone: (619)270-3103
San Diego, CA 92169 Fax: (619)270-9325
Publisher E-mail: mail@sdnews.com

Community newspaper. **Founded:** Oct. 1995. **Freq:** Weekly. **Print Method:** Web offset. **Cols./Page:** 5. **Col. Width:** 1 15/16 inches. **Col. Depth:** 15 3/4 inches. **Key Personnel:** David Mannis, Publisher; Kristen Collier, Editor-in-Chief; Terry Larsen, Advertising Dir. **Subscription Rates:** Free. **Remarks:** Combined advertising rates available with Beach and Bay Press, The Peninsula Beacon, and Golden Triangle News.
Ad Rates: BW: $1,278 **Circ:** Free 20,000
4C: $250

3271 La Prensa San Diego
La Prensa Munoz, Inc.
1950 5th Ave., Ste. 1-3 Phone: (619)231-2873
San Diego, CA 92101-2309 Fax: (619)231-9180
Publication E-mail: laprensa@lx.netcom.com

Community newspaper (Spanish and English). **Founded:** 1976. **Freq:** Weekly. **Print Method:** Offset. **Trim Size:** 13 x 21 1/2. **Cols./Page:** 6 and 8. **Col. Width:** 2 1/16 and 1 1/2 inches. **Col. Depth:** 21.5 and 21.5 inches. **Key Personnel:** Daniel H. Munoz, Jr., Editor, phone (619)231-2874; Daniel Munoz, Sr., Advertising Mgr., phone (619)231-9823, dmunoz1915@aol.com. **ISSN:** 0738-9183. **Subscription Rates:** $40 by mail. **Online:** Netcom. **URL:** http://www.laprensa-sandiego.org.
Ad Rates: GLR: $1.96 **Circ:** ‡30,000
BW: $3,354
4C: $3,654
SAU: $26
PCI: $26

3272 Latin American Business Review
Ahlers Center for International Business
5998 Alcala Park Phone: (619)260-4836
San Diego, CA 92110 Fax: (619)260-4891

Professional journal covering international business and economics. **Subtitle:** Journal of the Business Association of Latin American Studies (BALAS). **Founded:** 1998. **Freq:** Quarterly. **Print Method:** Sheetfed offset. **Trim Size:** 6 x 8 1/2. **Cols./Page:** 1. **Col. Width:** 4 3/8 inches. **Col. Depth:** 7 1/8 inches. **Key Personnel:** William Cohen, Publisher; Denise Dimon, Ph.D., Editor, dimon@acusd.edu; Sandy Jones Sickels, VP, Mktg., ssickels@haworthpressinc.com; Lori Beagell, Circulation Mgr.; Helen Mallon, VP, Journals Prod.; Kathleen McLeary, List Mgr. **ISSN:** 1234-3444. **Subscription Rates:** $50 individuals. **Remarks:** Accepts advertising.
Ad Rates: BW: $300 **Circ:** (Not Reported)

3273 Learning and Motivation
Academic Press
525 B St., Ste. 1900 Phone: (619)699-6557
San Diego, CA 92101-4495 Fax: (619)699-6305
Free: (800)894-3434
Publisher E-mail: apads@acad.com

Journal publishing original experimental research on the analysis of basic phenomena and mechanisms of learning, memory, and motivation. **Founded:** 1970. **Freq:** Quarterly. **Trim Size:** 5 7/8 x 9. **Key Personnel:** Steven Maier, Contact; Alison Ward, Advertising Coordinator. **ISSN:** 0023-9690. **Subscription Rates:** $141 U.S. and Canada; $182 other countries. **Remarks:** Accepts advertising. **URL:** http://www.aptnet.com.learningandmotivation.com.
Ad Rates: BW: $675 **Circ:** (Not Reported)
4C: $1,615

3274 The Log (Los Angeles/Ventura County Edition)
The Log Newspapers
2924 Emerson St., Ste. 200 Phone: (619)226-1608
San Diego, CA 92106 Fax: (619)226-0573
Free: (800)841-4377
Publisher E-mail: logledit@aol.com

Boating newspaper. **Subtitle:** Southern California's Boating Newspaper Si nce 1971. **Founded:** 1971. **Freq:** Biweekly. **Print Method:** Web offset. **Trim Size:** 10 1/4 x 16. **Cols./Page:** 4. **Col. Width:** 13.5 nonpareils. **Col. Depth:** 16 inches. **Key Personnel:** Joel Zlotnik, Editor, phone (619)226-6140, fax (619)226-1037. **Subscription Rates:** $24.95/yr. $2 single issue. **Remarks:** Accepts advertising.
Ad Rates: BW: $910 **Circ:** (Not Reported)

3275 The Log (Orange County Edition)
The Log Newspapers
2924 Emerson St., Ste. 200 Phone: (619)226-1608
San Diego, CA 92106 Fax: (619)226-0573
Free: (800)841-4377
Publisher E-mail: logledit@aol.com

Boating newspaper. **Founded:** 1971. **Freq:** Biweekly. **Cols./Page:** 4. **Col. Width:** 13.5 picas. **Col. Depth:** 16 inches. **Key Personnel:** Kevin Featherly, Editor. **Subscription Rates:** $53.95. $2 single issue. **Remarks:** Accepts advertising. **URL:** http://www.colin.dock//www.dot.con.
Ad Rates: BW: $757 **Circ:** (Not Reported)

3276 Macrobiotics Today
George Ohsawa Macrobiotic Foundation
4374 Hilldale Rd. Phone: (619)282-9003
San Diego, CA 92116 Fax: (619)282-8148

Magazine covering macrobiotics, health, and nutrition. **Founded:** 1960. **Freq:** Bimonthly. **Print Method:** Web press. **Trim Size:** 8 1/8 x 10 3/4. **Cols./Page:** 3. **Col. Width:** 2 1/4 inches. **Col. Depth:** 9 inches. **Key Personnel:** Bob Ligon, Editor, phone (619)282-9013, bkligon@home.com; Carl Ferre, Publisher. **Subscription Rates:** $20 individuals. **Remarks:** Advertising accepted; rates available upon request.
Circ: Paid 2,000
Controlled 5,000

3277 Metabolic Engineering
Academic Press
525 B St., Ste. 1900 Phone: (619)699-6557
San Diego, CA 92101-4495 Fax: (619)699-6305
Free: (800)894-3434
Publisher E-mail: apads@acad.com

Scholarly journal covering research in metabolic control analysis and related fields. **Key Personnel:** Gregory N. Stephanopoulos, Editor; Anthony J. Sinskey, Editor; Martin L. Yarmush, Editor. **Subscription Rates:** $195 U.S. and Canada; $230 elsewhere. **URL:** http://www.academicpress.com/mbe.

3278 Methods
Academic Press
525 B St., Ste. 1900 Phone: (619)699-6557
San Diego, CA 92101-4495 Fax: (619)699-6305
Free: (800)894-3434
Publisher E-mail: apads@acad.com

Scholarly journal covering recent techniques for laboratory researchers in the experimental biological and medical sciences. **Subtitle:** A Companion to Methods in Enzymology. **Key Personnel:** John N. Abelson, Editor; Kenneth W. Adolph, Editor. **ISSN:** 1046-2023. **Subscription Rates:** $210 U.S. and Canada; $250 elsewhere. **URL:** http://www.academicpress.com/methods.

3279 Methods in Immunology and Immunochemistry
Academic Press
525 B St., Ste. 1900 Phone: (619)699-6557
San Diego, CA 92101-4495 Fax: (619)699-6305
Free: (800)894-3434
Publisher E-mail: apads@acad.com

Journal containing information on new methods applicable to a number of disciplines for any modern laboratory. **Subtitle:** A Companion to Methods In Enzymology. **Founded:** 1994. **Freq:** Quarterly. **Trim Size:** 8 1/2 x 11. **Key Personnel:** John N. Abelson, Editor-in-Chief; Alison Ward, Advertising Coordinator. **ISSN:** 1046-2023. **Subscription Rates:** $100 individuals; $100 Canada; $124 other countries. **Remarks:** Accepts advertising. **Formerly**: Methods.
Ad Rates: BW: $800 **Circ:** (Not Reported)
4C: $1,740

3280 Microchemical Journal
Academic Press
525 B St., Ste. 1900 Phone: (619)699-6557
San Diego, CA 92101-4495 Fax: (619)699-6305
Free: (800)894-3434
Publisher E-mail: apads@acad.com

Focuses on microscale chemical analysis including clinically significant methods and procedures. **Subtitle:** Devoted to the Application of Microtechniques in all Branches of Chemistry. **Founded:** 1957. **Freq:** Bimonthly. **Trim Size:** 6 7/8 x 10. **Key Personnel:** Joseph Sheddon, Editor; Donald R. Bobbit, Advertising Mgr.; Alison Ward, Advertising Coordinator. **ISSN:** 0026-265X. **Subscription Rates:** $274 U.S. and Canada; $344 other countries. **Remarks:** Accepts advertising.
Ad Rates: BW: $800 **Circ:** (Not Reported)
4C: $1,740

3281 Microvascular Research
Academic Press
525 B St., Ste. 1900 Phone: (619)699-6557
San Diego, CA 92101-4495 Fax: (619)699-6305
Free: (800)894-3434
Publisher E-mail: apads@acad.com

Journal publishing information on research in the microvascular field and related fields. **Founded:** 1968. **Freq:** Bimonthly. **Trim Size:** 6 7/8 x 10. **Key Personnel:** David Shepro, Editor; Alison Ward, Advertising Coordinator. **ISSN:** 0026-2862. **Subscription Rates:** $330 U.S. and Canada; $395 other countries. **Remarks:** Accepts advertising.
Ad Rates: BW: $800 **Circ:** (Not Reported)
4C: $1,740

3282 Molecular and Cellular Neurosciences
Academic Press
525 B St., Ste. 1900 Phone: (619)699-6557
San Diego, CA 92101-4495 Fax: (619)699-6305
Free: (800)894-3434
Publisher E-mail: apads@acad.com

Journal containing information on molecular, cellular and tissue levels. **Founded:** 1994. **Freq:** 6/year. **Key Personnel:** P. Michael Conn, Editor-in-Chief. **ISSN:** 1044-7431. **Subscription Rates:** $267 individuals; $267 Canada; $295 other countries. **URL:** http://www.aptnetcom.molecularandcellularneurosciences.com.

3283 Molecular Phylogenetics and Evolution
Academic Press
525 B St., Ste. 1900 Phone: (619)699-6557
San Diego, CA 92101-4495 Fax: (619)699-6305
Free: (800)894-3434
Publisher E-mail: apads@acad.com

Journal containing information on a forum for molecular studies that advance our understanding of phylogeny and evolution. **Founded:** 1994. **Freq:** Quarterly. **Trim Size:** 8 1/2 x 11. **Key Personnel:** Morris Goodman, Editor-in-Chief; Alison Ward, Advertising Coordinator. **ISSN:** 1055-7903. **Subscription Rates:** $162 individuals; $162 Canada; $196 other countries. **Remarks:** Accepts advertising.
Ad Rates: BW: $800 **Circ:** (Not Reported)
4C: $1,740

3284 Neurobiology of Disease
Academic Press
525 B St., Ste. 1900 Phone: (619)699-6557
San Diego, CA 92101-4495 Fax: (619)699-6305
Free: (800)894-3434
Publisher E-mail: apads@acad.com

Scholarly journal covering basic and clinical neuroscience. **Key Personnel:** Dennis W. Choi, Editor-in-Chief; Jacques Mallet, Editor-in-Chief. **ISSN:** 0969-9961. **Subscription Rates:** $118 U.S. and Canada; $140 elsewhere. **URL:** http://www.academicpress.com/nbd.

3285 Neurobiology of Learning and Memory
Academic Press
525 B St., Ste. 1900 Phone: (619)699-6557
San Diego, CA 92101-4495 Fax: (619)699-6305
Free: (800)894-3434
Publisher E-mail: apads@acad.com

Journal publishing information on current neural-oriented behavioral research. Emphasizes the areas of neural plasticity and the mechanisms of learning and memory. **Founded:** 1972. **Freq:** Bimonthly. **Trim Size:** 8 1/2 x 11. **Key Personnel:** James L. McGaugh, Editor; William T. Greenough, Advertising Mgr.; Alison Ward, Advertising Coordinator. **ISSN:** 0163-1047. **Subscription Rates:** $304 U.S. and Canada; $376 other countries. **Remarks:** Accepts advertising.
Ad Rates: BW: $675 **Circ:** (Not Reported)
4C: $1,615

3286 NeuroImage
Academic Press
525 B St., Ste. 1900 Phone: (619)699-6557
San Diego, CA 92101-4495 Fax: (619)699-6305
Free: (800)894-3434
Publisher E-mail: apads@acad.com

Journal containing information on all neuroscientific data. **Freq:** Quarterly. **Trim Size:** 8 1/2 x 11. **Key Personnel:** Arthur W. Toga, Editor-in-Chief; Alison Ward, Advertising Coordinator. **ISSN:** 1053-8119. **Subscription Rates:** $235 individuals; $235 Canada; $261 other countries. **Remarks:** Accepts advertising.
Ad Rates: BW: $800 **Circ:** (Not Reported)
4C: $1,740

3287 NeuroProtocols
Academic Press
525 B St., Ste. 1900 Phone: (619)699-6557
San Diego, CA 92101-4495 Fax: (619)699-6305
Free: (800)894-3434
Publisher E-mail: apads@acad.com

Journal containing information on providing methodology of central significance to the neurosciences. **Subtitle:** A Companion to Methods in Neurosciences. **Founded:** 1994. **Freq:** 6/year. **Trim Size:** 8 1/2 x 11. **Key Personnel:** P. Michael Conn, Editor-in-Chief; Alison Ward, Advertising Coordinator. **ISSN:** 1058-6741. **Subscription Rates:** $148 individuals; $148 Canada; $186 other countries. **Remarks:** Accepts advertising.
Ad Rates: BW: $800 **Circ:** (Not Reported)
4C: $1,740

3288 Nitric Oxide
Academic Press
525 B St., Ste. 1900 Phone: (619)699-6557
San Diego, CA 92101-4495 Fax: (619)699-6305
Free: (800)894-3434
Publisher E-mail: apads@acad.com

Scholarly journal covering a variety of topics in biology and chemistry. **Subtitle:** Biology and Chemistry. **Key Personnel:** Louis J. Ignarro, Editor-in-Chief. **ISSN:** 1089-8603. **Subscription Rates:** $220 U.S. and Canada; $262 elsewhere. **URL:** http://www.academicpress.com/nox.

3289 Nuclear Data Sheets
Academic Press
525 B St., Ste. 1900 Phone: (619)699-6557
San Diego, CA 92101-4495 Fax: (619)699-6305
Free: (800)894-3434
Publisher E-mail: apads@acad.com

Journal publishing nuclear structure data evaluations and bibliography. **Subtitle:** Produced by the National Nuclear Data Center in affiliation with the International Network for Nuclear Structure Data Evaluation. **Founded:** 1966. **Freq:** Monthly. **Trim Size:** 8 1/2 x 11. **Key Personnel:** M.J. Martin, Editor; J.K. Tuli, Contact; Alison Ward, Advertising Coordinator. **ISSN:** 0090-3752. **Subscription Rates:** $426 U.S. and Canada; $510 other countries. **Remarks:** Accepts advertising.
Ad Rates: BW: $800 **Circ:** (Not Reported)
4C: $1,740

3290 Optical Fiber Technology
Academic Press
525 B St., Ste. 1900 Phone: (619)699-6557
San Diego, CA 92101-4495 Fax: (619)699-6305
Free: (800)894-3434
Publisher E-mail: apads@acad.com

Journal containing information on fiber amplifiers for the electronic regeneration. **Subtitle:** Materials, Devices and Systems. **Founded:** 1994. **Freq:** Quarterly. **Trim Size:** 8 1/2 x 11. **Key Personnel:** Emmanuel Desurvire, Editor-in-Chief; Alison Ward, Advertising Coordinator. **ISSN:** 1068-5200. **Subscription Rates:** $184 individuals; $184 Canada; $221 other countries. **Remarks:** Accepts advertising. **URL:** http://www.aptnet.com.opticalfibertechnology.com.
Ad Rates: BW: $675 **Circ:** (Not Reported)
4C: $1,615

3291 Organizational Behavior and Human Decision Processes
Academic Press
525 B St., Ste. 1900 Phone: (619)699-6557
San Diego, CA 92101-4495 Fax: (619)699-6305
Free: (800)894-3434
Publication E-mail: ap@acad.com
Publisher E-mail: apads@acad.com

Scientific journal publishing articles on research and development in human organizational psychology, including the decision processes. **Founded:** 1966. **Freq:** Monthly. **Trim Size:** 8 1/2 x 11. **Key Personnel:** Daniel R. Ilgen, Editor, phone (517)353-7205; Bonnie Baranoff, Advertising Coord. **ISSN:** 0749-5978. **Subscription Rates:** $975 U.S. and Canada; $1,075 other countries. **Remarks:** Accepts advertising. **URL:** http://www.academicpress.com/obhdp. **Formerly**: Organizational Behavior and Human Performance.
Ad Rates: BW: $675 **Circ:** (Not Reported)
4C: $1,615

3292 PennySaver/San Diego South
5575 Ruffin Rd. Phone: (619)576-6130
San Diego, CA 92123 Fax: (619)576-6040
Free: (888)736-6972

Shopper. **Founded:** 1964. **Freq:** Weekly. **Print Method:** Web offset. **Trim Size:** 7 1/2 x 10. **Cols./Page:** 4. **Col. Width:** 7 picas. **Col. Depth:** 9 3/16 inches. **Key Personnel:** Tim Sherman, General Manager, phone (619)576-6040. **Subscription Rates:** Free. **Remarks:** Advertising accepted; rates available upon request. **URL:** http://www.pennysaverusa.com.
Circ: Non-paid 1,057,000

3293 Pesticide Biochemistry and Physiology
Academic Press
525 B St., Ste. 1900 Phone: (619)699-6557
San Diego, CA 92101-4495 Fax: (619)699-6305
Free: (800)894-3434
Publisher E-mail: apads@acad.com

Journal publishing scientific articles pertaining to the mode action of plant protection agents, such as insecticides, fungicides, herbicides, similar compounds including nonlethal pest control agents, biosynthesis of phermones, hormones, and plant resistance agents. **Founded:** 1971. **Freq:** 9/year. **Trim Size:** 6 7/8 x 10. **Key Personnel:** Futimo Matsumura, Editor, phone (619)699-6825, fax (619)699-6380, apads@acad.com. **ISSN:** 0048-3575. **Subscription Rates:** $378 U.S. and Canada; $461 other countries. **Remarks:** Accepts advertising.
Ad Rates: BW: $850 **Circ:** (Not Reported)
4C: $1,895

3294 Plasmid
Academic Press
525 B St., Ste. 1900 Phone: (619)699-6557
San Diego, CA 92101-4495 Fax: (619)699-6305
Free: (800)894-3434
Publisher E-mail: apads@acad.com

Journal focuses on the biology of extrachromosoinal genetic elements in both prokaryotic eukaryotic systems, including their biological behavior, molecular structure, genetic function, their genetic products, and their use of genetic tools. **Subtitle:** A Journal Focused on Extrachromosomal Gene Systems and Mobile Genetic Elements in Prokaryotes and Eukaryotes. **Founded:** 1977. **Freq:** Bimonthly. **Trim Size:** 6 7/8 x 10. **Key Personnel:** Richard D. Kolodner, Editor; Francis L. Macrina, Editor; Alison Ward, Advertising Coordinator. **ISSN:** 0147-619X. **Subscription Rates:** $186 U.S. and Canada; $237 other countries. **Remarks:** Accepts advertising.
Ad Rates: BW: $800 **Circ:** (Not Reported)
4C: $1,740

3295 The Point
Point Loma Nazarene College
3900 Lomaland Dr. Phone: (619)221-2301
San Diego, CA 92106 Fax: (619)221-2566

Collegiate newspaper (tabloid). **Founded:** 1928. **Freq:** Weekly. **Print Method:** Uses mats. Offset. **Trim Size:** 11 x 14. **Cols./Page:** 4. **Col. Width:** 30 nonpareils. **Col. Depth:** 224 agate lines. **Key Personnel:** Craig Sturak, Editor. **Subscription Rates:** $35 individuals. **Remarks:** Color advertising not accepted.
Ad Rates: BW: $448 **Circ:** ‡2,300
PCI: $5

3296 Preventive Medicine
Academic Press
525 B St., Ste. 1900 Phone: (619)699-6557
San Diego, CA 92101-4495 Fax: (619)699-6305
Free: (800)894-3434
Publisher E-mail: apads@acad.com

Medical journal covering epidemiology and public health, with a clinical section geared toward physicians; emphasizes chronic "lifestyle-related" diseases. **Subtitle:** An International Journal Devoted to Practice and Theory. **Founded:** Mar. 1972. **Freq:** Bimonthly. **Trim Size:** 8 1/2 x 11. **Key Personnel:** Ernst L. Wynder, Editor; Jerome D. Cohen, Contact; Alison Ward, Advertising Coordinator. **ISSN:** 0091-7435. **Subscription Rates:** $216 U.S. and Canada; $260 other countries. **Remarks:** Accepts advertising.
Ad Rates: BW: $800 **Circ:** (Not Reported)
4C: $1,740

3297 The Professional Geographer
San Diego State University
Stuart C. Aitken and Janet Franklin
Dept. of Geography
San Diego State University
San Diego, CA 92182-4493
Publication E-mail: progeog@mail.sdsu.edu

Geographical journal. **Founded:** 1949. **Freq:** Quarterly. **Print Method:** Offset. **Trim Size:** 6 x 9. **Cols./Page:** 1. **Col. Width:** 29 nonpareils. **Col. Depth:** 43 agate lines. **Key Personnel:** Stuart C. Aitken, Co-editor; Annie Ross, Managing Editor, phone (619)594-8032, fax (619)594-4938; Serge Rey, Book Review Editor; Elisabeth S. Nelson, Cartographic Advisor; Richard D. Wright, Cartographic Advisor. **ISSN:** 0033-0124. **Subscription Rates:** $132 individuals; $154 out of country. **Remarks:** Accepts advertising.
Ad Rates: BW: $450 **Circ:** 8,000

3298 Protein Expression and Purification
Academic Press
525 B St., Ste. 1900 Phone: (619)699-6557
San Diego, CA 92101-4495 Fax: (619)699-6305
Free: (800)894-3434
Publisher E-mail: apads@acad.com

Journal containing information on aspects of protein purification. **Founded:** 1994. **Freq:** 6/year. **Trim Size:** 8 1/2 x 11. **Key Personnel:** Owen W. Griffith, Editor-in-Chief; Alison Ward, Advertising Coordinator. **ISSN:** 1046-5928. **Subscription Rates:** $170 individuals; $170 Canada; $198 other countries. **Remarks:** Accepts advertising. **URL:** http://www.aptnet.com.proteinexpressionandturification.com.
Ad Rates: BW: $800 **Circ:** (Not Reported)
4C: $1,740

3299 Quality Assurance
Academic Press
525 B St., Ste. 1900 Phone: (619)699-6557
San Diego, CA 92101-4495 Fax: (619)699-6305
Free: (800)894-3434
Publisher E-mail: apads@acad.com

Journal containing information on issues of quality assurance and quality control as they relate to biological, physical and engineering science and technology. **Subtitle:** Good Practice, Regulation and Law. **Founded:** 1994. **Freq:** Quarterly. **Trim Size:** 6 7/8 x 10. **Key Personnel:** Frederick Coulston, Editor; Alison Ward, Advertising Coordinator. **ISSN:** 1052-9411. **Subscription Rates:** $167 individuals; $167 Canada; $198 other countries. **Remarks:** Accepts advertising.
Ad Rates: BW: $800 **Circ:** (Not Reported)
4C: $1,740

3300 Quaternary Research
Academic Press
525 B St., Ste. 1900 Phone: (619)699-6557
San Diego, CA 92101-4495 Fax: (619)699-6305
Free: (800)894-3434
Publisher E-mail: apads@acad.com

Journal publishing articles from disciplines contributing to the knowledge of the Quaternary Period; including studies from geology, paleontology, and oceanography. **Subtitle:** An Interdisciplinary Journal. **Founded:** 1970. **Freq:** Bimonthly. **Trim Size:** 8 1/2 x 11. **Key Personnel:** Stephen C. Porter, Contact; Alison Ward, Advertising Coordinator. **ISSN:** 0033-5894. **Subscription Rates:** $192 U.S. and Canada; $232 other countries. **Remarks:** Accepts advertising.
Ad Rates: BW: $675 **Circ:** (Not Reported)
4C: $1,615

Rancho Bernardo News Journal - See Rancho Bernardo

3301 Real-Time Imaging
Academic Press
525 B St., Ste. 1900 Phone: (619)699-6557
San Diego, CA 92101-4495 Fax: (619)699-6305
Free: (800)894-3434
Publisher E-mail: apads@acad.com

Technical journal covering real-time imaging technologies and applications. **Key Personnel:** Phillip A. Laplante, Editor; Alexander D. Stoyen, Editor. **ISSN:** 1077-2014. **Subscription Rates:** $135 individuals. **URL:** http://www.academicpress.com/rti.

3302 Regulatory Toxicology and Pharmacology
Academic Press
525 B St., Ste. 1900 Phone: (619)699-6557
San Diego, CA 92101-4495 Fax: (619)699-6305
Free: (800)894-3434
Publisher E-mail: apads@acad.com

Journal presents significant development, public opinion, scientific data, ideas that bridge the gap between scientific information, legal aspects of Toxicological, and Pharmacological regulations. **Subtitle:** Official Journal of the International Society of Regulatory Toxicology and Pharmacology. **Founded:** 1981. **Freq:** Bimonthly. **Trim Size:** 8 1/2 x 11. **Key Personnel:** Frederick Coulston, Editor; Albert C. Kolbye, Jr., Editor; C. Jelleff Carr, Managing Editor. **ISSN:** 0273-2300. **Subscription Rates:** $180 U.S. and Canada; $236 other countries. **Remarks:** Accepts advertising.
Ad Rates: BW: $850 **Circ:** (Not Reported)
4C: $1,895

3303 Research in Economics/Ricerche Economiche
Academic Press
525 B St., Ste. 1900 Phone: (619)699-6557
San Diego, CA 92101-4495 Fax: (619)699-6305
Free: (800)894-3434
Publisher E-mail: apads@acad.com

Scholarly journal covering research in all fields of economics worldwide. **Subtitle:** An International Review of Economics. **Founded:** 1947. **Freq:** Quarterly. **Key Personnel:** Guglielmo Weber, Editor; Piero Gottardi, Assoc. Editor. **ISSN:** 1090-9443. **Subscription Rates:** $214 individuals. **URL:** http://www.academicpress.com/rie.

3304 Review of Economic Dynamics
Academic Press
525 B St., Ste. 1900 Phone: (619)699-6557
San Diego, CA 92101-4495 Fax: (619)699-6305
Free: (800)894-3434
Publisher E-mail: apads@acad.com

Scholarly journal covering economics for the Society for Economic Dynamics. **Freq:** Quarterly. **Key Personnel:** Thomas F. Cooley, Editor; David K. Levine, Editor; Ramon Marimon, Editor; Dale T. Mortensen, Editor; Edward C. Prescott, Editor; Thomas Sargent, Editor. **ISSN:** 1094-2025. **Subscription Rates:** $250 individuals. **URL:** http://www.academicpress.com/red.

3305 San Diego Bulletin
Metropolitan News Co.
210 S. Spring St. Phone: (213)628-4384
Los Angeles, CA 90012 Fax: (213)687-3886

Community newspaper. **Founded:** 1991. **Freq:** Weekly. **Print Method:** Offset. **Cols./Page:** 4. **Col. Width:** 15 picas. **Col. Depth:** 15 1/2 inches. **Key Personnel:** Roger M. Grace, Editor. **Remarks:** Accepts advertising.
Ad Rates: PCI: $6 **Circ:** Non-paid 1,000

3306 San Diego Business Journal
4909 Murphy Canyon Rd., No. 200 Phone: (619)277-6359
Fax: (619)571-3628
San Diego, CA 92123
Metropolitan business newspaper specializing in investigative and enterprise reporting on San Diego County businesses and related issues. **Founded:** June 1980. **Freq:** Weekly (Mon.). **Print Method:** Offset. **Trim Size:** 10 x 14. **Cols./Page:** 4. **Col. Width:** 27 nonpareils. **Col. Depth:** 196 agate lines. **Key Personnel:** Martin Hill, Editor; Ted Owen, Publisher; Charlie Chase, Advertising Dir. **ISSN:** 8750-6890. **Subscription Rates:** $58 individuals. **Remarks:** Accepts advertising. **Online:** DataTimes Corporation.
Ad Rates: BW: $2,730 **Circ:** ‡22,500
4C: $3,330

3307 San Diego Commerce
Daily Journal Corp.
PO Box 128579 Phone: (619)232-3486
San Diego, CA 92112-8579 Fax: (619)232-1159
Publication E-mail: san_diego@dailyjournal.com

Business and real estate newspaper. **Founded:** 1968. **Freq:** Daily. **Print Method:** Offset. **Trim Size:** 11 1/2 x 15. **Cols./Page:** 4. **Col. Width:** 2 3/8 inches. **Col. Depth:** 13 3/4 inches. **Key Personnel:** David K. Smith, Publisher, david_smith@dailyjournal.com; Rachael L. Frost, Editor, rachel_frost@dailyjournal.com; R. Yolanda Dominguez, Legal Advertising. **ISSN:** 1063-5513. **Subscription Rates:** $56. **Remarks:** Accepts advertising. **Formerly:** Back Country Trader.
Ad Rates: BW: $647 **Circ:** Paid 2,432
4C: $2,216 Free 209
PCI: $12

3308 San Diego Computer Journal
PC Specialists Inc.
7810 Trade St. Phone: (619)566-8200
San Diego, CA 92121
Publication focusing on business computing. **Founded:** 1987. **Freq:** Monthly. **Key Personnel:** Tobie Ann Smith, Editor; Bruse Geier, Publisher; Kevin Johnson, Advertising Dir. **Subscription Rates:** $10. Free single issue.
Circ: Combined 40,000

3309 San Diego County Physician
San Diego County Medical Society
3702 Ruffin Rd.
Box 23581
San Diego, CA 92193

Professional magazine for the San Diego county medical community. **Founded:** 1915. **Freq:** Monthly. **Trim Size:** 8 1/2 x 11. **Key Personnel:** Helen Westcott, Managing Editor. **Subscription Rates:** $25 individuals; $2.50 single issue. **Remarks:** Accepts advertising.
Ad Rates: BW: $500 **Circ:** Paid 2,800
4C: $1,400

3310 San Diego Daily Transcript
2131 3rd Ave. Phone: (619)232-4381
Box 85469 Fax: (619)239-5716
San Diego, CA 92101
Free: (800)697-6397
Publication E-mail: editor@sddt.com
Publisher E-mail: editor@sddt.com

Local business newspaper. **Founded:** 1886. **Freq:** Daily. **Print Method:** Offset. **Trim Size:** 13 1/4 x 21. **Cols./Page:** 6. **Col. Width:** 2 1/16 inches. **Col. Depth:** 21 inches. **Key Personnel:** Robert Loomis, Vice President, phone (619)232-4381, fax (619)239-5716, loomis@sddt.com; Melanie Potter, Vice President, potter@sddt.com; Andrew Kleske, Editor, phone (619)236-8126, fax (619)236-8126, kleske@sddt.com; Sara Wilensky, Advertising Dir., wilensky@sddt.com. **Subscription Rates:** $131 individuals. **Remarks:** Accepts advertising. **Online:** San Diego Source. **URL:** www.sddt.com.
Ad Rates: GLR: $1.68 **Circ:** Mon.-Fri. 6,404
BW: $2,746
4C: $3,386.32
SAU: $23.50

3311 San Diego Family Magazine
PO Box 23960 Phone: (619)685-6970
San Diego, CA 92193
Publication E-mail: sandiegofamily@family.com

Magazine. **Founded:** 1982. **Freq:** Monthly. **Print Method:** Web. **Trim Size:** 8 1/4 x 10 3/4. **Cols./Page:** 3. **Key Personnel:** Sharon Bay, Publisher. **Subscription Rates:** $16 individuals. **Remarks:** Accepts advertising. **URL:** http://www.sandiegofamily.com. **Formerly:** San Diego Family Press.
Circ: Free ‡119,862
Paid ‡143

3312 San Diego Law Review
San Diego Law Review Association
5998 University of San Diego, School of Law Phone: (619)260-4531
Fax: (619)260-4616
5998 Alcala Park
San Diego, CA 92110
Law journal. **Founded:** 1964. **Freq:** Quarterly. **Cols./Page:** 1. **Col. Width:** 6 1/2 inches. **Col. Depth:** 10 inches. **Key Personnel:** Brigid Bennett, fax (619)200-4753, bbennett@acusd.edu. **ISSN:** 0036-4037. **Subscription Rates:** $25 individuals; $43 other countries. **Remarks:** Accepts advertising. **Online:** LEXIS-NEXIS; Westlaw.
Ad Rates: BW: $150 **Circ:** 900

3313 San Diego Magazine
San Diego Magazine Publishing Co.
PO Box 85409 Phone: (619)230-9292
San Diego, CA 92186 Fax: (619)239-9220
Free: (800)600-2489

Regional magazine covering San Diego, California. **Founded:** 1948. **Freq:** Monthly. **Print Method:** Offset. **Trim Size:** 8 1/4 x 10 3/4. **Cols./Page:** 3. **Col. Width:** 27 nonpareils. **Col. Depth:** 138 agate lines. **Key Personnel:** James Fitzpatrick, C.E.O. & Publisher. **ISSN:** 0036-4045. **Subscription Rates:** $18 individuals; $3.50 single issue. **URL:** http://www.sandiego-online.com.
Ad Rates: BW: $3,275 **Circ:** Paid ★44,247
4C: $4,925

3314 San Diego Navy Dispatch
Western States Weeklies, Inc.
6312 Riverdale St
San Diego, CA 92160-0600

Newspaper for active and retired Navy and Marine Corps in San Diego county. **Founded:** 1961. **Freq:** Weekly. **Cols./Page:** 6. **Col. Width:** 9.5 picas. **Col. Depth:** 16 inches. **Subscription Rates:** Free. **Remarks:** Accepts advertising. **URL:** http://www.navydispatch.com.
Ad Rates: BW: $2,200 **Circ:** Non-paid 40,000

3315 San Diego Reader
P.O. Box 85803 Phone: (619)235-3000
San Diego, CA 92186 Fax: (619)231-0489
Publication E-mail: hrosen@spreader.com

Newspaper covering San Diego lifestyle emphasizing the arts, entertainment, and politics. Features comprehensive listings of movies, events, theater, and pop music; restaurant and film reviews; and free classified advertisements for its readers. **Founded:** Oct. 1972. **Freq:** Weekly (Thurs.). **Print Method:** Offset. **Trim Size:** 10 1/4 x 13. **Cols./Page:** 6. **Col. Width:** 1 1/2 inches. **Key Personnel:** Jim Holman, Editor and Publisher; Janis Walsh, Advertising Mgr. **Subscription Rates:** Free; $165 by mail. **Remarks:** Accepts advertising. **Available Online. URL:** http://www.sdreader.com.
Ad Rates: BW: $3,829 **Circ:** Free 160,000
4C: $5,770
PCI: $63.76

3316 The San Diego Union-Tribune
Union-Tribune Publishing Co.
350 Camino de la Renta Phone: (619)293-1211
San Diego, CA 92108 Fax: (619)293-1440

International, national, and local news. **Founded:** 1868. **Freq:** Daily. **Print Method:** Offset. **Cols./Page:** 6. **Col. Width:** 2 1/16 inches. **Col. Depth:** 21 1/2 inches. **Key Personnel:** Helen K. Copley, Publisher, phone (619)293-1106; Gene Bell, Pres./CEO, phone (293)-1101; Mack Quintana, Sales & Mrkt. Director, phone (293)-1500; Dexter La Pierre, Display Advertising Dir., phone (293)-1421; Rick Ott, Marketing Dir., phone (293)-1580; Karin Winner, Editor, phone (293)-1201; Neil Morgan, Assoc. Editor/Sr. Columnist, phone (293)-1301; Bill Gaspard, Sr. Editor/Visuals, phone (293)-1274; Doug Hope, Sr. Editor/Administration, phone (293)-1216; Todd Merriman, Sr. Editor/News, phone (293)-1049; Gina Lubrano, Readers Rep., phone (296)-1525; Lee Grant, Arts Dir., phone (293)-1281; Ray Kipp, Convention Editor, phone (293)-2235; Michael Crowell, Night & Day Editor, phone (293)-1018; Rick Levinson, Sr. Editor/Special projects, phone (293)-1246; Carol Goodhue, Training & Develpoment Editor, phone (293)-1261. **Subscription Rates:** $150.00 individuals. **Remarks:** Accepts advertising. **Online:** DataTimes Corporation. **URL:** http://www.uniontrib.com. **Alt. Formats:** CD-ROM, NewsBank, Inc. **Absorbed:** San Diego Tribune (1992). **Feature Editors:** Donald Bauder, *Financial/Business*, phone (293)-1523; Maureen Clancy, *Food*, phone (293)-1269; Alison DaRosa, *Travel*, phone (293)-2036; David Elliot, *Movie*, phone (293)-1268; John Freeman, *TV & Radio*, phone (293)-1521; Margaret King, *Food*, phone (293)-2229; Carl Larsen, *Garden/Home*, phone (293)-2075; Robert Laurence, *TV & Radio*, phone (293)-1892; Mike Smolens, *Political*, phone (293)-1256.
Ad Rates: GLR: $182.52 **Circ:** Mon.-Sat. **★378,112**
BW: $18450 Sun. **★450,646**
4C: $20250
PCI: $112.84

3317 The San Diego Voice and Viewpoint
The San Diego Voice & Viewpoint
1729 N. Euclid Ave. Phone: (619)266-2233
PO Box 95 Fax: (619)266-0533
San Diego, CA 92112-0095
Black American newspaper. **Founded:** 1960. **Freq:** Weekly (Thurs.). **Print Method:** Offset. Uses mats. **Cols./Page:** 5. **Col. Width:** 23 nonpareils. **Col. Depth:** 224 agate lines. **Key Personnel:** Earl Davis, Jr., Editor and Publisher. **Subscription Rates:** $25 individuals. **Remarks:** Accepts advertising.
Ad Rates: GLR: $.66 **Circ:** 13,000
BW: $1,373
4C: $1,748
SAU: $10.90

3318 S.D.T.A. Teacher Advocate
San Diego Teachers Association
10393 San Diego Mission Rd., No. 100 Phone: (619)283-4411
Fax: (619)282-7659
San Diego, CA 92108
Publication (tabloid) devoted to education. **Founded:** 1921. **Freq:** Monthly. **Print Method:** Offset. **Trim Size:** 8 1/2 x 11. **Cols./Page:** 3. **Col. Width:** 28 nonpareils. **Col. Depth:** 186 agate lines. **Key Personnel:** Suzanne Emery, Editor; Steven Kaplan, Advertising Mgr. **Remarks:** Color advertising not accepted.
Circ: Non-paid ‡8,000

3319 Seminars in Cell & Developmental Biology
Academic Press
525 B St., Ste. 1900 Phone: (619)699-6557
San Diego, CA 92101-4495 Fax: (619)699-6305
Free: (800)894-3434
Publisher E-mail: apads@acad.com

Scholarly journal covering cell and developmental biology for scientists. **Freq:** Bimonthly. **Key Personnel:** A. Colman, Editor. **ISSN:** 1084-9521. **Subscription Rates:** $175 individuals. **URL:** http://www.academicpress.com/semcdb.

3320 Senior World Newsmagazine
Kendall Communications
PO Box 1565 Phone: (619)593-2900
El Cajon, CA 92022 Fax: (619)442-4043

Newspaper (tabloid) for active older adults. **Founded:** 1973. **Freq:** Monthly. **Print Method:** Offset. **Cols./Page:** 5. **Col. Width:** 11.6 picas. **Col. Depth:** 16 inches. **Key Personnel:** Laura Impastato, Editor; Resa Trent, General Mgr. **Subscription Rates:** $10 individuals. **Remarks:** Accepts advertising. **Formerly:** Senior World of San Diego (1984).
Ad Rates: GLR: $6.50 **Circ:** Paid ‡900
BW: $2,713 Controlled ‡99,400
4C: $3,288

3321 Shooting Industry
Publishers Development Corp.
591 Camino de la Reina, Ste. 200 Phone: (619)297-8520
Fax: (619)297-5353
San Diego, CA 92108
Free: (800)633-8001

Magazine serving the firearms industry. **Founded:** 1955. **Freq:** Monthly. **Print Method:** Offset. **Trim Size:** 8 1/2 x 11. **Cols./Page:** 3. **Col. Width:** 26 nonpareils. **Col. Depth:** 140 agate lines. **Key Personnel:** Scott Farrell, Editor; George E. von Rosen, Publisher; Anita Carson, Advertising Mgr. **ISSN:** 0037-4148. **Subscription Rates:** Free to qualified subscribers; $25 individuals. **Remarks:** Accepts advertising.
Ad Rates: BW: $2,575 **Circ:** Paid ‡388
4C: $2,900 Non-paid ‡23,555
PCI: $165

3322 Simulation
Society for Computer Simulation
4838 Ronson Ct., Ste. L Phone: (619)277-3888
San Diego, CA 92111 Fax: (619)277-3930
Publication E-mail: simulation@scs.org
Publisher E-mail: scs@scs.org

Computer simulation technology journal containing technical articles, feature articles, calendar of events, columns, short courses listing, book reviews, and classified and display advertising. **Founded:** 1963. **Freq:** Monthly. **Print Method:** Offset. **Trim Size:** 8 1/2 x 11. **Cols./Page:** 2. **Col. Width:** 20 picas. **Col. Depth:** 54 picas. **Key Personnel:** Charles Shub, Editor-in-Chief; Lorrie Mowat, Managing Editor, lmowat@scs.org; Steve Branch, Advertising Mgr., branch@sdsc.edu. **ISSN:** 0037-5497. **Subscription Rates:** $165 individuals; $15 single issue. **Remarks:** Accepts advertising.
Ad Rates: GLR: $5 **Circ:** ‡3,800
BW: $997
4C: $1,400
PCI: $50

3323 Social Science Research
Academic Press
525 B St., Ste. 1900 Phone: (619)699-6557
San Diego, CA 92101-4495 Fax: (619)699-6305
Free: (800)894-3434
Publisher E-mail: apads@acad.com

Subtitle: A Quarterly Journal of Social Science Methodology and Quantitative Research. **Founded:** 1972. **Freq:** Quarterly. **Trim Size:** 6 x 9. **Key Personnel:** James D. Wright, Contact; Peter H. Rossi, Contact; Alison Ward, Advertising Coordinator. **ISSN:** 0049-089X. **Subscription Rates:** $132 U.S. and Canada; $175 other countries. **Remarks:** Accepts advertising.
Ad Rates: BW: $675 **Circ:** (Not Reported)
4C: $1,615

3324 Sociological Perspectives
Elseiver
Dept. of Sociology Phone: (619)594-1316
San Diego State University Fax: (619)584-1325
San Diego, CA 92182-4423
Publisher E-mail: fcentres@gpu.stv.ualberta.ca

Sociology journal. **Subtitle:** Official Journal of the Pacific Sociological Association. **Founded:** 1959. **Freq:** Quarterly. **Print Method:** Offset. **Trim Size:** 7 x 10. **Cols./Page:** 1. **Key Personnel:** Charles Hohm, Editor, cholm@mail.sdsu.edu. **ISSN:** 0731-1214. **Subscription Rates:** $185 institutions; $205 institutions, other countries; $225 institutions, other countries airmail; $80 individuals; $100 other countries; $120 other countries airmail; $47.50 single issue; $52.50 single issue other couuntries; $57.50 single issue other countries airmail. **Remarks:** Accepts advertising. **URL:** http://www.csus.edu/psa/journal.html.
Ad Rates: BW: $400 **Circ:** ‡1,200

3325 The Southern Cross
PO Box 81869 Phone: (619)490-8266
San Diego, CA 92138 Fax: (619)490-8355
Publisher E-mail: socross@diocese-sdiego.org

Roman Catholic newspaper. **Founded:** 1912. **Freq:** Semimonthly. **Print Method:** Offset. **Trim Size:** 62.5 pica x 96 pica. **Cols./Page:** 4. **Col. Width:** 19 nonpareils. **Col. Depth:** 224 agate lines. **Key Personnel:** Cyril Jones-Kellett, Editor; Most Rev. Robert H. Brom, Publisher; Lee Haralson, Dir. of Business Affairs; Kurt Bauer, Advertising, kbauer@diocese-sdiego.org. **ISSN:** 0745-0257. **Subscription Rates:** $20 individuals.
Ad Rates: PCI: $20 **Circ:** ‡31,000

3326 Theoretical Population Biology
Academic Press
525 B St., Ste. 1900 Phone: (619)699-6557
San Diego, CA 92101-4495 Fax: (619)699-6305
Free: (800)894-3434
Publisher E-mail: apads@acad.com

Journal presenting articles on the theoretical aspects of the biology of populations, particluarly in the areas of ecology, genetics, demography, and epidemiology. **Subtitle:** An International Journal. **Founded:** 1970. **Freq:** Bimonthly. **Trim Size:** 6 x 9. **Key Personnel:** M. Feldman, Editor; Alison Ward, Advertising Coordinator. **ISSN:** 0040-5809. **Subscription Rates:** $266 U.S. and Canada; $332 other countries. **Remarks:** Accepts advertising.
Ad Rates: BW: $800 **Circ:** (Not Reported)
4C: $1,740

3327 Thomas Jefferson Law Review
2121 San Diego Ave. Phone: (619)298-3111
San Diego, CA 92110 Fax: (619)692-8149

Journal covering law. **Founded:** 1996. **Freq:** Semiannual. **Subscription Rates:** $18 individuals. **Remarks:** Advertising not accepted. **Online:** Westlaw.
Circ: Combined 280

3328 Today in San Diego
3600 Mission Blvd. Phone: (619)488-0357
San Diego, CA 92109 Fax: (619)488-0357

Magazine (tabloid) distributed in hotel rooms, transportation centers, and visitor information areas in San Diego County containing articles and advertising on attractions, activities, shopping, and dining in San Diego, California. **Founded:** Jan. 1, 1965. **Freq:** Bimonthly. **Print Method:** Offset. **Trim Size:** 10 x 16. **Cols./Page:** 6. **Col. Width:** 10 picas. **Col. Depth:** 16 inches. **Key Personnel:** John B. Moriarty, Editor and Publisher. **Subscription Rates:** $15 individuals. **Remarks:** Accepts advertising.
Ad Rates: GLR: $1.25 **Circ:** Non-paid ‡80,000
BW: $745
4C: $900
PCI: $17.50

Today in San Diego - See San Diego

3329 Toxicology and Applied Pharmacology
Academic Press
525 B St., Ste. 1900 Phone: (619)699-6557
San Diego, CA 92101-4495 Fax: (619)699-6305
Free: (800)894-3434
Publisher E-mail: apads@acad.com

Journal publishing original scientific research on tissue structure or function resulting from the administration of chemicals, drugs, or natural products to animals or humans. **Subtitle:** Official Journal of the Society of Toxicology. **Founded:** 1959. **Freq:** Monthly. **Trim Size:** 8 1/2 x 11. **Key Personnel:** Edward Bresnick, Editor. **ISSN:** 0041-008X. **Subscription Rates:** $762 U.S. and Canada; $904 other countries. **Remarks:** Accepts advertising. **URL:** http://www.aptnet.com.toxicologyandappliedpharmacology.com.
Ad Rates: BW: $850 **Circ:** (Not Reported)
4C: $1,895

3330 Transactions of the Society for Computer Simulation International
Society for Computer Simulation
4838 Ronson Ct., Ste. L Phone: (619)277-3888
San Diego, CA 92111 Fax: (619)277-3930
Publication E-mail: transactions@scs.org
Publisher E-mail: scs@scs.org

Computer simulation technology journal containing refereed technical articles. **Subtitle:** Transactions of the Society for Computer Simulation. **Founded:** May 1984. **Freq:** Quarterly. **Print Method:** Offset. **Trim Size:** 8 1/2 x 11. **Cols./Page:** 2. **Key Personnel:** Bernard Zeigler, Editor-in-Chief; Lorrie Mo-

wat, Managing Editor, lmowat@scs.org. **ISSN:** 0740-6797. **Subscription Rates:** $145 individuals. **Remarks:** Advertising not accepted. **Formerly:** Transactions of the Society for Computer Simulation.
Circ: 1,000

3331 Truth Seeker
Truth Seeker Co., Inc.
16935 W. Bernardo Dr., Ste. 103 Phone: (619)676-0430 Fax: (619)676-0433
San Diego, CA 92127
Free: (800)321-9054
Publication E-mail: tsmarti@aol.com
Publisher E-mail: tsmelton@aol.com

Magazine devoted to freethought. **Subtitle:** The Journal of Independent Thought. **Founded:** 1873. **Freq:** Semiannual. **Print Method:** Offset. **Trim Size:** 8 1/2 x 11. **Cols./Page:** 2. **Col. Width:** 42 nonpareils. **Col. Depth:** 133 agate lines. **Key Personnel:** Bonnie Lange, President; William Lindley, Contact, tslindley@aol.com; Nancy Melton, Contact, tsmelton@aol.com; Marti Kranzberg, Contact, tsmarti@aol.com. **ISSN:** 0041-3712. **Subscription Rates:** $20 individuals; $35 other countries. **Remarks:** Advertising not accepted. **Online:** America Online, Inc.; Free Thought. **URL:** http://www.freethought.com; http://www.truth-seeker.com. **Alt. Formats:** Audio tape; Microform.
Circ: Non-paid 20,000

3332 Ultrasonic Imaging
Academic Press
525 B St., Ste. 1900 Phone: (619)699-6557
San Diego, CA 92101-4495 Fax: (619)699-6305
Free: (800)894-3434
Publisher E-mail: apads@acad.com

Journal publishing information on the development and application of ultrasonic techniques with an emphasis on medical diagnosis. **Subtitle:** An International Journal. **Founded:** 1979. **Freq:** Quarterly. **Trim Size:** 6 7/8 x 10. **Key Personnel:** Melvin Linzer, Editor; Alison Ward, Advertising Coordinator. **ISSN:** 0161-7346. **Subscription Rates:** $113 U.S. and Canada; $151 other countries. **Remarks:** Accepts advertising. **URL:** http://www.aptnet.com.ultrasonicimaging.com.
Ad Rates: BW: $800 **Circ:** (Not Reported)
4C: $1,740

3333 Update
Dawn Media
PO Box 33148 Phone: (619)229-0500
San Diego, CA 92163-3148 Fax: (619)229-6907
Free: (800)331-1751
Publisher E-mail: updateed@aol.com

General circulation newspaper serving the gay community. **Founded:** 1979. **Freq:** Weekly (Wed.). **Print Method:** Web offset. **Cols./Page:** 5. **Col. Width:** 2 inches. **Col. Depth:** 16 inches. **Key Personnel:** Tom Ellerbrock, Editor and Publisher. **Subscription Rates:** $75. **Remarks:** Accepts advertising.
Ad Rates: BW: $475 **Circ:** Paid ‡2,000
4C: $750 Free ‡25,000

3334 Uptown San Diego Examiner
Uptown Examiner Group
3605 30th St. Phone: (619)295-5432
PO Box 4368
San Diego, CA 92164
Community newspaper. **Subtitle:** Mid City's Journal of Community & Legal News. **Founded:** 1937. **Freq:** Semiweekly (Wed. and Fri.). **Trim Size:** 8 1/2 x 11. **Cols./Page:** 3. **Col. Depth:** 10 inches. **Key Personnel:** J. Specht, Editor; Art Specht, Publisher; Terence J. Burke, Associate Publisher. **ISSN:** 0898-4581. **Subscription Rates:** $25 individuals; $35 out of area. **Remarks:** Color advertising not accepted.
Ad Rates: BW: $183 **Circ:** Paid ⊕**275**
PCI: $5

3335 USIU Envoy
United States International University
10455 Pomerado Rd,. M-2 Phone: (619)635-4540
San Diego, CA 92131 Fax: (619)635-4843
Publication E-mail: Envoy@usiu.edu

College newspaper. **Founded:** 1990. **Freq:** Biweekly. **Trim Size:** 10 x 16. **Remarks:** Accepts advertising.
Ad Rates: BW: $325 **Circ:** Controlled 2,000
PCI: $6.75

3336 Viet Nam Hai Ngoai
Vietnam Hai Ngoal
PO Box 33627
San Diego, CA 92103-0580

Vietnamese magazine (Vietnamese). **Founded:** June 1, 1977. **Freq:** Monthly. **Print Method:** Offset. **Trim Size:** 5 1/2 x 8. **Cols./Page:** 2. **Col. Width:** 51 nonpareils. **Col. Depth:** 89 agate lines. **Key Personnel:** Dinh Thach Bich, Editor and Publisher; Vu Luc Thuy, Advertising Mgr. **Subscription Rates:** $43 individuals. **Remarks:** Accepts advertising.
Ad Rates: BW: $120 **Circ:** Paid ‡5,000
4C: $350 Non-paid ‡2,500

3337 Virology
Academic Press
525 B St., Ste. 1900 Phone: (619)699-6557
San Diego, CA 92101-4495 Fax: (619)699-6305
Free: (800)894-3434
Publisher E-mail: apads@acad.com

Scientific journal publishing research results in all branches of virology. **Founded:** 1955. **Freq:** 18/year. **Print Method:** Offset. **Trim Size:** 8 1/2 x 11. **Cols./Page:** 2. **Key Personnel:** W.K. Joklik, Editor; Alison Ward, Advertising Coord. **ISSN:** 0042-6822. **Subscription Rates:** $999 U.S and Canada; $1,232 other countries. **Remarks:** Accepts advertising. **URL:** http://www.aptnet.com.virology.com.
Ad Rates: BW: $800 **Circ:** (Not Reported)
4C: $1,740

3338 World Scanner Report
Commtronics Engineering
PO Box 262478-Gx Phone: (619)578-9247
San Diego, CA 92196-2478 Fax: (619)578-9247
Publication E-mail: ccheek@san.rr.com

Technical magazine on VHF-UHF scanning receivers. Covers the technology and engineering of scanning receivers and receiver processes. **Subtitle:** A Journal of VHF-UHF Radio Engineering & Technology. **Founded:** Jan. 1991. **Freq:** 10/year. **Print Method:** Offset. **Trim Size:** 8 1/2 x 11. **Cols./Page:** 3. **Col. Width:** 2 1/2 inches. **Col. Depth:** 10 inches. **Key Personnel:** W.D. Cheek, Editor, bcheek@san.rr.com; Cynthia Huebscher, Circulation Mgr. **ISSN:** 1061-9240. **Subscription Rates:** $35 individuals; $5 single issue. **Remarks:** Accepts advertising. **URL:** http://ourworld.compuserve.com/homepages/bcheek.
Ad Rates: GLR: $3 **Circ:** Paid 800
BW: $175 Non-paid 50
PCI: $6

3339 ZOONOOZ
Zoological Society of San Diego, Inc.
PO Box 551
San Diego, CA 92112-0551

Magazine on natural history, animal science, and conservation. **Founded:** 1926. **Freq:** Monthly. **Print Method:** Offset. **Trim Size:** 8 1/2 x 11. **Cols./Page:** 4 and 3. **Col. Width:** 20 and 27 nonpareils. **Col. Depth:** 136 agate lines. **Key Personnel:** Thomas L. Scharf, Editor. **ISSN:** 0044-5282. **Subscription Rates:** $15 domestic, 1 yr.; $40 domestic, 3 yrs.; $13 out of country; $50 out of country. **Remarks:** Advertising not accepted.
Circ: ‡200,000

3340 Country Cable Inc.
6839 Convoy Ct. Phone: (619)292-0415
San Diego, CA 92111 Fax: (619)292-1116

Founded: Aug. 1976. **Key Personnel:** Bruce Witte, President. **Cities Served:** Ramona, CA: subscribing households 2600; 95 channels.

3341 Cox Cable San Diego
5159 Federal Blvd. Phone: (619)263-9251
San Diego, CA 92105 Fax: (619)266-5555

Owner: Cox Cable Communications Inc., 1400 Lake Hearn Dr., Atlanta, GA 30319, (404)843-5000. **Key Personnel:** Robert McRann, General Mgr. **Cities Served:** Alpine, Chula Vista, City of San Diego, El Cajon, Imperial Beach, La Mesa, Lemon Grove, National City, Pine Valley, Poway, Santee, CA; San Diego County, CA: subscribing households 326,000; 77 channels; 3 community access channels; 380 hours per week community access programming.

3342 KBEST-FM - 94.9
1515 Murray Canyon Rd., Ste. 110 Phone: (619)297-1955 Fax: (619)543-1353
San Diego, CA 92108

Format: Oldies. **Founded:** 1960. **Formerly:** KWLT-FM (1988); KBZT-FM; KBZS-FM. **Operating Hours:** Continuous. **ADI:** San Diego, CA. **Key Personnel:** Mike Stafford, General Mgr.; Jim Infantine, Sales Mgr.; Chris Turner, Promotions Mgr. **Wattage:** 22,000.

3343 KBNT-TV - 19
5770 Ruffin Rd. Phone: (619)576-1919
San Diego, CA 92123-1013 Fax: (619)715-1919

Networks: Univision. **Founded:** 1990. **Operating Hours:** Continuous. **ADI:** San Diego, CA. **Key Personnel:** Philip Wilkinson, Pres./General Mgr.; Hector Molina, Station Mgr.; Mike Flynn, General Sales Mgr.; Jay Rabin, Local Sales Mgr.; Martha Barba, Research/Marketing Dir.; Lourdes Sandoval, News Dir. **Wattage:** 31.34 KW at 5,660 ft. AMSL. **Ad Rates:** $125-1,000 for 30 seconds.

3344 KCBQ-AM - 1170
PO Box 105.3 Phone: (619)286-1170
San Diego, CA 92112 Fax: (619)449-5398

Format: Oldies. **Networks:** Westwood One Radio. **Owner:** Compass Radio Group, at above address. **Founded:** 1946. **Operating Hours:** Continuous. **ADI:** San Diego, CA. **Key Personnel:** Robert J. Hughes, President & General Mgr.; Johathan D. Schwartz, Exec. VP/ CFO; Douglas P. Herman, Station Mgr.; Ellen Ascher, General Sales Mgr.; Kim Leeds, Promotions Dir.; Patty Hernandez, Business Mgr.; Jessie Bullet, Program Dir.; Bill Lipis, Chief Engineer; Kathy Allen, Traffic Mgr. **Wattage:** 50,000 day; 1,500 night. **Ad Rates:** Advertising accepted; rates available upon request.

3345 KCBQ-FM - 105.3
Box 105.3 Phone: (619)286-1170
San Diego, CA 92112 Fax: (619)449-5398

Format: Oldies. **Networks:** AP. **Owner:** Compass Radio Group, at above address, Fax: (619)449-8548. **Founded:** 1954. **Operating Hours:** Continuous. **ADI:** San Diego, CA. **Key Personnel:** Bob Ferro, General Sales Mgr.; Rich "Brother" Robin, Program Dir.; Julian Muschell, Sales Mgr.; Kim Leeds, Promotions Dir.; Jeff Stewart, Music Coord.; Dan Mitchinson, PSA Dir.; Mike Aiken, Asst. Promotions Dir.; Bill Lipis, Chief Engineer; Bob Hughes, General Mgr. **Wattage:** 29,000.

3346 KFMB-AM - 760
7677 Engineer Rd. Phone: (619)495-7536
San Diego, CA 92111 Fax: (619)279-7676
Free: (800)455-KFMB
E-mail: kfmb@cts.com

Format: Full Service; Talk. **Networks:** CBS. **Founded:** 1941. **Operating Hours:** Continuous. **ADI:** San Diego, CA. **Key Personnel:** Bob Bolinger, General Mgr.; Dave Sniff, Program Mgr.; Chuck Fritsch, News Dir.; Lori Ello, Promotions Mgr.; Dayna Monroe, Programming Asst. **Local Programs:** *Hudson & Bauer Show*, Steve Rooney, (619)495-7534; *The Stacy Taylor Show*, Phil Dietz; *The Ted Leitner Show*, John Dean, (619)495-7543. **Wattage:** 5000 day; 50,000 night. **URL:** http://www.760kfmb.com.

3347 KFMB-FM - 100.7
7677 Engineer Rd. Phone: (619)292-7600
San Diego, CA 92111-1582 Fax: (619)279-7676

Format: Adult Contemporary. **Networks:** Independent. **Founded:** 1959. **Operating Hours:** Continuous. **ADI:** San Diego, CA. **Key Personnel:** Bob Bolinger, Pres./Gen. Mgr.; Tracy Johnson, Operations Mgr.; Tom Gjerdrum, Program Dir.; Kelly Oden, Promotions Dir. **Wattage:** 36,000.

3348 KFMB-TV - 8
7677 Enigeer Rd. Phone: (619)571-8888
San Diego, CA 92111 Fax: (619)495-9369

Format: Commercial TV. **Networks:** CBS. **Founded:** 1949. **Operating Hours:** Continuous except 2 a.m.-6 a.m. Sat. and Sun. **ADI:** San Diego, CA. **Key Personnel:** Ed Trimble, General Mgr. **Local Programs:** *Assignment San Diego.*

3349 KFSD-FM - 94.1
600 W. Broadway, No. 2100 Phone: (619)239-9091
San Diego, CA 92101-3311 Fax: (619)236-0269

Format: Classical. **Networks:** Independent. **Owner:** Nationwide Communications, Inc., at above address. **Founded:** 1926. **Operating Hours:** Continuous. **ADI:** San Diego, CA. **Key Personnel:** Paul E. Palmer, General Mgr.; Kingsley McLaren, Program Dir.; Valerie Lindeman, Promotions Dir.; Angelica Go, Public Affairs Director. **Wattage:** 100,000. **Ad Rates:** $125-155 per unit.

3350 KGB-FM - 101.5
5745 Kearny Villa Rd., Ste. M Phone: (619)565-6006
San Diego, CA 92123-1136 Fax: (619)560-8090

Format: Classic Rock. **Founded:** 1956. **Formerly:** Nationwide. **Operating Hours:** Continuous. **ADI:** San Diego, CA. **Key Personnel:** Mike Glickenhaus, VP/GM; Todd Little, Program Dir. **Wattage:** 50,000. **Ad Rates:** Advertising accepted; rates available upon request. **URL:** http://www.101kgb.com.

3351 KGTV-TV - 10
Box 85347 Phone: (619)237-1010
San Diego, CA 92186 Fax: (619)262-1302

Format: Commercial TV. **Networks:** ABC. **Founded:** 1953. **ADI:** San Diego, CA. **Key Personnel:** Ed Quinn, General Mgr. **Local Programs:** *Good Morning San Diego.*

3352 KIFM-FM - 98.1
1615 Murray Canyon Rd., No. 710
San Diego, CA 92108
Phone: (619)297-3698
Fax: (619)543-1353
E-mail: webmaster@kifm.com

Format: Jazz. **Networks:** Independent. **Owner:** Jefferson Pilot Communications, at above address, (619)291-9797. **Founded:** 1960. **Operating Hours:** Continuous. **ADI:** San Diego, CA. **Key Personnel:** Mike Stafford, General Mgr., phone (619)718-7133, fax (619)543-1353; Bruce Walton, General Sales Mgr., phone (619)718-7140, bwalton@klfm.com. **Wattage:** 28,000. **Ad Rates:** $200-350 for 60 seconds. **URL:** http://www.kifm.com.

3353 KIOZ-FM - 105.3
5745 Kearny Villa Rd., Ste. M
San Diego, CA 92123
Phone: (619)565-6006
Fax: (619)569-7510

Format: Album-Oriented Rock (AOR). **Networks:** Independent. **Founded:** 1962. **Formerly:** KGMG-FM (1992); KCBQ-FM. **Operating Hours:** Continuous. **ADI:** San Diego, CA. **Key Personnel:** Mike Glickenhaus, General Mgr., phone (619)220-4218, fax (619)220-4288; Tim Dukes, Program Dir.; Shanon Leder, Music Dir.; Bob Iafrate, Dir. of Sales. **Local Programs:** *Dave, Shelly, & Chainsaw Morning Show*, Rich Berra, (619)565-6006, Fax (619)565-7510. **Wattage:** 29,000. **Ad Rates:** Advertising accepted; rates available upon request. **URL:** http://www.kioz.com.

3354 KJQY-FM 94.1 - 94.1
5745 Kearnyvilla Rd.
San Diego, CA 92123
Phone: (619)565-6006
E-mail: beachfm@adnc.com

Format: Adult Contemporary; Easy Listening. **Owner:** Jacor Broadcasting, 50 E. River Center Blvd., Covington, KY 41011, (606)655-2267, Fax: (606)655-9345. **Founded:** 1963. **Formerly:** KEZL-FM (1983); KSDO-FM; KSWV-FM; KCLX-FM; KKBH-FM. **Operating Hours:** Continuous; 100% local. **ADI:** San Diego, CA. **Wattage:** 100,000. **URL:** http://.

3355 KMCG-FM - 95.7
600 H. Broadway, Ste. 2150
San Diego, CA 92101
Phone: (619)615-9570
Fax: (619)615-9500
Free: (888)570-1957
E-mail: radio957@aol.com

Format: Adult Contemporary. **Networks:** Independent. **Founded:** 1965. **Formerly:** KKOS-FM; KUPR-FM. **Operating Hours:** Continuous. **ADI:** San Diego, CA. **Key Personnel:** Judy McNutt, Program Dir., phone (615)231-9570; Charlie Brown, Asst. Program Dir.; Irma B. Molina, Marketing and Promotions, fax (619)615-9507; Dennis M. Girazdon, General Mgr. **Local Programs:** *Gelder's Global Gig*, Jeff Gelder, (619)226-4033, Fax (619)226-4825; *Music without Boundaries*, Kenny Weisberg, (619)226-4033, Fax (619)226-4825.

3356 KNFR-FM - 96.1
750 B. St., Ste. 1920
San Diego, CA 92101

Format: Country. **Owner:** Triathlon Broadcasting, at above address. **Founded:** Oct. 1992. **Operating Hours:** Continuous. **ADI:** Spokane, WA. **Key Personnel:** Kosta Panidis, General Mgr.; Scott Shannon, Program Dir.; Mary Norton, Business Mgr.; Brenda Anderson, Traffic Dir. **Wattage:** 56,000. **Ad Rates:** Advertising accepted; rates available upon request.

3357 KNSD-TV - 39
8330 Engineer Rd.
San Diego, CA 92111
Phone: (619)279-3939
Fax: (619)279-1076

Format: Commercial TV. **Networks:** NBC. **Owner:** New World Communications of San Diego, at above address. **Founded:** 1965. **Formerly:** KAAR-TV (1966). **Operating Hours:** 5:15 a.m.-4:15 a.m.; 57% network, 43% local. **ADI:** San Diego, CA. **Key Personnel:** Neil Derrough, General Mgr.; Don Shafer, News Dir.; Penny Martin, Program Mgr.; Jim Laslavic, Sports Dir.; Doug Gilmore, Promotions Dir.; Darcey Gulen, Office Mgr.

3358 KOGO-AM - 600
5050 Murphy Canyon Rd.
San Diego, CA 92123
Phone: (619)278-1130
Fax: (619)715-3303

Format: Talk; News. **Networks:** CNN Radio; ABC. **Founded:** 1926. **Formerly:** KLZZ-AM; KKLQ-AM. **Operating Hours:** Continuous. **ADI:** San Diego, CA. **Key Personnel:** Kevin McCarthy, General Mgr., phone (619)285-4300, fax (619)285-4387; Hank Loeser, Sales Mgr., phone (619)285-3329, fax (619)285-4379; Jane Morton, News Dir., phone (619)560-6671, fax (619)715-3364; Cliff Albert, Program Dir., phone (619)715-3361; Sherry Toennies, Promotions Dir., phone (619)715-3340, fax (619)715-3372. **Local Programs:** *Alan Stock* 12 noon - 3 p.m., Tony Brittan; *Jim Alan* 11 p.m. - 2 a.m., Tony Brittan; *John Coleman* 9 a.m. - 12 noon, Tony Brittan. **Wattage:** 5000. **Ad Rates:** Advertising accepted; rates available upon request. KSDO-AM.

3359 KPBS-FM - 89.5
5200 Campanile
SDSU
San Diego, CA 92182-5400
Phone: (619)594-8100
Fax: (619)265-6478

Format: News; Public Radio. **Networks:** National Public Radio (NPR); American Public Radio (APR). **Founded:** 1960. **Operating Hours:** Continuous; 50% network, 50% local. **ADI:** San Diego, CA. **Key Personnel:** John Decker, Program Dir., phone (619)594-3037, fax (619)265-6417; Stefanie Levine, Contact; Stephanie Levine, Producer, phone (619)594-8072, fax (619)594-3099, slevine@mail.sdsu.edu; Mike Flaster, Program Dir., phone (619)594-4986, fax (619)265-6417, mflaster@mail.sdsu.edu; Mike Marotte, News Dir., phone (619)594-8141, marcotte@mail.sdsu.edu; Doug Myrland, General Mgr.; Jasbir Dhesi, Radio Producer, phone (619)594-8144, fax (619)594-3099, jdhesi@kpbs.org. **Local Programs:** *Taste of San Diego*, Kory Lueders; *These Days (Arts & Culture)*, Stefanie Levine; *These Days (Current Affairs)*, Kate Conccnnon. **Wattage:** 1750. **Ad Rates:** Noncommercial. **URL:** http://www.kpbs.org.

3360 KPBS-TV - 15
5200 Campanile Dr.
San Diego, CA 92182
Phone: (619)594-1515
Fax: (619)265-6417

Format: Public TV. **Networks:** Public Broadcasting Service (PBS). **Owner:** Board of Trustees, California State University, at above address. **Founded:** 1967. **Formerly:** KEBS-TV (1967). **Operating Hours:** 6:15 a.m.- 2am; 95% network, 5% local. **ADI:** San Diego, CA. **Key Personnel:** Doug Myrland, General Mgr., phone (619)594-2580, fax (619)265-6417; Michael Flaster, Assoc. Gen. Manager of Programming; Stephanie Bergsma, Assoc. Gen. Mgr./Development; John Folson, Engineering Mgr.; Gloria Penner Snyder, TV Program Production Dir.; Tom Karlo, Operations/Telecommunications Mgr.; Maura Grogan, Marketing and Communications Mgr. **Local Programs:** *Bloopy's Buddies*; *Debbi Fields' Great American Desserts*; *Liquid Stage*. **Wattage:** 3020. **Ad Rates:** Advertising accepted; rates available upon request.

3361 KPLN-FM - 103.7
8033 Linda Vista Rd
San Diego, CA 92111
Phone: (619)560-1037
Fax: (619)560-1881
Free: (888)388-1037

Networks: Independent. **Owner:** SFX Broadcasting, Inc., 650 Madison Ave., New York, NY 10022, (212)238-3100, Fax: (212)832-5121. **Founded:** 1965. **Formerly:** KOZN-FM (1981); KJQY-FM (1996); KMKX-FM. **Operating Hours:** Continuous. **ADI:** San Diego, CA. **Key Personnel:** Bob Bolinger, VP/Gen. Manager; Rich Hawkins, Program Dir., phone (619)467-4190; Lee McGowan, Chief Engineer, phone (619)467-4179, fax (619)571-0326; Peter Schwartz, General Sales Mgr., phone (619)467-4187, fax (619)560-1333; Joan Rubin, Controller, phone (619)467-4299; Beth Harris, Promotions Mgr., phone (617)467-4163, fax (619)571-0326; Cheri Olsen, Vendor Mgr., phone (619)467-4150, fax (619)571-0326. **Wattage:** 36,000. **Ad Rates:** Advertising accepted; rates available upon request. Combined advertising rates available with KYXY-FM. **URL:** http://www.planetfm.com.

3362 KPOP-AM - 1360
5050 Murphy Canyon Rd.
San Diego, CA 92123
Phone: (619)278-1130
Fax: (619)715-3379

Format: Big Band/Nostalgia. **Networks:** Westwood One Radio; CNN Radio. **Owner:** Jacor Communications, 50 E. Center Blvd., Covington, KY 41011, (606)655-2261. **Founded:** 1922. **Operating Hours:** Continuous. **ADI:** San Diego, CA. **Key Personnel:** Kevin McCarthy, General Mgr.; Jeff Williams, Program Dir.; Stephanie Morrissey, Promotions Dir. **Wattage:** 5000 day; 1000 night. **Ad Rates:** Advertising accepted; rates available upon request. CBR KOGO-AM, KSDO-AM. **URL:** http://www.kpopradio.com.

3363 KPRZ-AM - 1210
9255 Towne Centre Dr No. 535
San Diego, CA 92121
Phone: (619)535-1210
Fax: (619)535-1212
Free: (800)873-1210
E-mail: kprz_ radio@aol.com

Format: Religious; Talk. **Owner:** Salem Communications Corp., 4880 Santa Rosa Rd. No. 300, Camarillo, CA 93012, (805)987-0400, Fax: (805)482-8570. **Founded:** 1986. **Operating Hours:** Continuous. **ADI:** San Diego, CA. **Key Personnel:** Mark Larson, General Mgr.; Monica Murray, Operations Mgr.; Ellen Hinsch, Office Mgr. **Local Programs:** *Grapevine*, Monica Murray; *Larson Live!*, Mark Larson; *Master Trax*, David Manzi. **Wattage:** 20,000 day; 5000 night. **Ad Rates:** Advertising accepted; rates available upon request. **URL:** http://www.kprz.com.

3364 KSDO-AM - 1130
KSDO Bldg.
5050 Murphy Canyon Rd.
San Diego, CA 92123
Phone: (619)278-1130
Fax: (619)715-3303

Format: Talk; News. **Networks:** ABC. **Owner:** Jacor Broadcasting, 50 E. River Center Blvd., Covington, KY 41011, (606)655-2267, Fax: (606)655-9395. **Founded:** 1946. **Operating Hours:** Continuous; 30% network, 70% local. **ADI:** San Diego, CA. **Key Personnel:** Kevin McCarthy, V.P./General Mgr., phone (619)715-3300, fax (619)715-3387; Hank Loeser, Sales Mgr., phone (619)715-3329, fax (619)715-3379; Sherry Toennies, Promotions Dir., phone (619)715-3340, fax (619)715-3372; Mary Ayala, News Dir., phone (619)715-3318, fax (619)715-3372; Cliff Albert, Program Dir., phone (619)715-3361; Marcia Taylor, Traffic Mgr.; Bill Thompson, Chief Engineer, phone (619)715-3356, fax (610)715-3307. **Local Programs:** *KSDO Afternoon News*, Mary Ayala, News Dir.; *KSDO Morning News*, Mary Ayala, News Dir.; *Roger Hedgecock Show*, Jim Valentine, Producer. **Wattage:** 10,000. **Ad Rates:** Combined advertising rates available with KOGO-AM. **URL:** http://www.ksdo.com.

3365 KSDS-FM - 88.3
1313 12th Ave.
San Diego, CA 92101
Phone: (619)234-1062
Fax: (619)230-2212

Format: Jazz; Blues; World Beat. **Networks:** Independent. **Owner:** San Diego Community College District, 3375 Camino Del Rio South, San Diego, CA 92108, (619)584-6500. **Founded:** 1951. **Operating Hours:** Continuous; 100% local. **ADI:** San Diego, CA. **Key Personnel:** James Dark, General Mgr.; Mary Woodworth, Station Mgr.; Tony Sisti, Program Dir.; Joe Kocherhans, Music/Promotions Dir.; Hope Shaw, News Dir.; Fred Lewis, Sports Dir. **Wattage:** 831. **Ad Rates:** Noncommercial; underwriting available. **URL:** http://www.jazz88.org.

3366 KSON-FM - 97.3
PO Box 889004
San Diego, CA 92168
Phone: (619)291-9797
Fax: (619)543-1353

Format: Country. **Founded:** 1946. **ADI:** San Diego, CA. **Key Personnel:** Mike Stafford, General Mgr.; John Dimick, Operations Dir.; Greg Frey, Music Dir.; Steve Sapp, Promotions Dir.; Myra Has-Ellison, Contact; John A. Buffaloe, Chief Engineer. **Local Programs:** *SD Update*, Jack Smith, (619)291-9797, Fax (619)543-1353. **Wattage:** 50,000. **Ad Rates:** $110-500 per unit. Combined advertising rates available with KSON-AM:. **URL:** http://www.kson.com.

3367 KUSI-TV - 51
PO Box 719051
San Diego, CA 92171
Phone: (619)571-5151
Fax: (619)571-4852

Format: News; Talk. **Networks:** United Paramount Network. **Owner:** McKinnon Broadcasting Co., 4575 Viewridge Ave., San Diego, CA 92123. **Founded:** 1983. **Operating Hours:** 24 hrs. **ADI:** San Diego, CA. **Key Personnel:** Michael McKinnon, General Mgr.

3368 KYXY-FM - 96.5
8033 Linda Vista Rd.
San Diego, CA 92111-5170
Phone: (619)571-7600
Fax: (619)571-0326
Free: (888)560-9650

Format: Adult Contemporary. **Networks:** Independent. **Owner:** SFX Broadcasting, Inc., 650 Madison Ave., New York, NY 10022, (212)838-3100, Fax: (212)832-5121. **Founded:** 1960. **Operating Hours:** Continuous. **ADI:** San Diego, CA. **Key Personnel:** Bob Bolinger, VP/General Mgr., fax (619)560-1881; Rich Hawkins, Program Dir., phone (619)467-4190; Jean Arrollado, Promotions Dir., phone (619)467-4141; Joan Robin, Controller, phone (619)467-4188; Cathy Deary, General Sales Mgr., phone (619)467-4131, fax (619)560-4145; Jim Higgins, phone (619)467-4160, fax (619)560-1333; Lee McGowan, Chief Engineer, phone (619)467-4179; Sue Chaska, Vendor Mgr., phone (619)467-4132; Mira Simon, National Sales Mgr., phone (619)467-4169. **Wattage:** 41,000 ERP. **Ad Rates:** Combined advertising rates available with KYXY-AM. **URL:** http://www.kyxyfm.com.

3369 Time Warner Cable - San Diego
8949 Ware Ct.
San Diego, CA 92121
Phone: (619)695-3110
Fax: (619)566-6248
E-mail: jim.fellhauer@tvcable.com

Owner: Time Warner Cable, at above address, (619)578-2300, Fax: (619)566-6248. **Founded:** 1964. **Formerly:** Southwestern Cable TV (1998). **Key Personnel:** Jim Fellhauer, President. **Cities Served:** Clairemont, Del Mar Heights, La Jolla, Linda Vista, Mira Mesa, Mission Beach, North Poway, Pacific Beach, San Diego County, Tierrasanta, University City, CA; Bay Park, Carmel Mountain Ranch, Mission Valley, North City West, Poway, Rancho Bernardo, Rancho Penas Quitos, Sabre Springs, Serra Mesa, CA: subscribing households 205,000; 78 channels; 1 community access channel; 40 hours per week community access programming.

3370 XETV-TV - 6
8253 Ronson Rd. Phone: (619)279-6666
San Diego, CA 92111 Fax: (619)268-9388

Format: Commercial TV. **Networks:** Fox. **Owner:** Grupo Televisa, at above address. **Founded:** 1953. **Operating Hours:** 6 a.m.-2 a.m. **ADI:** San Diego, CA. **Key Personnel:** Joanie O'Laughlin, Vice President/General Manager, fax (619)277-5626, joanieo@compuserve.com; Chuck Dunning, General Sales Mgr., chuckdunig@aol.com; Bob Taylor, Vice President/CFO, fax (619)278-8253; Valerie Hoffman, Program Mgr., fax (619)571-3424; Judy Albrecht, Dir. Creative Services, fax (619)268-8351, jalbrecht@fox6.com; Bob Anderson, Operations Mgr.; Raff Ahlgren, Community Services Dir., fax (619)268-8351. **Local Programs:** *Fresh Point*; *Weekend with Raff Ahlgren*. **URL:** http://www.fox6.com.

3371 XHAS-TV - 33;49;57
6048 Cornerstone Ct. W., Ste. A Phone: (619)558-4646
San Diego, CA 92121 Fax: (619)558-0846

Format: Hispanic. **Networks:** Telemundo. **Founded:** 1990. **Operating Hours:** 6am-2am. **ADI:** San Diego, CA. **Key Personnel:** Fred Witt, General Mgr. **Local Programs:** *Buen Dia*; *Telenoticiero 33*; *Ultimo Minuto*. **Wattage:** 1,000,000 ERP. **URL:** http://www.amerimexmedi.com.

3372 XTRA-AM - 690
4891 Pacific Hwy. Phone: (619)291-9191
San Diego, CA 92110 Fax: (619)294-9362
E-mail: feedback@xtrasports.com

Format: Sports. **Networks:** ESPN Radio; CBS. **Founded:** 1934. **Operating Hours:** Continuous; 15% network, 85% local. **ADI:** San Diego, CA. **Key Personnel:** Kevin McCarthy, Exec. V.P./Gen. Mgr., phone (619)285-4300, fax (619)285-4387, kmccarthy@jacor.com; Doug Stewart, Promotions Dir., phone (619)220-4204, fax (619)220-4228; Jack Evans, Dir. of Programming/Operations; Tim Turner, General Sales Mgr., phone (619)220-4283, fax (619)220-4222; Joe Belshin, Natl. Sales Mgr., phone (619)220-4297, fax (619)218-7924; Dan Charleston, Nat'l Sales Mar., phone (619)220-4282, fax (619)218-7924. **Wattage:** 77,000 day, 50,000 night. **Ad Rates:** $200-300 per unit. **URL:** http://www.xtrasport690.com.

3373 XTRA-FM - 91.1
4891 Pacific Hwy. Phone: (619)291-9191
San Diego, CA 92110 Fax: (619)220-4288

Networks: Independent. **Owner:** Jacor Communications, 50 E. River Center, 12th Fl., Covington, KY 41011. **Founded:** 1981. **Formerly:** XETRA-FM. **Operating Hours:** Continuous. **ADI:** San Diego, CA. **Key Personnel:** Mike Glickenhaus, Vice Pres./Gen. Mgr., phone (619)220-4218, fax (619)220-4288, jacormike@aol.com; Bryan Schock, Program Dir., phone (619)220-4289, fax (619)291-3299, schlock91x@aol.co,; Joe Belshin, Natl. Sales Mgr., phone (619)220-4297, fax (619)718-7924; Joe Belshin, General Sales Mgr.; Bob lafrate, D.O.S. **Wattage:** 100,000. **Ad Rates:** $200-300 per unit.

SAN FERNANDO, pop. 17,731.

Los Angeles Co. (S). 20 m NW of Los Angeles. Citrus fruit and vegetable packing. Canning, preserving. Oil refinery. Cement pipe, olive oil, meat products, electronics, shirts, hosiery manufactured. Nurseries. Agriculture. Citrus fruit, vegetables.

3374 Record-Ledger
Mission Independent Corp.
1024 N. Maclay, Ste. 400 Phone: (818)365-3111
San Fernando, CA 91340
Newspaper with a Republican orientation. **Founded:** 1920. **Freq:** Weekly (Wed.). **Print Method:** Offset. **Cols./Page:** 6. **Col. Width:** 9.6 picas. **Col. Depth:** 14 inches. **Key Personnel:** Thelma Barrios, Publisher. **Remarks:** Accepts advertising.
Ad Rates: GLR: $.35 **Circ:** Paid 662
BW: $554 Free 10,000
4C: $679
PCI: $8.80

SAN FRANCISCO†, pop. 678,974.

City and County of San Francisco (W). On San Francisco Peninsula bounded by San Francisco Bay, Golden Gate and Pacific Ocean, has one of the finest harbor in the world. University of San Francisco. University of California at San Francisco. San Francisco State College. Other colleges. Law, dental, medical and many private schools. Gateway to the west, ranking in pacific waterborne commerce, financial center, wholesale trade. Printing and publishing houses. Manufactures paper boxes, confectionery, paints, chemicals, glass, leather, lumber, textiles, steel, clothing, bags, furniture, auto parts, electrical machinery, matches, clay, rubber products, tools, beverages. Coffee roasting, meat, fruit, vegetable packing, tea, spice, extract plants, shipyards, foundries, machine shops.

3375 Aberrations
Sirius Fiction
Box 460430
San Francisco, CA 94146-0430

Consumer magazine coverlng science fiction, fantasy, nonfiction, humor and reviews. **Founded:** Dec. 1991. **Freq:** Monthly. **Print Method:** Web offset. **Trim Size:** 5 1/4 x 8 3/8. **Cols./Page:** 2. **Col. Width:** 2 1/4 inches. **Col. Depth:** 7 1/2 inches. **Key Personnel:** Richard Blair, Editor. **ISSN:** 1058-2509. **Subscription Rates:** $31 individuals; $4.50 single issue. **Remarks:** Accepts advertising.
Ad Rates: BW: $60 **Circ:** Combined 1,500
4C: $90

3376 Action Sports
Miller Freeman, Inc.
600 Harrison St. Phone: (650)905-2200
San Francisco, CA 94107 Fax: (650)908-6604
Free: (800)227-4675
Publisher E-mail: techlearning_ editors@mfi.com

Retail magazine covering active lifestyle sports products and apparel. **Founded:** 1980. **Freq:** Monthly. **Print Method:** Offset. **Trim Size:** 8 3/8 x 10 7/8. **Cols./Page:** 3 and 2. **Col. Width:** 27 and 42 nonpareils. **Col. Depth:** 152 agate lines. **Key Personnel:** Sada Valov, Editor; Cathy Ruiz, Advertising Mgr. **ISSN:** 0199-4972. **Subscription Rates:** $25 individuals. **Remarks:** Accepts advertising. **Formerly:** Action Sports Retailer (1992).
Ad Rates: BW: $2,498 **Circ:** Paid ‡6,500
4C: $3,248 Controlled ‡1,500

3377 Aging Today
American Society on Aging
833 Market St., Ste. 511 Phone: (415)974-9600
San Francisco, CA 94103-1824 Fax: (415)974-0300
Publisher E-mail: info@asa.asaging.org

Newspaper (tabloid) for health, social service, and other professionals who work with older people. **Subtitle:** The bimonthly newspaper of the American Society on Aging. **Founded:** 1979. **Freq:** Bimonthly. **Print Method:** Offset. **Trim Size:** 11 1/4 x 15. **Cols./Page:** 4. **Col. Width:** 2 3/16 inches. **Col. Depth:** 13 inches. **Key Personnel:** Paul Kleyman, Editor, phone (415)974-9600, pkleyman@asa.asaging.org; Nancy Kaplan, Advertising Mgr., nkaplan@asa.asaging.org. **Subscription Rates:** $14.95 individuals; $24.95 two years. **Formerly:** The ASA Connection; The Aging Connection.
Ad Rates: BW: $1,075 **Circ:** Paid ‡12,500
4C: $2,075 Free ‡1,500

3378 AsianWeek
Pan Asia Venture Capital Corp.
809 Sacramento St. Phone: (415)397-0220
San Francisco, CA 94108 Fax: (415)397-7258
Publication E-mail: awsf@aol.com; asianweek@asianweek.com

Newspaper on Asian American interests. **Subtitle:** An English Language Journal for the Asian American Community. **Founded:** 1979. **Freq:** Weekly (Fri.). **Print Method:** Offset. **Trim Size:** 10 x 13. **Cols./Page:** 5. **Col. Width:** 24 nonpareils. **Col. Depth:** 196 agate lines. **Key Personnel:** James Carroll, Managing Editor; Erika Larson, Advertising Dir. **ISSN:** 0915-2056. **Subscription Rates:** $29 individuals. **Remarks:** Accepts advertising. **Available Online. Alt. Formats:** CD-ROM.
Ad Rates: BW: $1,323 **Circ:** ‡24,000
4C: $2,300

3379 BETA (Bulletin of Experimental Treatments for AIDS)
San Francisco AIDS Foundation
PO Box 426182 Phone: (415)487-8060
San Francisco, CA 94142-6182 Fax: (415)487-8066
Free: (800)367-2437
Publication E-mail: beta@sfaf.org

Magazine reporting medical information about treatment for HIV infection. **Subtitle:** Bulletin of Experimental Treatments for AIDS. **Founded:** June 1988. **Freq:** Quarterly. **Trim Size:** 8 3/8 x 10 7/8. **Cols./Page:** 2. **Col. Depth:** 10 inches. **Key Personnel:** Ron Baker, Editor, phone (415)487-8065, fax (415)487-8069, rbaker@sfaf.org; Mark Bowers, Managing Ed., phone (415)487-8067, fax (415)487-8069, mbowers@sfaf.org; Dave Robb, Subscriber Svcs., phone (415)487-8066, fax (415)487-8069, drobb@sfaf.org. **ISSN:** 1058-708X. **Subscription Rates:** $75 individuals; $165 institutions. **Remarks:** Advertising not accepted. **Online:** AEGIS BBS. **URL:** http://www.sfaf.org/beta.html.
Circ: Paid 1,500
Non-paid 18,500

3380 Black Sheets
Black Books
Box 31155 Phone: (415)431-0171
San Francisco, CA 94131 Fax: (415)431-0172
Publisher E-mail: blacksheets@blackbooks.com

Consumer magazine covering humor, sexuality, and popular culture. **Subtitle:** Kinky, Queer, Intelligent, Irreverant. **Founded:** 1993. **Freq:** Quarterly. **Print Method:** Web offset. **Trim Size:** 8 1/2 x 11. **Key Personnel:** Bill Brent, Publisher, bb@blackbooks.com. **ISSN:** 1071-5193. **Subscription Rates:** $20 individuals; $6 single issue. **Remarks:** Accepts advertising.
Circ: Paid 6,275

3381 Bright Lights
Box 420987 Phone: (510)601-5530
San Francisco, CA 94142-0987
Electronic journal covering film studies. **Founded:** Nov. 1995. **Freq:** Quarterly. **Key Personnel:** Gary Morris, Editor and Publisher, gmm@slip.net; George Brown, Webmaster. **Remarks:** Advertising not accepted. **URL:** http://www.slip.net/~gmm/bright.html.
Circ: (Not Reported)

3382 Business Valuation Review
American Society of Appraisers
660 Market St., No. 300 Phone: (415)986-1057
San Francisco, CA 94104 Fax: (415)392-6441

Technical journal for business valuers/appraisers and their clients. **Founded:** 1982. **Freq:** Quarterly. **Trim Size:** 8 1/2 x 11. **Cols./Page:** 1. **Key Personnel:** James H. Schilt, ASA, Editor; John E. Bakken, ASA, Publisher; Bradley A. Fowler, ASA, Contact; Shelly A. Chamberlain, Production Mgr. **ISSN:** 0882-2875. **Subscription Rates:** Free to qualified subscribers; $50. $12.50 single issue. **Remarks:** Accepts advertising. **Formerly:** Business Valuation News.
Ad Rates: BW: $250 **Circ:** Paid ‡1,100
Controlled ‡700

3383 CADENCE
Miller Freeman, Inc.
600 Harrison St. Phone: (650)905-2200
San Francisco, CA 94107 Fax: (650)908-6604
Free: (800)227-4675
Publisher E-mail: techlearning_ editors@mfi.com

News, reviews, techinical articles for auto CAD users. The world's largest independent AutoCAD Magazine. **Subtitle:** Using Autocad in the Professional Environment. **Founded:** 1986. **Freq:** Monthly. **Trim Size:** 8 x 10 7/8. **Cols./Page:** 3. **Key Personnel:** Johanna Kleepe, Publisher; Claire Goodhue, Associate Publisher. **ISSN:** 0887-9141. **Subscription Rates:** $39.95; $3.95 single issue. **Remarks:** Accepts advertising. **Online:** CompuServe.
Ad Rates: BW: $6,335 **Circ:** Paid 43,481
4C: $1,455 Controlled 31,565

3384 California Lawyer
Daily Journal Corp.
1145 Market St., 8th Fl. Phone: (415)252-0500
San Francisco, CA 94103 Fax: (415)252-0288

Law magazine. **Founded:** 1927. **Freq:** Monthly. **Print Method:** Offset. **Trim Size:** 8 1/4 x 10 3/4. **Cols./Page:** 3. **Col. Width:** 25 nonpareils. **Col. Depth:** 140 agate lines. **Key Personnel:** Peter Allen, Editor; Tema Goodwin, Managing Editor, tema_ goodwin@dailyjournal.com. **ISSN:** 0279-4063. **Subscription Rates:** $60 individuals; Free for licensed California attorneys. **Remarks:** Accepts advertising.
Ad Rates: BW: $5,610 **Circ:** Controlled ‡130,000
4C: $6,925

3385 California Legionnaire
The American Legion
Dept. of California Phone: (415)431-2400
117 Veterans War Memorial Bldg. Fax: (415)255-1571
401 Van Ness Ave.
San Francisco, CA 94102
Newspaper (tabloid) for veterans on legislation, the Veterans Administration, health fields, field operations, work of the legion and auxiliary in community affairs, and changes in post, unit, district, and department. **Founded:** 1920. **Freq:** Bimonthly. **Print Method:** Offset. **Trim Size:** 10 1/8 x 13. **Cols./Page:** 4. **Col. Width:** 2 1/4 inches. **Col. Depth:** 13 inches. **Key Personnel:** E. Paul Terry, Publishing Mgr.; Christopher Woodby, Editor. **Subscription Rates:** Free with CA American Legion membership; $15 nonmembers /year. **Remarks:** Accepts advertising.
Ad Rates: BW: $2,724 **Circ:** Paid 153,800
4C: $3,124 Free 1,000
PCI: $41

3386 California Official Reports
Bancraft-Whitney Co.
50 California St., 19th Fl. Fax: (415)732-8792
San Francisco, CA 94111-4624 Free: (800)537-2707

Publication containing opinions of the California Supreme Court and Court of Appeal. **Freq:** 3/month. **Print Method:** Offset. **Cols./Page:** 1. **Col. Width:** 45 nonpareils. **Col. Depth:** 98 agate lines. **Key Personnel:** Cynthia Sletto, Managing Editor, phone (415)732-8671, cynthia.sletto@westgroup.com.

Remarks: Advertising not accepted. **Online:** Westlaw. **Alt. Formats:** CD-ROM.
Circ: (Not Reported)

3387 California Voice
270 Francisco St. Fax: (415)931-0214
San Francisco, CA 94133-2012
Black community newspaper. **Founded:** 1919. **Freq:** Weekly (Fri.). **Print Method:** Letterpress. Uses mats. **Key Personnel:** Charles E. Belle, Editor. **Subscription Rates:** $9 individuals. **Remarks:** Accepts advertising.
Ad Rates: PCI: $12.85 **Circ:** Free 37,325

3388 California Wild
California Academy of Sciences
Golden Gate Park Phone: (415)750-7145
San Francisco, CA 94118 Fax: (415)221-4853
Free: (800)426-5411
Publication E-mail: calwild@calacademy.org

Consumer magazine. **Subtitle:** Natural Sciences for Thinking Animals. **Founded:** 1948. **Freq:** Quarterly. **Print Method:** Offset. **Trim Size:** 8 1/2 x 11. **Cols./Page:** 3. **Col. Width:** 27 nonpareils. **Col. Depth:** 114 agate lines. **Key Personnel:** Blake Edgar, Assoc. Editor; Douglas Corwin, Advertising Mgr.; Keith Howell, Editor, phone (415)750-7117; Gordy Slack, Associate Editor; Susan Schneider, Art Director. **ISSN:** 1094-3658. **Subscription Rates:** $12.95; $22 other countries; $11 agencies. **Remarks:** Accepts advertising. **Available Online. URL:** http://www.calacademy.org. **Alt. Formats:** Microform. **Formerly:** Pacific Discovery.
Ad Rates: BW: $2,150 **Circ:** ‡30,000
4C: $2,420

3389 California Wine Merchant's Gazette
Evento Gamina Publications
3237 Pierce Phone: (415)285-7333
PO Box 77291
San Francisco, CA 94107-0291
Wine magazine. **Founded:** 1982. **Freq:** Monthly. **Print Method:** Offset. **Cols./Page:** 1. **Col. Width:** 84 nonpareils. **Col. Depth:** 136 agate lines. **Subscription Rates:** $48 individuals.

3390 Chinese America
Chinese Historical Society of America
644 Broadway St., Ste. 402 Phone: (415)391-1188
San Francisco, CA 94133 Fax: (415)391-1150

Scholarly journal covering Chinese American history. **Subtitle:** History and Perspectives. **Founded:** 1987. **Freq:** Annual. **Subscription Rates:** $45 members; $15 single issue 8.5% for California residents. **Remarks:** Advertising not accepted.
Circ: (Not Reported)

3391 Chinese Times
686 Sacramento St. Phone: (415)982-0135
San Francisco, CA 94111 Fax: (415)982-3387

Ethnic community newspaper printed in Chinese. **Founded:** 1924. **Freq:** Daily (morn.). **Print Method:** Offset. Uses mats. **Trim Size:** 20 x 14. **Cols./Page:** 8. **Col. Width:** 16 nonpareils. **Col. Depth:** 315 agate lines. **Key Personnel:** Eva Chung, Editor; Dr. Stanley Hom, Publisher. **Subscription Rates:** $119.35 individuals; $.50 single issue. **Remarks:** Accepts advertising. **Formerly:** Gum Sun Times, Inc.
Ad Rates: GLR: $11.55 **Circ:** ‡11,000
PCI: $3.25

3392 Cinematograph
San Francisco Cinematheque
480 Potrero
San Francisco, CA 94110
Publication E-mail: cthegue@snfrns.com

Journal covering art film. **Founded:** 1985. **Freq:** Annual. **Key Personnel:** Steve Anker. **ISSN:** 0886-6570. **Subscription Rates:** $15 single issue; $25. **Remarks:** Accepts advertising.
Circ: Controlled 3,000

3393 Contact Point
University of the Pacific School of Dentistry
2155 Webster St. Phone: (415)929-6584
San Francisco, CA 94115-2333 Fax: (415)929-6654

College alumni and dental magazine. **Founded:** 1924. **Freq:** Quarterly. **Print Method:** Offset. **Cols./Page:** 3. **Col. Width:** 27 nonpareils. **Col. Depth:** 140 agate lines. **Key Personnel:** David W. Chambers, Editor; Sharon Wong, Advertising Mgr. **Remarks:** Accepts advertising.
Ad Rates: BW: $700 **Circ:** Non-paid ‡6,500
4C: $1,400

3394 The Culinarian
Chefs Association of the Pacific Coast, Inc.
1550 Bryant St., Ste. 810 Phone: (415)864-5627
San Francisco, CA 94103 Fax: (415)864-5628

Professional magazine for chefs. **Founded:** 1955. **Freq:** Monthly. **Print Method:** Offset. **Trim Size:** 11 x 17. **Cols./Page:** 3. **Col. Width:** 14 picas. **Col. Depth:** 60 picas. **Key Personnel:** Mary Forslund, Editor. **Subscription Rates:** $25. **Remarks:** Accepts advertising.
Ad Rates: BW: $230 **Circ:** ‡1,500
4C: $950

3395 Curator
California Academy of Sciences
Golden Gate Park Phone: (415)750-7145
San Francisco, CA 94118 Fax: (415)221-4853
Free: (800)426-5411
Publication E-mail: cresh@amnh.org

Scholarly publication for museum personnel. Contains black and white illustrations. **Subtitle:** The Museum Journal. **Founded:** 1958. **Freq:** Quarterly. **Trim Size:** 7 x 10. **Cols./Page:** 1 and 2. **Col. Width:** 4 and 2 5/8 inches. **Col. Depth:** 7 3/4 inches. **Key Personnel:** Samuel M. Taylor, Editor, phone (415)750-7383, fax (415)750-7372, staylor@casmail.calacademy.org; Mitch Allen, Publisher. **ISSN:** 0011-3069. **Subscription Rates:** $35; $65 industry; $40 other countries; $70 industry in other countries; $15 single issue. **Remarks:** Advertising not accepted. **Alt. Formats:** Microform.
Circ: Paid 1,600
Controlled 125

3396 Curve
Outspoken Enterprises, Inc.
1 Haight St., Ste. B Phone: (415)863-6538
San Francisco, CA 94102 Fax: (415)863-1609
Publication E-mail: curvemag@aol.com

National lesbian magazine covering news, politics, sports, arts, entertainment, and trends. Includes fiction, poetry, and profiles. **Subtitle:** Lesbian Magazine. **Founded:** 1991. **Freq:** Bimonthly. **Print Method:** Web press. **Trim Size:** 8 3/8 x 10 7/8. **Cols./Page:** 3. **Col. Width:** 2 1/2 inches. **Col. Depth:** 7 1/2 inches. **Key Personnel:** Frances Stevens, Publisher; Rebecca Alber, Managing Editor; Shannon Turner, Assistant Editor; Juliette Thompson, Dir. Marketing, phone (504)738-1021, fax (504)738-1022. **ISSN:** 1062-6247. **Subscription Rates:** $17.95; $4 single issue. **Remarks:** Accepts advertising. **Formerly:** Deneuve.
Ad Rates: BW: $2,455 **Circ:** Paid 68,000
4C: $3,559 Non-paid 305
PCI: $25

3397 Daily Pacific Builder
McGraw-Hill, Inc.
221 Main St., 8th Fl. Phone: (415)495-4200
San Francisco, CA 94105-1921 Fax: (415)495-0997
Free: (800)531-5439

Trade magazine for the building and engineering industry. **Founded:** 1890. **Freq:** Daily (morn.). **Print Method:** Offset. **Trim Size:** 11 1/2 x 17 1/2. **Cols./Page:** 5. **Col. Width:** 24 nonpareils. **Col. Depth:** 231 agate lines. **Key Personnel:** Susan K. Miller, Publisher; Carol Eaton, Editor. **Subscription Rates:** $1,200 individuals. **Remarks:** Accepts advertising.
Ad Rates: BW: $2,520 **Circ:** ‡1,800
4C: $3,170

3398 Diagnostic Imaging
Miller Freeman, Inc.
600 Harrison St. Phone: (650)905-2200
San Francisco, CA 94107 Fax: (650)908-6604
Free: (800)227-4675
Publisher E-mail: techlearning_ editors@mfi.com

News and analysis on clinical and economic developments in medical imaging. **Subtitle:** The Newsmagazine of Imaging, Innovation and Economics. **Founded:** Nov. 1979. **Freq:** Monthly. **Print Method:** Web offset. **Trim Size:** 8 1/8 x 10 7/8. **Cols./Page:** 3. **Col. Width:** 26 nonpareils. **Col. Depth:** 140 agate lines. **Key Personnel:** Peter L. Ogle, Editor; Sally Shankland, Publisher. **Subscription Rates:** $95 Nonqualified. **Remarks:** Accepts advertising. **URL:** http://www.dimag.com; http://www.mfi.com.
Ad Rates: BW: $4,940 **Circ:** Paid 978
4C: $7,030 Non-paid 30,283

3399 Disability Statistics Report
Disability Statistics Program
Institute for Health and Aging Phone: (415)502-5210
3333 California St., Rm 340 Fax: (415)476-9485
University of California
San Francisco, CA 94118
Magazine providing statistical data on disability in the U.S. as collected by the Disability Statistics Program. **Freq:** Irregular. **Subscription Rates:** No charge for single copies.

3400 The Dispatcher
International Longshoremen's and Warehousemen's Union
1188 Franklin St., 4th Fl. Phone: (415)775-0533
San Francisco, CA 94109 Fax: (415)775-1302

Newspaper containing union and labor news. **Subtitle:** Union Newspaper. **Founded:** 1942. **Freq:** Monthly. **Print Method:** Offset. **Cols./Page:** 4. **Col. Width:** 29 nonpareils. **Col. Depth:** 224 agate lines. **Key Personnel:** Kathy Wilkes, Editor; Steve Stallone, Asst. Ed. **ISSN:** 0012-3765. **Subscription Rates:** Free to union members.; $2.50 subscribers. **Remarks:** Advertising not accepted.
Circ: Non-paid ‡44,000

3401 Earth Island Journal
Earth Island Institute
300 Broadway, Ste. 28 Phone: (415)788-3666
San Francisco, CA 94133-3312 Fax: (415)788-7324
Publication E-mail: journal@eii.org

Magazine publishing environmental alerts and success stories from around the world. **Subtitle:** An International Environmental News Magazine. **Founded:** 1986. **Freq:** Quarterly. **Print Method:** Web offset. **Trim Size:** 10 7/8 x 8 1/2. **Cols./Page:** 3. **Col. Width:** 2 1/4 inches. **Key Personnel:** Gar Smith, Editor-in-Chief; Paige Sorvillo, Managing Editor; Sharon Skolnick, Art Dir.; Chris Clarke, Editor. **ISSN:** 1041-0406. **Subscription Rates:** Free to Earth Island Institute; $25 individuals; $4.50 single issue; $35 organizations; $3 newsstands; $4 Canada. **Remarks:** Accepts advertising. **URL:** http://www.earthisland.org/eii.
Ad Rates: BW: $600 **Circ:** Combined 14,000

3402 East Bay Guardian
The San Francisco Bay Guardian
520 Hampshire St. Phone: (415)255-3100
San Francisco, CA 94110 Fax: (415)255-8955

Community newspaper. **Founded:** 1990. **Freq:** Weekly.
Circ: Paid 2,000
Non-paid 70,000

3403 Educational Foundations
Caddo Gap Press
3145 Geary Blvd., No. 275 Phone: (415)922-1911
San Francisco, CA 94118 Fax: (415)440-4870
Publisher E-mail: caddogap@aol.com

Professional journal for the educational foundations fields. **Founded:** 1986. **Freq:** Quarterly. **Print Method:** Offset. **Trim Size:** 6 x 9. **Cols./Page:** 1. **Col. Width:** 27 picas. **Col. Depth:** 43 picas. **Key Personnel:** Alan H. Jones, Publisher. **ISSN:** 1047-8248. **Subscription Rates:** $60 institutions libraries; $40 individuals; $15 single issue. **Remarks:** Accepts advertising.
Ad Rates: BW: $200 **Circ:** 800

3404 El Bohemio News
4178 Mission St. Phone: (415)469-9579
San Francisco, CA 94112 Fax: (415)469-9481
Publisher E-mail: bohemio@ix.netcom.com

Newspaper (Spanish). **Founded:** 1971. **Freq:** Weekly. **Print Method:** Offset. **Cols./Page:** 6. **Col. Width:** 2 inches. **Col. Depth:** 21 inches. **Key Personnel:** Fred Rosado, Editor and Publisher, phone (415)469-9579, fax (415)469-9481. **Subscription Rates:** $60 individuals. **Remarks:** Accepts advertising.
Ad Rates: BW: $2,770 **Circ:** 42,300
4C: $3,445
SAU: $22
PCI: $25

3405 El Latino
San Francisco Latino Newspapers
348 Hayes St. Phone: (415)552-3031
San Francisco, CA 94102-4453 Fax: (415)552-2502

Spanish language newspaper serving San Francisco, Almeda, San Mateo, Santa Clara, Contra Costa, Napa, Solano, Sonoma, and Marin counties. **Founded:** Jan. 1993. **Freq:** Weekly (Wed.). **Trim Size:** 11 x 17. **Cols./Page:** 5. **Col. Width:** 2 1/16 inches. **Col. Depth:** 14 inches. **Key Personnel:** Roberto Heller, Publisher; Al Race, Editor; Carmen Ruiz, Account Exec. **ISSN:** 1054-5409. **Subscription Rates:** $52. **Remarks:** Accepts advertising. **Formerly:** San Francisco Latino.
Ad Rates: BW: $1,330 **Circ:** Non-paid 250
4C: $1,830 Paid 19,750
SAU: $10
PCI: $19

3406 Embedded Systems Programming
Miller Freeman, Inc.
600 Harrison St. Phone: (650)905-2200
San Francisco, CA 94107 Fax: (650)908-6604
Free: (800)227-4675
Publisher E-mail: techlearning_ editors@mfi.com

Magazine covering microprocessors and microcontrollers, high-level languages and real-time operating systems for design engineers, engineering managers, software developers, and programmers. **Founded:** Nov. 1988. **Freq:** Monthly including an additional issue in July. **Print Method:** Offset. **Trim Size:** 8 x 10 7/8. **Cols./Page:** 3. **Col. Width:** 13 picas. **Col. Depth:** 59 picas. **Key Personnel:** Lyndsey Vereen, Editor-in-Chief; Mike Flynn, Publisher; Sherri Gronli, Circula-

tion Mgr. **ISSN:** 4470-5662. **Subscription Rates:** Free to qualified subscribers; $55 individuals. **Remarks:** Accepts advertising. **URL:** http://www.embedded.com/. **Alt. Formats:** CD-ROM; Microfilm.
Ad Rates: BW: $2,595 **Circ:** 40,000
4C: $3,490

3407 Factsheet Five
PO Box 170099 Phone: (415)668-1781
San Francisco, CA 94117-0099
Magazine that lists and reviews alternative and underground periodicals, art, music, books, videos, and other pop culture flotsam and jetsam. **Subtitle:** The Definitive Guide to the Zine Revolution. **Founded:** 1982. **Freq:** Quarterly. **Print Method:** Sheetfed offset. **Trim Size:** 7 3/4 x 10 3/4. **Cols./Page:** 2. **Col. Width:** 3 1/2 inches. **Col. Depth:** 9 3/4 inches. **Key Personnel:** R. Seth Friedman, Editor, editor@factsheet5.com; f5seth@sirius.com. **ISSN:** 0890-6823. **Subscription Rates:** $20 bulk mail; $40 corporate; $45 other countries (Canada, Europe, U.K.); $55 other countries (Japan, Australia); $6 single issue. **Remarks:** Accepts advertising. **URL:** http://www.factsheet5.com.
Ad Rates: BW: $500 **Circ:** Combined ‡15,000
PCI: $40

3408 FAD Magazine
The R.J. Garbosky Co.
3450 3rd St., No. 2A-350 Phone: (415)647-7091
San Francisco, CA 94124 Fax: (415)285-2374
Publication E-mail: fadmag@aol.com

Fashion, art, and design megazine. **Subtitle:** Premiere Medium of the Avant-Garde. **Founded:** Dec. 1985. **Freq:** Quarterly. **Trim Size:** 10 x 12. **Key Personnel:** Dean Seven, Creative Dir. **ISSN:** 1066-6036. **Subscription Rates:** $20. **Remarks:** Accepts advertising. **URL:** http://www.fadmag.com.
Ad Rates: BW: $2,995 **Circ:** Paid ‡57,546
4C: $4,195

3409 Feminist Bookstore News
PO Box 882554 Phone: (415)642-9993
San Francisco, CA 94188 Fax: (415)642-9995
Publication E-mail: fbn@fembknews.com

Trade magazine for booksellers, librarians, and publishers interested in books by and about women. **Founded:** Oct. 1, 1976. **Freq:** Bimonthly. **Print Method:** Offset. **Trim Size:** 7 x 8 1/2. **Cols./Page:** 2. **Col. Width:** 3 inches. **Col. Depth:** 7 1/2 inches. **Key Personnel:** Carol Seajay, Editor and Publisher, carol@fembknews.com; Jenn Tust, Asst. Editor, jenn@fembknews.com; Kathryn Werhane, Advertising, kathryn@fembknews.com. **ISSN:** 0741-6555. **Subscription Rates:** $70 individuals; $6 single issue.
Ad Rates: BW: $770 **Circ:** Paid ‡800
Non-paid ‡50

3410 Filipinas Magazine
Filipinas Publishing, Inc.
655 Sutter St., Ste. 333 Phone: (415)563-5878
San Francisco, CA 94102 Fax: (415)292-5993
Free: (800)654-7777
Publication E-mail: filmagazin@aol.com

Magazine covering Filipino American interests and affairs. **Subtitle:** The Magazine for All Filipinos. **Founded:** 1992. **Freq:** Monthly. **Trim Size:** 8 1/2 x 11. **Key Personnel:** Rene Ciria-Cruz, Editor, phone (415)674-0964; Mona Lisa Yuchengco, Publisher, phone (415)674-0968. **ISSN:** 1063-4630. **Subscription Rates:** $24 U.S.; $39 Canada; $110 other countries. **Remarks:** Accepts advertising. **URL:** http://www.filipinasmag.com.
Ad Rates: BW: $2,500 **Circ:** Paid 24,126
4C: $3,000 Non-paid ★**2,727**

3411 Film/Tape World
Planet Communications
51 Federal St., Ste. 201 Phone: (415)543-6100
San Francisco, CA 94107
Trade magazine covering film, video and multimedia in Northern California for professionals. **Founded:** 1988. **Freq:** Monthly. **Print Method:** Web offset. **Trim Size:** 11 7/8 x 16 3/4. **Key Personnel:** Steve Goldstein, Editor, srgold@sirius.com; Michael Fox, Assoc. Publisher; Wes Dorman, Publisher. **Subscription Rates:** $35 individuals; $3.50 single issue. **Remarks:** Accepts advertising.
Ad Rates: BW: $900 **Circ:** Controlled 4,000
4C: $1,600

3412 Fourteen Hills
SFSU Phone: (415)338-3083
Dept. of Creative Writing
1600 Holloway Ave.
San Francisco, CA 94132-1722
Publication E-mail: hills@sfsu.edu
Publisher E-mail: hills@sfsu.edu

Magazine containing creative literary work. **Subtitle:** The SFSU Review. **Founded:** 1994. **Freq:** Semiannual. **Trim Size:** 6 x 9. **ISSN:** 1085-4576. **Subscription Rates:** $7 single issue. **Remarks:** Accepts advertising.
Circ: Paid 600

3413 France Today
France Press, Inc.
1051 Divisadero Phone: (415)921-5100
San Francisco, CA 94115 Fax: (415)921-0213
Free: (800)232-1549
Publisher E-mail: fpress@hooked.net

Magazine covering contemporary issues, events, trends, and travel in France. **Subtitle:** The Journal of French Travel & Culture. **Founded:** 1985. **Freq:** Bimonthly 10/year. **Key Personnel:** Lisel Fay, Office Mgr., phone (415)921-5100; Cara Ballard, Editorial Associate. **ISSN:** 0895-3651. **Subscription Rates:** $39 individuals; $5.50 single issue. **Remarks:** Accepts advertising. **Online:** American Cybercasting.
Circ: ‡25,000

3414 Generations, Journal of the American Society on Aging
American Society on Aging
833 Market St., Ste. 511 Phone: (415)974-9600
San Francisco, CA 94103-1824 Fax: (415)974-0300
Publisher E-mail: info@asa.asaging.org

Magazine for health, social service, and other professionals who work with older people; presenting in-depth view of a specific topic in aging emphasizing research and practice. **Founded:** 1976. **Freq:** Quarterly. **Print Method:** Offset. **Trim Size:** 7 1/2 x 10. **Cols./Page:** 2. **Col. Width:** 2 3/4 inches. **Col. Depth:** 8 3/4 inches. **Key Personnel:** Mary Tuckwiler Johnson, Editor; Nancy Ceridwyn, Advertising Mgr., phone (415)674-9615, nceridwyn@asa.asaging.org. **ISSN:** 0738-7806. **Subscription Rates:** $38 individuals. **Remarks:** Accepts advertising.
Ad Rates: BW: $1,225 **Circ:** Paid 14,200
Controlled 300

3415 Girljock
Rox-A-Tronic
PO Box 882723 Phone: (415)282-6833
San Francisco, CA 94188-2723 Fax: (415)282-6833

Publication focusing on the lives of women athletes and their admirers. **Founded:** 1990. **Freq:** Quarterly. **Subscription Rates:** $12. $5 single issue. **Remarks:** Advertising accepted; rates available upon request.
Circ: (Not Reported)

3416 Gnosis Magazine
PO Box 14217 Phone: (415)974-0600
San Francisco, CA 94114-0217 Fax: (415)974-0366
Publisher E-mail: gnosis@gnosismagazine.com

New Age magazine covering religion and spirituality. **Subtitle:** A Journal of the Western Inner Traditions. **Founded:** 1985. **Freq:** Quarterly. **Print Method:** Web offset. **Trim Size:** 8 1/4 x 10 3/4. **Key Personnel:** Jay Kinney, Editor and Publisher. **ISSN:** 0894-6159. **Subscription Rates:** $20 individuals; $25 other countries and institutions. **Remarks:** Accepts advertising. **URL:** http://www.gnosismagazine.com.
Ad Rates: BW: $865 **Circ:** Paid ⊕**16,000**
PCI: $85

3417 Golden Gate University Law Review
Golden Gate University School of Law
536 Mission St. Phone: (415)442-6690
San Francisco, CA 94105 Fax: (415)442-6609

Student-published law review, including Ninth Circuit Survey, Women's Law Forum, and Notes and Comments. **Founded:** 1970. **Freq:** Triennial. **Cols./Page:** 1. **Key Personnel:** Steven Lind, Subscriptions Coord. **ISSN:** 0363-0307. **Subscription Rates:** $22 individuals; $15 single issue. **Remarks:** Advertising not accepted. **Online:** West Online.
Circ: Paid 375

3418 Golden Gater
San Francisco State University
Dept. of Journalism Phone: (415)338-3123
1600 Holloway Ave. Fax: (415)338-3111
San Francisco, CA 94132
Publication E-mail: ggp@sfsu.edu

Collegiate newspaper. **Subtitle:** One of the Nation's Best College Newspapers. **Founded:** 1931. **Freq:** Semiweekly (Tues. and Thurs.). **Print Method:** Offset. **Trim Size:** 14 x 23. **Cols./Page:** 6. **Col. Width:** 2 1/16 inches. **Col. Depth:** 21 inches. **Key Personnel:** Douglas Allen, General Mgr. **Subscription Rates:** Free; $30 by mail. **Remarks:** Accepts advertising. **URL:** http://www.journalism.sfsu.edu.
Ad Rates: BW: $982.80 **Circ:** ‡10,000
4C: $1,632.80
PCI: $15.85

3419 The Guardsman
City College of San Francisco
50 Phelan Ave., V-67 Phone: (415)239-3446
San Francisco, CA 94112 Fax: (415)239-3884

Collegiate newspaper. **Founded:** 1935. **Freq:** Semiweekly. **Print Method:** Offset. **Cols./Page:** 5. **Col. Width:** 1 2/4 inches. **Col. Depth:** 16 inches. **Key Personnel:** J. Gonzales, Faculty Advisor. **Remarks:** Accepts advertising.
Circ: ‡10,000

3420 Harmony
Sea Fog Press, Inc.
447 20th Ave. Phone: (415)221-8527
PO Box 210056
San Francisco, CA 94121
Journal on social justice. **Subtitle:** Voices for a Just Future. **Founded:** 1987. **Freq:** Bimonthly. **Print Method:** Offset. **Trim Size:** 8 1/2 x 11. **Key Personnel:** Rose Evans, Managing Editor, roseevans@aol.com. **ISSN:** 0896-243X. **Subscription Rates:** $12. $2 single issue. **Remarks:** Advertising accepted; rates available upon request. **URL:** http://users.marble.net/~harmony.
Circ: Paid ‡1,000
Non-paid ‡100

3421 Hastings Communications and Entertainment Law Journal (COMM/ENT)
University of California, Hastings College of the Law
200 McAllister St. Phone: (415)551-4170
San Francisco, CA 94102-4978 Fax: (415)551-4110
Publication E-mail: comment@uchastings.edu

Law journal on the legal issues of Communications and entertainment law. **Subtitle:** COMM/ENT. **Founded:** 1977. **Freq:** Quarterly. **Print Method:** Offset. **Trim Size:** 6 3/4 x 9 3/4. **Key Personnel:** Albert Kaba, Scholarly Publications Coordinator. **ISSN:** 1061-6578. **Remarks:** Accepts advertising. **Available Online. URL:** http://www.uchastings.edu/pubs/comment/comment.html.
Ad Rates: BW: $200 **Circ:** Paid 1,050
Non-paid 150

3422 Health
Time Inc. Health
2 Embarcadero Center, Ste. 600 Phone: (415)248-2700
San Francisco, CA 94111 Fax: (415)248-2779

Consumer magazine covering medicine, health, and fitness issues. **Founded:** 1987. **Freq:** 7/year. **Print Method:** Web offset. **Trim Size:** 8 x 10 3/4. **Cols./Page:** 3. **Col. Width:** 2 1/4 inches. **Col. Depth:** 9 3/8 inches. **Key Personnel:** Barbara Paulsen, Editor-in-Chief, editor@health.com; Sheridan Warrick, Executive Editor. **ISSN:** 1047-0549. **Subscription Rates:** $18.00 individuals; $2.95 single issue. **Formerly:** In Health; Hippocrates.
Ad Rates: BW: $28,640 **Circ:** Paid ★**1,059,079**
4C: $36,290

3423 Hokubei Mainichi
Hokubei Mainichi, Inc.
1746 Post St. Phone: (415)567-7323
San Francisco, CA 94115 Fax: (415)567-1110
Publication E-mail: hokubei-editor@webjapan.com

General newspaper (Japanese and English). **Subtitle:** North American Daily. **Founded:** 1948. **Freq:** Tues.-Sat. (morn.). **Print Method:** Offset. **Cols./Page:** 8. **Col. Width:** 23 nonpareils. **Col. Depth:** 280 agate lines. **Key Personnel:** Ms. Atsuyo Hiramoto, Editor-in-Chief; Mr. J.K. Yamamoto, Editor; Chikako Moriya, Advertising Mgr. **Subscription Rates:** $125 1 year; $34 3 months; $65 6 months. **Remarks:** Accepts advertising.
Ad Rates: BW: $2,000 **Circ:** 10,000
4C: $3,500
PCI: $25

3424 H2SO4
Tentative Publications
Box 423354 Phone: (415)431-2135
San Francisco, CA 94142 Fax: (415)431-2135
Publication E-mail: h2so4@socrates.berkeley.edu

Literary journal covering fiction, reviews, humor, and the arts. **Founded:** Dec. 1992. **Freq:** Semiannual. **Trim Size:** 8 1/2 x 11. **Cols./Page:** 2 and 3. **Key Personnel:** Jill Stauffer, Editor and Publisher; Heidi Pollock, Assoc. Editor; Kamran Rastegar, Reviews. **ISSN:** 1083-3897. **Subscription Rates:** $10 individuals; $5 single issue. **Remarks:** Accepts advertising.
Ad Rates: BW: $200 **Circ:** Combined 600

3425 IABC Communication World
1 Hallidie Plaza, Ste. 600 Phone: (415)433-3400
San Francisco, CA 94102 Fax: (415)362-8762

Public relations/communication magazine. **Founded:** 1981. **Freq:** 9/year. **Print Method:** Offset. **Trim Size:** 8 3/8 x 10 7/8. **Cols./Page:** 3. **Col. Width:** 28 nonpareils. **Col. Depth:** 140 agate lines. **Key Personnel:** Gloria Gordon, Editor, phone

(415)544-4700, fax (415)540-4749, ggordan@labc.com. **ISSN:** 0744-7612. **Subscription Rates:** Included in membership. **Remarks:** Accepts advertising. **URL:** http://www.abc.com/cw/cwhome.htm. **Alt. Formats:** Mailing labels.
Ad Rates: BW: $1,430 **Circ:** Paid 14,506
4C: $2,055 Non-paid 657

3426 Intuition
PO Box 460773 Phone: (415)538-8171
San Francisco, CA 94146-0773 Fax: (415)538-8175
Publisher E-mail: intuitmag@aol.com

Consumer magazine covering New Age issues. **Subtitle:** A Magazine for the Higher Potential of the Mind. **Founded:** 1988. **Freq:** Bimonthly. **Key Personnel:** Colleen Mauro, Editor; Michael Gliksohn, Circulation Mgr.; Jody Stathakis, Advertising Mgr. **ISSN:** 1085-3529. **Subscription Rates:** $19.95 individuals; $4.95 single issue. **Remarks:** Accepts advertising.
Ad Rates: BW: $778 **Circ:** Paid 25,000
4C: $778

3427 Irish Focus News
The Irish Herald
3516 Geary Blvd. Phone: (415)752-7977
San Francisco, CA 94118 Fax: (415)750-9670
Publication E-mail: irishherald@msn.com

Irish community newspaper. **Subtitle:** The Irish Herald. **Founded:** 1962. **Freq:** Monthly. **Trim Size:** 10 x 16. **Cols./Page:** 5. **Col. Width:** 1 7/8 inches. **Col. Depth:** 16 inches. **Key Personnel:** Mikel O'Riordan, Publisher; Catherine Barry, Managing Editor. **ISSN:** 074 -0591. **Subscription Rates:** $20 individuals. **Remarks:** Accepts advertising. **Formerly**: The Irish Herald.
Ad Rates: BW: $1,190 **Circ:** Paid ⊕**4,000**
4C: $1,500 Non-paid ⊕**15,000**

3428 Jewish Star
109 Minna St., No. 323 Phone: (415)243-4313
San Francisco, CA 94105-3728 Fax: (415)243-0826

Magazine (tabloid) of book reviews of Jewish interest. **Founded:** 1947. **Freq:** Monthly. **Print Method:** Offset. **Trim Size:** 10 x 15 3/4. **Cols./Page:** 5. **Col. Width:** 24 nonpareils. **Col. Depth:** 182 agate lines. **Key Personnel:** Ne von Stuckey, Editor. **Subscription Rates:** $12 individuals. **Remarks:** Accepts advertising.
Ad Rates: GLR: $1 **Circ:** Paid 1,000
BW: $750 Non-paid 1,200
PCI: $15

3429 Journal Francais
France Press, Inc.
1051 Divisadero Phone: (415)921-5100
San Francisco, CA 94115 Fax: (415)921-0213
Free: (800)232-1549
Publisher E-mail: fpress@hooked.net

Magazine covering French history, politics, culture, and travel (French). **Founded:** 1965. **Freq:** Monthly. **Print Method:** Offset. **Trim Size:** 10 x 14. **Cols./Page:** 5. **Col. Width:** 21 nonpareils. **Col. Depth:** 190 agate lines. **Key Personnel:** Anne Prah Perochon, Editor; Marie Galanti, Publisher; Olivier Allegret, Advertising Dir. **ISSN:** 1089-1862. **Subscription Rates:** $39 individuals; $4.25 single issue. **Remarks:** Accepts advertising. **Online:** American Cybercasting; France Online. **Formerly**: Le Journal Francais d'Amerique.
Circ: ‡30,000

3430 Journal of IS Financial Management
IS Financial Management Association
PO Box 27543 Phone: (415)731-3706
San Francisco, CA 94127-0543
Professional magazine covering financial management of information services organizations. **Founded:** 1990. **Freq:** Triennial. **Trim Size:** 5 1/2 x 8 1/2. **Cols./Page:** 1. **Col. Width:** 4 1/2 inches. **Col. Depth:** 7 1/2 inches. **Key Personnel:** Susan Quinlan, Editor; Terence Quinlan, Editor. **ISSN:** 1092-1036. **Remarks:** Accepts advertising.
Circ: Controlled 750

3431 Journal of Neuro-AIDS
The Haworth Press, Inc.
San Francisco General Hospital Phone: (415)206-8297
Dept. of Neurology, Rm. 4M62 Fax: (415)476-5582
1001 Potrero Ave.
San Francisco, CA 94110
Publisher E-mail: getinfo@haworthpressinc.com

Journal on HIV/AIDS treatment and research. **Founded:** 1994. **Freq:** Quarterly. **Trim Size:** 6x8 1/2. **Key Personnel:** Richard W. Price, MD, Editor; Bill Cohen, Publisher. **ISSN:** 1069-7438. **Subscription Rates:** $45 individuals 30% more for Canada; 40% more for other countries; $60 institutions 30% more for Canada; 40% more for other countries; $125 libraries 30% more for Canada; 40% more for other countries. **Remarks:** Accepts advertising.
Ad Rates: BW: $300 **Circ:** Paid 74

3432 Journal of Psychoactive Drugs
Haight-Ashbury Publications
612 Clayton St. Phone: (415)565-1904
San Francisco, CA 94117-2958 Fax: (415)864-6162
Publication E-mail: hapjpd@aol.com

Professional journal on psychoactive drugs. **Subtitle:** A Multidisciplinary Forum. **Founded:** 1967. **Freq:** Quarterly. **Print Method:** Offset. **Trim Size:** 8 1/2 x 11. **Cols./Page:** 2. **Col. Width:** 19 picas. **Col. Depth:** 53 picas. **Key Personnel:** Richard B. Seymour, Managing Editor; David E. Smith, M.D., Publisher. **ISSN:** 0279-1072. **Subscription Rates:** $90 individuals; $160 institutions; $40 single issue. **Remarks:** Color advertising not accepted. **Formerly**: Journal of Psychedelic Drugs (1980).
Ad Rates: BW: $350 **Circ:** ‡1,100

3433 Journal of Thought
Caddo Gap Press
3145 Geary Blvd., No. 275 Phone: (415)922-1911
San Francisco, CA 94118 Fax: (415)440-4870
Publisher E-mail: caddogap@aol.com

Interdisciplinary journal for scholars, focusing on philosophy of education. **Founded:** 1966. **Freq:** Quarterly. **Print Method:** Offset. **Trim Size:** 6 x 9. **Cols./Page:** 1. **Col. Width:** 72 nonpareils. **Col. Depth:** 126 agate lines. **Key Personnel:** Alan Jones, Publisher. **ISSN:** 0022-5231. **Subscription Rates:** $40 individuals per year; $60 libraries; $60 institutions; $15 single issue. **Remarks:** Accepts advertising.
Ad Rates: BW: $200 **Circ:** ‡400

3434 Juxtapoz
High Speed Productions, Inc.
1303 Underwood Phone: (415)822-3083
San Francisco, CA 94124 Fax: (415)822-8359

Contains information on underground art and pop culture. **Founded:** 1993. **Freq:** Quarterly. **Print Method:** Offset. **Trim Size:** 8 1/8 x 10 7/8. **Cols./Page:** 3. **Col. Width:** 15 nonpareils. **Col. Depth:** 60 picas. **Key Personnel:** Kevin Thatcher, Editor and Publisher; Jamie Oshea, Managing Editor; Linsay Byrnes, Advertising Dir.; Edward H. Riggins, Publisher. **ISSN:** 1077-8411. **Subscription Rates:** $4.95 single issue; $14.95; $25 two years; $6.95 single issue Canada; $18.50 Canada; $25 other countries one year. **Remarks:** Accepts advertising.
Ad Rates: BW: $2,300 **Circ:** ‡54,000
4C: $2,950

3435 The Keeper's Log
U.S. Lighthouse Society
244 Kearny St., 5th Fl. Phone: (415)362-7255
San Francisco, CA 94108
Journal dedicated to the historical and contemporary aspects of lighthouses. **Founded:** 1984. **Freq:** Quarterly. **Print Method:** Offset. **Trim Size:** 7 1/4 x 9 1/4. **Cols./Page:** 3. **Col. Width:** 2 1/4 inches. **Col. Depth:** 9 3/8 inches. **Key Personnel:** Wayne Wheeler, Editor; W.C. Wheeler, Advertising Mgr. **ISSN:** 0883-0061. **Subscription Rates:** $25 individuals; $7 single issue.
Ad Rates: BW: $850 **Circ:** Paid ‡12,000
4C: $2,850 Non-paid ‡100

3436 KEY This Week San Francisco
L. Publishing, Inc.
PO Box 411107 Phone: (415)865-2300
San Francisco, CA 94141-1107 Fax: (415)252-1308
Publication E-mail: keysf@hooked.net

Magazine for visitors featuring San Francisco art, entertainment, shopping, restaurants, and special events information. **Founded:** 1918. **Freq:** Weekly (Fri.). **Print Method:** Web offset. **Trim Size:** 5 3/8 x 8 1/4. **Cols./Page:** 2. **Col. Width:** 26 nonpareils. **Col. Depth:** 105 agate lines. **Key Personnel:** Brian Stott, Editor; Kate Devereux, General Mgr.; Choppy Oshiro, Art Dir.; Janis McFarling, Marketing and Sales. **Subscription Rates:** $86 individuals; $2 single issue. **Remarks:** Accepts advertising. **URL:** http://www.keymag.com.
Ad Rates: BW: $820 **Circ:** Non-paid ‡22,000
4C: $1,025

3437 MacWeek
Ziff-Davis Publishing Co.
50 Beale St., 14th Fl. Phone: (415)243-3500
San Francisco, CA 94105 Fax: (415)243-3535
Publication E-mail: macweek@zd.com

Trade magazine (tabloid) for business users of Macintosh computers and other work stations. **Founded:** May 13, 1987. **Freq:** Weekly. **Print Method:** Offset. **Trim Size:** 10 3/4 x 14. **Cols./Page:** 4. **Col. Width:** 2 1/2 inches. **Col. Depth:** 10 inches. **Key Personnel:** Rick LePage, Publisher/Editor-in-Chief; David Morgenstern, Editor. **ISSN:** 0892-8118. **Subscription Rates:** $125 individuals; $225 Canada and Mexico; $350 other countries. **URL:** http://www.macweek.com.
Ad Rates: BW: $12,005 **Circ:** Controlled ‡85,000
4C: $14,955

3438 Macworld
International Data Group
501 2nd St., Ste. 500 Phone: (415)243-0505
San Francisco, CA 94107-1431 Fax: (415)442-0766
Publication E-mail: macworld@macworld.com

Magazine serving users of the Apple Macintosh personal computer, associated peripheral equipment, and software. **Subtitle:** The Essential Macintosh Resource. **Founded:** Feb. 1984. **Freq:** Monthly. **Print Method:** Offset. **Trim Size:** 11 x 13. **Cols./Page:** 3. **Col. Width:** 27 nonpareils. **Col. Depth:** 140 agate lines. **Key Personnel:** Colin Crawford, phone (415)267-1757, fax (415)974-7464, colin_crawford@macworld.com; Matt Sweeney, Publisher, phone (415)978-3271, fax (415)974-7464, matt_sweeney@macworld.com; Steve Plevin, Advertising Mgr., phone (415)978-3738, fax (415)924-7464, steve_plevin@macworld.com; Adrian Mello, Editor-in-Chief, phone (415)978-3246, adrian_mellow@macworld.com. **USPS:** 749-050. **Subscription Rates:** $30 individuals; $4.99 single issue. **Remarks:** Accepts advertising. **Online:** America Online, Inc.
Ad Rates: BW: $28,345 **Circ:** Paid 459,267
4C: $36,745 Non-paid 167,877

3439 Madrono
California Botanical Society
Dept. of Biology Phone: (415)338-1237
San Francisco State University Fax: (415)338-2295
San Francisco, CA 94132
Botanical journal. **Subtitle:** A West American Journal of Botany. **Founded:** May 20, 1916. **Freq:** Quarterly (Jan., April, July, Oct.). **Print Method:** Letterpress. Uses mats. **Cols./Page:** 1. **Col. Width:** 50 nonpareils. **Col. Depth:** 98 agate lines. **Key Personnel:** Robert Patterson, Editor. **ISSN:** 0024-9637. **Subscription Rates:** $50 individuals. **Remarks:** Advertising not accepted.
Circ: ‡1,200

3440 MediaFile
Media Alliance
814 Mission St., Suite 205 Phone: (415)546-6334
San Francisco, CA 94103 Fax: (415)546-6218
Publication E-mail: ma@igc.org
Publisher E-mail: info@media-alliance.org

Tabloid for northern California media workers. **Founded:** 1978. **Freq:** Bimonthly. **Trim Size:** 10 x 15 7/8. **Cols./Page:** 3 and 5. **Key Personnel:** Andrea Buffa, Editorial Team; Ben Clarke, Editorial Team, bcnc@media.alliance.org; Sandra Stewart, Editorial Team. **Subscription Rates:** $35. **Remarks:** Advertising not accepted. **URL:** http://www.media-alliance.org. **Formerly**: Propaganda Review.
Circ: 8,000

3441 Mercury
Astronomical Society of the Pacific
390 Ashton Ave. Phone: (415)337-1100
San Francisco, CA 94112 Fax: (415)337-5205
Free: (800)335-2624
Publisher E-mail: catalog@aspsky.org

Nontechnical magazine outlining new developments in astronomy, astronomy education, and public policy. **Subtitle:** The Journal of the Astronomical Society of the Pacific. **Founded:** Jan. 1972. **Freq:** Bimonthly. **Print Method:** Letterpress. **Trim Size:** 9 x 11. **Cols./Page:** 3. **Col. Width:** 27 nonpareils. **Col. Depth:** 135 agate lines. **Key Personnel:** James White, Editor, fax (415)337-5202, jwhite@physics.mtsu.edu. **ISSN:** 0047-6773. **Subscription Rates:** $35 individuals; $44 other countries; $25 students; $190 institutions Other countries. **Available Online. URL:** http://www.aspsky.org/html/mercury/mercury.html.
Ad Rates: BW: $800 **Circ:** Paid ‡7,000
PCI: $22 Non-paid ‡200

3442 Metro Reporter
270 Francisco St. Phone: (415)391-2030
San Francisco, CA 94133-2120 Fax: (415)391-2527

Black community newspaper. **Founded:** 1973. **Freq:** Daily. **Print Method:** Offset. **Cols./Page:** 6. **Col. Width:** 2 1/16 inches. **Col. Depth:** 21 inches. **Key Personnel:** Charles E. Belle, Editor; Carlton B. Goodlett, Publisher. **Subscription Rates:** $10 individuals.
Ad Rates: PCI: $10.50 **Circ:** Combined ‡108,895

3443 Microsoft Systems Journal
Miller Freeman, Inc.
600 Harrison St. Phone: (650)905-2200
San Francisco, CA 94107 Fax: (650)908-6604
Free: (800)227-4675
Publisher E-mail: techlearning_editors@mfi.com

Magazine focusing on the computer industry. **Online:** CompuServe Information Service.

3444 Mother Earth International Journal
Uniting the World Press
834 Brannan St., 2nd Flr. Phone: (415)522-9261
San Francisco, CA 94103 Fax: (415)552-9271

Journal of poetry and translations of poetry. **Founded:** 1991. **Key Personnel:** Herman Berlandt, Editor and Publisher. **Subscription Rates:** $18 individuals; $20 institutions; $20 out of country.

3445 Mother Jones
Foundation for National Progress
731 Market St., Ste. 600 Phone: (415)665-6637
San Francisco, CA 94103-2027 Fax: (415)665-6696

Magazine covering news, politics, and culture. **Subtitle:** Exposes and Politics. **Founded:** 1976. **Freq:** Bimonthly. **Print Method:** Offset. **Trim Size:** 8 1/4 x 10 1/2. **Cols./Page:** 3. **Col. Width:** 27 nonpareils. **Col. Depth:** 138 agate lines. **Key Personnel:** Jeffrey Klein, Editor; Jay Harris, Publisher. **ISSN:** 0362-8841. **Subscription Rates:** $18 individuals; $28 other countries. **Remarks:** Accepts advertising. **Online:** Nexis; Dialog; DataStar; Infonautics. **URL:** http://www.motherjones.com. **Alt. Formats:** Microform.
Ad Rates: BW: $4,880 **Circ:** Paid ★**130,276**
4C: $7,025
PCI: $185

3446 Multimedia World
International Data Group
501 2nd St. Phone: (415)281-8650
San Francisco, CA 94107 Fax: (415)281-3915
Publication E-mail: multimedia@pcworld.com

Magazine covering computer multimedia hardware and software. **Founded:** 1991. **Freq:** Monthly. **Trim Size:** 7 7/8 x 10 1/2. **Key Personnel:** Greg Mason, Publisher; Russell Glitman, Executive Editor; Mark Taussig, Associate Publisher. **Subscription Rates:** $17.97 individuals; $4.95 single issue. **Remarks:** Accepts advertising. **Online:** America Online, Inc. **URL:** http://www.mmworld.com. **Alt. Formats:** CD-ROM. **Formerly:** MPC World.
Ad Rates: BW: $12,175 **Circ:** 200,000
4C: $15,225

3447 Musical News
Musicians Union Local 6
116 Ninth St. Phone: (415)575-0777
San Francisco, CA 94103 Fax: (415)863-6173

Musicians' union newspaper. **Founded:** 1915. **Freq:** Monthly. **Print Method:** Letterpress. **Trim Size:** 7 1/2 x 10. **Cols./Page:** 3. **Key Personnel:** Melinda Wagner, Editor. **Subscription Rates:** $15 individuals. **Remarks:** Accepts advertising.
Ad Rates: BW: $150 **Circ:** Free ‡3,200
PCI: $7

3448 Network Magazine
Miller Freeman, Inc.
600 Harrison St. Phone: (650)905-2200
San Francisco, CA 94107 Fax: (650)908-6604
Free: (800)227-4675
Publisher E-mail: techlearning_ editors@mfi.com

Trade journal. **Subtitle:** The Competitive Advantage in Business Technology. **Founded:** 1986. **Freq:** Monthly. **Print Method:** Offset. **Trim Size:** 8 3/4 x 10 7/8. **Cols./Page:** 3. **Col. Width:** 13 picas. **Col. Depth:** 62 agate lines. **Key Personnel:** Steve Steinke, Editor-in-Chief, phone (415)905-2358, fax (415)905-2587; Elizabeth Clark, Executive Editor, phone (770)563-0116, fax (770)933-0666; Peter May, Publisher, phone (415)905-2345, fax (415)908-6602, jtoping@mfi.com; Liam Passmore, Marketing Mgr., phone (415)905-2516, fax (415)905-2587, lpassmore@mfi.com. **ISSN:** 0898-0012. **Remarks:** Accepts advertising. **Online:** CompuServe Information Service. **URL:** http://www.networkmagazine.com. **Formerly:** LAN Magazine.
Ad Rates: BW: $4,315 **Circ:** Paid ‡215,000
4C: $5,325

3449 New Directions for Child and Adolescent Development
Jossey-Bass Inc., Publishers
350 Sansome St. Phone: (415)433-1767
San Francisco, CA 94104 Fax: (800)605-2665
Free: (888)378-2537
Publication E-mail: webperson@jbp.com
Publisher E-mail: webperson@jbp.com

Developmental psychology journal. **Founded:** 1978. **Freq:** Quarterly. **Print Method:** Sheetfed offset. **Trim Size:** 6 x 9. **Cols./Page:** 1. **Col. Width:** 27 picas. **Col. Depth:** 45 picas. **Key Personnel:** William Damon, Editor, fax (650)725-8207. **ISSN:** 0195-2269. **Subscription Rates:** $67 individuals; $115 institutions. **Remarks:** Advertising not accepted. **Online:** OCLC. **URL:** http://www.josseybass.com. **Alt. Formats:** Microform. **Formerly:** New Directions for Child Development.
Circ: Paid 500
Non-paid 60

3450 New Directions for Evaluation
Jossey-Bass Inc., Publishers
350 Sansome St. Phone: (415)433-1767
San Francisco, CA 94104 Fax: (800)605-2665
Free: (888)378-2537
Publisher E-mail: webperson@jbp.com

Publication outlining techniques for conducting useful evaluation studies of programs. **Subtitle:** Journal of the American Evaluation Association. **Founded:** 1978. **Freq:** Quarterly. **Print Method:** Sheetfed offset. **Trim Size:** 5 7/8 x 9. **Cols./Page:** 1. **Col. Width:** 27 picas. **Col. Depth:** 45 picas. **Key Personnel:** Jennifer C. Greene, Editor-in-Chief, jcg8@cornell.edu; Gary T. Henry, Editor-in-Chief, gthenry@gsu.edu. **ISSN:** 0197-6736. **Subscription Rates:** $65 individuals; $115 institutions. **Remarks:** Advertising not accepted. **Online:** OCLC. **Alt. Formats:** Microform. **Formerly:** New Directions for Program Evaluation; New Directions Program Evaluation.
Circ: Paid 2,900
Non-paid 82

3451 Nob Hill Gazette
The Hearst Bldg., Ste. 222 Phone: (415)227-0190
5 3rd St. Fax: (415)974-5103
San Francisco, CA 94103
Publication E-mail: nancy@ndohillgazette.com

Regional magazine (tabloid) covering the arts, society, and business in the San Francisco Bay area. **Subtitle:** Nob Hill - An Attitude Not An Area. **Founded:** 1978. **Freq:** Monthly. **Print Method:** Offset. **Cols./Page:** 3. **Col. Width:** 36 nonpareils. **Col. Depth:** 224 agate lines. **Key Personnel:** Lois Lehrman, Publisher; Cindy Abbott, Publishers Assistant, cynthia@ndohillgazette.com. **Subscription Rates:** $35 individuals; $3 single issue. **Remarks:** Accepts advertising.
Ad Rates: BW: $5,100 **Circ:** Combined ❑**72,557**
4C: $6,970

3452 North Beach Now
350 Bay, Ste. 100-106 Phone: (415)391-1043
San Francisco, CA 94133 Fax: (415)398-2258
Publication E-mail: thenow@aol.com
Publisher E-mail: thenow@aol.com

Community newspaper serving North Beach and beyond. **Founded:** 1987. **Freq:** Monthly. **Print Method:** Web offset. **Trim Size:** 10 1/2 x 13. **Cols./Page:** 5. **Col. Width:** 1 3/4 inches. **Col. Depth:** 12 7/8 inches. **Key Personnel:** Georgann Leger, Managing Editor; Joan Dahlgren, Editor and Publisher. **Subscription Rates:** $28 individuals. **Remarks:** Accepts advertising.
Ad Rates: BW: $1625 **Circ:** Free ‡40,000
4C: $1900
PCI: $.45

3453 The Objector
CCCO Western Region
655 Sutter St., Ste. 514 Phone: (415)474-3002
San Francisco, CA 94102-1034 Fax: (415)474-2311
Free: (800)394-9544
Publisher E-mail: cccowr@igc.org

Subtitle: A Magazine of Conscience and Resistance. **Founded:** 1980. **Freq:** Quarterly. **Print Method:** Offset. Uses mats. **Trim Size:** 8 1/2 x 11. **Cols./Page:** 2. **Col. Width:** 27 nonpareils. **Col. Depth:** 140 agate lines. **Key Personnel:** Sam Diener, Editor. **ISSN:** 0279-103X. **Subscription Rates:** $17 individuals; $22 institutions and other countries; $3 single issue. **Remarks:** Advertising accepted; rates available upon request. **URL:** http://www.libertynet.org/~ccco.
Circ: ‡1,000

3454 Our Animals
San Francisco S.P.C.A.
2500 16th St. Phone: (415)554-3009
San Francisco, CA 94103 Fax: (415)431-6641
Publication E-mail: ouranimals@sfspca.org
Publisher E-mail: publicinfo@sfspca.org

Magazine containing news about cats, dogs, and SPCA programs that help them. **Subtitle:** The Journal of the San Francisco S.P.C.A. **Founded:** 1906. **Freq:** Quarterly. **Print Method:** Offset. **Trim Size:** 8 3/8 x 10 7/8. **Cols./Page:** 3. **Col. Width:** 2 3/8 inches. **Col. Depth:** 10 inches. **Key Personnel:** Paul Glassner, Editor. **ISSN:** 0030-6789. **Subscription Rates:** $25 Membership. **Remarks:** Accepts advertising.
Ad Rates: BW: $770 **Circ:** Paid ‡50,000
4C: $1,270 Non-paid ‡4,000

3455 OUT/LOOK, National Lesbian & Gay Quarterly
Out Look, National Lesbian & Gay Quarterly
1255 Post St. No. 948
San Francisco, CA 94109

Gay and lesbian magazine. **Founded:** Mar. 1988. **Freq:** Quarterly. **Print Method:** Offset. **Trim Size:** 8 1/2 x 11. **Cols./Page:** 2 and 3. **Col. Width:** 2 7/8 and 2 inches. **Col. Depth:** 8 7/8 inches. **Key Personnel:** Jan Zita Grover, Editor. **ISSN:** 0896-7733. **Subscription Rates:** $21; $29 institutions; $31 other countries. $5.95 single issue. **Remarks:** Accepts advertising.
Ad Rates: BW: $750 **Circ:** 17,000
4C: $2,500

3456 Pacific Bakers News
C.W. Soward
180 Mendell St. Phone: (415)826-2664
San Francisco, CA 94124-1740 Fax: (415)821-1070

Trade periodical for the retail and wholesale baking industry in the Western U.S. **Founded:** 1967. **Freq:** Monthly. **Trim Size:** 8 1/2 x 11. **Cols./Page:** 1. **Col. Width:** 5 inches. **Col. Depth:** 10 inches. **Key Personnel:** Cliff Soward, Editor and Publisher. **Subscription Rates:** $18 individuals; $2 single issue. **Remarks:** Accepts advertising.
Circ: Controlled 3,000

3457 Pacific Shipper
Primedia Information Inc.
225 Bush St., Ste. 353 Phone: (415)438-2165
San Francisco, CA 94104 Fax: (415)438-2139
Free: (800)221-8633
Publication E-mail: pacificshipper.com

Magazine covering the international shipping industry. **Subtitle:** The Newsweekly for All Coasts and All Modes. **Founded:** 1926. **Freq:** Weekly (Mon.). **Print Method:** Offset. **Trim Size:** 6 7/8 x 9 3/4. **Cols./Page:** 3. **Col. Width:** 21 nonpareils. **Col. Depth:** 124 agate lines. **Key Personnel:** Erik McMahon, Editor; John G. Capers III, Publisher, jcapers@primemediainfo.com. **ISSN:** 0300-8900. **Subscription Rates:** $199 individuals. **Remarks:** Accepts advertising.
Ad Rates: BW: $975 **Circ:** Paid ★**5,896**
4C: $1,990

3458 Palate and Spirit
2443 Filmore St., Ste. 347
San Francisco, CA 94115-1925

Periodical devoted to culinary travel. Features a seasonal directory of more than 100 culinary tours, food and wine programs at resorts and hotels, as well as cooking and wine schools. **Founded:** Feb. 1993. **Freq:** Quarterly. **Subscription Rates:** $49 individuals.

3459 PC WORLD
International Data Group
501 2nd St., Ste. 600 Phone: (415)243-0500
San Francisco, CA 94107-1437 Fax: (415)442-1891
Free: (800)PC-WORLD

Subtitle: The Magazine of Business Computing. **Founded:** Nov. 1983. **Freq:** Monthly. **Print Method:** Offset. **Trim Size:** 7 7/8 x 10 1/2. **Cols./Page:** 3. **Col. Width:** 12.5 picas. **Col. Depth:** 55 picas. **Key Personnel:** Phil Lemmons, Editorial Dir.; Jeff Edman, Publisher; Richard Marino, President/CEO; Cathryn Baskin, Editor-in-Chief. **ISSN:** 0737-8939. **Subscription Rates:** $29.90 individuals; $5.95 single issue. **Remarks:** Accepts advertising. **Online:** America Online, Inc.; Compuserve. **URL:** http://www.pcworld.com.
Ad Rates: BW: $45,735 **Circ:** Paid ★**1,147,034**
4C: $56,025
PCI: $680

Pennisula Reporter - See Millbrae

3460 Performance Computing
Miller Freeman, Inc.
600 Harrison St. Phone: (650)905-2200
San Francisco, CA 94107 Fax: (650)908-6604
Free: (800)227-4675
Publisher E-mail: techlearning_ editors@mfi.com

Magazine for professional users of UNIX and UNIX-like systems, and Windows NT. **Subtitle:** The UNIX and Windows NT Enterprise Magazine. **Founded:** 1983. **Freq:** Monthly 1 Special issue. **Print Method:** Offset. **Trim Size:** 8 x 10 7/8. **Cols./Page:** 2 and 3. **Col. Width:** 84 and 55 millimeters. **Col. Depth:** 254 millimeters. **Key Personnel:** Mark Hall, Editor, phone (650)655-4233, mhall@mfi.com; John Keough, Publisher, phone (650)655-4229, jkeough@mfi.com. **ISSN:** 0742-3136. **Subscription Rates:** Free to qualified subscribers; $55 Nonqualified. **Remarks:** Accepts advertising. **URL:** http://www.performance-computing.com. **Alt. Formats:** Braille; CD-ROM. **Former name:** UNIX Review (Apr. 1998).
Ad Rates: BW: $11,925 **Circ:** Controlled ‡89,000
4C: $14,225

3461 Pipelines
Plumbers - Steamfitters, UA Local 38
1621 Market St. Phone: (415)626-2000
San Francisco, CA 94103
Publication E-mail: pipelines@ualocal38.org
Publisher E-mail: ualocal38@ualocal38.org

Labor union newspaper. **Founded:** 1952. **Freq:** Monthly. **Col. Width:** 15 picas. **Key Personnel:** Rob Weinstein, Editor. **Subscription Rates:** Free. **Remarks:** Advertising not accepted.
Circ: Non-paid 2,500

3462 Poetry USA
National Poetry Association, Inc.
SOMAR Phone: (415)552-9261
934 Brannan St., 2nd Fl. Fax: (415)552-9271
San Francisco, CA 94103
Publication E-mail: poetryusa@aol.com
Publisher E-mail: gamuse@slip.net

Online poetry journal for a general audience. **Founded:** 1985. **Key Personnel:** Adam Shames, Managing Editor. **URL:** http://www.slip.net/~gamuse.

3463 Printed Circuit Design
Miller Freeman, Inc.
600 Harrison St. Phone: (650)905-2200
San Francisco, CA 94107 Fax: (650)908-6604
Free: (800)227-4675
Publisher E-mail: techlearning_ editors@mfi.com

Magazine for designers of PCB's and related technologies. **Subtitle:** The Definitive Journal of Printed Circuit Board Design. **Founded:** Sept. 1984. **Freq:** Monthly. **Print Method:** Offset. **Trim Size:** 8 3/8 x 10 7/8. **Cols./Page:** 3. **Col. Width:** 28 nonpareils. **Col. Depth:** 103 agate lines. **Key Personnel:** Pete Waddell, Editor-in-Chief; Frances Stewart, Publisher; Lisa Hamburg, Asst. Ed. **ISSN:** 0884-9862. **Subscription Rates:** Free to qualified subscribers; $60 institutions; $5 single issue. **Remarks:** Accepts advertising. **URL:** http://www.pcdmag.com/cybercafe/.
Ad Rates: GLR: $25 **Circ:** Paid 289
BW: $4575 Controlled 25,113
4C: $5570

3464 Prism
San Francisco State University
Dept. of Journalism Phone: (415)338-3123
1600 Holloway Ave. Fax: (415)338-3111
San Francisco, CA 94132
Publication E-mail: ggp@sfsu.edu

Collegiate publication. **Subtitle:** One of the Nation's Best College Magazines. **Founded:** 1968. **Freq:** Monthly. **Print Method:** Offset. **Trim Size:** 11 x 14. **Cols./Page:** 4. **Col. Width:** 2 1/4 inches. **Col. Depth:** 13 inches. **Key Personnel:** Douglas Allen, General Mgr. **Subscription Rates:** Free; $15 by mail. **Remarks:** Accepts advertising. **URL:** http://www.journalism.sfsu.edu. **Formerly**: Phoenix.
Ad Rates: BW: $436.80 **Circ:** Non-paid ‡10,000
4C: $1,086.80
PCI: $15.85

3465 Processed World
41 Sutter, Ste. 1829 Phone: (415)495-6823
San Francisco, CA 94104-4903 Fax: (415)626-2685

Publication reviewing the impact of technology on daily life. **Subtitle:** The Magazine With a Bad Attitude. **Founded:** 1981. **Freq:** Semiannual. **Print Method:** Web offset. **Trim Size:** 8 3/8 x 10 7/8. **Cols./Page:** 2 and 3. **Col. Width:** 3 1/2 and 2 inches. **Col. Depth:** 9 1/2 inches. **ISSN:** 0735-9381. **Subscription Rates:** $15; $18 libraries; $25 other countries. $5 single issue. **Remarks:** Advertising not accepted.
Circ: Paid 4,000
Non-paid 750

3466 Propaganda Review
Media Alliance
814 Mission St., Suite 205 Phone: (415)546-6334
San Francisco, CA 94103 Fax: (415)546-6218
Publisher E-mail: info@media-alliance.org

Publication analyzing many different aspects of corporate, media, and government propaganda. **Freq:** 2-3/year. **Subscription Rates:** $20; $40 Industry; $40 other countries.

3467 Publish
International Data Group
501 2nd St., Ste. 310 Phone: (415)243-0600
San Francisco, CA 94107 Fax: (415)975-2613

Magazine about the new technological tools of graphic design including information about how they are used and how they are evolving in the Design and Computer Age. **Subtitle:** Magazines for Electronic Publishing Professionals. **Founded:** Sept. 1986. **Freq:** Monthly. **Print Method:** Offset. **Trim Size:** 8 x 10 7/8. **Cols./Page:** 3. **Col. Width:** 2 3/8 inches. **Col. Depth:** 10 inches. **Key Personnel:** Jake Widman, Editor, editor@publish.com; Gene Gable, Publisher/President; Nathalie Valletter, Art Director; Batel Libes, Operations Mgr.; Rick Reynolds, Director; Ed Chittenden, Director; Mark Naman, Managing Editor; Peter Guastella, Circulation Director; Neil Versen, Assoc. Publisher/VP of Sales & Marketing. **ISSN:** 0897-6007. **Subscription Rates:** $39.90 individuals. **Remarks:** Accepts advertising. **URL:** http://www.publish.com.
Ad Rates: BW: $11,445 **Circ:** ‡98,819
4C: $14,880

3468 Puck
Permeable Press
2336 Market St., No. 14 Phone: (415)255-9765
San Francisco, CA 94114
Publication featuring fiction, book reviews, and news for publishers and writers. **Subtitle:** For Irrepressible Readers. **Founded:** 1984. **Freq:** Quarterly. **Trim Size:** 8 1/2 x 11. **Key Personnel:** Brian Clark, Editor, bcclark@igc.apc.org. **ISSN:** 1071-7633. **Subscription Rates:** $24 institutions; $15 individuals; $5 single issue. **Remarks:** Accepts advertising. **URL:** http://www.armory.com/~jay/permeable.html.
Ad Rates: BW: $150 **Circ:** Paid ‡100
Non-paid 2,000

3469 Pulp & Paper Forecaster
Miller Freeman, Inc.
600 Harrison St. Phone: (415)905-2337
San Francisco, CA 94107 Fax: (415)905-2240
Publication E-mail: subserv@mfs.com
Publisher E-mail: techlearning_ editors@mfi.com

Forecasting service of the pulp, paper, and paperboard industry. **Subtitle:** Bimonthly Analysis of the Pulp, Paper and Paperboard Industry. **Founded:** 1989. **Freq:** Bimonthly. **Print Method:** Offset. **Trim Size:** 8 1/2 x 11. **Cols./Page:** 2. **Col. Width:** 3 inches. **Col. Depth:** 8 3/4 inches. **Key Personnel:** Will Mies, Publisher; Ola Jane Gow, Assoc. Publisher; Harold Cody, Editoral Dir., phone (415)538-3801, fax (415)278-5371, hcody@mfi.com; Kurt Schaefer, Associate Director. **ISSN:** 0898-6886. **Subscription Rates:** $1,375 individuals; $230 single issue. **Remarks:** Advertising not accepted.
Circ: (Not Reported)

3470 Pulp & Paper International
Miller Freeman, Inc.
600 Harrison St. Phone: (650)905-2200
San Francisco, CA 94107 Fax: (650)908-6604
Free: (800)227-4675
Publisher E-mail: techlearning_ editors@mfi.com

Trade magazine covering pulp and paper manufacturing worldwide. **Freq:** Monthly. **Trim Size:** 210 x 297 mm. **Key Personnel:** Jim Kenny, Editor. **ISSN:** 0033-409X. **Subscription Rates:** $130 individuals; $15 single issue. **Remarks:** Accepts advertising.
Ad Rates: BW: $5,095 **Circ:** Controlled 15,134
4C: $7,595

3471 Raise the Stakes
Planet Drum Foundation
PO Box 31251 Phone: (415)285-6556
San Francisco, CA 94131 Fax: (415)285-6563
Publisher E-mail: planetdrum@igc.apc.org

Journal covering regional environmental issues. **Subtitle:** The Planet Drum Review. **Freq:** Semiannual. **Key Personnel:** Peter Borg, Editor. **Subscription Rates:** $25 individuals; $30 out of country. **Remarks:** Advertising not accepted.
Circ: Paid 630

3472 The Recorder
American Lawyer Media, L.P.
625 Polk St., Ste. 500 Phone: (415)749-5400
San Francisco, CA 94102-3368 Fax: (415)749-5449
Publication E-mail: recorder@counsel.com

Legal newspaper. **Subtitle:** The Bay Area's Legal Newspaper since 1877. **Founded:** 1877. **Freq:** Daily (morn.). **Print Method:** Offset. **Trim Size:** 11 1/2 x 17 1/2. **Cols./Page:** 10. **Col. Width:** 21 nonpareils. **Col. Depth:** 290 agate lines. **Key Personnel:** Peter Scheer, Publisher. **USPS:** 458-020. **Subscription Rates:** $369 individuals. **Remarks:** Accepts advertising. **URL:** http://www.callaw.com.
Ad Rates: BW: $1,495 **Circ:** 6,300
4C: $2,290
PCI: $70

3473 Release Print
Film Arts Foundation
346 9th St., 2nd. Fl. Phone: (415)552-8760
San Francisco, CA 94103 Fax: (415)552-0882

Trade magazine covering independent film and video. **Subtitle:** The Magazine of Film Arts Foundation. **Founded:** 1977. **Freq:** Monthly. **Print Method:** Sheetfed offset. **Trim Size:** 8 1/2 x 11. **Cols./Page:** 3. **Col. Width:** 2 7/16 inches. **Col. Depth:** 10 inches. **Key Personnel:** Karl Soehnlein, Information Pages; Thomas J. Powers, Editor; Andy Moore, Display Ad Sales. **ISSN:** 0890-5231. **Subscription Rates:** $45 individuals; $4.95 single issue. **Remarks:** Accepts advertising.
Ad Rates: BW: $500 **Circ:** Combined 8,500

3474 Research
Research Magazine, Inc.
2201 3rd St. Phone: (415)621-0220
San Francisco, CA 94107-0905 Fax: (415)621-0735
Publication E-mail: webmaster@researchmag.com

Magazine for stockbrokers including corporate profiles, financial data, articles on investment products, finance selling techniques and tools. **Subtitle:** Ideas for Today's Investment Professional. **Founded:** June 1978. **Freq:** Monthly. **Print Method:** Web. **Trim Size:** 8 1/4 x 10 3/4. **Cols./Page:** 3. **Col. Width:** 2 5/16 inches. **Col. Depth:** 9 3/4 inches. **Key Personnel:** Gil Weinreich, Managing Editor; Robert Tyndall, Publisher, phone (415)437-4205, rtyndall@researchmag.com. **ISSN:** 0192-172X. **Subscription Rates:** $35 individuals; $95 other countries. **Remarks:** Accepts advertising. **Available Online**.
Ad Rates: BW: $7,560 **Circ:** Paid 80
4C: $8,870 Non-paid 85,300

3475 San Francisco Art Institute Magazine
San Francisco Art Institute
800 Chestnut St. Phone: (415)749-4588
San Francisco, CA 94133 Fax: (415)749-4590

Magazine of the San Francisco Art Institute. **Freq:** Quarterly. **Key Personnel:** Ariege Arseguel, Assoc. Editor. **Subscription Rates:** Free to qualified subscribers. **Remarks:** Advertising not accepted.
Circ: Combined 5,000

3476 San Francisco Attorney Magazine
Bar Association of San Francisco
465 California St., Ste. 1100 Phone: (415)982-1600
San Francisco, CA 94104-1804
Professional journal covering law in San Francisco. **Subtitle:** Magazine of the Bar Association of San Francisco. **Founded:** 1937. **Freq:** Bimonthly. **Key Personnel:** James Hargarten, Editor-in-Chief; Pamela Adelman, Managing Editor, padelman@sfbar.org. **ISSN:** 0744-9348. **Subscription Rates:** $36 individuals. **Remarks:** Accepts advertising. **URL:** http://www.sfbar.org. **Former name**: San Francisco Bar; The Brief Case.
Circ: Paid 9,000

3477 The San Francisco and Bay Area Guide
San Francisco Guide, Inc.
2087 Union St. No. 1 Phone: (415)775-2212
San Francisco, CA 94123-4102 Fax: (415)441-7773
Publication E-mail: info@sfguide.com

Entertainment guide magazine. **Subtitle:** The Travelers Guide to the Bay Area Dining, Shopping, Maps, Theater, Events. **Founded:** 1970. **Freq:** Monthly. **Print Method:** Offset. **Trim Size:** 4 1/8 x 10. **Cols./Page:** 2. **Col. Width:** 1 7/8 inches. **Col. Depth:** 9 1/8 inches. **Key Personnel:** Eric Symons, Sales Mgr.; Linda Schreibman, Publisher/Contact. **Subscription Rates:** $12. **Online:** Internet.
Ad Rates: GLR: $25 **Circ:** Non-paid 130,000
BW: $1,275
4C: $1,550
PCI: $94

3478 The San Francisco Bay Guardian
520 Hampshire St. Phone: (415)255-3100
San Francisco, CA 94110 Fax: (415)255-8955

Alternative Newsweekly. **Founded:** Oct. 1966. **Freq:** Weekly. **Print Method:** Offset. **Cols./Page:** 5. **Col. Width:** 25 nonpareils. **Col. Depth:** 196 agate lines. **Key Personnel:** Bruce B. Brugmann, Editor and Publisher. **Subscription Rates:** Free; $32 by mail. **Remarks:** Accepts advertising. **Available Online**. **URL:** http://www.spbg.com.
Ad Rates: BW: $2,450 **Circ:** Non-paid ★**160,758**
4C: $3,100

3479 San Francisco Business Times
American City Business Journals
275 Battery St., Ste. 940 Phone: (415)989-2522
San Francisco, CA 94111 Fax: (415)398-2494
Publication E-mail: sanfrancisco@amcity.com

Local business newspaper (tabloid) serving the San Francisco Bay Area. **Subtitle:** Serving Alameda, Contra Costa, Marin, San Francisco and San Mateo Counties. **Founded:** Sept. 8, 1986. **Freq:** Weekly (Fri.). **Print Method:** Offset. **Trim Size:** 11 1/2 x 15. **Cols./Page:** 4. **Col. Width:** 28.5 nonpareils. **Col. Depth:** 14 inches. **Key Personnel:** Mary Huss, Publisher; Jamie Silver, Advertising Mgr. **ISSN:** 0890-0337. **Subscription Rates:** $75 individuals; $125 two years. **URL:** http://www.amcity.com/sanfrancisco. **Formerly**: San Francisco Business Journal.
Ad Rates: BW: $5,140 **Circ:** Paid ★**15,551**
4C: $5,740

3480 San Francisco Chronicle
Chronicle Publishing Co.
901 Mission St. Phone: (415)777-1111
San Francisco, CA 94103 Fax: (415)896-1107

General newspaper. **Founded:** 1865. **Freq:** Mon.-Sun. (morn.). **Print Method:** Flexography. **Cols./Page:** 6. **Col. Width:** 12 picas. **Col. Depth:** 301 agate lines. **Key Personnel:** Michael Bauer, Food Editor; John Carman, Television. **USPS:** 479-760. **Subscription Rates:** $14.40 individuals. **Remarks:** Accepts advertising. **Online:** DataTimes Corporation; CompuServe Information Service; LEXIS-NEXIS; Dialog (The Dialog Corporation). **Alt. Formats:** CD-ROM, NewsBank, Inc. **Feature Editors:** Michael Bauer, *Food*, phone (415)777-7044; John Carman, *TV*, phone (415)777-1111; Michael Kern, *Sports*, phone (415)777-7201; Scott Sommerdorf, *Photo*, phone (415)777-7077; Pat Steger, *Society*, phone (415)777-7160.
Ad Rates: BW: $28,251 **Circ:** Mon.-Fri. ★**475,324**
PCI: $224 Sat. ★**443,002**

3481 San Francisco Daily Journal
Daily Journal Corp.
1390 Market St., Ste. 1210 Phone: (415)252-0500
San Francisco, CA 94102 Fax: (415)252-0599

Newspaper for the legal community. **Founded:** 1893. **Freq:** Daily. **Print Method:** Offset. **Cols./Page:** 6. **Col. Width:** 2 1/4 inches. **Col. Depth:** 20 1/2 inches. **Key Personnel:** Philip Hager, Editor. **USPS:** 465-480. **Subscription Rates:** $298. **Remarks:** Accepts advertising. **Alt. Formats:** Microfilm. **Formerly**: San Francisco Banner; San Francisco Banner Daily Journal.
Ad Rates: BW: $865.92 **Circ:** Paid 6,571
4C: $1,465.92 Free 1,443
PCI: $7.04

3482 San Francisco Examiner
110 5th St. Phone: (415)777-2424
San Francisco, CA 94103-2918
General newspaper. **Founded:** 1887. **Freq:** Mon.-Sat. (eve.). **Print Method:** Letterpress. **Trim Size:** 13 x 21 1/2. **Cols./Page:** 6. **Col. Width:** 24 nonpareils. **Col. Depth:** 301 agate lines. **Key Personnel:** William R. Hearst III, Publisher; Frank Flood, Advertising Mgr. **USPS:** 479-780. **Remarks:** Combined advertising rates available with Chronicle. **Online:** Dialog (The Dialog Corporation); DataTimes Corporation; LEXIS-NEXIS. **URL:** http://www.sfgate.com. **Feature Editors:** Christine Barnes, *Lifestyle*, phone (415)777-7942; Mandy Behbehani, *Fashion*, phone (415)777-7944; Kandace Bender, *Metro*, phone (415)777-7881; Michael Brunker, *City*, phone (415)777-7850; George Cant, *Sunday*, phone (415)777-7966; Dave Dayton, *Entertainment*, phone (415)777-7941; Phil Elwood, *Music*, phone (415)525-0748; Jim Finefrock, *Editorials*, phone (415)777-7923; Don George, *Travel*, phone (415)777-8747; Rob Hurwitt, *Drama*, phone (415)777-7953; Jay Johnson, *News*, phone (415)777-7961; Jane Kay, *Environmental*, phone (415)777-8704; Bruce Koon, *Real Estate*, phone (415)777-7784; Lisa Krieger, *Medical*, phone (415)777-7867; Bob McLeod, *Photo*, phone (415)777-7840; Joyce Millman, *TV & Radio*, phone (415)777-7938; Katie Rabin, *Financial/Business*, phone (415)777-7927; Scott Rosenberg, *Movie*, phone (415)777-7766; Glenn Schwarz, *Sports*, phone (415)777-7750; Kathy Seligman, *Education*, phone (415)777-7882; Paul Wilner, *Features*, phone (415)777-7910; Jim Wood, *Food*, phone (415)777-7768.
Ad Rates: BW: $28,251 **Circ:** Mon.-Fri. ★**113,198**
PCI: $224 Sat. ★**83,466**

3483 San Francisco Independent
1201 Evans Ave. Phone: (415)826-1100
San Francisco, CA 94124 Fax: (415)826-5371

Community newspaper. **Subtitle:** San Francisco's Neighborhood Newspaper. **Founded:** 1972. **Freq:** 3/week. **Print Method:** Offset. **Cols./Page:** 6. **Col. Width:** 2 1/16 inches. **Col. Depth:** 21 inches. **Key Personnel:** Zoran Basich, Managing Editor; Wayne Wedgeworth, Advertising Dir.; Tom Trent, Natl. Ad. Mgr. **Remarks:** Accepts advertising.
Ad Rates: SAU: $40.45 **Circ:** Tues. 372,650
PCI: $53.50 Sat. 372,650
Thurs. 18,000

3484 San Francisco Magazine
243 Vallejo St. Phone: (415)398-2800
San Francisco, CA 94111 Fax: (415)398-6777

Regional interest magazine covering personalities, places, and events in the San Francisco Bay area. **Founded:** 1968. **Freq:** Monthly. **Print Method:** Offset. **Trim Size:** 8 1/8 x 10 7/8. **Cols./Page:** 3. **Col. Width:** 2.25 picas. **Col. Depth:** 10 inches. **Key Personnel:** Dale Eastman, Editor-in-Chief; Barney Fonzi, VP/Advertising Dir.; Steven Rivera, Publisher. **Subscription Rates:** $14.95 individuals; $2.95 single issue. **URL:** http://www.sanfran.com. **Formerly**: San Francisco Focus.
Ad Rates: BW: $7,555 **Circ:** Paid 158,990
4C: $10,515

3485 San Francisco Medicine
San Francisco Medical Society
1409 Satter St. Phone: (415)561-0861
San Francisco, CA 94109 Fax: (415)561-0833

Professional medical journal. **Freq:** Monthly. **Key Personnel:** Edare Carroll, Managing Editor. **Subscription Rates:** $40 individuals. **Remarks:** Accepts advertising. **URL:** http://www.sfms.org.
Ad Rates: BW: $490 **Circ:** (Not Reported)

3486 San Francisco Observer
PO Box 15102 Phone: (415)863-6397
San Francisco, CA 94115 Fax: (415)431-2021
Publisher E-mail: sfobserver@aol.com

Community newspaper. **Subtitle:** Serving the Heart of San Francisco. **Founded:** Feb. 1994. **Freq:** Monthly. **Cols./Page:** 5. **Col. Width:** 2 inches. **Key Personnel:** Michael Martin, Publisher. **Subscription Rates:** Free; $15 by mail. **Remarks:** Accepts advertising. **Formerly**: Western Edition (1998).
Ad Rates: BW: $1,295 **Circ:** Paid 100
4C: $1,545 Free 40,000
PCI: $17

3487 San Francisco Post
The Alameda Publishing Corp./Oakland Post
PO Box 1350 Phone: (510)763-1120
Oakland, CA 94604-1350 Fax: (510)763-9670

Black community newspaper. **Founded:** 1963. **Freq:** Semi-weekly (Wed. and Sun.). **Print Method:** Offset. **Cols./Page:** 6. **Col. Width:** 1 1/16 inches. **Col. Depth:** 21 1/2 inches. **Key Personnel:** Gail Berkley, Editor; Thomas Berkley, Publisher; Donald V. Welcher, Advertising Mgr. **Subscription Rates:** $42 individuals. **Remarks:** Accepts advertising.
Ad Rates: GLR: $43.73 **Circ:** Free ‡18,289
BW: $5,641.17

3488 SF Weekly
185 Berry St., No. 3800 Phone: (415)541-0700
San Francisco, CA 94107 Fax: (415)777-1839

Newsmagazine. **Subtitle:** Issues/Arts/Culture/Commentary. **Founded:** 1981. **Freq:** Weekly. **Print Method:** Web offset. **Trim Size:** 15 x 11 1/2. **Cols./Page:** 4 and 5. **Col. Width:** 14.5 and 11.5 picas. **Col. Depth:** 15 inches. **Key Personnel:** Jim Rizzi, Publisher; John Mecklin, Editor-in-Chief; Bill Wyman, Arts & Entertainment Editor; Chris Brand, Art Dir. **ISSN:** 1060-2526. **Subscription Rates:** $80 individuals. **Remarks:** Accepts advertising. **Formerly**: Calendar Magazine (1989).
Ad Rates: GLR: $2.60 **Circ:** Non-paid ★**118,234**
BW: $2,730
4C: $3,655
PCI: $34

3489 Sierra
Sierra Club
85 Second St., 2nd Fl. Phone: (415)977-5500
San Francisco, CA 94105-3441 Fax: (415)977-5793
Publication E-mail: sierra.letters@sierraclub.org
Publisher E-mail: planet@sierraclub.org

Magazine on conservation and the environment. **Subtitle:** The Magazine of the Sierra Club. **Founded:** 1893. **Freq:** Bimonthly. **Print Method:** Offset. **Trim Size:** 8 x 10 1/2. **Cols./Page:** 3. **Col. Width:** 27 nonpareils. **Col. Depth:** 128 agate lines. **Key Personnel:** Joan Hamilton, Editor, phone (415)977-5794; Robert Schildgen, Managing Editor, phone (415)977-5691, robert.schildgen@sieraclub.org; Frank Noto, Nat'l Adv. Dir., phone (415)977-5606, frank.noto@sierraclub.org. **USPS:** 495-920. **Subscription Rates:** $15 members; $2.95 single issue; $26 out of country. **Remarks:** Advertising not accepted for tobacco or for vehicles depicted off-road. **URL:** http://www.sierraclub.org. **Alt. Formats:** Microform.
Ad Rates: BW: $17,360 **Circ:** Paid ★**553,645**
4C: $25,460
PCI: $515

3490 Slap
High Speed Productions, Inc.
1303 Underwood Phone: (415)822-3083
San Francisco, CA 94124 Fax: (415)822-8359

Magazine covering skateboarding, music, art, and youth. **Founded:** Apr. 1992. **Freq:** Monthly. **Print Method:** Web offset. **Trim Size:** 8 3/8 x 10 7/8. **Key Personnel:** Lance Dawes, Editor; Dean Hultabo, Advertising Mgr.; Edward H. Riggins, Publisher. **ISSN:** 1076-9110. **Subscription Rates:** $16.50; $25 Canada; $30 other countries; $26 two years; $3.75 single issue; $5.25 single issue Canada. **Remarks:** Accepts advertising. **Formerly**: Slap Magazine.
Ad Rates: BW: $1,500 **Circ:** Paid 70,000
4C: $2,000

3491 Smith-Kettlewell Technical File
Smith-Kettlewell Eye Research Institute
2318 Fillmore St. Phone: (415)345-2124
San Francisco, CA 94115 Fax: (415)345-8455
Publication E-mail: rerc@skivs.ski.org

Magazine reporting on technology and devices for visually impaired persons. **Founded:** 1981. **Freq:** 4/2 years. **Key Personnel:** William Gerrey. **Subscription Rates:** $16 diskette; $18 braille; $14 talking book. **Remarks:** Advertising not accepted. **Alt. Formats:** Audio tape; Braille.
Circ: Paid 250

3492 Social Justice
Global Options
PO Box 40601 Phone: (415)550-1703
San Francisco, CA 94140-0601
Journal on crime and social issues. **Subtitle:** A Journal of Crime, Conflict, and World Order. **Founded:** 1974. **Freq:** Quarterly. **Print Method:** Offset. **Trim Size:** 6 x 9. **Cols./Page:** 1. **Col. Width:** 4 3/8 inches. **Col. Depth:** 6 7/8 inches. **Key Personnel:** Gregory Shank, Editor. **ISSN:** 0094-7571. **Subscription Rates:** $35; $75 institutions. **Formerly**: Crime and Social Justice (1989).
Ad Rates: BW: $250 **Circ:** Paid ‡3,000
Non-paid ‡50

3493 Software Development
Miller Freeman, Inc.
600 Harrison St. Phone: (650)905-2200
San Francisco, CA 94107 Fax: (650)908-6604
Free: (800)227-4675
Publisher E-mail: techlearning_ editors@mfi.com

Magazine for the computer programming industry. **Founded:** July 1984. **Freq:** Monthly. **Print Method:** Offset. **Trim Size:** 8 x 10 7/8. **Cols./Page:** 3. **Col. Width:** 12 picas. **Col. Depth:** 128 agate lines. **Key Personnel:** Rosaclaire Baisinger, Editorial Assistant, phone (415)356-3367, fax (415)905-4962, rbaisinger@mfi.com; Roger Smith, Technical Editor, phone (415)905-2280, fax (415)905-4962, rsmith@mfi.com; Barbara Hanscome, Editor-in-Chief, phone (415)905-2485, fax (415)905-4962, bhanscome@mfi.com; Marta McNair, Regional Sales Mgr., phone (415)905-2379, fax (415)905-4962, mmcnair@mfi.com; Greer Westerink, Regional Sales Mgr., phone (415)356-3362, fax (415)905-4962, gwesterink@mfi.com; Steve Nikkola, Regional Sales Mgr., phone (415)905-2256, fax (415)905-4962, snikkola@mfi.com; Lisa Kraus, Regional Sales Mgr., phone (212)615-2682, fax (212)279-3962, lkraus@mfi.com; Susan McDonald, Marketing Mgr., phone (415)905-2493, fax (415)905-4962, smcdonald@mfi.com. **ISSN:** 1070-8588. **Subscription Rates:** $39 individuals; $3.95 single issue. **Remarks:** Accepts advertising. **Available Online. Alt. Formats:** CD-ROM. **Formerly**: Computer Language.
Ad Rates: BW: $5,950 **Circ:** ‡72,000
4C: $7,045

3494 Sun-Reporter
Reporter Publications
1791 Vancroft Ave. Phone: (415)931-5778
San Francisco, CA 94124 Fax: (415)931-0214

Black community newspaper (tabloid). **Founded:** 1943. **Freq:** Weekly (Wed.). **Print Method:** Offset. **Cols./Page:** 5. **Col. Width:** 2 1/16 inches. **Col. Depth:** 14 inches. **Key Personnel:** Charles E. Belle, Editor; Carlton B. Goodlett, Ph.D., Publisher; Jack Kisbey, Advertising Mgr. **Subscription Rates:** $11 individuals. **Remarks:** Accepts advertising.
Ad Rates: SAU: $11.55 **Circ:** ‡11,249

3495 *Surface
7 Isadora Duncan Phone: (415)929-5100
San Francisco, CA 94102 Fax: (415)929-5103
Publication E-mail: surfacemag@surfacemag.com

Magazine covering fashion, arts, and entertainment. **Subtitle:** The American Avant-garde. **Founded:** Mar. 1994. **Freq:** Bimonthly. **Print Method:** Web offset. **Trim Size:** 9 x 10 7/8. **Key Personnel:** Richard Klein, Publisher, rklein@surfacemag.com; Riley John-Donnell, Publisher; Jeremy Lin, Editorial Dir.; Steve McDonald, Advertising Dir. **ISSN:** 1091-806X. **Subscription Rates:** $16. **Remarks:** Accepts advertising.
Ad Rates: BW: $5,867 **Circ:** Paid 96,000
4C: $7,337

3496 Swiss Journal
Swiss Journal Co.
548 Columbus Ave. Phone: (415)362-8072
PO Box 330082 Fax: (415)362-3159
San Francisco, CA 94133-2802
Swiss ethnic newspaper (English). **Founded:** 1918. **Freq:** Bimonthly. **Print Method:** Offset. **Trim Size:** 14 x 21. **Cols./Page:** 4. **Col. Width:** 3 inches. **Col. Depth:** 20 inches. **Key Personnel:** Louis M. Muschi, Exec. Editor; Anthony J. Muschi, Managing Editor. **ISSN:** 0039-7474. **Subscription Rates:** $26

individuals; $32 other countries. **Also known as:** Schweizer Journal.
Ad Rates: BW: $1,600 **Circ:** ‡10,000
PCI: $20

3497 Synapse
University of California, San Francisco
500 Parnassus Ave. Phone: (415)476-2211
Box 0376 Fax: (415)502-4537
San Francisco, CA 94143
Publication E-mail: synapse@itsa.ucsf.edu
Publisher E-mail: synapse@itsa.ucsf.edu

Collegiate newspaper (tabloid). **Founded:** 1956. **Freq:** Weekly. **Print Method:** Offset. **Trim Size:** 11 x 17. **Cols./Page:** 4. **Col. Width:** 27 nonpareils. **Col. Depth:** 224 agate lines. **Key Personnel:** Fred Gardner, Managing Editor, fred_gardner@quickmail.ucsf.edu. **ISSN:** 0887-4476. **Subscription Rates:** $20. **Remarks:** Accepts advertising. **URL:** http://itsa.ucsf.edu/~synapse.
Ad Rates: 4C: $1,835 **Circ:** 4,500
PCI: $8

3498 Teacher Education Quarterly
Caddo Gap Press
3145 Geary Blvd., No. 275 Phone: (415)922-1911
San Francisco, CA 94118 Fax: (415)440-4870
Publisher E-mail: caddogap@aol.com

Scholarly journal on teacher education. **Founded:** 1972. **Freq:** Quarterly. **Print Method:** Offset. **Trim Size:** 6 x 9. **Cols./Page:** 1. **Col. Width:** 27 picas. **Col. Depth:** 43 picas. **Key Personnel:** Alan H. Jones, Publisher. **ISSN:** 6737-4328. **Subscription Rates:** $40 individuals; $60 libraries institutions; $15 single issue. **Remarks:** Accepts advertising.
Ad Rates: BW: $200 **Circ:** 800

3499 Technology & Learning
Miller Freeman, Inc.
600 Harrison St. Phone: (650)905-2200
San Francisco, CA 94107 Fax: (650)908-6604
Free: (800)227-4675
Publication E-mail: editors@techlearning.com
Publisher E-mail: techlearning_editors@mfi.com

Magazine for educators (K-12) interested in the use of computers and other technology in schools. **Founded:** 1980. **Freq:** 10/year. **Print Method:** Offset. **Trim Size:** 7 7/8 x 10 7/8. **Cols./Page:** 3. **Col. Width:** 27 nonpareils. **Col. Depth:** 137 agate lines. **Key Personnel:** Judy Salpeter, Editor-in-Chief, phone (415)905-2643, fax (415)908-6604, jsalpeter@mfi.com; Jo-Ann McDevitt, Publisher, phone (415)905-2527, fax (415)908-6604, jmcdevitt@mfi.com. **ISSN:** 0746-4223. **Subscription Rates:** $24 individuals. **URL:** http://www.techlearning.com; http://www.millerfreeman.com. **Formerly:** Classroom Computer Learning.
Ad Rates: BW: $8,550 **Circ:** Paid ★13,378
4C: $10,785 Non-paid ★67,271

3500 Telemedicine and Telehealth Networks
600 Harrison St.
San Francisco, CA 94107

Trade publication covering integrated healthcare communications. **Freq:** Bimonthly. **Print Method:** Web offset. **Trim Size:** 8 1/8 x 10 7/8. **Key Personnel:** Deborah Dakins, Editor, ddakins@mfi.com; Sally Shankland, Publisher, sshankland@mfi.com; Karen Wertman, Advertising Mgr.; Lucinda Formydural, Circulation Mgr. **ISSN:** 1091-7853. **Remarks:** Accepts advertising. **URL:** http://www.telemedmag.com.
Ad Rates: BW: $3,090 **Circ:** Controlled 15,000
4C: $4,120

3501 THRASHER
High Speed Productions, Inc.
1303 Underwood Phone: (415)822-3083
San Francisco, CA 94124 Fax: (415)822-8359

Skateboard magazine. **Founded:** Dec. 1994. **Freq:** Quarterly. **Print Method:** Offset. **Trim Size:** 8 1/8 x 10 7/8. **Cols./Page:** 3 and 4. **Col. Width:** 15 and 11 nonpareils. **Col. Depth:** 60 picas. **Key Personnel:** Kevin J. Thatcher, Publisher; Edward H. Riggins, Publisher; Eben Sterling, Advertising. **ISSN:** 0889-0692. **Subscription Rates:** $18.50; $26 Canada; $35 other countries; $28 two years; $52 two years Canada; $3.95 single issue; $5.50 single issue Canada. **Remarks:** Accepts advertising. **Formerly:** THRASHER Skateboard Magazine (Jan. 1985).
Ad Rates: BW: $2,000 **Circ:** ‡250,000
4C: $3,000

3502 Tikkun
26 Fell St. Phone: (415)575-1200
San Francisco, CA 94102 Fax: (415)575-1434
Publisher E-mail: magazine@tikkun.org

Journal. **Subtitle:** A Bimonthly Jewish Critique of Politics, Culture and Society. **Founded:** June 1986. **Freq:** Bimonthly. **Print Method:** Web offset. **Trim Size:** 8 1/2 x 11. **Cols./Page:** 2 and 3. **Col. Width:** 37 1/2 and 24 nonpareils. **Col. Depth:** 129 1/2 agate lines. **Key Personnel:** Michael Lerner, Editor. **ISSN:** 0887-9982. **Subscription Rates:** $29 individuals; $5.95 single issue. **Remarks:** Accepts advertising. **URL:** http://www.tikkun.org.
Ad Rates: BW: $1,400 **Circ:** Combined 70,000
4C: $2,000

3503 Transactional Analysis Journal
International Transactional Analysis Association
450 Pacific Ave., Ste 250 Phone: (415)989-5640
San Francisco, CA 94133-4640 Fax: (415)989-9343
Publisher E-mail: itaa@itaa-net.org

Professional journal covering psychology. **Founded:** 1971. **Freq:** Quarterly. **Trim Size:** 7 x 10. **Cols./Page:** 2. **Col. Width:** 2 3/4 inches. **Col. Depth:** 7 inches. **Key Personnel:** Tony Tilney, Editor. **ISSN:** 0362-1537. **Subscription Rates:** $50 individuals. **Alt. Formats:** Microfilm. **Former name:** Transactional Analysis Bulletin.
Ad Rates: BW: $400 **Circ:** (Not Reported)

3504 TravelAge West
Reed Travel Group
49 Stevenson St., Ste. 460 Phone: (415)905-1155
San Francisco, CA 94105-2909 Fax: (415)905-1145

Magazine for retail travel agents in western U.S. and western Canada. **Founded:** Mar. 10, 1969. **Freq:** Weekly (Mon.). **Print Method:** Offset. **Trim Size:** 8 1/2 x 11. **Cols./Page:** 4. **Col. Width:** 20 nonpareils. **Col. Depth:** 140 agate lines. **Key Personnel:** Robert Carlsen, Editor, phone (415)905-1156; Evan Hirsch, Advertising Dir., phone (415)905-1166; Charles Sage, Advertising Mgr. **ISSN:** 0041-1973. **Subscription Rates:** Free to qualified subscribers; $25 individuals. **Remarks:** Accepts advertising.
Ad Rates: BW: $3,045 **Circ:** Controlled ‡34,001
4C: $4,465

3505 Underwriters' Report
657 Mission St., Ste. 300 Phone: (415)896-2660
San Francisco, CA 94105 Fax: (415)974-5041
Free: (800)527-5187

Magazine for agents, brokers, and insurer executives in the western states. **Subtitle:** The West's Leading Weekly Insurance News Magazine. **Founded:** 1905. **Freq:** Weekly (Thurs.). **Print Method:** Offset. **Trim Size:** 8 1/2 x 10 3/4. **Cols./Page:** 3. **Col. Width:** 27 nonpareils. **Col. Depth:** 133 agate lines. **Key Personnel:** Roy Pasini, Editor. **ISSN:** 0041-6622. **Subscription Rates:** $55 individuals; $2 single issue. **Remarks:** Accepts advertising. **URL:** http://www.uwreport.com.
Ad Rates: BW: $1,828 **Circ:** Combined 2,756
4C: $2,953
PCI: $85

3506 United States Lighthouse Society Bulletin and Keeper's Log (Qtrly Magazine)
U.S. Lighthouse Society
244 Kearny St., 5th Fl. Phone: (415)362-7255
San Francisco, CA 94108
Historical journal covering lighthouses, lightships and aids to navigation. **Founded:** 1984. **Freq:** Quarterly. **Cols./Page:** 3. **Key Personnel:** Wayne Wheeler, President/Editor. **ISSN:** 0883-0061. **Subscription Rates:** $25. **Remarks:** Accepts advertising.
Circ: Combined 10,030

3507 University of San Francisco Magazine
University of San Francisco
2130 Fulton St. Phone: (415)422-2698
San Francisco, CA 94117 Fax: (415)422-2696

University magazine. **Founded:** 1994. **Freq:** Semiannual. **Print Method:** Offset. **Trim Size:** 8 x 11. **Key Personnel:** Jim Mauo, Editor, mauo@usfca.edu. **Subscription Rates:** Free to qualified subscribers. **Remarks:** Advertising not accepted.
Circ: Controlled 65,000

3508 The Urban Latino News
3288 21st St. Phone: (415)821-4452
Box 9 Fax: (415)821-4452
San Francisco, CA 94110
Consumer lifestyle magazine for Hispanics. **Founded:** 1993. **Freq:** Semimonthly. **Print Method:** Web offset. **Trim Size:** 10 3/16 x 16 1/2. **Cols./Page:** 5. **Col. Width:** 18 inches. **Col. Depth:** 139 agate lines. **Key Personnel:** Gail E. Neira, Publisher. **Subscription Rates:** Free local only. **Remarks:** Accepts advertising.
Ad Rates: GLR: $20 **Circ:** Non-paid 20,000
BW: $2,520
4C: $3,145
PCI: $20

3509 Vehicle Leasing Today
National Vehicle Leasing Association
PO Box 281230 Phone: (650)548-9135
San Francisco, CA 94128-1230 Fax: (650)548-9155

Trade magazine covering the consumer and commercial automobile leasing markets. **Founded:** 1981. **Freq:** Quarterly. **Subscription Rates:** $40 individuals. **Remarks:** Accepts advertising.
Circ: (Not Reported)

3510 VIA
California State Automobile Association
150 Van Ness Ave. Phone: (415)565-2454
San Francisco, CA 94102 Fax: (415)552-5825
Free: (800)468-7563

Magazine covering worldwide and regional travel and recreation, restaurants, cars and car care, motorists issues, and traffic safety. **Subtitle:** Travel and News Magazine of the West. **Founded:** Aug. 1917. **Freq:** Bimonthly. **Print Method:** Offset. **Trim Size:** 8 x 10 7/8. **Cols./Page:** 3. **Col. Width:** 27 nonpareils. **Col. Depth:** 140 agate lines. **Key Personnel:** Lynn Ferrin, Editor; Kate MacIntyre, Advertising Mgr., phone (415)565-2455. **Subscription Rates:** $3.50 individuals; $.50 single issue. **Remarks:** Accepts advertising. **Formerly:** Motorland.
Ad Rates: BW: $22,195 **Circ:** Paid ★2,508,341
4C: $28,175

3511 Video Networks
Bay Area Video Coalition
2727 Mariposa St. Phone: (415)861-3282
San Francisco, CA 94110 Fax: (415)861-4316
Publisher E-mail: bavc@bavc.org

Magazine providing videographers with information on opportunities for grants, exhibition, distribution, festivals, and schools. **Founded:** 1977. **Freq:** Bimonthly. **Print Method:** Offset. **Trim Size:** 8 1/2 x 11. **Cols./Page:** 4. **Col. Width:** 1 7/8 inches. **Col. Depth:** 9 3/4 inches. **Key Personnel:** Karen Weiner, Managing Editor. **ISSN:** 0738-7563. **Subscription Rates:** $20 individuals. **URL:** http://www.bavc.org.
Ad Rates: BW: $400 **Circ:** Paid 2,000
Non-paid 50

3512 Vitae Schololasticae
Caddo Gap Press
3145 Geary Blvd., No. 275 Phone: (415)922-1911
San Francisco, CA 94118 Fax: (415)440-4870
Publisher E-mail: caddogap@aol.com

Scholarly journal covering research, scholarship, and other information about the study of biography in education. **Founded:** 1981. **Freq:** Semiannual. **Print Method:** Lithography. **Trim Size:** 6 x 9. **Cols./Page:** 1. **Col. Width:** 4 1/2 inches. **Col. Depth:** 7 inches. **Key Personnel:** Alan H. Jones, Publisher. **ISSN:** 0735-1909. **Subscription Rates:** $40 individuals; $60 libraries; $20 single issue. **Remarks:** Accepts advertising.
Ad Rates: BW: $200 **Circ:** Paid 125

3513 Wall Street Journal (Western Edition)
Dow Jones & Co., Inc.
201 California St., Ste. 1350 Phone: (415)986-6886
San Francisco, CA 94111 Fax: (415)956-0797

National business and finance newspaper. **Founded:** 1889. **Freq:** Daily (morn.). **Print Method:** Offset. **Cols./Page:** 6. **Col. Width:** 31 nonpareils. **Col. Depth:** 296 agate lines. **Key Personnel:** Paul Atkinson, Advertising Mgr.
Circ: Mon.-Fri. ★371,379

3514 The Western Journal of Medicine
Carden Jennings Publishing
California Medical Association Phone: (415)882-3374
221 Main St. Fax: (415)882-3379
PO Box 7602
San Francisco, CA 94120-7602
Publication E-mail: wjm@cjp.com

Journal featuring peer-reviewed articles for physicians and specialists on medical research, socioeconmics, and observation. **Founded:** 1902. **Freq:** Monthly. **Print Method:** Offset. **Trim Size:** 8 x 10 3/4. **Cols./Page:** 2. **Col. Width:** 3 1/2 inches. **Col. Depth:** 10 inches. **Key Personnel:** Taylor Bowen, MJ, Managing Editor; David Ern, Marketing Dir. **ISSN:** 0093-0415. **Subscription Rates:** $65 individuals U.S. and Canada; $120 two years; $20 students; $40 two years; $80 other countries; $145 two years other countries; $90 institutions; $160 two years institutions; $100 institutions, other countries; $175 two years institutions, other countries. **URL:** http://www.wjmed.com.
Ad Rates: GLR: $9 **Circ:** ‡45,000
BW: $1,150
4C: $1,840
PCI: $70

3515 Where San Francisco
Where Magazines International (San Francisco)
74 New Montgomery St., Ste. 320 Phone: (415)546-6101
San Francisco, CA 94105 Fax: (415)546-6108
Publication E-mail: robin.bruns@where-magazine.com

Consumer magazine covering tourist and travel information on San Francisco, California. **Founded:** July 1992. **Freq:** Monthly. **Cols./Page:** 3. **Key Personnel:** Susie McCormick, Publisher. **Subscription Rates:** $30 individuals; $5 single issue. **Remarks:** Accepts advertising.
Circ: (Not Reported)

3516 Wine & Spirits
818 Brannan St. Phone: (415)255-7736
San Francisco, CA 94103-4937 Fax: (415)255-9659
Publication E-mail: winespir@aol.com

Magazine containing consumer buying information on wine and spirits with in-depth articles on regions and trends in food and wine. **Subtitle:** The Practical Guide to Wine. **Founded:** 1981. **Freq:** 8/year. **Print Method:** Offset. **Trim Size:** 8 3/8 x 11. **Cols./Page:** 3. **Key Personnel:** Joshua Greene, Editor and Publisher, phone (212)695-4660. **ISSN:** 0890-0299. **Subscription Rates:** $26; $3.95 single issue. **Remarks:** Accepts advertising. **Formerly:** Wine & Spirits Buying Guide.
Ad Rates: BW: $3,805 **Circ:** ‡70,000
4C: $6,170

3517 Wired
Wired USA
520 3rd St., 4th Fl. Phone: (415)276-5000
San Francisco, CA 94107-1815 Fax: (415)276-5100
Free: (800)769-4733
Publication E-mail: info@wired.com

Consumer magazine focusing on the digital revolution's impact on business, culture, and society. **Subtitle:** The Magazine of the Digital Age. **Founded:** 1993. **Freq:** Monthly. **Print Method:** Web offset. **Trim Size:** 9 x 10 3/4. **Key Personnel:** Katrina Heron, Editor-in-Chief; Kevin Kelly, Editor; Dana Lyon, Publisher, dana@wired.com. **Subscription Rates:** $4.95 single issue; $5.95 single issue Canada. **Remarks:** Advertising accepted; rates available upon request. **Online:** America Online, Inc.
Circ: Paid ★511,478

3518 World Book of IABC Communicators
International Association of Business Communicators
1 Hallidie Plaza, Ste. 600 Phone: (415)433-3400
San Francisco, CA 94102 Fax: (415)362-8762

News magazine for public relations and organizational communication professionals. **Founded:** Nov. 1981. **Freq:** 8/year. **Trim Size:** 8 1/4 x 10 7/8. **Cols./Page:** 3. **Col. Width:** 2 3/8 inches. **Col. Depth:** 10 inches. **Key Personnel:** Gloria Gordon, Editor, ggordon@iabc.com. **ISSN:** 0744-7612. **Subscription Rates:** Available to members only. **Remarks:** Accepts advertising. **Alt. Formats:** Mailing labels.
Ad Rates: BW: $1,430 **Circ:** 15,000
4C: $2,055

3519 The World of Tribal Arts
Tribarts Inc.
2261 Market St., Ste. 644 Phone: (415)552-6884
San Francisco, CA 94114 Fax: (415)431-8321
Publisher E-mail: al@mediacity.com

Magazine covering tribal art worldwide. **Founded:** 1994. **Freq:** Quarterly. **Print Method:** Sheetfed offset. **Trim Size:** 210 x 297 mm. **ISSN:** 1354-2990. **Subscription Rates:** $53 individuals; $85 other countries; $14 single issue. **Remarks:** Accepts advertising. **URL:** http://www.tribalarts.com.
Ad Rates: 4C: $1900 **Circ:** Paid 3,000

3520 XLR8R
1388 Haight St. No. 105 Phone: (415)861-7583
San Francisco, CA 94117 Fax: (415)861-7584
Publication E-mail: xlr8r@xlr8r.com

Magazine covering dance and electronic music, fashion, and politics. **Subtitle:** Accelerating Music and Culture. **Founded:** Apr. 17, 1993. **Freq:** 8/year. **Print Method:** Web heat-set. **Trim Size:** 8.125 x 10.875. **Key Personnel:** Andrew Smith, Editor and Publisher, smith@xlr8r.com; Tomas Palermo, Managing Editor, tomas@xlr8r.com; Jennifer Cole, Advertising Mgr., jen@xlr8r.com. **Subscription Rates:** $12 individuals. **Remarks:** Accepts advertising. **URL:** http://www.xlr8r.com. **Alt. Formats:** CD-ROM.
Ad Rates: BW: $2,000 **Circ:** Paid 50,000
4C: $3,000

3521 Zine World
537 Jones St., No. 2386
San Francisco, CA 94102

Magazine containing reviews and news of interest to self-publishers. **Subtitle:** Freedom of the Press Is for Everyone. **Founded:** Nov. 1996. **Freq:** Bimonthly. **Print Method:** Offset. **Trim Size:** 5 1/2 x 8 1/2. **Cols./Page:** 2. **Key Personnel:** Doug Holland, Editor; E. Lampert, Circulation Mgr.; Kelli Williams, Art Director. **Subscription Rates:** $20 individuals; $3.50 single issue. **Remarks:** Accepts classified advertising. **Alt. Formats:** Audio tape.
Circ: Paid 180

3522 ZYZZYVA
41 Sutter St., Ste. 1400 Phone: (415)752-4393
San Francisco, CA 94104 Fax: (415)752-4391
Publication E-mail: zyzzyvainc@aol.com

Journal featuring West Coast writers and artists. **Subtitle:** The Last Word: West Coast Writers and Artists. **Founded:** 1985. **Freq:** Tri-quarterly. **Print Method:** Offset. **Trim Size:** 6 x 9. **Cols./Page:** 1. **Col. Width:** 60 nonpareils. **Col. Depth:** 108 agate lines. **Key Personnel:** Howard Junker, Editor, editor@zyzzva.org. **ISSN:** 8756-5633. **Subscription Rates:** $27 individuals; $10 single issue. **Remarks:** Color advertising not accepted. **Available Online. URL:** http://www.zyzzyva.org.
Ad Rates: BW: $500 **Circ:** Paid ‡2,500
Non-paid ‡1,000

3523 KABN-AM - 840
1255 Post St., Ste. 1011 Phone: (415)441-3377
San Francisco, CA 94109

Format: Talk. **Networks:** Westwood One Radio; CBS. **Owner:** American Radio Brokers, Inc., 9200 Lake Otis Pkwy., Anchorage, AK 99507, (907)344-5625, Fax: (907)344-5625. **Founded:** 1976. **Operating Hours:** Continuous. **ADI:** Anchorage, AK. **Key Personnel:** Chester Coleman, General Mgr./Program Dir., phone (415)441-3377; Susan Richards, Product Mgr.; Julie Zucchini, Music Dir.; Remington Noble, News Dir. **Wattage:** 50,000. **Ad Rates:** $22 for 15 seconds; $24 for 30 seconds; $25 for 60 seconds.

KADX-FM - See Anchorage, Alaska

3524 KALW-FM - 91.7
500 Mansell Phone: (415)841-4121
San Francisco, CA 94134
E-mail: kalwradio@aol.com

Format: Public Radio; Talk; Ethnic; News; Eclectic. **Networks:** National Public Radio (NPR); BBC World Service; Canadian Broadcasting Corporation (CBC)/Societe Radio-Canada (SRC). **Founded:** 1941. **Operating Hours:** Continuous; 70% network 30% local. **ADI:** San Francisco-Oakland-San Jose. **Key Personnel:** Michael Johnson, Contact, phone (415)841-4121, fax (415)841-4125. **Local Programs:** *Open Air*, Michael Johnson. **Wattage:** 1900. **Ad Rates:** Noncommercial. $60-100 for 30 seconds.

KAXX-AM - See Anchorage, Alaska

3525 KBHK-TV - 44
650 California St., 7th Fl. Phone: (415)249-4444
San Francisco, CA 94108 Fax: (415)397-1924
E-mail: upn@kbhk.com

Format: Commercial TV. **Networks:** United Paramount Network. **Owner:** United Television, Inc., 132 S. Rodeo Dr. 4th Fl., Beverly Hills, CA 90212, (310)281-4844, Fax: (310)281-4855. **Founded:** 1969. **Operating Hours:** 24 hrs. **ADI:** San Francisco-Oakland-San Jose. **Key Personnel:** Jerry Braet, General Mgr., phone (415)249-4400, jbraet@kbhktv.com; Tom Spitz, Program Dir., phone (415)249-4410, tspitz@kbhktv.com; Richard Jones, General Sales Mgr., phone (415)249-4400, fax (415)397-2140, rjones@kbhktv.com; George Brandt, Business Mgr., phone (415)249-4414, fax (415)249-4420, gbrandt@kbhktv.com. **Local Programs:** *Black Renaissance*, Tom Spitz, Mailing contact, (415)249-4410, Fax (415)397-1924; *El Amanecer*, Tom Spitz, Mailing contact, (415)249-4410, Fax (415)397-1924; *Susan Sikora Show*, Tom Spitz, Mailing contact. **Wattage:** 5,000,000 Video; 500,000 Audio. **URL:** http://www.upn44.com.

3526 KBLX-FM - 102.9
55 Hawthorne St. Ste. 900 Phone: (415)284-1029
San Francisco, CA 94105 Fax: (415)764-4959

Format: Jazz; Adult Contemporary. **Networks:** Independent. **Founded:** 1979. **Formerly:** KRE-FM. **Operating Hours:** Continuous. **ADI:** San Francisco-Oakland-San Jose. **Key Personnel:** Harvey Stone, Contact. **Local Programs:** *Bayview* 5:30 am - 6:00 am Sunday; *What's Going On* 9:35 am Monday-Friday. **Wattage:** 6600.

3527 KBPA-AM - 1220
114 Sansome St., Ste. 1410 Phone: (415)434-1220
San Francisco, CA 94104 Fax: (415)434-1280

Format: Educational. **Owner:** OIA License, L. L. C., at above address. **Operating Hours:** Continuous. **ADI:** San Francisco-Oakland-San Jose. **Key Personnel:** John Douglas, Chairman; Greg Douglas, President; Andy Whatley, V. P. of Marketing. **Wattage:** 5,000.

3528 KBWB - 20
2500 Marin St. Phone: (415)821-2020
San Francisco, CA 94124 Fax: (415)641-1163

Format: Commercial TV. **Founded:** 1960. **Formerly:** KOFY-TV. **Operating Hours:** Continuous. **ADI:** San Francisco-Oakland-San Jose. **Key Personnel:** Marty Edelman, General Mgr.; Michele Clerkley, Program Dir.; Mark Libby, Local; Lynne Simon, National; Karen Provenza, Promotions Mgr.

3529 KCBS-AM - 740
1 Embarcadero Center, Ste.3200 Phone: (415)765-4000
San Francisco, CA 94111-3768 Fax: (415)765-4152

Format: News; Information. **Networks:** CBS. **Owner:** CBS, 51 W. 52nd St., New York, NY 10019. **Founded:** 1909. **Formerly:** Radio San Jose. **Operating Hours:** Continuous. **ADI:** San Francisco-Oakland-San Jose. **Key Personnel:** Frank Oxarart, Vice President; Ed Cavagnaro, Contact; Gail Brooks, Contact; Hal Ramey, Sports Dir.; Ms. Jesse Waters, Contact; Lin Galliani, Contact; Stephen DiNardo, General Sales Mgr. **Wattage:** 50,000.

3530 KCNS-TV - 38
1550 Bryant St., Ste. 850 Phone: (415)863-3800
San Francisco, CA 94103 Fax: (415)863-3998

Format: Commercial TV; Ethnic. **Owner:** West Coast United Broadcasting Co., at above address. **Founded:** 1986. **Formerly:** KWBB-TV. **Operating Hours:** Continuous. **ADI:** San Francisco-Oakland-San Jose. **Key Personnel:** Martin Diaz, Dir. of Operations; Yvonne Clark, Controller; Skip Hamen, Chief Engineer; Michele Rosenfeld, Traffic Mgr.; Brent Scheiner, General Mgr. **Local Programs:** *Feng Shui*; *Inside China*. **Wattage:** 5,000,000.

3531 KDFC-FM - 102.1
455 Market St., Ste.2300 Phone: (415)975-5555
San Francisco, CA 94105 Fax: (415)975-5573

Format: Classical. **Networks:** Independent. **Founded:** 1947. **Operating Hours:** Continuous. **ADI:** San Francisco-Oakland-San Jose. **Key Personnel:** Dave Kendrick, General Mgr.; William O'Connell, Program Dir.; Tyler Phelps, Music Dir.; Linda Frame, General Sales Mgr.; Susan Wolin, Sales Mgr. **Wattage:** 33,000.

3532 KDTV-TV - 14
50 Freemont St., 41st Fl. Phone: (415)538-8000
San Francisco, CA 94105 Fax: (415)538-8053

Format: Commercial TV; Hispanic. **Networks:** Univision. **Owner:** Univision Television Group, Inc., at above address. **Founded:** 1975. **Formerly:** KEMO-TV (1975). **Operating Hours:** Continuous; 90% network, 10% local. **ADI:** San Francisco-Oakland-San Jose. **Key Personnel:** Maria Rodriguez, Traffic Mgr., fax (415)538-8029; Marcela Medina, General Mgr.; Chris Newgard, National Sales Mgr., fax (415)538-8036; Ernie Rizzuti, Local Sales Mgr., fax (415)538-8036. **Local Programs:** *Noticiero 14* 6 p.m. Monday-Friday, Tony LaGreca, Mailing contact. **Ad Rates:** $75-1,600 per unit.

3533 KEST-AM - 1450
145 natoma Phone: (415)978-5378
San Francisco, CA 94105 Fax: (415)978-5380

Format: New Age; Talk; Ethnic. **Simulcasts:** KOBO 1450 YUBA CITY-MARYSVILLE. **Networks:** Independent. **Founded:** 1926. **Operating Hours:** Continuous. **ADI:** San Francisco-Oakland-San Jose. **Key Personnel:** Julie Re, Business Mgr.; Tom Johnson, Program Dir.; Andrea Yamazaki, General Sales Mgr. **Wattage:** 1000. **Ad Rates:** Advertising accepted; rates available upon request.

3534 KFOG-FM - 104.5
55 Hawthorne St., Ste. 1100 Phone: (415)817-KFOG
San Francisco, CA 94105 Fax: (415)995-6867

Format: Album-Oriented Rock (AOR). **Simulcasts:** KFFG. **Networks:** Independent. **Founded:** 1963. **Operating Hours:** Continuous. **ADI:** San Francisco-Oakland-San Jose. **Key Personnel:** Tony Salvadore, Contact; Pat Evans, Program Dir. **Wattage:** 7900. **Ad Rates:** Advertising accepted; rates available upon request. **URL:** http://www.kfog.com.

3535 KFRC-AM - 610
500 Washington St., 2nd Fl. Phone: (415)391-9970
San Francisco, CA 94111-2919 Fax: (415)961-2329

Format: Oldies. **Founded:** 1924. **Operating Hours:** Continuous. **ADI:** San Francisco-Oakland-San Jose. **Key Personnel:** Will Schutte, General Mgr.; Brian Thomas, Program Dir. **Local Programs:** *Ron & Cammy Show* 3 p.m. - 7 p.m., Zak Parker, (415)951-2333, Fax (415)951-2329; *Sue Hall* 10 a.m. - 3 p.m., Sue Hall, (415)391-9970, ext. 711, Fax (415)951-2329. **Watt-**

age: 5000. **Ad Rates:** $10-650 per unit. **URL:** http://www.kfrc.com.

3536 KFRC-FM - 99.7
500 Washington, 2nd Fl. Phone: (415)391-9970
San Francisco, CA 94111 Fax: (415)951-2329

Format: Oldies. **Networks:** Independent. **Founded:** 1949. **Formerly:** KXXX-FM (1991). **Operating Hours:** Continuous. **ADI:** San Francisco-Oakland-San Jose. **Key Personnel:** W.I. Schultz, General Mgr.; Brian Thomas, Program Dir. **Wattage:** 45,000. **Ad Rates:** $10-650 per unit. **URL:** http://www.kfrc.com.

3537 KGO-AM - 810
900 Front St. Phone: (415)954-8100
San Francisco, CA 94111-1450 Fax: (415)362-5827

Format: News; Talk. **Networks:** ABC. **Founded:** 1924. **Operating Hours:** Continuous. **ADI:** San Francisco-Oakland-San Jose. **Key Personnel:** Michael Luckoff, Contact; Jack Swanson, Program Dir.; Bob Texeira, Sports Dir. **Wattage:** 50,000.

3538 KGO-TV - 7
900 Front St. Phone: (415)954-7777
San Francisco, CA 94111 Fax: (415)954-7289

Format: Commercial TV. **Networks:** ABC. **Operating Hours:** Continuous. **ADI:** San Francisco-Oakland-San Jose. **Key Personnel:** Jim Topping, General Mgr.

3539 KIOI-FM - 101.3
700 Montgomery St. Phone: (415)956-5101
San Francisco, CA 94111 Fax: (415)397-5101
E-mail: k101radio@aol.com

Format: Adult Contemporary. **Networks:** Independent. **Owner:** Evergreen Media Corporation, c/o 433 E. Las Colinas Blvd, Ste 1130, Irving, TX 75039, (214)869-9020, Fax: (214)869-3671. **Founded:** 1957. **Operating Hours:** Continuous. **ADI:** San Francisco-Oakland-San Jose. **Key Personnel:** Brent Osborne, General Mgr.; Carol Eckardt, Business Mgr. **Local Programs:** *The Don Bleu Show*, Bucky Whitaker, Producer. **Wattage:** 125,000.

3540 KIQI-AM - 1010
2601 Mission St. Phone: (415)695-1010
San Francisco, CA 94110 Fax: (415)695-1015

Format: Hispanic. **Owner:** Mr. Rene De La Rosa, at above address, Fax: (415)695-1023. **Founded:** 1957. **Operating Hours:** Continuous; 100% local. **ADI:** San Francisco-Oakland-San Jose. **Key Personnel:** Rene De La Rosa, President; Luu Quintzuilla, Program Dir.; Martha Alfonso, Traffic Mgr.; Micheal Sher, Nat'l Sales Mgr.; Richard Ferdinand, Station Mgr. **Wattage:** 10,000. **Ad Rates:** $60-88 for 30 seconds; $75-110 for 60 seconds.

3541 KISQ-FM - 98.1
750 Battery St., No. 200 Phone: (415)788-5225
San Francisco, CA 94111

Format: Blues. **Owner:** Chancellor Media, at above address. **Formerly:** KBGG-FM (1997). **Operating Hours:** Continuous. **ADI:** San Francisco-Oakland-San Jose. **Key Personnel:** Joe Bayliss, General Mgr.; Steve Watkins, General Sales Mgr.; Michael Erickson, Program Dir.; Sheri Nelson, Marketing Dir. **Wattage:** 100,000. **Ad Rates:** Advertising accepted; rates available upon request. **URL:** http://www.981kissfm.com.

3542 KITS-FM - 105.3
730 Harrison St., Ste. 300 Phone: (415)512-1053
San Francisco, CA 94107 Fax: (415)777-2284
Free: (800)696-1053

Format: Alternative/New Music/Progressive. **Founded:** 1986. **Operating Hours:** Continuous. **ADI:** San Francisco-Oakland-San Jose. **Key Personnel:** Richard Sands, Program Dir., phone (415)512-1053, fax (415)777-2284; Bill Lynch, General Sales Mgr. **Wattage:** 15,000. **Ad Rates:** $200-600 per unit.

3543 KKSF-FM - 103.7
340 Townsend St., 4th Fl. Phone: (415)975-5555
San Francisco, CA 94107-1633 Fax: (415)975-5573
E-mail: comments@kksf.tbo.com

Format: Jazz; Adult Contemporary. **Networks:** Independent. **Owner:** Chancellor Media, 340 Townsend St., 4th Fl., San Francisco, CA 94107. **Founded:** 1987. **Formerly:** KLOK-FM (1986). **Operating Hours:** Continuous. **ADI:** San Francisco-Oakland-San Jose. **Key Personnel:** Douglas F. Sterne, Vice Pres./General Mgr.; Steve Reedffe, General Sales Mgr.; Linda Frame, National Sales Mgr.; Sheri Mowbray, Local Sales Mgr.; Paul Goldstein, Program Dir.; Doug Irwin, Chief Engineer. **Wattage:** 7800. **Ad Rates:** $150-500 per unit. **URL:** http://www.kksf.com.

3544 KLLC-FM - 97.3
1 Embarcadero Center Phone: (415)765-4097
San Francisco, CA 94111 Fax: (415)765-4084
Free: (800)400-FM97
E-mail: studio@radioalice.com

Format: Adult Album Alternative; Adult Contemporary. **Networks:** CBS. **Owner:** Westinghouse, at above address, Fax: (415)781-3697. **Founded:** 1948. **Formerly:** KRQR-FM (1996). **Operating Hours:** Continuous. **ADI:** San Francisco-Oakland-San Jose. **Key Personnel:** Susan Seifert, General Sales Mgr., phone (415)765-4043, fax (415)765-4084, seifert@sfradio.cbs.com; Stephen DiNardo, Vice President, phone (415)765-4032, fax (415)765-4084, dinardo@sfradio.cbs.com; Liz Collier, Public Affairs, phone (415)765-4046, fax (415)765-4061, collier@sfradio.cbs.com; Louis Kaplan, Program Dir., phone (415)765-4187, fax (415)765-4084, kaplan@sfradio.cbs.com. **Wattage:** 82,000 ERP.

3545 KMEL-FM - 106.1
340 Townsend St., No. 5-106 Phone: (415)538-1061
San Francisco, CA 94107 Fax: (415)538-1060

Format: Contemporary Hit Radio (CHR). **Networks:** Independent. **Owner:** Evergreen Media Corp., at above address. **Founded:** 1960. **Operating Hours:** Continuous. **ADI:** San Francisco-Oakland-San Jose. **Key Personnel:** Richard Kelley, VP/Gen. Mgr.; Michelle Santosuosso, Program Dir.; Dan Haight, General Sales Mgr.; Katie Eyerly, Mktg. Dir. **Wattage:** 69,000. **URL:** http://www.106kmel@sirius.com.

3546 KNBR-AM - 680
55 Hawthorne St., Ste. 1100 Phone: (415)995-6800
San Francisco, CA 94105 Fax: (415)995-6867
E-mail: sports@knbrgb.com

Format: Sports; Talk. **Networks:** Westwood One Radio; CBS; ESPN Radio. **Founded:** 1922. **Operating Hours:** Continuous. **ADI:** San Francisco-Oakland-San Jose. **Key Personnel:** Tony Salvadore, General Mgr.; Bob Agnew, Program Dir.; Mike Jackson, Sales Mgr.; Brent Osborne, Contact. **Wattage:** 50,000.

3547 KNEW-AM - 910
750 Battery St., Ste. 200 Phone: (415)291-0202
San Francisco, CA 94111-1524 Fax: (415)395-9886
Free: (800)345-KNEW
E-mail: knew@aol.com

Networks: ABC. **Founded:** 1925. **Formerly:** KEWB-AM. **Operating Hours:** Continuous; 100% local. **ADI:** San Francisco-Oakland-San Jose. **Key Personnel:** Brent Osborne, General Mgr.; Ed Ely, Operations Mgr.; Bill Gillreath, General Sales Mgr.; David Isenberg, Promotions Dir.; Bob Hamilton, Program Dir. **Wattage:** 5000. **Ad Rates:** Advertising accepted; rates available upon request.

3548 KOIT-AM - 1260
455 Market St., No. 2300 Phone: (415)777-0965
San Francisco, CA 94105 Fax: (415)896-0965

Format: Adult Contemporary. **Networks:** AP; UPI. **Owner:** Bonneville International Corp., PO Box 1160, Salt Lake City, UT 84110-1160, (801)575-7500, Fax: (801)575-0965. **Operating Hours:** Continuous; 100% local. **ADI:** San Francisco-Oakland-San Jose. **Key Personnel:** Chuck Tweedle, Contact, ctweedle@koit.com; Sharon Warren, Contact, fax (415)546-5648, swarren@koit.com; Vickie Jenkins, Contact, vjenkins@koit.com; Bill Conway, Contact, bconway@koit.com; Mavis Sin, Contact, fax (415)357-0527, msin@koit.com; Louis Stolte, Contact, lstolte@koit.com; Dan Denton, Contact, ddenton@koit.com. **Wattage:** 5000.

3549 KOIT-FM - 96.5
455 Market St., No. 2300 Phone: (415)777-0965
San Francisco, CA 94105 Fax: (415)896-0965

Format: Adult Contemporary. **Networks:** AP; UPI. **Owner:** Bonneville International Corp., PO Box 1160, Salt Lake City, UT 84110-1160, (801)575-7500, Fax: (801)575-7548. **Operating Hours:** Continuous. **ADI:** San Francisco-Oakland-San Jose. **Key Personnel:** Chuck Tweedle, Contact, ctweedle@koit.com; Sharon Warren, Contact, fax (415)546-5648, swarren@koit.com; Vickie Jenkins, Contact, vjenkins@koit.com; Bill Conway, Contact, bconway@koit.com; Louise Stolte, Contact, lstolte@koit.com; Mavis Sin, Contact, fax (415)357-0527, msin@koit.com; Dan Denton, Contact, ddenton@koit.com. **Wattage:** 33,000.

3550 KPIX-TV - 5
855 Battery St. Phone: (415)362-5550
San Francisco, CA 94111-1597 Fax: (415)765-8844

Format: Commercial TV. **Networks:** CBS. **Founded:** 1940. **Operating Hours:** 5:30 a.m.-4 a.m. **ADI:** San Francisco-Oakland-San Jose. **Key Personnel:** Ralph Blansiardi, General Mgr.

3551 KPOO-FM - 89.5
PO Box 423030 Phone: (415)346-5373
San Francisco, CA 94142 Fax: (415)346-5173
E-mail: kpooradio@aol.com

Format: Full Service. **Networks:** Independent. **Operating Hours:** Continuous. **ADI:** San Francisco-Oakland-San Jose. **Key Personnel:** Jerome Parson, Program Dir.; Marylyn Fowler, Contact; Joe Rudolph, General Mgr. **Wattage:** 3000.

3552 KPTY-FM - 103.9
1710 Vallejo St.
San Francisco, CA 94123

Format: Contemporary Hit Radio (CHR). **Owner:** New Planet Radio, at above address. **Founded:** 1997. **Former name:** KBZR-FM (1997). **Operating Hours:** Continuous. **ADI:** Phoenix (Kingman, Prescott), AZ. **Key Personnel:** Mark Waters, General Mgr.; Mike Kennelley, General Sales Mgr.; Byron Kennedy, Program Dir. **Wattage:** 50,000. **Ad Rates:** $100-150 per unit. **URL:** http://www.partystationonline.com.

3553 KQED-FM - 88.5
2601 Mariposa St. Phone: (415)553-2129
San Francisco, CA 94110 Fax: (415)553-2241

Format: Public Radio. **Networks:** National Public Radio (NPR). **Founded:** 1969. **Operating Hours:** Continuous; 80% network, 20% local. **ADI:** San Francisco-Oakland-San Jose. **Key Personnel:** JoAnne Wallace, General Mgr.; Monty Carlos, Operations Dir.; Raul Ramirez, News Dir.; Jo Anne Wallace, Program Dir.; Cyrus Musiker, Assignment Editor; Sally Eisele, Sr., Producer. **Wattage:** 110,000. **Ad Rates:** $75-250 for 15 seconds. **URL:** http://www.kqed.org.

3554 KRON-TV - 4
1001 Van Ness Ave. Phone: (415)441-4444
San Francisco, CA 94109 Fax: (415)561-8759

Format: Commercial TV. **Networks:** NBC. **Owner:** Chronicle Broadcasting Co., at above address, Fax: (415)561-8136. **Founded:** 1949. **Operating Hours:** Continuous; 50% network, 50% local. **ADI:** San Francisco-Oakland-San Jose. **Key Personnel:** Amy McCombs, General Mgr.; E. Richard Cerussi, General Sales Mgr.; Al Holzer, News and Programming Dir.; Rick Swanson, Marketing and Programming Dir.; Janette Gitler, Community Relations; Jodie Chase, Media Relations Mgr. **Ad Rates:** $300-24,000 per unit.

3555 KSAN-FM - 94.9
750 Battery St., No. 200 Phone: (415)291-0202
PO Box 7448 Fax: (415)395-9886
San Francisco, CA 94111-1524

Format: Country. **Networks:** AP. **Founded:** 1954. **Operating Hours:** Continuous. **ADI:** San Francisco-Oakland-San Jose. **Key Personnel:** Lee Logan, Operations Mgr.; Bruce Blevins, General Mgr.; Richard Ryan, Music Dir.; Marlene Augustine, Contact; Julie Kahn, General Sales Mgr. **Wattage:** 60,000. **Ad Rates:** Advertising accepted; rates available upon request.

3556 KSFO-AM - 560
900 Front St. Phone: (415)398-5600
San Francisco, CA 94111-1450 Fax: (415)954-2795

Format: Oldies; Sports. **Networks:** Independent. **Founded:** 1925. **Operating Hours:** Continuous. **ADI:** San Francisco-Oakland-San Jose. **Key Personnel:** Ed Krampf, General Mgr.; Dave Anthony, Program Dir. **Wattage:** 5000. **Ad Rates:** $50-400 per unit.

3557 KTVO-AM - 1400
55 Hawthorne St., Ste. 900 Phone: (415)284-1029
San Francisco, CA 94105 Fax: (415)764-4959

Format: Ethnic. **Owner:** Inner City Broadcasting Corp., at above address. **Formerly:** KBLX-AM. **Operating Hours:** Continuous. **Key Personnel:** Harvey Stone, Pres./General Mgr.; Barry Rose, V. P./General Sales Mgr.; Paul Marks, Chief Engineer.

3558 KUSF-FM - 90.3
2130 Fulton St. Phone: (415)386-5873
San Francisco, CA 94117-1080
E-mail: kusf@usfca.edu

Format: Eclectic; Classical; Alternative/New Music/Progressive. **Networks:** Independent. **Owner:** University of San Francisco, at above address. **Founded:** 1962. **Formerly:** KCMA-FM (1973). **Operating Hours:** Continuous; 100% local. **ADI:** San Francisco-Oakland-San Jose. **Key Personnel:** Steve Runyon, General Mgr.; Kate Ingram, Program Dir.; Bill Ruck, Chief Engineer; Robert Barone, Fundraising Coordinator; Carrie Hourihan, Office Mgr. **Local Programs:** *Epicurean Corner*, Gina Snow, (415)563-0771; *Fighting Back*, Ralph Kessler, (510)845-9285; *Technation*, Dr. Moira Gunn, (415)386-2710. **Wattage:** 3000. **Ad Rates:** Underwriting available. $40 for 30 seconds. **URL:** http://web.usfca.edu/kusf.

3559 KUTO-AM - 1400
55 Hawthorne, Ste. 900 Phone: (415)284-1029
San Francisco, CA 94105 Fax: (415)764-4959
E-mail: inlanguage@compuserve.com

Format: Ethnic. **Networks:** Independent. **Founded:** 1922. **Formerly:** KRE-AM (1990); KBFN-AM; KBLX AM. **Operating Hours:** Continuous. **ADI:** San Francisco-Oakland-San Jose. **Key Personnel:** Harvey Stone, Contact. **Wattage:** 1,000. **Ad Rates:** $70-95 for 60 seconds. KVVN.

3560 KVVN-AM - 1430
55 Hawthorne St., Ste. 900 Phone: (415)284-1029
San Francisco, CA 94105 Fax: (415)764-4959

Format: Ethnic. **Owner:** Inner City Broadcasting Corp., at above address. **Formerly:** KNTA-AM. **Operating Hours:** Continuous. **Key Personnel:** Harvey Stone, Pres./General Mgr.; Barry Rose, V. P./General Sales Mgr.; Paul Marks, Chief Engineer.

3561 KYLD-FM - 94.9
750 Battery St., Ste. 200
San Francisco, CA 94111-1524

Format: Contemporary Hit Radio (CHR). **Owner:** Chancellor Media, at above address. **Formerly:** KSOL-FM. **Operating Hours:** Continuous. **ADI:** San Francisco-Oakland-San Jose. **Key Personnel:** Joe Cunningham, General Sales Mgr.; Dick Kelly, General Mgr.; Michael Martin, Program Dir. **URL:** http://www.wild949.com.

3562 TCI, San Francisco System
2055 Folsom St. Phone: (415)863-8500
San Francisco, CA 94110 Fax: (415)863-1659
Free: (800)945-2288

Founded: 1953. **Formerly:** Viacom Cable of San Francisco. **Key Personnel:** Douglas Schulz, Contact. **Cities Served:** San Francisco, CA: 54 channels; 1 community access channel; 56 hours per week community access programming.

3563 WILD-FM - 94.9
55 Green St., Ste. 200 Phone: (415)356-0949
San Francisco, CA 94111 Fax: (415)267-0949
Free: (800)333-9490

Format: Contemporary Hit Radio (CHR). **Networks:** Independent. **Founded:** 1967. **Formerly:** KSOL-FM (1987). **Operating Hours:** Continuous. **ADI:** San Francisco-Oakland-San Jose. **Key Personnel:** Bob Visotcky, General Mgr.; Michael Martin, Program Dir. **Wattage:** 8900. **Ad Rates:** Advertising accepted; rates available upon request. **Additional Contact Info: Mailing Address:** 90 Warren St., Boston, MA 02119-3248, (617)427-2222, fax: (617)427-2677.

SAN GABRIEL, pop. 30,072.

Los Angeles Co. (S). 5 m NE of Los Angeles. San Gabriel mission established 1771. Residential. Manufactures venetian blinds, wine, caskets, candied fruit, door chimes, cameras, toys. Agriculture. Fruit, vegetables, dairy and poultry products.

3564 Journal of Fuzzy Mathematics
International Fuzzy Mathmatics Institute
PO Box 639 Phone: (626)575-8466
San Gabriel, CA 91778 Fax: (626)575-0678
Publisher E-mail: ifmi@msn.com

Scholarly journal covering original research in mathematics. **Founded:** Mar. 1993. **Freq:** Quarterly. **Trim Size:** 7 x 10. **Key Personnel:** Prof. Hu Cheng-Ming, Editor. **ISSN:** 1066-8950. **Subscription Rates:** $120 individuals; $358 institutions; $120 individuals other countries; $358 institutions other countries. **Remarks:** Advertising not accepted.
Circ: (Not Reported)

SAN JACINTO, pop. 7,098.

Riverside Co. (SE). 32 m SE of Riverside. Food processing plants. Health resort, hot springs. Agriculture.

3565 The Hemet News
Donrey Media Group
474 W. Esplanada Ave. Phone: (909)487-2200
San Jacinto, CA 92583 Fax: (909)487-2250
Publication E-mail: hemetnew@koan.com

General newspaper. **Founded:** Dec. 1893. **Freq:** Tues.-Sun. **Print Method:** Offset. **Cols./Page:** 6. **Col. Width:** 25 nonpareils. **Col. Depth:** 301 agate lines. **Key Personnel:** Craig Shultz, Editor; Jim Fredericks, Publisher; Manny Padilla, Advertising Mgr. **Subscription Rates:** $56.03 individuals. **Remarks:** Accepts advertising.
Ad Rates: BW: $2,580 **Circ:** Tues.-Fri. 11,540
4C: $3,090 Sat. 11,540
SAU: $20 Sun. 12,439

SAN JOAQUIN

3566 San Joaquin Farm Bureau News
San Joaquin Farm Bureau Federation
PO Box 8444 Phone: (209)931-4931
Stockton, CA 95208-0444 Fax: (209)931-1433
Publication E-mail: bjsjstan@aol.com

Agricultural newspaper. **Founded:** 1944. **Freq:** Monthly. **Print Method:** Offset. **Trim Size:** 11.5 x 15. **Cols./Page:** 4. **Col. Width:** 2 1/4 inches. **Col. Depth:** 13 1/2 inches. **Key Personnel:** Debi Crawford, Advertising Manager, phone (209)474-1868, fax (209)474-1554; Russ Matthews, Business Mgr., phone (209)931-4931, fax (209)931-1433, matthews@cwws.net. **USPS:** 185-880. **Subscription Rates:** $.50 individuals; $5 nonmembers. **Remarks:** Accepts advertising.
Ad Rates: BW: $560 **Circ:** Paid ‡5,000
4C: $870
PCI: $14.20

SAN JOSE†, pop. 636,550.

Santa Clara Co. (W) 38 m SE of Oakland. California State University, at San Jose. West Coast center of research oriented electronic and space industries. Manufactures canning and dried fruit packing machinery; missiles, rocket boosters, computers, atomic electrical equipment, fruit, vegetable and fish cans; foundry, dairy products, chemicals, cement, aluminum, paint, fiberglass, matches, pumps, soaps, motors, cabinets, electronics. Automobile assembly plant. In extensive fruit, wine, nut, berry, grape and row crop growing region.

3567 ARTWEEK
2149 Paragon Dr., Ste. 100 Phone: (408)441-7065
San Jose, CA 95131 Fax: (408)441-9519
Free: (800)733-2916
Publisher E-mail: artweek@artweek.com

Magazine containing contemporary West Coast art reviews, commentary, features and interviews. **Founded:** Jan. 2, 1970. **Freq:** Monthly. **Print Method:** Offset. **Trim Size:** 11x14. **Cols./Page:** 5. **Key Personnel:** Kitty Spaulding, Publisher; Steven Jenkins, Editor-in-Chief; Patty An, Managing Editor. **ISSN:** 0004-4121. **Subscription Rates:** $32 individuals; $34 single issue Institutions; $50 other countries; $4.00 single issue. **Remarks:** Accepts advertising.
Ad Rates: GLR: $5 **Circ:** Paid ‡12,000
BW: $1,400 Non-paid ‡3,000
4C: $1,815

3568 The Beethoven Journal
American Beethoven Society
San Jose State University Phone: (408)924-4590
1 Washington Sq. Fax: (408)924-4715
San Jose, CA 95192-0171
Spotlights the life and works of Ludwig van Beethoven (1770-1827). Recurring features include letters to the editor, news of research, reports of meetings, book reviews, notices of publications available, and columns titled Audition Reports, Studies in Beethoven Bibliography, and Miscellanea. **Founded:** 1986. **Freq:** Semiannual. **Trim Size:** 8 1/2 x 11. **Key Personnel:** William Meredith, Editor, phone (408)924-4589, meredith@sjsu.edu. **ISSN:** 1087-8262. **Subscription Rates:** Free members; $25 institutions; $35 institutions, other countries. **Remarks:** Advertising not accepted. **URL:** http://www.music.sjsu.edu/Beethoven/index/caption.html. **Formerly:** The Beethoven Newsletter.
Circ: 1,000

3569 The California School Employee
California School Employees Association
2045 Lundy Ave. Phone: (408)263-8000
San Jose, CA 95131 Fax: (408)954-0948

Tabloid for school employees. **Founded:** Sept. 1931. **Freq:** Monthly. **Print Method:** Offset. **Trim Size:** 11x17. **Cols./Page:** 4. **Col. Width:** 28 nonpareils. **Col. Depth:** 126 agate lines. **Key Personnel:** Douglas Crooks, Public Relations Dir., dcrooks@csea.com. **ISSN:** 0008-1515. **Subscription Rates:** $5 nonmembers. **Remarks:** Accepts advertising.
Ad Rates: BW: $1,946 **Circ:** Controlled ‡130,000
4C: $2,696

3570 Construction Labor News
2102 Almaden Rd., Ste. 204 Phone: (408)265-6280
San Jose, CA 95125-2194 Fax: (408)265-7371
Publication E-mail: 71112.413@compuserve.com

Newspaper (tabloid) for labor unions. **Founded:** 1978. **Freq:** Monthly. **Print Method:** Offset. **Trim Size:** 11 x 14. **Cols./Page:** 5. **Col. Width:** 24 nonpareils. **Key Personnel:** Mindy Dravis-Gonzales, Publisher. **ISSN:** 0161-990X. **Subscription Rates:** $24 individuals.
Ad Rates: GLR: $3 **Circ:** Paid ‡25,000
BW: $1,200 Free ‡300
4C: $1,500
PCI: $25

3571 El Observador
1376 North 4th St., No. 100 Phone: (408)453-2944
San Jose, CA 95112-6311 Fax: (408)453-2979

Bilingual newspaper (Spanish and English). **Founded:** Oct. 1980. **Freq:** Weekly (Thurs.). **Print Method:** Offset. **Trim Size:** 13 x 21. **Cols./Page:** 6. **Col. Width:** 21 inches. **Col. Depth:** 21 inches. **Key Personnel:** Hilbert Morales, Publisher; Elizabeth Morales, Publisher; Monica Amador, Advertising Mgr. **Subscription Rates:** $35 individuals; $45 out of state. **Remarks:** Accepts display advertising. **Online:** EL-Observador.Com. **Alt. Formats:** CD-ROM.
Ad Rates: GLR: $2 **Circ:** Paid 72
BW: $2873 Free 10,708
4C: $3573
SAU: $23
PCI: $22.80

3572 India Currents
Box 21285 Phone: (408)274-6966
San Jose, CA 95151 Fax: (408)274-2733

The Complete Indian American Magazine. **Founded:** Apr. 1987. **Freq:** Monthly. **Print Method:** Offset. **Trim Size:** 8 1/4 x 10 1/2. **Cols./Page:** 3. **Col. Width:** 2 3/8 inches. **Col. Depth:** 9 3/4 inches. **Key Personnel:** Arvind Kumar, Editor, editor@indiacur.com; Ashok Jethanandani, Publisher, publisher@indiacur.com; Vandana Kumar, Managing Editor, mgeditor@indiacur.com. **ISSN:** 0896-095X. **Subscription Rates:** $19.95 by mail; $1.95 single issue. **Remarks:** Accepts advertising. **URL:** http://www.indiacur.com/indiacur/.
Ad Rates: BW: $540 **Circ:** Paid ‡2,050
4C: $960 Non-paid ‡21,000
PCI: $14

3573 Khang Chien Magazine
Khang Chien
PO Box 7826 Phone: (408)363-1078
San Jose, CA 95150 Fax: (408)363-1178

Vietnamese-language magazine covering events and developments in Vietnam. **Founded:** 1982. **Freq:** Quarterly. **Trim Size:** 10.50 x 8. **Key Personnel:** Nguyen Trong Thuc, Editor. **ISSN:** 0892-7588. **Subscription Rates:** $12 U.S.; $16 Canada; rates differ for other countries. **Remarks:** Advertising not accepted.
Circ: Paid 7,000
Non-paid 2,000

3574 La Oferta Review
1376 N. Fourth St. Phone: (408)436-7850
San Jose, CA 95112 Fax: (408)436-7861
Free: (800)336-7850
Publication E-mail: laoferta@bayarea.net

Community newspaper (English and Spanish). **Founded:** 1979. **Freq:** Weekly (Wed.). **Print Method:** Offset. **Trim Size:** 13 x 21. **Cols./Page:** 3. **Col. Width:** 6 inches. **Col. Depth:** 21 inches. **Key Personnel:** Frank Andrade, Publisher; Mary Andrade. **Subscription Rates:** $50. **Remarks:** Accepts advertising. **Available Online.**
Ad Rates: GLR: $30 **Circ:** ‡38,518
BW: $3,780
4C: $600
PCI: $30

3575 Metro
Metro Publishing, Inc.
550 S. 1st St. Phone: (408)298-8000
San Jose, CA 95113 Fax: (408)298-0602

Newspaper (tabloid) covering regional news, arts, and entertainment. **Subtitle:** Santa Clara Valley's Weekly Newspaper. **Founded:** Mar. 1985. **Freq:** Weekly (Thurs.). **Print Method:** Offset. **Trim Size:** 10 3/4 x 13 11/16. **Cols./Page:** 5. **Col. Width:** 26 nonpareils. **Col. Depth:** 196 agate lines. **Key Personnel:** Dan Pulcrano, Editor; David Cohen, Publisher; Scott Levander, Ad Dir. **Subscription Rates:** Free; $76 by mail. **Remarks:** Accepts advertising. **URL:** http://www.metroactive.com.
Ad Rates: BW: $2,597 **Circ:** Free 85,000
4C: $3,197

3576 Modern Liturgy
Resource Publications, Inc.
160 E. Virginia St., Ste. 290 Phone: (408)286-8505
San Jose, CA 95112-5876 Fax: (408)287-8748
Publication E-mail: mdrnlitrgy@aol.com
Publisher E-mail: info@rpinet.com

Creative idea journal for Roman Catholic church leaders, artists, and religious educators. **Founded:** 1973. **Freq:** 10/year. **Print Method:** Offset. **Trim Size:** 8 3/8 x 10 7/8. **Cols./Page:** 3. **Col. Width:** 13 1/2 picas. **Col. Depth:** 9 1/2 inches. **Key Personnel:** Nick Wagner, S.J., Editor, nick@rpinet.com; William Burns, Publisher, bill@rpinet.com; Kenneth Guentert, Dir. of Mktg. & Sales, ken@rpinet.com. **ISSN:** 0363-504X. **Subscription Rates:** $45 individuals. **Remarks:** Accepts

advertising. **URL:** http://www.rpinet.com. **Alt. Formats:** Mailing labels.
Ad Rates: BW: $996 **Circ:** Paid 20,000
4C: $1,476 Non-paid 10,000
PCI: $83

3577 Rosicrucian Digest
Rosicrucian Order, AMORC
Rosicrucian Park Phone: (408)947-3600
1342 Naglee Ave. Fax: (408)947-3677
San Jose, CA 95191
Magazine covering mysticism, science, and philosophy. **Founded:** 1915. **Freq:** Quarterly. **Print Method:** Offset. **Trim Size:** 7 1/2 x 10 1/4. **Cols./Page:** 2. **Col. Width:** 35 nonpareils. **Col. Depth:** 115 agate lines. **Key Personnel:** Robin Thompson, Editor. **ISSN:** 0035-8339. **Subscription Rates:** $12 individuals. **Remarks:** Advertising not accepted.
Circ: Combined ‡80,000

3578 San Jose Business Journal
American City Business Journals
96 N. 3rd St., Ste. 100 Phone: (408)295-3800
San Jose, CA 95112 Fax: (408)295-5028
Publication E-mail: sanjose@amcity.com

Business newspaper (tabloid). **Subtitle:** Serving San Jose and the Silicon Valley. **Founded:** May 2, 1982. **Freq:** Weekly (Fri.). **Print Method:** Offset. **Trim Size:** 10 3/4 x 14 1/2. **Cols./Page:** 4. **Col. Width:** 27 nonpareils. **Col. Depth:** 196 agate lines. **Key Personnel:** John Bowman, Editor, j.bowman@sjbj.com; Armon Mills, Publisher; Susan Wann, Advertising Dir.; Jeri Waxman, Director of Marketing/Circulation; Chip Jones, Director of Production; Linda Baker, Business Mgr.; Aldo Maragoni, Special Proj. Mgr. **ISSN:** 1048-8812. **Subscription Rates:** $69.95 individuals Per year; $1 single issue. **Remarks:** Accepts advertising. **URL:** http://www.amcity.com/sanjose. **Alt. Formats:** CD-ROM.
Ad Rates: GLR: $11.50 **Circ:** Paid ★13,664
BW: $4,620
4C: $5,220

3579 San Jose Mercury News
Knight-Ridder, Inc.
750 Ridder Park Dr. Phone: (408)920-5000
San Jose, CA 95190-0001 Fax: (408)288-8060

General newspaper. **Founded:** 1851. **Freq:** Mon.-Sun. (morn.). **Print Method:** Offset. **Trim Size:** 13 3/4 x 23. **Cols./Page:** 6. **Col. Width:** 25 nonpareils. **Col. Depth:** 298 agate lines. **Key Personnel:** Robert Ingle, Editor; Larry Jinks, Publisher. **Subscription Rates:** $28 Per month. **Remarks:** Accepts advertising. **Online:** America Online, Inc.; CompuServe Information Service; Dialog (The Dialog Corporation). **Alt. Formats:** CD-ROM. **Feature Editors:** Michael Antonucci, *TV & Radio*, phone (408)920-5690; Michalene Busico, *Family*, phone (408)920-5637; Robin Doussard, *Features*, phone (408)920-5642; David Early, *Lifestyle*, phone (408)920-5836; Rob Elder, *Editorials*, phone (408)920-5532; Mary Gottschalk, *Fashion*, phone (408)920-5607; Judith Green, *Drama*, phone (408)920-5914; Sam Gugino, *Food*, phone (408)920-5539; Holly Hayes, *Entertainment*, phone (408)920-5374; Paul Hertelendy, *Music*, phone (408)920-5656; Peter Hillan, *Financial/Business*, phone (408)920-5957; Joan Jackson, *Garden/Home*, phone (408)920-5518; Glenn Lovell, *Movie*, phone (408)920-5639; Geri Migielicz, *Photo*, phone (408)920-5090; Ron Miller, *TV & Radio*, phone (408)920-5000; Dick Nagel, *Sports*, phone (408)920-5863; Richard Scheinin, *Religion*, phone (408)920-5974; Mark Schwanhausser, *Real Estate*, phone (408)920-5078; Harry Sumrall, *Music*, phone (408)920-5046; Aleta Watson, *Education*, phone (408)920-5032; Zeke Wigglesworth, *Travel*, phone (408)920-5441.
Ad Rates: BW: $12,360 **Circ:** Mon.-Fri. ★290,885
PCI: $96.94 Sun. ★339,708
Sat. ★287,604

3580 San Jose Post-Record
Daily Journal Corp.
90 N. 1st St., Ste. 100 Phone: (408)287-4866
San Jose, CA 95113 Fax: (408)287-2544
Publication E-mail: sjpr@pacbell.net

Legal and business newspaper. **Subtitle:** A Publication of the Daily Journal Corporation. **Founded:** 1910. **Freq:** Tuesdays, Wednesdays, Fridays. **Print Method:** Offset. **Cols./Page:** 4. **Col. Width:** 2 1/2 inches. **Col. Depth:** 13 1/2 inches. **Key Personnel:** Joe Franklin, Editor; Fay Kenney, Publisher. **ISSN:** 0036-4185. **Subscription Rates:** $121 individuals. **Remarks:** Accepts advertising.
Ad Rates: BW: $330.48 **Circ:** 1,200
PCI: $6.12

3581 Senior Times
S.T. Publications
42 E. Santa Clara, Ste. 213 Phone: (408)288-5771
San Jose, CA 95113 Fax: (408)288-5794

Senior citizen newspaper. **Founded:** 1982. **Freq:** Monthly. **Print Method:** Web press. **Trim Size:** 10 x 16. **Cols./Page:** 5. **Col. Width:** 2 inches. **Col. Depth:** 16 inches. **Key Personnel:** Terry Wilbert, Editor. **Subscription Rates:** $15 individuals. **Remarks:** Accepts advertising.
Ad Rates: BW: $1,120 **Circ:** Paid 400
4C: $1,680 Controlled 34,400
PCI: $30

3582 Spartan Daily
San Jose State University
1 Washington Sq. Phone: (408)924-3280
San Jose, CA 95192-0149 Fax: (408)924-3282

Collegiate newspaper. **Founded:** 1934. **Freq:** Daily (morn.). **Print Method:** Offset. **Trim Size:** 14 x 22 3/4. **Cols./Page:** 6. **Col. Width:** 2 1/16 inches. **Col. Depth:** 20 3/4 inches. **Key Personnel:** Julia Wright, Editor; Doug Evans, Advertising Mgr. **Subscription Rates:** Free; $25 by mail. **Remarks:** Advertising not accepted for tobacco products.
Ad Rates: BW: $7,400 **Circ:** Paid 100
4C: $1,583 Free 5,900
SAU: $15.05
CNU: $9.26
PCI: $8.42

3583 Vietnam Daily Newspaper
Victorian Daily Newspaper
2350 S. 10th St. Phone: (408)292-3422
San Jose, CA 95112 Fax: (408)293-5153
Publication E-mail: dnn.batt.vietnamdaily.com

Community newspaper serving greater San Francisco area (Vietnamese). **Founded:** 1986. **Freq:** Daily. **Print Method:** Offset. **Trim Size:** 15 x 22. **Cols./Page:** 6. **Key Personnel:** Giang Nguyen, Publisher. **Remarks:** Accepts advertising.
Ad Rates: BW: $370 **Circ:** 10,000
PCI: $100

3584 KARA-FM - 105.7
750 Story Rd. Phone: (408)293-8030
PO Box 995 Fax: (408)293-6124
San Jose, CA 95108-0995

Format: Adult Contemporary. **Networks:** Independent. **Founded:** 1964. **Operating Hours:** Continuous. **ADI:** San Francisco-Oakland-San Jose. **Key Personnel:** Bob Kieve, General Mgr.; John McLeod, Program Dir. **Wattage:** 50,000.

3585 KAZA-AM - 1290
PO Box 1290 Phone: (408)984-1290
San Jose, CA 95108 Fax: (408)985-9322

Format: Hispanic. **Networks:** Lotus. **Founded:** 1967. **Operating Hours:** Sunrise-sunset. 6 a.m.-12 a.m. **ADI:** San Francisco-Oakland-San Jose. **Key Personnel:** Veronica Yanez, General Sales Mgr., radiokaza@aol.com; Manuel Reyes, Program Dir.; Deborah Romero, Promotions Mgr.; Filiberto Arteaga, Engineer. **Wattage:** 5000. **Ad Rates:** $64-80 for 30 seconds; $70-100 for 60 seconds.

3586 KBAY-FM - 94.5
PO Box 6616 Phone: (408)370-7377
San Jose, CA 95150 Fax: (408)364-4545

Format: Adult Contemporary; Soft Rock. **Networks:** Independent. **Owner:** United Broadcasting, at above address. **Founded:** 1963. **Formerly:** KEEN-FM (1965). **Operating Hours:** Continuous; 100% local. **ADI:** San Francisco-Oakland-San Jose. **Key Personnel:** David Burke, Contact; Bob Kohtz, Program Dir.; Frank Angelino, General Sales Mgr. **Wattage:** 1250. **Ad Rates:** $75-240 for 60 seconds. **URL:** http://www.kbay.com.

3587 KBRG-FM - 104.9
2905 S. King Rd. Phone: (408)274-1170
San Jose, CA 95122 Fax: (408)274-1818

Format: Hispanic. **Networks:** Independent. **Owner:** EXCL Communications, Inc., at above address. **Founded:** 1961. **Operating Hours:** Continuous; 100% local. **ADI:** San Francisco-Oakland-San Jose. **Key Personnel:** Athena Marks, General Mgr.; Jeffrey Liberman, Contact; Guillermo Prince, Contact. **Wattage:** 3000. **Ad Rates:** Advertising accepted; rates available upon request.

3588 KEZR-FM - 106.5
Box 2337 Phone: (408)287-5775
San Jose, CA 95109 Fax: (408)293-3341
Free: (800)499-1065

Format: Adult Contemporary. **Networks:** Independent. **Founded:** 1967. **Operating Hours:** Continuous. **ADI:** San Francisco-Oakland-San Jose. **Key Personnel:** John Levitt, General Mgr.; Jim Murphy, Program Dir. **Wattage:** 50,000.

3589 KFFG-FM - 97.7
50 Airport Parkway Phone: (408)817-KFOG
San Jose, CA 95134 Fax: (408)437-4926

Format: Contemporary Hit Radio (CHR). **Owner:** Susquehanna Radio Corp., P.O. Box 1432, York, PA 17405, (717)852-2132, Fax: (717)771-1436, Free: (800)876-1436. **Founded:** 1987. **Formerly:** KLZE-FM. **Operating Hours:** Continuous; 100% local. **ADI:** San Francisco-Oakland-San Jose. **Key Personnel:** Tony Salvadore, Vice President; Dwight Walker, Station Mgr.; Julie Kahn, Sales Mgr.; Joe Cunningham, Sales Mgr. **Wattage:** 1650.

3590 KICU-TV - 36
2102 Commerce Dr. Phone: (408)953-3636
San Jose, CA 95131 Fax: (408)953-3630
E-mail: sales@kicu.com

Format: Commercial TV. **Networks:** Independent. **Owner:** KICU, Inc., at above address. **Founded:** 1967. **Formerly:** KGSC-TV. **Operating Hours:** Continuous. **ADI:** San Francisco-Oakland-San Jose. **Key Personnel:** James H. Evers, President/GM, fax (408)953-3610, jevers@kicu.com; Melissa Tench-Stevens, Program Dir., mts@kicu.com; William S. Beeman, VP/Operations, berman@kicu.com; John W. DuBois, Exec. VP/General Sales Mgr., j.dubois@kicu.com; Valerie Williamson, Traffic Mgr., vtench@kicu.com; Scott McIver, Sales Mgr., s.mciver@kicu.com. **Local Programs:** *High School Sports Focus* 11:00 pm Friday; *Sports, San Jose Sharks, Golden State Warriors, Oakland A's, Sabercats (Indoor Football), Lasers (Soccar)*; *Silicon Valley Business This Week* 6:00 pm Sunday. **Wattage:** 4070kw GRP.

3591 KLEL-FM - 89.3
6677 Camden Ave. Phone: (408)268-6343
San Jose, CA 95120

Format: Album-Oriented Rock (AOR). **Networks:** Satellite Music Network. **Owner:** San Jose Unified School District, at above address. **Founded:** 1977. **ADI:** San Francisco-Oakland-San Jose. **Key Personnel:** Joe LoBue, General Mgr. **Wattage:** 100.

3592 KLIV-AM - 1590
PO Box 995 Phone: (408)293-8030
San Jose, CA 95108 Fax: (408)293-6124

Format: News. **Networks:** CNN Radio. **Owner:** Empire Broadcasting Corp., at above address. **Founded:** 1947. **Operating Hours:** Continuous; 100% local. **ADI:** San Francisco-Oakland-San Jose. **Key Personnel:** Robert Kieve, General Mgr.; Jane McMillan, Program/News Dir. **Wattage:** 5000.

3593 KLOK-AM - 1170
2905 S. King Rd. Phone: (408)274-1170
San Jose, CA 95122 Fax: (408)274-1818

Format: Hispanic. **Owner:** EXCL Communications, Inc., at above address. **Founded:** 1946. **Operating Hours:** Continuous. **ADI:** San Francisco-Oakland-San Jose. **Key Personnel:** Athena Marks, General Mgr.; Jeffrey Liberman, Station Mgr.; Mary McHernandez, General Sales Mgr.; Paul Millard, Controller; Martha Garza, Local Sales Mgr.; Guillermo Prince, Program and Music Dir.; Erwin Higueras, Production Dir. **Wattage:** 50,000 day; 5000 night. **Ad Rates:** Advertising accepted; rates available upon request.

3594 KNTV-TV - 11
645 Park Ave. Phone: (408)286-1111
San Jose, CA 95110 Fax: (408)295-5461

Format: Commercial TV. **Networks:** ABC. **Founded:** 1955. **Operating Hours:** Continuous. **ADI:** Salinas-Monterey, CA. **Key Personnel:** Stewart Park, Pres./Gen. Mgr.; Lisa Owen, Program Coord.; Terry McElhatton, News Dir., phone (408)297-8780, fax (408)286-1530; Christine Jenkins, General Sales Mgr., fax (408)286-0155. **Local Programs:** *Comunidad del Valle*; *Datebook*; *Good Morning San Jose*; *Midday San Jose*. **URL:** http://www.kntv.com.

3595 KOME-FM - 98.5
3031 Tisch Way, Ste. 3 Phone: (408)985-9800
Plaza West Fax: (408)296-8962
San Jose, CA 95128
E-mail: mantamarla@kome.com

Format: Alternative/New Music/Progressive. **Networks:** Independent. **Owner:** CBS Radio, 40 W. 57th St., 14th Fl., New York, NY 10019, (212)314-9200. **Founded:** 1968. **Formerly:** KRPM-FM (1971). **Operating Hours:** Continuous; 100% local. **ADI:** San Francisco-Oakland-San Jose. **Key Personnel:** James L. Hardy, General Mgr., fax ( )9858675, jhardy@kome.com; Ron Nenni, Operations Mgr., rnenni@kome.com; Jay Taylor, Program Dir., jtaylor@kome.com; Robin Rockwell, Promotions Dir., rockwell@kome.com; Marla Davies, Public Affairs Director, mdavies@kome.com; Nick Marnell, Station Mgr., fax ( )985-8675, nmarnell@kome.com. **Local Programs:** *Expressway Show*, Marla Davies; *Nocturnal Noise*. **Wattage:** 12,500 ERP. **URL:** www.kome.com.

3596 KRTY-FM - 95.3
750 Story Rd. Phone: (408)293-8030
San Jose, CA 95122-9510 Fax: (408)293-6124

Format: Country. **Networks:** Independent. **Founded:** 1966.

Formerly: KRVE-FM; KATD-FM. **Operating Hours:** Continuous; 100% local. **ADI:** San Francisco-Oakland-San Jose. **Key Personnel:** Bob Kieve, General Mgr.; Bill Macky, Program Dir.; Janice Festa, Sales Mgr.; Julie Stevens, Operations Mgr. **Wattage:** 850. **Ad Rates:** $120-150 per unit.

3597 KRZY-FM - 105.9
2905 S. King Rd. Phone: (408)837-1059
San Jose, CA 95122 Fax: (408)830-1190
E-mail: krzy1059@aol.com

Format: Hispanic. **Owner:** Excel Communication, at above address. **Operating Hours:** Continuous. **Key Personnel:** Karen Martinez, General Mgr.; Nancy Gaines, Business Mgr.; Gabriel Zavala, Promotions Dir. **Wattage:** 100,000. **Ad Rates:** Advertising accepted; rates available upon request.

3598 KSJS-FM - 90.5
HGH 130 Phone: (408)924-4548
San Jose, CA 95192-0094 Fax: (408)924-4583
E-mail: ksjs@ksjs.org

Format: Hip Hop; Eclectic; Alternative/New Music/Progressive. **Owner:** State of California, at above address. **Founded:** 1963. **Formerly**: KSJS-FM. **Operating Hours:** Continuous. **ADI:** San Francisco-Oakland-San Jose. **Key Personnel:** Sharon Jennings, General Mgr., phone (408)924-4549; Cathy Leyba, Asst. Promotions Dir., phone (408)924-4578; Michelle Guerrero, Asst. Production Dir., phone (408)924-4548; Kevin Ariente, Jazz Music Dir., phone (408)924-4547, fax (408)924-4558; Chris Minor, African American Music Dir., phone (408)924-4547, fax (408)924-4558; Mario Ovalles, Chicano Music Dir., phone (408)924-4547, fax (408)924-4558; Kara Moore, Marketing Dir., phone (408)924-7099; Robert Portnoy, Sports Dir. **Wattage:** 235. **Ad Rates:** $15-40 for 30 seconds. **URL:** http://www.ksjs.org.

3599 KSJX-AM - 1500
1420 Koll Circle Phone: (408)453-5400
San Jose, CA 95112 Fax: (408)452-1330
Free: (800)350-5756

Format: Ethnic. **Owner:** Baycom Partners, 50 Francisco St., Ste. 257, San Francisco, CA 94107, (415)421-0680, Fax: (415)421-0683. **Founded:** 1948. **Formerly**: KHTT-AM (1989). **Operating Hours:** Continuous. **ADI:** San Francisco-Oakland-San Jose. **Key Personnel:** John Sutherland, General Mgr.; Dana Jang, Program Mgr.; Paul Tonelli, News Dir.; Marybeth Powell, Traffic Mgr. **Wattage:** 10,000 day; 5000 night. **Ad Rates:** Advertising accepted; rates available upon request.

3600 KSTS-TV - 48
2349 Bering Dr. Phone: (408)435-8848
San Jose, CA 95131 Fax: (408)433-5921

Format: Commercial TV; Hispanic. **Networks:** Telemundo. **Operating Hours:** Continuous. **ADI:** San Francisco-Oakland-San Jose. **Key Personnel:** Paul Niedermeyer, General Mgr.; Lulu Ortiz, Program Dir.

3601 KTEH-TV - 54
1585 Schallenberger Rd. Phone: (408)795-5400
San Jose, CA 95131 Fax: (408)995-5446

Format: Public TV. **Networks:** Public Broadcasting Service (PBS). **Owner:** KIEH Foundation, at above address. **Founded:** 1964. **Operating Hours:** 6 a.m.-1 a.m. **ADI:** San Francisco-Oakland-San Jose. **Key Personnel:** Tom Fanella, Pres./CEO; Dann Parks, VP of Multi-Media; Danny McGuire, Executive Producer; Karen Roberts, Program Dir.; Michelle I. Muller, Dir. of Engineering. **Local Programs:** *Kid's Clubhouse*; *Malone*; *Pet Pourri*; *Real Science*. **Wattage:** 661 KW ERP. **Ad Rates:** Noncommercial. **URL:** http://www.kteh.org.

3602 KUFX-FM - 104.9
1420 Koll Cir. No. A Phone: (408)452-7900
San Jose, CA 95112-4601 Fax: (408)297-0359

Format: Classic Rock. **Networks:** Independent. **Founded:** 1970. **Formerly**: KWSS-FM (1991). **Operating Hours:** Continuous. **ADI:** San Francisco-Oakland-San Jose. **Key Personnel:** John Sutherland, General Mgr.; Dana Jang, Program Dir. **Wattage:** 50,000. **URL:** http://www.kufx.com.

SAN JUAN CAPISTRANO

3603 Capistrano Valley News
South Orange County News
PO Box 3629 Phone: (714)768-3631
Mission Viejo, CA 92690 Fax: (714)454-7354

Community newspaper. **Founded:** 1972. **Freq:** Weekly (Thurs.). **Print Method:** Offset. **Cols./Page:** 5. **Col. Width:** 12 1/16 inches. **Col. Depth:** 182 agate lines. **Key Personnel:** Sherrie Good, Editor; Mike Weaver, Publisher; Pat Norton, Advertising Mgr. **Subscription Rates:** $11 individuals. **Remarks:** Accepts advertising.
Ad Rates: PCI: $32.17 **Circ:** Controlled 5,493
Paid 3,283

3604 Grayson Report
Grayson Associates, Inc.
30481 Via Andalusia Phone: (949)487-9970
San Juan Capistrano, CA 92675 Fax: (949)487-9975

Academic journal written for consumer marketing practitioners. **Founded:** 1971. **Freq:** Bimonthly. **Print Method:** Offset. **Trim Size:** 8 1/2 x 11. **Cols./Page:** 2. **Col. Width:** 3.5 picas. **Col. Depth:** 10 inches. **Key Personnel:** Susan Grayson, Editor, grayson@durano.com; Robert A. Grayson, Publisher. **ISSN:** 0736-3761. **Subscription Rates:** $45 U.S. and Canada; $50 other countries. **Formerly**: Journal of Consumer Marketing (1992).

3605 Cox Communications
26181 Avenida Aeropuerto Phone: (714)240-8828
San Juan Capistrano, CA 92675 Fax: (714)661-7297
E-mail: cable.modem.oc@cox.com

Owner: Cox Communications, 1400 Lake Hearn Dr., Atlanta, GA 30319, (404)843-5000. **Founded:** 1968. **Formerly**: Dimension Cable. **Key Personnel:** Leo Brennan, VP & GM; Len White, Dir. Tech Opr.; Joe Rooney, Dir. Sales & Mktg. **Cities Served:** Dana Point, Irvine, Laguna Beach, Laguna Hills, Laguna Nigel, Lake Forest, Mission Viejo, Newport Beach, Orange, San Clemente, Tustin, CA; San Juan Capistrano, and County of Orange: subscribing households 227,000; 200 channels; 1 community access channel; 25 hours per week community access programming. **URL:** http://cox.com.

3606 KMRJ-FM - 99.5
25601 Paseo De La Paz Phone: (760)778-6995
San Juan Capistrano, CA 92675 Fax: (760)778-1249

Format: Alternative/New Music/Progressive. **Owner:** Mitchell Media, Inc., at above address. **Operating Hours:** Continuous. **Key Personnel:** Daniel P. Mitchell, President; Maurene Mitchell, Vice President; Thomas Mitchell, Program Dir.; Mark Moceri, Chief Engineer. **Wattage:** 3,000. **Ad Rates:** $6-35 for 30 seconds; $10-40 for 60 seconds.

SAN LEANDRO, pop. 63,952.

Alameda Co. (W) Adjoins Oakland. Residential. Manufactures tractors, calculating machines, alloy pistons, motor parts, lumber. Nurseries. Rock quarry.

Alameda County Observer - See Alameda

Hayward & Castro Valley Observer - See Hayward

3607 India West
India West Publications
933 Mac Arthur Blvd. Phone: (510)383-1140
San Leandro, CA 94577 Fax: (510)383-1155
Publication E-mail: indiawest@attmail.com

National newspaper specializing in news from India and about the Indian community in the U.S. **Founded:** 1975. **Freq:** Weekly (Fri.). **Print Method:** Offset. **Trim Size:** 11 x 17. **Cols./Page:** 5. **Col. Width:** 24 nonpareils. **Col. Depth:** 210 agate lines. **Key Personnel:** Bina Murarka, Editor, phone (510)383-1141; Ramesh Murarka, Publisher, phone (510)383-1151, fax (510)383-1154. **ISSN:** 0883-721X. **Subscription Rates:** $30 individuals. **Remarks:** Accepts advertising.
Ad Rates: BW: $1,200 **Circ:** 23,000
4C: $1,700
PCI: $12

Oakland Bay Area Observer - See Oakland

Piedmont & Berkeley Observer - See Piedmont

Sacramento Observer - See Sacramento

3608 San Leandro Observer
Observer Newspapers
Box 817
San Leandro, CA 94577

Community newspaper. **Founded:** May 22, 1972. **Freq:** Weekly (Fri.). **Print Method:** Offset. **Cols./Page:** 6. **Col. Width:** 10 picas. **Col. Depth:** 16 Inches. **Key Personnel:** Ad Fried, Managing Editor; Michael Robert, Publisher; R.A. Burrell, Advertising Mgr. **Subscription Rates:** $25 individuals. **Remarks:** Advertising not accepted for tobacco products. **Formerly**: San Leandro and South County Observer.
Ad Rates: BW: $3,000 **Circ:** ‡30,000
4C: $3,600
SAU: $40
PCI: $35

3609 KFTL-TV - 64
403 McCormick St. Phone: (510)632-5385
San Leandro, CA 94577 Fax: (510)632-8943
E-mail: kftl64@compuserve.com

Format: Religious; Commercial TV. **Networks:** Family Stations Radio. **Owner:** Family Stations Inc., at above address. **Founded:** 1988. **Operating Hours:** Continuous, except Sat. – 18 hrs. **ADI:** Sacramento-Stockton, CA. **Key Personnel:** Matt Tuter, Station Mgr.; John Tefertiller, Operations Mgr.; Lucy Nazareno, Traffic Dir.; Danny Angotti, Production Mgr. **Wattage:** 1,950,000.

SAN LUIS OBISPO†, pop. 34,252.

San Luis Obispo Co. (SW). 80 m NW of Santa Barbara. California Polytechnic State University. San Luis Obispo. Oil wells. Chromite deposits. Creameries, condensery, bottling, fertilizer works, electronics, motorcycle accessories, hot tub. Wineries. Ships produce. Dairy. Stock, fruit farms. Peas, lettuce, cauliflower. Almonds.

3610 Command Magazine
XTR Corp.
3547-D S. Higuera Phone: (805)546-9596
San Luis Obispo, CA 93401 Fax: (805)546-0570
Free: (800)488-2249
Publisher E-mail: perello@aol.com

Magazine profiling military strategies, analysis, and concepts. **Subtitle:** Military History, Strategy & Analysis. **Founded:** 1989. **Freq:** Bimonthly. **Print Method:** Web. **Trim Size:** 8 1/2 x 11. **Cols./Page:** 2. **Col. Width:** 20 picas. **Col. Depth:** 9 inches. **Key Personnel:** Ty Bomba, Editor, tyrone998@aol.comor; Chris Perello, Business/Advertising, perello@aol.com. **ISSN:** 1059-5651. **Subscription Rates:** $24.95 for one year; $12.95 for six months; $44.95 for two years. **Remarks:** Accepts advertising. **URL:** http://www.umahexagon.com; http://home.earthlink.net/~tonyzal.
Ad Rates: BW: $600 **Circ:** ‡24,000
4C: $720 Non-paid ‡100

3611 Design Methods
Design Methods Institute
Box 3
San Luis Obispo, CA 93406

Trade journal covering architecture and industrial design. **Founded:** 1966. **Freq:** Quarterly. **Trim Size:** 7 x 8 1/2. **Cols./Page:** 1. **Col. Width:** 5 inches. **Col. Depth:** 6 inches. **Key Personnel:** Donald P. Grant, Editor. **Subscription Rates:** $40 individuals; $10 single issue. **Remarks:** Advertising not accepted.
Circ: (Not Reported)

3612 Mustang Daily
California State Polytechnic University
San Luis Obispo, CA 93407 Phone: (805)756-1111
Fax: (805)756-1143

Collegiate newspaper. **Founded:** 1938. **Freq:** Daily. **Print Method:** Offset. **Cols./Page:** 5. **Col. Width:** 25 nonpareils. **Col. Depth:** 224 agate lines. **Key Personnel:** Published by students of California State Polytech University. **Subscription Rates:** $30 individuals. **Remarks:** Accepts advertising.
Ad Rates: BW: $604 **Circ:** Free 7,000
4C: $1,032

3613 New Times
197 Santa Rosa St. Phone: (805)546-8208
San Luis Obispo, CA 93405 Fax: (805)546-3641
Free: (800)215-0300
Publication E-mail: newtimes-slo@stooet.org
Publisher E-mail: mail@newtimes-slo.com

Newspaper. **Subtitle:** News Weekly. **Founded:** Aug. 1986. **Freq:** Weekly. **Trim Size:** 13 5/8 x 11. **Cols./Page:** 4. **Col. Width:** 2 3/8 inches. **Col. Depth:** 12 3/4 inches. **Key Personnel:** Steve Moss, Editor and Publisher; Bev Johnson, Advertising Director/Publisher. **Subscription Rates:** $37 individuals. **Remarks:** Accepts advertising. **URL:** http://www.newtimes-slo.com.
Circ: Free 39,395
Paid 44

3614 The San Luis Obispo County Telegram Tribune
Knight-Ridder, Inc.
3825 S. Higuera St. Phone: (805)781-7902
PO Box 112 Fax: (805)781-7905
San Luis Obispo, CA 93406-0112
Free: (800)456-8449
Publication E-mail: slott@scripps.com

General newspaper. **Founded:** Aug. 7, 1869. **Freq:** Daily and Sat. (morn.). **Print Method:** Offset. **Trim Size:** 12 1/2 x 22 3/4. **Cols./Page:** 6. **Col. Width:** 11 picas. **Col. Depth:** 301 agate

lines. **Key Personnel:** Jeff Brinley, Circulation Mgr., phone (805)781-7895, jbrinley@telegram-tribune.com; Butch Hughes, Advertising Dir., phone (805)781-7825, fax (805)781-7871, bhughes@telegram-tribune.com; Julia Aguilar, Publisher; Ron Godfrey, Production Dir. **Subscription Rates:** $144 individuals; $0.50 single issue; $1.00 Saturday. **Remarks:** Accepts advertising. **URL:** http://www.sanluisobispo.co.
Ad Rates: GLR: $1.80 BW: $2,472.61 4C: $2,772.61 PCI: $19.17 **Circ:** Mon.-Fri. ★34,659 Sat. ★41,566

3615 Senior Magazine
3565 S. Higuera St. Phone: (805)544-8711
San Luis Obispo, CA 93401 Fax: (805)544-4450

Magazine featuring topics of interest for seniors 4 color magazine. **Subtitle:** Central Coast Edition. **Founded:** June 1981. **Freq:** Monthly. **Print Method:** Offset. **Trim Size:** 13 x 10. **Cols./Page:** 3. **Col. Width:** 36 nonpareils. **Col. Depth:** 188 agate lines. **Key Personnel:** George Brand, Editor; Gary Suggs, Publisher. **Subscription Rates:** Free. **Remarks:** Accepts advertising.
Ad Rates: BW: $1,474 4C: $1,924 **Circ:** Controlled ‡50,000

3616 KCBX-FM - 90.1
4100 Vachell Ln. Phone: (805)781-3020
San Luis Obispo, CA 93401
E-mail: kcbx@kcbx.org

Format: Classical; Jazz; News; Information. **Networks:** National Public Radio (NPR). **Founded:** 1974. **Operating Hours:** 5:30 a.m.-1 a.m. **ADI:** Santa Barbara-Santa Maria-San Luis Obispo,CA. **Key Personnel:** Frank Lanzone, General Mgr. **Wattage:** 5600. **Ad Rates:** Noncommercial.

3617 KCPR-FM - 91.3
California Polytechnic State University Phone: (805)756-5277
San Luis Obispo, CA 93407 Fax: (805)756-2965
E-mail: kcpr@hertz.elec.cal.poly.edu

Format: Alternative/New Music/Progressive. **Networks:** BBC World Service. **Founded:** 1968. **Operating Hours:** Continuous; 5% network, 95% local. **ADI:** Santa Barbara-Santa Maria-San Luis Obispo,CA. **Key Personnel:** Phil Campbell, General Mgr.; Pedro Arroyo, Program Dir.; Jason Joyce, Music Dir.; Carver Cordes, Music Dir.; Katie Marzulo, News Dir.; Milos Nemeik, Chief Engineer, phone (805)756-5998; Rob Gaitan, Production Dir.; Allen Ng, Traffic Dir.; Melissa Underwood, Publicity Dir.; Nate Pontieus, Publicity Dir.; Trevor Gerhard, Marketing Dir.; Marcia Dallazen, Promotions Dir.; Cameron Jung, Promotions Dir. **Wattage:** 2000. **Ad Rates:** Noncommercial.

3618 KKJL-AM - 1400
PO Box 1400 Phone: (805)543-9400
San Luis Obispo, CA 93406 Fax: (805)543-0787

Format: Adult Contemporary. **Networks:** Westwood One Radio. **Owner:** Guy P. Hackman, at above address. **Founded:** 1962. **Formerly:** KKCB-AM (1992); KIXT-AM. **Operating Hours:** Continuous; 60% network, 40% local. **ADI:** Santa Barbara-Santa Maria-San Luis Obispo,CA. **Key Personnel:** Kyle Ronemus, Sales Mgr.; Fred Peterson, News Dir. **Wattage:** 1000. **Ad Rates:** $18 per unit.

3619 KLFF-FM - 89.3
PO Box 1561 Phone: (805)541-4343
San Luis Obispo, CA 93406 Fax: (805)541-9101
E-mail: klife@callamer.com

Format: Contemporary Christian. **Owner:** Logos Broadcasting Corp., at above address. **Operating Hours:** Continuous. **ADI:** Santa Barbara-Santa Maria-San Luis Obispo,CA. **Key Personnel:** Jon Fugcen, Pres./General Manager; Noonie Fugcen, Music Dir. **Wattage:** 4,400. **Ad Rates:** Noncommercial; underwriting available. **URL:** http://www.klife.org.

3620 KSBY-TV - 6
1772 Calle Joaquin Phone: (805)541-6666
San Luis Obispo, CA 93405 Fax: (805)541-5142
E-mail: ksby@ksby.com

Format: Commercial TV. **Networks:** NBC. **Owner:** SJL of California, L.P., at above address. **Founded:** 1953. **Operating Hours:** Continuous; 85% network, 15% local. **ADI:** Santa Barbara-Santa Maria-San Luis Obispo,CA. **Key Personnel:** Richard Armfield, Vice President; Dave Colby, News Dir.; Ty Ray, Sports Dir.; Shelley Appleby, Traffic Mgr.; Carl Edge, Program Dir.; Walt Ward, Technical Operations Director. **Wattage:** 100kw ERP. **Ad Rates:** $40-5,000 per unit. **URL:** http://www.ksby.com/ksby.

3621 KSLY-FM - 96.1
51 Zaca Ln., Ste.110 Phone: (805)545-0101
San Luis Obispo, CA 93401 Fax: (805)541-5303

Format: Top 40. **Owner:** Digisphere Broadcasting, at above address. **Founded:** 1962. **Operating Hours:** Continuous. **ADI:** Santa Barbara-Santa Maria-San Luis Obispo,CA. **Key Personnel:** Kathleen Marshall, Business Mgr.; Nancy Allison, Sales Mgr.; Greg Russo, Promotions Dir.; Dave Christopher, Operations Mgr., dc@ksly.com; Don Shore, General Mgr. **Wattage:** 5800. **Ad Rates:** $20-36 per unit. **URL:** http;//ksly.com.

3622 KVEC-AM - 920
1329 Chorro St. Phone: (805)543-8830
San Luis Obispo, CA 93401-4005 Fax: (805)781-2568
Free: (800)549-KVEC

Format: News; Sports; Talk. **Networks:** ABC; CNN Radio. **Owner:** Chorro Communications Inc., at above address. **Founded:** 1937. **Operating Hours:** Continuous; 40% network, 60% local. **ADI:** Santa Barbara-Santa Maria-San Luis Obispo,CA. **Key Personnel:** Frank Sheahan, President; Dan Clarkson, General Mgr.; Suzan Vaughan, News Dir. **Wattage:** 1000 day; 500 night. **Ad Rates:** $12-16 for 30 seconds; $12-20 for 60 seconds.

3623 KZOZ-FM - 93.3
4115 Broad St., Ste. B-4 Phone: (805)781-2750
San Luis Obispo, CA 93401 Fax: (805)781-2758
E-mail: tom@agmslo.com

Format: Classic Rock. **Owner:** American General Media, at above address. **Founded:** 1981. **Operating Hours:** Continuous; 100% local. **ADI:** Santa Barbara-Santa Maria-San Luis Obispo,CA. **Key Personnel:** Kathy Signorelli, General Mgr.; Mark Wilson, Program Dir.; Tom Keffury, Dir. of Operations. **Wattage:** 29,500. **Ad Rates:** $26-32 for 30 seconds.

3624 Sonic Cable TV of San Luis Obispo
PO Box 1205 Phone: (805)544-1962
San Luis Obispo, CA 93406 Fax: (805)541-6042

Owner: Sonic Communications, 235 Montgomery St., Ste. 400, San Francisco, CA 94104, (415)616-4600. **Founded:** 1977. **Key Personnel:** Jeffrey A. Smith, General Mgr. **Cities Served:** Arroyo Grande, Avila Beach, Cayucos, Grover Beach, Heritage Ranch, Morro Bay, Nipomo, Paso Robles, Pismo Beach, San Luis Obispo, San Miguel, CA: subscribing households 47,000; 60 channels; 1 community access channel.

3625 U.S. Cable TV of Jekyll Island
PO Box 4017 Phone: (805)546-9596
San Luis Obispo, CA 93407 Fax: (805)546-0570
Free: (800)488-2249

Owner: U.S. Cable, 28 W. Grand Ave., Montvale, NJ 07645, (201)930-9000. **Key Personnel:** Randall Houser, Contact; Roger Knotts, Contact; Lynda Buckingham, Office Mgr. **Cities Served:** subscribing households 650; 29 channels; 1 community access channel.

SAN MARCOS, pop. 17,479.

San Diego Co. (S) 85 m S of Los Angeles. Palomar Community College. Residential.

3626 Fast Times
810 Los Vallecitos Blvd., Ste.210 Phone: (760)591-9433
San Marcos, CA 92069-1449 Fax: (760)591-9105
Magazine for high school students to be used as part of classroom assignments in social studies. **Founded:** 1984. **Freq:** 8/year. **Print Method:** Web offset. **Trim Size:** 10 x 12. **Key Personnel:** Steven Posner, Editor; Jeff Lederman, Publisher; Elisabeth Cline, Advertising Mgr. **Subscription Rates:** Free. **Remarks:** Accepts advertising.
Ad Rates: BW: $17,000 4C: $23,000 **Circ:** Controlled ‡600,000

3627 San Marcos News Reporter
The News Reporter
815 W. Grand Ave., Ste. 103 Phone: (619)471-8701
San Marcos, CA 92069 Fax: (619)471-2630

Community newspaper serving San Marcos, Lake San Marcos, Twin Oaks Valley, Vista, Escondido, Mountain Meadows, and Bonsall. **Subtitle:** North San Diego County's Weekly Newspaper. **Founded:** 1971. **Freq:** Weekly (Thurs.). **Print Method:** Offset. **Trim Size:** 11 x 17. **Cols./Page:** 5. **Col. Width:** 1 7/8. inches. **Key Personnel:** W.F. Willoughby, Editor and Publisher. **Subscription Rates:** $52 individuals; $1 single issue. **Remarks:** Accepts advertising. **Formerly:** The Outlook.
Ad Rates: BW: $11 4C: $511 PCI: $6.75 **Circ:** 9,750

3628 Cox Communications
2790 Business Park Dr. Phone: (619)598-6666
Vista, CA 92083 Fax: (619)598-5601

Founded: 1972. **Formerly:** Cox Communications. **Cities Served:** San Diego County, Bonsall, Cardiff-by-the-Sea, Encinitas, Escondido, Leucadia, Oceanside, Ramona, Rancho Santa Fe, San Dieguito, Solana Beach, Vista, and Whispering Palms, CA.

SAN MARINO, pop. 13,307.

Los Angeles Co. (S). 5 m S of Pasadena. Residential.

3629 Huntington Library Quarterly
Huntington Library Press
1151 Oxford Rd. Phone: (626)405-2172
San Marino, CA 91108 Fax: (626)585-0794
Publisher E-mail: booksales@huntington.org

Scholarly journal featuring articles on the literature, history, and art of England and America, emphasizing the 16th through the 18th centuries. **Subtitle:** Studies on English and American History and Literature. **Founded:** May 1931. **Freq:** Quarterly. **Print Method:** Offset. **Trim Size:** 7 x 10. **Cols./Page:** 1. **Col. Width:** 5 inches. **Col. Depth:** 7.5 inches. **Key Personnel:** Susan Green, Editor, phone (626)405-2174, sgreen@huntington.org. **ISSN:** 0018-7895. **Subscription Rates:** $20 individuals; $40 institutions, other countries plus $8 for foreign plus postage. **Remarks:** Accepts advertising.
Ad Rates: BW: $200 **Circ:** Paid ‡800 Non-paid ‡150

3630 San Marino Tribune
2260 Huntington Dr. Phone: (626)282-5707
San Marino, CA 91108 Fax: (626)457-6436
Publication E-mail: smtnews@aol.com

Newspaper with a Republican orientation. **Founded:** 1928. **Freq:** Weekly (Thurs.). **Print Method:** Offset. **Cols./Page:** 6. **Col. Width:** 6 inches. **Col. Depth:** 21 1/2 inches. **Key Personnel:** Peter Day, Editor; Clifton Stanwood Smith, Jr., Publisher; Mary Smart, General Mgr., fax (626)282-3176. **Subscription Rates:** $36 individuals. **Remarks:** Accepts advertising.
Ad Rates: BW: $812.70 4C: $1,112.70 PCI: $6.30 **Circ:** Combined 3,892

SAN MATEO, pop. 77,561.

San Mateo Co. (W). On west side of San Francisco Bay, 20 m S of San Francisco. Residential. Tourism. Flower growing and shipping, printing, frozen foods, beverages, feed, precision instruments, rubber, steel products, drugs, paint, wine products, furniture, chemicals, electronics manufactured. Nurseries. Agriculture. Honey, artichokes, peas.

3631 Bass Player
Miller Freeman, Inc.
411 Borel Ave., Ste. 100 Phone: (415)358-9500
San Mateo, CA 94402 Fax: (415)358-8728
Publication E-mail: bassplayer@mfi.com
Publisher E-mail: techlearning_ editors@mfi.com

Magazine for electric and acoustic bass players. **Founded:** 1988. **Freq:** 12/year. **Print Method:** Web. **Trim Size:** 8 3/8 x 10 3/4. **Key Personnel:** Richard Johnson, Editor, rjohnston@mfi.com; Vicki Harfung, Publisher. **ISSN:** 1050-785X. **Subscription Rates:** $29.95 individuals; $4.95 single issue. **Remarks:** Accepts advertising. **Available Online. URL:** www.bassplayer.com.
Ad Rates: BW: $3,769 4C: $5,210 **Circ:** 45,000

3632 Coastside Chronicle
North County Publications
1080 S. Amphlett Blvd. Phone: (650)348-4321
PO Box 5400 Fax: (650)348-4446
San Mateo, CA 94402-1860
Newspaper. **Founded:** 1958. **Freq:** Semiweekly (Wed. and Sat.). **Print Method:** Offset. **Cols./Page:** 6. **Col. Width:** 26 nonpareils. **Col. Depth:** 301 agate lines. **Key Personnel:** Will Thomas, Editor; John H. Clinton, Jr., Publisher; Larry Boline, Advertising Mgr. **Subscription Rates:** Free. **Remarks:** Accepts advertising.
Ad Rates: BW: $1,606.05 4C: $1,906.05 SAU: $12.45 **Circ:** Paid 24 Free 7,401

Daly City Record - See Daly City

3633 Database Programming & Design
Miller Freeman, Inc.
411 Borel Ave., Ste. 100 Phone: (415)655-4292
San Mateo, CA 94402
Publication E-mail: dbpd@mfi.com

Publisher E-mail: techlearning_ editors@mfi.com

Computer magazine. **Founded:** 1987. **Freq:** Monthly. **Print Method:** Web offset. **Trim Size:** 8 x 10 7/8. **Cols./Page:** 3. **Col. Width:** 2 3/16 inches. **Col. Depth:** 9 3/4 inches. **Key Personnel:** David Stodder, Editor, dstodder@mfi.com; Donald A. Pazour, Publisher; Steve Schneideiman, Publisher; Jerry Okabe, Circulation Mgr.; Harvey Newquist, Publisher; Annalisa Chamberlain, Editor; Matt McCarthy, Editor. **ISSN:** 0895-4518. **Subscription Rates:** $47; $53 Canada; $62 other countries. $3.95 single issue. **Remarks:** Accepts advertising.
Ad Rates: BW: $3,225 **Circ:** Paid 25,427
4C: $4,215 Non-paid 1,683

3634 DBMS
Miller Freeman, Inc.—Entertainment Technology Group
411 Borel Ave., Ste. 100 Phone: (650)358-9500
San Mateo, CA 94402 Fax: (650)358-9966
Publication E-mail: dbms@mfi.com

Monthly magazine for developers and users of client-server database and internet/intranet applications. **Subtitle:** Tools and Strategies for I.S. Professionals. **Founded:** 1988. **Freq:** 13/year. **Print Method:** Web offset. **Trim Size:** 10 x 8 3/4. **Cols./Page:** 2 and 3. **Col. Width:** 3 1/2 and 3 inches. **Col. Depth:** 9 7/8 inches. **Key Personnel:** David Kalman, Publisher; Matt Stevens, Assoc. Editor, phone (650)655-4249, fax (650)358-9855; Philip Chapnick, Group Publisher. **ISSN:** 1041-5173. **Subscription Rates:** qualified controlled; $3.95 single issue. **Online:** CompuServe Information Service. **URL:** http://www.dbmsmag.com. **Formerly**: Business Software Magazine.
Ad Rates: BW: $8,839 **Circ:** Paid 17,210
4C: $10,139 Non-paid 57,123

3635 Dr. Dobb's Journal
Miller Freeman, Inc.—Entertainment Technology Group
411 Borel Ave., Ste. 100 Phone: (650)358-9500
San Mateo, CA 94402 Fax: (650)358-9966

Magazine. **Subtitle:** Software tools for the professional programmer. **Founded:** 1976. **Freq:** Monthly. **Print Method:** Offset, uses mats. **Trim Size:** 8 x 10 1/2. **Cols./Page:** 3. **Col. Width:** 27 nonpareils. **Col. Depth:** 140 agate lines. **Key Personnel:** Jonathan Erickson, Editor, phone (785)842-4818, fax (785)842-4524, jerickson@mfi.com; Peter Westerman, Publisher, phone (415)655-4231, pwesterman@mfi.com. **USPS:** 307-690. **Subscription Rates:** $34.95 individuals. **Remarks:** Accepts advertising. **Online:** CompuServe Information Service. **URL:** http://www.ddj.com. **Alt. Formats:** CD-ROM.
Ad Rates: BW: $9,200 **Circ:** 115,000
4C: $10,700

3636 Enterprise-Journal
North County Publications
1080 S. Amphlett Blvd. Phone: (650)348-4321
PO Box 5400 Fax: (650)348-4446
San Mateo, CA 94402-1860
Newspaper. **Founded:** 1895. **Freq:** Semiweekly (Wed. and Sat.). **Print Method:** Offset. **Cols./Page:** 6. **Col. Width:** 26 nonpareils. **Col. Depth:** 301 agate lines. **Key Personnel:** J. Hart Clinton, Publisher. **Subscription Rates:** $30 individuals. **Remarks:** Accepts advertising.
Ad Rates: SAU: $12.30 **Circ:** Paid 2,764
Free 13,986

3637 Guitar Player
Miller Freeman, Inc.—Entertainment Technology Group
411 Borel Ave., Ste. 100 Phone: (650)358-9500
San Mateo, CA 94402 Fax: (650)358-9966
Publication E-mail: guitplyr@mfi.com

Magazine featuring guitar-related articles. **Founded:** 1967. **Freq:** Monthly. **Print Method:** Offset. **Trim Size:** 8 1/8 x 10 3/4. **Cols./Page:** 3. **Col. Width:** 30 nonpareils. **Col. Depth:** 137 agate lines. **Key Personnel:** Michael Molenda, Editor; Cynthia Smith, Advertising Dir.; Ed Sengstack, Publisher. **ISSN:** 0017-5463. **Subscription Rates:** $29.95 individuals. **Remarks:** Accepts advertising. **URL:** http://www.guitarplayer.com/.
Ad Rates: BW: $4,555 **Circ:** Paid 130,379
4C: $6,865

3638 Infotainment World
Game Pro Media Group
951 Mariners Island Blvd., No. 700 Phone: (415)349-4300
Fax: (415)349-7482
San Mateo, CA 94404-1561
Publisher E-mail: gpmg@gamepro.com

Video game magazine. **Founded:** Apr. 1989. **Freq:** Monthly. **Trim Size:** 8 x 10 1/4. **Key Personnel:** John Rousseau, Pres./CEO, phone (415)286-2525; Cyndy Sandor, VP/Assoc. Publisher, phone (415)286-2515; Elaine Starling, Marketing Dir., phone (415)286-2590; Wes Nihei, Editor-in-Chief, phone (415)286-2543; Suzanne McCloskey, Circulation Dir. **Subscription Rates:** $19.97 individuals; $4.95 single issue. **Online:** America Online, Inc.
Ad Rates: BW: $10,800 **Circ:** 564,702
4C: $13,625

3639 InfoWorld
155 Bovet Rd., Ste. 800 Phone: (415)572-7341
San Mateo, CA 94402-3115 Fax: (415)358-1269

Weekly IS publication. **Subtitle:** The Voice of Personal Computing in the Enterprise. **Founded:** 1980. **Freq:** Weekly. **Print Method:** Offset. **Trim Size:** 10 5/8 x 15. **Cols./Page:** 5. **Col. Width:** 1 13/16 inches. **Col. Depth:** 13 inches. **Key Personnel:** Jim Martin, Publisher; Stewart Alsop, President; Michael Lowe, Editor-in-Chief; Patrick Crotty, Sr. VP Circulation/Research; Joel Deceuster, Vice President; Joel Deceuster, Assoc. Publisher. **Subscription Rates:** Free to qualified subscribers; $130 individuals. **Remarks:** Accepts advertising. **Online:** LEXIS-NEXIS.
Ad Rates: BW: $26,950 **Circ:** Controlled 250,000
4C: $31,950

3640 JADARA
PO Box 6956 Phone: (650)372-0620
San Mateo, CA 94403 Fax: (650)372-0661
Publisher E-mail: adaraorgn@aol.com

Journal focusing on original research, news, and resources on deafness and rehabilitation. **Subtitle:** A Journal for Professionals Networking for Excellence in Service Delivery for Individuals Who Are Deaf or Hard of Hearing. **Freq:** 3/year. **Trim Size:** 6 x 10. **Key Personnel:** Elizabeth Charlson. **ISSN:** 0899-9228. **Subscription Rates:** $60.00 nonmembers; $70 other countries. **Remarks:** Advertising accepted; rates available upon request. **URL:** http://www.adara.org.
Circ: Paid 1,200

3641 Junior Statement
Junior Statesmen of America
60 E. Third Ave., Ste. 320 Phone: (650)347-1600
San Mateo, CA 94401 Fax: (650)347-7200
Publisher E-mail: jsa@jsa.org

Trade magazine of the Junior State of America covering youth activities in politics and government. **Founded:** 1934. **Freq:** Quarterly. **Print Method:** Offset. **Trim Size:** 11 X 17. **Cols./Page:** 5. **Key Personnel:** Richard Prosser, Editor and Publisher. **Subscription Rates:** Included in membership. **Remarks:** Advertising not accepted.
Circ: Paid 10,000

3642 LAN Technology
411 Borel Ave., Ste. 100
San Mateo, CA 94402

Trade journal for the network integration marketplace. **Subtitle:** The Technical Resource for Network Specialists. **Founded:** 1988. **Freq:** Monthly. **Print Method:** Web offset. **Trim Size:** 8 x 10 1/2. **Cols./Page:** 3 and 2. **Col. Width:** 2 1/8 inches. **Col. Depth:** 9 1/2 inches. **Key Personnel:** Mark Hall, Editor; Michael Wiener, Publisher. **ISSN:** 1042-4695. **Subscription Rates:** $25. $3.95 single issue. **Online:** CompuServe Information Service.
Circ: ‡60,000

3643 New Media Magazine
Hyper Media Communications, Inc.
901 Mariner's Island Blvd., Ste. 365 Phone: (415)573-5170
Fax: (415)573-5131
San Mateo, CA 94404-1593
Magazine for the creators, producers, and deliverers of computer-generated presentations and multimedia business and educational products. **Freq:** Monthly. **Key Personnel:** David Bunnell, Editor; Bechy Waring, Advertising Mgr.; Richard Landry, Publisher; Sharon Van Lewen, Publisher. **Subscription Rates:** $24. $3.95 single issue.

San Bruno Herald - See San Bruno

3644 San Mateo Times
1080 S. Amphlett Blvd. Phone: (415)348-4321
San Mateo, CA 94402 Fax: (415)348-4446

General newspaper with Republican editorial. **Founded:** 1889. **Freq:** Mon.-Sat. (eve.). **Print Method:** Offset. **Cols./Page:** 6. **Col. Width:** 27 nonpareils. **Col. Depth:** 301 agate lines. **Key Personnel:** Michelle A. Carter, Managing Editor; John H. Clinton, Publisher; Joel Hall, Advertising Mgr. **Subscription Rates:** $60 individuals. **Remarks:** Accepts advertising.
Ad Rates: PCI: $22.90 **Circ:** Mon.-Sat. ★**34,331**

3645 Tiempo Latino News
The Urban Latino News
440 S. Norfolk St., No. 223
San Mateo, CA 94401-3013

Publication focusing on Hispanic/Latin issues in Northern California. **Founded:** 1976. **Freq:** Weekly. **Print Method:** Web offset. **Trim Size:** 13 x 21. **Cols./Page:** 6. **Col. Width:** 21 inches. **Col. Depth:** 139 agate lines. **Key Personnel:** Gail E. Neira, Publisher. **Subscription Rates:** Free local only. **Remarks:** Accepts advertising. **Also known as**: The Urban Latino.
Ad Rates: BW: $2,142 **Circ:** 30,000
4C: $2,767
SAU: $17
PCI: $17

3646 UPSIDE
UPSIDE Media Inc.
2015 Pioneer Ct. Phone: (650)377-0950
San Mateo, CA 94403-1736 Fax: (650)377-1961
Publication E-mail: edit@upside.com
Publisher E-mail: subs@upside.com

Consumer magazine covering business and technology. **Subtitle:** People Capital Technology. **Founded:** Oct. 1989. **Freq:** Monthly. **Print Method:** Web offset. **Trim Size:** 8 1/8 x 10 1/4. **Cols./Page:** 3. **Col. Width:** 2 inches. **Col. Depth:** 9 1/2 inches. **Key Personnel:** Richard Brandt, Editor; Jody Stathakis, Advertising Dir.; Frank Ha, Circulation Mgr. **ISSN:** 1052-0341. **Subscription Rates:** $29.95 individuals; $4.95 single issue. **Remarks:** Accepts advertising.
Circ: Controlled 129,000

3647 KCSM-FM - 91.1
1700 W. Hillsdale Blvd. Phone: (415)574-6427
San Mateo, CA 94402 Fax: (415)574-6675
E-mail: info@kcsm.phs.org

Format: Public Radio; Jazz; News. **Networks:** National Public Radio (NPR); American Public Radio (APR). **Owner:** San Mateo County Community College, 3401 CSM Dr., San Mateo, CA 94402, (415)574-6550, Fax: (415)574-6675. **Founded:** 1964. **Operating Hours:** Continuous; 20% network, 80% local. **ADI:** San Francisco-Oakland-San Jose. **Key Personnel:** Anne Weitzel, Station Mgr.; Melanie Berzon, Program Dir.; Dick Conte, Music and Operations Dir.; Claire Mack, Community Relations. **Wattage:** 14,000. **Ad Rates:** Noncommercial.

3648 KCSM-TV - 60
1700 W. Hillsdale Blvd. Phone: (415)574-6586
San Mateo, CA 94402 Fax: (415)574-6675
E-mail: info@kcsm.pbs.org

Format: Public TV. **Networks:** Public Broadcasting Service (PBS). **Owner:** San Mateo County Community College District, 3401 CSM Dr., San Mateo, CA 94402, (415)574-6550. **Founded:** 1964. **Operating Hours:** 24 hours Daily; 35% network, 65% local. **ADI:** San Francisco-Oakland-San Jose. **Key Personnel:** David Hosley, General Mgr.; Diane Nelson, Program Dir.; Claire Mack, Community Relations. **Local Programs:** *The Computer Chronicles*, Rick Zanardi; *A Higher Education*, Claire Mack, Community Relations; *Legal Currents*, Diane Nelson. **Wattage:** 1.5 million. **Ad Rates:** Underwriting available. **URL:** http://www.smcccd.cc.ca.us/smcccd/kcsm/kcsm.html.

SAN PABLO, pop. 19,750.

Contra Costa Co. (W). 2 m N of Richmond. Contra Costa College. Plumbers' supplies, automotive. Nurseries.

3649 The Advocate
Contra Costa College
2600 Mission Bell Dr. Phone: (510)235-7800
San Pablo, CA 94806 Fax: (510)235-NEWS
Publication E-mail: advocate@contracosta.cc.ca.us

Collegiate newspaper. **Founded:** 1950. **Freq:** Weekly. **Print Method:** Offset. **Cols./Page:** 6. **Col. Width:** 24 nonpareils. **Col. Depth:** 294 agate lines. **Key Personnel:** Marc Carig, Editor. **Subscription Rates:** Free. **Remarks:** Accepts advertising.
Ad Rates: GLR: $.34 **Circ:** Free ‡2,500
BW: $400
SAU: $7.50

SAN PEDRO

Los Angeles Co. (S). On San Pedro Bay, 24 m S of Los Angeles. Port of commerce. Point fermin historic light house. Shipyards and dry docks, fish canneries, oil refineries, lumber mills; paint, fertilizer, roofing material, oil well tool factories. Sardine, tuna, mackerel fisheries.

3650 Nocturnal Lyric
Box 115 Phone: (310)519-9220
San Pedro, CA 90733-0115
Publication E-mail: nlyric@webtv.net

Consumer magazine covering horror fiction and poetry. **Subtitle:** Journal of the Bizarre. **Founded:** 1987. **Freq:** Quarterly. **Key Personnel:** Susan Moon. **Subscription Rates:** $10

individuals; $3 single issue. **Remarks:** Accepts advertising. **URL:** http://www.angelfire.com/ca/nocturnallyric.
Circ: Paid 400

3651 Random Lengths/Harbor Independent News
Random Lengths, Inc.
1117 South Pacific Ave. Phone: (310)519-1016
San Pedro, CA 90731
Publication E-mail: 71632.201@compuserve.com

Alternative Newspaper. **Subtitle:** Harbor Independent News. **Founded:** Dec. 1979. **Freq:** Weekly. **Print Method:** Offset. **Trim Size:** 11 1/4 x 14. **Cols./Page:** 4. **Col. Width:** 14.5 picas. **Col. Depth:** 12 3/4 inches. **Key Personnel:** James P. Allen, Publisher; Tom Davidson, Advertising Mgr. **ISSN:** 0891-8627. **Subscription Rates:** $23.95 individuals; $39.50 two years; $1.95 single issue; $52.50 other countries. **Remarks:** Accepts advertising. **Available Online. URL:** http://www.laharbor.com/14days.htm.
Ad Rates: GLR: $2.65 **Circ:** Free ‡20,000
BW: $829
4C: $1,375
SAU: $10.45
PCI: $16.50

3652 Sri Swami Prem Digest
Intergalactic Culture Foundation
1569 Stonewood Ct. Phone: (310)831-4226
San Pedro, CA 90732-1502 Fax: (310)831-4226
Publication E-mail: ilcc@mailcity.com

Digest acquaints you with Prem Meditation; science of Yoga Therapy and others; commentaries on Galactic Chronicles, ancient Sutras and Classics; accomplishmen ts of various wisemen, yogis, and tantriks, and spiritually vibrant places from Himalayas to the lowlands. **Founded:** 1982. **Freq:** Annual. **Trim Size:** 5 1/2 x 8 1/2. **Cols./Page:** 2. **Col. Width:** 2 1/4 inches. **Col. Depth:** 6 3/4 inches. **Key Personnel:** Lucille Toland, Contact; Chris Osborne, Editor, phone (606)436-8538. **Subscription Rates:** $15; $25 other countries. **URL:** http://welcome.to/ilcc. **Formerly:** Lovetrance World Journal; Aum Namo Narayanaya Journal; The Hindu Digest.
Ad Rates: GLR: $25 **Circ:** (Not Reported)
SAU: $75
PCI: $50

SAN RAFAEL†, pop. 44,700.

Marin Co. (W). On San Pablo Straits, 18 m N of San Francisco. Residential. Dominican College of San Rafael (Cath. Manufactures diodes, oil burners, gloves, bricks, beverages, aluminium products, plastics, boats, fish oil, feed, creamery products. Diversified farming. Artichokes, peas, tomatoes.

3653 ASU Travel Guide
1525 Francisco Blvd. E. Phone: (415)459-0300
San Rafael, CA 94901 Fax: (415)459-0494
Publication E-mail: asu@asuguide.com

Magazine. **Subtitle:** The Guide for Airline Employee Discounts. **Founded:** 1970. **Freq:** Quarterly. **Print Method:** Offset. **Trim Size:** 8 1/4 x 5 1/4. **Cols./Page:** 2. **Col. Width:** 24 nonpareils. **Col. Depth:** 103 agate lines. **Key Personnel:** Christopher Gil, Managing Editor, chris@asuguide.com; Ron Folkenflik, Publisher, ronf@asuguide.com; Susan Sellers, Advertising Dir., susan@asuguide.com; Ron Heard, Vice Pres./Mktg.; Hank Sousa, Vice President/Advertising, hank@asuguide.com. **USPS:** 898-100. **Subscription Rates:** $34.95 individuals. **Remarks:** Accepts advertising. **Online:** CompuServe. **URL:** http://www.asuguide.com.
Ad Rates: BW: $3,095 **Circ:** ‡60,000
4C: $4,090

3654 Classified Gazette
The Classified Gazette, Inc.
716 4th St. Phone: (415)457-4888
San Rafael, CA 94901 Fax: (415)454-9849
Free: (800)794-4888
Publication E-mail: ads@classifiedgazette.com

Classified shopper (tabloid). **Founded:** 1968. **Freq:** Weekly (Wed. & Fri.). **Print Method:** Offset. Uses mats. **Trim Size:** 11 x 17. **Cols./Page:** 7. **Col. Width:** 1 3/8 inches. **Col. Depth:** 16 1/2 inches. **Key Personnel:** Barb Belanyi, General Mgr., phone (415)457-4151, fax (415)457-5731; Carol Gardella, Office Mgr., cgardella@classifiedgazette.com. **Subscription Rates:** Free; $93.60 by mail. **Remarks:** Accepts advertising.
Ad Rates: GLR: $2 **Circ:** Free ‡60,000
BW: $1,207
PCI: $12

3655 Grocers Report
Super Markets Productions Ltd.
PO Box 6124 Phone: (415)479-0211
San Rafael, CA 94903 Fax: (415)479-0211

Grocery industry magazine. **Founded:** 1978. **Freq:** Monthly. **Print Method:** Offset. **Trim Size:** 8 1/2 x 11. **Cols./Page:** 3. **Col. Width:** 27 nonpareils. **Col. Depth:** 140 agate lines. **Key Personnel:** Lori Abrams, Editor; J.M. Adlman, Publisher; Jon Adams, Advertising Mgr. **Subscription Rates:** Free to qualified subscribers. **Remarks:** Accepts advertising.
Ad Rates: BW: $2,500 **Circ:** Controlled ‡15,000
4C: $3,500

3656 Marin County Court Reporter
1010 Lootens Place No. 13 Phone: (415)458-1611
San Rafael, CA 94901 Fax: (415)458-1614
Publication E-mail: herald_ recorder@dailyjournal.com

Legal newspaper. **Founded:** 1967. **Freq:** Semiweekly (Tues. and Fri.). **Print Method:** Offset. **Cols./Page:** 4. **Col. Width:** 2 3/8 inches. **Col. Depth:** 15 inches. **Key Personnel:** Erik H. Cummins, Editor. **USPS:** 859-940. **Subscription Rates:** $93. **Remarks:** Advertising accepted; rates available upon request.
Circ: Paid ‡409
Free ‡9

3657 News Pointer
Marin Scope Community Newspapers, Inc.
PO Box T
San Rafael, CA 94903

Community newspaper serving San Rafael, Terra Linda, and Lucas Valley. **Freq:** Weekly (Wed.). **Print Method:** Offset. **Trim Size:** 13 x 21. **Cols./Page:** 8. **Col. Width:** 8.5 inches. **Col. Depth:** 2 inches. **Key Personnel:** Billie Anderson, Editor; Paul Anderson, Publisher. **Subscription Rates:** $20.
Ad Rates: 4C: $4 **Circ:** Combined ‡10,500
PCI: $12.75

3658 The Runner's Schedule
80 Mitchell Blvd. Phone: (415)472-7223
San Rafael, CA 94903 Fax: (415)472-7233
Free: (800)998-7904
Publication E-mail: editor@theschedule.com

Magazine covering running, racing, and fitness walking in the Western United States. **Founded:** 1982. **Freq:** Monthly. **Print Method:** Web offset. **Trim Size:** 8 3/8 x 10 7/8. **Cols./Page:** 3 and 3. **Col. Width:** 2.5 inches. **Col. Depth:** 9 7/8 inches. **Key Personnel:** Kees Tuinzing, Publisher, kees@theschedule.com; Dave Stringer, Editor, editor@theschedule.com. **ISSN:** 1087-4555. **Subscription Rates:** $17. **Remarks:** Accepts advertising. **Available Online. URL:** http://www.theschedule.com. **Formerly:** The Northern California Schedule.
Ad Rates: BW: $1,300 **Circ:** Paid ‡12,000
4C: $1,870

3659 Whole Earth
Point Foundation
1408 Mission Ave. Phone: (415)256-2800
San Rafael, CA 94901 Fax: (415)256-2808
Publication E-mail: wer@well.com

General interest magazine containing articles, commentary, and reviews of books, tools and ideas. **Subtitle:** Access to Tools and Ideas. **Founded:** 1974. **Freq:** Quarterly. **Print Method:** Web offset. **Trim Size:** 8 1/2 x 10 7/8. **Cols./Page:** 2. **Col. Width:** 17 picas. **Col. Depth:** 133 agate lines. **Key Personnel:** Andrew Gault, Publisher; Anna Lee, Business Mgr.; Peter Warshall, Editor. **ISSN:** 0749-5056. **Subscription Rates:** $24 individuals; $12 back issue; $30 Canada and Mexico; $40 other countries. **Remarks:** Accepts advertising. **Available Online. Formerly:** CoEvolution Quarterly; Whole Earth Review.
Ad Rates: BW: $1,000 **Circ:** ‡35,000
4C: $1,600

3660 Wines & Vines
The Hiaring Co.
1800 Lincoln Ave. Phone: (415)453-9700
San Rafael, CA 94901 Fax: (415)453-2517
Publication E-mail: geninfo@winesandvines.com

Wine trade magazine for the U.S., Canada, and Mexico. **Subtitle:** Authoritative Voice of the Grape and Wine Industry. **Founded:** 1919. **Freq:** Monthly. **Print Method:** Offset. **Trim Size:** 8 3/8 x 10 7/8. **Cols./Page:** 3 and 2. **Col. Width:** 27 and 42 nonpareils. **Col. Depth:** 140 agate lines. **Key Personnel:** Philip E. Hiaring, Publisher; Dottie Kubota-Cordery, President. **ISSN:** 0043-583X. **Subscription Rates:** $32.50 individuals; $5 single issue; $39 Canada and Mexico; $50 out of country. **Remarks:** Accepts advertising. **Alt. Formats:** Mailing labels.
Ad Rates: BW: $1,245 **Circ:** ‡3,200
4C: $2,335
PCI: $65

3661 KSRH-FM - 88.1
185 Mission Ave. Phone: (415)457-5774
San Rafael, CA 94901

Format: Contemporary Hit Radio (CHR); Album-Oriented Rock (AOR); Classic Rock; Urban Contemporary. **Networks:** Independent. **Owner:** San Rafael High School, at above address. **Founded:** 1980. **Operating Hours:** 9 a.m.-3 p.m. **Key Personnel:** Marianne Melnick, Contact. **Wattage:** 10. **Ad Rates:** Advertising accepted; rates available upon request.

SAN RAMON, pop. 4,300.

Contra Costa Co. (W) 16 m SE of Berkeley. Residential.

3662 Ed, The Official Publication of USDLA (United States Distance Learning Association)
ED, The Official Publication of USDLA
Box 5106 Phone: (510)606-5150
San Ramon, CA 94583-0906 Fax: (510)606-9410
Free: (800)829-3400

Journal covering applications of teleconferencing to education. **Subtitle:** Education at a Distance. **Founded:** 1985. **Freq:** Monthly. **Trim Size:** 8 1/2 x 11. **Cols./Page:** 2. **Key Personnel:** Corby Griffin, Director, corby@usdla.org; Dr. Elizabeth Perrin, Managing Editor; Donald Perrin, Managing Editor. **Subscription Rates:** $100. **URL:** http://www.usdla.org.
Ad Rates: 4C: $4,000 **Circ:** Paid 5,000

3663 The Nooner Magazine
Healthy Weight Journal
2491 San Ramon Valley Blvd.,
Ste. 1-355
San Ramon, CA 94583

Magazine containing information on entertainment, leisure, community, and business events in the TriValley area in the 580/680 Corridor. **Subtitle:** Fun Reading for Valley Business People. **Founded:** 1989. **Freq:** Monthly. **Print Method:** Web offset. **Trim Size:** 11 x 17. **Cols./Page:** 4. **Col. Width:** 2 1/4 inches. **Col. Depth:** 16 inches. **Key Personnel:** Karen Fagen, Editor and Publisher; Diane Sinclair, Editor; Diane Summers, Advertising; Mary Stark, Advertising. **Subscription Rates:** $12.99 individuals; $1.09 single issue.
Ad Rates: PCI: $27.50 **Circ:** Paid 11
Non-paid 16,000

3664 Teleconference Magazine
(ABC) Applied Business Telecommunications
Box 5106 Phone: (510)820-5563
San Ramon, CA 94583-0906 Fax: (510)820-5894
Publication E-mail: corby@usdla.org

Magazine including articles on teleconferencing applications and case studies, information about events, equipment, services, and people. **Subtitle:** The Business Communications Magazine. **Founded:** June 1981. **Freq:** Monthly. **Print Method:** Offset. **Trim Size:** 8 3/8 x 10 7/8. **Cols./Page:** 3. **Col. Width:** 27 nonpareils. **Col. Depth:** 137 agate lines. **Key Personnel:** Patrick Portway, Publisher; Andra Frantz, Editor. **Subscription Rates:** $60 Annual subscription; $10 single issue. **Remarks:** Accepts advertising. **URL:** http://www.usdla.org.
Ad Rates: BW: $1,500 **Circ:** Paid 10,000
4C: $1,800 Non-paid 15,000

SAN YSIDRO

San Diego Co.

3665 XEBG-AM - 1550
PO Box 430155 Phone: (619)595-7864
2630 E. Beyer Blvd., Ste. 265
San Ysidro, CA 92143
E-mail: vtacbc@mail.tij.cetys.mx

Format: Hispanic; Sports; News. **Owner:** Mario Mayans, at above address. **Founded:** Feb. 4, 1936. **Operating Hours:** Continuous. **ADI:** San Diego, CA. **Key Personnel:** Mario Mayans, President. **Wattage:** 1,000. **Ad Rates:** $28-41 for 30 seconds; $35-50 for 60 seconds.

3666 XEMB-AM - 1190
PO Box 430155 Phone: (619)595-7864
2630 E. Beyer Blvd., Ste. 265
San Ysidro, CA 92143
E-mail: vtacbc@mail.tis.cetys.mx

Format: Hispanic; Talk. **Networks:** Lotus. **Owner:** at above address, (619)425-9222. **Founded:** 1967. **Operating Hours:** 5 a.m.-1 a.m. **ADI:** El Centro, CA-Yuma, AZ. **Key Personnel:** Mario Mayans, General Mgr. **Wattage:** 500. **Ad Rates:** $21-37 for 30 seconds; $28-45 for 60 seconds.

3667 XEMM-AM - 800
PO Box 430155 Phone: (619)595-7864
San Ysidro, CA 92143
E-mail: vtacbc@mail.tij.cetys.mx

Format: Hispanic. **Owner:** Mario Mayans, at above address, (619)425-9222. **Founded:** May 1, 1960. **Operating Hours:** 5 a.m. - 12 a.m. **ADI:** San Diego, CA. **Key Personnel:** Mario Mayans, President. **Wattage:** 1,000. **Ad Rates:** $28-41 for 30 seconds; $35-50 for 60 seconds.

3668 XEWV-AM - 940
PO Box 430155 Phone: (619)595-7864
2630 E. Beyer Blvd., Ste. 265
San Ysidro, CA 92143
E-mail: vtacbc@mail.tij.cetys.mx

Format: Hispanic. **Networks:** Lotus. **Owner:** at above address, San Ysidro, CA 92143, (619)425-9222. **Founded:** 1955. **Operating Hours:** Continuous. **ADI:** El Centro, CA-Yuma, AZ. **Key Personnel:** Mario Mayans, President. **Wattage:** 1,000. **Ad Rates:** $21-37 for 30 seconds; $28-45 for 60 seconds.

3669 XEWV-FM - 106.7
PO Box 430155 Phone: (619)595-7864
2630 E. Beyer Blvd., Ste. 265 Fax: (619)425-9222
San Ysidro, CA 92143
E-mail: vtacbc@mail.tij.cetys.mx

Format: Hispanic. **Networks:** Lotus. **Owner:** at above address, San Ysidro, CA 92143, (619)425-9222. **Founded:** May 15, 1986. **Operating Hours:** Continuous. **ADI:** El Centro, CA-Yuma, AZ. **Key Personnel:** Mario Mayans, President. **Wattage:** 4500. **Ad Rates:** $21-37 for 30 seconds; $28-45 for 60 seconds.

3670 XEYX-AM - 820
PO Box 430155 Phone: (619)595-7864
2630 E. Beyer Blvd., Ste. 265
San Ysidro, CA 92143
E-mail: vtacbc@mail.tij.cetys.mx

Format: Hispanic; Sports; News. **Networks:** Lotus. **Owner:** at above address, (619)425-9222. **Founded:** May 1983. **Operating Hours:** 6 a.m.-12 a.m. **ADI:** El Centro, CA-Yuma, AZ. **Key Personnel:** Mario Mayans, President; Manuel Hurtado, Manager; Alicia Alvarez, Traffic Mgr. **Wattage:** 10,000. **Ad Rates:** $19-34 for 30 seconds; $25-41 for 60 seconds.

SANGER, pop. 12,558.

Fresno Co. (C). 14 m E of Fresno. Raisins, deciduous and citrus fruit packing houses, frozen food processing plants. Box making machinery, electric cables, cement pipes, overalls, wine manufactured. Agriculture. Grapes, citrus fruit, truck crops.

3671 El Sol Del Valle
718 N. St. Phone: (209)875-8771
Sanger, CA 93657
Bilingual community newspaper. **Founded:** 1986. **Freq:** Biweekly. **Trim Size:** 13 x 21. **Cols./Page:** 6. **Col. Depth:** 21 inches. **Key Personnel:** Kevin Kennedy, Editor and Publisher; Helena Kennedy, Editor and Publisher. **Subscription Rates:** $29.95. **Remarks:** Accepts advertising.
Ad Rates: GLR: $20 **Circ:** 24,400
BW: $2,268
4C: $2,593
PCI: $20

3672 Herald Advertiser
Sanger Herald, Inc.
740 N St. Phone: (209)875-2511
Sanger, CA 93657 Fax: (209)875-2521

Shopper. **Freq:** Weekly (Wed.). **Print Method:** Offset. **Cols./Page:** 6. **Col. Width:** 24 nonpareils. **Col. Depth:** 294 agate lines. **Key Personnel:** Rosemary Kallio, Publisher. **Remarks:** Advertising not accepted for tobacco products.
Ad Rates: BW: $938.70 **Circ:** Free ‡14,100
4C: $1,238.70
SAU: $7.45
PCI: $9.50

3673 Sanger Herald
Sanger Herald, Inc.
740 N St. Phone: (209)875-2511
Sanger, CA 93657 Fax: (209)875-2521

Community newspaper with a Republican orientation. **Founded:** 1889. **Freq:** Weekly (Thurs.). **Print Method:** Offset. **Cols./Page:** 6. **Col. Width:** 24 nonpareils. **Col. Depth:** 294 agate lines. **Key Personnel:** William Coleman, Editor; Rosemary Kallio, Publisher. **USPS:** 481-340. **Subscription Rates:** $16 individuals; $20 other countries. **Remarks:** Advertising not accepted for tobacco products.
Ad Rates: BW: $938.70 **Circ:** ‡3,200
4C: $1,238.70
SAU: $7.45
PCI: $9.50

SANTA ANA†, pop. 203,713.

Orange Co. (S). 36 m SE of Los Angeles. Santa Ana College. Manufactures sugar, glass products, plumbing material, foam rubber products, dehydrating, electronic, sport equipment, concentrates, extracts, agricultural machinery, perfumes, feed, cement pipes, soft drinks, rivets, fasteners. Canned and dried fruits and vegetables. Walnuts, oranges packed; hatchery.

3674 America's Network
Advanstar Communications
201 Sandpointe Ave., Ste. 600 Phone: (714)513-8400
Santa Ana, CA 92707 Fax: (714)513-8612
Free: (800)854-3112

Magazine serving telecommunications carrier companies, and other providers of telecommunications. Focuses on emerging technologies. **Subtitle:** Technology for the public network since 1909. **Founded:** Jan. 1909. **Freq:** Semimonthly. **Print Method:** Offset. **Trim Size:** 8 x 10.75. **Cols./Page:** 2 and 3. **Key Personnel:** Mary Slepicka, Ed.-in-Chief/Group Ed., phone (714)513-8400, fax (714)513-8634, mslepicka@americasnetwork.com; Danny Phillips, Group Publisher, phone (714)513-8400, fax (714)513-8634, dphillips@advanstar.com; Paul Semple, Publisher, phone (714)513-8400, fax (714)513-8634, psemple@advanstar.com; Annie Lindstrom, Sr. Editor, phone (212)951-6735, fax (212)683-4257, alindstrom@americasnetwork.com; Kurt Mackie, Managing Editor, phone (714)513-8400, fax (714)513-8634, kmackie@americasnetwork.com. **ISSN:** 1075-5292. **Subscription Rates:** $44 U.S.; $64 Canada and Mexico; $84 other countries. **Remarks:** Accepts advertising. **Available Online. URL:** http://www.americasnetwork.com. **Formerly:** Telephone Engineer & Managgement (TE&M).
Ad Rates: BW: $5,195 **Circ:** Paid 1,914
4C: $5,850 Non-paid 51,374

3675 Azteca News
PO Box 207
Santa Ana, CA 92702-0207

Community newspaper (Spanish). **Founded:** 1980. **Freq:** Weekly (Wed.). **Print Method:** Offset. **Trim Size:** 12 1/2 x 22. **Cols./Page:** 6. **Col. Width:** 2 inches. **Col. Depth:** 21 1/2 inches. **Key Personnel:** Fernando Velo, Editor and Publisher; Bill Reynoso, Editor. **Subscription Rates:** $48. **Remarks:** Accepts advertising. **Formerly:** Semanario Azteca (1986).
Ad Rates: BW: $1,548 **Circ:** Free ‡33,000
4C: $1,948
PCI: $12

3676 CADALYST
Advanstar Communications
201 Sandpointe Ave., Ste. 600 Phone: (714)513-8400
Santa Ana, CA 92707 Fax: (714)513-8612
Free: (800)854-3112
Publication E-mail: 70302.2531@compuserve.com

Magazine for AutoCAD users. **Subtitle:** Professional Management of AutoCAD Systems. **Founded:** 1984. **Freq:** Monthly. **Print Method:** Offset. **Trim Size:** 8 1/8 x 10 7/8. **Cols./Page:** 3. **Col. Width:** 13 picas. **Col. Depth:** 60.5 picas. **Key Personnel:** Gene Smarte, Editor-in-Chief; Jennifer Bauer, Production Mgr.; Dana Woodsmall, Publisher; Peggie Kegel, Circulation Mgr.; Lisa F. Anderson, Editor. **ISSN:** 0820-5450. **Subscription Rates:** $39 individuals; $4.95 single issue. **Remarks:** Accepts advertising. **URL:** http://www.cadonline.com.
Ad Rates: BW: $5,715 **Circ:** Paid 31,716
4C: $7,015 Non-paid 37,543

3677 Cartoonist and Comic Artist Magazine
2747 N. Grand Ave., No. 250 Phone: (714)550-9933
Santa Ana, CA 92705 Fax: (714)550-9933
Publication E-mail: cartoonmag@aol.com

Magazine for aspiring cartoonists. **Founded:** 1993. **Freq:** Quarterly. **Key Personnel:** Steve Pastis, Editor/Publisher and Advertising Mgr.; April Heath, Assoc. Editor. **Subscription Rates:** $20 individuals; $6 single issue. **Remarks:** Accepts advertising. **Former name:** The Aspiring Cartoonist.
Circ: Paid 2,000

3678 Comunicaciones
Advanstar Communications
201 Sandpointe Ave., Ste. 600 Phone: (714)513-8400
Santa Ana, CA 92707 Fax: (714)513-8612
Free: (800)854-3112

Trade magazine for telecommunications and information technology buyers in Mexico, the Caribbean, and South America (Spanish). **Freq:** Bimonthly. **Print Method:** Web offset. **Trim Size:** 8 x 10 3/4. **Key Personnel:** Mary Slepicka, Exec. Editor. **Subscription Rates:** Free to qualified subscribers; $45 individuals; $8 single issue. **Remarks:** Accepts advertising.
Ad Rates: BW: $4,695 **Circ:** Controlled 10,000
4C: $5,690

3679 Dealernews
Advanstar Communications
201 Sandpointe Ave., Ste. 600 Phone: (714)513-8400
Santa Ana, CA 92707 Fax: (714)513-8612
Free: (800)854-3112

Magazine covering dealers of motorcycles, watercraft, and other powersport vehicles. **Subtitle:** The Voice Of The Power Sports Vehicle Industry. **Founded:** 1965. **Freq:** 13/year. **Print Method:** Offset. **Trim Size:** 8 x 10 7/8. **Cols./Page:** 3. **Col. Width:** 27 nonpareils. **Col. Depth:** 140 agate lines. **Key Personnel:** Robin Hartfiel, Editor, phone (714)513-8423, fax (714)513-8414, rhartfiel@advanstar.com; John Murphy, Publisher, phone (717)513-8419, fax (714)513-8414, jmurphy@advanstar.com. **ISSN:** 0893-2522. **Subscription Rates:** $25. **Remarks:** Accepts advertising. **Formerly:** Motorcycle Dealernews.
Ad Rates: BW: $3,240 **Circ:** Paid 78
4C: $4,190 Non-paid 15,051

3680 Excelsior
117 W. 4th St. Phone: (714)704-4308
Santa Ana, CA 92701 Fax: (714)953-0345

Newspaper. **Freq:** Weekly. **Trim Size:** tabloid. **Cols./Page:** 5. **Key Personnel:** Tonnie Katz, Publisher; Catherine Reiland, Assoc. Publisher; Lydia Cano, Admin./Community Relations; Miguel Jimenez, Managing Editor; Mike Cano, Advertising Dir./Outside Sales; Mario Arreola, Advertising Dir./Inside Sales. **ISSN:** 1077-3916. **Remarks:** Accepts advertising.
Ad Rates: GLR: $27.18 **Circ:** Free ❑**41,078**
BW: $1,766.70
4C: $2,686.70
PCI: $27.18

3681 The Hellenic Calendar
2747 N. Grand Ave., No. 250 Phone: (714)550-9933
Santa Ana, CA 92705 Fax: (714)550-9933
Publication E-mail: greekpaper@aol.com

Community newspaper with items of interest to Greek-Americans of Southern California and the Southwest. **Founded:** Apr. 1979. **Freq:** Monthly. **Print Method:** Web offset. **Trim Size:** 11 x 17. **Key Personnel:** Steve Pastis, Editor/Publisher and Advertising Mgr.; April Heath, Assoc. Editor. **Subscription Rates:** $20 individuals. **Remarks:** Accepts advertising.
Ad Rates: BW: $400 **Circ:** Combined 10,000
4C: $700

3682 Hospitality Product News
Advanstar Communications
201 Sandpointe Ave., Ste. 600 Phone: (714)513-8400
Santa Ana, CA 92707 Fax: (714)513-8612
Free: (800)854-3112

Trade magazine serving the U.S. lodging industry. **Founded:** Sept. 1993. **Freq:** Bimonthly. **Print Method:** Web offset. **Trim Size:** 10 3/4 x 14 1/2. **Cols./Page:** 5. **Col. Width:** 1 3/4 inches. **Subscription Rates:** Free. **Remarks:** Accepts advertising.
Ad Rates: BW: $5,190 **Circ:** Non-paid 34,000
4C: $6,765

3683 InfoText
InfoText Publishing, Inc.
201 Sandpointe Ave., Ste. 600 Phone: (714)493-2434
Santa Ana, CA 92707-5761 Fax: (714)493-3018

Telecommunications trade publication. **Subtitle:** The Interactive Telephone Magazine. **Founded:** 1988. **Freq:** Monthly. **Print Method:** Sheetfed offset. **Trim Size:** 8 1/2 x 11. **Cols./Page:** 3. **Col. Width:** 2 3/8 inches. **Col. Depth:** 10 inches. **Key Personnel:** Jack Schember, Editor; Laura Dalton, Managing Editor; Kurt Indvik, Publisher; Bob Dale, Editor; Kip Ongstad, Advertising Mgr.; Monica Kollmann, Editor. **Subscription Rates:** $40; $100 Canada and Mexico; $150 other countries. **Remarks:** Accepts advertising.
Ad Rates: BW: $2,290 **Circ:** Controlled ‡18,000
4C: $3,015

3684 Landscape Architect and Specifier News
Landscape Communications, Ltd.
1560 Brookhollow Dr., No. 222 Phone: (714)979-5276
Santa Ana, CA 92705-5426 Fax: (714)979-3543

Trade magazine covering landscape architecture and planning for professionals. **Founded:** 1984. **Freq:** Monthly. **Trim Size:** 8 3/8 x 10 7/8. **Cols./Page:** 4. **Key Personnel:** Heather Lebus, Editor, hduval1@aol.com; Jennifer Knowles, Circulation Mgr.; George Schmok, Publisher, earthmanxatsaol.com. **ISSN:** 1060-9962. **Subscription Rates:** $29.95 individuals; $2.50 single issue. **Remarks:** Accepts advertising. **URL:** http://www.landscapeonline.com; landarchx@aol.com. **Former name:** Landscape Construction & Maintenance.
Ad Rates: BW: $3,195 **Circ:** Controlled 24,000
4C: $3,295

3685 Orange County Register
Freedom Communications Inc.
625 N. Grand Ave. Phone: (714)835-1234
PO Box 11626 Fax: (714)543-3904
Santa Ana, CA 92701-4347
Publication E-mail: ocregister@link.freedom.com

General newspaper. **Founded:** 1905. **Freq:** Daily (morn.). **Print Method:** Offset. **Trim Size:** 13 x 22 3/4. **Cols./Page:** 6. **Col. Width:** 25 nonpareils. **Col. Depth:** 129 agate lines. **Key Personnel:** R. David Threshie, Publisher; Tonnie Katz, Editor; N. Christian Anderson, Assoc. Publisher; John Schueler, Assoc. Publisher; Dick Cheverton, Managing Editor; Ken Brusic, Managing Editor. **Subscription Rates:** $90 individuals. **Remarks:** Accepts advertising. **Online:** DataTimes Corporation. **URL:** http://www.ocregister.com. **Alt. Formats:** CD-ROM, NewsBank, Inc. **Feature Editors:** Laura Bly, *Travel*, phone (714)953-7771; Blair Charnley, *News*, phone (714)953-2233; Jim Chute, *Music*, phone (714)953-7855; Joe Crea, *Food*, phone (714)953-2278; Cary Darling, *Music*, phone (714)953-7866; Lynne Domash, *Education, Environmental, Features, Political*, phone (714)953-3665; Jim Emerson, *Movie*, phone (714)953-7699; Ken Grubbs, *Editorials*, phone (714)953-7825; Nick Harder, *Garden/Home*, phone (714)953-7769; Cathy Lawhon, *Family*, phone (714)953-7772; Jeff Light, *City*, phone (714)953-4966; Ron Londen, *Photo*, phone (714)953-2289; Gary Lycan, *Radio*, phone (714)953-2203; Lisa Lytle, *Fashion*, phone (714)953-7854; Andre Mouchard, *Real Estate*, phone (714)953-7926; Tom O'Connor, *Drama*, phone (714)953-7979; Jean Pasco, *Aviation*, phone (714)834-5349; Susan Peterson, *Medical*, phone (714)953-7830; Ray Richmond, *TV*, phone (714)953-7868; Chris Smith, *Metro*, phone (714)953-2200; Mark Tomaszewski, *Sports*, phone (714)953-2299; Neil Wertheimier, *Financial/Business*, phone (714)953-7946; David Whiting, *Book, Entertainment*, phone (714)953-4987.
Ad Rates: BW: $18,318 **Circ:** Mon.-Sat. ★**356,953**
4C: $20,111 Sun. ★**413,349**
PCI: $142

3686 Pennysaver
Hart-Hanks Communications
1261 E. Dyer Rd., Ste. 100 Phone: (714)996-8900
Santa Ana, CA 92705-5605 Fax: (714)241-1049

Shopper. **Founded:** 1962. **Freq:** Weekly (Wed.). **Print Method:** Offset. **Cols./Page:** 4. **Col. Width:** 28 nonpareils. **Col. Depth:** 140 agate lines. **Key Personnel:** H. C. Van Ausdeln, Publisher. **Remarks:** Accepts advertising. **URL:** http://www.thepennysaver.com. **Formerly:** Quarter Tab.
Ad Rates: BW: $510 **Circ:** 220,000
4C: $5,920

3687 Response TV
201 E. Sandpointe Ave., Ste. 600 Phone: (714)513-8400
Fax: (714)513-8482
Santa Ana, CA 92707-5761
Free: (800)854-3112

Monthly trade magazine for the direct response TV, infomercial and interactive TV industries. **Subtitle:** The Information Leader for the Electronic Merchandising Industry. **Founded:** July 1992. **Freq:** Monthly. **Print Method:** Web offset. **Trim Size:** 8 x 10 7/8. **Cols./Page:** 3. **Key Personnel:** Jack Schember, Publisher, phone (714)513-8421, jschember@advanstar.com; David Nagel, Editor, phone (714)513-8453, dnagel@advanstar.com; Carol Neher, Assoc. Publisher, phone (714)513-8460, cneher@advanstar.com; Kellie Reagan, Assoc. Editor, phone (714)513-8460, kreagan@advanstar.com; Ellie Parvin, Publication Assistant, phone (714)513-8610, eparvin@advanstar.com. **Subscription Rates:** $39 individuals annual; $100 Foreign. **Remarks:** Accepts advertising. **URL:** http://www.responsetv.com.
Ad Rates: BW: $2880 **Circ:** Paid 700
4C: $3695 Non-paid 21,000

3688 Telecom Asia
Advanstar Communications
201 Sandpointe Ave., Ste. 600 Phone: (714)513-8400
Santa Ana, CA 92707 Fax: (714)513-8612
Free: (800)854-3112

Trade magazine for planning, engineering, and operational managers responsible for the design, installation, marketing, and maintenance of public and private telecom systems and networks in Asia and the Pacific Rim. **Founded:** 1990. **Freq:** Monthly. **Print Method:** Web offset. **Trim Size:** 8 x 10 3/4. **Key Personnel:** Robert Poe, Editor. **Subscription Rates:** Free to qualified subscribers; $120 individuals; $10 single issue. **Remarks:** Accepts advertising.
Ad Rates: BW: $5,136 **Circ:** Controlled 20,000
4C: $6,581

3689 Video Store
Advanstar Communications
201 E. Sandpointe Ave. Phone: (714)513-8447
Ste. 600 Fax: (714)513-8403
Santa Ana, CA 92707
Publication E-mail: vstore@aol.com

Business magazine for retailers of prerecorded video software, blank tapes, and accessories. **Founded:** 1978. **Freq:** Weekly. **Print Method:** Offset. **Trim Size:** 10 1/2 x 14. **Cols./Page:** 5. **Col. Width:** 11 picas. **Col. Depth:** 13 inches. **Key Personnel:** Thomas K. Arnold, Editor, tarnold@advanstar.coom; Don Rosenberg, Publisher, drossenberg@advanstar.com. **ISSN:** 0195-1770. **Subscription Rates:** $75 individuals; $150 Canada and Mexico; $185 other countries. **Remarks:** Accepts advertising.
Ad Rates: BW: $13,375 **Circ:** Non-paid 43,885
4C: $16,050 Paid 422
PCI: $245

3690 Comcast Cablevision
1830 E. Warner Ave. Phone: (562)799-7611
Santa Ana, CA 92705-5505 Fax: (562)799-7622

Owner: Comcast Cablevision, at above address, (714)338-2027, Fax: (714)871-8136. **Formerly:** Comcast Cablevision of Seal Beach. **Key Personnel:** Marilee Jackson, Production Mgr., mjack12744@aol.com. **Cities Served:** Buena Park, Fullerton, Newport Beach, Placentia, Santa Ana, Seal Beach, CA: subscribing households 225,000; 74 channels; 13 community access channels; 56 hours per week community access programming.

3691 KTBN-TV - 40
Box A Phone: (714)832-2950
Santa Ana, CA 92711 Fax: (714)665-2165

Format: Religious. **Networks:** Independent. **Operating Hours:** Continuous. **ADI:** Los Angeles (Corona & San Bernardino), CA. **Key Personnel:** John Reardon, Vice President.

3692 KWIZ-AM - 1480
3101 W. 5th St. Phone: (714)554-5000
Santa Ana, CA 92703-1829 Fax: (714)554-9362

Format: Hispanic. **Networks:** Independent. **Owner:** Liberman Broadcasting, at above address. **Founded:** 1926. **Operating Hours:** Continuous; 100% local. **Key Personnel:** Jose Liberman, Contact; Andrew Mars, General Mgr.; Al Southern, Sales Mgr.; David Gleason, Program Dir.; Victor Rosales, Promotions Dir. **Wattage:** 5000. **Ad Rates:** Advertising accepted; rates available upon request.

3693 WFGL-AM - 960
3000 W. McArthur Blvd. Phone: (714)549-8895
Santa Ana, CA 92704 Free: (800)272-9673
E-mail: wft@primenet.com

Format: Contemporary Christian. **Owner:** CSN International, PO Box 8000, Costa Mesa, CA 92628, Free: (800)272-WORD. **Founded:** 1950. **Formerly:** WXLO-AM. **Operating Hours:** Continuous. **Key Personnel:** George Small, Station Mgr., phone (508)342-5025, fax (508)342-0118, georgesmall@juno.com; Debbie Doran, Sales Mgr. **Wattage:** 2500 day, 1000 night. **Ad Rates:** $6-14 per unit.

SANTA BARBARA†, pop. 74,542.

Santa Barbara Co. (SW). On Pacific Ocean, 97 m NW of Los Angeles. University of California at Santa Barbara. City College. Westmont College. Private schools. research, light industrial, educational, medical, tourist and recreational center. Winter and summer resort. Oil-producing fields. Manufactures electronic products, plastics, aircraft parts, novelties. Oil refineries; meat packing, canning and frozen food processing plants; Nurseries. Ships cattle, lemons, beans, flowers, avocados, tomatoes.

3694 The Comedy Magazine
5290 Overpass Rd., No. 128 Phone: (805)964-7841
Santa Barbara, CA 93111 Fax: (805)964-1073

Humorous magazine covering various types of comedy, including stand-up, movies, and TV shows. **Founded:** Dec. 1993. **Freq:** Bimonthly. **Print Method:** Web press. **Trim Size:** 8 1/8 x 10 7/8. **Cols./Page:** 3. **Col. Width:** 2 1/4 inches. **Key Personnel:** Walter Jurek, Editor; Nancy Rothlein, Advertising Dir.; Monika Grant, Circulation Mgr. **ISSN:** 1080-4714. **Subscription Rates:** $19.95 individuals; $3.95 single issue. **Remarks:** Accepts advertising. **URL:** http://www.Earthchannel.com.
Ad Rates: BW: $1,600 **Circ:** Paid 14,000
4C: $2,700 Non-paid 200,000

3695 Current World Leaders: Almanac
International Academy at Santa Barbara
5385 Hollister Ave., Ste. 210 Phone: (805)964-0790
Santa Barbara, CA 93111-2305 Fax: (805)964-0890
Free: (800)530-2682
Publication E-mail: cwlinfo@iash.org
Publisher E-mail: info@iasb.org

Journal containing information about leaders of governments, colonies and key international organizations as well as demographic data. **Founded:** 1957. **Freq:** Bimonthly (3 Almanac issues, 3 Almanac Update issues). **Print Method:** Offset. **Trim Size:** 5 1/2 x 8 1/2. **Cols./Page:** 1. **Col. Width:** 25 picas. **Col. Depth:** 46 picas. **Key Personnel:** Thomas S. Garrison, Editorial Dir.; Joanne St. John, Publisher. **ISSN:** 0192-6802. **Subscription Rates:** $240 individuals; $290 institutions. **Remarks:** Advertising not accepted. **URL:** http://www.iasb.org/cwl.
Circ: 1,000

3696 Erosion Control
Forester Communications, Inc.
5638 Hollister No. 301 Phone: (805)681-1300
Santa Barbara, CA 93117 Fax: (805)681-1312
Publisher E-mail: publisher@erosioncontrol.net

Journal for professionals who create, implement, construct, and maintain projects in the field of erosion control. **Subtitle:** The Journal for Erosion and Sediment Control Professionals. **Founded:** Mar. 1994. **Freq:** 9/year. **Print Method:** Web offset. **Trim Size:** 8 1/8 x 10 7/8. **Cols./Page:** 3. **Col. Width:** 2 5/16 inches. **Col. Depth:** 9 3/4 inches. **Key Personnel:** John Trotti, Editor, editor@forester.net; Dan Waldman, Publisher, publisher@forester.net. **Subscription Rates:** $75; $15 single issue. **Remarks:** Accepts advertising.
Ad Rates: BW: $2,330 **Circ:** Controlled **20,000**
4C: $3,225

3697 Gender & Society
Sage Publications Inc.
University of California Phone: (805)893-7773
Santa Barbara, CA 93106 Fax: (805)893-3324
Publication E-mail: gendsoc@sscf.ucsb.edu
Publisher E-mail: info@sagepub.com

Journal covering theory and research in the study of gender as a primary social category and its relationship to social order; emphasizing the study of gender and feminist scholarship. **Founded:** Mar. 1987. **Freq:** Bimonthly 6/year. **Trim Size:** 5 1/2 x 8 1/2. **Cols./Page:** 1. **Col. Width:** 50 nonpareils. **Col. Depth:** 100 agate lines. **Key Personnel:** Beth Schneider, Editor; Cris Anderson, Circulation Mgr.; Judy Taylor, Managing Editor. **ISSN:** 0891-2432. **Subscription Rates:** $44 individuals; $117 institutions; $88 two years; $234 two years Institutions; $31 single issue; $30 single issue Institutions. **Remarks:** Accepts advertising.
Ad Rates: BW: $250 **Circ:** Paid ‡2,650
Non-paid ‡153

3698 Hispanic Business
425 Pine Ave. Phone: (805)964-4554
Santa Barbara, CA 93117-3709 Fax: (805)964-5539
Publisher E-mail: info@hbinc.com

English-language business magazine catering to Hispanic professionals, executives, and entrepreneurs. **Founded:** 1979. **Freq:** Monthly. **Print Method:** Offset. **Trim Size:** 7 7/8 x 10 1/2. **Cols./Page:** 3. **Col. Width:** 28 nonpareils. **Col. Depth:** 140 agate lines. **Key Personnel:** Jesus Chavarria, Publisher, jchavarria@mail.hbinc.com; Vaughn Hagerty, Managing Editor, vhagerty@mail.hbinc.com; Jeff D. Vitucci, Dir. of Research Services, jvitucci@mail.hbinc.com. **ISSN:** 0199-0349. **Subscription Rates:** $18 individuals; $2.95 single issue. **Remarks:** Accepts advertising. **URL:** http://www.hispanstar.com. **Alt. Formats:** Mailing labels.
Ad Rates: BW: $10,070 **Circ:** Paid 12,000
4C: $13,188 Controlled 200,000

3699 International Journal of Middle East Studies
Cambridge University Press
Univ. of California at Santa Barbara Phone: (805)893-2442
Fax: (805)893-8795
Santa Barbara, CA 93106-9410
Publication E-mail: ijmes@humanitas.ucsb.edu; journals_marketing@cup.org

Journal presenting research in social and cultural history of the Middle East. Published in cooperation with the middle east studies assoc. of North America. **Founded:** 1970. **Freq:** Quarterly. **Print Method:** Offset. **Trim Size:** 6 3/4 x 10. **Cols./Page:** 1. **Col. Width:** 58 nonpareils. **Col. Depth:** 106 agate lines. **Key Personnel:** R. Stephen Humphreys, Editor. **ISSN:** 0020-7438. **Subscription Rates:** $142. **Remarks:** Accepts advertising.
Ad Rates: BW: $500 **Circ:** Paid ‡3456
Non-paid ‡29

3700 Islands
Islands Publishing Co.
PO Box 4728 Phone: (805)745-7100
Santa Barbara, CA 93140-4728 Fax: (805)745-7105
Free: (800)322-1161
Publisher E-mail: islands@islandsmag.com

Publication on islands of the world and traveling. **Subtitle:** An International Magazine. **Founded:** Oct. 1981. **Freq:** Bimonthly. **Print Method:** Offset. **Trim Size:** 8 3/8 x 10 1/2. **Cols./Page:** 3. **Col. Width:** 25 nonpareils. **Col. Depth:** 133 agate lines. **Key Personnel:** Joan Tapper, Editor-in-Chief, phone (805)745-7110, fax (805)745-7102, jtapper@islandsmag.com; William Kasch, Publisher, phone (805)745-1199, fax (805)745-7105, wkasch@islandsmag.com; Michelle Gamble, Dir., Advertising, phone (805)745-7150, fax (805)745-7105, mgamble@islandsmag.com; Rina Viray, Production Mgr., phone (805)745-7131, fax (805)745-7102, rviray@idslandsmag.com; Barry Service, Circulation Dir., phone (805)745-7140, fax (805)745-7105, bservice@islandsmag.com. **ISSN:** 0745-7847. **Subscription Rates:** $24.00 individuals; $4.95 single issue. **Remarks:** Accepts advertising.
Ad Rates: BW: $12,795 **Circ:** Paid ★**216,110**
4C: $15,995

3701 The Journal of Services Marketing
Journal of Services Marketing, Inc.
108 Loma Media Rd. Phone: (805)564-1313
Santa Barbara, CA 93103-2178 Fax: (805)504-8800

Academic journal edited for practitioners. **Founded:** 1987. **Freq:** Quarterly. **ISSN:** 0887-6045. **Subscription Rates:** $60; $95 Industry; $100 other countries. $25 single issue.

3702 The Lightbulb/Invent! Journal
Inventors Workshop International
1029 Castillo St. Phone: (805)962-5722
Santa Barbara, CA 93101-3736 Fax: (805)899-4927

Journal for inventors, product developers, and creative individuals. **Founded:** 1972. **Freq:** Bimonthly. **Print Method:** Offset. **Trim Size:** 8-1/2 x 11. **Subscription Rates:** $24.95 individuals; $5 single issue. **Remarks:** Accepts advertising.
Ad Rates: BW: $600 **Circ:** Combined 6,000

3703 Photographer's Forum
Serbin Communications, Inc.
511 Olive St. Phone: (805)963-0439
Santa Barbara, CA 93101-1609 Fax: (805)965-0496

Photography magazine including profiles and consumer news for instructors and college photography students. **Founded:** 1977. **Freq:** Quarterly. **Print Method:** Offset. **Cols./Page:** 3. **Col. Width:** 27 nonpareils. **Col. Depth:** 140 agate lines. **Key Personnel:** Glen Serbin, Publisher; Jules Wartell, Advertising Mgr. **Subscription Rates:** $12 individuals. **Remarks:** Accepts advertising.
Ad Rates: BW: $1,760 **Circ:** ‡12,000
4C: $2,985

3704 Physics of Fluids
American Institute of Physics (AIP)
Editorial Office, Physics of Fluids Phone: (805)893-3200
Department of Chemical Engineering Fax: (805)893-5458
University of California
Santa Barbara, CA 93106
Publication E-mail: pof@engineering.ucsb.edu
Publisher E-mail: subs@aip.org

Journal focusing on fluid dynamics. **Founded:** 1958. **Freq:** Monthly. **Print Method:** Offset. **Trim Size:** 8 1/4 x 11 1/4. **Cols./Page:** 2. **Col. Width:** 41 nonpareils. **Col. Depth:** 138 agate lines. **Key Personnel:** Prof. Gary Leal, Editor, phone (805)893-3200, fax (805)893-5458; Prof. John Kim, Editor, phone (310)794-5576, fax (310)794-5599; Bonnie Alexander, Contact, phone (805)893-3200, fax (805)893-3200. **ISSN:** 0899-8213. **Subscription Rates:** $1,340. **Remarks:** Advertising accepted; rates available upon request. **Alt. Formats:** Microfiche. **Formerly:** Physics of Fluids A.
Circ: (Not Reported)

3705 Resorts & Great Hotels
Islands Publishing Co.
PO Box 4728 Phone: (805)745-7100
Santa Barbara, CA 93140-4728 Fax: (805)745-7105
Free: (800)322-1161
Publisher E-mail: islands@islandsmag.com

Magazine covering great resorts and hotels. **Subtitle:** The Connoisseur's Guide to the World's Best. **Founded:** Sept. 1987. **Freq:** Annual. **Key Personnel:** Dan Fox, Publisher; Annette Burden, Editor; Kelly Foy, Associate Editor; Shoshana Levy, Operations Mgr.; Mindy Sofro, Operations Mgr. **Subscription Rates:** $15 individuals. **Remarks:** Accepts advertising. **URL:** http://www.resortsandgreathotels.com. **Alt. Formats:** CD-ROM.
Ad Rates: 4C: $11,900 **Circ:** Paid ‡190,000

3706 Santa Barbara Independent
1221 State St., No. 200 Phone: (805)965-5205
Santa Barbara, CA 93101-2616 Fax: (805)965-5518
Publication E-mail: edit@indy.com; admin@indy.com

Community newspaper. **Founded:** 1986. **Freq:** Weekly (Thurs.). **Print Method:** Offset. **Trim Size:** 11 x 14. **Cols./Page:** 5. **Col. Width:** 11 picas. **Col. Depth:** 13 1/8 inches. **Key Personnel:** Marianne Partridge, Editor; George Thurlow, Publisher. **Subscription Rates:** $88 individuals per year. **Remarks:** Accepts advertising.
Ad Rates: BW: $1,283 **Circ:** Paid 23
4C: $1,933 Free 39,110
PCI: $15.50

3707 Santa Barbara News-Press
715 Anacapa St. Phone: (805)564-5200
PO Box 1359 Fax: (805)966-6258
Santa Barbara, CA 93102-1359
Publication E-mail: news@sbcoast.com

General newspaper. **Founded:** 1855. **Freq:** Mon.-Sun. (morn.). **Print Method:** Offset. **Cols./Page:** 6. **Col. Width:** 25 nonpareils. **Col. Depth:** 301 agate lines. **Key Personnel:** Allen Parsons, Editor; Steve Ainsley, Publisher; Tom Bolton, Managing Editor. **Subscription Rates:** $96 individuals. **Remarks:** Accepts advertising. **Available Online. URL:** http://www.sbcoast.com. **Feature Editors:** Melinda Johnson, *Book*, phone (805)564-5200.
Ad Rates: SAU: $19.82 **Circ:** Mon.-Sat. ★**44,956**
Sun. ★**50,000**

3708 Santa Barbara Review
104 La Vereda Ln.
Santa Barbara, CA 93108

Literary arts journal. **Subtitle:** Poetry, Fiction, Essays, Art, Book Reviews. **Founded:** 1993. **Freq:** Annual. **Print Method:** Offset. **Trim Size:** 6 x 9. **Cols./Page:** 2. **Key Personnel:** James T. Aeby, Managing Editor, jtaeby@west.net. **ISSN:** 1068-8617. **Subscription Rates:** $10 individuals; $10 single issue. **Remarks:** Accepts advertising.
Ad Rates: BW: $90 **Circ:** (Not Reported)

3709 Short Fuse
PO Box 90436
Santa Barbara, CA 93190

Literary magazine. **Founded:** 1983. **Freq:** 6/year. **Subscription Rates:** $9 individuals; Free Institutionalized persons; $1 single issue. **Remarks:** Advertising not accepted.
Circ: Combined 500

3710 The Veliger
California Malacozoological Society, Inc.
Santa Barbara Museum of Natural History Phone: (805)682-4711
Fax: (805)963-9679
2559 Puesta del Sol Rd.
Santa Barbara, CA 93105
Natural history magazine focusing on the various aspects of malacology (study of mollusks). **Founded:** 1957. **Freq:** Quarterly (Jan., April, July, Oct.). **Print Method:** Offset. **Trim Size:** 8 1/2 x 11. **Cols./Page:** 2. **Col. Width:** 42 nonpareils. **Col. Depth:** 112 agate lines. **Key Personnel:** Henry W. Chaney, Secretary; Barry Roth, Editor. **ISSN:** 0042-3211. **Subscription Rates:** $32 individuals; $38 Canada and Mexico; $44 other countries; $60 institutions; $66 Canada and Mexico Industry; $72 institutions other countries. **Remarks:** Advertising not accepted.
Circ: Paid ‡640
Non-paid ‡10

3711 KCSB-FM - 91.9
UCEN Rm. 3185 A Phone: (805)893-3757
Santa Barbara, CA 93106

Format: Alternative/New Music/Progressive; Eclectic. **Networks:** ABC; Pacific Mountain. **Owner:** Regents of the University of California, at above address. **Founded:** 1964. **Operating Hours:** Continuous. **ADI:** Santa Barbara-Santa Maria-San Luis Obispo,CA. **Key Personnel:** Elizabeth Robinson, Contact; Tom Archambault, Contact. **Local Programs:** *Cross Currents*, Chrystal Griffith; *Green Steward*, Phil LeVasseur; *Viewpoints*, Elizabeth Robinson. **Wattage:** 640. **Ad Rates:** Noncommercial.

3712 KDB - 93.7
23 W. Micheltorena Phone: (805)966-4131
Santa Barbara, CA 93101 Fax: (805)966-4788
E-mail: kdb@kdb.com

Format: Classical. **Networks:** Independent. **Founded:** 1926. **Formerly:** KDB-FM (1990). **Operating Hours:** Continuous. **Key Personnel:** R.C. Scott, Vice President. **Wattage:** 12,500. **Ad Rates:** $27-39 per unit.

3713 KEYT-TV - 3
730 Miramonte Dr. Phone: (805)882-3933
Santa Barbara, CA 93102 Fax: (805)882-3934
E-mail: keyt@aol.com

Format: Commercial TV. **Networks:** ABC. **Founded:** 1953. **Operating Hours:** Continuous; 60% network, 40% local. **ADI:** Santa Barbara-Santa Maria-San Luis Obispo,CA. **Key Personnel:** Byron Elton, General Mgr.; Bill Sally, Contact; Renee Foley, Program Dir.; Amy Feller, News Dir.; Don Katich, Production Mgr.; Pat Garrett, Chief Engineer; Jeff Martin, Promotions Mgr.; Mark Keenan, Business Mgr.

3714 KFAC-FM - 88.7
Box 77913 Phone: (213)514-1400
Los Angeles, CA 90007-0913 Fax: (213)747-9400
E-mail: kusc@kusc.org

Format: Classical; Public Radio. **Networks:** National Public Radio (NPR); Public Radio International (PRI). **Owner:** University of Southern California, at above address. **Founded:** 1985. **Operating Hours:** Continuous. **ADI:** Santa Barbara-Santa Maria-San Luis Obispo,CA. **Key Personnel:** Brenda Pennell, General Mgr., phone (213)514-1450, bpennell@kusc.org; James Russell, GM/Market Place Prod., phone (213)514-1500, fax (213)514-1506, jrussell@marketplace.org; Sheila Rue, phone (213)514-1430, srue@kusc.org. **Local Programs:** *Afternoon Music*, Steve Lama; *Marketplace*, David Brancaccio, (213)743-6555, Fax (213)747-0684; *The Morning Program*, Steve Lama; *Music 'til Midnight*, Jim Svejda. **Wattage:** 12,000. **Ad Rates:** Noncommercial. **URL:** http://www.kusc.org.

3715 KIST-AM - 1340
414 E. Cota St. Phone: (805)962-7800
Santa Barbara, CA 93101 Fax: (805)965-6001

Format: Oldies. **Founded:** 1946. **Operating Hours:** Continuous. **ADI:** Santa Barbara-Santa Maria-San Luis Obispo,CA. **Key Personnel:** Traci Claussen, Sales Mgr.; Tom Van Sant, PD; Mike Nicassio, Station Mgr. **Wattage:** 1000. **Ad Rates:** $25-40 for 30 seconds; $70-50 for 60 seconds. $10.40-$40 for 30 seconds; $13-$50 for 60 seconds. Combined advertising rates available with KMGQ-FM.

KLEI-AM - See Kailua, Hawaii

3716 KMGQ-FM - 106.3
414 East Cota St. Phone: (805)962-7800
Santa Barbara, CA 93101 Fax: (805)965-6001

Format: Adult Contemporary. **Founded:** 1982. **Operating Hours:** Continuous. **ADI:** Santa Barbara-Santa Maria-San Luis Obispo,CA. **Key Personnel:** Traci Claussen, Sales Mgr.; Vince Garcia, Program Dir.; Mike Nicassio, Station Mgr. **Local Programs:** *Abby & Mark* 6 a.m.-10 a.m.; *Mark Deanda* 10 a.m.-3 p.m.; *The Rendezvous Jazz Program* 7 p.m.-12 a.m. **Wattage:** 365. **Ad Rates:** $30-50 for 30 seconds; $50-90 for 60 seconds. $18.40-$54.40 for 30 seconds; $23-$68 for 60 seconds. Combined advertising rates available with KIST-AM.

3717 KQSB-AM - 990
414 East Cota St.
Santa Barbara, CA 93101
E-mail: info@amfm.com

Format: Talk; News. **Networks:** CNN Radio; Westwood One Radio. **Founded:** 1972. **Formerly:** KBBQ-AM (Oct. 1991); KTVN-AM (Feb. 1992); KSSM-AM (Nov. 1992). **Operating Hours:** Continuous. **ADI:** Santa Barbara-Santa Maria-San Luis Obispo,CA. **Key Personnel:** Jennifer VanDonge, General Sales Mgr.; Jim Watkins, Program Dir.; Paul Cavanagh, Operations Mgr., pcavanagh@jacor.com; David Hefferman, Promotions and Marketing Dir. **Wattage:** 5,000 day, 500 night.

3718 KSBL-FM - 101.7
414 East Cota St.
Santa Barbara, CA 93101
E-mail: info@amfm.com

Format: Adult Contemporary. **Founded:** 1981. **Formerly:** KLIT-FM. **Operating Hours:** Continuous. **ADI:** Santa Barbara-Santa Maria-San Luis Obispo,CA. **Key Personnel:** Jennifer VanDonge, General Sales Mgr.; Paul Cavanagh, Operations Mgr.; David Hefferman, Promotions and Marketing Dir.; Peter Bie, Program Dir. **Wattage:** 3100.

3719 KSPE-FM - 94.5
331 N. Milpas St. Ste. F Phone: (805)965-1490
Santa Barbara, CA 93103-3203 Fax: (805)966-7875

Format: Hispanic. **Founded:** 1989. **Formerly:** KCQR-FM. **Operating Hours:** Continuous. **ADI:** Santa Barbara-Santa Maria-San Luis Obispo,CA. **Key Personnel:** Richard Marsh, General Mgr.; James Farr, Sales Mgr.; Gerardo Lorenz, Program Dir.

3720 KTYD-FM - 99.9
414 East Cota St.
Santa Barbara, CA 93101
E-mail: info@amfm.com

Format: Classic Rock. **Networks:** Independent. **Founded:** 1972. **Operating Hours:** Continuous; 100% local. **ADI:** Santa Barbara-Santa Maria-San Luis Obispo,CA. **Key Personnel:** Jennifer VanDonge, General Sales Mgr.; Paul Cavanagh, Operations Mgr., pcavanagh@jacor.com; David Hefferman, Promotions and Marketing Dir. **Local Programs:** *Fear of Music*, Fear (Phil) Heiple; *The Jim Watkins Show*, Jim Watkins. **Wattage:** 34,000. **Ad Rates:** .

SANTA CLARA, pop. 87,746.

Santa Clara Co. (W). 3 m NW of San Jose. University of Santa Clara. Fruit packing, canning and drying. Sashes and doors, electronics, fiberglass, pottery, dairy products manufactured. Fruit farms. Apricots, prunes, pears, walnuts.

3721 CONNECT
3Com Corp.
5400 Bayfront Plaza Phone: (408)764-5000
Santa Clara, CA 95052-8145 Fax: (408)764-5001
Free: (800)NET-3CON

Subtitle: The Journal of Computer Networking. **Founded:** 1987. **Freq:** Quarterly. **Print Method:** Web offset. **Trim Size:** 8 3/8 x 10 7/8. **Cols./Page:** 3. **Key Personnel:** Suzanne Reed, Editor. **Subscription Rates:** $6 single issue. **Remarks:** Accepts advertising. **URL:** http://www.3com.//gg.
Ad Rates: BW: $5,700 **Circ:** Paid 110
4C: $1,000 Non-paid 52,637

3722 High Technology Careers Magazine
HTC
4701 Patrick Henry Dr., No. 1901 Phone: (408)970-8800
Fax: (408)980-5103
Santa Clara, CA 95054
Publisher E-mail: htc@vjf.com

Magazine (tabloid) containing employment opportunity information for the engineering and technical community. **Founded:** 1982. **Freq:** Monthly. **Print Method:** Web press. **Trim Size:** 11 x 13. **Cols./Page:** 4. **Col. Width:** 14 picas. **Col. Depth:** 10 inches. **Key Personnel:** Paul J. Burrowes, Publisher, burrowes@vjf.com. **ISSN:** 0749-2960. **Subscription Rates:** $43; Free; $3.50. **Remarks:** Accepts advertising. **URL:** http://www.vjf.com; http://www.hightechcareers.com.
Ad Rates: BW: $6,975 **Circ:** Non-paid ‡166,500
4C: $7,875
PCI: $3,800

3723 Kung Fu/Qigong
Pacific Rim Publishing, Inc.
PO Box 4657 Phone: (408)727-8989
Santa Clara, CA 95056 Fax: (408)727-9107
Free: (800)604-3332
Publication E-mail: tcmedia@aimnet.aimnet.com

Magazine featuring ancient Chinese holistic exercise for the body, mind, and breath. **Founded:** May 1992. **Freq:** Bimonthly. **Trim Size:** 8 x 10.875. **Key Personnel:** Gigi Oh, Publisher. **ISSN:** 1050-2173. **Subscription Rates:** $15; $3.50 single issue. **Remarks:** Accepts advertising. **URL:** http://www.tcmedia.com.
Ad Rates: BW: $800 **Circ:** Non-paid 70000
4C: $1300

3724 Potpourri
Potpourri Shoppers, Inc.
1350 Duane Ave. Phone: (408)562-9482
Santa Clara, CA 95054 Fax: (408)986-5350
Free: (800)479-4795
Publisher E-mail: info@potpourri.com

Shopper distributed in three San Francisco Bay area counties. **Founded:** July 7, 1970. **Freq:** Weekly (Wed.). **Print Method:** Offset. **Trim Size:** 11 1/4 x 12. **Cols./Page:** 6. **Col. Width:** 1 5/8 inches. **Col. Depth:** 11 inches. **Key Personnel:** Loren G. Dalton, President, phone (408)562-9480, fax (408)562-9474; Doug Thompsonn, CFO, phone (408)562-9446; John Frahm, Dir. of Ops., phone (408)562-9484; Howard Young, Dir. of Sales, phone (408)562-9486, fax (408)562-9487; Paul Corsaro, Dir. of Major Accts., phone (408)362-9487. **Subscription Rates:** Free. **Remarks:** Advertising accepted; rates available upon request. **Available Online.** **URL:** http://www.potpourri.com.
Circ: Free ‡1,100,000

3725 The Santa Clara
Santa Clara University
Box 3190 Phone: (408)554-4445
Santa Clara, CA 95053 Fax: (408)554-4673
Publication E-mail: dblanar@scuacc.scu.edu

University and alumni newspaper. **Founded:** 1922. **Freq:** Weekly (Thurs.). **Print Method:** Offset. **Trim Size:** 40. **Cols./Page:** 5. **Col. Width:** 18 nonpareils. **Col. Depth:** 224 agate lines. **Key Personnel:** Gordon Young, Adviser, phone (408)594-1890, gyoung@scn.edu; J. Lyons, Editor, jlyons@scn.edu. **Subscription Rates:** Free; $40 by mail. **Remarks:** Accepts advertising. **URL:** http://www-tsc.scu.edu.
Ad Rates: GLR: $8 **Circ:** Free ‡4,000
4C: $700
PCI: $6.80

3726 Santa Clara Computer and High Technology Law Journal
Santa Clara University School of Law
Santa Clara, CA 95053

Scholarly journal covering legal issues in high technology. **Founded:** 1984. **Freq:** Semiannual. **Subscription Rates:** $45 individuals; $25 single issue. **Remarks:** Advertising not accepted. **Online:** LEXIS-NEXIS; Westlaw. **URL:** http://www.techlaw.scu.edu.
Circ: Paid 463

3727 Santa Clara Law Review
Santa Clara University School of Law
Santa Clara, CA 95053

Professional legal journal. **Freq:** Quarterly. **Subscription Rates:** $40 individuals; $15 single issue. **Remarks:** Advertising not accepted.
Circ: (Not Reported)

3728 The Valley Catholic Newspaper
Roman Catholic Diocese of San Jose
900 Lafayette St., Ste. 301 Phone: (408)983-0260
Santa Clara, CA 95050-4966 Fax: (408)983-0268
Publication E-mail: valleycatholic@dsj.org

Newspaper for Catholics in Santa Clara County. **Founded:** 1982. **Freq:** Monthly (except July). **Print Method:** Offset. **Trim Size:** 10 1/4 x 12 1/2. **Cols./Page:** 5. **Col. Width:** 11 picas. **Col. Depth:** 177 agate lines. **Key Personnel:** Roberta M. Ward, Editor, ward@dsj.org; Most Rev. Pierre DuMaine, Bishop, Publisher, dumaine@dsg.org. **ISSN:** 8750-6238. **Subscription Rates:** $15 individuals; $16 out of area out of county. **Remarks:** Accepts advertising. **URL:** http://www.dsj.org/vc/valley.htm.
Ad Rates: BW: $382 **Circ:** Paid 25,189
4C: $814 Free 1,116
PCI: $20

3729 KSCU-FM - 103.3
500 El Camino Real - 3207 Phone: (408)554-4413
Santa Clara University
Santa Clara, CA 95053-3207

Format: Alternative/New Music/Progressive; Rap; Jazz; Blues. **Networks:** Independent. **Owner:** Santa Clara University, at above address. **Founded:** June 1966. **Operating Hours:** Connecticut. **Key Personnel:** Keith Schieron, General Mgr., phone (408)554-4414; Alison Lacy, Human Resources Dir., phone (408)551-1874; Kristi Martinez, Business Mgr., phone (408)551-1866; Steve Rubin, Chief Engineer, phone (408)551-1869; Yvonne Chen, Co-Music Dir., phone (408)554-4907; Alan Salmassian, Co-Music Dir., phone (408)554-4907. **Wattage:** 30. **Ad Rates:** $20-35 per unit.

SANTA CLARITA

3730 Black Belt Magazine
Rainbow Publications, Inc.
24715 Rockefeller Phone: (805)257-4066
PO Box 918 Fax: (805)257-3028
Santa Clarita, CA 91355
Free: (800)423-2874
Publisher E-mail: rainbow@rsabbs.com

Self-defense magazine featuring various martial arts, including how-to's, historical and current events in the martial arts. Audience ranges from pre-teens to 50's. **Founded:** Apr. 1961. **Freq:** Monthly. **Print Method:** Offset. **Trim Size:** 8 x 10 7/8. **Cols./Page:** 3. **Col. Width:** 13.5 picas. **Col. Depth:** 10 inches. **Key Personnel:** Jim Coleman, Editor; Michael James, Publisher; Barbara Lessard, Advertising Mgr. **ISSN:** 0277-3066. **Subscription Rates:** $28 individuals; $3.50 single issue; $4 single issue Canada. **Remarks:** Accepts advertising.
Ad Rates: BW: $1,521 **Circ:** ‡105,000
4C: $2,121

3731 The Flutist Quarterly
National Flute Association
c/o Myrna Brown Phone: (805)297-5287
PO Box 800597 Fax: (805)297-0753
Santa Clarita, CA 91380-0597
Official magazine of the National Flute Association covering the activities of professional flutists. Includes interviews and concert reviews. **Founded:** 1974. **Freq:** Quarterly. **Print Method:** Offset. **Trim Size:** 8 1/2 x 11. **Cols./Page:** 2. **Col. Width:** 3 3/8 inches. **Col. Depth:** 9 3/8 inches. **Key Personnel:** Glennis M. Stout, Editor, phone (313)668-6021; Victoria Jicha, Advertising Mgr., phone (708)835-5266. **ISSN:** 8756-8667. **Subscription Rates:** $25 includes membership; $15 students; $55 associate members. **Remarks:** Accepts advertising. **Formerly:** Newsletter of the National Flute Association (1984).
Ad Rates: BW: $275 **Circ:** ‡4,500

3732 MA Training
Rainbow Publications, Inc.
24715 Rockefeller Phone: (805)257-4066
PO Box 918 Fax: (805)257-3028
Santa Clarita, CA 91355
Free: (800)423-2874
Publisher E-mail: rainbow@rsabbs.com

Martial arts magazine. **Subtitle:** Martial Arts Training. **Founded:** June 1987. **Freq:** Bimonthly. **Print Method:** web offset. **Trim Size:** 8 x 10 7/8. **Cols./Page:** 3. **Col. Width:** 13 1/2 picas. **Col. Depth:** 10 inches. **Key Personnel:** Michael James, Publisher. **ISSN:** 0898-4786. **Subscription Rates:** $19.50; $2.95 single issue. **Remarks:** Accepts advertising. **Online:** Black Belt. **Formerly:** MA Weapons.
Ad Rates: BW: $900 **Circ:** Paid 35,000
4C: $1,300

3733 The Signal
Morris Newspapers, Inc.
PO Box 801870 Phone: (805)259-1234
Santa Clarita, CA 91380-1870 Fax: (805)254-8068
Publication E-mail: 24will@smartlink.net

General newspaper. **Founded:** 1919. **Freq:** Daily Tues.-Sun. (morn.). **Print Method:** Offset. **Trim Size:** 13 x 21 1/4. **Cols./Page:** 6. **Col. Width:** 2 1/16 inches. **Col. Depth:** 21 1/4 inches. **Key Personnel:** William H. Fleet, Publisher. **Subscription Rates:** $97.50 individuals annually. **Remarks:** Accepts advertising. **URL:** http://the-signal.com.
Ad Rates: GLR: $23.22 **Circ:** Combined 11,892
BW: $2,961.14
4C: $3,611.14
PCI: $21.91

3734 Unsearchable Riches
Concordant Publishing Concern, Inc.
15570 Knochaven Rd. Phone: (661)252-2112
Santa Clarita, CA 91350 Fax: (661)298-2758

Magazine presenting exposition of scripture, both Old and New Testaments. **Founded:** 1909. **Freq:** Bimonthly. **Print Method:** Offset. **Trim Size:** 5 x 7 1/2. **Cols./Page:** 1. **Col. Width:** 48 nonpareils. **Col. Depth:** 81 agate lines. **Key Personnel:** Dean Hough, Editor. **ISSN:** 0042-0476. **Subscription Rates:** $1 individuals. **Remarks:** Advertising not accepted.
Circ: ‡2,000

SANTA CRUZ†, pop. 41,483.

Santa Cruz Co. (W). On Pacific Ocean and Monterey Bay, 74 m S of San Francisco. University of California at Santa Cruz. Resort. Manufactures electronics, lime, wire, chewing gum, feed, redwood novelties, lumber. Fruits, vegetables, bulbs, fish packed. Nurseries. hatcheries, wineries. Limestone quarries. redwood timber. Fisheries. Agriculture. Artichokes, blueberries, apples, plums, grapes.

3735 Capitalism, Nature, Socialism
Guilford Publications, Inc.
c/o James O'Connor, Ph.D.
PO Box 8467
Santa Cruz, CA 95062
Publisher E-mail: info@guilford.com

Political journal. **Freq:** Quarterly. **Trim Size:** 6 x 9. **Key Personnel:** James O'Connor, Ph.D., Editor; Barbara Laurence, Managing Editor; Susan Pauliscat, Advertising, phone (212)431-9800. **ISSN:** 1045-5752. **Subscription Rates:** $27.50 individuals. **Remarks:** Accepts advertising.
Circ: Combined ‡1,983

3736 City on a Hill
City on a Hill Press
University of California Santa Cruz Phone: (831)459-4350
Fax: (831)459-4696
1156 High St.
Santa Cruz, CA 95064
Collegiate newspaper. **Founded:** 1966. **Freq:** Weekly (Thurs.). **Print Method:** Offset. **Cols./Page:** 5. **Col. Width:** 18 nonpareils. **Col. Depth:** 182 agate lines. **Key Personnel:** Nate Huff, phone (831)459-2430, natehyf@cats.ucsc.edu; Rafi Frankel, rasky@cats.ucsc.edu. **Subscription Rates:** $15 individuals. **Remarks:** Accepts advertising. **URL:** http://www.slugwire.org.
Ad Rates: GLR: $.55 **Circ:** Paid ‡500
BW: $557 Free ‡12,000
4C: $717
PCI: $13

3737 Highway 17 Almanack & Gazetteer
PO Box 3602 Phone: (831)479-3675
Santa Cruz, CA 95063-3602 Fax: (408)924-3229
Publication E-mail: hiway172lmanack@hotmail.com
Publisher E-mail: cogitator@hotmail.com

Almanac. **Founded:** 1992. **Freq:** 2/year. **Print Method:** Offset. **Trim Size:** 5 1/2 x 8 1/2. **Cols./Page:** 1. **Col. Width:** 4 1/2 inches. **Col. Depth:** 7 1/2 inches. **Key Personnel:** R.V. Leonard, Editor, rvleonard@hotmail.com; Harvey Gotliffe, Publisher, effitog@hotmail.com. **ISSN:** 1054-4585. **Subscription Rates:** $3.50 single issue. **Remarks:** Accepts advertising.
Ad Rates: BW: $400 **Circ:** Paid 3,500
Non-paid 1,500

3738 Judaism
American Jewish Congress
Kresge College
University of California
Santa Cruz, CA 95064
Publication E-mail: judaism@cats.ucsc.edu

Magazine dedicated to the creative discussion and exposition of the religious, moral, and philosophical concepts of Judaism and their relevance to the problems of modern society. **Subtitle:** A Quarterly Journal of Jewish Life and Thought. **Founded:** Jan. 1952. **Freq:** Quarterly. **Print Method:** Offset. Uses mats. **Trim Size:** 6 1/2 x 9 1/2. **Cols./Page:** 2 and 1. **Col. Width:** 30 and 54 nonpareils. **Col. Depth:** 108 agate lines. **Key Personnel:** Murray Baumgarten, Editor, phone (408)459-2586, fax (408)459-4424, judaism@cats.ucsc.edu. **ISSN:** 0022-5762. **Subscription Rates:** $20 individuals; $22 other countries; $6 single issue; $35 institutions; $10 single issue. **Remarks:** Accepts advertising. **Alt. Formats:** Microfilm; Microform.
Ad Rates: BW: $250 **Circ:** ‡5,500

3739 Santa Cruz County Sentinel
Santa Cruz Sentinel Publishers Co.
PO Box 638 Phone: (408)423-4242
Santa Cruz, CA 95061 Fax: (408)423-1154

Independent newspaper. **Founded:** June 14, 1856. **Freq:** Daily and Sunday (morn.). **Print Method:** Offset. **Cols./Page:** 6. **Col. Width:** 25 nonpareils. **Col. Depth:** 301 agate lines. **Key Personnel:** Tom Honig, Editor; Dave Regan, Publisher; Dorothy McCoy, Retail Mgr.; Karen Carnot, Advertising Dir. **Subscription Rates:** $126 individuals. **Remarks:** Accepts advertising. **Formerly:** Santa Cruz Sentinel.
Ad Rates: GLR: $1.44 **Circ:** Mon.-Sat. ★**27,620**
BW: $2,322 Sun. ★**30,158**
4C: $2,723
SAU: $18

3740 Stone Soup
Children's Art Foundation, Inc.
PO Box 83 Phone: (831)426-5557
Santa Cruz, CA 95063 Fax: (831)426-1161
Free: (800)447-4569
Publisher E-mail: editor@stonesoup.com

Literary magazine for children ages 8-14 years. **Subtitle:** The Magazine by Young Writers and Artists. **Founded:** May 1973. **Freq:** Bimonthly. **Print Method:** Offset. **Trim Size:** 7 x 10. **Cols./Page:** 2. **Col. Width:** 3 inches. **Col. Depth:** 8 inches. **Key Personnel:** Gerry Mandel, Editor; Laurie Gabriel, Fulfillment, lgabriel@cruznet.com. **ISSN:** 0094-579X. **Subscription Rates:** $32 individuals; $5.50 single issue. **Remarks:** Accepts advertising.
Ad Rates: BW: $500 **Circ:** Combined 19,000

3741 KSCO-AM - 1080
2300 Portola Dr. Phone: (408)475-1080
Santa Cruz, CA 95062 Fax: (408)475-2967

Format: News; Talk. **Networks:** AP. **Owner:** Michael Zwerling, at above address. **Founded:** 1947. **Formerly:** KSCO-AM (1988). **Operating Hours:** Continuous. **Key Personnel:** Michael Olson, General Mgr.; Don Husing, Contact; Michael Zwerling, Owner; Don Husing, Operations Mgr.; Rosemary Chalmers, Program Dir. **Local Programs:** *Eric Schoeck* 2-4 p.m., Rosemary Chalmers; *Good Afternoon Mont. Bay* 4-6 p.m., Paul Allen. **Wattage:** 10,000. **Ad Rates:** $25 for 30 seconds; $30 for 60 seconds. **URL:** http://www.ksco.com.

3742 KUSP-FM - 88.9
PO Box 423 Phone: (831)476-2800
203 8th Ave. Free: (800)695-5877
Santa Cruz, CA 95061
E-mail: kusp@kusp.org

Format: Public Radio; Full Service. **Networks:** National Public Radio (NPR). **Owner:** Pataphysical Broadcasting Foundation, at above address. **Founded:** 1972. **Operating Hours:** Continuous; 25% network, 75% local. **Key Personnel:** Peter Troxell, Station Mgr.; Johnny Simmons, Music Dir.; Larry Blood, Production Dir.; Barbara Diamond, Member Services; Dale Owen, Underwriting Dir.; Ray Price, Programming; Cherie Maitland, Bookkeeper; Stephen Slade, Develoment Director. **Local Programs:** *Prime Time*; *Radio Gram* 12:00 pm - 1:00 pm Monday, Eric Schoeck, Mailing contact; *State of the Arts* 12:00 pm - 1:00 pm Wednesday, Matt Howard; *Talk of the Bay* 6:30 pm Monday-Friday, Ray Price. **Wattage:** 1,200. **Ad Rates:** $18-28 per unit. **URL:** http://www.kusp.org.

SANTA FE SPRINGS, pop. 14,559.

Los Angeles Co. (S). 15 m SE of Los Angeles. Manufactures oil well tools and machinery, automotive equipment, chemicals, gas compressors. Oil refinery. Oil wells. Diversified farming.

3743 Asian Sources Computer Products
Asian Sources
10330 Pioneer Blvd., No. 240 Phone: (562)906-2320
PO Box 2118 Fax: (562)906-2420
Santa Fe Springs, CA 90670-8286
Publisher E-mail: service@asiansources.com

Trade magazine covering Asian sources of computer products and news. **Freq:** Monthly. **Print Method:** Web. **Trim Size:** 8 1/16 x 10 5/8. **Cols./Page:** 2. **Key Personnel:** Jonathan Bigelow, General Mgr., phone (562)946-6089, fax (562)944-9478; Dianna Corriero, Circulation Mgr., phone (562)906-2320, fax (562)906-2420. **Remarks:** Accepts advertising. **URL:** http://www.asiansources.com. **Absorbed:** Asian Sources Multimedia Products.
Circ: (Not Reported)

3744 Asian Sources Electronic Components
Asian Sources
10330 Pioneer Blvd., No. 240 Phone: (562)906-2320
PO Box 2118 Fax: (562)906-2420
Santa Fe Springs, CA 90670-8286
Publisher E-mail: service@asiansources.com

Trade magazine covering Asian sources of electronic components and news. **Freq:** Monthly. **Print Method:** Web. **Trim Size:** 8 1/16 x 10 5/8. **Cols./Page:** 2. **Key Personnel:** Jonathan Bigelow, General Mgr., phone (562)946-6089, fax (562)944-9478; Dianna Corriero, U.S. Line Mgr. **Subscription Rates:** $75 individuals; $20 single issue. **Remarks:** Accepts advertising. **URL:** http://www.asiansources.com. **Alt. Formats:** CD-ROM.
Circ: (Not Reported)

3745 Asian Sources Electronics
Asian Sources
10330 Pioneer Blvd., No. 240 Phone: (562)906-2320
PO Box 2118 Fax: (562)906-2420
Santa Fe Springs, CA 90670-8286
Publisher E-mail: service@asiansources.com

Trade magazine covering Asian sources of electronic news and products. **Freq:** Monthly. **Print Method:** Web. **Trim Size:** 8 1/16 x 10 5/8. **Cols./Page:** 2. **Key Personnel:** Jonathan Bigelow, General Mgr., phone (562)946-6089, fax (562)944-9478; Dianna Corriero, Circulation Mgr., phone (562)906-2320, fax (562)906-2420. **Subscription Rates:** $75 individuals; $20 single issue. **Remarks:** Accepts advertising. **URL:** http://www.asiansources.com. **Alt. Formats:** CD-ROM.
Circ: (Not Reported)

3746 Asian Sources Fashion Accessories & Supplies
Asian Sources
10330 Pioneer Blvd., No. 240 Phone: (562)906-2320
PO Box 2118 Fax: (562)906-2420
Santa Fe Springs, CA 90670-8286
Publisher E-mail: service@asiansources.com

Trade magazine covering Asian sources of fashion accessories, fabric, and manufacturing supplies and news. **Freq:** Monthly. **Print Method:** Web. **Trim Size:** 8 1/10 x 10 5/8. **Cols./Page:** 2. **Key Personnel:** Jonathan Bigelow, General Mgr., phone (562)946-6089, fax (562)944-9478; Dianna Corriero, Circulation Mgr., phone (562)906-2320, fax (562)906-2420. **Subscription Rates:** $75 individuals; $20 single issue. **Remarks:** Accepts advertising. **URL:** http://www.asiansources.com. **Alt. Formats:** CD-ROM.
Circ: (Not Reported)

3747 Asian Sources Gifts & Home Products
Asian Sources
10330 Pioneer Blvd., No. 240 Phone: (562)906-2320
PO Box 2118 Fax: (562)906-2420
Santa Fe Springs, CA 90670-8286
Publisher E-mail: service@asiansources.com

Trade magazine covering Asian sources of home products and gift items. **Freq:** Monthly. **Print Method:** Web. **Trim Size:** 8 1/16 x 10 5/8. **Cols./Page:** 2. **Key Personnel:** Jonathan Bigelow, General Mgr., phone (562)946-6089, fax (562)944-9478; Dianna Corriero, phone (562)906-2320, fax (562)906-2420. **Subscription Rates:** $75 individuals; $20 single issue. **Remarks:** Accepts advertising. **URL:** http://www.asiansources.com. **Alt. Formats:** CD-ROM.
Circ: (Not Reported)

3748 Asian Sources Hardwares
Asian Sources
10330 Pioneer Blvd., No. 240 Phone: (562)906-2320
PO Box 2118 Fax: (562)906-2420
Santa Fe Springs, CA 90670-8286
Publisher E-mail: service@asiansources.com

Trade magazine covering Asian sources of hardware products and news. **Freq:** Monthly. **Print Method:** Web. **Trim Size:** 8 1/16 x 10 5/8. **Cols./Page:** 2. **Key Personnel:** Jonathan Bigelow, General Mgr., phone (562)946-6089, fax (562)944-9478; Dianna Corriero, Circulation Mgr., phone (562)906-2320, fax (562)906-2420. **Subscription Rates:** $75 individuals; $20 single issue. **Remarks:** Accepts advertising. **URL:** http://www.asiansources.com.
Circ: (Not Reported)

3749 Asian Sources Telecom Sources
Asian Sources
10330 Pioneer Blvd., No. 240 Phone: (562)906-2320
PO Box 2118 Fax: (562)906-2420
Santa Fe Springs, CA 90670-8286
Publisher E-mail: service@asiansources.com

Trade magazine covering Asian sources of telecommunications products and news. **Freq:** Monthly. **Print Method:** Web. **Trim Size:** 8 1/16 x 10 5/8. **Cols./Page:** 2. **Key Personnel:** Jonathan Bigelow, General Mgr., phone (562)946-6089, fax (562)944-9478; Dianna Corriero, Circulation Mgr., phone (562)906-2320, fax (562)906-2420. **Subscription Rates:** $65 individuals; $20 single issue. **Remarks:** Accepts advertising. **URL:** http://www.asiansources.com.
Circ: (Not Reported)

3750 Asian Sources Timepieces
Asian Sources
10330 Pioneer Blvd., No. 240 Phone: (562)906-2320
PO Box 2118 Fax: (562)906-2420
Santa Fe Springs, CA 90670-8286
Publisher E-mail: service@asiansources.com

Trade magazine covering Asian sources of timepieces and news. **Freq:** Monthly. **Print Method:** Web. **Trim Size:** 8 1/16 x 10 5/8. **Cols./Page:** 2. **Key Personnel:** Jonathan Bigelow, General Mgr., phone (562)946-6089, fax (562)944-9478; Dianna Corriero, Circulation Mgr. **Subscription Rates:** $75 individuals; $20 single issue. **Remarks:** Accepts advertising. **URL:** http://www.asiansources.com. **Alt. Formats:** CD-ROM.
Circ: (Not Reported)

SANTA MARIA, pop. 39,685.

Santa Barbara Co. (SW). 75 m NW of Santa Barbara. Manufactures tire molds, electrical equipment power control cables, flexible cauplings, machine tools, aluminum products, frozen food processing, sugar refinery, Oil refining, & drilling. Cattle ranches. Vegetable farming.

3751 Central Coast This Week
Santa Maria Times
3200 Skyway Dr. Phone: (805)925-2691
PO Box 400 Fax: (805)928-5657
Santa Maria, CA 93455-1896
Community newspaper. **Founded:** 1984. **Freq:** Weekly (Tues.). **Print Method:** Offset. **Cols./Page:** 6. **Col. Width:** 24 nonpareils. **Col. Depth:** 231 agate lines. **Key Personnel:** Wayne Agner, Managing Editor; John Shields, Publisher; Tobey Anglin, Advertising Dir.; Annette Miller, Classified Mgr. **Subscription Rates:** Free; $6.50 by mail; $8.50 out of area; $9.50 out of state. **Remarks:** Accepts advertising.
Ad Rates: BW: $774.00 **Circ:** Free 14,500
4C: $1,154.00
SAU: $6.00
PCI: $6.00

3752 Santa Maria Times
3200 Skyway Dr. Phone: (805)925-2691
PO Box 400 Fax: (805)928-5657
Santa Maria, CA 93455-1896
Daily newspaper. **Founded:** 1882. **Freq:** morning 7 days a week. **Print Method:** Offset. **Cols./Page:** 6. **Col. Width:** 21 1/2 nonpareils. **Col. Depth:** 301 agate lines. **Key Personnel:** Wayne Agner, Managing Editor; John Shields, Publisher; Tobey Anglin, Advertising Director; Annette Miller, Classified

Mgr.; Ron Pidde, Retail Advertising Manager. **Subscription Rates:** $99 individuals. **Remarks:** Accepts advertising.
Ad Rates: GLR: $1.70 **Circ:** Mon.-Sat. 19,571
BW: $2,160.75 Sun. 21,067
4C: $2,540.75
SAU: $18.10
PCI: $16.75

3753 KBOX-FM - 104.1
Box 518 Phone: (805)922-1041
Santa Maria, CA 93456 Fax: (805)928-3069

Format: Adult Contemporary. **Networks:** NBC. **Founded:** 1968. **Formerly:** KLPC-FM (1984). **Operating Hours:** Continuous. **ADI:** Santa Barbara-Santa Maria-San Luis Obispo,CA. **Key Personnel:** Cliff Hunter, President; Mark Stevens, Operations Mgr. **Wattage:** 5700. **Ad Rates:** $27 for 30 seconds; $30 for 60 seconds.

3754 KCOY-TV - 12
1211 W. McCoy Ln. Phone: (805)925-1200
Santa Maria, CA 93455 Fax: (805)922-9830
E-mail: kcoy@kcoy.com

Format: Commercial TV. **Networks:** CBS. **Owner:** Benedak Corp., at above address. **Operating Hours:** 6 a.m.-2:07 a.m. **ADI:** Santa Barbara-Santa Maria-San Luis Obispo,CA. **Key Personnel:** Ted Utz, General Mgr.

KGDP-AM - See Orcutt

3755 KSBQ-AM - 1480
604 E. Chapel Phone: (805)922-3312
Santa Maria, CA 93454

Format: Hispanic. **Owner:** Jaime Bonilla Valdez, 269 H St., 3rd Fl., Chula Vista, CA 91910, (619)427-5877. **Founded:** 1961. **Operating Hours:** 24 hrs. **ADI:** Santa Barbara-Santa Maria-San Luis Obispo,CA. **Wattage:** 1000 day; 61 night. **Ad Rates:** $17-22 for 30 seconds; $19-24 for 60 seconds. KRQK-FM KJDJ-AM.

3756 KSMA-AM - 1240
Box 1240 Phone: (805)925-2582
Santa Maria, CA 93456 Fax: (805)928-1544
E-mail: ksni@pronet.net

Format: News; Talk; Sports; Information. **Networks:** CBS. **Owner:** Bayliss Broadcasting Company, 2215 Skyway Dr., Santa Maria, CA 93455. **Founded:** 1945. **Operating Hours:** Continuous. **ADI:** Santa Barbara-Santa Maria-San Luis Obispo,CA. **Key Personnel:** Alice Bayliss, Contact, ksni@pronet.net; Ed Krovitz, Sales Mgr., ksni@pronet.net. **Wattage:** 1000. **Ad Rates:** $9-22 for 30 seconds. **URL:** http://www.ksma.com.

3757 KSNI-FM - 102.5
2215 Skyway Dr. Phone: (805)925-2582
PO Box 1240 Fax: (805)928-1544
Santa Maria, CA 93456
E-mail: ksni@sunnycountry.com

Format: Country. **Networks:** Westwood One Radio. **Owner:** Bayliss Broadcasting Co., Inc., at above address. **Founded:** 1946. **Operating Hours:** Continuous. **ADI:** Santa Barbara-Santa Maria-San Luis Obispo,CA. **Key Personnel:** George Ballas, Program Dir.; Alice Bayliss, Owner/General Mgr.; Tony Gonzales, Public Service Dir.; Ed Krovitz, Sales Mgr.; Cindy Anderson, Traffic Mgr. **Wattage:** 10,000. **Ad Rates:** $25-50 per unit. **URL:** http://www.sunnycountry.com.

3758 KTA-TV - 7
1138 W. Church Phone: (805)928-7700
Santa Maria, CA 93458-4228 Fax: (805)928-8606

Format: Commercial TV. **Networks:** Univision. **Owner:** R&C Enterprises, at above address. **Founded:** 1987. **Operating Hours:** Continuous. **ADI:** Santa Barbara-Santa Maria-San Luis Obispo,CA. **Key Personnel:** Sandy Keefer, General Mgr.; Jose Guzman, Production Mgr.; Shannon Souza, Traffic Mgr.; Roy Keefer, Chief Engineer. **Wattage:** 10. **Ad Rates:** Advertising accepted; rates available upon request.

3759 KTAP-AM - 1600
104 West Chapel St. Phone: (805)928-4334
Santa Maria, CA 93454 Fax: (805)349-2765

Format: Hispanic. **Simulcasts:** Nights w/KIDI - FM. **Networks:** Independent. **Founded:** 1962. **Formerly:** KTAP-AM. **Operating Hours:** Continuous; 100% local. **ADI:** Santa Barbara-Santa Maria-San Luis Obispo,CA. **Key Personnel:** Steven J. Moffitt, General Mgr.; Laticia Dunes, Sales Mgr.; Enrique Uribe, Contact; Maricarmen Hernandez, Office Mgr.; Chava Ponce, Program Dir. **Wattage:** 500 day; 48 night. **Ad Rates:** $25 per unit.

3760 KUHL-AM - 1440
211 E. Fesler Phone: (805)922-7727
PO Box 1964 Fax: (805)349-0265
Santa Maria, CA 93456
Free: (800)549-5845

Format: Talk; News. **Networks:** ABC. **Owner:** Roger Blaemire, at above address. **Founded:** 1946. **Operating Hours:** Continuous; 40% network, 60% local. **ADI:** Santa Barbara-Santa Maria-San Luis Obispo,CA. **Key Personnel:** Rick Blaemire, Sales Mgr.; David Blaemire, Operations Mgr.; Flora Rodriquez, Traffic Mgr. **Wattage:** 5000 day; 1000 night. **Ad Rates:** $15-30 for 30 seconds; $17-35 for 60 seconds.

3761 KUHL/KTME - 1410
PO Box 1964 Phone: (805)735-1410
Santa Maria, CA 93456 Fax: (805)349-0165

Format: Oldies. **Simulcasts:** KUHL/KTME. **Networks:** ABC. **Owner:** Blackhawk Communications, PO Box 1964, Santa Maria, CA 93456, (805)922-7727, Free: (800)549-5845. **Founded:** 1958. **Formerly:** KNEZ-AM (1992); KCLL-AM; Mega Formula Broadcasting. **Operating Hours:** Continuous. **Key Personnel:** Bob Sharon, General Mgr. **Wattage:** 500. **Ad Rates:** $15-35 for 30 seconds; $20-40 for 60 seconds.

3762 KXFM-FM - 99.1
124 Carmen Lane, Ste. E Phone: (805)925-0101
Santa Maria, CA 93454 Fax: (805)348-3598

Format: Ethnic; Hispanic; News. **Networks:** Westwood One Radio. **Owner:** Bathysphere Broadcasting, L.P., at above address. **Founded:** 1946. **Operating Hours:** Continuous. **ADI:** Santa Barbara-Santa Maria-San Luis Obispo,CA. **Key Personnel:** Don Shore, General Mgr.; Nancy Allison, General Sales Mgr.; Dave Christopher, Operations Mgr.; Perla Pineda, Traffic Mgr. **Wattage:** 50,000 ERP. **Ad Rates:** $15-30 for 30 seconds; $17-35 for 60 seconds.

SANTA MONICA, pop. 88,314.

Los Angeles Co. (S). On Pacific Ocean, 16 m W of Los Angeles. Santa Monica College. Residential. Beach resort. Manufactures tools, dies, cosmetics, electronics, lubricating equipment.

3763 American Woman Motorscene
1510 11th St. Phone: (310)260-0192
Suite 201B Fax: (310)260-0175
Santa Monica, CA 90401
Automotive adventure and lifestyle magazine targeting working and active women. **Founded:** Jan. 1989. **Freq:** Bimonthly. **Print Method:** Web press. **Trim Size:** 10 3/8 x 7 3/8. **Key Personnel:** Courtney Caldwell, Publisher, courtney@americanwoman.com; BJ Killeen, Editor. **Subscription Rates:** $14.95; $20 two years two years; $2.95 single issue. **Remarks:** Accepts advertising. **Formerly:** American Woman Road Rider (1989); American Woman Road Riding (1990); American Woman Motorsports Magazine.
Ad Rates: BW: $1750 **Circ:** ‡100,000
4C: $3550
PCI: $45

3764 The City Scene
PO Box 1077 Phone: (310)319-1680
Santa Monica, CA 90406 Fax: (310)393-7988

Community newspaper. **Founded:** 1984. **Freq:** Monthly. **Cols./Page:** 5. **Col. Width:** 1.875 inches. **Col. Depth:** 13 inches. **Key Personnel:** Diane Margolin, Publisher. **Subscription Rates:** $10. **Remarks:** Accepts advertising. **Formerly:** On Montana.
Ad Rates: BW: $1,200 **Circ:** (Not Reported)
PCI: $35

3765 Drag Racing Monthly
General Media Automotive Group
3330 Ocean Park Blvd. Phone: (310)392-2998
Santa Monica, CA 90405-3211 Fax: (310)392-1171

Magazine for drag race enthusiasts. **Founded:** 1964. **Freq:** Monthly. **Print Method:** Offset. **Trim Size:** 8 x 10 1/2. **Cols./Page:** 3. **Col. Width:** 13 1/2 inches. **Col. Depth:** 9 3/8 inches. **Key Personnel:** Steve Collison, Editor, phone (609)768-0142, fax (609)768-5335. **Subscription Rates:** $17.95; $2.95 single issue. **Remarks:** Accepts advertising. **Formerly:** Super Stock & Drag Illustrated.
Ad Rates: BW: $1,640 **Circ:** Paid ★71,899
4C: $2,650

3766 Enclitic
Center for Media Literacy
Box 287 Fax: (310)394-1265
Santa Monica, CA 90406-0287
Journal featuring articles on politics, media, social/critical theory, and journalism. **Freq:** Quarterly. **Trim Size:** 7 1/2 x 10. **Cols./Page:** 2. **Col. Width:** 2 7/8 inches. **Col. Depth:** 8 1/4 inches. **Key Personnel:** John O'Kane, Editor and Publisher. **Remarks:** Accepts advertising.
Circ: Paid 6,000

3767 Entertainment Law Reporter; Movies Music Broadcasting Theater Publishing Multimedia Sports
Entertainment Law Reporter Publishing Co.
2118 Wilshire Blvd., No. 311 Phone: (310)829-9335
Santa Monica, CA 90403-5784 Fax: (310)829-9335
Publication E-mail: editor@entlawrpfr.com

Magazine focusing on local developments in motion pictures, television, radio, music, theatre, art, publishing, and sports. **Founded:** 1978. **Freq:** Monthly. **Key Personnel:** Lon Sobel, Publisher; Carol Sobel, Circulation Mgr., carolon@entlawrptr.com. **Subscription Rates:** $200. $15 single issue. **Remarks:** Accepts advertising. **Alt. Formats:** CD-ROM. **Formerly:** Entertainment Law Reporter; Motion Pictures, Television, Radio, Music Theater, Publishing, Sports.
Ad Rates: BW: $150 **Circ:** Paid 730

3768 Ergonomics in Design
Human Factors and Ergonomics Society
PO Box 1369 Phone: (310)394-1811
Santa Monica, CA 90406-1369 Fax: (310)394-2410
Publisher E-mail: hfes@compuserve.com

Trade magazine covering applied research in the design of user-friendly products, tools, and systems. **Subtitle:** The Magazine of Human Factors Applications. **Founded:** Jan. 1993. **Freq:** Quarterly. **Print Method:** Web offset. **Trim Size:** 8 1/2 x 11. **Cols./Page:** 2. **Key Personnel:** Lois Smith, Managing Editor. **ISSN:** 1064-8046. **Subscription Rates:** $39 individuals; $10 single issue. **Remarks:** Accepts advertising.
Ad Rates: BW: $1,540 **Circ:** Paid 5,600
4C: $2,440

3769 European Medical Device Manufacturer
Canon Communications LLC
3340 Ocean Park Blvd., Ste. 1000 Phone: (310)392-5509
Fax: (310)392-4920
Santa Monica, CA 90405-3216
Magazine on components, technologies, and service involved in medical device manufacturing. **Freq:** Bimonthly. **Key Personnel:** John Bethune, Editorial Dir., john.bethune@cancom.com; Norbert Sparrow, Editor, norbert.sparrow@cancom.com. **Remarks:** Accepts advertising. **URL:** http://www.devicelink.com. **Formerly:** International Medical Device & Diagnostic Industry (Jan. 1994).
Ad Rates: BW: $3,395 **Circ:** Non-paid 15,000
4C: $5,805

3770 Four Wheeler Magazine
General Media Automotive Group
3330 Ocean Park Blvd. Phone: (310)392-2998
Santa Monica, CA 90405-3211 Fax: (310)392-1171

Magazine on four-wheel-drive vehicles. **Founded:** Feb. 1, 1962. **Freq:** Monthly. **Print Method:** Offset. **Trim Size:** 8 x 10 3/4. **Cols./Page:** 3. **Col. Width:** 27 nonpareils. **Col. Depth:** 140 agate lines. **Key Personnel:** John Stewart, Editor; Chris Ballard, Advertising Mgr. **Subscription Rates:** $14.87 individuals. **Remarks:** Accepts advertising.
Ad Rates: BW: $5,265 **Circ:** Paid ★367,814
4C: $7,995

3771 The Good Life
Independent-Journal Newspapers
PO Box 1260 Phone: (213)393-0601
Santa Monica, CA 90406 Fax: (213)393-0606

Local newspaper. **Founded:** 1929. **Freq:** Weekly (Thurs.). **Print Method:** Offset. **Cols./Page:** 4. **Col. Width:** 20 nonpareils. **Col. Depth:** 294 agate lines. **Key Personnel:** Herb Chase, Jr., Editor. **Subscription Rates:** $45 individuals. **Remarks:** Accepts advertising.
Ad Rates: GLR: $1.25 **Circ:** Combined 40,000
BW: $1,200
4C: $1,700
SAU: $20
PCI: $20

3772 Human Factors
Human Factors and Ergonomics Society
PO Box 1369 Phone: (310)394-1811
Santa Monica, CA 90406-1369 Fax: (310)394-2410
Publisher E-mail: hfes@compuserve.com

Professional journal covering human factors and ergonomics research. **Subtitle:** The Journal of the Human Factors and Ergonomics Society. **Founded:** 1958. **Freq:** Quarterly. **Print Method:** Letterpress. **Trim Size:** 6 7/8 x 10. **Cols./Page:** 2. **Key Personnel:** William Vetter, Editorial Asst. **ISSN:** 0018-7208. **Subscription Rates:** $151 individuals; $38 single issue. **Remarks:** Advertising not accepted. **URL:** http://www.hfes.org.
Circ: Combined 6,300

3773 Medical Device & Diagnostic Industry
Canon Communications LLC
3340 Ocean Park Blvd., Ste. 1000 Phone: (310)392-5509 Fax: (310)392-4920
Santa Monica, CA 90405-3216
Publication E-mail: feedback@cancom.com

Magazine for manufacturers of medical devices and in vitro diagnostics. **Subtitle:** The Magazine for Medical Product Design, Manufacturing, and Marketing. **Founded:** 1979. **Freq:** Monthly. **Print Method:** Offset. **Trim Size:** 8 x 10 3/4. **Cols./Page:** 3. **Col. Width:** 13 picas. **Col. Depth:** 157 agate lines. **Key Personnel:** Steve Halasey, Exec. Editor, steve.halasey@cancom.com; Bill Cobert, Pub. and Pres., william.cobert@cancom.com; John Bethune, Editor, john.bethune@cancom.com; ED Sexton, Dir. of Sales & Marketing, ed.sexton@cancom.com. **ISSN:** 0194-844X. **Subscription Rates:** Free to qualified subscribers. **Remarks:** Accepts advertising. **URL:** http://www.devicelink.com.
Ad Rates: BW: $5560 **Circ:** Controlled 42,108
4C: $6985
PCI: $210

3774 Medical Product Manufacturing News
Canon Communications LLC
3340 Ocean Park Blvd., Ste. 1000 Phone: (310)392-5509 Fax: (310)392-4920
Santa Monica, CA 90405-3216
Magazine (tabloid) covering equipment, materials, components, and services for medical device and medical electronic manufacturers. **Subtitle:** The Magazine for Medical Product Design and Development. **Founded:** 1985. **Freq:** Monthly. **Print Method:** Offset. **Trim Size:** 11 x 16. **Cols./Page:** 4. **Col. Width:** 2 3/16 inches. **Col. Depth:** 207 agate lines. **Key Personnel:** William F. Cobert, Publisher; John Bethune, Editorial Dir; Amy Allen, Managing Editor; Willy Brujins-Miller, Circulation Mgr.; Ed Sexton, Director of Sales. **ISSN:** 0893-6250. **Subscription Rates:** Free to qualified subscribers. **Remarks:** Accepts advertising. **URL:** http://www.can.com/.
Ad Rates: GLR: $3.50 **Circ:** Controlled 30,050
BW: $5,995
4C: $7,420
PCI: $175

3775 Micro
Canon Communications LLC
3340 Ocean Park Blvd., Ste. 1000 Phone: (310)392-5509 Fax: (310)392-4920
Santa Monica, CA 90405-3216
Magazine dealing with contamination and defect analysis and control in semiconductor and advanced microelectronics industries. **Subtitle:** Contamination Identification, Analysis, and Control. **Founded:** 1983. **Freq:** 10/year. **Print Method:** Sheetfed offset. **Trim Size:** 8 x 10 3/4. **Cols./Page:** 2 and 3. **Col. Width:** 20 and 13 picas. **Key Personnel:** Tom Cheyney, Editor, tomcheyney@cancom.com. **ISSN:** 0738-713X. **Subscription Rates:** $10 single issue to qualified subscribers. **Remarks:** Accepts advertising. **URL:** http://www.cancom.com/micro. **Formerly:** Microcontamination.
Ad Rates: BW: $3965 **Circ:** Controlled 23,000
4C: $5115

3776 Muppet Babies
Harvey Comics Entertainment Inc.
100 Wilshire Blvd., Ste. 500 Phone: (310)451-3377
Santa Monica, CA 90401-1112 Fax: (310)458-6995

Comic book. **Freq:** Monthly. **Print Method:** Web offset. **Trim Size:** 6 1/8 x 10 1/8. **Key Personnel:** Sid Jacobson, Editor; Ed Shukin, Director; Kevin S. Bricklin, Director. **Subscription Rates:** $1.50 single issue.

3777 Neonatal Intensive Care
Goldstein & Associates
1150 Yale St., Ste. 12 Phone: (310)828-1309
Santa Monica, CA 90403 Fax: (213)829-1169

Subtitle: The Journal of Perinatalogy/Neonatology. **Founded:** 1988. **Freq:** Bimonthly. **Print Method:** Web offset. **Trim Size:** 8 3/8 x 10 7/8.

3778 Option
Supersonic Media, Inc.
1522 B Cloverfield Blvd. Phone: (310)449-0120
Santa Monica, CA 90404 Fax: (310)449-1153
Publication E-mail: optionmag@aol.com

Magazine. **Subtitle:** Music Culture. **Founded:** 1985. **Freq:** Bimonthly. **Print Method:** Web offset. **Trim Size:** 8 3/8 x 10 7/8. **Cols./Page:** 3. **Key Personnel:** Steve Appleford, Editor; Scott Becker, Publisher. **ISSN:** 0882-178X. **Subscription Rates:** $15.95 individuals; $21 Canada. **Remarks:** Accepts advertising.
Ad Rates: BW: $1,680 **Circ:** Paid ‡29,000
4C: $2,520

3779 Photo Lab Management
PLM Publishing Inc.
1312 Lincoln Blvd. Phone: (310)451-1344
PO Box 1700 Fax: (310)395-9058
Santa Monica, CA 90401-1706
Magazine covering photo lab process chemistries, digital imaging, equipment, personnel, and technicians for photo lab owners and managers. **Founded:** 1979. **Freq:** Monthly. **Print Method:** Offset. **Cols./Page:** 3 and 2. **Col. Width:** 27 and 42 nonpareils. **Col. Depth:** 140 agate lines. **Key Personnel:** Carolyn Ryan, Editor; Steve Sheanin, Publisher; Jerry Goldstein, Advertising Mgr. **USPS:** 467-030. **Subscription Rates:** Controlled; $15 individuals; $2.50 single issue. **Remarks:** Accepts advertising.
Ad Rates: BW: $3,580 **Circ:** Controlled ‡20,873
4C: $4,700
PCI: $115

3780 RAND Journal of Economics
RAND
1700 Main St. Phone: (310)393-0411
Santa Monica, CA 90401 Fax: (310)393-4818
Publication E-mail: rje@rand.org

Journal supports and encourages research in the behavior of regulated industries, the economic analysis of organizations, and, more generally, applied microeconomics. Both empirical and theoretical manuscripts in law and economics are encouraged. **Founded:** 1970. **Freq:** Quarterly. **Print Method:** Offset. **Trim Size:** 6 7/8 x 10. **Cols./Page:** 1. **Col. Width:** 65 nonpareils. **Col. Depth:** 125 1/2 agate lines. **Key Personnel:** James R. Hosek, Editor-in-Chief; Paula Larich, Managing Editor, larich@rand.org; Rae Archibald, Publisher. **ISSN:** 0741-6261. **Subscription Rates:** $60 individuals; $170 institutions; $185 other countries surface mail; $195 other countries airmail. **Remarks:** Advertising not accepted. **URL:** http://www.rje.org. **Alt. Formats:** Microfilm, UMI. **Formerly:** Bell Journal of Economics.
Circ: Paid ‡3,100
Non-paid ‡20

3781 RAND Review
RAND
1700 Main St. Phone: (310)393-0411
Santa Monica, CA 90401 Fax: (310)393-4818

Professional journal covering policy and research. **Freq:** Quarterly. **Print Method:** Offset lithography. **Trim Size:** 8 1/2 x 11. **Key Personnel:** John Godges, Editor, godges@rand.org; Christine Troncoso, Circulation Mgr. **Remarks:** Advertising not accepted. **URL:** http://www.rand.org/PUBS/rrr.html. **Former name:** RAND Research Review.
Circ: Controlled 15,000

3782 The RangeFinder
The RangeFinder Publishing Co., Inc.
1312 Lincoln Blvd. Phone: (310)451-8506
PO Box 1703 Fax: (310)395-9058
Santa Monica, CA 90406
Publication E-mail: jketts@earthlink.net

Trade publication for portrait, commercial and wedding photographers. **Subtitle:** The Magazine for Professional Photographers. **Founded:** July 1952. **Freq:** Monthly. **Print Method:** Offset. **Trim Size:** 8 3/8 x 10 13/16. **Cols./Page:** 3. **Col. Width:** 27 nonpareils. **Col. Depth:** 140 agate lines. **Key Personnel:** Bill Hurter, Editor; Steve Sheanin, Publisher; Jerry Goldstein, Advertising Dir. **ISSN:** 0033-9202. **Subscription Rates:** $18 individuals. **Remarks:** Accepts advertising.
Ad Rates: BW: $6,370 **Circ:** Paid 8,412
4C: $7,470 Controlled 40,959
PCI: $224

3783 Santa Monica College Corsair
Santa Monica Consair
1900 Pico Blvd. Phone: (310)452-9340
Santa Monica, CA 90405
Junior college newspaper. **Founded:** 1929. **Freq:** Weekly (Wed.). **Print Method:** Offset. **Cols./Page:** 6. **Col. Width:** 18 nonpareils. **Col. Depth:** 295 agate lines. **Key Personnel:** Alan Sturm, Advertising Mgr.
Circ: Free 5,000

3784 TradeShow & Exhibit Manager
Goldstein & Associates
1150 Yale St., Ste. 12 Phone: (310)828-1309
Santa Monica, CA 90403 Fax: (213)829-1169

Magazine for corporate exhibit managers and independent show organizers who are responsible for all facets of tradeshow activities, management, and expenditures. **Founded:** Feb. 1986. **Freq:** Bimonthly. **Print Method:** Offset. **Trim Size:** 8 3/8 x 10 7/8. **Cols./Page:** 3. **Col. Width:** 27 nonpareils. **Col. Depth:** 140 agate lines. **Key Personnel:** Les Plesko, Editorial Dir.; Steve Goldstein, Publisher. **ISSN:** 0893-2662. **Subscription Rates:** $58 individuals.
Ad Rates: BW: $2,387 **Circ:** 18,500
4C: $3,362

3785 World Tribune
World Tribune Press
525 Wilshire Blvd. Phone: (310)451-8811
Santa Monica, CA 90401 Fax: (310)260-8910
Publication E-mail: solcanews@aol.com

Newspaper covering Buddhism. **Founded:** 1964. **Freq:** Weekly. **Print Method:** Web. **Cols./Page:** 5. **Col. Width:** 11 picas. **Key Personnel:** Fred Zaitsu, Publisher; David McNeill, Managing Editor. **ISSN:** 0049-8165. **Subscription Rates:** $50 individuals. **Remarks:** Advertising not accepted.
Circ: Paid 29,000

3786 Century Communications
2939 Nebraska Ave. Phone: (310)829-7079
Santa Monica, CA 90404 Fax: (310)315-4450

Founded: 1967. **Formerly:** Century Southwest Cable. **Key Personnel:** Tom Belcher, phone (310)315-4441, fax (310)264-8017, tbelcher@centurycomm.com. **Cities Served:** Los Angeles and San Bernadino South Counties, Alta Loma, Bel Air, Bel Canyon, Beverly Crest, Beverly Hills, Boyle Heights, Cucamonga, Eagle Rock, El Segundo, El Sereno, Elysian Park, Glassell, Griffith Park, Highland Park, Hollywood, Lincoln Heights, Marina Del Ray, Mount Washington, Pacific Palisades, Santa Monica, Sherman Oaks, West Hollywood, West Los Angeles, and Westwood, CA.

3787 KACD-FM - 103.1
1425 5th St. Phone: (310)451-1031
Santa Monica, CA 90401 Fax: (310)395-8736

Format: Urban Contemporary. **Simulcasts:** KBCD-FM. **Networks:** Independent. **Founded:** 1960. **Formerly:** KSRF-FM (1960); KAJZ-FM. **Operating Hours:** Continuous; 100% local. **ADI:** Los Angeles (Corona & San Bernardino), CA. **Key Personnel:** Keith Cunningham, Program Dir.; Jim Murphy, Business Mgr. **Wattage:** 3000. **URL:** http://www.channel1031.com.

3788 KBLA-AM - 1580
1700 N. Alvarado St. Phone: (213)665-1580
Los Angeles, CA 90026 Fax: (213)660-1507

Format: Urban Contemporary. **Networks:** ABC; American Urban Radio; Unistar. **Founded:** 1947. **Formerly:** KDAY-AM (1991). **Operating Hours:** Continuous. **ADI:** Los Angeles (Corona & San Bernardino), CA. **Key Personnel:** Ed Kerby, General Mgr.; Rochelle Lucas, General Sales Mgr.; Jack Patterson, Program Dir.; Ron Russ, Chief Engineer; Ron Thompson, General Mgr. **Wattage:** 50,000. **Ad Rates:** $110.50-297.50 for 30 seconds; $130-350 for 60 seconds.

3789 KCRW-FM - 89.9
1900 Pico Blvd. Phone: (310)450-5183
Santa Monica, CA 90405 Fax: (310)450-7172

Format: Public Radio; Eclectic. **Simulcasts:** KCET. **Networks:** National Public Radio (NPR); Public Radio International (PRI). **Owner:** Santa Monica College, at above address. **Founded:** 1948. **Also known as:** KCRU-FM 89.1; KCRY-FM 89.3. **Operating Hours:** Continuous; 35% network, 65% local. **Key Personnel:** Ruth Seymour, General Mgr.; Jennifer Ferro, Asst. General Mgr., phone (310)314-4613, jennifer.ferro@kcrw.org; Nic Harcourt, Music Dir., phone (310)314-4646, nic.harcourt@kcrw.org; Steve Herbert, Chief Engineer, phone (310)314-4652, steve.herbert@kcrw.org; Sarah Spitz, Contact, phone (310)314-4627, sarah.spitz@kcrw.org; Gregory Hardison, Operations Dir., phone (310)314-4629; Howard Schlossberg, Contact, phone (310)314-4631, membership@kcrw.org; Cheryl Gee, Contact, phone (31-)314-4619, cheryl.gee@kcrw.org; Nan Sheri Lieberman, Contact, phone (310)314-4617, nan.sheri.lieberman@kcrw.org; Bob Carlson, Production Dir., phone (310)314-4610, bob.carlson@kcrw.org. **Local Programs:** *Good Food*, Jennifer Ferri; *Which Way LA*, Chris Douridas, Music Dir. **Wattage:** 7000. **Ad Rates:** Underwriting available. **URL:** http://www.kcrw.org.

SANTA PAULA, pop. 20,552.

Ventura Co. (SW). 15 m E of Ventura. Manufactures plastics, paper cartons, plastic cups, airplane parts. Fruit packing, canning and drying, walnuts packed, oil refineries. Oil wells. Agriculture. Lemons, oranges. Grapefruit. Avocados.

3790 KKZZ-AM - 1400
2284 S. Victoria Ave., Ste. 1-A Phone: (805)289-1400
Ventura, CA 93003 Fax: (805)644-4267

Format: Adult Contemporary. **Networks:** Westwood One Radio; CNN Radio. **Owner:** Gold Coast Broadcasting Company, at above address. **Founded:** 1948. **Operating Hours:** Continuous. **Key Personnel:** Carl Goldman, General Mgr.; Dan Carter, Sales Mgr.; Tom Spence, Operations Mgr. **Wattage:** 1000.

SANTA ROSA†, pop. 83,205.

Sonoma Co. (NW). 52 m NW of San Francisco. Fruit canning and drying, wineries, bottling, plating machine works, Shoes, lumber, chemical products, optical coating laboratories, electronics. Agriculture. Apples, grapes. Dairying.

3791 The California Surveyor
California Land Surveyors Association
PO Box 9098 Phone: (707)578-6016
Santa Rosa, CA 95405 Fax: (707)578-4406
Publisher E-mail: clsaco@aol.com

Land surveying magazine. **Founded:** 1967. **Freq:** Quarterly. **Print Method:** Offset. **Trim Size:** 8 1/2 x 11. **Cols./Page:** 3. **Col. Width:** 26 nonpareils. **Col. Depth:** 128 agate lines. **Key Personnel:** Thomas B. Mastin, PLS, Contact; Dorothy Calegari, Advertising Mgr. **Remarks:** Accepts advertising. **URL:** http://www.ca-surveyors.com.
Ad Rates: BW: $475 **Circ:** Non-paid ‡4,600

The Classified Gazette (Sonoma County Edition) - See Sonoma

3792 The Food & Beverage Industry
Journal Publications, Inc.
835 Piner Rd., Ste. A Phone: (707)568-5960
Santa Rosa, CA 95402 Fax: (707)568-5981

Trade magazine covering the food and beverage industry. **Freq:** Bimonthly. **Trim Size:** 10 x 13. **Key Personnel:** Michael Walsh, Publisher; Scott Clemens, Editor. **Subscription Rates:** $29.95 individuals; $.50 single issue. **Remarks:** Accepts advertising.
Ad Rates: BW: $3,000 **Circ:** (Not Reported)
4C: $3,500

3793 The Food & Beverage Journal
Journal Publications, Inc.
835 Piner Rd., Ste. A Phone: (707)568-5960
Santa Rosa, CA 95402 Fax: (707)568-5981
Publication E-mail: fbj@slip.net

Trade magazine for the food and beverage industry in the western U.S. **Freq:** Bimonthly. **Trim Size:** 10 x 13. **Key Personnel:** Scott Clemens, Editor; Michael Walsh, Publisher; Aldo Clamar, Sales Mgr. **Subscription Rates:** $29.95 individuals; $39.95 two years. **Remarks:** Accepts advertising.
Ad Rates: BW: $3,000 **Circ:** Combined 27,000
4C: $3,500

3794 Forum
Polebridge Press
PO Box 6144 Phone: (707)523-1323
Santa Rosa, CA 95406 Fax: (707)523-1350
Publisher E-mail: 103304.305@compuserve.com

Journal focusing on research on biblical and American traditions. **Founded:** 1981. **Freq:** Semiannual. **Trim Size:** 6 x 9. **Key Personnel:** Daryl D. Schmidt, Editor; Charlene Matejovsky, Managing Editor. **ISSN:** 0883-4970. **Subscription Rates:** $30 individuals; $15 single issue. **Remarks:** Advertising not accepted. **Formerly**: Foundations & Facets Forum.
Circ: Paid 805

3795 The Fourth R
Polebridge Press
PO Box 6144 Phone: (707)523-1323
Santa Rosa, CA 95406 Fax: (707)523-1350
Publisher E-mail: 103304.305@compuserve.com

Journal containing information about biblical and religious issues. **Founded:** 1981. **Freq:** Bimonthly. **Trim Size:** 8 1/2 x 11. **Key Personnel:** Culver H. Nelson, Editor; Bob Schwartz, Exec. Dir., bobschwartz@att.net. **ISSN:** 0893-1658. **Subscription Rates:** $25 individuals; $4.50 single issue. **Remarks:** Advertising not accepted.
Circ: Paid 1,500

3796 Maledicta
Maledicta Press
PO Box 14123 Phone: (707)523-4761
Santa Rosa, CA 95402-6123 Fax: (707)523-4761

Journal covering essays and glossaries of insults, curses, slurs, vulgarities and slang in all languages. **Subtitle:** The International Journal of Verbal Aggression. **Founded:** 1977. **Freq:** Irregular. **Print Method:** Offset. **Trim Size:** 5 1/2 x 8 1/2. **Cols./Page:** 1. **Col. Width:** 4 inches. **Col. Depth:** 6 3/4 inches. **Key Personnel:** Dr. Reinhold Aman, Editor and Publisher, aman@sonic.net. **ISSN:** 0363-3659. **Subscription Rates:** $18 single issue. **Remarks:** Advertising not accepted. **URL:** http://www.sonic.net/maledicta.
Circ: Paid 2,000

3797 Mother Baby Journal
1410 Neotomas, Ste. 107 Phone: (707)569-1415
Santa Rosa, CA 95405-7533 Fax: (707)569-0786
Publication E-mail: editorial@neonatalnetwork.com; mbj@neonatalnetwork.com

Professional magazine for nurses who work in Level I and II maternal-infant units, post-partum, labor, and delivery. **Subtitle:** The Journal of Family Centered Nursing. **Founded:** Jan. 1996. **Freq:** Bimonthly. **Trim Size:** 8 3/8 x 10 7/8. **Cols./Page:** 2. **Key Personnel:** Charles Rait, Publisher/Editor-in-Chief, crait@neonatalnetwork.com; Suzanne G. Rait, Managing Editor, srait@neonatalnetwork.com; Barbara E. Mansinne, Editorial Consultant. **ISSN:** 1084-6190. **Subscription Rates:** $24 individuals; $32 institutions; $32 Canada; $40 institutions Canada; $60 out of country. **Remarks:** Accepts advertising. **URL:** http://neonatalnetwork.com/mbj.
Ad Rates: GLR: $15 **Circ:** Combined 2,500
BW: $800
4C: $1,750

3798 Neonatal Network
Mother Baby Journal
1410 Neotomas, Ste. 107 Phone: (707)569-1415
Santa Rosa, CA 95405-7533 Fax: (707)569-0786
Publication E-mail: editorial@neonatalnetwork.com; neonatal82@aol.com

Professional medical journal for neonatal nurses and related health care professionals. **Subtitle:** The Journal of Neonatal Nursing. **Founded:** June 1982. **Freq:** 8/year. **Trim Size:** 8 3/8 x 10 7/8. **Cols./Page:** 2. **Key Personnel:** Charles Rait, Publisher/Editor-in-Chief, crait@neonatalnetwork.com; Suzanne G. Rait, Managing Editor, srait@neonatalnetwork.com; Barbara E. Mansinne, Editorial Consultant; Ute Berman, Advertising Mgr., advertising@neonatalnetwork.com. **ISSN:** 0730-0832. **Subscription Rates:** $38 individuals; $50 institutions; $8 single issue. **Remarks:** Accepts advertising. **URL:** http://neonatalnetwork.com.
Ad Rates: GLR: $15 **Circ:** Controlled 14,000
BW: $1,625
4C: $2,875

3799 Northwesterner
Northwestern Pacific Railroad Historical Society
PO Box 667 Phone: (707)539-9172
Santa Rosa, CA 95402-0667
Historical journal covering railroads. **Founded:** 1986. **Freq:** Semiannual. **Key Personnel:** Fred Codoni, Editor. **Subscription Rates:** $30 individuals. **Remarks:** Accepts advertising.
Ad Rates: BW: $135 **Circ:** Non-paid 700
4C: $300

3800 The Press Democrat
PO Box 910 Phone: (707)526-8585
Santa Rosa, CA 95402 Fax: (707)546-7538
Free: (800)675-5056

General newspaper. **Founded:** 1857. **Freq:** Mon.-Sun. (morn.). **Print Method:** Offset. **Trim Size:** 13 x 21. **Cols./Page:** 6. **Col. Width:** 25 nonpareils. **Col. Depth:** 294 agate lines. **Key Personnel:** Bruce Kyse, Exec. Editor, phone (707)521-5256, bkyse@pressdemo.com; Michael J. Parman, Publisher, phone (707)526-8596, fax (707)521-5302; Ken Svanum, Advertising Dir., phone (707)526-8575, fax (707)521-5493, ksvanum@pressdemocrat.com; Bob Swofford, Managing Editor, phone (707)521-5251, bswofford@pressdemo.com; Brad Bollinger, Business Editor, phone (707)521-5283, fax (707)521-5418, bbollinger@pressdemo.com; Jim Fremgen, News Editor, phone (707)521-5298, jfremgen@pressdemocrat.com; George Manes, Sports Editor, phone (707)521-8502, fax (707)521-5463, sports@pressdemo.com. **Subscription Rates:** $150 individuals. **Remarks:** Accepts advertising. **URL:** http://www.pressdemo.com. **Alt. Formats:** Microform.
Ad Rates: GLR: $3.83 **Circ:** Mon.-Sat. ★**93,015**
BW: $6,587 Sun. ★**102,622**
4C: $7,887
SAU: $52.28
CNU: $8
PCI: $53.55

3801 The Sonoma County Independent
Metrosa, Inc.
540 Mendocino Ave. Phone: (707)527-1200
Santa Rosa, CA 95401 Fax: (707)527-1298
Publication E-mail: indy@livewire.com

Newspaper. **Founded:** 1979. **Freq:** Weekly. **Print Method:** Web Press. **Trim Size:** 10 x 12 3/4. **Key Personnel:** Kelly Westby, Contact, fax (707)527-1288, k_westby@sjmetro.com. **Subscription Rates:** $25. **Formerly**: The Paper.
Ad Rates: BW: $1,205 **Circ:** Free 32,000
4C: $1,705 Paid 200

3802 Sonoma County Physician
Sonoma County Medical Association
3033 Cleveland Ave. Phone: (707)525-4325
Santa Rosa, CA 95403 Fax: (707)525-4289

Professional magazine of the Sonoma County Medical Association covering medicine. **Founded:** Jan. 1984. **Freq:** Bimonthly. **Trim Size:** 8 1/2 x 11. **Cols./Page:** 3. **Key Personnel:** Steve Osborn, Managing Editor, sosborn@rhs.org; Susan Gumucio, Advertising, sgumucio@rhs.org. **ISSN:** 1087-8807. **Subscription Rates:** $18 individuals; $3 single issue. **Remarks:** Accepts advertising. **URL:** http://www.scma.org.
Ad Rates: BW: $525 **Circ:** Combined 1,000
4C: $1,300

3803 Sonoma County Women's Voices
Women's Voices
PO Box 4448 Phone: (707)575-5654
Santa Rosa, CA 95402
Publication E-mail: wv@monitor.net

Periodical addressing issues and concerns of women in Sonoma County, CA. Includes calendar of events, news, features, poetry, and review. **Founded:** 1980. **Freq:** Monthly. **Print Method:** Web offset. **Cols./Page:** 3. **Col. Width:** 3 1/4 inches. **Col. Depth:** 16 inches. **Subscription Rates:** $15; $25. **Remarks:** Accepts advertising.
Ad Rates: BW: $430 **Circ:** Paid 300
PCI: $10 Non-paid 5,700

3804 Wine X Magazine
4184 Sonoma Mountain Rd. Phone: (707)545-0992
Santa Rosa, CA 95404 Fax: (707)542-7062
Free: (800)229-4639
Publisher E-mail: winex@wco.com

Consumer lifestyle magazine covering wine and food, music, video, beer, spirits coffee, fashion, the arts. **Subtitle:** Wine, Food, and an Intelligent Slice of Vice. **Founded:** July 1997. **Freq:** Bimonthly. **Print Method:** Web offset. **Trim Size:** 8 3/4 x 10 7/8. **Key Personnel:** Darryl M. Roberts, Editor and Publisher; Dan Eliason, Sales & Mktg. Dir., phone (707)537-8538, fax (707)539-9235, deliason@sonic.net. **Subscription Rates:** $18 individuals; $3.95 single issue. **Remarks:** Accepts advertising. **URL:** http://www.winexwired.com. **Formerly**: Wines International.
Ad Rates: BW: $3300 **Circ:** Controlled 35,000
4C: $3300

3805 KBBF-FM - 89.1
PO Box 7189 Phone: (707)545-8833
Santa Rosa, CA 95407-0189 Fax: (707)545-6642

Format: Hispanic. **Owner:** Bilingual Broadcasting Foundation Inc., at above address, Fax: (707)545-6244. **Founded:** 1973. **Operating Hours:** Continuous. **ADI:** San Francisco-Oakland-San Jose. **Key Personnel:** Maria Fincher, General Mgr.; Omar Vargas, Program Dir.; Miriam Gomez, Dir. of Finances; Crystal Rangel, Traffic Dir.; Hugo Mata, Development Director. **Local Programs:** *Mundo In Fantil* 10:00 am Saturday, Hugo Mata, Development Director, (707)545-8833, Fax (707)545-6244. **Wattage:** 1000. **Ad Rates:** Noncommercial. $10 for 30 seconds. **URL:** http://www.kbbf.org.

3806 KFGY-FM - 92.9
Box 2158 Phone: (707)543-0100
Santa Rosa, CA 95405-0158 Fax: (707)571-1097

Format: Country. **Networks:** Independent. **Founded:** 1979. **Formerly:** KREO-FM; KHTT-FM; KVVV-FM; KLCQ-FM. **Operating Hours:** Continuous; 100% local. **ADI:** San Francisco-Oakland-San Jose. **Key Personnel:** Rick Lee, General Mgr., phone (707)543-0129. **Ad Rates:** Advertising accepted; rates available upon request. **URL:** froggy929.com.

3807 KFTY-TV - 50
533 Mendocino Ave. Phone: (707)526-5050
PO Box 1150 Fax: (707)526-7429
Santa Rosa, CA 95402

Format: Commercial TV. **Networks:** Independent. **Owner:** KFTY Broadcasting, Inc., at above address. **Founded:** 1981. **Operating Hours:** Continuous. **ADI:** San Francisco-Oakland-San Jose. **Key Personnel:** John Burgess, General Mgr., jburgess@ackerley.com; Melanie Bartlett, Promotions Mgr.; Teresa McManus, Production Mgr.; Randy Rogers, General Sales Mgr.; Ron Wolfe, News Dir.; Eric Peter, Chief Engineer. **Local Programs:** *KFTY News* 7 & 10, Ron Wolfe. **Wattage:** 360. **Ad Rates:** $35-300 for 30 seconds. **URL:** http://www.ackerley.com/kfty.

3808 KMGG-FM - 97.7
PO Box 6673 Phone: (707)578-0977
Santa Rosa, CA 95406 Fax: (707)578-1736

Format: Oldies. **Networks:** Unistar. **Founded:** 1977. **Formerly:** KRJB-FM (1985). **Operating Hours:** Continuous. **ADI:** San Francisco-Oakland-San Jose. **Key Personnel:** Kent Bjugstad,

General Mgr.; Pat Gallagher, Public Service Director. **Wattage:** 25,000. **Ad Rates:** $24-36 per unit.

3809 KRRS-AM - 1460
PO Box 2277 Phone: (707)270-1460
Santa Rosa, CA 95405 Fax: (707)545-0112

Format: Hispanic. **Networks:** UPI. **Founded:** 1963. **Formerly:** KWFN-AM (1988). **Operating Hours:** Continuous. **ADI:** San Francisco-Oakland-San Jose. **Key Personnel:** Humberto Salinas, General Mgr.; Yesemia Deluna, Program Dir.; Ruben Muniz, Traffic Dir.; Nico Deluna, Production Mgr. **Wattage:** 1000. **Ad Rates:** $20.24-31 per unit.

3810 KSRO-AM - 1350
PO Box 2158 Phone: (707)543-0151
Santa Rosa, CA 95405-0158 Fax: (707)571-1097

Format: Talk; News. **Networks:** CNN Radio; NBC. **Owner:** Fuller Jeffrey Broadcasting, 8842 Quail Ln., Granite Bay, CA 95746, (916)791-3522. **Founded:** 1937. **Operating Hours:** Continuous. **ADI:** San Francisco-Oakland-San Jose. **Key Personnel:** Jose Diaz, Operations Mgr., phone (707)543-0100, fax (707)571-1097; Darryl Curtis, News Dir., phone (707)543-0100, fax (707)571-1097; Heidi Cordsen, Promotions Dir., phone (707)543-0100, fax (707)571-1097; Pete Walker, Sports Dir., phone (707)543-0100, fax (707)571-1097. **Local Programs:** *The Alan Stock Show*, Alan Stock. **Wattage:** 5000. **Ad Rates:** Advertising accepted; rates available upon request.

3811 KXFX-FM - 101.7
PO Box 2158 Phone: (707)543-0100
Santa Rosa, CA 95405 Fax: (707)571-1097

Format: Album-Oriented Rock (AOR). **Owner:** Fuller-Jeffrey Broadcasting Co., Inc., 8842 Quail Ln., Granite Bay, CA 95746. **Founded:** 1988. **Formerly:** KVRE-FM (1990). **Operating Hours:** Continuous. **ADI:** San Francisco-Oakland-San Jose. **Key Personnel:** Brian Hudson, Operations Mgr.; Steve Garland, Program Dir.; Jere Crosby, Promotions Dir.; Rick Lee, General Mgr. **Wattage:** 25,000 ERP. **Ad Rates:** Advertising accepted; rates available upon request. .

3812 KZST-FM - 100.1
3392 Mendecino Ave. Phone: (707)528-4434
Santa Rosa, CA 95403 Fax: (707)527-8216
E-mail: gz@kzst.com

Format: Adult Contemporary. **Networks:** Independent. **Owner:** Gordon Zlot, PO Box 100, Santa Rosa, CA 95402. **Founded:** 1971. **Operating Hours:** Continuous. **ADI:** San Francisco-Oakland-San Jose. **Key Personnel:** Tom Skinner, General Mgr.; Brent Farris, Program Dir. **Wattage:** 6,000. **Ad Rates:** $45-90 for 30 seconds; $50-100 for 60 seconds.

SARATOGA, pop. 29,261.

Santa Clara Co. (W). 10 m W of San Jose. Residential. Wine.

3813 EC.COM Magazine
PO Box 6 Phone: (408)867-6300
Saratoga, CA 95071-0006 Fax: (408)867-9800

Magazine for technical and corporate management that focuses on the technologies of electronic commerce and e-business. **Subtitle:** The Magazine For Electronic Commerce Management. **Founded:** Sept. 1995. **Freq:** Monthly. **Print Method:** Web offset. **Trim Size:** 8 3/8 x 10 7/8. **Cols./Page:** 2 and 3. **Key Personnel:** William H. Sleight, Publisher; Catherine Sleight, Editor-in-Chief. **ISSN:** 1084-6328. **Subscription Rates:** $48. **Remarks:** Accepts advertising. **URL:** http://www.ecmedia.com. **Formerly:** E-COMM Magazine.
Ad Rates: BW: $5,250 **Circ:** Controlled △**40,522**
4C: $6,275

3814 Norseman
West Valley College
14000 Fruitvale Phone: (408)867-2200
Saratoga, CA 95070-5697 Fax: (408)867-5033

Collegiate newspaper. **Founded:** 1963. **Freq:** Semimonthly. **Print Method:** Offset. **Cols./Page:** 6. **Col. Width:** 24 nonpareils. **Col. Depth:** 294 agate lines. **Remarks:** Accepts advertising.
Ad Rates: BW: $970 **Circ:** Free 4,000

3815 Saratoga News
Metro Publishing Inc.
14375 Saratoga Ave., Ste. E2 Phone: (408)867-6397
Saratoga, CA 95070 Fax: (408)867-1010
Publication E-mail: sn@vval.com

Community newspaper. **Founded:** 1955. **Freq:** Weekly (Wed.). **Print Method:** Offset. **Cols./Page:** 5. **Col. Width:** 2 1/16 inches. **Key Personnel:** Sue Fagaldelick, Editor; Dan Polcrano, President/Exec. Editor; David Cohen, Publisher. **ISSN:** 0745-6255. **Subscription Rates:** $26 individuals; $35 out of area. **Remarks:** Accepts advertising. **URL:** http://www.metro.active.com.
Ad Rates: BW: $695.75 **Circ:** Combined ‡9,500
4C: $1,074.75
PCI: $12.75

3816 Stanford French & Italian Studies
Dept. of French and Italian Phone: (408)741-1522
PO Box 876
Saratoga, CA 95071
Literature monograph series magazine. **Founded:** 1975. **Freq:** 5/year. **Print Method:** Offset. **Trim Size:** 6 x 9. **Cols./Page:** 1. **Col. Width:** 84 nonpareils. **Col. Depth:** 133 agate lines. **Key Personnel:** Anma Libri, Publisher. **Subscription Rates:** $46.50 single issue. **Remarks:** Advertising not accepted.
Circ: (Not Reported)

SAUSALITO, pop. 7090.

Marin Co. (W) 8 m NW of San Francisco. Residential.

3817 Marinscope Community Newspaper
Marin Scope Community Newspapers, Inc.
1050 Bridgeway Phone: (415)332-3778
Sausalito, CA 94965 Fax: (415)332-8714

Community newspaper serving Tiburon and Belvedere. **Freq:** Weekly (Tues.). **Print Method:** Offset. **Trim Size:** 13 x 21. **Key Personnel:** Billie Anderson, Editor; Paul Anderson, Publisher. **Subscription Rates:** 20. **Formerly:** Ebbtide.
Ad Rates: PCI: $8.75 **Circ:** Combined 45,000

SCOTTS VALLEY, pop. 6,891.

Santa Cruz (W) 7 m N of Santa Cruz. Residential.

3818 Senior Travel Tips
5281 Scotts Valley Dr. Phone: (408)438-6085
Scotts Valley, CA 95066-3514 Fax: (408)438-4705
Publisher E-mail: info@seniortraveltips.com

Trade magazine for tourism and travel planners of retired persons from the U.S. and Canada. **Founded:** May 1989. **Freq:** 8/year. **Print Method:** Web offset. **Trim Size:** 8 1/4 x 10 1/2. **Cols./Page:** 3. **Col. Width:** 2 1/4 inches. **Col. Depth:** 9 inches. **Key Personnel:** Elana Anderson, Editor and Publisher; Linnea Jessup, Managing Editor; Bill Strader, Marketing Dir. **Subscription Rates:** $26 individuals; Free to qualified subscribers. **Remarks:** Accepts advertising. **URL:** http://www.seniortraveltips.com.
Ad Rates: BW: $1,520 **Circ:** Controlled 11,000
4C: $2,120

SEAL BEACH, pop. 25,098.

Orange Co. (S). On Pacific Ocean, 6 mi. SE of Long Beach. Retirement Community. Marine recreation; surfing.

3819 Journal of Religion and Psychical Research
Academy of Religion and Psychical Research
14001 Thunderbird Dr., No. 4-K Phone: (562)493-0355
Seal Beach, CA 90740
Scholarly journal covering religion and psychical research. **Founded:** Jan. 1979. **Freq:** Quarterly. **Print Method:** Offset. **Trim Size:** 5 1/2 x 8 1/2. **Cols./Page:** 1. **Col. Width:** 4 1/2 inches. **Col. Depth:** 8 inches. **Key Personnel:** Claire G. Walker, Ph.D., Editor; Boyce Batey, Circulation Mgr. **ISSN:** 1731-2148. **Subscription Rates:** $35 individuals; $5 single issue. **Remarks:** Advertising not accepted.
Circ: Controlled 347

3820 The Leisure World Golden Rain News
PO Box 2338 Phone: (562)430-0534
Seal Beach, CA 90740 Fax: (562)598-1617

Official newspaper (tabloid) of the Golden Rain Foundation serving the retirement community of Seal Beach Leisure World. **Founded:** 1963. **Freq:** Weekly (Thurs.). **Print Method:** Offset. **Trim Size:** 11 3/8 x 17. **Cols./Page:** 5. **Col. Width:** 1 15/16 inches. **Col. Depth:** 16 inches. **Key Personnel:** David Saunders, Managing Editor. **Subscription Rates:** Free; $25 by mail. **Remarks:** Accepts advertising.
Ad Rates: BW: $872 **Circ:** Paid 6705
4C: $1,322 Free 2295
SAU: $10.90
PCI: $10.90

3821 Seal Beach Sun
The Sun Newspapers
216 Main St. Phone: (562)430-7555
PO Box 755 Fax: (562)430-3469
Seal Beach, CA 90740-6318
Community newspaper. **Founded:** 1967. **Freq:** Weekly (Thurs.). **Print Method:** Offset. **Cols./Page:** 5. **Col. Width:** 26 nonpareils. **Col. Depth:** 224 agate lines. **Key Personnel:** Gwen Parker, Publisher. **Subscription Rates:** $60 individuals. **Remarks:** Combined advertising rates available with Hunting Harbour Journal and The Rossmor Journal. **Formerly:** Seal Beach Journal (1992).
Ad Rates: GLR: $1.58 **Circ:** Paid 300
BW: $842 Free 13,700
4C: $1,240
PCI: $14.10

The Sun Journal - See Huntington Beach

SEBASTOPOL, pop. 5,500.

Sonoma Co. (NW). 7 m W of Santa Rosa. Fruit packing, canning and drying. Liquor, vinegar, pectin manufactured. Fruit, poultry, dairy farms. Apples, grapes, cherries.

3822 Sonoma West Exchange
Sonoma West Publishers, Inc.
PO Box 521 Free: (800)465-0780
Sebastopol, CA 95473-0521
Publication E-mail: news@sonomawest.com

Shopper. **Founded:** 1989. **Freq:** Weekly (Wed.). **Print Method:** Offset. **Cols./Page:** 6. **Col. Width:** 18 nonpareils. **Col. Depth:** 294 agate lines. **Former name:** Sebastopol Times & News Buyers Guide.
Circ: Free 11,300

3823 Sonoma West Times & News
Sonoma West Publishers, Inc.
PO Box 521 Free: (800)465-0780
Sebastopol, CA 95473-0521
Publication E-mail: new@sonomawest.com

Community newspaper. **Founded:** 1889. **Freq:** Weekly (Wed.). **Print Method:** Offset. **Cols./Page:** 6. **Col. Width:** 25 nonpareils. **Col. Depth:** 294 agate lines. **Key Personnel:** Barry Dugan, Editor; Rollic Atkinson, General Mgr. **Subscription Rates:** $25 individuals. **Remarks:** Accepts advertising. **Formerly:** Sebastopol Times & News.
Ad Rates: BW: $2,200 **Circ:** 6,000
4C: $2,630
SAU: $10.95
PCI: $17.50

SELMA, pop. 10,942.

Fresno Co. (C). 15 m SE of Fresno. Residential. Glass making raisin packing plants, machinery, wineries. Fruit, truck, dairy farms. Grapes, cotton, beef cattle, poultry.

3824 The Selma Enterprise
Community Newspaper, Inc.
2045 Grant St. Phone: (559)896-1976
PO Box 100 Fax: (559)896-9160
Selma, CA 93662
Community newspaper. **Founded:** 1886. **Freq:** Weekly (Wed.). **Print Method:** Offset. **Trim Size:** 14 x 21 3/4. **Cols./Page:** 6. **Col. Width:** 24 nonpareils. **Col. Depth:** 294 agate lines. **Key Personnel:** Jim Brock, Editor and Publisher; Joanne Heredia, Advertising Mgr. **Subscription Rates:** $20 individuals; $0.50 single issue. **Remarks:** Accepts advertising.
Ad Rates: BW: $670.80 **Circ:** ‡4,603
SAU: $5.20
PCI: $13.25

SHAFTER, pop. 7,010.

Kern Co. (S). 18 m NW of Bakersfield. Recreation. Potatoes, onions packed, cotton gins. Cement products, fertilizer manufactured. Truck, fruit, almond vineyards, poultry farms.

3825 Arvin Tiller
Reed Print, Inc.
107 E. Lerdo Hwy. Phone: (805)746-4942
Shafter, CA 93263-2701 Fax: (805)746-5571

Community newspaper. **Freq:** Weekly. **Cols./Page:** 6. **Key Personnel:** Roy Patrick, Managing Editor; Sue Hulsey, Office Mgr., phone (805)845-3704. **Subscription Rates:** $19 individuals. **Remarks:** Accepts advertising.
Ad Rates: PCI: $5.75 **Circ:** Paid 2,500

3826 Shafter Press
107 E. Lerdo Hwy. Phone: (805)746-4942
PO Bin A Fax: (805)746-5571
Shafter, CA 93263
Community newspaper. **Founded:** 1921. **Freq:** Weekly (Wed.). **Print Method:** Offset. **Cols./Page:** 6. **Col. Width:** 12 picas. **Col. Depth:** 21 inches. **Key Personnel:** Roy Patrick, Editor; Donald Reed, Publisher; Jerry Watts, Advertising Mgr. **USPS:** 419-700. **Subscription Rates:** $19 individuals; $21 out of area; $24 out of area. **Remarks:** Accepts advertising.
Ad Rates: BW: $693 **Circ:** ‡2,350
PCI: $5.75

3827 Shafter Shopper
107 E. Lerdo Hwy. Phone: (805)746-4942
PO Bin A Fax: (805)746-5571
Shafter, CA 93263
Shopper. **Founded:** 1921. **Freq:** Weekly. **Print Method:** Offset. **Cols./Page:** 6. **Col. Width:** 12 picas. **Col. Depth:** 21 inches. **Key Personnel:** Donald Reed, Publisher; Jerry Watts, Advertising Mgr. **Subscription Rates:** Free. **Remarks:** Accepts advertising.
Ad Rates: BW: $693 **Circ:** Free ‡4,000
PCI: $5.75

SHERMAN OAKS

3828 American Fitness
15250 Ventura Blvd.
Ste. 200
Sherman Oaks, CA 91403
Publisher E-mail: lpafaa@aol.com

Magazine covering trends in fitness, exercise programs, injury prevention, and nutrition. **Founded:** Oct. 1983. **Freq:** Bimonthly. **Print Method:** Offset. **Trim Size:** 8 1/8 x 10 7/8. **Cols./Page:** 5. **Key Personnel:** Peg Jordan, RN, Editor-in-Chief; Rhonda J. Wilson, Managing Editor; Roscoe K. Fawcett, Jr., Publisher; Cindy Schofield, Advertising Mgr. **ISSN:** 0893-5238. **Subscription Rates:** $27 individuals; $4.50 single issue. **Remarks:** Accepts advertising. **URL:** http://www.afaa.com. **Formerly:** Aerobics and Fitness (1990).
Ad Rates: BW: $1,565 **Circ:** Paid ‡35,000
4C: $3,300 Non-paid ‡879

3829 Country Connections
14431 Ventura Blvd., No. 407 Phone: (818)501-1896
Sherman Oaks, CA 91423 Fax: (818)501-1897
Free: (800)876-4326
Publication E-mail: connect@countryink.com

A journal presenting creative, credible alternatives in the areas of lifestyle, politics, culture, ecology and ethics. **Subtitle:** Seeking the Good Life - For the Common Good. **Founded:** Mar. 1995. **Freq:** Bimonthly. **Print Method:** Web. **Trim Size:** 11 3/4 x 17 1/2. **Key Personnel:** Catherine R. Leach, Contact. **ISSN:** 1082-0558. **Subscription Rates:** $16 individuals; $4 single issue.
Ad Rates: BW: $430 **Circ:** 2,000

3830 Eligible
PO Box 57466 Phone: (818)343-6514
Sherman Oaks, CA 91413 Fax: (818)774-1061

Consumer magazine exploring issues important to independent women and highlighting some of the most eligible bachelors in the country. **Subtitle:** For the independent woman. **Founded:** Mar. 16, 1994. **Freq:** Quarterly. **Print Method:** Web offset. **Trim Size:** 8 x 10 3/4. **Key Personnel:** Kathy Duliakas, Publisher, phone (818)343-6514. **ISSN:** 1073-256X. **Subscription Rates:** $11.50 individuals; $2.95 single issue. **Remarks:** Accepts advertising. **Formerly:** L.A.'s Eligible.
Ad Rates: BW: $3,000 **Circ:** Paid 50,000
4C: $3,500 Non-paid 5,000

3831 Spondylitis Plus
Spondylitis Association of America
PO Box 5872 Phone: (818)981-1616
Sherman Oaks, CA 91413 Fax: (818)981-9826
Free: (800)777-8189

Magazine providing a forum for exchange of information about spondylitis. **Freq:** Quarterly. **Subscription Rates:** $25 members. **Remarks:** Advertising not accepted. **Formerly:** Ankylosing Sponylitis News.
Circ: (Not Reported)

SIERRA MADRE, pop. 10,837.

Los Angeles Co. (S). 18 m NE of Los Angeles. Residential. Ceramics, tools, plastic manufactured. Residential.

3832 Freshwater & Marine Aquarium Magazine
R/C Modeler Corp.
144 W. Sierra Madre Blvd. Phone: (626)355-1476
PO Box 487 Fax: (626)355-6415
Sierra Madre, CA 91024-2435
Publication E-mail: remcorp@aol.com

Magazine featuring marine and tropical fish. **Founded:** Jan. 1978. **Freq:** Monthly. **Print Method:** Offset. **Trim Size:** 8 1/4 x 10 7/8. **Cols./Page:** 3. **Col. Width:** 27 nonpareils. **Col. Depth:** 140 agate lines. **Key Personnel:** Don Dewey, Editor; Barbara Richardson, Advertising Mgr. **ISSN:** 0160-4317. **Subscription Rates:** $22 individuals; $2.95 single issue; $27.50 other countries. **Remarks:** Accepts advertising. **URL:** http://www.mag-web.com.
Ad Rates: BW: $655 **Circ:** ‡48,000
4C: $940

3833 R/C Modeler
R/C Modeler Corp.
144 W. Sierra Madre Blvd. Phone: (626)355-1476
PO Box 487 Fax: (626)355-6415
Sierra Madre, CA 91024-2435
Magazine covering radio controlled model airplanes, boats, cars and helicopters. **Founded:** Oct. 1963. **Freq:** Monthly. **Print Method:** Offset. **Trim Size:** 8 1/4 x 10 7/8. **Cols./Page:** 3. **Col. Width:** 27 nonpareils. **Col. Depth:** 140 agate lines. **Key Personnel:** Patricia E. Crews, Editor; Kathy Acton, Advertising Mgr. **ISSN:** 0033-6866. **Subscription Rates:** $24 individuals; $32 other countries. **Remarks:** Accepts advertising.
Ad Rates: BW: $1,250 **Circ:** ‡220,000
4C: $1,570

3834 Sierra Madre News
49 S. Baldwin Ave. Phone: (818)355-3324
Sierra Madre, CA 91024 Fax: (818)355-2341

Local newspaper. **Founded:** 1906. **Freq:** Weekly (Thurs.). **Print Method:** Offset. **Cols./Page:** 8. **Col. Width:** 1 1/2 inches. **Col. Depth:** 21 inches. **Key Personnel:** Michael R. Dewees, Editor and Publisher. **USPS:** 495-960. **Subscription Rates:** $25 individuals; $28 Out of county. **Remarks:** Accepts advertising.
Ad Rates: BW: $840 **Circ:** Paid ‡3,500
4C: $940 Free ‡7,500
PCI: $7

SIMI VALLEY, pop. 77,500.

Ventura Co. (SW). 30 m NW of Los Angeles. Suburban community.

3835 The Enterprise
888 Easy St. Phone: (805)526-6211
Simi Valley, CA 93065-1812 Fax: (805)526-0479

General newspaper. **Founded:** Aug. 1, 1912. **Freq:** Daily (eve.), Sat. and Sun. (morn.). **Print Method:** Offset. **Trim Size:** 14 x 23. **Cols./Page:** 6. **Col. Width:** 25 nonpareils. **Col. Depth:** 301 agate lines. **Key Personnel:** Wayne Lee, Editor and Publisher; Sherrie Dowell, Advertising Mgr. **Subscription Rates:** $66 individuals. **Remarks:** Accepts advertising.
Ad Rates: GLR: $.76 **Circ:** Mon.-Sat. 14,297
BW: $1,071.99 Sun. 15,089
4C: $1,371.99
SAU: $9.23
PCI: $9.23

3836 Verve
Ron Reichick
Box 3205 Phone: (805)522-7575
Simi Valley, CA 93093 Fax: (805)527-2461

Journal covering poetry and short fiction. **Founded:** Jan. 1989. **Freq:** Semiannual. **Print Method:** Offset. **Trim Size:** 5 1/2 x 8 1/2. **Key Personnel:** Ron Reichick, Editor and Publisher; Marilyn Hochheiser, Editor; Virginia Anderson, Assoc. Editor. **Subscription Rates:** $12 two years; $3.50 single issue. **Remarks:** Advertising not accepted.
Circ: Controlled 700

SOLANA BEACH, pop. 5,023.

San Diego Co. (S). 20 m N of San Diego. Aero-space parts. Commercial flower growing. Nursery. Residential.

3837 Blade Citizen
Box A-F Phone: (619)755-1127
Solana Beach, CA 92075 Fax: (619)755-5107

Community newspaper. **Freq:** Semiweekly (Wed. and Fri.). **Trim Size:** 13 1/2 x 22. **Cols./Page:** 6. **Col. Width:** 12 1/2 picas. **Col. Depth:** 21 1/2 inches. **Key Personnel:** Scott Little, Publisher. **USPS:** 605-150. **Subscription Rates:** $12; $52 out of area. **Remarks:** Accepts advertising.
Ad Rates: GLR: $.78 **Circ:** ‡11,000
BW: $1,741.50
4C: $2,061.50
PCI: $13.60

3838 City Sports
City Sports, Inc.
214 S. Cedros Ave. Phone: (619)793-2711
Solana Beach, CA 92075 Fax: (619)793-2710

Regional magazine (tabloid) promoting an active lifestyle. Includes articles on participation sports such as cycling, skiing, running, inline skating, and outdoor adventure. **Founded:** 1974. **Freq:** Monthly. **Print Method:** Offset. **Trim Size:** 10 x 13 1/2. **Cols./Page:** 4. **Col. Width:** 2 1/8 inches. **Col. Depth:** 13 1/4 inches. **Key Personnel:** Lois Schwartz, Editor; Bob Babbitt; John Smith. **Subscription Rates:** $15 individuals. **Remarks:** Accepts advertising.
Circ: Non-paid 120,000
Non-paid 90,000

3839 Fitness Management Magazine
Leisure Publications
215 S. Hwy. 101, Ste. 110 Phone: (619)481-4155
PO Box 1198 Fax: (619)481-4228
Solana Beach, CA 92075
Publication E-mail: fmedit@fitnessworld.com; fitmgt@earthlink.net

Fitness, preventive health care, and management magazine for owners, managers, and program directors of physical fitness facilities. **Subtitle:** Issues and Solutions in Fitness Services. **Founded:** Mar. 1985. **Freq:** 13/year. **Print Method:** Offset. **Trim Size:** 8 3/8 x 10 7/8. **Cols./Page:** 3. **Col. Width:** 13 picas. **Col. Depth:** 10 inches. **Key Personnel:** Edward H. Pitts, Co-Publisher; David H. Levy, Co-Publisher; Ronale Tucker, Editor; Scott Christie, Director of Sales & Marketing. **ISSN:** 0882-0481. **Subscription Rates:** Free to qualified subscribers; $24 individuals; $45 other countries. **Remarks:** Accepts advertising. **URL:** http://www.fitnessworld.com.
Ad Rates: BW: $3,450 **Circ:** Paid 243
4C: $4,225 Controlled 26,000

SOLEDAD, pop. 5,928.

Monterey Co. (W). 26 m SE of Salinas. Residential. Historic Soledad mission. Winery. Agriculture. Dairying, beef cattle, carrots, lettuce.

3840 Gonzales Tribune
South Country Newspapers
635 Front St. Phone: (408)385-4880
Soledad, CA 93960 Fax: (408)385-4799

Community newspaper. **Founded:** 1891. **Freq:** Weekly (Wed.). **Print Method:** Offset. **Trim Size:** 14 x 22 3/4. **Cols./Page:** 6. **Col. Width:** 26 nonpareils. **Col. Depth:** 294 agate lines. **Key Personnel:** Bill Osterbrock, Editor; Harry Casey, Publisher; Julie Trescony, Advertising Mgr. **USPS:** 849-760. **Subscription Rates:** $15 individuals; $20 out of area. **Remarks:** Accepts advertising.
Ad Rates: SAU: $8.45 **Circ:** ‡705

3841 King City Rustler
South Country Newspapers
635 Front St. Phone: (408)385-4880
Soledad, CA 93960 Fax: (408)385-4799

Newspaper. **Founded:** 1901. **Freq:** Weekly (Wed.). **Print Method:** Offset. **Cols./Page:** 6. **Col. Width:** 26 nonpareils. **Col. Depth:** 294 agate lines. **Key Personnel:** Norman Nuck, Editor; Harry Casey, Publisher; John Robasciotti, Advertising Mgr. **Subscription Rates:** $23 within the county; $29 Out of Town. **Remarks:** Accepts advertising.
Ad Rates: SAU: $9.50 **Circ:** ‡3,225

3842 Soledad Bee
635 Front St. Phone: (408)678-2660
PO Box 95 Fax: (408)385-4799
Soledad, CA 93960
Community newspaper. **Founded:** 1909. **Freq:** Weekly (Wed.). **Print Method:** Offset. **Trim Size:** 14 x 22 3/4. **Cols./Page:** 6. **Col. Width:** 26 nonpareils. **Col. Depth:** 294 agate lines. **Key Personnel:** Patricia Stephens, Editor; Harry Casey, Publisher; Glends Bir, Advertising Mgr. **USPS:** 500-740.
Ad Rates: PCI: $8.45 **Circ:** 1,125

SOLVANG, pop. 2,004.

Santa Barbara Co. (SW). 40 m NW of Santa Barbara. Resort area. Cattle, horses, sheep ranching. Wineries, vineyards. Walnuts.

3843 Santa Ynez Valley News
Valley News
423 2nd St. Phone: (805)688-5522
PO Box 647 Fax: (805)688-7685
Solvang, CA 93464
Community newspaper. **Founded:** 1925. **Freq:** Semiweekly. **Print Method:** Offset. **Cols./Page:** 6. **Col. Width:** 21 nonpareils. **Col. Depth:** 126 agate lines. **Key Personnel:** Bert Etling, Editor; Sharry Bowers, Asst. to Publisher; Ronn Iverson, Advertising Dir. **Subscription Rates:** $18.50 individuals; $.35 single issue. **Remarks:** Accepts advertising.
Ad Rates: GLR: $12.85 **Circ:** Tues. 13,500
4C: $180 Thurs. 7,500
PCI: $11.42

3844 KSYV-FM - 96.7
1693 Mission Dr. Phone: (805)688-5798
Solvang, CA 93463 Fax: (805)688-2271
E-mail: ksyv@syv.com

Format: Adult Contemporary; News; Sports. **Networks:** ABC. **Owner:** Pacific Coast Broadcasting, at above address. **Founded:** 1982. **Operating Hours:** Continuous. **Key Personnel:** William O. Reelfs, Contact. **Wattage:** 5800.

SONOMA, pop. 6,054.

Sonoma Co. (NW). 21 m S of Santa Rosa. Residential. Wineries. automotive parts, cheese factories. Diversified farming. Grapes, poultry. Dairying. Retirement Community.

3845 Buyside
Buyside, Ltd.
PO Box 1329 Phone: (707)935-9200
Sonoma, CA 95476 Fax: (707)935-9300

Trade magazine covering investment ideas for money managers. **Subtitle:** Ideas for Today's Money Managers. **Founded:** Feb. 1994. **Freq:** Monthly. **Print Method:** Web offset. **Trim Size:** 8 3/8 x 10 7/8. **Cols./Page:** 2. **Col. Width:** 3 1/2 inches. **Col. Depth:** 9 3/8 inches. **Key Personnel:** Lauren Keyson, Editor; Darlene Christiansen, Production Mgr.; Jim Patrick, Sales Mgr.; Chris Brown, General Mgr.; Tracy Walling, Circulation Mgr. **Remarks:** Accepts advertising. **URL:** http://buyside.com.
Circ: Controlled 32,000

3846 The Classified Gazette (Sonoma County Edition)
The Classified Gazette, Inc.
532 College Ave Phone: (707)526-2437
Santa Rosa, CA 95404 Fax: (707)527-9251
Publication E-mail: santarosa@deltaworld.com

Classified shopper (tabloid). **Subtitle:** 1977. **Founded:** 1967. **Freq:** Weekly (Fri.). **Print Method:** Offset. Uses mats. **Cols./Page:** 7. **Col. Width:** 1 3/8 inches. **Col. Depth:** 16 1/2 inches. **Key Personnel:** Joseph F. Walsh, Editor, phone (415)457-4888, fax (415)457-5731, joega@deltaworld.com; Riley F. Hurd, Jr., Publisher; Richard Standard, Manager, phone (707)526-2434. **Subscription Rates:** Free; $1.80 Wk (mail). **Remarks:** Accepts advertising.
Ad Rates: GLR: $2 **Circ:** Free ‡26,854
BW: $1,095
PCI: $12

3847 The Sonoma Index-Tribune
PO Box C Phone: (707)938-2111
Sonoma, CA 95476 Fax: (707)938-1600
Publisher E-mail: billgsonomanews.com

Community newspaper. **Founded:** Apr. 17, 1879. **Freq:** Semiweekly (Tues. and Fri.). **Print Method:** Offset. **Trim Size:** 11 3/8 x 13 3/4. **Cols./Page:** 6. **Col. Width:** 11.6 picas. **Col. Depth:** 294 agate lines. **Key Personnel:** William E. Lynch, Editor/CEO, phone (707)933-2721, fax (707)938-1600, bill@sonomanews.com; Robert M. Lynch, Publisher, phone (707)933-2720, bob@sonomanews.com; Bill Hoban, News Editor, phone (707)933-2731, newsedit@sonomanews.com. **Subscription Rates:** $42 individuals. **Remarks:** Accepts advertising. **URL:** http://www.sonomanews.com.
Ad Rates: GLR: $1.21 **Circ:** Paid ❑11,539
BW: $2,129.40
4C: $2,379.40
PCI: $14

3848 Sonoma Valley News
The Sonoma Index-Tribune
PO Box C Phone: (707)938-2111
Sonoma, CA 95476 Fax: (707)938-1600
Publisher E-mail: billgsonomanews.com

Shopper. **Founded:** 1879. **Freq:** Weekly (Wed.). **Print Method:** Offset. **Trim Size:** 11 3/8 x 13 3/4. **Cols./Page:** 6. **Col. Width:** 11.6 picas. **Col. Depth:** 294 agate lines. **Key Personnel:** Robert M. Lynch, Publisher, phone (707)933-2720, bob@sonomanews.com; William E. Lynch, Editor/CEO, phone (707)933-2721, bill@sonomanews.com; Yatin Shah, General Mgr., ytin@sonomanews.com. **Subscription Rates:** Free; $25 by mail; $.50 single issue. **Remarks:** Accepts advertising. **Feature Editors:** Patricia Henley, *Food*, phone (707)933-2734, patricia@sonomanews.com.
Ad Rates: GLR: $1.05 **Circ:** Free ‡5,000

3849 Valley of the Moon Visitor's News
Sonoma Valley Publishing
PO Box C Phone: (707)938-2111
Sonoma, CA 95476 Fax: (707)938-1600
Publication E-mail: http://www.sonomanews.com

Tourist newspaper covering Sonoma Valley, California. **Founded:** 1987. **Freq:** Monthly. **Print Method:** Offset. **Cols./Page:** 4. **Col. Width:** 14 picas. **Col. Depth:** 13 inches. **Key Personnel:** Bill Hoban, News Editor, phone (707)933-2731, fax (707)938-1100, newsedit@sonomanews.com; Bill Lynch, Editor, phone (707)933-2721, bill@sonomanews.com. **Remarks:** Accepts advertising. **Feature Editors:** Patricia Healey, *Food*, phone (707)933-2734, patricia@sonomanews.com.
Ad Rates: BW: $399 **Circ:** Free 6,000
4C: $699

SONORA†, pop. 3,239.

Tuolumne Co. (EC). 50 m E of Stockton. Lumber, lime, foundry products, confectionery manufactured. Mountain resort. Gold mines. limestone quarries. timber. Agriculture. Cattle, apples, pears.

3850 Union-Democrat
Union Democrat Corp.
84 S. Washington St. Phone: (209)532-7151
Sonora, CA 95370-4711 Fax: (209)532-5139

General newspaper. **Founded:** 1854. **Freq:** Daily (eve.). **Print Method:** Offset. **Cols./Page:** 6. **Col. Width:** 24 nonpareils. **Col. Depth:** 294 agate lines. **Key Personnel:** Harvey C. McGee, Editor and Publisher. **Subscription Rates:** $60 individuals. **Remarks:** Accepts advertising. **Formerly**: Advertiser.
Ad Rates: GLR: $1.50 **Circ:** Mon.-Sat. ★11,823
BW: $830.76
4C: $1,040.76
SAU: $7.95

3851 KTUO-FM - 102.1
430 N. Washington St. Phone: (209)532-5511
Sonora, CA 95370 Fax: (209)533-1158

Format: Alternative/New Music/Progressive; Eclectic. **Networks:** Independent. **Owner:** Sonora Union High School District, at above address. **Founded:** 1979. **Operating Hours:** 12:35-1:06 p.m. and 7:00-8:a.m. Daily; 100% local. **Key Personnel:** Bix Beeman, Contact. **Wattage:** 30.

3852 KVML-AM - 1450
342 S. Washington St. Phone: (209)533-1450
Sonora, CA 95370-5020 Fax: (209)533-9520

Format: Talk; News. **Networks:** ABC. **Owner:** Clarke Broadcasting Corp., at above address. **Founded:** 1949. **Operating Hours:** 24 hr.; 80% network, 20% local. **Key Personnel:** H. Randolph Holder, Owner; Jim Cumberland, News Dir.; Lorree Sorrick, Program Dir.; Terrell Metheny, Jr., General Mgr.; Chris Davis, Operations Mgr. **Local Programs:** *Talk Back*, Lee Bottom. **Wattage:** 1000. **Ad Rates:** $14 for 30 seconds; $17.50 for 60 seconds. Combined advertising rates available with KZSQ-FM.

3853 KZSQ-FM - 92.7
342 S. Washington St. Phone: (209)533-1450
Sonora, CA 95370-5020 Fax: (209)533-9520

Format: Adult Contemporary. **Networks:** Independent. **Owner:** Clarke Broadcasting Corp., at above address. **Founded:** 1973. **Operating Hours:** Continuous; 100% local. **Key Personnel:** H. Randolph Holder, Owner; Jim Cumberland, News Dir.; Chris Davis, Operations Mgr.; Terrell Metheny, Jr., General Mgr. **Local Programs:** *Talk Back*, Lee Bottom. **Wattage:** 6000. **Ad Rates:** $16.50 for 30 seconds; $20.50 for 60 seconds. Combined advertising rates available with KVML-AM.

SOUTH LAKE TAHOE, pop. 20,681.

El Dorado Co. (EC). 100 m NE of Sacramento. Residential. Summer and winter resort area.

3854 Lake Tahoe Action Magazine
Tahoe Daily Tribune
3079 Harrison Ave. Phone: (530)541-3880
South Lake Tahoe, CA 96150 Fax: (530)541-0373

Lake Tahoe's entertainment guide. **Founded:** 1960. **Freq:** Weekly. **Trim Size:** 11 3/8 x 14. **Cols./Page:** 5. **Col. Depth:** 13 inches. **Key Personnel:** Denise Sloan, Entertainment/Arts Editor; Les Hill, Publisher. **Subscription Rates:** Free. **Remarks:** Accepts advertising. **Formerly**: Tahoe Action.
Ad Rates: 4C: $225 **Circ:** Paid ‡10,000
PCI: $18.50 Free ‡22,000

3855 Tahoe Daily Tribune
3079 Harrison Ave. Phone: (530)541-3880
South Lake Tahoe, CA 96150 Fax: (530)541-0373
Publication E-mail: tribune@tahoe.com

Community newspaper. **Founded:** 1958. **Freq:** Mon.-Fri.(morn.). **Print Method:** Offset. **Trim Size:** 13 x 21 1/8. **Cols./Page:** 6. **Col. Width:** 24 nonparells. **Col. Depth:** 301 agate lines. **Key Personnel:** Claipe Fortner, Editor, fortier@tahoe.com; Wiles Hill, Publisher; Pete Copeland, Advertising Dir. **Subscription Rates:** $102 individuals. **Remarks:** Accepts advertising.
Ad Rates: GLR: $9.10 **Circ:** Paid ‡9,134
BW: $1,818.90
4C: $1,847.50
SAU: $14.10
PCI: $18.00

3856 KOWL-AM - 1490
2435 Venice Dr. E. Phone: (916)541-6681
South Lake Tahoe, CA 96150 Fax: (916)541-4822

Format: Sports; Talk; News. **Simulcasts:** KRLT-FM. **Networks:** ABC. **Founded:** 1956. **Formerly**: Regency Communications. **Operating Hours:** Continuous. **Key Personnel:** Paul Middlebrook, General Mgr.; Brian Zappettini, Program Dir.; Jerry Hurwitz, News Dir. **Wattage:** 1000. **Ad Rates:** Advertising accepted; rates available upon request. Combined advertising rates available with KRLT-FM.

3857 KTHO-AM - 590
PO Box AM Phone: (916)542-5800
South Lake Tahoe, CA 96156 Fax: (916)544-0119

Format: News; Talk; Classic Rock. **Networks:** CBS. **Owner:** Emerald Broadcasting Co., at above address. **Founded:** 1963. **Operating Hours:** Continuous; 15% network, 85% local. **Wattage:** 2500. **Ad Rates:** Advertising accepted; rates available upon request.

SOUTH PASADENA

3858 American Cablevision of South Pasadena
909 El Centro St. Phone: (818)441-4559
South Pasadena, CA 91030-3115 Fax: (818)441-9730

Owner: Time Warner Cable, 300 First Stamford Pl., Stamford, CT 06902-6732, (203)328-0600, Fax: (203)328-0690. **Founded:** 1980. **Key Personnel:** Walt Kostrewski, General Mgr.; Gene Duenas, Chief Engineer; Karen Doss, Marketing Mgr.; Alfred Gonzalez, Customer Service Mgr.; Martha Welshans, Operations Mgr. **Cities Served:** San Marino, South Pasadena, CA: subscribing households 7,800; 50 channels; 1 community access channel; 6 hours per week community access programming.

SOUTH SAN FRANCISCO, pop. 49,393.

San Mateo Co. (W). 9 m S of San Francisco. Manufactures auto lifts, metal products, wire, flower pots, air conditioning units, chemicals, pastes, paint, scientific apparatus, airplane parts, radio equipment, magnesium products, plastics, electronics.

3859 Light Metal Age
Fellom Publishing Co.
170 S. Spruce Ave., Ste. 120 Phone: (415)588-8832
South San Francisco, CA 94080 Fax: (415)588-0901
Publication E-mail: lma@lightmetalage.com

Magazine serving primary and semi-fabrication metal plants that produce, semi-fabricate, process or manufacture the light metals: aluminum, magnesium, titanium, beryllium and their alloys, and/or the non-ferrous metals copper and zinc. **Subtitle:** The International Magazine of the Light Metal Industry. **Founded:** 1943. **Freq:** Bimonthly. **Print Method:** Offset. **Trim Size:** 8 1/4 x 11 1/8. **Cols./Page:** 3. **Col. Width:** 27 nonpareils. **Col. Depth:** 140 agate lines. **Key Personnel:** Wanda Fellom, Editor; Ann Marie Fellom, Publisher. **ISSN:** 0024-3345. **Subscription Rates:** $40 individuals.
Ad Rates: BW: $1,890 **Circ:** Paid 5,380
4C: $1,000
PCI: $100

3860 Philippine News
PO Box 2767 Phone: (415)872-3000
South San Francisco, CA 94083-2767 Fax: (415)872-0217
Free: (800)432-5877
Publication E-mail: pnewshq@aol.com

Newspaper for the Filipino community (six U.S. editions). **Founded:** 1961. **Freq:** Weekly. **Print Method:** Offset. **Cols./Page:** 6. **Col. Width:** 2 1/6 inches. **Col. Depth:** 21 1/2 inches. **Key Personnel:** Alex A. Esclamado, Publisher. **USPS:** 942-100. **Subscription Rates:** $30; $50 two years. **Remarks:** Accepts advertising. **Available Online**. **URL:** http://www.philippinenews.com.
Ad Rates: BW: $2,520 **Circ:** Paid 112,780
4C: $3,520 Free 7,500
SAU: $20

3861 Sing Tao Daily
Sing Tao Newspapers
215 Littlefield Ave. Phone: (650)872-1177
South San Francisco, CA 94080 Fax: (650)872-0234
Free: (800)SINGTAO

Newspaper (Chinese). **Founded:** 1938. **Freq:** Daily. **Trim Size:** 14 1/2 x 20. **Cols./Page:** 12. **Col. Width:** 1.125 inches. **Col. Depth:** 1 inches. **Key Personnel:** Tim S. Lau, Vice President, phone (650)872-2238, fax (650)872-0234; Wellington Cheng, Managing Editor. **USPS:** 497-120. **Subscription**

Rates: $165 individuals California edition; $155 out of state; $172 individuals Hawaii edition. **Remarks:** Accepts advertising. **Formerly:** Sing Tao Jih Pao.
Ad Rates: BW: $1,200 **Circ:** (Not Reported)
4C: $2,400
PCI: $5.2

SPRING VALLEY

3862 Spring Valley Bulletin
Forum Publications, Inc.
3434 Grove St. Phone: (619)469-0101
PO Box 127
Lemon Grove, CA 91946-1812
Community newspaper. **Founded:** 1948. **Freq:** Weekly (Thurs.). **Print Method:** Offset. **Trim Size:** 11 x 17. **Cols./Page:** 5. **Col. Width:** 11 1/2 picas. **Col. Depth:** 16 inches. **Key Personnel:** Steve Saint, Editor and Publisher. **Subscription Rates:** $15 individuals; $30 out of state. **Remarks:** Accepts advertising.
Ad Rates: BW: $1,000 **Circ:** ‡3,000
4C: $1,210
PCI: $12.50

SPRINGVILLE

3863 Tule River Times
PO Box 692 Phone: (209)539-3166
Springville, CA 93265 Fax: (209)539-2942

Community newspaper. **Subtitle:** Serving the Tule River Foothill and Mountain Communities. **Founded:** Aug. 1979. **Freq:** Weekly. **Print Method:** Offset. **Trim Size:** 10x13. **Cols./Page:** 5. **Col. Width:** 1 7/8 inches. **Col. Depth:** 13 inches. **Key Personnel:** Valeri McDonald, Editor and Publisher. **Subscription Rates:** $22; $25 out of county; $20 senior citizen. **Remarks:** Color advertising not accepted.
Ad Rates: BW: $308.75 **Circ:** Paid ‡2,000
PCI: $8.60 Free ‡100

STANFORD, pop. 8,691.

Santa Clara Co. (W). 14 m NW of San Jose. Residential. Stanford University. High tech industrial park.

3864 Birth of Tragedy Magazine
C.F.Y.
PO Box 6271 Phone: (650)324-9483
Stanford, CA 94309 Fax: (650)324-9495
Free: (800)742-6048
Publisher E-mail: eugene7@aol.com

Consumer magazine covering social issues. **Founded:** 1983. **Freq:** Semiannual. **Remarks:** Accepts advertising. **URL:** http://www.theoxbow.com.
Circ: Combined 6,000

3865 Journal of Economic Literature
American Economic Association
Stanford University Phone: (415)723-3741
Stanford, CA 94305
Publication E-mail: jel@leland.stanford.edu
Publisher E-mail: aeainfo@ctrvax.vanderbilt.edu

Economics journal. **Founded:** 1969. **Freq:** Quarterly. **Print Method:** Offset. **Cols./Page:** 1. **Col. Width:** 66 nonpareils. **Col. Depth:** 112 agate lines. **Key Personnel:** Prof. John Pencavel, Editor. **Subscription Rates:** $130. **Online:** Dialog (The Dialog Corporation). **Alt. Formats:** CD-ROM.
Ad Rates: BW: $875 **Circ:** ‡27,000

3866 Journal of Scientific Exploration
JSE Editorial Office Phone: (650)593-8581
PO Box 5848 Fax: (650)595-4466
Stanford, CA 94309-5848
Scholarly, refereed journal covering scientific advance in areas outside the established scientific discipline and anomalous phenomena. **Founded:** 1987. **Freq:** Quarterly. **Trim Size:** 6 x 9. **Key Personnel:** Marsha Sims, Exec. Editor, sims@jse.com; Dr. Bernhard Haisch, Editor-in-Chief. **ISSN:** 0892-3310. **Subscription Rates:** $50 individuals; $55 out of country; $100 institutions; $90 two years; $100 two years out of country; $175 two years institutional. **Remarks:** Advertising not accepted. **URL:** http://www.jse.com; http://www.catchword.com/register.htm.
Circ: Paid 3,000

3867 Stanford Business
Stanford Graduate School of Business
News & Publications Office Phone: (650)723-3157
Stanford, CA 94305-5015 Fax: (650)725-6750
Publication E-mail: gsb-newsline@gsb.stanford.edu

Magazine for business school alumni. **Founded:** 1931. **Freq:** Quarterly. **Print Method:** Offset. **Trim Size:** 8 1/2 x 11. **Key Personnel:** Cathy Castillo, Editor, phone (650)725-3238, castillo_cathy@gsb.stanford.edu; Nan Christensen, Production Mgr. **ISSN:** 0883-265X. **Subscription Rates:** $10 U.S. and Canada U.S. and Canada; $12 other countries; $12 out of country; $3 single issue single issue, other countries. **Remarks:** Advertising not accepted. **URL:** http://gsb-www.stanford.edu/gsbhome.html. **Formerly:** Stanford Business School Magazine.
Circ: Paid 18,000
Controlled 4,000

3868 The Stanford Daily
The Stanford Daily Publishing Corp.
Stanford University Phone: (650)725-2100
Storke Bldg. Fax: (650)725-1329
Stanford, CA 94305
Publication E-mail: letters@daily.stanford.edu
Publisher E-mail: business_manager@daily.stanford.edu

Collegiate newspaper. **Founded:** Sept. 1892. **Freq:** Daily (during the academic year); weekly (during the summer). **Print Method:** Offset. **Cols./Page:** 6. **Col. Width:** 25 nonpareils. **Col. Depth:** 294 agate lines. **Key Personnel:** Robin Tenold, Business Mgr.; Jim Tankersley, Editor. **USPS:** 518-420. **Subscription Rates:** $170. **Remarks:** Accepts advertising. **URL:** http://daily.stanford.org/.
Ad Rates: BW: $1,625.40 **Circ:** Free ‡13,500
4C: $2,060.40
PCI: $12.90

3869 Stanford Law Review
Stanford Law School
Stanford University Phone: (650)752-0183
Crown Quadrangle Fax: (650)723-0202
Stanford, CA 94305-8610
Journal covering law. **Founded:** 1948. **Freq:** Bimonthly. **Key Personnel:** Matthew Robison, President; Helen Nichols, Business Mgr. **Subscription Rates:** $40 individuals; $45 out of country; $14 single issue. **Remarks:** Accepts advertising. **Online:** LEXIS-NEXIS; Westlaw.
Ad Rates: BW: $600 **Circ:** Combined 2,167

3870 Stanford Lawyer
Stanford Law School
Stanford University Phone: (650)752-0183
Crown Quadrangle Fax: (650)723-0202
Stanford, CA 94305-8610
Publication E-mail: law.alum.pubs@forsythe.stanford.edu

Law school magazine for alumni, faculty, and students. **Founded:** 1966. **Freq:** Triennial. **Trim Size:** 8 x 11. **Key Personnel:** Constance Hellyer, Editor. **ISSN:** 0585-0576. **Subscription Rates:** Free to qualified subscribers. **Remarks:** Advertising not accepted. **Online:** Current Law Index; Dialog (The Dialog Corporation); Legal Trac. **Alt. Formats:** Microfiche, William S. Hein & Co.
Circ: Controlled 9,000

3871 Stanford Magazine
Stanford Alumni Association
Bowman Alumni House Phone: (650)725-0672
Stanford, CA 94305-4005 Fax: (650)725-8676

Alumni magazine. **Founded:** 1973. **Freq:** Bimonthly. **Print Method:** Offset. **Trim Size:** 8 1/8 x 10 3/4. **Cols./Page:** 3. **Col. Width:** 27 nonpareils. **Col. Depth:** 133 agate lines. **Key Personnel:** Ellen Williams, Business Mgr., phone (650)723-0863, ellenwi@leland.stanford.edu; Bob Cohn, Editor, phone (650)725-5109; Bambi Nicklen, Art Dir., phone (650)725-1085. **ISSN:** 1063-2778. **Subscription Rates:** $24 individuals; Free to qualified subscribers; $4 single issue. **Remarks:** Accepts advertising. **Online:** Internet. **URL:** http://www.stanfordmag.org.
Ad Rates: BW: $4,780 **Circ:** Controlled 100,000
4C: $6,830
PCI: $300

STOCKTON†, pop. 149,779.

San Joaquin Co. (C). An inland seaport on the San Joaquin River, 78 m E of San Francisco. University of the Pacific. San Joaquin Delta College. Manufactures boxboard, wooden and glass containers, auto windshields, window glass, pencil slats, doors, plows, feeds, fertilizers, bricks, scrapers, farm implement parts, concrete and steel pipes, structural iron and steel, cans, tire camelback, tire repair equipment, electrical equipment, paving machinery, cereal products, canned fruits and vegetables, motor boats, yachts, barges. Shipyards.

3872 The Catholic Lantern
Diocese of Stockton Phone: (209)466-5811
1105 N. Lincoln Fax: (209)941-9722
PO Box 4237
Stockton, CA 95203
Official newspaper (tabloid) of the Diocese of Stockton. **Founded:** 1982. **Freq:** Monthly. **Print Method:** Offset. **Cols./Page:** 6. **Col. Width:** 9.5 picas. **Col. Depth:** 12 1/2 inches. **Key Personnel:** Charles Goodman, Editor; Most Rev. Donald W. Montrose, Publisher; Richard Calderon, Advertising Dir. **Subscription Rates:** $12.50. **Remarks:** Accepts advertising.
Ad Rates: GLR: $9 **Circ:** Free 21,000
4C: $100
PCI: $10

3873 The Pacifican
University of the Pacific
3601 Pacific Ave. Phone: (209)946-2115
Hand Hall, 3rd Fl. Fax: (209)946-2195
Stockton, CA 95211
Publication E-mail: pacifican@uop.edu

Collegiate newspaper. **Founded:** 1908. **Freq:** Weekly (Thurs.). **Print Method:** Photo offset. **Trim Size:** 10 x 15. **Cols./Page:** 5. **Col. Width:** 1.875 inches. **Col. Depth:** 12 inches. **Key Personnel:** Trent Allen, Editor, phone (209)946-2114, ta0003@uop.edu. **Subscription Rates:** $30 individuals; $15 semester. **Remarks:** Accepts advertising. **URL:** http://www.pacifican@uop.edu.
Ad Rates: BW: $500 **Circ:** Free 5,000
4C: $660
PCI: $10

3874 The Record
530 E. Market St. Phone: (209)948-1702
PO Box 900 Fax: (209)547-8181
Stockton, CA 95202-3009
Free: (800)606-9742
Publication E-mail: newsroom@recordnet.com

General newspaper. **Founded:** 1895. **Freq:** Mon.-Sun. (morn.). **Print Method:** Letterpress. **Trim Size:** 13 3/4 x 22 3/4. **Cols./Page:** 6. **Col. Width:** 26 nonpareils. **Col. Depth:** 301 agate lines. **Key Personnel:** Jim Gold, Editor-in-Chief, phone (209)546-8251, fax (209)547-8186, jgold@recordnet.com; Sheldon Carpenter, AME/Design, phone (209)546-8274, fax (209)547-8186, sheldonc@recordnet.com; Thai Storm, Chief Librarian, phone (209)546-8286, fax (209)547-8186, thstorm@recordnet.com; Tony Sauro, Timeout Editor, phone (209)546-8267, fax (209)547-8186; Mike Klocke, Managing Editor, phone (209)546-8250, mklocke@recordnet.com. **USPS:** 522-240. **Subscription Rates:** $148.70 individuals. **Remarks:** Accepts advertising. **URL:** http://www.recordnet.com. **Formerly:** The Stockton Record. **Feature Editors:** Paul Feist, *Metro*, phone (209)943-8510, fax (209)547-8186, pfeist@recordnet.com; David Finch, *Photo*, phone (209)546-8268, fax (209)547-8186; Reed Fujii, *Features*, phone (209)546-8260, fax (209)547-8186, features@recordnet.com; Eric Grunder, *Financial/Business*, phone (209)546-8260, fax (209)547-8186, egrunder@recordnet.com; Kevin Parrish, *Editorials*, phone (209)546-8264, fax (209)547-8186, editor@recordnet.com; Sam Smith, *Sports*, phone (209)546-8282, fax (209)547-8187, ssmith@recordnet.com; Shari Spence, *TV*, *Travel*, phone (209)546-8277, fax (209)547-8186.
Ad Rates: GLR: $3.17 **Circ:** Mon.-Sat. 54,589
BW: $6,070.74 Sun. 68,970
4C: $6,946.74
SAU: $47.06
PCI: $47.06

San Joaquin Farm Bureau News - See San Joaquin

3875 Sun Diamond Grower
Sun Diamond Growers of California
1050 Diamond St. Phone: (209)467-6219
Stockton, CA 95205-7020 Fax: (209)467-6714

Magazine for producers of tree and vine crops. **Founded:** 1916. **Freq:** Quarterly. **Print Method:** Offset. **Trim Size:** 8 1/2 x 11. **Cols./Page:** 3. **Col. Width:** 29 nonpareils. **Col. Depth:** 134 agate lines. **Key Personnel:** Sandra J. McBride, Editor and Administration. **Remarks:** Accepts advertising.
Ad Rates: BW: $960 **Circ:** Controlled ‡10,000
4C: $1,450
PCI: $45

3876 Continental Cablevision
6505 Tam O'Shanter Phone: (209)473-4955
Stockton, CA 95210 Fax: (209)473-8177

Founded: 1973. **Cities Served:** San Joaquin County, French Camp, Lathrop, Lincoln Village West, Linden, and Manteca, CA.

3877 KCJH-FM - 90.1
9019 N. West Ln. Phone: (209)477-3690
Stockton, CA 95210

Format: Religious. **Networks:** USA Radio. **Owner:** Christian Life College, at above address. **Founded:** 1978. **Operating Hours:** Continuous. **ADI:** Sacramento-Stockton, CA. **Key Personnel:** Shirley Garner, General Mgr.; Adam Biddell, Music Dir.; Scott Mearns, Contact; Brent Regnart, Program Dir. **Wattage:** 26,000.

3878 KJOY-FM - 99.3
110 N. El Dorado St. Phone: (209)948-5529
Stockton, CA 95202-2308 Fax: (209)464-9999

Format: Adult Contemporary. **Owner:** Joseph Gamble Stations Inc., at above address. **Founded:** 1968. **Formerly**: KJAX-FM. **Operating Hours:** Continuous. **ADI:** Sacramento-Stockton, CA. **Key Personnel:** Joel Gamble, VP/Gen. Mgr.; Al Wilson, Station Mgr. **Wattage:** 3000. **Ad Rates:** Advertising accepted; rates available upon request.

3879 KLOC-AM - 920
6820 Pacific Ave., Ste. 2 Phone: (209)521-5562
Stockton, CA 95207-2604 Fax: (209)521-4131

Format: Hispanic. **Networks:** Independent. **Founded:** 1963. **Operating Hours:** Continuous; 100% local. **Wattage:** 2500.

3880 KMIX-AM - 1390
6820 Pacific Ave. Phone: (209)883-0433
Stockton, CA 95207 Fax: (209)883-4433

Format: Hispanic. **Networks:** Mutual Broadcasting System. **Founded:** 1949. **Operating Hours:** Continuous. **ADI:** Sacramento-Stockton, CA. **Key Personnel:** Tom Kelly, Program Dir.; Bob Salmon, General Mgr.; Bambi Clark, Sales Mgr. **Wattage:** 5000.

3881 KMIX-FM - 100.9
6820 Pacific Ave. Ste. 3 Phone: (209)474-0154
Stockton, CA 95207 Fax: (209)474-0136

Format: Hispanic. **Networks:** AP. **Owner:** Central Valley Communications, Inc., at above address. **Founded:** 1921. **Operating Hours:** Continuous. **ADI:** Sacramento-Stockton, CA. **Key Personnel:** Amadon Bustos, Contact, phone (916)646-4000, fax (916)646-3230; Juan Jose Ramirez, News Dir. **Wattage:** 6000. **Ad Rates:** Advertising accepted; rates available upon request.

3882 KQOD-FM - 100.1
1120 N. San Joaquin St. Phone: (209)462-5367
Stockton, CA 95202 Fax: (209)462-7959
Free: (800)500-8718

Format: Oldies. **Owner:** Carson-Group, Inc., at above address. **Founded:** 1980. **Formerly**: KFMR. **Operating Hours:** Continuous. **ADI:** Sacramento-Stockton, CA. **Key Personnel:** Susan Carson, Contact; Donna Cyr, Promotions Dir.; Arthur Morrison, Contact. **Wattage:** 6000.

3883 KSJC-FM - 89.5
5151 Pacific Ave. Phone: (209)474-5525
Stockton, CA 95207

Format: Eclectic; Ethnic. **ADI:** Sacramento-Stockton, CA. **Key Personnel:** Dave Alexander, General Mgr.

3884 KSTN-AM - 1420
2171 Ralph Ave. Phone: (209)948-5786
Stockton, CA 95206

Format: Contemporary Hit Radio (CHR). **Networks:** NBC. **Founded:** 1949. **Operating Hours:** Continuous. **ADI:** Sacramento-Stockton, CA. **Key Personnel:** Knox LaRue, Manager. **Wattage:** 5000 day; 1000 night.

3885 KSTN-FM - 107.3
2171 Ralph Ave. Phone: (209)948-5786
Stockton, CA 95206

Format: Ethnic; Hispanic. **Networks:** Cadena Radio Centro (CRC). **Founded:** 1956. **Operating Hours:** Continuous. **ADI:** Sacramento-Stockton, CA. **Key Personnel:** Knox LaRue, Manager. **Wattage:** 8100.

3886 KUOP-FM - 91.3
3601 Pacific Ave. Phone: (209)946-2582
Stockton, CA 95211 Free: (800)800-5867

Format: Public Radio; Eclectic. **Networks:** National Public Radio (NPR); Public Radio International (PRI). **Owner:** University of the Pacific, at above address, (209)946-2285. **Founded:** 1947. **Operating Hours:** Continuous; 25% network, 75% local. **ADI:** Sacramento-Stockton, CA. **Key Personnel:** Dennis L. Easter, Program Dir.; Jack Thomas, Public Affairs/News Director; Bridget Parks, Marketing; Carolyn Eades, Adm. Asst.; Jeff Crawford, Production Dir.; Scott Mearns, Chief Engineer. **Local Programs:** *Morning & Afternoon Classics*, Jeff Abbas, Mailing contact, (209)946-2379. **Wattage:** 7000. **Ad Rates:** Noncommercial.

3887 KWIN-FM - 97.7
6820 Pacific Ave., Ste.2 Phone: (209)476-1230
Stockton, CA 95207-2605 Fax: (209)957-1833

Format: Contemporary Hit Radio (CHR). **Simulcasts:** KWNN-FM. **Owner:** Front Line Communication Inc., at above address. **Founded:** 1959. **Formerly**: KWIN (1959). **Operating Hours:** Continuous. **ADI:** Sacramento-Stockton, CA. **Key Personnel:** Roy Williams, Contact, phone (209)476-1230, fax (209)957-1833; John Christian, Program Dir., phone (209)476-1230, fax (209)957-1833. **Wattage:** 3000.

3888 KWNN-FM - 98.3
6820 Pacific Ave. Phone: (209)476-1230
Stockton, CA 95207 Fax: (209)957-1833

Format: Contemporary Hit Radio (CHR). **Simulcasts:** KWIN-FM. **Owner:** Silverado Broadcasting, at above address. **Founded:** 1978. **Formerly**: KWNN (1996). **Operating Hours:** Continuous. **ADI:** Sacramento-Stockton, CA. **Key Personnel:** John Christian, Program Dir., phone (209)476-1230, fax (209)957-1833; Roy Williams, General Mgr.; John Buckley, Sales Mgr. **Wattage:** 3000.

3889 KYCC-FM - 89.1
9019 W. Lane Phone: (209)477-3690
Stockton, CA 95208 Fax: (209)477-2762

Format: Religious. **Networks:** USA Radio. **Owner:** Stockton Christian Life College, at above address. **Operating Hours:** Continuous. **Key Personnel:** Shirley Garner, General Mgr.; Brent Regnart, Program Dir.; Adam Biddel, Music Dir.; Marina Tahod, Office Mgr. **Wattage:** 6000. **Ad Rates:** Noncommercial. **URL:** http://www.kcjh@kcjh.org.

STUDIO CITY

3890 Money Making Opportunities
Success Publishing International
11071 Ventura Blvd. Phone: (818)980-9166
Studio City, CA 91604-3548 Fax: (818)980-7829

Magazine Source for small business opportunity seekers. **Founded:** 1959. **Freq:** 8/year. **Print Method:** Offset. **Cols./Page:** 3. **Col. Width:** 2 1/4 inches. **Col. Depth:** 140 agate lines. **Key Personnel:** Donald H. Perry, Publisher; Roger C. Perry, Account Exec. **Subscription Rates:** $8. **Remarks:** Advertising accepted; rates available upon request. **URL:** http://www.moneymakingopps.com.
Circ: Controlled ⊕**220,000**

SUISUN

3891 Journal of Wildlife Rehabilitation
International Wildlife Rehabilitation Council
4437 Central Pl., Ste. B4 Phone: (707)864-1761
Suisun, CA 94585-1663 Fax: (707)864-3106
Publisher E-mail: IWRC@inreach.com

Journal covering wildlife rehabilitation. **Founded:** 1978. **Freq:** Quarterly. **Trim Size:** 8 1/2 X 11. **Key Personnel:** Mary Reynolds. **ISSN:** 1071-2232. **Subscription Rates:** $40 individuals; $6 single issue; $50 family; $52 organization; $30 libraries and student. **Remarks:** Advertising not accepted. **Formerly**: Wildlife Journal.
Circ: Paid 2,000

SUN CITY, pop. 8,500.

Riverside Co. (SE). 25 m SE of Riverside. Retirement Community.

3892 Menifee Valley News
PO Box 310 Phone: (714)679-1191
Sun City, CA 92586 Fax: (714)679-2450

Community newspaper. **Founded:** 1988. **Freq:** Weekly. **Print Method:** Offset. **Trim Size:** 6 x 21. **Cols./Page:** 6. **Col. Depth:** 21 inches. **Key Personnel:** Joe Evans, Editor-in-Chief. **Subscription Rates:** $13; $32 out of country. **Remarks:** Accepts advertising. **Alt. Formats:** Microform.
Ad Rates: BW: $1,335.60 **Circ:** Paid 1,217
4C: $1,620.60 Non-paid 6,000
PCI: $10.98

3893 Sun City News
Community Publications Group
PO Box 310 Phone: (909)679-1191
Sun City, CA 92586 Fax: (909)679-2450

Retirement community newspaper. **Founded:** June 15, 1962. **Freq:** Weekly (Fri.). **Print Method:** Offset. **Trim Size:** 13 x 21 1/2. **Cols./Page:** 5. **Col. Width:** 26 nonpareils. **Col. Depth:** 301 agate lines. **Key Personnel:** Joe Hudon, General Mgr.; Joe Evans, Managing Editor. **Subscription Rates:** $13 individuals; $20 out of country. **Remarks:** Advertising not accepted for work at home. **Alt. Formats:** Microform.
Ad Rates: GLR: $1.38 **Circ:** Mon.-Sat. 3,200
BW: $902.16
4C: $1,187.16
PCI: $10.45

SUNLAND

3894 British-American Communications
7965 Foothill Blvd. Phone: (818)951-3900
Sunland, CA 91040-2958 Fax: (818)951-2951
Free: (800)278-3900

Founded: 1984. **Formerly**: British-Telecom, Inc. **Key Personnel:** Michael K. Bridges, President; John Cheeseman, Vice Pres./Chief Engineer; Diana N. Bridges, Secretary. **Cities Served:** Century City, Marina Del Ray, Studio City, West Los Angeles, CA; Riverside County & Los Angeles, CA: subscribing households 4,800; 62 channels; 1 community access channel; 20 hours per week community access programming.

SUNNYVALE, pop. 106,618.

Santa Clara Co. (W). 20 m NW of San Jose. Residential. Semi conductors, electronic components, computers, electrical heavy generating and control equipment, missile aerospace systems, paper products, chemicals. Nurseries. Fruit, canneries. Apricots, prunes, cherries.

3895 Austin-Healey Magazine
Austin-Healey Club
1160-B La Rochelle Terr. Phone: (408)541-9608
Sunnyvale, CA 94089 Fax: (408)541-9320
Publication E-mail: marka@infolane.com

Magazine for Austin-Healey owners. **Founded:** 1972. **Freq:** 10/year. **Trim Size:** 8 1/2 x 11. **Cols./Page:** 4. **Col. Width:** 3 inches. **Col. Depth:** 9 inches. **Key Personnel:** John Trifari, Contact, john4@home.net. **Subscription Rates:** $35. **Remarks:** Accepts advertising. **Available Online. URL:** http://www.healey.org. **Formerly**: Healy's Highlights.
Ad Rates: GLR: $10 **Circ:** Paid ‡1,550
BW: $200 Non-paid ‡100
4C: $250
PCI: $25

3896 Channel
Semiconductor Equipment & Materials International (SEMI)
Mathews & Clark Communications Phone: (408)736-1120
710 Lakeway, Ste. 170 Fax: (408)736-7880
Sunnyvale, CA 94086-4013
Publisher E-mail: semihq@semi.org

Trade magazine covering business and other news for suppliers of semiconductor equipment and materials. **Founded:** 1988. **Freq:** 6/yr. **Trim Size:** 8 x 11. **Cols./Page:** 4. **Col. Depth:** 10 inches. **Key Personnel:** Walter Mathews, Editor-in-Chief; Rose Eufinger, Managing Editor, reufinger@mathewsandclark.com. **Subscription Rates:** Free to qualified subscribers. **Remarks:** Accepts advertising. **URL:** http://www.semi.org.
Ad Rates: BW: $1,900 **Circ:** Controlled 13,000
4C: $2,500

3897 Employment Listings
Bay Area Employment Listings Magazine
PO Box 60935 Phone: (408)730-1970
Sunnyvale, CA 94088
Magazine covering employment listings for the Bay Area. **Founded:** Apr. 5, 1995. **Freq:** Weekly. **Print Method:** Newsprint. **Trim Size:** 8 1/2 x 10 3/8. **Cols./Page:** 3. **Key Personnel:** Lisa Zee. **Subscription Rates:** Free. **Remarks:** Accepts advertising. **Available Online.**
Ad Rates: GLR: $.80 **Circ:** (Not Reported)

3898 Interact
International Association of Hewlett-Packard Computer Users
1192 Borregas Ave. Phone: (408)747-0227
Sunnyvale, CA 94089 Fax: (408)747-0947

Magazine featuring in-depth articles of interest to users of Hewlett-Packard commercial computers. **Founded:** 1981. **Freq:** Monthly. **Print Method:** Offset. **Trim Size:** 8 1/2 x 11. **Cols./Page:** 3. **Col. Width:** 14 picas. **Col. Depth:** 10 inches. **Key Personnel:** Connie Wright, Editor and Publisher; Brian Hallin, Advertising Mgr. **ISSN:** 0279-2664. **Subscription Rates:** $49.50 individuals. **Remarks:** Accepts advertising.
Ad Rates: BW: $1,990 **Circ:** Paid ‡7,615
4C: $3,075 Controlled ‡4,000

3899 Nurseweek
Nurseweek Publishing
1156 Aster Ave., Ste. C Phone: (408)249-5877
Sunnyvale, CA 94086-6810 Fax: (408)249-8204
Free: (800)859-2691
Publication E-mail: editor@nurseweek.com
Publisher E-mail: nurseweek@nurseweek.com

Magazine (tabloid) featuring articles for R.N.'s. **Founded:** 1986. **Freq:** 32/year. **Print Method:** Web offset. **Trim Size:** 10 7/8 x 14. **Cols./Page:** 3. **Col. Depth:** 10 inches. **Key Personnel:** Whitney Wood, Managing Editor, fax (408)249-

3767, whitneyw@nurseweek.com; Andrew Baldwin, Publisher, fax (408)249-8670, andyb@nurseweek.com; Ray Riordan, National Advertising Dir., fax (972)488-8300, rayr@dhc.net; Barbara Bronson Gray, Editor-in-Chief, fax (818)889-2929, bbgray@ibm.net. **ISSN:** 1063-2859. **Remarks:** Accepts advertising. **URL:** http://www.nurseweek.com. **Alt. Formats:** Mailing labels. **Formerly:** California Nursing Review; California Nursing.
Ad Rates: GLR: $20.99 **Circ:** Controlled ‡225,000
PCI: $139.86

SUSANVILLE†, pop. 6,520.

Lassen Co. (NE). 80 m NW of Reno, Nev. Residential. Tourism. Beverages. Pine, fir timber. Dairy, stock, grain farms.

3900 Lassen County Times
Feather Publishing
800 Main St. Phone: (916)257-5321
Susanville, CA 96130 Fax: (916)257-0408
Publisher E-mail: featherpub@aol.com

Community newspaper. **Founded:** 1978. **Freq:** Weekly (Tues.). **Print Method:** Offset. **Cols./Page:** 6. **Col. Width:** 26 nonpareils. **Col. Depth:** 301 agate lines. **Key Personnel:** Michael Taborski, Publisher; Eve DeVeir, Managing Editor; Dave Moller, Editor. **Subscription Rates:** Free; $20 by mail. **Remarks:** Accepts advertising.
Ad Rates: BW: $709.50 **Circ:** Paid ‡5,767
4C: $400 Free ‡4,800
SAU: $5.50
PCI: $5.50

3901 KSUE-AM - 1240
3015 Johnstonville Rd. Phone: (916)257-2121
Susanville, CA 96130-8739 Fax: (916)257-6955
E-mail: radio@thegrid.net

Format: Full Service; Talk; Oldies; News. **Networks:** Mutual Broadcasting System. **Founded:** 1948. **Operating Hours:** Continuous; 25% network, 75% local. **ADI:** Reno, NV. **Key Personnel:** Rodney P. Chambers, Contact; Mike Smith, News Dir.; Hugh Hardaway, Program Dir. **Wattage:** 1000. **Ad Rates:** $7.00-10.50 for 30 seconds; $8.50-12.00 for 60 seconds. $7.00-$10.50 for 30 seconds; $8.50-$12.00 for 60 seconds. Combined advertising rates available with KSUE-FM.

3902 KSUE-FM - 93.3
3015 Johnstonville Rd. Phone: (916)257-2121
Susanville, CA 96130-8739 Fax: (916)257-6955
E-mail: radio@thegrid.net

Format: Country. **Networks:** Mutual Broadcasting System. **Founded:** 1976. **Operating Hours:** Continuous; 15% network, 85% local. **ADI:** Reno, NV. **Key Personnel:** Rodney P. Chambers, Contact; Mike Smith, News Dir.; Hugh Hardaway, Program Dir. **Wattage:** 100,000. **Ad Rates:** $7-10.50 for 30 seconds; $8.50-12 for 60 seconds. $7-$10.50 for 30 seconds; $8.50-$12 for 60 seconds. Combined advertising rates available with KSUE-AM.

SYLMAR

3903 Avatar
Pyx Press
PO Box 922648
Sylmar, CA 91392-2648

Publication series of single-author collections of fiction or poetry. **Founded:** 1994. **Freq:** 1-2/year. **Print Method:** Offset. **Key Personnel:** C. Darren Butler, Editor; Julie Thomas, Editor; Patricia Hatch, Manager. **Remarks:** Advertising not accepted.
Circ: (Not Reported)

3904 Magic Realism
Pyx Press
PO Box 922648
Sylmar, CA 91392-2648

Short fiction collections promoting magic realism as a North American literary form. **Founded:** 1994. **Freq:** 1-3/year. **Print Method:** Offset. **Key Personnel:** C. Daren Butler, Editor; Julie Thomas; Assoc. Editor; Patricia Hatch, Prod. Mgr. **Remarks:** Advertising not accepted. **Formerly:** North American Magic Realism.
Circ: (Not Reported)

3905 Strike Through The Mask
Pyx Press
PO Box 922648
Sylmar, CA 91392-2648

Journal consisting of a series of single-author collections of literary horror poetry or short fiction. **Founded:** 1994. **Freq:** 2/year. **Print Method:** Offset. **Key Personnel:** C. Darren Butler, Editor. **Remarks:** Advertising not accepted.
Circ: (Not Reported)

3906 A Theater of Blood
Pyx Press
PO Box 922648
Sylmar, CA 91392-2648

Magazine of bizarre and horrific short-short fiction and poetry. **Founded:** 1990. **Freq:** Annual. **Subscription Rates:** $7. $2.50 single issue. **Remarks:** Advertising accepted; rates available upon request.
Circ: Paid 150
Controlled 50

TAFT, pop. 5,316.

Kern Co. (S). 30 m SW of Bakersfield. Gasoline refineries. Oil pumps, tools, oil well equipment, pipe and steel manufactured. Oil, gas wells.

3907 Daily Midway Driller
Scripps League
PO Bin Z Phone: (805)763-3171
Taft, CA 93268-0046 Fax: (805)763-5638

General newspaper. **Founded:** 1910. **Freq:** Daily (eve.). **Print Method:** Offset. **Cols./Page:** 6. **Col. Width:** 24 nonpareils. **Col. Depth:** 298 agate lines. **Key Personnel:** John J. Byrne, Publisher. **Subscription Rates:** $38.40 individuals.

3908 Westside Shopping News
800 Center St. Phone: (805)763-3171
PO Box Z Fax: (805)763-3334
Taft, CA 93268
Shopper. **Founded:** 1910. **Freq:** Weekly. **Print Method:** Offset. **Cols./Page:** 6. **Col. Width:** 24 nonpareils. **Col. Depth:** 298 agate lines. **Key Personnel:** Dottie Parsons, Publisher. **Remarks:** Accepts advertising.
Ad Rates: SAU: $1.60 **Circ:** Free 4,600

TAHOE CITY, pop. 1,394.

Placer Co. (NE). On Lake Tahoe, 80 m NE of Sacramento. Machine shop. Resort.

3909 Tahoe World
PO Box 138 Phone: (916)583-3487
Tahoe City, CA 96145-0138 Fax: (916)583-7109
Publication E-mail: world@tahoe.com

Newspaper covering North Lake Tahoe, Truckee, Placer, and Nevada county. **Founded:** 1963. **Freq:** Weekly (Thurs.). **Print Method:** Offset. **Cols./Page:** 6. **Col. Width:** 18 nonpareils. **Col. Depth:** 301 agate lines. **Key Personnel:** Eric Henry, Editor; Bill Kunerth, Publisher; Janet Doherty, Promotions Mgr.; Suzi Higgins, Advertising; Micheal Smoot, Advertising. **Subscription Rates:** $34 individuals.
Ad Rates: GLR: $9 **Circ:** 6,000
4C: $235.00
PCI: $10.25

TAHOE VISTA, pop. 250.

Placer Co. (NE) 10 m N of Tahoe City. All year resort.

North Tahoe/Truckee Week - See Truckee

TARZANA

Los Angeles Co. (S). 25 m NW of Los Angeles. Residential. Commercial.

3910 RePlay Magazine
PO Box 7004 Phone: (818)776-2880
Tarzana, CA 91357 Fax: (818)776-2888

Trade magazine covering the amusement game industry. **Founded:** Oct. 1975. **Freq:** Monthly. **Print Method:** Sheetfed offset. **Trim Size:** 8 1/2 x 11. **Cols./Page:** 3. **Col. Width:** 2 1/4 inches. **Col. Depth:** 10 inches. **Key Personnel:** Marcus Webb, Editor, editor@replaymag.com; Barry Zwegen, Advertising Mgr. **ISSN:** 0360-7348. **Subscription Rates:** $65 individuals; $6 single issue. **Remarks:** Accepts advertising. **Formerly:** RePlay.
Ad Rates: BW: $1,190 **Circ:** Combined 5,770
4C: $1,690

TEHACHAPI, pop. 4,126.

Kern Co. (S). 46 m SE of Bakersfield. Resort area. Residential. Limestone quarries. Clay pits. Agriculture. wheat, barley, nectarines, peaches.

3911 Tehachapi News
Tehachapi News, Inc.
411 N. Mill St. Phone: (805)822-6828
PO Box 230 Fax: (805)822-4053
Tehachapi, CA 93561
Publisher E-mail: tni@tminet.com

Community newspaper. **Founded:** 1895. **Freq:** Weekly (Wed.). **Print Method:** Offset. **Cols./Page:** 6. **Col. Width:** 26 nonpareils. **Col. Depth:** 294 agate lines. **Key Personnel:** Mike White, Editor; William Mead, Publisher; Elizabeth Mead, Publisher. **USPS:** 536-740. **Subscription Rates:** $24 individuals; $29 out of county; $30 out of state.
Ad Rates: GLR: $10.38 **Circ:** ‡8,013
BW: $1,166
SAU: $11.40

TEMECULA, pop. 220.

Riverside Co. (S) 1 m S. of Murrieta. Residential.

3912 The Californian
28765 Single Oak Drive Ste. 100 Phone: (909)676-4315
Fax: (909)699-1467
Temecula, CA 92590
Publication E-mail: calnews@nctimes.com; day@scn.com

Newspaper. **Founded:** 1976. **Freq:** Daily (morn.). **Print Method:** Offset. **Cols./Page:** 6. **Col. Width:** 26 nonpareils. **Col. Depth:** 294 agate lines. **Key Personnel:** Kathy Day, Editor, fax (909)694-1215, day@nctimes.com; Claude Reinke, Pub. & Ad./Marketing Mgr.; Bette Webster, Circulation Mgr. **Subscription Rates:** $52 individuals. **Remarks:** Accepts advertising.
Ad Rates: GLR: $.39 **Circ:** Mon.-Sat. 12,485
BW: $941.70 Sun. 12,540
4C: $1,314.70

3913 KATY-FM - 101.3
27450 Ynez Rd., Ste. 316 Phone: (909)506-1222
Temecula, CA 92591 Fax: (909)506-1213
E-mail: katy@ez2.net

Format: Adult Contemporary. **Networks:** ABC. **Owner:** Kay Sadlier-Gill, at above address. **Founded:** Dec. 1, 1989. **Operating Hours:** Continuous. **Key Personnel:** Dave Carson, Station Mgr.; Cheri Nyman, Business Mgr.; Mike Rozof, Operations Mgr. **URL:** http://www.katyfm.com.

THOUSAND OAKS, pop. 77,797.

Ventura Co. (SW). 30 m SE of Ventura. Manufactures aircraft parts, electronic parts and parachutes, plastics. Horse breeding. Agriculture. Citrus fruit.

3914 Abstracts in Social Gerontology
Sage Publications Inc.
2455 Teller Rd. Phone: (805)499-0721
Thousand Oaks, CA 91320 Fax: (805)499-0871
Publisher E-mail: info@sagepub.com

Annotated bibliography of books, journal articles, and documents relevant to social gerontology. **Subtitle:** Current Literature on Aging. **Founded:** 1957. **Freq:** Quarterly. **Print Method:** Offset. **Trim Size:** 5 1/4 x 8 1/2. **Key Personnel:** Julie L. Moore, Editor; Janette Saquet, Co-Editor; Sara Miller McCune, Publisher; Paul V. McDowell, Documentation editor. **ISSN:** 1047-4862. **Subscription Rates:** $80 individuals; $21 single issue; $164 institutions, other countries and students.
Ad Rates: BW: $195 **Circ:** ‡8,400

3915 Administration & Society
Sage Publications Inc.
2455 Teller Rd. Phone: (805)499-0721
Thousand Oaks, CA 91320 Fax: (805)499-0871
Publisher E-mail: info@sagepub.com

Journal for social scientists and public administrators. **Founded:** 1969. **Freq:** Quarterly. **Print Method:** Offset. **Trim Size:** 5 1/2 x 8 1/2. **Cols./Page:** 1. **Col. Width:** 50 nonpareils. **Col. Depth:** 100 agate lines. **Key Personnel:** Gary L. Wamsley, Editor; Cris Anderson, Circulation Mgr. **ISSN:** 0095-3997. **Subscription Rates:** $55 individuals; $157 Industry; $110 two years; $314 two years, Industry; $15 single issue; $40 single issue, Industry; $37 single issue. **Remarks:** Accepts advertising.
Ad Rates: BW: $200 **Circ:** Paid ‡1,300
Non-paid ‡88

3916 AFFILIA: Journal of Women and Social Work
Sage Publications Inc.
2455 Teller Rd. Phone: (805)499-0721
Thousand Oaks, CA 91320 Fax: (805)499-0871
Publisher E-mail: info@sagepub.com

Journal following women in the social work field. **Founded:** 1986. **Freq:** Quarterly. **Print Method:** Offset. **Trim Size:** 5 1/2

x 8 1/2. **Cols./Page:** 1. **Col. Width:** 50 nonpareils. **Col. Depth:** 100 agate lines. **Key Personnel:** Cris Anderson, Circulation Mgr.; Carol H. Meyer, Editor; Cris Anderson, Advertising Mgr. **ISSN:** 0886-1099. **Subscription Rates:** $41 individuals; $113 Industry; $82 two years; $226 two years, Industry; $29 single issue, Industry. **Remarks:** Accepts advertising.
Ad Rates: BW: $250 **Circ:** Paid ‡1,250
Non-paid ‡110

3917 American Behavioral Scientist
Sage Publications Inc.
2455 Teller Rd. Phone: (805)499-0721
Thousand Oaks, CA 91320 Fax: (805)499-0871
Publisher E-mail: info@sagepub.com

Social and behavioral sciences journal. **Founded:** 1957. **Freq:** Bimonthly. **Print Method:** Offset. **Trim Size:** 5 1/2 x 8 1/2. **Cols./Page:** 1. **Col. Width:** 50 nonpareils. **Col. Depth:** 100 agate lines. **Key Personnel:** Cris Anderson, Circulation Mgr. **ISSN:** 0002-7642. **Subscription Rates:** $60 individuals; $200 institutions; $120 two years; $400 two years Institutions; $14 single issue; $28 single issue Institutions. **Remarks:** Accepts advertising.
Ad Rates: BW: $250 **Circ:** Paid 1,800
Non-paid 112

3918 American Politics Quarterly
Sage Publications Inc.
2455 Teller Rd. Phone: (805)499-0721
Thousand Oaks, CA 91320 Fax: (805)499-0871
Publisher E-mail: info@sagepub.com

Political science journal. **Founded:** 1973. **Freq:** Quarterly. **Print Method:** Offset. **Trim Size:** 5 1/2 x 8 1/2. **Cols./Page:** 1. **Col. Width:** 50 nonpareils. **Col. Depth:** 100 agate lines. **Key Personnel:** James C. Garand, Editor; Cris Anderson, Circulation Mgr.; Valerie Giramberk, Circulation Mgr. **ISSN:** 0044-7803. **Subscription Rates:** $48 individuals; $140 institutions; $96 two years; $280 two years Institutions; $36 single issue; $34 single issue Institutions. **Remarks:** Accepts advertising.
Ad Rates: BW: $250 **Circ:** Paid 1,250
Non-paid 92

3919 The Annals of the American Academy of Political and Social Science
Sage Publications Inc.
2455 Teller Rd. Phone: (805)499-0721
Thousand Oaks, CA 91320 Fax: (805)499-0871
Publisher E-mail: info@sagepub.com

Political and social science journal. **Founded:** 1890. **Freq:** Bimonthly. **Print Method:** Letterpress and offset. **Trim Size:** 6 1/4 x 9 1/4. **Cols./Page:** 1. **Key Personnel:** Richard D. Lambert, Editor; Cris Anderson, Circulation Mgr. **ISSN:** 0002-7162. **Subscription Rates:** $45 individuals; $145 two years Industry; $14 single issue; $25 single issue Industry. **Remarks:** Accepts advertising.
Ad Rates: BW: $250 **Circ:** Paid ‡5,800
Non-paid ‡186

3920 Behavior Modification
Sage Publications Inc.
2455 Teller Rd. Phone: (805)499-0721
Thousand Oaks, CA 91320 Fax: (805)499-0871
Publisher E-mail: info@sagepub.com

Psychology journal. **Founded:** 1977. **Freq:** Quarterly. **Print Method:** Offset. **Trim Size:** 5 1/2 x 8 1/2. **Cols./Page:** 1. **Col. Width:** 50 nonpareils. **Col. Depth:** 100 agate lines. **Key Personnel:** Michel Hersen, Editor; Alan Bellack, Advertising Mgr.; Cris Anderson, Circulation Mgr. **ISSN:** 0145-4455. **Subscription Rates:** $53 individuals; $155 institutions; $106 two years Institutions; $310 two years; $40 single issue Institutions. **Remarks:** Accepts advertising.
Ad Rates: BW: $200 **Circ:** Paid 1,500
Non-paid 115

3921 China Report: A Journal of East Asian Studies
Sage Publications Inc.
2455 Teller Rd. Phone: (805)499-0721
Thousand Oaks, CA 91320 Fax: (805)499-0871
Publisher E-mail: info@sagepub.com

Journal promoting the increased understanding of contemporary China and its East Asian neighbors, including articles on culture, methods of development, and impact on India and other South Asian countries. **Founded:** Feb. 1987. **Freq:** Quarterly. **Trim Size:** 6 1/4 x 9 1/2. **Key Personnel:** C.R.M. Rao, Editor; Cris Anderson, Circulation Mgr. **ISSN:** 0009-4455. **Subscription Rates:** $38 individuals; $74 institutions; $13 single issue; $22 single issue Institutions. **Remarks:** Advertising not accepted.
Circ: Paid 1,700

3922 Clinical Nursing Research
Sage Publications Inc.
2455 Teller Rd. Phone: (805)499-0721
Thousand Oaks, CA 91320 Fax: (805)499-0871
Publisher E-mail: info@sagepub.com

Journal on scholarly research focused on clinical practice. **Subtitle:** An International Journal. **Freq:** Quarterly. **Key Personnel:** Marilynn J. Wood, Editor; Patricia Hayes, Advertising Mgr.; Cris Anderson, Circulation Mgr. **ISSN:** 1054-7738. **Subscription Rates:** $41 individuals; $107 institutions.

3923 Communication Abstracts
Sage Publications Inc.
2455 Teller Rd. Phone: (805)499-0721
Thousand Oaks, CA 91320 Fax: (805)499-0871
Publisher E-mail: info@sagepub.com

Journal containing abstracts and references in communications. **Founded:** 1978. **Freq:** Bimonthly. **Print Method:** Offset. **Trim Size:** 5 1/2 x 8 1/2. **Cols./Page:** 1. **Col. Width:** 50 nonpareils. **Col. Depth:** 100 agate lines. **Key Personnel:** Thomas Gordon, Editor; Cris Anderson, Circulation Mgr.; Paul V. McDowell, Documentation editor; Robert G. Roberg, Associate editor. **ISSN:** 0162-2811. **Subscription Rates:** $125 individuals; $380 institutions; $23 single issue. **Remarks:** Accepts advertising.
Ad Rates: BW: $200 **Circ:** Paid 1,250
Non-paid 101

3924 Communication Research
Sage Publications Inc.
2455 Teller Rd. Phone: (805)499-0721
Thousand Oaks, CA 91320 Fax: (805)499-0871
Publisher E-mail: info@sagepub.com

Journal featuring writings on the impact of mass communications. **Founded:** 1974. **Freq:** Bimonthly. **Print Method:** Offset. **Trim Size:** 6 1/4 x 9 1/4. **Cols./Page:** 1. **Col. Width:** 50 nonpareils. **Col. Depth:** 100 agate lines. **Key Personnel:** Prof. Charles R. Berger, Editor; Sandra Ball-Rokeach, Advertising Mgr.; Cris Anderson, Circulation Mgr. **ISSN:** 0093-6502. **Subscription Rates:** $58 individuals; $205 institutions; $116 two years; $410 two years Institutions; $35 single issue single issue, Industry.; $33 single issue INS. **Remarks:** Accepts advertising.
Ad Rates: BW: $200 **Circ:** Paid 1,600
Non-paid 152

3925 Comparative Political Studies
Sage Publications Inc.
2455 Teller Rd. Phone: (805)499-0721
Thousand Oaks, CA 91320 Fax: (805)499-0871
Publisher E-mail: info@sagepub.com

Political science journal. **Founded:** 1968. **Freq:** Quarterly. **Print Method:** Offset. **Trim Size:** 5 1/2 x 8 1/2. **Cols./Page:** 1. **Col. Width:** 50 nonpareils. **Col. Depth:** 100 agate lines. **Key Personnel:** James A. Caporaso, Editor; Cris Anderson, Circulation Mgr. **ISSN:** 0010-4140. **Subscription Rates:** $47 individuals; $146 institutions; $94 two years; $292 two years two years, Industry; $37 single issue single issue, Industry; $36 single issue INS. **Remarks:** Accepts advertising.
Ad Rates: BW: $250 **Circ:** Paid ‡1,750
Non-paid ‡153

3926 Crime & Delinquency
Sage Publications Inc.
2455 Teller Rd. Phone: (805)499-0721
Thousand Oaks, CA 91320 Fax: (805)499-0871
Publisher E-mail: info@sagepub.com

Journal on policy studies in criminal justice. **Founded:** 1955. **Freq:** Quarterly. **Print Method:** Offset. **Trim Size:** 5 1/2 x 8 1/2. **Cols./Page:** 1. **Col. Width:** 50 nonpareils. **Col. Depth:** 100 agate lines. **Key Personnel:** Don C. Gibbons, Editor; Diane Irwin; Cris Anderson, Circulation Mgr. **ISSN:** 0011-1287. **Subscription Rates:** $157 individuals; $16 single issue Industry; $104 two years; $300 two years, Industry; $39 single issue, Industry. **Remarks:** Accepts advertising.
Ad Rates: BW: $200 **Circ:** Paid 2,900
Non-paid 151

3927 Criminal Justice and Behavior
Sage Publications Inc.
2455 Teller Rd. Phone: (805)499-0721
Thousand Oaks, CA 91320 Fax: (805)499-0871
Publisher E-mail: info@sagepub.com

Journal studying the effects of the criminal justice system on human behavior. **Founded:** 1974. **Freq:** Quarterly. **Print Method:** Offset. **Trim Size:** 5 1/2 x 8 1/2. **Cols./Page:** 1. **Col. Width:** 50 nonpareils. **Col. Depth:** 100 agate lines. **Key Personnel:** David S. Glenwick, Editor; Cris Anderson, Circulation Mgr. **ISSN:** 0093-8548. **Subscription Rates:** $47 individuals; $146 Industry; $94 two years; $280 two years, Industry; $36 single issue, Industry; $34 single issue. **Remarks:** Accepts advertising.
Ad Rates: BW: $250 **Circ:** Paid ‡1,950
Non-paid ‡177

3928 Cross-Cultural Research
Sage Publications Inc.
2455 Teller Rd. Phone: (805)499-0721
Thousand Oaks, CA 91320 Fax: (805)499-0871
Publisher E-mail: info@sagepub.com

Journal of cross-cultural research in the social and behavioral sciences. **Subtitle:** The Journal of Comparative Social Science. **Founded:** Feb. 1993. **Freq:** Quarterly. **Key Personnel:** Melvin Ember, Editor; Cris Anderson, Circulation Mgr. **ISSN:** 1069-3971. **Subscription Rates:** $45 individuals; $84 institutions.

3929 Economic Development Quarterly
Sage Publications Inc.
2455 Teller Rd. Phone: (805)499-0721
Thousand Oaks, CA 91320 Fax: (805)499-0871
Publisher E-mail: info@sagepub.com

Journal reporting on research programs, policies, and trends in economic development in large cities, small towns, rural areas, and overseas trade and expansion. **Founded:** Feb. 1987. **Freq:** Quarterly. **Print Method:** Offset. **Trim Size:** 8 1/2 x 11. **Cols./Page:** 1. **Key Personnel:** Richard Bingham, Editor; Cris Anderson, Circulation Mgr. **ISSN:** 0891-2424. **Subscription Rates:** $53 individuals; $148 Industry; $106 two years; $296 two years, Industry; $38 single issue, Industry; $36 single issue. **Remarks:** Accepts advertising.
Ad Rates: BW: $250 **Circ:** Paid ‡1,300
Non-paid ‡164

3930 Education and Urban Society
Corwin Press
2455 Teller Rd. Phone: (805)499-9734
Thousand Oaks, CA 91320 Fax: (805)499-5323
Publisher E-mail: info@corwinpress.com

Educational administration journal. **Founded:** 1968. **Freq:** Quarterly. **Print Method:** Offset. **Trim Size:** 5 1/2 x 8 1/2. **Cols./Page:** 1. **Col. Width:** 50 nonpareils. **Col. Depth:** 100 agate lines. **Key Personnel:** Edward R. Ducharme, Managing Editor; Mary K. Ducharme, Publisher, maryd@c4.net. **ISSN:** 0013-1245. **Subscription Rates:** $49 individuals; $15 single issue; $145 institutions; $12.50 single issue. **Remarks:** Accepts advertising.
Ad Rates: BW: $225 **Circ:** (Not Reported)

3931 Educational Administration Abstracts
Corwin Press
2455 Teller Rd. Phone: (805)499-0721
Thousand Oaks, CA 91320 Fax: (805)499-0871
Publication E-mail: order@corwin.sagepub.com
Publisher E-mail: info@corwinpress.com

Journal providing educational administration abstracts. **Founded:** 1966. **Freq:** Quarterly. **Print Method:** Offset. **Trim Size:** 5 1/2 x 8 1/2. **Cols./Page:** 1. **Col. Width:** 50 nonpareils. **Col. Depth:** 100 agate lines. **Key Personnel:** Paul V. McDowell, Editor; Gracia A. Alkema, Publisher. **ISSN:** 0013-1601. **Subscription Rates:** $95 individuals; $325 institutions one year; $190 two years; $640 institutions two years; $30 single issue; $90 single issue institutions. **Remarks:** Accepts advertising.
Ad Rates: BW: $225 **Circ:** Paid 708
Non-paid 37

3932 Educational and Psychological Measurement
Sage Publications Inc.
2455 Teller Rd. Phone: (805)499-0721
Thousand Oaks, CA 91320 Fax: (805)499-0871
Publisher E-mail: info@sagepub.com

Journal on problems and research in the areas of education, psychology, industry, and government. **Founded:** Mar. 1994. **Freq:** Quarterly. **Key Personnel:** Geraldine Thomas Sheehy, Editor; Cris Anderson, Circulation Mgr. **ISSN:** 0013-1644. **Subscription Rates:** $70 individuals; $70 institutions.

3933 Elvis International Forum
Creative Radio Network
PO Box 3373 Phone: (818)991-3892
Thousand Oaks, CA 91359 Fax: (818)991-3894

Consumer magazine covering entertainment. **Freq:** Quarterly. **Trim Size:** 8 1/2 x 11. **Cols./Page:** 3. **Key Personnel:** Darwin L. Lamm, Editor. **Subscription Rates:** $19.95 individuals; $6 single issue. **Remarks:** Accepts advertising.
Ad Rates: 4C: $3,500 **Circ:** Combined 90,800

3934 Evaluation & the Health Professions
Sage Publications Inc.
2455 Teller Rd. Phone: (805)499-0721
Thousand Oaks, CA 91320 Fax: (805)499-0871
Publisher E-mail: info@sagepub.com

Journal providing information relative to research and practice in health settings. **Founded:** 1978. **Freq:** Quarterly. **Print Method:** Offset. **Trim Size:** 5 1/2 x 8 1/2. **Cols./Page:** 1. **Col. Width:** 50 nonpareils. **Col. Depth:** 100 agate lines. **Key Personnel:** R. Barker Bausell, Editor; Cris Anderson, Circulation Mgr. **ISSN:** 0163-2787. **Subscription Rates:** $50 individuals; $144 Industry; $100 two years; $288 two years Institutions; $37 single issue Industry; $34 single issue INS. **Remarks:** Accepts advertising.
Ad Rates: BW: $195 **Circ:** Paid ‡1,100
Non-paid ‡161

3935 Evaluation Review
Sage Publications Inc.
2455 Teller Rd. Phone: (805)499-0721
Thousand Oaks, CA 91320 Fax: (805)499-0871
Publisher E-mail: info@sagepub.com

Journal containing evaluation studies. **Founded:** 1977. **Freq:** Bimonthly. **Print Method:** Offset. **Trim Size:** 5 1/2 x 8 1/2. **Cols./Page:** 1. **Col. Width:** 50 nonpareils. **Col. Depth:** 100 agate lines. **Key Personnel:** Richard A. Berk, Editor; Cris Anderson, Circulation Mgr. **ISSN:** 0193-841X. **Subscription Rates:** $63 individuals; $183 institutions; $126 two years; $366 two years Institutions; $32 single issue Industry; $30 single issue Institution. **Remarks:** Accepts advertising.
Ad Rates: BW: $200 **Circ:** Paid ‡1,600
Non-paid ‡208

3936 Family and Conciliation Courts Review
Sage Publications Inc.
2455 Teller Rd. Phone: (805)499-0721
Thousand Oaks, CA 91320 Fax: (805)499-0871
Publisher E-mail: info@sagepub.com

International communication forum to develop and improve the practice of conciliation counseling as a complement to judicial procedures. **Founded:** 1963. **Freq:** Quarterly. **Print Method:** Offset. **Trim Size:** 5 1/2 x 8 1/2. **Cols./Page:** 1. **Col. Width:** 50 nonpareils. **Col. Depth:** 100 agate lines. **Key Personnel:** Hugh McIsaac, Editor; Cris Anderson, Circulation Mgr. **ISSN:** 1047-5699. **Subscription Rates:** $47 individuals; $110 Industry; $94 two years; $220 two years, Industry; $29 single issue, Industry. **Remarks:** Accepts advertising.
Ad Rates: BW: $250 **Circ:** Paid 2,200
Non-paid 128

3937 Family and Consumer Sciences Research Journal
Sage Publications Inc.
2455 Teller Rd. Phone: (805)499-0721
Thousand Oaks, CA 91320 Fax: (805)499-0871
Publisher E-mail: info@sagepub.com

Home economics journal. **Founded:** 1971. **Freq:** Quarterly. **Print Method:** Offset. **Trim Size:** 6 7/8 x 9 15/16. **Cols./Page:** 2. **Col. Width:** 34 nonpareils. **Col. Depth:** 116 agate lines. **Key Personnel:** Dr. Rodney M. Cate, Editor; Cris Anderson, Circulation Mgr. **ISSN:** 0046-7774. **Subscription Rates:** $45 individuals; $80 Industry; $15 single issue; $22 single issue Industry. **Remarks:** Accepts advertising. **Formerly:** Home Economics Research Journal.
Ad Rates: BW: $250 **Circ:** Paid 2,300
Free 127

3938 Hispanic Journal of Behavioral Sciences
Sage Publications Inc.
2455 Teller Rd. Phone: (805)499-0721
Thousand Oaks, CA 91320 Fax: (805)499-0871
Publisher E-mail: info@sagepub.com

Journal publishes research articles, case histories, critical reviews, and scholarly notes that are of theoretical interest or deal with methodological issues related to Hispanic populations. **Founded:** Feb. 1989. **Freq:** Quarterly (February, May, August, and November). **Print Method:** Web press. **Trim Size:** 5 1/2 x 8 1/2. **Cols./Page:** 1. **Col. Width:** 50 nonpareils. **Col. Depth:** 100 agate lines. **Key Personnel:** Amado M. Padilla, Editor; Cris Anderson, Circulation Mgr. **ISSN:** 0739-9863. **Subscription Rates:** $51; $126 institutions; $15 single issue; $29 single issue Institutions; $84 two years. **Remarks:** Accepts advertising.
Ad Rates: BW: $250 **Circ:** Paid 1,250
Non-paid 163

3939 Human Communication Research
Sage Publications Inc.
2455 Teller Rd. Phone: (805)499-0721
Thousand Oaks, CA 91320 Fax: (805)499-0871
Publisher E-mail: info@sagepub.com

Interpersonal communication journal. **Founded:** 1974. **Freq:** Quarterly. **Print Method:** Offset. **Trim Size:** 6 x 9. **Cols./Page:** 1. **Col. Width:** 50 nonpareils. **Col. Depth:** 100 agate lines. **Key Personnel:** Prof. Howard Giles, Editor; Cris Anderson, Circulation Mgr. **ISSN:** 0360-3989. **Subscription Rates:** $54 individuals; $142 Industry; $108 two years; $284 two years Institutions; $37 single issue; $34 single issue INS. **Remarks:** Accepts advertising.
Ad Rates: BW: $250 **Circ:** Paid ‡3,850
Non-paid ‡96

3940 Human Resources Abstracts
Sage Publications Inc.
2455 Teller Rd. Phone: (805)499-0721
Thousand Oaks, CA 91320 Fax: (805)499-0871
Publication E-mail: info@sagepub.com
Publisher E-mail: info@sagepub.com

Journal providing abstracts refering to employment and labor relations. **Founded:** 1966. **Freq:** Quarterly. **Print Method:** Offset. **Trim Size:** 5 1/2 x 8 1/2. **Cols./Page:** 1. **Col. Width:** 50 nonpareils. **Col. Depth:** 100 agate lines. **Key Personnel:** Paul V. McDowell, Editor; Cris Anderson, Circulation Mgr. **ISSN:** 0099-2453. **Subscription Rates:** $118 individuals; $360 institutions; $236 two years; $720 two years institutions; $32 single issue; $92 single issue institutions. **Remarks:** Accepts advertising.
Ad Rates: BW: $200 **Circ:** Paid ‡800
Non-paid ‡76

3941 IB (Independent Business)
Group IV Communications, Inc.
125 Auburn Court, Ste. 100 Phone: (805)496-6156
Thousand Oaks, CA 91362-3617 Fax: (805)496-5469
Publication E-mail: gosmallbiz@aol.com

Magazine for small business owners. **Subtitle:** America's Small Business Magazine. **Founded:** 1989. **Freq:** Bimonthly. **Print Method:** Offset. **Trim Size:** 8 x 10 1/2. **Key Personnel:** Daniel Kehrer, Editor; Mike Carpenter, Publisher; Maryann Hammers, Managing Editor. **ISSN:** 1047-2347. **Subscription Rates:** Included with membership dues to Natl. Federation of Independent Business. **Remarks:** Accepts advertising.
Ad Rates: BW: $31,337 **Circ:** Non-paid △**550,000**
4C: $47,006

3942 Indian Economic and Social History Review
Sage Publications Inc.
2455 Teller Rd. Phone: (805)499-0721
Thousand Oaks, CA 91320 Fax: (805)499-0871
Publication E-mail: info@sagepub.com
Publisher E-mail: info@sagepub.com

Journal encompassing the history, economy, and society of India and South Asia, including comparative studies of world development. **Founded:** Mar. 1983. **Freq:** Quarterly. **Trim Size:** 6 1/4 x 9 1/2. **Key Personnel:** Dharma M. Kumar, Editor; Cris Anderson, Circulation Mgr. **ISSN:** 0019-4646. **Subscription Rates:** $50 individuals; $115 two years industry; $15 single issue; $31 single issue industry. **Remarks:** Advertising not accepted.
Circ: (Not Reported)

3943 The International Journal of Clinical and Experimental Hypnosis
Sage Publications Inc.
2455 Teller Rd. Phone: (805)499-0721
Thousand Oaks, CA 91320 Fax: (805)499-0871
Publisher E-mail: info@sagepub.com

Journal on research on hypnosis in various medical and dental specialities. The official publication of the Society for Clinical and Experimental Hypnosis. **Freq:** Quarterly. **Key Personnel:** Fred H. Frankel, Editor; Cris Anderson, Circulation Mgr. **ISSN:** 0020-7144. **Subscription Rates:** $57 individuals; $110 institutions.

3944 The International Journal of Supercomputer Applications
Sage Publications Inc.
2455 Teller Rd. Phone: (805)499-0721
Thousand Oaks, CA 91320 Fax: (805)499-0871
Publisher E-mail: info@sagepub.com

Journal provides an interdisciplinary forum for the exchange of experiences in supercomputing. **Founded:** Mar. 1987. **Freq:** Quarterly. **Trim Size:** 8 1/2 x 11. **Key Personnel:** Joanne L. Martin, Editor; Christine Lamb, Publisher; Laura Ayr, Advertising Mgr. **ISSN:** 0890-2720. **Subscription Rates:** $50 individuals; $100 institutions; $35 students. **Remarks:** Accepts advertising.
Ad Rates: BW: $400 **Circ:** (Not Reported)

3945 International Studies
Sage Publications Inc.
2455 Teller Rd. Phone: (805)499-0721
Thousand Oaks, CA 91320 Fax: (805)499-0871
Publisher E-mail: info@sagepub.com

Indian research journal in the field of international affairs and area studies. **Founded:** 1959. **Freq:** Quarterly. **Print Method:** Offset. **Trim Size:** 6 1/4 x 9 1/2. **Cols./Page:** 1. **Col. Width:** 50 nonpareils. **Col. Depth:** 100 agate lines. **Key Personnel:** P.A. Narasimha Murthy, Editor; Cris Anderson, Circulation Mgr. **ISSN:** 0020-8817. **Subscription Rates:** $38 individuals; $76 two years; $79 institutions; $158 two years INS.; $14 single issue; $24 single issue INS.

3946 Journal of Adolescent Research
Sage Publications Inc.
2455 Teller Rd. Phone: (805)499-0721
Thousand Oaks, CA 91320 Fax: (805)499-0871
Publisher E-mail: info@sagepub.com

Journal providing professionals with information on how individuals in the second decade of life (ages 10-20) develop, behave, and are influenced by societal and cultural perspectives. **Founded:** Jan. 1986. **Freq:** Quarterly. **Print Method:** Offset. **Trim Size:** 5 1/2 x 8 1/2. **Cols./Page:** 1. **Col. Width:** 50 nonpareils. **Col. Depth:** 100 agate lines. **Key Personnel:** E. Ellen Thornberg, Editor; Cris Anderson, Circulation Mgr. **ISSN:** 0743-5584. **Subscription Rates:** $45; $106 institutions; $15 single issue; $28 single issue Insitutions. **Remarks:** Accepts advertising.
Ad Rates: BW: $200 **Circ:** Paid ‡1,100
Non-paid ‡140

3947 Journal of Aging and Health
Sage Publications Inc.
2455 Teller Rd. Phone: (805)499-0721
Thousand Oaks, CA 91320 Fax: (805)499-0871
Publisher E-mail: info@sagepub.com

Journal presenting research relative to the social and behavioral factors related to aging and health. **Founded:** 1989. **Freq:** Quarterly. **Print Method:** Offset. **Trim Size:** 5 1/2 x 8 1/2. **Cols./Page:** 1. **Col. Width:** 50 nonpareils. **Col. Depth:** 100 agate lines. **Key Personnel:** Kyriakos S. Markides, Editor; Cris Anderson, Circulation Mgr. **ISSN:** 0898-2643. **Subscription Rates:** $50; $120 institutions; $16 single issue; $31 single issue Institutions. **Remarks:** Accepts advertising.
Ad Rates: BW: $200 **Circ:** Paid ‡1,300
Non-paid ‡178

3948 Journal of Applied Behavioral Science
Sage Publications Inc.
2455 Teller Rd. Phone: (805)499-0721
Thousand Oaks, CA 91320 Fax: (805)499-0871
Publisher E-mail: info@sagepub.com

Journal on research on behavioral science in application to social science. **Freq:** Quarterly. **Key Personnel:** Clayton P. Alderfer, Editor. **ISSN:** 0021-8863. **Subscription Rates:** $53 individuals; $116 institutions.

3949 Journal of the Association of Nurses in AIDS Care
Sage Science Press
2455 Teller Rd. Phone: (805)499-0721
Thousand Oaks, CA 91320 Fax: (805)499-0871
Publication E-mail: 73764.123@compuserve.com
Publisher E-mail: sagescience@sagepub.com

Professional magazine focusing on quality care for people with HIV/AIDS. **Founded:** 1991. **Freq:** Bimonthly. **Trim Size:** 8 3/8 x 11. **Cols./Page:** 2. **Key Personnel:** Susan Hansom, Executive Editor, phone (805)499-0721, susan_hanscom@sagcpub.com. **ISSN:** 1055-3290. **Subscription Rates:** $56 individuals; $145 institutions. **Remarks:** Accepts advertising.
Circ: Paid ‡4,500

3950 Journal of Black Psychology
Sage Publications Inc.
2455 Teller Rd. Phone: (805)499-0721
Thousand Oaks, CA 91320 Fax: (805)499-0871
Publisher E-mail: info@sagepub.com

Journal on the field of psychology with an Afrocentric perspective. Official publication of the Association of Black Psychologists. **Freq:** Quarterly. **Key Personnel:** Ann Kathleen Burlew, Editor; Cris Anderson, Circulation Mgr. **ISSN:** 0095-7984. **Subscription Rates:** $43 individuals; $113 institutions.

3951 Journal of Black Studies
Sage Publications Inc.
2455 Teller Rd. Phone: (805)499-0721
Thousand Oaks, CA 91320 Fax: (805)499-0871
Publisher E-mail: info@sagepub.com

Journal containing economic, historical, and philosophical research on black people. **Founded:** 1970. **Freq:** Bimonthly. **Print Method:** Offset. **Trim Size:** 5 1/2 x 8 1/2. **Cols./Page:** 1. **Col. Width:** 50 nonpareils. **Col. Depth:** 100 agate lines. **Key Personnel:** Molefi K. Asante, Editor; Sara Miller McCune, Publisher; Cris Anderson, Circulation Mgr. **ISSN:** 0021-9347. **Subscription Rates:** $69 individuals; $240 institutions; $138

two years; $480 two years institutions; $14 single issue; $42 single issue institutions. **Remarks:** Accepts advertising.
Ad Rates: BW: $250 — **Circ:** Paid ‡1,650, Non-paid ‡85

3952 Journal of Business and Technical Communications
Sage Publications Inc.
2455 Teller Rd. — Phone: (805)499-0721
Thousand Oaks, CA 91320 — Fax: (805)499-0871
Publisher E-mail: info@sagepub.com

Journal focusing on the improvement of communication practices in both industry and academe. **Founded:** 1987. **Freq:** Quarterly. **Print Method:** Offset. **Trim Size:** 5 1/2 x 8 1/2. **Cols./Page:** 1. **Col. Width:** 50 nonpareils. **Col. Depth:** 100 agate lines. **Key Personnel:** Thomas Kent, Editor; Cris Anderson, Circulation Mgr. **ISSN:** 0892-5720. **Subscription Rates:** $44 individuals; $110 Industry; $88 two years; $220 two years, Industry; $29 single issue, Industry. **Remarks:** Accepts advertising.
Ad Rates: BW: $250 — **Circ:** Paid 1,100, Non-paid 108

3953 Journal of Communication Inquiry
Sage Publications Inc.
2455 Teller Rd. — Phone: (805)499-0721
Thousand Oaks, CA 91320 — Fax: (805)499-0871
Publisher E-mail: info@sagepub.com

Academic journal concerning communication. **Founded:** 1974. **Freq:** Quarterly Jan., April, July, Oct. **Print Method:** offset. **Trim Size:** 6 x 9. **Key Personnel:** Jonathan Game, Editor, phone (319)335-5821, fax (319)335-5210, je-game@aol.com. **ISSN:** 0196–859. **Subscription Rates:** $75 institutions; $40 individual. **Remarks:** Accepts advertising.
Ad Rates: BW: $200 — **Circ:** (Not Reported)

3954 Journal of Contemporary Ethnography
Sage Publications Inc.
2455 Teller Rd. — Phone: (805)499-0721
Thousand Oaks, CA 91320 — Fax: (805)499-0871
Publisher E-mail: info@sagepub.com

Urban ethnography journal. **Founded:** 1972. **Freq:** Quarterly. **Print Method:** Offset. **Trim Size:** 5 1/2 x 8 1/2. **Cols./Page:** 1. **Col. Width:** 50 nonpareils. **Col. Depth:** 100 agate lines. **Key Personnel:** Spencer Cahill, Editor; Donileen Loseke, Editor; Sara Miller McCune, Publisher. **ISSN:** 0891-2416. **Subscription Rates:** $63 individuals; $211 institutions; $126 two years individual; $422 two years institutions; $18 single issue individual; $55 single issue institution. **Remarks:** Accepts advertising. **Formerly:** Urban Life (1988).
Ad Rates: BW: $200 — **Circ:** Paid ‡1,350, Non-paid ‡83

3955 Journal of Cross-Cultural Psychology
Sage Publications Inc.
2455 Teller Rd. — Phone: (805)499-0721
Thousand Oaks, CA 91320 — Fax: (805)499-0871
Publisher E-mail: info@sagepub.com

Cross-cultural psychology journal. **Founded:** 1970. **Freq:** Bimonthly. **Print Method:** Offset. **Trim Size:** 5 1/2 x 8 1/2. **Cols./Page:** 1. **Col. Width:** 50 nonpareils. **Col. Depth:** 100 agate lines. **Key Personnel:** Peter B. Smith, Editor; Walter J. Lonner, Senior Editor; Sara Miller McCune, Publisher. **ISSN:** 0022-0221. **Subscription Rates:** $65 individuals; $242 institutions; $130 two years; $484 two years institutions; $13 single issue; $42 single issue institutions. **Remarks:** Accepts advertising.
Ad Rates: BW: $250 — **Circ:** Paid ‡2,000, Non-paid ‡100

3956 Journal of Early Adolescence
Sage Publications Inc.
2455 Teller Rd. — Phone: (805)499-0721
Thousand Oaks, CA 91320 — Fax: (805)499-0871
Publisher E-mail: info@sagepub.com

Journal exploring development in children ages 10 to 14. **Founded:** 1980. **Freq:** Quarterly. **Print Method:** Offset. **Trim Size:** 5 1/2 x 8 1/2. **Cols./Page:** 1. **Col. Width:** 50 nonpareils. **Col. Depth:** 100 agate lines. **Key Personnel:** E. Ellen Thornburg, Editor; Cristine Anderson, Circulation Mgr. **ISSN:** 0272-4316. **Subscription Rates:** $45 individuals; $110 institutions; $90 two years; $220 institutions two years; $15 single issue; $29 institutions single issue. **Remarks:** Accepts advertising.
Ad Rates: BW: $200 — **Circ:** Paid 1,300, Non-paid 144

3957 Journal of Family Issues
Sage Publications Inc.
2455 Teller Rd. — Phone: (805)499-0721
Thousand Oaks, CA 91320 — Fax: (805)499-0871
Publisher E-mail: info@sagepub.com

Family studies journal. **Founded:** 1980. **Freq:** Bimonthly. **Print Method:** Offset. **Trim Size:** 5 1/2 x 8 1/2. **Cols./Page:** 1. **Col. Width:** 50 nonpareils. **Col. Depth:** 100 agate lines. **Key Personnel:** Wendy Link, Editor; Sara Miller McCune, Publisher; David Rigas, General Mgr. **ISSN:** 0192-513X. **Subscription Rates:** $70 individuals; $245 institutions; $140 two years; $490 two years institutions; $14 single issue; $43 single issue institutions. **Remarks:** Accepts advertising.
Ad Rates: BW: $250 — **Circ:** Paid ‡1,500, Non-paid ‡84

3958 Journal of Family Nursing
Sage Publications Inc.
2455 Teller Rd. — Phone: (805)499-0721
Thousand Oaks, CA 91320 — Fax: (805)499-0871
Publisher E-mail: info@sagepub.com

Scholarly journal on nursing issues pertaining to family health and illness. **Founded:** Feb. 1995. **Freq:** Quarterly. **Key Personnel:** Janice M. Bell, Editor; Cris Anderson, Circulation Mgr. **ISSN:** 1074-8407. **Subscription Rates:** $51 individuals; $125 institutions.

3959 Journal of Health Care for the Poor and Underserved
Sage Publications Inc.
2455 Teller Rd. — Phone: (805)499-0721
Thousand Oaks, CA 91320 — Fax: (805)499-0871
Publisher E-mail: info@sagepub.com

Journal covering the health problems of poor, elderly, rural and inner-city residents. **Founded:** 1990. **Freq:** Quarterly. **Trim Size:** 6 x 9. **Cols./Page:** 1. **Col. Width:** 4 3/4 inches. **Col. Depth:** 7 1/4 inches. **Key Personnel:** Srila Sen, Editor; Amy Cato, Pub./Managing Ed. **ISSN:** 1049-2089. **Subscription Rates:** $50 individuals; $118 institutions. **Remarks:** Advertising not accepted. **Alt. Formats:** Microfiche.
Circ: Paid ‡742, Non-paid ‡101

3960 Journal of Humanistic Psychology
Sage Publications Inc.
2455 Teller Rd. — Phone: (805)499-0721
Thousand Oaks, CA 91320 — Fax: (805)499-0871
Publisher E-mail: info@sagepub.com

Psychology journal. **Founded:** 1961. **Freq:** Quarterly. **Print Method:** Offset. **Trim Size:** 5 1/2 x 8 1/2. **Cols./Page:** 1. **Col. Width:** 50 nonpareils. **Col. Depth:** 100 agate lines. **Key Personnel:** Thomas Greening, Editor; Cris Anderson, Circulation Mgr. **ISSN:** 0022-1678. **Subscription Rates:** $54 individuals; $188 institutions; $108 two years; $376 two years institutions; $16 single issue individuals; $49 single issue institutions. **Remarks:** Accepts advertising.
Ad Rates: BW: $250 — **Circ:** Paid ‡3,000, Non-paid ‡133

3961 Journal of Interpersonal Violence
Sage Publications Inc.
2455 Teller Rd. — Phone: (805)499-0721
Thousand Oaks, CA 91320 — Fax: (805)499-0871
Publisher E-mail: info@sagepub.com

Journal focusing on the study and treatment of victims and perpetrators of violence. **Founded:** 1986. **Freq:** Quarterly. **Print Method:** Offset. **Trim Size:** 5 1/2 x 8 1/2. **Cols./Page:** 1. **Col. Width:** 50 nonpareils. **Col. Depth:** 100 agate lines. **Key Personnel:** Jon R. Conte, Editor; Cris Anderson, Circulation Mgr. **ISSN:** 0886-2605. **Subscription Rates:** $59 individuals; $189 institutions; $118 two years; $378 two years institutions; $12 single issue; $34 single issue institutions. **Remarks:** Accepts advertising.
Ad Rates: BW: $250 — **Circ:** Paid ‡6,250, Non-paid ‡157

3962 Journal of Language and Social Psychology
Sage Publications Inc.
2455 Teller Rd. — Phone: (805)499-0721
Thousand Oaks, CA 91320 — Fax: (805)499-0871
Publisher E-mail: info@sagepub.com

Journal on the social aspects of language. **Freq:** Quarterly. **Key Personnel:** James Bradac, Editor; Kathy Kellermann, Advertising Mgr.; Cris Anderson, Circulation Mgr. **ISSN:** 0261-927X. **Subscription Rates:** $62 individuals; $170 institutions.

3963 Journal of Planning Literature
Sage Publications Inc.
2455 Teller Rd. — Phone: (805)499-0721
Thousand Oaks, CA 91320 — Fax: (805)499-0871
Publisher E-mail: info@sagepub.com

Journal on the literature of city and regional planning. Includes reviews of articles on major issues, abstracts of books and articles, and title listings of additional publications. **Founded:** 1985. **Freq:** Quarterly. **Print Method:** Offset. **Trim Size:** 8 1/2 x 11. **Cols./Page:** 2. **Col. Width:** 32 nonpareils. **Col. Depth:** 114 agate lines. **Key Personnel:** Kenneth Pearlman, Editor; Cris Anderson, Circulation Mgr. **ISSN:** 0885-4122. **Subscription Rates:** $44; $113 institutions; $15 single issue; $29 single issue Institutions. **Remarks:** Accepts advertising.
Ad Rates: BW: $200 — **Circ:** Paid ‡900, Non-paid ‡157

3964 Journal of Research in Crime and Delinquency
Sage Publications Inc.
2455 Teller Rd. — Phone: (805)499-0721
Thousand Oaks, CA 91320 — Fax: (805)499-0871
Publisher E-mail: info@sagepub.com

Journal containing research in criminology. **Founded:** 1964. **Freq:** Quarterly. **Print Method:** Offset. **Trim Size:** 5 1/2 x 8 1/2. **Cols./Page:** 1. **Col. Width:** 50 nonpareils. **Col. Depth:** 100 agate lines. **Key Personnel:** James O. Finckenauer, Editor; Sara Miller McCune, Publisher; Cris Anderson, Circulation Mgr. **ISSN:** 0022-4278. **Subscription Rates:** $63 individuals; $198 institutions; $126 two years; $396 two years institutions; $18 single issue; $52 single issue institutions. **Remarks:** Accepts advertising.
Ad Rates: BW: $250 — **Circ:** Paid ‡1,750, Non-paid ‡77

3965 Journal of Sport & Social Issues
Sage Publications Inc.
2455 Teller Rd. — Phone: (805)499-0721
Thousand Oaks, CA 91320 — Fax: (805)499-0871
Publisher E-mail: info@sagepub.com

Journal on contemporary sports issues. The official journal of Northeastern University's Center for the Study of Sport in Society. **Founded:** Feb. 1994. **Freq:** Quarterly. **Key Personnel:** Lawrence Wenner, Editor; Cris Anderson, Circulation Mgr. **ISSN:** 0193-7325. **Subscription Rates:** $40 individuals; $90 institutions.

3966 Management Communication Quarterly
Sage Publications Inc.
2455 Teller Rd. — Phone: (805)499-0721
Thousand Oaks, CA 91320 — Fax: (805)499-0871
Publisher E-mail: info@sagepub.com

Journal reporting on communication research, with a focus on managerial and organizational effectiveness. **Founded:** Aug. 1987. **Freq:** Quarterly. **Print Method:** Offset. **Trim Size:** 5 1/2 x 8 1/2. **Cols./Page:** 1. **Col. Width:** 50 nonpareils. **Col. Depth:** 100 agate lines. **Key Personnel:** Patricia M. Buzzanell, Editor; Cris Anderson, Circulation Mgr.; Sarah Miller McCune, Publisher. **ISSN:** 0893-3189. **Subscription Rates:** $56 individuals; $190 institutions; $112 two years; $380 two years institutions; $16 single issue; $50 single issue institutions. **Remarks:** Accepts advertising.
Ad Rates: BW: $250 — **Circ:** Paid ‡1,300, Non-paid ‡84

3967 Modern China
Sage Publications Inc.
2455 Teller Rd. — Phone: (805)499-0721
Thousand Oaks, CA 91320 — Fax: (805)499-0871
Publisher E-mail: info@sagepub.com

Chinese society and modern history journal. **Founded:** 1975. **Freq:** Quarterly. **Print Method:** Offset. **Trim Size:** 5 1/2 x 8 1/2. **Cols./Page:** 1. **Col. Width:** 50 nonpareils. **Col. Depth:** 100 agate lines. **Key Personnel:** Philip C.C. Huang, Editor; Sara Miller McCune, Publisher. **ISSN:** 0097-7004. **Subscription Rates:** $67 individuals; $215 institutions; $134 two years; $430 two years institutions; $19 single issue; $73 single issue institutions. **Remarks:** Accepts advertising.
Ad Rates: BW: $200 — **Circ:** Paid ‡1,300, Non-paid ‡78

3968 Outburn
PO Box 3187 — Phone: (805)493-5861
Thousand Oaks, CA 91359-0187 — Fax: (805)493-5609
Publisher E-mail: outburn@outburn.com

Consumer magazine covering underground music. **Subtitle:** Subversive and Post-Alternative Music. **Founded:** Aug. 1996. **Freq:** 3/year. **Print Method:** Offset. **Trim Size:** 8 3/4 x 11 3/4. **Key Personnel:** Rodent Ek, Art Director/Co-Pulbsiher. **Subscription Rates:** $17 individuals; $5.50 single issue. **Remarks:** Accepts advertising. **URL:** http://www.outburn.com.
Ad Rates: BW: $800, 4C: $1,600 — **Circ:** (Not Reported)

3969 Peace Research Abstracts Journal
Sage Publications Inc.
2455 Teller Rd. — Phone: (805)499-0721
Thousand Oaks, CA 91320 — Fax: (805)499-0871
Publisher E-mail: info@sagepub.com

Journal abstracting articles on peace studies from around the world. **Founded:** Feb. 1994. **Freq:** Bimonthly. **Trim Size:** 8 1/2 x 11. **Cols./Page:** 2. **Key Personnel:** Cris Anderson, Circulation Mgr.; Monna Newcombe, Editor; Paul V. McDowell, Documentation editor. **ISSN:** 0031-3599. **Subscription**

Rates: $92 individuals; $313 institutions per year. **Remarks:** Advertising not accepted.
Circ: (Not Reported)

3970 Philosophy of the Social Sciences
Sage Publications Inc.
2455 Teller Rd. Phone: (805)499-0721
Thousand Oaks, CA 91320 Fax: (805)499-0871
Publisher E-mail: info@sagepub.com

Scholarly journal discussing topics in the social sciences. **Founded:** 1971. **Freq:** Quarterly. **Print Method:** Offset. **Trim Size:** 8 1/2 x 5 1/2. **Cols./Page:** 1. **Col. Width:** 54 nonpareils. **Col. Depth:** 101 agate lines. **Key Personnel:** I.C. Jarvie, Editor; Cris Anderson, Circulation Mgr. **ISSN:** 0048-3931. **Subscription Rates:** $47; $112 Industry; $15 single issue; $29 single issue Industry. **Remarks:** Accepts advertising.
Ad Rates: BW: $200 **Circ:** Paid ‡1,350
Non-paid ‡114

3971 Politics & Society
Sage Publications Inc.
2455 Teller Rd. Phone: (805)499-0721
Thousand Oaks, CA 91320 Fax: (805)499-0871
Publisher E-mail: info@sagepub.com

Journal on the social sciences of politics, sociology, and economics. **Freq:** Quarterly. **Key Personnel:** Cris Anderson, Circulation Mgr. **ISSN:** 0032-3292. **Subscription Rates:** $48 individuals; $127 institutions.

3972 Public Finance Quarterly
Sage Publications Inc.
2455 Teller Rd. Phone: (805)499-0721
Thousand Oaks, CA 91320 Fax: (805)499-0871
Publisher E-mail: info@sagepub.com

Public economy journal. **Founded:** 1973. **Freq:** Bimonthly. **Print Method:** Offset. **Trim Size:** 5 1/2 x 8 1/2. **Cols./Page:** 1. **Col. Width:** 50 nonpareils. **Col. Depth:** 100 agate lines. **Key Personnel:** J. Ronnie Davis, Editor; Sara Miller McCune, Publisher; Cris Anderson, Circulation Mgr. **ISSN:** 0048-5853. **Subscription Rates:** $74 individuals; $280 institutions; $148 two years; $560 two years institutions; $15 single issue; $49 single issue institutions. **Remarks:** Accepts advertising.
Ad Rates: BW: $200 **Circ:** Paid ‡1,500
Non-paid ‡84

3973 Research on Social Work Practice
Sage Publications Inc.
2455 Teller Rd. Phone: (805)499-0721
Thousand Oaks, CA 91320 Fax: (805)499-0871
Publisher E-mail: info@sagepub.com

Journal covering empirical research on the methods and outcomes of social work practice. **Founded:** 1991. **Freq:** Quarterly. **Print Method:** Offset. **Trim Size:** 5 1/2 x 8 1/2. **Cols./Page:** 1. **Col. Width:** 50 nonpareils. **Col. Depth:** 100 agate lines. **Key Personnel:** Bruce A. Thyer, PhD., Editor; Cris Anderson, Circulation Mgr. **ISSN:** 1049-7315. **Subscription Rates:** $46 individuals; $113 Industry; $92 two years; $226 two years, Industry; $29 single issue, Industry. **Remarks:** Accepts advertising.
Ad Rates: BW: $200 **Circ:** Paid ‡1,200
Non-paid 179

3974 Sage Family Studies Abstracts
Sage Publications Inc.
2455 Teller Rd. Phone: (805)499-0721
Thousand Oaks, CA 91320 Fax: (805)499-0871
Publisher E-mail: info@sagepub.com

Journal containing family studies abstracts. **Founded:** 1979. **Freq:** Quarterly. **Print Method:** Offset. **Trim Size:** 5 1/2 x 8 1/2. **Cols./Page:** 1. **Col. Width:** 50 nonpareils. **Col. Depth:** 100 agate lines. **Key Personnel:** Paul V. McDowell, Editor; Sara Miller McCune, Publisher; Nancy Hillegeist, Circulation Mgr. **ISSN:** 0164-0283. **Subscription Rates:** $102 individuals; $355 institutions; $204 two years; $710 two years institutions; $26 single issue; $91 single issue institutions. **Remarks:** Accepts advertising.
Ad Rates: BW: $200 **Circ:** Paid ‡750
Non-paid ‡71

3975 Sage Public Administration Abstracts
Sage Publications Inc.
2455 Teller Rd. Phone: (805)499-0721
Thousand Oaks, CA 91320 Fax: (805)499-0871
Publisher E-mail: info@sagepub.com

Journal containing abstracts on public administration. **Founded:** 1974. **Freq:** Quarterly. **Print Method:** Offset. **Trim Size:** 5 1/2 x 8 1/2. **Cols./Page:** 1. **Col. Width:** 50 nonpareils. **Col. Depth:** 100 agate lines. **Key Personnel:** Paul V. McDowell, Editor; Sara Miller McCune, Publisher. **ISSN:** 0094-6958. **Subscription Rates:** $98 individuals; $25 single issue; $295 institutions. **Remarks:** Accepts advertising.
Ad Rates: BW: $195 **Circ:** Paid ‡750
Non-paid ‡73

3976 Sage Urban Studies Abstracts
Sage Publications Inc.
2455 Teller Rd. Phone: (805)499-0721
Thousand Oaks, CA 91320 Fax: (805)499-0871
Publisher E-mail: info@sagepub.com

Journal containing abstracts on urban studies. **Founded:** 1973. **Freq:** Quarterly. **Print Method:** Offset. **Trim Size:** 5 1/2 x 8 1/2. **Cols./Page:** 1. **Col. Width:** 50 nonpareils. **Col. Depth:** 100 agate lines. **Key Personnel:** Paul V. McDowell, Editor; Sara Miller McCune, Publisher; Chris Anderson, Circulation Mgr. **ISSN:** 0090-5747. **Subscription Rates:** $110 individuals; $345 institutions; $30 single issue. **Remarks:** Accepts advertising.
Ad Rates: BW: $200 **Circ:** Paid ‡750
Non-paid ‡91

3977 Science, Technology & Human Values
Sage Publications Inc.
2455 Teller Rd. Phone: (805)499-0721
Thousand Oaks, CA 91320 Fax: (805)499-0871
Publisher E-mail: info@sagepub.com

Journal evaluating the ethics of science and technology. **Founded:** 1975. **Freq:** Quarterly. **Print Method:** Offset. **Trim Size:** 5 1/2 x 8 1/2. **Cols./Page:** 1. **Col. Width:** 50 nonpareils. **Col. Depth:** 100 agate lines. **Key Personnel:** Susan E. Cozzens, Editor; Cris Anderson, Circulation Mgr. **ISSN:** 0162-2439. **Subscription Rates:** $52 individuals; $128 Industry; $104 two years; $256 Industry, two years; $16 single issue; $33 Industry, single issue. **Remarks:** Accepts advertising.
Ad Rates: BW: $250 **Circ:** Paid 1,900
Non-paid 131

3978 SMR/Sociological Methods and Research
Sage Publications Inc.
2455 Teller Rd. Phone: (805)499-0721
Thousand Oaks, CA 91320 Fax: (805)499-0871
Publisher E-mail: info@sagepub.com

Sociology journal. **Founded:** 1972. **Freq:** Quarterly. **Print Method:** Offset. **Trim Size:** 5 1/2 x 8 1/2. **Cols./Page:** 1. **Col. Width:** 50 nonpareils. **Col. Depth:** 100 agate lines. **Key Personnel:** J. Scott Long, Editor; Edgar F. Borgatta, Advertising Mgr.; Sara Miller McCune, Publisher. **ISSN:** 0049-1241. **Subscription Rates:** $53 individuals; $142 institutions; $106 two years; $284 two years Institutions; $18 single issue; $38 single issue Institutions. **Remarks:** Accepts advertising.
Ad Rates: BW: $250 **Circ:** Paid ‡1,550
Non-paid ‡80

3979 Today's Family Life
Westlake Family Publisher
2219 E. Thousand Oaks Blvd., No. 465 Phone: (805)379-4905
Fax: (805)371-8909
Thousand Oaks, CA 91362
Monthly community magazine geared towards families and kids. **Founded:** Aug. 1994. **Freq:** Monthly. **Print Method:** Web. **Subscription Rates:** Free. **Remarks:** Accepts advertising. **Formerly:** Family Life Magazine of Ventury County.
Circ: Non-paid 15,000

3980 Urban Affairs Review
Sage Publications Inc.
2455 Teller Rd. Phone: (805)499-0721
Thousand Oaks, CA 91320 Fax: (805)499-0871
Publisher E-mail: info@sagepub.com

Urban studies journal. **Founded:** 1965. **Freq:** Quarterly. **Print Method:** Offset. **Trim Size:** 5 1/2 x 8 1/2. **Cols./Page:** 1. **Col. Width:** 50 nonpareils. **Col. Depth:** 100 agate lines. **Key Personnel:** Dennis R. Judd, Editor; Cris Anderson, Circulation Mgr. **ISSN:** 0042-0816. **Subscription Rates:** $50 individuals; $150 Industry; $100 two years; $300 two years Institutions; $39 Single issue, Industry; $35 single issue. **Remarks:** Accepts advertising. **Formerly:** Urban Affairs Quarterly.
Ad Rates: BW: $250 **Circ:** Paid ‡2,000
Non-paid ‡141

3981 Work and Occupations
Sage Publications Inc.
2455 Teller Rd. Phone: (805)499-0721
Thousand Oaks, CA 91320 Fax: (805)499-0871
Publisher E-mail: info@sagepub.com

Journal covering sociology as related to work, occupations, employment and labor relations. **Founded:** 1974. **Freq:** Quarterly. **Print Method:** Offset. **Trim Size:** 5 1/2 x 8 1/2. **Cols./Page:** 1. **Col. Width:** 50 nonpareils. **Col. Depth:** 100 agate lines. **Key Personnel:** Cris Anderson, Circulation Mgr.; Daniel B. Cornfield, Editor. **ISSN:** 0730-8884. **Subscription Rates:** $48 individuals; $133 Industry; $96 two years; $266 two years Two years, Industry; $34 single issue Single issue, Industry; $33 single issue INS. **Remarks:** Accepts advertising.
Ad Rates: BW: $200 **Circ:** Paid ‡1,250
Non-paid ‡133

3982 Written Communication
Sage Publications Inc.
2455 Teller Rd. Phone: (805)499-0721
Thousand Oaks, CA 91320 Fax: (805)499-0871
Publisher E-mail: info@sagepub.com

Journal presenting theory and methodology in the study of the written word. **Founded:** 1984. **Freq:** Quarterly. **Print Method:** Offset. **Trim Size:** 5 1/2 x 8 1/2. **Cols./Page:** 1. **Col. Width:** 50 nonpareils. **Col. Depth:** 100 agate lines. **Key Personnel:** Prof. Deborah Brandt, Editor; Prof. Martin Nystrand, Editor; Cris Anderson, Circulation Mgr. **ISSN:** 0741-0883. **Subscription Rates:** $50 individuals; $144 Industry; $16 single issue; $37 single issue Industry; $16 single issue; $34 single issue INS. **Remarks:** Accepts advertising.
Ad Rates: BW: $200 **Circ:** Paid ‡1,350
Non-paid ‡150

3983 Youth & Society
Sage Publications Inc.
2455 Teller Rd. Phone: (805)499-0721
Thousand Oaks, CA 91320 Fax: (805)499-0871
Publisher E-mail: info@sagepub.com

Journal on the culture and development of youth. **Founded:** 1969. **Freq:** Quarterly. **Print Method:** Offset. **Trim Size:** 5 1/2 x 8 1/2. **Cols./Page:** 1. **Col. Width:** 50 nonpareils. **Col. Depth:** 100 agate lines. **Key Personnel:** Margaret LeCompte, Editor; Kathryne Herr, Advertising Mgr.; Cris Anderson, Circulation Mgr. **ISSN:** 0044-118X. **Subscription Rates:** $48 individuals; $143 Industry; $16 single issue; $37 single issue Industry. **Remarks:** Accepts advertising.
Ad Rates: BW: $200 **Circ:** Paid ‡1,300
Non-paid ‡140

3984 KCLU-FM - 88.3
60 W. Olsen Rd. Phone: (805)493-3900
Thousand Oaks, CA 91360 Fax: (805)493-3982
E-mail: kclu@clunet.edu

Format: Jazz; Public Radio. **Owner:** California Lutheran University, at above address. **Founded:** Oct. 20, 1994. **Operating Hours:** Continuous. **Key Personnel:** Mary D. Olson, General Mgr.; Jeff Barry, Program Dir.; Judy Kaminsky, Sales. **Wattage:** 1300. **Ad Rates:** Advertising accepted; rates available upon request.

3985 KCPB-FM - 91.1
PO Box 77913 Phone: (213)514-1400
Los Angeles, CA 90007 Fax: (213)747-9400
E-mail: kusc@kusc.org

Format: Public Radio; Classical. **Networks:** National Public Radio (NPR); Public Radio International (PRI). **Owner:** University of Southern California Radio, at above address. **Founded:** 1982. **Operating Hours:** Continuous. **ADI:** Los Angeles (Corona & San Bernardino), CA. **Key Personnel:** Brenda Pennell, General Mgr., phone (213)514-1450, fax (213)514-1451, bpennell@kusc.org; James Russell, Gen.Mgr. MarkerPlace Prod., phone (213)514-1500, jrussell@marketplace.org; Sheila Rue, Program Dir., phone (213)514-1430, fax (213)514-1431, srue@kusc.org. **Local Programs:** *Afternoon Music*, Sheila Rue, Program Dir., (213)514-1430; *Marketplace*, David Brancaccio, (213)743-6555, Fax (213)747-0684; *The Morning Program*, Steve Lama; *Music 'til Midnight*, Jim Svejda. **Wattage:** 5000. **Ad Rates:** Noncommercial. **URL:** http://www.kusc.org.

THOUSAND PALMS

Riverside Co. (SC). 10 m W of Palm Springs.

3986 KPSL-AM - 1010
303 N. Indian Canyon Dr. Phone: (619)323-5775
Palm Springs, CA 92262 Fax: (619)320-6702
Free: (800)992-1010

Format: Sports; Talk. **Networks:** ABC. **Owner:** Franklin Communications Corp., at above address. **Founded:** 1987. **Operating Hours:** Continuous. **ADI:** Palm Springs, CA. **Key Personnel:** Milton Jones, President; Gene A. Pietragallo, Jr., General Mgr. **Local Programs:** *Judy A La Carte*, Judy Gilliard; *The Steamroom*, Bud Furillo; *Think Radio*, Clark Green. **Wattage:** 4,400 day; 400 night. **Ad Rates:** $15-20 for 30 seconds; $18-30 for 60 seconds.

TIBURON, pop. 6,685.

Marin Co. (W) 5 m N.W. of Sausalito. Residential.

3987 The Ark
The Ark Publishing Co.
Box 1054 Phone: (415)435-2652
Tiburon, CA 94920 Fax: (415)435-0849

Newspaper serving Strawberry, Tiburon, and Belvedere. **Founded:** 1973. **Freq:** Weekly. **Print Method:** Offset. **Trim Size:** 10 1/8 x 14. **Cols./Page:** 6. **Col. Width:** 19 nonpareils.

Col. Depth: 196 agate lines. **Key Personnel:** Marilyn Kessler, Editor and Publisher; Barbara Gnoss, Editor and Publisher; Steve McNamara, Publisher; Azi Najafi, Advertising Dir. **USPS:** 012-310. **Subscription Rates:** $35 individuals. **Remarks:** Accepts advertising.
Ad Rates: BW: $642.60 **Circ:** Free ‡40
PCI: $8.80

TOLUCA LAKE

The Tolucan Times - See Burbank

TORRANCE, pop. 131,497.

Los Angeles Co. (S). 16 m S of Los Angeles. El Camino College. Manufactures steel, aluminum, oil well machinery, paint, plumbing and heating fixtures, rubber goods, petroleum products, pistons, chemicals, plastics, brick, tile, aircraft, missiles, butter, cheese, insulating material, electronics, steel cable, synthetic rubber. Oil wells.

3988 Automotive Fleet
Bobit Publishing
21061 S Western Ave. Phone: (310)533-2400
Torrance, CA 90501 Fax: (310)533-2503

Automotive magazine covering the car and light truck fleet market. **Founded:** 1961. **Freq:** Monthly. **Print Method:** Offset. **Trim Size:** 8 x 10 7/8. **Cols./Page:** 3. **Col. Width:** 26 nonpareils. **Col. Depth:** 140 agate lines. **Key Personnel:** Edward J. Bobit, Editor and Publisher; Sherb Brown, Assoc. Publisher; Mike Antich, Executive Editor, mikea@bobit.com. **ISSN:** 0005-1519. **Subscription Rates:** $35 individuals; $42 Canada; $53 other countries. **Remarks:** Accepts advertising.
Ad Rates: BW: $5,445 **Circ:** Paid 252
4C: $6,645 Non-paid 21,706

3989 Chiropractic Products
Novicom, Inc.
20000 Mariner Ave., No. 480 Phone: (310)793-4141
Torrance, CA 90503 Fax: (310)793-4138
Publisher E-mail: novicom@earthlink.net

Magazine featuring new products and services available in the chiropractic field. **Founded:** 1985. **Freq:** 11/year. **Print Method:** Web offset. **Trim Size:** 8 3/8 x 10 7/8. **Cols./Page:** 3. **Key Personnel:** Laura Niznik, Editor; Marvin Rosenfeld, Publisher; Debra Schmitt, Advertising Mgr., phone (813)394-7077. **ISSN:** 1041-2360. **Subscription Rates:** $16. $2 single issue. **Remarks:** Accepts advertising. **URL:** http://www.novicom.com.
Ad Rates: BW: $1,545 **Circ:** Controlled 35,000
4C: $2,145

3990 Contemporary Orthopaedics
Bobit Publishing
21061 S Western Ave. Phone: (310)533-2400
Torrance, CA 90501 Fax: (310)533-2503

Medical magazine. **Founded:** 1978. **Freq:** Monthly. **Print Method:** Offset. **Trim Size:** 8 1/8 x 10 7/8. **Cols./Page:** 3. **Col. Width:** 35 nonpareils. **Col. Depth:** 156 agate lines. **Key Personnel:** Judi Prow, Editor; Thomas W. Bender, Publisher. **ISSN:** 0194-8458. **Subscription Rates:** $53 individuals; $63 Canada; $80 other countries; $5 single issue. **Remarks:** Accepts advertising.
Ad Rates: BW: $1,500 **Circ:** Non-paid 30,000
4C: $2,450

3991 Contemporary Surgery
Bobit Publishing
21061 S Western Ave. Phone: (310)533-2400
Torrance, CA 90501 Fax: (310)533-2503

Surgery journal. **Founded:** Oct. 1972. **Freq:** Monthly. **Print Method:** Offset. **Trim Size:** 8 x 10 7/8. **Cols./Page:** 2. **Col. Width:** 42 picas. **Col. Depth:** 60 picas. **Key Personnel:** Peggy Plendl, Editor; Thomas W. Bender, Publisher; Mary Reimer, Production Mgr. **Subscription Rates:** $53 individuals; $64 Canada; $80 other countries. **Remarks:** Accepts advertising.
Ad Rates: BW: $3,115 **Circ:** Combined 48,876
4C: $4,410 Combined 50,077

3992 Dental Surgery Products
Novicom, Inc.
20000 Mariner Ave., No. 480 Phone: (310)793-4141
Torrance, CA 90503 Fax: (310)793-4138
Publisher E-mail: novicom@earthlink.net

Trade magazine featuring product news releases and articles regarding dental surgery. **Founded:** Sept. 1996. **Freq:** 6/year. **Print Method:** Web offset. **Trim Size:** 8 1/8 x 10 7/8. **Cols./Page:** 3. **Key Personnel:** Christina Chang, Editor; April Hyatt, Advertising Dir., phone (602)353-5264, fax (602)953-5390. **Subscription Rates:** $12 U.S.; $30 other countries; $2 single issue. **Remarks:** Accepts advertising.
Ad Rates: BW: $1,310 **Circ:** Non-paid ⊕**13,000**
4C: $700

3993 Emergency
Bobit Publishing
21061 S Western Ave. Phone: (310)533-2400
Torrance, CA 90501 Fax: (310)533-2503
Publication E-mail: emg@bobit.com

Trade journal covering pre-hospital medical and rescue techniques for paramedics, firefighters, EMTS, RN's, EMS physicians and other emergency services. **Subtitle:** The Journal of Emergency Services. **Founded:** 1969. **Freq:** Monthly. **Print Method:** Offset. **Trim Size:** 8 3/8 x 10 7/8. **Cols./Page:** 3. **Col. Width:** 2 1/4 inches. **Col. Depth:** 10 inches. **Key Personnel:** Doug Fiske, Editor; Maurice S. Sutton, Publisher, msutton@bobit.com; Marianne Winfield, Asst. Editor, marianne@bobit.com; Vari MacNeil, Managing Editor, vari@bobit.com; Janet S. Pomerantz, National Sales Mgr., janetp@bobit.com. **ISSN:** 0162-5942. **Subscription Rates:** $23.95 individuals. **Remarks:** Accepts advertising. **Formerly:** Emergency Product News.
Ad Rates: GLR: $1.75 **Circ:** 29,000
BW: $2,320
4C: $3,120
PCI: $75

3994 Hawthorne/Gardena/Carson South Bay Extra
Breeze Newspapers
5215 Torrance Blvd.
Torrance, CA 90503-4009

Community newspaper covering reprints of articles published in *The Daily Breeze* and *The News-Pilot.*. **Freq:** Weekly. **Print Method:** Offset. **Cols./Page:** 5. **Col. Width:** 12 picas. **Col. Depth:** 78 picas. **Key Personnel:** Kathryn Martin, Editor. **Subscription Rates:** Free. **Remarks:** Accepts advertising. **Former name:** Redondo Reflex.
Circ: (Not Reported)

3995 Installation News
Bobit Publishing
21061 S Western Ave. Phone: (310)533-2400
Torrance, CA 90501 Fax: (310)533-2503

Technical journal of automotive electronics. Covers installation of autosound, security, cellular phones, and radar detectors. **Subtitle:** Serving the Mobile Electronics Industry. **Founded:** Nov. 1983. **Freq:** Monthly. **Print Method:** Offset. **Trim Size:** 8 3/8 x 11. **Cols./Page:** 3. **Col. Width:** 2 3/16 inches. **Col. Depth:** 10 inches. **Key Personnel:** Michele Guido, Editor; Mike'l Dornhecker, Publisher. **ISSN:** 0087-2287. **Subscription Rates:** Free to qualified subscribers. **Remarks:** Accepts advertising.
Ad Rates: BW: $2,920 **Circ:** Paid 103
4C: $3,820 Non-paid 23,528
PCI: $75

3996 The Lesbian News
PO Box 55
Torrance, CA 90507
Publication E-mail: theln@earthlink.net

Magazine of lesbian and gay-oriented articles, features, and cartoons. **Founded:** 1975. **Freq:** Monthly. **Print Method:** Web offset. **Trim Size:** 10 1/2 x 14 1/4. **Cols./Page:** 3. **Col. Width:** 3 1/4 inches. **Col. Depth:** 14 inches. **Key Personnel:** Ella Matthes, Publisher; Claudia Piras, Editor, phone (562)438-4444, fax (562)439-3375; Claudia Piras, Advertising Dir. **Subscription Rates:** $35 individuals; $65 two years. **Remarks:** Accepts advertising. **URL:** http://www.lesbiannews.com.
Ad Rates: BW: $990 **Circ:** ‡110,000
4C: $1,390

3997 Limousine & Chauffeur
Bobit Publishing
21061 S Western Ave. Phone: (310)533-2400
Torrance, CA 90501 Fax: (310)533-2503

Magazine for the limousine service industry. **Founded:** Mar. 1983. **Freq:** 7/year. **Print Method:** Offset. **Trim Size:** 8 x 10 7/8. **Cols./Page:** 3. **Col. Width:** 26 nonpareils. **Col. Depth:** 130 agate lines. **Key Personnel:** Sara Eastwood, Publisher; Donna Englander, Editor. **ISSN:** 8750-7374. **Subscription Rates:** $28 individuals; $38 Canada; $50 other countries. **Remarks:** Accepts advertising.
Ad Rates: BW: $1,850 **Circ:** Paid ‡4,135
4C: $2,650 Non-paid ‡7,189

3998 Metro Magazine
Bobit Publishing
21061 S Western Ave. Phone: (310)533-2400
Torrance, CA 90501 Fax: (310)533-2503
Publication E-mail: metromag@bobit.com

Magazine on public transportation. **Subtitle:** Serving Bus and Rail Transit and Motorcoach Operations Since 1904. **Founded:** 1904. **Freq:** 8/year. **Print Method:** Offset. **Trim Size:** 7 7/8 x 10 3/4. **Cols./Page:** 3. **Col. Width:** 26 nonpareils. **Col. Depth:** 140 agate lines. **Key Personnel:** Frank Di Giacomo, Publisher, phone (609)596-0999, fax (609)596-0168; Cliff Henke, Editor; Lenny Levine, Exec. Editor, lenny@bdbit.com; Mary Reimer, Production Mgr. **ISSN:** 0162-6221. **Subscription Rates:** $40 individuals; $6 single issue. **Remarks:** Accepts advertising. **URL:** http://www.transit-center.com.
Ad Rates: BW: $3,690 **Circ:** Controlled 18,000
4C: $4,490
PCI: $75

3999 Minority Business Entrepreneur
3528 Torrance Blvd., Ste. 101 Phone: (310)540-9398
Torrance, CA 90503-4826 Fax: (310)792-8263
Publisher E-mail: mbewbe@ix.netcom.com

Business magazine for ethnic minority and women business owners. **Founded:** 1984. **Freq:** Bimonthly. **Print Method:** Offset. **Trim Size:** 8 x 10 7/8. **Cols./Page:** 3. **Col. Width:** 13 picas. **Col. Depth:** 10 inches. **Key Personnel:** Jeanie M. Barnett, Editor; Ginger Conrad, Publisher. **ISSN:** 1048-0919. **Subscription Rates:** $16 individuals; Free to qualified subscribers. **Remarks:** Accepts advertising. **URL:** http://www.mbemag.com; ibjinx@netcom.com.
Ad Rates: BW: $3,675 **Circ:** 40,000
4C: $4,650
PCI: $70.00

4000 Physical Therapy Products
Novicom, Inc.
20000 Mariner Ave., No. 480 Phone: (310)793-4141
Torrance, CA 90503 Fax: (310)793-4138
Publisher E-mail: novicom@earthlink.net

Magazine featuring new products and services available in the physical therapy field. **Founded:** 1989. **Freq:** Bimonthly. **Print Method:** Web offset. **Trim Size:** 8 3/8 x 10 7/8. **Cols./Page:** 3. **Key Personnel:** Laura Niznik, Editor; Marvin Rosenfeld, Publisher; George Ross, Advertising Mgr. **ISSN:** 1059-096X. **Subscription Rates:** $12. $2 single issue. **Remarks:** Accepts advertising. **URL:** http;//www.novicom.com.
Ad Rates: BW: $1,755 **Circ:** Controlled 40,000
4C: $2,455

4001 Plastic Surgery Products
Novicom, Inc.
20000 Mariner Ave., No. 480 Phone: (310)793-4141
Torrance, CA 90503 Fax: (310)793-4138
Publisher E-mail: novicom@earthlink.net

Magazine featuring new products and services available in the plastic surgery field. **Founded:** 1991. **Freq:** 7/year. **Print Method:** Web offset. **Trim Size:** 8 3/8 x 10 7/8. **Key Personnel:** Ercon Diaz, Editor; April Hyatt, Advertising Mgr., phone (602)953-5264; Marvin Rosenfeld, Publisher. **Subscription Rates:** $12. $2 single issue. **Remarks:** Accepts advertising. **URL:** http://www.novicom.com.
Ad Rates: BW; $1,040 **Circ:** Controlled 18,000
4C: $1,640

4002 Podiatric Products
Novicom, Inc.
20000 Mariner Ave., No. 480 Phone: (310)793-4141
Torrance, CA 90503 Fax: (310)793-4138
Publisher E-mail: novicom@earthlink.net

Magazine featuring new products and services available in the podiatric field. **Founded:** 1984. **Freq:** 7/year. **Print Method:** Web offset. **Trim Size:** 8 3/8 x 10 7/8. **Cols./Page:** 3. **Key Personnel:** Christina Chang, Editor; Marvin Rosenfeld, Publisher; George Ross, Advertising Mgr. **ISSN:** 0890-3972. **Subscription Rates:** $12. $2 single issue. **Remarks:** Accepts advertising. **URL:** http://www.novicom.com.
Ad Rates: BW: $1,090 **Circ:** Controlled 13,000
4C: $1,690

4003 Police
Bobit Publishing
21061 S Western Ave. Phone: (310)533-2400
Torrance, CA 90501 Fax: (310)533-2503
Publication E-mail: police@bobit.com

Law enforcement magazine. **Subtitle:** The Law Enforcement Magazine. **Founded:** 1978. **Freq:** Monthly. **Print Method:** Offset. **Trim Size:** 7 7/8 x 10 3/4. **Cols./Page:** 3. **Col. Width:** 13 picas. **Col. Depth:** 9 1/4 inches. **Key Personnel:** Leslie Maris, Publisher/Nat'l Sales Mgr.; Dennis Hall, Exec. Ed.; Rebecca Stone, Senior Editor; Gary Thompson, Admin. and Ed. Asst. **ISSN:** 0893-8989. **Subscription Rates:** $23.95 individuals; $3 single issue. **Remarks:** Accepts advertising. **URL:** http://www.policemag.com. **Formerly:** Police Product News.
Ad Rates: BW: $2,825 **Circ:** ‡52,000
4C: $3,620
PCI: $3

4004 School Bus Fleet
Bobit Publishing
21061 S Western Ave. Phone: (310)533-2400
Torrance, CA 90501 Fax: (310)533-2503
Publication E-mail: sbf@bobit.com

Magazine on pupil transportation. **Founded:** 1956. **Freq:** 9/year. **Print Method:** Offset. **Trim Size:** 8 x 10 7/8. **Cols./Page:** 3. **Col. Width:** 26 nonpareils. **Col. Depth:** 140 agate lines. **Key Personnel:** Frank Di Giacomo, Publisher, phone (609)596-0999, fax (609)596-0168; Mary Reimer, Production Mgr., phone (310)533-2517; Steve Hirano, Editor, phone (310)533-2452, fax (310)533-2503. **ISSN:** 0036-6501. **Subscription Rates:** $25 individuals; $4 single issue. **Remarks:** Accepts advertising. **URL:** http://www.schoolbusfleet.com.
Ad Rates: BW: $4,600 **Circ:** Controlled 22,000
4C: $5,000 Paid 231
PCI: $75

4005 Security Sales
Bobit Publishing
21061 S Western Ave. Phone: (310)533-2400
Torrance, CA 90501 Fax: (310)533-2503
Publication E-mail: secsales@bobit.com

Magazine covering the security industry. **Subtitle:** Management Resource for The Professional Installing Dealer. **Founded:** Nov. 1979. **Freq:** Monthly. **Print Method:** Offset. **Trim Size:** 8 x 10 7/8. **Cols./Page:** 3. **Col. Width:** 13 picas. **Col. Depth:** 10 inches. **Key Personnel:** Jason Knott, Editor, phone (310)533-2538, jason@bobit.com. **ISSN:** 1204-831X. **Subscription Rates:** $35 individuals; $42 Canada; $53 other countries. **Remarks:** Accepts advertising. **Available Online.** **URL:** http://www.securitysales.com. **Formerly:** Alarm Installer and Dealer.
Ad Rates: BW: $3,180 **Circ:** 25,140
4C: $4,180

4006 Paragon Cable
1511 Cravens Ave. Phone: (310)618-9496
Torrance, CA 90501 Fax: (310)328-7628

Founded: 1984. **Key Personnel:** Paul Fisher, Contact; Bob Green, Contact. **Cities Served:** subscribing households 60,000; 60 channels; 12 community access channels.

TRACY, pop. 18,428.

San Joaquin Co. (C). 20 m SW of Stockton. Glass containers, milk products, food processing beet sugar factories, construction, sheathing, fruit, vegetable packing plants. Agriculture. Barley, Lima beans, tomatoes, asparagus, alfalfa, apricots, walnuts, almonds.

4007 Tracy Press
145 W. 10th St. Phone: (209)835-3030
PO Box 419 Fax: (209)835-0655
Tracy, CA 95376-3903
General newspaper. **Founded:** 1896. **Freq:** MXF (morn.). **Print Method:** Offset. **Cols./Page:** 6. **Col. Width:** 27 nonpareils. **Col. Depth:** 301 agate lines. **Key Personnel:** Thomas F. Matthews, Publisher; Samuel F. Matthews, Publisher. **Subscription Rates:** $34 individuals. **Remarks:** Accepts advertising.
Ad Rates: GLR: $.60 **Circ:** Mon.-Sat. ★**10,324**
BW: $1,118.43
4C: $1,368.43
SAU: $8.67
PCI: $8.67

4008 TCI Cable
305 W. 11th St. Phone: (209)835-4037
PO Box 530 Fax: (209)832-1148
Tracy, CA 95376

Founded: 1969. **Formerly:** UA Cablesystems of California (1992). **Key Personnel:** Lance Barnes, General Mgr., phone (707)447-3860, fax (707)446-4450, barnes.lance@tci.com. **Cities Served:** subscribing households 12,000; 65 channels; 1 community access channel; 12 hours per week community access programming.

TRONA, pop. 5,500.

San Bernardino Co. (NW) 140 m NW of San Bernardino. Manufactures chemicals, borax, lime, potash, bromine, soda ash.

4009 Trona Argonaut
PO Box 306 Phone: (760)372-4747
Trona, CA 93592 Fax: (760)372-4748
Free: (800)868-3526
Publisher E-mail: argonaut@ridgecrest.ca.us

Community newspaper. **Founded:** 1964. **Freq:** Weekly (Thurs.). **Print Method:** Offset. **Cols./Page:** 5. **Col. Width:** 2.05 inches. **Col. Depth:** 13 inches. **Key Personnel:** Joe Sonia, Publisher. **USPS:** 641-900. **Subscription Rates:** $20 in zips 93562 & 93592; $22 rest of USA. **Remarks:** Accepts advertising.
Ad Rates: GLR: $.20 **Circ:** ‡1,200
BW: $200
SAU: $4
PCI: $4.50

TRUCKEE, pop. 9,500.

Nevada Co. (NE). 32 m SW of Reno, Nev. Residential. Summer and winter resort. Lumbering.

4010 North Tahoe/Truckee Week
PO Box 49 Phone: (530)546-5995
Tahoe Vista, CA 96148 Fax: (530)546-8113

Magazine containing current events, entertainment, recreation, and sightseeing information for North Lake Tahoe visitors and residents. Includes classified ads. **Founded:** 1982. **Freq:** Weekly (Thurs.). **Print Method:** Offset. **Trim Size:** 11 x 14. **Cols./Page:** 6. **Col. Width:** 9 picas. **Col. Depth:** 14 inches. **Key Personnel:** Dave L. Good, Publisher. **Subscription Rates:** Free. **Remarks:** Accepts advertising. **Formerly:** North Tahoe Week (1990).
Ad Rates: PCI: $13 **Circ:** Controlled ‡20,000

4011 The Sierra Sun
Mount Rose Publishing Co.
PO Box 2973 Phone: (916)587-6061
Truckee, CA 96160 Fax: (916)587-3763
Publication E-mail: sun@tahoe.com

Local newspaper. **Founded:** 1869. **Freq:** Weekly (Thurs.). **Print Method:** Offset. **Cols./Page:** 6. **Col. Width:** 24 nonpareils. **Col. Depth:** 301 agate lines. **Key Personnel:** Peter Kostes, Editor; William Kunerth, Publisher. **Subscription Rates:** $25 individuals. **Remarks:** Accepts advertising.
Ad Rates: GLR: $10 **Circ:** 6,000
SAU: $4.94
PCI: $3

TUJUNGA

Los Angeles Co. (S). 12 m NW of Glendale. Residential. Health resort. Manufactures medical instruments, electronic products. Horse country. Light farming.

4012 Colony Communications, Inc.
10000 Commerce Ave. Phone: (818)352-7458
Tujunga, CA 91042 Fax: (818)352-7745

Founded: 1957. **Key Personnel:** Robert Brown, General Mgr.; Ranjan Mendonsa, Finance Manager. **Cities Served:** subscribing households 31,600; 61 channels; 3 community access channels.

TULARE, pop. 22,475.

Tulare Co. (SC). 45 m S of Fresno. Creameries. Cotton gins, winery. Diversified farming. Cotton, dairy products, beef cattle, deciduous fruit.

4013 Advance-Register & Times
Visalia Newspapers Inc.
PO Box 30 Phone: (209)688-0521
Tulare, CA 93275-0030
General newspaper. **Founded:** Dec. 11, 1882. **Freq:** Daily (eve.) and Sat. (morn.). **Print Method:** Offset. **Trim Size:** 14 1/2 x 23. **Cols./Page:** 6. **Col. Width:** 2 1/8 inches. **Col. Depth:** 21 1/2 inches. **Key Personnel:** Wayne Welch, Interim Editor; Connie Conway, Advertising Dir.; Lisa Patterson, Interim General Manager; Cliff Scott, Production Mgr. **Remarks:** Accepts advertising.
Ad Rates: PCI: $9.01 **Circ:** Mon.-Sat. ★**8,185**

4014 KGEN-AM - 1370-AM
PO Box 2040 Phone: (559)686-1370
Tulare, CA 93275 Fax: (559)685-1394

Format: Hispanic. **Owner:** Aztea Broadcasting Corp., 323 E. San Joaquin, Tulare, CA 93274. **Founded:** 1986. **Operating Hours:** Continuous. **Key Personnel:** Rolando Collantes, General Mgr.; Isabel Duran, Sales Mgr. **Wattage:** 1000. **Ad Rates:** Combined advertising rates available with KGEN-FM.

4015 KGEN-FM - 94.5
PO Box 2040 Phone: (559)686-1370
Tulare, CA 93275 Fax: (559)685-1394

Format: Ethnic. **Owner:** Rolando Collantes, at above address. **Founded:** 1986. **Former name:** KGEN-FM. **Operating Hours:** Continuous. **Key Personnel:** Isabel Duran, Sales and Promotions, phone (559)687-4881. **Wattage:** 6000.

4016 KJUG-AM - 1270
717 N. Mooney Blvd. Phone: (209)686-2866
Tulare, CA 93274-2411 Fax: (209)686-5265

Format: Country. **Founded:** 1945. **Formerly:** KCOK-AM (1945). **Operating Hours:** Continuous. **Key Personnel:** Larry W. Woods, President; Wayne Foster, General Mgr.; Dave Daniels, Program Dir.; Darrin Cantrell, News Dir. **Wattage:** 5000. **Ad Rates:** $10-60 for 30 seconds; $15-60 for 60 seconds. **URL:** http://www.kjug.com.

4017 KJUG-FM - 106.7
717 N. Mooney Blvd. Phone: (209)686-2866
Tulare, CA 93274-2411 Fax: (209)686-5265

Format: Contemporary Country. **Owner:** Larry W. Woods, at above address. **Founded:** 1959. **Formerly:** KWSM-FM (1959). **Operating Hours:** Continuous. **Key Personnel:** Larry W. Woods, President; Wayne Foster, General Mgr.; Sascha Rosen, Operations Mgr.; Darrin Cantrell, News Dir. **Wattage:** 50,000. **Ad Rates:** $10-60 for 30 seconds; $15-70 for 60 seconds.

TURLOCK, pop. 26,291.

Stanislaus Co. (C). 40 m SE of Stockton. California State University at Stanislaus. Turkey poultry processing plants, canning, dehydrating fruits and grapes, milk cartons, butter manufactured. Hatcheries. Nurseries. Poultry, fruit, dairy farms. Turkeys, grapes.

4018 The Signal
California State University, Stanislaus
801 W. Monte Vista Ave. Phone: (209)667-3410
Turlock, CA 95380 Fax: (209)667-3868
Publication E-mail: signal@toto.csustan.edu

Collegiate newspaper. **Founded:** 1971. **Freq:** Weekly (Wed.). **Print Method:** Offset. **Trim Size:** 10 x 12. **Cols./Page:** 4. **Col. Width:** 2.5 picas. **Col. Depth:** 182 agate lines. **Subscription Rates:** Free. **Remarks:** Color advertising not accepted. **URL:** http://lead.csustan.edu/commstudies/signal/signallead.html.
Ad Rates: BW: $211 **Circ:** Free ‡2,200
PCI: $4.50

4019 Turlock Journal
Central Valley Publishing
138 S. Center St. Phone: (209)634-9141
PO Box 800
Turlock, CA 95380-4508
Publisher E-mail: freelance@hollinet.com

General newspaper. **Founded:** 1904. **Freq:** Daily (eve.) and Sat. (morn.). **Print Method:** Offset. **Cols./Page:** 6. **Col. Width:** 24 nonpareils. **Col. Depth:** 301 agate lines. **Key Personnel:** Rob Cunningham, Editor; Ron Mix, Publisher; Darryl Clayman, Advertising Dir. **Subscription Rates:** $86.88 individuals. **Remarks:** Accepts advertising.
Ad Rates: GLR: $.57 **Circ:** Mon.-Fri. 7,300
BW: $1,171.80 Sat. 7,500
4C: $1,462.80
SAU: $7.98
PCI: $9.3

4020 KBDG-FM - 90.9
1600 E. Canal Dr. Phone: (209)667-0888
Turlock, CA 95380

Format: Educational. **Owner:** Turlock Joint Union High School District, at above address. **Founded:** 1977. **Key Personnel:** Robert G. Hoskins, Contact. **Wattage:** 150.

4021 KCSS-FM - 91.9
801 W. Monte Vista Ave Phone: (209)667-3378
Turlock, CA 95380 Fax: (209)667-3901
E-mail: kcss@toto.csustan.edu

Format: Blues; World Beat; Classical; Jazz; Alternative/New Music/Progressive; Blues; Rap. **Founded:** 1975. **Operating Hours:** 7 a.m. - 2 a.m. **Key Personnel:** Jeannie Pachelo, Station Mgr.; Kalons Saterfield, Promotions Dir.; Greg Jacquay, Chief Operator, phone (209)667-3427; Aril Buroker, Music Dir. **Wattage:** 151. **Ad Rates:** $8.50-10 per unit. **URL:** http://kcss.csustan.edu.

TUSTIN, pop. 32,073.

Orange Co. (S). 3 m E of Santa Ana. Suburban residential.

4022 Animation Journal
AJ Press
2011 Kingsboro Circle Phone: (714)544-6255
Tustin, CA 92780 Fax: (714)997-6700
Publisher E-mail: furniss@chapman.edu

Scholarly journal covering animation history and theory, film and television studies, popular culture and media studies. **Founded:** 1992. **Freq:** Semiannual. **Trim Size:** 5 3/8 x 8 1/2. **Cols./Page:** 1. **Col. Width:** 3 3/4 inches. **Key Personnel:** Maureen Furniss, Editor. **ISSN:** 1061-0308. **Subscription Rates:** $21.55 individuals; $43.10 institutions; $20 out of state individual; $40 out of state institution; $25 Canada and Mexico; $45 institutions, Canada and Mexico; $30 out of country; $50 institutions, other countries. **Remarks:** Advertising not accepted. **URL:** http://www.chapman.edu/animation.
Circ: Paid 200

4023 Racing & Sports Car Magazine
Pfanner Communications, Inc.
1371 E. Warner Ave., Ste. E Phone: (714)259-8240
Tustin, CA 92780 Fax: (714)259-1502

Public relations support publication for the Alfa Romeo distributors of North America. **Founded:** 1987. **Freq:** Quarterly. **Print Method:** Offset. **Trim Size:** 10 7/8 x 8 3/8. **Key Personnel:** Elyse Barrett, Editor. **Subscription Rates:** $5 single issue. **Remarks:** Advertising accepted; rates available upon request. **Formerly**: Quadrifoglio.
Circ: Controlled 13,000

4024 T.H.E. Journal
T. H. E. Journal
150 El Camino Real, No. 112 Phone: (714)730-4011
Tustin, CA 92780 Fax: (714)730-3739
Publisher E-mail: wladuke@thejournal.com

Application of technology journal for educators and administrators in higher ed ucation, K-12 and industry training. **Founded:** 1973. **Freq:** 11/year. **Print Method:** Offset. **Trim Size:** 7 7/8 x 10 1/2. **Cols./Page:** 3. **Col. Width:** 26 nonpareils. **Col. Depth:** 138 agate lines. **Key Personnel:** Bill Willis, Managing Editor, editorial@thejournal.com; Wendy LaDuke, Publisher, wladuke@thejournal.com. **ISSN:** 0192-592X. **Subscription Rates:** Free to qualified subscribers. **URL:** http://www.thejournal.com. **Also known as:** Technological Horizons in Education.
Ad Rates: BW: $9,200 **Circ:** Non-paid ★**166,500**
4C: $1,600

TWAIN HARTE

Tuolumne Co. (NW). 5 m N of Tuolumne.

4025 KKBN-FM - 93.5
22960 Vantage Pointe Dr. Phone: (209)586-1988
PO Box 708 Fax: (209)586-1111
Twain Harte, CA 95383

Format: Adult Contemporary. **Networks:** CBS; Mutual Broadcasting System. **Owner:** Clear Mountain Air Broadcasting Co., at above address. **Founded:** 1985. **Operating Hours:** Continuous; 20% network, 80% local. **ADI:** Sacramento-Stockton, CA. **Key Personnel:** Donald E. Leutz, Jr., Contact, don@cabinradio.com; Sylvia B. Leutz, Contact. **Wattage:** 6000. **Ad Rates:** $10-15 for 30 seconds; $12-18 for 60 seconds.

TWENTYNINE PALMS, pop. 14,000.

San Bernardino Co. (SE). 90 m E of San Bernardino. Health resort.

4026 The Desert Trail
Brehm Communications, Inc.
PO Box 159 Phone: (760)367-3577
Twentynine Palms, CA 92277 Fax: (760)367-1798
Publication E-mail: news@deserttrail.com
Publisher E-mail: 29trail@eee.org

Community newspaper. **Founded:** Apr. 18, 1935. **Freq:** Weekly (Thurs.). **Print Method:** Offset. **Cols./Page:** 6. **Col. Width:** 12 picas. **Col. Depth:** 21 1/2 inches. **Key Personnel:** Kelly O'Sullivan, Editor, kellyo@desterttrail.com; Jess Aured, Publisher, phone (760)365-3315, fax (760)365-8686, jaured@desertstar.com; Mark Miller, General Mgr., mmiller@desertrail.com. **USPS:** 155-020. **Subscription Rates:** $.50 individuals; $19.75 /year. **Remarks:** Accepts advertising.
Ad Rates: GLR: $3.10 **Circ:** ‡3,700
SAU: $14.10
PCI: $11.80

4027 KDHI-FM - 92.1
68474 29 Palms Hwy. Phone: (760)362-4264
Box 908 Fax: (760)362-4463
Twentynine Palms, CA 92277

Format: Contemporary Country. **Networks:** Jones Satellite. **Founded:** 1961. **Formerly**: KDHI-AM. **Operating Hours:** Continuous. **Key Personnel:** Duane Hoover, General Mgr.; Dorothy Hopko, Business Mgr.; Mike Hoover, Music Dir. **Wattage:** 6,000. **Ad Rates:** $11-15 per unit. Combined advertising rates available with KKJT-FM & KQYN-AM.

4028 KQYN-AM - 1250
68474 Twentynine Palms Hwy. Phone: (619)362-4264
PO Box 908 Fax: (619)362-4463
Twentynine Palms, CA 92277

Format: Big Band/Nostalgia. **Networks:** Westwood One Radio. **Owner:** Three D Radio Inc., at above address. **Founded:** 1965. **Operating Hours:** Continuous; 100% network. **Key Personnel:** Dorothy Hopko, Business Mgr.; Duane Hoover, General Mgr. **Wattage:** 1,000. **Ad Rates:** $8-15 for 30 seconds.

UKIAH†, pop. 12,035.

Mendocino Co. (NW). 60 m N of Santa Rosa. Residential. Fruit packing houses. Wineries, concrete pipe, sheet metal works, carpet mill lumber mills, masonite plant. Agriculture. Pears, grapes, cattle.

4029 Ukiah Daily Journal
Donrey Media Group
590 S. School St. Phone: (707)468-0123
PO Box 749 Fax: (707)468-3544
Ukiah, CA 95482-0749
Publication E-mail: udjpu@saber.net

General newspaper. **Founded:** 1860. **Freq:** Daily (eve.), Sunday (morn.). **Print Method:** Offset. **Cols./Page:** 6. **Col. Width:** 25 nonpareils. **Col. Depth:** 301 agate lines. **Key Personnel:** K. C. Meadows, Editor, phone (707)468-3526; Dennis Wilson, Publisher, phone (707)468-3505, fax (707)468-5780. **Subscription Rates:** $90 individuals. **Remarks:** Accepts advertising.
Ad Rates: GLR: $1.09 **Circ:** Mon.-Fri. ★**7,493**
BW: $2,109.15 Sun. ★**7,636**
4C: $2,409.15
SAU: $9
PCI: $10.90

4030 KDAC-AM - 1230
1400 Kuku Lane Phone: (707)466-5868
PO Box 539 Fax: (707)466-5852
Ukiah, CA 95482
E-mail: info@ukiahbroadcasting.com

Format: News; Talk. **Simulcasts:** KLLK-AM, KUKI-AM. **Networks:** AP. **Owner:** Charles Stone, at above address. **Founded:** 1948. **Operating Hours:** Continuous. **ADI:** San Francisco-Oakland-San Jose. **Key Personnel:** Jeanie Nord, Contact, jnord@inreach.com; Tove Sorensen, Program Dir., kuki@inreach.com; Dean Donos, News Dir. **Local Programs:** *Issues & Answers* 12:30 pm - 1:00 pm Saturday, Tove Sorensen, Program Dir.; *You're On The Air* 8:00 am - 9:00 am Monday-Friday, Dean Danos, (707)466-5865, Fax (707)466-5852; *The Kookie Sale-Swap Shop* 12:30 pm - 1:00 pm Monday-Friday, Jo-Lee V, Mailing contact. **Wattage:** 1000. **Ad Rates:** $18-25 for 30 seconds. Combined advertising rates available with KLLK-AM, KUKI-AM.

4031 KUKI-AM - 1400
1400 Kuki Ln.
PO Box 539
Ukiah, CA 95482
E-mail: info@ukiahbroadcasting.com

Format: News; Talk; Sports. **Networks:** ABC; CBS. **Founded:** 1951. **Operating Hours:** Continuous. **ADI:** San Francisco-Oakland-San Jose. **Key Personnel:** Jeanie Nord, General Mgr.; Tove Sorensen, Program Dir.; Dean Danos, News Dir. **Local Programs:** *Issues and Answers* 12:30 pm Saturday, Tove Sorenson; *You're On The Air* 8:00 am - 9:00 am Monday-Friday, Dean Danos, (707)466-5865, Fax (707)466-5852; *The Kookie Sale-Swap Shop* 12:30 pm - 1:00 pm Monday-Friday, Jo-Lee V, Mailing contact. **Wattage:** 1000. **Ad Rates:** $18-25 per unit. Combined advertising rates available with KDAC-AM.

4032 KUKI-FM - 103.3
1400 Kuki Ln. Phone: (707)466-5868
PO Box 539 Fax: (707)466-5852
Ukiah, CA 95482
E-mail: info@kukifm.com

Format: Country. **Networks:** ABC; CBS. **Owner:** Ukiah Broadcasting Corp., at above address. **Founded:** 1974. **Formerly**: KIAH-FM; KAFF-FM; KKTU-FM. **Operating Hours:** Continuous. **ADI:** San Francisco-Oakland-San Jose. **Key Personnel:** Jeanie Nord, General Mgr.; Tove Sorensen, Program Dir.; Dean Danos, News Dir. **Local Programs:** *Issues and Answers* 5:00 am - 6:00 am Sunday, Tove Sorensòn; *The Country Club* 7:00 pm - 12:00 midnight Friday, Tove Sorensen, Mailing contact, (707)466-5865; *Back In The Saddle* 12:00 noon - 3:00 pm Sunday, Tove Sorensen, (707)466-5865. **Wattage:** 2500. **Ad Rates:** $25-40 per unit.

4033 KWNE-FM - 94.5
2397 N. State St. Phone: (707)462-1451
Box 1056 Fax: (707)462-4670
Ukiah, CA 95482
E-mail: kwine@kwine.com

Format: Adult Contemporary; News; Information. **Networks:** ABC. **Founded:** 1968. **Formerly**: KLIL-FM (1968). **Operating Hours:** Continuous. **Key Personnel:** Guilford R. Dye, President; Michael A. Spencer, Station Mgr., capmikea@pacific.net; Bill Steele, Program Dir.; Gudrun Z. Dye, Contact. **Local Programs:** *Spanish Show*, Felix de Luna; *Wine Barrell Interview Program*, Bill Steele. **Wattage:** 2600. **Ad Rates:** $4-23 for 30 seconds; $5-28 for 60 seconds.

UNIVERSAL CITY

4034 Pratfall
PO Box 8341 Phone: (818)845-4048
Universal City, CA 91608
Magazine featuring Laurel and Hardy. **Founded:** 1969. **Freq:** Irregular. **Print Method:** Litho. **Trim Size:** 8 1/2 x 11. **Cols./Page:** 3. **Col. Width:** 2 1/8 inches. **Col. Depth:** 9 3/4 inches. **Key Personnel:** Lori S. Jones. **Subscription Rates:** $2 single issue. **Remarks:** Advertising not accepted.
Circ: 1,500

4035 Ship to Shore
Oceanic Navigation Research Society
PO Box 8005 Phone: (818)985-1345
Universal City, CA 91618-8005
Landscape formatted magazine featuring the history of ocean liner travel on the Atlantic, as well as other bodies of water. **Founded:** 1977. **Freq:** Quarterly. **Trim Size:** 8 1/2 x 11. **Cols./Page:** 3. **Key Personnel:** Charles Ira Sache, Editor. **ISSN:** 0738-6575. **Remarks:** Advertising accepted; rates available upon request. **URL:** http://www.titanic.org.
Circ: Controlled 300

VACAVILLE, pop. 43,367.

Solano Co. (NWC). 27 m SW of Sacramento. Food processing. Mobile homes. Light industry. Diversified farming.

4036 Teleconferencing Business Magazine
Business Teleconferencing
L. Dennis
Advertising Sales Director
Teleconferencing Business
Magazine
212 Raleigh Dr.
Vacaville, CA 95687

Magazine for news on the industry of teleconferencing. **Subtitle:** The Voice of the Teleconferencing Industry. **Founded:** Jan. 1995. **Freq:** 2x/mo. **Print Method:** Offset. **Trim Size:** 8 1/2 x 11. **Cols./Page:** 3. **Key Personnel:** Lucille Dennis, Advertising Dir., phone (707)451-8209, fax (707)451-4269, ldennis@communityonline.net; Paul Beatty, Publisher, beatty3atsjuno.com. **ISSN:** 1065-3007. **Subscription Rates:** $36; single issue; Free to qualified subscribers. **Remarks:** Accepts advertising.
Ad Rates: BW: $3,800 **Circ:** Non-paid ‡40,000
4C: $4,800

4037 The Weekly Star
The Reporter
916 Cotting Ln. Phone: (707)448-6401
Vacaville, CA 95696 Fax: (707)447-8411
Publication E-mail: newsroom@thereporter.com

Shopper, **Freq:** Weekly (Tues.). **Key Personnel:** Richard Rico, Publisher; Steve Huddleston, Publisher; Tom Hannon, Editor. **URL:** http://www.thereporter.com. **Formerly**: The Reporter Shopper (1990); The Weekly Leader.
Circ: Free ‡8,869

4038 KASK-FM - 91.5
160 Lighthouse Way Phone: (707)446-5500
Vacaville, CA 95688 Fax: (707)447-0630
E-mail: gdtop@castles.com

Format: Religious. **Owner:** Maranatha Broadcasting, at above address. **Founded:** Dec. 26, 1996. **Operating Hours:** Continuous. **Key Personnel:** Glenn D. Toppenberg, Pres./General Mgr. **Wattage:** 75. **Ad Rates:** Noncommercial. **URL:** http://www.kask.org.

4039 KUIC-FM - 95.3
600 E. Main St. Phone: (707)446-0200
Vacaville, CA 95688-3933 Fax: (707)446-0122
Free: (800)698-5842

Format: Adult Contemporary. **Networks:** Independent. **Owner:** Coast Radio Co., Inc., at above address. **Founded:** 1969. **Operating Hours:** Continuous; 100% local. **ADI:** Sacramento-Stockton, CA. **Key Personnel:** Jack Chunn, President, vbroadg@ix.netcom.com; Jim Hampton, Program Dir., jimh@kuicfm.com; Andrew Reed, Music Dir., andrew@kuicfm.com; Bob Breck, Station Mgr., bobb@kuicfm.com. **Local Programs:** *KUIC Morning Show*, Dave Paris. **Wattage:** 22,500. **Ad Rates:** $44-80 per unit. **URL:** http://www.kuicfm.com.

VALENCIA, pop. 12,200.

Los Angeles County. SW of Lake Hughes. Amusement park area.

4040 BMX Plus!
Hi-Torque Publishing Co., Inc.
25233 Anza Dr. Phone: (805)295-1910
Box 9502 Fax: (805)295-1278
Valencia, CA 91355
Free: (800)762-0345

Bicycle motocross magazine. **Founded:** 1978. **Freq:** Monthly. **Print Method:** Offset. **Trim Size:** 8 x 10 3/4. **Cols./Page:** 3. **Col. Width:** 27 nonpareils. **Col. Depth:** 140 agate lines. **Key Personnel:** Karl Rothe, Editor; R.S. Hinz, Publisher; Scott Wallenberg, Advertising Mgr. **ISSN:** 0195-0320. **Subscription Rates:** $18.98 individuals; $3.50 single issue.
Ad Rates: BW: $2,350 **Circ:** ‡47,615
4C: $3,450

4041 Dirt Bike Magazine
Hi-Torque Publishing Co., Inc.
25233 Anza Dr. Phone: (805)295-1910
Box 9502 Fax: (805)295-1278
Valencia, CA 91355
Free: (800)762-0345

Cycling magazine. **Founded:** 1971. **Freq:** Monthly. **Print Method:** Offset. **Trim Size:** 8 x 10 3/4. **Cols./Page:** 3. **Col. Width:** 26 nonpareils. **Col. Depth:** 140 agate lines. **Key Personnel:** Ron Lawson, Editor; Roland S. Hinz, Publisher; Scott Wallenberg, Advertising Mgr. **ISSN:** 0364-1546. **Subscription Rates:** $18.98 individuals; $3.50 single issue.
Ad Rates: BW: $4,995 **Circ:** Paid ★**100,060**
4C: $67,495

4042 Dirt Wheels
Hi-Torque Publishing Co., Inc.
25233 Anza Dr. Phone: (805)295-1910
Box 9502 Fax: (805)295-1278
Valencia, CA 91355
Free: (800)762-0345

ATV magazine. **Founded:** 1980. **Freq:** Monthly. **Print Method:** Offset. **Trim Size:** 8 x 10 3/4. **Cols./Page:** 3. **Col. Width:** 27 nonpareils. **Col. Depth:** 140 agate lines. **Key Personnel:** Dennis Cox, Editor; Roland Hinz, Publisher; Scott Wallenberg, Advertising Mgr. **ISSN:** 0745-0192. **Subscription Rates:** $18.98 individuals; $3.50 single issue.
Ad Rates: BW: $2,995 **Circ:** Paid 78,037
4C: $5,265

4043 Motocross Action
Hi-Torque Publishing Co., Inc.
25233 Anza Dr. Phone: (805)295-1910
Box 9502 Fax: (805)295-1278
Valencia, CA 91355
Free: (800)762-0345

Motocross racing magazine. **Founded:** 1973. **Freq:** Monthly. **Print Method:** Offset. Uses mats. **Trim Size:** 8 x 10 3/4. **Cols./Page:** 3. **Col. Width:** 26 nonpareils. **Col. Depth:** 140 agate lines. **Key Personnel:** Jody Weisel, Editor; Roland S. Hinz, Publisher; Scott Wallenberg, Advertising Mgr. **ISSN:** 0146-3292. **Subscription Rates:** $14.98 individuals; $2.50 single issue. **Remarks:** Accepts advertising.
Ad Rates: BW: $3,670 **Circ:** Paid ★**92,439**
4C: $5,925

4044 Mountain Bike Action
Daisy/Hi-Torque Publishing Co., Inc.
25233 Anca Dr. Phone: (805)295-1910
Valencia, CA 91355 Fax: (805)295-1278
Free: (800)767-0345

Magazine on off-road bicycling. **Founded:** 1986. **Freq:** Monthly. **Print Method:** Offset. **Trim Size:** 8 x 10 3/4. **Cols./Page:** 3. **Key Personnel:** Jody Weisel, Editor; R.S. Hinz, Publisher; Scott Wallenberg, Advertising Mgr. **Remarks:** Accepts advertising.
Ad Rates: BW: $1,295 **Circ:** Paid ★**86,302**

4045 3 & 4 Wheel Action
Hi-Torque Publishing Co., Inc.
25233 Anza Dr. Phone: (805)295-1910
Box 9502 Fax: (805)295-1278
Valencia, CA 91355
Free: (800)762-0345

Magazine designed for racing and recreational ATV riders. **Founded:** Nov. 1984. **Freq:** Monthly. **Print Method:** Offset. **Trim Size:** 8 x 10 3/4. **Cols./Page:** 3. **Key Personnel:** Ed Arnet, Editor; Roland Hinz, Publisher; Robert Rex, Advertising Mgr. **ISSN:** 0884-7126. **Subscription Rates:** $18.98 individuals; $3.50 single issue.
Ad Rates: BW: $1,850 **Circ:** Paid 36,826
4C: $2,995

4046 Traveling Times
Traveling Times, Inc.
25115 B-130 W. Ave. Stanford Phone: (661)295-1250
Valencia, CA 91355-3922 Fax: (661)295-8558

Travel journal. **Founded:** 1973. **Freq:** Quarterly. **Print Method:** Web offset. **Key Personnel:** Mirko A. Ilich, Editor and Publisher. **Remarks:** Advertising not accepted.
Circ: ‡1,650,000

VALLECITO

4047 Chalcedon Report
Chalcedon, Inc.
PO Box 158 Phone: (209)736-4365
Vallecito, CA 95251 Fax: (209)728-8522

Religious magazine containing articles that explore the relationship of Christian faith to the world. **Founded:** 1965. **Freq:** Monthly. **Print Method:** Offset. **Trim Size:** 8 3/4 x 10 3/4. **Cols./Page:** 2. **Col. Width:** 40 nonpareils. **Col. Depth:** 132 agate lines. **Key Personnel:** Andrew Sandlin, Editor, fax (209)728-8522. **Subscription Rates:** Free. **Remarks:** Advertising not accepted. **URL:** http://www.mother.com/~dlh/chalcedon.
Circ: Non-paid ‡10,700

VALLEJO, pop. 80,188.

Solano Co. (NWC). On Strait of Carquinez, 27 m NE of San Francisco. Manufactures dairy products, flour, beverages. Offshore oil drilling rigs. Planing mill, sheet metal works. Mare Island Naval Shipyard. Dairy, poultry, fruit farms.

4048 Vallejo Times-Herald
Donrey Media Group
440 Curtola Pkwy. Phone: (707)644-1141
PO Box 3188 Fax: (707)643-4322
Vallejo, CA 94590-0660
General newspaper. **Founded:** 1868. **Freq:** Mon.-Sun. (morn.). **Print Method:** Uses mats. Offset. **Cols./Page:** 6. **Col. Width:** 26 nonpareils. **Col. Depth:** 301 agate lines. **Key Personnel:** Donald Reynolds, Publisher. **Subscription Rates:** $6.50 Month; $12 by mail. **Remarks:** Accepts advertising.
Ad Rates: GLR: $15.50 **Circ:** Mon.-Sat. ★**20,362**
BW: $1,999.50 Sun. ★**21,946**
4C: $2,324.50

4049 KXBT-AM - 1630
3267 Sonoma Blvd. Phone: (707)644-8944
Vallejo, CA 94590 Fax: (707)644-3736
Free: (800)488-5842

Format: Urban Contemporary. **Networks:** Independent. **Owner:** Quick Broadcasting, Inc., 600 E. Main St., Vacaville, CA 95688. **Founded:** 1947. **Formerly:** KNBA-AM. **Operating Hours:** Continuous. **ADI:** San Francisco-Oakland-San Jose. **Key Personnel:** Diane DuBose, Station Mgr.; Andy Santamaria, President, phone (707)446-0200; Charlie Brock, Sales Mgr.; Chris Taylor, Programming Coordinator. **Wattage:** 10,000. **Ad Rates:** $50 per unit.

VALLEY CENTER

San Diego Co.

4050 Valley Roadrunner
Palomar Community Newspapers
PO Box 1529
Valley Center, CA 92082

Community newspaper for Valley Center, Pauma Valley, and Palomar Muontain. **Founded:** 1974. **Freq:** Weekly. **Cols./Page:** 6. **Col. Width:** 13 inches. **Col. Depth:** 21 inches. **Key Personnel:** David Ross, Editor; Dale Good, Publisher, publisher@valleycenter.com; Shirley Good, Publisher, publisher@valleycenter.com. **Subscription Rates:** $18; $.50 single issue.
Ad Rates: 4C: $250 **Circ:** Combined 3502
PCI: $9

VAN NUYS

Los Angeles Co. (S). 18 m NW of Los Angeles. Residential. Aircraft, auto body and trailers, cabinets, chemicals, dairy products, brick and tile, concrete block, pipes, guided missiles, toys, plastics manufactured. Automotive assembly plant. Nurseries.

4051 Adult Video News
6700 Valjean Ave. Phone: (818)786-4286
Van Nuys, CA 91406 Fax: (818)786-4287
Free: (800)521-2474
Publication E-mail: avnemail@aol.com
Publisher E-mail: sales@avn.com

Trade magazine for the adult entertainment industry. **Subtitle:** Adult Video News. **Founded:** 1983. **Freq:** Monthly plus annual entertainment guide. **Print Method:** Web. **Trim Size:** 8 3/8 x 10 7/8. **Cols./Page:** 3. **Col. Width:** 2 1/2 inches. **Col. Depth:** 10 1/4 inches. **Key Personnel:** Gene Ross, VP of Editorial Operations; Paul Fishbein, Editor and Publisher; Darren Roberts, Asst. Publisher; Jennifer Rosenblatt, Sales Director. **ISSN:** 0883-7090. **Subscription Rates:** $63; $7.95 single issue. **Remarks:** Accepts advertising. **URL:** http://www.avn.com.
Ad Rates: BW: $1,522 **Circ:** Paid ‡12,000
4C: $3,003 Controlled ‡28,000

Compton Metropolitan Gazette - See Compton

4052 Dialysis & Transplantation
Creative Age Publications, Inc.
7628 Densmore Ave. Phone: (818)782-7328
Van Nuys, CA 91406-2042 Fax: (818)782-7450
Free: (800)442-5667
Publication E-mail: dandT2@aol.com

Multi-disciplinary, peer-reviewed journal on clinical applications in dialysis, transplantation and nephrology for renal-care team. **Founded:** Nov. 1972. **Freq:** Monthly. **Print Method:** Offset. **Trim Size:** 8 x 10 3/4. **Cols./Page:** 3. **Col. Width:** 13.5 picas. **Col. Depth:** 60 picas. **Key Personnel:** Joseph G. Herman, Managing Editor; Deborah Carver, Publisher; Tom S. Blackstone, Assoc. Publisher, phone (972)238-3100, fax (972)238-0309. **ISSN:** 0090-2934. **Subscription Rates:** $35 individuals; $105 other countries. **Remarks:** Accepts advertising. **URL:** http://www.eneph.com.
Ad Rates: BW: $2,890 **Circ:** Non-paid △**19,394**
4C: $3,740

4053 Emergency Medical Services
Summer Communications, Inc.
7626 Densmore Ave. Phone: (818)786-4367
Van Nuys, CA 91406-2042 Fax: (818)786-9246
Free: (800)224-4367
Publication E-mail: emsmag@earthlink.net

Magazine covering emergency care, rescue and transportation. **Subtitle:** The Journal of Emergency Care, Rescue and Transportation. **Founded:** Nov. 1972. **Freq:** Monthly. **Print Method:** Offset. **Trim Size:** 8 x 10 3/4. **Cols./Page:** 3. **Col. Width:** 13 picas. **Col. Depth:** 60 picas. **Key Personnel:** Nancy Perry, Managing Editor; Carol Summer, Publisher. **ISSN:** 0094-6575. **Subscription Rates:** $19.95 individuals. **Remarks:** Accepts advertising. **Available Online. URL:** http://www.emsmagazine.com. **Alt. Formats:** Mailing lists.
Ad Rates: BW: $4,061 **Circ:** 48,125
4C: $5,221
PCI: $112

4054 Entertainment Employment Journal
5632 Van Nuys Blvd., Ste. 320 Phone: (818)920-0060
Van Nuys, CA 91401-4600 Free: (800)335-4335
Publication E-mail: editor@eej.com

Trade magazine covering business and technical careers in broadcast, electronic media, and motion pictures. **Founded:** 1992. **Freq:** Semimonthly. **Trim Size:** 8 5/16 x 10 7/8. **Cols./Page:** 3. **Col. Width:** 2 3/8 inches. **Col. Depth:** 10 inches. **Key Personnel:** Lawrence Haberman, Editor, editor@eej.com; G. Carbajal, Publisher, publisher@eej.com. **ISSN:** 1067-3970. **Subscription Rates:** $95 individuals; $125 institutions. **Remarks:** Accepts advertising.
Circ: (Not Reported)

4055 Import Automotive Parts & Accessories
Meyers Publishing
6211 Van Nuys Blvd. Phone: (818)785-3900
Van Nuys, CA 91401 Fax: (818)785-4397
Publisher E-mail: meyerspub@loop.com

Trade magazine for the automotive aftermarket. **Subtitle:** I.A.P.A. **Founded:** 1979. **Freq:** Monthly. **Print Method:** Offset. **Trim Size:** 8 x 10 7/8. **Cols./Page:** 3. **Col. Width:** 27 nonpareils. **Col. Depth:** 142 agate lines. **Key Personnel:** Steve Relyea, Editor; Len Meyers, Publisher; Lana R. Meyers, Advertising Dir.; Elyse Wilson, Operations Mgr. **ISSN:** 0199-4468. **Subscription Rates:** $50 Canada and Mexico; $85 other countries. **Remarks:** Accepts advertising.
Ad Rates: BW: $4,055 **Circ:** Paid 10
4C: $5,455 Controlled 34,017
PCI: $120

4056 La Guia Familiar
Latin Publications, Inc.
19804 Nordhoff Pl. Phone: (818)882-9200
PO Box 9190 Fax: (818)882-7200
Van Nuys, CA 91406-1309
Community newspaper (Spanish). **Founded:** Feb. 7, 1979. **Freq:** Weekly (Thurs.). **Print Method:** Offset. **Trim Size:** 8 1/4 x 10 9/16. **Cols./Page:** 5. **Col. Width:** 1 1/2 inches. **Col.**

Depth: 10 inches. **Key Personnel:** Arthur Lerner, Publisher. **Remarks:** Accepts advertising. **Formerly**: Variedades.
Ad Rates: BW: $3,062.50 **Circ:** Free ‡242,375
PCI: $61.25

4057 Location Update
7021 Hayvenhurst Ave. Phone: (818)785-6362
Van Nuys, CA 91406 Fax: (818)785-8092
Publisher E-mail: jt@ix.netcom.com

Magazine focusing on location filming. **Subtitle:** The Magazine of Film and Video Production. **Founded:** 1986. **Freq:** 12/year. **Print Method:** Web offset. **Key Personnel:** Andy Ozols, Associate Publisher; James Thompson, Publisher. **ISSN:** 1058-3238. **Subscription Rates:** $29.95; $39.95 Canada; $45.95 other countries. $3.95 single issue. **Remarks:** Advertising accepted; rates available upon request.
Circ: 24,000

Long Beach Express - See Long Beach

4058 Mundo L.A.
Latin Publications, Inc.
19804 Nordhoff Pl. Phone: (818)882-9200
PO Box 9190 Fax: (818)882-7200
Van Nuys, CA 91406-1309
Newspaper. **Founded:** Feb. 1, 1986. **Freq:** Weekly. **Print Method:** Offset. **Trim Size:** 11 x 13. **Key Personnel:** Arthur Lerner, Publisher. **Remarks:** Accepts advertising. **Formerly**: Tu Mundo.
Ad Rates: PCI: $141.39 **Circ:** Free 540,000

4059 The N.A. Way Magazine
World Service Office of Narcotics Anonymous, Inc.
PO Box 9999 Phone: (818)773-9999
Van Nuys, CA 91409 Fax: (818)700-0700
Publisher E-mail: info@wsoinc.com

Journal for and by recovering drug addicts. **Subtitle:** The International Journal of the Fellowship of Narcotics Anonymous. **Founded:** Sept. 1982. **Freq:** Quarterly. **Print Method:** Offset. **Trim Size:** 8 1/2 x 11. **Cols./Page:** 3. **Col. Width:** 14 picas. **Col. Depth:** 56 picas. **Key Personnel:** Cynthia Tooredman, Editor, cindytwso@aol.com; George Hollahan, Publisher. **ISSN:** 0896-9116. **Subscription Rates:** Free. **Remarks:** Advertising not accepted.
Circ: Non-paid 28,000

4060 Nailpro
Creative Age Publications, Inc.
7628 Densmore Ave. Phone: (818)782-7328
Van Nuys, CA 91406-2042 Fax: (818)782-7450
Free: (800)442-5667
Publication E-mail: nailpro@aol.com

Salon owners and nail technicians read Nailpro for continuing education in techniques and services, marketing and management tips, product information and industry news. **Founded:** 1989. **Freq:** Monthly plus special issue in April. **Print Method:** Web offset. **Trim Size:** 8 x 10 3/4. **Cols./Page:** 3. **Key Personnel:** Deborah Carver, Publisher; Linda W. Lewis, Editor; Kathy Kirkland, Exec. Ed. **ISSN:** 1049-4553. **Subscription Rates:** $31 individuals; $5 single issue; $24 students. **Remarks:** Accepts advertising.
Ad Rates: BW: $3,844 **Circ:** Paid 21,714
4C: $5,063 Non-paid 27,711

Pasadena Gazette - See Pasadena

San Fernando Gazette Express - See Pacoima

4061 Specialty Automotive Magazine
Meyers Publishing
6211 Van Nuys Blvd. Phone: (818)785-3900
Van Nuys, CA 91401 Fax: (818)785-4397
Publisher E-mail: meyerspub@loop.com

Trade magazine for the automotive aftermarket. **Subtitle:** S.A.M. **Founded:** 1983. **Freq:** Bimonthly. **Print Method:** Offset. **Trim Size:** 8 x 10 7/8. **Cols./Page:** 3. **Col. Width:** 27 nonpareils. **Col. Depth:** 142 agate lines. **Key Personnel:** Steve Relyea, Editor; Len Meyers, Publisher; Lana R. Meyers, Advertising Dir.; Elyse Wilson, Operations Mgr. **ISSN:** 0894-7414. **Subscription Rates:** $18 individuals; $5 single issue; $22 Canada; $47 other countries. **Remarks:** Accepts advertising.
Ad Rates: BW: $3,360 **Circ:** Controlled 26,530
4C: $4,760
PCI: $120

4062 Valley Star
Los Angeles Valley College
Journalism Dept. Phone: (818)781-1200
5800 Fulton Ave. Fax: (818)785-4672
Van Nuys, CA 91401-4096
Newspaper covering junior college student interests. **Founded:** 1949. **Freq:** Weekly (Thurs.). **Print Method:** Offset. **Cols./Page:** 6. **Col. Width:** 26 nonpareils. **Col. Depth:** 300 agate lines. **Key Personnel:** Kelli Morgan, Contact; Monica Lia, Advertising Assoc./Rep. **Subscription Rates:** Free. **Remarks:** Accepts advertising.
Ad Rates: BW: $660 **Circ:** Free ‡7,000
4C: $1,060
PCI: $8

4063 Win Magazine
Gambling Times, Inc.
16140 B. Valerio St. Phone: (818)781-9355
Van Nuys, CA 91406 Fax: (818)781-3125

Magazine featuring gambling, horseracing, lotteries, and casino games. **Founded:** Feb. 1977. **Freq:** Monthly. **Print Method:** Offset. **Trim Size:** 8 3/8 x 10 7/8. **Cols./Page:** 3. **Col. Width:** 27 nonpareils. **Col. Depth:** 140 agate lines. **Key Personnel:** Stanley Sludikoff, Editor and Publisher. **ISSN:** 0149-0214. **Subscription Rates:** $44 individuals; $4.95 single issue. **Remarks:** Accepts advertising. **URL:** http://www.gamblingtimes.com. **Formerly**: Gambling Times (1988).
Ad Rates: BW: $3,395 **Circ:** 50,604
4C: $4,195

4064 Winning Poker
Gambling Times, Inc.
16140 B. Valerio St. Phone: (818)781-9355
Van Nuys, CA 91406 Fax: (818)781-3125

Magazine for poker players. **Founded:** 1982. **Freq:** Monthly. **Print Method:** Offset. **Key Personnel:** Cecil Suzuki, Sr. Editor; Stanley Sludikoff, Editor; Bob Mason, Advertising Mgr. **Formerly**: Poker Player (Dec. 1990).

4065 KTLW-FM - 88.9
14820 Sherman Way Phone: (818)778-8400
Van Nuys, CA 91405 Fax: (818)778-8411
Free: (888)778-5859
E-mail: ktlw@livingway.org

Format: Contemporary Christian; Talk. **Networks:** SkyLight Satellite; Ambassador Inspirational Radio; Moody Broadcasting. **Owner:** Living Way Ministries, at above address. **Operating Hours:** Continuous. **Key Personnel:** Gary Curtis, Executive Dir., gcurtis@livingway.org; C. Olmstead, Operations Dir., colmstead@livingway.org. **Local Programs:** *Living Way*, Rita Medall. **Wattage:** 5,800. **Ad Rates:** Noncommercial. **URL:** http://www.ktlw.org.

4066 UAE
15055 Oxnard St. Phone: (818)781-1900
Van Nuys, CA 91411 Fax: (818)778-5235

Founded: 1986. **Formerly**: United Cable of ESFV; United Artists Cable. **Key Personnel:** Kurt Taylor, General Mgr., phone (818)778-5800; Larry D. Jones, Program Mgr.; Sheri Rubin, Public Relations Mgr. **Cities Served:** North Hollywood, San Fernando, Sherman Oaks, CA; Los Angeles County, CA: subscribing households 88,000; 78 channels; 2 community access channels; 280 hours per week community access programming.

VENICE

Los Angeles Co. (S). On Pacific Ocean, 1 m S of Santa Monica. Seaside resort. Residential.

4067 Venice Marina News
Copley Los Angeles Newspapers, Inc.
7776 Ivanhoe Ave.
La Jolla, CA 92037

Newspaper. **Founded:** 1928. **Freq:** Weekly (Wed.). **Print Method:** Offset. **Cols./Page:** 6. **Col. Width:** 26 nonpareils. **Col. Depth:** 301 agate lines. **Key Personnel:** Bertram Winrow, Publisher. **Subscription Rates:** $24 individuals. **Remarks:** Accepts advertising.
Ad Rates: GLR: $.65 **Circ:** Free 15,600

VENTURA†, pop. 75,000.

Ventura Co. (SW). 70 m N of Los Angeles. Summer and winter resort. Major oil production area. Manufactures gasoline, concrete pipe, electronics, food products, beverages. Ships flowers. Oil, gas wells. Agriculture. Citrus fruit, walnuts, lima beans. poultry, truck farms, cattle. Dairying.

4068 Art/Life
Art/Life Limited Editions
PO Box 23020 Phone: (805)648-4331
Ventura, CA 93002
Professional magazine featuring poetry, prose and art. **Subtitle:** Communication in Creative Ideas. **Founded:** 1981. **Freq:** 11/year. **Trim Size:** 8 1/2 x 11. **Key Personnel:** Joe Cardella, Editor; Pat Leddy, Advertising Mgr. **Subscription Rates:** $450. $50 single issue.

4069 Automated Builder
CMN Associates, Inc.
1445 Donlon St., Ste. 16 Phone: (805)642-9735
Ventura, CA 93003-5640 Fax: (805)642-8820

Covers factory-built housing industry. **Subtitle:** America's Housing Technology Transfer Magazine for Manufacturing and Marketing. **Founded:** 1964. **Freq:** Monthly. **Print Method:** Offset. **Trim Size:** 8 x 10 3/4. **Cols./Page:** 3. **Col. Width:** 2 3/16 picas. **Col. Depth:** 9 5/8 inches. **Key Personnel:** Don O. Carlson, Editor and Publisher; Lance Carlson, Advertising Mgr., lance@automatedbuilder.com. **ISSN:** 0899-5540. **Subscription Rates:** $50 individuals; $6 single issue; $100 other countries; $190 by mail overseas. **Remarks:** Accepts advertising. **Alt. Formats:** Microform. **Merged with:** Automation in Housing; Manufactured Home Dealer.
Ad Rates: BW: $3,745 **Circ:** Controlled 24,689
4C: $4,910

4070 Camcorder & Computer Video
Miller Magazines, Inc.
4800 Market St. Phone: (805)644-3824
Ventura, CA 93003-7783 Fax: (805)644-3875
Publication E-mail: camcoromg@aol.com

Magazine on home video and desktop video technology for consumers and prosumers. **Subtitle:** Video Photography and Desktop Video. **Founded:** 1985. **Freq:** Monthly. **Print Method:** Offset. **Trim Size:** 8 x 10 3/4. **Cols./Page:** 3. **Col. Width:** 2 1/2 inches. **Col. Depth:** 10 inches. **Key Personnel:** Bob Wolenik, Editor; James Miller, Publisher; Bonnie Jane Mason, Assoc. Editor/New Products Editor. **ISSN:** 1048-8804. **Subscription Rates:** $4.50; $4.95 Canada. **Remarks:** Accepts advertising. **Formerly**: Home Satellite TV; Super Television; Camcorder Report.
Ad Rates: BW: $1,550 **Circ:** ‡125,000
4C: $2,050
PCI: $77

4071 COINage
Miller Magazines, Inc.
4880 Market St. Phone: (805)644-3824
Ventura, CA 93003 Fax: (805)644-3875

Coin collecting magazine. **Founded:** 1964. **Freq:** Monthly. **Print Method:** Offset. **Trim Size:** 8 x 10 3/4. **Cols./Page:** 3. **Col. Width:** 27 nonpareils. **Col. Depth:** 140 agate lines. **Key Personnel:** Ed Reiter, Editor; James L. Miller, Publisher; Mike Gumpel, Advertising Mgr. **Subscription Rates:** $23 individuals; $33 other countries; $2.95 single issue. **Remarks:** Accepts advertising.
Ad Rates: BW: $1,050 **Circ:** (Not Reported)
4C: $1,550
PCI: $51.00

4072 Highways
TL Enterprises, Inc.
2575 Vista Del Mar Phone: (805)667-4100
Ventura, CA 93001 Fax: (805)667-4434
Free: (800)765-1912
Publication E-mail: goodsam@tl.com

Magazine for recreational vehicle owners. **Subtitle:** The Official Publication of the Good Sam Club. **Founded:** 1966. **Freq:** Monthly. **Print Method:** Offset. **Trim Size:** 8 x 10 3/4. **Cols./Page:** 3. **Col. Width:** 27 nonpareils. **Col. Depth:** 140 agate lines. **Key Personnel:** Susan Bray, Editorial Dir.; Ronald H. Epstein, Editor, reptein@tl.com; Kimberley Winters, Assoc. Editor, kwinters@tl.com; Terry Banister, Asst. Editor/Action Line, tbanister@tl.com; Jeanne Jones, Art Dir.; Bob Livingston, Technical Editor; Diane Fuller, Copy Editor; La Rae Lawson, Copy Editor; Sherman Goldenberg, Midwest Editor; Bruce Barnett, Contributing Editor; Bones Evers, Contributing Editor; Rich Johnson, Contributing Editor; Brenda Hutchinson, Production Mgr. **USPS:** 903-560. **Subscription Rates:** $2 single issue. **Remarks:** Accepts advertising. **URL:** http://www.goodsamclub.com/highways. **Formerly**: Good Sam's Hi-Way Herald (1989).
Ad Rates: BW: $17,840 **Circ:** ‡920,000
4C: $25,800

4073 Imaging News
Diamond Research Corp.
4864 Market St., Ste. C Phone: (805)650-9081
Ventura, CA 93003 Fax: (805)650-1607
Publisher E-mail: drc@west.net

Trade magazine covering imaging materials, technologies, and markets. **Freq:** Bimonthly. **Print Method:** Offset. **Trim Size:** 8 1/2 x 11. **Cols./Page:** 2 and 3. **Key Personnel:** Arthur S. Diamond, Editor and Publisher; Eve Diamond, Managing Editor; Dorothy Bacchilega, Vice President. **Subscription Rates:** $55 individuals. **Remarks:** Accepts advertising. **URL:** http://www.imagingnews.com/drc. **Former name**: R & R News.
Ad Rates: BW: $565 **Circ:** (Not Reported)
4C: $1,083

4074 Los Angeles Times—Ventura County Edition
The Times Mirror Co.
93 S. Chestnut St. Phone: (805)653-7566
Ventura, CA 93001 Fax: (805)653-7576
Publication E-mail: ventura@news.latimes.com

Community newspaper. **Founded:** Mar. 1987. **Freq:** Daily. **Key Personnel:** Bill Overend, Editor; Phyllis Jordan, City Editor.

4075 MotorHome
TL Enterprises, Inc.
2575 Vista Del Mar Phone: (805)667-4100
Ventura, CA 93001 Fax: (805)667-4434
Free: (800)765-1912

Magazine for motorhome enthusiasts. **Founded:** 1968. **Freq:** Monthly. **Print Method:** Offset. **Trim Size:** 7 7/8 x 10 1/2. **Cols./Page:** 3. **Col. Width:** 28 nonpareils. **Col. Depth:** 140 agate lines. **Key Personnel:** Bill Estes, Publisher; Barbara Leonard, Editorial Dir.; Terry Thompson, Natl. Sales Dir. **Subscription Rates:** $26 individuals; $3.99 single issue. **Remarks:** Accepts advertising. **Available Online. URL:** http://www.tl.com.
Ad Rates: BW: $6,905 **Circ:** Paid **★145,014**
4C: $9,925

4076 Power Electronic Systems
Adams/Intertec International Inc.
2472 Eastman Ave., No. 33 Phone: (805)650-7070
Ventura, CA 93003-5792 Fax: (805)650-7054
Publisher E-mail: info@pcim.com

"Provides in-depth technical information for power electronics designers; covering the components, technology and applications related to power electronic systems and subsystems.". **Founded:** 1975. **Freq:** Monthly. **Print Method:** Offset. **Trim Size:** 8 1/8 x 10 7/8. **Cols./Page:** 3. **Col. Width:** 13 picas. **Col. Depth:** 57 picas. **Key Personnel:** Dann Daggett, Publisher, dann@pcim.com; Judi Higgins, Advertising Asst. **ISSN:** 0885-0259. **Subscription Rates:** $175 other countries per year. **Remarks:** Accepts advertising. **URL:** http://www.pcim.com. **Formerly:** PCIM (Power Conversion & Intelligent Motion).
Ad Rates: BW: $4,310 **Circ:** Controlled 39,000
4C: $5,510

4077 Powerboat
1691 Spinnaker Dr., Ste. 206 Phone: (818)989-1820
Ventura, CA 93001-4378 Fax: (818)989-1823
Free: (800)738-5571
Publication E-mail: info@powerboatingmag.com

Magazine reporting news and trends in performance boating. Includes test reports on boats; technical reports on marine products, hull construction, and safety equipment; and water skiing and boat racing news. **Founded:** 1968. **Freq:** Monthly (Nov./Dec. combined issue). **Print Method:** Offset. **Trim Size:** 8 1/8 x 10 7/8. **Cols./Page:** 3. **Col. Width:** 13.5 picas. **Col. Depth:** 10 inches. **Key Personnel:** Gerald C. Nordskog, Publisher, phone (805)639-2226, fax (805)639-2225, sales@powerboatmag.com; Matt Trulio, Senior Editor, phone (805)677-3232, fax (805)639-2220, mtrulio@west.net; Doug Thompson, Senior Editor, phone (805)677-3227, fax (805)639-2220, dthomp321@aol.com; Victoria Newton, Ad Sales Mgr., phone (805)677-3228, fax (805)639-2220, vnewton@west.net; Jack Rothschild, Ad Sales Mgr., phone (805)677-3231, fax (805)639-2220, sales@powerboatmag.com; Robbie Destocki, Art Dir., phone (805)530-0316, fax (805)532-1460, robbied@west.net; Tosh Arimura, Circulation Mgr., phone (805)677-3230, fax (805)639-2220, tarimura@west.net. **ISSN:** 0032-6089. **Subscription Rates:** $27 individuals; $38 other countries. **Remarks:** Accepts advertising. **URL:** http://www.powerboatmag.com.
Ad Rates: BW: $3,135 **Circ:** 31,000
4C: $4,400
PCI: $132

4078 Rock & Gem
Miller Magazines, Inc.
4880 Market St. Phone: (805)644-3824
Ventura, CA 93003 Fax: (805)644-3875

Magazine about rocks, gold prosepecting, lapidary, and jewelry making. **Founded:** Mar. 1971. **Freq:** Monthly. **Print Method:** Offset. **Trim Size:** 8 x 10 3/4. **Cols./Page:** 3. **Col. Width:** 27 nonpareils. **Col. Depth:** 140 agate lines. **Key Personnel:** Alicia Morris, Managing Editor; James L. Miller, Publisher; Marlene Collier, Advertising Mgr. **Subscription Rates:** $24 individuals; $3.99 single issue. **Remarks:** Accepts advertising.
Ad Rates: BW: $688 **Circ:** ‡65,000
4C: $1,088

4079 RV Business
TL Enterprises, Inc.
2575 Vista Del Mar Phone: (805)667-4100
Ventura, CA 93001 Fax: (805)667-4434
Free: (800)765-1912
Publication E-mail: rvb@tl.com

Magazine about the business of manufacturing, distributing, and selling travel trailers, conversion vehicles, and motorhomes and related parts, accessories, and services. **Founded:** 1972. **Freq:** Monthly. **Print Method:** Offset. **Trim Size:** 8 x 10 3/4. **Cols./Page:** 2 and 3. **Col. Width:** 40 and 26 nonpareils. **Col. Depth:** 140 agate lines. **Key Personnel:** Sherman Goldenberg, Associate Publisher, phone (219)457-3370, fax (219)457-8925. **USPS:** 920-340. **Subscription Rates:** $48 individuals; $4 single issue ; free to trade. **Remarks:** Accepts advertising.
Ad Rates: BW: $3,115 **Circ:** Combined 15,900
4C: $4,490

4080 Thousand Oaks Star
Ventura County Star
5250 Ralston St. Phone: (805)650-2900
Ventura, CA 93003 Fax: (805)650-2944

General newspaper. **Founded:** 1954. **Freq:** Daily (morn.). **Print Method:** Offset. **Cols./Page:** 6. **Col. Width:** 25 nonpareils. **Col. Depth:** 301 agate lines. **Remarks:** Accepts advertising. **Formerly:** News Chronicles.
Ad Rates: SAU: $13.50 **Circ:** (Not Reported)
PCI: $12.50

4081 Trailer Life
TL Enterprises, Inc.
2575 Vista Del Mar Phone: (805)667-4100
Ventura, CA 93001 Fax: (805)667-4434
Free: (800)765-1912

Magazine for recreational vehicle (RV) enthusiasts. **Founded:** 1941. **Freq:** Monthly. **Print Method:** Offset. **Trim Size:** 7 7/8 x 10 1/2. **Cols./Page:** 3. **Col. Width:** 28 nonpareils. **Col. Depth:** 140 agate lines. **Key Personnel:** Bill Estes, Publisher; Barbara Leonard, Editorial Dir.; Janet Van Bibber, Advertising Dir. **Subscription Rates:** $22 individuals; $3.50 single issue. **Remarks:** Accepts advertising.
Ad Rates: BW: $6,245 **Circ:** Paid **★289,814**
4C: $9,045

4082 Ventura Bulletin
Metropolitan News Co.
210 S. Spring St. Phone: (213)628-4384
Los Angeles, CA 90012 Fax: (213)687-3886

Community newspaper. **Founded:** 1991. **Freq:** Weekly. **Print Method:** Offset. **Cols./Page:** 4. **Col. Width:** 15 picas. **Col. Depth:** 15 1/2 inches. **Key Personnel:** Roger M. Grace, Editor. **Remarks:** Accepts advertising.
Ad Rates: PCI: $6 **Circ:** Non-paid 1,000

4083 Ventura County & Coast Reporter
1567 Spinnaker Dr., No.202 Phone: (805)658-2244
Ventura, CA 93001 Fax: (805)658-7803

Weekly newspaper. **Founded:** 1977. **Freq:** Weekly (Thurs.). **Print Method:** Offset. **Trim Size:** 10 x 12. **Cols./Page:** 5. **Col. Width:** 1 7/8 inches. **Col. Depth:** 1 inches. **Key Personnel:** Nancy S. Cloutier, Editor and Publisher. **Subscription Rates:** Free; $50 by mail. **Remarks:** Accepts advertising.
Ad Rates: BW: $1,103 **Circ:** Paid ‡250
4C: $2,000 Free ‡35,000
PCI: $13.78

4084 Ventura County Star
5250 Ralston St. Phone: (805)650-2900
Ventura, CA 93003 Fax: (805)650-2944

General newspaper. **Founded:** 1875. **Freq:** Mon.-Sun. (morn.). **Cols./Page:** 6. **Col. Width:** 25 nonpareils. **Col. Depth:** 301 agate lines. **Key Personnel:** Tim Gallagher, Editor, phone (805)655-5838, fax (805)650-2950; Joe Howry, Managing Editor, phone (805)655-5801, fax (805)650-2950. **Subscription Rates:** $2.25 individuals per week. **Remarks:** Accepts advertising. **Formerly:** Ventura County Star Free Press. **Feature Editors:** Mike Blackwell, *Sports*, phone (805)655-5821, fax (805)650-2950; Colleen Cason, *Entertainment*, phone (805)655-1754, fax (805)650-2950; Timm Herdt, *Editorials*, phone (805)655-5802, fax (805)650-2950; Dave Mason, *TV*, phone (805)655-5831; Frank Moraga, *Financial/Business*, phone (805)987-5001, fax (805)650-2950; Rita Moran, *Women's*, phone (805)655-5831; Star Smith, *Features*, phone (805)655-1737, fax (805)650-2950.
Ad Rates: SAU: $14.13 **Circ:** Mon.-Sat. **★92,401**
Sun. **★104,607**

4085 Avenue TV Cable Service Inc.
1954 E. Main St. Phone: (805)643-9971
PO Box 1458 Fax: (805)643-1284
Ventura, CA 93002

Owner: John G. George, at above address. **Founded:** 1951. **Key Personnel:** Stephen George, System Mgr.; Pam Drake, Mktg. Dir.; Mike Rush, Chief Engineer. **Cities Served:** New Cuyama, Ventura, CA: subscribing households 10,500; 60 channels; 1 community access channel; 8 hours per week community access programming.

4086 Capp's TV Electronics Inc.
1399 Arundell Ave. Phone: (805)642-0241
Ventura, CA 93003 Fax: (805)650-1869
Free: (800)227-7747

4087 KBBY-FM - 95.1
6150 Olivas Park Dr. Phone: (805)644-9555
Ventura, CA 93003 Fax: (805)644-1966

Format: Adult Contemporary. **Networks:** Independent. **Founded:** 1962. **Operating Hours:** Continuous. **Key Personnel:** Marilyn Woods, General Mgr. **Wattage:** 28,000. **Ad Rates:** Advertising accepted; rates available upon request.

4088 KCAQ-FM - 104.7
2284 S. Victoria Ave. Phone: (805)289-1400
Ventura, CA 93003 Fax: (805)644-4257

Format: Contemporary Hit Radio (CHR). **Owner:** Gold Coast Broadcasting, at above address. **Founded:** 1958. **Formerly:** KACY-FM (1982); KPMJ-FM. **Operating Hours:** Continuous; 100% local. **Key Personnel:** Paul Smith, Promotions Dir.; Carl Goldman, President; Chip Ehrhardt, General Mgr.; Dan Garite, Program Dir.; Jacque Gonzalez, Music Dir. **Wattage:** 50,000. **Ad Rates:** $48-110 for 60 seconds. Combined advertising rates available with KKBE, KKZZ, KOLP, KTRO.

4089 KHAY-FM - 100.7
Box 699 Phone: (805)642-8595
Ventura, CA 93002 Fax: (805)656-5838

Format: Country. **Networks:** Independent. **Owner:** McDonald Media Group Inc., 1 Office Park Circle, Ste. 300, Birmingham, AL 35223-2585, (205)879-0456, Fax: (205)879-0479. **Founded:** 1962. **Operating Hours:** Continuous. **Key Personnel:** Thom King, General Mgr. **Wattage:** 39,000. **Ad Rates:** Advertising accepted; rates available upon request.

4090 KKBE-FM - 105.5
2284 Victoria Ave., Ste. 2M Phone: (805)289-1400
Ventura, CA 93003 Fax: (805)644-4257

Format: Country. **Founded:** 1960. **Formerly:** KTND-FM. **Operating Hours:** Continuous. **ADI:** Los Angeles (Corona & San Bernardino), CA. **Key Personnel:** Chip Ehrhardt, General Mgr., phone (805)289-1400. **Wattage:** 330. **Ad Rates:** Advertising accepted; rates available upon request.

KKZZ-AM - See Santa Paula

4091 KVEN-AM - 1450
Box 699 Phone: (805)642-8595
Ventura, CA 93002 Fax: (805)656-5838

Format: Talk. **Networks:** ABC; Mutual Broadcasting System; American Public Radio (APR). **Founded:** 1948. **Operating Hours:** Continuous. **Key Personnel:** Joe Armao, Contact. **Wattage:** 1000. **Ad Rates:** Advertising accepted; rates available upon request.

4092 KXBS-FM - 96.7
5200 Valentine Rd., No.230 Phone: (805)644-6800
Ventura, CA 93003 Fax: (805)644-6181
Free: (800)350-6800
E-mail: busrocks@isle.net

Format: Alternative/New Music/Progressive. **Networks:** Independent. **Owner:** KXBS, Inc., at above address. **Founded:** 1976. **Formerly:** KIEZ-FM. **Operating Hours:** Continuous. **Key Personnel:** Peter Daradics, General Mgr.; Stephanie Rose, Program/News Director. **Local Programs:** *Alternative Sub Zone*, Matt Cooper, Mailing contact; *Beginnings*, Jim Stone, Mailing contact; *Regional Riffs*, Aaron Parker, Mailing contact. **Wattage:** 3000. **Ad Rates:** $12-25 for 60 seconds.

4093 Lake Hughes Television Cable Service
1399 Arundell Ave. Phone: (805)642-0241
Ventura, CA 93003 Fax: (805)650-1869
Free: (800)227-7747

Owner: Capp's TV Electronics, at above address. **Founded:** 1960. **Key Personnel:** Earl C. Loughboro, President, cappsinc@aol.com; Charles Zych, Chief Engineer. **Cities Served:** Lake Hughes, CA: subscribing households 200; 23 channels; 1 community access channel.

VICTORVILLE, pop. 14,220.

San Bernardino Co. (SE). 42 m N of San Bernardino. Health resort. Dude ranches. Warehousing, electronics. Gold mines. Granite quarries. Agriculture. Alfalfa, cattle, turkeys.

4094 Daily Press
The Daily Press
PO Box 1389 Phone: (619)241-7744
Victorville, CA 92393 Fax: (619)241-7145
Free: (800)553-2006

General newspaper. **Founded:** Oct. 17, 1937. **Freq:** Mon.-Sun. (morn.). **Print Method:** Offset. **Cols./Page:** 6. **Col. Width:** 12 1/5 picas. **Col. Depth:** 21 1/2 inches. **Key Personnel:** Stephen M. Williams, Editor; Maureen Saltzer Brotherton, Publisher; Den Strella, Advertising Mgr. **ISSN:** 0739-0713. **Subscription Rates:** $111.80 individuals; $50.62 by mail per quarter. **Remarks:** Accepts advertising. **URL:** http.colin//www.vvdailypress.com.
Ad Rates: BW: $2,969.58 **Circ:** Wed. 38,000
4C: $3,344.58 Sun. 34,380
SAU: $23.02
PCI: $23.02

4095 Daily Press Preview
The Daily Press
PO Box 1389 Phone: (619)241-7744
Victorville, CA 92393 Fax: (619)241-7145
Free: (800)553-2006

Free Arts & Entertainment weekly. **Subtitle:** Victor Valley Edition. **Founded:** 1993. **Freq:** Weekly (Tues.). **Print Method:** Offset. **Trim Size:** 13 x 21 1/2. **Cols./Page:** 6. **Col. Width:** 2 1/16 inches. **Col. Depth:** 21 1/2 inches. **Key Personnel:** Lynn Tiffany, Editor, dpeditor@primnet.com; lmt@vvdailypress.com; Maureen S. Gawel, Publisher; Ray Marien, Advertising Mgr. **Subscription Rates:** Free. **Remarks:** Accepts advertising. **Formerly**: Sunday Extra.
Ad Rates: BW: $774 **Circ:** Tues. 34,000
4C: $1,159
SAU: $6.00
PCI: $6.00

4096 Hi-Desert Cablevision
12490 Business Center Dr., Ste. 1 Phone: (619)241-7848
Fax: (619)241-7659
Victorville, CA 92392
E-mail: hidescatv@aol.com

Owner: Booth American Co., 333 W.Fort St., Ste. 1200, Detroit, MI 48226, (313)202-3360, Fax: (313)202-3390. **Founded:** 1966. **Key Personnel:** Tom Burka, General Mgr.; Jeff Salkin, General Sales Mgr. **Cities Served:** Apple Valley, Hesperia, Spring Valley Lake, Victorville, CA: subscribing households 35,000; 62 channels.

4097 KATJ-FM - 100.7
PO Box 1428 Phone: (760)245-2212
15494 Palmdale Rd. Fax: (760)245-8012
Victorville, CA 92393

Format: Contemporary Country. **Networks:** Independent. **Owner:** Island Broadcasting, at above address. **Founded:** 1989. **Operating Hours:** 100% local. **ADI:** Los Angeles (Corona & San Bernardino), CA. **Key Personnel:** John Savidge, General Mgr. **Wattage:** 6000. **Ad Rates:** $13-40 for 30 seconds; $18-52 for 60 seconds. **URL:** http://www.katj.com.

4098 KHIZ-TV - 64
PO Box 6464 Phone: (619)241-5888
Victorville, CA 92393 Fax: (619)241-0056
E-mail: khiz@aol.com

Format: Commercial TV. **Networks:** Independent. **Founded:** 1987. **Formerly**: KVVT-TV (1992). **Operating Hours:** Continuous. **ADI:** Los Angeles (Corona & San Bernardino), CA. **Key Personnel:** Steve Sipe, General Sales Mgr.; Debbie Kershner, Program Dir.; Margaret Jackson, President. **Local Programs:** *Be Our Guest* 10 a.m. Monday-Friday; *Freddi Gold Show* 10:30 p.m. Monday-Friday. **Ad Rates:** $35-180 per unit. **URL:** http://vvo.com/khiz.htm.

4099 KIXW-AM - 960
12370 Hesperia Rd., Ste. 17 Phone: (619)241-1313
Victorville, CA 92392 Fax: (619)241-0205
Free: (800)278-4487

Format: Country. **Founded:** 1988. **Formerly**: KZXY-AM. **Operating Hours:** Continuous; 100% local. **Key Personnel:** Vicki Connor, Station Mgr.; Jay Stevens, Assist. Station Mgr.; David Wylie, News Dir. **Wattage:** 5000 AM. **Ad Rates:** Advertising accepted; rates available upon request.

4100 KROY-AM - 1590
15494 Palmdale Rd. Phone: (760)245-2212
PO Box 1428 Fax: (760)245-8012
Victorville, CA 92393

Format: Country. **Networks:** ABC. **Owner:** The Park Lane Group, at above address. **Founded:** 1961. **Operating Hours:** Continuous. **Key Personnel:** John Savidge, General Mgr. **Wattage:** 500. **Ad Rates:** $11.50-16 for 30 seconds; $14-20 for 60 seconds.

4101 KWRN-AM - 1550
15165 7th St., Ste. D Phone: (760)955-8722
PO Box 1283 Fax: (760)955-5751
Victorville, CA 92392

Format: Middle-of-the-Road (MOR); Hispanic. **Simulcasts:** 6 p.m.- 6a.m. **Owner:** KWRN Broadcasting, Inc., at above address. **Founded:** 1991. **Formerly**: KITH-AM; KAPL-AM. **Operating Hours:** Continuous. **ADI:** Los Angeles (Corona & San Bernardino), CA. **Key Personnel:** William Roberts, General Mgr.; Virginia Cruz-Roberts, Operations Mgr. **Local Programs:** *Morning Drive* Monday-Friday, Daniel Perez; *Romantic Program* Monday-Friday, Felipe Perdomo; *Viejitas pero Bonitas* 9-10am Saturday, Jose Luis Ruiz. **Wattage:** 5000 day; 500 night. **Ad Rates:** $10-15 for 30 seconds; $15-20 for 60 seconds.

4102 KZXY-FM - 102.3
12370 Hesperia Rd., Ste. 16 Phone: (760)241-1313
Victorville, CA 92392 Fax: (760)241-0205
E-mail: y102@highdesert.com

Format: Adult Contemporary. **Founded:** 1988. **Formerly**: KAVR-FM. **Operating Hours:** Continuous; 100% local. **Key Personnel:** John Covington, Station Mgr.; Gregg Thomas, Operations Mgr., athomas@mscomm.com; David Wylie, News Dir., newsman@mscomm.com. **Wattage:** 6000. **Ad Rates:** Advertising accepted; rates available upon request. $50 for 60 seconds.

VISALIA†, pop. 49,729.

Tulare Co. (SC). 42 m SE of Fresno. College of the Sequoias. Fruit canneries. Cheese, butter, transformers, milling products, electronic equipment, beverages manufactured. Walnuts, fruit packed. Diversified farming, Fruit, cattle, eggs.

4103 Visalia Times-Delta
Visalia Daily
330 N. West St. Phone: (209)734-5821
Visalia, CA 93291-6010 Fax: (209)733-0826

General newspaper. **Founded:** 1859. **Freq:** Mon.-Sat. (morn.). **Print Method:** Offset. **Cols./Page:** 6. **Col. Width:** 2 1/16 inches. **Key Personnel:** Janet C. Sanford Amandes, Publisher; Nancy Norton, Advertising Mgr. **Subscription Rates:** $67.60 individuals. **Remarks:** Accepts advertising.
Ad Rates: SAU: $16.28 **Circ:** Mon.-Fri. ★21,797
Sat. ★27,346

4104 Weekly Visalia Times-Daily
Visalia Daily
330 N. West St. Phone: (209)734-5821
Visalia, CA 93291-6010 Fax: (209)733-0826

Shopper. **Founded:** 1952. **Freq:** Weekly (Thurs.). **Print Method:** Offset. **Key Personnel:** Janet C. Sanford Amandes, Publisher; Tami Crawford, Advertising Dir. **Subscription Rates:** $15.55 individuals; $16.68 institutions. **Remarks:** Accepts advertising.
Ad Rates: GLR: $.15 **Circ:** Free 28,000
BW: $1,959.30
4C: $1,987.46
PCI: $3.60

4105 KARM-FM - 89.7
1300 S. Woodland Dr. Phone: (209)627-5276
Visalia, CA 93277 Fax: (209)627-5288
E-mail: karmradio@aol.com

Format: Religious. **Networks:** USA Radio. **Owner:** Harvest Broadcasting Co., at above address. **Founded:** 1990. **Operating Hours:** Continuous. **ADI:** Fresno-Visalia (Hanford), CA. **Key Personnel:** Chuck O'Dell, General Mgr.; Randy Stover, Chief Engineer; Tammy Teed, Program Dir.; Don Godman, Development Director. **Wattage:** 1000. **Ad Rates:** Noncommercial.

4106 KEYX-AM - 1400
3232 S. Mooney Blvd. Phone: (209)733-1400
Visalia, CA 93277 Fax: (209)251-3347

Format: Oldies. **Owner:** Americom Broadcasting, 6225 Sunset Blvd., Ste. 1900, Los Angeles, CA 90028. **Founded:** 1947. **Formerly**: KONG-AM (1981). **Operating Hours:** 5 a.m.-midnight; 0.5% network, 99.5% local. **ADI:** Fresno-Visalia (Hanford), CA. **Key Personnel:** Mike Bushey, Operations Mgr.; Art Nugent, News Dir.; Scott Seidenstricker, General Mgr. **Wattage:** 1000. **Ad Rates:** $10-30 per unit. Combined advertising rates available with KEYQ-AM: Combined rates also available with KF.

4107 KSEQ-FM - 97.1
617 W. Tulare Ave. Phone: (209)627-9710
Visalia, CA 93277-2552 Fax: (209)627-1590

Format: Adult Contemporary. **Networks:** Independent. **Owner:** Buckley Broadcasting, 166 W. Putnam, Greenwich, CT 06830. **Founded:** 1974. **Operating Hours:** Continuous; 100% local. **ADI:** Fresno-Visalia (Hanford), CA. **Key Personnel:** Ray MCarty, General Mgr.; Annette Christophe, News Dir.; Charlie Wolff, Operations Dir.; Clint Showalter, General Sales Mgr. **Wattage:** 17,000. **Ad Rates:** $26 for 30 seconds; $32 for 60 seconds.

VISTA, pop. 35,834.

San Diego Co. (SE). 32 m N of San Diego. Light manufacturing. Fruit. truck, poultry farms. Avocados.

4108 Good News Etc.
Good News Publishers Inc.
PO Box 2660 Phone: (760)724-3075
Vista, CA 92085 Fax: (760)724-8311
Publisher E-mail: comments@goodnewsetc.com

Community newspaper focusing on the christian community. **Founded:** 1984. **Freq:** Monthly. **Print Method:** Offset. **Trim Size:** 11x17. **Cols./Page:** 4. **Col. Width:** 2 3/8' inches. **Col. Depth:** 16' inches. **Key Personnel:** Rick Monroe, Editor and Publisher, rmonroe@goodnewsetc.com; Colleen Monroe, Publisher/Ad Director. **Subscription Rates:** $15. **Remarks:** Accepts advertising. **Available Online. URL:** http://www.goodnewstete.com.
Ad Rates: BW: $1,298 **Circ:** Combined 40,000
4C: $1,488

4109 Miata Magazine
Miata Club of America
1315 Buena Vista Dr.
Vista, CA 92083
Publisher E-mail: mdiasource@aol.com

Association magazine for Miata owners. **Founded:** 1989. **Freq:** 5/year. **Print Method:** Web offset. **Trim Size:** 8 1/8 x 10 7/8. **Key Personnel:** Norman H. Garrett III, Editor. **Subscription Rates:** $25. **Remarks:** Accepts advertising.
Ad Rates: BW: $1,750 **Circ:** Paid 28,000
4C: $3,540 Non-paid 10,000

4110 PennySaver
1300 Specialty Dr. Phone: (619)599-1400
Vista, CA 92083 Fax: (619)598-1113

Shopper. **Founded:** 1964. **Freq:** Weekly (Wed.). **Print Method:** Offset. Uses mats. **Trim Size:** 7 1/2 x 10. **Cols./Page:** 4. **Col. Width:** 7 picas. **Col. Depth:** 9 3/16 inches. **Key Personnel:** William Carman, President; David E. Clark, Dir. of Marketing. **Remarks:** Advertising accepted; rates available upon request. **URL:** http://www.thepennysaver.com.
Circ: Free ‡2,036,000

Cox Communications - See San Marcos

WALNUT, pop. 9978.

Los Angeles Co (S) 7 m SW of Pomona. Residential.

4111 Low Rider Magazine
Park Avenue Publishing, Inc
PO Box 648 Phone: (909)598-2300
Walnut, CA 91788-0648 Fax: (909)444-0162

Hispanic Automotive magazine. **Founded:** Dec. 1977. **Freq:** Monthly. **Print Method:** Offset. **Trim Size:** 8 x 10 7/8. **Cols./Page:** 3. **Col. Width:** 14 picas. **Col. Depth:** 60 picas. **Key Personnel:** Alberto Lopez, Publisher; Maria Brown, Advertising Dir.; David M. Cohen, Advertising Dir. **ISSN:** 0199-9362. **Subscription Rates:** $35 individuals. **Remarks:** Accepts advertising.
Ad Rates: BW: $3,654 **Circ:** Paid ★233,414
4C: $5,178

4112 The Mountaineer
Mt. San Antonio College
1100 N. Grand Ave. Phone: (909)594-5611
Walnut, CA 91789 Fax: (909)594-7661

Collegiate newspaper (tabloid). **Founded:** 1946. **Freq:** Monthly. **Print Method:** Offset. **Trim Size:** 10 x 15. **Cols./Page:** 5. **Col. Width:** 2 inches. **Col. Depth:** 182 agate lines. **Subscription Rates:** Free. **Remarks:** Advertising not accepted for Alcoholic beverages & tobacco products.
Ad Rates: BW: $350 **Circ:** Free ‡4,000
PCI: $6

4113 Official Magazine
International Association of Plumbing and Mechanical Officials
20001 Walnut Dr. S. Phone: (909)595-8449
Walnut, CA 91789-2825 Fax: (909)594-3690
Publisher E-mail: iapmo@earthlink.net

Trade publication containing articles of interest to anyone involved in the plumbing industry. **Founded:** 1958. **Freq:** Bimonthly. **Print Method:** Offset. **Trim Size:** 8 3/8 x 10 7/8. **Cols./Page:** 2. **Col. Width:** 3 1/2 inches. **Col. Depth:** 10 inches. **Key Personnel:** Kenneth S. Kochmann, Editor. **ISSN:** 0192-5784. **Subscription Rates:** $29. **Remarks:** Accepts advertising.
Ad Rates: BW: $585 **Circ:** Paid ‡5,000
4C: $1,385

4114 Jones Intercable Walnut Valley
20965 Lycoming St. Phone: (909)594-2729
Walnut, CA 91789 Fax: (909)598-0235

Owner: Glenn R. Jones, at above address. **Founded:** 1981. **Key Personnel:** Janet T. Spatz, General Mgr.; William R. Bradshaw, Marketing Mgr.; Mike Worrell, Engineering Mgr.; Karen Kennedy, Customer Service Mgr. **Cities Served:** Diamond Bar, Rowland Heights, CA: subscribing households 19,500; 57 channels; 6 community access channels; 20 hours per week community access programming.

WALNUT CREEK, pop. 53,643.

Contra Costa Co. (W). 15 m NE of Oakland. Manufactures canned goods, electronic equipment, food processing machinery, hand power tools, plastic coverings, walnut processing plant. Poultry, fruit, dairy farms. Walnuts, apricots, prunes. pears.

4115 Contra Costa News Register
1601 N. Main St., Ste. 107 Phone: (510)934-2780
PO Box 4779 Fax: (510)934-2532
Walnut Creek, CA 94596
Legal and business newspaper. **Founded:** 1955. **Freq:** Semiweekly (Tues. and Fri.). **Cols./Page:** 3. **Col. Width:** 28 nonpareils. **Col. Depth:** 182 agate lines. **Key Personnel:** Sandra Godsey, Editor; Noreen Clark, Publisher. **Subscription Rates:** $82; $135 two years. **Remarks:** Accepts advertising.
Ad Rates: PCI: $5 **Circ:** ‡1,000

4116 Contra Costa Times
Contra Costa Newspapers, Inc.
2640 Shadelands Dr. Phone: (925)935-2525
Walnut Creek, CA 94598-2513 Fax: (925)943-8362
Free: (800)465-0780

General newspaper. **Founded:** 1911. **Freq:** Daily (morn.). **Print Method:** Offset. **Cols./Page:** 6. **Col. Width:** 2 1/16 inches. **Col. Depth:** 21 1/2 inches. **Key Personnel:** George Riggs, Publisher & CEO; Pamela Henson, Vice Pres./Advertising; John Armstrong, Editor & Vice Pres. News; Mona Hatfield, News Research Manager. **Subscription Rates:** $99 individuals. **Remarks:** Accepts advertising. **Feature Editors:** Daniel Borenstein, *Political*; Jim Day, *News*; Jon Manlove, *Photo*.
Ad Rates: GLR: $3.71 **Circ:** Mon.-Sat. ★97,668
BW: $6,700 Sun. ★122,667
4C: $7,800
SAU: $51.98

4117 Diablo
Diablo Publications
2520 Camino Diablo, Ste. 200 Phone: (510)943-1111
Walnut Creek, CA 94596-3944 Fax: (510)943-1045
Publisher E-mail: diablospubs@aol.com

Neighborhood lifestyle publication for residents of San Francisco. **Subtitle:** The Magazine of the East Bay. **Founded:** 1979. **Freq:** Monthly. **Print Method:** Offset. **Trim Size:** 8 1/2 x 11. **Cols./Page:** 3. **Col. Width:** 27 nonpareils. **Col. Depth:** 140 agate lines. **Key Personnel:** Umberto Tosi, Editor; Steven J. Rivera, Publisher; Barney Fonzi, Advertising Mgr. **Subscription Rates:** $18 individuals. **Remarks:** Accepts advertising.
Ad Rates: BW: $3,450 **Circ:** Paid 402
4C: $3,750 Non-paid 42,197

4118 Diablo Business
Diablo Publications
2520 Camino Diablo, Ste. 200 Phone: (510)943-1111
Walnut Creek, CA 94596-3944 Fax: (510)943-1045
Publisher E-mail: diablospubs@aol.com

Business magazine covering East San Francisco bay region. **Founded:** July 1989. **Freq:** Semiannual. **Key Personnel:** Umberto Tosi, Editor; Stephen J. Rivera, Publisher. **Subscription Rates:** $3 single issue. **Remarks:** Accepts advertising. **URL:** http://www.diablo.com.
Ad Rates: BW: $2,588 **Circ:** Paid 561
Non-paid 7,649

4119 The Institutional Real Estate Letter
Institutional Real Estate, Inc.
1475 N. Broadway, Ste. 300 Phone: (925)933-4040
Walnut Creek, CA 94596 Fax: (925)934-4099
Publication E-mail: irel@irel.com
Publisher E-mail: irei@irei.com

Trade journal providing pension fund investment community with decision-making tools and information about real estate. **Subtitle:** The Information Source for Tax-Exempt Real Estate Investors. **Founded:** 1989. **Freq:** Monthly. **Print Method:** Sheet fed offset press. **Trim Size:** 8 1/2 x 11. **Cols./Page:** 3. **Key Personnel:** Geoffrey Dohrmann, Editor and Publisher; Jennifer Petch Babcock, Editor, j.petch@irel.com; Stacia Meadows, Advertising Dir.; Susan Sharpe, Production Mgr.; Nyia Dohrmann, Administration; Brett Monteith, Accounting/Finance; Larry Gray, Managing Editor. **ISSN:** 1044-1662. **Subscription Rates:** $1,495 individuals; $125 single issue. **Remarks:** Accepts advertising. **Available Online.**
Ad Rates: BW: $3,595 **Circ:** Paid 600
4C: $4,095 Non-paid 2,500

4120 Investment Property & Real Estate Capital Markets Report
Institutional Real Estate, Inc.
1475 N. Broadway, Ste. 300 Phone: (925)933-4040
Walnut Creek, CA 94596 Fax: (925)934-4099
Publisher E-mail: irei@irei.com

Trade journal covering commercial real estate investment. **Subtitle:** Reliable Source for Real Estate Capital Market Information. **Founded:** 1991. **Freq:** Monthly. **Print Method:** Sheet fed offset press. **Trim Size:** 8 1/2 x 11. **Key Personnel:** Geoffrey Dohrmann, Publisher and Editor-in-Chief; Larry Gray, Managing Editor; Steve Felix, Advertising Dir.; Susan Sharpe, Production Mgr.; Nyia Dohrmann, Administration; Ellie Samimi, Accounting/Finance. **ISSN:** 1064-1491. **Subscription Rates:** $495 individuals; $50 single issue. **Remarks:** Accepts advertising. **Online:** Teleres. **Formerly:** Real Estate Capital Markets Report.
Ad Rates: BW: $3,595 **Circ:** Paid 2,000
4C: $4,095 Non-paid 3,000

4121 Rossmoor News
Golden Rain Foundation
PO Box 2190 Phone: (510)988-7800
Walnut Creek, CA 94595 Fax: (510)935-8348
Publication E-mail: rossnews@ix.netcom.com

Community newspaper. **Subtitle:** For Seniors. **Founded:** 1965. **Freq:** Weekly (Wed.). **Print Method:** Offset. **Cols./Page:** 5. **Col. Width:** 24 nonpareils. **Col. Depth:** 192 agate lines. **Subscription Rates:** $35 individuals. **Remarks:** Accepts advertising.
Ad Rates: GLR: $.80 **Circ:** ‡6700
BW: $840
4C: $1,190
SAU: $12

WATERFORD, pop. 2,683.

Stanislaus Co. (C). 13 m E of Modesto. Residential. Diversified farming. Almonds, peaches, walnuts. Dairying.

4122 The Waterford News
Mid-Valley Publications
6950 Gerard St. Phone: (209)358-5311
Winton, CA 95388 Fax: (209)358-7108

Local newspaper. **Founded:** 1916. **Freq:** Weekly (Tues.). **Print Method:** Offset. **Trim Size:** 14 x 21. **Cols./Page:** 6. **Col. Width:** 2 inches. **Col. Depth:** 294 agate lines. **Key Personnel:** John Derby, Publisher, phone (209)874-1927. **Subscription Rates:** $19; $23 out of area.
Ad Rates: GLR: $7.95 **Circ:** ‡5,200
BW: $695
SAU: $10.95
PCI: $7.95

WATSONVILLE, pop. 23,543.

Santa Cruz Co. (W). 20 m N of Salinas. Fruit, Vegetables and lettuce packing houses, evaporating, cold storage, electronics plants, bottling works. Aluminum Extrusions, spray chemicals, vinegar, pectin, boxes, crates, manufactured. Agriculture. Apples, lettuce, berries.

4123 Register-Pajaronian
Watsonville Newspapers, Inc.
1000 Main St. Phone: (408)761-0611
PO Box 50055 Fax: (408)722-8386
Watsonville, CA 95077-3732
General newspaper. **Founded:** 1868. **Freq:** Daily (eve.) and Sat. (morn.). **Print Method:** Offset. **Cols./Page:** 6. **Col. Width:** 12 1/4 picas. **Col. Depth:** 21 inches. **Key Personnel:** Scott David Brennan, News Editor, fax (408)761-7338; Douglas Leifheit, Publisher, phone (408)761-7300. **USPS:** 669-540. **Subscription Rates:** $38 individuals; $40 other countries. **Remarks:** Accepts advertising.
Ad Rates: GLR: $.61 **Circ:** Mon.-Sat. ★8,204
BW: $1,476.72
4C: $1,744.72
SAU: $8.68
PCI: $126

4124 Sonic Cable TV of Santa Cruz
475 Airport Blvd. Phone: (408)724-1038
PO Box 508 Fax: (408)724-8387
Watsonville, CA 95077

Owner: Sonic Communications, Box 9371, Walnut Creek, CA 94598, (415)947-3700. **Founded:** 1965. **Key Personnel:** John Adams, General Mgr.; Curtis Kirby, Contact. **Cities Served:** subscribing households 14,400; 36 channels; 1 community access channel; 4 hours per week community access programming.

WEAVERVILLE†, pop. 5,950.

Trinity Co. (NW). 48 m NW of Redding. Sawmill. Pine, fir, cedar timber.

4125 Trinity Journal
PO Box 340 Phone: (530)623-2055
Weaverville, CA 96093 Fax: (530)623-2065

Community newspaper. **Founded:** 1856. **Freq:** Weekly (Wed.). **Print Method:** Offset. **Trim Size:** 13 x 21. **Cols./Page:** 6. **Col. Width:** 27 nonpareils. **Col. Depth:** 298 agate lines. **Key Personnel:** Mike Wenninger, Editor; Sarah Wenninger, Publisher. **USPS:** 673-220. **Subscription Rates:** $22 individuals; $30 out of area. **Remarks:** Accepts advertising.
Ad Rates: GLR: $5 **Circ:** ‡4,700
BW: $504

WEST COVINA

4126 Bayou Talk
Jo Val
PO Box 1344 Phone: (818)915-4211
West Covina, CA 91793-1344
Cajun Creole community newspaper. **Founded:** 1987. **Freq:** Monthly. **Cols./Page:** 5. **Col. Width:** 12 picas. **Col. Depth:** 13 inches. **Key Personnel:** Velma V. Conant Metoyer, Editor. **Subscription Rates:** $15. **Remarks:** Accepts advertising.
Ad Rates: PCI: $15 **Circ:** Paid 2,000
Non-paid 3,000

4127 San Gabriel Valley Tribune
San Gabriel Newspaper Group
1210 N. Azusa Canyon Rd.
West Covina, CA 91790
Publication E-mail: tribune@earthlink.net
Publisher E-mail: wdailynews@earthlink.net

Local newspaper. **Founded:** 1955. **Freq:** Daily. **Print Method:** Letterpress. **Cols./Page:** 6. **Col. Width:** 12 3/4 picas. **Col. Depth:** 301 agate lines. **Key Personnel:** Dorothy Reinhold, Vice Pres./Executive Managing Editor; Steve O'Sullivan, Managing Editor; Michael Coates, Asst. Managing Editor. **Subscription Rates:** $91 individuals. **Feature Editors:** Linda Alquist, *Food*; Tim Berger, *Photo*; Catherine Gaugh, *Features*; Steve Hunt, *Sports*; Rich Irwin, *Travel*; Vernor Rodgers, *Automotive*; Carla Sanders, *Fashion*; Steve Scauzillo, *Editorials*; Jason Schaff, *Financial/Business*; Liz Smilor, *Entertainment*.
Circ: Mon.-Fri. ★56,333
Mon.-Sat. ★58,102
Sun. ★59,331

WEST HOLLYWOOD, pop. 35,703.

Los Angeles Co. (SW). NE of Beverly Hills. Urban region.

4128 Art Issues
Foundation for Advanced Critical Studies, Inc.
8721 Santa Monica Blvd., Ste. 6 Phone: (323)876-4508
West Hollywood, CA 90069 Fax: (323)876-5061

Trade journal covering visual arts criticism. **Founded:** Jan. 1989. **Freq:** Bimonthly. **Print Method:** Sheetfed litho. **Trim Size:** 8 3/8 x 11. **Key Personnel:** Gary Kornblau, Editor. **ISSN:** 1046-8471. **Subscription Rates:** Free to qualified subscribers; $35 individuals; $5 single issue. **Remarks:** Accepts advertising.
Ad Rates: BW: $1,200 **Circ:** Non-paid 9,000

4129 Frontiers
Mercury Capital, Inc.
8380 Santa Monica Blvd., Ste. 200 Phone: (323)848-2222
Fax: (323)848-2321
West Hollywood, CA 90069
Publication E-mail: editor@frontiersweb.com

Consumer magazine covering gay and lesbian issues. **Founded:** May 1983. **Freq:** Biweekly. **Print Method:** Web offset. **Trim Size:** 10 3/8 x 13 1/4. **Key Personnel:** David Gardner, Advertising Dir., fax (323)848-9184, d_gardner@frontiersweb.com; Monica Trasandes, Editor; Bryan Newman, Circulation Mgr. **Subscription Rates:** $39 individuals. **Remarks:** Accepts advertising. **URL:** http://www.frontiersweb.com.
Ad Rates: BW: $1,375 **Circ:** Combined ❑**42,705**
4C: $1,800

4130 International Photographer Magazine
7715 Sunset Blvd., Ste. 300 Phone: (323)876-0160
West Hollywood, CA 90046 Fax: (323)878-1180
Publication E-mail: cameramag@aol.com

Trade magazine covering cinematography lighting techniques in film and video. **Founded:** 1929. **Freq:** Monthly. **Print Method:** Sheetfed offset. **Trim Size:** 8 1/2 x 11. **Key Personnel:** Suzanne R. Lezotte, Editor; John P. McCarthy, Advertising Sales; Teresa Ambriz, Circulation Mgr. **ISSN:** 0020-8299. **Subscription Rates:** $42 individuals; $4.95 single issue. **Remarks:** Accepts advertising.
Ad Rates: BW: $1,955 **Circ:** Combined ⊕**10,900**
4C: $2,985

4131 KYPA-AM - 1230
8730 Sunset Blvd. Phone: (310)289-7799
West Hollywood, CA 90069 Fax: (310)289-8070

Format: Talk. **Networks:** ABC. **Founded:** 1926. **Formerly:** KGFJ-AM (Apr. 18, 1996). **Operating Hours:** Continuous. **Key Personnel:** Andrew Whattey, Contact, andy.whattey@inteirnsfmei.com. **Wattage:** 1000. **Ad Rates:** Advertising accepted; rates available upon request.

WEST SACRAMENTO, pop. 12,002.

Yolo Co. (C). Adjacent to Sacramento. Manufactures box shooks. finger joints, moldings furniture, sawdust logs, building materials, boats. Light fixtures, truck trailers bodies, disinfectants, fertilizers, soil conditioning materials, rice millings, envelopes. Geophysical equipment.

4132 California Schools
California School Boards Association
3100 Beacon Blvd. Phone: (916)371-4691
PO Box 1660 Fax: (916)371-3407
West Sacramento, CA 95691
Free: (800)266-3382
Publisher E-mail: csba@csba.org

School management magazine covering educational issues and policies of vital importance to schools. **Founded:** 1942. **Freq:** Quarterly. **Print Method:** Offset. **Trim Size:** 8 1/2 x 11. **Cols./Page:** 3. **Col. Width:** 2 1/4 inches. **Col. Depth:** 9 inches. **Key Personnel:** Kevin Swartzendruber, Managing Editor, kswartzendruber@csba.org. **ISSN:** 0895-6073. **Subscription Rates:** $15 individuals; $28 two years; $5 single issue. **Remarks:** Accepts advertising. **Formerly:** California School Boards (1987).
Ad Rates: BW: $1,196 **Circ:** Paid ‡7,700
4C: $1,796 Non-paid ‡435

4133 News-Ledger
816 W. Acres Rd. Phone: (916)371-8030
PO Box 463
West Sacramento, CA 95691-3222
Publisher E-mail: editor@ireporting.com

Community newspaper. **Founded:** 1964. **Freq:** Weekly (Wed.). **Print Method:** Offset. **Cols./Page:** 6. **Col. Width:** 22 nonpareils. **Col. Depth:** 21 inches. **Key Personnel:** Michael P. Garten, Publisher; Steve Marschke, Editor. **USPS:** 388-320. **Subscription Rates:** $20 individuals; $25 out of area. **Remarks:** Accepts advertising.
Ad Rates: GLR: $5.75 **Circ:** 3,500
BW: $724.50
4C: $1,224.50

4134 Pulse!
Tower Records, Inc.
2500 Del Monte, Bldg. C. Phone: (916)373-2450
West Sacramento, CA 95691 Fax: (916)373-2480
Free: (800)525-5713

Magazine (tabloid) presenting qualitative and quantitative coverage of various forms of recorded sound. **Founded:** 1983. **Freq:** Monthly (except January). **Print Method:** Offset. **Trim Size:** 9 x 10 3/4. **Cols./Page:** 4. **Col. Width:** 12 1/2 picas. **Col. Depth:** 10 7/8 inches. **Key Personnel:** Suzanne Mikesel, Editor; Mike Farrace, Editor and Publisher; Anthony Howerton, Advertising Mgr. **Subscription Rates:** $29.95 2/year. **Remarks:** Accepts advertising. **URL:** http://www.towerrecords.com.
Circ: Non-paid ★**289,750**
Paid ★**2,288**

4135 KJAY-AM - 1430
5030 S. River Rd. Phone: (916)371-1459
West Sacramento, CA 95691

Format: Religious; Information. **Networks:** Independent. **Owner:** Jack L. Powell, at above address. **Founded:** 1963. **Operating Hours:** 6 a.m.-10 p.m. **Key Personnel:** Jack L. Powell, Contact; Gerald Sieber, Program Dir. **Wattage:** 500.

4136 KOVR-TV - 13
2713 KOVR Dr. Phone: (916)374-1313
West Sacramento, CA 95605 Fax: (916)364-1459
Free: (800)374-8813

Format: Commercial TV. **Networks:** CBS. **Founded:** 1954. **Operating Hours:** Continuous. **ADI:** Sacramento-Stockton, CA. **Key Personnel:** Steve Gigliotti, General Mgr.

4137 Sonic Cable Television of Northern California
1031 Triangle Ct. Phone: (916)372-2221
West Sacramento, CA 95605 Fax: (916)372-3865
Free: (888)997-6642

Owner: Sonic Communications, 1221 Broadway, 20th Fl., Oakland, CA 94612, (510)986-2255. **Founded:** 1977. **Key Personnel:** John Adams, General Mgr.; Barbara Beard, Office Mgr.; Heinz Ludke, Marketing Mgr.; Eric Brownell, Engineering Mgr. **Cities Served:** Placer County: 3 community access channels.

WEST WHITTIER

4138 Whittier Independent
Wave Community Newspapers
819 W. Whittier Blvd. Phone: (213)727-1117
Montebello, CA 90640-3623 Fax: (213)727-9515

Community Newspaper. **Founded:** 1922. **Freq:** 2/week (Wednesday & Saturday). **Print Method:** Uses mats. Offset. **Cols./Page:** 6. **Col. Width:** 21.5 nonpareils. **Col. Depth:** 301 agate lines. **Key Personnel:** Arthur V. Aguilar, Publisher. **Subscription Rates:** Free locally; $125 individuals. **Remarks:** Advertising accepted; rates available upon request. **Formerly:** West Whittier Independent.
Circ: Free ‡19,115

WESTLAKE VILLAGE, pop. 5,000.

Los Angeles Co. (SW). 3 m SE of Thousand Oaks.

4139 Crosscurrents, A Quarterly
2200 Glastonbury Rd. Phone: (818)991-1694
Westlake Village, CA 91361-3520 Fax: (818)707-3401
Literary magazine presenting poetry and fiction. **Founded:** 1980. **Freq:** Quarterly. **Print Method:** Offset. **Trim Size:** 6 x 9. **Key Personnel:** L.B. Michelson, Editor and Publisher. **ISSN:** 0739-2354. **Subscription Rates:** $18. $6 single issue. **Remarks:** Accepts advertising.
Ad Rates: BW: $70 **Circ:** ‡3,000

4140 MacTech Magazine
PO Box 5200 Phone: (805)494-9797
Westlake Village, CA 91359 Fax: (805)494-9798

Professional publication providing current and practical information on software programming and development for Macintosh computers. **Founded:** 1984. **Freq:** Monthly. **Print Method:** Web offset. **Trim Size:** 8 3/8 x 10 7/8. **Cols./Page:** 2. **Col. Width:** 4 3/16 inches. **Key Personnel:** Eric Gundrum, Editor-in-Chief; Jessica Courtney, Editor, editor@mactech.com; Neil Ticktin, Publisher, ceo@xplain.com. **Subscription Rates:** $5.85 single issue. **Remarks:** Accepts advertising. **URL:** http://www.mactech.com. **Alt. Formats:** CD-ROM. **Formerly:** MacTutor.
Ad Rates: BW: $1,275 **Circ:** Combined ‡15,488
4C: $2,395
PCI: $185

4141 Pacific Union Recorder
Pacific Union Conference of Seventh-day Adventists
PO Box 5005 Phone: (805)497-9457
Westlake Village, CA 91359 Fax: (805)495-2644
Publication E-mail: 74617,614@compuserve.com

Religious magazine. **Founded:** 1901. **Freq:** Monthly. **Print Method:** Web offset. **Trim Size:** 8 x 10 5/8. **Cols./Page:** 4. **Col. Width:** 21 nonpareils. **Col. Depth:** 130 agate lines. **Key Personnel:** C. Elwyn Platner, Editor. **ISSN:** 0744-6381. **Subscription Rates:** Free to qualified subscribers; $11 individuals; $15 other countries; $.85 single issue. **Remarks:** Accepts advertising. **Online:** Compuserve.
Ad Rates: BW: $1,695 **Circ:** Non-paid ‡59,000
4C: $2,850
PCI: $49.50

WESTMINSTER, pop. 71,133.

Orange Co. (S). 10 m W of Santa Ana. Residential. Light manufacturing. Diversified farming.

4142 Alba de America
Instituto Literario y Cultural Hispanico
8452 Furman Ave. Phone: (714)892-8285
Westminster, CA 92683 Fax: (714)892-8285

Literary magazine featuring Spanish language fiction, literary criticism, poetry, and essays. **Founded:** 1982. **Freq:** Annual. **Key Personnel:** Dr. Juana Arancibia, Editor, ilchja@aol.com. **ISSN:** 0888-3181. **Subscription Rates:** $48 individuals. **Remarks:** Advertising not accepted.
Circ: Paid 500

4143 Nguoi Viet Daily News
14891 Moran St. Phone: (714)892-9414
Westminster, CA 92683 Fax: (714)894-1381
Publication E-mail: nviet@ix.netcom.com; nvnews@aol.com

General newspaper (Vietnamese). **Founded:** Dec. 15, 1978. **Freq:** Mon.-Sun. (morn.). **Print Method:** Web. **Trim Size:** 13 x 21. **Cols./Page:** 6. **Col. Width:** 12 picas. **Key Personnel:** Do Ngoc Yen, Publisher. **Remarks:** Accepts advertising. **Formerly:** Nguoi Vet.
Ad Rates: BW: $659 **Circ:** 15,000
4C: $1,173
PCI: $11.75

4144 Westminister Herald
Westminister, Inc.
PO Box 428 Phone: (714)893-4501
Westminster, CA 92684 Fax: (714)893-4502

Newspaper. **Founded:** 1946. **Freq:** Weekly (Thurs.). **Print Method:** Uses mats. Letterpress. **Cols./Page:** 8. **Col. Width:** 22 nonpareils. **Col. Depth:** 294 agate lines. **Key Personnel:** L.W. Thomas, Editor and Publisher. **Subscription Rates:** $10 individuals. **Remarks:** Accepts advertising.
Ad Rates: GLR: $.28 **Circ:** (Not Reported)

WHITTIER, pop. 68,872.

Los Angeles Co. (S). 13 m SE of Los Angeles. Whittier College. Manufacturers oil tools, welding rods, alloy steel products, trailers, automobile polish, auto radiators, gas and oil burners, spray chemicals, tile, paper cartons, bullets, aircraft parts, boxes, cutlery, optical glass, plastics, women's apparel. Citrus fruit, mushrooms packed. Oil, gas wells. Fruit, dairy farms. Oranges, lemons, avocados, walnuts.

4145 Journal of the American Academy of Religion
Scholars Press
Department of Religious Studies Phone: (562)907-4200
Whittier College Fax: (562)907-4910
Whittier, CA 90605
Publication E-mail: sckolcomm@aol.com
Publisher E-mail: scholars@emory.edu

Journal containing articles on world religious traditions and research methodology studies. **Founded:** 1933. **Freq:** Quarterly. **Print Method:** Offset. **Trim Size:** 6 x 9. **Cols./Page:** 1. **Col. Width:** 54 nonpareils. **Col. Depth:** 96 agate lines. **Key Personnel:** Glenn Yocum, Editor, gyocum@whittier.edu; Leigh Anderson, Advertising Mgr., phone (409)727-2527. **ISSN:** 0002-7189. **Subscription Rates:** $60 institutions. **Remarks:** Accepts advertising. **Available Online. URL:** http://www.scholar.cc.emory.edu.
Ad Rates: BW: $450 **Circ:** 9,000

4146 Quaker Campus
Whittier College
Box 8613 Phone: (310)907-4254
Whittier, CA 90608 Fax: (310)945-5301

Collegiate newspaper. **Founded:** 1914. **Freq:** Weekly (Thurs.). **Print Method:** Offset. **Cols./Page:** 5. **Col. Width:** 24 nonpareils. **Col. Depth:** 210 agate lines. **Key Personnel:** Adam Pava, Editor-in-Chief; Greg Steele, Managing Editor, phone (310)907-5341. **Subscription Rates:** $26 Free; $26 by mail. **Remarks:** Accepts advertising. **Available Online. URL:** http://www.whittier.edu/ac/home.html.
Ad Rates: BW: $250 **Circ:** Free 1,800
4C: $550
PCI: $4.95

4147 Whittier Daily News
San Gabriel Newspaper Group
PO Box 581 Phone: (310)698-0955
Whittier, CA 90608 Fax: (310)698-0450
Publisher E-mail: wdailynews@earthlink.net

General newspaper. **Founded:** 1900. **Freq:** Daily (morn.). **Print Method:** Offset. **Cols./Page:** 6. **Col. Width:** 12 1/5

picas. **Col. Depth:** 301 agate lines. **Key Personnel:** William Bell, Editor and Publisher, phone (310)698-3015. **ISSN:** 0746-6188. **Subscription Rates:** $117; $.25 single issue. **Remarks:** Accepts advertising. **Formerly:** Daily News.
Ad Rates: BW: $4,980.45 **Circ:** Mon.-Fri. ★18,974
4C: $5,583.45 Mon.-Sat. ★19,275
SAU: $34.93 Sun. ★19,260
PCI: $15.70

WILLITS, pop. 4,008.

Mendocino Co. (NW). 110 m N of San Francisco. Manufactures redwood furniture and products, hydraulic cylinders. lumber, sawmills. Ranching.

4148 The Red Wood Crozier
The Redwood Crozier
24451 Sherwood Rd. Phone: (707)459-5710
Willits, CA 95490 Fax: (707)459-9070

Official newspaper of the Catholic Diocese of Santa Rosa. **Founded:** 1982. **Freq:** Monthly. **Cols./Page:** 3. **Col. Width:** 3 1/3 inches. **Col. Depth:** 13 inches. **Key Personnel:** Deacon Allan G. Bohner, Editor; Most Rev. G. Patrick Ziemann, Bishop, Publisher. **ISSN:** 0745-3248. **Subscription Rates:** $12. **Remarks:** Advertising not accepted.
Circ: Paid 12,000
Free 11,000

4149 The Willits News
1424 S. Main St. Phone: (707)459-4643
PO Box 628 Fax: (707)459-1664
Willits, CA 95490
Local newspaper. **Founded:** 1889. **Freq:** Semiweekly (Wed. and Fri.). **Print Method:** Offset. **Trim Size:** 14 x 22 1/4. **Cols./Page:** 6. **Col. Width:** 2 1/8 inches. **Col. Depth:** 21 inches. **Key Personnel:** Judi Pollace, Publisher, phone (707)263-5636, fax (707)263-0600; Debbie Clark, General Mgr., phone (707)459-4643, fax (707)459-1664. **USPS:** 685-140. **Subscription Rates:** $40 individuals. **Remarks:** Accepts advertising.
Ad Rates: GLR: $6.50 **Circ:** 3,800
SAU: $6.50

WILLOW CREEK, pop. 900.

Humboldt Co. (NW). On trinity River, 50 m NE OF Eureka. Recreation. Big foot country. Logging. Stud mill. Veneer and plywood mill.

4150 The Kourier
PO Box 355 Phone: (916)629-2811
Willow Creek, CA 95573
Local newspaper. **Founded:** Nov. 1967. **Freq:** Weekly (Wed.). **Print Method:** Offset. **Cols./Page:** 6. **Col. Width:** 12 picas. **Col. Depth:** 294 agate lines. **Key Personnel:** J.F. Garst, Jr., Editor and Publisher. **USPS:** 585-080. **Subscription Rates:** $19.50 individuals; $25 out of area. **Remarks:** Accepts advertising.
Ad Rates: BW: $466.20 **Circ:** ‡3,000

WILLOWS†, pop. 4,777.

Glenn Co. (NWC). 75 m NW of Sacramento. Manufactures cheese, butter, feed, beverages, roofing material. Rice drying plant. Diversified farming. Rice. sheep, cattle citrus fruit

4151 Orland Press-Register
Tri-County Newspapers, Inc.
101 Airport Rd. Phone: (530)934-6803
Willows, CA 95988 Fax: (530)934-6815

Community newspaper. **Founded:** 1898. **Freq:** Semiweekly (Tues. and Fri.). **Print Method:** Offset. **Cols./Page:** 6. **Col. Width:** 24 nonpareils. **Col. Depth:** 301 agate lines. **Key Personnel:** Martha Coe, Editor; Darrell Phillips, Publisher. **Subscription Rates:** $26 individuals; $38 out of area. **Remarks:** Accepts advertising.
Ad Rates: GLR: $.33 **Circ:** ‡2,250

4152 The Willows Journal
Morris Newspaper Corp.
PO Box 731 Phone: (916)934-6800
Willows, CA 95988 Fax: (916)934-6815

Newspaper. **Founded:** 1877. **Freq:** 3/week. **Print Method:** Offset. **Cols./Page:** 6. **Col. Width:** 24 nonpareils. **Col. Depth:** 301 agate lines. **Key Personnel:** Darrel Phillips, Publisher. **Subscription Rates:** $48 individuals. **Remarks:** Advertising not accepted.
Circ: (Not Reported)

4153 KIQS-AM - 1560
118 W. Sycamore Phone: (916)934-4654
PO Box 7 Fax: (916)934-4656
Willows, CA 95988

Format: Country. **Networks:** ABC. **Owner:** Kiqs, Inc, at above address. **Founded:** 1961. **Operating Hours:** Sunrise-sunset. **Key Personnel:** Anthony Rusnak, Gen. Mgr./Owner; Peggy Rusnak, Office/Production Mgr. **Local Programs:** *KIQS Talk Show*, Anthony Rusnak; *Swap Shop*, Peggy Rusnak. **Wattage:** 250. **Ad Rates:** $3.35 for 10 seconds; $3.75-5.95 for 30 seconds; $4.70-7.60 for 60 seconds.

WILMINGTON

4154 Wilmington Beacon
Rapid Publishing
349 W. Compton Phone: (213)774-0018
PO Box 4248
Compton, CA 90224
Black community newspaper. **Freq:** Weekly (Wed.). **Cols./Page:** 6. **Col. Width:** 12 1/2 picas. **Col. Depth:** 21 1/2 inches. **Key Personnel:** O. Ray Watkins, Publisher. **Remarks:** Accepts advertising.
Ad Rates: SAU: $10.65 **Circ:** (Not Reported)

4155 Copley/Colony Harbor Cablevision
605 E. G St. Phone: (310)513-0600
Wilmington, CA 90744 Fax: (310)549-5102

Owner: Colony Communications Inc., 20 Washington Pl., Providence, RI 02903, (401)277-7400. **Founded:** 1984. **Key Personnel:** Tim Kelley, General Mgr.; Randall Hicks, Marketing Mgr.; Moira Lane, Customer Service Mgr.; Rich Miller, Technician. **Cities Served:** Harbor City, Lomita, San Pedro, Torrance, Wilmington, CA: subscribing households 21,000; 60 channels.

WINCHESTER

4156 Hispanic Times Magazine
PO Box 579 Phone: (909)926-2119
Winchester, CA 92596
Magazine focusing on business and careers (English and Spanish). **Founded:** 1978. **Freq:** 5/year. **Print Method:** Offset. **Trim Size:** 8 1/8 x 10 7/8. **Cols./Page:** 3 and 2. **Col. Width:** 27 and 45 nonpareils. **Col. Depth:** 140 agate lines. **Key Personnel:** Gloria J. Davis, Editor, toxiekoji@aol.com; Humberto Salazar Lopez, Publisher. **ISSN:** 0892-1369. **Subscription Rates:** $30 individuals; $3.50 single issue. **Remarks:** Accepts advertising. **Online:** Ebasco; Softline.
Ad Rates: BW: $3,350 **Circ:** Paid ‡628
4C: $4,195 Controlled ‡60,000

WINTERS, pop. 2,652.

Yolo Co. (SC). 28 m W of Sacramento. Fruit drying and packing plants. Agriculture. Apricots, peaches, wheat, almonds.

4157 Winters Express
PO Box 608 Phone: (916)795-4551
312 Railroad Ave.
Winters, CA 95694-0608
Newspaper. **Founded:** 1884. **Freq:** Weekly (Thurs.). **Print Method:** Offset. **Cols./Page:** 6. **Col. Width:** 25 nonpareils. **Col. Depth:** 280 agate lines. **Key Personnel:** Charles Wallace, Editor and Publisher. **Subscription Rates:** $17.50 individuals. **Remarks:** Color advertising not accepted.
Ad Rates: BW: $516 **Circ:** ‡2,480
4C: $753
SAU: $4.40
PCI: $4.40

WINTON, pop. 4,995.

Merced Co. (C).

4158 Atwater's New Times
Mid-Valley Publications
6950 Gerard St. Phone: (209)358-5311
Winton, CA 95388 Fax: (209)358-7108

Shopping guide. **Founded:** 1967. **Freq:** Monthly. **Print Method:** Offset. **Key Personnel:** John Derby. **Subscription Rates:** $19; $23 out of area. **Remarks:** Accepts advertising.
Ad Rates: SAU: $7.95 **Circ:** Paid 2,800
PCI: $7.95

Denair Dispatch - See Denair

4159 Hilmar Times
Mid-Valley Publications
6950 Gerard St. Phone: (209)358-5311
Winton, CA 95388 Fax: (209)358-7108

Local newspaper. **Founded:** 1976. **Freq:** Weekly (Wed.). **Print Method:** Offset. **Trim Size:** 14 x 21. **Cols./Page:** 6. **Col. Width:** 2 inches. **Col. Depth:** 294 agate lines. **Key Personnel:** Jess Chamber, Editor, phone (209)632-4156; John M. Derby, Publisher. **Subscription Rates:** $19 individuals; $23 out of area. **Remarks:** Accepts advertising.
Ad Rates: GLR: $7.95 **Circ:** ‡4,000
BW: $695
4C: $995
SAU: $10.95
PCI: $7.95

Hughson Chronicle - See Hughson

4160 Merced County Times
Mid-Valley Publications
6950 Gerard St. Phone: (209)358-5311
Winton, CA 95388 Fax: (209)358-7108

Shopping guide. **Founded:** 1969. **Freq:** Monthly. **Print Method:** Offset. **Key Personnel:** Todder Smith, Editor. **Subscription Rates:** $19; $23 out of area; $.25 single issue. **Remarks:** Accepts advertising.
Ad Rates: BW: $795 **Circ:** Paid 5,600
4C: $1,100
SAU: $7.95
PCI: $7.95

The Waterford News - See Waterford

4161 Winton Times
Mid-Valley Publications
6950 Gerard St. Phone: (209)358-5311
Winton, CA 95388 Fax: (209)358-7108

Community newspaper. **Founded:** 1964. **Freq:** Weekly (Thurs.). **Print Method:** Offset. **Cols./Page:** 6. **Col. Width:** 10 picas. **Col. Depth:** 21 inches. **Key Personnel:** John M. Derby, Publisher. **Subscription Rates:** $19; $23 out of area.
Ad Rates: SAU: $10.95 **Circ:** ‡2,700
PCI: $7.95

WOODACRE

4162 Country Dance Lines
Drawer 139 Phone: (415)488-0154
Woodacre, CA 94973-0139 Fax: (415)488-4671
Publisher E-mail: cdl4cwdanc@aol.com

Consumer magazine covering Country Western dancing news and instruction. **Founded:** July 1984. **Freq:** Monthly. **Print Method:** Web offset. **Trim Size:** 8 x 11. **Cols./Page:** 3. **Col. Width:** 2 1/8 inches. **Col. Depth:** 9 5/8 inches. **Key Personnel:** Michael Hunt, Editor and Publisher; Barbara Romance, Advertising & Circulation. **ISSN:** 1083-3307. **Subscription Rates:** $20 individuals; $45 Canada individual/annual; $55 individuals Europe; $80 other countries; $5 single issue. **Remarks:** Accepts advertising.
Ad Rates: BW: $450 **Circ:** Paid 7,900
Non-paid 75

WOODLAND†, pop. 30,235.

Yolo Co. (C). 20 m NW of Sacramento. Manufactures mobile homes, trailers, farm implements plastics, draperies, lumber and wood products Cannery, Sugar refinery. Agriculture Tomatoes, sugar beets, rice barley walnuts, almonds.

4163 The Daily Democrat
Donrey Media Group
711 Main St. Phone: (916)662-5421
PO Box 730 Fax: (916)662-1288
Woodland, CA 95776
General newspaper. **Founded:** 1857. **Freq:** Daily (eve.), Sat. and Sun. (morn.). **Print Method:** Offset. **Cols./Page:** 6. **Col. Width:** 18 nonpareils. **Col. Depth:** 294 agate lines. **Key Personnel:** Jim Smith, Editor; Ted E. Dixon, Publisher; Neill Rabon, Advertising Mgr. **ISSN:** 0747-1890. **Subscription Rates:** $82.80 individuals including tax; $102.96 by mail including tax; $0.35 single issue.
Ad Rates: GLR: $1.80 **Circ:** Mon.-Sat. 9,887
BW: $1,419 Sun. 10,259
4C: $1,664
PCI: $11

WOODLAND HILLS

Los Angeles Co. (S). Suburb of Los Angeles. Residential. Commerical and industrial.

Daily News - See Los Angeles

4164 Exhibit Builder
Exhibit Builder, Inc.
22900 Ventura Blvd No. 245 Phone: (818)225-0100
PO Box 4144 Fax: (818)225-0138
Woodland Hills, CA 91365
Free: (800)356-4451

Magazine covering new product information and research related to the exhibit building, including museums and trade shows. **Founded:** 1983. **Freq:** 7/year. **Print Method:** Web offset. **Trim Size:** 8 x 10 3/4. **Cols./Page:** 3. **Col. Width:** 27 nonpareils. **Col. Depth:** 138 agate lines. **Key Personnel:** Judy Pomerantz, Editor; Jill Brookman, Publisher, jillb@xbuilder.com. **ISSN:** 0887-6878. **Subscription Rates:** $25; $50 three years. **Remarks:** Accepts advertising. **URL:** http://www.xbuilder.com.
Ad Rates: BW: $3,500 **Circ:** 14,500
4C: $920
PCI: $100

4165 Flex Magazines
Weider Publications
21100 Erwin St. Phone: (818)884-6800
Woodland Hills, CA 91367-3712 Fax: (818)704-5734
Free: (800)423-5590

Men's and women's competitive body building magazine. **Subtitle:** Voice of Champions. **Founded:** 1983. **Freq:** Monthly. **Print Method:** Offset. **Trim Size:** 7 7/8 x 10 1/2. **Cols./Page:** 3. **Col. Width:** 27 nonpareils. **Col. Depth:** 133 agate lines. **Key Personnel:** Jerry Kindela, Editor-in-Chief; George DePirro, Managing Editor; Bob Washburn, Publisher. **ISSN:** 8750-8915. **Subscription Rates:** $29.97 individuals; $4.95 single issue. **Remarks:** Accepts advertising.
Ad Rates: GLR: $45 **Circ:** Paid 140,244
BW: $4,535
4C: $5,975
PCI: $345

4166 For Patients Only
Dialysis, Inc.
6324 Variel Ave., Ste. 308 Phone: (818)704-5555
Woodland Hills, CA 91367 Fax: (818)704-6500
Publication E-mail: trademags@earthlink.net

Lifestyle magazine for dialysis and kidney transplantation patients. **Subtitle:** The Lifestyle Magazine for Renal Care Patients. **Founded:** 1989. **Freq:** Bimonthly. **Print Method:** Sheetfed offset. **Trim Size:** 8 1/4 x 10 7/8. **Cols./Page:** 3. **Col. Width:** 2 1/8 inches. **Col. Depth:** 10 inches. **Key Personnel:** Gordon Lore, Editor; Susan Summer, Assoc. Publisher and Marketing Dir.; Jerry Fisher, Publisher. **ISSN:** 0899-837X. **Subscription Rates:** $17. **Remarks:** Accepts advertising.
Ad Rates: BW: $1,975 **Circ:** Paid 4,300
4C: $2,825 Non-paid 6,700
PCI: $100

4167 ICS Cleaning Specialist
Business News Publishing Co. II, L.L.C.
22801 Ventura Blvd., Ste. 115 Phone: (818)224-8035
Woodland Hills, CA 91364-1222 Fax: (818)224-8042
Free: (800)835-4398
Publication E-mail: ics@bnp.com; http://www.icsmag.com

Trade magazine for the floor care and service industry. **Founded:** 1963. **Freq:** Monthly. **Print Method:** Heat-set web offset. **Trim Size:** 8 1/8 x 10 7/8. **Cols./Page:** 2 and 3. **Col. Width:** 40 and 26 nonpareils. **Col. Depth:** 140 agate lines. **Key Personnel:** Evan Kessler, Publisher, kesslere@bnp.com; Phil Johnson, Group Publisher; Arpi Lalbandian; Howard Olansky, Sr. Editor. **ISSN:** 1522-4708. **Subscription Rates:** $38 individuals; $38 Canada and Mexico; $60 other countries; $3.50 single issue. **Remarks:** Accepts advertising. **Available Online. Formerly**: Installation Specialist; Istallation & Cleaning Specialist.
Ad Rates: BW: $2,425 **Circ:** 27,000
4C: $3,420
PCI: $85

4168 Living Fit
Weider Publications
21100 Erwin St. Phone: (818)884-6800
Woodland Hills, CA 91367-3712 Fax: (818)704-5734
Free: (800)423-5590

A newstand-only publication for health and fitness fans. **Founded:** Sept. 1994. **Subscription Rates:** $2.50 single issue.
Circ: Paid 300,129

4169 Men's Fitness
Weider Publications
21100 Erwin St. Phone: (818)884-6800
Woodland Hills, CA 91367-3712 Fax: (818)704-5734
Free: (800)423-5590

Magazine devoted to health, nutrition, fitness and general lifestyle. **Subtitle:** Your Guide to Healthy Living. **Founded:** Aug. 1987. **Freq:** Monthly. **Print Method:** Offset. **Trim Size:** 7 7/8 x 10 1/2. **Cols./Page:** 3. **Col. Width:** 2 1/16 inches. **Col. Depth:** 9 3/8 inches. **Key Personnel:** Joe Weider, Publisher. **Subscription Rates:** $21.97 individuals; $3.50 single issue. **Remarks:** Accepts advertising. **URL:** http://www.mensfitness.com.
Ad Rates: BW: $12,585 **Circ:** Paid ★351,148
4C: $16,745

4170 Mission Valley Review
Los Angeles Newspaper Group
21221 Oxnard St. Phone: (818)713-3380
Woodland Hills, CA 91367 Fax: (818)713-3009

Shopper. **Founded:** 1973. **Freq:** Weekly (Wed.). **Print Method:** Offset. **Cols./Page:** 6. **Col. Width:** 21 1/2 nonpareils. **Col. Depth:** 294 agate lines. **Key Personnel:** Matt Hufman, Editor, phone (805)737-9027, fax (805)735-5118; Ron Hoffer, Publisher, phone (805)737-9030, fax (805)737-9037; Dick Bausman, Advertising Mgr., phone (805)737-9026, fax (805)736-5654. **Subscription Rates:** Free. **Remarks:** Accepts advertising.
Ad Rates: BW: $361.20 **Circ:** Free 8,048
4C: $706.20
SAU: $2.80
PCI: $2.80

4171 Muscle & Fitness
Weider Publications
21100 Erwin St. Phone: (818)884-6800
Woodland Hills, CA 91367-3712 Fax: (818)704-5734
Free: (800)423-5590

Physical fitness and lifestyle magazine. **Subtitle:** The Science of Living Super Fit. **Founded:** 1940. **Freq:** Monthly. **Print Method:** Perfect bound. **Trim Size:** 7 7/8 x 10 1/2. **Cols./Page:** 3. **Col. Width:** 27 nonpareils. **Col. Depth:** 140 agate lines. **Key Personnel:** Joe Weider, Publisher; Tom Deters, D.C., Editor-in-Chief, fax (818)595-0427. **ISSN:** 0744-5105. **Subscription Rates:** $3.95 single issue; $34.97 individuals. **Remarks:** Accepts advertising. **URL:** http://www.muscle-fitness.com.
Ad Rates: BW: $20,650 **Circ:** Paid ★455,981
4C: $25,780

4172 National Floor Trends Magazine
Business News Publishing Co. II, L.L.C.
22801 Ventura Blvd., Ste. 115 Phone: (818)224-8035
Woodland Hills, CA 91364-1222 Fax: (818)224-8042
Free: (800)835-4398
Publication E-mail: nft@bnp.com

Trade magazine for the floor covering industry. **Founded:** 1999. **Freq:** Monthly. **Print Method:** Offset, sheetfed. **Trim Size:** 8 1/2 x 10 7/8. **Cols./Page:** 2. **Col. Width:** 40 nonpareils. **Col. Depth:** 140 agate lines. **Key Personnel:** Phil Johnson, Group Publisher; Jeff Golden, Publisher & Editor, goldenj@bnp.com; Howard Olansky, Sr. Editor. **ISSN:** 1521-8031. **Subscription Rates:** $40 individuals; $52 Canada; $72 other countries; $6.50 SNG. **Remarks:** Accepts advertising. **Available Online. URL:** http://www.nflflrtrends.com. **Formerly**: Western Floors.
Ad Rates: BW: $4,775 **Circ:** 30,000
4C: $6,575
PCI: $120

4173 Prime Health & Fitness
Weider Publications
21100 Erwin St. Phone: (818)884-6800
Woodland Hills, CA 91367-3712 Fax: (818)704-5734
Free: (800)423-5590
Publication E-mail: primefit1@aol.com

Consumer magazine covering health, fitness, and lifestyle for men over 35 years. **Founded:** 1995. **Freq:** Quarterly. **Print Method:** Web offset. **Trim Size:** 7 7/8 x 10 1/2. **Cols./Page:** 2. **Key Personnel:** Bill Bush, Editor; David Kalmansohn, Senior Editor, phone (818)595-0572, fax (818)595-0575; Mike Carlson, Assoc. Editor. **ISSN:** 1083-0952. **Subscription Rates:** $9.97 individuals 6 issues. **Remarks:** Accepts advertising. **URL:** http://www.primehealth-fitness.com.
Ad Rates: BW: $4,800 **Circ:** Paid 161,332
4C: $6,000

4174 Shape
Weider Publications
21100 Erwin St. Phone: (818)884-6800
Woodland Hills, CA 91367-3712 Fax: (818)704-5734
Free: (800)423-5590

Magazine for women covering nutrition, weight control, physical fitness, psychology, fashion, beauty and travel. **Founded:** Sept. 1981. **Freq:** Monthly. **Print Method:** Offset. **Trim Size:** 7 3/4 x 10 1/2. **Cols./Page:** 3. **Col. Width:** 12 picas. **Col. Depth:** 62 picas. **Key Personnel:** Barbara S. Harris, Editor, phone (818)595-0593; Joe Weider, Publisher. **Subscription Rates:** $20 individuals; $2.99 single issue. **Remarks:** Accepts advertising. **URL:** http://www.shapemag.com.
Ad Rates: BW: $28,000 **Circ:** Paid ★1,143,409
4C: $35,845

4175 The Valley Vantage
23009 Ventura Blvd. Phone: (818)223-9545
Woodland Hills, CA 91364 Fax: (818)223-9552

Community newspaper. **Founded:** Feb. 1949. **Freq:** Weekly (Thurs.). **Print Method:** Offset. **Trim Size:** 10 1/4 x 14. **Cols./Page:** 5. **Col. Width:** 21 nonpareils. **Col. Depth:** 217 agate lines. **Key Personnel:** Rodger Sterling, Publisher; Kathleen Sterling, Publisher. **Subscription Rates:** Free; $30 by mail. **Remarks:** Accepts advertising. **Formerly**: Northridger News (1990).
Ad Rates: BW: $725 **Circ:** Free 60,000
4C: $1,400
PCI: $15

4176 Vecinos del Valle
Daily News of Los Angeles
21221 Oxnard St.
Woodland Hills, CA 91367

Hispanic oriented Community newspaper. **Subtitle:** Serimg the San Fernando Valley. **Founded:** Jan. 24, 1990. **Freq:** Weekly. **Cols./Page:** 5. **Col. Width:** 12 picas. **Col. Depth:** 21 inches. **Key Personnel:** Aida Ferrarone, Editor. **Subscription Rates:** $20 individuals. **Remarks:** Accepts advertising.
Ad Rates: GLR: $100 **Circ:** Free 48,371

4177 Western States Jewish History
Western States Jewish History Association
22711 Cass Ave. Phone: (818)225-9631
Woodland Hills, CA 91364 Fax: (818)225-8354
Publisher E-mail: david@inpubco.com

Magazine covering western Jewish history. **Founded:** Oct. 8, 1968. **Freq:** Quarterly. **Print Method:** Offset. **Trim Size:** 5 1/2 x 8 1/2. **Cols./Page:** 1. **Col. Width:** 51 nonpareils. **Col. Depth:** 93 agate lines. **Key Personnel:** Gladys Sturman, Editor/President, phone (818)222-4694, fax (818)591-0618. **ISSN:** 0043-4221. **Subscription Rates:** $25 individuals; $10 single issue. **Remarks:** Advertising not accepted.
Circ: Paid 1,200

YORBA LINDA, pop. 28,254.

Orange Co. (NE). 25 m SE of Los Angeles. Oil wells, citrus fruit.

4178 Western Birds
Western Field Ornithologists
6011 Saddletree Ln. Phone: (714)779-2201
Yorba Linda, CA 92886 Fax: (714)779-2202

Scholarly journal covering ornithology in the western U.S., Canada, and Mexico. **Founded:** 1973. **Freq:** Quarterly. **Trim Size:** 5 1/2 x 8 1/2. **Key Personnel:** Philip Unitt, Editor; Dori Myers, Manager. **ISSN:** 0160-1121. **Subscription Rates:** $20 individuals; $25 out of country. **Remarks:** Accepts advertising. **Former name**: California Birds.
Circ: Paid 1,000

4179 Century Communications
20409 Yorba Linda Blvd. Phone: (714)777-1313
Yorba Linda, CA 92686 Fax: (714)695-0075

Founded: 1991. **Formerly**: Yorba Linda Cable Television Co.; Empire Cable TV; Jones Spacelink Ltd. **Key Personnel:** Rod Hunt, Engineering Mgr., phone (714)695-1550; Karen Kennedy, General Mgr., phone (714)695-1550. **Cities Served:** Anaheim Hills, Yorba Linda, CA: subscribing households 18,000; 1 community access channel; 70 hours per week community access programming.

YREKA†, pop. 5,916.

Siskiyou Co. (N). 50 m S of Medford, Ore. Recreations. Light industry. Historic district. Creamery, bottling, cabinet works, logging, Gold mines. Pine timber. Dairy, stock, grain. Cattle ranching.

4180 Siskiyou Daily News
309 S. Broadway Phone: (530)842-5777
PO Box 129 Fax: (530)842-6787
Yreka, CA 96097-0129
Free: (800)540-5905
Publication E-mail: sisdaily@inreach.com

General newspaper. **Founded:** 1859. **Freq:** Daily (eve.). **Print Method:** Offset. **Cols./Page:** 6. **Col. Width:** 12 4/10 picas. **Col. Depth:** 301 agate lines. **Key Personnel:** Dale Andreasen, Editor and Publisher; Eric Grooters, Advertising Mgr.; Paul Shaw, Circulation Mgr.; Larry Vandemark, Production Supervisor. **Subscription Rates:** $72 individuals. **Remarks:** Accepts advertising. **URL:** http://www.siskiyoudaily.com. **Alt. Formats:** Microform.
Ad Rates: BW: $954.60 **Circ:** ‡6,000
4C: $1,179.60
PCI: $8.45

4181 KSYC-AM - 1490
316 Lawrence Ln. Phone: (916)842-4158
Yreka, CA 96097 Fax: (916)842-7635

Format: News; Talk; Oldies. **Networks:** Satellite Music Network; CBS. **Owner:** Siskiyou Radio Partners, Inc., at above address. **Founded:** 1945. **Operating Hours:** Continuous; 80% network, 20% local. **Key Personnel:** Al Blackmore, Gen. Mgr./Program Director; Rick Martin, News Dir.; Kevin Sponsor, Operations Mgr. **Wattage:** 1000. **Ad Rates:** $12.90-14.50 for 30 seconds; $16-18 for 60 seconds. Combined advertising rates available with KSYC-FM.

4182 KSYC-FM - 103.9
316 Lawrence Ln. Phone: (916)842-4158
Yreka, CA 96097 Fax: (916)842-7635

Format: Country. **Owner:** Siskiyou Radio Partners, Inc., at above address. **Founded:** 1983. **Operating Hours:** Continuous; 100% local. **ADI:** Medford, OR. **Key Personnel:** Al Blackmore, General Mgr/Program Director; Rich Martin, News Dir.; Kevin Sponsler, Operations Mgr. **Wattage:** 10.2 10,200. **Ad Rates:** $12.90-14.50 for 30 seconds; $16-18 for 60 seconds. Combined advertising rates available with KSYC-AM.

YUBA CITY†, pop. 18,736.

Sutter Co. (C). On Feather River, 40 m N of Sacramento. Fruit canning and drying. Fruit and nut packing house. Concrete pipe works. Creamery, feed mill, frozen food, seed cleaning plants. Diversified farming. Peaches, prunes, rice, beans.

4183 KUBA-AM - 1600
P.O. Drawer 232 Phone: (530)673-1600
Yuba City, CA 95992 Fax: (530)673-4768
E-mail: kuba@succeed.net

Format: News; Contemporary Country; Agricultural. **Networks:** CNN Radio. **Owner:** Ridge L. Harlan, at above address. **Founded:** 1948. **Operating Hours:** 19 hrs. Daily; 3% network, 97% local. **ADI:** Sacramento-Stockton, CA. **Key Personnel:** Robert R. Harlan, General Mgr.; Dave Bear, Operations Mgr.; Chris Gilbert, News Dir.; R.J. Blount, Station Mgr. **Wattage:** 5000. **Ad Rates:** $13.50-17 per unit. Combined advertising rates available with KXCL-FM.

4184 KXCL-FM - 103.9
P.O. Drawer 232 Phone: (530)673-1600
Yuba City, CA 95992 Fax: (530)673-4768
Free: (800)266-5104
E-mail: cool104@succeed.net

Format: Adult Contemporary; Soft Rock. **Networks:** Independent. **Owner:** Ridge L. Harlan, at above address. **Founded:** 1974. **Formerly:** KHEX-FM (1978); KXEZ-FM (1989). **Operating Hours:** 20 hrs. Daily; 100% local. **ADI:** Sacramento-Stockton, CA. **Key Personnel:** Robert R. Harlan, General Mgr.; Moe Howard, Program Dir.; Derek Moore, Music Dir.; Chris Gilbert, News Dir. **Wattage:** 25,000 ERP. **Ad Rates:** $19-24 per unit. Combined advertising rates available with KUBA-AM.

YUCAIPA, pop. 37,000.

San Bernardino Co. (SE). 9 m E of Redlands. Retirement living. Mobile home parks. Fruit, poultry, truck farms. Peaches, plums, tomatoes, apples.

4185 KLRD-FM - 90.1
PO Box 1000 Phone: (909)790-1848
Yucaipa, CA 92399

Format: Religious; Contemporary Hit Radio (CHR). **Networks:** USA Radio. **Owner:** Shepherd Communications, Inc., at above address. **Founded:** 1983. **Operating Hours:** Continuous; 5% network, 95% local. **ADI:** Los Angeles (Corona & San Bernardino), CA. **Key Personnel:** Candace Andrews, General Mgr.; Noonie Fugler, Network Program Dir.; Christie Reasons, Contact; Don Carson, Program Dir. **Wattage:** 300. **Ad Rates:** $35 per unit.

YUCCA VALLEY, pop. 14,200.

San Bernardino Co. (SE). 31 m N of Palm Springs. Desert and health resort.

4186 Hi-Desert Star
Hi Desert Publishing
56445 29 Palms Hwy. Phone: (760)365-3315
PO Box 880 Fax: (760)365-8686
Yucca Valley, CA 92286-2861
Community newspaper. **Founded:** 1957. **Freq:** Semiweekly. **Print Method:** Offset. **Trim Size:** 13 3/4 x 22 3/4. **Cols./Page:** 6 and 9. **Col. Width:** 2 and 1.25 inches. **Col. Depth:** 21.5 and 21.5 inches. **Key Personnel:** Susan Cchaney, Editor, schane@hidesertstar.com; Jess Allred, Publisher, jallred@hidesertstar.com; Judy Moore, Advertising Mgr., jmoore@hidesertstar.com. **Subscription Rates:** $27 individuals; $40 Out of county; $50 out of state. **Remarks:** Accepts advertising.
Ad Rates: GLR: $.97 **Circ:** ‡10,100
BW: $1,754.40
4C: $2,024.40

4187 Wheelers
Wheelers Publishing Co.
2015 Yellowknife Rd. Phone: (619)364-4317
Yucca Valley, CA 92284-4530
Magazine for, by, and about people with mobility impairments. **Freq:** 6/year. **Subscription Rates:** $20 individuals. **Remarks:** Advertising accepted; rates available upon request.
Circ: (Not Reported)

COLORADO

State Capital, DENVER

Colorado is bounded on the north by Nebraska and Wyoming, east by Nebraska and Kansas, south by Oklahoma and New Mexico, and west by Utah. Its breadth from east to west is 380 miles; length, 280 miles. The total land area is 103,730 square miles; its rank in area, eighth. The state, famous for its scenery, is intersected near the center by the main range of the Rocky Mountains, known as the Continental Divide, and includes its highest points. Among them are Mounts Elbert and Massive, the 2nd and 3rd highest peaks in the country, and famed Pike's Peak. The mountains enclose valleys or basins known as parks. Many are small but several are nearly 2,000 square miles in area. These parks are well-timbered, and abound with beautiful scenery, being diversified with low hills and ridges. All the great rivers which flow through the state have their origins in these hills. The average altitude of this state is over 6,800 feet above sea level, and the lowest altitude, along the Arkansas River in Prowers county, is 3,350 feet. There are 53 peaks towering to an altitude of 14,000 feet or more. In crossing the mountains, the height reached by rail is 10,856 feet. Timber is found in many places in Colorado at a height of 11,000 feet, and the snow line in summer is nearly 14,000 feet, while in the European Alps little arboreal growth is found at over 6,000 feet, and the line of perpetual snow is between 9,000 and 10,000 feet. In Colorado, wheat and oats have attained maturity at 7,000 to 8,000 feet, barley at over 10,000 feet, and apples, pears, plums, cherries, and small fruits between 7,000 and 8,000 feet. There are many mineral springs, some reputed to have medicinal value. Everywhere is unusual conformation and coloration. The eastern part of the state is an immense plain which was for many years devoted to cattle raising, but has now been developed into one of the finest agricultural districts in the country. The climate is warm in summer and cold in winter, but dry and healthful. The Weather Bureau at Denver gives the temperature (annual average) at 50.3; highest on record, 105, lowest on record, 29. Total annual precipitation (rain and snowfall) is 15.40 inches. The state is amply supplied with railway facilities, and freight tonnage and tourist travel are heavy. The U.S. Air Force Academy is located at Colorado Springs, the University of Colorado at Boulder, and the Colorado School of Mines at Golden.

POPULATION: 3,470,000 (1992). Rank among the states, 26th.

AGRICULTURE: Number of farms: 26,000 (1992). Farm acreage: 33,000,000 (1992). Cash receipts from farm marketings: crops, $1,097,000,000 (1991); livestock and products, $2,664,000,000 (1991).

FORESTS: Total forest land: 16,039,000 acres (1991). Principal woods: ponderosa pine, englemann spruce, lodgepole pine, douglas fir, white fir, cottonwood, aspen.

MINERALS: Value of production: $338,000,000 (1991). Principal minerals: molybdenum, sand and gravel, and cement. Value of petroleum production: $626,000,000 (1991).

MANUFACTURES: Value added by manufacture: $13,704,000,000 (1991). Leading industry groups: food and related products, printing and publishing, machinery (except electrical).

LIST OF COUNTIES

Total number of counties 63

County, Location on Map, and County Seat	Pop.
Adams (NEC), Brighton	265,038
Alamosa (S), Alamosa	13,617
Arapahoe (C), Littleton	391,511
Archuleta (S), Pagosa Springs	5,345
Baca (SE), Springfiled	4,556
Bent (SE), Las Animas	5,048
Boulder (N), Boulder	225,339
Chaffee (C), Salida	12,684
Cheyenne (E), Cheyenne Wells	2,397
Clear Creek (C), Georgetown	7,619
Conejos (S), Conejos	7,453
Costilla (S), San Luis	3,190
Crowley (SE), Ordway	3,946
Custer (SC), Westcliffe	1,926
Delta (W), Delta	20,980
Denver (NC), Denver	467,610
Dolores (S)W, Dove Creek	1,504
Douglas (C), Castle Rock	60,391
Eagle (NWC), Eagle	21,928
Elbert, (EC), Kiowa	9,646
El Paso (EC), Colorado Springs	397,014
Fremont (SC), Canon City	32,273
Garfield (W), Glenwood Springs	29,974
Gilpin (NC), Central City	3,070
Grand (N), Hot Sulphur Springs	7,966
Gunnison (W), Gunnison	10,273
Hinsdale (SW), Lake City	467
Huerfano (SW), Walsenburg	6,009
Jackson (N), Walden	1,605
Jefferson (NC), Golden	438,430
Kiowa (E), Eads	1,688
Kit Carson (E), Burlington	7,140
Lake (C), Leadville	6,007
La Plata (SW), Durango	32,284
Larimer (N), Fort Collins	186,136
Las Animas (SE), Trinidad	13,765
Lincoln (E), Hugo	4,529
Logan (NE), Sterling	17,567
Mesa (W), Grand Junction	93,145
Mineral (SW), Creede	558
Moffat (NW), Craig	11,357
Montezuma (SW), Cortez	18,672
Montrose (W), Montrose	24,423
Morgan (NE), Fort Morgan	21,939
Otero (SE), La Junta	20,185
Ouray (SW), Ouray	2,295
Park (C), Fairplay	7,174
Phillips (NE), Holyoke	4,189
Pitkin (W), Aspen	12,661
Prowers (SE), Lamar	13,347
Pueblo (C), Pueblo	123,051
Rio Blanco (NW), Meeker	5,972
Rio Grande (S), Del Norte	10,770
Routt (NW), Steamboat Springs	14,088
Saguache (SC), Saguache	4,619
San Juan (SW), Silverton	745
San Miguel (SW), Telluride	3,653
Sedgwick (NE), Julesburg	2,690
Summit (C), Breckenridge	12,881
Teller (C), Cripple Creek	12,468
Washington (NE), Akron	4,812
Weld (N), Greeley	131,821
Yuma (NE), Wray	8,954

STATISTICS

Newspapers

Period of Issue	
Daily	24
Evening Daily	18
Morning Daily	9
Daily with Sunday edition	12
Semiweekly	4
Weekly	110
Biweekly	1
Semimonthly	1
Monthly	4
Bimonthly	1

Quarterly 1
Free or partly free 13
Shopper 3
Total Newspapers 153

Periodicals

Period of Issue
Daily 1
Weekly 4
Biweekly 1
Semimonthly 4
Monthly 50
Bimonthly 37
Quarterly 55
Total Periodicals 211

Total number of publications 364

Radio Stations

AM Stations 57
FM Stations 96
Total Radio Stations 153

TV Stations

Total TV Stations 20

Cable Stations

Total Cable Systems 22

Total number of broadcast listings 195

AKRON†, pop. 1,716.

Washington Co. (NE). 40 m S of Sterling. Residential.

4188 The Akron News-Reporter
69 Main St. Phone: (970)345-2296
Akron, CO 80720 Fax: (970)345-6638
Publisher E-mail: akronews@ria.net

Local newspaper. **Founded:** 1929. **Freq:** Weekly (Thurs.). **Print Method:** Offset. **Trim Size:** 13 3/4 x 22 3/4. **Cols./Page:** 6. **Col. Width:** 25 nonpareils. **Col. Depth:** 297 agate lines. **Key Personnel:** Karen Ashley, Editor. **USPS:** 010-820. **Subscription Rates:** $21 by mail; $24 out of area. **Remarks:** Accepts advertising.
Ad Rates: BW: $475 **Circ:** Paid ‡2,500
SAU: $5 Free ‡30
PCI: $4

ALAMOSA†, pop. 6,830.

Alamosa Co. (S). 17 m S of Monte Vista.

4189 South Coloradan
Adams State College
College Center Phone: (719)589-7904
Alamosa, CO 81102 Fax: (719)589-7522

Collegiate newspaper (tabloid). **Founded:** 1925. **Freq:** Weekly. **Print Method:** Offset. **Cols./Page:** 5. **Col. Width:** 34 nonpareils. **Col. Depth:** 206 agate lines. **Key Personnel:** Valerie Lemoi, Editor; LisaAnn Stoner, Assoc. Ed.; Jack Morris, Adviser; Allison Barnes, Campus Life; Louise Piorder, News; Zach Odell, Sports; Bobbi Jo Heck, Ads; Sonya Rivera, Photography; Wendi McClaren, Copy Chief; Jefery Baldock, Promotions Mgr. **Subscription Rates:** Free. **Remarks:** Accepts advertising.
Ad Rates: GLR: $3.15 **Circ:** Free ‡2,000
BW: $175
PCI: $3.15

4190 The Valley Courier
Alamosa Newspapers, Inc.
401 State Ave. Phone: (719)589-2553
PO Box 1099 Fax: (719)589-6573
Alamosa, CO 81101
General newspaper. **Founded:** 1925. **Freq:** Tues.-Fri. (Morn.)and Sat. (Morn.). **Print Method:** Offset. **Trim Size:** 22 1/2 x 13 3/4. **Cols./Page:** 6. **Col. Width:** 2 5/32 inches. **Col. Depth:** 21 1/2 inches. **Key Personnel:** Keith R. Cerny, Publisher & Adv. Director, krc@fone.net; Tim Flowers, Editor; Vernon Trujillo, Production Mgr. **ISSN:** 1047-1170. **Remarks:** Accepts advertising.
Ad Rates: GLR: $1.32 **Circ:** Paid 5,500
BW: $1,193.25 Non-paid 100
4C: $1,493.25
PCI: $9.25

4191 KALQ-FM - 93.5
PO Box 179 Phone: (719)589-6644
Alamosa, CO 81101-0179 Fax: (719)589-0993

Format: Adult Contemporary. **Networks:** Unistar. **Owner:** Dale K. Burns, 400 N. Mesa, Los Alamos, NM 87544, (505)662-4342. **Founded:** 1969. **Formerly:** KGIW-FM (1976). **Operating Hours:** 6 a.m.-11 p.m.; 95% network, 5% local. **Key Personnel:** Mike Tanner, Program Dir.; Patsy Garcia, Promotions Dir.; Neil J. Hammer, General Mgr. **Wattage:** 3000. **Ad Rates:** $7.30 for 30 seconds; $12.60 for 60 seconds.

4192 KASF-FM - 90.9
c/o Adams State College Phone: (719)587-7871
Alamosa, CO 81102 Fax: (719)587-7522

Format: Eclectic. **Owner:** Adams State College, at above address. **Founded:** 1967. **Operating Hours:** 7 a.m.-2 a.m. all week. **Key Personnel:** David ColeBaca, Contact; David ColeBaca, General Mgr. **Wattage:** 1000.

4193 KGIW-AM - 1450
PO Box 179 Phone: (719)589-6644
Alamosa, CO 81101-0179 Fax: (719)589-0993

Format: Talk; News; Country; Religious; Agricultural. **Networks:** ABC. **Owner:** Dale K. Burns, 400 N. Mesa, Los Alamos, NM 87544, (505)662-4342. **Founded:** 1929. **Operating Hours:** 6 a.m.-11 p.m.; 35% network, 65% local. **Key Personnel:** Ron Loven, News Dir.; Neil Hammer, Sports Dir.; Helen Lozoya, Promotions Dir.; Neil Hammer, General Mgr. **Wattage:** 1000. **Ad Rates:** $7.50 for 30 seconds; $13 for 60 seconds.

4194 KRZA-FM - 88.7
528 9th St. Phone: (719)589-9057
Alamosa, CO 81101 Fax: (719)589-9258

Format: Public Radio; News; Jazz; Classical; Hispanic; Blues. **Networks:** National Public Radio (NPR). **Owner:** Equal Representation of Media Advocacy Corp., at above address. **Founded:** 1985. **Operating Hours:** MXF 5 a.m.-midnight; Saturday and Sunday 6 a.m.-midnight. **Key Personnel:** Kim Allison, Contact. **Wattage:** 5000. **Ad Rates:** Noncommercial.

ARVADA

4195 Cattle Guard
Colorado Cattlemen's Association
8833 Ralston Rd. Phone: (303)431-6422
Arvada, CO 80002-2839 Fax: (303)431-6446
Publisher E-mail: coloradocattlemen@juno.com

Magazine covering cattle industry news, including legislative updates and management techniques. **Subtitle:** The Official News Publication of the Colorado Cattlemen's Association. **Founded:** 1950. **Freq:** Monthly. **Print Method:** Offset. **Trim Size:** 8 1/2 x 11. **Cols./Page:** 3. **Col. Width:** 30 nonpareils. **Col. Depth:** 140 agate lines. **Key Personnel:** Pamela A. Gray, Editor and Publisher. **Subscription Rates:** $20 individuals. **URL:** http://www.yampa.com/cca.
Ad Rates: BW: $300 **Circ:** ‡3,000
PCI: $24

4196 The Plantagenet Connection
HT Communications
Box 1401 Phone: (303)657-2723
Arvada, CO 80001 Fax: (303)773-8962
Publisher E-mail: khf333@aol.com

Journal covering history and genealogy. **Subtitle:** History Through Genealogy. **Founded:** 1993. **Freq:** Semiannual. **Print Method:** Offset. **Trim Size:** 7 x 10. **Cols./Page:** 2. **Col. Width:** 3 inches. **Key Personnel:** Kenneth Harper Finton, Editor and Publisher, phone (303)420-4888, fax (303)420-4845, ichf333@aol.com. **ISSN:** 1081-1621. **Subscription Rates:** $24 individuals; $26 Canada; $32 other countries. **Remarks:** Accepts advertising. **Available Online.**
Ad Rates: BW: $150 **Circ:** Combined 1,150
PCI: $10

4197 KRMT-TV - 41
12014 W. 64th Ave. Phone: (303)423-4141
Arvada, CO 80004 Fax: (303)424-0571
E-mail: krmt.com

Format: Educational; Religious. **Networks:** Independent. **Owner:** Word of God Fellowship, 4201 Pool Rd., Colleyville, TX 76034, (817)571-1229, Fax: (817)571-7458. **Founded:** 1987. **Formerly:** KWBI-TV. **Operating Hours:** Continuous; 70% national, 30% local. **ADI:** Denver (Steamboat Springs), CO. **Key Personnel:** Ruben Mendez, General Mgr., krmt@poweronline.com; Brian Tetamore, Production Mgr.; Janice Smith, Sales Mgr.; Amy Wurtsbough, Traffic Mgr.; Sharon Metzger, Producer. **Local Programs:** *Off the Record with Lea* 11 a.m. Mon., 8 p.m. Wed.; *Rocky Mountain Celebration* 10 a.m. Monday-Friday; *Un Camino Mejor* 6:30 p.m. Sunday. **Wattage:** 2.2 million ERP. **Ad Rates:** Noncommercial. **URL:** http://www.krmt.com.

ASPEN†, pop. 3,678.

Pitkin Co. (W). 95 m E of Grand Junction. Winter and summer resort. Timber. Stock, grain, hay.

4198 Aspen Daily News
Ute City Tea Party Ltd.
517 E. Hopkins Phone: (970)925-2220
PO Box DD Fax: (970)920-2118
Aspen, CO 81611-1982
Publication E-mail: aspnews@sopris.net

General newspaper (tabloid). **Founded:** 1978. **Freq:** Daily and Sunday. **Print Method:** Web offset. **Trim Size:** 10 1/4 x 14. **Cols./Page:** 6. **Col. Width:** 1 9/16 inches. **Col. Depth:** 14 inches. **Key Personnel:** Ross Furukawa, General Mgr.; David Danforth, Publisher. **Subscription Rates:** Free. **Remarks:** Accepts advertising.
Ad Rates: BW: $399 **Circ:** Free 12,500
4C: $599
PCI: $5.40

4199 Aspen Magazine
Ridge Publications
Box G-3 Phone: (970)920-4040
Aspen, CO 81612 Fax: (970)920-4044
Publication E-mail: aspenmag@rof.net

Regional lifestyle magazine. **Founded:** 1974. **Freq:** Bimonthly. **Print Method:** Webb offset. **Trim Size:** 8 1/8 x 10 7/8. **Key Personnel:** Randy Beier, Publisher; Janet O'Grady, Editor; Nancy Mayer, Assoc. Publisher & Director of Sales; Michael Alvarez, Production Dir.; Paul Viola, Art Director; Jamie Miller, Managing Editor. **ISSN:** 1043-5085. **Subscription Rates:** $24; $45 other countries. $4.95 single issue. **Remarks:** Accepts advertising.
Ad Rates: BW: $2,240 **Circ:** Paid ‡5,500
4C: $2,635 Non-paid ‡10,500

4200 Aspen Times
310 E. Main St. Phone: (303)925-3414
Aspen, CO 81611 Fax: (303)925-6240

Community weekly newspaper (tabloid). **Founded:** 1881. **Freq:** Daily Daily M-F; Weekly F. **Print Method:** Offset. **Trim Size:** 10 1/4 x 16. **Cols./Page:** 5. **Col. Width:** 23 nonpareils. **Col. Depth:** 224 agate lines. **Key Personnel:** Candice Welch, Advertising Mgr.; Andy Stone, Editor-in-Chief; John Colson, Exec. Editor. **Subscription Rates:** $32 individuals. **Remarks:** Accepts advertising.
Ad Rates: BW: $480 **Circ:** ‡11,000
4C: $630
PCI: $6

4201 KSNO-FM - 103.9
421B Aspen Airport Business Center Phone: (970)925-7383
Aspen, CO 81611-1969 Fax: (970)920-4686

Format: Adult Album Alternative. **Owner:** Clifton Gardiner, PO Box 5559, Avon, CO 81620. **Founded:** 1985. **Formerly:** KTUS-FM (1986). **Operating Hours:** Continuous. **Key Personnel:** Jeff Hanle, General Mgr.; Tony Mauro, Program Dir., phone (970)949-0140, fax (970)949-0266; Alex Brady, News Dir., phone (970)949-0140, fax (970)949-0266. **Wattage:** 6000. **Ad Rates:** $14-18 for 30 seconds; $16-24 for 60 seconds.

4202 KSPN-FM - 97.7
225 N Mill St. Phone: (970)925-5776
Aspen, CO 81611-1503 Fax: (970)925-1142

Format: Adult Album Alternative. **Networks:** AP; CNN Radio. **Owner:** Charley Moss, at above address. **Founded:** 1970. **Operating Hours:** Continuous. **Key Personnel:** Jack Maley, General Mgr.; Carolyn Harvey, Music Dir.; Sally McClanahan, Sales Mgr.; Penny Torok, News Dir.; Tina Lutz, Program Dir.; Lisa Brickhouse, Production Dir.; Ryan Nargo, Promotions Dir.; Susan Terrall, Contact. **Wattage:** 3000. **Ad Rates:** $15-45 for 30 seconds.

4203 TCI Cablevision of Central Colorado
201 Aspen Airport Bus. Ctr. Phone: (970)925-4098
Aspen, CO 81611 Fax: (970)925-4106

Founded: 1967. **Formerly:** United Artists Cable (1992). **Cities Served:** subscribing households 10,289; 77 channels; 1 community access channel; 126 hours per week community access programming.

AURORA, pop. 158,588.

Arapahoe Co. and Adams Co. Adjoins Denver on east. Residential Manufactures fish hooks telephone parts and aircraft ejection seats.

4204 Authorship
The National Writers Association
3140 S. Peoria St., No. 295 Phone: (303)841-0246
Aurora, CO 80014-3155 Fax: (303)751-8593

Magazine for writers. **Founded:** 1937. **Freq:** Bimonthly. **Print Method:** Offset. **Trim Size:** 8 1/4 x 11. **Cols./Page:** 3. **Col. Width:** 27 nonpareils. **Col. Depth:** 140 agate lines. **Key Personnel:** Sandra Whelchel, Editor, sandywritr@aolco. **ISSN:** 1097-9347. **Subscription Rates:** $20 individuals. **Remarks:** Accepts advertising. **Available Online. URL:** http://www.nationalwriters.com.
Ad Rates: BW: $300 **Circ:** ‡4,000

4205 International Arabian Horse
International Arabian Horse Association
10805 E Bethany Dr. Phone: (303)450-4774
Aurora, CO 80014-2605 Fax: (303)450-5127
Publication E-mail: iaha@iaha.com

Magazine providing industry news and features to owners of purebred Arabians, Half-Arabians, and Anglo-Arabians. **Founded:** 1978. **Freq:** 8 x yr. **Print Method:** Web offset. **Trim Size:** 8 1/2 x 11. **Key Personnel:** Karen Karvonen, Editor, phone (303)696-4581, fax (303)696-4599, karenkarvonen@iaha.com. **Subscription Rates:** $24. **Remarks:** Accepts advertising. **Formerly:** Inside International.
Ad Rates: GLR: $.40 **Circ:** ‡30,000
BW: $500
4C: $775

4206 Model Railroading
Highlands Station, Inc.
2600 S. Parker Rd., Ste. 1-211 Phone: (303)338-1700
Aurora, CO 80014 Fax: (303)338-1949
Publication E-mail:
modelrringmag@modelrailroadingmag.com

Consumer magazine covering model trains for hobbyists. **Founded:** Dec. 1969. **Freq:** Monthly. **Print Method:** Web offset. **Key Personnel:** Randall B. Lee, Editor and Publisher; Chris Lane, National Sales Mgr.; Don Strait, Circulation Mgr. **Subscription Rates:** $31.95 individuals; $3.95 single issue. **Remarks:** Accepts advertising. **URL:** http://www.modelrailroadingmag.com.
Ad Rates: BW: $830 **Circ:** Combined ⊕**14,935**
4C: $1,140

4207 Prairie Dog
PO Box 470757
Aurora, CO 80047-0757

Literature, poetry, and art review. **Subtitle:** A Journal for the Somewhat Eccentric. **Founded:** 1988. **Freq:** Biennial. **Print Method:** Offset. **Trim Size:** 8 1/2 x 11. **Cols./Page:** 2. **Col. Width:** 3 3/4 inches. **Col. Depth:** 10 inches. **Key Personnel:** John Hart, Editor-in-Chief. **ISSN:** 1050-7280. **Subscription Rates:** $15 individuals; $5.95 single issue. **Remarks:** Accepts advertising. **Formerly:** Infinity Limited.
Ad Rates: BW: $120 **Circ:** Paid 300
PCI: $5 Non-paid 400

4208 Rocky Mountain Union Farmer
Rocky Mountain Farmers Union
10800 E. Bethany Dr., 4th Fl. Phone: (303)752-5800
Aurora, CO 80014-2632 Fax: (303)752-5810
Publisher E-mail: rmfu@aol.com

Agricultural magazine (tabloid) featuring articles on issues affecting family operated farms and ranches. **Founded:** 1912. **Freq:** 6x/year. **Print Method:** Offset. **Trim Size:** 11 1/2 x 17. **Cols./Page:** 4. **Col. Width:** 32 1/2 agate lines. **Col. Depth:** 218 agate lines. **Key Personnel:** Melissa Elliott, Editor; Dave Carter, Publisher. **ISSN:** 0035-7650. **Subscription Rates:** $7 individuals. **Remarks:** Advertising not accepted.
Circ: Paid ‡5,000
Controlled ‡500

4209 Software Publisher
WEBCOM Communications Corp.
4255 S. Buckley Rd., Ste. 314
Aurora, CO 80013

Magazine covering the latest developments in the software market. **Founded:** Jan. 1994. **Freq:** Monthly. **Key Personnel:** David Webster, Editor; Sheila Galatowitsch, Managing Editor. **Subscription Rates:** $60 individuals; $72 Canada and Mexico; $96 other countries. **Remarks:** Advertising accepted; rates available upon request.
Circ: (Not Reported)

4210 Southwestern Lore
Colorado Archaeological Society, Inc.
16551 E. 7th Place Phone: (303)360-5051
Aurora, CO 80011-7605 Fax: (303)985-2080

Archaeology journal. **Subtitle:** Archaeology of Colorado and the Southwest. **Founded:** 1935. **Freq:** Quarterly. **Print Method:** Letterpress. **Trim Size:** 6 x 9. **Cols./Page:** 1. **Col. Width:** 4 1/2 inches. **Col. Depth:** 7 1/4 inches. **Key Personnel:** Gordon C. Tucker, Jr., Editor, gtucker@golder.com. **ISSN:** 0038-4844. **Subscription Rates:** $2.50 single issue; $25 institutions; $12.50 individuals. **Remarks:** Advertising not accepted.
Circ: ‡1,000

4211 Star Trek Communicator
ST Communicator
Box 111000 Phone: (303)574-0907
Aurora, CO 80011 Fax: (303)547-9442
Free: (800)TRUE-FAN
Publisher E-mail: stcustservice@fanmedia.com

Consumer entertainment magazine covering all aspects of the film and television show, *Star Trek.*. **Founded:** 1980. **Freq:** Bimonthly. **Print Method:** Offset. **Trim Size:** 8 3/8 x 10 7/8. **Cols./Page:** 3. **Key Personnel:** Jon Bradley Snyder, Editor-in-Chief; David Latimer, Advertising Dir.; Dan Madsen, President/Publisher. **ISSN:** 1080-3793. **Subscription Rates:** $19.95 individuals; $4.50 single issue. **Remarks:** Accepts advertising.
Ad Rates: 4C: $5,000 **Circ:** Paid 250,000

4212 Leonard Communications Inc.
13780 E. Rice Pl. Phone: (303)693-0900
Aurora, CO 80015-1091 Fax: (303)690-4192

Key Personnel: Roger Leonard, President. **Cities Served:** Areas in Colorado, Kansas, Minnesota and Wyoming.

AVON

Eagle Co. (WC). 10 m SW of Vail.

4213 KZYR-FM - 103.1
PO Box 5559 Phone: (303)949-0140
Avon, CO 81620 Fax: (303)949-0266

Format: Adult Contemporary; Alternative/New Music/Progressive. **Founded:** 1984. **Operating Hours:** 100% local. **Key Personnel:** Clifton H. Gardiner, President; Simon Melser, General Sales Mgr.; Tony Mauro, Program Dir. **Wattage:** 12,000. **Ad Rates:** $16-24 for 30 seconds; $18-26 for 60 seconds.

BAILEY, pop. 175.

Park Co. (C). 72 m NE of Aspen. Residential.

4214 Park County Republican and The Fairplay Flume
Arkansas Valley Publishing Co.
PO Box 460 Phone: (303)838-4423
Bailey, CO 80421-0460 Fax: (303)838-8414
Free: (800)883-1154
Publication E-mail: theflume@rmi.net

Local newspaper. **Founded:** Feb. 20, 1879. **Freq:** Weekly (Fri.). **Print Method:** Offset. **Trim Size:** 5 x 16. **Cols./Page:** 5. **Col. Width:** 12 picas. **Col. Depth:** 16 inches. **Key Personnel:** Rockford M. Hayes, Editor; Merle Baranczyk, Publisher, phone (719)539-6691. **USPS:** 684-550. **Subscription Rates:** $19 individuals; $23 out of area; $26 out of state. **Remarks:** Accepts advertising. **Available Online. URL:** http://www.theflume.com.
Ad Rates: BW: $400 **Circ:** ‡3,500
4C: $500
PCI: $5.50

BERTHOUD, pop. 2,362.

Larimer Co. (N). 20 m. S. of Fort Collins. Manufactures store fixtures and displays, modular homes. Agriculture. Sugar beets, wheat, alfalfa. Livestock.

4215 The Old Berthoud Recorder
534 3rd Ave. Phone: (970)532-3715
PO Box J Fax: (970)532-3918
Berthoud, CO 80513
Community newspaper. **Founded:** 1892. **Freq:** Weekly (Thurs.). **Print Method:** Offset. **Trim Size:** 10 1/2 x 16. **Cols./Page:** 5. **Col. Width:** 11 1/2 picas. **Col. Depth:** 15 3/4 inches. **Key Personnel:** Anne Benson, Editor; Walter Kinderman, Publisher, phone (303)823-6625, fax (303)823-6633. **ISSN:** 0896-2812. **Subscription Rates:** $16; $30 out of county; $40 out of state. **Remarks:** Accepts advertising. **Formerly:** The Berthoud Recorder.
Ad Rates: GLR: $1.40 **Circ:** Paid ‡3,000
BW: $640
4C: $980
SAU: $5.50
PCI: $8.75

BOULDER†, pop. 76,685.

Boulder Co. (N). 32 m NW of Denver. Universit of Colorado. Tourism. Manufactures copy machines, chemicals, electronic devices, space hardware, cutlery, recreational equipment. Agriculture. Alfalfa, sugar beets.

4216 Abstracts with Programs
Geological Society of America, Inc.
3300 Penrose Pl. Phone: (303)447-2020
PO Box 9140 Fax: (303)447-1133
Boulder, CO 80301-9140
Free: (800)472-1988
Publication E-mail: pubs@geosociety.org
Publisher E-mail: pubs@geosociety.org

Journal containing abstracts of papers to be presented at Geological Society of America meetings. **Founded:** 1969. **Freq:** 6-7/year. **Print Method:** Offset, sheetfed. **Trim Size:** 8 3/8 x 10 7/8. **Key Personnel:** Donald M. Davidson, Jr., Editor; Ann Crawford, Advertising Mgr. **ISSN:** 0016-7592. **Subscription Rates:** $73. $20 single issue.
Ad Rates: BW: $800 **Circ:** 5,000
4C: $1,450

4217 American Music Research Center Journal
University of Colorado at Boulder
Campus Box 301
Boulder, CO 80309
Publisher E-mail: riis@spot.colorado.edu

Scholarly journal covering music in the U.S. **Founded:** 1991. **Freq:** Annual. **Key Personnel:** Thomas L. Riis, Editor, phone (303)492-7540. **ISSN:** 1058-3572. **Subscription Rates:** $10.50 individuals; $12.50 out of country; $10.50 single issue. **Remarks:** Advertising not accepted.
Circ: Combined 400

4218 American Suzuki Journal
Suzuki Association of Americas
PO Box 17310 Phone: (303)444-0948
Boulder, CO 80308-7310 Fax: (303)444-0984
Free: (888)378-9854
Publisher E-mail: suzuki@rmi.net

Music education journal. **Founded:** 1973. **Freq:** Quarterly. **Print Method:** Offset. **Trim Size:** 8 7/8 x 10 7/8. **Key Personnel:** Pamela Brasch, Exec. Admin., phone (303)444-0948. **ISSN:** 0193-5372. **Subscription Rates:** $45 members; $58 Canada; $45 other countries. **Remarks:** Accepts advertising.
Ad Rates: BW: $425 **Circ:** ‡6,500
4C: $900

4219 Blues Access
1455 Chestnut Place Phone: (303)443-7245
Boulder, CO 80304-3153 Fax: (303)939-9729

Magazine providing articles and information on blues musicians. **Subtitle:** The Distinctive Blues Magazine. **Founded:** 1990. **Freq:** Quarterly. **Print Method:** Web offset. **Trim Size:** 8 1/8 x 10 5/8. **Key Personnel:** Cary Wolfson, Publisher, roosterman@aol.com; Leland Rucker, Managing Editor, phone (303)494-6672, fax (303)494-1127, lrucker@earthlink.net; Jack Angus, Advertising Mgr., phone (206)767-9701, fax (206)768-9866, i2icom@earthlink.net. **ISSN:** 1066-4068. **Subscription Rates:** $15. **Remarks:** Accepts advertising. **URL:** http://www.bluesaccess.com.
Ad Rates: BW: $975 **Circ:** Paid ‡26,500
4C: $1,300 Non-paid ‡500

4220 Bulletin of Concerned Asian Scholars
3239 9th St.
Boulder, CO 80304-2112
Publication E-mail: tfenton@tgc.org

Asian studies journal. **Founded:** 1968. **Freq:** Quarterly. **Print Method:** Offset. **Trim Size:** 8 1/4 x 10. **Cols./Page:** 2. **Col. Width:** 42 nonpareils. **Col. Depth:** 130 agate lines. **Key Personnel:** Bill Doub, Editor and Publisher, doub@csf.colorado.edu; Nancy Doub, Managing Editor. **ISSN:** 0007-4810. **Subscription Rates:** $25 individuals add $ 1.00; $55 institutions add $ 1.00; $6 single issue. **Remarks:** Color advertising not accepted. **URL:** http://csf.colorado.edu/bcas/bcashome.html; http://www.cs.colorado.edu/bcas. **Alt. Formats:** Microform.
Ad Rates: BW: $110 **Circ:** Paid ‡1,300
Non-paid ‡100

4221 Campus Press
University of Colorado at Boulder
School of Journalism Phone: (303)492-8447
Campus Box 287 Fax: (303)492-0969
Boulder, CO 80309-0287
Publication E-mail: cpress@stripe.colorado.edu

Collegiate newspaper. **Subtitle:** CU's Student Produced Newspaper. **Founded:** Oct. 10, 1978. **Freq:** Weekly. **Print Method:** Offset web. **Cols./Page:** 5. **Col. Width:** 2 1/16 inches. **Col. Depth:** 13 inches. **Key Personnel:** Chris Mock, Advertising Dir. **Subscription Rates:** $50. **Remarks:** Accepts advertising. **Available Online. URL:** http://www.campuspress.colorado.edu.
Ad Rates: BW: $715 **Circ:** Controlled 6,000
4C: $425
PCI: $6

4222 CAUSE/EFFECT
EDUCAUSE
4772 Walnut St., Ste. 206 Phone: (303)449-4430
Boulder, CO 80301-2538 Fax: (303)440-0461
Publication E-mail: info@educause.edu
Publisher E-mail: info@cause.org

Contains information for people involved in managing and using information resources in higher education. **Subtitle:** A Practitioner's Journal About Managing and Using Information Resources On College and University Campuses. **Founded:** 1978. **Freq:** Quarterly. **Trim Size:** 8 1/2 x 11. **Key Personnel:** Julia A. Rudy, Editor, phone (303)939-0308, fax (303)440-0461, jrudy@educause.edu; Elizabeth Harris, Managing Editor, phone (303)939-0311, fax (303)440-0461, eharris@educause.edu. **ISSN:** 0164-534X. **Subscription Rates:** $52 members; $104 nonmembers; $72 members other countries; $104 nonmembers other countries. **Remarks:** Advertising not accepted. **URL:** http://www.educause.edu/pub/ce/cause-effect.html.
Circ: Paid 5,422
Free ⊕**170**

4223 Colorado Daily
Front Range Publishing
5505 Central Ave. Phone: (303)443-6272
PO Box 1719 Fax: (303)443-9357
Boulder, CO 80301-2820
Publication E-mail: tqalbot@bcn.boulder.co.us

Collegiate newspaper. **Founded:** Sept. 1, 1892. **Freq:** Monday thru Friday (morning). **Print Method:** Offset. **Trim Size:** 10 1/4 x 14. **Cols./Page:** 6. **Col. Width:** 19 nonpareils. **Col. Depth:** 196 agate lines. **Key Personnel:** Clint Talbott, Editor; Chris Harburg, Publisher; Jim Ditzel, Advertising Mgr. **Remarks:** Advertising not accepted for racist and sexist products/services.
Ad Rates: BW: $882.00 4C: $1362.00 PCI: $10.50
Circ: Mon.-Thurs. 15,608 Fri. 26,356

4224 Colorado Engineer
University of Colorado
Campus Box 422 Phone: (303)492-8635
Boulder, CO 80309-0422 Fax: (303)492-2199
Publication E-mail: cem@colorado.edu

Magazine for students, faculty, and alumni of the College of Engineering. **Founded:** 1904. **Freq:** 3 times a year. **Print Method:** Offset. **Trim Size:** 8 1/2 x 11. **Cols./Page:** 3. **Col. Width:** 28 nonpareils. **Col. Depth:** 134 agate lines. **Key Personnel:** Michael Niyompong, Contact, michael.niyompong@colorado.edu. **ISSN:** 0010-1583. **Subscription Rates:** $10 individuals. **Remarks:** Accepts advertising. **Available Online. URL:** http://cem.colorado.edu.
Ad Rates: BW: $1,000 4C: $1,800
Circ: Non-paid ‡5,000

4225 Colorado Ski Industry
Business Research Division
Campus Box 420 Phone: (303)492-8227
Boulder, CO 80309-0420 Fax: (303)492-3620

Monograph for the Colorado ski industry. **Subtitle:** Highlights of the 1997-98 Season. **Founded:** 1966. **Freq:** Annual. **Print Method:** Offset. **Trim Size:** 8 1/2 x 11. **Key Personnel:** C. R. Goeldner, Contact. **Subscription Rates:** $35 single issue. **Remarks:** Advertising not accepted.
Circ: (Not Reported)

4226 Daily Camera
Scripps Howard, Inc.
1048 Pearl Phone: (303)442-1202
Boulder, CO 80302 Fax: (303)442-1508

General newspaper. **Founded:** 1891. **Freq:** Mon.-Sun. (morn.). **Print Method:** Offset. **Trim Size:** 13 3/4 x 22 1/2. **Cols./Page:** 6. **Col. Width:** 2 1/16 inches. **Col. Depth:** 21 1/5 inches. **Key Personnel:** Barrie Hartman, Editor, phone (303)473-1390; Harold Higgens, Publisher, phone (303)473-1220. **Subscription Rates:** $93.60 individuals. **Remarks:** Advertising accepted; rates available upon request. **URL:** http://www.bouldernews.com.
Circ: Mon.-Sat. 34,927 Sun. 43,572

4227 Delicious! Magazine
New Hope Communications
1301 Spruce St. Phone: (303)939-8440
Boulder, CO 80302 Fax: (303)939-9559
Free: (800)839-7263
Publication E-mail: delicious@newhope.com
Publisher E-mail: sales@newhope.com

Magazine designed to be used as a merchandising and educational tool by natural food stores. **Founded:** 1985. **Freq:** 12/year. **Print Method:** Web offset. **Trim Size:** 8 x 10 3/4. **Key Personnel:** Kathryn Arnold, Editorial Director-Consumer Publications, ka@newhope.com; Nicola Ferrell, Production Dir.; Kim Paulsen, VP Publishing Division, kp@newhope.com. **Subscription Rates:** $24 individuals. **Remarks:** Accepts advertising. **Available Online. URL:** http:/www.newhope.com/delicious.
Ad Rates: BW: $6,070 4C: $7,715
Circ: Paid ★**445,484**

4228 English Language Notes
University of Colorado Phone: (303)492-7176
CB 226 Fax: (303)492-3521
Boulder, CO 80309
Publication E-mail: eln@stripe.colorado.edu

Journal discussing English language literature. **Founded:** Sept. 1963. **Freq:** Quarterly. **Print Method:** Offset. **Trim Size:** 6 x 9. **Cols./Page:** 1. **Col. Width:** 51 nonpareils. **Col. Depth:** 102 agate lines. **Key Personnel:** J. Wallace Donald, Editor, phone (303)492-8388. **ISSN:** 0013-8282. **Subscription Rates:** $22 U.S. and Canada; $28 other countries; $44 institutions USA and Canada; $50 institutions, other countries. **Remarks:** Accepts advertising.
Ad Rates: BW: $250
Circ: Paid ‡1,100 Non-paid ‡150

4229 Geological Society of America Bulletin
Geological Society of America, Inc.
3300 Penrose Pl. Phone: (303)447-2020
PO Box 9140 Fax: (303)447-1133
Boulder, CO 80301-9140
Free: (800)472-1988
Publisher E-mail: pubs@geosociety.org

Geology journal. **Founded:** 1888. **Freq:** Monthly. **Print Method:** Offset. **Trim Size:** 8 3/8 x 10 7/8. **Cols./Page:** 3 and 2. **Col. Width:** 28 and 43 nonpareils. **Col. Depth:** 130 agate lines. **Key Personnel:** Larry Bowlds, Managing Editor; J. Olsen, Director; Ann H. Crawford, Advertising Coord.; P. Lehr, Publications Mgr. **ISSN:** 0016-7606. **Subscription Rates:** $350 U.S., Canada, and Mexico; $360 other countries. **URL:** http://www.geosociety.org. **Alt. Formats:** CD-ROM. **Also known as:** GSA Bulletin.
Ad Rates: BW: $900 4C: $1,550
Circ: ‡6,000

4230 Geology
Geological Society of America, Inc.
3300 Penrose Pl. Phone: (303)447-2020
PO Box 9140 Fax: (303)447-1133
Boulder, CO 80301-9140
Free: (800)472-1988
Publisher E-mail: pubs@geosociety.org

Geology journal. **Founded:** 1973. **Freq:** Monthly. **Print Method:** Offset. **Trim Size:** 8 3/8 x 10 7/8. **Cols./Page:** 2 and 3. **Col. Width:** 43 and 28 nonpareils. **Col. Depth:** 130 agate lines. **Key Personnel:** A.H. Crawford, Advertising Coord.; J. Olsen, Production Mgr.; D.M. Davidson, Contact; P. Lehr, Publication Dir. **ISSN:** 0091-7613. **Subscription Rates:** $350 U.S., Canada, and Mexico; $360 other countries. **URL:** http://www.geosociety.org. **Alt. Formats:** CD-ROM.
Ad Rates: BW: $1,000 4C: $1,750
Circ: Paid ‡6,500

4231 Iron Feather Journal
Phun Inc.
Box 1905 Phone: (303)575-5652
Boulder, CO 80306
Consumer magazine covering alternative/underground electronic music. **Founded:** 1987. **Freq:** Quarterly. **Print Method:** Sheetfed offset. **Key Personnel:** Steven Prothero, Manager/Editor. **Subscription Rates:** $24 individuals; $6 single issue. **Remarks:** Accepts advertising. **URL:** http://mycal.net/ifj.
Ad Rates: BW: $100
Circ: Combined 3,500

4232 Journal of Clinical Orthodontics
JCO, Inc.
1828 Pearl St. Phone: (303)443-1720
Boulder, CO 80302 Fax: (303)443-9356

Dental journal. **Founded:** 1967. **Freq:** Monthly. **Print Method:** Offset. **Trim Size:** 8 1/4 x 10 7/8. **Cols./Page:** 2. **Col. Width:** 36 nonpareils. **Col. Depth:** 140 agate lines. **Key Personnel:** David Vogels, Managing Editor; Lynn Bollinger, Advertising Mgr.; Carol Varsos, Circulation Mgr. **Subscription Rates:** $130 individuals. **Remarks:** Accepts advertising. **Alt. Formats:** Mailing labels.
Ad Rates: BW: $1,800 4C: $3,420
Circ: Paid ‡10,445

4233 Journal of Energy and Development
International Research Center for Energy & Economic Development
909 14th St., Ste. 201 Phone: (303)492-7667
Boulder, CO 80302 Fax: (303)442-5042
Publication E-mail: iceed@stripe.Colorado.edu
Publisher E-mail: iceed@stripe.Colorado.EDU

Journal covering energy economics and policy, environment, and energy issues worldwide. **Founded:** 1975. **Freq:** Semiannual. **Print Method:** Offset. **Trim Size:** 6 1/2 x 9 1/2. **Key Personnel:** Dorothea H. ElMallakh, Managing Editor, phone (303)4421014; Suzanne Young, Advertising & Circulation Mgr.; Cecelia Lange, Book Review Editor. **ISSN:** 0361-4476. **Subscription Rates:** $42 individuals; $34 libraries; $22 students. **Remarks:** Accepts advertising.
Circ: Combined 1,000

4234 Loving More
Pep Publishing
PO Box 4358 Phone: (303)543-7540
Boulder, CO 80306 Free: (800)424-9561
Publication E-mail: lmm@lovemore.com

Magazine focusing on polyamory and new models for relationships. **Subtitle:** Loving More Magazine. **Founded:** 1983. **Freq:** Quarterly. **Trim Size:** 8 1/2 x 11. **Key Personnel:** Ryam Nearing, Editor, ryam@lovemore.com. **Subscription Rates:** $24 individuals; $6 single issue renewals. **Remarks:** Advertising accepted; rates available upon request. **URL:** http://www.lovemore.com. **Formerly:** Pep Talk - Group Marriage News.
Circ: ‡12,000

4235 Many Mountains Moving
420 22nd St. Phone: (303)545-9942
Boulder, CO 80302 Fax: (303)444-6510
Publisher E-mail: mmminc@concentric.net

Literary journal containing fiction, poetry, essays and art. **Subtitle:** A Literary Journal of Diverse Contemporary Voices. **Founded:** Dec. 1994. **Freq:** 3/year. **Print Method:** Web. **Trim Size:** 6 x 8 3/4. **Cols./Page:** 1. **Col. Width:** 4.4 inches. **Col. Depth:** 8 inches. **Key Personnel:** Naomi Horii, Editor; Marilyn Krysl, Editor; Luis Urrea, Contributing Editor; Kelley Jordan, Art Editor; Beth Nugert, Fiction Editor; Alissa Norton, Poetry Editor. **ISSN:** 1080-6474. **Subscription Rates:** $18 individuals; $15 students; $6.50 single issue. **Remarks:** Accepts advertising.
Ad Rates: BW: $200
Circ: Paid 1,800 Non-paid 200

4236 Masonry Society Journal
The Masonry Society
3970 Broadway, Ste. 201-D Phone: (303)939-9700
Boulder, CO 80304-1135 Fax: (303)541-9215
Publisher E-mail: info@masonrysociety.org

Trade journal covering masonry design and construction. **Founded:** 1982. **Freq:** Semiannual. **Print Method:** Offset. **Trim Size:** 8 1/2 x 11. **Cols./Page:** 2. **Col. Width:** 20 picas. **Key Personnel:** Rochelle C. Jaffe, Editor. **ISSN:** 0741-1294. **Subscription Rates:** $60 individuals; $30 single issue. **Remarks:** Advertising not accepted.
Circ: Controlled 850

4237 Natural Foods Merchandiser
New Hope Communications
1301 Spruce St. Phone: (303)939-8440
Boulder, CO 80302 Fax: (303)939-9559
Free: (800)839-7263
Publication E-mail: nfm@newhope.com
Publisher E-mail: sales@newhope.com

Natural foods industry trade magazine. **Founded:** Feb. 1979. **Freq:** Monthly. **Print Method:** Offset. **Trim Size:** 10 3/4 x 14 3/4. **Cols./Page:** 4. **Col. Width:** 27 nonpareils. **Col. Depth:** 140 agate lines. **Key Personnel:** Karen Raterman, Vice President, kraterman@newhope.com; Kim Paulsen, Publisher. **ISSN:** 0164-338X. **Subscription Rates:** $60 U.S., $75 Canada, $90 Surface foreign, $160 Air mail. **Remarks:** Accepts advertising. **URL:** http://www.newhope.com/nfm.
Ad Rates: BW: $2,835 4C: $4,740
Circ: Controlled ‡15,100

4238 On-Stage Studies
University of Colorado
Box 261 Fax: (303)492-7722
Boulder, CO 80309-0261
Journal covering theatre and dance in production. **Founded:** 1978. **Freq:** Annual. **Key Personnel:** Kim Axline, Editor; Charles Mitchell, Editor. **ISSN:** 0749-1549. **Subscription Rates:** $15 individuals. **Remarks:** Advertising accepted; rates available upon request.
Circ: (Not Reported)

4239 OR Manager
OR Reports
PO Box 17487 Phone: (505)982-1600
Boulder, CO 80308-0487 Fax: (505)983-0790
Publication E-mail: 75467.1545@compuserve.com
Publisher E-mail: 75467.1545@compuserve.com

Professional magazine covering operating room management in hospitals and ambulatory surgery centers. **Founded:** 1985. **Freq:** Monthly. **Print Method:** Offset. **Trim Size:** 8 1/4 x 11. **Cols./Page:** 3. **Col. Width:** 2 3/8 inches. **Col. Depth:** 10 inches. **Key Personnel:** Pat Patterson, Editor; John R. Schmus, Advertising Dir.; Elinor S. Schrader, Publisher. **ISSN:** 8756-8047. **Subscription Rates:** $86 individuals; $10 single issue. **Remarks:** Accepts advertising.
Ad Rates: BW: $1,150 4C: $2,150
Circ: Combined 3,500

4240 OR Reports
PO Box 17487 Phone: (505)982-1600
Boulder, CO 80308-0487 Fax: (505)983-0790
Publication E-mail: 65467.1545@compuserve.com
Publisher E-mail: 75467.1545@compuserve.com

Professional journal covering research and literature relating to the surgical operating room environment. **Founded:** 1992. **Freq:** Bimonthly. **Print Method:** Offset. **Trim Size:** 8 1/4 x 11. **Cols./Page:** 3. **Key Personnel:** Elinor S. Schrader, Publisher; Pat Patterson, Exec. Editor; Judith Mathias, Editor; Gordon L. Telford, MD, Consulting Editor. **ISSN:** 1065-8173. **Subscription Rates:** $88 individuals; $10 single issue. **Remarks:** Advertising not accepted.
Circ: Combined 1,000

4241 Premiere
Hachette Filipacchi
PO Box 55394 Phone: (303)604-7455
Boulder, CO 80323
Subtitle: The Movie Magazine. **Founded:** 1987. **Freq:** Monthly. **Print Method:** Offset. **Trim Size:** 10 x 12. **Cols./Page:** 4. **Col. Width:** 2 inches. **Col. Depth:** 10 5/8 inches. **Key Personnel:** Marian Schwindeman, Publisher; Susan Lyne, Editor. **USPS:** 089-492. **Subscription Rates:** $18. $2.25 single issue. **URL:** http://www.premiere.com.
Circ: Paid ★602,589

4242 Recording
Music Maker Publications, Inc.
5412 Idylwild Trail, Ste. 100 Phone: (303)516-9118
Boulder, CO 80301 Fax: (303)516-9119
Publication E-mail: recordin@idt.net; recordin@aol.com

Magazine geared toward helping musicians get the most out of their equipment to make the best recording possible. **Subtitle:** The Magazine for the Recording Musician. **Founded:** 1987. **Freq:** Monthly. **Print Method:** Web offset. **Trim Size:** 8 1/4 x 10 7/8. **Cols./Page:** 3. **Key Personnel:** Nick Batzdorf, Editor, phone (818)905-9101, fax (818)905-5434; Tom Hawley, Publisher; Brent Heintz, Assoc. Pub. **ISSN:** 1078-8352. **Subscription Rates:** $19.95; $3.95 single issue. **Remarks:** Accepts advertising. **URL:** http://www.recordingmag.com. **Alt. Formats:** CD-ROM. **Formerly:** Home & Studio Recording.
Ad Rates: BW: $1,815 **Circ:** Paid ‡21,512
4C: $2,415 Non-paid ‡4,000

4243 Rock & Ice
North South Publications
603 A South Broadway Phone: (303)499-8410
Boulder, CO 80303 Fax: (303)499-4131
Publication E-mail: mail@rockandice.com

Outdoor adventure magazine on mountaineering, rock climbing, and ice climbing. **Subtitle:** The World's Climbing Magazine. **Founded:** Mar. 1984. **Freq:** 8/year. **Print Method:** Web offset. **Trim Size:** 8 3/8 x 10 7/8. **Cols./Page:** 3. **Col. Width:** 27 nonpareils. **Col. Depth:** 131 agate lines. **Key Personnel:** Dougald MacDonald, Editor-in-Chief/Publisher, editorial@rockandice.com. **ISSN:** 0885-5722. **Subscription Rates:** $24; $42 two years; $4.95 single issue. **Remarks:** Accepts advertising. **URL:** http://www.rockandice.com.
Ad Rates: BW: $2,095 **Circ:** Paid ★37,276
4C: $2,895
PCI: $100

4244 Rocky Mountain Gardener
Westwind Publishing
PO Box 18537 Phone: (303)499-3228
Boulder, CO 80308 Fax: (303)499-3494
Publication E-mail: rocky@rmlife.com

Consumer magazine covering gardening in the Rocky mountain region. **Founded:** Dec. 1990. **Freq:** Quarterly. **Key Personnel:** Susan Martineau, Editor. **Subscription Rates:** $15 individuals; $4 single issue. **Remarks:** Accepts advertising.
Circ: Combined 7,000

4245 Ski
Times Mirror Magazines, Inc.
929 Pearl St., Ste. 200 Phone: (303)448-7600
Boulder, CO 80302 Fax: (303)448-7612

Magazine devoted to skiing. **Founded:** 1936. **Freq:** 8/year. **Print Method:** Offset. **Trim Size:** 8 1/2 x 11. **Cols./Page:** 3. **Col. Width:** 26 nonpareils. **Col. Depth:** 143 agate lines. **Key Personnel:** Andrew W. Bigford, Editor, awbig@kincf.com; Andrew W. Clurman, Publisher. **Subscription Rates:** $11.97 individuals; $2.95 single issue. **Remarks:** Accepts advertising. **URL:** http://www.skinet.com.
Ad Rates: BW: $21,630 **Circ:** Paid ★408,652
4C: $29,740

4246 Skiing
Times Mirror Magazines, Inc.
929 Pearl St., Ste. 200 Phone: (303)448-7600
Boulder, CO 80302 Fax: (303)448-7612
Publication E-mail: skiing@shinet.com

Skiing magazine. **Subtitle:** The Magazine of Winter Adventure. **Founded:** 1948. **Freq:** 7/year (issued monthly Sept. thru April). **Print Method:** Offset. **Trim Size:** 7 7/8 x 10 3/4. **Cols./Page:** 3. **Col. Width:** 27 nonpareils. **Col. Depth:** 140 agate lines. **Key Personnel:** Rick Kahl, Editor; Andrew W. Clurman, VP/Publisher. **ISSN:** 0037-6264. **Subscription Rates:** $13.94; $3.99. **Remarks:** Accepts advertising. **URL:** http://www.skinet.com/skiing.
Ad Rates: BW: $23,620 **Circ:** Paid ★403,189
4C: $32,480

4247 Skiing Trade News
Times Mirror Magazines, Inc.
929 Pearl St., Ste. 200 Phone: (303)448-7600
Boulder, CO 80302 Fax: (303)448-7612

Trade newspaper for the ski industry. Includes trade show previews, company news, retail trends, personnel changes, and miscellaneous news. **Founded:** 1948. **Freq:** (monthly Dec.-April; then every other month). **Trim Size:** 11 x 16. **Cols./Page:** 4. **Col. Width:** 13.5 picas. **Col. Depth:** 82 picas. **Key Personnel:** Arel Reilly, Publisher. **Subscription Rates:** $15 individuals. **Remarks:** Accepts advertising. **URL:** http://www.skinet.com. **Formerly:** Skiing Trade Monthly News (Jan. 1984).
Ad Rates: BW: $4,060 **Circ:** Free ‡16,875
4C: $6,170
PCI: $250

4248 Solar Today
American Solar Energy Society, Inc.
2400 Central Ave. G-1. Phone: (303)443-3130
Boulder, CO 80301 Fax: (303)443-3212
Publisher E-mail: ases@ases.org

Trade magazine covering solar energy for architects, builders, city planners, and consumers. **Founded:** Jan. 1987. **Key Personnel:** Maureen McIntyre, Editor. **ISSN:** 1042-0630. **Subscription Rates:** $29 individuals; $4 single issue. **Remarks:** Accepts advertising.
Circ: Paid 6,000

4249 Soldier of Fortune
Omega Group
5735 Arapahoe Ave. Phone: (303)449-3750
Boulder, CO 80303-1340 Fax: (303)444-5617
Publication E-mail: editor@sofmag.com

Monthly publication of military adventure and foreign intrigue. **Subtitle:** The Journal of Professional Adventurers. **Founded:** 1975. **Freq:** Monthly. **Print Method:** Offset. **Trim Size:** 8 x 10 7/8. **Cols./Page:** 3. **Col. Width:** 26 nonpareils. **Col. Depth:** 142 agate lines. **Key Personnel:** Robert K. Brown, Editor and Publisher; Dwight Swift, Managing Editor; John Walker, Advertising Dir.; Greg Peterson, CFO. **ISSN:** 0145-6784. **Subscription Rates:** $29.95 individuals; $4.95 single issue. **Remarks:** Accepts advertising. **URL:** http://www.sofmag.com.
Ad Rates: BW: $2,657 **Circ:** ‡98,000
4C: $3,623
PCI: $184

4250 VeloNews
Inside Communications, Inc.
1830 N. 55th St. Phone: (303)440-0601
Boulder, CO 80301 Fax: (303)444-6788
Publication E-mail: velonews@7dogs.com

Tabloid magazine for fans of mountain biking and road racing. **Subtitle:** Velonews: The Journal of Competitive Cycling. **Founded:** Mar. 1972. **Freq:** 20/year. **Print Method:** Web offset. **Trim Size:** 10 3/4 x 14. **Cols./Page:** 4 and 3. **Col. Width:** 2 1/4 and 3 1/8 inches. **Col. Depth:** 12 5/8 and 12 5/8 inches. **Key Personnel:** John Wilcockson, Editor, jwilcockson@7dogs.com; Alec Dinner, Advertising Dir., adinner@7dogs.com; Chuck Gestefield, Circulation Mgr., cgesterfield@7dogs.com. **ISSN:** 0161-1798. **Subscription Rates:** $39.97 individuals; $56 Canada; $102 out of country. **Remarks:** Advertising accepted; rates available upon request. **Available Online. URL:** http://www.velonews.com.
Circ: Paid ★37,141

4251 Vibe Magazine
Time Ventures
PO Box 59580 Phone: (303)678-8475
Boulder, CO 80322 Fax: (303)661-1181
Free: (800)477-3974

Publication focusing on popular music and culture. **Founded:** Sept. 1992. **Freq:** 10/year. **Print Method:** Offset. **Trim Size:** 10 x 12. **Key Personnel:** Jonathan Von Meter, Editor; Susan Cappo, Advertising Mgr.; Brendan Amyot, Circulation Mgr. **ISSN:** 1070-4701. **Subscription Rates:** $18. $2.50 single issue. **Remarks:** Accepts advertising. **URL:** http://www.vibe.com.
Ad Rates: BW: $10,500 **Circ:** Paid ★600,650
4C: $13,020

4252 Women's Sports & Fitness
Sports & Fitness, Inc.
2025 Pearl St. Phone: (303)440-5111
Boulder, CO 80302 Fax: (303)440-3313
Publication E-mail: kaasfp@aol.com

Magazine covering women's sports, fitness, nutrition, and health. **Founded:** 1974. **Freq:** 9/year. **Print Method:** Offset. **Trim Size:** 8 1/8 x 10 3/4. **Cols./Page:** 3. **Col. Width:** 27 nonpareils. **Col. Depth:** 121 agate lines. **Key Personnel:** Dagny Scott, Editor; Daemon Filson, Publisher. **ISSN:** 8750-653X. **Subscription Rates:** $19.97 individuals; $3.99 single issue. **Remarks:** Accepts advertising. **Alt. Formats:** Microform.
Ad Rates: BW: $10,500 **Circ:** Paid 216,958
4C: $14,000
PCI: $351

4253 KBCO-FM - 97.3
2500 Pearl St., Ste. 315 Phone: (303)444-5600
Boulder, CO 80302 Fax: (303)449-3057
E-mail: kbco@kbcoradio.com

Format: Adult Album Alternative. **Networks:** Independent. **Owner:** Jacor Broadcasting of Colorado, 1380 Lawrence St., Ste. 1300, Denver, CO 80204, (303)893-3699, Fax: (303)329-3699. **Founded:** 1977. **Operating Hours:** Continuous. **Key Personnel:** Don Howe, General Mgr.; Dave Benson, Program Dir.; Greg Hoffman, Sales Mgr., phone (303)694-6300, fax (303)694-4824; Rosemary Bennett, Natl. Sales Mgr. **Wattage:** 100,000. **Ad Rates:** $90-400 for 30 seconds. **URL:** http://www.kbcoradio.com.

4254 KBVI-AM - 1490
30085 Bluff St. Phone: (303)444-1490
Boulder, CO 80301 Fax: (303)442-6544
E-mail: radio@kvbi.com

Format: Full Service. **Networks:** Westwood One Radio; CNN Radio. **Owner:** Unicorn Productions, L.L.C., at above address. **Founded:** Nov. 1995. **Operating Hours:** Continuous. **ADI:** Denver (Steamboat Springs), CO. **Key Personnel:** Glen Gerberg, General Mgr.; Tony Kindelspire, Station Mgr., tkindelspire@kbvi.com; Lydia Smith, A. P. D., lsmith@kbvi.com. **Wattage:** 1000.

4255 KGNU-FM - 88.5
Box 885 Phone: (303)449-4885
Boulder, CO 80306

Format: Public Radio; Eclectic; News. **Networks:** National Public Radio (NPR); Public Radio International (PRI); Pacifica. **Owner:** Boulder Community Broadcasting Assn. Inc., at above address. **Founded:** 1978. **Operating Hours:** Continuous. **Key Personnel:** Marty Durlin, General Mgr.; Catherine Gallery, Music Dir.; Sam Fuqua, News Dir. **Wattage:** 1300. **Ad Rates:** Noncommercial.

4256 KVCU Radio 1190 - 1190 AM
Campus Box 207 Phone: (303)492-5031
Boulder, CO 80309 Fax: (303)492-1369
E-mail: kvcu-l@lists.colorado.edu

Format: Alternative/New Music/Progressive. **Founded:** 1978. **Formerly:** KUCB-AM (1998). **Operating Hours:** M-F 9-5. **Key Personnel:** Jason Mueller, Music Dir., phone (303)492-7405, fax (303)492-1369, kucb@usts.colorado.edu; Jim Musil, General Mgr., phone (303)492-5031, fax (303)492-1369; Stacey Thompson, General Mgr., phone (303)492-3243. **Wattage:** 5000 during day, 110 at night. **Ad Rates:** $10 for 30 seconds. **URL:** http://www.radio1190.com.

4257 TCI Cablevision of Colorado
Box 17610 Phone: (303)443-6836
Boulder, CO 80301-2514

Founded: 1965. **Cities Served:** Boulder County, CO.

BRECKENRIDGE†, pop. 1,200.

Summit Co. (C). 90 m SW of Denver. Summer & winter resort.

4258 Classic Cable
Box 1275 Phone: (303)453-7996
400 N Park Ave., Ste. 13 A Fax: (303)453-9251
Breckenridge, CO 80424
Free: (800)999-8876
E-mail: classicc@colorado.net

Formerly: Breckenridge Cable TV. **Key Personnel:** Danny Lingle, Plant Mgr. **Cities Served:** subscribing households 6,000; 36 channels; 1 community access channel.

4259 KSMT-FM - 102.3
130 Ski Hill Rd., Ste.110 Phone: (303)453-2234
Breckenridge, CO 80424 Fax: (303)453-5425

Format: Adult Contemporary; Alternative/New Music/Progressive. **Owner:** Rocky Mountain Radio Company, at above address. **Founded:** 1973. **Formerly:** KLGT-FM (1981). **Operating Hours:** Continuous; 99% local. **Key Personnel:** Mo Bennett, General Mgr. **Wattage:** 3000. **Ad Rates:** $16-35 per unit.

BREEN

4260 KLLV-AM - 550
14780 Hwy. 140 Phone: (970)259-5558
Breen, CO 81326

Format: Religious. **Owner:** Daystar Radio Ltd., at above address. **Founded:** 1984. **Key Personnel:** D. Williams, General Mgr.

BRIGHTON†, pop. 14,500.

Adams Co. (NEC). 20 m NE of Denver. Canning; beet sugar factories; mobile homes manufactured. Metal fabricating plants. Agriculture. Sugar beets, wheat, corn, cattle feeding; diversified farming.

4261 The Free Advertiser
Metrowest Newspapers
PO Box 646 Phone: (303)659-1141
Brighton, CO 80601 Fax: (303)659-2901

Shopping guide. **Freq:** Weekly. **Print Method:** Offset. **Cols./Page:** 6. **Col. Width:** 12 3/10 picas. **Col. Depth:** 21 inches. **Key Personnel:** Kathye Joens, Editor; Vi June, Publisher; Evelyn Duncan, Advertising Mgr. **Subscription Rates:** Free; $10 out of area.

4262 Standard Blade
Metrowest Newspapers
PO Box 646 Phone: (303)659-1141
Brighton, CO 80601 Fax: (303)659-2901

Community newspaper. **Founded:** 1902. **Freq:** Weekly Wed./Sat. **Print Method:** Offset. **Cols./Page:** 6. **Col. Width:** 12 3/10 picas. **Col. Depth:** 12 1/2 inches. **Key Personnel:** Annette Riesel, Editor. **Subscription Rates:** $29 individuals. **Remarks:** Accepts advertising. **Alt. Formats:** CD-ROM. **Formerly**: Standard Blade.
Ad Rates: GLR: $15 **Circ:** Paid 6,593
BW: $975 Non-paid 25,227
4C: $1200
SAU: $15
PCI: $15

4263 KLTT-AM - 670
2150 W. 29th Ave., Ste. 300 Phone: (303)458-8004
Denver, CO 80211 Fax: (303)433-7257
E-mail: klt670@aol.com

Format: Religious. **Networks:** AP. **Owner:** Crawford Broadcasting Inc., at above address, (303)433-5500, Fax: (303)433-1555. **Founded:** 1956. **Operating Hours:** Continuous. **ADI:** Denver (Steamboat Springs), CO. **Key Personnel:** Don Crawford, Jr., Exec. Director; Mike Triem, Sales Mgr. **Wattage:** 50,000.

BROOMFIELD, pop. 20,730.

Boulder, Adams & Jefferson Co. (NC). 15 m NW of Denver. Residential. Commercial, industrial and high tech centers.

4264 Sign Business
National Business Media, Inc.
PO Box 1416 Phone: (303)469-0424
Broomfield, CO 80020 Fax: (303)469-5730
Free: (800)669-0424

Subtitle: A National Business Media Publication. **Founded:** Oct. 1986. **Freq:** Monthly. **Print Method:** Offset. **Trim Size:** 8 x 11. **Cols./Page:** 3. **Col. Width:** 13.5 picas. **Col. Depth:** 10 inches. **Key Personnel:** Regan Dickinson, Editor; Ken Higgins, Publisher. **ISSN:** 0893-9888. **Subscription Rates:** $45 individuals; $75 Canada; $125 other countries; $95 Mexico; $5 single issue. **Remarks:** Accepts advertising. **URL:** http://www.nbm.com/signbusiness.
Ad Rates: BW: $2,677.50 **Circ:** Paid ‡12,006
4C: $3,485 Non-paid ‡4,508
PCI: $155

BRUSH, pop. 4,074.

Morgan Co. (NE). 61 E of Greeley. Retirement care centers. Manufacturers farm equipment, electronics. Hog processing plant. Livestock markets. Agriculture. Cattle, hogs, daires, horses, alfalfa, grain.

4265 Brush News-Tribune
PO Box 8 Phone: (970)842-5516
Brush, CO 80723 Fax: (970)842-5519
Publication E-mail: brushnew@ria.net

Community newspaper. **Founded:** 1894. **Freq:** Weekly (Wed.). **Print Method:** Offset. **Cols./Page:** 5. **Col. Width:** 25 nonpareils. **Col. Depth:** 182 agate lines. **Key Personnel:** Dave Graves, Editor and Publisher. **USPS:** 068-240. **Subscription Rates:** $17 individuals. **Remarks:** Accepts advertising.
Ad Rates: BW: $292.50 **Circ:** ‡2,400
4C: $322.50
SAU: $4.50
PCI: $3.95

BURLINGTON†, pop. 3,107.

Kit Carson Co. (EC). Sugar beets.

4266 Burlington Record & Plains Dealer
Burlington Record
PO Box 459 Phone: (719)346-5381
Burlington, CO 80807 Fax: (719)346-5514

Community newspaper with shopper. **Founded:** 1888. **Freq:** Weekly (Thurs.). **Print Method:** Web offset. **Cols./Page:** 8. **Col. Width:** 11 inches. **Col. Depth:** 21 inches. **Key Personnel:** Rol Hudler, Editor and Publisher. **Subscription Rates:** $19 individuals; $22 out of area. **Remarks:** Accepts advertising. **Formerly**: Burlington Record.
Ad Rates: GLR: $5.25 **Circ:** 7,500
BW: $882
4C: $1,002
PCI: $5.25

4267 KNAB-AM - 1140
17534 County Rd. 49 Phone: (719)346-8600
PO Box 516 Fax: (719)346-8656
Burlington, CO 80807

Format: Full Service; Adult Contemporary. **Networks:** ABC. **Owner:** Bette Bailly, at above address. **Founded:** 1967. **Operating Hours:** 12 hrs. Daily; 2% network, 98% local. **Key Personnel:** Glen Viehmeyer, Sales Mgr.; Bette Bailly, GM/President. **Wattage:** 1000. **Ad Rates:** $9.40-14.75 for 30 seconds; $17.40-23 for 60 seconds. Combined advertising rates available with KNAB-FM.

4268 KNAB-FM - 104.1
17534 County Rd. 49 Phone: (719)346-8600
PO Box 516 Fax: (719)346-8656
Burlington, CO 80807

Format: Full Service; Country. **Networks:** ABC. **Founded:** 1980. **Operating Hours:** Continuous; 2% network, 98% local. **Key Personnel:** Glen Viehmeyer, Sales Mgr.; Bette Baily, General Mgr. **Wattage:** 50,700. **Ad Rates:** $9.40-14.75 for 30 seconds; $17.00-23.00 for 60 seconds. Combined advertising rates available with KNAB-AM: $7.20-$10.80 for 20 seconds; $10-$13.80 for 30 seconds;.

CANON CITY†, pop. 13,037.

Fremont Co. (SC). On Arkansas River, 41 m W of Pueblo. Tourism. Royal Gorge. Light industry.

4269 Daily Record
Royal Gorge Publishing Corp.
701 S. 9th St. Phone: (719)275-7565
Canon City, CO 81212 Fax: (719)275-1353

Newspaper with an Indiana orientation. **Founded:** 1875. **Freq:** Daily (eve.). **Print Method:** Offset. **Cols./Page:** 6. **Col. Width:** 2 1/16 inches. **Col. Depth:** 21.5 picas. **Key Personnel:** Bob Helsley, Editor; Edward Lehman, Publisher; Terri Holloway, Advertising Mgr. **USPS:** 088-560. **Subscription Rates:** $84 individuals. **Remarks:** Accepts advertising.
Ad Rates: GLR: $.63 **Circ:** Mon.-Sat. 8,523
BW: $1,032
4C: $1,273.95
SAU: $8

4270 KRLN-AM - 1400
1615 Central Phone: (719)275-7488
Canon City, CO 81212 Fax: (719)275-5132

Format: Adult Contemporary; Oldies. **Networks:** CBS. **Owner:** Warner Inc.,, Box 30181, Lincoln, NE 68503, (402)475-4567, Fax: (402)479-1414. **Founded:** 1947. **Operating Hours:** Mon-Sat 5 am-midnight; Sun. 7 am-midnight; 10% network, 90% local. **Key Personnel:** Ed Norden, General Mgr.; Margaret Hitchcock, General Sales Mgr.; Kyle Horne, Sports Dir. **Local Programs:** *Morning Line*, Ed Norden. **Wattage:** 1000. **Ad Rates:** $9-17 for 30 seconds; $11-19 for 60 seconds. Combined advertising rates available with KGTY-FM.

4271 KSTY-FM - 103.9
1615 Central Phone: (719)275-7488
Canon City, CO 81212 Fax: (719)275-7488

Format: Country. **Owner:** Warner, Inc., PO Box 30181, Lincoln, NE 68503, (402)475-4567, Fax: (402)479-1414. **Founded:** 1975. **Formerly**: KSTX-FM; KRLN-FM. **Operating Hours:** Mon.-Sat. 5 am-midnight; Sun. 5 am-midnight; 10% network, 90% local. **Key Personnel:** Edward H. Norden, Gen. Mgr. & News Dir., fax (719)275-5132; Margaret Hitchcock, Sales Mgr., fax (719)275-5132; Kyle Horne, Sports Dir., fax (719)225-5132. **Wattage:** 3000. **Ad Rates:** $12.50-19 for 30 seconds; $14.20-23 for 60 seconds. $12.20-$19 for 30 seconds; $16.20-$23 for 60 seconds. Combined advertising rates available with KRLN-AM.

CARBONDALE, pop. 2,084.

Garfield Co. (W). 11 m S of Glenwood Springs.

4272 Climbing Magazine
Primedia
1101 Village Rd., Ste. LL-1B Phone: (970)963-9449
Carbondale, CO 81623 Fax: (970)963-9442
Publication E-mail: climbing@climbing.com

Magazine devoted to rock and mountain climbing. **Founded:** 1970. **Freq:** 9/year. **Print Method:** Web offset. **Trim Size:** 8 3/8 x 10 7/8. **Cols./Page:** 3. **Col. Width:** 13 picas. **Col. Depth:** 9 5/16 inches. **Key Personnel:** Duane Raleigh, Editor and Publisher; Julie Oldham, Advertising Dir. **ISSN:** 0045-7159. **Subscription Rates:** $29 individuals; $4.95 single issue; $38 Canada; $43 other countries. **URL:** http://www.climbing.com.
Ad Rates: BW: $1,995 **Circ:** Paid ★**47,514**
4C: $3,250

4273 KDNK-FM - 90.5
417 Main St. Phone: (970)963-0139
PO Box 1388 Fax: (970)963-0810
Carbondale, CO 81623
E-mail: kdnk@rof.net

Format: Public Radio; Full Service. **Networks:** National Public Radio (NPR). **Founded:** 1983. **Operating Hours:** 6 am-1 am weekdays; 7 am-1 am Saturday and Sunday; 20% network, 80% local. **Key Personnel:** Allen Scott, Station Mgr.; Skip Naft, Contact; Brenda Stolbach, Contact. **Wattage:** 215. **Ad Rates:** Noncommercial.

CASTLE ROCK†, pop. 3,913.

Douglas Co. (C). 20 m S. of Denver.

4274 Douglas County News Press
Douglas County Publishing
PO Box 1270 Phone: (303)688-3128
Castle Rock, CO 80104 Fax: (303)660-0240
Publication E-mail: dcnewspapers@aol.com

General newspaper. **Founded:** 1892. **Freq:** Weekly (Wed.). **Print Method:** Offset. **Cols./Page:** 6. **Col. Width:** 24 nonpareils. **Col. Depth:** 301 agate lines. **Key Personnel:** Gerald Heale, Publisher; Richard Bangs, Editor; John Thomas, Advertising Mgr. **Subscription Rates:** $26 individuals. **Remarks:** Accepts advertising. **Formerly**: Daily News Press.
Ad Rates: GLR: $162 **Circ:** Paid ‡7,245
BW: $2,475 Free ‡28,500
4C: $2,803
SAU: $19.65
PCI: $22.60

CENTER, pop. 1,630.

Saguache Co. (SWC). 60 m S.W. of Salida. Mining. Feed mills. Livestock. Agriculture. Grain, lettuce, potatoes.

4275 Center Post-Dispatch
SLV Publishing
PO Box 1059 Phone: (719)754-3172
Center, CO 81125-1059
Community newspaper. **Founded:** 1906. **Freq:** Weekly (Wed.). **Print Method:** Offset. **Trim Size:** 10 1/2 x 16. **Cols./Page:** 5. **Col. Width:** 2 inches. **Col. Depth:** 16 inches. **Key Personnel:** Becky Dillon, Editor; Keith Bray, Publisher. **USPS:** 775-900. **Subscription Rates:** $21 individuals. **Remarks:** Accepts advertising.
Ad Rates: BW: $484 **Circ:** Paid 556
PCI: $6.05 Free 9

4276 Center Municipal Cable System
400 S. Worth St. Phone: (719)754-3497
PO Box 400 Fax: (719)754-3379
Center, CO 81125

Founded: 1984. **Key Personnel:** Darrell T. Davis, Superintendent. **Cities Served:** Center, CO: subscribing households 627; 23 channels; 1 community access channel; 168 hours per week community access programming.

CENTRAL CITY†, pop. 329.

Gilpin Co. (NC). 30 m W of Denver. Gold, silver, lead, copper, zinc and uranium mines. Tourism.

4277 Weekly Register-Call
220 Spring St. Phone: (303)582-5333
PO Box 609 Fax: (303)582-3932
Central City, CO 80427-0609
General newspaper. **Founded:** July 28, 1862. **Freq:** Weekly (Fri.). **Print Method:** Offset. **Cols./Page:** 6. **Col. Width:** 26 nonpareils. **Col. Depth:** 280 agate lines. **Key Personnel:** Charlotte Taylor, Editor; William C. Russell, Jr., Publisher. **ISSN:** 0278-5838. **Subscription Rates:** $18 in county; $22 elsewhere in USA. **Remarks:** Accepts advertising.
Ad Rates: GLR: $.21 **Circ:** Paid 1,294
BW: $720 Non-paid 23
PCI: $6.50

CHEYENNE WELLS†, pop. 950.

Cheyenne Co. (EC).

4278 Cheyenne Range-Ledger
The Range-Ledger
PO Box 684 Phone: (719)767-5615
Cheyenne Wells, CO 80810 Fax: (719)767-5113

County newspaper. **Freq:** Weekly (Thurs.). **Cols./Page:** 8. **Col. Width:** 1 7/8 inches. **Col. Depth:** 21 inches. **Key Personnel:** Joyce Escudero, Editor and Publisher.
Circ: 1,300

COLORADO SPRINGS†, pop. 215,150.

El Paso Co. (EC). 68 m S of Denver. U.S. Air Force Academy. Colorado College. Union Printers' National Home. Health and Tourist resort. Sanatorium. Manufactures advertising film, granite, concrete, dairy products, brooms, novelties, chemicals, pottery, bricks, airplane engine mounts, machine tools, shell fuses, electric motors, gray and alloy castings, electronics, plastics, steel culverts. Chromium plating; meat packing; bookbinding; nuclear research.

4279 Academy Spirit
Gowdy Printcraft Press, Inc.
Headquarters USAFA, PAI Phone: (719)333-7496
Colorado Springs, CO 80840 Fax: (719)333-4094
Publisher E-mail: gowdyprint@aol.com

Military tabloid for personnel of the United States Air Force Academy. **Founded:** 1958. **Freq:** Weekly (Fri.). **Print Method:** Web offset. **Trim Size:** 11 1/4 x 17 1/4. **Cols./Page:** 6. **Col. Width:** 1 5/8 inches. **Col. Depth:** 16 inches. **Key Personnel:** Sr. A. Roy Utley, Editor, utleyrr.pa@usafa.af.mil; Fred Bernheim, Publisher; Phyllis Allen, Advertising Mgr. **Subscription Rates:** $45 individuals. **Remarks:** Accepts advertising. **URL:** http://www.usafa.af.mil/pa. **Formerly:** The Falcon FLyer; Falconnews.
Ad Rates: GLR: $.73 **Circ:** Free ‡7,500
BW: $816
4C: $1,176
PCI: $10.25

4280 Alliance Life
The Christian and Missionary Alliance
8595 Explorer Dr.
Colorado Springs, CO 80935
Publication E-mail: 70570.3457@compuserve.com

Religious magazine. **Subtitle:** A Journal of Christian Life and Missions. **Founded:** 1882. **Freq:** Semimonthly. **Print Method:** Offset. **Trim Size:** 8 3/8 x 10 7/8. **Cols./Page:** 3. **Col. Width:** 27 nonpareils. **Col. Depth:** 130 agate lines. **Key Personnel:** Stephen P. Adams, Editor; Michael Saunier, Assoc. Editor. **ISSN:** 1040-6794. **Subscription Rates:** $11.00; $16.00 Canada. **Remarks:** Advertising not accepted. **Alt. Formats:** Audio tape. **Formerly:** The Alliance Witness; The Alliance Weekly.
Circ: ‡60,000

4281 American Hockey Magazine
The Publishing Group, Inc.
1775 Bob Johnson Rd. Phone: (719)599-5500
Colorado Springs, CO 80906-4026 Fax: (719)599-5994
U.S.A. Hockey (sports association) magazine. **Founded:** 1973. **Freq:** 9/year. **Print Method:** Web offset. **Trim Size:** 11 x 14. **Cols./Page:** 3. **Col. Width:** 26 nonpareils. **Col. Depth:** 140 agate lines. **Key Personnel:** Darryl Seibel, Editor-in-Chief; Kris Pleimann, Editor. **Subscription Rates:** $13 individuals (included in membership). **Remarks:** Advertising accepted; rates available upon request.
Circ: Non-paid 220,000

4282 Breakaway Magazine
Focus on the Family
8605 Explorer Dr. Phone: (719)531-3400
Colorado Springs, CO 80920-1051 Fax: (719)548-5860
Free: (800)232-6459
Publication E-mail: corrdpt@fotf.org
Publisher E-mail: tifeditor@fotf.org

Christian magazine for teenage boys. **Founded:** 1990. **Freq:** Monthly. **Trim Size:** 8 1/8 x 11. **Key Personnel:** Greg Johnson, Editor. **Subscription Rates:** $15. $1.50 single issue. **Remarks:** Accepts advertising.
Ad Rates: 4C: $1,865 **Circ:** Paid 90,000

4283 CALF News Magazine
CALF News Magazine Ltd.
11425 Black Forest Rd., Ste. 8 Phone: (719)495-0303
PO Box 88312 Fax: (719)495-9204
Colorado Springs, CO 80908-8312
Magazine for commercial feedlot operators (1,000 head or more). **Subtitle:** Cattle Feeder. **Founded:** 1963. **Freq:** Monthly. **Print Method:** Offset. **Trim Size:** 8 1/2 x 11. **Cols./Page:** 3. **Col. Width:** 28 nonpareils. **Col. Depth:** 140 agate lines. **Key Personnel:** Steve Dittmer, Editor and Publisher. **Subscription Rates:** $29 individuals. **Remarks:** Accepts advertising.
Ad Rates: BW: $1,145 **Circ:** 4,675
4C: $1,985
PCI: $50

4284 CBA Marketplace
CBA Service Corp., Inc.
2620 Venetucci Blvd. Phone: (719)576-7880
PO Box 200 Fax: (719)576-0795
Colorado Springs, CO 80901
Free: (800)252-1950
Publisher E-mail: publications@cbaonline.org

A how-to magazine on the Christian retail industry. **Subtitle:** Official Magazine of CBA. **Founded:** June 1968. **Freq:** 12/year. **Print Method:** Letterpress and offset. **Trim Size:** 8 1/4 x 10 7/8. **Cols./Page:** 3. **Col. Width:** 27 nonpareils. **Col. Depth:** 138 agate lines. **Key Personnel:** Cindy Parolini, Publications Dir.; Bill Morr, Production Mgr.; Sue Grise, Editor; Debby Weaver, Managing Editor. **ISSN:** 0006-7563. **Subscription Rates:** $50 nonmembers; $43 CBA members; $7.50 single issue. **Remarks:** Accepts advertising. **URL:** http://www.cbaonline.org. **Formerly:** Bookstore Journal.
Ad Rates: BW: $1,504 **Circ:** Paid ‡8,514
4C: $2,084 Non-paid ‡567

4285 Christian Camp & Conference Journal
Christian Camping International/USA
405 W. Rockrimmon Blvd.
Colorado Springs, CO 80919
Publication E-mail: editor@cciusa.org
Publisher E-mail: cciusa@cciusa.org

Trade association magazine. **Founded:** 1958. **Freq:** Bimonthly. **Print Method:** Offset. **Trim Size:** 8 3/8 x 10 7/8. **Cols./Page:** 3. **Col. Width:** 27 nonpareils. **Col. Depth:** 140 agate lines. **Key Personnel:** Dean Ridings, Editor, editor@cciusa.org; John Ashmen, Publisher, john@cciusa.org; Robert Baylor, Advertising Mgr., advertising@cciusa.org. **Subscription Rates:** $24.95 individuals; $4.50 single issue. **Remarks:** Accepts advertising. **URL:** http://www.cciusa.org. **Formerly:** Journal of Christian Camping.
Ad Rates: BW: $650 **Circ:** ‡7,500
4C: $1,370

4286 Coaching Volleyball
American Volleyball Coaches Association
1227 Lake Plaza Dr., Ste. B Phone: (719)576-7777
Colorado Springs, CO 80906 Fax: (719)576-7778
Publication E-mail: kasher@avca.org; svivas@avca.org
Publisher E-mail: kasher@avca.org

Magazine for volleyball coaches. **Founded:** 1987. **Freq:** Bimonthly. **Print Method:** Web Press. **Trim Size:** 8 1/2 x 11. **Key Personnel:** Kinda Lenberg, Editor, phone (719)382-7672, fax (719)382-1127, kasher@avca.org. **ISSN:** 0894-4237. **Subscription Rates:** $20; $36 Industry. $4 single issue. **Alt. Formats:** Mailing labels.
Ad Rates: BW: $560 **Circ:** Paid 3,250
4C: $1,360

4287 Colorado Springs Gazette Telegraph
Freedom Newspapers, Inc.
30 S. Prospect Phone: (719)636-0266
Colorado Springs, CO 80903 Fax: (719)636-0202

General newspaper. **Founded:** Mar. 23, 1872. **Freq:** Mon.-Sun. (morn.). **Print Method:** Offset. **Trim Size:** 13 x 21 1/2. **Cols./Page:** 6. **Col. Width:** 2 1/16 inches. **Col. Depth:** 21.5 picas. **Key Personnel:** Steven A. Smith, Editor, phone (719)636-0105; Wayne Stewart, Asst. Editor, phone (719)636-0189; Gary Blakeley, Operations Dir., phone (719)636-0200; Mary Jacobus, Sales and Marketing Dir., phone (719)636-0104; Jane Ellis, Retail Advertising Dir., phone (719)636-0310; Cliff Foster, City Editor, phone (719)636-0363; Todd Hegert, Features Editor, phone (719)636-0273; Terri Fleming, Managing Editor; Jim Wright, Business Editor. **Subscription Rates:** $117.60 individuals; $168 out of area; $240 out of state. **Remarks:** Accepts advertising. Monday-Saturday: GLR: $5.03; BW: $8,925.51; 4C: $9,774.51; SAU: $69.19; Sunday: GLR: $6.16; BW: $10,291.62; 4C: $11,188.60; SAU: $79.78. **Online:** DataTimes Corporation. **URL:** http://www.usa.net/gazette/.
Circ: Mon.-Sat. ★99,473
Sun. ★120,117

4288 Currents
National Organization for Rivers
212 W. Cheyenne Mtn. Blvd. Phone: (719)579-8759
Colorado Springs, CO 80934 Fax: (719)576-6238
Publisher E-mail: nors@rmi.net

Magazine covering river conservation and access news for kayakers, rafters, and canoeists. **Subtitle:** Voice of the National Organization for Rivers. **Founded:** June 1979. **Freq:** Quarterly. **Print Method:** Offset. **Trim Size:** 8 1/2 x 11. **Cols./Page:** 3. **Col. Width:** 2 3/8 inches. **Col. Depth:** 9 inches. **Key Personnel:** Eric Leaper, Exec. Dir.; Greg Moore, Editor. **Subscription Rates:** $20 individuals; $1 single issue. **Remarks:** Accepts advertising.
Ad Rates: BW: $329 **Circ:** Paid ‡4,500
4C: $559 Non-paid ‡2,000

4289 Cycling Magazine
USA Cycling Inc.
1 Olympic Plaza Phone: (719)578-4581
Colorado Springs, CO 80909-5746 Fax: (719)578-4628
Free: (888)405-RACE
Publisher E-mail: media@usacycling.org

Official publication (tabloid) of the United States Cycling Federation. **Founded:** 1979. **Freq:** Bimonthly. **Print Method:** Letter press. **Trim Size:** 8 3/8 x 10 7/8. **Cols./Page:** 3. **Key Personnel:** Rich Wanninger, Editor, rwanninger@usacycling.org. **ISSN:** 1098-3724. **Subscription Rates:** $25 individuals; $40 other countries. **Remarks:** Accepts advertising. **Formerly:** Cycling USA; Norba News; Bike Racing Nation.
Ad Rates: 4C: $4,395 **Circ:** Paid ‡57,000
Non-paid ‡1,000

4290 Discipleship Journal
NavPress
PO Box 35004 Phone: (719)548-9222
Colorado Springs, CO 80935 Fax: (719)598-7128

Evangelical Christian magazine presenting biblical perspectives on Christian growth and ministry with an emphasis on putting principles into practice. **Founded:** Jan. 1981. **Freq:** Bimonthly. **Print Method:** Web offset. **Trim Size:** 8 1/4 x 10 3/4. **Cols./Page:** 3. **Col. Width:** 13.9 picas. **Col. Depth:** 58 picas. **Key Personnel:** Peter Mayberry, Assoc. Publisher, phone (719)531-3528; Susan Maycinik, Editor, phone (719)531-3529, smaycini@navigato.mhs.compuserve.com; Adam Holz, Assoc. Editor; Sue Kline, Managing Editor, phone (719)531-3514; Anne Meskey Elhajoui, Art Dir., phone (719)531-3527; Marcy Shultz, Asst. Dir., phone (719)531-3526; Dave Wilson, Advertising/Marketing Dir., phone (719)531-3579; Bob Yates, Adveristing Account Manager, phone (719)531-3558; June Whitely, Fulfillment Dir., phone (719)531-3501; Jon Killingsworth, Circulation Mgr., phone (719)531-3531; Diane Sevcik, Rights and Permissions, phone (719)531-3585. **ISSN:** 0273-5865. **Subscription Rates:** $21.97 individuals; $3.95 single issue; $27.97 out of country. **Remarks:** Accepts advertising. **URL:** http://www.navigators.org/djhome.html.
Ad Rates: BW: $2,735 **Circ:** Paid ‡105,436
4C: $3,235 Non-paid ‡886

4291 Eleventh Muse
Poetry West
Box 2413
Colorado Springs, CO 80901

Poetry journal. **Founded:** 1982. **Freq:** Semiannual. **Subscription Rates:** $8 individuals; $4 single issue. **Remarks:** Accepts advertising. **Alt. Formats:** Audio tape; Large-print.
Ad Rates: BW: $75 **Circ:** Paid 200

4292 Federal Rules Citations
Shepard's/McGraw-Hill
PO Box 35300 Phone: (719)481-7479
Colorado Springs, CO 80935-3530 Free: (800)525-2474
Publication covering citations within the U.S. reporter system for lawyers. **Freq:** Monthly. **Print Method:** Offset. **Trim Size:** 6 3/4 x 10. **Cols./Page:** 6. **Col. Width:** 1 inches. **Col. Depth:** 9 inches. **Key Personnel:** Lee Henry, Manager. **ISSN:** 1048-0838. **Subscription Rates:** $430 individuals. **Remarks:** Advertising not accepted. **Alt. Formats:** CD-ROM.
Circ: (Not Reported)

4293 Focus on the Family Clubhouse
Focus on the Family
8605 Explorer Dr. Phone: (719)531-3400
Colorado Springs, CO 80920-1051 Fax: (719)548-5860
Free: (800)232-6459
Publisher E-mail: tifeditor@fotf.org

Consumer Christian magazine for children ages 8-12 years. **Freq:** Monthly. **Key Personnel:** Jesse Florea, Editor; Annette Bourland, Asst. Editor. **Subscription Rates:** $15 individuals. **Remarks:** Advertising not accepted.
Circ: Paid 99,000

4294 Focus on the Family Clubhouse Jr.
Focus on the Family
8605 Explorer Dr. Phone: (719)531-3400
Colorado Springs, CO 80920-1051 Fax: (719)548-5860
Free: (800)232-6459
Publisher E-mail: tifeditor@fotf.org

Consumer Christian magazine for children ages 4 to 8 years. **Founded:** Dec. 1988. **Freq:** Monthly. **Key Personnel:** Jesse Florea, Editor; Kim Washburn, Asst. Editor. **ISSN:** 0895-1136. **Remarks:** Advertising not accepted.
Circ: Controlled 75,000

4295 Focus on the Family Magazine
Focus on the Family
8605 Explorer Dr. Phone: (719)531-3400
Colorado Springs, CO 80920-1051 Fax: (719)548-5860
Free: (800)232-6459
Publisher E-mail: tifeditor@fotf.org

Magazine containing marriage and parenting articles from a Christian perspective. **Founded:** 1977. **Freq:** Monthly. **Print Method:** Web offset. **Trim Size:** 8 x 10 1/2. **Cols./Page:** 3. **Col. Width:** 13 picas. **Key Personnel:** James C. Dobson, Ph.D, Publisher; Tom Neven, Editor, phone (719)548-5881, fax (719)548-3499; Kurt Bruner, Vice President of Periodicals; Timothy Jones, Senior Art Dir. **ISSN:** 0894-3346. **Subscription Rates:** Free to members. **Remarks:** Advertising not accepted. **URL:** http://www.family.org.
Circ: Free 2,600,000

4296 Insight
U.S. Association of Blind Athletes
33 N. Institute Phone: (719)630-0422
Colorado Springs, CO 80903 Fax: (719)630-0616
Publisher E-mail: usaba@usa.net

Magazine reporting on news and activities of the U.S. Association of Blind Athletes. **Freq:** Quarterly. **Key Personnel:** Carolina Bayon, Dir. of Communications, cbayon@iex.net; Charlie Huebner, Exec.Dir., chuebner@iex.net; Kim King, Dir. of Membership Srvcs., kking@iex.net; Mark Lucas, Asst. Exec. Dir. **Subscription Rates:** $30 individuals over 21 years old; $20 individuals under 21 years old; $10 volunteers. **Remarks:** Advertising not accepted. **Available Online. URL:** http://www.usaba.org. **Alt. Formats:** Audio tape. **Former name**: Vision.
Circ: Paid 3,000

4297 Journal of Regional Criticism
Arjuna Library Press
1025 Garner St., D, Space 18
Colorado Springs, CO 80905-1774

Scholarly publication covering Surrealism, mathematics, fine arts, and philosophy. **Founded:** 1979. **Freq:** Irregular. **Trim Size:** 8 1/2 x 11. **Key Personnel:** Prof. Joseph A. Uphoff, Jr., Director. **Remarks:** Accepts advertising.
Ad Rates: BW: $.10 **Circ:** (Not Reported)

4298 Juco Review
National Junior College Athletic Association
PO Box 7305 Phone: (719)590-9788
Colorado Springs, CO 80933-7305 Fax: (719)590-7324
Publisher E-mail: njcaa@ix.netcom,com

Sports and games magazine. **Founded:** Sept. 1954. **Freq:** 9/year. **Print Method:** Offset. **Trim Size:** 8 1/2 x 11. **Cols./Page:** 2. **Col. Width:** 42 nonpareils. **Col. Depth:** 140 agate lines. **Key Personnel:** George E. Killian, Editor/Administration. **ISSN:** 0047-2956. **Subscription Rates:** $25 individuals. **Remarks:** Accepts advertising.
Ad Rates: BW: $200 **Circ:** Paid 3,650
Non-paid 200

4299 Mountaineer
Gowdy Printcraft Press, Inc.
22 N. Sierra Madre Ave. Phone: (719)634-1593
PO Box 789 Fax: (719)632-0762
Colorado Springs, CO 80901-0789
Publisher E-mail: gowdyprint@aol.com

Military tabloid for personnel of Fort Carson. **Founded:** 1941. **Freq:** Weekly (Fri.). **Print Method:** Offset. Accepts mats. **Trim Size:** 11 1/4 x 17 1/4. **Cols./Page:** 6. **Col. Width:** 1 5/8 inches. **Col. Depth:** 16 inches. **Key Personnel:** Rick Emert, Editor; John Bernheim, Publisher; Phyllis Allen, Advertising Mgr. **Subscription Rates:** $45 individuals. **Remarks:** Accepts advertising.
Ad Rates: GLR: $0.75 **Circ:** Free ‡15,000
BW: $1,008
4C: $1,368
PCI: $10.50

4300 The Numismatist
American Numismatic Association
818 N. Cascade Ave. Phone: (719)632-2646
Colorado Springs, CO 80903-3279 Fax: (719)634-4085
Publisher E-mail: anaedi@money.org

Magazine for collectors of coins, medals, tokens, and paper money. **Subtitle:** For Collectors of Coins, Medals, Tokens and Paper Money. **Founded:** 1888. **Freq:** Monthly. **Print Method:** Offset. **Trim Size:** 7 3/8 x 9 1/4. **Cols./Page:** 3. **Col. Width:** 12 picas. **Col. Depth:** 46.5 picas. **Key Personnel:** Barbara Gregory, Editor and Publisher, anaedi@money.org; Rudy Bahr, Marketing and Advertising Dir. **ISSN:** 0029-6090. **Subscription Rates:** $31 individuals; $5 single issue. **Remarks:** Accepts advertising.
Ad Rates: BW: $456 **Circ:** Controlled 27,300

4301 The Olympian
U.S. Olympic Committee
One Olympic Plaza Phone: (719)578-4529
Colorado Springs, CO 80909 Fax: (719)578-4677

Magazine reporting the activities of the U.S. Olympic Committee. **Founded:** 1974. **Freq:** Bimonthly. **Print Method:** Web. **Trim Size:** 8 3/8 x 10 7/8. **Cols./Page:** 3. **Col. Width:** 11 picas. **Col. Depth:** 54 picas. **Key Personnel:** Bob Condron, Editor; H.O. Zimman, Publisher, phone (781)598-9230, fax (781)599-4018; David Zimman, Advertising Mgr. **ISSN:** 0094-9787. **Subscription Rates:** $19.98 individuals. **Remarks:** Accepts advertising. **URL:** http://www.olympic-usa.org; olympian. magazine@usoc.org.
Ad Rates: BW: $3,300 **Circ:** 125,000
4C: $4,800

4302 Physician Magazine
Focus on the Family
8605 Explorer Dr. Phone: (719)531-3400
Colorado Springs, CO 80920-1051 Fax: (719)548-5860
Free: (800)232-6459
Publisher E-mail: tifeditor@fotf.org

Magazine for medical professionals addressing personal and family growth, public policy and community involvement, patient care and research. **Subtitle:** A Publication of Focus on the Family. **Founded:** 1989. **Freq:** Bimonthly. **Print Method:** Offset. **Trim Size:** 8 1/2 x 11. **Key Personnel:** Susan Stevens, Editor, phone (719)548-5891, stevensm@macmail.fotf.org. **ISSN:** 1084-6905. **Subscription Rates:** Free to physicians. **Remarks:** Advertising not accepted. **Online:** America Online, Inc. **Formerly**: Focus on the Family Physician (1991).
Circ: ‡71,000

4303 Pikes Peak Journal
Pikes Peak Journal, Inc.
2113 W. Colorado Avenue Phone: (719)578-3085
Colorado Springs, CO 80904
Community newspaper (tabloid). **Founded:** May 24, 1882. **Freq:** Weekly (Fri.). **Print Method:** Offset. **Trim Size:** 11 x 17. **Cols./Page:** 5. **Col. Width:** 11 picas. **Col. Depth:** 15 inches. **Key Personnel:** Gail M. Bordeu, General Mgr.; Larry Ferguson, Managing Editor. **USPS:** 432-540. **Subscription Rates:** $15 individuals; $22 out of state. **Remarks:** Accepts advertising.
Ad Rates: GLR: $.58 **Circ:** Paid ‡1,600
BW: $540 Free ‡400
PCI: $4.30

4304 Prorodeo Sports News
Professional Rodeo Cowboys Association, Inc.
101 Prorodeo Dr. Phone: (719)593-8840
Colorado Springs, CO 80919-2301 Fax: (719)548-4889
Professional rodeo magazine. **Founded:** 1952. **Freq:** Biweekly. **Print Method:** Offset. **Trim Size:** 11 3/8 x 14 3/4. **Cols./Page:** 4. **Col. Width:** 2 3/8 inches. **Col. Depth:** 13 1/2 inches. **Key Personnel:** Paul Asay, Editor, pasay@prorodeo.com; D.D. DeLeo, Advertising Mgr. **ISSN:** 0161-5815. **Subscription Rates:** $36 individuals. **Remarks:** Accepts advertising. **URL:** http://www.prorodeo.com.
Ad Rates: BW: $860 **Circ:** ‡37,972
4C: $1,265
SAU: $17
PCI: $20

4305 RACQUETBALL Magazine
United States Racquetball Association
1685 West Uintah Phone: (719)635-5396
Colorado Springs, CO 80904-2921 Fax: (719)635-0685
Publication E-mail: rbzine@webaccess.net

The official publication of the United States Raquetball Association. **Founded:** Sept. 1, 1990. **Freq:** Bimonthly. **Trim Size:** 8 3/8 x 10 7/8. **Key Personnel:** Linda Mojer, Editor; Luke St. Onge, Publisher, usraadm@webaccess.net; Kevin Vicroy, Production Mgr., usrapr@webaccess.net. **ISSN:** 1060-877X. **Subscription Rates:** $15. $4.00 single issue. **Remarks:** Accepts advertising. **Available Online. URL:** http://www.racqmag.com.
Ad Rates: BW: $1,965 **Circ:** Paid 40,000
4C: $2,365
PCI: $80

4306 Space Observer
Gowdy Printcraft Press, Inc.
22 N. Sierra Madre Ave. Phone: (719)634-1593
PO Box 789 Fax: (719)632-0762
Colorado Springs, CO 80901-0789
Publisher E-mail: gowdyprint@aol.com

Military newspaper (tabloid) for personnel at Peterson Air Force Base, NORAD, Space Command, Falcon A.F.B., and the Canadian Defense Forces. **Founded:** June 1954. **Freq:** Weekly (Thurs.). **Print Method:** Web offset. **Trim Size:** 11 1/4 x 17 1/4. **Cols./Page:** 6. **Col. Width:** 1 5/8 inches. **Col. Depth:** 16 inches. **Key Personnel:** Kathy Buck, Editor; Fred Bernheim, Publisher; Michael Murt, Advertising Mgr. **Subscription Rates:** $45 individuals. **Remarks:** Accepts advertising.
Ad Rates: GLR: $0.68 **Circ:** Free ‡7,500
BW: $916
4C: $1,272
PCI: $9.55

4307 Teachers in Focus Magazine
Focus on the Family
8605 Explorer Dr. Phone: (719)531-3400
Colorado Springs, CO 80920-1051 Fax: (719)548-5860
Free: (800)232-6459
Publisher E-mail: tifeditor@fotf.org

Magazine for educators. **Founded:** 1992. **Freq:** 9/year. **Trim Size:** 8 x 10 3/4. **Cols./Page:** 2. **Col. Width:** 2 3/4 inches. **Col. Depth:** 9 1/2 inches. **Key Personnel:** Mark Hartwig, Editor, phone (719)548-5855, hartwimd@fotf.org. **ISSN:** 1065-5182. **Subscription Rates:** $20; $2.25 single issue. **Remarks:** Advertising not accepted. **Online:** America Online, Inc. **URL:** http://www.family.org/cforum/teachersmag.
Circ: 30,000

4308 Today's Christian Doctor
Christian Medical & Dental Society.
505 Baptist Rd. Phone: (719)481-8560
Colorado Springs, CO 80921 Fax: (719)481-8560

Medical journal. **Freq:** Quarterly. **Key Personnel:** David Biebel, Editor, davebiebel@aol.com; Patti Kowalchuk, Classified Adv. Sales; Rhonda Bauer, Display Adv. Sales. **ISSN:** 0009-546X. **Remarks:** Accepts advertising. **URL:** http://www.cmds.org. **Former name**: Christian Medical & Dental Society Journal.
Circ: (Not Reported)

4309 USA Hockey InLine Magazine
USA Hockey
1775 Bob Johnson Rd. Phone: (719)576-8724
Colorado Springs, CO 80906-4090 Fax: (719)538-1160
Free: (800)566-3288
Publisher E-mail: usah@usahockey.org

Magazine for inline hockey players, coaches, officials, and industry representatives offering tips on techniques, calendars of tournaments and special events, news of new products and services, and personality profiles. **Founded:** May 1995. **Freq:** Bimonthly. **Subscription Rates:** $10 members. **Remarks:** Advertising accepted; rates available upon request.
Circ: Paid 50,000

4310 USA Table Tennis Magazine
USA Table Tennis (USATT)
One Olympic Plaza Phone: (719)578-4583
Colorado Springs, CO 80909 Fax: (719)632-6071
Free: (800)326-8788
Publication E-mail: usatt2@iex.net
Publisher E-mail: usatt@iex.net

Magazine covering table tennis. **Founded:** 1933. **Freq:** Bimonthly. **Print Method:** Offset. **Trim Size:** 11 x 14 1/2. **Cols./Page:** 4. **Col. Width:** 22 nonpareils. **Col. Depth:** 192 agate lines. **Key Personnel:** Kevin Carlon, Exec. Dir. **ISSN:** 1089-1870. **Subscription Rates:** $17 individuals; $4 single issue. **Remarks:** Accepts advertising. **Formerly:** Table Tennis Topics; Spin; Table Tennis Today.
Ad Rates: BW: $450 **Circ:** Paid 7,000
4C: $930 Non-paid 800

4311 Western Horseman
Western Horseman, Inc.
PO Box 7980 Phone: (719)633-5524
Colorado Springs, CO 80933 Fax: (719)633-1392
Free: (800)874-6774

Magazine covering forms of horsemanship and all breeds of horses; emphasizing western stock horses and western lifestyle. **Founded:** Jan. 1936. **Freq:** Monthly. **Print Method:** Offset. **Trim Size:** 8 x 10 3/4. **Cols./Page:** 3. **Col. Width:** 26 nonpareils. **Col. Depth:** 96 agate lines. **Key Personnel:** Pat Close, Editor; Randy Witte, Publisher; Corliss Palmer, Advertising Dir. **ISSN:** 0043-3837. **Subscription Rates:** $20 individuals; $27 other countries; $2.95 single issue. **Remarks:** Accepts advertising.
Ad Rates: GLR: $3.30 **Circ:** Paid ★225,648
BW: $3,440
4C: $6,110
PCI: $190

4312 Colorado Springs Cablevision
213 N. Union Blvd. Phone: (719)457-4501
Colorado Springs, CO 80909-5705 Fax: (719)457-4503

Owner: Century Communications, 50 Locust Ave, New Canaan, CT 06840, (203)972-2000. **Founded:** 1967. **Key Personnel:** Dave Johnson, General Mgr., phone (719)457-4505; Jim Vack, Mktg. Mgr.; Jim Garcia, Tech. Oper. Mgr., phone (719)635-7873. **Cities Served:** subscribing households 85,000; 60 channels; 1 community access channel; 30 hours per week community access programming.

4313 KAFA-FM - 104.3
PO Box 6066 Phone: (719)333-5233
USAFA Fax: (719)333-6376
Colorado Springs, CO 80841

Format: Alternative/New Music/Progressive. **ADI:** Colorado Springs-Pueblo, CO. **Key Personnel:** Bill Scharton, Station Mgr. **Ad Rates:** Noncommercial.

4314 KCMN-AM - 1530
5050 Edison, Suite 218 Phone: (719)570-1530
Colorado Springs, CO 80915 Fax: (719)570-1007
E-mail: kbagdasar@aol.com

Format: Big Band/Nostalgia. **Networks:** CNN Radio; Westwood One Radio. **Founded:** 1963. **Operating Hours:** Sunrise-sunset. **ADI:** Colorado Springs-Pueblo, CO. **Key Personnel:** Chip Lusko, President, elway@nmia.com; Kent Bagdasar, Vice President, kbagdasar@aol.com; Pam Adams, General Mgr.; Tron Simpson, Operations Mgr., tronson@aol.com. **Wattage:** 3,000. **Ad Rates:** $14-25 for 30 seconds; $17-30 for 60 seconds. **URL:** http://www.netprobe.net/kcmn.

4315 KEPC-FM - 89.7
5675 S. Academy Blvd. Phone: (719)540-7489
Colorado Springs, CO 80904 Fax: (719)540-7487
E-mail: kepc@ppcc.colorado.edu

Format: Alternative/New Music/Progressive. **Networks:** Business Radio. **Owner:** Pikes Peak Community College, at above address. **Founded:** 1974. **Operating Hours:** Continuous. **ADI:** Colorado Springs-Pueblo, CO. **Key Personnel:** Kurt Grow, STA/Product. **Wattage:** 7880. **Ad Rates:** Noncommercial. **URL:** http://www.ppcc.cccoes.edu/dept/kepc/index.htm.

4316 KGFT-FM - 100.7
6760 Corporate Dr., Ste. 340 Phone: (719)531-5438
Colorado Springs, CO 80919 Fax: (719)531-5588

Format: Contemporary Hit Radio (CHR). **Networks:** ABC. **Founded:** 1986. **Formerly:** KATM-FM (1992). **Operating Hours:** Continuous; 2% network, 98% local. **ADI:** Colorado Springs-Pueblo, CO. **Key Personnel:** Tricia York, General Mgr.; Mark Blake, Program Dir.; Jennifer Bell, Contact; Roy Reeves, Promotions Mgr.; Jerry Cobb, Contact; Donna Huddleston, Contact. **Wattage:** 17,900. **Ad Rates:** $15-35 per unit.

4317 KILO-FM - 94.3
Box 2080 Phone: (719)634-4896
Colorado Springs, CO 80901 Fax: (719)634-5837

Format: Album-Oriented Rock (AOR). **Owner:** Bahakel Communications, at above address. **Founded:** 1966. **Operating Hours:** Continuous. **ADI:** Colorado Springs-Pueblo, CO. **Key Personnel:** Lou Mellini, General Mgr.; Pete Tonsits, General Sales Mgr.; Rich Hawk, Program Dir.; Don Jantzen, Music Dir.; Laura Roberts, Business Mgr.; Cindy Roadcap, Promotions Dir. **Wattage:** 83,000. **Ad Rates:** $5-70 per unit. **URL:** http://www.kilo943.com; http://www.kilob943.com.

4318 KKCS-AM - 1460
5145 Centennial Blvd., No. 200 Phone: (719)594-9000
Colorado Springs, CO 80919-4427 Fax: (719)594-9006

Format: Talk. **Founded:** 1956. **Operating Hours:** Continuous. **ADI:** Colorado Springs-Pueblo, CO. **Key Personnel:** Robert Gourley, General Mgr.; Bob Baronski, Sales Mgr.; Mike James, Program Dir.; Brian Leifker, News Dir.; Carla Cary, Promotions Dir. **Wattage:** 5000. **Ad Rates:** Advertising accepted; rates available upon request.

4319 KKCS-FM - 101.9
PO Box 39102 Phone: (719)594-9000
Colorado Springs, CO 80949 Fax: (719)594-9006

Format: Contemporary Country. **Founded:** 1967. **Operating Hours:** Continuous. **ADI:** Colorado Springs-Pueblo, CO. **Key Personnel:** Robert Gourley, General Mgr.; Bob Boronski, Sales Mgr.; Mike James, Program Dir.; Kayten Lee, News Dir.; Bobby Hiatt, Music Dir.; Carla Arnold, Promotions Dir. **Wattage:** 79,000.

4320 KKFM-FM - 98.1
6605 Corporate Dr., Ste. 130
Colorado Springs, CO 80919-1977

Format: Classic Rock. **Networks:** ABC. **Owner:** Citadel Communications Corp., at above address. **Founded:** 1958. **ADI:** Colorado Springs-Pueblo, CO. **Key Personnel:** Larry Wilson, President; Bob Proffitt, General Mgr. **Wattage:** 72,000.

4321 KKLI-FM - 106.3
6805 Corporate Dr., No. 130 Phone: (719)593-2700
Colorado Springs, CO 80919 Fax: (719)593-2727
E-mail: kkli@kkli.com

Format: Adult Contemporary. **Networks:** Independent. **Owner:** Citadel Communications, at above address. **Founded:** 1987. **Formerly:** KKQX-FM (1988). **Operating Hours:** Continuous. **ADI:** Colorado Springs-Pueblo, CO. **Key Personnel:** Brenda Goodrich, General Mgr., phone (719)593-2700, gm@kkli.com; Steve Larson, Program Dir., phone (719)593-2713, steve@kkli.com; Bill Bergenr, Sales Mgr., phone (719)593-2712, bill@kkli.com; Kevin Tanner, News Dir., kevin@kkli.com; Tori Martinez, Promotions Dir., phone (719)593-2682, tori@kkli.com; Cindy Dye, Office Mgr., phone (719)593-2761, cindy@kkli.com. **Wattage:** 50,000 ERP. **Ad Rates:** Advertising accepted; rates available upon request. **URL:** http://www.kkli.com.

4322 KKMG-FM - 98.9
6805 Corporate Dr., Ste. 130
Colorado Springs, CO 80919-1977

Format: Contemporary Hit Radio (CHR); Urban Contemporary. **Networks:** Independent. **Operating Hours:** Continuous. **ADI:** Colorado Springs-Pueblo, CO. **Key Personnel:** Rod Bogren, General Mgr.; Cathy Ehringer, General Sales Mgr.; Scooter "B", Program Dir.; Tina Blake, News Dir.; Brian Moore, Contact. **Wattage:** 100,000. **Ad Rates:** $36-50 per unit.

4323 KKTV-TV - 11
3100 N. Nevada Ave. Phone: (719)634-2844
Box 2110 Fax: (719)634-3741
Colorado Springs, CO 80907

Format: Commercial TV. **Networks:** CBS. **Founded:** 1952. **Operating Hours:** 5:30 a.m.-2 a.m. **ADI:** Colorado Springs-Pueblo, CO. **Key Personnel:** George Sanchez, Contact; Charlie Hogetvedt, General Mgr., fax (719)632-0808, chogetvedt@kktviinews.com. **Ad Rates:** $20-600 per unit. **URL:** http://www.kktv.com.

4324 KRCC-FM - 91.5
912 N. Weber St. Phone: (719)473-4801
Colorado Springs, CO 80903 Fax: (719)493-7863
E-mail: krcc@cc.colorado.edu

Format: News. **Networks:** National Public Radio (NPR). **Owner:** Colorado College, 14 E. Cache La Poudre St., Colorado Springs, CO 80903, (719)389-6000. **Founded:** 1951. **Operating Hours:** Continuous; 25% network, 75% local. **ADI:** Colorado Springs-Pueblo, CO. **Key Personnel:** Mario Valdes, Station Mgr., mvaldes@cc.colorado.edu; Sean Anglum, Development Dir., sanglum@cc.colorado.edu; Craig Koehn, Operations Mgr. **Wattage:** 2100. **URL:** http://www.krcc.org.

4325 KRDO-AM - 1240
PO Box 1457 Phone: (719)632-1515
Colorado Springs, CO 80901-1457 Fax: (719)635-8455

Format: Talk; Sports. **Networks:** ABC. **Owner:** Harry Hoth, at above address, (719)575-6301, Fax: (719)475-0729. **Founded:** 1947. **Operating Hours:** Continuous; 88% network,12% local. **ADI:** Colorado Springs-Pueblo, CO. **Key Personnel:** Patti L. Hoth, President, phone (719)575-6238, fax (719)579-6928; Mark Warren, Sales Mgr., phone (719)575-6289, fax (719)635-8455; Harry Hoth, CEO, phone (719)575-6301, fax (719)475-0729; Neil Klockziem, General Mgr., phone (719)575-6234, fax (719)635-8455; Baaron Pittenger, News Dir., phone (719)575-6203, fax (719)475-0815; Mike Lewis, Program Dir., phone (719)575-6245, fax (719)635-8455. **Wattage:** 1000. **Ad Rates:** $8-17 per unit. Combined advertising rates available with KRDO-FM, KSKX-FM.

4326 KRDO-FM - 95.1
PO Box 1457 Phone: (719)632-1515
Colorado Springs, CO 80901-1457 Fax: (719)635-8455

Format: Adult Contemporary. **Owner:** Harry Hoth, at above address. **Founded:** 1969. **Operating Hours:** Continuous; 100% local. **ADI:** Colorado Springs-Pueblo, CO. **Key Personnel:** Patti Hoth, President; Mark Warren, Sales Mgr.; Harry Hoth, CEO; Neil Klockziem, General Mgr.; Mike Lewis, Program Dir. **Wattage:** 96,000.

4327 KRDO-TV - 13
399 S. 8th St. Phone: (719)632-1515
PO Box 1457 Fax: (719)520-9374
Colorado Springs, CO 80905

Format: Commercial TV. **Networks:** ABC. **Owner:** Pike's Peak Broadcasting Co., at above address. **Founded:** 1953. **Operating Hours:** 18 hrs. Daily. **ADI:** Colorado Springs-Pueblo, CO. **Key Personnel:** Neil Klocksiem, General Mgr.; Kristen Reed, General Sales Mgr.; Matthew Walton, National Sales Mgr.; Lori Barber, Operations Mgr.; Tom Grinewich, Promotions Mgr.; Dave Rose, News Dir.; Charles Upton, Chief Engineer; Patti L. Hoth, President. **Wattage:** 282Kw. Visual E.R.P. DA.

4328 KRMH-AM - 1230
121 Alsace Way
Colorado Springs, CO 80906-3206

Format: Country. **Networks:** Unistar. **Owner:** Phoenix Broadcasting, at above address. **Founded:** 1960. **ADI:** Colorado Springs-Pueblo, CO. **Key Personnel:** Mike Lowery, Contact; Mike Garcia, Sports Dir. **Wattage:** 1000.

4329 KRMH-FM - 93.5
121 Alsace Way Phone: (719)486-3600
Colorado Springs, CO 80906-3206

Format: Adult Contemporary. **Owner:** Phoenix Broadcasting, at above address. **Founded:** 1985. **ADI:** Colorado Springs-Pueblo, CO. **Key Personnel:** Mike Lowery, Contact; Mike Garcia, Sports Dir. **Wattage:** 3000.

4330 KSKX-FM - 105.5
PO Box 1055 Phone: (719)578-1055
Colorado Springs, CO 80901 Fax: (719)520-9374

Format: Jazz. **Networks:** ABC. **Founded:** 1973. **Formerly:** KWYD-FM (Mar. 1, 1989); KHII-FM. **Operating Hours:** Continuous. **ADI:** Colorado Springs-Pueblo, CO. **Key Personnel:** Neil O. Klockziem, Station Mgr.; Michael Lewis, Program Dir. **Wattage:** 490. **Ad Rates:** Advertising accepted; rates available upon request.

4331 KSPZ-FM - 92.9
2864 S. Circle Dr., Ste. 150 Phone: (719)540-9200
Colorado Springs, CO 80906 Fax: (719)579-0882
Free: (800)522-0929
E-mail: oldies929@aol.com

Format: Oldies. **Owner:** Triathlon Broadcasting, at above address. **Founded:** 1960. **Operating Hours:** Continuous. **ADI:** Colorado Springs-Pueblo, CO. **Key Personnel:** Randy Hill, Gen. Mgr./Operations. **Wattage:** 76,000.

4332 KTLF-FM - 90.5
1665 Briargate Blvd., Ste. 100 Phone: (719)593-0600
Colorado Springs, CO 80920 Fax: (719)593-2399
Free: (800)428-1201
E-mail: ktlf@pcisys.net

Format: Religious. **Networks:** Moody Broadcasting. **Owner:** Education Communications of Colorado Springs, 1665 Briargate, Colorado Springs, CO 80920. **Founded:** 1989. **Operating Hours:** Continuous. **ADI:** Colorado Springs-Pueblo, CO. **Key Personnel:** Ronald Johnson, Contact; Larry Walters, General Mgr. **Local Programs:** *In Touch*, Larry Walters. **Wattage:** 50,000 ERP. **Ad Rates:** Noncommercial. **URL:** http://www.pcisys.net/~ktlf.

4333 KTWK-AM - 740
2864 S. Circle Dr., Ste. 150 Phone: (719)579-0880
Colorado Springs, CO 80906 Fax: (719)579-0884

Format: Big Band/Nostalgia. **Simulcasts:** KVOR-AM. **Owner:** Lakoduk Broadcasting Corp., at above address. **Founded:** 1955. **Formerly:** KSSS-AM. **ADI:** Colorado Springs-Pueblo, CO. **Key Personnel:** Greg Sher, Sales, phone (719)593-2767; Jim Arthur, Contact, phone (719)540-9200, fax (719)579-0882. **Wattage:** 3300 day; 1500 night. **Ad Rates:** $10-25 for 60 seconds.

4334 KVOR-AM - 1300
2864 S. Circle Dr., Ste. 150 Phone: (719)632-3536
Colorado Springs, CO 80906 Fax: (719)579-0882

Format: News; Talk. **Networks:** CBS; Mutual Broadcasting System. **Owner:** VOR/SPZ Inc., at above address. **Founded:** 1922. **Operating Hours:** Continuous. **ADI:** Colorado Springs-Pueblo, CO. **Key Personnel:** Jim Arthur, Dir. of Operations, phone (719)540-9200. **Local Programs:** *On the Carpet*, Jim Arthur. **Wattage:** 5000 day; 1000 night. **Ad Rates:** $50-75 for 60 seconds.

KVUU-FM - See Pueblo

4335 KWYD-AM - 1580
Box 5668 Phone: (719)392-4219
Colorado Springs, CO 80931

Format: Talk; Gospel; Religious. **Owner:** Patrick Communications II, at above address. **Founded:** 1988. **Formerly:** KPIK-AM (1988). **Operating Hours:** 13 hrs. Daily; 80% network, 20% local. **ADI:** Colorado Springs-Pueblo, CO. **Key Personnel:** Rick Martin, Station/Production Mgr.; John Boles, Public Service/News Dir.; Jody Ilett, Asst. Mgr. **Local Programs:** *Answer Line*, Gloria Frances, (719)392-4219; *PM Wynn Gospel Revue*, P. M. Wynn, (719)596-6002; *Public Pulse*, Jody Ilett, (719)392-4219. **Wattage:** 10,000. **Ad Rates:** $12-14 per unit.

4336 KXRM-TV - 21
560 Wooten Rd. Phone: (719)596-2100
PO Box 15789 Fax: (719)591-4180
Colorado Springs, CO 80935-5789

Format: Commercial TV. **Networks:** Fox. **Owner:** KXRM Partnership, at above address. **Founded:** 1985. **Operating Hours:** Continuous. **ADI:** Colorado Springs-Pueblo, CO. **Key Personnel:** Larry W. Douglas, General Mgr.; Tricia Lucero, Promotions Dir.; Kim Carlson, General Sales Mgr. **Local Programs:** *Fox 21 Sports Saturday*, Brian Jerman; *Village Voices*, Promise Lee. **Wattage:** 1,400,000. **Ad Rates:** $15-1,500 per unit. **URL:** www.kxrm21.com.

COPPER MOUNTAIN

4337 Copper Mountain Metropolitan District
513 Copper Rd. Phone: (970)968-2537
PO Box 3002
Copper Mountain, CO 80443

Founded: Nov. 1974. **Key Personnel:** Elizabeth Black, Manager; Sandy Summers, Chief Engineer. **Cities Served:** Copper Mountain, CO: subscribing households 880; 31 channels; 2 community access channels.

CORTEZ†, pop. 7,080.

Montezuma Co. (SW). 45 m W of Durango. Tourism. Manufactures match sticks. Oil wells. Pine timber. Agriculture. Fruit, dairy. Livestock.

4338 Montezuma Valley Journal
Cortez Newspapers Inc.
PO Box 0 Phone: (303)565-8527
Cortez, CO 81321 Fax: (303)565-8532

Newspaper with Report orientation. **Founded:** 1888. **Freq:** Semiweekly (Wed. and Fri.) Tuesday and Thursday. **Print Method:** Offset. **Cols./Page:** 6. **Col. Width:** 26 nonpareils. **Col. Depth:** 301 agate lines. **Key Personnel:** Jeanne Scrivner, Advertising Mgr.; Suzy Meyer, Editor; R.D. Brown, Publisher. **Subscription Rates:** $35 individuals. **Remarks:** Accepts advertising.
Ad Rates: GLR: $.40 **Circ:** ‡6,225
BW: $864.30
SAU: $7
PCI: $5.85

4339 Sentinel
Cortez Newspapers Inc.
PO Box 0 Phone: (303)565-8527
Cortez, CO 81321 Fax: (303)565-8532

Newspaper. **Founded:** 1928. **Freq:** Weekly (Sat.). **Print Method:** Offset. **Cols./Page:** 6. **Col. Width:** 26 nonpareils. **Col. Depth:** 301 agate lines. **Key Personnel:** R.D. Brown, Publisher; Jeanne Scrivner, Advertising Mgr.; Suzy Meyer, Editor. **Subscription Rates:** $35 individuals. **Remarks:** Accepts advertising.
Ad Rates: GLR: $.40 **Circ:** ‡6,200
BW: $864.30
4C: $1,224.30
SAU: $7
PCI: $5.85

4340 KISZ-FM - 97.9
Box 740 Phone: (303)565-3409
Cortez, CO 81321
E-mail: planet@cyberport.com

Format: Country. **Owner:** Roberts Radio, at above address, (505)327-4449, Fax: (505)327-5796. **Founded:** 1978. **Formerly:** KISS-FM (1994). **Operating Hours:** Continuous. **ADI:** Albuquerque (Santa Fe & Hobbs), NM. **Key Personnel:** Dave Schaeffer, Director; Diane Sanders, Traffic. **Local Programs:** *The Mark and Brian Radio Program* 6 - 10 a.m. Monday-Friday. **Wattage:** 100,000. **Ad Rates:** $12-22.50 for 30 seconds; $15-28 for 60 seconds. Combined advertising rates available with KRWN-FM; KENN-AM; KDGO-AM; KWXA-FM.

4341 KRTZ-FM - 98.7
2402 Hawkins St. Phone: (970)565-6565
Cortez, CO 81321 Fax: (970)565-8567
E-mail: libra@frontier.net

Format: Country. **Networks:** ABC. **Owner:** Cliff Gardiner, Rocky Mountain Radio Co., LLC, at above address, (970)949-3339. **Founded:** 1985. **Operating Hours:** Continuous; 99% network, 1% local. **Key Personnel:** Cliff Gardiner, Managing Partner; Lan DeGeneres, Sales Mgr.; D.C. Cavender, Program Dir.; Kelly Turner, News Dir./Operations Mgr.; Nihla McCabe, PSA Dir. **Wattage:** 27,000. **Ad Rates:** $6.90-13.20 for 30 seconds; $8.40-16 for 60 seconds.

4342 KSJD-FM - 91.5
33057 Hwy. 160 Phone: (303)565-8457
Box 970
Cortez, CO 81321

Format: Alternative/New Music/Progressive; Contemporary Hit Radio (CHR). **Networks:** National Public Radio (NPR); American Public Radio (APR). **Owner:** Basin Area Voc-Technical School, at above address, Fax: (303)565-8457. **Founded:** 1990. **Operating Hours:** 6 a.m.-midnight, Mon.-Fri. **Key Personnel:** Anthony Valdez, General Mgr. **Wattage:** 150.

4343 KVFC-AM - 740
PO Box 1299 Phone: (970)565-3409
Cortez, CO 81321 Fax: (970)565-8567
E-mail: londonbeat@hotmail.com

Format: Oldies; Sports; News. **Networks:** Westwood One Radio; CNN Radio. **Founded:** 1956. **Formerly:** KISZ-AM. **Operating Hours:** 5 a.m.-5 a.m., 85% network, 15% local. **ADI:** Albuquerque (Santa Fe & Hobbs), NM. **Key Personnel:** Lan Degeneres, General Mgr.; Lan DeGeneres, Sales Mgr.; Kelly Turner, News Dir.; Kelly Turner, Operations Mgr.; Nihla McCabe, PSA Director. **Wattage:** 1000. **Ad Rates:** $7.50-12 for 30 seconds.

CRAIG†, pop. 8,133.

Moffat Co. (NW). 213 m NW of Denver. Creamery. Ships livestock. Oil, gas wells. Stock, grain farms.

4344 Craig Daily Press
WorldWest Limited Liability Co.
466 Yampa Ave. Phone: (970)824-7031
Craig, CO 81625 Fax: (970)824-6810
Publication E-mail: dp_ edit@cmn.net

Community newspaper. **Founded:** 1904. **Freq:** Daily (eve.). **Print Method:** Offset. **Cols./Page:** 5. **Col. Width:** 24 nonpareils. **Col. Depth:** 224 agate lines. **Key Personnel:** Jim Files, Editor; Bill Muldoon, Publisher, bmuldoon@cmn.net. **ISSN:** 1440-6000. **Subscription Rates:** $72 individuals. **Remarks:** Accepts advertising. **Formerly:** Northwest Colorado Daily Press.
Ad Rates: BW: $720 **Circ:** Paid 2,971
4C: $960 Free 27
SAU: $5.50
PCI: $9

4345 KRAI-AM - 550
1111 W. Victory Way Phone: (970)824-6574
Craig, CO 81625 Fax: (970)826-4581
E-mail: 55country@krai.com

Format: Country. **Networks:** AP; CNN Radio. **Owner:** Wild West Radio Inc., at above address. **Founded:** 1948. **Operating Hours:** 5 a.m.-midnight. **ADI:** Denver (Steamboat Springs), CO. **Key Personnel:** Frank Hanel, General Mgr., frank@krai.com; Tammie Hanel, Station Mgr. **Wattage:** 5000. **Ad Rates:** $19.50-25.50 per unit.

4346 KRAI-FM - 93.7
1111 W. Victory Way Phone: (970)824-6574
PO Box 65 Fax: (970)879-3677
Craig, CO 81626-0065
E-mail: kraifm@krai.com

Format: Adult Contemporary. **Networks:** AP. **Owner:** Wild West Radio, Inc., at above address. **Founded:** 1976. **Operating Hours:** 5 a.m.-midnight. **ADI:** Denver (Steamboat Springs), CO. **Key Personnel:** Frank Hanel, General Mgr.; Rick Allen, Program Dir.; Tammie Hanel, Station Mgr. **Wattage:** 100,000. **Ad Rates:** $19.50-25.50 per unit.

CREEDE†, pop. 610.

Mineral Co. (SW). 21 m NW of South Fork. Residential. Mining.

4347 Mineral County Miner
SLV Publishing
PO Box 219 Phone: (719)658-2603
Creede, CO 81130
Community newspaper. **Founded:** Aug. 1975. **Freq:** Weekly (Thurs.). **Print Method:** Offset. **Trim Size:** 10 1/2 x 16. **Cols./Page:** 5. **Col. Width:** 2 inches. **Key Personnel:** Nate McMahon, Editor. **USPS:** 015-700. **Subscription Rates:** $25.95 individuals.
Ad Rates: BW: $504 **Circ:** Paid 956
SAU: $6.30 Free 15

CRESTED BUTTE, pop. 1,100.

Gunnison Co. (W). 28 m N of Gunnison. Western State College. Tourism. Recreation and ski area.

4348 Crested Butte Chronicle & Pilot
PO Box 369 Phone: (970)349-6114
Crested Butte, CO 81224 Fax: (970)349-6116
Publication E-mail: cbchronpilot@csn.net

Newspaper. **Founded:** 1963. **Freq:** Weekly (Fri.). **Print Method:** Offset. **Cols./Page:** 5. **Col. Width:** 12 picas. **Col. Depth:** 15 inches. **Key Personnel:** Mark Reaman, Editor; Roy Huffstetler, Advertising Mgr. **Subscription Rates:** $32 individuals; $40 out of country; $5 single issue. **Remarks:** Accepts advertising.
Ad Rates: PCI: $6 **Circ:** Paid ‡4,900
Free ‡40

4349 KBUT-FM - 90.3
Box 308 Phone: (303)349-5225
Crested Butte, CO 81224 Fax: (970)349-6440
E-mail: kbut@rmii.com

Format: Full Service. **Networks:** National Public Radio (NPR). **Founded:** 1986. **Operating Hours:** 6 a.m.-midnight. **Key Personnel:** Eileen Hughes, Program Dir.; Kim Carroll Bosler, General Mgr.; Kate Thomaidis, Underwriting Dir.; Mitzi Rapkin, News Reporter; Alex Fenlon, Music Dir. **Wattage:** 270.

CRESTONE

4350 Forefront
Spiritual Life Institute of America
PO Box 219 Phone: (719)256-4778
Crestone, CO 81131 Fax: (719)256-4719

Religious magazine. **Subtitle:** The Desert and the City. **Founded:** 1962. **Freq:** Quarterly. **Print Method:** Offset. **Trim Size:** 8 1/2 x 11. **Cols./Page:** 2 and 3. **Col. Width:** 3 7/8 inches. **Col. Depth:** 9 inches. **Key Personnel:** Connie Bielecki, Circulation Mgr.; David Denny, Editor. **ISSN:** 1076-304X. **Subscription Rates:** $16 individuals; $20 other countries; $4.50 single issue. **Remarks:** Advertising not accepted. **Formerly:** Desert Call.
Circ: Paid 2,200
Non-paid 200

CRIPPLE CREEK†, pop. 655.

Teller Co. (C). 20 m SW of Colorado Springs. Residential.

4351 The Gold Rush
Westward Communications/Douglas County Publishing
PO Box 839
Cripple Creek, CO 80813

Community newspaper (tabloid). **Founded:** 1891. **Freq:** Weekly (Wed.). **Print Method:** Offset. **Cols./Page:** 5. **Col. Width:** 11 1/2 picas. **Col. Depth:** 15 inches. **Key Personnel:** Bruce Schlabaugh, Publisher; Larry Ferguson, Editor; Steph Hilliard, Editor. **Subscription Rates:** $24 individuals; $40 out of area. **Remarks:** Accepts advertising. **Formerly:** The Teller County Times. **Additional Contact Info: Mailing Address:** 319 Perry St., PO Box 1270, Castle Rock, CO 80104, (719)687-3006, fax: (719)687-3009.
Ad Rates: BW: $256 **Circ:** ‡1,700
4C: $485
PCI: $4.95

DEER TRAIL, pop. 463.

Arapahoe Co. (NEC). 52 m E of Denver. Stock, grain farms. Wheat, beans, corn.

4352 Tri-County Tribune
PO Box 220 Phone: (303)769-4646
Deer Trail, CO 80105 Fax: (303)769-4650

Newspaper. **Founded:** 1899. **Freq:** Weekly (Thurs.). **Print Method:** Offset. **Cols./Page:** 4. **Col. Width:** 21 3/5 nonpareils. **Col. Depth:** 10 inches. **Key Personnel:** Harry L. Venter, Publisher. **Subscription Rates:** $18 individuals. **Remarks:** Accepts advertising.
Ad Rates: GLR: $.15 **Circ:** ‡400
PCI: $3

DELTA†, pop. 4,000.

Delta Co. (W). 44 m SE of Grand Junction. Tannery; flour mills; cannery. Spruce, fir timber. Agriculture.

4353 Delta County Independent
Leader Publishing Co., Inc.
401 Meeker St. Phone: (970)874-4421
Delta, CO 81416-1918 Fax: (970)874-4424
Publication E-mail: randydci@dci-press.com

Local newspaper. **Founded:** 1883. **Freq:** Weekly (Wed.). **Print Method:** Offset. **Cols./Page:** 6. **Col. Width:** 12 picas. **Col. Depth:** 21 inches. **Key Personnel:** Pat Sunderland, Editor, editor@dci-press.com; Norman Sunderland, Publisher; Roxanne McCormick, Advertising Mgr., ads@dci-press.com. **USPS:** 152-700. **Subscription Rates:** $17 individuals; $24 out of state; $20 out of country. **Remarks:** Accepts advertising. **URL:** http://www.dci-press.com.
Ad Rates: SAU: $4.95 **Circ:** 7,300
PCI: $4.95

DENVER†, pop. 491,396.

Denver Co. (NC). The State Capital. 112 m N of Pueblo. University of Denver; law, theology, vocational and other colleges and private schools. U. S. Mint. Meat packing; oil refineries; brewery; coffee roasters; vegetable and fruit canneries; food processing; printing and publishing houses. Uranium market center. Mining and farming machinery, rubber goods, fabricated metal, chemical and allied stone and clay products, western clothing, transportation equipment, scientific instruments, feed, flour, luggage manufactured.

4354 Africa Today
Lynne Rienner Publishers
University of Denver Phone: (303)871-3678
Graduate School of International Studies Fax: (303)871-2456
2201 S. Gaylord St.
Denver, CO 80208
Publication E-mail: afrtoday@du.edu

Journal on political, social, and economic conditions in Africa. **Founded:** Mar. 1954. **Freq:** Quarterly. **Print Method:** Offset. **Trim Size:** 6 x 9. **Cols./Page:** 1. **Col. Width:** 66 nonpareils. **Col. Depth:** 119 agate lines. **Key Personnel:** Angelique Haugerud, Editor, ahauger@du.edu; Michele S. Pietowski, Assoc. Editor. **ISSN:** 0001-9887. **Subscription Rates:** $28 individuals; $64 institutions. **Remarks:** Accepts advertising. **Alt. Formats:** Microform.
Ad Rates: BW: $175 **Circ:** Paid 1,800
Controlled 66

4355 AORN Journal
Association of Operating Room Nurses, Inc.
2170 S. Parker Rd., Ste. 300 Phone: (303)755-6300
Denver, CO 80231-5711 Fax: (303)750-3441
Free: (800)755-AORN
Publication E-mail: lcastle@aorn.org

Journal for perioperative nurses. **Founded:** 1960. **Freq:** Monthly. **Print Method:** Offset. **Trim Size:** 6 7/8 x 10. **Cols./Page:** 2. **Col. Width:** 32 nonpareils. **Col. Depth:** 112 agate lines. **Key Personnel:** Brenda Dawes, Editor, bs6d@aol.com. **ISSN:** 0001-2092. **Subscription Rates:** $80 individuals. **Remarks:** Accepts advertising. **URL:** http://www.aorn.org.
Ad Rates: GLR: $20 **Circ:** Paid 51,037
BW: $1,430 Controlled 155
4C: $2,195

Arizona Beverage Analyst - See Phoenix, Arizona

4356 Arthritis and Rheumatism
4200 E. 9th Ave., MS Rm. 2834 Phone: (303)315-6655
Box B-117 Fax: (303)315-7593
Denver, CO 80262
Publication E-mail: ginny.frazer@uchsc.edu

Medical journal covering current trends in treatment and investigation of arthritis. Peer-reviewed. **Subtitle:** The Official Journal of the American College of Rheumatology. **Founded:** 1958. **Freq:** Monthly. **Print Method:** Web offset. **Trim Size:** 8 1/2 x 11. **Cols./Page:** 2. **Col. Width:** 20 picas. **Col. Depth:** 51 picas. **Key Personnel:** Jane Diamond, Managing Editor, jdiamond@rheumatology.org; Michael Fiorillo, Advertising Sales; William P. Arend, MD, Editor, william.arend@uchsc.edu. **ISSN:** 0004-3591. **Subscription Rates:** $135 individuals; $65 students; $210 institutions. **Remarks:** Accepts advertising.
Ad Rates: BW: $1,690 **Circ:** ‡9,000

4357 The Bagpipe
American Highland Cattle Association
200 Livestock Exchange Bldg. Phone: (303)292-9102
4701 Marion St. Fax: (303)292-9171
Denver, CO 80216
Publisher E-mail: ahca@envisionet.net

Association publication about Highland cattle, marketing, management, promotion , national and regional news. **Founded:** 1990. **Freq:** Quarterly. **Key Personnel:** Chris Hawkins, Contact. **ISSN:** 1088-4122. **Subscription Rates:** $16 individuals. **Remarks:** Accepts advertising.
Circ: (Not Reported)

4358 Bible Advocate
Church of God (Seventh Day)
PO Box 33677 Phone: (303)452-7973
Denver, CO 80233-0677 Fax: (303)452-0657
Publication E-mail: cofgsd@denver.net

Bible-teaching magazine encouraging Christian growth and offering guidance on current issues. **Founded:** Aug. 10, 1863. **Freq:** Monthly. **Print Method:** Offset. **Trim Size:** 83/8 x 10 7/8. **Cols./Page:** 3. **Col. Width:** 26 nonpareils. **Col. Depth:** 132 agate lines. **Key Personnel:** Calvin Burrell, Editor; Sherri Langton, Assistant Editor. **ISSN:** 0746-0104. **Subscription Rates:** Free upon request. **Remarks:** Advertising not accepted. **URL:** http://www.denver.net/~baonline.
Circ: Controlled ‡12,200

4359 Bison World
National Bison Association
4701 Marion, Ste. 100 Phone: (303)292-2833
Denver, CO 80216 Fax: (303)292-2564
Publisher E-mail: info@nbabison.org

Magazine serving ranchers, farmers, and others interested in the American buffalo/bison. **Founded:** Sept. 1972. **Freq:** Quarterly. **Print Method:** Offset. **Trim Size:** 8 1/2 x 11. **Cols./Page:** 3. **Col. Width:** 27 nonpareils. **Col. Depth:** 136 agate lines. **Key Personnel:** Samuel W. Albrecht, Editor. **ISSN:** 1056-2400. **Subscription Rates:** members. **Remarks:** Accepts advertising. **URL:** http://www.nbabison.org.
Ad Rates: GLR: $.25 **Circ:** ‡2,300
BW: $520
4C: $595

4360 The Bloomsbury Review
PO Box 8928 Phone: (303)863-0406
Denver, CO 80201 Fax: (303)863-0408
Free: (800)283-3338
Publication E-mail: BloomsB@aol.com

Tabloid of book reviews, interviews with writers and poets, book-related essays, and original poetry. **Subtitle:** A Book Magazine. **Founded:** Dec. 1980. **Freq:** 6/year. **Print Method:** Offset. **Trim Size:** 11 1/4 x 15 1/4. **Cols./Page:** 4. **Col. Width:** 14 picas. **Col. Depth:** 168 agate lines. **Key Personnel:** Thomas M. Auer, Publisher. **ISSN:** 0276-1564. **Subscription Rates:** $16 individuals for 6 issues; $3 single issue. **Remarks:** Accepts advertising.
Ad Rates: BW: $3300 **Circ:** Paid ‡10,000
4C: $3,800 Controlled ‡40,000

4361 CED (Communications Engineering & Design)
600 S. Cherry St., No. 400 Phone: (303)393-7449
Denver, CO 80246 Fax: (303)393-6654
Free: (800)888-4824

Technical/business publication serving the engineering/management community within broadband/cable TV networks, telecommunications carriers, date and interactive networks. **Subtitle:** The Premier Magazine of Broadband Communications. **Founded:** 1975. **Freq:** Monthly. **Print Method:** Offset. **Trim Size:** 8 1/4 x 10 3/4. **Cols./Page:** 3. **Col. Width:** 25 nonpareils. **Col. Depth:** 136 agate lines. **Key Personnel:** Roger Brown, Editor, rbrown@cahners.com; Rob Stuehrk, Publisher, rstuehrk@cahners.com. **ISSN:** 0191-5428. **Subscription Rates:** $54 individuals. **Remarks:** Accepts advertising. **Available Online. URL:** http://www.cedmagazine.com. **Alt. Formats:** Mailing labels.
Ad Rates: BW: $4,592 **Circ:** Non-paid ‡22,500
4C: $6,067
PCI: $70

4362 The CF Apartment Reporter
Clayton-Fillmore Ltd.
PO Box 480894 Phone: (303)663-0606
Denver, CO 80248 Fax: (303)663-1616

Contains research, data, analysis, and narrative about apartment markets nationwide. **Founded:** 1995. **Freq:** Bimonthly. **Key Personnel:** Howard Treibitz, Editor, ht@clayfil.com. **Subscription Rates:** $179. **Remarks:** Advertising not accepted.
Circ: (Not Reported)

4363 The Citizen
Colorado Association of Public Employees
1390 Logan St., Ste. 402 Phone: (303)832-1001
Denver, CO 80203 Fax: (303)832-1004
Free: (800)245-2273
Publisher E-mail: capeinfo@aol.com

State government labor association newspaper (tabloid). **Founded:** 1941. **Freq:** Monthly. **Print Method:** Webpress. **Trim Size:** 11 1/4 x 17. **Cols./Page:** 4. **Col. Width:** 28 nonpareils. **Col. Depth:** 203 agate lines. **Key Personnel:** Phil Christie, Editor. **USPS:** 113-880. **Subscription Rates:** $7.50 individuals; $4.20 Association members. **Remarks:** Accepts advertising.
Ad Rates: BW: $500 **Circ:** Paid 10,400
Free 600

4364 The Clarion
University of Denver
Student Media Board Phone: (303)871-3131
Driscoll University Center Fax: (303)871-2568
2055 East Evans
Denver, CO 80208
Publication E-mail: clarion@du.edu

Collegiate newspaper. **Founded:** 1895. **Freq:** Weekly. **Print Method:** Offset. **Cols./Page:** 4. **Col. Width:** 2 1/4 inches. **Col. Depth:** 16 inches. **Key Personnel:** Kriti Arellano, Editor-in-Chief, clarion@du.edu. **Remarks:** Accepts advertising. **Available Online.**
Ad Rates: GLR: $.41 **Circ:** Free ‡4,000
BW: $525
PCI: $7.50

4365 Colorado Beverage Analyst
Bell Publications
2403 Champa St. Phone: (303)296-1600
Denver, CO 80205-2621 Fax: (303)295-2159

Trade magazine for the liquor, wine, and beer industries. **Founded:** 1936. **Freq:** Monthly. **Print Method:** Offset. **Trim Size:** 8 3/8 x 10 7/8. **Cols./Page:** 3. **Col. Width:** 28 nonpareils. **Col. Depth:** 120 agate lines. **Key Personnel:** Lawrence Bell, Publisher. **ISSN:** 0010-1516. **Subscription Rates:** $16 individuals. **Remarks:** Accepts advertising.
Ad Rates: BW: $570 **Circ:** Paid ‡345
4C: $1,120 Controlled ‡1,743

4366 Colorado Country Life
Colorado Rural Electric Association
PO Box 11338 Phone: (303)455-4111
Denver, CO 80211 Fax: (303)455-4807

Association journal. **Founded:** 1952. **Freq:** Monthly. **Print Method:** Offset. **Trim Size:** 8 1/8 x 10 7/8. **Cols./Page:** 3. **Col. Width:** 2 3/8 inches. **Col. Depth:** 10 inches. **Key Personnel:** Frank McCrea, Editor and Publisher; Mona Neeley, Managing Editor. **ISSN:** 1090-2503. **Subscription Rates:**

$12. **Remarks:** Color advertising accepted; rates available upon request.
Ad Rates: GLR: $4.93 **Circ:** 140,000
BW: $2,070.60
4C: $2,670.60
PCI: $69.02

4367 Colorado Editor
Colorado Press Association
1336 Glenarm Pl. Phone: (303)571-5117
Denver, CO 80204 Fax: (303)571-1803

Regional newspaper on journalism. **Founded:** 1923. **Freq:** Monthly. **Print Method:** Offset. **Cols./Page:** 5. **Col. Width:** 12 picas. **Col. Depth:** 12 inches. **Key Personnel:** Sardi Austin, Editor/Administration, saaustin@ri.net; Ed Otte, Publisher, cotte@csn.net. **ISSN:** 0162-0010. **Subscription Rates:** $5 individuals. **Remarks:** Accepts advertising.
Ad Rates: GLR: $.86 **Circ:** ‡1,100
BW: $384
PCI: $12

4368 Colorado Episcopalian
Diocese of Colorado
1300 Washington St. Phone: (303)837-1173
Denver, CO 80203-2008 Fax: (303)837-1311
Publisher E-mail: colarado@colaradodiocese.org

Religious tabloid. **Founded:** 1939. **Freq:** 6/year. **Print Method:** Web offset. **Cols./Page:** 5. **Col. Width:** 11 picas. **Col. Depth:** 150 agate lines. **Key Personnel:** Tom Beckwith, Editor, tom_beckwith@ecunet.org. **ISSN:** 0883-6728. **Subscription Rates:** Free. **Remarks:** Advertising not accepted. **URL:** http://www.coloradodiocese.org/.
Circ: Non-paid ‡14,600

4369 Colorado Expression
New West Publishing Inc.
10200 E. Girard Bldg B. Ste. 222 Phone: (303)751-0696
Fax: (303)751-6524
Denver, CO 80231
Magazine on Coloradoans and their lifestyles. **Founded:** 1991. **Freq:** Quarterly. **Print Method:** Web offset. **Trim Size:** 8 1/4 x 10 7/8. **Key Personnel:** Terry Vitale, President; Jacki Haynes, Operations Dir. **Subscription Rates:** $12 individuals; $4 single issue. **Remarks:** Accepts advertising.
Ad Rates: BW: $3,360 **Circ:** Controlled ⊕**25,000**
4C: $4,032

4370 The Colorado Lawyer
Colorado Bar Association
1900 Grant St., No. 940 Phone: (303)860-1115
Denver, CO 80203 Fax: (303)861-5274

Professional journal covering law in Colorado. **Founded:** Nov. 1971. **Freq:** Monthly. **Print Method:** Offset. **Key Personnel:** Arlene Abady, Managing Editor; Suellen Palcapis, Advertising Rep. **Subscription Rates:** $85 individuals. **Remarks:** Accepts advertising. **URL:** http://www.cobar.org.
Ad Rates: BW: $715 **Circ:** (Not Reported)

4371 The Colorado Leader
3480 W. 1st Ave. Phone: (303)922-0589
Denver, CO 80219 Fax: (303)922-2106

Community newspaper. **Founded:** 1919. **Freq:** Weekly. **Print Method:** Offset. **Cols./Page:** 5. **Col. Width:** 22 nonpareils. **Col. Depth:** 217 agate lines. **Key Personnel:** James Eitzen, Editor and Publisher. **Subscription Rates:** $16 individuals. **Remarks:** Accepts advertising.
Ad Rates: GLR: $.57 **Circ:** ‡2,065
BW: $450
PCI: $5.80

4372 Colorado Legionnaire
The American Legion, Dept. of Colorado
3003 Tejon Phone: (303)477-1655
Denver, CO 80211-3928 Fax: (303)477-2950

Magazine for veterans. **Founded:** 1967. **Freq:** 10/year. **Print Method:** Offset. Uses mats. **Cols./Page:** 6. **Col. Width:** 20 nonpareils. **Col. Depth:** 217 agate lines. **Key Personnel:** Charles Pat Smith, Editor and Publisher. **Remarks:** Accepts advertising.
Ad Rates: BW: $590 **Circ:** ‡33,000
PCI: $7.50

4373 Colorado Municipalities
Colorado Municipal League
1144 Sherman St. Phone: (303)831-6411
Denver, CO 80203-2207 Fax: (303)860-8175

Magazine covering items of interest to local government in Colorado. **Founded:** 1923. **Freq:** Bimonthly. **Print Method:** Offset. **Trim Size:** 8 1/4 x 10 3/4. **Cols./Page:** 3. **Col. Width:** 26 nonpareils. **Col. Depth:** 126 agate lines. **Key Personnel:** Steve Luther, Editor, sluther@cml.org. **USPS:** 123-140. **Subscription Rates:** $20 individuals /year; $35 /2 years.
Ad Rates: BW: $583 **Circ:** Paid 4,950
Controlled 350

4374 Colorado Outdoors
Colorado Division of Wildlife
6060 Broadway Phone: (303)291-7469
Denver, CO 80216-1000 Fax: (303)291-7109

Regional publication. **Founded:** 1938. **Freq:** Bimonthly. **Print Method:** Offset. **Trim Size:** 8 1/2 x 11. **Cols./Page:** 2. **Col. Width:** 26 nonpareils. **Col. Depth:** 102 agate lines. **Key Personnel:** Pat Trahey, Managing Editor, phone (303)291-7288, fax (303)291-7109, pat.trahey@state.co.us; Kathy McWright Barton, Circulation Mgr., fax (303)291-7109, kathy.mcwright-barton@state.co.us. **ISSN:** 0010-1699. **Subscription Rates:** $10.50 individuals; $19 two years. **Remarks:** Advertising not accepted. **URL:** http://www.dnr.state.co.us/wildlife.
Circ: Paid ‡43,576
Controlled ‡2,694

4375 The Daily Journal
McGraw-Hill, Inc.
2000 S. Colorado Blvd., Ste. 2000 Phone: (303)756-9995
Fax: (303)756-4465
Denver, CO 80222
Free: (800)323-2362

Construction news tabloid covering related legal, financial, real estate, and insurance information. **Founded:** May 22, 1897. **Freq:** Daily Mon.-Fri. **Print Method:** Offset. **Trim Size:** 10 x 16. **Cols./Page:** 5. **Col. Width:** 11 picas. **Col. Depth:** 16 inches. **Key Personnel:** Mark Shaw, Sr. Managing Editor, phone (303)584-6724; Al Slattery, Publisher, phone (303)584-6719. **Subscription Rates:** $1,384 individuals; $10 single issue. **Remarks:** Accepts advertising.
Ad Rates: BW: $1,920 **Circ:** Paid ‡1,206
4C: $2,795 Controlled ‡3,859
SAU: $24
PCI: $25

4376 The Denver Business Journal
American City Business Journals
1700 Broadway, Ste. 515 Phone: (303)837-3500
Denver, CO 80290 Fax: (303)837-3535
Publication E-mail: reporter@gnt.net

Local business newspaper. **Founded:** 1949. **Freq:** Weekly. **Print Method:** Web offset. **Trim Size:** 11 1/2 x 14 1/2. **Cols./Page:** 4. **Col. Width:** 2 3/8 inches. **Col. Depth:** 13 1/4 inches. **Key Personnel:** Henry Dubroff, Editor; Wayne Hicks, Managing Editor; Scott Bemis, Publisher. **ISSN:** 0893-7745. **Subscription Rates:** $61 individuals; $1.25 single issue. **Remarks:** Accepts advertising. **URL:** http://www.amcity.com/denver.
Ad Rates: BW: $3,900 **Circ:** Paid ★**14,398**
4C: $4,100

4377 Denver Catholic Register
Arch Bishop Newspaper
200 Josephine St. Phone: (303)388-4411
Denver, CO 80206-4710 Fax: (303)321-3693

Catholic newspaper (tabloid). **Subtitle:** Denver Catholic Register. **Founded:** 1900. **Freq:** Weekly (Wed.). **Print Method:** Offset. **Trim Size:** 10 1/4 x 14. **Cols./Page:** 6. **Col. Width:** 1 5/8 inches. **Col. Depth:** 14 inches. **Key Personnel:** Charlene Scott, Editor; J. Francis Stafford, Archbi, Publisher; Frank Vecchiarelli, Advertising Dir. **Subscription Rates:** $18.75 individuals. **Remarks:** Accepts advertising.
Ad Rates: GLR: $2.20 **Circ:** Paid 83,411
BW: $2,587.20 Free 500
4C: $3,187.20
PCI: $30.80

4378 Denver Herald-Dispatch
Barnum Publishing
47 S. Federal Phone: (303)935-2453
Denver, CO 80219 Fax: (303)936-0994

Newspaper (local news). **Founded:** 1926. **Freq:** Weekly (Thurs.). **Print Method:** Offset. **Cols./Page:** 6. **Col. Width:** 18 nonpareils. **Col. Depth:** 224 agate lines. **Key Personnel:** J.I. Rosenberg, Editor and Publisher. **Subscription Rates:** $25 individuals. **Remarks:** Accepts advertising.
Ad Rates: GLR: $1.10 **Circ:** 8,600
BW: $645
4C: $910
PCI: $18

4379 The Denver Post
1560 Broadway Phone: (303)820-1010
Denver, CO 80202 Fax: (303)820-1369
Free: (800)336-7678

General newspaper. **Founded:** 1892. **Freq:** Mon.-Sun. (morn.). **Print Method:** Letterpress. **Trim Size:** 13 x 22. **Cols./Page:** 6. **Col. Width:** 2 1/16 inches. **Col. Depth:** 22 inches. **Key Personnel:** Gil Spencer, Editor; Donald Hunt, Publisher. **Remarks:** Accepts advertising. Monday-Saturday: BW: $19,026; 4C: $21,471; PCI: $151; Sunday: BW: $25,380; 4C: $28,645; PCI: $205. **Online:** DataTimes Corporation; LEXIS-NEXIS. **URL:** http://www.denverpost.com. **Alt. Formats:** CD-ROM, NewsBank, Inc. **Feature Editors:** Jim Bates, *News*, phone (303)820-1270; Janet Bingham, *Education*, phone (303)820-1930; Fred Brown, *Political*, phone (303)820-1240; Diane Carman, *Entertainment, Lifestyle*, phone (303)820-1580; Jeannette Chavez, *Women's*, phone (303)820-1800; Mike Connelly, *Sports*, phone (303)820-1299; Virginia Culver, *Religion*, phone (303)820-1223; Joanne Davidson, *Society*, phone (303)820-1314; Helen Dollaghan, *Food*, phone (303)820-1440; Henry Dubroff, *Financial/Business*, phone (303)820-1306; Diane Eicher, *Medical*, phone (303)820-1483; Mary Ellen Botter, *Travel*, phone (303)820-1599; Todd Engdahl, *Metro*, phone (303)820-1650; Glenn Giffin, *Music*, phone (303)820-1624; Chuck Green, *Editorials*, phone (303)820-1935; Steve Larson, *Photo*, phone (303)820-1894; Giselle Massi, *TV*, phone (303)820-1210; Howie Movshovitz, *Movie*, phone (303)820-1480; Mark Obmassik, *Environmental*, phone (303)820-1415; Joanne Ostrow, *TV & Radio*, phone (303)820-1830; Cynthia Pasquale, *Features, Garden/Home*, phone (303)820-1368; Steve Raabe, *Rural Development*, phone (303)820-1948.
Circ: Mon.-Sat. ★**341,554**
Sun. ★**484,657**

4380 Denver Quarterly
University of Denver Phone: (303)871-2892
Dept. of English Fax: (303)871-2853
Denver, CO 80208
Creative writing journal. **Subtitle:** A Journal of Modern Culture. **Founded:** 1966. **Freq:** Quarterly. **Print Method:** Offset. **Trim Size:** 6 x 9. **Cols./Page:** 1. **Col. Width:** 4 inches. **Col. Depth:** 6 1/4 inches. **Key Personnel:** Bin Ramke, Editor, bramke@du.edu; Catherine L. Kasper, Managing Editor. **ISSN:** 0011-8869. **Subscription Rates:** $20 individuals; $6 single issue Institutions; $24 single issue other. **Remarks:** Accepts advertising. **Available Online. Alt. Formats:** Microform.
Ad Rates: BW: $150 **Circ:** Paid ‡700
Non-paid ‡200

4381 Denver University Law Review
7039 E. 18th Ave. Phone: (303)871-6172
Denver, CO 80220 Fax: (303)871-6411
Publication E-mail: solawrev@lib.law.du.edu

Legal magazine. **Founded:** 1923. **Freq:** Quarterly. **Print Method:** Offset. **Cols./Page:** 1. **Col. Width:** 54 nonpareils. **Col. Depth:** 112 agate lines. **Key Personnel:** Kent Modesitt, Editor-in-Chief, phone (303)871-6173, kmodesit@lib.law.du.edu; Chris Balch, Business & Online Editor, phone (303)871-6175, cbalch@lib.law.du.edu. **ISSN:** 0883-9409. **Subscription Rates:** $25 individuals; $30 other countries. **Remarks:** Advertising not accepted. **Available Online. URL:** http://www.du.edu/lawreview/home.html.
Circ: ‡600

4382 Focus on Exceptional Children
Love Publishing Co.
PO Box 22353 Phone: (303)221-7333
Denver, CO 80222 Fax: (303)221-7444
Publication E-mail: lovepublishing@compuserve.com
Publisher E-mail: lovepublishing@compuserve.com

Journal covering special education topics for teachers, professionals, and curriculum specialists. Each issue covers a single topic. **Founded:** July 1, 1969. **Freq:** 9/year. **Trim Size:** 8 1/2 x 11. **Key Personnel:** Tom Love, Contact. **ISSN:** 0015-511X. **Subscription Rates:** $30 individuals; $40 institutions. **Remarks:** Advertising not accepted.
Circ: (Not Reported)

4383 Highlander
Regis University
3333 Regis Blvd. Phone: (303)964-5391
Denver, CO 80221-1099 Fax: (303)964-5530

Collegiate newspaper. **Subtitle:** An Independent Weekly Student Publication. **Founded:** 1919. **Freq:** Weekly (during the academic year). **Print Method:** Offset. **Trim Size:** 11 x 17. **Cols./Page:** 5. **Col. Depth:** 1 3/4 inches. **Key Personnel:** Darcey Gehringer, Editor-in-Chief; Melinda Padilla, Bus. Manager. **Subscription Rates:** $35 /yr.
Ad Rates: BW: $230 **Circ:** 1,000
PCI: $7.50

4384 Interactive
5280 Publishing, Inc.
1554 Pennsylvania
Denver, CO 80203
Publication E-mail: danb@5280pub.com

Entertainment magazine serving Denver, Colorado. **Subtitle:** Denver's Mile-High Magazine. **URL:** http://www.5280pub.com/.

4385 Intermountain Jewish News
Intermountain and Jewish News
1275 Sherman St., Ste. 214 Phone: (303)861-2234
Denver, CO 80203-2299 Fax: (303)832-6942

Jewish interest newspaper. **Founded:** 1913. **Freq:** Weekly (Fri.). **Print Method:** Offset. **Trim Size:** 11 1/2 x 16 3/4. **Cols./Page:** 5. **Col. Width:** 11 1/2 picas. **Col. Depth:** 217 agate lines. **Key Personnel:** Mrs. Max Goldberg, Editor and Publisher. **ISSN:** 0047-0511. **Subscription Rates:** $48 individuals; $88 two years. **Remarks:** Accepts advertising.
Ad Rates: BW: $3,381.60 **Circ:** Paid ‡9,750
4C: $4,089.60 Free ‡165
SAU: $42.27

4386 Journal of the American Animal Hospital Association
American Animal Hospital Association
PO Box 150899 Phone: (303)986-2800
Denver, CO 80215-0899 Fax: (303)986-1700
Free: (800)252-2242
Publication E-mail: aahapubs@aol.com
Publisher E-mail: aaha@aol.com

Scientific and educational journal that publishes information for the practice of small animal medicine and surgery. **Founded:** 1965. **Freq:** Bimonthly. **Print Method:** Web offset. **Trim Size:** 8 3/8 x 10 7/8. **Cols./Page:** 2. **Col. Width:** 21 picas. **Col. Depth:** 52 picas. **Key Personnel:** Dr. Walt Ingwersen, Editor; Dr. John Albers, Publisher. **ISSN:** 0587-2871. **Subscription Rates:** $107 U.S. and Canada; $127 other countries. **Remarks:** Accepts advertising. **Alt. Formats:** Microform.
Ad Rates: BW: $1,425 **Circ:** 13,138
4C: $2,050

4387 Journal of the American Water Works Association
American Water Works Association
6666 W. Quincy Ave. Phone: (303)794-7711
Denver, CO 80235 Fax: (303)794-7310

Magazine dealingwith water supply resources, treatment, and distribution. **Founded:** 1914. **Freq:** Monthly. **Print Method:** Web offset. **Trim Size:** 8 1/8 x 10 7/8. **Cols./Page:** 3. **Col. Width:** 28 nonpareils. **Col. Depth:** 140 agate lines. **Key Personnel:** Nancy Zelig, Editor, phone (303)347-6277, fax (303)794-7310. **Subscription Rates:** $75.50 individuals. **Remarks:** Accepts advertising. **URL:** http://www.awwa.org.
Ad Rates: BW: $3,275 **Circ:** Paid ‡39,040
4C: $4,575 Controlled ‡3,993

4388 Journal of the ASFMRA
American Society of Farm Managers and Rural Appraisers (ASFMRA)
950 S. Cherry St., Ste. 508 Phone: (303)758-3513
Denver, CO 80246-2664 Fax: (303)758-0190
Publisher E-mail: asfmra@agri-associations.org; publications@agri-associations.org

Journal for agricultural professionals, including farm managers, rural appraisers, review appraisers, and agricultural consultants. **Founded:** 1937. **Freq:** Annual. **Print Method:** Sheetfed offset. **Trim Size:** 8 1/2 x 11. **Cols./Page:** 2. **Col. Width:** 3 1/2 inches. **Col. Depth:** 9 1/2 inches. **Key Personnel:** M. Peterson, Contact, mpeterson@agnassociations.org. **ISSN:** 0003-116X. **Subscription Rates:** $32 individuals. **Remarks:** Advertising not accepted.
Circ: Combined 3,500

4389 Journal of Environmental Health
National Environmental Health Association
720 S. Colorado Blvd., Ste. 970, South Tower Phone: (303)756-9090
Fax: (303)691-9490
Denver, CO 80246-1904
Publication E-mail: staff@neha.org
Publisher E-mail: staff@neha.org

Journal presenting environmental health and protection issues. **Subtitle:** Dedicated to the Advancement of the Environmental Health Professional. **Founded:** 1937. **Freq:** 10/year. **Print Method:** Offset. **Trim Size:** 8 1/2 x 11. **Cols./Page:** 3. **Col. Width:** 13.5 picas. **Col. Depth:** 10 inches. **Key Personnel:** Julie Collins, Contact, julie.collins@juno.com. **ISSN:** 0022-0892. **Subscription Rates:** Free to qualified subscribers; $90 individuals; single issues available. **Remarks:** Accepts advertising.
Ad Rates: GLR: $1 **Circ:** Paid 7,000
BW: $965 Controlled 3,000
4C: $1,680

4390 Journal of Financial Planning
Institute of Certified Financial Planners
3801 E. Florida Ave., Suite 708 Phone: (303)759-4900
Denver, CO 80210 Fax: (303)759-0749
Free: (800)322-4237
Publication E-mail: journal@icfp.org
Publisher E-mail: icfp@icfp.org

Trade journal for financial planning professionals. **Founded:** 1978. **Freq:** 8/yr. **Print Method:** Web press. **Trim Size:** 8 3/8 x 10 7/8. **Cols./Page:** 3. **Key Personnel:** Marvin W. Tuttle, Editor and Publisher, mtuttle@icfp.org; Maureen Irish, Managing Editor, mirish@icfp.org. **ISSN:** 1040-3981. **Subscription Rates:** $60 individuals. **Remarks:** Accepts advertising. **URL:** http://www.icfp.org/journal/jfpindex. **Formerly:** Institute of Certified Financial Planners.
Ad Rates: BW: $2,595 **Circ:** Controlled 25,000
4C: $3,445
PCI: $125

4391 Journal of Range Management
Society for Range Management
1839 York St. Phone: (303)355-7070
Denver, CO 80206-1213 Fax: (303)355-5059
Publication E-mail: srmden@ix.netcom.com

Journal focusing on the rangeland ecosystem. **Founded:** 1948. **Freq:** Bimonthly. **Print Method:** Offset. **Trim Size:** 8 1/2 x 11. **Cols./Page:** 3 and 2. **Col. Width:** 26 and 41 nonpareils. **Col. Depth:** 133 agate lines. **Key Personnel:** Gary Fraisier, Editor, phone (970)498-4232, fax (970)482-2909, gfrasier@lamar.colostate.edu; Patty Rich, Production Editor, rrich@circles.com or pmrich@ix.netcom.com. **ISSN:** 0022-409X. **Subscription Rates:** $56 individuals. **Remarks:** Accepts advertising. **Alt. Formats:** Microform.
Ad Rates: BW: $300 **Circ:** 3,400
4C: $700

4392 Law Enforcement Product News
General Communications, Inc.
100 Garfield St. Phone: (303)322-6400
Denver, CO 80206 Fax: (303)322-0627

Trade magazine covering products for law enforcement, corrections and security related professionals. **Founded:** 1990. **Freq:** Bimonthly. **Print Method:** Web offset. **Trim Size:** 10 7/8 x 15 3/4. **Cols./Page:** 3. **Col. Depth:** 15 inches. **Key Personnel:** Gregory Monroe, Editor; Michael George, Vice President, mlg@great.net. **ISSN:** 1060-5126. **Subscription Rates:** $24 individuals; $36 Canada; $48 other countries; Free to qualified subscribers. **Remarks:** Accepts advertising. **URL:** http://www.law-enforcement.com.
Ad Rates: BW: $3,120 **Circ:** Paid ★27,247
4C: $3,675
PCI: $150

4393 The Metropolitan
Metropolitan State College of Denver
Student Publications Phone: (303)556-8361
900 Auraria Pkwy, TV-313 Fax: (303)556-2596
1006 11st St.
PO Box 173362, Campus Box 57
Denver, CO 80204-2025
Collegiate newspaper. **Founded:** Feb. 19, 1979. **Freq:** Weekly (Fri.). **Print Method:** Offset. Uses mats. **Trim Size:** 10 1/4 x 14 1/2. **Cols./Page:** 4. **Col. Width:** 2 1/2 inches. **Col. Depth:** 14 inches. **Key Personnel:** Donna Hickey Jackson, Editor-in-Chief, hickeyd@mscd.edu; Kate B. Lutrey, Dir./Administration; Alisha Jeher, Sports Editor; John McDonough, Photo Editor. **Subscription Rates:** $15 individuals. **Remarks:** Accepts advertising. **URL:** http://www.mscd.edu/~themet.
Ad Rates: BW: $336 **Circ:** Free ‡10,000

4394 The Mining Record
Howell International Enterprise
PO Box 37510 Phone: (303)770-6791
Denver, CO 80237 Fax: (303)770-6796
Free: (800)441-4748

International mining industry newspaper. **Founded:** 1889. **Freq:** Weekly (Wed.). **Print Method:** Offset. **Trim Size:** 11 1/2 x 16 3/4. **Cols./Page:** 5. **Col. Width:** 22 nonpareils. **Col. Depth:** 210 agate lines. **Key Personnel:** D.E. Howell, Editor. **ISSN:** 0026-5241. **Subscription Rates:** $39 individuals. **Remarks:** Accepts advertising.
Ad Rates: BW: $1,200 **Circ:** ‡5,260
4C: $1,775
PCI: $25

4395 Mountain Geologist
Rocky Mountain Association of Geologists
820 16th St., No. 505
Denver, CO 80202-3218

Magazine covering geology. **Founded:** Jan. 1964. **Freq:** Quarterly. **Cols./Page:** 2. **Key Personnel:** Mark Longman, Executive Editor; Peggy Williams, Managing Editor. **ISSN:** 0027-254X. **Subscription Rates:** $34 individuals; $10 single issue. **Remarks:** Advertising not accepted.
Circ: Paid 2,200

4396 NARHA Strides
North American Riding for the Handicapped Association, Inc. (NARHA)
PO Box 33150 Phone: (303)452-1212
Denver, CO 80233 Fax: (303)252-4610
Free: (800)369-7433
Publication E-mail: narha@narha.org
Publisher E-mail: narha@narha.org

Promotes training for recreation and rehabilitation through horseback riding. Provides information about riding for people with disabilities, including news of the Association and its operating groups, and a calendar of events. **Founded:** Oct. 1995. **Freq:** Quarterly. **Trim Size:** 8 1/2 x 11. **Subscription Rates:** Free to qualified subscribers; $20. **Remarks:** Advertising accepted; rates available upon request. **Formerly:** NARHA News.
Circ: 4,100

4397 National Civic Review
National Civic League Press
1445 Market St., No. 300 Phone: (303)571-4343
Denver, CO 80202-1728 Fax: (303)571-4404
Free: (800)223-6004

Journal on local and state government. **Founded:** 1912. **Freq:** Quarterly. **Print Method:** Offset. **Trim Size:** 7 x 10. **Cols./Page:** 1. **Col. Width:** 6 inches. **Col. Depth:** 8 inches. **Key Personnel:** Mike McGrath, Editor. **ISSN:** 0027-9013. **Subscription Rates:** $30; $33 other countries. **Remarks:** Advertising accepted; rates available upon request. **Available Online. URL:** http://www.ncl.arg/ncl. **Alt. Formats:** CD-ROM.
Circ: ‡3,500

Nebraska Beverage Analyst - See Lincoln, Nebraska

New Mexico Beverage Analyst - See Santa Fe, New Mexico

4398 The New Review
2175 S. Jasmine, Ste. A Phone: (303)639-9000
Denver, CO 80222 Fax: (303)639-5125

Colorado media magazine. **Founded:** 1995. **Freq:** Monthly. **Print Method:** Offset. **Trim Size:** 8 1/2 x 11. **Cols./Page:** 3. **Col. Width:** 14 picas. **Col. Depth:** 10 inches. **Key Personnel:** Tom Pade, Editor; Curt Serveny, Publisher. **Subscription Rates:** $12.50 individuals. **Remarks:** Accepts advertising.
Ad Rates: BW: $575 **Circ:** ‡73,000
4C: $875
PCI: $35

4399 Newspapers & Technology
Mary L. Van Meter
1623 Blake St., Ste. 444 Phone: (303)575-9595
Denver, CO 80202 Fax: (303)575-9555
Publication E-mail: newsandtech.com

Trade journal. **Founded:** 1988. **Freq:** Monthly. **Trim Size:** 10 x 13. **Key Personnel:** Mary Van Meter, Publisher, vanmeternt@aol.com; Mike Tartar, Managing Editor. **Subscription Rates:** Free to qualified subscribers. **Remarks:** Advertising accepted; rates available upon request.
Circ: Non-paid ‡17,822

4400 Nuestras Raices/Our Roots
Genealogical Society of Hispanic America
Box 9606 Phone: (719)564-0631
Denver, CO 80209-0606 Fax: (310)202-1151
Publication E-mail: wrtrconsult@earthlink.net
Publisher E-mail: escritorio@compuserve.com

Journal covering Hispanic genealogy and history in the Southwestern U.S. and Mexico. **Founded:** 1988. **Freq:** Quarterly. **Cols./Page:** 2. **Key Personnel:** Maryellen Nead Salazar, emmysal@gte.net. **ISSN:** 1045-2524. **Subscription Rates:** $20 individuals. **Remarks:** Accepts advertising.
Ad Rates: BW: $22 **Circ:** Controlled 550

4401 Out Front Colorado
244 Washington St., 2nd Fl. Phone: (303)778-7900
Denver, CO 80203 Fax: (303)778-7978
Publication E-mail: outfrontc@aol.com

Biweekly newspaper. **Founded:** Apr. 1976. **Freq:** Biweekly. **Trim Size:** 10 1/4 x 13 1/2. **Key Personnel:** Gregory Montoya, Editor; David Beach, Advertising Dir. **Subscription Rates:** $65. **Remarks:** Accepts advertising.
Ad Rates: BW: $700 **Circ:** Free 25,000
4C: $1,180

4402 Parts & People
Automotive Counseling & Publishing Co., Inc.
450 Lincoln St., Ste. 110 Phone: (303)765-4664
Denver, CO 80203-3459 Fax: (303)765-4650
Free: (800)530-8557
Publication E-mail: partsandpeople.com

Trade magazine covering the automotive parts and service

industry in the Rocky Mountain and Midwestern U.S. regions. **Founded:** Aug. 1985. **Freq:** Monthly. **Print Method:** Web offset. **Cols./Page:** 4. **Col. Width:** 2 inches. **Col. Depth:** 13 inches. **Key Personnel:** Lance Buchner, Publisher, L_buchner@partsandpeople.com; Kevin Lowewn, Managing Editor, K_loewen@partsandpeople.com; Andy Dalzell, Associate Editor, a_dalzell@partsandpeople.com. **Subscription Rates:** Free to qualified subscribers; $25. **Remarks:** Accepts advertising.

Circ: Combined 31,000

4403 Public Safety Product News
General Communications, Inc.
100 Garfield St. Phone: (303)322-6400
Denver, CO 80206 Fax: (303)322-0627

Trade magazine covering products for firefighters, paramedics, 9-1-1, search and rescue, disaster, communications, investigators and security professionals. **Founded:** Nov. 1993. **Freq:** Bimonthly. **Print Method:** Web offset. **Trim Size:** 10 7/8 x 15 3/4. **Cols./Page:** 3. **Col. Depth:** 15 inches. **Key Personnel:** Gregory Monroe, Editor; Michael George, Vice President, mlg@great.net. **ISSN:** 1085-8822. **Subscription Rates:** $24 individuals; $36 Canada; $48 other countries; Free to qualified subscribers. **Remarks:** Accepts advertising. **URL:** http://www.publicsafety.com.
Ad Rates: BW: $3,439 **Circ:** Controlled ‡28,045
4C: $4,014
PCI: $200

4404 RCR-Radio Communications Report
RCR Publications, Inc.
777 E. Speer Blvd. Phone: (303)733-2500
Denver, CO 80203-4214 Fax: (303)733-2244
Publication E-mail: rcr@usa.net

Tabloid covering cellular, paging, land mobile radio, PCS paging, and SMR industries. **Subtitle:** The Newspaper for the Wireless Communications Industry. **Founded:** 1982. **Freq:** Weekly. **Print Method:** Offset. **Trim Size:** 11 x 14 1/2. **Cols./Page:** 5. **Col. Width:** 11 picas. **Col. Depth:** 230 agate lines. **Key Personnel:** Tracy Anderson-Ford, Editor; John Sudmeier, Publisher. **ISSN:** 0744-0618. **Subscription Rates:** $49 individuals; $3 single issue.
Ad Rates: BW: $4,550 **Circ:** Paid 10,000
4C: $5,390 Free 21,000

4405 Rock Garden Quarterly
North American Rock Garden Society
7530 E. Mississippi Dr. Phone: (303)368-7530
Denver, CO 80231
Trade journal covering horticulture. **Founded:** 1934. **Freq:** Quarterly. **Trim Size:** 6 x 9. **Key Personnel:** Gwen Kelaidis, Editor. **ISSN:** 1081-0765. **Subscription Rates:** $25 individuals; $7 single issue. **Remarks:** Accepts advertising. **Former name:** Bulletin of the Args.

Circ: Paid 5,000

4406 Rocky Mountain Motorist
AAA Colorado, Inc.
4100 E. Arkansas Ave. Phone: (303)753-8800
Denver, CO 80222 Fax: (303)758-8515

Magazine for members of the Colorado American Automobile Association. Contains articles on domestic and foreign travel as well as automotive issues. **Subtitle:** The Magazine for AAA Members and Travelers. **Founded:** 1922. **Freq:** Monthly. **Print Method:** Offset. **Trim Size:** 8 x 10 1/2. **Cols./Page:** 3. **Col. Width:** 2 1/4 inches. **Col. Depth:** 135 agate lines. **Key Personnel:** Kelly Eastlund, Managing Editor, phone (303)753-8800, fax (303)758-8515; Steve Seay, Publisher/President, phone (303)753-8800, fax (303)758-8515. **ISSN:** 0273-6772. **Subscription Rates:** Included in membership.
Ad Rates: BW: $6,301 **Circ:** Controlled ‡265,000
4C: $7,820

4407 Rocky Mountain News
Scripps Howard
400 W. Colfax Ave. Phone: (303)892-5000
PO Box 719 Fax: (303)892-5081
Denver, CO 80204
Free: (800)933-1990

General newspaper. **Founded:** Apr. 24, 1859. **Freq:** Mon.-Sun. (morn.). **Print Method:** Letterpress and offset. **Cols./Page:** 5. **Col. Width:** 2 1/16 inches. **Col. Depth:** 14 inches. **Key Personnel:** Jay Ambrose, Editor; Larry D. Strutton, Publisher, President; Vern Mallinen, Advertising Dir. **Subscription Rates:** $87 individuals. **Remarks:** Accepts advertising. **Online:** Dialog (The Dialog Corporation); CompuServe Information Service; DataTimes Corporation. **URL:** http://www.insidedenver.com. **Feature Editors:** Gale Baldwin, *City*, phone (303)892-5381; Amanda Covarrubias, *Education*, phone (303)892-5236; John Davidson, *News*, phone (303)892-2634; Janet Day, *Environmental*, phone (303)892-5346; Robert Denerstein, *Movie*, phone (303)892-5424; Bill Husted, *Society*, phone (303)892-5048; Karl Kuntz, *Photo*, phone (303)892-2626; Mike Madigan, *Sports*, phone (303)892-5326; Pam Maples, *Political*, phone (303)892-5212; Terry Mattingly, *Religion*, phone (303)892-5396; Lynde McCormick, *Financial/Business*, phone (303)892-5157; Marty Meitus, *Food*, phone (303)892-5229; Justin Mitchell, *Music*, phone (303)892-2562; Nancy Murray, *Fashion*, phone (303)892-5492; Kris Newcomer, *Medical*, phone (303)892-5371; Jean Otto, *Editorials*, phone (303)892-5478; Joe Rassenfoss, *Sunday*, phone (303)892-5052; John Rebchook, *Real Estate*, phone (303)892-5207; Rob Reuteman, *Rural Development*, phone (303)892-2658; Dusty Saunders, *TV & Radio*, phone (303)892-5137; Mim Swartz, *Travel*, phone (303)892-2552; Mary Winter, *Family, Features, Lifestyle, Women's*, phone (303)892-5169; Tom Wolfe, *Entertainment*, phone (303)892-5447.
Ad Rates: BW: $6,370 **Circ:** Mon.-Sat. ★**331,978**
4C: $7,745 Sun. ★**432,931**
SAU: $91

4408 Rocky Mountain Oyster
Mountaintop Publishing, Inc.
PO Box 27467 Phone: (303)985-3034
Denver, CO 80227 Fax: (303)986-5664
Publication E-mail: oyster@oyster.com

"Titillating publication" about sex with 100's of personal ads, photos,-articles for those over 21. **Subtitle:** Rocky Mountain Oyster and National Oyster. **Founded:** 1976. **Freq:** Weekly. **Print Method:** Web press. **Trim Size:** 11 1/2 x 17. **Cols./Page:** 4 and 6. **Col. Width:** 14 picas. **Col. Depth:** 15 1/4 inches. **Key Personnel:** Elaine Leass, Publisher, elaine@oyster.com; Dawn J. Smith, Assoc. Pub., dawn@oyster.com; Gary Scherman, Advertising/Distribution, gary@oyster.com. **Subscription Rates:** $99 yrly. **Remarks:** Accepts advertising. **URL:** http://www.oyster.com.
Ad Rates: GLR: $2 **Circ:** Paid 1,000
BW: $945 Non-paid 53,000
PCI: $35

4409 Seminars in Hearing
Thieme Medical Publishers, Inc.
4200 E. 9th Ave. Phone: (303)372-5850
B210 Fax: (303)372-5821
Denver, CO 80262
Publisher E-mail: journals@thieme.com

Medical journal. **Founded:** 1980. **Freq:** Quarterly. **Print Method:** Sheetfed offset. **Trim Size:** 7 x 10. **Cols./Page:** 2. **Col. Width:** 32 nonpareils. **Col. Depth:** 126 agate lines. **Key Personnel:** Mark Flanagan, Dir. of Production and Manufacturing; Brian Scanlan, Publisher. **ISSN:** 0734-9529. **Subscription Rates:** $65; $179 industry; $30 single issue. **Remarks:** Accepts advertising.
Ad Rates: BW: $700 **Circ:** Paid 2,155
4C: $825 Non-paid 78

4410 Star Wars Insider
Official Star Wars Fan Club
3720 Revere St.
Denver, CO 80239

Consumer magazine for *Star Wars* motion picture enthusiasts. **Founded:** 1987. **Freq:** Bimonthly. **Print Method:** Offset. **Trim Size:** 8 3/8 x 10 7/8. **Cols./Page:** 3. **Key Personnel:** Jon Bradley Snyder, Editor-in-Chief; David Latimer, Advertising Dir./Circulation Mgr. **ISSN:** 1041-5122. **Subscription Rates:** $19.95 individuals; $4.50 single issue. **Remarks:** Accepts advertising. **Former name:** The Lucasfilm Fan Club.
Ad Rates: 4C: $5,000 **Circ:** Paid 250,000

4411 State Education Leader
Education Commission of the States
707 17th St., No. 2700 Phone: (303)299-3600
Denver, CO 80202-3427 Fax: (303)296-8332
Publisher E-mail: ecs@ecs.org

Publication focusing on education policy making and trends. **Founded:** 1982. **Freq:** 3/year. **Print Method:** Offset. **Trim Size:** 11 x 17. **Cols./Page:** 2. **Col. Width:** 17 picas. **Col. Depth:** 60 picas. **Key Personnel:** Sherry Freeland Walker, Editor, swalker@ecs.org. **ISSN:** 0736-7511. **Subscription Rates:** $20 individuals; $8 single issue. **Remarks:** Advertising not accepted.

Circ: Paid 1,000
Controlled 4,000

4412 State Legislatures
National Conference of State Legislatures
1560 Broadway, No. 700 Phone: (303)830-2200
Denver, CO 80202-5140 Fax: (303)863-8003
Publication E-mail: sharon.randall@ncsl.org
Publisher E-mail: books@ncsl.org

Magazine bringing a national perspective to state politics and government by tracking legislation and issues, examining innovations and ideas, monitoring trends and developments, and exploring operations and procedures in the 50 state legislatures. **Subtitle:** The National Magazine of State Government and Policy. **Founded:** 1975. **Freq:** 10/year. **Print Method:** Offset. **Trim Size:** 8 1/2 x 10 7/8. **Cols./Page:** 3. **Col. Width:** 31 nonpareils. **Col. Depth:** 133 agate lines. **Key Personnel:** Karen Hansen, Editor, karen.hansen@ncsl.org; LeAnn Hoff, Advertising Mgr. **ISSN:** 0147-0641. **Subscription Rates:** $49 individuals.
Ad Rates: BW: $2,135 **Circ:** Paid ‡14,194
4C: $3,840 Non-paid ‡7,900

4413 Surgical Services Management
Association of Operating Room Nurses, Inc.
2170 S. Parker Rd., Ste. 300 Phone: (303)755-6300
Denver, CO 80231-5711 Fax: (303)750-3441
Free: (800)755-AORN
Publication E-mail: ssm@aorn.org

Professional magazine for health care managers and administrators who interact with the surgical services environment. **Founded:** Jan. 1995. **Freq:** Monthly. **Print Method:** Web offset. **Trim Size:** 8 1/2 x 11. **Key Personnel:** Joyce Merriman, Editorial Dir.; Crystal Nisly, Ad Sales; Suzanne F. Ward, Editor. **ISSN:** 1079-8269. **Subscription Rates:** $39.50 individuals; $65 out of country; $80 institutions; $6 single issue. **Remarks:** Accepts advertising.

Circ: Combined 14,000

4414 Technometrics
American Statistical Association
c/o Karen Kafadan Phone: (303)556-8463
University of Colorado-Denver Fax: (303)556-8550
Department of Mathematics
PO Box 173364
Denver, CO 80217-3364
Publisher E-mail: asainfo@mstat.org

Professional journal covering statistics for the physical, chemical and engineering sciences. **Founded:** 1958. **Freq:** Quarterly. **Trim Size:** 8 1/4 x 11. **Cols./Page:** 2. **Col. Width:** 21 picas. **Col. Depth:** 61 picas. **Key Personnel:** Nancy Epting, Production Editor, nancy@amstat.org. **ISSN:** 0041-1706. **Subscription Rates:** $22 individuals; $55 institutions; $25 single issue. **Remarks:** Advertising not accepted.

Circ: Combined ⊕**6,194**

4415 The Telephone Pioneer
Telephone Pioneers of America
P.O. Box 13888 Phone: (303)571-9274
Denver, CO 80201-3888 Fax: (303)572-0520
Free: (800)872-5995
Publication E-mail: rjt@alex.attmail.com

Membership newspaper. **Founded:** 1987. **Freq:** Quarterly. **Print Method:** Web offset. **Trim Size:** 10 1/2 x 13 1/2. **Cols./Page:** 4. **Key Personnel:** Bill Maroney, Editor; Bob Earl, Advertising Mgr. **Subscription Rates:** $20 institutions. **Remarks:** Accepts advertising. **URL:** http://www.telephone-pioneers.arg.
Ad Rates: GLR: $12 **Circ:** ‡756,350
BW: $7,770
4C: $9,960
PCI: $168

4416 TRENDS Magazine
American Animal Hospital Association
PO Box 150899 Phone: (303)986-2800
Denver, CO 80215-0899 Fax: (303)986-1700
Free: (800)252-2242
Publisher E-mail: aaha@aol.com

Professional magazine covering the management of small animal veterinary practices. **Founded:** Apr. 1985. **Freq:** Bimonthly. **Print Method:** Web offset. **Trim Size:** 8 3/8 x 10 7/8. **Cols./Page:** 3. **Key Personnel:** Kathleen Iiams Brown, Editor; Dr. John Albers, Publisher. **ISSN:** 1062-8266. **Subscription Rates:** $60 U.S. and Canada; $70 other countries. **Remarks:** Accepts advertising.
Ad Rates: BW: $1,850 **Circ:** 12,500
4C: $2,600

4417 Watch & Clock Review
Golden Bell Press
2403 Champa St. Phone: (303)296-1600
Denver, CO 80205 Fax: (303)295-2159

Magazine on watches and clocks. **Founded:** 1936. **Freq:** 10/year. **Print Method:** Offset. **Trim Size:** 8 3/8 x 10 7/8. **Cols./Page:** 3. **Col. Width:** 14 nonpareils. **Col. Depth:** 140 agate lines. **Key Personnel:** Lawrence Bell, Publisher; Bertram Kalisher, Advertising Mgr.; Dara Hinshaw, Managing Editor. **ISSN:** 0279-6198. **Subscription Rates:** $19.50; $3 single issue; foreign, add $10. **Remarks:** Accepts advertising. **Alt. Formats:** Microform.
Ad Rates: BW: $1,590 **Circ:** Paid ‡3,000
4C: $2,190 Non-paid ‡12,500
PCI: $40

4418 Welcome Home Magazine of Denver
Welcome Home Magazine
5944 S. Kipling St., Ste. 204 Phone: (303)972-2584
Littleton, CO 80127-2590 Fax: (303)972-2261

Magazine containing information for newly moved Denver,

CO, households. **Founded:** Mar. 1, 1990. **Freq:** Quarterly. **Print Method:** Web offset. **Trim Size:** 8 3/8 x 10 7/8. **Cols./Page:** 3. **Col. Width:** 13 picas. **Key Personnel:** James F. Sweeney, Publisher; Mary Sweeney, Editor. **Subscription Rates:** $12.58. **Remarks:** Accepts advertising.
Ad Rates: BW: $3,705 **Circ:** Controlled 31,000
4C: $4,440

4419 Western Livestock Journal
Crow Publications, Inc.
PO Box 9388 Phone: (303)722-7600
Denver, CO 80223-0388 Fax: (303)772-0155
Publication E-mail: wljj@aol.com

Newspaper (tabloid) covering activities of cattle industry and other livestock industry in the U.S. **Founded:** 1922. **Freq:** Weekly. **Print Method:** Offset. **Trim Size:** 11 1/2 x 16 3/4. **Cols./Page:** 6. **Col. Width:** 19 nonpareils. **Col. Depth:** 224 agate lines. **Key Personnel:** Fred Wortham, Editor; Dick Crow, Publisher; Pete Crow, Advertising Mgr. **ISSN:** 0094-6710. **Subscription Rates:** $27 individuals. **Remarks:** Advertising accepted; rates available upon request.
Circ: Paid ★19,452

4420 Westword
Westword Corp.
PO Box 5970 Phone: (303)296-7744
Denver, CO 80217 Fax: (303)296-5416
Publication E-mail: denver.editorial@westword.com

Metro newsweekly. **Founded:** Sept. 1977. **Freq:** Weekly. **Trim Size:** 11 x 14. **Cols./Page:** 8. **Col. Width:** 10 21/32 inches. **Col. Depth:** 14 inches. **Key Personnel:** Patricia Calhoun, Editor; Amy Cobb, Publisher, fax (303)296-5415, acobb@westword.com; Scott Tobias, Advertising Dir., fax (303)296-2457, stobias@westword.com. **Subscription Rates:** Free; $50 by mail. **Remarks:** Accepts advertising. **URL:** http://www.westword.com.
Ad Rates: BW: $2,998 **Circ:** Non-paid ★107,075
4C: $3,673.80
PCI: $22

4421 Wireless Week
600 S. Cherry St., No. 400 Phone: (303)393-7449
Denver, CO 80222 Fax: (303)399-2034

Trade tabloid covering the wireless industry including cellular, paging, satellite, and microwave. **Founded:** Oct. 1995. **Freq:** Weekly. **Key Personnel:** Judith Lockwood, Editor, jlockwood@chilton.net; Debby Denton, Ad Dir.; Ed Mott, Circulation Mgr. **Subscription Rates:** $59 individuals; $99 other countries. **Remarks:** Accepts advertising. **URL:** http://www.wirelessweek.com.
Ad Rates: BW: $5,145 **Circ:** Controlled ‡28,809
4C: $6,000
PCI: $75

4422 KALC-FM - 106
1200 17th St., Ste. 2300 Phone: (303)572-7000
Denver, CO 80202 Fax: (303)615-5393

Format: Adult Contemporary; Classic Rock. **Owner:** Chancellor Broadcasting Co., 12655 N. Central Expwy 405, Dallas, TX 75243, (214)239-6220. **Founded:** 1959. **Formerly:** KMJI-FM (1991); KBPI-FM (1994); KXLT-FM. **Operating Hours:** Continuous. **ADI:** Denver (Steamboat Springs), CO. **Key Personnel:** Gayle Shaw, General Mgr.; Brenda Goodrich, General Sales Mgr.; Anne Millison, Marketing Dir. **Wattage:** 100,000 ERP.

4423 KAZY-FM - 106.7
1380 Lawrence, Ste. 1300 Phone: (303)893-3699
Denver, CO 80204 Fax: (303)329-3699

Format: Album-Oriented Rock (AOR). **Networks:** ABC. **Owner:** Summit Broadcasting Corp., 115 Perimeter Center Pl., Ste. 1150, Atlanta, GA 30346, (404)394-0707. **Founded:** 1972. **Formerly:** KLZ-FM (1972). **Operating Hours:** Continuous; 5% network, 95% local. **ADI:** Denver (Steamboat Springs), CO. **Key Personnel:** Berkley Silver, Contact; Lynn Sornsen, Contact; Rich Gerber, Contact; Brian Taylor, Operations Mgr.; Beau Roberts, Music Dir.; Anne Millison, Promotions Dir.; Jack Tyson, Contact; Denny Moore, General Sales Mgr. **Wattage:** 100,000. **Ad Rates:** $100-300 for 60 seconds.

4424 KBCO-AM - 1190
8975 E. Kenyon Ave. Phone: (303)694-6300
Denver, CO 80237 Fax: (303)694-4919

Format: Talk. **Founded:** 1973. **Operating Hours:** Continuous. **ADI:** Denver (Steamboat Springs), CO. **Wattage:** 5000.

4425 KBDI-TV - 12
2900 Welton St., 1st Fl. Phone: (303)296-1212
Denver, CO 80205 Fax: (303)296-6650
Free: (800)727-8812

Format: Public TV. **Networks:** Public Broadcasting Service (PBS). **Owner:** Front Range Educational Media Corp., at above address. **Founded:** 1978. **Operating Hours:** Continuous. **ADI:** Denver (Steamboat Springs), CO. **Key Personnel:** Ted Krichels, General Mgr.; Paula Miller, Business Mgr. **Wattage:** 229,000.

4426 KBNO-AM - 1220
2727 Bryant St., Ste. 100 Phone: (303)292-5266
Denver, CO 80211-4154 Fax: (303)433-1330

Format: Hispanic. **Networks:** CNN Radio. **Owner:** at above address. **Founded:** 1954. **Operating Hours:** Continuous. **ADI:** Denver (Steamboat Springs), CO. **Key Personnel:** Zee Ferrufino, Pres./Gen. Mgr.; Alberto Alfonzo, Sales Mgr.; Eugenio Sepulveda, Program/News Dir. **Wattage:** 1000. **Ad Rates:** $40 for 30 seconds; $50 for 60 seconds.

4427 KCEC-TV - 50
777 Grant, Ste.110 Phone: (303)832-0050
Denver, CO 80203 Fax: (303)832-3410
E-mail: krecnews@aol.com

Format: Hispanic. **Networks:** Univision. **Founded:** 1990. **Operating Hours:** Continuous. **ADI:** Denver (Steamboat Springs), CO. **Key Personnel:** Yrma Rico, General Mgr., fax (303)832-7325; Sam Fuller, General Sales Mgr.; Fred Byers, National Sales Mgr. **Wattage:** 2,500,000. **Ad Rates:** Advertising accepted; rates available upon request.

4428 KCFR-FM - 90.1
2249 S. Josephine St. Phone: (303)871-9191
Denver, CO 80210 Fax: (303)733-3319
Free: (800)722-4449
E-mail: info@cpr.org

Format: Public Radio; Classical; News. **Networks:** National Public Radio (NPR). **Founded:** 1970. **Operating Hours:** Continuous; 35% network, 65% local. **ADI:** Denver (Steamboat Springs), CO. **Key Personnel:** Max Wycisk, President; Patricia Prevost, VP Development; Ed Trudeau, VP Broadcasting; Bob Hensler, VP Engineering; Jenny Gentry, VP Finance & Admin. **Wattage:** 50,000. **Ad Rates:** Noncommercial.

4429 KCNC-TV - 4
1044 Lincoln St. Phone: (303)861-4444
Denver, CO 80203 Fax: (303)830-6380

Format: Commercial TV. **Networks:** NBC. **Founded:** 1953. **ADI:** Denver (Steamboat Springs), CO. **Key Personnel:** Roger L. Ogden, Contact.

4430 KCUV-AM - 1150
1580 Lincoln, Ste. 700 Phone: (303)861-1156
Denver, CO 80203-1509 Fax: (303)861-1158

Format: Ethnic; Hispanic. **Founded:** 1987. **Formerly:** KJIM-AM (1992); KFRR-AM. **Operating Hours:** Continuous. **ADI:** Denver (Steamboat Springs), CO. **Key Personnel:** Vic Rumore, President; Manuel Fernandez, General Mgr.; Evelyn Casias, Station/Sales Mgr.; Robert Gaytan, Program Dir. **Wattage:** 5000 day; 1000 night. **Ad Rates:** $10-35 for 30 seconds; $15-55 for 60 seconds. $10-$35 for 30 seconds; $15-$55 for 60 seconds. Combined advertising rates available with KXRE-AM and KGRE-AM.

4431 KDVR-TV - 31
501 Wazee St. Phone: (303)595-3131
Denver, CO 80204 Fax: (303)595-8312

Format: Commercial TV. **Networks:** Fox. **Owner:** Fox Television Stations, Inc., 5746 Sunset Blvd., Los Angeles, CA 90028, (213)856-1000, Fax: (213)856-1659. **Founded:** 1983. **Operating Hours:** Continuous; 25% network, 75% local. **ADI:** Denver (Steamboat Springs), CO. **Key Personnel:** Glenn Dyer, General Mgr.; Ray Dowdle, General Sales Mgr.; John O'Laughlin, Program and Promotions Dir.; Sheryl Personett, Local Sales Mgr.; Catherine Andrey, National Sales Manager; Jim Hollinger, Chief Engineer. **URL:** www.fox31.com.

4432 KEZW-AM - 1430
10200 E. Girard Ave., Ste. B-130 Phone: (303)696-1714
Denver, CO 80231 Fax: (303)696-0522

Networks: Satellite Music Network; ABC. **Owner:** Tribune Broadcasting Company, at above address. **Founded:** 1954. **Formerly:** KOSI-AM (1981). **Operating Hours:** Continuous; 100% local. **ADI:** Denver (Steamboat Springs), CO. **Key Personnel:** David Juris, General Mgr.; Rick Crall, Station Mgr.; Ann Williams. **Local Programs:** *Hal & Murphy* 10 am-6 pm. **Wattage:** 10,000. **Ad Rates:** $70-100 per unit. Combined advertising rates available with KOSI-FM and KKHK-FM.

4433 KHIH-FM - 95.7
8975 E. Kenyon Ave. Phone: (303)694-6300
Denver, CO 80237

Format: Jazz. **Networks:** Mutual Broadcasting System. **Owner:** Noble Broadcast of Colorado, Inc., at above address. **Founded:** 1925. **Formerly:** KHOW-FM. **ADI:** Denver (Steamboat Springs), CO. **Key Personnel:** Dino Ianni, Contact; Mary Rawlins, General Sales Mgr.; Stacy Cantrell, Operations/Program Dir. **Wattage:** 5000.

4434 KHOW-AM - 630
8975 E. Kenyon Ave. Phone: (303)694-6300
Denver, CO 80237-1836 Fax: (303)694-4919

Format: Talk. **Networks:** Mutual Broadcasting System. **Owner:** Noble Broadcasting of Colorado, Inc., at above address. **Founded:** 1925. **Operating Hours:** Continuous. **ADI:** Denver (Steamboat Springs), CO. **Key Personnel:** Dino Ianni, General Mgr.; Mary Rawlins, General Sales Mgr.; Stacy Cantrell, Operations/Programming Dir. **Wattage:** 5000.

4435 KJME-AM - 1390
828 Santa Fe Dr. Phone: (303)623-1390
Denver, CO 80204-4345 Fax: (303)595-0131

Format: Hispanic; Ethnic. **Owner:** Jo-Mor Communications, Inc., at above address. **Founded:** 1987. **Operating Hours:** Continuous. **ADI:** Denver (Steamboat Springs), CO. **Key Personnel:** Andres Neidig, President; William Nerdig, Program Dir.; Kristina Roberts, General Sales Mgr. **Local Programs:** *Furia de los Supergrupos*, William Nerdig; *Radio Juventud*, Andrea Nerdig. **Wattage:** 5000. **Ad Rates:** $42 for 30 seconds; $53 for 60 seconds.

4436 KKHK-FM - 99.5
10200 E. Girard Ave., Ste. B131 Phone: (303)696-1714
Denver, CO 80231 Fax: (303)696-0522

Format: Classic Rock. **Owner:** Tribune Broadcasting Company, at above address. **Founded:** 1996. **Operating Hours:** Continuous. **ADI:** Denver (Steamboat Springs), CO. **Key Personnel:** David Juris, Vice Pres./Gen. Mgr.; Arthur N. Samuel, General Sales Mgr.; Lois Todd, Program Dir. **Wattage:** 100,000.

KLTT-AM - See Brighton

4437 KLZ-AM - 560
2150 W. 29th Ave., Ste. 300 Phone: (303)433-5500
Denver, CO 80211 Fax: (303)433-1555
E-mail: klz56@aol.com

Format: Contemporary Christian. **Owner:** Crawford Broadcasting Co., 591 Sippack Pike, Blue Bell, PA 19422-0735, (215)628-3500. **Founded:** 1922. **Operating Hours:** Continuous. **ADI:** Denver (Steamboat Springs), CO. **Key Personnel:** Donald B. Crawford, Jr., Contact; Jimmy Lakey, Program Dir./Contact. **Wattage:** 5000. **Ad Rates:** Advertising accepted; rates available upon request.

4438 KMGH-TV - 7
123 Speer Blvd. Phone: (303)832-7777
PO Box 5007 Fax: (303)839-8070
Denver, CO 80217

Format: Commercial TV. **Networks:** CBS. **Owner:** McGraw-Hill Broadcasting, 1221 Avenue of the Americas, New York, NY 10020, (212)512-2000. **Founded:** 1954. **Formerly:** KLZ-TV. **Operating Hours:** Continuous. **ADI:** Denver (Steamboat Springs), CO. **Key Personnel:** John B. Proffitt, Vice Pres./Gen. Mgr.; Christophebs Sehring, General Sales Mgr.; Carl Stieneker, Promotions/Mktg./Public Affairs Dir. **Local Programs:** *Crossroads*, Christine Oldroyd, (303)832-0229. **Wattage:** 316,000.

4439 KOA-AM - 850
1380 Lawrence St., Ste. 1300 Phone: (303)893-8500
Denver, CO 80204-2060 Fax: (303)892-4700

Format: News; Talk; Sports. **Networks:** ABC. **Owner:** Jacor Communications, 50 E. Rivercenter Blvd., 12th Fl., Covington, KY 41011, (606)655-2267, Fax: (606)655-9345. **Founded:** 1924. **Operating Hours:** Continuous. **ADI:** Denver (Steamboat Springs), CO. **Key Personnel:** Lee Larsen, Vice President; Robin Bertolucci, Program Dir.; Dick Carlson, General Sales Mgr. **Wattage:** 50,000. **Ad Rates:** Advertising accepted; rates available upon request.

4440 KOSI-FM - 101.1
10200 E. Girard Ave., Ste. B-130 Phone: (303)696-1714
Denver, CO 80231 Fax: (303)696-0522

Format: Adult Contemporary. **Networks:** Independent. **Owner:** Tribune Broadcasting Company, at above address. **Founded:** 1968. **Operating Hours:** Continuous. **ADI:** Denver (Steamboat Springs), CO. **Key Personnel:** David Juris, General Mgr.; Scott Taylor, Program Dir.; Jeff Schatz, General Sales Mgr. **Wattage:** 100,000. **Ad Rates:** Combined advertising rates available with KEZW-AM and KKHK-FM.

4441 KPXC-TV - 59
9805 E. Iliff Ave. Phone: (303)751-5959
Denver, CO 80231 Fax: (303)751-5993

Format: Commercial TV. **Owner:** Denver Channel 59 Corp., at above address. **Founded:** 1987. **Formerly:** KUBD-TV (1998). **Operating Hours:** Continuous. **Key Personnel:** Art Samuel, General Mgr. **Wattage:** 5,000,000. **Ad Rates:** $125-700 per unit.

4442 KRFX-FM - 103.5
1380 Lawrence St., Ste. 1300 Phone: (303)893-8500
Denver, CO 80204-2060 Fax: (303)892-4700

Format: Classic Rock. **Owner:** Jacor Communications of Colorado, at above address. **Founded:** 1945. **Formerly:** KOA-FM; KOAQ-FM. **Operating Hours:** Continuous; 100% local. **ADI:** Denver (Steamboat Springs), CO. **Key Personnel:** Don Howe, General Mgr.; Mark Remington, Contact; Jack Evans, Contact. **Wattage:** 100,000.

4443 KRMA-TV - 6
1089 Bannock St. Phone: (303)892-6666
Denver, CO 80204-4066 Fax: (303)620-5600
E-mail: krma.pbs.org

Format: Public TV. **Networks:** Public Broadcasting Service (PBS). **Owner:** Rocky Mountain Public Broadcasting Network, Inc., at above address. **Founded:** Jan. 30, 1956. **Operating Hours:** Continuous. 65% network, 5% local and 30% syndication. **ADI:** Denver (Steamboat Springs), CO. **Key Personnel:** Linda Rea, Production Dir., phone (303)620-5605; Dan Flenniken, Learning Services Dir., phone (303)620-5685; Trudy Fowler, Dir., Dev. & Mktg., phone (303)620-5688; Judy Persing, Finance Dir., phone (303)620-5668; Bud Rath, Engineering Dir., phone (303)620-5627, fax (303)620-5625; James Morgese, Pres./Gen. Mgr., phone (303)620-5662; Donna Sanford, Program Dir./Station Mgr., phone (303)6205617. **Local Programs:** *Life Wise* 4:30 p.m. Sunday, Trux Simmons; *State of Colorado* 7:30 p.m. Friday, Don Kinney. **Wattage:** 100,000. **Ad Rates:** Underwriting available. **URL:** http://www.krma.org.

4444 KRRF-AM - 1280
1560 Broadway, Ste. 1100 Phone: (303)832-5665
Denver, CO 80202 Fax: (303)832-7000
E-mail: am1280x@aol.com

Format: News; Talk. **Networks:** NBC; Westwood One Radio. **Founded:** 1948. **Formerly:** KXKL-AM. **Operating Hours:** Continuous. **Key Personnel:** David Burke, VP/General Mgr., bcfdave@aol.com; Mason Lewis, Program Dir./Operations Mgr., masonamfm@aol.com; Barbara Pooler, Traffic Mgr.; Dennis Douglass, General Sales Mgr., kxkldd@aol.com; Bill Harris, Chief Engineer. **Local Programs:** *Micros in the Morning* 5:00 am - 9:00 am Monday-Friday, Karen Rhoades, Exec. Producer. **Wattage:** 5000.

4445 KUSA-TV - 9
500 Speer Blvd. Phone: (303)871-9999
Denver, CO 80203 Fax: (303)698-4700

Format: Commercial TV. **Networks:** ABC. **Owner:** Gannett Co., 1100 Wilson Blvd., Arlington, VA 22234. **Formerly:** KBTV. **Operating Hours:** Continuous. **ADI:** Denver (Steamboat Springs), CO. **Key Personnel:** Joseph Franzgrote, President.

4446 KUVO-FM - 89.3
2900 Welton St., Ste. 200 Phone: (303)480-9272
Box 11111 Fax: (303)291-0757
Denver, CO 80205
E-mail: info@kuvo.org

Format: Jazz; Public Radio. **Networks:** National Public Radio (NPR); American Public Radio (APR). **Founded:** 1982. **Formerly:** KHUM-FM (1983). **Operating Hours:** Continuous; 100% local. **ADI:** Denver (Steamboat Springs), CO. **Key Personnel:** Florence Hernandez-Ramos, Contact; Carlos Lando, Program Dir.; Frank White, Contact; Tina Lujan, Contact. **Wattage:** 26,000. **Ad Rates:** $38 per unit. **URL:** http://www.kuvo.org.

4447 KVOD-FM - 92.5
1560 Broadway, Ste. 1100 Phone: (303)832-5665
Denver, CO 80202 Fax: (303)832-0964

Format: Classical. **Networks:** Independent. **Owner:** Chancellor Broadcasting, 1440 Ethan Way, Ste. 200, Sacramento, CA 95825, (916)929-5325, Fax: (916)929-1351. **Founded:** 1969. **Operating Hours:** Continuous. **ADI:** Denver (Steamboat Springs), CO. **Key Personnel:** Pam Kenny, General Mgr.; Jim Conder, Program Dir.; John Samson, Music Dir. **Local Programs:** *Down To Earth (folk)*, Joan Samson; *Mountain Aire*, Betsy Schwarm; *Pack Your Bags (travel)*, Jim Conder. **Wattage:** 74,000. **Ad Rates:** $60-125 per unit.

4448 KXKL-FM - 105.1
1560 Broadway, Ste. 1100 Phone: (303)832-5665
Denver, CO 80202 Fax: (303)832-7000

Format: Oldies. **Networks:** Independent. **Owner:** Chancellor, at above address. **Founded:** 1956. **Operating Hours:** Continuous. **ADI:** Denver (Steamboat Springs), CO. **Key Personnel:** Graham Satherlie, General Mgr.; Chris Hoffman, Program Dir.; Julie Mehrer, Production Dir.; Cathy Kennedy, Traffic Dir.; Dennis Douglass, General Sales Mgr.; Bill Harris, Chief Engineer. **Wattage:** 100,000.

4449 KYGO-AM - 1600
1095 S. Monaco Pkwy. Phone: (303)321-0950
Denver, CO 80224 Fax: (303)321-3383

Format: Country. **Owner:** Jefferson-Pilot Communications Co., 1 Julian Price Pl., Charlotte, NC 28208, (704)374-3500. **Operating Hours:** Continuous; 20% network, 80% local. **ADI:** Denver (Steamboat Springs), CO. **Key Personnel:** Robert Call, Contact; Steve Price, General Sales Mgr.; Jennifer Page, Music Dir.; Charles St. John, Program Dir.; Mark Etchason, Contact; Dawn Lehman, Contact; Brad Hart, Chief Engineer. **Wattage:** 5000. **Ad Rates:** Advertising accepted; rates available upon request.

4450 KYGO-FM - 98.5
1095 S. Monaco Pkwy. Phone: (303)321-0950
Denver, CO 80224 Fax: (303)321-3383

Format: Contemporary Country. **Owner:** Jefferson-Pilot Communications Co., 1 Julian Price Pl., Charlotte, NC 28208, (704)374-3500. **Operating Hours:** Continuous; 100% local. **ADI:** Denver (Steamboat Springs), CO. **Key Personnel:** Robert Call, Contact; Steve Price, General Sales Mgr.; John St. John, Program Dir.; Tad Svendson, Music Dir.; Mark Etchason, Contact; Dawn Lehman, Contact; Brad Hart, Chief Engineer. **Wattage:** 100,000. **Ad Rates:** Advertising accepted; rates available upon request.

4451 Mission Cable Co.
1873 S. Bellaire St., No. 1550 Phone: (303)756-5600
Denver, CO 80222-4348 Fax: (303)756-5774

Key Personnel: Robert C. Fanch, CEO; Thomas W. Binning, Contact; Bruce Tinney, Contact. **Cities Served:** Communities in Oklahoma, Arkansas, Texas, Arizona and Kansas .: subscribing households 80,000.

4452 Tele-Communications, Inc. (TCI)
PO Box 5630 Phone: (303)267-5500
Denver, CO 80217 Fax: (303)779-1228

Formerly: United Artists Cable Corp. (1992). **Cities Served:** subscribing households 2,752,726.

DILLON, pop. 1,200.

Summit Co. 80 m. W of Denver. Recreation. Mining.

4453 Binocular Vision & Strabismus Quarterly
Binoculus Publishing
740 Piney Acres Cir. Phone: (970)262-0753
PO Box 3727
Dillon, CO 80435-3727
Professional journal for physicians, surgeons, and other eye health care professionals. Cited online in Medline. **Founded:** 1985. **Freq:** Quarterly. **Trim Size:** 8 1/2 x 11. **Cols./Page:** 3. **Key Personnel:** Paul E. Romano, M.D., Editor; Judith Robinson, C.O., Ad and Circulation Mgr. **ISSN:** 1088-6281. **Subscription Rates:** $84 individuals; $156 two years; $28 single issue. **Remarks:** Accepts advertising. **Former name:** Binocular Vision & Eye Muscle Surgery.
Ad Rates: BW: $270 **Circ:** Combined 800
4C: $1,170

DOLORES, pop. 802.

Montezuma Co. (SW). 115 m S of Grand Junction. Manufactures plywood; saw mills; Ponderosa pine timber. Diversified farming. Sheep, cattle.

4454 Dolores Star
211 Railroad Ave. Phone: (970)882-4486
PO Box 660 Fax: (970)882-4476
Dolores, CO 81323-0660
Publication E-mail: dstar@hubwest.com

Community newspaper. **Founded:** 1897. **Freq:** Weekly (Thurs.). **Print Method:** Offset. **Cols./Page:** 4. **Col. Width:** 28 nonpareils. **Col. Depth:** 182 agate lines. **Key Personnel:** Robin Allmon, Publisher. **Subscription Rates:** $13 individuals; $20 out of area. **Remarks:** Color advertising accepted; rates available upon request.
Ad Rates: GLR: $4.50 **Circ:** Paid ‡1,400
BW: $180 Free ‡10

DOVE CREEK†, pop. 824.

Dolores Co. (SW). 80 m W of Durango. Recreational lake. Fishing and hunting. Uranium mining, oil and gas drilling. Pinto beans, wheat.

4455 Dove Creek Press
PO Box 598 Phone: (303)677-2214
Dove Creek, CO 81324
Newspaper with a Democratic orientation. **Founded:** 1939. **Freq:** Weekly (Thurs.). **Print Method:** Web. **Cols./Page:** 5. **Col. Width:** 22 nonpareils. **Col. Depth:** 196 agate lines. **Key Personnel:** Doug Funk, Publisher; Linda Funk, Publisher. **Subscription Rates:** $12 individuals. **Remarks:** Accepts advertising.
Ad Rates: BW: $150 **Circ:** Paid ‡1,100
SAU: $3.57 Free ‡58
PCI: $3.57

DURANGO†, pop. 11,426.

La Plata Co. (SW). 175 m SE of Grand Junction. Tourist resort. Gold, silver, lead, coal, uranium mines; oil, natural gas wells; pine timber; bottling works; nursery. Diversified farming. Hay, grain, fruit.

4456 Durango Herald
PO Drawer A-0950 Phone: (303)247-3504
Durango, CO 81302 Fax: (303)259-5011
Free: (800)530-8318

General newspaper. **Founded:** 1881. **Freq:** Tues.-Sun. (morn). **Print Method:** Offset. **Trim Size:** 22 3/4 x 13 1/2. **Cols./Page:** 6. **Col. Width:** 25 nonpareils. **Col. Depth:** 294 agate lines. **Key Personnel:** Morley C. Ballantine, Chmn./Editor; Richard Ballantine, Publisher; Sharon Hermes, Advertising Mgr.; Pat Jetton, Operations Manager. **USPS:** 162-960. **Subscription Rates:** $56 individuals; $68. **Remarks:** Accepts advertising.
Ad Rates: GLR: $1.71 **Circ:** Tues.-Fri. ★**9,222**
SAU: $7.45 Sat. ★**9,222**
PCI: $7.10 Sun. ★**10,834**

4457 KDUR-FM - 91.9
CUB 239 Phone: (303)247-7262
College Union Bldg. Fax: (303)247-7487
Fort Lewis College
Durango, CO 81301-3920

Format: Alternative/New Music/Progressive. **Networks:** Pacifica. **Owner:** Fort Lewis College, at above address. **Founded:** 1975. **Operating Hours:** Continuous; 25% network, 75% local. **ADI:** Grand Junction-Durango, CO. **Key Personnel:** Wynn Harris, Station Mgr.; Nancy Stoffer, Program Dir.; Kate Haspel, Office Mgr. **Wattage:** 150. **Ad Rates:** $10 for 30 seconds. **URL:** http://www.fortlewis.edu/kdur.

4458 KIQX-FM - 101.3
PO Box X Phone: (970)259-4444
Durango, CO 81302 Fax: (970)247-1005
E-mail: feb@frontier.net

Format: Adult Contemporary. **Networks:** CBS. **Owner:** Four Corners Broadcasting, at above address. **Founded:** 1981. **Operating Hours:** 5 a.m.-midnight; 2% network, 98% local. **ADI:** Grand Junction-Durango, CO. **Key Personnel:** Ward Holmes, General Mgr.; Mark Schelper, General Sales Mgr.; Tom Little, Program Mgr.; Bethany Hopp, Office Mgr. **Wattage:** 100,000. **Ad Rates:** $9-13 for 30 seconds; $11-16 for 60 seconds.

4459 KIUP-AM - 930
PO Box P Phone: (940)259-4444
Durango, CO 81302-3030 Fax: (940)247-1005
E-mail: feb@frontier.net

Format: Middle-of-the-Road (MOR). **Networks:** CBS; Mutual Broadcasting System. **Owner:** Four Corners Broadcasting LLC, at above address. **Founded:** 1935. **Operating Hours:** Continuous Daily; 35% network, 65% local. **ADI:** Albuquerque (Santa Fe & Hobbs), NM. **Key Personnel:** Ward S. Holmes, General Mgr., ward@frontier.net; Dave Bray, Program Dir.; Linda Wallace, News Dir. **Wattage:** 5000. **Ad Rates:** $9.50-18.70 for 30 seconds; $11.00-18.00 for 60 seconds. Combined advertising rates available with KIQX-FM, KRSJ-FM.

4460 KREZ-TV - 6
158 Bodo Dr. Phone: (303)259-6666
PO Box 2508 Fax: (303)247-8472
Durango, CO 81302
E-mail: krez@frontier.net

Format: Commercial TV. **Networks:** CBS. **Owner:** NM Broadcasting, 13 Broadcasting Pl., Albuquerque, NM 87104, (970)259-6666, Fax: (970)247-8472. **Founded:** 1963. **Operating Hours:** 4:30 a.m.-2 a.m. **ADI:** Albuquerque (Santa Fe & Hobbs), NM. **Key Personnel:** Jack Llewellyn, Operations/

Sales Mgr.; Doug Harris, Chief Engineer. **Ad Rates:** $50-250 per unit.

4461 KRSJ-FM - 100.5
PO Drawer P Phone: (970)259-4444
Durango, CO 81302 Fax: (970)247-1005
E-mail: fcb@frontier.net

Format: Country. **Networks:** ABC. **Founded:** 1972. **Formerly:** KIUP-FM (1974). **Operating Hours:** 19 hrs. Daily; 15% network, 85% local. **ADI:** Albuquerque (Santa Fe & Hobbs), NM. **Key Personnel:** Mark Simon, Sales Mgr.; Ward Holmes, General Mgr., ward@frontier.net; Kristin Maize, Office Mgr. **Wattage:** 100,000. **Ad Rates:** $8.50-16.50 for 30 seconds; $9.50-18.50 for 60 seconds. Combined advertising rates available with KIUP, KIQX.

EADS†, pop. 810.

Kiowa Co. (E). 110 m E of Pueblo. Stock, grain, poultry. Milo maize. Natural gas.

4462 Kiowa County Press
1208 Maine St. Phone: (719)438-5800
Box 248 Fax: (719)438-5352
Eads, CO 81036-0248
Publication E-mail: kcpnews@iguana.ruralnet.net
Publisher E-mail: kcpnews@ria.net

Community newspaper. **Founded:** 1887. **Freq:** Weekly (Fri.). **Print Method:** Offset. **Trim Size:** 8 x 10. **Cols./Page:** 4. **Col. Width:** 1.8 inches. **Col. Depth:** 10 inches. **Key Personnel:** Chris Sorensen, Editor; Connie McPherson, Circulation Mgr.; Marsha Beeson, Customer Service Rep. **ISSN:** 2959-4000. **Subscription Rates:** $19.50 individuals; $22 out of state. **Remarks:** Accepts advertising. **URL:** http://www.ruralnet.net/~kcpnews.
Ad Rates: BW: $232 **Circ:** Paid ‡1,100
PCI: $5.80 Free ‡50

EAGLE†, pop. 801.

Eagle Co. (NWC). 112 m W of Denver. Ski area. Gravel pits. Spruce, pine, cedar timber. Agriculture. Hay, grain, stock.

4463 The Eagle Valley Enterprise
Eagle Group Communications, Inc.
011 Eagle Park E. Dr. Phone: (303)328-6656
PO Box 450 Fax: (303)328-6393
Eagle, CO 81631
Publication E-mail: getnews@vail.net

Community newspaper. **Subtitle:** Legal Newspaper of Record/Eagle County. **Founded:** 1898. **Freq:** Weekly (Thurs.). **Print Method:** Offset. **Trim Size:** 11 x 17. **Cols./Page:** 4. **Col. Width:** 28 nonpareils. **Col. Depth:** 217 agate lines. **Key Personnel:** Nick Nickolich, Editor and Publisher. **USPS:** 163-860. **Subscription Rates:** $14 individuals; $17 Out of County. **Remarks:** Accepts advertising.
Ad Rates: BW: $434 **Circ:** Paid 3000
4C: $493 Free 300
PCI: $8.26

EATON, pop. 1,389.

Weld Co. (W). 7 m N of Greeley.

4464 North Weld Herald
206 1st St. Phone: (970)454-3466
Eaton, CO 80615 Fax: (970)454-3467

Community newspaper. **Freq:** Weekly (Thurs.). **Cols./Page:** 5. **Col. Width:** 1 inches. **Col. Depth:** 1 inches. **Key Personnel:** Gibb Green.; Bruce J. Bormann, Publisher. **Subscription Rates:** $16 individuals; $22 out of state. **Remarks:** Accepts advertising.
Ad Rates: PCI: $4.50 **Circ:** 2,200

ENGLEWOOD, pop. 33,695.

Arapahoe Co. (C). 7 m S of Denver. Retail, industrial, professional city. Manufactures electronic components, steel structures, tools. Greenhouses.

4465 American Salers
American Salers Association
7383 South Alton Way, Ste. 103 Phone: (303)770-9292
Englewood, CO 80112 Fax: (303)770-9302
Free: (888)972-5377
Publication E-mail: amsalers@aol.com

Trade magazine for the livestock industry. Represents Salers cattle breed offic ial publication of the American Salers Association. **Founded:** 1991. **Freq:** 9/year. **Trim Size:** 8 3/8 x 10 3/16. **Key Personnel:** Dean Pike, Manager. **Subscription Rates:** $50 Included in membership full member; $15 associate. **Remarks:** Accepts advertising.
Ad Rates: BW: $736 **Circ:** Paid ‡1,635
4C: $1,000

4466 Bariatrician
American Society of Bariatric Physicians
5600 S. Quebec, Ste. 109-A Phone: (303)770-2526
Englewood, CO 80111 Fax: (303)779-4834
Publication E-mail: bariatric@asbp.org
Publisher E-mail: bariatric@asbp.org

Professional journal covering the medical treatment of obesity and related conditions. **Founded:** 1984. **Freq:** Quarterly. **Print Method:** Web offset. **Trim Size:** 8 1/2 x 11. **Cols./Page:** 2. **Col. Width:** 3 1/2 inches. **Col. Depth:** 9 1/2 inches. **Key Personnel:** James Merker, CAE, Editor; J. P. Smith, Asst. Editor/Advertising Mgr., jpsmith@asbp.org. **ISSN:** 1099-4521. **Subscription Rates:** $48 individuals; $12 single issue; $72 other countries; $18 single issue. **Remarks:** Accepts advertising.
Ad Rates: BW: $850 **Circ:** Controlled 1,800
4C: $1,450

4467 Cable World
5680 Greenwood Plaza Blvd., Phone: (303)837-0900
Ste. 100 Fax: (303)837-0915
Englewood, CO 80111-2404
Magazine reporting news of the cable television industry. **Subtitle:** The Weekly Business News Magazine. **Founded:** Jan. 1989. **Freq:** Weekly. **Print Method:** Web offset. **Trim Size:** 8 1/4 x 10 3/4. **Cols./Page:** 3. **Col. Width:** 2 5/16 inches. **Key Personnel:** Matt Stump, Editorial Dir. **Subscription Rates:** $74 individuals. **Remarks:** Accepts advertising.
Ad Rates: BW: $6174 **Circ:** Paid 5,000
4C: $6724 Non-paid 15,000
PCI: $3067

4468 Colorado Medicine
Colorado Medical Society
7800 E. Dorado Pl. Phone: (303)779-5455
Englewood, CO 80111 Fax: (303)771-8657
Free: (800)654-5653
Publication E-mail: janet_ scardamaglia@cms.org

Magazine publishing news for physicians in Colorado. **Founded:** 1903. **Freq:** Monthly. **Print Method:** Offset. **Trim Size:** 8 1/2 x 11. **Cols./Page:** 3. **Col. Width:** 26 nonpareils. **Col. Depth:** 133 agate lines. **Key Personnel:** William S. Pierson, Editor, bill_ pierson@cms.org. **ISSN:** 0199-7343. **Subscription Rates:** $35 individuals. **Remarks:** Accepts advertising. **URL:** http://www.cms.org.
Ad Rates: GLR: $3 **Circ:** 5,500
BW: $850
4C: $1,250

4469 Cost Survey
Medical Group Management Association
104 Inverness Terr. E. Phone: (303)799-1111
Englewood, CO 80112-5306 Fax: (303)643-4439
Free: (888)608-5601

Professional magazine covering medical practice finances. **Founded:** 1956. **Freq:** Annual. **Trim Size:** 8 1/2 x 11. **Key Personnel:** David N. Gans, Survey Operations Dir.; James W. Margolis, Senior Project Dir. **ISSN:** 1064-4571. **Subscription Rates:** $300 single issue; Free to qualified subscribers. **Remarks:** Advertising not accepted.
Circ: Controlled 8,500

4470 Destinations
Air Group Publishing Corp.
6006 S. Holly St., Ste. 123
Englewood, CO 80111-4200

Inflight magazines for United Express focusing on the airlines' destinationcities in the Midwest, Mid-Atlantic states, and Colorado. **Founded:** 1984. **Freq:** Monthly. **Print Method:** Offset. **Trim Size:** 8 3/8 x 10 7/8. **Cols./Page:** 3. **Col. Width:** 34 nonpareils. **Col. Depth:** 135 agate lines. **Key Personnel:** Scott E. Dial, Editor-in-Chief; Karl Stout, President; Robert Greyhound, Advertising Mgr. **Subscription Rates:** $4 individuals. **Remarks:** Accepts advertising.
Ad Rates: BW: $1,500 **Circ:** Non-paid 12,000
4C: $1,875

4471 Healthcare Advertising Review
The Business Word
5350 S. Roslyn St. Phone: (303)290-8500
Ste. 400 Fax: (303)290-9025
Englewood, CO 80111-2125
Magazine for healthcare providers and advertising agencies reviewing print, direct mail, outdoor and television advertising done by healthcare institutions. **Subtitle:** Creative forum for the people who plan and create healthcare advertising programs. **Founded:** May 1, 1985. **Freq:** Bimonthly. **Print Method:** Offset. **Trim Size:** 8 x 13. **Cols./Page:** 2. **Col. Width:** 48 nonpareils. **Col. Depth:** 168 agate lines. **Key Personnel:** Jeannette Herrerid, Associate Editor, phone (303)290-8928, fax (303)967-0137, jeannette.herreria@businessword.com. **ISSN:** 8756-4513. **Subscription Rates:** $259 individuals; $50 single issue - nonsubscribers; $25 single issue - subscribers. **Remarks:** Advertising not accepted.
Circ: Paid ‡1,000

4472 Medical Group Management Journal
Medical Group Management Association
104 Inverness Terr. E. Phone: (303)799-1111
Englewood, CO 80112-5306 Fax: (303)643-4439
Free: (888)608-5601

Journal covering problems, questions, and issues of medical group practice management. **Founded:** 1953. **Freq:** Bimonthly. **Print Method:** Offset. **Trim Size:** 8 1/4 x 10 7/8. **Cols./Page:** 3. **Col. Width:** 2 3/8 inches. **Col. Depth:** 9 3/4 inches. **Key Personnel:** Pamela Moore, Senior Editor, plm@mgm.com; Sheila Tuitele, Advertising Mgr., sat@mgma.com. **ISSN:** 0025-7257. **Subscription Rates:** $48 individuals; $9.75 single issue. **Remarks:** Accepts advertising. **URL:** http://www.mgma.com.
Ad Rates: BW: $2,970 **Circ:** Paid 30,000
4C: $4,620 Controlled 2,000

4473 Mountain Living
Wiesner Publishing
7009 S. Potomac St. Phone: (303)397-7600
Englewood, CO 80112 Fax: (303)397-7619

Consumer magazine for mountain living. **Freq:** Bimonthly. **Print Method:** Web offset. **Trim Size:** 8 3/8 x 10 7/8. **Key Personnel:** Irene Rawlings, Editor; Eliza Castaneda, Publisher; Loneta Showell, Art Dir. **Subscription Rates:** $14.97 individuals; $3.95 single issue. **Remarks:** Accepts advertising.
Ad Rates: BW: $3,162 **Circ:** Paid 19,700
4C: $3,502 Non-paid 11,300

4474 Mountain Pilot
Wiesner Publishing
7009 S. Potomac St. Phone: (303)397-7600
Englewood, CO 80112 Fax: (303)397-7619
Publication E-mail: ed@mountainpilot.com

Magazine about aviation in the mountains and high altitude flying performance. **Founded:** 1985. **Freq:** Bimonthly. **Print Method:** Web offset. **Trim Size:** 8 3/8 x 10 7/8. **Cols./Page:** 3. **Col. Width:** 13.5 picas. **Col. Depth:** 9 1/2 inches. **Key Personnel:** Edward D. Huber, Editor and Publisher. **ISSN:** 1049-7781. **Subscription Rates:** $16.95 individuals; $2.95 single issue. **URL:** http://www.mountainpilot.com. **Formerly:** Wings West.
Ad Rates: BW: $1,140 **Circ:** Paid ‡5,500
4C: $1,340 Controlled ‡9,500
PCI: $95

4475 National Cattlemen
National Cattlemen's Beef Association
PO Box 3469
Englewood, CO 80155

Magazine covering beef-industry business management and issues. **Founded:** 1985. **Freq:** Monthly. **Print Method:** Offset. **Trim Size:** 8 1/2 x 11. **Cols./Page:** 3. **Key Personnel:** Kendal Frazier, Editor; Brett Erickson, Sales. **ISSN:** 0885-7679. **Subscription Rates:** $3 single issue. **Remarks:** Accepts advertising.
Ad Rates: BW: $2,500 **Circ:** Paid 41,600
4C: $3,325
PCI: $85

4476 The PRESS Magazine
Intertec Publishing
5680 Greenwood Plaza Blvd., Phone: (303)741-2901
Ste. 100 Fax: (720)489-3225
Englewood, CO 80111
Publication E-mail: press_ edit@intertec.com

Magazine (tabloid) serving the textile screenprinting, and custom apparel, industries. **Subtitle:** The Product and Technology Source for Textile Screenprinting. **Founded:** May 1979. **Freq:** Monthly. **Print Method:** Offset. Uses mats. **Trim Size:** 10 7/8 x 14. **Cols./Page:** 43. **Col. Width:** 13.5 nonpareils. **Col. Depth:** 78 picas. **Key Personnel:** Alan Farb, Editor, phone (720)489-3188, alah_ farb@iufevtec.com; Art Ellis, Publisher. **ISSN:** 0744-3161. **Subscription Rates:** $28 individuals; $35 Canada; $55 other countries; free to qualified U.S. subscribers. **URL:** http://www.intertec.com.
Ad Rates: BW: $5045 **Circ:** Controlled ‡27,512
4C: $5990

4477 Radio Resource
Pandata Corp.
14 Inverness Dr. E, Ste. D-136 Phone: (303)792-2390
Englewood, CO 80112 Fax: (303)792-2391
Free: (800)548-5536
Publication E-mail: edit@radioresourcemag.com
Publisher E-mail: info@radioresourcemag.com

Magazine for mobile radio system managers. **Subtitle:** System Solutions for Mobile Communications. **Founded:** 1986. **Freq:** 10/year. **Print Method:** Web offset. **Trim Size:** 8 1/8 x 10 7/8. **Key Personnel:** Stacey Skillern, Editor; Paulla Nelson-Shira, Publisher; Mark Shira, Vice President; Lola Friday, Traffic Mgr. **ISSN:** 1080-3025. **Remarks:** Accepts advertising.
Ad Rates: BW: $4,030 **Circ:** Non-paid 32,000
4C: $4,780
PCI: $85

4478 Rocky Mountain Baptist
Colorado Baptist General Convention
7393 S. Alton Way Phone: (303)771-2480
Englewood, CO 80112 Fax: (303)771-6272

Southern Baptist newspaper. **Founded:** 1956. **Freq:** Monthly. **Print Method:** Offset. **Trim Size:** 8 1/2 x 11. **Cols./Page:** 4. **Col. Width:** 29 nonpareils. **Col. Depth:** 224 agate lines. **Key Personnel:** Charles E. Sharp, Editor. **Subscription Rates:** $5 individuals.
Ad Rates: SAU: $6.63 **Circ:** ‡4,000

4479 Rocky Mountain Construction
ACP
9250 E. Costilla Ave., Ste. 400 Phone: (303)295-0630
Englewood, CO 80112-3647 Fax: (303)295-2159
Publisher E-mail: acppubs@cmgd.com

Magazine serving the construction industry of America's mountain regions. Topics covered include heavy engineering, building, landscaping, soil conservation, mining, and logging and federal, state, county, and city projects. Includes weekly construction reports. **Founded:** Jan. 1925. **Freq:** Semimonthly. **Print Method:** Offset. Uses mats. **Trim Size:** 8 1/8 x 10 7/8. **Cols./Page:** 3 and 2. **Col. Width:** 26 and 40 nonpareils. **Col. Depth:** 140 agate lines. **Key Personnel:** F. Hol Wagner, Jr., Editor, hol.wagner@cmdg.com; Chris Casey, Publisher, chris.casey@cmdg.com; John Krane, Contact, john.krane@cmdg.com. **USPS:** 468-980. **Subscription Rates:** Free to qualified subscribers; $40 individuals; $2 single issue. **Remarks:** Accepts advertising.
Ad Rates: BW: $980 **Circ:** Paid 53
4C: $1,430 Controlled 8,792
PCI: $32

4480 Satellite Communications
Intertec Publishing Corp.
5660 Greenwood Plaza Blvd., Ste. 350 Phone: (303)793-0448
Englewood, CO 80111 Fax: (303)793-0454
Free: (800)848-4273

Magazine for users and manufacturers in the commerical satellite industry. **Subtitle:** Technology to Connect a Worlwide Market. **Founded:** Oct. 1977. **Freq:** Monthly. **Print Method:** Web offset. **Trim Size:** 7 7/8 x 10 7/8. **Cols./Page:** 3. **Col. Width:** 26 nonpareils. **Col. Depth:** 128 agate lines. **Key Personnel:** Jim Gifford, Editor, phone (360)456-8610, fax (360)456-8699, jim_gifford@intertec.com; Amy C. Cosper, Assoc. Editor, phone (303)220-4287, amy_cosper@intertec.com; Melissa Henrie Cowan, Assoc. Publisher, melissa_henri@intertec.com. **ISSN:** 0147-7439. **Remarks:** Accepts advertising.
Ad Rates: PCI: $87 **Circ:** ‡22,107

4481 Stitches Magazine
Intertec Publishing Corp.
5660 Greenwood Plaza Blvd., Ste. 350 Phone: (303)793-0448
Englewood, CO 80111 Fax: (303)793-0454
Trade and business magazine for commercial embroiderers. **Subtitle:** Embroidery's Voice & Vision for 10 Years and More. **Founded:** May 1987. **Freq:** 15/year. **Print Method:** Offset. **Trim Size:** 8 3/8 x 10 7/8. **Cols./Page:** 3. **Col. Width:** 13 1/2 picas. **Col. Depth:** 10 inches. **Key Personnel:** Sylvia Lewis, Managing Editor, sylvia_lewis@intertec.com; John Torrey, Publisher, phone (913)979-1858, fax (913)967-1898, john_torrey@intertec.com. **ISSN:** 0899-5893. **Subscription Rates:** Free to qualified subscribers; $32; $37 Canada and Mexico; $45 other countries. **Remarks:** Accepts advertising.
Ad Rates: BW: $3,100 **Circ:** Combined △**18,289**
4C: $3,990
PCI: $1.70

4482 Twins Magazine
5350 S. Roslyn St., Ste. 400 Phone: (303)290-8500
Englewood, CO 80111-2125 Fax: (303)290-9025
Free: (800)328-3211
Publication E-mail: twins@businessword.com

International magazine providing support and information to parents of multiple-birth children. **Subtitle:** The Magazine for Parents of Multiples. **Founded:** 1984. **Freq:** Bimonthly. **Print Method:** Web offset. **Trim Size:** 8 x 10 3/4. **Cols./Page:** 3 and 2. **Col. Width:** 2 1/4 and 3 3/8 inches. **Col. Depth:** 9 1/2 and 9 1/2 inches. **Key Personnel:** Susan J. Alt, Editor; Donald E. L. Johnson, Publisher; Joel D. Gregg, Advertising Mgr.; Heather White, Asst. Editor; Marge D. Hansen, Managing Editor. **ISSN:** 0890-3077. **Subscription Rates:** $23.95. **URL:** http://www.twinsmagazine.com.
Ad Rates: BW: $2,926 **Circ:** Paid ★**36,643**
4C: $3,901 Non-paid ★**22,347**
PCI: $87

4483 www.industry.net
Industry.net Inc.
15 Inverness Way E., B106 Phone: (303)397-2383
Englewood, CO 80112-5776 Fax: (303)705-4205
Publication E-mail: newseditor@industry.net

News web site covering manufacturing and industrial equipment for engineering professionals. **Founded:** 1996. **Key Personnel:** Liz Maynard Prigge, Director, Editorial Content; Marty Farrell, VP, Sales; Eileen Quirk, COO; Rich Remington, Director of Technical and Prod. **Subscription Rates:** Free to qualified subscribers. **Remarks:** Advertising accepted; rates available upon request. **URL:** http://www.industry.net. **Former name:** IndustryNet Report.
Circ: Non-paid 500,000

KQKS-FM - See Longmont

4484 KRKS-AM - 990
7880 E. Berry Rd. Phone: (303)750-5687
Englewood, CO 80111 Fax: (303)696-8063
Free: (800)696-9673

Format: Religious; Talk; News; Information. **Networks:** CNN Radio; Sun Radio. **Founded:** 1953. **Operating Hours:** Continuous. **Ad Rates:** $40 for 30 seconds; $50 for 60 seconds.

4485 KTVD-TV - 20
11203 E. Peakview Ave. Phone: (303)792-2020
PO Box 6522 Fax: (303)790-4633
Englewood, CO 80111

Format: Commercial TV. **Networks:** United Paramount Network. **Owner:** FRFQ Fychaner, keys W Fullerton Chicago, at above address. **Founded:** 1988. **Operating Hours:** Continuous. **ADI:** Denver (Steamboat Springs), CO. **Key Personnel:** Greg Armstrong, General Mgr., phone (303)705-2330; Linda Larney, Contact, phone (303)705-2370. **Local Programs:** *Denver Talks*, Becky Alfrey, Mailing contact, (303)781-4946; *Focus on Colorado*. **Wattage:** 5 Million.

4486 KWGN-TV - 2
6160 S. Wabash Way Phone: (303)740-2222
Englewood, CO 80111 Fax: (303)740-2847

Format: Commercial TV. **Networks:** Warner Brothers Studios. **Owner:** Tribune Broadcasting Co., 435 N. Michigan Ave., Chicago, IL 60611, (312)222-3333. **Founded:** July 18, 1952. **Operating Hours:** Continuous; 100% local. **ADI:** Denver (Steamboat Springs), CO. **Key Personnel:** Bill Rosser, Contact, phone (303)740-2850, fax (303)796-3740, bross@tribune.com; Laura Nelson, Contact, phone (303)740-2854, fax (303)796-3743, lnelson@tribune.com; Steve Grund, News Dir., phone (303)740-2800, fax (303)740-2803, sgrund@tribune.com; George Riddell, Creative Services, phone (303)0740-2851, fax (303)796-3713, griddell@tribune.com; Beverly Martinez, Public Affair Contact, phone (303)740-2810, bmartinez@tribune.com; Derek Dalton, General Sales Mgr., phone (303)740-2856, ddalton@tribune.com. **Ad Rates:** Advertising accepted; rates available upon request.

4487 KYBG-AM - 1090
5660 Greenwood Plaza Blvd., Ste. 400 Phone: (303)721-9210
Englewood, CO 80111 Fax: (303)421-1435

Format: Sports; Talk. **Networks:** NBC; AP; CBS. **Owner:** KYBG, at above address. **Formerly:** KADX-FM (1987); KLSC-AM. **Operating Hours:** Continuous. **Key Personnel:** Ron Jamison, General Mgr.; John Vigil, Asst. Prod. Dir./News Dir.; Cindy Jamison, Public Affairs Dir.; Don Martin, Exec. Producer. **Wattage:** 50,000. **Ad Rates:** $35-125 per unit.

4488 KYBG-FM - 92.1
5660 Greenwood Plaza Blvd., Ste. 400 Phone: (303)721-9210
Englewood, CO 80111 Fax: (303)721-1435

Format: Sports; Talk. **Simulcasts:** KYBG-AM. **Networks:** NBC; AP; CBS. **Owner:** KYBG, at above address. **Founded:** 1978. **Formerly:** KZRZ-FM. **Operating Hours:** Continuous. **Key Personnel:** Ron Jamison, General Mgr.; John Vigil, Asst. Prod. Dir./News Dir.; Cindy Jamison, Public Affairs Dir.; Don Martin, Exec. Producer; Steve Gramzay, Program Dir. **Wattage:** 50,000. **Ad Rates:** $5-90 per unit.

4489 SUPERAUDIO Cable Radio Service
9697 E. Mineral Ave. Phone: (303)784-8256
Englewood, CO 80112 Fax: (303)784-8699
Free: (800)727-5663
E-mail: krice@superaudio.com

Founded: 1987. **Formerly:** Superadio (1991). **Key Personnel:** Jeff Wayne, President, phone (303)792-3111, fax (303)792-5608; Kathleen Rice, Product Manager, phone (303)784-8256, fax (303)792-5608, krice@superaudio.com. **Cities Served:** subscribing households 5,000,000; 9 channels.

4490 TCI of Colorado
6850 S. Tucson Way Phone: (303)778-2978
Englewood, CO 80112 Fax: (303)778-2912

Formerly: United Artist Cable. **Key Personnel:** Steve Santamaria, General Mgr.; Margaret Lejuste, Dir. Govt. and Community Affairs, phone (303)765-7278; Jon Bowman, Mgr. Govt. and Community Affairs, phone (303)765-7089. **Cities Served:** Twenty-three franchise areas in a six county area.: subscribing households 397,000; 60 channels.

ESTES PARK, pop. 2,703.

Larimer Co. (N). 62 m NW of Denver. Estes Park eastern gateway to Rocky Mountain National Park resort region.

4491 Trail Gazette
Box 1707 Phone: (970)586-3356
Estes Park, CO 80517 Fax: (970)586-9532

Newspaper. **Founded:** 1971. **Freq:** Semiweekly (Wed. and Fri.). **Print Method:** Offset. **Cols./Page:** 6. **Col. Width:** 12.3 picas. **Col. Depth:** 21 inches. **Key Personnel:** Tim Asbury, Managing Editor; Terence K. Licence, Publisher; Elizabeth Rogers, Advertising Mgr. **Subscription Rates:** $30 individuals; $41 in state; $49 out of state. **Remarks:** Accepts advertising. **URL:** http://www.eptrail.com.
Ad Rates: GLR: $.75 **Circ:** ‡5,877
BW: $1,323
4C: $1,673
PCI: $10.50

EVERGREEN, pop. 15,000.

Jefferson Co. (NC). 29 m W of Denver. Residential.

4492 Canyon Courier
Evergreen Newspapers, Inc.
PO Box 430 Phone: (303)838-4884
Evergreen, CO 80437 Fax: (303)674-4104
Publication E-mail: ccourier1@aol.com

Community newspaper (tabloid). **Founded:** Oct. 1958. **Freq:** Weekly (Wed.). **Print Method:** Offset. **Trim Size:** 10 1/4 x 16. **Cols./Page:** 4. **Col. Width:** 29 nonpareils. **Col. Depth:** 224 agate lines. **Key Personnel:** Tony Messenger, Editor; Kamal Eways, Publisher; John Ellis, Advertising Dir. **Subscription Rates:** $20 individuals; $24 out of area. **Remarks:** Accepts advertising.
Ad Rates: GLR: $.82 **Circ:** Paid ‡8,000
BW: $755.20 Free ‡400
4C: $855.60
SAU: $9.10
PCI: $11.80

FLAGLER, pop. 550.

Kit Carson Co. (E). 110 m SE of Denver. Feed mill; bird seed packaging plant. Livestock, dairy, farms. Wheat, corn, barley, proso.

4493 The Flagler News & Mile Save Shopper
The Flagler News
321 Main Ave. Phone: (719)765-4468
PO Box 188 Fax: (719)765-4517
Flagler, CO 80815
Newspaper with a Republican orientation. **Founded:** 1913. **Freq:** Weekly (Thurs.). **Print Method:** Offset. **Cols./Page:** 8. **Col. Width:** 11 picas. **Col. Depth:** 294 agate lines. **Key Personnel:** Thomas E. Bredehoft, Editor and Publisher. **USPS:** 199-580. **Subscription Rates:** $16 individuals; $19 out of state. **Remarks:** Accepts advertising. **Formerly:** The Flager News.
Ad Rates: GLR: $.22 **Circ:** 13,000
PCI: $3.50

FLORENCE

4494 Florence Citizen
200 S. Pikes Peak Phone: (719)784-6383
Florence, CO 81226
Community newspaper. **Founded:** 1898. **Freq:** Weekly (Thurs.). **Print Method:** Offset. **Trim Size:** 11 x 17. **Cols./Page:** 6. **Col. Width:** 9.6 picas. **Col. Depth:** 15 4/5 inches. **Key Personnel:** Robert M. and Susan E. Wood, Publisher. **Subscription Rates:** $13; $15 out of area. **Remarks:** Accepts advertising.
Ad Rates: BW: $250 **Circ:** ‡1,500
SAU: $5.41
PCI: $3.50

FORT COLLINS†, pop. 64,945.

Larimer Co. (N). 65 m N of Denver. Colorado State University. Manufactures sugar, flour, brick, tile, electronics, plastics, dental appliances, canned foods, machinery, beverages. Pine timber. Stock, grain, fruit, dairy farms. Sugar beets, lambs, alfalfa.

4495 Biology of Reproduction
Society for the Study of Reproduction
Animal Reproduction and Biotechnology Laboratory
Colorado State University
Fort Collins, CO 80523-1683
Phone: (970)491-2006
Fax: (970)491-2007
Publication E-mail: biorepro@cvmbs.colostate.edu
Publisher E-mail: ssr@ssr.org

Trade journal covering research on reproductive biology. **Founded:** 1967. **Freq:** Monthly. **Print Method:** Offset. **Trim Size:** 8 1/2 x 11. **Cols./Page:** 2. **Col. Width:** 3 1/2 inches. **Col. Depth:** 9 5/8 inches. **Key Personnel:** Dr. Gordon D. Niswender, Editor-in-Chief; Dr. Terry M. Nett, Assoc. Editor; Judith Jansen, Managing Editor. **ISSN:** 0006-3363. **Subscription Rates:** $250 individuals; $20 single issue. **Remarks:** Accepts advertising. **URL:** http://www.biolrepro.org.
Ad Rates: BW: $400 4C: $1,000 **Circ:** Controlled ⊕3,186

4496 Colorado Farmer-Stockman
Farm Progress Companies
200 E. Mulberry St.
Fort Collins, CO 80524
Phone: (970)416-7323
Fax: (970)416-6819

Farming and ranching magazine. **Founded:** 1947. **Freq:** Monthly. **Print Method:** Offset. **Trim Size:** 8 1/2 x 10 3/4. **Cols./Page:** 4. **Col. Width:** 26 nonpareils. **Col. Depth:** 190 agate lines. **Key Personnel:** Sara Wyant, Editorial Director/Publisher, swyant@farmprogress.com; Allan Johnson, President; Jerry Lucht, Sales Mgr.; Chuck Roth, Advertising Dir.; Joan Waldoch, Editor, jwaldoch@farmprogress.com. **ISSN:** 0010-1729. **Subscription Rates:** $14.98 individuals. **Formerly:** Colorado Rancher and Farmer.
Ad Rates: BW: $1,600 4C: $2,400 PCI: $65 **Circ:** Paid 3,421 Non-paid 6,690

4497 Colorado Review
Colorado State Unversity
Fort Collins, CO 80523
Phone: (970)491-5449
Publication E-mail: creview@vines.colostate.edu

Magazine covering poetry, fiction, nonfiction, and reviews. **Founded:** 1977. **Freq:** Semiannual. **Trim Size:** 6 x 9 1/4. **Cols./Page:** 1. **Col. Width:** 4 inches. **Col. Depth:** 6 1/2 inches. **Key Personnel:** David Milofsky, Editor; Karen Olson, Managing Editor; Nanette Rogers, Managing Editor; Jorie Graham, Poetry Editor; Donald Revell, Poetry Editor. **ISSN:** 1046-3348. **Subscription Rates:** $18 individuals; $9.50 single issue. **Remarks:** Advertising not accepted.
Circ: Paid 1,800,000

4498 Environ
Wary Canary Press
PO Box 2204
Fort Collins, CO 80522
Phone: (303)224-0083
Publication focusing on the production of a healthier environment by educating people about ecological lifestyles. **Subtitle:** A Magazine for Ecologic Living and Health. **Founded:** 1984. **Freq:** 2-3/year. **ISSN:** 0883-9719. **Subscription Rates:** $18 individuals; $30 industry. **Remarks:** Accepts advertising.
Ad Rates: BW: $6.00 **Circ:** Paid 2,000 Non-paid 3,000

4499 Forestry Research West
U.S. Forest Service
240 W. Prospect Rd.
Fort Collins, CO 80526
Phone: (970)498-1324
Fax: (970)498-1010
Publisher E-mail: rfletcher/rmvs@fs.fed.us

Journal covering research in forestry and natural resources in the western U.S. **Founded:** 1973. **Freq:** Quarterly. **Trim Size:** 7 3/4 x 10. **Cols./Page:** 3. **Col. Width:** 2 1/4 inches. **Col. Depth:** 6 inches. **Key Personnel:** Rick Fletcher, Editor, rfletcher/rmrs@fs.fed.us. **Subscription Rates:** Free to qualified subscribers. **Remarks:** Advertising not accepted.
Circ: Controlled 8,500

4500 Fort Collins Coloradoan
Gannett Co., Inc.
PO Box 1577
Fort Collins, CO 80522
Phone: (970)224-7730
Fax: (970)224-7899

General newspaper. **Founded:** 1873. **Freq:** Mon.-Sun. (morn.). **Print Method:** Offset. **Cols./Page:** 6. **Col. Width:** 24 nonpareils. **Col. Depth:** 301 agate lines. **Key Personnel:** David Greiling, Exec. Editor, phone (970)224-7755; Dorothy Bland, Publisher, phone (970)224-7783, fax (970)224-7726; P. J. Browning, Advertising Dir., phone (970)224-7714, fax (970)224-7726. **Subscription Rates:** $91 individuals. **Remarks:** Accepts advertising.
Ad Rates: SAU: $16.67 **Circ:** Mon.-Sat. ★29,050 Sun. ★36,180

4501 G.I.S. World
GIS World Inc.
400 N. College, Ste. 100
Fort Collins, CO 80524-2483
Phone: (970)221-0037
Fax: (970)221-5150
Publication E-mail: dee@gisworld.com
Publisher E-mail: info@gisworld.com

Professional magazine focusing on geographic information systems. **Subtitle:** The World's Leading Geographic Information Systems Publication. **Founded:** 1988. **Freq:** Monthly. **Print Method:** Offset. **Trim Size:** 8 3/8 x 10 7/8. **Cols./Page:** 3. **Col. Width:** 2 1/4 inches. **Col. Depth:** 9 1/2 inches. **Key Personnel:** John Hughes, Editor, hughes@gisworld.com. **ISSN:** 0897-5507. **Subscription Rates:** $72. **Remarks:** Accepts advertising. **URL:** http://www.geoplace.com.
Ad Rates: BW: $3,560 4C: $4,955 **Circ:** Paid 21,575

4502 International Dredging Review
PO Box 1487
Fort Collins, CO 80522-1487
Phone: (970)416-1903
Fax: (970)416-1878
Publication E-mail: idr@juno.com
Publisher E-mail: idr@juno.com

Magazine covering the dredging industry. **Founded:** Oct. 1981. **Freq:** 8/year. **Print Method:** Offset. Uses mats. **Trim Size:** 8 1/2 x 11. **Cols./Page:** 3 and 2. **Col. Width:** 26 and 40 nonpareils. **Col. Depth:** 140 agate lines. **Key Personnel:** Judith Powers, Editor and Publisher; Rob Francis, Advertising Mgr., phone (970)495-0635, francisr@juno.com; Mara Corti, Office Mgr. **ISSN:** 0737-8181. **Subscription Rates:** $45 individuals; $2.50 single issue; $75 out of country. **Remarks:** Accepts advertising. **URL:** http://www.dredgemag.com.
Ad Rates: BW: $1,250 4C: $1,850 PCI: $41.66 **Circ:** Paid 1,500 Controlled 1,450

4503 The Rocky Mountain Collegian
Colorado State University
Student Center Box 13
Colorado State University
Fort Collins, CO 80523-8033
Phone: (970)491-5267
Fax: (970)491-1690
Collegiate newspaper (broadsheet). **Founded:** 1891. **Freq:** Daily Daily during academic year. **Print Method:** Offset. **Trim Size:** 13 x 21 1/2. **Cols./Page:** 6. **Col. Width:** 12.2 picas. **Col. Depth:** 21 1/2 inches. **Key Personnel:** Chris Walsh, Editor, phone (970)491-1688; Larry Steward, General Mgr., phone (970)491-1781, lsteward@lamar.colostate.edu; Kim Blumhardt, Advertising Dir., phone (970)491-1146, kblumhardt@vines.colostate.edu. **Subscription Rates:** $55 individuals. **Remarks:** Accepts advertising. **Available Online.**
Ad Rates: BW: $941.70 4C: $1,101.70 PCI: $7.30 **Circ:** Free ‡11,500

4504 Statement (Fort Collins)
Colorado Language Arts Society
English Department
Colorado State University
Eddy Bldg.
Fort Collins, CO 80523
Phone: (970)491-5264
Fax: (970)491-5601
Journal for members of the Colorado Language Arts Society. **Founded:** 1963. **Freq:** Triennial. **Print Method:** Offset. **Trim Size:** 8 1/2 x 11. **Cols./Page:** 2. **Col. Width:** 3 1/4 inches. **Col. Depth:** 8 1/4 inches. **Key Personnel:** Louann Reid, Editor, lreid@vines.colostate.edu. **ISSN:** 1085-2549. **Subscription Rates:** $8 single issue. **Remarks:** Advertising not accepted.
Circ: Paid 850

4505 KCOL-AM - 1410
1612 Laporte Ave.
Fort Collins, CO 80522
Phone: (970)482-5991
Fax: (970)482-5994

Format: News; Talk. **Networks:** ABC; CNN Radio. **Owner:** Jacor Broadcasting, at above address, Fort Collins, CO 80521. **Founded:** 1947. **Operating Hours:** Continuous. **ADI:** Denver (Steamboat Springs), CO. **Key Personnel:** Stu Haskell, General Mgr.; Nina Hutchinson, Business and Traffic Dir. **Wattage:** 1000. **Ad Rates:** $6-14 for 30 seconds; $8-18 for 60 seconds. **URL:** www.kcol.com.

4506 KCSU-FM - 90.5
Lory Student Center
Colorado State University
Fort Collins, CO 80523
Phone: (303)491-7611
Fax: (303)491-7612

Format: Alternative/New Music/Progressive; Educational. **Owner:** State Board of Agriculture, Colorado State University, Fort Collins, CO 80523. **Founded:** 1964. **Operating Hours:** Continuous. **ADI:** Denver (Steamboat Springs), CO. **Key Personnel:** Mario Caballero, Broadcast Operations Adviser, phone (970)491-6643; Bob Terrill, Development & Training Adviser, phone (970)491-7613; William Hurt, Student Station Mgr., phone (970)491-7613; Sandy Campbell, Student News Dir., phone (970)491-1474; Deni LaRue, Student Program Dir., phone (970)491-7613; Judd Motchan, Student Music Dir., phone (970)491-1695; Kellie Straub, Development Dir., phone (303)491-7611. **Local Programs:** *AAA Music Mix*, Deni LaRue, Program Mgr.; *Bluegrass Show*, Bob Terrill, Music Dir.; *World Music*, Kellie Straub, Development Dir. **Wattage:** 10,000. **Ad Rates:** Noncommercial. $10 per unit. Underwriting available for .

4507 KIIX-AM - 600
1611 S. College, No. 211
PO Box 2047
Fort Collins, CO 80522
Phone: (970)484-5449
Fax: (970)484-5451

Format: Talk; News; Agricultural; Sports; Oldies. **Networks:** NBC. **Owner:** Tsunami Communications Inc., at above address, (970)484-5549. **Founded:** 1959. **Formerly:** KZIX-AM. **Operating Hours:** Continuous; 60% network, 40% local. **ADI:** Denver (Steamboat Springs), CO. **Key Personnel:** Stu Haskell, General Mgr.; Chris Adams, Program Dir.; Dick Andersen, Sales Mgr.; Wyatt Thompson. **Wattage:** 5000. **Ad Rates:** $10-25 per unit.

4508 KPAW-FM - 107.9
1612 Laporte Ave.
Fort Collins, CO 80521
Phone: (303)482-5991
Fax: (303)482-5994
E-mail: info@kpaw.com

Networks: ABC. **Owner:** Jacor Communications, at above address. **Founded:** 1971. **Formerly:** KIMN-FM. **Operating Hours:** Continuous. **Key Personnel:** Stu Haskell, General Mgr., phone (303)482-5991, fax (303)482-5994; Scott James, Operations Mgr., scott@kpaw.com; Nina Hutchinson, Business & Traffic Mgr., phone (303)482-5991, fax (303)482-5994. **Wattage:** 100,000. **Ad Rates:** KGLL, KCOL-AM, KIIX-AM. **URL:** http://www.kpaw.com.

4509 KTCL-FM - 93.3
Box 2047
Fort Collins, CO 80522
Phone: (303)484-5449

Format: Eclectic; Alternative/New Music/Progressive. **Owner:** Tsunami Communications Inc., at above address. **Founded:** 1965. **Formerly:** KIIX-FM. **Operating Hours:** Continuous. **ADI:** Denver (Steamboat Springs), CO. **Key Personnel:** Stu Haskell, General Mgr.; Linda Diehl, General Sales Mgr.; John Hayes, Program Dir. **Wattage:** 100,000.

4510 TCI of Fort Collins
1201 University Ave.
Fort Collins, CO 80521
Phone: (303)493-7400
Fax: (970)493-4958

Founded: 1978. **Key Personnel:** Bob Carnahan, General Mgr. **Cities Served:** subscribing households 30,000; 52 channels; 4 community access channels.

FORT LUPTON, pop. 4,700.

Weld Co. (N). 25 m N. of Denver. Residential. Oil, gas. Agricultural.

4511 Ft. Lupton Press
Metro West Publishing
PO Box 125
Fort Lupton, CO 80621
Phone: (303)857-4440
Fax: (303)659-2901

Community newspaper. **Founded:** 1906. **Freq:** Semiweekly (Wed. and Sat.). **Print Method:** Offset. **Cols./Page:** 6. **Col. Width:** 21 nonpareils. **Col. Depth:** 224 agate lines. **Key Personnel:** Bradley Womell, Editor. **Subscription Rates:** $29 individuals. **Remarks:** Accepts advertising.
Ad Rates: SAU: $6.75 **Circ:** Paid ‡1,100 Non-paid ‡4,400

FORT MORGAN†, pop. 7,594.

Morgan Co. (NE). 75 m NE of Denver. Manufactures modular homes; beet sugar processing; beef packing; nursery. Agriculture. Sugar beets, stock, corn, grain.

4512 The Fort Morgan Times
Eastern Colorado Publishing Co.
329 Main St.
PO Box 4000
Fort Morgan, CO 80701
Phone: (970)867-5651
Fax: (970)867-7448
Publication E-mail: fmtimes@ria.net

Newspaper with a community focus. **Founded:** 1884. **Freq:** Mon.-Sat. (eve.). **Print Method:** Offset. **Cols./Page:** 6. **Col. Width:** 25 nonpareils. **Col. Depth:** 301 agate lines. **Key Personnel:** Robert W. Spencer, Jr., Editor; Timi McCormick, Advertising Mgr.; Roy G. Robinson, Publisher; Tammy Nelson, Business Mgr.; Phillip K. Cummings, Circulation Mgr.; Wayne Wacker, Production Mgr. **USPS:** 205-940. **Subscription**

Rates: $108 individuals. **Remarks:** Advertising not accepted for X-rated material.
Ad Rates: GLR: $.66 **Circ:** Mon.-Sat. ★**4,572**
BW: $1,189.38
4C: $1,399.38
SAU: $9.55

4513 KBRU-FM - 101.7
PO Box 430 Phone: (970)867-5674
Fort Morgan, CO 80701 Fax: (970)842-1023

Format: Oldies. **Simulcasts:** KFTM. **Networks:** CBS. **Owner:** Arnold Broadcasting Co., Inc., PO Box 753, LaMar, CO 81052, (719)336-4227. **Founded:** 1949. **Operating Hours:** Continuous. **Key Personnel:** Pat Orourke, Sports Dir.; Jeff Lodding, News Dir.; Roger Morgan, Program Dir. **Local Programs:** *Morgan Talks* 7:00 am - 8:00 am Monday-Friday, Roger Morgan, (970)867-5674, Fax (970)867-5675, Jeff Lodding. **Wattage:** 3000. **Ad Rates:** $4.00-5.25 for 15 seconds; $5.75-7.00 for 30 seconds; $7.75-9.00 for 60 seconds. Combined advertising rates available with KSTC, KNNG.

4514 KFTM-AM - 1400
PO Box 430 Phone: (970)867-5674
Fort Morgan, CO 80701-0430 Fax: (970)542-1023
E-mail: kftm@sosinc.net

Format: Country. **Simulcasts:** KBRU. **Networks:** CBS. **Owner:** Arnold Broadcasting Co., Inc., PO Box 753, LaMar, CO 81052, (719)336-4227. **Founded:** 1949. **Operating Hours:** Continuous; 66.5% network, 33.5% local. **Key Personnel:** Pat Orourke, Sports Dir.; Jeff Lodding, News Dir. **Wattage:** 1000. **Ad Rates:** $5.25-8.75 for 15 seconds; $7.00-11.50 for 30 seconds; $9.00-15.50 for 60 seconds. Combined advertising rates available with KNNG; KSTC.

4515 KPRB-FM - 106.3
231 Main St. Phone: (970)867-7271
Fort Morgan, CO 80701 Fax: (970)867-2676
Free: (888)556-5747
E-mail: ksir@henge.com

Format: Adult Contemporary. **Owner:** JMS Broadcasting, L. L. C., at above address. **Operating Hours:** Continuous. **Key Personnel:** Wayne Johnson, General Mgr.; Kevin Shaffer, Sales Mgr.; Miki McRee, News Dir.; John Beltran, Sports Dir. **Wattage:** 3,000. **URL:** http://www.b106.net.

4516 KSIR-AM - 1010
231 Main St.
Fort Morgan, CO 80701
E-mail: ksir@henge.com

Format: Sports; Talk; Agricultural. **Networks:** ABC. **Founded:** 1977. **Formerly:** KKGZ-AM (1994). **Operating Hours:** Continuous. **Key Personnel:** Kevin M. Shaffer, President; Wayne Johnson, Vice President. **Local Programs:** *Coach's Corner*, Kevin Shaffer, (970)867-7271; *Morning Report* 6 a.m.-9 a.m., Wayne Johnson, (970)867-7271; *Sports Saturday*, Wayne Johnson, (970)867-7271. **Wattage:** 25,000. **Ad Rates:** Advertising accepted; rates available upon request. **URL:** http://www.ksir.com.

FOUNTAIN, pop. 8,324.

El Paso Co. (EC). 10 m SE of Colorado Springs. Nursery. Agriculture. Livestock, wheat, corn.

4517 El Paso County Advertiser & News
Shopper Press, Inc.
PO Box 400 Phone: (719)382-5611
120 E. Ohio Fax: (719)382-5614
Fountain, CO 80817
Community newspaper. **Founded:** Oct. 1958. **Freq:** Weekly (Wed.). **Print Method:** Offset. **Trim Size:** 11 x 17. **Cols./Page:** 7. **Col. Width:** 16 nonpareils. **Col. Depth:** 224 agate lines. **Key Personnel:** Kathryn A. Wiese, Publisher; Patricia St. Louis, Editor. **ISSN:** 0747-1920. **Subscription Rates:** $20 individuals. **Remarks:** Accepts advertising. **Former name:** Fountain Valley News.
Ad Rates: BW: $1,120 **Circ:** Paid 1,663
4C: $320
PCI: $10

4518 Fountain Valley News
Shopper Press, Inc.
PO Box 400 Phone: (719)382-5611
120 E. Ohio Fax: (719)382-5614
Fountain, CO 80817
Community newspaper. **Founded:** Oct. 1958. **Freq:** Weekly. **Print Method:** Offset. **Trim Size:** 11 x 17. **Cols./Page:** 7. **Col. Width:** 16 nonpareils. **Col. Depth:** 224 agate lines. **Key Personnel:** Kathryn A. Wiese, Publisher; Patricia St. Louis, Editor. **ISSN:** 0747-1920. **Subscription Rates:** $17; $20 elsewhere; $15 seniors-in state. **Remarks:** Accepts advertising. **Former name:** The Advertiser/The Security Advertiser.
Ad Rates: BW: $1,120 **Circ:** Paid 4,337
PCI: $10

FOWLER, pop. 1,217.

Otero Co. (SE). On Arkansas River, 36 m E of Pueblo. Cannery; meat plant. Agriculture. Alfalfa, tomatoes, corn, beans.

4519 Tribune
112 E. Cranston Phone: (719)263-5311
Fowler, CO 81039 Fax: (719)263-5100

Newspaper. **Founded:** 1897. **Freq:** Weekly (Thurs.). **Print Method:** Offset. **Cols./Page:** 5. **Col. Width:** 24 nonpareils. **Col. Depth:** 210 agate lines. **Subscription Rates:** $15 individuals; $18 Out of county. **Remarks:** Accepts advertising.
Ad Rates: GLR: $.47 **Circ:** ‡1,400
BW: $231.88
SAU: $3.75
PCI: $3.75

FREDERICK, pop. 855.

Weld Co. (N). 25 m N of Denver. Coal mines. Grain farms. Wheat, sugar beets.

4520 Farmer and Miner
Metro West Publishing, Inc.
Box 400 Phone: (303)833-2331
204 Oak St. Fax: (303)659-2901
Frederick, CO 80530
Community newspaper. **Founded:** 1932. **Freq:** Weekly (Thurs.). **Print Method:** Offset. **Cols./Page:** 6. **Col. Width:** 1 5/8 inches. **Col. Depth:** 14 inches. **Key Personnel:** Joe Rebel, Editor. **Subscription Rates:** $8.50 individuals. **Remarks:** Accepts advertising.
Ad Rates: PCI: $2.70 **Circ:** ‡1,300

FRISCO

4521 KYSL-FM - 93.9
PO Box 27 Phone: (970)668-0292
Frisco, CO 80443 Fax: (970)668-3667
E-mail: kysl@brecknet.com

Format: Adult Contemporary. **Networks:** ABC. **Owner:** Ann Penny Ogden, at above address. **Founded:** 1988. **Operating Hours:** Continuous. **Key Personnel:** Ann Penny Ogden, President; Marilyn Hogan, General Mgr. **Wattage:** 6,000. **Ad Rates:** $16-27 for 30 seconds; $20-35 for 60 seconds. **URL:** http://www.krystal93.com.

FRUITA, pop. 1,822.

Mesa Co. (C). 10 m NW of Grand Junction.

4522 Fruita Times
217 E. Aspen Ave. Phone: (970)858-3924
Fruita, CO 81521-2238 Fax: (970)858-7658

Community newspaper. **Founded:** 1892. **Freq:** Weekly (Wed.). **Print Method:** Offset. **Trim Size:** 17 x 11 3/8. **Cols./Page:** 4. **Col. Width:** 14 1/2 picas. **Col. Depth:** 16 inches. **Key Personnel:** Eugene Thomas, Editor and Publisher. **USPS:** 211-340. **Subscription Rates:** $20 individuals; $30 out of area.
Ad Rates: BW: $451.84 **Circ:** Paid 1,550
PCI: $7.06 Free 50

GLENWOOD SPRINGS†, pop. 4,637.

Garfield Co. (W). 150 m W of Denver. Recreation area. Coal mines. Ranching.

4523 Glenwood Post
2014 Grand Ave. Phone: (970)945-8515
Glenwood Springs, CO 81601 Fax: (970)945-4487

General newspaper. **Founded:** 1890. **Freq:** Daily. **Print Method:** Offset. **Trim Size:** 14 x 22 1/2. **Cols./Page:** 6. **Col. Width:** 2 1/16 inches. **Col. Depth:** 21 1/2 inches. **Key Personnel:** Dennis Webb, Managing Editor; Gary Dickson, Publisher; Bob Zanella, Advertising Mgr.; Mark Drudje, Circulation Mgr.; Norm Hephner, Production Mgr.; Mae Scott, Business Mgr. **ISSN:** 2202-2000. **Subscription Rates:** $96 individuals. **Available Online.**
Ad Rates: BW: $980.40 **Circ:** Paid ⊕**5,171**
4C: $934.50 Free ‡1,675
PCI: $7.60

4524 KGLN-AM - 980
Box 1028 Phone: (970)945-9124
Glenwood Springs, CO 81602 Fax: (970)945-5409
E-mail: kmts@kmts.com

Format: Oldies. **Networks:** CNN Radio. **Owner:** Colorado West Broadcasting Inc., at above address. **Founded:** 1951. **Operating Hours:** Continuous. **Key Personnel:** Gabe Chenoweth, General Mgr.; Kimberly Henrie, Dir. of Sales; Ron Milhorn, News Dir. **Wattage:** 1000. **Ad Rates:** $18-30 for 30 seconds; $23-35 for 60 seconds. $10-$18 for 30 seconds; $15-$23 for 60 seconds. Combined advertising rates available with KTMS-FM.

4525 KMTS-FM - 99.1
1322 1/2 Grand Phone: (970)945-9124
Glenwood Springs, CO 81601 Fax: (970)945-5409
E-mail: http://www.kmts.com; kmts@kmts.com

Format: Country. **Networks:** ABC. **Owner:** CO W. Broadcasting, at above address. **Founded:** 1977. **Formerly:** KGLS-FM (1978). **Operating Hours:** Continuous. **Key Personnel:** Gabe Chenoweth, General Mgr.; Kimberly Henrie, Dir. of Sales; Ron Milhorn, News Dir. **Wattage:** 10,000. **Ad Rates:** $18-30 for 30 seconds; $23-35 for 60 seconds. $10-$24 for 30 seconds; $15-$29 for 60 seconds. Combined advertising rates available with KGLN-AM: $20-$42 for 30 seconds; $25-.

GOLDEN†, pop. 12,237.

Jefferson Co. (C). 15 m W of Denver. Colorado School of Mines. Coal, gold mines; clay pits. Porcelain; fire-brick; brewery. Truck, dairy, stock, poultry farms.

4526 Advertising & Marketing Review
622 Gardenia Ct.
Golden, CO 80401

Professional magazine covering advertising and marketing news in Colorado. **Founded:** Sept. 1977. **Freq:** Monthly. **Print Method:** Offset. **Trim Size:** 8 3/8 x 10 7/8. **Cols./Page:** 3. **Col. Width:** 2 1/4 inches. **Col. Depth:** 9 inches. **Key Personnel:** Ken Custer, Editor and Publisher, phone (303)277-9840, fax (303)278-9909, kencuster@aol.com. **Subscription Rates:** $18 individuals; $2 single issue. **Remarks:** Accepts advertising. **URL:** http://www.ad-mkt-review.com.
Ad Rates: BW: $1,000 **Circ:** Combined 4,100
4C: $1,100

4527 Colorado School of Mines Quarterly
Colorado School of Mines
Golden, CO 80401 Phone: (303)273-3690
Fax: (303)273-3199
Free: (800)245-1060

Mineral engineering and earth science magazine. **Founded:** 1906. **Freq:** Quarterly. **Print Method:** Offset. **Cols./Page:** 2. **Col. Width:** 44 nonpareils. **Col. Depth:** 122 agate lines. **Subscription Rates:** $65; $70 other countries. **Remarks:** Advertising not accepted.
Circ: ‡600

4528 Dayspring
The Dayspring Press
18600 W 58th St.
Golden, CO 80403-1070

Academic journal of literary criticism. **Founded:** 1987. **Freq:** Quarterly. **Trim Size:** 5 1/2 x 8 1/2. **Cols./Page:** 1. **Col. Width:** 4 inches. **Col. Depth:** 7 inches. **Key Personnel:** Charlotte Campbell, Editor. **ISSN:** 0287-6772. **Subscription Rates:** $50 individuals; $5 single issue. **Remarks:** Accepts advertising. **Alt. Formats:** Large-print.
Ad Rates: GLR: $5 **Circ:** Paid 726
BW: $50

4529 Fiction Forum
The Dayspring Press
18600 W 58th St.
Golden, CO 80403-1070

Academic journal for writers of short and serial fiction. **Founded:** 1983. **Freq:** Monthly. **Trim Size:** 8 1/2 x 5 1/2. **Cols./Page:** 1. **Col. Width:** 4 inches. **Col. Depth:** 7 inches. **Key Personnel:** Charlotte L. Campbell, Editor. **ISSN:** 1287-6770. **Subscription Rates:** $50 individuals; $5 single issue. **Remarks:** Accepts advertising. **Alt. Formats:** Large-print.
Ad Rates: GLR: $5 **Circ:** Paid 608
BW: $35 Non-paid 12

4530 Golden Transcript
Golden Media, Inc.
1000 10th St. Phone: (303)279-5541
PO Box 987 Fax: (303)279-7157
Golden, CO 80401
Publication E-mail: tredltor@tesser.com

Community newspaper. **Founded:** 1866. **Freq:** Weekly (Fri.). **Print Method:** Offset. **Cols./Page:** 6. **Col. Width:** 2 1/16 inches. **Col. Depth:** 21 1/2 inches. **Key Personnel:** Vincent W. Bodiford, President/Publisher. **ISSN:** 0746-6382. **Subscription Rates:** $26 individuals. **Remarks:** Accepts advertis-

ing. **URL:** http://www.tesser.com/transcript/. **Formerly**: Colorado Transcript; Golden Daily Transcript.
Ad Rates: GLR: $1.15 **Circ:** Paid 3,843
BW: $2,016 Free 913
4C: $2,456
SAU: $18
PCI: $16

4531 The Jefferson County Transcript
Golden Media, Inc.
1000 10th St. Phone: (303)279-5541
PO Box 987 Fax: (303)279-7157
Golden, CO 80401
Publication E-mail: treditor@tesser.com

Community newspaper. **Founded:** 1983. **Freq:** Weekly. **Print Method:** Web offset. **Cols./Page:** 6. **Col. Width:** 2 inches. **Col. Depth:** 21 1/2 inches. **Key Personnel:** Vincent W. Bodiford, Publisher. **ISSN:** 1089-9200. **Subscription Rates:** Free. **Remarks:** Accepts advertising. **URL:** http://www.tesser.com/transcript. **Formerly**: The Weekly Transcript.
Ad Rates: BW: $1,806 **Circ:** Free ‡5,266
4C: $2,106
SAU: $14
PCI: $14

4532 Mines Magazine
Colorado School of Mines Press
Publications and Public Relations Dept. Phone: (303)273-3000
Fax: (303)273-3310
1500 Illinois St.
Golden, CO 80401
Free: (800)446-9488

Magazine containing campus research, feature stories related to school, business, technological development, and industry news of interest to alumni of the Colorado School of Mines. **Founded:** Jan. 1, 1910. **Freq:** Bimonthly. **Print Method:** Offset. **Trim Size:** 8 3/8 x 10 7/8. **Cols./Page:** 3. **Col. Width:** 2 1/4 inches. **Col. Depth:** 9 1/2 inches. **Key Personnel:** Charles Warren, Editor, cwarren@mines.edu. **ISSN:** 0096-4859. **Subscription Rates:** $39 individuals. **Remarks:** Accepts advertising. **URL:** http://www.mines.edu/beyond_ csm/alumni/.
Ad Rates: GLR: $1.33 **Circ:** ‡5,000
BW: $790
4C: $1,440

4533 Mines Oredigger
Colorado School of Mines Press
Publications and Public Relations Dept. Phone: (303)273-3000
Fax: (303)273-3310
1500 Illinois St.
Golden, CO 80401
Free: (800)446-9488

Collegiate newspaper. **Subtitle:** The Voice of the World's Foremost School of Mineral Engineering. **Founded:** 1919. **Freq:** Weekly (Tues.). **Print Method:** Web offset. **Trim Size:** 23 x 14. **Cols./Page:** 6. **Col. Width:** 2 inches. **Col. Depth:** 21 inches. **Key Personnel:** Tota Mukherjee, Editor; Jenny Falcone, Advertising Mgr. **Subscription Rates:** Free; $20 by mail. **Remarks:** Color advertising not accepted.
Ad Rates: BW: $921.60 **Circ:** Paid ‡500
PCI: $7 Free ‡3,000

4534 New Catholic Review
High Tech Distributors
18600 W 58th Ave.
Golden, CO 80403-1070

A monthly forum of Catholic fact and fiction. **Founded:** 1983. **Freq:** Monthly. **Print Method:** Photo offset. **Trim Size:** 5 1/2 x 8 1/2. **Cols./Page:** 1. **Col. Width:** 4 inches. **Col. Depth:** 7 inches. **Key Personnel:** Charlotte L. Campbell, General Mgr. **USPS:** 028-177. **Subscription Rates:** $50; $10 single issue. **Remarks:** Accepts advertising. **Alt. Formats:** Large-print.
Ad Rates: PCI: $10 **Circ:** Paid ‡620
Non-paid ‡72

4535 Poet's Forum
The Dayspring Press
18600 W 58th St.
Golden, CO 80403-1070

Academic journal for poets. **Founded:** 1988. **Freq:** Monthly. **Trim Size:** 5 1/2 x 8 1/2. **Cols./Page:** 1. **Col. Width:** 4 inches. **Col. Depth:** 7 inches. **Key Personnel:** Charlotte Campbell, General Mgr. **ISSN:** 0287-6773. **Subscription Rates:** $50 individuals; $5 single issue. **Remarks:** Advertising accepted; rates available upon request. **Alt. Formats:** Large-print.
Circ: Paid 516

4536 Production and Inventory Management Journal
APIS - The Educational Society for Resource Management
1826 Smith Rd. Phone: (303)279-7658
Golden, CO 80401 Fax: (303)273-3278

Trade refereed journal covering production and inventory management. **Founded:** 1960. **Freq:** Quarterly. **Print Method:** Offset. **Trim Size:** 8 1/2 x 11. **Cols./Page:** 2. **Col. Width:** 45 agate lines. **Col. Depth:** 126 agate lines. **Key Personnel:** R.E.D. Woolsey, Editor, phone (303)273-3484, fax (303)273-3278; Ronita E. Woolsey, Managing Editor. **ISSN:** 0897-8336. **Subscription Rates:** APICS members receive one subscription free; $50 second subscription; $110 nonmembers. **Remarks:** Advertising not accepted. **Formerly**: Production and Inventory Management.
Circ: Paid ‡70,000
Non-paid ‡700

4537 Sew News
Primedia Special Interest Publication
741 Corporate Circle Phone: (303)278-1010
Golden, CO 80401 Fax: (303)277-0370
Free: (800)881-6634
Publication E-mail: sewnews@aol.com

Magazine on fashion sewing news, products, and patterns. Includes interviews with designers. **Subtitle:** The Fashion Magazine for People Who Sew. **Founded:** 1980. **Freq:** Monthly. **Print Method:** Offset. **Trim Size:** 9 1/8 x 11 7/8. **Cols./Page:** 4. **Col. Width:** 27 nonpareils. **Col. Depth:** 192 agate lines. **Key Personnel:** Linda Griepentrog, Editor, snlindag@aol.com; Tina Battock, Publisher, tbattock@primediasi.com. **ISSN:** 0273-8120. **Subscription Rates:** $23.98 individuals; $4.95 single issue. **Remarks:** Accepts advertising. **URL:** http://www.sewnews.com.
Ad Rates: BW: $3,120 **Circ:** Paid ★168,593
4C: $4,690

GRANBY, pop. 973.

Grand Co. (N). 32 m W of Boulder. Tourism. Cattle ranching; mining.

4538 Sky-Hi News
Johnson Media, Inc.
PO Box 409 Phone: (970)726-5721
Granby, CO 80446 Fax: (970)726-8789

Newspaper. **Founded:** 1945. **Freq:** Weekly (Thurs.). **Print Method:** Offset. **Cols./Page:** 4. **Col. Width:** 28 nonpareils. **Col. Depth:** 224 agate lines. **Key Personnel:** Patrick Brower, Editor and Publisher. **Subscription Rates:** $19.50 individuals. **Remarks:** Accepts advertising.
Ad Rates: GLR: $.34 **Circ:** Paid 3,800
BW: $330 Free 7,500
4C: $700

4539 Winter Park Manifest
Johnson Media, Inc.
PO Box 409 Phone: (970)726-5721
Granby, CO 80446 Fax: (970)726-8789

Local newspaper. **Founded:** Mar. 1977. **Freq:** Weekly (Thurs.). **Print Method:** Offset. Uses mats. **Cols./Page:** 4. **Col. Width:** 28 nonpareils. **Col. Depth:** 140 agate lines. **Key Personnel:** Douglas M. Freed, Editor; William P. Johnson, Publisher; Barbara Slack, Advertising Mgr. **Subscription Rates:** $18. **Remarks:** Accepts advertising.
Ad Rates: BW: $400 **Circ:** Paid 2,900
PCI: $5.75 Free 800

GRAND JUNCTION†, pop. 27,071.

Mesa Co. (W). 250 m W of Denver. Mountain resort, skiing, hunting, fishing. Electronics. Oil shale, uranium, coal, precious metals. Diversified farming. Fruit, truck crops.

4540 The Daily Sentinel
734 S. 7th St. Phone: (303)242-5050
PO Box 668 Fax: (303)241-6860
Grand Junction, CO 81502-0668
Free: (800)332-5832

General newspaper. **Founded:** 1893. **Freq:** Daily (eve.). **Print Method:** Offset. **Cols./Page:** 6. **Col. Width:** 2 1/16 inches. **Col. Depth:** 21 inches. **Key Personnel:** George Orbanek, Editor and Publisher. **Subscription Rates:** $75.40 individuals.
Circ: Mon.-Sat. 30,340
Sun. 35,654

4541 Navioneer
American Navion Society
225 N. 5th St., Ste. 301 Phone: (303)243-8513
Grand Junction, CO 81501 Fax: (303)243-8503

Magazine containing information on Navion aircraft. **Founded:** 1960. **Freq:** Bimonthly. **Print Method:** Offset. **Trim Size:** 8 1/2 x 11. **Cols./Page:** 3. **Col. Width:** 7 1/2 inches. **Col. Depth:** 10 inches. **Key Personnel:** Jerry Feather, Editor. **Subscription Rates:** $25; $5 single issue. **Remarks:** Accepts advertising.
Circ: 1,200

4542 Penny Pincher
The Daily Sentinel
PO Box 2563 Phone: (303)243-9020
Grand Junction, CO 81502 Fax: (303)241-6860

Weekly classified. **Founded:** 1968. **Freq:** Weekly (Wed.). **Print Method:** Web. **Trim Size:** 10 3/4 x 13 1/2. **Cols./Page:** 4. **Col. Width:** 26 nonpareils. **Col. Depth:** 178 agate lines. **Key Personnel:** Ray Campbell, Publisher. **Remarks:** Accepts advertising. **Formerly**: Shopping News (1984).
Ad Rates: GLR: $.54 **Circ:** Free ‡18,500
BW: $225
4C: $275

4543 KBZS-AM - 620
660 Rood Ave. Phone: (970)242-5787
Grand Junction, CO 81501 Fax: (970)245-6585
E-mail: radiobuzz@radiobuzz.com

Format: Talk. **Networks:** NBC; Westwood One Radio. **Owner:** Leggett Broadcasting, Inc., at above address. **Founded:** 1957. **Formerly**: KSTR-AM (1993); KKTK-AM (1994); KKGM-AM (1996). **Operating Hours:** Continuous. **ADI:** Grand Junction-Durango, CO. **Key Personnel:** Brad Leggett, General Mgr.; Ken Pilling, Operations Mgr./Production Dir. **Wattage:** 5000. **Ad Rates:** Advertising accepted; rates available upon request. **URL:** http://www.radiobuzz.com.

4544 KCIC-FM - 88.5
3102 E Rd. Phone: (970)434-8391
Grand Junction, CO 81504

Format: Religious. **Networks:** Independent. **Owner:** Pear Park Baptist Schools, Inc., at above address, (303)434-4113. **Founded:** 1979. **Operating Hours:** 7 a.m.-8 p.m. **ADI:** Grand Junction-Durango, CO. **Key Personnel:** Harlan Larsen, President; Glenn Gardner, Program Dir., gfgardner@juno.com. **Wattage:** 450. **Ad Rates:** Noncommercial.

4545 KEKB-FM - 99.9
315 Kennedy Ave. Phone: (970)243-3699
Grand Junction, CO 81501 Fax: (970)243-0567

Format: Contemporary Country; Sports. **Owner:** Cumulus Broadcasting, at above address. **Founded:** 1998. **Formerly:** Jan Di Broadcasting, Inc. **Operating Hours:** Continuous. **ADI:** Grand Junction-Durango, CO. **Key Personnel:** Martiey Miller, General Sales Mgr., martiey.millerr@cobraclowest.com; Mike Shafer, Operations Dir., mike.shafer@coloradowest.com; Ron Peterson, Program Dir., ron.peterson@cobradowest.com; Michelle Marston, Music Dir., michelle.marston@coloradowest.com; Marie Petefish, Business Mgr., marie.petefish@cobradowest.com. **Wattage:** 80,000. **Ad Rates:** $15-85 for 30 seconds. **URL:** http://www.coloradowest.com.

4546 KEXO-AM - 1230
715 Horizon Dr. Phone: (970)243-1230
Ste. 430 Fax: (970)245-5858
Grand Junction, CO 81506

Format: Contemporary Christian. **Owner:** Mustang Broadcasting Co. KEXO/KKLY/KQIL/KQIX, at above address. **Founded:** 1948. **Operating Hours:** Continuous. **ADI:** Grand Junction-Durango, CO. **Key Personnel:** Paul Fee, General Mgr.; Dave Beck, Sales Mgr.; Robert St.John, Operations Mgr. **Wattage:** 1000. **Ad Rates:** Combined advertising rates available with KKNN-FM, KQIL-AM, KQIX-FM.

4547 KJCT-TV - 8
Box 3788 Phone: (303)245-8880
Grand Junction, CO 81502 Fax: (303)245-8249

Format: Commercial TV. **Networks:** ABC. **Founded:** 1954. **Operating Hours:** 5:55 a.m. -12:35 a.m. **Key Personnel:** Dan Mason, Station Mgr., danmason@kjct8.com; Rondi Spirz, Traffic Mgr.; Mike Murphy, Promotions Dir.; Roger Hightower, Chief Engineer; Dan McClintock, Creative Services Dir. **Ad Rates:** $10-500 for 30 seconds. **URL:** http://www.kjct8.com.

4548 KJOL-FM - 90.3
1206 Ute Ave. Phone: (303)243-4361
Grand Junction, CO 81501 Fax: (303)242-1309

Format: Contemporary Christian. **Networks:** Moody Broadcasting. **Owner:** 180 S. Garrison, Lakewood, CO 80226, (303)238-5386. **Founded:** 1982. **Operating Hours:** Continuous. **ADI:** Grand Junction-Durango, CO. **Key Personnel:** Ken Andrews, Manager; Scott McIntire, Program Dir. **Wattage:** 1500 ERP.

4549 KJYE-FM - 92.3
1360 E. Sherwood Dr. Phone: (970)241-9230
Grand Junction, CO 81501 Fax: (970)245-7551

Format: Easy Listening. **Owner:** MBC Grand Broadcasting, Inc., at above address. **Founded:** 1960. **Operating Hours:** Continuous. **ADI:** Grand Junction-Durango, CO. **Key Personnel:** Jim TerLouw, General Mgr. **Wattage:** 100,000 ERP.

4550 KKCO-TV - 11
2325 Interstate Ave. Phone: (970)243-1111
Grand Junction, CO 81505-8620 Fax: (970)243-1770
E-mail: tips@nbcllnews.com

Format: Commercial TV. **Networks:** NBC; United Paramount Network. **Owner:** Eagle III Broadcasting L.L.C., at above address. **Founded:** July 19, 1996. **Operating Hours:** Continuous. **ADI:** Grand Junction-Durango, CO. **Key Personnel:** Bill Varecha, CEO; Mike Moran, News Dir.; Mark Vannest, Chief Engineer. **Wattage:** 155,000. **Ad Rates:** $11.25-487.50 for 15 seconds; $15-650 for 30 seconds; $60-1300 for 60 seconds.

4551 KKNN-FM - 95.1
715 Horizon Dr. Phone: (970)243-1230
Ste. 430 Fax: (970)245-5858
Grand Junction, CO 81506
Free: (800)933-9653

Format: Contemporary Country. **Owner:** Mustiang Broadcasting Company, at above address. **Founded:** 1985. **Formerly:** KKLY-FM (1990). **Operating Hours:** Continuous. **ADI:** Grand Junction-Durango, CO. **Key Personnel:** Paul Fee, General Mgr.; Dave Beck, Sales Mgr.; Robert St. John, Operations Mgr. **Wattage:** 100,000. **Ad Rates:** Combined advertising rates available with KQIX-FM, KQIL-AM, KEXO-AM.

4552 KMSA-FM - 91.3
1175 Texas Ave. Phone: (303)248-1240
Grand Junction, CO 81502

Format: Alternative/New Music/Progressive. **Founded:** 1975. **Operating Hours:** 7 a.m. - 1 a.m. **ADI:** Grand Junction-Durango, CO. **Key Personnel:** Frank Bellavia, Contact, phone (970)248-1442, fax (970)248-1708. **Wattage:** 3000. **Ad Rates:** Noncommercial. **URL:** http://www.mesastate.edu/kmsa.

4553 KPRN-FM - 89.5
414 Main St. Phone: (303)241-5776
Grand Junction, CO 81501-2512 Fax: (303)245-8176

Format: News; Classical; Public Radio. **Networks:** National Public Radio (NPR). **Owner:** Public Broadcasting of Colorado Inc., at above address. **Founded:** 1985. **Operating Hours:** Continuous. **ADI:** Grand Junction-Durango, CO. **Key Personnel:** Mary Verdieck, KPRN Development. **Wattage:** 10,000. **Ad Rates:** Noncommercial.

4554 KQIL-AM - 1340
715 Horizon Dr Phone: (970)243-1230
Suite 430 Fax: (970)245-5858
Grand Junction, CO 81501

Format: Sports; Talk. **Networks:** ABC. **Owner:** Mustang Broadcasting Co., at above address. **Founded:** 1959. **Operating Hours:** Continuous. **ADI:** Grand Junction-Durango, CO. **Key Personnel:** Paul Fee, General Mgr.; Dave Beck, Sales Mgr.; Robert St.John, Operations Mgr. **Wattage:** 1000. **Ad Rates:** Combined advertising rates available with KQIX-FM.

4555 KQIX-FM - 93.1
715 Horizon Dr., Ste. 430 Phone: (970)243-1230
Grand Junction, CO 81506 Fax: (970)245-5858
Free: (800)933-0653

Format: Adult Contemporary. **Networks:** Independent. **Owner:** Mustang Broadcasting Company, at above address. **Founded:** 1973. **Operating Hours:** Continuous. **ADI:** Grand Junction-Durango, CO. **Key Personnel:** Paul Fee, General Mgr.; Dave Beck, Sales Mgr.; Robert St. John, Operations Mgr. **Wattage:** 100,000 ERP. **Ad Rates:** Combined advertising rates available with KQIL-AM, KKNN-FM, KEXO-AM.

4556 KREX-TV - 5
345 Hillcrest Manor Phone: (970)242-5000
Grand Junction, CO 81501 Fax: (970)242-0886
E-mail: accounts@krextv.com

Format: Commercial TV. **Networks:** CBS. **Founded:** 1954. **Operating Hours:** Continuous; 75% network, 25% local. **ADI:** Grand Junction-Durango, CO. **Key Personnel:** Ellen Miller, News Dir., fax (970)243-6397, newswest@krextv.com; Dylan Nardy, Promotions Dir.; June Worley, Program Dir.; Al Marra, General Mgr. **Ad Rates:** $35-425 per unit.

4557 KRGS-AM - 690
PO Box 60040 Phone: (970)241-6460
Grand Junction, CO 81506 Fax: (970)241-6452
E-mail: kiss@gj.net

Format: Oldies. **Networks:** Jones Satellite. **Owner:** Western Slope Communications, L.L.C., at above address. **Operating Hours:** Continuous. **ADI:** Grand Junction-Durango, CO. **Key Personnel:** Scott Uhl, Traffic Dir.; David Johnson, Station Mgr.; Jack Mitchell, News Dir.; Rick James, Music Dir.; Michelle Stanton, Office Mgr. **URL:** http://www.kissradio.com.

4558 KRYD-FM - 105
2325 Interstate Ave.
Grand Junction, CO 81505

Networks: NBC. **Owner:** Rocky III Investments, Inc., at above address. **Key Personnel:** W. M. Varecha, CEO, billv@nbcllnews.

KSTR-FM - See Montrose

GREELEY†, pop. 53,006.

Weld Co. (N). 50 m N of Denver. University of Northern Colorado and AIMS Junior College. Manufactures sugar, mobile homes, canned vegetables, butter, concrete products, machinery, potato sorters. Bottling works; meat packing plant; nursery; feed lots. Dairy products. Agriculture. Potatoes, sugar beets, alfalfa, grain, corn, beans.

4559 The Greeley Daily Tribune
Greeley Publishing Co.
501 8th Ave. Phone: (303)352-0211
PO Box 1138 Fax: (303)356-5780
Greeley, CO 80632
Free: (800)275-0321
Publication E-mail: gtribune@greeleytrib.com

General newspaper. **Founded:** 1870. **Freq:** Daily and Sunday (morn.). **Print Method:** Offset. **Cols./Page:** 6. **Col. Width:** 25 nonpareils. **Col. Depth:** 301 agate lines. **Key Personnel:** Chris Cobler, Editor; Jim Elsberry, Publisher, elsberry@greeleytrib.com. **USPS:** 228-040. **Subscription Rates:** $105 individuals. **Remarks:** Accepts advertising.
Ad Rates: BW: $20.75 **Circ:** Mon.-Sat. ★**23,817**
4C: $3,036.75 Sun. ★**24,556**
SAU: $12.65
PCI: $23.54

4560 Hispania
American Association of Teachers of Spanish and Portuguese, Inc.
University of Northern Colorado Phone: (970)351-1090
Butler Hancock, Rm. 210 Fax: (970)351-1095
Greeley, CO 80639
Educational journal (English, Portuguese, and Spanish). **Founded:** 1918. **Freq:** Quarterly. **Print Method:** Letterpress. **Trim Size:** 6 3/4 x 10. **Cols./Page:** 2. **Col. Width:** 54 nonpareils. **Col. Depth:** 105 agate lines. **Key Personnel:** Estelle Irizarry, Editor; Lynn A. Sandstedt, Publisher, lsandste@bentley.unco.edu; Elias Rodriguez, Advertising Mgr., phone (214)720-7300, fax (214)720-7330, egrdrgz@aol.com. **ISSN:** 0018-2133. **Subscription Rates:** $40. **Remarks:** Accepts advertising. **Alt. Formats:** CD-ROM; Mailing labels.
Ad Rates: BW: $275 **Circ:** Paid 13,000

4561 The Mirror
Student Media Corporation
823 16th St. Phone: (970)392-9270
Greeley, CO 80631 Fax: (970)392-9025

Collegiate newspaper. **Founded:** 1919. **Freq:** 3/week. **Print Method:** Offset. **Cols./Page:** 5. **Col. Width:** 24 nonpareils. **Col. Depth:** 223 agate lines. **Key Personnel:** Paula Cobler, General Mgr., phone (970)392-9286; Katherine Radosta, Advertising Mgr., phone (970)392-9323. **Subscription Rates:** $54 by mail. **Remarks:** Accepts advertising. **URL:** http://www.univnorthco.edu/mirror/mirror.htm; http://www.unco.edu/mirror.
Ad Rates: BW: $544 **Circ:** Free 10,000
4C: $944
SAU: $8.15
PCI: $6.80

4562 KGRE-AM - 1450
908 A 8th Ave., Ste. A Phone: (970)356-1452
Greeley, CO 80632-1104 Fax: (970)356-8522

Networks: Independent. **Owner:** Greeley Broadcasting Company, at above address. **Founded:** 1947. **Formerly:** KATR-AM (1989). **Operating Hours:** Continuous. **Key Personnel:** Ricardo Salazar, General/Sales Mgr. **Local Programs:** *Spanish Programming* 12 Noon - 12 Midnight. **Wattage:** 1000. **Ad Rates:** $15 for 30 seconds; $20 for 60 seconds.

4563 KSIR-FM - 107.1
822 7th St., Ste. 740 Phone: (970)353-6522
PO Box 2224
Greeley, CO 80632

Format: Easy Listening. **Networks:** Independent. **Owner:** KKDD-FM Broadcasters, at above address. **Founded:** 1978. **Formerly:** KKDD-FM (1991). **Operating Hours:** Continuous. **Key Personnel:** Robert D. Zellmer, General Mgr., phone (970)353-6522, fax (970)353-6523, bobz@ksir-fm.com. **Wattage:** 100,000. **Ad Rates:** Advertising accepted; rates available upon request.

4564 KUNC-FM - 91.5
University of Northern Colorado Phone: (303)351-2915
Greeley, CO 80639 Fax: (303)351-1780
E-mail: mail@kunc.org

Format: Full Service; Jazz; Alternative/New Music/Progressive; Classical; Public Radio. **Networks:** National Public Radio (NPR); Public Radio International (PRI). **Owner:** Trustees for the University of Northern Colorado, at above address. **Founded:** 1967. **Formerly:** KCBL-FM (1970). **Operating Hours:** Continuous; 25% network, 75% local. **Key Personnel:** Neil Best, General Product Manager, phone (970)351-1765, nbest@kunc.org; Linda Nelson, Underwriter Dir., lnelson@kunc.org; Ron Bailer, Chief Engineer, rbailer@kunc.org. **Wattage:** 100,000. **Ad Rates:** Noncommercial. **URL:** http://www.kunc.org.

GREENWOOD VILLAGE

4565 The Villager
8933 E. Union, Ste. 230 Phone: (303)773-8313
Greenwood Village, CO 80111 Fax: (303)773-8456

Local community newspaper. **Founded:** Nov. 1982. **Freq:** Weekly (Thurs.). **Print Method:** Offset. **Cols./Page:** 5. **Col. Width:** 1 7/8 inches. **Col. Depth:** 15.254 inches. **Key Personnel:** Bob Sweeney, Publisher; Gerri Sweeney, Editor and Publisher; Saundra Dorrance, Advertising Mgr. **Subscription Rates:** $36 individuals.
Ad Rates: BW: $1,705 **Circ:** Paid 3,650
4C: $1,705 Free 350
PCI: $22

4566 The Villager Office Park News
The Villager
8933 E. Union, Ste. 230 Phone: (303)773-8313
Greenwood Village, CO 80111 Fax: (303)773-8456

Newspaper for local businesspeople. **Founded:** 1992. **Freq:** Monthly. **Print Method:** Offset. **Cols./Page:** 5. **Col. Width:** 1 7/8 inches. **Col. Depth:** 15.254 inches. **Key Personnel:** Bob Sweeney, Publisher; Gerri Sweeney, Editor and Publisher; Saundra Dorrance, Advertising Mgr. **Subscription Rates:** $9 individuals; Free. **Remarks:** Combined advertising rates available with The Villager.
Ad Rates: BW: $1,162 **Circ:** Non-paid 5,000
4C: $1,562
SAU: $15
PCI: $15

GUNNISON†, pop. 5,785.

Gunnison Co. (W). On Gunnison River, 125 m SE of Grand Junction. Western State College of Colorado. Resort. Pine timber. Hay, cattle.

4567 Gunnison Country Times
Gunnison Communication, Inc.
218 N. Wisconsin Phone: (303)641-1414
PO Box 240 Fax: (303)641-6515
Gunnison, CO 81230
Community newspaper. **Founded:** 1975. **Freq:** Weekly (Wed.). **Print Method:** Offset. **Cols./Page:** 6. **Col. Width:** 26 nonpareils. **Col. Depth:** 294 agate lines. **Key Personnel:** Roger Morris, Managing Editor; John Thomas, Publisher. **USPS:** 092-113. **Subscription Rates:** $18 individuals; $24 Out of county. **Remarks:** Accepts advertising.
Ad Rates: GLR: $.62 **Circ:** ‡3,800
4C: $350
PCI: $7.44

4568 Crested Butte Cablevision/Gunnison Cablevision
412 W. Tomichi Ave. Phone: (303)641-6023
Gunnison, CO 81230 Fax: (303)641-6159

Owner: Rock & Associates, 5808 Lake Washington Blvd., Ste. 400, Kirkland, WA 98033. **Founded:** 1979. **Key Personnel:** Teri Tippett, Manager; Linda Land, Contact; Stephenie Morris, Office Mgr. **Cities Served:** subscribing households 3,086; 36 channels; 2 community access channels.

4569 KEJJ-FM - 98.3
234 N. Main Phone: (303)641-5000
Ste. 3D Fax: (303)641-3846
Gunnison, CO 81230

Format: Adult Contemporary. **Networks:** Jones Satellite. **Owner:** Steve Glasmannrks,LLC, PO Box 970, Montrose, CO 81402. **Founded:** 1980. **Formerly:** KGUC-FM (1992); KKYY-FM (1997). **Operating Hours:** Continuous. **Key Personnel:** Steve Glasmann, General Mgr.; Marty Weyl, Station Mgr.; Marc Pascoe, Marketing Consultant; Dawn Fakler, Account Executive. **Local Programs:** *Health Watch*, Leah Bougere, Mailing contact; *Sportsline*, Mike Stuart, Mailing contact. **Wattage:** 3000. **Ad Rates:** $10 for 30 seconds; $12 for 60 seconds. Combined advertising rates available with KKXK, KUBC.

4570 KPKE-AM - 1490
134 N. Main Phone: (970)641-4000
Gunnison, CO 81230 Fax: (970)641-3300

Format: Adult Contemporary; Full Service. **Networks:** ABC. **Owner:** J.H. Rees, at above address. **Founded:** June 1960. **Formerly:** KGUC-AM. **Operating Hours:** Continuous. **Key Personnel:** H. Rees, General Mgr. **Wattage:** 1000. **Ad Rates:** $8.50-15.50 for 30 seconds.

4571 KWSB-FM - 91.1
Western State College Phone: (303)943-7048
Gunnison, CO 81231 Fax: (303)943-7069

Format: Eclectic. **Networks:** AP. **Owner:** Associated Student Body of WSC, at above address, (303)943-3033. **Founded:** 1968. **Operating Hours:** 6 a.m.-midnight. **Key Personnel:** Jim Gelwicks, General Mgr.; Mandy Anderson, Station Mgr. **Wattage:** 135. **Ad Rates:** Noncommercial.

HAXTUN, pop. 1,014.

Phillips Co. (NE) 19 m NW of Holyoke. Residential.

4572 The Haxtun-Fleming Herald
PO Box 128 Phone: (970)774-6118
Haxtun, CO 80731 Fax: (970)774-7690
Publication E-mail: cjc@henge.com

Community newspaper. **Founded:** 1975. **Freq:** Weekly (Wed.). **Print Method:** Offset. **Trim Size:** Tabloid. **Cols./Page:** 5. **Col. Width:** 12 nonpareils. **Col. Depth:** 145 agate lines. **Key Personnel:** Jean Gray, Editor and Publisher; Carol Sheel, Advertising Mgr.; Lila Munday, Office Mgr. **USPS:** 120-650. **Subscription Rates:** $20 individuals; $22 out of area. **Remarks:** Accepts advertising. **URL:** http://www.hfherald.com. **Formerly:** The Haxtun Herald.
Ad Rates: BW: $334.10 **Circ:** ‡1,450
PCI: $5.14

HAYDEN, pop. 1,720.

Routt Co. (NW). 22 m E of Steamboat Springs. Logging, sawmills. Dairy, stock, poultry, grain farms.

4573 Hayden Valley Press
Yampa Valley Newpapers, Inc.
126 Walnut St. Phone: (303)276-3202
PO Box E Fax: (303)824-6810
Hayden, CO 81639-0160
Newspaper with a Republican orientation. **Founded:** 1904. **Freq:** Weekly (Thurs.). **Print Method:** Offset. **Cols./Page:** 5. **Col. Width:** 2 1/16 inches. **Col. Depth:** 223 agate lines. **Key Personnel:** Stefka White, Editor; Carol Brett-Beumer, Publisher. **ISSN:** 5780-6000. **Subscription Rates:** $14 individuals; $17 out of area. **Remarks:** Accepts advertising. **Online:** United Media.
Ad Rates: PCI: $6 **Circ:** ‡571

4574 KIDN-FM - 95.5
29587 Hwy. 40, Ste. 1 Phone: (303)870-0900
Steamboat Springs, CO 80487 Fax: (303)870-0300

Format: Adult Contemporary; Alternative/New Music/Progressive. **Networks:** UPI. **Founded:** 1983. **Formerly:** KRDZ-FM (1984); KKMX-FM (1991). **Operating Hours:** Continuous. **ADI:** Denver (Steamboat Springs), CO. **Key Personnel:** Cliff Gardiner, President; Penny Hawkins, Station Mgr.; Tony Mauro, Program Dir.; Tony Mauro, Program Dir. **Wattage:** 10,000. **Ad Rates:** Advertising accepted; rates available upon request.

HENDERSON

4575 Paws for Silence
International Hearing Dog, Inc. (IHDI)
5901 E. 89th Ave. Phone: (303)287-3277
Henderson, CO 80640-8315 Fax: (303)287-3425
Publisher E-mail: ihdi@aol.com
Magazine covering news of the International Hearing Dog, Inc. **Subtitle:** IHDI News. **Founded:** 1979. **Freq:** Quarterly. **Key Personnel:** Martha A. Foss, Pres./Dir. **Subscription Rates:** Free. **Remarks:** Advertising not accepted.
Circ: (Not Reported)

HOLYOKE†, pop. 2,092.

Phillips Co. (C). 48 m E of Sterling.

4576 Holyoke Enterprise
PO Box 297 Phone: (970)854-2811
Holyoke, CO 80734
Community newspaper. **Founded:** 1899. **Freq:** Weekly (Thurs.). **Print Method:** Offset. **Cols./Page:** 6. **Col. Width:** 12.2 picas. **Col. Depth:** 21.5 inches. **Key Personnel:** John Lindenberger, Editor; Loral Johnson, Publisher; Elna Johnson, Publisher; Brenda Brandt, Advertising Mgr./Pub. **USPS:** 248-120. **Subscription Rates:** $17.50 individuals; $21.50 out of area; $24.50 out of state. **Remarks:** Accepts advertising.
Ad Rates: SAU: $5.25 **Circ:** Paid 2,000
Free 20

HUGO†, pop. 776.

Lincoln Co. (E). 100 m E of Denver. Stock, grain, corn, wheat and barley.

4577 Eastern Colorado Plainsmen
329 4th St. Phone: (719)743-2371
Box 98
Hugo, CO 80821
Community newspaper. **Founded:** 1912. **Freq:** Weekly (Thurs.). **Print Method:** Offset. **Cols./Page:** 5. **Col. Width:** 26 nonpareils. **Col. Depth:** 186 agate lines. **Key Personnel:** Becky Osterwald, Publisher. **Subscription Rates:** $16 individuals in-state; $20 out of state. **Remarks:** Accepts advertising.
Ad Rates: GLR: $.23 **Circ:** Paid ‡1,315
BW: $5.25 Free ‡45
4C: $10
PCI: $4

IDAHO SPRINGS, pop. 2,093.

Clear Creek Co. (C). 33 m W of Denver. Fishing and skiing resort. Gold, silver, lead, copper mines. Hot mineral springs.

4578 The Clear Creek Courant
1634 Miner St. Phone: (303)567-4491
Box 2020 Fax: (303)567-4492
Idaho Springs, CO 80452-2020
Publication E-mail: cccourant@aol.com
Publisher E-mail: cccourant@bwn.net

Community newspaper (tabloid). **Founded:** Aug. 24, 1973. **Freq:** Weekly (Wed.). **Print Method:** Offset. **Trim Size:** 11 1/2 x 16 3/4. **Cols./Page:** 4. **Col. Width:** 14.5 picas. **Col. Depth:** 16 inches. **Key Personnel:** Cary Stiff, Editor and Publisher; Carol Wilcox, Editor and Publisher; Nancy Ego, Advertising Mgr. **USPS:** 052-610. **Subscription Rates:** $23 individuals; $28 out of area per year; $20 seniors. **Remarks:** Accepts advertising. **URL:** http://www.members.aol.com/cccourant.
Ad Rates: BW: $480 **Circ:** Paid 2,206
4C: $738
PCI: $10

IGNACIO

La Plata Co. (SW). 15 m SE of Durango.

4579 KSUT-FM - 91.3
PO Box 737 Phone: (970)563-0255
Ignacio, CO 81137 Fax: (970)563-0399

Format: Public Radio; Eclectic. **Networks:** National Public Radio (NPR); American Public Radio (APR). **Owner:** KUTE, Inc., at above address. **Founded:** 1976. **Operating Hours:** 5 a.m.-1 a.m.; 50% network, 50% local. **Key Personnel:** Beth Warren, Contact; Carlos Sena, General Mgr.; Steve Rauworth, Program Dir.; Scott D. Henning, Operations Dir.; Stasia Lanier, Music Dir. **Wattage:** 425. **Ad Rates:** Noncommercial; underwriting available.

4580 Rural Route Video
PO Box 640 Phone: (970)563-9593
Ignacio, CO 81137-0640 Fax: (970)563-9381

Owner: Microwave Distribution Services, Inc., at above address. **Founded:** 1983. **Key Personnel:** Chris May, President. **Cities Served:** subscribing households 400; 32 channels; 1 community access channel.

JOHNSTOWN, pop. 1,535.

Weld Co. (N). 18 m SW of Greeley. Agriculture. Cattle feeders and dairy operations. Sugar beets, grain, hay.

4581 Harris County Journal
PO Box 400
Johnstown, CO 80534-0400

Local newspaper. **Founded:** 1904. **Freq:** Weekly (Thurs.). **Print Method:** Offset. **Cols./Page:** 5. **Col. Width:** 11.5 picas. **Col. Depth:** 224 agate lines. **Key Personnel:** Cly de Briggs, Publisher. **Subscription Rates:** $14 individuals. **Remarks:** Accepts advertising.
Ad Rates: GLR: $.48 **Circ:** 2,600
BW: $307.20
SAU: $4.00
PCI: $4.48

JULESBURG†, pop. 1,578.

Sedgewick Co. (NE). On South Fork of Platte River, 135 m NE of Greeley. Manufactures beet sugar, fertilizer. Natural gas wells. Wheat, corn, beans.

4582 Julesburg Advocate
Eastern Colorado Publishing Co., Sub of The Denver Post Corp.
108-110 Cedar Phone: (970)474-3388
PO Box 46 Fax: (970)474-3389
Julesburg, CO 80737
Publisher E-mail: julesadv@ria.net

Community newspaper. **Founded:** 1899. **Freq:** Weekly (Thurs.). **Print Method:** Offset. **Trim Size:** 13 x 21 1/2. **Cols./Page:** 6. **Col. Width:** 12 1/2 picas. **Col. Depth:** 301 agate lines. **Key Personnel:** Sandi Austin, Publisher/ME. **USPS:** 230-160. **Subscription Rates:** $21 individuals; $24 out of area. **Remarks:** Accepts advertising.
Ad Rates: GLR: $0.38 **Circ:** Paid 1,850
BW: $478.80 Free 30
SAU: $5
PCI: $3.80

KERSEY

4583 The Voice
326 1st St. Phone: (303)356-7176
PO Box 130 Fax: (303)356-7176
Kersey, CO 80644
Community newspaper. **Founded:** 1979. **Freq:** Weekly (Thurs.). **Print Method:** Offset. **Cols./Page:** 6. **Col. Width:** 9 1/2 picas. **Col. Depth:** 13 1/2 inches. **Key Personnel:** James Noel, Publisher; Idella Noel, Publisher; Junita Johannes, Editor. **USPS:** 503-110. **Subscription Rates:** $14 individuals; $20 out of area; $25 out of state. **Remarks:** Accepts advertising.
Ad Rates: PCI: $5.15 **Circ:** 1,125

KREMMLING, pop. 1,250.

Grand Co. (N). 115 m NW of Denver. Tourism. Saw mill. Mining. Ranchers and stock farms.

4584 Middle Park Times
Box 476 Phone: (970)724-3350
Kremmling, CO 80459 Fax: (970)724-0879

Community newspaper. **Founded:** 1882. **Freq:** Weekly (Tues.). **Print Method:** Offset. **Cols./Page:** 4. **Col. Width:** 32 nonpareils. **Col. Depth:** 210 agate lines. **Key Personnel:** Patrick Brower, Publisher, phone (970)887-3334, fax (970)887-3204; Larry Banman, Editor/Advertising Mgr. **USPS:** 347-080. **Subscription Rates:** $15 individuals; $17 Out of county. **Remarks:** Accepts advertising.
Ad Rates: GLR: $.80 **Circ:** Paid ‡1,500
PCI: $6 Free ‡20

LA JARA, pop. 858.

Conejos Co. (S). 100 m SW of Pueblo. Fish hatchery. Agriculture. Dairy, stock, poultry, truck, grain farms.

4585 The Conejos County Citizen
SLV Publishing
517 Main St. Phone: (719)274-4192
PO Box 79
La Jara, CO 81140
Newspaper. **Founded:** 1892. **Freq:** Weekly (Thurs.). **Print Method:** Offset. **Trim Size:** 10 1/2 x 16. **Cols./Page:** 5. **Col. Width:** 2 inches. **Key Personnel:** Ray James, Editor; Steve Haynes, Publisher. **USPS:** 308-760. **Subscription Rates:** $14; $21 other countries. **Remarks:** Accepts advertising.
Ad Rates: BW: $484 **Circ:** Paid 700
PCI: $6.05 Free 7

LA JUNTA†, pop. 8,338.

Otero Co. (SE). On Arkansas River, 65 m E of Pueblo. Cannery; grain mill and elevator; livestock sales rings. Agriculture. Sugar beets, melons, grain, cattle.

4586 Ag Journal
PO Box 500 Phone: (719)384-8121
La Junta, CO 81050 Fax: (719)384-2867
Free: (800)748-1997
Publisher E-mail: journal@ria.net

Agricultural newspaper. **Founded:** 1949. **Freq:** Weekly (Fri.). **Print Method:** Offset. **Cols./Page:** 5. **Col. Width:** 25 nonpareils. **Col. Depth:** 196 agate lines. **Key Personnel:** Pat R. Ptolemy, General Mgr./Publisher; Andrea Rich, Editor; Mary Zimmerman, Advertising Mgr. **ISSN:** 0004-1890. **Subscription Rates:** $28 individuals; $30 out of state. **Remarks:** Accepts advertising. **Formerly:** Arkansas Valley Journal; Ag Almanac.
Ad Rates: BW: $605.63 **Circ:** ‡8,585
SAU: $8.50
PCI: $8.00

4587 La Junta Tribune-Democrat
La Junta Democrat Publishing Co.
422 Colorado Ave. Phone: (719)384-4475
PO Box 480 Fax: (719)384-4478
La Junta, CO 81050
General newspaper. **Founded:** 1897. **Freq:** Daily (eve.). **Print Method:** Offset. **Trim Size:** 11 3/8 x 14 1/2. **Cols./Page:** 5. **Col. Width:** 26 nonpareils. **Col. Depth:** 196 agate lines. **Key Personnel:** John B. Lowe, Publisher; Jack Lowe, General Mgr.; Wanda R. Lowe, Editor; Shelly Noe, Advertising Mgr.; Sherri White, Business Mgr.; Barb Romjoe, Circulation Mgr. **USPS:** 299-500. **Subscription Rates:** $45 individuals. **Remarks:** Accepts advertising.
Ad Rates: BW: $420 **Circ:** ‡3,787
4C: $685
SAU: $6

4588 KBLJ-FM - 92.1
PO Box 485 Phone: (719)384-5456
La Junta, CO 81050 Fax: (719)384-5450

Format: Country. **Networks:** InterMountain; Satellite Radio. **Owner:** Broadcast Management Inc., at above address. **Founded:** 1974. **Operating Hours:** Continuous. **Key Personnel:** Paul Coates, Contact. **Wattage:** 3000. **Ad Rates:** $4.50-21 for 60 seconds. KBZ3-AM.

4589 Total Local Communications Inc.
PO 929 Phone: (719)384-9898
La Junta, CO 81050 Fax: (719)384-7320
Free: (800)544-8524
E-mail: ppearce@secpa.com

Founded: 1980. **Key Personnel:** Rich Wilson, phone (719)384-9898, fax (719)384-7320, richw@secpa.com. **Cities Served:** Aguilar, Avondale, Boone, Cheraw, Crowley, Oak Creek, Olney Springs, Phippsburg, Stage Coach, Sugar City, CO: subscribing households 1,072; 20 channels; 4 community access channels.

LAFAYETTE

4590 Lafayette News
1285 Centaur Village Dr. Phone: (303)665-6515
Lafayette, CO 80026
Publication E-mail: twntlk@aol.com

Local newspaper. **Founded:** 1974. **Freq:** Semiweekly (Wed. and Sat.). **Print Method:** Offset. **Trim Size:** 10 7/8 x 16. **Cols./Page:** 6. **Col. Width:** 20 nonpareils. **Col. Depth:** 220 agate lines. **Key Personnel:** Douglas E. Conarroe, Publisher. **USPS:** 512-170. **Subscription Rates:** $25 individuals. **Remarks:** Accepts advertising. **URL:** http://www.adone.com/lafayette.
Ad Rates: GLR: $0.37 **Circ:** ‡2,400
BW: $504
4C: $758
SAU: $9.76
PCI: $7.50

LAKE CITY†, pop. 206.

Hinsdale Co. (SW). 60 m S.W. of Gunnison. Residential.

4591 Silver World
Silver Publishing Co.
PO Box 100 Phone: (970)944-2515
Lake City, CO 81235
Newspaper. **Founded:** 1978. **Freq:** Weekly (Fri.). **Print Method:** Uses mats. **Cols./Page:** 6. **Col. Width:** 20 nonpareils. **Col. Depth:** 186 agate lines. **Key Personnel:** Grant E. Houston, Editor and Publisher. **USPS:** 436-630. **Subscription Rates:** $26 individuals. **Remarks:** Accepts advertising.
Ad Rates: BW: $480 **Circ:** Paid ‡1450
PCI: $5 Free ‡10

LAKEWOOD, pop. 112,848.

Jefferson Co. (NC). 6 m SW of Denver. Residential. Commercial.

4592 American Penstemon Society Bulletin
American Penstemon Society
1569 S. Holland Ct. Phone: (303)986-8096
Lakewood, CO 80232
Journal covering flowers for the American Penstemon Society. **Founded:** 1946. **Freq:** Semiannual. **Subscription Rates:** $10 individuals; $15 out of country. **Remarks:** Accepts advertising.
Circ: Paid 500

4593 Community Pharmacist
5285 W. Louisiana Ave., Ste. 112 Phone: (303)975-0075
Fax: (303)975-0132
Lakewood, CO 80232-5976
Free: (800)922-8573

National magazine addressing the professional and business needs, concerns and continuing education of retail pharmacists practicing in independent, chain and supermarket pharmacies. **Founded:** 1908. **Freq:** Bimonthly. **Print Method:** Offset. **Trim Size:** 8 3/8 x 10 7/8. **Cols./Page:** 3. **Col. Width:** 26 nonpareils. **Col. Depth:** 135 agate lines. **Key Personnel:** Judith Lane, Publisher; Jennifer Lamb, Managing Editor; Jerry Lester, Advertising Sales; Ronald Quam, Publisher. **ISSN:** 0192-5792. **Subscription Rates:** Free to qualified subscribers; $25 institutions; $5 single issue. **Remarks:** Accepts advertising. **Formerly:** Southern Pharmacy Journal.
Ad Rates: BW: $4,900 **Circ:** Controlled ‡56,000
4C: $6,400

4594 HealthCare Distributor
ELF Publications
5285 W. Louisiana Ave., Ste. 112 Phone: (303)975-0075
Fax: (303)975-0132
Lakewood, CO 80232
Free: (800)922-8513

Magazine covering the issues and opportunities facing companies that distribute pharmaceuticals, medical/surgical products, and other health-care goods and services. **Founded:** 1948. **Freq:** Monthly. **Print Method:** Web offset. **Trim Size:** 8 3/8 x 10 7/8. **Cols./Page:** 3. **Col. Width:** 26 nonpareils. **Col. Depth:** 135 agate lines. **Key Personnel:** Judith Lane, Publisher; Ronald Quam, Publisher; Chuck Austin, Sr. Editor; Jennifer Lamb, Managing Editor; Jerry Lester, Account Mgr. **USPS:** 683-520. **Subscription Rates:** $30 individuals. **Remarks:** Accepts advertising. **Formerly:** Wholesale Drugs Magazine (Jan. 1997).
Ad Rates: BW: $2,475 **Circ:** ‡14,000
4C: $3,975

4595 Nurse Author and Editor
Hall Johnson Consulting
9737 W. Ohio Ave. Phone: (303)988-0056
Lakewood, CO 80226
Consumer magazine focusing on writing and editing in the field of nursing. **Founded:** 1991. **Freq:** Quarterly. **Key Personnel:** Suzanne Hall Johnson, Editor. **ISSN:** 1054-2353. **Subscription Rates:** $49. **Remarks:** Advertising accepted; rates available upon request.
Circ: Paid ‡500

4596 Pleiades Magazine
6677 W. Colfax Ave., Ste. D, Box 357 Phone: (303)237-1019
Lakewood, CO 80214-1805
Literary magazine covering poetry, fiction, music and related areas. **Founded:** 1958. **Freq:** Semiannual. **Key Personnel:** John L. Moravec, Editor and Publisher; Hadrian K. Sue; Cyril Osmond; Frank Klicpery. **Subscription Rates:** $9 individuals; $3.75 single issue; $2.50 single issue for universities. **Remarks:** Advertising accepted; rates available upon request.
Circ: Combined 10,000

4597 The Rock
Red Rocks Community College
13300 W. 6th Ave., Box 7 Phone: (303)914-6371
Lakewood, CO 80228-1255 Fax: (303)914-8154
Publisher E-mail: studentpubs@rrcc.cccoes.edu

Collegiate newspaper. **Subtitle:** The Rock. **Founded:** 1971. **Freq:** Semimonthly. **Print Method:** Offset. **Trim Size:** 11 1/2 x 17. **Cols./Page:** 4. **Col. Width:** 30 nonpareils. **Col. Depth:** 224 agate lines. **Key Personnel:** Beth Foster, Administration; Denise R. Palmateer, Editor. **Subscription Rates:** Free. **Remarks:** Accepts advertising. **Formerly:** Red Rocks Journal.
Ad Rates: BW: $288 **Circ:** Free ‡2,000
PCI: $5

4598 The Star
1235 Pierce St. Phone: (303)235-0116
Lakewood, CO 80214 Fax: (303)237-6080

Magazine covering the history, new models, events, and news about Mercedes-Benz autos; including technical information on maintenance, operation, and restoration. **Subtitle:** Magazine of the Mercedes-Benz Club of America. **Founded:** 1957. **Freq:** Bimonthly. **Print Method:** Offset. **Trim Size:** 8 3/8 x 10 7/8. **Cols./Page:** 3. **Col. Width:** 2 1/4 inches. **Col. Depth:** 10 inches. **Key Personnel:** Frank Barrett, Editor and Publisher, fbarrett@aol.com. **USPS:** 911-480. **Subscription Rates:** $35 individuals. **Remarks:** Accepts advertising.
Ad Rates: BW: $1,405 **Circ:** Paid ‡30,000
4C: $2,013 Non-paid ‡2,000

LAMAR†, pop. 7,797.

Prowers Co (SE). 110 m E of Pueblo. Lamar Community College. Manufactures portable grinders, hydraulic cylinders, buses, oil, gas. Alfalfa meal and feed meal. Agriculture. Grain, wheat. Livestock feed yards.

4599 Lamar Daily News and Holly Chieftain
Eastern Colorado Publishing Co.
310 S. 5th St. Phone: (719)336-2266
PO Box 1217 Fax: (719)336-2526
Lamar, CO 81052-1217
Publication E-mail: ldnews@iguana.ruralnet.net

Newspaper with an independent orientation. **Founded:** Aug. 7, 1907. **Freq:** Sunday Morning & Tuesday - Friday afternoons. **Print Method:** Offset. **Cols./Page:** 6. **Col. Width:** 26 nonpareils. **Col. Depth:** 294 agate lines. **Key Personnel:** Susan Mizell, Publisher. **ISSN:** 5855-6000. **Subscription Rates:** $84 individuals. **Remarks:** Accepts advertising.
Ad Rates: GLR: $.47 **Circ:** Mon.-Fri. ★**2,648**
BW: $874.41
4C: $1,041.41
SAU: $7.29
PCI: $7.29

4600 The Tri State Trader
Lamar Daily News
310 S. 5th St. Phone: (719)336-2266
PO Box 1217 Fax: (719)336-2526
Lamar, CO 81052
Shopper. **Founded:** 1970. **Freq:** Weekly (Wed.). **Print Method:** Offset. **Cols./Page:** 6. **Col. Width:** 2 1/16 inches. **Col. Depth:** 21 inches. **Key Personnel:** Susan Mizell, Publisher; Sandee Leighty, Advertising Mgr. **Subscription Rates:** $40 individuals. **Remarks:** Accepts advertising.
Ad Rates: SAU: $7.29 **Circ:** Free ‡14,000
PCI: $7.29

4601 KLMR-AM - 920
Box 890 Phone: (719)336-2206
Lamar, CO 81052 Fax: (719)336-7973
Free: (800)624-5766

Format: Country. **Networks:** ABC. **Owner:** A & B Broadcasting Inc., at above address. **Founded:** 1948. **Operating Hours:** Continuous. **Key Personnel:** Monte L. Spearman, President; Terry A. Reynolds, Sales Mgr.; Cory Lopez, News Dir.; Cory Alan Forgue, Sports Dir.; Lorrie Boyer, Agriculture Dir. **Wattage:** 5000.

4602 KSEC-FM - 93.3
Box 890 Phone: (719)336-2206
Lamar, CO 81052 Fax: (719)336-7973
Free: (800)624-5766
E-mail: klmr@iguana.ruralnet.net

Format: Adult Contemporary. **Networks:** Jones Satellite. **Owner:** A&B Broadcasting, Inc., at above address. **Founded:** 1978. **Operating Hours:** 24. **Key Personnel:** Monte L. Spearman, President; Terry Reynolds, Sales Mgr. **Local Programs:** *Anything Goes*, Dan Cochell; *High Plains Update*, Dan Cochell; *Valley Ag News*, Dan Cochell. **Wattage:** 100,000. **Ad Rates:** $5.25-7.50 for 15 seconds; $7.50-12.50 for 30 seconds; $9.75 for 60 seconds.

4603 KVAY-FM - 105.7
PO Box 1176 Phone: (719)336-8734
Lamar, CO 81052 Fax: (719)336-5977

Format: Country. **Founded:** 1987. **Formerly:** KNIC-FM. **Operating Hours:** 5 a.m.-midnight. **Key Personnel:** Larry E. Bauer, General Mgr.; Chris Bauer, Program Mgr.; Ron Bradburn, Sales Mgr.; Mike Patterson, News Dir. **Wattage:** 100,000. **Ad Rates:** $5.50-10.50 for 30 seconds.

LAS ANIMAS†, pop. 2,818.

Bent Co. (NWC). 20 m E of La Junta. Oil and gas wells; agriculture.

4604 Bent County Democrat
516 Carson Phone: (719)456-1333
PO Box 467 Fax: (719)456-1402
Las Animas, CO 81054
County newspaper. **Founded:** May 7, 1883. **Freq:** Weekly (Thurs.). **Print Method:** Offset. **Cols./Page:** 6. **Col. Width:** 2 1/16 inches. **Col. Depth:** 21 inches. **Key Personnel:** Jack

Lowe, Editor and Publisher. **Subscription Rates:** $20 individuals; $35 out of area.
Ad Rates: GLR: $5.75 **Circ:** Paid ‡1,200
BW: $725 Non-paid ‡800
PCI: $5.75

LIMON, pop. 1,805.

Lincoln Co. (E). 74 SE of Denver. Agriculture. Wheat, livestock.

4605 The Limon Leader
1062 Main St. Phone: (719)775-2064
Box 1300 Fax: (719)775-9082
Limon, CO 80828
Newspaper. **Founded:** 1910. **Freq:** Weekly (Thurs.). **Print Method:** Offset. **Cols./Page:** 6. **Col. Depth:** 21 inches. **Key Personnel:** Fred R. Lister, Publisher, lister@ria.net. **USPS:** 313-360. **Subscription Rates:** $17 individuals.
Ad Rates: BW: $441 **Circ:** ‡2,539
4C: $666
SAU: $3.50

LITTLETON†, pop. 34,000.

Arapahoe Co. (NEC). 10 m S of Denver. Arapahoe Community College. Manufactures trucks, fire extinguishers; dynamite, precision instruments, electronic and photo equipment. Nurseries, foundry. Residential.

4606 Activities, Adaptation & Aging
The Haworth Press, Inc.
6549 S. Lincoln St. Phone: (303)794-7676
Littleton, CO 80121 Fax: (303)794-7676
Publisher E-mail: getinfo@haworthpressinc.com

Professional quarterly journal. **Subtitle:** The Gerontological Journal of Activities. **Founded:** 1980. **Freq:** Quarterly. **Trim Size:** 4 3/8 x 7 1/8. **Key Personnel:** Phyllis M. Foster, ACC, Editor, phone (303)794-7676, pfoster2@juno.com; Bill Cohen, Publisher, phone (607)722-8273, fax (607)722-3487. **ISSN:** 0192-4788. **Subscription Rates:** $40; $175 industry; $200 libraries. **Remarks:** Accepts advertising. **Alt. Formats:** Microform.
Ad Rates: BW: $300 **Circ:** 737

4607 Boardwatch Magazine
8500 W. Bowles Ave., Ste. 210 Phone: (303)973-6038
Littleton, CO 80123 Fax: (303)933-3731
Free: (800)933-6038
Publication E-mail: info@boardwatch.com

Magazine covering the Internet and online service industries. **Subtitle:** Guide to Internet Access and World Wide Web. **Founded:** Mar. 1987. **Freq:** Monthly. **Print Method:** Web offset. **Trim Size:** 8 3/8 x 10 7/8. **Cols./Page:** 3. **Col. Width:** 2 5/16 inches. **Col. Depth:** 10 inches. **Key Personnel:** Jack Rickard, Editor and Publisher, jack.rickard@boardwatch.com; Bill Pettit, Dir., Sales, bill.pettit@boardwatch.com. **ISSN:** 1054-2760. **Subscription Rates:** $36 individuals; $5.95 single issue. **Remarks:** Accepts advertising. **URL:** http://www.boardwatch.com/.
Ad Rates: 4C: $5,900 **Circ:** Paid 20,764
Non-paid 7,692

4608 Democracy and Nature
Aigis Publications
PO Box 637
Littleton, CO 80160

Journal featuring articles on radical left politics, social theory, social ecology, and philosophy. **Subtitle:** The International Journal of Politics and Ecology. **Founded:** 1992. **Freq:** Irregular. **Trim Size:** 6 x 9. **Key Personnel:** Takis Fotopoulos, Intl. Mng. Editor. **ISSN:** 1085-5661. **Subscription Rates:** $25 individuals; $50 institutions; $9.50 single issue. **Remarks:** Accepts advertising.
Ad Rates: BW: $300 **Circ:** Paid 950
Controlled 50

4609 Journal of Applied Business Research
Western Academic Press
PO Box 620760 Phone: (303)904-4750
Littleton, CO 80162 Fax: (303)978-0413
Publisher E-mail: cluter@wapress.com

Applied business research magazine. **Founded:** 1985. **Freq:** Quarterly. **Print Method:** Offset. **Trim Size:** 7 1/4 x 10. **Cols./Page:** 2. **Col. Width:** 2 3/4 inches. **Col. Depth:** 7 3/4 inches. **Key Personnel:** Ronald C. Clute, Managing Editor, phone (303)972-6604, fax (303)978-0413, cluter@wapress.com. **ISSN:** 0892-7626. **Subscription Rates:** $35 individuals; $250 institutions. **Remarks:** Accepts advertising.
Ad Rates: PCI: $100 **Circ:** Paid ‡600
Controlled ‡100

4610 Journal of Legal Pluralism and Unofficial Law
William S. Hein & Co., Inc.
10368 W. Centennial Rd. Phone: (303)979-5657
Littleton, CO 80127 Fax: (303)979-0707
Free: (888)361-3255
Publisher E-mail: wsheinco@class.org

Scholarly journal covering legal pluralism and unofficial law worldwide. **Founded:** 1969. **Freq:** Semiannual. **Trim Size:** 6 3/4 x 9 3/4. **Cols./Page:** 1. **Col. Width:** 4 1/16 inches. **Col. Depth:** 8 1/4 inches. **Key Personnel:** Prof. Gordon R. Woodman, Editor-in-Chief, g.r.woodman@bham.ac.uk; Sheila Jarrett, Production Editor, sjarrett@rothman.com. **ISSN:** 0732-9113. **Subscription Rates:** $45 individuals. **Remarks:** Advertising not accepted.
Circ: Paid 313

4611 Littleton Independent
2329 W. Main St., Ste. 103 Phone: (303)794-7877
Littleton, CO 80120-8200 Fax: (303)794-1909

Community newspaper. **Founded:** 1888. **Freq:** Weekly (Thurs.). **Print Method:** Offset. **Cols./Page:** 5. **Col. Width:** 9.5 picas. **Col. Depth:** 13 inches. **Key Personnel:** Gerard J. Healey, Publisher, healey@southmetronews.com. **Subscription Rates:** $24.95. **Remarks:** Accepts advertising.
Ad Rates: SAU: $12.25 **Circ:** ‡10,500

4612 Minerals and Metallurgical Processing
Society for Mining, Metallurgy, and Exploration, Inc.
8307 Schaffer Pkwy. Phone: (303)973-9550
PO Box 625002 Fax: (303)973-3845
Littleton, CO 80162-5002
Free: (800)763-3132
Publisher E-mail: cs@smenet.org

Peer-reviewed journal providing technical and research information on minerals and metallurgical processing. **Founded:** May 20, 1984. **Freq:** Quarterly. **Print Method:** Offset. **Trim Size:** 8 1/8 x 10 7/8. **Cols./Page:** 2. **Col. Width:** 40 nonpareils. **Col. Depth:** 140 agate lines. **Key Personnel:** Roshan B. Bhappu, Editor; Joe Zullo, Publisher; Bill Yernberg, Associate Editor. **ISSN:** 0747-9182. **Subscription Rates:** $75 individuals. **Remarks:** Accepts advertising.
Ad Rates: BW: $800 **Circ:** ‡587
4C: $1,200

4613 Mining Engineering
Society for Mining, Metallurgy, and Exploration, Inc.
8307 Schaffer Pkwy. Phone: (303)973-9550
PO Box 625002 Fax: (303)973-3845
Littleton, CO 80162-5002
Free: (800)763-3132
Publisher E-mail: cs@smenet.org

Magazine for engineers and professionals engaged in exploration, underground and open pit mining, solution mining, rock mechanics, operations research, geological engineering, geohydrology, mineral processing, mineral, economics, and management. **Founded:** Jan. 1949. **Freq:** Monthly. **Print Method:** Offset. **Trim Size:** 8 1/8 x 10 7/8. **Cols./Page:** 3. **Col. Width:** 26 nonpareils. **Col. Depth:** 140 agate lines. **Key Personnel:** Tim O'Neil, Editor. **ISSN:** 0026-5187. **Subscription Rates:** $110 individuals. **Remarks:** Accepts advertising.
Ad Rates: BW: $2,890 **Circ:** Paid 17,057
4C: $4,090

4614 Review of Accounting Information Systems
Western Academic Press
PO Box 620760 Phone: (303)904-4750
Littleton, CO 80162 Fax: (303)978-0413
Publication E-mail: cluter@wapress.com
Publisher E-mail: cluter@wapress.com

Accounting Information Systems magazine. **Founded:** 1997. **Freq:** Quarterly. **Print Method:** Offset. **Trim Size:** 7 1/4 x 10. **Cols./Page:** 2. **Col. Width:** 2 3/4 inches. **Col. Depth:** 7 3/4 inches. **Key Personnel:** Ronald C. Clute, Managing Editor, phone (303)904-4750, fax (303)978-0413, cluter@wapress.com. **ISSN:** 1089-8670. **Subscription Rates:** $45 individuals; $225 institutions.
Ad Rates: PCI: $100 **Circ:** Paid ‡600
Controlled ‡100

4615 Texas Longhorn Journal
Texas Longhorn Journal, Inc.
2329 W. Main St., Ste. 102 Phone: (303)797-8522
Littleton, CO 80120 Fax: (303)797-8708
Publisher E-mail: spisales@iex.net

Livestock trade magazine. **Subtitle:** The Business Publication of the Texas Longhorn Industry. **Founded:** 1976. **Freq:** Bimonthly. **Print Method:** Sheetfed offset. **Trim Size:** 8 1/2 x 11. **Cols./Page:** 3 and 4. **Col. Width:** 2 3/8 and 2 inches. **Col. Depth:** 10 inches. **Key Personnel:** Charles B. Searle, Editor and Publisher; Becky Stairs, Sales Associate; Laurel Lane, Sales Associate. **ISSN:** 0747-1556. **Subscription Rates:** $29 individuals; $39 out of country. **Remarks:** Accepts advertising.
Ad Rates: BW: $950 **Circ:** ‡3,000
4C: $1,350
PCI: $40

Welcome Home Magazine of Denver - See Denver

Welcome Home Magazine of Las Vegas - See Las Vegas, Nevada

4616 TCI
7580 S. Pierce St., Unit 7 Phone: (303)930-2000
Littleton, CO 80123 Fax: (303)972-9417

Owner: TCI, 5619 DTC Pkwy., Englewood, CO 80111, (303)267-5500. **Founded:** 1972. **Formerly:** Evergreen Intercable, Inc. **Key Personnel:** Steve Santamaria, General Mgr., phone (303)603-5001, fax (303)603-5900; Joe Stackhouse, Operations Mgr., phone (303)603-5003, fax (303)603-5900; Ken Hillard, Engineering Mgr., phone (303)603-5041, fax (303)603-5900; Julie Seff, Marketing Mgr., phone (303)603-5501, fax (303)603-5940. **Cities Served:** Evergreen, Idledale, Kittredge, CO: subscribing households 3,500; 36 channels; 3 hours per week community access programming.

LONGMONT, pop. 42,942.

Boulder Co. (N). 34 m NW of Denver. Electronics, food products, building and construction, printing and publishing firms. Agriculture.

4617 Daily Times-Call
Lehman Communications Corp.
350 Terry St. Phone: (303)776-2244
PO Box 299 Fax: (303)678-8615
Longmont, CO 80502
Free: (800)796-8201
Publication E-mail: news@times-call.com

General newspaper. **Founded:** 1871. **Freq:** Daily and Sunday (morn.). **Print Method:** Offset. **Cols./Page:** 6. **Col. Width:** 26 nonpareils. **Col. Depth:** 301 agate lines. **Key Personnel:** Dean Lehman, Editor and President, fax (303)776-9271, dlehman@lehmancomm.com; Ed Lehman, Publisher, fax (303)776-0837; Mike Gugliotto, VP/General Mgr., fax (303)772-3759. **Subscription Rates:** $93 individuals. **Remarks:** Accepts advertising.
Ad Rates: BW: $1,652.49 **Circ:** Mon.-Sat. 20,950
4C: $2,067.49 Sun. 23,500
SAU: $14.04

4618 Vows
Grimes and Associates
522 Kimbark Phone: (303)776-3103
Longmont, CO 80501 Fax: (303)776-3798

Trade journal for bridal and wedding professionals. **Subtitle:** The Bridal and Wedding Business Journal. **Founded:** 1989. **Freq:** Bimonthly. **Print Method:** Web offset. **Trim Size:** 8 3/8 x 10 7/8. **Cols./Page:** 3. **Key Personnel:** Ginger Barry, Editor; Karl Nazarro, Art Dir. **Subscription Rates:** $25 individuals. **Remarks:** Accepts advertising.
Circ: (Not Reported)

4619 Comcast Communications
434 Kimbark St. Phone: (303)776-6600
Longmont, CO 80501 Fax: (303)678-5302

Founded: 1982. **Formerly:** Scripps Howard Cable Co. **Key Personnel:** Greg Griffin, General Mgr.; Brian Meier, Marketing Mgr.; Ian Thomas, Operations Mgr. **Cities Served:** Battlement Mesa, Berthoud, Ft. Lupton, Lafayette, Longmont, Louisville, Lovebud, Parachute, Superior, CO: subscribing households 45,000; 60 channels; 4 community access channels; 168 hours per week community access programming.

4620 KCDC-FM - 90.7
1200 S. Sunset St. Phone: (303)776-4696
Longmont, CO 80501-6595 Fax: (303)651-7446

Format: Adult Contemporary; Album-Oriented Rock (AOR). **Owner:** St. Urain Valley School District, at above address. **Founded:** 1975. **Operating Hours:** 100% local. **Key Personnel:** George N. Baskos, General Mgr.; James R. Boynton, Sr., Station Mgr., boynton_ james@stvrain.k12.co.us. **Wattage:** 100. **Ad Rates:** Noncommercial.

4621 KLMO-AM - 1060
614 Kimbark Phone: (303)776-2323
PO Box 799 Fax: (303)776-1377
Longmont, CO 80501-0799
Free: (888)345-1060
E-mail: klmoam1060@aol.com

Format: Hot Country. **Networks:** ABC. **Owner:** Pilgrim Communications, 54 Monument Circle, Ste. 250, Indianapolis, IN 46204, (317)655-9999, Fax: (317)655-9995. **Founded:** 1949.

Operating Hours: 6 a.m.-2 hours past sunset. **Key Personnel:** Bob Suarez, General Mgr., phone (303)776-2323, suarez442atsaol.com. **Wattage:** 10,000 (500 pre-sunrise). **Ad Rates:** $35-45 for 30 seconds; $40-50 for 60 seconds.

4622 KQKS-FM - 104.3
5660 Greenwood Plaza, Ste. 400 Phone: (303)721-9210
Englewood, CO 80111

Format: Contemporary Hit Radio (CHR). **Owner:** Western Cities Broadcasting Inc., at above address. **Founded:** 1964. **Operating Hours:** Continuous. **Key Personnel:** Ron Jamison, General Mgr. **Wattage:** 28,000.

LOVELAND, pop. 36,000.

Larimer Co. (N). 50 m N of Denver. Residential and commercial. Tourism. Manufactures electronic cameras & film products, measuring devices, computers, water chemical equipment, farm machinery. Canneries; creamery. Agriculture. Sugar beets, corn, wheat, cattle.

4623 American Paint and Coatings Journal
Douglas Publications, Inc.
4113 Fawn Trail Phone: (970)663-0241
Loveland, CO 80537 Fax: (970)663-0172

Magazine serving paint, varnish and lacquer manufacturers. **Founded:** 1916. **Freq:** Semimonthly except in June, July, August and December. **Print Method:** Offset. **Trim Size:** 5 1/2 x 8. **Cols./Page:** 2. **Col. Width:** 27 nonpareils. **Col. Depth:** 93 agate lines. **Key Personnel:** Mary Benke, Editor, mbenke@oneimage.com; Frank Johnson, Distribution Mgr., phone (212)639-1498, fax (212)639-1499. **ISSN:** 0098-5430. **Subscription Rates:** $35. **Remarks:** Accepts advertising.
Ad Rates: BW: $1,700 **Circ:** Paid 2,006
4C: $2,975 Non-paid 2,798

4624 Children's Ministry
Group Publishing, Inc.
1515 Cascade Ave. Phone: (970)669-3836
Loveland, CO 80538 Fax: (970)669-1994
Free: (800)447-1070
Publisher E-mail: @grouppublishing.com

Easy-to-do programming ideas, resources and helpful information for those who work in the church with kids from birth to 6th grade. **Founded:** Dec. 1990. **Freq:** 6/year. **Trim Size:** 8 x 10 3/4. **Key Personnel:** Thom Schultz, President; Tim Gilmour, Publisher; Christine Yount, Editor, cmeditor@ministrynet.usa.net; Kami Simianer, Advert. Mgr., fax (970)679-4370. **ISSN:** 1054-1144. **Subscription Rates:** $24.95 individuals; $4.95 single issue; $31.95 out of country. **Remarks:** Accepts advertising. **Online:** MinistryNet. **URL:** http://www.grouppublishing.com.
Ad Rates: BW: $3,345 **Circ:** Paid 55,000
4C: $3,345 Non-paid 5,000

4625 Group Magazine
Group Publishing, Inc.
1515 Cascade Ave. Phone: (970)669-3836
Loveland, CO 80538 Fax: (970)669-1994
Free: (800)447-1070
Publication E-mail: greditor@grouppublishing.com
Publisher E-mail: @grouppublishing.com

Magazine for youth ministers from all Christian denominations; deals with youth group philosophy, organization, activities, projects, programs, administration, workshop ideas, Bible studies, games, music, fund raising projects, service projects, resources, staff relationships and personal Christian growth. **Founded:** 1974. **Freq:** 6/year. **Print Method:** Heatset Web offset. **Trim Size:** 8 x 10 3/4. **Cols./Page:** 4. **Col. Width:** 9 1/2 picas. **Col. Depth:** 47 picas. **Key Personnel:** Thom Schultz, President; Tim Gilmour, Publisher; Shelley Richards, Advertising Mgr., fax (970)679-4370; Rick Lawrence, Editor; Kathy Dieterich, Asst. editor. **ISSN:** 0163-8971. **Subscription Rates:** $29.95 individuals; $5.95 single issue; $36.95 other countries. **Remarks:** Accepts advertising. **Available Online. URL:** http://www.grouppublishing.com.
Ad Rates: BW: $3245 **Circ:** ‡55,000
4C: $3245

4626 Handwoven
Herb Companion Press, LLC
201 E. 4th St. Phone: (970)669-7672
Loveland, CO 80537 Fax: (970)667-8317
Free: (800)272-2193

Magazine for weavers. **Founded:** 1979. **Freq:** 5/year. **Print Method:** Offset. **Trim Size:** 8 3/8 x 10 7/8. **Cols./Page:** 3. **Col. Width:** 30 nonpareils. **Col. Depth:** 134 agate lines. **Key Personnel:** Jean Scorgie, Editor; Linda C. Ligon, Publisher; Sharon Altergott, Advertising Mgr. **ISSN:** 0198-8212. **Subscription Rates:** $22 individuals; $4.50 single issue. **Remarks:** Accepts advertising.
Ad Rates: GLR: $1.50 **Circ:** ‡34,500
BW: $1,215
4C: $1,565
PCI: $55

4627 The Herb Companion
Herb Companion Press, LLC
201 E. 4th St.
Loveland, CO 80537
Publication E-mail: herbcompanion@hcpress.com

Magazine about the growing and using of herbs for food, fragrance, craft, and health. **Subtitle:** In Celebration of the Useful Plants. **Founded:** 1988. **Freq:** Bimonthly. **Print Method:** Web offset. **Trim Size:** 8 3/8 x 10 7/8. **Cols./Page:** 3. **Col. Width:** 13 picas. **Col. Depth:** 53 picas. **Key Personnel:** Robyn Griggs Lawrence, Editor; Suzanne De Atley, Advertising Mgr. **ISSN:** 1040-581X. **Subscription Rates:** $24. **Remarks:** Accepts advertising.
Ad Rates: BW: $3,950 **Circ:** 200,000
4C: $4,750
PCI: $115

4628 Loveland Daily Reporter-Herald
Lehman Communications Corp.
PO Box 59 Phone: (970)669-5050
Loveland, CO 80539 Fax: (970)667-1111
Free: (800)216-0680
Publication E-mail: news@reporter-herald.com; editor@todaysbiz.com

General newspaper. **Founded:** 1880. **Freq:** Daily (eve.), Sat. and Sun. (morn.). **Print Method:** Offset. **Trim Size:** 13 x 21 1/2. **Cols./Page:** 6. **Col. Width:** 18 nonpareils. **Col. Depth:** 301 agate lines. **Key Personnel:** Bob Rummel, Editor; Edward Lehman, Publisher; Sally Lee, Advertising Dir.; Ken Amundson, Managing Editor. **Subscription Rates:** $87 individuals. **Remarks:** Accepts advertising. **Alt. Formats:** Microform.
Ad Rates: GLR: $2.88 **Circ:** Mon.-Sat. ★**16,974**
BW: $1,738.92 Sun. ★**17,942**
4C: $2,123.92
PCI: $15.50

4629 NEWS/400
Duke Communications, Intl.
221 E. 29th St., Ste. 242 Phone: (303)663-4700
Loveland, CO 80538 Fax: (303)669-3016
Free: (800)621-1544
Publication E-mail: editors@news400.com

Trade magazine for programmers and data processing managers who use IBM AS/400. **Subtitle:** The 1 AS/400 Magazine Worldwide. **Founded:** 1982. **Freq:** 15/year. **Print Method:** Offset. Uses mats. **Trim Size:** 8 1/8 x 10 3/4. **Cols./Page:** 3 and 2. **Col. Width:** 13 picas. **Col. Depth:** 10 inches. **Key Personnel:** Wayne Madden, Publisher; David Duke, President; Kathy Nelson, Managing Editor. **ISSN:** 1084-7626. **Subscription Rates:** $129 individuals. **Online:** NEWSLINK. **URL:** http://www.news400.com. **Alt. Formats:** CD-ROM. **Formerly:** NEWS 3X/400.
Ad Rates: BW: $5,170 **Circ:** Paid ★**23,054**
4C: $6,600

4630 KLOV-AM - 1570
1570 W. 1st St. Phone: (970)667-1570
Box 8509 Fax: (970)667-1572
Loveland, CO 80537

Format: News; Talk; Sports. **Networks:** AP; Mutual Broadcasting System; USA Radio. **Owner:** Kraus Broadcasting Corp., at above address. **Founded:** 1955. **Operating Hours:** 24HRS ANR . **Key Personnel:** Melissa Kraus, Owner/Billing Accouints Rec & Payable; George Kraus, Operations Mgr.; Richard Judd, News/Sports Dir.; Philip Busby, Religious Programming; Dick Z. Auodny, Sunday Polka Show Host; Ciny Trammel, Sales. **Local Programs:** *Dick Zavodny Polka Show*; *News & Views*; *Sunday Morning Christian Broadcasting*. **Wattage:** 1000. **Ad Rates:** $8-12 for 30 seconds.

LYONS

4631 The Old Lyons Recorder
430 Main St. Phone: (303)823-6625
PO Box 1729 Fax: (303)823-6633
Lyons, CO 80540
Community newspaper. **Founded:** 1900. **Freq:** Weekly. **Print Method:** Offset. **Trim Size:** 10 1/2 x 16. **Cols./Page:** 5. **Col. Width:** 23 nonpareils. **Col. Depth:** 224 agate lines. **Key Personnel:** Walter J. Kinderman, Publisher. **Subscription Rates:** $16 U.S.; $30 in state; $40 out of state. **Remarks:** Accepts advertising.
Ad Rates: BW: $680 **Circ:** Paid ‡2,750
4C: $935
PCI: $8.50

MANCOS, pop. 872.

Montezuma Co. (SW). 17 m E. of Cortez. Saw mills. Mining. Farming. Ranching.

4632 Mancos Times Tribune
Cortez Newspapers Inc.
135 Grand Ave. Phone: (303)533-7766
PO Box 397 Fax: (303)565-8532
Mancos, CO 81328
Newspaper. **Founded:** 1892. **Freq:** Weekly (Wed.). **Print Method:** Offset. **Trim Size:** 11 x 17. **Cols./Page:** 5. **Col. Width:** 26 nonpareils. **Col. Depth:** 224 agate lines. **Key Personnel:** Suzy Meyer, Editor; R.D. Brown, Publisher; Jeanne Scrivner, Advertising Mgr. **Subscription Rates:** $15 individuals. **Remarks:** Accepts advertising.
Ad Rates: GLR: $.23 **Circ:** ‡992
BW: $360.36
4C: $720.36
SAU: $4.62

MEEKER†, pop. 2,400.

Rio Blanco Co. (NW). On White River, 40 m N of Rifle. Resort. Hunting, fishing, snowmobiling. Coal, uranium mines. Oil, natural gas wells. Oil shale. Pine timber. Agriculture. Cattle, sheep, hogs.

4633 The Meeker Herald
178 Main St. Phone: (970)878-4017
PO Box 720 Fax: (970)878-4016
Meeker, CO 81641
Newspaper. **Founded:** Aug. 15, 1885. **Freq:** Weekly (Thurs.). **Print Method:** Offset-Web. **Trim Size:** 15.5 x 23. **Cols./Page:** 6. **Col. Width:** 13.5 picas. **Col. Depth:** 21.5 inches. **Key Personnel:** Glenn R. Troester, Editor and Publisher; Donna L. Troester, General Mgr.; Debra Pettijohn, Circulation Admin. Mgr. **USPS:** 388-202. **Subscription Rates:** $25 individuals. **Remarks:** Accepts advertising.
Ad Rates: BW: $445 **Circ:** Paid ‡1,800
PCI: $5 Free ‡20

MONTE VISTA, pop. 4,110.

Rio Grande Co. (S).125m SW of Pueblo. Feed mill. Machine shops. Gold, silver mines. Spruce, pine timber. Dude ranches. Diversified farming, Potatoes, barley, lettuce, livestock.

4634 The Del Norte Prospector
SLV Publishing
229 Adams St. Phone: (719)852-3531
Monte Vista, CO 81144 Fax: (719)852-3387

Community newspaper. **Founded:** 1918. **Freq:** Weekly (Thurs.). **Print Method:** Offset. **Trim Size:** 10 1/2 x 16. **Cols./Page:** 5. **Col. Width:** 2 inches. **Col. Depth:** 16 inches. **Key Personnel:** Becky Dillon, Editor; Keith Bray, Publisher; Sarah Holmes, Reporter. **USPS:** 659-530. **Subscription Rates:** $25.95 individuals.
Ad Rates: BW: $504 **Circ:** Paid ‡630
SAU: $6.75 Free ‡5
PCI: $6.60

4635 The Monte Vista Journal
SLV Publishing
229 Adams St. Phone: (719)852-3531
Monte Vista, CO 81144 Fax: (719)852-3387

Newspaper. **Founded:** 1888. **Freq:** Weekly (Wed.). **Print Method:** Offset. **Trim Size:** 10 1/2 x 16. **Cols./Page:** 7. **Col. Width:** 2 inches. **Col. Depth:** 16 inches. **Key Personnel:** Sue Palmgren, Editor; Steve Haynes, Publisher. **USPS:** 360-660. **Subscription Rates:** $25.95 individuals. **Remarks:** Accepts advertising.
Ad Rates: BW: $540 **Circ:** Paid 2,086
SAU: $6.75 Free 33

4636 SLV Midweek
SLV Publishing
229 Adams St. Phone: (719)852-3531
Monte Vista, CO 81144 Fax: (719)852-3387

Community newspaper. **Founded:** 1978. **Freq:** Weekly (Wed.). **Print Method:** Offset. **Trim Size:** 10 1/2 x 16. **Cols./Page:** 5. **Col. Width:** 2 inches. **Key Personnel:** Steve Haynes, Publisher. **Subscription Rates:** Free. **Remarks:** Accepts advertising.
Ad Rates: BW: $820 **Circ:** Free ‡17,500
SAU: $10.25

4637 SLV Saturday Want Ads
SLV Publishing
229 Adams St. Phone: (719)852-3531
Monte Vista, CO 81144 Fax: (719)852-3387

Community newspaper. **Founded:** 1990. **Freq:** Weekly (Sat.). **Print Method:** Offset. **Trim Size:** 10 1/2 x 16. **Cols./Page:** 5. **Col. Width:** 2 inches. **Key Personnel:** Steve Haynes, Pub-

lisher. **Subscription Rates:** Free. **Remarks:** Accepts advertising.
Ad Rates: BW: $820 **Circ:** Free ‡11,588
SAU: $10.25

4638 KSLV-AM - 1240
109 Adams St. Phone: (719)852-3581
PO Box 631 Fax: (719)852-3583
Monte Vista, CO 81144
E-mail: kslv@amigo.net

Format: Country. **Networks:** ABC; Westwood One Radio. **Founded:** 1954. **Operating Hours:** Continuous. 92% network, 8% local. **ADI:** Colorado Springs-Pueblo, CO. **Key Personnel:** Gerald Vigil, General Mgr.; Damian Arellano, Music Dir.; Linda Pacheco, News Dir.; Karl Keller, Contact; Juanita Vigil, Traffic Mgr.; Jerry Medina, Contact. **Local Programs:** *KSLV Sports with Damian Arellano*; *Las Horas Latinas with Jerry Medina*; *Valley Views (public affairs program)*, Linda Pacheco, (719)852-3581, Fax (719)852-3583. **Wattage:** 1000.

4639 KSLV-FM - 95.3
109 Adams St. Phone: (719)852-3581
PO Box 631 Fax: (719)852-3583
Monte Vista, CO 81144
E-mail: kslv@amigo.net

Format: Soft Rock. **Networks:** Unistar; Westwood One Radio. **Founded:** 1986. **Operating Hours:** Continuous; 97% network, 3% local. **ADI:** Colorado Springs-Pueblo, CO. **Key Personnel:** Gerald Vigil, General Mgr.; Damian Arellano, Music Dir.; Linda Pacheco, News Dir.; Juanita Vigil, Traffic Mgr. **Wattage:** 6000.

MONTROSE†, pop. 8,668.

Montrose Co. (W). 59 m SE of Grand Junction. Black Canyon National Monument. Candy factory. Agriculture.

4640 Montrose Daily Press
535 S. 1st Phone: (303)249-3444
PO Box 850 Fax: (303)249-3331
Montrose, CO 81402-0850
General newspaper. **Founded:** 1908. **Freq:** Daily (eve.). **Print Method:** Offset. **Cols./Page:** 6. **Key Personnel:** Richard Day, Editor; William Prescott Allen III, Publisher; Jim Crouse, Advertising Mgr. **Subscription Rates:** $48 individuals.
Circ: ‡6,600

4641 KKXK-FM - 94.1
Box 970 Phone: (970)249-4546
Montrose, CO 81402 Fax: (970)249-2229
E-mail: staff@kubckkxk.com

Format: Contemporary Country. **Networks:** ABC. **Owner:** Woodland Communications Corp., at above address. **Founded:** 1977. **Operating Hours:** Continuous; 50% network, 50% local. **ADI:** Grand Junction-Durango, CO. **Key Personnel:** Steve Glasmann, General Mgr.; Wes Smith, Contact; Beg Haddock, Contact. **Local Programs:** *Classic Country* 2:00 pm - 5:00 pm Sunday, Del Abbott, Mailing contact. **Wattage:** 100,000. **Ad Rates:** $19-25 for 30 seconds; $25-35 for 60 seconds. Combined advertising rates available with KUBC-AM. **URL:** http://www.coloradioradio.com.

4642 KSTR-FM - 96.1
600 Rood Ave. Phone: (303)242-5787
Grand Junction, CO 81501 Fax: (303)245-6585
E-mail: kstr@kstr.com

Format: Album-Oriented Rock (AOR). **Owner:** Leggett Broadcasting Inc., at above address, (970)242-5787, Fax: (970)245-6585. **Founded:** 1980. **Operating Hours:** Continuous. **ADI:** Grand Junction-Durango, CO. **Key Personnel:** Brad Leggett, President; Ken Pilling, Operations Manager/Prog.Director. **Wattage:** 100,000. **Ad Rates:** Advertising accepted; rates available upon request. **URL:** http://www.kstr.com.

4643 KUBC-AM - 580
Box 970 Phone: (970)249-4546
Montrose, CO 81402 Fax: (970)249-2229
E-mail: staff@kubckkxk.com

Networks: ABC. **Owner:** Woodland Communications Corp., at above address. **Founded:** 1946. **Operating Hours:** Continuous; 90% network, 10% local. **ADI:** Grand Junction-Durango, CO. **Key Personnel:** Steve Glasmann, General Mgr.; Bee Haddock, Operations Mgr.; Dave Segal, News Dir.; Jim Frank, Chief Engineer. **Local Programs:** *Montrose Alive* 9:00 am - 10:00 am Thur., Fri., Ken Gale; *Nortena* 11:00 am - 2:00 pm Sunday, Maria Wells; *Window On Western Colorado* 9:00 am - 11:00 am Saturday, Del Abbott. **Wattage:** 5000. **Ad Rates:** $11-19 for 30 seconds; $16-25 for 60 seconds. Combined advertising rates available with KKXK-FM. **URL:** http://www.coloradoradio.com.

MONUMENT, pop. 690.

El Paso Co. (EC). 22 m N. of Colorado Springs.

4644 The Tribune
PO Box 488 Phone: (719)481-3423
Monument, CO 80132 Fax: (719)481-4172

Community newspaper. **Founded:** 1965. **Freq:** Weekly (Thurs.). **Print Method:** Offset. **Cols./Page:** 5. **Col. Width:** 22 nonpareils. **Col. Depth:** 219 agate lines. **Key Personnel:** William H. Kezziah, Editor and Publisher. **USPS:** 418-960. **Subscription Rates:** $17 individuals. **Remarks:** Accepts advertising.
Ad Rates: GLR: $.47 **Circ:** Paid ‡3,366
BW: $523.60 Free ‡145
PCI: $6.80

4645 Milestone Communications
1850 Woodmoor Dr., Ste. 200
Monument, CO 80132-9072

Owner: Milestone Media Mgt., 9600 Koger Blvd., Ste. 201, St. Petersburg, FL 33702. **Founded:** 1989. **Formerly:** Hoke Cable (1994). **Key Personnel:** Randy Mock, Engineering Supervisor; Randy Houso, Chief Technician; Robert Ortiz, Installer Technician. **Cities Served:** Hoke county: subscribing households 1,750; 39 channels.

4646 Tri-Lakes Cable
47 3rd St. Phone: (719)481-2451
Box 1929 Fax: (719)481-2211
Monument, CO 80132

Owner: Pioneer Cable Inc., at above address. **Founded:** 1982. **Key Personnel:** Rebecca Hendricks, Contact; Todd Lorenz, Contact. **Cities Served:** Gleneagle, Monument, CO: subscribing households 4,700; 54 channels.

MORRISON, pop. 478.

Jefferson Co. (NC). 12 m S. of Lakewood.

4647 NETA World
InterNational Electrical Testing Association
PO Box 687 Phone: (303)697-8441
Morrison, CO 80465 Fax: (303)697-8431
Publication E-mail: neta@netaworld.org
Publisher E-mail: neta@netaworld.org

Trade magazine for the electrical testing and maintenance industry. **Founded:** 1986. **Freq:** Quarterly. **Key Personnel:** Roderic Hageman, Technical Editor; Mary Jordan, Managing Editor; Jayne Hudson, Advertising Mgr. **Subscription Rates:** $28 individuals. **Remarks:** Accepts advertising.
Ad Rates: BW: $905 **Circ:** Controlled 6,000
4C: $1,730

4648 KWBI-FM - 91.1
16075 W. Belleview Ave. Phone: (303)697-5924
Morrison, CO 80465 Fax: (303)697-5944

Format: Religious. **Networks:** UPI; AP. **Owner:** Colorado Christian University, at above address, (303)202-0100. **Founded:** 1971. **Operating Hours:** Continuous. **Key Personnel:** Dr. Larry Donnithorne, President, phone (313)963-3350; Michael Brink, General Mgr. **Wattage:** 100,000. **Ad Rates:** Noncommercial. **URL:** http://www.kwbi.org.

NUCLA, pop. 1,027.

Montrose Co. (W). 9 m NW of Redvale. Residential.

4649 San Miguel Basin Forum
PO Box 9 Phone: (970)864-7425
Nucla, CO 81424 Fax: (970)864-7856
Publisher E-mail: wapiti@iti2.net

Local newspaper. **Founded:** 1897. **Freq:** Weekly (Thurs.). **Print Method:** Offset. **Cols./Page:** 5. **Col. Width:** 21 nonpareils. **Col. Depth:** 196 agate lines. **Key Personnel:** Roger Culver, Editor and Publisher; Kathy Reed, Advertising Mgr. **USPS:** 573-600. **Subscription Rates:** $20 individuals; $28 out of area. **Remarks:** Accepts advertising.
Ad Rates: GLR: $.36 **Circ:** ‡1,500
SAU: $5.90

ORDWAY†, pop. 1,135.

Crowley Co. (SE). 48 m E of Pueblo. Alfalfa meal mill. Agriculture. Livestock, cantaloupes, sugar beets, alfalfa, turkeys.

4650 The Ordway New Era
Rocky Ford Publishing Co.
223 Main St. Phone: (719)267-3576
Ordway, CO 81063 Fax: (719)267-4661

Community newspaper. **Founded:** 1902. **Freq:** Weekly (Tues.). **Print Method:** Offset. **Cols./Page:** 5. **Col. Width:** 25 nonpareils. **Col. Depth:** 200 agate lines. **Key Personnel:** John Cordsen, Editor; Mark Waugh, Sales Mgr. **USPS:** 410-680. **Subscription Rates:** $14 individuals; $16 out of area. **Remarks:** Accepts advertising.
Ad Rates: GLR: $.46 **Circ:** Paid ‡1,200
BW: $224.44 Free ‡200
SAU: $3.50

PAGOSA SPRINGS†, pop. 1,331.

Archuleta Co. (S). On San Juan River, 60 m E of Durango. Tourism, Skiing, biggame hunting & fishing. Hot springs. Cattle

4651 The Pagosa Springs Sun
Box 9 Phone: (303)264-2101
Pagosa Springs, CO 81147
Community newspaper. **Founded:** Dec. 3, 1909. **Freq:** Weekly (Thurs.). **Print Method:** Offset. **Cols./Page:** 6. **Col. Width:** 2 1/32 inches. **Col. Depth:** 21 inches. **Key Personnel:** David C. Mitchell, Editor and Publisher; Terri House, Advertising Mgr. **Subscription Rates:** $15 individuals; $24 Out of county. **Remarks:** Accepts advertising.
Ad Rates: SAU: $5.70 **Circ:** ‡3,400
PCI: $5.70

4652 KWUF-AM - 1400
PO Box 780 Phone: (970)264-1400
Pagosa Springs, CO 81147 Fax: (970)264-1063

Format: Country; Talk; Sports. **Networks:** NBC; Westwood One Radio. **Owner:** Stubbs Broadcasting Company, Inc., at above address. **Founded:** 1975. **Formerly:** KPAG-AM (1997). **Operating Hours:** Continuous. **Key Personnel:** Don Stubbs, General Mgr./Program Dir.; Chris Oliverez, Sports Dir./Operations Mgr.; Dianna Stubbs, Sales Mgr. **Local Programs:** *Big Game Hunters Show*; *Four Corners Ski Reports*; *Tradio*. **Wattage:** 1000. **Ad Rates:** $7 for 30 seconds. Combined advertising rates available with KWUF-FM.

4653 KWUF-FM - 106.3
PO Box 780 Phone: (970)264-1400
Pagosa Springs, CO 81147 Fax: (970)264-1063

Format: Oldies; Blues. **Networks:** NBC; Westwood One Radio. **Owner:** Stubbs Broadcasting Company, Inc., at above address. **Founded:** 1986. **Formerly:** KRQS-FM (1997). **Operating Hours:** Continuous. **Key Personnel:** Don Stubbs, General Mgr./Program Dir.; Chris Olivarez, Sports Dir.; Dianna Stubbs, Sales Mgr. **Wattage:** 3000. **Ad Rates:** $7 for 30 seconds.

PALISADE, pop. 1,551.

Mesa Co. (W). 15 m NE of Grand Junction. Residential. Recreation area. Mining. Agriculture.

4654 The Palisade Tribune and Valley Report
124 W. 3rd Phone: (970)464-5614
PO Box 8
Palisade, CO 81526
Community newspaper. **Founded:** 1903. **Freq:** Weekly (Thurs.). **Print Method:** Offset. **Trim Size:** 11 1/2 x 17 1/2. **Cols./Page:** 5. **Col. Width:** 11 1/2 picas. **Col. Depth:** 16 inches. **Key Personnel:** Bob Sweeney, Publisher; Bob Dougherty, Assoc. Publisher. **Subscription Rates:** $24 individuals; $29 out of area; $34 out of state.
Ad Rates: BW: $600 **Circ:** Paid ‡1,200
4C: $952.32 Free ‡3,000
PCI: $7.50

PAONIA, pop. 1,425.

Delta Co. (W). 28 m NE of Delta. Residential.

4655 High Country News
PO Box 1090 Phone: (970)527-4898
Paonia, CO 81428 Fax: (970)527-4897
Free: (800)905-1155
Publication E-mail: editor@hcn.org
Publisher E-mail: circulation@hcn.org

Journal covering natural resource and environmental issues in the Western U.S. **Founded:** 1970. **Freq:** Semimonthly. **Trim Size:** 11 x 17. **Col. Width:** 2 3/8 inches. **Key Personnel:** Ed Marston, Publisher, emarston@hcn.org; Betsy Marston, Editor, betsym@hcn.org. **ISSN:** 1091-5657. **Subscription Rates:** $28 individuals; $38 institutions; $1.50 single issue. **Remarks:**

Accepts advertising from members only. **URL:** http://www.hcn.org.
Ad Rates: GLR: $.50 **Circ:** Combined 19,800
PCI: $40

4656 KVNF-FM - 90.9
213 Grand Ave. Phone: (970)527-4866
PO Box 1350 Free: (800)284-5274
Paonia, CO 81428
E-mail: kvnf@kvnf.org

Networks: National Public Radio (NPR). **Owner:** North Fork Valley Public Radio, Inc., at above address. **Founded:** 1979. **Operating Hours:** 18 hours Daily; 15% network, 85% local. **Key Personnel:** Eric Truax, General Mgr.; Eb Wickes, Operations Mgr.; Candy Pennetta, Music Dir.; Barbara Phillips, underwriting director. **Wattage:** 3000. **Ad Rates:** Noncommercial.

PUEBLO†, pop. 97,453.

Pueblo Co. (SEC). On Arkansas River, 102 m S of Denver. University of Southern Colorado. Manufactures iron, steel, aluminum products, automotive pistons, storm sashes, plastic bags, windows, doors, auto trailers, brick, tile, lumber, compressed and liquified gases, dairy, concrete products. Clay plts. Stone quarries. Coal mines. Mineral insulation. Bottling works. Hatchery. Nursery.

4657 American Breweriana
American Breweriana Association, Inc.
4603 Castor Dr.
Pueblo, CO 81001
Publisher E-mail: breweriana@amigo.net

Journal for members of the American Breweriana Association, covering brewery history, advertising, and collectibles. **Subtitle:** Magizine of Brewery History and Advertising. **Founded:** 1980. **Freq:** Bimonthly. **Print Method:** Offset. **Trim Size:** 8.5 x 11. **Key Personnel:** Stan Galloway, Editor, breweriana@amigo.net. **ISSN:** 0748-8343. **Subscription Rates:** $25 included in membership fee. **Remarks:** Accepts advertising. **Formerly**: American Breweriana Journal.
Ad Rates: BW: $200 **Circ:** Controlled 3,400
4C: $300
PCI: $15

4658 The Colorado Tribune
Colorado Printing of Pueblo
447 Park Dr. Phone: (719)561-4008
Pueblo, CO 81005 Fax: (719)561-4007

Legal newspaper for Pueblo County. **Founded:** 1939. **Freq:** Weekly. **Print Method:** Offset. **Trim Size:** 10 3/16 x 15 7/8. **Cols./Page:** 5. **Col. Width:** 21 nonpareils. **Col. Depth:** 203 agate lines. **Key Personnel:** Rilda M. Cook, Editor; Jon F. Heaton, Publisher. **Subscription Rates:** $8 individuals; $16 other counties; $.25 single issue. **Remarks:** Accepts advertising.
Ad Rates: GLR: $.39 **Circ:** ‡374
BW: $75
4C: $520
SAU: $6.43
PCI: $5.46

4659 The Pueblo Chieftain
PO Box 4040 Phone: (719)544-3520
Pueblo, CO 81003 Fax: (719)546-3235

General newspaper. **Founded:** 1868. **Freq:** Mon.-Sun. (morn.). **Print Method:** Offset. **Cols./Page:** 6. **Col. Width:** 25 nonpareils. **Col. Depth:** 300 agate lines. **Key Personnel:** Robert H. Rawlings, Publisher. **Subscription Rates:** $96 individuals per year; $159 by mail in Colorado; $186 by mail outside of Colorado. **Remarks:** Accepts advertising.
Ad Rates: PCI: $41.35 **Circ:** Mon.-Sat. ★**51,705**
Sun. ★**55,216**

4660 USC Today
University of Southern Colorado
Dept. of Mass Communications Phone: (303)549-2818
2200 Bonforte Blvd. Fax: (719)549-2120
Pueblo, CO 81001-4901
Collegiate newspaper. **Founded:** 1972. **Freq:** Weekly (Wed.). **Print Method:** Offset. **Cols./Page:** 5. **Col. Width:** 26 nonpareils. **Col. Depth:** 182 agate lines. **Key Personnel:** Patricia Bowie Orman, Advertising Mgr.; Gail Binkly, Faculty Adviser. **Remarks:** Advertising not accepted for term paper services and catalogs.
Ad Rates: GLR: $3.50 **Circ:** Mon.-Thurs. 1,591,629
BW: $150 Fri. 2,008,940
PCI: $3.50

4661 KCSJ-AM - 590
3305 N. Elizabeth Phone: (719)543-5900
Pueblo, CO 81008 Fax: (719)543-7609
E-mail: kcsj@rm11.com

Format: News; Sports; Talk. **Networks:** CBS; NBC; Mutual Broadcasting System; ESPN Radio. **Owner:** Pueblo Broadcasters Inc., 1444 Wazee, Ste. 120, Denver, CO 80202. **Founded:** 1947. **Operating Hours:** Continuous. **ADI:** Colorado Springs-Pueblo, CO. **Key Personnel:** Tom Bruss, Sales Mgr.; Scott Jones, General Mgr. **Local Programs:** *Call of the Rled*, Eric Kelly, Mailing contact; *Prime Time Sports*, Dave Harroll, Mailing contact; *Sports-HS, USC*, Tony Wright, Mailing contact. **Wattage:** 1000. **Ad Rates:** Advertising accepted; rates available upon request. **URL:** http://www.puebloradio.com.

4662 KDZA-FM - 96.9
106 W. 24th St. Phone: (719)545-2080
Pueblo, CO 81003 Fax: (719)543-9898

Format: Country. **Founded:** 1975. **Operating Hours:** Continuous. **ADI:** Colorado Springs-Pueblo, CO. **Key Personnel:** Olene Greenwood, General Mgr. **Wattage:** 100,000.

4663 KOAA-TV - 5 & 30
2200 7th Ave. Phone: (719)544-5781
Pueblo, CO 81003 Fax: (719)544-7733
E-mail: news@koaa.com

Format: Commercial TV. **Networks:** NBC. **Owner:** Evening Post Publishing Co., 134 Columbus, Charleston, SC 29403, (803)577-7111. **Founded:** 1953. **Operating Hours:** Continuous; 67% network, 33% local. **ADI:** Colorado Springs-Pueblo, CO. **Key Personnel:** Evie Hudson, Business Mgr.; John O. Gilbert, General Mgr.; Phill Emertt, Sales Mgr.; Patricia Vaughan, Promotions; Paul Doll, National Sales Mgr.; Greg Boyce, News Dir.; Harv Holliday, Sports Dir.; Pat Friedell, Art Dir.; Quentin Henry, Chief Engineer. **Ad Rates:** $15-700 for 30 seconds; $30-1,400 for 60 seconds.

4664 KRMX-AM - 690
2829 Lowell Ave. Phone: (719)545-2883
Pueblo, CO 81003-1055 Fax: (719)545-2931

Format: Hispanic. **Networks:** Independent. **Owner:** Ventana Enterprises, Inc., at above address. **Founded:** 1958. **Formerly**: KAPI-AM. **Operating Hours:** Continuous. **ADI:** Colorado Springs-Pueblo, CO. **Key Personnel:** Dan Ramos, Sales Mgr.; Al Madril, News Dir. **Wattage:** 250. **Ad Rates:** $8-13 for 30 seconds; $10-17 for 60 seconds.

4665 KRRU-AM - 1480
4211 N. Elizabeth St. Phone: (719)542-4277
Pueblo, CO 81008

Networks: CBS; Jones Satellite. **Owner:** David Drucker, PO Box 1471, Evergreen, CO 80439, (303)526-1039, Fax: (303)670-5103. **Founded:** 1963. **Formerly**: KAYK-AM. **Operating Hours:** Continuous. **ADI:** Colorado Springs-Pueblo, CO. **Key Personnel:** Lloyd Evans, General Mgr.; Norm Smith, Engineer. **Wattage:** 1000. **Ad Rates:** $15-20 for 30 seconds; $20-30 for 60 seconds.

4666 KTSC-FM - 89.5
2200 Bonforte Blvd. Phone: (719)549-2822
Pueblo, CO 81001-4901 Fax: (719)549-2120

Format: Album-Oriented Rock (AOR). **Networks:** Independent. **Owner:** University of Southern CO, at above address, (303)549-2822. **Operating Hours:** 18 hours weekdays; 12 hours Saturday and Sunday; 100% local. **ADI:** Colorado Springs-Pueblo, CO. **Key Personnel:** Dave Birks, Contact; Bonnie Chyco, Contact. **Wattage:** 10,000.

4667 KTSC-TV - 8
2200 Bonforte Blvd. Phone: (719)543-8800
Pueblo, CO 81001-4901 Fax: (719)549-2208
Free: (800)388-6183

Format: Public TV. **Networks:** Public Broadcasting Service (PBS). **Founded:** 1971. **Operating Hours:** 6 a.m.-midnight; 95% network, 5% local. **ADI:** Colorado Springs-Pueblo, CO. **Key Personnel:** Tom Aube, Chief Engineer, phone (719)549-2994; Wynona Sullivan, Contact. **Local Programs:** *Horizons on Health* 7:30 p.m. Thursday, Roger Sajak; *Midlife Musings with Frances Weaver* Sat. 6:55 p.m. & Sun. 1:25 p.m; *Stand Off* 7 p.m. Thursday, Mike Aragon, Mailing contact. **Ad Rates:** $30 for 30 seconds. **URL:** http://www.ktsctv.org.

4668 KVUU-FM - 99.9
2864 S. Circle Dr., Ste. 150 Phone: (719)540-9200
Colorado Springs, CO 80906 Fax: (719)579-0884

Format: Adult Contemporary. **Founded:** 1976. **Operating Hours:** Continuous. **ADI:** Colorado Springs-Pueblo, CO. **Key Personnel:** Randy Hill, General Mgr., fax (719)579-0882; Lee Roberts, Contact, fax (719)579-0882; Paul Richards, News Dir., fax (719)579-0882. **Wattage:** 67,400. **Ad Rates:** $65-75 for 60 seconds.

4669 KYZX-FM - 104.5
3305 N Elizabeth Phone: (719)543-5900
Pueblo, CO 81008 Fax: (719)543-7609
E-mail: kcsj@rm11.com

Format: Country. **Networks:** Independent. **Owner:** Pueblo Broadcasters, Inc., at above address. **Founded:** 1979. **Formerly**: KCSJ-FM (1990). **Operating Hours:** Continuous. **ADI:** Colorado Springs-Pueblo, CO. **Key Personnel:** Scott Jones, General Mgr.; Tom Bruss, General Sales Mgr. **Wattage:** 50,000. **URL:** http://www.puebloradio.com.

4670 TCI Cablevision of Colorado
620 W. 9th St. Phone: (719)546-1090
Pueblo, CO 81003-2203 Fax: (719)546-1597
Free: (800)628-6876

Founded: 1970. **Cities Served:** Pueblo County.

PUEBLO WEST

4671 KFEL-AM - 970
30 N. Electronic Dr. Phone: (719)547-0411
Pueblo West, CO 81007 Fax: (719)547-9301

Format: Contemporary Christian. **Networks:** USA Radio. **Owner:** Metropolitan Radio Group, Inc., 1549 Greenbridge, Ozark, MO 65721, (417)581-5595. **Founded:** Aug. 1956. **Operating Hours:** Continuous. **ADI:** Colorado Springs-Pueblo, CO. **Key Personnel:** Gary L. Acker, President; Liliane St. Clair, General Mgr.; Henry Reyes, Sales Mgr.; Norm Smith, Chief Engineer. **Wattage:** 3,200.

4672 KNKN-FM - 107.1
30 N. Electronic Dr. Phone: (719)547-0411
Pueblo West, CO 81007 Fax: (719)547-9301
Free: (800)311-2217

Format: Hispanic. **Owner:** Metropolitan Radio Group, Inc., 1549 Greenbridge, Ozark, MO 65721. **Founded:** 1994. **Formerly**: KIKN. **Operating Hours:** Continuous. **ADI:** Colorado Springs-Pueblo, CO. **Key Personnel:** Liliane St. Clair, General Mgr.; Al Madril, Program Dir. **Wattage:** 50,000. **Ad Rates:** $10-20 for 30 seconds. Combined advertising rates available with KRMX-AM.

RANGELY, pop. 2,112.

Rio Blanco Co. (NW). On White River, 70 m N of Grand Junction. Oil refinery. Natural gas and oil wells. Coal mining. Grain, stock, dairy farms.

4673 Rangely Times
PO Box 460 Phone: (970)675-5033
Rangely, CO 81648 Fax: (970)675-8709
Publication E-mail: rtimes@amigo.net

Newspaper dedicated to local news, and sports info on area children. **Founded:** 1949. **Freq:** Weekly (Thurs.). **Print Method:** Offset. **Cols./Page:** 6. **Col. Width:** 13.5 picas. **Col. Depth:** 20.5 inches. **Key Personnel:** Rockford M. Hayes, Publisher. **USPS:** 605-540. **Subscription Rates:** $24 /year. **Remarks:** Accepts advertising. **Alt. Formats:** CD-ROM. **Formerly**: Rangely Driller.
Ad Rates: GLR: $.44 **Circ:** 1,250
BW: $500
PCI: $7.00

RIDGWAY

4674 Ouray County Plaindealer
The Ridgway Sun
PO Box 529 Phone: (970)626-5100
Ridgway, CO 81432 Fax: (970)626-5100

County newspaper (tabloid). **Subtitle:** The Newspaper That Refused to Diet. **Founded:** 1877. **Freq:** Weekly (Thurs.). **Print Method:** Offset. **Trim Size:** 10 1/4 x 13. **Cols./Page:** 6. **Col. Width:** 18 nonpareils. **Col. Depth:** 182 agate lines. **Key Personnel:** Beverly Corbell, Managing Editor, phone (970)325-4412, fax (970)325-4413, ouraypd@independence.net; David Mullings, Publisher, beverlyc@independence.net. **USPS:** 415-260. **Subscription Rates:** $26 individuals. **Remarks:** Accepts advertising.
Ad Rates: BW: $468 **Circ:** Paid 1,805
4C: $768 Free ‡41
PCI: $6

4675 The Ridgway Sun
PO Box 529 Phone: (970)626-5100
Ridgway, CO 81432 Fax: (970)626-5100

Tabloid covering community news. **Founded:** Apr. 2, 1980. **Freq:** Weekly (Thurs.). **Print Method:** Offset. **Trim Size:** 10 1/4 x 13. **Cols./Page:** 6. **Col. Width:** 18 nonpareils. **Col. Depth:** 182 agate lines. **Key Personnel:** David Mullings, Editor and

Publisher. **USPS:** 557-510. **Subscription Rates:** $23 individuals; $29 out of area.
Ad Rates: BW: $390 **Circ:** 925
4C: $690
PCI: $5

ROCKY FORD, pop. 4,859.

Otero Co. (SE). On Arkansas River, 53 m SE of Pueblo. Manufactures clothing, seed cleaning equipment, wire, apiary; seed processing plants. Agriculture. Seed raised. Alfalfa, corn, cattle, poultry.

4676 Rocky Ford Daily Gazette
912 Elm Ave. Phone: (719)254-3351
PO Box 430 Fax: (719)254-3354
Rocky Ford, CO 81067-1249
General newspaper. **Founded:** 1900. **Freq:** Daily (eve.). **Print Method:** Offset. **Cols./Page:** 6. **Col. Width:** 2 1/16 inches. **Col. Depth:** 21 inches. **Key Personnel:** Anne M. Thompson, Editor and Publisher. **USPS:** 468-900. **Subscription Rates:** $50 individuals. **Remarks:** Accepts advertising.
Ad Rates: BW: $510.30 **Circ:** ‡3,250
4C: $724.30
SAU: $4.05

SAGUACHE†, pop. 728.

Saguache Co. (SWC). 90 m SW of Pueblo. Lumbering. Gold, silver, copper, lead mines. Stock farms.

4677 Saguache Crescent
316 4th St. Phone: (719)655-2620
PO Box 195 Fax: (719)655-2620
Saguache, CO 81149
Community newspaper. **Founded:** 1879. **Freq:** Weekly (Thurs.). **Print Method:** Uses mats. Letterpress. **Cols./Page:** 6. **Col. Width:** 24 nonpareils. **Col. Depth:** 280 agate lines. **Key Personnel:** Marie O. Coombs, Editor; Dean I. Coombs, Publisher. **USPS:** 475-480. **Subscription Rates:** $12 individuals; $14 out of area. **Remarks:** Accepts advertising.
Ad Rates: SAU: $4.27 **Circ:** ‡665

SALIDA†, pop. 4,870.

Chaffee Co. (C). 75 m NW of Pueblo. Recreation, tourism, skiing. Bottling, sheet metal works. Limestone & molydenum mining. Calcium carbonate processing. Dairy, truck, poultry, cattle ranches.

4678 Chaffee County Times
Arkansas Valley Publishing Co.
125 E. 2nd St. Phone: (719)539-6691
PO Box 189 Fax: (719)539-6630
Salida, CO 81201-0189
Publication E-mail: mtnmail@rmii.com

Community newspaper. **Founded:** 1879. **Freq:** Weekly (Thurs.). **Print Method:** Offset. **Trim Size:** 11 1/2 x 16. **Cols./Page:** 5. **Col. Width:** 12 picas. **Col. Depth:** 15.5 inches. **Key Personnel:** Michael Bullock, Editor; Jane Hermann, Advertising Sales; Larkin Wiegert, Office Mgr. **Subscription Rates:** $22 individuals; $29 Out of county.
Ad Rates: BW: $448 **Circ:** ‡3,000
4C: $596
PCI: $5.60

4679 The Herald-Democrat
Arkansas Valley Publishing Co.
125 E. 2nd St. Phone: (719)539-6691
PO Box 189 Fax: (719)539-6630
Salida, CO 81201-0189
Newspaper. **Founded:** 1886. **Freq:** Weekly (Thurs.). **Print Method:** Offset. **Cols./Page:** 5. **Col. Width:** 25 nonpareils. **Col. Depth:** 196 agate lines. **Key Personnel:** Christine Barnett, Editor and Publisher; Grant Dunham, Editor; Merle Baranczyk, Publisher. **ISSN:** 0891-0197. **Subscription Rates:** $17 individuals; $25 Out of county. **Remarks:** Accepts advertising.
Ad Rates: GLR: $4.80 **Circ:** ‡2,700
BW: $384

4680 The Mountain Mail
Arkansas Valley Publishing Co.
125 E. 2nd St. Phone: (719)539-6691
PO Box 189 Fax: (719)539-6630
Salida, CO 81201-0189
Publication E-mail: mtnmail@rmii.com

General newspaper. **Founded:** 1880. **Freq:** Daily (morn.). **Print Method:** Offset. **Trim Size:** 11 3/8 x 16 3/4. **Cols./Page:** 5. **Col. Width:** 25 nonpareils. **Col. Depth:** 15 1/2 inches. **Key Personnel:** Merle Baranczyk, Editor and Publisher. **Subscription Rates:** $39 individuals. **Remarks:** Accepts advertising. **URL:** http://www.peaksnewsnet.com.
Ad Rates: GLR: $.35 **Circ:** Paid ‡2,900
BW: $375.88
4C: $615.88
SAU: $5
PCI: $4.85

4681 KVRH-AM - 1340
7600 County Rd. 120 Phone: (719)539-2575
Salida, CO 81201 Fax: (719)539-4851
E-mail: kbvc@amigo.net

Format: Full Service; Adult Contemporary. **Simulcasts:** KVRH-FM. **Networks:** AP. **Owner:** All Heart Radio, Inc., at above address. **Founded:** 1948. **Operating Hours:** 6 a.m.-10:10 p.m.; 8% network, 92% local. **Key Personnel:** William J. Murphy, President/GM; Patrick Lee, News Dir.; Michael Kay, Music/Sports Director. **Local Programs:** *KVRH Talk Show*, Patrick Lee; *Nancy Hale Show*, Nancy Hale. **Wattage:** 1000. **Ad Rates:** $8.80-10 for 30 seconds; $11-12.50 for 60 seconds. Combined advertising rates available with KVRH-FM. **URL:** http://www.vtinet.com/kvrh.

4682 KVRH-FM - 92.3
7600 County Rd. 120 Phone: (719)539-2575
Salida, CO 81201 Fax: (719)539-4851
E-mail: kbvc@amigo.net

Format: Full Service; Adult Contemporary. **Simulcasts:** KVRH-AM. **Networks:** AP. **Owner:** All Heart Radio, Inc., at above address. **Founded:** 1971. **Operating Hours:** 6 a.m.-10:10 p.m.; 8% network, 92% local. **Key Personnel:** William J. Murphy, President/GM; Patrick Lee, News Dir.; Michael Kay, Music/Sports Director. **Local Programs:** *KVRH Talk Show*, Patrick Lee; *Nancy Hale Show*, Nancy Hale. **Wattage:** 13,500. **Ad Rates:** $8.50-10 for 30 seconds; $11-12.50 for 60 seconds. Combined advertising rates available with KVRH-AM. **URL:** http://www.vtinet.com/kvrh.

SAN LUIS†.

Costilla Co. (SC).

4683 Costilla County Free Press
PO Box 306 Phone: (719)672-3764
San Luis, CO 81152 Free: (800)652-2181

Local newspaper. **Founded:** 1940. **Freq:** Weekly. **Print Method:** Offset. **Cols./Page:** 3. **Col. Width:** 2 inches. **Col. Depth:** 8 inches. **Key Personnel:** Iva L. Gallegos, Publisher; Renee M. Aragon, Editor. **Subscription Rates:** $15; $18 out of state. **Remarks:** Accepts advertising.
Ad Rates: BW: $100 **Circ:** Paid ‡275
PCI: $5 Free ‡25

SILT

4684 KKGD-AM - 810
PO Box 767 Phone: (303)625-5000
Silt, CO 81652-0767 Fax: (303)625-3031

Format: Country. **Owner:** Western Media, Inc., at above address. **Founded:** 1967. **Operating Hours:** 6 a.m.-midnight. **Key Personnel:** Lee Canterbury, General Mgr.; E.G. Edwards, General Sales Mgr.; Dick Hayes, Program Dir. **Wattage:** 1000. **Ad Rates:** $7 for 15 seconds; $10 for 60 seconds.

SILVERTON†, pop. 830.

San Juan Co. (SW). 120 m S of Grand Junction. Tourism. Lead, silver, gold, copper mines.

4685 The Silverton Standard and The Miner
1257 Greene St. Phone: (970)387-5477
Silverton, CO 81433-0008 Fax: (970)387-5291
Publisher E-mail: silvertonstd@frontier.net

Community newspaper. **Founded:** 1875. **Freq:** Weekly (Thurs.). **Print Method:** Offset. **Cols./Page:** 5. **Col. Width:** 23 nonpareils. **Col. Depth:** 182 agate lines. **Key Personnel:** Ethan Wortis, Editor and Publisher; Maureen Wortis, Publisher. **USPS:** 496-880. **Subscription Rates:** $23 individuals; $29 out of area. **Remarks:** Accepts advertising.
Ad Rates: GLR: $.33 **Circ:** Paid ‡1,400
BW: $357.50 Free ‡6
4C: $550
PCI: $5.50

SIMLA, pop. 460.

Elbert Co. (EC). 43 m NE of Colorado Springs. Industry. Waterbeds. Grain, stock, poultry, dairy farms. Wheat, corn, beans.

4686 Ranchland News
115 Sioux Ave. Phone: (719)541-2288
PO Box 307 Fax: (719)541-2289
Simla, CO 80835-0307
Community newspaper. **Founded:** 1901. **Freq:** Weekly (Thurs.). **Print Method:** Offset. **Trim Size:** 11 x 16. **Cols./Page:** 5. **Col. Width:** 11 1/2 picas. **Col. Depth:** 15 1/2 inches. **Key Personnel:** Fred Lister, Publisher; Tim Taylor, Editor; Susan Lister, Business Mgr., lister@ria.net. **USPS:** 455-020. **Subscription Rates:** $19 In El Paso, Elbert, and; Lincoln counties; $22 Elsewhere in Colorado; $27 out of state. **Remarks:** Accepts advertising. **Formerly:** Pikeview Farmer, Raunchland News, amd Simla Sun.
Ad Rates: BW: $461.12 **Circ:** (Not Reported)
PCI: $5.95

SOUTH FORK, pop. 250.

Rio Grande Co. (S). 28 m W of Monte Vista. Residential.

4687 South Fork Times
SLV Publishing
PO Box 158 Phone: (719)873-5592
South Fork, CO 81154-0158
Community newspaper. **Founded:** Dec. 1981. **Freq:** Weekly (Thurs.). **Print Method:** Offset. **Cols./Page:** 5. **Col. Width:** 2 inches. **Key Personnel:** Nate McMchan, Managing Editor; Stephen Haynes, Publisher. **USPS:** 659-530. **Subscription Rates:** $25.95 individuals.
Ad Rates: BW: $504 **Circ:** Paid 770
Free 7

STEAMBOAT SPRINGS†, pop. 6,500.

Routt Co. (NW). 160 m NW of Denver. Ski Town, U.S.A. Tourist resort. Mineral springs. Coal mines. Agriculture. Grain farms, cattle.

4688 Steamboat Pilot
1041 Lincoln Ave. Phone: (970)879-1502
PO Box 4488 Fax: (970)879-2888
Steamboat Springs, CO 80477
Local newspaper. **Founded:** 1885. **Freq:** Weekly (Thurs.). **Print Method:** Offset. **Cols./Page:** 6. **Col. Width:** 2 1/8 inches. **Col. Depth:** 21 1/2 inches. **Key Personnel:** Gary E. Maitland, Managing Editor, editor@stmbt-pilot.com; Suzanne Antinoro, Publisher. **Subscription Rates:** $24 individuals; $32 out of area. **Remarks:** Accepts advertising.
Ad Rates: GLR: $.44 **Circ:** ‡6,900
BW: $980.40
PCI: $7.60

4689 The Steamboat Whistle
Steamboat Pilot
PO Box 4827 Phone: (970)879-1502
Steamboat Springs, CO 80477 Fax: (970)879-2888

Newspaper (tabloid) providing tourist information on Steamboat Springs. **Founded:** 1962. **Freq:** Weekly (Fri.). **Print Method:** Offset. **Trim Size:** 11 1/4 x 15. **Cols./Page:** 4. **Col. Width:** 15 picas. **Col. Depth:** 14 inches. **Key Personnel:** Suzanne Antinoro, Publisher. **Subscription Rates:** Free. **Remarks:** Accepts advertising. **Online:** America Online, Inc.
Ad Rates: BW: $250 **Circ:** ‡5,000
PCI: $4.50

4690 KBCR-AM - 1230
PO Box 774050 Phone: (303)879-2270
Steamboat Springs, CO 80477 Fax: (303)879-1404

Format: Oldies; Talk; Sports. **Networks:** ABC. **Owner:** KBCR Inc., 815 Reed St., Lakewood, CO 80215, (303)233-8433, Fax: (303)825-9152. **Founded:** 1974. **Operating Hours:** Continuous. **ADI:** Denver (Steamboat Springs), CO. **Key Personnel:** John Gayer, President/G.M.; Terry Kottom, Program Dir., tkottom; John Larson, News Dir. **Local Programs:** *Country Western*, N. Rife. **Wattage:** 1000. **Ad Rates:** $8-15 for 30 seconds; $9-22.50 for 60 seconds.

4691 KBCR-FM - 96.9
Box 4050 Phone: (303)879-2270
Steamboat Springs, CO 80477 Fax: (303)879-1404

Format: Country. **Networks:** ABC. **Founded:** 1974. **Formerly:** KSBT-FM (1995). **Operating Hours:** Continuous. **ADI:** Denver (Steamboat Springs), CO. **Key Personnel:** Nathleen Rife, General Mgr., nathleen@kbcr.com; Terry Kottom, Program Dir., tkottom@cmn.net; Harper Louden, News Dir., harper@kbcr.com. **Wattage:** 10,000. **Ad Rates:** $25 per unit. Combined advertising rates available with AM 1230 KBCR.

4692 KFMU-FM - 104.1, 104.9, and 105.5
2955 Village Dr. Phone: (970)879-5368
Box 772850 Fax: (970)879-5843
Steamboat Springs, CO 80477

Format: Adult Album Alternative; Classic Rock; Adult Album Alternative. **Networks:** CBS. **Owner:** E.B.S.S. LLC, at above address. **Founded:** 1975. **Operating Hours:** Continuous; 15% network, 85% local. **ADI:** Denver (Steamboat Springs), CO. **Key Personnel:** Sean D. Waterman, General Mgr./General Sales Mgr., swaterman@kfmu.com; Tami Collari, Office Mgr., tcolari@kfmu.com; Erica Swissler, Program & Music Dir., eswiss@kfmu.com; Ron Bostwick, Promotions Dir., rbostwick@kfmu.com; Michelle Boles, News Dir., mbales@kfmu.com. **Local Programs:** *Outdoor Report*, Michelle Bales; *Ski Tips*, Michelle Bales. **Wattage:** 1200. **Ad Rates:** $16-36 per unit. **URL:** http://www.kfmu.com.

KIDN-FM - See Hayden

STERLING†, pop. 11,385.

Logan Co. (NE). 90 m NE of Greeley. Manufactures clothing, farm implements, sugar, beef processing plant. Alfalfa dehydrating. Diversified farming. Sugar beets, corn, wheat, beans.

4693 Journal-Advocate
504 N. 3rd St. Phone: (970)522-1990
PO Box 1272 Fax: (970)522-2320
Sterling, CO 80751
General newspaper. **Founded:** 1886. **Freq:** Daily (eve.) and Sat. (morn.). **Print Method:** Web offset. **Trim Size:** 13 3/4 x 21 1/2. **Cols./Page:** 6. **Col. Width:** 25 nonpareils. **Col. Depth:** 301 agate lines. **Key Personnel:** William H. Muldoon III, Publisher; Myron House, Advertising Mgr. **USPS:** 285-760. **Subscription Rates:** $72 individuals. **Remarks:** Accepts advertising.
Ad Rates: GLR: $0.70 **Circ:** Mon.-Sat. ★**5,223**
BW: $1,100.33
4C: $1,375.33
SAU: $8.53
PCI: $9.80

4694 KNNG-FM - 104.7
803 W. Main Phone: (303)522-1607
PO Box 830 Fax: (303)522-1322
Sterling, CO 80751
Free: (800)748-2220

Format: Hot Country. **Simulcasts:** KSTU 5:45am-9am, 12pm-1pm. **Networks:** ABC. **Owner:** KSTC, Inc., at above address. **Founded:** 1972. **Formerly:** KSTC-FM. **Operating Hours:** Continuous. **ADI:** Denver (Steamboat Springs), CO. **Key Personnel:** Bill Arnold, General Mgr.; Betty Carlson, Operations Mgr.; Tommy Witt, Public Service Dir. **Local Programs:** *Cross Talk*, Bill Arnold; *NE Colorado Sports Net*, Bill Arnold. **Wattage:** 100,000. **Ad Rates:** $9-19 for 60 seconds.

4695 KPMX-FM - 105.5
101 S. Division Phone: (303)522-4800
Sterling, CO 80751 Fax: (303)522-3997

Format: Adult Contemporary; Oldies. **Networks:** Jones Satellite; CNN Radio. **Owner:** Adams Enterainment Group, at above address. **Founded:** 1983. **Formerly:** KMXX-FM. **Operating Hours:** Continuous. **ADI:** Denver (Steamboat Springs), CO. **Key Personnel:** Phil Adams, General Mgr.; Diana Adams, Station Mgr.; Andy Rice, PD. **Local Programs:** *Andy & Darwin Mornings* 6 a.m.-10 a.m. Monday-Friday. **Wattage:** 3000. **Ad Rates:** $7.50-12 for 30 seconds; $11.25-16 for 60 seconds.

4696 KSTC-AM - 1230
803 W. Main Phone: (303)522-1607
PO Box 830 Fax: (303)522-1322
Sterling, CO 80751
Free: (800)748-2220

Format: Oldies. **Simulcasts:** 5:45-9am, 12:00-1pm. **Networks:** ABC. **Founded:** 1925. **Formerly:** KSEK (1975). **Operating Hours:** Continuous. **ADI:** Cheyenne, WY-Scottsbluff, NE (Sterling, CO). **Key Personnel:** Bill Arnold, General Mgr. **Wattage:** 1,000. **Ad Rates:** $9-19 for 11 seconds.

STRASBURG, pop. 900.

Adams & Arapahoe Co. (C) 5 m SE of Bennett. Residential. Home of Comanche Crossing. Museum and site where the rails first linked the east to the west.

4697 Eastern Colorado News
Eastern Colorado News, Inc.
1522 Main St. Phone: (303)622-4417
PO Box 555 Fax: (303)622-9717
Strasburg, CO 80136-0555
Community newspaper. **Founded:** 1916. **Freq:** Weekly (Thurs.). **Print Method:** Offset. **Cols./Page:** 6. **Col. Width:** 24 nonpareils. **Col. Depth:** 294 agate lines. **Key Personnel:** Mike Galarneau, Publisher. **USPS:** 165-666. **Subscription Rates:** $18 individuals; $20 out of state; $0.35 single issue. **Remarks:** Accepts advertising.
Ad Rates: SAU: $6.30 **Circ:** 1,978
PCI: $4.75

TELLURIDE†, pop. 1,000.

San Miguel Co. (SW). 87 m SE of Grand Junction. Tourist. Ski resort. Uranium mines. Ranching. Cattle and sheep.

4698 The Telluride Times-Journal
Wick Communications
PO Box 1765 Phone: (970)728-4488
Telluride, CO 81435 Fax: (970)728-6090
Publication E-mail: timesj@rmii.com

Community newspaper (tabloid). **Founded:** 1962. **Freq:** Weekly (Thurs.). **Print Method:** Offset. **Trim Size:** 10 x 16. **Cols./Page:** 5. **Col. Width:** 2 inches. **Col. Depth:** 15 9/10 inches. **Key Personnel:** Tom Bonfietti, Publisher. **USPS:** 537-360. **Subscription Rates:** $24 individuals.
Ad Rates: BW: $500 **Circ:** Paid 2,802
4C: $900 Free 884
PCI: $7.50

4699 KOTO-FM - 91.7
PO Box 1069 Phone: (970)728-4334
Telluride, CO 81435-1069 Fax: (970)728-4326
E-mail: koto@infozone.org

Format: Full Service. **Networks:** National Public Radio (NPR). **Owner:** San Miguel Educational Fund, at above address. **Founded:** 1975. **Operating Hours:** Continuous; 10% network, 90% local. **Key Personnel:** Ben Kerr, General Mgr.; Jon Kovash, News Dir.; Donna Santorelli, Music Dir.; Janice Zink, Events Coordinator. **Wattage:** 3000. **Ad Rates:** Noncommercial.

4700 Telluride Cablevision
220 S. Pine Phone: (970)728-4437
Box 979 Fax: (970)728-3687
Telluride, CO 81435

Owner: Century Communications, 50 Locust Ave., New Canaan, CT 06840-4737, (203)972-2000, Fax: (203)966-9228. **Founded:** 1980. **Key Personnel:** Bob Roberts, Contact, phone (970)928-4437, fax (970)728-3687. **Cities Served:** Ophir, Telluride, CO: subscribing households 1,500; 42 channels; 1 community access channel; 168 hours per week community access programming.

THORNTON, pop. 40,343.

Adams Co. (W). N of Denver.

4701 TCI
2190 E. 104th Ave. Phone: (303)930-2000
Thornton, CO 80233 Fax: (303)252-4419

Formerly: American Cablevision. **Cities Served:** Adams County, Arapahoe County, Douglas County, Jefferson County, North Glenn, Littleton, Thornton, and Wheat Ridge, CO.

TRINIDAD†, pop. 9,901.

Las Animas Co. (SE). On Purgatory River, 85 m SW of La Junta. Manufactures butter, sausage. Coal mines. Natural gas. Pine, aspen timber. Dairy farms. Pinto beans, barley, oats.

4702 Chronicle-News
The Shearman Group
200 Church St. Phone: (719)846-3311
PO Box 763 Fax: (719)846-3612
Trinidad, CO 81082-0763
General newspaper. **Founded:** 1877. **Freq:** Daily (eve.). **Print Method:** Offset. **Trim Size:** 13 x 21 1/2. **Cols./Page:** 6. **Col. Width:** 2 inches. **Col. Depth:** 21 1/2 inches. **Key Personnel:** Cosette Henritze, Editor; Hugh Shearman, Publisher. **Subscription Rates:** $36 individuals. **Remarks:** Accepts advertising.
Ad Rates: BW: $406.35 **Circ:** Mon.-Fri. 3,546
PCI: $4

4703 KCRT-AM - 1240
100 Fisher Dr. Phone: (719)846-3355
Trinidad, CO 81082 Fax: (719)846-4711
Free: (800)791-8028

Format: Country. **Networks:** ABC. **Owner:** Phillips Broadcasting, Inc., at above address. **Founded:** 1946. **Operating Hours:** Continuous. **Key Personnel:** Lory Phillips, General Mgr.; Robert Herrera, Chief Engineer; David Phillips, Contact; Robert Campbell, Sports Dir. **Wattage:** 250. **Ad Rates:** $4-9 for 30 seconds; $5-11 per unit. $4-$9 for 30 seconds;.

4704 KCRT-FM - 92.5
100 Fisher Dr. Phone: (719)846-3355
Trinidad, CO 81082 Fax: (719)846-4711
Free: (800)791-8028

Format: Adult Contemporary. **Networks:** ABC; Jones Satellite. **Owner:** Phillips Broadcasting, Inc., at above address. **Founded:** 1981. **Operating Hours:** Continuous. **Key Personnel:** Lory Phillips, Contact; David Phillips, Contact; Robert Herrera, Chief Engineer. **Wattage:** 15,000 ERP. **Ad Rates:** $6-11 for 30 seconds; $7-13 for 60 seconds.

VAIL, pop. 2,261.

Eagle Co. (NWC). 5m N of Minturn. Residential.

4705 Steamboat Magazine
Mac Media LLC
PO Box 1414 Phone: (970)949-9170
Vail, CO 81658 Fax: (970)949-9176
Publication E-mail: slindsay@mtnmags.com

Lifestyle magazine about Vail and Beaver Creek, Colorado. **Founded:** Nov. 1993. **Freq:** Semiannual. **Print Method:** Web. **Trim Size:** 8 3/8 x 10 7/8. **Cols./Page:** 3. **Key Personnel:** Rolly Wahl, Exec. Editor; Michael Barry, Publisher; Don Berger, Managing Editor, berger@vail.net. **Subscription Rates:** $12.50; $5.95 single issue. **Remarks:** Accepts advertising. **URL:** http://www.steamboatweb.com; http://www.macmediaweb.com. **Formerly:** Colorado's Front Range Quarterly.
Ad Rates: 4C: $3,970 **Circ:** Paid ‡3,000
Controlled ‡17,000

4706 Vail-Beaver Creek Magazine
Mac Media, Inc.
PO Box 368
Vail, CO 81658-0368

Regional consumer magazine. **Freq:** Semiannual. **Key Personnel:** Don Berger, Editor, bergerd@vail.net; Joel Schulman, Production Mgr., phone (970)879-5250, fax (970)879-4652, jschulm@mtnmags.com; Sandy Jacobs, Office Mgr., phone (970)879-5250, fax (970)879-4652, slindsay@mtnmags.com. **Subscription Rates:** $12.50 individuals; $9 single issue. **Remarks:** Accepts advertising. **URL:** http://www.vailweb.com.
Ad Rates: 4C: $3,626 **Circ:** (Not Reported)

4707 Vail Daily
PO Box 81 Phone: (970)949-0555
Vail, CO 81658 Fax: (970)949-7096

General tabloid newspaper. **Founded:** 1981. **Freq:** Mon.-Sun. (morn.). **Trim Size:** 10 1/2 x 16. **Cols./Page:** 5. **Col. Width:** 12 picas. **Col. Depth:** 16 inches. **Key Personnel:** Matt Fults, Editor; Robert Brown, Publisher. **Subscription Rates:** $30. **Remarks:** Accepts advertising. **Available Online. URL:** http://vaildaily.com.
Ad Rates: PCI: $6.50 **Circ:** ‡13,000

4708 KTUN-FM - 101.5
1000 Lionsridge Loop Phone: (303)476-7444
Vail, CO 81657 Fax: (303)476-8211

Format: Adult Album Alternative. **Networks:** CNN Radio. **Owner:** L & B Broadcasting II LLC, at above address. **Founded:** 1995. **Formerly:** KWLI-FM (1986); KQMT-FM (1995). **Operating Hours:** Continuous. **Key Personnel:** Massey Pitts, General Sales Mgr.; Don Taylor, Program Dir.; Carolyne Harvey, Music Dir. **Wattage:** 100,000 ERP. **Ad Rates:** $3-25 for 30 seconds; $5-30 for 60 seconds.

WALDEN†, pop. 947.

Jackson Co. (C). Coal mines, oil wells.

4709 Jackson County Star
PO Box 397 Phone: (970)723-4404
Walden, CO 80480 Fax: (970)723-4404
Publisher E-mail: thesstar@verinet.com

County newspaper. **Founded:** 1913. **Freq:** Weekly (Thurs.). **Print Method:** Offset. **Trim Size:** 10 x 16. **Cols./Page:** 6. **Col. Width:** 1 5/8 inches. **Col. Depth:** 16 inches. **Key Personnel:** Jim Dutin, Editor. **Subscription Rates:** $12 individuals; $15 out of area. **Remarks:** Color advertising not accepted.
Ad Rates: GLR: $4.20 **Circ:** Paid ‡1,150
BW: $408 Free ‡50
PCI: $4.20

WALSENBURG†, pop. 3,975.

Huerfano Co. (S). 50 m S of Pueblo. Tourism. Timber. Stock, grain farms.

4710 Huerfano World
111 W. 7th St. Phone: (719)738-1720
PO Box 191 Fax: (719)738-1727
Walsenburg, CO 81089
Community newspaper. **Founded:** 1887. **Freq:** Weekly (Thurs.). **Print Method:** Offset. **Cols./Page:** 6. **Col. Width:** 26 nonpareils. **Col. Depth:** 294 agate lines. **Key Personnel:** Jay D. Crook, Editor and Publisher; Vera Andreatta, Advertising

Mgr. **Subscription Rates:** $30 individuals. **Remarks:** Accepts advertising.
Ad Rates: GLR: $.50 BW: $882 4C: $1,500 SAU: $9.80 PCI: $9.80 **Circ:** Paid ‡2,975 Free ‡25

4711 KSPK-FM - 102.3
516 Main St. Phone: (719)738-3636
Walsenburg, CO 81089 Fax: (719)738-2010
E-mail: postmaster@kspk.com

Format: Country. **Networks:** ABC. **Owner:** Mainstreet Broadcasting Co., Inc., at above address. **Founded:** Mar. 1, 1985. **Operating Hours:** Continuous; 80% network, 20% local. **ADI:** Colorado Springs-Pueblo, CO. **Key Personnel:** Paul Richards, General Mgr., paul@kspk.com; Kim Lucero, Sales Mgr., kim@kspk.com. **Local Programs:** *Financial Strategies* 9:00 am Saturday, Sammy C. Brocato. **Wattage:** 17,000. **Ad Rates:** $10-17 for 30 seconds; $13-20 for 60 seconds. **URL:** http://kspk.com.

WESTCLIFFE†, pop. 324.

Custer Co. (SC). 62 m W of Pueblo. Recreation area. Silver, lead mines. Stock farms. Hay, grain, cattle.

4712 Wet Mountain Tribune
Little Publishing Co., Inc.
PO Box 300 Phone: (719)783-2361
Westcliffe, CO 81252 Fax: (719)783-2879
Publication E-mail: wmtrib@ris.net

Community newspaper. **Founded:** 1883. **Freq:** Weekly (Thurs.). **Print Method:** Offset. **Trim Size:** 10 1/8 x 16. **Cols./Page:** 6. **Col. Width:** 10 picas. **Col. Depth:** 224 agate lines. **Key Personnel:** James A. Little, Editor and Publisher. **USPS:** 681-200. **Subscription Rates:** $18 in county; $24 out of area. **Remarks:** Accepts advertising.
Ad Rates: GLR: $.30 BW: $384 PCI: $4 **Circ:** ‡2,820

WESTMINSTER, pop. 55,610.

Adams Co. (NEC). 8m NW of Denver. Residential.

4713 Denver Arts Center Programs
The Publishing House, Inc.
7380 Lowell Blvd. Phone: (303)428-9529
PO Box 215 Fax: (303)430-1676
Westminster, CO 80030
Magazine covering events held at the Denver Center for the Performing Arts. **Founded:** 1977. **Freq:** Monthly. **Print Method:** Offset. **Trim Size:** 8 1/4 x 10 3/4. **Cols./Page:** 3. **Col. Width:** 2 1/4 inches. **Col. Depth:** 9 3/4 inches. **Key Personnel:** Melanie Simonet, Editor; Wilbur Flachman, Publisher; Frank Debolt, Advertising Mgr. **Formerly:** Bravo.
Ad Rates: BW: $11,990 4C: $14,820 **Circ:** Non-paid ‡192,000 1,728,000

4714 Westminster Window
MetroNorth Newspapers, Inc.
PO Box 215 Phone: (303)426-6000
Westminster, CO 80030 Fax: (303)430-1676

Community newspaper. **Founded:** 1978. **Freq:** Weekly (Thurs.). **Print Method:** Offset. **Trim Size:** 11 1/4 x 13 3/4. **Cols./Page:** 5. **Col. Width:** 11.6 picas. **Col. Depth:** 12 3/4 inches. **Key Personnel:** Mikkel Kelly, Editor; Bruce G. Harper, General Mgr.; Jim May, Advertising Mgr.; Wilbur E. Flachman, President. **USPS:** 455-250. **Subscription Rates:** $24 individuals. **Remarks:** Accepts advertising.
Ad Rates: GLR: $1.30 BW: $990.68 4C: $1,500 PCI: $15.54 **Circ:** Paid 5,200 Non-paid 109

4715 KPOF-AM - 910
3455 W. 83rd Ave. Phone: (303)428-0910
Westminster, CO 80030 Fax: (303)429-0910
Free: (800)748-1775
E-mail: kpof@power-online.net

Format: Religious; Classical. **Networks:** Moody Broadcasting. **Owner:** Pillar of Fire, 1302 Sherman St., Denver, CO 80203, (303)839-1500, Fax: (303)429-0910, Free: (800)748-1775. **Founded:** 1928. **Operating Hours:** Continuous. **Key Personnel:** Robert B. Dallenbach, General Mgr., phone (303)427-5462, fax (303)428-6462, kpof@power-online.net; Barry Blue, Program/Religious Music Dir., phone (303)428-0910, fax (303)429-0910, kpof@power-online.net; Ray Rogers, Chief Engineer; Becky Ross, Classical Music Dir.; Pat Laplante, News Dir. **Local Programs:** *On the Air* 10:00 am Monday-Friday, Christy Gimer. **Wattage:** 5000 day; 1000 night. **Ad Rates:** Noncommercial. **URL:** http://www.kpof.org.

WHEAT RIDGE, pop. 30,293.

Jefferson Co. (NC). 5 m NW of Denver. Manufactures aluminum, containers, industrial supplies, office supplies. Nurseries, florists.

4716 Akita World
Hoflin Publishing Ltd.
4401 Zephyr St. Phone: (303)420-2222
Wheat Ridge, CO 80033-3299 Fax: (303)422-7000

Magazine for Akita dog fanciers. **Founded:** Feb. 1987. **Freq:** Bimonthly. **Trim Size:** 8.5x11. **Cols./Page:** 3. **Col. Width:** 2.375 inches. **Col. Depth:** 9.5 inches. **Key Personnel:** Donald R. Hoflin, Editor and Publisher; Cynthia L. Kersteins, Editor. **ISSN:** 0194-6323. **Subscription Rates:** $54 individuals; $63 other countries; $10 single issue. **URL:** http://www.hoflin.com.
Ad Rates: BW: $100 4C: $400 **Circ:** Paid 1,774 Non-paid 297

4717 The Borzoi Quarterly
Hoflin Publishing Ltd.
4401 Zephyr St. Phone: (303)420-2222
Wheat Ridge, CO 80033-3299 Fax: (303)422-7000

Magazine for lovers of the Borzoi dog breed. **Founded:** Jan. 1980. **Freq:** Quarterly. **Trim Size:** 8.5x11. **Cols./Page:** 3. **Col. Width:** 2.375 inches. **Col. Depth:** 9.5 inches. **Key Personnel:** Donald R. Hoflin, Editor and Publisher; Cynthia Kerstiens, Editor. **ISSN:** 0746-2875. **Subscription Rates:** $44 individuals; $48 other countries; $13 single issue. **URL:** http://www.hoflin.com.
Ad Rates: BW: $40 4C: $350 **Circ:** Paid 393 Non-paid 286

4718 The Boston Quarterly
Hoflin Publishing Ltd.
4401 Zephyr St. Phone: (303)420-2222
Wheat Ridge, CO 80033-3299 Fax: (303)422-7000

Magazine for fanciers of the Boston Terrier. **Founded:** Oct. 1986. **Freq:** Quarterly. **Trim Size:** 8.5 x 11. **Cols./Page:** 3. **Col. Width:** 2.375 inches. **Col. Depth:** 9.5 inches. **Key Personnel:** Donald R. Hoflin, Editor and Publisher; Cynthia L. Kersteins, Editor. **ISSN:** 0746-4088. **Subscription Rates:** $44 individuals; $48 other countries; $13 single issue. **URL:** http://www.hoflin.com.
Ad Rates: BW: $100 4C: $400 **Circ:** Paid 585 Non-paid 258

4719 The Coin Slot
Hoflin Publishing Ltd.
4401 Zephyr St. Phone: (303)420-2222
Wheat Ridge, CO 80033-3299 Fax: (303)422-7000

Antique coin-operated machines magazine. **Founded:** 1974. **Freq:** Quarterly. **Print Method:** Sheetfed offset. **Trim Size:** 8 1/2 x 11. **Cols./Page:** 3. **Col. Width:** 26 nonpareils. **Col. Depth:** 137 agate lines. **Key Personnel:** Donald R. Hoflin, Editor and Publisher. **ISSN:** 0745-8533. **Subscription Rates:** $44 individuals. **URL:** http://www.hoflin.com.
Ad Rates: BW: $120 4C: $420 **Circ:** ‡664

4720 Composites Technology
Ray Publishing, Inc.
4891 Independence St., Ste. 270 Phone: (303)467-1776 Fax: (303)467-1777
Wheat Ridge, CO 80033
Technical trade journal covering products employing FRP composites. **Subtitle:** Engineering & Manufacturing Solutions for Industry. **Founded:** May 1995. **Freq:** Bimonthly. **Print Method:** Offset. **Trim Size:** 8 3/8 x 10 7/8. **Key Personnel:** Judith Ray Hazen, Publisher, judy@raypubs.com; Paulette Whitcomb, Exec. Editor; Glenn Comar, Circulation Mgr./Marketing Dir.; Bill Parker, National Sales Mgr. **ISSN:** 1083-4117. **Subscription Rates:** $15 individuals; $6 single issue. **Remarks:** Accepts advertising.
Ad Rates: BW: $5,200 4C: $7,310 **Circ:** Controlled ‡25,000

4721 The Corgi Quarterly
Hoflin Publishing Ltd.
4401 Zephyr St. Phone: (303)420-2222
Wheat Ridge, CO 80033-3299 Fax: (303)422-7000

Magazine for fanciers of Welsh Corgi dogs. **Founded:** Nov. 1982. **Freq:** Quarterly. **Trim Size:** 8.5 x 11. **Cols./Page:** 3. **Col. Width:** 2.375 inches. **Col. Depth:** 9.5 inches. **Key Personnel:** Donald R. Hoflin, Editor and Publisher; Cynthia Kerstiens, Editor. **ISSN:** 0745-9734. **Subscription Rates:** $44 individuals; $48 other countries; $13 single issue. **URL:** http://www.hoflin.com.
Ad Rates: BW: $60 4C: $350 **Circ:** Paid 647 Non-paid 279

4722 The Dalmatian Quarterly
Hoflin Publishing Ltd.
4401 Zephyr St. Phone: (303)420-2222
Wheat Ridge, CO 80033-3299 Fax: (303)422-7000

Magazine for fanciers of Dalmatian Dogs. **Founded:** Jan. 1987. **Freq:** Quarterly. **Trim Size:** 8.5 x 11. **Cols./Page:** 3. **Col. Width:** 2.375 inches. **Col. Depth:** 9.5 inches. **Key Personnel:** Donald R. Hoflin, Editor and Publisher. **ISSN:** 0893-987X. **Subscription Rates:** $44 individuals; $48 other countries; $13 single issue. **URL:** http://www.hoflin.com.
Ad Rates: BW: $100 4C: $400 **Circ:** Paid 730 Non-paid 295

4723 Doberman World
Hoflin Publishing Ltd.
4401 Zephyr St. Phone: (303)420-2222
Wheat Ridge, CO 80033-3299 Fax: (303)422-7000

Founded: Jan. 1980. **Freq:** Quarterly. **Trim Size:** 8.5 x 11. **Cols./Page:** 3. **Col. Width:** 2.375 inches. **Col. Depth:** 9.5 inches. **Key Personnel:** Donald R. Hoflin, Editor and Publisher; Cynthia Kerstiens, Editor. **ISSN:** 0194-6323. **Subscription Rates:** $44 individuals; $48 other countries; $13 single issue. **URL:** http://www.hoflin.com. **Formerly:** The Doberman Quarterly.
Ad Rates: BW: $100 4C: $400 **Circ:** Paid 708 Non-paid 416

4724 Elkhound Annual
Hoflin Publishing Ltd.
4401 Zephyr St. Phone: (303)420-2222
Wheat Ridge, CO 80033-3299 Fax: (303)422-7000

Journal covering care and breeding of Norwegian Elkhounds for breeders and others. **Founded:** 1996. **Freq:** Annual. **Trim Size:** 8 1/2 x 11. **Key Personnel:** Don Hoflin, Editor. **Subscription Rates:** $44 individuals. **Remarks:** Accepts advertising.
Circ: (Not Reported)

4725 The English Cocker Quarterly
Hoflin Publishing Ltd.
4401 Zephyr St. Phone: (303)420-2222
Wheat Ridge, CO 80033-3299 Fax: (303)422-7000

Magazine for fanciers of English Cocker Spaniels. **Founded:** Nov. 1985. **Freq:** Quarterly. **Trim Size:** 8.5 x 11. **Cols./Page:** 3. **Col. Width:** 2.375 inches. **Col. Depth:** 9.5 inches. **Key Personnel:** Donald R. Hoflin, Editor and Publisher; Cyhthia Kerstiens, Editor. **ISSN:** 0746-4088. **Subscription Rates:** $44 individuals; $48 other countries; $13 single issue. **URL:** http://www.hoflin.com.
Ad Rates: BW: $60 4C: $350 **Circ:** Paid 617 Non-paid 295

4726 The German Shepherd Quarterly
Hoflin Publishing Ltd.
4401 Zephyr St. Phone: (303)420-2222
Wheat Ridge, CO 80033-3299 Fax: (303)422-7000

Magazine for German Shepherd owners and enthusiasts. **Founded:** Apr. 1983. **Freq:** Quarterly. **Trim Size:** 8.5x11. **Cols./Page:** 3. **Col. Width:** 2.375 inches. **Col. Depth:** 9.5 inches. **Key Personnel:** Donald R. Hoflin, Editor and Publisher; Cynthia L. Kersteins, Editor. **ISSN:** 0745-1849. **Subscription Rates:** $40 individuals; $44 other countries; $12 single issue. **URL:** http://www.hoflin.com.
Ad Rates: BW: $100 4C: $400 **Circ:** Paid ‡14,741 Non-paid ‡392

4727 High-Performance Composites
Ray Publishing, Inc.
4891 Independence St., Ste. 270 Phone: (303)467-1776 Fax: (303)467-1777
Wheat Ridge, CO 80033
Technical trade journal covering current application, design and manufacturing methods from products using advanced composite materials. **Subtitle:** Design and Manufacturing, Solutions for Industry. **Founded:** Sept. 1993. **Freq:** Bimonthly. **Print Method:** Offset. **Trim Size:** 8 3/8 x 10 7/8. **Key Personnel:** Judith Ray Hazen, Publisher, judy@raypubs.com; Paulette Whitcomb, Exec. Editor; Glenn Comar, Circulation Mgr./Marketing Dir.; Bill Parker, National Sales Mgr. **ISSN:** 1081-9223. **Subscription Rates:** $30 individuals; $6 single issue. **Remarks:** Accepts advertising.
Ad Rates: BW: $4,350 4C: $6,110 **Circ:** Controlled ‡20,000

4728 The Irish Wolfhound Quarterly
Hoflin Publishing Ltd.
4401 Zephyr St. Phone: (303)420-2222
Wheat Ridge, CO 80033-3299 Fax: (303)422-7000

Magazine for Irish Wolfhound owners and enthusiasts. **Founded:** Jan. 1980. **Freq:** Quarterly. **Trim Size:** 8.5 x 11. **Cols./Page:** 3. **Col. Width:** 2.375 inches. **Col. Depth:** 9.5 inches. **Key Personnel:** Donald R. Hoflin, Editor and Publisher; Cynthia L. Kersteins, Editor. **ISSN:** 0746-4087. **Subscrip-**

tion Rates: $44 individuals; $48 other countries; $13 single issue. **URL:** http://www.hoflin.com.
Ad Rates: BW: $100 **Circ:** Paid ‡717
4C: $400 Non-paid ‡279

4729 The Labrador Quarterly
Hoflin Publishing Ltd.
4401 Zephyr St. Phone: (303)420-2222
Wheat Ridge, CO 80033-3299 Fax: (303)422-7000

Magazine for Labrador retriever owners and enthusiasts. **Founded:** Jan. 1984. **Freq:** Quarterly. **Trim Size:** 8.5 x 11. **Cols./Page:** 3. **Col. Width:** 2.375 inches. **Col. Depth:** 9.5 inches. **Key Personnel:** Donald R. Hoflin, Editor and Publisher; Cynthia Kerstiens, Editor. **ISSN:** 8750-3557. **Subscription Rates:** $48 individuals; $46 other countries; $13 single issue. **URL:** http://www.hoflin.com.
Ad Rates: BW: $100 **Circ:** Paid ‡2235
4C: $400 Non-paid ‡288

4730 The Malamute Quarterly
Hoflin Publishing Ltd.
4401 Zephyr St. Phone: (303)420-2222
Wheat Ridge, CO 80033-3299 Fax: (303)422-7000

Magazine for Malamute dog owners and enthusiasts. **Founded:** Jan. 1980. **Freq:** Quarterly. **Trim Size:** 8.5 x 11. **Cols./Page:** 3. **Col. Width:** 2.375 inches. **Col. Depth:** 9.5 inches. **Key Personnel:** Donald R. Hoflin, Editor and Publisher; Cynthia Kerstiens, Editor. **ISSN:** 0746-4002. **Subscription Rates:** $44 individuals; $48 other countries; $13 single issue. **URL:** http://www.hoflin.com.
Ad Rates: BW: $65 **Circ:** Paid ‡538
4C: $350 Non-paid ‡337

4731 Quilter's Newsletter Magazine
Leman Publications, Inc.
6700 W. 44th Ave. Phone: (303)420-4272
Wheat Ridge, CO 80034 Fax: (303)420-7358

Magazine featuring quilting techniques, patterns, and designs; events, exhibitions, trade news, and suppliers' information. **Subtitle:** The Magazine for Quilt Lovers. **Founded:** Sept. 21, 1969. **Freq:** 10/year. **Print Method:** Offset. **Trim Size:** 8 3/8 x 10 7/8. **Cols./Page:** 2. **Col. Width:** 3 7/8 inches. **Col. Depth:** 10 inches. **Key Personnel:** Bonnie Leman, Editor and Publisher; Tina L. Battock, Advertising Mgr.; Robert Kaslik, President. **ISSN:** 0274-712X. **Subscription Rates:** $19.95 individuals; $36.95 two years 2 yrs. **Remarks:** Accepts advertising.
Ad Rates: BW: $3,235 **Circ:** Paid ★**187,116**
4C: $4,695

4732 Record Stockman
Record Stockman, Inc.
4800 Wadsworth Blvd., Ste. 200
PO Box 1209
Wheat Ridge, CO 80034

Tabloid reporting market and livestock news. **Founded:** 1889. **Freq:** Weekly. **Trim Size:** 11 1/2 x 16 3/4. **Cols./Page:** 5. **Col. Width:** 2 inches. **Col. Depth:** 15 3/4 inches. **Key Personnel:** Dan Green, Editor; Harry Green, Publisher. **Subscription Rates:** $35. **Remarks:** Color advertising accepted; rates available upon request.
Ad Rates: GLR: $.80 **Circ:** 12,000
BW: $1,920
4C: $450
PCI: $30

4733 The Rhodesian Ridgeback Quarterly
Hoflin Publishing Ltd.
4401 Zephyr St. Phone: (303)420-2222
Wheat Ridge, CO 80033-3299 Fax: (303)422-7000

Magazine for fanciers of Rhodesian Ridgeback dogs. **Founded:** Nov. 1984. **Freq:** Quarterly. **Trim Size:** 8.5 x 11. **Cols./Page:** 3. **Col. Width:** 2.375 inches. **Col. Depth:** 9.5 inches. **Key Personnel:** Donald R. Hoflin, Editor and Publisher. **ISSN:** 0745-6581. **Subscription Rates:** $44 individuals; $48 other countries; $13 single issue. **URL:** http://www.hoflin.com.
Ad Rates: BW: $65 **Circ:** Paid 442
4C: $350 Non-paid 246

4734 The Samoyed Quarterly
Hoflin Publishing Ltd.
4401 Zephyr St. Phone: (303)420-2222
Wheat Ridge, CO 80033-3299 Fax: (303)422-7000

Magazine for Samoyed dog fanciers. **Founded:** Jan. 1980. **Freq:** Quarterly. **Trim Size:** 8.5 x 11. **Cols./Page:** 3. **Col. Width:** 2.375 inches. **Col. Depth:** 9.5 inches. **Key Personnel:** Donald R. Hoflin, Editor and Publisher; Cynthia L. Kerstiens, Editor. **ISSN:** 8750-3557. **Subscription Rates:** $44 individuals; $48 other countries; $13 single issue. **URL:** http://www.hoflin.com.
Ad Rates: BW: $65 **Circ:** Paid 680
4C: $350 Non-paid 333

4735 The Siberian Quarterly
Hoflin Publishing Ltd.
4401 Zephyr St. Phone: (303)420-2222
Wheat Ridge, CO 80033-3299 Fax: (303)422-7000

Magazine for Siberian Husky fanciers. **Founded:** Dec. 1981. **Freq:** Quarterly. **Trim Size:** 8.5 x 11. **Cols./Page:** 3. **Col. Width:** 2.375 inches. **Col. Depth:** 9.5 inches. **Key Personnel:** Donald R. Hoflin, Editor and Publisher; Cynthia Kerstiens, Editor. **ISSN:** 0274-7286. **Subscription Rates:** $44 individuals; $48 other countries; $13 single issue. **URL:** http://www.hoflin.com.
Ad Rates: BW: $100 **Circ:** Paid 955
4C: $400 Controlled 354

4736 Southwest Stockman
PO Box 1209 Phone: (303)431-8911
Wheat Ridge, CO 80034 Free: (800)530-8539

Agricultural newspaper. **Founded:** 1958. **Freq:** Weekly (Fri.). **Print Method:** Offset. **Cols./Page:** 6. **Col. Width:** 25 nonpareils. **Col. Depth:** 221 agate lines. **Key Personnel:** Don Green, Editor; Harry E. Green, Jr., Publisher; Chris Brooks, Advertising Mgr. **Subscription Rates:** $15. **Remarks:** Accepts advertising.
Ad Rates: GLR: $1.15 **Circ:** 13,250

WHITEWATER

4737 Journal of Pyrotechnics
Journal of Pyrotechnics, Inc.
1775 Blair Rd. Phone: (970)245-0692
Whitewater, CO 81527-9513 Fax: (970)245-0692
Publication E-mail: kosankes@compuserve.com

Technical journal covering pyrotechnics, fireworks, special effects, propellants, rocketry, and civilian pyrotechnics. **Founded:** 1995. **Freq:** Semiannual. **Trim Size:** 8 x 11. **Cols./Page:** 2. **Col. Width:** 3 inches. **Col. Depth:** 9 inches. **Key Personnel:** Bonnie Kosanke, Publisher; Ken Kosanke, Managing Editor. **ISSN:** 1082-3999. **Subscription Rates:** $36 individuals; $21 single issue. **Remarks:** Accepts advertising $70/issue-includes name & address listing, plus 2 copies of the journal. **URL:** http://www.98.net/jop.
Circ: Combined 500

WINDSOR, pop. 4,470.

Weld Co. (WC).

4738 The Fence Post
Greeley Publishing Co.
423 Main St. Phone: (303)686-5691
Windsor, CO 80550 Fax: (303)686-5694
Free: (800)275-5646

Farm and ranch magazine. **Founded:** June 1980. **Freq:** Weekly (Mon.). **Print Method:** Offset. **Trim Size:** 8 x 10 3/4. **Cols./Page:** 4. **Col. Width:** 21 nonpareils. **Col. Depth:** 137 agate lines. **Key Personnel:** Andrea Galliher, Editor; John Walker, Publisher/Advertising Mgr. **Subscription Rates:** $14 individuals. **Remarks:** Accepts advertising.
Ad Rates: BW: $260 **Circ:** Paid ‡9,700
PCI: $15 Non-paid ‡400

4739 Windsor Beacon
425 Main St.
Windsor, CO 80550

General newspaper. **Founded:** Jan. 7, 1898. **Freq:** Weekly (Thurs.). **Cols./Page:** 6. **Col. Width:** 1.5625 inches. **Key Personnel:** Todd Vess, Editor; Roger Lipker, Publisher. **USPS:** 686–26. **Subscription Rates:** $15 individuals; $21 out of area.
Ad Rates: 4C: $532 **Circ:** Paid ‡3,000
PCI: $4.50

4740 KUAD-FM - 99.1
600 Main St. Phone: (303)686-2791
Windsor, CO 80550 Fax: (303)686-7491
Free: (800)860-9910
E-mail: pd@k99.com

Format: Country. **Founded:** 1971. **Operating Hours:** Continuous; 100% local. **ADI:** Denver (Steamboat Springs), CO. **Key Personnel:** Daniel F. Conway, General Mgr., phone (970)493-1170, fax (970)686-7491; Brian Gary, Music Dir., phone (970)493-1170, fax (970)686-7491, brian@k99.com; Dave Jensen, Program Dir., phone (970)493-1170, fax (970)686-7591, davej@k99.com; Todd Harding, News Dir. **Wattage:** 100,000. **Ad Rates:** $25 for 30 seconds; $35 for 60 seconds.

4741 KVVS-AM - 1170
1200 Carasel Dr., No. 124-K Phone: (970)686-1170
PO Box 698 Fax: (970)686-7700
Windsor, CO 80550

Format: Hispanic; News; Top 40. **Networks:** Independent. **Founded:** 1985. **Formerly:** KSGR-AM. **Operating Hours:** Daytime; 90% local, 10% national. **Key Personnel:** Veronica Sanchez-Velasco, Gen. Mgr./ Sales Mgr.; Antonio J. Velasco, Sports & Promotions Dir.; Betty Foos, Operations Mgr. **Local Programs:** *Monday's Hora Ranchera* mornings; *Saturday's Community Services Program.* **Wattage:** 1000. **Ad Rates:** $12 for 30 seconds; $18 for 60 seconds.

WOODLAND PARK, pop. 3,500.

Teller Co. (C). 18 m NW of Colorado Springs. Recreation area. Ranches.

4742 Ute Pass Courier
1200 E. Hwy. 24 Phone: (719)687-3006
PO Box 340 Fax: (719)687-3009
Woodland Park, CO 80863
Publication E-mail: wpcourier@aol.com

Newspaper. **Founded:** 1964. **Freq:** Weekly (Wed.). **Print Method:** Offset. **Cols./Page:** 5. **Col. Width:** 24 nonpareils. **Col. Depth:** 231 agate lines. **Key Personnel:** Jim Lovely, Editor; Mike Soule, General Mgr.; Rob Carrigan, Publisher, rcarrigan@aol.com. **Subscription Rates:** $19.95 individuals; $28 out of area. **Remarks:** Accepts advertising.
Ad Rates: GLR: $7.50 **Circ:** 3,750
BW: $5.94 11,000
4C: $175
PCI: $7.50

WRAY†, pop. 2,500.

Yuma Co. (EC). 65 m SE of Stirling.

4743 The Wray Gazette
411 Main St. Phone: (303)332-4846
PO Box 7 Fax: (303)332-4065
Wray, CO 80758-0007
Community newspaper. **Founded:** 1903. **Freq:** Weekly. **Print Method:** Offset. **Cols./Page:** 7. **Col. Width:** 12 picas. **Col. Depth:** 21 1/2 inches. **Key Personnel:** Maxine Wilkins, Editor; Kevin Wilkins, Publisher; Bryce Wilkins, Publisher. **USPS:** 693-260. **Subscription Rates:** $17 individuals; $19.50 out of area. **Remarks:** Accepts advertising.
Ad Rates: BW: $493.92 **Circ:** Paid 3,125
4C: $703.92 Free 40
PCI: $3.70

4744 KRDZ-AM - 1440
Box 466 Phone: (970)332-4171
Wray, CO 80758 Fax: (970)332-4172
E-mail: krdzkatr@plains.net

Format: Country; Oldies. **Networks:** ABC; Brownfield. **Founded:** 1978. **Operating Hours:** 4:50 a.m.-12 midnight. **Key Personnel:** Robert D. Zellmer, Jr., President; Robb Zellmer, Operations Mgr.; Howard Hale, Farm Director; Jim Bernhardt, News Dir.; Renee Stults, Sales Mgr. **Wattage:** 5000 day; 200 night. **URL:** http://www.plains.net/krdzkatr.

YUMA, pop. 2,824.

Yuma Co. (WC). 43 m SE of Sterling. Grain farms.

4745 Yuma Pioneer
207 S. Main St. Phone: (970)848-2174
PO Box 326 Fax: (970)848-2895
Yuma, CO 80759
General interest community newspaper. **Founded:** Dec. 25, 1886. **Freq:** Weekly. **Print Method:** Offset. **Trim Size:** 21 1/2 x 13 1/2. **Cols./Page:** 6. **Col. Width:** 13 picas. **Col. Depth:** 21 1/2 inches. **Key Personnel:** Roger K. Chance, Publisher; Anthony Rayl, Editor; Kimberly Johnson, Business Mgr. **Subscription Rates:** $20 individuals. **Remarks:** Accepts advertising.
Ad Rates: GLR: $.17 **Circ:** ‡2,850
BW: $434.70
SAU: $.68
PCI: $3.45

4746 KATR-FM - 98.3
804 S. Ash Phone: (970)848-3525
Yuma, CO 80759 Fax: (970)332-4172
E-mail: krdzkatr@plains.net

Format: Hot Country. **Networks:** ABC; Brownfield; Jones Satellite. **Owner:** New Directions Media, Inc., at above address, Yuma, CO 80759. **Founded:** 1983. **Formerly:** KRDZ-FM (1987). **Operating Hours:** Continuous. **Key Personnel:** Robert D. Zellmer, Pres./Gen. Mgr.; Robb Zellmer, Station Mgr.; Howard Hale, Farm Director; Jim Bernhardt, News Dir.; Renee Stults, Sales Mgr.; Gary Rightmire, Sports Dir. **Wattage:** 50,000 ERP. **URL:** http://www.plains.net/krdzkatr.

CONNECTICUT

State Capital, HARTFORD

Connecticut is bounded on the north by Massachusetts, east by Rhode Island, south by Long Island Sound, and west by New York. The average breadth from east to west is 86 miles; average length is 55 miles. The total land area is 4,845 square miles. The eastern part of the state has many ridges of low hills with fertile valleys. The Connecticut River valley, at a distance from the Sound, is very fertile. In the south the land is broken and soil sandy, but when well fertilized, yields good crops. The valleys of the Connecticut and Housatonic Rivers are immensely productive, the former primarily so in cigar leaf tobacco. In the west, the surface is rough and the hills abrupt, rising to an altitude of nearly 2,000 feet. The state has an abundant water supply for industrial uses. The Weather Bureau at Hartford gives the temperature (annual average) as 49.9; highest on record, 102; lowest on record, -18. Total annual precipitation is 44.14 inches. The State of Connecticut is noted for its manufacturing industries. Its capital city, Hartford, is noted for the extent and variety of its insurance interests. The state has many fine educational institutions, including Yale University at New Haven, founded in 1701. The Connecticut River is open to navigation from its mouth to Hartford.

POPULATION: 3,281,000 (1992). Rank among the states, 27th.

AGRICULTURE: Number of farms: 4,000 (1992). Farm acreage: less than 500,000 acres (1992). Cash receipts from farm marketings: crops, $255,000,000 (1991); livestock and products, $209,000,000 (1991).

FISHERIES: Total catch: 15,000,000 lbs. (1991), $45,000,000 value. Principal fish: oysters, lobsters, clams, flounder.

FORESTS: Total forest land: less than 500,000 acres (1990).

MINERALS: Value of production: $91,000,000 (1991). Principal minerals: stone, sand and gravel, feldspar.

MANUFACTURES: Value added by manufacture: $23,832,000,000 (1991). Leading industry groups: transportation equipment, machinery (except electrical), electrical machinery.

LIST OF COUNTIES

Total number of counties 8

County, Location on Map, and County Seat	Pop.
Fairfield (SW), Bridgeport and Danbury	827,645
Hartford (N), Hartford and New Britain	852,783
Litchfield (NW), Litchfield and Winsted	174,092
Middlesex (S), Middleton	143,196
New Haven (S), New Haven, Meriden, and Waterbury	804,219
New London (SE), New London and Norwich	254,957
Tolland (N), Rockville	128,699
Windham (NE), Putnam and Williamette	102,525

STATISTICS

Newspapers

Period of Issue	
Daily	20
Evening Daily	10
Morning Daily	10
Daily with Sunday edition	10
Semiweekly	9
Weekly	68
Semimonthly	2
Monthly	12
Free or partly free	18
Shopper	6
Total Newspapers	115

Periodicals

Period of Issue	
Weekly	3
Semimonthly	6
Monthly	58
Bimonthly	92
Quarterly	59
Total Periodicals	287

Total number of publications 402

Radio Stations

AM Stations	32
FM Stations	51
Total Radio Stations	83

TV Stations

Total TV Stations 14

Cable Stations

Total Cable Systems 17

Total number of broadcast listings 114

ANSONIA, pop. 19,039.

S. CT. New Haven Co. On Naugatuck River, 10 mi. NW of New Haven. Manufactures brass, copper, bronze products, elastic webbing, electrical supplies, foundry and screw machine products, insulated wire, machinery and machine tools, sheet metal specialties, sponge rubber, plastics.

4747 WADS-AM - 690
PO Box 110 Phone: (203)735-4606
Ansonia, CT 06401

Format: Adult Contemporary; Talk; Sports. **Networks:** Independent. **Founded:** 1956. **Operating Hours:** 5:30 a.m.-midnight. **Key Personnel:** Mario Sousa, General Mgr.; Sharon Lydem, Office Mgr. **Wattage:** 1000.

AVON, pop. 11,201.

WC CT. Hartford Co.

4748 Avon News
Imprint Newspapers
99 Main St. Phone: (860)236-3571
Bristol, CT 06010 Fax: (860)233-2080

Community newspaper (tabloid). **Founded:** 1981. **Freq:** Weekly. **Print Method:** Offset. **Trim Size:** 11 x 17. **Cols./Page:** 4. **Col. Width:** 15 nonpareils. **Col. Depth:** 16 inches. **Key Personnel:** Phyllis Hammer, Editor; Frank Chilinski, Publisher; Lori Levinson, Advertising Mgr. **USPS:** 667-090. **Subscription Rates:** $25 individuals; $21 Senior citizens. **Remarks:** Combined advertising rates available with other Imprint papers.
Circ: Paid 1,883
Non-paid 160

BETHEL, pop. 16,004.

SW CT. Fairfield Co. 8 mi. S. of Brookfield. Residential.

4749 Experimental Mechanics
Society for Experimental Mechanics
7 School St. Phone: (203)790-6373
Bethel, CT 06801 Fax: (203)790-4472
Publisher E-mail: sem@sem1.com

Archival journal for experimental mechanics focusing on techniques employed in the measurement of stresses and strains as applied to metals and other materials. **Freq:** Quarterly. **Trim Size:** 8 1/8 x 10 7/8. **Cols./Page:** 2. **Col. Width:** 19 picas. **Col. Depth:** 58 picas. **Key Personnel:** Kristin MacDonald, Publisher. **ISSN:** 0014-4851. **Subscription Rates:** $72 individuals. **Remarks:** Advertising not accepted.
Circ: 4,500

4750 Experimental Techniques
Society for Experimental Mechanics
7 School St. Phone: (203)790-6373
Bethel, CT 06801 Fax: (203)790-4472
Publisher E-mail: sem@sem1.com

Magazine on test techniques for solid mechanics programs. **Founded:** 1977. **Freq:** Bimonthly. **Print Method:** Offset. **Trim Size:** 8 1/8 x 10 7/8. **Cols./Page:** 3 and 2. **Col. Width:** 26 and 37 nonpareils. **Col. Depth:** 140 agate lines. **Key Personnel:** Patricia K. Brothers, Editor, journals@sem1.com; K. L. MacDonald, Publisher, kristin@sem1.com; Joni Virgilio, Advertising Sales, etexpos@sem1.com. **ISSN:** 0732-8818. **Subscription Rates:** $100 individuals.
Ad Rates: BW: $650 **Circ:** ‡4,380

BLACK ROCK

4751 Weston Voice
Hometown Publications, Inc.
1000 Bridgeport Ave.
Shelton, CT 06484
Publisher E-mail: homepubl@aol.com

Community newspaper. **Founded:** 1988. **Freq:** Weekly (Wed.). **Print Method:** Offset. **Trim Size:** 14 x 22 1/2. **Cols./Page:** 6. **Col. Width:** 1 3/8 inches. **Col. Depth:** 21 inches. **Key Personnel:** Chris Carroll, Editor; Ben Gumm, Publisher; Sally McLaren, Advertising Mgr. **Remarks:** Accepts advertising.
Ad Rates: GLR: $.875 **Circ:** Free 3,250
BW: $1,379
4C: $1,979
SAU: $12.26

BLOOMFIELD, pop. 18,608.

C. CT. Hartford Co. NNW of Hartford. Tobacco growing.

4752 Bloomfield Journal
Imprint Newspapers
99 Main St. Phone: (860)236-3571
Bristol, CT 06010 Fax: (860)233-2080

Community newspaper (tabloid). **Founded:** 1976. **Freq:** Weekly (Fri.). **Print Method:** Offset. **Trim Size:** 11 x 17. **Cols./Page:** 4. **Col. Width:** 15 nonpareils. **Col. Depth:** 16 inches. **Key Personnel:** Laura Manente, Editor; Frank Chilinski, Publisher; Lori Levinson, Director. **ISSN:** 0746-9632. **Subscription Rates:** $23 individuals; $18.50 Senior citizens. **Remarks:** Combined advertising rates available with other Imprint newspapers.
Ad Rates: PCI: $10.25 **Circ:** Paid 2,008
Non-paid 414

4753 The Catholic Transcript
The Catholic Transcript, Inc.
467 Bloomfield Ave. Phone: (860)286-2828
Bloomfield, CT 06002 Fax: (860)726-0000
Free: (800)726-2391

Official newspaper of the Archdiocese of Hartford. **Founded:** 1898. **Freq:** Monthly. **Print Method:** Offset. **Trim Size:** 11 3/8 x 17. **Cols./Page:** 5. **Col. Depth:** 16 inches. **Key Personnel:** Most Rev. Daniel A. Cronin, Publisher; Rev. Christopher M. Tiano, Exec. Editor; Elisa Hutcoe, Assoc. Editor; Carole Cronsell, Business Mgr. **USPS:** 094-540. **Subscription Rates:** $12. **Remarks:** Accepts advertising.
Ad Rates: BW: $1,080 **Circ:** Paid ⊕**67,000**
4C: $1,530 Non-paid ⊕**456**
PCI: $18

4754 WDRC-AM - 1360
869 Blue Hills Ave. Phone: (860)243-1115
Bloomfield, CT 06002 Fax: (860)286-8257
E-mail: mulligan@wdrc.com

Format: Adult Contemporary; Sports. **Simulcasts:** WMMW-AM. **Networks:** Independent. **Founded:** 1922. **Operating Hours:** Continuous; 60% network, 40% local. **ADI:** Hartford-New Haven (New London), CT. **Key Personnel:** Wayne G. Mulligan, VP/Gen. Mgr., mulligan@wdrc.com; Ron Pell, General Sales Mgr.; Laura Kittell, Operations Mgr. **Wattage:** 5000. **Ad Rates:** Combined advertising rates available with WDRC-FM, WWCO-AM, WSNG-AM. **URL:** http://www.wdrc.com.

4755 WDRC-FM - 102.9
869 Blue Hills Ave. Phone: (860)243-1115
Bloomfield, CT 06002 Fax: (860)286-8257
E-mail: bigd103@wdrc.com

Format: Oldies. **Networks:** Westwood One Radio. **Owner:** Buckley Broadcasting Corp., at above address. **Founded:** 1939. **Operating Hours:** Continuous. **ADI:** Hartford-New Haven (New London), CT. **Key Personnel:** Wayne G. Mulligan, General Mgr.; Ron Pell, General Sales Mgr.; Laura Kittell, Operations Mgr. **Wattage:** 19,500 ERP. **Ad Rates:** WDRC-AM, WWCO-AM, WMMW-AM, WSNG-AM.

4756 WJMJ-FM - 88.9
St. Thomas Seminary Phone: (203)242-8800
Bloomfield, CT 06002

Format: Classical; Easy Listening; Big Band/Nostalgia. **Networks:** ABC. **Founded:** 1976. **Operating Hours:** 5AM - 12MID. **Key Personnel:** John L. Ellinger, General Mgr.; Fred Swanson, Program Dir.; Ivor Hugh, Classical Music Dir. **Wattage:** 7200. **Ad Rates:** Noncommercial.

BOLTON

4757 The Community Voice Channel
200 Boston Tpke. Phone: (203)645-1454
PO Box 9171 Fax: (203)645-1454
Bolton, CT 06043

Founded: 1991. **Formerly**: Eastern Connecticut TV (1993). **Key Personnel:** Sandra Sprague, Exec. Dir. **Cities Served:** subscribing households 21,000; 2 community access channels; 25 hours per week community access programming.

BRANFORD, pop. 23,363.

S. CT. New Haven Co. 7 mi. S. of New Haven.

4758 Branford Review
Shore Line Newspapers
POB 829 Phone: (203)488-2535
230 E. Main St. Fax: (203)481-4125
Branford, CT 06405
Local news. **Founded:** 1928. **Freq:** Semiweekly (Wed. and Sat.). **Print Method:** Offset. **Cols./Page:** 6. **Col. Width:** 19 nonpareils. **Col. Depth:** 224 agate lines. **Key Personnel:** Silvio Albino, Managing Editor, phone (203)453-2711; Marianne Cipriano, Editor, phone (203)488-2535; Tony Santamaria, Advertising Mgr. **Subscription Rates:** $32 individuals.
Ad Rates: SAU: $9.25 **Circ:** Wed. ‡7,000
Sat. ‡6,000

4759 TCI Cable
Box 667 Phone: (203)481-3434
Branford, CT 06405-0667

Founded: 1975. **Cities Served:** New Haven County, East Haven, Guilford, Madison, North Branford, Northford, North Haven, and Wallingford, CT.

BRIDGEPORT†, pop. 142,546.

SW CT. Fairfield Co. Port of entry on Long Island Sound, 56 mi. NE of New York. University of Bridgeport, Fairfield University, Sacred Heart University, Bridgeport Engineering Institute and Housatonic Community College. Manufactures electrical appliances, ammunition, firearms, airplane engines, jet engine components, cutlery, brake linings, adding machines, machine tools, sewing machines, helicopters, airplane and aircraft accessories, hardware, machinery, brass, steel, asbestos products, valves and fittings, textiles.

4760 Auto Merchandising News
2370 North Ave., No. 2C Phone: (203)335-6181
Bridgeport, CT 06604-2326 Fax: (203)878-7319

Automotive trade magazine featuring auto news and trends, and new products, for the auto supply chains and mass-retailers. **Subtitle:** The National Business Publication for the Automotive Aftermarket. **Founded:** Sept. 1971. **Freq:** Monthly. **Print Method:** Offset. **Trim Size:** 8 1/2 x 11. **Cols./Page:** 3. **Col. Width:** 2 1/4 inches. **Col. Depth:** 10 inches. **Key Personnel:** Richard Burns, Editor; Bill Mortimer, Publisher; G. Watkins, Advertising Mgr. **USPS:** 560-350. **Subscription Rates:** $72 individuals; $6 single issue. **Remarks:** Accepts advertising. **Alt. Formats:** Mailing labels.
Ad Rates: BW: $4,975 **Circ:** Controlled ‡26,926
4C: $7,315

4761 Bridgeport News
Hometown Publications, Inc.
1000 Bridgeport Ave.
Shelton, CT 06484
Publisher E-mail: homepubl@aol.com

Community newspaper. **Founded:** 1987. **Freq:** Weekly (Thurs.). **Print Method:** Offset. **Trim Size:** 13 x 22 1/2. **Cols./Page:** 6. **Col. Width:** 1 7/8 inches. **Col. Depth:** 21 inches. **Key Personnel:** Rob Sullivan, Editor; Lorraine Bukowski, Advertising Mgr.; Regina Burkhart, Publisher; Henry S. Misiak, Jr., Advertising Dir. **Remarks:** Advertising accepted; rates available upon request. **Formerly**: North End News; Black Rock News.
Circ: Paid 11,400

4762 Connecticut Post
410 State St. Phone: (203)333-0161
Bridgeport, CT 06604-4501 Fax: (203)366-3373
Free: (800)423-8058
Publication E-mail: ctnews@snet.net

General newspaper. **Freq:** Mon.-Sun. (morn.). **Print Method:** Offset. **Trim Size:** 13 x 20 1/4. **Cols./Page:** 6. **Col. Width:** 12.4 picas. **Col. Depth:** 280 agate lines. **Key Personnel:** Rick Sayers, Editor/Assoc. Publisher, phone (203)330-6325, fax (203)367-8158; Mike Daly, Managing Editor, phone (203)330-6394; Todd Hollis, Asst. M.E./Technology, phone (203)330-6480; John Schwing, Fairfield County Editor, phone (203)330-6248; Mary Moran, New Heaven County/Valley Editor, phone (203)330-6224; Jim Shay, Sunday/Travel Editor, phone (230)330-6242; Linda Pinto, State Editor, phone (203)330-6496; Tom Caruso, Business Editor, phone (203)330-6351; Elaine Ficarra, F.E./Real Estate Editor, phone (203)330-6227; Gary Rogo, Sports Editor, phone (203)330-6210; Stephen J. Winters, Editorial Page Editor, phone (203)330-6203; Anita Lupariello, Community News, phone (203)330-6330; Patrick Quinn, Arts/Entertainment, phone (203)330-6381; Shelley Levi, Society Editor, phone (203)330-6432; Elaine Ficarra, Womanwise Editor, phone (203)330-6227; Jean Santopatre, Photo Editor, phone (203)330-6498; Cindy Simoneau, Asst. M.E., phone (203)330-6391. **Subscription Rates:** $90 Daily; $65 Sunday. **Remarks:** Accepts advertising. **Absorbed**: The Evening Sentinel. **Formerly**: The Bridgeport Post.
Ad Rates: GLR: $2.35 **Circ:** Mon.-Sat. ★**77,409**
PCI: $30 Sun. ★**93,201**

4763 Fairfield County Catholic
238 Jewett Ave. Phone: (203)372-4301
Bridgeport, CT 06606 Fax: (203)374-2044
Publication E-mail: fccatholic@snet.net

Official newspaper of the Roman Catholic Diocese of Bridgeport, (Fairfield county), CT. **Founded:** 1984. **Freq:** Monthly (except August). **Print Method:** Offset. **Trim Size:** 11 1/2 x 17. **Cols./Page:** 5. **Col. Width:** 2 inches. **Col. Depth:** 15 1/2

inches. **Key Personnel:** Dr. Joseph McAleer, Editor; Ralph Lazzaro, Advertising Mgr. **USPS:** 012-117. **Subscription Rates:** $15 individuals; $8 single issue. **Remarks:** Accepts advertising.
Ad Rates: GLR: $2.50 **Circ:** ‡90,000
BW: $1,900
CNU: $2
PCI: $25

4764 Publishing Research Quarterly
Transaction Publishers
Box 2423, Noble Sta. Phone: (203)380-0021
Bridgeport, CT 06608-0423 Fax: (203)380-1703
Publication E-mail: 70244.1532@compuserve.com
Publisher E-mail: trans@transactionpub.com

Journal publishing research and commentary on or about books, the publishing and book distribution process, and the social, political, economic, and technological conditions that help shape this process. **Founded:** 1986. **Freq:** Quarterly. **Print Method:** Offset. **Trim Size:** 6 3/4 x 10. **Cols./Page:** 1. **Col. Width:** 25 nonpareils. **Col. Depth:** 140 agate lines. **Key Personnel:** Albert Henderson, Editor. **ISSN:** 0741-6148. **Subscription Rates:** $54 individuals; $120 institutions; individuals other countries; $155 institutions, other countries; $96 two years individuals; $224 two years institutions. **Remarks:** Accepts advertising. **Formerly:** Book Research Quarterly.
Ad Rates: BW: $300 **Circ:** ‡1,000

4765 Cablevision of Southern Connecticut
122 River St. Phone: (203)846-4700
Bridgeport, CT 06604 Fax: (203)333-5883

Founded: 1977. **Formerly:** Southern Connecticut Cable (1983). **Key Personnel:** Glen Brown, Manager, phone (203)750-5606, fax (203)846-6331, gbrown@cablevision.com; Maryce Cunningham, Program Dir., phone (203)750-5774, fax (203)846-9412, mcunning@cablevision.com; Tom Appleby, News Dir., phone (203)750-5757, fax (203)849-1327. **Cities Served:** subscribing households 91,123; 110 channels; 3 community access channels; 96 hours per week community access programming.

4766 WCUM-AM - 1450
1862 State St. Phone: (203)335-1450
Bridgeport, CT 06605-2247 Fax: (203)331-9378

Format: Hispanic. **Networks:** Independent. **Owner:** Radio Cumbre Broadcasting Inc., at above address. **Founded:** 1941. **Formerly:** WJBX-AM (1989). **Operating Hours:** Continuous. **ADI:** New York, NY. **Key Personnel:** Migdalia R. Colon, Vice President; Madeline Perez, Traffic Mgr.; Pablo De Jesus Colon, President. **Local Programs:** *Flea Market on the Air*, Jose A. Colon; *Open Microphones*, Jose A. Colon; *Point of View*, Jose A. Colon. **Wattage:** 1000. **Ad Rates:** $32-60 for 30 seconds; $50-75 for 60 seconds. **URL:** http://www.radiocumbre.com.

4767 WEBE-FM - 107.9
2 Lafayette Sq. Phone: (203)333-9108
Bridgeport, CT 06604 Fax: (203)333-9107
Free: (800)WEB-E108

Format: Adult Contemporary. **Networks:** Independent. **Owner:** M.L. Media Partners, L.P., 350 Park Ave., 16th Fl., New York, NY 10022, (212)980-7110. **Founded:** 1984. **Formerly:** WDJF-FM. **Operating Hours:** Continuous; 100% local. **ADI:** New York, NY. **Key Personnel:** Vince Cremona, Vice President/Gen. Manager; Tim Quinn, News Dir.; Curtis Hansen, UP Operation. **Wattage:** 50,000. **Ad Rates:** $175-250 per unit. Combined advertising rates available with WICC-AM.

4768 WEDW-TV - 49
307 Atlantic St. Phone: (203)965-0440
Stamford, CT 06903-3524 Fax: (203)965-0447

Format: Public TV. **Simulcasts:** WEDH-TV. **Networks:** Public Broadcasting Service (PBS). **Operating Hours:** 6:45 a.m.-midnight. **ADI:** Hartford-New Haven (New London), CT. **Key Personnel:** Don Russell, General Mgr.; T. Wilder, News Dir. **Local Programs:** *Connecticut Town Meeting*, Lynn Laitman, General Mgr.; *Dr. Joyce Brothers Asks How's Your Life*, Lynn Laitman, General Mgr.; *Fairfield, CT, Documentary*, Lynn Laitman, General Mgr.

4769 WEZN-FM - 99.9
Park City Plaza Phone: (203)366-9321
10 Middle St. Fax: (203)336-9988
Bridgeport, CT 06604

Format: Adult Contemporary. **Networks:** Independent. **Founded:** 1973. **Operating Hours:** Continuous; 100% local. **ADI:** New York, NY. **Key Personnel:** James T. Morley, General Mgr.; John S. Ryan, General Sales Mgr.; Bill White, Operations Mgr.; Bob Michaels, News Dir. **Wattage:** 25,000. **Ad Rates:** $50-185 per unit.

4770 WICC-AM - 600
2 Lafayette Sq. Phone: (203)366-6000
Bridgeport, CT 06604-6000 Fax: (203)384-0600

Format: Adult Contemporary. **Networks:** AP. **Owner:** M.L. Media Partners, L.P., 645 5th Ave., New York, NY 10022, (212)980-7110. **Founded:** 1926. **Operating Hours:** Continuous. **ADI:** New York, NY. **Key Personnel:** Vince Cremona, Vice Pres./Gen. Mgr.; Anne Surface McManus, Vice Pres./Gen. Sales Mgr.; Curtis Hansen, Vice Pres./Operations/Production Mgr.; Tim Quinn, News Dir. **Local Programs:** *Coffee Break Chat* 9:30 a.m.; *Coffee Break Chat*; *Monday Town Meeting* 9-10 a.m.; *Monday Town Meeting* 9 a.m-10 a.m. Monday. **Wattage:** 1000. **Ad Rates:** $100-200 per unit.

4771 WPKN-FM - 89.5
244 University Ave. Phone: (203)576-4895
Bridgeport, CT 06601

Format: Eclectic. **Founded:** 1963. **ADI:** New York, NY. **Key Personnel:** Harry Minot, General Mgr. **Wattage:** 10,000. **Ad Rates:** Noncommercial.

BRISTOL, pop. 57,370.

N. CT. Hartford Co. 18 mi. SW of Hartford. Manufactures ball bearings, springs, clocks, watches, timing devices, chemicals, metal shapes, electrical resistance coils, variable transformers, electronic devices, electrical component parts, brass and aluminum forgings, sheet metal, wire rods, glass cutters, paper boxes, dairy, screw machine products, wall box dimmers, sports equipment, electro plating, cutlery.

Avon News - See Avon

Bloomfield Journal - See Bloomfield

4772 The Bristol Press
99 Main St. Phone: (203)584-0501
Bristol, CT 06010-6579 Fax: (203)584-2192

General newspaper. **Founded:** Mar. 9, 1871. **Freq:** Daily (eve.). **Print Method:** Offset. **Cols./Page:** 6. **Col. Width:** 25 nonpareils. **Col. Depth:** 301 agate lines. **Key Personnel:** Frank Keegan, Editor; Joseph H. Zersey IV, Publisher; Carolyn McCarthy, Advertising Mgr. **ISSN:** 0891-5563. **Subscription Rates:** $93.60 individuals. **Remarks:** Accepts advertising.
Ad Rates: SAU: $15.52 **Circ:** Mon.-Sat. ★15,936

4773 Broken Streets
57 Morningside Dr. E.
Bristol, CT 06010

Christian magazine. **Founded:** 1979. **Freq:** Biennial. **Trim Size:** 6 x 9. **Key Personnel:** Ron Grossman, Editor. **Subscription Rates:** $10; $4 single issue. **Remarks:** Accepts advertising.
Ad Rates: BW: $25 **Circ:** Paid 100
Non-paid 1,000

Canton News - See Canton

The Newington Town Crier - See Newington

4774 Rocky Hill Post
Imprint Newspapers
99 Main St. Phone: (860)236-3571
Bristol, CT 06010 Fax: (860)233-2080

Community newspaper. **Founded:** 1980. **Freq:** Weekly (Fri.). **Print Method:** Offset. **Cols./Page:** 4. **Col. Width:** 15 picas. **Col. Depth:** 16 inches. **Key Personnel:** Mark Romanow, Publisher; Keith Griffin, Editor. **Subscription Rates:** $25 individuals.
Ad Rates: SAU: $6 **Circ:** Paid 1,585
Non-paid 34

Simsbury News - See Simsbury

4775 West Hartford News
Imprint Newspapers
99 Main St. Phone: (860)236-3571
Bristol, CT 06010 Fax: (860)233-2080

Community newspaper. **Founded:** 1931. **Freq:** Weekly (Thurs.). **Print Method:** Offset. **Cols./Page:** 6. **Col. Width:** 10 picas. **Col. Depth:** 16 inches. **Key Personnel:** Frank Chilinski, Publisher; Keith Griffin, Editor; Laura Manente, Exec. Editor. **USPS:** 675-460. **Subscription Rates:** $32 individuals; $60 out of state. **Remarks:** Accepts advertising.
Ad Rates: SAU: $13.81 **Circ:** Paid 9,122
Non-paid 270

4776 Wethersfield Post
Imprint Newspapers
99 Main St. Phone: (860)236-3571
Bristol, CT 06010 Fax: (860)233-2080

Founded: 1957. **Freq:** Weekly (Fri.). **Print Method:** Offset. **Cols./Page:** 6. **Col. Width:** 10 picas. **Col. Depth:** 16 inches. **Key Personnel:** Keith Griffin, Imprint Managing Editor; Mark Romanow, Publisher. **Subscription Rates:** $25 individuals. **Remarks:** Accepts advertising.
Ad Rates: SAU: $12.49 **Circ:** Paid 3,817
Non-paid 188

Windsor Locks Journal - See Windsor

BROOKFIELD, pop. 12,872.

SW CT. Fairfield Co. 7 mi. N. of Danbury. Residential.

4777 Brookfield Journal
Housatonic Valley Publishing Co.
PO Box 268 Phone: (203)775-2533
Brookfield, CT 06804 Fax: (203)354-2645
Publisher E-mail: housvalpub@aol.com

Community newspaper. **Founded:** 1957. **Freq:** Weekly (Fri.). **Cols./Page:** 6. **Col. Width:** 2 1/16 inches. **Col. Depth:** 21 inches. **Key Personnel:** Mark Poirier, Editor; Arthur Cummings, Advertising Mgr.; Robert Mellis, Publisher; Jim Mills, Editor. **Subscription Rates:** $24.95; $34.95 out of county; $36.95 out of state. **Remarks:** Combined advertising rates available with other Housatonic Valley Publications.
Ad Rates: SAU: $9.35 **Circ:** Combined ♦2,424

4778 Journal of Vinyl and Additive Technology
Society of Plastics Engineers
14 Fairfield Dr. Phone: (203)775-0471
PO Box 0403 Fax: (203)775-8490
Brookfield, CT 06804-0403
Publisher E-mail: 4spemail@4spe.org

Journal containing technical articles on the processing and applications of vinyl (polyvinyl chloride). **Founded:** 1979. **Freq:** Quarterly. **Print Method:** Offset. **Trim Size:** 8 1/8 x 11. **Cols./Page:** 2. **Col. Width:** 39 nonpareils. **Col. Depth:** 99 agate lines. **Key Personnel:** Robert P. Braddicks, Jr., Editor, phone (914)664-7410. **ISSN:** 0193-7197. **Subscription Rates:** $95 members; $210 nonmembers. **Remarks:** Advertising not accepted. **URL:** http://www.4spe.org. **Formerly:** Journal of Vinyl Technology.
Circ: ‡535

4779 Plastics Engineering
Society of Plastics Engineers
14 Fairfield Dr. Phone: (203)775-0471
PO Box 0403 Fax: (203)775-8490
Brookfield, CT 06804-0403
Publisher E-mail: 4spemail@4spe.org

Plastics trade magazine. **Founded:** 1944. **Freq:** Monthly. **Print Method:** Web offset. **Trim Size:** 8 1/16 x 10 7/8. **Cols./Page:** 3 and 2. **Col. Width:** 28 and 42 nonpareils. **Col. Depth:** 140 agate lines. **Key Personnel:** Roger M. Ferris, Editor, rmferris@4spe.org; Daniel J. Domoff, Managing Editor, djdomoff@4spe.org; J.A. Forger, Publisher, jaforger@4spe.org; R.F. Mulligan, Advertising Dir., rfmulligan@4spe.org. **ISSN:** 0091-9578. **Subscription Rates:** $110 individuals; $190 two years. **Remarks:** Accepts advertising. **URL:** http://www.4spe.org.
Ad Rates: BW: $4,740 **Circ:** 32,035
4C: $7,170

4780 Polymer Engineering and Science
Society of Plastics Engineers
14 Fairfield Dr. Phone: (203)775-0471
PO Box 0403 Fax: (203)775-8490
Brookfield, CT 06804-0403
Publisher E-mail: 4spemail@4spe.org

Research and development in plastics and polymers materials. **Founded:** 1961. **Freq:** Semimonthly. **Print Method:** Offset. **Trim Size:** 8 1/8 x 11. **Cols./Page:** 2. **Col. Width:** 39 nonpareils. **Col. Depth:** 133 agate lines. **Key Personnel:** Robert A. Weiss, Editor-in-Chief. **ISSN:** 0032-3888. **Subscription Rates:** $220 members; $375 two years members; $320 nonmembers; $500 two years nonmembers; $700 corporations, institutions, libraries. **Remarks:** Advertising not accepted. **URL:** http://www.4spe.org.
Circ: 1,400

4781 ROTA.GENE
Print Shack
499 Federal Rd. Phone: (203)775-4515
Brookfield, CT 06804 Fax: (203)775-0180

Genealogical and historical magazine printed for the International Fellowship of Rotarians. **Founded:** 1980. **Freq:** Quarterly. **Trim Size:** 8 1/2 x 11. **Cols./Page:** 1 and 1. **Col. Width:**

7 and 7 inches. **Col. Depth:** 10 and 10 inches. **Key Personnel:** James R. High, Editor. **ISSN:** 0730-5168. **Subscription Rates:** $20 individuals. **Remarks:** Advertising accepted; rates available upon request.
Circ: Paid ‡300
Non-paid ‡150
Paid ‡100
Non-paid ‡105

4782 WINE-AM - 940
1004 Federal Rd. Phone: (203)775-1212
Brookfield, CT 06804-1123 Fax: (203)775-6452

Format: News. **Networks:** Connecticut Radio. **Founded:** 1964. **Operating Hours:** Sunrise-sunset; 5% network, 95% local. **Key Personnel:** Gary Starr, President; Pat Scully, News Dir.; Tony Savino, News, phone (203)775-2255. **Local Programs:** *Rick McDonald Show*, Rick McDonald. **Wattage:** 1000. **Ad Rates:** $15 for 30 seconds; $39 for 60 seconds.

4783 WRKI-FM - 95.1
1004 Federal Rd.
Brookfield, CT 06804-1123

Format: Album-Oriented Rock (AOR). **Founded:** 1957. **Operating Hours:** Continuous. **Key Personnel:** Gary J. Starr, President; Timothy J. Sheehan, Program Dir.; Thomas J. Principi, General Sales Mgr. **Wattage:** 50,000. **Ad Rates:** $30-190 for 60 seconds.

CANTON

4784 Canton News
Imprint Newspapers
99 Main St. Phone: (860)236-3571
Bristol, CT 06010 Fax: (860)233-2080

Community newspaper (tabloid). **Freq:** Weekly (Thurs.). **Print Method:** Offset. **Key Personnel:** Frank Chilinski, Publisher; Ellie Hart, Editor. **Subscription Rates:** $25; $21 senior citizens. **Remarks:** Combined advertising rates available with other Imprint Newspapers.
Circ: Paid 1,246
Non-paid 169

CHESHIRE, pop. 21,788.

S. CT. New Haven Co. 8 mi. SE of Waterbury. Manufactures stamped and pressed metals, wood products, machine tool accessories. Fruit, dairy, poultry, and bedding plant farms.

4785 The Cheshire Herald
The True Publishing Co.
PO Box 247 Phone: (203)272-5316
Cheshire, CT 06410 Fax: (203)250-7145
Publication E-mail: cheshireherald@snet.net

Community newspaper (tabloid). **Founded:** 1953. **Freq:** Weekly (Thurs.). **Print Method:** Offset. **Cols./Page:** 5. **Col. Width:** 2 inches. **Col. Depth:** 15 1/2 inches. **Key Personnel:** Dawn Miceli, Managing Editor; Joseph J. Jakubisyn, Publisher; Maureen Jakubisyn, Vice President. **Subscription Rates:** $19 individuals; $29 out of area. **Remarks:** Accepts advertising.
Ad Rates: GLR: $7.07 **Circ:** ‡7,200
PCI: $6.53

CLINTON, pop. 11,195.

S. CT. Middlesex Co. On Long Island Sound, 25 mi. E. of New Haven. Summer resort. Manufactures cosmetics, boats, plastics.

4786 Clinton Recorder
Shore Line Newspapers
PO Box 914 Phone: (860)669-5727
16-D W. Main St. Fax: (860)664-4531
Clinton, CT 06413
Newspaper. **Founded:** 1895. **Freq:** Semiweekly (Tues. and Sat.). **Print Method:** Offset. **Cols./Page:** 6. **Col. Width:** 19 nonpareils. **Col. Depth:** 224 agate lines. **Key Personnel:** William J. Rush, Publisher; Silvio Albino, Managing Editor. **USPS:** 682-330. **Subscription Rates:** $30 individuals.
Ad Rates: GLR: $17.15 (5 lines) **Circ:** Paid 4,292
PCI: $9.30

CROMWELL, pop. 11,210.

NW CT. Middlesex Co.

4787 The Cromwell Chronicle
Middlesex Magazine & Business Review
615 Main St. Phone: (203)635-1819
Cromwell, CT 06416 Fax: (203)632-7203

Community magazine. **Founded:** May 29, 1986. **Freq:** Monthly. **Print Method:** Offset. **Trim Size:** 8 x 10 1/2. **Cols./Page:** 3. **Col. Width:** 2 1/4 inches. **Col. Depth:** 9 1/2 inches. **Key Personnel:** Ron Nolan, Publisher; Clare Bearer, Publisher. **Subscription Rates:** $18. **Remarks:** Accepts advertising.
Ad Rates: BW: $975 **Circ:** Paid ‡15,000
PCI: $34

4788 Middlesex Magazine & Business Review
615 Main St.
Cromwell, CT 06416

Business journal/Consumer Mag. **Founded:** May 1991. **Freq:** Monthly. **Print Method:** Offset. **Trim Size:** 8 x 10 1/2. **Cols./Page:** 3. **Col. Width:** 2 3/8 inches. **Col. Depth:** 9 1/2 inches. **Key Personnel:** Ron Nolan, Publisher; Clare Bearer, Publisher. **Subscription Rates:** Free to qualified subscribers; $20. **Remarks:** Accepts advertising.
Ad Rates: BW: $975 **Circ:** Non-paid ‡7,500

DANBURY†, pop. 60,470.

SW CT. Fairfield Co. 21 mi. NW of Bridgeport. State College; State Trade School. Lake resort. Manufactures surgical instruments and supplies, electronic and railroad testing equipment, silverware, aluminum foil, aircraft parts, rubber tile, air conditioning equipment, steam generators, plastics, glue, textiles, ball and roller bearings, cardboard, fibre boxes. Agriculture. Dairying, poultry, truck farms.

4789 News-Times
333 Main St. Phone: (203)744-5100
Danbury, CT 06810 Fax: (203)792-8730

General newspaper. **Subtitle:** Community Newspaper. **Founded:** 1883. **Freq:** Mon.-Sun. (morn.). **Print Method:** Offset. **Trim Size:** 13 x 21. **Cols./Page:** 6. **Col. Width:** 25 nonpareils. **Col. Depth:** 300 agate lines. **Key Personnel:** Wayne J. Shepperd, Publisher. **Subscription Rates:** $106 individuals. **Remarks:** Accepts advertising. **URL:** http://www.newstimes.com.
Ad Rates: GLR: $16.86 **Circ:** Mon.-Sat. ★**35,512**
BW: $2,209 Sun. ★**42,450**
4C: $2,574
SAU: $17.53

4790 WDAQ-FM - 98.3
198 Main St. Phone: (203)744-4800
Danbury, CT 06810 Fax: (203)778-4655
E-mail: radio@98q.com

Format: Adult Contemporary. **Owner:** Berkshire Broadcasting Corp., at above address. **Founded:** 1954. **Operating Hours:** Continuous. **Key Personnel:** James B. Lee, Jr., President; Irving J. Goldstein, Contact. **Wattage:** 3000.

4791 WFAR-FM - 93.3
78 Liberty St. Phone: (203)748-0001
Danbury, CT 06810 Fax: (203)746-4262

Format: Ethnic; Religious. **Founded:** 1981. **Operating Hours:** Continuous; 50% network, 50% local. **Key Personnel:** David Abrantes, President; Antonio Botelho, Vice President; Helena Abrantes, Secretary. **Wattage:** 18.

4792 WLAD-AM - 800
198 Main St. Phone: (203)744-4800
Danbury, CT 06810 Fax: (203)778-4655
E-mail: radio80wlad@prodigy.com

Format: Full Service. **Networks:** Mutual Broadcasting System. **Owner:** Berkshire Broadcasting Corp., at above address. **Founded:** 1947. **Operating Hours:** Continuous. **ADI:** New York, NY. **Key Personnel:** James B. Lee, Jr., President; Irving J. Goldstein, Contact. **Wattage:** 1000 day; 287 night.

4793 WRNE-AM - 980
312 E Nine Mile Rd., Ste. 27 Phone: (904)478-6000
Pensacola, FL 32514-1475 Fax: (904)484-8080

Format: Urban Contemporary. **Networks:** Satellite Music Network; Southern Broadcasting. **Owner:** Media One Communications, at above address. **Founded:** 1957. **Formerly:** WFXP-AM (1992). **Operating Hours:** Continuous. **Key Personnel:** Robert Hill, General Mgr. **Wattage:** 2500 day; 1000 night. **Ad Rates:** $16-25 for 30 seconds; $22-31 for 60 seconds.

4794 WXCI-FM - 91.7
181 White St. Phone: (203)837-8635
Danbury, CT 06810-6845 Fax: (203)837-8599

Format: Alternative/New Music/Progressive. **Networks:** Independent. **Owner:** Campus Broadcast Assoc., at above address. **Founded:** 1973. **Formerly:** WSCT-FM (1973). **Operating Hours:** 6 a.m.-2 a.m.; 100% local. **Key Personnel:** Bill Repucci, General Mgr.; Jesse Gosselin, Program Dir.; Bob Marino, Music Dir.; Tonya White, Traffic Dir.; Nancy London, News Dir. **Wattage:** 3000. **Ad Rates:** Noncommercial.

DANIELSON, pop. 4,553.

SE CT. Windham Co. Borough in town of Killingly. Manunfactures paper products.

4795 Journal Transcript
Norwich Bulletin, Inc.
PO Box 299 Phone: (860)774-5563
Danielson, CT 06239 Fax: (860)774-5563

Community newspaper. **Founded:** 1981. **Freq:** Weekly. **Print Method:** Offset. **Trim Size:** 9 7/8 x 12 7/8. **Cols./Page:** 5. **Col. Width:** 11 picas. **Col. Depth:** 12 7/8 inches. **Key Personnel:** Vito J. Leo, Editor; David Whitehead, Publisher; Carol Tucker, Advertising Mgr.
Ad Rates: 4C: $575 **Circ:** Free ‡25,000
PCI: $8.30

DARIEN, pop. 18,892.

SW CT. Fairfield Co. 3 mi. NE of Stamford. Residential.

4796 Darien News-Review
6 Squab Ln. Phone: (203)655-7476
Darien, CT 06820 Fax: (203)655-1442
Publication E-mail: news@bcnnews.com

Newspaper. **Founded:** 1973. **Freq:** Weekly (Thurs.). **Print Method:** Offset. **Cols./Page:** 5. **Col. Width:** 22 nonpareils. **Col. Depth:** 224 agate lines. **Key Personnel:** B.V. Brooks, Publisher; Gary Larkin, Editor. **Subscription Rates:** $12 individuals. **Remarks:** Accepts advertising. **URL:** http://www.bcnnews.com. **Formerly**: News-Review.
Ad Rates: GLR: $.66 **Circ:** Thurs. 5,652
BW: $188.24
4C: $500
PCI: $9.24

4797 Friends of Animals Actionline
Friends of Animals, Inc.
777 Post Rd., Ste. 205 Phone: (203)656-1522
Darien, CT 06820-4721 Fax: (203)656-0267
Publisher E-mail: foa@igc.apc.org

Trade magazine covering animal issues for Friends of Animals, Inc. **Founded:** 1957. **Freq:** Quarterly. **ISSN:** 1072-2068. **Subscription Rates:** Included in membership. **Remarks:** Advertising not accepted. **URL:** http://www.friendsofanimals.org.
Circ: 150,000

4798 JAX FAX Travel Marketing Magazine
Jet Airtransport Exchange, Inc.
397 Post Rd. Phone: (203)655-8746
Darien, CT 06820 Fax: (203)655-6257
Free: (800)9-JAXFAX
Publication E-mail: tsjaxfax@aol.com

Travel planning magazine for travel agents. **Founded:** 1973. **Freq:** Monthly. **Print Method:** Offset. **Trim Size:** 8 1/8 x 10 7/8. **Cols./Page:** 2. **Col. Width:** 3 1/4 inches. **Col. Depth:** 10 inches. **Key Personnel:** Theresa Scanlon, Managing Editor; Clifton N. Cooke, Publisher; Barbara Mansone, Business Mgr.; Douglas Cooke, Asst. Pub. **ISSN:** 0148-9542. **Subscription Rates:** $15 year (12 issues). **Remarks:** Accepts advertising. **URL:** http://www.jaxfax.com.
Ad Rates: GLR: $18 **Circ:** Paid △**13,587**
BW: $3,400 Controlled △**13,124**
4C: $4,305

4799 Lamaze Parents' Magazine
Lamaze Institute for Family Education
9 Old Kings Hwy. S. Phone: (203)656-3600
Darien, CT 06820 Fax: (203)656-2221
Publisher E-mail: lamaze@lamaze.com

Magazine on childbirth and third trimester of pregnancy. **Founded:** 1983. **Freq:** 2/year. **Print Method:** Web offset. **Trim Size:** 7 7/8 x 10 3/4. **Key Personnel:** Carole Sherwood, VP of Editorial and Production. **Remarks:** Accepts advertising.
Ad Rates: BW: $82,800 **Circ:** Non-paid 2,400,000
4C: $107,900

4800 Lamazebaby
Lamaze Institute for Family Education
9 Old Kings Hwy. S. Phone: (203)656-3600
Darien, CT 06820 Fax: (203)656-2221
Publisher E-mail: lamaze@lamaze.com

Magazine covering an infant's first year of life. **Founded:** 1993. **Freq:** 2/year. **Print Method:** Web offset. **Trim Size:** 7 7/8 x 10 1/2. **Col. Width:** 2 1/4 inches. **Key Personnel:** Carole Sherwood, VP of Editorial and Production. **Remarks:** Accepts advertising.
Ad Rates: BW: $101,200 **Circ:** Non-paid 3,000,000
4C: $132,100

4801 Revista Lamaze Para Padres
Lamaze Publishing Co.
9 Old Kings Hwy. S Phone: (203)656-3600
Darien, CT 06820 Fax: (203)656-2221

Consumer magazine covering prenatal education in Spanish. **Freq:** Annual. **Print Method:** Offset. **Trim Size:** 7 7/8 x 10 1/2. **Subscription Rates:** Free. **Remarks:** Accepts advertising.
Circ: (Not Reported)

DERBY, pop. 12,346.

S. CT. New Haven Co. 7 mi. W. of New Haven. Manufactures tools and metal specialties, concrete vaults and tanks, dairy equipment, awning and radiator repairs, key blanks, locksmith supplies and tools, screw machine products, metal stampings, carburetors, organic chemicals, lumber and masonry supplies, covered wire and spiral boning, sponge and hard rubber products, and airplane parts.

4802 Shopping News
Valley Publishing Co.
7 Francis St. Phone: (203)735-6696
Derby, CT 06418 Fax: (203)735-0334

Shopping guide. **Founded:** 1960. **Freq:** Weekly (Tues.). **Key Personnel:** Blaze A. Garbatini, Publisher. **Remarks:** Combined advertising rates available with Valley Times.
Circ: Non-paid 18,189

EAST BERLIN

4803 Berlin Citizen
East Berlin Publishing House, LLC
230 Berlin St. Phone: (860)828-6942
East Berlin, CT 06023 Fax: (860)828-4998

Community newspaper. **Founded:** Jan. 8, 1997. **Freq:** Weekly. **Print Method:** Web offset. **Trim Size:** 11 x 17. **Cols./Page:** 5. **Col. Depth:** 15 inches. **Key Personnel:** Art Durity, Editor; Steven Cyr, Advertising Mgr.; David Durity, Circulation Mgr. **Subscription Rates:** $20 individuals; $40 out of area. **Remarks:** Accepts advertising.
Ad Rates: BW: $850 **Circ:** Controlled ⊕8,041
PCI: $13

EAST HADDAM, pop. 5,621.

S. CT. Middlesex Co. 10 mi. N. of Chester. Residential.

4804 KIND News
National Association for Humane and Environmental Education (NAHEE)
PO Box 362 Phone: (860)434-8666
East Haddam, CT 06423 Fax: (860)434-9579
Publication E-mail: kindnews@nahee.org
Publisher E-mail: nahee@nahee.org

In-classroom newspaper for children. **Subtitle:** Kids In Nature's Defense Club. **Founded:** 1983. **Freq:** 9/year. **Print Method:** Letterpress. **Cols./Page:** 3. **Col. Width:** 26 nonpareils. **Col. Depth:** 140 agate lines. **Key Personnel:** Bill DeRosa, Dir. of Publications, derosa@nahee.org; Dorothy Weller, Dir. of Outreach, fax (860)434-6282, weller@nahee.org. **ISSN:** 1050-8218. **Subscription Rates:** $25 (includes 32 copies per issue). **Remarks:** Advertising not accepted. **URL:** http://www.nahee.org; http://www.kindnews.org.
Circ: 1,216,000

4805 Show Magic
Goodspeed Opera House Foundation Inc.
PO Box 466 Phone: (860)873-8664
East Haddam, CT 06423-0466 Fax: (860)873-2329
Publisher E-mail: webmaster@goodspeed.org

Consumer magazine covering musical theatre. **Founded:** 1984. **Freq:** Quarterly. **Cols./Page:** 3. **Key Personnel:** John Pike, Editor; Sadie Mather, Subscriptions. **ISSN:** 8755-9560. **Subscription Rates:** $19 individuals; $5.95 single issue. **Remarks:** Accepts advertising.
Ad Rates: BW: $600 **Circ:** Controlled 5,000
4C: $1,500

4806 Show Music
Goodspeed Opera House Foundation Inc.
PO Box 466 Phone: (860)873-8664
East Haddam, CT 06423-0466 Fax: (860)873-2329
Publication E-mail: subscriptions@showmusic.org
Publisher E-mail: webmaster@goodspeed.org

Internationally acclaimed by professionals and fans as the premier magazine covering musical theatre around the world, SHOW MUSIC combines insightful interviews and reviews of productions, recordings, videos and books for a comprehensive quarterly look at news from on and off the musical stage. **Subtitle:** The Musical Theatre Magazine. **Founded:** 1982. **Freq:** Quarterly. **Trim Size:** 8 x 10 1/2. **Cols./Page:** 3. **Col. Width:** 2 1/8 inches. **Col. Depth:** 9 5/16 inches. **Key Personnel:** John Pike, Publisher, jpike@showmusic.org; Lisa Ryan, Production Mgr., lryan@showmusic.org; Max Opreeo, Editor, mpreeo@showmusic.org; Kate Pacowta, Advertising Dir., kpacowta@howmusic.org; Sadie Mather, Subscription Mgr., subscriptions@showmusic.org. **ISSN:** 8755-9560. **Subscription Rates:** $23 individuals; $8.95 single issue. **Remarks:** Accepts advertising. **URL:** http://www.goodspeed.org.
Ad Rates: BW: $620 **Circ:** Paid 5,000
4C: $1,500

EAST HARTFORD, pop. 52,563.

N. Ct. Hartford Co. 2 mi. E. of Hartford. Manufactures jet airplane engines, paper, stamping devices, furniture, confectionery, pickles. Bottling works. Dairy, stock, poultry farms.

4807 The Gazette
1171 Main St. Phone: (860)289-6468
East Hartford, CT 06108 Fax: (860)289-6469

Community newspaper. **Founded:** Oct. 1885. **Freq:** Weekly (Thurs.). **Print Method:** Offset. **Trim Size:** 10 3/8 x 12. **Cols./Page:** 5. **Col. Width:** 1 11/16 inches. **Col. Depth:** 12 inches. **Key Personnel:** William A. Doak, Editor; Marc Rommand, Publisher; N. Phaneuf, Advertising Mgr. **ISSN:** 8750-9156. **Subscription Rates:** $20 out of area. **Remarks:** Accepts advertising.
Ad Rates: GLR: $16.03 **Circ:** Paid ‡210
BW: $720 Free ‡19,750
4C: $795
SAU: $14.80

EASTON

4808 Easton Courier
Hometown Publications, Inc.
1000 Bridgeport Ave.
Shelton, CT 06484
Publisher E-mail: homepubl@aol.com

Community newspaper. **Founded:** 1979. **Freq:** Weekly (Thurs.). **Print Method:** Offset. **Trim Size:** 14 x 22 1/2. **Cols./Page:** 6. **Col. Width:** 1 3/8 inches. **Col. Depth:** 21 inches. **Key Personnel:** Beth Brashnahan, Editor; Regina Burkhart, Publisher; Robin Glowa, Advertising Mgr., fax (206)926-2092. **Subscription Rates:** $12 individuals. **Remarks:** Combined advertising rates available with other Hometown Publications.
Ad Rates: GLR: $.49 **Circ:** Combined ♦1,698
BW: $780.57
SAU: $6.94

ENFIELD, pop. 42,695.

N. CT. Hartford Co. 14 mi. N. of Hartford. Manufactures plastics, wood products, pumps, tools and dies, metal castings. Agriculture. Poultry, apples, potatoes.

4809 Enfield Reminder
Reminder Press
PO Box 27 Phone: (860)872-6648
130 Old Town Rd. Fax: (860)875-2089
Vernon, CT 06066
Local newspaper. **Freq:** Weekly. **Print Method:** Offset. **Cols./Page:** 6. **Col. Width:** 21 nonpareils. **Col. Depth:** 224 agate lines. **Key Personnel:** Kenneth A. Hovland, Publisher.

ESSEX, pop. 5,078.

S. Ct. Middlesex Co. 19 mi. SE of Middletown. Residential.

4810 Soundings
Trader Publishing Co.
35 Pratt St. Phone: (860)767-3200
Essex, CT 06426-1185 Fax: (860)767-0642
Publisher E-mail: soundings@worldnet.att.net

News magazine for recreational boaters. **Subtitle:** The Nation's Boating Newspaper. **Founded:** 1963. **Freq:** Monthly. **Print Method:** Offset. **Trim Size:** 11 x 14. **Cols./Page:** 4. **Key Personnel:** William Sisson, Editor, soundmgs@worldnet.att.net; Brad Thomas, Advertising Dir., fax (860)767-1048, soundingsads@worldnet.att.net. **USPS:** 527-030. **Subscription Rates:** $24.97 individuals; $3.95 single issue. **Remarks:** Advertising accepted; rates available upon request. **URL:** http://www.soundingspub.com.
Circ: Paid ‡73,487

4811 Woodshop News
Trader Publishing Co.
35 Pratt St. Phone: (860)767-8227
Essex, CT 06426 Fax: (860)767-0645
Free: (800)464-4793
Publication E-mail: woodshopnews@worldnet.att.net
Publisher E-mail: soundings@worldnet.att.net

Newspaper (tabloid) focusing on people and businesses involved in woodworking. **Founded:** Dec. 1986. **Freq:** Monthly. **Print Method:** Offset. **Trim Size:** 11 x 14 1/4. **Cols./Page:** 5. **Col. Width:** 1 13/16 inches. **Col. Depth:** 13 inches. **Key Personnel:** Thomas Clark, Editor; George Brooks, Publisher; Spencer Isola, Advertising Dir., phone (847)295-0051. **ISSN:** 0894-5403. **Subscription Rates:** $21.95 subscription; $3.95 single issue. **URL:** http://www.woodshopnews.com.
Ad Rates: BW: $3,870 **Circ:** Paid ⊕72,176
4C: $4,670 Free ⊕21,500

FAIRFIELD, pop. 54,849.

SW CT. Fairfield Co. 4 mi. W. of Bridgeport. Fairfield University (Jesuit coed); Sacred Heart Univ. (Cath. coed). Manufactures batteries, chemicals, drugs, roller bearings, auto accessories, computer graphics, hardware, plastics, machine tools; cement products, wire, guns, boilers. Bottling works. Resort.

4812 Cartoonist Profiles
PO Box 325 Phone: (203)227-2542
Fairfield, CT 06430-0325 Fax: (203)227-9508

Magazine profiling successful cartoonists. **Founded:** 1969. **Freq:** Quarterly. **Print Method:** Offset. **Trim Size:** 8 1/2 x 11. **Key Personnel:** Jud Hurd, Editor. **ISSN:** 0008-7068. **Subscription Rates:** $35. **Remarks:** Accepts advertising.
Ad Rates: BW: $350 **Circ:** (Not Reported)

4813 Fairfield Citizen-News
Brooks Community Newspapers, Inc.
220 Carter Henry Dr. Phone: (203)255-4505
Fairfield, CT 06430 Fax: (203)255-0456
Publisher E-mail: bcnews3@netakis.com

Newspaper. **Founded:** 1964. **Freq:** Semiweekly (Wed. and Fri.). **Print Method:** Offset. **Cols./Page:** 5. **Col. Width:** 27 nonpareils. **Col. Depth:** 224 agate lines. **Key Personnel:** Pat Hines, Editor; B.V. Brooks, Publisher; Kevin J. Lally, Advertising Mgr. **Subscription Rates:** $16 individuals. **Remarks:** Accepts advertising. **URL:** http://www.townline.com/brooks/brooks.htm.
Ad Rates: GLR: $.68 **Circ:** 9,627

4814 George Herbert Journal
Sacred Heart University
5151 Park Ave. Phone: (203)371-7810
Fairfield, CT 06432
Publication E-mail: spgottlieb@aol.com

Scholarly journal covering the work of George Herbert and related 17th century poets. **Founded:** 1977. **Freq:** Semiannual. **Print Method:** Photo offset. **Trim Size:** 5 1/2 x 8 1/2. **ISSN:** 0161-7435. **Subscription Rates:** $10 individuals; $25 institutions. **Remarks:** Accepts advertising.
Ad Rates: BW: $70 **Circ:** Combined 500

4815 Journal of Sustainable Agriculture
The Haworth Press, Inc.
Biology Dept. Phone: (203)254-4000
Fairfield Univ. Fax: (203)254-4253
Fairfield, CT 06430
Publication E-mail: getinfo@haworthpressinc.com
Publisher E-mail: getinfo@haworthpressinc.com

Journal whose goal is to promote the study and application of sustainable agriculture for solutions to the problems of resource depletion and environmental misuse. **Founded:** 1990. **Freq:** Quarterly. **Trim Size:** 6x8 1/2. **Cols./Page:** 1. **Col. Width:** 4 3/8 inches. **Col. Depth:** 7 1/8 inches. **Key Personnel:** Raymond Poincelot, PhD, Editor, rpoincelot@fair1.fairfield.edu; Bill Cohen, Publisher. **ISSN:** 1044-0046. **Subscription Rates:** $40 individuals; $52 individuals Canada; $56 individuals other countries; $160 libraries; $208 libraries Canada; $224 libraries other countries; $60 institutions; $78 institutions Canada; $84 institutions other countries. **Remarks:** Accepts advertising. **Alt. Formats:** Microform.
Ad Rates: BW: $300 **Circ:** Paid ‡775

4816 MacII Review
Comtech Group
360 Hunyadi Ave.
Fairfield, CT 06430

Magazine containing news and reviews dedicated to MacII products and applications. **Founded:** July 1988. **Freq:** Bimonthly. **Key Personnel:** Richard M. Coombs, Editor and Publisher. **Subscription Rates:** $23.70. $4.95 single issue. **Remarks:** Accepts advertising.
Ad Rates: BW: $1,650 **Circ:** 18,700

4817 Pi Mu Epsilon Journal
Fairfield University
c/o Russell Euler Phone: (660)562-1229
Northwest Missouri State University
Dept. of Math & Statistics
Maryville, MO 64468-6000
Publication E-mail: 0100120@acad.nwmissouri.edu

Professional mathematics journal. **Founded:** 1949. **Freq:** Semiannual. **Cols./Page:** 1. **Key Personnel:** Russell Euler, Editor, reuler@mail.nwmissouri.edu; Joan Weiss, Editor, weiss@fair1.fairfield.edu. **Subscription Rates:** $20 two years; $40 five years. **Remarks:** Advertising not accepted.
Circ: Controlled 3,600

4818 Soccer Jr.
Triplepoint Inc.
27 Unquowa Rd. Phone: (203)259-5766
Fairfield, CT 06430 Fax: (203)256-1119
Publication E-mail: soccerjrol@aol.com

Magazine about soccer. **Subtitle:** The Soccer Magazine for Kids. **Founded:** June 1992. **Freq:** Bimonthly. **Print Method:** Web offset. **Trim Size:** 8 1/8 x 10 7/8. **Key Personnel:** Joe Provey, Editor; Tom Mindrum, Publisher. **ISSN:** 1060-9911. **Subscription Rates:** $16.97. $3.75 single issue.
Ad Rates: BW: $4,944 **Circ:** Paid 110,000
4C: $6,180

4819 WSHU-FM - 91.1
5151 Park Ave. Phone: (203)371-7989
Fairfield, CT 06432-1023 Fax: (203)371-7991
Free: (800)937-6045

Format: Public Radio; Classical; News; Folk; New Age. **Networks:** National Public Radio (NPR); Beethoven Satellite; American Public Radio (APR). **Owner:** Sacred Heart University, at above address. **Founded:** 1964. **Operating Hours:** Continuous; 53% network, 47% local. **Key Personnel:** George Lombardi, General Mgr., lombardi@wshu.org; Chris Wienk, Program Dir., wienk@wshu.org; Tom Kuser, News Dir., kusar@wshu.org; Gillian Anderson, Development Dir., ganderson@wshu.org; Pam Mittendorff, Music Dir., mitty@wshu.org; Lori Miller, Underwriting Mktg. Mgr., lmiller@wshu.org; Geri Diorio, Production Mgr., diorio@wshu.org; Lynn Southard, Business Mgr. **Wattage:** 20,000. **Ad Rates:** Noncommercial. **URL:** http://www.wshu.org.

4820 WVOF-FM - 88.5
Fairfield University Phone: (203)254-4111
PO Box R Fax: (203)254-4267
Fairfield, CT 06430

Format: Eclectic; Full Service. **Networks:** Independent. **Founded:** 1974. **Operating Hours:** 6 a.m.-midnight Mon.-Thur., Continous Fri.-Sun. **Key Personnel:** Vic Sousa, Station Mgr.; Jon Sabol, Music Dir.; Kristi Olson, Music Dir.; Joe Fattenno, Program Dir.; Cris Ogis, News Dir.; Cindy Delnero, Public Affairs Dir.; MaryLou Albert, Publicity/Mktg. Dir.; John Mays, Format Dir. (Jazz). **Local Programs:** *Blue Grass Express*, Rob Lindally; *Breakfast Club*, Saul Nowitz; *Hip-Hop Club*, Cris Ogis. **Wattage:** 100. **Ad Rates:** Noncommercial.

FARMINGTON

4821 ACTA Anatomica
S. Karger Publishers, Inc.
26 W. Avon Rd. Phone: (860)675-7834
PO Box 529 Fax: (860)675-7302
Farmington, CT 06085
Publisher E-mail: karger@karger.ch

Scientific medical journal (English, French, and German). **Subtitle:** Journal of Anatomy, Embryology and Cell Biology. **Founded:** 1945. **Freq:** Monthly. **Print Method:** Offset. **Trim Size:** 210 x 280 mm. **Cols./Page:** 1. **Col. Width:** 99 nonpareils. **Col. Depth:** 155 agate lines. **Key Personnel:** AW. English, Editor; H.W. Denker, Editor. **ISSN:** 0001-5180. **Subscription Rates:** $1,353 plus $51 post/handling. **Remarks:** Color advertising accepted; rates available upon request.
Ad Rates: BW: $1,075 **Circ:** 1,200

4822 ACTA Haematologica
S. Karger Publishers, Inc.
26 W. Avon Rd. Phone: (860)675-7834
PO Box 529 Fax: (860)675-7302
Farmington, CT 06085
Publisher E-mail: karger@karger.ch

Scientific medical journal on functional morphology. **Founded:** 1948. **Freq:** 8/year. **Print Method:** Offset. **Trim Size:** 210 x 280 mm. **Cols./Page:** 1. **Col. Width:** 99 nonpareils. **Col. Depth:** 155 agate lines. **Key Personnel:** B. Ramot, Editor; I. Ben-Bassat, Editor. **ISSN:** 0001-5792. **Subscription Rates:** $532 plus $34 post/handling. **Remarks:** Color advertising accepted; rates available upon request.
Ad Rates: BW: $1,075 **Circ:** 1,600

4823 American Journal of Nephrology
S. Karger Publishers, Inc.
26 W. Avon Rd. Phone: (860)675-7834
PO Box 529 Fax: (860)675-7302
Farmington, CT 06085
Publisher E-mail: karger@karger.ch

Scientific medical journal on clinical information. **Founded:** 1981. **Freq:** Bimonthly. **Print Method:** Offset. **Trim Size:** 210 x 280 mm. **Cols./Page:** 1. **Col. Width:** 99 nonpareils. **Col. Depth:** 155 agate lines. **Key Personnel:** S.G. Massry, Editor. **ISSN:** 0250-8095. **Subscription Rates:** $423 plus $25.50 post/handling. **Remarks:** Color advertising accepted; rates available upon request.
Ad Rates: BW: $1,095 **Circ:** 2,900

4824 Analytische Psychologie
S. Karger Publishers, Inc.
26 W. Avon Rd. Phone: (860)675-7834
PO Box 529 Fax: (860)675-7302
Farmington, CT 06085
Publisher E-mail: karger@karger.ch

Scientific medical journal (German). **Subtitle:** Zeitchrift fur Analytische Psychologie und ihre Grenzgebiete. **Founded:** 1970. **Freq:** Quarterly. **Print Method:** Offset. **Trim Size:** 177 x 252 mm. **Cols./Page:** 1. **Col. Width:** 84 nonpareils. **Col. Depth:** 141 agate lines. **Key Personnel:** G. Bovensiepen, Editor; C.A. Meier, Editor. **ISSN:** 0301-3006. **Subscription Rates:** $75 plus $17 post/handling. **Remarks:** Color advertising accepted; rates available upon request.
Ad Rates: BW: $1,085 **Circ:** 1,700

4825 Annals of Nutrition and Metabolism
S. Karger Publishers, Inc.
26 W. Avon Rd. Phone: (860)675-7834
PO Box 529 Fax: (860)675-7302
Farmington, CT 06085
Publisher E-mail: karger@karger.ch

Scientific medical journal (English, French, and German). **Subtitle:** European Journal of Nutrition, Metabolic Diseases and Dietetics. **Founded:** 1959. **Freq:** Bimonthly. **Print Method:** Offset. **Trim Size:** 177 x 252 mm. **Cols./Page:** 1. **Col. Width:** 84 nonpareils. **Col. Depth:** 141 agate lines. **Key Personnel:** G. Wolfram, Editor. **ISSN:** 0250-6807. **Subscription Rates:** $276 plus $25.50 post/handling. **Remarks:** Color advertising accepted; rates available upon request.
Ad Rates: BW: $1,075 **Circ:** 1,250

4826 Audiology and Neuro-Otology
S. Karger Publishers, Inc.
26 W. Avon Rd. Phone: (860)675-7834
PO Box 529 Fax: (860)675-7302
Farmington, CT 06085
Publisher E-mail: karger@karger.ch

Scientific medical journal (English and French). **Subtitle:** Journal of Auditory Communication. **Founded:** 1962. **Freq:** Bimonthly. **Print Method:** Offset. **Trim Size:** 177 x 252 mm. **Cols./Page:** 1. **Col. Width:** 84 nonpareils. **Col. Depth:** 141 agate lines. **Key Personnel:** J.M. Aran, Editor-in-Chief. **ISSN:** 0020-6091. **Subscription Rates:** $240. **Remarks:** Accepts advertising. **Formerly:** Audiology.
Ad Rates: BW: $1,075 **Circ:** 1,650

4827 Biological Signals
S. Karger Publishers, Inc.
26 W. Avon Rd. Phone: (860)675-7834
PO Box 529 Fax: (860)675-7302
Farmington, CT 06085
Publisher E-mail: karger@karger.ch

Medical journal. **Founded:** 1992. **Freq:** Bimonthly. **Print Method:** Offset. **Trim Size:** 177 x 252 mm. **Cols./Page:** 1. **Col. Width:** 99 nonpareils. **Key Personnel:** S.F. Pang, Editor; T. Fujita, Editor; P.A. Ward, Editor. **ISSN:** 1016-0922. **Subscription Rates:** $266 plus $25.50 post/handling. **Remarks:** Accepts advertising.
Ad Rates: BW: $1,075 **Circ:** 800

4828 Biology of the Neonate
S. Karger Publishers, Inc.
26 W. Avon Rd. Phone: (860)675-7834
PO Box 529 Fax: (860)675-7302
Farmington, CT 06085
Publisher E-mail: karger@karger.ch

Scientific medical journal. **Subtitle:** Foetal and Neonatal Research. **Founded:** 1959. **Freq:** 12/year. **Print Method:** Offset. **Trim Size:** 177 x 252 mm. **Cols./Page:** 1. **Col. Width:** 84 nonpareils. **Col. Depth:** 141 agate lines. **Key Personnel:** J.P. Relier, Editor-in-Chief. **ISSN:** 0006-3126. **Subscription Rates:** $650 plus $25.50 post/handling. **Remarks:** Color advertising accepted; rates available upon request.
Ad Rates: BW: $1,075 **Circ:** 1,150

4829 Blood Purification
S. Karger Publishers, Inc.
26 W. Avon Rd. Phone: (860)675-7834
PO Box 529 Fax: (860)675-7302
Farmington, CT 06085
Publisher E-mail: karger@karger.ch

Scientific medical journal. **Subtitle:** Official Journal of the International Society of Blood Purification. **Founded:** 1983. **Freq:** Bimonthly. **Print Method:** Offset. **Trim Size:** 177 x 252 mm. **Cols./Page:** 1. **Col. Width:** 84 nonpareils. **Col. Depth:** 141 agate lines. **Key Personnel:** L.W. Henderson, Editor-in-Chief. **ISSN:** 0253-5068. **Subscription Rates:** $296 plus $25.50 post/handling. **Remarks:** Color advertising accepted; rates available upon request.
Ad Rates: BW: $1,085 **Circ:** 950

4830 Brain, Behavior and Evolution
S. Karger Publishers, Inc.
26 W. Avon Rd. Phone: (860)675-7834
PO Box 529 Fax: (860)675-7302
Farmington, CT 06085
Publisher E-mail: karger@karger.ch

Scientific medical journal. **Subtitle:** Official Organ of the J.B. Johnston Club. **Founded:** 1968. **Freq:** Monthly. **Print Method:** Offset. **Trim Size:** 210 x 280 mm. **Cols./Page:** 1. **Col. Width:** 84 nonpareils. **Col. Depth:** 141 agate lines. **Key Personnel:** Glenn Northcutt, Editor-in-Chief. **ISSN:** 0006-8977. **Subscription Rates:** $489 plus $25.50 post/handling. **Remarks:** Color advertising accepted; rates available upon request.
Ad Rates: BW: $1,085 **Circ:** 1,000

4831 Cardiology
S. Karger Publishers, Inc.
26 W. Avon Rd. Phone: (860)675-7834
PO Box 529 Fax: (860)675-7302
Farmington, CT 06085
Publisher E-mail: karger@karger.ch

Scientific medical journal. **Subtitle:** International Journal of Cardiovascular Medicine, Surgery and Pathology. **Founded:** 1937. **Freq:** Bimonthly. **Print Method:** Offset. **Trim Size:** 210 x 280. **Cols./Page:** 1. **Col. Width:** 99 nonpareils. **Col. Depth:** 155 agate lines. **Key Personnel:** J.S. Alpert, Editor-in-Chief. **ISSN:** 0008-6312. **Subscription Rates:** $615 plus $25.50 post/handling. **Remarks:** Color advertising accepted; rates available upon request.
Ad Rates: BW: $1,075 **Circ:** 1,300

4832 Caries Research
S. Karger Publishers, Inc.
26 W. Avon Rd. Phone: (860)675-7834
PO Box 529 Fax: (860)675-7302
Farmington, CT 06085
Publisher E-mail: karger@karger.ch

Professional journal. **Subtitle:** Journal of the European Organization for Caries Research (ORCA). **Founded:** 1967. **Freq:** Bimonthly. **Print Method:** Offset. **Trim Size:** 210 x 280 mm. **Cols./Page:** 1. **Col. Width:** 84 nonpareils. **Col. Depth:** 141 agate lines. **Key Personnel:** J. Terrovuo, Editor. **ISSN:** 0008-6568. **Subscription Rates:** $403 plus $25.50 post/handling. **Remarks:** Color advertising accepted; rates available upon request.
Ad Rates: BW: $1,075 **Circ:** 1,450

4833 Cellular Physiology and Biochemistry
S. Karger Publishers, Inc.
26 W. Avon Rd. Phone: (860)675-7834
PO Box 529 Fax: (860)675-7302
Farmington, CT 06085
Publisher E-mail: karger@karger.ch

Medical journal. **Subtitle:** International Journal of Experimental Cellular Physiology, Biochemistry, and Pharmacology. **Founded:** 1991. **Freq:** Bimonthly. **Print Method:** Offset. **Trim Size:** 210 x 280 mm. **Cols./Page:** 1. **Col. Width:** 99 nonpareils. **Key Personnel:** F. Lang, Managing Editor. **ISSN:** 1015-8987. **Subscription Rates:** $247 plus $25.50 post/handling. **Remarks:** Accepts advertising.
Ad Rates: BW: $1,085 **Circ:** ‡1,050

4834 Cerebrovascular Diseases
S. Karger Publishers, Inc.
26 W. Avon Rd. Phone: (860)675-7834
PO Box 529 Fax: (860)676-7302
Farmington, CT 06085
Publisher E-mail: karger@karger.ch

Medical journal. **Subtitle:** Official Journal of the European Stroke Council. **Founded:** 1991. **Freq:** Bimonthly. **Print Method:** Offset. **Trim Size:** 210 x 280 mm. **Cols./Page:** 1. **Col. Width:** 99 nonpareils. **Key Personnel:** J. Bogousslavsky,

Editor; M.G. Hennerici, Editor. **ISSN:** 1015-9770. **Subscription Rates:** $345 plus $25.50 post/handling. **Remarks:** Accepts advertising.
Ad Rates: BW: $1,085 **Circ:** ‡1,050

4835 Chemotherapy
S. Karger Publishers, Inc.
26 W. Avon Rd. Phone: (860)675-7834
PO Box 529 Fax: (860)675-7302
Farmington, CT 06085
Publisher E-mail: karger@karger.ch

Medical journal. **Subtitle:** International Journal of Experimental and Clinical Chemotherapy. **Founded:** 1960. **Freq:** Bimonthly. **Print Method:** Offset. **Trim Size:** 177 x 252 mm. **Cols./Page:** 1. **Col. Width:** 84 nonpareils. **Col. Depth:** 141 agate lines. **Key Personnel:** H. Schoenfeld, Editor. **ISSN:** 0009-3157. **Subscription Rates:** $354 plus $25.50 post/handling. **Remarks:** Color advertising accepted; rates available upon request.
Ad Rates: BW: $1,075 **Circ:** 1,300

4836 Cytogenetics and Cell Genetics
S. Karger Publishers, Inc.
26 W. Avon Rd. Phone: (860)675-7834
PO Box 529 Fax: (860)675-7302
Farmington, CT 06085
Publisher E-mail: karger@karger.ch

Scientific medical journal. **Founded:** 1962. **Freq:** 16/year. **Print Method:** Offset. **Trim Size:** 210 x 280 mm. **Cols./Page:** 1. **Col. Width:** 99 nonpareils. **Col. Depth:** 155 agate lines. **Key Personnel:** H.P. Klinger, Editor-in-Chief. **ISSN:** 0301-0171. **Subscription Rates:** $1,380 plus $68 post/handling. **Remarks:** Color advertising accepted; rates available upon request. **Formerly**: Cytogenetics.
Ad Rates: BW: $1,085 **Circ:** 1,800

4837 Dementia
S. Karger Publishers, Inc.
26 W. Avon Rd. Phone: (860)675-7834
PO Box 529 Fax: (860)675-7302
Farmington, CT 06085
Publisher E-mail: karger@karger.ch

Medical journal. **Founded:** 1990. **Freq:** Bimonthly. **Print Method:** Offset. **Trim Size:** 210 x 280 mm. **Cols./Page:** 1. **Col. Width:** 99 nonpareils. **Key Personnel:** V. Chan-Palay, Editor. **ISSN:** 1013-7424. **Subscription Rates:** $470 plus $25.50 post/handling. **Remarks:** Accepts advertising.
Ad Rates: BW: $1,085 **Circ:** ‡1,050

4838 Dermatology
S. Karger Publishers, Inc.
26 W. Avon Rd. Phone: (860)675-7834
PO Box 529 Fax: (860)675-7302
Farmington, CT 06085
Publisher E-mail: karger@karger.ch

Medical journal. **Subtitle:** Official Organ of Swiss and Belgian Society for Dermatology and Syphiligraphy. **Founded:** 1918. **Freq:** 8/year. **Print Method:** Offset. **Trim Size:** 210 x 280 mm. **Cols./Page:** 1. **Col. Width:** 84 nonpareils. **Col. Depth:** 141 agate lines. **Key Personnel:** J.H. Saurat, Editor-in-Chief. **ISSN:** 1018-8665. **Subscription Rates:** $532 plus $34 post/handling. **Remarks:** Color advertising accepted; rates available upon request. **Formerly**: Dermatologica (1992).
Ad Rates: BW: $1,095 **Circ:** ‡2,350

4839 Developmental Brain Dysfunction
S. Karger Publishers, Inc.
26 W. Avon Rd. Phone: (860)675-7834
PO Box 529 Fax: (860)675-7302
Farmington, CT 06085
Publisher E-mail: karger@karger.ch

Journal advancing the understanding of mental disorders. **Subtitle:** Mental Retardation, Malnutrition, and Aging. **Founded:** 1988. **Freq:** Bimonthly. **Print Method:** Offset. **Trim Size:** 177 x 252 mm. **Cols./Page:** 1. **Col. Width:** 99 inches. **Col. Depth:** 155 inches. **Key Personnel:** R. Ferri, Editor. **ISSN:** 1019-5815. **Subscription Rates:** $276 plus $25.50 post/handling. **Remarks:** Accepts advertising. **Formerly**: Brain Dysfunction (1992).
Ad Rates: BW: $1,075 **Circ:** 800
4C: $350

4840 Developmental Neuroscience
S. Karger Publishers, Inc.
26 W. Avon Rd. Phone: (860)675-7834
PO Box 529 Fax: (860)675-7302
Farmington, CT 06085
Publisher E-mail: karger@karger.ch

Medical journal. **Subtitle:** International Journal of Experimental and Clinical Neuroscience. **Founded:** 1979. **Freq:** Bimonthly. **Print Method:** Offset. **Trim Size:** 210 x 280 mm. **Cols./Page:** 1. **Col. Width:** 84 nonpareils. **Col. Depth:** 141 agate lines. **Key Personnel:** A.T. Campagnoni, Editor-in-Chief. **ISSN:** 0378-5866. **Subscription Rates:** $451 plus $25.50 post/handling. **Remarks:** Color advertising accepted; rates available upon request.
Ad Rates: BW: $1,075 **Circ:** 800

4841 Digestion
S. Karger Publishers, Inc.
26 W. Avon Rd. Phone: (860)675-7834
PO Box 529 Fax: (860)675-7302
Farmington, CT 06085
Publisher E-mail: karger@karger.ch

Medical journal. **Subtitle:** International Journal of Gastroenterology. **Founded:** 1968. **Freq:** Bimonthly. **Print Method:** Offset. **Trim Size:** 210 x 280. **Cols./Page:** 1. **Col. Width:** 84 nonpareils. **Col. Depth:** 141 agate lines. **Key Personnel:** R. Arnold, Editor-in-Chief. **ISSN:** 0012-2823. **Subscription Rates:** $975 plus $25.50 post/handling. **Remarks:** Color advertising accepted; rates available upon request.
Ad Rates: BW: $1,075 **Circ:** 1,250

4842 Digestive Diseases
S. Karger Publishers, Inc.
26 W. Avon Rd. Phone: (860)675-7834
PO Box 529 Fax: (860)675-7302
Farmington, CT 06085
Publisher E-mail: karger@karger.ch

Scientific medical journal. **Subtitle:** Current Concepts in Research and Practice. **Founded:** 1983. **Freq:** Bimonthly. **Print Method:** Offset. **Trim Size:** 177 x 252 mm. **Cols./Page:** 1. **Col. Width:** 84 nonpareils. **Col. Depth:** 141 agate lines. **Key Personnel:** S.R. Achem, Editor-in-Chief. **ISSN:** 0257-2753. **Subscription Rates:** $335 plus $25.50 post/handling. **Remarks:** Color advertising accepted; rates available upon request.
Ad Rates: BW: $1,075 **Circ:** 800

4843 Digestive Surgery
S. Karger Publishers, Inc.
26 W. Avon Rd. Phone: (860)675-7834
PO Box 529 Fax: (860)675-7302
Farmington, CT 06085
Publisher E-mail: karger@karger.ch

Scientific medical journal. **Subtitle:** Incorporating Surgical Gastroenterology. **Founded:** 1984. **Freq:** Bimonthly. **Print Method:** Offset. **Trim Size:** 210 x 280 mm. **Cols./Page:** 1. **Col. Width:** 99 nonpareils. **Col. Depth:** 155 agate lines. **Key Personnel:** E.H. Farthmann, Editor-in-Chief. **ISSN:** 0253-4886. **Subscription Rates:** $432 plus $25.50 post/handling. **Remarks:** Color advertising accepted; rates available upon request.
Ad Rates: BW: $1,095 **Circ:** 1,000

4844 European Journal of Human Genetics
S. Karger Publishers, Inc.
26 W. Avon Rd. Phone: (860)675-7834
PO Box 529 Fax: (860)675-7302
Farmington, CT 06085
Publisher E-mail: karger@karger.ch

Medical journal on genetic research. **Subtitle:** Official Journal of the European Society of Human Genetics. **Founded:** 1993. **Freq:** Bimonthly. **Print Method:** Offset. **Trim Size:** 7 x 9 7/8. **Key Personnel:** G. Romeo, Editor; M. Devoto, Advertising Mgr. **ISSN:** 1018-4813. **Subscription Rates:** $307 plus $25.50 post/handling.
Ad Rates: BW: $1,095 **Circ:** 1,000

4845 European Neurology
S. Karger Publishers, Inc.
26 W. Avon Rd. Phone: (860)675-7834
PO Box 529 Fax: (860)675-7302
Farmington, CT 06085
Publisher E-mail: karger@karger.ch

Scientific medical journal. **Founded:** 1968. **Freq:** 8/year. **Print Method:** Offset. **Trim Size:** 210 x 280 mm. **Cols./Page:** 1. **Col. Width:** 84 nonpareils. **Col. Depth:** 141 agate lines. **Key Personnel:** J. Bogousslavsky, Editor-in-Chief. **ISSN:** 0014-3022. **Subscription Rates:** $423 plus $25.50 post/handling. **Remarks:** Color advertising accepted; rates available upon request.
Ad Rates: BW: $1,085 **Circ:** 1,050

4846 European Surgical Research
S. Karger Publishers, Inc.
26 W. Avon Rd. Phone: (860)675-7834
PO Box 529 Fax: (860)675-7302
Farmington, CT 06085
Publisher E-mail: karger@karger.ch

Scientific medical journal. **Subtitle:** Clinical and Experimental Surgery. **Founded:** 1969. **Freq:** Bimonthly. **Print Method:** Offset. **Trim Size:** 177 x 252 mm. **Cols./Page:** 1. **Col. Width:** 84 nonpareils. **Col. Depth:** 141 agate lines. **Key Personnel:** K. Messmer, Editor-in-Chief. **ISSN:** 0014-312X. **Subscription Rates:** $335 plus $25.50 post/handling. **Remarks:** Color advertising accepted; rates available upon request.
Ad Rates: BW: $1,075 **Circ:** 800

4847 European Urology
S. Karger Publishers, Inc.
26 W. Avon Rd. Phone: (860)675-7834
PO Box 529 Fax: (860)675-7302
Farmington, CT 06085
Publisher E-mail: karger@karger.ch

Scientific medical journal. **Subtitle:** Official Organ of the European Association of Urology. **Founded:** 1975. **Freq:** 8/year. **Print Method:** Offset. **Trim Size:** 210 x 280 mm. **Cols./Page:** 1. **Col. Width:** 99 nonpareils. **Col. Depth:** 155 agate lines. **Key Personnel:** C.C. Schulman, Editor. **ISSN:** 0302-2838. **Subscription Rates:** $614 plus $34 post/handling. **Remarks:** Color advertising accepted; rates available upon request.
Ad Rates: BW: $1,095 **Circ:** 3,200

4848 Experimental and Clinical Immunogenetics
S. Karger Publishers, Inc.
26 W. Avon Rd. Phone: (860)675-7834
PO Box 529 Fax: (860)675-7302
Farmington, CT 06085
Publisher E-mail: karger@karger.ch

Scientific medical journal. **Founded:** 1984. **Freq:** Quarterly. **Print Method:** Offset. **Trim Size:** 177 x 252. **Cols./Page:** 1. **Col. Width:** 84 nonpareils. **Col. Depth:** 141 agate lines. **Key Personnel:** K. Bauer, Editor-in-Chief. **ISSN:** 0254-9670. **Subscription Rates:** $208 plus $17 post/handling. **Remarks:** Color advertising accepted; rates available upon request.
Ad Rates: BW: $1,075 **Circ:** 800

4849 Experimental Nephrology
S. Karger Publishers, Inc.
26 W. Avon Rd. Phone: (860)675-7834
PO Box 529 Fax: (860)675-7302
Farmington, CT 06085
Publisher E-mail: karger@karger.ch

Journal focusing on the biology of the kidney and renal diseases. Includes clinical studies. **Subtitle:** European Journal of Renal Research. **Founded:** 1993. **Freq:** Bimonthly. **Print Method:** Offset. **Trim Size:** 8 1/4 x 11. **Key Personnel:** Prof. L.G. Fine, Editor. **ISSN:** 1018-7782. **Subscription Rates:** $423 plus $25.50 post/handling. **Remarks:** Accepts advertising.
Ad Rates: BW: $1,085 **Circ:** 1,000

4850 Farmington Valley Herald
Bristol Press Publishing Co.
1522 Hopmeadow St. Phone: (203)658-4471
PO Box 477 Fax: (203)658-2898
Simsbury, CT 06070-1419
Newspaper. **Founded:** 1881. **Freq:** Weekly (Thurs.). **Print Method:** Letterpress and offset. **Trim Size:** 14 x 22. **Cols./Page:** 6. **Col. Width:** 20 nonpareils. **Col. Depth:** 175 agate lines. **Key Personnel:** Brian Kelly, Editor/General Mgr. **Subscription Rates:** $15 individuals. **Remarks:** Accepts advertising.
Ad Rates: BW: $350 **Circ:** ‡6,000
4C: $955.25
PCI: $10.90

4851 Fetal Diagnosis and Therapy
S. Karger Publishers, Inc.
26 W. Avon Rd. Phone: (860)675-7834
PO Box 529 Fax: (860)675-7302
Farmington, CT 06085
Publisher E-mail: karger@karger.ch

Scientific medical journal. **Subtitle:** Clinical Advances and Basic Research. Official Organ of the International Fetal Medicine and Surgery Society. **Founded:** 1986. **Freq:** Bimonthly. **Print Method:** Offset. **Trim Size:** 177 x 252 mm. **Cols./Page:** 1. **Col. Width:** 84 nonpareils. **Col. Depth:** 177 agate lines. **Key Personnel:** S. Uzan, Editor-in-Chief. **ISSN:** 1015-3837. **Subscription Rates:** $335 plus $25.50 post/handling. **Remarks:** Color advertising accepted; rates available upon request. **Formerly**: Fetal Therapy (1990).
Ad Rates: BW: $1,075 **Circ:** 800

4852 Folia Phoniatrica et Logopaedica
S. Karger Publishers, Inc.
26 W. Avon Rd. Phone: (860)675-7834
PO Box 529 Fax: (860)675-7302
Farmington, CT 06085
Publisher E-mail: karger@karger.ch

Medical journal. **Subtitle:** International Journal of Phoniatrics, Speech Therapy and Communication Pathology. **Founded:** 1947. **Freq:** Bimonthly. **Print Method:** Offset. **Trim Size:** 177 x 252 mm. **Cols./Page:** 1. **Col. Width:** 84 nonpareils. **Key Personnel:** E. Loebell, Editor. **ISSN:** 1021-7762. **Subscription Rates:** $208 plus $25.50 post/handling. **Remarks:** Color

advertising accepted; rates available upon request. **Formerly:** Folia Phoniatrica.
Ad Rates: BW: $1,075 **Circ:** 1,600

4853 Folia Primatologica
S. Karger Publishers, Inc.
26 W. Avon Rd. Phone: (860)675-7834
PO Box 529 Fax: (860)675-7302
Farmington, CT 06085
Publisher E-mail: karger@karger.ch

Scientific journal focussing on primatology. **Subtitle:** International Journal of Primatology. **Founded:** 1963. **Freq:** 8/year. **Print Method:** Offset. **Trim Size:** 177 x 252 mm. **Cols./Page:** 1. **Col. Width:** 84 nonpareils. **Col. Depth:** 141 agate lines. **Key Personnel:** R. H. Cromptonn, Editor. **ISSN:** 0015-5713. **Subscription Rates:** $336. **Remarks:** Accepts advertising.
Ad Rates: BW: $1,075 **Circ:** 850
4C: $1,400

4854 Gerontology
S. Karger Publishers, Inc.
26 W. Avon Rd. Phone: (860)675-7834
PO Box 529 Fax: (860)675-7302
Farmington, CT 06085
Publisher E-mail: karger@karger.ch

Medical journal. **Subtitle:** International Journal of Experimental and Clinical Gerontology. Organ of the International Association of Gerontology. **Founded:** 1957. **Freq:** Bimonthly. **Print Method:** Offset. **Trim Size:** 177 x 252 mm. **Cols./Page:** 1. **Col. Width:** 84 nonpareils. **Col. Depth:** 141 agate lines. **Key Personnel:** W. Meier-Rage, Managing Editor. **ISSN:** 0304-324X. **Subscription Rates:** $276 plus $25.50 post/handling. **Remarks:** Color advertising accepted; rates available upon request. **Formerly:** Gerontolgia Clinica.
Ad Rates: BW: $1,075 **Circ:** 1,250

4855 Gynaekologisch-geburtshilfliche Rundschau
S. Karger Publishers, Inc.
26 W. Avon Rd. Phone: (860)675-7834
PO Box 529 Fax: (860)675-7302
Farmington, CT 06085
Publisher E-mail: karger@karger.ch

Scientific medical journal (French, English, and German). **Founded:** 1964. **Freq:** Quarterly. **Print Method:** Offset. **Trim Size:** 215 x297. **Cols./Page:** 1. **Col. Width:** 84 nonpareils. **Col. Depth:** 141 agate lines. **Key Personnel:** H. Hepp, Editor; E. Reinhold, Editor; U. Haller, Editor. **ISSN:** 1018-8843. **Subscription Rates:** $238 plus $25.50 post/handling. **Remarks:** Color advertising accepted; rates available upon request. **Formerly:** Gynaekologische Rundschau (1992).
Ad Rates: BW: $1,085 **Circ:** 1,500

4856 Gynecologic and Obstetric Investigation
S. Karger Publishers, Inc.
26 W. Avon Rd. Phone: (860)675-7834
PO Box 529 Fax: (860)675-7302
Farmington, CT 06085
Publisher E-mail: karger@karger.ch

Scientific medical journal. **Founded:** 1970. **Freq:** 8/year. **Print Method:** Offset. **Trim Size:** 215 x 280 mm. **Cols./Page:** 1. **Col. Width:** 84 nonpareils. **Col. Depth:** 141 agate lines. **Key Personnel:** G. Zador, Editor. **ISSN:** 0378-7346. **Subscription Rates:** $614 plus $34 post/handling. **Remarks:** Color advertising accepted; rates available upon request.
Ad Rates: BW: $1,085 **Circ:** 950

4857 Haemostasis
S. Karger Publishers, Inc.
26 W. Avon Rd. Phone: (860)675-7834
PO Box 529 Fax: (860)675-7302
Farmington, CT 06085
Publisher E-mail: karger@karger.ch

Medical journal. **Subtitle:** International Journal on Haemostasis and Thrombosis Research. **Founded:** 1972. **Freq:** Bimonthly. **Print Method:** Offset. **Trim Size:** 177 x 252 mm. **Cols./Page:** 1. **Col. Width:** 84 nonpareils. **Col. Depth:** 141 agate lines. **Key Personnel:** H.C. Hemker, Editor. **ISSN:** 0301-0147. **Subscription Rates:** $296 plus $25.50 post/handling. **Remarks:** Color advertising accepted; rates available upon request.
Ad Rates: BW: $1,075 **Circ:** 1,150

4858 Hormone Research
S. Karger Publishers, Inc.
26 W. Avon Rd. Phone: (860)675-7834
PO Box 529 Fax: (860)675-7302
Farmington, CT 06085
Publisher E-mail: karger@karger.ch

Scientific medical journal. **Subtitle:** International Journal of Experimental and Clinical Endocrinology. Official Organ of the European Society for Paediatric Endocrinology. **Founded:** 1970. **Freq:** 12/year. **Print Method:** Offset. **Trim Size:** 210 x 280 mm. **Cols./Page:** 1. **Col. Width:** 84 nonpareils. **Col. Depth:** 141 agate lines. **Key Personnel:** J. Girard, Editor. **ISSN:** 0301-0163. **Subscription Rates:** $592 plus $51 post/handling. **Remarks:** Color advertising accepted; rates available upon request.
Ad Rates: BW: $1,085 **Circ:** 1,000

4859 Human Development
S. Karger Publishers, Inc.
26 W. Avon Rd. Phone: (860)675-7834
PO Box 529 Fax: (860)675-7302
Farmington, CT 06085
Publisher E-mail: karger@karger.ch

Scientific medical journal. **Founded:** 1958. **Freq:** Bimonthly. **Print Method:** Offset. **Trim Size:** 177 x 252 mm. **Cols./Page:** 1. **Col. Width:** 84 nonpareils. **Col. Depth:** 141 agate lines. **Key Personnel:** D. Kuhn, Editor. **ISSN:** 0018-716X. **Subscription Rates:** $200 plus $25.50 post/handling. **Remarks:** Color advertising accepted; rates available upon request.
Ad Rates: BW: $1,095 **Circ:** 2,200

4860 Human Heredity
S. Karger Publishers, Inc.
26 W. Avon Rd. Phone: (860)675-7834
PO Box 529 Fax: (860)675-7302
Farmington, CT 06085
Publisher E-mail: karger@karger.ch

Medical journal. **Subtitle:** International Journal of Human and Medical Genetics. **Founded:** 1950. **Freq:** Bimonthly. **Print Method:** Offset. **Trim Size:** 177 x 252 mm. **Cols./Page:** 1. **Col. Width:** 84 nonpareils. **Col. Depth:** 141 agate lines. **Key Personnel:** J. Ott, Editor. **ISSN:** 0001-5652. **Subscription Rates:** $307 plus $25.50 post/handling. **Remarks:** Color advertising accepted; rates available upon request.
Ad Rates: BW: $1,085 **Circ:** 1,000

4861 Indoor and Built Environment
S. Karger Publishers, Inc.
26 W. Avon Rd. Phone: (860)675-7834
PO Box 529 Fax: (860)675-7302
Farmington, CT 06085
Publisher E-mail: karger@karger.ch

Scientific journal. **Subtitle:** The Journal of Indoor Air International. **Founded:** 1992. **Freq:** Bimonthly. **Print Method:** Offset. **Trim Size:** 210 x 280 mm. **Cols./Page:** 1. **Col. Width:** 99 nonpareils. **Key Personnel:** D.F. Weetman, Editor. **ISSN:** 1016-4901. **Subscription Rates:** $146.50; $293 Industry. **Formerly:** Indoor Environment.
Ad Rates: BW: $1,085 **Circ:** 1,000

4862 Infusionstherapie und Transfusionsmedizin
S. Karger Publishers, Inc.
26 W. Avon Rd. Phone: (860)675-7834
PO Box 529 Fax: (860)675-7302
Farmington, CT 06085
Publisher E-mail: karger@karger.ch

Scientific medical journal (German and English). **Subtitle:** Internationale Zeitschrift fur Infusions- und Haemotherapie, klinische Ernahrung und Transfusionsmedizin. **Founded:** 1974. **Freq:** Bimonthly. **Print Method:** Offset. **Trim Size:** 210 x 297 mm. **Cols./Page:** 1. **Col. Width:** 99 nonpareils. **Col. Depth:** 163 agate lines. **Key Personnel:** H. Reissigl, Editor. **Subscription Rates:** $94 plus $25.50 post/handling. **Formerly:** Infusionstherapie (1992).
Circ: 11,000

4863 International Archives of Allergy and Immunology
S. Karger Publishers, Inc.
26 W. Avon Rd. Phone: (860)675-7834
PO Box 529 Fax: (860)675-7302
Farmington, CT 06085
Publisher E-mail: karger@karger.ch

Scientific medical journal. **Founded:** 1950. **Freq:** Monthly. **Print Method:** Offset. **Trim Size:** 210 x 297. **Cols./Page:** 1. **Col. Width:** 84 nonpareils. **Col. Depth:** 141 agate lines. **Key Personnel:** G. Wick, Editor. **ISSN:** 1018-2438. **Subscription Rates:** $1,383 plus $25.50 post/handling. **Remarks:** Color advertising accepted; rates available upon request. **Formerly:** International Archives of Allergy and Applied Immunology.
Ad Rates: BW: $1,075 **Circ:** 1,400

4864 Intervirology
S. Karger Publishers, Inc.
26 W. Avon Rd. Phone: (860)675-7834
PO Box 529 Fax: (860)675-7302
Farmington, CT 06085
Publisher E-mail: karger@karger.ch

Scientific medical journal. **Subtitle:** International Journal of Basic and Medical Virology. **Freq:** Bimonthly 8/year. **Print Method:** Offset. **Cols./Page:** 1. **Col. Width:** 84 nonpareils. **Col. Depth:** 141 agate lines. **Key Personnel:** R.W. Braun, Editor. **ISSN:** 0300-5526. **Subscription Rates:** $461 plus $25.50 post/handling. **Remarks:** Color advertising accepted; rates available upon request.
Ad Rates: BW: $1,075 **Circ:** 1,200

4865 Invasion and Metastasis
S. Karger Publishers, Inc.
26 W. Avon Rd. Phone: (860)675-7834
PO Box 529 Fax: (860)675-7302
Farmington, CT 06085
Publisher E-mail: karger@karger.ch

Scientific medical journal. **Subtitle:** Multichisciplinary Contributions on Non-Malignant and Malignant Phenotypes. **Founded:** 1981. **Freq:** Bimonthly. **Print Method:** Offset. **Trim Size:** 177 x 252 mm. **Cols./Page:** 1. **Col. Width:** 84 nonpareils. **Col. Depth:** 141 agate lines. **Key Personnel:** B. Sordat, Editor. **ISSN:** 0251-1789. **Subscription Rates:** $335 plus $25.50 post/handling. **Remarks:** Color advertising accepted; rates available upon request.
Ad Rates: BW: $1,075 **Circ:** 800

4866 Journal of Personality
Blackwell Publishers
Dept. of Psychiatry Phone: (860)679-3791
University of Connecticut Health Center Fax: (860)679-1146
263 Farmington Ave.
Farmington, CT 06030
Publisher E-mail: subscript@blackwellpub.com

Psychology journal. **Founded:** 1932. **Freq:** 6/year. **Print Method:** Offset. **Trim Size:** 6 x 9. **Cols./Page:** 1. **Col. Width:** 52 nonpareils. **Col. Depth:** 86 agate lines. **Key Personnel:** Howard Tennen, Editor, tennen@ns01.uchc.edu. **ISSN:** 0022-3506. **Subscription Rates:** $84 individuals North America; $270 institutions North America; $104 individuals elsewhere; $325 institutions elsewhere. **Remarks:** Accepts advertising Call publisher for rates. **URL:** http://www.blackwellpub.com. **Alt. Formats:** Microform.
Circ: ‡2,000

4867 Journal of Vascular Research
S. Karger Publishers, Inc.
26 W. Avon Rd. Phone: (860)675-7834
PO Box 529 Fax: (860)675-7302
Farmington, CT 06085
Publisher E-mail: karger@karger.ch

Scientific medical journal. **Founded:** 1964. **Freq:** Bimonthly. **Print Method:** Offset. **Trim Size:** 215 x 280 mm. **Cols./Page:** 1. **Col. Width:** 84 nonpareils. **Col. Depth:** 141 agate lines. **Key Personnel:** M.J. Mulvany, Editor. **ISSN:** 1018-1172. **Subscription Rates:** $383 plus $25.50 post/handling. **Remarks:** Color advertising accepted; rates available upon request. **Formerly:** Blood Vessels.
Ad Rates: BW: $1,085 **Circ:** 1,000

4868 Kidney and Blood Pressure Research
S. Karger Publishers, Inc.
26 W. Avon Rd. Phone: (860)675-7834
PO Box 529 Fax: (860)675-7302
Farmington, CT 06085
Publisher E-mail: karger@karger.ch

Scientific medical journal on the interdisciplinary approach to the mechanisms and regulation of renal functions. **Subtitle:** International Journal of Experimental Renal Physiology, Pathophysiology, Biochemistry and Pharmacology. **Founded:** 1979. **Freq:** Bimonthly. **Print Method:** Offset. **Trim Size:** 177 x 252 mm. **Cols./Page:** 1. **Col. Width:** 84 nonpareils. **Col. Depth:** 140 agate lines. **Key Personnel:** G.M. Berlyne, Editor; F. Lang, Editor. **ISSN:** 1011-6524. **Subscription Rates:** $321.50 by mail. **Remarks:** Color advertising accepted; rates available upon request. **Former name:** Renal Physiology (1989); Renal Physiology and Biochemistry.
Ad Rates: BW: $1,095 **Circ:** 800

4869 Medical Principles and Practice
S. Karger Publishers, Inc.
26 W. Avon Rd. Phone: (860)675-7834
PO Box 529 Fax: (860)675-7302
Farmington, CT 06085
Publisher E-mail: karger@karger.ch

Journal on recent advances made in basic medical sciences, clinical practice, and associated disciplines. **Subtitle:** International Journal of the Kuwait University Health Science Centre. **Founded:** 1988. **Freq:** Quarterly. **Print Method:** Offset. **Trim Size:** 177 x 252 mm. **Key Personnel:** B. Al-Nakib, Editor. **ISSN:** 1011-7571. **Subscription Rates:** $194. **Remarks:** Accepts advertising.
Ad Rates: BW: $1,085 **Circ:** 1,950
4C: $1400

4870 Mineral and Electrolyte Metabolism (MEM)
S. Karger Publishers, Inc.
26 W. Avon Rd. Phone: (860)675-7834
PO Box 529 Fax: (860)675-7302
Farmington, CT 06085
Publisher E-mail: karger@karger.ch

Scientific medical journal. **Founded:** 1978. **Freq:** Bimonthly. **Print Method:** Offset. **Trim Size:** 210 x 280 mm. **Cols./Page:** 1. **Col. Width:** 99 nonpareils. **Col. Depth:** 155 agate lines. **Key Personnel:** S.G. Massry, Editor. **ISSN:** 0378-0392. **Subscription Rates:** $412 plus $25.50 post/handling. **Remarks:** Color advertising accepted; rates available upon request.
Ad Rates: BW: $1,075 **Circ:** 850

4871 Natural Immunity
S. Karger Publishers, Inc.
26 W. Avon Rd. Phone: (860)675-7834
PO Box 529 Fax: (860)675-7302
Farmington, CT 06085
Publisher E-mail: karger@karger.ch

Medical research journal on the mechanisms of natural immune effectov cells and their clinical application. **Founded:** 1981. **Freq:** Bimonthly. **Print Method:** Offset. **Trim Size:** 177 x 252 mm. **Cols./Page:** 1. **Col. Width:** 84 nonpareils. **Col. Depth:** 141 agate lines. **Key Personnel:** R.B. Heberman, Editor. **ISSN:** 1018-8916. **Subscription Rates:** $266 plus $25.50 post/handling. **Remarks:** Color advertising accepted; rates available upon request. **Formerly**: Natural Immunity and Cell Growth Regulation.
Ad Rates: BW: $1,075 **Circ:** 800

4872 Nephron
S. Karger Publishers, Inc.
26 W. Avon Rd. Phone: (860)675-7834
PO Box 529 Fax: (860)675-7302
Farmington, CT 06085
Publisher E-mail: karger@karger.ch

Medical journal. **Founded:** 1964. **Freq:** 12/year. **Print Method:** Offset. **Trim Size:** 210 x 280 mm. **Cols./Page:** 1. **Col. Width:** 99 nonpareils. **Col. Depth:** 155 agate lines. **Key Personnel:** G.M. Berlyne, Editor; S. Giovannetti, Editor. **ISSN:** 0028-2766. **Subscription Rates:** $741 plus $51 post/handling. **Remarks:** Color advertising accepted; rates available upon request.
Ad Rates: BW: $1,095 **Circ:** 3,000

4873 Neuroendocrinology
S. Karger Publishers, Inc.
26 W. Avon Rd. Phone: (860)675-7834
PO Box 529 Fax: (860)675-7302
Farmington, CT 06085
Publisher E-mail: karger@karger.ch

Medical journal. **Subtitle:** International Journal for Basic and Clinical Studies on Neuroendocrine Relationships. **Founded:** 1965. **Freq:** 12/year. **Print Method:** Offset. **Trim Size:** 210 x 280 mm. **Cols./Page:** 1. **Col. Width:** 99 nonpareils. **Col. Depth:** 155 agate lines. **Key Personnel:** C. Kordon, Editor. **ISSN:** 0028-3835. **Subscription Rates:** $1,134 plus $51 post/handling. **Remarks:** Color advertising accepted; rates available upon request.
Ad Rates: BW: $1,085 **Circ:** 1,650

4874 Neuroepidemiology
S. Karger Publishers, Inc.
26 W. Avon Rd. Phone: (860)675-7834
PO Box 529 Fax: (860)675-7302
Farmington, CT 06085
Publisher E-mail: karger@karger.ch

Expert findings on the etiology and distribution of newological diseases. **Founded:** 1982. **Freq:** Bimonthly. **Print Method:** Offset. **Trim Size:** 177 x 252 mm. **Cols./Page:** 1. **Col. Width:** 84 nonpareils. **Col. Depth:** 140 agate lines. **Key Personnel:** M. Alter, Editor. **ISSN:** 0251-5350. **Subscription Rates:** $296. **Remarks:** Accepts advertising.
Ad Rates: BW: $1,075 **Circ:** 800
4C: $1400

4875 Neuropsychobiology
S. Karger Publishers, Inc.
26 W. Avon Rd. Phone: (860)675-7834
PO Box 529 Fax: (860)675-7302
Farmington, CT 06085
Publisher E-mail: karger@karger.ch

Medical journal on the neurobiological approach to behavior and mental disorders. **Subtitle:** International Journal of Experimental and Clinical Research in Biological Psychiatry, Pharmacopsychiatry, and Biological Psychology/Pharmacopsychology. **Founded:** 1975. **Freq:** 8/year. **Print Method:** Offset. **Trim Size:** 210 x 280 mm. **Cols./Page:** 1. **Col. Width:** 99 nonpareils. **Col. Depth:** 155 agate lines. **Key Personnel:** J. Mendlewiz, Editor; B. Saelfn, Editor; P. Melter, Editor; W.M. Hermann, Editor. **ISSN:** 0302-282X. **Subscription Rates:** $516 plus $34 post/handling. **Remarks:** Color advertising accepted; rates available upon request.
Ad Rates: BW: $1,085 **Circ:** 1,000

4876 Oncology
S. Karger Publishers, Inc.
26 W. Avon Rd. Phone: (860)675-7834
PO Box 529 Fax: (860)675-7302
Farmington, CT 06085
Publisher E-mail: karger@karger.ch

Medical journal presenting experimental and clinical findings. **Subtitle:** International Journal of Cancer Research and Treatment. **Founded:** 1948. **Freq:** Bimonthly. **Print Method:** Offset. **Trim Size:** 210 x 280 mm. **Cols./Page:** 1. **Col. Width:** 99 nonpareils. **Col. Depth:** 155 agate lines. **Key Personnel:** P.P. Carbone, Editor; S. Eckhardt, Advertising Mgr.; K. Munk, Editor; G.P. Murphy, Editor; H. Sugano, Advertising Mgr.; H. Wrba, Editor. **ISSN:** 0030-2414. **Subscription Rates:** $567. **Remarks:** Accepts advertising.
Ad Rates: BW: $1,075 **Circ:** 1,250
4C: $1400

4877 Onkologie
S. Karger Publishers, Inc.
26 W. Avon Rd. Phone: (860)675-7834
PO Box 529 Fax: (860)675-7302
Farmington, CT 06085
Publisher E-mail: karger@karger.ch

Medical journal (English). **Subtitle:** Zeischrift fur Krebsforschung und-behandlung. **Founded:** 1979. **Freq:** Bimonthly. **Print Method:** Offset. **Trim Size:** 210 x 297 mm. **Cols./Page:** 1. **Col. Width:** 99 nonpareils. **Col. Depth:** 164 agate lines. **Key Personnel:** W. Queisser, Editor; H. Huber, Editor. **ISSN:** 0378-584X. **Subscription Rates:** $94. **Remarks:** Advertising accepted; rates available upon request.
Circ: 11,000

4878 Ophthalmic Research
S. Karger Publishers, Inc.
26 W. Avon Rd. Phone: (860)675-7834
PO Box 529 Fax: (860)675-7302
Farmington, CT 06085
Publisher E-mail: karger@karger.ch

Research journal. **Subtitle:** Journal for Research in Experimental and Clinical Ophthalmology. **Founded:** 1970. **Freq:** Bimonthly. **Print Method:** Offset. **Trim Size:** 177 x 252 mm. **Cols./Page:** 1. **Col. Width:** 84 nonpareils. **Col. Depth:** 140 agate lines. **Key Personnel:** G.F.J.M. Vrensen, Editor. **ISSN:** 0030-3747. **Subscription Rates:** $383 plus $24 post/handling. **Remarks:** Color advertising accepted; rates available upon request.
Ad Rates: BW: $1,075 **Circ:** 850

4879 Ophthalmologica
S. Karger Publishers, Inc.
26 W. Avon Rd. Phone: (860)675-7834
PO Box 529 Fax: (860)675-7302
Farmington, CT 06085
Publisher E-mail: karger@karger.ch

Medical research journal (English, French, and German). **Subtitle:** International Journal of Ophthalmology. Organ of the Netherlands Ophthalmological Society. **Founded:** 1899. **Freq:** Bimonthly 8/year. **Print Method:** Offset. **Trim Size:** 210 x280. **Cols./Page:** 1. **Col. Width:** 84 nonpareils. **Col. Depth:** 140 agate lines. **Key Personnel:** Ch. Ohrloff, Editor. **ISSN:** 0030-3755. **Subscription Rates:** $461 plus $25.50 post/handling. **Remarks:** Color advertising accepted; rates available upon request.
Ad Rates: BW: $1,075 **Circ:** 1,250

4880 ORL
S. Karger Publishers, Inc.
26 W. Avon Rd. Phone: (860)675-7834
PO Box 529 Fax: (860)675-7302
Farmington, CT 06085
Publisher E-mail: karger@karger.ch

Medical journal. **Subtitle:** Journal for Oto-Rhino-Laryngology and Its Related Specialties. **Founded:** 1938. **Freq:** Bimonthly. **Print Method:** Offset. **Trim Size:** 210 x 280 mm. **Cols./Page:** 1. **Col. Width:** 84 nonpareils. **Col. Depth:** 140 agate lines. **Key Personnel:** W. Arnold, Editor. **ISSN:** 0301-1569. **Subscription Rates:** $408.5. **Remarks:** Accepts advertising.
Ad Rates: BW: $1,075 **Circ:** 850
4C: $1400

4881 Oto-Rhino-Laryngologia Nova
S. Karger Publishers, Inc.
26 W. Avon Rd. Phone: (860)675-7834
PO Box 529 Fax: (860)675-7302
Farmington, CT 06085
Publisher E-mail: karger@karger.ch

Medical journal. **Subtitle:** Europaishe Zeitschrift fur Praxis, Klinik, Forschung. **Founded:** 1991. **Freq:** Bimonthly. **Print Method:** Offset. **Trim Size:** 210 x 297 mm. **Cols./Page:** 1. **Col. Width:** 99 nonpareils. **Key Personnel:** W. Arnold, Editor; J.J. Manni, Editor; R.R. Probst, Editor. **ISSN:** 1014-8221. **Subscription Rates:** $346 plus $25.50 post/handling.
Ad Rates: BW: $1,075 **Circ:** ‡1,500

4882 Pathobiology
S. Karger Publishers, Inc.
26 W. Avon Rd. Phone: (860)675-7834
PO Box 529 Fax: (860)675-7302
Farmington, CT 06085
Publisher E-mail: karger@karger.ch

Scientific medical journal. **Subtitle:** Journal of Immune Pathology, Molecular and Cellular Biology. **Founded:** 1938. **Freq:** Bimonthly. **Print Method:** Offset. **Trim Size:** 210 x 280 mm. **Cols./Page:** 1. **Col. Width:** 84 nonpareils. **Col. Depth:** 141 agate lines. **Key Personnel:** J.M. Cruse, Editor-in-Chief. **ISSN:** 1015-2008. **Subscription Rates:** $489 plus $25.50 post/handling. **Remarks:** Color advertising accepted; rates available upon request. **Absorbed**: Pathology and Immunopathology Research. **Formerly**: Experimental Cell Biology (1990).
Ad Rates: BW: $1,085 **Circ:** 1,050

4883 Pediatric Neurosurgery
S. Karger Publishers, Inc.
26 W. Avon Rd. Phone: (860)675-7834
PO Box 529 Fax: (860)675-7302
Farmington, CT 06085
Publisher E-mail: karger@karger.ch

Medical journal. **Subtitle:** Official Organ of the American Society of Pediatric Neurosurgery. **Founded:** 1975. **Freq:** Bimonthly. **Print Method:** Offset. **Trim Size:** 210 x 280 mm. **Cols./Page:** 1. **Col. Width:** 99 nonpareils. **Col. Depth:** 155 agate lines. **Key Personnel:** F.J. Epstein, Editor. **ISSN:** 1016-2291. **Subscription Rates:** $284 plus $24 (postage & handling). **Remarks:** Accepts advertising. **Formerly**: Pediatric Neuroscience (1990).
Ad Rates: BW: $1,075 **Circ:** 1,150

4884 Pharmacology
S. Karger Publishers, Inc.
26 W. Avon Rd. Phone: (860)675-7834
PO Box 529 Fax: (860)675-7302
Farmington, CT 06085
Publisher E-mail: karger@karger.ch

Scientific journal. **Subtitle:** International Journal of Experimental and Clinical Pharmacology. **Founded:** 1959. **Freq:** 12/year. **Print Method:** Offset. **Trim Size:** 177 x 252 mm. **Cols./Page:** 1. **Col. Width:** 84 nonpareils. **Col. Depth:** 140 agate lines. **Key Personnel:** K. W. Sewing, Editor; E.S. Vesell, Editor; R. Kato, Editor. **ISSN:** 0031-7012. **Subscription Rates:** $701. **Remarks:** Accepts advertising. **Formerly**: Medicina Experimentis.
Ad Rates: BW: $1,075 **Circ:** 1,075
4C: $1400

4885 Phonetica
S. Karger Publishers, Inc.
26 W. Avon Rd. Phone: (860)675-7834
PO Box 529 Fax: (860)675-7302
Farmington, CT 06085
Publisher E-mail: karger@karger.ch

Scientific medical journal focussing on spoken language research. **Subtitle:** International Journal of Speech Science. **Founded:** 1957. **Freq:** Quarterly. **Print Method:** Offset. **Trim Size:** 177 x 252 mm. **Cols./Page:** 1. **Col. Width:** 84 nonpareils. **Col. Depth:** 140 agate lines. **Key Personnel:** K. Kohler, Editor. **ISSN:** 0031-8388. **Subscription Rates:** $245. **Remarks:** Accepts advertising.
Ad Rates: BW: $1,075 **Circ:** 1,150
4C: $1,400

4886 Psychopathology
S. Karger Publishers, Inc.
26 W. Avon Rd. Phone: (860)675-7834
PO Box 529 Fax: (860)675-7302
Farmington, CT 06085
Publisher E-mail: karger@karger.ch

Medical journal. **Subtitle:** International Journal of Descriptive Psychopathology, Phenomenology and Clinical Diagnostics. **Founded:** 1968. **Freq:** Bimonthly. **Print Method:** Offset. **Trim Size:** 177 x 252 mm. **Cols./Page:** 1. **Col. Width:** 84 nonpareils. **Col. Depth:** 140 agate lines. **Key Personnel:** P. Berner, Editor; E. Gabriel, Editor. **ISSN:** 0254-4962. **Subscription Rates:** $266 plus $25.50 post/handling. **Remarks:** Color advertising accepted; rates available upon request.
Ad Rates: BW: $1,075 **Circ:** 800

4887 Psychotherapy and Psychosomatics
S. Karger Publishers, Inc.
26 W. Avon Rd. Phone: (860)675-7834
PO Box 529 Fax: (860)675-7302
Farmington, CT 06085
Publisher E-mail: karger@karger.ch

Medical journal. **Founded:** 1953. **Freq:** 8/year. **Print Method:** Offset. **Trim Size:** 177 x 252 mm. **Cols./Page:** 1. **Col. Width:** 84 nonpareils. **Col. Depth:** 140 agate lines. **Key Personnel:** G. Fava, Editor. **ISSN:** 0033-3190. **Subscription Rates:** $380 plus $34 post/handling. **Remarks:** Color advertising accepted; rates available upon request.
Ad Rates: BW: $1,085 **Circ:** 1,000

4888 Respiration
S. Karger Publishers, Inc.
26 W. Avon Rd. Phone: (860)675-7834
PO Box 529 Fax: (860)675-7302
Farmington, CT 06085
Publisher E-mail: karger@karger.ch

Medical journal (English, French, German). **Subtitle:** International Review of Thoracic Diseases. **Founded:** 1944. **Freq:** Bimonthly. **Print Method:** Offset. **Trim Size:** 210 x 280 mm. **Cols./Page:** 1. **Col. Width:** 84 nonpareils. **Col. Depth:** 140 agate lines. **Key Personnel:** H. Herzog, Editor. **ISSN:** 0025-7931. **Subscription Rates:** $394 plus $25.50 post/handling. **Remarks:** Color advertising accepted; rates available upon request.
Ad Rates: BW: $1,075 **Circ:** 1,200

4889 Skin Pharmacology
S. Karger Publishers, Inc.
26 W. Avon Rd. Phone: (860)675-7834
PO Box 529 Fax: (860)675-7302
Farmington, CT 06085
Publisher E-mail: karger@karger.ch

Journal of pharmacological and biophysical research. **Subtitle:** The Official Journal of the Skin Pharmacology Society (SPS) and the International Society for Bioengineering and the Skin (ISBS). **Founded:** 1987. **Freq:** Quarterly. **Print Method:** Offset. **Trim Size:** 177 x 252 mm. **Key Personnel:** H. F. Merk, Editor. **ISSN:** 1011-0283. **Subscription Rates:** $187. **Remarks:** Accepts advertising.
Ad Rates: BW: $1,085 **Circ:** 1,000

4890 Stereotactic and Functional Neurosurgery
S. Karger Publishers, Inc.
26 W. Avon Rd. Phone: (860)675-7834
PO Box 529 Fax: (860)675-7302
Farmington, CT 06085
Publisher E-mail: karger@karger.ch

Scientific medical journal. **Subtitle:** Official Journal of the World and American Society for Stereotactic and Functional Neurosurgery. **Founded:** 1938. **Freq:** 8/year. **Print Method:** Offset. **Trim Size:** 177 x 252 mm. **Cols./Page:** 1. **Col. Width:** 84 nonpareils. **Col. Depth:** 141 agate lines. **Key Personnel:** P.L. Gildenberg, Editor. **ISSN:** 1011-6125. **Subscription Rates:** $320 plus $34 post/handling. **Remarks:** Color advertising accepted; rates available upon request.
Ad Rates: BW: $1,085 **Circ:** 1,085

4891 Tumor Biology
S. Karger Publishers, Inc.
26 W. Avon Rd. Phone: (860)675-7834
PO Box 529 Fax: (860)675-7302
Farmington, CT 06085
Publisher E-mail: karger@karger.ch

Journal on the basic biology of tumor markers–the crucial indicators of the the onset of cancer. **Subtitle:** The Journal of the International Society for Oncodevelopmental Biology and Medicine. **Founded:** 1980. **Freq:** Bimonthly. **Print Method:** Offset. **Trim Size:** 177 x 252 mm. **Key Personnel:** A.M. Neville, Editor. **ISSN:** 1010-4283. **Subscription Rates:** $335 plus $25.50 post/handling. **Remarks:** Accepts advertising.
Ad Rates: BW: $1,085 **Circ:** 1,000
4C: $350

4892 Urologia Internationalis
S. Karger Publishers, Inc.
26 W. Avon Rd. Phone: (860)675-7834
PO Box 529 Fax: (860)675-7302
Farmington, CT 06085
Publisher E-mail: karger@karger.ch

Medical practice-oriented research journal. **Founded:** 1955. **Freq:** 8/year. **Print Method:** Offset. **Trim Size:** 210 x 280 mm. **Cols./Page:** 1. **Col. Width:** 99 nonpareils. **Col. Depth:** 155 agate lines. **Key Personnel:** D. Hauri, Editor. **ISSN:** 0042-1138. **Subscription Rates:** $684. **Remarks:** Accepts advertising.
Ad Rates: BW: $1,085 **Circ:** 1,085
4C: $1400

4893 Verhaltenstherapie
S. Karger Publishers, Inc.
26 W. Avon Rd. Phone: (860)675-7834
PO Box 529 Fax: (860)675-7302
Farmington, CT 06085
Publisher E-mail: karger@karger.ch

Medical journal. **Subtitle:** Praxis, Forschung, Perspektiven. **Founded:** 1991. **Freq:** Quarterly. **Print Method:** Offset. **Trim Size:** 210 x 297 mm. **Cols./Page:** 1. **Col. Width:** 99 nonpareils. **Key Personnel:** I. Hand, Editor; H.U. Wittchen, Editor. **ISSN:** 1016-6262. **Subscription Rates:** $78 plus $17 post/handling. **Remarks:** Advertising accepted; rates available upon request.
Circ: ‡5,000

4894 Vox Sanguinis
S. Karger Publishers, Inc.
26 W. Avon Rd. Phone: (860)675-7834
PO Box 529 Fax: (860)675-7302
Farmington, CT 06085
Publisher E-mail: karger@karger.ch

Medical research journal. **Subtitle:** International Journal of Transfusion Medicine. Official Journal of the International Society of Blood Transfusion. **Founded:** 1956. **Freq:** 8/year. **Print Method:** Offset. **Trim Size:** 210 x 280 mm. **Cols./Page:** 1. **Col. Width:** 99 nonpareils. **Col. Depth:** 155 agate lines. **Key Personnel:** C.P. Engelfriet, Editor. **ISSN:** 0042-9007. **Subscription Rates:** $360. **Remarks:** Color advertising accepted; rates available upon request.
Ad Rates: BW: $1,095 **Circ:** 2,900

4895 WRCH-AM - 910
10 Executive Dr. Phone: (203)677-6700
Farmington, CT 06032 Fax: (203)678-7053

Format: News. **Networks:** Satellite Music Network; CNN Radio. **Founded:** 1949. **Formerly:** WRCQ-FM (1989); WNEZ-AM. **Operating Hours:** Continuous. **Key Personnel:** Enzo DeDominicis, President; Ronald Roy, Contact; Bill Buller, General Sales Mgr. **Wattage:** 5000. **Ad Rates:** $30-190 per unit. Combined advertising rates available with WRCH-FM:.

4896 WRCH-FM - 100.5
10 Executive Dr. Phone: (203)677-6700
Farmington, CT 06032-2841 Fax: (203)678-7053
E-mail: wrch1005@aol.com

Format: Adult Contemporary. **Networks:** Independent. **Founded:** 1968. **Operating Hours:** Continuous. **ADI:** Hartford-New Haven (New London), CT. **Key Personnel:** Suzanne McDonald, Market Mgr.; Chet Osadchey, Sales Mgr.; Jodi Long, General Mgr.; Allan Camp, Program Dir. **Wattage:** 50,000. **Ad Rates:** $50-500 per unit.

4897 WZMX-FM - 93.7
10 Executive Dr. Phone: (203)677-6700
Farmington, CT 06032-2837 Fax: (203)677-6799
E-mail: goods10@aol.com

Format: Adult Contemporary. **Founded:** 1939. **Formerly:** WLVH-FM (1992). **Operating Hours:** Continuous. **Key Personnel:** Suzanne Mcdonald, General Mgr.; Jodi Long, Sales Mgr. **Wattage:** 50,000.

GLASTONBURY, pop. 24,327.

N. Ct. Hartford Co. 10 mi. SE of Hartford. Manufactures machine tools, tubing. Nursery; hatchery. Poultry, tobacco, vegetable, fruit farms.

4898 The Glastonbury Citizen
The Glastonbury Citizen, Inc.
PO Box 373 Phone: (860)633-4691
87 Nutmeg Ln. Fax: (860)657-3258
Glastonbury, CT 06033
Publisher E-mail: newsbull@aol.com

Community newspaper (tabloid). **Founded:** 1948. **Freq:** Weekly (Thurs.). **Print Method:** Offset. **Trim Size:** 11 x 17. **Cols./Page:** 4 and 8. **Col. Width:** 2 1/4 and 1 3/16 inches. **Col. Depth:** 15 1/2 and 15 1/2 inches. **Key Personnel:** James Hallas, Publisher; Carole Saucier, Advertising Mgr.; Kathleen Stack, Editor; John Ultee, General Mgr. **Subscription Rates:** $20 individuals; $24 out of state. **Remarks:** Accepts advertising.
Ad Rates: GLR: $7 **Circ:** Combined ‡9,200
BW: $1,120
PCI: $10

4899 Rivereast News Bulletin
The Glastonbury Citizen, Inc.
PO Box 373 Phone: (860)633-4691
87 Nutmeg Ln. Fax: (860)657-3258
Glastonbury, CT 06033
Publisher E-mail: newsbull@aol.com

Community newspaper. **Founded:** 1982. **Freq:** Weekly. **Print Method:** Offset. **Trim Size:** 8 1/2 x 11. **Cols./Page:** 4 and 8. **Col. Width:** 2 1/2 and 1 3/16 inches. **Col. Depth:** 15 1/2 and 15 1/2 inches. **Key Personnel:** Jim Hallas, Editor and Publisher; Denise Dyment, Advertising Mgr. **Subscription Rates:** Free. **Remarks:** Accepts advertising.
Ad Rates: GLR: $.60 **Circ:** Free 24,000
BW: $770
PCI: $7

GREENS FARMS

4900 Extra Equity for Homebuyers
216 Greens Farms Sta. Phone: (203)254-1690
Greens Farms, CT 06436 Fax: (203)255-3707

Magazine for people who are about to move to a new home. **Founded:** Oct. 1983. **Freq:** 3/year. **Print Method:** Offset. **Trim Size:** 8 3/8 x 10 3/4. **Cols./Page:** 3. **Key Personnel:** William A. O'Brien, Publisher; Bob Griswold, Advertising Dir. **Remarks:** Accepts advertising.
Ad Rates: 4C: $13,072 **Circ:** Controlled 234,000

GREENWICH, pop. 59,578.

SW CT. Fairfield Co. 29 mi. NE of New York. Several private schools. Manufactures vacuum cleaners. Printing and publishing houses; engineering research.

4901 American Journal of Geriatric Cardiology
LeJacq Communications, Inc.
777 W. Putnam Ave. Phone: (203)531-0450
Greenwich, CT 06830-5014 Fax: (203)531-0533

Professional journal covering geriatric cardiology. **Founded:** 1991. **Freq:** Bimonthly. **Print Method:** Offset. **Trim Size:** 7 7/8 x 10 3/4. **Key Personnel:** Nancy Sharp, Managing Editor, fax (203)531-1713, managingeditor@lejacq.com; Sarah Howell, Corp. Publishing Dir., showell@lejacq.com; Jo-Ann Kalaka, Group Publisher, jkalaka@aol.com. **ISSN:** 1076-7460. **Subscription Rates:** $60 individuals; $12 single issue. **Remarks:** Accepts advertising.
Ad Rates: BW: $2,200 **Circ:** Controlled 20,000
4C: $3,295

4902 Cardiovascular Reviews & Reports
Cardiovascular Reviews & Reports, Inc.
777 W. Putnam Ave. Phone: (203)531-0450
Greenwich, CT 06830-5014 Fax: (203)531-0533

Journal. **Founded:** 1980. **Freq:** Monthly. **Print Method:** Offset. **Trim Size:** 7 7/8 x 10 3/4. **Cols./Page:** 2. **Col. Width:** 42 nonpareils. **Col. Depth:** 140 agate lines. **Key Personnel:** Louis F. LeJacq, Founder; JoAnn Kalaka, Publisher, jkalaka@aol.com; Nancy Sharp, Managing Editor, managingeditor@lejacq.com; Sarah Howell, Publishing Dir., showell@lejacq.com. **ISSN:** 0197-3118. **Subscription Rates:** $90 individuals; $105 institutions; $14 single issue.
Ad Rates: BW: $3,825 **Circ:** Controlled ‡81,107
4C: $5,000

4903 Congestive Heart Failure
LeJacq Communications, Inc.
777 W. Putnam Ave. Phone: (203)531-0450
Greenwich, CT 06830-5014 Fax: (203)531-0533
Publication E-mail: managingeditor@lejacq.com

Medical journal covering cardiology. **Founded:** 1994. **Freq:** Bimonthly. **Print Method:** Offset. **Trim Size:** 7 7/8 x 10 3/4. **Key Personnel:** Nancy Sharp, Managing Editor; Sarah Howell, Corp. Publishing Dir., showell@lejacq.com. **ISSN:** 1079-7998. **Subscription Rates:** $90 individuals; $14 single issue; $105 institutions, other countries. **Remarks:** Accepts advertising.
Ad Rates: BW: $2,960 **Circ:** Controlled ‡20,000
4C: $4,195

4904 Consultant
Cliggott Publishing Co.
55 Holly Hill Ln. Phone: (203)661-0600
PO Box 4010 Fax: (203)661-8163
Greenwich, CT 06831-0010
Medical journal for primary care, office-based physicians. **Subtitle:** Consultations in Primary Care. **Founded:** 1961. **Freq:** 12/year. **Print Method:** Offset. **Trim Size:** 7 3/4 x 10 5/8. **Cols./Page:** 3. **Col. Width:** 27 nonpareils. **Col. Depth:** 98 agate lines. **Key Personnel:** Jonathan L. Bigelow, Chief Operating Mgr.; Susan K. Lotstein, Editor; David S. March, Associate Publisher; Stephen K. Muruta, Editorial Director; Sarah Williams, Ph.D., Managing Editor; Frank T. Iorio, Group Publisher. **ISSN:** 0010-7069. **Subscription Rates:** $90 individuals; $105 other countries.
Ad Rates: BW: $5,520 **Circ:** Non-paid ‡154,900
4C: $7,960

4905 Flying
Hachette Filipacchi Magazines, Inc.
500 West Putnam Ave. Phone: (203)622-2700
Greenwich, CT 06830 Fax: (203)622-2725

General aviation magazine. **Founded:** 1927. **Freq:** Monthly. **Print Method:** Offset. **Trim Size:** 7 7/8 x 10 1/2. **Cols./Page:** 3. **Col. Width:** 27 nonpareils. **Col. Depth:** 140 agate lines. **Key Personnel:** J. Mac McClellan, Editor-In-Chief; Richard Koenig, Publisher; Wayne Lincourt. **Subscription Rates:** $26; $3.95 single issue. **Remarks:** Accepts advertising. **Online:** America Online, Inc.
Ad Rates: GLR: $32 **Circ:** Paid 311,671
BW: $14,915
4C: $22,385

4906 Global Custodian
Asset International, Inc.
125 Greenwich Ave. Phone: (203)629-5014
Greenwich, CT 06830 Fax: (203)629-5024
Publication E-mail: assetpub.com
Publisher E-mail: info@assetpub.com

Business journal for global investment and operations professionals. **Founded:** Sept. 1989. **Freq:** Quarterly. **Key Personnel:** Fergus Reid, Managing Editor, freid@assetpub.com. **Subscription Rates:** $100 individuals; $25 single issue. **Remarks:** Accepts advertising.
Circ: (Not Reported)

4907 Greenwich Time
20 E. Elm St. Phone: (203)625-4400
Greenwich, CT 06830-6529 Fax: (203)625-4419

General newspaper. **Founded:** 1877. **Freq:** Mon.-Sat. (eve.). **Print Method:** Offset. **Cols./Page:** 6. **Col. Width:** 2 1/16 inches. **Col. Depth:** 21 1/2 inches. **Key Personnel:** Kenneth H. Brief, Editor; William J. Rowe, Publisher; Joseph Pisani, Managing Editor; Michael R. Perry, Advertising Dir.; Jack A. Findley, Market, Vice President. **Subscription Rates:** $140.40 individuals.
Ad Rates: BW: $4,663.03 **Circ:** Mon.-Fri. ★**12,851**
4C: $5,088.03 Sat. ★**11,846**
PCI: $38.05 Sun. ★**14,095**

4908 Heart Failure
LeJacq Communications, Inc.
777 W Putnam Ave. Phone: (203)531-0450
Greenwich, CT 06830-5014 Fax: (203)531-0533
Publication E-mail: managingeditor@lejacq.com

Medical journal covering cardiology. **Founded:** 1984. **Freq:** Bimonthly. **Print Method:** Offset. **Key Personnel:** Nancy Sharp, Managing Editor, fax (203)531-1713, managingeditor@lejacq.com; Sarah Howell, Corporate Publishing Dir., showell@lejacq.com. **ISSN:** 8755-7673. **Subscription Rates:** $90 individuals; $14 single issue; $105 institutions. **Remarks:** Advertising not accepted.
Circ: (Not Reported)

4909 The Journal of Critical Illness
Cliggott Publishing Co.
55 Holly Hill Ln. Phone: (203)661-0600
PO Box 4010 Fax: (203)661-8163
Greenwich, CT 06831-0010
Professional journal presenting practical and authoritative information on the diagnosis and management of clinical problems in patients who have, are at risk for, are recovering from serious illness. **Subtitle:** Practical Inpatient and Outpatient Care. **Founded:** Jan. 1986. **Freq:** Monthly. **Print Method:** Offset. **Trim Size:** 7 3/4 x 10 3/4. **Cols./Page:** 3. **Col. Width:** 2 1/8 inches. **Col. Depth:** 10 inches. **Key Personnel:** Susan K. Lotstein, Editor; Maria Conforti, Advertising Coord.; Frank T. Iorio, Group Publisher; Ana Santiso Conlan, Publisher; Jonathan L. Bigelow, Chief Operating Officer; Stephen K. Lotstein, Editor; Sarah Williams, Ph.D., Managing Editor. **ISSN:** 1040-0257. **Subscription Rates:** $80 individuals; $95 other countries; $7 single issue. **Remarks:** Advertising accepted; rates available upon request.
Circ: Controlled ‡87,000

4910 The Journal of Musculoskeletal Medicine
Cliggott Publishing Co.
55 Holly Hill Ln. Phone: (203)661-0600
PO Box 4010 Fax: (203)661-8163
Greenwich, CT 06831-0010
Professional journal combining practical and authoritative information on diagnosis and management of a wide variety of common musculoskeletal disorders. **Founded:** Oct. 1983. **Freq:** Monthly. **Print Method:** Offset. **Trim Size:** 7 3/4 x 10 5/8. **Cols./Page:** 3. **Col. Width:** 2 1/8 inches. **Col. Depth:** 10 inches. **Key Personnel:** Leo Cristofar, Editor; Kenneth D. Watkins, Publisher; Diane Carpenteri, Advertising Sales Rep. **ISSN:** 0899-2517. **Subscription Rates:** $70 individuals; $90 other countries.
Ad Rates: BW: $3,680 **Circ:** Non-paid ‡91,789
4C: $5,055

4911 The Journal of Respiratory Diseases
Cliggott Publishing Co.
55 Holly Hill Ln. Phone: (203)661-0600
PO Box 4010 Fax: (203)661-8163
Greenwich, CT 06831-0010
Journal providing practical information about diagnosis and treatment pertaining to the respiratory system, both as the site of primary disease and as a complication of other clinical problems. **Founded:** 1979. **Freq:** Monthly. **Print Method:** Web offset. **Trim Size:** 7 3/4 x 10 3/4. **Cols./Page:** 3. **Col. Width:** 2 1/8 inches. **Col. Depth:** 8 5/8 inches. **Key Personnel:** Craig Borders, Editor; Molly K. Sawyer, Publisher; Andrea Perchak, Advertising Coordinator. **ISSN:** 0194-259X. **Subscription Rates:** $80 individuals; $7 single issue. **Remarks:** Advertising accepted; rates available upon request.
Circ: 86,998
Non-paid 86,000

4912 Plan Sponsor
Asset International, Inc.
125 Greenwich Ave. Phone: (203)629-5014
Greenwich, CT 06830 Fax: (203)629-5024
Publisher E-mail: info@assetpub.com

Trade magazine for pension fund and endowment executives. **Subtitle:** Insight on Plan Design & Investment Strategy. **Founded:** 1993. **Freq:** Monthly. **Print Method:** Web offset. **Trim Size:** 8 1/4 x 10 7/8. **Key Personnel:** Eric Laursen, Managing Editor; Mark Lee, Publisher. **Subscription Rates:** $150 individuals; Free to qualified subscribers. **Remarks:** Accepts advertising.
Ad Rates: BW: $8,610 **Circ:** Non-paid 35,000
4C: $11,655

4913 Yachting Magazine
Times Mirror Magazines, Inc.
20 E. Elm St. Phone: (203)625-4480
Greenwich, CT 06830 Fax: (203)625-4481
Publication E-mail: editor@yachtingnet.com

Yachting magazine for affluent, experienced sail and power yachtsmen. **Subtitle:** The Best of Today's Boats & Gear. **Founded:** 1907. **Freq:** Monthly. **Print Method:** Offset. **Trim Size:** 8 x 10 3/4. **Cols./Page:** 3 and 2. **Col. Width:** 24 and 27 nonpareils. **Col. Depth:** 132 agate lines. **Key Personnel:** Charles Barthold, Editor-in-Chief, cbarthold@yachtingnet.com; Peter Bechenbach, Publisher, phone (212)779-5085, fax (212)725-1035, pbechenbach@yachtingnet.com. **Subscription Rates:** $19.98 individuals; $3 single issue. **Remarks:** Accepts advertising. **URL:** http://www.yachtingnet.com.
Ad Rates: GLR: $18.95 **Circ:** Paid ★**135,207**
BW: $8,600
4C: $12,635

4914 Columbia International Inc.
PO Box 4624 Phone: (203)661-1509
9 Greenwich Office Park Fax: (203)661-7651
Greenwich, CT 06830

Founded: 1984. **Key Personnel:** Robert Rosencrans, President. **Cities Served:** Various communities in Michigan, Nevada, Oregon, Virginia, and Washington.: subscribing households 215,000; 40 channels; 2 community access channels; 20 hours per week community access programming.

4915 Paradigm Communications Inc.
300 Stanwich Rd. Phone: (203)622-1888
Greenwich, CT 06830-5317 Fax: (203)622-1887

Owner: Diversified Media Investors, at above address. **Founded:** 1979. **Key Personnel:** James Kingsdale, President. **Cities Served:** Anderson County, Greenville County, Pickens County, and West Pelzer, SC; Fentress County, Morgan County, Scott County, South Pittsburg, and Wartburg, TN.

4916 WGCH-AM - 1490
1490 Dayton Ave. Phone: (203)869-1490
Greenwich, CT 06830-1490 Fax: (203)869-3636

Format: News; Talk. **Simulcasts:** WVIP-AM. **Networks:** NBC. **Owner:** Greenwich Broadcasting Corp., at above address. **Founded:** 1964. **Operating Hours:** Continuous; 67% local, 33% network. **ADI:** New York, NY. **Key Personnel:** Peter Bernard, Assoc. Editor; John Connelly, Sports Dir.; William Hoover, Vice President; Jonathan Becker, General Sales Mgr. & President. **Local Programs:** *What's Cookin* 10:00 am - 12:00 noon Wednesday, Bob Small; *Morning Magazine* 10:00 - 12:00 noon Mon., Tues., Thurs., Fri., Nellie O'Brien, Mailing contact. **Wattage:** 1000. **Ad Rates:** $50-85 per unit. **URL:** http://www.wgcham.com.

GUILFORD, pop. 17,375.

S. CT. New Haven Co. On Long Island Sound, 15 mi. E. of New Haven. Summer resort. Manufactures ferrous and non-ferrous metals, tracing and reproduction cloths, honing stones, boats. Oysters, lobster fisheries. Agriculture. Roses, poultry, apples.

4917 Constructioneer
HES, Inc.
26 Long Hill Rd. Phone: (203)453-3717
PO Box 362 Fax: (203)453-4390
Guilford, CT 06437-0362
Free: (800)972-2001

Construction industry magazine covering New York, New Jersey, Pennsylvania, and Delaware. **Founded:** 1945. **Freq:** Semimonthly. **Print Method:** Offset. **Trim Size:** 8 1/2 x 10 7/8. **Cols./Page:** 3. **Col. Width:** 26 nonpareils. **Col. Depth:** 140 agate lines. **Key Personnel:** Sally Bahner, Managing Editor; Herbert E. Swartz, Publisher. **Subscription Rates:** Free to qualified subscribers; $50 individuals. **Remarks:** Accepts advertising.
Ad Rates: BW: $1,250 **Circ:** Paid 17
Non-paid 13,274

4918 New England Construction
HES, Inc.
26 Long Hill Rd. Phone: (203)453-3717
PO Box 362 Fax: (203)453-4390
Guilford, CT 06437-0362
Free: (800)972-2001

Trade magazine covering construction activities throughout the six New England states. **Founded:** 1946. **Freq:** Semimonthly. **Print Method:** Offset. **Trim Size:** 8 1/8 x 10 7/8. **Cols./Page:** 3. **Col. Width:** 13.5 picas. **Col. Depth:** 10 inches. **Key Personnel:** Sally Bahner, Managing Editor; Herbert Swartz, Publisher. **Subscription Rates:** Free to qualified subscribers; $50 others. **Remarks:** Accepts advertising.
Ad Rates: BW: $725 **Circ:** Paid 29
Non-paid 10,750

4919 Wire Journal International
Wire Association International, Inc.
1570 Boston Post Rd. Phone: (203)453-2777
Guilford, CT 06437 Fax: (203)453-8384

Wire and cable manufacturing and fabricators magazine. **Founded:** 1968. **Freq:** Monthly. **Print Method:** Offset. **Trim Size:** 8 1/8 x 10 7/8. **Cols./Page:** 3. **Col. Width:** 26 nonpareils. **Col. Depth:** 140 agate lines. **Key Personnel:** Paul Casteran, Publisher, pcasteran@wirenet.org; Anita Oliva, Dir., Publications, aoliva@wirenet.org; Mark Marselli, Editor, mmarselli@wirenet.org. **ISSN:** 0277-4275. **Subscription Rates:** $85 individuals. **Remarks:** Accepts advertising. **URL:** http://www.wirenet.org.
Ad Rates: PCI: $140 **Circ:** Controlled ‡14,097

HAMDEN, pop. 51,071.

S. CT. New Haven Co. 5 mi. N. of New Haven. Manufactures industrial machinery, precision tools, machine tools, paper products, communication equipment, cutlery, screw machine products, sewing machine parts, wood products, ceramics, automatic pistols, metal store fronts, structural steel fabricators, plastics, power transmission equipment, precision aircraft parts. Steel rolling mill.

4920 Connecticut Traveler
Connecticut Motor Club AAA
2276 Whitney Ave. Phone: (203)288-7441
Hamden, CT 06518-3505 Fax: (203)230-0182

Published for members of the Connecticut Motor Club-AAA who reside in some of Connecticut's most affluent areas. Editorial focuses on travel, with features ranging from regional daytrips to international destinations. Other regualr columns cover insurance, car care, traffic safety, local events and exclusive member savings. **Founded:** Dec. 1983. **Freq:** 12/year. **Print Method:** Offset. **Trim Size:** 11 1/2 x 14 1/2. **Cols./Page:** 4. **Col. Width:** 28 nonpareils. **Col. Depth:** 180 agate lines. **Key Personnel:** Annette Cormany, Director. **ISSN:** 0746-8636. **Subscription Rates:** $2.40 Included in membership. **Remarks:** Accepts advertising.
Ad Rates: BW: $4,590 **Circ:** 205,000

Rhode Island Beverage Journal - See Providence, Rhode Island

4921 WELI-AM - 960
495 Benham St. Phone: (203)281-9600
Hamden, CT 06514
E-mail: weli@weli.com

Format: News; Talk. **Networks:** Independent. **Founded:** 1937. **Operating Hours:** Continuous; 25% network, 75% local. **ADI:** Hartford-New Haven (New London), CT. **Key Personnel:** Faith Zila, General Mgr.; Jim Simomelli, Sales Mgr.; Mike Raub, Operations Mgr.; Daria Albinger, News Dir.; George Demaio, Sports Dir.; Barb Greco, Public Affairs Dir.; Fred Santore, Chief Engineer. **Local Programs:** *Telephone*

Talk, Paul Pacelli. **Wattage:** 5000. **Ad Rates:** $20-175 for 60 seconds. WKCI-FM, WAVZ-AM.

4922 WPLR-FM - 99.1
1191 Dixwell Ave. Phone: (203)287-9070
Hamden, CT 06514 Fax: (203)287-8997

Format: Album-Oriented Rock (AOR). **Networks:** Independent. **Founded:** 1944. **Operating Hours:** Continuous. **Key Personnel:** Rob Williams, General Mgr.; John Griffin, Program Dir.; Dona S. Goodman, National Sales Manager; Mike Juliano, General Sales Mgr.; Sam Tilery, Promotions Dir.; Margaret Wiecha, Business Mgr. **Wattage:** 50,000. **Ad Rates:** Combined advertising rates available with WYBC-FM. **URL:** http://www.wplr.com.

4923 WQAQ-FM - 98.1
555 New Rd. Phone: (203)281-0011
Box 59 Fax: (203)288-8098
Quinnipiac College
Hamden, CT 06518
E-mail: wqaq@quinnipiac.edu

Format: Full Service. **Owner:** Student Govt. Organization Of Quinnipac College, 555 New Rd., Hamden, CT 06518. **Founded:** 1969. **Operating Hours:** 7 a.m.-2 a.m. Mon.-Fri.; 9 a.m.-2 a.m. Sat. and Sun. **Key Personnel:** Sara Robertson, News Dir.; Jason Alexander, General Mgr.; John Mulhall, Program Dir.; James Ferrara, Promotions Dir.; Karyn Krein, Business Mgr.; Justin Louis, Production Dir.; Mike Fox, Music Dir.; Frank De Maria, Music Dir.; Rich Aroyya, Sports Dir.; Steve Glassman, P.B. **Wattage:** 10.

4924 WQUN-AM - 1220
Quinnipiac College Phone: (203)281-8984
275 Mount Carmel Ave. Fax: (203)287-5372
Hamden, CT 06518

Format: News; Information. **Networks:** CBS; Jones Satellite. **Owner:** Quinnipiac College, at above address. **Founded:** 1960. **Formerly:** WNNR-AM (1988); WXCT-AM. **Operating Hours:** Continuous. **ADI:** Hartford-New Haven (New London), CT. **Key Personnel:** Michael Collins, General Mgr.; Ray Andrewsen, Asst. G.M./Operations Director; Michelle Turner, News; Greg Little, News. **Wattage:** 1000 day; 330 night. **Ad Rates:** Advertising accepted; rates available upon request.

HARTFORD†, pop. 136,392.

N. CT. Hartford Co. On Connecticut River, midway between Boston and New York. The State Capital. Trinity College; St. Joseph College; Hartford College; University of Hartford; law, theological, and private schools. Home of United Technologies. Economy consisting of manufacturing, trade, finance, insurance, real estate. Insurance Cowing region.

4925 Campus Law Enforcement Journal
International Association of Campus Law Enforcement Administrators
638 Prospect Ave. Phone: (860)586-7517
Hartford, CT 06105-4298 Fax: (860)586-7550
Publisher E-mail: info@iaclea.org

Trade journal covering law enforcement on college campuses. **Freq:** Semimonthly. **Print Method:** Offset litho. **Trim Size:** 8 3/8 x 10 7/8. **Cols./Page:** 3. **Key Personnel:** Lisa A. Johnson, Managing Editor. **Subscription Rates:** $30 U.S., Canada, and Mexico; $35 other countries; $5 single issue. **Remarks:** Accepts advertising.
Circ: Paid 1,600

4926 CBIA News
CBIA Service Corp.
350 Church St. Phone: (860)244-1900
Hartford, CT 06103-1106 Fax: (860)278-8562

Association journal (tabloid) for business management. **Subtitle:** Journal of the Connecticut Business & Industry Association. **Founded:** 1923. **Freq:** 10/year. **Print Method:** Offset. **Trim Size:** 11 x 14 3/8. **Cols./Page:** 4. **Col. Width:** 27 nonpareils. **Col. Depth:** 219 agate lines. **Key Personnel:** Diane Edwards, Editor. **ISSN:** 0199-686X. **Subscription Rates:** $9 members; $12 nonmembers; $18 members two years; $22 nonmembers two years. **Remarks:** Accepts advertising.
Ad Rates: BW: $1,325 **Circ:** ‡10,000
4C: $1,725

4927 Connecticut Law Review
Connecticut Law Review Association
65 Elizabeth St.
Hartford, CT 06105-2290

Scholarly journal covering legal issues. **Founded:** 1975. **Freq:** Quarterly. **Key Personnel:** Ingrid Moll, Editor-in-Chief; Adam Golden, Advertising Editor. **ISSN:** 0010-6151. **Subscription Rates:** $28 individuals; $10 single issue. **Remarks:** Advertising not accepted.
Circ: Controlled 1,450

4928 Connecticut Motor Transport News
Motor Transport Association of Connecticut, Inc.
60 Forest St. Phone: (860)520-4455
Hartford, CT 06105 Fax: (860)520-4567

Trucking news magazine. **Founded:** 1932. **Freq:** Annual. **Print Method:** Offset. **Cols./Page:** 3. **Col. Width:** 26 nonpareils. **Col. Depth:** 140 agate lines. **Subscription Rates:** $2 individuals. **Remarks:** Accepts advertising.
Ad Rates: BW: $265 **Circ:** (Not Reported)
4C: $495

4929 Digest of Neurology and Psychiatry
400 Washington St. Phone: (860)545-7282
Hartford, CT 06106-3292 Fax: (860)545-7275

Digest containing abstracts of current literature in psychiatry, neurology, and related fields. **Freq:** Quarterly. **Subscription Rates:** $25 individuals USA; $30 elsewhere. **Remarks:** Advertising not accepted.
Circ: (Not Reported)

4930 The Hartford Courant
285 Broad St. Phone: (860)241-6200
Hartford, CT 06115 Fax: (860)520-3176

General newspaper. **Founded:** Oct. 29, 1764. **Freq:** Mon.-Sun. (morn.). **Print Method:** Offset. **Trim Size:** 13 1/2 x 21 3/4. **Cols./Page:** 6. **Col. Width:** 256 nonpareils. **Col. Depth:** 301 agate lines. **Key Personnel:** Michael E. Waller, Publisher and CEO; Marty Petty, GM/Senior V-P; David S. Barrett, Editor and Vice-President. **Subscription Rates:** $182 individuals. **Remarks:** Accepts advertising. **Online:** LEXIS-NEXIS. **Alt. Formats:** CD-ROM, NewsBank, Inc.
Ad Rates: BW: $21141 **Circ:** Mon.-Sat. ★**211,041**
4C: $22667 Sun. ★**303,399**
SAU: $139.31
PCI: $145.86

4931 Hartford Inquirer
Inquires Newspaper Group
PO Box 1260 Phone: (860)522-1462
Hartford, CT 06143 Fax: (860)522-3014

Black community newspaper. **Founded:** 1975. **Print Method:** Offset. **Trim Size:** 11 x 17. **Cols./Page:** 6. **Col. Width:** 9 1/2 inches. **Key Personnel:** Edward Laiscell, Editor; William R. Hales, Publisher. **Subscription Rates:** $27. **Remarks:** Accepts advertising.
Ad Rates: GLR: $3 **Circ:** 125,000
BW: $4,176
PCI: $43.50

4932 Human Development
The Jesuit Educational Center for Human Development
400 Washington St. Phone: (203)241-8041
Hartford, CT 06106 Fax: (203)241-8042

Journal updating psychological, psychiatric, medical, and theological information needed by persons fostering the full human development of others. **Founded:** 1980. **Freq:** Quarterly. **Trim Size:** 8 1/4 x 11 in. **Cols./Page:** 2. **Key Personnel:** James J. Gill, S.J., Editor. **Subscription Rates:** $24; $29 other countries.
Circ: Paid ‡10,000
Non-paid ‡300

4933 Managers Handbook
LIMRA International, Inc.
PO Box 208 Phone: (860)688-3358
Hartford, CT 06141-0208 Fax: (860)298-9555
Free: (800)235-4672

Magazine on financial services industry management. **Subtitle:** On-Target Ideas for Progressive Managers. **Founded:** 1996. **Freq:** Monthly. **Print Method:** Web press. **Trim Size:** 8 1/8 x 10 7/8. **Cols./Page:** 3. **Col. Width:** 24 nonpareils. **Col. Depth:** 112 agate lines. **Key Personnel:** Brad Ragaglia, Managing Editor, phone (860)298-3953, fax (860)298-3934, bragaglia@limra.com. **ISSN:** 0025-1968. **Subscription Rates:** $39.97 individuals; $7.50 single issue; $53.97 other countries. **Remarks:** Advertising not accepted. **Formerly:** Managers Magazine.
Circ: ‡8,000

4934 The Muslim World
Hartford Seminary
77 Sherman St. Phone: (860)509-9500
Hartford, CT 06105 Fax: (860)509-9509

Journal of Islamic studies, addressing Christian-Muslim relations. **Founded:** Jan. 1911. **Freq:** Quarterly. **Print Method:** Offset. **Trim Size:** 6 1/3 x 9 1/4. **Cols./Page:** 1. **Col. Width:** 51 nonpareils. **Col. Depth:** 108 agate lines. **Key Personnel:** Alwi Shihab, Contact, phone (860)509-9531; Dr. Ibrahim Abu-Rabi, Contact, phone (860)509-9530; Dr. Jane Idleman Smith, Contact, phone (860)509-9532, jismith@hartsem.edu. **ISSN:** 0027-4909. **Subscription Rates:** $30 individuals; $50 institutions; $5 single issue back issues only. **Remarks:** Accepts advertising. **URL:** http://www.hartsem.edu.
Ad Rates: BW: $100 **Circ:** ‡1,000

4935 The Trinity Tripod
Rare Reminders
Trinity College Phone: (860)297-2583
No. 702582 Fax: (860)297-5381
Hartford, CT 06106-3100
Publication E-mail: tripod@mail.trincoll.edu

Collegiate newspaper. **Founded:** 1901. **Freq:** Weekly (Tues.). **Print Method:** Offset. **Cols./Page:** 5. **Col. Width:** 24 nonpareils. **Col. Depth:** 224 agate lines. **Key Personnel:** Elizabeth Perry, Editor-in-Chief, phone (860)297-2583, tripod@mail.trincdl.edu; Owen W. Tripp, Business Mgr., phone (860)297-2584, fax (860)297-5361, owen.tripp@mail.trincoll.edu. **Subscription Rates:** Free; $15 individuals. **Remarks:** Accepts advertising. **URL:** http://www.trincoll.edu/info/pub_students/tripod.
Ad Rates: BW: $250 **Circ:** Paid 500
SAU: $4.15 Free 3,000
PCI: $7.26

4936 WCCC-AM - 1290
1039 Asylum Ave. Phone: (860)525-1069
Hartford, CT 06105 Fax: (860)246-9084
E-mail: fm107wccc@aol.com

Format: Classic Rock. **Simulcasts:** WCCC-FM. **Networks:** ABC. **Founded:** 1947. **Formerly:** Greater Hartford Communications Corp. **Operating Hours:** Sunrise-sunset. **ADI:** Hartford-New Haven (New London), CT. **Local Programs:** *The Morning Show*, Ron Dresner; *Rock Around New England*. **Wattage:** 1000. **Ad Rates:** Advertising accepted; rates available upon request. **URL:** http://www.wccc.com.

4937 WCCC-FM - 106.9
1039 Asylum Ave. Phone: (860)525-1069
Hartford, CT 06105 Fax: (860)246-9084
E-mail: fm107wccc@aol.com

Format: Classic Rock. **Simulcasts:** WCCC-AM. **Networks:** ABC. **Owner:** Greater Hartford Communications Corp., at above address. **Founded:** 1947. **Operating Hours:** Continuous. **ADI:** Hartford-New Haven (New London), CT. **Key Personnel:** Arnold E. Boyd, VP/GM; Jay Schultz, Director of Sales; Mike Karolyi, Program Dir.; Michael Picozzi, Program Dir.; Mike Karolyi, Music Dir. **Local Programs:** *The Morning Show*, Ron Dresner. **Wattage:** 50,000. **Ad Rates:** Advertising accepted; rates available upon request. **URL:** http://www.wccc.com.

4938 WEDH-TV - 24
240 New Britain Ave. Phone: (860)278-5310
Box 6240 Fax: (860)278-2157
Hartford, CT 06106-3185
E-mail: jerry_franklin@wedh.pbs.org

Format: Public TV. **Simulcasts:** WEDN-TV. **Networks:** Public Broadcasting Service (PBS). **Owner:** Connecticut Public Broadcasting, Inc., at above address, Fax: (860)244-9624. **Founded:** 1962. **Operating Hours:** 6:45 a.m.-midnight Daily; 8 a.m.-midnight Sat.; 7:30 a.m.-midnight Sun. **ADI:** Hartford-New Haven (New London), CT. **Key Personnel:** Jerry Franklin, Pres./CEO; Larry Rifkin, Exec. VP of Programming, larry_rifkin@wedh.pbs.org; Steve Futernick, Sr. VP, Community Development; Anita Ford Saunders, VP, Corporate Communications; John Berky, VP of Radio; Donna Collins, VP, Program Marketing; Meg Sakellarides, Chief Financial Officer; Jay Whitsett, VP Broadcast Oper. and Production Svcs. **Local Programs:** *Connecticut Journal*. **Wattage:** 55 KW. **Ad Rates:** Noncommercial.

WEDN-TV - See Norwich

WEDY-TV - See New Haven

4939 WFSB-TV - 3
3 Constitution Plaza Phone: (860)728-3333
Hartford, CT 06103 Fax: (860)728-0263
E-mail: wfsb@wfsb.com

Format: Commercial TV. **Networks:** CBS. **Owner:** Meredith Corporation, 3 Constitution Plaza, Hartford, CT 06103-1892. **Founded:** 1957. **Operating Hours:** Continuous. **ADI:** Hartford-New Haven (New London), CT. **Key Personnel:** Paul Virciglio, VP/General Mgr. **URL:** http://www.wfsb.com.

4940 WHCN-FM - 105.9
10 Columbus Blvd. Phone: (860)723-6080
Hartford, CT 06106 Fax: (860)723-6119

Format: Classic Rock. **Networks:** ABC. **Owner:** Atlantic Star Capstar Broadcasting, at above address. **Operating Hours:** Continuous. **ADI:** Hartford-New Haven (New London), CT.

Key Personnel: Rob Williams, Mktg. Mgr., phone (860)723-6002, fax (860)723-6034. **Wattage:** 50,000. **Ad Rates:** Advertising accepted; rates available upon request.

4941 WKSS-FM - 95.7
10 Columbus Blvd. Phone: (860)723-6160
Hartford, CT 06106-1944 Fax: (860)723-6198

Format: Contemporary Hit Radio (CHR). **Owner:** Atlantic Star-Division of Capstar Broadcasting, at above address. **Founded:** 1947. **Operating Hours:** Continuous. **ADI:** Hartford-New Haven (New London), CT. **Key Personnel:** Larry Hryb, Promotions Mgr., phone (860)723-6161; Rob Williams, Mktg. Mgr., phone (860)723-6002, fax (860)723-6034; Jeremy Savage, Operations Mgr., phone (860)723-6007, fax (860)723-6038; Dave Hilll, Program Dir., phone (860)723-6041, fax (860)723-6038; Paula Messina, DOS, phone (860)723-6004, fax (860)723-6037. **Wattage:** 50,000. **Ad Rates:** Advertising accepted; rates available upon request.

4942 WLAT-AM - 1230
86 Cedar St. Phone: (860)524-0001
Hartford, CT 06106 Fax: (860)548-1922

Format: Hispanic. **Founded:** 1939. **Formerly:** WNAQ-AM. **Operating Hours:** Continuous. **ADI:** Hartford-New Haven (New London), CT. **Key Personnel:** Oscar Nieves, Contact. **Wattage:** 5000. **Ad Rates:** $10-39 for 30 seconds; $13-45 for 60 seconds.

4943 WMRQ-FM - 104.1
Box 31-1410 Phone: (203)666-1411
Newington Branch Fax: (203)665-1175
Hartford, CT 06131
Free: (800)224-7827

Format: Adult Contemporary. **Networks:** Independent. **Founded:** 1967. **Formerly:** WIOF-FM (1992); WYSR-FM (1996). **Operating Hours:** Continuous; 100% local. **ADI:** Hartford-New Haven (New London), CT. **Key Personnel:** Tim Montgomery, Vice Pres./Gen. Mgr.; Jay Beau Jones, Program Dir.; Jay Schultz, Sales Mgr.; Rick Walsh, Chief Engineer. **Wattage:** 50,000. **Ad Rates:** Advertising accepted; rates available upon request.

WNPR-FM - See Norwich

4944 WPKT-FM - 90.5
240 New Britain Ave. Phone: (860)278-5310
PO Box 6240 Fax: (860)244-9624
Hartford, CT 06106
E-mail: radio90@prodigy.com

Format: Public Radio; Classical; News. **Networks:** National Public Radio (NPR); Public Radio International (PRI). **Owner:** Connecticut Public Broadcasting, at above address, Hartford, CT 06106, (203)278-2157. **Founded:** 1978. **Formerly:** WPBH-FM. **Operating Hours:** Continuous; 50% network; 50% local. **ADI:** Hartford-New Haven (New London), CT. **Key Personnel:** Jerry Franklin, General Mgr.; John F. Berky, Dir., Radio; Kim Grehn, Program Dir.; Audrey Rogers, Promotions Mgr. **Local Programs:** *Faith Middleton Show*, Faith Middleton, (203)777-7506, Fax (203)495-6444. **Wattage:** 19,000. **Ad Rates:** Noncommercial.

4945 WPOP-AM - 1410
10 Columbus Blvd. Phone: (860)723-6000
Hartford, CT 06106 Fax: (860)723-6038

Format: Sports. **Networks:** ESPN Radio. **Owner:** Atlantic Star-Capstar Broadcasting, at above address. **Founded:** 1935. **Formerly:** WNBC-AM. **Operating Hours:** Continuous; 5% network, 95% local. **ADI:** Hartford-New Haven (New London), CT. **Key Personnel:** Bob Plante, Program Dir., phone (860)723-6167; Rob Williams, V.P./General Mgr.; Rick Walsh, Chief Engineer; Lori Larson, Office Mgr. **Wattage:** 5000. **Ad Rates:** Advertising accepted; rates available upon request.

4946 WQTQ-FM - 89.9
Weaver High School Phone: (860)722-8661
415 Granby St. Fax: (860)286-9909
Hartford, CT 06112
E-mail: wqtq@uhavax.hartford.edu

Format: Urban Contemporary; Educational; Oldies; Gospel; Jazz; Rap; Reggae; Hip Hop. **Networks:** UPI. **Owner:** Hartford Board of Education, 153 Market St., 8th Fl., Hartford, CT 06103. **Founded:** Sept. 1971. **Operating Hours:** 6 a.m.-11 p.m.; M-F, 6 a.m.-12 a.m.; Sat., 9a.m.-9p.m. Sun. **ADI:** Hartford-New Haven (New London), CT. **Key Personnel:** Shirley Minnifield, Business Mgr.; Connie Coles, General Mgr.; Thomas Smith, Chief Operator. **Local Programs:** *A Different Perspective*, Anthony Price, (860)722-8660. **Wattage:** 115. **Ad Rates:** Noncommercial. **URL:** http://www.uhavax.hartford.edu/wgtg.

4947 WRDM TV - 13
886 Maple Ave. Phone: (860)956-1303
Hartford, CT 06114 Fax: (860)956-6834
E-mail: channel.13@net.net

Format: Hispanic. **Networks:** Telemundo. **Owner:** Channel 13 Television Inc., at above address. **Founded:** June 13, 1986. **Operating Hours:** Continuous. **ADI:** Hartford-New Haven (New London), CT. **Key Personnel:** Lucio C. Ruzzler, Sr., President; Gaetano Leone, General Mgr.; William Newton, President of Sales. **Local Programs:** *Adelante* 11:30 Friday, William Newton, (860)956-1303; *L'Italia D'America* 1:00 pm Sunday, Lucio C. Ruzzier, (860)956-1303; *L'ora Della Verita* 7:30 am Sunday, Lucio C. Ruzzier, (860)956-1303. **Wattage:** 18,000. **Ad Rates:** Advertising accepted; rates available upon request.

4948 WRTC-FM - 89.3
Trinity College Phone: (203)297-2450
300 Summit St. Fax: (203)297-5201
Hartford, CT 06106

Format: Eclectic; Jazz; Religious; Alternative/New Music/Progressive. **Owner:** Trinity College, at above address. **Founded:** 1948. **Operating Hours:** Continuous. **ADI:** Hartford-New Haven (New London), CT. **Key Personnel:** Patrice Evans, Station Mgr.; Yndia Lorick, Music Dir.; Bob Parzych, Jazz/Blues Director. **Wattage:** 350. **Ad Rates:** Noncommercial.

4949 WTIC-AM - 1080
1 Financial Plaza Phone: (203)522-1080
Hartford, CT 06103 Fax: (203)549-3431

Format: Full Service. **Networks:** CBS. **Founded:** 1925. **Operating Hours:** Continuous. **ADI:** Hartford-New Haven (New London), CT. **Key Personnel:** Suzanne McDonald, General Mgr.; Steve Salhancy, Operations Dir.; Jenneen Hull, Asst. Program. Dir., phone (860)522-1080. **Wattage:** 50,000.

4950 WTIC-FM - 96.5
1 Financial Plaza Phone: (860)522-1080
Hartford, CT 06103 Fax: (860)249-7509
E-mail: kktic@tiac.net

Format: Adult Contemporary. **Networks:** CBS. **Operating Hours:** Continuous. **ADI:** Hartford-New Haven (New London), CT. **Key Personnel:** Suzzane McDonald, General Mgr., fax (860)560-6307, suzannem@wtic.com; Steve Salhany, Operations Mgr., fax (860)549-3431; David Simpson, Music Dir.; John Capuano, Sales Mgr., fax (860)549-5746. **Wattage:** 50,000. **URL:** http://www.wtic.com.

4951 WTIC-TV - 61
One Corporate Center Phone: (860)527-6161
Hartford, CT 06103 Fax: (860)293-0178

Format: Commercial TV. **Networks:** Fox. **Owner:** Renaissance Communications, at above address. **Founded:** 1984. **Operating Hours:** Continuous. **ADI:** Hartford-New Haven (New London), CT. **Key Personnel:** Robert Gluck, General Mgr. **Wattage:** 5,000,000. **URL:** http://www.fox561.com.

4952 WTXX-TV - 20
One Corporate Center Phone: (860)527-6161
Hartford, CT 06103 Fax: (860)293-0178

Format: Commercial TV. **Networks:** Independent; United Paramount Network. **Owner:** Counterpoint Communications Inc., 15 Peach Orchard Rd., Prospect, CT 06712. **Founded:** 1982. **Operating Hours:** Continuous. **ADI:** Hartford-New Haven (New London), CT. **Key Personnel:** David L Brewer Jr, Contact. **Local Programs:** *CT Financial Review*, Clem Kasinskas, (203)758-3900, Fax (203)758-3908; *CT Financial Review*, Clem Kasinskas, (203)758-3900, Fax (203)758-3908. **Wattage:** 2240.

4953 WWYZ-FM - 92.5
10 Columbus Blvd. Phone: (860)723-6120
Hartford, CT 06106 Fax: (860)723-6130

Format: Country. **Networks:** Westwood One Radio. **Owner:** SFX Broadcasting, Inc., at above address. **Founded:** 1961. **Formerly:** WATR-FM (1972). **Operating Hours:** Continuous. **ADI:** Hartford-New Haven (New London), CT. **Key Personnel:** Greg Roche, Program Dir., phone (860)723-6121, fax (860)723-6130; John Victory, Sales Mgr., phone (860)723-6131. **Local Programs:** *Connecticut Top 30 Countdown.* **Wattage:** 50,000.

HEBRON, pop. 6,560.

SE CT. Tolland Co. 17 mi. SE of Hartford.

4954 Radiation Protection Management
RSA Publications
19 Pendelton Dr. Phone: (860)228-0824
Box 19 Fax: (860)228-4402
Hebron, CT 06248
Publisher E-mail: publish@radpro.com

Trade journal covering radiation, health, nuclear power, and industrial hygiene for nuclear professionals. **Subtitle:** The Journal of Applied Health Physics. **Founded:** Oct. 1983. **Freq:** Bimonthly. **Print Method:** Web offset. **Trim Size:** 8 1/2 x 11. **Cols./Page:** 3. **Key Personnel:** K. Paul Steinmeyer, Editor; Sharyn Mathews, Managing Editor. **ISSN:** 0740-0640. **Subscription Rates:** $49 individuals; $434 institutions; $10 single issue. **Remarks:** Accepts advertising.
Ad Rates: BW: $1,100 **Circ:** Paid 750
4C: $1,850

4955 RSO Magazine
RSA Publications
19 Pendelton Dr. Phone: (860)228-0824
Box 19 Fax: (860)228-4402
Hebron, CT 06248
Publisher E-mail: publish@radpro.com

Trade magazine covering industrial health and safety, nuclear medicine, and radiation for licensees and users of nuclear materials of all kinds. **Founded:** 1996. **Freq:** Bimonthly. **Print Method:** Web offset. **Trim Size:** 8 1/2 x 11. **Cols./Page:** 3. **Key Personnel:** K. Paul Steinmeyer, Editor; Sharyn L. Mathews, Managing Editor. **ISSN:** 1086-6353. **Subscription Rates:** $39 individuals; $125 institutions; $10 single issue. **Remarks:** Accepts advertising.
Ad Rates: BW: $750 **Circ:** Paid 950
4C: $1,500

HUNTINGTON

4956 Huntington Herald
Hometown Publications, Inc.
PO Box 332 Phone: (203)926-2080
Monroe, CT 06468 Fax: (203)926-2091
Free: (800)843-6791
Publisher E-mail: homepubl@aol.com

Community newspaper. **Founded:** 1981. **Freq:** Weekly (Wed.). **Print Method:** Offset. **Trim Size:** 13 x 21 3/4. **Cols./Page:** 6. **Col. Width:** 1 7/8 inches. **Col. Depth:** 21 inches. **Key Personnel:** Tom Henry, Editor; Regina Burkhart, Publisher; Robin Glowa, Advertising Mgr.; Hank Misiak, Advertising Dir. **Subscription Rates:** $12.00 individuals. **Remarks:** Combined advertising rates available with other Hometown Publications.
Ad Rates: BW: $1,522.08 **Circ:** Combined ♦6,835
4C: $2,122.08
PCI: $12.08

4957 The Motorcyclist's Post
11 Haven Ln. Phone: (203)929-9409
Huntington, CT 06484 Fax: (203)926-9347

Tabloid newspaper covering motorcycle activities and legislation. **Subtitle:** Voice of Northeast Motorcycle Riders. **Founded:** May 1967. **Freq:** Monthly. **Print Method:** Offset. **Trim Size:** 10 x 16 in. **Cols./Page:** 5. **Col. Width:** 2 inches. **Col. Depth:** 16 inches. **Key Personnel:** L. Castell, Editor, lcastell@snct.net. **ISSN:** 0164-9256. **Subscription Rates:** $20 individuals. **Remarks:** Accepts advertising.
Ad Rates: BW: $500 **Circ:** ‡10,060
4C: $650
SAU: $4.50
PCI: $8.50

KENSINGTON

4958 United Cable Television Services Corp.
222 New Park Dr. Phone: (203)677-9599
P.O. Box 4222 Fax: (203)829-3352
Kensington, CT 06037

Founded: 1975. **Key Personnel:** Ron Roe, General Mgr.; Jeff Cardoso, Plant Manager; Keith Froleiks, Business Manager. **Cities Served:** Bloomfield, East Hartford, Simsbury, West Hartford, Windsor, CT; Hartford County: subscribing households 151,500; 78 channels; 3 community access channels; 504 hours per week community access programming.

KENT

4959 Kent Good Times Dispatch
Housatonic Valley Publishing Co.
14 Main St. Phone: (860)927-4621
PO Box 430 Fax: (860)927-4622
Kent, CT 06757
Publication E-mail: housvalpub@aol.com
Publisher E-mail: housvalpub@aol.com

Community newspaper. **Founded:** 1952. **Freq:** Weekly (Fri.). **Print Method:** Offset. **Cols./Page:** 6. **Col. Width:** 2 1/16 inches. **Col. Depth:** 21 1/2 inches. **Key Personnel:** John Hetzler, General Mgr.; Alice Tessler, Editor; Lesly Ferris, Managing Editor. **Subscription Rates:** $19.95 individuals; $29.95 out of area. **Remarks:** Combined advertising rates available with other Housatonic Valley Publications.
Ad Rates: SAU: $3.55 **Circ:** Combined ♦**917**

LAKEVILLE, pop. 3,800.

NW CT. Litchfield Co. 26 mi. NW of Torrington. Resort. Light manufacturing. Dairy, poultry, horse farms.

4960 Lakeville Journal
The Lakeville Journal Co., LLC
33 Bissell St. Phone: (860)435-9873
PO Box 353 Fax: (860)435-0146
Lakeville, CT 06039
Community newspaper. **Founded:** 1897. **Freq:** Weekly (Thurs.). **Print Method:** Offset. **Cols./Page:** 7. **Col. Width:** 25 nonpareils. **Col. Depth:** 294 agate lines. **Key Personnel:** A. Whitney Ellsworth, Publisher; Jim Timpano, Assoc. Publisher; Kathryn Boughton, Editor; A.M. Kupferer, Advertising Mgr. **Subscription Rates:** $29.95; $38 out of area. **Remarks:** Accepts advertising.
Ad Rates: PCI: $8.00 **Circ:** Paid 4,571
Non-paid 14

4961 WQQQ-FM - 103.3
PO Box 1085 Phone: (203)435-3333
Lakeville, CT 06039 Fax: (203)435-3334

Format: Adult Contemporary. **Owner:** Ridgefield Broadcasting Corp., at above address. **Founded:** 1985. **Formerly:** WREF-AM (Oct. 1993). **Operating Hours:** Continuous; 100% local. **ADI:** New York, NY. **Key Personnel:** Dennis Jackson, President; Ron Lyon, General Mgr. **Local Programs:** *Marshall In The Morning,* Marshall Miles; *Rhoda Opum,* Rhoda Opum. **Wattage:** 3,700. **Ad Rates:** $15-23 for 30 seconds; $19-30 for 60 seconds. **URL:** http://www.wqqq.com.

LEWISBORO

4962 The Lewisboro Ledger
Hersam Acorn Newspapers, LLC
PO Box 1019 Phone: (203)438-6545
Ridgefield, CT 06877-9019
Publisher E-mail: newsroom@acorn-online.com

Community newspaper. **Founded:** 1976. **Freq:** Weekly (Wed.). **Print Method:** Offset. **Cols./Page:** 6. **Col. Width:** 2 1/16 inches. **Col. Depth:** 294 agate lines. **Key Personnel:** Andrew Viccora, Editor; Thomas B. Nash, Publisher. **Subscription Rates:** $30 individuals.
Ad Rates: BW: $850.50 **Circ:** Paid ♦**1,915**
PCI: $6.75 Non-paid ♦**51**

LITCHFIELD

4963 Litchfield Enquirer
Housatonic Valley Publishing Co.
43 West St.
PO Box 547
Litchfield, CT 06759
Publisher E-mail: housvalpub@aol.com

Community newspaper. **Founded:** 1825. **Freq:** Weekly (Fri.). **Print Method:** Offset. **Cols./Page:** 6. **Col. Width:** 26 nonpareils. **Col. Depth:** 294 agate lines. **Key Personnel:** T. Lip Rothschild, Publisher; John Norton, Vice President. **Subscription Rates:** $24.95 individuals; $34.95 Out of county; $36.95 out of state.
Ad Rates: SAU: $10.65 **Circ:** Combined ♦**2,012**

4964 WZBG-FM - 97.3
PO Box 1497 Phone: (860)567-3697
Litchfield, CT 06759 Fax: (860)567-3292
E-mail: mailwzbg@snet.net

Format: Adult Contemporary. **Networks:** CBS; Meadows Racing; Jones Satellite. **Owner:** Local Boys & Girls Broadcasting Corp., at above address. **Operating Hours:** Continuous. **Key Personnel:** Jennifer Parsons, General Mgr.; Dale Jones, Program Dir.; Jeff Zeiner, News Dir. **Local Programs:** *Swap Shop,* Mike Hand. **Wattage:** 3,000.

MADISON, pop. 14,031.

SE CT. New Haven Co. On Long Island Sound and Hammonasset River.

4965 Annals of Ophthalmology
Altier & Maynard Communications, Inc.
53 Oakwood Dr. Phone: (203)431-3454
Madison, CT 06443-1823
Ophtalmology journal. **Subtitle:** Official Publication of the American Society of Contemporary Ophthalmology. **Founded:** 1969. **Freq:** Monthly. **Print Method:** Offset. **Trim Size:** 7 7/8 x 10 3/4. **Cols./Page:** 2. **Col. Width:** 30 nonpareils. **Col. Depth:** 140 agate lines. **Key Personnel:** John G. Bellows, M.D., Editor; Bonnie Maynard, Advertising Mgr. **Subscription Rates:** $60; $75 Industry. **Remarks:** Accepts advertising.
Ad Rates: BW: $655 **Circ:** 8,844
4C: $1,480

4966 Black Health
Altier & Maynard Communications, Inc.
53 Oakwood Dr. Phone: (203)431-3454
Madison, CT 06443-1823
Subtitle: The First Health Magazine for Blacks. **Founded:** 1988. **Freq:** Quarterly. **Print Method:** Web offset. **Trim Size:** 8 1/8 x 10 3/4. **Key Personnel:** Bonnie Maynard, Publisher; Carlos Maynard, Publisher. **Subscription Rates:** Free to qualified subscribers; $10. $2.50 single issue. **Remarks:** Accepts advertising.
Ad Rates: BW: $6,000 **Circ:** Paid ‡2,340
4C: $7,000 Free ‡25,000

4967 Depression and Stress
International Universities Press, Inc.
59 Boston Post Rd. Phone: (203)245-4000
Madison, CT 06443-1524 Fax: (203)245-0775
Free: (800)TEL-EIUP
Publisher E-mail: office@iup.com

Journal covering the biological, psychosocial, and psychological aspects of depression and stress. **Founded:** 1994. **Freq:** Semiannual. **Key Personnel:** George H. Pollock, M.D., Editor. **Subscription Rates:** $45 individuals; $82 institutions.

4968 Gender and Psychoanalysis
International Universities Press, Inc.
59 Boston Post Rd. Phone: (203)245-4000
Madison, CT 06443-1524 Fax: (203)245-0775
Free: (800)TEL-EIUP
Publisher E-mail: office@iup.com

Subtitle: An Interdisciplinary Journal. **Founded:** 1996. **Freq:** Quarterly. **Trim Size:** 6 x 9. **Key Personnel:** James W. Barron, Ph.D., Editor. **Subscription Rates:** $40 individuals; $75 institutions. **Remarks:** Accepts advertising.
Ad Rates: BW: $360 **Circ:** (Not Reported)

4969 Integrative Psychiatry
International Universities Press, Inc.
59 Boston Post Rd. Phone: (203)245-4000
Madison, CT 06443-1524 Fax: (203)245-0775
Free: (800)TEL-EIUP
Publisher E-mail: office@iup.com

Journal focusing on the integration of psychiatry, medicine, and behavioral science for the benefit of research. **Subtitle:** The International Journal for the Synthesis of Medicine and Psychiatry. **Freq:** Quarterly. **Trim Size:** 8 1/4 x 11. **Key Personnel:** Alfred M. Freedman, M.D., Editor; Turan M. Itil M.D., Editor. **Subscription Rates:** $60 individuals; $115 industry. **Remarks:** Accepts advertising.
Ad Rates: BW: $300 **Circ:** (Not Reported)

4970 Journal of Clinical Psychoanalysis
International Universities Press, Inc.
59 Boston Post Rd. Phone: (203)245-4000
Madison, CT 06443-1524 Fax: (203)245-0775
Free: (800)TEL-EIUP
Publisher E-mail: office@iup.com

Journal exploring what really occurs in an analysis. **Founded:** 1992. **Freq:** Quarterly. **Trim Size:** 6 x 9. **Key Personnel:** Herbert M. Wyman, M.D., Editor; Stephen M. Rittenberg, M.D., Editor. **Subscription Rates:** $59 U.S.; $88 institutions. **Remarks:** Accepts advertising.
Ad Rates: BW: $580 **Circ:** (Not Reported)

4971 Journal of Developmental and Learning Disorders
International Universities Press, Inc.
59 Boston Post Rd. Phone: (203)245-4000
Madison, CT 06443-1524 Fax: (203)245-0775
Free: (800)TEL-EIUP
Publisher E-mail: office@iup.com

Journal concerned with the identification, prevention, and treatment of disorders that interfere with adaptive developmental and learning processes. **Founded:** 1997. **Freq:** Semiannual. **Trim Size:** 6 x 9. **Key Personnel:** Stanley Greenspan, M.D., Editor. **Subscription Rates:** $42 individuals; $70 institutions. **Remarks:** Accepts advertising.
Ad Rates: BW: $580 **Circ:** (Not Reported)

4972 Journal of Geriatric Psychiatry
International Universities Press, Inc.
59 Boston Post Rd. Phone: (203)245-4000
Madison, CT 06443-1524 Fax: (203)245-0775
Free: (800)TEL-EIUP
Publisher E-mail: office@iup.com

Journal discussing psychologic and psychiatric issues pertinant to the geriatric population. **Subtitle:** Official Journal of The Boston Society for Gerontologic Psychiatry. **Founded:** 1967. **Freq:** 2/year. **Trim Size:** 6 x 9. **Key Personnel:** Bennett Gurian, M.D., Editor; Margery Silver, Ed.D., Editor. **Subscription Rates:** $58 individuals; $84.50 institutions. **Remarks:** Accepts advertising.
Ad Rates: BW: $360 **Circ:** (Not Reported)

4973 Journal of Imago Relationship Therapy
Psychosocial Press
59 Boston Post Rd. Phone: (203)245-4000
PO Box 1524 Fax: (203)245-0775
Madison, CT 06443-1524
Free: (800)835-2487
Publisher E-mail: office@iup.com

Founded: 1996. **Freq:** Semiannual. **Trim Size:** 6 x 9. **Key Personnel:** Harville Hendrix, Ph.D., Editor. **Subscription Rates:** $44.25 individuals; $72 institutions. **Remarks:** Accepts advertising.
Ad Rates: BW: $360 **Circ:** (Not Reported)

4974 Psychoanalysis and Contemporary Thought
International Universities Press, Inc.
59 Boston Post Rd. Phone: (203)245-4000
Madison, CT 06443-1524 Fax: (203)245-0775
Free: (800)TEL-EIUP
Publication E-mail: office@iup.com
Publisher E-mail: office@iup.com

Psychoanalytic journal, broadening scientific and intellectual horizons. **Subtitle:** A Quarterly of Integrative and Interdisciplinary Thought. **Founded:** 1978. **Freq:** Quarterly. **Print Method:** Offset. **Trim Size:** 6 x 9. **Key Personnel:** Leo Goldberger, Editor, gberger@xp.psych.nyu.edu. **Subscription Rates:** $76.50 individuals; $130 institutions; $47 single issue. **Remarks:** Accepts advertising.
Ad Rates: BW: $325 **Circ:** 1,000

MANCHESTER, pop. 49,761.

N. CT. Hartford Co. 12 mi. E. of Hartford. Manufactures silk, rayon, paper, paper board, electrical instruments, soap, tools, reamers, friction clutches, reverse gears, parachutes. Nurseries. Dairy, tobacco farms.

4975 Journal Inquirer
Box 510
Manchester, CT 06045-0510

General newspaper. **Founded:** 1968. **Freq:** Daily (eve.) and Sat. (morn.). **Print Method:** Offset. Uses mats. **Cols./Page:** 5. **Col. Width:** 21 nonpareils. **Col. Depth:** 196 agate lines. **Key Personnel:** Elizabeth Ellis, Publisher; William Sybert, Advertising Mgr. **Subscription Rates:** $78 individuals. **Remarks:** Accepts advertising.
Ad Rates: BW: $1,676 **Circ:** Mon.-Sat. ★**46,281**
4C: $2,076
SAU: $23.95
PCI: $23.95

4976 Live Wire
Manchester Community College
MS 4 Phone: (203)647-6057
60 Bidwell St. Fax: (203)647-6238
Manchester, CT 06040
Collegiate newspaper. **Founded:** 1972. **Freq:** Semimonthly. **Print Method:** Offset. **Cols./Page:** 5. **Col. Width:** 22 nonpareils. **Col. Depth:** 224 agate lines. **Key Personnel:** Andy Buccino, Editor; Emily Carpenter, Section Editor; Michelle Connolly, Section Editor. **Remarks:** Accepts advertising. **Formerly:** The Cougar.
Ad Rates: BW: $350 **Circ:** Free ‡3,000
PCI: $4

4977 Manchester Reminder
Reminder Press
PO Box 27 Phone: (860)872-6648
130 Old Town Rd. Fax: (860)875-2089
Vernon, CT 06066
General newspaper. **Founded:** 1973. **Freq:** Weekly. **Print Method:** Offset. **Cols./Page:** 6. **Col. Width:** 20 nonpareils. **Col. Depth:** 196 agate lines. **Key Personnel:** Kenneth A. Hovland, Publisher. **Remarks:** Accepts advertising.
Ad Rates: GLR: $.36 **Circ:** (Not Reported)

4978 **Precision Shooting**
Precision Shooting, Inc.
222 Mckee St. Phone: (860)645-8776
Manchester, CT 06040 Fax: (860)643-8215

Magazine on target rifle shooting. **Founded:** 1956. **Freq:** Monthly. **Print Method:** Offset. **Cols./Page:** 3. **Col. Width:** 27 nonpareils. **Col. Depth:** 147 agate lines. **Key Personnel:** David D. Brennan, Editor; Kim Woble, Advertising Mgr. **ISSN:** 0048-5144. **Subscription Rates:** $3.95 single issue; $32 individuals. **Remarks:** Accepts advertising.
Ad Rates: BW: $445 **Circ:** 17,500
4C: $1000
PCI: $20

4979 **Cox Communications**
801 Parker St. Phone: (860)512-5000
Manchester, CT 06040 Fax: (860)512-5115

Owner: Cox Communications, at above address. **Founded:** 1975. **Formerly:** Cox Cable Greater Hartford, Inc. (1996). **Key Personnel:** Gary Perrelli, General Mgr.; John Wolfe, Government Affairs Dir.; Thorn Landers, Marketing Dir. **Cities Served:** Cheshire, Glastonbury, Manchester, Meriden, Newington, Rocky Hill, South Windsor, Southington, Wethersfeld, CT: subscribing households 101,500; 78 channels; 3 community access channels; 90 hours per week community access programming.

MERIDEN†, pop. 57,118.

S. CT. New Haven Co. 20 mi. S. of Hartford. Manufactures silverware, machine screws, lamps, plastics, electrical fixtures and appliances, auto parts, oil filters, automatic tools, telephones, switchboard equipment, airplane accessories, china, glassware, hardware.

4980 **Record-Journal**
The Record-Journal Publishing Co.
11 Crown St. Phone: (203)235-1661
PO Box 915 Fax: (203)639-0210
Meriden, CT 06450-0915
General newspaper. **Founded:** 1867. **Freq:** Mon.-Sun. (morn.). **Print Method:** Offset. **Cols./Page:** 6. **Col. Width:** 2 1/16 inches. **Col. Depth:** 21 1/2 inches. **Key Personnel:** James Smith, Exec. Editor; Don Schiller, Managing Editor; Eliot C. White, Publisher; Michael F. Killian, Vice President; Raymond U. Roy, Advertising Dir. **Subscription Rates:** $208 individuals; $232 out of county. **Remarks:** Accepts advertising. **URL:** http://www.record-journal.com.
Ad Rates: BW: $2,698.68 **Circ:** Mon.-Sat. ★**28,198**
4C: $3,073.68 Sun. ★**28,513**
PCI: $20.72

MIDDLEBURY

4981 **Business Digest of Greater Waterbury**
Four Stars Publishing Co., Inc.
197 Tranquility Rd.
Middlebury, CT 06762-2230

Magazine covering Greater Waterbury's business community. **Founded:** June 1989. **Freq:** Bimonthly. **Print Method:** Web offset. **Trim Size:** 8 3/8 x 10 7/8. **Cols./Page:** 3. **Col. Width:** 2 1/4 inches. **Col. Depth:** 9 3/4 inches. **Key Personnel:** Ferdinand Starbuck, Jr., Editor and Publisher. **ISSN:** 1046-168X. **Subscription Rates:** $15. $2.50 single issue. **Remarks:** Accepts advertising. **Formerly:** The Greater Waterbury Business Digest (1989).
Ad Rates: BW: $975 **Circ:** 6,000
4C: $1,375

4982 **Consumer Connection**
30 Nick Rd. Phone: (203)598-0745
Middlebury, CT 06762-2110
Shopper. **Founded:** 1987. **Freq:** Monthly. **Print Method:** Web offset. **Trim Size:** 11 1/2 x 13 1/2. **Cols./Page:** 5. **Col. Width:** 11.9 picas. **Col. Depth:** 12 inches. **Key Personnel:** Noa Silberberg, Publisher.
Ad Rates: BW: $500 **Circ:** Free 15,000

MIDDLETOWN†, pop. 39,040.

S. CT. Middlesex Co. On Connecticut River, 15 mi. S. of Hartford. Wesleyan University (coed); Middlesex Community College (coed). Retail, commercial and insurance center. Manufactures jet aircraft engines, brake linings. automotive parts, chemicals, webbing, fabricated metals, textiles, marine and industrial hardware, leather gaskets, tools, dies, office supplies, corrugated cartons, packing machines, electronics, plastic products. Agriculture. Tobacco, apples, dairy products.

4983 **Choice**
American Library Association (ALA)
100 Riverview Ctr. Phone: (860)347-6933
Middletown, CT 06457 Fax: (860)346-8586

Magazine of book and nonprint reviews of scholarly publications for undergraduate libraries, special and public libraries, librarians, faculty, students, and scholars. **Subtitle:** Current Reviews for Academic Libraries. **Founded:** Mar. 1964. **Freq:** Monthly (combined in July/Aug). **Print Method:** Offset. **Trim Size:** 8 1/2 x 11. **Cols./Page:** 2. **Col. Width:** 42 nonpareils. **Col. Depth:** 133 agate lines. **Key Personnel:** Irving E. Rickwood, Editor and Publisher; Stuart Foster, Advertising Mgr., phone (203)347-1387; Lisa M. Gross, Production Mgr. **ISSN:** 0009-4978. **Subscription Rates:** $177 individuals; $198 other countries; $21 single issue. **Remarks:** Accepts advertising. **Available Online.**
Ad Rates: BW: $1,485 **Circ:** Paid ‡4,350
4C: $2,420 Controlled ‡141

4984 **Garlinghouse Home Plans Guide**
L. F. Garlinghouse Co., Inc.
282 Main St. Phone: (203)343-5977
Middletown, CT 06457 Fax: (203)632-0712

Magazine featuring home plans for consumers. **Freq:** Quarterly. **Print Method:** Web offset. **Trim Size:** 8 x 10 7/8. **Key Personnel:** Whitney Garlinghouse, Editor and Publisher. **Subscription Rates:** $9.48. $3.95 single issue; $6.05 single issue other countries. **Remarks:** Accepts advertising.
Ad Rates: BW: $3,300 **Circ:** Non-paid ‡100,000
4C: $4,785

4985 **Wesleyan**
Wesleyan University
Middletown, CT 06459 Phone: (203)685-3699
Fax: (203)685-3601

University alumni magazine. **Subtitle:** The University Alumni Magazine. **Founded:** 1916. **Freq:** Quarterly. **Print Method:** Offset. **Cols./Page:** 3 and 2. **Col. Width:** 27 and 41 nonpareils. **Col. Depth:** 130 agate lines. **Key Personnel:** William Holder, Editor, wholder@wesleyan.edu. **USPS:** 674-760. **Remarks:** Advertising not accepted.
Circ: Controlled 30,000

4986 **The Wesleyan Argus**
Wesleyan University
PO Box 7055 Phone: (860)685-3325
Wesleyan Sta. Fax: (860)685-3411
Middletown, CT 06459
Publication E-mail: argus@wesleyan.edu

Collegiate newspaper. **Founded:** 1868. **Freq:** Semiweekly (Tues. and Fri.; during the academic year). **Print Method:** Uses mats. Offset. **Cols./Page:** 5. **Col. Width:** 22 nonpareils. **Col. Depth:** 224 agate lines. **Key Personnel:** Jeremy Dudd, Editor-in-Chief, phone (860)685-3952; Ike Walker, Editor-in-Chief. **USPS:** 674-680. **Subscription Rates:** $30 semester; $55 /year. **Remarks:** Accepts advertising.
Ad Rates: BW: $650 **Circ:** 3,200
4C: $800
PCI: $9.23

4987 **WESU-FM - 88.1**
Wesleyan Station Phone: (860)685-3668
Box 2300 Fax: (860)685-2411
Middletown, CT 06459
E-mail: wesu@wesleyan.edu

Format: Eclectic. **Owner:** Wesleyan Broadcasting Assoc., Inc., at above address. **Founded:** 1939. **Operating Hours:** Continuous. **Key Personnel:** Kim Wetzel, Station Mgr., kwetzel@wesleyan.edu; Rob Powers, Music Dir., rpowers@wesleyan.edu; Jonah Horwitz, Program Dir., jhorwitz@wesleyan.edu. **Local Programs:** *Gospel Express*, Marichal Monts; *Radio Avivamiento*, Sam Girong; *Reggae Bashment*, D. J. Derick. **Wattage:** 1,500. **Ad Rates:** Advertising accepted; rates available upon request.

MILFORD, pop. 50,898.

S. CT. New Haven Co. On Long Island Sound, 9 mi. SW of New Haven. Summer resort. Manufactures ball point pens, aerosol pressure cans, razors, locks, brass goods, rivets, metal novelties, screws, machine parts and tools, auto and marine hardware, thermostats, electric motors.

4988 **The Advertiser**
349 New Haven Ave. Phone: (203)876-6800
PO Box 5339 Fax: (203)877-4772
Milford, CT 06460
Free: (800)238-3226

Community newspaper. **Founded:** 1954. **Freq:** Weekly (Sat.). **Print Method:** Offset. **Cols./Page:** 6. **Col. Width:** 19 nonpareils. **Col. Depth:** 224 agate lines. **Key Personnel:** Denise Madera, Editor; Richard Barker, Publisher; William Flaucher, Advertising Mgr.
Ad Rates: SAU: $8.25 **Circ:** ‡17,500

4989 **The Bulletin**
Elm City Newspapers
349 New Haven Ave. Phone: (203)933-1000
PO Box 5339 Fax: (203)877-4772
Milford, CT 06460-6647
Free: (800)238-3226

Community newspaper (tabloid) serving Orange, Woodbridge, and Bethany. **Founded:** 1985. **Freq:** Weekly (Thurs.). **Print Method:** Photo offset. **Cols./Page:** 4. **Col. Width:** 18 nonpareils. **Col. Depth:** 133 agate lines. **Key Personnel:** Alan Olenick, Editor; Richard A. Barker, Publisher; William Flaucher, Advertising Dir. **Subscription Rates:** Free. **Remarks:** Accepts advertising. **Formerly:** Orange Bulletin.
Ad Rates: PCI: $7.70 **Circ:** Free ‡9,600

4990 **Elm City Citizen Newspaper**
ABC Capital City
349 New Haven Ave. Phone: (203)876-6800
PO Box 5339 Fax: (203)877-4772
Milford, CT 06460
Free: (800)238-3226

General newspaper. **Founded:** 1897. **Freq:** Daily (eve.), Sunday (morn.). **Print Method:** Offset. **Cols./Page:** 6. **Col. Width:** 19 nonpareils. **Col. Depth:** 210 agate lines. **Key Personnel:** Linda Bouvier, Editor; Ricki Smith-Coyne, Publisher. **Subscription Rates:** $63 individuals. **Remarks:** Accepts advertising.
Ad Rates: PCI: $8.45 **Circ:** Mon.-Fri. 6,496
Sun. 7,530

4991 **Milford Reporter**
Elm City Newspapers
349 New Haven Ave. Phone: (203)933-1000
PO Box 5339 Fax: (203)877-4772
Milford, CT 06460-6647
Free: (800)238-3226

Community newspaper (tabloid). **Founded:** 1963. **Freq:** Weekly (Fri.). **Print Method:** Photo offset. **Cols./Page:** 4. **Col. Width:** 18 nonpareils. **Col. Depth:** 133 agate lines. **Key Personnel:** Richard A. Barker, Publisher.
Ad Rates: GLR: $.79 **Circ:** Free ‡11,300
BW: $787.50
PCI: $8.75

4992 **National Development/Desarrollo Nacional**
Intercontinental Media Inc.
PO Box 3410 Phone: (203)874-1401
Milford, CT 06460 Fax: (203)874-1448

Magazine covering infrastructure development projects in the Middle East, Africa, Asia and South/Latin America. **Founded:** 1959. **Freq:** 6/year. **Print Method:** Offset. **Trim Size:** 10.75" x 10.75". **Cols./Page:** 4. **Col. Width:** 2 1/4 inches. **Col. Depth:** 10 inches. **Key Personnel:** Maria D'Aniello, Editor; James R. Coffey, Publisher. **ISSN:** 0730-0123. **Subscription Rates:** Free to qualified subscribers; $80 U.S.; $90 other countries. **Remarks:** Accepts advertising. **Absorbed:** Desarrollo Nacional.
Ad Rates: BW: $5,400 **Circ:** Controlled ‡21,000
4C: $6,350

4993 **Stratford Bard**
Elm City Newspapers
349 New Haven Ave. Phone: (203)876-6800
Milford, CT 06460 Fax: (203)877-4772
Publication E-mail: bard@juno.com

Community newspaper (tabloid). **Founded:** 1977. **Freq:** Weekly (Sat.). **Print Method:** Photo offset. **Key Personnel:** Erin Albren, Editor; William Rush, Publisher; Fred Carlson, Advertising Dir. **Subscription Rates:** Free. **Remarks:** Accepts advertising.
Ad Rates: PCI: $9 **Circ:** Free ‡17,000

West Haven News - See West Haven

4994 **WFIF-AM - 1500**
90 Kay Ave. Phone: (203)878-5915
Milford, CT 06460-5421
E-mail: wfif@juno.com

Format: Religious; Talk. **Networks:** USA Radio; Sun Radio; Ambassador Inspirational Radio. **Owner:** William Blount, c/o WARV, 19 Luther Ave., Warwick, RI 02886, (401)737-0700. **Founded:** 1965. **Operating Hours:** Sunrise-sunset; 50% network, 50% local. **Key Personnel:** William Blount, President; David Young, Vice President; Jennifer Hayden, Station Mgr.; William Barnett III, Chief Engineer. **Wattage:** 5000 day;500 post-sunset. **Ad Rates:** $10-12 for 30 seconds; $14-16 for 60 seconds. **URL:** http://www.lifechangingradio.com.

MONROE, pop. 14,010.

SW CT. Fairfield Co. 12 mi. N. of Bridgeport.

Huntington Herald - See Huntington

4995 LMT
LMT Communications, Inc.
731 Main St., Ste. A2 Phone: (203)459-2888
Monroe, CT 06468 Fax: (203)459-2889
Publication E-mail: info@lmtcommunications.com

Business strategies and marketing strategies magazine for dental laboratory owners and managers. **Subtitle:** Marketing/Technical/Business Strategies for Dental Laboratory Decision-Makers. **Founded:** 1984. **Freq:** 10/year. **Print Method:** Web offset. **Trim Size:** 10 7/8 x 14 1/2. **Cols./Page:** 5. **Col. Width:** 10 1/2 picas. **Col. Depth:** 74 picas. **Key Personnel:** Kelly Fessel-Carr, Editor, Kelly.carr@lmtcommunications.com; Judy Fishman, Publisher, judy.fishman@lmtcommunications.com; James Pouillard, Associate Publisher, james.pouilliard@lmtcommunications.com; Maribeth Marsico, Managing Editor, maribeth.marsico@lmtcommunications.com; Kim Molinaro, Associate Editor, kim.molinaro@lmtcommunications.com. **ISSN:** 8750-9539. **Subscription Rates:** $17.
Ad Rates: BW: $2,590 **Circ:** ‡17,934
4C: $3,890
PCI: $85

4996 WGRS-FM - 91.5
1014 Monroe Turnpike Phone: (203)268-9667
Monroe, CT 06468

Format: Classical; Big Band/Nostalgia; Folk. **Owner:** Monroe Board of Education, 375 Monroe Turnpike, Monroe, CT 06468. **Founded:** 1994. **Operating Hours:** Continuous. **Key Personnel:** Kurt Anderson, General Mgr.; Carol Babina, Development; Jane Stadler, Operations Dir. **Wattage:** 3,100.

4997 WGSK-FM - 90.1
1014 Monroe Turnpike Phone: (203)268-9667
Monroe, CT 06468

Format: Classical; Big Band/Nostalgia; Folk. **Owner:** Monroe Board of Education, 375 Monroe Turnpike, Monroe, CT 06468. **Operating Hours:** Continuous. **Key Personnel:** Kurt Anderson, General Mgr.; Carol Babina, Development; Jane Stadler, Operations Dir. **Wattage:** 258.

4998 WMNR-FM - 88.1
1014 Monroe Tpke. Phone: (203)268-9667
Monroe, CT 06468-1981

Format: Classical; Big Band/Nostalgia. **Networks:** Independent. **Owner:** Monroe Board of Education, 375 Monroe Turnpike, Monroe, CT 06468. **Operating Hours:** Continuous. **ADI:** New York, NY. **Key Personnel:** Kurt Anderson, General Mgr.; Carol Babina, Devolpment; Jane Stadler, Operations Dir.; Beatrice Asken, Music Dir. **Wattage:** 5000.

4999 WRXC-FM - 90.1
1014 Monroe Tpke. Phone: (203)268-9667
Monroe, CT 06468

Format: Jazz; Classical; Big Band/Nostalgia. **Networks:** Independent. **Owner:** Monroe Board of Education, 375 Monroe Turnpike, Monroe, CT 06468. **Founded:** 1982. **Operating Hours:** Continuous. **ADI:** New York, NY. **Key Personnel:** Kurt Anderson, General Mgr.; Carol Babina, Devolopment; Jane Stadler, Operations Dir.; Beatrice Asken, Music Dir. **Wattage:** 450.

MYSTIC, pop. 5,650.

SE CT. New London Co. 10 mi. E. of New London. Tourism.

5000 Log of Mystic Seaport
Mystic Seaport Museum, Inc.
75 Greenmanville Ave. Phone: (203)572-5347
PO Box 6000 Fax: (203)572-5326
Mystic, CT 06355-0990
Publisher E-mail: publications@mysticseaport.org

Journal on American maritime history and life. **Founded:** 1948. **Freq:** Quarterly. **Print Method:** Offset. **Trim Size:** 8 1/2 x 10 7/8. **Cols./Page:** 3. **Col. Width:** 28 nonpareils. **Col. Depth:** 129 agate lines. **Key Personnel:** Andrew W. German, Editor, andy@mysticseaport.org. **ISSN:** 0024-5828. **Subscription Rates:** $35 members; $2 single issue. **Remarks:** Advertising not accepted.
Circ: Paid 22,000
Controlled 300

5001 Religion Teacher's Journal
Twenty-Third Publications, Inc.
185 Willow St. Phone: (860)536-2611
PO Box 180 Fax: (800)572-0788
Mystic, CT 06355
Free: (800)321-0411
Publisher E-mail: ttpubs@aol.com

Trade magazine used as a training vehicle by pastors for laypersons working with them as church educators. **Founded:** 1967. **Freq:** 7/year. **Print Method:** Offset. Uses mats. **Trim Size:** 8 1/4 x 11. **Cols./Page:** 3. **Col. Width:** 27 nonpareils. **Col. Depth:** 140 agate lines. **Key Personnel:** Gwen Costello, Editor-in-Chief; William Holub, Rights & Permissions Contact; Susan Peowski, Advertising Mgr. **ISSN:** 0034-401X. **Subscription Rates:** $19.95 individuals; $17.95 2-5 individuals (each); $15.95 6-10 individuals (each); $13.95 11-20 individuals (each); $11.95 more than 20 individuals (each). **Remarks:** Accepts advertising. **Alt. Formats:** Microform.
Ad Rates: BW: $1,695 **Circ:** Paid 36,000
4C: $2,595

5002 Today's Parish
Twenty-Third Publications, Inc.
185 Willow St. Phone: (860)536-2611
PO Box 180 Fax: (800)572-0788
Mystic, CT 06355
Free: (800)321-0411
Publication E-mail: ttpubs@aol.com
Publisher E-mail: ttpubs@aol.com

Magazine which gives practical assistance in parish affairs for clergy, staff and lay workers in liturgy, music, education, computers, finance, administration and ministry in Catholic churches. **Founded:** 1969. **Freq:** 7/year. **Print Method:** Offset. **Trim Size:** 8 1/2 x 11. **Cols./Page:** 3. **Col. Width:** 26 nonpareils. **Col. Depth:** 140 agate lines. **Key Personnel:** Daniel Connors, Editor-in-Chief; William Holub, Rights and Permissions; Susan Peowski, Advertising Mgr. **ISSN:** 0040-8459. **Subscription Rates:** $22.95 individuals; $21.95 2-3 individuals (each); $19.95 4-10 individuals (each); $17.95 more than 10 individuals (each). **Remarks:** Accepts advertising.
Ad Rates: BW: $995 **Circ:** ‡15,000
4C: $1,795

NAUGATUCK, pop. 26,456.

S. CT. New Haven Co. 5 mi. S. of Waterbury. Manufactures chemicals, malleable iron castings, candy, aeronautical parts and fabricated metal products.

5003 Naugatuck Daily News
Daily News
71 Weid Dr. Phone: (203)729-2228
Naugatuck, CT 06770 Fax: (203)729-9099

General newspaper. **Founded:** 1885. **Freq:** Mon.-Sat. (eve.). **Print Method:** Offset. **Cols./Page:** 6. **Col. Width:** 22 nonpareils. **Col. Depth:** 308 agate lines. **Key Personnel:** Ronald Waer, Publisher; John Perritano, Editor. **Subscription Rates:** $87 individuals. **Remarks:** Accepts advertising.
Ad Rates: PCI: $6.15 **Circ:** 5,171

5004 WFNW-AM - 1380
700 Canal St.
Stamford, CT 06902

Format: Hispanic; Ethnic. **Founded:** 1961. **Key Personnel:** Gene Faltus, Chief Engineer. **Wattage:** 5000.

NEW BRITAIN†, pop. 73,840.

N. CT. Hartford Co. 10 mi. SW of Hartford. Central Connecticut State College. Manufacturing.

5005 The Herald
1 Herald Square Phone: (860)225-4601
PO Box 2050 Fax: (203)225-4601
New Britain, CT 06050-2050
General newspaper. **Founded:** 1880. **Freq:** Mon.-Sat. **Print Method:** Offset. **Cols./Page:** 6. **Col. Width:** 25 nonpareils. **Col. Depth:** 301 agate lines. **Key Personnel:** Judith W. Brown, Editor and Publisher. **USPS:** 377-920. **Subscription Rates:** $78 individuals. **Remarks:** Accepts advertising.
Ad Rates: GLR: $23.11 **Circ:** Mon.-Sat. 22,756
BW: $2535 Sun. 43,948
4C: $2845
SAU: $17.59
PCI: $19.65

5006 WFCS-FM - 97.9
1615 Stanley St. Phone: (860)225-8971
New Britain, CT 06053-2439 Fax: (860)225-4252

Format: Contemporary Hit Radio (CHR). **Networks:** Independent. **Founded:** 1950. **Formerly:** WTCC-AM (1972). **Operating Hours:** Continuous; 100% local. **Key Personnel:** Wayne Andrews, Program Dir.; Doug Turek, Promotions Mgr.; David Burke, Music Dir. **Wattage:** 100. **Ad Rates:** $8-12 for 30 seconds.

NEW CANAAN, pop. 17,931.

SW CT. Fairfield Co. 5 mi. NW of Norwalk. Residential.

5007 The Country Club
16 Forest St. Phone: (203)972-3892
New Canaan, CT 06840 Fax: (203)966-7268

Magazine edited exclusively for private country club members. **Founded:** Feb. 1986. **Freq:** Bimonthly. **Print Method:** Web offset. **Trim Size:** 8 3/8 x 10 7/8. **Cols./Page:** 3. **Key Personnel:** E. MacFarlan Moore, Editor and Publisher. **ISSN:** 0886-4462. **Subscription Rates:** Included with membership. **Remarks:** Accepts advertising. **Formerly:** The Golf Club.
Ad Rates: BW: $6,230 **Circ:** Non-paid ‡150,000
4C: $9,350

5008 Golf Range and Recreation Report
PO Box 1265 Phone: (203)972-6201
New Canaan, CT 06840 Fax: (203)972-1667
Publication E-mail: grraa@aol.com

Trade magazine catering to owners, operators, and developers of golf driving ranges, golf centers, and teaching academies. **Founded:** Jan. 1991. **Freq:** Bimonthly. **Print Method:** Web offset. **Trim Size:** 8 1/2 x 10 7/8. **Cols./Page:** 3. **Key Personnel:** Steven J. di Costanzo, President; Mark Silverman, Editor and Publisher. **Subscription Rates:** $75 U.S.; $125 other countries. **Remarks:** Accepts advertising. **URL:** http://www.golfshow.com/grraa.
Ad Rates: BW: $1300 **Circ:** Paid 640
4C: $1700 Controlled 5,600
PCI: $75

5009 New Canaan Advertiser
Hersam Publishing Co.
42 Vitti St. Phone: (203)966-9541
PO Box 605 Fax: (203)966-8006
New Canaan, CT 06840-4823
Community newspaper. **Founded:** July 25, 1908. **Freq:** Weekly (Thurs.). **Print Method:** Offset. **Trim Size:** 17 x 22 3/4. **Cols./Page:** 9. **Col. Width:** 21 nonpareils. **Col. Depth:** 294 agate lines. **Key Personnel:** E.J. Chrostowski, Editor; V. Donald Hersam, Jr., Publisher; Mary Anne Junget, Advertising Mgr. **Subscription Rates:** $20 individuals; $25 out of area; $12 Schoola. **Remarks:** Accepts advertising.
Ad Rates: GLR: $.37 **Circ:** Thurs. 6,462
BW: $926.10
4C: $1,826.10
PCI: $5.40

5010 WSLX-FM - 91.9
377 N. Wilton Rd. Phone: (203)966-5612
PO Box 1148
New Canaan, CT 06840

Format: Classical. **Networks:** Independent. **Owner:** St. Luke's Foundation, at above address. **Founded:** 1975. **Operating Hours:** 18 hrs. Daily; 100% local. **Key Personnel:** Daniel A. Mecca, Contact. **Wattage:** 10. **Ad Rates:** Noncommercial.

NEW HAVEN†, pop. 126,107.

S. CT. New Haven Co. On Long Island Sound. Yale University (coed); divinity, pharmacy, physical education and other colleges; private schools. Industrial center. Trap rock quarries. Shipyard. Manufactures guns, ammunition, hardware, tools, rubber goods, toys, sewing machine attachments, lamps, clocks, watches, textiles, asbestos insulated wire, airplane parts, paper boxboard. Agriculture.

5011 American Journal of Science
Yale University Phone: (203)432-3131
PO Box 208109 Fax: (203)432-5668
New Haven, CT 06520-8109
Journal focusing on geology and the geological sciences. **Founded:** 1818. **Freq:** 10/year. **Trim Size:** 6 x 9. **Cols./Page:** 1. **Col. Width:** 54 nonpareils. **Col. Depth:** 102 agate lines. **Key Personnel:** Marie Casey, Managing Editor. **Subscription Rates:** $40 individuals; $70 institutions. **Remarks:** Accepts advertising.
Ad Rates: BW: $100 **Circ:** 2,500

5012 L'Anello Che Non Tiene
Yale University
Box 4067, Yale Sta.
New Haven, CT 06520-4067

Journal covering Italian literature. **Subtitle:** Journal of Modern Italian Literature. **Freq:** Semiannual. **ISSN:** 0099-5273. **Subscription Rates:** $15 individuals. **Remarks:** Accepts advertising.
Ad Rates: BW: $100 **Circ:** (Not Reported)

5013 Business Times
Choice Media, LLC
PO Box 580 Phone: (203)782-1420
New Haven, CT 06513-0580 Fax: (203)782-3793
Publication E-mail: cbtimes@cfbusinesstimes.com

Business journal (tabloid). **Founded:** 1978. **Freq:** Monthly. **Print Method:** Web Offset. **Trim Size:** 11 x 13. **Cols./Page:** 4. **Col. Width:** 2 3/8 inches. **Col. Depth:** 12 1/2 inches. **Key Personnel:** Joel D. MacClaren, Publisher; Karen Brown, Advertising Mgr. **Subscription Rates:** $36 individuals per year. **Remarks:** Accepts advertising. **URL:** http://www.ctbusinesstimes.com.
Ad Rates: BW: $2,400 **Circ:** Non-paid ‡22,400
4C: $2,950

5014 Columbia
Knights of Columbus
1 Columbus Plaza Phone: (203)772-2130
New Haven, CT 06510-3326 Fax: (203)772-1923

International Catholic family magazine (French, Spanish, and English). **Subtitle:** Knights of Columbus Magazine. **Founded:** 1920. **Freq:** Monthly. **Print Method:** Offset. **Trim Size:** 8 1/4 x 10 3/4. **Cols./Page:** 3. **Col. Width:** 13.5 picas. **Col. Depth:** 60 picas. **Key Personnel:** Richard McMunn, Editor. **ISSN:** 0010-1869. **Subscription Rates:** $6 individuals. **Remarks:** Advertising not accepted.
Circ: ‡1,450,000

5015 Connecticut Medicine
Connecticut State Medical Society
160 St. Ronan St. Phone: (203)865-0587
New Haven, CT 06511 Fax: (203)492-4112
Publisher E-mail: csmg.org

Professional medical journal. **Subtitle:** The Journal of the Connecticut State Medical Society. **Founded:** 1936. **Freq:** Monthly. **Print Method:** Web offset. **Trim Size:** 8 x 11. **Cols./Page:** 2. **Col. Width:** 19 picas. **Col. Depth:** 9 inches. **Key Personnel:** Wanda Jacques-Gill, Managing Editor; Rhonda Hawes, Business Mgr. **ISSN:** 0010-6178. **Subscription Rates:** $25 individuals; $5 single issue. **Remarks:** Accepts advertising.
Ad Rates: BW: $395 **Circ:** (Not Reported)
4C: $1,100

5016 Connecticut Parent Magazine
Choice Media, LLC
PO Box 580 Phone: (203)782-1420
New Haven, CT 06513-0580 Fax: (203)782-3793
Publication E-mail: ctparent@family.com

Parenting magazine. **Founded:** 1984. **Freq:** Monthly. **Trim Size:** 11 x13. **Cols./Page:** 4. **Col. Width:** 2 3/8 inches. **Col. Depth:** 12 1/2 inches. **Key Personnel:** Joel D. MacClaren, Editor; Francesca Wood, Circulation Mgr.; Karen Brown, Assoc. Pub. **Subscription Rates:** $24 individuals. **Remarks:** Accepts advertising. **URL:** http://ctparent.com.
Ad Rates: BW: $1,560 **Circ:** Non-paid ‡48,500
4C: $2,110

5017 Fairfield County Business Times
Choice Media, LLC
P.O. Box 580 Phone: (203)782-1420
New Haven, CT 06513-0580 Fax: (203)782-3793
Publication E-mail: cbtimes@ctbusinesstimes.com

Business journal (tabloid). **Founded:** 1978. **Freq:** Monthly. **Print Method:** Web offset. **Trim Size:** 11 x 13. **Cols./Page:** 4. **Col. Width:** 2 3/8 inches. **Col. Depth:** 12 1/2 inches. **Key Personnel:** Joel D. MacClaren, Editor; Karen Brown, Advertising Mgr. **Subscription Rates:** $36 individuals. **Remarks:** Accepts advertising. **URL:** http://www.ctbusinesstimes.com.
Ad Rates: BW: $2,400 **Circ:** ‡7,400
4C: $2,950
PCI: $48

5018 Federal Sentencing Reporter
University of California Press/Journals
Yale Law School Phone: (203)334-1300
127 Wall St. Fax: (203)941-9407
New Haven, CT 06520
Publication E-mail: slyon@vera.org
Publisher E-mail: journal@ucop.edu

Law journal. **Key Personnel:** Daniel Freed, Editor; Alexis Agathocleous, Publication Mgr.; Marge Dean, Advertising & Circulation Mgr. **Subscription Rates:** $146 individuals; $90 Academic; $30 single issue. **Remarks:** Advertising not accepted.
Circ: (Not Reported)

5019 Imagination, Cognition and Personality
Baywood Publishing Co., Inc.
Dept. of Psychology Phone: (203)432-4527
Yale University Fax: (203)432-4608
Box 208205
New Haven, CT 06520-8205
Publisher E-mail: baywood@baywood.com

Journal focusing on the diverse uses of imagery, fantasy, and consciousness in psychotherapy, behavior modification, and related areas of sleep. **Subtitle:** Consciousness: Theory, Research, and Practice. **Founded:** 1981. **Freq:** Quarterly. **Trim Size:** 6 x 9. **Cols./Page:** 1. **Col. Width:** 4 1/2 inches. **Col. Depth:** 7 1/2 inches. **Key Personnel:** Jerome L. Singer, Ph.D., Editor, phone (203)432-4527, fax (203)432-4608, jerome.singer@yale.edu; Stuart Cohen, Ph.D., Publisher, phone (516)691-1270, fax (516)691-1770; Lisa Pagliaro, Managing Editor; Lorna Roher, Editor; S. Edwards, Circulation Mgr.; Kenneth S. Pope, Ph.D., Co-editor. **ISSN:** 0276-2366. **Subscription Rates:** $42.50 U.S. and Canada; $47.75 out of country; $122.50 Industry, U.S. & Canada; $127.35 Industry, other countries. **Remarks:** Advertising not accepted.
Circ: (Not Reported)

5020 The Inner City Newspaper
Penfield Communications, Inc.
50 Fitch St. Phone: (203)387-0354
New Haven, CT 06515 Fax: (203)387-2684

Community newspaper (tabloid). Includes some articles in Spanish. **Founded:** Sept. 1990. **Freq:** Weekly. **Print Method:** Web offset. **Trim Size:** 11 x 14 1/2. **Cols./Page:** 4. **Col. Width:** 2 5/16 inches. **Col. Depth:** 13 5/8 inches. **Key Personnel:** Thomas R. Ficklin, Editor-in-Chief, tomficklin@aol.com; John Thomas, Jr., Publisher. **Subscription Rates:** $35. **Remarks:** Accepts advertising.
Ad Rates: GLR: $35 **Circ:** Free ‡35,000
PCI: $19.50

5021 International Bulletin of Missionary Research
Overseas Ministries Study Center
490 Prospect St. Phone: (203)624-6672
New Haven, CT 06511-2196 Fax: (203)865-2857
Publication E-mail: ibmr@omsc.org

Professional journal on Christian mission and cross-cultural ministries. Examines contemporary issues and developments in the Christian world mission, employing interdenominational, interdisciplinary, and international perspectives. **Founded:** Jan. 1977. **Freq:** Quarterly. **Print Method:** Offset. **Trim Size:** 8 1/4 x 11. **Cols./Page:** 2 and 3. **Col. Width:** 22 and 13 1/2 picas. **Col. Depth:** 140 agate lines. **Key Personnel:** Gerald H. Anderson, Editor and Publisher, anderson@msc.org; Ruth E. Taylor, Advertising Dir., phone (207)799-4387; Gerald H. Anderson, Editor. **ISSN:** 0272-6122. **Subscription Rates:** $21 individuals; $6 single issue. **Remarks:** Color advertising not accepted. **Online:** EBSCO; Information Access Company; UMI. **Alt. Formats:** Microform. **Formerly:** Occasional Bulletin of Missionary Research.
Ad Rates: BW: $550 **Circ:** Paid 6,300
Non-paid 300

5022 Journal of Conflict Resolution
Sage Publications Inc.
Yale University Phone: (203)432-5235
Political Science Dept. Fax: (203)432-6196
New Haven, CT 06520-8301
Publication E-mail: jcr128@pantheon.yale.edu
Publisher E-mail: info@sagepub.com

Journal containing studies of war, peace, and international relations. **Subtitle:** Journal of the Peace Science Society (International). **Founded:** 1957. **Freq:** Bimonthly. **Print Method:** Offset. **Trim Size:** 5 1/2 x 8 1/2. **Cols./Page:** 1. **Col. Width:** 50 nonpareils. **Col. Depth:** 100 agate lines. **Key Personnel:** Bruce M. Russett, Editor, bruce.russett@yale.edu; Cris Anderson, Circulation Mgr. **ISSN:** 0022-0027. **Subscription Rates:** $78 individuals; $356 institutions; $15 single issue; $61 single issue Institutions. **Remarks:** Accepts advertising.
Ad Rates: BW: $250 **Circ:** Paid ‡2,363
Non-paid ‡114

5023 Journal of Marine Research
Yale University
PO Box 208109 Phone: (203)432-3154
New Haven, CT 06520-8109 Fax: (203)432-3134
Publication E-mail: jmr@yale.edu

Journal of interdisciplinary oceanographic research. **Founded:** 1937. **Freq:** Bimonthly. **Key Personnel:** George Veronis, Editor; Don Rice, Associate Editor. **ISSN:** 0022-2402. **Subscription Rates:** $110 individuals. **Remarks:** Advertising not accepted.
Circ: Paid 1,000

5024 Journal of Sustainable Forestry
The Haworth Press, Inc.
Yale Univ. School of Forestry, Phone: (203)432-5142
Greeley Mem. Lab Fax: (203)432-3929
370 Prospect St
New Haven, CT 06511
Publication E-mail: hmallon@haworthpressic.com; mcoch@haworthpress.com
Publisher E-mail: getinfo@haworthpressinc.com

Journal covering topics in biotechnology, physiology, silviculture, wood science, economics, and forest management. **Founded:** 1992. **Freq:** Quarterly. **Trim Size:** 6x8 1/2. **Key Personnel:** Graeme P. Berlyn, Ph.D., Editor, graeme@minerva.cis.yale.edu; Bill Cohen, Publisher, phone (607)722-5857, fax (607)722-1424. **ISSN:** 1054-9811. **Subscription Rates:** $45 individuals; $54 institutions; $103.50 libraries. **Remarks:** Accepts advertising. **Alt. Formats:** Microfiche.
Ad Rates: BW: $300 **Circ:** 148

5025 New Haven Advocate
1 Long Wharf Dr. Phone: (203)789-0010
New Haven, CT 06511-5991 Fax: (203)787-1418

Regional newspaper focusing on news, arts and entertainment. **Founded:** 1975. **Freq:** Weekly (Wed.). **Print Method:** Offset. **Trim Size:** 10 1/4 x 12 3/4. **Cols./Page:** 5. **Col. Width:** 11.5 picas. **Col. Depth:** 12 3/4 agate lines. **Key Personnel:** Josh Mamis, Editor, jmamis@newhavenadvocate.com; Gail Thompson, Publisher, gthompson@newhavenadvocate.com; Karen Unger, Listings Editor, kunger@newhavenadvocate.com; Susan Leighton, Sales Mgr., sleighton@newhavenadvocate.com. **Subscription Rates:** Free; $120 by mail. **Remarks:** Advertising accepted; rates available upon request. **URL:** http://www.newhavenadvocate.com.
Circ: Free 55,000

5026 New Haven Register
Long Wharf, 40 Sargent Dr. Phone: (203)789-5200
New Haven, CT 06511 Fax: (203)865-7894

General newspaper. **Founded:** Dec. 1812. **Freq:** Mon.-Sun. (morn.). **Print Method:** Offset. **Trim Size:** 13 x 21. **Cols./Page:** 6. **Col. Width:** 12.4 picas. **Col. Depth:** 21 inches. **Key Personnel:** William Rush, Publisher; Hank Misiak, Advertising Dir.; Abram Katz, Editor; Charles Kochakian, Editor; Jack Kramer, Editor; Michael Lynch, Marketing Director; Dave Butler, Editor; Michael Vanacore, National Manager; Tina Goodwin, Research Manager. **Remarks:** Accepts advertising. **URL:** http://www.ctcentral.com. **Feature Editors:** Joseph Amarante, *Editorials, TV & Radio*; Dianne Averill, *Women's*, phone (203)789-5673; D. Hayne Bayless, *Travel*, phone (203)789-5674; Jack Kramer, *Suburban*, phone (203)789-5708; Lloyd Thompson, *Science*.
Ad Rates: GLR: $4.80 **Circ:** Mon.-Sat. ★**100,062**
BW: $7,087.50 Sun. ★**112,318**
4C: $8,467.50
SAU: $56.25

5027 Saint Raphaels' Better Health
St. Raphael's Better Health
1450 Chapel St. Phone: (203)789-3972
New Haven, CT 06511 Fax: (203)789-4053

Health magazine. **Founded:** 1979. **Freq:** Bimonthly. **Print Method:** Offset. **Trim Size:** 8 1/8 x 10 3/4. **Cols./Page:** 3. **Col. Width:** 27 nonpareils. **Col. Depth:** 140 agate lines. **Key Personnel:** Magaly Olivero, Publishing Dir. **Subscription Rates:** $15 voluntary.
Ad Rates: BW: $2,500 **Circ:** Non-paid ★**132,971**
4C: $2,900

5028 Shore Line Times
Shore Line Newspapers
Sargent Dr. Phone: (203)453-2711
New Haven, CT 06511
Newspaper. **Founded:** 1877. **Freq:** Semiweekly (Wed. and Fri.). **Print Method:** Offset. **Cols./Page:** 6. **Col. Width:** 9.6 picas. **Col. Depth:** 16 inches. **Key Personnel:** William Rush, Publisher, phone (203)789-5200; Silvio Albino, Editor, phone (203)789-5617; Jim Gibbons, Advertising Mgr. **Subscription Rates:** $37 individuals; $55 out of country. **Remarks:** Accepts advertising.
Ad Rates: PCI: $9.30 **Circ:** Wed. ‡9,548
Fri. ‡9,548

5029 Theater (New Haven)
Yale University
222 York St. Phone: (203)432-8336
New Haven, CT 06520 Fax: (203)432-9664

Scholarly journal covering modern plays and theater. **Founded:** 1968. **Key Personnel:** Erika Munk, Editor. **ISSN:** 0616-0775. **Subscription Rates:** $22 individuals; $8 single issue. **Remarks:** Accepts advertising.
Ad Rates: BW: $250 **Circ:** Combined 2,400

5030 Yale Daily News
Yale Daily News Publishing Co., Inc.
PO Box 209007 Phone: (203)432-2414
Yale Sta. Fax: (203)432-7425
New Haven, CT 06520-9007
Publication E-mail: ydn@yale.edu; ydn.business@yale.edu

Collegiate newspaper. **Founded:** Jan. 1878. **Freq:** Daily (morn.) (during the academic year). **Print Method:** Offset. **Trim Size:** 12 x 21. **Cols./Page:** 6. **Col. Width:** 1.9 inches. **Col. Depth:** 21 inches. **Key Personnel:** Ephram Lustgarten, ephram.lustgarten@yaledailynews.com. **USPS:** 695-060. **Subscription Rates:** $.50 single issue; $75 out of area Free on campus. **Remarks:** Accepts advertising. **URL:** http://www.yaledailynews.com. **Alt. Formats:** CD-ROM.
Ad Rates: BW: $1764 **Circ:** Paid ‡1,000
4C: $2,262 Free ‡7,500
PCI: $16

5031 The Yale Herald
252 Park St. Phone: (203)432-7494
New Haven, CT 06511 Fax: (203)432-7559
Publication E-mail: herald@yale.edu

Collegiate newspaper. **Subtitle:** An Undergraduate Publication. **Founded:** Feb. 14, 1986. **Freq:** Weekly. **Trim Size:** 11.5 x 17. **Cols./Page:** 4. **Col. Width:** 2.5 inches. **Col. Depth:** 16 inches. **Key Personnel:** David Altschuler, Editor-in-Chief; Amanda McCaughley, Publisher. **Subscription Rates:** $45. **URL:** www.yale.edu/herald.
Ad Rates: BW: $625 **Circ:** Paid 250
4C: $900 Non-paid 5,000
PCI: $4.37

5032 The Yale Journal of Biology & Medicine
The Yale Journal of Biology and Medicine, Inc.
PO Box 208000 Phone: (203)785-4251
New Haven, CT 06520-8000 Fax: (203)785-4251
Publication E-mail: yjbm@yale.edu

Journal carrying original contributions, medical reviews, case reports, medical histories, biomedical symposia. **Founded:** Oct. 1928. **Freq:** Bimonthly. **Print Method:** Letterpress. **Trim Size:** 7 x 10. **Cols./Page:** 1. **Col. Width:** 5 inches. **Col. Depth:** 8 1/2 inches. **Key Personnel:** William C. Summers, M.D.,, Editor-in-Chief; Suzanne Lande, Publisher. **ISSN:** 0044-0086. **Subscription Rates:** $45 individuals; $90 institutions. **Remarks:** Advertising accepted; rates available upon request. **URL:** http://www.med.yale.edu/yjbm.
Circ: ‡600

5033 The Yale Journal of Criticism
PO Box 208298
New Haven, CT 06520

Journal of criticism covering literature and art. **Freq:** Semiannual. **Key Personnel:** Ian Baucom, Editor; Debarati Sawyal, Editor; Charles Musser, Editor; Maurice Wallace, Editor; Sarah Winter, Editor; Laura Wexler, Editor.

5034 Yale Journal of Law and Feminism
PO Box 208215 Phone: (203)432-4056
New Haven, CT 06520 Fax: (203)432-2592

Journal serving as a forum for the analysis of women's experience as affected by the law. **Founded:** 1989. **Freq:** Semiannual. **Print Method:** Offset. **Cols./Page:** 1. **ISSN:** 1043-9366. **Subscription Rates:** $20 individuals; $30 institutions; $30 industry. **Remarks:** Accepts advertising. **Online:** LEXIS and WESTLAW. **URL:** http://www.yale.edu/lawnfem/lawnfem.html.
Ad Rates: BW: $75 **Circ:** Paid 1,100

5035 The Yale Law Journal
Yale Law Journal Co.
PO Box 208215 Phone: (203)432-1666
New Haven, CT 06520-8215 Fax: (203)432-7482

Professional law journal. **Founded:** 1891. **Freq:** 8/year. **Print Method:** Letterpress. **Cols./Page:** 1. **Col. Width:** 57 nonpareils. **Col. Depth:** 105 agate lines. **Subscription Rates:** $40 individuals; $9 single issue. **Remarks:** Accepts advertising.
Ad Rates: BW: $175 **Circ:** ‡4,300

5036 The Yale Literary Magazine
PO Box 209087, Yale Stn. Phone: (203)432-4771
New Haven, CT 06520-7394
Literary magazine. **Subtitle:** An Undergraduate Publication. **Founded:** 1831. **Freq:** Semiannual. **Print Method:** Letterpress and offset. **Cols./Page:** 1. **Col. Width:** 60 nonpareils. **Col. Depth:** 112 agate lines. **Key Personnel:** Dana Goodyear, Co-Ed.; Chaudra Speeth, Co-Ed. **ISSN:** 0148-4605. **Subscription Rates:** Free; $15 individuals; $35 institutions. **Remarks:** Advertising not accepted.
Circ: Paid 130
Non-paid 2,500

5037 The Yale Review
Blackwell Publishers
Yale University Phone: (203)432-0499
Box 208243 Fax: (203)432-0510
Yale Sta.
New Haven, CT 06520
Publication E-mail: yalerev@yale.edu
Publisher E-mail: books@blackwellpub.com

Public affairs articles, literature, book reviews, poetry, and critical articles on literature and culture. **Founded:** 1911. **Freq:** Quarterly. **Print Method:** Offset. **Trim Size:** 6 x 9 1/8. **Cols./Page:** 1. **Col. Width:** 26 picas. **Col. Depth:** 44 picas. **Key Personnel:** J.D. McClatchy, Editor; Susan Bianconi, Managing Editor, susan.bianconi@yale.com. **ISSN:** 0044-0124. **Subscription Rates:** $27 individuals; $39 out of country Industry; $65 institutions; $73 institutions, other countries. **Remarks:** Accepts advertising.
Ad Rates: BW: $360 **Circ:** ‡6,000

5038 Yale Scientific Magazine
Yale Sta.
PO Box 209117
New Haven, CT 06520

Magazine on science and technology research at Yale. **Founded:** 1894. **Freq:** Quarterly. **Print Method:** Offset. **Trim Size:** 8 1/2 x 11 1/2. **Cols./Page:** 3. **Col. Width:** 2 1/4 inches. **Col. Depth:** 8 7/8 inches. **Key Personnel:** Elizabeth Arias, Editor-in-Chief. **ISSN:** 0091-0287. **Subscription Rates:** $12 individuals; $3 single issue; $24 other countries; $6 single issue other countries; $18 Canada; $4.50 single issue, Canada. **Remarks:** Accepts advertising. **URL:** http://www.yale.edu/scimag/.
Ad Rates: BW: $250 **Circ:** Paid ‡5,000
4C: $350 Non-paid ‡3,000
PCI: $15

5039 Comcast Cablevision
190 Whalley Ave. Phone: (203)865-0429
New Haven, CT 06511 Fax: (203)562-4331

Founded: 1964. **Formerly**: Storer Cable TV of Connecticut, Inc. **Cities Served:** New Haven County, Hamden, and West Haven, CT.

5040 WAVZ-AM - 1300
PO Box 85 Phone: (203)248-8814
New Haven, CT 06501 Fax: (203)281-2795

Format: Album-Oriented Rock (AOR). **Networks:** Satellite Music Network. **Owner:** Clear Channel Radio, Inc., 7710 Jones Maltsberger, No. 600, San Antonio, TX 78216. **Founded:** 1947. **Operating Hours:** Continuous. **ADI:** Hartford-New Haven (New London), CT. **Key Personnel:** Faith Zila, General Mgr.; Kelly Nash, Program Dir. **Wattage:** 1000. **Ad Rates:** $8-40 for 30 seconds; $10-50 for 60 seconds.

5041 WBNG-TV - 59
8 Elm St. Phone: (203)782-5900
New Haven, CT 06510 Fax: (203)782-5995
E-mail: @wb59.com

Format: Commercial TV. **Owner:** K-W TV, Inc., 4930 W. Oakton St., Skokie, IL 60077. **Founded:** Apr. 3, 1995. **Former name**: WTVU-TV. **Operating Hours:** Continuous. **ADI:** Hartford-New Haven (New London), CT. **Key Personnel:** Gail L. Brekke, VP/Station Mgr.; Greg Bendin, General Sales Mgr./News Mgr.; John Russo, LSM. **Wattage:** 5,000,000 ERP. **URL:** http://www.wb59.com.

5042 WEDY-TV - 65
c/o WEDH-TV Phone: (860)278-5310
240 New Britain Ave. Fax: (860)278-2157
Box 6240
Hartford, CT 06106-3185
Free: (800)683-1899

Format: Public TV. **Simulcasts:** WEDH-TV Hartford, CT. **Networks:** Public Broadcasting Service (PBS). **Founded:** 1962. **Operating Hours:** 7:00 a.m.-midnight Daily; 8 a.m.-midnight Sat & Sun. **ADI:** Hartford-New Haven (New London), CT. **Key Personnel:** Jerry Franklin, President & CEO, phone (860)278-5310, fax (860)244-9624, franklin@wedh.pbs.org; Larry Rifkin, Exec. VP of Programming, fax (860)278-2157; Steve Futernick, Sr. VP of Community Development; Anita Ford Saunders, VP of Creative Services, phone (860)278-5310, fax (860)244-9624, saunders@wedh.pbs.org; John Berky, VP of Radio, radio905@prodigy.com; Meg Sakellarides, CFO; JoAnn Freiberg-Regan, Dir. of ITRS; Jay Whitsett, VP Broadcast Oper. and Production svcs.; Paul Gagnon, Director of Membership, phone (860)278-5310, fax (860)244-9624. **Local Programs:** *Connecticut Lawmakers*, Steve Kotchco; *Connecticut This Week*, Mary Ollie Newman; *The Fourth Estate*; *On The Record*. **Wattage:** 55 KW. **Ad Rates:** Advertising not accepted.

5043 WKCI-FM - 101.3
PO Box 85 Phone: (203)248-8814
New Haven, CT 06501 Fax: (203)281-2795
E-mail: wkci@aol.comm

Format: Contemporary Hit Radio (CHR). **Networks:** Independent. **Founded:** 1969. **Operating Hours:** Continuous. **ADI:** Hartford-New Haven (New London), CT. **Key Personnel:** Faith Zila, General Mgr., phone (203)281-9600; Mike Raub, Operations Mgr., phone (203)281-9600; Jim Simenetti, Nat'l Sales Mgr., phone (203)281-9600. **Wattage:** 10,000. **Ad Rates:** $50-280 per unit.

5044 WTNH-TV - 8
Box 1859 Phone: (203)784-8888
New Haven, CT 06508 Fax: (203)773-1292
E-mail: wtnh@wtnh.com

Format: Commercial TV. **Networks:** ABC. **Operating Hours:** Continuous. **ADI:** Hartford-New Haven (New London), CT. **Key Personnel:** Hank Yaggi, Pres./Gen.Mgr. **URL:** http://www.wtnh.com.

5045 WYBC-FM - 94.3
165 Elm St. Phone: (203)432-4118
PO Box 209050 Fax: (203)432-4117
New Haven, CT 06520
E-mail: wybc@yale.edu

Format: Urban Contemporary. **Networks:** Satellite Music Network. **Founded:** 1941. **Operating Hours:** Continuous. **ADI:** Hartford-New Haven (New London), CT. **Key Personnel:** Wayne Schmidt, Ops. Dir. **Wattage:** 3000. **URL:** http://www.yale.edu/wybc.

NEW LONDON†, pop. 28,842.

SE CT. New London Co. On Long Island Sound at mouth of Thames River, 14 mi. S. of Norwich. Port of entry with deep harbor. Naval Coast Guard Service Center. Connecticut College; Univ. of Conn. U. S. Coast Guard Academy. Private schools. Manufactures toothpaste and tube containers, printing presses, diesel, marine and turbine engines, submarines, chemicals, floor covering, bed springs, mattresses, textiles, gear cutters, corrugated paper containers, paper products, thread, soap, wooden cabinets, safety razors. Shipyards.

5046 The College Voice
Connecticut College
270 Mohegan Ave. Phone: (203)439-2841
PO Box 4970 Fax: (203)439-2843
New London, CT 06320
Publisher E-mail: ccvoice@conncoll.edu

Collegiate newspaper. **Founded:** 1976. **Freq:** Weekly (Fri.). **Print Method:** Offset. **Trim Size:** 8 1/2 x 11. **Cols./Page:** 5. **Col. Width:** 24 nonpareils. **Col. Depth:** 238 agate lines. **Key Personnel:** Brian Bielvch, Editor-in-Chief; Josh Friedlander, Editor-in-Chief; Rob Knake, Managing Editor; Tim Herrick, Managing Editor. **Subscription Rates:** $40. **Remarks:** Accepts advertising.
Ad Rates: GLR: $4.50 **Circ:** Paid 100
BW: $300 Free 2,400

5047 The Day
Day Publishing Co.
47 Eugene O'Neill Dr. Phone: (203)442-2200
New London, CT 06320-1231 Fax: (203)442-5599
Free: (800)542-3354

General newspaper. **Founded:** 1881. **Freq:** Mon.-Sun. (morn.). **Print Method:** Offset. **Trim Size:** 13 x 21. **Cols./Page:** 6. **Col. Width:** 2 1/16 inches. **Col. Depth:** 21 inches. **Key Personnel:** Reid MacCluggage, Editor and Publisher, fax (203)447-1683, r.maccluggage@newlondonday.com; Alcino G. Almeida, General Mgr., fax (203)447-1683, a.almeida@newlondonday.com. **Subscription Rates:** $187.50 by mail. **Remarks:** Accepts advertising.
Ad Rates: GLR: $.91 **Circ:** Mon.-Sat. ★**41,192**
BW: $3,507.84 Sun. ★**46,977**
4C: $4,157.84
PCI: $15.70

5048 Nautical World
Primedia Enthusiast Publications
1 Whale Oil Row Phone: (860)444-0127
New London, CT 06320 Fax: (860)444-0129
Publication E-mail: nautworld@aol.com

Consumer magazine covering marine art, classic yachts, ocean liners, nautical books, and maritime history. **Founded:** Mar. 1994. **Freq:** Bimonthly. **Key Personnel:** Robert R. McKenna, Editor. **ISSN:** 1094-0170. **Subscription Rates:** $24.95 individuals; $3.50 single issue. **Remarks:** Accepts advertising.
Ad Rates: BW: $895 **Circ:** Paid **20,000**
4C: $1,600

5049 The Seal
Mitchell College
437 Pequot Ave. Phone: (860)443-2811
New London, CT 06320-4498 Fax: (860)437-0632
Free: (800)443-2811

Alumni newsletter. **Subscription Rates:** Free.
Circ: 10,000

5050 WCNI-FM - 91.1
Box 4972, Connecticut College Phone: (203)439-2853
270 Mohegan Ave. Fax: (860)439-2850
New London, CT 06320

Format: Eclectic. **Founded:** 1974. **Operating Hours:** Continuous. **ADI:** Hartford-New Haven (New London), CT. **Key Personnel:** Tom O'Connor, General Mgr.; Chucky Daddy, President. **Wattage:** 490. **Ad Rates:** Noncommercial.

5051 WQGN-FM - 105.5
7 Gov. Winthrop Blvd. Phone: (860)443-1980
New London, CT 06320 Fax: (860)444-7970
E-mail: q105@q105worldwide.com

Format: Contemporary Hit Radio (CHR). **Networks:** ABC; Westwood One Radio. **Founded:** 1971. **Formerly:** H & D Wireless LP; Q105. **Operating Hours:** Continuous. **Wattage:** 3000. **Ad Rates:** $30-75 per unit.

5052 WSUB-AM - 980
7 Governor Winthrop Blvd. Phone: (860)443-1980
New London, CT 06320-4360 Fax: (860)444-7970

Format: Talk; News; Sports. **Networks:** ABC; Talknet. **Owner:** Spring Broadcasting, 1750 Rockville Pine, S-20, Rockville, MD 20852, (301)770-4476, Fax: (301)770-5526. **Founded:** 1958. **Operating Hours:** Continuous. **ADI:** Hartford-New Haven (New London), CT. **Key Personnel:** Phil Jones, Station Mgr. **Local Programs:** *Feedback*, John Teehan; *Morning Magazine*, John Teehan; *Senior Focus*, Dale Callaghan. **Wattage:** 1000. **URL:** http://www.wsub.com.

5053 WTWS-TV - 26
3 Shaws Cove, Ste.226 Phone: (203)444-2626
New London, CT 06320 Fax: (203)440-2601

Format: Commercial TV. **Networks:** Independent. **Founded:** 1984. **Formerly:** WCLT-TV. **Operating Hours:** Continuous. **ADI:** Hartford-New Haven (New London), CT. **Key Personnel:** Bruce Fox, Station Mgr. & Sales Mgr.

NEW MILFORD, pop. 19,420.

NW CT. Litchfield Co. 16 mi. N. of Danbury. Manufactures disposable paper products, copper tubing, electronics equipment. Foundry. Summer resort. Dairy, poultry farms.

5054 New Milford Times
Housatonic Valley Publishing Co.
132 Danbury Rd. Phone: (860)354-2261
PO Box 1139 Fax: (860)354-2645
New Milford, CT 06776
Publisher E-mail: housvalpub@aol.com

Community newspaper. **Founded:** 1914. **Freq:** Weekly (Fri.). **Print Method:** Offset. **Cols./Page:** 6. **Col. Width:** 26 nonpareils. **Col. Depth:** 294 agate lines. **Key Personnel:** Arthur Cummings, Editor, edit@shippingdigest.com; Trip Rothschild, Publisher; John Norton, Vice President. **Subscription Rates:** $24.95 individuals; $34.95 Out of county; $36.95 out of state.
Ad Rates: SAU: $10.65 **Circ:** Combined ♦**5,896**

5055 The Patent Trader
Housatonic Valley Publishing Co.
132 Danbury Rd. Phone: (860)354-2261
PO Box 1139 Fax: (860)354-2645
New Milford, CT 06776
Publisher E-mail: housvalpub@aol.com

Community newspaper. **Founded:** 1956. **Freq:** Weekly (Thurs.). **Print Method:** Offset. **Cols./Page:** 6. **Col. Width:** 21 nonpareils. **Col. Depth:** 300 agate lines. **Key Personnel:** Carll Tucker, Editor and Publisher; Michael Enright, Editor. **Subscription Rates:** $45. **Remarks:** Accepts advertising.
Ad Rates: PCI: $14.50 **Circ:** Paid 6,702
Non-paid 1,830

5056 The Putnam County Courier
Housatonic Valley Publishing Co.
132 Danbury Rd. Phone: (860)354-2261
PO Box 1139 Fax: (860)354-2645
New Milford, CT 06776
Publisher E-mail: housvalpub@aol.com

Community newspaper. **Founded:** May 1841. **Freq:** Weekly (Wed.). **Print Method:** Offset. **Trim Size:** 11 1/2 x 17. **Cols./Page:** 5. **Col. Width:** 1 13/16 inches. **Col. Depth:** 16 inches. **Key Personnel:** Arthur Cummings, Editor; Robert Mellis, Publisher. **USPS:** 451-020. **Subscription Rates:** $18; $28 out of county; $30 out of state. **Remarks:** Color advertising not accepted . Combined advertising rates available with other Housatonic Valley publications.
Ad Rates: GLR: $1.50 **Circ:** Paid 4,875
BW: $412 Free 207
SAU: $5

Putnam Courier Trader - See Putnam

NEWINGTON, pop. 28,841.

N. CT. Hartford Co. 5 mi. SW of Hartford. Manufactures dies and tools, chemicals, bolts, nuts and screws, aircraft engines, motor vehicle parts, concrete blocks, bricks, heating equipment.

5057 The Newington Town Crier
Imprint Newspapers
99 Main St. Phone: (860)236-3571
Bristol, CT 06010 Fax: (860)233-2080

Community newspaper (tabloid). **Founded:** 1959. **Freq:** Weekly (Fri.). **Print Method:** Offset. Uses mats. **Cols./Page:** 6. **Col. Width:** 10 picas. **Col. Depth:** 16 inches. **Key Personnel:** Mark Romannow, Publisher; Keith Griffin, Editor; Gary Carra, News Editor. **USPS:** 618-380. **Subscription Rates:** $24 individuals; $20 Senior citizens. **Remarks:** Advertising accepted; rates available upon request.
Circ: Paid 2,993
Non-paid 32

5058 QST
American Radio Relay League, Inc.
225 Main St. Phone: (860)594-0200
Newington, CT 06111 Fax: (860)594-0259
Publication E-mail: qst@arrl.org; hqcarrl.org

Amateur radio magazine. **Subtitle:** Devoted Entirely to Amateur Radio. **Founded:** 1915. **Freq:** Monthly. **Print Method:** Offset. **Trim Size:** 8 3/16 x 10 7/8. **Cols./Page:** 3. **Col. Width:** 27 nonpareils. **Col. Depth:** 140 agate lines. **Key Personnel:** Mark Wilson, Editor; Hanan Suleiman, Advertising Mgr. **ISSN:** 0033-4812. **Subscription Rates:** $34 individuals. **Remarks:** Accepts advertising. **Alt. Formats:** Braille; CD-ROM; Microform.
Ad Rates: BW: $4,101 **Circ:** ‡168,975
4C: $4,651

5059 WRYM-AM - 840
1056 Willard Ave. Phone: (860)666-5646
Newington, CT 06111-3540 Fax: (860)666-5647

Format: Hispanic. **Networks:** Independent. **Owner:** Hartford County Broadcasting Corp., at above address. **Founded:** 1961. **Operating Hours:** Continuous. **ADI:** Hartford-New Haven (New London), CT. **Key Personnel:** Barry A. Kursman, General Mgr.; Omar Aguilera, Program Mgr.; Danny Delgado, Sports Dir. **Wattage:** 1000. **Ad Rates:** $23-28 for 30 seconds; $28-34 for 60 seconds.

NEWTOWN, pop. 19,107.

SW CT. Fairfield Co. 9 mi. E. of Danbury. Manufactures rubber hose, plastic molding, scientific instruments, business forms, paper boxes, wire. Nursery. Dairy, poultry, fruit farms.

5060 Antiques and the Arts Weekly
Bee Publishing Co., Inc.
5 Church Hill Rd. Phone: (203)426-3141
PO Box 5503 Fax: (203)426-1394
Newtown, CT 06470
Magazine featuring antiques. **Founded:** Oct. 1969. **Freq:** Weekly. **Print Method:** Offset. **Trim Size:** 11 1/2 x 17. **Cols./Page:** 5. **Col. Width:** 10 1/2 inches. **Col. Depth:** 217 agate lines. **Key Personnel:** R. Scudder Smith, Editor; Anita Maestas, Advertising Mgr. **Subscription Rates:** $38 individuals. **Remarks:** Accepts advertising. **Available Online. URL:** http://www.thebee.com.
Ad Rates: GLR: $7.70 **Circ:** Paid ‡24,255
PCI: $6.35 Non-paid ‡231

5061 Fine Cooking Magazine
Taunton Press
63 S. Main St., Box 5506 Fax: (203)270-6751
Newtown, CT 06470-5506 Free: (800)926-8776
Publication E-mail: finecook@taunton.com
Publisher E-mail: jchilds@taunton.com

Magazine focusing on food preparation. **Subtitle:** For People Who Love To Cook. **Founded:** 1994. **Freq:** 6/year. **Trim Size:** 8 7/8 x 10 7/8. **Key Personnel:** Christine Arrington, Publisher; Martha Holmberg, Editor. **ISSN:** 1072-5121. **Subscription Rates:** $30 per year (U.S.); $5.95 single issue.
Ad Rates: BW: $4,550 **Circ:** Paid 154,214
4C: $6,240
PCI: $240

5062 Fine Gardening
Taunton Press
63 S. Main St., Box 5506 Fax: (203)270-6751
Newtown, CT 06470-5506 Free: (800)926-8776
Publisher E-mail: jchilds@taunton.com

Hands-on magazine for avid gardeners of all skill levels. Filled with tips, ideas, information, and inspiration on garden design, gardening techniques, garden structures, and plants for the home landscape. **Founded:** May 1988. **Freq:** Bimonthly. **Print Method:** Web offset. **Trim Size:** 8 7/8 x 10 7/8. **Cols./Page:** 2 and 3. **Col. Width:** 3 1/8 and 2 inches. **Col. Depth:** 10.5 picas. **Key Personnel:** Suzanne Roman, Publisher, sueroman@taunton.com; Lee Ann White, Editor, fg@taunton.com; Jodie Delohery, Art Dir., jdelohery@art.taunton.com. **ISSN:** 0896-6281. **Subscription Rates:** $32; $5.95. **Remarks:** Accepts advertising. **URL:** http://www.taunton.com.
Ad Rates: BW: $6,695 **Circ:** Paid 183,556
4C: $9,866

5063 Fine Homebuilding
Taunton Press
63 S. Main St., Box 5506 Fax: (203)270-6751
Newtown, CT 06470-5506 Free: (800)926-8776
Publication E-mail: fh.taunton.com
Publisher E-mail: jchilds@taunton.com

Magazine for builders, architects, designers, and owner-builders. **Founded:** Feb. 1981. **Freq:** 8/year. **Print Method:** Web offset. **Trim Size:** 8 7/8 x 10 7/8. **Cols./Page:** 2 and 3. **Col. Width:** 22 and 14 picas. **Col. Depth:** 9 3/4 inches. **Key Personnel:** Kevin Ireton, Editor; Sam Vincent, Advertising; Jon Miller, Publisher, jmiller@taunton.com. **ISSN:** 0273-1398. **Subscription Rates:** $34 individuals; $6.95 single issue. **Remarks:** Accepts advertising.
Ad Rates: BW: $11,025 **Circ:** Paid 262,133
4C: $15,435

5064 Fine Woodworking
Taunton Press
191 S. Main St. Phone: (203)426-8171
Newtown, CT 06470 Fax: (203)270-6751
Free: (800)283-7252
Publication E-mail: fww@taunton.com
Publisher E-mail: jchilds@taunton.com

Technical magazine for the amateur and professional woodworker. **Founded:** 1975. **Freq:** Bimonthly. **Print Method:** Offset. **Trim Size:** 8 1/2 x 11. **Cols./Page:** 2. **Key Personnel:** Scott Gibson, Editor; James Chiavelli, Publisher; Dick West, Advertising Mgr. **ISSN:** 0730-0271. **Subscription Rates:** $32 individuals; $38 out of country. **Remarks:** Accepts advertising. **URL:** http://www.taunton.com.
Ad Rates: BW: $11,740 **Circ:** Paid 249,246
4C: $16,080

5065 Kitchen Garden
Taunton Press
63 S. Main St., Box 5506 Fax: (203)270-6751
Newtown, CT 06470-5506 Free: (800)926-8776
Publisher E-mail: jchilds@taunton.com

Gardening magazine for people who take pleasure and pride in their gardens and the food they prepare from them. Contains how-to information on growing, cooking, and preserving vegetables, herbs, and fruits. **Subtitle:** Growing and Cooking Great Food. **Founded:** Jan. 1996. **Freq:** Bimonthly. **Print Method:** Perfect Bound. **Trim Size:** 8 7/8 x 10 7/8. **Key Personnel:** Mary Morgan, Editor, phone (230)426-8191, kg@taunton.com; Suzanne Roman, Publisher, sueroman@taunton.com; Rosalind Wanke, Art Dir. **ISSN:** 1083-3072. **Subscription Rates:** $24 individuals; $4.95 single issue. **Remarks:** Accepts advertising. **URL:** http://www.taunton.com.
Ad Rates: BW: $3,725 **Circ:** ‡95,000
4C: $4,795

5066 The Newtown Bee
Bee Publishing Co., Inc.
5 Church Hill Rd. Phone: (203)426-3141
PO Box 5503 Fax: (203)426-1394
Newtown, CT 06470
Community newspaper. **Founded:** June 1877. **Freq:** Weekly (Fri.). **Print Method:** Offset. **Trim Size:** 17 x 23 1/2. **Cols./Page:** 9. **Col. Width:** 1 3/4 inches. **Col. Depth:** 20 1/2 inches. **Key Personnel:** R. Scudder Smith, Editor and Publisher, editor@thebee.com; Ed Turko, Advertising Mgr. **Subscription Rates:** $20 individuals. **URL:** http://www.thebee.com.
Ad Rates: GLR: $6.25 **Circ:** Paid ♦**6,986**
PCI: $5.16 Non-paid ♦**85**

5067 Threads
Taunton Press
63 S. Main St., Box 5506 Fax: (203)270-6751
Newtown, CT 06470-5506 Free: (800)926-8776
Publisher E-mail: jchilds@taunton.com

Magazine for sewers, knitters, and fabric and fiber craftspeople. Focus is on garment design, materials, and techniques.

Founded: Sept. 15, 1985. **Freq:** Bimonthly. **Print Method:** Offset. **Trim Size:** 8 7/8 x 10 7/8 in. **Cols./Page:** 3. **Col. Width:** 15 picas. **Col. Depth:** 7 inches. **Key Personnel:** Betsy Levine, Publisher; Amy Yanagi, Editor; Jan Wahlin, Publisher; Michelle Brown, Advertising Mgr. **ISSN:** 0882-7370. **Subscription Rates:** $26 two years; $58 Three years; $4.95 single issue. **Remarks:** Accepts advertising.
Ad Rates: BW: $4,805 **Circ:** ‡145,000
4C: $6,730
PCI: $180

NORTH HAVEN, pop. 22,080.

S. CT. New Haven Co. 6 mi. N. of New Haven. Chemical and aircraft plants.

5068 The Advisor
83 State St. Phone: (203)239-5404
Box 460 Fax: (203)239-7097
North Haven, CT 06473-0071
Community newspaper. **Founded:** 1965. **Freq:** Weekly (Tues.). **Print Method:** Offset. **Trim Size:** 11 1/4 x 16. **Cols./Page:** 6. **Col. Width:** 1 5/8 inches. **Col. Depth:** 15 3/4 inches. **Key Personnel:** Al Flagg, Publisher; Pat Flagg, Publisher. **Subscription Rates:** Free. **Remarks:** Accepts advertising.
Ad Rates: GLR: $.50 **Circ:** Free ‡31,500
BW: $600
4C: $800
SAU: $7
PCI: $6

5069 Nostalgiaworld
Nostalgia World
12 Drazen Dr. S. Phone: (203)239-4891
PO Box 231
North Haven, CT 06473-0231
Magazine on motion pictures, TV, recording stars, sports, and entertainment collectibles. **Founded:** 1979. **Freq:** Quarterly. **Print Method:** Offset. **Trim Size:** 8 x 10 1/2. **Cols./Page:** 2. **Col. Width:** 60 nonpareils. **Col. Depth:** 224 agate lines. **Key Personnel:** Bonnie Roth, Editor. **ISSN:** 0194-5041. **Subscription Rates:** $15 individuals. **Remarks:** Accepts advertising.
Ad Rates: BW: $95 **Circ:** Paid 2,500
4C: $500 Non-paid 4,000

5070 WNHC-AM - 1340
112 Washington Ave. Phone: (203)234-1340
North Haven, CT 06473-1707 Fax: (203)239-6712

Format: Urban Contemporary; Adult Contemporary. **Operating Hours:** Continuous; 100% local. **Key Personnel:** Edith Acabbo-Willis, Contact; Stan Boston, Program Dir.; Will Mebane, Sales Mgr. **Wattage:** 1000. **Ad Rates:** $36-60 per unit.

NORWALK, pop. 77,767.

SW CT. Fairfield Co. On Norwalk River, 45 mi. E. of New York. Manufactures pumps, textiles, astronomical instruments, electric signaling devices, air compressors, kitchen equipment, boats, stamped metal goods, neckties, wire cloth, cellophane, plastics, x-ray tubes, furniture, cosmetics, electronic equipment, office machines, duplicators, albums, and greeting cards. Oyster, lobster fisheries.

5071 Accessories
Business Journals, Inc.
50 Day St. Phone: (203)853-6015
PO Box 5550 Fax: (203)852-8175
Norwalk, CT 06856
Free: (800)521-0227

Trade magazine. **Founded:** 1908. **Freq:** Monthly. **Print Method:** Offset. **Cols./Page:** 6. **Key Personnel:** Linda Cohen, Publisher, phone (212)686-4412, fax (212)686-6821; Lorrie Frost, Assoc. Publisher; Susan Sommers, Editor-in-Chief. **Subscription Rates:** $35. $4 single issue. **Remarks:** Accepts advertising. **Available Online. URL:** fashionmall.com.
Ad Rates: BW: $5,170 **Circ:** Paid 11,000
4C: $6,260 Non-paid 11,000

5072 Easy & Fun Word Seek Puzzles
Penny Press, Inc.
6 Prowitt St. Phone: (203)866-6688
Norwalk, CT 06855 Fax: (203)854-5962

Magazine containing 63 word seek puzzles with solutions in back. **Freq:** Bimonthly. **Key Personnel:** Fran Danon, Editor. **Subscription Rates:** $5.88. $.99 single issue.

5073 The Environmental Magazine
Earth Action Network
28 Knight St.
Norwalk, CT 06851
Publication E-mail: info@emagazine.com

Clearinghouse of news, information and commentary on environmental issues. **Subtitle:** The Environmental Magazine. **Founded:** 1990. **Freq:** Bimonthly. **Print Method:** Web offset. **Trim Size:** 8 1/8 x 10 7/8. **Cols./Page:** 3. **Col. Width:** 2 1/8 inches. **Col. Depth:** 9 5/8 inches. **Key Personnel:** Doug Moss, Publisher, business@emagazine.com; Jim Motovalli, Editor. **ISSN:** 1046-8021. **Subscription Rates:** $20 individuals; $36 two years; $3.95 single issue. **Available Online. URL:** http://www.emagazine.com.
Ad Rates: GLR: $3.15 **Circ:** 56,000
BW: $2,100
4C: $3,155
PCI: $140

5074 Eyecare Business
Boucher Communications Inc.
200 Connecticut Ave., Ste. 5D Phone: (203)838-9100
Norwalk, CT 06854 Fax: (203)838-2550
Publication E-mail: name@cardinal.com

Magazine for eyecare professionals. **Subtitle:** Retail Strategies for Profitable Dispensing. **Founded:** 1986. **Freq:** Monthly. **Print Method:** Web press. **Trim Size:** 11 x 15. **Cols./Page:** 4. **Col. Width:** 13 1/2 picas. **Col. Depth:** 79 picas. **Key Personnel:** Stephanie Walter, Editor; Martin Cheifetz, Publisher. **ISSN:** 0885-9167. **Subscription Rates:** $75 individuals; $110 Canada; $175 other countries; $6 single issue. **Remarks:** Accepts advertising. **URL:** http://www.boucher1.com.
Ad Rates: GLR: $20 **Circ:** Non-paid 52,200
BW: $6160
4C: $7885

5075 Family Word Seek Puzzles
Penny Press, Inc.
6 Prowitt St. Phone: (203)866-6688
Norwalk, CT 06855 Fax: (203)854-5962

Magazine containing over 100 large-type puzzles and primary word seek puzzles. **Freq:** Quarterly. **Key Personnel:** Don Loiacano, Editor. **Subscription Rates:** $7.47. $1.99 single issue.

5076 Favorite Variety Puzzles and Games
Penny Press, Inc.
6 Prowitt St. Phone: (203)866-6688
Norwalk, CT 06855 Fax: (203)854-5962

Magazine containing over 250 puzzles including Double Trouble, Alphabet Soup, Flower Power, and more. **Freq:** Quarterly. **Key Personnel:** Fran Danon, Editor. **Subscription Rates:** $7.47. $1.99 single issue.

5077 Favorite Word Seek Puzzles
Penny Press, Inc.
6 Prowitt St. Phone: (203)866-6688
Norwalk, CT 06855 Fax: (203)854-5962

Magazine containing Word Seek and other puzzles. **Freq:** Bimonthly. **Key Personnel:** Don Loiacano, Editor. **Subscription Rates:** $5.88. $.99 single issue.

5078 Good Time Fill-in Puzzles
Penny Press, Inc.
6 Prowitt St. Phone: (203)866-6688
Norwalk, CT 06855 Fax: (203)854-5962

Magazine featuring word puzzles with larger type for easier reading. **Founded:** Apr. 1987. **Freq:** Quarterly. **Subscription Rates:** $7.50; $14.50 two years. $1.25 single issue.

5079 Good Time Word Seek Puzzles
Penny Press, Inc.
6 Prowitt St. Phone: (203)866-6688
Norwalk, CT 06855 Fax: (203)854-5962

Word puzzles magazine. **Founded:** Mar. 1987. **Freq:** Bimonthly. **Key Personnel:** Douglas Heller, Editor. **Subscription Rates:** $11.50; $21.50 two years.

5080 The Hour
The Hour Publishing Co.
346 Main Ave. Phone: (203)846-3281
Norwalk, CT 06851 Fax: (203)846-9897

General newspaper. **Founded:** 1871. **Freq:** Mon.-Sat. (eve.). **Print Method:** Offset. **Trim Size:** 13 x 22 3/4. **Cols./Page:** 6. **Col. Width:** 24 nonpareils. **Col. Depth:** 297 agate lines. **Key Personnel:** John P. Reilly, Editor; Jack H. Whitton, President; B.J. Frazier, Advertising Mgr. **USPS:** 398-200. **Subscription Rates:** $117.60 individuals. **Remarks:** Accepts advertising.
Ad Rates: GLR: $2.34 **Circ:** Mon.-Sat. ★**17,388**
BW: $1,625.63
PCI: $18.83

5081 Journal of Radiation Curing
Technology Marketing Corp.
1 Technology Plaza Phone: (203)852-6800
Norwalk, CT 06854 Fax: (203)853-2845
Free: (800)243-6002
Publisher E-mail: tmc@tmcnet.com

Scientific magazine on radiation curing. **Founded:** 1974. **Freq:** Quarterly. **Print Method:** Offset. **Trim Size:** 8 1/4 x 11. **Cols./Page:** 3. **Col. Width:** 45 nonpareils. **Col. Depth:** 140 agate lines. **Key Personnel:** Michael Hanrahan, Technology Editor; Nadji Tehrani, Publisher/Editor-in-Chief; Raymond Tompkins, Assoc. Publisher. **ISSN:** 1057-5715. **Subscription Rates:** $98 individuals; $113 other countries. **Remarks:** Accepts advertising. **Feature Editors:** Lynn Jones, *Features*.
Ad Rates: BW: $1,900 **Circ:** Paid 690
4C: $2,750 Non-paid 1,810

5082 Journal of Water Borne Coatings
Technology Marketing Corp.
1 Technology Plaza Phone: (203)852-6800
Norwalk, CT 06854 Fax: (203)853-2845
Free: (800)243-6002
Publisher E-mail: tmc@tmcnet.com

Magazine on waterborne coatings. **Founded:** 1978. **Freq:** Semiannual. **Print Method:** Offset. **Trim Size:** 8 1/4 x 11. **Cols./Page:** 3. **Col. Width:** 45 nonpareils. **Col. Depth:** 140 agate lines. **Key Personnel:** Michael J. Hanrahan, Technical Editor; Nadji Tehrani, Publisher; Raymond T. Tompkins, Publisher; Mark Hoag, Sales Mgr. **ISSN:** 0163-4526. **Subscription Rates:** $99 U.S. and Canada; $112 out of country. **Remarks:** Accepts advertising.
Ad Rates: BW: $1,700 **Circ:** Paid 250
4C: $2,550 Non-paid 750

5083 Modern Brewery Age
Business Journals, Inc.
50 Day St. Phone: (203)853-6015
PO Box 5550 Fax: (203)852-8175
Norwalk, CT 06856
Free: (800)521-0227

Magazine for the wholesale and brewing industry. **Founded:** 1933. **Freq:** Bimonthly. **Print Method:** Offset. **Cols./Page:** 3 and 2. **Col. Width:** 30 and 41 nonpareils. **Col. Depth:** 133 agate lines. **Key Personnel:** Peter V.K. Reid, Editor; Mac Brighton, Publisher. **Subscription Rates:** $85 individuals. **Remarks:** Accepts advertising.
Ad Rates: BW: $1,460 **Circ:** Paid ‡1,915
4C: $2,425

5084 Modern Brewery Age Tabloid Edition
Business Journals, Inc.
50 Day St. Phone: (203)853-6015
PO Box 5550 Fax: (203)852-8175
Norwalk, CT 06856
Free: (800)521-0227

Brewery industry tabloid. **Founded:** 1958. **Freq:** Weekly. **Print Method:** Offset. **Cols./Page:** 5. **Col. Width:** 24 nonpareils. **Col. Depth:** 182 agate lines. **Key Personnel:** Peter V.K. Reid, Editor, pete@breweryage.com; Brad Messerrly, Advertising Dir.; Mac Brighton, Publisher. **Subscription Rates:** $85 individuals. **Remarks:** Accepts advertising. **URL:** http://www.breweryage.com.
Ad Rates: BW: $1,370 **Circ:** ‡5,181
4C: $2,850

5085 New Canaan Lifestyles
Brooks Community Newspapers, Inc.
542 Westport Ave. Phone: (203)226-6311
Norwalk, CT 06851 Fax: (203)227-6864
Publisher E-mail: bcnews3@netakis.com

Community newspaper. **Freq:** Monthly. **Key Personnel:** Louise Lancaster-Keim, Editor; Kevin Lally, President; B. V. Brooks, Publisher. **Remarks:** Accepts advertising.
Ad Rates: BW: $3,200 **Circ:** 90,177
PCI: $40

5086 Norwalk Lifestyles
Brooks Community Newspapers, Inc.
542 Westport Ave. Phone: (203)849-1600
Norwalk, CT 06851 Fax: (203)840-4844
Publisher E-mail: bcnews3@netakis.com

Community newspaper. **Founded:** 1977. **Freq:** Monthly. **Print Method:** Offset. Uses mats. **Cols./Page:** 5. **Col. Width:** 27 nonpareils. **Col. Depth:** 224 agate lines. **Key Personnel:** Louise Lancaster-Keim, Editor; B.V. Brooks, Publisher; Jennifer Frey, Assistant Editor. **Subscription Rates:** Free. **Remarks:** Accepts advertising. **Formerly:** Norwalk News (1993).
Ad Rates: GLR: $.50 **Circ:** Free 15,059

5087 The Norwalk Weekly Life & Times
The Hour Publishing Co.
346 Main Ave. Phone: (203)846-3281
Norwalk, CT 06851 Fax: (203)846-9897

Community newspaper. **Freq:** Weekly (Thurs.). **Print Method:** Photo offset. **Key Personnel:** B. J. Frazier, Publisher. **Subscription Rates:** Free.
Circ: Non-paid 16,590

5088 Operations and Fulfillment
535 Connecticut Ave. Phone: (203)857-5656
Norwalk, CT 06854 Fax: (203)857-5654
Publication E-mail: ctannen@opsandfulfillment.com
Publisher E-mail: jspigardo@opsandfulfillment.com

Trade publication focusing on operations issues faced by catalog and direct response companies. Includes articles on order processing, warehousing, materials handling, and facilities management. **Subtitle:** Practical Solutions for Catalog and Direct Response Operations Management. **Founded:** 1993. **Freq:** Bimonthly. **Print Method:** Web offset. **Trim Size:** 8 1/8 x 10 7/8. **Cols./Page:** 3. **Key Personnel:** Rama Ramaswami, Editor, fax (203)854-2956, rramaswami@opsandfulfillment.com; Katherine Buchmayr, Natl. Sales Dir., phone (203)855-8959, kbuchmayr@opsandfulfillment.com; Kevin Sghia, Contact. **ISSN:** 1069-6083. **Subscription Rates:** $36 individuals; $8 single issue. **Remarks:** Accepts advertising. **URL:** http://www.opsandfulfillment.com.
Ad Rates: BW: $3,560 **Circ:** Paid ‡13,000
4C: $4,850

5089 Party & Paper Retailer
4 Ward Corp.
70 New Canaan Ave. Phone: (203)845-8020
Norwalk, CT 06850 Fax: (203)845-8022
Free: (800)825-0900
Publication E-mail: party@partypaper.com

Trade magazine for retailers of paper tableware, decorations, stationery, greeting cards, balloons, and other party-related items. **Founded:** Feb. 1986. **Freq:** Monthly. **Print Method:** Web offset. **Trim Size:** 8 1/4 x 10 7/8. **Cols./Page:** 3. **Col. Width:** 2 1/4 inches. **Col. Depth:** 7 inches. **Key Personnel:** Trisha McMahon Drain, Editor; Russell Ward, President; Gina Gavish, Publisher. **ISSN:** 0899-6008. **Subscription Rates:** $39 individuals; $6 single issue. **Remarks:** Accepts advertising. **URL:** http://www.partypaper.com. **Alt. Formats:** CD-ROM, Sourcebook.
Ad Rates: BW: $2,688 **Circ:** ‡20,000
4C: $3,463
PCI: $80

5090 Stamford Lifestyles
Brooks Community Newspapers, Inc.
542 Westport Ave. Phone: (203)226-6311
Norwalk, CT 06851 Fax: (203)227-6864
Publisher E-mail: bcnews3@netakis.com

Community newspaper. **Freq:** Monthly. **Key Personnel:** Louise Lancaster-Keim, Editor; Jennifer Frey, Asst. Editor; Kevin Lally, President; B. V. Brooks, Publisher.

5091 Teaching/K-8
40 Richards Ave. Phone: (203)855-2650
Norwalk, CT 06854-2509 Fax: (203)855-2656
Free: (800)249-9363
Publication E-mail: teachingk8@aol.com

Magazine for elementary teachers. **Subtitle:** The Professional Ideabook for Teachers. **Founded:** May 1971. **Freq:** 8/year. **Print Method:** Offset. **Trim Size:** 7 7/8 x 10 1/2. **Cols./Page:** 2 and 3. **Col. Width:** 2 1/4 inches. **Col. Depth:** 10 inches. **Key Personnel:** Patricia Broderick, Editorial Dir., pat@teachingk-8.com; Allen A. Raymond, Publisher, allen@teachingk-8.com. **ISSN:** 0891-4508. **Subscription Rates:** $24.97 individuals. **Remarks:** Accepts advertising. **Alt. Formats:** Microform. **Former name:** Early Years.
Ad Rates: BW: $5,955 **Circ:** Paid 102,130
4C: $7,445 Non-paid 3,736
PCI: $232

5092 Telemarketing & Call Center Solutions
Technology Marketing Corp.
1 Technology Plaza Phone: (203)852-6800
Norwalk, CT 06854 Fax: (203)853-2845
Free: (800)243-6002
Publisher E-mail: tmc@tmcnet.com

Magazine on telemarketing and business telecommunications technology. **Subtitle:** The Magazine of Integrated Marketing. **Founded:** 1982. **Freq:** Monthly. **Print Method:** Offset. **Trim Size:** 8 1/4 x 11. **Cols./Page:** 3. **Col. Width:** 26 nonpareils. **Col. Depth:** 140 agate lines. **Key Personnel:** Linda Driscoll, Editor; Nadji Tehrani, Publisher; Ray Tompkins, Assoc. Publisher. **ISSN:** 0730-6156. **Formerly:** Telemarketing.
Ad Rates: BW: $4,335 **Circ:** Paid 2,170
4C: $5,397 Non-paid 28,331

5093 Travelware
Business Journals, Inc.
50 Day St. Phone: (203)853-6015
PO Box 5550 Fax: (203)852-8175
Norwalk, CT 06856
Free: (800)521-0227

Travelware serves retailers and manufacturers of luggage, leather goods and travel accessories. **Subtitle:** The Independent Journal of Luggage, Leather Goods & Travel Accessories. **Founded:** 1898. **Freq:** 7/year. **Print Method:** Offset. **Trim Size:** 8 1/4 x 10 7/8. **Cols./Page:** 2 and 3. **Col. Width:** 27 and 40 nonpareils. **Col. Depth:** 120 agate lines. **Key Personnel:** Amanda Pernaa Kanaga, Publisher; Eileen Viglione Moseley, Editor-in-Chief; Sabrina L. Horne, Sr. Editor. **ISSN:** 0747-475X. **Subscription Rates:** $32 individuals; $3.50 single issue. **URL:** http://www.travelwaremag.com.
Ad Rates: BW: $3,100 **Circ:** Paid 661
4C: $3,915 Non-paid 11,778

5094 Turbomachinery International
Business Journals, Inc.
50 Day St. Phone: (203)853-6015
PO Box 5550 Fax: (203)852-8175
Norwalk, CT 06856
Free: (800)521-0227

Magazine for key management and engineering personnel in turbomachinery-using industries. Stimulates new approaches to energy conversion by providing technical concepts and details. **Founded:** 1959. **Freq:** Bimonthly. **Print Method:** Offset. **Trim Size:** 8 1/4 x 10 7/8. **Cols./Page:** 3 and 2. **Col. Width:** 26 and 40 nonpareils. **Col. Depth:** 140 agate lines. **Key Personnel:** Skip Ruch, Publisher; Thomas Barker, Editor. **ISSN:** 0149-4147. **Subscription Rates:** $49 individuals; $75 Canada. **Remarks:** Accepts advertising. **Alt. Formats:** Microfiche. **Formerly:** Gas Turbine International.
Ad Rates: BW: $3,920 **Circ:** Paid 1,597
4C: $4,745 Non-paid 9,479
PCI: $205

5095 Westport News
Brooks Community Newspapers, Inc.
542 Westport Ave. Phone: (203)226-6311
Norwalk, CT 06851 Fax: (203)227-6864
Publisher E-mail: bcnews3@netakis.com

Community newspaper. **Subtitle:** The Westport News. **Founded:** 1964. **Freq:** Semiweekly (Wed. and Fri.). **Print Method:** Offset. **Cols./Page:** 5. **Col. Width:** 27 nonpareils. **Col. Depth:** 224 agate lines. **Key Personnel:** Woody Klein, Editor; B.V. Brooks, Publisher; Kevin J. Lally, President. **Subscription Rates:** $21 individuals. **Remarks:** Accepts advertising. **Online:** Townline Information Services. **URL:** http://www.townline.com/westport/news/latenews.
Ad Rates: GLR: $.67 **Circ:** Combined 9,648

5096 Wilton Lifestyles
Brooks Community Newspapers, Inc.
542 Westport Ave. Phone: (203)226-6311
Norwalk, CT 06851 Fax: (203)227-6864
Publisher E-mail: bcnews3@netakis.com

Community newspaper. **Freq:** Monthly. **Key Personnel:** Louise Lancaster-Keim, Editor; Kevin Lally, President; Ida Culhane, Sales Mgr.; B. V. Brooks, Publisher. **Remarks:** Accepts advertising.
Ad Rates: BW: $3200 **Circ:** Combined 90,177
PCI: $40

5097 Cablevision of Connecticut LP
28 Cross St. Phone: (203)750-5600
Norwalk, CT 06851 Fax: (203)846-9412

Owner: Cablevision Systems Corp., 1 Media Crossways, Woodbury, NY 11797. **Founded:** 1982. **Key Personnel:** Maryce Cunningham, Program Dir., fax (203)750-3000, mcanning@cablevision.com; Tom Appleby, News Dir., fax (203)849-1327, tcappleby@ews12.com; Chris VanName, General Mgr., cvanname@cablevision.com. **Cities Served:** Darien, Easton, Fairfield County, Greenwich, New Canaan, Norwalk, Redding, Stamford, Weston, Westport, Wilton, CT: subscribing households 203,000; 110 channels; 1 community access channel; 168 hours per week community access programming. **URL:** http://www.news12.com; http://www.cablevision.com.

5098 WEFX-FM - 95.9
148 East Ave. Phone: (203)838-5566
Norwalk, CT 06851 Fax: (203)854-5116

Format: Classic Rock. **Founded:** 1975. **Formerly:** WDRN-FM (1977). **Operating Hours:** Continuous. **Key Personnel:** Frank Marro, News Dir.; Mike Fitzgerald, Program Dir.; Don Lacerenza, General Mgr. **Wattage:** 3000. **Ad Rates:** $80-100 per unit.

5099 WMRD-AM - 1150
167 N. Seir Hill Rd. Phone: (860)347-9673
Norwalk, CT 06850 Fax: (860)347-7704
E-mail: radio@wmrd.com

Format: Full Service. **Networks:** CBS; CNN Radio; CRN International; Westwood One Radio. **Owner:** Crossroads Communications, L. L. C., at above address. **Founded:** Dec. 1948. **Formerly:** WCNX-AM (1996). **Operating Hours:** 6:00 a.m.-12:00 a.m. **ADI:** Hartford-New Haven (New London), CT. **Key Personnel:** Don DeCesare, Pres./General Mgr., don@wmrd.com. **Wattage:** 2,500. **Ad Rates:** $8.75-19.50 for 30 seconds; $13-28.75 for 60 seconds; $51.75 per unit. **URL:** http://www.wmrd.com.

5100 WNLK-AM - 1350
148 East Ave. Phone: (203)838-5566
Norwalk, CT 06851 Fax: (203)854-5116

Format: Full Service. **Owner:** CRB of Norwalk, Inc., at above address. **Founded:** 1948. **Operating Hours:** Continuous; 5% network, 95% local. **Key Personnel:** Don Lacerenza, Contact; Mike Fitzgerald, Program Dir.; Frank Marro, News Dir. **Wattage:** 1000.

NORWICH, pop. 38,074.

SE CT. New London Co. 15 mi. N. of New London. Residential.

5101 Norwich Bulletin
66 Franklin St. Phone: (860)887-9211
Norwich, CT 06360 Fax: (860)887-9666
Free: (800)404-9211
Publication E-mail: norbull@bulletin.ctol.net

General newspaper. **Founded:** 1791. **Freq:** Daily and Sunday. **Print Method:** Offset. **Cols./Page:** 6. **Col. Width:** 2 inches. **Col. Depth:** 301 agate lines. **Key Personnel:** Keith Fontane, Exec. Ed., kfontaine@norwich.gannett.com; David A. Whitehead, Publisher, dwhitehead@norwich.gannett.com; Elliott Huron, Advertising Dir., ehuron@norwich.gannett.com. **Subscription Rates:** $143 individuals. **Remarks:** Accepts advertising.
Circ: Mon.-Sat. ★31,701
Sun. ★37,757

5102 WCTY-FM - 97.7
Cuprak Rd., POB 551 Phone: (203)887-3511
Norwich, CT 06360

Format: Country. **Networks:** ABC; CRN International; TNNR (The Nashville Network Radio). **Owner:** WICH, Inc., at above address. **Founded:** 1968. **Operating Hours:** Continuous. **Key Personnel:** Richard P. Reed, President; Karen F. Dole, Operations Dir. **Wattage:** 3000.

5103 WEDN-TV - 53
c/o WEDH-TV Phone: (860)278-5310
240 New Britain Ave. Fax: (860)278-2157
Hartford, CT 06106-3185

Format: Public TV. **Simulcasts:** WEDH-TV. **Networks:** Public Broadcasting Service (PBS). **Founded:** 1962. **Operating Hours:** 6:45 a.m.-midnight Daily; 8 a.m.-midnight Sat.; 7:30 a.m.-midnight Sun. **ADI:** Hartford-New Haven (New London), CT. **Key Personnel:** Jerry Franklin, President & CEO; Larry Rifkin, Exec. VP of Programming; Steve Futernick, Sr. VP of Community Development; Anita Ford Saunders, VP of Corporate Communications; John Berky, VP of Radio; Donna Collins, VP of Program Marketing; Meg Sakellarides, Chief Financial Officer; Jay Whitsett, VP Broadcast Oper. & Production Ser. **Local Programs:** *Connecticut Lawmakers*, Steve Kotcko; *Connecticut This Week*, Mary Ollie Newman; *The Fourth Estate*; *On The Record*. **Wattage:** 50 KW. **Ad Rates:** Advertising not accepted.

5104 WNPR-FM - 89.1
240 New Britain Ave. Phone: (860)278-5310
PO Box 260240 Fax: (860)244-9624
Hartford, CT 06106-0240
E-mail: radio905@aol.com

Format: Classical; News; Public Radio. **Networks:** National Public Radio (NPR); Public Radio International (PRI). **Owner:** Connecticut Public Broadcasting Inc., at above address. **Founded:** 1981. **Operating Hours:** Continuous. **ADI:** Hartford-New Haven (New London), CT. **Key Personnel:** John F. Berky, General Mgr.; Kim Grehn, Program Dir.; Eugene Amatruda, Operations Dir.; Audrey Rogers, Promotions Mgr. **Local Programs:** *Faith Middleton Show*, Faith Middleton, (203)777-7506. **Wattage:** 5100. **Ad Rates:** Noncommercial.

OAKVILLE, pop. 8,300.

NW CT. Litchfield Co. 4 mi. NW of Waterbury. Manufactures wire, screw machine products, hardware, plastics, nylon, synthetic yarns.

5105 Town Times
Prime Publishers
469 Main St. Phone: (860)274-6721
PO Box 1 Fax: (860)945-3116
Watertown, CT 06795
Community newspaper (tabloid). **Founded:** 1947. **Freq:** Weekly (Thurs.). **Print Method:** Offset. **Cols./Page:** 5. **Col. Width:** 1 3/4 inches. **Col. Depth:** 16 inches. **Key Personnel:** Thomas Valuckas, Editor; William E. Simmons, Publisher; Carolyn Priestmall, Advertising Mgr. **Subscription Rates:** $14 individuals; $16 out of area; $18 out of state. **Remarks:** Accepts advertising.
Ad Rates: BW: $384 **Circ:** Paid 240
PCI: $4.50 Free 3,532

OLD SAYBROOK, pop. 1,900.

SE CT. Middlesex Co. Residential.

5106 Pictorial-Gazette
Shore Line Newspapers
PO Box 813 Phone: (860)388-3441
Old Saybrook, CT 06475 Fax: (860)388-5613

Local newspaper covering a seven town area. **Freq:** Semi-weekly Tuesday and Saturday. **Trim Size:** 6 columns x 16. **Key Personnel:** Timothy Sawecke, Publisher; Beth Damarjian, Pictorial Editor; Rick Thurman, Directory of Sales. **Subscription Rates:** $32 individuals; $55 (Outside of Middlesex county). **Remarks:** Accepts advertising.
Ad Rates: GLR: $10 **Circ:** Paid ‡8,500
PCI: $10

5107 WLIS-AM - 1420
77 Springbrook Rd. Phone: (203)388-1420
PO Drawer W Fax: (203)388-2931
Old Saybrook, CT 06475
E-mail: radio@wlis.com

Format: Full Service; News; Sports; Soft Rock. **Simulcasts:** WMRD. **Networks:** CBS; CNN Radio; NBC. **Founded:** 1956. **Operating Hours:** 6 a.m.-midnight; 10% network, 90% local. **ADI:** Hartford-New Haven (New London), CT. **Key Personnel:** Chris Costelli, Program Dir.; Lisa Duffy, Sales Mgr.; Don DeCesare, Mng. Member; Art Barent, News Dir. **Local Programs:** *Mornings with Bob Muscatel*; *Shoreline Report*, Art Barent, News Dir.; *Swap Ship*. **Wattage:** 5000. **Ad Rates:** $15-20 for 30 seconds; $17-29 for 60 seconds. Combined advertising rates available with WMRD. **URL:** http://www.wlis.com.

ORANGE

5108 Good Day Sunshine
315 Derby Ave. Phone: (203)891-8131
Orange, CT 06477-1345 Fax: (203)891-8433
Publication E-mail: beatles@toursandevents.com
Publisher E-mail: beatletour@aol.com

Fan magazine featuring the Beatles and '60s British Rock. **Subtitle:** Beatles Fan Magazine. **Founded:** 1978. **Freq:** Quarterly 5/year. **Print Method:** Web offset. **Trim Size:** 8 x 10. **Key Personnel:** Charles F. Rosenay, Editor and Publisher, rosenay@aol.com; Bill Last, Editor; Mike Streeto, Contact; Mark Wallgren, Contact; Matt Hurwitz, Contact; Dana Whealn, Contact. **ISSN:** 1041-4118. **Subscription Rates:** $12; $16 Canada and Mexico; $22 other countries.
Ad Rates: BW: $98 **Circ:** Paid 5,200
4C: $325 Non-paid 800

PLAINVILLE

5109 The Belletrist Review
Marmarc Publications
Box 596 Phone: (860)747-2058
Plainville, CT 06062-0596
Literary magazine covering short fiction. **Founded:** 1992. **Freq:** Semiannual. **Trim Size:** 8 1/2 x 11. **Cols./Page:** 2. **Key Personnel:** Marlene Dube, Editor, mrlene@aol.com; Marc Sciegaert, Fiction Editor. **ISSN:** 1006-2332. **Subscription Rates:** $14.99 individuals; $7.99 single issue. **Remarks:** Advertising not accepted.
Circ: Paid 300

PROSPECT, pop. 6,807.

SC ST. New Haven Co. 3 mi. S. of Waterbury. Residential.

5110 Job Shop Technology
Edwards Publishing Co.
16 Waterbury Rd. Phone: (203)758-4474
PO Box 7193 Fax: (203)758-4475
Prospect, CT 06712
Publication E-mail: adjs@netcom.com

Trade magazine for the original equipment and product manufacturer. **Subtitle:** The Source Book for Outsourcing. **Founded:** Feb. 1984. **Freq:** Quarterly. **Print Method:** Offset. **Trim Size:** 8 1/8 x 10 7/8. **Cols./Page:** 2 and 3. **Col. Width:** 18.5 and 13.5 picas. **Col. Depth:** 140 agate lines. **Key Personnel:** John P. Wright, Editor; David B. Edwards, Publisher. **ISSN:** 0746-0881. **Subscription Rates:** Free to qualified subscribers; $20 individuals; $5 single issue. **URL:** http://www.jobshoptechnology.com.
Ad Rates: BW: $1,855 **Circ:** Controlled ‡32,000
4C: $2,455
PCI: $80

PUTNAM†, pop. 6,855.

NE CT. Windham Co. On Quinnebaug River, 28 mi. NW of Providence, RI. Manufactures phonograph needles, paper boxes, shoes, novelties, pointed steel goods. Silk, woolen mills; foundry. Dairy, poultry, fruit farms.

5111 Putnam Courier Trader
Housatonic Valley Publishing Co.
132 Danbury Rd. Phone: (860)354-2261
PO Box 1139 Fax: (860)354-2645
New Milford, CT 06776
Publisher E-mail: housvalpub@aol.com

Community newspaper. **Founded:** 1841. **Freq:** Weekly (Thurs.). **Key Personnel:** Barbara Gallo Farrell, Editor. **Subscription Rates:** Free. **Formerly:** The Putnam Trader; Putnam County Courier.
Circ: Non-paid 9,994
Paid 1,326

5112 Spring
PO Box 583 Phone: (860)974-3428
Putnam, CT 06260
Journal covering culture. **Subtitle:** A Journal of Archetype and Culture. **Freq:** Semiannual. **Key Personnel:** Barbara Shipley, Asst. Managing Editor. **ISSN:** 0362-0522. **Subscription Rates:** $35 individuals.

5113 WINY-AM - 1350
45 Pomfret St. Phone: (203)928-1350
Putnam, CT 06260 Fax: (203)928-7878

Format: Adult Contemporary. **Networks:** AP; Jones Satellite. **Owner:** Gerardi Broadcasting Corp., at above address. **Founded:** 1953. **Formerly:** WPCT-AM (1965). **Operating Hours:** Continuous. **ADI:** Providence, RI-New Bedford, MA. **Key Personnel:** Michael J. Gerardi, Contact; Gary W. Osbrey, General Mgr. **Local Programs:** *Gary O in the Morning* 6:00 am - 9:00 am Monday-Friday, Gary W. Osbrey; *The Talk Show with Dave Ward* 9:00 am - 11:00 am Monday-Friday, Dave Ward. **Wattage:** 5000. **Ad Rates:** $22-28 for 30 seconds.

RIDGEFIELD, pop. 20,120.

SW CT. Fairfield Co. 9 mi. S. of Danbury. Summer resort. Pharmaceutical, geological and optical research.

5114 Latin Mass Magazine
PO Box 993 Fax: (203)438-1305
Ridgefield, CT 06877
Catholic magazine for traditionalists. **Subtitle:** Chronicle of a Catholic Reform. **Founded:** Mar. 1992. **Freq:** Quarterly. **Print Method:** Offset. **Trim Size:** 8 1/4 x 11. **Cols./Page:** 3. **Key Personnel:** Roger A. McCaffrey, Editor and Publisher. **ISSN:** 1064-556X. **Subscription Rates:** $27.95; $7 single issue. **Remarks:** Accepts advertising.
Ad Rates: BW: $550 **Circ:** Paid 13,000
4C: $800 Non-paid 1,500

The Lewisboro Ledger - See Lewisboro

5115 Medicina Y Cultura
Mundo Medico USA, Inc
158 Danbury Rd., Ste. 8 Phone: (203)661-3680
Ridgefield, CT 06877-3200 Fax: (203)661-3889

Journal focusing on the needs of Hispanic physicians. **Founded:** June 1992. **Freq:** Monthly. **Remarks:** Accepts advertising.
Ad Rates: BW: $2,790 **Circ:** Controlled 41,000
4C: $4,480

5116 Model Airplane News
Air Age Publishing, Inc.
100 East Ridge Phone: (203)431-9000
Ridgefield, CT 06877 Fax: (203)431-3000

Magazine on radio-controlled model airplanes and helicopters. **Subtitle:** The World's Premier R/C Modeling Magazine. **Founded:** 1929. **Freq:** Monthly. **Print Method:** Offset. **Trim Size:** 8 1/4 x 10 7/8. **Cols./Page:** 3. **Col. Width:** 28 nonpareils. **Col. Depth:** 140 agate lines. **Key Personnel:** Tom Atwood, Editor; Louis De Francesco, Publisher. **ISSN:** 0026-7295. **Subscription Rates:** $27.95 individuals. **Remarks:** Accepts advertising.
Ad Rates: BW: $1,820 **Circ:** Paid ★78,403
4C: $2,450

5117 Radio Control Boat Modeler
Air Age Publishing, Inc.
100 East Ridge Phone: (203)431-9000
Ridgefield, CT 06877 Fax: (203)431-3000

Magazine for radio controlled power boat and sailboat modelers. **Founded:** 1986. **Freq:** 6/year. **Print Method:** Offset. **Trim Size:** 8 1/2 x 10 7/8. **Cols./Page:** 3. **Key Personnel:** Gerry Yarrish, Exec. Editor; Debra Sharp, Assoc. Editor; Sharon Warner, Advertising Dir.; L.V. DeFrancesca, Jr., Publisher. **ISSN:** 1043-8009. **Subscription Rates:** $19.95 individuals. **Remarks:** Advertising accepted; rates available upon request. **URL:** http://www.rcboatmodeler.com; http://www.airage.com.
Circ: 25,000

5118 The Redding Pilot
Hersam Acorn Newspapers, LLC
PO Box 1019 Phone: (203)544-9519
Ridgefield, CT 06877
Publication E-mail: newsroom@acorn-online.com
Publisher E-mail: newsroom@acorn-online.com

Community newspaper. **Founded:** 1966. **Freq:** Weekly (Thurs.). **Print Method:** Offset. **Cols./Page:** 6. **Col. Width:** 26 nonpareils. **Col. Depth:** 294 agate lines. **Key Personnel:** Sue Wolf, Editor; Thomas Nash, Publisher. **Subscription Rates:** $30 individuals.
Ad Rates: GLR: $8.50 **Circ:** Paid ♦**2,237**
BW: $926.10 Non-paid ♦**50**
PCI: $7.35

5119 The Ridgefield Press
Hersam Acorn Newspapers, LLC
16 Bailey Ave. Phone: (203)438-6544
Ridgefield, CT 06877 Fax: (203)438-3345
Free: (800)372-2790
Publication E-mail: newspaper@acron-online.com
Publisher E-mail: newsroom@acorn-online.com

Community newspaper. **Founded:** 1875. **Freq:** Weekly (Thurs.). **Print Method:** Offset. **Cols./Page:** 6. **Col. Width:** 12 picas. **Col. Depth:** 21 inches. **Key Personnel:** Macklin Reid, Editor; Jack Sanders, Executive Editor; Betty Irving, Circulation Mgr. **USPS:** 465-860. **Subscription Rates:** $30 individuals; $35 Out of county; $18 Military. **URL:** http://www.acorn-online.com. **Alt. Formats:** Microform.
Ad Rates: GLR: $8.50 **Circ:** Paid ♦**6,858**
BW: $882 Non-paid ♦**152**
4C: $1,250.50
SAU: $7

5120 WKRP-TV -
112 High Ridge Ave.
Ridgefield, CT 06877

Format: Commercial TV. **Owner:** Channel 29 of Charleston, Inc., at above address.

5121 WVSX-TV -
112 High Ridge Ave. Phone: (304)787-5959
Ridgefield, CT 06877

Format: Commercial TV. **Networks:** Fox. **Owner:** High Mountain Broadcasting Corp., at above address. **Operating Hours:** Continuous. **Key Personnel:** Gary O'Halloran, General Mgr. **Wattage:** 1,900,000.

ROCKVILLE†, pop. 13,500.

N. CT. Tolland Co. 16 mi. NE of Hartford. Population figure includes Vernon. Manufactures textile finishing, plastic products, electronics equipment, machine tools, chemicals, fish lines, envelopes, business forms, bank checks. Woodworking.

5122 The Broadcaster
Coventry Broadcaster, Inc.
Vernon Phone: (860)456-2211
PO Box 27 Fax: (860)872-4614
Rockville, CT 06066-0027
Shopper (tabloid). **Founded:** Feb. 1954. **Freq:** Weekly (Wed.). **Print Method:** Offset. **Trim Size:** 11 x 17. **Cols./Page:** 6. **Col. Width:** 1 5/8 inches. **Col. Depth:** 16 inches. **Key Personnel:** Joseph Duval, Advertising and General Manager; Marion Schultheiss, Publisher. **Subscription Rates:** Free. **Remarks:** Accepts advertising.
Ad Rates: BW: $624 **Circ:** Free 28,762
PCI: $6.50

ROCKY HILL, pop. 14,559.

NC CT. Hartford Co. 7 mi. E. of New Britain.

5123 Connecticut Pharmacist
Connecticut Pharmacists Association
35 Cold Spring Rd., Ste. 125 Phone: (203)563-4619
Rocky Hill, CT 06067-3167 Fax: (203)257-8241

Professional magazine. **Founded:** 1943. **Freq:** Quarterly. **Trim Size:** 8 1/2 x 11. **Key Personnel:** Marc S. McQuaid, Editor. **Subscription Rates:** $12. $3 single issue. **Remarks:** Accepts advertising.
Ad Rates: BW: $450 **Circ:** Controlled 1,500
4C: $1,100

SANDY HOOK

5124 Club Confidential
Paragon Publishing, Inc.
Box 200 Phone: (203)426-6533
Sandy Hook, CT 06482 Fax: (203)426-9533

Consumer magazine covering video reviews and other erotica for men. **Founded:** 1993. **Freq:** Monthly. **Key Personnel:** Steve Kolitz, Vice President, Circulation. **ISSN:** 1072-8060. **Subscription Rates:** $49 individuals; $5.99 single issue. **Remarks:** Accepts advertising.
Circ: (Not Reported)

5125 Club International Magazine
Paragon Publishing, Inc.
Box 200 Phone: (203)426-6533
Sandy Hook, CT 06482 Fax: (203)426-9533

Consumer magazine covering erotica for men. **Founded:** 1975. **Freq:** Monthly. **Key Personnel:** Steve Kolitz, Vice President, Circulation. **ISSN:** 0747-0819. **Subscription Rates:** $49 individuals; $5.99 single issue. **Remarks:** Accepts advertising.
Circ: (Not Reported)

5126 Club Specials Magazine
Paragon Publishing, Inc.
Box 200 Phone: (203)426-6533
Sandy Hook, CT 06482 Fax: (203)426-9533

Consumer magazine covering erotica for men. **Freq:** Monthly. **Key Personnel:** Steve Kolitz, Vice President, Circulation. **Remarks:** Accepts advertising.
Circ: (Not Reported)

5127 Mayfair Magazine
Mayfair Glen Publishing, Inc.
Box 815 Phone: (203)426-8992
Sandy Hook, CT 06482 Fax: (203)426-9533

Consumer magazine covering men's issues, erotica, and entertainment. **Freq:** Monthly. **Key Personnel:** Steve Kolitz, VP, Circulation. **Remarks:** Accepts advertising.
Circ: (Not Reported)

5128 Mayfair Specials
Mayfair Glen Publishing, Inc.
Box 815 Phone: (203)426-8992
Sandy Hook, CT 06482 Fax: (203)426-9533

Consumer magazine covering erotica for men. **Freq:** Monthly. **Key Personnel:** Steve Kolitz, Vice President, Circulation. **Remarks:** Accepts advertising.
Circ: (Not Reported)

5129 Men's World
Mayfair Glen Publishing, Inc.
Box 815 Phone: (203)426-8992
Sandy Hook, CT 06482 Fax: (203)426-9533

Consumer magazine covering erotica for men. **Freq:** Monthly. **Key Personnel:** Steve Kolitz, Vice President, Circulation. **Remarks:** Accepts advertising.
Circ: (Not Reported)

5130 Model Directory
Mayfair Glen Publishing, Inc.
Box 815 Phone: (203)426-8992
Sandy Hook, CT 06482 Fax: (203)426-9533

Consumer magazine covering erotica for men. **Freq:** Monthly. **Key Personnel:** Steve Kolitz, Vice President, Circulation. **Remarks:** Accepts advertising.
Circ: (Not Reported)

SEYMOUR, pop. 13,580.

SE CT. West New Haven Co. On Hoosotonic River, N. of Ansonia. Manufactures textiles, paper, brass.

5131 Tele-Media Company of Western Connecticut
80 Great Hill Rd. Phone: (203)736-2691
Seymour, CT 06483 Fax: (203)734-3425

Founded: 1972. **Formerly:** Valley Cable Vision, Inc. (1990). **Key Personnel:** William S. Dunlop, Vice President; Richard Brinker, Contact; Kevin Walsh, Ad. Sales Mgr.; M. Elizabeth Kennard, Program Dir.; Vence Caramanello, General Mgr. **Cities Served:** subscribing households 43,600; 74 channels; 30 community access channels.

SHARON, pop. 2,623.

NW CT. Litchfield Co. 7 mi. SW of Lakeville. Residential.

5132 WKZE-AM - 1020
Broadcast Center, Main St. Phone: (860)364-5800
PO Box 1020 Fax: (860)364-0129
Sharon, CT 06069
E-mail: wkze@snet.net

Format: Full Service; Country. **Networks:** USA Radio; CRN International. **Founded:** 1986. **Operating Hours:** 100% local. **Key Personnel:** Scott Johnson, Owner; Randy Milroy, Operations & Programming; Leah Shull, Station Mgr. **Local Programs:** *Tri State Countdown* 12:00 noon - 3:00 pm Saturday, Chuck Johnson. **Wattage:** 2500. **Ad Rates:** $16-36 per unit. Combined advertising rates available with WKZE-FM.

5133 WKZE-FM - 98.1
67 Main St. Phone: (860)364-5800
Sharon, CT 06069 Fax: (860)364-0129
E-mail: wkze@snet.net

Format: Full Service; Adult Album Alternative. **Networks:** USA Radio; AP. **Owner:** Johnson Development, Inc., at above address. **Founded:** 1992. **Operating Hours:** Continuous. **Key Personnel:** Scott Johnson, Owner; Randy Milroy, VP, Programming; Leah Shull, Station Mgr. **Local Programs:** *Frank's Picks* 8:00 pm 11:00 pm Friday, Frank Matheis, (860)364-5800; *Nite Jazz* 8:00 pm - 11:00 pm Sunday, Casey Mallinkrodt, (860)364-5800; *Theme & Variations* 9:00 - 12:00 noon Sunday, Herb Moore, (860)364-5800. **Wattage:** 6000. **Ad Rates:** $16-36 per unit. Combined advertising rates available with WKZE-AM.

SHELTON, pop. 31,314.

SW CT. Fairfield Co. 10 mi. N. of Bridgeport. Manufactures tools, dies, office machines, iron and steel forging, steel and foam rubber products, electronic controls. Dairy, poultry farms.

5134 American Biotechnology Laboratory
International Scientific Communications, Inc.
30 Controls Dr. Phone: (203)926-9300
PO Box 870 Fax: (203)926-9310
Shelton, CT 06484-0870
Publisher E-mail: iscpubs@iscpubs.com

Biotechnology magazine. **Founded:** 1983. **Freq:** 12/year. **Print Method:** Offset. **Trim Size:** 10 7/8 x 15. **Cols./Page:** 4. **Col. Width:** 12 picas. **Col. Depth:** 140 agate lines. **Key Personnel:** William N. Wham, Publisher; Dawn Kalman, Editor; Patricia Ekbatani, Managing Editor; Erin MacDonnell, Editorial Dir. **ISSN:** 0749-3223. **Subscription Rates:** $160 individuals. **Remarks:** Accepts advertising.
Ad Rates: BW: $5,650 **Circ:** Non-paid ‡70,792
4C: $1,620

5135 American Clinical Laboratory
International Scientific Communications, Inc.
30 Controls Dr. Phone: (203)926-9300
PO Box 870 Fax: (203)926-9310
Shelton, CT 06484-0870
Publisher E-mail: iscpubs@iscpubs.com

Technical magazine on clinical laboratory techniques. **Subtitle:** Serving Laboratory Management Professionals. **Founded:** 1982. **Freq:** 10/year. **Print Method:** Offset. **Trim Size:** 10 7/8 x 15. **Cols./Page:** 3. **Col. Width:** 13 picas. **Col. Depth:** 82 picas. **Key Personnel:** William N. Wham, Publisher; Brian Howard, Editor; Deanna Galello, Production Mgr.; Gina LaScola, Managing Editor. **ISSN:** 1041-3235. **Subscription Rates:** $237 individuals. **Remarks:** Accepts advertising. **URL:** http://www.iscpubs.com.
Ad Rates: BW: $4,890 **Circ:** Non-paid ‡54,273
4C: $6,200

5136 American Laboratory News
International Scientific Communications, Inc.
30 Controls Dr. Phone: (203)926-9300
PO Box 870 Fax: (203)926-9310
Shelton, CT 06484-0870
Publisher E-mail: iscpubs@iscpubs.com

Trade magazine for scientists. **Founded:** 1987. **Freq:** Monthly. **Print Method:** Offset. **Trim Size:** 10 7/8 x 15. **Cols./Page:** 4. **Col. Width:** 2 inches. **Col. Depth:** 12 7/8 inches. **Key Personnel:** William Wham, Publisher; Brian Howard, Editor; Maureen Jezierny, Production Mgr.; Susan Messinger, Managing Editor. **ISSN:** 0044-7749. **Subscription Rates:** $235. **Remarks:** Accepts advertising. **URL:** http://www.iscpubs.com.
Ad Rates: BW: $10,330 **Circ:** Non-paid 115,383
4C: $12,100

Bridgeport News - See Bridgeport

Easton Courier - See Easton

5137 European Clinical Laboratory
International Scientific Communications, Inc.
30 Controls Dr. Phone: (203)926-9300
PO Box 870 Fax: (203)926-9310
Shelton, CT 06484-0870
Publisher E-mail: iscpubs@iscpubs.com

Magazine for clinical laboratory scientists. **Founded:** 1982. **Freq:** Bimonthly. **Print Method:** Offset. **Trim Size:** 11 x 15 3/4. **Cols./Page:** 3. **Col. Width:** 12 picas. **Col. Depth:** 82 picas. **Key Personnel:** Brian Howard, Editor; William N. Wham, Publisher; Maureen Magner, Production Mgr. **ISSN:** 1047-5354. **Subscription Rates:** $193 individuals; $226 foreign. **Remarks:** Accepts advertising.
Ad Rates: BW: $7,625 **Circ:** Non-paid ‡31,774
4C: $8,995

5138 International Biotechnology Laboratory
International Scientific Communications, Inc.
30 Controls Dr. Phone: (203)926-9300
PO Box 870 Fax: (203)926-9310
Shelton, CT 06484-0870
Publisher E-mail: iscpubs@iscpubs.com

Biotechnology trade magazine. **Founded:** 1983. **Freq:** Bimonthly. **Print Method:** Offset. **Trim Size:** 11 x 15 3/4. **Cols./Page:** 3. **Col. Width:** 12 picas. **Col. Depth:** 82 picas. **Key Personnel:** Brian Howard, Editor; William N. Wham, Publisher; Maureen Magner, Production Mgr. **ISSN:** 0888-7225. **Subscription Rates:** $182 single issue; $150 other. **Remarks:** Accepts advertising.
Ad Rates: BW: $6,625 **Circ:** Controlled ‡36,957
4C: $8,185

5139 International Laboratory
International Scientific Communications, Inc.
30 Controls Dr. Phone: (203)926-9300
PO Box 870 Fax: (203)926-9310
Shelton, CT 06484-0870
Publisher E-mail: iscpubs@iscpubs.com

Scientific journal. **Founded:** 1971. **Freq:** 6/year. **Print Method:** Offset. **Trim Size:** 8 3/8 x 11. **Cols./Page:** 3. **Col. Width:** 24 nonpareils. **Col. Depth:** 140 agate lines. **Key Personnel:** Brian Howard, Editor; William N. Wham, Publisher; Maureen Magner, Production Dir. **ISSN:** 0010-2164. **Subscription Rates:** $165 individuals; $150 Europe. **Remarks:** Accepts advertising.
Ad Rates: BW: $7,835 **Circ:** Paid 86
4C: $10,570 Non-paid 58,535
PCI: $320

5140 Monroe Courier
Hometown Publications, Inc.
1000 Bridgeport Ave.
Shelton, CT 06484
Publication E-mail: homepubl@aol.com
Publisher E-mail: homepubl@aol.com

Community newspaper. **Founded:** 1972. **Freq:** Weekly (Thurs.). **Print Method:** Offset. **Trim Size:** 13 x 21 3/4. **Cols./Page:** 6. **Col. Width:** 1 7/8 inches. **Col. Depth:** 21 inches. **Key Personnel:** Nancy Doniger, Editor; Regina Burkhart, Publisher; Robin Glowa, Advertising Mgr., fax (206)926-2092; Hank Misiak, Advertising Dir. **Subscription Rates:** $12 individuals.
Ad Rates: BW: $1,253.70 **Circ:** Combined ♦4,496
4C: $1,853.70
PCI: $9.95

Stratford Star - See Stratford

5141 Trumbull Times
Hometown Publications, Inc.
1000 Bridgeport Ave.
Shelton, CT 06484
Publisher E-mail: homepubl@aol.com

Community newspaper. **Founded:** 1959. **Freq:** Weekly (Thurs.). **Print Method:** Offset. **Trim Size:** 14 x 22 1/2. **Cols./Page:** 6. **Col. Width:** 2 1/16 inches. **Col. Depth:** 21 inches. **Key Personnel:** Thomas Ebersold, Editor; Benjamin W. Gumm, Publisher; Sally McLaren, Advertising Mgr. **Subscription Rates:** $12.08 individuals.
Ad Rates: BW: $1,089.90 **Circ:** Combined ♦7,434
4C: $1,708.86
SAU: $10

Weston Voice - See Black Rock

SHERMAN

Rigel Communications Inc. - See Milledgeville, Georgia

SIMSBURY, pop. 21,161.

N. CT. Hartford Co. On Farmington River, 12 mi. W. of Hartford. Manufactures safety fuses, machine tools, gypsum insulation. Agriculture. Tobacco, dairy products.

Farmington Valley Herald - See Farmington

5142 Simsbury News
Imprint Newspapers
99 Main St. Phone: (860)236-3571
Bristol, CT 06010 Fax: (860)233-2080

Community newspaper (tabloid). **Freq:** Weekly (Thurs.). **Print Method:** Offset. **Cols./Page:** 6. **Col. Width:** 10 picas. **Col. Depth:** 16 inches. **Key Personnel:** Frank Chilinski, Publisher; Ellie Hart, Editor. **Subscription Rates:** $25; $21 senior citizens. **Remarks:** Combined advertising rates available with other Imprint Newspapers.
Circ: Paid 2,506
Non-paid 46

SOMERS, pop. 9,220.

NW CT. Tolland Co. E. of Enfield.

5143 WDJW-FM - 89.7
9th District Rd. Phone: (860)749-0719
Somers, CT 06071

Format: Album-Oriented Rock (AOR); Top 40. **Founded:** 1986. **Key Personnel:** Peter Stone, Contact. **Wattage:** 9.2. **Ad Rates:** Noncommercial.

SOUTH NORWALK

5144 Full Effect
Pilot Communications
29 Haviland St.
South Norwalk, CT 06854

Magazine featuring interviews and photos of R&B and hiphop artists. **Freq:** Bimonthly. **Key Personnel:** Crystal Brown, Editor; Roger Munford, Publisher. **Subscription Rates:** $2.95 single issue.

5145 National Relocation & Real Estate
The Relocation Information Service, Inc.
50 Water St. Phone: (203)855-1234
South Norwalk, CT 06854 Fax: (203)852-7208

Trade magazine focusing on the real estate and corporate relocation markets. **Subtitle:** "The Real Estate's News and Information Source". **Founded:** 1985. **Freq:** Bimonthly. **Trim Size:** 8 3/8 x 10 7/8. **Cols./Page:** 3. **Col. Width:** 18 nonpareils. **Col. Depth:** 140 agate lines. **Key Personnel:** Peter S. Featherston, Editor; Edward Finnegan, Advertising Mgr. **Subscription Rates:** $41.65. **Remarks:** Accepts advertising.
Ad Rates: GLR: $150 **Circ:** Paid ‡16,000
BW: $2,150 Controlled ‡14,000
4C: $3,250

5146 Travel World News Magazine
Travel Industry Network, Inc.
50 Washington St. Phone: (203)853-4955
South Norwalk, CT 06854 Fax: (203)866-1153
Publication E-mail: pgatt@travelworldnews.com

Magazine for the travel industry professional. **Founded:** 1988. **Freq:** Monthly. **Print Method:** Web offset. **Trim Size:** 8 1/8 x 10 7/8. **Cols./Page:** 3. **Col. Width:** 2 1/4 inches. **Col. Depth:** 7 inches. **Key Personnel:** Sara Southworth, Editor; Charles Gatt, Publisher. **ISSN:** 1044-4602. **Subscription Rates:** Free. **Remarks:** Accepts advertising.
Ad Rates: GLR: $890 **Circ:** Non-paid ‡30,000
BW: $4,400
4C: $6,200

SOUTH WINDSOR, pop. 17,198.

NC CT. Hartford Co. 5 mi. N. of Hartford. Residential.

5147 The Commercial Record
435 Buckland Rd. Phone: (860)644-3489
South Windsor, CT 06074-0902 Fax: (860)644-7363

Real estate and financial newspaper. **Founded:** 1882. **Freq:** Weekly (Fri.). **Print Method:** Offset. **Trim Size:** 11 3/8 x 16 7/8. **Cols./Page:** 4. **Col. Width:** 28 nonpareils. **Col. Depth:** 212 agate lines. **Key Personnel:** Walter Perry, Editor. **ISSN:** 0010-3098. **Subscription Rates:** $228 individuals. **Remarks:** Accepts advertising. **Available Online.**
Ad Rates: BW: $825 **Circ:** 3,200
4C: $1,075 Free 408
SAU: $32

SOUTHINGTON, pop. 36,879.

N. CT. Hartford Co. 7 mi. NW of Meriden. Manufactures hardware, tools, manifolds, forgings, airplane engines. Fruit, dairy, poultry farms. Apples, peaches.

5148 The Observer
The Step Saver, Inc.
PO Box 648 Phone: (860)621-6751
Southington, CT 06489-0648 Fax: (860)621-1841

Community newspaper. **Founded:** Dec. 1975. **Freq:** Weekly (Thurs.). **Print Method:** Offset. **Cols./Page:** 6. **Col. Width:** 12 picas. **Col. Depth:** 21 inches. **Key Personnel:** Robin Michel, Editor; Anthony L. Urillo, Publisher. **USPS:** 406-030. **Subscription Rates:** $22 individuals; $32 out of state; $100 out of country; single issue. **Remarks:** Combined advertising rates available with Step Saver.
Ad Rates: GLR: $.29 **Circ:** Paid 5,605
BW: $100 Non-paid 48
4C: $400
SAU: $7.50

5149 The Step Saver
The Step Saver, Inc.
PO Box 548 Phone: (860)628-9645
Southington, CT 06489-0548 Fax: (860)621-1841
Free: (800)378-3520

Shopper (tabloid). **Founded:** Apr. 10, 1963. **Freq:** Weekly (Tues.). **Print Method:** Offset. **Cols./Page:** 6. **Col. Width:** 10.5 picas. **Col. Depth:** 15 inches. **Key Personnel:** Anthony L. Urillo, Publisher. **Subscription Rates:** Free. **Remarks:** Combined advertising rates available with The Observer.
Ad Rates: GLR: $.41 **Circ:** Non-paid ♦**63,762**

5150 WNTY-AM - 990
PO Box 459 Phone: (860)628-0311
Southington, CT 06489 Fax: (860)276-9940

Format: Adult Contemporary. **Networks:** Sun Radio. **Founded:** 1969. **Operating Hours:** Continuous. **Key Personnel:** George Stevens, General Mgr. **Wattage:** 2500.

SOUTHPORT

SW CT. Fairfield Co. 55 mi. E. of New York.

5151 Gas Turbine World
Pequot Publishing, Inc.
PO Box 447 Phone: (203)259-1812
Southport, CT 06490-0447
Magazine containing technical and business information on the design application, operation, and maintenance of power plants for electrical generation, mechanical drive, oil and gas production and transmission, industrial process, CHP, and DHC applications. **Subtitle:** Serving industrial and electric utility power engineers. **Founded:** 1971. **Freq:** Bimonthly. **Print Method:** Web offset. **Trim Size:** 8 1/8 x 10 7/8. **Cols./Page:** 3. **Col. Width:** 2 1/16 inches. **Col. Depth:** 10 inches. **Key Personnel:** Peg Walker, Editor. **Subscription Rates:** $80. **Remarks:** Accepts advertising.
Ad Rates: BW: $3,490 **Circ:** Paid 910
4C: $4,385 Controlled 9,666

5152 The Small Press Book Review
PO Box 176 Phone: (203)332-7629
Southport, CT 06490 Fax: (203)332-7629

Magazine containing brief descriptive and critical book reviews, for librarians, distributors, general readers, and others in book trade. **Subtitle:** A Review of Books from Independent and Smaller Presses. **Founded:** 1985. **Freq:** Quarterly. **Print Method:** Electronic publishing. **Key Personnel:** Henry Berry, Editor, henryberry@aol.com. **ISSN:** 8756-7202. **Subscription Rates:** Free Controlled circulation. **Remarks:** Advertising not accepted.
Circ: (Not Reported)

STAFFORD SPRINGS, pop. 3,392.

N. CT. Tolland Co. 23 mi. NE of Hartford. Manufactures tools, dies, bottled soft drinks, chemicals. Woolens, worsted, cotton and silk mills.

5153 Tolland County Times
Toll and County Times
75 Gulf Rd
Stafford Springs, CT 06076

Community newspaper. **Founded:** 1989. **Freq:** Weekly (Thurs.). **Key Personnel:** William A. Johnson, Editor and Publisher; Lance C. Johnson, Publisher; Kathy McCarthy, Editor. **Subscription Rates:** $13; $10 senior citizens.

STAMFORD, pop. 102,453.

SW CT. Fairfield Co. On Long Island Sound, 35 mi. NE of New York. Manufactures chemicals, electrical equipment, pharmaceuticals, cosmetics, aircraft, metals, machinery, die casting, textiles, printing and publishing. Chemical, electronic research laboratories.

5154 The Advocate
Southern Connecticut Newspapers, Inc.
75 Tresser Blvd. Phone: (203)964-2200
PO Box 9307 Fax: (203)964-2345
Stamford, CT 06901-3304
General newspaper. **Founded:** 1829. **Freq:** Mon.-Sun. (morn.). **Print Method:** Offset. **Cols./Page:** 6. **Col. Width:** 2 1/16 inches. **Col. Depth:** 21 1/2 inches. **Key Personnel:** Barry Hoffman, Managing Editor; William J. Rowe, Publisher; Kenneth H. Brief, Editor; Michael R. Perry, Advertising Dir.; Jack A. Findley, Advertising Mgr. **Subscription Rates:** $140.40 individuals.
Ad Rates: BW: $4,687.54 **Circ:** Mon.-Fri. 28,514
4C: $5,112.54 Sat. 26,817
SAU: $43.95 Sun. 39,448

5155 American Demographics
PO Box 4274 Phone: (203)358-9900
Stamford, CT 06907 Fax: (203)358-5833
Free: (800)828-1133
Publication E-mail: editors@demographics.com
Publisher E-mail: editors@demographics.com

Tracks consumer, social, economic and demographic trends. **Subtitle:** Consumer Trends for Business Leaders. **Founded:** Jan. 1979. **Freq:** Monthly. **Print Method:** Offset. **Trim Size:** 8 3/8 x 11. **Cols./Page:** 3. **Col. Width:** 27 nonpareils. **Col. Depth:** 137 agate lines. **Key Personnel:** Shannon Dortch, Sr. Eitor; Michelle C. DeChant, Advertising Mgr. **ISSN:** 0163-4089. **Subscription Rates:** $69. **Remarks:** Accepts advertising. **Online:** LEXIS-NEXIS; Dow Jones News-Retrieval. **URL:** http://www.marketingtools.com.
Ad Rates: BW: $4,415 **Circ:** Paid 41,578
4C: $5,415

5156 Applied Behavioral Science Review
Elseiver
100 Prospect St. Phone: (203)323-9606
Stamford, CT 06901 Fax: (203)357-8446
Publication E-mail: 102062-2525@compuserve.com
Publisher E-mail: fcentres@gpu.stv.ualberta.ca

Psychology and sociology journal. **Founded:** 1992. **Freq:** Semiannual. **Print Method:** Offset. **Trim Size:** 7 x 10. **Cols./Page:** 1. **Col. Width:** 30 picas. **Col. Depth:** 49 picas. **Key Personnel:** Dr. David W. Britt, Editor. **ISSN:** 1068-8595. **Subscription Rates:** $75 individuals; $155 institutions; $175 institutions, other countries; $195 other countries air mail; $95 other countries; $115 other countries air mail; $80 single issue; $90 single issue, other countries; $100 single issue, other countries air mail. **Remarks:** Accepts advertising.
Ad Rates: BW: $400 **Circ:** ‡3,000

5157 Bowhunter Magazine
Cowles Enthusiast Media
4 High Ridge Park Phone: (203)322-2400
Stamford, CT 06905 Fax: (203)322-1966

The magazine is dedicated to the sport of Bowhunting. **Subtitle:** The Number One Bowhunting Magazine. **Founded:** Oct. 1971. **Freq:** 9/year. **Print Method:** Web offset. **Trim Size:** 8 1/4 x 10 3/4. **Cols./Page:** 3. **Key Personnel:** M.R. James, Editor, phone (406)756-9340, fax (406)756-1754; Fred Wallace, Advertising Dir., phone (502)773-3737, fax (502)773-3738; Richard Cochran, Editorial Director, phone (717)540-6717, fax (717)657-9552. **USPS:** 563-190. **Subscription Rates:** $27 individuals. **Remarks:** Accepts advertising.
Ad Rates: BW: $3,775 **Circ:** Paid ★**187,785**
4C: $5,795

5158 Catalog Age
Primedia Information
11 River Bend Dr. S Phone: (203)358-9900
PO Box 4949 Fax: (203)358-5811
Stamford, CT 06907-0949
Magazine serving the catalog marketing industry and its suppliers. **Founded:** 1984. **Freq:** 13/year. **Print Method:** Offset. Uses mats. **Trim Size:** 10 7/8 x 14 1/2. **Cols./Page:** 4. **Col. Width:** 26 nonpareils. **Col. Depth:** 182 agate lines. **Key**

Personnel: Laura M. Christiana, Editorial Dir. **Remarks:** Accepts advertising.
Ad Rates: BW: $3,760 **Circ:** Paid ★**2,161**
4C: $4,820 Non-paid ★**11,403**

5159 Country Journal
Cowles Enthusiast Media
4 High Ridge Park Phone: (203)322-2400
Stamford, CT 06905 Fax: (203)322-1966
Publication E-mail: cntryjrnl@aol.com

General resource publication on rural life, providing practical advice for the country dweller. **Subtitle:** For a Better Life With the Land. **Founded:** 1974. **Freq:** Bimonthly. **Print Method:** Offset. **Trim Size:** 8 x 10 7/8. **Cols./Page:** 3. **Col. Width:** 27 nonpareils. **Col. Depth:** 137 agate lines. **Key Personnel:** Toni Apgar, Publishing Dir.; Maryann Merion, Ad. Dir., mmerion@erols.com; Josh Garskof, Managing Editor. **ISSN:** 0094-0526. **Subscription Rates:** $21 individuals; $3.50 single issue. **Formerly:** Blair & Ketchum's Country Journal.
Ad Rates: BW: $5,445 **Circ:** Paid ★**145,182**
4C: $7,895

5160 Current Events
Weekly Reader Corp.
200 First Stamford Pl. Phone: (203)705-3500
PO Box 120023 Fax: (203)705-1661
Stamford, CT 06912-0023
Newspaper for junior and senior high school students. **Founded:** 1902. **Freq:** 26/year (during the academic year). **Trim Size:** 8 1/2 x 11. **Key Personnel:** Charles Piddock, Editor, phone (203)638-2619; Richard J. LeBrasseur, Advertising Mgr., phone (203)638-2667, fax (203)346-5994; Eric Ecker, Editor, phone (203)638-2423. **ISSN:** 0011-3492. **Subscription Rates:** $15.30 individuals less than 10 subscriptions; $7.65 individuals more than 10 subscriptions. **Remarks:** Advertising not accepted. **Alt. Formats:** Braille, American Printing Houe for the Blind; Microfilm, UMI.
Circ: ‡257,402

5161 Current Science
Weekly Reader Corp.
200 First Stamford Pl. Phone: (203)705-3500
PO Box 120023 Fax: (203)705-1661
Stamford, CT 06912-0023
Publication E-mail: science@weeklyreader.com

Science magazine for junior and senior high school students. **Founded:** 1927. **Freq:** Semimonthly (during the academic year). **Trim Size:** 8 1/2 x 11. **Key Personnel:** Dan Hogan, Managing Editor; Richard J. LeBrasseur, Publisher; Eric Ecker, Editor. **ISSN:** 0011-3905. **Subscription Rates:** $17.30 for two to nine copies; $8.65 more than ten subscriptions; $29.95 for one copy. **Remarks:** Advertising not accepted. **Alt. Formats:** Braille, American Printing House for the Blind; Microform, @UM.
Circ: ‡357,583

5162 Curriculum Administrator
Educational Media, LLC
992 High Ridge Rd. Phone: (203)322-1300
Stamford, CT 06905 Fax: (203)329-9177
Publication E-mail: camagazine@aol.com

Product magazine for K-12 curriculum administrators. **Subtitle:** Education, Trends, Issues Reources & Technology. **Founded:** 1986. **Freq:** 10/year. **Print Method:** Offset. **Trim Size:** 8 1/8 x 10 7/8. **Cols./Page:** 3. **Col. Width:** 12 1/2 picas. **Col. Depth:** 134 agate lines. **Key Personnel:** Jean Shields, Editor, jeans@edmediausa.com; Daniel Kinnaman, Publisher, dan@kinnaman.com; William Ziperman, General Mgr., billz@edmediausa.com. **ISSN:** 1082-5495. **Subscription Rates:** Free. **Remarks:** Advertising accepted; rates available upon request. **Formerly:** Curriculum Product News.
Circ: Controlled △**54,000**

5163 Directory World
Primedia Information
11 River Bend Dr. S Phone: (203)358-9900
PO Box 4949 Fax: (203)358-5811
Stamford, CT 06907-0949
Magazine for the telephone directory (yellow and white pages) industry. **Subtitle:** Business Solutions for the Yellow Pages and Directory Industry. **Founded:** 1989. **Freq:** Bimonthly 6/year. **Print Method:** Web offset. **Trim Size:** 8 1/2 x 11. **Key Personnel:** Kathleen M. Joyce, Editorial Director/Assoc. Publisher. **ISSN:** 1076-7258. **Subscription Rates:** Free to qualified subscribers. **Remarks:** Accepts advertising. **URL:** http://www.mediacentral.com/DirectoryWorld.
Ad Rates: BW: $2,730 **Circ:** Paid 1,074
4C: $4,025 Controlled 10,310

5164 Folio
Primedia Information
11 River Bend Dr. S Phone: (203)358-9900
PO Box 4949 Fax: (203)358-5811
Stamford, CT 06907-0949
Publishing industry trade magazine. **Subtitle:** The Magazine for Magazine Management. **Founded:** 1972. **Freq:** Monthly plus four special reports printed in April, July, Sept., & Nov. **Print Method:** Offset. **Trim Size:** 8 1/2 x 11. **Cols./Page:** 3. **Col. Width:** 27 nonpareils. **Col. Depth:** 140 agate lines. **Key Personnel:** Lisa Phillips, Editor-in-Chief, phone (203)358-4177, fax (203)358-5823, leppard@aol.com; Roberta Thomas, Publisher, phone (203)358-4183, fax (203)358-5822, robertathomas@cowlesbiz.com; Michael Dandrea, Ad Director, phone (203)683-3540, fax (203)683-4572, michael-dandrea@cowlesbiz.com. **Subscription Rates:** $96 individuals; $116 out of country; $6.50 single issue. **Remarks:** Accepts advertising. **Online:** America Online, Inc. **URL:** http://www.fourmag.com.
Ad Rates: BW: $4,480 **Circ:** Paid ★**8,816**
4C: $5,925 Non-paid ★**812**

5165 Journal of Income Distribution
Elseiver
100 Prospect St. Phone: (203)323-9606
Stamford, CT 06901 Fax: (203)357-8446
Publication E-mail: 102062.2525@compuserve.com
Publisher E-mail: fcentres@gpu.stv.ualberta.ca

Scientific journal. **Subtitle:** An International Journal of Social Economics. **Founded:** 1991. **Freq:** Semiannual. **Trim Size:** 7 x 10. **Cols./Page:** 1. **Col. Width:** 30 picas. **Col. Depth:** 42 picas. **Key Personnel:** J.T.J.M. van der Linden, Editor. **ISSN:** 0926-6437. **Subscription Rates:** $100 individuals; $190 institutions. **Remarks:** Accepts advertising.
Ad Rates: BW: $250 **Circ:** (Not Reported)

5166 Know Your World Extra
Weekly Reader Corp.
200 First Stamford Pl. Phone: (203)705-3500
PO Box 120023 Fax: (203)705-1661
Stamford, CT 06912-0023
Newspaper for junior and senior high school students. **Founded:** 1967. **Freq:** Semimonthly (during the academic year). **Trim Size:** 8 1/2 x 11. **Key Personnel:** W. Scott Ingram, Editor, phone (203)638-2441; Richard J. Le Brasseur, Publisher, phone (203)638-2667, fax (203)346-5994; Eric Ecker, Vice Pres./Group Product Developer, phone (203)638-2423. **ISSN:** 0163-4844. **Subscription Rates:** $17.90 (less than ten subscriptions); $8.95 (more than ten subscriptions). **Remarks:** Advertising not accepted. **Alt. Formats:** Braille, American Printing House for the Blind; Microfilm, UMI.
Circ: ‡172,109

5167 Motorcycle Tour & Cruiser
TAM Communications, Inc.
1010 Summer St., 3rd Fl. Phone: (203)425-8777
Stamford, CT 06905 Fax: (203)852-8775

Magazine featuring travel information from a motorcyclists' perspective. **Founded:** 1993. **Freq:** 9/year. **Trim Size:** 8 1/2 x 11. **Cols./Page:** 3. **Key Personnel:** Buzz Kanter, Publisher; Laura Brengelman, Editor. **ISSN:** 1069-2797. **Subscription Rates:** $19.94. **Remarks:** Accepts advertising. **Formerly:** Motorcycle Tour & Travel Adventure in Style; Motorcycle Tour & Travel.
Circ: Combined 30,000

5168 The Notebook
Catholic Movement for Intellectual & Cultural Affairs
31 Chesterfield Rd. Phone: (203)324-3573
Stamford, CT 06902
Journal of Catholic Professional Movement with world wide linkage. **Founded:** 1976. **Freq:** Quarterly. **Key Personnel:** Louisa D. Kirchner, Editor, kirchner@concenkric.net. **Subscription Rates:** $25. **Remarks:** Advertising not accepted.
Circ: (Not Reported)

5169 Race & Society
Elseiver
100 Prospect St. Phone: (203)323-9606
Stamford, CT 06901 Fax: (203)357-8446
Publication E-mail: 102062.2525@compuserve.com
Publisher E-mail: fcentres@gpu.stv.ualberta.ca

Journal that deals with race and society. **Founded:** 1997. **Freq:** Semiannual. **Trim Size:** 7 x 10. **Key Personnel:** Ronald L. Taylor, Editor. **ISSN:** 1090-9524. **Subscription Rates:** $70; $125 institutions. **Remarks:** Accepts advertising.
Circ: (Not Reported)

5170 Read
Weekly Reader Corp.
200 First Stamford Pl. Phone: (203)705-3500
PO Box 120023 Fax: (203)705-1661
Stamford, CT 06912-0023
Publication E-mail: edread@weeklyreader.com

A language arts magazine for junior & senior high school students, featuring award winning youngadult literature, classic adaptations, and history theme issues. **Founded:** 1951. **Freq:** Semimonthly during the academic year. **Print Method:** Offset. **Trim Size:** 5 3/4 x 8 1/2. **Key Personnel:** Scott Ingram, Managing Editor, phone (203)705-3479, singram@weeklyreader.com; Kate Davis, Editor, phone (203)705-3406, kdavis@weeklyreader.com; Ellen Florian, Assoc. Editor, phone (203)705-3449, eflorian@weeklyreader.com. **ISSN:** 0034-0359. **Subscription Rates:** $17.90 less than 10 subscriptions; $8.95 more than 10 subscriptions; $32.50 1 subscription. **Remarks:** Advertising not accepted. **Alt. Formats:** Microfilm, UMI; Microform.
Circ: ‡390,014

5171 Review of Financial Economics
Elseiver
100 Prospect St. Phone: (203)323-9606
Stamford, CT 06901 Fax: (203)357-8446
Publication E-mail: 102062.2525@compuserve.com
Publisher E-mail: fcentres@gpu.stv.ualberta.ca

Academic journal containing information on financial economics. **Founded:** 1992. **Freq:** Semiannual. **Trim Size:** 7 x 10. **Cols./Page:** 1. **Col. Width:** 30 picas. **Col. Depth:** 46 picas. **Key Personnel:** Gerald Whitney, Editor. **ISSN:** 1058-3300. **Subscription Rates:** $75; $155 institutions. **Remarks:** Accepts advertising.
Ad Rates: BW: $250 **Circ:** (Not Reported)

5172 Review of Radical Political Economics
Elseiver
100 Prospect St. Phone: (203)323-9606
Stamford, CT 06901 Fax: (203)357-8446
Publication E-mail: 102062.255@compuserve.com
Publisher E-mail: fcentres@gpu.stv.ualberta.ca

Academic journal containing information on radical political economics. **Founded:** 1968. **Freq:** Quarterly. **Trim Size:** 7 x 10. **Cols./Page:** 1. **Col. Width:** 30 picas. **Col. Depth:** 42 picas. **Key Personnel:** Hazel Gunn, Editor. **ISSN:** 0486-6134. **Subscription Rates:** $45; $165 institutions. **Remarks:** Accepts advertising.
Ad Rates: BW: $250 **Circ:** (Not Reported)

5173 The Sower
The Ukrainian Catholic Diocese of Stamford
14 Peveril Rd. Phone: (203)325-2116
Stamford, CT 06902-3019 Fax: (203)967-9948
Publication E-mail: basileos@aol.com

Official newspaper of Ukrainian Catholic Diocese of Stamford (Ukrainian and English). **Founded:** 1986. **Freq:** 20/year. **Print Method:** Offset. **Trim Size:** 11 1/2 x 17. **Cols./Page:** 4. **Col. Width:** 14 1/2 picas. **Col. Depth:** 16 inches. **Key Personnel:** Rev. Msgr. Leon A. Mosko, Editor, phone (203)358-9905. **ISSN:** 0896-6184. **Subscription Rates:** $15; $20 other countries. **Remarks:** Advertising not accepted.
Circ: Paid ‡8,220
Non-paid ‡140

5174 Symbolic Interaction
Elseiver
100 Prospect St. Phone: (203)323-9606
Stamford, CT 06901 Fax: (203)357-8446
Publication E-mail: 102062.255@compuserve.com
Publisher E-mail: fcentres@gpu.stv.ualberta.ca

Academic journal. **Subtitle:** Official Journal of the Society for the Study of Symbolic Interaction. **Founded:** 1968. **Freq:** Quarterly. **Trim Size:** 7 x 10. **Cols./Page:** 1. **Col. Width:** 30 picas. **Col. Depth:** 42 picas. **Key Personnel:** Michael Flaherty, Editor. **ISSN:** 0195-6068. **Subscription Rates:** $80; $185 institutions. **Remarks:** Accepts advertising.
Ad Rates: BW: $250 **Circ:** (Not Reported)

5175 Weekly Reader (Pre-K edition)
Weekly Reader Corp.
200 First Stamford Pl. Phone: (203)705-3500
PO Box 120023 Fax: (203)705-1661
Stamford, CT 06912-0023
Publication E-mail: weeklyreader.com

Educational newspaper for the pre-kindergarten classroom. **Founded:** Sept. 21, 1928. **Freq:** Weekly. **Trim Size:** 8 1/2 x 11. **Key Personnel:** Sandra Maccarone, Editor-in-Chief, phone (203)638-2452; Richard LeBrausseur, Publisher, phone (203)638-2667, fax (203)346-5994; Thaddeus Kozlowski, Vice President, phone (203)638-2425, fax (203)346-5964. **ISSN:** 0890-3174. **Subscription Rates:** $4.65 individuals. **Remarks:** Advertising not accepted. **Alt. Formats:** Braille, American Printing House for the Blind; Microform, UMI.
Circ: Paid 508,153

5176 American Cable Entertainment
4 Landmark Sq. Ste. 302 Phone: (203)323-1100
Stamford, CT 06901-2601 Fax: (203)325-3110

Owner: American Cable Entertainment, at above address. **Founded:** 1994. **Formerly:** Simmons Communications Inc. **Key Personnel:** Bruce A. Armstrong, Contact; John Flanagan, Contact. **Cities Served:** Various communities in NM, TX, OH, NB, ND, AR, CO, LA, CA, V A: subscribing households 76,200.

5177 Time Warner Communications
300 1st Stamford Pl. Phone: (203)328-0600
Stamford, CT 06902-6732 Fax: (203)328-0690

Founded: 1968. **Formerly:** American Television & Communications Corp. (1992). **Key Personnel:** Jimmy Doolittle, President. **Cities Served:** Alabama, Arkansas, California, Colorado, Connecticut, Florida, Georgia, Hawaii, Ilinois, Indiana, Iowa, Kansas, Kentucky, Louisiana, Maine.: subscribing households 4,700,000.

WEDW-TV - See Bridgeport

WFNW-AM - See Naugatuck

5178 WKHL-FM - 96.7
100 Prospect St. Phone: (203)327-1400
Stamford, CT 06901-1640 Fax: (203)359-9907

Format: Oldies. **Owner:** Q Broadcasting, Inc., at above address. **Founded:** 1947. **Formerly:** WYRS-FM (1990); KJAZ-AM. **Operating Hours:** Continuous. **Key Personnel:** Richard M. Brescia, Vice Pres./Gen. MNgr.; Charles Ponger, Vice Pres. of Sales; Mark Gaulke, Sales Mgr.; C.J. Haze, Program Dir. **Wattage:** 3000. **Ad Rates:** $65-100 per unit.

5179 WSTC-AM - 1400
100 Prospect St. Phone: (203)327-1400
Stamford, CT 06901-1640 Fax: (203)359-9907

Format: Full Service; News; Talk. **Networks:** ABC. **Owner:** Chase Broadcasting, 1 Financial Plaza, Hartford, CT, (203)522-1080. **Founded:** 1941. **Operating Hours:** Continuous. **Key Personnel:** John Fullam, General Mgr.; Al Tacca, General Sales Mgr.; Don Matsen, Program Dir. **Wattage:** 1000. **Ad Rates:** $85-125 per unit.

STORRS, pop. 10,691.

N. CT. Tollands Co. 8 mi. NW of Willmantic. University of Connecticut.

5180 The Public Perspective
Roper Center for Public Opinion Research
341 Mansfield Ave., U-164 Phone: (860)486-4440
Storrs, CT 06269-1164 Fax: (860)486-6308

Journal covering public opinion, public policy, social issues, and political science. **Subtitle:** A Roper Center Review of Public Opinion and Polling. **Founded:** Nov. 1989. **Freq:** Bimonthly. **Print Method:** Offset. **Key Personnel:** Everett Carll Ladd, Editor-in-Chief; David Wilber, Assoc. Editor; Lisa Ferraro Parmelee, Asst. Editor, lisap@opinion.isi.uconn.edu. **ISSN:** 1050-5067. **Subscription Rates:** $38.50 individuals; $105 institutions; $155 two years institutions; $55 libraries secondary schools; $6 single issue. **Remarks:** Advertising not accepted. **Online:** LEXIS-NEXIS; Dialog (The Dialog Corporation). **URL:** http://www.ropercenter.uconn.edu.
Circ: Combined 3,000

5181 Traditions
University of Connecticut
1266 Storrs Rd. Phone: (860)486-2377
Storrs, CT 06269-5144 Fax: (860)486-2063

Alumni magazine. **Founded:** 1995. **Freq:** Quarterly. **Key Personnel:** Gary E. Frank, Editor. **USPS:** 056-320. **Subscription Rates:** Free to qualified subscribers. **Remarks:** Advertising not accepted.
Circ: Controlled 120,000

STORRS MANSFIELD

5182 The Daily Campus
University of Connecticut
11 Dog Ln. Phone: (860)486-3407
Storrs Mansfield, CT 06268 Fax: (860)486-4388

Collegiate newspaper. **Founded:** 1896. **Freq:** Daily (morn.) (during the academic year). **Print Method:** Offset. **Trim Size:** 8 1/2 x 11. **Cols./Page:** 5. **Col. Width:** 1 7/8 inches. **Col. Depth:** 16 inches. **Key Personnel:** Kanru Martinson, Publisher; Alena Cybart, Editor; Michelle Notaro, Advertising Dir. **Subscription Rates:** $40 individuals. **Remarks:** Accepts advertising.
Ad Rates: GLR: $5 **Circ:** Combined ‡10,000
BW: $360
4C: $660

5183 The IMS Bulletin
Institute of Mathematical Statistics
Department of Statistics Phone: (860)486-4196
UCONN Fax: (860)486-4113
196 Auditorium Rd., U-120
Storrs Mansfield, CT 06269-3120
Publication E-mail: ims@stat.uconn.edu
Publisher E-mail: ims@imstat.org

Journal providing IMS news. **Founded:** 1972. **Freq:** Bimonthly. **Print Method:** Offset. **Trim Size:** 7 x 10. **Cols./Page:** 1. **Col. Width:** 5 inches. **Col. Depth:** 8 inches. **Key Personnel:** Dipak Dey, Editor. **ISSN:** 0146-3942. **Subscription Rates:** $50. **Remarks:** Accepts advertising. **URL:** http://www.stat.ucla.edu/ims/.
Ad Rates: BW: $250 **Circ:** Paid 4,200

5184 WHUS-FM - 91.7
Box U-8R Phone: (860)486-4007
2110 Hillside Rd. Fax: (860)486-2955
Storrs Mansfield, CT 06269-3008
E-mail: whusfm@uconnvm.uconn.edu

Format: Eclectic; Alternative/New Music/Progressive. **Networks:** AP. **Owner:** University of Connecticut, at above address. **Founded:** 1956. **Operating Hours:** Continuous. **Key Personnel:** John E. Murphy, General Mgr.; Mike Murphy, Operations Mgr.; Chris Sampson, Program Dir.; Dean Fiora, Production Dir.; John Zatowski, Chief Engineer; Barbara Becker, Business Mgr.; Nathan Phelps, Information Program Dir.; Rene Twarkins, Development Dir.; Sarah Morgenstein, Women's Affairs Dir.; Lily Cheung, Minority Affairs Dir.; David Estell, Training Dir. **Wattage:** 3160. **Ad Rates:** Noncommercial; underwriting available. **URL:** http://www.whusfm.saup.uconn.edu.

STRATFORD, pop. 50,541.

SW CT. Fairfield Co. 4 mi. SW of Milford. Residential.

5185 Bargain News
720 Baronum Ave. Phone: (203)377-3000
Stratford, CT 06497 Fax: (203)380-0741
Free: (800)288-4226
Publication E-mail: webmaster@bargainnews.com

Consumer weekly (tabloid) containing automotive classifieds and general news. **Founded:** Feb. 13, 1970. **Freq:** Weekly (Thurs.). **Print Method:** Offset. **Trim Size:** 11 x 17. **Cols./Page:** 6. **Col. Width:** 10 picas. **Col. Depth:** 95 1/2 picas. **Key Personnel:** John F. Roy, Publisher; David Reno, Advertising Mgr. **ISSN:** 7447-7353. **Subscription Rates:** $255. **Remarks:** Accepts advertising. **Available Online.** **URL:** http://www.bargainnews.com.
Ad Rates: BW: $1,204.88 **Circ:** Paid 42,000
PCI: $12.75

5186 Connecticut River Review
Connecticut Poetry Society
35 Lindsley Pl. Phone: (203)378-0755
Stratford, CT 06497
Poetry journal. **Founded:** 1978. **Freq:** Semiannual. **Print Method:** Web offset. **Trim Size:** 6 x 9. **Key Personnel:** Norah Christianson, Editor. **ISSN:** 0897-0998. **Subscription Rates:** $11 individuals; $6 single issue. **Remarks:** Advertising not accepted.
Circ: Paid 250

5187 Small Pond Magazine of Literature
Napoleon St. Cyr
PO Box 664 Phone: (203)378-4066
Stratford, CT 06615
Literary journal covering poetry and fiction. **Founded:** 1964. **Freq:** Triennial. **Print Method:** Offset. **Trim Size:** 5 1/2 x 8 1/2. **ISSN:** 0097-721X. **Subscription Rates:** $10 individuals; $4 single issue. **Remarks:** Accepts advertising.
Ad Rates: BW: $40 **Circ:** Combined 265

5188 Stratford Star
Hometown Publications, Inc.
1000 Bridgeport Ave.
Shelton, CT 06484
Publisher E-mail: homepubl@aol.com

Community newspaper. **Founded:** 1985. **Freq:** Weekly (Wed.). **Print Method:** Offset. **Trim Size:** 14 x 22 1/2. **Cols./Page:** 6. **Col. Width:** 1 3/8 inches. **Col. Depth:** 21 inches. **Key Personnel:** Chris Carroll, Editor; Ben Gumm, Publisher; Sally McLaren, Advertising Mgr. **Subscription Rates:** $12.50. **Remarks:** Combined advertising rates available with other Hometown Publications.
Ad Rates: GLR: $.80 **Circ:** Combined ♦**20,268**
BW: $1,263
4C: $1,863
SAU: $11.23

THOMASTON, pop. 6,276.

NW CT. Litchfield Co. 10 mi. N. of Waterbury. Manufactures clocks and clock crystals, brass screw machine products, glass, metal specialties. Dairy, truck, fruit farms.

5189 Thomaston Express
Bristol Acquisition Corp.
PO Box 250 Phone: (860)283-4355
Thomaston, CT 06787 Fax: (860)283-4356

Community newspaper. **Founded:** 1874. **Freq:** Weekly (Thurs.). **Print Method:** Offset. **Trim Size:** 10 1/2 x 12 1/2. **Cols./Page:** 5. **Col. Width:** 11.2 picas. **Col. Depth:** 11.5 inches. **Key Personnel:** Mike Chaiken, Editor; Marc Romanow, Publisher. **Subscription Rates:** $20 individuals; $26 in Connecticut; $32 out of state. **Remarks:** Accepts advertising.
Ad Rates: BW: $414.70 **Circ:** ‡1,900
PCI: $6.38

TOLLAND

5190 Connecticut Maple Leaf
French-Canadian Genealogical Society of Connecticut, Inc.
Box 928 Phone: (860)872-2597
Tolland, CT 06084-0928
Journal covering Frenoh-Canadian genealogy in Connecticut. **Founded:** June 1983. **Freq:** Semiannual. **Trim Size:** 8 1/2 x 11. **Cols./Page:** 1 and 2. **Col. Width:** 6 inches. **Col. Depth:** 9 inches. **Key Personnel:** Albert J. Marceau, Editor. **ISSN:** 1081-6275. **Subscription Rates:** Free to qualified subscribers. **Alt. Formats:** Microfiche.

5191 International Journal of Instructional Media (IM)
Westwood Press
149 Goose Ln.
Tolland, CT 06084

Journal featuring articles on instructional media and technology used in training. **Founded:** 1967. **Freq:** Quarterly. **Print Method:** Offset. **Trim Size:** 6 x 9. **Cols./Page:** 1. **Key Personnel:** Dr. Phillip J. Sleeman, Exec. Editor, phone (860)875-5484; Dick Lombard, Publisher. **ISSN:** 0092-1815. **Subscription Rates:** $130 individuals; $135 other countries. **Remarks:** Advertising not accepted. **Online:** EBSCO. **URL:** http://www.adprima.com/ijim.htm. **Alt. Formats:** Microform.
Circ: (Not Reported)

TORRINGTON, pop. 30,987.

NW CT. Litchfield Co. On Naugatuck River, 20 mi. N. of Waterbury. Manufactures industrial brushes, needles, bearings, universal joints, electronic computers, spring and mill machinery, venetian blinds, rotary pump, fans and blower wheels, castings, furniture, roller skates, sporting goods, machine screws and nuts, corrugated cardboard containers, lumber products, gaskets, textiles, hardware, tools.

5192 Foothills Trader
PO Box 665 Phone: (203)693-2990
Torrington, CT 06790
Community shopper covering the area west of Hartford from Avon to the Massachusetts border, south to Bristol, and west to New York state line. **Founded:** July 5, 1964. **Freq:** Weekly (Mon.). **Print Method:** Offset. **Trim Size:** 10 1/2 x 12. **Cols./Page:** 6. **Col. Depth:** 12 inches. **Key Personnel:** William T. Murray, Publisher. **Subscription Rates:** Free; $26 by mail.
Ad Rates: GLR: $6 **Circ:** Paid ‡25
BW: $1,008 Free ‡42,000

5193 The Register Citizen
Journal Register Inc.
190 Water St. Phone: (203)489-3121
PO Box 58 Fax: (203)489-6790
Torrington, CT 06790
Free: (800)489-1450

General newspaper. **Founded:** 1874. **Freq:** Mon.-Sat. (morn.). **Print Method:** Offset. **Trim Size:** 13 3/4 x 22 3/4. **Cols./Page:** 6. **Col. Width:** 12.3 picas. **Col. Depth:** 298 agate lines. **Key Personnel:** Mack Stewart, Publisher. **USPS:** 634-200. **Subscription Rates:** $99 individuals. **Remarks:** Accepts advertising.
Ad Rates: GLR: $.82 **Circ:** Mon.-Sat. ★**12,588**
BW: $1,454 Sun. ★**11,577**
4C: $1,654
SAU: $10.36
PCI: $11.40

TRUMBULL, pop. 32,989.

SW CT. Fairfield Co. 5 mi. S. of Bridgeport. Manufactures electronic components, silver and plated ware. Residential.

5194 Connecticut Magazine
Communications International
35 Nutmeg Dr. Phone: (203)380-6600
Trumbull, CT 06611 Fax: (203)380-6612
Publication E-mail: ctmag@pcnet.com

Magazine for Connecticut residents. Includes articles on politics, fashion, business, home interiors, restaurant reviews,

the arts, and real estate. **Founded:** Oct. 1971. **Freq:** Monthly. **Print Method:** Web offset. **Trim Size:** 8 x 10 3/4. **Cols./Page:** 3. **Col. Width:** 27 nonpareils. **Col. Depth:** 140 agate lines. **Key Personnel:** Charles Monagan, Editor; Michael Mims, Publisher. **ISSN:** 0889-7670. **Subscription Rates:** $18 individuals; $2.95 single issue; $30 other countries; $14.95 single issue other countries. **Remarks:** Accepts advertising. **URL:** http://www.connecticut.com.
Ad Rates: BW: $5,325 **Circ:** Paid ★88,639
4C: $7,825

5195 Cruising World Magazine
Cruising World Publications, Inc.
5520 Park Ave. Phone: (203)373-2102
Trumbull, CT 06611-0395
Boating magazine for those who enjoy cruising under sail. **Founded:** 1974. **Freq:** Monthly. **Print Method:** Printed web offset. **Trim Size:** 8 x 10 3/4. **Cols./Page:** 3. **Col. Width:** 13 picas. **Col. Depth:** 57 picas. **Key Personnel:** Bernadette Bernon, Editor; Gordon Medenica, Pres./Publisher; Sally Helme, Marine Ad. Sales Dir., phone (401)847-1588, fax (401)848-5048. **Subscription Rates:** $28; $3.50 single issue. **Remarks:** Accepts advertising.
Ad Rates: BW: $10,040 **Circ:** Paid ★152,368
4C: $14,610

5196 Golf Digest
New York Times Magazine Group
5520 Park Ave. Phone: (203)373-7000
Trumbull, CT 06611 Fax: (203)373-7111

International magazine for golfers. **Founded:** 1950. **Freq:** Monthly. **Print Method:** Offset. **Trim Size:** 9 x 10 7/8. **Cols./Page:** 3. **Col. Width:** 27 nonpareils. **Col. Depth:** 140 agate lines. **Key Personnel:** Jerry Tarde, Editor, phone (202)373-7198, fax (203)371-2162; Tom Brown, Publisher, phone (212)739-3019; Dan Govern, VP/National Sales Mgr., phone (203)371-2117. **ISSN:** 0017-176X. **Subscription Rates:** $27.94 individuals; $3.99 single issue. **Remarks:** Accepts advertising. **URL:** http://www.golfdigest.com.
Ad Rates: GLR: $112 **Circ:** Paid ★1,554,134
BW: $43,150
4C: $64,730
PCI: $1,530

5197 Golf Shop Operations
Golf Digest/Tennis, Inc.
5520 Park Ave. Phone: (203)373-7000
PO Box 0395 Fax: (203)371-2505
Trumbull, CT 06611-0395
Free: (800)451-2386

Magazine on golf shop operations. **Founded:** 1963. **Freq:** 10/year. **Print Method:** Offset. **Trim Size:** 10 3/4 x 14 1/2. **Cols./Page:** 4. **Col. Width:** 56 picas. **Col. Depth:** 182 agate lines. **Key Personnel:** Roger Casl, Publisher, phone (203)373-7122. **ISSN:** 0017-1824. **Subscription Rates:** $72 individuals; $10 individuals. **Remarks:** Accepts advertising.
Ad Rates: BW: $7,740 **Circ:** Controlled ‡17,907
4C: $10,850

5198 Journal of Texture Studies
Food & Nutrition Press, Inc.
6527 Main St. Phone: (203)261-8587
PO Box 374 Fax: (203)261-9724
Trumbull, CT 06611
Publisher E-mail: 72400.3517@compuserve.com

Journal for food industry and professionals. **Founded:** Nov. 1969. **Freq:** Bimonthly. **Print Method:** Offset. **Trim Size:** 6 x 9. **Key Personnel:** John J. O'Neil, Contact. **ISSN:** 0022-4901. **Subscription Rates:** $195 individuals. **Remarks:** Accepts advertising.
Ad Rates: BW: $300 **Circ:** (Not Reported)

5199 Restaurants, Resorts & Hotels
Trade Publishing Co.
PO Box 318 Phone: (203)279-0149
Trumbull, CT 06611
National business magazine serving the food service industry. **Founded:** May 1, 1983. **Freq:** Monthly. **Print Method:** Offset web. **Trim Size:** 8 1/2 x 11. **Cols./Page:** 3. **Col. Width:** 2 1/2 inches. **Col. Depth:** 10 inches. **Key Personnel:** James Martone, Editor; John P. Mortimer, Publisher. **Subscription Rates:** $30; $40 other countries. **Remarks:** Accepts advertising. **Formerly:** Restaurant Merchandising News (Jan. 1994).
Ad Rates: BW: $4,975 **Circ:** Paid ‡1,793
4C: $7,315 Controlled ‡61,000
PCI: $100

5200 Sport Shop News
Trade Publishing Co.
PO Box 318 Phone: (203)279-0149
Trumbull, CT 06611
National business magazine for the sporting goods retailer. **Founded:** 1989. **Freq:** Monthly. **Print Method:** Web offset. **Trim Size:** 8 1/2 x 11. **Cols./Page:** 3. **Col. Width:** 2 1/2 inches. **Col. Depth:** 10 inches. **Key Personnel:** James Martone, Editor; John Mortimer, Publisher. **Subscription Rates:** $36; $52 other countries. $5 single issue. **Remarks:** Accepts advertising.
Ad Rates: BW: $3,200 **Circ:** Paid ‡1,288
4C: $4,525 Controlled ‡22,121
SAU: $100

5201 Tennis
Golf Digest/Tennis, Inc.
5520 Park Ave. Phone: (203)373-7000
PO Box 0395 Fax: (203)371-2505
Trumbull, CT 06611-0395
Free: (800)451-2386

Tennis magazine. **Founded:** 1965. **Freq:** Monthly. **Print Method:** Offset. **Trim Size:** 8 x 10 7/8. **Cols./Page:** 3. **Col. Width:** 27 nonpareils. **Col. Depth:** 140 agate lines. **Key Personnel:** Donna Doherty, Editor; Gordon Medenica, Publisher; Rick Beispel, Advertising Mgr. **ISSN:** 0040-3423. **Subscription Rates:** $23.94 individuals; $2.95 single issue. **Remarks:** Accepts advertising. **Available Online. URL:** http://www.tennis.com.
Ad Rates: BW: $26,300 **Circ:** Paid ★775,486
4C: $31,560

5202 Tennis Buyer's Guide
Golf Digest/Tennis, Inc.
5520 Park Ave. Phone: (203)373-7000
PO Box 0395 Fax: (203)371-2505
Trumbull, CT 06611-0395
Free: (800)451-2386

Tennis buyers guide sent to tennis shop operators, retailers, buyers. **Founded:** 1984. **Freq:** Bimonthly. **Print Method:** Offset. **Trim Size:** 8 x 10 7/8. **Cols./Page:** 4. **Col. Width:** 21 nonpareils. **Col. Depth:** 182 agate lines. **Key Personnel:** Bill Grazi, Editor. **ISSN:** 0749-6478. **Subscription Rates:** $36 individuals; $8 single issue; $72 out of country; $10 single copy, foreign. **Remarks:** Accepts advertising. **Available Online. URL:** http://www.tennis.com.
Ad Rates: BW: $6,120 **Circ:** Controlled ‡10,836
4C: $8,570

5203 Tennis USTA
New York Times Magazine Group
5520 Park Ave. Phone: (203)373-7155
Trumbull, CT 06611 Fax: (203)371-2199

Magazine for U.S. Tennis Association members. **Founded:** Feb. 1990. **Freq:** Monthly. **Print Method:** Offset. **Trim Size:** 8 1/2 x 10 7/8. **Key Personnel:** Robert Moseley, Editor; Gordon Medenica, Publisher. **Subscription Rates:** Free to qualified subscribers. **Remarks:** Accepts advertising. **Formerly:** Tennis USA (1990).
Ad Rates: 4C: $12,000 **Circ:** Controlled ‡360,000

VERNON

NC CT. Tolland Co. 10 mi. SW of Rockville.

5204 Circuit Cellar INK
Circuit Cellar, Inc.
4 Park St. Phone: (860)875-2751
Vernon, CT 06066 Fax: (860)871-0411

Magazine providing practical, technical information for designers and builders of computer hardware and software applications. **Subtitle:** The Computer Applications Journal. **Founded:** 1988. **Freq:** Monthly. **Print Method:** Web offset. **Trim Size:** 8 1/8 x 10 7/8. **Cols./Page:** 3. **Col. Width:** 2 1/4 inches. **Col. Depth:** 9 5/8 inches. **Key Personnel:** Steve Ciarcia, Founder/Editorial Director; Ken Davidson, Editor-in-Chief; Daniel Rodrigues, Publisher. **ISSN:** 0896-8985. **Subscription Rates:** $21.95 individuals; $3.95 single issue. **Remarks:** Accepts advertising. **URL:** http://www.circellar.com/.
Ad Rates: BW: $2,100 **Circ:** Paid ‡34,000
4C: $2,350 Non-paid ‡6,800

5205 The Door Opener
An Open Door To The Inner Light, Inc.
70 Valley Falls Rd. Phone: (860)875-4101
Vernon, CT 06066 Fax: (860)648-1456
Publisher E-mail: anopendoor@aol.com

Publication focusing on holistic health and metaphysical lasses and workshops in Connecticut. **Subtitle:** Connecticut's Holistic Health and Metaphysical Networking Magazine. **Founded:** Nov. 1986. **Freq:** Quarterly. **Print Method:** Offset. **Trim Size:** 8 1/2 x 11. **Cols./Page:** 2. **Col. Width:** 3 5/8 inches. **Col. Depth:** 9 1/2 inches. **Key Personnel:** Jon Roe, Editor and Publisher. **ISSN:** 1069-6253. **Subscription Rates:** $12 individuals; $3 single issue. **Remarks:** Accepts advertising. **URL:** http://www.anopendoor.com.
Ad Rates: BW: $290 **Circ:** Paid 2,100
Non-paid 400

Enfield Reminder - See Enfield

Manchester Reminder - See Manchester

5206 Reminder
Reminder Press
PO Box 27 Phone: (860)872-6648
130 Old Town Rd. Fax: (860)875-2089
Vernon, CT 06066
Shopper. **Founded:** 1949. **Freq:** Weekly (Wed.). **Print Method:** Offset. **Cols./Page:** 6. **Col. Width:** 24 nonpareils. **Col. Depth:** 224 agate lines. **Key Personnel:** Kenneth A. Hovland, Publisher. **Remarks:** Accepts advertising.
Ad Rates: GLR: $.42 **Circ:** Free 23,071

Windsor Reminder - See Windsor

WALLINGFORD, pop. 37,274.

SC CT. New Haven Co. 5 mi. S. of Meriden. Choate School. Summer theatre. Manufactures silverware, chemicals, fancy hardware, tools, measuring instruments, electronics, textile factories. Fruit orchards.

5207 WWEB-FM - 89.9
Choate Rosemary Hall Foundation Phone: (203)697-2597
333 Christian St.
Wallingford, CT 06492
E-mail: wweb@qm.ch.ale.edu

Format: Full Service. **Networks:** Independent. **Owner:** Choate Rosemary Hall Foundation, at above address, (203)697-2000. **Founded:** 1969. **Operating Hours:** Continuous. **Key Personnel:** Chris Davies, Station Advisor; Alex Patrikis, Station Mgr., phone (203)6972000. **Wattage:** 10. **Ad Rates:** Noncommercial.

WATERBURY†, pop. 103,266.

S. CT. New Haven Co. 21 mi. NW of New Haven. Center of the brass industry. Manufactures brass and copper goods, clocks, watches, buckles, buttons, chemicals, toys, tools, metal novelties, lighting fixtures, machine shop products. Foundry.

5208 Alternative Energy Retailer
Zackin Publications, Inc.
70 Edwin Ave. Phone: (203)755-0158
PO Box 2180 Fax: (203)755-3480
Waterbury, CT 06722
Free: (800)325-6745

Trade magazine on solid fuel, pellet, and gas hearth heating. **Subtitle:** Dealer's Magazine. **Founded:** Nov. 1980. **Freq:** Monthly. **Print Method:** Offset. **Trim Size:** 8 1/2 x 11. **Cols./Page:** 3. **Col. Width:** 26 nonpareils. **Col. Depth:** 140 agate lines. **Key Personnel:** Dave Johnston, Managing Editor, johnston@aer-online.com; Henry Pacyna, Production Mgr.; David Zackin, Publisher; Linda R. Zackin, Advertising Dir. **ISSN:** 0273-8163. **Subscription Rates:** Free to qualified subscribers; $32 individuals. **Remarks:** Accepts advertising.
Ad Rates: BW: $2,430 **Circ:** Controlled ⊕9,837
4C: $3,400 Paid ⊕332

5209 Drycleaners News
Zackin Publications, Inc.
70 Edwin Ave. Phone: (203)755-0158
PO Box 2180 Fax: (203)755-3480
Waterbury, CT 06722
Free: (800)325-6745

Trade magazine (tabloid) for the drycleaning industry in the Northeastern U.S. **Subtitle:** The News and Management Magazine. **Founded:** 1951. **Freq:** Monthly. **Print Method:** Offset. **Trim Size:** 11 1/2 x 15. **Cols./Page:** 5. **Col. Width:** 24 nonpareils. **Col. Depth:** 196 agate lines. **Key Personnel:** David Zackin, Publisher; Linda Zackin, Advertising Dir.; Heather Bednar, Account Executive, bednar@dcn-online.com; Henry Pacyna, Production Mgr. **ISSN:** 0012-6802. **Subscription Rates:** Free to qualified subscribers; $36 Others. **Remarks:** Accepts advertising.
Ad Rates: BW: $1,025 **Circ:** Paid 41
4C: $1,755 Non-paid 8,698

5210 Northeast Outdoors
Woodall Publishing Co.
70 Edwin Ave. Phone: (203)755-0158
PO Box 2180 Fax: (203)755-3480
Waterbury, CT 06722-2180
Free: (800)325-3745
Publisher E-mail: emd@woodallpub.com

Consumer magazine (tabloid) covering recreational vehicles and camping in the northeastern U.S. **Subtitle:** The Northeast's Favorite Camping Publication. **Founded:** July 1968. **Freq:** Monthly. **Print Method:** Offset. **Trim Size:** 11 1/2 x 15. **Cols./Page:** 5. **Col. Width:** 24 nonpareils. **Col. Depth:** 196 agate lines. **Key Personnel:** Ann Emerson, Publisher; Brent Peterson, Editor, bpeterson@woodallpub.com; John Florian, Editorial Director. **ISSN:** 0199-8463. **Subscription Rates:** $8

individuals. **Remarks:** Accepts advertising. **URL:** http://www.woodalls.com.
Ad Rates: BW: $1,440 **Circ:** Paid ⊕**9,394**
4C: $2,090 Non-paid ⊕**1,365**

5211 Secondary Marketing Executive
LDJ Corp.
70 Edwin Ave. Phone: (203)755-0158
PO Box 2330 Fax: (203)755-3480
Waterbury, CT 06722
Free: (800)325-6745

Trade magazine (tabloid) covering the buying and selling of mortgages and mortgage servicing in the secondary market. **Subtitle:** Journal of Mortgage Banking Risk Management. **Founded:** Dec. 1986. **Freq:** Monthly. **Print Method:** Offset. **Trim Size:** 11 x 13 1/2. **Cols./Page:** 4. **Col. Width:** 13 3/5 picas. **Col. Depth:** 81 picas. **Key Personnel:** David Zackin, Publisher; Linda Zackin, Advertising Dir.; Linda Herrmann, Account Exec., herrmann@sme-online.com; Neil Morse, Editor, morse@sme-online.com. **ISSN:** 0891-2947. **Subscription Rates:** Free to qualified subscribers; $48 individuals. **Remarks:** Accepts advertising.
Ad Rates: BW: $4,110 **Circ:** Controlled ‡21,000
4C: $5,080

5212 Servicing Management
LDJ Corp.
70 Edwin Ave. Phone: (203)755-0158
PO Box 2330 Fax: (203)755-3480
Waterbury, CT 06722
Free: (800)325-6745

Trade magazine for mortgage professionals involved with mortgage loan servicing . **Subtitle:** The Magazine for Loan Servicing Administrators. **Founded:** 1989. **Freq:** Monthly. **Print Method:** Offset. **Trim Size:** 11 x 13 1/2. **Cols./Page:** 4. **Col. Width:** 2 1/4 inches. **Col. Depth:** 13 1/2 inches. **Key Personnel:** Linda Zackin, Advertising Dir.; Ruth Guillet Fields, Editor, fields@sm-online.com; Joyce Rubinstein, Account Exec., rubin@sm-online.com; David Zackin, Publisher; Henry Pacyna, Production Mgr. **ISSN:** 1044-1077. **Subscription Rates:** $48 individuals; $8 single issue. **Remarks:** Accepts advertising.
Ad Rates: BW: $3,360 **Circ:** Controlled ‡22,000
4C: $4,400

5213 The Waterbury Republican-American
American-Republican, Inc.
389 Meadow St. Phone: (203)574-3636
Waterbury, CT 06722 Fax: (203)596-9277
Free: (800)992-3232

General newspaper. **Founded:** 1844. **Freq:** Mon.-Sun. (morn.). **Print Method:** Offset. Uses mats. **Cols./Page:** 6. **Col. Width:** 12.5 picas. **Col. Depth:** 21 3/8 inches. **Key Personnel:** Robert D. Veillette, Managing Editor; William Southerland, Executive Editor; William J. Pape II, Publisher; Connie Lepore, Editorial Editor, phone (203)574-3636. **Subscription Rates:** $143 individuals. **Remarks:** Accepts advertising. **Feature Editors:** Suzan Bibisi, *City*; John Crowell, *Suburban*; Howard Fielding, *Financial/Business*; Robert Fredericks, *Metro*; Ed Goodman, *Entertainment, Society, Travel*; Thomas Hennick, *Suburban*; Thomas Kabelka, *Photo*; Colleen Kelly, *Real Estate, Religion*; Claire LaFleur, *Food, Women's*; Bill Leulchardt, *Political*; Lee Lewis, *Sports*; Jean Reid, *Food*; James V. Ruocco, *Fashion*; Russell Shaddox, *TV & Radio*; Robert Veillette, *News*.
Ad Rates: BW: $2,476.80 **Circ:** Mon.-Sat. ★**58,212**
4C: $2,956.80 Sun. ★**71,559**
SAU: $19.20

5214 Marcus Cable
695 Huntingdon Ave. Phone: (203)755-1178
Waterbury, CT 06708 Fax: (203)756-1321

Owner: Marcus Cable Partners, 2911 Turtle Creek Blvd., Ste. 1300, Dallas, TX 75219, (214)521-7898, Fax: (214)526-2154. **Founded:** 1975. **Formerly**: Sammons Communications. **Key Personnel:** Jeffrey A. Marcus, CEO/Pres.; Louis A. Borrelli, COO/Executive Vice Pres.; Thomas P. McMillin, CFO. **Cities Served:** Middlebury, Platts Mills, Plymouth, Prospect, Terryville, Wolcott, CT; Litchfield and New Haven counties: subscribing households 45,000; 78 channels; 3 community access channels; 40 hours per week community access programming.

5215 WATR-AM - 1320
1 Broadcast Ln. Phone: (203)755-1121
Waterbury, CT 06706 Fax: (203)574-3025

Format: News; Talk; Music of Your Life. **Networks:** CBS. **Owner:** WATR Inc., at above address. **Founded:** 1934. **Operating Hours:** Continuous. **ADI:** Hartford-New Haven (New London), CT. **Key Personnel:** Tom Chute, Gen. Manager/Program Dir. **Wattage:** 5000 day; 1000 night. **Ad Rates:** $19-37 for 30 seconds; $22-40 for 60 seconds.

5216 WWCO-AM - 1240
2 Mattoon Rd. Phone: (203)755-9926
PO Box 99 Fax: (203)753-8729
Waterbury, CT 06720

Format: Adult Contemporary. **Networks:** CNN Radio. **Owner:** Buckley Broadcasting Corp of CT, 869 Blue Hills Ave., Bloomfield, CT 06002, (860)243-1115, Fax: (860)286-8257. **Founded:** 1946. **Operating Hours:** Continuous;. **Key Personnel:** Wayne Mulligan, General Mgr.; Laura Kittell, Operations Mgr.; Walt Pinto, Program Dir. **Local Programs:** *Caruselo Italianio, Italian Pgm.* 10 a.m.-1 p.m. Sunday; *High School Sports.* **Wattage:** 1000. **Ad Rates:** $25-35 for 60 seconds. Combined advertising rates available with WDRC-AM, WSNG-AM.

WATERFORD, pop. 17,843.

SE CT. New London Co. 19 mi. S. of Montvilleo. Residential.

5217 Eastern Connecticut Cable Television, Inc.
61 Myrock Ave. Phone: (203)442-8525
PO Box 6001 Fax: (203)443-6031
Waterford, CT 06385

Founded: 1973. **Key Personnel:** Hugh O'Brien, System Mgr.; Mary Jane Rickard, Public Access Coord.; Edmond O'Brien, General Mgr.; Catherine M. Santaniello, Purchasing Contact; Janet B. Pawlikowski, Contact; L.J. Carroll, Tresurer. **Cities Served:** Newport, RI: subscribing households 44,446; 69 channels; 1 community access channel; 35 hours per week community access programming.

5218 Newport Cable TV Inc.
61 Myrock Ave. Phone: (203)442-8525
Box 6001 Fax: (203)443-6031
Waterford, CT 06385

Key Personnel: Edmund O'Brien, President; L. James Carroll, Treas. **Cities Served:** subscribing households 2,000.

5219 WTYD-FM - 100.9
90 Foster Rd. Phone: (860)442-5328
Waterford, CT 06385 Fax: (860)442-6532
E-mail: wtyd@hallradio.com

Format: Adult Contemporary; Soft Rock. **Networks:** Independent. **Owner:** Hall Communications, Inc., Cuprak Rd., Norwich, CT 06360. **Founded:** 1970. **Operating Hours:** Continuous. **ADI:** Hartford-New Haven (New London), CT. **Key Personnel:** Jim Reed, General Mgr.; Andy Russell, Station Mgr., arussell@hallradio.com. **Wattage:** 3000. **Ad Rates:** $30-78 for 60 seconds. **URL:** http://www.wtyd.com.

WATERTOWN, pop. 19,489.

NW CT. Litchfield Co. 5 mi. NW of Waterbury. Residential.

Town Times - See Oakville

WEST CORNWALL

5220 The Magazine of Fantasy & Science Fiction
Mercury Press, Inc.
143 Cream Hill Rd. Phone: (203)672-6376
West Cornwall, CT 06796 Fax: (203)672-2643
Publication E-mail: elfhill@aol.com

Science fiction magazine. **Founded:** 1949. **Freq:** Monthly. **Print Method:** Offset. **Trim Size:** 5 1/4 x 7 5/8. **Cols./Page:** 2. **Col. Width:** 2 1/4 inches. **Col. Depth:** 6 1/2 inches. **Key Personnel:** Edward L. Ferman, Publisher. **ISSN:** 0024-984X. **Subscription Rates:** $33.97 individuals; $3.50 single issue. **Remarks:** Accepts advertising.
Ad Rates: BW: $990 **Circ:** ‡51,000
4C: $3,250

WEST HARTFORD, pop. 68,031.

N. CT. Hartford Co. Adjacent to Hartford. St. Joseph College (Cath. women), University of Connecticut. Residential. Planetarium; aquarium; publishing houses.

5221 Communication Quarterly
West Virginia Wesleyan College
School of Communication Phone: (203)768-4633
University of Hartford
200 Bloomfield Ave.
West Hartford, CT 06117
Journal covering all forms of communication research. **Founded:** 1953. **Freq:** Quarterly. **Print Method:** Letterpress and offset. **Trim Size:** 7 x 10. **Cols./Page:** 1. **Col. Width:** 60 nonpareils. **Col. Depth:** 124 agate lines. **Key Personnel:** Robert L. Duran, Editor, phone (860)768-4604, duran@uhavax.hartford.edu. **ISSN:** 0146-3373. **Subscription Rates:** $25. **Remarks:** Accepts advertising.
Ad Rates: BW: $250 **Circ:** ‡2,700

5222 Connecticut Jewish Ledger
740 N. Main St. Phone: (860)231-2424
West Hartford, CT 06117 Fax: (860)231-2428
Publisher E-mail: ctjledger@aol.com

Jewish interest newspaper. **Founded:** 1929. **Freq:** Weekly (Thurs.). **Print Method:** Offset. **Trim Size:** 11 x 13 1/2. **Cols./Page:** 5. **Col. Width:** 1 7/8 inches. **Col. Depth:** 13 inches. **Key Personnel:** Nanci Fitzgerald, General Mgr. **Subscription Rates:** $29 individuals. **Remarks:** Accepts advertising. **Online:** America Online, Inc.; keyword Jewish.
Ad Rates: PCI: $39 **Circ:** ‡30,000

5223 ConnStruction
McHugh Design, Advertising & Publishing
62 Lasalle Rd., Ste. 211 Phone: (203)523-7518
West Hartford, CT 06107 Fax: (203)231-8808

Magazine for construction industry. **Subtitle:** Southern New England's Construction Journal. **Founded:** 1961. **Freq:** Quarterly. **Print Method:** Offset. **Trim Size:** 8 3/8 x 10 7/8. **Cols./Page:** 3 and 2. **Col. Width:** 27 and 42 nonpareils. **Col. Depth:** 154 agate lines. **Key Personnel:** Tracy E. McHugh, Publisher; Thomas Jakups, Production Editor. **ISSN:** 0893-5629. **Subscription Rates:** $28 individuals; $7.50 single issue. **Remarks:** Accepts advertising.
Ad Rates: BW: $650 **Circ:** Controlled ‡7,000
4C: $1,520

5224 The Hartford Automobiler
AAA Automobile Club of Hartford
815 Farmington Ave. Phone: (860)236-3261
West Hartford, CT 06119-1584 Fax: (860)523-1797
Free: (800)842-4320

Auto club magazine. **Subtitle:** The Motoring and Travel Magazine. **Founded:** 1902. **Freq:** Bimonthly. **Print Method:** Web. **Trim Size:** 8 3/8 x 10 7/8. **Key Personnel:** Jennifer Kyle, Editor, phone (860)570-4318. **ISSN:** 1077-5234. **Subscription Rates:** $2. **Remarks:** Accepts advertising.
Ad Rates: 4C: $4,961 **Circ:** 220,000

5225 Journal of HIV/AIDS Prevention and Education for Adolescents & Children
The Haworth Press, Inc.
University of Connecticut Phone: (860)570-9135
School of Social Work Fax: (860)570-9139
1798 Asylum Ave.
West Hartford, CT 06117-2698
Publisher E-mail: getinfo@haworthpressinc.com

Journal on HIV/AIDS for youths. **Founded:** 1994. **Freq:** Quarterly. **Trim Size:** 6x81/2. **Key Personnel:** Julio Morales, PHD, Editor; Bill Cohen, Publisher. **ISSN:** 1069-837X. **Subscription Rates:** $34 individuals 30% more for Canada; 40% more for other countries; $48 institutions 30% more for Canada; 40% more for other countries; $60 libraries 30% more for Canada; 40% more for other countries. **Remarks:** Accepts advertising. **Formerly:** Journal of HIV/AIDS Education and Prevention for Children and Adolescents.
Ad Rates: BW: $300 **Circ:** Paid 125

5226 Papyrus
Papyrus Literary Enterprises
102 LaSalle Rd.
PO Box 27097
West Hartford, CT 06127-0797
Publisher E-mail: readersndex.com/ple

Magazine featuring African American poetry, fiction, and nonfiction. Accepts book reviews. **Subtitle:** The Writer's Craftletter featuring the Black Experience. **Founded:** Sept. 1994. **Freq:** Quarterly. **Trim Size:** 8-1/2 x 11 81/2x11. **Cols./Page:** 2. **Col. Width:** 3 1/2 inches. **Col. Depth:** 8 inches. **Key Personnel:** Ginger Whitaker, Contact, gwhitaker@imagine.com. **ISSN:** 1078-5841. **Subscription Rates:** $8; $2.20 single issue; $1.75 for back issues; $1 sample copy. **Remarks:** Advertising accepted; rates available upon request. **Available Online. URL:** http://www.readersndex.com/papyrus.
Circ: 3,000,000

5227 WVIT-TV - 30
1422 New Britain Ave. Phone: (203)521-3030
West Hartford, CT 06110 Fax: (203)521-3110

Format: Commercial TV. **Networks:** NBC. **Founded:** 1953. **Formerly**: WHNB-TV; WNBC-TV; WKNB-TV. **Operating Hours:** Continuous. **ADI:** Hartford-New Haven (New London), CT. **Key Personnel:** Al Bova, Contact.

5228 WWUH-FM - 91.3
200 Bloomfield Ave. Phone: (860)768-4703
West Hartford, CT 06117 Fax: (860)768-5701
E-mail: wwuh@hartford.edu

Format: Eclectic; Ethnic; News; Folk; Talk; Jazz. **Networks:** Independent. **Owner:** University of Hartford, at above address, Fax: (860)768-5702. **Founded:** 1968. **Operating**

Hours: Continuous; 100% local. **Key Personnel:** John Ramsey, General Mgr.; Ann Carmody, Music Dir.; Susan Mullis, Contact; Nicole Godburn, Program Dir. **Wattage:** 1000. **URL:** http://www.wwuh.org.

WEST HAVEN, pop. 53,184.

S. CT. New Haven Co. Adjacent to New Haven. Residential. Summer resort. Manufactures aircraft parts, tools, gun parts, webbing, auto tires and tubes, fertilizer, perfumes, cellar and overhead doors, plastic, die castings, sheet metal and rubber products, elastic fabrics, pipe organs, rock drills, beer, and textiles.

5229 West Haven News
Elm City Newspapers
349 New Haven Ave. Phone: (203)933-1000
PO Box 5339 Fax: (203)877-4772
Milford, CT 06460-6647
Free: (800)238-3226

Community newspaper (tabloid). **Founded:** 1931. **Freq:** Weekly (Fri.). **Print Method:** Photo offset. **Key Personnel:** Alan Olenick, Editor; Richard A. Barker, Publisher; William Flaucher, Advertising Dir. **Subscription Rates:** Free.
Ad Rates: PCI: $7.70 **Circ:** Paid ‡550
Free ‡8,600

5230 WNHU-FM - 88.7
300 Orange Ave. Phone: (203)934-8888
West Haven, CT 06516
E-mail: wnhu@charger.newhaven.edu

Format: New Age; Jazz; Ethnic; Folk; Alternative/New Music/Progressive; Rap. **Networks:** AP. **Founded:** 1973. **Operating Hours:** 6 a.m.-2 a.m. **Key Personnel:** W. Vincent Burke, General Mgr., phone (203)934-8888. **Wattage:** 1,700. **Ad Rates:** Noncommercial.

WESTON, pop. 8,284.

SW CT. Fairfield Co. 10 mi. W. of Bridgeport. Residential.

5231 Troika
Lone Tout Publications, Inc.
PO Box 1006 Phone: (203)227-5377
Weston, CT 06883 Fax: (203)222-9332
Publisher E-mail: etroika@aol.com

Consumer lifestyle magazine. **Subtitle:** Wit, Wisdom & Wherewithal. **Founded:** Mar. 1994. **Freq:** Quarterly. **Print Method:** Web offset. **Trim Size:** 8 1/8 x 10 5/8. **Cols./Page:** 3. **Key Personnel:** Celia Meadow, Editor; Greg Weber, Advertising Mgr.; Alvin Averill, Circulation Mgr. **ISSN:** 1083-2335. **Subscription Rates:** $10 individuals; $3.50 single issue. **Remarks:** Accepts advertising. **URL:** troikamagazine.com.
Ad Rates: BW: $8,000 **Circ:** Paid 120,000
4C: $10,000

5232 The Weston Forum
Hersam Acorn Newspapers, LLC
PO Box 1185 Phone: (203)544-9990
Weston, CT 06883 Fax: (203)544-9153
Publisher E-mail: newsroom@acorn-online.com

Community newspaper. **Freq:** Weekly (Thurs.). **Cols./Page:** 6. **Col. Depth:** 2 1/16 inches. **Key Personnel:** Alicia Damia, Editor; Thomas B. Nash, Publisher. **Subscription Rates:** $20; $25 out of country.
Ad Rates: BW: $882 **Circ:** Paid ♦85
4C: $1,282 Non-paid ♦3,584
PCI: $7

WESTPORT, pop. 25,290.

SW CT. Fairfield Co. On Saugatuck River, 3 mi. NE of Norwalk. Manufactures chemicals, liquid soaps, embalming fluid. Residential.

5233 Architectural Designs
Architectural Designs, Inc.
274 Riverside Ave. Phone: (203)222-1113
Westport, CT 06880-4823 Fax: (203)221-9202
Publisher E-mail: JD1435@aol.com

Consumer magazine covering home plans. **Founded:** 1983. **Freq:** Bimonthly'. **Print Method:** Offset. **Trim Size:** 8 1/8 x 10 7/8. **Cols./Page:** 2. **Col. Width:** 3 3/8 inches. **Col. Depth:** 9 3/8 inches. **Key Personnel:** Carol Davis, Editor, cd1435@aol.com. **Subscription Rates:** $48.75 individuals; $4.95 single issue. **Remarks:** Accepts advertising. **URL:** http://www.architecturaldesigns.com. **Formerly**: Architectural Dreams.
Ad Rates: BW: $1,495 **Circ:** (Not Reported)
4C: $1,895

5234 Army Aviation Magazine
Army Aviation Publications, Inc.
49 Richmondville Ave. Phone: (203)226-8184
Westport, CT 06880-2000 Fax: (203)222-9863

Army aviation magazine. **Subtitle:** Official Publication of the Army Aviation Association of America (AAAA). **Founded:** 1953. **Freq:** 10/year. **Print Method:** Offset. **Trim Size:** 8 1/8 x 10 7/8. **Cols./Page:** 2. **Key Personnel:** William R. Harris, Jr., Editor-in-Chief; Lynn Coakley, Publisher; Robert C. Lachowski, Advertising Mgr.; Stephen Harding, Editor; Barbara Ross, Production Mgr. **ISSN:** 0004-2484. **Subscription Rates:** $30 individuals; $3.50 single issue. **Remarks:** Accepts advertising.
Ad Rates: BW: $3,500 **Circ:** ‡16,591
4C: $4,850

5235 Country Music
Silver Eagle Publishers
1 Turkey Hill Rd. S Phone: (203)221-4950
Westport, CT 06880 Fax: (203)221-4948

Consumer magazine covering country music. **Founded:** 1972. **Freq:** Bimonthly. **Print Method:** Web offset. **Trim Size:** 8 1/8 x 10 7/8. **Key Personnel:** Russell D. Barnard, Publisher; Leonard Mendelson, Assoc. Publisher/Advertising Dir.; Warren Beardow, Marketing Dir. **Subscription Rates:** $15.95 individuals; $3 single issue. **Remarks:** Accepts advertising.
Ad Rates: PCI: $640 **Circ:** Combined ⊕634,159

5236 Equity & Excellence in Education
Greenwood Publishing Group, Inc.
88 Post Rd. W. Phone: (203)226-3571
PO Box 5007 Fax: (203)226-6009
Westport, CT 06881-5007
Free: (800)225-5800
Publication E-mail: equity@educ.umass.edu
Publisher E-mail: prices@greenwood.com

Journal covering issues related to educational equity, educational quality, and school improvement. **Subtitle:** The University of Massachusetts School of Education Journal. **Founded:** 1963. **Freq:** 3/year. **Print Method:** Offset. **Trim Size:** 8 1/2 x 11. **Cols./Page:** 2. **Col. Width:** 43 nonpareils. **Col. Depth:** 60 agate lines. **Key Personnel:** Carolyn Peelle, Editor, phone (413)545-4185, fax (413)545-2879; Gerry Katz, Managing Editor, gkatz@greenwood.com. **ISSN:** 1066-5684. **Subscription Rates:** $35 individuals; $75 institutions. **Remarks:** Accepts advertising. **Formerly**: Integrateducation (1984).
Ad Rates: BW: $225 **Circ:** ‡1,500

5237 Global Business Review
Greenwood Publishing Group, Inc.
88 Post Rd. W. Phone: (203)226-3571
PO Box 5007 Fax: (203)226-6009
Westport, CT 06881-5007
Free: (800)225-5800
Publisher E-mail: prices@greenwood.com

International business journal focusing on global competition, coordination, and collaboration. **Founded:** 1994. **Freq:** Quarterly. **Subscription Rates:** $85.50 annual.

5238 Imaging Service Bureau News
PO Box 3149 Phone: (203)222-9310
Westport, CT 06880 Fax: (203)222-7871
Publisher E-mail: imagepub@furutis.net

Trade magazine for owners and executives in the business of performing document imaging services. **Founded:** Nov. 1986. **Freq:** Bimonthly. **Key Personnel:** David Miles, Editor and Publisher; Elizabeth Bergren, Asst. Editor/Website Mgr. **ISSN:** 1055-8098. **Subscription Rates:** $190 individuals; $35 single issue. **Remarks:** Accepts advertising.
Ad Rates: BW: $990 **Circ:** Combined 1,500

5239 Ireland of the Welcomes
The Mill Phone: (203)454-0344
49 Richmondville Ave. Fax: (203)454-8871
Westport, CT 06880
Magazine featuring the heritage, countryside, culture, and people of Ireland. **Founded:** 1952. **Freq:** Bimonthly. **Print Method:** Sheetfed. **Key Personnel:** Letitia Pollard, Editor; Donal Guilfoyle, Publisher. **USPS:** 480-190. **Subscription Rates:** $21. **Remarks:** Advertising accepted; rates available upon request.
Circ: ‡100,000

5240 Journal of Chemical Education
Centcom Ltd.
1599 Post Rd. E.
PO Box 231
Westport, CT 06880-5602

Magazine on chemical research and education. **Founded:** 1924. **Freq:** Monthly. **Print Method:** Offset. **Trim Size:** 8 1/8 x 11 1/8. **Cols./Page:** 3. **Col. Width:** 26 nonpareils. **Col. Depth:** 140 agate lines. **Key Personnel:** J.J. Lagowski, Editor; Edward Black, Advertising Mgr. **Subscription Rates:** $17 individuals. **Remarks:** Accepts advertising.
Ad Rates: BW: $2,250 **Circ:** 20,321
4C: $4,020

5241 MultiCultural Review
Greenwood Publishing Group, Inc.
88 Post Rd. W. Phone: (203)226-3571
PO Box 5007 Fax: (203)226-6009
Westport, CT 06881-5007
Free: (800)225-5800
Publication E-mail: mcreview@aol.com
Publisher E-mail: prices@greenwood.com

Magazine providing collection information to librarians and educators. **Subtitle:** Dedicated to a Better Understanding of Ethnic, Racial, & Religious Diversity. **Founded:** 1992. **Freq:** Quarterly. **Print Method:** Offset. **Trim Size:** 8 1/2 x 11. **Cols./Page:** 3. **Key Personnel:** Lyn Miller-Lachmann, Editor-in-Chief, phone (518)877-0906, fax (518)877-0906; Gerry Katz, Managing Editor, gkatz@greenwood.com; Lynda Harris, phone (203)226-3571, fax (203)226-6009, lharris@greenwood.com. **ISSN:** 1058-9236. **Subscription Rates:** $29.95 individuals; $59 institutions; $147 three years; $15 single back issue. **Remarks:** Accepts advertising.
Ad Rates: BW: $750 **Circ:** Paid ‡3,000
4C: $1,500

5242 NCJW Journal
National Council of Jewish Women, Inc.
6 Trailing Rock Ln. Phone: (203)256-1370
Westport, CT 06880
Publisher E-mail: mail@ncjw.org

Periodical reporting social policy issues of interest to NCJW members. **Freq:** Quarterly. **Print Method:** Web offset. **Trim Size:** 8 1/2 x 11. **Cols./Page:** 3. **Col. Width:** 2 6/8 inches. **Col. Depth:** 9 inches. **Key Personnel:** Lauren Schwartz Linfield, Editor. **ISSN:** 0161-2115. **Subscription Rates:** $2.50. **Remarks:** Accepts advertising. **Formerly**: Council Women.
Ad Rates: BW: $1,000 **Circ:** Paid 100,000
4C: $4,000
PCI: $60

5243 Remedy
Rx Remedy, Inc.
120 Post Rd. W. Phone: (203)341-7000
Westport, CT 06880 Fax: (203)221-4913
Publication E-mail: ldinerstein@rxremedy.com

Consumer magazine covering health and wellness for individuals over 50 years in the U.S. **Founded:** July 1992. **Freq:** Bimonthly. **Print Method:** Offset. **Key Personnel:** Joan Montgomery, National Sales Mgr.; Katherine G. Bell-Wills, Publisher; Valorie Weaver, Editor-in-Chief. **ISSN:** 1091-1146. **Subscription Rates:** $18 individuals; $3 single issue. **Remarks:** Accepts advertising.
Ad Rates: BW: $46,200 **Circ:** Controlled 2,200,000
4C: $55,000

5244 WMMM-AM - 1260
PO Box 511 Phone: (203)849-9955
Westport, CT 06881-0511 Fax: (203)840-1312
Free: (800)796-9666

Format: Oldies; Talk. **Networks:** USA Radio. **Owner:** Mark and Robert Graham, at above address. **Founded:** 1959. **Operating Hours:** 6 a.m.-8 p.m. **Key Personnel:** Walter G. Broadhurst, General Sales Mgr. **Local Programs:** *Connecticut Women in Business*, Carla Dietz. **Wattage:** 1000. **Ad Rates:** $20-40 for 30 seconds; $25-50 for 60 seconds.

5245 WWPT-FM - 90.3
Staples High School Phone: (203)226-9978
70 North Ave. Fax: (203)365-7669
Westport, CT 06880

Format: Eclectic. **Founded:** 1975. **Key Personnel:** Stephanie Ehrman, General Mgr.; Charles Bortunek, Program Dir. **Wattage:** 800. **Ad Rates:** Noncommercial.

WILLIMANTIC†, pop. 14,652.

NE CT. Windham Co. 30 mi. E. of Hartford. State College. Manufactures wire and cable, plastics, thread, non-woven fabric, braided fabric, insulation, mill and builders' supplies. Printing. Steel fabrication. Truck farms.

5246 Campus Lantern
Eastern Connecticut State College
83 Windham St. Phone: (203)465-4445
Willimantic, CT 06226-2308
Publication E-mail: lantern@ecsuc.ctstateu.edu

College campus-oriented newspaper (tabloid). **Founded:** 1949. **Freq:** Weekly (Wed.). **Print Method:** Offset. **Cols./Page:** 5. **Col. Width:** 2 1/4 inches. **Col. Depth:** 15 inches.

Key Personnel: Dan Lantos, Editor-in-Chief; Brian Moore, Managing Editor; Billy Hotchkiss, Advertising Mgr. **Subscription Rates:** Free; $9 by mail. **Remarks:** Accepts advertising.
Ad Rates: BW: $240 PCI: $6 **Circ:** Controlled ‡2,800

5247 The Chronicle
PO Box 148 Phone: (203)423-8466
1 Chronicle Rd. Fax: (203)423-7641
Willimantic, CT 06226-0148
Publication E-mail: chron@meca.com

General newspaper. **Founded:** Jan. 4, 1877. **Freq:** Daily (eve.) and Sat. (morn.). **Print Method:** Offset. **Cols./Page:** 6. **Col. Width:** 2 1/16 inches. **Col. Depth:** 21 inches. **Key Personnel:** George Geers, Editor; Lucy Bartlett Crosbie, Publisher; William Flaucher, Advertising Mgr. **USPS:** 684-960. **Subscription Rates:** $115.50 individuals. **Remarks:** Accepts advertising.
Ad Rates: GLR: $.31 **Circ:** Mon.-Sat. 10,103

5248 WECS-FM - 90.1
83 Windham St. Phone: (860)456-5354
Willimantic, CT 06226 Fax: (860)465-5073
E-mail: wecs@hotmail.com; wecs@hotmail.com

Format: Eclectic. **Networks:** National Public Radio (NPR). **Founded:** 1982. **Operating Hours:** Continuous. **Key Personnel:** John L. Zatowski, Contact, phone (860)465-4387. **Wattage:** 421. **Ad Rates:** Noncommercial.

5249 WILI-AM - 1400
720 Main St. Phone: (860)456-1111
Willimantic, CT 06226 Fax: (860)456-9501
E-mail: wili@com

Format: Full Service; Adult Contemporary. **Networks:** ABC; Satellite Music Network; Westwood One Radio. **Owner:** Nutmeg Broadcasting Co., at above address. **Founded:** 1957. **Operating Hours:** Continuous; 30% network, 70% local. **ADI:** Hartford-New Haven (New London), CT. **Key Personnel:** David M. Evan, General Mgr., dave@wili.com; Colin K. Rice, Vice President, colin@wili.com; Wayne Norman, Program Dir., norm@wili.com; Donna M. Evan, Sales Mgr., donna@wili.com; Mike Morrissette, News Dir., mikenews@wili.com; Gordon Smith, Production Mgr., guido@wili.com; Connie Warren, Traffic Dir., connie@wili.com; Craig Mellon, Chief Engineer, craig@wili.com; Michael Rice, Pres./CEO, mike@wili.com. **Local Programs:** *Issues '99* 11:00 - 12:00 Sunday, Mike Morrissette, (860)456-1111, Fax (860)456-9501; *Shawn Higgins Show* 12:00 noon - 6:00 pm Monday-Friday, Ron Carson, (860)456-1111, Fax (860)456-9501; *Wayne Norman Show* 6:00 amm - 10:00 am Monday-Friday, Wayne Norman, (860)456-1111, Fax (860)456-9501. **Wattage:** 1000. **Ad Rates:** $26-31 for 30 seconds; $34-38 for 60 seconds. $26-$31 for 30 seconds; $34-$38 for 60 seconds. Combined advertising rates available with WILI-FM.

5250 WILI-FM - 98.3
720 Main St. Phone: (860)456-1111
Willimantic, CT 06226 Fax: (860)456-9501
E-mail: wili@neca.com

Format: Adult Contemporary; Contemporary Hit Radio (CHR). **Owner:** Nutmeg Broadcasting Co., at above address. **Founded:** 1974. **Formerly:** WXLS-FM (1978); WNOU-FM (1985). **Operating Hours:** Continuous; 80% local, 20% network. **ADI:** Hartford-New Haven (New London), CT. **Key Personnel:** David M. Evan, Vice Pres./Gen. Mgr., dave@wili.com; Michael C. Rice, President, mike@wili.com; Colin K. Rice, Exec. Vice Pres., colin@wili.com; Donna M. Evan, Sales Mgr., donna@wili.com; Mike Morrissette, News Dir., mikenews@wili.com; Craig Mellon, Chief Engineer, craig@wili.com; Connie Warren, Traffic Dir., connie@wili.com; Gordon Lyle Smith, Production Mgr., guido@wili.com. **Wattage:** 3000 ERP. **Ad Rates:** $26-31 for 30 seconds; $34-38 for 60 seconds. WILI-AM.

WILTON, pop. 15,351.

SW CT. Fairfield Co. 5 mi. N. of Norwalk. Residential. Manufactures optical and electronic equipment, golf clubs. Nurseries.

5251 Critical Care International
GLOBETECH Publishing Inc.
8 Cannon Rd. Phone: (203)762-3432
Wilton, CT 06897 Fax: (203)762-8640

Professional magazine for the critical care field. **Founded:** Jan. 1994. **Freq:** Bimonthly. **Cols./Page:** 4. **Col. Width:** 65 millimeters. **Col. Depth:** 320 millimeters. **Key Personnel:** Jill Quigley Roberge, Editor; Eric Farmer, U.S. Advertising Mgr.; Tracie Bolack, Circulation Mgr. **ISSN:** 1068-1760. **Subscription Rates:** Free to qualified subscribers. **Remarks:** Accepts advertising.
Ad Rates: BW: $5,140 4C: $6,940 **Circ:** Controlled ‡26,000

5252 EMedia Professional
Online, Inc.
213 Danbury Rd. Phone: (203)761-1466
Wilton, CT 06897-4007 Fax: (203)761-1444
Free: (800)248-8466
Publication E-mail: emediapro@onlineinc.com
Publisher E-mail: info@onlineinc.com

Professional trade journal for CD publishers and developers using or considering CD-ROM, CD-Recordable, DVD, and other optical media. Contains product reviews and comparisons, surveys, newspages, columns, and interviews. **Subtitle:** Practical Solutions Using Optical Disc Technologies, Tools, and Services. **Founded:** 1987. **Freq:** Monthly. **Print Method:** Sheetfed. **Trim Size:** 8 1/2 x 11. **Cols./Page:** 2 and 3. **Col. Width:** 3 3/8 and 2 inches. **Col. Depth:** 9.5 picas. **Key Personnel:** Adam C. Pemberton, Publisher, adamp@onlineinc.com; Margaret Alexander, Sales Coord., margareta@onlineinc.com; Stephen Nathans, Managing Editor, stephenn@onlineinc.com; Jeff Partrka, Assoc. Editor, jeff.partyka@onlineinc.com. **ISSN:** 1090-946X. **Subscription Rates:** $55 individuals; $98 corporations. **Remarks:** Accepts advertising. **URL:** http://www.onlineinc.com/emedia. **Alt. Formats:** CD-ROM. **Formerly:** The Laserdisk Professional (1991); CD-ROM Professional.
Ad Rates: BW: $3,294 4C: $4,216 **Circ:** Combined △**30,277**

5253 Labmedica
GLOBETECH Publishing Inc.
8 Cannon Rd. Phone: (203)762-3432
Wilton, CT 06897 Fax: (203)762-8640

Professional magazine for managers of all kinds of laboratories. **Founded:** 1984. **Freq:** Bimonthly. **Trim Size:** 11 x 15 3/4. **Cols./Page:** 4. **Col. Width:** 244 in. inches. **Col. Depth:** 14 1/2 inches. **Key Personnel:** Marc Gueron, Publisher; Chrys Emery, Advertising Dir. **Subscription Rates:** Free to qualified subscribers. **Remarks:** Accepts advertising.
Ad Rates: BW: $4,750 4C: $6,350 **Circ:** Non-paid ‡26,000

5254 Running Times
Fitness Publishing, Inc.
213 Danbury Rd. Phone: (203)761-1113
Wilton, CT 06897 Fax: (203)761-9933

Sports magazine. **Founded:** 1977. **Freq:** Monthly. **Trim Size:** 8 1/2 x 11. **Cols./Page:** 3. **Key Personnel:** Carol Lasseter, Publisher, rtcarol@aol.com; Gordon Bakovus, Editor-in-Chief, rtbakoulis@aol.com. **ISSN:** 0147-2968. **Subscription Rates:** $24.95 individuals; $34.95 Canada; $50 out of country; $3.50 single issue. **Remarks:** Accepts advertising.
Ad Rates: BW: $3,240 4C: $5,490 **Circ:** Paid ★**48,532**

5255 Wilton Bulletin
Hersam Acorn Newspapers, LLC
PO Box 367 Phone: (203)762-3866
Wilton, CT 06897 Fax: (203)762-3120
Publication E-mail: bulletin@wilton-ct.com
Publisher E-mail: newsroom@acorn-online.com

Community newspaper. **Founded:** 1937. **Freq:** Weekly (Wed.). **Print Method:** Offset. Uses mats. **Cols./Page:** 6. **Col. Width:** 12 picas. **Col. Depth:** 21 inches. **Key Personnel:** Greg Bartlett, Editor; Thomas B. Nash, Publisher; John Hersam, Advertising Mgr. **USPS:** 685-780. **Subscription Rates:** $30 individuals; $35 Out of county; $18 Military.
Ad Rates: BW: $882 SAU: $7 **Circ:** Paid ♦**4,178** Non-paid ♦**125**

5256 The Wilton Villager
The Hour Publishing Co.
73 Old Ridgefield Rd., Ste. 4
Wilton, CT 06897

Community newspaper. **Founded:** 1996. **Freq:** Weekly (Thurs.). **Print Method:** Photo offset. **Key Personnel:** B. J. Frazie, Publisher.
Circ: Combined 6,310

WINDSOR

5257 Windsor Locks Journal
Imprint Newspapers
99 Main St. Phone: (860)236-3571
Bristol, CT 06010 Fax: (860)233-2080

Community newspaper (tabloid). **Founded:** 1880. **Freq:** Weekly (Fri.). **Cols./Page:** 6. **Col. Width:** 10 picas. **Col. Depth:** 16 inches. **Key Personnel:** Keith Griffin, Editor; Frank Chilinski, Publisher. **Subscription Rates:** $24; $20 senior citizens. **Remarks:** Accepts advertising.
Ad Rates: PCI: $3 **Circ:** Paid 1,594 Non-paid 32

5258 Windsor Reminder
Reminder Press
PO Box 27 Phone: (860)872-6648
130 Old Town Rd. Fax: (860)875-2089
Vernon, CT 06066
Local newspaper. **Founded:** 1968. **Freq:** Weekly. **Print Method:** Offset. **Cols./Page:** 6. **Col. Width:** 21 nonpareils. **Col. Depth:** 224 agate lines. **Key Personnel:** Kenneth A. Hovland, Publisher.

5259 WKND-AM - 1480
544 Windsor Ave. Phone: (203)688-6221
PO Box 1480 Fax: (203)688-0711
Windsor, CT 06095

Format: Full Service; Urban Contemporary. **Founded:** 1964. **Formerly:** WSOR-AM; WEHW-AM. **Operating Hours:** 6 a.m.-6 p.m. during winter; 6 a.m.-8:30 p.m. during summer. **Key Personnel:** Tony Guess, Program Dir.; Barbara Jones, Traffic Dir.; Thornton Anderson, General Mgr. **Local Programs:** *59 Minutes with Ben Andrews*, Ben Andrews, Mailing contact; *Urban Agenda*, Richard Legrier, Mailing contact; *What's on Your Mind*, Abdul Muhammad, Mailing contact. **Wattage:** 500. **Ad Rates:** $50-100 for 60 seconds.

WINSTED

NW CT. Litchfield Co. 15 mi. NW of New Hartford.

5260 Pegasus Cable Television
368 Main St. Phone: (203)379-9833
Winsted, CT 06098 Fax: (203)738-5088
Free: (800)827-8288

Key Personnel: Jennifer Garber, Operations Mgr.; John Dee, Contact. **Cities Served:** Barkhamsted, Colebrook, Harwinton, New Hartford, West Hartford, Winsted, CT; Belchertown, Charlton, Hadley, Lanesborough, MA; Moultonborough, NH: subscribing households 17,800; 35 channels; 1 community access channel.

WOODBRIDGE, pop. 7,761.

C. CT. New Haven Co. Residential.

5261 ABC News Index
Primary Source Media
12 Lunar Dr. Phone: (203)397-2600
Woodbridge, CT 06525 Fax: (203)397-3893
Free: (800)444-0799
Publication E-mail: sales@psmedia.com

Index of ABC news transcripts. **Freq:** Quarterly. **Trim Size:** 7 x 10. **Key Personnel:** Iren Whitney, Contact. **ISSN:** 0891-8775. **Remarks:** Advertising not accepted. **Alt. Formats:** CD-ROM.
Circ: (Not Reported)

WOODBURY, pop. 6,942.

NW CT. Litchfield Co. 8 mi. SW of Waterbury. Residential.

5262 Ski Area Management
Beardsley Publishing Corp.
45 Main St. N. Phone: (203)263-0888
PO Box 644 Fax: (203)266-0452
Woodbury, CT 06798-0644
Trade magazine. **Founded:** 1962. **Freq:** Bimonthly. **Print Method:** Sheetfed offset. **Trim Size:** 8 1/4 x 11 1/4. **Cols./Page:** 3. **Col. Width:** 13 picas. **Col. Depth:** 60 picas. **Key Personnel:** David Rowan, Editor and Publisher. **USPS:** 890-900. **Subscription Rates:** $26. single issue $4.25. **Remarks:** Accepts advertising.
Ad Rates: BW: $1,870 4C: $2,520 **Circ:** Paid ‡4,056

5263 Voices
Prime Publisher's, Inc.
90 Middle Quarter Mall Phone: (203)263-2116
Woodbury, CT 06798 Fax: (203)266-0199

Community newspaper serving Southbury, Heritage Village, South Britian, Woodbury, Bethlehem, Washington, New Preston, Middlebury, Oxford, Seymour, Shady Hook, Newtown, Monroe, and Bridgewater, CT. **Founded:** 1972. **Freq:** Semiweekly (Wed. and Sun.). **Print Method:** Offset. **Trim Size:** 11 1/2 x 16. **Cols./Page:** 5. **Col. Width:** 11.7 picas. **Col. Depth:** 210 agate lines. **Key Personnel:** Rudy Mazurosky, Publisher. **ISSN:** 0193-1474. **Subscription Rates:** $36 individuals. **Remarks:** Accepts advertising.
Ad Rates: GLR: $.79 BW: $661.50 4C: $1,377.50 SAU: $12.88 PCI: $11.06 **Circ:** Paid 465 Non-paid 26,279 Sun. 20,791

5264 VOICES Sunday-Weekly Star
Prime Publisher's, Inc.
90 Middle Quarter Mall Phone: (203)263-2116
Woodbury, CT 06798 Fax: (203)266-0199

Community newspaper serving Washington, Bethlehem, Woodbury, Middlebury, Oxford, Nangatuck, Southbury, Roxbury, and Bridgewater, Connecticut. **Founded:** May 20, 1985. **Freq:** Semiweekly (Wed. and Sat.). **Print Method:** Offset. **Trim Size:** 11 x 16 1/2. **Cols./Page:** 5. **Col. Width:** 11 picas. **Col. Depth:** 210 agate lines. **Key Personnel:** Rudy Mazurosky, Publisher. **ISSN:** 0193-1474. **Subscription Rates:** Free; $39 out of area. **Formerly:** The Weekly Star.
Ad Rates: GLR: $.79 **Circ:** Free 21,000
SAU: $12.88
PCI: $11.06

DELAWARE

State Capital, DOVER

Delaware is bounded on the north by Pennsylvania, east by the Delaware River and Bay and the Atlantic Ocean, south by Maryland, and west by Maryland and Pennsylvania. Its length from north to south is 110 miles; its breadth varies from about 9 miles to 36 miles. The total land area is 1,995 square miles, the second smallest state in area. The surface in the north is somewhat hilly, and southward the land is rolling, with fringes of marshes and swamp tracts along the indentations of Delaware Bay. The southern portion is a sandy region, but by skillful farming has been made highly productive. The soil of the interior is light and easily cultivated. The Weather Bureau at Wilmington gives the temperature (annual average) at 54.2; highest on record, 107; lowest on record, -12. Total annual precipitation is 40.84 inches. The manufacturing center of the state is Wilmington, a port on the Delaware River. It is close to the Delaware and Chesapeake Canal, a waterway which crosses the state and connects the two bays of the same names, facilitating shipping between Philadelphia and Baltimore and other ports in Maryland and Virginia. Other harbors are Lewes and New Castle. The University of Delaware is located at Newark.

POPULATION: 689,000 (1992). Rank among the states, 46th.

AGRICULTURE: Number of farms: 3,000 (1992). Farm acreage: 1,000,000 (1992). Cash receipts from farm marketings: crops, $181,000,000 (1991); livestock and products, $438,000,000 (1991).

FISHERIES: Total catch: 8,000,000 lbs. (1991), $4,000,000 value. Principal fish: menhaden, clams.

FORESTS: Total forest land: 398,000 acres (1987). Total value forest products: $2,750,000 (1987).

MINERALS: Value of production: $5,000,000 (1991). Principal minerals: sand and gravel and gemstones.

MANUFACTURES: Value added by manufacture: $4,231,000,000 (1991). Leading industry groups: chemicals and allied products, food and related products, apparel and related products.

LIST OF COUNTIES

Total number of counties 3

County, Location on Map, and County Seat	Pop.
Kent (C), Dover	110,993
New Castle (N), Wilmington	441,946
Sussex (S), Georgetown	113,229

STATISTICS

Newspapers

Period of Issue	
Daily	2
Morning Daily	2
Daily with Sunday edition	2
Semiweekly	3
Weekly	13
Bimonthly	1
Free or partly free	5
Shopper	1
Total Newspapers	18

Periodicals

Period of Issue	
Monthly	4
Bimonthly	3
Quarterly	4
Total Periodicals	17

Total number of publications 35

Radio Stations

AM Stations	11
FM Stations	14
Total Radio Stations	25

Cable Stations

Total Cable Systems 3

Total number of broadcast listings 28

BETHANY BEACH

5265 The Wave
Atlantic Publications
Rte. 1 Lem Hichman Plaza Phone: (302)537-1881
Bethany Beach, DE 19930
Community newspaper. **Founded:** 1987. **Freq:** Weekly (Wed.). **Print Method:** Photo offset. **Key Personnel:** Janet Eaton, Office Mgr. **Remarks:** Combined advertising rates available with Delaware Coast Press.
Circ: Paid 352

CLAYMONT

5266 WJBR-AM - 1290
3001 Philladlphia Pike Phone: (302)791-4110
Claymont, DE 19703 Fax: (302)529-9536
E-mail: info@wjbr.com

Format: Big Band/Nostalgia. **Networks:** Westwood One Radio; CNN Radio. **Owner:** Atlantic Star Communications, 500 5th Ave., Ste. 3000, New York, NY 10110, (212)302-2727, Fax: (212)302-6457. **Founded:** 1947. **Formerly:** WTUX-AM. **Operating Hours:** Continuous; 100% local. **ADI:** Philadelphia, PA. **Key Personnel:** Jay Sterin, General Mgr.; Michael Waite, Program Dir.; Dave Banks, Music Dir.; Valerie Mack, News Dir.; Joe Robinson, Public Service; Bill Kaye, Contact. **Wattage:** 2500. **Ad Rates:** $50-120 per unit.

5267 WJBR-FM - 99.5
3001 Philladelphia Pike Phone: (302)791-4110
Claymont, DE 19703 Fax: (302)791-9669
Free: (800)275-9527
E-mail: info@wjbr.com

Format: Adult Contemporary. **Networks:** AP. **Founded:** 1957. **Operating Hours:** Continuous. **ADI:** Philadelphia, PA. **Key Personnel:** Michael Waite, General Mgr., fax (303)791-9669, mwaite@wjbr.com; Michael Waite, Program Dir.; Valerie Mack, News Dir.; Joe Robinson, Public Service. **Wattage:** 50,000. **Ad Rates:** Advertising accepted; rates available upon request. **URL:** http://www.wjbr.com.

DAGSBORO

5268 American Cable TV of Lower Delaware
N. Dupont Hwy. Phone: (302)732-6600
PO Box 144A Fax: (302)732-6616
Dagsboro, DE 19939

Founded: 1968. **Formerly:** Simmons Cable TV of Lower Delaware. **Cities Served:** Sussex County, Bethany Beach, Clarksville, Dagsboro, Frankford, Millville, Ocean View, Omar, Roxana, Selbyville, and Slaughter Beach, DE; Worcester County and Bishopville, MD.

DOVER†, pop. 23,512.

C. DR. Kent Co. 42 mi. S. of Wilmington. The State Capital. State College, Wesley College, Delaware Technical and Community College. Manufactures dry and canned goods, processed chocolate, soft drinks, refrigerators, textiles, paper products, latex paint, brick. Dairy; foundry; bottling works; feed mill. Agriculture. Wheat, corn, vegetables, fruit.

5269 The Airlifter
Delaware State News
436 AW/PA Phone: (302)677-3373
Dover AFB
Dover, DE 19902-5154
Local military base newspaper. **Founded:** 1965. **Freq:** Weekly (Fri.). **Print Method:** Offset. **Trim Size:** 11 1/2 x 15. **Cols./Page:** 5. **Col. Width:** 11.5 picas. **Col. Depth:** 14 inches. **Key Personnel:** Sr. Airman Jennifer Hall, Editor; Helen Downing, Advertising Mgr. **Subscription Rates:** Free. **Remarks:** Accepts advertising.
Ad Rates: BW: $630 **Circ:** Free 7,500
4C: $870
PCI: $9

5270 Delaware State News
Independent Newspapers, Inc.
PO Box 737 Phone: (302)674-3600
Dover, DE 19903 Fax: (302)741-8252
Publication E-mail: dsnnews@newszap.com

Community newspaper. **Subtitle:** the downstate daily. **Founded:** 1953. **Freq:** Mon.-Sun. **Print Method:** Offset. **Trim Size:** 13 1/2 x 22 1/2. **Cols./Page:** 6. **Col. Width:** 24 nonpareils. **Col. Depth:** 21 1/2 inches. **Key Personnel:** Andrew West, Editor, phone (302)674-3600, fax (302)741-8252; Helen Downing, Advertising Mgr., phone (302)741-8282, fax (302)741-8261. **USPS:** 152-160. **Subscription Rates:** $130 individuals. **Remarks:** Accepts advertising. Monday-Saturday: GLR: $1.85; BW: $2,747.70; 4C: $3,347.70; PCI: $21.30; Sunday: GLR: $2.25; BW: $3,354; 4C: $4,055; PCI: $26. **URL:** http://www.newszap.com. **Merged with:** The Daily Whale (June 1997).
Circ: Mon.-Sat. 18,368
Sun. 26,879

5271 Dover Post
Dover Post Co.
PO Box 664 Phone: (302)678-3616
Dover, DE 19903 Fax: (302)678-8291
Free: (800)942-1616

Community newspaper. **Founded:** Apr. 30, 1975. **Freq:** Weekly (Wed.). **Print Method:** Offset. **Trim Size:** 11 1/2 x 17. **Cols./Page:** 6. **Col. Width:** 9 1/2 picas. **Col. Depth:** 16 inches. **Key Personnel:** Don Flood, Editor; Jim Flood, Sr., Publisher; Fred Kaltreider, Advertising Mgr.; Jim Flood, Jr., General Mgr. **Subscription Rates:** Free; $33.80 individuals; $0.50 single issue.
Ad Rates: GLR: $.56 **Circ:** Free 24,485
BW: $651 Paid 1,953
4C: $1,026
SAU: $11.30
PCI: $7.75

5272 Sussex Countian
Dover Post Co.
PO Box 664 Phone: (302)678-3616
Dover, DE 19903 Fax: (302)678-8291
Free: (800)942-1616

County newspaper. **Founded:** Apr. 1886. **Freq:** Weekly (Wed.). **Print Method:** Offset. Uses mats. **Trim Size:** 11 1/2 x 17. **Cols./Page:** 6. **Col. Width:** 24 nonpareils. **Col. Depth:** 336 agate lines. **Key Personnel:** Carolyn M. O'Neal, General Mgr.; William T. Spencer, Managing Editor. **USPS:** 530-120. **Subscription Rates:** $18 individuals; $22 out of state. **Remarks:** Accepts advertising.
Ad Rates: GLR: $0.33 **Circ:** ‡4,740
BW: $691.20
4C: $952.40
SAU: $9.60
PCI: $7.20

The Sussex Post - See Georgetown

5273 WDOV-AM - 1410
Denny's Rd. Phone: (302)674-1410
Dover, DE 19901 Fax: (302)674-8621

Format: News; Talk. **Networks:** CNN Radio. **Founded:** 1956. **Operating Hours:** Continuous. **ADI:** Philadelphia, PA. **Key Personnel:** Christopher John Walus, General Mgr.; Phil Feliciangeli, News Dir.; Martha Burns, General Sales Mgr. **Local Programs:** *Delaware News Magazine*; *The Morning Report*, Rick Gaidls. **Wattage:** 5400. **Additional Contact Info: Mailing Address:** PO Drawer B, Dover, DE 19903.

5274 WDSD-FM - 94.7
5595 Denneys Rd. Phone: (302)734-5816
Dover, DE 19904-1362 Fax: (302)674-8621

Format: Country. **Founded:** 1956. **Operating Hours:** Continuous. **ADI:** Philadelphia, PA. **Key Personnel:** Christopher John Walus, General Mgr.; Sky Phillips, Program Dir.; Martha Burns, General Sales Mgr.; Phil Feliciangeli, News Dir. **Wattage:** 50,000.

5275 WKEN-AM - 1600
Walker Rd. Phone: (302)674-1234
PO Box 553 Fax: (302)674-5407
Dover, DE 19903-0553

Format: Talk; News. **Networks:** ABC; Mutual Broadcasting System; Talknet. **Owner:** First State Broadcasting, Inc., PO Box 553, Dover, DE 19903. **Founded:** 1957. **Operating Hours:** 5 a.m.-1 a.m.; 10% network, 90% local. **Key Personnel:** Joe Farley, General Mgr. **Wattage:** 5000. **Ad Rates:** $8-17 for 30 seconds; $11-20 for 60 seconds.

5276 WQVL-AM - 1600
400 Walker Rd. Phone: (302)730-1600
PO Box 553 Fax: (302)730-9398
Dover, DE 19901
E-mail: heaven1600at.juno.com

Format: Gospel; Religious. **Networks:** Sun Radio. **Owner:** Vin-Lor Broadcasting, Inc., at above address. **Founded:** May 11, 1998. **Former name:** WKEN-AM (1997). **Operating Hours:** Continuous. **Key Personnel:** Pastor Lott, General Mgr.; Harvey Bullock, Program Dir.; Joyce Lott, PSA. **Wattage:** 5000. **Ad Rates:** $15 for 30 seconds; $30 for 60 seconds.

GEORGETOWN†, pop. 1,710.

S DE. Sussex Co. 35 mi. S. of Dover. Saw mills. Food processing. Agriculture.

5277 The Sussex Post
Independent Newspapers, Inc.
PO Box 1130 Phone: (302)934-9261
Dover, DE 19903 Fax: (302)629-6700

Local newspaper. **Founded:** 1972. **Freq:** Weekly (Wed.). **Print Method:** Offset. **Trim Size:** 13.5 x 22.88. **Cols./Page:** 6. **Col. Width:** 24 nonpareils. **Col. Depth:** 301 agate lines. **Key Personnel:** Lauren Finnerty, Editor, phone (302)629-5505, fax (302)629-6700; Debra West, Advertising Mgr., phone (302)629-5505 ext. 2012, fax (302)629-6700. **Subscription Rates:** Free; $10 by mail. **Remarks:** Accepts advertising.
Ad Rates: GLR: $2 **Circ:** Free 18,513
BW: $1,715.70
4C: $1,915.70
PCI: $13.30

5278 WDTS-AM - 620
Delaware Tech Phone: (302)856-5400
PO Box 610
Georgetown, DE 19947

Format: Alternative/New Music/Progressive; Top 40; Jazz; Blues; Classic Rock. **Operating Hours:** 8:30 a.m.-3:30 p.m., Daily; closed during summer semester. **Key Personnel:** Tamera Postles, Music Dir./Gen. Mgr., tpostles@outland.dtcc.edu. **Wattage:** 10. **Ad Rates:** Noncommercial.

5279 WSSR-AM - 900
701 N. Dupont Hwy. Phone: (302)856-2567
Georgetown, DE 19947 Fax: (302)856-6839

Format: Big Band/Nostalgia; Oldies. **Networks:** Satellite Music Network; ABC. **Founded:** 1951. **Formerly:** WSEA-AM. **Operating Hours:** Continuous. **Key Personnel:** Cathy Delgham, General Mgr.; Jack Dawhack, Operations Mgr.; Jim McHugh, Program Dir. **Local Programs:** *Art Curleys* Noon-3 p.m.; *Beach Perspective*; *Johnny Williams Show*. **Wattage:** 10,000.

5280 WZBH-FM - 93.5
701 N. Dupont Hwy. Phone: (302)856-2567
PO Box 111 Fax: (302)856-7633
Georgetown, DE 19947
Free: (888)780-0970

Format: Album-Oriented Rock (AOR). **Owner:** Great Scott Broadcasting, at above address. **Founded:** 1969. **Formerly:** WSEA-FM. **Operating Hours:** Continuous. **Key Personnel:** John Allen, Program Dir.; John Allen, Music Dir.; Cathy Dieghand, General Mgr.; Steve Frene, General Sales Mgr. **Wattage:** 25,000.

HARRINGTON, pop. 2,405.

S DE. Kent Co. 7 mi. W. of Milford.

5281 Harrington Journal
Independent Newspapers Inc.
PO Box 239 Phone: (302)674-3600
Harrington, DE 19952 Fax: (302)741-8252

Newspaper on women's interests. **Founded:** 1913. **Freq:** Weekly (Wed.). **Print Method:** Offset. **Cols./Page:** 6. **Col. Width:** 17 nonpareils. **Col. Depth:** 294 agate lines. **Key Personnel:** Michael Pelrine, Regional Executive Editor. **Subscription Rates:** $15 individuals.
Circ: ‡2,300

LEWES, pop. 2,197.

S DE. Sussex Co. 5 mi. N. of Rehoboth Beach.

5282 Cape Gazette
PO Box 213 Phone: (302)645-7700
Lewes, DE 19958 Fax: (302)645-1664
Publication E-mail: capegaz@dmv.com
Publisher E-mail: dnf@capegazette.com

Community newspaper. **Subtitle:** Delaware's Cape Region. **Founded:** 1993. **Freq:** Weekly Fri. **Print Method:** Offset. **Cols./Page:** 5. **Col. Width:** 1 7/8 inches. **Key Personnel:** Dennis Forney, Publisher; Carol Mawyer Fehrenbach, Advertising Dir., carolf@capegazette.com. **USPS:** 010-294. **Subscription Rates:** $.50 single issue; $25; $40 out of country. **Remarks:** Accepts advertising.
Ad Rates: GLR: $.59 **Circ:** Combined ⊕**7,300**
BW: $399
SAU: $8.30
PCI: $8.30

5283 Decoy Magazine
PO Box 787 Phone: (302)644-9001
Lewes, DE 19958 Fax: (302)644-9003

Magazine for decoy collectors and enthusiasts. **Founded:** 1979. **Freq:** Bimonthly. **Print Method:** Sheet fed. **Trim Size:** 8

1/2 x 11. **Cols./Page:** 3. **Col. Width:** 2 7/16 inches. **Col. Depth:** 9 11/16 inches. **Key Personnel:** Joe Engers, Editor and Publisher. **ISSN:** 1055-0364. **Subscription Rates:** $36; $40 Canada; $70 other countries; $7 single issue. **Remarks:** Accepts advertising.
Ad Rates: BW: $525 **Circ:** Paid ‡2,800
4C: $750 Non-paid ‡100

MIDDLETOWN

5284 Middletown Transcript
Dover Post Co.
PO Box 228 Phone: (302)378-9531
Middletown, DE 19709 Fax: (302)378-0647

Community newspaper. **Founded:** 1868. **Freq:** Weekly (Thurs.). **Cols./Page:** 6. **Col. Width:** 9.5 picas. **Col. Depth:** 16 inches. **Key Personnel:** Scott Lawrence, Editor; Jim Flood, Sr., Publisher. **USPS:** 347-560. **Subscription Rates:** $18.95 individuals; $28.95 out of area.
Ad Rates: BW: $619.20 **Circ:** Paid 3,550
SAU: $9.80 Controlled 550

MILFORD, pop. 5,356.

S DE. Sussex Co. 60 mi. S. of Wilmington. Manufactures electronic equipment, cement blocks, bricks, garments, canned foods. Truck farms.

5285 WAFL-FM - 97.7
PO Box 808 Phone: (302)422-7575
Milford, DE 19963-0808 Fax: (302)422-3069
E-mail: staff@dol.net

Format: Adult Contemporary. **Networks:** Independent. **Founded:** 1971. **Operating Hours:** Continuous; 100% local. **Key Personnel:** Anthony Iannini, Program Dir.; Mary Lou Schuster, News Dir.; Jeff Farrow, Music Dir.; Alex Kolobielski, Vice President. **Local Programs:** *Dan Gaffney Morning Show*, Dan Gaffney. **Wattage:** 6000. **Ad Rates:** $36-42 for 30 seconds; $46-54 for 60 seconds. $25-$36 for 30 seconds; $32-$45 for 60 seconds. Combined advertising rates available with WYUS-AM. **URL:** http://www.eagle977.com.

5286 WXPZ-FM - 101.3
PO Box K Phone: (302)424-1013
Milford, DE 19963 Fax: (302)424-2358
Free: (800)314-1013
E-mail: lightfm@wxpz.com

Format: Adult Contemporary; Contemporary Christian. **Owner:** Samson Communications Inc., at above address, Free: (800)314-1013. **Founded:** 1990. **Operating Hours:** Continuous. **ADI:** Salisbury, MD. **Key Personnel:** William T. Sammons, Jr., President, bsammons@wxpz.com; Beth Addonizio, General Sales Mgr., baddoniz@wxpz.com; Denise Harper, General Mgr., dharper@wxpz.com. **Wattage:** 3000. **Ad Rates:** $16-20 for 30 seconds; $18 for 60 seconds. **URL:** http://www.wxpz.com.

5287 WYUS-AM - 930
PO Box 808 Phone: (302)422-7575
Milford, DE 19963 Fax: (302)422-3069

Format: Hispanic. **Founded:** 1953. **Formerly**: WTHD-AM (1981). **Operating Hours:** 5:45 a.m.-midnight. **Key Personnel:** Rafael Dossman, Program Dir.; Eloina Alonso, News Dir.; Alex Kolobielski, Vice President. **Local Programs:** *Local Spanish Talk*; *Panorama* Noon-1 p.m. Monday-Friday, Rafael Dossmann, (302)422-2428, Fax (302)422-3069. **Wattage:** 500. **Ad Rates:** $15-25 for 30 seconds; $19-31 for 60 seconds. $15-$25 for 30 seconds; $19-$31 for 60 seconds. Combined advertising rates available with WAFL-FM.

MILLSBORO, pop. 1,233.

S DE. Sussex Co. 13 mi. SW of Rehoboth Beach.

5288 American Cable TV
PO Box 440 Phone: (302)732-6600
Millsboro, DE 19966 Fax: (302)732-6616

Formerly: Simmons Cable TV of Lower Delaware (1992); American Cable. **Key Personnel:** David T. Kane, General Mgr.; Bruce Redden, Contact; Elizabeth Butler, Office Mgr. **Cities Served:** subscribing households 23,138; 29 channels.

NASSAU

5289 Rescue-EMS Magazine
Lifesaving Communications, Inc.
111 Highway One, Ste. 6
PO Box 100
Nassau, DE 19969-0100

Magazine (tabloid) serving the emergency medical services directors and field personnel. **Founded:** Sept. 1983. **Freq:** Bimonthly. **Print Method:** Heatset. **Cols./Page:** 3. **Col. Width:** 3 inches. **Col. Depth:** 9 inches. **Key Personnel:** Steve Stevenson, Editor; Bill Stevenson, Assoc. Editor; David C. McLaughlin, Publisher. **Subscription Rates:** $15 individuals; $2.50 single issue. **Remarks:** Accepts advertising.
Ad Rates: BW: $1,675 **Circ:** Paid ‡3,299
4C: $2,200 Non-paid ‡19,626

NEW CASTLE, pop. 4,907.

N DE. New Castle Co. On Delaware River, 6 mi. S. of Wilmington. Tourism. National historic landmark. Manufactures fibre products, steel castings, furnaces, chemicals, cement blocks. Refineries.

5290 New Castle Weekly
203 Delaware St. Phone: (302)328-6005
New Castle, DE 19720
Community newspaper. **Founded:** 1991. **Freq:** Weekly (Wed.). **Print Method:** Offset. **Trim Size:** 13 1/2 x 22. **Cols./Page:** 8. **Col. Width:** 1 5/8 inches. **Col. Depth:** 21 inches. **Key Personnel:** Mimi Carpenter, Editor/Owner. **ISSN:** 0746-0376. **Subscription Rates:** $12 individuals. **Remarks:** Accepts advertising.
Ad Rates: BW: $630 **Circ:** ‡1,200
PCI: $3.75

5291 The News Journal
950 W. Basin Rd. Phone: (302)324-2617
PO Box 15505 Fax: (302)324-5518
New Castle, DE 19720
Free: (800)235-9100
Publication E-mail: newsroom@newsjournal.com

General newspaper. **Founded:** 1871. **Freq:** Mon.-Sun. **Print Method:** Offset. **Cols./Page:** 6. **Col. Width:** 14 nonpareils. **Col. Depth:** 300 agate lines. **Remarks:** Accepts advertising.
Ad Rates: PCI: $71.85 **Circ:** Mon.-Sat. 125,241
Sun. 149,162

5292 Suburban Cable of New Castle County
4008 N. DuPont Hwy. Phone: (302)652-1454
New Castle, DE 19720-6325 Fax: (302)655-0774

Owner: Suburban Cable, 200 Cresson Blvd., Oaks, PA 19456. **Founded:** 1969. **Formerly**: TCI Cable of New Castle County (1996). **Key Personnel:** Joanne Courtney, General Mgr.; Don Pitman, Plant Engineer; Edward Higgins, Program Mgr. **Cities Served:** Arden, Ardencroft, Ardentown, Bellefonte, Elsmere, New Castle, Neward, Newport, DE; New Castle County: subscribing households 144,000; 53 channels; 1 community access channel; 85 hours per week community access programming.

NEWARK, pop. 25,247.

N DE. New Castle Co. 15 mi. SW of Wilmington. University of Delaware. Manufactures food, cosmetics, pharmaceuticals, fibre products, paper, chemical containers, automobiles, concrete blocks, buttons. Agriculture. Corn, wheat, apples.

5293 The History of Family
Elseiver
University of Delaware Phone: (302)831-6500
101 Alison Hall Fax: (302)831-3080
Newark, DE 19716
Publication E-mail: 102062.2525@compuserve.com
Publisher E-mail: fcentres@gpu.stv.ualberta.ca

Scholarly journal of research on historical family patterns, marriage, kinship, the life course, and demography. **Subtitle:** An International Quarterly. **Founded:** 1996. **Freq:** Quarterly. **Trim Size:** 7 x 10. **Cols./Page:** 1. **Col. Width:** 30 picas. **Col. Depth:** 46 picas. **Key Personnel:** Tamara Hareven, Editor, phone (302)831-6500, fax (302)831-3080; Andrejs Plakans, Editor, phone (515)292-9538, fax (515)292-6045. **ISSN:** 1081-602X. **Subscription Rates:** $70 individuals; $165 institutions. **Remarks:** Accepts advertising.
Ad Rates: BW: $250 **Circ:** (Not Reported)

5294 International Journal of Conflict Management
University of Delaware
150 S. College Phone: (302)831-1422
Newark, DE 19716 Fax: (302)831-1445

Scholarly journal covering conflict in management. **Founded:** 1988. **Freq:** Monthly. **Key Personnel:** Dr. M. Afzalur Rahim. **ISSN:** 1044-4068. **Subscription Rates:** $169 individuals; $49 students; $59 Professional. **Remarks:** Accepts advertising.
Circ: Paid 500

5295 Journal of Adolescent & Adult Literacy
International Reading Association
800 Barksdale Rd. Phone: (302)731-1600
PO Box 8139 Fax: (302)731-1057
Newark, DE 19714-8139
Free: (800)336-7323
Publication E-mail: journals@reading.org

Scholarly journal of secondary and adult reading education. **Founded:** Oct. 1957. **Freq:** 8/year. **Print Method:** Offset. **Trim Size:** 8 3/8 x 10 7/8. **Cols./Page:** 2 and 3. **Col. Width:** 20 and 13.5 picas. **Col. Depth:** 54 picas. **Key Personnel:** John Elkins, Editor; Linda Hunter, Advertising Mgr., lhunter@reading.org; Allan Luke, Editor. **ISSN:** 1081-3004. **Subscription Rates:** $45 individuals; $6 single issue; $90 institutions. **Remarks:** Accepts advertising. **Alt. Formats:** Microfiche. **Formerly**: Journal of Reading.
Ad Rates: BW: $475 **Circ:** ‡15,000
4C: $1,075

5296 Lectura y Vida
International Reading Association
800 Barksdale Rd. Phone: (302)731-1600
PO Box 8139 Fax: (302)731-1057
Newark, DE 19714-8139
Free: (800)336-7323

Spanish language journal for teachers and researchers in reading education. **Founded:** 1980. **Freq:** Quarterly. **Print Method:** Offset. **Trim Size:** 7 3/4 x 11. **Cols./Page:** 2. **Col. Width:** 18 picas. **Col. Depth:** 58 picas. **Key Personnel:** Maria Elena Rodriguez, Editor, mer@iralyv.publi.com. **ISSN:** 0325-8637. **Subscription Rates:** $38; $41 US; $19 other countries; $9 single issue. **Remarks:** Advertising accepted; rates available upon request.
Circ: Paid 1,900
Controlled 30

5297 Reading Today
International Reading Association
800 Barksdale Rd. Phone: (302)731-1600
PO Box 8139 Fax: (302)731-1057
Newark, DE 19714-8139
Free: (800)336-7323
Publication E-mail: readingtoday@reading.org

Professional newspaper of the International Reading Association. **Founded:** June 1983. **Freq:** Bimonthly. **Print Method:** Web offset. **Trim Size:** 11 3/8 x 16 1/2. **Cols./Page:** 4. **Col. Width:** 2 1/2 inches. **Col. Depth:** 15 1/2 inches. **Key Personnel:** John Micklos, Jr., Editor, jmicklos@reading.org; Linda Hunter, Advertising Mgr. **ISSN:** 0737-4208. **Subscription Rates:** $30. **Remarks:** Accepts advertising. **Alt. Formats:** Microform.
Ad Rates: BW: $2,375 **Circ:** Paid 90,000
4C: $3,375
PCI: $125

5298 The Review
University of Delaware
150 S. College Ave Phone: (302)451-2771
Newark, DE 19711-5215 Fax: (302)831-1440

Collegiate newspaper (tabloid). **Founded:** 1882. **Freq:** Semiweekly (Tues. and Fri.; during the academic year). **Print Method:** Offset. **Cols./Page:** 5. **Col. Width:** 24 nonpareils. **Col. Depth:** 189 agate lines. **Key Personnel:** Doug Donovan, Contact. **Subscription Rates:** $15 individuals. **Remarks:** Accepts advertising.
Ad Rates: BW: $485 **Circ:** (Not Reported)
SAU: $4.73

5299 WNRK-AM - 1260
496 Walther Rd., Box 8152 Phone: (302)737-5200
Newark, DE 19702 Fax: (302)737-7466

Format: Full Service; Oldies. **Networks:** Mutual Broadcasting System; NBC; ABC. **Owner:** ARC Broadcasting, Inc., at above address. **Founded:** 1964. **Operating Hours:** Continuous; 95% local. **Key Personnel:** Al R. Campagnone, General Mgr.; Jim Hicks, Contact; Dan Casey, Sports Dir.; Shawn Higer, Traffic Mgr. **Wattage:** 1000. **Ad Rates:** $19.95-28.80 for 30 seconds; $24.95-35.95 for 60 seconds.

5300 WVUD-FM - 91.3
Universtiy of Delaware Phone: (302)831-2701
Perkins Student Center Fax: (302)831-1399
Newark, DE 19716
E-mail: wvud@mvs.udel.edu

Format: Eclectic; Full Service. **Networks:** AP. **Founded:** 1968. **Formerly**: WXDR-FM (1993). **Operating Hours:** Continuous; 5% network, 95% local. **Key Personnel:** Chuck Tarver, Station Mgr., phone (302)831-2701, nero@udel.edu; Dave MacKenzie, Contact, davemack@udel.edu. **Wattage:** 1000.

OCEAN VIEW

5301 WRKE-FM - 101.7
Q-Tone Broadcasting Corp. Phone: (302)539-2600
63 Atlantic Ave.
Rte. 1, Box 24
Ocean View, DE 19970-9801

Format: Top 40. **Networks:** NBC. **Owner:** Q-Tone Broadcasting Corp., at above address. **Founded:** 1986. **Formerly:** WOVU-FM (1990). **Operating Hours:** Continuous. **Key Personnel:** Anthony J. Quartarone, Owner/V.P./Gen. Mgr.; Charles A. Stephens, Brodcast Coord.; Manuel Mena, Music Dir. **Wattage:** 3000. **Ad Rates:** $16-24 for 30 seconds; $17-27 for 60 seconds.

REHOBOTH BEACH, pop. 1,730.

S DE. Sussex Co. 5 mi. SE of Lewes.

5302 Delaware Beachcomber
Thomson Publishing
PO Box 309 Phone: (302)227-9466
Rehoboth Beach, DE 19971 Fax: (302)227-9469
Publication E-mail: dcp@shore-source.com

Vacation entertainment guide. **Founded:** 1966. **Freq:** Weekly. **Print Method:** Web offset. **Cols./Page:** 5. **Col. Width:** 10 13/16 inches. **Col. Depth:** 13 inches. **Key Personnel:** Susan Lyons, General Mgr.; Rob Rector, Editor. **Subscription Rates:** $35. **Remarks:** Accepts advertising. **Alt. Formats:** Microform.
Ad Rates: SAU: $9 **Circ:** Free ‡25,000

5303 Delaware Coast Press
Thomson Publishing
PO Box 309 Phone: (302)227-9466
Rehoboth Beach, DE 19971 Fax: (302)227-9469
Publication E-mail: dcp@dmv.com

Community newspaper (tabloid). **Founded:** 1899. **Freq:** Weekly (Wed.). **Print Method:** Offset. **Cols./Page:** 5. **Col. Width:** 10 13/16 inches. **Col. Depth:** 13 inches. **Key Personnel:** Jane Meleady, Gen. Mgr./Advertising Dir.; Terry Plowman, Editor. **Subscription Rates:** $35 individuals. **Remarks:** Accepts advertising.
Ad Rates: 4C: $231 **Circ:** Free 16,000
SAU: $9
PCI: $7.30

5304 WGMD-FM - 92.7
Box 530 Phone: (302)945-2050
Rehoboth Beach, DE 19971 Fax: (302)945-3781
E-mail: listen@wgmd.com

Format: Full Service. **Networks:** AP; ABC. **Founded:** 1980. **Operating Hours:** Continuous. **Key Personnel:** Marie Moulinier, Sales Mgr.; Mechell Burgette, Operations Dir.; Sandy Shipe, Office Mgr. **Wattage:** 3000.

SEAFORD, pop. 5,256.

S DE. Sussex Co. On Nanticoke River, 20 mi. N. of Salisbury, MD. Manufactures nylon, baskets, boxes, crates, concrete blocks, feed, and garments. Truck and fruit farms.

5305 Leader & State Register
Chesapeake Publishing Corp.
616 Water St. Phone: (302)629-5505
PO Box 1130 Fax: (302)629-6700
Seaford, DE 19973
Community newspaper. **Founded:** 1891. **Freq:** Semiweekly (Wed. and Fri.). **Print Method:** Offset. **Cols./Page:** 6. **Col. Width:** 2 1/16 inches. **Col. Depth:** 21 inches. **Key Personnel:** Bryant L. Richardson, Editor; Milt Mitchell, Advertising Dir.; Jim Klinedinst, Advertising Mgr. **Subscription Rates:** $23.50 individuals; $37. **Remarks:** Accepts advertising.
Ad Rates: BW: $1209.60 **Circ:** 10,000
4C: $1459.60
SAU: $9.60
PCI: $9.60

5306 WJPX-AM - 1280
1039 S. Dual Hwy. Phone: (302)629-6636
Seaford, DE 19973 Fax: (302)846-9898

Format: Adult Contemporary. **Networks:** Unistar. **Owner:** Beach Broadcasting Corp., at above address, (906)653-1400. **Founded:** 1954. **Operating Hours:** Continuous; 100%. **Key Personnel:** Frank Bradley, Program/Gen. Mgr. **Local Programs:** *Market Place*, Frank Bradley. **Wattage:** 1000. **Ad Rates:** $10-24 for 30 seconds; $14-28 for 60 seconds.

5307 WSUX-FM - 98.3
1039 S. Dual Hwy. Phone: (302)629-6636
Seaford, DE 19973 Fax: (302)846-9898

Format: Adult Contemporary. **Networks:** Unistar. **Owner:** South Jersey Radio, at above address, (906)653-1400. **Founded:** 1971. **Operating Hours:** Continuous; 100% network. **Key Personnel:** Frank Bradley, Program/Gen. Mgr. **Local Programs:** *Market Place*, Frank Bradley. **Wattage:** 3000. **Ad Rates:** $10-24 for 30 seconds; $14-28 for 60 seconds.

SELBYVILLE

5308 WSBL-FM - 97.9
PO Box 379 Phone: (302)436-9725
Selbyville, DE 19975 Fax: (302)436-9726

Format: Country. **Networks:** CNN Radio; Westwood One Radio. **Owner:** Anchor Broadcasting Ltd., at above address. **Founded:** 1993. **Operating Hours:** Continuous. **ADI:** Salisbury, MD. **Key Personnel:** Walt Barcus, Station Mgr.; John Johnson, Sales Mgr. **Wattage:** 3000. **Ad Rates:** $21-25 for 30 seconds; $26-35 for 60 seconds.

SMYRNA

5309 Smyrna/Clayton Sun-Times
Dover Post Co.
25 W. Commerce St. Phone: (302)653-2083
PO Box 327 Fax: (302)653-8821
Smyrna, DE 19977
Local newspaper (tabloid). **Founded:** July 1854. **Freq:** Weekly (Wed.). **Print Method:** Offset. **Trim Size:** 11 1/2 x 15. **Cols./Page:** 6. **Col. Width:** 9 1/2 picas. **Col. Depth:** 16 inches. **Key Personnel:** Ben Mace, Editor; Fred Kaltreider, Editor. **Subscription Rates:** $16.95; $29.95 out of state. **Remarks:** Accepts advertising. **Formerly:** Smyrna Clayton Sun (July 1987); Smyrna Times.
Ad Rates: BW: $652.80 **Circ:** Paid ‡3,200
4C: $677.60
PCI: $6.80

WILMINGTON†, pop. 70,195.

N DE. New Castle Co. On Delaware River, 25 mi. SW of Philadelphia. Brandywine College; Goldey Beacom College. Port of entry and important trading center. Manufactures chemicals, leather and rubber products, textiles, tile, floor coverings, cork products and railroad cars.

5310 Archaeological Society of Delaware Bulletin
Archaeological Society of Delaware
Box 12483
Wilmington, DE 19850

Professional journal covering archaeology and history in Delaware. **Founded:** 1933. **Freq:** Annual. **Print Method:** Offset. **Trim Size:** 8 1/2 x 11. **Key Personnel:** Barbara Silber, Editor. **Subscription Rates:** $10 individuals; $15 institutions. **Remarks:** Advertising not accepted.
Circ: Paid 100

5311 Big Shout Magazine
1120 West St. Phone: (302)888-2929
Wilmington, DE 19801 Fax: (302)888-2926
Publication E-mail: bigshout@magpage.com

Entertainment magazine of the Delaware Valley region. Contains artist profiles, band showcases, a calendar of events, information on music, and monthly columns. **Freq:** Bimonthly. **Subscription Rates:** $20 individuals; single issue free. **Remarks:** Advertising accepted; rates available upon request. **URL:** http://www.magpage.com/bigshout/swnew/mon.html.
Circ: (Not Reported)

5312 The Crafts Report
Crafts Report
300 Water St. Phone: (302)656-2209
Wilmington, DE 19801 Fax: (302)656-4894
Free: (800)777-7098
Publication E-mail: marketing@craftsreport.com

Business Magazine for Professional Craft Community. **Subtitle:** The Business Journal for the Crafts Industry. **Founded:** 1975. **Freq:** 12/year. **Print Method:** Web. **Trim Size:** 8 1/8 x 10 7/8. **Cols./Page:** 3. **Col. Width:** 2 5/16 inches. **Col. Depth:** 10 inches. **Key Personnel:** Bernadette Finnerty, Editor; Lammot Copeland, Publisher; Larry Hornug, Advertising Mgr.; Dana Williams, Mktg. Dir. **Subscription Rates:** $29 individuals; $5 single issue. **Remarks:** Accepts advertising. **URL:** http://www.craftsreport.com/.
Ad Rates: BW: $1,135 **Circ:** (Not Reported)
4C: $1,530

5313 Delaware Genealogical Society Journal
Delaware Genealogical Society
505 Market St. Mall
Wilmington, DE 19801

Journal covering genealogy. **Founded:** 1980. **Freq:** Semiannual. **Print Method:** Photo offset. **Trim Size:** 6 x 9. **Cols./Page:** 1. **Key Personnel:** Mary Fallon Richards, Editor, phone (302)475-3616, mfallonr@ix.netcom.com; John C. Richards, Pub. Coordinator; Edward E. Gray, Business Mgr. **Subscription Rates:** Free to qualified subscribers; $4 single issue (back issues); $14.50 others (vol. of 4 issues). **Remarks:** Advertising not accepted. **URL:** http://www.delgensoc.org.
Circ: Paid 700

5314 Delaware Journal of Corporate Law
Widener University
Box 7286 Phone: (302)477-2145
Wilmington, DE 19803 Fax: (302)477-2042
Publication E-mail: law.review@law.widener.edu

Professional journal covering corporate law. **Founded:** 1976. **Freq:** 3/year. **Key Personnel:** James M. Kron, Business Mgr., phone (302)477-2261; Linda J. Hahs, Circulation Mgr., linda.j.hahs@law.widener.edu. **Subscription Rates:** $50 two years; $77.40 two years overseas. **Remarks:** Accepts advertising. **Online:** LEXIS-NEXIS; Westlaw.
Ad Rates: BW: $425 **Circ:** Paid 997

5315 Delaware Medical Journal
Medical Society of Delaware
1925 Lovering Ave. Phone: (302)658-7596
Wilmington, DE 19806-2166 Fax: (302)658-9669
Publisher E-mail: info-msd@medsocdel.org

Medical journal. **Subtitle:** Official Publication of the Medical Society of Delaware. **Founded:** 1929. **Freq:** Monthly. **Print Method:** Offset. **Trim Size:** 8 1/2 x 11. **Cols./Page:** 2. **Col. Width:** 32 nonpareils. **Col. Depth:** 126 agate lines. **Key Personnel:** G. Stephen DeCherney, M.D., Editor; Peter V. Rocca, M.D., Asst. Editor; Kristine M. Riccardino, Managing Editor, kmr@medsocdel.org. **ISSN:** 0011-7781. **Subscription Rates:** $25 individuals; $2.50 single issue; $40 other countries. **Remarks:** Accepts advertising.
Ad Rates: BW: $225 **Circ:** Paid 1,630
4C: $675 Controlled 17

5316 Delaware Today
3301 Lancaster Pike, Ste. 5-C Phone: (302)656-1809
Wilmington, DE 19805-1436 Fax: (302)656-5843
Free: (800)285-0400
Publication E-mail: editors@delawaretoday.com
Publisher E-mail: delawaretoday.com

Regional interest magazine. **Founded:** 1962. **Freq:** Monthly. **Print Method:** Offset. **Trim Size:** 8 3/16 x 10 7/8. **Cols./Page:** 3. **Col. Width:** 27 nonpareils. **Col. Depth:** 140 agate lines. **Key Personnel:** Marsha Mah, Editor; Robert F. Martinelli, Publisher, robpub@aol.com; Carmen Host, Ass. Pub./Advertising. **ISSN:** 1086-8380. **Subscription Rates:** $18 individuals; $2.95 single issue. **Remarks:** Accepts advertising.
Ad Rates: BW: $2,550 **Circ:** Paid ★**21,202**
4C: $3,595

5317 The Dialog
Catholic Press of Wilmington, Inc.
PO Box 2208 Phone: (302)254-0645
1925 Delaware Ave. Fax: (302)573-2397
Wilmington, DE 19899-2208
Publication E-mail: thedialog@aol.com

Religious newpaper. **Founded:** 1965. **Freq:** Weekly (Thurs.). **Print Method:** Offset. **Trim Size:** 11 x 13 1/2. **Cols./Page:** 5. **Col. Width:** 26 nonpareils. **Col. Depth:** 301 agate lines. **Key Personnel:** Daniel Medinger, Advertising Mgr.; James Grant, Editor. **USPS:** 152-440. **Subscription Rates:** $15 individuals. **Remarks:** Accepts advertising.
Ad Rates: GLR: $1.02 **Circ:** ‡50,695
BW: $1,795.50
4C: $2,700
PCI: $29

5318 Family Times
Family Times, Inc.
1900 Superfine Ln. Phone: (302)575-0935
Wilmington, DE 19802 Fax: (302)575-0933
Free: (800)969-2666
Publisher E-mail: ftimes@family.com

Parenting magazine. **Founded:** 1991. **Freq:** Monthly. **Print Method:** Web press. **Trim Size:** 11 1/2 x 14. **Cols./Page:** 4. **Col. Width:** 2 3/8 inches. **Col. Depth:** 12 3/8 inches. **Key Personnel:** James Tomey, Publisher; Joe Nudge, Advertising; Denise Yearian, Editor. **Subscription Rates:** $18 individuals. **Remarks:** Accepts advertising.
Ad Rates: BW: $1,600 **Circ:** Combined ❑**34,821**
4C: $1,900

5319 Worddance
Playful Productions, Inc.
PO Box 10804 Phone: (302)322-6699
Wilmington, DE 19850 Fax: (302)322-4531

Consumer magazine for and by young people that includes poetry, fiction, and art. **Founded:** 1991. **Freq:** Quarterly. **Trim**

Size: 6 x 9. **Key Personnel:** Stuart Ungar, Director. **ISSN:** 1071-6602. **Subscription Rates:** $18 individuals. **Remarks:** Advertising not accepted.
Circ: (Not Reported)

5320 WDEL-AM - 1150
2727 Shipley Rd. Phone: (302)478-2700
PO Box 7492 Fax: (302)478-0100
Wilmington, DE 19803
Free: (800)544-1150
E-mail: wdel@dpnet.net

Format: News; Talk. **Networks:** CNN Radio; AP; ESPN Radio. **Owner:** Delmarva Broadcasting, at above address. **Founded:** 1922. **Operating Hours:** Continuous. **ADI:** Philadelphia, PA. **Key Personnel:** Julian H. Booker, Pres./Gen. Mgr., fax (309)478-7929, peteb@dpnet.net; John Rago, Program Dir.; Chris Walns, General Sales Mgr.; Cynthia Morgan, Sales & Mktg. Dir.; Janette Johnson, Mktg. Dir. **Local Programs:** *The John Radio Show* 10:00 am - 12:00 noon Monday-Friday, Kpjm Rago, Program Dir. **Wattage:** 5000. **URL:** http://www.wdel.com.

5321 WILM-AM - 1450
1215 French St. Phone: (302)656-9800
Wilmington, DE 19801 Fax: (302)655-1450

Format: News. **Networks:** CBS; Mutual Broadcasting System; AP; Wall Street Journal Radio. **Owner:** Sally V. Hawkins, at above address. **Founded:** 1923. **Operating Hours:** Continuous; 20% network, 80% local. **Key Personnel:** Sally V. Hawkins, General Mgr.; Allan Loudell, Program Mgr.; Fred Hosier, News Dir.; Bridget Bartholow, Sales Mgr.; Tom Byrne, Sports Dir. **Wattage:** 1000.

5322 WMPH-FM - 91.7
5201 Washington St. Phone: (302)762-7199
Wilmington, DE 19809-2198 Fax: (302)762-7042
E-mail: radio@wmph.org

Format: Eclectic; Top 40. **Owner:** Brandywine School District, 1000 Pennsylvania Ave., Claymont, DE 19703, (302)792-3800, Fax: (302)792-3814. **Founded:** 1969. **Operating Hours:** Continuous. **Key Personnel:** Clint Dantinne, General Mgr., phone (302)762-7199, cdantin@den.k12.de.us; Tom Lapinski, Chairman, tlapins@den.k12.de.us; Robert Fioretti, Jr., Program Dir.; Mike Pullig, Music Dir.; Jennifer Melvin, Operations Mgr.; Ariel Adams, News Dir.; Warren Racine, Chief Engineer. **Local Programs:** *Brandywine Bulletin Board* 5:30 pm Monday-Friday, Jennifer Melvin; *Brandywine Sports Corner* 9:00 - 10:00 pm Monday, Marshall Manlove. **Wattage:** 100. **Ad Rates:** Noncommercial. **URL:** http://www.wmph.org.

5323 WQJZ-FM - 97.1
PO Box 7492 Phone: (302)436-9007
Wilmington, DE 19803 Fax: (302)436-4485
E-mail: dtgm@wqjz.com

Format: Jazz. **Networks:** Jones Satellite. **Owner:** Delmarva Broadcasting, at above address. **Founded:** 1994. **Operating Hours:** Continuous. **Key Personnel:** Michael Reath, General Mgr., phone (410)742-3212, dbcone@dmv.com; Joe Beail, General Sales Mgr., phone (410)742-3212; Derek Allen, Operations Mgr. **Wattage:** 4600. **URL:** http://www.wqjz.com.

5324 WSTW-FM - 93.7
2727 Shipley Rd. Phone: (302)478-2700
PO Box 7492 Fax: (302)478-0100
Wilmington, DE 19803
Free: (800)544-9370
E-mail: wstw@dpnet.net

Format: Adult Contemporary; Contemporary Hit Radio (CHR). **Networks:** Independent. **Owner:** Delmarva Broadcasting, at above address. **Founded:** 1950. **Operating Hours:** Continuous; 100% local. **ADI:** Philadelphia, PA. **Key Personnel:** Julian H. Booker, General Mgr., fax (302)478-7929, peters@dpnet.net; Cynthia Morgan, Dir. of Sales, fax (302)479-1544, cynthiam@dpnet.net; Chris Walus, General Sales Mgr., chrisw@dpnet.net; John Wilson, Program Dir., wstw@dpnet.net; Janette Johnson, Mktg. Dir., wstw@dpnet.net. **Wattage:** 50,000. **URL:** http://www.wstw.com.

5325 WXJN-FM - 105.9
PO Box 7492
Wilmington, DE 19803

Format: Country. **Owner:** Delmarva Broadcasting Co., at above address. **Founded:** 1992. **Operating Hours:** Continuous. **Key Personnel:** Michael Reath, General Mgr., dbcone@dmv.com; Joe Beail, General Sales Mgr.; Joe Edwards, Operations Mgr. **Wattage:** 6000.

WINTERTHUR

5326 Winterthur Portfolio
University of Chicago Press
Publications Division Phone: (302)888-4613
Winterthur Museum Fax: (302)888-4950
Winterthur, DE 19735
Free: (800)448-3883

Journal covering the history of American art and artifacts. **Subtitle:** A Journal of American Material Culture. **Founded:** 1964. **Freq:** 3/year. **Print Method:** Offset. **Trim Size:** 8 1/2 x 11. **Cols./Page:** 2. **Key Personnel:** Lisa Lock, Editor, llock@winterthur.org; Tim Hill, Advertising Mgr. **ISSN:** 0084-0416. **Subscription Rates:** $28.05 individuals; $84.15 Industry; $38.05 Individual other countries; $88.20 Industry other countries; $10 single issue. **Remarks:** Accepts advertising. **URL:** http://www.winterthur.org.
Ad Rates: BW: $220 **Circ:** Paid ‡1,600

DISTRICT OF COLUMBIA

The District of Columbia is enclosed by the state of Maryland and is bounded on the west by the Potomac River, which separates it from the state of Virginia. Its land area is 61 square miles. It is the seat of the Federal Government of the United States and most of its activities center around the departments of the Government. These divisions are housed in spacious and attractive buildings that give the city distinction, invite the inspection of an enormous number of visitors, and add to the beauty of a place which abounds in trees, flowers, and natural scenery. Across the Potomac there are additional sights that draw the attention of those who visit the District: Arlington, the National Cemetery, and the Tomb of the Unknown Soldier, Mt. Vernon and Alexandria, all rich in national and historical interest. Industrial activity had been primarily for local consumption. The Potomac, which flows into Chesapeake Bay, is navigable and wide and deep enough to accommodate large vessels. The Weather Bureau gives the temperature (annual average) of the city ad 58.0; highest on record, 106; lowest, -15. Total annual precipitation is 38.63 inches.

POPULATION: 589,000 (1992).

MANUFACTURES: Value added by manufacture: $1,573,000,000 (1991). Leading industry groups: printing and publishing, food and related products, stone, clay, and glass products.

STATISTICS

Newspapers

Period of Issue	
Daily	2
Morning Daily	2
Daily with Sunday edition	2
Semiweekly	2
Weekly	14
Biweekly	3
Monthly	12
Bimonthly	4
Quarterly	3
Free or partly free	2
Total Newspapers	45

Periodicals

Period of Issue	
Semiweekly	1
Weekly	23
Biweekly	4
Semimonthly	5
Monthly	111
Bimonthly	104
Quarterly	175
Variant	0
Total Periodicals	517

Total number of publications 562

Radio Stations

AM Stations	4
FM Stations	12
Total Radio Stations	16

TV Stations

Total TV Stations 6

Cable Stations

Total Cable Systems 2

Total number of broadcast listings 24

WASHINGTON, pop. 637,651.

On Potomac River, 38 mi. from Baltimore, 136 mi. from Philadelphia, 234 mi. from New York, 104 mi. from Richmond. Capitol of the United States. Eight bridges to suburban cities, Arlington, Alexandria, and Fairfax County in Virginia. George Washington, Georgetown, American, Catholic and Howard Universities; many other educational institutions. About 27 percent of Washington workers are employed by the Federal or District Government. United States Capitol and other Government buildings; National Cathedral. Has some of the finest libraries, museums, art galleries, historical shrines and memorials in the world. Draws a large number of tourists each year. Headquarters of many nonprofit organizations.

5327 AARP Bulletin
American Association of Retired Persons (AARP)
601 East St., NW Phone: (202)434-3340
Washington, DC 20049 Fax: (800)424-3410
Publication E-mail: bulletin@aarp.org
Publisher E-mail: aarp1@aol.com

Newspaper for mature Americans. **Founded:** 1959. **Freq:** Monthly. **Print Method:** Rotogravure. **Trim Size:** 9 3/4 x 11 1/2. **Cols./Page:** 4. **Col. Width:** 27 nonpareils. **Col. Depth:** 133 agate lines. **Key Personnel:** Elliot Carlson, Editor; Martha Ramsey, Acting Pub. Dir., phone (202)434-6850; Patricia Mondello, Advertising Dir., phone (212)599-1880, fax (212)986-8167. **ISSN:** 1044-1123. **Subscription Rates:** Included in membership. **Remarks:** Advertising accepted; rates available upon request. **URL:** http://www.aarp.org. **Alt. Formats:** Audio tape. **Formerly**: AARP News Bulletins.
Circ: Paid **★20,357,541**

5328 AASHTO Quarterly
American Association of State Highway & Transportation Officials
444 N. Capitol St. NW, Ste. 249 Phone: (202)624-5800
Washington, DC 20001 Fax: (202)624-5806
Free: (800)231-3475
Publisher E-mail: aashto@aashto.org

Highway and transportation journal. **Founded:** 1921. **Freq:** Quarterly. **Print Method:** Letterpress and offset. **Trim Size:** 8 1/2 x 11. **Cols./Page:** 3. **Col. Width:** 26 nonpareils. **Col. Depth:** 133 agate lines. **Key Personnel:** Sunny Mays Schust, Editor, sunnys@intergate.dot.gov. **Subscription Rates:** Free to qualified subscribers; $10 individuals; $11.25 other countries. **Remarks:** Advertising not accepted.
Circ: Paid ‡1,000
Controlled ‡5,200

5329 AAUW Outlook
American Association of University Women
1111 16th St. NW Phone: (202)785-7700
Washington, DC 20036 Fax: (202)872-1425
Free: (800)326-AAUW
Publisher E-mail: info@aauw.org

Magazine covering women's concerns including current family, education and legislative issues. **Founded:** Jan. 1989. **Freq:** Quarterly. **Print Method:** Web offset. **Trim Size:** 8 1/4 x 10 7/8. **Cols./Page:** 4. **Col. Width:** 2 3/8 inches. **Col. Depth:** 10 inches. **Key Personnel:** Jackie Zakrewsky, Editor, phone (202)785-7734, editor@aauw.org. **ISSN:** 0161-5661. **Subscription Rates:** $15 individuals. **Formerly**: Graduate Women.
Ad Rates: BW: $2,900 **Circ:** Controlled ‡150,000
4C: $4,200
PCI: $125

5330 ABA Consumer Credit Delinquency Bulletin
American Bankers Association
1120 Connecticut Ave. NW Phone: (202)663-5374
Washington, DC 20036 Fax: (202)828-4540
Free: (800)338-0626

Magazine comparing bank consumer loan delinquency rates and repossessions nationwide on a state by state basis. **Founded:** 1948. **Freq:** Quarterly. **Trim Size:** 8 1/2 x 11. **Key Personnel:** Jane Yao, Editor. **ISSN:** 1058-8841. **Subscription Rates:** $200 nonmembers; $110 members. **Remarks:** Advertising not accepted.
Circ: (Not Reported)

5331 Academe: Bulletin of the AAUP
American Association of University Professors
1012 14th St. NW, Ste. 500 Phone: (202)737-5900
Washington, DC 20005 Fax: (202)737-5526
Free: (800)424-2973
Publisher E-mail: aaup@aaup.org

Higher education magazine for college and university professors. **Founded:** 1915. **Freq:** Bimonthly. **Print Method:** Offset. Uses mats. **Trim Size:** 8 1/2 x 11. **Cols./Page:** 3. **Col. Width:** 2 1/4 inches. **Col. Depth:** 9 3/4 inches. **Key Personnel:** John Lyons, Editor; Bonnie Gardner, Managing Editor. **ISSN:** 0190-2946. **Subscription Rates:** $59 individuals; $69 out of country. **Remarks:** Accepts advertising.
Ad Rates: BW: $1,775 **Circ:** ‡44,000
4C: $2,275

5332 Academic Medicine
Association of American Medical Colleges
2450 N. St. NW
Washington, DC 20037-1126
Publication E-mail: acadmed@aamc.org

Medical journal publishing scholarly and research articles on all aspects of the education of physicians. **Founded:** 1926. **Freq:** Monthly. **Print Method:** Offset. **Trim Size:** 8.5 x 11. **Cols./Page:** 2. **Col. Width:** 31 nonpareils. **Key Personnel:** Addeane S. Caelleigh, Editor, phone (202)828-0540; Diane R. Sherel, Advertising Mgr. **ISSN:** 0022-2577. **Subscription Rates:** $70 U.S., Latin America, and; Canada; $120 other countries; $7 single issue; $8 single issue Other countries. **Remarks:** Color advertising accepted; rates available upon request. **URL:** http://www.aanc.org. **Formerly**: Journal of Medical Education (1988).
Ad Rates: BW: $1,050 **Circ:** ‡5,900
4C: $1,775

5333 ACCA Docket
American Corporate Counsel Association
1025 Connecticut Ave. NW, Ste. 200 Phone: (202)293-4103
Fax: (202)293-4701
Washington, DC 20036-5425
Publisher E-mail: acca@acca.com

Professional journal covering law. **Subtitle:** The Journal of the American Corporate Counsel Association. **Founded:** 1983. **Freq:** Bimonthly. **Print Method:** Sheetfed offset. **Trim Size:** 8 1/4 x 11. **Cols./Page:** 2. **Col. Width:** 18 picas. **Col. Depth:** 52 picas. **Key Personnel:** Deneen Stambore, Publisher, stambone@acca.com; Heidi Vierow, Editor, vierow@acca.com; Lisa Woodward, Production Mgr., woodward@acca.com; Iain Mitchell, Advertising Mgr., mitchell@acca.com. **ISSN:** 0895-9544. **Subscription Rates:** $175 individuals; $200 out of country; $30 single issue; $75 law students. **Remarks:** Accepts advertising. **Online:** LEXIS-NEXIS; Westlaw. **URL:** http://www.acca.com.
Ad Rates: BW: $2,500 **Circ:** Paid ⊕**10,500**
4C: $4,500

5334 Access America
Architectural and Transportation Barriers Compliance Board (Access Board)
1331 F St. NW, Ste. 1000 Phone: (202)272-5434
Washington, DC 20004-1111 Fax: (202)272-5447
Free: (800)USA-ABLE
Publication E-mail: info@access-board.gov

Newsletter featuring news and activities of the Architectural and Transportation Barriers Compliance Board. **Subtitle:** Access Currents. **Freq:** Bimonthly. **Key Personnel:** Dave Yanchulis, yanchulis@access-board.gov. **Subscription Rates:** Free. **Remarks:** Advertising not accepted. **URL:** http://www.access-board.gov. **Alt. Formats:** Audio tape; Braille; Diskette; Large-print.
Circ: Non-paid 10,000

5335 The Activist Guide
Drug Reform Coordination Network (DRCNet)
2000 P St. NW, Ste. 615 Phone: (202)362-0030
Washington, DC 20036-6920 Fax: (202)362-0032
Publisher E-mail: drcinfo@drcnet.org

Contains information regarding drug law enforcement and policies for politicians and activists. **Subscription Rates:** $25. **URL:** http://www.drcnet.org/pubs/guide/10-95/guide10-95.html.

5336 Adult Education Quarterly
American Association for Adult & Continuing Education
1200 19th St. NW, Ste. 300 Phone: (202)429-5131
Washington, DC 20036 Fax: (202)223-4579
Publication E-mail: drewallbritten@sba.com

Journal of theory and research in adult and continuing education. **Founded:** 1950. **Freq:** Quarterly. **Trim Size:** 6 x 9. **Key Personnel:** Ron Cervero, Editor; Sharan Merriam, Advertising Mgr.; Jeanette Smith, Dir, of Communications. **Subscription Rates:** $34 individuals; $41 other countries. **Remarks:** Accepts advertising.
Ad Rates: BW: $250 **Circ:** 5,000

5337 Adult Learning
American Association for Adult & Continuing Education
1200 19th St. NW, Ste. 300 Phone: (202)429-5131
Washington, DC 20036 Fax: (202)223-4579
Publication E-mail: drewallbritten@sba.com

Journal covering instructional techniques and issues relating to adult and continuing education. **Founded:** 1989. **Freq:** Bimonthly. **Print Method:** Sheet fed offset. **Trim Size:** 8 1/2 x 11. **Cols./Page:** 3. **Col. Width:** 2 1/4 inches. **Col. Depth:** 9 1/8 inches. **Key Personnel:** Jeanette Smith, Editor. **ISSN:** 0740-0578. **Subscription Rates:** $27. **Remarks:** Accepts advertising.
Ad Rates: BW: $475 **Circ:** ‡6,000
4C: $875

5338 Agricultural Aviation
National Agricultural Aviation Association
1005 E St. SE Phone: (202)546-5722
Washington, DC 20003 Fax: (202)546-5726
Publisher E-mail: naaa@aol.com

Magazine covering trends in the agricultural aviation industry. **Founded:** Mar. 1974. **Freq:** 6/year. **Print Method:** Web press. **Trim Size:** 8 3/8 x 10 7/8. **Cols./Page:** 3 and 3. **Col. Width:** 2 1/4 and 2 inches. **Col. Depth:** 9 3/4 inches. **Key Personnel:** Natalie Lutz, Editor; Peggy Knizner, Ad Sales. **ISSN:** 0745-4864. **Subscription Rates:** Free to qualified subscribers; $30 individuals; $45 other countries. **Remarks:** Accepts advertising.
Ad Rates: BW: $1,185 **Circ:** Controlled 6,000
4C: $1,845

5339 Air Jobs Digest
World Air Data
Box 42724 Phone: (301)990-6800
Washington, DC 20015 Fax: (301)990-8484

Newspaper covering job listings in aviation and aerospace worldwide. **Founded:** 1986. **Freq:** Monthly. **Key Personnel:** Ellis Hammond, President. **ISSN:** 1056-5051. **Subscription Rates:** $96 individuals. **Remarks:** Accepts advertising.
Circ: Combined 40,000

5340 Air & Space Smithsonian
901 D St. SW, 10th Fl. Phone: (202)287-3733
Washington, DC 20024 Fax: (202)287-3163
Publication E-mail: airspacedt@aol.com

Aviation and aerospace magazine. **Founded:** 1986. **Freq:** Bimonthly. **Trim Size:** 8 3/8 x 10 7/8. **Cols./Page:** 3. **Col. Width:** 28 nonpareils. **Col. Depth:** 140 agate lines. **Key Personnel:** George C. Larson, Editor; Ron Walker, Publisher; Louis Kolenda, Advertising Dir. **ISSN:** 0886-2257. **Subscription Rates:** $20 individuals. **Remarks:** Accepts advertising. **URL:** http://www.airspacemag.com/.
Ad Rates: GLR: $40 **Circ:** Paid **★251,077**
BW: $9,435
4C: $14,085

5341 Alam Attijarat (The World of Business)
2700 Virginia Ave. NW, Ste. 107 Phone: (202)337-2413
Washington, DC 20037 Fax: (202)337-3383

Magazine focusing on business in the Middle East. Printed in Arabic. **Founded:** 1966. **Freq:** Monthly. **Print Method:** Offset. **Trim Size:** 8 1/8 x 10 7/8. **Cols./Page:** 3. **Col. Width:** 26 nonpareils. **Col. Depth:** 140 agate lines. **Key Personnel:** Robert Herlihy, Publisher; Barbara Stagnitta, Advertising Mgr.; Dr. Nadim Makdisi, Editor-in-Chief. **USPS:** 538-910. **Subscription Rates:** $60; free to qualified executives in 18 Middle East countries. **Remarks:** Accepts advertising.
Ad Rates: BW: $3,590 **Circ:** Non-paid ‡20,954
4C: $4,840

5342 America Work
AFL-CIO
815 16th St. NW, Rm. 402 Phone: (202)637-5010
Washington, DC 20006 Fax: (202)508-6908

Labor magazine. **Founded:** 1996. **Freq:** 11/year. **Trim Size:** 10 X 12. **Key Personnel:** Tula Conneh, Editor. **Subscription Rates:** $10 individuals. **Remarks:** Advertising not accepted. **URL:** http://www.aflcio.org.
Circ: ‡65,000

5343 American
American University Press
4400 Massachusetts Ave. NW Phone: (202)885-3409
Washington, DC 20016-8046 Fax: (202)885-3226
Free: (800)462-6420

Magazine for University alumni and friends. **Founded:** 1948. **Freq:** Quarterly. **Print Method:** Offset. **Trim Size:** 8 1/2 x 11. **Cols./Page:** 3. **Col. Width:** 38 nonpareils. **Col. Depth:** 112 agate lines. **Key Personnel:** Trudi Rishikof, Director, trishik@american.edu. **Remarks:** Advertising not accepted.
Circ: ‡55,000

5344 American Advertising
American Advertising Federation (AAF)
1101 Vermont Ave. NW, Suite 500 Phone: (202)898-0089
Fax: (202)898-0159
Washington, DC 20005
Free: (800)999-2231
Publisher E-mail: aaf@aaf.org

Association magazine covering the advertising/marketing communications business and AAF programs. **Subtitle:** The

American Advertising Federation Magazine. **Founded:** Apr. 1984. **Freq:** Quarterly. **Print Method:** Offset. **Trim Size:** 8 3/8 x 10 7/8. **Cols./Page:** 3. **Col. Width:** 2 1/4 inches. **Col. Depth:** 9 5/8 inches. **Key Personnel:** Kevin Smith, Ad Sales, ksmith@aaf.org; Florence Jones, Art Dir., phone (202)371-2307, fjones@aaf.org. **Subscription Rates:** Free to members of the American Advertising Federation.
Ad Rates: GLR: $4.50 **Circ:** Non-paid ‡45,000
BW: $5,400
4C: $7,426
PCI: $150

5345 American Annals of the Deaf
Conference of Educational Administrators Serving the Deaf
KDES, PAS-6 Phone: (202)651-5340
800 Florida Ave. NE Fax: (202)651-5708
Washington, DC 20002
Free: (800)526-9105

Magazine focusing on education of the deaf. **Founded:** 1847. **Freq:** 5/year. **Print Method:** Offset. Uses mats. **Trim Size:** 8 1/2 x 11. **Cols./Page:** 2. **Col. Width:** 42 nonpareils. **Col. Depth:** 121 agate lines. **Key Personnel:** Donald Moores, Editor; Constance Toliver, Managing Editor. **ISSN:** 0002-726X. **Subscription Rates:** $50 individuals; $55 Canada; $65 other countries.
Ad Rates: GLR: $4 **Circ:** ‡3,500
BW: $395

5346 American Antiquity
Society for American Archaeology
900 2nd St. NE, No. 12 Phone: (202)789-8200
Washington, DC 20002-3557 Fax: (202)789-0284
Publisher E-mail: publications@saa.org

Journal on the archaeology of the New World. **Founded:** 1935. **Freq:** Quarterly. **Print Method:** Offset. **Trim Size:** 7 x 10. **Cols./Page:** 2. **Col. Width:** 16.5 picas. **Col. Depth:** 140 agate lines. **Key Personnel:** Lynne Goldstein, Editor; Rick Peterson, Advertising Mgr., rick_ peterson@saa.org. **ISSN:** 0002-7316. **Subscription Rates:** Free to qualified subscribers; $175 institutions. **Remarks:** Accepts advertising. **Alt. Formats:** Microform; Mailing labels.
Ad Rates: BW: $480 **Circ:** ‡6,200

5347 American Art
Smithsonian Institution
601 Indiana Ave., Ste. 200 Phone: (202)357-1812
Washington, DC 20004 Fax: (202)633-9637

Scholarly journal covering the history of U.S. art, architecture, landscape design, photography, film, video, and other visual media. **Founded:** 1987. **Freq:** 3/year. **Key Personnel:** Theresa Slowik, Managing Editor, phone (202)357-4512; Katherine Manthorne, Exec. Editor, phone (202)357-2233, fax (202)633-9189, kmanthor@nmaa.si.edu. **ISSN:** 0890-4901. **Subscription Rates:** $35 individuals; $15 single issue. **Remarks:** Accepts advertising. **URL:** http://www.nmaa.si.edu/journal. **Former name:** Smithsonian Studies in American Art.
Ad Rates: BW: $250 **Circ:** Paid 2,000
4C: $500

5348 American Educational Research Journal
American Educational Research Association
1230 17th St. NW Phone: (202)223-9485
Washington, DC 20036-3078 Fax: (202)775-1824

Educational research journal. **Founded:** 1964. **Freq:** Quarterly. **Print Method:** Web offset. **Trim Size:** 6 x 9. **Cols./Page:** 1. **Col. Width:** 54 nonpareils. **Col. Depth:** 98 agate lines. **Key Personnel:** William B. Thomas, Editor; Patricia Ashton, Editor; James Algina, Editor; Thomas J. Campbell, Director; Meredith Scott, Director; Donna Curd, Managing Editor; Kevin Morah, Assoc. Ed. **ISSN:** 0002-8312. **Subscription Rates:** $41 individuals; $15 single issue; $50 out of country; $56 institutions. **Remarks:** Color advertising not accepted.
Ad Rates: BW: $600 **Circ:** ‡19,800

5349 American Educator
American Federation of Teachers
555 New Jersey Ave. NW Phone: (202)879-4430
Washington, DC 20001-2079 Fax: (202)879-2014
Publisher E-mail: afteditor@aol.com

Magazine on education. **Founded:** 1967. **Freq:** Quarterly. **Trim Size:** 8 1/4 x 10 7/8. **Cols./Page:** 2. **Key Personnel:** Liz McPike, Editor. **Subscription Rates:** $8. **Remarks:** Accepts advertising.
Ad Rates: BW: $7,240 **Circ:** ‡630,000
4C: $9,240

5350 The American Enterprise
American Enterprise Institute
1150 17th St. NW Phone: (202)862-5800
Washington, DC 20036-4670 Fax: (202)862-7177

Economics, domestic and foreign policy, politics, and public opinion magazine. **Subtitle:** A National Magazine of Politics, Business, and Culture. **Founded:** Jan. 1990. **Freq:** Bimonthly. **Print Method:** Offset. Uses mats. **Trim Size:** 9 x 10 7/8. **Cols./Page:** 3 and 2. **Col. Width:** 46 picas. **Col. Depth:** 117 agate lines. **Key Personnel:** Scott Walter, Editor, phone (202)862-5887, fax (202)862-7178; Christopher C. DeMuth, Publisher. **ISSN:** 1047-3572. **Subscription Rates:** $29 individuals; $56 corporate; $5 single issue. **Remarks:** Accepts advertising.
Ad Rates: BW: $2,000 **Circ:** Paid 15,000
4C: $2,700

5351 American Forests
PO Box 2000 Phone: (202)955-4500
Washington, DC 20013 Fax: (202)955-4588
Free: (800)368-5748
Publisher E-mail: member@amfor.org

Forest conservation magazine. **Subtitle:** The Magazine of Trees & Forests. **Founded:** 1895. **Freq:** Quarterly. **Print Method:** Offset. **Trim Size:** 8 x 10 7/8. **Cols./Page:** 3. **Col. Width:** 28 nonpareils. **Col. Depth:** 140 agate lines. **Key Personnel:** Dan Smith, VP Communications, dsmith@amfor.org; Michelle Robbins, Editor, mrobbins@amfor.org. **ISSN:** 0002-8541. **Subscription Rates:** $25 individuals. **Remarks:** Accepts advertising. **URL:** http://www.americaforests.org.
Ad Rates: BW: $1,372 **Circ:** ‡25,000
4C: $2,118
PCI: $92

5352 American Institute for Conservation of Historic and Artistic Works Journal
American Institute for Conservation of Historic & Artistic Works (AIC)
1717 K St. NW, Ste. 301 Phone: (202)452-9545
Washington, DC 20006 Fax: (202)452-9328
Publisher E-mail: infoaic@aol.com

Journal covering historic and artistic works conservation. **Founded:** 1960. **Freq:** 3/year. **Print Method:** Web offset. **Trim Size:** 7 1/2 x 9 3/4. **Cols./Page:** 2. **Col. Width:** 2 1/2 inches. **Col. Depth:** 7 3/4 inches. **Key Personnel:** Chandra L. Reedy, Editor-in-Chief; Paul Whitmore, Senior Editor; Jennifer Guff, Production Editor, jgoffaic@aol.com; Jeanette Spencer, Advertising Mgr., spencernic@aol.com. **ISSN:** 0197-1360. **Subscription Rates:** $75 individuals; $95 out of country. **Remarks:** Accepts advertising.
Ad Rates: BW: $495 **Circ:** Paid 3,700
4C: $850

5353 American Journal of Addictions
American Psychiatric Press, Inc.
1400 K St. NW, Ste. 1101 Phone: (202)682-6262
Washington, DC 20005 Fax: (202)789-2648
Free: (800)368-5777
Publisher E-mail: apa@psych.org

Journal covering all scientific and clinical aspects of alcohol and drug addictions. **Founded:** 1992. **Freq:** Quarterly. **Trim Size:** 6 7/8 x 10. **Key Personnel:** Sheldon Miller, Editor. **ISSN:** 1055-0496. **Subscription Rates:** $99. **Remarks:** Advertising accepted; rates available upon request. **Alt. Formats:** CD-ROM.
Circ: Paid 1,400
Non-paid 25

5354 American Journal of International Law
American Society of International Law (ASIL)
2223 Massachusetts Ave. NW Phone: (202)939-6000
Washington, DC 20008 Fax: (202)797-7133
Publication E-mail: services@asil.org

Legal journal including research articles, current developments, judicial decisions, and book reviews written by leading scholars and practitioners of international law. **Founded:** 1907. **Freq:** Quarterly. **Print Method:** Offset. **Trim Size:** 6 7/8 x 10 1/4. **Cols./Page:** 1. **Col. Width:** 55 nonpareils. **Col. Depth:** 108 agate lines. **ISSN:** 0002-9300. **Subscription Rates:** $140 individuals; $45 single issue; $155 out of country. **Remarks:** Color advertising not accepted. **Online:** Lexis/Nexis, Westlaw and JSTOR.
Ad Rates: BW: $460 **Circ:** ‡6,800

5355 American Journal on Mental Retardation
American Association on Mental Retardation
444 N. Capitol St. NW, Ste. 846 Phone: (202)387-1968
Washington, DC 20001-1512 Fax: (202)387-2193
Free: (800)424-3688
Publication E-mail: drouth@umiami.ir.miami.edu
Publisher E-mail: mailbox@aamr.org

Journal concerning research about mental retardation. **Founded:** 1896. **Freq:** 6/year. **Print Method:** 6 7/8 x 9 3/4. **Key Personnel:** Stephen Stidinger, Contact, stephens@aamr.org. **ISSN:** 0895-8017. **Subscription Rates:** $135 nonmembers.
Ad Rates: BW: $520 **Circ:** Combined 10,000

5356 American Journal of Psychiatry
American Psychiatric Press, Inc.
1400 K St. NW, Ste. 1101 Phone: (202)682-6262
Washington, DC 20005 Fax: (202)789-2648
Free: (800)368-5777
Publication E-mail: ajp@psych.org
Publisher E-mail: apa@psych.org

Psychiatry journal. **Founded:** 1844. **Freq:** Monthly. **Print Method:** Uses mats. Offset. **Trim Size:** 8 1/8 x 10 7/8. **Cols./Page:** 2. **Col. Width:** 44 nonpareils. **Col. Depth:** 140 agate lines. **Key Personnel:** Nancy C. Anderson M.D., Ph.D., Editor. **ISSN:** 0002-953X. **Subscription Rates:** $70 individuals; $100 institutions; $35 students. **Online:** Ovid. **Alt. Formats:** CD-ROM, American Psychiatric Electronic Library, CMC Research.
Ad Rates: BW: $2,920 **Circ:** Paid ‡45,633
4C: $4,220 Non-paid ‡700

5357 American Journal of Public Health
American Public Health Association
1015 15th St. NW Phone: (202)789-5600
Washington, DC 20005 Fax: (202)789-5661

Public health journal. **Founded:** 1911. **Freq:** Monthly. **Print Method:** Offset. **Trim Size:** 8 1/4 x 11. **Cols./Page:** 2. **Col. Width:** 40 nonpareils. **Col. Depth:** 126 agate lines. **Key Personnel:** Dr. Merbyn Susser, M.D., Editor; Mary Beth Schultz, Advertising Mgr. **ISSN:** 0090-0036. **Subscription Rates:** $100 individuals; $160 institutions. **Remarks:** Accepts advertising. **URL:** http://www.apha.org.
Ad Rates: BW: $1,185 **Circ:** ‡36,000
4C: $1,985

5358 American Mathematical Monthly
Mathematical Association of America
1529 18th St. NW Phone: (202)387-5200
Washington, DC 20036 Free: (800)741-9415
Publisher E-mail: epedreir@nadd.org

A journal of mathematical exposition. Each issue includes articles on new developments on mathematical research, reviews of fields that are in interesting states of development, shorter mathematical notes that display interesting viewpoints on parts of mathematics. **Founded:** 1894. **Freq:** 10/year. **Print Method:** Offset. **Cols./Page:** 1. **Col. Width:** 65 nonpareils. **Col. Depth:** 115 agate lines. **Key Personnel:** Herbert S. Wilf, Editor; E. Sullivan, Advertising Mgr. **Subscription Rates:** $90 individuals. **Remarks:** Accepts advertising.
Ad Rates: BW: $650 **Circ:** ‡20,000

5359 American Mineralogist
Mineralogical Society of America
1015 18th St., NW, Ste. 601 Phone: (202)775-4344
Washington, DC 20036-5274 Fax: (202)775-0018
Publisher E-mail: business@minsocam.org

Scholarly journal covering mineralogy, crystallography, petrology, and geochemistry. **Subtitle:** An International Journal of Earth and Planetary Materials. **Founded:** 1916. **Freq:** Bimonthly. **Trim Size:** 7 3/4 x 10 1/4. **Cols./Page:** 2. **Key Personnel:** Anne M. Hofmeister, Editor, phone (314)935-7440, hofmeist@leuce.wustl.edu; Robert Dyne, Editor, phone (314)935-5344, bdo_ d@rocdoc.wustl.edu; Rachel Russell, Managing Editor, phone (202)862-1608, fax (202)775-0018, rrussell@miusocam,org. **ISSN:** 0003-004X. **Subscription Rates:** $30 individuals; $430 institutions. **Remarks:** Advertising not accepted.
Circ: Paid 3,200

5360 The American Nurse
American Nurses Association
600 Maryland Ave. SW, Ste. 100 W. Phone: (202)651-7024
Fax: (202)651-7005
Washington, DC 20024-2571
Free: (800)274-4262

Newspaper (tabloid) for the nursing profession. **Founded:** Feb. 1972. **Freq:** 8/year. **Print Method:** Web/heat-set. **Trim Size:** 11 3/8 x 16. **Cols./Page:** 4. **Col. Width:** 28 nonpareils. **Col. Depth:** 200 agate lines. **Key Personnel:** Connie Helmlinger, Editor, taneditor@ana.org; Elizabeth McNamara, Advertising/Sales. **ISSN:** 0098-1486. **Subscription Rates:** $10 students; $20 nonmembers; $30 other countries. **Remarks:** Accepts advertising. **Alt. Formats:** Microfilm.
Ad Rates: GLR: $17 **Circ:** ‡210,000
BW: $4,740
4C: $5,840
PCI: $117

5361 American Political Science Review
American Political Science Association
1527 New Hampshire Ave. NW Phone: (202)483-2512
Washington, DC 20036-1206 Fax: (202)483-2657
Publication E-mail: apsr@ssc.msu.edu
Publisher E-mail: apsa@apsanet.org

Scholarly journal. **Founded:** 1906. **Freq:** Quarterly. **Print Method:** Offset. **Trim Size:** 7 3/16 x 9 3/4. **Cols./Page:** 2.

Col. Width: 20 picas. **Col. Depth:** 56 1/2 picas. **Key Personnel:** Ada Finifter, Editor; Mark Linbach, Book Review Editor; Lauren Harris, Advertising Mgr. **Online:** J-Stor.
Ad Rates: BW: $655 **Circ:** ‡16,000

5362 The American Postal Worker
American Postal Workers Union, AFL-CIO
1300 L St. NW Phone: (202)842-4200
Washington, DC 20005 Fax: (202)842-4297

AFL-CIO postal labor. **Founded:** 1903. **Freq:** Monthly. **Print Method:** Offset. **Trim Size:** 11 1/2 x 17. **Cols./Page:** 4. **Col. Width:** 33 nonpareils. **Col. Depth:** 187 agate lines. **Key Personnel:** Moe Biller, Editor. **ISSN:** 0044-7811. **Subscription Rates:** $3 individuals. **Remarks:** Advertising not accepted.
Circ: 300,000

5363 American Psychological Association Monitor
American Psychological Association
750 1st St. NE Phone: (202)336-5500
Washington, DC 20002-4242 Fax: (202)336-5568
Free: (800)374-2721
Publication E-mail: letters.monitor@apa.org
Publisher E-mail: webmaster@apa.org

Journal that presents research issues and theories in psychology. **URL:** http://www.apa.org/monitor/monitor.html.

5364 American Psychologist
American Psychological Association
750 1st St. NE Phone: (202)336-5500
Washington, DC 20002-4242 Fax: (202)336-5568
Free: (800)374-2721
Publisher E-mail: webmaster@apa.org

Official journal of the Association. Publishes empirical, theoretical, and professional articles. **Founded:** 1946. **Freq:** Monthly. **Print Method:** Offset. **Trim Size:** 8 1/4 x 11. **Cols./Page:** 2. **Col. Width:** 46 nonpareils. **Col. Depth:** 126 agate lines. **Key Personnel:** Raymond D. Fowler, Editor; Susan Knapp, Exec. Editor; Jodi Ashcraft, Advertising Mgr.; Juanita Brodie, Circulation Mgr.; Terri Pilkerton, Advertising Sales Rep. **ISSN:** 0003-066X. **Subscription Rates:** Free to qualified subscribers; $189 nonmembers; $349 institutions. **Remarks:** Accepts advertising.
Ad Rates: BW: $1,045 **Circ:** ‡105,500

5365 American Quarterly
Johns Hopkins University Press
Department of English Phone: (202)687-7539
Georgetown University Fax: (202)687-1923
Washington, DC 20057
Publication E-mail: aq@gusun.georgetown.edu
Publisher E-mail: jlinfo@jhupress.jhu.edu

Journal on American culture. **Subtitle:** Official Publication of the American Studies Association. **Founded:** 1949. **Freq:** Quarterly. **Print Method:** Offset. **Trim Size:** 6 x 9. **Cols./Page:** 1. **Col. Width:** 26 picas. **Col. Depth:** 7 inches. **Key Personnel:** Tara Dorai-Berry, Advertising Mgr.; Lucy Maddox, Editor. **ISSN:** 0003-0678. **Subscription Rates:** $62 institutions; Subscription free to ASA members.
Ad Rates: BW: $395 **Circ:** ‡6,240

5366 American Railway Engineering Association Bulletin
American Railway Engineering Association
50 F St. NW Phone: (202)639-2190
Washington, DC 20001 Fax: (202)639-2183

Magazine of the American Railway Engineering Association. Contains technical committee reports; proposed changes to the Manual for Railway Engineering and Portfolio of Trackwork Plans; reports on railway engineering, construction, and maintenance; results of research investigations and service tests; and proceedings of the Annual Technical Conference. **Founded:** 1899. **Freq:** 5/year. **Print Method:** Offset. **Trim Size:** 6 x 9. **Cols./Page:** 1. **Col. Width:** 27 picas. **Col. Depth:** 47 picas. **Key Personnel:** A.C. Parker, Advertising Mgr. **ISSN:** 0003-0694. **Subscription Rates:** $81 individuals.
Ad Rates: BW: $690 **Circ:** 38,000
4C: $1,475

5367 American Rehabilitation
Rehabilitation Services Administration (RSA)
Mary Switzer Bldg., Rm. 3030 Phone: (202)205-8296
330 C St. SW Fax: (202)205-9874
Washington, DC 20202-2531
Publication E-mail: frank_romano@ed.gov

Magazine on rehabilitation of the handicapped. **Founded:** 1975. **Freq:** Quarterly. **Print Method:** Offset. **Cols./Page:** 3. **Col. Width:** 27 nonpareils. **Col. Depth:** 116 agate lines. **Key Personnel:** Frank Romano, Editor and Publisher, frank_romano@ed.gov. **ISSN:** 0362-4048. **Subscription Rates:** $8 individuals U.S.; $10 out of country. **Remarks:** Advertising not accepted. **URL:** http://www.ed.gov/pubs/American Rehab. **Alt. Formats:** Audio tape. **Formerly:** Rehabilitation Record (1975).
Circ: 3,700

5368 The American Scholar
Phi Beta Kappa Society
1785 Massachusetts Ave., NW, 4th Fl. Phone: (202)265-3808
Fax: (202)265-0083
Washington, DC 20036
Publisher E-mail: scholar@pbk.org

Journal containing articles and essays on intellectual, artistic, literary, and scientific subjects; includes serious discussion, argument, and humor. **Founded:** 1932. **Freq:** Quarterly. **Print Method:** Web Offset. **Trim Size:** 6 7/8 x 10. **Cols./Page:** 2. **Col. Width:** 31 nonpareils. **Col. Depth:** 112 agate lines. **Key Personnel:** Anne Fadiman, Editor; Peggy Ferrin, Advertising Mgr., phone (210)497-1914, fax (210)497-1982, mferrin000@aol.com. **ISSN:** 0003-0937. **Subscription Rates:** $25 individuals; $6.95 single issue; $9.95 single issue other countries.
Ad Rates: GLR: $35 **Circ:** ‡26,500
BW: $730

5369 American Studies International
George Washington University Phone: (202)994-7368
2108 G St. NW Fax: (202)994-8651
Washington, DC 20052
Publication E-mail: asi@gwu.edu

Academic journal publishing bibliographic and scholarly essays on American Studies including history, literature, folklore, politics, religion, and art. Conferences, publications, fellowships, and grants announcements included. **Founded:** 1962. **Freq:** 3/year (Feb., June, Oct.). **Print Method:** Offset. **Trim Size:** 6 x 9. **Cols./Page:** 3. **Col. Width:** 26 nonpareils. **Col. Depth:** 132 agate lines. **Key Personnel:** Bernard Mergen, Editor; Brian Finnegan, Editor. **ISSN:** 0003-1321. **Subscription Rates:** $30 individuals; $40 institutions; $40 other countries; $8 single issue (Journal); $3 single issue (Newsletter). **Remarks:** Accepts advertising.
Ad Rates: BW: $150 **Circ:** ‡2,000

5370 American Teacher
American Federation of Teachers
555 New Jersey Ave. NW Phone: (202)879-4430
Washington, DC 20001-2079 Fax: (202)879-2014
Publication E-mail: wleague74@aol.com
Publisher E-mail: afteditor@aol.com

Newspaper focusing on issues of education and the labor union. **Founded:** 1916. **Freq:** 8/year. **Print Method:** Offset. **Trim Size:** 10 7/8 x 14. **Cols./Page:** 5. **Col. Width:** 11 nonpareils. **Col. Depth:** 169 agate lines. **Key Personnel:** Trish Gorman, Editor, phone (202)879-4430, tgorman@aft.org; Mike Rose, Editor, mrose@aft.org. **ISSN:** 0003-1380. **Subscription Rates:** $12 individuals (for non-union members). **Remarks:** Accepts advertising.
Ad Rates: BW: $10,230 **Circ:** Paid 850,000
4C: $12,502

5371 The American University Law Review
Joe Christensen, Inc.
4801 Massachusetts Ave. NW, No. 621 Phone: (202)274-4433
Fax: (202)274-0773
Washington, DC 20016
Legal journal. **Founded:** 1951. **Freq:** Bimonthly. **Print Method:** Offset. **Trim Size:** 6 5/8 x 10. **Cols./Page:** 1. **Col. Width:** 57 nonpareils. **Col. Depth:** 112 agate lines. **Key Personnel:** Martine Tavakoli, Editor, mtavako@wcl.american.edu. **ISSN:** 0003-1453. **Subscription Rates:** $35 individuals; $40 other countries. **Remarks:** Accepts display advertising. **Online:** Lexis, Westlaw. **Alt. Formats:** Microform.
Ad Rates: BW: $100 **Circ:** Paid ‡570
Non-paid ‡700

5372 American Visions
American Visions Media, Inc.
1156 15th St. NW, Ste 615 Phone: (202)496-9593
Washington, DC 20005 Fax: (202)496-9851

Subtitle: The Magazine of Afro-American Culture. **Founded:** Jan. 1986. **Freq:** Bimonthly. **Print Method:** Offset. **Trim Size:** 8 1/4 x 10 7/8. **Cols./Page:** 3. **Col. Width:** 13 picas. **Col. Depth:** 50 picas. **Key Personnel:** Gary Puckrein, President; Joanne Harris, Editor; Mel Fellis, Advertising Mgr. **ISSN:** 0884-9390. **Subscription Rates:** $18 individuals. **Remarks:** Accepts advertising. **Alt. Formats:** Microfiche.
Ad Rates: BW: $4,800 **Circ:** Paid 125,000
4C: $7,000 Controlled 5,000

5373 The Americas
The Academy of American Franciscan History
The Catholic University of America Phone: (202)319-5890
Fax: (202)319-5569
620 Michigan Ave. NE
B-17 Gibbons Hall
Washington, DC 20064
Publication E-mail: americas@cua.edu

Journal on Inter-American cultural history. **Subtitle:** Inter-American Cultural History. **Founded:** 1944. **Freq:** Quarterly. **Print Method:** Offset. Uses mats. **Trim Size:** 7 x 10. **Cols./Page:** 1. **Col. Width:** 57 nonpareils. **Col. Depth:** 112 agate lines. **Key Personnel:** Dr. Vincent Peloso, Editor. **ISSN:** 0003-1615. **Subscription Rates:** $22 other countries; $95 institutions; $38 individuals; $20 students; $25 single issue. **Remarks:** Accepts advertising. **URL:** http://www.cua.edu/www/org/tam/index.htm.
Ad Rates: PCI: $4.50 **Circ:** ‡1,000

5374 Animal Sheltering Magazine
Humane Society of the United States (HSUS)
2100 L St. NW Phone: (202)452-1100
Washington, DC 20037 Fax: (202)258-3081
Publication E-mail: asm@ix.netcom.com

Magazine covering animal shelter operation, care of animals, pet adoptions, and other animal issues. **Subtitle:** The Community Animal Care, Control, and Protection Resource. **Founded:** Apr. 1, 1978. **Freq:** 6/year. **Trim Size:** 8 1/2 x 11. **Key Personnel:** Scott Kirkwood, Editor, phone (301)548-7732; Nancy Lawson, Asst. Editor, phone (301)548-7775. **ISSN:** 0734-3078. **Subscription Rates:** $8 individuals. **Remarks:** Accepts advertising. **Formerly:** Shelter Sense.
Circ: Paid 5,000

5375 Annual Energy Review 1997
U.S. Energy Information Administration
James Forrestal Bldg., Rm. 1F-048 Phone: (202)586-8800
Fax: (202)586-0727
Washington, DC 20585
Publisher E-mail: infoctr@eia.doe.gov

Government publication covering energy and fuel data. **Founded:** May 1983. **Freq:** Annual. **Key Personnel:** Leigh Carleton, phone (202)586-1132, leigh.carleton@eia.doe.gov. **Subscription Rates:** $31 single issue. **Remarks:** Advertising not accepted. **URL:** http://www.eia.doe.gov. **Alt. Formats:** CD-ROM, Energy InfoDisc. **Formerly:** Annual Report to Congress, Vol. II.
Circ: (Not Reported)

5376 Anthropological Quarterly
CUA Press
Catholic University Phone: (202)319-5080
Washington, DC 20064 Fax: (202)319-4782
Publication E-mail: anth-qrt@cua.edu

Journal publishing articles, reviews, and lists of recently published books in all areas of socio-cultural anthropology. **Founded:** 1928. **Freq:** Quarterly. **Trim Size:** 7 1/2 x 9 1/2. **Cols./Page:** 2. **Col. Width:** 33 nonpareils. **Col. Depth:** 115 agate lines. **Key Personnel:** Phyllis Pease Chock, Editor; Gordon A. Conner, Business Mgr. **ISSN:** 0003-5491. **Subscription Rates:** $28 individuals; $38 institutions; $9 single issue. **Formerly:** Primitive Man.
Ad Rates: BW: $150 **Circ:** Paid ‡794
Non-paid ‡91

5377 Antimicrobial Agents and Chemotherapy
American Society for Microbiology
1325 Massachusetts Ave. NW Phone: (202)737-3600
Washington, DC 20005 Fax: (202)942-9342
Publisher E-mail: journals@asmusa.org

Journal devoted exclusively to all aspects of antimicrobial, antiviral, antiparasitic, and antimicrobial agents and chemotherapy. **Founded:** 1972. **Freq:** Monthly. **Print Method:** Offset. Uses mats. **Trim Size:** 8 1/4 x 11. **Cols./Page:** 2. **Col. Width:** 42 nonpareils. **Col. Depth:** 127 agate lines. **Key Personnel:** George A. Jacoby, Jr., Editor-in-Chief. **ISSN:** 0066-4804. **Subscription Rates:** $55 members; $311 nonmembers. **Remarks:** Accepts advertising. **Available Online. URL:** http://www.journals.asm.org.
Ad Rates: BW: $1,575 **Circ:** Paid ‡7,400
4C: $1,525 Non-paid ‡30

5378 APA Monitor
American Psychological Association
750 1st St. NE Phone: (202)336-5500
Washington, DC 20002-4242 Fax: (202)336-5568
Free: (800)374-2721
Publisher E-mail: webmaster@apa.org

Official newspaper of the APA. Reports on the science, profession, and social responsibility of psychology, including latest legislative developments affecting mental health, education, and research support. **Founded:** 1970. **Freq:** Monthly. **Print Method:** Offset. **Trim Size:** 11 3/8 x 16 7/8. **Cols./Page:**

5. **Col. Width:** 224 agate lines. **Col. Depth:** 24 nonpareils. **Key Personnel:** Rhea K. Farberman, Executive editor; Jodi Ashcraft, Advertising Mgr.; Tyrone Ingram, Advertising Sales Rep. **ISSN:** 0001-2114. **Subscription Rates:** Free to qualified subscribers; $32 nonmembers; $37 institutions. **Remarks:** Accepts advertising.
Ad Rates: GLR: $7.25 **Circ:** ‡102,350
BW: $4,595
PCI: $5,395

5379 APF Reporter
Alicia Patterson Foundation
1730 Pennsylvania Ave. NW, Ste. 850 Phone: (202)393-5995
Washington, DC 20006 Fax: (301)951-8512
Publication E-mail: afpengel@charm.net

Professional magazine for journalists. **Founded:** 1961. **Freq:** Quarterly. **Key Personnel:** Margaret Engel, Editor, apfengel@charm.net. **ISSN:** 0913-4562. **Subscription Rates:** Free to qualified subscribers. **Remarks:** Advertising not accepted. **URL:** http://www.aliciapatterson.org.
Circ: Controlled 4,000

5380 Applied and Environmental Microbiology
American Society for Microbiology
1325 Massachusetts Ave. NW Phone: (202)737-3600
Washington, DC 20005 Fax: (202)942-9342
Publication E-mail: journals@asmusa.org
Publisher E-mail: journals@asmusa.org

Journal emphasizing food microbiology, industrial microbiology, biotechnology, physiological microbial ecology, ecosystem research, and ecological studies of algae, fungi, protozoa, and viruses. **Founded:** 1953. **Freq:** Monthly. **Print Method:** Offset. Uses mats. **Trim Size:** 8 1/4 x 11. **Cols./Page:** 2. **Col. Width:** 42 nonpareils. **Col. Depth:** 127 agate lines. **Key Personnel:** Judy D. Wall, Editor-in-Chief. **ISSN:** 0099-2240. **Subscription Rates:** $58 members; $347 nonmembers institutions. **Remarks:** Accepts advertising. **Available Online.** **URL:** http://www.journals.asm.org.
Ad Rates: BW: $1,210 **Circ:** Paid ‡8,450
4C: $2,420 Non-paid ‡35

5381 Applied Optics
Optical Society of America
2010 Massachusetts Ave. NW Phone: (202)223-8130
Washington, DC 20036 Fax: (202)223-1096
Free: (800)762-6960
Publication E-mail: goed@osa.org
Publisher E-mail: info@usa.org

Journal covering all varieties and applications of optics including lasers, optical engineering, holography, quantum electronics, information processing, and meteorology. **Founded:** 1962. **Freq:** 3/month. **Print Method:** Offset. **Trim Size:** 8 1/4 x 11 1/4. **Cols./Page:** 2. **Col. Width:** 40 nonpareils. **Col. Depth:** 140 agate lines. **Key Personnel:** John R. Murray, Editor-in-Chief; Stephen O'Connor, Advertising Sales Coord. **ISSN:** 0003-6935. **Subscription Rates:** $790 individuals. **Remarks:** Advertising not accepted. **Available Online.** **URL:** http://192.239.26.3. **Alt. Formats:** CD-ROM.
Circ: ‡7,000

5382 Arab Studies Quarterly
Association of Arab-American University Graduates, Inc.
4201 Connecticut Ave. NW, No. 305 Phone: (202)237-8312
Washington, DC 20008 Fax: (202)237-8313
Magazine covering Arab affairs, the Middle East, and U.S. foreign policy. **Founded:** 1979. **Freq:** Quarterly. **Trim Size:** 6 x 9. **Key Personnel:** William W. Haddad, Editor. **ISSN:** 0271-3519. **Subscription Rates:** $24; $40 institutions. $6 single issue. **Remarks:** Accepts advertising. **Alt. Formats:** Microform.
Ad Rates: BW: $250 **Circ:** Paid ‡1,500
Non-paid ‡300

5383 Archives of Environmental Health
Heldref Publications
Helen Dwight Reid Educational Foundation Phone: (202)296-6267
1319 18th St. NW Fax: (202)296-5149
Washington, DC 20036-1802
Free: (800)365-9753
Publication E-mail: aeh@heldref.org
Publisher E-mail: revu@heldref.org

Journal providing objective documentation of the effects of environmental agents on human health. Official publication of the Society for Occupational and Environmental Health. **Subtitle:** An International Journal. **Founded:** 1950. **Freq:** Bimonthly. **Print Method:** Offset. Uses mats. **Trim Size:** 8 1/2 x 11. **Cols./Page:** 2. **Col. Width:** 3 3/8 inches. **Col. Depth:** 10 inches. **Key Personnel:** Grant Williams, Adv. Production Mgr., advertise@heldref.org; Douglas Kirkpatrick, Director; Fred Huber, Circulation Mgr., subscribe@heldref.org; Jean Kline, Fulfillment Mgr., subscribe@heldref.org; Pat McCready, Managing Editor. **ISSN:** 0003-9896. **Subscription Rates:** $137 individuals; other countries add $20 postage. **Remarks:** Accepts advertising. **Online:** EBSCO; Healthgate; Infonautics; Ovid Technologies, Inc.; Information Access; Institute for Scientific Information; UMI. **URL:** http://www.heldref.org. **Alt. Formats:** CD-ROM.
Ad Rates: BW: $515 **Circ:** Paid ‡1,600

5384 Arms Control Today
Arms Control Association
1726 M St. NW, Ste. 201 Phone: (202)463-8270
Washington, DC 20036 Fax: (202)463-8273
Publication E-mail: act@armscontrol.org

Magazine focusing on arms control issues. **Founded:** 1972. **Freq:** 10/year. **Print Method:** Offset. **Trim Size:** 8 1/2 x 11. **Cols./Page:** 3. **Col. Width:** 28 nonpareils. **Col. Depth:** 98 agate lines. **Key Personnel:** Tom Pfeiffer, Editor; John Springer, Managing Editor. **ISSN:** 0196-125X. **Subscription Rates:** $50 individuals; $60 other countries; $60 Institutions; $25 students. **Remarks:** Accepts advertising. **Available Online.** **URL:** http://www.armscontrol.org.
Ad Rates: BW: $200 **Circ:** ‡4,000

5385 Arts Education Policy Review
Heldref Publications
Helen Dwight Reid Educational Foundation Phone: (202)296-6267
1319 18th St. NW Fax: (202)296-5149
Washington, DC 20036-1802
Free: (800)365-9753
Publication E-mail: aepr@heldref.org
Publisher E-mail: revu@heldref.org

Journal covering major policy issues in arts education. **Founded:** 1879. **Freq:** Bimonthly. **Print Method:** Offset. Uses mats. **Trim Size:** 8 1/2 x 11. **Cols./Page:** 3. **Col. Width:** 2 1/8 inches. **Col. Depth:** 9 5/8 inches. **Key Personnel:** Grant Williams, Adv. Production Mgr., advertise@heldref.org; Douglas Kirkpatrick, Director; Fred Huber, Circulation Mgr., subscribe@heldfref.org; Jean Kline, Fulfillment Mgr., subscribe@heldref.org; Leila Saad, Managing Editor. **ISSN:** 1063-2913. **Subscription Rates:** $39 individuals; $69 institutions Industry; other countries add $15 postage. **Remarks:** Accepts advertising. **Online:** EBSCO; Infonautics; Information Access; UMI. **URL:** http://www.heldref.org.
Ad Rates: BW: $455 **Circ:** ‡1,061

5386 ASA Employment Bulletin
American Sociological Association
1722 N St. NW Phone: (202)833-3410
Washington, DC 20036 Fax: (202)785-0146
Free: (800)877-2693
Publication E-mail: eb@asanet.org
Publisher E-mail: executive.office@asanet.org

Bulletin covering sociology positions in academic and in-practice settings and fellowships. **Founded:** 1968. **Freq:** Monthly. **Cols./Page:** 3. **Col. Width:** 2 1/2 inches. **Col. Depth:** 9 1/2 inches. **Key Personnel:** Karen Edwards. **Subscription Rates:** $20 individuals; $3 single issue. **Remarks:** Accepts advertising. **URL:** http://www.asanet.asanet.org.
Ad Rates: PCI: $110 **Circ:** Controlled 3,500

5387 ASAE Association Law and Policy
American Society of Association Executives
1575 I St. NW Phone: (202)626-2723
Washington, DC 20005 Fax: (202)408-8825
Publication E-mail: legalsec@asaenet.otg
Publisher E-mail: asae@asaenet.org

Professional journal covering law issues. **Founded:** 1987. **Freq:** Semimonthly. **Key Personnel:** George E. Constantine, II,Esq, Editor, phone (202)626-2818, fax (202)371-1673, gconstan@asaenet.org. **Subscription Rates:** Included in membership. **Remarks:** Advertising not accepted.
Circ: Non-paid 1,200

5388 ASEE Prism
American Society for Engineering Education
1818 N St., NW, Ste. 600 Phone: (202)331-3500
Washington, DC 20036 Fax: (202)265-8504
Publication E-mail: l.castien@asee.org

Professional magazine for educators in the field of engineering. **Founded:** 1991. **Freq:** 10/year. **Print Method:** Offset. **Trim Size:** 8 1/4 x 11. **Key Personnel:** Robert Blake, Pub. Mgr.; Tim Delaney, Advertising Mgr.; Kirstin Peters, Classified Mgr. **ISSN:** 0022-0809. **Subscription Rates:** Free to qualified subscribers; $69 individuals. **Remarks:** Accepts advertising. **Available Online.** **URL:** http://www.asee.org/PRISM.
Ad Rates: BW: $855 **Circ:** ‡12,000
4C: $1,825

5389 ASHE-ERIC Higher Education Reports
ERIC Clearinghouse on Higher Education
George Washington University Phone: (202)296-2597
1 Dupont Circle, Ste. 630 Fax: (202)452-1844
Washington, DC 20036-1183
Free: (800)773-3742
Publication E-mail: pubs@eric-he.edu

Monograph series providing literature review and issue analysis in higher education. Specializes in administrative, governance and teaching issues. **Founded:** 1972. **Freq:** 8/year. **Print Method:** Offset. **Trim Size:** 6 x 9. **Cols./Page:** 1. **Col. Width:** 31 picas. **Col. Depth:** 45 picas. **Key Personnel:** Adrianne J. Kezar, Editor, akezar@eric. **ISSN:** 0884-0040. **Subscription Rates:** $144 individuals; $24 single issue. **Remarks:** Advertising not accepted. **URL:** http://www.ericHe.org. **Alt. Formats:** Microform.
Circ: ‡4,000

5390 Asian Affairs
Heldref Publications
Helen Dwight Reid Educational Foundation Phone: (202)296-6267
1319 18th St. NW Fax: (202)296-5149
Washington, DC 20036-1802
Free: (800)365-9753
Publication E-mail: aa@heldref.org
Publisher E-mail: revu@heldref.org

Journal focusing on U.S. policy in Asia, as well as on the domestic politics, economics, and international relations of Asian countries. **Subtitle:** An American Review. **Founded:** 1973. **Freq:** Quarterly. **Print Method:** Offset. **Trim Size:** 6 x 9. **Cols./Page:** 1. **Col. Width:** 4 1/2 inches. **Col. Depth:** 7 inches. **Key Personnel:** Grant Williams, Adv. Production Mgr., advertise@heldref.org; Douglas Kirkpatrick, Director; Fred Huber, Circulation Mgr., subscribe@heldref.org; Jean Kline, Fulfillment Mgr., subscribe@heldref.org; Martha Yager, Managing Editor. **ISSN:** 0092-7678. **Subscription Rates:** $40 individuals; $80 institutions Foreign add $13; $20 single issue. **Remarks:** Accepts advertising. **Online:** EBSCO; Infonautics; Information Access; UMI. **URL:** http://www.heldref.org.
Ad Rates: BW: $170 **Circ:** ‡358

5391 ASID Professional Designer
The American Society of Interior Designers
608 Massachusetts Ave., NE Phone: (202)546-3480
Washington, DC 20002 Fax: (202)546-3240
Publisher E-mail: asid@asid.org

Magazine for members of the interior design industry. **Founded:** 1975. **Freq:** Bimonthly. **Print Method:** Web offset. **Trim Size:** 8 1/4 x 10 7/8. **Cols./Page:** 3. **Key Personnel:** Rachel Zanardi, Editor, rzanardi@asid.org. **Remarks:** Accepts advertising. **Formerly:** The ASID Report.
Ad Rates: BW: $3,085 **Circ:** Controlled 33,000
4C: $3,465

5392 ASM News
American Society for Microbiology
1325 Massachusetts Ave. NW Phone: (202)737-3600
Washington, DC 20005 Fax: (202)942-9342
Publisher E-mail: journals@asmusa.org

Magazine for microbiologist. Includes letters addressing scientific and nonscientific topics; reports from ASM's active committees on meetings, publications, education, and branch activities; general microbiology interest articles; book reviews; and employment opportunities. **Founded:** 1935. **Freq:** Monthly. **Print Method:** Offset. Uses mats. **Trim Size:** 8 1/4 x 10 7/8. **Cols./Page:** 3. **Col. Width:** 27 nonpareils. **Col. Depth:** 129 agate lines. **Key Personnel:** Michael I. Goldberg, Editor-in-Chief. **ISSN:** 0044-7897. **Subscription Rates:** $50 nonmembers; $3 single issue. **Remarks:** Accepts advertising.
Ad Rates: BW: $2,150 **Circ:** Paid ‡42,684
4C: $3,425 Non-paid ‡50

5393 Association Management
American Society of Association Executives
1575 I St. NW Phone: (202)626-2723
Washington, DC 20005 Fax: (202)408-8825
Publisher E-mail: asae@asaenet.org

Articles address issue, programs, news and trends important to not-for-profit organizations of all sizes and scopes. **Subtitle:** The Magazine for Association Executives. **Founded:** 1949. **Freq:** Monthly. **Print Method:** Offset. **Trim Size:** 8 1/4 x 10 7/8. **Cols./Page:** 3. **Col. Width:** 27 nonpareils. **Col. Depth:** 140 agate lines. **Key Personnel:** Ann Mahoney, Editor-in-Chief; Keith Skillman, Exec. Editor. **ISSN:** 0004-5578. **Subscription Rates:** $24 members included in dues; $30 nonmembers; $5 single issue. **Remarks:** Accepts advertising.
Ad Rates: BW: $6,310 **Circ:** Paid ★24,505
4C: $8,715

5394 Azure
The Shalem Center
1140 Connecticut Ave. NW, Ste. 801 Phone: (202)887-1270
Fax: (202)887-1277
Washington, DC 20036
Publisher E-mail: shalemorder@shalem.org.il

Journal covering various aspects of Israeli and Jewish thought, society, and politics, as well as research on Jewish history and philosophy (English and Hebrew). **Subtitle:** Ideas for the Jewish Nation. **Founded:** 1996. **Freq:** Quarterly. **Key Personnel:** Ofir Haivrey, Editor-in-Chief; Yoram Hazony, Editor; Joshua Weinstein, Editor; David Hazony, Production Mgr. **Subscription Rates:** $26 by mail.

5395 Bank & Corporate Governance Law Reporter
1601 Connecticut Ave., NW, No. 602 Phone: (202)467-5755
Fax: (202)328-2430
Washington, DC 20009
Publisher E-mail: lawre[illegible]t@aol.com

Professional journal covering corporate governance and securities law. Available in print format or via e-mail. **Founded:** 1988. **Freq:** Monthly. **Print Method:** Photo offset. **Trim Size:** 8 1/2 x 11. **Cols./Page:** 2. **Col. Width:** 3 1/2 inches. **Col. Depth:** 8 inches. **Key Personnel:** Neil Cohen, Editor. **ISSN:** 1072-8643. **Subscription Rates:** $1,750 individuals. **Remarks:** Advertising not accepted. **Former name**: Mergers & Acquisitions Law Reporter.
Circ: (Not Reported)

5396 Bank Marketing Magazine
Bank Marketing Association
1120 Connecticut Ave., NW Phone: (202)663-5378
Washington, DC 20036-3902 Fax: (202)828-4540
Free: (800)433-9013
Publication E-mail: ksherida@aba.com

Magazine containing information on bank marketing, advertising, and public relations. **Founded:** Feb. 1916. **Freq:** Monthly. **Print Method:** Offset. **Trim Size:** 8 1/4 x 10 7/8. **Cols./Page:** 3. **Col. Width:** 2 1/8 inches. **Col. Depth:** 10 inches. **Key Personnel:** Kevin Sheridan, Editor, ksherida@aba.com; Larry Price, Publisher, phone (202)663-5378, lprice@aba.com. **ISSN:** 0888-3194. **Subscription Rates:** $120 nonmembers; $150 other countries. **Remarks:** Accepts advertising.
Ad Rates: BW: $2,200 **Circ:** Paid ‡4,003
4C: $3,100

5397 Behavioral Medicine
Heldref Publications
Helen Dwight Reid Educational Foundation Phone: (202)296-6267
Fax: (202)296-5149
1319 18th St. NW
Washington, DC 20036-1802
Free: (800)365-9753
Publication E-mail: bmed@heldref.org
Publisher E-mail: revu@heldref.org

Interdisciplinary journal focusing on research and management of problem-stress. Includes basic and clinical medical science as well as social and behavioral science approaches. **Founded:** 1975. **Freq:** Quarterly. **Print Method:** Sheetfed offset. **Trim Size:** 8 1/2 x 11. **Cols./Page:** 2. **Col. Width:** 3 3/8 inches. **Col. Depth:** 10 inches. **Key Personnel:** Grant Williams, Production Mgr., advertise@heldref.org; Fred Huber, Circulation Mgr., subscribe@heldref.org; Jean Kline, Fulfillment Mgr., subscribe@heldref.org; Martha Wedeman, Managing Editor. **ISSN:** 0896-4289. **Subscription Rates:** $48 individuals; $90 institutions; other countries add $13 postage. **Remarks:** Accepts advertising. **Online:** Healthgate; EBSCO; Infonautics; Ovid Technologies, Inc.; Information Access; Institute of Scientific Information; UMI; Responsive DataBase Services, Inc. **URL:** http://www.heldref.org. **Alt. Formats:** CD-ROM.
Ad Rates: BW: $250 **Circ:** ‡682

5398 Behavioral Neuroscience
American Psychological Association
750 1st St. NE Phone: (202)336-5500
Washington, DC 20002-4242 Fax: (202)336-5568
Free: (800)374-2721
Publisher E-mail: webmaster@apa.org

Journal presenting research in the broad field of the biological bases of behavior. **Founded:** Feb. 1983. **Freq:** Bimonthly. **Print Method:** Offset. **Trim Size:** 8 1/4 x 11. **Cols./Page:** 2. **Col. Width:** 46 nonpareils. **Col. Depth:** 126 agate lines. **Key Personnel:** Michela Gallagher, PhD, Editor; Susan Knapp, Exec. Editor; Jodi Ashcraft, Advertising Mgr.; Juanita Brodie, Circulation Mgr.; Terri Pilkerton, Advertising Sales Rep. **ISSN:** 0735-7044. **Subscription Rates:** $90 members; $181 nonmembers; $362 institutions. **Remarks:** Accepts advertising.
Ad Rates: BW: $175 **Circ:** ‡1,850

5399 Biometrics
The International Biometric Society
1444 I Street NW, Ste. 700 Phone: (202)712-9050
Washington, DC 20005-2210 Fax: (202)216-9646
Publisher E-mail: ibs@bostromdc.com

Statistical methodology journal. **Founded:** Feb. 1945. **Freq:** Quarterly. **Print Method:** Letterpress and offset. **Trim Size:** 6 7/8 x 10 1/4. **Cols./Page:** 1. **Col. Width:** 56 nonpareils. **Col. Depth:** 112 agate lines. **Key Personnel:** Charles McGrath, Contact, phone (202)712-9025, cmcgrath@bostromdc.com. **ISSN:** 0006-341X. **Subscription Rates:** $110 individuals. **Remarks:** Color advertising not accepted.
Ad Rates: BW: $635 **Circ:** ‡8,500

5400 BioScience
American Institute of Biological Sciences
1444 Eye St. NW, Ste. 200 Phone: (202)628-1500
Washington, DC 20005 Fax: (202)628-1509
Free: (800)992-2427
Publication E-mail: bioscience@aibs.org

Review journal for biologists, containing articles, book reviews, reviews, features, and announcements. **Founded:** Jan. 1951. **Freq:** Monthly. **Print Method:** Offset. **Trim Size:** 8 1/8 x 10 7/8. **Cols./Page:** 3. **Col. Width:** 27 nonpareils. **Col. Depth:** 133 agate lines. **Key Personnel:** Rebecca Chasan, Editor. **ISSN:** 0006-3568. **Subscription Rates:** $70 individuals; $195 institutions; $12.50 single issue. **Remarks:** Advertising accepted; rates available upon request. **URL:** http://www.aibs.org/bioscience.html.
Circ: Paid ‡9,000
Non-paid ‡402

5401 B'nai B'rith International Jewish Monthly
B'nai B'rith
1640 Rhode Island Ave. NW Phone: (202)857-6600
Washington, DC 20036 Fax: (202)296-1092
Publisher E-mail: ijm@bnaibrith.org

Jewish family interest magazine. **Founded:** 1886. **Freq:** 6/year. **Print Method:** Offset. **Trim Size:** 8 1/2 x 11. **Cols./Page:** 3. **Col. Width:** 28 nonpareils. **Col. Depth:** 140 agate lines. **Key Personnel:** Eric Rozenman, Executive Editor, phone (202)857-6646, erozenman@bnaibrith.org; Stacey Free, Managing Editor, phone (202)857-2708. **ISSN:** 0279-3415. **Subscription Rates:** $2 single issue. **Remarks:** Accepts advertising. **Available Online. URL:** http://bnaibrith.org/ijm. **Alt. Formats:** Microform.
Ad Rates: GLR: $7.58 **Circ:** Paid ‡169,434
BW: $3,106 Non-paid ‡2,042
4C: $5,016

5402 Braille Book Review
National Library Service for the Blind and Physically Handicapped
1291 Taylor St., NW Phone: (202)707-5100
Washington, DC 20542 Fax: (202)707-0712
Free: (800)424-8567
Publisher E-mail: nls@loc.gov

Bibliography of publications for the visually and physically handicapped (braille and large print). **Founded:** 1932. **Freq:** Bimonthly. **Print Method:** Offset. **Trim Size:** 10 3/8 x 8 5/8. **Cols./Page:** 2. **Col. Width:** 42 nonpareils. **Col. Depth:** 99 agate lines. **ISSN:** 0006-873X. **Subscription Rates:** Free to registered patrons of NLS. **Remarks:** Advertising not accepted. **Available Online. Alt. Formats:** Braille; Diskette.
Circ: Non-paid ‡15,000

5403 Braille Forum
American Council of the Blind
1155 15th St. NW, Ste. 720 Phone: (202)467-5081
Washington, DC 20005 Fax: (202)467-5085
Free: (800)424-8666
Publisher E-mail: info@acb.org

Magazine reporting on news of the American Council of the Blind. **Founded:** 1961. **Freq:** Monthly. **Key Personnel:** Nolan Crabb, Editor, ncrabb@erols.com. **Subscription Rates:** Free for individuals in US; $25 for companies & overseas members. **Remarks:** Advertising not accepted. **URL:** http://www.acb.org. **Alt. Formats:** Audio tape; Braille; Diskette; Large-print.
Circ: Non-paid 22,000

5404 Broadcasting and Cable
Cahners Publishing Co.
Entertainment Division Phone: (202)659-2340
1705 DeSales St. NW Fax: (202)429-0651
Washington, DC 20036
News magazine covering The Fifth Estate (radio, TV, cable, and satellite), and the regulatory commissions involved. **Founded:** 1931. **Freq:** Weekly. **Print Method:** Offset. **Trim Size:** 7 7/8 x 10 1/2. **Cols./Page:** 3. **Col. Width:** 13 picas. **Col. Depth:** 9 3/4 inches. **Key Personnel:** Donald V. West, Editor; Harry Jessell, Exec. Editor. **ISSN:** 0007-2028. **Subscription Rates:** $129 individuals; $4.95 single issue. **Remarks:** Accepts advertising. **URL:** http://www.broadcastingcable.com. **Formerly**: Broadcasting (1992).
Ad Rates: BW: $5,960 **Circ:** Paid ★25,752
4C: $8,010 Non-paid ★10,151

5405 The Brookings Review
Brookings Institution Press
1775 Massashusetts Ave. NW Phone: (202)797-6000
Washington, DC 20036 Fax: (202)797-6004
Free: (800)275-1447
Publication E-mail: review@brook.edu
Publisher E-mail: BIBOOKS@BROOK.EDU

Magazine presenting to a general audience, artcles on economics, foreign policy gonernmental and business. **Founded:** 1982. **Freq:** Quarterly. **Print Method:** Sheetfed offset. **Trim Size:** 8 1/2 x 11. **Cols./Page:** 2. **Col. Width:** 20.5 picas. **Col. Depth:** 58 picas. **Key Personnel:** Brenda B. Szittya, Editor, bszittya@brook.edu; Robert L. Faherty, Publisher; Jill Bernstein, Marketing Advisor, phone (202)797-6254, fax (202)797-6195. **ISSN:** 0745-1253. **Subscription Rates:** Free to qualified subscribers; $17.95 individuals; $24.95 other countries. **Remarks:** Accepts advertising.
Ad Rates: BW: $2,250 **Circ:** Paid ‡6,000
4C: $3,500 Controlled ‡10,000

5406 Builder
Hanley-Wood, Inc.
1 Thomas Circle, Ste. 600 Phone: (202)452-0800
Washington, DC 20005 Fax: (202)785-1974

Magazine covering housing and construction industry. **Subtitle:** The Magazine of the National Association of Home Builders. **Founded:** 1947. **Freq:** Monthly. **Print Method:** Offset. **Trim Size:** 8 x 10 1/2. **Key Personnel:** Mike Tucker, Executive V.P., Group Publisher, mtucker@hanley-wood.com; Warren Nesbitt, Publisher, wnesbitt@hanley-wood.com; Boyce Thompson, Editor-in-Chief, bthompso@hanley-wood.com. **ISSN:** 0744-1193. **Subscription Rates:** $29.95 individuals. **Remarks:** Accepts advertising. **URL:** http://www.builderonline.com. **Alt. Formats:** CD-ROM.
Ad Rates: BW: $11,565 **Circ:** Paid 194,000
4C: $14,030 Controlled 30,000
PCI: $345

5407 Building Products
Hanley-Wood, Inc.
1 Thomas Cir., Ste. 600 Phone: (202)736-3301
Washington, DC 20005 Fax: (202)785-1974

Trade magazine for the home-building industry and allied fields. **Founded:** Mar. 1990. **Freq:** Quarterly. **Print Method:** Web offset. **Trim Size:** 11 x 14. **Cols./Page:** 4. **Key Personnel:** Jean Dimeo, Editor. **ISSN:** 1055-0216. **Subscription Rates:** Free to qualified subscribers. **Remarks:** Advertising accepted; rates available upon request. **URL:** http://www.builderonline.com. **Alt. Formats:** CD-ROM.
Circ: Controlled ‡70,000

5408 Bulletin of the American Astronomical Society
American Institute of Physics (AIP)
2000 Florida Ave. NW, Ste. 400 Phone: (202)328-2010
Washington, DC 20009-1231 Fax: (202)234-2560
Publication E-mail: aas@aas.org
Publisher E-mail: subs@aip.org

Journal presenting abstracts of meeting papers and annual reports from observatories. **Founded:** 1968. **Freq:** Quarterly. **Print Method:** Offset. **Trim Size:** 8 1/2 x 11. **Cols./Page:** 2. **Col. Width:** 40 nonpareils. **Col. Depth:** 138 agate lines. **Key Personnel:** R.M. Milkey, Editor. **ISSN:** 0002-7537. **Subscription Rates:** $50. **Remarks:** Advertising not accepted. **Available Online. URL:** http://www.aas.org/publications/baas/baas.html.
Circ: ‡1,665

5409 The Business Advocate
U.S. Chamber of Commerce
1615 H St. NW Phone: (202)463-5460
Washington, DC 20062-2000 Fax: (202)463-3114

Magazine reporting economic and business trends affecting the national business community and the economy. Supplement to Nation's Business. **Founded:** 1926. **Freq:** Bimonthly. **Print Method:** Offset. **Trim Size:** 8 x 10 3/4. **Cols./Page:** 3. **Col. Width:** 2 1/4 inches. **Col. Depth:** 10 inches. **Key Personnel:** Mary McElveen, Editor; Bob Gotshall, Advertising Dir. **Subscription Rates:** $50. **Remarks:** Accepts advertising.
Ad Rates: BW: $6,300 **Circ:** 200,000
4C: $9,450

5410 Business Economics
National Association for Business Economics
1233 20th St., Ste. 505 Phone: (202)463-6223
Washington, DC 20036 Fax: (202)463-6239
Publisher E-mail: nabe@nabe.com

Professional journal of the National Association of Business

Economists covering topics such as macro and microeconomics, monetary and fiscal policy, business forecasting, international economics, and deregulation. **Founded:** 1965. **Freq:** Quarterly. **Print Method:** Sheetfed offset. **Trim Size:** 8 1/2 x 11. **Cols./Page:** 2. **Col. Width:** 40 nonpareils. **Col. Depth:** 138 agate lines. **Key Personnel:** Edmund A. Mennis, Editor, edmennis@instanet.com; Susan Doolittle, Advertising Mgr., doolittle@nabe.com. **ISSN:** 0007-666X. **Subscription Rates:** $55 individuals; $70 other countries; $18 single issue. **Remarks:** Accepts advertising. **URL:** http://www.nabe.com.
Ad Rates: BW: $550 **Circ:** ‡4,700

5411 CAQ (Covert Action Quarterly)
C. A. Publications, Inc.
1500 Massachusetts Ave. NW, No. 732 Phone: (202)331-9763
Washington, DC 20005 Fax: (202)331-9751
Publication E-mail: caq@igc.org

Political analysis magazine researching and documenting U.S. activities worldwide. **Founded:** 1978. **Freq:** Quarterly. **Print Method:** Web. **Trim Size:** 8 1/2 x 11. **Cols./Page:** 2. **Col. Width:** 3 1/2 inches. **Col. Depth:** 9 1/2 inches. **Key Personnel:** Terry Allen, Editor. **ISSN:** 0275-309X. **Subscription Rates:** $22 individuals; $38 two years; $27 Canada and Mexico; $48 two years Canada and Mexico; $35 other countries; $63 two years other countries. **Remarks:** Advertising accepted; rates available upon request. **URL:** http://www.mediafilter.com. **Alt. Formats:** Microfiche. **Formerly:** Covert Action Information Bulletin; Covert Action Quarterly.
Circ: ‡10,000

5412 Caring
National Association for Home Care
228 Seventh St. Phone: (202)547-7424
Washington, DC 20003 Fax: (202)547-3540
Publication E-mail: caring@nahc.org; caring@nahs.org

Journal concerning home care. **Founded:** Oct. 1982. **Freq:** Monthly. **Trim Size:** 8 1/8 x 10 7/8. **Cols./Page:** 2. **Col. Width:** 3 3/8 inches. **Col. Depth:** 9 1/2 inches. **Key Personnel:** Heather Dittbrenner, Senior Editor; Nancy Hoffmann, Managing Editor; Chris Adams, Advertising Dir. **ISSN:** 0738-467X. **Subscription Rates:** $45 individuals. **Remarks:** Accepts advertising. **Online:** National Association for Home Care Homepage. **Formerly:** National Association for Home Care.
Ad Rates: BW: $1,235 **Circ:** Paid 7,000
4C: $1,735

5413 Caring People
National Association for Home Care
228 Seventh St. Phone: (202)547-7424
Washington, DC 20003 Fax: (202)547-3540

Magazine spotlighting individuals who care and service others. **Founded:** 1986. **Freq:** Annual. **Print Method:** Offset. **Trim Size:** 8 1/8 x 10 7/8. **Cols./Page:** 3. **Col. Width:** 2 1/8 inches. **Col. Depth:** 9 1/4 inches. **Key Personnel:** Val Halamandaris, Publisher; Heather Dittbrenner, Editor. **ISSN:** 1041-4959. **Subscription Rates:** $7.50 single issue. **Remarks:** Advertising accepted; rates available upon request.
Circ: (Not Reported)

5414 The Carpenter
United Brotherhood of Carpenters and Joiners of America, AFL-CIO
101 Constitution Ave. NW Phone: (202)546-6206
Washington, DC 20001 Fax: (202)547-8979

Official magazine of the Carpenters' Union. **Founded:** 1881. **Freq:** Bimonthly. **Print Method:** Offset. **Trim Size:** 8 5/16 x 11. **Cols./Page:** 3. **Col. Width:** 13 picas. **Col. Depth:** 58 picas. **Key Personnel:** Andris Silins, Editor; David Patterson, Advertising Mgr., dpatter867@aol.com; Monte Byers, Communication Dir.; Dave Ransom, Managing Editor. **ISSN:** 0008-6843. **Subscription Rates:** $10 individuals; $2 single issue. **Remarks:** Accepts advertising.
Ad Rates: BW: $11,400 **Circ:** 473,104
4C: $19,950

5415 Catering Industry Employee
Hotel Employees and Restaurant Employees International Union
1219 28th St. NW Phone: (202)393-4373
Washington, DC 20007-3389 Fax: (202)965-2958

Trade journal for culinary and hospitality workers. Official publication of the Hotel Employees and Restaurant Employees International Union. **Founded:** 1893. **Freq:** Bimonthly. **Print Method:** Offset. **Trim Size:** 8 1/2 x 11. **Cols./Page:** 3. **Col. Width:** 13 picas. **Col. Depth:** 57 inches. **Key Personnel:** Ted T. Hansen, Editor; Donald J. Byers, Managing Editor. **ISSN:** 0008-7815. **Subscription Rates:** $5 individuals. **Remarks:** Advertising not accepted. **URL:** http://www.hereunion.org.
Circ: ‡215,000

5416 Cathedral Age
Washington National Cathedral
Massachusetts & Wisconsin Aves. NW Phone: (202)537-5681
Fax: (202)364-6600
Washington, DC 20016-5098
Publication E-mail: cathedral_ age@cathedral.org

Magazine on activities at the Washington National Cathedral and other general religious topics. **Founded:** 1925. **Freq:** Quarterly. **Print Method:** Offset. **Trim Size:** 8 1/2 x 11. **Cols./Page:** 3. **Col. Width:** 13 inches. **Col. Depth:** 58 inches. **Key Personnel:** Craig Stapert, Editor, cstapert@cathedral.org. **ISSN:** 0008-7874. **Subscription Rates:** $15 individuals; $3.75 single issue. **Remarks:** Advertising not accepted. **Alt. Formats:** Microform.
Circ: ‡28,800

5417 The Catholic Biblical Quarterly
Catholic Biblical Association of America
Catholic University of America Phone: (202)319-5519
Leahy Hall, Rm. 297 Fax: (202)3[illegible]-1799
Washington, DC 20064
Publisher E-mail: cua-cathbib@cua.edu

Magazine presenting scholarly investigation of Scripture and related fields, including exegesis, biblical theology, archeology, textual and literary criticism, Near Eastern history, and comparative religion as related to the Bible. **Founded:** 1939. **Freq:** Quarterly. **Print Method:** Offset. **Trim Size:** 6 x 9. **Cols./Page:** 1. **Col. Width:** 54 nonpareils. **Col. Depth:** 102 agate lines. **Key Personnel:** Rev. Aelred Cody, Editor; Joseph Jensen, Advertising Mgr., jensen@cua.ebll. **ISSN:** 0008-7912. **Subscription Rates:** $25 individuals. **Remarks:** Color advertising not accepted.
Ad Rates: BW: $175 **Circ:** Paid ‡4,200
Non-paid ‡56

5418 The Catholic Historical Review
CUA Press
240 Leahy Catholic University Phone: (202)319-5052
Washington, DC 20064 Fax: (202)319-4985

Magazine on all areas of church history. **Subtitle:** Official Organ of the American Catholic Historical Assn. **Founded:** Apr. 1915. **Freq:** Quarterly. **Print Method:** Offset. **Trim Size:** 6 x 9. **Cols./Page:** 1. **Col. Width:** 53 nonpareils. **Col. Depth:** 93 agate lines. **Key Personnel:** Rev. Robert Trisco, Editor, phone (202)319-5079, fax (202)319-4967, trisco@cua.edu; Gordon A. Conner, Business Mgr., phone (202)319-5052, fax (202)319-4985, conner@cua.edu. **ISSN:** 0008-8080. **Subscription Rates:** $40 individuals & institutions; $10 single issue. **Remarks:** Accepts advertising.
Ad Rates: BW: $150 **Circ:** Paid ‡1,926
Non-paid ‡166

5419 Catholic University Law Review
Columbus School of Law - Catholic University of America Phone: (202)319-5159
Fax: (202)319-4459
2600 John McCormick Rd.
Washington, DC 20064
Journal of legal scholarship. **Founded:** 1950. **Freq:** Quarterly. **Print Method:** Letterpress. **Cols./Page:** 1. **Col. Width:** 60 nonpareils. **Col. Depth:** 122 agate lines. **Key Personnel:** Siobhan Rausch, Executive editor; Ann Boeckman, Editor-in-Chief. **ISSN:** 0008-8390. **Subscription Rates:** $28 individuals. **Online:** Westlan; LEXIS-NEXIS.
Ad Rates: BW: $125 **Circ:** ‡1,400

5420 Catholic Woman
National Council of Catholic Women
1275 K St. NW, Ste. 975 Phone: (202)682-0334
Washington, DC 20005 Fax: (202)682-0338
Free: (800)506-9407
Publisher E-mail: nccw@us.net

Magazine informing membership about programs and policies. **Founded:** 1973. **Freq:** Bimonthly. **Trim Size:** 8 1/2 x 11. **Cols./Page:** 3. **Key Personnel:** Annette Kane, Exec. Dir.; Marie Wood, Editor. **ISSN:** 0270-3610. **Subscription Rates:** $12. **Remarks:** Advertising not accepted.
Circ: 10,500

5421 Change
Heldref Publications
Helen Dwight Reid Educational Foundation Phone: (202)296-6267
Fax: (202)296-5149
1319 18th St. NW
Washington, DC 20036-1802
Free: (800)365-9753
Publication E-mail: ch@heldref.org
Publisher E-mail: revu@heldref.org

Magazine dealing with contemporary issues in higher learning. **Subtitle:** The Magazine of Higher Learning. **Founded:** 1969. **Freq:** Bimonthly. **Print Method:** Offset. Uses mats. **Trim Size:** 8 1/8 x 10 7/8. **Cols./Page:** 3. **Col. Width:** 2 1/4 inches. **Col. Depth:** 9 3/4 inches. **Key Personnel:** Nanette Wiese, Managing Editor; Douglas Kirkpatrick, Director; Grant Williams, Advertising Production Mgr., advertise@heldref.org; Lorraine Sekera, Associate Editor; Fred Huber, Circulation Mgr., subscribe@heldref.org; Jean Kline, Fulfillment Mgr., subscribe@heldref.org. **ISSN:** 0009-1383. **Subscription Rates:** $40 individuals; $82 institutions; $15 out of country add; $14 single issue. **Remarks:** Accepts advertising. **Online:** EBSCO; Infonautics; Information Access; Institute of Scientific Information; UMI; Responsive DataBase Services, Inc. **URL:** http://www.heldref.org. **Alt. Formats:** CD-ROM.
Ad Rates: BW: $2,150 **Circ:** Combined ‡15,000
4C: $3,370

5422 Chemical Regulation Reporter
Bureau of National Affairs, Inc. (BNA)
1231 25th St. NW Phone: (202)452-4323
Washington, DC 20037 Fax: (202)452-7773
Free: (800)372-1033
Publisher E-mail: bnaplus@bna.com

Newspaper covering administrative, regulatory, legislative, and developments affecting use of chemicals. **Founded:** 197[illegible]. **Freq:** [illegible]ekly. **Key Personnel:** Bernard Chabel, Managing Editor; Martha Canan, S[illegible]or Copy Editor. **Re**[illegible] Advertising not accepted.
Ci[illegible] (Not Reported)

5423 Chemical Waste Litigation Reporter
1601 Connecticut Ave., NW, No. 602
Washington, DC 20009
Publication E-mail: lawreport@aol.com

Professional journal covering environmental law. Available in print format or via e-mail. **Founded:** 1982. **Freq:** Monthly. **Print Method:** Photo offset. **Trim Size:** 8 1/2 x 11. **Cols./Page:** 2. **Col. Width:** 3 1/2 inches. **Col. Depth:** 8 inches. **Key Personnel:** Susan Bernard, Editor. **ISSN:** 0889-0633. **Subscription Rates:** $1,700 individuals. **Remarks:** Advertising not accepted. **Former name:** Chemical and Radiation Waste Litigation Reporter.
Circ: (Not Reported)

5424 ChemMatters
American Chemical Society
1155 16th St. NW Phone: (202)872-4505
Washington, DC 20036 Fax: (202)872-8727
Free: (800)227-5558
Publication E-mail: chemmatters@acs.org
Publisher E-mail: edit.cen@acs.org

Magazine for high school chemistry students. **Subtitle:** Demystifying Everyday Chemistry. **Founded:** Feb. 1983. **Freq:** Quarterly. **Trim Size:** 8 1/2 x 11. **Cols./Page:** 3. **Key Personnel:** Michael Shea, Editor, phone (202)872-6341, fax (202)833-7732. **ISSN:** 0736-4687. **Subscription Rates:** $10 individuals. **Remarks:** Advertising not accepted. **URL:** http://www.chemcenter.org.
Circ: Paid ⊕40,000

5425 Child Welfare
Transaction Publishers
440 1st St. NW, Ste. 310 Phone: (202)638-2952
Washington, DC 20001 Fax: (202)638-4004
Publication E-mail: journal@cwla.org
Publisher E-mail: trans@transactionpub.com

Child welfare services journal. **Subtitle:** Journal of Policy, Practice, and Program. **Founded:** 1920. **Freq:** Bimonthly. **Print Method:** Offset. **Trim Size:** 6 x 9. **Cols./Page:** 1. **Col. Width:** 60 nonpareils. **Col. Depth:** 110 agate lines. **Key Personnel:** Carl Schoenberg, Senior Editor; Eve Malakoff-Klein, Managing Editor. **ISSN:** 0009-4021. **Subscription Rates:** $66 individuals two years; $90 institutions; $98 individuals; $122 institutions, other countries; $120 individuals; $156 two years institutions; $42 students.
Ad Rates: GLR: $12 **Circ:** ‡12,000
BW: $525
PCI: $90

5426 Children's Voice
Child Welfare League of America, Inc. (CWLA)
440 1st St. NW, 3rd Fl. Phone: (202)638-2952
Washington, DC 20001-2085 Fax: (202)638-4004
Free: (800)407-6273
Publication E-mail: voice@cwla.org
Publisher E-mail: books@cwla.org

Magazine providing information on child welfare programs and policy developments. **Founded:** 1991. **Freq:** Quarterly. **Print Method:** Sheetfed. **Trim Size:** 8 1/2 x 11. **Cols./Page:** 2. **Key Personnel:** Steve Boehm, Editor, phone (202)942-0326; Tiffany Lindsley, Advertising Mgr., phone (202)942-0318, tlindsle@cwla.org. **ISSN:** 1057-736X. **Subscription Rates:** $50. **Remarks:** Accepts advertising.
Ad Rates: BW: $1,010 **Circ:** 15,000
4C: $1,660

5427 The China Business Review
U.S. China Business Council
1818 N. St. NW, Ste. 200 Phone: (202)429-0340
Washington, DC 20036 Fax: (202)833-9027
Publication E-mail: info@uschina.org
Publisher E-mail: info@uschina.org

International business magazine. **Subtitle:** The American Journal of Business in China & Hong Kong. **Founded:** Jan. 1974. **Freq:** Bimonthly. **Print Method:** Offset. **Trim Size:** 8 1/2 x 11. **Cols./Page:** 3. **Col. Width:** 26 nonpareils. **Col. Depth:** 137 agate lines. **Key Personnel:** Gregory S. Heslin, Business Mgr., fax (202)833-9027, gheslin@uschina.org; Catherine Gelb, Editor-in-Chief, cgelb@uschina.org. **ISSN:** 0163-7169. **Subscription Rates:** $99 individuals; $150 other countries. **Remarks:** Accepts advertising. **Online:** Data Times; CCA; Chamber World Network; Lexis-Nexis; Infonantics. **URL:** http://www.uschina.org/cbr. **Alt. Formats:** Mailing labels. **Formerly:** The China Business Forum.
Ad Rates: GLR: $10 **Circ:** Paid ‡5,600
BW: $1,850 Non-paid ‡100
4C: $3,400

5428 Christian Social Action: General Board of Church and Society, The United Methodist Church
General Board of Church and Society, The United Methodist Church
100 Maryland Ave. NE Phone: (202)488-5621
Washington, DC 20002 Fax: (202)488-1617
Free: (800)967-0880
Publication E-mail: sboyant@umc-gbcs.org

Magazine on Christian social issues. **Founded:** 1973. **Freq:** Monthly. **Print Method:** Web offset. **Trim Size:** 8 1/2 x 11. **Cols./Page:** 2. **Col. Width:** 28 nonpareils. **Col. Depth:** 100 agate lines. **Key Personnel:** Lee Ranck, Editor, lranck@umc-gbcs.org. **ISSN:** 0897-0459. **Subscription Rates:** $15 individuals. **Remarks:** Accepts advertising. **Formerly:** Engage, Social Action.
Ad Rates: BW: $325 **Circ:** Paid ‡2,000
Non-paid ‡1,000

5429 The Chronicle of Higher Education
1255 23rd St. NW, Ste. 700 Phone: (202)466-1000
Washington, DC 20037-1125 Fax: (202)296-2691

Higher education magazine (tabloid). **Founded:** Nov. 23, 1966. **Freq:** Weekly. **Print Method:** Offset. **Trim Size:** 11 3/8 x 15. **Cols./Page:** 5. **Col. Width:** 23 nonpareils. **Col. Depth:** 189 agate lines. **Key Personnel:** Corbin Gwaltney, Editor; Robinette D. Ross, Publisher. **ISSN:** 0009-5982. **Subscription Rates:** $75 individuals; $3.25 single issue. **Remarks:** Accepts advertising. **Online:** Nexis. **URL:** http://chronicle.com.
Ad Rates: BW: $4,940 **Circ:** Paid ★**94,859**
4C: $7,805
PCI: $52.70

5430 The Chronicle of Philanthropy
The Chronicle of Philanthrophy
1255 23rd St. NW, Ste. 700 Phone: (202)466-1200
Washington, DC 20037 Fax: (202)466-2078

Magazine covering fundraising, philanthropy, and non-profit organizations. Includes information on tax rulings, new grants, and statistics, reports on grant makers, and profiles of foundations. **Subtitle:** The Newspaper of the Non-Profit World. **Founded:** 1988. **Freq:** Biweekly. **Print Method:** Offset. **Trim Size:** 11 3/8 x 15. **Cols./Page:** 5. **Col. Width:** 1 7/8 inches. **Col. Depth:** 15 inches. **Key Personnel:** Stacy Palmer, Managing Editor; Robinette Davis Ross, Publisher. **ISSN:** 1040-676X. **Subscription Rates:** $67.50 individuals. **Remarks:** Accepts advertising. **URL:** http://www.philanthropy.com. **Alt. Formats:** CD-ROM.
Ad Rates: BW: $4,070 **Circ:** Paid ★**39,925**
4C: $5,165

5431 Church & State
Americans United for Separation of Church & State
1816 Jefferson Place, N.W. Phone: (202)466-3234
Washington, DC 20036 Fax: (202)466-2587
Publication E-mail: americansunited@au.org
Publisher E-mail: americansunited@au.org

Magazine on church-state relations. **Founded:** 1948. **Freq:** 11/year. **Print Method:** Offset. **Trim Size:** 8 3/8 x 10 7/8. **Cols./Page:** 3. **Col. Width:** 40 nonpareils. **Col. Depth:** 136 agate lines. **Key Personnel:** Joseph L. Conn, Editor; Barry Lynn, Publisher; Robert Boston, Assist. editor. **ISSN:** 0009-6334. **Subscription Rates:** $18 individuals; $2 single issue; $25 other countries (execpt Canada & Mexico). **Remarks:** Advertising not accepted. **URL:** http://www.au.org.
Circ: Paid ‡33,000
Controlled ‡2,600

5432 Civilization
666 Pennsylvania Ave. SE, Ste. 303 Phone: (202)546-6600
Fax: (202)546-6632
Washington, DC 20003
Publication E-mail: letters@civmag.com

Magazine for members of the Library of Congress. **Founded:** Nov. 1994. **Freq:** Bimonthly. **Key Personnel:** Sara Sklaroff, Managing Editor. **Remarks:** Advertising accepted; rates available upon request.
Circ: Paid ★**281,721**

5433 Class Action Reports
Class Actions Reports, Inc.
4900 Massachusetts Ave. NW, Ste. 230 Phone: (202)364-1031
Fax: (202)363-6912
Washington, DC 20016
Publisher E-mail: ClassActionRep@erols.com

Professional journal covering state and federal class action decisions in all areas of law. **Founded:** 1972. **Freq:** Bimonthly. **Print Method:** Offset. **Key Personnel:** Beverly C. Moore, Jr., Editor; Stuart J. Logan, Assoc. Editor; Deanna I. Moore, Business Mgr. **ISSN:** 0746-7168. **Subscription Rates:** $350 individuals; $50 single issue. **Remarks:** Accepts advertising. **URL:** http://www.ClassActionReports.com.
Ad Rates: BW: $1,200 **Circ:** Controlled 700

5434 The Clearing House
Heldref Publications
Helen Dwight Reid Educational Foundation Phone: (202)296-6267
Fax: (202)296-5149
1319 18th St. NW
Washington, DC 20036-1802
Free: (800)365-9753
Publication E-mail: tch@heldref.org
Publisher E-mail: revu@heldref.org

Educational journal of interest to middle level and high school teachers and administrators. **Subtitle:** A Journal of Educational Research, Controversy, & Practices. **Founded:** 1925. **Freq:** Bimonthly. **Print Method:** Offset. **Trim Size:** 8 1/2 x 11. **Cols./Page:** 2. **Col. Width:** 3 1/2 inches. **Col. Depth:** 10 inches. **Key Personnel:** Grant Williams, Advertising Production Mgr., advertise@heldref.org; Douglas Kirkpatrick, Director; Fred Huber, Circulation Mgr., subscribe@heldfref.org; Jean Kline, Fulfillment Mgr., subscribe@heldref.org; Judy Cusick, Managing Editor. **ISSN:** 0009-8655. **Subscription Rates:** $35 individuals; $64 institutions add $15 for foreign postage. **Remarks:** Accepts advertising. **Online:** EBSCO; Infonautics; Information Access; UMI. **URL:** http://www.heldref.org/. **Alt. Formats:** CD-ROM.
Ad Rates: BW: $525 **Circ:** ‡2,000

5435 Clinical and Diagnostic Laboratory Immunology
American Society for Microbiology
1325 Massachusetts Ave. NW Phone: (202)737-3600
Washington, DC 20005 Fax: (202)942-9342
Publication E-mail: editorialservices.jmls@asmusa.org
Publisher E-mail: journals@asmusa.org

Scholarly journal covering clinical laboratory immunology for medical professionals. **Founded:** Jan. 1994. **Freq:** Bimonthly. **Trim Size:** 8 1/4 x 11. **Key Personnel:** Steven D. Douglas, M.D., Editor-in-Chief. **ISSN:** 1071-412X. **Subscription Rates:** $51 members U.S.; $15 single issue members. **Remarks:** Accepts advertising. **URL:** http://www.journals.asm.org. **Alt. Formats:** CD-ROM.
Ad Rates: BW: $900 **Circ:** Paid 1,360
4C: $1800

5436 Clinical Laboratory News
American Association for Clinical Chemistry
2101 L St. NW, Ste. 202 Phone: (202)857-0717
Washington, DC 20037-1526 Fax: (202)887-5093
Free: (800)892-1400
Publication E-mail: cln@aacc.org
Publisher E-mail: info@aacc.org

Scholarly magazine providing current news in the field of clinical laboratory science. **Subtitle:** The Primary Source for the Clinical Laboratorian. **Founded:** 1974. **Freq:** Monthly. **Print Method:** Offset. **Trim Size:** 10 7/8 x 16 1/4. **Cols./Page:** 4. **Col. Width:** 28 nonpareils. **Col. Depth:** 210 agate lines. **Key Personnel:** Nancy Sasavage, Ph.D., Editor. **ISSN:** 0161-9640. **Subscription Rates:** $30; $4 single issue; $65 out of country. **Remarks:** Accepts advertising. **Available Online. URL:** http://www.aacc.org. **Formerly:** Clinical Chemistry News (1993).
Ad Rates: BW: $3,750 **Circ:** Controlled 25,000
4C: $4,700

5437 Clinical Microbiology Reviews
American Society for Microbiology
1325 Massachusetts Ave. NW Phone: (202)737-3600
Washington, DC 20005 Fax: (202)942-9342
Publisher E-mail: journals@asmusa.org

Journal reviewing work in clinical microbiology field. **Founded:** 1988. **Freq:** Quarterly. **Print Method:** Offset. **Trim Size:** 8 1/4 x 11. **Cols./Page:** 2. **Col. Width:** 3 1/4 inches. **Col. Depth:** 9 1/2 inches. **Key Personnel:** Betty A. Forbes, Editor-in-Chief. **ISSN:** 0893-8512. **Subscription Rates:** $40 members U.S.; $53 members Europe; $54 members Latin Ameria; $55 members ROW; $146 nonmembers U.S.; $168 nonmembers Europe; $169 nonmembers Latin America; $170 nonmembers ROW. **Remarks:** Accepts advertising. **URL:** http://www.journals.asm.org. **Alt. Formats:** CD-ROM.
Ad Rates: BW: $1,175 **Circ:** ‡9,412
4C: $2,350

5438 Club Director
National Club Association
1 Lafayette Centre Phone: (202)822-9822
1120 20th St. NW, No. 725 Fax: (202)822-9808
Washington, DC 20036
Free: (800)625-6221

Private club magazine for members. **Subtitle:** The Magazine of the National Club Association (NCA). **Founded:** 1962. **Freq:** Bimonthly. **Print Method:** Litho offset. **Trim Size:** 8 1/2 x 10 7/8. **Cols./Page:** 3. **Col. Width:** 2 5/16 inches. **Col. Depth:** 7 inches. **Key Personnel:** Mary Barnes Embody, Editor, embody@natlclub.org; George Evanko, Advertising Dir., evanko@natlclub.org. **ISSN:** 1050-8600. **Subscription Rates:** $18 individuals; $3 single issue. **Remarks:** Accepts advertising. **URL:** http://www.natlclub.org. **Former name:** Perspective.
Ad Rates: BW: $1,150 **Circ:** Controlled ⊕**9,058**

5439 Cold War International History Project
1000 Jefferson Dr. SW Phone: (202)357-2967
Washington, DC 20560 Fax: (202)357-4439

Journal covering historical war issues. **Founded:** 1992. **Freq:** Semiannual. **Key Personnel:** Christian Ostermann, Editor. **Subscription Rates:** Free to qualified subscribers. **Remarks:** Advertising not accepted. **URL:** http://www.cw.hp.si.edu.
Circ: (Not Reported)

5440 College Mathematics Journal
Mathematical Association of America
1529 18th St. NW Phone: (202)387-5200
Washington, DC 20036 Free: (800)741-9415
Publisher E-mail: epedreir@nadd.org

Journal providing articles for undergraduate college math students. **Freq:** 5/year. **Key Personnel:** Gerald Alexanderson, Editor; Elaine Sullivan, Advertising Mgr. **Subscription Rates:** $60 individuals. **Remarks:** Accepts advertising.
Ad Rates: BW: $360 **Circ:** (Not Reported)

5441 College Teaching
Heldref Publications
Helen Dwight Reid Educational Foundation Phone: (202)296-6267
Fax: (202)296-5149
1319 18th St. NW
Washington, DC 20036-1802
Free: (800)365-9753
Publication E-mail: ct@heldref.org
Publisher E-mail: revu@heldref.org

Journal covering faculty development for college teachers and administrators. **Founded:** 1953. **Freq:** Quarterly. **Print Method:** Offset. **Trim Size:** 8 1/2 x 11. **Cols./Page:** 2. **Col. Width:** 3 3/8 inches. **Col. Depth:** 9 1/2 inches. **Key Personnel:** Grant Williams, Production Mgr., advertis@heldref.org; Douglas Kirkpatrick, Director; Fred Huber, Circulation Mgr., subs@heldref.org; Jean Kline, Fulfillment Mgr. **ISSN:** 8756-7555. **Subscription Rates:** $33.50 individuals; $60 institutions; other countries add $13 postage. **Remarks:** Accepts advertising. **Online:** EBSCO; Infonautics; Information Access; UMI. **URL:** http://www.heldref.org. **Alt. Formats:** CD-ROM.
Ad Rates: BW: $300 **Circ:** Paid ‡1,945
4C: $395

5442 Command Information Package
Chief of Public Affairs
Command Information Unit Phone: (703)697-0050
1500 Army Pentagon 2D622 Fax: (703)697-5746
Washington, DC 20310-1500
Publisher E-mail: papaorg@meade-emh2.ftmeade.army.mil

Publication covering information of interest to Army officers, NCOs, and enlisted soldiers. Includes articles on aspects of Army life including professional development and personal affairs. **Freq:** 2/year. **Trim Size:** 8 x 11. **Key Personnel:** Willard K. Morris, Editor, morriwk@hgda.army.mil. **Subscription Rates:** Free.
Circ: Controlled 177,000

5443 Commodity Markets and the Developing Countries
The World Bank
1818 H St., NW Phone: (202)473-3854
Washington, DC 20433 Fax: (202)522-3564
Publisher E-mail: books@worldbank.org

Magazine analyzing the production, consumption, and trade patterns of certain commodities. Also details the current market trends for food, agricultural raw materials, metals and minerals, energy, and fertilizer. **Subtitle:** A World Bank Quarterly. **Founded:** Dec. 1993. **Freq:** Quarterly. **Trim Size:** 8 1/2 x 11. **Cols./Page:** 2. **Col. Width:** 16 inches. **Col. Depth:** 55 inches. **Key Personnel:** Antony Kamal Sayess, Contact, phone (202)473-2209, fax (202)522-2631. **ISSN:** 1020-0967. **Subscription Rates:** $150. **Remarks:** Advertising not accepted. **Available Online. URL:** http://www.worldbank.org.
Circ: Paid 350
Non-paid 600

5444 Communio-International Catholic Review
PO Box 4557 Phone: (202)526-0251
Washington, DC 20017 Fax: (202)526-1934
Publisher E-mail: communio@aol.com

Journal on theology, philosophy, and culture promoting authentic renewal within the Catholic Church. **Founded:** 1974. **Freq:** Quarterly. **Print Method:** Sheetfed offset. **Trim Size:** 6 x 9. **Key Personnel:** Dr. David L. Schindler, Editor. **ISSN:** 0094-2065. **Subscription Rates:** $27 individuals; $31 Canada; $35 other countries; $49 institutions. **Remarks:** Accepts advertising.
Ad Rates: BW: $300 **Circ:** Paid ‡2,500
Non-paid ‡150

5445 Community College Journal
American Association of Community Colleges (AACC)
1 Dupont Circle NW, Ste. 410 Phone: (202)728-0200
Washington, DC 20036 Fax: (202)223-9390
Free: (800)250-6557
Publisher E-mail: aaccpub@pmds.com

Educational magazine. **Founded:** Oct. 1930. **Freq:** Bimonthly. **Print Method:** Offset. **Trim Size:** 8 1/4 x 11. **Cols./Page:** 3. **Col. Width:** 26 nonpareils. **Col. Depth:** 130 agate lines. **Key Personnel:** James Roche, Sr. Editor, jroche@aacc.nche.edu. **ISSN:** 1067-1803. **Subscription Rates:** $28 individuals; $21 10+ to same address in U.S.; $36 other countries; $31 10+ to same address in other countries; $4 single issue. **Remarks:** Accepts advertising. **URL:** http://www.aacc.nche.edu.
Ad Rates: BW: $1,910 **Circ:** Paid ‡12,800
4C: $2,895 Controlled ‡21

5446 Computational Seismology
American Geophysical Union
2000 Florida Ave. NW Phone: (202)462-6900
Washington, DC 20009 Fax: (202)328-0566
Free: (800)966-2481
Publisher E-mail: service@agu.org

Journal covering Russian translations of applications of modern mathematics and computer science to seismology and related earth science studies. **ISSN:** 0733-5792. **Remarks:** Advertising not accepted.
Circ: (Not Reported)

5447 Computer Law Reporter
1601 Connecticut Ave., NW, No. 602 Phone: (202)462-5755
Fax: (202)328-2430
Washington, DC 20009
Publication E-mail: lawreport@aol.com
Publisher E-mail: lawreport@aol.com

Professional journal covering computer law, patent law, and trademark law. Available in print format or via e-mail. **Founded:** 1981. **Freq:** Monthly. **Print Method:** Photo offset. **Trim Size:** 8 1/2 x 11. **Cols./Page:** 2. **Col. Width:** 3 1/2 inches. **Col. Depth:** 8 inches. **Key Personnel:** John Noble, Editor. **ISSN:** 0739-7771. **Subscription Rates:** $1,600 individuals. **Remarks:** Advertising not accepted.
Circ: (Not Reported)

5448 Congress in Print
Congressional Quarterly
1414 22nd St. NW Phone: (202)887-8500
Washington, DC 20037 Fax: (800)380-3810
Free: (800)638-1710

News on Congressional documents. **Founded:** 1977. **Freq:** Weekly (Tues.). **Print Method:** Offset. **Trim Size:** 8 1/2 x 11. **Cols./Page:** 3. **Col. Width:** 29 nonpareils. **Col. Depth:** 140 agate lines. **Key Personnel:** Michele Hatty, Editor; Bob Merry, Publisher. **Subscription Rates:** $198 individuals. **Remarks:** Advertising not accepted. **Available Online. URL:** http://www.cq.com.
Circ: (Not Reported)

5449 Congressional Digest
Congressional Digest Corp.
3231 P St. NW Phone: (202)333-7332
Washington, DC 20007-2772 Fax: (202)625-6670

Unique "Pro & Con" analysis shows you both sides of important Congressional controversies. Topics recently covered include Chemical Weapons Control, Deficit Reduction and Affirmation Action. Annual subscription features 12 issues plus a free cumulative index spanning more than 15 years. **Founded:** 1921. **Freq:** 10/year. **Print Method:** Offset. **Trim Size:** 8 1/2 x 11. **Cols./Page:** 2. **Col. Width:** 42 nonpareils. **Col. Depth:** 140 agate lines. **Key Personnel:** Griff Thomas, President; Sarah Orrick, Editor; Page B. Robinson, Publisher; Madelyn Von Sternberg, Circulation Mgr. **ISSN:** 0010-5899. **Subscription Rates:** $45 individuals; $86 two years; $126 three year. **Remarks:** Accepts advertising.
Circ: (Not Reported)

5450 Conscience
Catholics for a Free Choice
1436 U St. NW, No. 301 Phone: (202)986-6093
Washington, DC 20009-3997
Publisher E-mail: cffc@igc.apc.org

Journal devoted to the exploration of reproductive health and gender issues, with a focus on ethics. **Subtitle:** A Newsjournal of Prochoice Catholic Opinion. **Founded:** 1980. **Freq:** Quarterly. **Print Method:** Web press. **Trim Size:** 8 1/4 x 10 1/2. **Cols./Page:** 3. **Col. Width:** 2 1/8 inches. **Col. Depth:** 9 inches. **Key Personnel:** Maggie Hume, Editor. **ISSN:** 0740-6835. **Subscription Rates:** $10. $3.50 single issue. **Remarks:** Advertising accepted; rates available upon request. **Alt. Formats:** Microform.
Circ: Combined 10,000

5451 Construction & Modernization Report
American Hotel & Motel Association
1201 New York Ave. NW, Ste. 600 Phone: (202)289-3100
Fax: (202)289-3199
Washington, DC 20005-3931
Publisher E-mail: infoctr@ahma.com

Lists new hotel/motel construction and renovation projects throughout the US and Canada. **Freq:** Monthly. **Key Personnel:** Karin Mastrangeld, Assoc. Dir., kmastraneglo@ahma.com. **Subscription Rates:** Membership only. **Remarks:** Advertising not accepted.
Circ: (Not Reported)

5452 CONSTRUCTOR
Associated General Contractors Information
1957 E St. NW Phone: (202)393-2040
Washington, DC 20006-5107 Fax: (202)628-7369

Magazine with information for contractors. **Subtitle:** The Construction Management Magazine. **Founded:** 1919. **Freq:** Monthly. **Print Method:** Web. **Trim Size:** 8 1/8 x 10 7/8. **Cols./Page:** 3. **Col. Width:** 24 nonpareils. **Col. Depth:** 119 agate lines. **Key Personnel:** Bob Herring, Editor, phone (202)383-2768, herringb@agc.org; Donald Scott, Publisher, phone (202)383-2755, scottd@agc.org; Rich Bohan, Production Mgr., phone (202)383-2752, bohanr@agc.org; Debbie Owens, Reader Service. **ISSN:** 0162-6191. **Subscription Rates:** $15 members; $135 nonmembers; $4 single issue. **Remarks:** Accepts advertising. **URL:** http://www.agc.org.
Ad Rates: GLR: $1.25 **Circ:** (Not Reported)
BW: $3,450
4C: $3,850

5453 Consulting Psychology Journal: Practice and Research
Educational Publishing Foundation
750 1st St. NE Phone: (202)336-5600
Washington, DC 20002-4242 Fax: (202)336-5568

Journal including theoretical/conceptual articles with implications for consulting, original research regarding consultation, reviews in specific areas of practice, and case studies. **Founded:** 1949. **Freq:** Quarterly. **Print Method:** Offset. **Trim Size:** 7 x 10. **Cols./Page:** 2. **Col. Width:** 20 picas. **Col. Depth:** 56 picas. **Key Personnel:** Richard Diedrich, Ph.D, Editor; Susan Knapp, Contact; Jodi Ashcraft, Contact. **ISSN:** 1061-4087. **Subscription Rates:** $30 members; $58 nonmembers; $88 institutions.
Ad Rates: BW: $175 **Circ:** Paid ‡1,050

5454 Consumers' Research
800 Maryland Ave. NE Phone: (202)546-1713
Washington, DC 20002 Fax: (202)546-1638

Magazine that investigates issues of consumer concern, including health, finance, automobiles, nutrition, and government regulation. **Subtitle:** Analyzing products, services, and consumer issues. **Founded:** 1927. **Freq:** Monthly. **Print Method:** Offset. **Cols./Page:** 2. **Col. Width:** 37 nonpareils. **Col. Depth:** 133 agate lines. **Key Personnel:** Peter L. Spencer, Editor; M. Stanton Evans, Publisher; Guy Murdoch, Managing Editor. **ISSN:** 0095-2222. **Subscription Rates:** $24 individuals. **Remarks:** Accepts advertising. **Alt. Formats:** Braille; CD-ROM. **Feature Editors:** Katy Abraham, *Garden/Home*; Beatrice Trum Hunter, *Food.*
Ad Rates: BW: $855 **Circ:** ‡12,000
4C: $1,080

5455 Contemporary Psychology
American Psychological Association
750 1st St. NE Phone: (202)336-5500
Washington, DC 20002-4242 Fax: (202)336-5568
Free: (800)374-2721
Publisher E-mail: webmaster@apa.org

Journal presenting critical reviews of books, films, tapes, and other media representing a cross section of psychological literature. **Subtitle:** A Journal of Reviews. **Founded:** Jan. 1956. **Freq:** Monthly. **Print Method:** Offset. **Trim Size:** 8 1/4 x 11. **Cols./Page:** 3. **Col. Width:** 30 nonpareils. **Col. Depth:** 136 agate lines. **Key Personnel:** John Harvey, Editor; Susan Knapp, Exec. Editor; Jodi Ashcraft, Advertising Mgr.; Juanita Brodie, Circulation Mgr.; Terri Pilkerton, Advertising Sales Rep. **ISSN:** 0010-7549. **Subscription Rates:** $75 members; $150 nonmembers; $300 institutions. **Remarks:** Accepts advertising.
Ad Rates: BW: $445 **Circ:** ‡3,400

5456 Contingencies
American Academy of Actuaries
1100 17th St., NW, 7th Fl. Phone: (202)223-8196
Washington, DC 20036 Fax: (202)872-1948
Publication E-mail: contingencies@actuary.org
Publisher E-mail: info@actuary.org

Magazine on actuarial science and its relevance to current business problems and social issues. **Subtitle:** The Magazine of the Actuarial Profession. **Founded:** 1989. **Freq:** Bimonthly. **Print Method:** Web offset. **Trim Size:** 8 1/8 x 10 7/8. **Cols./Page:** 3. **Col. Width:** 2 3/8 inches. **Col. Depth:** 9 7/16 inches. **Key Personnel:** Steve Sullivan, Editor, sullivan@actuary.org; Lee Jernstadt, Contributing Editor, jernstadt@actuary.org. **ISSN:** 1048-9851. **Subscription Rates:** $24. **Remarks:** Accepts advertising.
Ad Rates: BW: $2,770 **Circ:** Paid ‡13,000
4C: $3,950 Controlled ‡10,000

5457 Cooperative Business Journal
National Cooperative Business Association (NCBA)
1401 New York Ave. NW, Ste. 1100 Phone: (202)638-6222
Fax: (202)638-1374
Washington, DC 20005
Publisher E-mail: ncba@ncba.org

Trade magazine covering business. **Founded:** 1987. **Freq:** Monthly 10/year. **Trim Size:** 11 x 17. **Key Personnel:** Leta Mach, Editor, phone (202)383-5450, lmach@ncba.org. **ISSN:** 0893-3391. **Subscription Rates:** $15 individuals; $25 out of country including Canada.
Ad Rates: GLR: $7.50 **Circ:** (Not Reported)
BW: $1,315

5458 The Corridor Real Estate Journal
The Daily Record Co.
1025 Vermont Ave., N.W., Ste. 1110 Phone: (202)737-6860
Fax: (202)737-6848
Washington, DC 20005
Free: (800)878-5627

Commercial real estate journal for managers and property owners of offices, retail and industrial space, and multi-family residential units. **Founded:** 1989. **Freq:** Weekly. **Print Method:** Web offset. **Trim Size:** 11 x 15. **Cols./Page:** 5. **Col. Width:** 2 inches. **Col. Depth:** 14 inches. **Key Personnel:** Tom Smith, Editor, tjs@reji.com; Keith Rosenbaum, Publisher, keithr@reji.com. **ISSN:** 1048-7948. **Subscription Rates:** $104; $3 single issue. **Remarks:** Accepts advertising. **Absorbed**: Property Management Monthly. **Formerly**: Washington Real Estate News.
Ad Rates: BW: $1,695 **Circ:** Paid ‡5,000
4C: $2,095 Controlled ‡3,000

5459 County News
Research Foundation, Inc.
440 1st St. NW Phone: (202)393-6226
Washington, DC 20001-2080 Fax: (202)393-2630
Publication E-mail: cnews@naco.org

Newspaper focusing on county government for elected and appointed county officials. **Founded:** 1971. **Freq:** Biweekly. **Print Method:** Offset. **Trim Size:** 10 x 13. **Cols./Page:** 5. **Col. Width:** 2 inches. **Col. Depth:** 189 agate lines. **Key Personnel:** Beverly Schlotterbeck, Editor; Larry Naake, Publisher. **ISSN:** 0744-9798. **Subscription Rates:** $85 individuals; $42.50 Free. **Remarks:** Accepts advertising. **Available Online. URL:** http://www@naco.org/news/news.htm.
Ad Rates: BW: $2,744 **Circ:** Paid 25,000
4C: $3,194 Free 2,500
PCI: $43

5460 The CQ Researcher
Congressional Quarterly
1414 22nd St. NW Phone: (202)887-8500
Washington, DC 20037 Fax: (800)380-3810
Free: (800)638-1710
Publication E-mail: cqresearcher@cq.com

Magazine examining world affairs, science, and community welfare. **Subtitle:** Weekly Reports on Current Affairs. **Founded:** 1923. **Freq:** Weekly. **Print Method:** Offset. **Trim Size:** 8 1/2 x 11. **Cols./Page:** 2. **Col. Width:** 21 picas. **Col. Depth:** 9 inches. **Key Personnel:** Sandra Stencel, Editor, phone (202)887-8631, sstencel@cq.com; Robert Merry, Publisher, phone (202)887-8564, rmerry@cq.com. **ISSN:** 0013-0958. **Subscription Rates:** $340. **Remarks:** Advertising not accepted. **Available Online. URL:** http://library.cq.com. **Alt. Formats:** Microform. **Formerly:** Editorial Research Reports.
Circ: Paid ‡5,000

5461 CQ Weekly
Congressional Quarterly
1414 22nd St. NW Phone: (202)887-8500
Washington, DC 20037 Fax: (800)380-3810
Free: (800)638-1710

Congressional and political news research service. **Founded:** 1945. **Freq:** Weekly (Sat.). **Print Method:** Offset. **Trim Size:** 8 1/2 x 11. **Cols./Page:** 2. **Col. Width:** 42 nonpareils. **Col. Depth:** 126 agate lines. **Key Personnel:** David Rapp, Exec. Editor; Deborah McGregor, Managing Editor; Robert W Merry, Publisher. **Subscription Rates:** $1,220 individuals. **URL:** http://www.cq.com. **Former name:** Congressional Quarterly Weekly Report.
Ad Rates: BW: $7,700 **Circ:** Paid 8,009
4C: $10,500 Non-paid 1,385

5462 Crisis Magazine
The Morley Institute
1814 1/2 N St., NW Phone: (202)861-7790
Washington, DC 20036 Fax: (202)861-7788
Free: (800)852-9962
Publication E-mail: mail@crisismagazine.com

Magazine focusing on politics, culture, the arts, and the Church. **Founded:** 1982. **Freq:** 11/year. **Trim Size:** 8 1/8 x 10 3/4. **Cols./Page:** 2. **Col. Depth:** 8 7/8 inches. **Key Personnel:** Deal W. Hudson, Editor-in-Chief; Michelle Delaney, Dir. of Communications. **ISSN:** 0084-1705. **Subscription Rates:** $29.95; $4 single issue. **Remarks:** Accepts advertising. **URL:** http://www.crisis.magazine.com.
Ad Rates: PCI: $25 **Circ:** Paid 12,000
Non-paid 3,000

5463 Critique
Heldref Publications
Helen Dwight Reid Educational Foundation Phone: (202)296-6267
Fax: (202)296-5149
1319 18th St. NW
Washington, DC 20036-1802
Free: (800)365-9753
Publication E-mail: crit@heldref.org
Publisher E-mail: revu@heldref.org

Journal publishing closely focused critical essays on contemporary fiction. **Subtitle:** Studies in Contemporary Fiction. **Founded:** 1956. **Freq:** Quarterly. **Print Method:** Offset. **Trim Size:** 6 x 9. **Cols./Page:** 1. **Col. Width:** 4 1/2 inches. **Col. Depth:** 7 inches. **Key Personnel:** Grant Williams, Adv. Production Mgr., advertise@heldref.org; Douglas Kirkpatrick, Director; Fred Huber, Circulation Mgr., subscribe@heldref.org; Jean Kline, Fulfillment Mgr., subscribe@heldref.org; Helen Strong, Managing Editor. **ISSN:** 0011-1619. **Subscription Rates:** $37 individuals; $66 institutions; other countries add $13 postage. **Remarks:** Accepts advertising. **Online:** EBSCO; Infonautics; Information Access; Institute for Scientific Information; UMI. **URL:** http://www.heldref.org. **Alt. Formats:** CD-ROM.
Ad Rates: BW: $265 **Circ:** Paid 1,100

5464 C.U.A. Magazine
Catholic University of America
620 Michigan Ave. NE Phone: (202)319-5600
McMahon Hall, Rm. 311 Fax: (202)319-4440
Washington, DC 20064
Publication E-mail: cua-magazine@cua.edu

University magazine for alumni. **Founded:** 1989. **Freq:** 3/year. **Key Personnel:** Anne Smith, Editor-in-Chief, phone (202)319-6977, fax (202)319-4440, smitha@cua.edu. **Subscription Rates:** Free to qualified subscribers. **Remarks:** Advertising not accepted. **URL:** http://www.cua.edu. **Former name:** Envoy (1989).
Circ: Non-paid 50,000

5465 Current
Heldref Publications
Helen Dwight Reid Educational Foundation Phone: (202)296-6267
Fax: (202)296-5149
1319 18th St. NW
Washington, DC 20036-1802
Free: (800)365-9753
Publisher E-mail: revu@heldref.org

Journal that reprints articles on education, politics, and other social issues. **Founded:** 1960. **Freq:** 10/year. **Print Method:** Offset. **Trim Size:** 7 x 10. **Cols./Page:** 1. **Col. Width:** 6 inches. **Col. Depth:** 8 1/2 inches. **Key Personnel:** Grant Williams, Advertising Mgr., adverts@heldref.org; Douglas Kirkpatrick, Director; Fred Huber, Circulation Mgr.; Jean Kline, Fulfillment Manager, subs@heldref.org. **ISSN:** 0011-3131. **Subscription Rates:** $32 individuals; $60 institutions; add $17 for postage outside the United States. **Remarks:** Advertising accepted; rates available upon request. **Online:** EBSCO; Infonautics; Information Access; Inst. Scient. Info.; UMI. **URL:** http://www.heldref.org/. **Alt. Formats:** CD-ROM.
Circ: ‡2,174

5466 Current Antarctic Literature
The Library of Congress
Science & Technology Division Phone: (202)707-1181
Washington, DC 20540 Fax: (202)707-1925

Comprehensive abstracts journal. **Founded:** Sept. 1972. **Freq:** Monthly. **Print Method:** Offset. **Trim Size:** 8 1/2 x 11. **Cols./Page:** 2. **Col. Width:** 38 nonpareils. **Col. Depth:** 121 agate lines. **Key Personnel:** Stuart G. Hibben, Editor. **ISSN:** 0096-879X. **Subscription Rates:** Free to qualified subscribers. **Remarks:** Advertising not accepted. **Available Online.**
Circ: Controlled ‡1,100

5467 Currents
Council for Advancement and Support of Education (CASE)
11 Dupont Circle, Ste. 400 Phone: (202)328-5900
Washington, DC 20036-1261 Fax: (202)387-4973
Free: (800)554-8536
Publisher E-mail: casebooks@case.org

Magazine covering fundraising techniques. **Founded:** Sept. 1975. **Freq:** Monthly. **Print Method:** Web offset. **Trim Size:** 8 1/4 x 11. **Cols./Page:** 3. **Col. Width:** 13 1/2 picas. **Col. Depth:** 9 inches. **Key Personnel:** Karla Taylor, Editor; Sue Partyke, Advertising Mgr. **ISSN:** 0748-478X. **Subscription Rates:** $95 individuals. **Remarks:** Accepts advertising. **URL:** http://www.case.org. **Alt. Formats:** Microform. **Absorbed:** Case Currents (1992).
Ad Rates: BW: $1,760 **Circ:** ‡15,000
4C: $2,735

5468 Custom Home
Hanley-Wood, Inc.
1 Thomas Circle, Ste. 600 Phone: (202)452-0800
Washington, DC 20005 Fax: (202)785-1974

Trade publication. **Subtitle:** The Art and Craft of Custom Home Building. **Founded:** Feb. 1991. **Freq:** Bimonthly. **Print Method:** Web offset. **Trim Size:** 9 x 11. **Key Personnel:** Leslie Ensor, Editor; Jack Brannigan, Publisher. **ISSN:** 1055-3479. **Subscription Rates:** $24 individuals; $10 single issue; $36 other countries. **Remarks:** Accepts advertising.
Ad Rates: BW: $4,000 **Circ:** ‡40,000
4C: $5,475

5469 The Custom Tailor
Custom Tailors and Designers Association of America, Inc.
PO Box 53052 Phone: (202)387-7220
Washington, DC 20009-9052 Fax: (202)387-7713

Custom tailoring magazine. **Founded:** 1912. **Freq:** 3 year. **Print Method:** Offset. **Trim Size:** 8 1/2 x 10 7/8. **Cols./Page:** 2. **Col. Width:** 34 nonpareils. **Col. Depth:** 112 agate lines. **Key Personnel:** Suzanne Kilgore, Editor. **Subscription Rates:** $50 individuals. **Remarks:** Accepts advertising.
Ad Rates: BW: $650 **Circ:** ‡500
4C: $1,575

5470 Daughters of the American Revolution Magazine
National Society Daughters of the American Revolution
1776 D St. NW Phone: (202)879-3286
Washington, DC 20006-5392 Fax: (202)879-3283

Official magazine of the DAR. **Founded:** 1892. **Freq:** 10/year. **Print Method:** Offset. **Trim Size:** 8 1/8 x 10 7/8. **Cols./Page:** 3. **Col. Width:** 27 nonpareils. **Col. Depth:** 140 agate lines. **Key Personnel:** Mary Rose Hall, Editor; Mary Rose Hall, Editor. **ISSN:** 0011-7013. **Subscription Rates:** $12 individuals. **Remarks:** Accepts advertising. **Alt. Formats:** Microform.
Ad Rates: BW: $600 **Circ:** ‡40,000
4C: $1,495
PCI: $45

5471 DEFENDERS Magazine
Defenders of Wildlife
1101 14th St. NW, Ste. 1400 Phone: (202)682-9400
Washington, DC 20005 Fax: (202)682-1331
Publisher E-mail: info@defenders.com

Wildlife conservation magazine. **Founded:** 1926. **Freq:** Quarterly. **Print Method:** Offset. **Trim Size:** 8 1/4 x 10 7/8. **Cols./Page:** 3. **Col. Width:** 30 nonpareils. **Col. Depth:** 132 agate lines. **Key Personnel:** James G. Deane, Editor. **ISSN:** 0162-6337. **Subscription Rates:** $20 members; $3 single issue. **Remarks:** Advertising not accepted.
Circ: ‡130,000

5472 Defense Monitor
Center for Defense Information
1779 Massachusetts Ave., NW Phone: (202)332-0600
Washington, DC 20036 Fax: (202)462-4559
Publisher E-mail: info@cdi.org

Journal reporting defense information. **Founded:** 1972. **Freq:** 10/year. **Print Method:** Offset. **Trim Size:** 10 3/4 x 8 1/8. **Cols./Page:** 3. **Key Personnel:** David Johnson, Contact, djohnson@cdi.org; Jeffrey W. Mason, Research Analyst/Librarian. **ISSN:** 0195-6450. **Subscription Rates:** $1 single issue for back issues; $35 /year. **Remarks:** Advertising not accepted. **URL:** http://www.cdi.org.
Circ: (Not Reported)

5473 Demokratizatsiya
Heldref Publications
Helen Dwight Reid Educational Foundation Phone: (202)296-6267
Fax: (202)296-5149
1319 18th St. NW
Washington, DC 20036-1802
Free: (800)365-9753
Publication E-mail: dem@heldref.org
Publisher E-mail: revu@heldref.org

Journal covering past and current political, economical, social, and legal changes and developments in the Soviet Union and its successor states. **Subtitle:** The Journal of Post-Soviet Democratization. **Founded:** 1992. **Freq:** Quarterly. **Trim Size:** 6 x 9. **Key Personnel:** Douglas Kirkpatrick, Director; Grant Williams, Advertising Mgr., advertise@heldref.org; Fred Huber, Circulation Mgr.; Jean Kline, Fulfillment Manager, subscribe@heldref.org. **ISSN:** 1074-6846. **Subscription Rates:** $48 individuals; $83 institutions; add $15 for postage outside the United States. **Online:** EBSCO; Infonautics; UMI.
Ad Rates: BW: $255 **Circ:** Paid 300

5474 Destinations
American Bus Association
1100 New York Ave. NW, Ste. 1050 Phone: (202)842-1645
Fax: (202)842-0850
Washington, DC 20005-3934
Free: (800)283-2877

Subtitle: The Magazine of North American Motorcoach Tours and Travel. **Founded:** 1979. **Freq:** Monthly. **Print Method:** Offset. **Trim Size:** 8 1/2 x 11. **Cols./Page:** 3. **Key Personnel:** Veronica Chao, Editor-in-Chief; Jackie McKone, Advertising Mgr. **ISSN:** 0279-8468. **Subscription Rates:** $25 individuals; $30 Canada; $3 single issue. **Remarks:** Accepts advertising.
Ad Rates: BW: $1595 **Circ:** Paid ‡3,379
4C: $2295 Controlled ‡2,621

5475 Developmental Psychology
American Psychological Association
750 1st St. NE Phone: (202)336-5500
Washington, DC 20002-4242 Fax: (202)336-5568
Free: (800)374-2721
Publisher E-mail: webmaster@apa.org

Journal presenting empirical contributions that advance knowledge and theory about human psychological growth and development from infancy to old age. **Founded:** Jan. 1969. **Freq:** Bimonthly. **Print Method:** Offset. **Trim Size:** 8 1/4 x 11. **Cols./Page:** 2. **Col. Width:** 46 nonpareils. **Col. Depth:** 126 agate lines. **Key Personnel:** Carolyn Zahn-Waxler, Editor; Susan Knapp, Exec. Editor; Jodi Ashcraft, Advertising Mgr.; Terri Pilkerton, Advertising Sales Rep. **ISSN:** 0012-1649. **Subscription Rates:** $80 members; $155 nonmembers; $310 institutions. **Remarks:** Accepts advertising.
Ad Rates: BW: $245 **Circ:** ‡5,400

5476 Developments
American Resort Development Association
1220 L St. NW, Ste. 500 Phone: (202)371-6700
Washington, DC 20005 Fax: (202)289-8544
Publication E-mail: pubcomm@arda.org
Publisher E-mail: webmaster@arda.org

Magazine for resort developers, suppliers, and related industries. **Founded:** 1979. **Freq:** 11/year. **Print Method:** Offset. **Trim Size:** 8 3/8 x 10 7/8. **Cols./Page:** 3. **Col. Width:** 2 5/16 inches. **Col. Depth:** 9 5/8 inches. **Key Personnel:** Sheila Morris, Director of Publications; Michel Soudee, Managing

Editor; Romain Falloux, Asst. Ed. **Subscription Rates:** Included in membership. **Remarks:** Accepts advertising.
Ad Rates: BW: $1,030 **Circ:** 2,800
4C: $1,630

5477 Distribution Channels
American Wholesale Marketers Association
1128 16th St. NW Phone: (202)463-2124
Washington, DC 20036 Fax: (202)467-0559

For service based distributors marketing to the retail trade. **Subtitle:** AWMA's Magazine for Candy, Tobacco, Grocery and General Merchandiser Marketers. **Founded:** Dec. 1948. **Freq:** 10/year. **Print Method:** Web offset. **Trim Size:** 8 1/4 x 10 7/8. **Cols./Page:** 3. **Col. Width:** 2 1/4 inches. **Col. Depth:** 10 inches. **Key Personnel:** Joyce Grimley O'Brien, Executive Editor & Publisher, joyceg@awmanet.org. **ISSN:** 0162-5136. **Subscription Rates:** $36 individuals; $46 other countries; $5 single issue. **Remarks:** Accepts advertising. **URL:** http://www.awmanet.org/awma/. **Formerly:** Candy Wholesaler.
Ad Rates: BW: $3,275 **Circ:** Paid 3,754
4C: $4,675 Controlled 8,323

5478 District Energy
International District Energy Association
1200 19th St. NW, Ste. 300 Phone: (202)429-5111
Washington, DC 20036-2422 Fax: (202)429-5113
Publisher E-mail: idea@dc.sba.com

District heating and cooling magazine. **Founded:** 1915. **Freq:** Quarterly. **Print Method:** Offset. **Trim Size:** 8 1/2 x 11. **Cols./Page:** 2. **Col. Width:** 40 nonpareils. **Col. Depth:** 133 agate lines. **Key Personnel:** John L. Fiegel, Publisher, john_fiegel@dc.sba.com; Marie Williams, Associate Publisher, marie_williams@dc.sba.com; Troy Foreman, Subscriptions, troy_foreman@dc.sba.com. **ISSN:** 0885-6621. **Subscription Rates:** $50 individuals; $75 other countries. **Remarks:** Accepts advertising. **Formerly:** District Heating & Cooling.
Ad Rates: BW: $800 **Circ:** ‡3,520
4C: $1,460

5479 The Eagle-News
American University Press
4400 Massachusetts Ave. NW Phone: (202)885-3409
Washington, DC 20016-8046 Fax: (202)885-3226
Free: (800)462-6420
Publication E-mail: eagle@american.edu; eic@mail.egal.american.edu

Collegiate newspaper. **Founded:** 1925. **Freq:** Weekly (Mon.). **Print Method:** Offset. **Cols./Page:** 6. **Col. Width:** 13 picas. **Col. Depth:** 294 agate lines. **Subscription Rates:** Free; $60 by mail. **Remarks:** Accepts advertising. **URL:** http://www.egal.american.edu.
Ad Rates: BW: $987 **Circ:** Paid ‡150
4C: $1,447 Free ‡10,000
PCI: $8.75

5480 East Asian Executive Reports
International Executive Reports, Ltd.
717 D St. NW, No. 300 Phone: (202)628-6900
Washington, DC 20004-2807 Fax: (202)628-6618
Publication E-mail: execrep@aol.com
Publisher E-mail: execrep@aol.com

Financial and legal magazine covering business in and with East Asia. **Founded:** 1979. **Freq:** Monthly. **Print Method:** Offset. **Trim Size:** 8 1/2 x 11. **Cols./Page:** 2. **Col. Width:** 40 nonpareils. **Col. Depth:** 140 agate lines. **Key Personnel:** William C. Hearn, Editor and Publisher; Lloyd B. Gibson, Advertising Mgr. **ISSN:** 0272-1589. **Subscription Rates:** $455 individuals; $465 other countries. **Remarks:** Accepts advertising. **Online:** Westlaw; LEXIS-NEXIS. **URL:** http://www.dealnet.com/manda.
Ad Rates: BW: $275 **Circ:** Paid ‡400
Non-paid 500

5481 EBRI Issue Brief
Johns Hopkins University Press
2121 K St. NW, Ste. 600 Phone: (202)659-0670
Washington, DC 20037 Fax: (202)775-6312
Publication E-mail: publications@ebri.org
Publisher E-mail: jlinfo@jhupress.jhu.edu

Publication printing summaries and reports on benefit topics (covers one topic per issue). **Freq:** Monthly. **Key Personnel:** Dallas Salisbury, President, phone (202)775-6322; Maureen Richmond, Managing Editor, phone (202)775-6341, richmond@ebri.org. **ISSN:** 0887-137X. **Remarks:** Advertising not accepted.
Circ: (Not Reported)

5482 EBRI Quarterly Pension Investment Report
Employee Benefit Research Institute
2121 K St. NW, Ste. 600 Phone: (202)659-0670
Washington, DC 20037-1896 Fax: (202)775-6312
Publisher E-mail: publications@ebri.org

Report on private and public pension funds and pension investment perrformance. **Founded:** 1986. **Freq:** Quarterly. **Print Method:** Offset. **Trim Size:** 8 1/2 x 11. **Key Personnel:** Dallas Salisbury, President, phone (202)775-6322, fax (202)775-6312, salisbury@ebn.org; Maureen Richmond, Managing Editor, phone (202)775-6314, fax (202)775-6312, richmond@ebri.org. **ISSN:** 0889-4396. **Subscription Rates:** Available to EBRI members; only. **Remarks:** Advertising not accepted.
Circ: ‡350

5483 Educational Evaluation and Policy Analysis
American Educational Research Association
1230 17th St. NW Phone: (202)223-9485
Washington, DC 20036-3078 Fax: (202)775-1824

Educational evaluation and policy analysis journal. **Founded:** 1979. **Freq:** Quarterly. **Print Method:** Sheetfed offset. **Trim Size:** 6 3/4 x 10. **Cols./Page:** 2. **Col. Width:** 32 nonpareils. **Col. Depth:** 116 agate lines. **Key Personnel:** Marvin Alkin, Editor; Thomas J. Campbell, Director; Lennan Harding, Managing Editor; Meredith Scott, Advertising Mgr. **ISSN:** 0162-3737. **Subscription Rates:** $41 individuals; $15 single issue; $50 out of country; $56 institutions.
Ad Rates: BW: $400 **Circ:** ‡6,000

5484 Educational Record
American Council on Education (ACE)
1 Dupont Circle, Ste. 800 Phone: (202)939-9300
Washington, DC 20036 Fax: (202)833-4760

Magazine publishes articles on issues affecting higher education; provides a forum for the presentation of ideas and information for college and university administrators and faculty. **Subtitle:** The Magazine of Higher Education. **Founded:** 1920. **Freq:** Quarterly. **Print Method:** Offset. **Trim Size:** 8 1/2 x 11. **Cols./Page:** 3. **Col. Width:** 26 nonpareils. **Col. Depth:** 140 agate lines. **Key Personnel:** Wendy Bresler, Editor-in-Chief; Jamie Weyandt, Editor. **ISSN:** 0013-1873. **Subscription Rates:** $10 single issue; $45 other countries. **Remarks:** Accepts advertising.
Ad Rates: BW: $850 **Circ:** Paid ‡1150
4C: $1,550 Non-paid ‡6350

5485 Educational Researcher
American Educational Research Association
1230 17th St. NW Phone: (202)223-9485
Washington, DC 20036-3078 Fax: (202)775-1824

Educational research journal. **Founded:** 1972. **Freq:** 9/year. **Print Method:** Offset. Uses mats. **Trim Size:** 8 3/8 x 10 3/4. **Cols./Page:** 3. **Col. Width:** 25 nonpareils. **Col. Depth:** 140 agate lines. **Key Personnel:** Robert Donmoyer, Editor; Thomas J. Campbell, Director; Leannah Harding, Managing Editor; Meredith Scott, Advertising Mgr. **ISSN:** 0013-189X. **Subscription Rates:** $41 individuals; $8 single issue; $56 institutions; $50 out of country; Free to members of AERA.
Ad Rates: BW: $1,050 **Circ:** ‡23,800
4C: $1500

5486 Electric Perspectives
Edison Electric Institute
701 Pennsylvania Ave. NW Phone: (202)508-5000
Washington, DC 20004 Fax: (202)508-5759

Magazine for managers of U.S. investor-owned electric utilities. **Founded:** 1976. **Freq:** Bimonthly. **Print Method:** Web offset. **Trim Size:** 8 1/8 x 10 7/8. **Cols./Page:** 3. **Key Personnel:** Erie Blume, Associate Editor; Bill Mambert, Advertising Mgr.; Jane Nunnlee, Publisher. **ISSN:** 0364-474X. **Subscription Rates:** $50; $5 single issue. **Remarks:** Accepts advertising.
Ad Rates: BW: $3,830 **Circ:** Paid 308
4C: $5,280 Controlled 18,200

5487 Employee Benefit Notes
Johns Hopkins University Press
2121 K St. NW, Ste. 600 Phone: (202)659-0670
Washington, DC 20037 Fax: (202)775-6312
Publisher E-mail: jlinfo@jhupress.jhu.edu

Report printing news and developments in employee benefits. Includes updates on legislation, regulations, corporate trends, surveys, and book reviews. **Freq:** Monthly. **Key Personnel:** Dallas Salisbuy, EBRI President, phone (202)775-6322; Maureen Richmond, Managing Editor, phone (202)775-6341, richmond@ebri.org. **ISSN:** 0887-1388. **Remarks:** Advertising not accepted.
Circ: (Not Reported)

5488 Energy Prices and Taxes
Organization for Economic Cooperation and Development (OECD)
2001 L St. NW, Ste. 650 Phone: (202)785-6323
Washington, DC 20036-4922 Fax: (202)785-0350
Free: (800)456-6323
Publisher E-mail: washington.contact@oecd.org

Tabloid presenting energy price and tax information. **Founded:** 1984. **Freq:** Quarterly. **Print Method:** Offset. **Trim Size:** 7 7/8 x 10 5/8. **ISSN:** 0256-2332. **Subscription Rates:** $230 individuals; $252 by air mail. **Remarks:** Advertising not accepted.
Circ: (Not Reported)

5489 Engineers
American Association of Engineering Societies
1111 19th St. NW, Ste. 403 Phone: (202)296-2237
Washington, DC 20036 Fax: (202)296-1151
Free: (888)400-AAES
Publication E-mail: arabon@aaes.org
Publisher E-mail: agoldman@aaes.org

Professional magazine covering careers in engineering. **Subtitle:** Providing Information on Jobs, Salaries, and Other Engineering Workforce Issues. **Founded:** 1992. **Freq:** Quarterly. **Cols./Page:** 4. **Key Personnel:** Amy Goldman, Marketing Mgr., agoldman@aaes.org; Tom Price, Executive Dir., tprice@aaes.org; Matthew Doster, Editor, mdoster@aaes.org. **ISSN:** 1079-7211. **Subscription Rates:** $100. **Remarks:** Advertising not accepted.
Circ: Controlled 1,200

5490 Environment
Heldref Publications
Helen Dwight Reid Educational Foundation Phone: (202)296-6267
Fax: (202)296-5149
1319 18th St. NW
Washington, DC 20036-1802
Free: (800)365-9753
Publication E-mail: env@heldref.org
Publisher E-mail: revu@heldref.org

Articles on critical environmental issues, by leading scientists and policymakers. **Founded:** 1958. **Freq:** 10/year. **Print Method:** Offset. Uses mats. **Trim Size:** 8 1/8 x 10 7/8. **Cols./Page:** 3. **Col. Width:** 2 1/4 inches. **Col. Depth:** 9 3/16 inches. **Key Personnel:** Barbara T. Richman, Managing Editor, env@heldref.org; Douglas Kirkpatrick, Director; Fred Huber, Circulation Mgr., subscribe@heldref.org; Jean Kline, subscribe@heldref.org. **ISSN:** 0013-9157. **Subscription Rates:** $39 individuals; $79 institutions; add $17 for postage outside the United States. **Remarks:** Accepts advertising. **Online:** EBSCO; Infonautics; Information Access; Inst. Scient. Info.; UMI. **URL:** http://www.heldref.org/. **Alt. Formats:** CD-ROM.
Ad Rates: BW: $1,460 **Circ:** Paid ‡6,000
4C: $2,595 Non-paid ‡1,000

5491 The Environmental Forum
Environmental Law Institute
1616 P St. NW, Ste. 200 Phone: (202)939-3800
Washington, DC 20036 Fax: (202)939-3868
Free: (800)433-5120
Publication E-mail: dujack@eli.org

Professional journal covering environmental law, policy, and management. **Founded:** May 1982. **Freq:** Bimonthly. **Print Method:** Sheetfed offset. **Trim Size:** 8 1/8 x 10 7/8. **Cols./Page:** 2. **Col. Width:** 2 7/10 inches. **Col. Depth:** 8 9/10 inches. **Key Personnel:** Stephen Dujack, Editor, dujack@eli.org; Mary Swan, Advertising Mgr. **ISSN:** 0731-5732. **Subscription Rates:** $75 standard rate; $50 government and academic individuals; $20 public interest employee rate. **Remarks:** Accepts advertising.
Ad Rates: BW: $850 **Circ:** Controlled 3,900

5492 EOS
American Geophysical Union
2000 Florida Ave. NW Phone: (202)462-6900
Washington, DC 20009 Fax: (202)328-0566
Free: (800)966-2481
Publication E-mail: eosnews@agu.org
Publisher E-mail: service@agu.org

Professional newspaper containing refereed articles on current geophysical research and on the relationship of geophysics to social and political questions. **Subtitle:** Transactions. **Founded:** 1919. **Freq:** Weekly. **Print Method:** Offset. **Trim Size:** 11 3/4 x 17. **Cols./Page:** 4. **Col. Width:** 2 1/4 inches. **Col. Depth:** 15 1/2 inches. **Key Personnel:** Maria Lebron, Manager News and New Media Publishing; Penny Kriese, Advertising Mgr. **ISSN:** 0096-3941. **Subscription Rates:** $160 individuals. **URL:** http://www.agu.org.
Ad Rates: GLR: $9.00 **Circ:** 35,000
BW: $3,150
4C: $4,550
PCI: $75

5493 EPA Administrative Law Reporter
1601 Connecticut Ave., NW, No. 602 Phone: (202)462-5755
Fax: (202)328-2430
Washington, DC 20009
Publisher E-mail: lawreport@aol.com

Professional journal covering environmental law. Available in print format or via e-mail. **Founded:** 1993. **Freq:** Monthly. **Trim Size:** 8 1/2 x 11. **Cols./Page:** 2. **Col. Width:** 2 1/2 inches. **Col. Depth:** 8 inches. **Key Personnel:** Mark Cohen,

Editor. **ISSN:** 1072-8635. **Subscription Rates:** $1,250 individuals. **Remarks:** Advertising not accepted.
Circ: (Not Reported)

5494 The Explicator
Heldref Publications
Helen Dwight Reid Educational Foundation
1319 18th St. NW
Washington, DC 20036-1802
Phone: (202)296-6267
Fax: (202)296-5149
Free: (800)365-9753
Publisher E-mail: revu@heldref.org

Journal offering insightful literary interpretations. **Founded:** 1942. **Freq:** Quarterly. **Print Method:** Offset. **Trim Size:** 6 x 9. **Cols./Page:** 1. **Col. Width:** 4 3/4 inches. **Col. Depth:** 7 inches. **Key Personnel:** Grant Williams, Advertising Mgr., advertise@heldref.org; Douglas Kirkpatrick, Director; Fred Hurber, Circulation Mgr., subscribe@heldref.org; Jean Kline, Advertising Dir., subscribe@heldref.org; Beverly Glover-Wood. **ISSN:** 0014-4940. **Subscription Rates:** $35 individuals; $66 institutions; add $13 for postage outside the United States. **Online:** EBSCO; Infonautics; Information Access; Inst. Scient. Info.; UMI. **URL:** http://www.heldref.org/. **Alt. Formats:** CD-ROM.
Ad Rates: BW: $295 **Circ:** Paid ‡1,700

5495 Export Today Magazine
Trade Communications, Inc.
733 15th St. NW, Ste. 1100
Washington, DC 20005
Phone: (202)737-1060
Fax: (202)783-5966
Publication E-mail: julie@ekpurttoday.com

Magazine for executives, providing "how-to" strategies for doing business outside the U.S. **Founded:** 1985. **Freq:** 12/year. **Print Method:** Web offset. **Trim Size:** 8 1/8 x 10 3/4. **Cols./Page:** 2. **Key Personnel:** John Mooney, Publisher; Patricia Steele, Associate Publisher. **ISSN:** 0882-4711. **Subscription Rates:** $49 individuals; $84 other countries. **Available Online. URL:** exporttoday.com.
Ad Rates: BW: $5,230 **Circ:** ‡72,000
4C: $7,475

5496 FAA Aviation News
DOT/FAA
AFS-805
800 Independence Ave., S.W.
Washington, DC 20591
Phone: (202)267-8017
Fax: (202)267-9463
Magazine containing aviation safety information. **Subtitle:** A DOT/ Flight Standards Safety Publication. **Founded:** 1961. **Freq:** 8/year. **Print Method:** Web. **Trim Size:** 8 1/2 x 11. **Cols./Page:** 3. **Col. Width:** 30 nonpareils. **Col. Depth:** 136 agate lines. **Key Personnel:** Phyllis Duncan, Editor, phyllis.duncan@faa.dot.gov. **Subscription Rates:** $16 individuals; $20 other countries. **Remarks:** Advertising not accepted. **URL:** http://www.faa.gov/avr/news/newshome.htm.
Circ: Paid 18,000
Controlled 13,000

5497 Facts about Coal
National Mining Association
1130 17th St. NW
Washington, DC 20036-4677
Phone: (202)463-2619
Fax: (202)857-0135

Trade magazine covering historical data, statistics, and other information about coal production, transportation, and use. **Freq:** Annual. **Trim Size:** 5 1/2 x 8. **Key Personnel:** Jeanne Chircop, Editor; Elizabeth Roca-Crooks, Editorial Asst. **Subscription Rates:** $15 individuals. **Remarks:** Advertising not accepted.
Circ: (Not Reported)

5498 Family Economics and Nutrition Review
U.S. Department of Agriculture
1120 20th St., NW, Ste. 200, N Lobby
Washington, DC 20036
Phone: (202)418-0243
Fax: (202)208-2321
Journal covering economic and nutritional issues related to families. **Founded:** 1943. **Freq:** Quarterly. **Key Personnel:** Julia M. Dinkins, Assoc. Editor; Jane W. Fleming, Managing Editor. **Subscription Rates:** $10 individuals. **Remarks:** Advertising not accepted. **Former name**: Family Economics Review.
Circ: Paid 1,500
Non-paid 3,500

5499 Family Systems
Georgetown Family Center
4400 MacArthur Blvd. NW, Ste. 102
Washington, DC 20007
Phone: (202)965-0730
Fax: (202)337-6801
Publisher E-mail: gtfamctr@georgetownfamilycenter.org

Professional journal covering biology and family behavior and evolution. **Subtitle:** A Journal of Natural Systems Thinking in Psychiatry and the Sciences. **Founded:** 1994. **Freq:** Semiannual. **Print Method:** Offset. **Trim Size:** 7 x 10. **Cols./Page:** 1. **Col. Width:** 4 1/2 inches. **Col. Depth:** 8 1/8 inches. **Key Personnel:** Michael E. Kerr, M.D., Editor; Ruth Riley Sagar, M.A., Managing Editor; Elizabeth Utschig, Production Editor. **ISSN:** 1070-0609. **Subscription Rates:** $28 individuals; $40 institutions. **Remarks:** Advertising not accepted.
Circ: Combined 680

5500 Family Therapy News
American Association for Marriage and Family Therapy
1133 15th St.,NW No. 300
Washington, DC 20005
Phone: (202)467-5118
Fax: (202)223-2329

Newspaper for professionals in family therapy and mental health-related issues. **Founded:** 1970. **Freq:** Bimonthly. **Print Method:** Offset. **Trim Size:** 11 1/2 x 15. **Cols./Page:** 4. **Col. Width:** 2.25 picas. **Col. Depth:** 14 inches. **Key Personnel:** Calli Schmidt, Editor, cschmidt@aamft.org. **USPS:** 575-470. **Subscription Rates:** $25.00 individuals; $40.00 institutions, Canada; $35.00 other countries; $4.00 single issue. **Remarks:** Accepts advertising.
Ad Rates: BW: $1,500 **Circ:** 22,000
4C: $1,950

5501 Fast Forward
The Washington Post
1150 15th St. NW
Washington, DC 20071-2400
Phone: (202)334-6160
Fax: (202)334-5693
Free: (800)627-1150
Publisher E-mail: ffwd@washpost.com

Journal about home entertainment and information technology. **Founded:** Aug. 31, 1994. **Freq:** Weekly. **Remarks:** Accepts advertising.
Circ: (Not Reported)

5502 The Federal Lawyer
Federal Bar Association
2215 M St., NW
Washington, DC 20037
Phone: (202)785-1614
Fax: (202)785-1568
Publication E-mail: pubs@fedbar.org
Publisher E-mail: pubs@fedbar.org

Magazine devoted to federal legal issues. **Founded:** 1981. **Freq:** 10/year. **Print Method:** Web offset. **Trim Size:** 8 3/8 x 10 7/8. **Cols./Page:** 3. **Col. Width:** 28 nonpareils. **Col. Depth:** 136 agate lines. **Key Personnel:** Jane Peterson, Editor; Cathleen Barrie, Managing Editor. **ISSN:** 1080-675X. **Subscription Rates:** $30 individuals; $5 single issue; $40 single issue foreign. **Remarks:** Accepts advertising. **Online:** Westlaw. **Formerly**: The Federal Bar News and Journal.
Ad Rates: BW: $800 **Circ:** ‡15,000
4C: $1,420

5503 Federal Mine Safety and Health Review
U.S. Federal Mine Safety and Health Review Commission
1730 K St. NW, 6th Fl.
Washington, DC 20006

Publication covering decisions of the Federal Mine Safety & Health Review Commission. **Freq:** Monthly. **Subscription Rates:** $102 individuals.

5504 Federal Register Index
Office of the Federal Register
National Archives & Records Admin.
Washington, DC 20408-0001
Phone: (202)523-5227
Fax: (202)523-6866
Publisher E-mail: info@fedreg.nara.gov

Index to the Federal Register. **Founded:** 1936. **Freq:** Monthly. **Print Method:** Letterpress. **Cols./Page:** 3. **Col. Width:** 6 nonpareils. **Col. Depth:** 126 agate lines. **ISSN:** 0364-1406. **Subscription Rates:** $25 individuals; $31.25 other countries. **Remarks:** Advertising not accepted. **URL:** http://www.nara.gov/fedreg.
Circ: (Not Reported)

5505 Finance & Development
International Monetary Fund
700 19th St. NW
Washington, DC 20431
Phone: (202)623-7430
Fax: (202)623-7201
Publication E-mail: fandd@imf.org; pgleason@imf.org
Publisher E-mail: jlavin@imf.org

Magazine explaining work and policies of the Bretton Woods institutions. Carries articles and book reviews on financial and developmental issues. Published in seven languages (English, French, Spanish, Arabic, and Chinese). **Founded:** 1964. **Freq:** Quarterly. **Print Method:** Offset. **Trim Size:** 8 1/2 x 11. **Cols./Page:** 2. **Col. Width:** 19 1/2 picas. **Col. Depth:** 53 picas. **Key Personnel:** Ian S. McDonald, Editor-in-Chief, phone (202)623-7090, fax (202)623-6149, imcdonald@imf.org; Linda Marx, Dir. of Sales, phone (212)252-0222, fax (212)252-1020. **ISSN:** 0015-1947. **Subscription Rates:** Free (surface mail); $20 (air mail). **Remarks:** Accepts advertising. **Available Online. URL:** http://www.imf.org/fandd.
Ad Rates: GLR: $133 **Circ:** Controlled 100,000
BW: $6,000
4C: $7,000

5506 Financial Market Trends
Organization for Economic Cooperation and Development (OECD)
2001 L St. NW, Ste. 650
Washington, DC 20036-4922
Phone: (202)785-6323
Fax: (202)785-0350
Free: (800)456-6323
Publisher E-mail: washington.contact@oecd.org

Publication containing analyses and examinations of financial market developments in OECD countries. **Founded:** 1977. **Freq:** 3/year. **Print Method:** Offset. **ISSN:** 0378-651X. **Subscription Rates:** $67 individuals; $72 by air mail. **Remarks:** Advertising not accepted.
Circ: (Not Reported)

5507 Financial Statistics
Organization for Economic Cooperation and Development (OECD)
2001 L St. NW, Ste. 650
Washington, DC 20036-4922
Phone: (202)785-6323
Fax: (202)785-0350
Free: (800)456-6323
Publisher E-mail: washington.contact@oecd.org

Magazine providing statistics on financial markets and balances in OECD countries. **Freq:** Monthly. **Print Method:** Offset. **ISSN:** 0304-3371. **Subscription Rates:** $430 individuals; $469 by mail air mail. **Remarks:** Advertising not accepted.
Circ: (Not Reported)

5508 Focus: Carrying Capacity Selections
Carrying Capacity Network, Inc.
2000 P St. NW, Ste. 240
Washington, DC 20036
Phone: (202)296-4548
Fax: (202)296-4609
Free: (800)466-4866
Publication E-mail: ccn@us.net

Scholarly journal covering literature on environment, population, and immigration. **Founded:** 1991. **Freq:** 2 x yr. **Trim Size:** 11 x 18. **Key Personnel:** David Durham, Exec. Editor; Kathleen McNeilly, Managing Editor. **ISSN:** 1062-7472. **Subscription Rates:** $20 individuals; $5 single issue. **Remarks:** Advertising not accepted.
Circ: Combined 1,100

5509 Food Chemical News
1725 K St. NW, Ste. 506
Washington, DC 20006
Phone: (202)887-6320
Fax: (202)887-6335

Magazine covering food safety and regulation. **Founded:** 1959. **Freq:** Weekly. **Key Personnel:** Paul Shread, Editor. **Subscription Rates:** $1,200 individuals. **Remarks:** Accepts advertising.
Circ: (Not Reported)

5510 Food Marketing Industry Speaks
Food Marketing Institute
800 Connecticut Ave. NW, Ste. 400
Washington, DC 20006
Phone: (202)452-8444
Fax: (202)429-4529
Publisher E-mail: fmi@fmi.org

Trade magazine covering grocery industry indicators. **Freq:** Annual. **Subscription Rates:** $30 members; $75 nonmembers. **Remarks:** Advertising not accepted.
Circ: (Not Reported)

5511 Foreign Policy
Carnegie Endowment for International Peace
1779 Massachusetts Ave. NW
Washington, DC 20036
Phone: (202)939-2230
Fax: (202)483-4430
Publication E-mail: feditor@ciep.org
Publisher E-mail: ceip@ceip.org

Magazine on U.S. foreign policy. **Founded:** 1970. **Freq:** Quarterly. **Print Method:** Offset. **Trim Size:** 6 x 9. **Cols./Page:** 1. **Col. Width:** 4 1/8 inches. **Col. Depth:** 7 inches. **Key Personnel:** Moises Naim, Editor; Pat Baggott, Circulation Mgr., phone (202)939-2236, pbaggott@ceip.org; Elisa Graham, Assoc. Publisher & GM, phone (202)939-2241, ligraham@ceip.org. **ISSN:** 0015-7228. **Subscription Rates:** $33 individuals; $8.50 single issue. **Remarks:** Color advertising not accepted. **URL:** http://www.foreignpolicy.com. **Alt. Formats:** CD-ROM.
Ad Rates: BW: $825 **Circ:** Paid 25,000
4C: $1,250 Non-paid 3,500

5512 Foreign Service Journal
American Foreign Service Association
2101 E. St., NW
Washington, DC 20037
Phone: (202)338-4045
Fax: (202)338-8244
Publication E-mail: journal@afsa.org
Publisher E-mail: afsa@afsa.org

Magazine for professionals in foreign affairs (State Department, AID, USIA). **Subtitle:** The Magazine for Foreign Affairs Professionals. **Founded:** 1924. **Freq:** Monthly. **Print Method:** Offset. **Trim Size:** 8 1/2 x 11. **Cols./Page:** 3. **Col. Width:** 31 nonpareils. **Col. Depth:** 136 agate lines. **Key Personnel:** Robert Guldin, Managing Editor; Kathleen Currie, Contact;

Maureen Herman, Asst. Ed.; Ed Miltenberger, Advertising & Circulation Mgr. **ISSN:** 0015-7279. **Subscription Rates:** $40 individuals; $3.50 single issue. **URL:** htpp://www.afsa.org.
Ad Rates: BW: $986 **Circ:** ‡13,500
4C: $1,412

5513 Foreign Trade by Commodities, Series C
Organization for Economic Cooperation and Development (OECD)
2001 L St. NW, Ste. 650 Phone: (202)785-6323
Washington, DC 20036-4922 Fax: (202)785-0350
Free: (800)456-6323
Publisher E-mail: washington.contact@oecd.org

Magazine on the value of trade flows of OECD countries. **Freq:** 5/year. **ISSN:** 0474-540X. **Subscription Rates:** $490 individuals; $537 by air mail. **Remarks:** Advertising not accepted.
Circ: (Not Reported)

5514 Foundation News & Commentary
Council on Foundations
1828 L St. NW, Ste. 300 Phone: (202)466-6512
Washington, DC 20036 Fax: (202)785-3926
Publication E-mail: fncsubs@cof.org

Magazine for foundations and grantseekers. **Founded:** 1958. **Freq:** Bimonthly. **Print Method:** Offset. **Trim Size:** 8 1/4 x11. **Cols./Page:** 3. **Col. Width:** 2 1/4 inches. **Col. Depth:** 8 1/2 inches. **Key Personnel:** Jody Curtis, Editor. **ISSN:** 0015-8976. **Subscription Rates:** $48 individuals; $8 single issue. **Remarks:** Accepts advertising. **Online:** Council on Foundations. **URL:** http://www.cof.org; http://www.co7.org. **Formerly:** Foundation News.
Ad Rates: BW: $1,350 **Circ:** ‡13,000
4C: $2,200
PCI: $50

5515 France Magazine
Maison Francaise
4101 Reservoir Rd., NW Phone: (202)944-6069
Washington, DC 20007 Fax: (202)944-6072

Magazine covering French culture, society and business for Francophiles. **Founded:** 1985. **Freq:** Quarterly. **Key Personnel:** Renee Schettler, Editorial Asst.; Nathalie Daubress-Read, Advertising; Karen Taylor, Editor. **Subscription Rates:** Free. **Remarks:** Accepts advertising.
Circ: Non-paid 40,000

5516 Franchising World
International Franchise Association
1350 New York Ave. NW, Ste. 900 Phone: (202)628-8000
Fax: (202)628-0812
Washington, DC 20005-4709
Free: (800)543-1038
Publisher E-mail: ifa@franchise.org

Trade magazine covering topics of interest to franchise company executives and the business world. **Founded:** 1971. **Freq:** Bimonthly. **Print Method:** Offset. **Trim Size:** 8 3/8 x 10 7/8. **Cols./Page:** 3. **Col. Width:** 13.5 picas. **Col. Depth:** 203 agate lines. **Key Personnel:** Polly Larson, Editor, polly@franchise.org; Gary Voudrie, Advertising Dir. **ISSN:** 1041-7311. **Subscription Rates:** $18 individuals; $3.50 single issue. **Remarks:** Accepts advertising.
Ad Rates: BW: $3,140 **Circ:** Paid ‡500
4C: $3,800 Controlled ‡9,500

5517 Front Lines
Office of Legislative and Public Affairs
Publications Division Phone: (202)647-4330
U.S. Agency for International Development, Rm. 4889 Fax: (202)647-3945
Washington, DC 20523-0056
Publication E-mail: bsnead@usaid.gov

Newspaper on aid to other countries and international development. **Founded:** 1962. **Freq:** Monthly. **Print Method:** Offset. **Trim Size:** 8 1/2 x 11. **Cols./Page:** 4. **Col. Width:** 28 nonpareils. **Col. Depth:** 204 agate lines. **Key Personnel:** Suzanne Chase, Editor, phone (202)712-4142, fax (202)216-3035, schase@usaid.gov. **Subscription Rates:** Free. **Remarks:** Advertising not accepted.
Circ: Free ‡10,000

5518 GAMA International Journal
1922 F St. NW Phone: (202)331-6088
Washington, DC 20006-4389 Fax: (202)785-5712
Free: (800)345-2687

Trade magazine for field managers in life insurance and financial services industries. **Subtitle:** A Practitioner's Guide to Field Managers. **Founded:** 1976. **Freq:** Bimonthly. **Trim Size:** 8 x 10 7/8. **Cols./Page:** 3. **Col. Width:** 2 1/8 inches. **Col. Depth:** 10 inches. **Key Personnel:** Connie Creswell, Editor; Lisa Niedzielak, Advertising Dir. **Subscription Rates:** $18 members; $30 nonmembers; $3.50 single issue members; $5.50 single issue non-members. **Remarks:** Accepts advertising. **URL:** http://www.gamaweb.com. **Former name:** GAMA News Journal.
Ad Rates: BW: $900 **Circ:** Controlled 7,500
4C: $1,600

5519 Gargoyle Magazine
Atticus Books
1508 U St. NW Phone: (202)667-8148
Washington, DC 20009 Fax: (202)657-0892
Publisher E-mail: atticus@radix.net

Literary magazine.

5520 Genetic, Social, and General Psychology Monographs
Heldref Publications
Helen Dwight Reid Educational Foundation Phone: (202)296-6267
Fax: (202)296-5149
1319 18th St. NW
Washington, DC 20036-1802
Free: (800)365-9753
Publisher E-mail: revu@heldref.org

Journal dealing with biological, behavioral, and social aspects of psychology. **Founded:** 1925. **Freq:** Quarterly. **Print Method:** Offset. Uses mats. **Trim Size:** 6 x 9. **Cols./Page:** 1. **Col. Width:** 5 inches. **Col. Depth:** 7 1/2 inches. **Key Personnel:** Grant Williams, Advertising Mgr., advertis@heldref.org; Douglas Kirkpatrick, Director; Fred Huber, Circulation Mgr., subs@heldref.org; Jean Kline, Fulfillment Manager, subscribe@heldref.org; Doris Chalfin. **ISSN:** 8756-7547. **Subscription Rates:** $115 individuals; $28.75 single issue; add $13 for postage outside the United States. **Online:** EBSCO; Healthgate; Infonautics; Information Access; Inst. Scient. Info.; UMI. **URL:** http://www.heldref.org/. **Alt. Formats:** CD-ROM.
Ad Rates: BW: $170 **Circ:** Paid ‡450

5521 Geomagnetism and Aeronomy International
American Geophysical Union
2000 Florida Ave. NW Phone: (202)462-6900
Washington, DC 20009 Fax: (202)328-0566
Free: (800)966-2481
Publisher E-mail: service@agu.org

Journal with Russian translations of research in geomagnetism and aeronomy. **Freq:** Bimonthly. **ISSN:** 1091-6539.

5522 George Washington Journal of International Law and Economics
National Law Center
2008 G St. NW
Washington, DC 20052

Professional journal covering international law. **Freq:** Triennial. **Key Personnel:** Brett Sagel, Editor-in-Chief; Stephanie Roches, Exec. Managing Editor. **Remarks:** Advertising not accepted.
Circ: (Not Reported)

5523 The George Washington Law Review
2008 G St. NW, 2nd Fl. Phone: (202)676-3868
Washington, DC 20052 Fax: (202)676-3876
Publication E-mail: gwlr@gwis2.circ.gwv.eu

Collective law journal. **Founded:** 1932. **Freq:** Bimonthly. **Print Method:** Offset. Uses mats. **Cols./Page:** 1. **Col. Width:** 55 nonpareils. **Col. Depth:** 115 agate lines. **Key Personnel:** Rachel Stein, Contact, gwlr@gwu.edu. **ISSN:** 0016-8076. **Subscription Rates:** $36 individuals; $34 subscription co.; $40 U.S. and other countries 40; $38 subscription co. **Remarks:** Accepts advertising. **Online:** Lexis-Nexis. **Alt. Formats:** Microform.
Ad Rates: BW: $200 **Circ:** ‡2,000

5524 The Georgetown Current
The Current Newspapers
5125 Macarthur Blvd., NW, Ste. 18 Phone: (202)244-7223
Fax: (202)363-9850
Washington, DC 20016
Free: (202)363-9850
Publication E-mail: current@erold.com

Community newspaper. **Founded:** 1967. **Freq:** Weekly. **Cols./Page:** 5. **Col. Width:** 2 inches. **Col. Depth:** 13 inches. **Key Personnel:** Shari Madden, Editor. **Subscription Rates:** $52 individuals. **Remarks:** Accepts advertising.
Ad Rates: BW: $1,350 **Circ:** Combined 37,000
4C: $1,750

5525 Georgetown Magazine
Georgetown University
Office of Alumni & University Relations Phone: (202)687-4317
Fax: (202)687-2311
2115 Wisconsin Ave., Ste. 500
Washington, DC 20057
Publication E-mail: gumag@gunet.georgetown.edu

Magazine for alumni, parents, faculty, and staff of Georgetown University. **Founded:** 1947. **Freq:** Quarterly. **Print Method:** Offset. **Cols./Page:** 2 and 3. **Col. Width:** 13 and 20 nonpareils. **Col. Depth:** 54 picas. **Key Personnel:** Nancy Freiberg-Robertson, Editor. **ISSN:** 0745-9009. **Subscription Rates:** Free. **Remarks:** Accepts advertising.
Ad Rates: BW: $1,900 **Circ:** Free ‡113,000
4C: $4,700

5526 The Georgetown Voice
Georgetown University
PO Box 571066 Phone: (202)687-6780
Georgetown University Fax: (202)687-6763
Washington, DC 20057-1066
Publication E-mail: voice@gusun.georgetown.edu

Collegiate newspaper. **Subtitle:** Georgetown University's Weekly Newsmagazine. **Founded:** Mar. 1969. **Freq:** Weekly (Thurs.). **Print Method:** Offset. **Trim Size:** 13 x 20. **Cols./Page:** 4. **Col. Width:** 2.5 inches. **Key Personnel:** Nicole Gesualdo, Editor-in-Chief, gesualdn@gusun.georgetown.edu; Katherine McCue, Managing of Business, mccueka@gusun.georgetown.edu. **Subscription Rates:** $30 individuals; $20 students for one semester; $35 students, other countries one semester overseas; $70 students, other countries one year overseas. **Remarks:** Advertising not accepted for abortions, condoms, or ghostwriting paper services. **URL:** http://www.georgetown.edu/publications/voice.
Ad Rates: BW: $572 **Circ:** Free ‡8,400
4C: $772
PCI: $12

5527 The Germanic Review
Heldref Publications
Helen Dwight Reid Educational Foundation Phone: (202)296-6267
Fax: (202)296-5149
1319 18th St. NW
Washington, DC 20036-1802
Free: (800)365-9753
Publication E-mail: ger@heldref.org
Publisher E-mail: revu@heldref.org

Journal devoted to the study of Germanic languages and literatures. **Subtitle:** Literature, Culture, Theory. **Founded:** 1925. **Freq:** Quarterly. **Print Method:** Offset. **Trim Size:** 6 x 9. **Cols./Page:** 2. **Col. Width:** 3 1/2 inches. **Col. Depth:** 10 inches. **Key Personnel:** Grant Williams, Advertising Production Mgr., advertise@heldref.org; Fred Huber, Circulation Mgr., subscribe@heldref.org; Jean Kline, Fulfillment Mgr., subscribe@heldref.org; Mary O'Donnell; Douglas Kirkpatrick, Director. **ISSN:** 0016-8890. **Subscription Rates:** $41 individuals; $83 institutions $13 foreign postage. **Remarks:** Accepts advertising. **Online:** EBSCO. **URL:** http://www.heldref.org. **Alt. Formats:** CD-ROM.
Ad Rates: BW: $260 **Circ:** Paid ‡950

5528 The Gerontologist
Gerontological Society of America
1030 15th St., NW, Ste. 250 Phone: (202)842-1275
Washington, DC 20005-1503 Fax: (202)842-1150
Publication E-mail: gerontologist@maxwell.syr.edu
Publisher E-mail: geron@geron.org

Multidisciplinary peer-reviewed journal presenting new concepts, clinical ideas, and applied research in gerontology. Includes book and audiovisual reviews. **Founded:** 1961. **Freq:** Bimonthly. **Print Method:** Web offset. **Trim Size:** 8 3/8 x 10 7/8. **Cols./Page:** 2. **Col. Width:** 34 nonpareils. **Col. Depth:** 119 agate lines. **Key Personnel:** Vernon L. Greene, Editor, phone (315)443-5455; Heather Worley, Publications and Advertising Dir.; Jennifer Campi, Production Editor. **ISSN:** 0016-9013. **Subscription Rates:** $77 individuals; $145 institutions; $87 individuals foreign; $155 institutions foreign. **Remarks:** Accepts advertising. **Alt. Formats:** Microfilm.
Ad Rates: BW: $730 **Circ:** Paid ‡7,400
4C: $1,465

5529 GFWC Clubwoman Magazine
General Federation of Women's Clubs
1734 N St. NW Phone: (202)347-3168
Washington, DC 20036 Fax: (202)835-0246
Publication E-mail: gfwc@gfwc.org

Magazine covering women's clubs news and community service projects. **Founded:** 1897. **Freq:** Bimonthly. **Print Method:** Offset. **Trim Size:** 8 1/4 x 10 7/8. **Cols./Page:** 3. **Col. Width:** 2 1/8 inches. **Col. Depth:** 9 5/8 inches. **Key Personnel:** Nancy E. Hoffmann, Editor; Joshua Moglia, Asst. Editor. **ISSN:** 0745-2209. **Subscription Rates:** $6 individuals. **Remarks:** Accepts advertising.
Ad Rates: BW: $850 **Circ:** ‡18,000
4C: $1,350

5530 Gifted Child Quarterly
National Association for Gifted Children
1707 L St. NW, No. 550 Phone: (202)785-4268
Washington, DC 20036 Fax: (202)785-4248

Professional journal covering education for gifted students. **Founded:** 1954. **Freq:** Quarterly. **Trim Size:** 8 1/2 x 11. **Cols./Page:** 2. **Key Personnel:** Tracy Cross, Editor, phone

(765)285-7455. **ISSN:** 0016-9862. **Subscription Rates:** $50 individuals. **Remarks:** Advertising accepted; rates available upon request.
Circ: Paid 6,500

5531 Governing Magazine
Times Publishing Co.
1100 Conneticut Ave. NW, Ste. 1300 Phone: (202)862-8802
Washington, DC 20036 Fax: (202)862-0032
Free: (800)944-0922
Publication E-mail: mailbox@governing.com

Magazine serving the public sector of federal, state and local government. **Subtitle:** The Magazine of States and Localities. **Founded:** 1987. **Freq:** Monthly Web Offset. **Trim Size:** 8 1/4 x 10 7/8. **Key Personnel:** Peter Harkness, Publisher. **Subscription Rates:** $39.95 individuals Annual; $4.50 single issue; $9.95 students, other countries; $59.95 Foreign. **Remarks:** Accepts advertising. **Online:** Congressional Quarterly Inc. (CQ). **Alt. Formats:** Microform.
Ad Rates: BW: $10,275 **Circ:** Controlled 86,000
4C: $12,410

5532 Government Executive
National Journal
1501 M St. NW, Ste. 300 Phone: (202)739-8400
Washington, DC 20005 Fax: (202)833-8069
Publication E-mail: govexec@govexec.com
Publisher E-mail: njdc@njdc.com

Magazine for government executives. **Founded:** Mar. 1968. **Freq:** 12/year. **Print Method:** Offset. **Trim Size:** 8 3/16 x 10 7/8. **Cols./Page:** 3. **Col. Width:** 27 nonpareils. **Col. Depth:** 140 agate lines. **Key Personnel:** Tim Clark, Editor and Publisher, phone (202)739-8506, fax (202)739-8511, tclark@njdc.com. **ISSN:** 0017-2626. **Subscription Rates:** Free to qualified subscribers; $48 individuals. **Remarks:** Accepts advertising. **Available Online. URL:** http://govexec.com.
Ad Rates: BW: $8,200 **Circ:** Paid 900
4C: $10,750 Controlled 60,450

5533 GraphiCommunicator
Graphic Communications International Union
1900 L St. NW Phone: (202)462-1400
Washington, DC 20036 Fax: (202)331-9516

Trade newspaper of the Graphic Communications International Union. **Founded:** 1983. **Freq:** 8/year. **Print Method:** Offset. **Trim Size:** 11 x 16. **Cols./Page:** 4. **Col. Width:** 14 1/2 picas. **Col. Depth:** 90 picas. **Key Personnel:** James J. Norton, Editor; Herald Grandstaff, Managing Editor. **USPS:** 410-750. **Subscription Rates:** $12 individuals; $15 elsewhere. **Remarks:** Advertising not accepted.
Circ: ‡160,000

5534 Greenpeace Magazine
Greenpeace USA
1436 U St. NW Phone: (202)462-1177
Washington, DC 20009 Fax: (202)483-8683
Free: (800)326-0959
Publication E-mail: gp@sharewest.com

Magazine covering environmental issues and the activities of Greenpeace. **Founded:** 1981. **Freq:** 3x/year. **Print Method:** Web offset. **Trim Size:** 8 1/8 x 10 7/8. **Cols./Page:** 3. **Col. Width:** 2 1/16 inches. **Col. Depth:** 9 5/8 inches. **Key Personnel:** David Barre, Editor-in-Chief, phone (202)319-2486, davidbarre@wdc.greenpeace.org; Naomi Perian s, Writer/Assoc. Editor, phone (202)319-2422, naomi.perian@wdc.greenpeace.org; Rob King, Production Coord., phone (202)319-2460, rob.king@wdc.greepeace.org; Jay Townsend, Editor-in-Chief. **ISSN:** 0899-0190. **Subscription Rates:** $30. **Remarks:** Advertising not accepted. **URL:** http://www.greenpeaceusa.org.
Circ: Paid ‡400,000

5535 The GW Hatchet
George Washington University
2140 G St. NW Phone: (202)994-7550
Washington, DC 20052 Fax: (202)994-1309

Collegiate newspaper (tabloid). **Founded:** 1904. **Freq:** 2/week (during the academic year). **Print Method:** Offset. **Trim Size:** 10 13/16 x 14. **Cols./Page:** 5. **Col. Width:** 24 nonpareils. **Col. Depth:** 192.5 agate lines. **Key Personnel:** Steven Morse, General Mgr.; Elissa Leibowitz, Editor. **Subscription Rates:** $40 individuals Per year. **Remarks:** Accepts advertising.
Ad Rates: BW: $679 **Circ:** Paid ‡150
4C: $1,000 Free ‡10,000
PCI: $9.70

5536 The Health Insurance Underwriter
National Association of Health Underwriters
1000 Connecticut Ave., No. 810 Phone: (202)223-5533
Washington, DC 20036-5302 Fax: (202)785-2274

Trade magazine covering health insurance for members. **Freq:** Monthly (combined Jul/Aug issue). **Trim Size:** 8 1/8 x 10 7/8. **Cols./Page:** 3. **Key Personnel:** Patricia Tyler, Editor. **ISSN:** 0017-9019. **Subscription Rates:** Included in membership; $25 nonmembers. **Remarks:** Accepts advertising.
Ad Rates: BW: $1,290 **Circ:** Paid 14,500
4C: $2,152

5537 Health Psychology
American Psychological Association
750 1st St. NE Phone: (202)336-5500
Washington, DC 20002-4242 Fax: (202)336-5568
Free: (800)374-2721
Publisher E-mail: webmaster@apa.org

Journal exploring the relationship between behavioral principles and physical health. **Founded:** 1981. **Freq:** Bimonthly. **Print Method:** Offset. **Key Personnel:** David S. Krantz, PhD, Editor; Jodi Ashcraft, Advertising Mgr.; Juanita Brodie, Circulation Mgr.; Terri Pilkerton, Advertising Sales Rep. **ISSN:** 0278-6133. **Subscription Rates:** $38; $77 nonmembers; $180 Industry. **Remarks:** Accepts advertising.
Ad Rates: BW: $355 **Circ:** 9,500

5538 Health & Social Work
National Association of Social Workers
750 1st St. NE, Ste. 700 Phone: (202)408-8600
Washington, DC 20002-4241 Fax: (202)336-8312
Free: (800)638-8799
Publication E-mail: press@naswdc.org

Journal on social work practices in the health field. **Subtitle:** A Journal of the National Association of Social Workers. **Founded:** 1976. **Freq:** Quarterly. **Print Method:** Offset. **Trim Size:** 7 x 10. **Cols./Page:** 2. **Col. Width:** 17 picas. **Col. Depth:** 53 picas. **Key Personnel:** Paula Delo, Managing Editor, pdelo@naswdc.org. **ISSN:** 0360-7283. **Subscription Rates:** $45 members; $70 nonmembers; $87 institutions; $30 students. **Remarks:** Accepts advertising.
Ad Rates: BW: $525 **Circ:** 6,500

5539 Healthplan Magazine
American Association of Health Plans
1129 20th St. NW, Ste. 600 Phone: (202)778-3245
Washington, DC 20036 Fax: (202)331-7487
Publication E-mail: jproctor@aahp.org

Trade magazine covering news and analysis of managed health care for HMO and PPO executives. **Subtitle:** The Magazine of Trends, Insights, and Best Practices. **Freq:** Bimonthly. **Key Personnel:** Diana Madden, Managing Editor, phone (202)778-3200, dmadden@aahp.org; Jennifer Proctor, Asst. Editor, phone (202)778-3200, jproctor@aahp.org. **ISSN:** 1087-3678. **Subscription Rates:** $75 /year. **Remarks:** Accepts advertising. **URL:** http://www.aahp.org.
Ad Rates: BW: $1,998 **Circ:** Paid ‡6,700

5540 Higher Education Management
Organization for Economic Cooperation and Development (OECD)
2001 L St. NW, Ste. 650 Phone: (202)785-6323
Washington, DC 20036-4922 Fax: (202)785-0350
Free: (800)456-6323
Publisher E-mail: washington.contact@oecd.org

Journal covering goverment and national systems, international structures, evaluation and performance indicators, planning, resources and finance, and staff policies and training in higher education management. **Freq:** 3/year. **Print Method:** Offset. **ISSN:** 1013-851X. **Subscription Rates:** $65 individuals; $69 by air mail. **Remarks:** Advertising not accepted.
Circ: (Not Reported)

5541 The Hill
733 15th St. NW, No. 1140 Phone: (202)628-8500
Washington, DC 20005 Fax: (202)628-8503
Free: (800)284-3437
Publication E-mail: hillnews@aol.com

Newspaper covering Capitol Hill. **Founded:** Sept. 1994. **Freq:** Weekly. **Key Personnel:** Jerry Finklestein, Chairman; Martin Tolchin, Editor-in-Chief. **Subscription Rates:** $100 individuals; $175 two years. **Remarks:** Accepts advertising. **URL:** http://www.hillnews.com.
Circ: 22,500

5542 Historic Preservation Forum
National Trust for Historic Preservation
1785 Massachusetts Ave. NW Phone: (202)588-6296
Washington, DC 20036-2117 Fax: (202)588-6223
Free: (800)944-6847
Publication E-mail: forum@nthp.org

Journal covering historic preservation. **Freq:** Quarterly. **Key Personnel:** Byrd Wood, phone (202)588-6189, fax (202)588-6223, byrd_wood@nthp.org. **Subscription Rates:** $110 individuals. **Remarks:** Advertising not accepted. **URL:** http://www.nationaltrust.org.
Circ: Paid 3,800

5543 Historical Methods
Heldref Publications
Helen Dwight Reid Educational Foundation Phone: (202)296-6267 Fax: (202)296-5149
1319 18th St. NW
Washington, DC 20036-1802
Free: (800)365-9753
Publication E-mail: hm@heldref.org
Publisher E-mail: revu@heldref.org

Journal on quantitative methods for historical research. **Subtitle:** A Journal of Quantitative and Interdisciplinary History. **Founded:** Dec. 1967. **Freq:** Quarterly. **Print Method:** Offset. Uses mats. **Trim Size:** 8 1/2 x 11. **Cols./Page:** 2. **Col. Width:** 3 1/2 inches. **Col. Depth:** 10 inches. **Key Personnel:** Grant Williams, Advertising Mgr., advertise@heldref.org; Douglas J. Kirkpatrick, Director; Fred Huber, Circulation Mgr., subs@heldref.org; Gwen Arnold, Marketing Dir.; Barbara Kahn, Managing Editor. **ISSN:** 0161-5440. **Subscription Rates:** $43 individuals; $94 institutions; add $13 for postage outside the United States. **Online:** EBSCO; Infonautics; Information Access; Inst. Scient. Info.; UMI. **URL:** http://www.heldref.org/. **Alt. Formats:** CD-ROM.
Ad Rates: BW: $255 **Circ:** Paid ‡450

5544 History
Heldref Publications
Helen Dwight Reid Educational Foundation Phone: (202)296-6267 Fax: (202)296-5149
1319 18th St. NW
Washington, DC 20036-1802
Free: (800)365-9753
Publication E-mail: his@heldref.org
Publisher E-mail: revu@heldref.org

Journal providing reviews of new history books. **Subtitle:** Reviews of New Books. **Founded:** 1972. **Freq:** Quarterly. **Print Method:** Offset. **Trim Size:** 8 1/2 x 11. **Cols./Page:** 3. **Col. Width:** 2 1/3 inches. **Col. Depth:** 10 inches. **Key Personnel:** Grant Williams, Advertising Mgr., advertise@heldref.org; Douglas Kirkpatrick, Director; Fred Huber, Circulation Mgr., subscribe@heldref.org; Jean Kline, Fulfillment Manager, subscribe@heldref.org; Michael McCarthy, Managing Editor. **ISSN:** 0361-2759. **Subscription Rates:** $50 individuals; $100 institutions; add $13 for postage outside the United States. **Online:** EBSCO; Infonautics; Information Access; UMI. **URL:** http://www.heldref.org/. **Alt. Formats:** CD-ROM.
Ad Rates: BW: $175 **Circ:** Paid ‡460

5545 Hospital Topics
Heldref Publications
Helen Dwight Reid Educational Foundation Phone: (202)296-6267 Fax: (202)296-5149
1319 18th St. NW
Washington, DC 20036-1802
Free: (800)365-9753
Publication E-mail: ht@heldref.org
Publisher E-mail: revu@heldref.org

Journal for upper and middle management in the changing hospital and health care industry. **Founded:** 1922. **Freq:** Quarterly. **Print Method:** Letterpress and offset. **Trim Size:** 8 1/2 x 11. **Cols./Page:** 3. **Col. Width:** 2 1/4 inches. **Col. Depth:** 9 3/8 inches. **Key Personnel:** Grant Williams, Advertising Mgr., advertise@heldref.org; Douglas Kirkpatrick, Director; Fred Huber, Circulation Mgr., subscribe@heldref.org; Jean Kline, Fulfillment Manager, subscribe@heldref.org; Julia Goodwin, Managing Editor. **ISSN:** 0018-5868. **Subscription Rates:** $35 individuals; $64 institutions; add $13 for postage outside the United States. **Remarks:** Accepts advertising. **Online:** Healthgate; EBSCO; Infonautics; Ovid; UMI; Responsive Database Services, Inc. **URL:** http://www.heldref.org/. **Alt. Formats:** CD-ROM.
Ad Rates: BW: $175 **Circ:** Paid ‡900

5546 Housing Policy Debate
Fannie Mae Foundation
4000 Wisconsin Ave. NW, North Tower, Ste. 1 Phone: (202)274-8000 Fax: (202)274-8111
Washington, DC 20016-2804
Publisher E-mail: fmfpubs@fanniemaefoundation.org

Journal covering research and policy analysis on housing and community development. **Founded:** 1990. **Freq:** Quarterly. **Key Personnel:** James H. Carr, Editor; Steven P. Hornburg, Managing Editor; Carol A. Bell, Publications Editor. **ISSN:** 1051-1482. **Subscription Rates:** Free. **Remarks:** Advertising not accepted. **URL:** http://www.fanniemaefoundation.org.
Circ: Non-paid 7,000

5547 Howard Journal of Communications
Taylor & Francis
The Howard Journal of Communications Phone: (202)806-4039 Fax: (202)232-8305
P.O. Box 471
Howard University
Washington, DC 20059
Publication E-mail: wstarosta@howard.edu

Publisher E-mail: info@taylorandfrancis.com

Examines ethnicity, gender, and culture as domestic and international communication concerns. **Founded:** 1989. **Freq:** Quarterly. **Print Method:** Offset. **Key Personnel:** Carolyn Stroman, Editor, phone (202)806-6711, cstroman@fac.howard.edu. **ISSN:** 1064-6175. **Remarks:** Accepts advertising. **Online:** Taylor and Francis.
Ad Rates: BW: $200 **Circ:** (Not Reported)
4C: $1,100

5548 The HOYA
Georgetown University
421 Leavey Student Center Phone: (202)687-3415
POBOX 571065 Fax: (202)687-3929
Washington, DC 20057-1065
Publication E-mail: advertising@thehoya.com

Collegiate newspaper. **Subtitle:** Georgetown's Newspaper of Record Since 1920. **Founded:** 1920. **Freq:** Semiweekly (during the academic year) Tues. and Fri. **Print Method:** Offset. **Trim Size:** 13 3/8 x 20. **Cols./Page:** 6. **Col. Width:** 14 picas. **Col. Depth:** 20 inches. **Key Personnel:** Matt Axelrod, Advertising Mgr., phone (202)687-3947, fax (202)687-2741. **Subscription Rates:** Free; $45 by mail; $70 other countries. **URL:** http://www.thehoya.com.
Ad Rates: GLR: $8 **Circ:** Paid ‡500
BW: $1,008 Free ‡8,400
PCI: $8

5549 H.S.M.A.I. Marketing Review
Hospitality Sales and Marketing Association International (HSMAI)
1300 L. St. NW, No. 1020 Phone: (202)789-0089
Washington, DC 20005 Fax: (202)789-1725

Professional magazine covering sales and marketing information for the hospitality industry. **Founded:** 1982. **Freq:** Quarterly. **Key Personnel:** Ilsa Whittemore, Editor. **USPS:** 677-730. **Subscription Rates:** $65 individuals; $16.25 single issue; Free to qualified subscribers. **Remarks:** Accepts advertising.
Circ: Controlled 6,500

5550 HSUS News
Humane Society of the United States (HSUS)
2100 L St. NW Phone: (202)452-1100
Washington, DC 20037 Fax: (202)258-3081

Magazine reporting on the activities of the Humane Society. **Freq:** Quarterly. **Print Method:** Web offset. **Trim Size:** 8 1/2 x 10 7/8. **Key Personnel:** Deborah Salem, Editor. **Subscription Rates:** Free to members who contribute $10 or more. **Remarks:** Advertising not accepted.
Circ: (Not Reported)

5551 Human Events
Eagle Publishing Inc.
One Massachusetts Ave. NW Phone: (202)216-0600
Washington, DC 20001 Fax: (202)216-0610

Foreign and domestic political news tabloid. **Subtitle:** The National Conservative Weekly. **Founded:** Feb. 2, 1944. **Freq:** Weekly. **Print Method:** Offset. **Trim Size:** 11 1/2 x 14. **Cols./Page:** 4. **Col. Width:** 27 nonpareils. **Col. Depth:** 176 agate lines. **Key Personnel:** Thomas S. Winter, Editor-in-Chief, twinter@eaglepub.com; Mark Ziebarth, Marketing and Advertising, mziebarth@eaglepub.com; Terence Jeffrey, Editor, tjeffrey@eaglepub.com. **Subscription Rates:** $69.95 individuals. **Remarks:** Accepts advertising. **Alt. Formats:** Microform.
Ad Rates: BW: $1,158 **Circ:** ‡50,000

5552 IBEW Journal
International Brotherhood of Electrical Workers, AFL-CIO
1125 15th St. NW Phone: (202)728-6014
Washington, DC 20005 Fax: (202)728-7664

Labor magazine for local union members. **Founded:** 1891. **Freq:** Monthly. **Key Personnel:** C. James Spellane, Director. **Subscription Rates:** $4 individuals. **Remarks:** Advertising not accepted. **Former name:** Electrical Workers Journal.
Circ: Paid 700,000

5553 ICSID Review
Johns Hopkins University Press
1818 H. St., NW Phone: (202)458-1751
World Bank, Rm. U11-051 Fax: (202)522-2615
Washington, DC 20433
Publisher E-mail: jlinfo@jhupress.jhu.edu

Law journal focusing on foreign investment issues. **Subtitle:** Foreign Investment Law Journal. **Founded:** 1986. **Freq:** Semiannual. **Print Method:** Offset. **Trim Size:** 7 x 10. **Cols./Page:** 1. **Col. Width:** 26 picas. **Col. Depth:** 7 inches. **Key Personnel:** Tara Dorai-Berry, Advertising Mgr.; Ibrahim F.I. Shihata, Editor. **ISSN:** 0258-3690. **Subscription Rates:** $57. **Remarks:** Accepts advertising.
Ad Rates: BW: $175 **Circ:** ‡470

5554 The IDB
Inter-American Development Bank
1250 H St. NW Phone: (202)942-8132
Washington, DC 20577 Fax: (202)942-8254

Business journal covering opportunities in procurement of goods and services for projects financed by the Inter-American Development Bank. **Founded:** Aug. 1995. **Freq:** Monthly. **Trim Size:** 8 1/2 x 11. **Cols./Page:** 2. **Key Personnel:** B. Rietveld, Chief of Publications. **ISSN:** 1076-8424. **Subscription Rates:** $150 individuals. **Remarks:** Accepts advertising.
Circ: Paid 1,000

5555 In Transit
Amalgamated Transit Union, AFL-CIO, CLC
5025 Wisconsin Ave. NW Phone: (202)537-1645
Washington, DC 20016-4139 Fax: (202)244-7824

Amalgamated transit union magazine. **Founded:** 1892. **Freq:** 6/year. **Print Method:** Offset. **Trim Size:** 8 1/2 x 11. **Cols./Page:** 4. **Col. Width:** 13 picas. **Col. Depth:** 60 picas. **Key Personnel:** Shawn T. Perry, Editor. **Remarks:** Advertising not accepted.
Circ: Non-paid 160,000

5556 Indicators of Industrial Activity
Organization for Economic Cooperation and Development (OECD)
2001 L St. NW, Ste. 650 Phone: (202)785-6323
Washington, DC 20036-4922 Fax: (202)785-0350
Free: (800)456-6323
Publisher E-mail: washington.contact@oecd.org

Report presenting industrial indicators for business and government interests. **Freq:** Quarterly. **Print Method:** Offset. **Trim Size:** 7 7/8 x 10 5/8. **Cols./Page:** 1. **Col. Width:** 84 nonpareils. **Col. Depth:** 133 agate lines. **ISSN:** 0250-4278. **Subscription Rates:** $80 individuals; $88 by air mail. **Remarks:** Advertising not accepted.
Circ: (Not Reported)

5557 Industrial Biotech News
Devo Enterprises, Inc.
1003 K. St. NW, Ste. 570 Phone: (202)857-0244
Washington, DC 20001-4425 Fax: (202)857-0237

Trade magazine covering biotechnology for manufacturing applications and environment clean-up. **Founded:** Jan. 1998. **Freq:** Bimonthly. **Key Personnel:** K. Devine, Editor; Terri Stewart, Circulation; Steve Castle, Advertising. **Subscription Rates:** $215 individuals. **Remarks:** Accepts advertising. **Former name:** Biotreatment News.
Ad Rates: BW: $600 **Circ:** (Not Reported)

5558 Infection and Immunity
American Society for Microbiology
1325 Massachusetts Ave. NW Phone: (202)737-3600
Washington, DC 20005 Fax: (202)942-9342
Publisher E-mail: journals@asmusa.org

Journal of articles on the state of disease, with an emphasis on infections caused by pathogenic bacteria, fungi, and unicellular parasites; ecology and epidemiology of pathogenic microbes; virulence factors such as toxins and surface structures; nonspecific factors in host resistance and susceptibility to infection; immunology of microbial infection; and vaccine development and evaluation. **Founded:** 1970. **Freq:** Monthly. **Print Method:** Offset. Uses mats. **Trim Size:** 8 1/4 x 11. **Cols./Page:** 2. **Col. Width:** 42 nonpareils. **Col. Depth:** 127 agate lines. **Key Personnel:** Vincent A. Fischetti, Editor-in-Chief. **ISSN:** 0019-9567. **Subscription Rates:** $63 members; $436 nonmembers. **Remarks:** Accepts advertising. **Available Online. URL:** http://www.journals.asm.org.
Ad Rates: BW: $1,210 **Circ:** Paid ‡6,684
4C: $1,210 Non-paid ‡50

5559 Information Outlook
Special Libraries Association
1700 18th St. NW Phone: (202)234-4700
Washington, DC 20009-2514 Fax: (202)234-2442
Publication E-mail: magazine@sla.org
Publisher E-mail: sla@sla.org

Official magazine of the Special Libraries Association. Includes articles on the administration, organization, and operation of special libraries and information centers; research reports in librarianship, documentation, education, information science and technology; and articles on such concerns as professional standards, salary information, education, and public relations. **Founded:** 1997. **Freq:** Monthly. **Print Method:** Offset. **Trim Size:** 8 1/8 x 10 7/8. **Cols./Page:** 12. **Key Personnel:** Susan W. Broughton, Managing Editor, phone (202)939-3674, fax (202)265-9317, susan@sla.org. **ISSN:** 1091-0808. **Subscription Rates:** $75 individuals; $90 other countries. **Remarks:** Accepts advertising. **Formerly:** Special Libraries (1997).
Ad Rates: BW: $2,000 **Circ:** ‡15,000
4C: $3,000

5560 Initiatives
National Association for Women in Education
1325 18th St. NW, Ste. 210 Phone: (202)659-9330
Washington, DC 20036-6511 Fax: (202)457-0946
Publisher E-mail: nawe@clark.net

Journal focusing on education and the personal and professional development of women. Subtitle: Journal of NAWE. **Founded:** 1937. **Freq:** Quarterly. **Trim Size:** 8 x 11. **Key Personnel:** Lynn M. Gangone, fax (202)457-0946. **ISSN:** 0094-3460. **Subscription Rates:** $50; $75 other countries. $15 single issue. **Remarks:** Accepts advertising.
Ad Rates: BW: $125 **Circ:** Paid 3000

5561 Innovations in Aging
National Council on the Aging, Inc. (NCOA)
409 3rd St. SW, 2nd Fl. Phone: (202)479-1200
Washington, DC 20024 Fax: (202)479-0735

Magazine exploring significant developments in the field of aging. **Founded:** 1986. **Freq:** Quarterly. **Key Personnel:** Michael Reinemer, Editor, phone (202)479-6975, michael.reinemer@ncoa.org. **Subscription Rates:** $90 individuals; $175 institutions; $8 single issue. **Remarks:** Advertising accepted; rates available upon request.
Circ: Paid 8,000

5562 Insight
The Washington Times Corp.
3600 New York Ave. NE Phone: (202)636-3000
Washington, DC 20002-1947 Fax: (202)636-3000
Free: (800)822-2822

General interest news magazine covering geopolitics, business, science, health, law, and culture. **Subtitle:** On the News. **Founded:** 1985. **Freq:** Weekly. **Print Method:** Offset. **Trim Size:** 8 x 10 1/2. **Cols./Page:** 3. **Col. Width:** 3 1/4 inches. **Col. Depth:** 10 3/4 inches. **Key Personnel:** Paul Rodriguez, Managing Editor; Peter Gogan, Business Dir. **ISSN:** 0884-9285. **Subscription Rates:** $53. **Remarks:** Accepts advertising. **Alt. Formats:** CD-ROM, NewsBank, Inc.
Ad Rates: BW: $12,500 **Circ:** 439,687
4C: $15,000

5563 Inter-American Review of Bibliography
Organization of American States
1889 F St. NW, Ste. 200-A Phone: (202)458-3140
Washington, DC 20006 Fax: (202)458-6115
Publication E-mail: rib@oas.org

Journal covering research in progress, publications of the U.S. Congress on Latin America and the Carribean, recent articles, book reviews, and doctoral dissertations in the social sciences and humanities concerning Latin America and the Carribbean in English, Spanish, French and Portuguese. **Founded:** Mar. 1951. **Freq:** Quarterly. **Print Method:** Letterpress. **Trim Size:** 6 3/4 x 9. **Cols./Page:** 1. **Col. Width:** 56 nonpareils. **Col. Depth:** 103 agate lines. **Key Personnel:** Sarah Meneses, Ph.D., General Editor, smeneses@oas.org. **ISSN:** 0250-6262. **Subscription Rates:** $30 individuals. **Remarks:** Advertising not accepted.
Circ: Paid ‡1,100
Non-paid ‡250

5564 Intergovernmental Perspective
U.S. ACIR
TechWorld Plaza, S. Bldg.
800 K St. NW, Ste. 450
Washington, DC 20575

Magazine featuring articles relating to intergovernmental issues, public finance, and ACIR research. **Founded:** 1975. **Freq:** Quarterly. **Print Method:** Offset. **Trim Size:** 8 1/2 x 11. **Cols./Page:** 2. **Col. Width:** 42 nonpareils. **Col. Depth:** 128 agate lines. **Key Personnel:** Joan Casey, Editor. **ISSN:** 0362-8507. **Subscription Rates:** Free. **Remarks:** Advertising not accepted.
Circ: Free ‡18,000

5565 INTERMISSION
K Communications
6205 Redwood Ln. Phone: (703)971-7530
Alexandria, VA 22310
Reviews and previews of performing arts in Washington DC, Virginia, and Maryland. **Subtitle:** Performing Arts News Magazine. **Founded:** 1970. **Freq:** Monthly. **Print Method:** Offset. **Trim Size:** 8 x 11. **Cols./Page:** 3. **Col. Width:** 13 picas. **Col. Depth:** 140 agate lines. **Key Personnel:** Verna A. Kerans, Editor and Publisher; Charles Spicka, Editor. **Subscription Rates:** $12 individuals. **Formerly:** The Review; Rosslyn Review.
Ad Rates: BW: $400 **Circ:** Paid ‡1,000
4C: $700 Non-paid ‡9,000
PCI: $12

5566 International Coal
National Mining Association
1130 17th St. NW Phone: (202)463-2625
Washington, DC 20036-4677 Fax: (202)833-9636

Trade journal covering statistics and reference information on coal worldwide. **Founded:** 1976. **Freq:** Annual. **Trim Size:** 8 1/2 x 11. **Key Personnel:** Leslie Coleman, Editor, phone (202)463-9780, lcoleman@policy.nma.org. **Subscription Rates:** $150 individuals; Free to qualified subscribers. **Remarks:** Advertising not accepted.
Circ: (Not Reported)

5567 The International Economy
The International Economy Publications, Inc.
1133 Connecticut Ave. NW, Ste. 901 Phone: (202)861-0791
Fax: (202)861-0790
Washington, DC 20036-4305
Magazine. **Subtitle:** The Magazine of International Economic Policy. **Founded:** 1987. **Freq:** Bimonthly. **Print Method:** Web offset. **Trim Size:** 8 1/4 x 10 7/8. **Cols./Page:** 2. **Key Personnel:** David Smick, Publisher. **ISSN:** 0898-4336. **Subscription Rates:** $72. $12 single issue. **Remarks:** Advertising accepted; rates available upon request.
Circ: (Not Reported)

5568 International Fire Fighter
International Association of Fire Fighters
1750 New York Ave. NW Phone: (202)737-8484
Washington, DC 20006-5395 Fax: (202)737-8418

Union tabloid. **Founded:** Jan. 1918. **Freq:** Bimonthly. **Print Method:** Offset. **Trim Size:** 11 1/2 x 15 1/2. **Cols./Page:** 4. **Col. Width:** 14 picas. **Col. Depth:** 84 picas. **Key Personnel:** Alfred K. Whitehead, Editor; Kelly Press, Publisher; George Burke, Communications Dir. **ISSN:** 0020-6773. **Subscription Rates:** Free to qualified subscribers; $18 individuals. **Remarks:** Advertising not accepted.
Circ: Non-paid 195,000

5569 The International Journal of Action Methods: Psychodrama, Skill Training, and Role Playing
Heldref Publications
Helen Dwight Reid Educational Foundation Phone: (202)296-6267
Fax: (202)296-5149
1319 18th St. NW
Washington, DC 20036-1802
Free: (800)365-9753
Publication E-mail: ijams@heldref.org
Publisher E-mail: revu@heldref.org

Journal featuring articles on the application of action methods to the fields of psychotherapy, counseling, and education. **Founded:** 1947. **Freq:** Quarterly. **Print Method:** Offset. **Trim Size:** 6 x 9. **Cols./Page:** 1. **Col. Width:** 4 1/2 inches. **Col. Depth:** 7 inches. **Key Personnel:** Grant Williams, Advertising Mgr., advertis@heldref.org; Douglas Kirkpatrick, Director; Fred Huber, Circulation Mgr., subs@heldref.org; Jean Kline, Fulfillment Manager, subs@heldref.org. **ISSN:** 1096-7680. **Subscription Rates:** $45 individuals; $73 institutions; add $12 for postage outside the United States. **Remarks:** Color advertising not accepted. **Online:** Healthgate; EBSCO; Healthgate; EBSCO; Infonautics; Information Access; UMI. **URL:** http://www.heldref.org/. **Alt. Formats:** CD-ROM. **Formerly:** Journal of Group Psychotherapy, Psychodrama, and Sociometry.
Ad Rates: BW: $260 **Circ:** Combined ‡1,054

5570 International Journal of Government Auditing
c/o General Accounting Office, Rm. 7806 Phone: (202)512-4707
Fax: (202)512-4021
441 G St. NW
Washington, DC 20548-0001
Publisher E-mail: oil@gao.gov

Financial management journal printed in Arabic, French, German, Spanish, and English. **Founded:** 1974. **Freq:** Quarterly. **Print Method:** Letterpress. **Trim Size:** 8 1/2 x 11. **Key Personnel:** Don R. Drach, Editor, ddrach@gao.gov. **ISSN:** 0047-0724. **Subscription Rates:** $5 individuals. **Remarks:** Advertising not accepted.
Circ: (Not Reported)

5571 International Journal of Legal Informations
International Association of Law Libraries
Box 5709 Phone: (202)707-9866
Washington, DC 20016-1309 Fax: (202)707-1820

Professional journal covering foreign, comparative, and international law. **Founded:** 1973. **Freq:** 3/year. **Key Personnel:** Marie-Louise H. Bernal, Editor, mber@loc.gov. **ISSN:** 0731-1265. **Subscription Rates:** $55 individuals; $80 institutions; $225. **Remarks:** Advertising not accepted. **URL:** http://www.iall.org. **Alt. Formats:** Microform. **Former name:** International Journal of Law Libraries.
Circ: Paid 600

5572 International Legal Materials
American Society of International Law (ASIL)
2223 Massachusetts Ave. NW Phone: (202)939-6000
Washington, DC 20008 Fax: (202)797-7133

Documentary journal includes treaties, national legislation, national and international judicial decisions, and reports and resolutions of international organizations. **Founded:** 1962. **Freq:** Bimonthly. **Print Method:** Offset. **Trim Size:** 8 1/2 x 11. **Key Personnel:** David A. Levy, Interim Ed., phone (202)939-6036; Elizabeth Fabrizio, Assistant Ed. **ISSN:** 0020-7829. **Subscription Rates:** $190; $210 other countries. **Remarks:** Accepts advertising. **Online:** Westlaw, Lexis. **Alt. Formats:** Microform.
Ad Rates: BW: $300 **Circ:** Paid 2,111

5573 International Notices to Airmen
U.S. Department of Transportation
800 Independence Ave., SW Phone: (202)426-8790
Washington, DC 20591-0002
Flight standards safety publication. **Founded:** 1975. **Freq:** Semiweekly. **Print Method:** Letterpress. **Cols./Page:** 2. **Col. Width:** 38 nonpareils. **Col. Depth:** 130 agate lines. **ISSN:** 0364-6742. **Subscription Rates:** $35 single issue members; $150 nonmembers; $10 single issue ASM members; $40 single issue ASM members; $40 single issue nonmembers.

5574 Interservice
American Logistics Association
1133 15th St. NW, Ste. 640 Phone: (202)466-2520
Washington, DC 20005 Fax: (202)296-4419

Journal for the military resale industry. **Founded:** Sept. 1980. **Freq:** Quarterly. **Print Method:** Offset. **Trim Size:** 8 1/2 x 11. **Cols./Page:** 3. **Col. Width:** 39 nonpareils. **Col. Depth:** 142 agate lines. **Key Personnel:** Herman Marshall, Editor; Jim Heald, Advertising Mgr. **ISSN:** 0273-7485. **Subscription Rates:** $20 individuals; $25 other countries. **Remarks:** Accepts advertising. **Formerly:** Quartermaster's Review.
Ad Rates: BW: $1,600 **Circ:** Paid ‡10,000
4C: $2,750

5575 The InTowner
InTowner Publishing Corp.
1730-B Corcoran St., NW Phone: (202)234-1717
Washington, DC 20009
Publication E-mail: intowner@intowner.com
Publisher E-mail: intowner@intowner.com

Community newspaper for residents of downtown neighborhoods. **Founded:** 1968. **Freq:** Monthly. **Print Method:** Offset. **Trim Size:** 11 1/4 x 15. **Cols./Page:** 4. **Col. Width:** 2 1/4 inches. **Col. Depth:** 13 7/8 inches. **Key Personnel:** P. L. Wolff, Editor and Publisher, plwolff@intowner.com. **ISSN:** 0887-9400. **Subscription Rates:** $25 individuals; $35 other countries; $2 single issue. **Remarks:** Accepts advertising. **URL:** http://www.intowner.com.
Ad Rates: BW: $975 **Circ:** Paid 100
4C: $1,375 Free 32,000
PCI: $17.41

5576 The Ironworker
International Association of Bridge, Structural & Ornamental Iron Workers
1750 New York Ave. NW, St. 400 Phone: (202)383-4878
Fax: (202)638-4856
Washington, DC 20006
Magazine reporting industry news for ironworkers. **Founded:** 1901. **Freq:** Monthly. **Print Method:** Offset. **Trim Size:** 8 1/2 x 11. **Key Personnel:** W.M. Lawbaugh, Editor.

5577 ITE Journal
Institute of Transportation Engineers
525 School St. SW, Ste. 410 Phone: (202)554-8050
Washington, DC 20024-2797 Fax: (202)863-5486

Technical magazine focusing on the plan, design, and operation of surface transportation systems. **Founded:** 1930. **Freq:** Monthly. **Print Method:** Offset. **Trim Size:** 8 1/4 x 11. **Cols./Page:** 3. **Col. Width:** 13 picas. **Col. Depth:** 130 agate lines. **Key Personnel:** Shannon Gore Peters, Editor, speters@vax.ite.org; Marianne Wool, Advertising Mgr., mwool@vax.ite.org. **ISSN:** 0162-8178. **Subscription Rates:** $60 U.S. and Canada; $80 other countries. **Remarks:** Accepts advertising. **URL:** http://www.ite.org.
Ad Rates: BW: $860 **Circ:** ‡14,000
4C: $1,660

5578 IUE News
International Union of Electronic, Electrical, Salaried, Machine and Furniture Workers, AFL-CIO
1126 16th St. NW Phone: (202)785-7208
Washington, DC 20036-4866 Fax: (202)785-7448
Publication E-mail: iuenews@iue.org
Publisher E-mail: info@iue.org

Labor newspaper. **Founded:** 1949. **Freq:** Bimonthly. **Key Personnel:** Lauren Asplen, Editor, phone (202)785-7230. **Remarks:** Advertising not accepted.
Circ: Paid 165,000

5579 Japan-U.S. Business Report
Japan Economic Institute
1000 Connecticut Ave. NW, Ste. 211 Phone: (202)296-5633
Fax: (202)296-8333
Washington, DC 20036
Publisher E-mail: jei@jei.org

Business publication covering activities of U.S. companies in Japan and Japanese companies in the U.S. **Founded:** 1974. **Freq:** Monthly. **Print Method:** Offset. **Trim Size:** 8 1/2 x 11. **Cols./Page:** 2. **Col. Width:** 3 1/2 inches. **Col. Depth:** 9 1/4 inches. **Key Personnel:** Susan MacKnight, Editor-in-Chief. **ISSN:** 0888-5702. **Subscription Rates:** $185 individuals North America; $195 other countries. **Remarks:** Advertising not accepted. **Online:** Predicast.
Circ: 500

5580 The Jewish Veteran
1811 R St. NW Phone: (202)265-6280
Washington, DC 20009 Fax: (202)234-5662
Publication E-mail: jwv@erols.com
Publisher E-mail: jwv@erols.com

Subtitle: National Publication of the Jewish War Veterans of the USA. **Founded:** 1896. **Freq:** 5/year. **Print Method:** Offset. **Trim Size:** 8 3/8 x 10 3/4. **Cols./Page:** 3. **Col. Width:** 26 nonpareils. **Col. Depth:** 154 agate lines. **Key Personnel:** Kevin Barney, Managing Editor; Ian Lipner, Managing Editor. **ISSN:** 0047-2018. **Subscription Rates:** $7.50 individuals. **URL:** http://www.penfed.org/jwv/home.htm.
Ad Rates: BW: $1,000 **Circ:** Paid 40,000
PCI: $150 Non-paid 5,000

5581 Jewish Woman
Jewish Women International
1828 L. St. NW Ste. 250 Phone: (202)857-1300
Washington, DC 20036 Fax: (202)857-1380
Publication E-mail: editor@jwi.org
Publisher E-mail: jwi@jwi.org

Jewish women's magazine. **Founded:** 1951. **Freq:** Quarterly. **Trim Size:** 8 1/4 x 10 3/4. **Key Personnel:** Susan Tomchin, Editor. **ISSN:** 1098-7347. **Subscription Rates:** Included in membership dues. **Remarks:** Advertising accepted; rates available upon request. **Formerly:** Women's World.
Circ: Combined ‡75,000

5582 Journal of Abnormal Psychology
American Psychological Association
750 1st St. NE Phone: (202)336-5500
Washington, DC 20002-4242 Fax: (202)336-5568
Free: (800)374-2721
Publisher E-mail: webmaster@apa.org

Journal presenting articles on basic research and theory in the broad field of abnormal behavior. **Founded:** 1906. **Freq:** Quarterly. **Print Method:** Offset. **Trim Size:** 8 1/4 x 11. **Cols./Page:** 2. **Col. Width:** 46 nonpareils. **Col. Depth:** 126 agate lines. **Key Personnel:** Susan Mineka, Editor; Susan Knapp, Exec. Editor; Jodi Ashcraft, Advertising Mgr.; Juanita Brodie, Circulation Mgr.; Terri Pilkerton, Advertising Sales Rep. **ISSN:** 0021-843X. **Subscription Rates:** $27 members; $67 nonmembers; $138 institutions. **Remarks:** Accepts advertising.
Ad Rates: BW: $235 **Circ:** ‡7,900

5583 Journal of Agricultural Lending
American Bankers Association
1120 Connecticut Ave. NW Phone: (630)637-0199
Washington, DC 20036 Fax: (630)637-0198
Publisher E-mail: countryside-mktg@worldnet.att.net

Trade journal for agricultural credit specialists/managers. **Founded:** 1986. **Freq:** Quarterly. **Key Personnel:** Carroll Merry, Editor; Joan Blanchfield, Publisher, phone (202)663-5100. **Subscription Rates:** $60 members; $90 nonmembers. **Remarks:** Advertising not accepted.
Circ: Paid 580

5584 Journal of American College Health
Heldref Publications
Helen Dwight Reid Educational Foundation Phone: (202)296-6267
Fax: (202)296-5149
1319 18th St. NW
Washington, DC 20036-1802
Free: (800)365-9753
Publication E-mail: jach@heldref.org
Publisher E-mail: revu@heldref.org

Journal covering developments and research in the college healthcare field. **Founded:** 1952. **Freq:** Bimonthly. **Print Method:** Offset. **Trim Size:** 8 1/2 x 11. **Cols./Page:** 2. **Col. Width:** 3 3/8 inches. **Col. Depth:** 9 1/2 inches. **Key Personnel:** Grant Williams, Advertising Mgr., advertise@heldref.org; Douglas Kirkpatrick, Director; Fred Huber, Circulation Mgr., subscribe@heldref.org; Jean Kline, Fulfillment Manager, sub-

scribe@heldref.org; Martha Wedeman, Managing Editor. **ISSN:** 0744-8481. **Subscription Rates:** $56 individuals; $98 institutions; add $15 for postage ouside the United States. **Remarks:** Accepts advertising. **Online:** HealthGate; EBSCO; Infonautics; Information Access; UMI; Responsive DataBase Services, Inc. **URL:** http://www.heldref.org/. **Alt. Formats:** CD-ROM.
Ad Rates: BW: $350 **Circ:** Combined ‡2,800
4C: $2,100

5585 Journal of the American Pharmaceutical Association
American Pharmaceutical Association
2215 Constitution Ave., NW Phone: (202)429-7557
Washington, DC 20037 Fax: (202)628-5425
Free: (800)237-2742
Publication E-mail: japha@mail.aphanet.org

Journal for pharmacy professionals. **Founded:** 1912. **Freq:** Bimonthly. **Print Method:** Web offset. **Trim Size:** 8 1/4 x 10 7/8. **Cols./Page:** 4. **Col. Depth:** 125 agate lines. **Key Personnel:** Rick Harding, Dir. of Periodicals; L. Michael Posey, Pharmacy Ed.; Ron Teeter, Senior Ed.; Elizabeth Kniska Keyes, Continuing Education Ed.; Kathleen Solomon, Copy Ed.; Elfriede Malone, Editorial Asst.; Sharon L. Ruckdeschel, Advertising Mgr.; Mary Jane Hickey, Art and Production Dir.; Gray McD. Siegel, Graphics Mgr.; Christopher K. Baker, Graphic Designer. **ISSN:** 1086-5802. **Subscription Rates:** $30 Included in membership; $175 individuals; $200 out of country; $35 single issue. **URL:** http://www.aphanet.org. **Formerly:** American Pharmacy.
Ad Rates: BW: $2,915 **Circ:** Paid ‡50,000
4C: $4,505

5586 Journal of Applied Psychology
American Psychological Association
750 1st St. NE Phone: (202)336-5500
Washington, DC 20002-4242 Fax: (202)336-5568
Free: (800)374-2721
Publisher E-mail: webmaster@apa.org

Journal presenting research on applications of psychology in work settings such as industry, correction systems, government, and educational institutions. **Founded:** Mar. 1917. **Freq:** Bimonthly. **Print Method:** Offset. **Trim Size:** 8 1/4 x 11. **Cols./Page:** 2. **Col. Width:** 46 nonpareils. **Col. Depth:** 126 agate lines. **Key Personnel:** Kevin R. Murphy, PhD, Editor; Susan Knapp, Exec. Editor; Jodi Ashcraft, Advertising Mgr.; Juanita Brodie, Circulation Mgr.; Terri Pilkerton, Advertising Sales Rep. **ISSN:** 0021-9010. **Subscription Rates:** $73 members; $145 nonmembers; $290 institutions. **Remarks:** Accepts advertising.
Ad Rates: BW: $225 **Circ:** ‡5,500

5587 The Journal of Arts Management, Law, and Society
Heldref Publications
Helen Dwight Reid Educational Foundation Phone: (202)296-6267
Fax: (202)296-5149
1319 18th St. NW
Washington, DC 20036-1802
Free: (800)365-9753
Publication E-mail: jamls@heldref.org
Publisher E-mail: revu@heldref.org

Journal seeks to increase communication and foster understanding among artists, public and private policymakers, cultural administrators, trustees, patrons, scholars, educators, and lawyers. **Founded:** 1970. **Freq:** Quarterly. **Print Method:** Offset. **Trim Size:** 6 x 9. **Cols./Page:** 1. **Col. Width:** 4 1/2 inches. **Col. Depth:** 7 inches. **Key Personnel:** Grant Williams, Advertising Mgr., advertise@heldref.org; Douglas J. Kirkpatrick, Director; Fred Huber, Circulation Mgr., subscribe@heldref.org; Jean Kline, Fulfillment Manager, subscribe@heldref.org; Michael McCarthy, Managing Editor. **ISSN:** 1063-2921. **Subscription Rates:** $50 individuals; $100 institutions (foreign add $13); $25 single issue. **Online:** EBSCO; Infonautics; Information Access; Inst. Scientific Info.; UMI. **URL:** http://www.heldref.org/. **Alt. Formats:** CD-ROM. **Former name:** Journal of Arts Management and Law.
Ad Rates: BW: $175 **Circ:** Paid ‡437

5588 Journal of the Association for Communication Administration (JACA)
Association for Community Based Education
1805 Florida Ave. NW Phone: (202)462-6333
Washington, DC 20009
Communication administration magazine. **Founded:** 1972. **Freq:** 3/year. **Print Method:** Offset. **Trim Size:** 6 1/2 x 10. **Key Personnel:** Ronald Applbaum, Editor. **ISSN:** 0360-0939. **Subscription Rates:** $75; $60 libraries. $18 single issue. **Remarks:** Accepts advertising. **Formerly:** ACA Bulletin.
Ad Rates: BW: $150 **Circ:** ‡400

5589 Journal of Bacteriology
American Society for Microbiology
1325 Massachusetts Ave. NW Phone: (202)737-3600
Washington, DC 20005 Fax: (202)942-9342
Publisher E-mail: journals@asmusa.org

Journal publishing articles about bacteria and other microorganisms, including fungi and other unicellular, eucaryotic organisms. **Founded:** 1916. **Freq:** Semimonthly. **Print Method:** Offset. Uses mats. **Trim Size:** 8 1/4 x 11. **Cols./Page:** 2. **Col. Width:** 42 nonpareils. **Col. Depth:** 127 agate lines. **Key Personnel:** Graham C. Walker, Editor-in-Chief. **ISSN:** 0021-9193. **Subscription Rates:** $82 members; $448 nonmembers institutions. **Remarks:** Accepts advertising. **URL:** http://www.journals.asm.org.
Ad Rates: BW: $1,175 **Circ:** Paid ‡6,400
4C: $2,350 Non-paid ‡35

5590 Journal of Broadcasting & Electronic Media
Broadcast Education Association
1771 N St. NW
Washington, DC 20036-2805

Scholarly journal on broadcasting and the electronic media. **Founded:** 1956. **Freq:** Quarterly. **Print Method:** Offset. **Trim Size:** 6 x 9. **Cols./Page:** 1. **Col. Width:** 54 nonpareils. **Col. Depth:** 102 agate lines. **Key Personnel:** W. James Potter, Editor. **ISSN:** 0883-8151. **Subscription Rates:** $40; $25 students; $50 other countries. **Remarks:** Accepts advertising. **Formerly**: Journal of Broadcasting (1985).
Circ: Paid ‡2,230
Non-paid ‡120

5591 Journal of Clinical Microbiology
American Society for Microbiology
1325 Massachusetts Ave. NW Phone: (202)737-3600
Washington, DC 20005 Fax: (202)942-9342
Publisher E-mail: journals@asmusa.org

Journal publishing primary research in microbiological aspects of human and animal infections and infestations, with particular emphasis on their etiologic agents, diagnosis, and epidemiology. **Founded:** 1975. **Freq:** Monthly. **Print Method:** Offset. Uses mats. **Trim Size:** 8 1/4 x 11. **Cols./Page:** 2. **Col. Width:** 42 nonpareils. **Col. Depth:** 127 agate lines. **Key Personnel:** Richard C. Tilton, Editor-in-Chief. **ISSN:** 0095-1137. **Subscription Rates:** $55 members; $312 nonmembers. **Remarks:** Accepts advertising. **Available Online**. **URL:** http://www.journals.asm.org.
Ad Rates: BW: $1,825 **Circ:** Paid ‡13,327
4C: $3,350 Non-paid ‡50

5592 Journal of Comparative Psychology
American Psychological Association
750 1st St. NE Phone: (202)336-5500
Washington, DC 20002-4242 Fax: (202)336-5568
Free: (800)374-2721
Publisher E-mail: webmaster@apa.org

Journal reporting on laboratory and field studies of the behavioral patterns of various species as they relate to evolution, development, ecology, control, and functional significance. **Founded:** Mar. 1983. **Freq:** Quarterly. **Print Method:** Offset. **Trim Size:** 8 1/4 x 11. **Cols./Page:** 2. **Col. Width:** 46 nonpareils. **Col. Depth:** 126 agate lines. **Key Personnel:** Charles T. Snowdon, PhD, Editor; Susan Knapp, Exec. Editor; Jodi Ashcraft, Advertising Mgr.; Juanita Brodie, Circulation Mgr.; Terri Pilkerton, Advertising Sales Rep. **ISSN:** 0735-7036. **Subscription Rates:** $29 members; $58 nonmembers; $116 institutions. **Remarks:** Accepts advertising.
Ad Rates: BW: $175 **Circ:** ‡1,500

5593 The Journal of Consulting and Clinical Psychology
American Psychological Association
750 1st St. NE Phone: (202)336-5500
Washington, DC 20002-4242 Fax: (202)336-5568
Free: (800)374-2721
Publisher E-mail: webmaster@apa.org

Journal presenting abstracts from subscriber-selected journals in the area of clinical psychology. **Founded:** 1980. **Freq:** Bimonthly. **Print Method:** Offset. **Trim Size:** 8 1/4 x 11. **Cols./Page:** 2. **Col. Width:** 47 nonpareils. **Col. Depth:** 127 agate lines. **Key Personnel:** Phillip C. Kendall, PhD, Exec. Editor; Jodi Ashcraft, Advertising Mgr.; Maurine Jackson, Operations Dir.; Terri Pilkerton, Advertising Sales Rep. **ISSN:** 0022-006X. **Subscription Rates:** $87 members; $174 nonmembers; $349 institutions. **Remarks:** Accepts advertising. **Formerly**: PsycScan: Clinical Psychology.
Ad Rates: BW: $395 **Circ:** ‡9,650

5594 Journal of Democracy
Johns Hopkins University Press
National Endowment for Democracy Phone: (202)293-0300
Fax: (202)223-6042
1101 15th St., NW, Ste. 802
Washington, DC 20005
Publication E-mail: jod@ned.org
Publisher E-mail: jlinfo@jhupress.jhu.edu

Journal covering democratic regimes and movements around the world. **Founded:** 1990. **Freq:** Quarterly. **Trim Size:** 6 x 9. **Key Personnel:** Marc F. Plattner, Editor; Tara Dorai-Berry, Advertising Mgr.; Larry Diamond, Editor. **ISSN:** 1045-5736. **Subscription Rates:** $29 individuals; $70 Industry. **Remarks:** Accepts advertising. **Available Online**. **URL:** http://www.press.jhu.edu/journals/journals_of_democracy/.
Ad Rates: BW: $235 **Circ:** 3,400

5595 The Journal of Economic Education
Heldref Publications
Helen Dwight Reid Educational Foundation Phone: (202)296-6267
Fax: (202)296-5149
1319 18th St. NW
Washington, DC 20036-1802
Free: (800)365-9753
Publication E-mail: jece@heldref.org
Publisher E-mail: revu@heldref.org

Journal for educators of introductory through graduate level economics. **Founded:** 1969. **Freq:** Quarterly. **Print Method:** Offset. **Trim Size:** 6 x 9. **Cols./Page:** 1. **Col. Width:** 4 1/2 inches. **Col. Depth:** 7 inches. **Key Personnel:** Grant Williams, Advertising Mgr., adverts@heldref.org; Douglas Kirkpatrick, Director; Fred Huber, Circulation Mgr., subscribe@heldref.org; Jean Klein, Fulfillment Manager, subscribe@heldref.org; Rosalind Springsteen, Managing Editor. **ISSN:** 0022-0485. **Subscription Rates:** $41 individuals; $82 institutions; foreign, add $13. **Remarks:** Accepts advertising. **Online:** EBSCO; Infonautics; Information Access; Inst. Scient. Info.; UMI. **URL:** http://www.heldref.org/.
Ad Rates: BW: $340 **Circ:** Paid ‡1,100

5596 Journal of Education for Business
Heldref Publications
Helen Dwight Reid Educational Foundation Phone: (202)296-6267
Fax: (202)296-5149
1319 18th St. NW
Washington, DC 20036-1802
Free: (800)365-9753
Publication E-mail: jeb@heldref.org
Publisher E-mail: revu@heldref.org

Journal for business teachers, featuring business fundamentals, career and distributive education, consumer economics, management and trends in communications, information systems, and knowledge systems for business. **Founded:** 1924. **Freq:** Bimonthly. **Print Method:** Offset. **Trim Size:** 8 1/2 x 11. **Cols./Page:** 4. **Col. Width:** 3 3/8 inches. **Col. Depth:** 4 5/8 inches. **Key Personnel:** Grant Williams, Advertising Mgr., advertise@heldref.org; Douglas Kirkpatrick, Director; Fred Huber, Circulation Mgr.; Jean Kline, Fulfillment Manager, subscribe@heldre.org; Isabella Owen, Managing Editor. **ISSN:** 0883-2323. **Subscription Rates:** $38 individuals; $64 institutions; add $15 for postage outside the United States. **Remarks:** Accepts advertising. **Online:** EBSCO; Infonautics; Information Access; UMI; Responsive Database Services, Inc. **URL:** http://www.heldref.org/. **Alt. Formats:** CD-ROM.
Ad Rates: BW: $700 **Circ:** Paid ‡1,297
4C: $1240

5597 Journal of Educational Psychology
American Psychological Association
750 1st St. NE Phone: (202)336-5500
Washington, DC 20002-4242 Fax: (202)336-5568
Free: (800)374-2721
Publisher E-mail: webmaster@apa.org

Journal presenting articles dealing with learning, especially as related to instruction, development, and adjustment. **Founded:** 1910. **Freq:** Quarterly. **Print Method:** Offset. **Trim Size:** 8 1/4 x 11. **Cols./Page:** 2. **Col. Width:** 46 nonpareils. **Col. Depth:** 126 agate lines. **Key Personnel:** Michael Pressley, Ph.D., Editor; Susan Knapp, Exec. Editor; Jodi Ashcraft, Advertising Mgr.; Juanita Brodie, Circulation Mgr.; Terri Pilkerton, Advertising Sales Rep. **ISSN:** 0022-0663. **Subscription Rates:** $51 members; $102 nonmembers; $204 institutions. **Remarks:** Accepts advertising.
Ad Rates: BW: $225 **Circ:** ‡5,100

5598 The Journal of Educational Research
Heldref Publications
Helen Dwight Reid Educational Foundation Phone: (202)296-6267
Fax: (202)296-5149
1319 18th St. NW
Washington, DC 20036-1802
Free: (800)365-9753
Publication E-mail: jer@heldref.org
Publisher E-mail: revu@heldref.org

Educational research journal for teachers, counselors, supervisors, administrators, planners, and educational researchers. **Founded:** 1920. **Freq:** Bimonthly. **Print Method:** Offset. **Trim Size:** 8 1/2 x 11. **Cols./Page:** 2. **Col. Width:** 20 picas. **Key Personnel:** Grant Williams, Advertising Mgr., advertise@heldref.org; Fred Huber, Circulation Mgr., subscribe@heldref.org; Jean Kline, Fulfillment Manager, sub-

scribe@heldref.org; Jeanne Bebo, Managing Editor. **ISSN:** 0022-0671. **Subscription Rates:** $44 individuals add $15 for postage outside the United States; $88 institutions. **Online:** EBSCO; Infonautics; Info. Access; Inst. Scient. Info.; UMI. **URL:** http://www.heldref.org/. **Alt. Formats:** CD-ROM.
Ad Rates: BW: $35 **Circ:** Paid ‡2,900

5599 The Journal of Environmental Education
Heldref Publications
Helen Dwight Reid Educational Foundation
1319 18th St. NW
Washington, DC 20036-1802
Phone: (202)296-6267
Fax: (202)296-5149
Free: (800)365-9753
Publication E-mail: jee@heldref.org
Publisher E-mail: revu@heldref.org

Environmental education journal for department chairpersons and directors of programs in outdoor education. **Founded:** 1969. **Freq:** Quarterly. **Print Method:** Offset. **Trim Size:** 8 1/2 x 11. **Cols./Page:** 2. **Col. Width:** 3 1/4 inches. **Col. Depth:** 10 inches. **Key Personnel:** Grant Williams, Production Mgr., advertise@heldref.org; Douglas Kirkpatrick, Director; Fred Huber, Circulation Mgr., subscribe@heldref.org; Jean Kline, Fulfillment Mgr., subscribe@heldref.org; Catherine Simon, Managing Editor. **ISSN:** 0095-8964. **Subscription Rates:** $40 individuals; $79 institutions; other countries add $13 postage. **Remarks:** Accepts advertising. **Online:** UMI; EBSCO; Infonautics. **URL:** http://www.heldref.org/. **Alt. Formats:** CD-ROM.
Circ: Paid ‡1,300

5600 The Journal of Experimental Education
Heldref Publications
Helen Dwight Reid Educational Foundation
1319 18th St. NW
Washington, DC 20036-1802
Phone: (202)296-6267
Fax: (202)296-5149
Free: (800)365-9753
Publication E-mail: jxe@heldref.org
Publisher E-mail: revu@heldref.org

Journal focusing on formal and scientific studies in education and the methodology of behavioral science research. **Founded:** 1932. **Freq:** Quarterly. **Print Method:** Offset. **Trim Size:** 6 x 9. **Cols./Page:** 1. **Col. Width:** 5 inches. **Col. Depth:** 7 1/2 inches. **Key Personnel:** Grant Williams, Adv. Production Mgr., advertise@heldref.org; Douglas Kirkpatrick, Director; Fred Huber, Circulation Mgr., subscribe@heldref.org; Jean Kline, Fulfillment Mgr., subscribe@heldref.org; Paige Jackson, Managing Editor. **ISSN:** 0022-0973. **Subscription Rates:** $38 individuals; $75 institutions; other countries add $13 for postage. **Remarks:** Accepts advertising. **Online:** EBSCO; Infonautics; Information Access; Institute of Scientific Information; UMI. **URL:** http://www.heldref.org. **Alt. Formats:** CD-ROM.
Ad Rates: BW: $260 **Circ:** Paid ‡1,100

5601 Journal of Experimental Psychology: Animal Behavior Processes
American Psychological Association
750 1st St. NE
Washington, DC 20002-4242
Phone: (202)336-5500
Fax: (202)336-5568
Free: (800)374-2721
Publisher E-mail: webmaster@apa.org

Journal presenting experimental studies on the basic mechanisms of perception, learning, motivation, and performance, especially in nonhuman animals. **Founded:** Jan. 1975. **Freq:** Quarterly. **Print Method:** Offset. **Trim Size:** 8 1/4 x 11. **Cols./Page:** 2. **Col. Width:** 46 nonpareils. **Col. Depth:** 126 agate lines. **Key Personnel:** Mark E. Bouton, Ph.D., Editor; Susan Knapp, Exec. Editor; Jodi Ashcraft, Advertising Mgr.; Juanita Brodie, Circulation Mgr.; Terri Pilkerton, Advertising Sales Rep. **ISSN:** 0097-7403. **Subscription Rates:** $36 members; $73 nonmembers; $145 institutions. **Remarks:** Accepts advertising.
Ad Rates: BW: $175 **Circ:** ‡1,900

5602 Journal of Experimental Psychology: General
American Psychological Association
750 1st St. NE
Washington, DC 20002-4242
Phone: (202)336-5500
Fax: (202)336-5568
Free: (800)374-2721
Publisher E-mail: webmaster@apa.org

Journal presenting longer, more integrative reports of interest to all experimental psychologists. **Founded:** Mar. 1975. **Freq:** Quarterly. **Print Method:** Offset. **Trim Size:** 8 1/4 x 11. **Cols./Page:** 2. **Col. Width:** 46 nonpareils. **Col. Depth:** 126 agate lines. **Key Personnel:** Nora S. Newcombe, Ph.D., Editor; Susan Knapp, Exec. Dir.; Jodi Ashcraft, Advertising Mgr.; Juanita Brodie, Circulation Mgr.; Terri Pilkerton, Advertising Sales Rep. **ISSN:** 0096-3445. **Subscription Rates:** $29 members; $58 nonmembers; $116 institutions. **Remarks:** Accepts advertising.
Ad Rates: BW: $175 **Circ:** ‡3,000

5603 Journal of Experimental Psychology: Human Perception and Performance
American Psychological Association
750 1st St. NE
Washington, DC 20002-4242
Phone: (202)336-5500
Fax: (202)336-5568
Free: (800)374-2721
Publisher E-mail: webmaster@apa.org

Journal presenting studies of perception, verbal and motor performance, and related cognitive processes in humans. **Founded:** 1975. **Freq:** Bimonthly. **Print Method:** Offset. **Trim Size:** 8 1/4 x 11. **Cols./Page:** 2. **Col. Width:** 46 nonpareils. **Col. Depth:** 126 agate lines. **Key Personnel:** Thomas H. Carr, Editor; Susan Knapp, Exec. Editor; Jodi Ashcraft, Advertising Mgr.; Juanita Brodie, Circulation Mgr.; Terri Pilkerton, Advertising Sales Rep. **ISSN:** 0096-1523. **Subscription Rates:** $109 members; $200 nonmembers; $391 institutions. **Remarks:** Accepts advertising.
Ad Rates: BW: $175 **Circ:** ‡2,500

5604 Journal of Experimental Psychology: Learning, Memory and Cognition
American Psychological Association
750 1st St. NE
Washington, DC 20002-4242
Phone: (202)336-5500
Fax: (202)336-5568
Free: (800)374-2721
Publisher E-mail: webmaster@apa.org

Journal presenting experimental studies on fundamental encoding, transfer, memory, and cognitive processes in human behavior. **Founded:** Jan. 1975. **Freq:** Bimonthly. **Print Method:** Offset. **Trim Size:** 8 1/4 x 11. **Cols./Page:** 2. **Col. Width:** 46 nonpareils. **Col. Depth:** 126 agate lines. **Key Personnel:** James H. Neely, Ph.D., Editor; Susan Knapp, Exec. Editor; Jodi Ashcraft, Advertising Mgr.; Juanita Brodie, Circulation Mgr.; Terri Pilkerton, Advertising Sales Rep., phone (202)3310-5524. **ISSN:** 0278-7393. **Subscription Rates:** $109 members; $200 nonmembers; $391 institutions. **Remarks:** Accepts advertising.
Ad Rates: BW: $175 **Circ:** ‡3,300

5605 Journal of Family Psychology
American Psychological Association
750 1st St. NE
Washington, DC 20002-4242
Phone: (202)336-5500
Fax: (202)336-5568
Free: (800)374-2721
Publisher E-mail: webmaster@apa.org

Journal reporting on theory, research, and clinical practice in family psychology; including articles on family and marital theory and concepts, research and evaluation, therapeutic frameworks and methods, and policies and legal matters concerning family and marriage. **Founded:** Sept. 1987. **Freq:** Quarterly. **Print Method:** Offset. **Trim Size:** 6 3/4 x 10. **Cols./Page:** 1. **Col. Width:** 50 nonpareils. **Col. Depth:** 100 agate lines. **Key Personnel:** Ross D. Parke, PhD, Editor; Susan Knapp, Exec. Editor; Jodi Asheraft, Advertising Mgr.; Terri Pilkerton, Advertising Sales Rep. **ISSN:** 0893-3200. **Subscription Rates:** $44 members; $87 nonmembers; $113 institutions. **Remarks:** Accepts advertising. **Former name:** Journal of Family Issues.
Ad Rates: BW: $195 **Circ:** ‡4,700

5606 The Journal of General Psychology
Heldref Publications
Helen Dwight Reid Educational Foundation
1319 18th St. NW
Washington, DC 20036-1802
Phone: (202)296-6267
Fax: (202)296-5149
Free: (800)365-9753
Publication E-mail: gen@heldref.org
Publisher E-mail: revu@heldref.org

Psychology journal devoted to experimental, physiological, and comparative psychology. **Founded:** 1927. **Freq:** Quarterly. **Print Method:** Offset. Uses mats. **Trim Size:** 6 x 9. **Cols./Page:** 1. **Col. Width:** 5 inches. **Col. Depth:** 7 1/2 inches. **Key Personnel:** Douglas Kirkpatrick, Director; Grant Williams, Production Mgr., advertise@heldref.org; Fred Huber, Circulation Mgr., subscribe@heldref.org; Jean Kline, Fulfillment Mgr.; Jeannie Carlick, Managing Editor. **ISSN:** 0022-1309. **Subscription Rates:** $114 individuals; other countries add $13 postage. **Remarks:** Accepts advertising. **Online:** Health Gate; EBSCO; Infonautics; Institute of Scientific Information; UMI; Information Access. **URL:** http://www.heldref.org. **Alt. Formats:** CD-ROM.
Ad Rates: BW: $255 **Circ:** Paid ‡1,100

5607 The Journal of Genetic Psychology
Heldref Publications
Helen Dwight Reid Educational Foundation
1319 18th St. NW
Washington, DC 20036-1802
Phone: (202)296-6267
Fax: (202)296-5149
Free: (800)365-9753
Publication E-mail: gnt@heldref.org
Publisher E-mail: revu@heldref.org

Psychology journal devoted to research and theory in developmental and clinical psychology. **Founded:** 1891. **Freq:** Quarterly. **Print Method:** Offset. Uses mats. **Trim Size:** 6 x 9. **Cols./Page:** 1. **Col. Width:** 5 inches. **Col. Depth:** 7 1/2 inches. **Key Personnel:** Grant Williams, Advertising Mgr., advertise@heldref.org; Douglas Kirkpatrick, Director; Fred Huber, Circulation Mgr., subscribe@heldref.org; Jean Kline, subscribe@heldref.org; Elizabeth Bruce, Managing Editor. **ISSN:** 0022-1325. **Subscription Rates:** $115 individuals; add $13 for postage outside the United States. **Online:** Healthgate; EBSCO; Infonautics; Information Access; Inst. Scient. Info.; UMI. **URL:** http://www.heldref.org/. **Alt. Formats:** CD-ROM.
Ad Rates: BW: $260 **Circ:** Paid ‡847

5608 Journal of Geophysical Research
American Geophysical Union
2000 Florida Ave. NW
Washington, DC 20009
Phone: (202)462-6900
Fax: (202)328-0566
Free: (800)966-2481
Publication E-mail: service@kosmos.agu.org
Publisher E-mail: service@agu.org

Journal containing original contributions on the physics and chemistry of the Earth, its environment, and the solar system. Separate sections devoted to space science, solid-earth geophysics, the oceans, the atmosphere, and planets. **Founded:** 1896. **Freq:** 72/year. **Print Method:** Letterpress and offset. **Cols./Page:** 2. **Col. Width:** 39 nonpareils. **Col. Depth:** 132 agate lines. **ISSN:** 0148-0227. **Subscription Rates:** $4,598 institutions. **Remarks:** Advertising not accepted. **Alt. Formats:** Microfiche.
Circ: (Not Reported)

5609 Journal of Hospitality & Tourism Research
Council on Hotel, Restaurant, and Institutional Education
1200 17th St. NW
Washington, DC 20036
Phone: (202)331-5990
Fax: (202)785-2511
Publisher E-mail: alliance@access.digex.net

Scholarly journal covering research on hospitality and tourism education. **Freq:** Quarterly. **Trim Size:** 6 x 9. **Cols./Page:** 1. **Key Personnel:** Lori Pierelli, Publications Mgr. **Subscription Rates:** $65 individuals; $125 libraries. **Remarks:** Advertising not accepted.
Circ: (Not Reported)

5610 Journal of Housing and Community Development
National Association of Housing and Redevelopment Officials
630 I St. NW
Washington, DC 20001-3736
Phone: (202)289-3500
Fax: (202)289-8181
Publisher E-mail: nahro@nahro.org

Housing and community development information for association members, practitioners in the field, and academicians. **Founded:** 1944. **Freq:** Bimonthly. **Print Method:** Offset. **Trim Size:** 8 1/2 x 11. Offset. **Cols./Page:** 3. **Col. Width:** 13 picas. **Col. Depth:** 58 picas. **Key Personnel:** Terence K. Cooper, Editor; Richard Smith, Advertising Rep.; Francis Hart, Advertising Dir.; Deborah Erlanson, President; LaTonya C. Rajah-Gibbs, Editorial Assistant; Angela Callahan, Assistant Editor. **Subscription Rates:** $24 individuals. **Formerly:** Journal of Housing.
Ad Rates: BW: $1,320 **Circ:** Non-paid 13,000
4C: $1,760

5611 Journal of Housing Research
Fannie Mae Foundation
4000 Wisconsin Ave. NW, North Tower, Ste. 1
Washington, DC 20016-2804
Phone: (202)274-8000
Fax: (202)274-8111
Publisher E-mail: fmfpubs@fanniemaefoundation.org

Trade magazine covering research on housing and mortgage finance issues. **Founded:** 1990. **Freq:** Semiannual. **Key Personnel:** James H. Carr, Editor, phone (202)274-8060, jcarr@fanniemaefoundation.org; Amy S. Bogdon, Managing Editor, phone (202)274-8192, amy_bogdon@fanniemaefoundation.org; Carol A. Bell, Publications Editor, phone (202)274-8075, cbell@fanniemaefoundation.org. **ISSN:** 1052-7001. **Subscription Rates:** Free to qualified subscribers. **Remarks:** Advertising not accepted. **URL:** http://www.fanniemaefoundation.org.
Circ: Non-paid 6,200

5612 The Journal of Indo-European Studies
Institute for the Study of Man
1133 13th St. NW, No. C-2
Washington, DC 20005
Phone: (202)371-2700
Fax: (202)371-1523

Journal of anthropology, archaeology, mythology, and historical linguistics. **Founded:** 1973. **Freq:** Quarterly. **Print Method:** Offset. **Trim Size:** 6 x 9. **Cols./Page:** 1. **Col. Width:** 50 nonpareils. **Col. Depth:** 98 agate lines. **Key Personnel:** Roger Pearson, Editor; Edgar C. Polome, Contact; James Mallory, Editor. **ISSN:** 0092-2323. **Subscription Rates:** $47

individuals; $110 Institutions; $32.50 students. **Remarks:** Accepts advertising.
Ad Rates: BW: $200 **Circ:** Paid ‡880
Non-paid ‡50

5613 Journal of International Business Studies
3240 Prospect St. NW Phone: (202)944-3755
Washington, DC 20007 Fax: (202)944-3762
Publication E-mail: jibs@gunet.georgetown.edu

Scholarly business journal. **Founded:** 1970. **Freq:** Quarterly. **Key Personnel:** Thomas L. Brewer, Editor. **ISSN:** 0047-2506. **Subscription Rates:** $57 individuals; $63 out of country; $14.50 single issue. **Remarks:** Accepts advertising.
Ad Rates: BW: $400 **Circ:** Paid 4,200

5614 Journal of the International Union of Bricklayers & Allied Craftworkers
815 15th St. NW Phone: (202)383-3136
Washington, DC 20005 Fax: (202)737-2708

Tabloid for trade union members. **Founded:** 1890. **Freq:** Monthly. **Print Method:** Offset. **Trim Size:** 11 x 15. **Cols./Page:** 4. **Col. Width:** 14 picas. **Key Personnel:** Craig Weir, Editor. **ISSN:** 0362-3696. **Subscription Rates:** $1.50 individuals; Included in membership. **Remarks:** Advertising not accepted. **URL:** http://www.bacweb.org.
Circ: Paid ‡2,000
Controlled ‡110,000

5615 Journal of Latin American Affairs
Box 3726
Washington, DC 20007

Academic journal covering Latin American affairs and policy. **Founded:** 1993. **Freq:** Semiannual. **Key Personnel:** Jorge Daniel Taillant, Editor-in-Chief. **ISSN:** 1072-7701. **Subscription Rates:** $17 individuals. **Remarks:** Accepts advertising.
Circ: (Not Reported)

5616 Journal of Motor Behavior
Heldref Publications
Helen Dwight Reid Educational Foundation Phone: (202)296-6267
Fax: (202)296-5149
1319 18th St. NW
Washington, DC 20036-1802
Free: (800)365-9753
Publication E-mail: jmb@heldref.org
Publisher E-mail: revu@heldref.org

Research journal on motor behavior. **Founded:** 1969. **Freq:** Quarterly. **Print Method:** Offset. **Trim Size:** 8 1/2 x 11. **Cols./Page:** 1. **Col. Width:** 7 inches. **Col. Depth:** 10 inches. **Key Personnel:** Fred Huber, Circulation Mgr., subscribe@heldref.org; Grant Williams, Advertising Mgr., advertise@heldref.org; Jean Kline, Fulfillment Mgr.; Douglas Kirkpatrick, Director; Betty Adelman, Managing Editor. **ISSN:** 0022-2895. **Subscription Rates:** $65 individuals; $130 institutions; other countries add $18 postage. **Remarks:** Accepts advertising. **Online:** Health Gate; EBSCO; Infonautics; Information Access; Institute of Scientific Information; UMI. **URL:** http://www.heldref.org/. **Alt. Formats:** CD-ROM.
Ad Rates: BW: $260 **Circ:** Paid ‡1,100

5617 The Journal of Negro Education
Journal of Negro Education
Howard University Phone: (202)806-8120
PO Box 311 Fax: (202)806-8434
Washington, DC 20059
Publication E-mail: jne.law.howard.edu

Educational research journal devoted to black and minority education. **Founded:** 1932. **Freq:** Quarterly. **Print Method:** Letterpress. **Trim Size:** 7 x 10. **Cols./Page:** 1. **Col. Width:** 5 1/2 inches. **Col. Depth:** 7 1/2 inches. **Key Personnel:** Dr. Sylvia T. Johnson, Editor, phone (202)806-8127; Mahmoud Gudarzi, Advertising Mgr., phone (202)806-8122. **ISSN:** 0022-2984. **Subscription Rates:** $16 individuals; $20 Institutions; $24 other countries; $6 single issue. **Remarks:** Color advertising not accepted.
Ad Rates: BW: $200 **Circ:** Paid ‡2,300
Controlled ‡100

5618 Journal of Neuropsychiatry and Clinical Neurosciences
American Psychiatric Press, Inc.
1400 K St. NW, Ste. 1101 Phone: (202)682-6262
Washington, DC 20005 Fax: (202)789-2648
Free: (800)368-5777
Publisher E-mail: apa@psych.org

Journal concentrating on the latest research in neuropsychiatry and clinical neurosciences. **Freq:** Quarterly. **Subscription Rates:** $85 individuals; $135 institutions; $42.50 students. **Remarks:** Advertising accepted; rates available upon request.
Circ: Paid 1,700

5619 Journal of the Optical Society of America A: Optics and Image Science
Optical Society of America
2010 Massachusetts Ave. NW Phone: (202)223-8130
Washington, DC 20036 Fax: (202)223-1096
Free: (800)762-6960
Publication E-mail: atourt@osa.org
Publisher E-mail: info@usa.org

Journal covering atmospheric optics, color vision and diffraction, image processing, scattering and coherence theory, machine vision, physiological optics, statistical optics. **Founded:** 1984. **Freq:** Monthly. **Print Method:** Offset. **Trim Size:** 8 1/4 x 11 1/4. **Cols./Page:** 2. **Col. Width:** 38 nonpareils. **Col. Depth:** 123 agate lines. **Key Personnel:** James R. Fienup, Editor. **ISSN:** 0740-3232. **Subscription Rates:** $917 institutions. **Remarks:** Advertising not accepted. **Available Online. URL:** http.//192.239.36.3. **Alt. Formats:** CD-ROM; Microform.
Circ: Paid 3,012

5620 Journal of the Optical Society of America B: Optical Physics
Optical Society of America
2010 Massachusetts Ave. NW Phone: (202)223-8130
Washington, DC 20036 Fax: (202)223-1096
Free: (800)762-6960
Publication E-mail: jbed@osa.org
Publisher E-mail: info@usa.org

Journal covering modern quantum optics, optical physics, laser physics, nonlinear optics, optical coherent transients, multiphoton processes, spectroscopy, advances in nonlinear optical materials, science, and technology. **Founded:** Jan. 1984. **Freq:** Monthly. **Print Method:** Offset. **Trim Size:** 8 1/4 x 11. **Cols./Page:** 2. **Col. Width:** 38 nonpareils. **Col. Depth:** 123 agate lines. **Key Personnel:** Tony Heinz, Editor. **ISSN:** 0740-3224. **Subscription Rates:** $917 individuals. **Remarks:** Advertising not accepted. **Available Online. URL:** http://192.239.36.3. **Alt. Formats:** CD-ROM.
Circ: (Not Reported)

5621 Journal of Palestine Studies
Institute for Palestine Studies
3501 M St. NW Phone: (202)342-3990
Washington, DC 20007 Fax: (202)342-3927
Free: (800)874-3614
Publication E-mail: bookorders@ipsjps.org
Publisher E-mail: ips-dc@ipsjps.org

English language quarterly exclusively devoted to Palestinian affairs and the Arab-Israeli conflict. **Founded:** 1971. **Freq:** Quarterly. **Trim Size:** 6 3/4 x 10. **Key Personnel:** Philip Mattar, Editor, pmattan@ipsjps.org. **ISSN:** 0377-919X. **Subscription Rates:** $36 individuals; $72 institutions; $21 students and seniors; $10 single issue. **Remarks:** Accepts advertising. **Alt. Formats:** Microform.
Ad Rates: BW: $275 **Circ:** Paid 3,500

5622 Journal of Personality and Social Psychology
American Psychological Association
750 1st St. NE Phone: (202)336-5500
Washington, DC 20002-4242 Fax: (202)336-5568
Free: (800)374-2721
Publisher E-mail: webmaster@apa.org

Journal presenting research in three major areas: attitudes and social cognition; interpersonal relations and group processes; and personality processes and individual differences. **Founded:** 1965. **Freq:** Monthly. **Print Method:** Offset. **Trim Size:** 8 1/4 x 11. **Cols./Page:** 2. **Col. Width:** 46 nonpareils. **Col. Depth:** 126 agate lines. **Key Personnel:** Ed Diener, PhD, Editor; Norman Miller, Advertising Mgr.; Russell Geen, Editor; Terri Pilkerton, Advertising Sales Rep. **ISSN:** 0022-3514. **Subscription Rates:** $155 members; $310 nonmembers; $679 institutions. **Remarks:** Accepts advertising.
Ad Rates: BW: $225 **Circ:** ‡5,600

5623 Journal of Pharmaceutical Sciences
American Pharmaceutical Association
2215 Constitution Ave., NW Phone: (202)429-7557
Washington, DC 20037 Fax: (202)628-5425
Free: (800)237-2742

Professional journal publishing research articles in the pharmaceutical sciences. **Founded:** 1912. **Freq:** Monthly. **Print Method:** Offset. **Trim Size:** 8 1/4 x 11 5/16. **Cols./Page:** 2. **Col. Width:** 3 1/2 inches. **Col. Depth:** 9 1/2 inches. **Key Personnel:** Bruce Poorman, Advertising, phone (216)331-5151, fax (216)331-3432. **ISSN:** 0022-3549. **Remarks:** Accepts advertising. **URL:** http://pubs.acs.org.
Ad Rates: BW: $1,020 **Circ:** Paid ‡5,000
Non-paid ‡120

5624 Journal of Popular Film and Television
Heldref Publications
Helen Dwight Reid Educational Foundation Phone: (202)296-6267
Fax: (202)296-5149
1319 18th St. NW
Washington, DC 20036-1802
Free: (800)365-9753
Publication E-mail: jpft@heldref.org
Publisher E-mail: revu@heldref.org

Journal on film and television addressed from a sociocultural perspective. **Founded:** 1971. **Freq:** Quarterly. **Print Method:** Offset. **Trim Size:** 8 1/2 x 11. **Cols./Page:** 2. **Col. Width:** 4 1/2 inches. **Col. Depth:** 7 inches. **Key Personnel:** Douglas Kirkpatrick, Director; Grant Williams, Advertising Mgr., advertise@heldref.org; Fred Huber, Circulation Mgr., subscribe@heldref.org; Jean Kline, Fulfillment Manager, subscribe@heldref.org; Julia Goodwin, Managing Editor. **ISSN:** 0195-6051. **Subscription Rates:** $36 individuals; $70 institutions; add $13 for postage outside the United States. **Online:** EBSCO; Infonautics; Information Access; Inst. Scientific Info.; UMI; Responsive DataBase Services, Inc. **URL:** http://www.heldref.org/. **Alt. Formats:** CD-ROM.
Ad Rates: BW: $195 **Circ:** Paid ‡780

5625 Journal of Psychiatric Research
American Psychiatric Press, Inc.
1400 K St. NW, Ste. 1101 Phone: (202)682-6262
Washington, DC 20005 Fax: (202)789-2648
Free: (800)368-5777
Publisher E-mail: apa@psych.org

Journal for practicing and research psychotherapists. **Founded:** 1992. **Freq:** Quarterly. **Trim Size:** 6 7/8 x 10. **Key Personnel:** Jerald Kay, M.D., Editor. **ISSN:** 1055-050X. **Subscription Rates:** $85. **Remarks:** Advertising accepted; rates available upon request. **Alt. Formats:** CD-ROM. **Formerly:** Journal of Psychotheraphy Practice and Research.
Circ: Paid 1,600
Non-paid 25

5626 The Journal of Psychology
Heldref Publications
Helen Dwight Reid Educational Foundation Phone: (202)296-6267
Fax: (202)296-5149
1319 18th St. NW
Washington, DC 20036-1802
Free: (800)365-9753
Publication E-mail: jrl@heldref.org
Publisher E-mail: revu@heldref.org

Psychology journal which publishes a variety of research and theoretical articles. **Subtitle:** Interdisciplinary and Applied. **Founded:** 1935. **Freq:** Bimonthly. **Print Method:** Offset. Uses mats. **Trim Size:** 6 x 9. **Cols./Page:** 1. **Col. Width:** 5 inches. **Col. Depth:** 7 1/2 inches. **Key Personnel:** Grant Williams, Advertising Mgr., advertise@heldref.org; Fred Huber, Circulation Mgr., subscribe@heldref.org; Douglas Kirkpatrick, Director; Jean Kline, Fulfillment Manager, subscribe@heldref.org; Doris Chalfin, Managing Editor. **ISSN:** 0022-3980. **Subscription Rates:** $130 individuals and institutions; foreign, add $15. **Online:** Healthgate; EBSCO; Infonautics; Information Access; Inst. Scientific Info.; UMI. **URL:** http://www.heldref.org/. **Alt. Formats:** CD-ROM. **Formerly:** The Journal of Psychology: Interdisciplinary and Applied.
Ad Rates: BW: $260 **Circ:** Paid ‡1,400

5627 Journal of Social, Political & Economic Studies
Council for Social and Economic Studies
1133 13 St. NW, Ste. C-2 Phone: (202)371-2700
Washington, DC 20005 Fax: (202)371-1523

Journal on current and international social, political, and economic issues. **Founded:** 1976. **Freq:** Quarterly. **Print Method:** Offset. **Trim Size:** 6 x 9. **Cols./Page:** 1. **Col. Width:** 50 nonpareils. **Col. Depth:** 98 agate lines. **Key Personnel:** Roger Pearson, Ph.D., Editor. **ISSN:** 0193-5941. **Subscription Rates:** $40; $80 Institutions and libraries. **Remarks:** Accepts advertising. **Alt. Formats:** CD-ROM.
Ad Rates: BW: $175 **Circ:** Paid ‡1,200
Non-paid ‡80

5628 The Journal of Social Psychology
Heldref Publications
Helen Dwight Reid Educational Foundation Phone: (202)296-6267
Fax: (202)296-5149
1319 18th St. NW
Washington, DC 20036-1802
Free: (800)365-9753
Publication E-mail: soc@heldref.org
Publisher E-mail: revu@heldref.org

Psychology journal of experimental, empirical, and field studies of groups, cultural effects, cross-national problems, language, and ethnicity. **Founded:** 1929. **Freq:** Bimonthly. **Print Method:** Offset. **Trim Size:** 6 x 9. **Cols./Page:** 1. **Col. Width:** 5 inches. **Col. Depth:** 7 1/2 inches. **Key Personnel:** Grant Williams, Advertising Mgr., advertise@heldref.org; Douglas

Kirkpatrick, Director; Fred Huber, Circulation Mgr., subscribe@heldref.org; Jean Kline, Fulfillment Manager, subscribe@heldref.org; Elisa Subin, Managing Editor. **ISSN:** 0022-4545. **Subscription Rates:** $130 individuals; add $15 for postage outside the United States. **Online:** Healthgate; EBSCO; Infonautics; Information Access; Inst. Scient. Info.; UMI; Responsive DataBase Services. **URL:** http://www.heldref.org/. **Alt. Formats:** CD-ROM.
Ad Rates: BW: $295 **Circ:** Paid ‡1,700

5629 Journal of Virology
American Society for Microbiology
1325 Massachusetts Ave. NW Phone: (202)737-3600
Washington, DC 20005 Fax: (202)942-9342
Publisher E-mail: journals@asmusa.org

Journal on viruses of bacteria, plants, and animals. **Founded:** 1967. **Freq:** Monthly. **Print Method:** Offset. Uses mats. **Trim Size:** 8 1/4 x 11. **Cols./Page:** 2. **Col. Width:** 42 nonpareils. **Col. Depth:** 127 agate lines. **Key Personnel:** Thomas E. Shenk, Editor-in-Chief. **ISSN:** 0022-538X. **Subscription Rates:** $99 members; $482 nonmembers institutions. **Remarks:** Accepts advertising. **Available Online. URL:** http://www.journals.asm.org.
Ad Rates: BW: $1,175 **Circ:** Paid ‡5,100
4C: $2,190 Non-paid ‡30

5630 The Journals of Gerontology; Psychological Sciences & Social Sciences
Gerontological Society of America
1030 15th St., NW, Ste. 250 Phone: (202)842-1275
Washington, DC 20005-1503 Fax: (202)842-1150
Publisher E-mail: geron@geron.org

Two journals under one cover presenting scientific articles and research in the fields of biology and medicine, as they relate to aging. **Subtitle:** Series A: Biological Sciences and Medical Sciences. **Founded:** 1946. **Freq:** Bimonthly. **Print Method:** Web offset. **Trim Size:** 8 3/8 x 10 7/8. **Cols./Page:** 2. **Col. Width:** 30 nonpareils. **Col. Depth:** 116 agate lines. **Key Personnel:** Elizabeth Borgen, Contact; Bettie Donley, Contact. **ISSN:** 1079-5006. **Subscription Rates:** $95 individuals; $195 institutions. **Remarks:** Accepts advertising. **Alt. Formats:** Microform. **Formerly**: The Journal of Gerontology.
Ad Rates: BW: $660 **Circ:** Paid ‡5,600
4C: $1,360

5631 Journeyman Roofer and Waterproofer
United Union of Roofers
1660 L St. NW, Ste. 800 Phone: (202)463-7663
Washington, DC 20036-5603 Fax: (202)463-6906

Trade journal. **Founded:** 1925. **Freq:** Monthly. **Key Personnel:** John A. McConaty, Editor. **Subscription Rates:** $2. $.20 single issue. **Formerly**: Journeyman Roofer.
Circ: 23,000

5632 Kennedy Institute of Ethics Journal
Johns Hopkins University Press
Joseph & Rose Kennedy Institute of Ethics Phone: (202)687-6790
Georgetown Univ. Fax: (202)687-8089
Washington, DC 20057
Publisher E-mail: jlinfo@jhupress.jhu.edu

Journal featuring opinions and analysis of bioethics. **Founded:** 1991. **Freq:** Quarterly. **Trim Size:** 6 3/4 x 10. **Cols./Page:** 1. **Col. Width:** 4 3/4 inches. **Col. Depth:** 7 1/2 inches. **Key Personnel:** Jessica Rigdon, Editor, phone (410)516-6982, jrigdon@mail.press.jhu.edu; Tara Dorai-Berry, Advertising Mgr.; Carol Mason Spicer, Editor, spicerca@gunet.georgetown.edu. **ISSN:** 1054-6863. **Subscription Rates:** $53 individuals; $91 institutions; $35 students. **Remarks:** Accepts advertising.
Ad Rates: BW: $250 **Circ:** 2,000

5633 Kerem
3035 Porter St. NW Phone: (202)364-3006
Washington, DC 20008 Fax: (202)364-3806

Religious, literary journal on Jewish themes. **Subtitle:** Creative Explorations in Judaism. **Founded:** 1992. **Freq:** Annual. **Trim Size:** 6 x 9. **Key Personnel:** Gilah Langner, Editor, phone (202)364-3006, fax (202)364-3806, langner@erols.com; Sara R. Horowitz, Editor. **ISSN:** 1068-6975. **Subscription Rates:** $8.50 individuals. **Remarks:** Advertising accepted; rates available upon request.
Circ: (Not Reported)

5634 Kiplinger's Personal Finance Magazine
Kiplinger Washington Editors, Inc.
1729 H St. NW Phone: (202)887-6491
Washington, DC 20006 Fax: (202)887-6542
Free: (800)544-0155
Publication E-mail: magazine@kiplinger.com

Personal finance magazine featuring new and existing products and services providing information on investments, insurance, taxes, home ownership, recreation, education, automobiles, healthcare, and career and retirement planning. **Founded:** 1947. **Freq:** Monthly. **Print Method:** Offset. **Trim Size:** 8 x 10 13/16. **Cols./Page:** 3. **Col. Width:** 13 picas. **Col. Depth:** 140 agate lines. **Key Personnel:** Theodore J. Miller, Editor; Knight Kiplinger, Publisher; Roger Steckler, Advertising Mgr. **ISSN:** 0009-143X. **Subscription Rates:** $18. $2.50 single issue. **Remarks:** Accepts advertising. **Formerly**: Changing Times (1992).
Ad Rates: GLR: $58.30 **Circ:** Paid ★**1,029,386**
BW: $18,000
4C: $25,500

5635 Kitchen & Bath Showroom
Hanley-Wood, Inc.
1 Thomas Circle, Ste. 600 Phone: (202)452-0800
Washington, DC 20005 Fax: (202)785-1974

Trade magazine for kitchen and bath showroom dealers. **Founded:** 1990. **Freq:** 4/year. **Key Personnel:** Bob Hoffman, Editor; Jean Dimeo, Business editor; Nina Patel, Products editor. **Remarks:** Accepts advertising. **URL:** http://www.remodeling.hw.net. **Formerly**: Kitchen & Bath Design Guide.
Circ: (Not Reported)

5636 The Laborer
Laborers' International Union of North America
905 16th St. NW Phone: (202)737-8320
Washington, DC 20006 Fax: (202)737-2754

Trade magazine for union members. **Freq:** Quarterly. **Key Personnel:** Arthur A. Coia, Editor. **ISSN:** 0023-6888. **Remarks:** Advertising not accepted.
Circ: (Not Reported)

5637 Lambda Book Report
Lambda Literary Foundation
PO Box 73910 Phone: (202)462-7924
Washington, DC 20056 Fax: (202)462-5264
Publication E-mail: lbreditor@aol.com

Magazine covering gay and lesbian literature. **Subtitle:** A Review of Contemporary Gay and Lesbian Literature. **Founded:** 1987. **Freq:** Monthly. **Print Method:** Web offset. **Trim Size:** 8 1/4 x 10 3/4. **Cols./Page:** 3. **Col. Width:** 2 3/8 inches. **Col. Depth:** 9 7/8 inches. **Key Personnel:** Jim Marks, Managing Editor; Kanani Kauka, Senior Editor; Terrance Harps, Assistant Editor; Robert Costello, Advertising Dir. **ISSN:** 1048-9487. **Subscription Rates:** $34.95; $4.95 single issue. **Remarks:** Accepts advertising. **Online:** America Online, Inc. **Alt. Formats:** CD-ROM; Microform, UMI. **Formerly**: Lambda Rising Book Report.
Ad Rates: BW: $650 **Circ:** Paid 8,000
SAU: $300 Non-paid 150
PCI: $40

5638 LAN Life Association News
National Association of Life Underwriters
1922 F St. NW Phone: (202)331-6070
Washington, DC 20006-4387 Fax: (202)835-9608
Free: (800)247-4074
Publication E-mail: lanadv@nalu.org; lanedit@nalu.org

Service and Educational magazine for life insurance agents and financial advisors. **Founded:** 1906. **Freq:** Monthly. **Print Method:** Offset. **Trim Size:** 8 1/8 x 10 7/8. **Cols./Page:** 3. **Col. Width:** 26 nonpareils. **Col. Depth:** 136 agate lines. **Key Personnel:** Afsoon Namini, Publisher; Jeffery R. Kosnett, Editor. **ISSN:** 0024-3078. **Subscription Rates:** $7 by mail; $22 other countries. **Remarks:** Accepts advertising.
Ad Rates: BW: $5,100 **Circ:** ‡123,957
4C: $6,100

5639 Landscape Architecture
American Society of Landscape Architects
636 Eye St., NW Phone: (202)898-2444
Washington, DC 20001-3736 Fax: (202)898-1185

Professional magazine covering land planning and design. **Founded:** 1910. **Freq:** Monthly. **Print Method:** Offset. **Trim Size:** 8 7/8 x 10 7/8. **Cols./Page:** 2. **Col. Width:** 17 picas. **Col. Depth:** 60 picas. **Key Personnel:** Lee Fleming, Managing Editor; James G. Trulove, Publisher; Lee Ann Moody, Advertising Dir. **ISSN:** 0023-8031. **Subscription Rates:** $42 individuals; $7 single issue; $9 single issue (Canada). **Remarks:** Accepts advertising. **Available Online.**
Ad Rates: BW: $2,230 **Circ:** ‡25,000
4C: $2,955

5640 Latin American Antiquity
Society for American Archaeology
900 2nd St. NE, No. 12 Phone: (202)789-8200
Washington, DC 20002-3557 Fax: (202)789-0284
Publisher E-mail: publications@saa.org

Journal covering the archaeology of Mesoamerica, Central and South America, and the Caribbean (English and Spanish). **Founded:** 1990. **Freq:** Quarterly. **Print Method:** Offset. **Trim Size:** 7 x 10. **Cols./Page:** 2. **Col. Width:** 16.5 picas. **Col. Depth:** 140 agate lines. **Key Personnel:** Katherine Schreiber, Editor; Rick Peterson, Advertising Mgr. **ISSN:** 1045-6635. **Subscription Rates:** Free to qualified subscribers; $115 institutions. **Alt. Formats:** Mailing labels.
Ad Rates: BW: $184 **Circ:** ‡1,500

5641 Law Briefs
Office of General Counsel
U.S. Catholic Conference Phone: (202)541-3300
3211 Fourth St. NE Fax: (202)541-3337
Washington, DC 20017
Law journal. **Freq:** Monthly. **Key Personnel:** Michael F. Moses, Editor.

5642 Law and Policy in International Business
Law Center
600 New Jersey Ave. NW Phone: (202)662-9300
Washington, DC 20001 Fax: (202)662-9313

Professional journal covering international law. **Founded:** 1968. **Freq:** Quarterly. **Key Personnel:** Robert T. C. Vermylen, Editor-in-Chief; Todd M. Coltman, Exec. Editor; Marianne C. Fiorelli, Managing Editor; Eleanor Santson Tyler, Managing Editor; Lisa Cantos, Administrative Editor. **ISSN:** 0023-9208. **Subscription Rates:** $35 individuals; $12.50 single issue. **Remarks:** Accepts advertising. **Online:** LEXIS-NEXIS; Westlaw. **URL:** http://www.LPIB.edu.
Circ: (Not Reported)

5643 Leader in Action
American Association of University Women
1111 16th St. NW Phone: (202)785-7700
Washington, DC 20036 Fax: (202)872-1425
Free: (800)326-AAUW
Publication E-mail: editor@mail.aauw.com
Publisher E-mail: info@aauw.org

National leadership magazine for AAUW leaders. **Subtitle:** AAUW's National Leadership Magazine. **Founded:** 1980. **Freq:** 3/year. **Print Method:** Offset. **Trim Size:** 8 1/2 x 11. **Cols./Page:** 2. **Col. Width:** 2 1/2 inches. **Key Personnel:** Jodi Lipson, Editor, phone (202)785-7737, fax (202)872-1425, lipsonj@mail.aauw.org. **ISSN:** 8755-2620. **Subscription Rates:** $15 members; $20 nonmembers. **Remarks:** Advertising not accepted. **Alt. Formats:** Audio tape.
Circ: Non-paid 18,000

5644 Legal Times
American Lawyer Media, L.P.
1730 M St. NW, Ste. 802 Phone: (202)457-0686
Washington, DC 20036 Fax: (202)785-4539
Publication E-mail: legal.times@counsel.com

Legal magazine covering law, lobbying, and politics in Washington, DC. **Subtitle:** Law and Lobbying in the Nation's Capital. **Founded:** 1978. **Freq:** Weekly. **Print Method:** Offset. **Trim Size:** 11 3/8 x 16. **Cols./Page:** 4. **Col. Width:** 14.3 picas. **Col. Depth:** 14.5 inches. **Key Personnel:** Eric Effron, Editor and Publisher; Tom Watson, Exec. Editor; Jon Groner, Managing Editor; Ann Pelham, Associate Publisher; Mari Hotchkiss, Production Dir.; Laura McFarland, Advertising Mgr. **Subscription Rates:** $669. **Remarks:** Accepts advertising. **Online:** LEXIS-NEXIS; Counsel Connect.
Ad Rates: BW: $2,858 **Circ:** ‡75,000
4C: $3,558

5645 Liberal Education
Association of American Colleges & Universities
1818 R St. NW Phone: (202)387-3760
Washington, DC 20009 Fax: (202)265-9532
Free: (800)297-3775

Magazine promoting liberal education and the undergraduate curiculum. **Founded:** 1915. **Freq:** Quarterly. **Print Method:** Offset. **Trim Size:** 8 1/2 x 11. **Cols./Page:** 2. **Col. Width:** 48 nonpareils. **Col. Depth:** 134 agate lines. **Key Personnel:** Bridget Puzon, Editor, phone (202)884-7416, fax (202)265-9532, puzon@aacu.nw.dc.us; Joann Stevens, Vice President for Communications, phone (202)884-7416, fax (202)265-3775, stevens@aacu.nw.dc.us. **ISSN:** 0024-1822. **Subscription Rates:** $36 members; $42 nonmembers; $10 single issue. **Remarks:** Advertising not accepted. **URL:** http://www.aacu-edu.org. **Alt. Formats:** Microfiche.
Circ: Paid ‡900
Controlled ‡3,200

5646 Lincoln Review
The Lincoln Institute for Research and Education, Inc.
1001 Connecticut Ave. NW, Ste. 1135 Phone: (202)223-5112
Washington, DC 20036-5504
Black public policy journal. **Founded:** 1979. **Freq:** Quarterly. **Print Method:** Offset. **Trim Size:** 6 x 9. **Cols./Page:** 1. **Key Personnel:** J.A. Parker, Editor and Publisher. **ISSN:** 0192-5083. **Subscription Rates:** $12 individuals.
Circ: Non-paid ‡7,000

5647 The Living Light
Office of the Executive Editor Phone: (202)319-5705
Caldwell 345 Fax: (202)635-4871
Catholic University of America
Washington, DC 20064
Publication E-mail: marthaler@cua.edu

Journal of United States Catholic Conference Department of Education promoting dialogue with Catholic educators in the fields of catechetics in school programs, and religious education and formation. **Founded:** 1964. **Freq:** Quarterly. **Trim Size:** 6 x 9. **Cols./Page:** 2. **Key Personnel:** Rev. Berard L. Marthaler, Editor, fax (202)319-5704; Timothy D. Delaney, Advertising Mgr. **ISSN:** 0024-5275. **Subscription Rates:** $29.95 individuals; $39.95 outside U.S. and Canada; $8.95 single issue. **Remarks:** Accepts advertising.
Ad Rates: BW: $200 **Circ:** Paid 1,200

5648 Lodging Magazine
American Hotel & Motel Association
1201 New York Ave. NW, Ste. 600 Phone: (202)289-3100
Fax: (202)289-3199
Washington, DC 20005-3931
Publication E-mail: llodgers@aol.com
Publisher E-mail: infoctr@ahma.com

Magazine directed to the management staff of hotels and motels. **Founded:** Sept. 1975. **Freq:** Monthly. **Print Method:** Web offset. **Trim Size:** 8 3/8 x 10 7/8. **Cols./Page:** 3. **Col. Width:** 2 3/8 inches. **Col. Depth:** 10 inches. **Key Personnel:** Larry Wilhelm, Publisher, phone (202)289-3163, lwilhelm@ahma.com; Philip Hayward, Editor, phone (202)289-3169, phayward@ahma.com; John Paul Boukis, Bus. Mgr., phone (202)289-3150. **ISSN:** 0360-9235. **Subscription Rates:** $49 individuals; $9 single issue; $85 other countries. **Remarks:** Accepts advertising.
Ad Rates: BW: $5,700 **Circ:** Paid 4,885
4C: $6,900 Non-paid 48,568

5649 Main Economic Indicators
Organization for Economic Cooperation and Development (OECD)
2001 L St. NW, Ste. 650 Phone: (202)785-6323
Washington, DC 20036-4922 Fax: (202)785-0350
Free: (800)456-6323
Publication E-mail: washcont@oecd.org
Publisher E-mail: washington.contact@oecd.org

Report graphing changes in the economies of OECD member countries. **Freq:** Monthly. **Print Method:** Offset. **Trim Size:** 7 7/8 x 10 5/8. **Cols./Page:** 1. **Col. Width:** 84 nonpareils. **Col. Depth:** 133 agate lines. **ISSN:** 0474-5523. **Subscription Rates:** $290 individuals; $327 by air mail. **Remarks:** Advertising not accepted.
Circ: (Not Reported)

5650 Main Science & Technology Indicators
Organization for Economic Cooperation and Development (OECD)
2001 L St. NW, Ste. 650 Phone: (202)785-6323
Washington, DC 20036-4922 Fax: (202)785-0350
Free: (800)456-6323
Publisher E-mail: washington.contact@oecd.org

Magazine examining resources devoted to research and development, and the output and impact of scientific and technological activity. **Freq:** Semiannual. **Print Method:** Offset. **ISSN:** 1011-792X. **Subscription Rates:** $55 individuals; $58 by air mail. **Remarks:** Advertising not accepted.
Circ: (Not Reported)

5651 The Mankind Quarterly
Scott-Townsend Publishers
PO Box 34070 Phone: (202)371-2700
Washington, DC 20043 Fax: (202)371-1523

Anthropology journal. **Founded:** 1959. **Freq:** Quarterly. **Print Method:** Offset. **Trim Size:** 8 1/2 x 6. **Cols./Page:** 1. **Col. Width:** 50 nonpareils. **Col. Depth:** 98 agate lines. **Key Personnel:** Hans Jurgen, Editor; Richard Lynn, Editor; Brunetto Chiarelli, Editor; Edgar C. Polome, Editor; Glayde Whitney, Editor. **ISSN:** 0025-2344. **Subscription Rates:** $40 individuals; $80 institutions; $25 students. **Remarks:** Accepts advertising. **URL:** http://mankind.org.
Ad Rates: BW: $200 **Circ:** Paid ‡1,020
Non-paid ‡60

5652 Mathematics Magazine
Mathematical Association of America
1529 18th St. NW Phone: (202)387-5200
Washington, DC 20036 Free: (800)741-9415
Publisher E-mail: epedreir@nadd.org

Magazine featuring informal mathematical articles and notes designed to appeal to faculty and students at the undergraduate level. Also contains a problems section, a reviews section, a news and letters section featuring early publication of problems and solutions from Olympiads and Putnam Competitions. **Founded:** 1925. **Freq:** Bimonthly. **Print Method:** Offset. **Cols./Page:** 1. **Col. Width:** 65 nonpareils. **Col. Depth:** 115 agate lines. **Key Personnel:** G.L. Alexanderson, Editor; E. Sullivan, Advertising Mgr. **Subscription Rates:** $35 individuals. **Remarks:** Accepts advertising.
Ad Rates: BW: $360 **Circ:** (Not Reported)

5653 Mediation Quarterly
Jossey-Bass Inc., Publishers
6242 29th St. NW
Washington, DC 20015
Publisher E-mail: webperson@jbp.com

Publication offering information on applications, techniques, and concerns in the family mediation field. **Subtitle:** Journal of the Academy of Family Mediator. **Founded:** 1983. **Freq:** Quarterly. **Print Method:** Sheetfed offset. **Trim Size:** 6 x 9. **Cols./Page:** 1. **Col. Width:** 27 picas. **Col. Depth:** 45 picas. **Key Personnel:** Peter R. Maida, Ph.D, Editor. **ISSN:** 0739-4098. **Subscription Rates:** $49 individuals; $82 institutions. **Remarks:** Advertising not accepted.
Circ: Paid ‡2,108
Non-paid ‡98

5654 Mental Retardation
American Association on Mental Retardation
444 N. Capitol St. NW, Ste. 846 Phone: (202)387-1968
Washington, DC 20001-1512 Fax: (202)387-2193
Free: (800)424-3688
Publication E-mail: staylo01@mailbox.syr.edu
Publisher E-mail: mailbox@aamr.org

Magazine featuring articles on mental retardation for professionals and parents. **Founded:** 1964. **Freq:** Bimonthly. **Trim Size:** 6 7/8 x 9 3/4. **Key Personnel:** Stephen Stidinger, Contact, phone (202)387-1968, fax (202)387-2193. **ISSN:** 0047-6765. **Subscription Rates:** $115 nonmembers.
Ad Rates: BW: $520 **Circ:** Paid 10,000

5655 Microbiology and Molecular Biology Reviews
American Society for Microbiology
1325 Massachusetts Ave. NW Phone: (202)737-3600
Washington, DC 20005 Fax: (202)942-9342
Publisher E-mail: journals@asmusa.org

Broad-based review journal covering microbiology, immunology, and molecular and cellular biology. **Founded:** 1937. **Freq:** Quarterly. **Print Method:** Offset. Uses mats. **Trim Size:** 8 1/4 x 11. **Cols./Page:** 2. **Col. Width:** 42 nonpareils. **Col. Depth:** 127 agate lines. **Key Personnel:** Catherine L. Squires, Editor-in-Chief. **ISSN:** 1092-2172. **Subscription Rates:** $45 members; $151 nonmembers institutions. **Remarks:** Accepts advertising. **URL:** http://asmusa.org. **Formerly:** Microbiological Reviews.
Ad Rates: BW: $1,525 **Circ:** Paid ‡11,171
4C: $1,095 Non-paid ‡50

5656 Middle East Executive Reports
International Executive Reports, Ltd.
717 D St. NW, No. 300 Phone: (202)628-6900
Washington, DC 20004-2807 Fax: (202)628-6618
Publication E-mail: execrep@aol.com
Publisher E-mail: execrep@aol.com

Magazine on legal, technical, and financial requirements for business in the Mid East. **Founded:** Sept. 1978. **Freq:** Monthly. **Print Method:** Offset. **Trim Size:** 8 1/2 x 11. **Cols./Page:** 2. **Col. Width:** 3 1/2 inches. **Col. Depth:** 9 3/8 inches. **Key Personnel:** William Hearn, Publisher; Mimi Mann, Editor; Lloyd Gibson, Advertising Mgr. **ISSN:** 0271-0498. **Subscription Rates:** $455; $195 non-profit Industry. **Remarks:** Accepts advertising. **Online:** LEXIS-NEXIS; Westlaw.
Ad Rates: BW: $425 **Circ:** Paid ‡500
Non-paid ‡400

5657 Middle East Insight
1200 18th St. NW, Ste. 305 Phone: (202)466-2146
Washington, DC 20036 Fax: (202)466-2147

Journal covering politics and business of the Middle East. **Founded:** 1980. **Freq:** Bimonthly. **ISSN:** 0731-9371. **Subscription Rates:** $27 individuals; $10 single issue. **Remarks:** Accepts advertising.
Circ: (Not Reported)

5658 The Middle East Journal
Middle East Institute
1761 N St. NW Phone: (202)785-1141
Washington, DC 20036 Fax: (202)331-8861
Publication E-mail: mej@mideasti.org
Publisher E-mail: mej@mideasti.org

Journal covering social, political, and economic aspects of the Middle East. **Founded:** Jan. 1947. **Freq:** Quarterly. **Print Method:** Offset. **Trim Size:** 6 1/2 x 9 1/2. **Cols./Page:** 1. **Col. Width:** 30 nonpareils. **Col. Depth:** 96 agate lines. **Key Personnel:** Michael Collins Dunn, Editor, fax (202)452-8876, editor@mideasti.org. **ISSN:** 0026-3141. **Subscription Rates:** $36 individuals; $48 institutions; $65.50 two years.
Ad Rates: BW: $400 **Circ:** ‡3,500

5659 Middle East Report
Middle East Research & Information Project
1500 Massachusetts Ave. NW, Ste. 119 Phone: (202)223-3677
Fax: (202)223-3604
Washington, DC 20005
Publisher E-mail: merip@igc.org

Publication focusing on Middle Eastern politics and societal issues. **Founded:** 1971. **Freq:** Quarterly. **Trim Size:** 8 1/4 x 10 3/4. **Key Personnel:** Beth Golatzki, Business Mgr.; Geoff Hartman, Editor. **ISSN:** 0899-2851. **Subscription Rates:** $32 individuals; $59 two years; $58 institutions, other countries; $100 two years Institutions, other countries. **Remarks:** Advertising not accepted.
Circ: 4,000

5660 Mining Voice
National Mining Association
1130 17th St. NW Phone: (202)463-2619
Washington, DC 20036-4677 Fax: (202)857-0135

Trade magazine covering political, business, environmental, and social trends affecting mining in the U.S. **Subtitle:** The Magazine of the National Mining Association. **Founded:** Mar. 1995. **Freq:** Bimonthly. **Trim Size:** 8 1/2 x 11. **Cols./Page:** 2. **Key Personnel:** Jeanne Chircop, Editor, jchircop@pr.nma.org; Elizabeth Roca-Crooks, Editorial Asst., phone (202)463-2640, lroca-crooks@nma.org; Gloria Castro, Circulation Supervisor, phone (202)463-2624, gcastro@pr.nma.org. **ISSN:** 1080-6121. **Subscription Rates:** $36 individuals; $72 out of country. **Remarks:** Accepts advertising. **URL:** http://www.nma.org.
Ad Rates: BW: $1,975 **Circ:** Paid 10,000
4C: $2,725

5661 Mississippi Monitor
American Rivers
1025 Vermont Ave. NW, Ste. 720 Phone: (202)347-7550
Fax: (202)347-9240
Washington, DC 20005
Publisher E-mail: amrivers@amrivers.org

Community newspaper. **Subtitle:** The Newspaper Dedicated to the Mississippi River. **Founded:** Mar. 1997. **Freq:** Monthly. **Trim Size:** 11 1/2 x 12. **Key Personnel:** Scott Faber, Contact. **Subscription Rates:** Free. **URL:** http://www.amrivers.org/msmonhom.html.
Circ: Non-paid 5,200

5662 Mobile Communications Report
Warren Publishing, Inc.
2115 Ward Ct. NW Phone: (202)872-9200
Washington, DC 20037 Fax: (202)293-3435
Publisher E-mail: warrenpub@mindspring.com

Publication covering the mobile satellite industry. **Subtitle:** The Authoritative Report on Aeronautical, Maritime, Land Mobile Satellites, and Radio Determination. **Founded:** 1987. **Freq:** Biweekly. **Key Personnel:** Albert Warren, Publisher; Betty Alvine, Circulation Mgr.; Gary Madderom, Marketing Dir. **ISSN:** 0146-6061. **Subscription Rates:** $549 U.S.; $572 other countries. **Remarks:** Advertising not accepted. **Available Online**. **Formerly**: Mobile Satallite Reports.
Circ: (Not Reported)

5663 Mobility
Employee Relocation Council (ERC)
1720 N St. NW Phone: (202)857-0857
Washington, DC 20036 Fax: (202)467-4012
Publisher E-mail: info@erc.org

Magazine for professionals in the relocation industry. **Subtitle:** The total relocation magazine. **Founded:** 1980. **Freq:** Monthly. **Print Method:** Web press. **Trim Size:** 8 1/8 x 10 7/8. **Cols./Page:** 3. **Col. Width:** 13 picas. **Col. Depth:** 58 picas. **Key Personnel:** Jerry Holloman, Editor and Publisher, jholloma@erc.org; Richard McGuire, Advertising Mgr., rmcguire@erc.org. **ISSN:** 0195-8194. **Subscription Rates:** $48 individuals; $5 single issue. **Remarks:** Accepts advertising. **URL:** http://www.erc.org.
Ad Rates: BW: $2,000 **Circ:** Paid ‡11,970
4C: $2,950 Non-paid ‡498

5664 Modern Maturity
American Association of Retired Persons (AARP)
601 E St. NW Phone: (202)434-2277
Washington, DC 20049 Fax: (202)434-6451
Publisher E-mail: aarp1@aol.com

Magazine for persons fifty and older. **Founded:** 1957. **Freq:** Bimonthly. **Print Method:** Roto Gravure and Web Offset. **Trim Size:** 8 1/8 x 10 3/4. **Cols./Page:** 3 and 2. **Col. Width:** 26 and 43 nonpareils. **Col. Depth:** 143 agate lines. **Key Personnel:** Henry Fenwick, Editor. **ISSN:** 0026-8046. **Subscription**

Rates: $8 individuals. **Remarks:** Accepts advertising. **Alt. Formats:** Audio tape.
Ad Rates: BW: $215,880 **Circ:** Paid ★**20,534,357**
4C: $239,200

5665 Molecular and Cellular Biology
American Society for Microbiology
1325 Massachusetts Ave. NW Phone: (202)737-3600
Washington, DC 20005 Fax: (202)942-9342
Publisher E-mail: journals@asmusa.org

Journal providing information on the molecular biology of eucaryotic cells, of both microbial and higher organisms. **Founded:** 1981. **Freq:** Monthly. **Print Method:** Offset. Uses mats. **Trim Size:** 8 1/4 x 11. **Cols./Page:** 2. **Col. Width:** 42 nonpareils. **Col. Depth:** 127 agate lines. **Key Personnel:** Alan M. Weiner, Editor-in-Chief. **ISSN:** 0270-7306. **Subscription Rates:** $84 members; $450 nonmembers institutions. **Remarks:** Accepts advertising. **Available Online. URL:** http://www.journals.asm.org.
Ad Rates: BW: $1,175 **Circ:** Paid ‡5,500
4C: $1,175 Non-paid ‡35

5666 Momentum
National Catholic Educational Association
1077 30th St. NW, Ste. 100 Phone: (202)337-6232
Washington, DC 20007 Fax: (202)333-6706

Journal for educators. **Subtitle:** Official Journal of National Catholic Educational Association. **Founded:** 1970. **Freq:** Quarterly. **Print Method:** Offset. **Trim Size:** 8 1/2 x 11. **Cols./Page:** 3. **Key Personnel:** Patricia Feistritzer, Editor. **ISSN:** 0026-914X. **Subscription Rates:** Free to qualified subscribers; $20 individuals. **Remarks:** Accepts advertising. **Alt. Formats:** Microform; Mailing labels.
Ad Rates: BW: $2,600 **Circ:** Paid ‡24,500
4C: $3,800

5667 Monthly Statistics of Foreign Trade
Organization for Economic Cooperation and Development (OECD)
2001 L St. NW, Ste. 650 Phone: (202)785-6323
Washington, DC 20036-4922 Fax: (202)785-0350
Free: (800)456-6323
Publisher E-mail: washington.contact@oecd.org

Statistical report on foreign trade of OECD countries. **Freq:** Monthly. **Print Method:** Offset. **Trim Size:** 7 7/8 x 10 5/8. **Cols./Page:** 1. **Col. Width:** 84 nonpareils. **Col. Depth:** 133 agate lines. **ISSN:** 0474-5388. **Subscription Rates:** $190 individuals; $214 by air mail. **Remarks:** Advertising not accepted.
Circ: (Not Reported)

5668 Mortgage Banking Magazine
Mortgage Bankers Association of America
1125 15th St. NW Free: (800)793-MBAA
Washington, DC 20005
Magazine of the real estate finance industry. **Subtitle:** The Magazine of Real Estate Finance. **Founded:** 1939. **Freq:** Monthly. **Print Method:** Offset. **Trim Size:** 8 1/2 x 10 7/8. **Cols./Page:** 3. **Col. Width:** 26 nonpareils. **Col. Depth:** 140 agate lines. **Key Personnel:** Janet Reilley Hewitt, Editor-in-Chief, phone (202)861-6592, fax (202)861-0736, janet_hewitt@mbaa.org; Lesley Hall, Associate Editor, phone (202)861-1930, lesley_hall@mbaa.org; Mildred Jones, Advertising Mgr., phone (202)861-6555, mildred_jones@mbaa.org. **ISSN:** 0730-0212. **Subscription Rates:** $45 individuals. **Remarks:** Accepts advertising. **URL:** http://www.mbaa.org. **Alt. Formats:** Microform.
Ad Rates: BW: $2,842 **Circ:** ‡10,204
4C: $3,832
PCI: $65.00

5669 Multinational Monitor
Essential Information, Inc.
PO Box 19405 Phone: (202)387-8030
Washington, DC 20036 Fax: (202)234-5176
Publication E-mail: monitor@essential.org

Magazine reporting on the impact of multinational corporations on labor, Third World development, women, and politics. **Founded:** 1979. **Freq:** Monthly. **Print Method:** Offset. **Trim Size:** 8 1/2 x 11. **Cols./Page:** 2. **Key Personnel:** Robert Weissman, Editor; John Richard, Managing Editor; Cynthia Renfro, Business Mgr. **ISSN:** 0197-4637. **Subscription Rates:** $25 individuals; $30 nonprofit orgs.; $40 businesses. **Remarks:** Accepts advertising. **URL:** gopher.
Ad Rates: BW: $700 **Circ:** Paid ‡10,000
Non-paid ‡2,000

5670 Museum News
American Association of Museums
1575 I St. NW, Ste. 400 Phone: (202)289-1818
Washington, DC 20005 Fax: (202)289-6578
Publisher E-mail: aaminfo@aam-us.org

Magazine for museum employees, trustees, and volunteers. **Founded:** Jan. 1, 1924. **Freq:** Bimonthly. **Print Method:** WEB. **Trim Size:** 8 1/2 x 11. **Cols./Page:** 3. **Col. Width:** 27 nonpareils. **Col. Depth:** 134 agate lines. **Key Personnel:** John Strand, Editor and Publisher; Bart Ecker, Advertising Mgr.; Jane Lusaka, Managing Editor. **ISSN:** 0027-4089. **Subscription Rates:** $38 individuals; $7 single issue. **Remarks:** Accepts advertising.
Ad Rates: BW: $1,935 **Circ:** ‡14,500
4C: $3,125

5671 Musical Mainstream
National Library Service for the Blind and Physically Handicapped
1291 Taylor St., NW Phone: (202)707-5100
Washington, DC 20542 Fax: (202)707-0712
Free: (800)424-8567
Publisher E-mail: nls@loc.gov

General music magazine available only in braille and large print, and on 8 rpm disk formats. **Founded:** 1977. **Freq:** Quarterly. **Print Method:** Offset. **Cols./Page:** 2. **Col. Width:** 72 nonpareils. **Col. Depth:** 146 agate lines. **Key Personnel:** Shirley P. Emanuel, Editor. **ISSN:** 0364-7501. **Subscription Rates:** Free to eligible persons. **Remarks:** Advertising not accepted. **Alt. Formats:** Braille; Diskette; Large-print.
Circ: Non-paid ‡3,600

5672 Nabe News
National Association for Business Economics
1233 20th St., Ste. 505 Phone: (202)463-6223
Washington, DC 20036 Fax: (202)463-6239
Publisher E-mail: nabe@nabe.com

Publication focusing on news of the National Association of Business Economists. **Freq:** Bimonthly. **Key Personnel:** Susan Doolittle, Contact. **Subscription Rates:** $7.50 single issue (Subscription available only with NABE membership). **Remarks:** Accepts advertising.
Circ: (Not Reported)

5673 Nabe Quarterly Surveys
National Association for Business Economics
1233 20th St., Ste. 505 Phone: (202)463-6223
Washington, DC 20036 Fax: (202)463-6239
Publisher E-mail: nabe@nabe.com

Journal of National Association for Business Economists. **Founded:** 1965. **Freq:** Quarterly. **Key Personnel:** Susan Doolittle, Contact. **Subscription Rates:** Included in membership.

5674 National Alliance
National Alliance of Postal and Federal Employees
1628 11th St. NW Phone: (202)939-6325
Washington, DC 20001 Fax: (202)939-6389

Magazine for postal and federal employees. **Founded:** 1913. **Freq:** Monthly. **Print Method:** Offset. **Trim Size:** 8 1/2 x 11. **Cols./Page:** 3. **Col. Width:** 28 nonpareils. **Col. Depth:** 133 agate lines. **Key Personnel:** Jacquelyn C. Moore, Editor, jmoore@patriot.net. **ISSN:** 0027-8513. **Subscription Rates:** $10 individuals. **Remarks:** Accepts advertising. **URL:** http://www.napfe.com.
Ad Rates: BW: $420 **Circ:** ‡14,700

5675 National Business Woman
Business and Professional Women's Foundation
2012 Massachusetts Ave. NW Phone: (202)293-1200
Washington, DC 20036 Fax: (202)861-0298

Magazine for working women that promotes workplace equity issues. **Founded:** 1919. **Freq:** Quarterly. **Print Method:** Web offset. **Trim Size:** 8 1/8 x 10 3/4. **Cols./Page:** 3. **Col. Width:** 2 1/4 inches. **Col. Depth:** 10 3/4 inches. **Key Personnel:** A. Antoanela Barcutian, Senior Editor, phone (202)293-1100, abarcutain@bpwusa.org. **ISSN:** 0027-8831. **Subscription Rates:** $29. **Remarks:** Accepts advertising.
Ad Rates: BW: $2,500 **Circ:** Controlled ‡75,000
4C: $3,000
PCI: $200

5676 National Environmental Enforcement Journal
National Association of Attorneys General
750 1st St. NE, Ste. 1100 Phone: (202)326-6000
Washington, DC 20002 Fax: (202)408-7014

Trade journal covering law and environmental enforcement. **Founded:** 1986. **Freq:** Monthly. **Key Personnel:** Judith E. McKee, Editor, phone (202)326-6044, jmckee@naag.org. **Subscription Rates:** $95 libraries and government; $195 individuals. **Remarks:** Advertising not accepted. **Online:** Lexis.
Circ: Controlled 750

5677 National Geographic
National Geographic Society
1145 17th St. NW Phone: (202)857-6112
Washington, DC 20036 Fax: (202)775-6141
Free: (800)638-6400
Publisher E-mail: natgeo1@aol.com

Magazine designed to teach individuals about history, culture, the environment, science, and themselves. **Subtitle:** Official Journal of the National Geographic Society. **Founded:** 1888. **Freq:** Monthly. **Print Method:** Offset. **Trim Size:** 6 3/4 x 10. **Cols./Page:** 2. **Col. Width:** 32 nonpareils. **Col. Depth:** 122 agate lines. **Key Personnel:** Gilbert M. Grosvenor, Chairman of the Board of Trustees; Reg Murphy, President; William L. Allen, Editor. **ISSN:** 0027-9358. **Subscription Rates:** $25 individuals; $5 single issue. **Remarks:** Accepts advertising. **Online:** America Online, Inc. **URL:** http://www.nationalgeographic.com. **Alt. Formats:** CD-ROM.
Circ: Paid ★**8,612,102**

5678 National Geographic Traveler
National Geographic Society
1145 17th St. NW Phone: (202)857-6112
Washington, DC 20036 Fax: (202)775-6141
Free: (800)638-6400
Publication E-mail: traveler@nationalgeographic.com
Publisher E-mail: natgeo1@aol.com

Travel magazine emphasizing practical information about U.S. and foreign destinations. **Founded:** 1984. **Freq:** 8/year. **Print Method:** Offset. **Trim Size:** 8 1/4 x 11. **Cols./Page:** 4. **Col. Width:** 15 picas. **Col. Depth:** 57 picas. **Key Personnel:** Keith Bellows, Editor; Dawn Drew, Advertising Dir. **Subscription Rates:** $17.95; $3.95 single issue. **Remarks:** Accepts advertising. **URL:** http://www.nationalgeographic.com.
Ad Rates: BW: $23,860 **Circ:** Paid 724,094
4C: $31,810

5679 National Geographic WORLD
National Geographic Society
1145 17th St. NW Phone: (202)857-6112
Washington, DC 20036 Fax: (202)775-6141
Free: (800)638-6400
Publisher E-mail: natgeo1@aol.com

Magazine featuring factual stories on outdoor adventure, natural history, sports, science, and history for children ages 8 through 13. **Founded:** Sept. 1975. **Freq:** Monthly. **Print Method:** Offset. **Trim Size:** 8 1/2 x 10 3/4. **Cols./Page:** 3. **Col. Width:** 14 picas. **Key Personnel:** Susan Tejada, Editor, phone (202)828-6651, fax (202)775-6112, stejada@ngs.org. **ISSN:** 0361-5499. **Subscription Rates:** $17.95 individuals; $2.50 single issue. **Remarks:** Advertising not accepted.
Circ: Paid ‡1,246,210
Free ‡13,334

5680 National Guard Magazine
1 Massachusetts Ave. NW Phone: (202)789-0031
Washington, DC 20001 Fax: (202)682-9358
Free: (888)226-4287
Publication E-mail: magazine@ngaus.org
Publisher E-mail: ngaus@ngaus.org

Magazine for Army and Air National Guard Officers. **Founded:** 1947. **Freq:** Monthly. **Print Method:** Offset. **Cols./Page:** 3 and 2. **Col. Width:** 26 and 40 nonpareils. **Col. Depth:** 138 agate lines. **Key Personnel:** Major General Richard Alexander, RET., Publisher; John Goheen, Dir of Communications, phone (202)408-4892, pakane@ngaus.org; Capt. Kevin McAndrews, Business Mgr., phone (202)408-5897, kmcandre@ngaus.org; Capt. Bonnie Carter, Circulation Mgr., phone (202)408-5215, bcarter@ngaus.org; M. Catherine Casper, CPA, Controller; Kristin Patterson, News Editor. **ISSN:** 0163-3945. **Subscription Rates:** $25 individuals. **Remarks:** Accepts advertising. **URL:** http://www.ngaus.org. **Formerly:** The National Guardsman.
Ad Rates: BW: $2,600 **Circ:** ‡69,500
4C: $3,600

5681 The National Interest
National Affairs, Inc.
1112 16th St. NW, Ste. 540 Phone: (202)785-8555
Washington, DC 20036 Fax: (202)467-0006

Journal covering foreign policy. **Founded:** 1985. **Freq:** Quarterly. **Print Method:** Web. **Trim Size:** 7 x 10. **Cols./Page:** 2. **Col. Width:** 2 3/4 inches. **Col. Depth:** 10 inches. **Key Personnel:** Kristen Yessayan, Managing Editor; Owen Harries, Editor. **ISSN:** 0884-9382. **Subscription Rates:** $26 individuals; $36 other countries; $7 single issue.
Ad Rates: BW: $500 **Circ:** Combined ‡9,000

5682 National Jesuit News
1424 16th St. NW, No. 300 Phone: (202)986-5461
Washington, DC 20036 Fax: (202)328-9212

Newspaper reporting on the activities of American Jesuits and national and international issues affecting their ministries. **Founded:** 1971. **Freq:** Monthly. **Print Method:** Offset. **Trim**

Size: 11 1/4 x 14 5/8. **Cols./Page:** 4. **Col. Width:** 15 picas. **Col. Depth:** 13 3/8 inches. **Key Personnel:** Rev. Thomas M. Lucas, S.J., Editor; Elizabeth O'Keefe, Managing Editor. **ISSN:** 0199-0284.
Circ: Non-paid ‡6,000

5683 National Journal
1501 M St. NW, Ste. 300 Phone: (202)739-8400
Washington, DC 20005 Fax: (202)833-8069
Publisher E-mail: njdc@njdc.com

National news magazine. **Subtitle:** The Weekly on Politics and Government. **Founded:** 1969. **Freq:** Weekly (Sat.). **Print Method:** Offset. **Trim Size:** 8 1/2 x 11. **Cols./Page:** 3. **Col. Width:** 25 nonpareils. **Col. Depth:** 126 agate lines. **Key Personnel:** Richard Frank, Editor; John Fox Sullivan, Publisher. **ISSN:** 0360-4217. **Subscription Rates:** $839 individuals; $99 individuals full-time faculty. **Remarks:** Accepts advertising. **Online:** Legi-Slate, Inc.; LEXIS-NEXIS.
Ad Rates: BW: $6,500 **Circ:** Paid 5,418
4C: $8,600 Non-paid 2,029

5684 National NOW Times
National Organization for Women, Inc.
1000 16th St. NW, Ste. 700 Phone: (202)331-0066
Washington, DC 20036 Fax: (202)785-8576
Publication E-mail: nnt@now.org
Publisher E-mail: now@now.org

Feminist magazine. **Freq:** Quarterly. **Key Personnel:** Patricia Ireland, Editor; Lisa Bennett-Higney, Managing Editor. **ISSN:** 0149-4740. **Subscription Rates:** $35. **Remarks:** Accepts advertising. **URL:** http://www.now.org.
Ad Rates: PCI: $65 **Circ:** 250,000

5685 National Parks
National Parks & Conservation Association
1776 Massachusetts Ave. N.W. Phone: (202)223-6722
Washington, DC 20036
Magazine on issues affecting our National Parks. **Subtitle:** The Magazine of the National Parks and Conservation Association. **Founded:** 1919. **Freq:** Bimonthly. **Print Method:** Offset. **Trim Size:** 8 1/8 x 10 7/8. **Cols./Page:** 2. **Col. Width:** 13.5 picas. **Col. Depth:** 127 agate lines. **Key Personnel:** Leslie Happ, Editor-in-Chief. **ISSN:** 0276-8186. **Subscription Rates:** $25 individuals; $2.50 single issue. **Remarks:** Accepts advertising. **Online:** American Online (key word: parks).
Ad Rates: BW: $8,984 **Circ:** Paid ★406,718
4C: $13,240

5686 The National Voter
League of Women Voters of the United States (LWVUS)
1730 M St. NW, Ste. 1000 Phone: (202)429-1965
Washington, DC 20036-4508 Fax: (202)429-0854
Publisher E-mail: lwv@lwv.org

Official journal of the League of Women Voters encouraging active citizen involvement in goverment. **Founded:** 1951. **Freq:** Quarterly. **Print Method:** Web offset. **Trim Size:** 8 3/8 x 10 7/8. **Cols./Page:** 3. **Col. Width:** 13.5 picas. **Col. Depth:** 58.5 picas. **Key Personnel:** Meg S. Duskin, Editor, megd@lwv.org. **ISSN:** 0028-0372. **Subscription Rates:** Included in membership; $15 individuals; $2.50 single issue. **Remarks:** Accepts advertising. **Available Online. URL:** http://www.lwv.org.
Ad Rates: GLR: $3.15 **Circ:** Paid ‡102,000

5687 Nation's Building News
Nations Building News
1201 15th St. NW Phone: (202)822-0525
Washington, DC 20005-2800 Fax: (202)861-2131

Trade magazine (tabloid) covering home building and all related industries. **Founded:** 1985. **Freq:** Semimonthly. **Print Method:** Offset. **Trim Size:** 10 1/4 x 14. **Cols./Page:** 4. **Col. Width:** 27 nonpareils. **Col. Depth:** 196 agate lines. **Key Personnel:** Tim Ahern, Editor; John M. Hemsworth, Publishing Dir. **ISSN:** 8750-6580. **Remarks:** Accepts advertising.
Ad Rates: BW: $3,800 **Circ:** 150,000
4C: $4,880

5688 Nation's Business
U.S. Chamber of Commerce
1615 H St. NW Phone: (202)463-5460
Washington, DC 20062-2000 Fax: (202)463-3114

Business magazine for small businesses. **Subtitle:** The Small Business Adviser. **Founded:** Sept. 1912. **Freq:** Monthly. **Print Method:** Offset. **Trim Size:** 8 3/16 x 10 7/8. **Cols./Page:** 3. **Col. Width:** 13.5 picas. **Col. Depth:** 140 agate lines. **Key Personnel:** Mary McElveen, Editor; David A. Roe, Publisher; Pete McCutchen, Advertising Dir. **ISSN:** 0028-047X. **Subscription Rates:** $22 individuals; $2.50 single issue. **Remarks:** Accepts advertising.
Ad Rates: BW: $35,690 **Circ:** Paid ★858,718
4C: $53,350

5689 Nation's Cities Weekly
National League of Cities
1301 Pennsylvania Ave. NW, Phone: (202)626-3000
Ste 550 Fax: (202)626-3043
Washington, DC 20004-1763
Publication E-mail: weekly@nlc.org
Publisher E-mail: pa@nlc.org

Tabloid newspaper covering municipal government and urban affairs. **Founded:** 1978. **Freq:** Weekly. **Print Method:** Offset. **Trim Size:** 11 3/8 x 14 1/2. **Cols./Page:** 5. **Col. Width:** 27 nonpareils. **Col. Depth:** 189 agate lines. **Key Personnel:** Jeff Fletcher, Editor, phone (202)626-3123, fletcher@nlc.org; Julianne Ryder, Managing Editor, phone (202)626-3047, ryder@nlc.org. **ISSN:** 0164-5935. **Subscription Rates:** $96 individuals; $149 two years; $192 For 3 years. **Remarks:** Accepts advertising. **Online:** UMI. **Feature Editors:** Elaine Harris, *Features*, phone (202)626-3048, harris@nlc.org.
Ad Rates: GLR: $12 **Circ:** ‡30,000
BW: $3,635
4C: $4,135

5690 The Nation's Health
American Public Health Association
1015 15th St. NW Phone: (202)789-5600
Washington, DC 20005 Fax: (202)789-5661
Publication E-mail: nations.health@apha.org

Public health policy, research and legislation news. **Founded:** 1971. **Freq:** 11/year. **Print Method:** Offset. **Trim Size:** tabloid. **Cols./Page:** 5. **Col. Width:** 1 5/8 inches. **Col. Depth:** 76 picas. **Key Personnel:** Trish Nicholson, Editor; Michele Late, Asst. Ed.; Ashell Alston, Adv. Mgr. **ISSN:** 0028-0496. **Subscription Rates:** $25 individuals. **Remarks:** Accepts advertising.
Ad Rates: GLR: $2.50 **Circ:** Paid ‡32,000
BW: $1,725 Non-paid ‡1,200
4C: $2,525

5691 Nature International Weekly Journal of Science
Nature Publishing Co.
968 National Press Bldg. Phone: (202)737-2355
529-14 St. NW Fax: (202)628-1609
Washington, DC 20045
Publication E-mail: nature@natureny.com
Publisher E-mail: nature@nature.com

Magazine covering science and technology, including the fields of biology, biochemistry, genetics, medicine, earth sciences, physics, pharmacology, and behavioral sciences. **Subtitle:** International Weekly Journal of Science. **Founded:** Nov. 4, 1869. **Freq:** Weekly. **Print Method:** Offset. **Trim Size:** 8 1/4 x 11. **Cols./Page:** 3. **Col. Width:** 2 3/16 inches. **Col. Depth:** 9 3/4 inches. **Key Personnel:** Philip Campbell, Editor; Mary Waltham, President; Laura Garwin, North American Ed. **ISSN:** 0028-0836. **Subscription Rates:** $145 individuals; $495 institutions. **Remarks:** Accepts advertising. **URL:** http://www.nature.com.
Ad Rates: BW: $3,585 **Circ:** Paid 53,861
4C: $4,760 Non-paid 686

5692 Navy Civil Engineer
Naval Facilities Engineering Command
Washington Navy Yard Phone: (202)685-9008
1322 Patterson Ave., SE, Ste. 1000 Fax: (202)685-1484
Washington, DC 20374-5065
Magazine for Navy Civil Engineer Corps and other professional civil engineers. **Founded:** 1960. **Freq:** Tri-annually. **Print Method:** Offset. **Trim Size:** 8 1/2 x 11. **Cols./Page:** 3 and 2. **Col. Width:** 25 and 40 nonpareils. **Col. Depth:** 145 agate lines. **Key Personnel:** Sharon Luckett, luckettsl@maufac.navy.mil. **ISSN:** 0096-9419. **Subscription Rates:** $6.50 individuals. **Remarks:** Advertising not accepted.
Circ: Paid ‡200
Non-paid ‡16,000

5693 NBA Magazine
National Bar Association
1225 11th St., NW Phone: (202)842-3900
Washington, DC 20001 Fax: (202)289-6170

Professional magazine covering law. **Founded:** 1983. **Freq:** Bimonthly. **Trim Size:** 8 1/8 x 10 7/8. **Cols./Page:** 3. **Col. Width:** 2 3/16 inches. **Col. Depth:** 9 5/8 inches. **Key Personnel:** John Crump, Editor-in-Chief; Maurice Foster, Managing Editor; Carol Hobson, Senior Editor. **Subscription Rates:** $60 individuals. **Remarks:** Accepts advertising.
Circ: (Not Reported)

5694 NEA Today
National Education Association (NEA)
1201 16th St., NW Phone: (202)833-4000
Washington, DC 20036 Fax: (202)822-7974
Free: (800)229-4200
Publisher E-mail: plibz@aol.com

Education magazine. **Founded:** Oct. 1982. **Freq:** 8/year. **Print Method:** Offset. **Trim Size:** 10 x 14. **Cols./Page:** 4. **Col. Width:** 28 nonpareils. **Col. Depth:** 187 agate lines. **Key Personnel:** Bill Fischer, Editor; Sam Pizzigati, Publisher; Suzanne Wade, Advertising Coord. **Subscription Rates:** $75 (included in membership dues). **Remarks:** Accepts advertising.
Ad Rates: BW: $33,035 **Circ:** Paid 2,140,876
4C: $37,795
PCI: $895

5695 Negro History Bulletin
Association for the Study of Afro-American Life and History
1407 14th St. NW Phone: (202)667-2822
Washington, DC 20005-3704 Fax: (202)387-9802

Magazine profiling black history through feature articles and biographies. **Founded:** 1937. **Freq:** Quarterly or Bi-annually. **Trim Size:** 8 1/2 x 11. **Key Personnel:** Dr. Cynthia Neverdon-Morton, Editor. **ISSN:** 0028-2529. **Subscription Rates:** $25 individuals. **Remarks:** Advertising not accepted.
Circ: ‡10,000

5696 Neuropsychology
American Psychological Association
750 1st St. NE Phone: (202)336-5500
Washington, DC 20002-4242 Fax: (202)336-5568
Free: (800)374-2721
Publisher E-mail: webmaster@apa.org

Journal focusing on basic and clinical research, the integration of basic and applied findings, and improving practice in the field of neuropsychology. **Founded:** 1987. **Freq:** Quarterly. **Print Method:** Offset. **Trim Size:** 8 1/4 x 11. **Key Personnel:** Laird S. Cermak, PhD, Editor; Jodi Ashcraft, Advertising Mgr.; Juanita Brodie, Circulation Mgr.; Terri Pilkerton, Advertising Sales Rep. **ISSN:** 0894-4105. **Subscription Rates:** $44; $87 nonmembers; $113 Industry. **Remarks:** Accepts advertising.
Ad Rates: BW: $175 **Circ:** 5,000

5697 Neuropsychology Abstracts
American Psychological Association
750 1st St. NE Phone: (202)336-5500
Washington, DC 20002-4242 Fax: (202)336-5568
Free: (800)374-2721
Publisher E-mail: webmaster@apa.org

This publication includes abstracts drawn from the psyc info database on neuropsychology. **Founded:** 1992. **Freq:** Quarterly. **Print Method:** Offset. **Trim Size:** 8 1/2 x 11. **Cols./Page:** 2. **Col. Width:** 20 picas. **Col. Depth:** 55 picas. **Key Personnel:** Dennis Auld, Exec. Editor; Jodi Ashcraft, Advertising Mgr.; Maurine Jackson, Operations Dir.; Terri Pilkerton, Advertising Sales Rep. **ISSN:** 1083-4915. **Subscription Rates:** $24 members; $49 nonmembers; $99 institutions. **Remarks:** Accepts advertising. **Formerly:** PsycSCAN: Neuropsychology and Neuropsychology Abstracts.
Ad Rates: BW: $185 **Circ:** ‡2,850

5698 New Directions Magazine
1250 Connecticut Ave. NW
Washington, DC 20008

Literary magazine. **Founded:** Oct. 1973. **Freq:** Quarterly. **Print Method:** Offset. **Trim Size:** 8 1/2 x 11. **Cols./Page:** 3. **Col. Width:** 30 nonpareils. **Col. Depth:** 112 agate lines. **Key Personnel:** Abdulkadir N. Said, Editor. **USPS:** 906-980. **Remarks:** Accepts advertising.
Ad Rates: BW: $3,074 **Circ:** Non-paid ‡10,000
4C: $4,972

5699 New Homes Guide
Housing Data Reports, Inc.
1010 Wisconsin Ave. Phone: (202)342-0410
Washington, DC 20007 Fax: (202)342-0515

Magazine covering new home real estate in metropolitan Washington, DC. **Subtitle:** Washington Area's Only Complete Guide to Every New Home Community. **Founded:** 1974. **Freq:** Bimonthly. **Print Method:** Offset. **Trim Size:** 5 1/2 x 7 1/8. **Key Personnel:** Charles Browning, Publisher. **ISSN:** 0195-0940. **Subscription Rates:** Free. **Remarks:** Accepts advertising. **URL:** http://www.newhomes.com.
Ad Rates: BW: $4,550 **Circ:** Non-paid ‡50,000
4C: $5,550

5700 New Observer
811 Florida Ave. NW Phone: (202)232-3060
Washington, DC 20001 Fax: (202)232-1711

Black community newspaper. **Key Personnel:** Michael Angelo Graham, Editor.

5701 The New Republic
New Republic, Inc.
1220 19th St. NW Phone: (202)331-7494
Suite 600 Fax: (202)331-0275
Washington, DC 20036
Publication E-mail: tnr@aol.com

Journal featuring current events comments and reviews. **Subtitle:** A Journal of Politics and the Arts. **Founded:** 1914. **Freq:** Weekly (Mon.). **Print Method:** Offset. **Trim Size:** 8 x 10 3/4. **Cols./Page:** 3. **Col. Width:** 2 1/4 inches. **Col. Depth:** 134 agate lines. **Key Personnel:** Martin Peretz, Editor-in-Chief; Joan M. Stapleton, Publisher. **ISSN:** 0028-6583. **Subscription Rates:** $69.67 individuals; $84.97 Canada; $99.97 other countries; $2.95 single issue. **Remarks:** Accepts advertising. **Alt. Formats:** CD-ROM.
Ad Rates: BW: $5,790 **Circ:** Paid ★**94,552**
4C: $8,380
PCI: $95

5702 The NFIB Foundation Small Business Economic Trends
The NFIB Education Foundation
600 Maryland Ave. SW, Ste. 700 Phone: (202)554-9000
Fax: (202)484-1567
Washington, DC 20024
Free: (800)634-2669

Publication reporting on various small business economic conditions gleaned from random sample surveys of NFIB members. **Founded:** Oct. 1973. **Freq:** Monthly. **Key Personnel:** Valerie Mascari, Contact. **ISSN:** 0362-3548. **Subscription Rates:** $250 individuals. **Remarks:** Advertising not accepted. **Formerly**: The NFIB Foundation Quarterly Economic Report for Small Business.
Circ: 1,000

5703 NICHCY News Digest
National Information Center for Children and Youth With Disabilities (NICHCY)
PO Box 1492 Phone: (202)884-8200
Washington, DC 20013-1492 Fax: (202)884-8441
Free: (800)695-0285
Publisher E-mail: nichcy@aed.org

Magazine for parents of children with special needs and the professionals who work with and care for them. **Founded:** 1985. **Freq:** 3/year. **Trim Size:** 8 1/2 x 11. **Key Personnel:** Suzanne Ripley, Director, sripley@aed.org. **Remarks:** Advertising not accepted. **URL:** http://www.nichcy.org. **Alt. Formats:** Diskette.
Circ: (Not Reported)

5704 The Northwest Current
The Current Newspapers
5125 Macarthur Blvd., NW, Ste. 18 Phone: (202)244-7223
Fax: (202)363-9850
Washington, DC 20016
Free: (202)363-9850
Publication E-mail: current@crols.com

Community newspaper. **Founded:** 1967. **Freq:** Weekly. **Print Method:** Offset. **Cols./Page:** 5. **Col. Width:** 11.5 picas. **Col. Depth:** 13 inches. **Key Personnel:** Davis Kennedy, Publisher. **Subscription Rates:** $52. **Remarks:** Accepts advertising.
Ad Rates: BW: $1,350 **Circ:** Combined ‡37,000
4C: $1,750
PCI: $22

5705 Occupational Outlook Quarterly
U.S. Government Printing Office
U.S. Department of Labor Phone: (202)606-5700
2 Massachusetts Ave. NE, RM. 2135 Fax: (202)606-5745
Washington, DC 20212
Magazine providing occupational and employment information. **Founded:** 1958. **Freq:** Quarterly. **Print Method:** Letterpress. **Cols./Page:** 2. **Col. Width:** 40 nonpareils. **Col. Depth:** 128 agate lines. **Key Personnel:** Kathleen Green, Contact, green_k@bls.gov. **ISSN:** 0199-4786. **Subscription Rates:** $8. **Remarks:** Advertising not accepted.
Circ: Paid ⊕**26,175**

5706 OECD Economic Studies
Organization for Economic Cooperation and Development (OECD)
2001 L St. NW, Ste. 650 Phone: (202)785-6323
Washington, DC 20036-4922 Fax: (202)785-0350
Free: (800)456-6323
Publisher E-mail: washington.contact@oecd.org

Magazine containing articles on macroeconomics and economic policy in international and national settings. **Freq:** Semiannual. **Print Method:** Offset. **ISSN:** 0255-0822. **Subscription Rates:** $65 individuals; $69 by air mail. **Remarks:** Advertising not accepted.
Circ: (Not Reported)

5707 OECD Observer
Organization for Economic Cooperation and Development (OECD)
2001 L St. NW, Ste. 650 Phone: (202)785-6323
Washington, DC 20036-4922 Fax: (202)785-0350
Free: (800)456-6323
Publisher E-mail: washington.contact@oecd.org

Magazine on economic affairs, science, and technology. **Founded:** 1962. **Freq:** Bimonthly. **Print Method:** Offset. **Trim Size:** 9 x 11 5/8. **Key Personnel:** Ulla Ranhall-Reyners, Editor. **ISSN:** 0029-7054. **Subscription Rates:** $30 individuals; $38 by air mail. **Remarks:** Advertising not accepted.
Circ: (Not Reported)

5708 Off Our Backs
Off Our Backs: A Women's News Journal
2337 18th St. NW Phone: (202)234-8072
Washington, DC 20009 Fax: (202)234-8092
Publication E-mail: 73613.1256@compuserve.com
Publisher E-mail: offourback@compuserve.com

Feminist newsjournal featuring articles by, for, and about women. **Subtitle:** A Women's Newsjournal. **Founded:** Feb. 1970. **Freq:** Monthly 11/year. **Print Method:** Offset. **Trim Size:** 13 x 17 1/2. **Cols./Page:** 4. **Col. Width:** 35 nonpareils. **Col. Depth:** 228 agate lines. **ISSN:** 0030-0071. **Subscription Rates:** $25 individuals; $50 institutions Industry; $33 out of country; $3 single issue. **Remarks:** Accepts advertising. **Alt. Formats:** Braille; Braille; Microform.
Ad Rates: BW: $400 **Circ:** Paid 2,500
PCI: $20 Non-paid 18,000

5709 The Officer
The Reserve Officers Association
1 Constitution Ave. NE Phone: (202)479-2200
Washington, DC 20002 Fax: (202)479-0416

Magazine for active and reserve officers of all military branches. **Founded:** 1924. **Freq:** Monthly. **Print Method:** Offset. **Cols./Page:** 4. **Col. Width:** 10 picas. **Col. Depth:** 58 picas. **Key Personnel:** Carol Wilson-Bunn, USAF, Acting Editor; Major Gen. Roger W. Sandler, AUS(R), Publisher. **ISSN:** 0030-0268. **Subscription Rates:** $12 individuals; $1.15 single issue. **Remarks:** Accepts advertising.
Ad Rates: BW: $2,750 **Circ:** 100,000
4C: $4,050
PCI: $110

5710 Oil, Gas, Coal and Electricity Quarterly Statistics
Organization for Economic Cooperation and Development (OECD)
2001 L St. NW, Ste. 650 Phone: (202)785-6323
Washington, DC 20036-4922 Fax: (202)785-0350
Free: (800)456-6323
Publisher E-mail: washington.contact@oecd.org

Report providing statistics on oil and gas supply and demand in the OECD area. **Freq:** Quarterly. **Print Method:** Offset. **Trim Size:** 7 5/8 x 10 5/8. **Cols./Page:** 1. **Col. Width:** 84 nonpareils. **Col. Depth:** 133 agate lines. **ISSN:** 0378-6536. **Subscription Rates:** $235 individuals; $254 by air mail. **Remarks:** Advertising not accepted. **Formerly**: Quarterly Oil Statistics and Energy Balances.
Circ: (Not Reported)

5711 OPASTCO Roundtable
Organization for Promotion and Advancement of Small Telecommunications Companies (OPASTCO)
21 Dupont Circle NW, Ste. 700 Phone: (202)659-5990
Washington, DC 20036 Fax: (202)659-4619
Publication E-mail: roundtable@opastco.org

Provides practical how-to information to help small independent telephone companies compete in the telecommunications industry. **Subtitle:** Ideas for Small Telecommunications Companies. **Founded:** 1988. **Freq:** Bimonthly. **Print Method:** Sheetfed offset. **Trim Size:** 8 1/4 x 11. **Cols./Page:** 3. **Key Personnel:** Martha K. Silver, Editor, mks@opastco.org. **ISSN:** 1043-6073. **Subscription Rates:** $35; $20 members. **Remarks:** Accepts advertising.
Ad Rates: BW: $1,910 **Circ:** Paid ‡2,900
4C: $2,810 Non-paid ‡600

5712 Optics & Photonics News
Optical Society of America
2010 Massachusetts Ave. NW Phone: (202)416-1420
Washington, DC 20036 Fax: (202)416-6130
Publication E-mail: opn@osa.org
Publisher E-mail: info@usa.org

Magazine covering the field of optics and photonics from theory to instrumentation and systems applications; research, industry trends; fiber optics, laser research and applications. **Founded:** 1975. **Freq:** Monthly. **Print Method:** Web offset. **Trim Size:** 8 1/8 x 10 7/8. **Cols./Page:** 3. **Col. Width:** 26 nonpareils. **Col. Depth:** 140 agate lines. **Key Personnel:** Andrea Pendleton, Editor; Stephen O'Connor, Advertising Coord. **ISSN:** 1047-6938. **Subscription Rates:** $99 individuals; $15 single issue. **Remarks:** Accepts advertising. **URL:** http://www.osa.org. **Formerly**: Optics News.
Ad Rates: BW: $1,955 **Circ:** Paid ‡11,516
4C: $3,265 Non-paid ‡7,466

5713 PA Times
American Society for Public Administration
1120 G St. NW, No. 700 Phone: (202)393-7878
Washington, DC 20005 Fax: (202)638-4952
Publisher E-mail: dcaspa@aol.com

Public administration newspaper (tabloid). **Founded:** 1978. **Freq:** Monthly. **Print Method:** Offset. **Trim Size:** 11 1/2 x 15. **Cols./Page:** 4. **Col. Width:** 28 nonpareils. **Col. Depth:** 185 agate lines. **Key Personnel:** Mary Hamilton, Editor-in-Chief; John Larkin, Editor. **ISSN:** 0149-8797. **Subscription Rates:** $30 individuals. **Alt. Formats:** Mailing labels.
Ad Rates: BW: $500 **Circ:** 13,500
4C: $900
PCI: $25

5714 PAN*NET
United States Pan Asian American Chamber of Commerce (USPAACC)
1329-18th St. NW Phone: (202)296-5221
Washington, DC 20036 Fax: (202)296-5225
Publisher E-mail: uspaacc@his.com

Publication concerning USPAACC issues. **Subtitle:** East-West Report. **Founded:** 1991. **Freq:** Quarterly. **Trim Size:** 8 x 10. **Cols./Page:** 3. **Col. Width:** 2 inches. **Key Personnel:** Susan Au Allen, President, susanallen@uspaacc.org; James Epp, Executive Director, jamesepp@uspaacc.org. **Subscription Rates:** $25. **Remarks:** Accepts advertising.
Ad Rates: BW: $1,000 **Circ:** Paid ‡1,800
Non-paid ‡3,200

5715 Paper, Paperboard, and Wood Pulp Monthly Statistical Summary
American Forest and Paper Association
Forest & Paper Information Center Phone: (202)463-2700
Fax: (202)463-2785
1111 19th St. NW, Ste. 700
Washington, DC 20036
Publication E-mail: garrj@diantech.com

Magazine covering statistical and economic trends in paper, paperboard, and wood pulp. **Founded:** 1920. **Freq:** Monthly. **Print Method:** Offset. **Cols./Page:** 1. **Col. Width:** 86 nonpareils. **Col. Depth:** 125 agate lines. **Key Personnel:** Stan Lancey, Editor. **Subscription Rates:** $450 domestic; $480 overseas. **Remarks:** Advertising not accepted. **URL:** http://www.poeitech.com.
Circ: (Not Reported)

5716 Parenting for High Potential
National Association for Gifted Children
1707 L St. NW, No. 550 Phone: (202)785-4268
Washington, DC 20036 Fax: (202)785-4248

Consumer magazine covering parenting issues. **Founded:** Sept. 1996. **Freq:** Quarterly. **Trim Size:** 8 1/2 x 11. **Key Personnel:** Peter Rosenstein, Publisher; James Alvino, Editor. **Subscription Rates:** $25 institutions. **Remarks:** Advertising accepted; rates available upon request.
Circ: Combined 15,000

5717 Parking Magazine
National Parking Association
1112 16th St. NW, Ste. 300 Phone: (202)296-4336
Washington, DC 20036 Fax: (202)331-8523
Free: (800)647-PARK

Parking industry magazine. **Subtitle:** A Publication of the National Parking Association. **Founded:** 1952. **Freq:** 10/year. **Print Method:** Sheetfed offset. **Trim Size:** 8 1/4 x 11. **Col. Depth:** 9 3/4 inches. **Key Personnel:** Lourie Reichenberg, Managing Editor. **ISSN:** 0031-2193. **Subscription Rates:** $95 individuals; $125 other countries. **Remarks:** Accepts advertising.
Ad Rates: BW: $1,045 **Circ:** 5,000
4C: $1,545

5718 Passenger Transport
American Public Transit Association
1201 New York Ave. NW, Ste. 400 Phone: (202)898-4000
Fax: (202)898-4029
Washington, DC 20005
Newspaper covering the public transit industry in the U.S. and Canada. **Subtitle:** The Weekly Newspaper of the Transit Industry. **Founded:** 1943. **Freq:** Weekly (Mon.). **Print Method:** Offset. **Trim Size:** 10 3/4 x 12 5/8. **Cols./Page:** 4. **Col. Width:** 28 nonpareils. **Col. Depth:** 139 agate lines. **Key Personnel:** Rhonda Goldberg, Managing Editor, phone (202)898-4120, rgoldberg@apta.com; Cecilia Barber, Advertising Mgr., phone (202)898-4122, cbarber@apta.com; Susan Berlin, Assoc. Editor, phone (202)898-4047, sberlin@apta.com. **ISSN:** 0364-345X. **Subscription Rates:** $65

individuals; $2 single issue. **Remarks:** Accepts advertising. **URL:** www.apta.com.
Ad Rates: GLR: $7.75 BW: $2,290 4C: $3,277 PCI: $67 **Circ:** Paid 4,535 Free 401

5719 Pastoral Music
National Association of Pastoral Musicians
225 Sheridan St. NW Phone: (202)723-5800
Washington, DC 20011 Fax: (202)723-2262
Publisher E-mail: npmsing@aol

Pastoral music magazine. **Founded:** 1976. **Freq:** Bimonthly. **Print Method:** Offset. **Trim Size:** 8 1/2 x 11. **Cols./Page:** 3 and 2. **Col. Width:** 26 and 40 nonpareils. **Col. Depth:** 136 agate lines. **Key Personnel:** Dr. Gordon E. Truitt, Managing Editor; Rev. Virgil C. Funk, Publisher; Nancy Chvatal, Advertising Mgr. **ISSN:** 0363-6569. **Subscription Rates:** $24 individuals. **Remarks:** Accepts advertising.
Ad Rates: BW: $625 PCI: $100 **Circ:** 9000

5720 Perspectives in Education and Deafness
Gallaudet University Press
800 Florida Ave. NE Phone: (202)651-5488
Washington, DC 20002 Fax: (202)651-5489
Free: (800)621-2736

Journal for parents and professionals concerned with the education of hearing impaired students. **Founded:** 1982. **Freq:** 5/year (Sept., Nov., Jan., March, and May). **Print Method:** Sheetfed offset. **Trim Size:** 8 1/2 x 11. **Cols./Page:** 3. **Col. Width:** 14 picas. **Col. Depth:** 53 picas. **Key Personnel:** Mary E. Abrams, Editor; Marteal Pitts, Circulation Mgr. **ISSN:** 1051-6204. **Subscription Rates:** $15. $3.50 single issue. **Remarks:** Accepts advertising. **Formerly:** Perspectives for Teachers of the Hearing Impaired (1989).
Ad Rates: BW: $400 4C: $850 PCI: $75 **Circ:** Paid ‡3,000 Controlled ‡1,000

5721 Perspectives on Political Science
Heldref Publications
Helen Dwight Reid Educational Foundation Phone: (202)296-6267 Fax: (202)296-5149
1319 18th St. NW
Washington, DC 20036-1802
Free: (800)365-9753
Publication E-mail: pps@heldref.org; subscribe@heldref.og
Publisher E-mail: revu@heldref.org

Journal reviewing new books on government, politics, and international affairs, and publishing articles emphasizing the philosophical assumptions of politics. **Founded:** 1972. **Freq:** Quarterly. **Print Method:** Letterpress. Uses mats. **Trim Size:** 8 1/2 x 11. **Cols./Page:** 2. **Col. Width:** 3 1/2 inches. **Col. Depth:** 10 inches. **Key Personnel:** Grant Williams, Advertising Mgr., advertise@heldref.org; Douglas Kirkpatrick, Director; Fred Huber, Circulation Mgr.; Jean Kline, Fulfillment Manager. **ISSN:** 1045-7097. **Subscription Rates:** $49 individuals; $98 institutions; foreign, add $13. **Online:** EBSCO; Infonautics; Information Access; UMI. **URL:** http://www.heldref.org. **Alt. Formats:** CD-ROM.
Ad Rates: BW: $155 **Circ:** Paid ‡530

5722 Petroleum Independent
Independent Petroleum Association of America
1101 16th St. NW Phone: (202)857-4774
Washington, DC 20036 Fax: (202)857-4799
Free: (800)433-2851

Magazine for the independent exploration and production sector of the petroleum industry. Includes political and business trends. **Founded:** 1930. **Freq:** Bimonthly. **Print Method:** Offset. **Trim Size:** 8 1/4 x 11. **Cols./Page:** 3 and 2. **Col. Width:** 28 and 40 nonpareils. **Col. Depth:** 140 agate lines. **Key Personnel:** Bruce A. Wells, Editor. **ISSN:** 0747-2528. **Subscription Rates:** $100 individuals. **Remarks:** Accepts advertising. **Online:** Information Access Company.
Ad Rates: BW: $2,300 4C: $3,490 **Circ:** ‡8,000

5723 Pharmacy Today
American Pharmaceutical Association
2215 Constitution Ave., NW Phone: (202)429-7557
Washington, DC 20037 Fax: (202)628-5425
Free: (800)237-2742

Reports on current news and opinions for pharmacists. **Subtitle:** Pharmaceutical Care News and Analysis. **Founded:** 1995. **Freq:** Monthly. **Trim Size:** 11 x 15. **Key Personnel:** William J. Reynolds, Advertising Dir., phone (202)429-7582, fax (202)628-5425, pharmtoday@mail.aphanet.org; Rick Harding, Dir. of Periodicals, phone (202)429-7557. **Remarks:** Accepts advertising.
Ad Rates: BW: $7,170 4C: $9,115 **Circ:** 95,693

5724 Population Bulletin
Population Reference Bureau
1875 Connecticut Ave. NW, Ste. 520 Phone: (202)483-1100 Fax: (202)328-3937
Washington, DC 20009
Free: (800)877-9881
Publisher E-mail: popref@prb.org

Journal on population studies. **Founded:** Sept. 1945. **Freq:** Quarterly. **Print Method:** Offset. **Trim Size:** 7 x 9 1/4. **Cols./Page:** 2. **Col. Width:** 28 nonpareils. **Col. Depth:** 100 agate lines. **Key Personnel:** Mary Mederios Kent, Editor, phone (202)939-5418, mkent@prb.org. **ISSN:** 0032-468X. **Subscription Rates:** $49 members; $7 single issue. **Remarks:** Advertising not accepted.
Circ: ‡5,000

5725 Postal Record
National Association of Letter Carriers
100 Indiana Ave. NW Phone: (202)393-4695
Washington, DC 20001-2144 Fax: (202)737-1540

Magazine for active and retired letter carriers. **Founded:** 1889. **Freq:** Monthly. **Print Method:** Web press. **Trim Size:** 8 1/4 x 11. **Cols./Page:** 3. **Col. Width:** 26 nonpareils. **Col. Depth:** 133 agate lines. **Key Personnel:** Vincent R. Sombrotto, Editor. **ISSN:** 0032-5376. **Subscription Rates:** Included in membership. **Remarks:** Advertising not accepted.
Circ: 310,000

5726 Preservation
National Trust for Historic Preservation
1785 Massachusetts Ave. NW Phone: (202)588-6296
Washington, DC 20036-2117 Fax: (202)588-6223
Free: (800)944-6847

Newspaper featuring historic preservation and architecture. **Founded:** 1961. **Freq:** Monthly. **Print Method:** Offset. **Trim Size:** 11 x 15. **Cols./Page:** 4. **Col. Width:** 34 nonpareils. **Col. Depth:** 210 agate lines. **Key Personnel:** Arnold Berke, Editor; Bob Barron, Advertising Mgr. **ISSN:** 0032-7735. **Subscription Rates:** $15 membership. **Remarks:** Accepts advertising. **Formerly:** Historic Preservation News.
Ad Rates: BW: $3,675 **Circ:** Paid ★212,799

5727 Preventing School Failure
Heldref Publications
Helen Dwight Reid Educational Foundation Phone: (202)296-6267 Fax: (202)296-5149
1319 18th St. NW
Washington, DC 20036-1802
Free: (800)365-9753
Publication E-mail: psf@heldref.org; subscribe@heldref.org
Publisher E-mail: revu@heldref.org

Journal for educators and parents, focusing on students with learning and behavioral problems. Includes information on programs and practices that help students with special needs. **Founded:** 1956. **Freq:** Quarterly. **Trim Size:** 8 1/2 x 11. **Cols./Page:** 1. **Col. Width:** 7 1/4 inches. **Col. Depth:** 9 1/2 inches. **Key Personnel:** Douglas Kirkpatrick, Director; Grant Williams, Advertising Production Mgr., advertise@heldref.org; Fred Huber, Circulation Mgr.; Jean Kline, Fulfillment Mgr., subs@heldref.org. **ISSN:** 1045-988X. **Subscription Rates:** $38 individuals; $78 institutions; foreign, add $13. **Remarks:** Accepts advertising. **Online:** EBSCO. **URL:** http://www.heldref.org. **Alt. Formats:** CD-ROM.
Ad Rates: BW: $175 **Circ:** Paid ‡630

5728 Problems of Post-Communism
M.E. Sharpe, Inc.
2013 G St. NW, Ste. 401 Phone: (202)994-3962
Washington, DC 20052 Fax: (202)994-5436
Publication E-mail: popc@gwu.edu
Publisher E-mail: mes@usa.net

Scholarly journal focusing on communist and post-communist societies. **Founded:** 1951. **Freq:** Bimonthly. **Print Method:** Letterpress. **Trim Size:** 8 1/2 x 10 1/2. **Cols./Page:** 2. **Col. Width:** 40 nonpareils. **Col. Depth:** 122 agate lines. **Key Personnel:** James R. Millar, Editor; Barbara Ladd, Advertising Mgr. **ISSN:** 0032-941X. **Subscription Rates:** $130 other countries; $170 other countries; $45 individuals. **Formerly:** Problems of Communism (1994).
Ad Rates: BW: $750 **Circ:** (Not Reported)

5729 Proceedings of the Entomological Society of Washington
Entomological Society of Washington
Smithsonian Institution Phone: (202)382-1786
Dept. of Entomology
Washington, DC 20560-0168
Scientific journal for publication of original research on insects. **Founded:** Mar. 31, 1886. **Freq:** Quarterly. **Print Method:** Offset. **Trim Size:** 6 7/8 x 10. **Cols./Page:** 2. **Col. Width:** 31 1/2 nonpareils. **Col. Depth:** 112 agate lines. **Key Personnel:** David R. Smith. **ISSN:** 0013-8797. **Subscription Rates:** $60 institutions; $70 other countries; $25 individuals. **Remarks:** Advertising accepted; rates available upon request.
Circ: ‡800

5730 Proceedings of the National Academy of Sciences of the United States of America
National Academy of Sciences
2101 Constitution Ave. Phone: (202)334-2672
Washington, DC 20418 Fax: (202)334-2738
Publication E-mail: pnas@nas.edu

Journal of multidisciplinary sciences. **Founded:** 1915. **Freq:** Biweekly. **Print Method:** Offset. **Trim Size:** 8 3/8 x 10 7/8. **Cols./Page:** 2. **Col. Width:** 20 picas. **Col. Depth:** 58 1/2 picas. **Key Personnel:** Nicholas R. Cozzarelli, Editor; Kenneth R. Fulton, Publisher; Diane M. Sullenberger, Executive Ed. **ISSN:** 0027-8424. **Subscription Rates:** $165 individuals; $90 students; $125 postdoctoral; $685 institutions; $265 other countries; $190 other countries student; $225 other countries postdoctoral; $785 institutions, other countries. **Remarks:** Accepts advertising. **Available Online. URL:** http://www.pnas.org. **Alt. Formats:** Microform.
Ad Rates: BW: $1,840 4C: $2,935 **Circ:** Paid 6,400 Non-paid 1,300

5731 Professional Psychology: Research and Practice
American Psychological Association
750 1st St. NE Phone: (202)336-5500
Washington, DC 20002-4242 Fax: (202)336-5568
Free: (800)374-2721
Publisher E-mail: webmaster@apa.org

Journal presenting articles on techniques and practices used in the application of psychology, including applications of research, standards of practice, interprofessional relations, delivery of services, and training. **Founded:** 1969. **Freq:** Bimonthly. **Print Method:** Offset. **Trim Size:** 8 1/4 x 11. **Cols./Page:** 2. **Col. Width:** 46 nonpareils. **Col. Depth:** 126 agate lines. **Key Personnel:** Patrick H. DeLeon, PhD, Editor; Susan Knapp, Exec. Editor; Jodi Ashcraft, Advertising Mgr.; Juanita Brodie, Circulation Mgr.; Terri Pilkerton, Advertising Sales Rep. **ISSN:** 0735-7028. **Subscription Rates:** $44 members; $87 nonmembers; $174 institutions. **Remarks:** Accepts advertising.
Ad Rates: BW: $245 **Circ:** ‡7,800

5732 Professional Report
Society of Industrial and Office Realtors
700 11th St. NW, Ste. 510 Phone: (202)737-1150
Washington, DC 20001-4511 Fax: (202)737-8796
Free: (888)891-7467

Trade magazine for commercial real estate brokerage. **Founded:** Jan. 1991. **Freq:** Quarterly. **Trim Size:** 8 1/2 x 11. **Cols./Page:** 2 and 3. **Col. Width:** 4 1/4 and 2 1/2 inches. **Col. Depth:** 9 1/2 and 9 1/2 inches. **Key Personnel:** Linda Nasvaderani, Contact, phone (202)737-8783, lnasvaderani@mail.sior.com. **USPS:** 324-270. **Subscription Rates:** $25. **Remarks:** Accepts advertising. **URL:** http://www.sior.com.
Ad Rates: BW: $800 4C: $1,600 **Circ:** Paid 3,500

5733 ProSales
Hanley-Wood, Inc.
1 Thomas Circle, Ste. 600 Phone: (202)452-0800
Washington, DC 20005 Fax: (202)785-1974

Trade publication covering construction and retail sales. **Founded:** 1989. **Freq:** 12/year. **Print Method:** Web offset. **Trim Size:** 8 1/4 x 11 1/8. **Cols./Page:** 3. **Key Personnel:** Greg Brooks, Editor; Hilary Kanter, Managing Editor, phone (202)736-3316, fax (202)785-1974, hkanter@hanley-wood.com. **ISSN:** 1055-3444. **Remarks:** Accepts advertising.
Ad Rates: BW: $5,100 4C: $6,000 PCI: $135 **Circ:** Controlled 40,000

5734 Provider
American Health Care Association
1201 L St. NW Phone: (202)842-4444
Washington, DC 20005 Fax: (202)842-3860

Magazine. **Subtitle:** For Long Term Care Professionals. **Founded:** 1975. **Freq:** Monthly. **Print Method:** Web offset. **Trim Size:** 8 1/8 x 10 7/8. **Cols./Page:** 3. **Col. Width:** 13 picas. **Col. Depth:** 58 picas. **Key Personnel:** Lynn Wagner, Editor-in-Chief, phone (202)898-2819, fax (202)842-3860, lwagner@ahca.org; Mike DiSanto, Sales Director, phone (202)898-2838. **ISSN:** 0888-0352. **Subscription Rates:** $48 nonmembers. **Formerly:** American Health Care Association Journal (Mar. 1986).
Ad Rates: BW: $3400 4C: $4700 PCI: $150 **Circ:** 44,778

5735 PS: Political Science & Politics
American Political Science Association
1527 New Hampshire Ave. NW Phone: (202)483-2512
Washington, DC 20036-1206 Fax: (202)483-2657
Publication E-mail: ps@apsanet.org
Publisher E-mail: apsa@apsanet.org

Political science journal. **Founded:** 1968. **Freq:** Quarterly. **Print Method:** Web press. **Trim Size:** 8 1/2 x 11. **Cols./Page:** 3. **Key Personnel:** Robert J.P. Hauck, Editor; Laura Barrantes, Advertising Mgr. **ISSN:** 1049-0965. **Subscription Rates:** $10 single issue Subscriptions available to; members only.; $15 single issue. **Remarks:** Accepts advertising. **URL:** http://www.apsaet.org.
Ad Rates: BW: $545 **Circ:** ‡16,000

5736 Psychiatric News
American Psychiatric Press, Inc.
1400 K St. NW, Ste. 1101 Phone: (202)682-6262
Washington, DC 20005 Fax: (202)789-2648
Free: (800)368-5777
Publication E-mail: pnews@psych.org
Publisher E-mail: apa@psych.org

Professional magazine of the American Psychiatric Assn. **Founded:** 1966. **Freq:** Semimonthly. **Print Method:** Offset. Uses mats. **Trim Size:** 11 1/4 x 16. **Cols./Page:** 4. **Col. Width:** 28 nonpareils. **Col. Depth:** 205 agate lines. **Key Personnel:** Herbert M. Gant, Exec. Editor, phone (202)682-6133, hgant@psych.org. **ISSN:** 0033-2704. **Subscription Rates:** $40 individuals. **Remarks:** Accepts advertising. **URL:** http://www.psch.org/pnews/.
Ad Rates: BW: $3,300 **Circ:** Paid ‡37,436
4C: $4,550 Non-paid ‡1,219

5737 Psychiatric Services
American Psychiatric Association
1400 K St. NW Phone: (202)682-6000
Washington, DC 20005 Fax: (202)682-6347
Publication E-mail: psjournal@psych.org

Interdisciplinary mental health journal covering clinical, legal, and public policy issues. **Founded:** 1950. **Freq:** Monthly. **Print Method:** Offset. Uses mats. **Trim Size:** 8 1/4 x 10 7/8. **Cols./Page:** 3. **Col. Width:** 12 3/5 picas. **Col. Depth:** 55 picas. **Key Personnel:** John A. Talbott, M.D., Editor, phone (202)682-6070, fax (202)682-6189; Teddye Clayton, Managing Editor, phone (202)682-6070, fax (202)682-6189, tclayton@psych.org. **ISSN:** 1075-2730. **Subscription Rates:** $45 individuals; $75 institutions. **Remarks:** Accepts advertising. **URL:** http://www.appl.org/psjournal. **Alt. Formats:** CD-ROM, American Psychiatric Press Electronic Library; Microform. **Formerly:** Hospital and Community Psychiatry (Jan. 1, 1995).
Ad Rates: GLR: $8.50 **Circ:** Paid ‡12,885
BW: $2,030 Non-paid ‡9,339
4C: $3,130

5738 Psychiatry
Guilford Publications, Inc.
George Washington University Phone: (202)994-2636
Medical Center Fax: (202)994-4812
2300 Eye St. NW
Washington, DC 20037
Publisher E-mail: info@guilford.com

Journal covering interpersonal and biological processes. **Subtitle:** Interpersonal and Biological Processes. **Founded:** 1938. **Freq:** Quarterly. **Print Method:** Offset. **Trim Size:** 7 x 10. **Cols./Page:** 2. **Col. Width:** 16 picas. **Col. Depth:** 47 picas. **Key Personnel:** David Reiss, Editor. **ISSN:** 0033-2747. **Subscription Rates:** $35; $105 institutions. **Remarks:** Accepts advertising. **Alt. Formats:** Microfilm.
Ad Rates: BW: $250 **Circ:** 2,017

5739 Psychological Abstracts
American Psychological Association
750 1st St. NE Phone: (202)336-5500
Washington, DC 20002-4242 Fax: (202)336-5568
Free: (800)374-2721
Publisher E-mail: webmaster@apa.org

Journal containing nonevaluative summaries of the serial's literature in psychology and related disciplines. The abstracts are listed under 22 major classification categories. **Founded:** 1927. **Freq:** Monthly. **Print Method:** Offset. **Trim Size:** 8 1/2 x 11. **Cols./Page:** 2. **Col. Width:** 46 nonpareils. **Col. Depth:** 126 agate lines. **Key Personnel:** Denny Auld, Exec. Editor; Maurine Jackson, Operations Dir. **ISSN:** 0033-2887. **Subscription Rates:** $700 members; $1,399 nonmembers; $1,399 institutions. **Remarks:** Advertising not accepted.
Circ: ‡2,000

5740 Psychological Assessment
American Psychological Association
750 1st St. NE Phone: (202)336-5500
Washington, DC 20002-4242 Fax: (202)336-5568
Free: (800)374-2721
Publisher E-mail: webmaster@apa.org

Journal presenting original empirical articles concerning clinical assessment and evaluations. **Founded:** 1989. **Freq:** Quarterly. **Print Method:** Offset. **Trim Size:** 8 1/4 x 11. **Key Personnel:** Stephen N. Haynes, PhD, Editor; Susan Knapp, Exec. Editor; Jodi Ashcraft, Advertising Mgr.; Juanita Brodie, Circulation Mgr.; Terri Pilkerton, Advertising Sales Rep. **ISSN:** 1040-3590. **Subscription Rates:** $44 members; $87 nonmembers; $174 institutions. **Remarks:** Accepts advertising.
Ad Rates: BW: $235 **Circ:** Paid ‡5,700

5741 Psychological Bulletin
American Psychological Association
750 1st St. NE Phone: (202)336-5500
Washington, DC 20002-4242 Fax: (202)336-5568
Free: (800)374-2721
Publisher E-mail: webmaster@apa.org

Journal presenting comprehensive and integrative reviews and interpretations of critical substantive and methodological issues and practical problems from all the diverse areas of psychology. **Founded:** 1904. **Freq:** Bimonthly. **Print Method:** Offset. **Trim Size:** 8 1/4 x 11. **Cols./Page:** 2. **Col. Width:** 46 nonpareils. **Col. Depth:** 126 agate lines. **Key Personnel:** Nancy Eisenberg, PhD, Editor; Susan Knapp, Exec. Editor; Jodi Ashcraft, Advertising Mgr.; Juanita Brodie, Circulation Mgr.; Terri Pilkerton, Advertising Sales Rep. **ISSN:** 0033-2909. **Subscription Rates:** $73 members; $145 nonmembers; $290 institutions. **Remarks:** Accepts advertising.
Ad Rates: BW: $245 **Circ:** ‡6,800

5742 Psychological Review
American Psychological Association
750 1st St. NE Phone: (202)336-5500
Washington, DC 20002-4242 Fax: (202)336-5568
Free: (800)374-2721
Publisher E-mail: webmaster@apa.org

Journal presenting articles that make theoretical contributions to all areas of scientific psychology. **Founded:** 1894. **Freq:** Quarterly. **Print Method:** Offset. **Trim Size:** 8 1/4 x 11. **Cols./Page:** 2. **Col. Width:** 46 nonpareils. **Col. Depth:** 126 agate lines. **Key Personnel:** Robert A. Bjork, PhD, Editor; Susan Knapp, Exec. Editor; Jodi Ashcraft, Advertising Mgr.; Juanita Brodie, Circulation Mgr.; Terri Pilkerton, Advertising Sales Rep. **ISSN:** 0033-295X. **Subscription Rates:** $54 members; $109 nonmembers; $203 institutions. **Remarks:** Accepts advertising.
Ad Rates: BW: $225 **Circ:** ‡5,900

5743 Psychology of Addictive Behaviors
Educational Publishing Foundation
750 1st St. NE Phone: (202)336-5600
Washington, DC 20002-4242 Fax: (202)336-5568

Journal including original research related to the psyhological aspects of addictive behaviors, such as alcoholism, drug abuse, eating disorders, and other compulsive behaviors. **Founded:** 1987. **Freq:** Quarterly. **Print Method:** Offset. **Trim Size:** 6 3/4 x 10. **Cols./Page:** 2. **Col. Width:** 16 picas. **Col. Depth:** 50 picas. **Key Personnel:** H. Miles Cox, Editor; Susan Knapp, Contact; Jodi Ashcraft, Contact. **ISSN:** 0893-164X. **Subscription Rates:** $45 members; $45 nonmembers; $60 institutions.
Ad Rates: BW: $150 **Circ:** Paid ‡725

5744 Psychology and Aging
American Psychological Association
750 1st St. NE Phone: (202)336-5500
Washington, DC 20002-4242 Fax: (202)336-5568
Free: (800)374-2721
Publisher E-mail: webmaster@apa.org

Journal presenting original articles on adult development and aging. Represents both research and practice on the subject of psychogerontology. **Founded:** Mar. 1986. **Freq:** Quarterly. **Print Method:** Offset. **Trim Size:** 8 1/4 x 11. **Cols./Page:** 2. **Col. Width:** 46 nonpareils. **Col. Depth:** 126 agate lines. **Key Personnel:** Leah L. Light, Ph.D., Editor; Jodi Ashcraft, Advertising Mgr.; Juanita Brodie, Circulation Mgr.; Terri Pilkerton, Advertising Sales Rep. **ISSN:** 0882-7974. **Subscription Rates:** $51 members; $102 nonmembers; $203 institutions. **Remarks:** Accepts advertising.
Ad Rates: BW: $175 **Circ:** ‡3,200

5745 Psychosomatics
American Psychiatric Press, Inc.
1400 K St. NW, Ste. 1101 Phone: (202)682-6262
Washington, DC 20005 Fax: (202)789-2648
Free: (800)368-5777
Publisher E-mail: apa@psych.org

Journal publishing peer-reviewed articles and research reports on medical psychiatry. **Subtitle:** The Journal of the Academy of Psychosomatic Medicine. **Founded:** 1960. **Freq:** Bimonthly. **Print Method:** Offset. **Trim Size:** 6 7/8 x 10. **Cols./Page:** 3. **Col. Width:** 26 nonpareils. **Col. Depth:** 140 agate lines. **Key Personnel:** John McDuffie, Managing Editor. **ISSN:** 0033-3182. **Subscription Rates:** $99 individuals; $149 institutions. **Remarks:** Accepts advertising.
Ad Rates: BW: $700 **Circ:** Paid 1,747
4C: $1,400 Non-paid 781

5746 PsycSCAN: Applied Psychology
American Psychological Association
750 1st St. NE Phone: (202)336-5500
Washington, DC 20002-4242 Fax: (202)336-5568
Free: (800)374-2721
Publisher E-mail: webmaster@apa.org

Journal presenting abstracts from subscriber-selected journals in the area of applied psychology. **Founded:** 1981. **Freq:** Quarterly. **Print Method:** Offset. **Trim Size:** 8 1/2 x 11. **Cols./Page:** 2. **Col. Width:** 47 nonpareils. **Col. Depth:** 127 agate lines. **Key Personnel:** Denny Auld, Exec. Editor; Jodi Ashcraft, Advertising Mgr.; Maurine Jackson, Operations Dir.; Terri Pilkerton, Advertising Sales Rep. **ISSN:** 0271-7506. **Subscription Rates:** $19.50 members; $33 nonmembers; $66 institutions. **Remarks:** Accepts advertising.
Ad Rates: BW: $185 **Circ:** ‡3,000

5747 PsycSCAN: Behavior Analysis & Therapy
American Psychological Association
750 1st St. NE Phone: (202)336-5500
Washington, DC 20002-4242 Fax: (202)336-5568
Free: (800)374-2721
Publisher E-mail: webmaster@apa.org

Journal on basic and applied behavior analysis. Developed jointly by APA and Division of Experimental Analysis of Behavior (Division 25). **Founded:** Mar. 1995. **Freq:** Quarterly. **Print Method:** Offset. **Trim Size:** 8 1/2 x 11. **Key Personnel:** Dennis Auld, Editor; Jodi Ashcraft, Advertising Mgr.; Juanita Brodie, Circulation Mgr.; Terri Pilkerton, Advertising Sales Rep. **ISSN:** 1078-3946. **Subscription Rates:** $19.50 members; $49 nonmembers; $99 institutions. **Remarks:** Accepts advertising.
Ad Rates: BW: $185 **Circ:** Paid 2,400

5748 PsycSCAN: Clinical Psychology
American Psychological Association
750 1st St. NE Phone: (202)336-5500
Washington, DC 20002-4242 Fax: (202)336-5568
Free: (800)374-2721
Publisher E-mail: webmaster@apa.org

Journal presenting abstracts from subscriber-selected journals in the area of developmental psychology. **Founded:** 1980. **Freq:** Quarterly. **Print Method:** Offset. **Trim Size:** 8 1/2 x 11. **Cols./Page:** 2. **Col. Width:** 47 nonpareils. **Col. Depth:** 127 agate lines. **Key Personnel:** Denny Auld, Exec. Editor; Jodi Ashcraft, Advertising Mgr.; Maurine Jackson, Operations Dir.; Terri Pilkerton, Advertising Sales Rep. **ISSN:** 0197-1484. **Subscription Rates:** $21 members; $35 nonmembers; $69 institutions. **Remarks:** Accepts advertising.
Ad Rates: BW: $205 **Circ:** ‡7,900

5749 PsycSCAN: LD/MR
American Psychological Association
750 1st St. NE Phone: (202)336-5500
Washington, DC 20002-4242 Fax: (202)336-5568
Free: (800)374-2721
Publisher E-mail: webmaster@apa.org

Journal presenting abstracts from subscriber-selected journals in the area of learning disabilities, mental retardation, and communication disorders. **Founded:** 1982. **Freq:** Quarterly. **Print Method:** Offset. **Trim Size:** 8 1/2 x 11. **Cols./Page:** 2. **Col. Width:** 47 nonpareils. **Col. Depth:** 127 agate lines. **Key Personnel:** Denny Auld, Exec. Editor; Jodi Ashcraft, Advertising Mgr.; Maurine Jackson, Operations Dir.; Terri Pilkerton, Advertising Sales Rep. **ISSN:** 0730-1928. **Subscription Rates:** $21 members; $35 nonmembers; $69 institutions. **Remarks:** Accepts advertising.
Ad Rates: BW: $185 **Circ:** ‡1,800

5750 Public Administration Review
American Society for Public Administration
1120 G St. NW, No. 700 Phone: (202)393-7878
Washington, DC 20005 Fax: (202)638-4952
Publication E-mail: jlarkin@aspanet.org
Publisher E-mail: dcaspa@aol.com

Public administration journal. **Founded:** 1940. **Freq:** Bimonthly. **Print Method:** Offset. **Trim Size:** 6 1/2 x 9. **Cols./Page:** 2. **Col. Width:** 38 nonpareils. **Col. Depth:** 125 agate lines. **Key Personnel:** Irene Rubin, Editor-in-Chief. **ISSN:** 0033-3352. **Subscription Rates:** $90 individuals; $130 foreign. **Remarks:** Accepts advertising.
Ad Rates: BW: $575 **Circ:** ‡16,000
PCI: $50

5751 The Public Employee Magazine
American Federation of State, County & Municipal Employees
1625 L St. NW Phone: (202)429-1144
Washington, DC 20036-5687 Fax: (202)429-1120
Publication E-mail: pubaffairs@afscme.org

Magazine providing news and features of concern to members of AFSCME. **Founded:** 1936. **Freq:** Bimonthly. **Print Method:** Offset. **Trim Size:** 8 1/2 x 11. **Cols./Page:** 3. **Col. Width:** 14 picas. **Col. Depth:** 58 picas. **Key Personnel:** Jeff Rubin, Editor. **ISSN:** 1062-5992. **Remarks:** Advertising not accepted. **URL:** http://www.asscme.org.
Circ: ‡1,400,000

5752 The Public Interest
National Affairs, Inc.
1112 16th St. NW, Ste. 540 Phone: (202)785-8555
Washington, DC 20036 Fax: (202)467-0006
Publication E-mail: bertschj@aol.com

Magazine focusing on sociology, political economics, and domestic policy. **Founded:** 1965. **Freq:** Quarterly. **Print Method:** Offset. **Trim Size:** 6 x 9 1/8. **Cols./Page:** 1. **Col. Width:** 50 nonpareils. **Col. Depth:** 106 agate lines. **Key Personnel:** Irving Kristol, Co-Editor; Nathan Glazer, Co-Editor. **ISSN:** 0033-3557. **Subscription Rates:** $25 individuals. **Remarks:** Advertising not accepted.
Circ: 8,000

5753 Public Management (PM)
International City/County Management Association
777 N. Capitol St. NE, Ste. 500 Phone: (202)289-4262
Washington, DC 20002-4201 Fax: (202)962-3500
Free: (800)745-8780

Magazine for local government administrators. **Founded:** 1919. **Freq:** Monthly. **Print Method:** Offset. **Trim Size:** 8 1/4 x 10 7/8. **Cols./Page:** 3 and 2. **Col. Width:** 26 and 40 nonpareils. **Col. Depth:** 116 agate lines. **Key Personnel:** Beth Payne, Editor, phone (202)962-3619, bpayne@icma.org. **ISSN:** 0033-3611. **Subscription Rates:** $32 individuals; $48 other countries; $4 single issue. **Remarks:** Accepts advertising. **URL:** http://www.icma.org.
Ad Rates: BW: $1,210 **Circ:** Controlled ‡14,000
4C: $2,110

5754 Public Power
American Public Power Association (APPA)
2301 M St. NW Phone: (202)467-2900
Washington, DC 20037-1484 Fax: (202)467-2910

Official magazine of the American Public Power Association serving publicly-owned electric utility markets. **Founded:** Jan. 1942. **Freq:** Bimonthly. **Print Method:** Sheet-fed offset. **Trim Size:** 8 x 10 7/8. **Cols./Page:** 3. **Col. Width:** 26 nonpareils. **Col. Depth:** 133 agate lines. **Key Personnel:** Jeanne Wickline LaBella, Editor and Publisher, jlabella@appanet.org; James M. Bartlett, Art Director; Wanda D. Rakes-Harrell, Advertising Coordinator. **ISSN:** 0033-3654. **Subscription Rates:** $50 individuals. **Remarks:** Accepts advertising. **URL:** http://www.apaanet.org.
Ad Rates: BW: $1,960.00 **Circ:** Controlled 14,700
4C: $3,005.00 Paid 138

5755 Quality Advocate
The American Health Quality Association
1140 Connecticutt Ave., N.W., Ste. 1050 Phone: (202)331-5790
Fax: (202)331-9334
Washington, DC 20036
Publisher E-mail: ahqa@ahqa.org

Professional magazine covering quality improvement in health care. **Founded:** 1995. **Freq:** Quarterly. **Key Personnel:** Laura Kaloi, Contact. **Remarks:** Advertising not accepted. **Former name:** AMPRA Review.
Circ: Paid 1,500

5756 Quarterly Labour Force Statistics
Organization for Economic Cooperation and Development (OECD)
2001 L St. NW, Ste. 650 Phone: (202)785-6323
Washington, DC 20036-4922 Fax: (202)785-0350
Free: (800)456-6323
Publisher E-mail: washington.contact@oecd.org

Report providing statistics on the short term development of the major components of the labor force in the U.S. and 12 other OECD countries. **Founded:** 1979. **Freq:** Quarterly. **Print Method:** Offset. **Trim Size:** 7 7/8 x 10 5/8. **Cols./Page:** 1. **Col. Width:** 84 nonpareils. **Col. Depth:** 133 agate lines. **ISSN:** 0255-3627. **Subscription Rates:** $60 individuals; $67 by air mail. **Remarks:** Advertising not accepted.
Circ: (Not Reported)

5757 Quarterly National Accounts
Organization for Economic Cooperation and Development (OECD)
2001 L St. NW, Ste. 650 Phone: (202)785-6323
Washington, DC 20036-4922 Fax: (202)785-0350
Free: (800)456-6323
Publisher E-mail: washington.contact@oecd.org

Report compiling income statistics on U.S. and 11 other OECD countries. **Freq:** Quarterly. **Print Method:** Offset. **Trim Size:** 7 7/8 x 10 5/8. **Cols./Page:** 1. **Col. Width:** 84 nonpareils. **Col. Depth:** 133 agate lines. **ISSN:** 0304-3738. **Subscription Rates:** $90 individuals; $104 by air mail. **Remarks:** Advertising not accepted.
Circ: (Not Reported)

5758 Quotarian
Quota International
1420 21st St. NW Phone: (202)331-9694
Washington, DC 20036 Fax: (202)331-4395
Publisher E-mail: staff@quota.org

Member magazine for non-profit international service organizations. **Freq:** Annual. **Trim Size:** 8 x 11. **Key Personnel:** Kathleen W. Treiber, CAE, Editor and Publisher; Christy F. Herz, Managing Editor. **ISSN:** 0747-2072. **Subscription Rates:** $10 individuals. **Remarks:** Advertising not accepted. **Former name:** Quota International Connection.
Circ: Controlled ⊕**8,322**

5759 Radio Science
American Geophysical Union
2000 Florida Ave. NW Phone: (202)462-6900
Washington, DC 20009 Fax: (202)328-0566
Free: (800)966-2481
Publisher E-mail: service@agu.org

Journal covering scientific contributions on all aspects of electromagnetic phenomena related to physical problems. **Freq:** Bimonthly. **ISSN:** 0048-6604. **Subscription Rates:** $61 individuals; $20 single issue. **Remarks:** Advertising not accepted.
Circ: (Not Reported)

5760 RE:view
Heldref Publications
Helen Dwight Reid Educational Foundation Phone: (202)296-6267
Fax: (202)296-5149
1319 18th St. NW
Washington, DC 20036-1802
Free: (800)365-9753
Publication E-mail: subscribe@heldref.org
Publisher E-mail: revu@heldref.org

Journal for educators, researchers, parents, and others concerned with services for visually handicapped children, youth, and adults. **Subtitle:** Rehabilitation and Education for Blindness and Visual Impairment. **Founded:** 1969. **Freq:** Quarterly. **Print Method:** Offset. **Trim Size:** 6 x 9. **Cols./Page:** 1. **Col. Width:** 5 inches. **Col. Depth:** 7 1/2 inches. **Key Personnel:** Grant Williams, Advertising Mgr., advertise@heldref.org; Douglas Kirkpatrick, Director; Fred Huber, Circulation Mgr.; Jean Kline, Fulfillment Manager. **ISSN:** 0899-1510. **Subscription Rates:** $34 individuals; $68 institutions; Foreign add $12. **Online:** EBSCO; Infonautics; Information Access; UMI. **URL:** http://www.heldref.org. **Alt. Formats:** Audio tape; CD-ROM. **Formerly:** Re:VIEW .
Ad Rates: BW: $330 **Circ:** Combined ‡4,900

5761 Real Estate Finance Today
Real Estate Finance Press
1125 15th St. NW Phone: (202)861-6989
Washington, DC 20005 Fax: (202)861-0736
Free: (800)793-MBAA

Tabloid tracing economic trends and government actions that affect mortgage lenders. **Founded:** Mar. 1984. **Freq:** Weekly. **Print Method:** Offset. **Trim Size:** 10 x 15. **Cols./Page:** 4. **Col. Width:** 14.4 picas. **Col. Depth:** 189 agate lines. **Key Personnel:** Marshall Taylor, Editor, fax (202)429-9524; Peter House, Advertising Dir., phone (202)861-1946. **ISSN:** 0742-0021. **Subscription Rates:** $98 individuals. **Remarks:** Accepts advertising.
Ad Rates: GLR: $10 **Circ:** Paid ‡7,000
BW: $2,185 Non-paid ‡1,000
4C: $2,860
PCI: $55

5762 Reality
PO Box 50 Phone: (703)836-0565
Washington, DC 20044
Religious magazine. **Founded:** 1966. **Freq:** Monthly. **Print Method:** Letterpress and offset. **Cols./Page:** 3. **Col. Width:** 25 nonpareils. **Col. Depth:** 143 agate lines. **Key Personnel:** Lois Rader, Editor and Publisher. **USPS:** 378-630. **Remarks:** Advertising not accepted. **Alt. Formats:** Microfiche.
Circ: ‡2,000

5763 Realtor News
National Association of Realtors
700 11th St. NW Phone: (202)383-1193
Washington, DC 20001-4507 Fax: (202)383-1231
Publisher E-mail: narpubs.nar@notes.compuserve.com

Real estate magazine. **Founded:** 1967. **Freq:** Monthly. **Print Method:** Offset. **Trim Size:** 8 x 10 1/2. **Cols./Page:** 3. **Col. Width:** 2 3/8 inches. **Col. Depth:** 8 1/2 inches. **Key Personnel:** Marjorie Green, Publisher; William Adkinson, Publisher. **ISSN:** 0279-6309. **Subscription Rates:** $48 individuals.
Ad Rates: BW: $22,870 **Circ:** Paid 727,360
4C: $28,390 Free 1,376

5764 Recreation News
PO Box 32335 Phone: (202)965-6960
Washington, DC 20007-0635 Fax: (202)965-6964
Publication E-mail: recreation_ news@mcimail.com

Newspaper focusing on recreational activities in the Washington, D.C. area. **Founded:** Oct. 1, 1983. **Freq:** Monthly. **Print Method:** Offset. **Trim Size:** 11 1/2 x 15. **Cols./Page:** 6. **Col. Width:** 1 1/2 inches. **Col. Depth:** 14 inches. **Key Personnel:** Henry Dunbar, Editor; Michael T. Kapsa, Publisher. **ISSN:** 1056-9294. **Subscription Rates:** $15 annually.
Ad Rates: BW: $3677.52 **Circ:** Non-paid ‡104,000
4C: $4722.52
PCI: $43.78

5765 Recycling Times
Environmental Industry Associations
4301 Connecticut Ave., Ste. 300 Phone: (202)244-4700
Washington, DC 20008 Fax: (202)966-4868
Free: (800)424-2869
Publication E-mail: rct@envasns.org

Newspaper (tabloid) covering waste recycling and markets. **Subtitle:** The Newspaper For Recycling and Waste Professionals. **Founded:** Mar. 1989. **Freq:** Biweekly. **Trim Size:** 11 1/4 x 15. **Cols./Page:** 4. **Col. Width:** 2 5/16 inches. **Col. Depth:** 13 1/4 inches. **Key Personnel:** John T. Aquino, Editor-in-Chief; Jenny Heumann, Editor. **ISSN:** 1042-0614. **Subscription Rates:** $99 individuals. **Remarks:** Accepts advertising.
Ad Rates: BW: $1,300 **Circ:** 5,000
4C: $1,785

5766 Regulation
Cato Institute
1000 Massachusetts Ave. NW Phone: (202)842-0200
Washington, DC 20001-5403 Fax: (202)842-3490
Free: (800)767-1241
Publisher E-mail: catl@cato.org

Goverment regulation. **Subtitle:** Cato Review of Business & Government. **Founded:** July 1977. **Freq:** Quarterly. **Print Method:** Offset. **Trim Size:** 8 1/2 x 11. **Cols./Page:** 2. **Col. Width:** 38 nonpareils. **Col. Depth:** 134 agate lines. **Key Personnel:** Edward L. Hudgins, Editor; Edward H. Crane, Publisher; Ricardo Reyes, Managing Editor, rrayes@cato.org. **ISSN:** 0147-0590. **Subscription Rates:** Free to qualified subscribers; $18 individuals; $28 libraries and institutions. **Remarks:** Accepts advertising. **URL:** http://cato.org.
Ad Rates: BW: $800 **Circ:** Paid 1,500
4C: $1,250 Controlled 6,000

5767 Remodeling
Hanley-Wood, Inc.
1 Thomas Circle, Ste. 600 Phone: (202)452-0800
Washington, DC 20005 Fax: (202)785-1974

Trade magazine for the professional remodeling industry. **Founded:** May 1985. **Print Method:** Offset. **Trim Size:** 8 1/8 x 10 7/8. **Cols./Page:** 3. **Col. Width:** 13 picas. **Col. Depth:** 58 picas. **Key Personnel:** Paul Deffenbaugh, Editor-in-Chief, phone (202)736-3359; Jack Brannigan, Publisher, phone (847)267-1080, fax (847)267-1088. **ISSN:** 0885-8039. **Subscription Rates:** $24.95 individuals; $8 single issue. **Remarks:** Accepts advertising. **URL:** http://www.remodeling.hw.net.
Ad Rates: 4C: $11,340 **Circ:** Paid 1,056
Controlled 80,000

5768 Research News Reporter
Institute for Women's Policy Research
1400 20th St. NW, Ste. 104 Phone: (202)785-5100
Washington, DC 20036 Fax: (202)833-4362

Periodical of reprinted newspaper articles from the New York Times, Wall Street Journal, and Washington Post on women's policy issues subdivided into the following sections: work and education; poverty and income; politics and society; family life; health and reproductive issues. **Founded:** 1989. **Freq:** Monthly. **Key Personnel:** Anna Rockett, Editor, anna@www.iwpr.org. **Subscription Rates:** $175; $295 Corporations. **Remarks:** Advertising not accepted.
Circ: Paid 250

5769 Research-Technology Management
Industrial Research Institute, Inc.
1550 M. St. NW Phone: (202)296-8811
Washington, DC 20005 Fax: (202)776-0756

Magazine for managers of research, development, and technology implementation. **Founded:** 1958. **Freq:** Bimonthly. **Print Method:** Offset. **Trim Size:** 8 1/2 x 11. **Cols./Page:** 2 and 3. **Key Personnel:** Michael F. Wolff, Editor, phone (212)722-6551, fax (212)831-8594, mwolff3877@aol.com; Charles F. Larson, Publisher. **ISSN:** 0895-6308. **Subscription Rates:** $60 individuals; $140 industry, libraries and corporations; $20 single issue. **Remarks:** Advertising not accepted. **URL:** http://www.iriinc.org. **Alt. Formats:** Microform. **Formerly**: Research Management.
Circ: Paid ‡4,200
Non-paid ‡800

5770 The Responsive Community
The Reponsive Community
703 Gelman Library Phone: (202)994-8194
The George Washington University Fax: (202)994-1606
Washington, DC 20052
Free: (800)245-7460
Publication E-mail: comnet@gwis2.circ.gwu.edu

Journal Dedicated to exploring the relationships between individual rights and community responsibilities, and the foundations of a new moral/social order. **Subtitle:** Rights and Responsibilities. **Founded:** Jan. 1991. **Freq:** Quarterly. **Print Method:** Offset. **Trim Size:** 6 x 9. **Cols./Page:** 1. **Key Personnel:** Amitai Etzioni, Editor, phone (202)994-8190; Dan Doherty, Managing Editor, phone (202)994-8194, ddoherty@gwu.edu; Becca Merrill, Circulation Mgr., phone (202)994-4355. **ISSN:** 1053-0754. **Subscription Rates:** $27; $70 institutions; $7.95 single issue. **Remarks:** Accepts advertising.
Ad Rates: BW: $500 **Circ:** Paid 2,500
Non-paid 500

5771 Restaurant Information Abstracts
National Restaurant Association
1200 17th St. NW Phone: (202)331-5960
Washington, DC 20036 Fax: (202)331-5950
Free: (800)424-5156
Publication E-mail: isal@restaurant.org

Periodical containing abstracts of restaurant magazines. **Freq:** Biweekly. **Subscription Rates:** $50 members; $100. **Remarks:** Advertising not accepted. **Formerly**: Foodservice Information Abstracts (1998).
Circ: 250

5772 Restaurants USA
National Restaurant Association
1200 17th St. NW Phone: (202)331-5960
Washington, DC 20036 Fax: (202)331-5950
Free: (800)424-5156

How-to magazine for restaurant owners and managers. Includes industry trends, operational pointers, management principles, and association activities. **Subtitle:** The Monthly Magazine of the National Restaurant Assn. **Founded:** Nov. 1981. **Freq:** Monthly. **Print Method:** Web offset. **Trim Size:** 8 1/2 x 11. **Cols./Page:** 3 and 2. **Col. Width:** 13.5 and 10 picas. **Col. Depth:** 130 agate lines. **Key Personnel:** Jennifer Batty, Editor. **ISSN:** 0890-5584. **Subscription Rates:** $125 individuals. **Remarks:** Advertising not accepted. **URL:** http://www.restaurant.org.
Circ: Non-paid 39,000

5773 Retirement Life
National Association of Retired Federal Employees
1533 New Hampshire Ave. NW Phone: (202)234-0832
Washington, DC 20036 Fax: (202)797-9698

Magazine for federal civil service retirees and employees. **Subtitle:** A NARFE Publication for Current and Retired Federal Employees. **Founded:** 1954. **Freq:** Monthly. **Print Method:** Web offset. **Trim Size:** 8 x 10 1/2. **Cols./Page:** 3. **Col. Width:** 26 nonpareils. **Col. Depth:** 136 agate lines. **Key Personnel:** Kathleen E. Delaney, Editor. **ISSN:** 0034-6197. **Subscription Rates:** Included in membership; $25 nonmembers. **Remarks:** Accepts advertising.
Ad Rates: BW: $6,355 **Circ:** ‡450,000
4C: $7,400

5774 Review of Educational Research
American Educational Research Association
1230 17th St. NW Phone: (202)223-9485
Washington, DC 20036-3078 Fax: (202)775-1824

Journal of reviews of research literature relating to education. **Founded:** 1931. **Freq:** Quarterly. **Print Method:** Web offset. **Trim Size:** 6 x 9. **Cols./Page:** 1. **Col. Width:** 54 nonpareils. **Col. Depth:** 98 agate lines. **Key Personnel:** Carl Grant, Editor; Thomas J. Campbell, Director; Meredith Scott, Advertising Mgr.; Beth Graue, Assoc. Editor; Russell Burnett, Managing Editor. **ISSN:** 0034-6543. **Subscription Rates:** $41 individuals; $15 single issue; $56 institutions; $50 other countries. **URL:** http://www.aera.net. **Alt. Formats:** Microform.
Ad Rates: BW: $600 **Circ:** ‡18,400

5775 Review of Metaphysics
Philosophy Education Society
The Review of Metaphysics Phone: (202)635-8778
The Catholic University of America Fax: (202)319-4484
Washington, DC 20064
Free: (800)255-5924
Publication E-mail: mail@reviewofmetaphysics.org

Journal containing philosophical articles, abstracts, book reviews, announcements, and annual notices. **Founded:** 1947. **Freq:** Quarterly. **Print Method:** Offset. **Trim Size:** 4 5/8 x 7 3/4. **Cols./Page:** 1. **Col. Width:** 55 nonpareils. **Col. Depth:** 103 agate lines. **Key Personnel:** Jude P. Dougherty, Editor. **ISSN:** 0034-6632. **Subscription Rates:** $28 individuals; $45 institutions; $100 sustaining institutions; $18 students; $12 single issue; $18 retirees. **Remarks:** Accepts advertising.
Ad Rates: BW: $200 **Circ:** ‡2,500

5776 Reviews of Geophysics
American Geophysical Union
2000 Florida Ave. NW Phone: (202)462-6900
Washington, DC 20009 Fax: (202)328-0566
Free: (800)966-2481
Publisher E-mail: service@agu.org

Professional journal covering scientific work in geophysics. **Freq:** Quarterly. **ISSN:** 8755-1209. **Subscription Rates:** $28 individuals. **Remarks:** Advertising not accepted.
Circ: (Not Reported)

5777 ReVision
Heldref Publications
Helen Dwight Reid Educational Foundation Phone: (202)296-6267
Fax: (202)296-5149
1319 18th St. NW
Washington, DC 20036-1802
Free: (800)365-9753
Publisher E-mail: revu@heldref.org

Interdisciplinary journal that advances inquiry and research in philosophy, religion, psychology, social theory, science, and the arts. **Subtitle:** A Journal of Consciousness and Transformation. **Founded:** 1978. **Freq:** Quarterly. **Print Method:** Offset. **Trim Size:** 8 1/2 x 11. **Cols./Page:** 3. **Col. Width:** 2 1/4 inches. **Col. Depth:** 10 inches. **Key Personnel:** Celia Dubois, Managing Editor; Douglas Kirkpatrick, Director; Grant Williams, Advertising Mgr., advertise@heldref.org; Mary McGann Ealley, Sales Rep. **ISSN:** 0275-6935. **Subscription Rates:** $35 individuals; $60 institutions; out of country add $13. **Remarks:** Accepts advertising. **Online:** EBSCO; Infonautics; Information Access; UMI. **URL:** http://www.heldref.org. **Alt. Formats:** CD-ROM.
Ad Rates: BW: $500 **Circ:** Paid ‡900

5778 Revista Panamericana de Salud Publica
Pan American Health Organization
Publications Program, PAHO Phone: (202)974-3086
525 23rd St. NW Fax: (202)338-0869
Washington, DC 20037
Publication E-mail: publiper@paho.org
Publisher E-mail: sales@paho.org

Multilingual public health journal providing information on medical and health progress in the Americas. **Founded:** 1997. **Freq:** Monthly. **Print Method:** Offset. **Trim Size:** 8 1/2 x 11. **Cols./Page:** 3. **Col. Width:** 43.5 nonpareils. **Key Personnel:** Dr. Maria Luisa Clark, Editor-in-Chief, phone (202)974-3083. **ISSN:** 1020-4989. **Subscription Rates:** $68 U.S. and Canada; $85 other countries; $10 single issue; $38 Latin America/Caribbean. **Remarks:** Advertising not accepted. **URL:** http://www.paho.org. **Also known as**: Pan American Journal of Public Health. **Formerly**: Bulletin of the Pan American Health Organization.
Circ: ‡12,000

5779 RICO Law Reporter
1601 Connecticut Ave., NW, No. 602 Phone: (202)462-5755
Fax: (202)328-2430
Washington, DC 20009
Publisher E-mail: lawreport@aol.com

Professional journal covering securities law. Available in print format or via e-mail. **Founded:** 1985. **Freq:** Monthly. **Print Method:** Photo offset. **Trim Size:** 8 1/2 x 11. **Cols./Page:** 2. **Col. Width:** 3 1/2 inches. **Col. Depth:** 8 inches. **Key Personnel:** Mary Lyons, Editor. **ISSN:** 0889-0461. **Subscription Rates:** $1,500 individuals. **Remarks:** Advertising not accepted.
Circ: (Not Reported)

5780 Rocks & Minerals
Heldref Publications
Helen Dwight Reid Educational Foundation Phone: (202)296-6267
Fax: (202)296-5149
1319 18th St. NW
Washington, DC 20036-1802
Free: (800)365-9753
Publication E-mail: rm@heldref.org
Publisher E-mail: revu@heldref.org

Magazine for students of mineralogy, geology, and paleontology. **Founded:** 1926. **Freq:** Bimonthly. **Print Method:** Offset. **Trim Size:** 8 3/8 x 11. **Cols./Page:** 2. **Col. Width:** 3 1/2 inches. **Col. Depth:** 9 1/2 inches. **Key Personnel:** Grant Williams, Advertising Mgr., advertise@heldref.org; Douglas Kirkpatrick, Director; Fred Huber, Circulation Mgr., subscribe@heldref.org; Mary McGann Ealley, Sales Rep.; Leila Saad, Managing Editor. **ISSN:** 0035-7529. **Subscription Rates:** $38 individuals; $74 institutions; foreign, add $10. **Remarks:** Accepts advertising. **Online:** EBSCO; Infonautics; Info. Access; UMI. **URL:** http://www.heldref.org/. **Alt. Formats:** CD-ROM.
Ad Rates: BW: $500 **Circ:** Paid ‡3,100
4C: $1,100 Controlled 1,000

5781 Roll Call
Roll Call, Inc.
900 2nd St. NE, Ste. 107 Phone: (202)289-4900
Washington, DC 20002 Fax: (202)289-2205

Contains the news of Congress from an unique insider perspective. **Subtitle:** The Newspaper of Capitol Hill. **Founded:** June 16, 1955. **Freq:** Semiweekly (Mon. and Thurs.). **Print Method:** Offset. **Trim Size:** 11 3/8 x 16. **Cols./Page:** 4. **Col. Width:** 2.25 picas. **Col. Depth:** 14 inches. **Key Personnel:** Stacy Mason, Editor; Laurie Battaglia, Publisher; Karen Whitman, Advertising Dir.; Katherine Feeling, Circulation Dir. **ISSN:** 0035-788X. **Subscription Rates:** $210; $3 single issue. **Remarks:** Accepts advertising. **Online:** LEXIS-NEXIS. **URL:** http://www.rollcall.com.
Ad Rates: BW: $6,400 **Circ:** Paid 5,161
4C: $7,400 Non-paid 12,244

5782 Romance Quarterly
Heldref Publications
Helen Dwight Reid Educational Foundation Phone: (202)296-6267
Fax: (202)296-5149
1319 18th St. NW
Washington, DC 20036-1802
Free: (800)365-9753
Publication E-mail: rq@heldref.org
Publisher E-mail: revu@heldref.org

Periodical publishing historical and interpretive articles on French, Spanish, Catalan, Italian, Portuguese, and Brazilian literature, and romance linguistics. **Founded:** 1953. **Freq:** Quarterly. **Trim Size:** 6 x 9. **Key Personnel:** Grant Williams, Advertising Mgr., advertise@heldref.org; Fred Huber, Circulation Mgr., subscribe@heldref.org; Jean Kline, Fulfillment Manager, subscribe@heldref.org; Douglass Kirkpatrick, Director; Beverly Glover-Wood, Managing Editor. **ISSN:** 0883-1157. **Subscription Rates:** $40 individuals; $74 institutions; add $13 for postage outside the United States. **Online:** EBSCO; Infonautics; UMI. **Alt. Formats:** CD-ROM.
Ad Rates: BW: $160 **Circ:** Paid 422

5783 RTNDA Communicator
Radio-Television News Directors Association
1000 Conneticut Avenue NW, Ste. 615 Phone: (202)659-6510
Fax: (202)223-4007
Washington, DC 20036
Free: (800)807-8632
Publication E-mail: rtnda@rtnda.org

Radio and television news trade publication. **Subtitle:** The Magazine for Electronic Journalists. **Founded:** 1946. **Freq:** Monthly. **Print Method:** Offset. **Trim Size:** 8 3/8 x 10 7/8. **Cols./Page:** 3. **Col. Width:** 27 nonpareils. **Col. Depth:** 145 agate lines. **Key Personnel:** Barbara S. Cochran, Pres./Publisher, phone (202)467-5205, fax (202)223-4007, barbarac@rtnda.org; Leslie Sansam Emery, Communications Dir., phone (202)467-5203, fax (202)223-4007, noreenw@rtnda.org; Ron Bardach, Advertising Dir., phone (202)467-5208, fax (202)203-4007, ronb@rtnda.org; Bryan Moffett, Managing Editor, phone (202)467-5210, fax (202)224-4007, bryanb@rtnda.org. **Subscription Rates:** Included in membership; $75 nonmembers; $8 single issue. **URL:** http://www.rtnda.org/rtnda/.
Ad Rates: BW: $1,555 **Circ:** ‡4,700
4C: $2,135

5784 Rural Development Perspectives
Department of Agriculture/ERS
1800 M St. NW Phone: (202)694-5050
Washington, DC 20036
Publisher E-mail: service@econ.ag.gov

Trade magazine covering rural issues. **Freq:** Semiannual.

Subscription Rates: $19 individuals; $38 out of country. **Remarks:** Advertising not accepted.
Circ: (Not Reported)

5785 Rural Telecommunications
National Telephone Cooperative Association
2626 Pennsylvania Ave. NW Phone: (202)298-2300
Washington, DC 20037-1695 Fax: (202)298-2320
Publication E-mail: frs@ntca.org

Trade publication devoted to rural telecommunications industry. **Founded:** 1981. **Freq:** Bimonthly. **Print Method:** Offset. **Trim Size:** 8 1/2 x 11. **Cols./Page:** 3. **Col. Width:** 27 nonpareils. **Col. Depth:** 133 agate lines. **Key Personnel:** Jennifer Mayne, Managing Editor, phone (202)298-2311, fax (202)965-4967, jmayne@ntca.org; David Bolton, Editor, phone (202)298-2331, dbolton@ntca.org; Jill O'Rourke, Publications Manager. **ISSN:** 0744-2548. **Subscription Rates:** $20 members; $40 nonmembers. **Remarks:** Accepts advertising. **Online:** EBSCO CASIAS.INC. **Alt. Formats:** Microform.
Ad Rates: BW: $1375 **Circ:** Paid ‡4,090
4C: $2200 Non-paid ‡250

5786 Salary Survey
National Association for Business Economics
1233 20th St., Ste. 505 Phone: (202)463-6223
Washington, DC 20036 Fax: (202)463-6239
Publisher E-mail: nabe@nabe.com

Publication that provides data on income levels by educational attainment, industry and location. **Freq:** Every other year. **Subscription Rates:** $30 single issue. **Remarks:** Advertising not accepted.
Circ: (Not Reported)

5787 Science
American Association for the Advancement of Science
1200 New York Ave., NW Phone: (202)326-6626
Washington, DC 20005 Fax: (202)289-4950

Magazine devoted to science, scientific research, and public policy. **Founded:** July 3, 1880. **Freq:** Weekly (Fri.). **Print Method:** Offset. **Trim Size:** 8 1/4 x 10 1/2. **Cols./Page:** 3. **Col. Width:** 26 nonpareils. **Col. Depth:** 139 agate lines. **Key Personnel:** Floyd Bloom, Editor; Richard S. Nicholson, Publisher; Beth Rosner, Associate Publisher; Susan Meredith, Advertising Mgr.; Janis Crowley, Recruitment Advertising Mgr. **ISSN:** 0036-8075. **Subscription Rates:** $105 individuals; $7 single issue. **Remarks:** Accepts advertising. **URL:** htpp://www.sciencemag.org.
Ad Rates: BW: $6,530 **Circ:** Paid ★156,712
4C: $7,980
PCI: $495

5788 Science Activities
Heldref Publications
Helen Dwight Reid Educational Foundation Phone: (202)296-6267
Fax: (202)296-5149
1319 18th St. NW
Washington, DC 20036-1802
Free: (800)365-9753
Publication E-mail: sa@heldref.org
Publisher E-mail: revu@heldref.org

Journal providing a source of elementary, junior high, and high school science projects and activities. **Founded:** 1962. **Freq:** Quarterly. **Print Method:** Offset. **Trim Size:** 8 1/2 x 11. **Cols./Page:** 2. **Col. Width:** 3 1/2 inches. **Col. Depth:** 10 inches. **Key Personnel:** Grant Williams, Advertising Mgr., advertise@heldref.org; Douglas Kirkpatrick, Director; Fred Huber, Circulation Mgr., subscribe@heldref.org; Betty Bernard, Managing Editor. **ISSN:** 0036-8121. **Subscription Rates:** $35 individuals; $64 institutions; foreign, add $13 for postage. **Online:** EBSCO; Infonautics; Info. Access; UMI. **URL:** http://www.heldref.org/. **Alt. Formats:** CD-ROM.
Ad Rates: BW: $255 **Circ:** ‡1,112

5789 Science Books & Films
American Association for the Advancement of Science
1200 New York Ave., NW Phone: (202)326-6626
Washington, DC 20005 Fax: (202)289-4950
Publication E-mail: sb&f@aaas.org

Professional journal reviewing science books, AV materials, and software made for general audiences, teachers, and students from kindergarten to college. **Founded:** 1965. **Freq:** 9/year. **Print Method:** Offset. **Trim Size:** 8 1/2 x 11. **Cols./Page:** 3. **Key Personnel:** Maria Sosa, Editor-in-Chief, phone (202)326-6453, msosa@aaas.org; Barbara Walthall, Editor, phone (202)326-6646, bwalthal@aaas.org; Janet Aldrich, Assoc. Ed., phone (202)326-6626; Chickona Royster, Subscriptions, phone (202)326-6454, croyster@aaas.org. **ISSN:** 0098-342X. **Subscription Rates:** $40 individuals; $7 single issue. **Remarks:** Advertising not accepted.
Circ: Paid ‡4,500
Non-paid ‡600

5790 Science News
Science Service, Inc.
1719 N St. NW Phone: (202)785-2255
Washington, DC 20036 Fax: (202)785-1243
Free: (800)347-6969
Publisher E-mail: sciedu@sciserv.org

Reports on new findings in physical, biological and behavioral sciences. **Subtitle:** The Weekly Newsmagazine of Science. **Founded:** 1926. **Freq:** Weekly (Sat.). **Print Method:** Offset. **Trim Size:** 8 1/8 x 10 7/8. **Cols./Page:** 3. **Col. Width:** 27 nonpareils. **Col. Depth:** 140 agate lines. **Key Personnel:** Julie Ann Miller, Editor, fax (202)659-0365; Donald Harless, Publisher. **ISSN:** 0036-8423. **Subscription Rates:** $49.50 individuals; $2 single issue. **Remarks:** Accepts advertising. **Online:** Compuserve. **Alt. Formats:** Audio tape; Braille; CD-ROM.
Ad Rates: BW: $5,933 **Circ:** Paid ★181,961
4C: $8,308

5791 The Scottish Rite Journal (Southern Jurisdiction, USA)
Supreme Council of the 33rd Degree, A&A Scottish Rite
1733 16th St. NW Phone: (202)232-3579
Washington, DC 20009-3103 Fax: (202)387-1843
Free: (800)776-2766
Publisher E-mail: council@srmason-sj.org

Masonic magazine. **Founded:** 1904. **Freq:** Monthly. **Print Method:** Offset. **Trim Size:** 5 1/4 x 7 1/4. **Cols./Page:** 2. **Col. Width:** 25 nonpareils. **Col. Depth:** 85 agate lines. **Key Personnel:** C. Fred Kleinknecht, Editor-in-Chief; Dr. John W. Boettjer, Managing Editor. **Subscription Rates:** Free to qualified subscribers; $4 institutions. **Remarks:** Advertising not accepted. **URL:** http://www.srmason-sj.org. **Formerly:** The New Age.
Circ: Non-paid ‡430,000

5792 Scrap
Institute of Scrap Recycling Industries
1325 G. St. NW, Ste. 1000 Phone: (202)737-1770
Washington, DC 20005 Fax: (202)626-0900

Magazine for the scrap processing and recycling industry. **Founded:** 1943. **Freq:** Bimonthly. **Print Method:** Offset. **Trim Size:** 8 1/8 x 10 7/8. **Cols./Page:** 3. **Col. Width:** 13.5 picas. **Col. Depth:** 60 picas. **Key Personnel:** Kent Kiser, Editor, phone (202)662-8547, fax (202)626-0947; James E. Fowler, Publisher, phone (202)662-8544, fax (202)626-0944. **ISSN:** 0036-9527. **Subscription Rates:** $32.95 individuals. **URL:** http://www.scrap.org. **Formerly:** Scrap Processing and Recycling.
Ad Rates: BW: $1,770 **Circ:** Paid 7322
4C: $2,500
PCI: $65

5793 Sculpture
International Sculpture Center
1050 17th St. NW, Ste. 250 Phone: (202)785-1144
Washington, DC 20036 Fax: (202)785-0810
Publication E-mail: sculpt@dgsys.com
Publisher E-mail: isc@aitswire.org

Magazine for sculptors, artists, contemporary sculpture experts, arts professionals, and enthusiasts. **Founded:** 1982. **Freq:** 10/year (monthly, except May/June & July/August). **Print Method:** Web offset. **Trim Size:** 8 1/4 x 10 7/8. **Cols./Page:** 3. **Col. Width:** 14 picas. **Col. Depth:** 58 picas. **Key Personnel:** Glenn Harper, Editor; Anne Harnish, Managing Editor; Kim Kerker, Advertising Dir. **ISSN:** 0889-728X. **Subscription Rates:** $50 individuals; $6 single issue. **Remarks:** Accepts advertising. **URL:** http://www.sculpture.org.
Ad Rates: BW: $1,400 **Circ:** Paid ‡11,000
4C: $2,250 Non-paid ‡5,000

5794 SEC Docket
U.S. Securities and Exchange Commission
450 Fifth St. NW
Washington, DC 20549

Professional journal covering orders and releases issued by the Securities and Exchange Commission. **Founded:** 1970. **Freq:** Weekly. **Remarks:** Advertising not accepted. **Available Online.**
Circ: (Not Reported)

5795 Section 504 Compliance Handbook
Thompson Publishing Group
1725 K St. NW, Ste. 700 Phone: (202)872-4000
Washington, DC 20006 Fax: (202)739-9578
Publication E-mail: sfch@thompson.com

Magazine covering new developments in disability law. **Freq:** Monthly. **Subscription Rates:** $218 individuals. **Remarks:** Advertising not accepted.
Circ: (Not Reported)

5796 Securities Reform Act Litigation Reporter
1601 Connecticut Ave., NW, No. 602 Phone: (202)462-5755
Fax: (202)328-2430
Washington, DC 20009
Publication E-mail: lawreport@aol.com
Publisher E-mail: lawreport@aol.com

Professional journal covering securities law. Available in print format or via e-mail. **Founded:** 1995. **Freq:** Monthly. **Print Method:** Photo offset. **Trim Size:** 8 1/2 x 11. **Cols./Page:** 2. **Col. Width:** 3 1/2 inches. **Col. Depth:** 8 inches. **Key Personnel:** Mary Lyons, Managing Editor. **Subscription Rates:** $1,000 individuals. **Remarks:** Advertising not accepted.
Circ: (Not Reported)

5797 Shakespeare Quarterly
The Folger Shakespeare Library
201 E. Capitol St. SE Phone: (202)544-7077
Washington, DC 20003-1094 Fax: (202)544-4623

Journal containing scholarly interpretations of Shakespeare in a variety of intellectual, social, artistic, and historical contexts. **Founded:** 1950. **Freq:** Quarterly. **Print Method:** Offset. **Trim Size:** 6 7/8 x 10. **Cols./Page:** 1. **Col. Width:** 30 picas. **Col. Depth:** 46 1/2 picas. **Key Personnel:** Dr. Barbara A. Mowat, Editor; Mary Tonkinson, Advertising Mgr.; Jean Ferrick, Contact; Toni Krieger, Contact. **ISSN:** 0037-3222. **Subscription Rates:** $45 individuals; $60 institutions; $50 other countries; $65 institutions, other countries; $8 single issue. **Remarks:** Color advertising not accepted.
Ad Rates: BW: $225 **Circ:** Paid ‡3,400
Non-paid ‡250

5798 Share the Word
Paulist National Catholic Evangelization Association
3031 4th St. NE Phone: (202)832-5022
Washington, DC 20017 Fax: (202)269-0209
Free: (800)237-5515
Publisher E-mail: pncea@pncea.org

Magazine on Catholic interpretation of the Sunday lectionary readings. **Subtitle:** Scripture Reflections for Today's Desciples. **Founded:** 1979. **Freq:** Seasonal. **Print Method:** Offset. **Trim Size:** 5 1/4 x 7 3/4. **Cols./Page:** 2. **Col. Width:** 2 inches. **Col. Depth:** 6 1/8 inches. **Key Personnel:** Paula Diehl, Editor, pauladiehl@pncea.org. **ISSN:** 0199-5049. **Subscription Rates:** $17.50; $25.50 Canada; $27.50 other countries. **Remarks:** Accepts advertising. **Alt. Formats:** Mailing lists.
Ad Rates: BW: $316.80 **Circ:** Paid ‡13,000
4C: $601.80

5799 Shofar
B'nai B'rith Youth Organization
1640 Rhode Island Ave. NW Phone: (202)857-6633
Washington, DC 20036-3278 Fax: (202)857-6568

Jewish youth newspaper. **Founded:** 1925. **Freq:** Quarterly. **Print Method:** Offset. **Cols./Page:** 4. **Col. Width:** 28 nonpareils. **Col. Depth:** 205 agate lines. **Key Personnel:** Jeff Hoffman, Editor. **ISSN:** 0745-9327. **Subscription Rates:** $1 individuals. **Remarks:** Accepts advertising.
Circ: ‡30,000

5800 Sister City News
Sister Cities International
1300 Pennsylvania Ave. NW, Ste. 250 Phone: (202)312-1200
Fax: (202)312-1201
Washington, DC 20004-3002
Publisher E-mail: info@sister-cities.org

Newspaper (tabloid) covering economic, cultural, and social programs initiated and managed by municipal, civic, and government officials and their international counterparts. **Founded:** 1961. **Freq:** Bimonthly. **Print Method:** Web offset. **Trim Size:** 11 1/4 x 15. **Cols./Page:** 4. **Col. Width:** 28 nonpareils. **Col. Depth:** 194 agate lines. **Key Personnel:** Richard Oakland, Editor; Carol Lynn Greene, Publisher. **Subscription Rates:** $10. **Remarks:** Accepts advertising.
Ad Rates: BW: $1,150 **Circ:** Paid ‡11,312
4C: $1,400 Free ‡2,000

5801 Skylines
Building Owners & Managers Association International
1201 New York Ave. SW, Ste. 300 Phone: (202)408-2662
Fax: (202)371-0181
Washington, DC 20005
Magazine on the commercial real estate industry. **Subtitle:** News of the Commercial Real Estate Industry. **Founded:** 1908. **Freq:** Monthly. **Print Method:** Offset. **Trim Size:** 8 1/2 x 11. **Cols./Page:** 2. **Col. Width:** 17 nonpareils. **Col. Depth:** 190 agate lines. **Key Personnel:** Stephanie J. Opppenheimer, Editor, phone (202)326-6315, soppen@boma.org; Lisa Prats, Publisher, phone (202)326-6351, lprats@boma.org. **ISSN:** 0892-7847. **Subscription Rates:** $75 nonmembers. **Remarks:** Accepts advertising. **URL:** http://www.boma.org.
Ad Rates: 4C: $3,525 **Circ:** Paid 16,067

5802 Smithsonian Magazine
900 Jefferson Dr., SW Phone: (202)786-2900
Washington, DC 20560
Publication E-mail: edletters@aol.com

General interest magazine. **Founded:** 1970. **Freq:** Monthly. **Print Method:** Offset. **Trim Size:** 8 3/8 x 10 7/8. **Cols./Page:** 3. **Col. Width:** 28 nonpareils. **Col. Depth:** 140 agate lines. **Key Personnel:** Don Moser, Editor, fax (202)786-2564, dmoser@simag.si.edu; Ron Walker, Publisher, fax (202)633-9454, rwalker@simag.si.edu; David Cator, Advertising Dir., phone (212)916-1313, fax (212)986-4259. **ISSN:** 0037-7333. **Subscription Rates:** $24. **Remarks:** Accepts advertising. **Online:** AOL, MSN, Compuserve. **Alt. Formats:** Audio tape.
Ad Rates: BW: $47,495 **Circ:** Paid ★**2,041,134**
4C: $69,595

5803 Social Education
National Council for the Social Studies (NCSS)
3501 Newark St., NW Phone: (202)966-7840
Washington, DC 20016 Fax: (202)966-2061
Publisher E-mail: publications@ncss.org

Official journal of the National Council for the Social Studies. **Founded:** 1937. **Freq:** 7/year. **Print Method:** Web offset. **Trim Size:** 8 1/8 x 10 7/8. **Cols./Page:** 3. **Col. Width:** 2 1/8 inches. **Col. Depth:** 8 1/2 inches. **Key Personnel:** Bill Doran, Advertising Dir., phone (301)277-7342, fax (301)864-8772; Michael Simpson, Editor, msimpson@ncss.org; Terri Ackerman, Managing Editor, tackerman@ncss.org; Jennifer Truran Rothwell, Associate Editor, jrothwell@ncss.org. **ISSN:** 0037-7724. **Subscription Rates:** $50 individuals; $7.50 single issue plus shipping and handling; $59 institutions. **Online:** ERIC. **URL:** http://www.ncss.org; http://www.socialstudies.org. **Alt. Formats:** Microform.
Ad Rates: BW: $1,800 **Circ:** Paid ‡29,000

5804 Social Security Bulletin
U.S. Government Printing Office
Office of Research and Statistics Phone: (202)282-7138
Van Ness Centre, Rm. 209 Fax: (202)282-7219
4301 Connecticut Ave. NW
Washington, DC 20008
Bulletin reporting data on the operations of the Social Security Administration and the results of research and analysis pertinent to the social security program. **Founded:** 1938. **Freq:** Quarterly. **Print Method:** Offset. Uses mats. **Cols./Page:** 2. **Col. Width:** 20 nonpareils. **Col. Depth:** 130 agate lines. **ISSN:** 0037-7910. **Subscription Rates:** $13. **Remarks:** Advertising not accepted.
Circ: (Not Reported)

5805 The Social Studies
Heldref Publications
Helen Dwight Reid Educational Foundation Phone: (202)296-6267
Fax: (202)296-5149
1319 18th St. NW
Washington, DC 20036-1802
Free: (800)365-9753
Publication E-mail: tss@heldref.org
Publisher E-mail: revu@heldref.org

Journal for teachers and administrators in the social studies field. **Founded:** 1909. **Freq:** Bimonthly. **Print Method:** Offset. Uses mats. **Trim Size:** 8 1/2 x 11. **Cols./Page:** 4. **Col. Width:** 2 1/4 inches. **Col. Depth:** 7 inches. **Key Personnel:** Grant Williams, Advertising Mgr., advertise@heldref.org; Douglas Kirkpatrick, Director; Fred Huber, Circulation Mgr., subscribe@heldref.org; Jean Kline, Fulfillment, subs@heldref.org. **ISSN:** 0037-7996. **Subscription Rates:** $38 individuals; $64 institutions; add $15 for postage outside the United States. **Online:** EBSCO; Infonautics; Information Access; UMI. **URL:** http://www.heldref.org/. **Alt. Formats:** CD-ROM.
Ad Rates: BW: $375 **Circ:** Paid ‡1,950

5806 Social Work
National Association of Social Workers
750 1st St. NE, Ste. 700 Phone: (202)408-8600
Washington, DC 20002-4241 Fax: (202)336-8312
Free: (800)638-8799
Publication E-mail: press@naswda.org

Magazine for social workers. **Subtitle:** Journal of the National Association of Social Workers. **Founded:** 1956. **Freq:** Bimonthly. **Print Method:** Offset. **Trim Size:** 7 x 10. **Cols./Page:** 2. **Col. Width:** 17 picas. **Col. Depth:** 50 picas. **Key Personnel:** Paula Delo, Executive Editor, pdelo@naswdc.org. **ISSN:** 0037-8046. **Subscription Rates:** members free; $71 nonmembers; $98 institutions. **Remarks:** Accepts advertising.
Ad Rates: BW: $1,465 **Circ:** 165,000

5807 Social Work in Education
National Association of Social Workers
750 1st St. NE, Ste. 700 Phone: (202)408-8600
Washington, DC 20002-4241 Fax: (202)336-8312
Free: (800)638-8799

Journal. **Subtitle:** A Journal for Social Workers in Schools. **Founded:** 1978. **Freq:** Quarterly. **Print Method:** Offset. **Trim Size:** 7 x 10. **Cols./Page:** 2. **Col. Width:** 13 1/2 picas. **Col. Depth:** 48 picas. **Key Personnel:** Paula Delo, Managing Editor, pdelo@naswdc.org. **ISSN:** 0162-7961. **Subscription Rates:** $39 members; $62 nonmembers; $84 institutions; $26 students. **Remarks:** Accepts advertising.
Ad Rates: BW: $480 **Circ:** 3,700

5808 Social Work Research
National Association of Social Workers
750 1st St. NE, Ste. 700 Phone: (202)408-8600
Washington, DC 20002-4241 Fax: (202)336-8312
Free: (800)638-8799
Publication E-mail: press@naswdc.org

Research journal for social workers. **Founded:** 1977. **Freq:** Quarterly. **Print Method:** Offset. **Trim Size:** 7 x 10. **Cols./Page:** 2. **Col. Width:** 16 picas. **Col. Depth:** 53 picas. **Key Personnel:** Paula Delo, Managing Editor, pdelo@naswdc.org. **ISSN:** 1070-5309. **Subscription Rates:** $40 members; $63 nonmembers; $87 institutions; $28 students. **Remarks:** Accepts advertising. **Formerly**: Social Work Research & Abstracts.
Ad Rates: BW: $465 **Circ:** Paid 3,000

5809 Sojourners
Sojourners
2401 15th St. NW Phone: (202)328-8842
Washington, DC 20009 Fax: (202)328-8757
Free: (800)714-7474

Independent, economical christian magazine which anal faith, politics, and culture from a progressive, justice-oriented perspective. **Subtitle:** Faith, Politics, and Culture. **Founded:** 1971. **Freq:** Bimonthly. **Print Method:** Offset. **Trim Size:** 8 1/4 x 10 7/8. **Cols./Page:** 3. **Col. Width:** 2 5/16 inches. **Col. Depth:** 9 7/8 inches. **Key Personnel:** James Wallis, Editor; Joseph Roos, Publisher; Karen L. Lattea, Managing Editor; David Wade, Marketing Dir.; Anne O'Rourke, Development Dir. **ISSN:** 0364-2097. **Subscription Rates:** $3.95 single issue. **Remarks:** Accepts advertising. **Available Online. URL:** www.sojourners.com/sojourners.
Ad Rates: BW: $1,375 **Circ:** Paid ‡24,000
4C: $1,495 Non-paid ‡3,000

5810 Solar Industry Journal
Solar Energy Industries Association
122 C. St. NW, 4th Fl. Phone: (202)383-2600
Washington, DC 20001 Fax: (202)383-2670
Publisher E-mail: info@seia.org

Professional journal for the solar industry. **Founded:** 1989. **Freq:** Quarterly. **Key Personnel:** Linda Ladas, Editor; Anne Snyder, Asst. Editor/Advertising Mgr. **Subscription Rates:** $25 individuals. **Remarks:** Accepts advertising.
Circ: (Not Reported)

5811 Spiritual Life
Washington Province of Discalced Carmelite Friars, Inc.
2131 Lincoln Rd. NE Phone: (202)832-8489
Washington, DC 20002-1199 Fax: (202)832-8967
Free: (800)832-8489

Catholic journal of spirituality. **Subtitle:** A Quarterly of Contemporary Spirituality. **Founded:** 1955. **Freq:** Quarterly. **Print Method:** Offset. **Trim Size:** 6 x 9. **Cols./Page:** 1. **Col. Width:** 54 nonpareils. **Col. Depth:** 98 agate lines. **Key Personnel:** Brother Edward O'Donnell, Editor, edodonnell@aol.com; Bryan Paquette, Business Mgr.; Michael Stoegbauer, Promotion & Circulation Mgr., stoegbauer@juno.com. **ISSN:** 0038-7630. **Subscription Rates:** $16 individuals; $4.50 single issue. **Remarks:** Advertising not accepted. **Alt. Formats:** Microform.
Circ: 12,000

5812 The Spotlight
Liberty Lobby
300 Independence Ave. SE Phone: (202)544-1794
Washington, DC 20003
Publisher E-mail: libertylob@aol.com

Newspaper covering public affairs. **Founded:** Sept. 17, 1975. **Freq:** Weekly (Thurs.). **Print Method:** Offset. **Trim Size:** 11 1/2 x 15. **Cols./Page:** 4. **Col. Width:** 29 nonpareils. **Col. Depth:** 88 agate lines. **Key Personnel:** Frederick V. Blahut, Managing Editor; Andrew Arnold, Editor. **ISSN:** 0191-6270. **Subscription Rates:** $40 individuals; $74 two years. **URL:** http://www.spotlight.org.
Ad Rates: BW: $3,187.95 **Circ:** ‡100,000

5813 STI Review
Organization for Economic Cooperation and Development (OECD)
2001 L St. NW, Ste. 650 Phone: (202)785-6323
Washington, DC 20036-4922 Fax: (202)785-0350
Free: (800)456-6323
Publisher E-mail: washington.contact@oecd.org

Magazine containing articles which link the topics of technology, science, production structures, the role of government and industry, and economic growth. **Freq:** Semiannual. **Print Method:** Offset. **ISSN:** 1010-5247. **Subscription Rates:** $55 individuals; $58 by air mail. **Remarks:** Advertising not accepted.
Circ: (Not Reported)

5814 Stone Review
National Stone Association
1415 Elliot Pl. NW Phone: (202)342-1100
Washington, DC 20007-2599 Fax: (202)342-0702
Free: (800)342-1415

Trade magazine for stone producers and suppliers of equipment to the aggregates industry. **Founded:** Feb. 1985. **Freq:** Bimonthly. **Print Method:** Offset. **Trim Size:** 8 1/4 x 10 3/4. **Cols./Page:** 3 and 2. **Col. Width:** 13.5 and 21.5 picas. **Col. Depth:** 10 inches. **Key Personnel:** R.A. "Gus" Edwards, Exec. Editor; Jennifer Joy Wilson, Publisher; Frank Atlee, Editor, fatlee@aggregates.org. **ISSN:** 8750-9210. **Subscription Rates:** $48 individuals; $8 single issue.
Ad Rates: BW: $1,300 **Circ:** Paid ‡2,558
4C: $2,000 Non-paid ‡1,412

5815 Stores
NRF Enterprises, Inc.
Liberty Place Phone: (202)783-7971
325 7th St. NW, Ste. 1000 Fax: (202)737-2849
Washington, DC 20004-2802
Free: (800)NRF-HOW2
Publication E-mail: publisher@nrf.com; editor@nrf.com

Subtitle: The Magazine for Retail Decision Makers. **Founded:** 1912. **Freq:** Monthly. **Print Method:** Offset. **Trim Size:** 8 1/2 x 10 7/8. **Cols./Page:** 3. **Col. Width:** 26 nonpareils. **Col. Depth:** 140 agate lines. **Key Personnel:** Rick Gallagher, V.P. & Publisher, phone (202)626-8103, publisher@nrf.com; Harrison Donnelly, Executive Editor, phone (202)626-8163, editor@nrf.com; Mary Alice Elmer, Managing Editor; Amy B. Clotworthy, Editorial Assistant, clotworthya@nrf.com. **ISSN:** 0039-1867. **Subscription Rates:** $49; $79 other countries. **Remarks:** Accepts advertising. **Available Online. URL:** http://www.stores.org.
Ad Rates: BW: $6,895 **Circ:** Paid 15,776
4C: $8,890 Non-paid 19,966

5816 Sulphur in Agriculture
Sulphur Institute
1140 Connecticut Ave., NW,
Ste. 612
Washington, DC 20036

Journal covering the use of sulphur in agriculture. **Founded:** 1977. **Freq:** Semiannual. **Key Personnel:** Donald L. Messick, Editor. **ISSN:** 0160-0680. **Subscription Rates:** $5 single issue. **Remarks:** Advertising not accepted.
Circ: (Not Reported)

5817 SYMPHONY
American Symphony Orchestra League
1156 15th NW, Suite 800 Phone: (202)776-0212
Washington, DC 20005-1704 Fax: (202)776-0224
Publication E-mail: editor@symphony.org
Publisher E-mail: league@symphony.org

Magazine with news and articles for symphony orchestra managers, trustees, conductors, volunteers, and musicians. **Founded:** 1989. **Freq:** Bimonthly. **Print Method:** Offset. **Trim Size:** 8 1/4 x 10 7/8. **Cols./Page:** 3. **Col. Width:** 2.25 picas. **Col. Depth:** 10 inches. **Key Personnel:** Melinda Whiting, Editor, melinda@symphony.org; Laura Tucker, Advertising Rep., ltucker@symphony.org; Chester Lane, Senior Editor, chesterl@symphony.org. **ISSN:** 0271-2687. **Subscription Rates:** $35 individuals. **Remarks:** Accepts advertising. **Former name**: Symphony Magazine; Symphony News.
Ad Rates: BW: $1,905 **Circ:** ‡18,500
4C: $2,630
PCI: $90

5818 Symposium
Heldref Publications
Helen Dwight Reid Educational Foundation Phone: (202)296-6267
Fax: (202)296-5149
1319 18th St. NW
Washington, DC 20036-1802
Free: (800)365-9753
Publication E-mail: sym@heldref.org
Publisher E-mail: revu@heldref.org

Journal on modern literature from other countries. **Subtitle:** A Quarterly Journal in Modern Foreign Literatures. **Founded:** 1947. **Freq:** Quarterly. **Print Method:** Offset. Uses mats. **Trim Size:** 6 x 9. **Cols./Page:** 1. **Col. Width:** 4 1/4 inches. **Col. Depth:** 7 3/8 inches. **Key Personnel:** Grant Williams, Advertising Mgr., advertise@heldref.org; Douglas Kirkpatrick, Director; Fred Huber, Circulation Mgr., subscribe@heldref.org; Jean Kline, Fulfillment Manager, subscribe@heldref.org. **ISSN:** 0039-7709. **Subscription Rates:** $39 individuals; $78 institutions; foreign, add $13. **Remarks:** Advertising accepted; rates available upon request. **Online:** EBSCO; Infonautics;

Information Access; Inst. Scient. Info.; UMI. **URL:** http://www.heldref.org/. **Alt. Formats:** CD-ROM.
Circ: Paid ‡611

5819 Systems & Procedures Exchange Center (SPEC) Kit
ARL Publications
Dept. No. 0692 Phone: (202)296-8656
Washington, DC 20073-0692 Fax: (202)872-0884
Publisher E-mail: arlhq@arl.org

Journal pertaining to research library management practices. **Founded:** Nov. 1973. **Trim Size:** 8 1/1 x 11. **Key Personnel:** Lee Anne George, Contact, leeanne@arl.org. **ISSN:** 0160-3582. **Subscription Rates:** $40 nonmembers; $25 members. **Remarks:** Advertising not accepted. **Online:** ERIC Clearinghouse on Information and Technology. **URL:** http://www.arl.org/spec/surveys/.
Circ: Paid 550
Non-paid 10

5820 Talking Book Topics
National Library Service for the Blind and Physically Handicapped
Publications & Media Section Phone: (202)707-9281
NLS/BPH Fax: (202)707-0712
Washington, DC 20542
Publisher E-mail: nls@loc.gov

Catalog of books available to the visually and physically handicapped. Also produces a recorded edition and a large print edition. **Founded:** 1936. **Freq:** Bimonthly. **Print Method:** Offset. **Trim Size:** 8 1/2 x 11. **Cols./Page:** 2. **Col. Width:** 42 nonpareils. **Col. Depth:** 99 agate lines. **Key Personnel:** George Thuronyi, Editor, phone (202)707-9281, fax (202)707-0712, gthu@loc.gov. **ISSN:** 0039-9183. **Subscription Rates:** Free. **Remarks:** Advertising not accepted. **URL:** http://www.loc.gov/nls. **Alt. Formats:** Audio tape; Braille; Large-print.
Circ: Free ‡286,000

5821 The Tax Executive
Tax Executives Institute, Inc.
1200 G. St. NW, Ste. 300 Phone: (202)638-5601
Washington, DC 20005-3814 Fax: (202)638-5607
Publication E-mail: asktei@tei.org

Professional journal covering business tax issues. **Founded:** 1948. **Freq:** Bimonthly. **Print Method:** Web offset. **Trim Size:** 8 1/2 x 11. **Cols./Page:** 3. **Col. Width:** 20.5 picas. **Col. Depth:** 55.5 picas. **Key Personnel:** Timothy McCormally, Editor. **ISSN:** 0040-0025. **Subscription Rates:** $115 individuals; $22 single issue. **Remarks:** Accepts advertising.
Ad Rates: BW: $925 **Circ:** Combined 5,556
4C: $1,700

5822 The Tax Management International Forum
Tax Management Inc.
1250 23rd St. NW Phone: (202)833-7240
Washington, DC 20037 Free: (800)372-1033

Publication presenting a comparative discussion of international tax law problems by practitioners in major industrial countries. **Founded:** Jan. 1980. **Freq:** Quarterly. **Print Method:** Offset. **Trim Size:** 8 1/4 x 11 3/4. **Key Personnel:** Nick Webb, Contact. **ISSN:** 0143-7941. **Subscription Rates:** $405 individuals. **Remarks:** Advertising not accepted.
Circ: (Not Reported)

5823 Tax Practice Adviser
Tax Management Inc.
1250 23rd St. NW Phone: (202)833-7240
Washington, DC 20037 Free: (800)372-1033
Publication E-mail: tm@bna.com

Monthly report covering tax management. **Founded:** 1990. **Freq:** Monthly. **Print Method:** Offset. **Trim Size:** 8 1/2 x 11. **Key Personnel:** Glenn B. Davis, Managing Editor. **Subscription Rates:** $951 individuals. **Remarks:** Advertising not accepted. **Formerly:** IRS Practice and Policy.
Circ: Paid 1,000
Non-paid 279

5824 Teaching and Change
Corwin Press
1201 16th St. NW Phone: (202)822-7256
Washington, DC 20036 Fax: (202)822-7206
Publication E-mail: neapub9@aol.com
Publisher E-mail: info@corwinpress.com

Journal on the adaption of teaching institutions to changing social factors. **Founded:** 1993. **Freq:** Quarterly. **Trim Size:** 6 x 9. **Key Personnel:** Alice Humbertson, Journals Mgr., phone (805)499-9734, fax (805)499-5323, alice.humbertson@corwinpress.com; Barbara Pape, Managing Editor, phone (202)724-0124, fax (202)632-0957. **ISSN:** 1068-378X. **Subscription Rates:** $45 single issue; $160 institutions; $40 individuals; $20 single issue. **Remarks:** Accepts advertising. **Online:** OCLC First Search. **Alt. Formats:** Mailing labels.
Circ: Paid 750
Non-paid 20

5825 The Teamster
International Brotherhood of Teamsters
25 Louisiana Ave. NW Phone: (202)624-6800
Washington, DC 20001-2198 Fax: (202)624-6918

Labor union magazine. **Founded:** 1902. **Freq:** 8/year. **Print Method:** Web. **Trim Size:** 8 1/2 x 11. **Cols./Page:** 3. **Col. Width:** 13 picas. **Col. Depth:** 133 agate lines. **Key Personnel:** Matt Witt, Editor. **ISSN:** 1083-2394. **Subscription Rates:** $12 individuals; $2 single issue. **Remarks:** Advertising not accepted. **URL:** http://www.teamster.org. **Formerly:** The International Teamster; The New Teamster.
Circ: ‡1,886,230

5826 TechTrends: for Leaders in Education & Training
Association for Educational Communications and Technology (AECT)
1025 Vermont Ave. NW, Ste. 820 Phone: (202)347-7834
Fax: (202)347-7839
Washington, DC 20005
Publisher E-mail: aect@aect.org

Professional magazine for educators and trainers. **Founded:** 1956. **Freq:** Bimonthly. **Print Method:** Offset. Uses mats. **Trim Size:** 8 1/2 x 11. **Cols./Page:** 3. **Col. Width:** 26 nonpareils. **Col. Depth:** 133 agate lines. **Key Personnel:** Mary Twillman, Director of Publications, maryt@aect.org. **ISSN:** 8756-3894. **Subscription Rates:** Free to AECT members; $40 nonmembers; $44 other countries. **Remarks:** Accepts advertising. **Alt. Formats:** Mailing labels.
Ad Rates: BW: $1,300 **Circ:** ‡8,000

5827 Tectonics
American Geophysical Union
2000 Florida Ave. NW Phone: (202)462-6900
Washington, DC 20009 Fax: (202)328-0566
Free: (800)966-2481
Publisher E-mail: service@agu.org

Scientific journal covering tectonics and earth sciences. **Freq:** Bimonthly. **ISSN:** 0278-7407. **Remarks:** Advertising not accepted.
Circ: (Not Reported)

5828 TeleTimes
United States Telephone Association (USTA)
1401 H St. NW, Ste. 600 Phone: (202)326-7300
Washington, DC 20005-2164 Fax: (202)326-7333
Free: (800)646-8782

Magazine for management of local exchange carriers and other companies providing products and services to the telecom industry. **Founded:** 1987. **Freq:** 6/year. **Print Method:** Sheetfed. **Trim Size:** 8 1/2 x 11. **Key Personnel:** Cheryl Sullivan, Editor, phone (202)326-7265, csulliva@usta.org; Amy Lambert, Editorial Asst., phone (202)326-7372, alambert@usta.org; Kim McDonald, Editorial Asst., phone (202)326-7278, kmcdonald@usta.org. **ISSN:** 1074-5823. **Subscription Rates:** $20 members; $60 nonmembers; $85 other countries. **Remarks:** Accepts advertising.
Ad Rates: BW: $1,547 **Circ:** 5,000
4C: $2,347

5829 Television & Cable Factbook
Warren Publishing, Inc.
2115 Ward Ct. NW Phone: (202)872-9200
Washington, DC 20037 Fax: (202)293-3435
Publication E-mail: factbook@warrenpub.com
Publisher E-mail: warrenpub@mindspring.com

Publication focusing on television, cable, and support industries. **Founded:** 1951. **Freq:** 1/year. **Print Method:** Offset. **Trim Size:** 8 1/2 x 11. **Cols./Page:** 3. **Key Personnel:** Albert Warren, Publisher; Michael Taliaferro, Managing Editor. **Subscription Rates:** $495. **Remarks:** Advertising accepted; rates available upon request. **Alt. Formats:** CD-ROM, Factbook on CD-ROM.
Circ: (Not Reported)

5830 Textile Museum Journal
Textile Museum
2320 S St. NW Phone: (202)667-0441
Washington, DC 20008 Fax: (202)483-0994
Publisher E-mail: info@textilemuseum.org

Journal covering textile history. **Founded:** 1962. **Freq:** Annual. **Print Method:** Litho. **Trim Size:** 8 1/2 x 11. **Cols./Page:** 2. **Col. Width:** 16 picas. **Col. Depth:** 56 picas. **Key Personnel:** Carol Bier, Editor; Ann Rowe, Editor; Sumru Krody, Managing Editor. **Subscription Rates:** $15 single issue; Free to qualified subscribers. **Remarks:** Advertising not accepted. **URL:** http://www.textilemuseum.org.
Circ: (Not Reported)

5831 THEOLOGICAL STUDIES
Theological Studies, Inc.
Georgetown University Phone: (202)338-0754
37th & O Sts. NW Fax: (202)687-7679
Washington, DC 20057-1136
Theological journal. **Founded:** 1940. **Freq:** Quarterly. **Print Method:** Offset. **Trim Size:** 6 x 9. **Cols./Page:** 1. **Col. Width:** 52 nonpareils. **Col. Depth:** 91 agate lines. **Key Personnel:** Michael A. Fahey, S.J., Editor; John R. Keating, S.J., Manager. **ISSN:** 0040-5639. **Subscription Rates:** $23 individuals; $33 institutions; $30 individuals other countries; $40 institutions, other countries. **Available Online. Alt. Formats:** CD-ROM; Microform, University Microfilms, Information Access, Uncover Co.
Ad Rates: BW: $340 **Circ:** ‡4,704

5832 The Thomist
Dominican Fathers, Province of St. Joseph
487 Michigan Ave. NE Phone: (202)529-5300
Washington, DC 20017 Fax: (202)636-4460

Journal promoting inquiry into contemporary philosophical and theological questions. **Subtitle:** A Spectulative Quarterly Review. **Founded:** 1939. **Freq:** Quarterly. **Trim Size:** 6 x 9. **Cols./Page:** 1. **Key Personnel:** Rev. J.A. DiNoia, O.P., Editor. **ISSN:** 0040-6325. **Subscription Rates:** $25 individuals; $35; $45 institutions; $12.50 single issue. **Remarks:** Accepts advertising. **URL:** http://www.thomist.org. **Alt. Formats:** Microform.
Ad Rates: BW: $175 **Circ:** Paid 1000
Controlled 50

5833 Thought & Action
National Education Association of the United States
1201 16th St. NW Phone: (202)822-7214
Washington, DC 20036 Fax: (202)822-7206

Journal covering higher education. **Subtitle:** The NEA Higher Education Journal. **Founded:** 1984. **Freq:** Semiannual. **Key Personnel:** Con Lehane, Editor, clehane@nea.org. **Subscription Rates:** $30 individuals; Free to qualified subscribers. **Remarks:** Advertising not accepted. **URL:** http://www.nea.org/he.
Circ: Paid 80,000

5834 Today's Internist
American Society of Internal Medicine
2011 Pennsylvania Ave. NW, Ste. 800 Phone: (202)835-2746
Fax: (202)835-0441
Washington, DC 20006-1834
Publication E-mail: asimeditor@asim.org
Publisher E-mail: asim@asim.org

Magazine on internal medicine practice, health policy, and related socio-economic issues. **Subtitle:** The Magazine of the American Society of Internal Medicine. **Founded:** 1959. **Freq:** 6/year. **Print Method:** Offset. **Trim Size:** 8 3/8 x 10 7/8. **Cols./Page:** 3. **Col. Width:** 24 nonpareils. **Col. Depth:** 137 agate lines. **Key Personnel:** C. Burns Roehrig, M.D., Editor, editor@asim.org; Javy Awan, Managing Editor, jawan@asim.org. **ISSN:** 0020-9546. **Subscription Rates:** $24 individuals; $12 for retired ASIM members; $30 other countries. **Remarks:** Accepts advertising. **URL:** http://www.asim.org/ti_home.htm. **Formerly:** The Internist: Health Policy in Practice (Jan. 1, 1997); The Internist.
Ad Rates: BW: $1,037 **Circ:** Paid ‡20,979
4C: $2,147 Non-paid ‡15,013

5835 Today's Realtor
National Association of Realtors
700 11th St. NW Phone: (202)383-1193
Washington, DC 20001-4507 Fax: (202)383-1231
Publisher E-mail: narpubs.nar@notes.compuserve.com

Real estate magazine. **Founded:** 1979. **Freq:** Monthly. **Print Method:** Offset. **Trim Size:** 8 x 10 1/2. **Cols./Page:** 3. **Col. Width:** 7 inches. **Col. Depth:** 9 1/2 inches. **Key Personnel:** Pamela Geurds Kabati, Editorial Dir.; Annette Cohen, Publisher. **ISSN:** 1086-8054. **Subscription Rates:** $48 individuals. **Remarks:** Accepts advertising. **URL:** http://www.judds.com/tr.htm.
Ad Rates: BW: $23,560 **Circ:** Paid 725,000
4C: $29,250 Free 1,323

5836 The Tower
Sun Newspapers
400A UCW, Catholic University Phone: (202)319-5778
Washington, DC 20064 Fax: (202)319-5529
Publication E-mail: mcgonagle@cua.edu

University newspaper. **Founded:** 1922. **Freq:** Weekly. **Cols./Page:** 5. **Col. Width:** 1.75 inches. **Col. Depth:** 13 inches. **Key Personnel:** Jennifer C. Zoghby, Editor-in-Chief; Carrie Drummond, Managing Editor; Jonathan M. Daigle, Operations Mgr.; Matthew Sweeney, Business Mgr. **Subscription Rates:** Free on campus; $15 students per semester. **Remarks:** Accepts advertising.
Ad Rates: BW: $422.50 **Circ:** Free 5,000
PCI: $7

5837 TransCaucasus, A Chronology
Lucine Kasbarian
888 17th St. NW, Ste. 904 Phone: (202)775-1981
Washington, DC 20006 Fax: (202)775-5648
Publication E-mail: anca-dc@ix.netcom.com

Chronological summary of the significant social, economic, and political events in the lower caucasus, as reported by local and international media and selected sources in the region. **Subtitle:** A Chronology. **Founded:** 1992. **Freq:** Monthly. **Key Personnel:** Christopher M. Hekimian, Editor; Richard Giragosian, Writer. **ISSN:** 1078-3113. **Subscription Rates:** Free to qualified subscribers. **Remarks:** Advertising not accepted.
Circ: 2,000

5838 Transportation Quarterly
Eno Transportation Foundation, Inc.
One Farragut Square South Phone: (202)879-4700
Suite 500 Fax: (202)879-4719
Washington, DC 20006-4003
Trade magazine on transportation. **Founded:** 1947. **Freq:** Quarterly. **Print Method:** Letterpress and offset. **Trim Size:** 7 x 10. **Cols./Page:** 2. **Key Personnel:** Carolyn Fields, Circulation Mgr., phone (202)879-4704, fax (202)879-4719, Carolyn@enotrons.com. **ISSN:** 0278-9434. **Subscription Rates:** $45 individuals; $65 out of country. **Remarks:** Advertising not accepted.
Circ: Controlled ‡3,000

5839 TRIAL
Association of Trial Lawyers of America
1050 31st. St. NW Phone: (202)965-3500
Washington, DC 20007-4499 Fax: (202)965-0030
Free: (800)424-2725

Legal magazine. **Subtitle:** Journal of the Association of Trial Lawyers of America. **Founded:** 1964. **Freq:** Monthly. **Print Method:** Offset. **Trim Size:** 8 1/4 x 10 7/8. **Cols./Page:** 3. **Col. Width:** 27 nonpareils. **Col. Depth:** 134 agate lines. **Key Personnel:** Elizabeth Yeary, Editor, betty.yeary@atlahq.org; Judith Lewis, Advertising Mgr., phone (202)944-2870, judy.lewis@atlahq.org. **ISSN:** 0041-2538. **Subscription Rates:** $79 individuals; $7.50 single issue. **Remarks:** Accepts advertising. **URL:** http://www.atlanet.org.
Ad Rates: GLR: $30 **Circ:** Paid 44,537
BW: $3,095 Non-paid 6,275
4C: $3,895

5840 Troubling Company Prospector
Beard Group, Inc.
PO Box 9867 Phone: (301)951-6400
Washington, DC 20016 Fax: (301)951-3621
Publisher E-mail: chris@beard.com

Professional magazine covering businesses showing signs of financial strain. **Subtitle:** Profiles of Firms in Transition. **Founded:** 1992. **Freq:** Weekly. **Key Personnel:** Christopher Beard, Publisher. **ISSN:** 1062-2330. **Subscription Rates:** $1150. **Remarks:** Advertising not accepted.
Circ: (Not Reported)

5841 Trusteeship
Association of Governing Boards of Universities and Colleges
1 Dupont Circle, Ste. 400 Phone: (202)296-8400
Washington, DC 20036 Fax: (202)223-7053

Professional magazine covering higher education for board members and chief executives. **Founded:** 1993. **Freq:** Bimonthly. **Print Method:** Web offset. **Key Personnel:** Daniel J. Levin, Editor, danl@agb.org; Deborah Bongiorno, Managing Editor. **ISSN:** 1068-1027. **Subscription Rates:** $65 nonmembers; $40 members. **Remarks:** Advertising not accepted. **URL:** http://www.agb.org. **Former name**: AGB Reports.
Circ: Paid 32,000

5842 21st Century Science & Technology
21st Century Science Associates, Inc.
PO Box 16285 Phone: (703)777-7473
Washington, DC 20041-6285 Fax: (703)777-8853
Publication E-mail: tcs@mediasoft.net

Science magazine. **Founded:** 1988. **Freq:** Quarterly. **Print Method:** Offset. **Trim Size:** 8 1/4 x 10 1/2. **Cols./Page:** 3. **Col. Depth:** 9 inches. **Key Personnel:** Marjorie Mazel Hecht, Managing Editor. **ISSN:** 0895-6420. **Subscription Rates:** $25; $3.50 single issue. **Remarks:** Accepts advertising.
Ad Rates: BW: $1,000 **Circ:** Paid 25,000

5843 U.A. Journal
United Association of Journeymen & Apprentices of the Plumbing & Pipefitting Industry of the U.S. & Canada
901 Massachusetts Ave. NW Phone: (202)628-5823
Washington, DC 20001 Fax: (202)628-5024

Labor magazine. **Founded:** 1889. **Freq:** Monthly. **Print Method:** Web offset. **Trim Size:** 8 1/4 x 11 7/8. **Cols./Page:** 4. **Col. Width:** 11 picas. **Col. Depth:** 60 picas. **Key Personnel:** Thomas H. Patchell, Editor. **ISSN:** 0095-7763. **Remarks:** Advertising not accepted. **URL:** http://www.ua.org.
Circ: Controlled 330,000

5844 United Mine Workers Journal
United Mine Workers of America
900 15th St. NW Phone: (202)842-7200
Washington, DC 20005 Fax: (202)842-7227
Publication E-mail: journal@umwa.org

Magazine emphasizing energy, coal, labor, and legislation. **Founded:** 1891. **Freq:** Bimonthly. **Print Method:** Offset. **Trim Size:** 9 1/4 x 11 1/4. **Cols./Page:** 3. **Col. Width:** 30 nonpareils. **Col. Depth:** 140 agate lines. **Key Personnel:** Doug Gibson, Editor, phone (202)842-7241, dgibson@umwa.org. **ISSN:** 0041-7327. **Subscription Rates:** $10 individuals; $25 institutions; $100 Corporations. **Remarks:** Advertising not accepted.
Circ: (Not Reported)

5845 U.S. Medicine
2021 L St. NW, Ste. 400 Phone: (202)463-6000
Washington, DC 20036-3362 Fax: (202)223-2849
Publisher E-mail: usmedicine@usmedicine.com

Medical newspaper intended for physicians and pharmacists practicing in local, state, and federal governments, and private-sector managed care. **Founded:** Jan. 1, 1965. **Freq:** Monthly. **Print Method:** Offset. **Trim Size:** 11 x 15 3/4. **Cols./Page:** 4. **Col. Width:** 37 nonpareils. **Col. Depth:** 205 agate lines. **Key Personnel:** Nancy Tomich, Editor and Publisher; Frank Best, Chairman. **ISSN:** 0191-6246. **Subscription Rates:** $135 individuals. **Remarks:** Accepts advertising.
Ad Rates: GLR: $45 **Circ:** Paid 96
BW: $5,800 Free 43,518
4C: $7,325

5846 U.S. News & World Report
2400 N St. NW Phone: (202)955-2000
Washington, DC 20037-1196 Fax: (202)955-2049

National and international news magazine. **Founded:** 1933. **Freq:** Weekly (Mon.). **Print Method:** Offset. **Trim Size:** 8 x 10 1/2. **Cols./Page:** 3. **Col. Width:** 27 nonpareils. **Col. Depth:** 140 agate lines. **Key Personnel:** James Fallows, Editor; Pat Hagerty, Advertising Mgr.; Tom Evans, Publisher. **Subscription Rates:** $39.75 individuals; $2.50 single issue. **Remarks:** Accepts advertising. **Online:** DataTimes Corporation; LEXIS-NEXIS. **URL:** http://wwwz.USN.com/usnews/.
Circ: Paid 2,224,003

5847 Update (Library of Congress)
National Library Service for the Blind and Physically Handicapped
1291 Taylor St., NW Phone: (202)707-5100
Washington, DC 20542 Fax: (202)707-0712
Free: (800)424-8567
Publisher E-mail: nls@loc.gov

Magazine reporting on current information on library services for disabled individuals. **Freq:** Quarterly. **Subscription Rates:** Free. **Remarks:** Advertising not accepted. **Alt. Formats:** Braille.
Circ: Non-paid 7,600

5848 Upgrade
Software Publishers Association
1730 M St., NW, No. 700 Phone: (202)452-1600
Washington, DC 20036-4510 Fax: (202)223-8756

Professional magazine covering technology and computers. **Freq:** Monthly. **Print Method:** Sheetfed offset. **Trim Size:** 8 1/2 x 11. **Cols./Page:** 2. **Key Personnel:** Kathleen Rakestraw, Editor, krakestraw@spa.org. **ISSN:** 1083-4605. **Subscription Rates:** $79 individuals. **Remarks:** Accepts advertising. **Former name:** SPA News.
Ad Rates: BW: $1,805 **Circ:** Paid 6,000
4C: $2,205

5849 Urban Land Magazine
Urban Land Institute
1025 Thomas Jefferson, NW, Phone: (202)624-7000
500 W Fax: (202)624-7140
Washington, DC 20007-5201
Free: (800)321-5011
Publisher E-mail: bookstore@uli.org

Professional magazine for land use and development practitioners. **Founded:** 1941. **Freq:** Monthly. **Key Personnel:** Kristina Kessler, Editor; John McKenzie, Advertising Dir. **ISSN:** 0042-0891. **Subscription Rates:** Included with a membership in the Urban Land Institute. $5 single issue. **Remarks:** Accepts advertising.
Ad Rates: BW: $3,250 **Circ:** Paid 12,400
4C: $4,565

5850 Valuation
American Society of Appraisers
PO Box 17265 Phone: (703)478-2228
Washington, DC 20041 Fax: (703)742-8471
Free: (800)ASA-VALU
Publisher E-mail: asainfo@appraisers.org

Professional journal covering appraising. **Founded:** 1984. **Freq:** Semiannual. **Print Method:** Offset. **Trim Size:** 6 x 9. **Cols./Page:** 1. **Col. Width:** 4 3/4 inches. **Col. Depth:** 8 1/4 inches. **Key Personnel:** Rebecca Ewing Mavey, Editor. **ISSN:** 0042-238X. **Subscription Rates:** $15 single issue; Free to qualified subscribers. **Remarks:** Accepts advertising.
Ad Rates: BW: $700 **Circ:** Combined 8,000

5851 Valve Magazine
Valve Manufacturers Association of America (VMA)
1050 17th St. NW, Ste. 280 Phone: (202)331-8105
Washington, DC 20036-5503 Fax: (202)296-0378
Publisher E-mail: vma@vma.org

Trade magazine covering valves. **Founded:** 1989. **Freq:** Quarterly. **ISSN:** 1057-2813. **Subscription Rates:** $28 individuals. **Remarks:** Accepts advertising.
Circ: (Not Reported)

5852 Vital Issues
Bethune-Dubois Publications
600 New Hampshire Ave. NW, Phone: (202)625-2900
Ste. 1125 Fax: (202)625-0499
Washington, DC 20037
Journal presenting major speeches by professional leaders. **Subtitle:** The Journal of African American Speeches. **Founded:** 1991. **Freq:** Quarterly. **Cols./Page:** 7. **Key Personnel:** Dr. Teta V. Banks, Editor. **ISSN:** 1056-6368. **Subscription Rates:** $49 individuals; $88 two years. **Remarks:** Advertising accepted; rates available upon request.
Circ: Paid 1,500
Non-paid 500

5853 The Volta Review
Alexander Graham Bell Association for the Deaf
3417 Volta Pl. NW Phone: (202)337-5220
Washington, DC 20007-2778 Fax: (202)337-8314
Publisher E-mail: agbell2@aol.com

Journal on educating the deaf. **Founded:** 1898. **Freq:** 5/year. **Print Method:** Offset. **Trim Size:** 6 x 9. **Cols./Page:** 1. **Col. Width:** 54 nonpareils. **Col. Depth:** 105 agate lines. **Key Personnel:** Nancy Tye-Murray, PhD, Editor, nancy_tyc-murray@cldmac.wustl.edu; Margaret Messina, Managing Editor, mamolline@aol.com; Elizabeth Quigley, Advertising Mgr., agbell2@aol.com. **ISSN:** 0042-8639. **Subscription Rates:** $52 institutions; $50 members; $30 students. **Remarks:** Accepts advertising. **Alt. Formats:** Mailing labels.
Ad Rates: BW: $479 **Circ:** ‡3,450

5854 Volta Voices
Alexander Graham Bell Association for the Deaf
3417 Volta Pl. NW Phone: (202)337-5220
Washington, DC 20007-2778 Fax: (202)337-8314
Publisher E-mail: agbell2@aol.com

Magazine providing news of interest to the hearing impaired. **Founded:** 1994. **Freq:** 6/year. **Print Method:** Offset. **Trim Size:** 8 1/2 x 11. **Key Personnel:** Margaret Messina, Editor, mamoline@aol.com. **ISSN:** 1074-8016. **Subscription Rates:** $52 individuals; $50 members; $40 parents; $30 students. **Remarks:** Accepts advertising. **Formerly**: Newsounds, Our Kids Magazine.
Ad Rates: BW: $519 **Circ:** Paid ⊕**4,200**
4C: $1,200

5855 The Washington Blade
1408 U St. NW, 2nd Fl. Phone: (202)797-7000
Washington, DC 20009 Fax: (202)797-7040

Tabloid presenting gay and lesbian community and national news. **Subtitle:** The Gay Weekly of the Nation's Capital. **Founded:** Oct. 1969. **Freq:** Weekly. **Print Method:** Web offset. **Trim Size:** 9 3/4 x 13 1/2. **Cols./Page:** 4. **Col. Width:** 14 picas. **Col. Depth:** 13 1/4 inches. **Key Personnel:** Lisa M. Keen, Editor; Donald J. Michaels, Publisher; Mark Sullivan, Managing Editor; Colleen Marzec, Asst. Managing Editor. **ISSN:** 0278-9892. **Subscription Rates:** $45 individuals. **Remarks:** Accepts advertising. **Available Online. URL:** http://www.washblade.com.
Ad Rates: BW: $1,020 **Circ:** Free ❑**41,446**
4C: $1,475 Paid ❑**1,346**
PCI: $35

5856 Washington Business Journal
American City Business Journals
2000 14th St. N., Ste. 500 Phone: (703)875-2200
Arlington, VA 22201-2566 Fax: (703)875-2231
Publication E-mail: wbizjrhl@aol.com

Metropolitan business newspaper (tabloid). **Founded:** 1982. **Freq:** Weekly. **Print Method:** Offset. **Cols./Page:** 4. **Col.**

Width: 27 nonpareils. **Col. Depth:** 196 agate lines. **Key Personnel:** Alex Orfinger, Publisher; Ellen Duhamel, Business Mgr.; Kent Hoover, Editor; D'Arcy Kelner, Circulation/ Mktg. Dir.; Rick Baierlein, Advertising Dir.; Molly Zlokovitz, Art Director. **ISSN:** 0737-3147. **Subscription Rates:** $69 individuals. **Remarks:** Accepts advertising. **URL:** http:// www.amcity.com/washington.
Ad Rates: BW: $3,785 **Circ:** Paid ★**15,617**
4C: $4,385

5857 Washington History
Historical Society of Washington, D.C.
1307 New Hampshire NW Phone: (202)785-2068
Washington, DC 20036-1507 Fax: (202)887-5785

Historical journal covering local history. **Subtitle:** Magazine of the Historical Society of Washington D.C. **Founded:** 1989. **Freq:** Semiannual. **Trim Size:** 7 x 10. **Cols./Page:** 2. **Col. Width:** 2 5/8 inches. **Col. Depth:** 8 inches. **Key Personnel:** Jane Freundel Levey, Editor. **ISSN:** 1042-9719. **Subscription Rates:** $30 individuals; $7 single issue. **Remarks:** Accepts advertising.
Ad Rates: BW: $400 **Circ:** Paid 3,000

5858 The Washington Informer
3117 Martin Luther King Jr. Ave. SE Phone: (202)561-4100
Fax: (202)574-3785
Washington, DC 20032-1537
Newspaper (tabloid) serving Washington's metropolitan area black community. **Founded:** Oct. 16, 1964. **Freq:** Weekly (Thurs.). **Print Method:** Offset. **Cols./Page:** 5. **Col. Width:** 2 1/16 inches. **Col. Depth:** 13 inches. **Key Personnel:** Denise Rouard Barnes, Editor and Publisher. **Subscription Rates:** $15 individuals. **Remarks:** Accepts advertising. **Available Online.**
Ad Rates: GLR: $1.28 **Circ:** ‡27,000
BW: $1,170
4C: $1,470
PCI: $18

5859 The Washington Lawyer
The District of Columbia Bar
1250 H St. NW, 6th Fl. Phone: (202)737-4700
Washington, DC 20005 Fax: (202)626-3470

Forum for articles and news items for the Washington legal community. **Subtitle:** Official Journal of the District of Columbia Bar. **Founded:** 1986. **Freq:** Bimonthly. **Print Method:** Web. **Trim Size:** 8 1/4 x 10 7/8. **Cols./Page:** 3. **Col. Width:** 13.5 picas. **Col. Depth:** 64 agate lines. **Key Personnel:** Jane Ottenberg, Editor-in-Chief; Tim Lowry, Advertising Mgr.; Katherine Mazzaferri, Publisher; Wendy Jordan, Editor. **ISSN:** 0890-8761. **Subscription Rates:** $30 annually. **Remarks:** Accepts advertising. **Formerly:** District Lawyer.
Ad Rates: BW: $3,195 **Circ:** Paid 65,000
4C: $4,395 Non-paid 800

5860 The Washington Monthly
1611 Connecticut Ave. NW, Ste. 4A Phone: (202)462-0128
Fax: (202)332-8413
Washington, DC 20009
Publication E-mail: washmonth@aol.com
Publisher E-mail: washmonth@aol.com

Political and public policy opinion magazine. **Subtitle:** Indepth Coverage of Government, Politics, and Media. **Founded:** Feb. 1969. **Freq:** 10/year. **Print Method:** Offset. **Trim Size:** 7 1/2 x 9 3/4. **Cols./Page:** 2. **Col. Width:** 18 picas. **Col. Depth:** 50 picas. **Key Personnel:** Charles Peters, Editor-in-Chief; Kathleen A. Nuccetelli, Publisher; Robet Worth, Editor; Michelle Cottle, Editor; Sheryl Sherwin, Business Mgr. **ISSN:** 0043-0633. **Subscription Rates:** $29.95 individuals; $3.95 single issue. **Remarks:** Advertising not accepted for cigarettes and tobacco products. **Online:** ALTERNET.
Ad Rates: BW: $2,500 **Circ:** Paid 22,000
4C: $4,000 Non-paid 4,000

5861 The Washington New Observer
The Washington New Observer Corp.
811 Florida Ave. NW Phone: (202)232-3060
Washington, DC 20001-3017 Fax: (202)232-1711

Black community newspaper. **Founded:** 1957. **Freq:** Weekly (Thurs.). **Print Method:** Tabloid. Offset. **Cols./Page:** 5. **Col. Width:** 24 nonpareils. **Col. Depth:** 196 agate lines. **Key Personnel:** Robert T. Newton, Editor; Lauren Newton Johnson, Advertising Mgr. **Subscription Rates:** $24 individuals. **Remarks:** Accepts advertising.
Ad Rates: BW: $945 **Circ:** ‡20,000
4C: $1,345
PCI: $13.50

5862 The Washington Opera Magazine
The Washington Opera
Kennedy Center Phone: (202)416-7815
Washington, DC 20566 Fax: (202)416-7857

Magazine presenting background information on opera productions presented at Kennedy Center by the Washington Opera. **Founded:** 1974. **Freq:** 3/year. **Print Method:** Web offset. **Trim Size:** 8 1/2 x 11. **Cols./Page:** 3. **Key Personnel:** Mark Lyons, Managing Editor. **ISSN:** 5147-1000. **Subscription Rates:** Free to qualified subscribers; $8. **Remarks:** Accepts advertising.
Ad Rates: BW: $2,570 **Circ:** Controlled 58,000
4C: $3,250

5863 The Washington Post
1150 15th St. NW Phone: (202)334-6160
Washington, DC 20071-2400 Fax: (202)334-5693
Free: (800)627-1150
Publisher E-mail: ffwd@washpost.com

General newspaper. **Founded:** 1877. **Freq:** Mon.-Sun. (morn.). **Print Method:** Letterpress and offset. Uses mats. **Cols./Page:** 6. **Col. Width:** 26 nonpareils. **Col. Depth:** 308 agate lines. **Key Personnel:** Donald E. Graham, Publisher; Boisfeuillet Jones, Jr., President & General Manager; Leonard Downie, Exec. Editor; Meg Greenfield, Editorial Page Editor; Stephen S. Rosenfeld, Deputy Editorial Page Editor; Robert Kaiser, Managing Editor; Michael Getler, Deputy Managing Editor; Ben Bradlee, Vice-President. **Subscription Rates:** $9.80 individuals 4 weeks. **Remarks:** Accepts advertising. **Online:** Dow Jones News-Retrieval; LEXIS-NEXIS. **Alt. Formats:** CD-ROM. **Feature Editors:** Peter Behr, *Financial/ Business*, phone (202)334-7320; Ken Bredemeier, *Real Estate*, phone (202)334-7124; David Broder, *Political*, phone (202)334-7444; John Carmody, *TV & Radio*, phone (202)334-7568; Milton Coleman, *Metro*, phone (202)334-6224; Joe Elbert, *Photo*, phone (202)334-7383; Mary Hadar, *Features*, phone (202)334-6030; Linda Halsey, *Travel*, phone (202)334-7591; Nina Hyde, *Fashion*, phone (202)334-7548; Majorie Hyer, *Religion*, phone (202)334-7334; Robert Kaiser, *News*, phone (202)334-7549; Rita Kempley, *Movie*, phone (202)334-7565; Margaret Mason, *Family*, phone (202)334-6565; Joseph McLellan, *Music*, phone (202)334-7565; Henry Mitchell, *Garden/Home*, phone (202)334-7570; Donnie Radcliffe, *Society*, phone (202)334-7556; Phyllis Richman, *Food*, phone (202)334-7590; Ward Sinclair, *Rural Development*, phone (202)334-7440; George Solomon, *Sports*, phone (202)334-7367; Bob Thompson, *Sunday*, phone (202)334-6468; Abigail Trafford, *Medical*, phone (202)334-5011; Judy Weintraub, *Living*, phone (202)334-6291.
Ad Rates: BW: $45,530.76 **Circ:** Mon.-Fri. ★**759,122**
4C: $49,768.86 Sat. ★**709,578**
PCI: $344.93 Sun. ★**1,099,174**

5864 The Washington Post Magazine
The Washington Post
1150 15th St. NW Phone: (202)334-6160
Washington, DC 20071-2400 Fax: (202)334-5693
Free: (800)627-1150
Publisher E-mail: ffwd@washpost.com

Magazine covering Washington personalities and issues affecting the city, the Virginia and Maryland suburbs, and the nation. **Founded:** 1961. **Freq:** Weekly. **Print Method:** Offset. **Trim Size:** 8 x 10 1/2. **Cols./Page:** 3. **Col. Width:** 2 1/4 inches. **Col. Depth:** 10 inches. **Key Personnel:** Anne Karalekas, Publisher; Steve Coll, Editor. **ISSN:** 0190-8286. **Subscription Rates:** Included in subscription to the Washington Post.
Ad Rates: GLR: $60 **Circ:** Paid ★**80,077**
BW: $22,330
4C: $27,068
PCI: $620

5865 The Washington Quarterly
The MIT Press
1800 K St. NW, Ste. 400 Phone: (202)775-3251
Washington, DC 20006 Fax: (202)463-7218
Publisher E-mail: webmistress@mitpress.mit.edu

Journal of international affairs focusing on the full set of political, economic, and security issues related to the international engagement of the UnitedStates and their policy implications. **Founded:** 1978. **Freq:** Quarterly. **Print Method:** Offset. **Trim Size:** 6 3/4 x 10. **Cols./Page:** 2. **Col. Width:** 30 nonpareils. **Col. Depth:** 98 agate lines. **Key Personnel:** Eric R. Peterson, Editor-in-Chief; Michael J. Mazarr, Editor; Monica C. Neal, Assoc. Editor; Nicholas Koukopoulos, Asst. Editor. **ISSN:** 0163-660X. **Subscription Rates:** $36 individuals; $95 institutions; $24 students; $55.64 Canada; $118.77 institutions, Canada; $42.80 students, Canada; $52 other countries; $111 institutions, other countries; $40 students, other countries; $10 single issue. **Remarks:** Accepts advertising. **Online:** LEXIS-NEXIS. **URL:** http://www.mitpress.mit.edu/jrnls-catalog/washington.html.
Ad Rates: BW: $300 **Circ:** Paid ‡4,000
Non-paid ‡250

5866 Washington Review
Friends of the Washington Review of the Arts, Inc.
PO Box 50132 Phone: (202)638-0515
Washington, DC 20091-0132
Trade journal covering arts and literature. **Founded:** 1975. **Freq:** Bimonthly. **Print Method:** Web offset. **Trim Size:** 11 1/4 x 16. **Cols./Page:** 3. **Col. Width:** 3 1/2 inches. **Col. Depth:** 16 inches. **Key Personnel:** Clarissa Wittenber, Contact; Mary Swift, Manager/Advertising. **ISSN:** 1630-903X. **Subscription Rates:** $15 individuals; $2.50 single issue. **Remarks:** Accepts advertising. **URL:** http://www.erols.com/rotaylor/washrev. **Former name:** Washington Review of Arts & Literature.
Ad Rates: BW: $250 **Circ:** Controlled 800
PCI: $15

5867 Washington Technology
Post-Newsweek Business Information
8500 Leesburg Pkwy., Ste. 7500
Vienna, VA 22182
Publication E-mail: wtonline@wtonline.com

Magazine for technology industry professionals in the government marketplace. **Subtitle:** The Business Newspaper for Government Systems Integrators. **Founded:** 1986. **Freq:** Semimonthly. **Print Method:** Web offset. **Trim Size:** 10 3/8 x 13. **Cols./Page:** 4. **Col. Width:** 2 3/8 inches. **Col. Depth:** 12 1/4 inches. **Key Personnel:** Scott Lewis, Publisher; Trish Gilmartin Williams, Editor. **Subscription Rates:** Free to qualified subscribers. **URL:** http://www.wtonline.com.
Ad Rates: GLR: $120 **Circ:** Controlled 40,000
BW: $6,955
4C: $8,905

5868 The Washington Times
News World Communications
3600 New York Ave. NE Phone: (202)636-3000
Washington, DC 20002 Fax: (202)529-2471
Publication E-mail: wtnews@wt.infi.net

Newspaper with a Report orientation. **Founded:** May 17, 1982. **Freq:** Mon.-Sun. (morn.). **Print Method:** Offset. **Trim Size:** 14 x 22 3/4. **Cols./Page:** 6. **Col. Width:** 24 nonpareils. **Col. Depth:** 294 agate lines. **Key Personnel:** Wesley Pruden, Editor-in-Chief; Bill Giles, Managing Editor; Preston E. Innerst, Sr., Deputy Managing Editor; Francis Coombs, Deputy Managing Editor; Ted Agres, Deputy Asst. Managing Editor; Barbara Taylor, Asst. Managing Editor; Mary Lou Forbes, Communentary Editor; Tod Lindberg, Editorial Page Editor; Kenneth Hanner, National Desk Editor; David Jones, Foreign Desk Editor; Ken McIntyre, Metro Desk Editor; Bob Menaker, Business Desk Editor; Gary Hopkins, Sports Editor; Glen Stubbe, Dir. of Photography. **ISSN:** 0732-8494. **Subscription Rates:** $26 13 weeks; $52 26 weeks; $104 52 weeks; $175 52 via mail. **Remarks:** Accepts advertising. **Online:** DataTimes Corporation; Dialog (The Dialog Corporation); LEXIS-NEXIS. **URL:** http://www.washtimes.com. **Alt. Formats:** CD-ROM, Wayzata Technology Inc.
Ad Rates: GLR: $6.68 **Circ:** Mon.-Fri. ★**100,536**
BW: $7,875 Sat. ★**69,216**
4C: $8,875 Sun. ★**56,632**

5869 Washington View
Viewcomm, Inc.
6856 Eastern Ave. NW, No. 309
Washington, DC 20012-2165

Magazine for upscale blacks living in the Washington area. **Founded:** June 1989. **Freq:** Bimonthly. **Print Method:** Web offset. **Trim Size:** 8 1/4 x 10 3/4. **Cols./Page:** 3. **Key Personnel:** Effie Upshaw, Managing Editor; Malcolm Beech, Publisher. **ISSN:** 1042-4229. **Subscription Rates:** $12. $2.95 single issue. **Remarks:** Accepts advertising.
Ad Rates: BW: $2,875 **Circ:** 40,000
4C: $3,560

5870 Washingtonian Magazine
Washington Magazine, Inc.
1828 L St. NW, Ste. 200 Phone: (202)296-1246
Washington, DC 20036-5104
Publication E-mail: editorial@washingtonian.com

Metropolitan interest magazine. **Founded:** 1965. **Freq:** Monthly. **Print Method:** Offset. **Trim Size:** 8 1/4 x 10 7/8. **Cols./Page:** 3. **Col. Width:** 2 1/4 inches. **Col. Depth:** 10 inches. **Key Personnel:** John A. Limpert, Editor, phone (202)296-3600; Philip Merrill, Publisher; Eleanor Merrill, Assoc. Publisher; Edward P. Mansfield, Jr., Advertising Dir. **ISSN:** 0043-0897. **Subscription Rates:** $24 individuals; $34.95 out of area; $2.95 single issue. **Remarks:** Accepts advertising. **Available Online. URL:** http:// www.washingtonian.com.
Ad Rates: BW: $10,245 **Circ:** Paid ★**158,096**
4C: $15,715

5871 Waste Age
Environmental Industry Associations
4301 Connecticut Ave., Ste. 300 Phone: (202)244-4700
Washington, DC 20008 Fax: (202)966-4868
Free: (800)424-2869
Publication E-mail: wasteage@envasns.org

Magazine containing news on solid and hazardous wastes, recycling, and pollution control. **Subtitle:** The Authoritative Voice of Waste Systems and Technology. **Founded:** 1970. **Freq:** Monthly. **Print Method:** Offset. **Trim Size:** 8 1/8 x 10 7/8. **Cols./Page:** 2. **Col. Width:** 40 nonpareils. **Col. Depth:** 140

agate lines. **Key Personnel:** John T. Aquino, Editor-in-Chief; Jerry Schwartz, Publisher, phone (516)755-2222. **ISSN:** 0043-1001. **Subscription Rates:** $55 by mail. **Remarks:** Accepts advertising. **URL:** http://www.wasteage.com.
Ad Rates: BW: $3,135 **Circ:** Paid △**222**
4C: $4,610 Non-paid △**39,037**

5872 Water Resources Research
American Geophysical Union
2000 Florida Ave. NW Phone: (202)462-6900
Washington, DC 20009 Fax: (202)328-0566
Free: (800)966-2481
Publisher E-mail: service@agu.org

Interdisciplinary sciences journal containing original contributions on physical, chemical, biological, and sociological aspects of water science as well as water law. **Founded:** 1965. **Freq:** Monthly. **Print Method:** Offset. **Trim Size:** 8 1/4 x 11 1/4. **Cols./Page:** 2. **Col. Width:** 20 picas. **Col. Depth:** 57.5 picas. **Key Personnel:** Samuel C. Colbeck, Editor. **ISSN:** 0043-1397. **Subscription Rates:** $119 individuals Annual AGU members; $20 single issue AGU members; $720 institutions; $65 single issue institutions; $59 students AGU students. **Remarks:** Advertising not accepted. **URL:** http://www.agu.org.com. **Alt. Formats:** Microform.
Circ: (Not Reported)

5873 Weatherwise
Heldref Publications
Helen Dwight Reid Educational Foundation Phone: (202)296-6267
Fax: (202)296-5149
1319 18th St. NW
Washington, DC 20036-1802
Free: (800)365-9753
Publication E-mail: ww@heldref.org
Publisher E-mail: revu@heldref.org

Popular weather magazine for students, teachers, and professionals. **Founded:** 1948. **Freq:** Bimonthly. **Print Method:** Offset. **Trim Size:** 8 1/8" x 10 7/8". **Cols./Page:** 3. **Col. Width:** 2 1/4 inches. **Col. Depth:** 9 3/4 inches. **Key Personnel:** Doyle Rice, Editor, ww@heldref.org; Douglas Kirkpatrick, Director; Kimberly Cutlip, Assistant Editor, ww@heldref.org; Fred Huber, Circulation Mgr., subscribe@heldref.org; Grant Williams, Advertising Mgr., advertise@heldref.org; Jean Kline, Fulfillment Manager, subscribe@heldref.org. **ISSN:** 0043-1672. **Subscription Rates:** $29 individuals; $62 institutions; add $15 for postage outside the United States. **Remarks:** Accepts advertising. **Online:** EBSCO; Infonautics; Information Access; UMI. **URL:** http://www.heldref.org/; http://www.weatherwise.org. **Alt. Formats:** CD-ROM.
Ad Rates: BW: $1240 **Circ:** Controlled 15,000
4C: $2100 Paid 9,900

5874 The Weekly Standard
1150 17th St. NW, No. 505 Phone: (202)293-4900
Washington, DC 20036 Fax: (202)293-4901

Consumer magazine covering political issues. **Founded:** Sept. 18, 1995. **Freq:** Weekly. **Key Personnel:** William Kristol, Editor and Publisher; David Bass, Deputy Publisher; Jennifer Felten, Business Mgr. **ISSN:** 1083-3013. **Subscription Rates:** $78 individuals; $3.50 single issue. **Remarks:** Advertising accepted; rates available upon request. **Online:** LEXIS-NEXIS.
Circ: Combined ⊕**85,895**

5875 WETA Magazine
WETA Publishing
Box 2626 Phone: (703)845-8085
Washington, DC 20013-2626 Fax: (703)998-3412

Member magazine of public television channel 26 and radio station WETA/FM 91 in the metropolitan Washington, DC area. **Subtitle:** WETA Magazine. **Founded:** 1987. **Freq:** Monthly. **Print Method:** Web offset. **Trim Size:** 8 x 10 7/8. **Cols./Page:** 3. **Col. Width:** 2 1/8 inches. **Col. Depth:** 10 inches. **Key Personnel:** Pat Good, Editor, phone (703)845-8084, pgood@weta.com; Ingrid Bond, Advertising Mgr. **Subscription Rates:** $30 individuals. **Remarks:** Accepts advertising. **Formerly:** Dial Weta.
Ad Rates: BW: $3,245 **Circ:** Paid ‡125,000
PCI: $4,865 Non-paid ‡1,500

5876 Where Washington
1225 19th St. NW, Ste. 510 Phone: (202)463-4550
Washington, DC 20036 Fax: (202)463-4553
Publication E-mail: wheredc@mindspring.com
Publisher E-mail: wheredc@mindspring.com

Consumer magazine covering tourist information for Washington, DC. **Founded:** June 1965. **Key Personnel:** Rick Mellineaux, Publisher; Jean Cohen, Editor; Kecia Jenkins, Circulation Mgr.; Julie DeVol, Advertising Dir. **Subscription Rates:** $55 individuals; $5 single issue. **Remarks:** Accepts advertising.
Circ: Controlled 95,500

5877 Who Cares
Who Cares Inc.
1511 K St. N.W., Ste.412 Phone: (202)628-1691
Washington, DC 20005 Fax: (202)628-2063
Free: (800)628-1692
Publication E-mail: info@whocares.org
Publisher E-mail: info@whocares.org

Publication designed to help individuals create and manage non-profit organizations. **Subtitle:** The Tool Kit fo Social Change. **Founded:** Oct. 1993. **Freq:** Bimonthly. **Trim Size:** 8 3/8 x 11. **Key Personnel:** Leslie Crutchfield, Editor, crutch@whocares.org; Angela Wheeler, Publisher. **ISSN:** 1070-7255. **Subscription Rates:** $15 individuals; $30 individuals foreign; $3.95 single issue. **Remarks:** Accepts advertising. **URL:** http://www.whocares.org. **Formerly:** Who Cares: A Journal of Service & Action; Who Cares: The Magazie for People Who Do.
Ad Rates: BW: $3,000 **Circ:** 50,000
4C: $3,600
PCI: $3.95

5878 The Wilson Quarterly
Woodrow Wilson Center Press
One Woodrow Wilson Plaza Phone: (202)691-4010
1300 Pennsylvania Ave. NW Fax: (202)691-4001
Washington, DC 20523
Publisher E-mail: wwcem166@sivm.si.edu

News magazine on the world of ideas. Covers world affairs, history, art, theater, television, and popular culture. **Founded:** 1976. **Freq:** Quarterly. **Print Method:** Offset. **Trim Size:** 7 x 10. **Cols./Page:** 2. **Col. Width:** 2 3/4 inches. **Col. Depth:** 8 Inches. **Key Personnel:** Stephen Lagerfeld, Acting Editor; Kathy Read, Publisher. **ISSN:** 0363-3276. **Subscription Rates:** $6 single issue. **Remarks:** Accepts advertising. **URL:** http://wwics.si.edu/wq.
Ad Rates: BW: $3,400 **Circ:** Paid ‡60,000
4C: $5,000

5879 Women's Political Times
National Women's Political Caucus
1630 Connecticut Ave. NW, Ste. 201 Phone: (202)785-1100
Fax: (202)785-3605
Washington, DC 20009
Publisher E-mail: mailnwpc@aol.com

Magazine covering politics, feminism and women's issues for members, subscribers, and donors. **Subtitle:** Womens Political Times. **Freq:** Quarterly. **Subscription Rates:** $35 individuals. **Remarks:** Advertising not accepted.
Circ: (Not Reported)

5880 Working America
United Food and Commercial Workers International Union
1775 K St. NW Phone: (202)223-3111
Washington, DC 20006
Labor union magazine. **Founded:** 1979. **Freq:** Bimonthly. **Print Method:** Offset. **Trim Size:** 8 1/4 x 10 7/8. **Cols./Page:** 3. **Col. Width:** 26 nonpareils. **Col. Depth:** 134 agate lines. **Key Personnel:** Douglas H. Dority, Editor; Greg Denier, Managing Editor. **ISSN:** 0195-0363. **Subscription Rates:** Distributed to UFCW members; and selected labor relations; specialists. **Remarks:** Advertising not accepted.
Circ: Controlled ‡1,000,000

5881 World Affairs
Heldref Publications
Helen Dwight Reid Educational Foundation Phone: (202)296-6267
Fax: (202)296-5149
1319 18th St. NW
Washington, DC 20036-1802
Free: (800)365-9753
Publication E-mail: wa@heldref.org
Publisher E-mail: revu@heldref.org

International relations journal. **Founded:** 1834. **Freq:** Quarterly. **Print Method:** Offset. **Trim Size:** 8 1/2 x 11. **Cols./Page:** 3. **Col. Width:** 3 1/4 inches. **Col. Depth:** 7 inches. **Key Personnel:** Grant Williams, Advertising Production Mgr., advertise@heldref.org; Fred Huber, Circulation Mgr., subscribe@heldref.org; Jean Kline, Fulfillment Mgr., subscribe@heldref.org; Douglas Kirkpatrick, Director. **ISSN:** 0043-8200. **Subscription Rates:** $40 individuals; $67 institutions (foreign add $13). **Remarks:** Accepts advertising. **Online:** EBSCO. **URL:** http://www.heldref.org. **Alt. Formats:** CD-ROM.
Ad Rates: BW: $175 **Circ:** Paid ‡600

5882 World Around You
Gallaudet University Press
800 Florida Ave. NE Phone: (202)651-5488
Washington, DC 20002 Fax: (202)651-5489
Free: (800)621-2736

News magazine presenting information for hearing-impaired teens. Teacher's edition available. **Founded:** Sept. 1978. **Freq:** 5/year. **Trim Size:** 8 1/2 x 11. **Key Personnel:** Cathryn Carroll, Editor. **ISSN:** 0199-8293. **Subscription Rates:** $7; $12 other countries. **Remarks:** Advertising not accepted.
Circ: 5,300

5883 The World Bank Economic Review
The World Bank
1818 H St., NW Phone: (202)473-1056
Washington, DC 20433 Fax: (202)522-0304
Publisher E-mail: books@worldbank.org

Magazine detailing research that emphasizes empirical applications. **Founded:** Sept. 1986. **Freq:** Triennial. **Trim Size:** 7 x 10. **Cols./Page:** 1. **Col. Width:** 5 inches. **Col. Depth:** 8 1/4 inches. **Key Personnel:** Antony Kamal Sayess, Marketing Contact, phone (202)473-2209, fax (202)522-2631. **ISSN:** 0258-6770. **Subscription Rates:** $30 individuals; $50 institutions; Free to non-OCED countries; $55 two years individual; $95 two years institutions. **Remarks:** Advertising not accepted. **Available Online. URL:** http://www.worldbank.org//. **Alt. Formats:** Microform.
Circ: Paid 1,800
Non-paid 10,000

5884 World Bank Research Observer
The World Bank
1818 H St., NW Phone: (202)473-1056
Washington, DC 20433 Fax: (202)522-0304
Publisher E-mail: books@worldbank.org

Magazine which provides information on research in the field of development economics. **Founded:** Jan. 1986. **Freq:** Biennial February and August. **Trim Size:** 7 x 10. **Cols./Page:** 1. **Col. Width:** 5 inches. **Col. Depth:** 8 1/4 inches. **Key Personnel:** Antony Kamal Sayess, Marketing Contact, phone (202)473-2209, fax (202)522-2631. **ISSN:** 0257-3032. **Subscription Rates:** $25 individuals; $40 institutions; $45 two years individual; $75 two years institutions; free to readers in non-OECD (developing) countries. **Remarks:** Advertising not accepted. **Available Online. URL:** http://www.worldbank.org/. **Alt. Formats:** Microform.
Circ: Paid 1,800
Non-paid 10,000

5885 The World & I
The Washington Times Corp.
3600 New York Ave. NE Phone: (202)635-4059
Washington, DC 20002 Fax: (202)269-9353
Free: (800)822-2822
Publication E-mail: theworldandi@mcimail.com; 276-1932@mcimail.com; wandimag@ids2.idsonline.com

Encyclopedic journal including world news; developments in science, the arts, and philosophy; book reviews; photo essays. **Subtitle:** The Magazine for Serious Readers. **Founded:** Jan. 1986. **Freq:** Monthly. **Print Method:** Offset. **Trim Size:** 7 1/2 x 10 1/8. **Cols./Page:** 3. **Col. Width:** 2 1/4 inches. **Col. Depth:** 8 3/4 inches. **Key Personnel:** Michael Marshall, Executive Editor, phone (202)635-4006, fax (202)269-9353; Morton A. Kaplan, Editor and Publisher, phone (202)635-4001, fax (202)269-9353; Eric Olsen, Assoc. Exec. Editor, phone (202)635-4040, fax (202)269-9353; Lee Edwards, Senior Editor, phone (202)635-4091, fax (202)269-9353; Diane M. Falk, Director of Research/Contact. **ISSN:** 5669-8721. **Subscription Rates:** $45 individuals; $7.95 single issue. **URL:** http://www.worldandi.com. **Alt. Formats:** Braille; CD-ROM, Newsbank. **Feature Editors:** Dinshaw Dadachanii, *Science*; Linda Fomstal, *Living*; Stephen Kenkin, *Art*, phone (202)636-3365, fax (202)526-3497; Clark Munsell, *Book*; Susan Osmond, *Art*, phone (202)635-4059, fax (202)269-9353; Susan Reno, *Book*; Glenn C. Strait, *Science*.
Ad Rates: BW: $1,012 **Circ:** Paid 20,056
4C: $1,417 Non-paid 2,781

5886 World M&A Network
717 D. St. NW, No. 300 Phone: (202)628-7767
Washington, DC 20004-2807 Fax: (202)628-6618
Free: (800)809-0666
Publication E-mail: manda@dealnet.com

Lists companies for sale, companies seeking to purchase other companies, and sources of acquisition financing. **Founded:** 1988. **Freq:** Monthly. **Trim Size:** 6 1/2 x 10. **Cols./Page:** 2. **Col. Width:** 2 3/4 inches. **Col. Depth:** 8 1/2 inches. **Key Personnel:** John Bailey, Publisher, jbailey@worldm-anetwork.com. **ISSN:** 1046-4778. **Subscription Rates:** $395 U.S.; $425 out of country. **URL:** http://www.worldm-anetwork.com.
Ad Rates: BW: $350 **Circ:** Paid 1,000
Non-paid 14,000

5887 World Watch
Worldwatch Institute
1776 Massachusetts Ave. NW Phone: (202)452-1999
Washington, DC 20036 Fax: (202)296-7365
Free: (800)555-2028
Publication E-mail: wwpub@worldwatch.org
Publisher E-mail: worldwatch@worldwatch.org

Magazine reporting on ecological protection and economic

development worldwide. **Subtitle:** A Bimonthly Magazine of the Worldwatch Institute. **Founded:** 1988. **Freq:** Bimonthly. **Print Method:** Web offset. **Trim Size:** 8 1/2 x 11. **ISSN:** 0896-0615. **Subscription Rates:** $20. **Remarks:** Advertising not accepted. **URL:** http://www.worldwatch.org.
Circ: Paid ‡30,000
Non-paid ‡3,000

5888 Worldwatch Paper Series
Worldwatch Institute
1776 Massachusetts Ave. NW Phone: (202)452-1999
Washington, DC 20036 Fax: (202)296-7365
Free: (800)555-2028
Publication E-mail: worldwatch@worldwatch.org
Publisher E-mail: worldwatch@worldwatch.org

Series of monographs on different environmental topics. **Founded:** 1974. **Freq:** 7/year. **Print Method:** Offset. **Trim Size:** 5 1/2 x 8 1/2. **Cols./Page:** 1. **Col. Width:** 26 picas. **Col. Depth:** 34 picas. **Key Personnel:** Ed Ayres, Editor. **Subscription Rates:** Free to qualified subscribers; $25. $4 single issue. **Remarks:** Advertising not accepted. **URL:** http://www.world.org; http://www.worldwatch.org.
Circ: Paid ‡14,000
Non-paid ‡1,000

5889 Young Children
National Association for the Education of Young Children
1509 16th St. NW Phone: (202)232-8777
Washington, DC 20036-1426 Fax: (202)328-1846
Free: (800)424-2460
Publication E-mail: editorial@naeyc.org
Publisher E-mail: naeyc@naeyc.org

Professional journal on the education of young children (up to age 8). **Founded:** 1944. **Freq:** Bimonthly. **Print Method:** Heatset web. **Trim Size:** 8 3/8 x 10 7/8. **Cols./Page:** 3 and 2. **Col. Width:** 28 and 42 nonpareils. **Col. Depth:** 134 agate lines. **Key Personnel:** Polly Greenberg, Editor. **ISSN:** 0044-0728. **Subscription Rates:** $30 individuals; $5 single issue. **Remarks:** Accepts advertising.
Ad Rates: BW: $1,325 **Circ:** ‡104,790
4C: $2,300

5890 Youth Today
American Youth Work Center
1200 17th St. NW, 4th Fl. Phone: (202)785-0764
Washington, DC 20036 Fax: (202)728-0657
Publication E-mail: hn2759@handsnet.org
Publisher E-mail: HN2759@handsnet.org

National newspaper focused on out-of-school programs and services in operation in the U.S. Reports on news, policy formulation, decision-making, and emerging technology affecting youth-serving agencies. **Subtitle:** The Newspaper on Youth Work. **Founded:** Sept. 1992. **Freq:** Bimonthly. **Cols./Page:** 4. **Col. Width:** 2.25 inches. **Col. Depth:** 12 inches. **Key Personnel:** Bill Treanor, Publisher; William Howard, Editor. **Subscription Rates:** Free to qualified subscribers.
Ad Rates: BW: $1,225 **Circ:** Controlled 58,000
4C: $2,075

5891 ZooGoer
Friends of the National Zoo
National Zoological Park Phone: (202)673-4711
Washington, DC 20008 Fax: (202)673-4738

Magazine for members of Friends of the National Zoo. **Freq:** Bimonthly. **Print Method:** Web offset. **Trim Size:** 8 3/8 x 10 7/8. **Cols./Page:** 3. **Key Personnel:** Susan Lumpkin, Editor, phone (202)673-4993, susan@fonz.org; Robert Mall, robtmall@fonz.org. **ISSN:** 0163-416X. **Subscription Rates:** $25 individuals. **Remarks:** Accepts advertising. **URL:** http://www.fonz.org.
Ad Rates: 4C: $1,650 **Circ:** Paid 27,000
SAU: $3,000

5892 The ZPG Reporter
Zero Population Growth, Inc.
1400 16th St. NW, Ste. 320 Phone: (202)332-2200
Washington, DC 20036 Fax: (202)332-2302
Free: (800)767-1956
Publication E-mail: zpgcomm@igc.apc.org; zpg@igc.apc.org

Paper promoting a sustainable balance of population, resources, and the environment. **Founded:** 1968. **Freq:** Bimonthly. **Trim Size:** 11 x 14. **Cols./Page:** 3 and 4. **Key Personnel:** Tim Cline, Editor; Lee Polansky, Managing Editor; Joy Fishel, Research Specialist. **ISSN:** 0199-0071. **Remarks:** Advertising not accepted. **URL:** http://www.zpg.org.
Circ: Paid 55,000

5893 District Cablevision, Inc.
900 Michigan Ave. NE Phone: (202)635-5100
Washington, DC 20017 Fax: (202)462-4064

Founded: 1985. **Key Personnel:** Frances Turner, General Mgr.; Margaret King, Customer Service Mgr.; Fitzroy Francis, Plant Mgr.; Lau Wilson, Business Mgr.; Althea Purnell, Human Resource Mgr.; Frank Loney, Security; Jeanine Taylor, Marketing Mgr.; George Williams, Special Product Mgr. **Cities Served:** subscribing households 79,000; 58 channels.

5894 WAMU-FM - 88.5
American University/Brandywine Phone: (202)885-1200
Washington, DC 20016-8082
E-mail: feedback@wamu.org

Format: News; Information; Talk; Folk; Bluegrass. **Networks:** National Public Radio (NPR); BBC World Service; Public Radio International (PRI). **Founded:** 1961. **Operating Hours:** Continuous. **ADI:** Washington, DC. **Key Personnel:** Laura Murray, Business Mgr., lmurray@wamu.org; F. Kim Hodgson, General Mgr., khodgson@wamu.org; Steve Martin, Program Dir., smartin@wamu.org; Donna Clark, P.I. Director, dclark@wamu.org; Mike Byrnes, Chief Engineer, mbyrnes@wamu.org; Kathy Merritt, News Dir., kmerritt@wamu.org. **Local Programs:** *Derek McGinty Show*, Elaine Bole, (202)885-1226, Fax (202)885-1217; *Diane Rehm Show*, Daray Bacon, (202)885-1231, Fax (202)885-1216; *Metro Connection*, Kathy Merritt, (202)885-3825, Fax (202)885-1269. **Wattage:** 50,000. **Ad Rates:** Noncommercial.

5895 WASH-FM - 97.1
3400 Idaho Ave. NW Phone: (202)895-5000
Washington, DC 20016 Fax: (202)895-5103

Format: Adult Contemporary. **Founded:** 1948. **Operating Hours:** Continuous. **ADI:** Washington, DC. **Key Personnel:** Steve Streit, Program Dir.; Mark O'Brien, General Mgr.; Melissa Houston, Sales Mgr. **Wattage:** 23,500.

5896 Washington Cable
700 7th St. SW Phone: (202)646-1600
Washington, DC 20024-2484 Fax: (202)479-4396

Founded: 1979. **Key Personnel:** Joseph Klein, General Mgr.; Perry Klein, Vice President. **Cities Served:** Washington, DC; Chevy Chase, MD; Fairfax, VA: subscribing households 4,000; 30 channels; 1 community access channel.

5897 WDCA-TV - 20
5202 River Rd. Phone: (301)986-9322
Bethesda, MD 20816 Fax: (301)654-3517
E-mail: upn2owdca@paramount.com

Format: Commercial TV. **Networks:** United Paramount Network. **Owner:** Paramount Stations Group, 5555 Melrose Ave., Billy Wilder Bldg., Hollywood, CA 90038, (213)956-8100, Fax: (213)862-0121. **Founded:** Apr. 1966. **Operating Hours:** Continuous. **ADI:** Washington, DC. **Key Personnel:** John Long, Vice Pres./Gen. Mgr., phone (301)986-9322, fax (301)654-3517; Michael Schroeder, Program Mgr.; Pedro Perez, Chief Engineer; Leisa Weir, Public Affairs Dir.; Karen Stokes, Business Mgr.; Shaun McDonald, General Sales Mgr. **Local Programs:** *Making a Difference* 8:00 am Sunday, Lisa Weir, Dir. of Public Affairs. **Wattage:** 4 mega watts. **URL:** http://www.upn20wdca.com.

5898 WDCU-FM - 90.1
4200 Connecticut Ave. NW Phone: (202)274-5090
Washington, DC 20008 Fax: (202)274-6174

Format: Jazz; Public Radio. **Owner:** University of the District of Columbia, at above address. **Founded:** 1982. **Operating Hours:** Continuous. **ADI:** Washington, DC. **Key Personnel:** Edith Smith, General Mgr.; Debbie Akwei, Promotions Dir.; Candy Shannon, Program Dir.; Ernest White, Marketing Director. **Wattage:** 6800. **Ad Rates:** Noncommercial.

5899 WETH-FM - 89.1
PO Box 2626
Washington, DC 20013

Format: Public Radio; Classical; News. **Networks:** National Public Radio (NPR). **Owner:** Greater Washington Educational Telecommunications Assoc., 2775 S. Quincy St., Arlington, VA 22206, (703)998-2790, Fax: (703)824-7288. **Operating Hours:** Continuous. **Key Personnel:** Arthur Cohen, V. P./General Mgr.; Dan DeVanu, Program Dir. **Ad Rates:** Noncommercial. **URL:** http://www.weta.org.

5900 WFTY-TV - 50
2121 Wisconsin Ave., NW Phone: (202)965-0050
Washington, DC 20007

Format: Commercial TV. **Networks:** Independent. **Founded:** 1986. **Formerly:** WCQR-TV (1986). **Operating Hours:** 6:30 a.m.-6:00 a.m. **ADI:** Washington, DC. **Key Personnel:** Don Hazen, Production Mgr.; Curtis Garris, Chief Engineer; Michelle Dowd, Contact; Andy Ockershausen, General Mgr.; Andy Zmindinski, Contact; Terri Bornstein, General Sales Mgr.

5901 WGMS-FM - 103.5
3400 Idaho Ave., NW Phone: (202)895-5000
Washington, DC 20016-3069 Fax: (202)895-4168
E-mail: classical@wgms.com

Format: Classical. **Founded:** 1947. **Operating Hours:** Continuous. **ADI:** Washington, DC. **Key Personnel:** Kari Winston, General Mgr., kwinston@wgms.com; Jim Allison, Program Dir., jallison@wgms.com; Chris Broullire, Dir. of Sales, cbroullire@wgms.com; Steve Nicklin, Dir. of Marketing, snicklin@wgms.com. **Wattage:** 46,000 ERP.

5902 WHMM-TV - 32
2222 4th St. NW Phone: (202)806-3200
Washington, DC 20059 Fax: (202)806-3300

Format: Public TV. **Networks:** Public Broadcasting Service (PBS). **Founded:** 1980. **Operating Hours:** 8 a.m-12:30 a.m.; 60% network, 40% local. **ADI:** Washington, DC. **Key Personnel:** Edward Jones, Jr., General Mgr.; William Pratt, Contact.

5903 WHUR-FM - 96.3
529 Bryant St. NW Phone: (202)806-3500
Washington, DC 20059 Fax: (202)806-3522

Format: Urban Contemporary; Adult Contemporary. **Networks:** CBS. **Founded:** 1971. **Operating Hours:** Continuous. **ADI:** Washington, DC. **Key Personnel:** Millard J. Watkins III, General Mgr.; Hector Hannizal, Program Dir.; S. Jeannette Tyce, General Sales Mgr.; Barbara Jacobs, Traffic Mgr.; Alaina Moss, Promotions Dir.; John Thomas, Chief Engineer. **Wattage:** 24,000 ERP.

5904 WJLA-TV - 7
3007 Tilden St. NW Phone: (202)364-7777
Washington, DC 20008 Fax: (202)362-1124

Format: Commercial TV. **Networks:** ABC. **Owner:** Allbritton Communications Co., 808 17th St. NW, Ste. 300, Washington, DC 20006, (202)789-2130, Fax: (202)822-6749. **Founded:** Oct. 3, 1947. **Formerly:** WMAL-TV. **Operating Hours:** Continuous. **ADI:** Washington, DC. **Key Personnel:** Terrence J. Connelly, Pres./Gen. Mgr., phone (202)364-7800, fax (202)364-1943, tconnelly@wjla.com. **URL:** http://www.abc7dc.com.

5905 WJZW-FM - 105.9
4400 Jenifer St. NW Phone: (202)686-3100
Washington, DC 20015-2113

Format: Jazz. **Networks:** Independent. **Founded:** 1958. **Formerly:** WCXR-FM. **Operating Hours:** Continuous. **Key Personnel:** Jim Robinson, General Mgr.; Kenny King, Program Dir., phone (202)895-2440, fax (202)686-3070, kenneth.king@abc.com; Don Culp, Engineer, phone (202)895-2324, fax (202)686-3064, donald.s.culp@abc.com; Denise Smith, Promotions Dir., phone (202)895-2446, fax (202)686-3064, denise.s.smith@abc.com; Thomas Grooms, News Dir. **Local Programs:** *Spectrum*, Thomas Grooms. **Wattage:** 28,000 @650 FT HAAT.

5906 WKYS-FM - 93.9
4001 Nebraska Ave. NW Phone: (202)686-9300
Washington, DC 20016-2733 Fax: (202)686-2028

Format: Adult Contemporary; Contemporary Hit Radio (CHR). **Networks:** Independent. **Owner:** Albimar Communications, at above address. **Founded:** 1947. **Operating Hours:** Continuous; 100% local. **ADI:** Washington, DC. **Key Personnel:** Skip Finley, President; Barbara Prieto, Program Dir.; John Irving, News Dir.; Richard F. Boland, V. Pres./CFO; Peggy Miles, Creative Services Dir. **Wattage:** 25,000.

5907 WMAL-AM - 630
4400 Jenifer St. NW Phone: (202)686-3100
Washington, DC 20015-2113 Fax: (202)537-0009

Format: Full Service. **Networks:** ABC. **Owner:** Capital Cities/ABC, Inc., 125 West End Ave., New York, NY 10019, (212)887-7777. **Founded:** 1925. **Operating Hours:** Continuous. **ADI:** Washington, DC. **Key Personnel:** Zemira Jones, General Sales Mgr., phone (202)895-2342; Tom Bresnahan, Pres./Gen. Mgr., phone (202)895-2302; Jim Gallant, Operations Mgr., phone (202)895-2325; John Butler, News Dir., phone (202)686-3100; Amy Musher, Promotions Dir., phone (202)895-2363; Jeanne DuBell, Public Sevice Dir. **Wattage:** 5000.

5908 WMMJ-FM - 102.3
400 H St. NE Phone: (202)675-4800
Washington, DC 20002 Fax: (202)675-4842

Format: Oldies. **Networks:** ABC. **Founded:** 1987. **Operating Hours:** Continuous. **ADI:** Washington, DC. **Key Personnel:** Catherine L. Hughes, Contact; Alfred Liggins, President; Jack Malloy, CFO; Tony Washington, General Mgr.; Lawrence G. Jones, Program Dir.; Betty Fuller, Contact; Mike Jones, Promotions Dir.; Jim Allen, News Dir. **Local Programs:**

Encore Performance, Lawrence G. Jones; *Saturday Nite Flashback Dance Party*, Lawrence G. Jones. **Wattage:** 3000.

5909 WMZQ-FM - 98.7
5513 Connecticut Ave. NW Phone: (202)362-8330
Washington, DC 20015-2607 Fax: (202)966-2679

Format: Contemporary Country. **Networks:** Independent. **Founded:** 1968. **Formerly**: WMOD-FM (1975). **Operating Hours:** Continuous. **ADI:** Washington, DC. **Key Personnel:** Mac Daniels, Program Dir.; Charlie Ochs, General Mgr. **Wattage:** 50,000.

5910 WPFW-FM - 89.3
2390 Champlain St., NW, 2nd Fl. Phone: (202)588-0999
Washington, DC 20009 Fax: (202)588-0561
E-mail: bmwpfw@aol.com

Format: Jazz; Ethnic; News. **Networks:** Pacifica. **Owner:** Pacifica Foundation, 1929 Martin Luther King Jr. Way, Berkeley, CA 94704, (415)848-6767, (510)843-0130, Fax: (510)845-0289. **Founded:** 1977. **Operating Hours:** Continuous. **ADI:** Washington, DC. **Key Personnel:** Bessie M. Wash, General Mgr.; Lou Hankins, Program Dir.; Joanne Meredith Jackson, Development Dir.; Bob Daughtry, Operations Dir.; Rita Henderson, Office Mgr. **Wattage:** 50,000. **Ad Rates:** Noncommercial.

5911 WPGC-AM - 1580
6301 Ivy Ln., Ste. 800 Phone: (301)441-3500
Greenbelt, MD 20770-1416 Fax: (202)432-1583

Format: Gospel. **Networks:** CBS; AP. **Founded:** 1954. **Operating Hours:** Continuous; 50% network, 50% local. **Key Personnel:** Glenn Brooks, Station Mgr.; Benjamin Hill, General Mgr.; Matt Anderson, Program Dir. **Local Programs:** *Community Focus*, Gene Harley; *On-Track*, Gene Harley; *Robin Breeson Show*, Gene Harley. **Wattage:** 50,000 day; 292 night. **Ad Rates:** $15-55 per unit.

5912 WPGC-FM - 95.5
6301 Ivy Ln., Ste. 800 Phone: (301)441-3500
Greenbelt, MD 20770 Fax: (301)441-9555

Format: Contemporary Hit Radio (CHR); Urban Contemporary. **Founded:** 1959. **Formerly**: WCLY-FM (1987). **Operating Hours:** Continuous. **Key Personnel:** Jay Stevens, Program Dir.; Benjamin Hill, General Mgr.; Gene Harley, P.R. Dir.; Sam Rogers, Sales Mgr. **Local Programs:** *Community Focus*, Gene Harley; *Public File*, Gene Harley; *Yo Listen Up*, Gene Harley. **Wattage:** 50,000. **Ad Rates:** Advertising accepted; rates available upon request.

5913 WRC-TV - 4
4001 Nebraska Ave. NW Phone: (202)885-4000
Washington, DC 20016 Fax: (202)885-5022

Format: Commercial TV. **Networks:** NBC. **Operating Hours:** Continuous. **ADI:** Washington, DC. **Key Personnel:** Allan S. Horlick, Contact.

5914 WRQX-FM - 107.3
4400 Jenifer St. NW Phone: (202)686-3100
Washington, DC 20015-2113 Fax: (202)364-9668

Format: Adult Contemporary. **Networks:** ABC. **Founded:** 1948. **Formerly**: WMAL-FM (1979). **Operating Hours:** Continuous. **ADI:** Washington, DC. **Key Personnel:** Jim Robinson, General Sales Mgr.; Steve Kosbau, Program Dir., phone (202)895-2402; Chilli Amar, News Dir., phone (202)895-2436, fax (202)686-3070, chilli.amaralphabetical.com; Carol Parker, Music Dir., phone (202)895-2404; George Longwell, Contact; Don Culp, Chief Engineer. **Wattage:** 50,000. **Ad Rates:** Advertising accepted; rates available upon request.

5915 WTOP-AM - 1500
3400 Idaho Ave. NW Phone: (202)895-5000
Washington, DC 20016-3046 Fax: (202)895-5140

Format: News; Sports. **Networks:** CBS; AP. **Founded:** 1926. **Operating Hours:** Continuous. **ADI:** Washington, DC. **Key Personnel:** Tom McKinley, V.P./Gen. Mgr.; Hal Brown, News Dir.; Mark O'Brien, Sales Mgr.; Dave Garner, Chief Engineer. **Wattage:** 50,000.

5916 WTTG-TV - 5
5151 Wisconsin Ave. NW Phone: (202)244-5151
Washington, DC 20016 Fax: (202)244-1745

Format: Commercial TV. **Networks:** Fox. **Owner:** Fox Television Stations Inc., 1999 S. Bundy Dr., Los Angeles, CA 90035. **Operating Hours:** Continuous. **ADI:** Washington, DC. **Key Personnel:** Gene McHugh, General Mgr.; Gregg Kelley, General Sales Mgr.; David Levy, Program Dir.; Linda Spero, Promotions Dir. **Local Programs:** *Redskins Playbook*.

5917 WUSA-TV - 9
4100 Wisconsin Ave. NW Phone: (202)364-5999
Washington, DC 20016 Fax: (202)364-6163

Format: Commercial TV. **Networks:** CBS. **Owner:** Gannett Co., at above address. **Formerly**: WDVM-TV; WTOP-TV. **Operating Hours:** Continuous. **ADI:** Washington, DC. **Key Personnel:** Henry Yaggi, Contact; Dave Pearce, Contact; Sandra Butler Jones, Contact; Kevin O'Tool, Contact.

5918 WYCB-AM - 1340
1025 Vermont Ave., NW, Ste. 1030 Phone: (202)737-6400
Washington, DC 20005 Fax: (202)638-3027

Format: Gospel; Religious. **Networks:** Mutual Broadcasting System. **Founded:** 1978. **Operating Hours:** Continuous. **ADI:** Washington, DC. **Key Personnel:** Karen Jackson, General Mgr.; Don Miller, Program Dir. **Wattage:** 1000. **Ad Rates:** $25 for 30 seconds.

5919 WZHF-AM - 1390
5513 Connecticut Ave. NW Phone: (202)362-8330
Washington, DC 20015 Fax: (202)966-2679

Format: Country. **Simulcasts:** WMZQ-FM. **Networks:** Independent. **Founded:** 1947. **Formerly**: WEAM-AM. **Operating Hours:** Continuous. **ADI:** Washington, DC. **Key Personnel:** Steve Chaconas, Program Dir.; Charlie Ochs, General Mgr. **Wattage:** 5000. **Ad Rates:** Advertising accepted; rates available upon request.

FLORIDA

State Capital, TALLAHASSEE

Florida is bounded on the north by Alabama and Georgia, on the east by the Atlantic Ocean, on the west by the Gulf of Mexico. A 50-mile stretch of the Perdido River on the northwest edge completes the circuit. These boundaries enclose a land area of 54,153 square miles and 4,511 square miles of water–a total area of 53,997 square miles. The general coastline measures 1,197 miles around the state. The extreme distance from east to west across Florida measures 467 miles, while the extreme length from the 31st parallel to the southernmost keys is about 444 miles. In general, Florida vegetation is divided among seven distinct areas: flatwoods, scrub lands, grassy swamps, savannas, salt marshes, hammocks, and high pinelands. While Florida contains more varieties of native trees than any other region in America, only five are the true natives: oak, pine, cypress, palm, and mangrove trees. The pine, from the stunted sand pine to the stately open-crown longleaf variety, is the most common tree in Florida. Over 30,000 lakes and bays dot the state, headed by mammoth Lake Okeechobee, 730 square miles of shallow fresh water, roughly triangular in shape and 25 to 31 miles across. Okeechobee overflows today through great levees and flood gates into canals and into the sea. For centuries, the lake simply overflowed its banks into the beginning of the Indian-named "River of Grass," the Everglades. Altogether 858,500 acres of land and 370,000 acres of water and swamps compose the Everglades National Park. There are no high elevations in the state. The area in Walton County near De Funiak Springs in the northwest corner of the state is listed as the highest at 345 feet. Iron Mountain, 325 feet, is the highest point in peninsular Florida. Climate is semi-tropical, but temperatures do not reach extremes. The Weather Bureau at Miami list the temperature (annual average) at 75.9. Florida's economy is based on agriculture, industry, and tourism. The citrus growing and processing activities in Florida outrank all other U.S. citrus production. The larger educational institutions include the University of Florida in Gainesville, Florida State University in Tallahassee, and University of Miami in Coral Gables.

POPULATION: 13,488,000 (1992). Rank among the states, 4th.

AGRICULTURE: Number of farms: 39,000 (1992). Farm acreage: 11,000,000 (1992). Cash receipts from farm marketings: crops, $4,969,000,000 (1991); livestock and products, $1,172,000,000 (1991).

FISHERIES: Total catch: 162,000,000 lbs. (1991). Principal fish: shrimp, catfish and bullheads, mullet, red snapper, crabs, oysters.

FORESTS: Total forest land: 1,246,000 acres (1991). Principal woods: southern yellow pine, cypress, red and sap gum, oak, black and tupelo gum, yellow poplar, ash, eastern cedar, maple, hickory, walnut, elm.

MINERALS: Value of production: $1,396,000,000 (1991). Principal minerals: phosphate rock, stone, cement.

MANUFACTURES: Value added by manufacture: $29,055,000,000 (1991). Leading industry groups: food and related products, chemicals and allied products, paper and allied products.

LIST OF COUNTIES

Total number of counties 67

County, Location on Map, and County Seat	Pop.
Alachua (N), Gainesville	181,596
Baker (NE), Macclenny	18,456
Bay (NW), Panama City	126,994
Bradford (NC), Starke	22,515
Brevard (E), Titusville	398,978
Broward (S), Fort Lauderdale	1,255,488
Calhoun (NW), Blountstown	11,011
Charlotte (SW), Punta Gorda	110,975
Citrus (WC), Inverness	93,515
Clay (NE), Green Cove Springs	105,986
Collier (S), Naples	152,099
Columbia (N), Lake City	42,613
Dade (S), Miami	1,937,094
De Soto (SW), Arcadia	23,865
Dixie (N), Cross City	10,585
Duval (NE), Jacksonville	672,971
Escambia (NW), Pensacola	262,798
Flagler (NE), Bunnell	28,701
Franklin (NW), Apalachicola	8,967
Gadsden (NW), Quincy	41,105
Gilchrist (N), Trenton	9,667
Glades (S), Moore Haven	7,591
Gulf (NW), Wewahitchka	11,504
Hamilton (N), Jasper	10,930
Hardee (C), Wauchula	19,499
Hendry (SC), La Belle	25,773
Hernando (WC), Brooksville	101,115
Highlands (C), Sebring	68,432
Hillsborough (WC), Tampa	834,054
Holmes (NW), Bonifay	15,778
Indian River (E), Vero Beach	90,208
Jackson (NW), Marianna	41,375
Jefferson (N), Monticello	11,296
Lafayette (N), Mayo	5,578
Lake (C), Tavares	152,104
Lee (S), Fort Myers	335,113
Leon (N), Tallahassee	912,493
Levy (W), Bronson	25,923
Liberty (NW), Bristol	5,569
Madison (N), Madison	16,569
Manatee (WC), Bradenton	211,707
Marion (NC), Ocala	194,833
Martin (E), Stuart	100,900
Monroe (S), Key West	78,024
Nassau (NE), Fernandina Beach	43,941
Okaloosa (NW), Crestview	143,776
Okeechobee (EC), Okeechobee	29,627
Orange (EC), Orlando	677,491
Osceola (C), Kissimmee	107,728
Palm Beach (SE), West Palm Beach	863,518
Pasco (WC), Dade City	281,131
Pinellas (WC), Clearwater	851,659
Polk (C), Bartow	405,382
Putnam (NE), Palatka	65,070
St. Johns (NE), St. Augustine	83,824
St. Lucie (SE), Fort Pierce	150,171
Santa Rosa (NW), Milton	81,608
Sarasota (SW), Sarasota	277,776
Seminole (EC), Sanford	287,529
Sumter (C), Bushnell	31,577
Suwanee (N), Live Oak	26,780
Taylor (N), Perry	17,111
Union (N), Lake Butler	10,252
Volusia (E), De Land	370,712
Wakulla (NW), Crawfordville	14,202
Walton (NW), De Funiak Springs	27,760
Washington (NW), Chipley	16,919

STATISTICS

Newspapers

Period of Issue	
Daily	44
Evening Daily	9
Morning Daily	28
Daily with Sunday edition	30
Triweekly	1
Semiweekly	25

Weekly	173
Biweekly	9
Semimonthly	4
Monthly	17
Bimonthly	2
Quarterly	2
Free or partly free	57
Shopper	37
Total Newspapers	292

Periodicals

Period of Issue	
Weekly	12
Biweekly	7
Semimonthly	3
Monthly	97
Bimonthly	52
Quarterly	76
Total Periodicals	327

Total number of publications	619

Radio Stations

AM Stations	156
FM Stations	185
Total Radio Stations	341

TV Stations

Total TV Stations	67

Cable Stations

Total Cable Systems	32

Total number of broadcast listings	440

ALTAMONTE SPRINGS, pop. 21,493.

EC FL. Seminole Co. 10 mi. NE of Orlando.

5920 Internal Auditor
Institute of Internal Auditors, Inc.
249 Maitland Ave. Phone: (770)442-8633
Altamonte Springs, FL 32701-4201 Fax: (770)442-9742
Free: (877)867-4957
Publisher E-mail: iiapubs@pbd.com

Internal auditing. **Founded:** 1944. **Freq:** Bimonthly. **Print Method:** Offset. **Trim Size:** 8 x 10 7/8. **Cols./Page:** 3. **Col. Width:** 28 nonpareils. **Col. Depth:** 140 agate lines. **Key Personnel:** JoAn Schultz, Advertising Coordinator, jbell@theiia.org; Gretchen Gorfine, Production Administrator, ggorfine@theiia.org; Christy Chapman, Exec. Ed., cchapman@theiia.org. **ISSN:** 0020-5745. **Subscription Rates:** $60 individuals; $10 single issue; $84 other countries. **Remarks:** Accepts advertising. **Available Online.**
Ad Rates: BW: $2,718 **Circ:** 46,500
4C: $4,919

5921 WTLN-AM - 1520
400 W. Lake Brantley Rd. Phone: (407)682-9494
Altamonte Springs, FL 32714-2715 Fax: (407)682-7005

Format: Religious. **Networks:** Independent. **Owner:** Alton Rainbow Corp., at above address. **Founded:** 1964. **Operating Hours:** Continuous; 75% satellite; 25% local, or syndicated tape programs. **Key Personnel:** T.H. Moffit, Jr., General Mgr.; Janice Willis, Station Mgr.; Lou Mueller, Chief Engineer; Chris Shenk, News Dir. **Wattage:** 5000 / 350W night. **Ad Rates:** Advertising accepted; rates available upon request.

5922 WTLN-FM - 95.3
400 W. Lake Brantley Rd. Phone: (407)682-9494
Altamonte Springs, FL 32714 Fax: (407)682-7005
E-mail: joyful953@aol.com

Format: Religious. **Networks:** Independent. **Owner:** Alton Rainbow Corp., at above address. **Founded:** 1968. **Operating Hours:** Continuous;100% local. **Key Personnel:** T.H. Moffit, Jr., General Mgr.; Janice Willis, Station Mgr.; Lou Mueller, Chief Engineer; Chris Shenk, News Director. **Wattage:** 6000. **Ad Rates:** Advertising accepted; rates available upon request.

5923 WXXL-FM - 106.7
337 S. North Lake Blvd., Ste. 1024 Phone: (407)339-1067
Fax: (407)332-9613
Altamonte Springs, FL 32701

Format: Contemporary Hit Radio (CHR). **Networks:** Independent. **Founded:** 1990. **Formerly**: WCAT-FM (1988). **Operating Hours:** Continuous. **Key Personnel:** Randall Rahe, General Mgr.; Adam Cook, Program Dir. **Wattage:** 100,000.

APALACHICOLA†, pop. 2,565.

NW FL. Franklin Co. On Gulf Mexico, at mouth of Apalachiola River, 65 mi. SW of Tallahassee. Boat connections. Seafood cannery. Manufactures turpentine, cigar boxes, army tents, barrels, boats. Fish, shrimp, crab, oyster fisheries; hardwood timber. Poultry farms.

5924 WOYS-FM - 100.5
35 Island Dr., No. 16 Phone: (904)670-8450
Eastpoint, FL 32328-3222 Fax: (904)670-8450
E-mail: manager@oysterradio.com

Format: Adult Contemporary. **Networks:** ABC. **Founded:** 1988. **Operating Hours:** 24 hours. **Key Personnel:** Howard Wesson, General Mgr. **Wattage:** 10,000. **Ad Rates:** $3-12.75 for 30 seconds. **URL:** http://www.oysterradio.com.

APOLLO BEACH

5925 East Bay Breeze
Sunbelt Newspapers, Inc.
1507 Sun City Center Plaza Phone: (813)634-3007
Sun City Center, FL 33573-5300 Fax: (813)634-8420

Community newspaper. **Founded:** 1983. **Freq:** Weekly (Wed.). **Print Method:** Offset. **Trim Size:** 5 x 15. **Cols./Page:** 5. **Col. Width:** 20 nonpareils. **Col. Depth:** 238 agate lines. **Key Personnel:** Carla Rockwell, General Mgr., phone (813)6897764, fax (813)689-9685. **Subscription Rates:** Free. **Remarks:** Accepts advertising.
Ad Rates: GLR: $2.50 **Circ:** Free 16,000
BW: $708.75
4C: $948.75
PCI: $9.45

APOPKA, pop. 6,019.

EC FL. Orange Co. 10 mi. NW of Orlando. Nurseries. Citrus fruit, poultry and truck farms.

5926 The Apopka Chief
439 W. Main St. Phone: (407)886-2777
Apopka, FL 32712 Fax: (407)889-4121

Community newspaper. **Founded:** 1923. **Freq:** Weekly (Fri.). **Print Method:** Offset. **Cols./Page:** 6. **Col. Width:** 26 nonpareils. **Col. Depth:** 301 agate lines. **Key Personnel:** John R. Peery, Editor; John E. Ricketson, Publisher; Jacqulyne Trefler, Advertising Mgr. **Subscription Rates:** $18 individuals; $23 out of area. **Remarks:** Accepts advertising. **Alt. Formats:** Mailing labels.
Ad Rates: GLR: $6.60 **Circ:** Paid 3,600
BW: $851.40
4C: $986.40
SAU: $6.60
PCI: $6.60

5927 Bow & Swing
34 E. Main St. Fax: (407)886-7151
Apopka, FL 32703
Publisher E-mail: rgb@gdi.net

Trade magazine covering square and round dancing in Florida. **Founded:** 1952. **Freq:** Monthly. **Print Method:** Offset. **Trim Size:** 5 x 8. **Cols./Page:** 2. **Subscription Rates:** $12 individuals. **Remarks:** Accepts advertising.
Ad Rates: BW: $75 **Circ:** Paid 1,250
Non-paid 200

5928 The Planter Newspaper
439 W. Main St. Phone: (407)886-2777
Apopka, FL 32712 Fax: (407)889-4121
Publication E-mail: apopkachief@earthlink.net

Local newspaper. **Founded:** 1965. **Freq:** Weekly (Thurs.). **Print Method:** Offset. **Cols./Page:** 6. **Col. Width:** 26 nonpareils. **Col. Depth:** 301 agate lines. **Key Personnel:** John R. Peery, Editor; John E. Ricketson, Publisher; Jacquelyne Trefcer, Advertising Mgr. **Subscription Rates:** $50 individuals. **Remarks:** Accepts advertising. **Alt. Formats:** Mailing labels.
Ad Rates: GLR: $8 **Circ:** Free 10,000
BW: $1,032
4C: $1,272
SAU: $8.80
PCI: $8

ARCADIA†, pop. 6,002.

SW FL. De Soto Co. 50 mi. E. of Sarasota. Manufactures electrical transformers. Phosphate mining. Citrus fruit, cattle.

5929 The Arcadian
PO Drawer 670 Phone: (813)494-2434
Arcadia, FL 33821 Fax: (813)494-3533

Newspaper. **Founded:** 1924. **Freq:** Weekly (Thurs.). **Print Method:** Offset. **Key Personnel:** Timothy Adamson, Editor; Donna S. Latimer, Publisher; Judie Huffman, Advertising Mgr. **Subscription Rates:** $11.50 individuals; $13.50 out of county. **Remarks:** Accepts advertising.
Ad Rates: SAU: $7.50 **Circ:** ‡9,500

5930 De Soto Sun Herald
Sun Coast Media Group
PO Drawer 670 Phone: (941)494-7600
Arcadia, FL 33821 Fax: (941)494-3533

Community newspaper. **Freq:** Weekly (Thurs.). **Cols./Page:** 6. **Col. Width:** 12 2/5 picas. **Col. Depth:** 21.5 picas. **Key Personnel:** Patti Magee, Editor; Derek Dunn-Rankin, Publisher. **Subscription Rates:** $15. **Remarks:** Accepts advertising.
Ad Rates: BW: $833.18 **Circ:** ‡9,800
4C: $1,173.18
SAU: $6.65

5931 WKGF-FM - 98.3
201 W. Asbury St. Phone: (813)494-2525
PO Box 794 Fax: (813)494-9444
Arcadia, FL 33821
Free: (800)367-9543

Format: Contemporary Christian. **Networks:** USA Radio. **Owner:** Dakos Broadcasting, at above address. **Founded:** 1977. **Formerly**: WOKD-AM (1990); WOKD-FM. **Operating Hours:** 6 a.m.-midnight. **Key Personnel:** Gilbert Sullivan, General Mgr. **Wattage:** 3000 ERP. **Ad Rates:** $10-18 for 30 seconds; $12-22 for 60 seconds.

AUBURNDALE, pop. 6,501.

C FL. Polk Co. 41 mi. NE of Tampa.

5932 Canada News
PO Box 1729 Phone: (941)967-6450
Auburndale, FL 33823 Fax: (941)967-1954
Free: (800)535-6788

Newspaper for resident and vacationing Canadians in the southern U.S. **Founded:** 1982. **Freq:** Weekly (Nov.-April); Monthly: June, July, Aug., and Sept. **Print Method:** Offset. **Trim Size:** 11 1/2 x 17. **Cols./Page:** 5. **Col. Width:** 12 picas. **Col. Depth:** 224 agate lines. **Key Personnel:** David Perks, Publisher; Andy Steinbergs, Advertising Dir. **USPS:** 696-250. **Subscription Rates:** $1.25 individuals weekly by mail. **Remarks:** Accepts advertising.
Ad Rates: GLR: $1.36 **Circ:** Paid ‡18,310
BW: $1,520 Free ‡2,096
4C: $2,070
PCI: $19

AVON PARK, pop. 8,026.

C FL. Highlands Co. 43 mi. SE of Lakeland. South Florida Junior College. Citrus packing plants; bottling works. Timber. Citrus, stock, truck farms.

5933 Prensa Hispana (Hispanic Press)
Hispanic Press
PO Box 29 Phone: (941)452-6162
Avon Park, FL 33826-0029 Fax: (941)452-1006

Spanish language newspaper. **Founded:** Jan. 1995. **Trim Size:** 11 x 17. **Key Personnel:** Roberto Cubero, Editor/Owner, rcubero@strato.net. **Subscription Rates:** $15. **Remarks:** Advertising accepted; rates available upon request.
Circ: Free 10,000

5934 WAVP-AM - 1390
PO Box 29 Phone: (941)452-6162
Avon Park, FL 33826-0029 Fax: (941)452-1006

Format: Hispanic. **Networks:** Cadena Radio Centro (CRC); CNN Radio. **Owner:** Histed Media Group, at above address. **Founded:** 1958. **Formerly**: WKHF-AM (1994). **Operating Hours:** Continuous; 90% local, 10% network. **ADI:** Tampa- St. Petersburg (Lakeland, Sarasota),FL. **Key Personnel:** Robert Cubero, President, rcubero@strato.net. **Wattage:** 1000. **Ad Rates:** $10-13 for 30 seconds; $15-20 for 60 seconds.

BAKER

WTJT-FM - See Crestview

BARTOW†, pop. 14,824.

C FL. Polk Co. 12 mi. SE of Lakeland. Fruit and vegetable shipping. Phosphate mines. Citrus fruit, cattle, and truck farms.

5935 Bartow Shopper
Stauffer Communications
650 6th St. SW
PO Box 1440
Winter Haven, FL 33880-3325

Shopping guide (tabloid). **Founded:** 1952. **Freq:** Weekly (Wed.). **Print Method:** Offset. **Trim Size:** 11 1/3 x 17 1/2. **Cols./Page:** 5. **Key Personnel:** Curtis Lamb, Publisher. **Subscription Rates:** Free. **Remarks:** Color advertising accepted; rates available upon request. **Formerly**: Polk Shopper (1990).
Ad Rates: GLR: $.48 **Circ:** Combined 6,671
BW: $536
PCI: $670

5936 The Citrus Industry
Associated Publications Corp.
495 E. Summerlin St. Phone: (813)533-4114
Bartow, FL 33830 Fax: (813)534-1758

Citrus fruit industry magazine. **Founded:** 1920. **Freq:** Monthly. **Print Method:** Offset. **Trim Size:** 8 1/2 x 11. **Cols./Page:** 3. **Col. Width:** 26 nonpareils. **Col. Depth:** 140 agate lines. **Key Personnel:** Ernie Neff, Editor, phone (941)533-4114, fax (941)534-1758; Mariann Holland, Publisher; Debbie Williams, Advertising Mgr., fax (941)533-6924. **Subscription Rates:** $18 individuals. **Remarks:** Accepts advertising.
Ad Rates: BW: $1,315 **Circ:** ‡10,000
4C: $1,915

5937 WBAR-AM - 1460
1355 Maple Ave. Phone: (941)533-9227
PO Box 820 Fax: (941)519-9514
Bartow, FL 33830

Format: Country; Bluegrass; Gospel. **Owner:** J.R. Livesay, at above address. **Founded:** 1953. **Operating Hours:** 6 a.m.-7 p.m. **Key Personnel:** Elmer White, Station Mgr. **Wattage:**

1000. **Ad Rates:** $4-4.75 for 30 seconds; $5.25-6.95 for 60 seconds.

5938 WWBF-AM - 1130
1130 Radio Rd. Phone: (941)533-0744
Bartow, FL 33830 Fax: (941)533-8546
E-mail: tomthorn@gate.net

Format: Oldies. **Networks:** Mutual Broadcasting System; Florida Radio; Motor Racing. **Owner:** Thornburg Communications, Inc., at above address. **Founded:** 1969. **Formerly:** WPUL-AM (1984). **Operating Hours:** Continuous. 10% network, 90% local. **ADI:** Tampa-St. Petersburg (Lakeland, Sarasota), FL. **Key Personnel:** Thomas N. Thornburg, General Mgr., tomthorn@gate.net; Susan E. Thornburg, Office Mgr.; Jeffrey A. Thornburg, Chief Engineer, jat@gate.net. **Local Programs:** *Bartow High School Sports*, Tom Thornburg; *Wake Up Easy Show*, Tom Thornburg; *WBF Shopper*, Jeff Thornburg. **Wattage:** 2500 day; 500 night. **Ad Rates:** $10-13 for 30 seconds; $15-21 for 60 seconds. **URL:** http://www.wwbf.net.

BELLE GLADE, pop. 17,000.

Palm Beach Co. (NW). On SE shore of Lake Okeechobee.

5939 The Sun
Independent Newspapers, Inc.
417 NW 16th St. Phone: (407)996-4404
Belle Glade, FL 33430 Fax: (561)996-2209

Community newspaper. **Founded:** 1923. **Freq:** Weekly (Thurs.). **Print Method:** Offset. **Cols./Page:** 6. **Col. Width:** 12 nonpareils. **Col. Depth:** 28 agate lines. **Key Personnel:** Brenda Bunting, Editor. **USPS:** 005-026. **Subscription Rates:** $15.90 individuals. **Remarks:** Accepts advertising. **Formerly:** Belle Glade Sun; Belle Glade Herald; Belle Glade-Pahokee Sun.
Ad Rates: BW: $1,011.36 **Circ:** Paid ‡2,200
4C: $1,086.36
SAU: $7.84
PCI: $9.33

5940 WBGF-FM - 93.5
715 State Rd. Phone: (407)996-2063
Box 1505 Fax: (407)996-1852
Belle Glade, FL 33430

Format: Adult Contemporary; Oldies. **Networks:** ABC; Jones Satellite. **Founded:** 1951. **Formerly:** WSWN-FM (1951). **Operating Hours:** Continuous. **Key Personnel:** Vern Thacker, General Mgr.; Jane Hobbs, Program Dir. **Wattage:** 5000. **Ad Rates:** $5-10 for 30 seconds; $7.50-15 for 60 seconds.

5941 WSWN-AM - 900
2001 State Rd. 715 Phone: (561)996-2063
PO Box 1505 Fax: (561)996-1852
Belle Glade, FL 33430

Format: Urban Contemporary. **Networks:** ABC; Florida Radio. **Founded:** 1947. **Operating Hours:** Continuous; 2% network, 98% local. **Key Personnel:** Phil Haire, General Mgr.; Dave Smith, Program Dir. **Wattage:** 1000. **Ad Rates:** $11.75-15 for 30 seconds; $14.75-22.50 for 60 seconds.

BELLEVIEW, pop. 1,913.

NC FL. Marion Co. 11 mi. S. of Ocala.

5942 Voice of South Marion
PO Box 700 Phone: (904)245-3161
Belleview, FL 34421
Publication E-mail: vosm@aol.com

Community newspaper. **Founded:** Oct. 21, 1969. **Freq:** Weekly (Thurs.). **Print Method:** Offset. **Trim Size:** 10 x 15. **Cols./Page:** 4. **Col. Width:** 28 nonpareils. **Col. Depth:** 196 agate lines. **Key Personnel:** Jim Waldron, Editor and Publisher. **Subscription Rates:** $10 individuals. **Remarks:** Accepts advertising.
Ad Rates: BW: $140 **Circ:** 2,700
PCI: $5

BIG PINE KEY

Monroe Co. (S). One of the Florida Keys, just below Marathon.

5943 WWUS-FM - 104.7
30336 Oversea Hwy. Phone: (305)872-9100
Big Pine Key, FL 33043 Fax: (305)872-8930

Format: Album-Oriented Rock (AOR); Adult Contemporary. **Networks:** CNN Radio. **Owner:** Crain Communications, Inc., 1400 Woodbridge Ave., Detroit, MI 48207, (313)446-6080. **Founded:** 1980. **Operating Hours:** Continuous. **Key Personnel:** Bob Soos, General Mgr.; Gene Michaels, Station Mgr.; Steve Miller, Program Dir.; Bill Becker, News Dir.; Nancy Rouan, Traffic Mgr. **Wattage:** 100,000.

BLOUNTSTOWN†.

Calhoun Co. (NW). 10 m S of Calhoun.

5944 The County Record
PO Box 366 Phone: (904)674-5041
Blountstown, FL 32424 Fax: (904)674-5008

Community newspaper. **Founded:** 1907. **Freq:** Weekly (Thurs.). **Print Method:** Web offset. **Cols./Page:** 6. **Col. Width:** 2 inches. **Col. Depth:** 21 1/2 inches. **Key Personnel:** Robert A. Turner, Editor. **USPS:** 110-810. **Subscription Rates:** $14.98; $17.76 out of county. **Remarks:** Accepts advertising. **Formerly:** Blounstown County Record (1992).
Ad Rates: BW: $3.75 **Circ:** 3,000
SAU: $3.75

5945 WPHK-FM - 102.3
269 Kelly Ave. Phone: (904)674-5101
Blountstown, FL 32424 Fax: (904)674-2965

Format: Country. **Networks:** Jones Satellite. **Owner:** Blountstown Communications, Inc., at above address. **Founded:** 1973. **Formerly:** WRTM-FM (1987). **Operating Hours:** Continuous. **ADI:** Panama City, FL. **Key Personnel:** Harry Hagan, News/Sales/General Mgr.; Cathy Hagan, Program Dir. **Wattage:** 3000. **Ad Rates:** $6-8 for 30 seconds; $8-10 for 60 seconds.

5946 WYBT-AM - 1000
269 Kelly Ave. Phone: (904)674-5101
Blountstown, FL 32424 Fax: (904)674-2965

Format: Country; Gospel. **Networks:** Independent. **Owner:** Blountstown Communications, Inc., at above address. **Founded:** 1962. **Formerly:** WKMK-AM (1987). **Operating Hours:** Sunrise-sunset. **ADI:** Panama City, FL. **Key Personnel:** Harry Hagan, Contact; Cathy Hagan, Program Dir.; Charlett Sumerlin, Music Dir. **Wattage:** 1000. **Ad Rates:** $4.75-6.30 for 30 seconds; $5.95-7.90 for 60 seconds.

BOCA RATON, pop. 49,505.

SE FL. Palm Beach Co. On Atlantic Ocean, 25 mi. S. of West Palm Beach. Florida Atlantic University; College of Boca Raton. Computer center. Truck, poultry, and dairy farms.

5947 Boca Raton Magazine
JES Publishing Corp.
6413 Congress Ave., Ste. 100 Phone: (561)997-8683
Boca Raton, FL 33487 Fax: (561)997-8909
Publication E-mail: bocamag@aol.com

Publication showcases life in Southern Florida; includes features on food, fashion, interior design, the arts, entertainment, and travel. **Subtitle:** Florida At Its Best. **Founded:** Oct. 1981. **Freq:** Bimonthly. **Print Method:** Offset. **Trim Size:** 8 3/8 x 10 7/8. **Cols./Page:** 3. **Col. Width:** 13.5 picas. **Col. Depth:** 58.5 picas. **Key Personnel:** Marie Speed, Editor; Margaret Mary Shuff, Publisher/Pres.; Lisa Ocker, Managing Editor; Libby Good, Dir. of Advertising; Susan Surnamer Rosser, Design Dir. **ISSN:** 0740-2856. **Subscription Rates:** $19.95 individuals; $4.95 single issue. **Remarks:** Accepts advertising. **Formerly:** Florida Style (Jan. 1986).
Ad Rates: BW: $2,570 **Circ:** Paid ‡16,331
4C: $3,330 Non-paid ‡3,993

5948 The Boca Raton News
33 SE 3rd St. Phone: (407)395-8300
Boca Raton, FL 33432 Fax: (407)338-4944

General newspaper. **Founded:** 1955. **Freq:** Mon.-Sun. (morn.). **Print Method:** Offset. **Cols./Page:** 6. **Col. Width:** 2 inches. **Key Personnel:** Michael Martin, Publisher. **Remarks:** Accepts advertising. **Formerly:** The News; Delray Beach News.
Ad Rates: SAU: $14.25 **Circ:** Mon.-Sat. 14,248
Sun. 17,411

5949 Boca Raton Thursday Times
SFNN, Inc.
601 Fairway Dr. Phone: (954)574-5300
Deerfield Beach, FL 33441 Fax: (954)429-1207
Free: (800)275-8820
Publication E-mail: dtom@netrunner.net
Publisher E-mail: bukley@gate.net

Community newspaper (tabloid). **Founded:** 1965. **Freq:** Weekly (Thurs.). **Print Method:** Offset. **Cols./Page:** 6. **Col. Width:** 1 5/8 inches. **Col. Depth:** 16 inches. **Key Personnel:** Scott Patterson, Publisher; Ron Bukley, Editor. **Subscription Rates:** $69. **Remarks:** Accepts advertising.
Ad Rates: PCI: $26.70 **Circ:** Combined 24,870

5950 Boca's Best
Gulfstream Newspapers, Inc.
PO Box 223580
Hollywood, FL 33022-3580

Shopper. **Freq:** Weekly. **Key Personnel:** Dick Lewkowicz, Publisher; David Goldstein, Editor.

5951 Corporate & Incentive Travel
Coastal Communications Corp.
2600 N. Military Trail Phone: (561)989-0600
Boca Raton, FL 33431-6309 Fax: (561)989-9509

Magazine for corporate executives with the responsibility for staging and planning meetings, incentive travel programs, conferences, and conventions. **Founded:** 1983. **Freq:** Monthly. **Print Method:** Offset. **Trim Size:** 8 1/8 x 10 7/8. **Cols./Page:** 3. **Col. Width:** 26 nonpareils. **Col. Depth:** 98 agate lines. **Key Personnel:** Harvey Grotsky, Editor and Publisher. **ISSN:** 0739-1587. **Subscription Rates:** $55. **Remarks:** Accepts advertising.
Ad Rates: BW: $7,925 **Circ:** Paid ★46,077
4C: $10,375

5952 Globe
Globe Communications
5401 NW Broken Sound Blvd. Phone: (561)997-7733
Boca Raton, FL 33487-3587 Fax: (561)241-5689
Free: (800)749-7733

Consumer magazine (tabloid). **Founded:** 1975. **Freq:** Weekly. **Trim Size:** 9 7/8 x 11 3/8. **Cols./Page:** 6. **Col. Width:** 1 7/16 inches. **Col. Depth:** 10 7/8 inches. **Key Personnel:** Mike Rosenbloom, Publisher; Jack Linder, Advertising Mgr. **USPS:** 347-840. **Subscription Rates:** $29.75 individuals. **Remarks:** Accepts advertising.
Ad Rates: GLR: $13 **Circ:** Paid ★835,175
BW: $11,856
4C: $13,215
PCI: $182

5953 HVAC/R Distribution Today
Air-Conditioning and Refrigeration Wholesalers Association
1650 S. Dixie Hwy., 5th Fl. Phone: (305)755-7000
Boca Raton, FL 33432-7462 Fax: (305)491-8100
Publisher E-mail: mail@arw.org

Trade magazine covering all aspects of the HVAC/R distribution channel. **Freq:** Bimonthly. **Trim Size:** 11 x 17. **Subscription Rates:** $45 individuals; $100 corporate and library; $15 single issue. **Remarks:** Accepts advertising.
Circ: Paid 500
Non-paid 250

5954 Insurance Meeting Management
Coastal Communications Corp.
2600 N. Military Trail Phone: (561)989-0600
Boca Raton, FL 33431-6309 Fax: (561)989-9509

Trade magazine covering the insurance industry for professionals responsible for meeting destination; site selection; convention and incentive travel programming; and incentive merchandise purchasing. **Founded:** Nov. 1994. **Freq:** Bimonthly. **Print Method:** Web offset. **Trim Size:** 8 1/8 x 10 7/8. **Cols./Page:** 3. **Col. Width:** 2 1/8 inches. **Col. Depth:** 10 inches. **Key Personnel:** Harvey Grotsky, Publisher. **ISSN:** 1078-7666. **Subscription Rates:** $40 individuals; $6 single issue; Free to qualified subscribers. **Remarks:** Accepts advertising. **Former name:** Insurance Meetings & Incentives.
Ad Rates: BW: $2,380 **Circ:** Controlled 5,309
4C: $3,680

5955 Journal of Environmental Pathology, Toxicology & Oncology
CRC Press, Inc.
2000 Corporate Blvd. NW Phone: (561)994-0555
Boca Raton, FL 33431 Fax: (561)998-9114
Publisher E-mail: orders@crcpress.com

Science journal. **Founded:** Sept. 1977. **Freq:** Bimonthly. **Print Method:** Offset. **Trim Size:** 6 3/4 x 9 3/4. **Cols./Page:** 1. **Col. Width:** 60 nonpareils. **Col. Depth:** 120 agate lines. **Subscription Rates:** $97 individuals; $135 institutions; $116 other countries; $140 institutions OTC.
Circ: Paid ‡1,730
Non-paid ‡320

5956 Medical Marketing & Media
CPS Communications, Inc.
7200 W. Camino Real, Ste. 215 Phone: (561)368-9301
Boca Raton, FL 33433 Fax: (561)368-7870
Publisher E-mail: webmaster@cpsnet.com

Magazine containing medical and pharmaceutical marketing news. **Founded:** 1966. **Freq:** 13/year. **Print Method:** Offset. **Trim Size:** 8 1/4 x 10 7/8. **Cols./Page:** 3. **Col. Width:** 26 nonpareils. **Col. Depth:** 140 agate lines. **Key Personnel:** David Gideon, Publisher; Steve Selinger, Advertising Mgr.

Subscription Rates: $75 individuals; $90 Canada; $120 other countries; $7 single issue. **Remarks:** Accepts advertising.
Ad Rates: BW: $2,225 **Circ:** Controlled ‡10,000
4C: $3,250

5957 National Examiner
Globe Communications
5401 NW Broken Sound Blvd. Phone: (561)997-7733
Boca Raton, FL 33487-3587 Fax: (561)241-5689
Free: (800)749-7733

Tabloid featuring articles on celebrities, human interest, and the supernatural. **Freq:** Weekly. **Print Method:** Offset. **Trim Size:** 11 1/2 x 10. **Cols./Page:** 6. **Col. Width:** 9 1/5 picas. **Col. Depth:** 158 agate lines. **Key Personnel:** William Burt, Editor; Tony Miles, Exec. Publisher; Jack Linder, Advertising Mgr. **Subscription Rates:** $22 U.S. and Canada; $41 other countries.
Circ: Paid ★456,223

5958 Powerline
Electrical Generating Systems Association (EGSA)
1650 S. Dixie Hwy. Phone: (954)755-2677
Boca Raton, FL 33432-7462
Trade magazine for the on-site power generating industry. **Key Personnel:** Gordon Johnson, Technical Editor; Jalane Kellough, Advertising Mgr. **Subscription Rates:** Free to qualified subscribers. **Remarks:** Accepts advertising. **URL:** http://www.arw.org.
Circ: (Not Reported)

5959 Produce Business
Phoenix Media Network Inc.
PO Box 811768 Phone: (561)447-0810
Boca Raton, FL 33481 Fax: (561)368-9125
Publication E-mail: producebiz@aol

International magazine covering buying end of the fruit, vegetable, and floral industry. **Founded:** 1985. **Freq:** Monthly. **Print Method:** Web offset. **Trim Size:** 8 3/8 x 10 7/8. **Cols./Page:** 3. **Col. Width:** 2 5/16 inches. **Col. Depth:** 10 1/8 inches. **Key Personnel:** Alexandra Salas-Rujas, Editor; James E. Prevor, Editor-in-Chief; Kenneth Whitacre, Publisher. **ISSN:** 0886-5663. **Subscription Rates:** $48. $4.95 single issue. **Remarks:** Accepts advertising.
Ad Rates: BW: $3,450 **Circ:** Paid ‡7,706
4C: $4,825 Non-paid ‡12,170

5960 SalesDoctors Magazine
5455 N. Federal Hwy., Ste. Q Phone: (561)997-9345
Boca Raton, FL 33487 Fax: (561)997-9375
Publisher E-mail: salesdoctors@worldnet.att.net

Online magazine about sales and marketing. **Subtitle:** Seeking Cures for the Common Close. **Founded:** 9, 1995. **Freq:** Weekly. **Key Personnel:** Art Siegel, Publisher; Donna Siegel, Managing Editor. **ISSN:** 1086-9476. **Subscription Rates:** Free. **Remarks:** Accepts advertising. **URL:** http://salesdoctors.com.
Circ: 40,000

5961 Today's Boca Woman News Magazine
Gold Coast Marketing
2520 Boca Raton Blvd. Phone: (407)750-7765
Boca Raton, FL 33431 Fax: (407)750-7049

Magazine (tabloid) promoting awareness of women's issues. **Subtitle:** South Florida's Good Parenting Publication. **Founded:** 1992. **Freq:** 10/year. **Print Method:** Web offset. **Trim Size:** 10 1/2 x 13. **Cols./Page:** 4. **Col. Width:** 2 1/4 inches. **Col. Depth:** 12.5 inches. **Key Personnel:** Peter Davidson, Editor and Publisher; Fanny Glance Davidson, Publisher. **Subscription Rates:** $25 individuals. **Remarks:** Accepts advertising. **URL:** http://www.todayswoman.com. **Formerly:** Florida Parent Magazine (1992).
Ad Rates: BW: $1,265 **Circ:** Paid ‡590
4C: $1,545 Non-paid ‡25,000
PCI: $25.30

5962 Your Health
Globe Communications
5401 NW Broken Sound Blvd. Phone: (561)997-7733
Boca Raton, FL 33487-3587 Fax: (561)241-5689
Free: (800)749-7733
Publication E-mail: yhealth@aol.com

Health news magazine. **Subtitle:** A Lifetime of Health and Fitness. **Founded:** 1963. **Freq:** 8x/per yr. **Print Method:** Offset. **Trim Size:** 8 1/2 x 11. **Cols./Page:** 3. **Key Personnel:** Susan Gregg, Editor, phone (561)989-1182; Len Seminara, Advertising Mgr., phone (561)989-1222. **ISSN:** 0889-4329. **Subscription Rates:** $12.95 individuals; $23.25 two years. **Remarks:** Advertising accepted; rates available upon request. **URL:** http://yourhealthmag.com. **Formerly:** Your Health & Medical Bulletin (Sept. 1983).
Circ: Paid 47,288

5963 Adelphia Cable Communication
23123A State Rd. 7
Boca Raton, FL 33428

Formerly: West Boca Cablevision Inc. **Key Personnel:** John Gash, General Mgr. **Cities Served:** Palm Beach County.

5964 WSBR-AM - 740
6699 Federal Hwy. Phone: (407)997-0074
Boca Raton, FL 33487-4011 Fax: (407)997-0476

Format: Sports; Information; News. **Networks:** ABC; Unistar. **Founded:** 1965. **Operating Hours:** 5:30 a.m.-midnight. **Key Personnel:** Susan Goldsmith, Contact; Bob Morency, General Mgr.; Alison Gardner, Program Dir. **Wattage:** 2500 day; 940 night.

5965 WWNN-AM - 980
6699 N. Federal Highway Phone: (407)997-0074
Boca Raton, FL 33487 Fax: (407)997-0076

Format: News. **Networks:** Winners News (WNN). **Founded:** 1987. **Formerly:** WBSS-AM (1987); WWHR-AM. **Operating Hours:** Continuous; 90% network, 10% local. **ADI:** Miami (Ft. Lauderdale), FL. **Key Personnel:** Joseph Nuckols, Contact. **Wattage:** 5000.

BONIFAY†, pop. 2,500.

Holmes Co. (SE). 96 m ENE of Pensacola. Timber, diversified farming.

5966 Holmes County Advertiser
Woodham Family Publications
112 E. Virginia Ave. Phone: (850)547-2270
Bonifay, FL 32425 Fax: (850)547-9200

Community newspaper. **Founded:** 1892. **Freq:** Weekly (Wed.). **Print Method:** Offset. **Cols./Page:** 6. **Col. Width:** 12 picas. **Col. Depth:** 21 inches. **Key Personnel:** Kathy Foster, Editor. **Subscription Rates:** $19.08 individuals. **Remarks:** Accepts advertising.
Ad Rates: BW: $441 **Circ:** Free ‡4,200
4C: $841
SAU: $5.50
PCI: $3.50

BONITA SPRINGS, pop. 5,400.

Lee Co. (S). 22 m S of Ft. Myers on Gulf Coast.

5967 Bonita Banner
Scripps Howard, Inc.
PO Box 40 Phone: (941)992-2110
Bonita Springs, FL 33959 Fax: (941)992-7819

Community newspaper. **Subtitle:** Bonita Banner. **Founded:** 1959. **Freq:** Semiweekly (Wed. and Sat.). **Print Method:** Offset. **Cols./Page:** 6. **Col. Width:** 2 1/4 inches. **Col. Depth:** 22 1/4 inches. **Key Personnel:** Todd Pratt, Editor; Cathy Cottrill, Managing Editor; Steve Akers, General Mgr. **Subscription Rates:** Free; $36 by mail. **Remarks:** Accepts advertising.
Ad Rates: BW: $1,415.10 **Circ:** Free 33,000
4C: $1,615
SAU: $10.60
PCI: $10.60

BOSTWICK

5968 Cinevue Worldwide Talent Directory
Steve Postal Productions
Carraway St. Phone: (904)325-9356
PO Box 428
Bostwick, FL 32007
Trade journal for motion picture, television, radio, and theater producers. **Founded:** Jan. 1988. **Freq:** Quarterly. **Print Method:** Offset. **Trim Size:** 8 1/2 x 11. **Cols./Page:** 2. **Key Personnel:** Gail Postal, Editor; Steve Postal, Advertising Mgr. **Subscription Rates:** Free to qualified subscribers; $20. $5 single issue. **Remarks:** Accepts advertising.
Ad Rates: BW: $250 **Circ:** Paid ‡2,000
4C: $495 Controlled ‡2,000

BOYNTON BEACH

Palm Beach Co. (SE). 10 m N of Delray Beach.

5969 Boynton Beach Times
SFNN, Inc.
601 Fairway Dr. Phone: (954)574-5300
Deerfield Beach, FL 33441 Fax: (954)429-1207
Free: (800)275-8820
Publisher E-mail: bukley@gate.net

Community newspaper (tabloid). **Founded:** 1979. **Freq:** Weekly (Wed.). **Print Method:** Offset. **Trim Size:** 11 3/8 x 17 1/2. **Cols./Page:** 6. **Col. Width:** 1 5/8 inches. **Col. Depth:** 16 inches. **Key Personnel:** Scott Patterson, Publisher. **Subscription Rates:** $17. **Remarks:** Accepts advertising.
Ad Rates: PCI: $18.90 **Circ:** Free 23,624

5970 Eastern Aftermarket Journal
Stan Hubsher, Inc.
8211 Horseshoe Bay Rd. Phone: (561)733-8799
Boynton Beach, FL 33437
Magazine for automotive jobbers and wholesalers who manage aftermarket business. **Founded:** 1957. **Freq:** Bimonthly. **Print Method:** Offset. **Trim Size:** 8 1/2 x 11. **Cols./Page:** 3 and 2. **Col. Width:** 14 and 21 picas. **Col. Depth:** 72 picas. **Key Personnel:** Stan Hubsher, Editor and Publisher; Ruth Williams, Editor. **ISSN:** 0192-3595. **Subscription Rates:** $33 for 3 year subscription. **Remarks:** Accepts advertising.
Ad Rates: BW: $1,970 **Circ:** Controlled 10,150
4C: $2,575

5971 WRMB-FM - 89.3
1511 W. Boynton Beach Blvd. Phone: (407)737-9762
Boynton Beach, FL 33436 Fax: (407)737-9899
E-mail: 76117,1026@compuserve.com

Format: Religious. **Networks:** Moody Broadcasting. **Owner:** Moody Bible Institute, 820 N. LaSalle Dr., Chicago, IL 60610, (312)329-4305. **Founded:** 1979. **Operating Hours:** Continuous; 36% network, 64% local. **Key Personnel:** Mike Bingham, Station Mgr.; Chuck Conlon, Chief Engineer; Ken Senes, Asst. Mgr. **Local Programs:** *Breakaway*, Boyce Tate; *Clock Watcher*, Ken Senes; *South Florida Edition*, Robin Wright. **Wattage:** 100,000. **Ad Rates:** Noncommercial.

5972 WXEL-TV - 42
3401 S. Congress Ave. Phone: (561)737-8000
Boynton Beach, FL 33426 Fax: (561)369-3067

Format: Public TV. **Networks:** Public Broadcasting Service (PBS). **Owner:** South Florida Public Telecommunications, Inc., at above address. **Founded:** 1982. **Formerly:** WHRS-TV (1984). **Operating Hours:** 18 hrs. Daily. **ADI:** West Palm Beach-Ft. Pierce-Vero Beach, FL. **Key Personnel:** Mary Souder, President/CEO; John LaBonia, Executive VP/COO; Paul Rose, VP of Operations; Phil DiComo, V.P. of External Affairs.

BRADENTON†, pop. 30,170.

WC FL. Manatee Co. On Manatee River, 41 mi. S. of Tampa. Fruit and vegetable shipping; grapefruit cannery; bottling works; crate mill. Winter resort. Pine timber. Diversified farming.

5973 Bradenton Herald
Knight-Ridder, Inc.
102 Manatee Ave. W Phone: (941)748-0411
PO Box 921 Fax: (941)745-7097
Bradenton, FL 34206
General newspaper. **Founded:** 1922. **Freq:** Mon.-Sun. (morn.). **Print Method:** Offset. **Trim Size:** 13 x 21 1/4. **Cols./Page:** 6. **Col. Width:** 2 1/32 inches. **Col. Depth:** 297 agate lines. **Key Personnel:** Wayne H. Poston, Editor; Craig D. Wells, Publisher; Robert G. Turner, Jr., General Mgr. **Subscription Rates:** $112.95 individuals; $234 out of area. **URL:** http://www.bhlp.com.
Circ: Mon.-Sat. 45,902
Sun. 58,680

5974 Bradenton Shopping Guide
Florida Sun Publications
116 6th Ave. E. Phone: (941)748-4344
Bradenton, FL 34208 Fax: (941)747-3699

Shopper (tabloid). **Founded:** 1953. **Freq:** Weekly (Wed.). **Print Method:** Offset. **Trim Size:** 10 5/8 x 15. **Cols./Page:** 7. **Col. Width:** 8.5 picas. **Col. Depth:** 15 inches. **Key Personnel:** Dianna Herron, General Mgr. **Subscription Rates:** Free. **Remarks:** Accepts advertising.
Ad Rates: BW: $1,180 **Circ:** Non-paid 54,962
4C: $1,580
CNU: $1,239
PCI: $11.50

5975 East European Quarterly
PO Box 10039 Phone: (941)753-4782
Bradenton, FL 34282-0039 Fax: (941)753-4782

Journal studying the history, politics, economics, and civilization of Eastern Europe. **Founded:** Mar. 1967. **Freq:** Quarterly. **Print Method:** Offset. **Trim Size:** 5 1/2 x 8 1/2. **Cols./Page:** 1. **Col. Width:** 66 nonpareils. **Col. Depth:** 119 agate lines. **Key Personnel:** Stephen Fischer-Galati, Editor. **ISSN:** 0012-8449. **Subscription Rates:** $15 individuals; $20 institutions (Foreign add $2.75 postage); $12 students; $5 single issue. **Remarks:** Accepts advertising.
Ad Rates: BW: $100 **Circ:** ‡1,000

5976 WJIS-FM - 88.1
6469 Parkland Dr. Phone: (813)753-0401
Sarasota, FL 34243 Fax: (813)753-2963

Format: Religious. **Owner:** WJIS FM Radio, at above address. **Founded:** 1986. **ADI:** Tampa- St. Petersburg (Lakeland, Sarasota),FL. **Key Personnel:** James Campbell, President; Jeff MacFarlane, Jr., General Mgr. **Wattage:** 100,000.

BRANDON, pop. 65,000.

WC FL. Hillsborough Co. 10 mi. E. of Tampa. Manufactures concrete blocks and bricks. Poultry farms. Citrus fruits.

5977 The Gazette
WordsPlus, Inc.
Box 2650 Phone: (813)689-7566
Brandon, FL 33509-2650 Fax: (813)654-6995

Consumer magazine for gay and lesbian Floridians. **Subtitle:** Florida's Gay and Lesbian News. **Founded:** 1988. **Freq:** Monthly. **Print Method:** Web offset. **Key Personnel:** Rand Hall, Editor; Sue Cummings, Manager. **Subscription Rates:** $24 individuals. **Remarks:** Accepts advertising.
Ad Rates: BW: $360 **Circ:** (Not Reported)
4C: $645

BRANFORD, pop. 820.

Suwannee Co. (S). 23 m S of Live Oak.

5978 The Branford News
Branford News, Inc.
PO Box 148 Phone: (904)935-1427
Branford, FL 32008 Fax: (904)935-3043

Community newspaper. **Founded:** Aug. 3, 1967. **Freq:** Weekly (Thurs.). **Print Method:** Offset. **Cols./Page:** 9. **Col. Width:** 2 inches. **Col. Depth:** 21 1/2 inches. **Key Personnel:** George Petrena, Editor; Shirley W. Hatch, Publisher; Peggy Terry, Advertising Mgr. **USPS:** 063-280. **Subscription Rates:** $15 Free; $18 by mail other; $.50 single issue. **Remarks:** Accepts advertising.
Ad Rates: BW: $470.85 **Circ:** Paid ‡2,000
PCI: $4.33

BRISTOL

5979 The Calhoun-Liberty Journal
Summers Road
PO Box 536 Phone: (850)643-3333
Bristol, FL 32321 Fax: (850)643-3334

Community newspaper. **Founded:** 1981. **Freq:** Weekly (Wed.). **Print Method:** Offset. **Cols./Page:** 5. **Col. Width:** 12 picas. **Col. Depth:** 15 1/2 inches. **Key Personnel:** Teresa Eubanks, Editor; Johnny Eubanks, Publisher. **USPS:** 012-367. **Subscription Rates:** $18; $.50 single issue. **Remarks:** Accepts advertising. **Formerly:** The Weekly Journal (1992); Liberty Journal.
Ad Rates: BW: $360 **Circ:** 4,650
PCI: $4

BRONSON

5980 Levy County Journal
PO Box 159 Phone: (352)486-2312
Bronson, FL 32621 Fax: (352)486-5042

Community newspaper. **Founded:** 1930. **Freq:** Weekly (Thurs.). **Print Method:** Offset. **Cols./Page:** 7. **Col. Width:** 2 inches. **Col. Depth:** 21 inches. **Key Personnel:** Elton Cobb, Editor and Publisher. **USPS:** 310-708. **Subscription Rates:** $10 individuals. **Remarks:** Accepts advertising.
Ad Rates: PCI: $1.50 **Circ:** Paid 1,100

BROOKSVILLE†, pop. 5,582.

WC FL. Hernando Co. 50 mi. N. of Tampa. Manufactures electronic components and furniture. Citrus fruit, poultry, and stock farms. Horse breeding.

5981 Hernando Today
15299 Cortez Blvd. Phone: (352)796-1949
Brooksville, FL 34613 Fax: (352)799-5246

Community newspaper. **Founded:** 1987. **Freq:** Mon.-Sat. **Print Method:** Offset. **Cols./Page:** 6. **Col. Width:** 12.3 picas. **Col. Depth:** 125 picas. **Key Personnel:** Duane Chichester, Publisher. **ISSN:** 0000-6285. **Subscription Rates:** $34.45 individuals. **Remarks:** Accepts advertising. **Formerly:** Green Sheet.
Ad Rates: GLR: $1.39 **Circ:** Free ‡12,000
BW: $2,142 Paid ‡15,000
4C: $2,507
SAU: $17.00
PCI: $11.75

5982 WWJB-AM - 1450
PO Box 1507 Phone: (904)796-7469
Brooksville, FL 34605 Fax: (904)796-5074

Format: Country; Talk. **Networks:** ABC. **Owner:** Hernando Broadcasting Co., at above address. **Founded:** 1958. **Operating Hours:** Continuous. **Key Personnel:** Katie Bare, Office Mgr.; Chris Howard, Program Dir.; Dennis Miller, Sales Mgr. **Wattage:** 1000.

BUNNELL†, pop. 1,816.

NE FL. Flagler Co. 65 mi. SE of Jacksonville. Pine, cypress timber. Agriculture. Citrus fruits, corn, vegetables.

5983 Flagler/Palm Coast News-Tribune
The News-Journal Corp.
901 6th St. Phone: (904)252-1511
Daytona Beach, FL 32117-8099 Fax: (904)258-8465

Newspaper with a Democratic orientation. **Founded:** 1913. **Freq:** Semiweekly (Wed. and Sat.). **Print Method:** Offset. **Trim Size:** 13 3/4 x 22. **Cols./Page:** 6. **Col. Width:** 23 nonpareils. **Col. Depth:** 294 agate lines. **Key Personnel:** Tippen Davidson, Publisher; Robert Hughes, Marketing Dir. **Subscription Rates:** $16.70 individuals; $30.16 out of state. **Remarks:** Accepts advertising. **URL:** http://www.news-journalonline.com.
Ad Rates: BW: $951.30 **Circ:** ‡7,828
4C: $1,211.30
SAU: $7.55

5984 Flagler Pennysaver
Volusia Pennysaver, Inc.
2A McCormick Dr. Phone: (904)437-5971
Bunnell, FL 32110
Shopper. **Freq:** Weekly (Wed.).
Circ: Free ‡7,480

BUSHNELL†, pop. 1,000.

C FL. Sumter Co. 63 mi. NE of Tampa. Agriculture. Cattle, tomatoes, cucumbers, watermelons.

5985 Sumter County Times
Landmark Community Newspapers, Inc.
204 E. McCollum Ave. Phone: (352)793-2161
Bushnell, FL 33513 Fax: (352)793-1486

Community newspaper. **Founded:** 1881. **Freq:** Weekly (Thurs.). **Print Method:** Offset. **Cols./Page:** 6. **Col. Width:** 2 inches. **Col. Depth:** 1 inches. **Key Personnel:** Bob Reichman, Editor; Gerry Mulligan, Publisher. **Subscription Rates:** $16.43 individuals; $29.15 out of state. **Remarks:** Accepts advertising.
Ad Rates: BW: $645 **Circ:** ‡4,800
4C: $1,026.57
SAU: $7.10
PCI: $5

CALLAHAN, pop. 850.

NE FL. Nassau Co. 20 mi. NW of Jacksonville. Pine, cypress timber. Manufactures veneer. Naval stores. Diversified farming. Poultry, livestock, potatoes, truck crops.

5986 Nassau County Record
PO Box 609 Phone: (904)879-2727
Callahan, FL 32011-0609 Fax: (904)879-5155

Community newspaper. **Founded:** 1930. **Freq:** Weekly (Thurs.). **Print Method:** Offset. **Cols./Page:** 6. **Col. Width:** 27 nonpareils. **Col. Depth:** 301 agate lines. **Key Personnel:** Jennifer Wise, Publisher. **USPS:** 371-640. **Subscription Rates:** $10 individuals; $17 out of Nassau, Duval, or; Charlton counties. **Remarks:** Accepts advertising.
Ad Rates: GLR: $.29 **Circ:** ‡5,000
BW: $580.50
SAU: $4.25
PCI: $4.50

CAPE CORAL, pop. 31,884.

S FL. Lee Co. 10 mi. SW of Fort Myers.

5987 The Cape Coral Daily Breeze
Breeze Publishing Co.
PO Box 151306 Phone: (813)574-1110
Cape Coral, FL 33915-1306 Fax: (813)574-3403

General newspaper. **Freq:** Daily (eve.). **Print Method:** Offset. **Cols./Page:** 8. **Col. Width:** 9 picas. **Col. Depth:** 21 1/2 inches. **Key Personnel:** Christopher Strine, Managing Editor. **Remarks:** Accepts advertising.
Ad Rates: PCI: $4.95 **Circ:** ‡5,500

5988 Lee County Shopper
Breeze Publishing Co.
PO Box 151306 Phone: (813)574-1110
Cape Coral, FL 33915-1306 Fax: (813)574-3403

Shopper. **Founded:** 1976. **Freq:** Weekly (Wed.). **Print Method:** Offset. **Cols./Page:** 6. **Col. Width:** 20 nonpareils. **Col. Depth:** 224 agate lines. **Key Personnel:** Joel Jenkins, General Mgr.; Jack Glarrow, Advertising Mgr. **Subscription Rates:** free. **Remarks:** Accepts advertising.
Ad Rates: GLR: $.992 **Circ:** Free 105,000
BW: $1,334.40
4C: $1,554.40
PCI: $13.90

The Pine Island Eagle - See Pine Island

5989 WFTX-TV - 36/4
621 SW Pine Island Rd. Phone: (813)574-3636
Cape Coral, FL 33991 Fax: (813)574-4803
Free: (800)846-6397

Format: Commercial TV. **Networks:** Fox. **Founded:** 1986. **Formerly:** Wabash Valley Broadcasting, Inc. **Operating Hours:** 6 a.m.-2 a.m. **ADI:** Fort Myers-Naples, FL. **Key Personnel:** Chris Andrews, General Mgr., phone (941)574-3636, fax (941)574-2025; Mark Pierce, Station Mgr.

CAROL CITY

5990 WEDR-FM - 99.1
Box 551748 Phone: (305)623-7711
Carol City, FL 33055 Fax: (305)624-2736

Format: Urban Contemporary. **Networks:** Independent. **Founded:** 1963. **Operating Hours:** Continuous. **ADI:** Miami (Ft. Lauderdale), FL. **Key Personnel:** Jerry Rushin, Contact. **Wattage:** 70,000.

CARROLLWOOD

5991 Carrollwood News
Sunbelt Newspapers, Inc.
5501 W. Waters Ave., Ste. 404
Tampa, FL 33634-1229

Community newspaper. **Founded:** 1980. **Freq:** Weekly (Wed.). **Print Method:** Offset. **Cols./Page:** 5. **Col. Width:** 20 nonpareils. **Col. Depth:** 238 agate lines. **Key Personnel:** Carla Rockwell, General Mgr. **Subscription Rates:** Free. **Remarks:** Accepts advertising.
Ad Rates: BW: $691.05 **Circ:** Free 31,951
4C: $916.05
PCI: $8.13

CASSELBERRY, pop. 15,247.

EC FL. Seminole Co. 10 mi. N. of Orlando.

5992 WONQ-AM - 1030
1033 Semoran Blvd., No. 253 Phone: (407)830-0800
Casselberry, FL 32707-5758 Fax: (407)260-6100
E-mail: wonq1030@gdi.net

Format: Hispanic. **Networks:** CNN Radio. **Founded:** 1985. **Operating Hours:** Continuous. **ADI:** Orlando-Daytona Beach-Melbourne, FL. **Key Personnel:** George M. Arroyo, Contact; Esperanza Arroyo, General Mgr.; George Mier, Program Dir.; Hector Bauza, Sales Mgr.; Agustin Galaria, Operations Dir.; Sandra Carrasquillo, Traffic Dir.; Nitza Conquet, Contact. **Local Programs:** *Asunto Publico*, Mr. Josivan Padilla; *Buenos Dias, Buen Dia*, Ms. Maritza Beltran. **Wattage:** 39,000. **Ad Rates:** $12-15 for 15 seconds; $19-22 for 30 seconds; $24-26 for 60 seconds.

5993 WRMQ-AM - 1140
1033 E. Semoran Blvd., Ste. 253 Phone: (407)830-0800
Fax: (407)260-6100
Casselberry, FL 32707
E-mail: wonq1030@aol.com

Format: Hispanic. **Networks:** Sun Radio. **Owner:** Florida Broadcasters, at above address. **Founded:** 1985. **Formerly:** WONQ-AM (1992). **Operating Hours:** Sunrise-sunset. **ADI:** Orlando-Daytona Beach-Melbourne, FL. **Key Personnel:** George Arroyo, Pres./General Mgr.; Tonya Arroyo, Vice

President; Tito Galarza, Program Dir.; Hector Bauza, Sales Mgr. **Local Programs:** *Quedate con Miguel*, Miguel A. Negron; *El Destape Mananero*, Willie Ruiz. **Wattage:** 5,000.

CHATTAHOOCHEE, pop. 5,332.

NW FL. Gadsden Co. On Apalachicola River, 40 mi. NW of Tallahassee. Grist mill. Agriculture. Tobacco, truck crops.

5994 Twin City News
The Chattahoochee Publishing Corp.
PO Box 505 Phone: (904)663-2255
Chattahoochee, FL 32324 Fax: (904)663-8102

Community newspaper. **Founded:** 1946. **Freq:** Weekly (Thurs.). **Print Method:** Offset. **Cols./Page:** 6. **Col. Width:** 23 nonpareils. **Col. Depth:** 300 agate lines. **Key Personnel:** Stanley J. Ramsey, Editor and Publisher, stanr@mailer.gadcomm.net. **USPS:** 645-240. **Subscription Rates:** $18.85 individuals. **Remarks:** Accepts advertising.
Ad Rates: SAU: $3.75 **Circ:** ‡1,700

5995 WTCL-AM - 1580
PO Box 157 Phone: (904)663-2323
Chattahoochee, FL 32324-0814

Format: Urban Contemporary. **Networks:** USA Radio. **Founded:** 1963. **Formerly:** WENO-AM (1989). **Operating Hours:** Daytime. **Key Personnel:** John Blessinger, General Mgr. **Wattage:** 10,000. **Ad Rates:** $4.68-6.17 for 30 seconds; $5.86-7.75 for 60 seconds.

CHIEFLAND

Levy Co. (NW). 5 m N of Bronson.

5996 Chiefland Citizen
PO Box 980 Phone: (904)493-4796
Chiefland, FL 32626 Fax: (904)493-9336

Community newspaper. **Founded:** 1950. **Freq:** Weekly (Thurs.). **Trim Size:** 16 x 22 3/4. **Cols./Page:** 7. **Col. Width:** 2 inches. **Col. Depth:** 21 1/2 inches. **Key Personnel:** Terry Witt, Editor; Walter Wilson, Publisher. **Subscription Rates:** $1605 individuals local; $2105 out of area. **Remarks:** Accepts advertising.
Ad Rates: GLR: $.37 **Circ:** 3,600
BW: $781.10
SAU: $3.66
PCI: $5.19

5997 WLQH-AM - 940
PO Box 99 Phone: (904)493-4011
Chiefland, FL 32626-0099 Fax: (904)493-9909

Format: News; Country; Contemporary Country; Bluegrass; Gospel. **Networks:** CNN Radio. **Owner:** White Construction, at above address. **Founded:** 1967. **Operating Hours:** 6 a.m.-midnight. **Key Personnel:** Robert Moody, Gen. Mgr./Program Dir. **Wattage:** 1000. **Ad Rates:** $5-10 for 30 seconds; $7.50-10 for 60 seconds.

5998 WLQH-FM - 97.3
PO Box 99 Phone: (904)493-4940
Chiefland, FL 32626 Fax: (904)493-9909

Format: Country; Gospel; Bluegrass. **Networks:** CNN Radio. **Owner:** White Construction, at above address. **Founded:** 1992. **Operating Hours:** 6 a.m.-midnight. **Key Personnel:** Robert Moody, Gen. Mgr./Program Dir. **Wattage:** 6000. **Ad Rates:** $5.50 for 30 seconds; $7.50 for 60 seconds.

5999 WTBH-FM - 91.5
Rte. 2, PO Box 497 Phone: (904)493-2650
Chiefland, FL 32626 Fax: (904)493-7352
Free: (800)344-9824

Format: Religious. **Owner:** Long Pond Baptist Church, at above address. **Founded:** 1988. **Operating Hours:** Continuous. **Key Personnel:** Ron Cason, President; Rhonda Cook, News Dir. **Wattage:** 3,000.

CHIPLEY†, pop. 3,330.

NW FL. Washington Co. 36 mi. S. of Dothan, AL. Manufactures lumber, spools. Agriculture. Cotton, peanuts, watermelons.

6000 Washington County News
PO Box 627 Phone: (904)638-0212
Chipley, FL 32428 Fax: (904)638-4601

Community newspaper. **Founded:** 1924. **Freq:** Semiweekly (Mon. and Thurs.). **Print Method:** Offset. **Cols./Page:** 6. **Col. Width:** 24 nonpareils. **Col. Depth:** 301 agate lines. **Key Personnel:** M. Pujol, Editor; Maurice Pujol, Jr., Publisher. **Subscription Rates:** $15 individuals.

6001 WBGC-AM - 1240
901 S. Blvd W. Phone: (904)638-0234
Chipley, FL 32428 Fax: (904)638-4333

Format: Country. **Networks:** UPI; Florida Radio. **Founded:** 1956. **Key Personnel:** Homer Rhoden, Owner/Gen. Mgr.; Charles P. Wooten, Chief Engineer; Kathy Chesser, Traffic/Office Mgr. **Wattage:** 1,000. **Ad Rates:** Advertising accepted; rates available upon request.

CLEARWATER†, pop. 85,450.

WC FL. Pinellas Co. On Gulf of Mexico, 25 mi. W. of Tampa. Tourist resort. Fishing. Citrus fruit, flowers.

6002 Interiorscape
Brantwood Publications, Inc.
2410 Northside Dr. Phone: (813)796-3877
Clearwater, FL 33761-2216 Fax: (813)791-4126

Interior landscape design magazine. **Founded:** 1981. **Freq:** Bimonthly. **Print Method:** Offset. **Cols./Page:** 3. **Col. Width:** 27 nonpareils. **Col. Depth:** 140 agate lines. **Key Personnel:** Jeffrey A. Morey, Publisher. **Subscription Rates:** $12 individuals; $3 single issue.

6003 Jewish Press of Pinellas County
Jewish Press Group of Tampa Bay (FL), Inc.
PO Box 6970 Phone: (727)535-4400
Clearwater, FL 34618-6970 Fax: (727)530-3039
Publication E-mail: jptb@aol.com
Publisher E-mail: jptb@aol.com

Jewish community newspaper. **Founded:** 1986. **Freq:** Biweekly. **Print Method:** Offset. **Cols./Page:** 5. **Col. Width:** 2 inches. **Col. Depth:** 15 3/4 inches. **Key Personnel:** Jim Dawkins, Publisher/Advertising Mgr.; Karen Dawkins, Managing Editor. **Subscription Rates:** $8 individuals. **Remarks:** Accepts advertising.
Ad Rates: GLR: $17 **Circ:** Controlled 5,350
BW: $1,000
4C: $1,250
SAU: $10
PCI: $10

6004 Jewish Press of Tampa
Jewish Press Group of Tampa Bay (FL), Inc.
PO Box 6970 Phone: (727)535-4400
Clearwater, FL 34618-6970 Fax: (727)530-3039
Publisher E-mail: jptb@aol.com

Jewish community newspaper. **Founded:** 1988. **Freq:** Biweekly. **Print Method:** Offset. **Cols./Page:** 5. **Col. Width:** 2 inches. **Col. Depth:** 15 3/4 inches. **Key Personnel:** Jim Dawkins, Publisher/Advertising Mgr.; Karen Dawkins, Managing Editor. **ISSN:** 3763-1792. **Subscription Rates:** $8 individuals; $15 out of state. **Remarks:** Accepts advertising.
Ad Rates: BW: $1,000 **Circ:** Controlled 5,118
4C: $1,250
PCI: $9

6005 Nursery Business Retailer
Brantwood Publications, Inc.
2410 Northside Dr. Phone: (813)796-3877
Clearwater, FL 33761-2216 Fax: (813)791-4126

Wholesale and retail nursery operations magazine. **Founded:** 1955. **Freq:** Bimonthly. **Print Method:** Offset. **Trim Size:** 8 1/2 x 11. **Cols./Page:** 3 and 2. **Col. Width:** 27 and 36 nonpareils. **Col. Depth:** 140 agate lines. **Key Personnel:** Jeffrey A. Morey, Editor; Richard W. Morey, Publisher. **Subscription Rates:** $15 individuals; $3 single issue. **Remarks:** Accepts advertising.
Ad Rates: BW: $820 **Circ:** Paid ‡1,806
4C: $985 Non-paid ‡5,932

6006 Southern Golf
Brantwood Publications, Inc.
2410 Northside Dr. Phone: (813)796-3877
Clearwater, FL 33761-2216 Fax: (813)791-4126

Golf course operations magazine. **Founded:** 1969. **Freq:** Bimonthly. **Print Method:** Offset, sheetfed. **Trim Size:** 8 1/2 x 11. **Cols./Page:** 3 and 2. **Col. Width:** 27 and 36 nonpareils. **Col. Depth:** 140 agate lines. **Key Personnel:** Richard W. Morey, Editor and Publisher. **Subscription Rates:** $9 individuals; $3 single issue. **Remarks:** Accepts advertising.
Ad Rates: BW: $780 **Circ:** (Not Reported)
4C: $935

6007 Tampa Bay Magazine
Tampa Bay Publications, Inc.
2531 Landmark Dr., Ste. 101 Phone: (813)791-4800
Clearwater, FL 34621 Fax: (813)796-0527

City lifestyle publication. **Founded:** June 1, 1986. **Freq:** Bimonthly. **Print Method:** Web. **Trim Size:** 8 1/8 x 10 7/8. **Cols./Page:** 3. **Col. Width:** 2 1/16 inches. **Col. Depth:** 9 1/2 inches. **Key Personnel:** Aaron Fodiman, Publisher; Mike Stoveken, Sales Mgr. **Subscription Rates:** $12 individuals; $3.95 single issue. **Remarks:** Accepts advertising.
Ad Rates: BW: $2,500 **Circ:** Paid ‡17,371
4C: $3,200 Controlled ‡13,200

6008 WBDN-AM - 760
1915 N. Date Mabry Hwy., Ste. 200 Phone: (813)871-1819
Fax: (813)871-1155
Clearwater, FL 34622-5552
E-mail: wbdn@aol.com

Founded: 1995. **Formerly:** WEND-AM (1994). **Operating Hours:** Continuous;. **ADI:** Tampa-St. Petersburg (Lakeland, Sarasota), FL. **Key Personnel:** Francisco Luciano, General Mgr.; Sybil Ortiz, Sales Mgr.; Flor Vazquez, Manager; Al Fuentes, Program Dir. **Wattage:** 10,000. **Ad Rates:** $55 for 60 seconds.

6009 WCLF-TV - 22
PO Box 6922 Phone: (813)535-5622
Clearwater, FL 34618

Networks: Christian Television. **Owner:** Christian Television Corp., Inc., at above address. **Founded:** 1979. **Operating Hours:** Continuous; 65% network, 35% local. **ADI:** Tampa-St. Petersburg (Lakeland, Sarasota), FL. **Key Personnel:** Robert R. D'Andrea, President; Jack Jarvis, Production Dir.; Robert T. Kennedy, Dir. of Special Proj./Cable Relations; Carl Berger, Chief Engineer; Cardin A. Hesselton, Sales/Program Mgr.; Arthelene Rippy, Music Dir. **Local Programs:** *Action 60's* 10 a.m., Herman Bailey; *The Good Life* 12:30 p.m., Lon Barclay; *Together Again* 4 p.m. Monday-Friday, Jim Gates.

6010 WPSO-AM - 1500
27873 US 19 N. Phone: (813)725-3500
Clearwater, FL 34621 Fax: (813)724-5997

Format: Talk; Public Radio; News. **Owner:** Soprios Agelatos, at above address. **Founded:** 1963. **Formerly:** WGUL-AM (1985). **Operating Hours:** Sunrise-sunset;. **ADI:** Tampa-St. Petersburg (Lakeland, Sarasota), FL. **Key Personnel:** Soprios Agelatos, President; Timothy Adkins, Contact. **Wattage:** 250. **Ad Rates:** $20 for 30 seconds; $25 for 60 seconds.

6011 WTAN-AM - 1340
200 Pierce Blvd. Phone: (813)447-9826
Clearwater, FL 34616 Fax: (813)447-7709

Format: Talk. **Networks:** USA Radio; Westwood One Radio. **Owner:** Drenick Communication, at above address. **Founded:** 1948. **Operating Hours:** Continuous. 100% local. **ADI:** Tampa-St. Petersburg (Lakeland, Sarasota), FL. **Key Personnel:** Robert Yagoda, Station Mgr., yagodab@aol.com; Ted Drettakis, Manager. **Local Programs:** *Le Cher at Large*, Charles LeCher, Mailing contact; *Nite Talk*, Robert Yagoda, Mailing contact, (813)447-9826. **Wattage:** 1,000. **Ad Rates:** $39 for 30 seconds; $59 for 60 seconds.

6012 WXTB-FM - 97.9
13577 Feather Sound Dr., Ste. 550 Phone: (813)572-9808
Fax: (813)572-0935
2 Corporate Dr., Ste. 550
Clearwater, FL 34622-5550

Format: Album-Oriented Rock (AOR). **Owner:** Jacor Comm., One E. 4th St., 6th Fl., Cincinnati, OH 45202, (513)562-8000. **Founded:** 1967. **Formerly:** WKRL-FM (1990). **Operating Hours:** Continuous. **ADI:** Tampa-St. Petersburg (Lakeland, Sarasota), FL. **Key Personnel:** Daniel V. DiLoreto, Contact; Brad Hardin, Operations Mgr. **Local Programs:** *Bubba the Love Sponge* 6 a.m. - 10 a.m., Mike Oliviero; *Scott Ledjer* 2 p.m. - 6 p.m., Mike Oliviero; *Ted Kamikazi* 10 a.m. - 2 p.m., Mike Oliviero. **Wattage:** 100,000. **Ad Rates:** Advertising accepted; rates available upon request.

CLERMONT, pop. 5,461.

C FL. Lake Co. 22 mi. W. of Orlando. Steel fabrication. Manufactures cabinets, pillows, boats, garden furniture. Citrus fruit, truck and poultry farms.

6013 South Lake Press
Republic Newspapers, Inc.
787 8th St. Phone: (352)394-2183
Clermont, FL 34711 Fax: (352)394-8001
Publication E-mail: slpress@aol.com

Newspaper. **Founded:** 1913. **Freq:** Weekly (Wed.). **Print Method:** Offset. Uses mats. **Trim Size:** 13 x 21 1/2. **Cols./Page:** 6. **Col. Width:** 2 inches. **Col. Depth:** 21 1/2 inches. **Key Personnel:** Patti Bryan, General Mgr.; Loretta Lynn,

Editor. **USPS:** 503-560. **Subscription Rates:** $15 individuals. **Remarks:** Accepts advertising. **Formerly:** Zephyrhills News.
Ad Rates: GLR: $1 **Circ:** Paid 2,800
BW: $896 Free 76
4C: $300
SAU: $6
CNU: $6
PCI: $6.95

6014 Zephyrhills Shopper
Republic Newspapers, Inc.
787 8th St. Phone: (352)394-2183
Clermont, FL 34711 Fax: (352)394-8001

Local Newspaper. **Founded:** 1911. **Freq:** Weekly. **Cols./Page:** 6. **Col. Width:** 2.2 inches. **Col. Depth:** 21.5 inches. **Key Personnel:** Chris Drews, Publisher. **USPS:** 699-080. **Subscription Rates:** $14. **Remarks:** Accepts advertising. **Formerly:** East Pasco Weekend Shopping Guide (1995).
Ad Rates: SAU: $8.40 **Circ:** Paid ‡5,500

CLEWISTON, pop. 6,000.

SC FL. Hendry Co. On Lake Okeechobee, 55 mi. W. of West Palm Beach. Raw sugar, mills. Agriculture. Sugar cane, beans, tomatoes, watermelons, cucumbers. Beef cattle.

6015 Clewiston News
Independent Newspapers, Inc.
PO Box 1236 Phone: (941)983-9148
Clewiston, FL 33440 Fax: (941)983-7537
Publication E-mail: clewnews@gate.net

Newspaper. **Founded:** 1928. **Freq:** Weekly (Wed.). **Print Method:** Offset. **Cols./Page:** 6. **Col. Width:** 12 nonpareils. **Col. Depth:** 301 agate lines. **Key Personnel:** Richard Hitt, Publisher, phone (941)465-4213, fax (941)465-4046, okeeman@aol.com; Rose Aroyo, Advertising Mgr.; Kerry R. Faunce, General Mgr. **USPS:** 117-920. **Subscription Rates:** $26 individuals. **Remarks:** Accepts advertising.
Ad Rates: BW: $415 **Circ:** ‡3,500
4C: $655
PCI: $10.26

6016 Cablevision Industries
306 S. Bond St. Phone: (813)983-9131
Clewiston, FL 33440-3812 Fax: (813)983-5556

Founded: 1989. **Key Personnel:** Douglas Kelly, Contact. **Cities Served:** subscribing households 3,780; 34 channels.

6017 WAFC-AM - 590
530 E. Alverdez Phone: (941)983-6106
Clewiston, FL 33440 Fax: (941)983-6109
Free: (800)330-1063
E-mail: radiofiesta@net.gate

Format: Hispanic. **Owner:** Glades Media Company, at above address, Clewiston, FL 33440. **Founded:** 1988. **Operating Hours:** Continuous; 90% local, 10% network. **ADI:** Fort Myers-Naples, FL. **Key Personnel:** Robbie Castellanos, General Mgr., robbie@gate.net; Francisco Arne, Operations Dir., poncho@gate.net. **Wattage:** 1000. **Ad Rates:** $11.75-16.95. per unit. **URL:** http://www.wafcfm.com.

6018 WAFC-FM - 106.3
116 Commercio St. Phone: (813)983-6106
PO Box 2109 Fax: (813)983-6109
Clewiston, FL 33440
E-mail: robbiec@gate.net

Format: Contemporary Country. **Networks:** NBC. **Owner:** Robert Castellanos, at above address, Clewiston, FL 33440. **Founded:** 1979. **Operating Hours:** Continuous. **ADI:** Fort Myers-Naples, FL. **Key Personnel:** Robbie Castellanos, Sales/Gen. Mgr.; Debbie Pattison, Operations Dir. **Local Programs:** *Dial 'n' Deal*, Robbie Castellanos; *Focus on the Glades*, Gail Castellanos. **Wattage:** 6000. **Ad Rates:** $13-18 for 60 seconds. Combined advertising rates available with WAFC-AM. **URL:** http://www.radiofiesta.com.

COCOA

6019 The Capsule
Brevard Community College
1519 Clearlake Rd. Phone: (407)632-1111
Cocoa, FL 32922 Fax: (407)633-4565
Publication E-mail: capsule.c@a1.brevard.cc.fl.us

Collegiate newspaper (tabloid). **Founded:** 1963. **Freq:** Semimonthly. **Print Method:** Offset. **Trim Size:** 11 x 17. **Cols./Page:** 5. **Col. Width:** 11.5 picas. **Col. Depth:** 15 inches. **Key Personnel:** Sam Stanley, Advisor; Glenn Danforth, Managing Editor. **Subscription Rates:** $5/col in ; National rates $8/col in. **Remarks:** Advertising accepted; rates available upon request color advertising not accepted.
Circ: ‡4,000

6020 WBCC-TV - 68
1519 Clearlake Rd. Phone: (407)632-1111
Cocoa, FL 32922 Fax: (407)634-3724
E-mail: wallacep@brevard.cc.fl.us

Format: Educational. **Networks:** Independent. **Owner:** Brevard Community College, at above address. **Founded:** 1988. **Formerly:** WRES-TV. **Operating Hours:** 18 hours Daily. **ADI:** Orlando-Daytona Beach-Melbourne, FL. **Key Personnel:** Thomas E. Gamble, President; Joe Williams, General Mgr.; Philip T. Wallace, Station Mgr., wallace.p@brevard.cc.fl.us; Bob Gilbert, Production Dir.; Art Carlson, Chief Engineer. **Wattage:** 60,000. **URL:** www.brevard.cc.fl.us/wbcc/.

6021 WMIE-FM - 91.5
1150 W. King St. Phone: (407)632-1000
Cocoa, FL 32922-8618

Format: Religious. **Owner:** National Christian Network, at above address. **Founded:** 1984. **Operating Hours:** Continuous; 100% local. **Key Personnel:** Tom Shaw, Operations Dir.; Ray Kassis, General Mgr.; Tom Shaw, General Sales Mgr. **Wattage:** 20,000. **Ad Rates:** Noncommercial.

6022 WWBC-AM - 1510
1150 W. King St. Phone: (407)632-1510
Cocoa, FL 32922-8618

Format: Religious. **Owner:** Astro Enterprises, at above address. **Founded:** 1965. **Operating Hours:** Continuous. **Key Personnel:** Tom Shaw, Contact; Ray Kassis, General Mgr. **Wattage:** 1000. **Ad Rates:** $3.25-6.50 for 30 seconds; $5.75-11.50 for 60 seconds. $3.25-$6.50 for 30 seconds; $5.75-$11.50 for 60 seconds. Combined advertising rates available with WMIE-FM.

6023 WWHL-AM - 1350
2405 Broadcast Ct. Phone: (407)636-4411
Cocoa, FL 32922 Fax: (407)636-4380

Format: News; Sports. **Networks:** CNN Radio. **Owner:** EZY Communications, Inc., at above address. **Founded:** 1959. **Formerly:** WEZY-AM (1987). **Operating Hours:** Continuous; 98% network, 2% local. **Key Personnel:** Tanya Klepper, Contact. **Wattage:** 1000. **Ad Rates:** $15-65 per unit.

COCONUT GROVE

Dade Co. (SE). South suburban section of Miami.

6024 WTMI-FM - 93.1
3225 Aviation Ave. Phone: (305)856-9393
Coconut Grove, FL 33133 Fax: (305)854-0783

Format: Classical; Jazz. **Networks:** Concert Music Network (CMN). **Founded:** 1971. **Formerly:** WKAT-FM (1971). **Operating Hours:** Continuous. **Key Personnel:** John Burkavage, General Mgr.; Lyn Farmer, Program Dir.; Woody Tanger, CEO; Todd Tanger, General Sales Mgr. **Wattage:** 100,000. **URL:** http://www.wtmi.com.

COOPER CITY

6025 Lacja's World
E.R. Publishing, Inc.
1911 N.W. 114 Ave. Phone: (954)431-0161
Cooper City, FL 33026 Fax: (954)431-4661
Publisher E-mail: erpublish@aol.com

In-flight magazine for Lacja Airlines (Spanish and English). **Founded:** 1985. **Freq:** Bimonthly. **Print Method:** Web and sheetfed offset. **Trim Size:** 8 1/2 x 11. **Cols./Page:** 3. **Key Personnel:** Ed Rippen, Editor. **Subscription Rates:** Free to qualified subscribers; $26. **Remarks:** Accepts advertising. **Formerly:** LAP's Dimension (1991).
Ad Rates: BW: $1,850 **Circ:** Controlled 20,000
4C: $2,000

CORAL GABLES, pop. 47,000.

S FL. Dade Co. On Atlantic Ocean at mouth of Biscayne Bay. University of Miami. Resort. Manufactures cosmetics, garments, furniture, fertilizer, radio equipment, paper boxes, fiberglass boats.

6026 Aboard Magazine
North-South Net, Inc.
100 Almeria Ave., Ste. 220 Phone: (305)441-9744
Coral Gables, FL 33134-6027 Fax: (305)441-9739
Publisher E-mail: aboard@worldnet.att.net

Bilingual (English and Spanish) in-flight magazine for eleven Central and South American airlines: Aviateca (of Guatemala), Saeta (of Ecuador), Nica Air, Lloyd Aero Boliviano (LAB), Lineas Aereas Paraguayas (LAP), Taca (of El Salvador), Lanchile, Dominicana, Aeroperu, Pluna (of Uruguay), Sansa (of Honduras). Aeropostal, Tam. **Founded:** 1976. **Freq:** Bimonthly. **Print Method:** Offset. **Trim Size:** 8 3/8 x 10 7/8. **Cols./Page:** 3. **Col. Width:** 27 nonpareils. **Col. Depth:** 140 agate lines. **Key Personnel:** Diana G. Bethel, Publisher. **Remarks:** Accepts advertising.
Ad Rates: BW: $900 **Circ:** Non-paid ‡6,625
4C: $1,125

6027 Artes Graficas
Carvajal International
901 Ponce de Leon Blvd., Ste. 901 Phone: (305)448-6875
Free: (800)622-6657
Coral Gables, FL 33134
Publication E-mail: zedcoast@.aol.com; rymresource@gospel.com.net

Technical trade magazine for the printing, newspaper, and graphic arts professionals throughout Latin America (spanish). **Subtitle:** The Monthly Graphic Arts Magazine for all of Latin America. **Founded:** Oct. 1967. **Freq:** Monthly. **Print Method:** Web offset. **Trim Size:** 8 1/8 x 10 7/8. **Cols./Page:** 3. **Col. Width:** 2 1/16 inches. **Key Personnel:** Marcia Cardenas, Editor; Juan Carlos Gayoso, Publisher, gayosa@carvajal-usa.com. **ISSN:** 1054-2434. **Subscription Rates:** $50; $50 Free to qualified subscribers. **Remarks:** Accepts advertising. **URL:** http://www.gospelcom.net/ligonier. **Formerly:** Industria Grafica & Artes Graficas.
Ad Rates: BW: $3,980 **Circ:** 28,000
4C: $4,855
PCI: $105

6028 Coral Gables News
Community Newspapers
PO Box 43-1970 Phone: (305)667-7481
Miami, FL 33143 Fax: (305)661-0954
Publication E-mail: communitynewspapers.com
Publisher E-mail: cnedor@gate.net

Community newspaper (tabloid). **Founded:** 1958. **Freq:** 3/week. **Print Method:** Offset. **Trim Size:** 10 1/4 x 17. **Cols./Page:** 6. **Col. Width:** 1 1/2 inches. **Col. Depth:** 16 inches. **Key Personnel:** Michael Miller, Editor; Grant Miller, Publisher. **Subscription Rates:** $12 individuals. **Remarks:** Accepts advertising.
Ad Rates: GLR: $.72 **Circ:** Free ‡12,000
BW: $1,350
4C: $2,400
PCI: $13.50

6029 Entertainment & Sports Law Review
University of Miami School of Law
PO Box 248087 Phone: (305)284-4456
Coral Gables, FL 33124 Fax: (305)284-2861

Journal covering entertainment and sports related topics within the law. **Founded:** 1984. **Freq:** Semiannual. **Key Personnel:** David T. Lupo, Editor-in-Chief. **Subscription Rates:** $35 single issue. **Remarks:** Advertising not accepted. **Formerly:** Entertainment & Sports Law Journal.
Circ: (Not Reported)

6030 International Journal for Housing Science and Its Applications
Ural and Associates, Inc.
Box 340525 Phone: (305)446-9462
Coral Gables, FL 33134 Fax: (305)461-0921

Scientific journal covering architecture, engineering, financing and planning. **Founded:** 1978. **Freq:** Quarterly. **Key Personnel:** Prof. Oktay Ural, Editor-in-Chief. **ISSN:** 0146-6518. **Subscription Rates:** $225 individuals. **Remarks:** Accepts advertising.
Ad Rates: BW: $250 **Circ:** Controlled 700

6031 James Joyce Literary Supplement
University of Miami
Box 248145 Phone: (305)284-3140
Coral Gables, FL 33124 Fax: (305)284-5635
Publication E-mail: jjls@umiami.ir.miami.edu

Scholarly journal covering the works of James Joyce and his contemporaries. **Founded:** May 1987. **Freq:** Semiannual. **Key Personnel:** Blake Hobby, Managing Editor; Zack Bowen, Editor. **ISSN:** 0899-3114. **Subscription Rates:** $10 individuals; $6 single issue. **Remarks:** Accepts advertising.
Ad Rates: BW: $500 **Circ:** Combined 475

6032 Journal of the Academy of Marketing Science
Sage Publications Inc.
University of Miami Phone: (305)284-6673
School of Business Administration Fax: (305)284-3762
PO Box 248012
Coral Gables, FL 33124
Publisher E-mail: info@sagepub.com

Professional journal on the science of marketing. **Founded:** 1973. **Freq:** Quarterly. **Print Method:** Offset. **Trim Size:** 8 1/2 x 11. **Cols./Page:** 2. **Key Personnel:** A. Parasuraman, Editor,

phone (305)284-3515, parsu@miami.edu; Sally Sultan, Coordinator, ssultan@exchange.sba.miami.edu. **ISSN:** 0092-0703. **Subscription Rates:** $60 individuals; $125 institutions. **Remarks:** Color advertising not accepted. **Additional Contact Info: Advertising:** JAI Press, Inc., 55 Old Post Rd., No. 2, PO Box 1678, Greenwich, CT 06836-1678, (203)661-7602.
Ad Rates: BW: $300 **Circ:** ‡1,500

6033 Journal of Religious Gerontology
The Haworth Press, Inc.
University of Miami Phone: (305)284-4733
PO Box 248264 Fax: (305)284-2772
Coral Gables, FL 33124-4672
Publisher E-mail: getinfo@haworthpressinc.com

Journal of scholastic and practical articles on religion and aging issues. **Founded:** 1990. **Freq:** Quarterly. **Trim Size:** 6 x 8 1/2. **Key Personnel:** Stephen Sapp, Ph.D., Editor, ssapp@miami.edu; Bill Cohen, Publisher. **ISSN:** 1050-2289. **Subscription Rates:** $40 individuals; $75 institutions; $140 libraries. **Remarks:** Accepts advertising. **Alt. Formats:** Microfiche. **Formerly:** Journal of Religion and Aging.
Ad Rates: BW: $300 **Circ:** 691

6034 The Miami Hurricane
University of Miami
PO Box 248132 Phone: (305)284-4401
Coral Gables, FL 33124 Fax: (305)284-4404

Collegiate newspaper. **Founded:** 1927. **Freq:** Semiweekly (during the academic year). **Print Method:** Offset. **Cols./Page:** 6. **Col. Width:** 24 nonpareils. **Col. Depth:** 315 agate lines. **Key Personnel:** Lynn Carnillo, Editor, ldc@hurricane.miami.edu; Greg Kanton, Business Mgr. **Subscription Rates:** Free; $25 by mail. **Remarks:** Accepts advertising. **Online:** Miami Hurricane. **URL:** http://www.hurricane.miami.edu.
Ad Rates: GLR: $.57 **Circ:** Free ‡10,000
BW: $1,080
4C: $350
PCI: $8

6035 Res Ipsa Loquitur
University of Miami School of Law
PO Box 248087 Phone: (305)284-4456
Coral Gables, FL 33124 Fax: (305)284-2861
Publication E-mail: resipsa@resipsa.org

Collegiate journal for the law school. **Subtitle:** The Bi-Weekly Journal of the University of Miami School of Law. **Founded:** 1940. **Freq:** Biweekly. **Print Method:** Offset. **Trim Size:** 11 x 16. **Cols./Page:** 4. **Col. Width:** 25 nonpareils. **Col. Depth:** 224 agate lines. **Key Personnel:** Richard Fower, Managing; Jonathan Neuman, Managing Editor. **Subscription Rates:** Free. **Remarks:** Accepts advertising. **URL:** http://www.resipsa.org/resipsa. **Formerly:** The Slip Sheet.
Ad Rates: BW: $400 **Circ:** Free 2,000
4C: $500
PCI: $15

6036 South Florida
Florida Media Affiliates, Inc.
800 Dougals Rd., Ste. 500 Phone: (305)445-4500
Coral Gables, FL 33134 Fax: (305)445-4600
Publication E-mail: southfla@shadow.net

Regional magazine covering entertainment, fashion, home and garden, politics, and business. **Founded:** Oct. 1, 1975. **Freq:** Monthly. **Print Method:** Offset. **Trim Size:** 8 1/8 x 10 7/8. **Cols./Page:** 3. **Col. Width:** 13 picas. **Col. Depth:** 57 picas. **Key Personnel:** Nancy Moore, Publisher; Leslie Sternlieb, Editor; Odalys Garcia, Circulation Dir.; Ralph Obert, Production Mgr.; Michael Perham, Operations Dir. **Subscription Rates:** $19.95 individuals; $3.95 single issue. **Remarks:** Accepts advertising. **URL:** http./www.interactive.line.com/sf. **Formerly:** South Florida Magazine.
Ad Rates: BW: $5,100 **Circ:** Paid ‡44,872
4C: $6,370
PCI: $165

6037 Tecnologia del Plastico
C.C. International Publishing, Inc.
901 Ponce de Leon Blvd., Ste. 901 Phone: (305)448-6875
Fax: (305)448-9942
Coral Gables, FL 33134
Free: (800)622-6657
Publisher E-mail: gayoso@carvajal-usa.com

Plastics industry magazine. Coverage includes makers, suppliers, and users of machinery, raw materials, molds, injection, extrusion, blow molding, thermoforming transformation, plastics products, and packaging. **Founded:** 1984. **Freq:** 10 times a year. **Print Method:** Web offset. **Trim Size:** 8 1/4 x 10 7/8. **Cols./Page:** 3. **Col. Width:** 13 picas. **Key Personnel:** Juan Carlos Gayoso, Publisher, gayoso@carvajal-usa.com. **Remarks:** Accepts advertising.
Ad Rates: BW: $4,245 **Circ:** Controlled △**15,102**
4C: $5,390
PCI: $135

6038 Vista Magazine
Vista Publications
999 Ponce de Leon Blvd., Ste. 600 Phone: (305)442-2462
Fax: (305)443-7650
Coral Gables, FL 33134
Magazine supplement in major daily English language newspapers. **Subtitle:** The Magazine for All Hispanics. **Founded:** Sept. 1985. **Freq:** Monthly. **Print Method:** Gravure. **Trim Size:** 9 1/8 x 11. **Key Personnel:** Gustavo Godoy, Publisher; Carmen Teresa Roiz, Regional Editor, carmentere@aol.com; Julia Lobaco, Editor, jlobaco@aol.com. **Remarks:** Accepts advertising.
Ad Rates: BW: $30,100 **Circ:** Non-paid ★**973,729**
4C: $36,300

6039 The Wine News
T.E. Smith Inc.
PO Box 14-2096 Phone: (305)444-7250
Coral Gables, FL 33114 Fax: (305)444-5706
Publication E-mail: wineline@aol.com

Consumer magazine covering wine, food, and travel. **Founded:** May 1985. **Freq:** Bimonthly. **Print Method:** Sheetfed offset. **Trim Size:** 10 x 13. **Cols./Page:** 3. **Key Personnel:** Kathy Sinners, Managing Editor; Tom Smith, Publisher; Elizabeth Smith, Advertising. **ISSN:** 1065-4895. **Subscription Rates:** $24 individuals; $5 single issue. **Remarks:** Accepts advertising.
Ad Rates: BW: $3,700 **Circ:** Combined 57,000
4C: $5,000

6040 WVUM-FM - 90.5
Box 248191 Phone: (305)284-3131
Coral Gables, FL 33124 Fax: (305)284-3132
E-mail: wvum@miami.edu

Format: Alternative/New Music/Progressive. **Networks:** Independent. **Owner:** University of Miami, at above address. **Founded:** 1967. **Operating Hours:** Continuous; 100% local. **ADI:** Miami (Ft. Lauderdale), FL. **Key Personnel:** LaFontaine Oliver, General Mgr., phone (305)284-3474, fax (305); James Eiselman, Program Dir., phone (305)284-3460; Eric Rasco, Music Dir., phone (302)284-6383; Jose Rodriquiez, News Dir., phone (305)284-3451; Dan Laing, Sports Dir., phone (305)284-3451; Rufus Wells, Underwriting Dir., phone (305)284-3482; Jesse Swinger, Production Dir., phone (305)284-3955; Suzette Espinosa, Public Service Dir., phone (305)284-3451; Vicky Garza, Public Relations Dir., phone (305)284-3955; Aramis Israel, Promotions Dir., phone (305)284-3482; Ken Naylor, Training Dir., phone (305)284-3460; Bryan Daste, Engineer, phone (305)284-3955; Arely Carballo, Traffic Dir., phone (305)284-3955; Roy Silverstein, Web Master, phone (305)284-3955. **Wattage:** 1,300. **Ad Rates:** Noncommercial.

CORAL SPRINGS, pop. 38,769.

S FL. Broward Co. 38 mi. N. of Miami.

6041 Bachelor Book Magazine
Bachelor International Enterprises, Inc.
8222 Wiles Rd., Ste. 111 Phone: (954)341-8801
Coral Springs, FL 33067 Fax: (954)341-8982
Publication E-mail: info@bachelorbook.com
Publisher E-mail: bachlor@msn.com

Magazine for women that profiles single, eligible men in the U.S. and Canada. Plus stories and topics geared towards enrichment and empowerment of the lives of single women. **Subtitle:** The Magazine for Today's Single Woman. **Founded:** June 1991. **Freq:** 3/year. **Print Method:** Offset. **Trim Size:** 8 1/2 x 11. **Cols./Page:** 3. **Col. Width:** 2 1/4 inches. **Col. Depth:** 10 inches. **Key Personnel:** Mindi F. Rudan, Publisher; Paul Gallota, Publisher; Nina L. Diamond, Managing Editor; Gary Lampner, Food Editor; Anise Hartman, Travel Editor; Arron Barberian, Wine Editor; Parker Lewis, Health Editor; Pam Atertonian, Music Editor; Lisa Hall, New Products Editor; Hank Rudan, Finance Editor; Rick Lesser, Beauty Editor; Hank Rudan, Tech and Computer Editor; Tracy Damus, Fitness Editor; Mindi Rudan, Gardening and Hobby Editor. **Subscription Rates:** $31.25 for 5 issues; $8 single issue. **Remarks:** Accepts advertising. **URL:** http://www.bachelorbook.com.
Ad Rates: BW: $2,380 **Circ:** Paid 90,000
4C: $3,395
PCI: $100

6042 Bachelorette Book Magazine
Bachelor International Enterprises, Inc.
8222 Wiles Rd., Ste. 111 Phone: (954)341-8801
Coral Springs, FL 33067 Fax: (954)341-8982
Publication E-mail: info@bachelorbook.com
Publisher E-mail: bachlor@msn.com

Lifestyle magazine for men that profiles 75-100 single eligible women in the U.S. and Canada. Plus stories and topics of special interest to today's single gentleman. **Subtitle:** The Magazine For Today's Single Gentleman. **Founded:** June 1994. **Freq:** Every 3-4 months. **Print Method:** Offset. **Trim Size:** 8 1/2 x 11. **Cols./Page:** 3. **Col. Width:** 2 1/4 inches. **Col. Depth:** 10 inches. **Key Personnel:** Mindi F. Rudan, Publisher; Paul Gallotta, Sr. Editor; Nina L. Diamond, Manager/Contributing Editor; Gary Lampner, Food Editor; Anise Hartman, Travel Editor; Arron Barberian, Wine Editor; Parker Lewis, Health Editor; Pam Athertonian, Music Editor; Lisa Hall, New Products Editor; Hank Rudan, Finance Editor; Rick Lesser, Beauty Editor; Hank Rudan, Tech and Computer Editor; Tracy Damus, Fitness Editor; Mindi Rudan, Gardening and Hobby Editor. **Subscription Rates:** $31.25 for 5 issues; $8 single issue. **URL:** http://www.bachelorbook.com.
Ad Rates: BW: $2,380 **Circ:** Paid 45,000
4C: $3,395
PCI: $100

6043 Coral Springs News
Gulfstream Newspapers, Inc.
PO Box 223580
Hollywood, FL 33022-3580

Community newspaper. **Founded:** 1949. **Freq:** Weekly (Wed.). **Print Method:** Offset. **Cols./Page:** 6. **Col. Width:** 21 nonpareils. **Col. Depth:** 230 agate lines. **Key Personnel:** Gary Curreri, Editor; James Bouldin, Publisher; Richard Lewkowicz, Advertising Mgr. **Remarks:** Accepts advertising.
Ad Rates: BW: $345 **Circ:** Free ‡22,500
PCI: $5.65

Margate/Coconut Creek Forum - See Margate

6044 Tamarac/North Lauderdale Forum
SFNN, Inc.
9660 W. Sample Rd., Ste. 203 Phone: (954)752-7474
Coral Springs, FL 33065 Fax: (954)752-7855
Publisher E-mail: bukley@gate.net

Community newspaper (tabloid). **Founded:** 1969. **Freq:** Weekly (Thurs.). **Print Method:** Offset. **Cols./Page:** 6. **Col. Width:** 1 5/8 inches. **Col. Depth:** 16 inches. **Key Personnel:** Suzanne Pemper, Publisher. **Subscription Rates:** Free. **Remarks:** Accepts advertising. **Formerly:** Coral Springs Forum/Margate Forum.
Ad Rates: GLR: $22.75 **Circ:** Non-paid 18,165
BW: $2,184
4C: $2,679

6045 Advanced Cable Communications
12409 NW 35th St. Phone: (305)753-0100
Coral Springs, FL 33065 Fax: (305)345-8164
Free: (800)275-6767

Founded: 1975. **Formerly:** Cable TV of Coral Springs. **Key Personnel:** Wally Snedeker, Contact, phone (954)752-7244, fax (954)345-8164; Rick Scheller, Contact; Michelle Fitzpatrick, Contact; Mike Milo, Production Dir. **Cities Served:** Coral Springs, FL: subscribing households 32,500; 80 channels; 1 community access channel.

CRAWFORDVILLE†, pop. 10,694.

NW FL. Wakulla Co. 23 mi. S. of Tallahassee.

6046 The Leon County News
PO Box 307 Phone: (904)656-7627
Crawfordville, FL 32326-0307
County newspaper. **Founded:** 1977. **Freq:** Weekly (Thurs.). **Print Method:** Offset. **Cols./Page:** 6. **Col. Width:** 12 picas. **Col. Depth:** 21 1/2 inches. **Key Personnel:** Stacie M. Phillips, Publisher; Shannon P. Turnbull, General Mgr. **Subscription Rates:** $12.64 individuals. **Remarks:** Accepts advertising.
Ad Rates: GLR: $.15 **Circ:** ‡100

6047 The Wakulla News
Wakulla Publishing Co.
PO Box 307 Phone: (904)926-7102
Crawfordville, FL 32326 Fax: (904)926-3815

Community newspaper. **Founded:** 1895. **Freq:** Weekly (Thurs.). **Print Method:** Offset. **Cols./Page:** 6. **Col. Width:** 12 picas. **Col. Depth:** 21 1/2 inches. **Key Personnel:** Stacie Phillips, Editor; Shannon Turnbull, Managing Editor. **Subscription Rates:** $22 individuals. **Remarks:** Accepts advertising.
Ad Rates: GLR: $.21 **Circ:** ‡5,200
BW: $580.50
PCI: $5.25

CRESCENT CITY, pop. 1,722.

NE FL. Putnam Co. 60 mi. S. of Jacksonville. Boat works; tool and die plant; seafood packing house. Fisheries. Dairy farms.

6048 Crescent City Courier-Journal
Florida Publishing Co.
330 N. Summit St. Phone: (904)698-1644
Crescent City, FL 32112 Fax: (904)698-1994

Newspaper. **Founded:** 1946. **Freq:** Weekly (Wed.). **Print Method:** Offset. **Cols./Page:** 6. **Col. Width:** 24 nonpareils. **Col. Depth:** 301 agate lines. **Key Personnel:** Al Krombach, Editor; Ronnie Hughes, Publisher; Ricki Smith, Advertising Mgr. **USPS:** 451-140. **Subscription Rates:** $12 individuals; $14 out of county. **Remarks:** Accepts advertising.
Ad Rates: GLR: $.29 **Circ:** Paid 2,250
BW: $523.74 Free 5,800
PCI: $4.06

CRESTVIEW†, pop. 7,617.

NW FL. Okaloosa Co. 45 mi. NE of Pensacola. Sawmills. Ships pecans. Diversified agriculture. Cattle, cotton, corn.

6049 North Okaloosa Bulletin
Okaloosa Publishing Co.
301 N. Main St. Phone: (904)682-6524
PO Box 447 Fax: (904)682-2246
Crestview, FL 32536
Publication E-mail: cnl@cn-leader.com

Community newspaper (tabloid). **Founded:** 1975. **Freq:** Weekly (Wed.). **Print Method:** Offset. **Trim Size:** 11 5/8 x 17. **Cols./Page:** 6. **Col. Width:** 20 nonpareils. **Col. Depth:** 224 agate lines. **Key Personnel:** David J. Hein, Editor; James Knudsen, Publisher. **Subscription Rates:** Free; $52 by mail. **Remarks:** Accepts advertising. **URL:** http://www.cn-leader.com.
Ad Rates: BW: $307.20 **Circ:** Free ♦12,169
4C: $707.20
PCI: $3.30

6050 WAAZ-FM - 104.9
PO Box 267 Phone: (904)682-4623
Crestview, FL 32536 Fax: (904)682-5232

Format: Country. **Networks:** CBS. **Owner:** Crestview Broadcasting Co., at above address. **Founded:** 1965. **Operating Hours:** 5 a.m.-midnight. **Key Personnel:** James T. Whitaker, Contact; Dutch Van buskirk, Sales Mgr.; Gladys K. Fountain, Traffic Dir. **Wattage:** 3000.

6051 WJSB-AM - 1050
PO Box 267 Phone: (904)682-4623
Crestview, FL 32536 Fax: (904)682-5232

Format: Country; Middle-of-the-Road (MOR). **Networks:** CBS. **Owner:** Crestview Broadcasting Co., at above address. **Founded:** 1954. **Key Personnel:** James T. Whitaker, Contact; Sallie Stapleton, Promotions Mgr. **Wattage:** 5000.

6052 WTJT-FM - 90.1
PO Box 189 Phone: (904)537-2009
Baker, FL 32531 Fax: (904)537-4663

Format: Religious. **Networks:** USA Radio. **Owner:** Okaloosa Public Radio Inc., at above address. **Founded:** 1987. **Operating Hours:** 24 hrs. **Key Personnel:** Robert Williamson, General Mgr.; Randy Henry, Chief Engineer. **Wattage:** 20,000.

CROSS CITY†.

Dixie Co. (NW). 10 m NE of Shamrock.

6053 Dixie County Advocate
PO Box 5030 Phone: (904)498-3312
Cross City, FL 32628 Fax: (904)498-0420

Community newspaper. **Founded:** 1923. **Freq:** Weekly (Thurs.). **Print Method:** Offset. **Cols./Page:** 8. **Col. Width:** 10 picas. **Col. Depth:** 21 1/2 inches. **Key Personnel:** Skipper K. Jones, Editor and Publisher. **Subscription Rates:** $16.05 individuals; $21.40 out of state. **Remarks:** Accepts advertising.
Ad Rates: GLR: $2 **Circ:** ‡3,000
SAU: $2.29

6054 WDFL-AM - 1240
PO Box 2220 Phone: (904)498-0304
Cross City, FL 32628-2220 Fax: (904)498-0304

Format: Contemporary Country. **Networks:** CNN Radio. **Founded:** 1986. **Operating Hours:** Continuous; 8% network, 92% local. **Key Personnel:** Jerry Prater, General Mgr.; Ray Stanfield, Program Dir. **Wattage:** 1000. **Ad Rates:** $6 for 30 seconds; $8 for 60 seconds.

6055 WDFL-FM - 106.3
PO Box 2220 Phone: (904)498-0304
Cross City, FL 32628-2220

Format: Contemporary Country. **Networks:** CNN Radio. **Founded:** 1987. **Operating Hours:** Continuous; 8% network, 92% local. **Key Personnel:** Jerry Prater, General Mgr.; Ray Staqnfield, Program Dir. **Wattage:** 3000. **Ad Rates:** $6 for 30 seconds; $8 for 60 seconds.

CRYSTAL RIVER, pop. 2,778.

W FL. Citrus Co. 35 mi. SW of Ocala.

6056 Citrus County Chronicle
Landmark Community Newspapers, Inc.
1624 N. Meadowcrest Blvd. Phone: (904)563-6363
Crystal River, FL 34429
General newspaper. **Founded:** 1890. **Freq:** Mon.-Sun. (morn.). **Print Method:** Offset. Uses mats. **Cols./Page:** 6. **Col. Width:** 12.3 picas. **Col. Depth:** 21.5 inches. **Key Personnel:** Jim Hunter, Editor; Gerard Mulligan, Publisher; David Ernest, Advertising V.P. **Subscription Rates:** $77 individuals. **Remarks:** Accepts advertising.
Ad Rates: BW: $1,548 **Circ:** Mon.-Sat. ★**22,048**
4C: $1,798 Sun. ★**25,172**
SAU: $12

6057 WXCV-FM - 95.3
PO Box 1408 Phone: (904)795-9595
Crystal River, FL 34423 Fax: (904)795-7220
Free: (800)330-9595
E-mail: citrus95@xtalwind.net

Format: Adult Contemporary. **Networks:** AP; ABC. **Owner:** Steve Manuel/Jim Kimbrough/Bruce Snow, at above address. **Founded:** 1983. **Operating Hours:** Continuous; 10% network, 90% local. **Key Personnel:** Glynn Naw, General Mgr.; John Harrison, Program & News Dir.; Denise Pierce, Traffic Mgr. **Wattage:** 6,000. **Ad Rates:** $17-23 per unit.

DADE CITY†, pop. 4,923.

WC FL. Pasco Co. 30 mi. NW of Lakeland. Manufactures concrete water pipes, lumber. Citrus fruit, truck, and poultry farms.

6058 Pasco News
Sunpress Publications, Inc.
13032 U.S. Hwy. 301 Phone: (352)567-5639
PO Box 187 Fax: (352)567-5640
Dade City, FL 33525
Community newspaper. **Subtitle:** Pasco News. **Founded:** 1904. **Freq:** Weekly (Thurs.). **Print Method:** Offset. **Cols./Page:** 8. **Col. Width:** 28 nonpareils. **Col. Depth:** 301 agate lines. **Key Personnel:** Carlene Ellberg, Editor; J.W. Owens, Publisher, owens@pasconews.com. **Subscription Rates:** $14.84 individuals. **Remarks:** Accepts advertising. **Alt. Formats:** CD-ROM.
Ad Rates: GLR: $0.67 **Circ:** ‡5,000
PCI: $4.92

6059 Pasco Shopper
Sunpress Publications, Inc.
13032 U.S. Hwy. 301 Phone: (352)567-5639
PO Box 187 Fax: (352)567-5640
Dade City, FL 33525
Shopper. **Founded:** 1948. **Freq:** Weekly (Wed.). **Print Method:** Offset. **Trim Size:** 10 x 16 1/2. **Cols./Page:** 6. **Col. Width:** 10 picas. **Col. Depth:** 16 inches. **Key Personnel:** J.W. Owens, Publisher. **Subscription Rates:** Free. **Remarks:** Accepts advertising. **Alt. Formats:** CD-ROM.
Ad Rates: GLR: $.49 **Circ:** Free ‡223,167
BW: $603.90
4C: $703.90
PCI: $8.34

6060 WDCF-AM - 1350
37905 WDCF Dr. Phone: (904)567-1350
Dade City, FL 33525 Fax: (904)567-5532

Format: Country. **Networks:** NBC; Florida Radio. **Founded:** 1954. **Operating Hours:** Continuous; 25% network, 75% local. **Key Personnel:** Jeff Collins, General Mgr.; Lori Collins, News Dir.; Tyke Newton, Sports Dir.; Jay Price, Gospel Music Dir. **Local Programs:** *Community Corner*, David Sharp; *Sports Talk*, Tyke Newton, Sports Dir.; *20/20 News*, Lori Collins, News Dir. **Wattage:** 1000 day; 500 night. **Ad Rates:** $5.95-10.95 for 60 seconds.

DAVIE

Broward Co. (SE). 5 m W of Hollywood.

6061 The Observer
Broward Community College
3501 S.W. Davie Rd. Phone: (954)475-6700
Davie, FL 33314 Fax: (954)423-6405

Collegiate newspaper (tabloid). **Founded:** 1986. **Freq:** Biweekly. **Print Method:** Offset. **Trim Size:** 10 1/4 x 16. **Cols./Page:** 5. **Col. Width:** 11.5 picas. **Col. Depth:** 224 agate lines. **Key Personnel:** Wanda De Marzo, Editor-in-Chief, phone (954)475-6700; Greta Penenori, Advertising Mgr., phone (954)973-2237; Tom Lassiter, Advisor, phone (954)-475-6700. **Subscription Rates:** Free. **Remarks:** Accepts advertising. **Formed by the merger of:** The Polaris (1986); The Phoenix (1986); New Horizons (1986).
Ad Rates: BW: $400 **Circ:** Free 10,000
4C: $700
PCI: $10

6062 WAVS-AM - 1170
6360 SW 41st Place Phone: (954)584-1170
Davie, FL 33314 Fax: (954)581-6441

Format: Ethnic. **Networks:** Independent. **Owner:** Radio WAVS, Inc., 950 N. Federal Hwy., Pompano Beach, FL 33062, (954)781-6060. **Founded:** 1971. **Operating Hours:** Continuous; 100% local. **ADI:** Miami (Ft. Lauderdale), FL. **Key Personnel:** Roy H. Bresky, President; Winsome Charlton, Office/Traffic Mgr.; Winston Barnes, Program/News Dir.; Tony Blair, Sales Mgr.; Ray A. Hooper, General Mgr. **Wattage:** 5000. **Ad Rates:** $55 for 30 seconds; $65 for 60 seconds.

DAYTONA BEACH, pop. 50,830.

E FL. Volusia Co. On Halifax River, 91 mi. S. of Jacksonville. Bethune Cookman College; Embry-Riddle Aeronautical University; Daytona Beach Community College. Summer and winter resort. Sport and commercial fishing. Stock car racing. Agriculture. Citrus fruit, truck crops.

6063 Daytona Times
Daytona Times, Inc.
427 S. Dr. M. L. King Jr. Blvd. Phone: (904)253-0321
Daytona Beach, FL 32114 Fax: (904)254-7510

Black community newspaper. **Founded:** Aug. 1978. **Freq:** Weekly (Thurs.). **Print Method:** Offset. **Cols./Page:** 6. **Col. Width:** 2 1/16 inches. **Col. Depth:** 21 inches. **Key Personnel:** Charles W. Cherry II, Editor and Publisher. **Subscription Rates:** $35 individuals. **Remarks:** Accepts advertising.
Ad Rates: GLR: $.82 **Circ:** ‡20,150
BW: $1,973.16
4C: $2,223.16
PCI: $16.44

Flagler/Palm Coast News-Tribune - See Bunnell

6064 Halifax Magazine
Hanson Media, Inc.
405 N. Clyde Morris Blvd. Phone: (904)255-1860
Daytona Beach, FL 32114 Fax: (904)255-2860
Publication E-mail: hfxmag@n-jcenter.com

Consumer lifestyle and business magazine. **Subtitle:** Journal of Florida's Funcoast. **Founded:** Dec. 1995. **Freq:** 10/year. **Print Method:** Web. **Trim Size:** 8 3/8 x 10 7/8. **Cols./Page:** 3. **Col. Width:** 2 1/4 inches. **Col. Depth:** 10 inches. **Key Personnel:** Bev Hanson, Editor; Lenny DiMinno, Advertising Dir.; Diane Connett, Circulation Mgr. **Subscription Rates:** $18.55 individuals; $1.95 single issue. **Remarks:** Accepts advertising. **Online:** Global Data Link. **URL:** http://www.halifaxmagazine.com. **Former name:** New Volusia.
Ad Rates: BW: $1,525 **Circ:** Combined 67,000
4C: $1,850

6065 The News-Journal
The News-Journal Corp.
901 6th St. Phone: (904)252-1511
Daytona Beach, FL 32117-8099 Fax: (904)258-8465

Newspaper with a Democratic orientation. **Founded:** 1904. **Freq:** Mon.-Sun. (morn.). **Print Method:** Offset. **Trim Size:** 13 3/4 x 22. **Cols./Page:** 6. **Col. Width:** 26 nonpareils. **Col. Depth:** 294 agate lines. **Key Personnel:** Tippen Davidson, Publisher & Co-Editor; Josephine Davidson, Editor; Georgia Kaney, General Mgr.; Dick Dunkel, Managing Editor; Mike Czeczot, Managing Editor; Don Lindley, Editor; Tom Brown, Business Editor; Natalie Dix, Editoral page editor; Linda Trimble, Education Editor; Suzy Kridner, Entertainment & Home editor; Judy Liberi, Fashion editor; Suzy Kridner, Travel & Women's editor; Cathy Klasne, Food editor; Suzy Kridner, Lifestyle editor; Warren Baslee, Outdoor editor; Lydia Hinshaw, Sports editor; Robert Hughes, Marketing director; Katie Carlson, Promotions Dir.; Kathy Coughlin, Advertising Dir.; Bryan Stephens, Classified Mgr.; Robert Kearley, Circulation director. **USPS:** 149-820. **Subscription Rates:** $118.51 indi-

viduals. **Remarks:** Accepts advertising. Sunday: BW: $8,637.30; 4C: $10,262.30.
Ad Rates: BW: $7,680.80 **Circ:** Mon.-Sat. 102,406
4C: $9,285.80 Sun. 123,005
SAU: $60.80

6066 Our World
Our World Publishing Corp.
1104 N. Nova Rd., Ste. 251 Phone: (904)441-5367
Daytona Beach, FL 32117 Fax: (904)441-5604
Publication E-mail: ourworldmg@aol.com

Travel magazine. **Subtitle:** The International Gay & Lesbian Travel Magazine. **Founded:** 1989. **Freq:** 10/year. **Print Method:** Web offset. **Trim Size:** 8 x 10 3/4. **Cols./Page:** 3. **Col. Width:** 2 1/4 inches. **Col. Depth:** 9 3/4 inches. **Key Personnel:** Wayne Whiston, Editor. **ISSN:** 1044-6699. **Subscription Rates:** $35 individuals; $45 other countries; $4.95 single issue. **Remarks:** Accepts advertising. **URL:** http://www.ourworldmag.com.
Ad Rates: BW: $1,100 **Circ:** ‡50,000
4C: $2,080

6067 PC Presentations Productions
Pisces Publishing Group Inc.
1400 S. Nova Rd., Ste. 303 Phone: (904)253-6480
Daytona Beach, FL 32114-5814 Fax: (904)253-6480
Publisher E-mail: piscespub@piscespub.com

Consumer PC magazine. **Subtitle:** The Electronic Magazine Windows Graphics and Digital Video. **Founded:** Sept. 1993. **Freq:** Weekly. **Key Personnel:** Don Johnson, Editor; Douglas Finlay, Managing Editor. **ISSN:** 1065-9699. **Remarks:** Advertising accepted; rates available upon request. **URL:** http://www.piscespub.com/pcpp.html.
Circ: Non-paid ‡3,000

6068 Public Safety Communications
APCO International, Inc.
2040 S. Ridgewood Ave. Phone: (904)322-2500
Daytona Beach, FL 32119-8437 Fax: (904)322-2501
Free: (888)272-6911
Publication E-mail: bulletin@apcointl.org

Public safety communications magazine. **Subtitle:** APCO Bulletin. **Founded:** 1935. **Freq:** Monthly. **Print Method:** Web offset. **Trim Size:** 8 1/8 x 10 7/8. **Cols./Page:** 3. **Col. Width:** 28 nonpareils. **Col. Depth:** 140 agate lines. **Key Personnel:** Cindy Lorow, Editor, lorowc@apcointl.org; Kathy O' Connell, Production Mgr.; Terry Diehl, Advertising Mgr., diehlt@apcointl.org. **ISSN:** 0001-2165. **URL:** http://www.apcointl.org. **Formerly**: APCO BULLETIN (Jan. 1, 1999).
Ad Rates: BW: $1,460 **Circ:** Paid ‡11,765
4C: $2,530 Controlled ‡199

6069 Voice
Bethune-Cookman College
640 2nd Ave. Phone: (904)255-1401
Daytona Beach, FL 32115 Fax: (904)258-8951

Black collegiate newspaper. **Subtitle:** Voice. **Founded:** 1974. **Freq:** Monthly. **Print Method:** Offset. **Trim Size:** 11 x 17. **Cols./Page:** 4. **Col. Width:** 22 nonpareils. **Col. Depth:** 196 agate lines. **Key Personnel:** E.W. Wanjohi, Editor/Advisor; Sharhonda Ford, Editor-in-Chief; Kathryn Guzzman, Advertising Dir. **Subscription Rates:** Free; $10 individuals. **Remarks:** Accepts advertising. **Alt. Formats:** Mailing labels.
Ad Rates: 4C: $216 **Circ:** ‡3,000
PCI: $6

6070 WAPN-FM - 91.5
1508 State Ave. Phone: (904)677-4272
250311 Fax: (904)673-3715
Daytona Beach, FL 32125

Format: Religious. **Owner:** Public Radio, Inc., at above address. **Founded:** 1985. **Operating Hours:** Continuous. **ADI:** Orlando-Daytona Beach-Melbourne, FL. **Key Personnel:** Gordon C. Lund, General Mgr.; Earlyne Lund, Program Dir. **Wattage:** 1800.

6071 WCEU-TV - 15
PO Box 9245 Phone: (904)254-4415
Daytona Beach, FL 32120-9245
E-mail: wceu_tv@wceu.pbs.org

Networks: Public Broadcasting Service (PBS). **Owner:** Coastal Educational Broadcasters, Inc., at above address, Fax: (904)254-4427, Free: (800)638-9238. **Founded:** 1987. **Operating Hours:** 6 a.m. - 12:30 a.m. **ADI:** Orlando-Daytona Beach-Melbourne, FL. **Key Personnel:** Don A. Thigpen, General Mgr.; Sandra Session-Robertson, Asst. Gen. Mgr. Prog. & Communications; Scot Creveling, Dir. of Underwriting; Pete Miniscalco, Program Dir.; George Clark, Business Manager/PRDD; Bill Schwartz, Chief Engineer; Sanoma Robertson, Dir. of Major Giving. **Wattage:** 708,000. **URL:** http://www.wceu.org.

6072 WGTR-FM - 107.9
PO Box 2860
Daytona Beach, FL 32120

Format: Country. **Networks:** Meadows Racing. **Owner:** Root Communications Group, L. P., 4841 Hwy. 17 Bypass S., Myrtle Beach, SC 29577, (843)293-0107. **Operating Hours:** Continuous. **Key Personnel:** Theresa Miller, Market Mgr.; Lori Lathrup, General Sales Mgr.; Ken Slotnick, Local Sales Mgr.; Scrap Jackson, Operations Mgr. **Wattage:** 50,000. **Ad Rates:** $25-35 for 30 seconds; $35-45 for 60 seconds.

6073 WNDB-AM - 1150
126 W. International Speedway Blvd. Phone: (904)257-1150
Fax: (904)239-0966
Daytona Beach, FL 32114

Format: Talk; News; Sports. **Networks:** CBS. **Owner:** Black Crow Broadcasting, at above address. **Founded:** Apr. 1948. **Formerly:** WDNJ-AM. **Operating Hours:** Continuous; 70% network, 30% local. **ADI:** Orlando-Daytona Beach-Melbourne, FL. **Key Personnel:** Mike Moltane, General Sales Mgr.; Rory O'Neill, News Dir.; Dave Wrenn, Chief Engineer; Taft Moore, General Mgr. **Local Programs:** *Marc Bernier Show*, Marc Bernier, (904)257-1150; *Sports Scene*, Mike Scudeiro, (904)257-1150. **Wattage:** 1000. **Ad Rates:** $22-30 for 30 seconds; $30-45 for 60 seconds. **URL:** http://www.wndb.com.

6074 WROD-AM - 1340
PO Box 991 Phone: (904)253-0000
Daytona Beach, FL 32115 Fax: (904)225-3178

Format: Big Band/Nostalgia. **Networks:** ABC. **Owner:** La Paz Broadcasting, 136 Heritage Circle, Ormond Beach, FL 32174. **Founded:** 1947. **Operating Hours:** Continuous; 40% network, 60% local. **ADI:** Orlando-Daytona Beach-Melbourne, FL. **Key Personnel:** Anthony Welch, Pres./Gen. Mgr.; Jim Underwood, General Sales Mgr.; Bob Edwards, News Dir.; Catheriue Welch, Music Dir. **Wattage:** 1000. **Ad Rates:** $25-35 for 30 seconds; $30-40 for 60 seconds.

6075 WWSK-FM - 107.1
PO Box 2860
Daytona Beach, FL 32120

Format: Classic Rock. **Owner:** Root Communications Group, L. C., 4841 Hwy. 17 Bypass S., Myrtle Beach, SC 29577, (843)293-0107. **Formerly**: WCIG-FM. **Operating Hours:** Continuous. **Key Personnel:** Theresa Miller, Market Mgr.; Lori Lathrup, General Sales Mgr.; Ken Slotnick, Local Sales Mgr.; Scrap Jackson, Operations Mgr. **Wattage:** 50,000. **Ad Rates:** $25-40 for 30 seconds; $35-50 for 60 seconds.

6076 WWXM-FM - 97.7
PO Box 2860
Daytona Beach, FL 32120

Format: Contemporary Hit Radio (CHR). **Owner:** Root Communications Group, L. P., 4841 Hwy. 17 Bypass S., Myrtle Beach, SC 29577, (843)293-0107. **Operating Hours:** Continuous. **Key Personnel:** Theresa Miller, Market Mgr.; Lori Lathrop, General Sales Mgr.; Ken Slotnick, Local Sales Mgr.; Scrap Jackson, Operations Mgr. **Wattage:** 100,000. **Ad Rates:** $30-40 for 30 seconds; $40-50 for 60 seconds.

DE FUNIAK SPRINGS

6077 De Funiak Herald
Woodham Family Publications
14-16 Baldwin Ave. Phone: (904)892-3232
PO Box 1546 Fax: (904)894-2270
De Funiak Springs, FL 32433
Community newspaper. **Founded:** 1890. **Freq:** Weekly (Thurs.). **Print Method:** Offset. **Cols./Page:** 6. **Col. Width:** 12 2/5 picas. **Col. Depth:** 21 inches. **Key Personnel:** John P. Jones, Editor; Gary and Cindy Woodham, Publisher. **USPS:** 149-900. **Subscription Rates:** $19.26 individuals; $20 out of area. **Formerly**: De Funiak Herald-Breeze (1992).
Ad Rates: PCI: $3.50 **Circ:** 7,500

6078 The Herald Breeze
PO Box 1546 Phone: (904)892-3232
De Funiak Springs, FL 32433 Fax: (904)892-2270
Publication E-mail: herald@dfs.wwia.net

Community newspaper. **Founded:** 1990. **Freq:** Weekly. **Print Method:** Offset. **Trim Size:** 14 x 23. **Cols./Page:** 6. **Col. Width:** 12 picas. **Col. Depth:** 21 inches. **Key Personnel:** Dianna Van Horn, Editor; Brenda Peters, Advertising Mgr.; Gary Woodham, Publisher. **Subscription Rates:** $12.72; $15 (outside Florida). **Remarks:** Accepts advertising. **Alt. Formats:** Mailing labels. **Formerly**: The Beach Breeze.
Ad Rates: BW: $476.28 **Circ:** Paid 877
PCI: $3.78 Free 3,500

DE LAND

6079 The New Volusian
The News-Journal Corp.
111 S. Alabama Ave. Phone: (904)734-3661
Box 1119 Fax: (904)736-8972
De Land, FL 32721
Community newspaper. **Founded:** 1964. **Freq:** Semiweekly (Wed. and Sat.). **Print Method:** Offset. **Cols./Page:** 6. **Col. Width:** 2 1/16 inches. **Col. Depth:** 21 inches. **Key Personnel:** David Wiggins, Editor; Thomas M. Lindley, General Mgr.; Robert MacDonald, Advertising Dir.; Will Arington, Circulation Mgr. **Subscription Rates:** $18; $35 (mail). **Remarks:** Combined advertising rates available with Sun News. **URL:** http://www.news-journalonline.com. **Formerly**: The Deltona Enterprise (1991); The Enterprise (1992); Four Towns Enterprise.
Ad Rates: GLR: $4 **Circ:** ‡4,500

6080 Skydiving
1725 N. Lexington Ave. Phone: (904)736-4793
De Land, FL 32724 Fax: (904)736-9786
Publication E-mail: skydivng@interserv.com; skydivng@totcon.com

Magazine (tabloid) for skydiving enthusiasts. **Founded:** June 29, 1979. **Freq:** Monthly. **Print Method:** Offset. **Trim Size:** 13 1/2 x 15. **Cols./Page:** 4. **Col. Width:** 14 picas. **Col. Depth:** 81 picas. **Key Personnel:** Sue Clifton, Editor; Michael Truffer, Publisher; Troy White, Advertising Mgr. **ISSN:** 0192-7361. **Subscription Rates:** $20 individuals; $5 single issue. **Remarks:** Accepts advertising.
Ad Rates: BW: $817 **Circ:** ‡14,200
4C: $1,307

6081 West Volusia Pennysaver
Volusia Pennysaver, Inc.
PO Box 3536
De Land, FL 32723-3536
Publication E-mail: readwvps@n-jcenter.com

Shopper. **Founded:** 1971. **Freq:** Semiweekly (Wed. and Sat.). **Print Method:** Offset. **Cols./Page:** 6. **Col. Width:** 9 picas. **Col. Depth:** 13 inches. **Key Personnel:** Stephen Blais, Gen. Mgr./Adv. Dir. **Subscription Rates:** Free. **Remarks:** Accepts advertising. **Formerly**: De Land Pennysaver (1992).
Ad Rates: GLR: $.82 **Circ:** Non-paid **50,000**
BW: $897
4C: $300
PCI: $12.30

6082 WXVQ-AM - 1490
220 E. Hubbard Ave. Phone: (904)734-9386
PO Box 1777 Fax: (904)734-9361
De Land, FL 32721

Format: News; Talk; Sports. **Networks:** ABC; Florida Radio. **Founded:** 1948. **Formerly**: WJBS-AM (1985). **Operating Hours:** Continuous; 50% network, 50% local. **ADI:** Orlando-Daytona Beach-Melbourne, FL. **Key Personnel:** Rick Green, General Mgr.; Pat Green, Program Mgr.; Al Everson, News Dir. **Wattage:** 1000. **Ad Rates:** $15 for 60 seconds.

6083 WYND-AM - 1310
316 E. Taylor Rd. Phone: (904)734-1310
De Land, FL 32724 Fax: (968)734-1315

Format: Religious; News; Talk. **Owner:** at above address. **Founded:** 1956. **Key Personnel:** Al Richards, General Mgr. **Wattage:** 5,000 day; 95 night. **Ad Rates:** $10-20 for 60 seconds.

DEERFIELD BEACH, pop. 39,193.

SE FL. Broward Co. 5 mi. N. of Pompano Beach.

Boca Raton Thursday Times - See Boca Raton

Boynton Beach Times - See Boynton Beach

6084 Broward Jewish Journal
SFNN, Inc.
601 Fairway Dr. Phone: (954)574-5300
Deerfield Beach, FL 33441 Fax: (954)429-1207
Free: (800)275-8820
Publication E-mail: ptom@netrunner.net
Publisher E-mail: bukley@gate.net

Jewish interest newspaper (tabloid). **Founded:** 1965. **Freq:** Weekly (Thurs.). **Print Method:** Offset. **Cols./Page:** 6. **Col. Width:** 1 5/8 inches. **Col. Depth:** 16 inches. **Key Personnel:** Andrew Polin, Editor; Rabbi Bruce Warshal, Publisher. **Subscription Rates:** Free. **Remarks:** Accepts advertising.
Ad Rates: PCI: $74.75 **Circ:** Free 75,000

6085 Deerfield Beach Shoppers Guide
Gulfstream Newspapers, Inc.
PO Box 223580
Hollywood, FL 33022-3580

Shopper. **Founded:** 1949. **Freq:** Weekly (Wed.). **Print Method:** Offset. **Trim Size:** 10 1/4 x 16 1/2. **Cols./Page:** 6. **Col. Width:** 1 5/8 inches. **Col. Depth:** 16 1/2 inches. **Key Personnel:** James Bouldin, Publisher; Richard Lewkowicz, Advertising Mgr. **Remarks:** Accepts advertising.
Ad Rates: BW: $400 **Circ:** Free ‡18,400
PCI: $5.40

6086 Deerfield Beach Times
SFNN, Inc.
601 Fairway Dr. Phone: (954)574-5300
Deerfield Beach, FL 33441 Fax: (954)429-1207
Free: (800)275-8820
Publication E-mail: dtom@netrunner.net
Publisher E-mail: bukley@gate.net

Community newspaper (tabloid). **Founded:** 1965. **Freq:** Weekly (Thurs.). **Print Method:** Offset. **Cols./Page:** 6. **Col. Width:** 1 5/8 inches. **Col. Depth:** 16 inches. **Key Personnel:** Scott Patterson, Publisher. **Subscription Rates:** Free. **Remarks:** Accepts advertising.
Ad Rates: PCI: $15.35 **Circ:** Free 18,841

Delray Beach Times - See Delray Beach

6087 Eastsider
South Florida Newspaper Network
601 Fairway Dr. Phone: (305)698-6397
Deerfield Beach, FL 33441 Fax: (305)429-0556
Free: (800)575-8820
Publication E-mail: bukley@gate.net
Publisher E-mail: binkley@gate.net

Community newspaper. serving Broward County, FL. **Freq:** Weekly. **Key Personnel:** Arnold Simon, Art Critic; Bette Kozarak, Theater Critic; Mitch Miller, Design Editor; Joe Marshall, Photo Editor. **Subscription Rates:** Free.
Circ: Controlled 26,901

6088 Hi-Riser
SFNN, Inc.
601 Fairway Dr. Phone: (954)574-5300
Deerfield Beach, FL 33441 Fax: (954)429-1207
Free: (800)275-8820
Publisher E-mail: bukley@gate.net

Community newspaper. **Freq:** Weekly (Thurs.). **Cols./Page:** 68. **Col. Width:** 1 7/8 inches. **Col. Depth:** 13 inches. **Key Personnel:** Scott Patterson, Publisher.
Ad Rates: PCI: $19.75 **Circ:** Combined 18,214

6089 Jewish Journal Dade
South Florida Newspaper Network
601 Fairway Dr. Phone: (305)698-6397
Deerfield Beach, FL 33441 Fax: (305)429-0556
Free: (800)575-8820
Publisher E-mail: binkley@gate.net

Jewish interest newpaper serving Dade County, FL. **Freq:** Weekly. **Cols./Page:** 5. **Col. Width:** 1 7/8 inches. **Col. Depth:** 13 inches. **Key Personnel:** Ed Wilder, Circulation Mgr.; Sharon Patterson, Ad. Mgr. **Subscription Rates:** Free. **Remarks:** Accepts advertising.
Ad Rates: PCI: $27.35 **Circ:** Combined 20,828

6090 Mutual Funds Magazine
2200 SW 10th St. Phone: (954)421-1000
Deerfield Beach, FL 33442-8799 Fax: (954)570-8200
Free: (800)818-8973
Publication E-mail: gkp@mfmag.com

Magazine providing information on choosing mutual funds. **Subtitle:** Your Monthly Guide To America's Best Investments. **Founded:** Sept. 1994. **Freq:** Monthly. **Print Method:** Offset. **Trim Size:** 8x 10 3/4. **Cols./Page:** 3 and 3. **Col. Width:** 2 1/4 and 4 5/8 inches. **Col. Depth:** 10 and 4 7/8 inches. **Key Personnel:** Norman Fosback, Editor-in-Chief; Edward C. Frey, Publisher. **ISSN:** 1079-0039. **Subscription Rates:** $14.97 individuals; $2.50 single issue. **Remarks:** Accepts advertising. **URL:** http://www.mfmag.com.
Ad Rates: BW: $24,795 **Circ:** Paid ★**782,115**
4C: $34,715

6091 Observer Community Newspaper
Deerfield Publishers
43 NE 2nd St. Phone: (954)428-9045
Deerfield Beach, FL 33441 Fax: (954)428-9096

Community newspaper. **Founded:** 1961. **Freq:** Weekly (Thurs.). **Print Method:** Web offset. **Trim Size:** 10 x 16. **Cols./Page:** 6. **Col. Width:** 10 1/2 picas. **Col. Depth:** 16 inches. **Key Personnel:** Judy Wilson, Managing Editor; Joan Durbin, Editor; Jim Canavan, Advertising Dir. **Subscription Rates:** $60. **Remarks:** Accepts advertising.
Ad Rates: 4C: $1,000 **Circ:** 25,000
PCI: $8

6092 Palm Beach Jewish Journal North
SFNN, Inc.
601 Fairway Dr. Phone: (954)574-5300
Deerfield Beach, FL 33441 Fax: (954)429-1207
Free: (800)275-8820
Publisher E-mail: bukley@gate.net

Jewish community newspaper. **Founded:** 1986. **Freq:** Weekly (Tues.). **Trim Size:** 10 1/8 x 16. **Cols./Page:** 5. **Col. Width:** 1 5/8 inches. **Col. Depth:** 13 inches. **Key Personnel:** Andy Polin; Rabbi Bruce Warshal; Ed Wilder. **Subscription Rates:** Free. **Remarks:** Accepts advertising. **Formerly:** Palm Beach Jewish Journal.
Ad Rates: BW: $875 **Circ:** Combined 21,467
4C: $1,275
SAU: $9.10

Palm Beach Jewish Journal South - See West Palm Beach

6093 West Boca Times
SFNN, Inc.
601 Fairway Dr. Phone: (954)574-5300
Deerfield Beach, FL 33441 Fax: (954)429-1207
Free: (800)275-8820
Publisher E-mail: bukley@gate.net

Community newspaper (tabloid). **Founded:** 1965. **Freq:** Weekly (Wed.). **Print Method:** Offset. **Cols./Page:** 5. **Col. Width:** 1 7/8 inches. **Col. Depth:** 13 inches. **Key Personnel:** Andrew Polin, Editor; Scott Patterson, Publisher. **Subscription Rates:** $69. **Remarks:** Accepts advertising.
Ad Rates: PCI: $15.10 **Circ:** Non-paid 22,411

DEFUNIAK SPRINGS†.

Walton Co. (NW). 30 m SW of Bonifay.

6094 WZEP-AM - 1460
PO Box 627 Phone: (850)892-3158
DeFuniak Springs, FL 32435 Fax: (850)892-9675
E-mail: wzep@access.aic-fl.com

Format: Full Service; News; Country; Oldies. **Networks:** NBC; Florida Radio. **Owner:** Walton County Broadcasting, Inc, at above address. **Founded:** 1955. **Operating Hours:** Continuous. **ADI:** Panama City, FL. **Key Personnel:** Arthur F. Dees, Owner/Pres.; Martha K. Dees, Owner/Vice President; Karen Hoehne, News Dir.; Rod Hughes, Sports Dir.; Richard Lovelling, Operations Mgr. **Local Programs:** *Hi Neighbor* 6 a.m.-9 a.m. Monday-Friday, Art Dees, (904)892-3158, Fax (904)892-9675; *Musical Memories* 3 p.m.-5:30 p.m. Monday-Friday, Sonny Yates, (904)892-3158, Fax (904)892-9675. **Wattage:** 5000. **Ad Rates:** Advertising accepted; rates available upon request. **URL:** http://www.aic-fl.com/wzep.

DELRAY BEACH, pop. 34,325.

SE FL. Palm Beach Co. On Atlantic Ocean, 17 mi. S. of West Palm Beach. Tourist resort. Nurseries. Agriculture.

6095 Delray Beach Times
SFNN, Inc.
601 Fairway Dr. Phone: (954)574-5300
Deerfield Beach, FL 33441 Fax: (954)429-1207
Free: (800)275-8820
Publisher E-mail: bukley@gate.net

Community newspaper (tabloid). **Founded:** 1977. **Freq:** Weekly. **Print Method:** Offset. **Trim Size:** 11 3/8 x 17 1/2. **Cols./Page:** 6. **Col. Width:** 1 5/8 inches. **Col. Depth:** 16 inches. **Key Personnel:** Ron Bukley, Editor; Scott Patterson, Publisher. **Subscription Rates:** $17. **Remarks:** Accepts advertising.
Ad Rates: PCI: $15.35 **Circ:** Combined 17,427

6096 Infection Control & Sterilization Technology
Midway Publishing Corp.
100 E. Linton Blvd., Ste. 502A Phone: (561)330-0920
Delray Beach, FL 33483 Fax: (561)330-0970
Publication E-mail: edmayworm@aol.com
Publisher E-mail: midway.cst@aol.com

Professional magazine for infection control practitioners and people who make purchasing decisions concerned with decontamination, disinfection, and sterilization in health care settings. **Founded:** Jan. 1995. **Freq:** Monthly. **Print Method:** Web offset. **Trim Size:** 8 x 10 3/4. **Key Personnel:** Suzanne Rehor, VP Publishing; Bobbi Levien, Editor-in-Chief. **ISSN:** 1078-8972. **Subscription Rates:** $49 individuals; $6.50 single issue. **Remarks:** Accepts advertising. **Former name:** Journal of Health Care Material Management.
Ad Rates: BW: $2,830 **Circ:** Paid △**25,000**
4C: $3,980

6097 Journal of Healthcare Resource Management
Midway Publishing Corp.
100 E. Linton Blvd., Ste. 502A Phone: (561)330-0920
Delray Beach, FL 33483 Fax: (561)330-0970
Publisher E-mail: midway.cst@aol.com

Trade magazine for senior healthcare personnel responsible for taking costs out of the system while improving outcomes. **Subtitle:** Managing the Business of Healthcare. **Founded:** 1983. **Freq:** Monthly. **Print Method:** Offset. **Trim Size:** 8 x 10 3/4. **Cols./Page:** 3. **Col. Width:** 26 nonpareils. **Col. Depth:** 140 agate lines. **Key Personnel:** Roxann Marshburn, Editor, edmayworm@aol.com; Jeff Mayworm, Vice President; Don Heidkamp, Assoc. Pubisher; Daniel Mayworm, Publisher. **ISSN:** 1078-9537. **Subscription Rates:** $49 individuals; $6.5 single issue; $58 Canada; $98 other countries. **Remarks:** Accepts advertising. **Formerly:** Journal of Healthcare Material Management; Journal of Resource Management.
Ad Rates: BW: $2,575 **Circ:** Paid 4,000
4C: $3,725 3825 Controlled 20,000
PCI: $100.00

6098 WDBF-AM - 1420
2710 W. Atlantic Ave. Phone: (407)278-1420
Box 1420 Fax: (407)278-1898
Delray Beach, FL 33445

Format: Big Band/Nostalgia; Jazz. **Networks:** CBS. **Owner:** Vic Knight, at above address. **Founded:** 1952. **Operating Hours:** Continuous. **ADI:** West Palm Beach-Ft. Pierce-Vero Beach, FL. **Key Personnel:** George Mills, General Mgr.; Paul Dunn. **Wattage:** 5000.

DELTONA

6099 Motorcycle Shopper
Payne Corp.
1353 Herndon Ave. Phone: (407)860-1989
Deltona, FL 32725-9046 Fax: (407)574-1014
Free: (800)982-4599
Publication E-mail: mshopper@iag.net

Magazine for buying, selling, and trading motocycles. **Subtitle:** The Source for Motorcycles, Parts, Accessories, Sidecars, Tools, Clubs, Events, and More!. **Founded:** May 1990. **Freq:** Monthly. **Print Method:** Web offset. **Trim Size:** 8 1/8 x 10 7/8. **Cols./Page:** 3. **Col. Width:** 2 1/4 inches. **Col. Depth:** 9 3/4 inches. **Key Personnel:** Luis Hernandez, Publisher; Tracy E. Hardy, Associate Publisher. **ISSN:** 1075-2447. **Subscription Rates:** $19.95 individuals; $2.99 single issue; $3.99 single issue out of country; $42 Canada; $60 other countries. **Remarks:** Accepts advertising. **Available Online. URL:** http:// www.motorcycleshopper.com.
Ad Rates: BW: $731.25 **Circ:** Paid 37,000
4C: $925

DESTIN, pop. 3,600.

NW FL. Okaloose Co. 6 mi. S. of Fort Walton Beach. Tourist resort.

6100 The Destin Log
Destin Log
PO Box 957 Phone: (850)837-2828
Destin, FL 32540 Fax: (904)654-5982
Publication E-mail: emeraldcoast@destin.com
Publisher E-mail: emeraldcoast@destin.com

Newspaper. **Founded:** 1974. **Freq:** Semiweekly (Wed. and Sat.). **Print Method:** Offset. **Cols./Page:** 6. **Col. Width:** 25 nonpareils. **Col. Depth:** 301 agate lines. **Key Personnel:** Michael A. Levi, Publisher, phone (850)654-8422, emeraldcast@destin.com; Kenneth Books, Managing Editor, kbooks@destin.net. **Subscription Rates:** $38 individuals; $44.45 out of state; $0.50 single issue. **Feature Editors:** Charlotte Potthast, *Features*, phone (850)654-8445, newsroom@destin.net.
Ad Rates: GLR: $9.69 **Circ:** ‡8,500
PCI: $9.27

DUNEDIN, pop. 30,203.

WC FL. Pinellas Co. 21 mi. W. of Tampa. Winter resort. Manufactures canning machinery, citrus packing equipment, furniture. Citrus fruit, truck crops.

6101 The Dunedin Times/The Palm Harbor Sounder
Dunedin Times Co.
PO Box 493 Phone: (727)447-8353
Dunedin, FL 34697-0493 Fax: (727)736-1854

Community newspaper (broadsheet). **Founded:** Feb. 1923. **Freq:** Biweekly. **Print Method:** Offset. **Trim Size:** 13 x 21 1/2. **Cols./Page:** 5. **Col. Width:** 13 picas. **Col. Depth:** 21 inches. **Key Personnel:** Russell G. Boaeuf, Editor and Publisher. **Subscription Rates:** Free; $20 by mail.
Ad Rates: BW: $600 **Circ:** Paid 250
4C: $220 Free 15,000
SAU: $5
PCI: $6.50

DUNNELLON

Marion Co. (NC). 10 m SW of Ocala.

6102 Contemporary South Asia
Carfax Publishing Co.
PO Box 2025
Dunnellon, FL 34430-2025

Journal covering policy issues and historical articles on South Asia. **Founded:** 1992. **Freq:** 3/year. **Key Personnel:** Gowher Rizvi, Editor; Robert Cassen, Advertising Mgr.; Subrata Mitra, Editor; Tom Jannuzi, Editor; Iftikhar Malik, Advertising Mgr.; Kazi Shahidullah, Editor; Bishnu Mohapatra, Editor; Sridhar K. Khatri, Advertising Mgr. **ISSN:** 0958-4935. **Subscription Rates:** $150. $66 single issue. **Remarks:** Advertising accepted; rates available upon request.
Circ: (Not Reported)

6103 Nanobiology: Journal of Research in Nanoscale Living
Carfax Publishing Co.
PO Box 2025
Dunnellon, FL 34430-2025

Journal covering all aspects of cellular systems in coherence. Emphasizes processes acting on nanomechanisms, such as repair, replication, and where the cytoskeleton acts as an operator. **Freq:** Quarterly. **Key Personnel:** Per Anders Hansson, Editor; Hirokazu Hotani, Advertising Mgr.; Stuart R. Hameroff, Editor; P.I. Lazarev, Editor; W.R. Adey, Advertising Mgr.; Antonio Lazcano, Editor; Vladimir Kislov, Editor; Steen Rasmussen, Advertising Mgr. **ISSN:** 0958-3165. **Subscription Rates:** $280. **Alt. Formats:** Microfiche.

6104 Technology Analysis and Strategic Management
Carfax Publishing Co.
PO Box 2025
Dunnellon, FL 34430-2025

Journal linking the analysis of science and technology with the strategic needs of policy makers and management. **Founded:** 1989. **Freq:** Quarterly. **Key Personnel:** Steve Gutwistle. **ISSN:** 0953-7325.

EASTPOINT

WOYS-FM - See Apalachicola

ENGLEWOOD, pop. 5,108.

SW FL. Sarasota & Charlotte Co. On Gulf of Mexico and Lemon Bay, 30 mi. S. of Sarasota. Tourist resort. Boat yard. Boating and fishing. Citrus fruit farms.

6105 WENG-AM - 1530
1355 S. River Rd. Phone: (941)474-3231
PO Box 2908 Fax: (941)475-2205
Englewood, FL 34295
E-mail: radio@thewave1530am.com

Format: Talk; News; Sports. **Networks:** ABC; Florida Radio. **Founded:** 1964. **Operating Hours:** Sunrise-sunset; 10% network, 90% local. **Key Personnel:** S. Capaccio, Station Mgr., sal@thewave1530am.com; Brenda Chaisson, Sales Mgr., brenda@thewave1530am.com; Salvatore A. Capaccio, Production/P.S.A./Sports Mgr.; Ellen Greenaway, Office Mgr., ellen@thewave1530am.com. **Local Programs:** *Breakfast Club* 8:00 am - 9:00 am Monday-Friday, Sal Capaccio, Mailing contact. **Wattage:** 1000. **Ad Rates:** $10-14 for 30 seconds; $16-22 for 60 seconds.

6106 WSEB-FM - 91.3
517 Paul Morris Dr., Ste. C4-2 Phone: (813)475-9732
Englewood, FL 34223 Fax: (813)473-1797

Format: Religious. **Networks:** Voice of Christian Youth America. **Owner:** Suncoast Educational Broadcasting Corp., at above address. **Founded:** 1989. **Operating Hours:** Continuous; 40% network, 60% local. **Key Personnel:** Wallis C. Metts, President. **Wattage:** 62,000. **Ad Rates:** Noncommercial.

ESTERO

Lee Co. (SW). 10 m SW of Ft. Myers.

6107 WRXK-FM - 96.1
PO Box 9600 Phone: (941)495-2100
Estero, FL 33928 Fax: (941)992-8165
Free: (800)346-7625

Networks: ABC. **Owner:** Beasley Broadcast Group, 3033 Rivera Dr., Ste. 200, Naples, FL 33940, (941)263-5000, Fax: (941)263-8191. **Founded:** 1976. **Formerly**: WLEQ-FM (1986). **Operating Hours:** Continuous; 3% network, 97% local. **Key Personnel:** Brad Beasley, General Mgr.; Robert Hallman, General Sales Mgr.; John Rozz, Program Dir.; Roxanne McVay, Music Dir.; Ron Kabansky, Promotions Dir. **Local Programs:** *Stan & Haney* 3:00 pm - 7:00 pm Monday-Friday, Mike Spiwak, Producer; *Liquid Lunch* 12:00 noon - 1:00 pm Monday-Friday, Roxanne McVay, Air personality. **Wattage:** 100,000.

EUSTIS

Lake Co. (NC). 5 m NW of Mt. Dora.

6108 WKIQ-AM - 1240
1057 N. Palm Circle Phone: (352)357-1240
Eustis, FL 32726 Fax: (352)357-4250

Format: Talk; News; Sports. **Networks:** NBC; People's Network; Westwood One Radio. **Owner:** Christianson Broadcasting, Inc, at above address. **Founded:** 1942. **Formerly**: WLCF-AM; WEUS-AM; WWLB-AM. **Operating Hours:** Continuous. **Key Personnel:** Carl Christianson, Contact; Larry King, Operations Mgr. **Local Programs:** *Rise & Shine with Carl & Maggie*; *Sports Talk*, Bill Gier, Mailing contact; *Talk Track with Bob Green*, Bob Green, Mailing contact. **Wattage:** 1000. **Ad Rates:** $5-14 for 30 seconds. **URL:** http://www.wkiq.com; http://www.graveline.com.

FERNANDINA BEACH†, pop. 7,224.

NE FL. Nassau Co. On Amelia Island, 25 mi. NE of Jacksonville. Manufactures wood pulp, fish oil, meal fertilizer. Shrimp packing. Shrimp, oyster, fisheries; pine timber.

6109 News-Leader
Ocala Star - Banner
PO Box 766 Phone: (904)261-3696
Fernandina Beach, FL 32035 Fax: (904)261-3698

Newspaper. **Founded:** 1854. **Freq:** Weekly (Wed.). **Print Method:** Offset. **Cols./Page:** 6. **Col. Width:** 2 1/16 inches. **Col. Depth:** 21 1/2 inches. **Key Personnel:** Anthony Quesada, Editor; Foy R. Maloy, Jr., Publisher. **Subscription Rates:** $19.29 individuals; $45 out of area. **Remarks:** Accepts advertising. **URL:** http://www.fbnewsleader.com.
Ad Rates: BW: $1,647.33 **Circ:** Wed. ★**9,899**
4C: $1,942.33
PCI: $12.77

6110 Media One
1600 S. 14th St. Phone: (904)261-3624
Fernandina Beach, FL 32034 Fax: (904)277-2590

Formerly: Fernandina Cablevision. **Key Personnel:** Gordon Baker, General Mgr., phone (904)261-3625. **Cities Served:** Amelia Island, Callghan, Fernandina, Folkston, Hilliard, Kings Bay, Nahunta, Plantation, GA: subscribing households 7,200; 60 channels; 1 community access channel; 50 hours per week community access programming.

FORT LAUDERDALE†, pop. 153,256.

S FL. Broward Co. On Atlantic Ocean, 25 mi. N. of Miami. Broward Community College; Fort Lauderdale College of Business and Finance. Tourist resort. Manufactures cement products, fertilizer, mattresses, furniture, aircraft fittings, electronic equipment, fibre glass, chemicals, plastics, aluminum and concrete products, boats.

6111 American Firearms Industry
National Association of Federally Licensed Firearms Dealers
2455 E. Sunrise Blvd., Ste. 916 Phone: (954)561-3505
Fort Lauderdale, FL 33304 Fax: (954)561-4129
Publisher E-mail: afi@amfire.com

Magazine of the American firearms industry. **Founded:** 1973. **Freq:** 12/year. **Trim Size:** 8 1/2 x 11. **Cols./Page:** 3. **Col. Width:** 3 inches. **Col. Depth:** 10 inches. **Key Personnel:** Edward A. Conyers, Nat'l Adv. Mgr.; Andrew Molchan, Publisher. **Subscription Rates:** $25 individuals individual; $5 single issue. **URL:** http://www.amfire.com.
Ad Rates: BW: $2,850 **Circ:** Combined 50,000
4C: $3,450

6112 Angler Magazine
Holmes Communications
941 NE 19th Ave., Ste. 212 Phone: (954)763-1705
Fort Lauderdale, FL 33304 Fax: (954)763-4605
Publication E-mail: so.kingfish@worldnet.att.net

Magazine for saltwater fishing enthusiasts for members of The Southern Kingfish and Saltwater Anglers Associations. **Founded:** 1990. **Freq:** Monthly. **Print Method:** Photo offset. **Trim Size:** 10 1/8 x 13 1/4. **Cols./Page:** 5. **Col. Width:** 11 picas. **Col. Depth:** 12 inches. **Key Personnel:** Jack Holmes, Editor and Publisher; Deona Holmes, Advertising Dir. **Subscription Rates:** $18 association member; $45 competition member; $60 families. **Remarks:** Accepts advertising.
Ad Rates: BW: $1250 **Circ:** ‡30,000
4C: $2,060

6113 Blockbuster
Blockbuster Entertainment Corp.
1 Blockbuster Plaza Phone: (954)832-3000
Fort Lauderdale, FL 33301 Fax: (954)832-4525

Subtitle: The Video Magazine. **Founded:** 1989. **Freq:** Monthly. **Print Method:** Web offset. **Trim Size:** 8 1/4 x 10 7/8. **Cols./Page:** 3. **Col. Width:** 2 1/4 inches. **Key Personnel:** J.P. Faber, Editor; Ron Castell, Publisher. **Remarks:** Accepts advertising.
Ad Rates: BW: $15,770 **Circ:** Non-paid 970,000
4C: $19,700

6114 Broward Daily Business Review
American Lawyer Media, L.P.
633 S. Andrews Ave. Phone: (954)468-2600
Fort Lauderdale, FL 33301 Fax: (305)944-9451
Free: (800)777-7300
Publication E-mail: review@floridabiz.com

Publication of enterprise, real estate, and law in the Broward area. **Founded:** 1966. **Freq:** Daily. **Print Method:** Web offset. **Trim Size:** 11 3/8 x 17. **Cols./Page:** 4. **Col. Width:** 2 3/8 inches. **Col. Depth:** 15 inches. **Key Personnel:** Edward Wasserman, Editor, phone (305)347-6612, fax (305)347-6626; T. Alicia Coya, Publisher, phone (305)347-6632, fax (305)374-8474; Mike Vogel, Editor, phone (954)468-2620, fax (954)468-2630, mvogel@floridabus.com. **ISSN:** 0887-4751. **Subscription Rates:** $179. **Remarks:** Accepts advertising. **Alt. Formats:** Diskette; Mailing labels. **Formerly**: Broward Review.
Ad Rates: BW: $1,500 **Circ:** Paid 9,624
4C: $2,075.50 Non-paid 206
PCI: $26.12

6115 Business in Broward
Lauderdale Publishing Co.
PO Box 460669
Fort Lauderdale, FL 33346-0699
Publication E-mail: sfbiz@mindspring.com

Business magazine focusing on business development in Broward County, Florida. **Founded:** Jan. 1987. **Freq:** 8/year. **Print Method:** Offset. **Trim Size:** 8 1/2 x 11. **Cols./Page:** 3. **Col. Width:** 2.25 picas. **Col. Depth:** 8 3/8 inches. **Key Personnel:** Sherry Friedlander, Publisher; Cathy Dube, Editor. **Subscription Rates:** $32 individuals. **Remarks:** Accepts advertising. **Available Online. URL:** http://www.bizflorida.com//.
Ad Rates: BW: $1,800 **Circ:** Paid ‡14,200
4C: $2,400 Controlled ‡5,800

6116 City Link
Sun Sentinel
200 E. Las Olas Blvd. Phone: (954)356-4943
Fort Lauderdale, FL 33301 Fax: (954)356-4949

Newspaper. **Founded:** Mar. 1991. **Freq:** Weekly. **Print Method:** Offset. **Cols./Page:** 5. **Col. Width:** 2 1/16 inches. **Col. Depth:** 13 inches. **Key Personnel:** Megan Burns, Advertising Mgr., phone (954)356-4028, fax (954)356-4093, mburns@tribune.com; Michael Farver, Editor, phone (954)359-4946, mfarver@citylink.com. **Remarks:** Accepts advertising. **Online:** America Online, Inc. **URL:** http://www.citylink.com. **Former name**: XS Magazine.
Ad Rates: GLR: $30 **Circ:** Non-paid ★**50,840**
BW: $1,950
BW: $1,300
4C: $2,479.42
4C: $1,700
PCI: $23
PCI: $20

6117 College and Research Libraries
Association of College and Research Libraries
3301 College Ave. Phone: (954)262-4620
Fort Lauderdale, FL 33314-7796 Fax: (954)262-3805
Publisher E-mail: acrl@ala.org

Journal for ACRL members. **Founded:** Dec. 1939. **Freq:** Bimonthly. **Print Method:** Offset. **Trim Size:** 6 1/8 x 9 1/4. **Cols./Page:** 2. **Col. Width:** 29 nonpareils. **Col. Depth:** 105 agate lines. **Key Personnel:** Donald Riggs, Editor, driggs@nsu.nova.edu; Stuart Foster, Advertising Mgr., phone (203)347-3764. **ISSN:** 0010-0870. **Subscription Rates:** $60 nonmembers. **Remarks:** Accepts advertising.
Ad Rates: BW: $935 **Circ:** ‡12,000
4C: $1,710

6118 El Nuevo Herald
Hometown Herald
1520 E. Sunrise Blvd. Phone: (954)527-8940
Fort Lauderdale, FL 33304 Fax: (954)527-8955

Spanish-language newspaper. **Founded:** Mar. 29, 1976. **Freq:** Mon.-Sun. (morn.). **Print Method:** Offset. **Trim Size:** 13 x 22 1/2. **Cols./Page:** 6. **Col. Width:** 2 1/16 inches. **Col. Depth:** 22 1/2 inches. **Key Personnel:** Barbara Gutierrez, Editor; Robert Suarez, Publisher; Roberto Oliva, Advertising Dir. **Subscription Rates:** $3.46 weekly. **Remarks:** Accepts advertising. **Formerly:** El Miami Herald (Nov. 1987).
Ad Rates: GLR: $42 **Circ:** Mon.-Sat. 102,194
BW: $5,231.25 Sun. 127,113
4C: $6,181.25
SAU: $36.25

6119 Fort Lauderdale Downtown
Fort Lauderdale Downtown, Inc.
PO Box 1596 Phone: (954)565-6561
Fort Lauderdale, FL 33305 Fax: (954)467-2642

Community newspaper. **Subtitle:** Serving Fort Lauderdale Downtown. **Founded:** May 1988. **Freq:** Monthly. **Print Method:** Offset. **Trim Size:** 11 x 14. **Cols./Page:** 4. **Col. Width:** 27 nonpareils. **Col. Depth:** 140 agate lines. **Key Personnel:** Helen Ditzler, Publisher.
Ad Rates: BW: $450 **Circ:** ‡5,000

6120 Hometown Herald
1520 E. Sunrise Blvd. Phone: (954)985-4595
Fort Lauderdale, FL 33304 Fax: (954)985-4687

Community newspaper. **Founded:** 1964. **Freq:** Semiweekly (Thurs. and Sun.). **Print Method:** Letterpress. **Cols./Page:** 6. **Col. Width:** 26 nonpareils. **Col. Depth:** 315 agate lines. **Key Personnel:** Dorothy Klein, Editor; Fred Benson, Advertising Mgr. **Remarks:** Accepts advertising. **Formerly:** Broward Neighbors.
Circ: Paid ‡42,200

6121 Journal of Child and Adolescent Substance Abuse
The Haworth Press, Inc.
Nova Southeastern University Phone: (954)262-5806
Ctr. for Psychological Studies Fax: (954)262-1592
3301 College Ave.
Fort Lauderdale, FL 33314
Free: (800)342-9678
Publisher E-mail: getinfo@haworthpressinc.com

Journal covering strategies for chemically dependent adolescents and their families. **Founded:** 1993. **Freq:** Quarterly. **Trim Size:** 6x81/2. **Key Personnel:** Frank DePiano, PhD, Editor, phone (954)262-5733; Vincent B. VanHassett, PhD, Editor, phone (954)262-5752; Bill Cohen, Publisher. **ISSN:** 1067-828X. **Subscription Rates:** $36 individuals; $75 institutions; $145 libraries. **Remarks:** Accepts advertising.
Ad Rates: BW: $300 **Circ:** Paid 325

6122 Journal of Developmental and Physical Disabilities
Plenum Publishing Corp.
Nova Southeastern University Phone: (305)476-4773
3301 College Ave.
Fort Lauderdale, FL 33314
Publisher E-mail: info@plenum.com

Professional journal. **Freq:** Quarterly. **Print Method:** Offset. **Key Personnel:** Vincent B. Van Hassett, Editor; Michael Hersen, Advertising Mgr.; Sophia Conyers, Editor. **ISSN:** 1056-263X. **Subscription Rates:** $40 individuals; $140 institutions. **Remarks:** Advertising accepted; rates available upon request. **Formerly:** Journal of the Multihandicapped Person (1992).
Circ: (Not Reported)

6123 Journal of Psychotherapy in Independent Practice
The Haworth Press, Inc.
Center for Psychological Studies Phone: (954)262-5806
Nova Southeast University Fax: (954)202-3093
3301 College Ave.
Fort Lauderdale, FL 33314
Publisher E-mail: getinfo@haworthpressinc.com

Journal for private practice psychotherapists. **Subtitle:** Innovations In Clinical Methods and Assessment, Consultation and Practice Management. **Founded:** 1983. **Freq:** Quarterly. **Key Personnel:** Frank DePiano, Ph.D., Editor; Bill Cohen, Publisher. **ISSN:** 0731-7158. **Subscription Rates:** $45; $145 libraries; $160 industry. **Remarks:** Accepts advertising. **Formerly:** Psychotherapy in Private Practice.
Ad Rates: BW: $300 **Circ:** 399

6124 Journal of Segmentation in Marketing
The Haworth Press, Inc.
Nova Southeastern University Phone: (954)262-5097
School of Business and Entrepreneurship Fax: (954)424-5933
c/o Art Weinstein, Editor
3100 SW 9th Ave.
Fort Lauderdale, FL 33315
Free: (800)672-7223
Publisher E-mail: getinfo@haworthpressinc.com

Professional journal covering marketing. **Subtitle:** Innovations in Market Identification and Targeting. **Founded:** 1997. **Freq:** Semiannual. **Trim Size:** 6 x 8 1/2. **Cols./Page:** 1. **Key Personnel:** Art Weinstein, Ph.D., Editor, art@sbe.nova.edu. **ISSN:** 1091-1340. **Subscription Rates:** $25 individuals; $40 institutions; $65 libraries. **Remarks:** Advertising accepted; rates available upon request.
Circ: (Not Reported)

6125 New River Waterway Times
Waterfront Publishing, Inc.
11 Tommie Terrace Phone: (954)761-1937
Fort Lauderdale, FL 33312 Fax: (954)785-5228

Local magazines covering the waterfront community. **Founded:** 1983. **Freq:** Monthly. **Print Method:** Web offset. **Trim Size:** 8 1/2 x 11. **Cols./Page:** 3. **Col. Width:** 2 3/8 inches. **Col. Depth:** 10 inches. **Key Personnel:** Wanda Zubak, Editor; Terrance L. Willard, Publisher. **Subscription Rates:** $15; $25 two years.
Ad Rates: BW: $808 **Circ:** Paid 1,400
4C: $1,050 Non-paid 18,600
PCI: $30

6126 South Florida Business Journal
American City Business Journals
1050 Lee Wagener Blvd. No. 302 Phone: (305)594-2100
Fax: (305)359-2135
Fort Lauderdale, FL 33315-3500
Newspaper covering business in Miami, Fort Lauderdale, and West Palm Beach. **Founded:** Sept. 15, 1980. **Freq:** Weekly (Fri.). **Print Method:** Web offset. **Trim Size:** 11 x 15. **Cols./Page:** 4. **Col. Width:** 2.58 inches. **Col. Depth:** 14 inches. **Key Personnel:** Gary Press, Publisher, phone (704)359-2121, fax (704)359-2135; Ross Nethery, Editor, phone (704)359-2120; Joel Welker, Advertising Mgr., phone (704)359-2122. **ISSN:** 0746-2271. **Subscription Rates:** $69 individuals 1 year; $105 2 year; $139 3 year.
Ad Rates: GLR: $4 **Circ:** Paid ★8,053
BW: $3,003
4C: $3,603

6127 Sun-Sentinel
Sun-Sentinel Co.
200 E. Las Olas Blvd. Phone: (954)356-4000
Fort Lauderdale, FL 33301-2293 Fax: (954)356-4559

Newspaper. **Founded:** 1960. **Freq:** Mon.-Sun. (morn.). **Print Method:** Offset. **Cols./Page:** 6. **Col. Width:** 25 nonpareils. **Col. Depth:** 297 agate lines. **Key Personnel:** Earl Maucker, Editor, phone (954)356-4600; Ellen Soeteber, Managing Editor, phone (954)356-4602. **Subscription Rates:** $144.42 Broward County; $157.10 Palm Beach County; $136.15 South Broward. **Remarks:** Accepts advertising. **Online:** Dialog (The Dialog Corporation); CompuServe Information Service. **URL:** http://www.sunsentinel.com; http://www.sun-sentinel.com. **Alt. Formats:** CD-ROM, NewsBank, Inc.; CD-ROM, On Newsbank. **Formerly:** Fort Lauderdale News. **Feature Editors:** Gail DeGeorge, *Financial/Business*, phone (954)356-4661, fax (954)356-4680; John Dolen, *Entertainment*, phone (954)356-4701, fax (954)456-4624; Kingsley Guy, *Editorials*, phone (954)356-4616, fax (954)356-4624; Rod Hagwood, *Fashion*, phone (954)356-4721, fax (954)356-4624; Deborah Hartz, *Food*, phone (954)356-4723, fax (954)356-4624; Charlyne Varkonyi, *Garden/Home*, phone (954)356-4729, fax (954)356-4624; Jack Zink, *Drama*, phone (954)356-4706, fax (954)356-4624.
Ad Rates: GLR: $255.85 **Circ:** Mon.-Sat. ★243,950
BW: $32,237.10 Sun. ★353,998
4C: $35,382.10
SAU: $255.85
PCI: $259.99

6128 Voice (Ft. Lauderdale)
Cary-Joy Communications
PO Box 030397
Fort Lauderdale, FL 33303-0397
Publication E-mail: voice.hab.net

Newspaper covering rehabilitation and physical disabilities. **Subtitle:** Medical Rehab Networking Newspaper. **Founded:** 1987. **Freq:** Monthly. **Print Method:** Web. **Cols./Page:** 4. **Col. Width:** 2 1/8 inches. **Col. Depth:** 14 inches. **Key Personnel:** Melanie Glick, Advertising Mgr.; Ray Brasted, Editor. **Subscription Rates:** $25 individuals. **Remarks:** Accepts advertising. **URL:** http://www.voicepaper.com.
Ad Rates: BW: $1,195 **Circ:** (Not Reported)

6129 The Voice Newspaper
The Voice of Florida
PO Box 030397 Phone: (954)463-5556
Fort Lauderdale, FL 33303-0397 Fax: (954)463-2674
Publication E-mail: voicehab@gate.net

Paper for persons with disabilities and referral resources. **Founded:** 1987. **Freq:** Monthly. **Print Method:** Web. **Trim Size:** 10 x 14. **Cols./Page:** 4. **Col. Width:** 2 7/16 inches. **Col. Depth:** 14 inches. **Key Personnel:** Ray Brasted, Editor; Melanie Brasted, Advertising Mgr. **Subscription Rates:** $25 individuals. **Remarks:** Accepts advertising. **Available Online. Formerly:** The Voice.
Ad Rates: BW: $1,195 **Circ:** (Not Reported)

6130 Waterfront News
Ziegler Publishing Co., Inc.
1523 S. Andrews Ave. Phone: (954)524-9450
Fort Lauderdale, FL 33316-2507 Fax: (954)524-9464
Free: (800)226-9464
Publication E-mail: h2onews@aol.com

Community newspaper . **Subtitle:** South Florida's Nautical Newspaper. **Founded:** Mar. 1984. **Freq:** Monthly. **Print Method:** Offset. **Trim Size:** 11 x 17. **Cols./Page:** 3. **Col. Width:** 3 1/3 inches. **Col. Depth:** 16 inches. **Key Personnel:** John Ziegler, Publisher; Jennifer Heit, Editor. **ISSN:** 8756-0038. **Subscription Rates:** $12 by mail. **Remarks:** Accepts advertising. **Available Online. URL:** http://waterfront-news.com.
Ad Rates: GLR: $5 **Circ:** Paid ‡750
BW: $1,000 Free ‡35,000
4C: $1,400
PCI: $30

6131 Westside Gazette
PO Box 5304 Phone: (954)523-5115
Fort Lauderdale, FL 33310 Fax: (954)522-2553
Free: (800)371-6310

Black community newspaper. **Founded:** 1971. **Freq:** Semiweekly (Thurs. and Sun.). **Print Method:** Offset. **Cols./Page:** 6. **Col. Width:** 24 nonpareils. **Col. Depth:** 294 agate lines. **Key Personnel:** Yvonne Henry, Editor; Levi Henry, Jr., Publisher. **Subscription Rates:** $20 individuals. **Remarks:** Accepts advertising.
Ad Rates: GLR: $.75 **Circ:** Paid ‡7,000
SAU: $10.50 Free ‡14,500

6132 Comcast Communications, Inc.
644 S. Andrews Ave. Phone: (954)527-6620
Fort Lauderdale, FL 33301 Fax: (954)523-4247

Founded: 1979. **Formerly:** Selkirk Communications Inc. **Key Personnel:** Mary J. Colletti, General Mgr.; Cindy Stoddart, Dir. of Public & Government Relations; Jo Rudy, Production Mgr., fax (954)764-2182; Nancy Valle Harrington, Ad Sales Mgr., fax (954)227-7716; Mike Rodriguez, Technical Operations Mgr., fax (954)523-4052. **Cities Served:** Aventura, Hallandale, Lauderdale-by-the-Sea, Oakland Park, Sea Ranch Lakes, FL; Broward County: subscribing households 105,000; 81 channels; 1 community access channel; 50 hours per week community access programming.

6133 WEXY-AM - 1520
412 W. Oakland Park Blvd. Phone: (305)561-1520
Fort Lauderdale, FL 33311-1712 Fax: (305)561-9830
Free: (800)648-8063

Format: Religious; Urban Contemporary. **Founded:** 1963. **Operating Hours:** Continuous. **ADI:** Miami (Ft. Lauderdale), FL. **Key Personnel:** Henry Greene, Program Dir.; Doug DeVos, Operations Mgr. **Wattage:** 3500 day; 250 night. **Ad Rates:** $18-34 for 30 seconds; $23-54 for 60 seconds.

6134 WHYI-FM - 100.7
1975 E. Sun Blvd., 4th Fl. Phone: (954)463-9299
Fort Lauderdale, FL 33304 Fax: (954)524-7002

Format: Contemporary Hit Radio (CHR). **Networks:** Independent. **Owner:** Clear Channel Metroplex Communications, PO Box 659512, San Antonio, TX 78265, (210)822-2828. **Founded:** 1960. **Operating Hours:** Continuous. **ADI:** Miami (Ft. Lauderdale), FL. **Key Personnel:** David Ross, General Mgr., driggs@nsu.nova.edu. **Wattage:** 100,000. **Ad Rates:** $100-400 for 60 seconds.

6135 WSRF-AM - 1580
3000 SW 60th Ave. Phone: (305)587-1035
Fort Lauderdale, FL 33314 Fax: (305)581-1301
Free: (305)581-1580

Format: Ethnic. **Networks:** Independent. **Founded:** 1955. **Operating Hours:** 6 a.m.-midnight. **ADI:** Miami (Ft. Lauderdale), FL. **Key Personnel:** Gary Lewis, General Mgr.; Michael Scarlett, Business Mgr.; Tony Bourne, Program Dir. **Wattage:** 10,000 day; 5000 night. **Ad Rates:** $15 for 30 seconds; $25 for 60 seconds.

FORT MEADE, pop. 5,546.

C FL. Polk Co. 50 mi. SE of Tampa. Phosphate mining. Citrus growing and processing. Cattle.

6136 The Fort Meade Leader
Frisbie Publishing
25 W. Broadway Phone: (941)285-8625
PO Box 893 Fax: (941)285-7634
Fort Meade, FL 33841
Free: (941)285-7634
Publication E-mail: polkdemo@aol.com

Local newspaper. **Founded:** 1910. **Freq:** Tuesday and Friday. **Print Method:** Offset. **Trim Size:** 16 x 22 3/4. **Cols./Page:** 7. **Col. Width:** 2 1/8 inches. **Col. Depth:** 21 inches. **Key Personnel:** S.L. Frisbie IV, Publisher, polkdemo@aol.com; Linda Holcomb, Advertising Mgr. **USPS:** 907-620. **Subscription Rates:** $20 individuals in county; $30 out of area; $35 out of state. **Remarks:** Accepts advertising.
Ad Rates: BW: $767.34 **Circ:** ‡1,285
SAU: $5.55

FORT MYERS†, pop. 40,000.

S FL. Lee Co. On Caloosahatchee River, 120 mi. SE of Tampa. Edison Community College. Resort area. Manufactures trailers, boats, surgical and medical supplies, lumber, cigars, electronic equipment. Ships fruit and vegetables.

6137 AFSM International Professional Journal
AFSM International
1342 Colonial Blvd., Ste. 25 Phone: (941)275-7887
Fort Myers, FL 33907-1007 Fax: (941)275-0794
Free: (800)333-9786
Publisher E-mail: afsmi@afsmi.org

Journal for executives, managers, and professionals in the high technology services and support industry. **Founded:** Nov. 1975. **Freq:** Monthly. **Print Method:** Offset. **Trim Size:** 8 x 10 7/8. **Cols./Page:** 2 and 3. **Col. Width:** 19 and 12 picas. **Col. Depth:** 55.5 picas. **Key Personnel:** David Henault, Publisher, dhenault@afsmi.org; Suzanne Tissier, Editor, stissier@afsmi.org; Susan Davidson, Advertising Mgr., sdavidson@afsmi.org. **ISSN:** 1049-2135. **Subscription Rates:** $125 individuals; $12 single issue available to members only.; Available to members only. **Remarks:** Accepts advertising. **URL:** http://www.afsmi.org.
Ad Rates: BW: $2,520 **Circ:** 20,000
4C: $3,320

6138 High Technology Services Management
The Association for Services Management International
1342 Colonial Blvd., Ste. 25 Phone: (941)275-7887
Fort Myers, FL 33907 Fax: (941)275-0794
Free: (800)333-9786
Publisher E-mail: afsmi@afsmi.org

Journal on high technology services. **Founded:** 1976. **Freq:** Monthly. **Print Method:** 8 x 10 7/8. **Key Personnel:** David Henault, Publisher; Suzanne Tissier, Editor; Susan Davidson, Advertising Mgr. **Subscription Rates:** $125 members. **Remarks:** Accepts advertising. **Available Online. URL:** http://www.afsmi.org.
Ad Rates: BW: $2,520 **Circ:** Controlled 22,000
4C: $3,320

6139 SignCraft
Signcraft Publishing Co. Inc.
PO Box 60031 Phone: (941)939-4644
Fort Myers, FL 33906 Fax: (941)939-0607
Free: (800)204-0204
Publisher E-mail: signcraft@signcraft.com

Trade magazine. **Subtitle:** World's No. 1 Sign Magazine. **Founded:** Apr. 1, 1980. **Freq:** Bimonthly. **Print Method:** Web offset. **Trim Size:** 8 1/8 x 10 7/8. **Cols./Page:** 3. **Col. Width:** 28 nonpareils. **Col. Depth:** 140 agate lines. **Key Personnel:** Tom McIltrot, Editor and Publisher; Dennis McIltrot, Publisher; Bill McIltrot, Advertising Mgr. **ISSN:** 0270-4757. **Subscription Rates:** $28 individuals; $5.50 single issue. **Remarks:** Accepts advertising.
Ad Rates: BW: $2,532 **Circ:** Paid ★15,502
4C: $3,382

6140 Jones Intercable
2212 McGregor Blvd. Phone: (941)334-8055
Box 1360 Fax: (941)334-7023
Fort Myers, FL 33902

Owner: Jones Intercable Inc., 9697 E. Mineral Ave., Englewood, CO 80112, (303)792-3111. **Founded:** 1961. **Formerly:** Southern Cablevision (1985). **Key Personnel:** Gary McDonald, General Mgr.; Beverly Wall, Marketing Mgr., phone (941)334-8678, fax (941)334-7954; Gregg Wood, Chief Engineer, phone (941)334-8595, fax (941)334-8575; Paul Gregg, New Media Sales Mgr., phone (441)334-7855, fax (941)334-8575. **Cities Served:** Briarcliff, East Lee County, Fort Myers, Gateway, Iona, South Fort Myers, FL; Lee County: subscribing households 45,000; 61 channels; 1 community access channel; 16 hours per week community access programming.

6141 WARO-FM - 94.5
2824 Palm Beach Blvd. Phone: (941)337-2346
Fort Myers, FL 33916 Fax: (941)332-0767

Format: Classic Rock. **Owner:** Meridian Broadcasting, Inc., at above address. **Operating Hours:** Continuous. **Key Personnel:** Joseph C. Schwartzel, President. **Wattage:** 100,000.

6142 WAYF-FM - 88.1
PO Box 61275 Phone: (941)936-1929
Fort Myers, FL 33906 Free: (888)936-1929
E-mail: wayfm@wayfm.com

Format: Contemporary Christian. **Owner:** WAY-FM Media Group, Inc., at above address. **Founded:** 1987. **Operating Hours:** Continuous. **ADI:** Fort Myers-Naples, FL. **Key Personnel:** Bob Augsburg, President; Todd Stack, Operations Dir.; Kym McCleary, Business Admin.; Pati Sprague, Admin. Asst. **Wattage:** 50,000. **Ad Rates:** Noncommercial. **URL:** http://www.wayfm.com.

6143 WAYJ-FM - 88.7
1860 Boy Scout Dr., Ste. 202 Phone: (941)936-1929
Fort Myers, FL 33907 Fax: (941)936-5433
Free: (888)936-1929
E-mail: wayjradio@aol.com

Format: Religious; Contemporary Christian. **Networks:** USA Radio. **Owner:** WAYJ Radio, at above address. **Founded:** 1987. **Operating Hours:** Continuous; 90% network, 10% local. **ADI:** Fort Myers-Naples, FL. **Key Personnel:** Todd Stack, Station Mgr., waytodd@aol.com; Chad Clemens, Production, waychad@aol.com; Pati Sprague, Office Mgr., waypati@aol.com; Kym McCleary, Business Administration. **Local Programs:** *The New Morning Show* 7:00 am - 9:00 am Monday-Friday, Todd Stack, Mailing contact; *Afternoon Drive* 4:00 pm - 7:0 pm Monday-Friday, Chad Clemens. **Wattage:** 50,000. **Ad Rates:** Noncommercial. **URL:** http://www.wayfm.com.

6144 WBBH-TV - 20
PO Box 7578 Phone: (941)939-2020
Fort Myers, FL 33911 Fax: (941)936-7771
E-mail: nbc-2@water.net

Format: Commercial TV. **Networks:** NBC. **Founded:** 1968. **Operating Hours:** Continuous. **ADI:** Fort Myers-Naples, FL. **Key Personnel:** Steve Pontius, General Mgr. **URL:** water.net.

6145 WCRM-AM - 1350
3448 Canal St. Phone: (941)332-1350
Fort Myers, FL 33916-6513 Fax: (941)332-8890

Format: Gospel; Ethnic. **Networks:** CNN Radio. **Owner:** Jesus Christ is Lord, Inc., at above address. **Founded:** 1964. **Formerly:** WHYS-AM; WWWQ-AM. **Operating Hours:** Continuous. **ADI:** Fort Myers-Naples, FL. **Key Personnel:** Salvador Santana, General Mgr., phone (941)332-1350, fax (941)332-8890. **Local Programs:** *Emmanuel*, Abel Navanjo; *Talk of Town*, Veronica Shoemaker; *Voz de Pentecostez*, Ebenezer Pastor. **Wattage:** 2000. **Ad Rates:** Advertising accepted; rates available upon request.

6146 WDRR-FM - 98.5
7290 College Pkwy., Ste. 100 Phone: (941)275-9377
Fort Myers, FL 33907 Fax: (941)275-0962

Format: Jazz. **Owner:** Ruth Communications Corp., at above address. **Operating Hours:** Continuous. **Key Personnel:** Ruth H. Ray, Pres./General Mgr., ruth@wdrr.com; Todd Johnston, Sales Mgr., toddj@wdrr.com; Bill Bruun, Program Dir., billb@wdrr.com; Gerry Tussey, Traffic Dir. **Ad Rates:** Advertising accepted; rates available upon request. **URL:** http://www.wdrr.com.

6147 WGCU-FM - 90.1
Florida Gulf Coast University Phone: (941)590-2500
10501 FGCU Blvd. S. Fax: (941)590-2511
Fort Myers, FL 33965-6565
Free: (888)314-9090

Format: Jazz; News; Classical; Public Radio. **Networks:** National Public Radio (NPR). **Owner:** Florida Board of Regents, at above address. **Founded:** 1983. **Formerly:** WSFP-AM. **Operating Hours:** Continuous; 34% network, 66% local. **ADI:** Fort Myers-Naples, FL. **Key Personnel:** Barney Bogue, Underwriting Mgr., phone (941)590-2522, bbogue@fgcu.edu; Gene Craven, Station Mgr., phone (941)590-2505, gcraven@fgcu.edu; Valerie Alker, News Dir., phone (941)590-2518, fax (941)590-2520, valker@fgcu.edu; Glenn Sabatka, Radio Reading Service Mgr., phone (941)590-2530, gsabatka@fgcu.edu; Jill Erickson, Dir., Development and Promotions, phone (941)590-2508. **Wattage:** 100,000. **Ad Rates:** Noncommercial; underwriting available.

6148 WGCU-TV - 30
19501 Ben Hill Griffin Pkwy. Phone: (941)598-9737
Fort Myers, FL 33965-6565 Fax: (941)598-2598
Free: (800)522-9737

Format: Public TV. **Networks:** Public Broadcasting Service (PBS). **Owner:** Florida Board of Regents, at above address. **Founded:** 1983. **Formerly:** WSFP-TV (1996). **Operating Hours:** Continuous. (5 days); 95% network, 5% local. **ADI:** Fort Myers-Naples, FL. **Key Personnel:** Toby Ann Cooke, Communications Dir., toby_ cooke@wgcu.pbs.org; Terry Dugas, Program Dir.; Deborah Ward, Contact; Kirk Lehtomaa, Station Mgr.; Sheri Colemand, Production Mgr.; Sharon Striker, Operations Mgr.; Ken St. Hill, Business Mgr. **Local Programs:** *Florida Close to Home*, Cleo Garcia, (941)598-9737; *Florida Gulf Coast University*, Bill Doughty, (941)598-9737. **Ad Rates:** $90 for 15 seconds. **URL:** www.wgcu.org.

6149 WINK-AM - 1240
2824 Palm Beach Rd. Phone: (941)337-2346
Fort Myers, FL 33916-1590 Fax: (941)332-0767

Format: Talk; News. **Networks:** CBS. **Owner:** Fort Myers Broadcasting Co., at above address. **Founded:** 1940. **Operating Hours:** Continuous. **ADI:** Fort Myers-Naples, FL. **Key Personnel:** Joe Schwartzel, General Mgr.; Wayne Simons, Dir. of Sales; Bob Grissinger, Dir. of Programming. **Local Programs:** *Rich King*, Mary Heath. **Wattage:** 1000. **Ad Rates:** Advertising accepted; rates available upon request.

6150 WINK-FM - 96.9
2824 Palm Beach Blvd. Phone: (941)337-2346
Fort Myers, FL 33916-1590 Fax: (941)332-0767

Format: Adult Contemporary. **Owner:** Fort Myers Broadcasting Co., at above address. **Founded:** 1964. **Operating Hours:** Continuous. **ADI:** Fort Myers-Naples, FL. **Key Personnel:** Joe Schwartzel, General Mgr.; Wayne Simons, Dir. of Sales; Bob Grissinger, Dir. of Programming. **Wattage:** 100,000.

6151 WINK-TV - 11
2824 Palm Beach Blvd. Phone: (941)334-1111
Fort Myers, FL 33916 Fax: (941)334-0744

Format: Commercial TV. **Networks:** CBS. **Owner:** Fort Myers Broadcasting Co., at above address. **Founded:** 1954. **Operating Hours:** Continuous. **ADI:** Fort Myers-Naples, FL. **Key Personnel:** Gary Gardner, General Mgr.; Liz Combs, News Dir./Chief Eng.; Mark Gilson, Promotions Mgr.; Tim Briggs, Production Mgr.; Maxine Johnson, Business Mgr. **Local Programs:** *Live at Five*. **Wattage:** 316.

6152 WJBX-FM - 99.3
12995 S. Cleveland Ave., Ste. 258 Phone: (813)275-9980
Fort Myers, FL 33907-7714 Fax: (813)275-5611

Format: Adult Album Alternative. **Networks:** AP. **Owner:** Schefflera, Inc., at above address. **Founded:** 1983. **Formerly:** WCZR-FM (1993). **Operating Hours:** Continuous. **ADI:** Fort Myers-Naples, FL. **Key Personnel:** John Linn, General Mgr.; Bernie Green, General Sales Mgr. **Wattage:** 50,000. **Ad Rates:** $55 per unit.

6153 WJST-FM - 106.3
12995 S. Cleve Ave., No. 258 Phone: (813)275-9980
Fort Myers, FL 33907 Fax: (813)275-5611

Networks: ABC. **Founded:** 1983. **Formerly:** WSUV-FM (1994); WROC-FM. **Operating Hours:** Continuous. **ADI:** Fort Myers-Naples, FL. **Key Personnel:** Joe Bell, General Sales Mgr. **Local Programs:** *Jones Music of Your Life* 10:00 am - 6:00 am Monday-Saturday, Cliff Shell; *Breakfast Club* 6:00 am

- 9:00 am Monday-Friday. **Wattage:** 6,000. **Ad Rates:** $50 for 60 seconds.

6154 WMYR-AM - 1410
2835 Hanson St. Phone: (813)332-2102
Fort Myers, FL 33901 Fax: (813)332-3135

Format: Gospel; Country. **Owner:** Robert Hecksher, at above address. **Founded:** 1952. **Operating Hours:** Continuous. **ADI:** Fort Myers-Naples, FL. **Key Personnel:** K. Hecksher, Sales Mgr.; Simon Train, Program Dir. **Local Programs:** *Indy 500 Race Network*; *Live coverage: High School Football & Basketball*. **Wattage:** 5000. **Ad Rates:** $8.25-10.25 for 15 seconds; $26-35 for 30 seconds; $34-47 for 60 seconds.

6155 WNOG-AM - 1270
2824 Palm Beach Blvd. Phone: (941)337-2346
Fort Myers, FL 33916 Fax: (941)332-0767

Format: Talk; News. **Simulcasts:** WINK-AM. **Networks:** CBS. **Owner:** Meridian Broadcasting, Inc. p, 2824 Palm Blvd., Fort Myers, FL 33916. **Founded:** 1954. **Operating Hours:** Continuous. **ADI:** Fort Myers-Naples, FL. **Key Personnel:** Joe Schwartzel, General Mgr.; Frank Kinsman, News Dir. **Wattage:** 5000.

6156 WPRW-FM - 93.5
2824 Palm Beach Blvd. Phone: (941)337-2346
Fort Myers, FL 33916 Fax: (941)332-0767

Format: Top 40. **Owner:** Meridian Broadcasting, Inc., at above address. **Operating Hours:** Continuous. **Key Personnel:** Joseph Schwartzer, President. **Wattage:** 3,000.

6157 WSOR-FM - 90.9
940 Tarpon St. Phone: (941)334-1393
Fort Myers, FL 33916 Fax: (941)334-0596
E-mail: wsor@moody.edu

Format: Religious. **Networks:** USA Radio. **Owner:** Moody Bible Institute of Chicago, MBI, 820 N. Labelle, Chicago, IL 60610, (312)329-4310, (312)329-8980, Free: (800)DLM-OODY. **Founded:** 1971. **Formerly:** WLSF-FM. **Operating Hours:** Continuous. **ADI:** Fort Myers-Naples, FL. **Key Personnel:** Bill Simon, General Mgr., wsimon@moody.edu; Ron Maxwell, Contact. **Wattage:** 36,000. **Ad Rates:** Noncommercial.

6158 WTLQ-AM - 1200
2824 Palm Beach Blvd. Phone: (941)337-2346
Fort Myers, FL 33916 Fax: (941)332-0767

Format: Talk. **Owner:** Fort Meyers Broadcasting Co., at above address. **Operating Hours:** Continuous. **ADI:** Fort Myers-Naples, FL. **Wattage:** 10,000.

6159 WWGR-FM - 101.9
4210 Metro Pkwy., No. 210 Phone: (941)936-2599
Fort Myers, FL 33916 Fax: (941)936-0977

Format: Country. **Networks:** Independent. **Owner:** Renda Broadcasting Corp., at above address. **Founded:** 1969. **Formerly:** WHEW-FM. **Operating Hours:** Continuous. **ADI:** Fort Myers-Naples, FL. **Wattage:** 100,000. **Ad Rates:** $8.25-10.50 for 15 seconds; $26-35 for 30 seconds; $34-47 for 60 seconds.

6160 WZVN-TV - 26
PO Box 7087 Phone: (941)939-2020
Fort Myers, FL 33911-7087 Fax: (941)939-4801
E-mail: kunk@water.net

Format: Commercial TV. **Networks:** ABC. **Owner:** Montclair Communications, 4001 N. Tamiami Trail, North Ste. 370, Naples, FL 34103, (941)939-6236, Fax: (941)939-4801. **Formerly:** WEVU-TV (1995). **Operating Hours:** Continuous. **ADI:** Fort Myers-Naples, FL. **Key Personnel:** Lara Kunkler, General Mgr., phone (941)939-6236, fax (941)939-4801, kunk@water.net; Dvid McKelvey, Chief Engineer, phone (941)643-3400; David McKelvey, Chief Engineer. **URL:** http://www.abc-7.com.

FORT MYERS BEACH

6161 Fort Myers Beach Bulletin
Breeze Publishing Co.
19260 San Carlos Blvd. Phone: (941)463-4421
Fort Myers Beach, FL 33931 Fax: (941)463-1402
Publisher E-mail: bchbulletin@aol.com

Arts and entertainment. **Founded:** Dec. 1951. **Freq:** Weekly (Fri.). **Print Method:** Offset. **Trim Size:** 10 3/8 x 16. **Cols./Page:** 6. **Col. Width:** 1 5/8 inches. **Col. Depth:** 16 inches. **Key Personnel:** Julia Campbell, Editor; Morgan Newcomb, General Mgr. **Subscription Rates:** Free; $9 by mail; $30 out of area; $38 Canada. **Remarks:** Accepts advertising.
Ad Rates: GLR: $.33 **Circ:** Paid ‡16,000
BW: $331.20 Free ‡14,500
4C: $531.20
PCI: $4.25

FORT PIERCE

6162 The Tribune
Freedom Communications Inc.
600 Edwards Rd. Phone: (561)461-2050
PO Box 69 Fax: (561)461-4447
Fort Pierce, FL 34954
Free: (800)444-TRIB

General newspaper. **Founded:** 1903. **Freq:** Mon.-Sun. (morn.). **Print Method:** Offset. **Trim Size:** 13 3/4 x 22 3/4. **Cols./Page:** 6. **Col. Width:** 25 nonpareils. **Col. Depth:** 301 agate lines. **Key Personnel:** Harold Muddiman, Editor, harold_muddiman@link.freedom.com; Maureen Saltzer Gawel, Publisher, maureen_saltzer@link.freedom.com. **Subscription Rates:** $85.80 individuals. **Remarks:** Accepts advertising. Monday-Saturday: BW: $2,031.75; 4C: $2,486.75; SAU: $15.75; Sunday: SAU: $16.97. **Formerly:** News Tribune.
Circ: Mon.-Sat. 28,681
Sun. 31,128

6163 WAVW-FM - 101.7
PO Box 39 Phone: (561)567-1055
Fort Pierce, FL 34954 Fax: (561)595-0214

Format: Country. **Networks:** ABC. **Founded:** 1973. **Operating Hours:** Continuous. **ADI:** West Palm Beach-Ft. Pierce-Vero Beach, FL. **Key Personnel:** Charlie DiToro, General Mgr.; Jeanette W. Pagano, Sales Mgr.; Lynn Wasson, Office Mgr. **Wattage:** 6000. **Ad Rates:** $40 for 30 seconds; $45 for 60 seconds.

6164 WQCS-FM - 88.9
3209 Virginia Ave. Phone: (407)468-4744
Fort Pierce, FL 34981 Fax: (407)462-4743

Format: Public Radio; Classical. **Networks:** National Public Radio (NPR); AP; American Public Radio (APR). **Owner:** Indian River Community College, at above address. **Founded:** 1982. **ADI:** West Palm Beach-Ft. Pierce-Vero Beach, FL. **Key Personnel:** Jim Holmes, Station Mgr.; George Dyer, Music Dir. **Wattage:** 100,000. **Ad Rates:** Noncommercial.

FORT WALTON BEACH

6165 Emerald Coast Living
Foxdale Publications
PO Box 336 Phone: (850)243-9011
Fort Walton Beach, FL 32549 Fax: (850)243-4390

Magazine (tabloid) featuring real estate and tourism news. **Founded:** Sept. 1984. **Freq:** Monthly. **Print Method:** Offset. **Trim Size:** 10 1/4 x 16. **Cols./Page:** 7. **Col. Width:** 1.25 picas. **Col. Depth:** 16 inches. **Key Personnel:** Garry Fox, Editor; Garfield L. Fox, Publisher. **Remarks:** Accepts advertising.
Ad Rates: BW: $448 **Circ:** Controlled ‡25,000
4C: $828
PCI: $4.50

6166 Northwest Florida Daily News
Freedom Communications Inc.
200 Racetrack Rd. NW Phone: (904)863-1111
Fort Walton Beach, FL 32548 Fax: (904)862-5230
Free: (800)755-1185

Local newspaper. **Founded:** Feb. 1946. **Freq:** Mon.-Sun. (morn.). **Print Method:** Offset. **Trim Size:** 13 3/4 x 23. **Cols./Page:** 6. **Col. Width:** 25 nonpareils. **Col. Depth:** 301 agate lines. **Key Personnel:** Tom Conner, Editor; Marvin DeBolt, Publisher; Sam Childs, Advertising Dir. **ISSN:** 0898-168X. **Subscription Rates:** $96 individuals; $145 out of area. **Remarks:** Accepts advertising.
Ad Rates: GLR: $3.02 **Circ:** Mon.-Sat. 39,195
BW: $1,244.85 Sun. 51,226
4C: $1,664.85
PCI: $15.85

6167 N.W. Florida Business Journal
Foxdale Publications
PO Box 336 Phone: (850)243-9011
Fort Walton Beach, FL 32549 Fax: (850)243-4390

Journal with business editorials directed toward owners and CEOs. **Founded:** Jan. 28, 1988. **Freq:** Monthly. **Print Method:** Offset. **Trim Size:** 10 1/4 x 13. **Cols./Page:** 7. **Col. Width:** 1 1/4 inches. **Col. Depth:** 13 inches. **Key Personnel:** Garfield L. Fox, Publisher. **Remarks:** Accepts advertising. **Formerly:** Nutty Rosie's Coupon Savers.
Ad Rates: BW: $819 **Circ:** Paid ‡12,000
4C: $1,394
PCI: $4.46

6168 Okaloosa County Reporter
Foxdale Publications
PO Box 336 Phone: (850)243-9011
Fort Walton Beach, FL 32549 Fax: (850)243-4390

Community newspaper. **Founded:** Aug. 20, 1967. **Freq:** Weekly. **Print Method:** Offset. **Key Personnel:** Garry Fox, Editor; Garfield Fox, Publisher. **Subscription Rates:** $20. individuals; $60. out of area; $120. other countries. **Remarks:** Accepts advertising. **Formerly:** Okaloosa County TV-News Shopper.
Ad Rates: BW: $600 **Circ:** Combined ‡15,000
4C: $1,000
PCI: $5

6169 Emerald Coast Cable Television
784 N. Beal Pkwy. Phone: (904)862-4142
Drawer 2827 Fax: (904)862-1708
Fort Walton Beach, FL 32549

Founded: 1963. **Key Personnel:** Michelle Oswalt, Contact. **Cities Served:** subscribing households 58,300; 45 channels; 1 community access channel; 10 hours per week community access programming.

6170 WFGX-TV - 35
105 Beach Dr., Ste. B1 Phone: (904)863-3235
Fort Walton Beach, FL 32547 Fax: (904)862-7659
E-mail: wfgx@emeraldcoast.com

Format: Commercial TV. **Networks:** Warner Brothers Studios. **Operating Hours:** 6 a.m.-3 a.m. **ADI:** Mobile, AL-Pensacola, FL. **Key Personnel:** Carl Leahy, General Mgr.; John Merrill, Sales Mgr.

6171 WFTW-AM - 1260
PO Box 2347 Phone: (904)243-7676
Fort Walton Beach, FL 32549-2347 Fax: (904)664-0203
E-mail: wftw@radiopeople.net

Format: News; Talk; Information. **Networks:** Unistar; Talknet. **Founded:** 1953. **Operating Hours:** Continuous. **ADI:** Mobile, AL-Pensacola, FL. **Key Personnel:** Georgia Edmiston, General Mgr., ga@radiopeople.net. **Wattage:** 2500. **URL:** http://www.wftw.com.

6172 WKSM-FM - 99.5
225 N.W. Hollywood Blvd. Phone: (904)243-7676
PO Box 2347 Fax: (904)664-0203
Fort Walton Beach, FL 32549-2347
E-mail: wksm@radiopeople.net

Format: Album-Oriented Rock (AOR). **Owner:** Holladay Broadcasting, at above address. **Founded:** 1965. **Formerly:** WFTW-FM (1988). **Operating Hours:** Continuous. **ADI:** Mobile, AL-Pensacola, FL. **Key Personnel:** Georgia Edmiston, General Mgr. **Wattage:** 50,000. **URL:** http://www.wksm.com.

6173 WMMK-FM - 92.1
21 Miracle Strip Pkwy. Phone: (850)244-1400
Fort Walton Beach, FL 32548 Fax: (850)243-1471

Format: Oldies. **Owner:** Emerald Coast Radio Corp., at above address, (904)664-2400, Fax: (904)664-2552. **Founded:** 1981. **Operating Hours:** Continuous; 100% local. **Key Personnel:** Ron Hale, Sr., General Mgr.; Dean Crumly, Program Dir.; Skip Davis, Music Dir. **Wattage:** 25,000. **Ad Rates:** $19-39 per unit.

6174 WPSM-FM - 91.1
13 Kelly Ave. Phone: (904)244-7667
Fort Walton Beach, FL 32548 Fax: (904)244-3254
E-mail: mtgflorida@aol.com

Format: Contemporary Christian. **Founded:** 1985. **Operating Hours:** Continuous; 2% network, 98% local. **Key Personnel:** L.M. Thorne, President; Terry Thorne, Manager; Mark Giles, Music Dir./Prog. Dir. **Wattage:** 5000. **Ad Rates:** Noncommercial. **URL:** http://www.wpsm.com.

FROSTPROOF

6175 Frostproof News
Sunshine Printing
19 S. Scenic Hwy. Phone: (941)635-2171
PO Box 67 Fax: (941)635-4265
Frostproof, FL 33843
Local newspaper. **Founded:** 1914. **Freq:** Weekly (Thurs.). **Print Method:** Offset. **Cols./Page:** 6. **Col. Width:** 12 picas. **Col. Depth:** 21.5 inches. **Key Personnel:** Brooke Vantlook,

Editor. **USPS:** 211-260. **Subscription Rates:** $15.90 individuals; $21.20 out of area; $7.95 individuals for 6 months; $10.60 out of area for 6 months. **Remarks:** Accepts advertising.
Ad Rates: BW: $285.00 **Circ:** ‡2,000
PCI: $6.19

FRUITLAND PARK

6176 Sumter Shopper
Mid-Florida Publications, Inc.
407 Hwy. 27-441 Phone: (352)748-2424
Fruitland Park, FL 34731
Shopper. **Founded:** 1966. **Freq:** Weekly. **Cols./Page:** 6. **Col. Width:** 10 inches. **Col. Depth:** 16 1/2 inches. **Subscription Rates:** Free. **Remarks:** Accepts advertising.
Ad Rates: 4C: $100 **Circ:** Free ‡13,044

GAINESVILLE†, pop. 81,371.

N FL. Alachua Co. 72 mi. SW of Jacksonville. University of Florida; Sante Fe Community College. Manufactures electronics, sporting goods, sailboats, heavy equipment. Corn, soybeans, sunflower seeds.

6177 Art Reference Services Quarterly
The Haworth Press, Inc.
University of Florida Phone: (904)392-0222
201 Fine Arts Bldg. A
Gainesville, FL 32611
Publisher E-mail: getinfo@haworthpressinc.com

Covers art and architectural library references. **Founded:** 1992. **Freq:** Quarterly. **Trim Size:** 6x8 1/2. **Cols./Page:** 1. **Key Personnel:** Edward H. Teague, Editor; Bill Cohen, Publisher. **ISSN:** 1050-2548. **Subscription Rates:** $38 individuals; $75 institutions; $75 libraries. **Alt. Formats:** Microfiche; Microfilm.
Ad Rates: BW: $300 **Circ:** 321

6178 Business & Professional Ethics Journal
Center for Applied Philosophy Phone: (352)392-2084
Box 118545 Fax: (352)392-5577
Univ. Of Florida
Gainesville, FL 32611
Interdisciplinary journal on ethics in business and the professions. **Founded:** 1981. **Freq:** Quarterly. **Trim Size:** 6 x 9. **Cols./Page:** 1. **Col. Width:** 4 inches. **Col. Depth:** 7 inches. **Key Personnel:** Robert J. Baum, Editor, phone (352)392-2084, ext. 332, rbaum@phil.ufl.edu. **ISSN:** 0277-2027. **Subscription Rates:** $30 individuals; $90 institutions and corporations. **Remarks:** Accepts advertising.
Ad Rates: BW: $200 **Circ:** 750

6179 Buyers' Guide
Buyers Guide
239 W. University Ave., Ste. C Phone: (904)372-5468
PO Box 1081 Fax: (904)373-9178
Gainesville, FL 32602
Free: (800)372-5468

Shopping guide. **Founded:** 1971. **Freq:** Weekly (Wed.). **Print Method:** Offset. **Cols./Page:** 4. **Col. Width:** 14 picas. **Col. Depth:** 13 inches. **Key Personnel:** Suzanne Olson, General Mgr. **Remarks:** Accepts advertising.
Ad Rates: GLR: $2.50 **Circ:** Free ‡40,000
BW: $525
4C: $625

6180 Contributions on Entomology International
Associated Publishers
PO Box 140103 Phone: (352)371-4071
Gainesville, FL 32614-0103 Fax: (352)371-4071
Publisher E-mail: assopubl@yahoo.com

Professional journal covering insects worldwide. **Founded:** 1995. **Freq:** Irregular Published in parts and mailed as published. **Print Method:** Offset. **Trim Size:** 7 x 10. **Cols./Page:** 1. **Col. Width:** 5 2/10 inches. **Col. Depth:** 8 inches. **Key Personnel:** V. K. Gupta, Editor and Publisher, vkgupta@yahoo.com. **ISSN:** 1084-0745. **Subscription Rates:** $60 individuals and Libraries. **Remarks:** Advertising not accepted.
Circ: (Not Reported)

6181 Counterpoise
Alternatives in Print Task Force of the Social Responsibilities Round Table
1716 SW Williston Rd. Phone: (352)335-2200
Gainesville, FL 32608
Publication E-mail: willett@afn.org

Journal reviewing alternative publications which "develop a sense of human rights and liberties, or oppose authoritarian values, or promote social responsibility." Strives to review works which other review journals have not included. **Subtitle:** For Social Responsibilities, Liberty and Dissent. **Founded:** Jan. 1997. **Freq:** Quarterly. **Trim Size:** 8 1/2 x 11. **Key Personnel:** Charles Willett, Editor, willett@gnv.fdt.net. **ISSN:** 1092-0714. **Subscription Rates:** $35 institutions; $25 individuals; $15 students and retired people. **Remarks:** Accepts advertising.
Ad Rates: BW: $275 **Circ:** (Not Reported)

6182 Delos
University of Florida
2346 NPB 118440 Phone: (352)377-1560
Gainesville, FL 32611 Fax: (352)392-0524

Literary journal. **Subtitle:** A Journal of Translation and International Literature. **Founded:** 1988. **Freq:** Semiannual. **Print Method:** Offset. **Trim Size:** 6 x 9 1/4. **Cols./Page:** 1. **Key Personnel:** Harold P. Hanson, Editor, hanson@.phys.ufl.edu. **ISSN:** 0011-7951. **Subscription Rates:** $15; $10 students; $20 Industry; $25 two years; $35 Industry two years. **Remarks:** Advertising not accepted.
Circ: Paid 400
Controlled 25

6183 Florida Environments
Florida Environments Publishing, Inc.
4010-F Newberry Rd. Phone: (352)373-1401
Gainesville, FL 32607 Fax: (352)373-1405
Publisher E-mail: info@enviroworld.com

Monthly environmental newsmagazine. **Subtitle:** Florida's 1 Environmental News Source. **Founded:** 1987. **Freq:** Monthly. **Print Method:** Web offset. **Trim Size:** 11 3/8 x 17. **Cols./Page:** 4. **Col. Width:** 2 1/3 inches. **Col. Depth:** 15 1/2 inches. **Key Personnel:** David Newport, Editor and Publisher, phone (904)373-1401, fax (904)373-1405. **ISSN:** 0894-9743. **Subscription Rates:** $18.95. **Remarks:** Accepts advertising. **URL:** http://www.enviroworld.com.
Ad Rates: GLR: $1.50 **Circ:** Paid ⊕**11,271**
BW: $1,172 Free 3,000
4C: $1,910
PCI: $72

6184 Florida International Law Journal
University of Florida
141 Bruton Geer Phone: (352)392-4980
Gainesville, FL 32611-7635 Fax: (352)392-9641
Publisher E-mail: fjil@law.ufl.edu

Scholarly journal covering law. **Founded:** 1986. **Freq:** Irregular. **Key Personnel:** Azim Sajn, Editor; Ava Delorenzo, Staff Sec. **ISSN:** 0882-6420. **Subscription Rates:** $25 individuals. **Remarks:** Advertising not accepted. **Online:** LEXIS-NEXIS; Westlaw.
Circ: Combined 285

6185 Florida Leader for High School Students
Oxendine Publishing, Inc.
PO Box 14081 Phone: (352)373-6907
Gainesville, FL 32604-2081 Fax: (352)373-8120
Publication E-mail: 75143.2043@compuserve.com

Magazine for college campus leaders at 343 public high schools in Florida. **Founded:** 1991. **Freq:** Quarterly. **Print Method:** Offset. **Trim Size:** 8 1/2 x 11. **Cols./Page:** 3. **Col. Width:** 13 1/2 picas. **Col. Depth:** 60 picas. **Key Personnel:** W.H. Oxendine, Jr., Publisher; Kay Quinn, Managing Editor; Teresa L. Beard, Asst. Ed.; Jeffrey Riemersa, Art Dir. **Subscription Rates:** $20. $3.50 single issue. **Remarks:** Accepts advertising. **Available Online.**
Ad Rates: BW: $4,900 **Circ:** 100
4C: $4,900 Paid 25,000

6186 Florida Leader Magazine
Oxendine Publishing, Inc.
PO Box 14081 Phone: (352)373-6907
Gainesville, FL 32604-2081 Fax: (352)373-8120
Publication E-mail: 75143.2043@compuserve.com

Publication distributed at 74 institutions of higher education and at 343 high schools. **Subtitle:** Florida's College Magazine. **Founded:** Aug. 1983. **Freq:** 6/year (Aug., Sept., Jan. - April). **Print Method:** Web offset. **Trim Size:** 8 3/8 x 10 7/8. **Cols./Page:** 3. **Col. Width:** 28 nonpareils. **Col. Depth:** 140 agate lines. **Key Personnel:** W.H. "Butch" Oxendine, Jr., Editor and Publisher; Kay Quinn, Managing Editor; Teresa L. Beard, Asst. Ed.; Jeffrey Riemersa, Art Dir. **ISSN:** 0898-4387. **Subscription Rates:** $20 Free to qualified subscribers; $4.50 single issue. **Remarks:** Accepts advertising. **Online:** CompuServe.
Ad Rates: BW: $3,484 **Circ:** Controlled ‡25,000
4C: $3,484

6187 Florida Water Resources Journal
5200 NW 43rd St. No. 102-301 Phone: (352)374-4946
Gainesville, FL 32606
Water, wastewater, and environmental magazine. **Founded:** 1949. **Freq:** Monthly. **Print Method:** Letterpress and offset. Uses mats. **Trim Size:** 8 1/4 x 11. **Cols./Page:** 3. **Col. Width:** 26 nonpareils. **Col. Depth:** 140 agate lines. **Key Personnel:** John D. Crane, Editor, jcrane@concentric.net. **ISSN:** 0896-1794. **Subscription Rates:** $24 individuals. **Remarks:** Accepts advertising.
Ad Rates: BW: $600 **Circ:** ‡8,300
4C: $1,290
PCI: $50

6188 FloridAgriculture
Florida Farm Bureau Federation
PO Box 147030 Phone: (352)374-1523
Gainesville, FL 32614-7030 Fax: (352)374-1530

Newspaper for members of the Florida Farm Bureau Federation. **Founded:** 1943. **Freq:** Monthly. **Print Method:** Offset. **Trim Size:** 11 3/8 x 13 3/4. **Cols./Page:** 4. **Col. Width:** 28 nonpareils. **Col. Depth:** 182 agate lines. **Key Personnel:** Mary Ward, Editor, phone (352)374-1521; G.B. Crawford, Asst. Editor, phone (352)374-1517; Judy Plock, phone (904)374-1521; Mary Griffis, Advertising Mgr.; Tom Lampert, Advertising Representative. **ISSN:** 0015-3869. **Remarks:** Accepts advertising.
Ad Rates: BW: $1,950 **Circ:** Paid ‡92,000
4C: $2,580 Free ‡1,500
PCI: $50

6189 The Gainesville Iguana
PO Box 14712
Gainesville, FL 32604

Journal focused on feminist, anti-racist, labor, and progressive local news. **Founded:** Oct. 1986. **Freq:** Monthly. **Print Method:** Web offset. **Trim Size:** 8 3/8 x 10 7/8. **Cols./Page:** 3. **Col. Width:** 2 1/4 inches. **Col. Depth:** 9 1/8 inches. **Key Personnel:** Joe Courter, Editor; Jenny Brown, Advertising Mgr.; Pete Self, Editor. **Subscription Rates:** Free; $10 (mail). **Remarks:** Accepts advertising.
Ad Rates: BW: $80 **Circ:** Paid 700
PCI: $5 Non-paid 3,000

6190 The Gainesville Sun
PO Box 147147
Gainesville, FL 32614

General newspaper. **Founded:** 1876. **Freq:** Mon.-Sun. (morn.). **Print Method:** Offset. **Trim Size:** 13 3/4 x 22. **Cols./Page:** 6. **Col. Width:** 2 1/16 inches. **Col. Depth:** 21 inches. **Key Personnel:** John W. Fitzwater, Exec. Editor; Jim Osteen, Exec. Editor; Curt Pierson, Advertising Mgr.; Buddy Collings, High School Sports Editor. **ISSN:** 0163-4925. **Subscription Rates:** $182 individuals. **Remarks:** Accepts advertising. **URL:** http://www.sunone.com. **Feature Editors:** Pete Aldrich, *Sports*; Diane Chun, *Features*, phone (904)374-5041; Ron Cunningham, *Editorials*, phone (904)374-5075; Tim Davis, *Photo*, phone (904)374-5029; Lillian Guevara-Castro, *Financial/Business*, phone (904)374-5039; Darrell Hartman, *Metro*, phone (904)374-5085; Bill Lever, *News*, phone (904)374-5056; Jacki Levine, *Features*, phone (904)374-5000; Noel Nash, *Sports*, phone (904)374-5066; Mitch Stacy, *Metro*, phone (904)374-5085; Jim Trebilcock, *News*.
Ad Rates: GLR: $2.28 **Circ:** Mon.-Sat. ★**51,493**
BW: $300 Sun. ★**59,675**
4C: $540
SAU: $49.63
PCI: $41.24

6191 Holarctic Lepidoptera
Association for Tropical Lepidotera
Box 141210 Phone: (352)372-3505
Gainesville, FL 32614-1210 Fax: (352)373-3249

Scientific journal covering Lepidoptera of North American and Eurasia. **Founded:** 1994. **Freq:** Semiannual. **Trim Size:** 8 x 11. **Cols./Page:** 2. **Col. Width:** 3 5/8 inches. **Col. Depth:** 9 inches. **Key Personnel:** Dr. J. B. Heppner, Editor/Executive Dir. **ISSN:** 1070-4140. **Subscription Rates:** $45 individuals. **Remarks:** Advertising not accepted. **URL:** http://www.troplep.org.
Circ: Combined 425

6192 The Human Quest
4300 N.W. 23rd Ave. Phone: (813)894-0097
PO Box 203
Gainesville, FL 32614-7050
Publisher E-mail: chasmagg@aol.com

Journal. **Subtitle:** A Humanist Approach to Religion, Ethics and Education. **Founded:** 1804. **Freq:** Bimonthly. **Print Method:** Offset. **Trim Size:** 8 1/2 x 10. **Cols./Page:** 3. **Col. Width:** 27 nonpareils. **Col. Depth:** 140 agate lines. **Key Personnel:** Charles S. Gregg, Managing Editor. **ISSN:** 0009-6628. **Subscription Rates:** $18 individuals. **Remarks:** Accepts advertising.
Ad Rates: BW: $180 **Circ:** ‡2,200
PCI: $10

6193 The Independent Florida Alligator
Campus Communications, Inc.
PO Box 14257 Phone: (352)376-4446
Gainesville, FL 32604-2257 Fax: (352)376-4556
Publication E-mail: advert@atlantic.net

Collegiate newspaper. **Founded:** Oct. 1906. **Freq:** Daily (morn.). **Print Method:** Offset. **Trim Size:** 11 x 14. **Cols./Page:** 5. **Col. Width:** 2 1/16 inches. **Col. Depth:** 13 inches. **Key Personnel:** C.E. Barber, Contact; Patricia Carey, Contact. **ISSN:** 0015-3877. **Subscription Rates:** Free; $35 (U.S. mail). **Remarks:** Accepts advertising. **Available Online. URL:** http://www.alligator.org.
Ad Rates: GLR: $1.71 **Circ:** Paid ‡93
BW: $1,560 Free ‡31,907
4C: $1,910
SAU: $24
PCI: $24

6194 Jazziz
Jazziz Magazine, Inc.
3620 NW 43rd St. Phone: (352)375-3705
Gainesville, FL 32606 Fax: (352)375-7268
Publication E-mail: jazziz@sprintmail.com
Publisher E-mail: mail@jazziz.com

Music magazine focusing on all aspects of improvisational and instrumental music for sophisticated listeners. Comes monthly with audio and multimedia CD featuring new, classic and exclusive music. **Subtitle:** Art for your ears. **Founded:** Dec. 1983. **Freq:** Monthly. **Print Method:** Offset. **Trim Size:** 8 1/2 x 10 1/2. **Cols./Page:** 3. **Col. Width:** 2 1/8 inches. **Col. Depth:** 9 1/4 inches. **Key Personnel:** Larry Blumenfeld, Editor-in-Chief, lblu@aol.com; Michael Fagien, Publisher, mfagien@jazziz.com; Lori Fagien, Publisher, lfagien@jazziz.com. **ISSN:** 0074-5885. **Subscription Rates:** $69.95 individuals; $99.95 other countries; $5 single issue with no CD; $79.95 Canada and Mexico. **Remarks:** Accepts advertising. **Available Online. URL:** http://www.jazziz.com. **Alt. Formats:** CD-ROM; Mailing labels.
Ad Rates: BW: $3,495 **Circ:** Paid ‡150,000
4C: $4,875 Non-paid ‡65,000

6195 Journal of Aging Studies
Elseiver
University of Florida
P.O. Box 117330
Gainesville, FL 32611-7330
Publication E-mail: 102062-2525@compuserve.com
Publisher E-mail: fcentres@gpu.stv.ualberta.ca

Journal of aging studies. **Founded:** 1987. **Freq:** Quarterly. **Print Method:** Offset. **Trim Size:** 6 7/8 x 10. **Cols./Page:** 1. **Key Personnel:** Jaber F. Gubrium, Editor, jaber@nervm.nercd.ufl.edu. **ISSN:** 0890-4065. **Subscription Rates:** $180 institutions; $200 institutions, other countries; $220 institutions, other countries airmail; $80 individuals; $100 other countries; $120 other countries airmail; $47.50 single issue; $52.50 single issue other countries; $57.50 single issue other countries airmail. **Remarks:** Accepts advertising.
Ad Rates: BW: $300 **Circ:** (Not Reported)

6196 Journal of the American Society of Nephrology
Lippincott Williams & Wilkins
University of Florida Phone: (352)392-4007
Division of Nephrology Fax: (352)846-0441
PO Box 100224
Gainesville, FL 32610-0224
Journal covering kidney functions and renal diseases. **Subtitle:** Official Journal of the American Society of Nephrology. **Founded:** 1990. **Freq:** Monthly. **Print Method:** Offset. **Trim Size:** 8 1/8 x 10 7/8. **Key Personnel:** C. Craig Tosher, M.D., Editor; Steve Tauber, Advertising Mgr.; Sherry Reed, Rep., phone (410)528-8553, sreed@wwilkins.com. **ISSN:** 1046-6673. **Subscription Rates:** $255 individuals; $330 other countries. **Remarks:** Accepts advertising. **Alt. Formats:** Mailing labels.
Ad Rates: BW: $980 **Circ:** Paid 6,720
4C: $1,995 Non-paid 274

6197 Journal of Clinical Monitoring
Box 100254
Dept. of Anesthesiology
College of Medicine
University of Florida
Gainesville, FL 32610-0254
Publication E-mail: davis@anest.ufl.edu.usa; nynke.coutinho@wkap.nl; astrid.huizer@wkap.nl
Publisher E-mail: loes.wils@wkap.nl

Medical journal for anesthesiologists and designers of patient and drug monitoring equipment. **Subtitle:** Official Journal of the Society for Technology in Anesthesia. **Founded:** Jan. 1985. **Freq:** 8/year. **Print Method:** Offset. **Trim Size:** 8 1/8 x 10 7/8. **Cols./Page:** 2. **Col. Width:** 3 3/8 inches. **Col. Depth:** 10 inches. **Key Personnel:** J.S. Gravenstein, Editor, jgravens@anest2.anest.ufl.edu; William V. Ferguson, Advertising Mgr. **ISSN:** 0748-1977. **Subscription Rates:** $107 individuals. **Remarks:** Accepts advertising.
Ad Rates: GLR: $0.65 **Circ:** Paid 1,300
BW: $690
4C: $1640

6198 Journal of College and University Student Housing
Association of College and University Housing Officers-International (ACUHO-I)
c/o Norbert W. Dunkel, Editor Phone: (352)392-2171
University of Florida Fax: (352)392-6819
University Housing
PO Box 112100
Gainesville, FL 32611-2100
Publication E-mail: norbd@neufhou.mail.ufl.edu
Publisher E-mail: osuachuho@postbox.acs.ohio-state.edu

Scholarly journal covering housing research for housing officers. **Founded:** 1980. **Freq:** Semiannual. **Trim Size:** 7 x 9 5/8. **Cols./Page:** 2. **Col. Width:** 2 5/8 inches. **Col. Depth:** 8 3/8 inches. **Key Personnel:** Mary Ellerbrock, Communications Coord. **ISSN:** 0161-827X. **Subscription Rates:** $20 members; $30 nonmembers; $12.50 members single copy; $17 nonmembers single copy. **Remarks:** Advertising not accepted.
Circ: (Not Reported)

6199 Librarians at Liberty
1716 SW Williston Rd. Phone: (352)335-2200
Gainesville, FL 32608
Magazine featuring articles critical of mainstream publishing, bookselling, and librarianship. **Founded:** 1993. **Freq:** Semiannual. **Trim Size:** 8 1/2 x 11. **Cols./Page:** 2. **Col. Width:** 3 inches. **Col. Depth:** 9 inches. **Key Personnel:** Charles Willett, Editor, willett@fdt.net. **ISSN:** 1069-0832. **Subscription Rates:** $10 individuals; $5 single issue.
Ad Rates: BW: $140 **Circ:** (Not Reported)

6200 Oriental Insects
Associated Publishers
PO Box 140103 Phone: (352)371-4071
Gainesville, FL 32614-0103 Fax: (352)371-4071
Publisher E-mail: assopubl@yahoo.com

Professional journal covering insects of the Tropics. **Subtitle:** A Journal of Taxonomy & Zoogeography of Old World. **Founded:** 1967. **Freq:** Annual. **Print Method:** Offset. **Trim Size:** 7 x 11. **Cols./Page:** 1. **Col. Width:** 5 2/10 inches. **Key Personnel:** V. K. Gupta, Publisher, vkgupta@yahoo.com. **ISSN:** 0030-5316. **Subscription Rates:** $60 to Libraries; $40 individuals. **Remarks:** Accepts advertising.
Ad Rates: BW: $100 **Circ:** (Not Reported)

6201 Plant Protection News
Department of Agriculture and Consumer Services
1911 SW 34th St. Phone: (352)372-3505
PO Box 147100 Fax: (352)372-2300
Gainesville, FL 32614-7100
Publication E-mail: mcconm@doacs.state.fl.us
Publisher E-mail: dixonw@doacs.state.fl.us

Government magazine covering division programs and regulations for industry, government, and the general public. **Freq:** Semiannual. **Trim Size:** 6 x 9. **Cols./Page:** 2. **Key Personnel:** Maeve McConnell, Contact. **ISSN:** 0015-4008. **Subscription Rates:** Free. **Remarks:** Advertising not accepted. **Former name:** Plant Industry News.
Circ: Non-paid 14,000

6202 Play Magazine
Milor Entertainment Group
3620 NW 43rd St. Phone: (352)375-3705
Gainesville, FL 32606 Fax: (352)375-7268

Consumer magazine that reviews the latest in music, video, books, multimedia, toy and game technology for children and the family. **Subtitle:** Quality Entertainment for Your Children. **Founded:** Nov. 1992. **Freq:** Bimonthly. **Print Method:** Offset. **Trim Size:** 8 1/2 x 11. **Cols./Page:** 3. **Col. Width:** 2 1/4 inches. **Col. Depth:** 10 inches. **Key Personnel:** Michael Fagien, Editor-in-Chief; Lori Fagien, Publisher. **Subscription Rates:** $12. $3.95 single issue. **Remarks:** Accepts advertising. **Alt. Formats:** CD-ROM; Microform.
Ad Rates: BW: $3,500 **Circ:** 110,000
4C: $4,500

6203 Professional Ethics
University of Florida
Center for Applied Philosophy Phone: (352)392-2084
PO Box 118545 Fax: (352)392-5577
University of Florida
Gainesville, FL 32604
Publication E-mail: applied@philiu.ufl.edu

Interdisciplinary journal on professional ethics. **Subtitle:** A Multidisciplinary Journal. **Founded:** 1992. **Freq:** Quarterly. **Trim Size:** 6 x 9. **Cols./Page:** 1. **Col. Width:** 4 inches. **Col. Depth:** 7 inches. **Key Personnel:** Robert J. Baum, Editor, rbaum@phil.ufl.edu. **ISSN:** 1063-6579. **Subscription Rates:** $30 individuals; $60 institutions. **Remarks:** Accepts advertising. **URL:** http://web.phil.ufl.edu/applied.
Ad Rates: BW: $200 **Circ:** Paid 700

6204 The Record Farm & Ranch
Sante Fe Publishing Co., Inc.
PO Box 806 Phone: (352)377-2444
Gainesville, FL 32602 Fax: (352)338-1986
Publication E-mail: record620@aol.com

Agricultural newspaper and local business edition. **Founded:** 1969. **Freq:** Weekly. **Print Method:** Offset. **Trim Size:** 11 1/2 x 16. **Cols./Page:** 5. **Col. Width:** 11.5 picas. **Col. Depth:** 15 inches. **Key Personnel:** Dick Canaday, Editor; Constance D. Rowe, Publisher. **USPS:** 086-430. **Subscription Rates:** $20 individuals; $24 out of state. **Remarks:** Accepts advertising. **Formerly:** Independent Farmer and Rancher.
Ad Rates: GLR: $.84 **Circ:** ‡5,000
BW: $726.08
4C: $1,026.08
PCI: $9.68

6205 The Record-Local
The Record Farmer and Ranch-Statewide
PO Box 806 Phone: (352)377-2444
620 N. Main St. Fax: (352)338-1986
Gainesville, FL 32602
Publisher E-mail: record620@aol.com

Community and business newspaper. **Founded:** 1989. **Freq:** Weekly. **Print Method:** Offset. **Cols./Page:** 5. **Col. Width:** 1 7/8 inches. **Col. Depth:** 15 inches. **Key Personnel:** Connie Rowe, Publisher; Richard Canaday, Editor. **USPS:** 086-430. **Subscription Rates:** $20 individuals; $24 out of state. **Formerly:** Independent Farmer and Rancher.
Ad Rates: GLR: $.41 **Circ:** ‡5,000
BW: $575.66
4C: $875.66
PCI: $6.96

6206 Relationships Today
Romantic Lifelines
1224 NW 9th Ave.
Gainesville, FL 32601-4942

Magazine teaching people how to improve the quality of their relationships. **Founded:** Apr. 1988. **Freq:** Monthly. **Key Personnel:** Lyle Benjamin, Editor and Publisher. **Subscription Rates:** $24. $2.95 single issue. **Remarks:** Accepts advertising.
Ad Rates: BW: $3,480 **Circ:** 160,000

6207 Republican Liberty
2508 S.W. 35th Place No. 41 Phone: (904)378-1548
Gainesville, FL 32608 Fax: (904)337-9888
Free: (800)RLC-9660
Publication E-mail: afn14454@afn.org; 76025.1244@compuserve.com

Magazine covering the libertarian Republican movement. Contains reviews, satire, letters, and articles. **Founded:** 1990. **Freq:** 6/year. **Trim Size:** 8-1/2 x 11. **Key Personnel:** Mike Holmes, Contact; Phil Blumel, Contact. **Subscription Rates:** $20 individuals; Free for sample copy. **Remarks:** Advertising not accepted.
Circ: Paid 600
Non-paid 100

6208 Tri-ology Technical Report
Department of Agriculture and Consumer Services
1911 SW 34th St. Phone: (352)372-3505
PO Box 147100 Fax: (352)372-2300
Gainesville, FL 32614-7100
Publisher E-mail: dixonw@doacs.state.fl.us

Government, scientific publication covering plant pests and disease. **Founded:** 1961. **Freq:** Bimonthly. **Trim Size:** 8 1/2 x 11. **Key Personnel:** Dr. Nancy Coile, Contact, fax (352)955-2300, coilen@doacs.state.fl.us. **Subscription Rates:** Free. **Remarks:** Advertising not accepted.
Circ: Non-paid 880

6209 Tropical Lepidoptera
Association for Tropical Lepidotera
Box 141210 Phone: (352)372-3505
Gainesville, FL 32614-1210 Fax: (352)373-3249

Scientific journal covering Lepidoptera of worldwide tropical regions and the Southern Hemisphere. **Founded:** 1990. **Freq:** Semiannual. **Trim Size:** 8 x 11. **Cols./Page:** 2. **Col. Width:** 3 5/8 inches. **Col. Depth:** 9 inches. **Key Personnel:** Dr. J. B. Heppner, Editor/Executive Dir., jbhatl@aol.com. **ISSN:** 1048-8138. **Subscription Rates:** $45 individuals. **Remarks:** Advertising not accepted. **URL:** http://www.troplep.org.
Circ: Combined 805

📖 **6210 University of Florida Today Magazine**
University of Florida National Alumni Association
PO Box 113075 Phone: (352)392-0186
Gainesville, FL 32604 Fax: (352)392-3358
Publisher E-mail: ufalumni@uff.ufl.edu

Collegiate magazine for alumni. **Founded:** 1927. **Freq:** Quarterly. **Print Method:** Offset. **Trim Size:** 8 3/8 x 10 7/8. **Cols./Page:** 3. **Col. Width:** 27 nonpareils. **Col. Depth:** 126 agate lines. **Key Personnel:** Wayne McDaniel, Advertising Mgr, phone (352)3921905, fax (352)3928736; John Lester, Editor, phone (352)3920186, fax (352)3920186, jclester@ufl.edu; Liesl O'Dell, Assistant Editor, liesll@ufl.edu. **Remarks:** Accepts advertising.
Ad Rates: BW: $600 **Circ:** Controlled ‡27,000
4C: $800

🎙 **6211 WAJD-AM - 1390**
7120 SW 24th Ave. Phone: (352)331-2200
Gainesville, FL 32607-3705 Fax: (352)331-0401
Free: (800)330-1053
E-mail: kiss1053@aol.com

Format: Alternative/New Music/Progressive. **Networks:** AP. **Owner:** Gillen Broadcasting Corp., at above address. **Founded:** 1961. **Formerly:** WDVH-AM; WMGI-AM. **Operating Hours:** Continuous. **ADI:** Gainesville (Ocala), FL. **Key Personnel:** Doug Gillen, President. **Wattage:** 5000 day; 51 night. **URL:** http://www.kiss1053.

🎙 **6212 WCJB-TV - 20**
6220 NW 43rd St. Phone: (904)377-2020
Gainesville, FL 32606 Fax: (352)373-6516
E-mail: wcjb@wcjb.com

Format: Commercial TV. **Networks:** ABC. **Founded:** Apr. 7, 1971. **Operating Hours:** 6 a.m.-1:30 a.m. weekdays; 6 a.m.-2:30 a.m. Fri. and Sat. **ADI:** Gainesville (Ocala), FL. **Key Personnel:** Carolyn Catlin, General Mgr.; Alan Chatman, General Sales Mgr.; Alan Johns, Production Mgr.; Bob Williams, News Dir. **Wattage:** 2.8 MW. **URL:** http://www.wcjb.com.

🎙 **WFVR-AM** - See Valdosta, Georgia

🎙 **6213 WLUS-AM - 980**
3135 SE 27th St. Phone: (352)372-2528
Gainesville, FL 32601 Fax: (352)372-2520

Format: Middle-of-the-Road (MOR); Talk. **Networks:** ABC; Precision Racing; Meadows Racing. **Owner:** Alliance Broadcasting Co, at above address. **Founded:** 1954. **Formerly:** WDVH-AM. **Operating Hours:** 6 a.m.-10 p.m.; 70% network, 30% local. **ADI:** Gainesville (Ocala), FL. **Key Personnel:** William E. Morris, Contact; Jim Brand, Program Dir. **Local Programs:** *Gene Rockford Show*, Gene Rockford; *Nascar Racing*, Bill Morris; *OJ Show*, Jim Brand. **Wattage:** 5000. **Ad Rates:** $14-19 for 30 seconds; $17-22 for 60 seconds. Combined advertising rates available with WDJY-FM.

🎙 **6214 WRRX-FM - 97.7**
900 NW 8th Ave. Phone: (904)376-1230
Gainesville, FL 32601 Fax: (904)376-2666

Format: Classic Rock. **Networks:** NBC; Florida Radio. **Owner:** Gator Broadcasting Co., at above address. **Founded:** 1984. **Formerly:** WGGG-FM (1991). **Operating Hours:** Continuous. **ADI:** Gainesville (Ocala), FL. **Key Personnel:** John Starr, Contact; Liz Mattox, Sales Mgr. **Wattage:** 6,000. **Ad Rates:** $15-30 per unit.

🎙 **6215 WRUF-AM - 850**
University of Florida Phone: (352)392-0771
3200 Weimer Hall Fax: (352)392-0519
PO Box 14444
Gainesville, FL 32604
E-mail: gm@wruf.com

Format: News; Sports; Talk. **Networks:** CBS; CNN Radio. **Owner:** College of Journalism - University of Florida, at above address. **Founded:** 1928. **Operating Hours:** Continuous; 50% network, 50% local. **ADI:** Gainesville (Ocala), FL. **Key Personnel:** Robert H. Clarke, Contact, bclarke@wruf.com; Tom Krynski, Contact, tkrynsi@wruf.com. **Local Programs:** *850 Live*, Tom Krynski. **Wattage:** 5000. **Ad Rates:** Advertising accepted; rates available upon request. Combined advertising rates available with WRUF-FM. **URL:** http://www.wruf.com.

🎙 **6216 WRUF-FM - 103.7**
University of Florida Phone: (352)392-0771
POB 14444 Fax: (352)392-0519
3200 Weimer Hall
Gainesville, FL 32604
E-mail: gm@wruf.com

Format: Album-Oriented Rock (AOR). **Owner:** University of Florida Board of Regents, at above address. **Founded:** 1948. **Operating Hours:** Continuous; 100% local. **ADI:** Gainesville (Ocala), FL. **Key Personnel:** Robert H. Clarke, Contact, bclarke@wruf.com; Harry Guscott, Station Mgr. **Local Programs:** *Alternative Revolution*, H. Guscott, Mailing contact; *5 O'Clock Rock Block*, H. Guscott, Mailing contact; *Lunchtime Classics*, H. Guscott, Mailing contact. **Wattage:** 100,000. **Ad Rates:** Combined advertising rates available with WRUF-AM. **URL:** http://www.rock104.com.

🎙 **6217 WUFT-FM - 89.1**
University of Florida, Gainesville Phone: (352)392-5200
2206 Weimer Hall Fax: (352)392-5741
Gainesville, FL 32611

Format: Public Radio; Classical; News; Jazz. **Networks:** National Public Radio (NPR); American Public Radio (APR). **Owner:** University of Florida Board of Regents, at above address. **Founded:** 1981. **Operating Hours:** Continuous; 40% network, 60% local. **ADI:** Gainesville (Ocala), FL. **Key Personnel:** Steve Seipp, Operations Mgr., sseipp@jou.fl.edu; William A. Beckett, Program Dir., bbeckett@jou.ufl.edu; Kevin Allen, News Dir., kallen@jou.ufl.edu; Manis Samons, Chief Engineer, msamons@jou.ufl.edu; Henri Pensis, Station Mgr., hpensis@jou.ufl.edu; Rick Lehner, General Mgr., lehnerr@nervm.nerdc.ufl.edu. **Local Programs:** *Conner Calling*, Hank Conner, Mailing contact; *Florida First*, Kevin Allen, Mailing contact; *Sikorski's Attic*, John Sikorski, Mailing contact. **Wattage:** 100,000. **Ad Rates:** Noncommercial.

🎙 **6218 WUFT-TV - 5**
University of Florida Phone: (904)392-5551
1200 Weimer Hall Fax: (904)392-5731
Gainesville, FL 32611
E-mail: gm@wuft.org

Format: Public TV. **Networks:** Public Broadcasting Service (PBS). **Owner:** University of FL, at above address. **Founded:** 1958. **Operating Hours:** 6 a.m.-midnight; 95% network and acquired, 5% local. **ADI:** Gainesville (Ocala), FL. **Key Personnel:** Richard A. Lehner, General Mgr.; Lyn Ganz, Station Mgr.; Vickie Villies, Program Mgr. **Wattage:** 100,000.

🎙 **6219 WYKS-FM - 105.3**
7120 SW 24th Ave. Phone: (352)331-2200
Gainesville, FL 32607 Fax: (352)331-0401
Free: (800)330-1053
E-mail: kiss1053@aol.com

Format: Contemporary Hit Radio (CHR). **Networks:** AP. **Founded:** 1970. **Operating Hours:** Continuous. **ADI:** Gainesville (Ocala), FL. **Key Personnel:** Rondre Adams, Production Mgr.; Jeri Banta, Program Dir.; Doug Gillen, President; Laura Banta, Business Mgr.; Nick Vance, APD. **Local Programs:** *The Perimeter* 8 p.m. - midnight Sunday, Drew Hawkins, Mailing contact, (352)331-2200, Fax (352)331-0401. **Wattage:** 6000. **Ad Rates:** $15-40 for 30 seconds. **URL:** http://www.kiss1053.

GENEVA

📖 **6220 Higher & Higher**
PO Box 829 Phone: (407)349-BLUE
Geneva, FL 32732 Fax: (407)349-5236
Publication E-mail: hhemail@aol.com
Publisher E-mail: hhemail@aol.com

Magazine for fans of the music group The Moody Blues. **Subtitle:** The Moody Blues Magazine. **Founded:** 1983. **Freq:** 3/year. **Trim Size:** 8 1/2 x 11. **Key Personnel:** Mark Murley, Editor and Publisher; Randy Salas, Editor. **Subscription Rates:** $30. **Remarks:** Accepts advertising. **URL:** http://www.moodies-magazine.com.
Ad Rates: BW: $350 **Circ:** Combined 3,500
4C: $550

GRACEVILLE, pop. 2,918.

NW FL. Jackson Co. 20 mi. S. of Dothan, AL. Lumber mills, cotton ginning. Agriculture. Cotton, watermelons, peanuts.

📖 **6221 The Graceville News**
PO Box 187 Phone: (904)263-6015
Graceville, FL 32440 Fax: (904)263-1042
Publisher E-mail: grnews@wfeca.net

Community newspaper. **Founded:** 1903. **Freq:** Weekly (Thurs.). **Print Method:** Offset. **Cols./Page:** 6. **Col. Width:** 24 nonpareils. **Col. Depth:** 126 agate lines. **Key Personnel:** Ferrin Cox, Publisher; Sharon Taylor, Advertising Editor. **Subscription Rates:** $14 individuals; $12 senior citizens. **Remarks:** Accepts advertising.
Ad Rates: SAU: $2.67 **Circ:** ‡1750

GREEN COVE SPRINGS†, pop. 4,154.

NE FL. Clay Co. On St. Johns River, 26 mi. S. of Jacksonville. Health resort. Commercial and sport fishing.

🎙 **6222 WAYR-AM - 550**
2500 Russell Rd. Phone: (904)284-1111
Green Cove Springs, FL 32043-9492
E-mail: wayradioam@aol

Format: Religious. **Networks:** Voice of Christian Youth America. **Owner:** Good Tidings Trust, Inc., at above address. **Founded:** 1960. **Operating Hours:** Continuous; 10% network, 90% local. **ADI:** Jacksonville (Brunswick), FL. **Key Personnel:** Dick Weer, Contact; Bart Wagner, Contact. **Wattage:** 5000 day; 500 night. **Ad Rates:** Noncommercial.

🎙 **6223 WJBT-FM - 92.7**
10592 E Balmoral Car,Ste. 1 Phone: (904)696-1015
Jacksonville, FL 32218 Fax: (904)696-1011

Networks: CBS. **Owner:** Jacor Broadcasting of FLA, Inc., at above address. **Founded:** 1978. **ADI:** Jacksonville (Brunswick), FL. **Key Personnel:** Bruce Demps, Vice President; Nate Bell, Program Dir. **Wattage:** 3,000.

GRETNA

🎙 **6224 WGWD-FM - 100.7**
100A N. Madison Phone: (904)627-7086
PO Box 919 Fax: (904)627-3422
Quincy, FL 32351

Format: Soft Rock. **Founded:** 1989. **Key Personnel:** Monte Bitner, Contact; Tony Woods, Program Dir. **Wattage:** 3,000.

GULF BREEZE, pop. 5,457.

NW FL. Santa Rosa Co. On Gulf of Mexico, 3 mi. S. of Pensacola.

📖 **6225 The Gulf Breeze Sentinel**
Gulf Breeze Publishing Co.
1200 Gulf Breeze Pky. Phone: (904)934-1200
Gulf Breeze, FL 32561 Fax: (904)932-8765

Newspaper. **Founded:** Dec. 1960. **Freq:** Weekly (Thurs.). **Cols./Page:** 6. **Col. Width:** 24 nonpareils. **Col. Depth:** 294 agate lines. **Key Personnel:** Marlin Osborn, Publisher; Eloise Lautier, Editor. **Subscription Rates:** $18 individuals. **Remarks:** Accepts advertising.
Ad Rates: GLR: $.57 **Circ:** ‡5,500
BW: $1,290
4C: $1,590
SAU: $10
PCI: $8

📖 **6226 Mexico Business Journal**
Gulf Breeze Publishing Co.
1200 Gulf Breeze Pky. Phone: (904)934-1200
Gulf Breeze, FL 32561 Fax: (904)932-8765

Publication providing news and information on doing business in Mexico. **Founded:** Sept. 1, 1993. **Freq:** Weekly.

📖 **6227 Perido Pelican**
Gulf Breeze Publishing Co.
1200 Gulf Breeze Pky. Phone: (904)934-1200
Gulf Breeze, FL 32561 Fax: (904)932-8765

Community newspaper. **Founded:** 1989. **Freq:** Semimonthly. **Print Method:** Offset. **Trim Size:** 11 3/8 x 13 1/2. **Cols./Page:** 5. **Col. Width:** 12 picas. **Key Personnel:** Fran Thompson, Editor and Publisher. **Remarks:** Accepts advertising.
Ad Rates: GLR: $9 **Circ:** Non-paid ‡8,000

📖 **6228 Russia & Eurasia Armed Forces Review Annual**
Academic International Press
PO Box 1111 Fax: (850)934-0953
Gulf Breeze, FL 32562-1111
Publisher E-mail: aipress@aol.com

Professional publication covering military developments in Russia and other former Soviet Union states. **Founded:** 1977. **Freq:** Annual. **Trim Size:** 6 x 9. **Subscription Rates:** $177 single issue; $97 single issue non standing order basis. **Remarks:** Advertising not accepted.
Circ: (Not Reported)

📖 **6229 Russia & Eurasia Documents Annual**
Academic International Press
PO Box 1111 Fax: (850)934-0953
Gulf Breeze, FL 32562-1111
Publisher E-mail: aipress@aol.com

Scholarly journal covering Russia and Eurasia. **Founded:** 1987. **Freq:** Annual. **Subscription Rates:** $97 individuals; $77 individuals standing order. **Remarks:** Advertising not accepted. **Former name:** USSR Documents Annual.
Circ: (Not Reported)

6230 Multivision Cable TV
4435 Gulf Breeze Pkwy. Phone: (904)932-9233
Gulf Breeze, FL 32561 Fax: (904)932-9237
Free: (800)239-8411

Owner: Multivision Cable TV Corp., 321 Railroad Ave., Greenwich, CT 06830, (203)622-4860. **Founded:** 1978. **Key Personnel:** Terry A. Messner, Contact; Norris Mayberry, Contact; Robyn Roy, Contact. **Cities Served:** subscribing households 18,916; 35 channels; 1 community access channel; 20 hours per week community access programming.

HAINES CITY, pop. 10,799.

C FL. Polk Co. 20 mi. NE of Lakeland. Citrus fruit canning and packing. Fruit, truck, stock farms.

6231 WLVF-AM - 930
110 W. Scenic Hwy. Phone: (813)422-9583
Haines City, FL 33844 Fax: (813)422-0110
Free: (888)422-9583
E-mail: wlvf@gate.net

Format: Gospel. **Simulcasts:** WLVF-FM. **Networks:** USA Radio. **Founded:** 1960. **Operating Hours:** Sunrise-sunset. **Key Personnel:** Randy Daniel, Station Mgr., wlvf@gate.net; Kevin Campbell, Marketing Dir.; Steven Carter, Program Dir., fax (941)422-0110; Travis Lane, Music Dir. **Wattage:** 500. **Ad Rates:** Advertising accepted; rates available upon request.

6232 WLVF-FM - 90.3
110 W. Scenic Hwy. Phone: (941)422-9583
Haines City, FL 33844 Fax: (941)422-0110
Free: (888)422-9583
E-mail: wlvf@gate.net

Format: Religious. **Networks:** USA Radio. **Founded:** 1986. **Operating Hours:** Continuous. **Key Personnel:** Kevin Campbell, Marketing Dir., phone (941)422-9583; Steve Carter, Program Dir., phone (941)422-5195, fax (941)422-0110; Richard Lemon, Music Dir., phone (941)421-1227; Randy Daniel, Station Mgr., phone (941)422-9583. **Local Programs:** *As It is on Earth*, Phil Stringer, (941)422-6493. **Wattage:** 1200. **Ad Rates:** Noncommercial.

HALLANDALE, pop. 36,460.

S FL. Broward Co. On Atlantic Ocean, 15 mi. N. of Miami. Retirement community. Tourists. Race tracks.

6233 The Digest
Box 785 Phone: (305)457-8029
Hallandale, FL 33009-0785 Fax: (305)457-1284

Newspaper. **Founded:** 1963. **Freq:** Weekly (Thurs.). **Print Method:** Offset. **Cols./Page:** 8. **Col. Width:** 33 nonpareils. **Col. Depth:** 168 agate lines. **Key Personnel:** Peter Bluesten, Editor and Publisher. **Subscription Rates:** $78 individuals. **Remarks:** Accepts advertising. **Formerly:** Hallandale Digest.
Ad Rates: GLR: $.50 **Circ:** Free ‡48,000
BW: $1,100
SAU: $9.99
PCI: $11.50

6234 Textile Rental Magazine
Textile Rental Services Association of America
1130 E. Hallandale Beach Blvd. Phone: (954)457-7555
Hallandale, FL 33009 Fax: (954)457-3890

Magazine focusing on industrial and commercial laundering and linen supply. **Subtitle:** Uniform and Linen Service Management Trends. **Founded:** 1917. **Freq:** Monthly. **Print Method:** Offset. **Trim Size:** 8 1/4 x 10 7/8. **Cols./Page:** 3. **Col. Width:** 26 nonpareils. **Col. Depth:** 140 agate lines. **Key Personnel:** John R. Massey, Exec. Ed., jmassey@trsa.org; Nancy J. Rhodes, Assoc. Ed./Prod. Mgr., nrhodes@trsa.org; Candi Pillitteri, Art Director; Steven Feldman, Advertising Mgr., sfeldman@trsa.org; Debra Dean, Traffic Coord., dean@trsa.org; Leslie Melvin, Acctg., lmelvin@trsa.org; Sharon O'Connor, soconner@trsa.org. **ISSN:** 0195-0118. **Subscription Rates:** $110 individuals for first subscription; $35 for additional subscriptions to same company. **Remarks:** Accepts advertising. **URL:** http://www.trsa.org.
Ad Rates: BW: $1,750 **Circ:** ‡5,900
4C: $2,750

HAVANA, pop. 2,932.

NW FL. Gadsden Co. 15 mi. N. of Tallahassee. Lumber. Agriculture. Tobacco, corn, tomatoes, livestock.

6235 Havana Herald
Priority News, Inc.
103 W. 7th Ave. Phone: (904)539-6586
Havana, FL 32333 Fax: (904)539-0454
Publication E-mail: hherald@gcn.scri.fsu.edu

Newspaper with agricultural coverage. **Founded:** Feb. 7, 1947. **Freq:** Weekly (Thurs.). **Print Method:** Offset. **Cols./Page:** 6. **Col. Width:** 12 picas. **Col. Depth:** 301 agate lines. **Key Personnel:** John N. Bert, Publisher; Billy Blackman, Editor. **USPS:** 237-340. **Subscription Rates:** $17.3 individuals; $20.4 out of county. **Remarks:** Accepts advertising.
Ad Rates: GLR: $.29 **Circ:** Paid ⊕2600
BW: $516 Free ⊕25
4C: $976
SAU: $4
PCI: $4

HEATHROW

6236 Al Dia
Pepperdine Enterprises
1367 Tadsworth Terr.
Heathrow, FL 32746

Trade magazine covering Latin American trade. **Founded:** 1991. **Freq:** Bimonthly. **Print Method:** Offset. **Key Personnel:** Noemi T. Pepperdine. **Subscription Rates:** $15 individuals; $45 out of country. **Remarks:** Accepts advertising.
Ad Rates: BW: $2,900 **Circ:** (Not Reported)
4C: $3,700

HERNANDO

6237 WRZN-AM - 720
3988 N. Roscoe Rd. Phone: (352)726-7221
Hernando, FL 34442 Fax: (352)726-3172

Format: Big Band/Nostalgia; Middle-of-the-Road (MOR). **Networks:** Satellite Music Network. **Owner:** Management and Marketing Synergy Inc., at above address, (850)671-5151, Fax: (850)671-5030. **Founded:** 1989. **Operating Hours:** 6 a.m.-12 midnight. **ADI:** Gainesville (Ocala), FL. **Key Personnel:** Mark Varney, Operations Mgr.; Linda Tilley, General Sales Mgr.; Chet Forbush, Office/Traffic Mgr. **Local Programs:** *Memorys & Music*, Peter Mallon, (352)726-7221; *P.M. in the A.M.*, Peter Mallon, (352)726-7221. **Wattage:** 10,000 day; 250 night. **Ad Rates:** Advertising accepted; rates available upon request.

6238 WXOF-FM - 96.3
2480 N. Essex Ave. Phone: (904)746-0090
Hernando, FL 34442 Fax: (904)746-4344
Free: (888)418-9963

Format: Hot Country. **Networks:** NBC. **Owner:** Heart of Citrus Broadcasting, at above address. **Founded:** Oct. 1, 1992. **Formerly:** WPDS-FM. **Operating Hours:** Continuous. **ADI:** Tampa- St. Petersburg (Lakeland, Sarasota),FL. **Key Personnel:** Carl Marcocci, President; Johnny "O", Program/News and Promotion Director; Rick Parrish, Production Dir. **Wattage:** 6,000. **Ad Rates:** $18-35 for 30 seconds.

HIALEAH, pop. 145,254.

S FL. Dade Co. On Miami Canal, 7 mi. NW of Miami. Hialeah Park Race Track. Manufactures furniture, chemicals, machinery, glass, textiles, aluminum, concrete, paper, food, leather, electronic products, boats, plastics.

6239 El Sol de Hialeah
Sol de Hialeah Publishing Co.
436 Palm Ave. Phone: (305)887-8324
Hialeah, FL 33010 Fax: (305)887-8324

Community newspaper (Spanish). **Founded:** 1969. **Freq:** Weekly (Thurs.). **Cols./Page:** 6. **Col. Width:** 1 5/8 inches. **Col. Depth:** 17 inches. **Key Personnel:** Raul Martinez, Editor. **Remarks:** Accepts advertising.
Ad Rates: BW: $714 **Circ:** Non-paid ‡24,000
4C: $1,400
SAU: $7

6240 Plumpers and Big Women
Firestone Publishing Corp.
14411 Commerce Way, Ste. 420 Phone: (305)557-0071
Hialeah, FL 33016-1598 Fax: (305)557-6005
Free: (800)641-4062
Publisher E-mail: dugent@dugent.com

Consumer magazine covering full-figured women for men. **Founded:** 1993. **Freq:** Monthly. **Trim Size:** 8 1/2 x 11. **Key Personnel:** Steve Dorfman, Editor, steved@dugent.com. **Subscription Rates:** $24 individuals; $6.99 single issue.

6241 Media One of South Florida
2151 W. 62nd St. Phone: (305)456-4200
Hialeah, FL 33016-2624 Fax: (305)819-5218

Owner: Continental Cablevision, Pilot House, Lewis Wharf, Boston, MA 02110, (617)742-9500, Free: (800)225-6248. **Founded:** 1978. **Key Personnel:** Cele Seldon, Local Sales Mgr./Advertising, phone (305)819-5217; Renee Pollack, General Sales Mgr./Advertising; Phil Gallub, General Mgr., phone (305)828-4236. **Cities Served:** Coral Gables, Doral, Fountainbleau, Hialeah, Hialeah Gardens, Medley, Miami Lakes West, Miami Springs, Sweetwater, Virginia Gardens, West Miami, FL: subscribing households 90,000; 22 channels; 3 community access channels; 72 hours per week community access programming.

6242 WSCV-TV - 51
2340 W. 8th Ave. Phone: (305)888-5151
Hialeah, FL 33010-2019 Fax: (305)888-9270

Format: Commercial TV. **Networks:** Telemundo. **Owner:** Telemundo Group, at above address. **Operating Hours:** 20 hours daily. **ADI:** Miami (Ft. Lauderdale), FL. **Key Personnel:** J. Manuel Calvo, Contact; Ramon Pineda, General Sales Mgr.; Jose Franchi, Contact. **Ad Rates:** $75-1,000 per unit.

HIGH SPRINGS, pop. 2,491.

N FL. Alachua Co. On Santa Fe River, 22 mi. NW of Gainesville. Manufactures plastic pipe, transformers, air compressors. Phosphate mine. Tobacco, watermelons, peanuts.

6243 The High Springs Herald
The Herald Publishing Co., Inc.
PO Box 745
High Springs, FL 32655-0745
Publication E-mail: hsherald@freenet.ufl.edu; hsherald@afn.org

Newspaper. **Founded:** 1952. **Freq:** Weekly (Thurs.). **Print Method:** Offset. **Trim Size:** 13 3/4 x 22. **Cols./Page:** 6. **Col. Width:** 18 nonpareils. **Col. Depth:** 294 agate lines. **Key Personnel:** Ed Barber, Publisher; Bo Turner, General Mgr./Ed. **ISSN:** 0746-1046. **Subscription Rates:** $12 individuals; $15 out of county; $17 out of state.
Ad Rates: GLR: $.50 **Circ:** Paid ‡3,600
BW: $882
4C: $1,182
SAU: $7
PCI: $7

6244 Cable Florida
2025 NE Santa Fe Blvd. Phone: (904)454-2299
Box 905 Free: (800)881-9740
High Springs, FL 32643

Key Personnel: Jim Morris, Contact. **Cities Served:** Municipal/Marion County: subscribing households 6,800; 46 channels.

6245 WYOC-FM - 104.9
PO Box 1646 Phone: (352)372-4487
High Springs, FL 32643 Fax: (352)372-9400
Free: (800)781-WYOC

Format: Oldies. **Networks:** CNN Radio; Westwood One Radio. **Owner:** Millstone Broadcasting, 3720 NW 43rd St., Gainesville, FL 32606. **Founded:** 1995. **Formerly:** WKAE-FM. **Operating Hours:** Continuous; 75% network, 25% local. **ADI:** Gainesville (Ocala), FL. **Key Personnel:** Don Boyd, General Mgr.; Michael Johnson, Program Dir.; Don Boyd, Sales Mgr.; Rebecca Birx, VP Station Operations. **Local Programs:** *Florida Marlins Baseball*, Tom Kenney. **Wattage:** 6,000. **Ad Rates:** $10-30 per unit.

HOLLYWOOD, pop. 117,188.

S FL. Broward Co. On Atlantic Ocean and Intracoastal Waterway, 20 mi. N. of Miami. Resort. Race tracks. Boating and water skiing. Manufactures concrete blocks, furniture, electronic equipment, game equipment, aluminum castings, plastics, jewelry, boats.

Boca's Best - See Boca Raton

6246 Community News
Community News Publishing Co.
6836 Stirling Rd. Phone: (954)963-4000
Hollywood, FL 33024 Fax: (954)964-2000

Community newspaper. **Founded:** 1987. **Freq:** Weekly (Wed.). **Print Method:** Web offset. **Cols./Page:** 6. **Col. Width:** 9.5 picas. **Col. Depth:** 16 inches. **Key Personnel:** Roger Clark, Publisher. **Subscription Rates:** $65 individuals. **Remarks:** Accepts advertising.
Ad Rates: PCI: $30 **Circ:** Free 71,384

Coral Springs News - See Coral Springs

Deerfield Beach Shoppers Guide - See Deerfield Beach

6247 Diet & Fitness
Lifetime Periodicals, Inc.
2131 Hollywood Blvd. Phone: (954)925-5242
Hollywood, FL 33020 Fax: (954)925-5244
Publisher E-mail: lifetime@shadow.net

Consumer magazine covering health, diet, and fitness. **Freq:** Quarterly. **Key Personnel:** Donald Lessne, President. **Remarks:** Accepts advertising.
Circ: (Not Reported)

6248 Electronic Commerce World
2021 Coolidge St. Phone: (305)925-5900
Hollywood, FL 33020-2427 Fax: (305)925-7533
Free: (800)336-4889
Publication E-mail: ecomworld@ix.netcom.com

Magazine emphasizing electronic commerce, including EDI. **Subtitle:** Business Solution Through Technology Integration. **Founded:** 1991. **Freq:** Monthly. **Print Method:** Offset. **Trim Size:** 8 3/8 x 10 3/4. **Cols./Page:** 3 and 2. **Col. Width:** 27 and 42 nonpareils. **Col. Depth:** 140 agate lines. **Key Personnel:** Michael McGarr, Editor; Richard D'Alessandro, Publisher; Eileen Baldwin, National Sales Manager; Rachel Sessa, Advertising Production Mgr. **ISSN:** 0274-9874. **Subscription Rates:** $29.95 individuals; $4 single issue; $5 single, Canada. **Remarks:** Accepts advertising. **URL:** http://ecomworld.com. **Formerly**: EDI World.
Ad Rates: BW: $5,355 **Circ:** Paid ‡44,000
4C: $6,380
PCI: $120

6249 Fell's U.S. Coins Magazine
Lifetime Periodicals, Inc.
2131 Hollywood Blvd. Phone: (954)925-5242
Hollywood, FL 33020 Fax: (954)925-5244
Publisher E-mail: lifetime@shadow.net

Consumer magazine covering coins and collecting. **Subtitle:** Quarterly Investment Guide. **Freq:** Quarterly. **Key Personnel:** Donald Lessne, President. **ISSN:** 1041-6951. **Remarks:** Accepts advertising.
Circ: (Not Reported)

6250 Landscape and Nursery Digest
Betrock Information Systems, Inc.
7770 Davie Rd. Ext. Phone: (954)981-2821
Hollywood, FL 33024 Fax: (954)981-2823
Free: (800)627-3819
Publisher E-mail: betrock@betrock.com

Trade magazine for the landscape and nursery industry in the Southeast U.S. **Founded:** 1970. **Freq:** Monthly. **Print Method:** Sheetfed offset. **Trim Size:** 8 1/2 x 11. **Cols./Page:** 3. **Key Personnel:** Irv Betrock, Ph.D., Publisher; Lissie Allen, Art Dir.; Linda Thorne, Editor. **Subscription Rates:** $29.95 individuals; $5 single issue. **Remarks:** Accepts advertising. **Formerly**: Nursery Digest.
Ad Rates: BW: $1,200 **Circ:** Controlled 13,380
4C: $2,000

6251 Le Soleil de la Floride
Worldwide Publications No. 1, Inc.
2020 Scott St. Phone: (305)923-4510
Hollywood, FL 33020 Fax: (305)923-4533

Newspaper (tabloid) featuring Florida attractions for vacationing Canadians (French). **Subtitle:** Florida's Unique French Newspaper. **Founded:** Aug. 1983. **Freq:** Monthly. **Print Method:** Offset. **Cols./Page:** 7. **Col. Width:** 1 5/16 inches. **Col. Depth:** 11 1/4 inches. **Key Personnel:** Jean Laurac, Editor, jeanl@icanect.net; Denyse Chartrand, Advertising Mgr.; Barry Sacharow, Editor. **ISSN:** 0835-1805. **Subscription Rates:** $18 U.S. and Canada. **Remarks:** Accepts advertising. **URL:** http:planete.oc.ca/soleil.
Ad Rates: GLR: $1.60 **Circ:** Paid 40,000
BW: $1,000 Controlled 10,000
4C: $1,500
PCI: $22.40

6252 MoneyLines Magazine
Lifetime Periodicals, Inc.
2131 Hollywood Blvd. Phone: (954)925-5242
Hollywood, FL 33020 Fax: (954)925-5244
Publisher E-mail: lifetime@shadow.net

Consumer magazine covering investment opportunities. **Freq:** Quarterly. **Key Personnel:** Donald Lessne, President. **Remarks:** Accepts advertising.
Circ: (Not Reported)

6253 Reach Out Magazine
3090 Sheridan St., Ste. 207 Phone: (954)985-0319
Hollywood, FL 33021 Fax: (954)985-0483
Free: (888)660-8338
Publication E-mail: reachout@reachoutmag.com

Magazine by and for people with disabilities. Features personal ads, human interest stories, articles, advice, support group listings, and humor. **Subtitle:** Full Feature Personal Ad Magazine By/For People With Disabilities. **Founded:** 1991. **Freq:** Quarterly. **Trim Size:** 8 1/2 x 11. **Key Personnel:** Jim Jakubek, Publisher, jim@reachoutmag.com. **Subscription Rates:** $10.60 U.S., Canada, and Mexico three years; $30 other countries three years; $20 per year for online version. **Remarks:** Accepts display and classified advertising. **URL:** http://www.reachoutmag.com.
Ad Rates: BW: $425 **Circ:** Paid ‡3,000

6254 Specialty Cooking Magazine
Lifetime Periodicals, Inc.
2131 Hollywood Blvd. Phone: (954)925-5242
Hollywood, FL 33020 Fax: (954)925-5244
Publisher E-mail: lifetime@shadow.net

Consumer magazine covering cooking, health and fitness. **Freq:** Quarterly. **Key Personnel:** Donald Lessne, President. **Remarks:** Accepts advertising.
Circ: (Not Reported)

6255 WDZL-TV - 39
2055 Lee St. Phone: (954)925-3939
Hollywood, FL 33020 Fax: (954)922-3965

Format: Commercial TV. **Owner:** Tribune Broadcasting Company, 435 N. Michigan Ave., Chicago, IL 60611. **Founded:** 1982. **Operating Hours:** Continuous. **ADI:** Miami (Ft. Lauderdale), FL. **Key Personnel:** Jeanette Jordan, Public Affairs Dir.; Harvey Cohen, General Mgr.; Gary Zenobi, General Sales Mgr.; Alan Rosenfeld, Local Sales Mgr.; Ed Perl, National Sales Mgr.; Diana Swords, Program Mgr.; Eric Berkowitz, Creative Service Dir.; Mark Ryan, Controller; Steve Ellis, Chief Engineer; Jeff Eggleston, Operations Mgr. **Local Programs:** *Between the Lines*; *Lift Every Voice.* **Wattage:** 5,000,000. **URL:** http://www.wb39.com.

6256 WFLC-FM - 97.3
2741 N. 29th Ave. Phone: (954)584-7117
Hollywood, FL 33020 Fax: (954)847-3230

Format: Adult Contemporary. **Networks:** Independent. **Owner:** Cox Radio, Inc., 1400 Lake Hearn Dr. NE, Atlanta, GA 30319, (404)843-5000. **Founded:** 1963. **Formerly**: WAIA-FM (1986); WGTR-FM. **Operating Hours:** Continuous; 100% local. **ADI:** Miami (Ft. Lauderdale), FL. **Key Personnel:** Robert Green, VP/Gen. Mgr.; Tip Landay, Program Dir.; John Lynch, Sales Mgr.; Daryl Leoce, Nat'l. Sales Mgr.; Mitch Wein, Chief Engineer; John Saavedra, Controller. **Wattage:** 100,000. **Ad Rates:** $200-300 per unit.

6257 WKIS-FM - 99.9
9881 Sheridan St. Phone: (954)431-6200
Hollywood, FL 33024 Fax: (954)437-2466
Free: (800)255-9956

Format: Country. **Owner:** Beasley FM Acquisitions, Inc., at above address. **Founded:** 1965. **Formerly**: WKQS-FM (1987). **Operating Hours:** Continuous. **ADI:** Miami (Ft. Lauderdale), FL. **Key Personnel:** Dave Donahue, General Mgr.; Bob McKay, Program Dir. **Wattage:** 100,000. **URL:** http://wkis.com.

HOLMES BEACH, pop. 4,023.

SW FL. Manatee Co. On Gulf Coast, 10 mi. N. of Sarasota. Resorts. Shopping centers.

6258 School Intervention Report
Safe Schools Coalition, Inc.
5351 Gulf Dr. Phone: (941)778-6652
Box 1338 Fax: (941)778-6818
Holmes Beach, FL 34218-1338
Free: (800)537-4903
Publication E-mail: 102630.2245@compuserve.com

Journal providing information and resources to educators regarding problems in school, including suicide, drug/alcohol abuse, teenage pregnancy, child abuse, truancy, vandalism, and peer assaults. **Founded:** Sept. 1, 1987. **Freq:** Quarterly. **Print Method:** Offset. **Trim Size:** 8 1/2 x 11. **Cols./Page:** 2. **Col. Width:** 3 1/4 inches. **Col. Depth:** 9 inches. **Key Personnel:** Alan McEvoy, Editor; Ruth Erickson, Managing Editor. **ISSN:** 0894-5152. **Subscription Rates:** $22 nonmembers; Free Included in membership. **Remarks:** Accepts advertising. **URL:** http://www.ed.mtu.edu/safe.
Ad Rates: BW: $200 **Circ:** Paid ‡1,700
Non-paid ‡1,000

HOMESTEAD, pop. 20,668.

S FL. Dade Co. 28 mi. SW of Miami. Homestead Air Force Base. Fertilizer factory. Citrus fruit, truck farms. Tomatoes, okra, beans, squash, potatoes.

6259 Florida Entomologist
Florida Entomological Society
University of Florida, TREC Phone: (305)246-7040
18905 SW 280 St. Fax: (305)246-7003
Homestead, FL 33031
Entomological journal containing abstracts (English and Spanish). **Subtitle:** An International Journal for the Americas. **Founded:** 1917. **Freq:** Quarterly. **Print Method:** Offset. **Trim Size:** 6 x 9. **Cols./Page:** 1. **Key Personnel:** R. M. Baranowski, Editor, rmb@gnv.ifas.ufl.edu. **ISSN:** 0015-4040. **Subscription Rates:** $30 individuals; $7.50 single issue. **Remarks:** Advertising not accepted.
Circ: ‡1,000

6260 Palmetto Bay News
Community Newspapers
PO Box 43-1970 Phone: (305)667-7481
Miami, FL 33143 Fax: (305)661-0954
Publisher E-mail: cnedor@gate.net

Community newspaper (tabloid). **Founded:** 1968. **Freq:** 3/week. **Print Method:** Offset. **Trim Size:** 10 1/4 x 16. **Cols./Page:** 6. **Col. Width:** 19 nonpareils. **Col. Depth:** 238 agate lines. **Key Personnel:** Michael Miller, Editor; Grant Miller, Publisher. **Subscription Rates:** $78 individuals. **Remarks:** Accepts advertising. **URL:** http://communitynewspapers.com. **Formerly**: Homestead-Florida City News.
Ad Rates: GLR: $.72 **Circ:** Free 6,000
BW: $1,350
4C: $2,400
PCI: $13.50

6261 South Dade News Leader
15 NE 1st Rd. Phone: (305)245-2311
Homestead, FL 33030 Fax: (305)248-0596

General newspaper. **Founded:** 1912. **Freq:** Triweekly. **Print Method:** Offset. **Cols./Page:** 6. **Col. Width:** 25 nonpareils. **Col. Depth:** 21.5 inches. **Key Personnel:** Pat L. Hollinger, Editor; Richard A. Hackney, Publisher. **Subscription Rates:** $72.80 individuals. **Remarks:** Accepts advertising.
Ad Rates: GLR: $6.60 **Circ:** Combined ‡12,514
BW: $800
4C: $960
PCI: $18.90

6262 WOIR-AM - 1430
100 Blair Rd.
Oyster Bay, NY 11771

Format: Ethnic; Hispanic. **Owner:** Omni-Lingual Broadcasting Corp., at above address. **Founded:** 1957. **Key Personnel:** Aurelio Duque Estrada, Operations Mgr.; Jose A. Marques, News Dir. **Wattage:** 5,000.

ISLAMORADA

6263 Free Press
PO Box 469 Phone: (305)664-2266
Islamorada, FL 33036 Fax: (305)664-8411
Free: (800)926-8412
Publication E-mail: dead.bait@aol.com

Feature newspaper of general interest for the Florida Keys. **Subtitle:** The Countywide Feature Newspaper for the Florida Keys. **Founded:** Jan. 1987. **Freq:** Monthly. **Print Method:** Web Offset. **Trim Size:** 11 x 17. **Cols./Page:** 5. **Col. Width:** 22 1/2 nonpareils. **Col. Depth:** 224 agate lines. **Key Personnel:** Sandra Kay Barrett, Editor and Publisher; Stanley Becker, Publisher. **Subscription Rates:** Free; $17 (mail). **Remarks:** Accepts advertising. **Formerly**: Island Navigator.
Ad Rates: BW: $945 **Circ:** Paid ‡500
4C: $1,155 Free ‡19,500
PCI: $13

JACKSONVILLE†, pop. 609,860.

NE FL. Duval Co. Located on Atlantic Ocean an equal distance from Miami and Atlanta. Edward Waters College; Jones College; Jacksonville University; Florida Junior College at Jacksonville. Center of commerce, finance and insurance with three large naval facilities.

6264 American Shipper
PO Box 4728 Phone: (904)355-2601
Jacksonville, FL 32201-4728 Fax: (904)791-8836
Free: (800)874-6422
Publisher E-mail: amshpjx1@aol.com

Transportation and shipping magazine. **Founded:** 1959. **Freq:** Monthly. **Print Method:** Offset. **Trim Size:** 8 1/4 x 10 7/8. **Cols./Page:** 3 and 2. **Col. Width:** 27 and 41 nonpareils. **Col. Depth:** 140 agate lines. **Key Personnel:** David A. Howard, Editor; Hayes H. Howard, Publisher; Nancy Barry, Asst. Advertising Mgr.; Clinton W. Alphen, Assoc Pub.; Joseph A. Bonney, Managing Editor. **ISSN:** 0160-225X. **Subscription**

Rates: $48 Free to qualified subscribers; $120 air mail delivery domestic or foreign. **Remarks:** Accepts advertising.
Ad Rates: BW: $3,310 **Circ:** Paid 2,359
4C: $4,435 Controlled ‡11,757

6265 Florida Baptist Witness
1230 Hendricks Ave. Phone: (904)396-2351
Jacksonville, FL 32207 Fax: (904)346-0696
Free: (800)226-8584
Publisher E-mail: witness@flbaptist.org

Baptist newspaper. **Founded:** 1884. **Freq:** Weekly (Thurs.). **Print Method:** Offset. **Trim Size:** 11 x 17. **Cols./Page:** 5. **Col. Width:** 2 inches. **Col. Depth:** 16 inches. **Key Personnel:** Michael D. Chute, Editor, phone (904)396-2351, fax (904)396-6470. **USPS:** 700-940. **Subscription Rates:** $11 individuals. **Remarks:** Color advertising not accepted.
Ad Rates: BW: $3,160 **Circ:** Paid ‡71,000
PCI: $39.50 Free ‡1,500

6266 Florida Star Times
PO Box 40629 Phone: (904)766-8834
Jacksonville, FL 32203-0629 Fax: (904)765-1673

Black community newspaper. **Founded:** Apr. 1951. **Freq:** Weekly. **Print Method:** Offset. **Cols./Page:** 6. **Col. Width:** 2 1/4 inches. **Col. Depth:** 21 1/2 inches. **Key Personnel:** Mary Wooten Simpson, Publisher. **Subscription Rates:** $41.60; $21.58 6 months. **Remarks:** Accepts advertising.
Ad Rates: GLR: $11 **Circ:** Thurs. 2,400
PCI: $14

6267 The Florida Times-Union
Morris Communications Corp.
1 Riverside Ave. Phone: (904)359-4111
Jacksonville, FL 32202-4904 Fax: (904)359-4478
Publisher E-mail: 73711.1232@compuserve.com

General newspaper. **Founded:** 1864. **Freq:** Mon.-Sun. (morn.). **Print Method:** Letterpress and offset. **Trim Size:** 13 3/4 x 22 3/4. **Cols./Page:** 6. **Col. Width:** 25 nonpareils. **Col. Depth:** 301 agate lines. **Key Personnel:** Richard T. Allport, Exec. Editor; Frederick W. Hartmann, Editor; Carl N. Cannon, Publisher; Raymond P. Dallman, Dir. of Advertising & Marketing. **Subscription Rates:** $104 individuals. **Remarks:** Accepts advertising. **Online:** DataTimes Corporation. **URL:** http://www.jacksonville.com. **Feature Editors:** Roger Bull, *Family, Features, Lifestyle, Saturday, Sunday*, phone (904)359-4296; David Crumpler, *Movie*, phone (904)359-4164; Linda Hanks Stem, *Food, Garden/Home*, phone (904)359-4102; Beau Helton, *Education*, phone (904)359-4390; Foster Marshall, *Photo*, phone (904)359-4287; Nancy McAlister, *TV & Radio*, phone (904)359-4370; Theresa McTammans, *Fashion, Society*, phone (904)359-4155; Mark Middlebrook, *Environmental, Metro, News, Political*, phone (904)359-4504; Mike Ricites, *Sports*, phone (904)359-4438; Mike Romaner, *Financial/Business, Real Estate, Rural Development*, phone (904)359-4282; Scott Simpson, *Drama, Entertainment, Music, Travel*, phone (904)359-4521; Bill Sweisgood, *Editorials*, phone (904)359-4307; Barbara White, *Religion*, phone (904)359-4272.
Ad Rates: GLR: $8.03 **Circ:** Mon.-Fri. 182,136
BW: $14,493.15 Sat. 208,916
4C: $16,139.15 Sun. 256,710
PCI: $112.35

6268 Jacksonville Shopping Guide
CAN Media Jacksonville, Inc.
3801 University Blvd. W. Phone: (904)737-7320
Jacksonville, FL 32217 Fax: (904)737-2274

Shopper (tabloid). **Founded:** 1971. **Freq:** Weekly (Wed.). **Print Method:** Offset. **Trim Size:** 11 1/4 x 16. **Cols./Page:** 6. **Col. Width:** 19 nonpareils. **Col. Depth:** 210 agate lines. **Key Personnel:** Terry Mitton, General Mgr.; Joyce Lydon, Publisher. **Remarks:** Color advertising not accepted.
Ad Rates: BW: $2,375 **Circ:** Free ‡88,000

6269 Jacksonville Today
White Publishing Co.
1032 Hendricks Phone: (904)396-8666
Jacksonville, FL 32207
City lifestyle magazine. **Founded:** Feb. 1985. **Freq:** 10/year. **Print Method:** Offset. **Trim Size:** 8 1/4 x 11. **Cols./Page:** 3. **Col. Width:** 14 1/2 picas. **Col. Depth:** 10 inches. **Key Personnel:** Larry Marscheck, Director; James L. White III, Publisher. **ISSN:** 0885-4769. **Subscription Rates:** $13.25. **Remarks:** Accepts advertising.
Ad Rates: BW: $1,995 **Circ:** Paid 14,535
4C: $2,795 Free 6,613

6270 Kalliope
Florida Community College at Jacksonville
3939 Roosevelt Blvd. Phone: (904)381-3511
Jacksonville, FL 32205
Journal containing women's poetry, fiction, interviews, reviews, and artwork. **Subtitle:** A Journal of Women's Literature and Art. **Founded:** 1978. **Freq:** 3/yer. **Print Method:** Offset, Perfect Bound. **Trim Size:** 7 1/4 x 8 1/2. **Cols./Page:** 1. **Key Personnel:** Mary Sue Koeppel, Editor. **ISSN:** 0735-7885. **Subscription Rates:** $15 individuals; $21.95 other countries; $23.50 institutions; $29.97 institutions, other countries; $7 single issue. **Remarks:** Advertising not accepted. **Alt. Formats:** Audio tape; Microform.
Circ: Paid 1,500
Non-paid 100

6271 The Party Shopper
Festivities Publications, Inc.
815 Haines St. Phone: (904)634-1902
Jacksonville, FL 32206 Fax: (904)633-8764
Free: (800)729-6338
Publication E-mail: readermail@aol.com

Magazine covering the special event/party planning industry. Includes articles on business, decorating ideas, and suppliers. **Founded:** 1994. **Freq:** Bimonthly. **Print Method:** Web offset. **Trim Size:** 8 1/8 x 10 7/8. **Key Personnel:** Debra Paulk, Editor and Publisher; Sheryl Martin, Prod./Editorial Mgr.; Holly Hunter, Marketing Dir.; Kathy Horak, Editor. **ISSN:** 1049-9970. **Subscription Rates:** $29.95 individuals; $10 single issue. **Remarks:** Accepts advertising.
Circ: Paid 3,000
Controlled 7,000

6272 South Asian Review
South Asian Library Association
University of North Florida
Jacksonville, FL 32224

Scholarly journal covering South Asian literature and studies. **Founded:** 1976. **Freq:** Annual. **Cols./Page:** 2. **Key Personnel:** Satya S. Pachori, Editor. **ISSN:** 0275-9527. **Subscription Rates:** $15 individuals; $17 out of country. **Remarks:** Advertising not accepted.
Circ: Controlled 150

6273 Southern Genealogists Exchange Quarterly
Southern Genealogist's Exchange Society, Inc.
PO Box 2801 Phone: (904)387-9142
Jacksonville, FL 32203
Publisher E-mail: jbilly@freewwweb.com

Genealogical and historical magazine. **Founded:** 1957. **Freq:** Quarterly. **Trim Size:** 8 1/2 x 11. **Cols./Page:** 1. **Key Personnel:** Mary-Louise Howard, Editor; Richard B. Cardell, President; Doris R. Wilson, Corresponding Secretary. **ISSN:** 0584-4487. **Subscription Rates:** $20 individuals; $6 single issue. **Remarks:** Accepts advertising.
Circ: Controlled 500

6274 The Tomahawk
Alpha Sigma Phi Fraternity
112 W. Adams St., Ste. 1616 Phone: (904)359-0048
Jacksonville, FL 32202
Fraternity tabloid. **Founded:** 1847. **Freq:** Quarterly. **Print Method:** Offset. **Cols./Page:** 3. **Col. Width:** 36 nonpareils. **Col. Depth:** 154 agate lines. **Key Personnel:** Jeffrey R. Hoffman, Editor. **USPS:** 007-964. **Subscription Rates:** Free to qualified subscribers; $30. **Remarks:** Advertising not accepted.
Circ: ‡37,000

6275 Continental Cablevision
5934 Richard St. Phone: (904)731-7700
Box 17613 Fax: (904)636-0521
Jacksonville, FL 32245-8810

Founded: 1979. **Key Personnel:** Michael Harper, Program Mgr. **Cities Served:** subscribing households 248,000; 78 channels; 49 community access channels.

6276 WAPE-FM - 95.1
9090 Hogan Rd. Phone: (904)642-1055
Jacksonville, FL 32216-4648 Fax: (904)641-3297

Format: Contemporary Hit Radio (CHR). **Networks:** Independent. **Founded:** 1949. **Operating Hours:** Continuous; 100% local. **ADI:** Jacksonville (Brunswick), FL. **Key Personnel:** Mark Schwartz, Contact; Rich Rectanus, General Sales Mgr.; Jeff McCartney, Program Dir. **Wattage:** 100,000. **Ad Rates:** $75-310 per unit.

6277 WAWS-TV - 30
8675 Hogan Rd. Phone: (904)642-3030
Jacksonville, FL 32216 Fax: (904)646-0115

Format: Commercial TV. **Networks:** Fox. **Founded:** 1981. **Operating Hours:** 5 a.m.-1:30 a.m. **ADI:** Jacksonville (Brunswick), FL. **Key Personnel:** Josh McGraw, General Mgr.; Phil Waterman, General Sales Mgr.; Doreen Morgan, Promotions Dir.; Russ Rockwell, Chief Engineer; Lynn Defoor, Contact. **Ad Rates:** $30-3,000 per unit.

6278 WBWL-AM - 600
6869 Lenox Ave. Phone: (904)783-3711
Box 6877 Fax: (904)786-1529
Jacksonville, FL 32236

Format: Sports. **Networks:** CBS. **Owner:** PRISM Radio Partners, L.P., at above address. **Formerly:** WPDQ-AM (Nov. 1997). **Operating Hours:** Continuous. **ADI:** Jacksonville (Brunswick), FL. **Key Personnel:** Mark Schwartz, General Mgr.; Rich Rectanus, Dir. of Sales; Mike Dorwart, Program Dir.; Jill Gosett, Local Sales Mgr.; Cat Thomas, Operations Mgr.; Jennifer Davies, Promotions Dir. **Wattage:** 5000.

6279 WEJZ-FM - 96.1
1896 Corporate Sq. Blvd. Phone: (904)727-9696
Jacksonville, FL 32216 Fax: (904)721-9322

Format: Adult Contemporary. **Networks:** Independent. **Owner:** Renda Broadcasting, 1459 Crane Ave., Pittsburgh, PA 15220-4098. **Founded:** 1949. **Operating Hours:** Continuous. **ADI:** Jacksonville (Brunswick), FL. **Key Personnel:** Buc Weatherby, General Mgr.; Ron Foster, Program Dir. **Wattage:** 100,000. **Ad Rates:** $135-160 per unit.

6280 WFYV-FM - 104.5
9090 Hogan Rd. Phone: (904)642-1055
Jacksonville, FL 32216-4648 Fax: (904)641-3297

Format: Album-Oriented Rock (AOR). **Networks:** Independent. **Founded:** 1979. **Operating Hours:** Continuous. **ADI:** Jacksonville (Brunswick), FL. **Key Personnel:** Mark Schwartz, General Mgr.; David Moore, Program Dir.; Cat Thomas, Operations Mgr.; Rich Rectanus, Dir. of Sales; Lindley Tolbert, Local Sales Mgr.; Chase Kennedy, News Dir.; Jennifer Davies, Promotions Dir. **Wattage:** 100,000.

6281 WIVY-FM - 102.9
6869 Lenox Ave. Phone: (904)783-3711
Jacksonville, FL 32205 Fax: (904)786-1529

Format: Adult Contemporary. **Networks:** Independent. **Founded:** 1965. **Operating Hours:** Continuous; 100% local. **ADI:** Jacksonville (Brunswick), FL. **Key Personnel:** Mark Schwartz, General Mgr.; Rich Rectanus, DOS; Andy Fisher, Local Sales Mgr.; Cat Thomas, Operations Mgr./PD; Roxy Tyler, News Dir.; Jennifer Davies, Promotions Dir. **Wattage:** 100,000.

6282 WJAX-AM - 1220
5353 Arlington Expy. Phone: (904)744-0049
Jacksonville, FL 32211-5540

Format: Big Band/Nostalgia. **Networks:** Mutual Broadcasting System. **Owner:** Mr. Jack H. Jones, at above address, (904)743-1122. **Founded:** 1964. **Operating Hours:** Sunrise-sunset. **ADI:** Jacksonville (Brunswick), FL. **Key Personnel:** Wayne Mashburn, General Mgr. **Wattage:** 1000.

WJBT-FM - See Green Cove Springs

6283 WJCT-FM - 89.9
100 Festival Pk. Ave. Phone: (904)353-7770
Jacksonville, FL 32202 Fax: (904)358-6352

Format: News; Classical; Jazz. **Networks:** National Public Radio (NPR). **Founded:** 1972. **Operating Hours:** Continuous. **ADI:** Jacksonville (Brunswick), FL. **Key Personnel:** David R. Anderson, General Mgr. **Wattage:** 100,000. **Ad Rates:** Noncommercial.

6284 WJCT-TV - 7
100 Festival Park Ave. Phone: (904)353-7770
Jacksonville, FL 32202-1397 Fax: (904)354-6846

Format: Public TV. **Networks:** Public Broadcasting Service (PBS). **Owner:** WJCT, Inc., at above address. **Founded:** 1958. **Operating Hours:** 5:30 a.m.-1 a.m.; 80% network, 20% local. **ADI:** Jacksonville (Brunswick), FL. **Key Personnel:** Vic DiGenti, Vice Pres./Special Events, phone (904)358-6346; Carla Marlier, Vice President, phone (904)358-6329; Stephen C. Travis, Vice Pres., Finance, phone (904)358-6335; Kathy Bargar, Director, Special Events, Marketing, phone (904)358-6317; Marjorie Brown, Vice Pres., Sales, phone (904)358-6342; William G. Dresser, Pres./Gen. Mgr., phone (904)358-6343; Rick Johnson, Sr. Vice President, Broadcasting, phone (904)358-6394; Ellyne Lonergan, Developmental National Productions, phone (904)358-6324. **Local Programs:** *Picture* 8:30 pm Thursday, Ellyne Lonergan; *The Pollcats* 7:30 p.m. Saturday, Tom Bronakoski. **Ad Rates:** Noncommercial. **URL:** http://www.wjct.org.

6285 WJFR-FM - 88.7
2611 WERD Radio Dr. Phone: (904)389-9088
Jacksonville, FL 32204

Format: Religious. **Founded:** 1987. **ADI:** Jacksonville (Brunswick), FL. **Key Personnel:** Jim Beck, General Mgr.; Craig Hulsebos, Program Dir. **Wattage:** 8000.

6286 WJGR-AM - 1320
5555 Radio Ln. Phone: (904)388-7711
Jacksonville, FL 32205 Fax: (904)384-0859
E-mail: wjgram@cis.com; wjgram@prodigy.com; wjgram@compuserve.com

Format: News; Talk; Sports. **Networks:** ABC; Mutual Broadcasting System; Westwood One Radio. **Owner:** Jacor Communications, Inc., 2o1 E. 5th St., 1300 Central Trust Center, Cincinnati, OH 45202, (513)621-1300. **Founded:** 1957. **Formerly**: WVOJ-AM (Apr. 1, 1994); WQIK-AM. **Operating Hours:** Continuous; 95% network, 5% local. **ADI:** Jacksonville (Brunswick), FL. **Key Personnel:** Larry Stevens, Program Dir.; Hartley Adkins, Sales Mgr.; Martha Philpot, Business Mgr.; Jeff Jones, Regional Sales Mgr.; Berneida Owens, Contact; Les Samuels, General Mgr. **Local Programs:** *Justice Coalition's Victim's Advocate*, Ted Hires, Mailing contact, (904)783-6312, Fax (904)783-4172; *Race Report with Donnie Helmly*, Donnie Helmly, Mailing contact, (904)285-2702, Fax (904)280-9074. **Wattage:** 5000.

6287 WJWB-TV - 17
9117 Hogan Rd. Phone: (904)641-1700
Jacksonville, FL 32216 Fax: (904)641-0306

Format: Commercial TV. **Founded:** 1966. **Formerly**: WJKS-TV (Feb. 12, 1997). **Operating Hours:** Continuous. **ADI:** Jacksonville (Brunswick), FL. **Key Personnel:** Michael A. Liff, Pres. & Gen. Mgr.; Marty Miller, General Sales Mgr.; Traci O'Neill, Program Dir.; Scott McAninch, Marketing Dir.; George Birnbaum, Operations Mgr. **Ad Rates:** $30-1,500 per unit.

6288 WJXR-FM - 92.1
PO Box 1 Phone: (904)259-2292
Jacksonville, FL 32234 Fax: (904)358-2265

Format: Country. **Networks:** ABC. **Owner:** WJXR Inc., at above address, Fax: (904)259-4488. **Founded:** 1978. **Formerly**: WBKF-FM (1984). **Operating Hours:** Continuous; 5% network, 95% local. **ADI:** Jacksonville (Brunswick), FL. **Key Personnel:** Greg Perich, Contact; Sarah Perich, Corporate Sec./Treasurer. **Wattage:** 25,000. **Ad Rates:** $20 for 30 seconds; $25 for 60 seconds.

6289 WJXT-TV - 4
Box 5270 Phone: (904)399-4000
Jacksonville, FL 32247 Fax: (904)399-1828
E-mail: news@wjxt.com

Format: Commercial TV. **Networks:** CBS. **Owner:** Post-Newsweek Stations, Inc., 3 Constitution Plaza, Hartford, CT 06103-1892, (860)493-6530. **Founded:** 1949. **Formerly**: WMBR-TV (1953). **Operating Hours:** Continuous; 60% network, 40% local. **ADI:** Jacksonville (Brunswick), FL. **Key Personnel:** Sherry Burns, Vice Pres./Gen. Mgr.; Peggy Madigan, General Sales Mgr.; Mike Stutz, News Dir.; Ann Sutton, Vice Pres./Program Mgr. **Local Programs:** *Eyewitness News* 5:30a.m., noon, 5, 5:30, 6, 11, Sharon Siegel; *Eyewitness News Daybreak* 6-7a.m., Kelly Clemons. **Wattage:** 100 Kw. **Ad Rates:** Advertising accepted; rates available upon request. **URL:** http://www.wjxt.com.

6290 WKQL-FM - 96.9
6869 Lennox Ave. Phone: (904)783-3711
Box 6877 Fax: (904)786-1529
Jacksonville, FL 32205

Format: Oldies. **Networks:** Independent. **Formerly**: WAIV-FM. **Operating Hours:** Continuous; 100% local. **ADI:** Jacksonville (Brunswick), FL. **Key Personnel:** Heather White, News Dir.; Angie Pinto, Promo Dir.; Cat Thomas, PD/Operations Mgr.; Andy Fisher, Local Sales Mgr. **Wattage:** 100,000. **Ad Rates:** $75-160 per unit.

6291 WKTZ-FM - 90.9
5353 Arlington Expressway Phone: (904)743-2400
Jacksonville, FL 32211-5587

Format: Easy Listening. **Networks:** Mutual Broadcasting System. **Owner:** Jones College, at above address. **Founded:** 1964. **Operating Hours:** Continuous. **ADI:** Jacksonville (Brunswick), FL. **Key Personnel:** Wayne Mashburn, General Mgr. **Wattage:** 50,000. **Ad Rates:** Noncommercial.

6292 WNCM-FM - 88.1
2361 Cortez Rd. Phone: (904)641-9626
Jacksonville, FL 32216 Fax: (904)645-9626

Format: Religious; Contemporary Christian. **Networks:** Sun Radio. **Founded:** 1984. **Operating Hours:** Continuous. **ADI:** Jacksonville (Brunswick), FL. **Key Personnel:** Calvin Grabau, Contact. **Wattage:** 1000. **Ad Rates:** $12 for 30 seconds; $15 for 60 seconds.

6293 WNZS-AM - 930
8386 Baymeadows Rd., Ste. 107 Phone: (904)636-0507
Jacksonville, FL 32256 Fax: (904)636-7971

Format: Sports. **Networks:** CBS. **Owner:** Paxson Broadcasting, at above address. **Formerly**: WRXJ-AM (1991). **Operating Hours:** Continuous; 50% network, 50% local. **ADI:** Jacksonville (Brunswick), FL. **Key Personnel:** Tommy Charles, Program Dir.; David Lamm, Sports Dir.; Linda Byrd, V. Pres./Gen. Mgr. **Local Programs:** *Lamm at Large*, Tommy Charles; *Sports Talk Today*, Tommy Charles. **Wattage:** 5000. **Ad Rates:** $5-25 per unit.

6294 WOBS-AM - 1530
5900 Picketville Rd. Phone: (904)783-1530
Jacksonville, FL 32205 Fax: (904)695-1631

Format: Religious. **Networks:** Independent. **Founded:** 1976. **Formerly**: WJGR-AM; WCRJ-AM. **Operating Hours:** Daytime. **Key Personnel:** Michael Craft, General Mgr., phone (941)954-1280, fax (940)955-9062; Chris Morris, Program Dir. **Wattage:** 50,000. **Ad Rates:** $13-22 for 30 seconds.

6295 WQIK-FM - 99.1
5555 Radio Ln. Phone: (904)388-7711
Jacksonville, FL 32205 Fax: (904)384-0859

Format: Contemporary Country. **Networks:** ABC. **Owner:** Jacor Communications, Inc., 1300 Central Trust Center, 201 E. 5th St., Cincinnati, OH 45202, (513)621-1300. **Founded:** 1954. **Operating Hours:** Continuous. **ADI:** Jacksonville (Brunswick), FL. **Key Personnel:** Rebecca Turner, News Dir.; Gail Austin, Program Dir.; Les Samuels, General Mgr.; Hartley Adkins, General Sales Mgr.; Jeff Jones, Contact; Martha Philpot, Contact; Berneida Owens, Contact; John Scott, Music Dir. **Wattage:** 100,000.

6296 WROS-AM - 1050
5590 Rio Grande Ave. Phone: (904)353-1050
Jacksonville, FL 32254 Fax: (904)353-7076

Format: Religious. **Owner:** Elwyn Hall, at above address, (904)353-7076. **Founded:** 1980. **Formerly**: WQIK-AM. **Operating Hours:** 6 a.m.-sundown. **ADI:** Jacksonville (Brunswick), FL. **Key Personnel:** Elwyn Hall, Owner; Jeremy Methuin, Promotions Mgr.; Valerie. Anthony, Contact; Loretta Whitley, Manager; Dean Hall, Vice President. **Wattage:** 5000. **Ad Rates:** $20 for 30 seconds; $13-22 for 60 seconds.

6297 WSOL-FM - 101.5
10592 E. Balmoral Circle, Ste. 1 Phone: (904)696-1015
Jacksonville, FL 32218 Fax: (904)696-1011

Format: Adult Contemporary. **Owner:** Jacor Broadcasting Co., at above address. **Founded:** 1966. **Operating Hours:** Continuous. **ADI:** Jacksonville (Brunswick), FL. **Key Personnel:** Rik Rogers, General Mgr.; Sandra Rockwell, Contact; Mickey Johnson, Program Dir.; Mark Tyree, General Sales Mgr. **Wattage:** 100,000 ERP.

6298 WSVE-AM - 1280
4343 Spring Grove Rd. Phone: (904)766-1211
Jacksonville, FL 32209-3629 Fax: (904)766-1332

Format: Religious. **Networks:** Mutual Broadcasting System. **Owner:** Willis Broadcasting Corp., 645 Church St., Ste. 400, Norfolk, VA 23510, (804)622-4600. **Founded:** 1982. **Formerly**: WEXI-AM. **Operating Hours:** Continuous. **ADI:** Jacksonville (Brunswick), FL. **Key Personnel:** Charles McGeathey, Reciever/Gen. Mgr.; Emily Timmons, Nat. Sal. **Wattage:** 5000. **Ad Rates:** $20 for 30 seconds; $35 for 60 seconds.

6299 WTEV-TV - 47
11700 Central Pkwy. Phone: (904)355-4741
Jacksonville, FL 32224-2600 Fax: (904)353-8400

Format: Commercial TV. **Networks:** United Paramount Network. **Formerly**: WNFT-TV. **Operating Hours:** Continuous. **ADI:** Jacksonville (Brunswick), FL. **Key Personnel:** Josh McGraw, General Mgr.; Paige Dietz, Program Dir.; Tony Sotelo, Production Mgr.

6300 WTLV-TV - 12
1070 E. Adams St. Phone: (904)354-1212
Jacksonville, FL 32202 Fax: (904)354-3299

Format: Commercial TV. **Networks:** NBC. **Founded:** 1957. **Operating Hours:** Continuous. **ADI:** Jacksonville (Brunswick), FL. **Key Personnel:** Ken Tonning, General Mgr.; Roz Fields, Program Dir.

6301 WVOJ-AM - 970
2427 University Blvd. N. Phone: (904)743-6234
Jacksonville, FL 32211 Fax: (904)745-0331
Free: (888)743-6970

Format: Sports; Talk. **Founded:** 1969. **Formerly**: WOZN-AM (1984). **Operating Hours:** 18 hrs. daily. **ADI:** Jacksonville (Brunswick), FL. **Key Personnel:** Robin Raphael, Pres., Owner & Asst. Prog. Dir. **Local Programs:** *Game*; *Greg Larson Show*; *Trivia Wizard*, John Simon. **Wattage:** 1000. **Ad Rates:** $15 for 30 seconds; $20 for 40 seconds; $30 for 60 seconds.

6302 WZAZ-AM - 1400
10592 E. Balmoral, Ste. 1 Phone: (904)696-1015
Jacksonville, FL 32218 Fax: (904)696-1011
E-mail: prayazclub@aol.com

Format: Gospel. **Networks:** CBS; ABC. **Founded:** 1984. **Formerly**: WERD-AM (1984); UNC Media of Jacksonville. **Operating Hours:** Continuous. **ADI:** Jacksonville (Brunswick), FL. **Key Personnel:** Ralph Christian, General Mgr.; Doc Wynter, Program Dir.; Mincy Pollock, Music Dir., phone (904)696-1143, fax (904)714-4487. **Wattage:** 1000.

JACKSONVILLE BEACH†, pop. 15,462.

NE FL. Duval Co. 15 mi. E. of Jacksonville. Beach resort.

6303 Beaches Leader
The Leader Group
PO Box 50129 Phone: (904)249-9033
Jacksonville Beach, FL 32240
Newspaper. **Founded:** 1963. **Freq:** Semiweekly (Wed. and Fri.). **Print Method:** Offset. **Trim Size:** 11 1/2 x 13 1/2. **Cols./Page:** 6. **Col. Width:** 25 nonpareils. **Col. Depth:** 21 1/2 inches. **Key Personnel:** Kathleen Feindt-Bailey, Editor; Thomas H. Wood, Publisher; Linda Borgstde, Dir. of Sales. **Subscription Rates:** $20 individuals. **Remarks:** Advertising accepted; rates available upon request.
Circ: ‡11,500

6304 The Mirror
The Beaches Leader, Inc.
1114 Beach Blvd. Phone: (904)249-9033
Jacksonville Beach, FL 32250
Publication E-mail: mayportmir@aol.com

Civilian newspaper published for Military and Civilian personnel and their dependents at Mayport, Florida. **Founded:** 1957. **Freq:** Weekly (Fri.). **Print Method:** Web press. **Cols./Page:** 5. **Col. Width:** 24 nonpareils. **Col. Depth:** 231 agate lines. **Key Personnel:** Hal Newsome, Editor; Thomas H. Wood, Publisher; Linda Borgstede, Advertising Dir., phone (904)249-9033. **Subscription Rates:** $40 individuals. **Remarks:** Accepts advertising.
Ad Rates: SAU: $7.84 **Circ:** Free ‡9,700
PCI: $8.23

6305 Sun-Times
The Leader Group
PO Box 50129 Phone: (904)249-9033
Jacksonville Beach, FL 32240
Local newspaper. **Subtitle:** The Beaches Newspaper. **Founded:** Apr. 1, 1981. **Freq:** Weekly (Wed.). **Print Method:** Offset. **Trim Size:** 11 1/2 x 17. **Cols./Page:** 5. **Col. Width:** 27 nonpareils. **Col. Depth:** 231 agate lines. **Key Personnel:** Jay Smith, Editor; Tom Wood, Publisher; Kenneth Lynam, Advertising Mgr. **Subscription Rates:** Free; $12 by mail. **Remarks:** Accepts advertising.
Ad Rates: GLR: $.71 **Circ:** Free ‡23,500
BW: $815
4C: $1,010.10
SAU: $9.88

JUPITER, pop. 9,388.

SE FL. Palm Beach Co. 18 mi. N. of West Palm Beach.

6306 International Desalination and Water Reuse Quarterly
Lineal Publishing Co.
306 Eagle Dr. Phone: (561)746-5566
Jupiter, FL 33477 Fax: (561)746-5599
Publication E-mail: dwrdesal@aol.com

Trade magazine covering water treatment and reuse. **Founded:** 1991. **Freq:** Quarterly. **Print Method:** Offset. **Trim Size:** 8 1/8 x 10 7/8. **Key Personnel:** Irv Lineal, Publisher; Paul Green, Publisher, phone (203)227-6500; Gordon Leitner, Editor. **ISSN:** 1022-5404. **Subscription Rates:** $40 individuals; $10 single issue. **Remarks:** Accepts advertising.
Ad Rates: BW: $3,530 **Circ:** Controlled 8,000
4C: $4,530

6307 The Jupiter Courier
Soripps Howard, Inc.
PO Box 1486 Phone: (407)746-5111
Jupiter, FL 33468-1486 Fax: (407)743-0673

Local newspaper. **Founded:** 1973. **Freq:** Semiweekly (Wed. and Sun.). **Print Method:** Offset. **Cols./Page:** 6. **Col. Width:** 26 nonpareils. **Col. Depth:** 301 agate lines. **Key Personnel:**

Jerry Rupar, Director. **USPS:** 985-980. **Subscription Rates:** $48 individuals per year; $72 by mail per year. **Remarks:** Accepts advertising.
Ad Rates: BW: $2,231.70 **Circ:** Paid ‡8,000
4C: $2,681.70 Free ‡17,000
PCI: $17.30

KENDALL

6308 Kendall News
Community Newspapers
PO Box 43-1970 Phone: (305)667-7481
Miami, FL 33143 Fax: (305)661-0954
Publication E-mail: communitynewspapers.com
Publisher E-mail: cnedor@gate.net

Community newspaper (tabloid). **Founded:** 1958. **Freq:** 3/week. **Print Method:** Offset. **Trim Size:** 10 1/4 x 16. **Cols./Page:** 6. **Col. Width:** 19 nonpareils. **Col. Depth:** 238 agate lines. **Key Personnel:** Michael Miller, Editor; Grant Miller, Publisher. **Subscription Rates:** $78 individuals. **Remarks:** Accepts advertising.
Ad Rates: GLR: $.72 **Circ:** Free ‡15,000
BW: $1,350
4C: $2,400
PCI: $413.50

KENNETH CITY

6309 The Suncoast Compass
Compass Productions
PO Box 28421 Phone: (813)547-4903
Kenneth City, FL 33709 Fax: (813)547-4903

Christian newspaper covering local, national, and international news. **Founded:** May 1997. **Freq:** Monthly. **Print Method:** Web offset. **Trim Size:** 11 x 17. **Cols./Page:** 4. **Col. Width:** 2 1/2 inches. **Col. Depth:** 16 inches. **Key Personnel:** Pamela Page-Bellis, Editor; Robin Brown, Managing Editor. **Subscription Rates:** $12 individuals. **Remarks:** Accepts advertising.
Ad Rates: BW: $500 **Circ:** Controlled 20,000

KEY BISCAYNE, pop. 5,489.

S FL. Dade Co. 6 mi. S. of Miami Beach.

6310 The Islander News
104 Crandon Blvd., No. 301 Phone: (305)361-3333
Key Biscayne, FL 33149 Fax: (305)361-5051

Community newspaper. **Subtitle:** The Life and Times of Key Biscayne, Florida. **Founded:** Nov. 2, 1966. **Freq:** Weekly (Thurs.). **Print Method:** Offset. **Trim Size:** 11 1/4 x 17 1/2. **Cols./Page:** 4. **Col. Width:** 2 3/8 inches. **Col. Depth:** 10 inches. **Key Personnel:** Nancye Ray, Editor and Publisher. **USPS:** 007-287. **Subscription Rates:** $15 individuals; $45 out of area. **Remarks:** Accepts advertising.
Ad Rates: BW: $350 **Circ:** Paid ‡3,100
PCI: $20 Free ‡600

KEY LARGO

Monroe Co. (SE). 5 m N of Tavernier.

6311 Catamaran Sailor
Ram Press
PO Box 2060 Phone: (305)451-3287
Key Largo, FL 33037 Fax: (305)453-0255
Publisher E-mail: ram5@icanect.net

Newspaper for catamaran sailors. **Founded:** Feb. 1995. **Freq:** 10/year. **Trim Size:** 8 1/2 x 11. **Cols./Page:** 3. **Col. Width:** 2 1/4 inches. **Key Personnel:** Mary Wells, Editor and Publisher; Rick White, Advertising Mgr. **Subscription Rates:** $10 individuals. **URL:** http://www.catsailor.com/.
Ad Rates: BW: $180 **Circ:** Paid 1,500
Non-paid 1,000

6312 WKLG-FM - 102.1
99343 Oversea Hwy. Phone: (305)451-2202
Key Largo, FL 33037 Fax: (305)453-0289
Free: (800)726-3419

Format: Adult Contemporary. **Networks:** ABC. **Owner:** WKLG Inc., Box 457, Key Largo, FL 33037. **Founded:** 1984. **Operating Hours:** Continuous. **ADI:** Miami (Ft. Lauderdale), FL. **Key Personnel:** Doug LaRue, Pres. and CEO. **Local Programs:** *Hook, Line & Sinker*, Bonnie Harrison, General Mgr. **Wattage:** 50,000. **Ad Rates:** $45-50 for 30 seconds; $75-80 for 60 seconds.

KEY WEST†, pop. 24,292.

S FL. Monroe Co. On Gulf of Mexico, 153 mi. S. of Miami. Florida Keys Community College. Tourist resort. Fisheries. Shrimp factories; sponge industry; bottling works.

6313 Cayo
PO Box 4516
Key West, FL 33041

Literary magazine covering fiction, poetry and photography in Key West. **Subtitle:** Reflections of Life in the Keys. **Founded:** May 1995. **Freq:** Quarterly. **Print Method:** Offset. **Key Personnel:** Alysan Matley, Editor; Kevin Crean, Photo Editor; Kirby Congdon, Poetry Editor. **Subscription Rates:** $16 individuals; $2 single issue. **Remarks:** Accepts advertising.
Circ: (Not Reported)

6314 Journal of Women and Aging
The Haworth Press, Inc.
PO Box 830 Phone: (305)744-9913
Key West, FL 33041-0830 Fax: (305)744-9835
Publication E-mail: infokeys@aol.com
Publisher E-mail: getinfo@haworthpressinc.com

Journal for professionals concerned with the health and well-being of the aging woman. **Founded:** 1989. **Freq:** Quarterly. **Trim Size:** 6x8 1/2. **Key Personnel:** J. Dianne Garner, DSW, Editor; Bill Cohen, Publisher. **ISSN:** 0895-2841. **Subscription Rates:** $40 individuals; $90 institutions; $175 libraries. **Remarks:** Accepts advertising. **Alt. Formats:** Microfiche.
Ad Rates: BW: $300 **Circ:** 467

6315 Key West Citizen
3420 Northside Dr. Phone: (305)294-6641
PO Box 1800 Fax: (305)294-0768
Key West, FL 33040
Local newspaper. **Subtitle:** Monroe County's Only Daily Newspaper. **Founded:** 1879. **Freq:** Daily and Sunday (morn.). **Print Method:** Offset. **Trim Size:** 13 x 21 1/2. **Cols./Page:** 9. **Col. Width:** 26 nonpareils. **Col. Depth:** 301 agate lines. **Key Personnel:** William Barry, Publisher; Bernard Hunt, Editor; Randy Erickson, Advertising Dir. **USPS:** 294-240. **Subscription Rates:** $99.51 individuals. **Remarks:** Accepts advertising.
Ad Rates: GLR: $.69 **Circ:** Mon.-Fri. ★9,541
BW: $1,489.95 Sun. ★11,588
4C: $1,744.95
PCI: $11.55

6316 WEOW-FM - 92.5
5016 5th Ave. Phone: (305)294-2523
PO Box 4500 Fax: (305)296-0358
Key West, FL 33041-2523

Format: Contemporary Hit Radio (CHR); Album-Oriented Rock (AOR). **Networks:** Independent. **Owner:** Peter Arnow, at above address. **Founded:** 1978. **Formerly:** WIIS-FM (1990). **Operating Hours:** Continuous; 100% local. **ADI:** Miami (Ft. Lauderdale), FL. **Key Personnel:** Peter Arnow, President; Melody Agliardo, Vice Pres. of Operations; Bill Bravo, Program Dir.; Todd Swofford, General Mgr. **Wattage:** 100,000. **Ad Rates:** $16-40 for 30 seconds; $18-50 for 60 seconds.

6317 WIIS-FM - 107.1
1075 Duval St., Ste. C17 Phone: (305)292-1133
Key West, FL 33040 Fax: (305)292-6936
E-mail: island107@cis.compuserve.com

Owner: Keyed Up Communications, 2734 Polk St., Hollywood, FL 33020. **Founded:** 1978. **Operating Hours:** Continuous. **Key Personnel:** Jeff Underwood, General Mgr.; David Wurmlinger. **Wattage:** 6000. **Ad Rates:** $12-20 for 30 seconds; $18-24 for 60 seconds.

6318 WJIR-FM - 90.9
1209 United St. Phone: (305)296-5773
Key West, FL 33040-3409 Fax: (305)294-9547

Format: Religious. **Networks:** Independent. **Founded:** 1986. **Operating Hours:** Continuous; 50% network, 50% local. **Key Personnel:** Ernest De Loach, President; Martha Menendez, Contact; Paul Hitchcock, Chief Engineer. **Wattage:** 300. **Ad Rates:** Noncommercial.

6319 WKRY-FM - 93.5
3820 N. Roosevelt Blvd. Phone: (305)296-2435
Key West, FL 33040 Fax: (305)296-1155
E-mail: wkry@conch.net

Format: Adult Contemporary. **Networks:** Independent. **Owner:** Paxson Communications Corp., 93351 Overseas Hwy., Tavernier, FL 33070, (305)852-9085, Fax: (305)852-5586. **Founded:** 1986. **Operating Hours:** Continuous. **Key Personnel:** Sherry J. Russo, General Mgr.; Gary Branson, Operations Mgr.; Simon Hendrix, Music Dir. **Wattage:** 31,500. **Ad Rates:** $15.00-18.00 for 30 seconds; $18.00-21.00 for 60 seconds. **URL:** http://www.wkry@conch.net.

6320 WKWF-AM - 1600
5016 5th Ave. Phone: (305)294-2523
PO Box 4500 Fax: (305)296-0358
Key West, FL 33040

Format: Oldies. **Networks:** CBS; Florida Radio. **Owner:** Drexel Hill Associates of Florida, at above address. **Founded:** 1959. **Formerly:** WKIZ-AM. **Operating Hours:** Continuous. **Key Personnel:** Peter Arnow, President; Todd Swofford, General Mgr.; Melody Agliardo, Contact. **Wattage:** 250.

6321 WOZN-FM - 98.7
PO Box 14369 Phone: (305)293-9898
Tallahassee, FL 32317-4369 Fax: (305)293-9654

Format: Album-Oriented Rock (AOR). **Founded:** 1986. **Operating Hours:** Continuous. **ADI:** Miami (Ft. Lauderdale), FL. **Key Personnel:** Bruce Timm, President; Daniel P. Amann, Production Dir. **Wattage:** 100,000. **Ad Rates:** $10-16 for 15 seconds; $12-18 for 30 seconds; $14-20 for 60 seconds.

KEYSTONE HEIGHTS

Clay Co. (NE). 20 m SE of Starke.

6322 WYFB-FM - 90.5
5553 SE 3rd Ave. Phone: (352)473-7077
Keystone Heights, FL 32656 Fax: (352)473-7077
E-mail: wyfb@aol.com

Format: Religious. **Networks:** Bible Broadcasting; AP. **Founded:** 1985. **Operating Hours:** Continuous; 90% network, 10% local. **Key Personnel:** Lowell Davey, President; Tom Penalver, Station Mgr.; Tom Penal, Manager. **Wattage:** 100,000. **Ad Rates:** Noncommercial.

KISSIMMEE†, pop. 15,331.

C FL. Osceola Co. On Lake Tohopekalige, 8 mi. E. of Walt Disney World. Plastic factory. Sawmills. Boat building. Naval stores. Fruit, cattle, beans, potatoes.

6323 Florida Cattleman and Livestock Journal
Florida Cattleman's Association
PO Box 421403 Phone: (407)846-8025
Kissimmee, FL 34742-1403 Fax: (407)933-8209
Free: (800)647-0026
Publisher E-mail: fcmfca@aol.com

Livestock news. **Founded:** 1936. **Freq:** Monthly. **Print Method:** Offset. **Trim Size:** 8 1/4 x 11. **Cols./Page:** 3. **Col. Width:** 26 nonpareils. **Col. Depth:** 140 agate lines. **Key Personnel:** Barbara Starcher, Production Coordinator. **ISSN:** 0015-3958. **Subscription Rates:** $35 individuals. **Remarks:** Accepts advertising.
Ad Rates: BW: $595 **Circ:** Paid 4,383
4C: $895 Non-paid 205
PCI: $27

6324 Osceola News-Gazette
Florida Sun Publications
PO Box 422068 Phone: (407)846-7600
Kissimmee, FL 34742-2068 Fax: (407)846-8516
Publication E-mail: osceolang@aol.com

Community newspaper. **Founded:** 1897. **Freq:** Semiweekly (Thurs. & Sat.). **Print Method:** Offset. **Trim Size:** 13 x 20 1/2. **Cols./Page:** 8. **Col. Width:** 18 nonpareils. **Col. Depth:** 287 agate lines. **Key Personnel:** Bill Orben, Editor; Dan Autrey, Publisher; Paula Stark, Advertising Mgr. **USPS:** 513-540. **Subscription Rates:** $30 individuals. **Remarks:** Accepts advertising. **URL:** http://www.osnewsgazette.com.
Ad Rates: BW: $1,218 **Circ:** Non-paid 27,493
4C: $1,443 Paid 1,088
PCI: $7.25

6325 Osceola Shopper
Florida Sun Publications
PO Box 422068 Phone: (407)846-7600
Kissimmee, FL 34742-2068 Fax: (407)846-8516

Shopper. **Freq:** Weekly (Wed.). **Print Method:** Photo offset. **Key Personnel:** Charles Onken, Circulation Mgr. **Subscription Rates:** Free.
Circ: Non-paid 32,323

6326 South Orange News
Florida Sun Publications
PO Box 422068 Phone: (407)846-7600
Kissimmee, FL 34742-2068 Fax: (407)846-8516

Community newspaper. **Founded:** 1994. **Freq:** Weekly (Thurs.). **Print Method:** Photo offset. **Key Personnel:** Charles Onken, Circulation Mgr.
Circ: Non-paid 19,625

6327 American Cablevision Services Inc.
900 Towne Center Dr. Phone: (407)933-5308
Kissimmee, FL 34759-3438 Fax: (407)870-5006

Owner: AVATAR Properties, at above address. **Founded:** 1971. **Key Personnel:** Jeff Pashley, President; Richard Leibe, General Mgr.; Tim Blydenburgh, Plant Supervisor; Tracy Wivestad, Advt. Insertion Mgr. **Cities Served:** Kissimmee, Poinciana, FL; Osceola and Polk Counties: subscribing households 3,800; 35 channels; 1 community access channel.

6328 WFIV-AM - 1080
1080 Country Blvd. Phone: (407)847-4422
Kissimmee, FL 34741 Fax: (407)932-1688

Format: Hispanic. **Owner:** Edward C. Allmon, at above address. **Founded:** 1964. **Operating Hours:** 14 hours daily. **ADI:** Orlando-Daytona Beach-Melbourne, FL. **Key Personnel:** Edward C. Allmon, Contact. **Wattage:** 10,000. **Ad Rates:** $25 for 60 seconds.

6329 WOTS-AM - 1220
5770 W. Vine St., Ste. 150 Phone: (407)396-1220
Kissimmee, FL 34746 Fax: (407)396-1042

Format: Information. **Founded:** 1977. **Formerly**: WMJK-AM (1994). **Operating Hours:** Continuous;100% local. **ADI:** Orlando-Daytona Beach-Melbourne, FL. **Key Personnel:** Deac Hundley, General Mgr.; Terry Mason, Station Mgr.; Lisa Grabowski, Business Mgr.; Mike Zimmer, Sales Mgr.; Mike Singer, Engineer. **Wattage:** 1000. **Ad Rates:** $15 for 30 seconds; $20 for 60 seconds.

LA BELLE†, pop. 2,294.

SC FL. Hendry Co. On Caloosahatchee River, 32 mi. NE of Fort Myers. Oil field. Agriculture. Citrus, cattle, honey.

6330 Caloosa Belle
The Caloose Belle
PO Box 518 Phone: (813)675-2541
La Belle, FL 33935-0518 Fax: (813)675-1449

Community newspaper. **Founded:** 1923. **Freq:** Weekly (Wed.). **Print Method:** Offset. **Cols./Page:** 6. **Key Personnel:** Richard Schuster, Editor and Publisher; Martha Puletti, Advertising Mgr. **Subscription Rates:** $16 individuals. **Remarks:** Accepts advertising.
Ad Rates: GLR: $.40 **Circ:** Free 6,500
BW: $844.95
SAU: $6.55

6331 Immokalee Bulletin
The Caloose Belle
PO Box 518 Phone: (813)675-2541
La Belle, FL 33935-0518 Fax: (813)675-1449

Community newspaper. **Freq:** Weekly (Thurs.). **Cols./Page:** 6. **Col. Width:** 2 1/16 inches. **Col. Depth:** 21.5 picas. **Key Personnel:** Louise Blanchard, Editor. **Subscription Rates:** Free; $5 (mail); $10 out of area. **Remarks:** Accepts advertising.
Ad Rates: PCI: $5.65 **Circ:** Free ‡4,500

LADYSMITH

6332 Mid-Atlantic Cable
Box 22 Phone: (904)448-0166
Ladysmith, FL 22501 Fax: (904)448-9347

Owner: Mid-Atlantic Cable, 5335 Wisconsin Ave., Ste. 750, Washington, DC 20015. **Founded:** 1989. **Key Personnel:** Carole DiRubba-Lewis, Customer Service Mgr.; Damon Bragg, Chief Engineer. **Cities Served:** Caroline and King William counties: subscribing households 1,200; 40 channels; 1 community access channel; 168 hours per week community access programming.

LAKE CITY†, pop. 9,257.

N FL. Columbia Co. 60 mi. W. of Jacksonville. Lake City Community College. Manufactures turpentine, mobile homes, lumber. Poultry and stock.

6333 Lake City Reporter
126 E. Duval St. Phone: (904)752-1293
PO Box 1709 Fax: (904)752-9400
Lake City, FL 32055-4025
Newspaper (Democratic). **Founded:** 1874. **Freq:** Daily (eve.). **Print Method:** Offset. **Cols./Page:** 6. **Col. Width:** 26 nonpareils. **Col. Depth:** 301 agate lines. **Key Personnel:** Russ Roberts, Editor; Don Caldwell, Publisher; Andy Caldwell, Advertising Mgr. **Subscription Rates:** $51 individuals. **Remarks:** Accepts advertising.
Ad Rates: GLR: $.76 **Circ:** Mon.-Thurs. ★**8,823**
BW: $1,393.20 Fri. ★**10,212**
4C: $1,711.20
PCI: $10.80

6334 News Advertiser
508 N. 1st St. Phone: (904)752-8280
Lake City, FL 32055 Fax: (904)758-5869

Regional shopper-news. **Subtitle:** Lake City News-Advertiser. **Founded:** Jan. 1959. **Freq:** Weekly. **Print Method:** Offset. **Trim Size:** 11 x 16. **Cols./Page:** 6. **Col. Width:** 20 nonpareils. **Col. Depth:** 210 agate lines. **Key Personnel:** Don Dockery, Publisher. **Subscription Rates:** Free; $18 by mail. **Remarks:** Accepts advertising.
Ad Rates: GLR: $.65 **Circ:** Paid ‡3,265
BW: $819 Free ‡22,519
4C: $1,419
SAU: $12.18

6335 WDSR-AM - 1340
3507 S. Marion St. Phone: (904)752-1340
PO Box 3299 Fax: (904)755-9369
Lake City, FL 32056
E-mail: wnfb@mix943.com

Format: Sports; Talk. **Networks:** CBS. **Owner:** Newman Media, Inc., at above address. **Founded:** 1946. **Operating Hours:** Continuous; 100% network. **ADI:** Jacksonville (Brunswick), FL. **Key Personnel:** Suzi Abbott, General Mgr.; Austin Reed, Program Dir. **Wattage:** 1000. **Ad Rates:** $8-12 for 30 seconds; $10-15 for 60 seconds. Combined advertising rates available with WNFB.

6336 WGRO-AM - 960
Rte. 13 Phone: (904)752-0960
PO Box 318 Fax: (904)752-9861
Lake City, FL 32055

Format: Country. **Owner:** Louis D. Bolton, 3821 Cove Dr., Birmingham, AL 35213, (205)879-1587. **Founded:** 1958. **Operating Hours:** Continuous; 100% local. **Key Personnel:** Robert Hendrickson, Contact; Scott Berns, Operations Mgr. **Wattage:** 500 day; 1000 night. **Ad Rates:** $4.60 for 30 seconds; $9.50 for 60 seconds.

6337 WNFB-FM - 94.3
PO Box 3299 Phone: (904)752-9436
Lake City, FL 32056 Fax: (904)755-9369
E-mail: wnfb@mix943.com

Format: Adult Contemporary. **Networks:** CBS; Florida Radio. **Owner:** Newman Media, Inc., at above address, (407)298-4000, Fax: (407)297-4077. **Founded:** 1969. **Formerly:** WQPD-FM. **Operating Hours:** Continuous; 100% local. **ADI:** Jacksonville (Brunswick), FL. **Key Personnel:** Renita Boyer, Office Mgr.; Suzi Abbott, General Mgr., suziabbott@mix943.com; Austin Reed, Program Dir., austinreed@mix943.com; Ron Keiter, Technical Dir., ronkeiter@mix943.com; Steve Johnson, Sales Mgr., stevejohnson@mix943.com. **Wattage:** 50,000. **Ad Rates:** $15-20 for 30 seconds; $20-32 for 60 seconds. Combined advertising rates available with WDSR-AM. **URL:** http://www.ix943.com.

6338 WOLR-FM - 91.3
Rt. 2, Box 667 Phone: (904)935-3300
Lake City, FL 32055 Fax: (904)673-3715

Format: Adult Contemporary; Religious. **Networks:** Independent. **Owner:** WOLR 91.3 FM, Inc., at above address. **Founded:** 1986. **Operating Hours:** Continuous; 100% local. **Key Personnel:** Gordon Lund, Station Mgr. **Wattage:** 18,000. **Ad Rates:** Noncommercial.

LAKE MARY

Seminole Co. (NC). 2 m W of Sanford.

6339 Charisma
Strang Communications Co.
600 Rinehart Rd. Phone: (407)333-0600
Lake Mary, FL 32746 Fax: (407)333-7133
Publication E-mail: charisma@strang.com

Religious. **Subtitle:** And Christian Life. **Founded:** 1975. **Freq:** Monthly. **Print Method:** Offset. **Trim Size:** 8 x 10 3/4. **Cols./Page:** 3. **Col. Width:** 27 nonpareils. **Col. Depth:** 140 agate lines. **Key Personnel:** Stephen Strang, Publisher; J. Lee Grady, Editor, grady@strang.com; Jimmy Stewart, Managing Editor, stewart@strang.com; Billy Bruce, News Editor, bruce@strang.com. **ISSN:** 0895-156X. **Subscription Rates:** $22.97 individuals. **Remarks:** Accepts advertising. **Online:** Strang Communications. **URL:** http://www.charismamag.com.
Ad Rates: BW: $6,850 **Circ:** Paid 220,000
4C: $7,450 Non-paid 2,000

6340 Christian Retailing
Strang Communications Co.
600 Rinehart Rd. Phone: (407)333-0600
Lake Mary, FL 32746-4968 Fax: (407)333-7100
Publication E-mail: retailing@strang.com

Tabloid on retailing Christian merchandise. **Founded:** Dec. 15, 1986. **Freq:** 20/year. **Print Method:** Offset. **Trim Size:** 10 3/4 x 14 3/4. **Cols./Page:** 4. **Col. Width:** 2.25 picas. **Col. Depth:** 14 inches. **Key Personnel:** Marcia Ford, Managing Editor, mford@strang.com; Bob Minotti, Advertising Dir., minotti@strang.com. **ISSN:** 0027-6782. **Subscription Rates:** Free to bookstores; $75 individuals.
Ad Rates: BW: $1,843 **Circ:** Controlled ‡10,500
4C: $2,418

6341 WJHM-FM - 101.9
37 Skyline Dr., Ste. 4200 Phone: (407)333-0072
Lake Mary, FL 32746 Fax: (407)333-2919
E-mail: fm102jamz@aol.com

Format: Urban Contemporary. **Owner:** Chancellor Media Corp., 433 E. Las Colinas Blvd., Ste. 1130, Irving, TX 75039, (972)869-9020, Fax: (972)869-3671. **Founded:** 1988. **Formerly**: WCFI-FM (1986). **Operating Hours:** Continuous; 3% network, 100% local. **ADI:** Orlando-Daytona Beach-Melbourne, FL. **Key Personnel:** Mike Gonick, General Mgr., fax (407)333-2191, xl1067fm@aol.com; Mary Ann Kaplan, General Sales Mgr., fax (407)333-2342, maskjamz@aol.com; Russ Allen, Program Dir., fax (407)333-2342, playaruss@aol.com. **Wattage:** 61,000.

6342 WOFL-TV - 35
35 Skyline Dr. Phone: (407)644-3535
Lake Mary, FL 32746 Fax: (407)333-3535

Format: Commercial TV. **Networks:** Independent; Fox. **Operating Hours:** Continuous. **ADI:** Orlando-Daytona Beach-Melbourne, FL. **Key Personnel:** Tom Calato, Contact.

6343 WOGX-TV - 51
35 Skyline Dr. Phone: (407)741-5095
Lake Mary, FL 32746 Fax: (407)333-0234

Format: Commercial TV. **Networks:** Fox. **Owner:** Meredith Corp., Locust at 17th. St, Des Moines, IA 50309-3023, (515)284-3000. **Founded:** 1983. **Formerly:** WBSP-TV (1986). **Operating Hours:** Continuous. **ADI:** Gainesville (Ocala), FL. **Key Personnel:** Bill Avery, Program Dir.; Sandy Wagner, Sales Mgr.; Tom Calato, General Mgr.; Don Holt, Production Mgr.; John Jones, Chief Engineer; John McThompson, Contact. **Ad Rates:** $30-1100 per unit.

LAKE PARK, pop. 6,909.

SE FL. Palm Beach Co. 5 mi. N. of W. Palm Beach. Resort area.

6344 Kidstuff
Guidelines Press
1307 S. Killian Dr. Phone: (407)842-9411
Lake Park, FL 33403-1918 Fax: (407)842-2237

Language arts programming resource for preschool and K-3 teachers, daycare workers, and childrens' librarians. **Subtitle:** A Treasury of Early Childhood Enrichment Materials. **Founded:** 1981. **Freq:** Monthly. **Print Method:** Offset. **Trim Size:** 8 1/2 x 11. **Cols./Page:** 2. **Col. Width:** 3 1/2 inches. **Col. Depth:** 139 agate lines. **Key Personnel:** Sheila H. Debs, Editor; Howard R. Debs, Publisher. **ISSN:** 0278-632X. **Subscription Rates:** $24 individuals. **Remarks:** Advertising accepted; rates available upon request.
Circ: 10,000

LAKE PLACID, pop. 963.

C FL. Highlands Co. 34 mi. NW of Okeechobee. Nursery. Caladium capitol of the World. Tourism. Agriculture. Truck farms, citrus fruit, cattle.

6345 Journal
232 N. Main St. Phone: (813)465-2433
PO Box 696 Fax: (813)699-0331
Lake Placid, FL 33852-9624
Publication E-mail: wupy@up.net

Community newspaper. **Founded:** 1959. **Freq:** Weekly (Thurs.). **Print Method:** Offset. **Cols./Page:** 8. **Col. Width:** 19 nonpareils. **Col. Depth:** 301 agate lines. **Key Personnel:** Mathew Delaney, Editor; Constance Delaney, Publisher; Mark Delaney, Advertising Mgr. **Subscription Rates:** $10.50 individuals; $12.50 out of state. **Remarks:** Color advertising accepted; rates available upon request.
Ad Rates: GLR: $.25 **Circ:** 4,900

LAKE WALES, pop. 8,466.

C FL. Polk Co. 30 mi. SE of Lakeland. Tourist resort. Ships citrus fruits. Manufactures boats, fertilizer, mattresses, concrete products, ceramic tile, canned fruits and vegetables. Citrus fruit packed; grapefruit cannery. Agriculture. Oranges, grapefruit, cattle.

6346 The Lake Wales News
The Lake Wales News, Inc.
140 Stuart Ave. Phone: (941)676-3467
Lake Wales, FL 33853 Fax: (941)676-3468

Community newspaper. **Founded:** June 1926. **Freq:** Weekly (Thurs.). **Print Method:** Offset. **Trim Size:** 16 1/8 x 22. **Cols./Page:** 8. **Col. Width:** 20 nonpareils. **Col. Depth:** 21 inches. **Key Personnel:** S.L. Frisbie IV, Editor and Publisher, phone (941)533-4183, fax (941)533-0402. **USPS:** 302-900. **Subscription Rates:** $15 local; $18 out of country; $.25 single issue. **Remarks:** Accepts advertising.
Ad Rates: BW: $504 **Circ:** Paid ‡2,977
PCI: $3.75 Free ‡25

6347 WIPC-AM - 1280
630 Mt. Lake Cutoff Rd. Phone: (813)676-9179
Lake Wales, FL 33853-7854

Networks: Talknet. **Founded:** 1951. **Formerly:** WKZJ-AM (1991). **Operating Hours:** Continuous. **Key Personnel:** Cecil Underwood, General Mgr. **Wattage:** 1000. **Ad Rates:** $9.75-12 for 30 seconds; $15-19.50 for 60 seconds.

LAKE WORTH, pop. 26,107.

SE FL. Palm Beach Co. Adjoins West Palm Beach on the south. Manufactures storage batteries, chemicals, paint. Nurseries. Winter resort.

6348 Lake Worth Herald
Lake Worth Herald Press
130 S. H St. Phone: (561)585-9387
Lake Worth, FL 33460 Fax: (561)585-5434
Publication E-mail: talk@wjml.com

General newspaper. **Founded:** Feb. 1912. **Freq:** Weekly (Thurs.). **Print Method:** Offset. **Trim Size:** 11 1/4 x 17 1/2. **Cols./Page:** 6. **Col. Width:** 20 nonpareils. **Col. Depth:** 224 agate lines. **Key Personnel:** Jay Kravetz, Editor. **Subscription Rates:** $15 individuals. **Remarks:** Accepts advertising. **Alt. Formats:** CD-ROM.
Ad Rates: BW: $696 **Circ:** Paid 955
4C: $295 Free 26,283
PCI: $7.25

6349 National Enquirer
600 East Coast Ave. Phone: (561)586-1111
Lake Worth, FL 33464-0002 Fax: (561)540-1009
Publication E-mail: letters@nationalenquirer.com

General editorial. **Founded:** 1926. **Freq:** Weekly. **Print Method:** Letterpress (Rotogravure). **Trim Size:** 9 3/8 x 11 3/8. **Cols./Page:** 5. **Col. Width:** 23 nonpareils. **Col. Depth:** 154 agate lines. **Key Personnel:** Steve Coz, Editor, fax (561)540-1010; Tony Hoyt, Publisher, phone (212)888-3320. **ISSN:** 1056-3482. **Subscription Rates:** $19.95 individuals. **Remarks:** Accepts advertising. **URL:** http://www.nationalenquirer.com.
Ad Rates: BW: $39,500 **Circ:** Paid ★2,244,213
4C: $49,800

6350 RAG
RAG Publications
PO Box 6768 Phone: (561)968-1888
Lake Worth, FL 33466-6768
All music-magazine featuring interviews, biographies, and trade and technical articles. **Founded:** July 1977. **Freq:** Monthly. **Print Method:** Offset. **Trim Size:** 8 1/2 x 11. **Cols./Page:** 4. **Col. Width:** 1 3/4 inches. **Col. Depth:** 9 3/4 inches. **Key Personnel:** Sandy Husted, Editor; Dino Fedele, Publisher. **ISSN:** 1061-9879. **Subscription Rates:** $15; $25 two years. **Remarks:** Accepts advertising.
Ad Rates: GLR: $1.60 **Circ:** 20,000
BW: $870.40
4C: $1,395.40

6351 WLVS-AM - 1380
1939 7th Ave. N. Phone: (561)585-5533
Lake Worth, FL 33461-3898 Fax: (561)585-0131

Format: Hispanic. **Networks:** CNN Radio. **Founded:** 1959. **Formerly:** WLIZ-AM (1987). **Operating Hours:** Continuous; 100% local. **ADI:** West Palm Beach-Ft. Pierce-Vero Beach, FL. **Key Personnel:** Max Hopkins, Regional Mgr., mhopkins@gladesmedia.com; James Garza, Sales. **Local Programs:** *Radio Fiesta*, Paco Alba, (561)585-5533, Fax (561)585-0131. **Wattage:** 1000. **Ad Rates:** $15 for 30 seconds; $25 for 60 seconds.

6352 WPBR-AM - 1340
PO Box 1340 Phone: (561)582-7401
Lake Worth, FL 33460-1340 Fax: (561)582-9254

Format: Talk. **Networks:** Mutual Broadcasting System. **Owner:** Emil Antonoff, at above address. **Founded:** 1988. **Operating Hours:** Continuous. **Key Personnel:** Frank R. Shaheen, Business Mgr. **Wattage:** 1000. **Ad Rates:** $16-44 for 30 seconds; $20-55 for 60 seconds.

LAKELAND, pop. 52,500.

C FL. Polk Co. 32 mi. E. of Tampa. Florida Southern College. Manufactures fertilizer, beverages, batteries, furniture, food machinery, ceramic tile. Phosphate mines. Citrus fruit packing and canning. Fruit, truck, poultry farms.

6353 Florida Living Magazine
Florida Media, Inc.
3235 Duff Rd. Phone: (941)858-7244
Lakeland, FL 33810 Fax: (941)859-5297
Publication E-mail: flliving@earthlink.net

Statewide lifestyle magazine. **Subtitle:** Florida Living Magazine. **Founded:** 1981. **Freq:** Monthly. **Print Method:** Web offset. **Trim Size:** 8 x 10 7/8. **Cols./Page:** 3. **Col. Width:** 13 picas. **Col. Depth:** 10 inches. **Key Personnel:** E. Douglas Cifers, Publisher, fax (941)859-3197; Kristen Crane, Managing Editor. **ISSN:** 0888-9600. **Subscription Rates:** $21.95 individuals; $31.95 other countries. **Remarks:** Accepts advertising. **URL:** http://www.floridaliving.org. **Formerly:** Florida Living.
Ad Rates: BW: $4,900 **Circ:** Paid ‡168,475
4C: $7,938 Non-paid ‡4,209

6354 The Ledger
33815 W. Lime St. Phone: (941)802-7000
PO Box 408 Fax: (941)687-7090
Lakeland, FL 33802
Publication E-mail: online@theledger.com

General newspaper. **Founded:** 1924. **Freq:** Mon.-Sun. (morn.). **Print Method:** Offset. **Trim Size:** 17 x 24. **Cols./Page:** 6. **Col. Width:** 25 nonpareils. **Col. Depth:** 301 agate lines. **Key Personnel:** Louis Michael Perez, Exec. Editor; Don R. Whitworth, Publisher. **Subscription Rates:** $75.40 individuals. **Remarks:** Accepts advertising. **URL:** http://www.theledger.com. **Feature Editors:** Tom Arthur, *City, Metro, Rural Development*, phone (813)687-7000; Brad Beahan, *Drama*, phone (813)687-7000; Carol Blair, *Garden/Home*, phone (813)687-7000; Lynne Cooke, *Family, Features, Lifestyle, Society, Women's*, phone (813)687-7000; K. Darcy Hanzlik, *Education*, phone (813)687-7000; Barry Friedman, *News, Saturday, Sunday*, phone (813)687-7000; Mary Jo Rappana, *Fashion*, phone (813)687-7000; Jeff Kline, *Financial/Business, Real Estate*, phone (813)687-7000; Tom Palmer, *Environmental*, phone (813)687-7000; Michael Peltier, *Aviation*, phone (813)687-7000; Marialice Quinn, *Radio, Religion, TV, Travel*, phone (813)687-7000; Tony Ranze, *Photo*, phone (813)687-7000; Trent Rowe, *Food*, phone (813)687-7000; Bill Rufty, *Political*, phone (813)687-7000; Dave Schultz, *Editorials*, phone (813)687-7000; John Valerino, *Sports*, phone (813)687-7000; Steve Webb, *Book, Entertainment, Movie, Music*, phone (813)687-7000; Robin Williams, *Medical*, phone (813)687-7000.
Ad Rates: PCI: $34.63 **Circ:** Mon.-Sat. 80,482
Sun. 98,571

6355 Onionhead Literary Quarterly
Lakeland Center for Creative Arts
115 N. Kentucky Ave. Phone: (941)680-2787
Lakeland, FL 33801
Literary magazine. **Founded:** Jan. 1989. **Freq:** Quarterly. **Trim Size:** 5 1/2 x 8 1/2. **Key Personnel:** Susan Crawford, Editor; Dot Davis, Editor; Brenda Patterson, Editor. **Subscription Rates:** $8 individuals; $16 out of country; $3 single issue. **Remarks:** Advertising not accepted.
Circ: Combined 320

6356 The Southern
Florida Southern College
111 Lake Hollingsworth Dr. Phone: (941)680-4170
Lakeland, FL 33801-5698 Fax: (941)680-6244

Collegiate newspaper. **Founded:** 1923. **Freq:** Biweekly. **Print Method:** Letterpress and offset. **Cols./Page:** 5. **Col. Width:** 11 picas. **Col. Depth:** 90 picas. **Key Personnel:** Benjamin Anderson, Advisor. **Subscription Rates:** $5 individuals. **Remarks:** Accepts advertising.
Ad Rates: BW: $375 **Circ:** Free ‡2,500
PCI: $5

6357 People's Cable Inc.
3705 Hwy. 98 S Phone: (813)647-5226
Lakeland, FL 33813

Founded: 1991. **Key Personnel:** Patrick D. McConnell, President; John W. Gilman, General Sales Mgr. **Cities Served:** Barton, Lakeland, Mulberry, Winter Haven, FL: subscribing households 11,000; 33 channels. **Additional Contact Info: Mailing Address:** PO Box 5620, Lakeland, FL 33807-5620.

6358 WLKF-AM - 1430
404 W. Lime St. Phone: (941)682-4191
Lakeland, FL 33815-4651 Fax: (941)682-3143
E-mail: hottalk@wlkf.com

Format: News; Talk. **Networks:** NBC; ABC. **Owner:** Hall Communications, 404 W. Lime St., PO Box 2038, Lakeland, FL 33806, (941)682-8184, Fax: (941)683-2409. **Founded:** 1936. **Formerly:** WLAK-AM. **Operating Hours:** Continuous. **ADI:** Tampa- St. Petersburg (Lakeland, Sarasota),FL. **Key Personnel:** Lowell Shumaker, Operations Mgr.; Arthur Rowbotham, President; Steve Howard, General Mgr. **Wattage:** 5000. **Ad Rates:** Advertising accepted; rates available upon request. **URL:** http://www.wlkf.com.

6359 WONN-AM - 1230
404 W. Lime St. Phone: (941)682-8184
PO Box 2038 Fax: (941)683-2409
Lakeland, FL 33801
Free: (800)227-9797

Networks: CNN Radio. **Owner:** Hall Communications, Inc., at above address. **Founded:** 1949. **Operating Hours:** Continuous; 10% network, 90% local. **ADI:** Tampa- St. Petersburg (Lakeland, Sarasota),FL. **Key Personnel:** Art Rowbotham, General Mgr., arowbotham@hallradio.com; Dick Goleno, Sports Dir./PD; Tom O'Brien, News Dir.; Steve Howard, Station Mgr., showard@hallradio.com. **Wattage:** 1000. **Ad Rates:** $10 for 30 seconds; $25 for 60 seconds.

6360 WPCV-FM - 97.5
PO Box 2038 Phone: (941)682-8184
Lakeland, FL 33806 Fax: (941)683-2409
Free: (800)227-9787
E-mail: wpcv.com

Format: Contemporary Country. **Owner:** Hall Communications, Inc., at above address. **Founded:** 1963. **Formerly:** WINT-FM (1966). **Operating Hours:** Continuous. **ADI:** Tampa-St. Petersburg (Lakeland, Sarasota), FL. **Key Personnel:** Art Rowbotham, General Mgr., arowbotham@hallradio.com; Nancy Cattarius, General Sales Mgr.; Steve Howard, Station Mgr., showard@hallradio.com; Dave Wright, Program/Promotions Dir., decjay@gatener.com; Dave Wright. **Wattage:** 100,000. **Ad Rates:** Advertising accepted; rates available upon request. **URL:** http://www.wpcv.com.

6361 WTWB-AM - 1570
777 Carpenters Way Phone: (941)858-3805
PO Box 95020 Fax: (941)859-0171
Lakeland, FL 33804-5020
Free: (800)742-3969
E-mail: wtwb1570@aol.com

Format: Gospel; Southern Gospel. **Networks:** ABC. **Founded:** 1956. **Operating Hours:** 24Hrs. **ADI:** Tampa- St. Petersburg (Lakeland, Sarasota),FL. **Key Personnel:** Shane Simmons, General Mgr. **Local Programs:** *Gospel Home Coming*, Dick Shiftlett; *Time to Live*, Tim Thomas. **Wattage:** 5000. **Ad Rates:** $9.00 for 30 seconds; $12.00 for 60 seconds.

6362 WWAB-AM - 1330
1203 West Chase St. Phone: (813)682-2998
PO Box 65 Fax: (813)687-4000
Lakeland, FL 33802-0065

Format: Urban Contemporary; Blues. **Networks:** American Urban Radio. **Founded:** 1957. **Operating Hours:** Sunrise-sunset. **ADI:** Tampa- St. Petersburg (Lakeland, Sarasota),FL. **Key Personnel:** Dee Van Pelt, General Mgr. **Wattage:** 1000. **Ad Rates:** $10 for 30 seconds; $15 for 60 seconds.

LANTANA, pop. 8,048.

SE FL. Palm Beach Co. 10 mi. S. of Palm Beach.

6363 Amerikan Uutiset
Amerikan Uutiset Inc.
PO Box 8147 Phone: (561)588-9770
Lantana, FL 33462 Fax: (561)588-3229
Publication E-mail: amuutiset@aol.com

Ethnic newspaper (Finnish). **Founded:** 1932. **Freq:** Weekly (Thurs.). **Print Method:** Offset. Uses mats. **Cols./Page:** 6. **Col. Width:** 1 5/8 inches. **Col. Depth:** 16 inches. **Key Personnel:** Sakri Viklund, Editor-in-Chief. **ISSN:** 0745-9971. **Subscription Rates:** $32 individuals. **Remarks:** Accepts advertising.
Ad Rates: GLR: $.21 **Circ:** 5,000
BW: $460.80
4C: $556.80
PCI: $8

6364 Soap Opera Magazine
Soap Opera Magazine, Inc.
600 SE Coast Ave.
Lantana, FL 33462

Magazine reporting on daytime television soap operas. **Freq:** Weekly. **Key Personnel:** Joseph Pollcy, Editor. **Subscription Rates:** $39.84 individuals; $1.49 single issue. **Remarks:** Advertising accepted; rates available upon request.
Circ: Paid 300,267

LARGO, pop. 60,000.

WC FL. Pinellas Co. 12 mi. NW of St. Petersburg. Small Industries. Nurseries.

6365 The Battery Man
Independent Battery Manufacturers Association, Inc.
100 Larchwood Dr. Phone: (813)586-1408
Largo, FL 33770-2811 Fax: (813)586-1400
Free: (800)237-6126
Publication E-mail: thebatteryman@juno.com
Publisher E-mail: thebatteryman@juno.com

International trade journal for the battery industry and related areas. **Founded:** 1921. **Freq:** Monthly. **Print Method:** Offset. **Trim Size:** 8 1/2 x 11. **Cols./Page:** 3. **Col. Width:** 27 nonpareils. **Col. Depth:** 140 agate lines. **Key Personnel:** David Pfleeger, Editor; Suzanne Kellerman, Advertising/Circulation. **ISSN:** 0005-6359. **Subscription Rates:** $20 individuals; $3 single issue; $22 other countries; $55 airmail. **Remarks:** Accepts advertising.
Ad Rates: BW: $610 **Circ:** 4,100
4C: $1,214

6366 Oasis
Box 626 Phone: (727)449-2186
Largo, FL 33779-0626
Publisher E-mail: oasislit@aol.com

Literary magazine. **Founded:** Sept. 1992. **Freq:** Quarterly. **Key Personnel:** Neal Storrs, Editor and Publisher. **ISSN:** 1064-6299. **Subscription Rates:** $20 individuals; $7.50 single issue. **Remarks:** Advertising not accepted.
Circ: Combined 290

6367 Value Retail News
Off-Price Specialists, Inc.
11701 S. Belchir Rd., St. 130 Phone: (941)536-4047
Largo, FL 34640 Fax: (941)536-4389
Free: (800)669-1020

Trade magazine. **Subtitle:** The Outlet/Off-Price Journals. **Founded:** Jan. 1983. **Freq:** Monthly. **Print Method:** Sheetfed offset. **Trim Size:** 11 x 15. **Cols./Page:** 4. **Col. Width:** 13.25 picas. **Col. Depth:** 13 3/4 inches. **Key Personnel:** Kris Hundley, Executive Editor, phone (ext).470; Tom Kirwan, Senior Editor, phone (ext)471; Linda Humphers, Senior Editor, phone (ext).472; Dan Cochran, V.P. General Mgr. **Subscription Rates:** $144 individuals; $72 for second and subsequent subs; criptions. **Remarks:** Accepts advertising. **URL:** http://www.outletsource.com.
Ad Rates: BW: $2,870 **Circ:** ‡5,000
4C: $3,935
PCI: $150.00

LEESBURG, pop. 13,191.

C FL. Lake Co. 40 mi. NW of Orlando. Lake-Sumter Community College. Manufactures concrete products, mobile homes. Packs citrus fruit. Fishing resort. Truck and citrus farms.

6368 Comcast
8130 County Rd. 44, Leg A Phone: (904)787-7875
Leesburg, FL 34788-3704 Fax: (904)365-6279

Founded: 1968. **Formerly:** Lake County Cablevision. **Key Personnel:** Philip Yapkowitz, General Mgr., phone (352)787-9601, fax (352)326-8492. **Cities Served:** Eustis, Fruitland Park, Howey-in-the-Hills, Lady Lake, Lake County, Montverde, Mount Dora, Mount Plymouth, Sorrento, Tavares, Umatilla, FL: subscribing households 57,000; 45 channels.

6369 Leesburg Lakeshore Mobile Home Park
1208 N. Lee St. Phone: (352)787-5683
Leesburg, FL 34748 Fax: (352)787-1561

Owner: Tom Grizzard and Sally Reeves, at above address. **Founded:** 1947. **Key Personnel:** Tom Grizzard, General Partner; Sally Reeves, General Partner. **Cities Served:** subscribing households 184; 13 channels.

LEHIGH ACRES, pop. 16,000.

S FL. Lee Co. 12 mi. E. of Fort Myers. Semi retirement community.

6370 News-Star
News Star Publications
PO Box 908 Phone: (941)369-2191
Lehigh Acres, FL 33970-0908 Fax: (941)369-1396
Publication E-mail: newsstar@mindspring.com

Community newspaper. **Founded:** Feb. 15, 1962. **Freq:** Weekly (Wed.). **Print Method:** Offset. **Trim Size:** 10 1/2 x 12.5. **Cols./Page:** 6. **Col. Width:** 9.5 picas. **Col. Depth:** 12.5 inches. **Key Personnel:** Tom Wason, Editor, editorialstar@mindsping.com; Curt Middleton, General Mgr., publisherstar@mindspring.com. **Subscription Rates:** Free; $28 out of area mail. **Remarks:** Accepts advertising.
Ad Rates: GLR: $8.85 **Circ:** Paid 8,393
BW: $663.75 Free 6,889
4C: $813.75
PCI: $6

LITHIA

6371 Farm and Ranch News
Farm & Ranch News
PO Box 160 Phone: (813)737-6397
Lithia, FL 33547-0160 Fax: (813)737-6397
Publication E-mail: flabest@aol.com

Trade publication covering agribusiness issues for commercial farmers and ranchers. **Founded:** Oct. 1974. **Freq:** Monthly. **Print Method:** Web offset. **Trim Size:** 11 x 13 3/4. **Cols./Page:** 6. **Col. Width:** 1 7/8 inches. **Col. Depth:** 13 1/2 inches. **Key Personnel:** George Parker, Jr., Publisher, fla.best@aol.com. **USPS:** 111-230. **Subscription Rates:** $12.50. **Remarks:** Accepts advertising.
Ad Rates: BW: $510 **Circ:** Paid 6,000
4C: $750 Controlled 13,000
PCI: $7.50

LIVE OAK†.

Suwannee Co. (NC). 20 m NW of Lake City.

6372 The Jasper News
Live Oak Publications
211 Howard St. E Phone: (904)362-1734
PO Box 370 Fax: (904)364-5578
Live Oak, FL 32060
Local newspaper. **Founded:** 1870. **Freq:** Weekly (Thurs.). **Print Method:** Offset. **Trim Size:** 13 x 21 1/2. **Cols./Page:** 6. **Col. Width:** 2 inches. **Col. Depth:** 21 1/2 inches. **Key Personnel:** Michael Coulter, Publisher; Gail Newsome, General Mgr. **Subscription Rates:** $12 individuals; $19 out of area. **Remarks:** Accepts advertising.
Ad Rates: GLR: $8.50 **Circ:** Paid 2,100
SAU: $6.25 Free 300
PCI: $6.37

6373 Live Oak Suwannee Democrat
Live Oak Publications
211 Howard St. E Phone: (904)362-1734
PO Box 370 Fax: (904)364-5578
Live Oak, FL 32060
Publication E-mail: lonews1@alltel.net

Community newspaper. **Founded:** 1884. **Freq:** Semiweekly (Wed. and Fri.). **Trim Size:** Offset press. **Cols./Page:** 6. **Col. Width:** 12 picas. **Col. Depth:** 21 1/2 inches. **Key Personnel:** Susan Lamb, Editor, phone (904)364-2132; Michael Coulter, Publisher, phone (904)364-2125. **Subscription Rates:** $25. **Remarks:** Accepts advertising. **Feature Editors:** Vivian Sterling, *Sports*, phone (904)364-2131.
Ad Rates: PCI: $8.67 **Circ:** 5,500

6374 WLVO-FM - 106.1
PO Box 1061 Phone: (904)364-1061
Live Oak, FL 32064 Fax: (904)362-3148

Format: Oldies. **Owner:** Leon F. Patterson, at above address. **Founded:** Sept. 1, 1998. **Operating Hours:** Continuous. **Ad Rates:** $8-11 for 30 seconds; $12-17 for 60 seconds.

6375 WQHL-AM - 1250
Box 130 Phone: (904)362-1250
Live Oak, FL 32060 Fax: (904)364-3504
Free: (800)242-9810

Format: Talk; News; Sports; Sports. **Networks:** ABC. **Owner:** Day Communications, Inc., at above address. **Founded:** 1949. **Formerly:** WNER-AM (1988). **Operating Hours:** 6 a.m.-1 a.m.; 10% local, 90% network. **ADI:** Jacksonville (Brunswick), FL. **Key Personnel:** George Day, Contact; Shannon Day, Vice President; Dean Blackwell, Sales Mgr.; N. Shannon Day, Program Dir. **Wattage:** 1000. **Ad Rates:** $3 for 15 seconds; $5 for 30 seconds; $8 for 60 seconds.

6376 WQHL-FM - 98.1
1305 E. Helvenston St. Phone: (904)362-1250
PO Box 130 Fax: (904)364-3504
Live Oak, FL 32060
Free: (800)242-9810

Format: Hot Country. **Networks:** ABC. **Owner:** Day Communications, Inc., at above address. **Founded:** 1973. **Operating Hours:** Continuous. **ADI:** Jacksonville (Brunswick), FL. **Key Personnel:** George R. Day, Jr., President; N. Shannon Day, Vice President; Dean Blackwell, Sales Mgr. **Wattage:** 50,000. **Ad Rates:** $5-5.88 for 15 seconds; $10-12 for 30 seconds; $18-21 for 60 seconds.

LONGBOAT KEY

6377 Black Tie
The Longboat Observer, Inc.
5570 Gulf of Mexico Dr. Phone: (941)387-0345
Longboat Key, FL 34228 Fax: (941)383-7193

Consumer magazine covering society and the arts. **Subtitle:** The Magazine of Society and the Arts. **Key Personnel:** Lisa Walsh, Editor and Publisher.

LONGWOOD, pop. 10,029.

Seminole Co. (C). 10 m N of Orlando.

6378 Bull & Bear Financial Report
Bull & Bear Financial Newspaper
PO Box 917179 Phone: (407)682-6170
Longwood, FL 32791 Fax: (407)775-1760
Free: (800)336-BULL

Newspaper featuring a comprehensive digest of what the top performing investment advisory newsletters are recommending as well as general financial news. Includes articles pertaining to precious metals, stocks, mutual funds, and the economy. **Founded:** May 1974. **Freq:** Monthly. **Print Method:** Web offset. **Cols./Page:** 4. **Col. Width:** 14 1/2 picas. **Col. Depth:** 15 1/2 inches. **Key Personnel:** David J. Robinson, Editor and Publisher; Valerie Waters, Advertising Mgr. **ISSN:** 0319-1362. **Subscription Rates:** $29 individuals. **Remarks:** Accepts advertising.
Ad Rates: PCI: $51 **Circ:** Paid 38,000
Non-paid 17,000

6379 Jam Magazine
135 W. Jessup Ave. Phone: (407)767-8377
Longwood, FL 32750 Fax: (407)767-0533
Publication E-mail: mail@floridajam.com

Consumer magazine covering music. **Founded:** Mar. 1987. **Freq:** Semimonthly. **Trim Size:** 8 1/8 x 10 1/2. **Key Personnel:** George Biggers, Editor and Publisher; Jennifer Sametini, Assignment Editor/Editorial Coord.; David Smith, Music Editor. **Subscription Rates:** $42 individuals. **Remarks:** Accepts advertising. **Online:** Digital City Orlando. **URL:** http://www.floridajam.com.
Ad Rates: BW: $1,500 **Circ:** (Not Reported)

6380 Pageantry
Pageantry, Talent & Entertainment Services, Inc.
1855 W. State Rd., No. 434,
Ste. 254
Longwood, FL 32750
Publication E-mail: pageantmag@aol.com
Publisher E-mail: pageant@magicnet.net

Trade magazine covering the pageant, fashion, talent and modeling industries. **Founded:** 1980. **Freq:** Quarterly. **Print Method:** Web offset. **Trim Size:** 8 3/8 x 10 7/8. **Cols./Page:** 3. **Col. Width:** 2 7/16 inches. **Col. Depth:** 10 1/8 inches. **Key Personnel:** Lisa Nees, Editor; Carl Dunn, Advertising Mgr. **ISSN:** 1075-3133. **Subscription Rates:** $18 individuals; $30 two years; $6 single issue. **Remarks:** Accepts advertising. **URL:** http://www.pageantrymagazine.com.
Ad Rates: GLR: $3 **Circ:** Combined 68,000
BW: $1,518
4C: $2,418

6381 Tow Times
T.T. Publications, Inc.
PO Box 522020 Phone: (407)327-4817
Longwood, FL 32752-2020 Fax: (407)327-2603
Publication E-mail: towtimes@towtimes.com

Trade magazine. **Subtitle:** The Publication for and by the Professionals of the Towing and Recovery Industry. **Founded:** Sept. 1983. **Freq:** Monthly. **Print Method:** Offset. **Trim Size:** 8 1/8 x 10 7/8. **Cols./Page:** 3. **Col. Width:** 2 1/4 inches. **Col. Depth:** 10 inches. **Key Personnel:** Tim Jackson, Editor, editorial@towtimes.com; Clarissa Powell, Publisher, publisher@towtimes.com; Eleanor Joyce, Advertising Mgr. **Subscrip-**

tion Rates: $34 individuals. **Remarks:** Accepts advertising. **Available Online. URL:** http://www.towtimes.com.
Ad Rates: BW: $2,852 **Circ:** Paid 10,490
4C: $3,752 Controlled 18,152
PCI: $75

6382 WOCL-FM - 105.9
2101 State Rd. 434, Ste. 305 Phone: (407)682-2121
Longwood, FL 32779-5034 Fax: (407)682-2902
E-mail: woclradio@aol.com

Format: Oldies. **Networks:** Independent. **Founded:** 1986. **Operating Hours:** Continuous; 100% local. **Key Personnel:** Dan Wachs, General Mgr., woclradio@aol.com; Bill Fries, Program Dir., billfries@mindspring.com; Nick Puddicombe, Dir. of Sales, nickapudd@mindspring.com; Ed Allen, Chief Engineer, eda1373@aol.com; Nancy McMann, Office Mgr., macnanc@aol.com. **Wattage:** 100,000.

LUTZ

6383 The Lutz Community News
15431 N. Florida Ave. Phone: (813)963-1918
Tampa, FL 33613 Fax: (813)963-3910

Community newspaper. **Freq:** Weekly. **Cols./Page:** 6. **Col. Width:** 1 9/16 inches. **Col. Depth:** 16 inches. **Key Personnel:** Charlie Reese, Editor. **Subscription Rates:** Free; $5.95 by mail. **Remarks:** Accepts advertising. **Formerly:** Lutz Partyline.
Ad Rates: PCI: $8.34 **Circ:** Free 9,500

MACCLENNY

6384 The Baker County Press
104 S. 5th St. Phone: (904)259-2400
PO Box 598 Fax: (904)259-6502
Macclenny, FL 32063-0598
Local newspaper. **Founded:** 1929. **Freq:** Weekly (Thurs.). **Print Method:** Offset. **Cols./Page:** 6. **Col. Width:** 27 nonpareils. **Col. Depth:** 301 agate lines. **Key Personnel:** James C. McGauley, Editor and Publisher; Jeanie Shadd, Advertising Mgr. **Subscription Rates:** $16 individuals; $20 out of area. **Remarks:** Accepts advertising.
Ad Rates: GLR: $.32 **Circ:** ‡5,400
BW: $567
SAU: $4
PCI: $4.80

MADEIRA BEACH

6385 Booth Communications
420 150th Ave. Phone: (813)392-0660
Madeira Beach, FL 33708 Fax: (813)397-6854

Owner: Booth American Co., 333 W. Fort St., Detroit, MI 48226, (313)202-3360, Fax: (313)202-3390. **Founded:** 1980. **Key Personnel:** Terry A. Messner, General Mgr.; Kay Curran, Office Mgr.; Brian Chase, Chief Technician. **Cities Served:** Madeira Beach, North Redington Beach, Redington Beach, Redington Shores, FL: subscribing households 5,865; 62 channels; 0 community access channels; 0 hours per week community access programming.

MADISON†, pop. 3,487.

N FL. Madison Co. 28 mi. S. of Valdosta, GA. Sawmills. Agriculture. Tobacco, cotton, corn, peaches, watermelons, cattle and hogs.

6386 Madison County Carrier
Tommy Greene Publishing Co., Inc.
PO Drawer 772 Phone: (850)973-4141
Madison, FL 32341 Fax: (850)973-4121

Community newspaper. **Founded:** Aug. 5, 1964. **Freq:** Semiweekly (Wed. and Fri.). **Print Method:** Offset. **Trim Size:** 13 3/4 x 23. **Cols./Page:** 6. **Col. Width:** 12 picas. **Col. Depth:** 21 1/2 inches. **Key Personnel:** Tommy Greene, Publisher; Emerald G. Kinsley, General Mgr. **USPS:** 324-800. **Subscription Rates:** $20 individuals. **Remarks:** Accepts advertising.
Ad Rates: BW: $645 **Circ:** ‡4,100
4C: $795
PCI: $5

6387 Madison Enterprise-Recorder
PO Box 722 Phone: (904)973-6361
Madison, FL 32341 Fax: (904)973-6491

Newspaper. **Founded:** 1865. **Freq:** Weekly (Wed.). **Print Method:** Offset. **Cols./Page:** 6. **Col. Width:** 16 nonpareils. **Col. Depth:** 301 agate lines. **Key Personnel:** Michael Coulter, Publisher; Susan K. Lamb, Publisher; Linda Rye, Advertising Mgr. **Subscription Rates:** $18 individuals; $21 out of county. **Remarks:** Accepts advertising.
Ad Rates: GLR: $.375 **Circ:** ‡2,475
SAU: $5.25

MAITLAND, pop. 8,763.

EC FL. Orange Co. 5 mi. N. of Orlando.

6388 Personal Investing News
531 Versailles Dr., Ste. 110 Phone: (407)629-9229
Maitland, FL 32751-4591 Fax: (407)629-6719

Financial newspaper (tabloid). **Founded:** 1985. **Freq:** Bimonthly. **Print Method:** Web offset. **Trim Size:** 10 7/8 x 8 3/8. **Cols./Page:** 3. **Key Personnel:** Charles Arnold, Publisher. **Subscription Rates:** $24.95 individuals. **Remarks:** Accepts advertising.
Ad Rates: 4C: $6,000 **Circ:** Paid ‡50,000

6389 WJRR-FM - 101.1
2500 Maitland Center Pkwy., Ste. 401 Phone: (407)661-1100
Maitland, FL 32751 Fax: (407)660-1623

Format: Album-Oriented Rock (AOR). **Networks:** Independent. **Owner:** Paxson Communications Corp., 601 Clearwater Park Blvd., West Palm Beach, FL 33401, (407)659-4122, Fax: (407)659-4252. **Founded:** 1985. **Formerly:** WCKS-FM (1991); WSTF-FM. **Operating Hours:** Continuous. **Key Personnel:** Jenny Sue Rhoades, Pres. and General Mgr.; Dick Sheetz, Program Dir.; Schanae Wright, Contact; David Murray, Contact. **Wattage:** 100,000.

6390 WSHE-FM - 100.3
2500 Maitland Center Pkwy., No. 401 Phone: (407)916-7800
Maitland, FL 32751 Fax: (407)916-7510
Free: (888)916-1003

Founded: 1971. **Formerly:** WDIZ-FM (1996). **Operating Hours:** Continuous. **ADI:** Orlando-Daytona Beach-Melbourne, FL. **Key Personnel:** Jenny Sue Rhoades, Pres./General Mgr., fax (407)660-1623; Katherine Brown, Program Dir., katherinebrown@shee100.com. **Wattage:** 100,000. **Ad Rates:** $40-225 per unit. **URL:** http://www.she100.com.

MALABAR

6391 WIRB-TV - 56
6525 Babcock St. SE Phone: (407)725-0056
Malabar, FL 32950-1137 Fax: (407)951-2669

Format: Public TV. **Networks:** Independent. **Founded:** 1985. **Formerly:** WAKY-TV (1985). **Operating Hours:** 6 a.m.-1 a.m.; 100% local. **ADI:** Orlando-Daytona Beach-Melbourne, FL. **Key Personnel:** Jim Richards, General Mgr.; Robert Rich, President; Bill Lobean, Production Mgr.; Wayne Fleenor, Program Dir. **Ad Rates:** $35-100 per unit.

MARATHON, pop. 9,872.

S FL. Monroe Co. On Gulf of Mexico, 45 mi. NE of Key West. Fisheries. Tourist resort.

6392 Florida Keys Keynoter
3015 Overseas Hwy. Phone: (305)743-5551
PO Box 158 Fax: (305)743-9586
Marathon, FL 33050
Publication E-mail: keynoter@aol.com

Community newspaper (tabloid). **Founded:** Feb. 1953. **Freq:** Semiweekly (Wed. and Sat.). **Print Method:** Letterpress and flexo. **Trim Size:** 10 1/4 x 12.85. **Cols./Page:** 5. **Col. Width:** 11.6 picas. **Col. Depth:** 12.85 inches. **Key Personnel:** Tom Schumaker, Publisher; Tom Tuell, Editor; Charlotte Sikora, Marketing Director. **ISSN:** 8756-6427. **Subscription Rates:** $30 individuals; $40 out of area. **Remarks:** Accepts advertising. **URL:** http://www.keynoter.com.
Ad Rates: GLR: $2.54 **Circ:** Wed. ❑9,730
BW: $922.35 Sat. ❑10,539
4C: $1,267.35
PCI: $14.19

6393 The Keys Advertiser
Marathon/Big Pine Key Free Press
9709 Overseas Hwy. Phone: (305)743-8766
Marathon, FL 33050 Fax: (305)743-9977

Community newspaper. **Founded:** 1990. **Freq:** Weekly. **Print Method:** Photo offset. **Trim Size:** 11 1/2 x 12. **Cols./Page:** 5. **Col. Width:** 1 13/16 inches. **Col. Depth:** 11 1/2 inches. **Key Personnel:** John Thacker, General Mgr. **Subscription Rates:** Free. **Remarks:** Accepts advertising.
Ad Rates: BW: $425 **Circ:** Free 10,200
4C: $600
PCI: $8.50

6394 WAVK-FM - 105.5
11399 Overseas Hwy. Phone: (305)743-3434
Marathon, FL 33050 Fax: (305)743-9091

Format: Adult Contemporary. **Networks:** Satellite Music Network. **Owner:** Clear Channel Comms., 93351 Overseas Hwy., Marathon, FL 33050, (305)852-9085. **Founded:** 1985. **Formerly:** WPLC-FM (1986). **Operating Hours:** Continuous; 80% network, 20% local. **Key Personnel:** Shannon Butler, Gen./Sales Mgr., phone (305)743-3434, fax (305)743-9091, shannon@reefnet.com; Jon Huff, Program/Sports Dir.; Harry Thomas, News Dir., jhuff305@aol.com. **Local Programs:** *Good Morning Marathon*, Jon Huff; *Marathon's Best Catch Fishing Show*, Jon Huff. **Wattage:** 26,000. **Ad Rates:** $6-8 for 30 seconds; $6-10 for 60 seconds. Combined advertising rates available with WKRY, WFKZ.

MARCO ISLAND, pop. 8,000.

S FL. Collier Co. On Gulf of Mexico, 45 mi. S. of Fort Myers.

6395 Marco Island Eagle
PO Box 579 Phone: (813)394-7592
Marco Island, FL 33969 Fax: (813)394-8552
Publication E-mail: marcoeagle@aol.com

Community newspaper. **Founded:** 1968. **Freq:** Weekly (Wed.). **Print Method:** Offset. **Cols./Page:** 5. **Col. Width:** 27 nonpareils. **Col. Depth:** 238 agate lines. **Key Personnel:** Ron Delhomme, Editor; Cheryl Ferrara, Publisher. **Subscription Rates:** $15 individuals; $30 out of area; $63 out of state. **Remarks:** Accepts advertising. **Available Online. URL:** http://www.marcoeagle.com.
Ad Rates: GLR: $.40 **Circ:** Wed. ★8,838
BW: $935
4C: $1,185
PCI: $11

MARGATE, pop. 39,610.

S FL. Broward Co. 10 mi. NE of Fort Lauderdale.

6396 Dealer Communicator
Fichera Publications
777 S. State Rd. Phone: (954)971-4360
Margate, FL 33068 Fax: (954)971-4362
Free: (800)327-8999

Trade journal (tabloid) for the printing industry. **Subtitle:** The Dealer News Journal. **Founded:** 1980. **Freq:** Monthly. **Print Method:** Offset. Uses mats. **Trim Size:** 11 x 17. **Cols./Page:** 4. **Col. Width:** 29 nonpareils. **Col. Depth:** 196 agate lines. **Key Personnel:** O. Mike Fichera, Publisher, omike@dealercommunicator.com. **Subscription Rates:** $30 individuals. **Remarks:** Accepts advertising. **Online:** America Online, Inc. **URL:** http://www.dealercommunicator.com.
Ad Rates: BW: $6,465 **Circ:** Controlled ‡13,136
4C: $7,460
PCI: $355

6397 Margate/Coconut Creek Forum
SFNN, Inc.
9660 W. Sample Rd., Ste. 203 Phone: (954)752-7474
Coral Springs, FL 33065 Fax: (954)752-7855
Publisher E-mail: bukley@gate.net

Community newspaper (tabloid). **Founded:** 1965. **Freq:** Weekly (Thurs.). **Print Method:** Offset. **Cols./Page:** 6. **Col. Width:** 1 5/8 inches. **Col. Depth:** 16 inches. **Key Personnel:** Suzanne Pemper, PUB, Publisher. **Subscription Rates:** Free. **Remarks:** Accepts advertising.
Ad Rates: PCI: $20.80 **Circ:** Combined 21,070

MARIANNA†, pop. 6,974.

NW FL. Jackson Co. On Chipola River, 60 mi. NW of Tallahassee. Chipola Junior College. Recreation area. Manufactures furniture, textiles, commercial laundry equipment. Limestone quarries. Agriculture.

6398 Marianna Jackson County Floridan
Thomson Newspapers
4403 Constitution Ln. Phone: (904)526-3614
Marianna, FL 32446 Fax: (904)482-4470

General newspaper. **Founded:** 1922. **Freq:** Tues.-Fri. (eve.); Sun. (morn.). **Print Method:** Offset. **Cols./Page:** 6. **Col. Width:** 25 nonpareils. **Col. Depth:** 301 agate lines. **Key Personnel:** Judy Green, Editor; S. Jane Benton, Publisher. **Subscription Rates:** $94.25 individuals. **Remarks:** Accepts advertising.
Ad Rates: 4C: $233 **Circ:** Tues.-Fri. ★5,967
SAU: $8.41 Sun. ★6,736

6399 WJAQ-FM - 100.9
140 W. Lafayette St., Ste. A Phone: (904)482-3046
PO Box 569 Fax: (904)526-7702
Marianna, FL 32446

Format: Contemporary Country. **Networks:** Westwood One Radio. **Owner:** MFR, Inc., PO Box 569, Marianna, FL 32446, Fax: (904)482-3049. **Founded:** 1964. **Operating Hours:**

Continuous;. **ADI:** Panama City, FL. **Key Personnel:** Rick James, General Mgr.; Don Moore, News Dir. **Wattage:** 6,000. **Ad Rates:** $8.5-10 for 30 seconds; $9.6-13.5 for 60 seconds.

6400 WJNF-FM - 91.1
PO Box 450 Phone: (904)526-4477
Marianna, FL 32446 Fax: (904)526-1831
E-mail: wjnf@phonl.com

Format: Religious. **Networks:** USA Radio; Moody Broadcasting; Ambassador Inspirational Radio; SkyLight Satellite. **Owner:** Marianna Educational Broadcast Foundation Inc., at above address. **Founded:** May 1985. **Operating Hours:** 6 a.m.-11 p.m. **Key Personnel:** Quinton Hollis, Program Dir.; Shellie F. Hollis, Manager. **Local Programs:** *Force of Faith*, Flovious Pittman. **Wattage:** 383. **Ad Rates:** Noncommercial.

6401 WTOT-AM - 980
4376 Lafayette St. Phone: (904)482-3046
PO Box 569 Fax: (904)482-3249
Marianna, FL 32446

Format: News; Talk. **Networks:** Westwood One Radio. **Owner:** MFR, Inc., at above address. **Founded:** 1958. **Operating Hours:** Continuous. **ADI:** Panama City, FL. **Key Personnel:** Rick James, General Mgr.; Don Moore, News Dir. **Wattage:** 1000. **Ad Rates:** $9-12 for 30 seconds; $13-17 for 60 seconds.

6402 WTYS-AM - 1340
PO Box 777 Phone: (904)482-2131
2725 Jefferson St. Fax: (904)526-3687
Marianna, FL 32447-0777
E-mail: wtysb94@phonl.com

Format: News; Talk. **Simulcasts:** WBNF-FM. **Networks:** Westwood One Radio; NBC. **Founded:** 1948. **Operating Hours:** Continuous. **ADI:** Dothan, AL. **Key Personnel:** W. F. Dunkle III, General Mgr.; Tom O'Brien, Operations Mgr.; Autem Day, News Dir. **Local Programs:** *Classified*, Bill Dunkle; *Morning Magazine*, Bill Dunkle. **Wattage:** 1000. **Ad Rates:** Combined advertising rates available with WBNF-FM.

6403 WTYS-FM - 94.1
PO Box 777 Phone: (850)482-2131
Marianna, FL 32447 Fax: (850)526-3687
E-mail: wtysradio@phonl.com

Format: Southern Gospel. **Networks:** Westwood One Radio; Florida Radio. **Owner:** James L. Adams, Jr., at above address. **Founded:** Aug. 1995. **Formerly:** WBNF-FM. **Operating Hours:** Continuous. **ADI:** Dothan, AL. **Key Personnel:** James L. Adams, Jr., General Mgr.; Tom O' Brien, Operations Mgr.; Autem Day, News Dir.; Shirley Sims, Office Mgr. **Wattage:** 2,200. **Ad Rates:** Advertising accepted; rates available upon request. **URL:** http://www.phonl.com/wtys.

MAYO†, pop. 891.

N FL. Lafayette Co. 63 mi. NW of Gainesville. Manufactures lumber, boats, ethanol, concrete blocks. Timber. Agriculture. Tobacco, dairy products, poultry.

6404 The Mayo Free Press
Mayo Tree Press
PO Box 248 Phone: (904)294-1210
Mayo, FL 32066 Fax: (904)294-2666

Community newspaper. **Founded:** 1888. **Freq:** Weekly (Thurs.). **Print Method:** Offset. **Cols./Page:** 6. **Col. Width:** 21 nonpareils. **Col. Depth:** 294 agate lines. **Key Personnel:** Lori France, Editor; Shirley Hatch, Publisher. **USPS:** 334-600. **Subscription Rates:** $15 individuals; $18. **Remarks:** Accepts advertising.
Ad Rates: BW: $457.95 **Circ:** ‡1,650
4C: $450
SAU: $3
PCI: $3.55

MELBOURNE, pop. 46,536.

E FL. Brevard Co. On Indian River and Atlantic Ocean, 35 mi. S. of Kennedy Space Center. Florida Institute of Technology. Resort. Aerospace industry. Manufactures electronic components. Citrus fruit, vegetables.

6405 The Champion
PO Box 362173 Phone: (407)242-8491
Melbourne, FL 32936-2173
Christian newspaper (tabloid) for university audience. Articles apply the tenets of Christianity to contemporary issues. **Subtitle:** America's Christian Campus Newspaper. **Founded:** 1994. **Freq:** Quarterly. **Print Method:** Web press. **Trim Size:** 11 x 17. **Cols./Page:** 3. **Col. Width:** 3 1/4 inches. **Col. Depth:** 15 inches. **Key Personnel:** Jay Rodgers, Editor; Jay Rogers, Editor. **Subscription Rates:** Free; $15 (mail). **Remarks:** Accepts advertising. **Formerly:** The Forerunner (1994).
Ad Rates: BW: $675 **Circ:** Paid ‡3,000
4C: $750 Free ‡2,000

6406 Florida Today
Cape Publications, Inc.
Gannett Plaza Phone: (407)242-3500
PO Box 419000 Fax: (407)242-6620
Melbourne, FL 32941-9000
Free: (800)633-8449

General newspaper. **Founded:** Mar. 21, 1966. **Freq:** Mon.-Sun. (morn.). **Print Method:** Offset. Uses mats. **Cols./Page:** 6. **Col. Width:** 2 1/16 inches. **Col. Depth:** 21 inches. **Key Personnel:** Bennie Ivory, Editor; Michael Coleman, Publisher. **Subscription Rates:** $143 local; $208 out of area. **Remarks:** Accepts advertising. **Feature Editors:** Amy Clark, *Fashion*, phone (407)242-3784; Robin Footlick, *Features*; Hanna Krause, *Family*, phone (407)242-3779; Colleen Moore, *Entertainment*, phone (407)242-3717.
Ad Rates: GLR: $3.95 **Circ:** Mon.-Fri. 90,167
SAU: $43.10 Sun. 117,215
PCI: $36.75

6407 WAOA-FM - 107.1
1775 W. Hibiscus Blvd., Ste. 301 Phone: (407)984-1000
Fax: (407)724-1565
Melbourne, FL 32901

Format: Contemporary Hit Radio (CHR). **Networks:** Independent. **Owner:** GEM Broadcasting Inc., at above address. **Founded:** 1971. **Formerly:** WTAI-FM (1976); WRTI-FM. **Operating Hours:** Continuous; 3% network, 97% local. **ADI:** Orlando-Daytona Beach-Melbourne, FL. **Key Personnel:** Jeff Kimmell, General Mgr.; Paul Brooks, Contact; Dan Deaton, Program Dir.; Wayne West, News Dir. **Wattage:** 100,000.

6408 WCIF-FM - 106.3
702 E. New Haven Ave. Phone: (407)725-9243
Box 366
Melbourne, FL 32902

Format: Religious. **Owner:** First Baptist Church of Melbourne, at above address. **Founded:** 1980. **Operating Hours:** Continuous. **ADI:** Orlando-Daytona Beach-Melbourne, FL. **Key Personnel:** Lee J. Martinez, General Mgr.; Martha Root, Operations Mgr. **Wattage:** 4200.

6409 WFIT-FM - 89.5
150 W. University Blvd. Phone: (407)674-8140
Melbourne, FL 32901 Fax: (407)984-8461
E-mail: wfit@iv.net

Format: Jazz; Public Radio. **Networks:** National Public Radio (NPR). **Owner:** The Florida Institute of Technology, at above address. **Founded:** 1975. **Operating Hours:** 5 a.m.-12 a.m. **Key Personnel:** Terri Wright, General Mgr.; Todd Kennedy, Operations Dir.; Barbara Bingnear, Development. **Wattage:** 4600. **Ad Rates:** $20-35 for 30 seconds.

6410 WGGD-FM - 95.1
2221 Front St. Phone: (407)723-1240
Melbourne, FL 32901 Fax: (407)725-6821

Format: Oldies. **Networks:** Independent. **Owner:** City Broadcasting Co., Inc., at above address. **Founded:** 1966. **Formerly:** WYRL-FM (1986). **Operating Hours:** Continuous; 100% local. **ADI:** Orlando-Daytona Beach-Melbourne, FL. **Key Personnel:** David P. Franco, Contact; Ken Holiday, Program Dir. **Wattage:** 6000.

6411 WLRQ-FM - 99.3
1388 S. Babcock St. Phone: (407)636-4411
Melbourne, FL 32901-3009 Fax: (407)636-4380

Format: Adult Contemporary. **Networks:** CNN Radio. **Owner:** EZY Communications, Inc., at above address. **Founded:** 1959. **Formerly:** WEZY-FM (1987). **Operating Hours:** Continuous; 2% network, 98% local. **Key Personnel:** Tanya Klepper, Contact. **Wattage:** 50,000. **Ad Rates:** $15-65 per unit.

6412 WMMB-AM - 1240
2221 Front St. Phone: (407)723-1240
Melbourne, FL 32901 Fax: (407)725-6821

Format: Middle-of-the-Road (MOR); Big Band/Nostalgia. **Networks:** ABC; Mutual Broadcasting System; Florida Radio. **Owner:** City Broadcasting Co., Inc., at above address. **Founded:** 1947. **Operating Hours:** Continuous; 8% network, 92% local. **ADI:** Orlando-Daytona Beach-Melbourne, FL. **Key Personnel:** David P. Franco, Contact; Larry Brewer, Program Dir.; Roz Postell, News Dir. **Wattage:** 1000.

6413 WTAI-AM - 1560
1775 W. Hibiscus Blvd., Ste. 301 Phone: (407)984-1000
Fax: (407)724-1565
Melbourne, FL 32901

Format: Talk; News. **Networks:** ABC. **Owner:** GEM Broadcasting Inc., at above address, (407)984-1234. **Founded:** 1967. **Operating Hours:** 6 a.m.-8 p.m.; 85% network, 15% local. **ADI:** Orlando-Daytona Beach-Melbourne, FL. **Key Personnel:** Jeffrey C. Kinmel, General Mgr.; Paul Brooks, Natl. Sales Mgr.; Jon Roberts, Program Dir. **Wattage:** 5000.

MIAMI†, pop. 377,000.

S FL. Dade Co. On Biscayne Bay, 355 mi. S. of Jacksonville. Miami Christian University; Miami-Dade Community College; Barry College. Winter and summer resort. Shipyards. Manufactures airplane parts, canned fruits and vegetables, furniture, mattresses, garments, pharmaceuticals, paint, fertilizers, cement, plastics, electronic components, cigars, water heaters, leather products.

6414 Automundo Magazine
AutoMundo Productions, Inc.
2960 S.W. 8th St., 2nd Fl. Phone: (305)541-4198
Miami, FL 33135-2827 Fax: (305)541-5138

Automotive magazine (Spanish). Editorial focus on innovative concepts in the industry. Contains special racing circuit sections. **Founded:** Oct. 1982. **Freq:** Monthly. **Print Method:** Offset. **Trim Size:** 8 1/2 x 11. **Cols./Page:** 3. **Col. Width:** 26 nonpareils. **Col. Depth:** 140 agate lines. **Key Personnel:** Jorge Koechlin, Editor, phone (305)541-4198, fax (305)541-5138, jorgek@automundo.com. **Subscription Rates:** $19.95 individuals; $3.95 single issue. **Remarks:** Accepts advertising. **Available Online. URL:** http://www.automundo.com.
Ad Rates: BW: $3,352 **Circ:** Paid 25,000
4C: $4,482 Non-paid 25,000

Barry Magazine - See Miami Shores

6415 Bienvenidos a Miami
Welcome Publishing Co., Inc.
1751 NE 162nd St. Phone: (305)944-9444
Box 630-518 Fax: (305)949-0544
North Miami Beach, FL 33162-4757
Magazine for Spanish speaking tourists (Spanish). **Founded:** 1975. **Freq:** Biweekly. **Print Method:** Offset. **Trim Size:** 5 3/8 x 8 3/8. **Cols./Page:** 2. **Col. Width:** 26 nonpareils. **Col. Depth:** 45 agate lines. **Key Personnel:** Alan Levine, Publisher. **Subscription Rates:** $35 individuals; $.35 single issue. **Remarks:** Accepts advertising.
Ad Rates: BW: $400 **Circ:** Non-paid ‡16,000
4C: $525

6416 Buenhogar
Editorial Televisa
6355 NW 36th St. Phone: (305)871-6400
Miami, FL 33166-7099 Fax: (305)871-4939
Publisher E-mail: cosmo@editorial-televisa.com

Magazine for the homemaker featuring articles of general interest and e ntertainment (Spanish). **Founded:** 1965. **Freq:** Biweekly. **Print Method:** Offset. **Trim Size:** 8 5/8 x 10 7/8. **Cols./Page:** 3. **Col. Width:** 13.5 picas. **Col. Depth:** 59.5 picas. **Key Personnel:** Mirta Blanco, Editor; Enrique J. Perez, Advertising Sales Dir.; Mario A. Freude, Vice Pres. Sales. **Subscription Rates:** $24.95 individuals; $2.95 single issue. **Remarks:** Accepts advertising.
Ad Rates: BW: $1,200 **Circ:** ‡18,449
4C: $1,600

6417 Caribbean Review
Caribbean Review Inc.
9700 SW 67th Ave. Phone: (305)284-8466
Miami, FL 33156 Fax: (305)284-1019

Magazine dedicated to the Caribbean, Latin America, and their emigrant groups. **Founded:** Jan. 1969. **Freq:** Quarterly. **Print Method:** Offset. **Trim Size:** 8 1/2 x 11. **Cols./Page:** 3. **Key Personnel:** Barry B. Levine, Editor and Publisher. **ISSN:** 0008-6525. **Subscription Rates:** $20 individuals. **Remarks:** Accepts advertising.
Ad Rates: BW: $750 **Circ:** Paid ‡5,000
4C: $975 Non-paid ‡2,000

6418 The Chief of Police
National Association of Chiefs of Police
3801 Biscayne Blvd. Phone: (305)573-0070
Miami, FL 33137 Fax: (305)573-9819
Free: (800)527-1517
Publisher E-mail: policeinfo@aphf.org

Professional journal covering law enforcement. **Founded:** 1967. **Freq:** Bimonthly. **Key Personnel:** Jim Gordon, Exec.

Editor. **ISSN:** 0889-9207. **Subscription Rates:** $18 individuals. **Remarks:** Accepts advertising.
Ad Rates: BW: $1,400 **Circ:** (Not Reported)
4C: $1,940

Coral Gables News - See Coral Gables

6419 Cosmopolitan en Espanol
Editorial Televisa
6355 NW 36th St. Phone: (305)871-6400
Miami, FL 33166-7099 Fax: (305)871-4939
Publisher E-mail: cosmo@editorial-televisa.com

Magazine for the young modern Hispanic woman; covering fashion, relationships, travel, entertainment, and career (Spanish). **Founded:** 1973. **Freq:** Monthly. **Print Method:** Offset. **Trim Size:** 8 x 10 7/8. **Cols./Page:** 3. **Col. Width:** 13 picas. **Col. Depth:** 58.5 picas. **Key Personnel:** Sara Maria Castany, Editor, fax (305)871-4939; Enrique J. Perez, Advertising Sales Dir. **Subscription Rates:** $19.50 individuals; $2.50 single issue. **Remarks:** Accepts advertising.
Ad Rates: BW: $2,250 **Circ:** Paid ★42,278
4C: $3,000

6420 Daily Business Review
American Lawyer Media, L.P.
1 SE 3rd Ave., Ste. 900 Phone: (305)377-3721
Miami, FL 33131 Fax: (305)374-8474
Free: (800)777-7300
Publication E-mail: review@floridabiz.com

Daily newspapers covering business, real estate and law in South Florida. **Founded:** 1926. **Freq:** Daily. **Print Method:** Offset. **Trim Size:** 11 3/8 x 17. **Cols./Page:** 4. **Col. Width:** 2 3/8 inches. **Col. Depth:** 15 inches. **Key Personnel:** Edward Wasserman, Editor-in-Chief; Eva Rodriquez, Managing Editor; Jacqueline Bueno, Assoc. Editor; Patrick Danner, Assoc. Editor; Tony Doris, Assoc. Editor; Mary Hladky, Assoc. Editor; David P. Sedore, Assoc. Editor; Charles Buhman, Exec. News Editor; Jay Rees, News Editor; Julie Calsi, Copy Editor; Jim D. Pamplin, COO/CFO; T. Alicia Coya, Publisher; Jay Ducassi, Exec. Editor. **ISSN:** 0888-0263. **Subscription Rates:** $179. **Remarks:** Accepts advertising. **Formerly:** Miami Review.
Ad Rates: BW: $3,300 **Circ:** Paid 10,184
Controlled 286

6421 Diario las Americas
The Americas Publishing Co.
2900 NW 39th St. Phone: (305)633-3341
Miami, FL 33142-5149 Fax: (305)635-7668

General interest newspaper (Spanish). **Founded:** July 4, 1953. **Freq:** Tues.-Sun.(morn.). **Print Method:** Offset. **Trim Size:** 13 x 21. **Cols./Page:** 6. **Col. Width:** 2 1/16 inches. **Col. Depth:** 21 inches. **Key Personnel:** Horacio Aguirre, Editor and Publisher; Miguel A. Suzrez, Advertising Dir. **Subscription Rates:** $57 individuals; $91 out of area. **Remarks:** Accepts advertising. **Feature Editors:** Miguel A. Suarez, *Travel*, phone (305)633-3341; Chichi Aloy, *Society*, phone (305)633-3341; Luis B. De Lima, *Sports*, phone (305)633-3341; Buddy Clarke, *Movie*, phone (305)633-3341; Vivian Crucet, *Entertainment*, phone (305)633-3341; Luis Felipe Marsans, *Music*, phone (305)633-3341; Yolanda Gonzales Alfaro, *City*, *Metro*, phone (305)633-3341; Magda Gonzalez, *Fashion*, *Lifestyle*, *Living*, *Women's*, phone (305)633-3341; Alex Gort, *Photo*, phone (305)633-3341; Oscar Grau, *Garden/Home*, *Real Estate*, phone (305)633-3341; Enrique Llaca, *Financial/Business*, phone (305)633-3341; Luis Mario, *News*, phone (305)633-3341; Ariel Remos, *Political*, phone (305)633-3341; Carmencita San Miguel, *Food*, phone (305)633-3341.
Ad Rates: GLR: $2.00 **Circ:** Mon.-Fri. ‡65,670
BW: $3,528 Sun. ‡69,580
4C: $4,728
PCI: $28.00

6422 Dolphin Digest
Curtis Publishing Co.
8033 NW 36th St., No. S-438 Phone: (305)594-0508
Miami, FL 33166-6644 Fax: (305)594-0518
Free: (800)334-4005

Sports publication (tabloid) reporting on the activities of the Miami Dolphins. **Founded:** 1972. **Freq:** Weekly (Tues.). **Print Method:** Offset. **Trim Size:** 9 3/4 x 13. **Cols./Page:** 4. **Col. Width:** 13.5 picas. **Key Personnel:** Andy Cohen, Editor; Thomas Curtis, Publisher; Miriam Mato, Circulation Mgr.; Ken Keidel, Advertising Coord. **ISSN:** 0744-3226. **Subscription Rates:** $39.95 individuals; $2 single issue. **Remarks:** Accepts advertising.
Ad Rates: BW: $1,045 **Circ:** Paid 30,000
4C: $1,345 Non-paid 500

6423 El Nuevo Patria
El Nuevo Patria Publishing Co.
850 N Miami Ave., No. 102 Phone: (305)530-8787
Miami, FL 33136 Fax: (305)577-8989

Hispanic community newspaper (tabloid; Spanish). **Subtitle:** South Florida's First Hispanic Weekly. **Founded:** July 25, 1959. **Freq:** Weekly (Thurs.). **Print Method:** Offset. **Trim Size:** 10 x 16. **Cols./Page:** 6. **Col. Width:** 1 9/16 inches. **Col. Depth:** 16 inches. **Key Personnel:** Eladio Jose Armesto, Publisher; Carlos Diaz Lujan, PhD, Editor-in-Chief; Rosa Maria Armeto, Associate Ed.; Omar R. Rosa, Production Dir.; Alejandro Casuso, MD, Medical Editor; Augustin Blanco, Photography Dir.; Miriam Gonzalez, Advertising Dir. **USPS:** 014-458. **Subscription Rates:** Free; $24 by mail; $36 other countries. **Remarks:** Accepts advertising. **Feature Editors:** Sandra Baroja, *Food*; Alejandro Casusa, MD, *Medical*; Sarvelio Del Valle, *Sports*; James Dobson, PhD, *Family*; Alexis Gandara, *Automotive*; Ralph Garcia, *Book*; Arturo Garrote, *Political*; Jose Marmol, *Editorials*; Ernesto Martinez-Gil, *Financial/Business*; Vidal A. Ramos, *Entertainment*; Madeline Sandoval, *Features*.
Ad Rates: BW: $1569.60 **Circ:** Paid ‡12,800
PCI: $15 Free ‡15,200

6424 Entertainment News & Views
PO Box 38-1817
Miami, FL 33238
Publication E-mail: staff@entnews.com
Publisher E-mail: hsalus@entnews.com

Local dining, arts, and entertainment newspaper. **Subtitle:** South Florida's Premier Arts, Dining, and Entertainment Weekly. **Founded:** 1980. **Freq:** Weekly. **Print Method:** Web offset. **Trim Size:** 10 x 16. **Cols./Page:** 6. **Col. Width:** 1 5/8 inches. **Col. Depth:** 1 inches. **Key Personnel:** Howard Salus, Publisher, hsaulus@entnews.com; Sarah Churchill, Editor, sara@entnews.com. **Subscription Rates:** $45. **Remarks:** Accepts advertising. **URL:** http://www.entnews.com.
Ad Rates: BW: $1200 **Circ:** Free 50,000
4C: $1500
PCI: $12

6425 Exito
Sun Sentinel
8323 NW 12 St. No. 212 Phone: (305)597-5000
Miami, FL 33126 Fax: (305)597-5035

Community newspaper. **Founded:** Nov. 20, 1991. **Freq:** Weekly. **Cols./Page:** 5. **Col. Width:** 2 1/16 inches. **Col. Depth:** 1 inches. **Key Personnel:** Cristina Beauvoir, Advertising Dir.; Alfredo Duran, Publisher. **Remarks:** Accepts advertising.
Ad Rates: GLR: $36.20 **Circ:** Free 79,414
4C: $530

6426 The Florida Catholic
9401 Biscayne Blvd.
Miami, FL 33138

Catholic interest magazine (English and Spanish). **Founded:** 1959. **Freq:** Semimonthly. **Print Method:** Offset. **Cols./Page:** 4. **Col. Width:** 28 nonpareils. **Col. Depth:** 189 agate lines. **Key Personnel:** Robert L. O'Steen, Editor. **Subscription Rates:** $10 individuals. **Formerly:** The Voice.

6427 The Florida Newspaper
PO Box 971490 Phone: (305)254-3400
Miami, FL 33197-1490 Fax: (305)254-6007
Free: (800)445-1746

Community newspaper. **Founded:** 1927. **Freq:** Weekly. **Print Method:** Offset. **Cols./Page:** 5. **Col. Width:** 24 nonpareils. **Col. Depth:** 224 agate lines. **Key Personnel:** Joan C. Teglas, Editor and Publisher. **ISSN:** 1053-5713. **Subscription Rates:** $8 individuals per year. **Remarks:** Accepts advertising. **Formerly:** The Floridian Newspaper.
Ad Rates: GLR: $.80 **Circ:** Paid ‡8,000
BW: $896 Free ‡200
4C: $1,296
PCI: $13.60

6428 The Florida Shipper Magazine
1401 Biscayne Blvd.
Miami, FL 33132

Shipping trade magazine. **Founded:** Sept. 25, 1975. **Freq:** Weekly (Mon.). **Print Method:** Offset. **Trim Size:** 7 3/4 x 10 3/4. **Cols./Page:** 3. **Col. Width:** 31 nonpareils. **Col. Depth:** 137 agate lines. **Key Personnel:** Brian Neuhart, Publisher. **ISSN:** 0884-8548. **Subscription Rates:** $40 individuals.
Ad Rates: BW: $684 **Circ:** Paid ★1,675
4C: $1,079

6429 Florida Sports Magazine
Florida Sports Inc.
PO Box 558090 Phone: (305)265-0060
Miami, FL 33255 Fax: (305)265-0906
Free: (800)932-2118

Newspaper (tabloid) covering Florida's participatory sports; featuring sports profiles, event coverage, training suggestions, nutrition, sports medicine, travel, and sports calendar. **Subtitle:** The Magazine for Active Florida. **Founded:** Feb. 1987. **Freq:** 10/year. **Print Method:** Web offset. **Trim Size:** 10 x 13. **Cols./Page:** 4. **Col. Width:** 2 3/16 inches. **Col. Depth:** 182 agate lines. **Key Personnel:** Jim Woodman, Jr., Editor and Publisher, jwoodman@floridasports.com. **ISSN:** 0891-7949. **Subscription Rates:** $15. **Remarks:** Accepts advertising. **URL:** http://www.floridasports.com. **Formerly:** Florida Sports Review (1989).
Ad Rates: BW: $2,095 **Circ:** Non-paid 130,000
4C: $2,790
PCI: $40

6430 Florida Sportsman
Wickstrom Publishers
5901 SW 74th St., Ste. 310 Phone: (305)661-4222
Miami, FL 33143 Fax: (305)284-0277
Publication E-mail: editor@flsportsman.com

Boating, fishing, camping, hunting, and conservation magazine. **Founded:** July 1969. **Freq:** Monthly. **Print Method:** Offset. **Trim Size:** 8 1/4 x 10 7/8. **Cols./Page:** 3. **Col. Width:** 27 nonpareils. **Col. Depth:** 140 agate lines. **Key Personnel:** Glenn Law, Editor; Karl Wickstrom, Publisher; Robert L. Mitchell, Advertising Mgr. **ISSN:** 0015-3885. **Subscription Rates:** $24.95 individuals; $3.95 single issue. **Remarks:** Accepts advertising. **URL:** http://www.flsportsman.com.
Ad Rates: BW: $3,280 **Circ:** Paid 108,054
4C: $4,435

6431 The Flyer
Community Newspaper Company
11900 SW 128th St. Phone: (305)232-4115
Miami, FL 33186 Fax: (305)251-5141
Publisher E-mail: townonline.com

Advertiser (English and Spanish). **Founded:** Nov. 1977. **Freq:** Weekly (Wed.). **Print Method:** Offset. **Trim Size:** 7 3/4 x 10 3/4. **Cols./Page:** 4. **Col. Width:** 43 nonpareils. **Col. Depth:** 139 agate lines. **Key Personnel:** Carlos Guzman, President. **Remarks:** Advertising accepted; rates available upon request.
Circ: Non-paid ‡1,018,449

6432 Football News
Football News, Inc.
8033 NW 36 St. Phone: (305)594-0508
Miami, FL 33166 Fax: (305)594-0518
Free: (800)334-4005

Sports magazine covering college and professional football. **Founded:** 1939. **Freq:** 20/year. **Print Method:** Offset. **Trim Size:** 10 1/8 x 13 1/4. **Cols./Page:** 4. **Col. Width:** 27 nonpareils. **Col. Depth:** 189 agate lines. **Key Personnel:** Tom Curtis, Publisher; Andy Cohen, General Mgr. **Subscription Rates:** $39.95. **Remarks:** Accepts advertising.
Ad Rates: BW: $2,000 **Circ:** Paid 75,000
4C: $3,150 Non-paid 875

6433 Geomundo
Editorial Televisa
6355 NW 36th St. Phone: (305)871-6400
Miami, FL 33166-7099 Fax: (305)871-4939
Publisher E-mail: cosmo@editorial-televisa.com

Magazine on travel, geography, and flora and fauna (Spanish). **Founded:** 1977. **Freq:** Monthly. **Print Method:** Offset. **Trim Size:** 7 3/4 x 10 11/16. **Cols./Page:** 3. **Col. Width:** 13 picas. **Col. Depth:** 58.5 picas. **Key Personnel:** Elvira Mendoza, Editor; Enrique J. Perez, Advertising Sales Dir. **Subscription Rates:** $25.50 individuals; $3 single issue. **Remarks:** Accepts advertising.
Ad Rates: BW: $1,050 **Circ:** (Not Reported)
4C: $1,400

6434 Harper's Bazaar en Espanol
Editorial Televisa
6355 NW 36th St. Phone: (305)871-6400
Miami, FL 33166-7099 Fax: (305)871-4939
Publisher E-mail: cosmo@editorial-televisa.com

Hispanic edition of Harper's Bazaar (Spanish). **Founded:** 1980. **Freq:** 8/year. **Print Method:** Offset. **Trim Size:** 8 5/8 x 10 7/8. **Cols./Page:** 3. **Col. Width:** 14 picas. **Col. Depth:** 60 picas. **Key Personnel:** Sara Castany, Editor; Enrique J. Perez, Advertising Mgr.; Mario A. Freude, Editor. **Subscription Rates:** $24.95 individuals; $2.95 single issue. **Remarks:** Accepts advertising.
Ad Rates: BW: $800 **Circ:** ‡13,108
4C: $1,200

6435 Hialea-Opa Locka News
Community Newspapers
PO Box 43-1970 Phone: (305)667-7481
Miami, FL 33143 Fax: (305)661-0954
Publisher E-mail: cnedor@gate.net

Newspaper. **Founded:** 1971. **Freq:** Semiweekly (Mon. & Fri.). **Print Method:** Offset. **Cols./Page:** 6. **Col. Width:** 19 nonpareils. **Col. Depth:** 238 agate lines. **Key Personnel:** Michael Miller, Editor; Grant Miller, Publisher. **Subscription Rates:** $26 individuals. **Remarks:** Accepts advertising. **Formerly:** Carol City-Opa Locka News.
Ad Rates: GLR: $.72 **Circ:** Free ‡7,000

6436 The Hispanic American Historical Review
Duke University Press
Florida International University Phone: (305)348-4247
206 Chemistry & Physics Bldg. Fax: (305)348-3053
University Park
Miami, FL 33199
Journal focusing on Latin-American history. **Founded:** 1921. **Freq:** Quarterly. **Print Method:** Offset. **Trim Size:** 6 x 9. **Cols./Page:** 1. **Col. Width:** 52 nonpareils. **Col. Depth:** 98 agate lines. **Key Personnel:** Mark Szuchman, Editor; Nancy Kimberly, Advertising Mgr., kimberly@acpub.duke.edu; Steve Cohn, Editor. **ISSN:** 0018-2168. **Subscription Rates:** $40 individuals; $105 institutions; $20 students. **Remarks:** Accepts advertising. **Available Online. URL:** http://www.duke.edu/web/dupress/dup.htm. **Alt. Formats:** Mailing labels.
Ad Rates: BW: $300 **Circ:** ‡2,400

6437 Hombre Internacional
Editorial Televisa
6355 NW 36th St. Phone: (305)871-6400
Miami, FL 33166-7099 Fax: (305)871-4939
Publisher E-mail: cosmo@editorial-televisa.com

Magazine for upscale men covering business, politics, travel, fashion, arts, and sports (Spanish). **Founded:** 1975. **Freq:** Monthly. **Print Method:** Offset. **Trim Size:** 8 x 10 7/8. **Cols./Page:** 3. **Col. Width:** 13 picas. **Col. Depth:** 58.5 picas. **Key Personnel:** Mrs. Romeo Franco Caputi, Editor; Enrique Perez, Advertising Mgr.; Mario Freude, General Mgr. **Subscription Rates:** $22.50. $2.50 single issue. **Remarks:** Accepts advertising.
Ad Rates: BW: $1,425 **Circ:** ‡12,749
4C: $1,900

6438 Hora de Cierra
IAPA Press Institute
2911 NW 39th St. Phone: (305)634-2465
Miami, FL 33142 Fax: (305)635-2272

Spanish-language trade magazine covering the newspaper and magazine publishing industry in Latin America. **Founded:** Jan. 1970. **Freq:** Quarterly. **Print Method:** Offset. **Trim Size:** 8 3/8 x 10 7/8. **Cols./Page:** 3. **Col. Width:** 2 1/4 inches. **Col. Depth:** 9 7/8 inches. **Key Personnel:** Noel Leon, Editor, nleon@sipiapa.com. **ISSN:** 1021-9641. **Subscription Rates:** $24 individuals; $6 single issue. **Remarks:** Accepts advertising. **Former name**: El Boletin (Oct. 1992).
Ad Rates: BW: $1,285 **Circ:** Controlled 7,800
4C: $2,140

6439 Ideas para Su Hogar (Ideas for Your Home)
Editorial Televisa
6355 NW 36th St. Phone: (305)871-6400
Miami, FL 33166-7099 Fax: (305)871-4939
Publisher E-mail: cosmo@editorial-televisa.com

Magazine for homemakers; including articles on cooking, decorating, gardening, and patterns (Spanish). **Founded:** 1978. **Freq:** Monthly. **Print Method:** Offset. **Trim Size:** 8 x 10 7/8. **Cols./Page:** 3. **Col. Width:** 13 picas. **Col. Depth:** 58.5 picas. **Key Personnel:** Gloria Ramos, Editor; Enrique J. Perez, Advertising Mgr.; Mario A. Freude, Editor. **Subscription Rates:** $20.95 individuals; $2.50 single issue. **Remarks:** Accepts advertising.
Ad Rates: BW: $825 **Circ:** ‡10,848
4C: $1,100

6440 International Journal of Mathematical and Statistical Sciences
Thesaurus Publishing
141 NE 3rd Ave., No 604
Miami, FL 33132-2221
Publication E-mail: ijmss@guarany.cpd.unb.br

Scholarly journal covering mathematical and statistical sciences. **Founded:** June 1992. **Freq:** Semiannual. **Trim Size:** 15.5 x 22.5 cm. **Col. Width:** 11.5 centimeters. **Col. Depth:** 18.5 centimeters. **Key Personnel:** Prof. Pushpa N. Rathie, Managing Editor. **ISSN:** 1055-7490. **Subscription Rates:** $50 individuals; $100 institutions. **Remarks:** Accepts advertising.
Ad Rates: BW: $200 **Circ:** (Not Reported)

6441 ITM - Industria Turistica Magazine
Charles Francis Publishers
PO Box 521898 Phone: (305)551-8493
Miami, FL 33152-1898 Fax: (305)551-0141

Magazine concerning Latin American travel and industry (Spanish and English). **Founded:** 1957. **Freq:** Monthly. **Print Method:** Offset. **Trim Size:** 8 1/2 x 11. **Cols./Page:** 2 and 3. **Col. Width:** 27 and 40 nonpareils. **Col. Depth:** 140 agate lines. **Key Personnel:** L. Francis, Editor; Charles Francis, Publisher. **Subscription Rates:** $10 individuals. **Remarks:** Accepts advertising.
Ad Rates: BW: $2,200 **Circ:** Non-paid ‡9,500
4C: $2,500

6442 Journal of Interamerican Studies and World Affairs
School of International Studies
1541 Brescia Ave. Phone: (305)284-5554
Coral Gables, FL 33146-3010 Fax: (305)284-4406
Publication E-mail: jiswa@sis.miami.edu

Journal of Interamerican Studies and World Affairs. **Founded:** 1959. **Freq:** Quarterly. **Print Method:** Offset. **Trim Size:** 6x9. **Cols./Page:** 1. **Col. Width:** 50 nonpareils. **Col. Depth:** 100 agate lines. **Key Personnel:** William C. Smith, Editor; Eleanor Lahn, Managing Editor. **ISSN:** 0022-1937. **Subscription Rates:** $45 individuals; $22 students USA; $98 institutions. **URL:** http://www.rienner.com/jis.htm. **Alt. Formats:** Microform.
Ad Rates: BW: $250 **Circ:** Paid 1,300
Controlled 202

6443 Journal of Personality Disorders
Guilford Publications, Inc.
5400 S.W. 99th Terrace Phone: (305)284-3361
Miami, FL 33156 Fax: (305)661-8888
Publisher E-mail: info@guilford.com

Journal devoted to the diagnosis and treatment of clinically significant personality disorders. **Subtitle:** Official Journal of the International Society for the Study of Personality Disorders. **Founded:** 1986. **Freq:** Quarterly. **Print Method:** Offset. **Trim Size:** 7 x 10. **Cols./Page:** 1. **Col. Width:** 72 nonpareils. **Col. Depth:** 126 agate lines. **Key Personnel:** Allen J. Frances, M.D., Editor; Theodore Millon, Ph.D., Editor. **ISSN:** 0885-579X. **Subscription Rates:** $35; $105 institutions; $30 Amer. Psychoanalytic Asn. **Remarks:** Accepts advertising. **Alt. Formats:** Microfilm.
Ad Rates: BW: $250 **Circ:** 1,313

6444 Journal of Security Administration
BLSS, Inc.
Box 164509 Phone: (305)253-9933
Miami, FL 33116-4509 Fax: (305)254-9662
Publication E-mail: mbtitus@herald.infi.net

Journal covering security administration topics. **Founded:** 1978. **Freq:** Semiannual. **Trim Size:** 5 1/2 x 8 1/2. **ISSN:** 0195-9425. **Subscription Rates:** $25 individuals; $20 single issue. **Remarks:** Accepts advertising.
Circ: Paid 2,500

Kendall News - See Kendall

6445 Latin Trade
200 S. Biscayne Blvd., No. 1150 Phone: (305)358-8373
Miami, FL 33131 Fax: (305)358-9761
Publication E-mail: lattrade@aol.com

Trade publication featuring business news and analysis on Latin America and the Caribbean. **Founded:** Jan. 1993. **Freq:** Monthly. **Print Method:** Web Offset. **Trim Size:** 8 1/8 x 10 7/8. **ISSN:** 1087-0857. **Subscription Rates:** $36 individuals; $58 two years; $3.95 single issue. **Remarks:** Accepts advertising. **URL:** http://www.latintrade.com. **Formerly**: U.S./Latin Trade.
Ad Rates: BW: $8,170 **Circ:** Paid ‡37,552
4C: $10,525 Controlled ‡49,119

6446 Libre
LIBRE
904 SW 23rd Ave. Phone: (305)643-4888
Miami, FL 33135 Fax: (305)649-2767

Community newspaper (tabloid, Spanish). **Founded:** 1966. **Freq:** Weekly (Fri.). **Print Method:** Offset. **Trim Size:** 10 x 16 1/2. **Cols./Page:** 6. **Key Personnel:** Demetrio Perez, Jr., Publisher & Director. **Subscription Rates:** $24. **Remarks:** Accepts advertising. **Formerly**: El Matancero Libre.
Ad Rates: GLR: $9 **Circ:** Paid 3,900
BW: $19 Free 28,000
4C: $12
PCI: $9

6447 Mecanica Popular
Editorial Televisa
6355 NW 36th St. Phone: (305)871-6400
Miami, FL 33166-7099 Fax: (305)871-4939
Publisher E-mail: cosmo@editorial-televisa.com

Magazine covering automobiles, electronics, science, photography, audio and video equipment, and workshop projects (Spanish). **Founded:** 1947. **Freq:** Monthly. **Print Method:** Offset. **Trim Size:** 7 3/4 x 10 11/16. **Cols./Page:** 3. **Col. Width:** 13 picas. **Col. Depth:** 58.5 picas. **Key Personnel:** Santiago J. Villazon, Editor; Enrique J. Perez, Advertising Sales Dir.; Mario A. Freude, V.P. Sales. **Subscription Rates:** $23.50 individuals; $2.50 single issue. **Remarks:** Accepts advertising.
Ad Rates: BW: $825 **Circ:** ‡14,977
4C: $1,100

6448 Miami Daily Business Review
American Lawyer Media, L.P.
1 SE 3rd Ave., Ste. 900 Phone: (305)377-3721
Miami, FL 33131 Fax: (305)347-8474
Free: (800)777-7300
Publication E-mail: review@floridabiz.com

Publication of enterprise, real estate, and law in the Miami area. **Founded:** 1926. **Freq:** Daily. **Print Method:** Web offset. **Trim Size:** 11 3/8 x 17. **Cols./Page:** 4. **Col. Width:** 2 3/8 inches. **Col. Depth:** 15 inches. **Key Personnel:** Edward Wasserman, Editor-in-Chief, phone (305)347-6612, fax (305)347-6626; Jim D. Pamplin, COO/CFO; T. Alicia Coya, Publisher; Jay Ducassi, Exec. Editor; Eva Rodriquez, Managing Editor; Jacqueline Bueno, Assoc. Editor; Patrick Danner, Assoc. Editor; Tony Doris, Assoc. Editor; Mary Hladky, Assoc. Editor; David P. Sedore, Assoc. Editor; Charles Buhman, Exec. News Editor; Jay Rees, News Editor; Julie Calsi, Copy Editor. **ISSN:** 0888-0263. **Subscription Rates:** $179. **Remarks:** Accepts advertising. **Alt. Formats:** Diskette; Mailing labels. **Formerly**: Miami Review.
Ad Rates: BW: $3,300 **Circ:** Paid 9,363
Non-paid 236

6449 The Miami Herald
Knight-Ridder, Inc.
1 Herald Plaza Phone: (305)350-2111
Miami, FL 33132-1693
General newspaper. **Founded:** 1910. **Freq:** Mon.-Sun. (morn.). **Print Method:** Letterpress, offset, and flexography. **Cols./Page:** 6. **Col. Width:** 22.5 nonpareils. **Col. Depth:** 315 agate lines. **Key Personnel:** Jim Hampton, Editor, phone (305)376-2287; David Lawrence, Publisher; Jim Roos, V.P./Marketing. **Subscription Rates:** $114.41 individuals. **Remarks:** Accepts advertising. **Online:** Dialog (The Dialog Corporation); CompuServe Information Service; America Online, Inc. **Alt. Formats:** CD-ROM, Dialog (The Dialog Corporation). **Feature Editors:** Paul Anger, *Sports*, phone (305)376-3499; Hal Boedeker, *TV & Radio*, phone (305)376-3652; Ellie Brecher, *Fashion*, phone (305)376-3631; Jay Clarke, *Travel*, phone (305)376-3655; Bill Cosford, *Movie*, phone (305)376-3661; Tom Fiedler, *Political*, phone (305)376-3477; Felicia Gressette, *Food*, phone (305)376-3636; Peggy Landers, *Religion*, phone (305)376-3472; Susan Olds, *News*, phone (305)376-3620; Ileana Oroza, *News*, phone (305)376-3579; Leonard Pitts, *Music*, phone (305)376-3658; Steve Rice, *Photo*, phone (305)376-3747; Max Roberts, *Garden/Home, Real Estate*, phone (305)376-3520; Jim Roos, *Music*, phone (305)376-3656; Rex Seline, *Financial/Business*, phone (305)376-3610; Georgia Tasker, *Garden/Home*, phone (305)376-3643; Elissa Vanaver, *Features*, phone (305)376-3628.
Ad Rates: GLR: $15.21 **Circ:** Mon.-Sat. ★**630.251**
BW: $28,755 Sun. ★**440,252**
4C: $31,955
SAU: $213

6450 Miami New Times
New Times
2800 Biscayne Blvd., Ste. 100 Phone: (305)576-8000
PO Box 011591 Fax: (305)571-7677
Miami, FL 33137
Alternative Weekly. **Subtitle:** Miami's News and Arts Weekly. **Founded:** 1987. **Freq:** Weekly (Thurs.). **Print Method:** Offset. **Trim Size:** 10 x 12 7/8. **Cols./Page:** 8. **Col. Width:** 1 1/16 inches. **Col. Depth:** 10 inches. **Key Personnel:** Jim Mullin, Editor; Tom Finkel, Managing Editor; Michael B. Cohen, Publisher. **Subscription Rates:** Free. **Remarks:** Accepts advertising. **URL:** http://www.miaminewtimes.com. **Formerly**: New Times of Miami; New Times.
Circ: Non-paid 106,692
Paid 41

6451 Miami Shores News
Community Newspapers
PO Box 43-1970 Phone: (305)667-7481
Miami, FL 33143 Fax: (305)661-0954
Publisher E-mail: cnedor@gate.net

Community newspaper (tabloid). **Founded:** 1972. **Freq:** Semiweekly (Mon. and Fri.). **Print Method:** Offset. **Trim Size:** 10 1/4 x 16. **Cols./Page:** 6. **Col. Width:** 19 nonpareils. **Col. Depth:** 238 agate lines. **Key Personnel:** Michael Miller, Editor; Grant Miller, Publisher. **Subscription Rates:** $52 individuals. **Remarks:** Accepts advertising.
Ad Rates: GLR: $.72 **Circ:** Free ‡4,000
BW: $1,350
4C: $2,400

6452 The Miami Times
900 NW 54th St. Phone: (305)757-1147
Miami, FL 33127 Fax: (305)757-5770

Black community newspaper. **Founded:** Sept. 1, 1923. **Freq:** Weekly (Thurs.). **Print Method:** Offset. **Trim Size:** 13 3/4 x 22. **Cols./Page:** 6. **Col. Width:** 2 1/16 inches. **Col. Depth:** 21 inches. **Key Personnel:** Rachel J. Reeves, Publisher; Mohamad Hamaludin, Editor; Garth C. Reeves, Publisher. **USPS:**

344-340. **Subscription Rates:** $35 individuals. **Remarks:** Accepts advertising.
Ad Rates: GLR: $1.36 **Circ:** Thurs. 16,464
BW: $2,646
4C: $3,546
PCI: $21

6453 Miami Today
Today Enterprises, Inc.
PO Box 1368 Phone: (305)358-2663
Miami, FL 33101
Newspaper (tabloid) covering business and community information targeted to the upper management levels. **Founded:** June 2, 1983. **Freq:** Weekly (Thurs.). **Print Method:** Offset. **Trim Size:** 11 1/4 x 17 1/2. **Cols./Page:** 5. **Col. Width:** 12.5 picas. **Col. Depth:** 16 inches. **Key Personnel:** Michael Lewis, Editor and Publisher; Carmen Betancourt Lewis, Vice President, phone (305)358-4008. **USPS:** 012-964. **Subscription Rates:** $60 individuals; $1 single issue. **Remarks:** Accepts advertising. **Alt. Formats:** Microform.
Ad Rates: BW: $4,800 **Circ:** Controlled △**33,511**
4C: $5,300 Paid △**643**

6454 The New Times
New Times
2800 Biscayne Blvd., Ste. 100 Phone: (305)576-8000
PO Box 011591 Fax: (305)571-7677
Miami, FL 33137
A monthly newspaper focusing on personal growth, spirituality, and holistic approaches to wellness and our environment. **Subtitle:** Changing and Enriching Lives Since 1985. **Founded:** June 1985. **Freq:** Monthly. **Print Method:** Web offset. **Cols./Page:** 6. **Col. Width:** 2 inches. **Col. Depth:** 21 inches. **Key Personnel:** Deverick Martin, Publisher; David A. Young, Editor, dyoung@speakeasy.org. **ISSN:** 1044-2782. **Subscription Rates:** $15 individuals. **Remarks:** Accepts advertising. **URL:** http://www.speakeasy.org/newtimes/. **Absorbed:** Inner Woman (1992). **Formerly:** Spiritual Women's Times (1990).
Ad Rates: SAU: $18 **Circ:** Paid ‡1,500
PCI: $18 Free ‡21,500

North Miami Beach News - See North Miami Beach

6455 Occupational Therapy in Health Care
The Haworth Press, Inc.
Dept. of Occupational Therapy Phone: (305)348-3105
University Park Campus Fax: (305)348-1240
Miami, FL 33199
Publication E-mail: kaplans@fiu.edu
Publisher E-mail: getinfo@haworthpressinc.com

Journal for occupational therapists. **Subtitle:** A Journal of Contemproary Practice. **Founded:** 1984. **Freq:** Quarterly. **Trim Size:** 4 3/8 x 7 1/8. **Key Personnel:** Susan Heling Kaplan, Editor, phone (305)348-3105, fax (305)348-1240, Kaplans@fiu.edu; Bill Cohen, Publisher. **ISSN:** 0738-0577. **Subscription Rates:** $40 individuals; $75 institutions; $105 libraries. **Remarks:** Advertising not accepted. **Alt. Formats:** Microfiche; Microfilm.
Circ: 650

Palmetto Bay News - See Homestead

6456 Pleasure Boatings Caribbean Sports & Travel Magazine
Graphcom Publishing, Inc.
1995 NE 150 St., Ste. 107 Phone: (305)945-7403
Miami, FL 33181-1185 Fax: (305)947-6410

Vacation guide. **Founded:** 1971. **Freq:** Quarterly. **Print Method:** Web offset. **Trim Size:** 8 x 10 3/4. **Cols./Page:** 3. **Col. Width:** 2.25 picas. **Col. Depth:** 10 inches. **Key Personnel:** Jeff Green, Managing Editor; Don Zern, Exec. Editor; Robert L. Ulrich, Publisher; Connie Frocchi, Advertising Dir. **Subscription Rates:** $8 individuals; $2.50 single issue. **Remarks:** Accepts advertising.
Ad Rates: BW: $1,580 **Circ:** Paid ‡21,775
4C: $2,330 Non-paid ‡3,475

6457 Reggae Report
RR International Magazine, Inc.
21300 NE 24 Ct. Phone: (305)933-1178
Miami, FL 33180 Fax: (305)933-9918
Publication E-mail: ReggaeRprt@aol.com

Consumer magazine covering Caribbean and world music. **Founded:** Aug. 1983. **Freq:** Bimonthly. **Print Method:** Sheetfed offset. **Trim Size:** 8 1/2 x 11. **Cols./Page:** 3. **Key Personnel:** Peggy Quattro, Publisher, Reggaerprt@aol.com; Sara Gurgen, Editor, SaraGurgen@aol.com. **ISSN:** 1065-3023. **Subscription Rates:** $20 individuals. **Remarks:** Accepts advertising.
Circ: (Not Reported)

6458 St. Thomas Law Review
St. Thomas University School of Law
16400 NW 32nd Ave. Phone: (305)623-2380
Miami, FL 33054 Fax: (305)623-2390
Free: (800)228-5030

Legal journal. **Founded:** 1988. **Freq:** Triennial. **Key Personnel:** Nancy Campiglia, Editor-in-Chief. **Subscription Rates:** $27.50 single issue; $10 single issue. **Remarks:** Advertising not accepted. **Online:** LEXIS-NEXIS; Westlaw.
Circ: (Not Reported)

6459 Score Magazine
Quad International, Inc.
13360 SW 128th St. Phone: (305)662-5459
Miami, FL 33186
Consumer men's sophisticate magazine. **Founded:** June 1992. **Freq:** 13/year. **Print Method:** Offset. **Trim Size:** 8 x 10 7/8. **Cols./Page:** 3. **Col. Width:** 2 1/4 inches. **Col. Depth:** 10 inches. **Key Personnel:** John C. Fox, Publisher/Editor-in-Chief, FoxJ@scoregroup.com. **ISSN:** 1073-2438. **Subscription Rates:** $49.95 individuals. **Remarks:** Accepts advertising. **URL:** http://www.scoreland.com.
Ad Rates: BW: $1,800 **Circ:** Paid ‡60,959

6460 Social
Good News Publishing Co.
7022 SW 53rd Ln. Phone: (305)665-8101
Miami, FL 33155 Fax: (305)666-1449

Consumer magazine covering local society. **Founded:** Mar. 1982. **Freq:** Monthly. **Trim Size:** 7 x 10. **Cols./Page:** 3. **Key Personnel:** Joan Nielson, Editor and Publisher; Rosalind Moore, Contact. **Subscription Rates:** $24 individuals; $2.95 single issue. **Remarks:** Accepts advertising.
Ad Rates: BW: $800 **Circ:** (Not Reported)
4C: $1100

6461 South Florida Jewish Tribune Broward Edition
Jewish Media Group, Inc.
540 NW 165th St. Phone: (305)919-9340
Miami, FL 33169 Fax: (305)919-8344

Newspaper serving the Jewish community of Ft. Lauderdale and Hollywood, Florida. **Founded:** 1986. **Freq:** Weekly. **Print Method:** Offset. **Trim Size:** 11 x 13 5/8. **Cols./Page:** 6. **Col. Width:** 9 picas. **Col. Depth:** 75 picas. **Key Personnel:** Maureen Berkowitz, Editor; Jerome E. Libbin, Publisher. **Subscription Rates:** Free; $13 by mail. **Formerly:** Broward Jewish World.

6462 South Miami News
Community Newspapers
PO Box 43-1970 Phone: (305)667-7481
Miami, FL 33143 Fax: (305)661-0954
Publisher E-mail: cnedor@gate.net

Community newspaper (tabloid). **Founded:** 1968. **Freq:** 3/week. **Print Method:** Offset. **Trim Size:** 10 1/4 x 16. **Cols./Page:** 6. **Col. Width:** 19 nonpareils. **Col. Depth:** 238 agate lines. **Key Personnel:** Michael Miller, Editor; Grant Miller, Publisher. **Subscription Rates:** $78 individuals. **Remarks:** Accepts advertising.
Ad Rates: GLR: $.72 **Circ:** ‡8,000
BW: $1,350
4C: $2,400
PCI: $13.50

6463 Southeast Travel Professional
1200 NW 78th Ave., Ste. 216 Phone: (305)592-6133
Miami, FL 33126 Fax: (305)592-9741

Travel newspaper (tabloid). **Founded:** May 1988. **Freq:** Monthly. **Print Method:** Offset. **Trim Size:** 9 3/4 x 13. **Cols./Page:** 4. **Col. Width:** 14 picas. **Key Personnel:** Larry Cafiero, Editor, caftravel@aol.com; John A. Deveraux, Publisher; Roz Kornblum, Associate Publisher/Marketing. **Subscription Rates:** $12. **Remarks:** Accepts advertising. **Formerly:** Florida Travel Professional.
Ad Rates: BW: $1,270 **Circ:** Paid 450
4C: $1,670 Controlled 11,000
PCI: $40

6464 Southern Beverage Journal
14337 SW 119 Ave. Phone: (305)233-7230
Miami, FL 33186 Fax: (305)252-2580
Publication E-mail: sobevjrnl@aol.com

Alcohol beverage trade journal. **Founded:** 1947. **Freq:** Monthly. **Print Method:** Offset. **Trim Size:** 8 1/4 x 10 7/8. **Cols./Page:** 3 and 2. **Col. Width:** 27 and 42 nonpareils. **Col. Depth:** 140 agate lines. **Key Personnel:** Wanda Rowe, Editor; Richard Pierce, Advertising Mgr. **ISSN:** 0193-0613. **Subscription Rates:** $30 individuals. **Remarks:** Color advertising accepted; rates available upon request.
Ad Rates: BW: $2,995 **Circ:** ‡25,000

6465 Tequesta
Historical Association of Southern Florida
101 W. Flagler St. Phone: (305)375-1492
Miami, FL 33130 Fax: (305)375-1609
Publisher E-mail: publications@historical-museum.org

Journal covering local history. **Subtitle:** The Journal of the Historical Association of Southern Florida. **Founded:** 1941. **Freq:** Annual. **Print Method:** Offset. **Trim Size:** 6 x 9. **Cols./Page:** 1. **Col. Width:** 4 1/4 inches. **Col. Depth:** 7 1/8 inches. **Key Personnel:** Paul George, Ph.D., Editor; Jamie Welch, Managing Editor. **Subscription Rates:** Free to qualified subscribers; $5 single issue. **Remarks:** Advertising not accepted.
Circ: Paid 3,600

6466 Thoughts for All Seasons
Valley Press
478 NE 56th St. Phone: (305)756-8800
Miami, FL 33137-2621
Consumer magazine covering literature and humor. **Subtitle:** The Magazine of Epigrams. **Founded:** 1976. **Freq:** Irregular. **Print Method:** Offset. **Trim Size:** 6 x 9. **Key Personnel:** Michel Paul Richard, Editor. **ISSN:** 0886-6481. **Subscription Rates:** $6 single issue. **Remarks:** Accepts advertising.
Ad Rates: BW: $125 **Circ:** Non-paid 1,000

6467 Tu Internacional
Editorial Televisa
6355 NW 36th St. Phone: (305)871-6400
Miami, FL 33166-7099 Fax: (305)871-4939
Publisher E-mail: cosmo@editorial-televisa.com

Magazine providing the young woman with information on beauty, fashion, entertainment, decorating, and cooking (Spanish). **Founded:** 1981. **Freq:** Monthly. **Print Method:** Offset. **Trim Size:** 8 x 10 7/8. **Cols./Page:** 3. **Col. Width:** 13 picas. **Col. Depth:** 58.5 picas. **Key Personnel:** Nahyr Alcosta, Editor; Enrique J. Perez, Advertising Mgr.; Mario A. Freude, Editor. **Subscription Rates:** $20.95 individuals; $2.50 single issue. **Remarks:** Accepts advertising.
Ad Rates: BW: $825 **Circ:** ‡11,452
4C: $1,100

6468 TV y Novelas
Editorial Televisa
6355 NW 36th St. Phone: (305)871-6400
Miami, FL 33166-7099 Fax: (305)871-4939
Publisher E-mail: cosmo@editorial-televisa.com

Magazine covering the spanish-language soap operas lifestyles of entertainers; including photos and interviews (Spanish). **Founded:** 1982. **Freq:** Biweekly. **Print Method:** Offset. **Trim Size:** 7 3/4 x 10 11/16. **Cols./Page:** 3. **Col. Width:** 13 picas. **Col. Depth:** 58.5 picas. **Key Personnel:** Dora Luz Vargas, Editor; Enrique J Perez, Advertising Mgr.; Mario A. Freude, Editor. **Subscription Rates:** $27.95 individuals; $1.75 single issue. **Remarks:** Accepts advertising.
Ad Rates: BW: $2,325 **Circ:** Paid 155,507
4C: $3,100

6469 Up Front Drug Information
Street Pharmocologists Update
5701 Biscayne Blvd., Ste. 9PH Phone: (305)757-2566
Miami, FL 33137 Fax: (305)758-4677

Magazine giving information on drugs and drug referrals. **Freq:** Quarterly.

6470 Vanidades Continental
Editorial Televisa
6355 NW 36th St. Phone: (305)871-6400
Miami, FL 33166-7099 Fax: (305)871-4939
Publisher E-mail: cosmo@editorial-televisa.com

Women's fashion and beauty magazine (Spanish). **Founded:** 1961. **Freq:** Biweekly. **Print Method:** Offset. **Trim Size:** 8 5/8 x 10 7/8. **Cols./Page:** 3. **Col. Width:** 13.5 picas. **Col. Depth:** 59.5 picas. **Key Personnel:** Sara Barcelo de Castany, Editor; Enrique J. Perez, Advertising Sales Dir.; Mario A. Freude, V.P. Sales. **Subscription Rates:** $46 individuals; $2.95 single issue. **Remarks:** Accepts advertising.
Ad Rates: BW: $3,375 **Circ:** Paid ★**83,761**
4C: $4,500

6471 The Weekly News
The Weekly News, Inc.
901 NE 79th St. Phone: (305)757-6333
Miami, FL 33138 Fax: (305)756-6488
Publisher E-mail: info@theweeklynews.org

Shopper. **Founded:** May 22, 1958. **Freq:** Weekly (Wed.). **Print Method:** Offset. **Trim Size:** 11 x17. **Cols./Page:** 6. **Col. Width:** 20 nonpareils. **Col. Depth:** 238 agate lines. **Key Personnel:** Bette Kissick, Editor; John Mayo, Publisher. **Remarks:** Accepts advertising. **Formerly:** The Weekly.
Ad Rates: BW: $377.40 **Circ:** Free 13,000
SAU: $8.70

6472 The Weekly News
The Weekly News, Inc.
901 NE 79th St. Phone: (305)757-6333
Miami, FL 33138 Fax: (305)756-6488
Publisher E-mail: info@theweeklynews.org

Gay newspaper on news and issues. **Subtitle:** TWN. **Founded:** Aug. 22, 1977. **Freq:** Weekly (Wed.). **Print Method:** Web offset. **Trim Size:** 10 1/4 x 13. **Cols./Page:** 4. **Col. Width:** 14 picas. **Col. Depth:** 13 inches. **Key Personnel:** Bill Watson, Publisher. **ISSN:** 0898-1477. **Subscription Rates:** $39 by mail six months. **URL:** http://www.twnmag.com.
Ad Rates: BW: $1,025 **Circ:** Free ‡32,000
4C: $1,525
PCI: $40

6473 Welding Journal
American Welding Society (AWS)
550 LeJeune Rd. NW Phone: (305)443-9353
PO Box 351040 Fax: (305)443-5951
Miami, FL 33135
Free: (800)443-9353
Publisher E-mail: info@aws.org

Trade magazine. **Subtitle:** Published by the American Welding Society to advance the science, technology and application of welding. **Founded:** Jan. 1922. **Freq:** Monthly. **Print Method:** Offset. **Trim Size:** 8 1/8 x 10 7/8. **Cols./Page:** 3. **Col. Width:** 26 nonpareils. **Col. Depth:** 140 agate lines. **Key Personnel:** Jeff Weber, Publisher, jweber@awsparc.amweld.org; Rob Saltzstein, Advertising Mgr.; Andrew Cullison, Editor. **ISSN:** 0043-2296. **Subscription Rates:** $90 individuals; $130 other countries; $4.50 single issue members; $6 single issue non-members. **Remarks:** Accepts advertising.
Ad Rates: BW: $3,812 **Circ:** Paid 47,719
4C: $4,747
PCI: $90

6474 The Wild Wood Reader
National Alliance of Short Story Authors (NASSA)
7505 SW 82nd St., No. 222 Phone: (305)668-2283
Miami, FL 33143 Fax: (305)668-0636

Consumer magazine covering short fiction. **Founded:** Jan. 1997. **Freq:** Quarterly. **Print Method:** Offset. **Trim Size:** 5 1/2 x 8 1/2. **Key Personnel:** Alex Gonzalez, Editor. **Subscription Rates:** $15 individuals; $25 institutions; $10 students; $5 single issue. **Remarks:** Accepts advertising. **Alt. Formats:** Large-print.
Ad Rates: BW: $250 **Circ:** Paid 2,000
Non-paid 500

6475 Miami Tele-Communications, Inc.
1306 NW 7th Ave. Phone: (305)325-1370
Miami, FL 33136 Fax: (305)325-8741

Founded: 1984. **Key Personnel:** Maureen O'Neill, General Mgr.; Bonnie Lopez, Business Operations Mgr.; Jorge Gonzalez, Technical Operations Mgr. **Cities Served:** Miami, Opa-Locka, FL: subscribing households 65,000; 61 channels; 2 community access channels; 168 hours per week community access programming.

6476 TCI Cable TV
9825 SW 72nd St. Phone: (305)595-0924
Miami, FL 33173 Fax: (305)598-3944

Founded: 1979. **Formerly:** Dade Cable TV. **Cities Served:** Dade County, FL.

6477 TCI of South Florida
18601 NW 2nd Ave. Phone: (305)653-5541
Miami, FL 33169 Fax: (305)614-6718

Owner: Tele-Communications, Inc. (TCI), at above address. **Founded:** 1978. **Formerly:** Storer Cable (1992). **Key Personnel:** Tony Genova, General Mgr. **Cities Served:** Communities in Dade and Broward counties.: subscribing households 125,000; 40 channels; 1 community access channel; 40 hours per week community access programming.

6478 WAMR-FM - 107.5
2828 Coral Way Phone: (305)441-2073
Miami, FL 33145-3204 Fax: (305)445-8908

Format: Adult Contemporary; Ethnic; Hispanic. **Founded:** 1971. **Formerly:** WJOK-FM (1979); WQBA-FM. **Operating Hours:** Continuous; 100% local. **ADI:** Miami (Ft. Lauderdale), FL. **Key Personnel:** Luis Diaz-Albertiny, General Mgr.; Tony Campos, Production Mgr. **Wattage:** 100,000. **Ad Rates:** $225 for 30 seconds; $300 for 60 seconds.

6479 WAXY-FM - 105.9
20450 NW 2nd Ave. Phone: (305)653-8811
Miami, FL 33169-2505 Fax: (305)652-5385

Format: Adult Contemporary; Oldies. **Networks:** AP. **Owner:** Clear Channel Radio, 200 Concord Plaza, No. 600, San Antonio, TX 78216. **Founded:** 1960. **Operating Hours:** Continuous. **ADI:** Miami (Ft. Lauderdale), FL. **Key Personnel:** David Ross, General Mgr. **Wattage:** 100,000. **Ad Rates:** $15-220 per unit.

6480 WBFS-TV - 33
16550 NW 52nd Ave. Phone: (305)621-3333
Miami, FL 33014 Fax: (305)628-3448

Format: Commercial TV. **Networks:** Independent; United Paramount Network. **Founded:** 1982. **Operating Hours:** Continuous. **ADI:** Miami (Ft. Lauderdale), FL. **Key Personnel:** Bill Ballard, Contact; Tracy Swann, Program Dir.; Kathy Sparks, Sales Mgr.; Bernie Diaz, Contact.

6481 WCIX-TV - 6
8900 NW 18th Terr. Phone: (305)593-0606
Miami, FL 33172 Fax: (305)477-3040

Format: Commercial TV. **Networks:** CBS. **Operating Hours:** Continuous. **ADI:** Miami (Ft. Lauderdale), FL. **Key Personnel:** Alan Shaklan, General Mgr.

6482 WDNA-FM - 88.9
PO Box 558636 Phone: (305)662-8889
Miami, FL 33255 Fax: (305)662-1975
E-mail: wdna@paradise.net

Format: Public Radio; Jazz. **Networks:** Independent; Public Radio International (PRI). **Owner:** Bascomb Memorial Broadcasting Foundation, at above address. **Founded:** 1971. **Operating Hours:** Continuous; 100% local. **ADI:** Miami (Ft. Lauderdale), FL. **Key Personnel:** Margarita Pelleya, General Mgr.; Raymond M. Ball, Jr., Chief Engineer; Arturo Gomez-Cruiz, Music Dir. **Wattage:** 7,400. **Ad Rates:** Noncommercial. $30 per unit.

6483 WINZ-AM - 940
194 NW 187th St. Phone: (305)654-9494
Miami, FL 33169 Fax: (305)654-9090
Free: (800)603-9494

Format: News. **Networks:** ABC. **Owner:** Paxson Communications Corp., 601 Clearwater Park Rd., West Palm Beach, FL 33401, (407)659-4122, Fax: (407)659-4252, Free: (800)648-7296. **Founded:** 1946. **Operating Hours:** Continuous. **ADI:** Miami (Ft. Lauderdale), FL. **Key Personnel:** Ronna Woulfe, President; Roger Koch, VP, Sales; Wendy Harmon, Business Mgr.; Dimitri Dixon-Goss, Traffic Mgr.; Peter Bolger, Program Dir.; Phil Latzman, Sports Dir.; Cary Alfonso, Promotions Dir. **Wattage:** 50,000. **URL:** http://www.940winz.com.

6484 WIOD-AM - 610
194 NW 187th St. Phone: (305)654-9494
Miami, FL 33169 Fax: (305)654-9090
Free: (800)603-9494

Networks: AP; ABC. **Founded:** 1926. **Operating Hours:** Continuous. **ADI:** Miami (Ft. Lauderdale), FL. **Key Personnel:** Amy Farley, Controller, phone (305)999-6255; Peter Bolger, Program Dir., phone (305)999-6260, fax (305)654-0094; Ronna Woulfe, General Mgr., phone (305)999-6225, fax (305)652-2161. **Wattage:** 10,000. **URL:** http://www.newsradio610.com.

6485 WLQY-AM - 1320
11645 Biscayne Blvd., Ste. 102-B Phone: (305)891-1729
Miami, FL 33181-3138 Fax: (305)891-1583

Format: Religious; Hispanic; Ethnic. **Founded:** 1953. **Operating Hours:** Continuous. **ADI:** Miami (Ft. Lauderdale), FL. **Key Personnel:** Sandra B. Herzberg, General Mgr.; Rick Santos, Station Mgr. **Wattage:** 5000.

6486 WLRN-FM - 91.3
172 NE 15th St. Phone: (305)995-1717
Miami, FL 33132-1349 Fax: (305)995-2299

Format: Public Radio; Eclectic. **Networks:** National Public Radio (NPR). **Founded:** 1948. **Formerly:** WTHS-FM (1967). **Operating Hours:** Continuous (except 2 a.m.-6 a.m. Sun.). **ADI:** Miami (Ft. Lauderdale), FL. **Key Personnel:** Gustavo Sagasoume, General Mgr., phone (305)995-2260; W. Theodore Fudredge, Station Mgr., phone (305)995-2206, fax (305)995-2221, teldredge@wlrn.org; Joseph Cooper, Program Dir.; Michael Peyton, Sales Mgr., phone (305)995-2268, fax (305)995-2227, mpeyton@wlrn.org. **Wattage:** 100,000. **Ad Rates:** Noncommercial.

6487 WLRN-TV - 17
172 NE 15th St. Phone: (305)995-1717
Miami, FL 33132 Fax: (305)995-2299
E-mail: info@wlrn.org

Format: Public TV. **Networks:** Public Broadcasting Service (PBS). **Founded:** 1969. **Operating Hours:** 7 a.m.-midnight. **ADI:** Miami (Ft. Lauderdale), FL. **Key Personnel:** Gustavo Sagastume, General Mgr.; Carmen Salman, Communications Dir. **Ad Rates:** Noncommercial. **URL:** http://www.wlrn.org.

6488 WLTV-TV - 23
9405 NW 41st Phone: (305)471-3900
Miami, FL 33178 Fax: (305)471-4160

Format: Commercial TV. **Networks:** Univision. **Owner:** Univision Television Group, 605 3rd Ave., 12th Fl., New York, NY 10158, (212)455-5200, Fax: (212)867-6710. **Founded:** 1971. **Operating Hours:** 21 hours daily; 80% network, 20% local. **ADI:** Miami (Ft. Lauderdale), FL. **Key Personnel:** Tomas T. Johansen, General Mgr.; Olga M. Luis, Station Mgr.; Stephanie Kontzamanys, Local Sales Mgr.; Matt Boxer, Nat'l Sales Mgr.; Marilyn Hansen, General Sales Mgr. **Local Programs:** *Marlins Major League Games*; *Miami Ahora (Public Affairs)*. **Ad Rates:** $190-4,000 per unit.

6489 WLVE-FM - 93.9
194 NW 187th St. Phone: (305)654-9494
Miami, FL 33169 Fax: (305)654-9090
Free: (800)603-9494
E-mail: jazz@love94.com

Format: Adult Contemporary; Jazz. **Simulcasts:** WWLV-FM. **Networks:** Independent. **Owner:** Clear Channel Communications, 200 Concord Plz., No. 600, San Antonio, TX 78216, (210)822-2828, Fax: (210)822-2299. **Founded:** 1955. **Formerly:** WWWL-FM (1987). **Operating Hours:** Continuous; 100% local. **ADI:** Miami (Ft. Lauderdale), FL. **Key Personnel:** Ronna Fink-Woulfe, President, phone (305)999-6225, fax (305)654-9090, rwoulfe@ccmiami.com; Bret Michael, Program Dir., phone (305)999-6202, bmichael@ccmiami.com; Toni Shreffler, Promotions Mgr., phone (305)999-6229, fax (305)654-0094, tshreffler@ccmiami.com; Joanne Rice, News/ Public Service/Director, phone (305)999-6251, fax (305)654-0094, trice@ccmiami.com; Joanne Rice, News Dir. **Wattage:** 100,000. **URL:** http://www.love94.com.

6490 WLYF-FM - 101.5
20450 NW 2nd Ave. Phone: (305)653-8811
Miami, FL 33169-2505 Fax: (305)652-0098
E-mail: litefm@wlyf.com

Format: Soft Rock; Adult Contemporary. **Founded:** 1970. **Operating Hours:** Continuous. **ADI:** Miami (Ft. Lauderdale), FL. **Key Personnel:** Dennis Collins, General Mgr.; Rob Sidney, Program Dir. **Wattage:** 100,000. **URL:** http://www.wlyf.com.

6491 WMCU-FM - 89.7
330 Biscayne Blvd., Ste. 600 Phone: (305)381-7400
Miami, FL 33132 Fax: (305)381-7413

Format: Contemporary Christian. **Networks:** USA Radio; AP. **Owner:** Trinity Evangelical Divinity School, 2065 Half Day Rd., Deerfield, FL 60015. **Founded:** Aug. 1970. **Operating Hours:** Continuous. **ADI:** Miami (Ft. Lauderdale), FL. **Key Personnel:** Steve James, Station Mgr.; Merryan Padrou, Assistant Mgr.; Dr. Ken Meyer, President; Dwight Taylor, Operations Mgr.; Uri Katz, News Dir. **Wattage:** 100,000. **Ad Rates:** Noncommercial; underwriting available. **URL:** http://www.wmcuradio.com.

6492 WMRZ-AM - 790
20450 NW 2nd Ave. Phone: (305)653-8811
Miami, FL 33169 Fax: (305)652-5385

Format: News; Talk. **Networks:** ABC. **Founded:** 1947. **Formerly:** WNWS-AM (1990). **Operating Hours:** Continuous. **ADI:** Miami (Ft. Lauderdale), FL. **Key Personnel:** Dennis Collins, General Mgr.; Don Kearns, Production Mgr.; Rick Charnack, Sales Mgr.; Kelly Silva, Contact; Naomi Wright, Contact. **Wattage:** 25,000.

6493 WMXJ-FM -
20450 NW 2nd Ave. Phone: (305)651-1027
Miami, FL 33169 Fax: (305)652-3032
Free: (800)226-1027
E-mail: majic@gate.net

Format: Oldies. **Networks:** Independent. **Owner:** Jefferson Pilot Communications, PO Box 21008, Greensboro, NC 27420, (910)691-3890, Fax: (910)691-3311. **Founded:** 1985. **Formerly:** WCKO-FM. **Operating Hours:** Continuous; 100% local. **ADI:** Miami (Ft. Lauderdale), FL. **Key Personnel:** Ed Scarborough, Program Dir.; Lori Sheffield, Promotions Dir.; Dennis Collins, General Mgr.; Rick Charnack, General Sales Mgr.; Mindy Lang, Music Dir.; Joe Johnson, Production Dir.; David Stonecipher, CEO; Theresa Stone, President; Jim Yelton, Chief Engineer. **Wattage:** 100,000. **Ad Rates:** $50-400 per unit.

6494 WOCN-AM - 1450
350 N.E. 71st St. Phone: (305)759-7280
Miami, FL 33138 Fax: (305)759-2276

Format: Hispanic. **Networks:** Independent. **Founded:** 1984. **Operating Hours:** Continuous; 100% local. **ADI:** Miami (Ft. Lauderdale), FL. **Key Personnel:** Pablo Vega, President; Richard Vega, Contact; Sebastian Bega, Vice President. **Wattage:** 1000.

6495 WPBT-TV - 2
14901 NE Sesame St. Phone: (305)949-8321
Miami, FL 33181 Fax: (305)944-4211

Format: Public TV. **Networks:** Public Broadcasting Service (PBS). **Founded:** Aug. 12, 1955. **Operating Hours:** 6 a.m.-3a.m. **ADI:** Miami (Ft. Lauderdale), FL. **Key Personnel:** George Dooley, President and CEO; Dave Mullins, VP, Marketing; Michael Boylan, Sr. VP, Production; Linda O'Bryon, Sr. VP; John Reynolds, Sr. VP; Diana Arlotta, VP, Administrative Services; Shirley Carroll, VP, Finance/Corporate Treasurer; Jack Gibson, VP, Programming; Graham Simmons, VP, Engineering. **Local Programs:** *Issues and the Media*; *New Florida*; *The Nightly Business Report*. **Wattage:** 100 KW. **Ad Rates:** $650 for 30 seconds. **URL:** http://www/channel2.org.

6496 WPLG-TV - 10
3900 Biscayne Blvd. Phone: (305)576-1010
Miami, FL 33137 Fax: (305)325-2480

Format: Commercial TV. **Networks:** ABC. **Operating Hours:** Continuous. **ADI:** Miami (Ft. Lauderdale), FL. **Key Personnel:** John Garwood, General Mgr.

6497 WPLL-FM - 103.5
194 NW 187th St. Phone: (305)654-9494
Miami, FL 33169 Fax: (305)654-9090

Format: Adult Contemporary. **Owner:** Paxson Communications Corp., 601 Clearwater Park Rd., West Palm Beach, FL 33401, (407)659-4122, Fax: (407)659-4252, Free: (800)648-7296. **Founded:** 1959. **Formerly:** WSHE-FM. **Operating Hours:** 0% network, 100% local. **ADI:** Miami (Ft. Lauderdale), FL. **Key Personnel:** Ronna Woulfe, V. Pres./Gen. Mgr.; Dave Stewart, Program Dir.; Roger Koch, General Sales Mgr.; Terri Lynn, Public Affairs Dir. **Wattage:** 100,000.

6498 WPOW-FM - 96.5
20295 NW 2nd Ave. Phone: (305)653-6796
Miami, FL 33169 Fax: (305)770-1456

Format: Top 40. **Owner:** Greg Reed, at above address. **Founded:** 1985. **Operating Hours:** Continuous. **ADI:** Miami (Ft. Lauderdale), FL. **Key Personnel:** Greg Reed, Contact; Kid Curry, Program Dir.; Kenny Bernstein, Promotions Dir.; Matthew Bell, General Sales Mgr. **Wattage:** 100,000.

6499 WQAM-AM - 560
20295 NW 2nd Ave. Phone: (305)653-6796
Miami, FL 33169 Fax: (305)770-1456
E-mail: wq@mc.com

Format: Sports; Talk; Adult Contemporary; Oldies. **Networks:** ESPN Radio. **Owner:** Beasley Reed Broadcasting, at above address. **Founded:** 1921. **Operating Hours:** Continuous. **ADI:** Miami (Ft. Lauderdale), FL. **Key Personnel:** Greg Reed, General Mgr.; Ray Perry, Sales Mgr. **Local Programs:** *First Team with Former Miami Dolphin Jose Rose, Jeff DeForest, & Steve Goldstein* 6-10 a.m. Monday-Friday, Duff Lindsey, Exec. Producer; *Hank Goldberg* 3-7 p.m., Josh Darrow, Exec. Producer; *Mid-day with Joe Zagachie & Dave O'Brien* 10 a.m. - 12 noon, Chris Visser, Exec. Producer. **Wattage:** 5000. **Ad Rates:** Advertising accepted; rates available upon request. **URL:** http://wqam.com.

6500 WQBA-AM - 1140
2828 Coral Way Phone: (305)441-2073
Miami, FL 33145 Fax: (305)445-8908

Format: Full Service; Talk; Hispanic. **Founded:** 1967. **Formerly:** WMIE-AM (1966). **Operating Hours:** Continuous; 100% local. **ADI:** Miami (Ft. Lauderdale), FL. **Key Personnel:** Claudia Puig, General Mgr.; Augustin Acosta, Station Mgr. **Wattage:** 50,000. **Ad Rates:** $100 for 30 seconds; $150 for 60 seconds.

6501 WRHC-AM - 1550
330 SW 27th Ave., Ste. 207 Phone: (305)541-3300
Miami, FL 33135-2957 Fax: (305)643-6224

Format: News; Talk; Hispanic. **Networks:** Independent. **Founded:** 1963. **Operating Hours:** Continuous. **ADI:** Miami (Ft. Lauderdale), FL. **Key Personnel:** Jorge A. Rodriguez, President; Ana Vidal Rodriguez, Vice President; Carlos Carreras, Sr., Treasurer. **Local Programs:** *Amanacer Azul*, Frank Ramirez; *La Pena Azul*, Salvador Lew; *Por Nuestra Comunidad*, Jose Marmol. **Wattage:** 10,000 day; 250 night.

6502 WSUA-AM - 1260
2100 Coral Way Phone: (305)285-1260
Miami, FL 33145 Fax: (305)858-5907

Format: Hispanic. **Networks:** Independent. **Owner:** El Dorado Communication, at above address. **Founded:** 1996. **Operating Hours:** Continuous; 100% local. **ADI:** Miami (Ft. Lauderdale), FL. **Key Personnel:** Gerardo Reyes, President; William Restrepo, News Dir.; Silvio Cortez, Finance VP; Frank Guerra, Chief Engineer. **Wattage:** 5000. **Ad Rates:** $120 for 60 seconds. **URL:** http://www.caracolusa.com.

6503 WSVN-TV - 7
1401 79th St. Phone: (305)751-6692
PO Box 1118 Fax: (305)795-2715
Miami, FL 33138
E-mail: 7news@wsvn.com

Format: Commercial TV. **Networks:** Fox; Independent. **Owner:** Sunbeam Television Corp., at above address. **Founded:** 1956. **Formerly:** WCKT-TV. **Operating Hours:** Continuous. **ADI:** Miami (Ft. Lauderdale), FL. **Key Personnel:** Robert Leider, Contact, phone (305)7952602, fax (305)7952738; Bert Medina, Contact; John Bak, Chief Engineer; Robert Holtzer, General Sales Mgr., phone (305)7952795; Charlie Folds, Contact; Jim Ladas, Contact; Alice Jacobs, News Dir.; Dianna Stuver, Business Mgr., phone (305)7952620. **Ad Rates:** Noncommercial. **URL:** http://www.wsvn.com.

6504 WTVJ-TV - 6
316 N. Miami Ave. Phone: (305)379-6666
Miami, FL 33128 Fax: (305)789-4202
E-mail: nbc6.nbc.com

Format: Commercial TV. **Networks:** NBC. **Founded:** 1949. **Operating Hours:** Continuous. **ADI:** Miami (Ft. Lauderdale), FL. **Key Personnel:** Donald V. Browne, Contact; Barry Allenuck, Contact; Deborah Collura, News Dir.; Karla Nelson, Contact; Carol DeVane, Contact; Donald Ramsey, Contact; Paul Russell, Contact. **Wattage:** 100 kw. **Ad Rates:** $100-12,000 per unit.

6505 WXDJ-FM - 95.7
3191 Coral Way, Suite 1000 Phone: (305)447-9595
Miami, FL 33145 Fax: (305)448-4735

Format: Hispanic. **Networks:** Independent. **Founded:** 1987. **Operating Hours:** Continuous; 100% local. **ADI:** Miami (Ft. Lauderdale), FL. **Key Personnel:** Kymm Abrahamson, General Mgr.; Maggie Rodriguez, General Sales Mgr.; Jesus Salas, Productions Director. **Wattage:** 100,000.

6506 WZTA-FM - 94.9
194 N.W. 187th St. Phone: (305)654-9494
Miami, FL 33169 Fax: (305)654-9090
Free: (800)603-9494

Networks: Independent. **Operating Hours:** Continuous. **ADI:** Miami (Ft. Lauderdale), FL. **Key Personnel:** Gregg Steele, Program Dir., phone (305)999-6250, fax (305)654-9090, gsteele@ccmiami.com; Ronna Woulfe, General Mgr., phone (305)999-6225, fax (305)652-2161. **Wattage:** 100,000. **URL:** http://www.949zeta.com.

MIAMI BEACH, pop. 96,298.

S FL. Dade Co. 3 mi. SE of Miami. Summer and winter resort.

6507 Chai Today
Chai Publications
420 Lincoln Rd., Ste. 409 Phone: (305)672-1937
Miami Beach, FL 33139 Fax: (305)673-1283

Magazine promoting an understanding of the principles of Judaism. **Founded:** 1989. **Freq:** Bimonthly. **Print Method:** Web offset. **Trim Size:** 8 3/8 x 10 7/8. **Cols./Page:** 3. **Key Personnel:** Michael Lozenik, Editor. **Subscription Rates:** $18; $24 two years. $2.50 single issue. **Remarks:** Accepts advertising.
Ad Rates: BW: $3,045 **Circ:** Paid ‡168,000
4C: $4,350

6508 Marine Business Journal
Marine Business Journal, Inc.
1766 Bay Rd. Phone: (305)538-0700
Miami Beach, FL 33139 Fax: (305)532-8657
Publication E-mail: sboating@iconect.net

Trade magazine. **Subtitle:** The Voice of the Marine Industries Nationwide. **Founded:** 1987. **Freq:** Bimonthly. **Print Method:** Web press. **Trim Size:** 8 1/2 x 10 7/8. **Cols./Page:** 3. **Col. Width:** 13 picas. **Col. Depth:** 9 inches. **Key Personnel:** George Strickland; Skip Allen, Publisher; George Allen, Advertising Mgr. **ISSN:** 0192-3579. **Subscription Rates:** $15 individuals; $25 other countries; $2.95 single issue. **Remarks:** Accepts advertising. **URL:** http://www.conect.net/comm/sboating.
Ad Rates: BW: $3,380 **Circ:** Paid 27,000
4C: $4,505 Controlled 1,426
PCI: $70

6509 Show Continental
Impact of Miami, Inc.
PO Box 402039 Phone: (305)532-6710
Miami Beach, FL 33140 Fax: (305)672-8511

Entertainment magazine (Spanish). **Founded:** 1984. **Freq:** Monthly. **Print Method:** Offset. **Trim Size:** 8 1/2 x 11. **Cols./Page:** 4. **Key Personnel:** Graciela A. Ricciardi, Editor, showmagz@icanect.net; Alberto A. Micheli, Publisher. **Subscription Rates:** $18.72. **Remarks:** Accepts advertising.
Ad Rates: BW: $890 **Circ:** ‡65,000
4C: $1,500

6510 The Sun Post
Post Newspaper Group, Inc.
1688 Meridian Ave. No. 702 Phone: (305)538-9700
PO Box 19-1870
Miami Beach, FL 33139
Publication E-mail: sunposted@aol.com

Local newspaper. **Founded:** Jan. 1, 1986. **Freq:** Weekly. **Print Method:** Offset. **Trim Size:** 11 x 17. **Cols./Page:** 6. **Col. Width:** 1 1/2 inches. **Col. Depth:** 16 1/2 inches. **Key Personnel:** Felix Stark, Editor and Publisher; Jeannette Stark, Editor. **Subscription Rates:** $35. **Remarks:** Accepts advertising. **Formerly:** Sun Reporter/Sunrise Mirror (Jan. 1, 1986).
Ad Rates: BW: $1,050 **Circ:** Paid ‡2,000
4C: $1,500 Free ‡45,000
SAU: $10.50

6511 WMBM-AM - 1490
814 1st St. Phone: (305)672-1100
Miami Beach, FL 33139 Fax: (305)673-1194
E-mail: wmbm@wmbm.com

Format: Gospel. **Networks:** American Urban Radio; Westwood One Radio. **Owner:** New Birth Broadcasting Corp., at above address. **Founded:** Mar. 1995. **Operating Hours:** Continuous. **ADI:** Miami (Ft. Lauderdale), FL. **Key Personnel:** Victor T. Curry, General Mgr.; Horac Straws, Program Dir. **Wattage:** 1000. **Ad Rates:** $70-85 for 30 seconds; $98-160 for 60 seconds. **URL:** http://www.wmbm.com.

MIAMI LAKES

6512 Recommend
Worth International Communications Corp.
5979 NW, 151 St., Ste. 120 Phone: (305)828-0123
Miami Lakes, FL 33014 Fax: (305)826-6950
Free: (800)447-0123

Travel industry magazine. **Subtitle:** Helping Travel Agents Sell Travel. **Founded:** Mar. 1967. **Freq:** Monthly. **Print Method:** Offset. **Trim Size:** 8 3/8 x 10 7/8. **Cols./Page:** 3. **Col. Width:** 2 1/4 inches. **Col. Depth:** 10 inches. **Key Personnel:** Hal Herman, President/Editor-in-Chief; Laurel Herman, Editor and Publisher. **ISSN:** 0034-1452. **Subscription Rates:** Free to industry affiliate; $48 institutions. **Remarks:** Accepts advertising. **URL:** http://www.gotravel.com.
Ad Rates: BW: $6,840 **Circ:** Non-paid △**60,895**
4C: $9,270

MIAMI SHORES, pop. 8,960.

Dade Co. (NE). 9 m N of Miami.

6513 Barry Magazine
Barry University
11300 NE 2nd Ave. Phone: (305)899-3188
Miami, FL 33161 Fax: (305)899-3186

Collegiate magazine. **Founded:** 1994. **Freq:** 3/year. **Print Method:** Web offset. **Trim Size:** 8 1/2 x 10 7/8. **Key Personnel:** Joseph McQuay, Editor, mcquay@jeanne.barry.edu. **Remarks:** Advertising not accepted. **Formerly:** The Flame.
Circ: Non-paid 40,000

6514 La Voz Catolica
Archdiocese of Miami
9401 Biscayne Blvd. Phone: (305)758-3399
Miami Shores, FL 33138 Fax: (305)754-1797

Community newspaper (Spanish). **Founded:** 1959. **Freq:** Monthly. **Print Method:** Offset. **Trim Size:** 9 3/4 x 13 1/4. **Cols./Page:** 5. **Col. Width:** 2 inches. **Col. Depth:** 12 inches. **Key Personnel:** Araceli Cantero, Editor, fax (305)762-1130; Gloria M. Sori, Advertising Dir., phone (305)762-1201, fax (305)762-1223; Edith Garcia, Editor, phone (305)762-1127. **ISSN:** 1044-1883. **Subscription Rates:** $25 other countries per year; $12 individuals per year. **Remarks:** Accepts advertising. **URL:** http://www.vozcat1@march.org; http://www.vozcat.com. **Formerly:** Insert of The Voice (1982).
Ad Rates: BW: $960 **Circ:** ⊕**48,000**
4C: $1,310
PCI: $16

MIAMI SPRINGS, pop. 12,350.

S FL. Dade Co. 10 mi. W. of Miami.

6515 Airline, Ship & Catering ONBOARD SERVICES Magazine
Club Publications
665 La Villa Dr. Phone: (305)887-1701
Miami Springs, FL 33166-6029 Fax: (305)885-1923
Free: (800)887-2550

Air and cruise line food, onboard services, and duty free industries trade magazine (tabloid). **Founded:** 1974. **Freq:** 9/year. **Print Method:** Offset. **Trim Size:** 11 x 14. **Cols./Page:** 5. **Col. Width:** 24 nonpareils. **Col. Depth:** 196 agate lines. **Key Personnel:** Jim O'Neal, Editor; Alex Morton, Publisher; Donna Wood-Beney, Advertising Mgr. **ISSN:** 0892-4236. **Subscription Rates:** $25 individuals. **Remarks:** Accepts advertising.
Ad Rates: BW: $2,750 **Circ:** Paid ★18
4C: $3,995 Non-paid ★3,730

6516 City & Country Club Life
Club Publications
665 La Villa Dr. Phone: (305)887-1701
Miami Springs, FL 33166-6029 Fax: (305)885-1923
Free: (800)887-2550

Publication covering fashion, travel, profiles, interiors, and entertaining. **Subtitle:** The Social Magazine for South Florida. **Founded:** 1985. **Freq:** Bimonthly. **Print Method:** Offset. **Trim Size:** 11 1/8 x 14 1/4. **Cols./Page:** 3. **Col. Width:** 2 7/4 inches. **Col. Depth:** 12 inches. **Key Personnel:** Alex Morton, Publisher; Rachael Britipaja, Account Exec. **ISSN:** 0897-4926. **Subscription Rates:** $15 individuals. **Remarks:** Accepts advertising.
Ad Rates: BW: $1,950 **Circ:** Paid 793
4C: $2,800 Non-paid 13,903

MIDWAY

6517 WTLH-TV - 49
PO Box 949 Phone: (904)942-4900
Midway, FL 32343-0949 Fax: (904)942-0062

Format: Commercial TV. **Networks:** Fox. **Founded:** 1989. **Operating Hours:** 5:30 a.m. Monday - 1 a.m. Sunday. **ADI:** Tallahassee, FL-Thomasville (Bainbridge), GA. **Key Personnel:** Frank Watson, General Mgr.; Donald Abel, Program Dir.; Jay Haller, Sales Mgr.; Jan Wheeless, Promotions Mgr.; Sue Schultz, Contact.

MILTON†, pop. 7,206.

NW FL. Santa Rosa Co. On Blackwater River, 25 mi. NE of Pensacola. Naval stores, lumber, chemical, fiber industries. Pine timber. Agriculture. Cotton, corn, soybeans.

6518 Santa Rosa Free Press
Press Gazette
531 SW Elva St. Phone: (904)623-3616
Milton, FL 32570 Fax: (904)623-2007
Publication E-mail: srpgazette@aol.com

Community newspaper serving Santa Rosa County. **Freq:** Weekly (Thurs.). **Print Method:** Offset. **Cols./Page:** 9. **Col. Width:** 17 nonpareils. **Col. Depth:** 301 agate lines. **Key Personnel:** Jim Fletcher, Editor; Jimmie D. Hill, Publisher; Sam Dougherty, Advertising Mgr. **Remarks:** Accepts advertising.
Ad Rates: GLR: $.429 **Circ:** Free ‡21,500

6519 Santa Rosa Press Gazette
Press Gazette
531 SW Elva St. Phone: (904)623-3616
Milton, FL 32570 Fax: (904)623-2007

Community newspaper serving Santa Rosa County. **Founded:** 1907. **Freq:** Semiweekly (Mon. and Thurs.). **Print Method:** Offset. **Trim Size:** 13 x 21 1/2. **Cols./Page:** 6. **Key Personnel:** James Fletcher, Editor; Jimmie D. Hill, Publisher; Jim T. Martin, Advertising Mgr. **Subscription Rates:** $24 individuals; $17 Senior citizens; $30 out of area. **Remarks:** Accepts advertising.
Ad Rates: BW: $1,148.10 **Circ:** ‡6,700
SAU: $10.15
PCI: $10.15

6520 WEBY-AM - 1330
7179 Printers Alley Phone: (850)623-1330
Milton, FL 32583

Format: News; Talk. **Networks:** ABC; USA Radio. **Owner:** Byrd Mapoles, at above address. **Founded:** 1985. **Operating Hours:** 6 a.m.-6 p.m. **Key Personnel:** Byrd Mapoles, General Mgr.; Joyce Campbell, General Mgr.; Lisa Dailey, Office Mgr. **Local Programs:** *Byrd Mapoles Local News.* **Wattage:** 5000. **Ad Rates:** $5 for 30 seconds; $10 for 60 seconds.

6521 WECM-AM - 1490
703 Berryhill Rd. Phone: (904)623-1490
Milton, FL 32570 Fax: (904)623-5444

Format: Gospel; News. **Networks:** USA Radio. **Owner:** Faith Bible College, 1207 Hamilton Bridge Rd., Milton, FL 32570. **Founded:** 1989. **Formerly:** WCKC-AM. **Operating Hours:** 6 a.m.-10 p.m. **Key Personnel:** Mac Johnson, General Mgr.; John C. Gunton, Contact. **Local Programs:** *Breakfast Table* 6:45 a.m.-8 a.m., Ken Johnson, (904)623-1455; *Suppertime Gospel* 4 p.m.-5 p.m., Lloyd Fowler, (904)623-1490; *Voice of the People* 5 p.m.-6 p.m., Marty Davis, (904)626-6529; *Voice of Victory* 8:03 a.m.-8:15 a.m., Dr. Mac Johnson, (904)623-1455. **Wattage:** 1000. **Ad Rates:** $3.75 for 30 seconds; $6.25 for 60 seconds.

MIRAMAR

Broward Co. (SE). 20 m W of Hallandale.

6522 WYHS-TV - 69
10306 USA Today Way Phone: (954)435-6900
Miramar, FL 33025 Fax: (954)435-7406

Format: Commercial TV. **Owner:** Silver King Broadcasting, at above address. **Founded:** 1988. **Formerly:** WYSH-TV (1969). **Operating Hours:** Continuous; 88% network, 12% local. **ADI:** Miami (Ft. Lauderdale), FL. **Key Personnel:** Lily Guzman, Operations Mgr.; Mike Kuszewski, Chief Engineer. **Wattage:** 5 megawatts.

MONTICELLO†, pop. 2,994.

N FL. Jefferson Co. 25 mi. NE of Tallahassee. Light industry. Nurseries. Timber. Agriculture. Watermelon seeds, pecans, hogs.

6523 Monticello News
100 W. Dogwood St. Phone: (904)997-3568
PO Box 428 Fax: (904)997-3774
Monticello, FL 32344
Community newspapers. **Subtitle:** Community Newspaper. **Founded:** 1869. **Freq:** Semiweekly (Wed. and Fri.). **Print Method:** Offset. **Cols./Page:** 6. **Col. Width:** 24 nonpareils. **Col. Depth:** 294 agate lines. **Key Personnel:** Ron Cichon, Publisher. **ISSN:** 0746-5297. **Subscription Rates:** $30 individuals; $35 out of state. **Remarks:** Accepts advertising.
Ad Rates: GLR: $.37 **Circ:** ‡3,000
BW: $620.48
4C: $300
PCI: $5.48

MOORE HAVEN†, pop. 1,250.

S FL. Glades Co. On Lake Okeechobee, 75 mi. W. of West Palm Beach. Fishing resort area. Agriculture. Beans, cabbage, tomatoes. Cattle and dairy farms.

6524 Glades County Democrat
PO Box 70 Phone: (941)946-0511
Moore Haven, FL 33471-0070 Fax: (941)983-7537

Community newspaper. **Founded:** 1922. **Freq:** Weekly (Thurs.). **Print Method:** Offset. **Cols./Page:** 5. **Col. Width:** 12 nonpareils. **Col. Depth:** 301 agate lines. **Key Personnel:** Tracy Whirls, Editor; Richard Hitt, Publisher; Kerry Faunce, Advertising Mgr. **ISSN:** 0745-4120. **Subscription Rates:** $18 individuals. **Remarks:** Accepts advertising.
Ad Rates: BW: $185 **Circ:** ‡1,500
SAU: $6.13

MULBERRY, pop. 2,950.

C FL. Polk Co. 10 mi. S. of Lakeland. Phosphate mines. Fruit, truck, and poultry farms.

6525 Mulberry Press
Polk County Press
1020 N. Church Ave. Phone: (813)425-3411
Highway 37 N.
Mulberry, FL 33860
Community newspaper. **Founded:** 1909. **Freq:** Weekly (Wed.). **Print Method:** Offset. **Cols./Page:** 6. **Col. Width:** 2 1/16 inches. **Col. Depth:** 21 inches. **Key Personnel:** William Histed, Editor and Publisher; Robert Histed, Contact. **USPS:** 367-780. **Subscription Rates:** $24 annual.
Ad Rates: GLR: $.30 **Circ:** Paid ‡4,500
BW: $450 Non-paid ‡300
SAU: $6.50

NAPLES†, pop. 17,581.

S FL. Collier Co. On Gulf of Mexico, 30 mi. S. of Fort Myers. Resort. Shrimp fisheries. Agriculture.

6526 Everglades Echo
Tuff Publications, Inc.
2301 County Rd. 951, Ste. C Phone: (941)353-0444
Naples, FL 34116-6524 Fax: (941)353-9040
Publisher E-mail: tuffpub@aol.com

Community newspaper. **Founded:** 1979. **Freq:** Weekly (Tues.). **Print Method:** Offset. **Trim Size:** 11 x 17. **Cols./Page:** 5. **Col. Width:** 2 1/8 inches. **Col. Depth:** 16 1/2 inches. **Key Personnel:** R.W. Tuff, Editor and Publisher. **USPS:** 681-690. **Subscription Rates:** $23.32 individuals in county; $28.62 individuals out of county; $30 out of country. **Remarks:** Accepts advertising.
Ad Rates: BW: $1,120 **Circ:** 1,000
4C: $1,420
PCI: $4

6527 Gulfshore Life Magazine
Gulfshore Communications
2975 S. Horseshoe Dr., Ste. 100 Phone: (941)643-3933
Fax: (941)643-5017
Naples, FL 34104-6133
Free: (800)220-4853
Publication E-mail: gulfshore@olusa.com
Publisher E-mail: gulfshore1@aol.com

Lifestyle magazine. **Subtitle:** The Magazine of Southwest Florida. **Founded:** Jan. 1, 1970. **Freq:** 10/year (combined issues May/June and July/August). **Print Method:** Webb. **Trim Size:** 8 3/8 x 10 7/8. **Cols./Page:** 3. **Col. Width:** 42 picas. **Col. Depth:** 60.3 picas. **Key Personnel:** Elizabeth Heath, Editor; Charles Colletti, Publisher. **ISSN:** 0745-0079. **Subscription Rates:** $25 individuals. **Remarks:** Accepts advertising.
Ad Rates: BW: $1,800 **Circ:** Paid ‡12,000
4C: $2,500 Non-paid ‡12,000

6528 Home & Condo
Gulfshore Communications
2975 S. Horseshoe Dr., Ste. 100 Phone: (941)643-3933
Fax: (941)643-5017
Naples, FL 34104-6133
Free: (800)220-4853
Publisher E-mail: gulfshore1@aol.com

S.W. Florida's resource for home & garden ideas. **Subtitle:** Southwest Florida's Resource for Home & Garden Ideas. **Founded:** 1980. **Freq:** 7/year. **Print Method:** Web offset. **Trim Size:** 8 3/8 x 10 7/8. **Key Personnel:** Helene LeComte, Editor; Charles Colletti, Publisher. **ISSN:** 0745-0089. **Subscription Rates:** $14.45; $2.95 single issue. **Remarks:** Accepts advertising.
Ad Rates: BW: $2,355 **Circ:** Paid ‡6,000
4C: $3,050 Controlled ‡29,000

6529 Link
Distributor's Link Inc.
4297 Corporate Sq. N. Phone: (941)643-2713
Naples, FL 34104 Fax: (941)643-5220
Free: (800)356-1639
Publication E-mail: linkmagazine@msn.com

Trade magazine for the fastener industry. **Founded:** 1976. **Freq:** Quarterly. **Key Personnel:** Leo J. Coar, Contact. **Subscription Rates:** $30 individuals. **Remarks:** Advertising accepted; rates available upon request. **URL:** http://www.linkmagazine.com.
Circ: Paid 13,000

6530 Naples Daily News
Collier County Publishing Co.
1075 Central Ave. Phone: (941)263-4770
Naples, FL 34102 Fax: (941)263-4817

General newspaper. **Subtitle:** Daily Newspaper. **Founded:** 1923. **Freq:** Mon.-Sun. (morn.). **Print Method:** Offset. **Cols./Page:** 6. **Col. Width:** 25 nonpareils. **Col. Depth:** 22 1/4 inches. **Key Personnel:** Corbin A. Wyant, Publisher, phone (941)263-4837; J. Patrick Berling, Advertising Dir., phone (941)263-4758. **Subscription Rates:** $17 individuals. **Remarks:** Accepts advertising. **URL:** http://www.naplesnews.com.
Ad Rates: BW: $4,278.68 **Circ:** Mon.-Sat. ★41,029
4C: $3,755.14 Sun. ★53,498
PCI: $32.05

6531 Naples Guide
947 4th Ave. S Phone: (941)262-6524
Naples, FL 34102 Fax: (941)262-3468
Publication E-mail: stugrang@aol.com

Magazine covering arts, entertainment, shopping, dining, beauty, health, home and garden, and real estate in Naples, FL, and the surrounding areas. **Subtitle:** The Magazine of Arts, Entertainment, and More. **Founded:** 1953. **Freq:** Monthly 12/year. **Print Method:** Web. **Trim Size:** 5 1/2 x 8 1/2. **Cols./Page:** 2. **Col. Width:** 13 picas. **Col. Depth:** 45 picas. **Key Personnel:** Alyce Mathias, Editor and Publisher. **Sub-**

scription Rates: $25; $2 single issue. **Remarks:** Accepts advertising.
Ad Rates: BW: $1,144 **Circ:** Controlled ‡320,000
4C: $1,495

6532 Naples Shopper
Tuff Publications, Inc.
2301 County Rd. 951, Ste. C Phone: (941)353-0444
Naples, FL 34116-6524 Fax: (941)353-9040
Publisher E-mail: tuffpub@aol.com

Shopper containing news. **Founded:** 1978. **Freq:** Biweekly. **Print Method:** Web offset. **Trim Size:** 11 x 17. **Cols./Page:** 5. **Col. Width:** 2 1/8 inches. **Col. Depth:** 16 inches. **Key Personnel:** R.W. Tuff, Editor. **Subscription Rates:** Free. **Remarks:** Accepts advertising. **Formerly:** Shoppers' Special; Naples Area Shopper.
Ad Rates: PCI: $14 **Circ:** Free ‡26,500

6533 Continental Cablevision
Box 413018 Phone: (941)793-9600
Naples, FL 33941-3018 Fax: (941)793-1317

Owner: US West Media, at above address. **Founded:** 1967. **Key Personnel:** Ken Fuchs, District Mgr.; Larry Hoepfner, Dir. of Mktg; David Elliot, Dir. of Local Sales/Prg. **Cities Served:** Everglades City, Ft. Myers, Naples, Sanibel, FL: subscribing households 130,000; 50 channels; 1 community access channel; 168 hours per week community access programming.

6534 WAVV-FM - 101.1
11800 Tamiami Trail E. Phone: (941)775-9288
Naples, FL 34113-7985 Fax: (941)793-7000

Format: Easy Listening. **Networks:** AP. **Owner:** Alpine Broadcasting Corp., at above address, (941)793-1011, Fax: (941)793-7000. **Founded:** 1987. **Operating Hours:** Continuous. **ADI:** Fort Myers-Naples, FL. **Key Personnel:** Norman Alpert, President, phone (941)793-1011, fax (941)793-7000; Jeff Alpert, General Mgr.; Kenny Lamb, Operations Mgr.; Donna Alpert, Business Mgr.; Al Baxa, Chief Engineer; Michelle Herrera, Office Mgr. **Local Programs:** *Sunday Champagne Jazz Brunch* 9am-12pm. **Wattage:** 100,000. **Ad Rates:** $39-72 for 30 seconds; $49-84 for 60 seconds.

6535 WPJS-AM - 1330
3033 Riviera Dr., No. 200 Phone: (813)248-9040
Naples, FL 33940-4134

Format: Urban Contemporary. **Founded:** 1945. **Formerly:** WLAT-AM (1988). **Operating Hours:** Continuous; 10% network, 90% local. **ADI:** Fort Myers-Naples, FL. **Key Personnel:** Randall Ramsey, Station Mgr.; Michael Burgess, Program Dir.; Rahim Akram, Music Dir.; Cherly Hall, Promotions Dir. **Wattage:** 5000. **Ad Rates:** $5-16 for 30 seconds; $7-20 for 60 seconds.

6536 WSGL-FM - 103.1
2500 Airport Rd. S., Ste 211 Phone: (813)793-1031
Naples, FL 33962 Fax: (813)793-7329
Free: (800)349-1031

Format: Adult Contemporary. **Networks:** Independent. **Owner:** Timm Enterprises, at above address. **Founded:** 1980. **Operating Hours:** Continuous; 100% local. **ADI:** Fort Myers-Naples, FL. **Key Personnel:** Joe Landon, General Mgr.; Chuck Gaffney, Program Dir.; David Rosato, Gen. Sales Mgr.; Janet Manzelli, News Dir.; Marty Simpson, Music Dir.; Chuck Thomas, PSA Dir. **Local Programs:** *70's-80's Saturday Night* 6 p.m.-10 p.m. Saturday, Phil Beckman, (941)732-9745; *Traffic Jam* 5 p.m. Monday-Friday, Ann Rae. **Wattage:** 14,000. **Ad Rates:** $20-34 per unit.

NEW PORT RICHEY, pop. 11,196.

WC FL. Pasco Co. 18 mi. N. of Clearwater. Citrus fruit.

6537 Suncoast News (Friday Edition)
West Pasco Press
PO Box 785 Phone: (813)849-7500
New Port Richey, FL 34652-0785 Fax: (813)847-2902
Subscription Community newspaper. **Founded:** 1916. **Freq:** Weekly (Fri.). **Print Method:** Offset. **Cols./Page:** 6. **Col. Width:** 22 nonpareils. **Col. Depth:** 231 agate lines. **Key Personnel:** Carl Orth, Editor; Rich Litowchak, Publisher. **Subscription Rates:** $10.48 individuals. **Remarks:** Advertising accepted; rates available upon request.
Circ: ‡2,500

6538 Tarpon Springs Leader
6214 Hwy. 19 Phone: (813)937-6101
New Port Richey, FL 34652-2528
Shopper. **Founded:** 1906. **Freq:** Weekly. **Print Method:** Offset. **Cols./Page:** 6. **Col. Width:** 22 nonpareils. **Col. Depth:** 231 agate lines. **Key Personnel:** Derek Dunn Rankin, Publisher. **Subscription Rates:** $10.48 individuals.
Circ: Free ‡19,000

6539 West Pasco Press
6214 US Hwy. 19 Phone: (813)849-7500
New Port Richey, FL 34652 Fax: (813)847-2902

Community newspaper. **Founded:** 1916. **Freq:** Weekly (Fri.). **Print Method:** Offset. **Cols./Page:** 6. **Col. Width:** 22 nonpareils. **Col. Depth:** 231 agate lines. **Key Personnel:** Rich Litowchak, General Mgr., rlitowchak@tampatrib.com; Bob Fransen, Display Sales Manager; Gwen Stevenson, Editorial Dir. **USPS:** 381-980. **Subscription Rates:** $10 individuals. **Remarks:** Accepts advertising.
Ad Rates: GLR: $4.05 **Circ:** Paid ⊕1,500
BW: $263.25
4C: $503.25

NEW SMYRNA BEACH, pop. 13,557.

E FL. Volusia Co. On North Indian River, 14 mi. S. of Daytona Beach. Tourist resort. Shrimp and crab fisheries. Citrus fruit.

6540 New Smyrna Pennysaver
Volusia Pennysaver, Inc.
237 Canal St. Phone: (904)423-2300
Box 767 Fax: (904)426-2807
New Smyrna Beach, FL 32170
Publication E-mail: nsbpennl@n-jcenter.com

Shopper. **Founded:** 1982. **Freq:** Weekly (Wed.). **Print Method:** Offset. **Trim Size:** 11 x 13 3/4. **Cols./Page:** 6. **Col. Width:** 18 nonpareils. **Col. Depth:** 182 agate lines. **Key Personnel:** Doug Hodson, General Mgr. **Subscription Rates:** Free.
Ad Rates: GLR: $647.40 **Circ:** Free ‡26,000
BW: $631.80
4C: $827.40
PCI: $8.30

6541 The Observer
823 S. Dixie Fwy. Phone: (904)428-2441
PO Box 10 Fax: (904)428-1265
New Smyrna Beach, FL 32170
General newspaper. **Founded:** 1913. **Freq:** Tues. & Sat. **Print Method:** Offset. **Trim Size:** 13 x 21 1/2. **Cols./Page:** 6. **Col. Width:** 2 1/16 inches. **Col. Depth:** 21 1/2 inches. **Key Personnel:** David Crawley, Publisher; Jim Jones, Editor. **USPS:** 382-200. **Subscription Rates:** $67. **Remarks:** Accepts advertising. **Formerly:** News & Observer (1987).
Ad Rates: GLR: $.70 **Circ:** Paid 5,992
SAU: $9.22

6542 WSBB-AM - 1230
PO Box 130 Phone: (904)428-9091
New Smyrna Beach, FL 32170 Fax: (904)428-7853
Free: (877)449-6793
E-mail: wsbb@volusia.com

Format: Middle-of-the-Road (MOR); Oldies. **Networks:** Westwood One Radio. **Owner:** Brian Tolby, at above address. **Founded:** 1951. **Operating Hours:** Continuous. **Key Personnel:** Brian Tolby, General Mgr., tolbyb@aol.com. **Wattage:** 1000. **Ad Rates:** $20 for 30 seconds; $28 for 60 seconds.

NICEVILLE

6543 The Bay Beacon
1181 E. John Sims Pkwy. Phone: (850)678-1080
Niceville, FL 32578 Fax: (850)729-3225
Publication E-mail: baybeacon@aol.com

Community newspaper. **Founded:** Apr. 22, 1992. **Freq:** Weekly. **Print Method:** Web offset. **Cols./Page:** 6. **Col. Width:** 12.2 picas. **Col. Depth:** 21 1/2 inches. **Key Personnel:** Stephen Kent, Editor and Publisher; Sara Kent, Advertising Mgr. **USPS:** 016-224. **Subscription Rates:** $45.95 individuals. **Remarks:** Accepts advertising.
Ad Rates: BW: $780 **Circ:** 13,250
4C: $1,075
SAU: $7.25

NOKOMIS, pop. 2,500.

SW FL. Sarasota Co. 20 mi. S. of Sarasota.

6544 Communications News
Nelson Publishing, Inc.
2500 Tamiami Tr. N. Phone: (941)966-9521
Nokomis, FL 34275-3482 Fax: (941)966-2590
Publication E-mail: info@comnews.com
Publisher E-mail: nelpub@ix.netcom.com

Magazine featuring networking communications technology applications. **Subtitle:** Solutions for Today's Networking Decision Makers. **Founded:** Oct. 1964. **Freq:** Monthly. **Print Method:** Offset. **Trim Size:** 8 x 10 3/4. **Cols./Page:** 3 and 2. **Col. Width:** 26 and 40 nonpareils. **Col. Depth:** 140 agate lines. **Key Personnel:** Vern Nelson, Group Publisher; Ripley Hotch, Editor, ripley@comnews.com. **ISSN:** 0010-3632. **Subscription Rates:** $74; $126 other countries; $8.50 single issue. **Remarks:** Accepts advertising. **Available Online. URL:** http://www.comnews.com.
Ad Rates: BW: $7,995 **Circ:** ‡80,001
4C: $9,945
PCI: $175

6545 EE Evaluation Engineering
Nelson Publishing, Inc.
2500 Tamiami Tr. N. Phone: (941)966-9521
Nokomis, FL 34275-3482 Fax: (941)966-2590
Publication E-mail: ee@nelsonpub.com
Publisher E-mail: nelpub@ix.netcom.com

Trade magazine covering electronic engineering, evaluation and test. **Subtitle:** The Magazine of Electronic Evaluation & Test. **Founded:** Mar. 1962. **Freq:** Monthly. **Print Method:** Offset. **Trim Size:** 8 x 10 3/4. **Cols./Page:** 3 and 2. **Col. Width:** 26 and 40 nonpareils. **Col. Depth:** 140 agate lines. **Key Personnel:** Paul Milo, Editor, pmilo@nelsonpub.com; Stephen Berlin, Publisher, sberlin@nelsonpub.com. **ISSN:** 0149-0370. **Subscription Rates:** $99 individuals; $140 other countries; $9.50 single issue. **Remarks:** Accepts advertising. **URL:** http://www.nelsonpub.com/ee/.
Ad Rates: BW: $5,630 **Circ:** Non-paid ‡76,049
4C: $6,925
PCI: $145

6546 Modern Applications News (MAN)
Nelson Publishing, Inc.
2500 Tamiami Tr. N. Phone: (941)966-9521
Nokomis, FL 34275-3482 Fax: (941)966-2590
Publisher E-mail: nelpub@ix.netcom.com

Trade magazine covering metalworking engineering, design, and manufacturing. **Subtitle:** The Metalworking Idea Magazine. **Founded:** 1967. **Freq:** Monthly. **Print Method:** Web offset. **Trim Size:** 8 1/8 x 10 7/8. **Cols./Page:** 3 and 2. **Col. Width:** 26 and 40 nonpareils. **Col. Depth:** 140 agate lines. **Key Personnel:** A.V. Nelson, Group Publisher, phone (941)966-9521, fax (941)966-2590; Bob Olree, Associate Publisher, phone (941)966-9521, fax (941)966-2590; Larry Olson, Editor, phone (941)966-9521, fax (941)966-2590, larry@mansite.com. **Subscription Rates:** Free to qualified subscribers; $97 individuals; $115 other countries; $9.50 single issue. **Remarks:** Accepts advertising. **URL:** http://www.mansite.com.
Ad Rates: BW: $4,771 **Circ:** Controlled ‡80,001
4C: $6,265 Free ‡27
PCI: $165 Paid ‡107

NORTH MIAMI

6547 FIU Hospitality
Florida International University
151st St. and Biscayne Blvd.
North Miami, FL 33181

Trade journal covering hospitality management. **Freq:** Quarterly. **Trim Size:** 7 x 10. **Cols./Page:** 1. **Col. Width:** 5 inches. **Col. Depth:** 8 inches. **Key Personnel:** Anthony Marshall, Publisher; William O'Brien, Editor. **ISSN:** 0739-7011. **Subscription Rates:** $15 individuals. **Remarks:** Accepts advertising. **URL:** www.fiu.edu/~review.
Ad Rates: BW: $1,000 **Circ:** Controlled 7,000

6548 WKAT-AM - 1360
13499 Biscayne Blvd., Ste. 1 Phone: (305)949-9528
North Miami, FL 33181 Fax: (305)944-4788

Format: Hispanic. **Networks:** Independent. **Owner:** Howard Broadcasting Inc., at above address. **Founded:** 1937. **Operating Hours:** Continuous; 100% local. **Key Personnel:** Ilene Premer, Promotions Dir., phone (305)891-7026; Howard Premer, President; Arnie Premer, V.P./Station; Sam Stoddart, Chief Engineer. **Local Programs:** *RCN*. **Wattage:** 10,000. **Ad Rates:** $40-70 per unit.

NORTH MIAMI BEACH, pop. 35,000.

S FL. Dade Co. 10 mi. N. of Miami. Marinas. Tourist resort. Light manufacturing.

Bienvenidos a Miami - See Miami

6549 North Miami Beach News
Community Newspapers
PO Box 43-1970 Phone: (305)667-7481
Miami, FL 33143 Fax: (305)661-0954
Publication E-mail: communitynewspapers.com
Publisher E-mail: cnedor@gate.net

Community newspaper (tabloid). **Founded:** 1970. **Freq:** Semiweekly (Mon. and Fri.). **Print Method:** Offset. **Trim Size:** 10 1/4 x 16. **Cols./Page:** 6. **Col. Width:** 19 nonpareils. **Col.**

Depth: 238 agate lines. **Key Personnel:** Michael Miller, Editor; Grant Miller, Publisher. **Subscription Rates:** $52 individuals. **Remarks:** Accepts advertising.
Ad Rates: GLR: $.72 **Circ:** Free ‡13,000
BW: $1,350
4C: $2,400
PCI: $13.50

6550 Welcome to Miami and the Beaches
Welcome Publishing Co., Inc.
1751 NE 162nd St. Phone: (305)944-9444
Box 630-518 Fax: (305)949-0544
North Miami Beach, FL 33162-4757
Visitor's guide directing tourists on where to dine, shop, and sightsee in Miami. **Founded:** 1970. **Freq:** Weekly. **Print Method:** Offset. **Trim Size:** 5 3/8 x 8 3/8. **Cols./Page:** 2. **Col. Width:** 2 1/8 inches. **Col. Depth:** 7 1/2 inches. **Key Personnel:** Kaplan Tina, Editor; Alan Levine, Publisher. **Subscription Rates:** Free; $35. **Remarks:** Accepts advertising.
Ad Rates: BW: $400 **Circ:** Non-paid △**16,000**
4C: $525

NORTH PALM BEACH, pop. 11,344.

SE FL. Palm Beach Co. 8 mi. N. of Palm Beach. Commercial area.

6551 National PAL CopsnKids Chronicles
National Police Athletic League
618 U.S. Hwy. 1, Ste. 201 Phone: (516)844-1823
North Palm Beach, FL 33408 Fax: (516)863-6120
Publication E-mail: copnkid1@aol.com

Newspaper on crime prevention and items regarding the Police Athletic League. **Founded:** 1984. **Freq:** Quarterly. **Print Method:** Desktop. **Trim Size:** 11 1/4 x 13 3/4. **Cols./Page:** 5. **Col. Width:** 2 inches. **Col. Depth:** 12 3/4 inches. **Key Personnel:** Shirley A. McCoy, Editor/Production. **ISSN:** INS -. **Subscription Rates:** Free. **Remarks:** Accepts advertising. **Former name:** National PAL Update.
Ad Rates: BW: $950 **Circ:** Controlled 22,000
4C: $1,450

NORTH PORT, pop. 6,200.

Sarasota Co. (SE).

6552 North Port Sun Herald
Sun Coast Media Group
13644 S. Tamiami Tr. Phone: (941)426-9544
North Port, FL 34287-2055 Fax: (941)423-2318

Community newspaper. **Founded:** 1977. **Freq:** Semiweekly (Wed. and Sun.). **Print Method:** Offset. **Cols./Page:** 6. **Col. Width:** 2 1/16 inches. **Col. Depth:** 21 inches. **Key Personnel:** Valarie Harring, Editor; Jeff Dunn-Rankin, Publisher. **Subscription Rates:** $27 individuals. **Remarks:** Accepts advertising.
Ad Rates: BW: $831.60 **Circ:** Paid 3,200
4C: $1,061.60 Free 5,000
SAU: $7.75

OCALA†, pop. 37,170.

NC FL. Marion Co. 38 mi. S. of Gainesville. Central Florida Community College. Limestone and phosphate mines. Vegetables, melons.

6553 Ocala Star-Banner
Star Banner
2121 SW 19th Ave. Phone: (904)867-4010
Rte. 32674, PO Box 490 Fax: (904)867-4018
Ocala, FL 34478
Free: (800)541-2171

General newspaper. **Founded:** 1866. **Freq:** Mon.-Sun. (morn.). **Print Method:** Offset. **Trim Size:** 13 x 21 1/2. **Cols./Page:** 6. **Col. Width:** 26 nonpareils. **Col. Depth:** 301 agate lines. **Key Personnel:** Mark Mathes, Exec. Editor; Foy Maloy, Advertising Dir. **Subscription Rates:** $114 individuals. **Remarks:** Accepts advertising. **URL:** http://www.thezone.com; http://www.theocone.com. **Feature Editors:** Lucy Beebe, *Environmental*, phone (904)867-4119; Cherie Beers, *Metro, News*, phone (904)867-4103; Alwyn Cassil, *Education*, phone (904)867-4123; David Cyril, *Drama, Fashion, Religion*, phone (904)867-4134; Kyle Danaceau, *Photo*, phone (904)867-4151; Rima Firrone, *Book*, phone (904)867-4156; Jim French, *Radio, TV*, phone (904)867-4108; Patti Griffiths, *City*, phone (904)867-4105; Mark Hollis, *Political*, phone (904)867-4112; Diane Howe, *Entertainment, Movie, Music*, phone (904)867-4157; Laura Knight, *Medical, Science*, phone (904)867-4134; Mark Pino, *Sports*, phone (904)867-4141; Marta Salij, *Suburban*, phone (904)867-4107; Denise Slaughter, *Family, Features, Food, Lifestyle, Living, Society, Travel, Women's*, phone (904)867-4130; Tyler Ward, *Aviation, Consumer Affairs, Farm, Financial/Business, Garden/Home, Real Estate*, phone (904)867-4128; Bernard Watts, *Editorials*, phone (904)867-4101.
Ad Rates: GLR: $4.48 **Circ:** Mon.-Sat. ★**46,529**
BW: $3,786.15 Sun. ★**50,092**
4C: $4,506.15
SAU: $29.35

6554 Cox Cable Greater Ocala
Box 2318 Phone: (904)237-1111
Ocala, FL 34478 Fax: (904)237-6706

Owner: Cox Cable Communications, 1400 Lake Hearn Dr., Atlanta, GA 30319, (404)843-5000, Fax: (404)843-5775. **Founded:** 1978. **Formerly:** Cox Cable Ocala (1990). **Key Personnel:** Gary Cassard, Vice Pres./Gen. Mgr.; Janet Barnard, Dir. of Finance; Jaime Cherlin, Operations Dir.; Dana Nemenyi, Dir. of Marketing; Ken Williams, Dir. of Technical Operations. **Cities Served:** Ocala, Silver Springs, FL: subscribing households 28,911; 38 channels.

6555 WMFQ-FM - 92.9
3357 SW 7th St. Phone: (352)732-2442
Ocala, FL 34474 Fax: (352)622-6675

Format: Adult Contemporary; Soft Rock. **Owner:** Asterisk Communications, at above address. **Founded:** 1965. **Operating Hours:** Continuous; 100% local. **ADI:** Gainesville (Ocala), FL. **Key Personnel:** John Rutledge, Contact; Tommy Rockwell, Program Dir.; Shirley Sopp, Business Mgr. **Wattage:** 50,000. **Ad Rates:** Advertising accepted; rates available upon request. Combined advertising rates available with WTRS, WYGC.

6556 WMOP-AM - 900
343 NE 1st Ave. Phone: (904)732-2010
Ocala, FL 34470 Fax: (904)629-1614
E-mail: wmopam@aol.com

Format: Sports; Talk. **Networks:** ESPN Radio. **Owner:** Florida Sports Talk, Inc., at above address. **Founded:** 1953. **Operating Hours:** Continuous. 5% network, 95% local. **ADI:** Gainesville (Ocala), FL. **Key Personnel:** Gordon Smith, General Mgr.; Jeff Frances, Operations Mgr.; Buddy Martin, Program Dir.; William Boyer, Chief Engineer. **Wattage:** 5000. **Ad Rates:** $15-25 for 30 seconds; $20-30 for 60 seconds. **URL:** http://www.floridasportstalk.com.

6557 WOCA-AM - 1370
1515 E. Silver Springs Blvd., Ste. 190 W. Phone: (352)732-8000
Ocala, FL 34470 Fax: (352)732-0174
E-mail: woca@woca.com

Format: News; Talk. **Networks:** ABC. **Owner:** Greater Ocala Broadcasting Corp., at above address. **Founded:** 1965. **Formerly:** WWKE-AM (1981). **Operating Hours:** 6 a.m.-8 p.m.; 65% network, 35% local. **ADI:** Gainesville (Ocala), FL. **Key Personnel:** Robert M. Hauck, Contact; Tishia A. Moeller, Contact; Elsa Cabrera, Traffic Mgr. **Local Programs:** *Chamber Talk*, Bill Ashford; *Health Talk*, Bill Ashford; *Ocala on the Air*, Bill Ashford, (352)732-0174, Fax (352)732-8000. **Wattage:** 5000. **Ad Rates:** $13-15 for 30 seconds; $14-18 for 60 seconds. **URL:** http://www.woca.com.

6558 WOGK-FM - 93.7
3602 NE 20th Pl. Phone: (352)622-5600
PO Box 70229 Fax: (352)622-7822
Ocala, FL 34470

Format: Country. **Networks:** ABC. **Owner:** Ocala Broadcasting, Inc., at above address. **Founded:** 1985. **Formerly:** WMMZ-FM. **Operating Hours:** Continuous. **ADI:** Gainesville (Ocala), FL. **Key Personnel:** Jim Robertson, General Mgr.; Bill Kramer, Program Dir. **Wattage:** 100,000. **Ad Rates:** $35-80 per unit.

6559 WTMC-AM - 1290
3621 NW 10th St. Phone: (352)622-9862
Ocala, FL 34475 Fax: (352)622-8648
E-mail: am1290@aol.com

Format: News; Talk. **Networks:** CNN Radio. **Owner:** News, at above address. **Founded:** 1939. **Operating Hours:** Continuous; 90% network/10% local. **ADI:** Gainesville (Ocala), FL. **Key Personnel:** Larry Whitler, Contact; Gin Swab, News Dir.; Ken Jones, Sales Mgr. **Wattage:** 5000 day; 1000 night. **Ad Rates:** $9-11.25 for 30 seconds; $11.50-14 for 60 seconds.

6560 WTRS-FM - 102.3
3357 SW 7th St. Phone: (904)732-9877
Ocala, FL 34474 Fax: (904)622-6675

Format: Contemporary Country; Country. **Networks:** Independent. **Owner:** Asterisk Communications, Inc., at above address. **Founded:** 1969. **Operating Hours:** Continuous. **ADI:** Gainesville (Ocala), FL. **Key Personnel:** John Rutledge, Manager; Shane Finch, Program Dir.; Dave Tyler, Music Dir. **Local Programs:** *Walter Scott Live*, Ron Morgan. **Wattage:** 50,000. **Ad Rates:** $30-45 for 30 seconds; $35-50 for 60 seconds. Combined advertising rates available with WMFQ, WYGC.

ODESSA

6561 WWS/World Wide Shipping
World Wide Shipping Guide, Inc.
16302 Byrnwyck Ln. Phone: (813)920-4788
Odessa, FL 33556 Fax: (813)920-8268

Magazine reporting trends, developments, and government regulations effecting the shipping business. Serves ports, carriers, shippers, formwalers, customs brokers, distributors, agents, stevedores, and terminal operators. **Founded:** 1914. **Freq:** 8/year. **Print Method:** Letterpress and offset. **Trim Size:** 8 3/8 x 10 7/8. **Cols./Page:** 3. **Col. Width:** 26 nonpareils. **Col. Depth:** 140 agate lines. **Key Personnel:** Lee Di Paci, Publisher, lee@wwship.com. **ISSN:** 1060-7900. **Subscription Rates:** $32 individuals. **Remarks:** Accepts advertising. **URL:** http://www.wwhip.com. **Formerly:** World Ports – American Seaports; American Seaports; WWS/World Ports.
Ad Rates: BW: $2,600 **Circ:** Paid 893
4C: $3,525 Non-paid 12,000

OKEECHOBEE†, pop. 4,225.

EC FL. Okeechobee Co. At head of Lake Okeechobee, 60 mi. NW of West Palm Beach. Vegetable canning and packing plants. Commercial fishing. Agriculture. Cattle and dairy farms.

6562 Okeechobee News
Independent Newspapers, Inc.
PO Box 639 Phone: (941)763-3134
Okeechobee, FL 34973 Fax: (941)763-5901

Community newspaper. **Founded:** 1917. **Freq:** Mon.-Sun. **Print Method:** Offset. Uses mats. **Trim Size:** 22 3/4 x 13 1/4. **Cols./Page:** 6. **Col. Width:** 2 1/16 inches. **Col. Depth:** 301 agate lines. **Key Personnel:** Phil Divece, Editor; Judy Kasten, Publisher, kast1ja@okeechobee.com. **USPS:** 406-160. **Subscription Rates:** $117.70 individuals; $201.43 out of county. **Remarks:** Accepts advertising.
Ad Rates: BW: $1,483.50 **Circ:** Sun. ‡4,000
4C: $1,733.50
PCI: $11.50

6563 Okeechobee Shoppers Guide
Florida Sun Publications
105 W. South Park Phone: (941)763-1171
Okeechobee, FL 34972 Fax: (941)763-7680

Shopper. **Founded:** 1977. **Freq:** Weekly (Wed.). **Print Method:** Offset. **Trim Size:** 11 1/2 x 16. **Cols./Page:** 6. **Col. Width:** 26 nonpareils. **Col. Depth:** 210 agate lines. **Key Personnel:** Scott Akers, Publisher. **Subscription Rates:** Free.
Ad Rates: BW: $450 **Circ:** Free 14,000
4C: $650
PCI: $5

6564 Adelphia
107 NW 7th Ave. Phone: (941)763-5566
Okeechobee, FL 34972 Fax: (941)467-7776

Formerly: Cablevision Industries; Harte Hanks Cable; Time Warner Cable. **Key Personnel:** Karen Aldridge, Manager, phone (941)763-9391. **Cities Served:** Belle Glade, Clewiston, Lakeport, Morehaven, Okeechobee, Pahokee, South Beach, FL: subscribing households 17,000; 52 channels.

6565 WOKC-AM - 1570
3101 S. U.S. 441 South Phone: (941)763-3181
PO Box 1247 Fax: (941)763-6036
Okeechobee, FL 34974

Format: Country. **Networks:** NBC. **Owner:** Rick Stokes, 3103 SE 25th St., Okeechobee, FL 34974, (941)467-8061, Fax: (941)763-6036. **Founded:** 1962. **Operating Hours:** 6 a.m.-11 p.m. **Key Personnel:** J.D. Chadwick, Music Dir.; Al Stokes, CEO; Rick Stokes, General Mgr.; Charles Murphy, News Dir.; Robert Lightsey, Sales Mgr. **Local Programs:** *The Country Store*, Rick Stokes, Mailing contact, (941)763-3181, Fax (941)763-6036; *Wonderful Weekend*, J.D. Chadwidk, Mailing contact, (941)763-3443, Fax (941)763-6036. **Wattage:** 1000. **Ad Rates:** $12 per unit.

ORANGE PARK

6566 Clay Today
ADD, Inc.
1564 Kingsley Ave. Phone: (904)264-3200
Drawer 1209 Fax: (904)269-6958
Orange Park, FL 32073-4594
Publisher E-mail: addinc@earthlink.net

Community newspaper serving Clay County, FL. **Founded:** Dec. 16, 1974. **Freq:** Weekly. **Print Method:** Web offset. **Key Personnel:** Jon Cantrell, Editor, phone (904)264-8962. **Sub-**

scription Rates: $25; $34 out of area; $.50 single issue. **Remarks:** Accepts advertising.
Ad Rates: GLR: $.10 **Circ:** Paid ‡3,000
BW: $800 Non-paid ‡21,635
4C: $950
SAU: $13

ORLANDO†, pop. 125,700.

EC FL. Orange Co. 100 mi. NE of Tampa. University of Central Florida; Orlando Naval Training Center. Walt Disney World. Manufactures electronics, weapons systems, missiles. Citrus fruit and truck farms.

6567 The Central Florida Future
11875 High Tech Ave., Suite 250 Phone: (407)823-8054
Orlando, FL 32817 Fax: (407)823-9495
Publication E-mail: cffurture@gdi.net

Collegiate newspaper (tabloid). **Founded:** 1968. **Freq:** Twice weekly Tues and Thurs. **Print Method:** Offset. Uses mats. **Trim Size:** 10 x 16. **Cols./Page:** 5. **Col. Width:** 2 inches. **Col. Depth:** 218 agate lines. **Key Personnel:** Sean Perry, Editor; Steve Norris, Publisher. **Subscription Rates:** $50 per semester. **Remarks:** Accepts advertising. **URL:** http://www.gdi.net/cff/cff.html.
Ad Rates: PCI: $7.25 **Circ:** Free ‡10,000

6568 Communications on Applied Nonlinear Analysis
International Publications
12046 Coed Dr. Phone: (407)282-5476
Orlando, FL 32826
Scholarly journal covering research in applied mathematical nonlinear analysis. **Founded:** Jan. 1994. **Freq:** Quarterly. **Trim Size:** 8 1/2 x 11. **Key Personnel:** Ram U. Verma. **ISSN:** 1074-133X. **Subscription Rates:** Free to qualified subscribers; $75 individuals; $150 libraries; $35 single issue. **Remarks:** Accepts advertising.
Ad Rates: BW: $200 **Circ:** Combined 100

6569 Faulkner Journal
University of Central Florida
PO Box 161346 Phone: (407)823-5152
Orlando, FL 32816-1346 Fax: (407)823-6532
Publication E-mail: faulkner@pegasus.cc.ucf.edu

Academic journal covering the work of William Faulkner. **Founded:** 1985. **Freq:** Semiannual. **Key Personnel:** Dawn Trouard, Managing Editor; Linda Hargreaves, Editorial Asst. **ISSN:** 0084-2949. **Subscription Rates:** $12 institutions U.S./Canada/Mexico; $19 individuals Foreign; $25 institutions Foreign. **Remarks:** Advertising not accepted.
Circ: (Not Reported)

6570 The Florida Catholic
PO Box 609512 Phone: (407)423-3438
Orlando, FL 32860-9512 Fax: (407)660-2977
Free: (800)377-3438

Official newspaper (tabloid) of the Diocese of Orlando. **Founded:** 1939. **Freq:** Weekly. **Print Method:** Offset. **Cols./Page:** 4. **Col. Width:** 14 picas. **Col. Depth:** 224 agate lines. **Key Personnel:** Henry Libersat, Editor/General Mgr., phone (407)660-9141, sdemontrichard@flcath.org; Steve Paradis, Managing Editor, sparadis@flcath.org. **Subscription Rates:** $10; $20 other countries; $16; $20 U.S.; $42 /year foreign. **Remarks:** Accepts advertising. **URL:** http://www.flcath.org.
Ad Rates: GLR: $1.96 **Circ:** ⊕142,000

6571 Florida Realtor
Florida Association of Realtors
7025 Augusta Nat'l Dr. Phone: (407)438-1400
Orlando, FL 32822-5017 Fax: (407)438-1411
Publication E-mail: flrealtor@fl.realtorusa.com

Real estate magazine. **Founded:** 1925. **Freq:** 11/year. **Print Method:** Web offset. **Trim Size:** 8 x 10 3/4. **Cols./Page:** 3. **Col. Width:** 14 picas. **Col. Depth:** 140 agate lines. **Key Personnel:** Jamie Floerefield, Editor-in-Chief; Jeffrey M. Zipper, Publisher; Tracey Lawton, Assoc. Editor; Jim Angel, Designer; Joseph A. Bono, Advertising Mgr. **ISSN:** 0199-5839. **Subscription Rates:** $15 individuals; $1 single issue. **Remarks:** Accepts advertising. **Available Online.**
Ad Rates: BW: $3,090 **Circ:** Paid ‡60,000
4C: $3,865 Non-paid ‡362

6572 Florida Review
University of Central Florida
PO Box 161346 Phone: (407)823-5152
Orlando, FL 32816-1346 Fax: (407)823-6532

Literary magazine covering fiction, nonfiction and poetry. **Founded:** 1972. **Freq:** Semiannual. **Print Method:** Offset. **Trim Size:** 6 3/4 x 9 3/4. **Key Personnel:** Russ Kesler, Editor. **ISSN:** 0742-2466. **Subscription Rates:** $10 individuals; $15 two years; $6 single issue. **Remarks:** Advertising not accepted.
Circ: Controlled 550

6573 GOLFWEEK
Golfweek
7657 Commerce Center Dr. Phone: (407)345-5500
Orlando, FL 32819 Fax: (407)345-9404

Journal of record for competitive golf. Delivers the most complete news and information about the game, the people and the industry, to golf's most important audience. **Subtitle:** America's Golf Newspaper. **Founded:** Mar. 1975. **Freq:** Weekly. **Print Method:** Offset. **Trim Size:** 11 x 14 1/4. **Cols./Page:** 4. **Col. Width:** 2 1/4 inches. **Col. Depth:** 13 3/4 inches. **Key Personnel:** Ken Henson, President, phone (407)345-5510, fax (407)345-9404, khanson@golfweek.com; Jim Nugent, Publisher, jnugent@golfweek.com; Dave Seanor, Editor, phone (407)345-5536, fax (407)345-9945, dseanor@golfweek.com. **ISSN:** 0745-7464. **Subscription Rates:** $69.95 individuals. **Remarks:** Accepts advertising. **URL:** http://www.golfweek.com.
Ad Rates: BW: $8,048 **Circ:** 87,500
4C: $12,555

6574 La Semana
2413-B E. South St. Phone: (407)895-4171
Orlando, FL 32803 Fax: (407)895-0435

Community newspaper (Spanish). **Founded:** 1981. **Freq:** Weekly. **Print Method:** Offset. **Trim Size:** Standard. **Cols./Page:** 6. **Col. Width:** 2 1/4 inches. **Col. Depth:** 21 1/2 inches. **Key Personnel:** Raul Delgado-Baguer, Editor and Publisher; John Cobb, Editor. **Remarks:** Accepts advertising.
Ad Rates: BW: $645 **Circ:** 16,500
4C: $745
PCI: $5

6575 NASPA Technical Support
2123 S. Kirkman Rd., No. 175 Phone: (407)296-5050
Orlando, FL 32811 Fax: (407)296-0870
Publication E-mail: editor@naspa.net

Trade publication serving computing network and systems professionals in medium- to large-scale computing centers. **Subtitle:** Supporting Enterprise Networks and Operating Environments. **Founded:** May 1986. **Freq:** Monthly. **Print Method:** Offset. **Trim Size:** 8 1/4 x 10 3/4. **Key Personnel:** Amy Novotny, Editor; Jerry Seefeldt, Advertising Mgr., jerry@naspa.net; Meg Marradeth, Circulation Mgr. **ISSN:** 1079-3135. **Subscription Rates:** $19.98 individuals. **Remarks:** Accepts advertising. **URL:** http://www.naspa.net. **Alt. Formats:** CD-ROM.
Ad Rates: BW: $4,600 **Circ:** Paid ‡22,767
4C: $4,600 Controlled ‡21,356

6576 Orlando Business Journal
American City Business Journals
315 E. Robinson St., Ste. 250 Phone: (407)649-8470
Orlando, FL 32801-1949 Fax: (407)649-8469

Newspaper (tabloid) covering local business news, trends, and ideas of interest to industry, trade, agribusiness, finance, and commerce. **Founded:** June 1984. **Freq:** Weekly. **Print Method:** Offset. **Trim Size:** 11 3/8 x 12 3/4. **Cols./Page:** 4. **Col. Width:** 2 1/4 inches. **Col. Depth:** 12 3/4 inches. **Key Personnel:** Kent Hoover, Editor; Robert Roe, Publisher; Joan Watts, Advertising Dir. **ISSN:** 8750-8656. **Subscription Rates:** $45 individuals plus sales tax. **Remarks:** Accepts advertising.
Ad Rates: BW: $2,160 **Circ:** Paid ★8,559
4C: $2,660 Controlled 5,300

6577 The Orlando Sentinel
Orlando SentinelCommunications
633 N. Orange Ave. Phone: (407)420-5000
Orlando, FL 32801-1300 Fax: (407)420-5661

General newspaper. **Founded:** June 6, 1876. **Freq:** Mon.-Sun. (morn.). **Print Method:** Offset. **Cols./Page:** 6. **Col. Width:** 24 nonpareils. **Col. Depth:** 294 agate lines. **Key Personnel:** Jane Healy, Managing Editor, jhealy@orlandosentinel.com; Manning Pynn, Editor of Editorial Page, mpynn@orlandosentinel.com; Bill Dunn, Associate Managing Editor, bdunn@orlandosentinel.com; Jim Clark, Staff Development Editor, jclark@orlandosentinel.com; John Huff, Editor of New Technology, jhuff@orlandosentinel.com. **Subscription Rates:** $180 individuals. **Remarks:** Accepts advertising. Monday-Saturday: GLR: $12.60; BW: $22,226; 4C: $24,743; PCI: $176.40; Sunday: GLR: $16.39; BW: $28,912; 4C: $31,797; PCI: $229.46. **Online:** Dialog (The Dialog Corporation); DataTimes Corporation; LEXIS-NEXIS; CompuServe Information Service. **Alt. Formats:** CD-ROM, NewsBank, Inc.
Circ: Mon.-Sat. ★249,714
Sun. ★369,881

6578 The Orlando Times
4403 Vineland Rd., Ste. B-5 Phone: (407)841-3710
PO Box 555339 Fax: (407)849-0434
Orlando, FL 32855-5339
Black community newspaper. **Founded:** 1975. **Freq:** Weekly (Thurs.). **Cols./Page:** 6. **Col. Width:** 2 1/16 inches. **Col. Depth:** 129 picas. **Key Personnel:** Lottie Collins, Editor; Calvin Collins, Jr., Publisher. **Subscription Rates:** $26.50 individuals; $14.84 six months; $30 out of state; $.53 single issue. **Available Online.**
Ad Rates: BW: $14 **Circ:** 11,000
4C: $484
SAU: $6
PCI: $14

6579 The Paper
Valencia Community College
1800 S. Kirkman Rd. Phone: (407)299-5000
PO Box 3028 Fax: (407)299-5000
Orlando, FL 32802
Publication E-mail: jgismdi@valenciasonvce.com

Collegiate newspaper (tabloid). **Subtitle:** Valencia Source. **Founded:** 1967. **Freq:** Semimonthly. **Print Method:** Offset. Uses negatives. **Trim Size:** 10 1/8 x 16. **Cols./Page:** 5. **Col. Width:** 22 nonpareils. **Col. Depth:** 224 agate lines. **Key Personnel:** Joe Gisondi, Faculty Advisor, jgisondi@mail.valencia.cc.fl.us; Darren Iozia, Editor-in-Chief; Chris Warg, Managing Editor. **Subscription Rates:** $300 full page; $200 1/2 page; $100 1/4 page; $50 1/8 page. **Remarks:** Accepts advertising. **Formerly:** The Paper.
Ad Rates: GLR: $.45 **Circ:** Free ‡6,000
BW: $300
4C: $600
PCI: $5

6580 Plating & Surface Finishing
American Electroplaters and Surface Finishers Society
12644 Research Pkwy. Phone: (407)281-6441
Orlando, FL 32826-3298 Fax: (407)281-6446
Free: (800)793-8076
Publisher E-mail: journal@aeof.org

Magazine. **Subtitle:** Journal of the American Electroplaters and Surface Finishers Society. **Founded:** 1912. **Freq:** Monthly. **Print Method:** Web press. **Trim Size:** 8 1/8 x 11. **Cols./Page:** 3. **Col. Width:** 26 nonpareils. **Col. Depth:** 140 agate lines. **Key Personnel:** Sylvia L. Baxley, Editor; Ted Witt, Publisher; Anne Gaither, Advertising Mgr. **ISSN:** 0360-3164. **Subscription Rates:** $60 individuals; $80 other countries. **Remarks:** Accepts advertising.
Ad Rates: BW: $2,000 **Circ:** Paid ‡7,803
4C: $3,400
PCI: $50

6581 Senior News
1412 W. Colonial Dr., No. 100B Phone: (954)977-7770
Orlando, FL 32804-7119 Fax: (954)977-7779

Community newspaper for seniors (50). **Founded:** Feb. 1995. **Freq:** Monthly. **Print Method:** Offset. **Trim Size:** 10 1/4 x 13. **Cols./Page:** 6. **Col. Width:** 1 5/8 inches. **Key Personnel:** Harvey Lustig, Publisher. **Subscription Rates:** Free; $15 mailed. **Formerly:** Local News & Shopper (Nov. 1986).
Ad Rates: GLR: $10.35 **Circ:** Free ‡20,000
4C: $300 additional
PCI: $10.35

6582 Tabletalk
Ligonier Ministries
PO Box 547500 Phone: (407)333-4244
Orlando, FL 32854 Fax: (407)333-4233
Publication E-mail: ttorlando@aol.com
Publisher E-mail: rymresource@gospelcom.net

Magazine featuring articles on Christian studies. **Founded:** May 1977. **Freq:** Monthly. **Print Method:** Web press. **Trim Size:** Digest. **Key Personnel:** R.C. Sproul, Chairman of the Board, ligonier@gospelcom.net; R.C. Sproul, Jr., Editor-in-Chief, phone (540)475-6064, covamdude@aol.com; Robert Barnes, Assoc. Ed., phone (407)435-4343, rymresource@gospelcom.net. **ISSN:** 1064-881X. **Subscription Rates:** $18 individuals annual; $2.00 single issue; $30 out of country. **Remarks:** Advertising not accepted. **URL:** http://www.ligonier.org.
Circ: Paid ⊕50,000
Non-paid ⊕10,000

6583 Technical Support
NaSPA
PO Box 616711 Phone: (407)296-5050
Orlando, FL 32861 Fax: (407)296-0870
Publication E-mail: editor@naspa.net

Professional magazine for computer network and systems professionals. **Freq:** Monthly. **Cols./Page:** 3. **Key Personnel:** Jerry Seefeldt, Publisher; Amy Novotny, Editor. **ISSN:** 1079-

3135. **Subscription Rates:** $29.95 individuals. **Remarks:** Accepts advertising. **URL:** http://www.naspa.net.
Ad Rates: BW: $4,122.50 **Circ:** Controlled 44,113
4C: $4,122.50

6584 Worldwide Challenge
Campus Crusade for Christ
100 Sunport Ln. Phone: (407)826-2390
Orlando, FL 32809 Fax: (407)826-2374
Free: (800)688-4992
Publication E-mail: wchallenge@aol.com

Religion and theology magazine. **Founded:** Jan. 1974. **Freq:** Bimonthly. **Print Method:** Offset. **Trim Size:** 8 1/2 x 10 3/4. **Cols./Page:** 3. **Col. Width:** 27 nonpareils. **Col. Depth:** 133 agate lines. **Key Personnel:** Sherry M. Cumpstone, Mktg./Circulation, phone (407)826-2389, cumpstone@cci.org. **ISSN:** 0746-9241. **Subscription Rates:** $12.95 individuals; $17.45 other countries; $3 single issue. **Remarks:** Advertising not accepted. **Online:** America Online, Inc. **URL:** http://www.ccci.org/wwwc.
Circ: 95,000

6585 Time Warner Cable of Florida
3767 All American Blvd. Phone: (407)295-9119
Orlando, FL 32810 Fax: (407)578-0979

Owner: Time Warner Cable, at above address. **Founded:** 1975. **Formerly:** Cablevision of Central Florida (1985). **Key Personnel:** David Spencer, VP/Gen. Mgr.; Johnny Langley, Production Mgr., phone (407)667-5201. **Cities Served:** Orange, Osceala, and Seminole counties.: subscribing households 230,000; 81 channels; 1 community access channel; 15 hours per week community access programming.

6586 WACX-TV - 55
4520 Parkbreeze Ct. Phone: (407)298-5555
Orlando, FL 32808

Format: Commercial TV. **Owner:** Assoc. Christian Television System, Inc., at above address. **Founded:** 1982. **Formerly:** WIYE-TV (1988). **Operating Hours:** Continuous; 75% network, 25% local. **ADI:** Orlando-Daytona Beach-Melbourne, FL. **Key Personnel:** Claud Bowers, Contact; Angela Courte, Contact; John Wasson, Chief Engineer; Linda Jarrell, Program Dir. **Wattage:** 5,000,000. **Ad Rates:** $55-85 for 30 seconds. **URL:** http://wwspn.com.

6587 WAJL-AM - 1190
1160 S.Semoran BLVD Phone: (407)380-9255
Ste A Fax: (407)382-7565
Orlando, FL 32807
Free: (800)981-9255
E-mail: wajl@wajl.com

Format: Talk. **Networks:** NBC. **Owner:** Lapcom Communications, 1160 S. Semonan Blvd., Ste. A, Orlando, FL 32807, Free: (800)855-8885. **Founded:** 1977. **Operating Hours:** Sunrise-sunset. **ADI:** Orlando-Daytona Beach-Melbourne, FL. **Key Personnel:** Steve Lapa, Owner; Scott Fallows, Sales/Programming Mgr.; Mindy Linkous, Promotions Mgr./News Dir.; Sirrelle Smith, Operations/Production Mgr. **Local Programs:** *Christian Consumer Advocate*, Jim Paris; *Life in the Kingdom*, Laurel Hughes. **Wattage:** 5000. **Ad Rates:** $50 for 30 seconds.

6588 WCFB-FM - 94.5
4192 John Young Pkwy. Phone: (407)297-0945
Orlando, FL 32804 Fax: (407)291-4879

Format: Adult Contemporary. **Networks:** Independent. **Founded:** 1952. **Formerly:** WWLV-FM. **Operating Hours:** Continuous; 100% local. **ADI:** Orlando-Daytona Beach-Melbourne, FL. **Key Personnel:** Angela Brilis, Promotions; Steve Holbrook, Operations Mgr.; Richard C. Reis, General Mgr.; Tom Bohannon, Chief Engineer; Bill Hendrich, General Sales Mgr. **Wattage:** 100,000. **Ad Rates:** $100 per unit.

6589 WCPX-TV - 6
4466 John Young Parkway Phone: (407)521-1200
Orlando, FL 32804 Fax: (407)521-1204

Format: Commercial TV. **Networks:** CBS. **Owner:** Post Newsweek Stations, 3 Constitution Plz., Hartford, CT 06103. **Founded:** 1954. **Formerly:** WDBO-TV. **Operating Hours:** 24Hrs. a Day. **ADI:** Orlando-Daytona Beach-Melbourne, FL. **Key Personnel:** Kathleen Keefe, General Mgr., phone (407)521-1271; John McKay, General Sales Mgr., phone (407)521-1248; Lena Sadiwskyj, News Dir.; Richard Moore, News Dir. **URL:** http://www.wcpx.com; http://www.feedback@wkmg.com.

6590 WDBO-AM - 580
4192 John Young Pkwy. Phone: (407)295-5858
Orlando, FL 32804 Fax: (407)291-4879

Format: Talk; News; Sports. **Networks:** ABC. **Founded:** 1924. **Operating Hours:** Continuous. **ADI:** Orlando-Daytona Beach-Melbourne, FL. **Key Personnel:** Bill Hendrich, General Mgr.; Pete Spriggs, Program Dir.; Jackie Rinker, General Sales Mgr. **Wattage:** 50,000.

6591 WESH-TV - 2
PO Box 547697 Phone: (407)645-2222
Orlando, FL 32854 Fax: (407)539-7823

Format: Commercial TV. **Networks:** NBC. **Founded:** 1956. **Operating Hours:** Continuous. **ADI:** Orlando-Daytona Beach-Melbourne, FL. **Key Personnel:** William Bauman, Contact. **Wattage:** 100.

6592 WFTV-TV - 9
490 E. South St. Phone: (407)841-9000
Orlando, FL 32801-2841 Fax: (407)244-8302
Free: (800)972-9388
E-mail: wftvch9@aol.com

Format: Commercial TV. **Networks:** ABC. **Owner:** Cox Enterprises, 1400 Lake Hearn Dr. NE, Atlanta, GA 30319, (404)843-2000. **Founded:** 1958. **Operating Hours:** Continuous; 41% network, 59% local. **ADI:** Orlando-Daytona Beach-Melbourne, FL. **Key Personnel:** Bill Hoffman, General Sales Mgr., fax (407)841-8259; Chip Reif, Production Mgr., phone (407)244-8338, fax (407)245-3692; David B. Lippoff, Vice Pres./General Mgr., phone (407)244-8300, fax (407)481-9902, david_lippoff@wftv.com; Lauren Watkins, News Dir., phone (407)244-8383, fax (407)244-8372; Susan Adams Lloyd, Program Dir., phone (407)244-8337, fax (407)481-9902, susan.lloyd@wftv.com; Donna Dalymple, Marketing Dir., phone (407)244-8355; Paul Warnock, Chief Engineer, fax (407)841-8259. **Local Programs:** *Eyewitness News* 6 a.m., noon, 5 & 5:30, 6 & 11 Monday-Friday, Lauren Watkins; *Health Documentaries*, Skip Skiffington. **Ad Rates:** $75-4000 per unit.

6593 WHOO-AM - 990
200 S. Orange Ave., Ste. 2240 Phone: (407)422-9696
Orlando, FL 32801 Fax: (407)422-5883

Format: Big Band/Nostalgia. **Networks:** ABC; Satellite Music Network. **Owner:** Cox Radio, Inc., 1400 Lake Hearn Dr., Atlanta, GA 30319, (404)843-5000. **Founded:** 1952. **Operating Hours:** Continuous. **ADI:** Orlando-Daytona Beach-Melbourne, FL. **Key Personnel:** Tim Robisch, General Sales Mgr., fax (407)422-0917, trobish@coxorlando.com; Bob Rose, Promotions Dir., brose@coxorlando.com; Bruce McGregor, Program Dir.; Ron Louis, Production Dir., rlouis@coxorlando.com. **Wattage:** 50,000.

6594 WHTQ-FM - 96.5
200 S. Orange Ave., Ste. 2240
Orlando, FL 32801

Format: Sports; Album-Oriented Rock (AOR). **Networks:** NBC. **Owner:** TK Communications, 110 SE 6th St., Fort Lauderdale, FL 33301, (305)525-8500. **Founded:** 1952. **Operating Hours:** Continuous. **Key Personnel:** Frank Tenore, Contact; Jim Steel, Contact; Robert Valois, General Sales Mgr.; Paul Proly, Contact; Joe Finger, News Dir.; Jennifer Lichtenwald, Contact; Bruce Cherry, Contact. **Wattage:** 100,000. **Ad Rates:** $64-120 per unit.

6595 WMFE-TV - 24
11510 E. Colonial Dr. Phone: (407)273-2300
Orlando, FL 32817 Fax: (407)273-3613
E-mail: viewresp@wmfe.pbs.org

Format: Public TV. **Networks:** Public Broadcasting Service (PBS). **Founded:** Mar. 1965. **Operating Hours:** 7:15 a.m.-midnight. **ADI:** Orlando-Daytona Beach-Melbourne, FL. **Key Personnel:** Stephen M. Steck, President. **Local Programs:** *Assignment*, Alice Tall, Producer. **Ad Rates:** Noncommercial. **URL:** http://www.pbs.org/wmfe.

6596 WMMO-FM - 98.9
200 S. Orange Ave., Ste. 2240 Phone: (407)422-9890
Orlando, FL 32801 Fax: (407)422-6538

Format: Soft Rock; Adult Contemporary. **Owner:** Cox Radio, Inc., 1400 Lake Hearn Dr., Atlanta, GA 30319, (404)843-5000. **Founded:** 1990. **Operating Hours:** Continuous. **ADI:** Orlando-Daytona Beach-Melbourne, FL. **Key Personnel:** Debbie A. Morel, Vice Pres./General Mgr., fax (407)422-8844, dmorel@coxorlando.com; Fleetwood Gruver, Operations Mgr., fax (407)422-8844, fgruver@coxorlando.com; Pete DeSimone, General Sales Mgr., pdesimone@coxorlando.com. **Wattage:** 38,000. **Ad Rates:** Advertising accepted; rates available upon request. **URL:** http://www.wmmo.com.

6597 WOKB-AM - 1600
8263 Conroy Windmere Rd. Phone: (407)523-2770
Orlando, FL 32801 Fax: (407)523-2888

Format: Gospel. **Owner:** Rama Communications, Inc., 4938 W. Colonial Dr., Orlando, FL 32808. **Operating Hours:** Continuous. **ADI:** Orlando-Daytona Beach-Melbourne, FL. **Key Personnel:** Joe Fisher, V.P./General Mgr. **Wattage:** 5,000. **Ad Rates:** $40 for 30 seconds; $50 for 60 seconds.

6598 WRBW-TV - 65
2000 Universal Studios, Ste. 200 Phone: (407)248-6500
Orlando, FL 32819 Fax: (407)248-6520
E-mail: wrbw@wrbw.com

Format: Commercial TV. **Networks:** United Paramount Network. **Owner:** Rainbow Broadcasting Ltd., at above address. **Founded:** 1993. **Operating Hours:** Continuous. **ADI:** Orlando-Daytona Beach-Melbourne, FL. **Key Personnel:** Joseph Rey, General Mgr.; Susan Jaramillo, Station Mgr.; David Schwartz, VP, Sales; Jay Rosenthal, Local Sales Mgr. **Wattage:** 5,000,000. **URL:** http://www.upn-65.com.

6599 WTGL-TV - 52
653 W. Michigan St. Phone: (407)423-5200
Orlando, FL 32805 Fax: (407)422-0120
E-mail: wtgltv52@ix.netcom.com

Networks: Christian Television. **Owner:** Good Life Broadcasting, Inc., at above address, Fax: (407)423-8153. **Founded:** 1982. **Operating Hours:** Continuous Sat.-Thurs.; 1 a.m.-6 a.m. Fri. **ADI:** Orlando-Daytona Beach-Melbourne, FL. **Key Personnel:** Annette Smith, Program Dir.; Kathy Mikesell, Office Mgr.; Laura Rooks, Producer; Gene Polino, Chm.; Ken Mikesell, Pres./Gen. Mgr.; Lisa Edwards, Finance Dir.; Keith Roberts, Chief Engineer. **Local Programs:** *The Bottom Line*; *Central Florida Live*; *Today's Family*. **Wattage:** 5 million. **Ad Rates:** $100 for 30 seconds; $160 for 60 seconds.

6600 WUCF-FM - 89.9
PO Box 162199 Phone: (407)823-0899
Orlando, FL 32816-2199 Fax: (407)823-6364
E-mail: wucf@pegasus.cc.ucf.edu

Format: Jazz. **Networks:** Public Radio International (PRI); National Public Radio (NPR). **Owner:** University of Central Florida, at above address. **Founded:** 1977. **Operating Hours:** Continuous. **ADI:** Orlando-Daytona Beach-Melbourne, FL. **Key Personnel:** Paul Thomas, Music Dir.; Rafael Gonzalez, Marketing Dir.; Kayonne Riley, Station Mgr.; Terry Rensel, Program Dir. **Local Programs:** *Drivetime Jazz*, Wayne Perkins, (407)823-6364; *WUCF in the Morning*, Peter Carroll. **Wattage:** 40,000. **Ad Rates:** Noncommercial; underwriting available. **URL:** http://wucf.ucf.edu/.

6601 WWKA-FM - 92.3
4192 John Young Pkwy. Phone: (407)298-9292
Orlando, FL 32804 Fax: (407)291-4879

Format: Contemporary Country. **Networks:** Independent. **Owner:** Cox Radio Inc., 1400 Lake Hearn Dr., Atlanta, GA 30319, (404)843-5200. **Founded:** Jan. 1983. **Formerly:** WDBO-FM (1983). **Operating Hours:** Continuous; 100% local. **ADI:** Orlando-Daytona Beach-Melbourne, FL. **Key Personnel:** Bill Hendrich, General Mgr.; Mike Moore, Program Dir.; Cindy Revisore, General Sales Mgr. **Wattage:** 100,000.

6602 WXTO-AM - 1600
PO Box 680889 Phone: (407)291-1395
Orlando, FL 32868 Fax: (407)578-1734

Format: Hispanic. **Networks:** ABC; Spanish Information Service. **Owner:** Champion Broadcasting of Florida, Inc., at above address. **Founded:** 1980. **Formerly:** WOKB-AM. **Operating Hours:** Continuous. **ADI:** Orlando-Daytona Beach-Melbourne, FL. **Key Personnel:** Jose D. Ricci, General Mgr.; Pedro Sanchez, Program Dir. **Wattage:** 5000. **Ad Rates:** $10-15 for 30 seconds; $19-26 for 60 seconds.

ORMOND BEACH, pop. 21,378.

E FL. Volusia Co. 7 mi. N. of Daytona Beach. Tourist resort.

6603 Daytona Pennysaver
Volusia Pennysaver, Inc.
454 S. Young St. Phone: (904)677-4262
PO Box 67 Fax: (904)672-7453
Ormond Beach, FL 32174
Community shopper. **Founded:** 1976. **Freq:** Weekly (Wed.). **Print Method:** Tabloid. Offset. Uses mats. **Cols./Page:** 6. **Col. Width:** 21 nonpareils. **Col. Depth:** 182 agate lines. **Key Personnel:** Thomas M. Lindley, Publisher. **Remarks:** Accepts advertising.
Ad Rates: GLR: $.50 **Circ:** Free ‡57,660
SAU: $8

6604 Foreign Tax Law Bi-Weekly Bulletin
Foreign Tax Law, Inc.
PO Box 2189 Phone: (904)253-5785
Ormond Beach, FL 32175-2189 Fax: (904)257-3003
Publisher E-mail: ftlp@foreignlaw.com

Professional journal covering proposed legislation on business and tax law from non-US jurisdictions translated into English. **Freq:** Biweekly. **Trim Size:** 8 x 11. **Cols./Page:** 1. **Key Personnel:** Sondra Yananra, Editor. **ISSN:** 0095-7291. **Sub-**

scription Rates: $175 individuals; $20 single issue. **Remarks:** Advertising not accepted.
Circ: (Not Reported)

6605 WELE-AM - 1380
432 S. Nova Rd. Phone: (904)677-4122
Ormond Beach, FL 32174 Fax: (904)677-4123

Format: Religious; News; Talk. **Networks:** NBC. **Founded:** 1957. **Formerly:** WDAT-AM. **Operating Hours:** 24hrs. **Key Personnel:** Doug Wilhite, General Mgr.; Doug Wilhite II, Program Dir. **Wattage:** 5000 day; 2500 night. **Ad Rates:** $30 for 30 seconds; $35 for 60 seconds.

6606 WFKS-FM - 99.9
801 W. Granada Blvd. Phone: (904)672-9210
Ormond Beach, FL 32174 Fax: (904)677-2252
Free: (800)672-9210

Founded: 1981. **Formerly:** WNFI-FM (1981). **Operating Hours:** Continuous. **ADI:** Orlando-Daytona Beach-Melbourne, FL. **Key Personnel:** Jim Davis, General Mgr., jdavis@n-jcenter.com. **Wattage:** 100,000. **Ad Rates:** Advertising accepted; rates available upon request. **URL:** http://www.radiokiss.com.

PACE

6607 WXBM-FM - 102.7
1687 Quintet Rd. Phone: (904)994-5357
Pace, FL 32571 Fax: (904)994-7191

Format: Country. **Networks:** Mutual Broadcasting System. **Owner:** Patterson broadcasting, Inc., 400 Perimeter center Terrace, N.E., Ste 410, Atlanta, GA 30346. **Founded:** 1964. **Operating Hours:** Continuous. **Key Personnel:** Dave Cobb, General Mgr.; Ron Bird, General Sales Mgr. **Wattage:** 100,000.

PALATKA†, pop. 9,890.

NE FL. Putman Co. On St. Johns River, 52 mi. S. of Jacksonville. Saint Johns River Community College. Fisheries. Lumber. Citrus fruit.

6608 Palatka Daily News
The Daily News
1825 St. Johns Ave. Phone: (904)328-2721
PO Box 777 Fax: (904)325-0663
Palatka, FL 32178-4400
General newspaper. **Founded:** 1885. **Freq:** Daily (eve.). **Print Method:** Offset. **Cols./Page:** 6. **Col. Width:** 25 nonpareils. **Col. Depth:** 301 agate lines. **Key Personnel:** James R. Brown, Editor; John E. Newhouse II, Publisher. **USPS:** 418-500. **Subscription Rates:** $45 individuals. **Remarks:** Accepts advertising.
Ad Rates: SAU: $10.20 **Circ:** Mon.-Fri. ★11.771

6609 Putnam Pennysaver
Volusia Pennysaver, Inc.
PO Box 220 Phone: (904)328-4649
Palatka, FL 32178 Fax: (904)325-4617

Shopper serving Putnam County and adjacent communities. **Founded:** Nov. 1, 1984. **Freq:** Weekly (Wed.). **Print Method:** Offset. **Trim Size:** 11 x 14. **Cols./Page:** 6. **Col. Width:** 1 1/2 inches. **Col. Depth:** 13 inches. **Key Personnel:** Thom Giordano, General Mgr. **Subscription Rates:** $52 individuals. **Remarks:** Accepts advertising.
Ad Rates: BW: $460.20 **Circ:** Free ‡26,015
4C: $640.20
PCI: $5.90

6610 WIYD-AM - 1260
900 River St. Phone: (904)325-4556
Palatka, FL 32177

Format: Country; Contemporary Country. **Networks:** ABC; Florida Radio. **Owner:** Ronnie and Suzanne Tumlin, at above address. **Founded:** 1947. **Formerly:** WWPF-AM (1980). **Operating Hours:** Continuous. **Key Personnel:** Mary Makie, Contact; Bob Henry, Contact. **Local Programs:** *Mid Morning Show* 9:40 am - 10:25 am Monday-Friday, Mary Mackie, (904)325-4556. **Wattage:** 1000. **Ad Rates:** $8-10 for 30 seconds; $10-15 for 60 seconds.

6611 WPLK-AM - 800
PO Box 335 Phone: (904)325-5800
Palatka, FL 32178-0335 Fax: (904)328-8725

Format: Country. **Networks:** ABC. **Owner:** Radio Palatka, Inc., at above address. **Founded:** 1957. **Formerly:** WSUZ-AM (1990). **Operating Hours:** Continuous; 10% network, 90% local. **ADI:** Jacksonville (Brunswick), FL. **Key Personnel:** George Duck, Contact; Wayne Bullock, General Mgr. **Wattage:** 1000. **Ad Rates:** $6-8 for 30 seconds; $8-12.50 for 60 seconds.

PALM BEACH, pop. 10,415.

SE FL. Palm Beach Co. Across Lake Worth from West Palm Beach. Resort area.

6612 Palm Beach Daily News
Palm Beach Newspapers, Inc.
265 Royal Pionciana Way Phone: (561)820-3800
Palm Beach, FL 33480-4007 Fax: (561)655-4594

General newspaper. **Founded:** 1894. **Freq:** Mon.-Sun. (morn.). **Print Method:** Offset. **Trim Size:** 13 x 22 1/2. **Cols./Page:** 6. **Col. Width:** 2 1/16 inches. **Col. Depth:** 22 1/2 inches. **Key Personnel:** Joyce Reingold, Publisher, phone (561)820-3838, fax (561)820-3836; Susan Dufour, Advertising Dir., phone (561)820-3820. **USPS:** 418-660. **Subscription Rates:** $57.80 individuals; $103.71 out of area. **Remarks:** Accepts advertising.
Ad Rates: BW: $25.63 **Circ:** Paid ‡6,827
PCI: $22.64 Free ‡2,764

6613 Palm Beach Society Magazine
Box 591 Phone: (561)659-5555
240 Worth Ave. Fax: (561)655-6209
Palm Beach, FL 33480
Free: (800)452-7066
Publication E-mail: pbsocmag@southern.net

Society magazine. **Subtitle:** The Social Pictorial. **Founded:** 1953. **Freq:** Weekly. **Print Method:** Offset. **Trim Size:** 10 13/16 x 13. **Cols./Page:** 5. **Col. Width:** 2 1/16 inches. **Col. Depth:** 13 inches. **Key Personnel:** James Jennings Sheeran, Editor and Publisher. **ISSN:** 1045-7259. **Subscription Rates:** $36 individuals; $2.50 single issue. **Formerly:** The Social Pictorial.
Ad Rates: GLR: $13 **Circ:** Paid 4,500
BW: $900 Non-paid 500
4C: $1,500
PCI: $13

6614 WPTV-TV - 5
PO Box 510 Phone: (407)655-5455
Palm Beach, FL 33480 Fax: (407)655-8947
E-mail: wptv.com; wptv@aol.com

Format: Commercial TV. **Networks:** NBC. **Founded:** Aug. 22, 1954. **Operating Hours:** Continuous. **ADI:** West Palm Beach-Ft. Pierce-Vero Beach, FL. **Key Personnel:** William Brooks, Contact. **Wattage:** 100KW.

PALM BEACH GARDENS

6615 Selling
The Dartnell Corp.
360 Hiatt Dr. Fax: (561)622-2423
Palm Beach Gardens, FL 33418 Free: (800)621-5463
Publisher E-mail: dartnell@dartnellcorp.com

Magazine covering information for sales professionals in all areas. **Subtitle:** The Front Line of Business. **Founded:** Aug. 1993. **Freq:** Monthly. **Trim Size:** 8 X 10. **Key Personnel:** Tracy Butzko, phone (773)564-3150, tbutzko@dartnellcorp.com; T.B. Zabon, phone (773)564-3155, fax (773)561-4842, tzabonAatsdartnellcorp.com. **Subscription Rates:** $79 individuals. **Remarks:** Accepts advertising. **Formerly:** Selling Magazine.
Ad Rates: 4C: $5,000 **Circ:** (Not Reported)

6616 Media Partners
A Division of Adelphia Phone: (561)844-3211
2001 W Blue Heron Blvd. Fax: (561)844-6733
Riviera Beach, FL 33404

Founded: 1967. **Formerly:** Adelphia Communications (Jan. 1997). **Key Personnel:** Mark Galloway, Regional General Mgr., phone (561)863-5701, fax (561)845-7709; Howard Hackley, Regional Advt. Sales Dir., fax (561)969-7315; Beth Stull, National Sales Mgr.; Sally Harper, Local Sales Mgr., phone (561)637-2750, fax (561)637-2754; Pablo Ortiz, Local Sales Mgr.; Joseph Koker, Client Services Mgr.; Jerry Styes, Traffic Mgr., fax (561)881-4531. **Cities Served:** Palm Beach Gardens, FL: subscribing households 100,000; 62 channels.

6617 WPBF-TV - 25
3970 RCA Blvd., Ste. 7007 Phone: (407)694-2525
Palm Beach Gardens, FL 33410 Fax: (407)624-1089
E-mail: wpbfpromo@aol.com

Format: Commercial TV. **Networks:** ABC. **Owner:** Paxson Communications, 601 Clearwater Park Rd., West Palm Beach, FL 33401. **Founded:** 1989. **Operating Hours:** Continuous. **ADI:** West Palm Beach-Ft. Pierce-Vero Beach, FL. **Key Personnel:** Doug Barker, General Mgr., phone (561)694-2525, fax (561)627-6738; Jean Waldstein, Traffic and Programming Manager, fax (561)624-8093; Linda LaManna, Promotion & Marketing Director, fax (561)627-6738; Shawn Bartlett, Local Sales Manager, fax (561)625-0538; Caroline Scollard, National Sales Manager, fax (561)625-0538; Cliff Thomas, Chief Engineer, fax (561)627-6738; Bill Burke, News Dir., fax (561)624-1089. **Local Programs:** *PBF News in Review*, Su Jackson-Ross, Producer. **Wattage:** 5,000,000.

PALM CITY, pop. 950.

E FL. Martin Co. 2 mi. SW of Stuart.

6618 Fore Florida
1025 SW Martin Downs Blvd., Phone: (561)288-7499
Ste. 102A Fax: (561)288-1963
Palm City, FL 34990
Publisher E-mail: forefl@gate.net

Regional golf magazine. **Founded:** Jan. 1996. **Freq:** Bimonthly. **Print Method:** Web offset. **Trim Size:** 8 1/8 x 10 7/8. **Key Personnel:** Daniel Shube, Publisher; Ruth Hauser, General Mgr. **Subscription Rates:** Free to qualified subscribers; $9 individuals. **Remarks:** Accepts advertising.
Ad Rates: BW: $1,495 **Circ:** Paid 100
4C: $1,995 Non-paid 40,000

PALM COAST

Flagler Co.

6619 Palm Coast Cablevision Ltd.
211 St. Joe Plaza Dr. Phone: (904)445-5464
Palm Coast, FL 32137 Fax: (904)445-5434

Formerly: Palm Cable Inc. **Key Personnel:** Rosa Rosas, General Mgr., rrosas@kingwoodcable.com. **Cities Served:** Volusia, CO; Palm Coast, FL: subscribing households 10,000; 65 channels; 1 community access channel.

PALM HARBOR

6620 Algebras, Groups & Geometries
Hadronic Press, Inc.
35246 U.S. 19 N., Ste. 115 Phone: (813)934-9593
Palm Harbor, FL 34684 Fax: (813)934-9275
Publisher E-mail: ibr@gte.net

Scholarly journal covering mathematics for graduate and post graduate students. **Freq:** Quarterly. **Trim Size:** 7 /14 x 9. **Key Personnel:** Prof. Ruggero Santilli, Editor; Pamela Fleming, Circulation Mgr. **ISSN:** 0741-9937. **Subscription Rates:** $160 individuals. **Remarks:** Advertising not accepted.
Circ: Paid 200

6621 Hadronic Journal
Hadronic Press, Inc.
35246 U.S. 19 N., Ste. 115 Phone: (813)934-9593
Palm Harbor, FL 34684 Fax: (813)934-9275
Publisher E-mail: ibr@gte.net

Scholarly journal covering physics for graduate and post-graduate students. **Freq:** Semimonthly. **Trim Size:** 7 1/4 x 9. **Key Personnel:** Prof. Ruggero Santilli, Editor; Pamela Fleming, Circulation Mgr. **ISSN:** 0162-5519. **Subscription Rates:** $260 individuals. **Remarks:** Advertising not accepted. **URL:** http://home1.gte.net/ibr.
Circ: Paid 150

6622 Hadronic Journal Supplement
Hadronic Press, Inc.
35246 U.S. 19 N., Ste. 115 Phone: (813)934-9593
Palm Harbor, FL 34684 Fax: (813)934-9275
Publisher E-mail: ibr@gte.net

Scholarly journal covering physics for graduate and post-graduate students. **Freq:** Quarterly. **Trim Size:** 7 1/4 x 9. **Key Personnel:** Prof. Ruggero Santilli, Editor; Pamela Fleming, Circulation Mgr. **ISSN:** 0882-5396. **Subscription Rates:** $150 individuals. **Remarks:** Advertising not accepted.
Circ: Paid 100

6623 WGUL-AM - 860
35048 US Highway 19 Phone: (813)442-4027
Palm Harbor, FL 34684 Fax: (813)781-4375
Free: (800)332-9485

Format: Music of Your Life; Easy Listening; Big Band/Nostalgia; Jazz. **Simulcasts:** WGUL-FM. **Networks:** UPI. **Owner:** Carl J. Marcocci, at above address. **Founded:** 1985. **Operating Hours:** Continuous; 40% network, 60% local. **ADI:** Tampa-St. Petersburg (Lakeland, Sarasota), FL. **Key Personnel:** Steven J. Schurdell, Contact; Paul Mueller, Chief Engineer. **Wattage:** 2000. **Ad Rates:** $40-50 for 30 seconds; $50-60 for 60 seconds.

6624 WGUL-FM - 96.1
35048 U.S. Hwy. 19 Phone: (813)442-4027
Palm Harbor, FL 34684 Fax: (813)781-4375

Format: Music of Your Life; Easy Listening; Big Band/Nostalgia; Jazz. **Simulcasts:** WGUL-AM. **Networks:** UPI. **Owner:**

Carl J. Marcocci, at above address. **Founded:** 1985. **Operating Hours:** Continuous; 40% network, 60% local. **ADI:** Tampa-St. Petersburg (Lakeland, Sarasota), FL. **Key Personnel:** Steven J. Schurdell, Contact; Paul Mueller, Chief Engineer. **Wattage:** 6000. **Ad Rates:** $40-50 for 30 seconds; $50-60 for 60 seconds.

6625 WLVU-AM - 1470
2625 County Rd. 95 Phone: (813)786-9588
Palm Harbor, FL 34684

Format: Ethnic. **Networks:** Independent. **Founded:** 1955. **Operating Hours:** Continuous. **ADI:** Tampa-St. Petersburg (Lakeland, Sarasota), FL. **Key Personnel:** Frank Ferrei, General Mgr. **Wattage:** 5000 day; 500 night.

PANAMA CITY†, pop. 33,346.

NW FL. Bay Co. On St. Andrews Bay and Gulf of Mexico, 98 mi. E. of Pensacola. Gulf Coast Community College. Resort area. Manufactures boats, concrete products, lumber, textiles, auto disc pads, and beverages.

6626 The Journal of Ideas
Institute for Memetic Research, Inc.
PO Box 16327
Panama City, FL 32406-1327
Publisher E-mail: publications@aiga.org

Journal covering the evolution of ideas, discovery of creative processes, memetics, and abstract evolution. **Founded:** 1990. **Freq:** Quarterly. **Print Method:** Offset. **Trim Size:** 8 1/2 x 11. **Cols./Page:** 2. **Col. Width:** 2 3/4 inches. **Col. Depth:** 9 inches. **Key Personnel:** Dr. Elan Moritz, Editor. **ISSN:** 1049-6335. **Subscription Rates:** $46; $138 Industry. $26 single issue. **Remarks:** Advertising not accepted.
Circ: ‡200

6627 News Herald
Freedom Communications Inc.
501 W. 11th St. Phone: (904)763-7621
Panama City, FL 32402 Fax: (904)763-4636

Community newspaper. **Founded:** 1931. **Freq:** Mon.-Sun. (morn.). **Print Method:** Offset. **Trim Size:** 13 3/4 x 22 3/4. **Cols./Page:** 6. **Col. Width:** 25 1/2 nonpareils. **Col. Depth:** 301 agate lines. **Key Personnel:** Bill Salter, Editor; Scott Fischer, Publisher; Scott Walker, Advertising Mgr. **USPS:** 419-560. **Subscription Rates:** $85.80 individuals; $102 out of area. **Remarks:** Accepts advertising.
Ad Rates: GLR: $.52 **Circ:** Mon.-Sat. 34,935
BW: $1,475.76 Sun. 40,026
4C: $1,925.76
SAU: $11.44

6628 WFSG-TV - 56
1600 Red Barber Plaza Phone: (850)487-3170
Tallahassee, FL 32310 Fax: (850)487-3093
Free: (800)322-9378

Format: Public TV. **Simulcasts:** WFSU-TV Tallahassee, FL. **Networks:** Public Broadcasting Service (PBS). **Owner:** Florida Board of Regents, at above address. **Founded:** Nov. 1988. **Operating Hours:** 5 a.m.-11:00 p.m. **ADI:** Panama City, FL. **Key Personnel:** Pat Keating, General Mgr.; Donna Landrum, Business Mgr.; Rebecca Crawford, Teleconferencing; Charles Allen, Dir. of Development. **Local Programs:** *Body Electric*, Donna Landrum, (904)487-3170; *Florida Face to Face*, Beth Switzer, (904)487-3170. **URL:** http://www.fsu.edu/˜wfsu_tv/.

6629 WFSY-FM - 98.5
PO Box 759 Phone: (904)769-6161
Panama City, FL 32402-0759 Fax: (904)769-6164

Format: Contemporary Hit Radio (CHR). **Networks:** ABC. **Owner:** The Woodfin Group, at above address. **Founded:** 1986. **Formerly:** WGNE-FM. **Operating Hours:** Continuous; 1% network, 99% local. **ADI:** Panama City, FL. **Key Personnel:** Jim Dooley, Operations Dir.; Joe Crews, News Dir.; Karen Tucker, Promotions Dir.; Randy Sheffield, General Mgr.; Rob Ashe, Station Mgr.; Patsy Sellers, Office Mgr. **Wattage:** 100,000. **Ad Rates:** $20-38 for 30 seconds; $25-47.50 for 60 seconds.

6630 WGNE-AM - 590
2615 E. 15th St. Phone: (904)769-6161
Panama City, FL 32405 Fax: (904)769-6164
E-mail: oasis@interor.com

Format: Jazz. **Owner:** B Radio Inc., at above address. **Founded:** 1986. **Formerly:** WDLP-AM. **Operating Hours:** Continuous; 1% network, 99% local. **ADI:** Panama City, FL. **Key Personnel:** Tim O'Brien, General Mgr. **Wattage:** 1700 day; 2500 night. **Ad Rates:** $9 for 30 seconds; $11 for 60 seconds.

6631 WLTG-AM - 1430
3216 W. Highway, 390 No. B Phone: (850)784-9873
Panama City, FL 32405-2718 Fax: (850)784-6908

Format: Information; News; Talk; Sports. **Networks:** Sun Radio; Chancellor Broadcasting. **Owner:** Hour Group Broadcasting, Inc., PO Box 15635, Panama City, FL 32406. **Founded:** 1949. **Formerly:** WPCF-AM (1978). **Operating Hours:** Continuous. **ADI:** Panama City, FL. **Key Personnel:** John Gay, General Mgr.; John Gay, Program Dir.; Peggy Gay, Office Mgr.; Rex Ogburn, News and PSA Dir. **Wattage:** 5000.

6632 WMBB-TV - 13
613 Harrison Ave. Phone: (850)769-2313
Box 1340 Fax: (850)769-8231
Panama City, FL 32402
E-mail: admin@wmbb.com

Format: Commercial TV. **Networks:** ABC. **Owner:** Spartan Communications, Inc., PO Box 1717, Spartanburg, SC 29304, (864)576-7777. **Founded:** 1973. **Formerly:** WDTB-TV. **Operating Hours:** 75% network, 25% local. **ADI:** Panama City, FL. **Key Personnel:** Hugh Roche, General Mgr.; Teri Basford, Promotions Dir.; Tim Kelley, Sports Dir.; Patti Clements, Program Dir., pclements@wmbb.com; Larche Hardy, News Dir.; Cherise Ierardi, Production Mgr.; Elizabeth Parker, Business Mgr.; Bill Byrd, Sales Mgr.; Wendell Nelson, Chief Engineer; Letitia Williams, Traffic Mgr. **Wattage:** 316.

6633 WPAP-FM - 92.5
1834 Lisenby Ave. Phone: (904)769-1408
PO Box 2288 Fax: (904)769-0659
Panama City, FL 32402-2288

Format: Country. **Networks:** Independent. **Operating Hours:** Continuous; 100% local. **ADI:** Panama City, FL. **Key Personnel:** Rick Braswell, Program Dir.; Tom Gardner, News Dir.; Reed Kenny, Contact; Bo Bowman, General Mgr. **Wattage:** 100,000. **Ad Rates:** $36-60 for 30 seconds; $40-70 for 60 seconds.

PANAMA CITY BEACH

6634 Beach Bay News
Woodham Family Publications
17214 Back Beach Rd. Phone: (904)234-6990
Panama City Beach, FL 32413 Fax: (904)234-3054

Community newspaper. **Founded:** 1978. **Freq:** Weekly (Wed.). **Print Method:** Offset. **Cols./Page:** 6. **Col. Width:** 12 picas. **Col. Depth:** 294 agate lines. **Key Personnel:** Adrian Savelle, Editor; Larry Woodham, Publisher; Leigh Rushing, Office Assistant, Advertising; Beth McCann, Advertising Mgr. **Subscription Rates:** Free; $20 by mail. **Remarks:** Accepts advertising.
Ad Rates: BW: $661.50 **Circ:** Free 10,000
SAU: $6.86
PCI: $5.25

6635 Jones Spacelink
603 Camellia St. Phone: (904)235-2980
Panama City Beach, FL 32407 Fax: (904)234-7344

Founded: 1980. **Formerly:** Jones Intercable. **Key Personnel:** Ray Kistler, General Mgr.; Bill Dorsey, Chief Engineer; Lisa Renaker, Marketing Mgr.; Pamm Cox, Business Mgr. **Cities Served:** Panama City Beach, FL: subscribing households 8,500; 63 channels; 1 community access channel; 168 hours per week community access programming.

6636 WILN-FM - 105.9
8317 Front Beach Rd., Ste. 21 Phone: (904)233-6606
Panama City Beach, FL 32407 Fax: (904)233-1541

Format: Contemporary Hit Radio (CHR). **Owner:** Empire Broadcasting System, LLP, PO Box 1790, Panama City, FL 32402. **Founded:** 1985. **Formerly:** WLVV-FM (1987). **Operating Hours:** Continuous; 100% local. **ADI:** Panama City, FL. **Key Personnel:** Chris Murray, General Mgr. **Wattage:** 50,000. **Ad Rates:** $25 per unit.

6637 WJHG-TV - 7
8195 Front Beach Rd. Phone: (904)234-2125
Panama City Beach, FL 32407 Fax: (904)233-6647
E-mail: wjhg@aol.com

Format: Commercial TV. **Networks:** NBC. **Owner:** Gray Communications Systems, Inc, PO Box 48, Albany, GA 31703, (912)888-9378. **Founded:** 1953. **Formerly:** WJDM-TV (1960). **Operating Hours:** Continuous. **ADI:** Panama City, FL. **Key Personnel:** Terry Cole, President/General Mgr.; Jim Crump, General Sales Mgr.; Desiree Landers, News Dir.; Kathy Fultz. **Ad Rates:** Advertising accepted; rates available upon request.

6638 WPFM-FM - 107.9
6906 W. Hwy. 98 Phone: (904)234-8858
Panama City Beach, FL 32407 Fax: (904)234-6592

Format: Contemporary Hit Radio (CHR). **Networks:** Independent. **Owner:** Root Communications, Ltd., at above address. **Founded:** 1963. **Operating Hours:** Continuous; 100% local. **ADI:** Panama City, FL. **Key Personnel:** Tom Dibacco, General Mgr.; Darrell Johnson, Sales Mgr.; Mike Stone, Contact; Charlie Wooten, Contact. **Wattage:** 100,000. **Ad Rates:** $14-20 for 30 seconds; $16-30 for 60 seconds. $10-$14 for 30 seconds; $12-$16 for 60 seconds. Combined advertising rates available with WDRK-FM.

6639 WTBB-FM - 97.7
8317 Front Beach Rd., Ste. 21 Phone: (904)233-6606
Panama City Beach, FL 32407 Fax: (904)233-1541

Format: Album-Oriented Rock (AOR). **Owner:** Group M Communications, Inc., PO Box 1790, Panama City, FL 32402. **Founded:** 1983. **Operating Hours:** Continuous. **ADI:** Panama City, FL. **Key Personnel:** Chris Murray, Manager. **Wattage:** 100,000. **Ad Rates:** $20 per unit. Combined advertising rates available with WILN-AM.

PEMBROKE PARK

Broward Co.

6640 WHFT-TV - 45
3324 Pembroke Rd. Phone: (305)962-1700
Pembroke Park, FL 33021 Fax: (305)962-2817

Format: Religious. **Founded:** 1973. **Formerly:** WFCB-TV (1977). **Operating Hours:** Continuous; 65% network, 6% local, 29% paid programming. **ADI:** Miami (Ft. Lauderdale), FL. **Key Personnel:** Michael S. Everett, General Mgr.; Robin Downing, Production Mgr.; Jacques Morisset, Chief Engineer; Elizabeth M. Crespo, Contact. **Ad Rates:** Noncommercial.

PEMBROKE PINES

6641 Health & Beauty Magazine
8551 NW 10 St. Phone: (954)434-3885
Pembroke Pines, FL 33084-3224 Fax: (954)437-4580

Magazine covering the health and beauty industry. **Founded:** 1990. **Freq:** 10/year. **Print Method:** Web Offset. **Trim Size:** 8 1/4 x 11. **Key Personnel:** Marie Provernzaico, Contact. **Subscription Rates:** $16 individuals; $3 single issue. **Remarks:** Advertising accepted; rates available upon request. **Formerly:** Salon Technologies.
Circ: (Not Reported)

PENSACOLA†, pop. 57,619.

NW FL. Escambia Co. On Pensacola Bay, 7 mi. from Gulf of Mexico, 61 mi. SE of Mobile, AL. Pensacola Junior College; University of West Florida; U.S. Naval Air Station. Port of entry with deep harbor and considerable commerce. Manufactures boats, nylon, chemicals, cottonseed oil, lumber, fertilizer, furniture, beverages, and paper products.

6642 The Escambia Sun-Press
Escambia Sun-Press, Inc.
PO Box 4625 Phone: (904)456-3121
Pensacola, FL 32507 Fax: (904)456-0103

Local newspaper. **Founded:** Oct. 1946. **Freq:** Weekly. **Print Method:** Offset. **Cols./Page:** 9. **Col. Width:** 10 1/2 picas. **Col. Depth:** 21 inches. **Key Personnel:** Denise Messer, Editor; Michael J. Driver, Publisher. **Subscription Rates:** $10.50 individuals. **Remarks:** Accepts advertising.
Ad Rates: PCI: $4.50 **Circ:** 3,500

6643 Half Tones to Jubilee
Pensacola Junior College
1000 College Blvd.
Pensacola, FL 32504

Literary journal covering poetry and fiction. **Founded:** 1986. **Freq:** Annual. **Key Personnel:** Walter F. Spara, Senior Editor, phone (850)484-1418. **Subscription Rates:** $4 individuals. **Remarks:** Advertising not accepted.
Circ: (Not Reported)

6644 The Ketch Pen
Washington Cattlemen's Association
Box 34257 Phone: (904)934-1200
Pensacola, FL 32507
Livestock. **Founded:** 1937. **Freq:** Bimonthly. **Print Method:** Offset. **Trim Size:** 10 13/16 x 13. **Cols./Page:** 3. **Col. Width:** 7 1/4 inches. **Col. Depth:** 13 inches. **Key Personnel:** Carolyn

Hunt, Editor. **ISSN:** 0889-2857. **Subscription Rates:** $30. **Remarks:** Accepts advertising.
Ad Rates: BW: $565 **Circ:** ‡3,000
4C: $745
PCI: $30

6645 Pensacola History Illustrated
Pensacola Historical Society
117 E. Government St. Phone: (850)434-5455
Pensacola, FL 32501
Publisher E-mail: phstaff@freent.com

Journal covering local history. **Founded:** 1983. **Freq:** Semiannual. **Print Method:** Offset. **Trim Size:** 8 1/2 x 11. **Cols./Page:** 2. **Col. Width:** 3 1/4 inches. **Col. Depth:** 9 1/2 inches. **Key Personnel:** Virginia Parks, Editor; Sandra Johnson, Editor. **ISSN:** 1082-5193. **Subscription Rates:** $25 individuals. **Remarks:** Advertising not accepted. **Former name:** Echo and Pensacola Historical Society Quarterly.
Circ: Controlled 700

6646 Pensacola News Journal
1 News-Journal Plaza Phone: (904)435-8500
Pensacola, FL 32501-5670 Fax: (904)435-8633

General newspaper. **Founded:** 1889. **Freq:** Mon.-Sun. (morn.). **Print Method:** Letterpress. **Trim Size:** 13 1/2 x 22 3/4. **Cols./Page:** 6. **Col. Width:** 24 nonpareils. **Col. Depth:** 301 agate lines. **Key Personnel:** Anne Saul, Exec. Editor; Kenneth W. Andrews, Publisher; George Gutierrez, Advertising Mgr.; Gayle Pryor. **Subscription Rates:** $143.40 individuals. **Remarks:** Accepts advertising. **Feature Editors:** Sandra Burnett, *Food*, phone (904)435-8655; Susan Catron, *Features, Lifestyle, Medical, Travel*, phone (904)435-8621; Alice Crann, *Fashion*, phone (904)435-8632; Mike Mika, *Financial/Business*, phone (904)435-8517.
Ad Rates: BW: $6,524.82 **Circ:** Mon.-Fri. ★**61,050**
4C: $7,125.82 Sat. ★**68,350**
SAU: $50.58 Sun. ★**83,037**

6647 Pensacola Voice
213 E. Yonge St. Phone: (904)434-6963
Pensacola, FL 32503-3766 Fax: (904)469-8745

Black community newspaper. **Founded:** 1966. **Freq:** Weekly. **Cols./Page:** 6. **Col. Width:** 2 inches. **Col. Depth:** 21 inches. **Subscription Rates:** $10. **Remarks:** Accepts advertising.
Ad Rates: BW: $1,060.92 **Circ:** ‡35,896
4C: $1,460.92
PCI: $8.42

6648 SCUBA Times
GBP, Inc.
14110 Perdido Key Dr., Ste. 16 Phone: (904)492-7805
Pensacola, FL 32507 Fax: (904)492-7807

Magazine containing articles about domestic and foreign dive locations, resorts, and equipment, and personalities in diving. **Subtitle:** The Active Diver's Magazine. **Founded:** 1979. **Freq:** Bimonthly. **Print Method:** Offset. **Trim Size:** 8 x 10 7/8. **Key Personnel:** Fred D. Garth, Publisher; Robert D. Garth, Publisher; Christopher Grant, Editor. **Subscription Rates:** $13; $18 other countries; $22 two years; $36 other countries, two years. **Remarks:** Accepts advertising. **URL:** http://www.scubatimes.com.
Ad Rates: BW: $1,875 **Circ:** ‡46,000
4C: $2,720

6649 Voyager
University of West Florida
11000 University Pkwy. Phone: (850)474-2191
Pensacola, FL 32514-5751 Fax: (850)474-2109
Publication E-mail: vgerbus@uwf.edu; voyager@uwf.edu

Collegiate newspaper. **Founded:** 1968. **Freq:** Weekly. **Print Method:** Web offset. **Trim Size:** 10 3/8 x 12 7/8. **Cols./Page:** 4. **Col. Width:** 2 3/8 inches. **Col. Depth:** 196 agate lines. **Key Personnel:** Neil Reichmuth, Advertising Mgr., voyager@uwf_edu; Raychell Shoemoe, Business Mgr.; Terry Latham, Advisor, phone (850)474-2194. **Subscription Rates:** Free on campus; $25 by mail. **Remarks:** Accepts advertising. **URL:** http://www.uwf.edu/~voyager.
Ad Rates: BW: $384 **Circ:** Free ‡8,000
4C: $704
PCI: $8.25

6650 Cox Cable TV of Pensacola
2205 La Vista Ave. Phone: (904)477-2695
Pensacola, FL 32504 Fax: (904)479-3912

Founded: 1969. **Cities Served:** Escambia County, FL.

6651 WBQP-TV - 2
3101 North R St. Phone: (850)433-1210
Pensacola, FL 32505 Fax: (850)433-2537
E-mail: wbqp@wbqp.com

Format: Commercial TV. **Owner:** Watson Broadcasting, at above address. **Founded:** July 1992. **Operating Hours:** Continuous. **Key Personnel:** Vernon Watson, General Mgr.; Gary Montgomery, Station Mgr. **Wattage:** 31,100. **Ad Rates:** Advertising accepted; rates available upon request.

6652 WBSR-AM - 1450
Box 8057 Phone: (904)438-4982
Pensacola, FL 32505-0057 Fax: (904)433-7932
E-mail: wbsr@dotstar.net; wbsr@www.wbsr.com

Format: Adult Contemporary. **Networks:** Unistar; CNN Radio. **Founded:** 1946. **Formerly:** Frederic T.C. Brewer. **Operating Hours:** Continuous. **ADI:** Mobile, AL-Pensacola, FL. **Key Personnel:** Gene Pfalzer, Manager. **Wattage:** 1000. **URL:** http://www.wbsr.com.

6653 WCOA-AM - 1370
PO Box 12487 Phone: (904)478-6011
Pensacola, FL 32573-2487 Fax: (904)478-3971

Format: News; Talk. **Networks:** ABC. **Founded:** 1926. **Operating Hours:** Continuous; 60% network, 40% local. **ADI:** Mobile, AL-Pensacola, FL. **Key Personnel:** Darrell Tate, Contact. **Wattage:** 5000. **Ad Rates:** $26-42 for 30 seconds; $31-47 for 60 seconds.

6654 WEAR-TV - 3
4990 Mobile Hwy. Phone: (904)456-3333
Pensacola, FL 32506 Fax: (904)455-0159
E-mail: wear3@weartv.com

Format: Commercial TV. **Networks:** ABC. **Founded:** 1953. **Operating Hours:** Local programming: Channel 3 news at 5, 6, and 10. **ADI:** Mobile, AL-Pensacola, FL. **Key Personnel:** Carl Leahy, General Mgr., cleahy@wear.com; Landon Smith, Program Dir., jsmith@weartv.com. **Wattage:** 100kw visual.

6655 WJLQ-FM - 100.7
6565 N. W St. Phone: (904)478-6011
Pensacola, FL 32505 Fax: (904)478-3971

Format: Adult Contemporary; Urban Contemporary. **Founded:** 1966. **Operating Hours:** Continuous. **ADI:** Mobile, AL-Pensacola, FL. **Key Personnel:** Darrell Tate, General Mgr.; Greg Gordon, Program Dir. **Wattage:** 100,000. **Ad Rates:** $25-57 for 30 seconds; $30-63 for 60 seconds.

6656 WMEZ-FM - 94.1
Box 8057 Phone: (904)432-4775
Pensacola, FL 32505 Fax: (904)433-7932
Free: (800)471-6914

Format: Adult Contemporary; Soft Rock. **Networks:** Unistar; CNN Radio. **Owner:** Frederic T.C. Brewer, at above address. **Operating Hours:** Continuous. **Key Personnel:** Gene Pfalzer, Manager. **Wattage:** 100,000.

WRNE-AM - See Danbury, Connecticut

6657 WSRE-TV - 23
1000 College Blvd. Phone: (904)484-1200
Pensacola, FL 32504-8998 Fax: (904)484-1255

Format: Public TV. **Networks:** Public Broadcasting Service (PBS). **Founded:** 1967. **Operating Hours:** 5:45 a.m.-12:30 a.m.; 90% network, 10% local. **ADI:** Mobile, AL-Pensacola, FL. **Key Personnel:** Allan A. Pizzato, General Mgr.; Steve Agerton, Chief Engineer.

6658 WSWL-AM - 790
3801 N. Pace Blvd. Phone: (904)433-1141
PO Box 8127 Fax: (904)433-1142
Pensacola, FL 32505

Format: News. **Networks:** CNN Radio. **Formerly:** WPFA-AM. **Operating Hours:** Continuous; 100% network. **Key Personnel:** Don Schroeder, Contact. **Wattage:** 1000. **Ad Rates:** $10-35 for 30 seconds; $20-40 for 60 seconds.

6659 WTKX-FM - 101.5
111 N. Baylen St. Phone: (904)438-7543
Pensacola, FL 32501 Fax: (904)432-1466

Format: Album-Oriented Rock (AOR). **Networks:** Independent. **Owner:** Southern Broadcasting Co., at above address, FL. **Founded:** 1971. **Operating Hours:** Continuous; 100% local. **Key Personnel:** Howard Seaton, General Mgr.; Mike Strummer, Program Dir. **Wattage:** 100,000.

6660 WUWF-FM - 88.1
University of West Florida Phone: (850)474-2787
11000 University Pkwy. Fax: (850)474-3283
Pensacola, FL 32514-5750
Free: (800)239-9893
E-mail: pcrawfor@uwf.edu

Format: Classical; Jazz; Alternative/New Music/Progressive; News; Public Radio. **Networks:** National Public Radio (NPR); Public Radio International (PRI). **Owner:** University of West Florida, at above address. **Founded:** 1981. **Operating Hours:** Continuous; 30% network, 70% local. **Key Personnel:** Patrick Crawford, General Mgr., pcrawfor@uwf.edu; Rebecca Baltas, Program Dir., bbaltas@uwf.edu; Walt Gillette, Finance & Development Dir., wgillett@uwf.edu; Kassy Tyler, Contact, ktyler@uwf.edu; Susan Watson, Ed. Outreach Coord., spwatson@uwf.edu. **Local Programs:** *Interlude*, John Macdonell. **Wattage:** 100,000. **URL:** http://www.wuwf.org.

6661 WYCL-FM - 107.3
6485 Pensacola Blvd. Phone: (850)473-0400
Pensacola, FL 32505 Fax: (850)473-0907

Format: Oldies. **Owner:** Clear Channel Broadcasting, 200 Concord Plaza, Ste. 600, San Antonio, TX 78216, (210)822-2828, Fax: (210)829-8080. **Founded:** 1996. **Formerly:** WOWW-FM. **Operating Hours:** Continuous. **Key Personnel:** Jeannie Hufford, General Mgr., jhufford@gulf.net; Patty Gilroy, General Sales Mgr., pgilroy@cool107.com; John Weeks, Program Dir., kok@cool107.com; Polly Weeks, Business Mgr., pweeks@gulf.net. **Wattage:** 100,000. **Ad Rates:** Advertising accepted; rates available upon request. Combined advertising rates available with WTKX-FM. **URL:** http://www.cool107.com.

PERRY†, pop. 8,254.

N FL. Taylor Co. 52 mi. SE of Tallahassee. Manufactures lumber, forestry products, marine products, pyrotechnics, snack foods. Commercial fishing. Stock and poultry farms. Tobacco, peanuts, potatoes.

6662 Perry News-Herald
Perry Newspapers, Inc.
PO Box 888 Phone: (904)584-5513
Perry, FL 32347 Fax: (904)838-1566
Publisher E-mail: perrynews@perrygulfnet.com

Community newspaper serving Taylor County. **Founded:** 1889. **Freq:** Semiweekly (Wed. and Fri.). **Print Method:** Offset. **Cols./Page:** 6. **Col. Width:** 23 nonpareils. **Col. Depth:** 301 agate lines. **Key Personnel:** Donald D. Lincoln, Publisher; Carolyn DuBose, Advertising Mgr. **ISSN:** 0747-2358. **Subscription Rates:** $20 individuals; $32 out of area. **Remarks:** Accepts advertising.
Ad Rates: BW: $896.55 **Circ:** 9,000
PCI: $6.95

6663 Perry Taco Times
Perry Newspapers, Inc.
PO Box 888 Phone: (904)584-5513
Perry, FL 32347 Fax: (904)838-1566
Publisher E-mail: perrynews@perrygulfnet.com

Community newspaper serving Taylor County. **Founded:** 1961. **Freq:** Semiweekly. **Print Method:** Offset. **Trim Size:** 13 x 21 1/2. **Cols./Page:** 6. **Col. Width:** 2 inches. **Col. Depth:** 21 1/2 inches. **Key Personnel:** Susan H. Lincoln, Managing Editor; Donald D. Lincoln, Publisher; Carolyn DuBose, Advertising Mgr. **ISSN:** 0747-2358. **Subscription Rates:** $20 individuals; $32 out of area. **Remarks:** Color advertising not accepted.
Ad Rates: BW: $580.50 **Circ:** ‡5,000
PCI: $4.75

6664 WNFK-FM - 105.5
PO Box 779 Phone: (904)584-2972
Perry, FL 32347 Fax: (904)584-4616

Format: Country. **Simulcasts:** WPRY-AM. **Networks:** NBC; Florida Radio. **Owner:** RAHU Broadcasting, Inc., 1 Broadcast Pl., Hwy. 27 E., Perry, FL 32347. **Founded:** 1990. **Operating Hours:** 6 a.m.-midnight. **Key Personnel:** Don W. Hughes, Contact; Bill Stephens, Sales Mgr.; Linda Thurman, Contact; Amy Hughes, Program Mgr. **Wattage:** 3000. **Ad Rates:** $3-6 for 15 seconds; $4-7 for 30 seconds; $5-9 for 60 seconds.

6665 WPRY-AM - 1400
PO Box 779 Phone: (904)584-2972
Perry, FL 32347 Fax: (904)584-4616

Format: Country. **Simulcasts:** WNFK-FM. **Networks:** NBC; Florida Radio. **Owner:** RAHU Broadcasting, Inc., 1 Broadcast Pl., Hwy. 27 E., Perry, FL 32347. **Founded:** 1953. **Operating Hours:** 6 a.m.-midnight. **Key Personnel:** Don W. Hughes, Contact; Bill Stephens, Sales Mgr.; Linda Thurman, Contact; Amy Hughes, Program Mgr. **Wattage:** 1000. **Ad Rates:** $2-4 for 15 seconds; $2.50-5 for 30 seconds; $3-6 for 60 seconds.

PINE ISLAND

Island off W coast of Lee Co. Orange groves, resort.

6666 The Pine Island Eagle
Breeze Publishing Co.
2510 Del Prado Phone: (941)574-1110
Cape Coral, FL 33904 Fax: (941)574-5693

Community newspaper. **Founded:** Apr. 1976. **Freq:** Weekly.

Print Method: Offset. **Cols./Page:** 6. **Col. Depth:** 16 inches. **Key Personnel:** Maureen Milne Donald, Editor; Vicky L. Estes, Advertising Representative. **Subscription Rates:** Free; $30 by mail. **URL:** http://www.flguide.com.
Ad Rates: BW: $229 **Circ:** Free ‡8,500
4C: $429
PCI: $5.15

PINELLAS PARK, pop. 32,811.

WC FL. Pinellas Co. 10 mi. NW of Saint Petersburg. Manufactures air conditioners, plastics, and medical equipment.

6667 Polish Heritage
American Council For Polish Culture
6507 107th Terr. N Phone: (727)541-7875
Pinellas Park, FL 33782-2432 Fax: (727)541-7875

Magazine focusing on Polish heritage and culture. **Founded:** 1948. **Freq:** Quarterly. **Print Method:** Offset. **Trim Size:** 8 1/2 x 11. **Cols./Page:** 3. **Col. Width:** 34 nonpareils. **Col. Depth:** 150 agate lines. **Key Personnel:** Wallace M. West, Editor. **Subscription Rates:** $10 individuals. **Remarks:** Accepts advertising.
Ad Rates: BW: $375 **Circ:** ‡4,500
PCI: $15

PLANT CITY, pop. 19,056.

WC FL. Hillsborough Co. 22 mi. E. of Tampa. Manufactures mobile homes, fertilizer, crates, boxes, and concrete blocks. Agriculture. Cattle, strawberries, citrus fruits, vegetables.

6668 The Courier
Sunbelt Newspapers, Inc.
101 N. Wheeler St. Phone: (813)752-3113
Plant City, FL 33566 Fax: (813)754-3725

Community newspaper. **Founded:** 1884. **Freq:** Weekly (Thurs.). **Print Method:** Offset. **Cols./Page:** 5. **Col. Width:** 20 nonpareils. **Col. Depth:** 238 agate lines. **Key Personnel:** Carla Rockwell, General Mgr. **Subscription Rates:** $17. $.25 single issue. **Remarks:** Accepts advertising.
Ad Rates: BW: $807 **Circ:** (Not Reported)
4C: $947
PCI: $10.76

6669 Plant City Shopper
Sunbelt Newspapers, Inc.
101 N. Wheeler St. Phone: (813)752-3113
Plant City, FL 33566 Fax: (813)754-3725

Shopper. **Founded:** 1946. **Freq:** Weekly (Wed.). **Print Method:** Offset. **Cols./Page:** 5. **Col. Width:** 20 nonpareils. **Col. Depth:** 238 agate lines. **Key Personnel:** Carla Rockwell, General Mgr.; Joyce Jordan, Adv. Mgr. **Subscription Rates:** Free. **Remarks:** Accepts advertising.
Ad Rates: BW: $1,079.25 **Circ:** Free 26,800
4C: $1,219.25
PCI: $14.39

PLANTATION

6670 Loafer's Choice
1400-G NW 65th Ave. Phone: (954)791-3224
PO Box 16928 Fax: (954)581-3463
Plantation, FL 33318
Publisher E-mail: pennysvr@bellsouth.net

Subtitle: West Broward's Free Weekly Newspaper for Everyone. **Founded:** 1986. **Freq:** Weekly (Fri.). **Print Method:** Offset. **Trim Size:** 10 1/4 x 12 7/8. **Cols./Page:** 4. **Col. Width:** 2 5/16 inches. **Col. Depth:** 12 inches. **Key Personnel:** Bernie Grossman, Publisher; Ruth Rice, Operations Mgr., phone (954)791-3224, fax (954)581-3463. **Subscription Rates:** Free.
Ad Rates: BW: $550 **Circ:** Non-paid 19,000

6671 Pennysaver
1400-G NW 65th Ave. Phone: (954)792-1151
PO Box 16928 Fax: (954)581-3463
Plantation, FL 33318
Publication E-mail: pennysvr@bellsouth.net

Shopper. **Founded:** 1977. **Freq:** Biweekly Monday's. **Print Method:** Offset. **Trim Size:** 10 1/2 x 12 1/2 in. **Cols./Page:** 3. **Col. Width:** 3 inches. **Col. Depth:** 12 1/2 inches. **Key Personnel:** Bernie Grossman, Publisher, phone (954)792-1159; Ruth Rice, Operations Mgr., phone (954)792-1147. **Subscription Rates:** Free.
Ad Rates: BW: $400 **Circ:** Free 62,500

POMPANO BEACH, pop. 52,618.

S FL. Broward Co. On Atlantic Ocean, 9 mi. N. of Fort Lauderdale. Resort area. Light industry and manufacturing. Manufactures boats, computer-related products, concrete products, lighting fixtures, venetian blinds, metal awnings. Agriculture. Citrus fruits, vegetables.

6672 Florida Fireman
Florida State Firemen's Association, Inc.
4921 NW 76th Pl. Phone: (954)426-1068
Pompano Beach, FL 33073 Fax: (954)426-5162
Publisher E-mail: fsfal@juno.com

Magazine for fire fighters. **Founded:** 1933. **Freq:** Monthly. **Print Method:** Letterpress and offset. **Cols./Page:** 3. **Col. Width:** 28 nonpareils. **Col. Depth:** 140 agate lines. **Key Personnel:** Olga Kwielien, Editor, oak264@aol.com. **Subscription Rates:** $25 individuals. **Remarks:** Accepts advertising.
Ad Rates: BW: $245 **Circ:** ‡5,900

6673 Paul's Record Magazine
713 Gardens Dr., Apt. 203
Pompano Beach, FL 33069-0951

Consumer magazine covering rock and rhythm & blues music, artists, and record labels. **Founded:** July 1975. **Freq:** Irregular. **Key Personnel:** Paul Bezanker, Editor and Publisher, bezanker@aol.com. **ISSN:** 0360-2109. **Subscription Rates:** $10 single issue. **Remarks:** Advertising not accepted.
Circ: (Not Reported)

6674 The Pompano Ledger
The Pompano Ledger Publishing Co.
2500 S.E. 5th Court Phone: (954)532-2000
Pompano Beach, FL 33062
Publication E-mail: 72747.502@compuserve.com
Publisher E-mail: the_ ledger@compuserve

Community newspaper. **Founded:** 1980. **Freq:** Weekly (Thurs.). **Print Method:** Web offset. **Trim Size:** 13 x 21 1/2. **Cols./Page:** 6. **Col. Width:** 20 nonpareils. **Col. Depth:** 301 agate lines. **Key Personnel:** Edward J. Foley III, Editor; Karen Foley, Publisher. **USPS:** 011-588. **Subscription Rates:** $26.50 individuals; $13.78 local. **Remarks:** Accepts advertising. **URL:** http://www.ourworld.compuserve.com/homepages/the_ ledger.
Ad Rates: GLR: $.93 **Circ:** Paid ‡27,500
BW: $1,670.55 Free ‡500
4C: $1,940.55
SAU: $17.95

6675 Media One
141 NW 16th St. Phone: (305)946-7011
Box 1689 Fax: (305)782-5781
Pompano Beach, FL 33061

Founded: 1975. **Formerly:** Continental Cablevision. **Cities Served:** Broward County, FL: subscribing households 180,000.

PONTE VEDRA BEACH

6676 Actuarial Digest
PO Box 1127 Phone: (904)273-1245
Ponte Vedra Beach, FL 32004
Trade magazine for actuarial professionals. **Founded:** Feb. 1982. **Freq:** Bimonthly. **Print Method:** Web offset. **Trim Size:** 8 1/2 x 11. **Key Personnel:** Eugene F. Hubbard, Editor. **Subscription Rates:** $24 individuals U.S. only. **Remarks:** Accepts advertising.
Ad Rates: BW: $1,995 **Circ:** Controlled 16,100
4C: $2,695

6677 International Journal of Logistics Management
International Logistics Research Inc.
PO Box 2166 Phone: (904)880-8653
Ponte Vedra Beach, FL 32004-2166 Fax: (904)880-8654
Publication E-mail: mkuhn@gw.unf.edu

Mathematics journal. **Key Personnel:** Dr. Douglas M. Lambert, Editor; Martin Christopher, Editor. **ISSN:** 0957-4093. **Subscription Rates:** $85 individuals.

PORT CHARLOTTE

Charlotte Co. (SW). 2 m NW of Punta Gorda.

6678 The Charlotte Sun Herald
Sun Coast Media Group, Inc.
23170 Harborview Rd.
Port Charlotte, FL 33980

General newspaper. **Freq:** Mon.-Sun. (morn.). **Print Method:** Offset. **Trim Size:** 22 x 27 1/2. **Cols./Page:** 6. **Col. Width:** 2 1/16 inches. **Col. Depth:** 290 1/2 agate lines. **Key Personnel:** Jim Gouvellis, Editor; Derek Dunn-Rankin, Publisher. **Subscription Rates:** $48. **Remarks:** Accepts advertising.
Ad Rates: SAU: $9.60 **Circ:** Mon.-Sat. ★**30,234**
Sun. ★**32,895**

6679 WVIJ-FM - 91.7
3279 Sherwood Rd. Phone: (813)624-5000
Port Charlotte, FL 33980 Fax: (813)625-5364

Format: News; Gospel; Southern Gospel; Eclectic. **Networks:** USA Radio. **Owner:** Port Charlotte Educational Broadcasting Foundation Inc., at above address. **Founded:** 1987. **Operating Hours:** Continuous; 25% network, 75% local. **Key Personnel:** Dan Kolenda, Jr., Contact; John Kolenda, Program Dir.; James Kolenda, Production Dir. **Wattage:** 380. **Ad Rates:** Noncommercial.

PORT ORANGE, pop. 18,756.

E FL. Volusia Co. 10 mi. S. of Daytona Beach.

6680 WMFJ-AM - 1450
4295 Ridgewood Ave. Phone: (904)672-1450
Port Orange, FL 32127

Format: Religious. **Networks:** SkyLight Satellite; USA Radio. **Owner:** Cornerstone Broadcast Corp., at above address, (904)756-9000. **Founded:** 1935. **Operating Hours:** Continuous; 60% network, 40% local. **Key Personnel:** William A. Leisner, Contact, phone (904)756-9000. **Wattage:** 1000. **Ad Rates:** $5-12 for 30 seconds; $7-15 for 60 seconds.

PORT RICHEY

Pasco Co. (WC). 2 m W of Land O'Lakes.

6681 WLPJ-FM - 91.5
8410 U.S. 19, Ste. 109 Phone: (813)848-9150
Port Richey, FL 34668 Fax: (813)848-1233
Free: (800)456-8910
E-mail: joy@joyfm.com

Format: Contemporary Christian. **Owner:** Radio Training Network, 5015 S. Florida Ave., Ste. 104, Lakeland, FL 33813, (941)644-3464, Fax: (941)646-5326. **Founded:** 1985. **Operating Hours:** Continuous. **ADI:** Tampa-St. Petersburg (Lakeland, Sarasota), FL. **Key Personnel:** Rob Dempsey, Station Mgr. **Wattage:** 2750. **Ad Rates:** Noncommercial.

6682 WLVU-FM - 106.3
6214 Springer Dr. Phone: (813)845-1063
Port Richey, FL 34668-5339

Format: Middle-of-the-Road (MOR). **Networks:** AP. **Founded:** 1979. **Operating Hours:** Continuous. **ADI:** Tampa-St. Petersburg (Lakeland, Sarasota), FL. **Key Personnel:** Frank Ferreri, General Mgr. **Wattage:** 3000.

6683 WYFE-FM - 88.9
16310-1 U.S. Hwy. 19 Phone: (727)862-9323
Port Richey, FL 34667 Fax: (727)862-9323
Free: (800)888-7077
E-mail: wyfefm@aol.com

Format: Religious. **Networks:** Bible Broadcasting. **Founded:** 1988. **Formerly:** WFCE-FM (1988). **Operating Hours:** Continuous; 93% network, 7% local. **Key Personnel:** Dr. Jack Long, General Mgr. **Wattage:** 60,000. **Ad Rates:** Noncommercial. **URL:** http://www.amen.net/bbn.

PORT ST. JOE

6684 The Star
Box 308 Phone: (904)227-1278
Port St. Joe, FL 32456 Fax: (904)227-7212

Newspaper. **Founded:** 1937. **Freq:** Weekly (Thurs.). **Print Method:** Offset. **Trim Size:** 6 x 21. **Cols./Page:** 6. **Col. Width:** 21 nonpareils. **Col. Depth:** 308 agate lines. **Key Personnel:** Wesley R. Ramsey, Editor and Publisher. **Subscription Rates:** $20 individuals. **Remarks:** Accepts advertising.
Ad Rates: PCI: $5 **Circ:** ‡4,000

PORT ST. LUCIE

6685 WPSL-AM - 1590
8245 Business Park Dr. Phone: (561)340-1590
Port St. Lucie, FL 34952-7950 Fax: (561)340-3245
Free: (888)792-1590
E-mail: wpsl@gate.net

Format: Talk. **Networks:** CBS; ABC; ESPN Radio. **Founded:** 1985. **Operating Hours:** Continuous. **ADI:** West Palm Beach-Ft. Pierce-Vero Beach, FL. **Key Personnel:** Carol Wyatt, President/CEO/General Sales Manager; Greg Wyatt, V.P./Gen. Mgr.; Clif Desmond, News Dir. **Local Programs:**

Computer Talk, Tony Zanini; *Internet Today*, Mark Gibbs; *Swap Shop*, Clif Desmond. **Wattage:** 5000. **Ad Rates:** $22-26 for 30 seconds; $28-32 for 60 seconds. **URL:** http://www.wpsl.com.

6686 WQOL-FM - 103.7
PO Box 0093 Phone: (561)335-9300
Port St. Lucie, FL 34985 Fax: (561)335-3291
Free: (800)486-0103

Format: Adult Contemporary. **Networks:** Independent. **Owner:** Wayne Dillon, at above address. **Founded:** 1986. **Operating Hours:** Continuous; 100% local. **ADI:** West Palm Beach-Ft. Pierce-Vero Beach, FL. **Key Personnel:** Bill West, Program Dir.; Judy Davis, General Sales Mgr.; Sally Dillon, Promotions Dir. **Wattage:** 50,000. **Ad Rates:** $22-40 for 30 seconds; $26-47 for 60 seconds.

6687 WZZR-FM - 92.7
PO Box 0093 Phone: (407)335-9300
Port St. Lucie, FL 34985 Fax: (407)335-3291

Format: Album-Oriented Rock (AOR). **Formerly:** WRIT-FM (1987). **Operating Hours:** Continuous; 5% network, 95% local. **Key Personnel:** Charlie DiToro, General Mgr.; Rich Dickerson, Program Dir.; Barbara Marshall, Business Mgr. **Wattage:** 50,000.

PUNTA GORDA†, pop. 10,000.

SW FL. Charlotte Co. On Charlotte Harbor Bay, 23 mi. NW of Fort Myers. Retirement Area. Yachting and fishing resort. Agriculture.

6688 Charlotte Shopping Guide
Cape Coral Daily Breeze
128 W. Charlotte Ave. Phone: (941)639-1136
Punta Gorda, FL 33950 Fax: (941)639-4832

Shopper. **Founded:** Feb. 26, 1959. **Freq:** Weekly (Wed.). **Print Method:** Offset. **Trim Size:** 10 5/8 x 17. **Cols./Page:** 6. **Col. Width:** 16 agate lines. **Col. Depth:** 210 agate lines. **Key Personnel:** Larry Mc Donald, Advertising Mgr. **Remarks:** Accepts advertising.
Ad Rates: BW: $729.60 **Circ:** Free ‡38,000
4C: $879.60
PCI: $9.55

6689 WCCF-AM - 1580
4810 Deltona Dr. Phone: (813)639-1188
Punta Gorda, FL 33950 Fax: (813)639-6742
Free: (800)749-9290

Format: Talk. **Networks:** ABC. **Owner:** InterMart Broadcasting Southwest Florida, Inc, at above address. **Founded:** 1961. **Operating Hours:** Continuous; 75% network, 25% local. **Key Personnel:** Michael Moody, General Mgr.; David Ayres, General Sales Mgr. **Wattage:** 1,250. **Ad Rates:** $25.00 for 60 seconds.

6690 WEEJ-FM - 100.1
3151 Cooper St., No. 56 Phone: (941)639-1112
Punta Gorda, FL 33950 Fax: (941)637-6187

Format: Oldies. **Networks:** CNN Radio; Unistar. **Founded:** 1976. **Operating Hours:** Continuous. **Key Personnel:** Hal Kneller, General Mgr.; Steve Johnson, General Sales Mgr. **Wattage:** 100,000. **Ad Rates:** $26 for 60 seconds.

6691 WIKX-FM - 92.9
4810 Deltona Dr. Phone: (813)639-1188
Punta Gorda, FL 33950 Fax: (813)639-6742
Free: (800)749-9290

Format: Country. **Simulcasts:** WKZY-FM. **Networks:** ABC. **Owner:** Intermart Broadcasting of Southwest Florida, Inc., 4810 Deltona Dr., Punta Gorda, FL 33950, (941)639-1188, Fax: (941)639-6742, Free: (800)749-9290. **Founded:** 1982. **Formerly:** WQLM-FM. **Operating Hours:** Continuous; 5% network, 95% local. **ADI:** Fort Myers-Naples, FL. **Key Personnel:** Michael Moody, General Mgr.; David Ayres, General Sales Mgr. **Wattage:** 50,000. **Ad Rates:** $45.00 per unit.

6692 WKII-AM - 1070
3151 Cooper St., Ste. 56 Phone: (941)639-1112
Punta Gorda, FL 33950 Fax: (941)637-6187

Format: Middle-of-the-Road (MOR). **Networks:** CNN Radio. **Founded:** 1986. **Operating Hours:** Continuous; 5% network, 95% local. **ADI:** Fort Myers-Naples, FL. **Key Personnel:** Harold M. Kneller, Jr., General Mgr.; Steve Johnson, General Sales Mgr.; Pat Wasson, News Dir. **Wattage:** 5000. **Ad Rates:** $11-40 per unit.

QUINCY†, pop. 8,591.

NW FL. Gadsden Co. 26 mi. W. of Tallahassee. SManufactures wire, lumber, furniture, tobacco. Bottling works. Diversified agriculture.

6693 Gadsden County Times
PO Box 790 Phone: (904)627-7649
Quincy, FL 32353 Fax: (904)627-7191

Community newspaper. **Founded:** 1901. **Freq:** Weekly (Thurs.). **Print Method:** Offset. **Cols./Page:** 6. **Col. Width:** 26 nonpareils. **Col. Depth:** 285 agate lines. **Key Personnel:** Alice DuPont, Editor; Michael O'Halloran, Publisher; Bev Kirk, Advertising Mgr. **Subscription Rates:** $12 individuals. **Remarks:** Accepts advertising.
Ad Rates: GLR: $.42 **Circ:** Paid ⊕4,345
BW: $704.34 Free ⊕759
4C: $929.34
PCI: $5.74

WGWD-FM - See Gretna

RIVIERA BEACH

Palm Beach Co. (SE). 4 m N of Palm Beach.

6694 Adelphia Cable
2129 Congress Phone: (561)863-5701
Riviera Beach, FL 33404 Fax: (561)845-7709

Founded: 1979. **Formerly:** National Cable. **Key Personnel:** Geoffrey Gil, Contact; Bob Altman, Contact; Phil Lynch, Contact. **Cities Served:** subscribing households 48,500; 45 channels; 2 community access channels.

Media Partners - See Palm Beach Gardens

ROCKLEDGE

6695 WRFB-AM - 860
PO Box 561270 Phone: (407)631-6827
Rockledge, FL 32956 Fax: (407)631-6866

Format: Middle-of-the-Road (MOR); Music of Your Life. **Owner:** Breunnd Broadcasting, Inc., at above address. **Founded:** 1952. **Formerly:** WWKO-AM (1994). **Operating Hours:** Continuous. **Wattage:** 1000 day; 121 night.

RUSKIN

6696 Shopper Observer News
PO Box 7
Ruskin, FL 33570
Publication E-mail: sccobserver@aol.com

Newspaper. **Founded:** 1958. **Freq:** Weekly (Wed.). **Print Method:** Offset. **Cols./Page:** 5. **Col. Width:** 1 7/8 inches. **Col. Depth:** 14.5 inches. **Key Personnel:** Brenda Knowles, Editor and Publisher. **Subscription Rates:** $18 individuals. **Remarks:** Accepts advertising. **Online:** America Online.
Ad Rates: BW: $425 **Circ:** Free 18,200
4C: $500
PCI: $10.20

ST. AUGUSTINE

6697 The National Culinary Review
American Culinary Federation, Inc.
10 San Bartola Dr. Phone: (904)824-4468
St. Augustine, FL 32085 Fax: (904)825-4758
Free: (800)624-9458
Publisher E-mail: acf@aug.com

Trade magazine covering food and cooking. **Subtitle:** The Authority on Cooking in America. **Founded:** 1929. **Freq:** Monthly. **Key Personnel:** Wendy Philcox, Editor. **ISSN:** 0747-7716. **Subscription Rates:** $50 individuals; $3 single issue. **Remarks:** Accepts advertising.
Ad Rates: BW: $2,596 **Circ:** (Not Reported)
4C: $3,368

6698 The St. Augustine Record
Morris Communications Corp.
PO Box 1630 Phone: (904)829-6562
St. Augustine, FL 32085-1630 Fax: (904)829-6664
Publisher E-mail: 73711.1232@compuserve.com

General newspaper. **Founded:** 1894. **Freq:** Daily (eve.), Sat. and Sun. (morn.). **Print Method:** Offset. **Cols./Page:** 6. **Col. Width:** 12.5 picas. **Col. Depth:** 21 inches. **Key Personnel:** Ron Hughes, Publisher, phone (904)829-6562, fax (904)829-6664; Jim Sutton, Editor; Grover Ford, Advertising Dir.; Steve Carswell, Production Dir.; Lee Hutchins, Circulation Director; Zoe Ann Moss, Division Controller; Gail Cumiskey, Comp. Sup.; John Studwell, Photo Chief. **Subscription Rates:** $95.40 individuals. **Remarks:** Accepts advertising.
Ad Rates: GLR: $2.85 **Circ:** Mon.-Fri. ★14,679
BW: $1,549.80 Sat. ★17,151
4C: $1,809.80 Sun. ★16,101
SAU: $12.30

6699 St. John's Pennysaver
Volusia Pennysaver, Inc.
1740 A1A South Phone: (904)471-8488
PO Box 500 Fax: (904)471-4519
St. Augustine, FL 32085
Publication E-mail: sjpenny@aol.com

Shopper. **Founded:** 1987. **Freq:** Weekly (Thurs.). **Print Method:** Photo offset. **Trim Size:** 11 x 14. **Cols./Page:** 6. **Col. Width:** 1 1/2 inches. **Col. Depth:** 13 inches. **Key Personnel:** Paula Freeman, General Mgr., phone (904)471-8507. **Remarks:** Accepts advertising.
Ad Rates: BW: $705.90 **Circ:** Free **25,222**
4C: $885.90
PCI: $9.05

6700 WFOY-AM - 1240
1 Radio Rd. Phone: (904)829-3416
St. Augustine, FL 32084 Fax: (904)829-8051
E-mail: wfoy@aug.com

Format: Talk; News. **Networks:** CBS; Florida Radio; Mutual Broadcasting System; Unistar; Westwood One Radio; EFM. **Owner:** Douglas D. Shull, at above address. **Founded:** 1936. **Operating Hours:** Continuous. **Key Personnel:** Douglas D. Shull, Contact; Laurie Jones, Contact; Al Brennan, News Dir.; David Shull, Program Dir. **Local Programs:** *On Time St. Augustine*, Laurie Jones. **Wattage:** 1000. **Ad Rates:** $14-18 for 60 seconds.

6701 WSOS-FM - 94.1
2715 Stratton Blvd. Phone: (904)824-0833
St. Augustine, FL 32095 Fax: (904)825-0105
Free: (877)829-9767

Format: Adult Contemporary. **Networks:** Westwood One Radio. **Owner:** WSOS-FM, Inc., at above address. **Founded:** 1982. **Formerly:** WMKM-FM. **Operating Hours:** Continuous. **ADI:** Jacksonville (Brunswick), FL. **Key Personnel:** Anita Roberts, Traffic Mgr.; Joe Roberts, Program Dir.; Alan Alsobrook, Chief Engineer; Joe Roberts, Sales Mgr. **Wattage:** 25,000. **Ad Rates:** $20 for 30 seconds; $25 for 60 seconds.

ST. PETERSBURG

6702 Copyright Law Reports
CCH Inc.
10100 Ninth St. N. Phone: (813)576-3189
St. Petersburg, FL 33716 Fax: (813)577-0301
Free: (800)TELL-CCH

Copyright law publication. **Founded:** 1978. **Freq:** Monthly. **Print Method:** Offset. Uses mats. **Trim Size:** 6 x 9. **Cols./Page:** 2. **Col. Width:** 40 nonpareils. **Col. Depth:** 133 agate lines. **Key Personnel:** Janette Spencer-Davis, Editor; Kathleen Larrison, Managing Editor. **USPS:** 006-843. **Subscription Rates:** $500 individuals yearly. **Remarks:** Advertising not accepted.
Circ: ‡950

6703 The duPont Registry: A Buyer's Gallery of Fine Automobiles
duPont Publishing, Inc.
3051 Tech Dr. Phone: (727)573-9339
St. Petersburg, FL 33716 Fax: (727)572-5523
Free: (800)233-1731
Publication E-mail: dupreg@aol.com; mobordo@earthlink.net

Glossy, full-color magazine featuring the finest classic, luxury, and exotic cars in the world for sale. **Founded:** Apr. 1985. **Freq:** Monthly. **Print Method:** Offset. **Trim Size:** 8 x 10 7/8. **Key Personnel:** Ron Barreto, General Mgr., ron@dupontregistry.com; Thomas L. duPont, Publisher, phone (727)572-4946, tldupont@dupontregistry.com; Steven B. Chapman, President, steve@dupontregistry.com; Jerry A. Britt, COO, phone (727)561-0505, jerry@dupontregistry.com; John Chapman, National Sales Mgr., johnc@dupontregistsry.com; Chris Castelitz, Public Relations Dir., chriscc@dupontregistsry.com. **ISSN:** 0890-362X. **Subscription Rates:** $49.95 individuals; $5.95 single issue; $6.95 single issue other countries. **Remarks:** Accepts advertising. **Available Online. URL:** www.dupontregistsry.com.
Ad Rates: 4C: $7,245 **Circ:** Paid ★90,048

6704 The duPont Registry: A Buyer's Gallery of Fine Boats
duPont Publishing, Inc.
3051 Tech Dr. Phone: (727)573-9339
St. Petersburg, FL 33716 Fax: (727)572-5523
Free: (800)233-1731
Publication E-mail: mobordo@eartlink.net

Magazine featuring worldwide luxury sail and sport boats for sale. **Founded:** Feb. 1997. **Freq:** Bimonthly. **Print Method:** Web offset. **Trim Size:** 8 x 10 7/8. **Cols./Page:** 2. **Key Personnel:** Tim Breaux, Editor-in-Chief, fax (813)571-1812, tim@dupontregistry.com. **Subscription Rates:** Free to qualified subscribers; $29.95 individuals; $44.95 Canada; $69.95 other countries; $4.95 single issue. **Remarks:** Accepts advertising. **URL:** http://www.dupontregistry.com.
Ad Rates: BW: $2,700 **Circ:** Paid 16,000
Controlled 38,000

6705 The duPont Registry: A Buyer's Gallery of Fine Homes
duPont Publishing, Inc.
3051 Tech Dr. Phone: (727)573-9339
St. Petersburg, FL 33716 Fax: (727)572-5523
Free: (800)233-1731

Magazine featuring worldwide luxury homes for sale. **Founded:** Aug. 1995. **Freq:** Bimonthly. **Print Method:** Web offset. **Trim Size:** 8 x 10 7/8. **Cols./Page:** 2. **Key Personnel:** Eric Kennedy, Editor-in-Chief; Jerry Britt, Circulation Mgr. **Subscription Rates:** Free to qualified subscribers; $29.95 individuals; $44.95 Canada; $69.95 other countries; $4.95 single issue. **Remarks:** Accepts advertising.
Ad Rates: 4C: $4,320 **Circ:** Paid 31,000
Controlled 26,000

6706 Florida Marine Research Institute Technical Reports
Florida Marine Research Institute
100 8th Ave. SE Phone: (727)896-8626
St. Petersburg, FL 33701-5095 Fax: (727)823-0166

Scientific journal covering marine resource topics, especially marine resource management. **Founded:** 1995. **Freq:** Irregular. **Print Method:** Sheetfed offset. **Trim Size:** 8 1/2 x 11. **Cols./Page:** 2. **Col. Width:** 20 picas. **Col. Depth:** 54 picas. **Key Personnel:** James F. Quinn, Scientific Editor; Llyn French, Production, french_l@epic7.dep.state.fl.us; Jan Boyett, Circulation Mgr., boyett_j@epic7.dep.state.fl.us. **ISSN:** 1092-194X. **Subscription Rates:** Free to qualified subscribers. **Remarks:** Advertising not accepted.
Circ: Non-paid 600

6707 Florida Marine Research Publications
Florida Marine Research Institute
100 8th Ave. SE Phone: (727)896-8626
St. Petersburg, FL 33701-5095 Fax: (727)823-0166

Scientific journal covering marine resource topics. **Founded:** Dec. 1973. **Freq:** Irregular. **Print Method:** Sheetfed offset. **Trim Size:** 8 1/2 x 11. **Cols./Page:** 2. **Col. Width:** 20 picas. **Col. Depth:** 54 picas. **Key Personnel:** James F. Quinn, Jr., Scientific Editor; Llyn French, Production, french_l@epic7.dep.state.fl.us; Jan Boyett, Circulation Mgr., boyett_j@epic7.dep.state.fl.us. **ISSN:** 0095-0157. **Subscription Rates:** Free to qualified subscribers. **Remarks:** Advertising not accepted.
Circ: Non-paid 600

6708 Florida Trend
Trend Book Division
PO Box 611 Phone: (727)821-5800
St. Petersburg, FL 33731 Fax: (727)822-5083
Publisher E-mail: lkeever@flrend.com

Business. **Subtitle:** The Magazine of Florida Business. **Founded:** 1958. **Freq:** Monthly. **Print Method:** Offset. **Trim Size:** 8 1/4 x 10 7/8. **Cols./Page:** 3. **Col. Width:** 13.5 picas. **Col. Depth:** 60 agate lines. **Key Personnel:** Mark Howard, Editor, mhoward@fltrend.com; Lynda Keever, Publisher, lkeever@fltrend.com. **ISSN:** 0015-4326. **Subscription Rates:** $29.95 individuals; $2.95 single issue. **Remarks:** Accepts advertising. **Available Online**. **URL:** http://www.floridatrend.com.
Ad Rates: BW: $7,225 **Circ:** Paid 50,000
4C: $9,390 Non-paid 10,371

6709 Florida Underwriter
EDT Phone: (727)576-1101
9887 4th St. N. Fax: (727)577-4002
Ste. 230
St. Petersburg, FL 33702
Magazine for insurance agents and executives in Florida. **Founded:** May 1984. **Freq:** Monthly. **Print Method:** Offset. **Trim Size:** 8 1/2 x 11. **Cols./Page:** 3. **Col. Width:** 2 1/4 inches. **Col. Depth:** 9 inches. **Key Personnel:** James E. Seymour, Editor; Joseph Maty, Advertising Mgr., phone (727)578-1515, fax (727)578-1516. **ISSN:** 0743-3441. **Subscription Rates:** $16.50 individuals; $2 single issue. **Remarks:** Accepts advertising.
Ad Rates: BW: $1,451 **Circ:** Paid ★**1,336**
4C: $2,281 Non-paid ★**8,024**

6710 Labor Law Journal
CCH Inc.
10100 ML King St. Phone: (813)576-3189
St. Petersburg, FL 33716 Fax: (813)577-0301

Business journal. **Founded:** 1949. **Freq:** Monthly. **Print Method:** Offset. **Trim Size:** 6 x 9. **Cols./Page:** 1. **Col. Width:** 30 picas. **Key Personnel:** Ronald Miller, Managing Editor. **USPS:** 300-460. **Subscription Rates:** $164 individuals; $14 single issue. **Remarks:** Advertising not accepted.
Circ: ‡2,075

6711 Maddux Report
Maddux Publishing, Inc.
PO Box 202 Phone: (813)823-4394
St. Petersburg, FL 33731 Fax: (813)821-1645
Free: (800)226-4394
Publisher E-mail: maddux@packet.net

Magazine on business and real estate activities in the seven-county Tampa Bay region. **Subtitle:** The Business of Tampa Bay. **Founded:** Feb. 1984. **Freq:** Monthly. **Print Method:** Web offset. **Trim Size:** 8 1/8 x 10 7/8. **Cols./Page:** 3. **Col. Width:** 2.25 picas. **Col. Depth:** 10 inches. **Key Personnel:** Carlen Maddux, Editor and Publisher, maddux@packet.net. **Subscription Rates:** Free to qualified subscribers; $45 institutions; $4.95 single issue. **Remarks:** Accepts advertising.
Ad Rates: BW: $2,395 **Circ:** Paid 1,040
4C: $2,990 Controlled 13,180

6712 Memoirs of the Hourglass Cruises
Florida Marine Research Institute
100 8th Ave. SE Phone: (727)896-8626
St. Petersburg, FL 33701-5095 Fax: (727)823-0166

Scientific journal covering marine resource and marine research topics. **Founded:** Mar. 1969. **Freq:** Irregular. **Print Method:** Sheetfed offset. **Trim Size:** 8 1/4 x 10 3/4. **Cols./Page:** 1. **Col. Width:** 39 picas. **Col. Depth:** 54 picas. **Key Personnel:** James F. Quinn, Scientific Editor; Llyn French, Production, french_l@epic7.dep.state.fl.us; Jan Boyett, Circulation Mgr., boyett_j@epic7.dep.state.fl.us. **ISSN:** 0085-0683. **Subscription Rates:** Free to qualified subscribers. **Remarks:** Advertising not accepted.
Circ: Non-paid 600

6713 Pinellas News
Potter Media Inc.
538 4th St. N Phone: (813)894-2411
St. Petersburg, FL 33701 Fax: (813)894-2522
Publication E-mail: pinellas_news@msn.com; pinellas-news@msn.com

Community newspaper serving Pinellas County with community news and legal advertising. **Founded:** Feb. 3, 1963. **Freq:** Weekly (Fri.). **Print Method:** Offset. **Cols./Page:** 6. **Col. Width:** 2 1/16 inches. **Key Personnel:** Robert M. Potter, Editor and Publisher. **ISSN:** 1072-3307. **Subscription Rates:** $20 by mail. **Remarks:** Accepts advertising. **Formerly**: Pinellas Park News.
Ad Rates: GLR: $10 **Circ:** (Not Reported)
BW: $882

6714 St. Petersburg Times
Times Publishing Co.
490 1st Ave. S. Phone: (727)893-8111
PO Box 1121 Fax: (727)893-8675
St. Petersburg, FL 33701
Free: (800)333-7505

General newspaper. **Founded:** 1884. **Freq:** Daily (morn.). **Print Method:** Offset. **Trim Size:** 13 x 21 1/2. **Cols./Page:** 6. **Col. Width:** 2 1/16 inches. **Col. Depth:** 21 1/2 inches. **Key Personnel:** Andy Barnes, Editor, phone (727)893-8625; Paul Tash, Exec. Editor, phone (727)893-8887; Tom Rawlins, Senior Editor, phone (727)893-8420; Chris Lavin, World Editor, phone (727)893-8739; Ron Dupont, Web Editor/Asst. Metro Editor, phone (727)893-8628; Phil Gailey, Editor, phone (727)893-8268; Margo Hammond, Editor, phone (727)893-8768; Jack Sheppard, AME/Sports, phone (727)893-8495; Nancy Waclawek, AME/Features, phone (727)893-8780; Rob Hooker, Metro Editor/Business Editor, phone (727)893-8780; Sonya Doctorian, AME/Photo, phone (727)893-8231; Susan Taylor Martin, Sr. Correspondent, phone (727)893-8642; Neil Brown, Managing Editor, phone (727)893-8441; Neville Green, Managing Editor/Tampa, phone (813)226-3370; Joe Childs, Managing Editor/Clearwater, phone (727)445-4186. **USPS:** 477-200. **Subscription Rates:** $102.85 individuals. **Remarks:** Accepts advertising. **Online:** DataTimes Corporation; Dialog (The Dialog Corporation); LEXIS-NEXIS. **URL:** http://www.sptimes.com. **Alt. Formats:** CD-ROM, NewsBank, Inc.
Ad Rates: GLR: $14 **Circ:** Mon.-Sat. ★**323,355**
BW: $29,283 Sun. ★**411,445**
4C: $1,654
SAU: $196
PCI: $240

6715 The Seed Pod
American Hibiscus Society
PO Box 12073 Phone: (813)896-1081
St. Petersburg, FL 33733-2073 Fax: (813)823-0054

Professional horticultural magazine covering Hibiscus care and showing. **Founded:** 1956. **Freq:** Quarterly. **Print Method:** Offset. **Trim Size:** 5 x 8. **Key Personnel:** Katie McClain, Editor. **USPS:** 687-170. **Remarks:** Accepts advertising. **URL:** http://www.trop-hibiscus.com.
Ad Rates: BW: $100 **Circ:** Controlled 1,200
4C: $350

6716 Travel News
Travel Agents International, Inc.
11006 4th St. N., No. 27 Phone: (813)576-8241
St. Petersburg, FL 33716-2945 Fax: (813)579-0529

Travel publication. **Founded:** 1981. **Freq:** Monthly. **Print Method:** Web offset. **Trim Size:** 11 x 17. **Cols./Page:** 4. **Col. Width:** 15 picas. **Col. Depth:** 15 inches. **Key Personnel:** Matthew Wiseman, Editor. **Subscription Rates:** Free. **Remarks:** Accepts advertising.
Ad Rates: BW: $2,100 **Circ:** 200,000
4C: $3,600
PCI: $35.60

6717 The Weekly Challenger
2500 9th St. S. Phone: (813)896-2922
St. Petersburg, FL 33705
Black community newspaper. **Founded:** Sept. 1967. **Freq:** Weekly. **Print Method:** Offset. **Trim Size:** 8 x 21 1/2. **Cols./Page:** 8. **Col. Width:** 1 1/2 inches. **Col. Depth:** 21 1/2 inches. **Key Personnel:** Cynthia Armstrong, Editor; Cleveland Johnson, Publisher; William Blackshear, Advertising Mgr. **Subscription Rates:** $15 individuals; $22 out of county. **Remarks:** Accepts advertising.
Ad Rates: 4C: $320 **Circ:** 32,000
SAU: $8.40

6718 The Wooden Horse
St. Petersburg Junior College
PO Box 13489 Phone: (813)341-3676
St. Petersburg, FL 33733
Collegiate newspaper. **Founded:** 1927. **Freq:** Monthly. **Print Method:** Offset. **Cols./Page:** 5. **Col. Width:** 22 nonpareils. **Col. Depth:** 210 agate lines. **Key Personnel:** Pamela Page Bellis, Inst. Associate. **Subscription Rates:** Free. **Remarks:** Accepts advertising.
Ad Rates: BW: $450 **Circ:** Free 6,000
4C: $700
PCI: $7.05

6719 WBHS-TV - 50
12425 28th St. N., Ste. 301 Phone: (813)573-5550
St. Petersburg, FL 33716 Fax: (813)571-1931

Format: Commercial TV. **Networks:** Home Shopping Network. **Operating Hours:** Continuous. **ADI:** Tampa-St. Petersburg (Lakeland, Sarasota), FL. **Key Personnel:** Jim Goodman, General Mgr.; Allen McCarty, Chief Engineer; Cheryl Barron, Program Mgr.

6720 WECX-FM - 99.9
Campus Box D Phone: (813)864-8419
4200 54th Ave. S.
St. Petersburg, FL 33711
E-mail: wecx@eckerd.edu

Format: Alternative/New Music/Progressive. **Founded:** 1977. **Formerly**: WECR-AM. **Operating Hours:** Continuous. **ADI:** Tampa- St. Petersburg (Lakeland, Sarasota),FL. **Ad Rates:** Noncommercial. **URL:** http://www.wecx.eckerd.edu.

6721 WHNZ-AM - 570
11300 4th St. N., Ste. 318 Phone: (813)577-7131
St. Petersburg, FL 33716 Fax: (813)578-8569

Format: News; Information; Talk. **Networks:** CBS; AP. **Owner:** Paxson Communications, Inc., 601 Clearwater Park Rd., West Palm Beach, FL 33401, (561)659-4122, Fax: (561)655-7246. **Founded:** 1961. **Formerly**: WPLP-AM (1992); WTKN-AM. **Operating Hours:** Continuous; 70% network, 30% local. **ADI:** Tampa-St. Petersburg (Lakeland, Sarasota), FL. **Key Personnel:** Skip Schmidt, Pres./Gen. Mgr., fax (813)578-2477; Linda Stacy, General Sales Mgr., fax (813)576-7570; Gene Lindsey, Program Dir., phone (813)579-2007, fax (813)578-2477, glindsey@cctampa.com; Melanie Knous, Exec. Admin.; Gordon Byrd, News Dir., phone (813)522-6397, gbyrd@cctampa.com. **Local Programs:** *Gator Football, Bas-*

ketball; Orlando Magic Basketball. **Wattage:** 5000 day; 10,000 night. **URL:** http://www.tampabayradio.com.

6722 WHPT-FM - 102.5
11300 4th St. N., Ste. 318 Phone: (813)577-7131
St. Petersburg, FL 33716 Fax: (813)578-2477

Format: Adult Contemporary; Album-Oriented Rock (AOR). **Networks:** Independent. **Owner:** Paxson Communications, Inc., 601 Clearwater Park Rd., West Palm Beach, FL 33401, (561)659-4122, Fax: (561)659-4252. **Founded:** 1973. **Formerly**: WAVE-FM (1986). **Operating Hours:** Continuous. **ADI:** Tampa-St. Petersburg (Lakeland, Sarasota), FL. **Key Personnel:** Rose E. Bobier, Promotions Dir.; Drew M. Rashbaum, General Mgr.; Linda Stacy, General Sales Mgr.; Chuck Beck, Program Dir.; Melanie Knous, Contact; Carson Cooper, News Dir. **Local Programs:** *House of Blues Hour & Break; Letterman Top 10.* **Wattage:** 100,000.

6723 WQYK-AM - 1010
9450 Koger Blvd. Phone: (813)576-6055
St. Petersburg, FL 33702 Fax: (813)577-1324
Free: (800)992-3699

Format: Talk. **Networks:** Westwood One Radio. **Operating Hours:** Continuous; 100% local. **ADI:** Tampa-St. Petersburg (Lakeland, Sarasota), FL. **Key Personnel:** Jay Miller, General Mgr.; Dave Hutchinson, General Sales Mgr.; Tom Rivers, Program Dir. **Wattage:** 50,000.

6724 WQYK-FM - 99.5
9450 Koger Blvd. Phone: (813)576-6055
St. Petersburg, FL 33702 Fax: (813)577-1324

Format: Contemporary Country. **Networks:** Independent. **Operating Hours:** Continuous; 100% local. **ADI:** Tampa-St. Petersburg (Lakeland, Sarasota), FL. **Key Personnel:** Jay Miller, General Mgr.; Dave Hutchison, Contact; Tom Rivers, Operations Dir. **Wattage:** 100,000.

6725 WRXB-AM - 1590
1700 34th St. S. Phone: (813)327-9792
St. Petersburg, FL 33711-3833 Fax: (813)321-3025

Format: Urban Contemporary. **Networks:** American Urban Radio. **Owner:** J. Eugene Danzey, at above address. **Founded:** 1976. **Operating Hours:** Continuous. **ADI:** Tampa-St. Petersburg (Lakeland, Sarasota), FL. **Key Personnel:** J. Eugene Danzey, Owner/Gen. Mgr.; Michael Danzey, Vice President; Valorie D. Garner, Station Mgr.; Robert Sanchez, Music/Program Dir. **Wattage:** 5000 day; 1000 night. **Ad Rates:** $20-40 for 30 seconds; $30-50 for 60 seconds.

6726 WSJT-FM - 94.1
11300 4th St. N., No. 318 Phone: (813)577-7131
St. Petersburg, FL 33716 Fax: (813)578-2477
E-mail: smoothjazz@wsjt.com

Networks: Independent. **Founded:** 1967. **Formerly**: WVFM-FM; WEZY-FM. **Operating Hours:** Continuous. **ADI:** Tampa-St. Petersburg (Lakeland, Sarasota),FL. **Key Personnel:** Skip Schmidt, General Mgr. **Wattage:** 100,000. **Ad Rates:** $125-175 for 30 seconds; $150-200 for 60 seconds. Combined advertising rates available with WHNZ, WHPT, WZTM, WRBQ-AM, WRBQ-FM, WSSR, WILV. **URL:** http://www.wsjt.com.

6727 WSUN-AM - 620
877 Executive Center Dr. W., No. 300 Phone: (813)576-1073
Fax: (813)576-8098
St. Petersburg, FL 33702-8444
Free: (800)525-2662

Format: Talk; Sports. **Founded:** 1927. **Operating Hours:** Continuous; 100% local. **ADI:** Tampa- St. Petersburg (Lakeland, Sarasota),FL. **Wattage:** 10,000. **Ad Rates:** Advertising accepted; rates available upon request.

6728 WTIS-AM - 1110
311 112th Ave. NE Phone: (813)576-2234
St. Petersburg, FL 33716 Fax: (813)577-3814

Format: Religious. **Networks:** Independent. **Founded:** 1946. **Operating Hours:** Sunrise-sunset. **ADI:** Tampa-St. Petersburg (Lakeland, Sarasota), FL. **Key Personnel:** Mike Smith, Contact; Mike Smith, Operations Dir.; Dave Guerin, Program Dir. **Wattage:** 10,000. **Ad Rates:** $30 per unit.

6729 WTOG-TV - 44
365 105th Terr. NE Phone: (813)576-4444
St. Petersburg, FL 33716 Fax: (813)577-1806

Format: Commercial TV. **Networks:** United Paramount Network. **Owner:** Paramount Stations Group, 5555 Melrose Ave., Hollywood, CA 90038-3197, (213)956-8100, Fax: (213)862-0121. **Founded:** 1968. **Operating Hours:** Continuous; 100% local. **ADI:** Tampa-St. Petersburg (Lakeland, Sarasota), FL. **Key Personnel:** Mike Conway, Vice President; Jim LaBranche, News Dir.; Barbara Burley, Program Dir.; Bryan Slonaker, Promotions Dir.; Steve Wilkerson, General Sales Mgr.; Mike Rajewski, Sales Mgr.; John Kays, Chief Engineer; Marge Smelt, Business Mgr.; Rhonda Romano, Community Relations Director. **Wattage:** 1,000,000.

6730 WTSP-TV - 10
11450 Gandy Blvd. Phone: (727)577-1010
Box 10000 Fax: (727)576-6924
St. Petersburg, FL 33702

Format: Commercial TV. **Networks:** CBS. **Founded:** 1965. **Formerly**: WLCY-TV. **Operating Hours:** Continuous, except Sun. night. **ADI:** Tampa-St. Petersburg (Lakeland, Sarasota), FL. **Key Personnel:** Norean Parker, Contact. **Ad Rates:** Advertising accepted; rates available upon request. **URL:** http://www.wtsp.com.

6731 WWRM-FM - 94.9
877 Executive Center W., Ste. 300 Phone: (813)576-1073
Fax: (813)576-8098
St. Petersburg, FL 33702-8444

Format: Adult Contemporary. **Formerly**: WWBA-FM (1988). **Operating Hours:** Continuous; 100% local. **ADI:** Tampa- St. Petersburg (Lakeland, Sarasota),FL. **Wattage:** 100,000. **Ad Rates:** Advertising accepted; rates available upon request.

6732 WYUU-FM - 92.5
9721 Executive Center Dr., No. 200 Phone: (813)221-2925
Fax: (813)579-9111
St. Petersburg, FL 33702
Free: (800)966-2925

Format: Oldies. **Networks:** Independent. **Owner:** Entercom, 100 Presidential Blvd., Bala Cynwyd, PA 19004, (215)667-1226. **Formerly**: WXCR-FM (1989). **Operating Hours:** Continuous. **ADI:** Tampa-St. Petersburg (Lakeland, Sarasota), FL. **Key Personnel:** David A. Trusty, Contact; Nancy Benach, General Sales Mgr.; Dennis Anderson, Program Dir.; Dennis Andersen, Operations Mgr. **Wattage:** 50,000. **Ad Rates:** Advertising accepted; rates available upon request.

SANFORD

6733 Brown Gold Magazine
NTM Publications
1000 E. 1st St. Phone: (407)323-3430
Sanford, FL 32771-1487 Fax: (407)330-0376
Publication E-mail: ntm@ntm.org

Tribes mission religious magazine. **Founded:** 1943. **Freq:** Monthly. **Print Method:** Offset. **Trim Size:** 7 5/8 x 10 1/2. **Cols./Page:** 2. **Col. Width:** 36 nonpareils. **Col. Depth:** 126 agate lines. **Key Personnel:** Macon G. Hare, Editor. **ISSN:** 0007-2494. **Subscription Rates:** $7 individuals. **Remarks:** Advertising not accepted.
Circ: Paid 38,582
Controlled 12,344

6734 Sanford Herald
300 N. French Ave. Phone: (407)322-2611
Sanford, FL 32771
General newspaper. **Founded:** 1908. **Freq:** Daily (eve.), Sunday (morn.). **Print Method:** Offset. **Cols./Page:** 6. **Col. Width:** 25 nonpareils. **Col. Depth:** 301 agate lines. **Key Personnel:** Ron Hosie, Managing Editor; Wayne D. Doyle, Publisher; Laura Sollien, Advertising Dir. **Subscription Rates:** $57 individuals. **Remarks:** Accepts advertising.
Ad Rates: SAU: $7.95 **Circ:** Paid ‡9,500

6735 WTRR-AM - 1400
PO Box 1448 Phone: (407)322-1400
Sanford, FL 32772-1448 Fax: (407)330-7571
E-mail: wtrr1400@gate.net

Format: Adult Contemporary. **Owner:** J & V Communications Co., at above address. **Founded:** 1947. **Formerly**: WKUS-AM (1990); WUEZ-AM; WNSI-AM. **Operating Hours:** Continuous. **ADI:** Orlando-Daytona Beach-Melbourne, FL. **Key Personnel:** Joe Episcopo, General Mgr., wtrr1400@iag.net. **Local Programs:** *Amor* 9:00 am - 6:00 am Monday-Friday, Joe Episcopo, General Mgr. **Wattage:** 1000. **Ad Rates:** $12-26 for 30 seconds. Combined advertising rates available with WPRD-AM 1440, WOTS-AM 1220. **URL:** http://www.wtrr.com.

SANIBEL

6736 Island Life Magazine
Hooper Publishing Co.
PO Box 929 Phone: (941)433-4090
Sanibel, FL 33957
Lifestyle magazine focusing on the barrier islands of Florida's west coast, from Marco Island to Sarasota. **Founded:** 1983. **Freq:** Quarterly. **Print Method:** Offset. **Trim Size:** 8 1/2 x 11. **Cols./Page:** 3. **Col. Depth:** 10 inches. **Key Personnel:** Joan Hooper, Editor; Van B. Hooper, Publisher; William Farnsworth, Advertising and Business Manager. **Subscription Rates:** $14 individuals; $3 single issue. **Remarks:** Accepts advertising.
Ad Rates: 4C: $2,300 **Circ:** ‡15,000

6737 Island Reporter
PO Box 809 Phone: (941)472-1587
Sanibel, FL 33957 Fax: (941)472-8398

Local newspaper. **Founded:** 1973. **Freq:** Weekly (Fri.). **Print Method:** Offset. **Cols./Page:** 6. **Col. Width:** 20 nonpareils. **Col. Depth:** 224 agate lines. **Key Personnel:** Michelle Moran, Editor; Morgan Newcomb, General Mgr., phone (941)482-7111, fax (941)482-6365; Gwenda Hiett, Contact. **Subscription Rates:** $28 individuals. **Remarks:** Accepts advertising.
Ad Rates: GLR: $.22 **Circ:** 8,500
BW: $6,966
4C: $846
PCI: $7.25

6738 The Islander
Breeze Publishing Co.
PO Box 56
Sanibel, FL 33957-0056

Community newspaper. **Founded:** 1961. **Freq:** Weekly. **Cols./Page:** 6. **Col. Width:** 9.5 picas. **Col. Depth:** 16 inches. **Key Personnel:** Christopher Strine, Editor; Joel Jenkins, General Mgr. **Subscription Rates:** $19.75 individuals; $26 out of state. **Remarks:** Accepts advertising.
Ad Rates: PCI: $5.90 **Circ:** ‡6,000

SARASOTA

6739 Accounting Review
American Accounting Association
5717 Bessie Dr. Phone: (941)921-7747
Sarasota, FL 34233 Fax: (941)923-4093
Publisher E-mail: aaahq@packnet.net

Accounting education, research, financial reporting, and book reviews. **Founded:** 1926. **Freq:** Quarterly. **Print Method:** Offset. **Trim Size:** 7 x 10. **Cols./Page:** 1. **Col. Depth:** 110 agate lines. **Key Personnel:** Linda Bamber, Editor. **ISSN:** 0001-4826. **Subscription Rates:** $100 individuals. **Remarks:** Accepts advertising.
Ad Rates: BW: $750 **Circ:** 11,000

6740 The Beach Weekly
Florida Sun Publications
3755 S. Tuttle Ave. Phone: (813)923-2544
Sarasota, FL 34239 Fax: (813)924-1866

Community newspaper. **Founded:** 1984. **Freq:** Weekly (Fri.). **Print Method:** Offset. **Cols./Page:** 6. **Col. Width:** 20 nonpareils. **Col. Depth:** 217 agate lines. **Key Personnel:** John Mayo, Publisher. **Remarks:** Accepts advertising.
Ad Rates: BW: $840.72 **Circ:** Free 50,000
4C: $1,190.72

6741 The Bulletin
2490 Dr. Martin Luther King, Jr. Way Phone: (941)953-3990
PO Box 2560
Sarasota, FL 34230-2560
Black community newspaper. **Founded:** 1959. **Freq:** Weekly (Fri.). **Print Method:** Offset. **Cols./Page:** 6. **Col. Width:** 2 1/16 inches. **Col. Depth:** 126 agate lines. **Key Personnel:** Richard Wright, Editor; Rosalind J. Bacon, Managing Editor; Fred L. Bacon, Advertising Mgr. **Subscription Rates:** $26 individuals; $.25 single issue. **Remarks:** Accepts advertising.
Ad Rates: 4C: $180.00 **Circ:** Paid 16,500
PCI: $10.75

6742 Chips from Many Trees and Growing Roots
ACETO Bookmen
5721 Antietam Dr. Phone: (941)924-9170
Sarasota, FL 34231
Genealogical magazine covering families in Canada and the U.S. **Founded:** 1997. **Freq:** Quarterly. **Trim Size:** 8 1/2 x 11. **Cols./Page:** 1. **Col. Width:** 7 inches. **Col. Depth:** 10 inches. **Key Personnel:** Charles D. Townsend, Editor/Manager. **ISSN:** 1091-9473. **Subscription Rates:** $20 individuals; $25 Canada; $30 elsewhere. **Remarks:** Accepts advertising.
Circ: Combined 225

6743 Library & Archival Security
The Haworth Press, Inc.
One Ben Franklin Dr., Apt. 51 Phone: (941)388-3157
Sarasota, FL 34236
Publication E-mail: schlimazel@aol.com
Publisher E-mail: getinfo@haworthpressinc.com

Journal dealing with crime and security problems in libraries. **Founded:** 1974. **Freq:** 2/year. **Trim Size:** 6 x8 1/2. **Key Personnel:** Bruce A. Shuman, PhD, Editor; Bill Cohen, Publisher. **ISSN:** 0196-0075. **Subscription Rates:** $40 indi-

viduals; $115 institutions; $115 libraries. **Remarks:** Accepts advertising.
Ad Rates: BW: $300 **Circ:** Paid 480

6744 New Writer's Magazine
PO Box 5976 Phone: (941)953-7903
Sarasota, FL 34277 Fax: (941)953-7903
Free: (800)249-0658
Publication E-mail: newriters@aol.com

Magazine covering the craft of writing. **Founded:** 1986. **Freq:** Bimonthly. **Print Method:** Offset. **Trim Size:** 8 1/2 x 11. **Cols./Page:** 3. **Col. Width:** 2 1/4 inches. **Col. Depth:** 9 3/4 inches. **Key Personnel:** George J. Haborak, Editor and Publisher. **ISSN:** 0895-6510. **Subscription Rates:** $15 individuals; $25 two years; $3 single issue. **Remarks:** Accepts advertising. **URL:** http://www.newriters.com.
Ad Rates: BW: $300 **Circ:** ‡5,000
PCI: $30

6745 Pelican Press
230 Avenida Madera Phone: (941)349-4949
Sarasota, FL 34242 Fax: (941)346-7118

Community newspaper (tabloid) serving Sarasota and coastal regions. **Founded:** Mar. 1971. **Freq:** Weekly. **Print Method:** Offset. **Trim Size:** 10 7/8 x 16 1/2. **Cols./Page:** 6. **Col. Width:** 9.5 picas. **Col. Depth:** 217 agate lines. **Key Personnel:** Anne H. Johnson, Editor; John B. Davidson, Publisher; Sally Baxter, General Mgr. **Subscription Rates:** $32 by mail. **Remarks:** Accepts advertising.
Ad Rates: BW: $1,152 **Circ:** Paid ‡800
4C: $1,427 Free ‡23,500
PCI: $12

6746 Sarasota Herald-Tribune
The New York Times Co.
801 S. Tamiami Trail Phone: (941)953-7755
Sarasota, FL 34236 Fax: (941)957-5276
Free: (800)282-9425
Publisher E-mail: name@nytimes.com

General newspaper. **Founded:** 1925. **Freq:** Mon.-Sun. (morn.). **Print Method:** Offset. **Cols./Page:** 6. **Col. Width:** 26 nonpareils. **Col. Depth:** 294 agate lines. **Key Personnel:** Diane H. McFarlin, Exec. Editor; Thomas Tryon, Editor; Lynn O. Matthews, Publisher; Harold Bubil, Quest Editor, phone (941)957-5103. **Remarks:** Accepts advertising. **Feature Editors:** Scott Peterson, *Sports*, phone (941)957-5172; Susan Rite, *Features*, phone (941)957-5271; Janet Uffinger, *Fashion*, phone (941)957-5417; Joel Welin, *Entertainment*, phone (941)957-5175.
Circ: Mon.-Sat. ★**98,1031**
Sun. ★**121,698**

6747 Sarasota Magazine
Clubhouse Publishing, Inc.
601 S. Osprey Ave. Phone: (813)366-8225
Sarasota, FL 34236-7526 Fax: (813)365-7272

Business publication covering Sarasota and Manatee County inserted into monthly city magazine. **Founded:** 1983. **Freq:** Monthly. **Print Method:** Offset. **Cols./Page:** 3. **Col. Width:** 27 nonpareils. **Col. Depth:** 137 agate lines. **Key Personnel:** Pam Daniel, Editor; Daniel Denton, Publisher; Jimmy Dean, Advertising Mgr. **Subscription Rates:** $18 individuals. **Remarks:** Accepts advertising.
Ad Rates: BW: $1,200 **Circ:** Combined ‡13,000
4C: $1,800

6748 SEE Beaches
Miles Media Group, Inc.
3675 Clark Rd. Phone: (941)922-3575
Sarasota, FL 34233-2358 Fax: (941)923-6309
Free: (800)683-0010
Publisher E-mail: mmg@netline.net

Consumer travel guides. **Founded:** 1954. **Freq:** Annual. **Key Personnel:** Patti Upton, Publisher, phone (800)683-1000; Errol Croft, Editorial Dir. **Subscription Rates:** Free. **Remarks:** Accepts advertising.
Ad Rates: 4C: $570 **Circ:** Non-paid 125,000

6749 SEE Emerald Coast
Miles Media Group, Inc.
3675 Clark Rd. Phone: (941)922-3575
Sarasota, FL 34233-2358 Fax: (941)923-6309
Free: (800)683-0010
Publisher E-mail: mmg@netline.net

Consumer magazine covering visitor information and travel. **Founded:** Jan. 13, 1955. **Freq:** Quarterly. **Key Personnel:** Rick Seevers, Account Exec. **Remarks:** Accepts advertising. **URL:** http://www.see-florida.com.
Circ: (Not Reported)

6750 See Florida Keys
Miles Media Group, Inc.
3675 Clark Rd. Phone: (941)922-3575
Sarasota, FL 34233-2358 Fax: (941)923-6309
Free: (800)683-0010
Publisher E-mail: mmg@netline.net

Tourist magazine for the Florida Keys. **Founded:** 1988. **Freq:** 3 TIMES PER YEAR. **Print Method:** Web offset. **Trim Size:** 5 1/4 x 7 1/2. **Cols./Page:** 2. **Col. Width:** 13 picas. **Col. Depth:** 41 picas. **Key Personnel:** Shelley Sisko, Assoc. Publisher; John Criswell, Publisher. **Subscription Rates:** Free. **Remarks:** Accepts advertising. **Online:** Florida On-Line BBS. **Formerly:** The Keys Guide (1990).
Ad Rates: BW: $2,856 **Circ:** Non-paid 600,000
4C: $3,563.20

6751 Writer's Guidelines Magazine
Independent Publishing Co.
PO Box 18566 Phone: (941)924-3201
Sarasota, FL 34276 Fax: (941)925-4468

Publishing magazine featuring market information. **Subtitle:** A Roundtable For Writers And Editors. **Founded:** 1988. **Freq:** Bimonthly. **Trim Size:** 8 1/2 x 11. **Cols./Page:** 2. **Key Personnel:** E.P. Ned Burke, Editor. **ISSN:** 1053-1793. **Subscription Rates:** $16 individuals; $25 two years; $4 single issue. **Remarks:** Accepts advertising. **Formerly:** Guidelines (1990).
Ad Rates: BW: $95 **Circ:** Paid ‡750
Non-paid ‡250

6752 Yesterday's Magazette
Independent Publishing Co.
PO Box 18566 Phone: (941)924-3201
Sarasota, FL 34276 Fax: (941)925-4468
Publication E-mail: YMagazette@aol.com

Consumer magazine covering nostalgia. **Subtitle:** The Original Magazine of Memories. **Founded:** 1973. **Freq:** Bimonthly. **Print Method:** Offset. **Trim Size:** 8 1/2 x 11. **Cols./Page:** 3. **Col. Width:** 7 inches. **Col. Depth:** 10 inches. **Key Personnel:** E. P. "Ned" Burke, Editor. **Subscription Rates:** $18 individuals; $3 single issue. **Remarks:** Accepts advertising.
Ad Rates: PCI: $35 **Circ:** Paid 1,500

6753 Comcast Cable
5205 Fruitville Rd. Phone: (813)371-4444
Box 1178 Fax: (813)371-5097
Sarasota, FL 34232

Founded: 1962. **Formerly:** Sterer Cable TV of Florida, Inc. **Cities Served:** Manatee and Sarasota counties, FL.

6754 WBSV-TV - 62
2065 Cantu Ct. Phone: (941)379-0062
Sarasota, FL 34232 Fax: (941)378-9224

Format: Classical. **Owner:** DeSoto Channel 62 Associates Limited Partnership, at above address. **Founded:** May 3, 1991. **Operating Hours:** Continuous. **ADI:** Tampa- St. Petersburg (Lakeland, Sarasota),FL. **Key Personnel:** Danford L. Sawyer, President; David Jahns, General Sales Mgr.; Patrick Pierce. **Local Programs:** *62 Town Hall*, Sheryl Greene, Tom Wilson. **Wattage:** 5,000,000. **Ad Rates:** $30.00-300.00 for 30 seconds.

WJIS-FM - See Bradenton

6755 WKXY-AM - 930
2500 10th St. Phone: (941)366-4422
Sarasota, FL 34237
E-mail: wkxy@usa.net

Format: News; Talk. **Networks:** Westwood One Radio; CBS. **Founded:** 1949. **Operating Hours:** Continuous. **ADI:** Tampa-St. Petersburg (Lakeland, Sarasota),FL. **Key Personnel:** Charles L. Fernandez, General and Commerical Mgr. **Wattage:** 5000 day; 2500 night. **Ad Rates:** Advertising accepted; rates available upon request.

6756 WKZM-FM - 105.5
PO Box 7627 Phone: (941)371-3163
Sarasota, FL 34278-7627 Fax: (941)377-8575

Format: Religious. **Networks:** Independent. **Owner:** Christian Fellowship Radio, Inc., at above address. **Founded:** 1974. **Operating Hours:** Continuous; 100% local. **ADI:** Tampa- St. Petersburg (Lakeland, Sarasota),FL. **Key Personnel:** Lowell A. Brubaker, General Mgr.; Roy Mazeline, Chief Engineer. **Wattage:** 3000. **Ad Rates:** Noncommercial.

6757 WQSA-AM - 1220
1991 Main St., No. 184 Phone: (941)955-1946
Sarasota, FL 34236-5914 Fax: (941)366-7778
E-mail: wqsa1220@aol.com

Format: Sports. **Networks:** Westwood One Radio. **Owner:** Alliance Broadcasting, at above address. **Founded:** 1961. **Operating Hours:** Continuous; 80% network, 20% local. **ADI:** Tampa- St. Petersburg (Lakeland, Sarasota),FL. **Key Personnel:** Jennifer Rowe, Traffic/Prod. Dir.; Drew Ryan, Sports Dir.; Scott Hayes, Account Mgr. **Wattage:** 1000. **Ad Rates:** $10-25 for 30 seconds; $10-25 for 60 seconds.

6758 WSPB-AM - 1450
1713 Ken Thompson Pkwy. Phone: (941)388-3936
Sarasota, FL 34236 Fax: (941)388-3720

Format: News; Talk. **Simulcasts:** WFLA-AM. **Founded:** 1939. **Operating Hours:** Continuous. **ADI:** Tampa- St. Petersburg (Lakeland, Sarasota),FL. **Key Personnel:** Brian Holmes, Operations Mgr.; Sheila Diamond, Corporate Sales Dir. **Wattage:** 1000. **URL:** http://www.wspb.com.

6759 WSRZ-FM - 106.5
1713 Ken Thompson Parkway Phone: (941)388-3936
Sarasota, FL 34236 Fax: (941)388-6408
E-mail: wsrz.com

Format: Oldies. **Networks:** Independent. **Founded:** 1986. **Operating Hours:** Continuous. **ADI:** Tampa- St. Petersburg (Lakeland, Sarasota),FL. **Key Personnel:** Laura Brennan, Traffic Mgr.; Mark Stough, General Sales Mgr.; Pete Jarrett, Program Dir./Operations Mgr.; Robin Ross, Business Mgr.; Frank Lischak, General Mgr. **Wattage:** 25,000. **Ad Rates:** $20-100 per unit. Combined advertising rates available with WYNF-FM, WSPB-AM.

6760 WTMY-AM - 1280
2101 Hammock Pl. Phone: (941)954-1280
Sarasota, FL 34235 Fax: (941)953-9062

Format: Talk. **Owner:** Metropolitan Radio Group, Inc., 1549 Greenbridge, Ozark, MO 65721, (417)581-5595. **Founded:** Dec. 2, 1961. **Operating Hours:** Continuous. **ADI:** Tampa-St. Petersburg (Lakeland, Sarasota), FL. **Key Personnel:** Gary L. Acker, President; T. Michael Craft, General Mgr.; Valerie Silver, Public Affairs Dir.; Jim Grant, Chief Engineer. **Wattage:** 500.

6761 WWSB-TV -
5725 Lawton Dr. Phone: (941)923-8840
Sarasota, FL 34233 Fax: (941)924-3971

Format: Commercial TV. **Networks:** ABC. **Founded:** 1971. **Formerly:** WXLT-TV. **Operating Hours:** Continuous. **ADI:** Tampa- St. Petersburg (Lakeland, Sarasota),FL. **Key Personnel:** J. Manuel Calvo, General Mgr/VP; Ken Long, Business Mgr.; Kim Urbuteit, General Sales Mgr.; Vann Smith, Local Sales Mgr.; Julie Shaffer, National Sales Mgr.; Deanna Goins, Promotions Mgr.; Julie Ford, News Dir.; Terry Douma, Operations Mgr.; Mike Burnham, Chief Engineer; Colleen Marone, Administrative Asst. **Ad Rates:** Advertising accepted; rates available upon request.

SEBRING

6762 The News-Sun
The News-Sun, Inc.
2227 U.S. 27 S. Phone: (941)385-6155
Sebring, FL 33870 Fax: (941)385-1954

Newspaper with a focus on community news and events. **Founded:** 1919. **Freq:** Triweekly (Wed., Fri., and Sun.). **Print Method:** Offset. Uses mats. **Cols./Page:** 6. **Col. Width:** 21 nonpareils. **Col. Depth:** 301 agate lines. **Key Personnel:** Tim Thompson, Publisher; Romona Washington, Exec. Editor. **Subscription Rates:** $36 individuals. **Remarks:** Advertising accepted; rates available upon request.
Circ: Wed. ★**12,133**
Fri. ★**11,379**
Sun. ★**13,085**

6763 Sebring Shopping Guide
Florida Sun Publications
1010 US 27 N. Phone: (941)382-1141
Sebring, FL 33870 Fax: (941)382-3046

Shopper. **Founded:** 1974. **Freq:** Weekly (Wed.). **Print Method:** Offset. **Cols./Page:** 6. **Col. Width:** 20 nonpareils. **Col. Depth:** 238 agate lines. **Key Personnel:** Sharon A. Lind, General Mgr.; Wayne Abbott, Circulation Mgr. **Subscription Rates:** Free. **Remarks:** Accepts advertising.
Ad Rates: GLR: $6.20 **Circ:** Non-paid 19,066
BW: $489
4C: $650
PCI: $6.20

6764 WWLL-FM - 105.7
2411 U.S. 27 S. Phone: (813)385-5151
Sebring, FL 33870 Fax: (813)385-5511
E-mail: cohanradio@hotmail.com

Format: Classic Rock. **Networks:** CNN Radio. **Owner:** Roper Broadcasting, at above address, (941)302-1063, Fax: (941)382-1982, Free: (800)991-9965. **Founded:** 1967. **For-**

merly: WCAC. **Operating Hours:** Continuous. **ADI:** Tampa-St. Petersburg (Lakeland, Sarasota), FL. **Key Personnel:** Celeste Chung, Operations Dir.; Jeffrey M. Gooda II. **Wattage:** 20,000. **Ad Rates:** $5-15 for 30 seconds; $6.50-18 for 60 seconds.

6765 WWOJ-FM - 99.1
3750 U.S. 27 N., Ste. 1 Phone: (941)382-1063
Sebring, FL 33870 Fax: (941)382-1982
E-mail: oj-tk@digital.net

Format: Country. **Networks:** CBS. **Owner:** Cohan Radio Group, Inc., at above address, (941)382-9999. **Founded:** 1984. **Operating Hours:** Continuous; 1% network, 99% local. **ADI:** Tampa-St. Petersburg (Lakeland, Sarasota), FL. **Key Personnel:** Pete Coughlin, Contact; Celeste Chung, Program Dir. **Wattage:** 10,000. **Ad Rates:** $14.50-25.00 for 60 seconds.

6766 WWTK-AM - 730
3750 U.S. 27 N., Ste. 1 Phone: (941)382-TALK
Sebring, FL 33870 Fax: (941)382-1982
E-mail: oj-tk@digital.net

Format: Talk. **Networks:** CBS; EFM; Mutual Broadcasting System. **Owner:** Cohen Radio Group, Inc., at above address. **Founded:** 1989. **Operating Hours:** Continuous. **ADI:** Tampa-St. Petersburg (Lakeland, Sarasota), FL. **Key Personnel:** Pete Coughlin, Owner/Manager; Barry Foster, News Dir. **Local Programs:** *Barry Foster* 9:00 am - 11:00 am Monday-Friday, Barry Foster. **Wattage:** 500.

SOUTH DAYTONA

6767 WPUL-AM - 1590
PO Box 4010 Phone: (904)767-1131
South Daytona, FL 32121-4010 Fax: (904)254-7510

Format: Jazz; Urban Contemporary; Oldies. **Networks:** Independent. **Founded:** 1988. **Formerly:** WZIP-AM. **Operating Hours:** 6 a.m.-12 a.m. **Key Personnel:** Charles W. Cherry, Station/General Mgr. **Wattage:** 1000. **Ad Rates:** $18 for 30 seconds; $25 for 60 seconds.

SOUTH MIAMI

6768 Today's Grocer
Florida Grocer Publications, Inc.
PO Box 430760 Phone: (305)441-1138
South Miami, FL 33243-0760 Fax: (305)661-6720
Free: (800)440-3067

Trade journal serving the Florida food industry. **Founded:** 1956. **Freq:** Monthly. **Print Method:** Offset. Uses mats. **Trim Size:** 13 x 22. **Cols./Page:** 6. **Col. Width:** 1 1/8 inches. **Col. Depth:** 21 inches. **Key Personnel:** Dennis M. Kane, Editor; Jack Nobles, Publisher. **USPS:** 432-630. **Subscription Rates:** Free to qualified subscribers; $29. **Remarks:** Accepts advertising. **Alt. Formats:** Mailing labels. **Formerly**: Florida Grocer.
Ad Rates: BW: $2,600 **Circ:** Controlled ‡19,500
4C: $3,100

6769 Vacation Industry Review
Interval International
6262 Sunset Dr., Penthouse 1 Phone: (305)666-1861
South Miami, FL 33143 Fax: (305)668-3408
Free: (800)622-1861

Trade magazine on development, finance, marketing, and management of timeshare resorts. **Founded:** 1984. **Freq:** Bimonthly. **Trim Size:** 8 1/2 x 11. **Cols./Page:** 3. **Col. Width:** 2 3/16 inches. **Col. Depth:** 9 inches. **Key Personnel:** George Leposky, Editor, gleposky@interval-intl.com; Marilyn Castro, Advertising Mgr., fax (305)668-3413, mcastro@interval.intl.com. **Subscription Rates:** Free. **Remarks:** Accepts advertising. **URL:** http://www.interval-intl.com.
Ad Rates: BW: $1,465 **Circ:** Controlled 15,000
4C: $2,020

SPARR

6770 The International Permaculture Solutions Journal
Yankee Permaculture
PO Box 52
Sparr, FL 32192-0052
Publication E-mail: yankeePerm@aol.com
Publisher E-mail: permacultur@aol.com

Journal covering the environment and permaculture. **Founded:** 1983. **Freq:** Irregular. **Key Personnel:** Dan Hemenway, Editor; Cynthia Hemenway, Editor. **ISSN:** 1046-8366. **Subscription Rates:** $25 single issue. **Remarks:** Advertising not accepted. **Former name:** The International Permaculture Species Yearbook.
Circ: (Not Reported)

6771 Permaculture Review, Overview and Digest
Yankee Permaculture
PO Box 52
Sparr, FL 32192-0052
Publisher E-mail: permacultur@aol.com

Periodical covering food systems and the environment. **Founded:** 1996. **Freq:** Irregular. **Key Personnel:** Dan Hemenway, Editor; Cynthia Hemenway, Editor. **Remarks:** Advertising not accepted.
Circ: (Not Reported)

STARKE

6772 Bradford County Telegraph
Bradford Telegraph
135 W. Call St. Phone: (904)964-6305
PO Drawer A Fax: (904)964-8628
Starke, FL 32091
Community newspaper. **Founded:** 1879. **Freq:** Weekly (Thurs.). **Cols./Page:** 6. **Col. Width:** 12 picas. **Col. Depth:** 21 inches. **Key Personnel:** John Miller, Publisher; Marcia Goodge, Editor. **Subscription Rates:** $20 individuals; $22 out of country.
Ad Rates: BW: $686.70 **Circ:** 6,000
PCI: $5.45

6773 Lake Region Monitor
Bradford Telegraph
135 W. Call St. Phone: (904)964-6305
PO Drawer A Fax: (904)964-8628
Starke, FL 32091
Community newspaper. **Founded:** 1973. **Freq:** Weekly (Thurs.). **Cols./Page:** 6. **Col. Width:** 12 picas. **Col. Depth:** 21 inches. **Key Personnel:** John M. Miller, Publisher; Lesley Peters, Editor. **Subscription Rates:** $20 individuals; $22 out of country.
Ad Rates: BW: $516.60 **Circ:** 2,250
PCI: $4.10

6774 Union County Times
PO Drawer A Phone: (904)496-2261
Starke, FL 32091 Fax: (904)964-8268

Local newspaper. **Founded:** 1921. **Freq:** Weekly. **Print Method:** Offset. **Cols./Page:** 6. **Col. Width:** 13 picas. **Col. Depth:** 21 inches. **Key Personnel:** Linda Griffis, Editor; John M. Miller, Publisher. **Subscription Rates:** $20 individuals in county; $22 out of country.
Ad Rates: BW: $592.20 **Circ:** Paid 2250
PCI: $4.70 Free 300

STUART†, pop. 9,380.

E FL. Martin Co. On St. Lucie River, 38 mi. N. of West Palm Beach. Tourist resort. Commercial fishing.

6775 Flashes Shopping Guide
Flashes, Inc.
17 W. Flagler Ave. Phone: (561)287-0650
Stuart, FL 34994 Fax: (561)283-5090

Shopper. **Founded:** 1951. **Freq:** Weekly (Wed.). **Print Method:** Offset. **Cols./Page:** 6. **Col. Width:** 10 picas. **Col. Depth:** 16 inches. **Key Personnel:** Gary L. Hawken, Publisher. **Subscription Rates:** Free.
Ad Rates: BW: $1,403 **Circ:** Free 61,300
PCI: $14.62

6776 The Stuart News
PO Box 9009 Phone: (561)287-1550
Stuart, FL 34995-9009 Fax: (561)221-4250

General newspaper. **Founded:** 1913. **Freq:** Mon.-Sun. (morn.). **Print Method:** Offset. **Trim Size:** 13 3/4 x 22 3/4. **Cols./Page:** 6. **Col. Width:** 24 nonpareils. **Col. Depth:** 301 agate lines. **Key Personnel:** Thomas E. Weber, Jr., Editor; Greg Anderson, Advertising Dir., phone (561)221-4275; Rebecca Freeman, Business Mgr., phone (561)221-4131, fax (561)221-4132. **Subscription Rates:** $79.80 individuals. **Remarks:** Accepts advertising.
Ad Rates: GLR: $5.89 **Circ:** Mon.-Sat. ★32,786
BW: $3,148.89 Sun. ★42,014
4C: $480
PCI: $24.41

6777 WCNO-FM - 89.9
177 S.W. Monterey Rd. Phone: (407)221-1100
Stuart, FL 34994-4641

Format: Religious. **Founded:** 1989. **Operating Hours:** Continuous; 100% local. **ADI:** West Palm Beach-Ft. Pierce-Vero Beach, FL. **Key Personnel:** Ray Kassis, General Mgr.; Tom Craton, General Sales Mgr. **Wattage:** 100,000. **Ad Rates:** Noncommercial.

6778 WRBD-AM - 1470
PO Box 626 Phone: (954)731-4800
Stuart, FL 34995-0626 Fax: (954)739-7917

Format: Gospel; Urban Contemporary. **Networks:** American Urban Radio. **Owner:** WRBD Inc., at above address. **Founded:** 1959. **Operating Hours:** Continuous. **Key Personnel:** James Thomas, Program/Music Director; Greg Cooper, Assistant Program Director; Hank Mosby, Sales Mgr.; Jerry Rushin, General Mgr. **Wattage:** 50,000. **Ad Rates:** $27-39 for 15 seconds; $35-51 for 30 seconds; $42-60 for 60 seconds.

6779 WSTU-AM - 1450
1000 NW Alice Ave. Phone: (407)692-1000
Stuart, FL 34994 Fax: (407)692-2231

Format: Oldies. **Networks:** ABC. **Owner:** MMM Broadcasting, Inc., 6699 N. Federal Hwy., Boca Raton, FL 33487. **Founded:** 1969. **Operating Hours:** Continuous. **ADI:** West Palm Beach-Ft. Pierce-Vero Beach, FL. **Key Personnel:** Tom Teter, Contact; Barry G. Marsh, Operations Mgr.; Barbara Clifton, Promotions Dir.; Patricia A. Larschan, General Sales Mgr. **Wattage:** 1000. **Ad Rates:** Advertising accepted; rates available upon request.

SUN CITY CENTER

East Bay Breeze - See Apollo Beach

6780 The Sun
Sunbelt Newspapers, Inc.
1507 Sun City Center Plaza Phone: (813)634-9258
Sun City Center, FL 33573 Fax: (813)634-8420

Community newspaper. **Founded:** 1973. **Freq:** Weekly (Wed.). **Print Method:** Offset. **Trim Size:** 5 x 15. **Cols./Page:** 5. **Col. Width:** 20 nonpareils. **Col. Depth:** 238 agate lines. **Key Personnel:** Carla Rockwell, General Mgr., phone (813)689-7764, fax (813)689-9685. **Subscription Rates:** Free. **Remarks:** Accepts advertising. **Formerly**: Sunbelt Publilshing Co.
Ad Rates: GLR: $2.50 **Circ:** Combined 11,500
BW: $941.25
4C: $1,181.25
PCI: $12.55

SUNRISE, pop. 52,740.

Broward Co. (NE). Suburb of Ft. Lauderdale.

6781 The Broward Informer
PO Box 130207 Phone: (954)370-6009
Sunrise, FL 33313
Publication E-mail: informer@interpoint.net

Local with empyhasis on travel and consumer protection, and seniors' affairs news. **Subtitle:** Condo Informer Travel Magazine. **Founded:** 1975. **Freq:** Biweekly. **Print Method:** Offset. Accepts mats. **Trim Size:** 10 1/4 x 16. **Cols./Page:** 6. **Col. Width:** 1 9/16 inches. **Col. Depth:** 16 inches. **Key Personnel:** Steve Mangerian, Editor of food, travel, entertainment; Mayda Mangerian, Editor-in-Chief; Michael Gaines, Office Mgr. **Subscription Rates:** $20 individuals. **Remarks:** Accepts advertising. **URL:** http://www.browardinformer.com. **Formerly**: Sunrise News (1990); Broward Sunrise Informer (1992); Condo Informer.
Ad Rates: BW: $576 **Circ:** Paid ‡2,000
4C: $800 Free ‡80,000
SAU: $6
PCI: $6.75

6782 South Florida Parenting
South Florida Parenting, Inc.
5555 Nob Hill Rd. Phone: (954)747-3050
Sunrise, FL 33351 Fax: (954)747-3055
Free: (800)244-8447
Publication E-mail: kbochi@tribune.com

Parenting magazine. **Founded:** Aug. 1990. **Freq:** Monthly. **Trim Size:** 8 1/4 x 10 1/4. **Cols./Page:** 3. **Key Personnel:** Lisa Goodlin, Advertising and Marketing Dir., phone (954)747-3051, lgoodlin@tribune.com. **Subscription Rates:** Free. **Remarks:** Accepts advertising.
Ad Rates: BW: $2,055 **Circ:** Combined ❑110,467
4C: $3,360

TALLAHASSEE†, pop. 80,800.

N FL. Leon Co. 160 mi. NW of Jacksonville. State Capital. Florida State University; Florida Agricultural and Mechanical University. Manufactures lumber, boats, pine extracts pulpwood, feed, insecticides, and pre-stressed concrete. Diversified agriculture.

6783 Capital Outlook
Capitol Outlook
602 N. Adams St. Phone: (904)681-1852
Tallahassee, FL 32301-1114 Fax: (904)681-1093

Black community newspaper. **Founded:** 1964. **Freq:** Weekly. **Cols./Page:** 6. **Col. Depth:** 21 1/2 inches. **Key Personnel:** Roosevelt Wilson, Editor and Publisher. **Subscription Rates:** $30. **Remarks:** Accepts advertising.
Ad Rates: GLR: $9 **Circ:** 11,333
BW: $1,064.25

6784 Dive Notes
Florida Association of Dive Operators
2320 Apalache Pkwy. Phone: (904)656-3483
Tallahassee, FL 32301 Fax: (904)656-5732

Trade magazine for dive store owners and equipment manufacturers. **Freq:** Bimonthly. **Key Personnel:** Susan Trainor, Editor; John McBride, Advertising Mgr.
Circ: 500

6785 Elder Update
Department of Elder Affairs
4040 Esplanade Way Phone: (904)414-2000
Tallahassee, FL 32399-7000 Fax: (904)414-2008

Newspaper (tabloid) providing Florida's senior citizens with consumer information. **Founded:** 1991. **Freq:** Monthly. **Print Method:** Offset. **Trim Size:** 11 1/4 x 13 5/8. **Cols./Page:** 4. **Key Personnel:** Kit Bauman, Editor. **USPS:** 403-710. **Subscription Rates:** Free. **Alt. Formats:** Audio tape; Braille. **Formerly:** The Senior Consumer (1992).
Circ: Free ‡73,000

6786 The Famuan
Florida A&M University
Tallahassee, FL 32307 Phone: (904)599-3159
Fax: (904)561-2570

College newspaper. **Founded:** 1919. **Freq:** Weekly. **Print Method:** Offset. **Trim Size:** 11 1/2 x 17 1/2. **Cols./Page:** 4. **Col. Width:** 26 nonpareils. **Col. Depth:** 196 agate lines. **Key Personnel:** Louise R. Ritchie, Contact, phone (904)599-3840. **Subscription Rates:** Free; $30 by mail. **Remarks:** Accepts advertising.
Ad Rates: GLR: $1 **Circ:** Free ‡5,000
BW: $448
PCI: $8

6787 Florida Administrative Weekly
Darby Printing
Florida Dept. of State Phone: (850)488-8427
Bureau of Administration Fax: (850)575-8852
PO Box 2235
Tallahassee, FL 32399-0250
Publication E-mail: faw@mail.municode.com
Publisher E-mail: subs@darbyprinting.com

State administration magazine. **Subtitle:** Florida Administrative Weekly. **Founded:** 1975. **Freq:** Weekly. **Print Method:** Offset. **Trim Size:** 8 1/2 x 11. **Cols./Page:** 2. **Col. Width:** 27 nonpareils. **Col. Depth:** 120 agate lines. **Key Personnel:** Liz Cloud, Editor/Sales Mgr. of Dept. of State; Dana Martin, Sales Rep. of Municipal Code Corp. **Subscription Rates:** $184.50 individuals plus tax; $6.00 single issue. **Online:** Internet.
Ad Rates: GLR: $.74 **Circ:** Paid ‡2,600
Non-paid ‡190

6788 Florida Banking
QP Publishing
Florida Bankers Assn. Phone: (850)224-2265
PO Box 1360 Fax: (850)224-2423
Tallahassee, FL 32302-1360
Publication E-mail: fba!wbarager@tbamail.attmail.com

Trade journal for Florida bankers. **Founded:** Sept. 1974. **Freq:** Bimonthly. **Trim Size:** 8 1/4 x 10 3/4. **Cols./Page:** 3. **Key Personnel:** Wendy A. Barager, Editor. **Subscription Rates:** $15 individuals. **Remarks:** Accepts advertising. **URL:** http://www.tallynet.com/bizpages/flbanking. **Former name:** Banking Today; Florida Banker.
Ad Rates: BW: $1,145 **Circ:** (Not Reported)

6789 The Florida Bar Journal
The Florida Bar
650 Apalachee Pkwy. Phone: (850)561-5600
Tallahassee, FL 32399-2300 Fax: (850)561-5817
Free: (800)342-8060
Publication E-mail: journal@flabar.org

Legal journal. **Founded:** Aug. 1927. **Freq:** Monthly. **Print Method:** Offset. **Trim Size:** 8 1/8 x 10 7/8. **Cols./Page:** 3. **Col. Width:** 13.5 picas. **Col. Depth:** 58 picas. **Key Personnel:** Judson Orrick, Editor, phone (850)561-5680, jorrick@flabar.org; John F. Harkness, Jr., Publisher; Cassandra Dixon, Advertising Mgr., phone (850)561-5601, dixon@flabar.org. **ISSN:** 0015-3915. **Subscription Rates:** $40 individuals; $2 single issue. **Remarks:** Accepts advertising. **Online:** Westlaw. **URL:** http://www.flabar.org. **Alt. Formats:** Microform.
Ad Rates: BW: $1,850 **Circ:** △58,085
4C: $2,500

6790 Florida Contractor
Florida Association of PHCC
PO Box 13089 Phone: (904)878-3134
Tallahassee, FL 32317 Fax: (904)878-1291
Publication E-mail: emsfl@juno.com

Plumbing, heating, cooling magazine. **Founded:** 1941. **Freq:** Monthly. **Print Method:** Offset. **Cols./Page:** 3. **Col. Width:** 26 nonpareils. **Col. Depth:** 140 agate lines. **Key Personnel:** Marian Smith, Editor; Norm Jensen, Advertising Mgr. **Subscription Rates:** $15 individuals. **Remarks:** Accepts advertising.
Ad Rates: BW: $380 **Circ:** (Not Reported)

6791 Florida CPA Today
Florida Institute of Certified Public Accountants, Inc.
PO Box 5437 Phone: (904)224-2727
Tallahassee, FL 32314 Fax: (904)222-8190

Magazine covering issues relating to Florida's CPA Profession. **Founded:** Jan. 1985. **Freq:** 1XM (February and March are combined). **Print Method:** Web offset. **Trim Size:** 8 3/8 x 10 7/8. **Key Personnel:** Michael Delaney, Director; Lloyd "Buddy" Turman, Exec. Editor; Kriss Foss, Editor; Katrina Campbell, Classified Advertising. **Subscription Rates:** Subscriptions not available. **Remarks:** Accepts advertising. **Available Online. URL:** http://www.ficpa.org.
Ad Rates: BW: $1,411 **Circ:** Controlled 19,400
4C: $2,020

6792 Florida Engineering Society Journal
Florida Engineering Society
PO Box 750 Phone: (904)224-7121
Tallahassee, FL 32302 Fax: (904)222-4349

Professional magazine covering engineering in Florida. **Founded:** 1917. **Freq:** Monthly. **Print Method:** Offset. **Trim Size:** 8 1/2 x 11. **Cols./Page:** 3. **Col. Width:** 2 3/8 inches. **Col. Depth:** 9 7/8 inches. **Key Personnel:** Patricia Sunseri, Editor; Randy Traynor, Advertising Mgr. **ISSN:** 0015-4032. **Subscription Rates:** $50 individuals. **Remarks:** Accepts advertising.
Ad Rates: BW: $765 **Circ:** Paid ‡4,500
4C: $1,370

6793 Florida Field Naturalist
Florida Ornithological Society
Tall Timbers Research Sta. Phone: (850)893-4153
Rt. 1, Box 678 Fax: (850)668-7781
Tallahassee, FL 32312-9712
Ornithology journal. **Founded:** 1973. **Freq:** Quarterly. **Print Method:** Offset. **Trim Size:** 6 x 9. **Cols./Page:** 1. **Col. Width:** 45 nonpareils. **Col. Depth:** 75 agate lines. **Key Personnel:** R. Todd Engstrom, Editor, engstrom@bio.fsu.edu. **ISSN:** 0738-999X. **Subscription Rates:** $15 individuals; $10 students. **Remarks:** Color advertising not accepted.
Ad Rates: BW: $100 **Circ:** ‡575

6794 Florida Flambeau
Florida Flambeau Foundation, Inc.
Florida State University Phone: (904)681-6692
505 S. Woodward, Box 20287 Fax: (904)681-3577
Tallahassee, FL 32316
Publication E-mail: floridaflambeau@nettally.com

Collegiate newspaper. **Founded:** 1915. **Freq:** Daily. **Print Method:** Offset. **Trim Size:** 5 x 13. **Cols./Page:** 6. **Col. Width:** 19 nonpareils. **Col. Depth:** 182 agate lines. **Key Personnel:** Amre Klimchak, Editor; Greg Colovos, General Mgr.; Ken Biderman, Advertising Mgr. **Subscription Rates:** $115 individuals. **Remarks:** Accepts advertising. **URL:** http://www.florida.flambeau.com.
Ad Rates: GLR: $1.65 **Circ:** Non-paid ‡21,000
BW: $854.75
4C: $979.75
PCI: $13.15

6795 Florida Funeral Director
Florida Funeral Directors Services, Inc.
502 E. Jefferson St. Phone: (850)224-1969
PO Box 6009 Fax: (850)224-7965
Tallahassee, FL 32314
Publication E-mail: ffda@tallynet.com; ffdamember@bigplanet.com
Publisher E-mail: ffda@tallynet.com

Trade professional magazine. **Subtitle:** The Official Publication of the Florida Funeral Directors Association. **Founded:** 1932. **Freq:** Monthly. **Print Method:** Offset. **Col. Depth:** 133 agate lines. **Key Personnel:** Diana Hull, Editor. **ISSN:** 0273-9747. **Subscription Rates:** $30 individuals. **Remarks:** Accepts advertising.
Ad Rates: BW: $225 **Circ:** Paid 1,000
4C: $725 Non-paid 50

6796 Florida Hotel & Motel Journal
Accommodations, Inc., Subsidiary
200 W. College Ave. Phone: (904)224-2888
Tallahassee, FL 32301 Fax: (904)222-1752
Free: (800)476-FHMA

Professional management journal for hotel owners and executives. **Subtitle:** The Official Publication of the Florida Hotel and Motel Association. **Founded:** Oct. 1978. **Freq:** 10/year. **Print Method:** Web offset. **Trim Size:** 8 3/8 x 10 7/8. **Key Personnel:** Jayleen Woods, Editor; Janet Litherland, Assoc. Editor; Michelle Cyr, Advertising Mgr., fax (407)891-9985, mcyr@email.msn.com. **ISSN:** 8750-6807. **Subscription Rates:** $24 individuals; $2.40 single issue. **Remarks:** Accepts advertising.
Ad Rates: BW: $1,560 **Circ:** Controlled **8,000**
4C: $2,240

6797 Florida Market Bulletin
Florida Dept. of Agriculture & Consumer Services
545 East Tennessee St. Phone: (850)487-8000
Tallahassee, FL 32308 Fax: (850)922-2189
Free: (800)435-7352
Publication E-mail: landw@doacs.state.fl.us

Agricultural publication. **Founded:** 1917. **Freq:** Monthly. **Cols./Page:** 4. **Col. Width:** 2 1/4 inches. **Col. Depth:** 12 inches. **Key Personnel:** Mary Pichard, Classified Advertising Manager; Galen Moses, Editor. **USPS:** 330-180. **Subscription Rates:** Free to Florida residents; $10 others. **Remarks:** Advertising not accepted. **URL:** http://doacs.state.fl.us; http://www.fmb-subs.doccs.state.fl.us.
Circ: Controlled ‡18,000

6798 Florida Medical Association
Florida Medical Association, Inc.
PO Box 10269 Phone: (904)224-6496
Tallahassee, FL 32302-2269 Fax: (904)224-6627
Publisher E-mail: medone_ info@medone.org

Tabloid newspaper covering issues of the Florida Medical Association. **Freq:** Bimonthly. **Key Personnel:** Glenn S. Hooper, M.D., Editor; Marie Dowling, Managing Editor; Francine A. Walker, VP, Communications and Education. **Remarks:** Advertising accepted; rates available upon request. **URL:** http://www.medone.org.
Circ: (Not Reported)

6799 Florida Music Director
Florida Music Educators Association
2305 Kilkenny Dr. W Phone: (904)644-4412
Tallahassee, FL 32308 Fax: (904)644-2033

Music magazine. **Subtitle:** Includes Florida Music Teacher. **Founded:** 1947. **Freq:** 10/year. **Print Method:** Offset. **Trim Size:** 8 1/2 x 11. **Cols./Page:** 3. **Col. Width:** 28 nonpareils. **Col. Depth:** 140 agate lines. **Key Personnel:** Michael Allen, Editor; Judith D. Stone, Exec. Dir., judystone@mindspring.com; Misti L. Pittenger, Advertising Mgr. **ISSN:** 0046-4155. **Subscription Rates:** $15 individuals; $2.50 single issue. **Remarks:** Accepts advertising.
Ad Rates: BW: $275 **Circ:** Paid ‡4,500
4C: $550

6800 Florida Pharmacy Today
Florida Pharmacy Association
610 N. Adams St. Phone: (850)222-2400
Tallahassee, FL 32301-1114 Fax: (850)561-6758
Publication E-mail: fpa@pharmview.com
Publisher E-mail: mtg584@aol.com

Professional pharmacy journal. **Founded:** 1937. **Freq:** Monthly. **Print Method:** Offset. **Trim Size:** 8 3/8 x 10 7/8. **Cols./Page:** 3. **Col. Width:** 40 nonpareils. **Col. Depth:** 140 agate lines. **Key Personnel:** Julia Hanway, Editor, phone (850)928-2405, fax (850)926-2411, mtg584@aol.com. **ISSN:** 0161-746X. **Subscription Rates:** $36 individuals; $70 institutions. **Remarks:** Accepts advertising.
Ad Rates: BW: $582 **Circ:** ‡3,000
4C: $1,082

6801 Florida Psychologist
Florida Psychological Association
408 Office Plaza Dr. Phone: (850)656-2222
Tallahassee, FL 32301-2757 Fax: (850)942-4586

Membership magazine for psychologists. **Freq:** Quarterly. **Print Method:** Offset. **Key Personnel:** Antonio Carvajal, Editor. **Subscription Rates:** Free to qualified subscribers. **Remarks:** Accepts advertising.
Ad Rates: BW: $425 **Circ:** Controlled 1,800

6802 Florida Rental Association News
Florida Rental Association
335 Beard St. Phone: (904)222-6000
Tallahassee, FL 32303 Fax: (904)681-2890
Publication E-mail: tony@assocofc.attmail.com

Trade magazine for rental equipment dealers in Florida.

Founded: 1989. **Freq:** Bimonthly. **Remarks:** Advertising accepted; rates available upon request.
Circ: 1600

6803 Florida Truck News
Florida Trucking Association, Inc.
350 E. College Ave. Phone: (904)222-9900
Tallahassee, FL 32301-1565 Free: (800)435-7365

Trucking industry association magazine. **Founded:** June 10, 1947. **Freq:** Monthly. **Print Method:** Offset. **Trim Size:** 8 1/2 x 11. **Cols./Page:** 3 and 2. **Col. Width:** 26 and 42 nonpareils. **Col. Depth:** 140 agate lines. **Key Personnel:** Rivers H. Buford III, Managing Editor; Tom B. Webb, Publisher; Ed Pooser, Advertising Mgr. **ISSN:** 0015-4334. **Subscription Rates:** $25 individuals; $5 single issue. **Remarks:** Accepts advertising.
Ad Rates: BW: $460 **Circ:** Paid ‡1,600
4C: $910 Controlled ‡800
PCI: $35

6804 Focal Point
Professional Opticians of Florida
335 Beard St. Phone: (850)222-6000
Tallahassee, FL 32303 Fax: (850)681-2890

Trade magazine for licensed opticians. **Freq:** Quarterly. **Print Method:** saddle-stitched. **Trim Size:** 8 1/4 x 10 7/8. **Key Personnel:** Mark A. Miller, Advertising Mgr., mark@hmgnet.com; Michelle Cyr, Advertising Mgr., michelle@hmgnet.com. **Remarks:** Accepts advertising. **URL:** http://www.pof.org.
Ad Rates: GLR: $133 **Circ:** 1,200
BW: $275
4C: $664

6805 Grape Times
Florida Grape Growers Association
335 Beard St.
Tallahassee, FL 32303

Magazine for wine enthusiasts and those working in wineyards and wineries. **Freq:** Bimonthly. **Key Personnel:** Peter Lohrengel, Editor; John McBride, Advertising Mgr.
Circ: 200

6806 The Journal of the Academy of Florida Trial Lawyers
218 S. Monroe Phone: (850)224-9403
Tallahassee, FL 32301 Fax: (850)224-4254
Publisher E-mail: aftl@ix.netcom.com

Case reference periodical forum for discussion of legislative & legal issues. **Founded:** 1961. **Freq:** Monthly. **Print Method:** Offset. **Trim Size:** 8 1/2 x 11. **Cols./Page:** 2. **Key Personnel:** S. Victor Tipton, Editor; Jan Thomason, Contact; Kathy Wilson, Dir.; Samantha Strickland, Coordinator. **Subscription Rates:** $7.50 single issue. **Remarks:** Accepts advertising. **URL:** http://www.aftl.org.
Ad Rates: BW: $450 **Circ:** Paid 4,000
4C: $750

6807 Journal of Geography
National Council for Geographic Education
Dept. of Geography Phone: (904)644-8375
Florida State University
Tallahassee, FL 32306-2050
Publisher E-mail: ncge-org@grove.iup.edu

Journal for geography instructors at all educational levels. **Founded:** 1896. **Freq:** Bimonthly. **Print Method:** Letterpress and offset. **Trim Size:** 8 1/2 x 11. **Cols./Page:** 2. **Col. Width:** 40 nonpareils. **Col. Depth:** 133 agate lines. **Key Personnel:** Jonathan Leib, Editor, jleib@garnet.acns.fsu.edu. **ISSN:** 0022-1341. **Subscription Rates:** $20 students; $40 individuals. **Remarks:** Accepts advertising. **URL:** geog.tamu.edu.
Ad Rates: BW: $400 **Circ:** ‡4,500
4C: $1,000

6808 On Track
Florida Economic Development Council
335 Beard St.
Tallahassee, FL 32303

Trade magazine for economic development professionals and chambers of commerce. **Freq:** Quarterly. **Key Personnel:** Peter Lohrengel, Editor; John McBride, Advertising Mgr.
Circ: 300

6809 Psychomusicology
Florida State University
Tallahassee, FL 32306-1180 Phone: (850)644-5786
Fax: (850)644-6100

Scholarly journal covering research in music. **Founded:** 1981. **Freq:** Semiannual. **Print Method:** Offset. **Trim Size:** 6 x 9. **Col. Width:** 4 inches. **Col. Depth:** 7 inches. **Key Personnel:** Jack A. Taylor, Editor, taylor@cmr.fsu.edu; Jerry P. Wood, Business Mgr., jpw@cmr.fsu.edu. **ISSN:** 0275-3987. **Subscription Rates:** $27 individuals; $33 other countries; $18 single issue U.S.; $21 single issue other countries. **Remarks:** Advertising not accepted. **URL:** http://otto.cmr.fsu.edu/psychomus.
Circ: (Not Reported)

6810 Quality Cities
Florida League of Cities
201 Park Ave. W. Phone: (904)222-9684
PO Box 1757 Fax: (904)222-3806
Tallahassee, FL 32302-1757
Publication E-mail: tmccants@flcitiess.com

Magazine covering issues of interest to Florida's municipal officials. **Founded:** Apr. 1928. **Freq:** 11/year. **Print Method:** Offset. **Trim Size:** 8 1/2 x 11. **Cols./Page:** 3. **Col. Width:** 13 picas. **Col. Depth:** 55 picas. **Key Personnel:** Michael Sittig, Publisher; Lydia Markley, Art & Ad.Man., lmarkley@flcities.com. **ISSN:** 0892-4171. **Subscription Rates:** $20 individuals. **Remarks:** Accepts advertising.
Ad Rates: BW: $477 **Circ:** Paid ‡3,786
4C: $1,165 Non-paid ‡1,179

6811 Relay Magazine
Florida Municipal Electric Association, Inc.
PO Box 10114
Tallahassee, FL 32302
Publication E-mail: swatFMEA@aol.com
Publisher E-mail: swatfmea@aol.com

Trade magazine covering the electric utility industry in Florida. **Founded:** 1957. **Freq:** Monthly. **Print Method:** Offset. **Trim Size:** 8 x 11. **Key Personnel:** Stephanie Wolanski, Editor, swolanski@publicpower.com; Brenda Thompson, Circulation Mgr., bthompson@publicpower.com. **Subscription Rates:** Free to qualified subscribers. **Remarks:** Accepts advertising.
Ad Rates: 4C: $700 **Circ:** Controlled 2,200

6812 Rental Guide
Rental Guide Magazine
1600 Capital Circle SW Phone: (904)574-2111
Tallahassee, FL 32310-9246 Fax: (904)574-2525
Free: (800)277-7800

Rental guide magazine for the Seattle/Puget Sound Area. **Freq:** Quarterly. **Key Personnel:** Tom Scardino, Vice Pres./Publishing. **Subscription Rates:** Free. **Remarks:** Advertising accepted; rates available upon request. **URL:** http://www.homes.com.
Circ: Non-paid 128,926

6813 Scuba Retailer
Scuba Retailers Association
335 Beard St.
Tallahassee, FL 32303

Trade magazine for dive store owners and equipment manufacturers. **Freq:** Bimonthly. **Key Personnel:** Peter Lohrengel, Editor; John McBride, Advertising Mgr.
Circ: 3,000

6814 Social Theory and Practices
Florida State University
151 Dodd Hall Phone: (850)644-0220
Tallahassee, FL 32306-1500 Fax: (850)644-3832
Publisher E-mail: journals@mailer.fsu.edu

Scholarly journal covering social philosophy worldwide. **Founded:** 1970. **Freq:** Triennial. **Print Method:** Offset. **Trim Size:** 6 x 9 1/4. **Cols./Page:** 1. **Col. Width:** 4 1/4 inches. **Col. Depth:** 7 1/4 inches. **Key Personnel:** R. M. Dancy, Editor; Margaret Dancy, Managing Editor. **ISSN:** 0037-802X. **Remarks:** Accepts advertising. **URL:** http://www.fsu.edu/~philo/STP.
Ad Rates: BW: $80 **Circ:** Combined 700

6815 Studies in Art Education
National Art Education Association
Dept of Art Ed Phone: (904)644-1915
126 MCH-3014 Fax: (904)644-5067
Florida St. Univ.
Tallahassee, FL 32306-3014
Publisher E-mail: naea@dgs.dgsys.com

Journal of research in visual art education. **Founded:** 1959. **Freq:** Quarterly. **Trim Size:** 6 x 9. **Cols./Page:** 1. **Col. Width:** 28 picas. **Col. Depth:** 7 1/2 inches. **Key Personnel:** Carol May, Managing Editor. **ISSN:** 0039-3541. **Subscription Rates:** $25. $9 single issue. **Remarks:** Advertising not accepted.
Circ: Paid ‡4,197
Non-paid ‡30

6816 The Tallahassee Advertiser
PO Box 3696 Phone: (904)385-3547
Tallahassee, FL 32315-3696 Fax: (904)385-6177
Publisher E-mail: tta19@mail.idt.net

Local community newspaper. **Founded:** Nov. 26, 1976. **Freq:** Weekly (Thurs.). **Print Method:** Offset. **Trim Size:** 11.25 x 13. **Cols./Page:** 6. **Col. Width:** 1 9/16 inches. **Col. Depth:** 13 inches. **Key Personnel:** Curtis Lamb, General Mgr. **ISSN:** 0744-4400. **Subscription Rates:** $49 individuals. **Remarks:** Accepts advertising. **URL:** http://www.tallahasseeadvertiser.com.
Ad Rates: GLR: $9 **Circ:** Paid 8,120
BW: $702 Free 1,880
4C: $827
PCI: $9

6817 Tallahassee Democrat
Knight-Ridder, Inc.
277 N. Magnolia Dr. Phone: (850)599-2100
PO Box 990 Fax: (850)599-2295
Tallahassee, FL 32301-0990
General newspaper. **Founded:** Mar. 3, 1905. **Freq:** Mon.-Sun. (morn.). **Print Method:** Offset. **Trim Size:** 13 11/16 x 22 3/4. **Cols./Page:** 6. **Col. Width:** 2 1/16 inches. **Col. Depth:** 21 1/2 inches. **Key Personnel:** Lou Heldman, Sr. V.P./Exec. Editor; J. Carrol Dadisman, Publisher; Thomas E. Privett, V.P. Mktg. **ISSN:** 0738-5153. **Subscription Rates:** $134.16 individuals; $218.40 out of state. **Remarks:** Accepts advertising. **URL:** http://www.tdo.com. **Feature Editors:** Chuck Beard, *Travel*, phone (904)599-2207; Bill Berlow, *Education*, *Environmental*, phone (904)599-2257; Dorothy Clifford, *Real Estate*, phone (904)599-2208; Bill Cotterell, *Political*, phone (904)222-6729; Byron Dobson, *City*, *Metro*, phone (904)599-2256; Lorrie Guttman, *Food*, phone (904)599-2315; Barbara Laughlin, *Consumer Affairs*, phone (904)599-2312; J. M. Pudlow, *News*, phone (904)599-2293; Ron Morris, *Sports*, phone (904)599-2160; Janie Nelson, *Drama*, *Entertainment*, *Family*, *Features*, *Garden/Home*, *Lifestyle*, *Living*, *Medical*, *Movie*, *Music*, *Radio*, *Science*, *Society*, phone (904)599-2170; Zilpha Underwood, *Book*, *Fashion*, *Religion*, *Women's*, phone (904)599-2314.
Ad Rates: GLR: $2.33 **Circ:** Mon.-Sat. **★52,188**
BW: $4,207.98 Sun. **★71,129**
4C: $4,717.98
PCI: $32.62

6818 Tallahassee Magazine
Rowland Publishing, Inc.
PO Box 1837 Phone: (904)878-0554
Tallahassee, FL 32302 Fax: (904)656-1871

Magazine focusing on lifestyles in Tallahassee, FL. **Founded:** Mar. 1979. **Freq:** Bimonthly. **Print Method:** Web offset. **Trim Size:** 8 3/8 x 10 7/8. **Cols./Page:** 3. **Col. Width:** 2 1/4 inches. **Col. Depth:** 10 inches. **Key Personnel:** Brian Rowland, Publisher; Larry Pilkington, Sales Mgr.; Kathy Grobe, Managing Editor. **Subscription Rates:** $16.85 individuals; $2.95 single issue.
Ad Rates: BW: $1560 **Circ:** Controlled 17,300
4C: $1940

6819 Thanatos
Florida Funeral Directors Services, Inc.
502 E. Jefferson St. Phone: (850)224-1969
PO Box 6009 Fax: (850)224-7965
Tallahassee, FL 32314
Publication E-mail: ffda@tallynet.com
Publisher E-mail: ffda@tallynet.com

Subtitle: A Realistic Journal Concerning Dying, Death and Bereavement. **Founded:** 1975. **Freq:** Quarterly. **Print Method:** Offset. **Trim Size:** 8 1/2 x 11. **Cols./Page:** 3. **Key Personnel:** Jan Scheff, Editor. **ISSN:** 0160-8681. **Subscription Rates:** $16 individuals; $21 other countries; $4 single issue. **Remarks:** Advertising not accepted.
Circ: Paid ‡7,000
Non-paid ‡200

6820 Today's FDA
Florida Dental Association
1111 E Tennessee St. Phone: (850)681-3629
Tallahassee, FL 32308-6914 Fax: (850)561-0504
Publisher E-mail: fda@floridadental.org

Professional journal for members of Florida Dental Association. **Founded:** 1989. **Freq:** Monthly. **Print Method:** Web offset. **Trim Size:** 11 1/4 x 15 1/2. **Cols./Page:** 4. **Key Personnel:** Karen Thurston Chavez, Managing Editor. **ISSN:** 1048-5317. **Subscription Rates:** Included in membership. **Remarks:** Accepts advertising. **Former name:** Florida Dental Journal; Dental Times Dispatch.
Circ: (Not Reported)

6821 Trial Advocate Quarterly
Florida Defense Lawyers Association
c/o Claire Hamner Matherro
Florida State University
College of Law
425 W. Jefferson St.
Tallahassee, FL 32306-1034

Professional journal covering law in Florida. **Founded:** 1981. **Freq:** Quarterly. **Trim Size:** 8 1/4 x 11. **Cols./Page:** 2. **Col. Width:** 3 7/16 inches. **Col. Depth:** 9 11/16 inches. **Key Personnel:** Claire Hamner Matherro, Editor. **Subscription**

Rates: $40 individuals; $10 single issue. **Remarks:** Accepts advertising.
Ad Rates: BW: $250 **Circ:** Combined 1,500

6822 WAMF-FM - 90.5
Florida A&M University Phone: (904)599-3083
PO Box 6202 Fax: (904)561-2829
Tallahassee, FL 32312

Format: Jazz; Ethnic; Urban Contemporary. **Networks:** Independent. **Owner:** Florida A&M University, at above address. **Founded:** 1977. **Operating Hours:** 7 am-1 pm Sun-Thur, 7 am-4 pm Fri and Sat; 100% local. **ADI:** Tallahassee, FL-Thomasville (Bainbridge), GA. **Key Personnel:** Darryl Smith, General Mgr.; Phillip Keirstead, News Dir., phone (904)5612601, fax (904)5612829. **Local Programs:** *Classic Showcase*, Carl McBride; *Meet the Professor*, John Omachonu; *Musica Caliente*, John Omachonu. **Wattage:** 1600. **Ad Rates:** Noncommercial.

6823 WANM-AM - 1070
PO Box 14369 Phone: (904)222-1070
Tallahassee, FL 32317-4369 Fax: (904)877-1040

Format: News. **Networks:** CNN Radio. **Founded:** 1974. **Operating Hours:** Sunrise-sunset. **ADI:** Tallahassee, FL-Thomasville (Bainbridge), GA. **Key Personnel:** Vernon Arnold, Operations Mgr. **Local Programs:** *Smoke This (Cigar Show)*, Vernon Arnold; *Sounds of Faith (Urban Gospel)* Sunday, Vernon Arnold. **Wattage:** 10,000. **Ad Rates:** $10 for 30 seconds; $14 for 60 seconds.

6824 WBZE-FM - 98.9
109B Ridgeland Rd. Phone: (904)385-1156
Tallahassee, FL 32312 Fax: (904)224-8329

Format: Soft Rock. **Founded:** 1962. **Formerly:** WBGM-FM; HVS Partners. **Operating Hours:** Continuous. **ADI:** Tallahassee, FL-Thomasville (Bainbridge), GA. **Key Personnel:** Jon Hill, General Mgr. **Wattage:** 100,000. **URL:** http://www.989breeze.com.

6825 WCTV-TV - 6
Box 3048 Phone: (904)893-6666
Tallahassee, FL 32315 Fax: (904)893-5193

Format: Commercial TV. **Networks:** CBS. **Owner:** Gray Communication Systems, Inc., PO Box 3048, Tallahassee, FL 32315. **Founded:** Sept. 15, 1955. **Operating Hours:** Continuous. **ADI:** Tallahassee, FL-Thomasville (Bainbridge), GA. **Key Personnel:** Melvin H. Blank, Operations Mgr.; Jack Donahue, Director of Sales & Marketing; Mike Smith, News & Production Director; Elliot Toole, Promotions Mgr.; Jere Pique, President. **Wattage:** 97,500.

6826 WCVC-AM - 1330
117 1/2 Henderson Rd. Phone: (850)386-7133
Tallahassee, FL 32312-2337 Fax: (850)386-2138
Free: (888)386-9282

Format: Religious; Contemporary Christian. **Networks:** Ambassador Inspirational Radio; USA Radio. **Founded:** 1953. **Formerly:** WMEN-AM (1976). **Operating Hours:** Sunrise-sunset. **ADI:** Tallahassee, FL-Thomasville (Bainbridge), GA. **Key Personnel:** Wendell Borrink, General Mgr.; Alan McCall, Local Sales Mgr., phone (850)486-1330, fax (850)386-2138. **Local Programs:** *Morning Lite* 6:30 a.m. Monday-Friday, Alan McCall, Sales Coord., (850)386-1330, Fax (850)386-2138; *Sunday Praise* 7 a.m. Sunday; *Town Meeting* 5 p.m. Monday-Friday; *Family Alive* 1:00 pm Saturday. **Wattage:** 5000. **Ad Rates:** $10 for 30 seconds; $13 for 60 seconds.

WFSG-TV - See Panama City

6827 WFSQ-FM - 91.5
1600 Red Barber Plaza Phone: (904)487-3086
Tallahassee, FL 32310 Fax: (904)487-3293
Free: (800)829-8809
E-mail: wfsufm@sfsu.org

Format: Classical. **Networks:** National Public Radio (NPR). **Founded:** 1990. **Formerly:** WFSU-FM. **Operating Hours:** Continuous. **ADI:** Tallahassee, FL-Thomasville (Bainbridge), GA. **Key Personnel:** Caroline Austin, Station Mgr., fax (904)487-3086, caustin@mailer.fsu.edu; Ben Wilcox, News Dir., bwilcoxmaineler.fsu.edu. **Wattage:** 100,000. **Ad Rates:** Noncommercial. **URL:** http://www.wfsu.org.

6828 WFSU-FM - 88.9
1600 Red Barber Plaza Phone: (904)487-3086
Tallahassee, FL 32310 Fax: (904)487-3293
Free: (800)829-8809
E-mail: wfsufm@wfsu.org

Format: Public Radio; News; Information. **Networks:** American Public Radio (APR); National Public Radio (NPR). **Founded:** 1954. **Operating Hours:** Continuous; 80% network, 20% local. **ADI:** Tallahassee, FL-Thomasville (Bainbridge), GA. **Key Personnel:** Caroline Austin, Station Mgr., fax (904)487-2611, caustin@mailer.fsu.edu; Ben Wilcox, News Dir., bwilcox@fsu.edu. **Local Programs:** *People's Editorial*, Ben Wilcox. **Wattage:** 95,000. **Ad Rates:** Noncommercial. **URL:** http://www.wfsu.org.

6829 WFSU-TV - 11
1600 Red Barber Plaza Phone: (904)487-3170
Tallahassee, FL 32310 Fax: (904)487-3093
Free: (800)322-9378
E-mail: wfsu-tv@mailer.fsu.edu

Format: Public TV. **Networks:** Public Broadcasting Service (PBS). **Founded:** 1960. **Operating Hours:** 6:45 a.m.-1 a.m.; 95% network, 5% local. **ADI:** Tallahassee, FL-Thomasville (Bainbridge), GA.

6830 WGLF-FM - 104.1
1310 Paul Russell Rd. Phone: (904)878-1104
Tallahassee, FL 32301 Fax: (904)877-1040
E-mail: jocks@gu1f104.com

Format: Album-Oriented Rock (AOR). **Networks:** Independent. **Founded:** 1969. **Operating Hours:** Continuous; 100% local. **ADI:** Tallahassee, FL-Thomasville (Bainbridge), GA. **Key Personnel:** Kim McAllister, General Mgr.; Paul Davis, Program Dir.; Rick Flagg, News Dir. **Local Programs:** *Gulf 104 Morning Show*, T.C. McGuire, (904)878-1104, Fax (904)877-1040. **Wattage:** 100,000. **Ad Rates:** $40-60 per unit. **URL:** gu1f104.com.

6831 WHBT-AM - 1410
109B Ridgeland Rd. Phone: (904)385-1156
Tallahassee, FL 32312 Fax: (904)224-8329

Format: Religious. **Founded:** 1959. **Formerly:** WBGM-AM (1991); HVS Partners. **Operating Hours:** Continuous. **ADI:** Tallahassee, FL-Thomasville (Bainbridge), GA. **Key Personnel:** Jon Hill, General Mgr. **Wattage:** 5,000.

6832 WHBX-FM - 96.1
109-B Ridgeland Rd. Phone: (904)385-1156
Tallahassee, FL 32312 Fax: (904)224-8329

Format: Urban Contemporary. **Networks:** Satellite Music Network. **Founded:** 1981. **Formerly:** WTMG-FM (1992). **Operating Hours:** Continuous. **ADI:** Tallahassee, FL-Thomasville (Bainbridge), GA. **Key Personnel:** Jon Hill, Market Mgr. **Ad Rates:** Advertising accepted; rates available upon request. WBZE, WWLD, WGLF.

6833 WMLO-FM - 104.9
3360 Capital Circle N.E. Phone: (904)668-6600
Tallahassee, FL 32308 Fax: (904)422-1070
Free: (800)560-5448
E-mail: wompam@weir.net

Format: Adult Contemporary. **Networks:** Wall Street Journal Radio; CNN Radio. **Owner:** Ed Winton, at above address. **Founded:** 1987. **Operating Hours:** Continuous. **ADI:** Tallahassee, FL-Thomasville (Bainbridge), GA. **Key Personnel:** Linda Winton, General Mgr. **Wattage:** 50,000. **Ad Rates:** $18-38 per unit.

6834 WNLS-AM - 1270
Bldg. G Phone: (850)422-3107
325 John Knox Rd. Fax: (850)514-4441
Tallahassee, FL 32303

Format: Sports; Talk. **Networks:** ESPN Radio. **Owner:** Clear Channel Communications, Inc., PO Box 659512, San Antonio, TX 78265-9512. **Founded:** 1935. **Operating Hours:** Continuous. **ADI:** Tallahassee, FL-Thomasville (Bainbridge), GA. **Key Personnel:** David Manning, General Mgr., dmanning@cctall.com; Lee Bowen, Program Dir., lbowen@cctall.com. **Wattage:** 5000. **Ad Rates:** Advertising accepted; rates available upon request. Combined advertising rates available with WTNT-FM, WXSR-FM, WOKL-FM, WJZT-FM. **URL:** http://www.sportsworld.com.

WOZN-FM - See Key West

6835 WTNT-FM - 94.9
325 John Knox Rd. Phone: (850)422-3107
Bldg. G Fax: (850)383-0747
Tallahassee, FL 32303

Format: Contemporary Country. **Networks:** Independent. **Owner:** Clear Chanel Radio, at above address. **Founded:** 1967. **Operating Hours:** Continuous; 100% local. **ADI:** Tallahassee, FL-Thomasville (Bainbridge), GA. **Key Personnel:** David Manning, General Mgr.; Judy Bailey, Sales Mgr. **Wattage:** 100,000. **Ad Rates:** $60-70 for 60 seconds.

6836 WTWC-TV - 40
8440 Deerlake Rd. Phone: (850)893-4140
Tallahassee, FL 32312 Fax: (850)893-6974

Format: Commercial TV. **Networks:** NBC. **Owner:** Guy Gannett Communications, at above address. **Operating Hours:** Continuous. 22. **ADI:** Tallahassee, FL-Thomasville (Bainbridge), GA. **Key Personnel:** William Anderson, General Mgr.; Dave Greubel, General Sales Mgr.; Rob Gwinn, Traffic Mgr.; Paige Dietz, Program Mgr. **Wattage:** 3,100,000.

6837 WTXL-TV - 27
8927 Thomasville Rd. Phone: (904)893-3127
Tallahassee, FL 32312 Fax: (904)668-1460
E-mail: wtxl.com

Format: Commercial TV. **Networks:** ABC. **Owner:** Media Venture Management, Inc, at above address. **Founded:** 1976. **Formerly:** WECA-TV (1984). **Operating Hours:** Continuous. **ADI:** Tallahassee, FL-Thomasville (Bainbridge), GA. **Key Personnel:** Brian Cobb, Owner; Janice Gargus, Program Dir.; Christine Boldt, Business Mgr.; Dan Akens, General Mgr. **Ad Rates:** $20-2000 per unit.

6838 WUMX-FM - 103.1
PO Box 13909 Phone: (904)386-5141
Tallahassee, FL 32317-3549 Fax: (904)878-3292

Format: Adult Contemporary. **Networks:** AP. **Founded:** 1976. **Formerly:** WTHZ-FM (1991). **Operating Hours:** Continuous. **ADI:** Tallahassee, FL-Thomasville (Bainbridge), GA. **Key Personnel:** Howard B. Dolgoff, General Mgr. **Wattage:** 50,000. **Ad Rates:** $75 for 30 seconds.

6839 WVFS-FM - 89.7
420 Diffenbaugh Bldg. Phone: (904)644-3871
Tallahassee, FL 32306 Fax: (904)644-8642

Format: Alternative/New Music/Progressive. **Founded:** 1986. **Operating Hours:** Continuous. **ADI:** Tallahassee, FL-Thomasville (Bainbridge), GA. **Key Personnel:** Lee Stepina, Station Mgr.; Christopher White, Contact; Maria Bakkalappo, Operations Dir.; Ken O'Leary, News Dir. **Wattage:** 299. **Ad Rates:** Noncommercial.

6840 WXSR-FM - 101.5
3360 Capital Circle NE Phone: (904)385-0101
Tallahassee, FL 32308 Fax: (904)386-7363
E-mail: x1015@aol.com

Format: Adult Album Alternative. **Networks:** Westwood One Radio. **Owner:** Paxson Communications, at above address. **Founded:** 1990. **Formerly:** WFHT-FM (1993). **Operating Hours:** Continuous. **ADI:** Tallahassee, FL-Thomasville (Bainbridge), GA. **Key Personnel:** Rick Schmidt, Program Dir.; Dave Lowe, General Mgr.; Belinda Beninger, General Sales Mgr. **Wattage:** 50,000.

TAMPA†, pop. 271,523.

WC FL. Hillsborough Co. At head of Hillsboro Bay, 24 mi. from Gulf of Mexico. University of Tampa; University of South Florida; Florida College. Mac Dill A.F.B. Resort area. Leading port in shipping phosphate and citrus fruit. Manufactures cigars, fertilizer, feed, cement, beverages, clothing, paint, glass, chemicals, aluminum products, and pharmaceuticals. Fruit and vegetable packing and canning.

6841 AAA Going Places
AAA Auto Club South
1515 N. Westshore Blvd. Phone: (813)289-5923
Tampa, FL 33607 Fax: (813)289-6245

Magazine for auto club members and the travel market. **Subtitle:** The Magazine for Today's Traveler. **Founded:** Mar. 1982. **Freq:** Bimonthly. **Print Method:** Offset. **Trim Size:** 8 x 10 1/2. **Cols./Page:** 3. **Col. Width:** 2 3/16 inches. **Col. Depth:** 9 3/8 inches. **Key Personnel:** Phyllis W. Zeno, Editor; Bob Sharp, Publisher; Michael Eisman, Advertising Mgr., phone (813)289-5431. **Subscription Rates:** $1 individuals. **Remarks:** Accepts advertising. **Available Online. Alt. Formats:** Braille; CD-ROM.
Ad Rates: BW: $36,488 **Circ:** Paid 2,300
4C: $39,900

6842 BBC Music Magazine
Warner Enterprises
PO Box 61099
Tampa, FL 33661

Publication that reviews popular CD's and features articles on numerous musicians. Each issue includes a full-length CD. **Freq:** Monthly. **Subscription Rates:** $36.

Carrollwood News - See Carrollwood

6843 Design Cost Data
DC & D Technologies, Inc.
8602 N. 40th St. Phone: (813)989-9300
Tampa, FL 33604 Fax: (813)980-3982
Free: (800)533-5680
Publication E-mail: info@dcd.com

Publication providing real cost data case studies of various

types completed around the country for design and building professionals. **Subtitle:** Cost Estimating Magazine for Design and Construction. **Founded:** Mar. 1958. **Freq:** Bimonthly. **Print Method:** Web offset. **Trim Size:** 8 1/2 x 11. **Cols./Page:** 3. **Col. Width:** 2 1/4 inches. **Col. Depth:** 10 inches. **Key Personnel:** Barbara Castelli, Publisher, barb@dcd.com. **ISSN:** 0739-3946. **Subscription Rates:** $78.40 individuals. **Remarks:** Accepts advertising. **Available Online. URL:** http://www.dcd.com. **Alt. Formats:** CD-ROM.
Ad Rates: BW: $1,950 **Circ:** Controlled ‡15,000
4C: $2,750

6844 Financial Management
Financial Management Association
School of Business Phone: (813)974-2084
University of South Florida Fax: (813)974-3318
Tampa, FL 33620-5500
Publisher E-mail: fma@bsn01.bsn.usf.edu

Magazine covering business, economics, finance and management. **Subtitle:** The Journal of the Financial Management Association. **Founded:** 1972. **Freq:** Quarterly. **Print Method:** Offset. **Trim Size:** 8 1/4 x 10 7/8. **Cols./Page:** 2. **Col. Width:** 38 nonpareils. **Col. Depth:** 118 agate lines. **Key Personnel:** Douglas R. Emery, Editor; John D. Finnerty, Editor. **ISSN:** 0046-3892. **Subscription Rates:** $95 individuals; $20 single issue. **Remarks:** Accepts advertising.
Ad Rates: BW: $500 **Circ:** ‡12,000

6845 The Florida Anthropologist
Florida Anthropological Society, Inc.
PO Box 82255 Phone: (813)991-4643
Tampa, FL 33682
Publisher E-mail: tsimpson@luna.cas.usf.edu

Journal focusing on anthropology and archaeology. **Founded:** 1948. **Freq:** Quarterly. **Print Method:** Letterpress and offset. **Trim Size:** 8 1/2 x 11. **Cols./Page:** 2. **Col. Width:** 56 nonpareils. **Col. Depth:** 102 agate lines. **Key Personnel:** Robert J. Austin, Editor, phone (813)677-2280, fax (813)671-8416, bob@searchinc.com. **ISSN:** 0015-3893. **Subscription Rates:** included with membership. **Remarks:** Accepts advertising.
Ad Rates: BW: $100 **Circ:** ‡950

6846 Florida Sentinel-Bulletin
2207-21st Ave. Phone: (813)248-1921
PO Box 3363 Fax: (813)248-4507
Tampa, FL 33601
Black community newspaper (tabloid). **Founded:** 1945. **Freq:** Semiweekly (Tues. and Fri.). **Print Method:** Offset. **Trim Size:** 10 x 15. **Cols./Page:** 5. **Col. Width:** 2 inches. **Col. Depth:** 15 inches. **Key Personnel:** C. Blythe Andrews, Jr., Publisher; Sybil Andrews Wells, General Mgr. **Subscription Rates:** $31 individuals. **Remarks:** Color advertising not accepted.
Ad Rates: GLR: $.72 **Circ:** ‡23,345
PCI: $10

6847 The Flyer
201 Kelsey Ln. Phone: (813)626-9430
Tampa, FL 33619 Fax: (813)626-8923

Shopper. **Founded:** 1977. **Freq:** Weekly (Wed.). **Print Method:** Offset. **Trim Size:** 7 3/4 x 10. **Cols./Page:** 2. **Col. Width:** 30 nonpareils. **Col. Depth:** 168 agate lines. **Key Personnel:** Jim Kendall, Publisher, phone (813)626-4812. **Remarks:** Accepts advertising.
Ad Rates: GLR: $17 **Circ:** Free 675,000

6848 Free Press
Free Press Publishing Co.
1010 Cass St. Phone: (813)254-5888
Tampa, FL 33606 Fax: (813)251-0511

Community newspaper. **Founded:** 1911. **Freq:** Weekly. **Print Method:** Offset. **Cols./Page:** 8. **Col. Width:** 9 1/2 picas. **Col. Depth:** 20 inches. **Key Personnel:** John N. Harrison III, Publisher. **Subscription Rates:** $12 individuals.
Circ: ‡1,040

6849 HAWKEYE
Hillsborough Community College
PO Box 5096 Phone: (813)253-7664
Tampa, FL 33675-5096 Fax: (813)253-7622

Collegiate newspaper. **Founded:** 1969. **Freq:** Semimonthly. **Print Method:** Offset. **Trim Size:** 10 x 16. **Cols./Page:** 4. **Col. Width:** 14 picas. **Col. Depth:** 16 inches. **Key Personnel:** Leigh M. Caldwell, Editor. **Remarks:** Accepts advertising. **Available Online. URL:** http://www.hcc.cc.fl.us.
Ad Rates: SAU: $10.50 **Circ:** Free ‡5,000
PCI: $7.03

6850 Health Science
American Natural Hygiene Society
PO Box 30630 Phone: (813)855-6607
Tampa, FL 33630
Health and natural hygiene magazine, for members of ANHS. **Subtitle:** Living in Harmony with Nature. **Founded:** 1978. **Freq:** Bimonthly. **Print Method:** Offset. **Cols./Page:** 3. **Col. Width:** 27 nonpareils. **Col. Depth:** 133 agate lines. **Key Personnel:** James Michael Lennon, Editor. **ISSN:** 0883-8216. **Subscription Rates:** $25 U.S. and Canada; $45 other countries. **Remarks:** Advertising not accepted.
Circ: 6,000

6851 Journal of Behavioral Health Services & Research
Sage Publications Inc.
Louis de la Parte Florida Mental Health Institute Phone: (813)974-6400
Fax: (813)974-6257
University of South Florida
13301 Bruce B. Downs Blvd.
Tampa, FL 33612-3807
Publisher E-mail: info@sagepub.com

Journal on the organization, financing, delivery, and outcome of behavioral health services. **Founded:** 1972. **Freq:** Quarterly. **Trim Size:** 7 x 10. **Key Personnel:** Dr. Bruce L. Levin, Editor, levin@fmhi.usf.edu. **ISSN:** 0092-8623. **Subscription Rates:** $58 individuals; $15 single issue; $130 institutions; $24 single copy, institutions. **Remarks:** Accepts advertising. **URL:** http://www.fmhi.usf.edu/jbhsr/jbhsrmain.html. **Alt. Formats:** Microform. **Formerly:** Journal of Mental Health Administration.
Ad Rates: BW: $250 **Circ:** Paid 2,500
Non-paid 100

6852 The Journal of Craniofacial Surgery
Lippincott Williams & Wilkins
Tampa Bay Craniofacial Center Inc. Phone: (813)238-0409
Fax: (813)238-0400
801 W. Dr. Martin Luther King Jr. Blvd.
Tampa, FL 33603
Free: (800)783-0409

Medical journal concerning the field of facial skeletal surgery. **Subtitle:** Official Journal of American Assoc. of Pedatric Plastic Surgeons, Intl. Soc. of Craniofacial Surgery & European Society of Craniofacial Surgery. **Founded:** Jan. 1985. **Freq:** 6/year. **Print Method:** Offset. **Trim Size:** 8 1/8 x 10 7/8. **Cols./Page:** 2. **Col. Width:** 3 3/8 inches. **Col. Depth:** 10 inches. **Key Personnel:** Mutaz Habal, M.D., Editor, fax (813)238-1119, mbhabal@gte.net. **ISSN:** 1049-2275. **Subscription Rates:** $288 individuals; $56 single issue. **URL:** http://www.mhabal.com/plasticsurgery.
Ad Rates: GLR: $200 **Circ:** Paid 900

6853 Journal of the International Association of Jazz Record Collectors
International Association of Jazz Record Collectors (IAJRC)
9027 Navajo Ave. Phone: (813)985-1894
Tampa, FL 33637
Publisher E-mail: wdrake@gte.net

Magazine for record collectors. **Founded:** 1965. **Freq:** Quarterly. **Print Method:** Offset. **Trim Size:** 8 1/2 x 11. **Cols./Page:** 2. **Key Personnel:** Roberta Drake, Corresponding Sec., wdrake@gte.net. **ISSN:** 0098-9487. **Subscription Rates:** $25 members; $25 other countries air freight; $40 libraries. **Remarks:** Accepts advertising.
Ad Rates: BW: $100 **Circ:** ‡2,000

6854 Journal of Mental Health and Aging
Springer Publishing Co.
c/o Donna Cohen, Ph.D., Editor Phone: (813)974-4665
University of South Florida
Department of Aging and Mental Health
13301 Bruce B. Downs Blvd.
Tampa, FL 33612-3899
Publisher E-mail: springer@springerpub.com

Scholarly journal covering aging population for mental health professionals. **Founded:** 1995. **Freq:** 3/year. **Trim Size:** 7 x 10. **Cols./Page:** 1. **Col. Width:** 5 inches. **Col. Depth:** 8 inches. **Key Personnel:** Donna Cohen, Ph.D., Editor, cohen@hal.finh.usf.edu; Rafael Ortiz, Advertising Mgr.; Cory Sklaire, Circulation Mgr.; Matt Fenton, Production Mgr. **ISSN:** 1078-4470. **Subscription Rates:** $39 individuals; $69 two years; $44 individuals out of country; $79 two years out of country; $78 institutions; $129 institutions two years; $87 institutions out of country; $149 institutions two years out of country; $15 single issue. **Remarks:** Accepts advertising.
Ad Rates: BW: $300 **Circ:** Combined 200

6855 Journal of Theoretical Probability
Plenum Publishing Corp.
Dept. of Math Phone: (813)974-2664
University of South Florida Fax: (813)974-2700
Tampa, FL 33620
Publication E-mail: arun@math.usf.edu
Publisher E-mail: info@plenum.com

Mathematics journal. **Founded:** Jan. 1988. **Freq:** Quarterly. **Print Method:** Offset. **Key Personnel:** A. Mukherjea, Editor, arun@math.usf.edu; Sophia Conyers, Advertising Mgr. **ISSN:** 0894-9840. **Remarks:** Advertising accepted; rates available upon request.
Circ: Paid 350

6856 La Gaceta
La Gaceta Publishing Inc.
PO Box 5536
Tampa, FL 33675
Publication E-mail: lagaceta@aol.com

Community newspaper (Spanish, English, Italian). **Founded:** 1922. **Freq:** Weekly (Fri.). **Print Method:** Offset. **Cols./Page:** 5. **Col. Width:** 22 nonpareils. **Col. Depth:** 231 agate lines. **Key Personnel:** Roland Manteiga, Editor and Publisher. **USPS:** 299-240. **Subscription Rates:** $15 individuals. **Remarks:** Accepts advertising.
Ad Rates: BW: $701.25 **Circ:** ‡18,079
4C: $1,126.25
PCI: $8.50

6857 The Laker
15431 N. Florida Ave. Phone: (813)963-1918
Tampa, FL 33613-1243 Fax: (813)963-3910
Free: (888)320-6397
Publication E-mail: webeacon@gte.net

Community newspaper (tabloid). **Founded:** 1981. **Freq:** Weekly (Wed.). **Print Method:** Offset. **Trim Size:** 11 1/4 x 17. **Cols./Page:** 6. **Col. Width:** 1 inches. **Col. Depth:** 16 1/2 inches. **Key Personnel:** Anne McKenna, Publisher. **Remarks:** Accepts advertising.
Ad Rates: PCI: $6.50 **Circ:** Free ‡21,500

The Lutz Community News - See Lutz

6858 Medical Business Gulf Coast Edition
MBWC, Inc.
1211 N Westshore Blvd., No. 713 Fax: (813)288-8268
Free: (800)327-3736
Tampa, FL 33607
Publication E-mail: L.gibson@worldnet.att.net

Professional magazine covering healthcare business news. **Founded:** Sept. 1995. **Freq:** Biweekly. **Key Personnel:** Lynda Gibson, Managing Editor; Brian Foster, Publisher; Chris Gomont, Circulation Mgr.; Ann Staats, Manager. **Subscription Rates:** $85.20 individuals. **Remarks:** Accepts advertising.
Ad Rates: BW: $2,374 **Circ:** (Not Reported)
4C: $3,124

6859 Oracle
University of South Florida
CPR 472 Phone: (813)974-6242
Tampa, FL 33620-5600 Fax: (813)974-4887
Publication E-mail: editor@zephyr.oracle.usf.edu

Collegiate newspaper. **Founded:** 1966. **Freq:** Daily. **Print Method:** Offset. **Trim Size:** 5 x 13. **Cols./Page:** 5. **Col. Width:** 19 nonpareils. **Col. Depth:** 224 agate lines. **Key Personnel:** Mary Fearn, Business Mgr., phone (813)974-6265; John Wing, Editor-in-Chief, phone (813)974-5190. **Subscription Rates:** $10.95; $15 individuals semester; $10 individuals summer. **Remarks:** Accepts advertising. **URL:** http://www.oracle.osf.edu. **Alt. Formats:** CD-ROM.
Ad Rates: SAU: $11.50 **Circ:** Paid ‡150
Free ‡16,850

6860 Pharmaceutical Engineering
International Society for Pharmaceutical Engineering, Inc.
3816 W. Linebaugh Ave., Ste. 412 Phone: (813)960-2105
Fax: (813)264-2816
Tampa, FL 33624-4702
Magazine on the health care manufacturing industry. **Founded:** 1980. **Freq:** Bimonthly. **Print Method:** Offset. **Trim Size:** 8 3/8 x 10 7/8. **Cols./Page:** 2 and 3. **Col. Width:** 39 and 24 nonpareils. **Col. Depth:** 140 agate lines. **Key Personnel:** Lynda Goldbach, Publications Manager; David Hall, Sales Mgr.; Gloria ESoda, Editor. **ISSN:** 0273-8139. **Subscription Rates:** $60 individuals; $78 other countries; $30 single issue. **Remarks:** Accepts advertising. **URL:** ispe.org.
Ad Rates: GLR: $80 **Circ:** Paid 11,579
BW: $2,320 Non-paid 5,905
4C: $3,370
PCI: $70

6861 Physician Executive
American College of Physician Executives
4890 W. Kennedy Blvd., Ste. 200 Phone: (813)287-2000
Fax: (813)287-8993
Tampa, FL 33609
Free: (800)562-8088

Journal focusing on health care management and medical management for physician executives. **Subtitle:** Journal of Management. **Founded:** July 1976. **Freq:** Bimonthly. **Print Method:** Offset. **Trim Size:** 8 1/2 x 11. **Cols./Page:** 3. **Col. Width:** 27 nonpareils. **Col. Depth:** 140 agate lines. **Key**

Personnel: Susan Sasenick, Editor, sazmac@att.net. **ISSN:** 0898-2759. **Subscription Rates:** Free to qualified subscribers; $72 institutions; $10 single issue; $84 other countries. **Remarks:** Accepts advertising.
Ad Rates: BW: $15 **Circ:** Paid ‡300
4C: $2,350 Controlled ‡13,000
PCI: $50

6862 Renalife
American Association of Kidney Patients, Inc.
100 S. Ashley Dr., Ste. 280 Phone: (813)223-7099
Tampa, FL 33602 Fax: (813)223-0001
Free: (800)749-2257
Publication E-mail: aakpnat@aol.com
Publisher E-mail: aakpnat@aol.com

Magazine covering news and information for kidney patients. **Freq:** Quarterly. **Subscription Rates:** $25 individuals; $150 institutions. **Remarks:** Advertising accepted; rates available upon request. **Formerly:** Renalife Bulletin.
Circ: Paid 20,000

6863 The Tampa Tribune
Tampa Tribune
202 S. Parker St. Phone: (813)259-7711
PO Box 191 Fax: (813)259-7676
Tampa, FL 33606-2395
Free: (800)382-5588

General newspaper. **Founded:** Jan. 1, 1895. **Freq:** Mon.-Sun. (morn.). **Print Method:** Offset. **Cols./Page:** 6. **Col. Width:** 25 nonpareils. **Col. Depth:** 294 agate lines. **Key Personnel:** Jack Butcher, Publisher. **Subscription Rates:** $91 individuals. **Remarks:** Accepts advertising. **URL:** http://www.tampatrib.com. **Feature Editors:** Walt Belcher, *TV*, phone (813)259-7654; Deanna Bellandi, *Medical*, phone (813)259-7807; Lyn Billitteri, *News*, phone (813)259-7760; Phillip Booth, *Music*, phone (813)259-7570; Bob Bowden, *Automotive, Food*, phone (813)259-7679; Gail Cadow (Home), *Garden/Home*, phone (813)259-7651; John Coffeen, *Photo*, phone (813)259-7873; Beth Dolan (Garden), *Garden/Home*, phone (813)259-7562; Michael Dunn, *Real Estate*, phone (813)259-7801; Martha Durrance, *Drama, Features*, phone (813)259-7810; Booth Gunter, *Environmental*, phone (813)259-7854; Dave Hardin, *News*, phone (813)259-7699; Ray Locker, *Political*, phone (904)259-7667; Karen Long, *Religion*, phone (813)259-7613; Steve Matthews, *Financial/Business*, phone (813)259-7865; Edwin Roberts, *Editorials*, phone (813)259-7784; Bob Ross, *Movie*, phone (813)259-7605; Amy Scherzer, *Society*, phone (813)259-7660; Dorothy Smiljanich, *Travel*, phone (813)259-7650; Paul Smith, *Sports*, phone (813)259-7831; Judie Taggart, *Fashion, Women's*, phone (813)259-7617; Vickey Williams, *Metro*, phone (813)259-7943.
Ad Rates: BW: $12,474 **Circ:** Mon.-Sat. ★**221,812**
4C: $13,799 Sun. ★**312,306**
SAU: $88
PCI: $99

The Temple Terrace Beacon - See Temple Terrace

6864 Town'n Country News
Sunbelt Newspapers, Inc.
5501 W. Waters Ave., Ste. 404
Tampa, FL 33634-1229

Community newspaper. **Founded:** 1989. **Freq:** Weekly (Wed.). **Print Method:** Offset. **Cols./Page:** 5. **Col. Width:** 20 nonpareils. **Col. Depth:** 238 agate lines. **Key Personnel:** Carla Rockwell, General Mgr. **Subscription Rates:** Free. **Remarks:** Accepts advertising.
Ad Rates: BW: $621.35 **Circ:** Free 22,000
4C: $846.35
PCI: $7.31

6865 World of Fandom
Box 9421 Phone: (813)933-7424
Tampa, FL 33604
Consumer entertainment magazine covering movies, music, television and related topics. **Founded:** 1985. **Freq:** Quarterly. **Print Method:** Web offset. **Trim Size:** 8 1/4 x 10 7/8. **Cols./Page:** 3. **Key Personnel:** Allen Shevy, wofshevy@gate.net. **Subscription Rates:** $15 individuals; $5 single issue. **Remarks:** Accepts advertising. **URL:** http://www.zipmoll.com/wofmag.
Ad Rates: BW: $400 **Circ:** Controlled 30,000
4C: $600

6866 WAKS-FM - 100.7
4002 Gandy Blvd. Phone: (813)839-9393
Tampa, FL 33611

Format: Adult Contemporary. **Owner:** Jacor Communications, Inc., 50 E. River Center Blvd., Ste. 1200, Covington, KY 41011. **Founded:** 1947. **Formerly:** WUSA-FM (1995). **Operating Hours:** Continuous. **ADI:** Tampa-St. Petersburg (Lakeland, Sarasota), FL. **Key Personnel:** Dan Oi'Loretto, General Mgr., fax (813)839-5969; Russell Link, Controller, fax (813)831-4475; Mason Dixon, Operations Mgr., fax (813)832-6325. **Wattage:** 100,000. **Ad Rates:** $200-400 for 60 seconds.

6867 WAMA-AM - 1550
PO Box 151300 Phone: (813)875-0086
Tampa, FL 33684-1300

Format: Hispanic. **Networks:** UPI. **Owner:** Efrain Archilla, at above address. **Founded:** 1961. **Operating Hours:** 6 a.m.-midnight. **ADI:** Tampa-St. Petersburg (Lakeland, Sarasota), FL. **Key Personnel:** Manuel Enrique Semprit, Station Mgr. **Local Programs:** *Good Morning Tampa* Monday-Friday, M. Semprit, Mailing contact, (813)875-0086; *Morning & Afternoon Discothches*; *1550 News* 7 a.m - 8 a.m. Monday-Friday. **Wattage:** 10,000. **Ad Rates:** $28-34 for 30 seconds; $32-41 for 60 seconds.

6868 WBVM-FM - 90.5
3816 Morrison Ave. Phone: (813)289-8040
Tampa, FL 33629 Fax: (813)282-3580
Free: (800)223-9286

Format: Religious; Classical. **Owner:** Bishop of Catholic Diocese of St. Petersburg, PO Box 40200, St. Petersburg, FL 33743-0200, (813)344-1611. **Founded:** 1985. **Operating Hours:** Continuous. **ADI:** Tampa-St. Petersburg (Lakeland, Sarasota), FL. **Key Personnel:** Thomas W. Derzypolski, General Mgr.; Susan D. Thomas, Program Dir. **Wattage:** 100,000.

6869 WDAE-AM - 1250
4002 Grandy Blvd. Phone: (813)839-9393
Tampa, FL 33611 Fax: (813)831-3299
E-mail: wdae1250@aolcom

Format: Sports. **Networks:** ESPN Radio. **Owner:** Jacor Communications, 50 E. River Center Blvd., 12th Fl., Covington, KY 41011, (606)655-2267, Fax: (606)655-9352. **Founded:** 1922. **Operating Hours:** 50% network, 50% local. **ADI:** Tampa-St. Petersburg (Lakeland, Sarasota), FL. **Key Personnel:** Gabe Hobbs, Program Dir., pad920@aol.com; David Reinhart, General Mgr., fax (813)839-5969; Russell Link, Controller, fax (813)831-4475. **Wattage:** 5000. **Ad Rates:** $100-150 for 60 seconds.

6870 WDUV-FM - 103.5
4002 W. Gandy Blvd., No. A Phone: (813)839-9393
Tampa, FL 33611-3410

Format: Easy Listening. **Owner:** Jacor Communications Inc., 50 E. River Center Blvd., Ste. 1200, Covington, KY 41011, (606)655-2267. **Founded:** 1963. **Operating Hours:** Continuous. **ADI:** Tampa- St. Petersburg (Lakeland, Sarasota),FL. **Key Personnel:** David Reinhart, General Mgr., fax (813)839-5969; Russell Link, Controller, fax (813)831-4475; Gabe Hobbs, Operations Mgr., fax (813)831-3299. **Wattage:** 100,000. **Ad Rates:** $125-250 for 60 seconds.

6871 WEDU-TV - 3
1300 North Blvd. Phone: (813)254-9338
Tampa, FL 33607 Fax: (813)253-0826

Format: Public TV. **Networks:** Public Broadcasting Service (PBS). **Owner:** Florida West Coast Public Broadcasting, Inc., at above address. **Founded:** 1956. **Operating Hours:** 7:30 a.m.-1 a.m. **ADI:** Tampa-St. Petersburg (Lakeland, Sarasota), FL. **Key Personnel:** Stephen L. Rogers, Contact; Stephen Strouf, Program Mgr.; Paul Dietrich, Contact; Christina Beyer, Contact; Elsie Garner, Contact; Leah Rickenbacker, Contact; Gustavo Sagastume, Contact; Frank Wolynski, Chief Engineer; Richard Delaney, Production Mgr.

6872 WFLA-AM - 970
4002A Gandy Blvd. Phone: (813)839-9393
Tampa, FL 33611 Fax: (813)831-3299

Format: News; Talk. **Networks:** ABC. **Owner:** Jacor Communications, Inc., 50 E. River Center Blvd., Ste. 1200, Covington, KY 41011, (606)655-2267. **Founded:** 1924. **Operating Hours:** Continuous. **ADI:** Tampa-St. Petersburg (Lakeland, Sarasota), FL. **Key Personnel:** David Reinhart, General Mgr., fax (813)839-5969; Russell Link, Controller, fax (813)831-4475; Gabe Hobbs, Operations Mgr. **Wattage:** 5000. **Ad Rates:** $250-400 for 60 seconds.

6873 WFLA-TV - 8
905 E. Jackson St., Box 1410 Phone: (813)228-8888
Tampa, FL 33601 Fax: (813)221-5787
Free: (800)824-1695
E-mail: kpilcher@wfla.com

Format: Commercial TV. **Networks:** NBC. **Owner:** Media General Broadcast Group, PO Box 85333, Richmond, VA 23293-0001, (804)649-6000, Fax: (804)649-6524. **Founded:** 1955. **Formerly:** WXFL-TV (1988). **Operating Hours:** Continuous. **ADI:** Tampa-St. Petersburg (Lakeland, Sarasota), FL. **Key Personnel:** Paul Catoe, Pres./Gen. Mgr.; Dan Bradley, News Dir., fax (813)225-2770; Jack Lyons, General Sales Mgr., fax (813)223-3244; Melinda Bacon, Marketing Dir., fax (812)221-5787; Veda Jo Martin, Community Affairs Dir., fax (813)221-5787. **Local Programs:** *Harris Live* 12:30 p.m.-1:30 p.m. Monday-Friday, Joe LoNigro, Producer. **Wattage:** 360. **URL:** http://www.wfla.com.

6874 WFLZ-FM - 93.3
4002A Gandy Blvd. Phone: (813)839-9393
Tampa, FL 33611 Fax: (813)831-3299

Format: Contemporary Hit Radio (CHR). **Owner:** Jacor Communications, Inc., 50 E. River Center Blvd., Ste. 1200, Covington, KY 41011. **Founded:** 1948. **Formerly:** WPDS-FM (1987). **Operating Hours:** Continuous. **ADI:** Tampa-St. Petersburg (Lakeland, Sarasota), FL. **Key Personnel:** B.J. Harris, Program Dir.; David Reinhart, General Mgr., fax (813)839-5969; Russell Link, Controller, fax (813)831-4475. **Wattage:** 100,000. **Ad Rates:** $300-400 for 60 seconds.

6875 WFTS-TV - 28
4045 N Himes Ave. Phone: (813)623-2828
Tampa, FL 33607-6607 Fax: (813)744-2828

Format: Commercial TV. **Networks:** ABC. **Owner:** Scripps Howard Broadcasting, at above address. **Founded:** 1981. **Operating Hours:** Continuous. **ADI:** Tampa-St. Petersburg (Lakeland, Sarasota), FL. **Key Personnel:** Jim Major, Contact; Larry Jopek, General Sales Mgr.; Marsha Kidd-Collins, Contact; Paul Wilson, Contact; Joseph Logsdon, Contact; Michael Barich, Contact; Chris Raynor, Promotions Mgr.; Wanda Cooley, Traffic Mgr.; Lee Melvin, Contact; Joy Petit, Contact; Lu Romero, Production Mgr.

6876 WMNF-FM - 88.5
1210 E. M.L.K. Jr. Blvd. Phone: (813)238-8001
Tampa, FL 33603 Fax: (813)238-1802
E-mail: wmnf.org

Format: Eclectic. **Networks:** National Public Radio (NPR). **Founded:** 1979. **Operating Hours:** Continuous; 10% network, 90% local. **ADI:** Tampa- St. Petersburg (Lakeland, Sarasota),FL. **Key Personnel:** Randy Wynne, Program Dir.; Rob Lorei, News Dir.; Richard Eiswerth, Station Mgr., rich@wmnf.org. **Local Programs:** *Morning Show*, Randy Wynne; *60's Show*, Randy Wynne; *Traffic Jam*, Randy Wynne. **Wattage:** 70,000. **Ad Rates:** Noncommercial. **URL:** www.wmnf.org.

6877 WQBN-AM - 1300
PO Box 151300 Phone: (813)871-1333
Tampa, FL 33684-1300 Fax: (813)876-1333

Format: Hispanic. **Networks:** CNN Radio. **Owner:** Radio Tropical, Inc., at above address. **Founded:** 1950. **Formerly:** WSOL-AM (1985). **Operating Hours:** 6 a.m.-midnight. **ADI:** Tampa-St. Petersburg (Lakeland, Sarasota), FL. **Key Personnel:** Marc L. Vila, Vice Pres./General Mgr.; Manuel Semprit, Program Dir. **Local Programs:** *Flea Martket Radial* 10:30-11:00 a.m., Margaret Granados; *Le Pena Deportiva*, Ricky Martinez; *Morning Talk with Carlos* 8:30 a.m., Carlos Martinez. **Wattage:** 5000 day; 1000 night. **Ad Rates:** $45-60 for 30 seconds; $30-65 for 60 seconds. **Additional Contact Info: Mailing Address:** PO Box 151300, Tampa, FL 33684-1300.

6878 WRBQ-AM - 1380
5510 W. Gray St., Ste. 130 Phone: (813)287-1047
Tampa, FL 33609 Fax: (813)287-0041

Format: Urban Contemporary. **Networks:** ABC; Satellite Music Network. **Founded:** 1954. **Formerly:** WTSP-AM; WLCY-AM; WNSI-AM. **Operating Hours:** Continuous. **ADI:** Tampa-St. Petersburg (Lakeland, Sarasota), FL. **Key Personnel:** Ronnie Lane, Program Dir.; David F. Manning, Contact; Laura Daigle, Contact; Teddi Lewis, Contact. **Wattage:** 5000.

6879 WRBQ-FM - 104.7
5510 W. Gray St., Ste. 130 Phone: (813)287-1047
Tampa, FL 33609 Fax: (813)287-0041

Format: Country. **Networks:** ABC. **Founded:** 1954. **Formerly:** WPKM-FM (1971). **Operating Hours:** Continuous. **ADI:** Tampa-St. Petersburg (Lakeland, Sarasota), FL. **Key Personnel:** David Manning, Vice Pres./Gen. Mgr.; Laura Daigle, Business Mgr.; Teddi Lewis, National Sales Manager; Ron Lane, Program Dir. **Wattage:** 100,000.

6880 WSSR-FM - 95.7
5510 W. Gray St., Ste. 130 Phone: (813)261-2957
Tampa, FL 33609-1088 Fax: (813)261-2909

Format: Adult Contemporary. **Networks:** Independent. **Founded:** 1963. **Formerly:** WNLT-FM (1991); WMTX-FM. **Operating Hours:** Continuous. **ADI:** Tampa-St. Petersburg (Lakeland, Sarasota), FL. **Key Personnel:** Skip Schindler, General Mgr.; Sherri Blakely, Contact. **Wattage:** 100,000.

6881 WTMP-AM - 1150
5207 Washington Blvd. Phone: (813)620-1300
Tampa, FL 33619 Fax: (813)628-0713

Format: Urban Contemporary. **Networks:** American Urban Radio. **Founded:** 1954. **Operating Hours:** Continuous. **ADI:** Tampa-St. Petersburg (Lakeland, Sarasota), FL. **Key Personnel:** Ronald M. Jordan, General Mgr.; Chris Turner, Program Dir. **Wattage:** 5000. **Ad Rates:** $30-95 for 30 seconds; $30-95 for 60 seconds.

6882 WTTA-TV - 38
5510 W. Gray St., No. 38 Phone: (813)289-3838
Tampa, FL 33609 Fax: (813)289-0000

Format: Commercial TV. **Networks:** Independent; Florida Contemporary Radio. **Owner:** Bay Television Inc., 2000 W. 41st St., Baltimore, MD 21211, (410)467-5043. **Founded:** 1985. **Operating Hours:** Continuous. **ADI:** Tampa-St. Petersburg (Lakeland, Sarasota), FL. **Key Personnel:** Steve Hess, Chief Engineer; Tom Watson, General Mgr.; Jennifer Beaver, Program Dir. **Local Programs:** *"bolt.net"*; *Lighting Strikes*, Terry Crisp; *Tampa Bay Lightning*.

6883 WTVT-TV - 13
3213 W. Kennedy Blvd. Phone: (813)876-1313
Tampa, FL 33609 Fax: (813)875-8329
E-mail: 13@wtvt.com

Format: Commercial TV. **Networks:** Fox. **Owner:** Fox Television Stations, Inc., 1999 S. Bundy Dr.,, Los Angeles, CA 90025-5235, (310)584-2000. **Founded:** 1955. **Operating Hours:** Continuous. **ADI:** Tampa-St. Petersburg (Lakeland, Sarasota), FL. **Key Personnel:** David Boylan, V.P./Gen. Mgr., phone (813)870-9601, fax (813)870-9775; Phil Metlin, Vice President, phone (813)870-9701, fax (813)870-9894; Brian Fields, Dir., Programming & Research, phone (813)870-7119, fax (813)870-9724; Mike House, V.P., Creative Services, phone (813)870-9704, fax (813)870-9648; Bob Linere, V.P., Sales, phone (813)870-9606, fax (813)870-9724. **Wattage:** 318k. **Ad Rates:** Advertising accepted; rates available upon request. **URL:** http://www.wtvt.com.

6884 WUSF-FM - 89.7
University of South Florida, WRB 219 Phone: (813)974-4890
4202 E. Fowler Ave. Fax: (813)974-5016
Tampa, FL 33620-6860
Free: (800)741-9090

Format: Public Radio; Jazz; News; Classical. **Networks:** National Public Radio (NPR). **Owner:** Florida Board of Regents, at above address. **Founded:** 1963. **Operating Hours:** Continuous. **ADI:** Tampa- St. Petersburg (Lakeland, Sarasota),FL. **Key Personnel:** Mary Diana, Music Dir., mdiana@wusf.usf.edu; Brian McCabe, Operations Mgr., bmccabe@wusf.usf.edu; James Heck, General Mgr., jheck@wsuf.usf.edu; Susan Johnson, Program Dir., sjohnson@wusf.usf.edu; JoAnn Urofsky, Station Mgr., jurofsky@wusfusf.edu; Ginnie Mikula, Development and Mktg. Dir., gmikula@wusf.usf.edu; Connie McDonnell, Promotions Mgr., cmcdonnell@wusf.usf.edu; Evelyn Massaro, Membership Manager, emassaro@wusf.usf.edu. **Wattage:** 100,000. **Ad Rates:** Noncommercial; underwriting available. **URL:** http://www.wusf.usf.edu.

6885 WUSF-TV - 16
University of South Florida Phone: (813)974-4000
4202 Fowler Ave. Fax: (813)974-4806
Tampa, FL 33620
Free: (800)654-3703

Format: Public TV. **Networks:** Public Broadcasting Service (PBS). **Owner:** Florida Board of Regents, at above address. **Founded:** 1966. **Operating Hours:** 6:00 a.m.-2 a.m. **ADI:** Tampa-St. Petersburg (Lakeland, Sarasota), FL. **Key Personnel:** James Heck, General Mgr.; Susan Geiger, Program Dir.; William Buxton, Station Mgr. **Wattage:** 1.2 million. **Ad Rates:** Underwriting available.

6886 WUTZ-AM - 1075
University of Tampa Phone: (813)253-3333
401 W. Kennedy Blvd.
Tampa, FL 33606

Format: Alternative/New Music/Progressive. **Operating Hours:** 11 A.M. - 11 P.M.Daily. **ADI:** Tampa- St. Petersburg (Lakeland, Sarasota),FL. **Key Personnel:** Mike Mullarkey, General Mgr.; Jacob Nickerson, Music Dir. **Wattage:** 250. **Ad Rates:** Noncommercial.

6887 WWWB-TV - 32
7201 E. Hillsborough Ave. Phone: (813)626-3232
Tampa, FL 33610 Fax: (813)622-7732

Format: Commercial TV. **Founded:** 1986. **Formerly:** WTMV-TV (Sept. 16, 1996). **Operating Hours:** Continuous. **ADI:** Tampa-St. Petersburg (Lakeland, Sarasota), FL. **Key Personnel:** Michael E. Schuch, VP/General Mgr.; Lynne Conlan, Creative Services Dir., fax (813)626-1961; Joe Pauly, Program Dir., fax (813)626-1961; Ken Lucas, General Sales Mgr., fax (813)622-9032; John Norvel, Chief Engineer, fax (813)626-1961; Wanda Snyder, Traffic Mgr., fax (813)622-7732; Nicole Zittman, National Sales Mgr., fax (813)622-7732; Scott Lilly, Sales Mgr., fax (813)622-7732. **Wattage:** 5,000,000.

TAVERNIER

6888 WFKZ-FM - 103.1
93351 Overseas Hwy. Phone: (305)852-9085
Tavernier, FL 33070 Fax: (305)852-5586

Format: Adult Contemporary. **Owner:** Key Chain, Inc., at above address. **Founded:** 1983. **Operating Hours:** Continuous. **ADI:** Miami (Ft. Lauderdale), FL. **Key Personnel:** K.C. Stewart, Program Dir.; Jack Niedbalski, Contact. **Local Programs:** *Lunchtime- Saturday Night At The Oldies*, Jack Niedbalski, (305)852-9085; *On The Water With Capt. Skip Bradeen*, Jack Niedbalski, (305)852-9085; *Turtle Club-The Radio Show*, Jack Niedbalski, (305)852-9085. **Wattage:** 25,000. **Ad Rates:** $12-16 for 30 seconds; $14-23 for 60 seconds.

TEMPLE TERRACE

6889 The Temple Terrace Beacon
15431 N. Florida Ave. Phone: (813)963-1918
Tampa, FL 33613 Fax: (813)963-3910
Publisher E-mail: webeacon@gfe.net

Community newspaper. **Freq:** Weekly. **Cols./Page:** 6. **Col. Width:** 1 9/16 inches. **Col. Depth:** 16 inches. **Key Personnel:** Anne McKenna, Editor. **Subscription Rates:** Free; $60 by mail. **Remarks:** Accepts advertising.
Ad Rates: PCI: $8.40 **Circ:** Free 10,000

TITUSVILLE†, pop. 31,910.

E FL. Brevard Co. On Indian River, 42 mi. E. of Orlando. Resort area. Kennedy Space Center. Citrus fruit farms.

6890 PhotoPro
Patch Communications
5211 S. Washington Ave. Phone: (407)268-5010
Titusville, FL 32780-7315 Fax: (407)267-1894

Professional photography magazine. **Founded:** 1990. **Freq:** Bimonthly. **Print Method:** Web offset. **Trim Size:** 8 1/8 x 10 7/8. **Cols./Page:** 3. **Col. Width:** 2 1/4 inches. **Col. Depth:** 9 1/2 inches. **Key Personnel:** Christi Ashby, Publisher; Eileen Tedder, Editor; Marcia Aubry, Director. **ISSN:** 1049-8974. **Subscription Rates:** $16.95. **Remarks:** Accepts advertising.
Ad Rates: BW: $3,095 **Circ:** Paid 26,919
4C: $3,990 Non-paid 11,977

6891 Shutterbug
Patch Communications
5211 S. Washington Ave. Phone: (407)268-5010
Titusville, FL 32780-7315 Fax: (407)267-1894

Photography magazine. **Founded:** 1971. **Freq:** Monthly. **Print Method:** Offset. **Trim Size:** 10 x 13. **Cols./Page:** 4. **Col. Width:** 22 nonpareils. **Col. Depth:** 182 agate lines. **Key Personnel:** Bob Shell, Editor; Bonnie Paulk, Editorial Director; Don Welk, Publisher. **Subscription Rates:** $16 individuals. **Remarks:** Accepts advertising.
Ad Rates: BW: $2,295 **Circ:** Paid ★82,860
4C: $3,295

6892 Shutterbug's Outdoor & Nature Photography
Patch Communications
5211 S. Washington Ave. Phone: (407)268-5010
Titusville, FL 32780-7315 Fax: (407)267-1894

Consumer magazine covering photography. **Founded:** Dec. 1, 1995. **Freq:** Quarterly. **Print Method:** Web offset. **Trim Size:** 8 1/2 x 11. **Cols./Page:** 3. **Key Personnel:** Peter K. Burian, Editor, PBurian@aol.com; Jospeh Laurino, Advertising Mgr.; Bonnie Paulk, Editorial Dir. **Subscription Rates:** $9.95 individuals; $3.99 single issue. **Remarks:** Advertising accepted; rates available upon request.
Circ: Combined 37,200

6893 Star Advocate
Gannett Co., Inc.
1100 S. Hopkins Ave. Phone: (407)267-4711
Titusville, FL 32780 Fax: (407)264-2228

Newspaper. **Founded:** 1880. **Freq:** Weekly (Wed.). **Print Method:** Offset. **Cols./Page:** 6. **Col. Width:** 26 nonpareils. **Col. Depth:** 312 agate lines. **Key Personnel:** R.H. Hudson, Editor and Publisher. **Subscription Rates:** $13 by mail. **Remarks:** Accepts advertising.
Ad Rates: GLR: $.50 **Circ:** Free 22,500

6894 WAMT-AM - 1060
3909 Champion Rd. Phone: (407)264-1060
Titusville, FL 32796

Format: News; Talk. **Networks:** CNN Radio. **Owner:** Radio Brevard, Inc., at above address. **Operating Hours:** Continuous. **Key Personnel:** Greg Sherlock, Operations Mgr.; Connie Fishbaugh, Sales Mgr. **Local Programs:** *Town Talk*, Connie Fishbaugh. **Wattage:** 10,000. **Ad Rates:** $10 for 30 seconds.

6895 WPGS-AM - 840
805 N. Dixie Ave. Phone: (407)383-1000
Titusville, FL 32796 Fax: (407)383-0814
Free: (877)683-1580
E-mail: wpgs@wpgs.com

Format: Talk; News; Sports; Religious. **Simulcasts:** WNTF 1580. **Owner:** WPGS Inc., at above address. **Founded:** 1984. **Formerly:** WNUY-AM. **Operating Hours:** Daytime. **ADI:** Orlando-Daytona Beach-Melbourne, FL. **Key Personnel:** Ed Shiflett, Manager; John S. Rowan, Chief Engineer; Marie Doherty, Office Mgr. **Wattage:** 250. **Ad Rates:** $7.50 for 30 seconds; $10 for 60 seconds. Combined advertising rates available with WNTF 1580 AM. **URL:** http://www.wpgs.com.

TRENTON†, pop. 1,131.

N FL. Gilchrist Co. 30 mi. W. of Gainesville. Naval stores. Saw, grist mills. Agriculture.

6896 Gilchrist County Journal
PO Box 127 Phone: (352)463-7135
Trenton, FL 32693 Fax: (352)463-7393

Community Newspaper. **Founded:** 1932. **Freq:** Weekly (Thurs.). **Print Method:** Offset. **Cols./Page:** 8. **Col. Width:** 18 nonpareils. **Col. Depth:** 294 agate lines. **Key Personnel:** J. Min Ayers, Editor and Publisher. **Subscription Rates:** $15 individuals; $20 out of area plus tax; $20 out of state plus tax. **Remarks:** Accepts advertising.
Ad Rates: GLR: $.07 **Circ:** 4,000
PCI: $2.25

VALPARAISO

Okaloosa Co. (NW). 2 m N of Elgin Air Force Base.

6897 Valparaiso Communication Systems
Box 296 Phone: (904)729-5404
Valparaiso, FL 32580 Fax: (904)678-4553

Founded: 1976. **Key Personnel:** Burt B. Bennett, Manager. **Cities Served:** Valparaiso, FL: subscribing households 1620; 72 channels; 1 community access channel; 168 hours per week community access programming.

VENICE, pop. 12,153.

SW FL. Sarasota Co. On Gulf of Mexico, 18 mi. S. of Sarasota. Resort area.

6898 The Advertiser
Sun Coast Media
200 E. Venice Ave. Phone: (813)484-2611
Venice, FL 34285 Fax: (813)485-3036

Shopper. **Freq:** Semiweekly (Wed. and Sat.). **Print Method:** Offset. **Cols./Page:** 6. **Col. Width:** 22 nonpareils. **Col. Depth:** 231 agate lines. **Key Personnel:** Don Moore, Editor; Derek Dunn-Rankin, Publisher; Lang Capasso, Advertising Mgr.
Circ: Free 131,900

6899 Florida Mariner
PO Box 1220 Phone: (941)488-9307
Venice, FL 34284 Fax: (941)488-9309
Free: (800)388-9307
Publication E-mail: flmariner@earthlink.net

Recreational boats, related products and services magazine. **Subtitle:** The Boater's Guide to Florida. **Founded:** 1984. **Freq:** Biweekly. **Print Method:** Offset. **Trim Size:** 11 x 15. **Cols./Page:** 5. **Col. Width:** 11 picas. **Col. Depth:** 14 inches. **Key Personnel:** Ken Brothwell, Publisher, kbrothwell@earthlink.net. **Subscription Rates:** $39.95 Free; $99.95 Canada. **Remarks:** Accepts advertising. **Formerly:** Gulf Mariner; Gulf/Atlantic Mariner.
Ad Rates: BW: $999 **Circ:** Paid 381
4C: $1,299 Free 24,350

6900 The Venice Gondolier
Sun Coast Media
200 E. Venice Ave. Phone: (813)484-2611
Venice, FL 34285 Fax: (813)485-3036

Newspaper. **Founded:** 1946. **Freq:** 3/week. **Print Method:** Offset. Cols 6. **Key Personnel:** Don Moore, Editor; Derek

Dunn-Rankin, Publisher; Carol Moore, Advertising Mgr. **Subscription Rates:** $23.
Circ: Wed. ★**11,057**
Sat. ★**12,206**

6901 Venice Weekly
Florida Sun Publications
504 E. Venice Ave. Phone: (813)485-5425
Venice, FL 34292 Fax: (813)488-4577

Shopper. **Founded:** 1956. **Freq:** Weekly (Wed.). **Print Method:** Offset. **Cols./Page:** 6. **Col. Width:** 22 nonpareils. **Col. Depth:** 238 agate lines. **Key Personnel:** Steve Sachkar, Editor and Publisher. **Subscription Rates:** Free.
Ad Rates: GLR: $.49 **Circ:** Non-paid 29,198

6902 Wild Dog
1327 Whispering Ln.
Venice, FL 34292-1449

Literary magazine. **Subtitle:** An Erratic Publication of Unconventional Excellence. **Founded:** Jan. 1992. **Freq:** Quarterly 4/year. **Print Method:** Offset. **Trim Size:** 8 1/2 x 11. **Cols./Page:** 1. **Key Personnel:** Jack D. Welch, phone (941)484-8505. **Subscription Rates:** $25 annual; $7 single issue. **Remarks:** Accepts advertising.
Circ: Paid ‡250
Non-paid ‡500

6903 WAMR-AM - 1320
282 N. Auburn Rd. Phone: (813)484-2636
Venice, FL 34292 Fax: (813)488-4159

Format: News; Sports. **Networks:** NBC. **Owner:** Asterisk Radio, Inc., 1429 N. Federal Hwy., Fort Lauderdale, FL 33304-1492, (305)566-7559. **Founded:** 1960. **Operating Hours:** Continuous; 70% network, 30% local. **ADI:** Tampa- St. Petersburg (Lakeland, Sarasota),FL. **Key Personnel:** Dave McClure, Contact; Dennis Scott, Contact. **Wattage:** 5000. **Ad Rates:** $21 for 30 seconds; $40 for 60 seconds.

6904 WCTQ-FM - 92.1
282 N. Auburn Rd. Phone: (813)484-2636
Venice, FL 34292 Fax: (813)488-4159

Format: Country. **Networks:** NBC. **Owner:** Asterisk Radio, Inc., 1429 N. Federal Hwy., Fort Lauderdale, FL 33304-1492, (305)566-7559. **Founded:** 1974. **Formerly:** WRAV-FM (1988). **Operating Hours:** Continuous; 5% network, 95% local. **ADI:** Tampa- St. Petersburg (Lakeland, Sarasota),FL. **Key Personnel:** Dave McClure, General Mgr.; Ed Couzens, Program Dir. **Wattage:** 6000. **Ad Rates:** $25-40 for 30 seconds; $28-50 for 60 seconds.

VENICE BEACH

6905 Englewood Sun Herald
200 E. Venice Phone: (813)484-2611
Venice Beach, FL 34285 Fax: (813)485-3036

Newspaper. **Founded:** 1955. **Freq:** 3/week. **Print Method:** Offset. **Cols./Page:** 6. **Col. Width:** 26 nonpareils. **Col. Depth:** 301 agate lines. **Key Personnel:** Richard R. Rogoski, Editor; Lang Lupasso, General Mgr. **Subscription Rates:** $26 individuals. **Remarks:** Accepts advertising.
Ad Rates: BW: $1,064.70 **Circ:** ‡4,500
4C: $1,294.70
SAU: $8.45

VERO BEACH†, pop. 16,176.

E FL. Indian River Co. On Indian River, 72 mi. N. of West Palm Beach. Winter resort. Citrus fruit.

6906 Antitrust Law and Economics Review
ALER, Inc.
ALER, Inc. Fax: (561)461-6007
PO Box 3532
Vero Beach, FL 32964-3532
Economics journal. **Founded:** 1967. **Freq:** Quarterly. **Print Method:** Offset. **Cols./Page:** 1. **Col. Width:** 54 nonpareils. **Col. Depth:** 98 agate lines. **Key Personnel:** Charles E. Mueller, Editor. **ISSN:** 0003-6048. **Subscription Rates:** $119.50 individuals. **Remarks:** Advertising not accepted.
Circ: (Not Reported)

6907 Florida Real Estate
Florida Real Estate Magazine, L.P.
PO Box 4258
Vero Beach, FL 32964

Trade magazine for realtors. **Founded:** 1987. **Freq:** Quarterly. **Subscription Rates:** Free to qualified subscribers.
Circ: Non-paid ‡77,622

6908 Press-Journal
PO Box 1268 Phone: (561)562-2315
Vero Beach, FL 32961 Fax: (561)978-2365

General newspaper. **Founded:** 1919. **Freq:** Daily and Sunday (morn.). **Print Method:** Offset. **Cols./Page:** 6. **Col. Width:** 12.6 picas. **Col. Depth:** 318 agate lines. **Key Personnel:** Darryl K. Hicks, President, fax (561)978-2395. **Subscription Rates:** $125.19 individuals; $216 out of area. **Remarks:** Accepts advertising.
Ad Rates: GLR: $18.46 **Circ:** Mon.-Sat. ★**29,173**
BW: $2,381.34 Sun. ★**32,838**
4C: $2,951.34
PCI: $18.46

6909 WAXE-AM - 1370
Box 39 Phone: (561)567-1055
Vero Beach, FL 32961-0039 Fax: (561)595-0214
E-mail: waxe@bloomberg.net

Format: News; Talk. **Owner:** Southern Star Communications, at above address. **Founded:** 1954. **Operating Hours:** Continuous. **ADI:** West Palm Beach-Ft. Pierce-Vero Beach, FL. **Key Personnel:** Charlie DiToro, General Mgr. **Wattage:** 1000.

6910 WGYL-FM - 93.7
1235 16th St. Phone: (561)567-0937
Vero Beach, FL 32961 Fax: (561)562-4747

Format: Adult Contemporary; Jazz. **Networks:** ABC. **Founded:** Dec. 18, 1970. **Operating Hours:** Continuous. **ADI:** West Palm Beach-Ft. Pierce-Vero Beach, FL. **Key Personnel:** Jim Hoffman, General Mgr.; Gary B. Duglin, Station Mgr.; Neal Stannard, Operations Mgr.; Mikeg Fitzgerald, Program Dir.; Christopher Myers, Chief Engineer. **Local Programs:** *The Morning Show* 6:00 am - 9:00 am Monday-Friday. **Wattage:** 50,000. **Ad Rates:** $25-35 for 30 seconds; $35-50 for 60 seconds.

6911 WTTB-AM - 1490
1235 16th St. Phone: (561)569-1490
Vero Beach, FL 32960 Fax: (561)562-4747

Format: Talk. **Networks:** ABC. **Founded:** 1954. **Operating Hours:** Continuous. **ADI:** West Palm Beach-Ft. Pierce-Vero Beach, FL. **Key Personnel:** Gary B. Duglin, Station Mgr.; Jim Hoffman, General Mgr.; Neal Stannard, Operations Mgr.; Christopher Myers, Chief Engineer. **Local Programs:** *Let's Go to the Movies* 7:00 pm - 8:00 pm Monday, Gary B. Duglin, Station Mgr.; *Your Point of View* 8:00 pm - 9:00 pm Wednesday; *Tradio* 12:15 pm - 1:00 pm Monday-Friday. **Wattage:** 1000. **Ad Rates:** $17-27 for 30 seconds; $7.77-30 for 60 seconds.

WAUCHULA†, pop. 2,986.

C FL. Hardee Co. 40 mi. S. of Lakeland. Parks. Truck, fruit, stock farms. Citrus groves.

6912 The Herald Advocate
The Herald-Advocate Publishing Co., Inc.
113 S. 7th Ave. Phone: (941)773-3255
PO Box 338 Fax: (941)773-0657
Wauchula, FL 33873
County seat newspaper. **Founded:** 1900. **Freq:** Weekly (Thurs.). **Print Method:** Offset. **Cols./Page:** 6. **Col. Width:** 25 nonpareils. **Col. Depth:** 21 1/2 inches. **Key Personnel:** Jim Kelly, Editor and Publisher. **Subscription Rates:** $25 individuals; $33 out of area; $40 out of state. **Remarks:** Accepts advertising. **Merged with:** The Florida Advocate.
Ad Rates: GLR: $.30 **Circ:** ‡5,350
BW: $435.15
SAU: $4.20
PCI: $4

6913 WAUC-AM - 1310
PO Box 471 Phone: (813)773-5008
Wauchula, FL 33873-0908 Fax: (813)773-2032

Format: Top 40; Agricultural; Sports. **Networks:** Florida Radio; Satellite Music Network. **Owner:** Ted Hite, at above address. **Founded:** 1958. **Operating Hours:** 19 hours daily; 5% network, 95% local. **Key Personnel:** Ted Hite, Sr., Contact; Ted Hite, Jr., Contact; Woody Woods, Contact. **Wattage:** 5000. **Ad Rates:** $6-10 for 30 seconds; $10-15 for 60 seconds.

WELLINGTON

6914 Polo
Polo Publications, Inc.
3500 Fairlane Farms Rd. Phone: (407)793-9524
Wellington, FL 33414 Fax: (407)793-9576
Publication E-mail: polomag@aol.com

Magazine containing feature articles, tournament reports, current events, and Polo Association news. **Founded:** May 1975. **Freq:** 10/year. **Print Method:** Offset. **Trim Size:** 8 1/2 x 10 3/4. **Cols./Page:** 3. **Col. Width:** 28 nonpareils. **Col. Depth:** 138 agate lines. **Key Personnel:** Peter Rizzo, Editor and Publisher; Ami Shinitzky, Founding Editor; Gwen Rizzo, Managing Editor. **ISSN:** 0146-4574. **Subscription Rates:** $40 individuals. **Remarks:** Accepts advertising.
Ad Rates: BW: $1,435 **Circ:** ‡7,000
4C: $2,185

WEST PALM BEACH†, pop. 62,530.

SE FL. Palm Beach Co. On Lake Worth opposite Palm Beach, with bridge connections. Port of entry with deep harbor. Resort area. Commercial fisheries. Manufactures data processing systems, aircraft engines and parts, electronic components, transistors, tools and dies, furniture, mattresses, aluminum doors, and concrete products.

6915 Ancestry
Palm Beach County Genealogical Society, Inc.
Box 1746
West Palm Beach, FL 33402-1746

Genealogical magazine. **Freq:** Quarterly. **Trim Size:** 8 1/2 x 11. **Key Personnel:** Jane M. Allen, Circulation. **Subscription Rates:** $15 individuals; $2.50 single issue. **Remarks:** Advertising not accepted.
Circ: Combined 400

6916 Corporate Real Estate Executive
(NACORE) International Association of Corporate Real Estate Executives
440 Columbia Dr., Ste. 100 Phone: (561)683-8111
West Palm Beach, FL 33409 Fax: (561)697-4853
Publication E-mail: publications@flinet.com

Real estate deal-making techniques magazine. **Founded:** Aug. 1972. **Freq:** 9/year. **Print Method:** Offset. **Trim Size:** 8 1/2 x 11. **Cols./Page:** 4. **Col. Width:** 14 picas. **Col. Depth:** 10 inches. **Key Personnel:** Kathleen B. Dempsey, Editor and Publisher; Steve Katon, Asst. Editor. **ISSN:** 1042-9115. **Subscription Rates:** $65 individuals per year; $75 Canada; $95 by mail Overseas.
Ad Rates: BW: $3,225 **Circ:** Paid 3,800
4C: $4,820

6917 Palm Beach Daily Business Review
American Lawyer Media, L.P.
100 S. Dixie Hwy. Phone: (407)820-2060
West Palm Beach, FL 33401 Fax: (407)944-0605
Free: (800)777-7300

Publication of enterprise, real estate, and law in the Palm Beach area. **Founded:** 1978. **Freq:** Daily. **Print Method:** Web offset. **Trim Size:** 11 3/8 x 17 1/2. **Cols./Page:** 4. **Col. Width:** 2 3/8 inches. **Col. Depth:** 16 inches. **Key Personnel:** Edward Wasserman, Editor; Donna Trainer-Stutts, Publisher. **ISSN:** 0884-8785. **Subscription Rates:** $224 annually; $160 semi-annually. **Remarks:** Accepts advertising. **Alt. Formats:** Diskette; Mailing labels. **Formerly:** Palm Beach Review.
Ad Rates: BW: $1,170 **Circ:** Paid 2,100
4C: $1,835.50 Non-paid 266
PCI: $21.69

6918 Palm Beach Jewish Journal South
SFNN, Inc.
601 Fairway Dr. Phone: (954)574-5300
Deerfield Beach, FL 33441 Fax: (954)429-1207
Free: (800)275-8820
Publication E-mail: dtom@netrunner.net
Publisher E-mail: bukley@gate.net

Jewish community newspaper (tabloid). **Founded:** 1986. **Freq:** Weekly (Tues.). **Print Method:** Offset. **Trim Size:** 10 1/8 x 16. **Cols./Page:** 6. **Col. Width:** 1 5/8 inches. **Col. Depth:** 16 inches. **Key Personnel:** Andy Polin, Managing Editor; Alan Goch, Editor; Ed Wilder, Circulation Mgr.; Charlie Schwartz, Sales Mgr.; Rabbi Bruce Warshal, Publisher. **Subscription Rates:** Free. **Remarks:** Accepts advertising. **Formerly:** Palm Beach Jewish Journal.
Ad Rates: SAU: $9.10 **Circ:** Combined 26,813
PCI: $53.35

6919 The Palm Beach Post
2751 S. Dixie Hwy. Phone: (407)820-4401
West Palm Beach, FL 33405 Fax: (407)820-4407
Free: (800)432-7595

General newspaper. **Founded:** 1916. **Freq:** Mon.-Sun. (morn.). **Print Method:** Offset. **Trim Size:** 13 1/2 x 23 9/16. **Cols./Page:** 6. **Col. Width:** 2.17 inches. **Col. Depth:** 22 1/2 inches. **Key Personnel:** Tom Guiffrida, Publisher, phone (407)820-4124; Edward Sears, Editor, phone (407)820-4133; Jan Tuckwood, Assoc. Editor, phone (407)820-4519, fax (407)820-4445. **Subscription Rates:** $132.60 individuals. **Remarks:** Accepts advertising. **Online:** Dialog (The Dialog Corporation); CompuServe Information Service; LEXIS-NEXIS. **Alt. Formats:** CD-ROM, NewsBank, Inc. **Feature**

Editors: Cheryl Blackerby, *Travel*, phone (407)820-4727, fax (407)820-4445; Tim Burke, *Sports*, phone (407)820-4480; Joe Chudicek, *Financial/Business*, fax (407)820-4578; Pete Cross, *Photo*, phone (407)820-4490; Brian Crowley, *Political*, phone (407)820-4723, fax (407)820-4407; Steve Gushet, *Religion*, phone (407)820-4721, fax (407)820-4445; Carl Hardy, *Radio*, phone (407)820-4483; Jan Norris, *Food*, phone (407)820-4737; Price Patton, *Metro*, phone (407)820-4400; Nicole Piscopo, *Lifestyle*, phone (407)820-4704; Bill Rose, *Metro*, phone (407)820-4402, fax (407)820-4407; Gary Schwan, *Movie*, phone (407)820-4574; Kevin Thompson, *TV*, phone (407)820-4436; Ava Van de Water, *Garden/Home*, *Society*, phone (407)820-4722, fax (407)820-4445.
Ad Rates: GLR: $77.35 **Circ:** Mon.-Sat. 187,943
BW: $10,442.25 Sun. 238,334
4C: $12,196.25

6920 Welcome!
(NACORE) International Association of Corporate Real Estate Executives
440 Columbia Dr., Ste. 100 Phone: (561)683-8111
West Palm Beach, FL 33409 Fax: (561)697-4853
Publication E-mail: nacor@flanet.com

Symposium program for annual education conference. **Subtitle:** NACORE Annual Symposium and Exposition Program. **Founded:** 1983. **Freq:** Annual. **Key Personnel:** Kathleen Dempsey, Editor; Steve Katon, Asst. Editor. **Remarks:** Accepts advertising. **Formerly**: NACORE Annual Symposium and Exposition Program.
Ad Rates: BW: $2,995 **Circ:** Controlled 3,000
4C: $3,590

6921 WBZT-AM - 1290
4763 10th Ave. N. Phone: (407)965-9211
PO Box 20389 Fax: (407)965-9233
West Palm Beach, FL 33416

Format: News; Talk; Sports. **Networks:** ABC. **Founded:** 1947. **Formerly**: WPCK-AM (1992); WIRK-AM; WPBG-AM. **Operating Hours:** Continuous. **ADI:** West Palm Beach-Ft. Pierce-Vero Beach, FL. **Key Personnel:** Lee K. Strasser, Manager; Marie Turner, Program Dir. **Wattage:** 5000.

6922 WCLB-FM - 95.5
901 N. Point Pkwy., Ste. 201 Phone: (561)838-4300
West Palm Beach, FL 33407 Fax: (561)838-4357

Format: Country. **Operating Hours:** Continuous. **ADI:** West Palm Beach-Ft. Pierce-Vero Beach, FL. **Key Personnel:** Chet Tart, General Mgr.; Eric Chaney, Program Dir.; David Nau, Promotions Dir. **Wattage:** 100,000.

6923 WEAT-AM - 850
2406 S. Congress Ave. Phone: (561)439-1111
West Palm Beach, FL 33406 Fax: (561)965-1102
E-mail: radio1@radio1.com

Format: News; Sports. **Networks:** AP; CBS. **Founded:** 1948. **Operating Hours:** Continuous. **ADI:** West Palm Beach-Ft. Pierce-Vero Beach, FL. **Key Personnel:** E. Reso, Business Mgr.; David D'Eugenio, General Mgr.; Ken Harris, Local Sales/Operations Mgr. **Local Programs:** *In Touch with South Florida*, Karen Curtis, (561)965-5500, Fax (561)965-1102. **Wattage:** 5000 day; 1000 night. **Ad Rates:** Combined advertising rates available with WOLL-FM, WKGR-FM.

6924 WEAT-FM - 104.3
701 Northpoint Parkway, Ste. 500
West Palm Beach, FL 33407
E-mail: sunny1043.com

Format: Adult Contemporary; Soft Rock. **Networks:** Independent. **Founded:** 1969. **Formerly**: Chancellor LMA to American Radio Systems. **Operating Hours:** Continuous. **ADI:** West Palm Beach-Ft. Pierce-Vero Beach, FL. **Key Personnel:** Lee R. Strassero, Vice Pres./Gen. Mgr.; Les Jacoby, Program Dir.; Jeff Greenwald, General Sales Mgr. **Wattage:** 100,000.

6925 WFLX-TV - 29
4119 W. Blue Heron Blvd. Phone: (561)845-2929
West Palm Beach, FL 33404 Fax: (561)863-1238

Format: Commercial TV. **Networks:** Fox. **Owner:** Malrite Communications Group, Inc., at above address. **Founded:** 1982. **Operating Hours:** Continuous. **ADI:** West Palm Beach-Ft. Pierce-Vero Beach, FL. **Key Personnel:** Murray Green, General Mgr.; Ken Beedle, Station Mgr. **Wattage:** 5,000,000.

6926 WIRK-FM - 107.9
4763 10th Ave. N. Phone: (407)965-9211
PO Box 20389 Fax: (407)965-9233
West Palm Beach, FL 33416

Format: Country. **Owner:** American Radio Systems, at above address. **Founded:** 1965. **Operating Hours:** Continuous. **ADI:** West Palm Beach-Ft. Pierce-Vero Beach, FL. **Key Personnel:** Lee K. Strasser, Manager; Ron Brooks, Program Dir. **Wattage:** 100,000.

6927 WJNA-AM - 1230
2406 S. Congress Ave. Phone: (561)432-5100
West Palm Beach, FL Fax: (561)432-5111

Format: Big Band/Nostalgia. **Networks:** ABC. **Owner:** James Crystal Holdings, at above address. **Formerly**: WJNO-AM (1997). **Operating Hours:** Continuous. **Key Personnel:** AL Baker, Operations/Public Service. **Wattage:** 5,100.

6928 WJNO-AM - 1230
1540 Latham Rd. Phone: (407)838-4300
West Palm Beach, FL 33409 Fax: (407)838-4357
E-mail: wjnochet@filnet.com

Format: News; Talk. **Simulcasts:** 1330. **Networks:** ABC. **Owner:** Fairbanks Communications, at above address. **Founded:** 1936. **Operating Hours:** Continuous. **ADI:** West Palm Beach-Ft. Pierce-Vero Beach, FL. **Key Personnel:** Chet Tart, General Mgr.; Jim Edwards, Program Dir. **Wattage:** 1000.

6929 WJWA-AM - 1040
PO Box 189
West Palm Beach, FL 33402

Format: Urban Contemporary. **Networks:** Southern Broadcasting; ABC. **Founded:** 1974. **Operating Hours:** Continuous. **ADI:** Miami (Ft. Lauderdale), FL. **Key Personnel:** Gary Lewis, Contact; Mike James, Program Dir. **Wattage:** 25,000.

6930 WKGR-FM - 98.7
3071 Continental Dr. Phone: (561)616-6600
West Palm Beach, FL 33407 Fax: (561)616-6677
E-mail: radio1@radio1.com

Format: Classic Rock. **Networks:** Independent. **Founded:** 1961. **Operating Hours:** Continuous. **ADI:** West Palm Beach-Ft. Pierce-Vero Beach, FL. **Key Personnel:** Skip Schmidt, General Mgr., schmidt@cctampa.com; William Brown, Local Sales Mgr.; David Denver, Program Dir., ddenver@clearchamel.com. **Wattage:** 100,000. **URL:** http://www.gater.com.

6931 WLVJ-AM - 640
1601 Belvedere Rd., Ste. 204 E. Phone: (561)688-9585
West Palm Beach, FL 33406-1543 Fax: (561)688-9601
Free: (800)655-9585
E-mail: wlvj@gate.net

Format: Religious; News. **Simulcasts:** WMKL-FM. **Networks:** USA Radio; International Broadcasting. **Owner:** South Florida Radio, 1601 Belvedere Rd Ste. 204E, West Palm Beach, FL 33406. **Founded:** 1986. **Operating Hours:** 24Hrs.,32% network, 12% local. **ADI:** West Palm Beach-Ft. Pierce-Vero Beach, FL. **Key Personnel:** Ron G. Smith, General Mgr.; Alex MacDonald, Program Dir.; Bert Williams, Office Mgr.; Matt Beaty, Traffic Mgr. **Local Programs:** *Bethesda By the Sea*; *Closer Look*, Steve Forsythe. **Wattage:** 25,000 day; 4500 night.

6932 WMBX-FM - 102.3
701 Northpoint Pkwy., Ste. 500 Phone: (561)686-9505
West Palm Beach, FL 33407 Fax: (561)640-9065

Format: Adult Contemporary. **Owner:** Palm Beach Radio Broadcasting, Inc., at above address. **Founded:** 1980. **Formerly**: WHLG-FM. **Operating Hours:** Continuous. **ADI:** West Palm Beach-Ft. Pierce-Vero Beach, FL. **Key Personnel:** Patricia A. Larschan, General Mgr.; Mark Krieger, General Sales Mgr.; Pam Crosby, News Dir.; Barbara Clifton, Promotions Dir.; Kevin Callahan, Program Dir. **Wattage:** 50,000. **Ad Rates:** Advertising accepted; rates available upon request.

6933 WMFL-FM - 88.5
1601 Belvedere Rd. Phone: (305)245-9300
West Palm Beach, FL 33406 Fax: (305)852-7396
E-mail: wmfl@familyvalue.net

Format: Educational. **Owner:** South Florida Educational Broadcasters, at above address. **Founded:** Oct. 1997. **Operating Hours:** Continuous. **Key Personnel:** Carl Quel, President, phone (561)688-9585, wlrj@gate.net; Ron Smith, General Mgr., phone (561)688-9585; Corky Toth, Station Mgr., phone (305)245-9300. **Wattage:** 8000. **Ad Rates:** Underwriting available.

6934 WMKL-FM - 91.7
1601 Belvedere Rd., Ste. 2046 Phone: (305)852-4470
West Palm Beach, FL 33406 Fax: (305)852-7396
E-mail: wmkl@familyvalue.net

Format: Educational; Religious. **Owner:** South Florida Educational Broadcasters, at above address. **Founded:** Oct. 1997. **Operating Hours:** Continuous. **ADI:** Miami (Ft. Lauderdale), FL. **Key Personnel:** Carl Quel, President, phone (561)688-9585, wlrj@gate.net; Ron Smith, General Mgr., phone (561)688-9585; Corky Toth, Station Mgr., phone (305)245-9300. **Wattage:** 40,000. **Ad Rates:** Underwriting available. **URL:** http://www.familyvalue.net.

6935 WOLL-FM - 94.3
2406 S. Congress Ave. Phone: (561)439-1111
West Palm Beach, FL 33406 Fax: (561)965-1102
E-mail: radio1@radio-1.com

Format: Oldies. **Networks:** Independent. **Founded:** 1971. **Formerly**: WNJY-FM (1989); WMXQ-FM. **Operating Hours:** Continuous. **ADI:** West Palm Beach-Ft. Pierce-Vero Beach, FL. **Key Personnel:** David D'Eugenio, General Mgr.; David Denver, Program Dir.; Bill Brown, Sales Mgr. **Wattage:** 6000. **Ad Rates:** Combined advertising rates available with WBZT-AM, WKGR-FM. **URL:** http://www.943beach.com.

6936 WPEC-TV - 12
PO Box 198512 Phone: (561)844-1212
West Palm Beach, FL 33419-8512 Fax: (561)842-1212

Format: Commercial TV. **Networks:** CBS. **Owner:** Freedom Communications, at above address. **Founded:** 1955. **Formerly**: WEAT-TV. **Operating Hours:** Continuous. **ADI:** West Palm Beach-Ft. Pierce-Vero Beach, FL. **Key Personnel:** William B. Peterson, VP/Gen. Mgr.; Jay Mitchell, News Dir.; Donn Colee, Jr., Promotions Mgr.; John Heislman, NSM; John Gee, LSM; Doug Wolfmueller, General Sales Mgr. **Ad Rates:** $25-3000 per unit.

6937 WPOM-AM - 1600
5033 Okeechobee Blvd. Phone: (561)687-1960
West Palm Beach, FL 33417-4533 Fax: (561)687-4221

Format: Urban Contemporary. **Founded:** 1958. **Operating Hours:** Continuous; 100% local. **ADI:** West Palm Beach-Ft. Pierce-Vero Beach, FL. **Key Personnel:** Dennis G. Mobley, General Mgr. **Wattage:** 5000. **Ad Rates:** $30-60 per unit.

6938 WRLX-FM - 92.1
901 Northpoint Pkwy., Ste 201 Phone: (561)478-9688
West Palm Beach, FL 33407

Format: Easy Listening. **Founded:** 1978. **Formerly**: WNGS-FM (1992). **Operating Hours:** Continuous. **ADI:** West Palm Beach-Ft. Pierce-Vero Beach, FL. **Key Personnel:** Steve Lapa, General Mgr.; Paul Dunn, Program Dir. **Local Programs:** *South Florida Forum*, Al Baker. **Wattage:** 7,200.

6939 WRMF-FM - 97.9
1540 Latham Rd. Phone: (561)838-4300
West Palm Beach, FL 33409-5181 Fax: (561)687-4187
E-mail: wjnochet@filnet.com

Format: Adult Contemporary. **Networks:** Independent. **Owner:** Richard M. Fairbanks, at above address. **Founded:** 1957. **Operating Hours:** Continuous. **ADI:** West Palm Beach-Ft. Pierce-Vero Beach, FL. **Key Personnel:** Chet Tart, General Mgr.; Ken Payne, Program Dir. **Wattage:** 100,000. **URL:** http://www.wrmf.com.

6940 WXEL-FM - 90.7
PO Box 6607 Phone: (561)737-8000
West Palm Beach, FL 33405 Fax: (561)369-3067

Format: Public Radio; News; Classical. **Networks:** National Public Radio (NPR). **Owner:** South Florida Public Telecommunications, Inc., at above address. **Founded:** 1969. **Formerly**: WHRS-FM (1985). **Operating Hours:** Continuous. **ADI:** West Palm Beach-Ft. Pierce-Vero Beach, FL. **Key Personnel:** Mary Souder, President/CEO; John LaBonia, Executive VP/COO; Phil DiComo, VP/External Affairs; Paul Rose, VP of Operations. **Wattage:** 25,000. **Ad Rates:** Noncommercial.

WEWAHITCHKA†, pop. 1,742.

NW FL. Gulf Co. On Apalachicola River, 35 mi. E. of Panama City. Boat connections. Retirement area. Naval stores; sawmill. Pine, cypress timber. Diversified agriculture.

6941 The Gulf County Breeze
Breeze Publishing Co.
118 N. 2nd St. & Osceola Ave. Phone: (904)639-2706
PO Box 218
Wewahitchka, FL 32465
Community newspaper. **Founded:** 1925. **Freq:** Weekly (Thurs.). **Print Method:** Letterpress. **Trim Size:** 12 x 18. **Cols./Page:** 5. **Col. Width:** 12 millimeters. **Col. Depth:** 16 1/2 inches. **Key Personnel:** Edward A. Bandjough, Editor and Publisher; Nell L. Bandjough, Advertising Mgr. **USPS:** 213-

800. **Subscription Rates:** $12 individuals; $15 out of area; $20 out of state. **Remarks:** Accepts advertising.
Ad Rates: GLR: $.375 BW: $426 SAU: $5.25 **Circ:** Paid ‡1,300 Free ‡200

WILDWOOD

6942 WHOF-AM - 640
6833 N. E. 79th
Wildwood, FL 34785
Phone: (352)748-6164
Fax: (352)748-8834

Format: Religious; Information. **Networks:** USA Radio. **Owner:** Walker Heart of Florida Broadcasting, Inc., at above address. **Operating Hours:** Continuous. **Key Personnel:** Keith Walker, Pres./General Mgr.; Joe Ruggiero, Operations Mgr.

WILLISTON, pop. 2,240.

N FL. Levy Co. 20 mi. S. of Gainesville.

6943 Williston Sun-Suwannee Valley News
PO Box Q
Phone: (352)528-6397
Williston, FL 32696
Local newspaper. **Founded:** 1879. **Freq:** Weekly (Thurs.). **Print Method:** Offset. **Cols./Page:** 8. **Col. Width:** 20 nonpareils. **Col. Depth:** 301 agate lines. **Key Personnel:** Nick Williams, Editor; Bess E. Williams Publisher. **Subscription Rates:** $10 individuals. **Remarks:** Accepts advertising.
Ad Rates: PCI: $2 **Circ:** ‡2,300

WINTER GARDEN, pop. 6,789.

EC FL. Orange Co. On Lake Apopka, 10 mi. W. of Orlando. Resort area. Citrus fruit, vegetable packing and shipping. Agriculture. Fruits, vegetables. Nurseries.

6944 Folkart Treasures
Forkart Treasures
14212 El Pico St.
Winter Garden, FL 34787-9414

Magazine focuses on country living products. **Freq:** Quarterly. **Key Personnel:** Jennifer Winquist, Editor. **Subscription Rates:** $19.95. $4 single issue.

6945 West Orange Times
PO Box 770309
Winter Garden, FL 34777
Phone: (407)656-2121
Fax: (407)656-6075

Community newspaper. **Founded:** 1913. **Freq:** Weekly (Thurs.). **Print Method:** Offset. **Cols./Page:** 6. **Col. Width:** 24 nonpareils. **Col. Depth:** 301 agate lines. **Key Personnel:** Anne Bailey, Editor; Andrew Bailey, Publisher. **Subscription Rates:** $12.50 individuals; $15 out of area. **Remarks:** Accepts advertising.
Ad Rates: BW: $774 4C: $954 SAU: $6 **Circ:** 7,000

WINTER HAVEN, pop. 21,119.

Polk Co. (C). 14 m E of Lakeland. Winter resort. Cypress Gardens. Manufactures citrus by-products, alcohol, molasses, feed, nutfood products, cigars, roofing, paper boxes, fertilizer. Crate, planing mills; sheet metal, bottling works; fruit packing and canning. Nurseries. Citrus fruit groves.

Bartow Shopper - See Bartow

6946 Financial Studies of the Small Business
Financial Research Associates Inc.
510 Ave. J. SE
Winter Haven, FL 33880
Phone: (941)299-3969
Fax: (941)299-2131

Trade magazine covering financial standards for small businesses. **Founded:** 1978. **Freq:** Annual. **Remarks:** Accepts advertising.
Circ: (Not Reported)

6947 Journal of Food Science
Institute of Food Technologists
PO Box 3065
Winter Haven, FL 33885-3065
Phone: (941)293-6519
Fax: (941)299-8244
Publisher E-mail: info@ift.org

Journal containing original research papers and articles relating to food science. **Founded:** Jan. 1961. **Freq:** Bimonthly. **Print Method:** Offset. **Trim Size:** 8 1/2 x 11. **Cols./Page:** 2. **Col. Width:** 21 picas. **Col. Depth:** 59 picas. **Key Personnel:** Dr. Robert E. Berry, Editor; Dan Weber, Publisher; Fran Katz, Advertising Mgr. **ISSN:** 0022-1947. **Subscription Rates:** $150. **Remarks:** Advertising not accepted.
Circ: ‡10,550

6948 La Prensa Newspaper
News Chief Publishing Group
650 Sixth St. SW
Winter Haven, FL 33882
Phone: (941)294-7731
Fax: (941)294-2008
Publisher E-mail: nchief@gate.net

Newspaper (tabloid) serving the Hispanic community of Central and South Florida (Spanish). **Founded:** Aug. 21, 1981. **Freq:** Weekly (Thurs.). **Print Method:** Offset. **Trim Size:** 11 1/2 x 17. **Cols./Page:** 5. **Col. Width:** 2 1/16 inches. **Col. Depth:** 16 inches. **Key Personnel:** Dora Cassanova, Editor; Manuel A. Toro, Publisher; Brenda Lopez, Advertising Dir.; Maria Melendez, Accounting Mgr. **Subscription Rates:** Free; $25 by mail. **Remarks:** Accepts advertising.
Ad Rates: BW: $1,360 4C: $1,660 SAU: $17 **Circ:** Free ‡19,828

6949 Lake Wales Highlander
PO Box 1440
Winter Haven, FL 33882-1440

General newspaper. **Founded:** 1916. **Freq:** Daily (eve.). **Print Method:** Offset. **Trim Size:** Broadsheet. **Cols./Page:** 6. **Col. Width:** 1 9/16 inches. **Col. Depth:** 301 agate lines. **Key Personnel:** Jan Mayo Kahler, Editor; Larry Beasley, Publisher. **USPS:** 143-160. **Subscription Rates:** $45 individuals. **Remarks:** Accepts advertising.
Ad Rates: BW: $574.05 4C: $734.05 SAU: $4.59 PCI: $4.59 **Circ:** Paid 2,798

6950 Newschief
Morris Communication Corp.
PO Box 1440
Winter Haven, FL 33882-1440
Phone: (941)294-7731
Fax: (941)294-2008
Publication E-mail: nchief@gate.net

Community newspaper. **Founded:** Apr. 2, 1953. **Freq:** Weekly (Thurs.). **Print Method:** Offset. **Trim Size:** 12 3/4 x 21 1/2. **Cols./Page:** 6. **Col. Width:** 2 inches. **Col. Depth:** 21 1/2 inches. **Key Personnel:** Curtis Lamb, Editor and Publisher; Philip Pettus, Managing Editor. **USPS:** 586-700. **Subscription Rates:** $13 individuals; $15 out of area. **Formerly:** Auburndale Star.
Ad Rates: GLR: $.45 BW: $516 4C: $900 PCI: $3.85 **Circ:** Combined 2,104

6951 North Lakeland Shopper
Stauffer Communications
650 6th St. SW
PO Box 1440
Winter Haven, FL 33880-3325

Shopping guide (tabloid). **Founded:** 1952. **Freq:** Weekly (Wed.). **Print Method:** Offset. **Trim Size:** 11 1/3 x 17 1/2. **Cols./Page:** 5. **Col. Width:** 10.5 picas. **Key Personnel:** Curtis Lamb, Publisher. **Subscription Rates:** Free. **Remarks:** Accepts advertising.
Ad Rates: GLR: $.48 BW: $536 PCI: $670 **Circ:** Combined 28,339

6952 Senior Times Magazine
PO Box 7325
Winter Haven, FL 33883-7325
Phone: (941)294-9376
Fax: (941)293-2505

Magazine devoted to educating senior citizens on recreational, political, health and financial issues. **Founded:** Oct. 1, 1991. **Freq:** Monthly. **Print Method:** Webb. **Trim Size:** 8 1/2 x 11. **Cols./Page:** 2. **Col. Width:** 3 1/2 inches. **Col. Depth:** 10 inches. **Key Personnel:** Judy A. Kahler, Editor; Bill Bowen, Antiques; Jim Geladas, Humor; Christopher Desrochers, Legal; Sharon Kiser, Assoc. Editor; Judy Kahler, Travel and History; Drew Snell, Profiles. **Subscription Rates:** $15 individuals.
Ad Rates: BW: $825.00 4C: $1,025.00 **Circ:** Paid ‡100 Non-paid ‡19,900

6953 Shopper
Lake Wales Highlander
PO Box 1440
Winter Haven, FL 33882-1440

Shopper. **Founded:** 1973. **Freq:** Weekly (Wed.). **Print Method:** Offset. **Cols./Page:** 6. **Col. Width:** 21 nonpareils. **Col. Depth:** 238 agate lines. **Key Personnel:** Kevin Cruess, Publisher. **Remarks:** Accepts advertising.
Ad Rates: GLR: $.26 **Circ:** Free 16,000

6954 South Lakeland Shopper
Stauffer Communications
650 6th St. SW
PO Box 1440
Winter Haven, FL 33880-3325

Shopping guide (tabloid). **Founded:** 1952. **Freq:** Weekly (Wed.). **Print Method:** Offset. **Trim Size:** 11 1/3 x 17 1/2. **Cols./Page:** 5. **Col. Width:** 10.5 picas. **Key Personnel:** Curtis Lamb, Publisher. **Subscription Rates:** Free. **Remarks:** Color advertising accepted; rates available upon request.
Ad Rates: GLR: $.48 BW: $536 PCI: $670 **Circ:** Free 28,152

6955 The Water Skier
USA Waterski
799 Overlook Dr.
Winter Haven, FL 33884
Phone: (941)324-4341
Fax: (941)325-8259
Free: (800)533-2972
Publication E-mail: usawsmagazine@worldnet.att.net
Publisher E-mail: usawaterski@usawaterski.org

Water skiing magazine. **Subtitle:** Official Publication of USA Water Ski. **Founded:** 1951. **Freq:** 9/year. **Print Method:** Offset. **Trim Size:** 8 3/8 x 10 7/8. **Cols./Page:** 3. **Col. Width:** 13 picas. **Col. Depth:** 57 picas. **Key Personnel:** Greg Nixon, Publisher/Editor, gnixon@usawaterski.org; Dan Justman, Advertising Mgr., djustman@usawaterski.org; Scott Atkinson, Managing Editor, satkinson@usawaterski.org. **ISSN:** 0049-7002. **Subscription Rates:** $25. **Remarks:** Accepts advertising. **URL:** http://www.usawaterski.org.
Ad Rates: BW: $1,097 4C: $1,701 PCI: $63 **Circ:** Paid ‡30,000 Non-paid ‡500

6956 Winter Haven News Chief
Stauffer Communications
PO Box 1440
Winter Haven, FL 33882

General newspaper. **Founded:** 1911. **Freq:** Daily (eve.). **Print Method:** Offset. **Trim Size:** 13 3/4 x 22 3/4. **Cols./Page:** 6. **Col. Width:** 24 nonpareils. **Col. Depth:** 301 agate lines. **Key Personnel:** Gary E. Maitland, Exec. Editor; Larry T. Beasley, Publisher; Janice Saunders, Advertising Mgr. **USPS:** 687-160. **Subscription Rates:** $132.08 individuals. **Remarks:** Accepts advertising.
Ad Rates: BW: $1,188.09 4C: $1,608.09 SAU: $9.21 **Circ:** Combined 11,026

6957 Winter Haven Shopper
News Chief Publishing Group
650 Sixth St. SW
Winter Haven, FL 33882
Phone: (941)294-7731
Fax: (941)294-2008
Publisher E-mail: nchief@gate.net

Shopper. **Founded:** 1952. **Freq:** Weekly (Wed.). **Print Method:** Offset. **Trim Size:** 11 1/3 x 17 1/2. **Cols./Page:** 5. **Col. Width:** 10.5 picas. **Key Personnel:** Larry Beasley, Publisher. **Remarks:** Color advertising accepted; rates available upon request.
Ad Rates: GLR: $.48 BW: $380 4C: $680 PCI: $4.75 **Circ:** Free ‡33,000

6958 WHNR-AM - 1360
1505 Dundee Rd.
PO Box 7742
Winter Haven, FL 33884-1013
Phone: (813)299-1141
Fax: (813)293-6397

Format: Middle-of-the-Road (MOR); News; Talk. **Networks:** ABC. **Formerly:** WYXY-AM (1990). **Operating Hours:** 5 a.m.-midnight. **Key Personnel:** B.J. Nielson, General Mgr. **Wattage:** 5000 day; 2500 night.

6959 WSIR-AM - 1490
665 Lake Howard Dr. SW
Winter Haven, FL 33880-2577
Phone: (941)294-4111
Fax: (941)452-1006

Format: Adult Contemporary; Hispanic. **Networks:** Cadena Radio Centro (CRC). **Owner:** William Mark Histed, at above address. **Founded:** 1947. **Operating Hours:** Continuous. **ADI:** Tampa-St. Petersburg (Lakeland, Sarasota), FL. **Key Personnel:** Robert Cubero, General Manager, Prog. Director, rcubero@strato.net; Brenda Histed-Searle, News Dir. **Wattage:** 1000. **Ad Rates:** $15 for 30 seconds; $20 for 60 seconds.

WINTER PARK, pop. 22,314.

Orange Co. (EC). 3 m NE of Orlando. Residential. Rollins College. U.S. Navy training center. Tourist resort.

6960 AngelWatch
AngelWatch, Inc.
1850 Lee Rd., No. 334 Phone: (407)629-4811
Winter Park, FL 32789 Fax: (407)628-4255
Publication E-mail: rwpfl@aol.com

Magazine for people interested in angels. **Subtitle:** Searching for God Through the Work of the Angels. **Founded:** Aug. 1992. **Freq:** Bimonthly. **Print Method:** Offset. **Trim Size:** 8 1/2 x 11. **Cols./Page:** 3. **Col. Width:** 14 picas. **Col. Depth:** 9 inches. **Key Personnel:** Patricia Proechel, Editor, rwpfl@aol.com. **ISSN:** 1063-8962. **Subscription Rates:** $19. **Remarks:** Advertising not accepted.
Circ: Paid 10,462
Non-paid 25

6961 Caribbean Travel and Life
Caribbean Travel and Life, Inc.
330 West Canton Ave. Phone: (407)628-4802
Winter Park, FL 32789 Fax: (407)628-7061
Publication E-mail: sb3@worldzine.com

Magazine covering travel, culture, and leisure in the Caribbean. **Founded:** Jan. 1986. **Freq:** 8x/yr. **Print Method:** Web offset. **Trim Size:** 8 1/8 x 10 7/8. **Cols./Page:** 3. **Col. Width:** 13 picas. **Col. Depth:** 72 picas. **Key Personnel:** Steve Blount, Editor; Sue Gilman, Publisher. **ISSN:** 0891-9496. **Subscription Rates:** $23.95 individuals. **Remarks:** Accepts advertising. **Available Online**. **URL:** http://www.carib.com.
Ad Rates: BW: $5,306 **Circ:** Paid ★**117,137**
4C: $7,920
PCI: $190

6962 Florida Forum
FRSA
4111 Metric Dr. Phone: (407)671-3772
PO Box 4850 Fax: (407)679-0010
Winter Park, FL 32793
Free: (800)767-3772

Roofing, sheet metal, and air conditioning magazine. **Founded:** Jan. 1, 1961. **Freq:** Monthly. **Print Method:** Offset. **Trim Size:** 8 1/4 x 11. **Cols./Page:** 3 and 2. **Col. Width:** 27 and 40 nonpareils. **Col. Depth:** 140 agate lines. **Key Personnel:** Bonnie B. Pierce, Editor; Steve Munnell, Executive Director. **ISSN:** 0191-4618. **Subscription Rates:** $25 tax. **Remarks:** Accepts advertising.
Ad Rates: BW: $1,060 **Circ:** Controlled ‡5,000
4C: $1,760
PCI: $30

6963 Florida Grower
Meister Publishing Co.
1555 Howell Branch Rd., No. C-204 Phone: (407)539-6552
Fax: (407)539-6544
Winter Park, FL 32789
Publisher E-mail: info@meisternet.com

Agricultural magazine. **Founded:** 1907. **Freq:** Monthly. **Print Method:** Offset. **Trim Size:** 8 1/2 x 11. **Cols./Page:** 3. **Col. Width:** 27 nonpareils. **Col. Depth:** 140 agate lines. **Key Personnel:** William J. Miller II, Publishing Dir.; Frank Garner, Editor; Jon Miducki, Associate Publisher/Advertising Dir.; Rick Melnick, Group Editor. **ISSN:** 0015-4091. **Subscription Rates:** Free; $35 by mail; $45 out of area; $50 other countries. **Formerly:** Florida Grower & Rancher.
Ad Rates: GLR: $4.70 **Circ:** Controlled 13,396
BW: $1,633
4C: $3,283
PCI: $66

6964 The Florida Naturalist
Florida Audubon Society
1331 Palmetto Ave., Ste. 110 Phone: (407)539-5700
Winter Park, FL 32789 Fax: (407)539-5701
Publication E-mail: audubonfla@aol.com; sbogan@audubon.org

Magazine on Florida's natural history. **Founded:** 1927. **Freq:** Quarterly. **Print Method:** Offset. **Trim Size:** 8 3/8 x 10 7/8. **Cols./Page:** 3. **Col. Width:** 26 nonpareils. **Col. Depth:** 136 agate lines. **Key Personnel:** Sandra Bogan, Editor. **ISSN:** 0015-4172. **Subscription Rates:** $25 individuals; $18 libraries; $3 single issue. **Remarks:** Accepts advertising.
Ad Rates: BW: $1595.00 **Circ:** 30,000
4C: $1,950

6965 Florida Specifier
National Technical Communications Co., Inc. (NTCC)
PO Box 2027 Phone: (407)671-7777
Winter Park, FL 32790 Fax: (407)671-7757
Free: (800)881-6822

Monthly tabloid covering water, wastewater, hazardous waste, solid waste, air quality, and pollution prevention in Florida. **Subtitle:** Practical Information for Environmental Professionals. **Founded:** 1979. **Freq:** Monthly. **Print Method:** Offset. **Trim Size:** 11 1/4 x 17. **Cols./Page:** 4. **Col. Width:** 27 nonpareils. **Col. Depth:** 224 agate lines. **Key Personnel:** Melora Grattan, Editor; Mike Eastman, Publisher, mreast@enviro-net.com; Dee Main, Advertising Mgr. **ISSN:** 0740-1973. **Subscription Rates:** $24.95 individuals; $5 single issue. **Remarks:** Accepts advertising. **Available Online**. **URL:** http://www.enviro-net.com.
Ad Rates: BW: $1,255 **Circ:** Paid ‡1,000
4C: $1,950 Controlled ‡12,500
PCI: $50

6966 Latitudes
Caribbean Travel and Life, Inc.
330 West Canton Ave. Phone: (407)628-4802
Winter Park, FL 32789 Fax: (407)628-7061
Publication E-mail: affcarib@aol.com

In-flight magazine for American Eagle airlines' San Juan, PR, and Miami, FL hubs (English and Spanish). **Freq:** Quarterly 6x/yr. **Cols./Page:** 3. **Col. Width:** 2 1/4 inches. **Col. Depth:** 10 inches. **Key Personnel:** Steve Blount, Editor; Jane Mcallister, Publisher. **Remarks:** Accepts advertising. **URL:** http://www.carib.com.
Ad Rates: BW: $4,228 **Circ:** Controlled 105,000
4C: $6,300

6967 Marlin
World Publications, Inc.
330 W. Canton Ave. Phone: (407)628-4802
Winter Park, FL 32789 Fax: (407)628-7061
Publication E-mail: marlin@worldzine.com

Covers offshore sport-fising for billfish and other large pelagics. **Subtitle:** The International Sportingfishing Magazine. **Founded:** 1981. **Freq:** Bimonthly. **Print Method:** Web offset. **Trim Size:** 8 1/8 x 10 3/4. **Cols./Page:** 3. **Col. Width:** 2 3/16 inches. **Col. Depth:** 10 inches. **Key Personnel:** Glenn Hughes, Publisher, gh1@worldzine.com; David Ritchie, Editor, dr1@worldzine.com. **ISSN:** 0749-2006. **Subscription Rates:** $24.95; $3.95 single issue. **Remarks:** Accepts advertising. **URL:** http://www.marlinmag.com.
Ad Rates: GLR: $60 **Circ:** Paid 40,000
BW: $3,445 Non-paid 10,000
4C: $5,100

6968 Moneyworld
Gulf/Atlantic Publishing, Inc.
1947 Lee Rd. Phone: (407)628-5700
Winter Park, FL 32789-2165 Fax: (407)628-0807
Free: (800)444-4980
Publication E-mail: money_world@money-world.net

Investment magazine (tabloid). **Founded:** 1987. **Freq:** Monthly. **Print Method:** Web offset. **Trim Size:** 11 x 13. **Cols./Page:** 3. **Col. Width:** 14 picas. **Key Personnel:** Donald R. Philpott, Managing Editor, don_philpott@money-world.net; Roberto E. Veitia, Publisher; Jessica Klarp, Editor, jessica_klarp@money-world.net. **Subscription Rates:** $29. **Remarks:** Accepts advertising.
Ad Rates: BW: $12,600 **Circ:** Paid 40,000
4C: $18,000 Free 260,000

6969 Ornamental Outlook
Meister Publishing Co.
1555 Howell Branch Rd., No. C-204 Phone: (407)539-6552
Fax: (407)539-6544
Winter Park, FL 32789
Publisher E-mail: info@meisternet.com

Trade magazine for the environmental horticulture industry. **Subtitle:** Your Connection to the South's Horticulture Industry. **Founded:** 1977. **Freq:** Monthly. **Trim Size:** 8 1/2 x 11. **Cols./Page:** 3. **Col. Width:** 28 nonpareils. **Col. Depth:** 182 agate lines. **Key Personnel:** William J. Miller II, Publishing Dir.; Joe Monahan, Associate Publisher/Advertising Dir.; Kris Sweet, Editor; Delilah Onofrey, Group Editor. **Subscription Rates:** $30 individuals in Florida; $37 out of state; $57.50 other countries.
Ad Rates: BW: $1,118 **Circ:** 13,175
4C: $1,743

6970 Rollins Sandspur
Rollins College
Box 2742 Phone: (407)646-2696
Winter Park, FL 32789 Fax: (407)646-1530

Collegiate newspaper. **Founded:** 1894. **Freq:** Weekly. **Print Method:** Offset. **Trim Size:** 11 x 16. **Cols./Page:** 5. **Col. Width:** 22 nonpareils. **Col. Depth:** 217 agate lines. **Key Personnel:** Chris Smith, Editor; Adam Long, Advertising Mgr. **Subscription Rates:** $20 individuals. **Remarks:** Accepts advertising.
Ad Rates: PCI: $5 **Circ:** ‡2,500

6971 Sport Fishing
World Publications, Inc.
330 W. Canton Ave. Phone: (407)628-4802
Winter Park, FL 32789 Fax: (407)628-7061
Publication E-mail: sportfish@worldzine.com

Magazine about saltwater fishing. **Subtitle:** The Magazine of Saltwater Fishing. **Founded:** 1986. **Freq:** 9/year. **Print Method:** Web offset. **Trim Size:** 8 1/8 x 10 3/4. **Cols./Page:** 3. **Col. Width:** 2 3/16 inches. **Col. Depth:** 10 inches. **Key Personnel:** Terry Snow, President; Dean Travis Clarke, Exec. Editor; Glenn Hughes, Publisher, gh1@worldzine.com. **ISSN:** 0896-7369. **Subscription Rates:** $19.97 individuals; $3.95 single issue. **Remarks:** Accepts advertising.
Ad Rates: BW: $8,219 **Circ:** Paid ★**127,096**
4C: $11,745 Non-paid ★**26,845**

6972 Sunshine Artist
Palm House Publishing, Inc.
2600 Temple Dr. Phone: (407)539-1399
Winter Park, FL 32789-1371 Fax: (407)539-1499
Free: (800)597-2573
Publication E-mail: sunart@magicnet.net
Publisher E-mail: business@sunshineartist.com

Trade magazine covering arts and crafts shows and festivals. **Founded:** 1972. **Freq:** Monthly. **Print Method:** Web offset. **Trim Size:** 8 1/8 x 10 7/8. **Cols./Page:** 3. **Col. Width:** 2 1/4 inches. **Col. Depth:** 9 3/4 inches. **Key Personnel:** David Cook, Publisher; Amy Detwiler, Editor. **ISSN:** 0199-9370. **Subscription Rates:** $29.95 individuals; $4.95 single issue. **Remarks:** Accepts advertising. **URL:** http://www.sunshineartist.com.
Ad Rates: BW: $830 **Circ:** Combined ⊕**30,000**
4C: $1,255

6973 Waterski Magazine
World Publications, Inc.
330 W. Canton Ave. Phone: (407)628-4802
Winter Park, FL 32789 Fax: (407)628-7061
Publication E-mail: waterski@worldzine.com

Magazine on waterskiing. **Subtitle:** The World's Leading Water Ski Magazine. **Founded:** 1978. **Freq:** 9/year. **Print Method:** Web offset. **Trim Size:** 8 1/8 x 10 3/4. **Cols./Page:** 3. **Col. Width:** 2 3/16 inches. **Col. Depth:** 10 inches. **Key Personnel:** Terry L. Snow, Publisher; John McEver, Jr., Advertising Dir.; Pierce Hoover, Editor. **ISSN:** 0883-7813. **Subscription Rates:** $19.97. $3.95 single issue. **Remarks:** Accepts advertising. **Formerly:** World Waterskiing.
Ad Rates: GLR: $39 **Circ:** Paid ★**101,512**
BW: $5,800
4C: $8,685

6974 Windsurfing
World Publications, Inc.
330 W. Canton Ave. Phone: (407)628-4802
Winter Park, FL 32789 Fax: (407)628-7061

Windsurfing magazine. **Founded:** 1981. **Freq:** 8/year. **Print Method:** Offset. **Cols./Page:** 3. **Col. Width:** 26 nonpareils. **Col. Depth:** 140 agate lines. **Key Personnel:** Debbie Snow, Editor; Terry Snow, Publisher; Susan Gilman, Advertising Mgr. **Subscription Rates:** $18.97 individuals.

6975 WLOQ-FM - 103.1
170 W. Fairbanks Ave. Phone: (407)647-5557
Winter Park, FL 32789 Fax: (407)647-4495
E-mail: general@wloq.com

Format: Jazz. **Networks:** Independent. **Owner:** Herb Gross, at above address. **Founded:** 1966. **Operating Hours:** Continuous; 5% network, 95% local. **Key Personnel:** JoAnn McGilvray, Business Mgr., fax (407)647-8815; Kim McFadden, General Mgr.; Deborah Crowley, Program Dir.; Ben Schilling, Mktg./Promotions Dir.; James Gross, General Sales Mgr. **Wattage:** 25,000. **URL:** http://www.wloq.com.

6976 WOMX-FM - 105.1
1801 Lee Rd., Ste. 270 Phone: (407)629-5105
Winter Park, FL 32789 Fax: (407)647-6515
Free: (800)282-9649

Format: Adult Contemporary. **Owner:** Chancellor Media Corp., 300 Crescent Ct., Ste. 600, Dallas, TX 75201, (214)922-8700, Fax: (214)922-8701. **Founded:** 1967. **Formerly:** WBJW-FM (1989). **Operating Hours:** Continuous. **ADI:** Orlando-Daytona Beach-Melbourne, FL. **Key Personnel:** Tim Baldwin, Music Dir.; David Isreal, Program Dir., davidmix@aol.com; Pam Roberts, Traffic Dir.; Dan Wachs, General Mgr.; Dennis Sloatman, Dir. of Engineers; Al Romanie, Business Mgr.; Angela Gooslin, Promotions Dir. **Wattage:** 100,000. **Ad Rates:** $75-250 per unit.

6977 WPRK-FM - 91.5
1000 Holt Ave. Phone: (407)646-2241
Rollins College Fax: (407)646-1560
Box 2745
Winter Park, FL 32789
E-mail: wprkfm@rollins.edu

Format: Eclectic. **Founded:** 1952. **Operating Hours:** Continuous Daily. **Key Personnel:** Dr. Susan Cohn Lackman, General Mgr., phone (407)646-2400, fax (407)646-2533, slackman@rollins.edu; Nellie Lackman, Promotions Dir., elackman@rollins.edu; Myrna Caban, mcaban@rollins.edu;

Destin Berthelot, Director; Matt Donnelly, Program Dir., dberthelot@rollins.edu; Andrew Greenwood, Public Service Dir. **Wattage:** 1300. **Ad Rates:** Noncommercial. **URL:** http://tars.rollins.edu/wprk.

GEORGIA

State Capital, ATLANTA

Georgia is bounded on the north by Tennessee and North Carolina, northeast by South Carolina, southeast by the Atlantic Ocean, south by Florida, and west by Alabama. Extreme length from north to south is 315 miles, extreme breadth, 250 miles. Total land area is 57,919 square miles. The surface is varied. Along the coast it is intersected by numerous rivers and sounds; the country for miles inland is a succession of ridges of pines and live oaks and swamps of cypress. The great Okefenokee swamp is in the southeast. Back from the coast is a stretch of sandy land, mostly pine barrens yielding quantities of timber and naval stores. A series of terraces bring the region in the middle of the state to about 575 feet above tidewater, from which elevation it rises toward the north more rapidly, until it becomes mountainous, being there crossed by spurs of the Appalachians. The Weather Bureau at Atlanta gives the temperature (annual average) as 61.3; highest on record, 103; lowest on record, -9. The total annual precipitation is 50.77 inches. Savannah is one of the chief south Atlantic seaports and has an important foreign and domestic commerce. There are numerous mineral springs in Georgia, of which the Indian Spring in Butts county and Lithia Springs in Douglas County are among the best known. The University of Georgia, located at Athens, the Georgia Institute of Technology, Georgia State College, and Emory University, all in Atlanta, are the largest institutions of higher education in the state.

POPULATION: 6,751,000 (1992). Rank among the states, 11th.

AGRICULTURE: Number of farms: 46,000 (1992). Farm acreage: 12,000,000 (1992). Cash receipts from farm marketings: crops, $1,825,000,000 (1991); livestock and products, $2,153,000,000 (1991).

FISHERIES: Total catch: 16,000,000 lbs. (1991), $24,000,000 value. Principal fish: shrimp, crabs, shad.

FORESTS: Total forest land: 1,846,000 acres (1991). Principal woods: southern yellow pine, yellow poplar, red and sap gum, oak, black and tupelo gum, cypress, ash, maple, sycamore, hickory, cottonwood and aspen, elm.

MINERALS: Value of production: $1,495,000,000 (1991). Principal minerals: clays, stone, and cement.

MANUFACTURES: Value added by manufacture: $36,576,000,000 (1991). Leading industry groups: textile mill products, transportation equipment, food and related products, paper and allied products.

LIST OF COUNTIES

Total number of counties 159

County, Location on Map, and County Seat	Pop.
Appling (SE), Baxley	15,744
Atkinson (S), Pearson	6,213
Bacon (SE), Alma	9,566
Baker (SW), Newton	3,615
Baldwin (C), Milledgeville	39,530
Banks (NE), Homer	10,308
Barrow (NE), Winder	29,721
Bartow (NW), Cartersville	55,915
Ben Hill (S), Fitzgerald	16,245
Berrien (S), Nashville	14,153
Bibb (C), Macon	150,137
Bleckley (C), Cochran	10,430
Brantley (SE), Nahunta	11,077
Brooks (S), Quitman	15,398
Bryan (SE), Pembroke	15,438
Bulloch (E), Statesboro	43,125
Burke (E), Waynesboro	20,579
Butts (C), Jackson	15,326
Calhoun (SW), Morgan	5,013
Camden (SE), Woodbine	30,167
Candler (E), Metter	7,744
Carroll (W), Carrollton	71,422
Catoosa (NW), Ringgold	42,464
Charlton (SE), Folkston	8,496
Chatham (SE), Savannah	216,774
Chattahoochee (W), Cussetta	16,934
Chattooga (NW), Summerville	22,242
Cherokee (NW), Canton	90,204
Clarke (NE), Athens	87,594
Clay (SW), Fort Gaines	3,364
Clayton (NWC), Jonesboro	182,052
Clinch (S), Homerville	6,160
Cobb (NW), Marietta	447,745
Coffee (S), Douglas	29,592
Colquitt (S), Moultrie	36,645
Columbia (E), Appling	66,031
Cook (S), Adel	13,456
Coweta (W), Newnan	53,853
Crawford (WC), Knoxville	8,991
Crisp (SWC), Cordele	20,011
Dade (NW), Trenton	13,147
Dawson (N), Dawsonville	9,429
Decatur (SW), Bainbridge	25,517
DeKalb (NWC), Decatur	25,517
Dodge (SC), Eastman	17,607
Dooly (SC), Vienna	9,901
Dougherty (SW), Albany	96,321
Douglas (W), Douglasville	71,120
Early (SW), Blakely	11,854
Echols (S), Statenville	2,334
Effingham (S), Springfield	25,687
Elbert (NE), Elberton	18,949
Emanuel (E), Swainsboro	20,546
Evans (SE), Claxton	8,724
Fannin (N), Blue Ridge	15,992
Fayette (W), Fayetteville	62,415
Floyd (NW), Rome	81,251
Forsyth (N), Cumming	44,083
Franklin (NE), Carnesville	16,650
Fulton (NW), Atlanta	648,779
Gilmer (N), Elijay	13,368
Glascock (E), Gibson	2,357
Glynn (SE), Brunswick	62,496
Gordon (NW), Calhoun	35,067
Grady (SW), Cairo	20,279
Greene (NEC), Greensboro	11,793
Gwinnett (NC), Lawrenceville	352,910
Habersham (NE), Clarkesville	27,622
Hall (N), Gainesville	95,434
Hancock (NEC), Sparta	8,908
Haralson (NW), Buchanan	21,966
Harris (W), Hamilton	17,788
Hart (NE), Hartwell	19,712
Heard (W), Franklin	8,628
Henry (NWC), McDonough	58,741
Houston (C), Perry	89,208
Irwin (S), Ocilla	8,649
Jackson (NE), Jefferson	30,005
Jasper (NC), Monticello	8,453
Jeff Davis (SE), Hazlehurst	12,032
Jefferson (E), Louisville	17,408
Jenkins (E), Millen	8,247
Johnson (EC), Wrightsville	8,329
Jones (C), Gray	20,739
Lamar (W), Barnesville	13,038
Lanier (S), Lakeland	5,531
Laurens (C), Dublin	39,988
Lee (SW), Leesburg	16,250
Liberty (SE), Hinesville	52,745
Lincoln (NE), Lincolntown	7,442

Long (SE), Ludowici 6,202
Lowndes (S), Valdosta 75,981
Lumpkin (N), Dahlonega 14,573
Macon (SWC), Oglethorpe 13,114
Madison (NE), Danielsville 21,050
Marion (W), Buena Vista 5,590
McDuffie (E), Thomson 20,119
McIntosh (SE), Darien 8,634
Meriwither (W), Greenville 22,411
Miller (SW), Colquitt 6,280
Mitchell (SW), Camilla 20,275
Monroe (C), Forsyth 17,113
Montgomery (SEC), Mount Vernon 7,379
Morgan (NC), Madison 12,883
Murray (NW), Chatsworth 26,147
Muscogee (W), Columbus 179,278
Newton (NC), Covington 41,808
Oconee (N), Watkinsville 17,618
Oglethorpe (N), Lexington 9,763
Paulding (NW), Dallas 41,611
Peach (C), Fort Valley 21,189
Pickens (N), Jasper 14,432
Pierce (SE), Blackshear 13,328
Pike (W), Zebulon 10,224
Polk (NW), Cedartown 33,185
Pulaski (C), Hawkinsville 8,108
Putnam (C), Eatonton 14,137
Quitman (SW), Georgetown 2,209
Rabun (NE), Clayton 11,648
Randolph (SW), Cuthbert 8,023
Richmond (E), Augusta 189,719
Rockdale (NC), Conyers 54,091
Schely (W), Ellaville 3,588
Screven (E), Sylvania 13,843
Seminole (SW), Donalsonville 9,010
Spalding (W), Griffin 54,457
Stephens (NE), Toccoa 23,251
Stewart (SW), Lumpkin 5,654
Sumter (SWC), Americus 30,228
Talbot (W), Talbotton 6,524
Taliaferro (NE), Crawfordville 1,915
Tattnall (SE), Reidsville 17,722
Taylor (W), Butler 7,642
Telfair (SC), McRae 11,000
Terrell (SW), Dawson 10,653
Thomas (SW), Thomasville 38,943
Tift (S), Tifton 34,998
Toombs (SEC), Lyons 24,072
Towns (N), Hiawassee 6,754
Treutlen (SEC), Soperton 5,994
Troup (W), La Grange 55,532
Turner (S), Ashburn 8,703
Twiggs (C), Jefferson 9,806
Union (N), Blairsville 11,993
Upson (W), Thomaston 26,300
Walker (NW), La Fayette 58,340
Walton (NC), Monroe 38,586
Ware (SE), Waycross 35,471
Warren (E), Warrentown 6,078
Washington (EC), Sandersville 19,112
Wayne (SE), Jesup 22,356
Webster (W), Preston 2,263
Wheeler (SEC), Alamo 4,903
White (N), Cleveland 13,006
Whitfield (NW), Dalton 72,462
Wilcox (SC), Abbeville 7,008
Wilkes (NE), Washington 10,597
Wilkinson (C), Irwinton 10,228
Worth (S), Sylvester 19,744

STATISTICS

Newspapers

Period of Issue
Daily 25
Evening Daily 17
Morning Daily 8
Daily with Sunday edition 11
Triweekly 2
Semiweekly 15
Weekly 176
Biweekly 3
Semimonthly 2
Monthly 11
Bimonthly 3
Quarterly 2
Free or partly free 49
Shopper 18
Total Newspapers 251

Periodicals

Period of Issue
Weekly 6
Biweekly 1
Semimonthly 1
Monthly 63
Bimonthly 32
Quarterly 50
Total Periodicals 195

Total number of publications 446

Radio Stations

AM Stations 141
FM Stations 133
Total Radio Stations 274

TV Stations

Total TV Stations 36

Cable Stations

Total Cable Systems 46

Total number of broadcast listings 356

ACWORTH

6978 Acworth Neighbor
Neighbor Newspapers, Inc.
580 Fairground St. Phone: (770)428-9411
PO Box 449 Fax: (770)428-7945
Marietta, GA 30060
Community newspaper. **Founded:** 1969. **Freq:** Weekly (Thurs.). **Print Method:** Offset. **Cols./Page:** 6. **Col. Width:** 26 nonpareils. **Col. Depth:** 301 agate lines. **Key Personnel:** Betty Schmidt, Editor; Otis A. Brumby, Jr., Publisher; R. Terry Smith, Vice President. **USPS:** 951-780. **Subscription Rates:** Free; $12 institutions; $18 out of area; $24 out of state.
Ad Rates: GLR: $1 **Circ:** Combined 17,904
BW: $1,806
4C: $2,131
SAU: $14

6979 Food People
Olson Publications, Inc.
5137 Highway 92 Phone: (404)974-1077
Acworth, GA 30102 Free: (800)647-3724
Publication E-mail: foodpeopl3@aol.com

Trade tabloid covering the retail food industry. **Founded:** Feb. 1981. **Freq:** Monthly. **Print Method:** Offset. **Trim Size:** 11 1/2 x 15. **Cols./Page:** 5. **Col. Width:** 22 nonpareils. **Col. Depth:** 196 agate lines. **Key Personnel:** Ms. Johnnie Nelson, Managing Editor; Tom Olson, Publisher. **ISSN:** 0279-9839. **Subscription Rates:** $28 individuals; $2.50 single issue. **Remarks:** Accepts advertising.
Ad Rates: BW: $3,250 **Circ:** Paid 335
4C: $4,750 Non-paid 42,149

ADAIRSVILLE

6980 North Bartow News
321B N. Main St. Phone: (770)773-3754
PO Box 374 Fax: (770)773-3754
Adairsville, GA 30103
Community newspaper. **Freq:** Weekly (Tues.). **Print Method:** Offset. **Trim Size:** 14 x 22 3/4. **Cols./Page:** 6. **Col. Width:** 12 1/2 picas. **Col. Depth:** 21 1/2 inches. **Key Personnel:** Charles Hurley, Publisher. **Subscription Rates:** Free; $25 by mail. **Remarks:** Accepts advertising.
Ad Rates: BW: $451.50 **Circ:** Free ‡6,100
4C: $671.50
SAU: $3.50
CNU: $548.25

ADEL

6981 Adel News-Tribune
Quitman
PO Box 312 Phone: (912)896-2233
Adel, GA 31620 Fax: (912)896-7237
Publisher E-mail: iant@surfsouth.com

Community newspaper. **Founded:** 1889. **Freq:** Weekly (Wed.). **Print Method:** Offset. **Cols./Page:** 6. **Col. Width:** 12 1/2 picas. **Col. Depth:** 21 inches. **Key Personnel:** Bill Grant, General Mgr. **ISSN:** 0746-0716. **Subscription Rates:** $15.90. **Remarks:** Accepts advertising.
Ad Rates: SAU: $3.60 **Circ:** 3,200

6982 Quitman Free Press
Quitman
PO Box 312 Phone: (912)896-2233
Adel, GA 31620 Fax: (912)896-7237
Publisher E-mail: iant@surfsouth.com

Community newspaper. **Founded:** 1876. **Freq:** Weekly (Wed.). **Cols./Page:** 6. **Col. Width:** 2 inches. **Col. Depth:** 21 inches. **Key Personnel:** Bob Tribble, Publisher. **Subscription Rates:** $18. **Remarks:** Accepts advertising.
Ad Rates: BW: $75 **Circ:** 3,400
SAU: $3.95

6983 WDDQ-FM - 92.1
1200 W. 4th St. Phone: (912)896-4572
Adel, GA 31620 Fax: (912)896-4710
Free: (800)701-8845

Format: Soft Rock. **Networks:** Georgia Radio. **Owner:** Williams Investment Co., at above address. **Founded:** 1979. **Operating Hours:** Continuous; 100% local. **Key Personnel:** John L. Williams, Contact; Aubrey Smith, Manager. **Wattage:** 6000. **Ad Rates:** $7 for 30 seconds. Combined advertising rates available with WBIT-AM.

ALAMO†, pop. 993.

SEC GA. Wheeler Co. 70 mi. SE of Macon. Little Ocmulgee State Park. Naval stores. Manufactures garments. Feed mill. Pine poplar timber. Agriculture. Cotton, tobacco, watermelons.

6984 The Wheeler County Eagle
PO Box 409 Phone: (912)529-6624
Alamo, GA 30411-0409 Fax: (912)529-5399

Newspaper. **Founded:** 1913. **Freq:** Weekly (Wed.). **Print Method:** Offset. **Cols./Page:** 6. **Col. Width:** 26 nonpareils. **Col. Depth:** 294 agate lines. **Key Personnel:** S. DuBose Porter, Editor. **Subscription Rates:** $15.90 individuals; $26.50 out of area. **Remarks:** Accepts advertising.
Ad Rates: GLR: $.27 **Circ:** ‡2,100
BW: $485.10
4C: $745.10
SAU: $1.68
PCI: $3.78

ALBANY†, pop. 73,934.

SW GA. Dougherty Co. On Flint River, 89 mi. SE of Columbus. Albany State College; Albany Junior College. Manufactures cottonseed oil, house trailers, farm implements, and fertilizer. Lumber mills; bottling works; meat packing; peanuts, pecan shelling. Radium spring. Pine timber. Agriculture. Pecans, peanuts, cotton.

6985 Albany Area Advertiser
Southwest Georgia Shoppers, Inc.
212 N. Washington St Phone: (912)888-7653
Albany, GA 31701 Fax: (912)438-7593
Free: (800)676-0414
Publication E-mail: aaateri@surfsouth.com

Shopper. **Founded:** 1979. **Freq:** Weekly (Tues.). **Print Method:** Web offset. **Trim Size:** 10 1/4 x 12. **Cols./Page:** 6. **Col. Width:** 9 picas. **Col. Depth:** 12 inches. **Key Personnel:** Teri Underwood, GM and Advertising Mgr., phone (912)431-0133. **Subscription Rates:** $15 individuals. **Remarks:** Accepts advertising.
Ad Rates: GLR: $1 **Circ:** Free 44,000
BW: $760.50
4C: $885.50
PCI: $9.75

6986 The Albany Herald
PO Box 48
Albany, GA 31702

Daily newspaper. **Founded:** 1891. **Freq:** Daily (morn.). **Print Method:** Offset. **Trim Size:** 13 1/2 x 22 3/4. **Cols./Page:** 6. **Col. Width:** 26 nonpareils. **Col. Depth:** 301 agate lines. **Key Personnel:** Kay Read, Editor; Gary W. Boley, President & Publisher. **USPS:** 012-320. **Subscription Rates:** $144 individuals. **Remarks:** Accepts advertising.
Ad Rates: GLR: $23.25 **Circ:** Mon.-Fri. 34,067
BW: $2,999.25 Sun. 40,732
4C: $3,396.25
SAU: $16.98
PCI: $23.25

6987 The Albany Journal
PO Box 1628 Phone: (912)435-6222
Albany, GA 31702-1628 Fax: (912)435-0557
Publication E-mail: ajournal@isoa.net

General newspaper. **Founded:** 1939. **Freq:** Weekly. **Print Method:** Offset. **Cols./Page:** 6. **Col. Width:** 12 picas. **Col. Depth:** 21 1/2 inches. **Key Personnel:** P.A. Davis, Publisher; Debbie Estevez, Managing Editor. **Subscription Rates:** $24.13 individuals; $0.50 single issue. **Remarks:** Color advertising not accepted.
Ad Rates: GLR: $14 **Circ:** Mon.-Sat. 32,185
BW: $1,806 Sun. 37,408
4C: $2,226
PCI: $15.40

6988 WALB-TV - 10
PO Box 3130 Phone: (912)883-0154
Albany, GA 31706-3130 Fax: (912)434-8768

Format: Commercial TV. **Networks:** NBC. **Founded:** Apr. 15, 1954. **Operating Hours:** 6:30 a.m.-2 a.m. **ADI:** Albany (Valdosta & Cordele), GA. **Key Personnel:** James R. Wilcox, Pres. & General Mgr. **Local Programs:** *Dialogue*, Nicole Bailey; *Today in Georgia*, Robert Hydrick; *Town & Country*, Ruthie Garner. **Ad Rates:** Advertising accepted; rates available upon request.

6989 WALG-AM - 1590
Box 2407 Phone: (912)436-7233
Albany, GA 31703-2407 Fax: (912)888-6018

Format: Talk. **Founded:** 1940. **Operating Hours:** Continuous. **ADI:** Albany (Valdosta & Cordele), GA. **Key Personnel:** Bob Roddy, General Mgr. **Wattage:** 5000 day; 1000 night.

6990 WANL-AM - 1250
2804 N. Jefferson St. Phone: (912)432-1250
Albany, GA 31701 Fax: (912)432-1927

Format: Religious. **Networks:** SkyLight Satellite. **Owner:** Lifeline Radio Corp., PO Box 90, Thomasville, GA 31799. **Founded:** 1962. **Formerly:** WQDE-AM (1987). **Operating Hours:** Continuous; 5% network, 95% local. **ADI:** Albany (Valdosta & Cordele), GA. **Key Personnel:** Sherry Jackson, Station Mgr. **Wattage:** 1000. **Ad Rates:** $6 for 30 seconds; $9 for 60 seconds.

6991 WFXL-TV - 31
1211 N. Slappey Blvd. Phone: (912)435-3100
PO Box 4050 Fax: (912)435-0485
Albany, GA 31706
Free: (800)284-5501
E-mail: wfxl@wfxl.com

Format: Commercial TV. **Networks:** Fox; Independent. **Founded:** 1982. **Formerly:** WTSG-TV. **Operating Hours:** Continuous. **ADI:** Albany (Valdosta & Cordele), GA. **Key Personnel:** John Bennett, General Sales Mgr.; Bill Parks, General Mgr.; Acklin Stone, LSM; Roger Jones, Natl. Sales Mgr; Daniel Dayton, General Mgr. **Local Programs:** *Fox News at 10 p.m.*, Heather Childers, News Dir. **Ad Rates:** $35-800 per unit. **URL:** http://www.wfxl.com.

6992 WGPC-AM - 1450
2011 Gillionville Rd. Phone: (912)883-6500
Albany, GA 31707 Fax: (912)883-1450

Format: Full Service. **Networks:** CBS; Gannett News. **Owner:** Albany Broadcasting Company, at above address. **Founded:** 1933. **Operating Hours:** Continuous. **ADI:** Albany (Valdosta & Cordele), GA. **Key Personnel:** L.M. George, President. **Wattage:** 1000.

6993 WGPC-FM - 104.5
2011 Gillionville Rd. Phone: (912)883-6500
Albany, GA 31707 Fax: (912)883-1450

Format: Full Service. **Networks:** CBS; Gannett News. **Owner:** Albany Broadcasting Co., at above address. **Founded:** 1963. **Operating Hours:** Continuous. **ADI:** Albany (Valdosta & Cordele), GA. **Key Personnel:** L.M. George, President. **Wattage:** 100,000 ERP.

6994 WKAK-FM - 101.7
Dunbar Ln., POB W Phone: (912)436-7233
Albany, GA 31702 Fax: (912)888-6018

Format: Contemporary Country. **Networks:** ABC. **Owner:** Radio One: WKAK Inc., at above address. **Founded:** 1972. **Operating Hours:** Continuous. **ADI:** Albany (Valdosta & Cordele), GA. **Key Personnel:** Bob Roddy, General Mgr.; Dave Cobb, Sales Mgr. **Wattage:** 3000.

6995 WMGR-FM - 97.3
PO Box 3106 Phone: (912)439-9704
Albany, GA 31706-3106 Fax: (912)439-1509
Free: (800)789-0973

Format: Contemporary Hit Radio (CHR). **Owner:** Peterson Broadcasting, Inc., at above address. **Founded:** 1960. **Formerly:** WJAD-FM (1994). **Operating Hours:** Continuous. **ADI:** Albany (Valdosta & Cordele), GA. **Key Personnel:** John Dawson, Program Dir.; Jim Squires, General Sales Mgr.; Bill West, Operations Dir. **Local Programs:** *John & Melissa Morning Show*. **Wattage:** 100,000. **Ad Rates:** $32 for 30 seconds; $42 for 60 seconds.

6996 WOBB-FM - 100.3
PO Box 3106 Phone: (912)439-9704
Albany, GA 31706-3106 Fax: (912)439-1509
Free: (800)567-1003

Format: Country. **Networks:** Unistar. **Owner:** Peterson Broadcasting, Inc., at above address. **Founded:** 1970. **Formerly:** WSGY-FM (1994); WCUP-FM. **Operating Hours:** Continuous; 100% local. **ADI:** Albany (Valdosta & Cordele), GA. **Key Personnel:** Jim Squires, General Mgr.; Bill West, Operations Mgr.; Steve King, Production Mgr.; Bill West, Operations Mgr. **Local Programs:** *Wild Billk & Radio Boy Morning Show*. **Wattage:** 100,000. **Ad Rates:** $32 for 30 seconds; $42 for 60 seconds.

6997 WQVE-FM - 105.5
Box 484 Phone: (912)434-9010
Albany, GA 31702 Fax: (912)434-9099
E-mail: eturner.velvet105@juno.com

Format: Adult Contemporary. **Networks:** ABC. **Founded:** 1976. **Formerly:** WOFF-FM (1990). **Operating Hours:** Continuous; 75% Local 25% Network. **ADI:** Albany (Valdosta & Cordele), GA. **Key Personnel:** Edward E. Turner, General Mgr., eturner.velvet105@juno.com; Jackie Hargrow, Program Dir. **Wattage:** 6000. **Ad Rates:** Advertising accepted; rates available upon request.

ALMA†, pop. 3,756.

SE GA. Bacon Co. 65 mi. NW of Brunswick. Manufactures carpet fiber, clothing, optical lenses, manufactured homes. Agriculture. Tobacco, soybean, corn, wheat. Blueberries, peaches. Cattle, swine.

6998 Alma Times-Statesman
South Fire News
PO Box 428 Phone: (912)632-7201
Alma, GA 31510-0428 Fax: (912)632-4156

Local newspaper. **Founded:** 1906. **Freq:** Weekly (Thurs.). **Print Method:** Offset. **Cols./Page:** 6. **Col. Width:** 25 nonpareils. **Col. Depth:** 301 agate lines. **Key Personnel:** Max Gardner, Editor and Publisher; Helen Gardner, Editor and Publisher. **Subscription Rates:** $11.66. **Remarks:** Accepts advertising.
Ad Rates: GLR: $.23 **Circ:** ‡3,492
BW: $415.38
4C: $748.71

6999 Dixie Cable TV
Box 97 Phone: (912)632-4241
Alma, GA 31510 Fax: (912)632-4519

Key Personnel: Teddy Solomon, President; Kevin Brooks, Manager. **Cities Served:** Bacon County: subscribing households 1,802; 54 channels.

ALPHARETTA, pop. 3,128.

NW GA. Fulton Co. 20 mi. N. of Atlanta. Residential. Light industry.

7000 Alpharetta Neighbor
Neighbor Newspapers, Inc.
10479 Alpharetta St., Ste. 10 Phone: (770)993-7400
Roswell, GA 30075 Fax: (770)518-6062

Community newspaper. **Founded:** 1968. **Freq:** Weekly (Wed.). **Print Method:** Offset. **Cols./Page:** 6. **Col. Width:** 26 nonpareils. **Col. Depth:** 301 agate lines. **Key Personnel:** Otis A. Brumby, Jr., Publisher. **USPS:** 071-770. **Subscription Rates:** Free; $12 institutions; $18 out of area; $24 out of state.
Ad Rates: GLR: $.99 **Circ:** Combined 41,496
BW: $1,793.10
4C: $2,118.10
SAU: $13.90

7001 Aquarius
163 Norcross St., Ste. 105
Alpharetta, GA 30201-1970

Newspaper focusing on personal growth. **Founded:** June 1993. **Freq:** Monthly. **Trim Size:** 10 x 12. **Cols./Page:** 4. **Key Personnel:** Gloria Parker, Publisher; Dan Liss, Editor. **Subscription Rates:** $25 annual.
Ad Rates: BW: $715 **Circ:** Paid 200
Non-paid 50,000

7002 Bracket Racing USA
CSK Publishing Co., Inc.
3003 Maple Ln. Phone: (404)442-0376
Alpharetta, GA 30201 Fax: (404)410-1585

Magazine for participating bracket racers and late model performance cars who prefer elapsed time racing over oval track. **Subtitle:** BRUSA. **Founded:** 1989. **Freq:** 8/year. **Print Method:** Offset. **Trim Size:** 8 x 10 7/8. **Cols./Page:** 3. **Col. Width:** 2 1/3 inches. **Col. Depth:** 10 inches. **Key Personnel:** Dale Wilson, Editor; Ralph Monti, Publisher; Mads C. Buck, Advertising Mgr. **Subscription Rates:** $16. $3.25 single issue. **Remarks:** Accepts advertising.
Ad Rates: BW: $1,290 **Circ:** Paid ‡30,000
4C: $1,725

7003 CE News
Civil Engineering News, Inc.
4005 Windward Plz. Dr., No. 580 Phone: (770)664-2812
Fax: (770)664-7319
Alpharetta, GA 30005
Trade magazine serving civil engineers and land surveyors engaged in land development, highways, bridges, structural, environmental, geotechnical, water resources, and industrial engineering projects including surveying. **Founded:** Feb. 1989. **Freq:** Monthly. **Print Method:** Heatset. **Trim Size:** 7 7/8 x 10 3/4. **Cols./Page:** 3. **Col. Width:** 2 3/16 inches. **Col. Depth:** 9 3/4 inches. **Key Personnel:** Lissa Piorot, Editor, editor@cenews.com; Jack Eller, Advertising Mgr., advertising@cenews.com; Gloria Gregory, Circulation Mgr., subscriptions@cenews.com. **ISSN:** 1051-9629. **Subscription Rates:** Free to qualified subscribers; $36 individuals; $3 single issue. **Remarks:** Accepts advertising. **Formerly:** Civil Engineering News.
Ad Rates: BW: $3,900 **Circ:** Paid 5,306
4C: $5,095 Controlled 44,133
PCI: $130

AMERICUS†, pop. 16,131.

SW GA. Sumter Co. 35 mi. N. of Albany. Georgia Southwestern College. Manufactures metal products, cottonseed oil, light fixtures, furniture, textiles. Vegetable packing. Pine timber. Agriculture. Cotton, fruit, peanuts, livestock.

7004 Habitat World
Habitat for Humanity International, Inc.
121 Habitat St. Phone: (912)924-6935
Americus, GA 31709-3498 Fax: (912)924-6541

Newspaper covering the activities of the Habitat for Humanity. **Founded:** Mar. 1984. **Freq:** Bimonthly. **Print Method:** Web offset. **Trim Size:** 9 3/4 x 11. **Cols./Page:** 4. **Col. Width:** 2 inches. **Col. Depth:** 9 inches. **Key Personnel:** Milana McLead, Editor. **ISSN:** 0890-958X. **Remarks:** Advertising not accepted.
Circ: Free 1,050,000

7005 Journal of Third World Studies
Association of Third World Studies, Inc.
PO Box 1232 Phone: (912)931-2078
Americus, GA 31709 Fax: (912)931-2960

Scholarly journal covering Third World problems, issues, and developments. **Founded:** 1984. **Freq:** Semiannual. **Key Personnel:** Dr. Harold Isaacs, Editor, hisaacs@canes.gsw.edu. **ISSN:** 8755-3449. **Subscription Rates:** $45 individuals; $23 single issue. **Remarks:** Accepts advertising.
Ad Rates: BW: $250 **Circ:** Paid 815

7006 The Sou'Wester
Georgia Southwestern State University
GSW Box 1199
800 Wheatley
Americus, GA 31709

Collegiate newspaper (tabloid). **Subtitle:** "The Voice of Georgia Southwestern". **Founded:** 1936. **Freq:** Weekly (during the academic year). **Print Method:** Offset. **Trim Size:** 10 x 13 1/2. **Cols./Page:** 5. **Col. Width:** 2 inches. **Col. Depth:** 196 agate lines. **Key Personnel:** Sharon Daniel, Editor-in-Chief. **Subscription Rates:** $12 per semester. **Remarks:** Accepts advertising. **URL:** http://canes.gsw.peachnet.edu. **Formerly:** The Gale.
Ad Rates: GLR: $5 **Circ:** Free ‡1,500
BW: $300
4C: $600
PCI: $5

7007 WDEC-AM - 1290
605 McGarrah St. Phone: (912)924-1290
Americus, GA 31709 Fax: (912)928-3579

Format: Ethnic. **Networks:** Satellite Music Network. **Founded:** 1947. **Key Personnel:** A.J. Butch Guest, Contact; Victoria Guest, General Sales Mgr. **Wattage:** 1000.

7008 WDEC-FM - 94.7
215 Hwy. 30 W. Phone: (912)324-6500
PO Box 727 Fax: (912)928-2337
Americus, GA 31709

Format: Adult Contemporary. **Networks:** ABC. **Founded:** 1968. **Formerly:** WADZ-FM (1987). **Operating Hours:** Continuous. **ADI:** Columbus, GA (Opelika, AL). **Key Personnel:** Steve Lashley, General Mgr. **Wattage:** 25,000.

7009 WISK-AM - 1390
Hwy. 30 W. Phone: (912)924-1390
PO Box 727 Fax: (912)928-2337
Americus, GA 31709

Format: Talk; News. **Networks:** ABC; Georgia Radio. **Founded:** 1962. **Operating Hours:** 6 a.m.-midnight. **ADI:** Columbus, GA (Opelika, AL). **Key Personnel:** Steve Lashley, General Mgr. **Wattage:** 5000.

7010 WISK-FM - 98.7
Hwy. 30 W. Phone: (912)924-1390
PO Box 727 Fax: (912)928-2337
Americus, GA 31709

Format: Country. **Networks:** ABC; Gannett News. **Founded:** 1973. **Formerly:** WPUR-FM (1992). **Operating Hours:** continuous. **ADI:** Columbus, GA (Opelika, AL). **Key Personnel:** Steve Lashley, General Mgr. **Wattage:** 25,000.

ASHBURN

7011 The Wiregrass Farmer
Ashburn Newspapers
109 Gordon St. Phone: (912)567-3655
Ashburn, GA 31714
Publication E-mail: wiregras@surfsouth.com

Community newspaper. **Founded:** 1899. **Freq:** Weekly (Wed.). **Cols./Page:** 6. **Col. Width:** 13 picas. **Col. Depth:** 21 1/2 inches. **Key Personnel:** Ben Baker, Editor; Jerry Lavender, Advertising Mgr.; Lisa Wiley, Classified Ads. **USPS:** 687-460. **Subscription Rates:** $26.50 individuals. **Remarks:** Accepts advertising. **URL:** http://www.tifton.com/˜wiregras/html/.
Ad Rates: GLR: $4.55 **Circ:** 3,000
BW: $528.90
PCI: $4.10

ATHENS†, pop. 42,549.

NE GA. Clarke Co. On Oconee River, 70 mi. NE of Atlanta. University of Georgia; U.S. Navy Supply Corps School. Manufactures fertilizer, textiles, clocks, transformers, electronics, cottonseed products, furniture. Timber. Food and poultry processing center. Agriculture producing and marketing center. Livestock, poultry farms.

7012 Athens Magazine
Morris Communications Corp.
PO Box 912 Phone: (706)208-2331
Athens, GA 30603-0912 Fax: (706)208-2339
Free: (800)533-4252
Publication E-mail: athmag@onlineathens.com
Publisher E-mail: 73711.1232@compuserve.com

Regional magazine for Athens, Georgia. **Subtitle:** The Lifestyle Magazine of Northwest Georgia. **Founded:** Mar. 1989. **Freq:** Bimonthly. **Print Method:** Offset. **Trim Size:** 8 1/8 x 10 7/8. **Cols./Page:** 3. **Col. Width:** 2 1/4 inches. **Col. Depth:** 9 1/2 inches. **Key Personnel:** Elaine Kabler, Editor; Carey M. Almund II, Sales Mgr. **ISSN:** 1053-6300. **Subscription Rates:** $14.95 individuals; $3.75 single issue. **Remarks:** Accepts advertising.
Ad Rates: BW: $1,202 **Circ:** 6,500
4C: $1,563

7013 Athens Observer
445 N. Milledge Ave.
Athens, GA 30601

Community newspaper. **Founded:** 1974. **Freq:** Weekly (Thurs.). **Print Method:** Offset. **Cols./Page:** 6. **Col. Width:** 2 1/16 I nonpareils. **Col. Depth:** 21 agate lines. **Key Personnel:** Carley Wetherington, News Dir.; Shannon Frye, Entertainment Ed.; Johnnie Ellis, Advertising Mgr.; Tina Van Why, Office Manager. **Subscription Rates:** $25 individuals. **Remarks:** Accepts advertising.
Ad Rates: GLR: $1 **Circ:** ‡3,300
BW: $1,393.56
4C: $1,653.56
PCI: $11.06

7014 Athens Star
Morris Communications Corp.
PO Box 912 Phone: (706)549-0123
Athens, GA 30603-0912 Fax: (706)543-5234
Publisher E-mail: 73711.1232@compuserve.com

Local newspaper. **Founded:** May 1, 1969. **Freq:** Weekly (Wed.). **Print Method:** Offset. **Cols./Page:** 6. **Col. Width:** 26 nonpareils. **Col. Depth:** 298 agate lines. **Key Personnel:** Kevin Price, Editor; A. Mark Smith, Publisher; Carey Almond, Advertising Mgr. **Remarks:** Accepts advertising.
Ad Rates: GLR: $.33 **Circ:** Free ‡30,185

7015 Berkeley Democrat
PO Box 792
Athens, GA 30603

Community newspaper. **Founded:** 1918. **Freq:** Weekly (Wed.). **Print Method:** Offset. **Subscription Rates:** $11. **Remarks:** Accepts advertising.
Ad Rates: GLR: $.32 **Circ:** Combined 11,806
BW: $491.40
PCI: $4.50

7016 College Student Affairs Journal
402 Aderhold Hall Phone: (706)542-4120
University of Georgia Fax: (706)542-4130
Athens, GA 30605
Journal covering college student affairs research and program planning. **Freq:** Semiannual. **Key Personnel:** Dr. Diane L. Cooper, Editor, dlcooper@coe.uga.edu. **ISSN:** 0888-210X. **Subscription Rates:** $25 individuals; $15 single issue. **Remarks:** Advertising not accepted.
Circ: Paid 1,100

7017 Communications in Soil Science and Plant Analysis
Marcel Dekker, Inc.
183 Paradise Blvd., Ste. 104 Phone: (706)613-7813
Athens, GA 30607 Fax: (706)613-7573
Publisher E-mail: journals@dekker.com

Journal on soil chemistry, fertility, soil testing, soil crop nutrition, plant analysis, plant physiology, and liming. **Found-**

ed: 1970. **Freq:** 20/year. **Print Method:** Offset. **Trim Size:** 5 7/8 x 9. **Cols./Page:** 1. **Col. Width:** 54 nonpareils. **Col. Depth:** 103 agate lines. **Key Personnel:** Dr. H. A. Mills, Executive Editor, hamills@aol.com. **ISSN:** 0010-3624. **Subscription Rates:** $612.50; $1,225 Industry.
Ad Rates: BW: $665 4C: $1,455 **Circ:** ‡800

7018 Das Fenster Nach Druben
Die Hausfrau, Inc.
1060 Gaines School Rd., Ste. C-3 Phone: (706)548-4382
Athens, GA 30605 Fax: (706)548-8856
Free: (800)398-7753
Publisher E-mail: dasfenster@earthlink.net

Magazine for Germans in the U.S. and Canada (German). **Founded:** 1904. **Freq:** Monthly. **Print Method:** Offset. **Trim Size:** 8 1/4 x 10 7/8. **Cols./Page:** 2 and 3. **Col. Width:** 3 3/4 and 2 inches. **Col. Depth:** 10 and 10 inches. **Key Personnel:** Roswitha Shapland, Editor, dasfenster@earthlink.net'; V. George Mazeika, Publisher; Alex Mazcika, Business Mgr. **ISSN:** 1073-6832. **Subscription Rates:** $19.95 by mail; $2.95 single issue. **Remarks:** Accepts advertising. **Formerly:** Die Hausfrau.
Ad Rates: GLR: $26.50 BW: $795 4C: $1,395 PCI: $26.50 **Circ:** Paid ‡18,000 Free ‡780

7019 Flagpole Magazine
PO Box 1027 Phone: (706)549-9523
Athens, GA 30603 Fax: (706)548-8981
Publication E-mail: flagpole@negia.net

Magazine covering the arts, entertainment, politics, and news in Athens, GA; also reports on the international music scene. **Founded:** 1987. **Freq:** Weekly. **Print Method:** Web press. **Trim Size:** 11 3/8 x 15. **Cols./Page:** 4. **Col. Width:** 2 3/8 inches. **Col. Depth:** 13 inches. **Key Personnel:** Pete McCommons, Editor; Robin Littlefield, Man. Ed. & Business Mgr.; Alicia Nickles, Advertising Dir.; Larry Tenner, Production Dir. **Subscription Rates:** $38. **Remarks:** Accepts advertising. **URL:** http://www.flagpole.com.
Ad Rates: BW: $580 4C: $880 **Circ:** Combined 13,803

7020 Georgia Business and Economic Conditions
University of Georgia
Selig Center Economic Growth, Terry College of Business Phone: (706)542-4085
Athens, GA 30602 Fax: (706)542-3858
Journal publishing information on business and economic research. **Founded:** 1947. **Freq:** Bimonthly. **Print Method:** Offset. **Trim Size:** 8 1/2 x 11. **Cols./Page:** 2. **Col. Width:** 38 nonpareils. **Col. Depth:** 112 agate lines. **Key Personnel:** Lorena M. Akioka, Editor. **ISSN:** 0297-3857. **Subscription Rates:** Free. **Remarks:** Advertising not accepted. **Available Online. URL:** http://www.selig.uga.edu.
Circ: Free ‡3,500

7021 Georgia Historical Quarterly
301 LeConte Hall Phone: (706)542-6300
University of Georgia Fax: (706)542-2455
Athens, GA 30602
Historical magazine. **Founded:** 1917. **Freq:** Quarterly. **Print Method:** Uses mats. Letterpress and offset. **Cols./Page:** 1. **Col. Width:** 51 nonpareils. **Col. Depth:** 91 agate lines. **Key Personnel:** John C. Inscoe, Editor, jinscoe@arches.uga.edu. **Subscription Rates:** $35 individuals. **Remarks:** Accepts advertising.
Ad Rates: BW: $150 **Circ:** ‡2,800

7022 Georgia Law Review
University of Georgia
Athens, GA 30602 Phone: (706)542-7286

Professional journal covering law. **Freq:** Quarterly. **Subscription Rates:** $28 individuals. **Remarks:** Advertising not accepted. **Online:** LEXIS-NEXIS; Westlaw.
Circ: (Not Reported)

7023 Georgia Magazine
University of Georgia
University Communications Phone: (706)542-3354
Alumni House Fax: (706)542-9492
Athens, GA 30602-4370
Magazine serving the interests of university alumni. **Founded:** 1920. **Freq:** Quarterly. **Print Method:** Offset. **Trim Size:** 8 3/8 x 10 7/8. **Cols./Page:** 3. **Col. Width:** 27 nonpareils. **Col. Depth:** 140 agate lines. **Key Personnel:** Kent Hannon, Editor; Pamela Leed, Marketing Director. **ISSN:** 0016-8130. **Subscription Rates:** $25 individuals. **Remarks:** Accepts advertising. **Formerly:** Georgia Alumni Record.
Ad Rates: BW: $1,000 4C: $1,300 **Circ:** ‡30,000

7024 Georgia Music News
Georgia Music Educators Association
University of Georgia Phone: (706)542-3737
School of Music Fax: (706)542-2773
Athens, GA 30602
Publisher E-mail: gmea@mindspring.com

Music education journal. **Founded:** 1940. **Freq:** Quarterly. **Print Method:** Offset. **Trim Size:** 8 1/2 x 11. **Cols./Page:** 3. **Col. Width:** 28 nonpareils. **Col. Depth:** 140 agate lines. **Key Personnel:** Mary Leglar, Editor, phone (706)542-2763, mleglar@arches.uga.edu. **ISSN:** 0046-5789. **Subscription Rates:** $4 members; $16 nonmembers. **Remarks:** Accepts advertising.
Ad Rates: BW: $170 **Circ:** 2,500

7025 The Georgia Review
The University of Georgia Phone: (706)542-3481
Athens, GA 30602-9009 Fax: (706)542-0047

Literary journal. **Founded:** Mar. 21, 1947. **Freq:** Quarterly. **Print Method:** Letterpress. **Trim Size:** 6 3/4 x 10. **Cols./Page:** 1. **Col. Width:** 28 picas. **Col. Depth:** 42 picas. **Key Personnel:** Stanley W. Lindberg, Editor; Charlotte W. Mealor, Advertising Mgr., cmealor@arches.uga.edu. **ISSN:** 0016-8386. **Subscription Rates:** $18 individuals; $7 single issue; $23 other countries. **Remarks:** Color advertising not accepted. **Alt. Formats:** Microform.
Ad Rates: BW: $350 **Circ:** Combined ‡6,500

7026 Journal of Agricultural and Applied Economics
Conner Hall Phone: (706)542-0747
University of Georgia Fax: (706)542-0739
Athens, GA 30602-7509
Publisher E-mail: jaee@agecon.uga.edu

Professional journal covering scholarly and other work in agricultural economics. **Founded:** Dec. 1969. **Freq:** Semiannual. **Trim Size:** 7 x 10. **Cols./Page:** 2. **Col. Width:** 17 picas. **Col. Depth:** 52 picas. **Key Personnel:** Chung L. Huang, Editor; Michael E. Wetzstein, Editor. **ISSN:** 1074-0708. **Subscription Rates:** $20 individuals; $25 out of country; $10 single issue. **Remarks:** Accepts advertising. **URL:** http://www.agecon.uga.edu/˜jaae/jaae.htm. **Formerly:** Southern Journal of Agricultural Economics.
Ad Rates: BW: $400 **Circ:** Paid 750

7027 Journal of Foraminiferal Research
Cushman Foundation for Foraminiferal Research
c/o Susan Goldstein
Department of Geology
University of Georgia
Athens, GA 30602

Scholarly journal covering Foraminiferida and allied groups of organisms. **Founded:** 1971. **Freq:** Quarterly. **Trim Size:** 8 1/2 x 11. **Cols./Page:** 2. **Key Personnel:** Susan Goldstein, Editor. **ISSN:** 0096-1191. **Subscription Rates:** $40 individuals; $80 institutions. **Remarks:** Advertising not accepted.
Circ: (Not Reported)

7028 Journal of Geriatric Drug Therapy
The Haworth Press, Inc.
Univ. of Georgia Phone: (706)542-5325
College of Pharmacy Fax: (706)542-5373
Athens, GA 30602
Publisher E-mail: getinfo@haworthpressinc.com

Journal addressing drug therapy and related issues in the geriatric population. **Founded:** 1986. **Freq:** Quarterly. **Trim Size:** 6x8 1/2. **Key Personnel:** Bill Cohen, Publisher. **ISSN:** 8756-4629. **Subscription Rates:** $48 individuals; $110 institutions; $225 libraries. **Remarks:** Accepts advertising. **URL:** http://www.haworth.com. **Alt. Formats:** Microform.
Ad Rates: BW: $300 **Circ:** 366

7029 Journal of Learning Disabilities
PRO-ED, Inc.
School of Professional Studies Phone: (706)542-4506
570 Aderhold Hall Fax: (706)542-5872
University of Georgia
Athens, GA 30602
Publisher E-mail: proedrd2@aol.com

Special education journal. **Founded:** 1968. **Freq:** 6/year. **Print Method:** Offset. **Trim Size:** 8 3/8 x 10 7/8. **Cols./Page:** 3. **Col. Width:** 28 nonpareils. **Col. Depth:** 134 agate lines. **Key Personnel:** J. Lee Wiederholt, Editor; Judith K. Voress, Advertising Mgr.; Donald Hammill, Publisher; Judith M. Kroese, Editorial Asst. **ISSN:** 0022-2194. **Subscription Rates:** $49 individuals; $105 institutions; $115 other countries. **Remarks:** Accepts advertising.
Ad Rates: BW: $800 **Circ:** ‡8,500

7030 The Red and Black
The Red and Black Publishing Co.
University of Georgia Phone: (404)543-1809
Alumni House Fax: (404)542-9492
Athens, GA 30606-4370
College newspaper for University of Georgia students and faculty. **Founded:** 1892. **Freq:** Tues.-Fri. (during academic year). **Print Method:** Offset. **Cols./Page:** 6. **Col. Width:** 21 nonpareils. **Col. Depth:** 301 agate lines. **Subscription Rates:** Free on campus; $24 institutions. **Remarks:** Accepts advertising.
Ad Rates: BW: $1,549 4C: $1,849.80 **Circ:** Free 16,000

7031 Social Studies and the Young Learner
National Council for the Social Studies (NCSS)
c/o Sherry Field, Editor Phone: (706)542-7265
217 Tucker Hall
University of Georgia
Athens, GA 30602-7014
Publication E-mail: ssyl@ncss.org
Publisher E-mail: publications@ncss.org

Magazine covering social studies education for grades K-6. **Founded:** 1988. **Freq:** Quarterly. **Print Method:** Web offset. **Trim Size:** 8 1/8 x 10 7/8. **Cols./Page:** 3. **Col. Width:** 2 1/8 inches. **Col. Depth:** 8 1/2 inches. **Key Personnel:** Sherry Field, Editor; Jennifer Truran Rothwell, Assoc. Editor. **ISSN:** 1056-0300. **Subscription Rates:** $50 individuals; $67 institutions; $7.50 single issue. **Remarks:** Accepts advertising. **Online:** ERIC; Dialog (The Dialog Corporation). **URL:** http://www.socialstudies.org. **Alt. Formats:** Microform, University Microfilms International (UMI).
Ad Rates: BW: $625 4C: $1,225 **Circ:** Paid 6,000

7032 Southeastern Geographer
Association of American Geographers, Southeastern Division
Department of Geography Phone: (706)542-2350
University of Georgia Fax: (706)542-2388
Athens, GA 30602-2502
Scholarly journal covering geographical topics, especially the Southern U.S. **Founded:** 1961. **Freq:** Semiannual. **Print Method:** Sheetfed offset. **Trim Size:** 6 x 9. **Cols./Page:** 1. **Col. Width:** 4 3/5 inches. **Col. Depth:** 7 inches. **Key Personnel:** James O. Wheeler, Editor, jowheel@uga.edu. **ISSN:** 0038-366X. **Subscription Rates:** $25 nonmembers; $30 institutions; Free to qualified subscribers. **Remarks:** Accepts advertising.
Circ: Combined 800

7033 Southeastern Journal of Music Education
University of Georgia
250 River Rd. Phone: (706)542-3737
Athens, GA 30602 Fax: (706)542-2773
Publication E-mail: mleglar@arches.uga.edu

Professional journal covering music education and music research. **Founded:** 1989. **Freq:** Annual. **Print Method:** Photo offset. **Key Personnel:** Mary A. Leglar. **ISSN:** 1047-9635. **Subscription Rates:** $20 institutions; $15 individuals. **Remarks:** Advertising not accepted.
Circ: Paid 300

7034 State and Local Government Review
Carl Vinson Institute of Government
201 N. Milledge Ave. Phone: (706)542-2736
Athens, GA 30602-5482 Fax: (706)542-6239
Publisher E-mail: cviog@uga.edu

Journal covering research and views of state and local government. **Freq:** Triennial. **Trim Size:** 7 x 10. **Key Personnel:** Karen Pou, Circulation; Richard W. Campbell, Editor, campbell@igs.cviog.uga.edu; Ann Allen, Advertising. **ISSN:** 0160-323X. **Subscription Rates:** $16 individuals. **Remarks:** Advertising not accepted. **URL:** http://www.cviog.uga.edu/projects/slgr.
Circ: Controlled 1,000

7035 OCB Cablevision Inc.
3706 Atlanta Hwy., Ste. 2 Phone: (706)353-2972
Athens, GA 30606 Fax: (706)549-8496

Key Personnel: Terry Kelly, General Mgr. **Cities Served:** Athens and Watkinsville, GA.

7036 TCI Cablevision of Georgia
495 Hawthorne Ave., Ste. 102 Phone: (706)543-6585
Athens, GA 30606 Fax: (706)354-8027

Founded: 1964. **Cities Served:** Clarke, Madison, and Oconee counties, GA.

7037 WBKZ-AM - 880
548 Hawthorne Ave. Phone: (706)548-8800
PO Box 88 Fax: (706)549-8800
Athens, GA 30606
Free: (800)375-9000

Format: Urban Contemporary; Gospel. **Networks:** Mutual Broadcasting System; Southern Broadcasting. **Owner:** Brown Broadcasting System, Inc., 386 N. Milledge Ave., Athens, GA 30601, (706)543-8074, Free: (800)375-9080. **Founded:** July 1994. **Operating Hours:** Sunrise-sunset. **ADI:** Atlanta (Athens & Rome), GA. **Key Personnel:** Melvin C. Geter II, General Mgr. **Local Programs:** *Community Forum* 9:00 am - 10:30 am Saturday, Rick Dunn, Host; *Cross Roads* 10:00 am Thursday, Melvin C. Geter; *Gospel Music Show Case* 9:00 Sunday, L. Cooper, Producer. **Wattage:** 5000. **Ad Rates:** $11-17 for 30 seconds; $15-23 for 60 seconds.

7038 WGAU-AM - 1340
850 Bobbin Mill Rd. Phone: (706)549-1340
Athens, GA 30610 Fax: (706)546-0441

Format: News; Talk; Sports. **Networks:** AP; Mutual Broadcasting System; Unistar. **Owner:** Clarke Broadcasting Corp, at above address. **Founded:** 1938. **Operating Hours:** Continuous. **ADI:** Atlanta (Athens & Rome), GA. **Key Personnel:** Larry England, General Mgr.; Mark Leopold, Sales Mgr. **Wattage:** 1000. **Ad Rates:** $25 for 30 seconds; $30 for 60 seconds.

7039 WNGC-FM - 95.5
850 Bobbin Mill Rd. Phone: (706)549-1340
Athens, GA 30606 Fax: (706)546-0441

Format: Country. **Networks:** NBC; Unistar. **Owner:** Clarke Broadcasting Corp., at above address. **Founded:** 1969. **Formerly**: WGAU-FM (1969). **Operating Hours:** Continuous; 100% local. **ADI:** Atlanta (Athens & Rome), GA. **Key Personnel:** Larry England, General Mgr.; Mark Leopold, Sales Mgr. **Wattage:** 100,000. **Ad Rates:** $50 for 30 seconds; $60 for 60 seconds. Combined advertising rates available with WGAU-AM.

ATLANTA†, pop. 496,973.

NE GA. Fulton Co. 60 mi. SW of Athens. The State Capital. Georgia State University; Georgia Institute of Technology; Emory University; Atlanta University; other colleges and private schools. Finance, transportation, distribution and telephone communication center. Manufactures batteries, textiles, fertilizers, furniture, chemicals, cottonseed oil, flour,building products. Printing and publishing; automobile, aircraft assembly plants.

7040 Abstract Bulletin of the Institute of Paper Science and Technology
Institute of Paper Science & Technology
500 10th St. NW Phone: (404)894-5700
Atlanta, GA 30318 Fax: (404)894-4778
Free: (800)558-6611

Abstract journal featuring pulp and paper chemistry, technology, and allied fields material. **Founded:** Sept. 1930. **Freq:** Monthly. **Print Method:** Offset. **Trim Size:** 8 1/4 x 10 3/4. **Cols./Page:** 2. **Key Personnel:** Rosanna M. Bechtel, Editor, phone (404)8947866, fax (404)8944778, rosanna.betchel@ipst.edu. **ISSN:** 0020-3033. **Subscription Rates:** $2050. **Remarks:** Advertising not accepted. **Online:** DIALOG, STN. **Alt. Formats:** CD-ROM. **Formerly**: Abstract Bulletin of the Institute of Paper Chemistry.
Circ: Paid ‡660
Controlled ‡90

7041 Access Control & Security Systems Integration
Intertec Publishing Corp.
6151 Powers Ferry Rd.
Atlanta, GA 30339

Magazine covering security products and services in application-based articles. **Subtitle:** No. 1 Source for Security Applications. **Founded:** 1958. **Freq:** Monthly. **Print Method:** Offset. **Trim Size:** 11 x 14 1/2. **Cols./Page:** 4. **Col. Width:** 14 nonpareils. **Col. Depth:** 140 agate lines. **Key Personnel:** Tina D'Aversa-Williams, Publisher, tdaversa@mindspring.com; Larry Anderson, Editor; Gregg Herring, Group Publisher; George Partington, Assoc. Editor; Kate Doherty, Asst. Editor. **ISSN:** 0894-6639. **Subscription Rates:** $42 individuals. **Remarks:** Accepts advertising. **URL:** http://www.securitysolutions.com. **Alt. Formats:** Mailing labels. **Formerly:** Access Control (1995).
Ad Rates: GLR: $12 **Circ:** Paid ‡262
BW: $3,855 Controlled ‡31,000
4C: $5,325
PCI: $150

7042 Adhesives Age
Intertec Publishing Corp.
6151 Powers Ferry Rd., NW Phone: (770)618-0113
Atlanta, GA 30339 Fax: (770)618-0349

Magazine containing news and technology for those engaged in the manufacturing, application, research, and marketing of adhesives, sealants, and related products. **Founded:** 1958. **Freq:** Monthly. **Print Method:** Offset. **Trim Size:** 7 7/8 x 10 7/8. **Cols./Page:** 3 and 2. **Col. Width:** 2 1/8 and 3 3/8 inches. **Col. Depth:** 10 inches. **Key Personnel:** Ann Barker, Editor, ann_barker@intertec.com; Claudia Hine, Managing Editor, claudia_hine@intertec.com. **ISSN:** 0001-821X. **Subscription Rates:** $60 individuals. **Remarks:** Accepts advertising. **Online:** CIS; Dow Jones; EBSCO; Information Access; Lexis-Nexis; UMI Co.; W. Wilson Co.; Individual Inc. **Alt. Formats:** Microform.
Ad Rates: BW: $4,190 **Circ:** Paid 1,727
4C: $5,525 Controlled 24,962
PCI: $145

7043 AIDS Weekly Plus
C.W. Henderson
PO Box 5528 Fax: (770)507-7788
Atlanta, GA 30307 Free: (800)633-4931
Publisher E-mail: cwhender@hendersonnet.atl.ga

Presents information about AIDS/HIV research. **Subscription Rates:** $1,900. **URL:** http://www.newsfile.com/homepage/1a.htm.

7044 Alternatives
PO Box 56682 Phone: (404)303-1873
Atlanta, GA 30356 Fax: (404)303-1871

Newspaper focusing on environmental, health and social issues worldwide. **Freq:** Monthly. **Key Personnel:** Rochel Haigh Blehr, Publisher; Caroline Hubbard, Copy Editor. **Subscription Rates:** $15 annual. **Remarks:** Advertising accepted; rates available upon request.
Circ: (Not Reported)

7045 American City and County
Argus: A Division of Intertec Publishing
6151 Powers Ferry Rd NW Phone: (770)955-2500
Atlanta, GA 30339 Fax: (770)618-0349

Municipal and county administration magazine. **Founded:** 1909. **Freq:** Monthly. **Print Method:** Offset. **Trim Size:** 8 1/8 x 10 7/8. **Cols./Page:** 3. **Col. Width:** 26 nonpareils. **Col. Depth:** 140 agate lines. **Key Personnel:** Janet Ward, Editor, janet_ward@intertec.com. **ISSN:** 0149-337X. **Subscription Rates:** $67 individuals. **Remarks:** Accepts advertising. **URL:** http://www.localgov.com.
Ad Rates: BW: $4,985 **Circ:** Paid 420
4C: $6,360 Controlled 74,000
PCI: $160

7046 American Papermaker
Roger's American Papermaker
57 Executive Park S., Ste. 310 Phone: (404)325-9153
Atlanta, GA 30329-2213 Fax: (404)325-9581

Magazine for paper manufacturing industry. **Founded:** 1938. **Freq:** Monthly. **Print Method:** Offset. **Trim Size:** 8 x 10 3/4. **Cols./Page:** 3. **Col. Width:** 28 nonpareils. **Col. Depth:** 140 agate lines. **Key Personnel:** Jerome Koncel, Editor; Phillip J. Boyd, Exec. Publisher. **ISSN:** 1056-4772. **Subscription Rates:** $30 individuals; $45 other countries.
Ad Rates: BW: $3,120 **Circ:** Paid 809
4C: $5,470 Non-paid 29,232
PCI: $55

7047 APICS-The Performance Advantage
Lionheart Publishing Inc.
2555 Cumberland Pkwy., Ste. 299 Phone: (404)431-0867
Atlanta, GA 30339 Fax: (404)432-6969
Free: (800)392-7294
Publication E-mail: lpi@lionhrtpub.com
Publisher E-mail: info@lionhrtpub.com

Manufacturing sector publication. **Founded:** 1991. **Freq:** Monthly. **Print Method:** Web offset. **Trim Size:** 8 1/8 x 10 7/8. **Cols./Page:** 3. **Col. Width:** 13 picas. **Key Personnel:** David Greenfield, Editor. **Subscription Rates:** $47 individuals; $8 single issue. **Remarks:** Accepts advertising.
Ad Rates: BW: $6,150 **Circ:** Paid ‡82,000
4C: $7,335
PCI: $215

7048 Apparel Industry International
Bill Communications, Inc.
6255 Barfield Rd., Ste. 200 Phone: (404)252-8831
Atlanta, GA 30328-4300 Fax: (404)252-4436
Free: (800)241-9034
Publication E-mail: mcorthzar@aiimag.com

Trade magazine covering the Latin American apparel industry in Spanish. **Subtitle:** The State-of-the Art Magazine About the Latin American Apparel Industry. **Founded:** 1991. **Freq:** Bimonthly. **Print Method:** Web offset. **Trim Size:** 8 1/8 x 10 7/8. **Cols./Page:** 4. **Col. Width:** 13 picas. **Col. Depth:** 9 7/8 inches. **Key Personnel:** Mercedes Cortazar, Editor, mcortazar@ziimag.com; Sean McGinnis, Publisher, mginnis@ui-atl.com; Kitty Brigham, Circulation Dir., kbrigham@sui-atl.com; Calvin Ashley, Advertising Production Coord., cashley@sui-atl.com. **ISSN:** 1089-4322. **Subscription Rates:** $47 individuals; $70 Canada and Mexico; $7.50 single issue. **Remarks:** Accepts advertising. **URL:** http://www.aiimag.com.
Ad Rates: BW: $2,940 **Circ:** Controlled 15,000
4C: $3,750

7049 Art & Antiques
Trans World Publishing, Inc.
2100 Powers Ferry Rd. Phone: (770)955-5656
Atlanta, GA 30339 Fax: (770)952-0669
Free: (800)827-0818
Publication E-mail: artantqmag@aol.com

Consumer magazine for those interested in the fine and decorative arts and their settings. **Founded:** 1978. **Freq:** 11/year. **Print Method:** Offset. **Trim Size:** 9 x 10 7/8. **Cols./Page:** 3. **Col. Width:** 27 nonpareils. **Col. Depth:** 154 agate lines. **Key Personnel:** Douglas C. Billian, Publisher; Barbara S. Tapp, Editor-in-Chief; Patti Verbanas, Managing Editor. **Subscription Rates:** $35 individuals. **Remarks:** Accepts advertising.
Ad Rates: BW: $9,900 **Circ:** Paid ★196,171
4C: $11,990

7050 Art Material Trade News
Argus Business
6151 Powers Ferry Rd.
Atlanta, GA 30339-2941
Publication E-mail: mgibbs@mindspirngs.com

Arts and crafts materials magazine. **Subtitle:** A Magazine About Art Supply Retailing. **Founded:** Apr. 1948. **Freq:** Bimonthly. **Print Method:** Offset. **Trim Size:** 8 1/8 x 10 7/8. **Cols./Page:** 3. **Col. Width:** 13 picas. **Col. Depth:** 60 picas. **Key Personnel:** Ben W. Johnson, Editor; Gregg Herring, Publisher; Claire Feiner, Advertising Mgr. **ISSN:** 0004-3265. **Subscription Rates:** Free to qualified subscribers; $42 individuals. **Remarks:** Accepts advertising. **URL:** http://www.internetview.com.
Ad Rates: BW: $2,395 **Circ:** Paid 168
4C: $3,100 Non-paid 8,100
PCI: $190

7051 ART PAPERS
Atlanta Art Papers, Inc.
PO Box 5748 Phone: (404)588-1837
Atlanta, GA 31107 Fax: (404)588-1836

Journal featuring articles on contemporary art and artists, reviews, newsbriefs, letters, and a classified listing section. **Founded:** 1977. **Freq:** Bimonthly. **Print Method:** Web offset. **Trim Size:** 10 x 13 1/2. **Cols./Page:** 4. **Col. Width:** 1 11/16 inches. **Col. Depth:** 12 inches. **Key Personnel:** Larisa Gray, Exec. Dir.; Michele Slater, Asst. Dir., mslater@pd.org; Michael Piltari, Editor. **Subscription Rates:** $30. $5.50 single issue. **Alt. Formats:** Microfiche; Mailing labels.
Ad Rates: GLR: $.40 **Circ:** Paid 15,000
BW: $480 90,000
4C: $645

7052 Arthritis Today
Arthritis Foundation
1330 W. Peachtree St. Phone: (404)872-7100
Atlanta, GA 30309 Fax: (404)872-9559
Free: (800)283-7800

Consumer magazine on living with arthritis; updates on research and treatments as well as general health and lifestyle topics. **Subtitle:** The Magazine for Help and Hope. **Founded:** Jan. 1987. **Freq:** Bimonthly. **Print Method:** Offset. **Trim Size:** 8 1/4 x 10 3/4. **Cols./Page:** 3. **Col. Width:** 2 1/4 inches. **Col. Depth:** 140 agate lines. **Key Personnel:** Cindy T. McDaniel, Editor; William M. Otto, Publisher; Tracy Ballew, Managing Editor. **ISSN:** 0890-1120. **Subscription Rates:** Free to one-year members of the Arthritis Foundation. **Remarks:** Accepts advertising. **Online:** Electronic Newsstand. **Formerly**: National Arthritis News.
Ad Rates: BW: $15,047 **Circ:** Paid ★625,405
4C: $21,539 Non-paid ★46,863

7053 ASHRAE Journal
American Society of Heating, Refrigerating and Air-Conditioning Engineers, Inc. (ASHRAE)
1791 Tullie Circle NE Phone: (404)636-8400
Atlanta, GA 30329 Fax: (404)321-5478
Free: (800)5AS-HRAE
Publisher E-mail: orders@ashrae.org

Magazine for the heating, refrigeration, and air conditioning trade. **Founded:** Mar. 1, 1957. **Freq:** Monthly. **Print Method:** Offset. **Trim Size:** 8 1/4 x 10 7/8. **Cols./Page:** 3 and 2. **Col.**

Width: 26 and 40 nonpareils. **Col. Depth:** 140 agate lines. **Key Personnel:** Fred Turner, Editor, fturner@ashrae.org; Edwin F. Farley, Assoc. Publisher, efarley@ashrae.org. **ISSN:** 0001-2491. **Subscription Rates:** $59 individuals; $8 single issue. **Remarks:** Accepts advertising.
Ad Rates: BW: $4,760 **Circ:** Paid ★**35,829**
4C: $1,200 Non-paid ★**19,968**

7054 ATI America's Textiles International
Billian Publishing, Inc.
2100 Powers Ferry Rd. Phone: (770)955-5656
Atlanta, GA 30339 Fax: (770)952-0669
Free: (800)533-8484

Magazine for the textile industry; including fiber producers, carpet mills, dyeing and finishing plants, and spinning, weaving, and knitting operations. **Founded:** 1887. **Freq:** Monthly. **Print Method:** Offset. **Trim Size:** 8 x 10 3/4. **Cols./Page:** 3. **Col. Width:** 26 nonpareils. **Col. Depth:** 140 agate lines. **Key Personnel:** Monte Plott, Editor. **Subscription Rates:** Free to qualified subscribers; $43 institutions. **Remarks:** Accepts advertising. **URL:** http://www.billian.com/textile. **Alt. Formats:** Microform.
Ad Rates: BW: $4,220 **Circ:** Paid 269
4C: $5,990 Controlled 33,920
PCI: $95

7055 Atlanta Baby
4330 Georgetown Sq. II, No. 506 Phone: (770)454-7599
Fax: (770)454-7699
Atlanta, GA 30338-6217
Publisher E-mail: atlparnt@family.com

Consumer magazine covering family issues. **Founded:** Oct. 1983. **Freq:** Monthly. **Print Method:** Offset. **Trim Size:** 8 1/4 x 10 3/4. **Cols./Page:** 3. **Col. Width:** 2 1/4 inches. **Col. Depth:** 10 inches. **Key Personnel:** Liz White, Publisher; Peggy Middendorf, Editor. **Subscription Rates:** $12 individuals. **Remarks:** Accepts advertising.
Ad Rates: BW: $1,685 **Circ:** Controlled 76,000
4C: $2,135

7056 Atlanta Bulletin
1655 Peachtree St., Ste. 1003 Phone: (404)874-1968
Atlanta, GA 30309 Fax: (404)874-1950

Community newspaper serving Atlanta and the surrounding counties. Multicultural. **Founded:** Aug. 1974. **Freq:** Weekly (Sat.). **Print Method:** Offset. **Trim Size:** 9 1/2 x 14. **Cols./Page:** 4. **Col. Width:** 15 picas. **Col. Depth:** 2 centimeters. **Key Personnel:** JoAnn Smith, Editor and Publisher; Diona H. McKenzie, Manager; Annette Johnson, Editor. **Subscription Rates:** Free; $30 out of area. **Remarks:** Accepts advertising. **Formerly:** Metro Atlanta Community Bulletin.
Ad Rates: GLR: $10 **Circ:** Controlled 50,000
BW: $1,945.44
4C: $2,270.44
PCI: $34.74

7057 Atlanta Business Chronicle
American City Business Journals
1801 Peachtree St. NE, Ste. 150 Phone: (404)249-1000
Fax: (404)249-1058
Atlanta, GA 30309
Publication E-mail: bizchron@mindspring.com; atlanta@amcity.com

Local business newspaper. **Founded:** 1978. **Freq:** Weekly. **Print Method:** Web offset. **Trim Size:** 11 3/8 x 16. **Cols./Page:** 4. **Col. Width:** 2 1/4 inches. **Col. Depth:** 14 inches. **Key Personnel:** David Rubinger, Editor, phone (404)249-1024; Ed Baker, Publisher, fax (404)249-1048; Nancy Kenerly, Advertising Mgr., phone (404)249-1030, fax (404)249-1048. **ISSN:** 0164-8071. **Subscription Rates:** $66 individuals. **Remarks:** Accepts advertising. **URL:** http://www.amcity.com/atlanta.
Ad Rates: BW: $2,959 **Circ:** Paid ★**28,268**
4C: $3,550 Non-paid ★**469**
PCI: $80

7058 Atlanta Daily World
145 Auburn Ave. NE Phone: (404)659-1110
Atlanta, GA 30335-1201
Publisher E-mail: publisher@atlantadailyworld.com

Black community newspaper. **Founded:** 1928. **Freq:** 2/wk. (Thurs. and Sun.). **Print Method:** Offset. **Cols./Page:** 6. **Col. Width:** 1 5/8 inches. **Col. Depth:** 21 inches. **Key Personnel:** Alexis Scott, Editor and Publisher. **Subscription Rates:** $55.25. **Remarks:** Accepts advertising.
Ad Rates: GLR: $.70 **Circ:** ‡18,000
BW: $1,600
4C: $2,200
PCI: $12.70

7059 Atlanta History
Atlanta Historical Society, Inc.
130 W. Paces Ferry Rd. Phone: (404)814-4085
Atlanta, GA 30305 Fax: (404)814-2041

Journal covering local history. **Subtitle:** A Journal of Georgia and the South. **Founded:** 1927. **Freq:** Quarterly. **Print Method:** Offset. **Trim Size:** 8 1/2 x 11. **Cols./Page:** 3. **Key Personnel:** Kim Blass, Managing Editor, kblass@atlhist.org; Brad Rice, Editor; Andy Ambrose, Assoc. Editor. **ISSN:** 0896-3975. **Subscription Rates:** $20 individuals; $5 single issue. **Remarks:** Accepts advertising. **Former name:** Atlanta Historical Journal.
Ad Rates: BW: $275 **Circ:** Paid 5,500

7060 Atlanta Homes and Lifestyles
Wiesner Inc.
1100 Johnson Ferry Rd. NE, Ste. 595 Phone: (404)252-6670
Fax: (404)252-6673
Atlanta, GA 30342
Free: (800)264-2456
Publication E-mail: althomes@aol.com

Magazine on shelter and design topics, gardening, remodeling and entertaining. **Founded:** 1983. **Freq:** 8/year. **Print Method:** Web offset. **Trim Size:** 8 3/8 x 10 7/8. **Cols./Page:** 3. **Col. Width:** 13.5 picas. **Col. Depth:** 132 agate lines. **Key Personnel:** Oma Blaise, Editor, phone (404)965-4469; Gina Schreiber, Publisher, phone (404)965-4414, vschreiber@aol.com. **ISSN:** 0887-1523. **Subscription Rates:** $18.95 individuals; $3.95 single issue. **Remarks:** Accepts advertising. **Formerly:** Southern Homes.
Ad Rates: BW: $3,625 **Circ:** ‡33,828
4C: $4,960

7061 The Atlanta Inquirer
947 Martin Luther King Jr. Dr. NW Phone: (404)523-6086
Fax: (404)523-6088
Atlanta, GA 30314
Black community newspaper. Distributed each Thursday with a Saturday publication date. **Founded:** 1960. **Freq:** Weekly (Thurs.). **Print Method:** Offset. **Trim Size:** 13 x 21.5. **Cols./Page:** 6. **Col. Width:** 2 1/16 inches. **Col. Depth:** 21 inches. **Key Personnel:** Christopher Weems, Associate Editor; John B. Smith, Advertising Dir.; Sallie Pope Howard, Advertising Dir.; Kimberly Bryant, Advertising Dir. **Subscription Rates:** $52 individuals. **Available Online. URL:** http://www.mindspring.com/cweem/inq.html.
Ad Rates: GLR: $1.80 **Circ:** Paid 61,082
BW: $2,600.64
4C: $2,900.64
SAU: $19.04
PCI: $25.20

7062 The Atlanta Journal and Constitution
72 Marietta St. NW Phone: (404)526-5151
PO Box 4689 Fax: (404)526-5746
Atlanta, GA 30302-4689
Free: (800)846-6672
Publication E-mail: constitution@ajc.com; journal@ajc.com

General newspaper. **Founded:** June 16, 1868. **Freq:** Mon.-Sun. (morn.). **Print Method:** Offset. **Cols./Page:** 6. **Col. Width:** 25 nonpareils. **Col. Depth:** 297 agate lines. **Key Personnel:** Ron Martin, Editor; Roger Kintzel, Publisher; Susan Soper, Asst. Mng. Editor, phone (404)526-5441. **ISSN:** 0093-1179. **Subscription Rates:** $53.03 individuals Monday-Friday; $174.20 out of area; $293.80 out of state. **Remarks:** Accepts advertising. **Online:** DataTimes Corporation; Dialog (The Dialog Corporation); LEXIS-NEXIS; CompuServe Information Service. **URL:** http://www.accessatlanta.com. **Alt. Formats:** CD-ROM. **Formed by the merger of:** The Atlanta Journal; The Atlanta Constitution. **Feature Editors:** Ron Feinberg, *Religion*; Connie Green, *Garden/Home*; Jennifer Hill, *Financial/Business*; Kathy Janich, *Entertainment*; Bob Longino, *Features*; Howard Pousner, *Travel*; Susan Puckett, *Food*; Eleanor Ringel, *Movie*; Frank Rizzo, *Features*; Nick Tate, *Medical, Science*.
Ad Rates: GLR: $5.60 **Circ:** Mon.-Thurs. ★**409,970**
BW: $5,236 Fri. ★**476,990**
4C: $5,696 Sat. ★**509,754**
SAU: $167.44 Sun. ★**677,019**
PCI: $46.81

7063 Atlanta Magazine
Emmis Publishing Corp.
2 Midtown Plaza Phone: (404)872-3100
1360 Peachtree St., Ste. 1800 Fax: (404)870-6230
Atlanta, GA 30309
City magazine. **Founded:** 1961. **Freq:** Monthly. **Print Method:** Offset. **Trim Size:** 8 x 10 7/8. **Cols./Page:** 3. **Col. Width:** 2.25 picas. **Col. Depth:** 10 inches. **Key Personnel:** Lee Walburn, Editor-in-Chief; Susie Love, Publisher. **ISSN:** 0004-6701. **Subscription Rates:** $18 individuals; $2.95 single issue. **Remarks:** Accepts advertising. **URL:** http://atlantamag.atlanta.com.
Ad Rates: BW: $5,455 **Circ:** Paid ★**67,406**
4C: $7,180

7064 Atlanta Parent
Atlanta Parent, Inc.
2346 Perimeter Park Dr., Ste. 101 Phone: (770)454-7599
Fax: (770)454-7699
Atlanta, GA 30341
Publication E-mail: atlparnt@family.com

Parenting magazine. **Founded:** 1983. **Freq:** Monthly. **Print Method:** Web offset. **Trim Size:** 8 1/4 x 10 3/4. **Cols./Page:** 3. **Col. Width:** 2 1/4 inches. **Col. Depth:** 10 inches. **Key Personnel:** Liz White, Editor and Publisher. **Subscription Rates:** $30 individuals. **Remarks:** Accepts advertising. **Available Online. URL:** http://www.ztlontaparent.com.
Ad Rates: BW: $1,500 **Circ:** Free ❑**72,379**
4C: $1,950 Paid ❑**30**
PCI: $71

7065 Atlanta Sports & Fitness Magazine
Atlanta Sports & Fitness Magazine, Inc.
359 E. Paces Ferry Rd. NE, Ste. 101 Phone: (404)842-0359
Fax: (404)816-5215
Atlanta, GA 30305
Publisher E-mail: asfmag1@aol.com

General interest sports, health, and fitness journal. Journal includes a feature called *Atlanta Health and Beauty* every month. **Subtitle:** Atlanta's Guide to Healty and Active Living. **Founded:** May 1990. **Freq:** Monthly. **Key Personnel:** Jim Robinson, Publisher; Laura Weldon, Editor; Sherri Adair, Executive Director; Suzanne Klarer, Director of Events; Kris Burnett, Business Mgr. **Subscription Rates:** Free. **Remarks:** Advertising accepted; rates available upon request. **Formerly:** Atlanta Health & Fitness Magazine (Mar. 1993).
Circ: 900,000

7066 The Atlanta Voice
633 Pryor St. SW Phone: (404)524-6426
Box 92405 Fax: (404)523-7853
Atlanta, GA 30314-0405
Black community newspaper. **Founded:** 1966. **Freq:** Weekly (Thurs.). **Print Method:** Web. **Cols./Page:** 6. **Col. Depth:** 14 inches. **Key Personnel:** Stan Washington, Editor; Janis Ware, Publisher. **Subscription Rates:** $39. **Remarks:** Accepts advertising.
Ad Rates: GLR: $6.50 **Circ:** 133,000
BW: $5,805
SAU: $45

7067 AUC Digest
Atlanta University Center
PO Box 3191 Phone: (404)523-6136
Atlanta, GA 30302 Fax: (404)523-5467

Collegiate newspaper (tabloid). **Founded:** 1973. **Freq:** Weekly (Mon.). **Print Method:** Offset. **Cols./Page:** 4. **Col. Width:** 27 nonpareils. **Col. Depth:** 196 agate lines. **Key Personnel:** Lo Jelks, Editor and Publisher. **Subscription Rates:** $28 individuals. **Remarks:** Accepts advertising.
Ad Rates: GLR: $.70 **Circ:** Paid ‡100
BW: $587 Non-paid ‡15,000

7068 Aurora Rising
5835 Allen Ct. Phone: (404)303-0072
Atlanta, GA 30328 Fax: (404)303-0072
Free: (800)368-9026

Magazine concerned with consciousness, creativity, and spiritual growth, with focuses on healing and the arts. **Subtitle:** The Magazine for a New World. **Founded:** Apr. 1, 1992. **Freq:** Quarterly. **Print Method:** Web offset. **Trim Size:** 8 1/2 x 10 7/8. **Key Personnel:** Karen Willis, Editor and Publisher; Karen S. Adler, Editor. **Subscription Rates:** $16 individuals; $4.50 single issue. **Remarks:** Accepts advertising.
Ad Rates: BW: $390 **Circ:** Paid 7,000
4C: $690 Non-paid 3,000

7069 Automotive & Transportation Interiors
Bill Communications, Inc.
6255 Barfield Rd., Ste. 200 Phone: (404)252-8831
Atlanta, GA 30328-4300 Fax: (404)252-4436
Free: (800)241-9034

Trade magazine for the automotive interiors industry worldwide. **Founded:** 1994. **Freq:** Monthly. **Print Method:** Offset. **Trim Size:** 8 1/8 x 10 7/8. **Cols./Page:** 3. **Col. Width:** 2 1/4 inches. **Col. Depth:** 10 inches. **Key Personnel:** Richard Lebovitz, Co-Publisher/Editor, rlebovitz@autointeriors.com; Artie Bernstein, Co-Publisher/National Sales Mgr., abernstein@autointeriors.com,; Kitty Brigham, Circulation Dir., kbrigham@autointeriors.com. **ISSN:** 1071-1430. **Subscription Rates:** $47 individuals; $7 single issue. **Remarks:** Accepts advertising. **URL:** http://www.autointeriors.com.
Ad Rates: BW: $3,645 **Circ:** Controlled ‡13,093
4C: $5,595

7070 babysue
PO Box 8989 Phone: (404)320-1178
Atlanta, GA 31106-8989
Consumer magazine covering satire, music, and humor.

Founded: Jan. 1983. **Freq:** Quarterly. **Print Method:** Web offset. **Trim Size:** 8 1/2 x 11. **Cols./Page:** 3. **Key Personnel:** Don W. Seven, Editor. **ISSN:** 1076-8890. **Subscription Rates:** $12 individuals; $3 single issue. **Remarks:** Accepts advertising. **URL:** http://www.babysue.com. **Formerly:** babysue review.
Ad Rates: BW: $150 **Circ:** Controlled 5,000

7071 Best Sellers Collection
Drawing Board Atlanta, Inc.
PO Box 15556 Phone: (404)624-3999
Atlanta, GA 30333-0556 Fax: (404)624-4063
Publisher E-mail: dbahomeplans@mindspring.com

Trade magazine for the architecture and homebuilding industry. **Founded:** Oct. 9, 1989. **Freq:** Quarterly. **Print Method:** Web offset. **Trim Size:** 8 1/2 x 11. **Cols./Page:** 3. **Key Personnel:** P. A. Jessup, Editor. **Subscription Rates:** $12 individuals; $5 single issue; Free to qualified subscribers. **Remarks:** Accepts advertising.
Circ: Combined 5,200

7072 BioWorld Magazine
American Health Consultants, Inc.
3525 Piedmont Rd., Bldg. 6, Ste. 400 Phone: (404)262-7436
Fax: (404)262-7837
Atlanta, GA 30305
Free: (800)688-2421
Publisher E-mail: customerservice@ahcpub.com

Magazine covering the biotechnology industry. **Subtitle:** The Business of Biotechnology. **Founded:** 1990. **Freq:** 10/year. **Print Method:** Saddlestitch. **Trim Size:** 8 1/8 x 10 7/8. **Key Personnel:** Cliff Barney, Editor; David Bunnell, Publisher; Bob LaPointe, Advertising Mgr. **Subscription Rates:** Free to qualified subscribers; $75 other countries. **Remarks:** Accepts advertising.
Ad Rates: BW: $2,400 **Circ:** Controlled ‡10,000
4C: $3,400

7073 Black Employment and Education Magazine
Hamdani Communications Inc.
Bldg. 56, Ste. 282 Phone: (404)469-5891
2625 Piedmont Rd.
Atlanta, GA 30324
Periodical for black college and trade school students and professors. **Subtitle:** Blacks in Healthcare Administration. **Founded:** 1990. **Freq:** Bimonthly. **Trim Size:** 8 1/2 x 11. **Cols./Page:** 3. **Col. Width:** 2 1/8 inches. **Col. Depth:** 9 1/2 inches. **Key Personnel:** S. Barry Hamdani, Editor and Publisher. **ISSN:** 1053-704X. **Subscription Rates:** $15. $3 single issue. **Remarks:** Advertising accepted; rates available upon request.
Circ: Paid ‡25,000
Controlled ‡150,000

7074 Blood Weekly
C.W. Henderson
PO Box 5528 Fax: (770)507-7788
Atlanta, GA 30307 Free: (800)633-4931
Publisher E-mail: cwhender@hendersonnet.atl.ga

Contains information on blood-related topics, with an emphasis on the blood banking industry. **Founded:** Apr. 1996. **Subscription Rates:** $300 quarterly. **URL:** http://www.newsfile.com/x1b.htm.

7075 Boating World
Trans World Publishing, Inc.
2100 Powers Ferry Rd. Phone: (770)955-5656
Atlanta, GA 30339 Fax: (770)952-0669
Free: (800)827-0818

Magazine directed to active-lifestyle boaters in the up-to-35 ft. powerboat market. Provides articles and features on all aspects of the boating industry for the novice to the experienced boater. **Founded:** 1979. **Freq:** 10/year. **Print Method:** Offset. **Trim Size:** 8 x 10 3/4. **Cols./Page:** 3. **Col. Width:** 27 nonpareils. **Col. Depth:** 139 1/4 agate lines. **Key Personnel:** Joe Skorupa, Editor; Douglas Billian, Publisher; Jay Perkins, Publisher. **ISSN:** 1059-5155. **Subscription Rates:** $28; $31 other countries; $3.50 single issue. **Remarks:** Accepts advertising. **Formerly:** Small Boat Journal (1992); Boat Journal.
Ad Rates: BW: $5,510 **Circ:** Paid ★96,103
4C: $8,520 Non-paid ★20,700
PCI: $89

7076 Bulletin of the American Schools of Oriental Research
Scholars Press
118 Trimble Hall Phone: (404)727-0807
Emory University Fax: (404)727-2903
Atlanta, GA 30322
Publisher E-mail: scholars@emory.edu

Journal on Near Eastern studies. **Founded:** 1919. **Freq:** Quarterly. **Print Method:** Offset. **Trim Size:** 8 1/2 x 11. **Cols./Page:** 2. **Col. Width:** 36 nonpareils. **Col. Depth:** 120 agate lines. **Key Personnel:** Prof. Albert Leonard, Jr., Editor. **ISSN:** 0003-097X. **Subscription Rates:** $60; $80 institutions. **Remarks:** Accepts advertising.
Ad Rates: BW: $300 **Circ:** ‡2,100

7077 Business Atlanta
Argus Business
6151 Powers Ferry Rd.
Atlanta, GA 30339-2941
Publication E-mail: mcibbs@mindspring.com

Business magazine. **Subtitle:** and the International South. **Founded:** Mar. 1980. **Freq:** Monthly. **Print Method:** Offset. **Trim Size:** 8 1/8 x 10 7/8. **Cols./Page:** 3. **Col. Width:** 28 nonpareils. **Col. Depth:** 140 agate lines. **Key Personnel:** John Sequerth, Editor; Thomas C. Kaleta, Publisher. **ISSN:** 0192-0855. **Subscription Rates:** $39 individuals. **Remarks:** Accepts advertising. **URL:** http://www.internetview.com.
Ad Rates: BW: $3,170 **Circ:** Paid 1,694
4C: $4,070 Controlled 35,759

7078 CALC Report
Clergy & Laity Concerned
92 Piedmont Ave. NE Phone: (404)377-1983
Atlanta, GA 30303-2528 Fax: (404)377-5367

Liberal religious magazine. **Subtitle:** People of Faith and Conscience Working for Justice and Peace. **Freq:** Quarterly. **Print Method:** Offset. **Trim Size:** 8.25 x 10.75 inches. **Cols./Page:** 3. **Col. Width:** 2.25 inches. **Col. Depth:** 9 inches. **Key Personnel:** Leslie Withers, Editor. **Subscription Rates:** $30 individuals; $40 other countries. **Remarks:** Advertising accepted; rates available upon request.
Circ: ‡11,000

7079 The Christian Index
1585 S. Ponce De Leon Ave. NE Phone: (770)261-0600
Fax: (770)261-0610
Atlanta, GA 30307
Free: (877)424-6339
Publication E-mail: cindex@compuserve.com
Publisher E-mail: editor@christianindex.org

News magazine for the Georgia Baptist Convention. **Founded:** 1822. **Freq:** Weekly (Thurs.) every other week during the summer. **Print Method:** Letterpress and offset. **Cols./Page:** 5. **Col. Width:** 1 7/8 inches. **Col. Depth:** 13 1/2 inches. **Key Personnel:** Dr. William T. Neal, Editor. **ISSN:** 0362-0832. **Subscription Rates:** $10 individuals. **Remarks:** Accepts advertising.
Ad Rates: BW: $1,360 **Circ:** Paid 62,000
4C: $1,700 Non-paid 2,000
PCI: $18

7080 Cinema Journal
University of Texas Press
c/o Frank Tomasulo Phone: (404)651-3200
Department of Communication Fax: (404)651-1409
Georgia State University
Atlanta, GA 30303
Publication E-mail: cj@cinemastudies.org
Publisher E-mail: cj@cinemastudies.org

Scholarly journal covering film and television history, criticism, news, events, and aesthetics. **Founded:** 1961. **Freq:** Quarterly. **Print Method:** Offset. **Trim Size:** 6 x 9. **Key Personnel:** Frank Tomasulo, Editor. **ISSN:** 0009-7101. **Subscription Rates:** $25 individuals; $8 single issue. **Remarks:** Accepts advertising.
Ad Rates: BW: $195 **Circ:** Combined ⊕2,076

7081 CLA Journal
College Language Association
Morehouse College Phone: (404)681-2800
Atlanta, GA 30314 Fax: (404)215-7266

Journal containing articles on language and literature. **Founded:** 1957. **Freq:** Quarterly. **Print Method:** Offset. **Trim Size:** 6 x 9. **Cols./Page:** 1. **Col. Width:** 54 nonpareils. **Col. Depth:** 94 agate lines. **Key Personnel:** Dr. Cason L. Hill, Editor. **ISSN:** 0007-8549. **Subscription Rates:** $40 individuals; $41.50 Canada; $45.50 other countries; $20 other. **Remarks:** Color advertising not accepted.
Ad Rates: BW: $300 **Circ:** Paid ‡1,500
Controlled ‡10

7082 Clark Atlanta University Magazine
Atlanta University
223 James P. Brawley Drive SW Phone: (404)880-8680
Atlanta, GA 30314
College alumni magazine. **Founded:** 1989. **Freq:** Semiannual. **Key Personnel:** Toni Mosley, Editor. **Subscription Rates:** Free to qualified subscribers.
Circ: Controlled 18,000

7083 Commuter Air International
6151 Powers Ferry Rd. NW Phone: (404)955-2500
Atlanta, GA 30339-2941 Fax: (404)618-0343

Subtitle: The International Magazine for Regional, Commuter, and Short Haul Airlines. **Founded:** 1978. **Freq:** Monthly. **Print Method:** Offset. **Trim Size:** 8 1/8 x 10 7/8. **Cols./Page:** 3. **Col. Width:** 26 nonpareils. **Col. Depth:** 140 agate lines. **Key Personnel:** Justin Powers, Editor; David Premo, Publisher. **ISSN:** 1054-7436. **Subscription Rates:** Free to qualified subscribers; $45 institutions. **Remarks:** Accepts advertising.
Ad Rates: BW: $4,835 **Circ:** Paid 650
4C: $6,005 Controlled 32,000
PCI: $130

7084 Configurations
Johns Hopkins University Press
School of Literature, Communication and Culture
Georgia Institute of Technology
Atlanta, GA 30332-0165
Publisher E-mail: jlinfo@jhupress.jhu.edu

Journal on the humanities. **Subtitle:** A Journal of Literature, Science and Technology. **Freq:** 3/year. **Print Method:** Offset. **Trim Size:** 6 x 9. **Cols./Page:** 1. **Col. Width:** 26 picas. **Col. Depth:** 7 inches. **Key Personnel:** Jim Bono, Editor; T. Hugh Crawford, Editor; Paula Findlen, Editor; Tara Dorai-Berry, Advertising Coordinator. **ISSN:** 1063-1801. **Subscription Rates:** $30 individuals; $64 institutions. **Remarks:** Accepts advertising. **Available Online. URL:** http://www.press.jhu.edu/press/gournak/titles/con.html.
Ad Rates: BW: $190 **Circ:** Paid 1000

7085 Consumer Technology
Jaye Communications, Inc.
2841 Akers Mill Rd. SE Phone: (770)984-9444
Atlanta, GA 30339-3104 Fax: (770)933-9072
Publication E-mail: editorial@jaye.com

Technology and business publication for the SOUTHEAST. **Freq:** Monthly. **Key Personnel:** Mike Adkinson, Editor and Publisher, mike.adkinson@jaye.com; Colleen Hinsberg, Assoc. Editor, colleen.hinsberg@jaye.com. **Subscription Rates:** $24 individuals; $15 single issue. **Remarks:** Accepts advertising. **URL:** http://www.jaye.com. **Formerly:** Technology South.
Circ: (Not Reported)

7086 Corporate Cashflow
6151 Powers Ferry Rd. NW Phone: (404)618-0198
Atlanta, GA 30339-2941
Trade journal for corporate treasury managers. **Subtitle:** The Magazine of Treasury Management. **Founded:** June 1980. **Freq:** Monthly. **Print Method:** Web offset. **Trim Size:** 8 1/8 x 10 7/8. **Cols./Page:** 3. **Col. Width:** 13 picas. **Key Personnel:** Richard Gamble, Editor; Peggie Elgin, Editor; Patti-Ann Zielinski, Editor. **ISSN:** 1040-0311. **Remarks:** Accepts advertising. **Formerly:** Cash Flow.
Ad Rates: BW: $6,410 **Circ:** Controlled 40,000
4C: $7,855

7087 Creative Loafing
750 Willoughby Way Phone: (404)688-5623
Atlanta, GA 30312 Fax: (404)614-3599
Free: (800)953-5623
Publication E-mail: webmaster.creativeloafing@.com

Alternative news weekly newspaper (tabloid). **Founded:** 1972. **Freq:** Weekly (Wed.). **Print Method:** Offset. **Trim Size:** 10 x 12 7/8. **Cols./Page:** 4. **Col. Width:** 1 7/16 inches. **Col. Depth:** 12 7/8 inches. **Key Personnel:** Deborah Eason, Publisher; Ken Edlestin, Editor; Howard Landsman, General Sales Mgr., phone (404)614-1227, fax (404)614-1227, howard.landsman@cln.com. **Subscription Rates:** Free; $40. **Remarks:** Accepts advertising. **URL:** http://www.creativeloafing.com.
Ad Rates: BW: $5,873 **Circ:** Free 165,000
4C: $7,448 Paid 346

7088 Defense & Security Electronics
Intertec Publishing
6151 Powers Ferry Rd. Phone: (770)955-2500
Atlanta, GA 30339 Fax: (770)618-0348
Free: (800)323-8905
Publication E-mail: mgibbs@mindspring.com

Defense and security electronics magazine. **Founded:** 1969. **Freq:** Monthly. **Print Method:** Offset. **Trim Size:** 8 1/8 x 10 7/8. **Cols./Page:** 3. **Col. Width:** 27 nonpareils. **Col. Depth:** 140 agate lines. **Key Personnel:** Roger Lesser, Editor; Kathy Walsh, Publisher. **ISSN:** 0278-3479. **Subscription Rates:** $38 individuals. **Remarks:** Accepts advertising. **URL:** http://www.internetview.com. **Absorbed:** Microwave Systems News. **Formerly:** Defense Electronics.
Ad Rates: BW: $5,450 **Circ:** Paid 1,681
4C: $6,400 Non-paid 43,000

7089 Drug Abuse Update
National Families in Action
2957 Clairmont Rd., Ste. 150 Phone: (404)248-9676
Atlanta, GA 30329 Fax: (404)248-1312
Publication E-mail: pkemp@mindspring.com
Publisher E-mail: nfia@mindspring.com

Online magazine covering substance abuse. **Founded:** 1982. **Freq:** Quarterly. **Key Personnel:** Paula C. Kemp, Editor. **ISSN:** 0739-6562. **Subscription Rates:** $30 individuals. **Remarks:** Advertising not accepted. **URL:** http://www.emory.edu/NFIA.
Circ: Combined 7,000

7090 Economic Review
Federal Reserve Bank of Atlanta
104 Marietta St. Phone: (404)521-8269
Atlanta, GA 30303-2713 Fax: (404)521-8050

Journal presenting research on finance topics, economics in the southeastern U.S. and the nation, and macroeconomic and international monetary issues. **Subtitle:** Economic Review. **Founded:** 1914. **Freq:** Bimonthly. **Print Method:** Sheetfed press. **Trim Size:** 8 1/2 x 11. **Cols./Page:** 2. **Col. Width:** 19 picas. **Col. Depth:** 54 picas. **Key Personnel:** Joycelyn T. Woolfolk, Editor. **ISSN:** 0732-1813. **Subscription Rates:** Free. **Remarks:** Advertising not accepted. **URL:** http://www.frbatlanta.org.
Circ: Controlled ‡23,000

7091 EMC Test & Design
Argus Business
6151 Powers Ferry Rd.
Atlanta, GA 30339-2941

Professional magazine for engineers and their managers focusing on electromagnetic compatability. **Founded:** Nov. 1990. **Freq:** Monthly. **Key Personnel:** Ellen M. Millen, Editor. **ISSN:** 1054-5816. **Subscription Rates:** $39. $5 single issue. **Remarks:** Advertising accepted; rates available upon request.
Circ: (Not Reported)

7092 Emerging Infectious Diseases
U.S. National Center for Infectious Diseases
1600 Clifton Rd., Mailstop C-12 Phone: (404)639-4856
Atlanta, GA 30333 Fax: (404)639-3039
Publication E-mail: eideditor@cdc.gov

Medical journal covering infectious diseases. **Founded:** Jan. 1995. **Freq:** 4-6/year. **Trim Size:** 8 1/2 x 11. **Key Personnel:** Joseph E. McDade, Ph.D., Editor-in-Chief. **ISSN:** 1080-6040. **Subscription Rates:** Free. **Remarks:** Advertising not accepted. **URL:** http://www.cdc.gov/EID/.
Circ: (Not Reported)

7093 Emory Magazine
Emory University
1655 N. Decatur Rd. Phone: (404)727-7872
Atlanta, GA 30322 Fax: (404)727-0169
Publication E-mail: emorymag@emory.edu

Magazine for university alumni. **Founded:** 1924. **Freq:** Quarterly 4/year. **Print Method:** Web offset. **Trim Size:** 8 1/2 x 11. **Cols./Page:** 3 and 2. **Col. Width:** 13 and 20 nonpareils. **Col. Depth:** 147 agate lines. **Key Personnel:** Andrew W.M. Beierle, Editor. **ISSN:** 0013-6727. **Subscription Rates:** Free to University donors/Alumni. **Remarks:** Advertising not accepted. **Available Online. URL:** http://www.emory.edu/emory_magazine.
Circ: Non-paid ‡78,000

7094 The Emory Wheel
Emory University
Drawer W. Phone: (404)727-6178
Atlanta, GA 30322 Fax: (404)727-3613
Publication E-mail: wheel@emory.edu

Collegiate newspaper (tabloid). **Founded:** 1918. **Freq:** Semiweekly (Tues. and Fri.; during the academic year). **Print Method:** Offset. **Trim Size:** 11 1/2 x 15. **Cols./Page:** 5. **Col. Width:** 22 nonpareils. **Col. Depth:** 196 agate lines. **Key Personnel:** Kimberly L. Freeman, Editor-in-Chief; Erin Bruce, Executive Editor; James Furdell, Managing Editor; Shyam Reddy, General Mgr.; Matthew Pinzur, News Editor; Marc Sher, Editorials Editor; Alastair Gamble, A&E Editor; Kathleen Chapman, Features Editor; Childs Walker, Sports Editor; Romy Ribitzky, Photo Editor. **Subscription Rates:** $65 individuals. **Remarks:** Accepts advertising. **Available Online. URL:** http://www.emory.edu/wheel.
Ad Rates: BW: $557 **Circ:** Combined 7,500
4C: $796.50
PCI: $7.95

7095 Environmental Technology
Adams Green Industry Publishing
2110 Powers Ferry Rd., Ste. 460 Phone: (770)937-0222
Atlanta, GA 30339 Fax: (770)937-0303
Trade publication for environmental and pollution control professionals. **Founded:** Sept. 1991. **Freq:** Bimonthly 7/year. **Print Method:** Web offset. **Trim Size:** 8 x 10 3/4. **Cols./Page:** 2 and 3. **Key Personnel:** Chris Bryon Campbell, Publisher; Michael Hilts, Editor; Roger DiGregorio, Circulation Mgr. **ISSN:** 1067-2583. **Remarks:** Accepts advertising. **Formerly:** The National Environmental Journal.
Ad Rates: BW: $5,290 **Circ:** Paid ‡37
4C: $6,525 Non-paid ‡65,472
PCI: $115

7096 Etcetera Magazine
151 Renaissance Pkwy. Phone: (404)888-0063
Atlanta, GA 30308 Fax: (404)888-0910
Publication E-mail: etc@mindspring.com

Magazine for gays and lesbians. **Founded:** June 1985. **Freq:** Weekly. **Print Method:** Web press. **Trim Size:** 5 1/4 x 8 1/4. **Cols./Page:** 3. **Col. Width:** 1 1/2 inches. **Col. Depth:** 7 5/8 inches. **Key Personnel:** Jack Pelham, Editor, etced-it@mindspring.com; Jim Heverly, Publisher; Ron Whalen, Advertising Mgr., etccads@mindspring.com; Rob Nixon, News Editor; Elizabeth Elkins, Events Editor. **Subscription Rates:** $65 individuals; $2 single issue. **Remarks:** Accepts advertising. **URL:** http://www.etcmag.com.
Ad Rates: BW: $383 **Circ:** Non-paid 23,000
4C: $533

7097 Farmers & Consumers Market Bulletin
Georgia Dept. of Agriculture
Georgia Dept. of Agriculture Phone: (404)656-3682
Agriculture Bldg., Capitol Sq., Rm. 226 Fax: (404)651-7957
19 Martin Luther King Jr. Dr.
Atlanta, GA 30334-4250
Free: (800)2825852

State agriculture and consumer newspaper. **Founded:** 1917. **Freq:** Weekly (Wed.). **Print Method:** Web offset. **Trim Size:** 11 1/4 x 15. **Cols./Page:** 5. **Col. Width:** 22 nonpareils. **Col. Depth:** 215 agate lines. **Key Personnel:** Carlton Moore, Editor. **ISSN:** 0889-5619. **Subscription Rates:** $10 out of state. **Remarks:** Advertising not accepted. **URL:** http://www.agr.state.ga.us.
Circ: Free 270,000

7098 Feminist Issues
Transaction Publishers
Emory University
History Dept., Bowden Hall
561 Kilgo Cir.
Atlanta, GA 30322
Publisher E-mail: trans@transactionpub.com

Journal on feminism in daily life. **Founded:** 1980. **Freq:** 2/year. **Key Personnel:** Elizabeth Fox-Genovese, Editor. **ISSN:** 0270-6679. **Subscription Rates:** $40 individuals; $56 other countries; $80 institutions; $96 other countries institutions; $72 two years individuals; $144 two years institutions. **Remarks:** Accepts advertising.
Ad Rates: BW: $200 **Circ:** Paid 500

7099 Forest Landowner
Forest Landowners Association
PO Box 95385 Phone: (404)325-2954
Atlanta, GA 30347-0385 Fax: (404)325-2955
Free: (800)325-2954

Forestry magazine. **Founded:** 1941. **Freq:** Bimonthly. **Print Method:** Offset. **Trim Size:** 8 1/2 x 11. **Cols./Page:** 3. **Col. Width:** 28 nonpareils. **Col. Depth:** 133 agate lines. **Key Personnel:** Matt Workman, Asst. Editor. **ISSN:** 0015-7406. **Subscription Rates:** $40 individuals; $2.50 single issue. **Remarks:** Accepts advertising. **Formerly:** Forest Farmer Magazine.
Ad Rates: BW: $790 **Circ:** 9,600
4C: $1,240

7100 Fulton County Daily Report
Daily Report Co.
190 Pryor St. SW Phone: (404)521-1227
Atlanta, GA 30303 Fax: (404)523-5924

Law newspaper (tabloid) reporting state news affecting the legal and business communities; including articles and digests of recent opinions from appellate and federal courts. **Founded:** 1890. **Freq:** Daily (eve.). **Print Method:** Offset. **Trim Size:** 11 3/8 x 17 1/2. **Cols./Page:** 4. **Col. Width:** 29 nonpareils. **Col. Depth:** 220 agate lines. **Key Personnel:** S. Richard Gard, Jr., Editor and Publisher, phone (404)521-1227, fax (404)523-5924; Arthur Hahn, Advertising Dir. **USPS:** 211-640. **Subscription Rates:** $245 individuals.
Ad Rates: GLR: $230 **Circ:** Paid 5,270
BW: $1,200 Non-paid 552
4C: $1,650
PCI: $20

7101 Georgia Bar Journal
State Bar of Georgia
800 The Hurt Bldg. Phone: (404)527-8700
50 Hurt Plaza Fax: (404)527-8717
Atlanta, GA 30303
Free: (800)334-6865
Publication E-mail: journal@gabar.org

Law journal. **Founded:** 1938. **Freq:** Bimonthly. **Print Method:** Offset. **Trim Size:** 8 3/8 x 10 7/8. **Cols./Page:** 3. **Col. Width:** 27 nonpareils. **Col. Depth:** 133 agate lines. **Key Personnel:** Jennifer M. Davis, Managing Editor, phone (404)527-8736, jendavis@gabar.org; Amy Williams, Advertising Coordinator, phone (404)527-8792, journal@gabar.org. **Subscription Rates:** $36 individuals; $6 single issue. **Remarks:** Accepts advertising. **URL:** http://www.gabar.org. **Formerly:** Georgia State Bar Journal.
Ad Rates: BW: $1,323 **Circ:** 27,000
4C: $3,393

7102 The Georgia Bulletin
680 W. Peachtree St. NW Phone: (404)888-7832
Atlanta, GA 30308-1984 Fax: (404)888-7849

Religious newspaper (tabloid) for the Catholic Archdiocese of Atlanta. **Founded:** 1962. **Freq:** Weekly (Thurs.). **Print Method:** Offset. **Trim Size:** 10 1/4 x 13 1/2. **Col. Depth:** 196 agate lines. **Key Personnel:** Gretchen Keiser, Editor, phone (401)885-7832; Archbishop John Donoghue, Publisher; Tom Aisthorpe, Advertising Mgr., phone (404)885-7213; Kathi Stearns, Exec. Editor. **Subscription Rates:** $18 individuals; $40 other countries. **Remarks:** Accepts advertising.
Ad Rates: BW: $1,663.20 **Circ:** 66,000
PCI: $14

7103 Georgia Future Farmer
Georgia Association of Future Farmers of America
Dept. of Vocational Education Phone: (404)656-2562
Twin Towers East, Rm. 1766 Fax: (404)651-8984
Atlanta, GA 30334
Agricultural magazine. **Founded:** 1933. **Freq:** Quarterly. **Print Method:** Offset. **Cols./Page:** 3. **Col. Width:** 27 nonpareils. **Col. Depth:** 129 agate lines. **Key Personnel:** John K. Wilkinson, Editor.

7104 Georgia Professional Engineer
Magnolia Studios
120 Interstate N. Parkway Blg. 400 Phone: (770)988-9551
Suite 444 Fax: (770)988-9539
Atlanta, GA 30339
Free: (800)788-3984
Publisher E-mail: mstudios@mindspring.com

Engineering journal. **Founded:** 1944. **Freq:** Bimonthly. **Print Method:** Letterpress and offset. **Trim Size:** 8 1/2 x 11. **Cols./Page:** 3. **Col. Width:** 28 nonpareils. **Col. Depth:** 140 agate lines. **Key Personnel:** Pamela Peterson-Frey. **Subscription Rates:** $25 individuals.
Ad Rates: BW: $800 **Circ:** Controlled 6,000
4C: $900

7105 Georgia Tech Alumni Magazine
Georgia Tech Alumni Association
190 North Ave. NW Phone: (404)894-2391
Atlanta, GA 30313 Fax: (404)894-5113
Publication E-mail: editor@alumni.gatech.edu

Alumni magazine covering management of technology. **Founded:** Mar. 1923. **Freq:** Quarterly. **Print Method:** Web. **Trim Size:** 8 1/8 x 10 7/8. **Key Personnel:** John C. Dunn, Editor; Hoyt Coffee, Assoc. Editor; Robb Stanek, Marketing Dir. **ISSN:** 1061-9747. **Subscription Rates:** $10 individuals. **Remarks:** Accepts advertising.
Ad Rates: BW: $1,505 **Circ:** Paid ⊕**27,500**
4C: $2,065

7106 Georgia Technology Sourcebook
Jaye Communications, Inc.
2841 Akers Mill Rd. SE Phone: (770)984-9444
Atlanta, GA 30339-3104 Fax: (770)933-9072

Publication listing Georgia's high technology firms. **Founded:** 1985. **Freq:** 1/year. **Key Personnel:** Mike Adkinson, Editor and Publisher. **Subscription Rates:** $27. $15.95 single issue. **Remarks:** Advertising accepted; rates available upon request. **Available Online. URL:** http://www.jaye.com.
Circ: (Not Reported)

7107 Golf World
Billian Publishing, Inc.
2100 Powers Ferry Rd. Phone: (770)955-5656
Atlanta, GA 30339 Fax: (770)952-0669
Free: (800)533-8484

Magazine covering tournament golf at all levels of play internationally; also features travel articles, analysis, and instruction. **Founded:** 1947. **Freq:** Weekly. **Print Method:** Offset. **Trim Size:** 8 1/2 x 11. **Cols./Page:** 3. **Col. Width:** 26

nonpareils. **Col. Depth:** 140 agate lines. **Key Personnel:** Richard S. Taylor, Editor; Douglas C. Billian, Publisher. **Subscription Rates:** $22 individuals; $1 single issue. **Remarks:** Accepts advertising.
Ad Rates: BW: $3,830 **Circ:** Paid ★153,432
4C: $6,330 Non-paid ★7,707

7108 Health Management Technology
Intertec Publishing
6151 Powers Ferry Rd. Phone: (770)955-2500
Atlanta, GA 30339 Fax: (770)618-0348
Free: (800)323-8905

Business magazine for healthcare information systems professionals and managers. **Founded:** 1980. **Freq:** Monthly. **Trim Size:** 3/8 x 10 7/8. **Cols./Page:** 3. **Col. Width:** 27 nonpareils. **Col. Depth:** 134 agate lines. **Key Personnel:** Thomas J. Wall, Editor, tom_wall@intertec.com; Michael Gossman, Publisher, phone (770)618-0249. **ISSN:** 0745-1075. **Subscription Rates:** $42 individuals per year. **Remarks:** Accepts advertising. **Available Online. URL:** http://www.healthmgttech.com. **Formerly:** Computers in Healthcare.
Ad Rates: BW: $4,195 **Circ:** Paid 3,000
4C: $5,045 Non-paid 35,000

7109 Healthcare Marketing Report
HMR Publications Group, Inc.
PO Box 76002
Atlanta, GA 30358-1002

Newspaper covering health care marketing in the U.S. **Founded:** 1982. **Freq:** Monthly. **Subscription Rates:** $175 individuals; $13 single issue. **Remarks:** Accepts advertising.
Circ: (Not Reported)

7110 Hogan's Alley
PO Box 47684 Phone: (770)458-2624
Atlanta, GA 30362
Publication E-mail: 71061.43@compuserve.com

Journal covering comics, editorial cartoons, and animated entertainment. **Subtitle:** The Magazine of the Cartoon Arts. **Founded:** Aug. 1994. **Freq:** Semiannual. **Print Method:** Offset. **Trim Size:** 8 3/8 x 10 3/4. **Cols./Page:** 3. **Col. Width:** 2.25 inches. **Col. Depth:** 9 1/2 inches. **Key Personnel:** Rick Marschall, Editor; Tom Heintjes, Editor. **ISSN:** 1074-7354. **Subscription Rates:** $21.95; $6.95 single issue. **Remarks:** Accepts advertising. **URL:** http://www.cagle.com/hogan.
Ad Rates: BW: $250 **Circ:** Paid 5000
4C: $400

7111 Hooters Magazine
1815 The Exchange Phone: (770)951-2040
Atlanta, GA 30339 Fax: (770)618-7049

Consumer magazine of Hooters restaurants. **Founded:** 1987. **Freq:** Quarterly. **Print Method:** Web offset. **Trim Size:** 8 1/2 x 10 7/8. **Key Personnel:** Rick Hammell, Editor and Publisher. **Subscription Rates:** $13.95 individuals; $3.95 single issue. **Remarks:** Accepts advertising.
Ad Rates: 4C: $2,130 **Circ:** Paid 32,000

7112 IAL News
International Association of Laryngectomees (IAL)
1599 Clifton Rd. NE Phone: (404)320-3333
Atlanta, GA 30329-4250 Fax: (404)636-5567

Magazine for persons rehabilitating from laryngectomies. **Freq:** 3/year. **Subscription Rates:** Free. **Remarks:** Advertising not accepted.
Circ: Non-paid 15,000

7113 International Journal of Heating, Ventilating, Air-Conditioning and Refrigeration Research (HVAC & R Research)
American Society of Heating, Refrigerating and Air-Conditioning Engineers, Inc. (ASHRAE)
1791 Tullie Circle NE Phone: (404)636-8400
Atlanta, GA 30329 Fax: (404)321-5478
Free: (800)5AS-HRAE
Publication E-mail: rjournal@me.engr.wisc.edu
Publisher E-mail: orders@ashrae.org

Trade journal covering research and development in heating, refrigeration and air-conditioning engineering. **Founded:** Jan. 1995. **Freq:** Quarterly. **Cols./Page:** 1. **Key Personnel:** John Mitchell, Ph.D., Editor. **ISSN:** 1078-9669. **Subscription Rates:** $145 individuals. **Alt. Formats:** CD-ROM.

7114 International Studies in Philosophy
Scholars Press
PO Box 15399
Atlanta, GA 30333-0399
Publisher E-mail: scholars@emory.edu

Scholarly journal covering philosophy for an international audience. **Founded:** 1969. **Freq:** Quarterly. **Key Personnel:** Pat Johnston, Subscriber Svcs. Mgr. **ISSN:** 0270-5664.
Circ: Paid 400

7115 Intertrade and Investment
A.I.M. Communications, Inc.
119 Pharr Rd. NW, Ste. A-4 Phone: (404)239-9225
Atlanta, GA 30305 Fax: (404)816-9264
Publication E-mail: aim@aimlink.com

Tabloid. **Subtitle:** The U.S. International Business Resource. **Founded:** Nov. 1992. **Freq:** Monthly. **Print Method:** Web offset. **Trim Size:** 9 x 12. **Cols./Page:** 4. **Col. Width:** 13 picas. **Col. Depth:** 66 picas. **Key Personnel:** Ken Anderberg, Editor. **Subscription Rates:** $195; $20 single issue. **Remarks:** Accepts advertising. **URL:** http://www.aimlink.com. **Formerly:** Atlanta International Magazine.
Ad Rates: BW: $1,615 **Circ:** Paid ‡500
4C: $2,260 Controlled ‡7,500

7116 Journal of American Ethnic History
Transaction Publishers
School of History, Technology and Society Phone: (404)894-6834
Fax: (404)894-0535
Georgia Institute of Technology
250 North Ave.
Atlanta, GA 30332
Publisher E-mail: trans@transactionpub.com

Journal addressing various aspects of American immigration and ethnic history including background of emigration, ethnic and racial groups, native Americans, and immigration policies. **Founded:** 1981. **Freq:** Quarterly. **Print Method:** Offset. **Trim Size:** 6 x 9. **Key Personnel:** Ronald H. Bayor, Editor, rb2@prism.gatech.edu. **ISSN:** 0278-5927. **Subscription Rates:** $30 individuals; $62 other countries individuals; $15 students; $72 institutions; $104 other countries institutions; $55 two years individuals; $138 two years institutions. **Remarks:** Accepts advertising. **Alt. Formats:** Braille.
Ad Rates: BW: $300 **Circ:** 1,100

7117 Journal of the History of Philosophy
Journal of the History of Philosophy, Inc.
Emory University Phone: (404)727-9765
Dept. of Philosophy
Atlanta, GA 30322
History journal of Western philosophy (English, French, German, and Italian). **Founded:** Oct. 1963. **Freq:** Quarterly. **Print Method:** Offset. **Trim Size:** 6 1/4 x 10. **Cols./Page:** 1. **Col. Width:** 30 picas. **Col. Depth:** 45.5 picas. **Key Personnel:** Gerald Press, Editor. **ISSN:** 0022-5053. **Subscription Rates:** $25 individuals; $65 institutions; $73 by mail overseas; $16.50 single issue. **Remarks:** Accepts advertising.
Ad Rates: BW: $200 **Circ:** 1,600

7118 Journal of the Medical Association of Georgia
1330 W. Peachtree St., No. 500 Phone: (404)881-5065
Atlanta, GA 30309 Fax: (404)881-5021
Free: (800)282-0224

Medical journal. **Founded:** 1911. **Freq:** Quarterly. **Print Method:** Offset. **Trim Size:** 8 1/4 x 11. **Cols./Page:** 3. **Col. Width:** 39 nonpareils. **Col. Depth:** 133 agate lines. **Key Personnel:** Melissa Connor, MD, Managing Editor, phone (404)325-0558, fax (404)325-1690, plusone@mindspring.com. **ISSN:** 0025-7028. **Subscription Rates:** $60 individuals. **Remarks:** Accepts advertising.
Ad Rates: BW: $1,250 **Circ:** 8,000
4C: $1,825

7119 Journal of Negro History
Association for the Study of Afro-American Life and History
Morehouse College Phone: (404)215-2620
Box 20 Fax: (404)215-2715
Atlanta, GA 30314
Afro-American history journal. **Founded:** Jan. 1916. **Freq:** Quarterly. **Print Method:** Offset. **Cols./Page:** 1. **Col. Width:** 51 nonpareils. **Col. Depth:** 112 agate lines. **Key Personnel:** Dr. Alton Hornsby, Jr., Editor, hornsbya@morehouse.edu; hornsbya@aol.com. **ISSN:** 0022-2922. **Subscription Rates:** $30 individuals; $6.50 single issue. **Remarks:** Accepts advertising.
Ad Rates: BW: $350 **Circ:** Paid ‡3,700
4C: $600 Non-paid ‡300

7120 Journal of Nursing Measurement
Springer Publishing Co.
c/o Ora L. Strickland, Ph.D., Editor
Nell Hodgson Woodruff School of Nursing
Emory University
Atlanta, GA 30322
Publisher E-mail: springer@springerpub.com

Scholarly journal covering tools, approaches, or procedures for the measurement of variables for nursing practice, education, and research. **Founded:** 1993. **Freq:** Semiannual. **Trim Size:** 7 x 10. **Cols./Page:** 1. **Col. Width:** 5 inches. **Col. Depth:** 10 inches. **Key Personnel:** Ora L. Strickland, Ph.D., Editor; Rafael Ortiz, Advertising Mgr.; Cory Sklaire, Circulation Mgr.; Matt Fenton, Production Mgr. **ISSN:** 1061-3749. **Subscription Rates:** $33 individuals; $56 two years; $38 individuals out of country; $66 two years out of country; $67 institutions; $106 institutions two years; $72 institutions out of country; $124 institutions two years out of country; $20 single issue. **Remarks:** Accepts advertising.
Ad Rates: BW: $300 **Circ:** Combined 300

7121 KNOW Atlanta Magazine
New South Publishing Inc.
1303 Hightower Trail, Ste. 101 Phone: (770)650-1102
Atlanta, GA 30350 Fax: (770)650-2848
Free: (800)536-5669
Publication E-mail: knowmag@aol.com

Magazine about Atlanta. **Founded:** 1986. **Freq:** Quarterly. **Print Method:** Web offset. **Trim Size:** 81/8 x 10 7/8. **Cols./Page:** 3. **Col. Width:** 1 3/4 inches. **Col. Depth:** 10 inches. **Key Personnel:** Susan Thompson, President; Larry Lebovitz, Vice President. **Subscription Rates:** $3.50 single issue. **Remarks:** Accepts advertising. **Online:** AOL.
Ad Rates: BW: $3,160 **Circ:** Controlled ⊕45,000
4C: $5,300

7122 LOMA Resource
Life Office Management Association
LOMA 2300 Windy Ridge Pkwy. Phone: (770)951-1770
Suite 600 Fax: (770)984-6417
Atlanta, GA 30339-8443
Free: (800)275-5662

Life insurance industry management magazine. **Founded:** 1975. **Freq:** Monthly. **Print Method:** Offset. **Trim Size:** 8 1/8 x 10 7/8. **Cols./Page:** 3. **Col. Width:** 26 nonpareils. **Col. Depth:** 140 agate lines. **Key Personnel:** Ron Clark, Editor/Administration. **Subscription Rates:** $36 individuals; $3 single issue; $48 students Foreign. **Remarks:** Accepts advertising. **URL:** http://www.loma.org.
Ad Rates: BW: $2,200 **Circ:** Non-paid 27,000
4C: $3,195

7123 Mangajin
Mangajin, Inc.
212 14th St. NW Phone: (404)724-0895
Atlanta, GA 30318-5304 Fax: (404)724-0897
Free: (800)552-3206

Magazine of Japanese pop culture and language learning. **Subtitle:** Japanese Pop Culture and Language Learning. **Founded:** June 1990. **Freq:** 10/year. **Print Method:** Web offset. **Trim Size:** 8 1/4 x 10 3/4. **Cols./Page:** 3. **Col. Width:** 2 1/4 inches. **Col. Depth:** 9 3/4 inches. **Key Personnel:** Vaughan P. Simmons, Editor, vaughan@mangajin.com; Kazuo Nishizaki, Advertising Mgr., kazuo@mangajin.com; Alton Wallace, Business Mgr., alton@mangajin.com. **ISSN:** 1051-8177. **Subscription Rates:** $39.95 U.S.; $80 other countries; $5.50 single issue. **Remarks:** Accepts advertising.
Ad Rates: BW: $2,500 **Circ:** Paid ‡27,721
4C: $2,900 Controlled ‡344
PCI: $8

7124 Midwest Poetry Review
PO Box 20236 Phone: (404)350-0714
Atlanta, GA 30325-0236 Fax: (404)352-8417

Poetry review. **Founded:** 1980. **Freq:** Quarterly. **Print Method:** Offset. **Trim Size:** 5 1/2 x 8 1/2. **Cols./Page:** 1. **Col. Width:** Var inches. **Col. Depth:** Var inches. **Key Personnel:** John K. Ottley, Jr., Publisher. **ISSN:** 0745-8738. **Subscription Rates:** $20 U.S.; $5.78 single issue. **Remarks:** Accepts advertising.
Ad Rates: BW: $100 **Circ:** ‡240

7125 Modern Paint and Coatings
Argus Business
6151 Powers Ferry Rd.
Atlanta, GA 30339-2941

Trade magazine on paint and coatings plants management, research, and development. **Subtitle:** Today's Technology For Performance and Compliance. **Founded:** 1910. **Freq:** Monthly. **Print Method:** Offset. **Trim Size:** 8 1/8 x 10 7/8. **Cols./Page:** 3. **Col. Width:** 27 nonpareils. **Col. Depth:** 130 agate lines. **Key Personnel:** Larry Anderson, Editor; Joseph M. Palmer, Publisher. **ISSN:** 0098-7786. **Subscription Rates:** $48 individuals; $68 other countries; $4.50 single issue. **Remarks:** Accepts advertising.
Ad Rates: BW: $2,435 **Circ:** Paid 397
4C: $3,635 Non-paid 17,636

7126 Molecular Pharmacology, an International Journal
Lippincott Williams & Wilkins
Emory University School of Medicine Phone: (404)727-0362 Fax: (404)727-4242
Department of Pharmacology, Rm. 5033
1510 Clifton Rd.
Atlanta, GA 30322-3090
Medical journal. **Founded:** 1965. **Freq:** Monthly. **Print Method:** Offset. **Trim Size:** 8 3/8 x 10 7/8. **Cols./Page:** 2. **Col. Width:** 32 nonpareils. **Col. Depth:** 119 agate lines. **Key Personnel:** Raymond J. Dingledine, Ph.D, Editor; Rich Dodenhoff, Pub. Direc. s, dodenhof@aspet.faseb.org; Esmeralda Galan, Managing Editor, phone (404)727-0362, fax (404)727-4242, galan@pharm.emory.edu. **Subscription Rates:** $130 individuals; $175 other countries. **Remarks:** Accepts advertising. **Available Online. URL:** http://www.molpharm.org. **Alt. Formats:** Mailing labels.
Ad Rates: BW: $565 **Circ:** Paid ‡1,460
4C: $1,305 Non-paid ‡87

7127 Morbidity and Mortality Weekly Report
Centers for Disease Control and Prevention
Epidemiology Program Office Fax: (404)639-3880
1600 Clifton Rd. NE
Mail Stop C08
Atlanta, GA 30333
Publication E-mail: mmwrq@cdc.gov

Magazine focusing on public health problems and diseases. **Subtitle:** Morbidity and Mortality Weekly Report. **Founded:** 1878. **Freq:** Weekly. **Trim Size:** 5 15/16 x 8 1/2. **Remarks:** Advertising not accepted. **URL:** http://www.cdc.gov/epo/mmwr/mmwr.html. **Alt. Formats:** Microform. **Formerly:** MMWR.
Circ: Combined 44,000

7128 Mundo Hispanico
PO Box 13808 Phone: (404)881-0441
Atlanta, GA 30324-0808 Fax: (404)881-6085
Publication E-mail: mundohispanico@mundohispanico.com

Newspaper (tabloid) for the Hispanic community (English and Spanish). **Founded:** 1979. **Freq:** Weekly. **Print Method:** Web offset. **Cols./Page:** 5. **Col. Width:** 1 15/16 inches. **Col. Depth:** 13 3/4 inches. **Key Personnel:** Lino H. Donminguez, Publisher, ldominguez@mundohispanico.com; Fabiola Dortch, General Mgr., fdortch@mundohispanico.com. **ISSN:** 1051-4147. **Subscription Rates:** $75 individuals; $100 industry. **Remarks:** Accepts advertising. **Alt. Formats:** CD-ROM.
Ad Rates: BW: $1,031.25 **Circ:** Paid 110
4C: $1,753.12 Free 17,000
PCI: $17.50

7129 National Real Estate Investor
Intertec Publishing Corp.
6151 Powers Ferry Rd., Ste. 200 Phone: (770)955-2500 Fax: (770)618-0348
Atlanta, GA 30339
Publication E-mail: mgibbs@mindspring.com

Magazine on commercial real estate investment, development and management. **Founded:** 1959. **Freq:** Monthly. **Print Method:** Offset. **Trim Size:** 8 1/8 x 10 7/8. **Cols./Page:** 3. **Col. Width:** 26 nonpareils. **Col. Depth:** 140 agate lines. **Key Personnel:** Ben Johnson, Publisher, phone (770)618-0215, fax (770)618-0343; John Davis, Group Publisher. **ISSN:** 0027-9994. **Subscription Rates:** $132 individuals; $9.50 single issue; $92 students, other countries. **Available Online. URL:** http://www.internetreview.com.
Ad Rates: BW: $4,755 **Circ:** Paid ‡3,971
4C: $6,310 Controlled ‡29,075
PCI: $210

7130 Net News
New South Publishing Inc.
1303 Hightower Trail, Ste. 101 Phone: (770)650-1102
Atlanta, GA 30350 Fax: (770)650-2848
Free: (800)536-5669
Publication E-mail: knowmag@aol.com

Tennis news magazine. **Subtitle:** Official Publication of the Atlanta Lawn Tennis Association (ALTA). **Founded:** 1963. **Freq:** Bimonthly. **Print Method:** Web offset. **Trim Size:** 8 1/8 x 10 7/8. **Cols./Page:** 3. **Key Personnel:** Susan Thompson, Publisher; John Hanna, Assoc. Publisher; Cheryl Fenton, Editor. **Subscription Rates:** Free to paying members. **Remarks:** Accepts advertising.
Ad Rates: BW: $2,590 **Circ:** Paid 50,000
4C: $3,380

7131 New Vico Studies
Philosophy Documentation Center
c/o Donald Phillip Verene
Emory University
Atlanta, GA 30322
Publisher E-mail: phildoc@opie.bgsu.edu
Scholarly journal covering the philosophy of Giambattista Vico. **Founded:** 1983. **Freq:** Annual. **Key Personnel:** Donald Phillip Verene, Editor. **ISSN:** 0733-9542. **Subscription Rates:** $21. **Remarks:** Accepts advertising.
Circ: (Not Reported)

7132 Northside Neighbor/Sandy Springs Neighbor
Neighbor Newspapers, Inc.
5290 Roswell Rd. NW, Ste. M Phone: (404)256-3100
Atlanta, GA 30342 Fax: (404)256-3292

Community newspaper. **Founded:** 1968. **Freq:** Weekly (Wed.). **Print Method:** Offset. **Cols./Page:** 6. **Col. Width:** 26 nonpareils. **Col. Depth:** 301 agate lines. **Key Personnel:** Otis A. Brumby, Jr., Publisher; Faye Edmundson, News Editor; Stephanie deJarnette, Advertising Mgr. **USPS:** 865-620. **Subscription Rates:** $112; $.50 single issue. **Remarks:** Accepts advertising.
Ad Rates: BW: $3,433.50 **Circ:** Paid 133
4C: $3,783.50 Non-paid 24,352
SAU: $17.10
PCI: $27.75

7133 Openings
Scholars Press
PO Box 15399 Phone: (404)727-2343
Atlanta, GA 30333-0399 Fax: (404)727-5140
Publication E-mail: openings@emory.edu
Publisher E-mail: scholars@emory.edu

Electronic publication of professional job listings for religious scholars. **Founded:** 1985. **Freq:** Monthly. **Key Personnel:** Miki McBride-Sala, Manager. **Subscription Rates:** Free to members of AAR and SBL. **URL:** http://scholar.cc.emory.edu.
Circ: 14,000

7134 Our Kids Atlanta
Our Kids Atlanta Magazine
2255 Cumberland Pkwy., No. 1900 Phone: (404)438-1400
Atlanta, GA 30339
Newspaper. **Freq:** Monthly. **Subscription Rates:** $12.
Circ: Free ❑**74,700**
Paid ❑**46**

7135 PEI Magazine
PPA Publications & Events, Inc.
229 Peachtree St. NE, Ste. 2200 Phone: (404)522-8600 Fax: (404)614-6405
International Tower
Atlanta, GA 30303
Digital Imaging for novices to professionals. **Subtitle:** Photo Electronic Imaging. **Founded:** 1958. **Freq:** Monthly. **Print Method:** Offset. **Trim Size:** 8 x 10 7/8. **Cols./Page:** 3. **Col. Width:** 27 nonpareils. **Col. Depth:** 140 agate lines. **Key Personnel:** Kim Brady, Editorial Dir.; Kristen Delaney, Advertising and Circulation Mgr.; Andrew N. Foster, Jr., Publisher; Donna McMahon, Director. **ISSN:** 0146-0153. **Subscription Rates:** $4 News stand; $20 U.S. and other countries; $33 Canada; $50 U.S. and other countries. **Remarks:** Accepts advertising. **URL:** http://www.peimag.com. **Formerly:** Photomethods; Photo Electronic Imaging.
Ad Rates: BW: $5,050 **Circ:** Paid 5,177
4C: $1,200 Non-paid 38,252
PCI: $220

7136 PENSION Management
Intertec Publishing
6151 Powers Ferry Rd. Phone: (770)955-2500
Atlanta, GA 30339 Fax: (770)618-0348
Free: (800)323-8905

Magazine on pension investment and fund administration. **Founded:** 1964. **Freq:** Monthly. **Print Method:** Offset. **Trim Size:** 8 1/8 x 10 7/8. **Cols./Page:** 3. **Col. Width:** 26 nonpareils. **Col. Depth:** 140 agate lines. **Key Personnel:** Lindsay Wyatt, Editor. **ISSN:** 0098-1753. **Subscription Rates:** $68 individuals. **Remarks:** Accepts advertising. **Formerly:** PENSION WORLD.
Ad Rates: BW: $5,195 **Circ:** Combined 28,927
4C: $6,550
PCI: $180

7137 Point of Purchase Magazine
Bill Communications, Inc.
6255 Barfield Rd., Ste. 200 Phone: (404)252-8831
Atlanta, GA 30328-4300 Fax: (404)252-4436
Free: (800)241-9034

Industry publication providing news, market trends, issues, research, and analysis on the point of purchase industry from the perspective of brand marketers and retailers. **Founded:** Oct. 1995. **Freq:** 10/year. **Print Method:** Web offset. **Trim Size:** 10 7/8 x 14 1/2. **Key Personnel:** Stan Berman, Publisher, phone (954)726-5690, fax (954)726-5731; Laurie Najjar, Editor, lnajjar@popmag.com; John Sawyer, Natl. Sales Mgr., jsawyer@popmag.com; Kitty Brigham, Circulation Dir., kbrigham@svi-atl.com. **Subscription Rates:** $70 U.S.; $85 Canada; $95 other countries surface; $190 other countries airmail. **Remarks:** Accepts advertising. **URL:** http://www.popmag.com.
Ad Rates: BW: $4,315 **Circ:** Controlled 18,500
4C: $5,360

7138 Porsche Panorama
Porsche Club of America
912 Lullwater Rd. Phone: (404)378-9823
Atlanta, GA 30307 Fax: (404)377-7041

Magazine for Porsche owners and members of the Porsche Club of America. **Founded:** 1955. **Freq:** Monthly. **Print Method:** Web offset. **Trim Size:** 7 x 9 3/4. **Cols./Page:** 2. **Col. Width:** 2 3/4 inches. **Col. Depth:** 8 3/4 inches. **Key Personnel:** Betty Jo Turner, Editor. **ISSN:** 0147-3565. **Subscription Rates:** $36 members.
Ad Rates: BW: $938 **Circ:** Paid ‡45,000
4C: $1,690 Non-paid ‡2,000

7139 Professional Photographer Storytellers
Professional Photographers of America, Inc.
229 Peachtree St. NE, Ste. 2200 Phone: (404)522-8600 Fax: (404)614-6405
International Tower
Atlanta, GA 30303
Free: (800)786-6277
Publication E-mail: ppaeditor@aol.com
Publisher E-mail: info@ppa-world.org

Subtitle: The Business Magazine of Professional Photography. **Founded:** 1907. **Freq:** Monthly. **Print Method:** Offset. **Trim Size:** 8 1/2 x 11. **Cols./Page:** 3. **Col. Width:** 26 nonpareils. **Col. Depth:** 140 agate lines. **Key Personnel:** Kimberly Brady, Editorial Dir.; E. Sapwater, Exec. Editor; Donna McMahon, Director; Andrew N. Foster, Jr., Publisher; Kristen Delaney, Advertising and Circulation Mgr. **ISSN:** 0033-0167. **Subscription Rates:** $27 individuals; $45 Canada; $66 other countries. **Remarks:** Accepts advertising. **URL:** http://www.ppa-world.org. **Formerly:** Professional Photographer.
Ad Rates: BW: $2,995 **Circ:** Paid 25,332
4C: $1,200
PCI: $165

7140 Resource
Life Office Management Association
2300 Windy Ridge Pkwy., Ste. 600 Phone: (770)951-1770 Fax: (770)984-6417
Atlanta, GA 30339-8443
Free: (800)275-5662

Trade magazine for the life insurance industry. **Freq:** Monthly. **Print Method:** Web offset. **Trim Size:** 8 1/8 x 10 7/8. **Subscription Rates:** Free to qualified subscribers. **Remarks:** Accepts advertising.
Ad Rates: BW: $2,200 **Circ:** Non-paid 27,000
4C: $3,225

7141 Retail Ink
International Specialty Shops Association
PO Box 14456 Phone: (404)237-2907
Atlanta, GA 30324 Fax: (404)237-0093

Consumer magazine covering the retail market. **Founded:** 1992.

7142 RF Design
Intertec Publishing
6151 Powers Ferry Rd. Phone: (770)955-2500
Atlanta, GA 30339 Fax: (770)618-0348
Free: (800)323-8905

Magazine covering the R.F. engineering field. **Subtitle:** Engineering Principles and Practice. **Founded:** 1978. **Freq:** Monthly. **Print Method:** Offset. **Trim Size:** 7 7/8 x 10 7/8. **Cols./Page:** 3. **Col. Width:** 13.5 picas. **Col. Depth:** 58.5 picas. **Key Personnel:** Don Bishop, Editor; Gregg Miller, Contact; Pat Werner, Contact. **ISSN:** 0163-321X. **Subscription Rates:** $42 individuals; $62 other countries; $102 by mail airmail. **Remarks:** Accepts advertising.
Ad Rates: BW: $4,185 **Circ:** Paid 200
4C: $4,960 Non-paid 40,000

7143 SCLC National Magazine
Southern Christian Leadership Conference (SCLC)
334 Auburn Ave. NE Phone: (404)522-1420
Atlanta, GA 30303 Fax: (404)524-7957
Free: (800)421-0472

Publication directed toward black and Civil Rights communities. **Subtitle:** The National Publication of the Southern Christian Leadership Conference. **Freq:** Bimonthly. **Trim Size:** 8 1/2 x 11. **Cols./Page:** 2. **Key Personnel:** Dr. Steven W. Blood, Sr., Publisher; Mike Dejoie, Editor; Marcia Nobler, Advertising Dir.; Janet Walz, Office Mgr.
Circ: 400,000

7144 Shopping Center World
Intertec Publishing
6151 Powers Ferry Rd. Phone: (770)955-2500
Atlanta, GA 30339 Fax: (770)618-0348
Free: (800)323-8905

Publication focusing on the retail commercial real estate industry. **Founded:** 1972. **Freq:** Monthly. **Print Method:** Web offset. **Trim Size:** 8 1/8 x 10 7/8. **Cols./Page:** 3. **Col. Width:** 13 picas. **Col. Depth:** 60 picas. **Key Personnel:** Teresa DeFranks, Editor, teresa-defranks@intertec.com; John Davis, Publisher, john-davis@intertec.com; Walter Coward, Circulation Mgr., walter-coward@intertec.com. **Subscription Rates:** $79 individuals; $10 single issue. **Remarks:** Accepts advertising. **URL:** http://www.internetreview.com.
Circ: Paid 830
Controlled 35,000

7145 South Atlantic Review
South Atlantic Modern Language Association
Georgia State University Phone: (404)651-2693
University Plaza Fax: (404)651-2858
Atlanta, GA 30303-3083
Publisher E-mail: engdjr@panther.gsu.edu

Scholarly journal containing articles and essays on the modern languages and literatures by members of the South Atlantic Modern Language Association. **Founded:** 1935. **Freq:** Quarterly. **Print Method:** Offset. **Trim Size:** 6 x 9. **Cols./Page:** 1. **Col. Width:** 50 nonpareils. **Col. Depth:** 112 agate lines. **Key Personnel:** Matthew Roudane, Editor. **ISSN:** 0277-335X. **Subscription Rates:** $25; $35 other countries. **Remarks:** Accepts advertising.
Ad Rates: BW: $150 **Circ:** Paid ‡3,800
Non-paid ‡200

7146 Southeast Food Service News
Southeast Publishing Co., Inc.
PO Box 47719 Phone: (770)452-1807
Atlanta, GA 30362 Fax: (770)457-3829
Publication E-mail: sfns@ewdro.com
Publisher E-mail: sfsn@mjn.com

Magazine (tabloid) serving the food industry. **Founded:** Nov. 1977. **Freq:** Monthly. **Print Method:** Offset-Web. **Trim Size:** 11 x 15. **Cols./Page:** 5. **Col. Width:** 1 3/4 inches. **Col. Depth:** 13 3/4 inches. **Key Personnel:** David Noel, Editor; R. Dal Rasmussen, Publisher; Elliott Fischer, Newspaper Advertising Mgr. **ISSN:** 0199-2805. **Subscription Rates:** $32 individuals. **Remarks:** Accepts advertising.
Ad Rates: BW: $2,452 **Circ:** Paid ‡2,091
4C: $3,427 Controlled ‡22,597
PCI: $41.25

7147 The Southern Journal of Optometry
Southern Council of Optometrists, Inc.
4661 N. Shallowford Rd. Phone: (770)451-8206
Atlanta, GA 30338-6322 Fax: (770)451-3156

Optometry journal. **Founded:** 1959. **Freq:** Annual. **Print Method:** Offset. **Trim Size:** 8 3/8 x 11. **Cols./Page:** 2. **Col. Width:** 33 nonpareils. **Col. Depth:** 119 agate lines. **Key Personnel:** Lyman Norden, O.D., Editor; Sam J. Galloway, Jr., Advertising Mgr. **Subscription Rates:** $16 individuals. **Remarks:** Accepts advertising.
Ad Rates: BW: $715 **Circ:** Paid 5,437
4C: $1,465 Non-paid 347

7148 Southern Voice
Window Media
1095 Zonolite Rd., Ste. 100 Phone: (404)876-1819
Atlanta, GA 30306 Fax: (404)876-2709
Publication E-mail: southvoice@aol.com

Newspaper covering lesbian and gay issues. **Subtitle:** All the News for Your Life. And Your Style. **Founded:** Mar. 1, 1988. **Freq:** Weekly. **Trim Size:** 11 x 13 1/2. **Cols./Page:** 4. **Col. Width:** 2 1/4 inches. **Col. Depth:** 11 1/2 inches. **Key Personnel:** Chris Crain, Editor and Publisher; Rick Ellsasser, Publisher. **Subscription Rates:** $.75 single issue; $80 individuals annual. **URL:** http://www.sovo.com; http://www.southernvoice.com.
Ad Rates: BW: $745 **Circ:** Controlled ‡30,000

7149 Sporting Goods Dealer
Bill Communications, Inc.
6255 Barfield Rd., Ste. 200 Phone: (404)252-8831
Atlanta, GA 30328-4300 Fax: (404)252-4436
Free: (800)241-9034

Magazine which offers expert reporting on trends affecting team dealers and ret ailers who service schools, colleges, pro and local teams. **Subtitle:** The Voice of Team Dealers Since 1899. **Founded:** Oct. 1899. **Freq:** Monthly. **Print Method:** Offset. **Trim Size:** 10 7/8 x 8 3/8. **Cols./Page:** 4. **Col. Width:** 10 1/2 picas. **Col. Depth:** 59 picas. **Key Personnel:** Darren Drevik, Editor-in-Chief. **ISSN:** 0038-8017. **Subscription Rates:** Free to qualified subscribers; $100. $6 single issue. **Remarks:** Accepts advertising. **URL:** http://www.sgdealer.com.
Ad Rates: BW: $2,860 **Circ:** Controlled ‡18,000
4C: $3,700
PCI: $105

7150 Swimming Pool/Spa Age
Intertec Publishing Corp.
6151 Powers Ferry Rd. Phone: (770)618-0279
Atlanta, GA 30339 Fax: (770)618-0343

Magazine providing feature articles, products, and news designed to help pool/spa builders, dealers, retailers, and service technicians. **Founded:** 1926. **Freq:** Monthly. **Print Method:** Offset. **Trim Size:** 11 x 15. **Cols./Page:** 4. **Col. Width:** 13 1/2 picas. **Col. Depth:** 14 inches. **Key Personnel:** Michael Grossman, Publisher; Mike Pallerino, Editor; David Premo, Group Pub. **ISSN:** 0899-1022. **Subscription Rates:** $48 individuals; $4.25 single issue. **Remarks:** Accepts advertising.
Ad Rates: BW: $2,155 **Circ:** Controlled 17,064
4C: $2,771

7151 Symbol
Pasco Publishing, Inc.
120 Interstate N. Pkwy. E., No. 445 Phone: (770)956-1207
Atlanta, GA 30339 Fax: (770)988-8976
Free: (888)679-6265
Publication E-mail: symbolmag@aol.com

Lifestyle magazine. **Subtitle:** Of Southern Lifestyle. **Founded:** 1986. **Freq:** Monthly. **Print Method:** Web offset. **Trim Size:** 8 3.75 x 10.875. **Cols./Page:** 3. **Col. Width:** 2 1/4 inches. **Col. Depth:** 10 inches. **Key Personnel:** Jane Gaston, Managing Editor, gastonpeac@aol.com; Gregory A. Caccavale, Publisher. **Subscription Rates:** $24 individuals; $3.95 single issue. **Remarks:** Accepts advertising. **Formerly:** Peachtree Magazine (May 1998).
Ad Rates: BW: $2,500 **Circ:** ‡110,000
4C: $4,000

7152 TAPPI JOURNAL
Technical Association of Pulp and Paper Industry (TAPPI)
Technology Park/Atlanta Phone: (770)446-1400
PO Box 105113 Fax: (770)209-7400
Atlanta, GA 30348-5113
Free: (800)332-8686
Publication E-mail: tj@tappi.org

Magazine on pulp and paper research, production, conversion, and packaging. **Founded:** 1949. **Freq:** Monthly. **Print Method:** Offset. **Trim Size:** 8 1/8 x 10 7/8. **Cols./Page:** 3 and 2. **Col. Width:** 26 and 39 nonpareils. **Col. Depth:** 140 agate lines. **Key Personnel:** Don Meadows, Editor, phone (770)209-7214, dmeadows@tappi.org; Mary Beth Bennett, Business Mgr., phone (770)209-7210, mbennett@tappi.org; Beth R. Puett, Advertising Dir., phone (770)209-7216, fax (720)209-7517, bpuetl@tappi.org. **ISSN:** 0734-1415. **Subscription Rates:** $95 included in membership fee; $7.50 single issue; $11 single issue to nonmembers. **Remarks:** Accepts advertising. **URL:** http://www.tappi.org. **Alt. Formats:** CD-ROM; Microfiche; Microform.
Ad Rates: BW: $4,875 **Circ:** Paid 29,707
4C: $7,100 Non-paid 10,313
PCI: $100

7153 Tech Notes
Jaye Communications, Inc.
2841 Akers Mill Rd. SE Phone: (770)984-9444
Atlanta, GA 30339-3104 Fax: (770)933-9072

Publication featuring a calander of high technology events. **Freq:** Weekly. **Key Personnel:** Mike Adkinson, Editor and Publisher; William Pollock, Managing Editor. **Subscription Rates:** $27. $15.95 single issue. **Remarks:** Advertising accepted; rates available upon request. **Available Online. URL:** http://www.jaye.com.
Circ: (Not Reported)

7154 Tech Topics
Georgia Tech Alumni Association
190 North Ave. NW Phone: (404)894-2391
Atlanta, GA 30313 Fax: (404)894-5113
Publication E-mail: editor@alumni.gatech.edu

Alumni newspaper. **Founded:** Sept. 1971. **Freq:** Quarterly. **Print Method:** Web offset. **Trim Size:** 11 x 15. **Cols./Page:** 4. **Key Personnel:** John C. Dunn, Editor; Hoyt Coffee, Assoc. Editor; Robb Stanek, Marketing & Advertising Dir. **ISSN:** 1062-077X. **Subscription Rates:** Free to qualified subscribers. **Remarks:** Accepts advertising.
Ad Rates: BW: $1,505 **Circ:** Controlled **80,000**
4C: $2,065

7155 The Technique
Georgia Institute of Technology
353 Ferst Dr., Rm. 137 Phone: (404)894-2831
Atlanta, GA 30332-0290 Fax: (404)894-1650
Publication E-mail: editor@technique.gatech.edu

Collegiate newspaper. **Subtitle:** The South's Livliest College Newspaper. **Founded:** 1911. **Freq:** Weekly (Fri.). **Print Method:** Offset. **Trim Size:** 5 x 15. **Cols./Page:** 5. **Col. Width:** 25 nonpareils. **Col. Depth:** 192 agate lines. **Key Personnel:** Greg Scherrer, Editor; Rose Mary Wells, Publications Mgr., rosemary.wells@vpss.gated.edu. **Subscription Rates:** $25 individuals. **Remarks:** Advertising not accepted for alcoholic beverages and tobacco products. **Available Online. URL:** http://www.gatech.edu/nique.
Ad Rates: GLR: $.50 **Circ:** Paid ‡300
BW: $900 Non-paid ‡10,700
4C: $1,300
SAU: $12
PCI: $12

7156 Textile World
Intertec Publishing
6151 Powers Ferry Rd. Phone: (770)955-2500
Atlanta, GA 30339 Fax: (770)618-0348
Free: (800)323-8905

International magazine on textile manufacturing and man-made fiber products. **Founded:** 1868. **Freq:** Monthly. **Print Method:** Offset. **Trim Size:** 8 x 10 3/4. **Cols./Page:** 3. **Col. Width:** 24 nonpareils. **Col. Depth:** 123 agate lines. **Key Personnel:** McAllister Isaacs, Editor, mac-is-sacs@intertec.com; Gary De Hart, Assoc. Pub./Sales, phone (770)618-0465, gary-dehart@intertec.com. **ISSN:** 0040-5213. **Subscription Rates:** $45 individuals; $80 foreign, surface mail; $110 foreign, air mail; Free to qualified subscribers. **Remarks:** Accepts advertising.
Ad Rates: BW: $5,150 **Circ:** Paid 617
4C: $6,950 Controlled 31,803

7157 Textiles Panamericanos
Billian Publishing, Inc.
2100 Powers Ferry Rd. Phone: (770)955-5656
Atlanta, GA 30339 Fax: (770)952-0669
Free: (800)533-8484

Textile manufacturing magazine. Printed in Spanish. (Latin American circulation.). **Founded:** 1941. **Freq:** Quarterly. **Print Method:** Offset. **Trim Size:** 8 x 10 3/4. **Cols./Page:** 3. **Col. Width:** 26 nonpareils. **Col. Depth:** 140 agate lines. **Key Personnel:** J.A. Woodroffe, Editor; Connie Somozo, Advertising Mgr. **Subscription Rates:** $40 individuals; $448 other countries; $15 single issue. **Remarks:** Accepts advertising.
Ad Rates: BW: $2,810 **Circ:** Paid ‡30
4C: $4,420 Controlled ‡11,243
PCI: $85

7158 Truck Accessory News
Bill Communications, Inc.
6255 Barfield Rd., Ste. 200 Phone: (404)252-8831
Atlanta, GA 30328-4300 Fax: (404)252-4436
Free: (800)241-9034

Trade magazine covering product specifics for truck and automotive aftermarket retailers in the light-truck accessory market. **Subtitle:** Product and Trends for Aftermarket Retailers. **Founded:** 1993. **Freq:** Bimonthly. **Print Method:** Web offset. **Trim Size:** 8 1/8 x 10 7/8. **Cols./Page:** 3. **Key Personnel:** Alfreda Vaughn, Editor, avaughn@svi-atl.com; Randy Easton, Publisher/National Sales Mgr.; Kitty Brigham, Circulation Dir. **ISSN:** 1075-8178. **Subscription Rates:** $37 individuals; $3 single issue. **Remarks:** Accepts advertising.
Ad Rates: BW: $2,465 **Circ:** Controlled ‡10,000
4C: $1,510

7159 Veranda
Veranda Publications Inc.
455 East Paces Ferry Rd., Ste. 216 Phone: (404)261-3603
Atlanta, GA 30305 Fax: (404)364-9772
Free: (800)767-5863

Consumer magazine featuring interiors, gardens, flowers, antiques, architecture, cuisine, designer interviews, travel and literary excerpts. **Founded:** Mar. 1987. **Freq:** Bimonthly. **Print Method:** Offset. **Trim Size:** 8 3/8 x 10 7/8. **Key Personnel:** Lisa Newsom, Editor. **ISSN:** 1040-8150. **Subscription Rates:** $28 individuals; $52 other countries; $5.50 single issue. **Remarks:** Accepts advertising.
Ad Rates: BW: $20,310 **Circ:** Paid ★**354,783**
4C: $26,380

7160 Veterans' Bulletin
Georgia Dept. of Veterans Service
Floyd Veterans Bldg., 970-E Phone: (404)656-5933
Atlanta, GA 30334 Fax: (404)656-7006

Magazine for veterans, their dependents, and retired citizens. **Founded:** 1948. **Freq:** Quarterly. **Print Method:** Offset. **Trim**

Size: 8 1/2 x 11. **Key Personnel:** Preston Charles, Editor. **Remarks:** Advertising not accepted.
Circ: Controlled ‡2,500

7161 Waste Age
Intertec Publishing
6151 Powers Ferry Rd. Phone: (770)955-2500
Atlanta, GA 30339 Fax: (770)618-0348
Free: (800)323-8905

Waste removal and disposal magazine. **Subtitle:** The Business Magazine for Waste Management Professionals. **Founded:** 1958. **Freq:** Monthly. **Print Method:** Offset. **Trim Size:** 8 1/8 x 10 7/8. **Cols./Page:** 3. **Col. Width:** 26 nonpareils. **Col. Depth:** 140 agate lines. **Key Personnel:** William M. Wolpin, Editor and Publisher, phone (770)618-0112, fax (770)618-0349, bill_ wolpin@intertec.com. **ISSN:** 0161-035X. **Subscription Rates:** $55 individuals. **Remarks:** Accepts advertising. **Formerly:** World Wastes.
Ad Rates: BW: $2,475 **Circ:** Paid 1,000
4C: $3,605 Non-paid 42,000
PCI: $75

7162 Wesleyan Christian Advocate
Wesleyan Christian Advocate, Inc.
159 Ralph McGill Blvd. NE Phone: (404)659-8809
PO Box 54455 Fax: (404)659-1727
Atlanta, GA 30308
Publication E-mail: wcadvocate@mindspring.com

Tabloid. **Subtitle:** Official News Weekly of Georgia United Methodism. **Founded:** 1836. **Freq:** Weekly. **Print Method:** Offset. **Trim Size:** 11 3/8 x 15. **Cols./Page:** 5. **Col. Width:** 28 nonpareils. **Col. Depth:** 195 agate lines. **Key Personnel:** Rev. Mike Morgan, Editor. **USPS:** 674-700. **Subscription Rates:** $16 individuals.
Ad Rates: BW: $625 **Circ:** ‡21,000
PCI: $24

7163 Cox Enterprises
1400 Lake Hearn Dr. Phone: (404)843-5000
Atlanta, GA 30319 Fax: (404)843-5775

Key Personnel: James Robbins, President. **Cities Served:** Gainsville, Ocala, Pensacola, FL; Cedar Rapids, IA; Quint Cities, IL; Saginaw, MI; Roanoke, NC; Omaha, NE; Cleveland, OH; Oklahoma City, OK; Virginia Beach, VA.

KCJZ-FM - See San Antonio, Texas

7164 KJSR-FM - 103.3
1400 Lake Hearn Dr., N. E. Phone: (918)493-3434
Atlanta, GA 30319

Format: Classic Rock. **Owner:** Cox Radio, Inc., at above address. **Formerly:** KTFX-FM. **Operating Hours:** Continuous. **ADI:** Tulsa (Bartlesville), OK. **Key Personnel:** Laurie Harbison, General Sales Mgr.; Chuck Browning, V. P./ General Mgr.; Steve Fernandez, Program Dir.; Cy Valanejad, Marketing Dir.; LaDonna Ervin, Traffic Dir. **Wattage:** 100,000.

7165 Time Warner Cable
115 Perimeter Center Pl. NE, Ste. 550 Phone: (770)394-8837
Fax: (404)698-0228
Atlanta, GA 30346-1238

Formerly: MetroVision Inc. **Key Personnel:** Henry Harris, President.

7166 WABE-FM - 90.1
740 Bismark Rd. NE Phone: (404)827-8900
Atlanta, GA 30324-4102 Fax: (404)827-8956

Format: Public Radio; News; Classical. **Networks:** National Public Radio (NPR). **Owner:** Atlanta Board of Education, at above address. **Founded:** 1948. **Operating Hours:** Continuous; 40% network, 60% local. **ADI:** Atlanta (Athens & Rome), GA. **Key Personnel:** Earl Johnson, Manager, phone (404)827-8989, ejohnson@wabe.org; Lois Reitzes, Program Dir., phone (404)827-8984, lois@wabe.org; Eric Weston, Promotions, phone (404)827-8950, eweston@wabe-wpba.org. **Wattage:** 100,000. **Ad Rates:** Noncommercial.

7167 WAEC-AM - 860
1465 Northside Dr., Ste. 114 Phone: (404)355-8600
Atlanta, GA 30318 Fax: (404)355-4156

Format: Religious. **Networks:** Independent. **Founded:** 1947. **Operating Hours:** Continuous. **ADI:** Atlanta (Athens & Rome), GA. **Key Personnel:** Paul Ploener, General Mgr.; Larry Young, Program Dir. **Wattage:** 5000. **Ad Rates:** $30-45 for 30 seconds; $40-55 for 60 seconds.

7168 WAFS-AM - 920
1827 Powers Ferry Rd., Ste. 200 Phone: (770)226-0920
Fax: (770)226-0927
Atlanta, GA 30339
E-mail: wafs@moody.edu

Format: Religious. **Networks:** USA Radio; Moody Broadcasting. **Owner:** Moody Bible Institute of Chicago, 820 North LaSalle Blvd., Chicago, IL 60610, (312)329-4000. **Founded:** 1989. **Operating Hours:** Continuous. **ADI:** Atlanta (Athens & Rome), GA. **Key Personnel:** Chuck Burge, Production Dir.; Mary Jo Kneiser, Announcer; Sharon Oliver, Admin. Asst.; Bob Lipscomb, Chief Engineer; Ray Hashley, Station Mgr.; Tracy Haney, News. **Local Programs:** *New Day Atlanta*, Chuck Burge; *Prime Time Atlanta*, Tracy Haney. **Wattage:** 5000 day; 1000 night. **Ad Rates:** Noncommercial.

7169 WAGA-TV - 5
1551 Briarcliff Rd. NE Phone: (404)875-5555
Atlanta, GA 30306 Fax: (404)898-0238
E-mail: fox5@atlanta.com

Format: Commercial TV. **Networks:** Fox. **Owner:** New World Comunications, 3200 Windy Hill RD., Ste 1100 West, Atlanta, GA 30339, (770)955-0045, Fax: (770)563-9600. **Founded:** 1949. **Operating Hours:** Continuous. **ADI:** Atlanta (Athens & Rome), GA. **Key Personnel:** Gene McHugh, Vice Pres./GM, phone (404)898-0235, fax (404)898-0238; Bill Schneider, Vice President, phone (404)898-0297, fax (404)898-0277; John Kukla, Creative Services Dir., phone (404)898-0191, fax (404)898-0293; Budd McEntee, Vice Pres. News, phone (404)898-0110, fax (404)898-0169; David Jones, Vice Pres. Engineering/OPS, phone (404)890-0215, fax (404)724-4400; Kathy Soifer, Vice Pres. Programming & Promotion, phone (404)898-0246; Michael Holmes, Vice Pres. Finance, phone (404)898-0200, fax (404)898-0206. **Wattage:** 100,000. **Ad Rates:** $125-35,000 per unit. **URL:** http://www.wagatv.com.

7170 WALR-FM - 104.7
209 CNN Center Phone: (404)688-0068
Atlanta, GA 30303 Fax: (404)688-4262

Format: Adult Contemporary; Urban Contemporary. **Networks:** ABC. **Owner:** David Dickey, at above address. **Founded:** 1986. **Formerly:** WAGO-FM (1989). **Operating Hours:** Continuous. **ADI:** Atlanta (Athens & Rome), GA. **Key Personnel:** David Dickey, General/Station Mgr.; Matt Ross, Sales Mgr.; Kris McClendon, Program Dir.; Sheree Rosende, Business Mgr. **Local Programs:** *Issues & Answers*, Ron Sailor; *Music of Praise & Worship*, Reggie Gay. **Wattage:** 50,000.

7171 WAOK-AM - 1380
1201 Peachtree St. Phone: (404)898-8900
Ste.800 Fax: (404)898-8916
Atlanta, GA 30361

Format: Gospel. **Networks:** NBC. **Founded:** 1954. **Operating Hours:** Continuous. **ADI:** Atlanta (Athens & Rome), GA. **Key Personnel:** Rick Caffey, Contact, phone (404)898-8921, fax (404)898-8915, caffeyr@cbsradio.com. **Wattage:** 5,000. **Ad Rates:** Advertising accepted; rates available upon request.

7172 WATL-TV - 36
1 Monroe Pl. Phone: (404)881-3600
Atlanta, GA 30324 Fax: (404)881-3635

Format: Commercial TV. **Networks:** Warner Brothers Studios. **Owner:** QWest Broadcasting, 1661 Canal St., New Orleans, LA 70112, (504)525-3838, Fax: (504)564-0952. **Founded:** 1969. **Operating Hours:** 6 a.m.-2 a.m. daily; 2 a.m.-6 a.m. Tue.-Sat. **ADI:** Atlanta (Athens & Rome), GA. **Key Personnel:** Don Hess, Program Mgr.; Veon Mynatt, Research Dir.; JoAnna Hemleb, General Sales Mgr. **Wattage:** 2,030,000 video; 204,500 audio. **Ad Rates:** Advertising accepted; rates available upon request. **URL:** http://www.wb36.com.

7173 WCLK-FM - 91.9
111 James P. Brawley Dr. SW Phone: (404)880-8273
Atlanta, GA 30314-4207 Fax: (404)880-8869

Format: Public Radio; Jazz. **Networks:** National Public Radio (NPR). **Owner:** Clark Atlanta University, Fair at James P. Brawley Dr., Atlanta, GA 30314, (404)880-8000. **Founded:** 1974. **Operating Hours:** Continuous; 30% network, 70% local. **ADI:** Atlanta (Athens & Rome), GA. **Key Personnel:** Wendy Williams, Station Mgr.; Ben Fagan, Program Dir.; Cherry Ann Holder, Promotions & Public Affairs; Shenita Vanish, Membership; Deb Moore, Music Dir.; Ben Casey, Program Dir. **Wattage:** 2500. **Ad Rates:** Noncommercial. **URL:** http://www.cau-wclk.com.

WCLP-TV - See Chatsworth

7174 WCNN-AM - 680
209 CNN Center Phone: (404)688-0068
Atlanta, GA 30303-2705 Fax: (404)688-4262

Format: Talk; Urban Contemporary; Sports. **Owner:** Lewis Dickey, at above address. **Founded:** 1967. **Formerly:** WGTW-AM (1987). **Operating Hours:** Continuous. **ADI:** Atlanta (Athens & Rome), GA. **Key Personnel:** Lewis Dickey, Jr, General Mgr.; Shelia O'Connor, General Sales Mgr.; Yolanda Y. Nasttburn, Office Mgr.; Erica Thornton, Business Mgr.; Kris McClendon, FM Programming; Mike Thompson, AM Programming; Rick Cafey, Station Mgr. **Local Programs:** *Herb & Terrence*; *M&M Guys*; *"Steak" Shapiro/AJ & Bean.* **Wattage:** 50,000.

7175 WDWD-AM - 590
210 Interstate N. Pkwy.101 Phone: (770)541-0590
6th Fl. Fax: (770)952-7461
Atlanta, GA 30339

Networks: ABC. **Owner:** ABC, Inc., 77 W. 66th St., New York, NY 10023, (212)456-7777. **Founded:** 1938. **Formerly:** WPLO-AM (1986); WKHX-AM. **Operating Hours:** Continuous; 100% local. **ADI:** Atlanta (Athens & Rome), GA. **Key Personnel:** Victor Sansone, President/General Mgr.; Kathleen Seguin, Operations Dir.; Kellie Welborn, Operations Coord.; Bill Massey, Chief Engineer. **Wattage:** 5000. **Ad Rates:** Advertising accepted; rates available upon request. Combined advertising rates available with WYAY-FM.

7176 WFOX-FM - 97.1
2000 Riveredge Pkwy., Ste. 797 Phone: (770)953-9369
Atlanta, GA 30328-4682 Fax: (770)955-5483

Format: Oldies. **Networks:** Independent. **Founded:** 1965. **Operating Hours:** Continuous. **ADI:** Atlanta (Athens & Rome), GA. **Key Personnel:** Marv Nyren, Vice President, phone (770)953-9369, fax (770)955-5483, mnyren971@aol.com. **Local Programs:** *Perspective*, Greg Black; *Randy & Spiff Show*, Mitch Elliott. **Wattage:** 100,000. **Ad Rates:** $250 for 30 seconds; $500 for 60 seconds.

7177 WGKA-AM - 1190
2999 Piedmont Rd. NE Phone: (404)231-2395
Atlanta, GA 30305 Fax: (404)231-1200
E-mail: wgka@mindspring.com

Format: Classical; Educational; Information. **Networks:** Concert Music Network (CMN). **Owner:** WGKA, Inc., at above address. **Founded:** 1955. **Operating Hours:** Sunrise-sunset. **ADI:** Atlanta (Athens & Rome), GA. **Key Personnel:** Joe Weber, President; Alex Buckellew, Office Mgr./Traffic; Mike Rose, General Mgr. **Local Programs:** *Atlanta Arts Calendar*, *Atlanta Symphony Preview*, *Consumer Forum*. **Wattage:** 10,000. **Ad Rates:** $28-48 for 30 seconds; $35-60 for 60 seconds.

7178 WGNX-TV - 46
1810 Briarcliff Rd. NE Phone: (404)325-4646
Atlanta, GA 30329-4097 Fax: (404)327-3003
E-mail: wgnxtv@aol.com

Format: Commercial TV. **Networks:** CBS. **Owner:** Tribune Broadcasting Co., 435 N. Michigan Ave., Ste. 1900, Chicago, IL 60611-4041, (312)222-3333. **Founded:** 1971. **Formerly:** WANX-TV. **Operating Hours:** Continuous. **ADI:** Atlanta (Athens & Rome), GA. **Key Personnel:** Herman Ramsey, General Mgr.; Michael Norton, Sales Mgr.; Mike Dreaden, News Dir.

7179 WGST-AM - 640
550 Pharr Rd. NE, No. 400 Phone: (404)233-0640
Atlanta, GA 30363 Fax: (404)237-5856

Format: Talk; News. **Networks:** ABC; CBS. **Operating Hours:** Continuous; 35% network, 65% local. **ADI:** Atlanta (Athens & Rome), GA. **Key Personnel:** Bob Houghton, Contact; Eric Seidel, Station Mgr.; Steve Yaulios, General Sales Mgr. **Wattage:** 50,000.

7180 WGST-FM - 105.7
50 Pharr Rd. NE Phone: (404)233-0640
Atlanta, GA 30363 Fax: (404)237-5856

Format: Country. **Networks:** ABC. **Founded:** 1957. **Absorbed:** WCHK-FM. **Operating Hours:** Continuous. **ADI:** Atlanta (Athens & Rome), GA. **Key Personnel:** Byron L. Dobbs, Vice-President. **Wattage:** 50,000. **Ad Rates:** $26-38 for 30 seconds; $34-48 for 60 seconds.

7181 WKHX-FM - 101.5
210 Interstate North Pkwy., 6th Fl. Phone: (770)955-0101
Fax: (770)953-4612
Atlanta, GA 30339

Format: Country. **Networks:** ABC. **Owner:** ABC, Inc., 77 W. 66th St., New York, NY 10023, (212)456-7777. **Founded:** 1950. **Formerly:** WBIE-FM (1981). **Operating Hours:** Continuous; 100% local. **ADI:** Atlanta (Athens & Rome), GA. **Key Personnel:** Victor Sansone, President/General Manager; Neil H. McGinley, Operations Mgr.; Jacque Colletti, Sales Director; Deborah Richards, News Dir.; Bill Massey, Chief Engineer; Susan B. Flinchum, Office Mgr.; Tobi Lyons, Promotions Dir. **Wattage:** 100,000. **Ad Rates:** Advertising accepted; rates available upon request. Combined advertising rates available with WYAY-FM.

7182 WKLS-FM - 96.1
1800 Century Blvd. NE, Ste. 1200 Phone: (404)325-0960
Atlanta, GA 30345-3268 Fax: (404)325-8715
E-mail: bhelbusk@96rock.com

Format: Album-Oriented Rock (AOR); Classic Rock. **Networks:** Independent. **Founded:** 1960. **Operating Hours:** Continuous; 100% local. **ADI:** Atlanta (Athens & Rome), GA. **Key Personnel:** Tom Connolly, Pres./Gen. Mgr.; Alan Rothenberg, General Sales Mgr.; Pat Envin, Promotions Dir.; Beth Kepple, Music/News Dir.; Bob Helbush, Chief Engineer, bhelbush@96rock.com. **Wattage:** 100,000. **URL:** http://www.96rock.com.

7183 WNGM-TV - 34
200 N. Cobb Pkwy., No. 114 Phone: (770)528-1400
Marietta, GA 30062 Fax: (770)528-1403

Format: Commercial TV. **Networks:** Independent. **Owner:** Whitehead Media, Inc., 3970 RCA Blvd., Ste. 7007, Palm Beach Gardens, FL 33410-4231, (561)686-3434, Fax: (561)691-1177. **Founded:** 1989. **Operating Hours:** Continuous. **ADI:** Atlanta (Athens & Rome), GA. **Key Personnel:** Eddie Whitehead, General Mgr.; Jack Crumpler, Program Executive/Gen. Sales Mgr.; Bill Owens, Production Mgr./Promotions Dir.; Al Saltzman, Chief Engineer; Michelle L. Kirkbride, Accounting Mgr.; M. Wynn Westmoreland, Business Mgr. **Local Programs:** *Mornings With Meg*; *North Georgia Gospel*; *30 Minutes of Rock*. **Ad Rates:** $40 for 30 seconds.

7184 WNNX-FM - 99.7
3405 Piedmont Rd., Ste. 500 Phone: (404)266-0997
Atlanta, GA 30305 Fax: (404)364-5855

Format: Alternative/New Music/Progressive. **Owner:** Susquehanna Broadcasting Co., PO Box 2026, York, PA 17405, (717)848-5500, Free: (800)876-1436. **Founded:** Oct. 1993. **Formerly:** WAPW-FM (1986). **Operating Hours:** Continuous; 3% network, 97% local. **ADI:** Atlanta (Athens & Rome), GA. **Key Personnel:** Reed Haggard, General Sales Mgr., rhaggard@99x.com; Mark Renier, General Mgr.; Leslie Fram, Program Dir.; John Riemensschneider, Local Sales Manager, jriemens@99x.com. **Local Programs:** *Viewpoint Atlanta*, Melissa Carter. **Wattage:** 100,000 ERP. **URL:** http://www.com/99X.

7185 WPBA-TV - 30
740 Bismarck Rd. NE Phone: (404)827-8900
Atlanta, GA 30324 Fax: (404)827-8956

Format: Public TV. **Networks:** Public Broadcasting Service (PBS). **Founded:** 1958. **Formerly:** WETV-TV. **Operating Hours:** Continuous. **ADI:** Atlanta (Athens & Rome), GA. **Key Personnel:** Eric Weston, Contact; Milton C. Clipper, Jr, General Mgr.; Joanne Cox, Program Mgr.; Jeffrey Bennett, Business Mgr. **Local Programs:** *King Festival*; *Laymen Lawyer*.

7186 WPCH-FM - 94.9
1819 Peachtree Rd., Ste. 700 Phone: (404)367-0949
Atlanta, GA 30309 Fax: (404)362-9490

Format: Soft Rock. **Networks:** Independent. **Founded:** 1972. **Operating Hours:** Continuous. **ADI:** Atlanta (Athens & Rome), GA. **Key Personnel:** Vance Dillard, Station Mgr.; Tom Connolly, General Mgr.; Steve Goss, Program Dir.; Kari Dean, News Dir. **Wattage:** 100,000. **URL:** http://www.peach949.com.

7187 WQXI-AM - 790
1 Capital City Plaza Phone: (404)261-2970
3350 Peachtree Rd,. Penthouse Ste. Fax: (404)365-9026
Atlanta, GA 30326
E-mail: inewkirk@wqxi.com

Format: Sports; Talk. **Networks:** NBC. **Founded:** 1947. **Operating Hours:** Continuous. **ADI:** Atlanta (Athens & Rome), GA. **Key Personnel:** Mark Kanov, General Mgr.; Ike Newkirk, Program Dir., inewkirk@wqxi.com. **Local Programs:** *Illumination*, Ike Newkirk; *Open Line*, Ike Newkirk. **Wattage:** 25,000 day; 1000 night. **URL:** http://www.wqxi.com.

7188 WRAS-FM - 88.5
University Plaza Phone: (404)651-2240
Georgia State University Fax: (404)651-2184
Atlanta, GA 30303

Format: Alternative/New Music/Progressive. **Networks:** ABC. **Owner:** Georgia State University, at above address, (404)651-2202. **Founded:** 1971. **Operating Hours:** Continuous. **ADI:** Atlanta (Athens & Rome), GA. **Key Personnel:** Jeff Walker, General Mgr. **Wattage:** 100,000.

7189 WREK-FM - 91.1
Georgia Institue of Technology Phone: (404)894-2468
165 8th St. NW Fax: (404)894-6872
Atlanta, GA 30332
E-mail: wrek@mordred.gatech.edu

Format: Eclectic. **Founded:** 1968. **Operating Hours:** Continuous; 100% local. **ADI:** Atlanta (Athens & Rome), GA. **Key Personnel:** Brent Harris, General Mgr.; Stephen Fenton, Program Dir.; Rahul Bali, News Dir. **Wattage:** 40,000. **Ad Rates:** Noncommercial. **URL:** http://www.gatech.edu/wrek.

7190 WRFG-FM - 89.3
1083 Austin Ave. NE Phone: (404)523-3471
Atlanta, GA 30307
E-mail: wrfg@mindspring.com

Format: Eclectic; Ethnic. **Networks:** Pacifica. **Owner:** Radio Free Georgia Broadcasting Foundation, Inc., at above address. **Founded:** 1973. **Operating Hours:** Continuous; 95% local. **ADI:** Atlanta (Athens & Rome), GA. **Key Personnel:** B. Kai Aiyetoro, Contact, phone (404)5233471. **Local Programs:** *Good Morning Blues*, Tom Davis, (404)523-3471; *R&B on RFG*, Abdul Mannan, (404)523-3471; *World Party*, Abdul Mannan, (404)523-3471. **Wattage:** 100,000. **Ad Rates:** Noncommercial; underwriting available. **URL:** http://www.wrfg.org.

7191 WSB-AM - 750
1601 W. Peachtree St. NE Phone: (404)897-7500
Atlanta, GA 30309 Fax: (404)897-7363

Format: Talk; News. **Networks:** AP. **Owner:** Cox Broadcasting, 1400 Lake Hearn Dr. NE, Atlanta, GA 30319, (404)843-5000. **Founded:** 1922. **Operating Hours:** Continuous. **ADI:** Atlanta (Athens & Rome), GA. **Key Personnel:** David Meszaros, Station Mgr.; Chris Camp, News Dir.; Jill Cook, Promotions Dir., phone (404)897-7556, fax (404)897-6211; Greg Moceri, Operations Mgr., phone (404)897-6232, fax (404)897-2226; Marc W. Morgan, Vice President, phone (404)897-6230; Lori Rechin-Sheridan, General Sales Mgr., phone (404)897-7545, fax (404)897-6211, lrechin@mindspring.com; Neil Williamson, Marketing Dir., phone (404)897-7595, fax (404)897-6211. **Wattage:** 50,000.

7192 WSB-FM - 98.5
1601 W. Peachtree St. NE Phone: (404)897-7500
Atlanta, GA 30309 Fax: (404)897-7363

Format: Adult Contemporary. **Owner:** Cox Broadcasting, 1400 Lake Hearn Dr. NE, Atlanta, GA 30319, (404)843-5000. **Founded:** 1948. **Operating Hours:** Continuous. **ADI:** Atlanta (Athens & Rome), GA. **Key Personnel:** Neal Mazier, General Sales Mgr., phone (404)897-7565, fax (404)897-6211; Will Gara, Promotions Dir., phone (404)897-7858, guhgoob@prodigy.com; Tom Paleveda, Program Dir., phone (404)897-7591. **Local Programs:** *Morning Show*, Keith Whitaker, (404)897-7364. **Wattage:** 100,000. **Ad Rates:** Advertising accepted; rates available upon request.

7193 WSB-TV - 2
1601 W. Peachtree St. NE 30309 Phone: (404)897-7000
Atlanta, GA 30309 Fax: (404)897-7525

Format: Commercial TV. **Networks:** ABC. **Founded:** 1948. **Operating Hours:** Continuous. **ADI:** Atlanta (Athens & Rome), GA. **Key Personnel:** Greg Stone, General Mgr.; Bill Spell, Sales Mgr.; A.R. Vancawtfort, Program Dir.; David Lippoff, News Dir.; Mark Engel, Contact. **Ad Rates:** Advertising accepted; rates available upon request.

7194 WSTR-FM - 94.1
3350 Peachtree Rd., Penthouse Ste. Phone: (404)261-2970
Atlanta, GA 30326 Fax: (404)365-9026
E-mail: star94.com

Format: Adult Contemporary. **Networks:** Independent. **Founded:** 1966. **Formerly:** WQXI-FM (1992). **Operating Hours:** Continuous. **ADI:** Atlanta (Athens & Rome), GA. **Key Personnel:** Dan Bowen, Program Dir.; Mark Kanov, VP/Gen. Mgr. **Wattage:** 100,000.

7195 WSVH-FM - 91.1
260 14th St. NW Phone: (912)598-3300
Atlanta, GA 30318 Free: (800)673-7332
E-mail: wsuh@earthlink.net

Format: Public Radio; Classical; Jazz; News; Information. **Networks:** National Public Radio (NPR); Public Radio International (PRI); Peach State Public Radio. **Owner:** Georgia Public Telecommunications Commission, 260 14th St., NW, Atlanta, GA 30318, (404)685-2400, Fax: (404)685-2684, Free: (800)654-3038. **Founded:** 1981. **Operating Hours:** Continuous; 50% network, 50% local. **ADI:** Savannah, GA. **Key Personnel:** Deborah Weppelman, Station Mgr.; Susan Curry Brun, Operations Dir.; Carroll V. Baker, Chief Engineer. **Wattage:** 100,000. **Ad Rates:** Noncommercial.

7196 WTBS-TV - 17
1 CNN Center Phone: (404)827-1717
PO Box 105366 Fax: (404)885-4947
Atlanta, GA 30348-5366

Format: Commercial TV. **Networks:** Independent. **Owner:** Turner Broadcasting System, at above address, (404)827-1500. **Founded:** 1976. **Operating Hours:** Continuous. **ADI:** Atlanta (Athens & Rome), GA. **Key Personnel:** Bill Burke, President.

7197 WUPA-TV - 69
2700 NE Expy., BLDG. A Phone: (404)325-6929
Atlanta, GA 30345 Fax: (404)633-4567
E-mail: wupa@paramount.com

Format: Commercial TV. **Networks:** United Paramount Network. **Owner:** Viacom International, Inc., at above address, (212)258-6000, Fax: (212)258-6100. **Founded:** 1981. **Formerly:** WVEU-TV. **Operating Hours:** Continuous. **ADI:** Atlanta (Athens & Rome), GA. **Key Personnel:** Linda Danna, VP/General Manager; Eric Lassberg, General Sales Mgr.; Steve Brown, Local Sales Mgr.; Eileen Beam, Traffic Mgr.; Sarb Sewak Khalsa, Business Mgr.; Walter Naar, Operations Mgr.; Keith Grant, Chief Engineer; Michel Pelletier, Promotions Mgr. **Local Programs:** *American Rap Makers* 11:00 pm Saturday, Arnell Freeman; *Focus Atlanta* 7:00 am Saturday, Keisha Williams, Public Affairs Dir., (404)728-4610; *The Planet Rocks* 12:00 midnight Saturday. **Wattage:** 2630. **Ad Rates:** $50-3500 per unit.

7198 WXIA-TV - 11
1611 W. Peachtree St. NE Phone: (404)892-1611
Atlanta, GA 30309

Format: Commercial TV. **Networks:** NBC. **Founded:** 1951. **Formerly:** WQXI-TV. **Operating Hours:** Continuous. **ADI:** Atlanta (Athens & Rome), GA. **Key Personnel:** Bob Walker, Contact; Brien Kennedy.

7199 WYAY-FM - 106.7
210 Interstate North Pkwy 6th Fl. Phone: (770)955-0106
Atlanta, GA 30339 Fax: (770)952-7461
Free: (800)248-1067

Format: Contemporary Country. **Networks:** ABC. **Owner:** ABC, Inc., 77 West 66th, New York, NY 10023, (212)456-7777. **Operating Hours:** Continuous; 100% local. **ADI:** Atlanta (Athens & Rome), GA. **Key Personnel:** Cyndi Caldwell, Local Sales Mgr.; Tobi Lyons, Promotions Dir.; Victor Sansone, President/General Mgr.; Neil McGinley, Program Dir. **Wattage:** 100,000. **Ad Rates:** $30-350 per unit. Combined advertising rates available with WDWD-AM.

7200 WZGC-FM - 92.9
1100 Johnson Ferry Rd., Ste. 593 Phone: (404)851-9393
Atlanta, GA 30342 Fax: (404)843-3541
E-mail: zmail@z93.com

Format: Classic Rock. **Networks:** Unistar; Westwood One Radio. **Founded:** 1965. **Operating Hours:** Continuous. **ADI:** Atlanta (Athens & Rome), GA. **Key Personnel:** Gary Lewis, General Mgr.; Elaine Saunders, National Sales Mgr.; Barry Levin, General Sales Mgr.; Dwight Douglas, Program Dir.; Marcia Shipley, News/Public Service Dir.; Scott Keithley, Promotions Dir.; Brian Birr, Asst. Promotions Dir.; Robin Henderson, Business Mgr. **Local Programs:** *Eye on Atlanta*, Marcia Shipley. **Wattage:** 100,000. **URL:** http://www.293.com.

AUGUSTA†, pop. 59,864.

E. GA. Richmond Co. On Savannah River, at head of navigation on Georgia/South Carolina border. Medical College of Georgia; Augusta College; Paine College (black); Georgia School of Dentistry. Manufactures textiles, vehicles, plastics, brick, tile, pharmaceuticals, cottonseed oil, paper products, chemicals, fertilizers. Timber. Kaolin deposits.

7201 The Augusta Chronicle
News Bldg. Phone: (706)724-0851
725 Broad St. Fax: (706)722-7403
PO Box 1928
Augusta, GA 30903
Publisher E-mail: newsroom@augustachronicle.com

Daily newspaper. **Founded:** 1785. **Freq:** Mon.-Sun. (morn.). **Print Method:** Offset. **Cols./Page:** 6. **Col. Width:** 24 nonpareils. **Col. Depth:** 301 agate lines. **Key Personnel:** Dennis Sodomka, Exec. Editor; W.S. Morris III, Publisher. **Subscription Rates:** $108 individuals. **Remarks:** Accepts advertising. **URL:** http://www.augustachronicle.com. **Feature Editors:** E. Adams, *Women's*, phone (706)724-0851; Elizabeth Adams, *Family*, *Fashion*, *Lifestyle*, phone (706)724-0851, eadams@augustachronicle.com; Rob Carr, *Photo*, phone (706)724-0851, Augphoto@augustachronicle.com; Sylvia Cooper, *Political*, phone (706)724-0851; Tom Corwin,

Medical, phone (706)724-0851; Rob Davey, *Environmental*, phone (706)724-0851; T. Giddens, *TV & Radio, Travel*, phone (706)724-0851; Tharon Giddens, *Book, Garden/Home, Real Estate*, phone (706)724-0851; Dale Hokrein, *Financial/Business*, phone (706)724-0851, bized@augustachronicle.com; Faith Johnson, *Education*, phone (706)724-0851; Phil Kent, *Editorials*, phone (706)724-0851; Kent Kimes, *Drama, Entertainment, Movie, Music*, phone (706)724-0851; Jennifer Miller, *City, Metro, Rural Development*, phone (706)724-0851; Virginia Norton, *Religion*, phone (706)724-0851.
Ad Rates: BW: $4,731.72 **Circ:** Mon.-Thurs. ★**71,639**
4C: $5,444.72 Fri. ★**90,556**
PCI: $36.68 Sat. ★**88,426**
Sun. ★**100,045**

7202 Augusta Focus
The Augusta Focus
PO Box 10112 Phone: (706)722-7327
Augusta, GA 30903 Fax: (706)724-6969
Free: (800)531-0542

General newspaper. **Founded:** Oct. 1981. **Freq:** Weekly (Thurs.). **Print Method:** Web Offset. **Cols./Page:** 6. **Col. Width:** 2 inches. **Col. Depth:** 21 inches. **Key Personnel:** Frederick Benjamin, Editor; Charles W. Walker, Publisher; Dot Ealyhill, Advertising Mgr. **Subscription Rates:** $11.75 individuals. **Remarks:** Accepts advertising.
Ad Rates: GLR: $1 **Circ:** Paid ‡19,500
BW: $1,025.64 Free ‡1,000
4C: $1,207.08
PCI: $9.58

7203 Gray's Sporting Journal
Morris Magazines
735 Broad St. Phone: (706)722-6060
Augusta, GA 30901 Fax: (706)823-3641

Hunting and fishing magazine. **Founded:** 1975. **Freq:** Bimonthly. **Print Method:** Web offset. **Trim Size:** 8 1/8 x 10 7/8. **Cols./Page:** 2. **Col. Width:** 35 nonpareils. **Col. Depth:** 9 5/16 inches. **Key Personnel:** David Foster, Editor/General Mgr.; Heather Rhodes, List Services Mgr.; Lea Cocherham, fax (706)724-3873; Leslie Nelson, Managing Editor. **ISSN:** 0273-6691. **Subscription Rates:** $36.95 individuals; $6.95 single issue. **Remarks:** Accepts advertising.
Ad Rates: BW: $2,700 **Circ:** Paid ★**30,119**
4C: $3,540

7204 The Metro Courier
314 Walton Way
Augusta, GA 30903

Black community newspaper. **Founded:** 1983. **Freq:** Weekly (Wed.). **Print Method:** Offset. **Trim Size:** 6 x 21. **Cols./Page:** 6. **Col. Width:** 24 nonpareils. **Col. Depth:** 294 agate lines. **Key Personnel:** Barbara A. Gordon, Editor and Publisher. **Subscription Rates:** $25 individuals; $30 out of state. **Formerly**: Metro County Courier; The County Courier.
Ad Rates: GLR: $95 **Circ:** ‡23,660
BW: $100
4C: $400
PCI: $1450

7205 SPUR MAGAZINE
Morris Magazines
735 Broad St. Phone: (706)722-6060
Augusta, GA 30901 Fax: (706)823-3641

Magazine for horse owners, breeders, trainers, and enthusiasts. Features articles on thoroughbred racing, steeplechasing, polo, foxhunting, showing, three-day eventing and the lifestyles of these sports. **Subtitle:** The Magazine of Equestriah and Country Life. **Founded:** 1965. **Freq:** Bimonthly. **Print Method:** Web. **Trim Size:** 8 1/4 x 11. **Cols./Page:** 3. **Col. Width:** 2 1/4 inches. **Col. Depth:** 10 inches. **Key Personnel:** Cathy Laws, Editor. **ISSN:** 0098-5422. **Subscription Rates:** $24.95 individuals.
Ad Rates: BW: $3,320 **Circ:** 25,000
4C: $4,985

7206 WACG-FM - 90.7
2500 Walton Way Phone: (706)737-1661
Augusta, GA 30904-2200 Fax: (706)737-1773

Format: News; Classical; Public Radio; Jazz. **Networks:** National Public Radio (NPR). **Owner:** Peach State Public Radio, 260 14th St., NW, Atlanta, GA 30318, (404)756-4730, Free: (800)654-3038. **Founded:** June 2, 1970. **Operating Hours:** 6 a.m.-midnight; 75% network, 25% local. **ADI:** Augusta, GA. **Key Personnel:** Alan Cooke, Station Mgr., acooke@aug.edu; Jeanie Allen, Promotions/Development Dir., phone (706)733-0602; Jennifer Bannister, Secretary, RRS Coordinator, jbannist@aug.edu. **Local Programs:** *SoundScapes*. **Wattage:** 30,000. **Ad Rates:** Noncommercial.

7207 WAGT-TV - 26
905 Broad St. Phone: (706)826-0026
PO Box 1526 Fax: (706)724-7491
Augusta, GA 30903-1526

Format: Commercial TV. **Networks:** NBC. **Operating Hours:** 6 a.m.-2:15 weekdays; 6 a.m.-1 a.m. Saturday and Sunday. **ADI:** Augusta, GA. **Key Personnel:** Hal Edwards, General Mgr.; Eric Baker, Contact.

7208 WAKB-FM - 96.9
PO Box 10003 Phone: (706)854-0440
Augusta, GA 30903 Fax: (706)854-1055

Format: Urban Contemporary. **Networks:** ABC. **Founded:** 1979. **Formerly**: WRDW-FM (1991). **Operating Hours:** Continuous. **ADI:** Augusta, GA. **Key Personnel:** Dianne Wilkinson, General Mgr. **Local Programs:** *Doug Banks* 2 p.m.-7 p.m.; *Tom Joyner Morning Show* 6 a.m.-10 a.m. **Wattage:** 25,000. **Ad Rates:** $30-40 for 30 seconds; $35-45 for 60 seconds. Combined advertising rates available with WAEG-FM.

7209 WBBQ-FM - 104.3
PO Box 2066
Augusta, GA 30903-2066

Format: Adult Contemporary; News. **Simulcasts:** WBBQ AM. **Networks:** ABC. **Owner:** WBBQ AM/FM, at above address. **Founded:** 1947. **Operating Hours:** Continuous; 5% network, 95% local. **ADI:** Augusta, GA. **Key Personnel:** Birnie Florie, General Mgr.; Jim DeFontes, News Dir.; John Patrick, Program Dir.; Tanya McLendon, Traffic Dir. **Wattage:** 100,000. **Ad Rates:** Combined advertising rates available with WBBQ-AM.

7210 WFAM-AM - 1050
552 Laney-Walker Phone: (706)722-6077
Augusta, GA 30901 Fax: (706)722-7066

Format: Religious; Gospel. **Founded:** 1960. **Formerly**: WIGL-AM (1985). **Operating Hours:** 6:00-9:00 p.m.-midnight; 10% network, 90% local. **ADI:** Augusta, GA. **Wattage:** 5000. **Ad Rates:** $7.50-15 for 30 seconds; $10-20 for 60 seconds.

7211 WGOR-FM - 93.9
PO Box 211045 Phone: (706)855-9494
Augusta, GA 30917-1594 Fax: (706)860-9343
E-mail: wqac@wqac.com

Format: Oldies. **Networks:** CNN Radio. **Founded:** 1983. **Formerly**: WMTZ-FM (1992). **Operating Hours:** Continuous. **ADI:** Augusta, GA. **Key Personnel:** Kent Dunn, General Mgr.; Don MacNeil, Program Dir.; Tina Adcock, Business Mgr.; Harley Drew, Operations Dir. **Wattage:** 25,000. **URL:** http://www.gabn.net/coolfm.

WGPH-FM - See Vidalia

7212 WJBF-TV - 6
1001 Reynolds St. Phone: (706)722-6664
PO Box 1404 Fax: (706)722-0022
Augusta, GA 30903
E-mail: wjbftv6@aol.com

Format: Commercial TV. **Networks:** ABC. **Founded:** 1953. **Operating Hours:** 5;30 a.m.-2 a.m. weekend Sat.-Sun./Continuous Mon.-Fri. **ADI:** Augusta, GA. **Key Personnel:** Louis Wall, General Mgr.; Charles Coleman, General Sales Mgr.; Mary Jones, Program Dir. **Wattage:** 100,000. **Ad Rates:** $25-750 for 30 seconds. **URL:** http://www.wjbf.com.

7213 WKZK-AM - 1600
PO Box 1454 Phone: (706)738-9191
Augusta, GA 30903 Fax: (706)738-9191

Format: Gospel. **Networks:** American Urban Radio. **Owner:** Gospel Radio Inc., PO Box 1454, Augusta, GA 30903. **Founded:** 1962. **Formerly**: WFNL-AM (1979). **Operating Hours:** 6 a.m.-sunset. **ADI:** Augusta, GA. **Key Personnel:** Garfield Turner, General Sales Mgr. and Program Dir.; Walter B. Robinson, Jr., President; Dora Clayton, National Ad. Agency; Vonghett Oatis, Music Dir./Traffic Mgr./Public Service. **Local Programs:** *Deliverance Hour*, Walter Kearse, Mailing contact; *Hour of Truth*, Roy Myles, Mailing contact; *Voices of Reason, Voices of Hope*, Nathaniel Irvin, Mailing contact. **Wattage:** 500. **Ad Rates:** $9 for 30 seconds; $18 for 60 seconds.

7214 WRDW-AM - 1480
1480 Eisenhower Dr. Phone: (706)667-8999
Augusta, GA 30904 Fax: (706)481-0092

Format: Sports. **Owner:** Advertisement Network System, Inc, at above address, (706)724-0916. **Founded:** 1930. **Operating Hours:** Continuous. **ADI:** Augusta, GA. **Key Personnel:** Don Beard, General Mgr.; April Beard, Program Dir. **Wattage:** 5000. **Ad Rates:** $15-25 for 30 seconds; $20-30 for 60 seconds.

7215 WRDW-TV - 12
PO Drawer 1212 Phone: (912)278-1212
Augusta, GA 30903-1212 Fax: (912)279-8316
E-mail: wrdw.com

Format: Commercial TV. **Networks:** CBS. **Owner:** Gray Communications, 126 N. Washington St., Albany, GA 31701, (912)888-9378, Fax: (912)888-9374. **Founded:** 1954. **Operating Hours:** Continuous 7 days a week/52 weeks a year. **ADI:** Augusta, GA. **Key Personnel:** John Ray, VP/GM, phone (803)278-1212, fax (803)279-8316; Joe Thomting, Sales Mgr.; Gwen McGrady, Production Mgr.; Estelle Parsley, News Dir.; Bonita Pitts, Promotions Dir.; Brian Zittlau, Chief Engineer. **Local Programs:** *Music and Things* 10:30-11 a.m. Sunday, Oscar Brown; *Paine College Presents* 10:30-11 a.m., Therese Griffin. **Wattage:** 300,000. **URL:** http://wrdw.com.

7216 WTHB-AM - 1550
Box 1584
Augusta, GA 30903-1584

Format: Gospel. **Networks:** ABC; CBS. **Founded:** 1960. **Operating Hours:** Sunrise-sunset. **ADI:** Augusta, GA. **Key Personnel:** William S. Jaeger, General Mgr.; Carroll Redd, Jr., Contact; James L. Alexander, Operations Mgr.; Richard Burkeen, General Sales Mgr. **Wattage:** 5000.

AUSTELL

7217 Austell Neighbor
Neighbor Newspapers, Inc.
580 Fairground St. Phone: (770)428-9411
PO Box 449 Fax: (770)428-7945
Marietta, GA 30060
Community newspaper. **Founded:** 1969. **Freq:** Weekly (Thurs.). **Subscription Rates:** $12; $18 out of area; $24 out of state. **Remarks:** Combined advertising rates available with other Neighbor Newspapers.
Circ: Combined 21,474

7218 WAOS-AM - 1460
c/o WAOS Radio Phone: (770)944-6684
5815 Westside Rd. Fax: (770)944-9794
PO Box 746
Austell, GA 30001

Format: Hispanic. **Networks:** Independent. **Founded:** 1964. **Formerly**: WJYA-AM (1991); WLKQ-AM. **Operating Hours:** Sunrise-sunset, network news. **Key Personnel:** Samuel Zamarron, President. **Wattage:** 5000. **Ad Rates:** $30 for 30 seconds; $40 for 60 seconds.

7219 WXEM-AM - 1460
5815 Westside Rd. Phone: (770)944-0900
PO Box 746 Fax: (770)944-9794
Austell, GA 30001

Owner: La Favorita, Inc., at above address.

BAINBRIDGE†, pop. 10,553.

SW GA. Decatur Co. On Flint River, 67 mi. SW of Albany. Fuller's earth mines. Manufactures bottle washing machinery, crates, boxes, asphalt, molded plastics, automotive ignition harnesses, lumber, mattresses, polypropylene fabrics. Tobacco packing; pecans shelling; cotton ginning. Pine timber. Diversified farming.

7220 The Post-Searchlight
The Bainbridge Post-Searchlight, Inc.
301 N. Crawford St. Phone: (912)246-2827
PO Box 277 Fax: (912)246-7665
Bainbridge, GA 31717-3612
Free: (800)521-5232
Publisher E-mail: postsrch@surfsouth.com

Newspaper. **Founded:** 1907. **Freq:** Semiweekly (Wed. and Sat.). **Print Method:** Offset. **Trim Size:** 13 3/4 x 22 3/4. **Cols./Page:** 6. **Col. Width:** 12.5 nonpareils. **Col. Depth:** 301 agate lines. **Key Personnel:** Sam Griffin, Editor; Sam M. Griffin, Jr., Publisher; David Maxwell, Advertising Mgr. **USPS:** 439-920. **Subscription Rates:** $29 individuals. **Remarks:** Accepts advertising. **Alt. Formats:** Microform.
Ad Rates: GLR: $.375 **Circ:** ‡7,000
BW: $714.66
4C: $864.66
SAU: $5.54
PCI: $5.54

7221 The Post-Searchlight Extra
The Bainbridge Post-Searchlight, Inc.
301 N. Crawford St. Phone: (912)246-2827
PO Box 277 Fax: (912)246-7665
Bainbridge, GA 31717-3612
Free: (800)521-5232
Publisher E-mail: postsrch@surfsouth.com

Shopper. **Freq:** Weekly (Wed.). **Print Method:** Offset. **Cols./**

Page: 6. **Col. Width:** 25 nonpareils. **Col. Depth:** 301 agate lines. **Key Personnel:** Sam M. Griffin, Jr., Editor and Publisher; David C. Maxwell, Advertising Mgr. **Subscription Rates:** $23.66 individuals; $35.36 out of area. **Remarks:** Accepts advertising.
Ad Rates: GLR: $.31 **Circ:** Paid ‡6,000
BW: $460.53 Free ‡15,500

7222 WMGR-AM - 930
1609 E. Shotwell St. Phone: (912)246-1650
Bainbridge, GA 31717 Fax: (912)248-0975

Format: Middle-of-the-Road (MOR); Talk; Gospel. **Networks:** ABC. **Owner:** Peterson Broadcasting Corp., 225 Green St., Ste. 906, Fayetteville, NC 28301. **Founded:** 1946. **Operating Hours:** 6 a.m.-midnight. **ADI:** Tallahassee, FL-Thomasville (Bainbridge), GA. **Key Personnel:** Jim Squires, General Mgr.; Lenoris Clary, Program Dir.; Diane Strickland, Station Mgr. **Wattage:** 5000.

BARNESVILLE†, pop. 4,887.

W. GA. Lamar Co. 45 mi. S. of Atlanta. Manufactures tire fabrics, childrens clothing, wood products, lumber. Flour mill. Agriculture. Cotton, peaches, pecans, soybeans.

7223 The Herald-Gazette
PO Box 220 Phone: (404)358-0754
509 Greenwood St. Fax: (404)358-0756
Barnesville, GA 30204
Local newspaper. **Founded:** 1867. **Freq:** Weekly (Tues.). **Print Method:** Offset. **Cols./Page:** 6. **Col. Width:** 28 nonpareils. **Col. Depth:** 298 agate lines. **Key Personnel:** Walter B. Geiger, Jr., Editor and Publisher, walterg@barnesville.com; Laura M. Geiger, Advertising Mgr. **USPS:** 506-810. **Subscription Rates:** $16.05 individuals. **Remarks:** Accepts advertising. **Available Online. URL:** http://www.barnesville.com.
Ad Rates: GLR: $5 **Circ:** ‡5,000
4C: $400
PCI: $5

7224 WBAF-AM - 1090
645 Forsyth St. Phone: (404)358-1090
Barnesville, GA 30204

Format: Country; Religious. **Networks:** Georgia Radio; NBC. **Owner:** Barnesville Broadcasting Inc., at above address. **Founded:** 1966. **Operating Hours:** Sunrise-sunset; 10% network, 10% local, 80% other. **Key Personnel:** Charles Waters, Contact; Ken Green, News Dir. **Wattage:** 1000. **Ad Rates:** $3.50 for 30 seconds; $5 for 60 seconds.

BAXLEY†, pop. 3,586.

SE GA. Appling Co. 45 mi. N. of Waycross. Manufactures mobile homes, garments, steel fabricated buildings, lumber. Naval stores. Truck, stock farms. Cotton, tobacco, blueberries, vegetables.

7225 The Baxley News-Banner
PO Box 410 Phone: (912)367-2468
Baxley, GA 31515 Fax: (912)367-0277
Publication E-mail: baxbnr@baxleynewsbanner.com

Newspaper with a Bipartisan orientation. **Subtitle:** Bipartisan. **Founded:** 1884. **Freq:** Weekly (Wed.). **Print Method:** Offset. **Trim Size:** 14 x 22 1/2. **Cols./Page:** 6. **Col. Width:** 24 nonpareils. **Col. Depth:** 301 agate lines. **Key Personnel:** Max Gardner, Editor and Publisher. **USPS:** 385-960. **Subscription Rates:** $21.20 individuals. **Remarks:** Accepts advertising. **URL:** http://www.baxleynewsbanner.com.
Ad Rates: GLR: $.31 **Circ:** ‡4,400
BW: $559.86
4C: $739.86
SAU: $4.34
PCI: $4.50

7226 Cable-Vue TV Inc.
PO Box 660 Phone: (912)367-9811
Baxley, GA 31515-0660

Key Personnel: Carroll Morris, General Mgr. **Cities Served:** Baxley, GA.

7227 WBYZ-FM - 94.5
Box 389 Phone: (912)367-3000
Baxley, GA 31513 Fax: (912)367-9779
E-mail: wbyz@altamaha.net

Format: Country. **Networks:** ABC. **Founded:** 1982. **Operating Hours:** Continuous. **Key Personnel:** Peggy Miles, General Mgr. **Wattage:** 100,000. **Ad Rates:** $10 for 30 seconds; $12 for 60 seconds.

7228 WUBI-TV - 34
201 E. Jekyll Rd. Phone: (912)367-3434
Baxley, GA 31513 Fax: (912)367-5299

Format: Commercial TV. **Networks:** United Paramount Network. **Owner:** Southern TV Corp., at above address. **Founded:** 1991. **Operating Hours:** Continuous. **ADI:** Savannah, GA. **Key Personnel:** Dan L. Johnson, Pres./CEO; Jo Johnson, VP/Station Mgr. **Wattage:** 316,000. **Ad Rates:** Advertising accepted; rates available upon request.

7229 WUFE-AM - 1260
PO Box 390 Phone: (912)367-3000
Baxley, GA 31515 Fax: (912)367-9779

Format: Gospel. **Networks:** ABC. **Owner:** South Georgia Broadcasters, Inc., at above address. **Founded:** 1954. **Operating Hours:** 6:00 a.m.-6:00 p.m. **ADI:** Savannah, GA. **Key Personnel:** Peggy Miles, General Mgr. **Wattage:** 5,000. **Ad Rates:** $4 for 30 seconds; $6 for 60 seconds.

BIG CANOE

7230 Big Canoe Cable TV System
591 Big Canoe Phone: (706)268-3333
Big Canoe, GA 30143 Fax: (706)268-3413

Key Personnel: Mike McShane, General Mgr. **Cities Served:** Big Canoe, GA.

BLACKSHEAR†, pop. 3,112.

SE GA. Pierce Co. 8 mi. NE of Waycross. Utility-Industrial Park. Naval store industries. Manufactures fertilizer, lumber products, textiles, knives. Yellow pine timber. Agriculture. Tobacco, corn. pecans, livestock.

7231 Times
638 Gordon St. Phone: (912)449-6693
PO Box 410 Fax: (912)449-1719
Blackshear, GA 31516
Community newspaper. **Founded:** 1867. **Freq:** Weekly (Wed.). **Print Method:** Offset. **Cols./Page:** 6. **Col. Width:** 27 nonpareils. **Col. Depth:** 294 agate lines. **Key Personnel:** Rose Aldridge, News Editor; Robert M. Williams, Jr., Publisher; Chery Williams, General Mgr. **Subscription Rates:** $18 individuals; $256 out of area. **Remarks:** Accepts advertising.
Ad Rates: GLR: $.25 **Circ:** 3,000
BW: $516
4C: $716
PCI: $4

7232 WGIA-AM - 1350
245 E. Main St. Phone: (912)449-3442
PO Box 619 Fax: (912)449-1266
Blackshear, GA 31516

Format: Religious; Contemporary Christian. **Networks:** USA Radio. **Owner:** Christian Media Network Inc., at above address. **Founded:** 1983. **Formerly:** WIEZ-AM. **Operating Hours:** 7 am-6 pm winter, 7am-8:30pm summer; 50% network, 50% local. **Key Personnel:** Joe Chalk, General Mgr.; James McKinnon, Sales. **Wattage:** 2500. **Ad Rates:** $2.50-5 for 15 seconds; $3-8 for 30 seconds; $5-9.50 for 60 seconds.

BLAIRSVILLE†, pop. 530.

N. GA. Union Co. 85 mi. NE of Atlanta. Timber. Farming. Industrial.

7233 North Georgia News
PO Box 2029 Phone: (706)745-6343
Blairsville, GA 30514 Fax: (706)745-1830

Newspaper. **Founded:** 1923. **Freq:** Weekly (Wed.). **Print Method:** Offset. **Cols./Page:** 6. **Col. Width:** 27 nonpareils. **Col. Depth:** 301 agate lines. **Key Personnel:** Barbara Ward, Office Mgr.; Wanda R. West, Publisher; Kenneth West, General Mgr.; Norman Cooper, News Editor. **Subscription Rates:** $35 other countries. **Remarks:** Accepts advertising.
Ad Rates: GLR: $.17 **Circ:** Paid ‡9,700
BW: $330.24 Free ‡5,000
4C: $500
SAU: $5.50
PCI: $3.25

BLAKELY†, pop. 5,880.

SW GA. Early Co. 50 mi. W. of Albany. Manufactures metal, paper products, textiles, farming machinery, truck trailers.Grist mills. Pine, hardwood timber. Agriculture. Cotton, peanuts, corn.

7234 Early County News
The Early County News
PO Box 748 Phone: (912)723-4376
Blakely, GA 31723 Fax: (912)723-6097

Community newspaper. **Founded:** 1859. **Freq:** Weekly (Thurs.). **Print Method:** Offset. **Cols./Page:** 6. **Col. Width:** 25 nonpareils. **Col. Depth:** 301 agate lines. **Key Personnel:** W.W. Fleming, Editor and Publisher. **ISSN:** 1640-6000. **Subscription Rates:** $15.75 individuals; $27.30 out of area. **Remarks:** Accepts advertising.
Ad Rates: GLR: $.25 **Circ:** ‡3,900
BW: $451.50
4C: $851.50
SAU: $3.50

7235 Southern Festivals
107 S. Main St. Phone: (912)723-2778
Blakely, GA 31723 Fax: (912)723-2779
Free: (800)558-3378

A statewide newspaper covering travel and tourism. **Subtitle:** The South's Festival Newspaper. **Founded:** Dec. 1992. **Freq:** Bimonthly. **Trim Size:** 10 x 13 1/2. **Cols./Page:** 5. **Col. Width:** 1 7/8 inches. **Key Personnel:** Lollie C. Taylor, Publisher; J.S. Taylor, Editor and Publisher, jtaylor@sowega.net. **Subscription Rates:** $14; $25 two years. **Remarks:** Accepts advertising. **URL:** http://www.southernfestivals.com. **Alt. Formats:** Microform.
Ad Rates: BW: $1012 **Circ:** Paid 3,000
PCI: $15 Non-paid 20,000

7236 Blakely Cable Television, Inc.
41 Court Sq. Phone: (912)723-3555
Blakely, GA 31723 Fax: (912)723-3800

Founded: 1979. **Key Personnel:** W.C. Deloach, Jr., President; Bill Dyer, Contact. **Cities Served:** Columbia, AL: 33 channels.

BLOOMINGDALE

EC GA. Chatham Co. 20 mi. NW of Savannah.

7237 WYFS-FM - 89.5
156 Falcon Ln. Phone: (912)748-0031
Bloomingdale, GA 31302
E-mail: wfys@aol.com

Format: Religious. **Networks:** Bible Broadcasting. **Owner:** Bible Broadcasting Network, Inc., PO Box 1818, Charlotte, NC 28241-7300, (704)523-5555. **Founded:** 1986. **Operating Hours:** Continuous; 97.5% network, 2.5% local. **Key Personnel:** Lowell Davey, President; Harold Richards, Contact; Will Wonsang, Station Mgr., phone (912)748-0031, wyfs@aol.com; Leo T. Galletta, Contact. **Local Programs:** *Insight*, William Wonsang. **Wattage:** 100,000. **Ad Rates:** Noncommercial. **URL:** http://www.amen.net/bbn.

BLUE RIDGE†, pop. 1,376.

SC GA. Fannin Co.

7238 The News Observer
PO Box 989 Phone: (706)632-2019
Blue Ridge, GA 30513 Fax: (706)632-2577

Community newspaper. **Founded:** 1990. **Freq:** Weekly (Wed.). **Print Method:** Offset. **Trim Size:** 13 x 21 1/2. **Cols./Page:** 6. **Col. Width:** 12.5 picas. **Key Personnel:** Glenn Harbison, Publisher; Stacy S. Chastain, Editor. **Subscription Rates:** $25. **Remarks:** Accepts advertising. **Formerly:** The Observer.
Ad Rates: BW: $735.30 **Circ:** 10,200
4C: $1,000.30
PCI: $6.71

7239 WPPL-FM - 103.9
PO Box 938 Phone: (706)632-9775
Blue Ridge, GA 30513 Fax: (706)632-5922
Free: (888)632-9775

Format: Country. **Networks:** Georgia Radio; Meadows Racing; Satellite Music Network; Capitol Sports. **Founded:** 1971. **Operating Hours:** Sun-Sat 6a.m.-10p.m. **Key Personnel:** Daton Davis, Gen.Mgr./Sales Mgr.; Rebecca St. John, Program Dir./Music Dir.; Vicky Burk, Traffic Dir./Office Mgr.; Jody Nicholson, Music Dir.; Kenneth Ferguson, Chief Engineer. **Wattage:** 6,000. **Ad Rates:** $18-15 per unit.

BOGART

NC GA. Oconee and Clarke Co. 10 mi. W. of Athens.

7240 WPUP-FM - 103.7
1010 Tower Place Phone: (706)549-6222
Bogart, GA 30622 Fax: (706)353-1967

Format: Album-Oriented Rock (AOR). **Owner:** Southern Broadcasting, Inc., at above address. **Founded:** 1988. **Formerly:** WBIC-FM (1990). **Operating Hours:** Continuous. **ADI:** Atlanta (Athens & Rome), GA. **Key Personnel:** Traci Jahn, General Mgr.; Benji Kurtz, Program Dir., kjallen@g-net.net; Tammy Goldstein, Sales Mgr. **Wattage:** 25,000. **Ad Rates:** $23.50 for 30 seconds; $27 for 60 seconds. **URL:** http://www.rock1037.com/.

7241 WRFC-AM - 960
1010 Tower Place Phone: (706)549-6222
Bogart, GA 30622 Fax: (706)353-1967
E-mail: athens96@aol.com

Format: News; Talk; Sports. **Networks:** ABC; ESPN Radio; CBS. **Owner:** AM 96, Inc., at above address. **Founded:** 1948. **Operating Hours:** Continuous; 50% network, 50% local. **ADI:** Atlanta (Athens & Rome), GA. **Key Personnel:** Traci John, General Mgr.; Tommy Goldstein, Sales Mgr.; Allen Tibbets, Program Dir. **Local Programs:** *Weak Minds Wandering* 9 a.m.-10 a.m. Monday-Friday, Hugh Christian. **Wattage:** 5000. **Ad Rates:** $8-16 for 30 seconds; $11-19 for 60 seconds. **URL:** http://www.wrfc.com/.

BOWDON, pop. 1,743.

W. GA. Carroll Co. 52 mi. SW of Atlanta. Grist mills; textile works. Pine timber. Agriculture. Cotton, corn.

7242 Bowdon Bulletin
118 City Hall Ave. Phone: (404)258-2146
Bowdon, GA 30108 Fax: (404)258-9747

Newspaper with a Democratic orientation. **Founded:** 1890. **Freq:** Weekly (Thurs.). **Cols./Page:** 6. **Col. Width:** 21 nonpareils. **Col. Depth:** 287 agate lines. **Key Personnel:** Tom Overton, Contact. **Subscription Rates:** $20 individuals.

BREMEN, pop. 4,280.

SE GA. Haralson Co. 40 mi. W. of Atlanta.

7243 The Haralson Gateway Beacon
Paxton Media Group
PO Box 685 Phone: (770)537-2434
Bremen, GA 30110 Fax: (770)537-0826

Community newspaper. **Freq:** Weekly (Thurs.). **Print Method:** Offset. **Cols./Page:** 6. **Col. Width:** 2 1/16 inches. **Col. Depth:** 21 1/2 inches. **Key Personnel:** Bruce Browning, Editor, phone (770)832-6631, fax (770)834-9991; Judy Westmoreland, Classifieds/OFM; Bill Agan, Retail Advertising Rep. **ISSN:** 0746-4169. **Subscription Rates:** $20 individuals; $27.50 out of area; $31 out of state. **Remarks:** Accepts advertising.
Ad Rates: BW: $646.38 **Circ:** ‡6,500
PCI: $5.13

7244 WGMI-AM - 1440
613 Tallapoosa St. Phone: (770)537-0840
Bremen, GA 30110 Fax: (770)537-0220

Format: Southern Gospel. **Founded:** 1957. **Formerly:** WSLE-AM; WBKI-AM. **Operating Hours:** 7 a.m.-7 p.m.; 100% local. **Key Personnel:** Horace Garner, General Mgr.; Scott Garner, Prg. Dir./Sale Mgr.; Peggy Garner, Office Mgr. **Local Programs:** *Gospel Greats*, Scott Garner; *Your Story Hour* Noon Saturday, Scott Garner. **Wattage:** 2500. **Ad Rates:** $6-8 for 30 seconds; $10-14 for 60 seconds.

BRUNSWICK†, pop. 19,585.

SE GA. Glynn Co. 60 mi. N. of Jacksonville. Seaport. Tourism. Manufactures plastics, sheet rock, turpentine, resin, lumber, paint, steam boilers, caustic soda, chlorine. Seafood and auto processing. Shrimp fisheries. Pine timber.

7245 The Brunswick News
Brunswick News Publishing Co.
3011 Altama Ave. Phone: (912)265-8320
PO Box 1557 Fax: (912)264-4973
Brunswick, GA 31521
General newspaper. **Founded:** Sept. 1902. **Freq:** Mon.-Sat. **Print Method:** Offset. **Cols./Page:** 6. **Col. Width:** 2 1/16 inches. **Col. Depth:** 21 inches. **Key Personnel:** C.H. Leavy III, Editor; Ron Maulden, General Mgr.; Hank Rowland, Managing Editor. **USPS:** 068-180. **Subscription Rates:** $60 individuals; $76 out of area; $0.35 single issue.
Ad Rates: BW: $1,028.16 **Circ:** ‡16,284
4C: $1,313.16
SAU: $8.16

7246 Harbor Sound
1326 Newcastle St. Phone: (912)264-4521
PO Box 606 Fax: (912)264-4531
Brunswick, GA 31521
Community newspaper. **Subtitle:** The Harbor Sound. **Founded:** June 1, 1983. **Freq:** Weekly (Tues.). **Print Method:** Offset. **Trim Size:** 10 1/4 x 15. **Cols./Page:** 6. **Col. Width:** 9.5 picas. **Col. Depth:** 15 inches. **Key Personnel:** James H. Dryden, Editor and Publisher. **Subscription Rates:** Free; $30 by mail. **Remarks:** Accepts advertising.
Ad Rates: GLR: $2 **Circ:** Free ‡31,000
BW: $795
PCI: $8.58

7247 Century Communication
Box 1336 Phone: (912)264-2288
Brunswick, GA 31521 Fax: (912)264-4618

Founded: 1986. **Key Personnel:** Robert Hymson, General Mgr.; Julie Boatright, Office Mgr. **Cities Served:** Nassau County: subscribing households 1,970; 33 channels; 1 community access channel.

7248 WMOG-AM - 1490
3833 U.S. Hwy. 82 Phone: (912)262-9664
Brunswick, GA 31523-7735 Fax: (912)264-5462

Format: News; Sports; Middle-of-the-Road (MOR); Oldies. **Networks:** ABC. **Founded:** 1940. **Operating Hours:** Continuous; 20% local. **Key Personnel:** George Sample, General Mgr., phone (912)267-1025, fax (912)264-5462; Scott Ryfun, News Dir. **Wattage:** 600. **Ad Rates:** $8-15 for 30 seconds; $11-21 for 60 seconds. $8-$15 for 30 seconds; $11-$21 for 60 seconds.

7249 WSFN-AM - 790
7515 Blythe Island Hwy. Phone: (912)264-6251
Brunswick, GA 31525

Format: Sports. **Networks:** CNN Radio; ABC; ESPN Radio. **Owner:** MarMac Communications, L.L.C., at above address. **Former name:** WPIQ-AM. **Operating Hours:** Continuous. **Key Personnel:** Gary Marmitt, General Mgr.; Sharon McKeand, Business Mgr.; Gary Moss, Program Dir. **Wattage:** 500. **URL:** http://www.wsfn.com.

7250 WWSN-FM - 103.3
3833 U.S. Hwy. 82 Phone: (912)267-1025
Brunswick, GA 31525 Fax: (912)264-5462

Format: Adult Contemporary. **Networks:** Independent. **Founded:** 1972. **Formerly:** WHFX (1988); WFGD (1998). **Operating Hours:** Continuous; 100% local. **Key Personnel:** George Samyle, General Mgr.; Dennis Abercrombie, Program Dir. **Wattage:** 100,000. **Ad Rates:** $20.00-25.00 for 30 seconds; $25.00-40.00 for 60 seconds.

BUENA VISTA†, pop. 1,544.

W. GA. Marion Co. 35 mi. SE of Columbus. Lumber, grist mills; cotton ginning. Dairy, stock, poultry, fruit farms. Cotton, corn, peanuts.

7251 Patriot-Citizen
Rolin Press Group
PO Box 108 Phone: (912)887-3674
Buena Vista, GA 31803
Founded: 1876. **Freq:** Weekly (Thurs.). **Print Method:** Offset. **Trim Size:** 6 x 21 1/2. **Cols./Page:** 6. **Col. Width:** 13 inches. **Col. Depth:** 301 agate lines. **Key Personnel:** Ron Provencher, Publisher, phone (912)887-3675; Linda Provencher, Editor, phone (912)887-3674. **USPS:** 329-760. **Subscription Rates:** $15.75 individuals; $23.65 out of county; $30 out of state.
Ad Rates: GLR: $.29 **Circ:** ‡1250
BW: $516
4C: $709.55
SAU: $4
PCI: $4

BUFORD

NC GA. Gwinnett and Hall Co. 15 mi. N. of Swannee.

7252 WLKQ-FM - 102.3
6449 Radio Park Dr. Phone: (770)945-9953
Buford, GA 30518-3558 Fax: (770)932-0988

Format: Oldies. **Networks:** Mutual Broadcasting System; Georgia Radio. **Founded:** 1970. **Formerly:** WGCO-FM (1985). **Operating Hours:** Continuous; 5% network, 95% local. **ADI:** Atlanta (Athens & Rome), GA. **Key Personnel:** Jaqueline A. Joseph, General Mgr.; Al Garner, General Sales Mgr.; Mark Joseph, Operations Mgr. **Wattage:** 3300. **Ad Rates:** $26 for 30 seconds.

BUTLER

7253 Taylor County News
Taylor News
PO Box 550 Phone: (912)862-5101
Butler, GA 31006 Fax: (912)862-9668

Community newspaper. **Freq:** Weekly (Thurs.). **Print Method:** Offset. **Cols./Page:** 6. **Col. Width:** 13 picas. **Col. Depth:** 21 1/2 inches. **Key Personnel:** Jim Cosey, Editor and Publisher; Valori Moore, Asst. Publisher. **Subscription Rates:** $15 individuals.
Ad Rates: SAU: $2.94 **Circ:** 2,350

CAIRO†, pop. 8,777.

SW GA. Grady Co. 6 mi. E. of Whigham. Residential.

7254 Cairo Messenger
Cairo Messenger Inc.
31-35 1st Ave. NE Phone: (912)377-2032
PO Box 30 Fax: (912)377-4640
Cairo, GA 31728-2193
Publication E-mail: cmessngr@rose.net

Community newspaper. **Founded:** 1904. **Freq:** Weekly (Wed.). **Print Method:** Offset. **Cols./Page:** 6. **Col. Width:** 12.04 picas. **Col. Depth:** 21 inches. **Key Personnel:** Robert H. Wind, Editor and Publisher. **USPS:** 888-260. **Subscription Rates:** $13.50 local; $18.50 in GA; $20.50 outside GA. **Remarks:** Accepts advertising.
Ad Rates: BW: $567 **Circ:** 6,200
PCI: $1.90

7255 South Georgia Shopper
Phillips Publishing
PO Box 502
Cairo, GA 31728-0642

Shopper (tabloid). **Founded:** Oct. 1973. **Freq:** Weekly (Tues.). **Print Method:** Offset. **Trim Size:** 11 1/2 x 15. **Cols./Page:** 6. **Col. Width:** 9 picas. **Col. Depth:** 16 inches. **Key Personnel:** Charles Sewell, Contact. **Subscription Rates:** Free. **Remarks:** Accepts advertising.
Ad Rates: BW: $273 **Circ:** Free ‡40,000
4C: $513
PCI: $4.50

CALHOUN†, pop. 6,000.

NW GA. Gordon Co. 60 mi. N. of Atlanta. Manufactures carpets, rugs, ball bearings, concrete mixers, outboard motors. Lumber. Agriculture. Corn, hay. Poultry.

7256 The Calhoun Times
News Publishing Co.
PO Box 8 Phone: (706)629-2231
Calhoun, GA 30703 Fax: (706)625-0899

Newspaper with a Democratic orientation. **Founded:** 1870. **Freq:** Semiweekly (Wed. and Sat.). **Print Method:** Offset. **Cols./Page:** 6. **Col. Width:** 21 nonpareils. **Col. Depth:** 301 agate lines. **Key Personnel:** Jim Hobgood, Publisher. **Subscription Rates:** $24 individuals. **Remarks:** Accepts advertising.
Ad Rates: BW: $867 **Circ:** Paid 9,200
4C: $905.34
PCI: $6.50

7257 WEBS-AM - 1110
PO Box 1299 Phone: (706)629-2238
Calhoun, GA 30703 Fax: (706)629-7092

Format: Adult Contemporary; News; Oldies. **Networks:** NBC. **Owner:** Radio WEBS, Inc., at above address. **Founded:** 1966. **Operating Hours:** Sunrise-sunset; 10% network, 90% local. **ADI:** Atlanta (Athens & Rome), GA. **Key Personnel:** Kenyon D. Payne, Contact; Elva Payne, Contact; Carolyn Glaze, Contact. **Wattage:** 250. **Ad Rates:** $8 for 30 seconds; $10 for 60 seconds.

7258 WJTH-AM - 900
PO Box 1119 Phone: (706)629-6397
Calhoun, GA 30703-1119 Fax: (706)629-8463
E-mail: wjth@nwga.com

Format: Country. **Networks:** ABC. **Owner:** Cherokee Broadcasting Co., at above address. **Founded:** 1977. **Operating Hours:** 6 a.m.-10 p.m.; 2% network, 98% local. **ADI:** Atlanta (Athens & Rome), GA. **Key Personnel:** Keith Thomas, Contact; Sam Thomas, General Mgr. **Wattage:** 1000. **Ad Rates:** $8.25-8.82 for 30 seconds; $11.47-12.05 for 60 seconds.

CAMILLA†, pop. 5,414.

SW GA. Mitchell Co. 26 mi. S. of Albany. Manufactures

fertilizer, cottonseed oil, textiles. Poultry and peanut processing; lumber mills. Pine timber. Stock, cattle, poultry, truck farms. Cotton, corn, soybeans, peanuts, pecans.

7259 The Camilla Enterprise
PO Box 365 Phone: (912)336-5265
Camilla, GA 31730-0365 Fax: (912)336-8476

Newspaper with a Democratic orientation. **Founded:** 1903. **Freq:** Semiweekly (Wed. and Fri.). **Print Method:** Offset. **Cols./Page:** 6. **Col. Width:** 26 nonpareils. **Col. Depth:** 301 agate lines. **Key Personnel:** Mike Tabb, Editor; Roger Ann Jones, Publisher. **Subscription Rates:** $17.85 individuals; $22.05 out of state. **Remarks:** Accepts advertising.
Ad Rates: GLR: $.16 **Circ:** ‡4,000
BW: $387
4C: $602
PCI: $3.50

CANTON†, pop. 3,654.

NW GA. Cherokee Co. On Etowah River, 35 mi. NW of Atlanta. Cotton mills. Chicken processing plants. Pine, poplar timber. Agriculture. Corn, poultry, livestock.

7260 WCHK-AM/WNSY-FM - 1290
2189 Marietta Hwy. Phone: (770)479-2101
PO Box 231
Canton, GA 30114

Format: Country; News; Oldies. **Networks:** Georgia Radio; USA Radio. **Owner:** Cherokee Broadcasting Co., Inc., at above address. **Founded:** 1957. **Operating Hours:** Continuous. **Key Personnel:** Michael D. Searcy, General Mgr. **Wattage:** 6000. **Ad Rates:** $10-15 for 30 seconds; $15-20 for 60 seconds.

CARROLLTON†, pop. 15,000.

W. GA. Carroll Co. 50 mi. SW of Atlanta. West Georgia College; Carroll County Area Voc-Tech.; John Tanner State Park. Fishing, boating and swimming. Manufactures wire and cable products, auto body parts, stainless steel pipes & tubing, textiles.

7261 Christianity and Literature
State University of West Georgia
Carrollton, GA 30118-2200 Phone: (770)830-2261
Fax: (770)836-6512

Scholarly journal covering Christianity and literature. **Founded:** 1951. **Freq:** Quarterly. **Trim Size:** 6 x 9. **Key Personnel:** Dr. Robert Snyder, Editor, rsnyder@westga.edu. **ISSN:** 0148-3331. **Subscription Rates:** $25 members; $35 institutions members; $45 members two years; $65 two years institutional members; $35 members individual/out of country. **Remarks:** Accepts advertising.
Ad Rates: BW: $200 **Circ:** Paid 1,000

7262 The Times-Georgian
PO Box 460 Phone: (404)834-6631
Carrollton, GA 30117-0460 Fax: (404)834-9991

General newspaper. **Founded:** 1945. **Freq:** Tues.-Sun. (morn.). **Print Method:** Offset. **Cols./Page:** 6. **Col. Width:** 25 nonpareils. **Col. Depth:** 301 agate lines. **Key Personnel:** Fred Lister, Publisher. **Subscription Rates:** $75 individuals. **Remarks:** Accepts advertising.
Ad Rates: BW: $1,510.46 **Circ:** Paid ♦9,792
4C: $1,730.46 Non-paid ♦248
SAU: $10.74
PCI: $12.22

7263 Women & Politics
The Haworth Press, Inc.
Political Science Dept. Phone: (770)836-6504
State University of West Georgia Fax: (770)836-4665
Carrollton, GA 30118
Publication E-mail: wandp@westga.edu

Research journal on gender issues and politics. **Subtitle:** A Journal of Research and Policy Studies. **Founded:** 1980. **Freq:** Quarterly. **Trim Size:** 6x8 1/2. **Key Personnel:** Dr. Janet M. Clark, Editor, jclark@westga.edu; Bill Cohen, Publisher, phone (607)656-7981. **ISSN:** 0195-7732. **Subscription Rates:** $40 individuals; $140 institutions; $250 libraries. **Remarks:** Accepts advertising. **URL:** http://www.westga.edu/~wandp/w+p.html.
Ad Rates: BW: $300 **Circ:** 635

7264 WBTR-FM - 92.1
101 Commercial Ave. Phone: (770)832-9685
PO Box 569 Fax: (770)830-7625
Carrollton, GA 30117

Format: Country. **Networks:** Georgia Radio; Motor Racing. **Owner:** Carroll County Media Inc., at above address, Carrollton, GA 30117. **Founded:** 1964. **Operating Hours:** Continuous; 100% local. **ADI:** Atlanta (Athens & Rome), GA. **Key Personnel:** Greg Gerard, General Mgr. **Local Programs:** *Carroll County High School Football Game of the Week*, Tom Cooper. **Wattage:** 3000 ERP. **Ad Rates:** $9-12 for 30 seconds; $11-15 for 60 seconds.

7265 WWGC-FM - 90.7
State University of West Georgia Phone: (404)836-6731
Carrollton, GA 30118 Fax: (404)830-2244

Format: Public Radio. **Networks:** Public Radio International (PRI); National Public Radio (NPR); Peach State Public Radio. **Founded:** 1973. **Operating Hours:** 6 a.m.-midnight; 40% local. **Key Personnel:** Brooks Robinson, Operations Mgr.; Erroll Crane, Music Dir.; Kevin Sanders, General Mgr.; Sean Gilbert, Production Mgr. **Local Programs:** *The Jazz and Blues Show*, Erroll Crane, (770)836-6731, Fax (770)830-2244; *Velvet Soup (Acoustic)*, Brooks Robinson, (770)836-6731, Fax (770)830-2244. **Wattage:** 500. **Ad Rates:** Noncommercial.

CARTERSVILLE†, pop. 9,508.

NW GA. Bartow Co. 40 mi. NW of Atlanta. Manufactures plastic bags. Carpet and knitting mills. Limestone, barium, iron ore, manganese mines; pine timber. Livestock.

7266 The Daily Tribune News
Cartersville Newspapers
PO Box 70 Phone: (404)382-4545
251 South Tenn. St. Fax: (404)382-2711
Cartersville, GA 30120-0070
General newspaper. **Founded:** 1946. **Freq:** Daily (eve.). **Print Method:** Offset. **Trim Size:** 14 x 22 3/4. **Cols./Page:** 6. **Col. Width:** 26 nonpareils. **Col. Depth:** 301 agate lines. **Key Personnel:** Charles Hurley, Editor and Publisher. **USPS:** 146-740. **Subscription Rates:** $60 individuals; $90 out of county; $130 out of state. **Remarks:** Accepts advertising. **Alt. Formats:** CD-ROM.
Ad Rates: BW: $848.82 **Circ:** 102,000
4C: $1,118.82
PCI: $6.58

7267 Herald-Tribune
Cartersville Newspapers
PO Box 70 Phone: (404)382-4545
251 South Tenn. St. Fax: (404)382-2711
Cartersville, GA 30120-0070
General newspaper. **Founded:** 1919. **Freq:** Weekly (Tues.). **Print Method:** Offset. **Trim Size:** 14 x 22 3/4. **Cols./Page:** 6. **Col. Width:** 26 nonpareils. **Col. Depth:** 301 agate lines. **Key Personnel:** Charles Hurley, Editor and Publisher. **USPS:** 598-940. **Subscription Rates:** $20 individuals; $28 out of county. **Remarks:** Accepts advertising.
Ad Rates: BW: $774 **Circ:** Free ⊕29,673
4C: $974
PCI: $6

7268 Prestige Cable TV
156 Morningside Dr. Phone: (404)382-0531
Box 785 Fax: (404)386-2540
Cartersville, GA 30120

Owner: Jon Oscher, at above address. **Founded:** 1971. **Key Personnel:** Hershel Wisebram, Contact; Grady Ireland, President; Dick Caswell, Vice President. **Cities Served:** Canton, Cartersville, GA; Mooresville, NC; Fredericksburg, Garrisonville, Warrenton, VA; Forsyth County, GA; Orange County, VA; Carroll County, MD.: subscribing households 93,887; 54 channels; 2 community access channels.

7269 WCCV-FM - 91.7
PO Box 1000 Phone: (770)387-0917
Cartersville, GA 30120 Fax: (770)387-2856
E-mail: ibn@ibnetwork.org

Format: Religious. **Networks:** Moody Broadcasting; Ambassador Inspirational Radio; SkyLight Satellite. **Owner:** Immanuel Broadcasting Network, Inc., at above address. **Founded:** 1983. **Operating Hours:** 95% local, 5% network. **Key Personnel:** Neil Hopper, Operations Mgr.; Ed Tuter, President. **Wattage:** 910. **Ad Rates:** Noncommercial. **URL:** http://www.ibnetwork.org.

7270 WYXC-AM - 1270
1410 Hwy. 411 NE Phone: (770)382-1270
Cartersville, GA 30121 Fax: (770)386-7350

Format: Country. **Networks:** CBS. **Owner:** Empire Radio Ltd., at above address. **Founded:** 1961. **Formerly:** WKRW-AM (1981). **Operating Hours:** 24 hrs; 5% network, 95% local. **ADI:** Atlanta (Athens & Rome), GA. **Key Personnel:** Julia N. Frew, Manager. **Wattage:** 500. **Ad Rates:** $5.25 for 30 seconds; $6.60 for 60 seconds.

CATAULA

7271 WYFK-FM - 89.5
75 Raymond Dr. Phone: (706)322-1980
Cataula, GA 31804-9666

Format: Religious. **Networks:** Bible Broadcasting. **Owner:** Bible Broadcasting Network, Inc., PO Box 1818, Charlotte, NC 28201, (704)523-5555, (704)522-1967, Free: (800)888-7077. **Founded:** 1987. **Operating Hours:** Continuous; 97.5% network, 2.5% local. **Key Personnel:** Lowell Davey, President; Harold Richards, Satelite Program Mgr.; Mark Andrews, Station Mgr.; Leo T. Galletta, Network Operations Mgr. **Wattage:** 50,000. **Ad Rates:** Noncommercial.

CEDARTOWN†.

NW GA. Polk Co. 40 mi. SW of Rome.

7272 The Cedartown Standard
News Publishing Co.
PO Box 308 Phone: (770)748-1520
Cedartown, GA 30125 Fax: (770)748-1524

Community newspaper. **Founded:** 1869. **Freq:** Semiweekly (Tues. and Thurs.). **Print Method:** Offset. **Trim Size:** 13 3/4 x 22 3/4. **Cols./Page:** 6. **Col. Width:** 2 1/16 inches. **Col. Depth:** 21 1/4 inches. **Key Personnel:** Jim Penney, Editor, jpenney@npco.com; Jim Penney, Publisher. **Subscription Rates:** $24 local. **Remarks:** Accepts advertising.
Ad Rates: GLR: $6.79 **Circ:** Paid ‡3,400
BW: $480.68
4C: $680.68
SAU: $6
PCI: $6.79

7273 WGAA-AM - 1340
413 Lakeview Dr. Phone: (770)748-1340
PO Box 167 Fax: (770)748-4539
Cedartown, GA 30125

Format: Country; News; Talk; Adult Contemporary; Country; Contemporary Country; Religious; Gospel. **Networks:** NBC. **Owner:** Burgess Broadcasting Corp., at above address. **Founded:** 1941. **Operating Hours:** 17 hours Daily. **ADI:** Atlanta (Athens & Rome), GA. **Key Personnel:** Frank H. Burgess, Sr, Pres. & Station Mgr.; Van Cowart, News Dir.; Jim Schliestett, Chief Engineer. **Local Programs:** *Local News*, Ross Shackleford; *Local Sports*, Frank Burgess, Sr.; *Oldies Shows Contests*, Allen Ray, Mailing contact. **Wattage:** 1000. **Ad Rates:** $5.50-10.50 for 30 seconds; $6.50-11.50 for 60 seconds.

CHAMBLEE

7274 Chamblee De Kalb Neighbor
Neighbor Newspapers, Inc.
580 Fairground St. Phone: (770)428-9411
PO Box 449 Fax: (770)428-7945
Marietta, GA 30060
Community newspaper. **Founded:** 1975. **Freq:** Weekly (Wed.). **Print Method:** Offset. **Cols./Page:** 6. **Col. Width:** 26 nonpareils. **Col. Depth:** 301 agate lines. **Key Personnel:** Otis A. Brumby, Jr., Publisher. **USPS:** 951-740. **Subscription Rates:** Free; $12 institutions; $18 out of area; $24 out of state.
Ad Rates: GLR: $.97 **Circ:** Combined 20,590
BW: $1,741.50
4C: $2,066.50
SAU: $13.50

CHATSWORTH†, pop. 2,493.

NW GA. Murray Co. 38 mi. SE of Chattanooga, TN. Summer resort. Manufactures textiles, talc products. Talc mines; pine timber. Agriculture. Corn, cotton, hay.

7275 Chatsworth Times
Walls Newspapers
224 N. 3rd Ave. Phone: (706)695-4646
PO Box 130 Fax: (706)695-7181
Chatsworth, GA 30705
Newspaper. **Founded:** 1890. **Freq:** Weekly (Thurs.). **Print Method:** Offset. **Cols./Page:** 6. **Col. Width:** 21 nonpareils. **Col. Depth:** 287 agate lines. **Key Personnel:** David L. Shelton, Editor and Publisher. **Subscription Rates:** $15.75 individuals; $28 out of area. **Remarks:** Accepts advertising.
Ad Rates: BW: $586.95 **Circ:** Paid 5,400
4C: $786.95
SAU: $6
PCI: $4.55

7276 Chatsworth Cablevision Co.
Box 1443 Phone: (706)695-2727
Chatsworth, GA 30705 Fax: (706)695-3459

Owner: Helecion Cable Communication, 927 Hwy. 52 Alt., PO Box 1443, Chatsworth, GA 30705. **Founded:** July 25, 1996.

Formerly: C-4 Media Cable; Frontier Vision. **Key Personnel:** Pamela Foxworth, Contact; Rich Donahue, General Mgr. **Cities Served:** Murray County: subscribing households 5,032; 37 channels; 1 community access channel.

7277 WCLP-TV - 18
c/o WGTV-TV Phone: (404)756-2400
1540 Stewart Ave. SW Fax: (404)756-2407
Atlanta, GA 30310
Free: (800)222-6006

Format: Public TV. **Networks:** Public Broadcasting Service (PBS); Georgia Public Television. **Owner:** Georgia Public Telecommunications Commission, at above address. **Founded:** 1967. **Operating Hours:** 6 a.m.-midnight; 100% network. **ADI:** Chattanooga (Cleveland), TN. **Key Personnel:** Werner Rogers, Contact; Frank Bugg, Contact; Kent Steele, Program Dir.; Babette Davidson, Program Mgr.; Marcia Kilingsworth, Contact. **Local Programs:** *Georgia Outdoors*; *The Lawmakers*. **Ad Rates:** Noncommercial.

CHEROKEE

7278 Cherokee Plus
Neighbor Newspapers, Inc.
580 Fairground St. Phone: (770)428-9411
PO Box 449 Fax: (770)428-7945
Marietta, GA 30060
Community newspaper. **Founded:** 1986. **Freq:** Semiweekly (Wed. and Sun.). **Subscription Rates:** Free. **Formerly**: South Cherokee Neighbor (July 1989).
Circ: Non-paid 18,500

CLARKESVILLE†, pop. 1,500.

NE GA. Habersham Co. 80 mi. NE of Atlanta. Saw, planing, grist, knitting mills; poultry processing plant. Manufactures electrical products, furniture, textiles. Walnut, pine timber. Fruit, truck farms. Peaches, apples, beans.

7279 WCHM-AM - 1490
PO Box 368 Phone: (404)754-6272
Clarkesville, GA 30523 Fax: (404)754-8621

Format: Southern Gospel. **Networks:** USA Radio. **Founded:** 1975. **Formerly**: WLTA-AM (1979). **Operating Hours:** Continuous; 5% network, 95% local. **Local Programs:** *Radio Market* 8:35 am - 9:00 am Mon. - Sat., Brian Rothell, Mailing contact. **Wattage:** 1000. **Ad Rates:** $7 for 30 seconds; $9 for 60 seconds.

CLAXTON†, pop. 2,694.

SE GA. Evans Co. 50 mi. W. of Savannah. Residential.

7280 The Enterprise
PO Box 218 Phone: (912)739-2132
Claxton, GA 30417 Fax: (912)739-2140
Free: (800)794-3924

Local newspaper. **Founded:** 1912. **Freq:** Weekly (Wed.). **Print Method:** Offset. **Cols./Page:** 6. **Col. Width:** 26 nonpareils. **Col. Depth:** 294 agate lines. **Key Personnel:** Mitchell E. Peace, Publisher; Vicky Whitehead, Editor/Gen. Mgr., vwhiteh849@aol.com. **Subscription Rates:** $18 locally; $24 out of state. **Remarks:** Accepts advertising. **Online:** America Online, Inc.
Ad Rates: BW: $504 **Circ:** ‡3,500
4C: $629
PCI: $5.75

7281 WCLA-AM - 1470
316 N. River St. Phone: (912)739-3035
Box 427 Fax: (912)739-0050
Claxton, GA 30417
E-mail: wcla@g-net.net

Format: Gospel. **Networks:** Georgia Radio. **Owner:** Progressive United Comm., at above address. **Founded:** 1958. **Operating Hours:** Continuous. **ADI:** Savannah, GA. **Key Personnel:** Paschell Mix, Contact; Econuel Ingram, Contact; Pat Collins, Contact. **Local Programs:** *Legends of Gospel* 12:00 noon Sat., Sun., Pat Collins, Business Mgr. **Wattage:** 1000 day; 260 night. **Ad Rates:** $6-8 for 30 seconds; $9-10 for 60 seconds. Combined advertising rates available with WCLA-FM.

7282 WCLA-FM - 107.3
316 N. River St. Phone: (912)739-3035
Claxton, GA 30417 Fax: (912)739-0050
E-mail: wcla@g-net.net

Format: Classical. **Networks:** ABC. **Owner:** Progressive United Comm., at above address. **Founded:** 1972. **Operating Hours:** Continuous. **ADI:** Savannah, GA. **Key Personnel:** Paschell Mix, Contact; Econuel Ingram, Contact; Pat Collins, Contact. **Wattage:** 25,000. **Ad Rates:** $8-10 for 30 seconds; $11-12 for 60 seconds. Combined advertising rates available with WCLA-AM.

CLAYTON†, pop. 1,838.

NE GA. Rabun Co. 45 mi. NE of Gainesville. Tourist resort. Skiing, whitewater rafting. Manufactures textiles, fabricated metal products, carpets. Saw mills. Pine, hardwood timber. Agriculture.

7283 Northland Cable TV
PO Box 2008 Phone: (706)782-4249
Clayton, GA 30525 Fax: (706)782-3707

Formerly: Rabun Cablevision. **Key Personnel:** Rick Marchman, General Mgr. **Cities Served:** Clayton, GA.

7284 WRBN-FM - 104.1
PO Box 1149 Phone: (706)782-4251
Clayton, GA 30525 Fax: (706)782-4252

Format: Adult Contemporary. **Networks:** ABC. **Founded:** 1989. **Formerly**: WQXJ-FM (1996). **Operating Hours:** Continuous. **ADI:** Atlanta (Athens & Rome), GA. **Key Personnel:** Jan Lunsford, Operations Mgr.; Wayne O'Kelley, News Dir.; Tom Stanwood, General Mgr. **Wattage:** 6000. **Ad Rates:** $6-12 for 30 seconds; $8-14 for 60 seconds.

CLEVELAND†.

NE GA. White Co. 30 mi. N. of Clermont.

7285 WRWH-AM - 1350
Hood St. Phone: (706)865-3181
PO Box 181 Fax: (706)865-0421
Cleveland, GA 30528
E-mail: ddyer@ngweb.net

Format: Country; Religious. **Networks:** NBC; Gannett News. **Owner:** Newsic, Inc., at above address. **Founded:** 1958. **Operating Hours:** 6 a.m.-sunset. **ADI:** Atlanta (Athens & Rome), GA. **Key Personnel:** Dean Dyer, Contact; Bonnie Dyer, Music Dir. **Local Programs:** *Public Forum*, Dean Dyer; *Swap Shop*, Dean Dyer. **Wattage:** 1000. **Ad Rates:** $5.20 for 30 seconds; $6.10 for 60 seconds.

COCHRAN†, pop. 5,161.

C. GA. Bleckley Co. 40 mi. S. of Macon. Manufactures textiles, fluorescent lighting fixtures. Planing mill; cotton ginning. Pine timber. Agriculture. Cotton, corn, peaches, peanuts.

7286 The Cochran Journal
The Cochran Journal Inc.
PO Box 232 Phone: (912)934-6303
Cochran, GA 31014 Fax: (912)934-6800
Publisher E-mail: journal@accucomm.net

Community newspaper. **Subtitle:** Official Organ of Bleckley County Since 1908. **Founded:** 1908. **Freq:** Weekly (Wed.). **Print Method:** Offset. **Cols./Page:** 6. **Col. Width:** 13.5 picas. **Col. Depth:** 21.5 picas. **Key Personnel:** Jerry Gunn, Editor, phone (912)934-6303, journal@accucomm.net; Bob Tribble, Publisher, phone (912)825-2432, ltpeachpub@aol.com. **Subscription Rates:** $19.26; $23.85 out of area; $30 out of state. **Remarks:** Accepts advertising. **Feature Editors:** Rebecca Holland, *Sports*, bholland@accucumm.net.
Ad Rates: GLR: $4 **Circ:** ‡3,600
BW: $5
SAU: $5.30
PCI: $5

7287 Kernel
Middle Georgia College
Cochran, GA 31014 Phone: (912)934-3393
Fax: (912)934-3342

Collegiate newspaper. **Founded:** 1930. **Freq:** 5/college semester. **Print Method:** Offset. **Cols./Page:** 5. **Col. Width:** 22 nonpareils. **Col. Depth:** 196 agate lines. **Key Personnel:** Jennifer Brannon, Advisor, jbrannon@warrior.mgc.peadinet.edu. **Remarks:** Accepts advertising.
Ad Rates: GLR: $.15 **Circ:** Free ‡1,000

7288 WVMG-AM - 1440
PO Box 570 Phone: (912)934-4548
Cochran, GA 31014-0570

Format: Country; Gospel; Sports. **Networks:** NBC; Georgia Radio. **Founded:** 1988. **Operating Hours:** 6 a.m.-midnight; 4% network, 96% local. **Key Personnel:** Charles G. Hill, Contact; Martha Shirah, Sales Mgr. **Wattage:** 1000. **Ad Rates:** $4-6 for 30 seconds; $5-7 for 60 seconds.

7289 WVMG-FM - 96.7
PO Box 570 Phone: (912)934-4548
Cochran, GA 31014 Free: (800)962-9864

Format: Country; Religious; Gospel; Sports. **Networks:** NBC; Georgia Radio. **Founded:** 1988. **Operating Hours:** Continuous; 4% network, 96% local. **Key Personnel:** Tom Kirk, General Mgr. **Wattage:** 6,000. **Ad Rates:** $5-7 for 30 seconds; $6-9 for 60 seconds.

COLQUITT†, pop. 2,065.

SW GA. Miller Co. 30 mi. N. of Decatur. Cotton ginning. Manufactures timber, fertilizer, plaster. Dairy, stock, poultry farms. Cotton, corn, peanuts.

7290 Miller County Liberal
157 E. Main St. Phone: (912)758-5549
PO Box 37 Fax: (912)758-5540
Colquitt, GA 31737-0037
Newspaper with a Democratic orientation. **Founded:** 1897. **Freq:** Weekly (Thurs.). **Print Method:** Web offset. **Trim Size:** 13 3/4 x 21 1/2. **Cols./Page:** 6. **Col. Width:** 12 picas. **Col. Depth:** 21 1/2 inches. **Key Personnel:** Terry Toole, Editor and Publisher, terryt@surfsouth.com; Betty Jo Toole, Advertising Mgr. **USPS:** 349-700. **Subscription Rates:** $14 individuals; $22 out of country. **Remarks:** Accepts advertising. **Alt. Formats:** CD-ROM.
Ad Rates: GLR: $4.00 **Circ:** ‡2,900
BW: $516
4C: $785
SAU: $4.00
PCI: $4.00

COLUMBUS†, pop. 168,598.

W. GA. Muscogee Co. On Chattahoochee River, at head of navigation, 95 mi. SW of Atlanta. U.S. Infantry School. Convention & trade center. Historic district. Manufactures textiles, fiber bags, hand tools, electric capacitors, brick. Iron works; foundries; machine shops; bottling works; meat packing.

The Benning Leader - See Fort Benning

7291 Columbus Ledger-Enquirer
Knight-Ridder, Inc.
PO Box 711 Phone: (706)324-5526
Columbus, GA 31994 Fax: (706)576-6290

General newspaper. **Founded:** 1930. **Freq:** Mon.-Sun. (morn.). **Print Method:** Offset. **Cols./Page:** 6. **Col. Width:** 25 nonpareils. **Col. Depth:** 301 agate lines. **Key Personnel:** Al Johnson, Exec. Editor; Dick Stone, Advertising Mgr. **Subscription Rates:** $143.52 individuals. **Remarks:** Accepts advertising. **URL:** http://www.l-e-o.com. **Feature Editors:** Skip Connett, *Religion*, phone (404)571-8565; Chuck Crouch, *Photo*, *Science*, phone (404)571-8565; Jeff Davison, *City*, *Education*, *Metro*, *News*, *Political*, phone (404)571-8566; Ken Edelstein, *Environmental*, phone (404)571-8516; George Henry, *Sports*, phone (404)571-8565; Sandra Okamoto, *Drama*, *Entertainment*, *Movie*, *Music*, phone (404)571-8585; Baxter Omohurdro, *Editorials*, phone (404)571-8583; Jim Poole, *Consumer Affairs*, *Farm*, *Financial/Business*, *Garden/Home*, *Real Estate*, *Rural Development*, phone (404)571-8513; Kaffie Sledge, *Family*, *Fashion*, *Features*, *Lifestyle*, *Living*, *Medical*, *Society*, *Women's*, phone (404)571-8585; Louise Smith, *Food*, phone (404)571-8565; Chris Turner, *TV*, phone (404)571-8565; Mick Walsh, *Radio*, *TV*, phone (404)571-8565.
Ad Rates: BW: $4,369.23 **Circ:** Mon.-Thurs. ★**49,282**
4C: $5,044.23 Fri. ★**57,519**
SAU: $33.87 Sat. ★**56,705**
PCI: $33.87 Sun. ★**66,250**

7292 The Columbus Times
Columbus Times
2230 Buena Vista Rd. Phone: (706)324-2404
Columbus, GA 31906 Fax: (706)596-0657

Black community newspaper. **Founded:** 1958. **Freq:** Weekly (Wed.). **Print Method:** Offset. Broadsheet. **Trim Size:** 13 x 21 1/2. **Cols./Page:** 6. **Col. Width:** 2 1/16 inches. **Col. Depth:** 21 1/2 inches. **Key Personnel:** Ophelia Devore Mitchell, Editor and Publisher, phone (706)324-2464, fax (706)596-0657, coltimas@ldl.net; Helmut Gerdes, Advertising Mgr. **Subscription Rates:** $31.46 individuals. **Remarks:** Accepts advertising.
Ad Rates: BW: $1,733.76 **Circ:** ‡20,000
4C: $2,048.76
SAU: $15.69

7293 TCI Cablevision of Georgia
Box 1678 Phone: (706)324-2288
Columbus, GA 31902 Fax: (706)324-4031
Free: (800)210-8882

Founded: 1970. **Cities Served:** Harris County, Muscogee County, and Bibb City, GA.

7294 TeleCable of Columbus, Inc.
6700 Macon Rd. Phone: (706)569-5900
Columbus, GA 31907 Fax: (706)568-8270

Founded: 1970. **Cities Served:** Muscogee County, GA.

7295 WCGQ-FM - 107.3
1353 13th Ave. Phone: (706)327-1217
Columbus, GA 31901 Fax: (706)596-4600

Format: Adult Contemporary. **Founded:** 1973. **Operating Hours:** Continuous. **ADI:** Columbus, GA (Opelika, AL). **Key Personnel:** C.A. McClure, Jr., Owner, mclure@ldl.net; Joseph W. McClure, Owner; Margaret M. Moore, Owner; Charles A. McClure, Jr., President/General Manager; Helen Neal, General Sales Mgr. **Wattage:** 100,000. **Ad Rates:** $30-50 for 30 seconds; $36-60 for 60 seconds. $25-$45 for 30 seconds; $35-$55 for 60 seconds. Combined advertising rates available with WRCG-AM.

7296 WDAK-AM - 540
PO Box 1640 Phone: (706)596-5100
Columbus, GA 31994

Format: Sports; Talk. **Networks:** ABC; NBC; ESPN Radio. **Owner:** Solar Broadcasting, Inc., at above address. **Founded:** 1940. **Operating Hours:** Continuous. **ADI:** Columbus, GA (Opelika, AL). **Key Personnel:** Jim Powey, V. P./General Mgr.; John Cage, Program and Traffic Dir. **Local Programs:** *The Upper Deck* 7:00 a.m.-9:00 a.m., J. Powell; *Sport Lunch* 12:00 p.m.-1:00 p.m., J. Powell. **Wattage:** 5,000. **Ad Rates:** $15 for 30 seconds; $20 for 60 seconds.

7297 WEAM-AM - 1580
PO Box 766 Phone: (706)298-1590
Columbus, GA 31902 Fax: (706)298-7800

Format: Gospel. **Networks:** USA Radio. **Founded:** 1980. **Operating Hours:** 6 a.m. - midnight. **ADI:** Columbus, GA (Opelika, AL). **Key Personnel:** Charyn Cannon. **Local Programs:** *Morning Magazine*, Margaret Dawson; *Morning Magazine*, Margaret Dawson, (334)298-1580; *Valley Viewpoints*, Margaret Dawson, (334)298-1580. **Wattage:** 2300 day; 1000 night. **Ad Rates:** Advertising accepted; rates available upon request.

7298 WGSY-FM - 100.1
PO Box 687 Phone: (706)576-3000
Columbus, GA 31902-0687 Fax: (706)576-3010

Format: Adult Contemporary. **Networks:** ABC. **Founded:** 1971. **Formerly:** WXLE-FM; WEIZ-FM. **Operating Hours:** Continuous; 100% local. **ADI:** Columbus, GA (Opelika, AL). **Key Personnel:** Jim Martin, Market Mgr.; Susan Breazeale, Dir. of Sales; Brian Waters, Operations Mgr.; Mollie Norris, Promotions; Chuck Leonard, News Dir.; Alan Jeffries, Production Mgr. **Wattage:** 6000. **Ad Rates:** Advertising accepted; rates available upon request.

7299 WLTZ-TV - 38
PO Box 12289 Phone: (706)561-3838
Columbus, GA 31917-2289 Fax: (706)563-8467
E-mail: wltz38@fiac.net

Format: Commercial TV. **Networks:** NBC. **Owner:** Lewis Broadcasting Corp., at above address. **Founded:** 1970. **Formerly:** WYEA-TV (1970). **Operating Hours:** Continuous. **ADI:** Columbus, GA (Opelika, AL). **Key Personnel:** Charles Collins, Operations Mgr., wltz@knology.net; Tom Breazeale, General Mgr.; Jim Davis, General Sales Mgr.; Jim Devitt, Promotions Mgr. **Local Programs:** *NBC 38 Coffee Break.* **Wattage:** 1,070,000. **Ad Rates:** Advertising accepted; rates available upon request.

7300 WPNX-AM - 1460
PO Box 687 Phone: (706)576-3000
Columbus, GA 31902-0687 Fax: (706)576-3010

Format: Southern Gospel. **Networks:** ABC. **Founded:** 1952. **Formerly:** WPNX-AM (1989). **Operating Hours:** 6 a.m - 12 p.m.; 65% network, 35% local. **ADI:** Columbus, GA (Opelika, AL). **Key Personnel:** Jim Martin, Manager; Jerry Northington, Sales Mgr. **Wattage:** 5000. **Ad Rates:** $12 for 30 seconds; $18 for 60 seconds.

7301 WRBL-TV - 3
1350 13th AVE. 31901 Phone: (706)323-3333
P.O. Box 270 Fax: (706)327-6655
Columbus, GA 31902-0270

Format: Commercial TV. **Networks:** CBS. **Owner:** TCS Television Partners, L.P., at above address. **Founded:** 1953. **Operating Hours:** Continuous. **ADI:** Columbus, GA (Opelika, AL). **Key Personnel:** Ray Chumley, General Mgr.; Albert Parsons, General Sales Mgr.; Alice Upshaw, Program Dir. **Ad Rates:** $10-700 for 30 seconds.

WRFS-AM - See Alexander City, Alabama

7302 WSTH-FM - 106.1
PO Box 687 Phone: (706)576-3000
Columbus, GA 31902-0687 Fax: (706)576-3010
E-mail: wayout@mindspring.com

Format: Country. **Networks:** ABC. **Founded:** 1986. **Formerly:** WRFS-FM. **Operating Hours:** Continuous. **ADI:** Columbus, GA (Opelika, AL). **Key Personnel:** Jim Martin, Market Mgr.; Susan Breazeale, Dir. of Sales; Brian Waters, Operations Mgr.; Mollie Norris, Promotions; Chuck Leonard, News Dir.; Alan Jeffries, Production Mgr. **Wattage:** 100,000. **Ad Rates:** $35-58 for 60 seconds. Combined advertising rates available with WDAK, WRFS.

7303 WTVM-TV - 9
1909 Wynnton Rd Phone: (706)324-6471
Columbus, GA 31906 Fax: (706)322-7527

Format: Commercial TV. **Networks:** ABC. **Founded:** 1953. **Operating Hours:** Continuous. **ADI:** Columbus, GA (Opelika, AL). **Key Personnel:** Lee Brantley, General Mgr. **Ad Rates:** Advertising accepted; rates available upon request.

7304 WXTX-TV - 54
PO Box 12188 Phone: (706)561-5400
Columbus, GA 31917 Fax: (706)561-6505

Format: Commercial TV. **Networks:** Fox. **Founded:** 1983. **Operating Hours:** Continuous. **ADI:** Columbus, GA (Opelika, AL). **Key Personnel:** Stephen F. Thomas, General Mgr.; Sharon Davlin, Program Dir.; Elsie Haden, Traffic Mgr.; Frank Williams, General Sales Mgr.; Kelley Mitchell, Promotions; Larry Stephens, Production.

COMER, pop. 930.

NE GA. Madison Co. 17 mi. NE of Athens. Textiles factories. Agriculture. Poultry products.

7305 The Comer News
PO Box 7 Phone: (706)783-2553
1976 Main St. Fax: (706)783-2553
Comer, GA 30629
Weekly community newspaper. **Founded:** 1909. **Freq:** Weekly (Thurs.). **Print Method:** Offset. **Cols./Page:** 6. **Col. Width:** 12 picas. **Col. Depth:** 21 inches. **Key Personnel:** J.C. Ayers, Editor and Publisher. **Subscription Rates:** $15 individuals. **Remarks:** Advertising not accepted for lottery, alcohol, and tobacco products.
Ad Rates: GLR: $.20 **Circ:** ‡1,700
BW: $352.80
4C: $652.80
PCI: $2.80

COMMERCE, pop. 4,092.

NE GA. Jackson Co. 18 mi. N. of Athens. Manufactures textiles, hydraulic pumps, electronic products, cotton goods, lumber. Farming. Peach orchards.

7306 The Commerce News
Jackson Herald, Inc.
1672 S. Broard St. Phone: (706)335-2927
PO Box 459
Commerce, GA 30529
Community newspaper. **Founded:** 1875. **Freq:** Weekly (Wed.). **Print Method:** Offset. Uses mats. **Cols./Page:** 6. **Col. Width:** 26 nonpareils. **Col. Depth:** 294 agate lines. **Key Personnel:** Herman Buffington, Publisher. **Subscription Rates:** $12.72 individuals. **Remarks:** Color advertising accepted; rates available upon request.
Ad Rates: BW: $599.85 **Circ:** ‡4,600
PCI: $4.65

7307 WJJC-AM - 1270
220 Little St. Phone: (706)335-3155
PO Box 379 Fax: (706)335-7622
Commerce, GA 30529

Format: Country; Southern Gospel; Sports. **Networks:** NBC; Georgia Radio. **Founded:** 1957. **Operating Hours:** 12a.m.-12:00 p.m.; 8% network, 92% local. **ADI:** Atlanta (Athens & Rome), GA. **Key Personnel:** Gerald Jordan, General Mgr.; Rob Jordan, Sales Mgr.; Bill Carson, Chief Engineer/Public Dir.; Rick Bennett, Sports Dir.; Keith Parnell, Music Dir.; Denise Jordan, Office Mgr. **Local Programs:** *Fabulous Football Fridays*; *Obituary's*; *Trading Post.* **Wattage:** 173. **Ad Rates:** $7-10 for 30 seconds; $8-10 for 60 seconds.

CONYERS†, pop. 6,567.

NC GA. Rockdale Co. 20 mi. SE of Atlanta. Manufactures tires, mattresses, business forms, fluorescent fixtures, food products, fabricated steel, aluminum screens, awnings, clothing, plastics. Meat packing plant. Pine timber. Agriculture.

7308 East Metro Plus
Rockdale Citizen
969 Main St. Phone: (404)483-7108
PO Box 136 Fax: (904)483-2955
Conyers, GA 30207
Shopper. **Founded:** 1953. **Freq:** Weekly (Wed.). **Print Method:** Offset. **Cols./Page:** 6. **Col. Width:** 24 nonpareils. **Col. Depth:** 301 agate lines. **Key Personnel:** Fred Turner, Editor; Elizabeth H. Staples, Publisher; Jane O. Patterson, Advertising Mgr. **Remarks:** Accepts advertising. **Formerly:** This Week in East Metro.
Ad Rates: BW: $857.85 **Circ:** Free ‡22,000
SAU: $6.65

7309 Rockdale Citizen
969 Main St. Phone: (404)483-7108
PO Box 136 Fax: (904)483-2955
Conyers, GA 30207
General newspaper. **Founded:** 1953. **Freq:** Daily (eve.). **Print Method:** Offset. **Cols./Page:** 6. **Col. Width:** 24 nonpareils. **Col. Depth:** 301 agate lines. **Key Personnel:** Barry King, Editor; Joe Cunningham, Publisher; Ernie Yarbrough, Advertising Mgr. **Subscription Rates:** $0.50 single issue. **Remarks:** Accepts advertising.
Ad Rates: SAU: $4.60 **Circ:** Combined ♦**10,575**

7310 WPBS-AM - 1050
1381 Rockbridge Rd. Phone: (770)483-1000
Conyers, GA 30207 Fax: (770)483-1099

Format: Religious. **Networks:** USA Radio. **Owner:** Midway Holiness Church Inc., at above address, (404)483-1000. **Founded:** 1979. **Formerly:** WTPO-AM (1989). **Operating Hours:** Continuous. **Key Personnel:** Erich Janzen, General Mgr. **Wattage:** 1000. **Ad Rates:** $3-15 for 30 seconds; $4-20 for 60 seconds.

CORDELE†, pop. 10,914.

SWC GA. Crisp Co. 65 mi. S. of Macon. Manufactures phosphate, lumber, fertilizer, textiles, air conditioners, concrete products, foundry products, feeds. Timber. Diversified farming. Cotton, peanuts, pecans, watermelons.

7311 Cordele Dispatch
McLeansboro Times-Leader
306 13th Ave. W. Phone: (912)273-2277
PO Box 1058 Fax: (912)273-7239
Cordele, GA 31015-1058
Publisher E-mail: press@excel.net

General newspaper. **Founded:** 1908. **Freq:** Daily (eve.). **Print Method:** Offset. **Trim Size:** 13 x 21 1/2. **Cols./Page:** 6. **Col. Width:** 2 1/16 inches. **Col. Depth:** 301 agate lines. **Key Personnel:** Randy Cox, Publisher; Shane Belton, Advertising Dir. **Subscription Rates:** $88.40 individuals. **Remarks:** Accepts advertising.
Ad Rates: GLR: $0.58 **Circ:** ‡6,000
BW: $1,056.51
4C: $1,286.51
SAU: $8.19

7312 Cover Story
Cordele Dispatch
306 13th Ave. W
Cordele, GA 31015

Shopper. **Freq:** Weekly (Wed.). **Print Method:** Offset. **Trim Size:** 13 x 21 1/2. **Cols./Page:** 6. **Col. Width:** 26 nonpareils. **Col. Depth:** 301 agate lines. **Key Personnel:** Randy Cox, Publisher; Shane Belton, Advertising Dir. **Remarks:** Accepts advertising.
Ad Rates: GLR: $0.21 **Circ:** Free ‡3,000
BW: $387
4C: $617
SAU: $3

7313 Southeastern News
South Georgia News
302 W. 16th Ave., Ste. D Phone: (912)273-6714
Cordele, GA 31015 Fax: (912)273-6714

Black community newspaper. **Founded:** May 5, 1995. **Freq:** Monthly. **Trim Size:** 7 1/4 X 10. **Subscription Rates:** $12 individuals; $.25 single issue. **Remarks:** Accepts advertising.
Ad Rates: PCI: $10 **Circ:** (Not Reported)

7314 WSST-TV - 55
PO Box 917 Phone: (912)273-0001
Cordele, GA 31015 Fax: (912)273-8894
E-mail: wsst@sowega.net

Format: Commercial TV. **Networks:** Independent. **Owner:** Sunbelt-South Tele-Communications, Ltd., at above address. **Founded:** June 1, 1989. **Operating Hours:** Continuous. **ADI:** Albany-Schenectady-Troy, NY. **Key Personnel:** Bill Goodson, General Mgr./General Partner; Phil Streetman, Station Mgr.; Sara Howell, Sales Mgr.; Lee Wright, Program Dir.; Ricky

Smarr, Production Mgr. **Wattage:** 100,000. **Ad Rates:** $30 for 30 seconds.

CORNELIA

NE GA. Habersham Co. 5 mi. W. of Mt. Airy.

7315 The Northeast Georgian
Community Newspaper
PO Box 190 Phone: (404)778-4215
Cornelia, GA 30531-0190 Fax: (706)778-4114

Community newspaper. **Founded:** 1892. **Freq:** Weekly (Tues.). **Print Method:** Offset. **Cols./Page:** 6. **Col. Width:** 12 picas. **Col. Depth:** 21 1/2 inches. **Key Personnel:** Steve Avery, Publisher. **Subscription Rates:** $15. **Remarks:** Accepts advertising. **Formerly:** Cornelia Northeast Georgian (1992).
Ad Rates: BW: $645 **Circ:** 8,100
4C: $860
PCI: $5.55

7316 WCON-AM - 1450
540 N. Main St. Phone: (706)778-2241
PO Box 100 Fax: (706)778-0576
Cornelia, GA 30531

Format: Gospel; Country. **Networks:** ABC; Georgia Radio. **Owner:** Habersham Broadcasting Co., at above address. **Founded:** 1953. **Operating Hours:** Continuous. **Key Personnel:** Bobbie C. Foster, Contact; Ted Taylor, News Dir. **Wattage:** 1000. **Ad Rates:** $4-5 for 30 seconds; $6-7 for 60 seconds.

7317 WCON-FM - 99.3
540 N. Main St. Phone: (706)778-2241
PO Box 100 Fax: (706)778-0576
Cornelia, GA 30531

Format: Country. **Networks:** ABC; Georgia Radio. **Owner:** Habersham Broadcasting Co., at above address. **Founded:** 1965. **Operating Hours:** Continuous. **Key Personnel:** Bobbie C. Foster, General Mgr. **Wattage:** 50,000. **Ad Rates:** $6-8 for 15 seconds; $8-10 for 30 seconds; $10-12 for 60 seconds.

COVINGTON†, pop. 10,586.

NC GA. Newton Co. 36 mi. SE of Atlanta. Manufactures automotive moulding, industrial adhesive, corrugated boxes, wire screening, olefin fiber, plastic bags and foam products. Pine, oak, poplar timber. Diversified farming.

7318 Covington News
Covington Newspaper Co., Inc.
PO Box 1249 Phone: (770)786-3401
1148 Monticello St. Fax: (770)786-6451
Covington, GA 30209-1249
Community newspaper. **Founded:** 1864. **Freq:** Triweekly. **Print Method:** Offset. **Cols./Page:** 6. **Col. Width:** 26 nonpareils. **Col. Depth:** 301 agate lines. **Key Personnel:** Ron Stokes, Publisher; David Emmons, Marketing Mgr.; Ross Norton, Managing Editor. **Subscription Rates:** $41.34 individuals. **Remarks:** Accepts advertising.
Ad Rates: BW: $896.55 **Circ:** ‡7,450
4C: $1,271.55
PCI: $7.90

7319 Multi-County Star
Covington Newspaper Co., Inc.
PO Box 1249 Phone: (770)786-3401
1148 Monticello St. Fax: (770)786-6451
Covington, GA 30209-1249
Community newspaper. **Founded:** 1976. **Freq:** Weekly (Tues.). **Print Method:** Offset. **Cols./Page:** 6. **Col. Width:** 26 nonpareils. **Col. Depth:** 301 agate lines. **Key Personnel:** Denny Hill, Editor and Publisher; Sam Knox, Advertising Mgr. **Subscription Rates:** Free. **Remarks:** Accepts advertising.
Ad Rates: GLR: $.74 **Circ:** Free ‡26,300
BW: $1,180.35
4C: $1,630.35
SAU: $9.15

7320 City of Covington CATV
1167 Pace St. Phone: (404)385-2044
PO Box 1527 Fax: (404)385-2045
Covington, GA 30209

Founded: 1980. **Key Personnel:** Gary Curtis, General Mgr. **Cities Served:** Newton County: subscribing households 6,271; 36 channels; 1 community access channel.

7321 WGFS-AM - 1430
1151 Hendricks St. Phone: (770)786-1430
PO Box 869 Fax: (770)784-9892
Covington, GA 30209

Format: Country. **Networks:** CBS; Georgia Radio. **Founded:** 1946. **Operating Hours:** 6 a.m.-8 p.m. **ADI:** Atlanta (Athens & Rome), GA. **Key Personnel:** Chris Elder, General Mgr.; Susan J. Fuller, News Dir. **Local Programs:** *Healthtalk*, Steve Aldridge; *Super Trivia Spectacular*, Bill Dolan. **Wattage:** 5000. **Ad Rates:** $5.45-7.05 for 30 seconds; $7.66-10.33 for 60 seconds. **URL:** http://www.wgfs.com.

CRAWFORDVILLE†, pop. 594.

C. GA. Taliaferro Co.

7322 Crawfordville Advocate-Democrat
The Herald Journal
Rte. 1 Phone: (706)453-7988
PO Box 124 Fax: (706)453-2311
Crawfordville, GA 30631
Community newspaper. **Founded:** 1911. **Freq:** Weekly. **Cols./Page:** 6. **Col. Width:** 2 inches. **Col. Depth:** 21 inches. **Key Personnel:** Barbara M. Darden, Editor; Carey Williams, Jr., Publisher. **Subscription Rates:** $5 individuals. **Remarks:** Accepts advertising.
Ad Rates: GLR: $2.50 **Circ:** Paid 790
PCI: $6.40 Free 10

CUMMING†, pop. 2,094.

N. GA. Forsythe Co. 35 mi. N. of Atlanta. Residential.

7323 Forsyth County News
PO Box 210 Phone: (770)887-3126
Cumming, GA 30130 Fax: (770)889-6017

Community newspaper. **Founded:** 1908. **Freq:** Tri-weekly (Wed., Fri., Sun.). **Print Method:** Offset. Uses sheets. **Cols./Page:** 6. **Col. Width:** 26 nonpareils. **Col. Depth:** 301 agate lines. **Key Personnel:** Karleen Chaulker, Editor; Dennis Stockton, Publisher. **Subscription Rates:** $30 individuals; $50 out of country.
Ad Rates: BW: $1449 **Circ:** Wed. ♦**13,836**
4C: $1674 Sun. ♦**15,009**
SAU: $11.50 Fri. ♦**13,750**

7324 WMLB-AM - 1170
1107 Atlanta Hwy. Phone: (770)889-1170
Cumming, GA 30040-6405 Fax: (770)887-3333

Owner: Lanier Broadcasting, Inc., at above address. **Founded:** 1961. **Formerly:** WSNE-AM (1980); WHNE-AM. **Operating Hours:** Sunrise-sunset; 10% network; 90% local. **Key Personnel:** Amy Rives McCollum, General Mgr.; Greg Bolan, Sales Mgr.; David Stone, Program Dir., dave@wmlb.com; Jim Dean, Contact. **Local Programs:** *MRN Racing*; *Party Line*; *Swap Shop*. **Wattage:** 5000. **Ad Rates:** $12 for 30 seconds; $20 for 60 seconds. **URL:** http://www.wmlb.com.

7325 WWEV-FM - 91.5
PO Box 248 Phone: (770)781-9150
Cumming, GA 30028 Fax: (770)781-5003
Free: (800)522-9150

Format: Religious; Contemporary Christian. **Networks:** USA Radio. **Founded:** 1981. **Operating Hours:** Continuous; 100% local. **ADI:** Atlanta (Athens & Rome), GA. **Key Personnel:** N. Barry Holt, General Mgr.; Larry Grover, Music Dir. **Local Programs:** *Powersource*, Tim Bagley; *Southern Breeze*, Larry Grover, Music Dir. **Wattage:** 9000. **Ad Rates:** Noncommercial.

CUTHBERT†, pop. 3,620.

SW GA. Randolph Co. 46 mi. NW of Albany. Manufactures projectors, lumber, baskets, textiles, soft drinks. Cotton ginning. Pine, oak, gum, poplar timber. Agriculture. Cotton, peanuts, corn.

7326 Peach State Cablevision
Box 304 Phone: (912)732-3744
Cuthbert, GA 31740 Fax: (912)732-6026
Free: (800)342-8405

Owner: Cooke Cablevision, Box 4200, Woodland Hills, CA 91365, (818)713-3800. **Formerly:** Cooke Cablevision (1992). **Key Personnel:** Sonny Seneker, General Mgr. **Cities Served:** Cuthbert, GA.

DAHLONEGA†, pop. 2,800.

C. GA. Lumpkin Co. North Georgia College. Gold mining, trading, and poultry production.

7327 The Dahlonega Nugget
1074 W. Main St. Phone: (706)864-3613
PO Box 36 Fax: (706)864-4360
Dahlonega, GA 30533
Publication E-mail: thenug@stc.net

Local newspaper. **Founded:** May 1, 1890. **Freq:** Weekly (Wed.). **Print Method:** Offset. **Cols./Page:** 6. **Col. Width:** 12.2 picas. **Col. Depth:** 21 1/2 inches. **Key Personnel:** Terrie Ellerbee, Editor; John Solesbee, Publisher, phone (706)778-4215, fax (706)778-4114; Lynn Clark, Advertising Mgr. **Subscription Rates:** $17 individuals; $33 out of area. **Remarks:** Accepts advertising.
Ad Rates: BW: $499.23 **Circ:** ‡5,050
4C: $799.23
CNU: $4.25
PCI: $5.20

7328 WKHC-FM - 104.3
1376 Ben Higgins Rd. Phone: (706)867-9542
Dahlonega, GA 30533
E-mail: gold_104@stc.net

Format: Country. **Networks:** ABC. **Owner:** Southern Radio, Inc., at above address. **Founded:** Dec. 16, 1996. **Operating Hours:** Continuous. **ADI:** Atlanta (Athens & Rome), GA. **Key Personnel:** Ashley Croom, Sales Mgr.; Kevin Croom, General Mgr. **Wattage:** 6000. **Ad Rates:** $15 for 30 seconds; $18 for 60 seconds. **URL:** http://www.gold104.com.

DALLAS†, pop. 2,508.

C. GA. Paulding Co. 30 mi. WNW of Atlanta. Lumber and cotton mills.

7329 Dallas New Era
121 W. Spring St. Phone: (404)445-3379
PO Box 530
Dallas, GA 30132
Local newspaper. **Founded:** 1882. **Freq:** Weekly. **Print Method:** Offset. **Cols./Page:** 8. **Col. Width:** 11 millimeters. **Col. Depth:** 21.5 inches. **Key Personnel:** T.E. Parker, Editor/Administration; J.T. Parker, Publisher; J.S. Parker, Publisher. **Subscription Rates:** $0.25 single issue. **Remarks:** Accepts advertising.
Ad Rates: GLR: $.19 **Circ:** Paid 6,900
BW: $457.52 Free 125
PCI: $2.30

The Paulding Neighbor - See Paulding

DALTON†, pop. 20,743.

NW GA. Whitfield Co. 30 mi. SE of Chattanooga, TN. Manufactures carpets, lumber, concrete blocks, septic tanks, tile, textiles. Talc mines. Pine, oak timber. Agriculture. Cotton, corn, poultry.

7330 The Daily Citizen-News
Thomson Newspapers
308 S. Thornton Phone: (404)278-1011
PO Box 1167 Fax: (404)275-6641
Dalton, GA 30720-8268
Publication E-mail: dcnnews@vol.com

General newspaper. **Founded:** 1962. **Freq:** Daily and Sunday (morn.). **Print Method:** Offset. **Trim Size:** 13 x 21 1/2. **Cols./Page:** 6. **Col. Width:** 12.4 nonpareils. **Col. Depth:** 301 agate lines. **Key Personnel:** Frank Sayles, Jr., Publisher, fsayles@vol.com; Jeff Mutter, Advertising Mgr. **Subscription Rates:** $10.50 per month carrier; $99 by mail. **Remarks:** Accepts advertising.
Ad Rates: BW: $1,567.35 **Circ:** Mon.-Fri. 14,443
4C: $1,817.35 Wed. 13,714
SAU: $8.43 Sun. 12,691

7331 WBLJ-AM - 1230
PO Box 809 Phone: (404)278-3300
Dalton, GA 30722-0809 Fax: (706)272-7966

Format: Full Service; Adult Contemporary; Oldies; Gospel. **Networks:** ABC; Georgia Radio. **Owner:** Carmen Trevitt, P.O. Box 809, Dalton, GA 30722-0809. **Founded:** 1940. **Operating Hours:** Continuous; 20% network, 80% local. **ADI:** Chattanooga (Cleveland), TN. **Key Personnel:** Bill Holloway, Production Mgr., phone (404)279-1230; Barbara Wilson, General Mgr., phone (404)278-2149; Pat Mahoney, News Dir., phone (404)278-4097; Clancy Graham, Contact, phone (404)279-1230. **Local Programs:** *Hispanuic Program*, Barbara Wilson, Mailing contact; *Sports Rock*, Stephen Gregg, Mailing contact. **Wattage:** 1000. **Ad Rates:** $8-13.95 for 30 seconds; $19.85 for 60 seconds.

7332 WDAL-AM - 1430
PO Box 1284 Phone: (706)278-5511
Dalton, GA 30722 Fax: (706)278-9917

Format: News; Talk. **Networks:** CBS; Sun Radio. **Owner:** Radio Center Dalton, Inc., at above address. **Founded:** 1953. **Formerly:** WRCD-AM (1987); WLSQ-AM. **Operating Hours:** Continuous; 75% network, 25% local. **ADI:** Chattanooga (Cleveland), TN. **Key Personnel:** Paul Fink, General Mgr.; Larry Gibson, Contact; Deborah Parker, Sales Mgr. **Local Programs:** *Floor Radio*; *Open Line*. **Wattage:** 2500. **Ad Rates:** $8 for 30 seconds; $14 for 60 seconds.

7333 WQMT-FM - 98.9
945 Riverbend Rd. Phone: (706)278-9950
Dalton, GA 30720 Fax: (706)272-7966

Format: Country; Gospel. **Networks:** ABC. **Founded:** 1977. **Operating Hours:** Continuous; 2.3% network, 97.7% local. **ADI:** Chattanooga (Cleveland), TN. **Key Personnel:** Terresa Trevitt, V.P. of Operations & Finance; Barbara Wilson, Sales Mgr.; Tom Phillips, Music Dir.; Jim Pirkle, News Dir. **Local Programs:** *Barbara Wilson Show.* **Wattage:** 6000. **Ad Rates:** $7-17 for 30 seconds; $9-22 for 60 seconds.

DANIELSVILLE†, pop. 354.

NE GA. Madison Co. 16 mi. NE of Athens. Farming. Dairy, poultry products.

7334 Monitor
PO Box 279 Phone: (706)795-3102
140 Court House Square Fax: (706)783-2553
Danielsville, GA 30633
Community newspaper. **Founded:** 1882. **Freq:** Weekly (Fri.). **Print Method:** Offset. **Cols./Page:** 6. **Col. Width:** 12 picas. **Col. Depth:** 21 inches. **Key Personnel:** J.C. Ayers, Editor and Publisher, phone (706)783-2553. **Subscription Rates:** $15 individuals. **Remarks:** Advertising not accepted for lottery, alcohol, and tobacco products. **Alt. Formats:** Microfilm.
Ad Rates: GLR: $.20 **Circ:** ‡1,800
BW: $352.80
4C: $652.80
PCI: $2.80

DARIEN†, pop. 1,731.

SE GA. McIntosh Co. 18 mi. N. of Brunswick. Historical area. Shoe factory; seafood cannery. Shad, crabs, catfish, sturgeon, shrimp fisheries. Pulpwood. Truck, dairy farms.

7335 The Darien News
PO Box 496 Phone: (912)437-4251
Darien, GA 31305 Fax: (912)437-2299
Publication E-mail: darprint@darientel.net

Newspaper covering Darien and McIntosh County. **Founded:** June 1951. **Freq:** Weekly (Thurs.). **Print Method:** Offset. **Cols./Page:** 6. **Col. Width:** 21 1/2 nonpareils. **Col. Depth:** 301 agate lines. **Key Personnel:** Kathleen Russell, Exec. Editor. **USPS:** 566-040. **Subscription Rates:** $19.08 individuals; $24.38 out of area; $28 out of state. **Remarks:** Accepts advertising.
Ad Rates: GLR: $.25 **Circ:** ‡3,420
BW: $451.50
4C: $651.50
SAU: $4

DAWSON†, pop. 5,699.

C. GA. Terrell Co. 22 mi. NW of Albany. Lumber, peanuts.

7336 The Dawson News
139 W. Lee St. Phone: (912)995-2175
PO Box 350 Fax: (912)995-2176
Dawson, GA 31742
Community newspaper. **Founded:** Mar. 1867. **Freq:** Weekly. **Print Method:** Offset. **Trim Size:** 13 x 21 1/2. **Cols./Page:** 6. **Col. Width:** 2 1/8 inches. **Col. Depth:** 21 inches. **Key Personnel:** William Thomas Rountree, Editor and Publisher. **USPS:** 149-480. **Subscription Rates:** $18 in Terrell County; $23 in state; $27 out of state. **Remarks:** Accepts advertising.
Ad Rates: BW: $661.50 **Circ:** ‡2,800
4C: $886.50
SAU: $5.25
PCI: $5.25

7337 Southern Connection
125 N. Main St.
Dawson, GA 31742-1417

Shopping guide. **Founded:** 1990. **Freq:** Weekly. **Print Method:** Web offset. **Cols./Page:** 7. **Col. Width:** 8 picas. **Col. Depth:** 15 inches. **Key Personnel:** Diane Waters, Publisher. **Subscription Rates:** Free. **Remarks:** Advertising accepted; rates available upon request. **Formerly:** Dawson Buyers Guide.
Circ: Free ‡12,898

7338 WACS-TV - 25
Rte. 1 Box 75A Phone: (912)623-4883
Parrott, GA 31777 Free: (800)222-6006

Format: Public TV. **Networks:** Public Broadcasting Service (PBS); Georgia Public Television. **Owner:** Georgia Public Telecommunications Commission, at above address. **Founded:** 1967. **Operating Hours:** 6 a.m.-midnight; 100% local. **ADI:** Columbus, GA (Opelika, AL). **Key Personnel:** Richard E. Ottinger, Contact; Frank Bugg, Contact; Kent Steele, Program Dir.; Al Korn, Contact. **Ad Rates:** Noncommercial.

DAWSONVILLE†, pop. 342.

N. GA. Dawson Co. 22 mi. NW of Gainesville. North Georgia College; Gainesville Junior College; Lanier Tech. Blackburn State Park. Camping, fishing, swimming. Manufactures carpet yarn, textiles. Book binding; feed mill; newspaper, commercial printing.

7339 Dawson County Advertiser and News
PO Box 225 Phone: (706)265-2345
Dawsonville, GA 30534 Fax: (706)265-7842
Publication E-mail: dcadvert@stc.net

Community newspaper. **Subtitle:** Your Hometown Newspaper. **Founded:** 1887. **Freq:** Weekly (Thurs.). **Print Method:** Web. **Trim Size:** 11 x 16. **Cols./Page:** 6. **Col. Width:** 12.4 picas. **Col. Depth:** 21 1/2 inches. **Key Personnel:** Chyrl Waldrip, Editor; Don Waldrip, Publisher. **USPS:** 149-420. **Subscription Rates:** $10 individuals inside county; $15 outside county; $20 out of state. **Remarks:** Accepts advertising.
Ad Rates: BW: $658.40 **Circ:** ‡4,700
4C: $853.40
PCI: $4.60

DECATUR†, pop. 18,404.

NWC GA. DeKalb Co. Adjacent to Atlanta. Agnes Scott College (women); Columbia Theological Seminary. Residential. Dairy, poultry, truck farms.

7340 Agnes Scott Alumnae Magazine
Agnes Scott College
141 E. College Ave. Phone: (404)471-6301
Decatur, GA 30030-3797 Fax: (404)471-6177

College alumni magazine. **Founded:** 1924. **Freq:** Semiannual. **Print Method:** Sheetfed offset. **Trim Size:** 8 3/8 x 10 7/8. **Cols./Page:** 4. **Col. Width:** 1 inches. **Col. Depth:** 8 1/4 inches. **Key Personnel:** Mary Alma Durrett, Editor, fax (404)471-6298, mdurrett@agnesscott.edu. **Subscription Rates:** Free to qualified subscribers. **Remarks:** Advertising not accepted. **URL:** http://www.agnesscott.edu/publications. **Former name:** Agnes Scott Quarterly.
Circ: Non-paid 12,000

7341 Decatur De Kalb Neighbor
Neighbor Newspapers, Inc.
580 Fairground St. Phone: (770)428-9411
PO Box 449 Fax: (770)428-7945
Marietta, GA 30060
Community newspaper. **Founded:** 1970. **Freq:** Weekly (Wed.). **Subscription Rates:** $12; $18 out of area; $24 out of state. **Remarks:** Combined advertising rates available with other Neighbor Newspapers.
Circ: Combined 45,551

7342 Decatur De Kalb News/Era
Decatur News Publishing Co., Inc.
613 Church St. Phone: (404)373-4488
Decatur, GA 30033-5701 Fax: (404)373-0971

Community newspaper. **Subtitle:** The Business and Financial Review. **Founded:** 1948. **Freq:** Weekly (Thurs.). **Print Method:** Offset. **Trim Size:** 14 1/2 x 22 3/4. **Cols./Page:** 6. **Col. Width:** 26 nonpareils. **Col. Depth:** 301 agate lines. **Key Personnel:** Joe Hiett, Editor and Publisher; Stein Griffin, Advertising Mgr. **USPS:** 898-660. **Subscription Rates:** $15.75 individuals.
Ad Rates: GLR: $.58 **Circ:** Paid 6,804
BW: $1,078.56 Non-paid 217
4C: $1,347.64
SAU: $8.56
PCI: $8.56

7343 Dixie Contractor
Associated Construction Publications
209-A Swanton Way Phone: (404)377-2683
Box 280 Fax: (404)371-1509
Decatur, GA 30030-3271
Magazine for the Southeastern construction industry. **Founded:** 1926. **Freq:** Semimonthly. **Print Method:** Offset. **Trim Size:** 8 x 10 7/8. **Cols./Page:** 3. **Col. Width:** 26 nonpareils. **Col. Depth:** 140 agate lines. **Key Personnel:** Steve Hudson, Editor; J.O. Bowen, Jr., Publisher; Francis J. Aaron, Advertising Mgr. **ISSN:** 0012-4281. **Subscription Rates:** $15 individuals. **Remarks:** Accepts advertising.
Ad Rates: BW: $960 **Circ:** Paid 1,076
4C: $1,403 Non-paid 8,557

7344 The Profile
Agnes Scott College
141 E. College Ave. Phone: (404)471-6301
Decatur, GA 30030-3797 Fax: (404)471-6177

Collegiate newspaper. **Founded:** 1916. **Freq:** Bimonthly. **Print Method:** Webpress. **Trim Size:** 11 x 14. **Cols./Page:** 5. **Col. Width:** 22 nonpareils. **Col. Depth:** 210 agate lines. **Key Personnel:** Jennifer Jensen, Editor-in-Chief; Beth Godbee, Advertising Mgr. **Subscription Rates:** $20 individuals. **Remarks:** Accepts advertising.
Ad Rates: BW: $280 **Circ:** Paid ‡75
PCI: $4.10 Free ‡925

7345 Young Horizons Indigo
PO Box 371595 Phone: (404)241-5003
Decatur, GA 30037-1595
Publication E-mail: gigattyhi@aol.com

Newsmagazine for parents and teachers of African-American youth containing articles of general interest. **Founded:** 1989. **Freq:** Monthly. **Cols./Page:** 4. **Col. Width:** 2 3/8 inches. **Key Personnel:** Terry Williams, Sr. Editor. **Subscription Rates:** $15 individuals.
Ad Rates: BW: $1,250.00 **Circ:** Paid 15,000
4C: $1,500.00

7346 WXLL-AM - 1310
4287 Memorial Dr. Phone: (404)299-8933
Suite H Fax: (404)288-4697
Decatur, GA 30032

Format: Religious. **Networks:** Independent. **Owner:** Margery J. Watson, at above address. **Founded:** 1964. **Operating Hours:** Daytime. **Key Personnel:** Margary J. Watson, General Mgr. **Local Programs:** *Cathedral Vineyard Ministries.* **Wattage:** 500. **Ad Rates:** $12-24 for 30 seconds; $15-30 for 60 seconds.

DEMOREST

7347 The American Genealogist
PO Box 398 Phone: (706)865-6440
Demorest, GA 30535-0398 Fax: (706)865-6440
Publisher E-mail: amgen@stc.net

Scholarly genealogy journal. **Founded:** 1922. **Freq:** Quarterly. **Print Method:** Offset. **Trim Size:** 6 x 9. **Cols./Page:** 1. **Col. Width:** 55 nonpareils. **Col. Depth:** 103 agate lines. **Key Personnel:** David L. Greene, Editor and Publisher; Robert C. Anderson, Editor; A. Jane McFerrin, Managing Editor. **ISSN:** 0002-8592. **Subscription Rates:** $25 individuals; $48 two years; $70 for 3 years; $7 single issue. **Remarks:** Advertising not accepted. **Alt. Formats:** Microform.
Circ: ‡1,850

7348 Habersham Review
Piedmont College
Box 10 Phone: (706)778-3000
Demorest, GA 30535
Literary journal with Southeastern US focus. **Founded:** 1991. **Freq:** Semiannual. **Key Personnel:** Frank Gannon, Editor; Stephen R. Whited, Poetry Editor. **ISSN:** 1060-0469. **Subscription Rates:** $12 individuals; $6 single issue. **Remarks:** Accepts advertising.
Ad Rates: BW: $350 **Circ:** (Not Reported)

DONALSONVILLE†, pop. 3,320.

SW GA. Seminole Co. 32 mi. E. of Dothan. Peanut, saw, planing mills. Pine timber. Agriculture. Cotton, peanuts, cattle, hogs, velvet beans, corn, vegetables.

7349 Donalsonville News
PO Box 338 Phone: (912)524-2343
Donalsonville, GA 31745 Fax: (912)524-2343

Community newspaper. **Founded:** 1916. **Freq:** Weekly (Thurs.). **Print Method:** Offset. **Cols./Page:** 6. **Col. Width:** 12 picas. **Col. Depth:** 301 agate lines. **Key Personnel:** Waldo L. McLeod, Publisher. **Subscription Rates:** $18 individuals. **Remarks:** Accepts advertising.
Ad Rates: GLR: $.19 **Circ:** ‡3,600
SAU: $3

DORAVILLE

7350 Doraville De Kalb Neighbor
Neighbor Newspapers, Inc.
580 Fairground St. Phone: (770)428-9411
PO Box 449 Fax: (770)428-7945
Marietta, GA 30060
Community newspaper. **Founded:** 1975. **Freq:** Weekly (Wed.). **Subscription Rates:** $12; $18 out of area; $24 out of state. **Remarks:** Combined advertising rates available with other Neighbor Newspapers.
Circ: Combined 20,590

DOUGLAS†, pop. 10,980.

S. GA. Coffee Co. 36 mi. NW of Waycross. South Georgia College. Manufactures mobile homes, farm machinery, concrete, lumber, turpentine, ice, asphalt, feed. Bottling works; garment plants; printers; poultry & egg processing. Timber. Agriculture. Tobacco, poultry, peanuts, corn, swine, cattle.

7351 Coffee County News
Coffee County News & Shopper, Inc.
213 N. Peterson Ave. Phone: (912)384-9112
Douglas, GA 31533 Fax: (912)384-4220
Publication E-mail: nuzshoper@almatel.net

Community newspaper. **Founded:** Oct. 10, 1990. **Freq:** Weekly (Fri.). **Print Method:** Offset. **Trim Size:** 10 1/2 x 15. **Cols./Page:** 5. **Col. Width:** 11 picas. **Col. Depth:** 15 inches. **Key Personnel:** William H. Kibbey, Editor; Carlene S. Phelps, Publisher; Elaine Fox, Advertising Mgr. **USPS:** 013-808. **Subscription Rates:** $18 individuals; $30 out of area. **Formerly**: Douglas News.
Ad Rates: GLR: $1 **Circ:** Paid ‡7,800
BW: $375
4C: $475
PCI: $5.00

7352 The Douglas Enterprise
1823 S. Peterson Ave. Phone: (912)384-2323
PO Box 551 Fax: (912)283-0218
Douglas, GA 31533
Newspaper. **Founded:** Apr. 1888. **Freq:** Semiweekly (Wed. and Sun.). **Print Method:** Offset. **Cols./Page:** 6. **Col. Width:** 25 nonpareils. **Col. Depth:** 294 agate lines. **Key Personnel:** Thomas H. Frier, Jr., Editor; Jim Merritt, Publisher. **USPS:** 160-360. **Subscription Rates:** $4.25 individuals; $0.50 single issue. **Remarks:** Accepts advertising. **Alt. Formats:** CD-ROM.
Ad Rates: GLR: $.63 **Circ:** ‡8,500
BW: $630
4C: $780
PCI: $5

7353 The Douglas Shopper
Coffee County News & Shopper, Inc.
213 N. Peterson Ave
Douglas, GA 31533
Publication E-mail: nuzshopr@almatel.net

Shopper. **Founded:** July 23, 1980. **Freq:** Weekly (Tues.). **Print Method:** Offset. **Trim Size:** 10 1/2 x 15. **Cols./Page:** 6. **Col. Width:** 9 picas. **Col. Depth:** 15 inches. **Key Personnel:** Carlene S. Phelps, Editor and Publisher; Elaine Fox, Advertising Mgr. **Subscription Rates:** $15. **Remarks:** Accepts advertising.
Ad Rates: GLR: $1 **Circ:** Free ‡18,700
BW: $450
4C: $550
PCI: $5

7354 Cablevision
Box 1223 Phone: (912)384-4675
Douglas, GA 31533 Fax: (912)384-4132

Key Personnel: David Richardson, General Mgr. **Cities Served:** Coffee County: subscribing households 6,200; 48 channels; 1 community access channel.

7355 WDMG-AM - 860
620 E. Ward St. Phone: (912)384-3250
Douglas, GA 31533-3915 Fax: (912)383-8552

Format: Adult Contemporary; Top 40. **Networks:** Georgia Radio; Satellite Music Network. **Owner:** WDMG, Inc., PO Box 1874, Tallahassee, FL 32302-1874. **Founded:** 1947. **Operating Hours:** 5 a.m.-midnight Mon.-Sat.; 6 a.m.-11 p.m. Sun. **Key Personnel:** B.F.J. Timm, President; Roy L. Jones, Jr., Contact; John Higgs, News Dir. **Wattage:** 5000. **Ad Rates:** $8-13.50 for 30 seconds; $12-15 for 60 seconds.

7356 WOKA-AM - 1310
PO Box 471 Phone: (912)384-1310
Douglas, GA 31533 Fax: (912)383-6328

Format: Religious. **Networks:** NBC; Georgia Radio. **Operating Hours:** 6 a.m.-sundown; 4% network, 96% local. **ADI:** Albany (Valdosta & Cordele), GA. **Key Personnel:** Grady Seawright, Contact; Tim Seawright, Contact. **Wattage:** 1000. **Ad Rates:** $4.50-5.65 for 30 seconds; $5.50-6.65 for 60 seconds.

7357 WOKA-FM - 106.7
PO Box 471 Phone: (912)384-8153
Douglas, GA 31533 Fax: (912)383-6328

Format: Country. **Networks:** NBC; Georgia Radio. **Founded:** 1962. **Operating Hours:** Continuous. 4% network, 96% local. **ADI:** Albany (Valdosta & Cordele), GA. **Key Personnel:** Dave Hedrick, General Mgr.; Arthur Hutto, News Dir. **Local Programs:** *Coffee Break*, Arthur Hutto; *Exchange Show*, Walter Minix, (912)389-1067. **Wattage:** 100,000. **Ad Rates:** $10 for 30 seconds; $12 for 60 seconds. Combined advertising rates available with WOKA-AM.

DOUGLASVILLE†, pop. 7,274.

W. GA. Douglas Co. 20 mi. W. of Atlanta. Chemical research. Manufactures textile products, metal fabrication. Asphalt refinery; lumber mills; quarries. Pine, hardwood timber.

7358 Douglas County Sentinel
Douglas County Tri-County News
6405 Fairbyrn Rd. Phone: (404)942-6571
PO Box 1586 Fax: (404)949-7556
Douglasville, GA 30134-6911
General newspaper. **Founded:** 1902. **Freq:** Daily (eve.). **Print Method:** Offset. **Cols./Page:** 6. **Col. Width:** 25 nonpareils. **Col. Depth:** 301 agate lines. **Key Personnel:** Jeff Durham, Editor; Fred Lister, Publisher; Susan Kiser, Advertising Mgr. **Subscription Rates:** $38 individuals; $42 out of area. **Remarks:** Accepts advertising.
Ad Rates: SAU: $6.89 **Circ:** ‡9,000

7359 WDCY-AM - 1520
8451 S. Cherokee Blvd., Ste. B Phone: (770)920-1520
Douglasville, GA 30134-2520 Fax: (770)920-4600

Format: Gospel; Southern Gospel. **Founded:** 1963. **Formerly:** WDGL-AM (1984). **Operating Hours:** Sunrise-sunset; 100% local. **Key Personnel:** Sandy Johns, Program Dir.; Ken Johnsr, General Mgr. **Wattage:** 2500.

7360 Wometco Cable
5979 Fairburn Rd. Phone: (404)942-0010
Douglasville, GA 30134 Fax: (404)949-7010

Owner: Wometco Cable Corp., at above address. **Founded:** Aug. 1978. **Key Personnel:** R.A. Madsen, General Mgr.; Angela Reid, Business Mgr.; Bill Naivar, Plant Mgr.; Steven Barlow, Marketing Mgr. **Cities Served:** Douglasville, Lithia Springs, GA: subscribing households 17,450; 56 channels; 1 community access channel.

DUBLIN†, pop. 15,143.

C. GA. Laurens Co. On Oconee River, 50 mi. SE of Macon. Manufactures furniture, textiles, carpets, aluminum products, fertilizer, lumber, farm implements. Meat packing; recycling plant; cotton warehouses. Timber. Agriculture. Cotton.

7361 The Courier Herald
Griffin Lovett
PO Drawer B, Court Sq. Sta. Phone: (912)272-5522
Dublin, GA 31040-2449 Fax: (912)272-2189
Free: (800)833-8504

General newspaper. **Founded:** 1913. **Freq:** Daily (eve.) and Sat. (morn.). **Print Method:** Offset. **Cols./Page:** 6. **Col. Width:** 25 nonpareils. **Col. Depth:** 301 agate lines. **Key Personnel:** DuBose Porter, Editor; Griffin Lovett, Publisher. **Subscription Rates:** $52 individuals. **Remarks:** Accepts advertising. **Available Online.**
Ad Rates: GLR: $2 **Circ:** Mon.-Sat. ★**11,623**
BW: $1,290
4C: $1,530
SAU: $11.85
PCI: $10

7362 WKKZ-FM - 92.7
Glenwood Rd. Phone: (912)272-9270
Box 967 Fax: (912)275-3592
Dublin, GA 31040-0967

Format: Adult Contemporary. **Networks:** CBS. **Founded:** 1964. **Formerly**: WXLI-FM. **Operating Hours:** Continuous; 10% network, 90% local. **Key Personnel:** Mike Kirby, Contact; Ray Beck, Manager; Steve O'Neal, Music Dir. **Wattage:** 50,000. **Ad Rates:** $8-14 for 30 seconds; $12-16 for 60 seconds.

7363 WMLT-AM - 1330
807 Bellevue Ave. Phone: (912)272-4422
Dublin, GA 31021 Fax: (912)275-4657
E-mail: wqzy@accucomm.net

Format: Oldies; News. **Networks:** ABC; Georgia Radio. **Owner:** State Broadcasting Corp., PO Box 130, Dublin, GA 31040, (912)272-8896. **Founded:** 1945. **Operating Hours:** Continuous.; 40% network, 60% local. **Key Personnel:** Mac Davis, General Mgr.; Yvonne Lamb Castillo, News Dir.; Jeff Kidd, Program Dir.; Anne Everly, Sales Mgr. **Wattage:** 5000. **Ad Rates:** $4.60-7.25 for 30 seconds; $5.70-9 for 60 seconds.

7364 WQZY-FM - 95.9
807 Bellevue Ave. Phone: (912)272-8896
PO Box 130 Fax: (912)275-4657
Dublin, GA 31021
E-mail: wqzy@accucomm.net

Format: Country. **Networks:** NBC. **Owner:** State Broadcasting Corp., at above address, (912)272-4422. **Founded:** 1976. **Operating Hours:** Continuous; 5% network, 95% local. **ADI:** Macon, GA. **Key Personnel:** Mac Davis, General Mgr.; Charlie Edwards, Program Dir.; Yvonne Lamb Castillo, News Dir. **Wattage:** 100,000. **Ad Rates:** $10-12 for 30 seconds; $15-20 for 60 seconds.

7365 WXLI-AM - 1230
Glenwood Rd. Phone: (912)272-4282
Box 967 Fax: (912)275-3592
Dublin, GA 31040-0967

Format: Contemporary Country. **Networks:** CBS. **Founded:** 1958. **Operating Hours:** Continuous. **Key Personnel:** Mike Kirby, General Mgr.; Ray Beck, Sales Mgr.; Steve O'Neal, Music Dir. **Wattage:** 1000. **Ad Rates:** $5-9 for 30 seconds; $7-11 for 60 seconds.

DULUTH, pop. 6,140.

NW GA. Gwinett Co.

7366 Pipeline
Georgia Association of Plumbing, Heating and Cooling Contractors
3338 Gwinnett Plantation Way Fax: (404)476-7802
Duluth, GA 30136-4647
Plumbing industry magazine. **Founded:** 1954. **Freq:** 4/year. **Print Method:** Offset. **Trim Size:** 8 1/2 x 11. **Key Personnel:** Robert Sumner, Editor. **Formerly**: Plumb.
Ad Rates: BW: $275 **Circ:** 3,000

7367 Shuttle Spindle & Dyepot
Handweavers Guild of America, Inc.
3327 Duluth Hwy., Ste. 201 Phone: (770)495-7702
Duluth, GA 30096-3339 Fax: (770)495-7703
Publisher E-mail: 73744.202@compuserve.com

Magazine on fiber arts. **Founded:** 1969. **Freq:** Quarterly. **Print Method:** Offset. **Trim Size:** 8 1/2 x 11. **Cols./Page:** 3. **Col. Width:** 26 nonpareils. **Col. Depth:** 140 agate lines. **Key Personnel:** Sandra Bowles, Editor. **ISSN:** 0049-0423. **Subscription Rates:** $35 individuals; $7 single issue. **Remarks:** Accepts advertising. **URL:** http://www.weavespindye.org.
Ad Rates: BW: $850 **Circ:** 15,000
4C: $1215

7368 Prime Star Inc.
3483 Satellite Blvd., Ste. 210 Phone: (770)622-5411
Duluth, GA 30096 Fax: (770)622-5413

Formerly: GCTV (Georgia Cable TV & Communications). **Key Personnel:** William R. Proud, Contact; Collie Burnett, Jr., Vice President. **Cities Served:** subscribing households 206,000; 52 channels; 1 community access channel.

DUNWOODY, pop. 4,400.

NW GA. DeKalb Co. 22 mi. N. of Atlanta.

7369 The Chattahoochee Review
Georgia Perimeter College
2101 Womack Rd. Phone: (770)551-3019
Dunwoody, GA 30338-4497
Literary review. **Founded:** 1980. **Freq:** Quarterly. **Print Method:** Offset. **Trim Size:** 6 x 9. **Cols./Page:** 1. **Key Personnel:** Lawrence Hetrick, Editor; JoAnn Adkins, Managing Editor; Collie Owens, Poetry Editor. **ISSN:** 0741-9155. **Subscription Rates:** $16 individuals; $5 single issue. **Remarks:** Advertising not accepted.
Circ: Paid 185
Non-paid 1,250

7370 Dunwoody De Kalb Neighbor
Neighbor Newspapers, Inc.
580 Fairground St. Phone: (770)428-9411
PO Box 449 Fax: (770)428-7945
Marietta, GA 30060
Community newspaper. **Founded:** 1975. **Freq:** Weekly (Wed.). **Subscription Rates:** $12; $18 out of area; $24 out of state. **Remarks:** Combined advertising rates available with other Neighbor Newspapers.
Circ: Combined 20,590

EAST COBB

7371 The East Cobb Neighbor
Neighbor Newspapers, Inc.
580 Fairground St. Phone: (770)428-9411
PO Box 449 Fax: (770)428-7945
Marietta, GA 30060
Community newspaper. **Founded:** 1977. **Freq:** Weekly (Thurs.). **Print Method:** Offset. **Cols./Page:** 6. **Col. Width:** 26 nonpareils. **Col. Depth:** 301 agate lines. **Key Personnel:** Otis A. Brumby, Jr., Publisher. **USPS:** 398-050. **Subscription Rates:** $12 individuals; $18 out of area; $24 out of state. **Remarks:** Accepts advertising.
Ad Rates: GLR: $1.05 **Circ:** Paid 21
BW: $1,902.75 Non-paid 42,960
4C: $2,192.75
SAU: $14.75

EAST POINT, pop. 37,486.

NW GA. Fulton Co. 5 mi. S. of Atlanta. Manufactures textiles, paint, glass, paper products, fertilizer, chemicals, concrete products, machinery, auto batteries. Agriculture. Cotton, corn, dairying.

7372 WTJH-AM - 1260
2146 Dodson Dr. Phone: (404)344-2233
East Point, GA 30344-1050 Fax: (404)346-0647

Format: Religious. **Owner:** Willis Broadcasting, 645 Church St., Ste. 400, Norfolk, VA 23501, (800)873-4600. **Operating Hours:** Continuous. **Key Personnel:** Rhodell Lewis, Program Dir.; Valencia Williams, Office Mgr.; Kevin Jones, Music Dir. **Wattage:** 5000. **Ad Rates:** $25 for 30 seconds; $30 for 60 seconds.

EASTMAN†, pop. 5,330.

C. GA. Dodge Co. 52 mi. SE of Macon. Tobacco, timber, cotton, corn.

7373 Times Journal Spotlight
The Time Journal & Spotlight
PO Drawer 4189 Phone: (912)374-5562
Eastman, GA 31023 Fax: (912)374-3464

Community newspaper. **Founded:** 1871. **Freq:** Weekly. **Print Method:** Offset. **Cols./Page:** 6. **Col. Width:** 12 picas. **Col. Depth:** 21 inches. **Key Personnel:** Julia J. Roberts, Editor and Publisher; Barbara Williams, General Mgr.; Joe Roberts, Advertising Dir.; John I. Roberts, Assoc. Editor; Barbara Williams, General Mgr. **Subscription Rates:** $15.00 individuals; $20.00 out of area; $24.00 out of state. **Remarks:** Accepts advertising.
Ad Rates: GLR: $.30 **Circ:** ‡4,950
BW: $529.20
4C: $769.20
PCI: $4.20

7374 WUFF-AM - 710
731 College Phone: (912)374-3437
Box 4097 Fax: (912)374-3585
Eastman, GA 31023-2205

Format: Country. **Networks:** NBC. **Owner:** Farnell O'Quinn, at above address, (912)374-3438. **Founded:** 1961. **Formerly:** WPFE-AM. **Operating Hours:** 6 a.m.-sunset; 3% network, 97% local. **Key Personnel:** Gene Rogers, Manager; Joy Henderson, Contact; Bob Scott, Program Dir. **Wattage:** 2500. **Ad Rates:** $4 for 30 seconds; $5 for 60 seconds.

7375 WUFF-FM - 92.1
Box 4097 Phone: (912)374-3437
Eastman, GA 31023

Format: Country. **Key Personnel:** Gene Rogers, Manager. **Wattage:** 6000.

EATONTON†, pop. 4,448.

C. GA. Putnam Co. 41 mi. NE of Macon. Resort. Manufactures feed, mobile homes. Dairying. Timber. Diversified farming. Horses, cattle.

7376 The Eatonton Messenger
Putnam Printing Co., Inc.
PO Box 4027 Phone: (706)485-3501
Eatonton, GA 31024 Fax: (706)485-4166
Free: (888)485-3501
Publication E-mail: msgr@msgr.com

General newspaper. **Founded:** 1867. **Freq:** Weekly (Thurs.). **Print Method:** Offset. **Cols./Page:** 6. **Key Personnel:** Michele Smith, Editor and Publisher; Janet Wilson, Business Mgr. **Subscription Rates:** $20 in county; $23.32 out of area; $28.62 out of state. **Remarks:** Combined advertising rates available with Messenger Plus.
Ad Rates: BW: $353 **Circ:** Paid ‡4,000
4C: $440

7377 Messenger Plus
Putnam Printing Co., Inc.
PO Box 4027 Phone: (706)485-3501
Eatonton, GA 31024 Fax: (706)485-4166
Free: (888)485-3501
Publication E-mail: msgr@mail.oconee.com

Shopper. **Founded:** 1985. **Freq:** Weekly (Mon.). **Print Method:** Offset. **Cols./Page:** 6. **Col. Width:** 12 picas. **Col. Depth:** 21 inches. **Key Personnel:** Michele Smith, Editor; Janet Wilson, Business Mgr. **Remarks:** Combined advertising rates available with The Eatonton Messenger.
Ad Rates: BW: $6.12 **Circ:** Non-paid ‡8,300
SAU: $3.55
PCI: $6.12

7378 Communi Comm Services
PO Box 3668 Phone: (706)485-2288
Eatonton, GA 31024 Fax: (706)485-0118
Free: (800)554-3235

Formerly: GEM Communications; Southern Cable View. **Key Personnel:** Larry Angel, General Mgr.; Mark Beaubien, Contact; Dianne Simmons, Office Mgr.

ELBERTON†, pop. 7,000.

NE GA. Elbert Co. 70 mi. NW of Augusta. Extensive granite works. Manufactures lumber, silk, cotton, cottonseed products, tools. Granite quarries; pine, oak timber. Agriculture. Cotton, corn, oats.

7379 The Elberton Star
14 N. Oliver St. Phone: (404)283-3100
PO Box 280 Fax: (404)283-7841
Elberton, GA 30635-0280
Community newspaper. **Founded:** 1887. **Freq:** Weekly (Wed.). **Print Method:** Offset. Uses mats. **Cols./Page:** 6. **Col. Width:** 24 3/4 nonpareils. **Col. Depth:** 297 1/2 agate lines. **Key Personnel:** Steve Carswell, General Mgr.; Peggy Vickery, Accounting. **ISSN:** 8750-6734. **Subscription Rates:** $16 individuals. **Remarks:** Accepts advertising.
Ad Rates: BW: $650.25 **Circ:** Paid ‡5,400
4C: $825.25 Free ‡50
SAU: $5.10

7380 WEHR-FM - 105.1
14 S. Public Sq., Ste. 200 Phone: (706)213-1051
Elberton, GA 30635 Fax: (706)213-6955
E-mail: todays105@dj.net

Format: Adult Contemporary. **Networks:** ABC. **Owner:** Chase Broadcasting Inc., at above address. **Founded:** May 1998. **Former name:** WDDA-FM (1998). **Operating Hours:** Continuous. **Key Personnel:** Scott Smith, General Mgr., todays105@dj.net. **Ad Rates:** $8 for 30 seconds; $10 for 60 seconds.

7381 WWRK-FM - 92.1
Box 638 Phone: (706)283-1714
Elberton, GA 30635-0638 Fax: (706)283-8710

Format: Contemporary Country. **Networks:** Jones Satellite. **Founded:** 1972. **Formerly:** WSGC-FM (1975). **Operating Hours:** Continuous; 40% network, 60% local. **Key Personnel:** Mickey Palmer, Contact; Scott Smith, Music Dir.; Mel Stovall, News Dir.; Nate Hirsch, President. **Wattage:** 3000. **Ad Rates:** $5 for 15 seconds; $7 for 30 seconds; $8.50 for 60 seconds.

ELLIJAY†, pop. 1,510.

N. GA. Gilmer Co. 65 mi. N. of Atlanta. Resort. Poultry processing. Pine, oak timber. Farming. Corn, cabbage, apples.

7382 Times-Courier
Times-Courier Pub.
PO Box 1076 Phone: (706)635-4313
Ellijay, GA 30540 Fax: (706)635-7006
Publication E-mail: courier@ellijay.comm

Community newspaper. **Founded:** 1875. **Freq:** Weekly (Wed.). **Print Method:** Offset. **Cols./Page:** 6. **Col. Width:** 10.5 picas. **Col. Depth;** 21 inches. **Key Personnel:** George N. Bunch, Editor and Publisher. **USPS:** 639-280. **Subscription Rates:** $18 individuals. **Alt. Formats:** CD-ROM.
Ad Rates: GLR: $4.50 **Circ:** Paid 6,900
BW: $498.48 Non-paid 35
4C: $698.48
SAU: $4.50
PCI: $4.50

FAYETTEVILLE†, pop. 4,430.

C. GA. Fayette Co.

7383 Fayette County News
Fayette Newspapers, Inc.
180 Church St. Phone: (770)461-6317
PO Box 96 Fax: (770)460-8172
Fayetteville, GA 30214
Community newspaper. **Founded:** Nov. 1886. **Freq:** 3/week. **Print Method:** Offset. **Trim Size:** 13 x 21 1/2. **Cols./Page:** 6. **Col. Width:** 2 1/8 inches. **Col. Depth:** 21 1/2 inches. **Key Personnel:** Pat Cooper, Editor; Robert Tribble, Publisher; Gary Cornwell, Advertising Mgr. **ISSN:** 5818-6957. **Subscription Rates:** $26.25; $20.40 senior citizens. **Remarks:** Accepts advertising.
Ad Rates: GLR: $.24 **Circ:** ‡4,600
BW: $445.05
4C: $815.05
SAU: $3.60

FITZGERALD†, pop. 10,250.

S. GA. Ben Hill Co. 152 mi. S. of Atlanta. Manufactures carpet yarn, mobile homes, automotive batteries, irrigation equipment, aluminum casting, concrete products. Peanut processing; garment factories; sawmills; meat packing plant; metal works. Diversified farming.

7384 The Herald-Leader
Pryor Publications, Inc.
Drawer 40 Phone: (912)423-9331
Fitzgerald, GA 31750 Fax: (912)423-6533

Community newspaper. **Founded:** Dec. 20, 1895. **Freq:** Weekly (Wed.). **Print Method:** Offset. **Trim Size:** 7 1/2 x 11 1/2. **Cols./Page:** 6. **Col. Width:** 12 1/2 picas. **Col. Depth:** 21 inches. **Key Personnel:** Tim Anderson, Editor and Publisher. **Subscription Rates:** $18.55 individuals Fitzgerald & adjoining counties; $30.21 elsewhere in Georgia; $35 out of state. **Remarks:** Accepts advertising.
Ad Rates: BW: $441 **Circ:** ‡5,341
4C: $641
PCI: $4.50

7385 WBHB-AM - 1240
601 W. Roanoke Dr. Phone: (912)423-2077
PO Box 100 Fax: (912)423-8313
Fitzgerald, GA 31750-3633

Format: Adult Contemporary. **Networks:** NBC; Georgia Radio. **Owner:** M & M Broadcasting, at above address. **Founded:** 1946. **Operating Hours:** 5 a.m.-midnight Daily, 6 a.m.-midnight Saturday and Sunday. **Key Personnel:** Charley Ridgeway, Sports Dir.; Mike Roberts, Operations Mgr. **Wattage:** 1000. **Ad Rates:** $4-4.50 for 15 seconds; $5.50-6.75 for 30 seconds; $7.50-8.75 for 60 seconds.

7386 WKAA-FM - 97.7
601 W. Roanoke Dr., No. 100 Phone: (912)423-2077
Fitzgerald, GA 31750-9633 Fax: (912)423-8313

Format: Oldies. **Networks:** Jones Satellite. **Owner:** Tony W. Mooney, at above address. **Founded:** 1982. **Formerly:** WSPX-FM (1990). **Operating Hours:** Continuous. **ADI:** Albany (Valdosta & Cordele), GA. **Key Personnel:** Danny Hogan, Operations Mgr.; Tony Mooney, General Mgr. **Wattage:** 3000. **Ad Rates:** $6 for 30 seconds; $10 for 60 seconds.

FLOWERY BRANCH

7387 Certified Engineering Technician
American Society of Certified Engineering Technicians
Box 1348 Phone: (770)967-9173
Flowery Branch, GA 30542-0023 Fax: (770)967-8049

Professional magazine covering engineering technology. **Founded:** 1964. **Freq:** Bimonthly. **Trim Size:** 8 1/2 x 11. **Key Personnel:** Kurt H. Schuler, General Mgr. **ISSN:** 0746-6641. **Subscription Rates:** $12 individuals; $20 Canada; $40 other countries. **Remarks:** Accepts advertising.
Ad Rates: BW: $450 **Circ:** Controlled 2,000

FOLKSTON†, pop. 2,243.

SE GA. Charlton Co. 35 mi. S. of Waycross. Manufactures staves, textiles, lumber, turpentine. Pine, hardwood timber. Titanium mining. Cattle and hogs. Agriculture. Tobacco, cotton, corn.

7388 Charlton County Herald
Thompson Publishing, Inc.
102 1/2 W. Love St. Phone: (912)496-3585
PO Box 398 Fax: (912)496-4585
Folkston, GA 31537
Newspaper. **Founded:** 1898. **Freq:** Weekly (Wed.). **Print Method:** Offset. **Cols./Page:** 6. **Col. Width:** 21 1/2 nonpareils. **Col. Depth:** 129 agate lines. **Key Personnel:** David L. Thompson, Editor. **Subscription Rates:** $14.98; $18.19 out of area. **Remarks:** Accepts advertising. **Alt. Formats:** CD-ROM.
Ad Rates: BW: $516 **Circ:** 3000
4C: $856
PCI: $4

FOREST PARK

7389 Ornamental Miscellaneous Metal Fabricator
National Ornamental and Miscellaneous Metals Association
804 Main St., Ste. F Phone: (404)363-4009
Forest Park, GA 30297 Fax: (404)366-1852
Publisher E-mail: nomma2@aol.com

Magazine for ornamental and miscellaneous metals fabrication industry. **Founded:** 1959. **Freq:** Bimonthly. **Trim Size:** 8 1/4 x 11. **Cols./Page:** 3. **Key Personnel:** Todd Daniel, Editor; Dawn Sikes, Ed. Assist. **ISSN:** 0191-5940. **Subscription**

Rates: $24 individuals; $6 single issue. **Remarks:** Accepts advertising. **Online:** Internet.
Ad Rates: BW: $1,035 **Circ:** Combined ‡10,000
4C: $1,350

7390 Parnassus Literary Journal
Kudzu Press
Box 1384
Forest Park, GA 30051

Poetry journal. **Founded:** 1975. **Freq:** Triennial. **Trim Size:** 5 1/2 x 8 1/2. **Key Personnel:** Denver Stull, Editor and Publisher. **ISSN:** 0748-8787. **Subscription Rates:** $18 individuals; $6 single issue. **Remarks:** Advertising not accepted.
Circ: (Not Reported)

FORSYTH†, pop. 4,624.

C. GA. Monroe Co. 25 mi. NW of Macon. Tift College of Mercer University (women). Textiles, lumber and wood products.

7391 Monroe County Reporter
PO Box 795 Phone: (912)994-2358
Forsyth, GA 31029 Fax: (912)994-2359

Newspaper. **Founded:** 1972. **Freq:** Weekly (Wed.). **Print Method:** Offset. **Cols./Page:** 6. **Col. Width:** 27 nonpareils. **Col. Depth:** 301 agate lines. **Key Personnel:** Wanda M. Belknap, Publisher; Diane Crosby, Editor; Kathy Shealy, Advertising Mgr. **Subscription Rates:** $19.00 individuals local; $36.00 out of area. **Remarks:** Accepts advertising.
Ad Rates: BW: $8.20 **Circ:** 4,000
4C: $308.20
PCI: $8.20

FORT BENNING, pop. 32,567.

W. GA. Chattahoochee Co. 8 mi. S. of Columbus.

7392 The Benning Leader
PO Box 711 Phone: (706)571-8574
Columbus, GA 31902 Fax: (706)576-6290

Newspaper distributed to personnel of Ft. Benning as well as residents of the military community. **Founded:** 1991. **Freq:** Weekly (Fri.). **Print Method:** Letterpress and offset. Uses mats. **Cols./Page:** 5. **Col. Width:** 2 1/16 inches. **Col. Depth:** 13 inches. **Key Personnel:** Tony Adams, Editor, phone (706)571-8754, fax (706)576-6290; Rodney Mahone, Advertising Mgr. **Subscription Rates:** $12 individuals. **Remarks:** Accepts advertising.
Ad Rates: BW: $1,662.81 **Circ:** Free 25,000
4C: $1,927.81
SAU: $12.89

7393 Infantry
U.S. Army Infantry School
PO Box 52005 Phone: (706)545-2350
Fort Benning, GA 31995-2005
Magazine containing current information on infantry organization, weapons, equipment, tactics, and techniques; includes relevant historical articles and book reviews. **Founded:** 1921. **Freq:** Bimonthly. **Print Method:** Letterpress and offset. **Trim Size:** 8 1/2 x 11. **Cols./Page:** 3 and 2. **Col. Width:** 30 and 40 nonpareils. **Col. Depth:** 133 agate lines. **Key Personnel:** Russell A. Eno, Editor; Marie B. Edgerton, Deputy Editor. **ISSN:** 0019-9532. **Subscription Rates:** $12 individuals; $2.50 single issue. **Remarks:** Advertising not accepted.
Circ: Paid ‡3,700
Controlled ‡10,360

FORT GORDON

E. GA. Richmond Co. SW of Augusta.

7394 Army Communicator
U.S. Army Signal Regiment
USASC & FG, Bldg 29808A Phone: (706)791-7204
(Signal Towers), Rm. 707 Fax: (706)791-3917
Fort Gordon, GA 30905
Magazine providing information technology to the Signal Regiment and industry partners, allied signal services, other U.S. armed forces, ROTC and JROTC cadets. **Subtitle:** Voice of the Signal Regiment. **Founded:** 1976. **Freq:** Quarterly. **Print Method:** Offset. **Trim Size:** 8 1/2 x 11. **Cols./Page:** 3. **Col. Width:** 15 picas. **Col. Depth:** 64 picas. **Key Personnel:** Lisa Alley, Editor-in-Chief, alleyl@emh.gordon.army.mil. **ISSN:** 0362-5745. **Subscription Rates:** Free upon request. **Remarks:** Advertising not accepted. **Available Online. URL:** http://www.gordon.army.mil/ocos/bmdiv/ac/default.htm.
Circ: Controlled ‡5,000

FORT OGLETHORPE, pop. 5,443.

NW GA. Catoosa-Walker Co. 6 mi. S. of Chattanooga, TN. Residential.

7395 Busy Shopper
Busy Shopper, Inc.
1819 Cross St. Phone: (706)866-1020
Fort Oglethorpe, GA 30742 Fax: (706)866-1128

Shopper (tabloid). **Subtitle:** North Georgia Busy Shopper, East Ridge Busy Shopper. **Founded:** 1966. **Freq:** Weekly (Wed.). **Print Method:** Offset. **Trim Size:** 11 1/2 x 15. **Cols./Page:** 6. **Col. Width:** 20 nonpareils. **Col. Depth:** 194 agate lines. **Key Personnel:** Larry Boyer, Publisher. **Subscription Rates:** Free.
Ad Rates: GLR: $.52 **Circ:** Non-paid 39,760
BW: $685.86
4C: $885.86
PCI: $8.17

FORT VALLEY†, pop. 9,000.

C. GA. Peach Co. 29 mi. SW of Macon. Fort Valley State College (black). Manufactures cottonseed oil, baskets, farm implements, chemicals, ventilating fans, truck and bus bodies. Pine timber. Agriculture. Peaches, corn, grain, asparagus.

7396 The Camellia Journal
American Camellia Society
Massee Lane Gardens Phone: (912)967-2358
100 Massee Ln. Fax: (912)967-2083
Fort Valley, GA 31030-9100
Publisher E-mail: acs@mail.peach.public.lib.ga.us

Journal for Camellia growers. **Founded:** Apr. 1946. **Freq:** Quarterly. **Print Method:** Letterpress and offset. **Trim Size:** 11 x 8 1/2. **Cols./Page:** 3. **Col. Width:** 30 nonpareils. **Col. Depth:** 135 agate lines. **Key Personnel:** Ann Blair Brown, Editor/Administration. **ISSN:** 0065-762X. **Subscription Rates:** $25 individuals. **Remarks:** Accepts advertising.
Ad Rates: BW: $304 **Circ:** ‡5,000
4C: $395

7397 Fort Valley Herald
Atlantic Communications of Georgia, Inc.
315 N. Camellia Blvd. Phone: (912)822-9714
PO Box 899 Fax: (912)232-8666
Fort Valley, GA 31030
Free: (800)236-0060

Black community newspaper. **Founded:** 1986. **Freq:** Weekly (Wed.). **Print Method:** Offset. **Trim Size:** 13 x 21 1/2 in. **Cols./Page:** 6. **Col. Width:** 2 inches. **Key Personnel:** Robert E. James, Editor and Publisher. **Subscription Rates:** $15; $17 out of state. **Remarks:** Accepts advertising.
Ad Rates: GLR: $.86 **Circ:** ‡6,000
PCI: $12

7398 Leader- The Tribune
Leader-Tribune, Inc.
PO Box 1060 Phone: (912)825-2432
Fort Valley, GA 31030-1060 Fax: (912)825-4130
Publisher E-mail: ltpeachpub@aol.com

Community newspaper. **Founded:** 1889. **Freq:** Weekly (Wed.). **Print Method:** Web press. **Cols./Page:** 6. **Col. Width:** 12.4 picas. **Col. Depth:** 21 1/2 inches. **Key Personnel:** Vicky Whitehead, General Mgr. **Subscription Rates:** $21.60 individuals discount for seniors; $29.15 out of area; $45 out of state. **Remarks:** Accepts advertising. **Alt. Formats:** CD-ROM. **Formerly:** Fort Valley Leader-Tribune (1991).
Ad Rates: GLR: $6.45 **Circ:** 4,200
BW: $645
4C: $800
PCI: $7.25

7399 Piedmont Cable Corp.
Rte. 2, Box 1085 Phone: (912)825-3578
Fort Valley, GA 31030 Fax: (912)825-3611

Owner: D. Mark Baxter, at above address. **Founded:** Oct. 1989. **Key Personnel:** Denice Morgan, General Mgr. **Cities Served:** Byron, Fort Valley, Lizella, GA: subscribing households 600; 40 channels; 1 community access channel; 24 hours per week community access programming.

7400 Valley Cable TV Inc.
PO Box 508 Phone: (912)825-3626
Fort Valley, GA 31030

Founded: 1970. **Key Personnel:** Fletcher Barnes, President; Jimmy Barnes, Vice President; Bobby Barnes, Vice President. **Cities Served:** subscribing households 650; 29 channels; 1 community access channel.

7401 WFXM-FM - 100.1
Atl Hwy. 341 Phone: (912)827-1273
Fort Valley, GA 31030 Fax: (912)742-8299

Format: Urban Contemporary. **Networks:** American Urban Radio; Mutual Broadcasting System. **Founded:** 1973. **Formerly:** WFNE-FM. **Operating Hours:** Continuous. **Key Personnel:** Albert E. Smith, General Mgr.; George Threatt, Operations Mgr.; Sharon Wilson, Traffic Mgr.; Patricia Glass, Sales Mgr.; Wanda Harvey, Office Mgr. **Wattage:** 3000.

7402 WKXK-FM - 97.9
Hwy. 341 N. Phone: (912)825-5547
PO Box 1150 Fax: (912)742-8299
Fort Valley, GA 31030

Format: Country. **Networks:** American Urban Radio; Mutual Broadcasting System. **Founded:** 1989. **Formerly:** WXKO-FM (1989). **Operating Hours:** Continuous. **ADI:** Macon, GA. **Key Personnel:** Albert E. Smith, General Mgr.; George Threatt, Operations Mgr.; Patricia Glass, Sales Mgr.; Sharon Wilson, Traffic Dir.; Wanda Harvey, Office Mgr. **Wattage:** 6000.

7403 WXKO-AM - 1150
Hwy. 341 N. Phone: (912)825-5547
PO Box 1150 Fax: (912)742-8299
Fort Valley, GA 31030-1150

Format: Religious; Ethnic. **Founded:** 1951. **Formerly:** WFPM-AM (1981). **Operating Hours:** 6 a.m.-sunset. **ADI:** Macon, GA. **Key Personnel:** Wanda Harvey, Office Mgr.; Sharon Wilson, Traffic Mgr.; Albert E. Smith, General Mgr.; Jarrett Reagan, Operations Mgr.; Rudy Carson, Sales Mgr.; Patricia Glass, Sales Mgr.; George Threatt, Operations Mgr. **Wattage:** 1000 day; 72 night.

FRANKLIN

7404 The News & Banner
The News & Banner, Inc.
PO Box 97 Phone: (706)675-3374
Franklin, GA 30217
Community newspaper. **Freq:** Weekly (Wed.). **Cols./Page:** 6. **Col. Width:** 12.4 picas. **Col. Depth:** 21 inches. **Key Personnel:** Berrien T. McCutchen, Editor and Publisher.
Circ: 1,100

GAINESVILLE†, pop. 15,280.

N. GA. Hall Co. 48 mi. NE of Atlanta. Brenau College (women); Gainesville Junior College. Manufactures textiles, furniture, gasoline turbine engines, nylon thread, bricks. Poultry, egg production and processing plant. Hardwood timber. Agriculture.

7405 Poultry and Egg Marketing
Gannett Co., Inc.
PO Box 1338 Phone: (770)536-2476
Gainesville, GA 30503 Fax: (770)532-4894
Publication E-mail: ptpub@mindspring.com

Marketing magazine (tabloid) covering the poultry and egg trade. **Founded:** 1920. **Freq:** Bimonthly. **Print Method:** Offset. **Trim Size:** 11 x 13 1/4. **Cols./Page:** 4. **Col. Width:** 28 nonpareils. **Col. Depth:** 182 agate lines. **Key Personnel:** Chris Hill, Editor, ptedit@mindspring.com; Randall Smallwood, Publisher, ptpubassistantmindspring.com. **ISSN:** 0032-5716. **Subscription Rates:** Free. **Remarks:** Accepts advertising.
Ad Rates: BW: $1,425 **Circ:** Controlled ‡11,600
4C: $1,825
PCI: $29

7406 Poultry Times
Gannett Co., Inc.
PO Box 1338 Phone: (770)536-2476
Gainesville, GA 30503 Fax: (770)532-4894

Magazine covering the poultry and eggs industries. **Founded:** 1954. **Freq:** Biweekly. **Print Method:** Offset. **Trim Size:** 11 x 13 1/4. **Cols./Page:** 5. **Col. Width:** 23 nonpareils. **Col. Depth:** 13 inches. **Key Personnel:** Chris Hill, Editor, ptedit@mindspring.com; Randall Smallwood, Publisher, ptpub@mindspring.com; Charles McEachern, Advertising Dir., ptadvert@mindspring.com. **ISSN:** 0885-3371. **Subscription Rates:** $9 individuals; $17 two years; $18 other countries; $32 two years other countries. **Remarks:** Accepts advertising.
Ad Rates: GLR: $4.80 **Circ:** Paid ★12,307
BW: $3,188
4C: $3,663
PCI: $51

7407 Shelby Report of the Southeast
Shelby Publishing Co., Inc.
517 Green St. Phone: (770)534-8380
Gainesville, GA 30501 Fax: (770)535-0110
Publication E-mail: shelbypub@aol.com
Publisher E-mail: shelbypub@aol.com

Retail and wholesale food trade newspaper. **Founded:** 1968. **Freq:** Monthly. **Print Method:** Offset. **Trim Size:** 11 1/8 x 15. **Cols./Page:** 5. **Col. Width:** 11 nonpareils. **Col. Depth:** 196 agate lines. **Key Personnel:** Chuck Gilmer, Editor; Gary G. Shelby, Publisher; Ileen Bloch, Vice President. **ISSN:** 0194-

1968. **Subscription Rates:** $25 individuals. **Remarks:** Accepts advertising.
Ad Rates: BW: $2,940 — **Circ:** Paid 2,215
4C: $4,140 — Controlled 23,470
PCI: $42 — Non-paid 3,481

7408 Shelby Report of the Southwest
Shelby Publishing Co., Inc.
517 Green St. Phone: (770)534-8380
Gainesville, GA 30501 Fax: (770)535-0110
Publisher E-mail: shelbypub@aol.com

Retail and wholesale food trade newspaper. **Founded:** 1977. **Freq:** Monthly. **Print Method:** Offset. **Trim Size:** 11 1/8 x 15. **Cols./Page:** 5. **Col. Width:** 11 picas. **Col. Depth:** 13 7/8 inches. **Key Personnel:** Chuck Gilmer, Editor; Gary G. Shelby, Publisher; Ileen Bloch, Vice President. **ISSN:** 0192-916X. **Subscription Rates:** $25 individuals.
Ad Rates: BW: $2,940 — **Circ:** Paid ‡1,846
4C: $4,140 — Controlled ‡20,357
PCI: $42 — Non-paid ‡3,638

7409 Sunbelt Foodservice
Shelby Publishing Co., Inc.
517 Green St. Phone: (770)534-8380
Gainesville, GA 30501 Fax: (770)535-0110
Publisher E-mail: shelbypub@aol.com

Trade newspaper (tabloid) covering the food industry geared toward restaurant operators. **Founded:** Sept. 1984. **Freq:** Monthly. **Print Method:** Offset. **Trim Size:** 8 1/4 x 11. **Cols./Page:** 4. **Col. Width:** 11 picas. **Col. Depth:** 10 inches. **Key Personnel:** Chuck Gilmer, Editor; Gary G. Shelby, Publisher; Stormie Ellwanger, Advertising Mgr. **Subscription Rates:** $25 individuals. **Remarks:** Accepts advertising. **URL:** shelbypub@aol.com.
Ad Rates: BW: $1,840 — **Circ:** Paid 1,650
4C: $3,040 — Controlled 28,350

7410 The Times
PO Box 838 Phone: (770)532-1234
Gainesville, GA 30503 Fax: (770)532-7085
Publication E-mail: 102432.3532@compuserve

General newspaper. **Founded:** 1947. **Freq:** Daily (eve.), Sat. and Sun. (morn.). **Print Method:** Offset. **Trim Size:** 13 x 21 1/2. **Cols./Page:** 6. **Col. Width:** 25 nonpareils. **Col. Depth:** 301 agate lines. **Key Personnel:** Chris Jensen, Publisher; Rebecca Johnson, Market Development Director, fax (770)532-1368; Cindy McCurry-Ross, Executive Editor, fax (770)532-0457; Brenda Bohn, Advertising Dir., fax (770)532-8187. **Subscription Rates:** $156 individuals home delivery. **Remarks:** Accepts advertising. **Feature Editors:** Micheal Beard, *Entertainment, Living.*
Ad Rates: GLR: $4.18 — **Circ:** Mon.-Sat. 22,624
BW: $3,229 — Sun. 26,918
4C: $3,649
PCI: $25.03

7411 Intermedia
1102 Thompson Bridge Rd. NE Phone: (770)532-9961
Box 2535 Fax: (770)532-0455
Gainesville, GA 30503

Owner: InterMedia Partners, 235 Montgomery St., Ste. 435, San Francisco, CA 94104. **Formerly:** Gainesville Cablevision. **Key Personnel:** Danny Jobe, Operations Mgr.; Liz Dycus, Plant Mgr.; Susan Beem, Sales Mgr. **Cities Served:** Buford, Flowery Branch, Gainesville, Oakwood, GA: subscribing households 24,500; 33 channels.

7412 WBCX-FM - 89.1
Brenau University, 1 Centennial Cir. Phone: (770)538-4708
Fax: (770)538-4701
Gainesville, GA 30501
E-mail: rbigalke@lib.brenau.edu

Format: Classical; Jazz. **Networks:** Jones Satellite; Public Radio International (PRI). **Owner:** Brenau University, at above address. **Founded:** 1975. **Operating Hours:** Continuous; satellite/local. **ADI:** Atlanta (Athens & Rome), GA. **Key Personnel:** Rob Bigalke, Director, rbigalke@lib.brenau.edu. **Local Programs:** *Brenau News Forum* Thurs., 5:30 pm; Fri. 7:00 am, Rob Bigalke, Mailing contact, (770)538-4708, Fax (770)538-4701; *Focus on Classics* 6:00 pm Thursday, Mandy Wade, Mailing contact; *Jazz Street With Dr. Jazz* 7:00 pm - 10:00 pm Friday, Rob Bigalke. **Wattage:** 835. **Ad Rates:** Noncommercial.

7413 WDUN-AM - 550
1102 Thompson Bridge Rd. Phone: (770)532-9921
PO Box 10 Fax: (770)532-0506
Gainesville, GA 30503
Free: (800)552-WDUN
E-mail: radiocenter@applied.com

Format: News; Talk; Sports. **Networks:** ABC. **Owner:** John W. Jacobs, III, at above address. **Founded:** 1949. **Operating Hours:** Continuous; 25% network, 75% local. **ADI:** Atlanta (Athens & Rome), GA. **Key Personnel:** John W. Jacobs, Jr., Chairman; John W. Jacobs III, Gen. Mgr./Pres.; Bill Maine, Station Mgr.; Ken Stanford, News Dir.; John Parks, Operations Mgr. **Local Programs:** *Fun at Four & Five*, B. Brewer; *Morning Show/Morning Talk*, Bill Maine, Station Mgr.; *Topical Talk at 10*, Bill Maine. **Wattage:** 10,000 day; 2500 night. **Ad Rates:** $12-29 for 30 seconds; $22-39 for 60 seconds. **URL:** http://www.wdun.com.

7414 WGGA-AM - 1240
PO Box 10 Phone: (404)532-9921
Gainesville, GA 30503 Fax: (404)532-0506

Format: Gospel; Southern Gospel; Big Band/Nostalgia. **Networks:** CBS. **Owner:** WGGA Radio of Gainesville, Inc., at above address. **Founded:** 1941. **Operating Hours:** Continuous. **Key Personnel:** Glenda Voiles, General Mgr.; Tom Israel, Operations Mgr.; Carol Israel, Office Mgr. **Wattage:** 1000. **Ad Rates:** $6-20 per unit.

7415 WKZD-AM - 1330
1864 Thompson Bridge Rd. Phone: (770)531-1330
Gainesville, GA 30501 Fax: (770)718-0551

Format: Adult Contemporary; Oldies. **Networks:** CNN Radio. **Owner:** Georgia Mountains Communications, Inc., Box 2255, Gainesville, GA 30503. **Founded:** 1986. **Operating Hours:** 6 a.m.-sunset; 100% local. **ADI:** Atlanta (Athens & Rome), GA. **Key Personnel:** Sam Davis, Program Dir.; Mike Wofford, Sports Dir.; Dave Puckett, Station Mgr.; Carol McAboy, News Dir. **Wattage:** 1000. **Ad Rates:** $7.50 for 30 seconds; $10 for 60 seconds.

7416 WLBA-AM - 1130
311 Green St., Ste. 200 Phone: (770)532-6331
Gainesville, GA 30501 Fax: (770)532-2672

Format: Contemporary Country. **Networks:** NBC. **Owner:** Bennie Hewett, at above address, (404)536-3890. **Founded:** 1957. **Formerly:** WNRJ-AM (1978). **Operating Hours:** 6 a.m.-8 p.m.; 20% network, 80% local. **Wattage:** 10,000. **Ad Rates:** $5-11 for 30 seconds; $8-14 for 60 seconds.

7417 WMJE-FM - 102.9
PO Box 10 Phone: (770)532-9921
Gainesville, GA 30503 Fax: (770)532-0506
Free: (800)273-0103
E-mail: radiocenter@applied.com

Format: Adult Contemporary. **Networks:** Unistar; Westwood One Radio. **Owner:** WGGA Radio of Gainesville, Inc., at above address. **Founded:** 1990. **Formerly:** WGGA-FM. **Operating Hours:** 24 hours. **ADI:** Atlanta (Athens & Rome), GA. **Key Personnel:** John W. Jacobs IV, Pres./CEO; Bill Maine, Station Mgr.; Jay Andrews, Program Dir. **Local Programs:** *Jay Andrews Afternoon Show*, Jay Andrews; *Wake-Up Service*, Bill Maine, Program Dir. **Wattage:** 25,000. **Ad Rates:** $5-13 for 30 seconds; $8-16 for 60 seconds. **URL:** http://www.wdun.com.

7418 WSTE-FM - 106.1
340 Jesse Jewell Pky., Ste. 525 Phone: (770)534-8106
Gainesville, GA 30501 Fax: (770)534-2614

Format: Country. **Networks:** Motor Racing. **Owner:** Southern Broadcasting Companies, Inc., 3428 Rilman Rd., Atlanta, GA 30327. **Founded:** 1946. **Formerly:** WLET-FM (1985). **Operating Hours:** Continuous; 100% local. **ADI:** Atlanta (Athens & Rome), GA. **Key Personnel:** Dan Gorby, General Mgr./General & Local Sales Mgr.; Joel Williams, Program Dir.; B.J. Williams, News Dir.; Deborah Reece, Production Dir. **Wattage:** 100,000. **Ad Rates:** Advertising accepted; rates available upon request. **URL:** http://www.south106.com.

GLENNVILLE, pop. 4,144.

SE GA. Tattnall Co. 20 mi. S. of Collins. Residential. Import and export industry. Rotary mowers.

7419 WKIG-AM - 1580
226 E. Bolton St. Phone: (912)654-3580
Glennville, GA 30427 Fax: (912)654-3580
E-mail: wkigfm@pineland.net

Format: Gospel. **Networks:** NBC. **Owner:** Tattnall County Broadcasting Co., PO Box 98, Glennville, GA 30427. **Founded:** 1961. **Operating Hours:** Sunrise-sunset; 98% network, 2% local. **Key Personnel:** Judy W. Cobb, Station Mgr. **Wattage:** 1000. **Ad Rates:** $4.00-5.70 for 30 seconds; $5.15-6.65 for 60 seconds.

7420 WKIG-FM - 106.3
226 E. Bolton St.
Glennville, GA 30427
E-mail: wkigfm@pineland.net

Format: Adult Contemporary. **Networks:** Satellite Music Network. **Founded:** 1977. **Operating Hours:** Continuous. **Key Personnel:** Judy W. Cobb, Manager; Roy L. Woods, News and Program Dir. **Wattage:** 6000. **Ad Rates:** $4-5.75 per unit.

GLENWOOD

7421 Scripps Howard Cable
PO Box 615 Phone: (912)523-5100
Glenwood, GA 30428-0615 Fax: (912)523-5591

Key Personnel: Jim Sherman, Operations Mgr.; Martin O'Keefe, Contact. **Cities Served:** subscribing households 1,465; 25 channels.

GORDON

7422 Wilkinson County News
Box 205 Phone: (912)946-2218
Irwinton, GA 31042 Fax: (912)946-2218

Community newspaper. **Founded:** 1922. **Freq:** Weekly (Thurs.). **Print Method:** Offset. **Cols./Page:** 6. **Col. Width:** 21 nonpareils. **Col. Depth:** 301 agate lines. **Key Personnel:** Edwin Boone, Editor/Administration; Joe Boone, Publisher. **Subscription Rates:** $12.50 individuals; $14.50 out of area; $15.50 out of state. **Remarks:** Advertising not accepted for tobacco products.
Ad Rates: GLR: $.12 — **Circ:** Paid ‡2,650
BW: $315
4C: $590
PCI: $2.50

GRAY†, pop. 2,145.

C. GA. Jones Co. 14 mi. NE of Macon. Agriculture. Corn, cotton, peaches.

7423 The Jones County News
PO Box 1538 Phone: (912)986-3929
Gray, GA 31032 Fax: (912)986-1935
Publication E-mail: jcnews@bigfoot.com

Local newspaper. **Founded:** 1895. **Freq:** Weekly (Thurs.). **Print Method:** Offset. **Cols./Page:** 6. **Col. Width:** 24 nonpareils. **Col. Depth:** 301 agate lines. **Key Personnel:** T. Moore, Editor; G.B. Moore III, Publisher. **Subscription Rates:** $19.26 individuals; $21.40 out of state. **Remarks:** Accepts advertising.
Ad Rates: GLR: $.18 — **Circ:** 5,500
BW: $332.80
PCI: $2.60

GREENSBORO†, pop. 2,985.

NE GA. Greene Co. 30 mi. S. of Athens. Residential.

7424 The Herald-Journal
PO Box 149 Phone: (706)453-7988
Greensboro, GA 30642 Fax: (404)453-2311

Newspaper with a Democratic orientation. **Freq:** Weekly (Thurs.). **Print Method:** Letterpress and offset. **Cols./Page:** 6. **Col. Width:** 12 picas. **Col. Depth:** 21 1/2 inches. **Key Personnel:** Carey Williams, Jr., Editor and Publisher. **Subscription Rates:** $15.90 individuals. **Remarks:** Accepts advertising.
Ad Rates: BW: $516 — **Circ:** ‡4,400
4C: $876
PCI: $4

GRIFFIN†, pop. 20,728.

W. GA. Spalding Co. 40 mi. S. of Atlanta. Manufactures textiles. Fruit, dairy farms. Cotton, peppers, wheat.

7425 The Fayette Neighbor
Neighbor Newspapers, Inc.
323 E. Solomon St. Phone: (770)227-3276
P.O. Box M Fax: (404)412-1678
Griffin, GA 30224
Community newspaper. **Founded:** 1978. **Freq:** Daily (eve.), Sat. and Sun. (morn.). **Print Method:** Offset. **Cols./Page:** 6. **Col. Width:** 26 nonpareils. **Col. Depth:** 301 agate lines. **Key Personnel:** John Payne, Jr., Editor; Otis Raybon, Jr., Publisher; Jeffrey Jones, Advertising Mgr. **USPS:** 405-590. **Subscription Rates:** $18 out of area; $24 out of state.
Ad Rates: GLR: $.68 — **Circ:** Paid 21
BW: $1,482.21 — Non-paid 19,714
4C: $1,787.21
SAU: $9.50
PCI: $11.49

7426 Griffin Daily News
323 E. Solomon St. Phone: (404)227-3276
PO Box M Fax: (404)412-1678
Griffin, GA 30224
Newspaper with a Democratic orientation. **Founded:** 1871. **Freq:** Mon.-Sat. (eve.). **Print Method:** Offset. **Cols./Page:** 6. **Col. Width:** 2 inches. **Col. Depth:** 301 agate lines. **Key Personnel:** Bill Knight, Editor; Otis Raybon, Jr., Publisher; William P. Krakoff, Advertising Mgr. **Subscription Rates:** $75.60 individuals. **Remarks:** Accepts advertising.
Ad Rates: GLR: $9.04 **Circ:** Mon. ★**13,476**
BW: $1,116.16 Tues.-Fri. ★**11,784**
4C: $1,416.16 Sat. ★**11,734**
PCI: $9.04 Sun. ★**11,672**

7427 Insight Communications
1150 Everee Inn Rd. Phone: (770)228-3333
Griffin, GA 30223 Fax: (770)228-1982

Owner: Insight Communications Co., L.P., 126 E. 56th, New York, NY 10022, (212)371-2266. **Founded:** 1969. **Key Personnel:** Ann Cherrette, General Mgr. **Cities Served:** Griffin, Orchard Hill, Sunny Side, Spalding County, GA.: subscribing households 12,200; 47 channels; 1 community access channel; 10 hours per week community access programming.

7428 KLCU-FM - 92.5
1523 Kell Ln., Ste. 1 Phone: (770)412-8700
Griffin, GA 30223 Fax: (770)412-8080
E-mail: thebear92@aol.com

Format: Country. **Networks:** Meadows Racing. **Owner:** Spalding Broadcasting, L.P., at above address. **Founded:** Dec. 31, 1995. **Operating Hours:** Continuous. **ADI:** Atlanta (Athens & Rome), GA. **Key Personnel:** Les Reed, General Mgr.; Carl Pruett, Sales Mgr.; Geogia Gregory, News Dir.; Stan Watson, Program Dir. **Wattage:** 6000. **URL:** http://www.bear92.com.

7429 WHIE-AM - 1320
PO Drawer G Phone: (404)227-9451
Griffin, GA 30224 Fax: (404)227-8822

Format: Country; News; Talk. **Founded:** 1952. **Operating Hours:** 6 a.m.-11 p.m. **Key Personnel:** Fred Watkins, Contact. **Local Programs:** *Community Comment*, Bonnie Pfrogner; *Shop Talk*, Bonnie Pfrogner. **Wattage:** 5000.

7430 WKEU-AM - 1450
1000 Memorial Dr. Phone: (404)227-5507
PO Box 997 Fax: (404)229-2291
Griffin, GA 30224

Format: Middle-of-the-Road (MOR). **Networks:** ABC. **Founded:** 1934. **Operating Hours:** 19 hours Daily; 5% network, 95% local. **ADI:** Atlanta (Athens & Rome), GA. **Key Personnel:** Bill Taylor, General Mgr.; Barry Clark, Sales Mgr.; Stan Watson, PD.; Sam Stacy, Chief Financial Officer; Eddie Whitlock, News Dir. **Wattage:** 1000. **Ad Rates:** $6.25 for 30 seconds; $12.50 for 60 seconds.

7431 WQUL-FM - 97.7
PO Box 997 Phone: (404)227-5507
1000 Memorial Dr. Fax: (404)229-2291
Griffin, GA 30224
Free: (800)441-0097

Format: Oldies. **Networks:** ABC. **Founded:** 1966. **Formerly:** WKEU-FM (1990). **Operating Hours:** 5 a.m.-midnight; 60% network, 40% local. **ADI:** Atlanta (Athens & Rome), GA. **Key Personnel:** Leonard Bolton, General Mgr.; Joe Beail, Station Mgr. **Wattage:** 3300. **Ad Rates:** $6.25-11.25 for 30 seconds; $7.75-12.75 for 60 seconds.

GROVETOWN

7432 Cencom Cable Television
PO Box 329 Phone: (706)860-1580
536 E. Robinson Ave. Fax: (706)868-9399
Grovetown, GA 30813-0329

Owner: Cencom Cable Associates, 635 Maryville Cent Ste. 300, St. Louis MO 63141, Chesterfield, MO. **Formerly:** American Cablevision. **Key Personnel:** Christopher Carson, Contact. **Cities Served:** subscribing households 3,480; 41 channels.

HAMPTON

7433 21st Century Adventures
256 Red Maple Dr. Phone: (770)946-3392
Hampton, GA 30228 Fax: (770)946-4173

Travel magazine for those seeking adventure. Articles, written by freelance travelers, offer detailed information on specific destinations. **URL:** http://www.10e-design.com/centadv/.

HARTWELL†, pop. 4,855.

NE GA. Hart Co. 21 mi. E. of Anderson, SC. Recreational area. Manufactures textiles, flour. Textile plant. Agriculture. Cotton, grain, clover, poultry, livestock.

7434 The Hartwell Sun
Southern Cresent News
PO Box 700
Hartwell, GA 30643

Newspaper. **Founded:** 1876. **Freq:** Weekly (Thurs.). **Print Method:** Offset. **Cols./Page:** 6. **Col. Width:** 20 nonpareils. **Col. Depth:** 301 agate lines. **Key Personnel:** Steve F. Carswell, Editor; Rita Chapman, Advertising Mgr.; Peggy Vickery, Advertising Mgr. **Subscription Rates:** $18 individuals. **Remarks:** Accepts advertising.
Ad Rates: GLR: $.18 **Circ:** ‡6,000
BW: $650.25
4C: $825.25
PCI: $5.10

7435 WKLY-AM - 980
PO Box 636 Phone: (706)376-2233
Hartwell, GA 30643 Fax: (706)376-3100

Format: Country; Religious. **Networks:** NBC; Georgia Radio. **Owner:** WKLY Broadcasting Co., at above address. **Founded:** 1948. **Operating Hours:** 6:00 a.m.-9:00 p.m.; 10% network, 90% local. **Key Personnel:** Edward Hicks, Contact; Frances Hicks, Contact; Harris E. Brown, Program Dir.; Mike Atkins, Contact, phone (706)376-2233; Bruce Hicks, Contact; Bryan Hicks, GM/CON. **Local Programs:** *Cookin' with Frances* 10:15 am Mon., Tues., Thurs., Frances Hicks; *Weekly Sports Rap* 3:15 pm Monday-Friday, Harris Brown; *Weekly Swap Shop* 10:30 am Monday-Friday, Mike Atkins, (706)376-3363. **Wattage:** 1000 day; 149 night. **Ad Rates:** $7-8 for 30 seconds; $12-14 for 60 seconds.

HAWKINSVILLE†, pop. 4,372.

C. GA. Pulaski Co. On Ocmulgee River, 40 mi. S. of Macon. Harness horse training tracks. Manufactures cotton towels and yarn, lumber. Pine timber. Diversified farming. Cotton, corn, peanuts.

7436 Hawkinsville Dispatch and News
Hawkinsville Publishing Co.
329 Commerce St. Phone: (912)783-1291
PO Box 30 Fax: (912)783-1293
Hawkinsville, GA 31036
Community newspaper. **Founded:** 1867. **Freq:** Weekly (Wed.). **Print Method:** Offset. **Cols./Page:** 6. **Col. Width:** 12 picas. **Col. Depth:** 21 1/2 inches. **Key Personnel:** Chuck Southerland, Publisher. **USPS:** 237-900. **Subscription Rates:** $18 individuals plus tax. **Remarks:** Accepts advertising.
Ad Rates: BW: $438.60 **Circ:** Paid ‡2,910
SAU: $3.40 Non-paid ‡50
PCI: $3.40

7437 WCEH-FM - 103.9
Eastman Hwy., PO Box 1398 Phone: (912)892-9061
Hawkinsville, GA 31036-0489 Fax: (912)892-9063

Format: Adult Contemporary; Oldies; Middle-of-the-Road (MOR). **Networks:** ABC; Georgia Radio. **Owner:** Tri-County Broadcasting, Inc., at above address. **Founded:** 1968. **Operating Hours:** Continuous. **ADI:** Macon, GA. **Key Personnel:** Jay Braswell, General Mgr.; Tom Kirk, News Dir.; Bill Boys, Program Dir. **Wattage:** 25,000.

HAZLEHURST†, pop. 4,249.

SE GA. Jeff Davis Co. 50 mi. N. of Waycross. Manufactures carpet backing, sporting goods, textiles, refrigeration filter dryer, tobacco and naval stores industries. Yellow pine timber. Agriculture. Tobacco, cotton, corn.

7438 Jeff Davis Ledger
12 Latimer St. Phone: (912)375-4225
PO Box 338 Fax: (912)375-3704
Hazlehurst, GA 31539
Publication E-mail: jdleder@altamaha.net

Community newspaper. **Founded:** 1900. **Freq:** Weekly (Wed.). **Print Method:** Offset. **Cols./Page:** 6. **Col. Width:** 26 nonpareils. **Col. Depth:** 294 agate lines. **Key Personnel:** Thomas H. Purser, Editor and Publisher, phone (912)3754225. **Subscription Rates:** $15 individuals. **Remarks:** Accepts advertising. **Available Online. Alt. Formats:** CD-ROM.
Ad Rates: GLR: $0.29 **Circ:** ‡3,800
BW: $504
SAU: $4.20

7439 WVOH-AM - 920
PO Box 757 Phone: (912)375-4511
Hazlehurst, GA 31539 Fax: (912)375-4512

Format: Country; Religious. **Networks:** NBC; Georgia Radio. **Owner:** Jeff Davis Broadcasters, Inc., at above address. **Founded:** 1962. **Operating Hours:** 24Hrs. 40% network, 60% local. **Key Personnel:** John I. Hulett, Sr., Contact; Wilbur G. Heath, Contact; Bruce Bostwick, Contact; Ronnie Williams, Music Dir.; John Davis, Contact. **Wattage:** 500 day; 39 night. **Ad Rates:** $3.00 for 15 seconds; $4.00 for 30 seconds; $4.50 for 60 seconds. WVOH-FM.

7440 WVOH-FM - 93.5
PO Box 757 Phone: (912)375-4511
Hazlehurst, GA 31539 Fax: (912)375-4512

Format: Country. **Networks:** NBC; Georgia Radio. **Owner:** Jeff Davis Broadcasters, Inc., at above address. **Founded:** 1976. **Operating Hours:** 24Hrs; 50% network, 50% local. **Key Personnel:** John I. Hulett, Sr., Contact; Wilbur G. Heath, Contact; Bruce Bostwick, Contact; Ronnie William, Music Dir.; Joan Davis, Contact. **Wattage:** 50,000. **Ad Rates:** $3.00 for 15 seconds; $4.00 for 30 seconds; $4.50 for 60 seconds.

HENRY

7441 The Henry Neighbor
Neighbor Newspapers, Inc.
580 Fairground St. Phone: (770)428-9411
PO Box 449 Fax: (770)428-7945
Marietta, GA 30060
Community newspaper. **Founded:** 1978. **Freq:** Weekly (Thurs.). **Print Method:** Offset. **Cols./Page:** 6. **Col. Width:** 26 nonpareils. **Col. Depth:** 301 agate lines. **Key Personnel:** Otis A. Brumby, Jr., Publisher. **USPS:** 405-570. **Subscription Rates:** $12 individuals; $18 out of country; $24 out of state.
Ad Rates: GLR: $.77 **Circ:** Paid 19
BW: $1,393.20 Non-paid 21,196
4C: $1,683.20
SAU: $10.80

HIAWASSEE†, pop. 491.

N. GA. Towns Co. 90 mi. NE of Atlanta. Hardwood timber. Diversified farming. Corn, wheat, apples.

7442 Towns County Herald
Box 365 Phone: (706)896-4454
Hiawassee, GA 30546 Fax: (706)745-1830

Community newspaper. **Founded:** 1928. **Freq:** Weekly (Thurs.). **Print Method:** Offset. **Cols./Page:** 6. **Col. Width:** 24 nonpareils. **Col. Depth:** 301 agate lines. **Key Personnel:** Wanda R. West, Editor and Publisher; Kenneth West, General Mgr.; Donna Corn, Contact. **Subscription Rates:** $15 individuals; $20 out of area. **Remarks:** Accepts advertising.
Ad Rates: GLR: $.17 **Circ:** ‡3,500
BW: $419.25
4C: $919.25
PCI: $4

HINESVILLE†, pop. 12,000.

SE GA. Liberty Co. 35 mi. SW of Savannah. Fort Steward. Manufactures paper. Timber.

7443 The Coastal Courier
PO Box 498 Phone: (912)876-0156
Hinesville, GA 31313 Fax: (912)368-6329
Publisher E-mail: ccourier@infoave.net

Newspaper. **Founded:** 1871. **Freq:** 3/week. **Print Method:** Offset. **Trim Size:** 13 x 21 1/2. **Cols./Page:** 6. **Col. Width:** 24 nonpareils. **Col. Depth:** 301 agate lines. **Key Personnel:** Pat Watkins, Editor, pwatkins@infoave.net; Mark Griffin, Publisher. **USPS:** 311-680. **Subscription Rates:** $15.50 individuals. **URL:** http://www.hinesvillenews.com.
Ad Rates: GLR: $.34 **Circ:** 5,500
BW: $826.89
SAU: $6.41

7444 Tri-County Penny Saver
PO Box 498 Phone: (912)876-0156
Hinesville, GA 31313 Fax: (912)368-6329

Shopper. **Founded:** 1980. **Freq:** Weekly (Tues.). **Print Method:** Offset. **Trim Size:** 10 1/4 x 13. **Cols./Page:** 6. **Col. Width:** 12 1/2 picas. **Col. Depth:** 13 inches. **Key Personnel:** Goldie Myers, Advertising Mgr.; Mark Griffin, General Mgr. **Subscription Rates:** $39 individuals. **Remarks:** Accepts advertising.
Ad Rates: GLR: $8.50 **Circ:** Free 21,500
BW: $663
4C: $888
PCI: $8.50

7445 Bresnan Communications Co.
1050 Kacey Dr. Phone: (912)427-6364
Hinesville, GA 31313-5369 Fax: (912)427-0513

Owner: Bresnan Communications Co., 709 West Chester Ave., White Plains, NY 10604, (914)993-6600. **Key Personnel:** Jon W. Lash, General Mgr.; William T. Porter, Area Mgr.; Edward Dice, Technical Mgr.; Donna R. Wainwright, Operations Mgr. **Cities Served:** Allenhurst, Flemington, Gardi, Hinesville, Jesup, Ludowici, Odum, Richmond Hill, Screven, Walthourville, Woodbine, GA: subscribing households 22,000; 42 channels.

7446 WGML-AM - 990
PO Box 615 Phone: (912)368-3399
Hinesville, GA 31313-3611 Fax: (912)368-4191

Format: Ethnic; Religious. **Owner:** Powerhouse Broadcasting, PO Box 93, Hinesville, GA 31313, (912)368-0617, Fax: (912)368-0620. **Founded:** 1958. **Operating Hours:** Daytime. **Key Personnel:** James Smith, General Mgr. **Wattage:** 250. **Ad Rates:** $4-8 for 30 seconds; $6-12 for 60 seconds.

7447 WHVL-FM - 104.7
120 Liberty St./CD-104 Phone: (912)369-4852
Hinesville, GA 31313 Fax: (912)876-6920
Free: (800)888-6499

Format: Adult Contemporary. **Owner:** Bullie Broadcasting Corp., at above address. **Founded:** 1993. **Operating Hours:** Continuous. **ADI:** Savannah, GA. **Wattage:** 25,000. **Ad Rates:** $6-8 for 30 seconds; $8-10 for 60 seconds.

HOGANSVILLE, pop. 3,362.

W. GA. Troup Co. 50 mi. SW of Atlanta. Residential.

7448 The Hogansville Herald
Rolin Press Group
PO Box 250 Phone: (912)887-3674
Richland, GA 31825 Fax: (912)887-2800

Community newspaper. **Founded:** 1944. **Freq:** Weekly (Thurs.). **Print Method:** Offset. **Trim Size:** 11 1/2 x 14. **Cols./Page:** 6. **Col. Width:** 12 picas. **Col. Depth:** 301 agate lines. **Key Personnel:** Laurie Lewis, Editor; Bob Tribble, Publisher. **Subscription Rates:** $15 individuals; $23.63 out of area; $30 out of state. **Remarks:** Accepts advertising.
Ad Rates: GLR: $.29 **Circ:** ‡1,150
BW: $509.55
4C: $664.40
SAU: $3.95
PCI: $3.95

HOMERVILLE†, pop. 3,112.

S. GA. Clinch Co. 26 mi. W. of Waycross. Manufactures plastic and metal containers. Lithography. Pine timber.

7449 WBTY-FM - 105.5
Box 577 Phone: (912)487-3412
Homerville, GA 31634 Fax: (912)487-3414

Format: Classic Rock. **Founded:** 1979. **Operating Hours:** Continuous. **Key Personnel:** Nancy Strickland, Manager; Jane Welch, Operations Mgr. **Wattage:** 3000. **Ad Rates:** $2.50 for 30 seconds; $4.75 for 60 seconds.

IRWINTON†, pop. 841.

C. GA. Wilkinson Co. 30 mi. SE of Macon. Pine timber; kaolin deposits. Agriculture.

Wilkinson County News - See Gordon

7450 WVKX-FM - 103.7
PO Box 569 Phone: (912)946-3445
Irwinton, GA 31042 Fax: (912)946-2406

Format: Urban Contemporary; Blues. **Owner:** Wilkinson Broadcasting, at above address. **Operating Hours:** Continuous. **ADI:** Macon, GA. **Key Personnel:** Reggie Smith, Manager; George Threatt, Operations and Music Dir.; James Thomas, Gospel and Religious Coor.; Stan Carter, General Mgr. **Wattage:** 6,000. **Ad Rates:** $16 for 30 seconds; $20 for 60 seconds.

JACKSON†, pop. 4,043.

C. GA. Butts Co. 45 mi. SE of Atlanta. Sheet metal fabrication. Timber. Cattle farms.

7451 Jackson Progress-Argus
PO Box 249 Phone: (770)775-3107
Jackson, GA 30233 Fax: (770)775-3855

Newspaper. **Founded:** 1873. **Freq:** Weekly (Wed.). **Print Method:** Offset. **Cols./Page:** 6. **Col. Width:** 12 picas. **Col. Depth:** 21 1/2 inches. **Key Personnel:** Larry Stanford, Editor; W. Herman Cawthon, Publisher. **USPS:** 272-140. **Subscription Rates:** $20 individuals; $36 out of county. **Remarks:** Accepts advertising.
Ad Rates: BW: $1,006.20 **Circ:** ‡4,100
4C: $300
PCI: $7.80

7452 WJGA-FM - 92.1
PO Box 3878 Phone: (770)775-3151
Jackson, GA 30233 Fax: (770)775-3151

Format: Adult Contemporary; Urban Contemporary. **Networks:** Independent. **Founded:** 1967. **Operating Hours:** 6 a.m.-1 a.m. **Key Personnel:** Don Earnhart, General Mgr. **Wattage:** 3000. **Ad Rates:** $8.80 for 30 seconds; $11 for 60 seconds.

JASPER†, pop. 1,556.

N. GA. Pickens Co. 50 mi. N. of Atlanta. Manufactures shoes, industrial rubber products. Marble mining and processing. Agriculture.

7453 Pickens County Progress
PO Box 67 Phone: (706)692-2457
Jasper, GA 30143 Fax: (706)692-9738
Publication E-mail: progress@ellijay.com

Newspaper with a Democratic orientation. **Founded:** 1886. **Freq:** Weekly (Thurs.). **Print Method:** Offset. **Cols./Page:** 6. **Col. Width:** 20 nonpareils. **Col. Depth:** 294 agate lines. **Key Personnel:** Martha E. Pool, Editor; John R. Pool, Publisher; William E. Pool, Advertising Mgr. **Subscription Rates:** $15.90 individuals; $23.32 Georgia Counties; $28.62 out of state. **Remarks:** Accepts advertising.
Ad Rates: BW: $3.00 **Circ:** ‡6,700

7454 WYYZ-AM - 1490
PO Box 280 Phone: (706)692-4100
Jasper, GA 30143 Fax: (706)692-4012

Format: Country; Gospel. **Networks:** CBS. **Owner:** Hellinger Broadcasting, Inc., at above address. **Operating Hours:** Continuous. **Key Personnel:** Mark Hellinger, President; Faye Hitt, Music Dir./Sales Mgr.; N. Vollrath, Program Dir.; Jennifer Tigwor, Office Mgr. **Local Programs:** *Gospel Time*, Faye Hitt. **Wattage:** 1,000. **Ad Rates:** $6 for 30 seconds; $8 for 60 seconds.

JEFFERSON†, pop. 2,000.

NE GA. Jackson Co. 65 mi. SE of Macon. Cotton mills. Dairy products. Agriculture. Soybeans, corn, cattle, poultry.

7455 Banks County News
MainStreet Newspapers Inc.
PO Box 908 Phone: (706)367-5233
Jefferson, GA 30549-0908 Fax: (706)367-8056

Newspaper. **Founded:** Dec. 1968. **Freq:** Weekly. **Print Method:** Offset. **Cols./Page:** 6. **Col. Width:** 27 nonpareils. **Col. Depth:** 301 agate lines. **Key Personnel:** Mike Buffington, Editor; Herman Buffington, Publisher; Scott Buffington, Advertising Mgr. **Subscription Rates:** $16.66 individuals; $22.20 out of area in state; $35.35 out of state. **Remarks:** Accepts advertising.
Ad Rates: GLR: $2.20 **Circ:** 6,700

7456 The Jackson Herald
MainStreet Newspapers Inc.
PO Box 908 Phone: (706)367-5233
Jefferson, GA 30549-0908 Fax: (706)367-8056

Newspaper with an independent orientation. **Founded:** June 1875. **Freq:** Weekly (Wed.). **Print Method:** Offset. **Cols./Page:** 6. **Col. Width:** 27 nonpareils. **Col. Depth:** 301 agate lines. **Key Personnel:** Mike Buffington, Editor, fax (706)367-8050; Herman Buffington, Publisher; Scott Buffington, Advertising Mgr. **Subscription Rates:** $16.66 local; $22.20 state; $35.35 out of state. **Remarks:** Accepts advertising.
Ad Rates: PCI: $3.50 **Circ:** ‡6,800

JEFFERSONVILLE†, pop. 1,473.

C. GA. Twiggs Co. 20 mi. SE of Macon. Residential.

7457 Twiggs County New Era
The Twiggs County
PO Box 292 Phone: (912)945-3566
Jeffersonville, GA 31044 Fax: (912)986-1935

Local newspaper. **Founded:** 1928. **Freq:** Weekly (Wed.). **Print Method:** Offset. **Cols./Page:** 6. **Col. Width:** 13 picas. **Col. Depth:** 21 inches. **Key Personnel:** Mark Watkins, Editor; Robert Tribbie, Publisher. **Subscription Rates:** $14.70 individuals; $19.50 out of area; $25.00 out of state. **Remarks:** Accepts advertising. **URL:** http://www.accucom.net/~mwatkins/era.htm.
Ad Rates: GLR: $.21 **Circ:** Paid 2009
BW: $441.00 Free 50
4C: $532.80
SAU: $2.60
PCI: $3.50

JESUP†, pop. 10,500.

SE GA. Wayne Co. 40 mi. NE of Waycross. Manufactures lumber, turpentine, textiles, furniture. Timber. Grain, truck, poultry, stock farms. Tobacco, corn.

7458 The Press-Sentinel
PO Box 607 Phone: (912)427-4246
Jesup, GA 31545 Fax: (912)427-4092

General newspaper. **Founded:** 1865. **Freq:** Semiweekly (Wed. and Sun.). **Print Method:** Offset. **Trim Size:** 14 x 22 3/4. **Cols./Page:** 6. **Col. Width:** 12.25 picas. **Col. Depth:** 301 agate lines. **Key Personnel:** J.H. (Sandy) Sanders, Publisher. **Subscription Rates:** $18.95 individuals. **Remarks:** Accepts advertising.
Ad Rates: BW: $690.15 **Circ:** 7,200
4C: $990.15
SAU: $5.35

7459 The Speedy Bee
PO Box 998 Phone: (912)427-4018
Jesup, GA 31598 Fax: (912)427-8447

Monthly trade newspaper for the beekeeping and honey industry. **Subtitle:** The Beekeeper's Newspaper. **Founded:** 1972. **Freq:** Monthly. **Print Method:** Offset. **Trim Size:** 11 x 17. **Cols./Page:** 5. **Col. Width:** 24 nonpareils. **Col. Depth:** 182 agate lines. **Key Personnel:** Troy H. Fore, Jr., Editor and Publisher, tfore@veta.jusupnet.com. **ISSN:** 0190-6798. **Subscription Rates:** $17.25 individuals. **Remarks:** Accepts advertising.
Ad Rates: BW: $845 **Circ:** ‡4,000

7460 Bresnan Communications Co.
Box 676 Phone: (912)427-6364
Jesup, GA 31545 Fax: (912)427-0513
Free: (800)627-6364

Founded: 1967. **Key Personnel:** Jon W. Lash, Southern Area Mgr. **Cities Served:** Wayne, Liberty, Camden and McIntosh Counties.: subscribing households 7,300; 42 channels.

7461 WIFO-FM - 105.5
PO Box 647 Phone: (912)427-3712
Jesup, GA 31598-0647 Fax: (912)530-7717

Format: Country. **Networks:** ABC; Georgia Radio. **Founded:** 1968. **Operating Hours:** 6 a.m.-12 a.m.; 5% network, 95% local. **ADI:** Savannah, GA. **Key Personnel:** Bob Morgan, News/Sports Dir.; Charles W. Hubbard, Jr., Program Dir.; Jim Cote, Engineer. **Wattage:** 3000. **Ad Rates:** $9.41 for 30 seconds; $13.53 for 60 seconds.

7462 WLOP-AM - 1370
PO Box 647 Phone: (912)427-3711
Jesup, GA 31598-0647 Fax: (912)530-7717

Format: Country. **Networks:** ABC; Georgia Radio. **Founded:** 1949. **Operating Hours:** 6 a.m.-12 a.m.; 5% network, 95% local. **ADI:** Savannah, GA. **Key Personnel:** Bob Morgan, News/Sports Dir.; Charles W. Hubbard, Jr., Program Dir. and Sales Mgr.; Jim Cote, Chief Engineer. **Wattage:** 5000 day; 36 night. **Ad Rates:** $9.41 for 30 seconds; $13.53 for 60 seconds.

JONESBORO†, pop. 4,132.

NWC GA. Clayton Co. 15 mi. S. of Atlanta. Manufactures furniture, machinery, hardware, dies, sheet metal, concrete, wood products.

7463 Clayton News/Daily
News Daily
136 Church St. Phone: (770)478-5753
PO Box 368 Fax: (770)473-9032
Jonesboro, GA 30237
General newspaper. **Founded:** 1971. **Freq:** Daily. **Print Method:** Offset. **Cols./Page:** 6. **Col. Width:** 24 nonpareils. **Col. Depth:** 301 agate lines. **Key Personnel:** Steve Jones, Managing Editor; Chuck Martin, Publisher; Colleen Mitchell, Advertising Dir., cmitch@mindspring-com. **Subscription Rates:** $21.00 individuals 3 months; $33.98 out of state/3 months.
Ad Rates: BW: $1,277.10 **Circ:** Wed. 26,200
4C: $1,577.10 Fri. 17,550
PCI: $9.90

7464 Wometco Cable
6435 Tara Blvd., Ste. 22 Phone: (404)478-0010
Jonesboro, GA 30236 Fax: (404)471-6639

Owner: Us West, at above address. **Key Personnel:** Chris Cafty, General Mgr.; Nancy Hauser, Marketing Manager. **Cities Served:** Clayton, Fulton, & Henry Counties, GA: subscribing households 45,000; 57 channels.

KENNESAW

7465 Kennesaw Neighbor
Neighbor Newspapers, Inc.
580 Fairground St. Phone: (770)428-9411
PO Box 449 Fax: (770)428-7945
Marietta, GA 30060
Community newspaper. **Founded:** 1969. **Freq:** Weekly (Thurs.). **Cols./Page:** 6. **Col. Depth:** 21 inches. **Subscription Rates:** Free; $12; $18 out of area; $24 out of state. **Remarks:** Combined advertising rates available with other Neighbor Newspapers.
Ad Rates: PCI: $18.10 **Circ:** Combined 17,904

KINGSLAND, pop. 2,008.

SE GA. Camden Co. 36 mi. NE of Jacksonville, FL. Navy submarine base. Chemical factory. Timber. Agriculture. Stock, poultry, dairying.

7466 The Southeast Georgian
The Tribune/Georgian
PO Box 1429 Phone: (912)729-5231
Kingsland, GA 31548 Fax: (912)729-1589

Newspaper. **Founded:** 1894. **Freq:** Weekly (Wed.). **Print Method:** Offset. **Trim Size:** 22 3/4 x 14. **Cols./Page:** 6. **Col. Width:** 13 picas. **Col. Depth:** 21 1/2 inches. **Key Personnel:** Mark Jicha, Editor and Publisher. **Subscription Rates:** $14.50 individuals; $25 out of area. **Remarks:** Accepts advertising.
Ad Rates: BW: $554.70 **Circ:** ‡5,000
4C: $804.70
SAU: $4
PCI: $4.30

7467 Kings Bay Communications, Inc.
PO Box 1267 Phone: (912)729-3777
Kingsland, GA 31548

Founded: 1978. **Key Personnel:** Don Trednick, General Mgr. **Cities Served:** Camden County, Kingsland, GA: subscribing households 3,650; 50 channels; 1 community access channel; 10 hours per week community access programming.

7468 WATY-FM - 91.3
PO Box 1448 Phone: (912)496-7964
Kingsland, GA 31548 Fax: (912)496-4086

Format: Educational; Easy Listening. **Owner:** Okefenokee Education Foundation, at above address. **Founded:** 1998. **Key Personnel:** Jack Mays, President, maysj@planttel.net. **Wattage:** 600. **Ad Rates:** $10 for 30 seconds; $12 for 60 seconds. **URL:** http://www.planttec.net.

7469 WKBX-FM - 106.3
111 N. Grove Blvd. Phone: (912)729-6106
PO Box 2525 Fax: (912)729-4106
Kingsland, GA 31548
E-mail: wkbx@k-bay106.com

Format: Country; News. **Networks:** ABC. **Founded:** 1987. **Operating Hours:** Continuous. **ADI:** Jacksonville (Brunswick), FL. **Key Personnel:** James U. Steele, Contact; Doug Vaught, Local Sales Manager; John Fleury, Program Mgr.; Dave Smith, News Dir. **Local Programs:** *Country Chaos*, Randy Horn, (912)729-6000. **Wattage:** 6000. **Ad Rates:** $4-10 for 30 seconds; $6-15 for 60 seconds. **URL:** http://www.k-bay106.com.

7470 WOKF-FM - 92.5
PO Box 1448 Phone: (912)882-2925
Kingsland, GA 31548 Fax: (912)882-2853
Free: (800)762-5087
E-mail: wokf@aol.com

Format: Oldies; Talk. **Networks:** Jones Satellite; NBC. **Owner:** Folkston Broadcasters, Inc., at above address. **Founded:** Nov. 6, 1989. **Operating Hours:** Continuous. **ADI:** Jacksonville (Brunswick), FL. **Key Personnel:** Jack Mays, General Mgr. **Wattage:** 6000. **Ad Rates:** $10 for 30 seconds; $12 for 60 seconds.

LA FAYETTE†, pop. 6,714.

C. GA. Walker Co. 18 mi. WSW of Dalton. Agricultural trading center, textile mills.

7471 Walker County Messenger
News Publishing Co.
120 E. Patton St. Phone: (706)638-1859
La Fayette, GA 30728 Fax: (706)638-7045

County newspaper. **Founded:** 1877. **Freq:** Semiweekly. **Print Method:** Offset. **Trim Size:** 13 3/4 x 22 3/4. **Cols./Page:** 6. **Col. Width:** 2 1/16 inches. **Col. Depth:** 21 1/4 inches. **Key Personnel:** Don Stilwell, Editor; Nancy DeBond, Advertising Mgr. **Subscription Rates:** $24 within the county. **Remarks:** Accepts advertising.
Ad Rates: GLR: $6.80 **Circ:** Paid ‡4,050
BW: $867
4C: $1,117
SAU: $6.08
PCI: $6.80

7472 WQCH-AM - 1590
PO Box 746 Phone: (706)638-3276
Warthen St. Fax: (706)638-3896
La Fayette, GA 30728

Format: Country. **Networks:** UPI. **Owner:** Radix Broadcasting, Inc., PO Box 746, Lafayette, GA 30728. **Founded:** 1954. **Formerly:** WLFA-AM (1988). **Operating Hours:** 6 a.m.-sundown; 2% network, 98% local. **ADI:** Chattanooga (Cleveland), TN. **Key Personnel:** Rich Gwyn, General Mgr.; Joan Butler, News Dir. **Wattage:** 5000. **Ad Rates:** $4-5.50 for 15 seconds; $4.60-6.60 for 30 seconds; $6.80-9.60 for 60 seconds.

LA GRANGE†.

WC GA. Troup Co. 30 mi. W. of Meriwether.

7473 Charter Com Inc.
208 Ridley Ave. Phone: (706)882-4329
La Grange, GA 30240

Owner: Charter Communications Inc., 12444 Powerscourt Dr., Ste. 550, St. Louis, MO 63131. **Founded:** May 1, 1994. **Key Personnel:** Randy Hughes, State Mgr.; Linda Fulcher, Office Mgr.; Clayton Jennings, Chief Engineer; David Troxel, Regional Mgr. **Cities Served:** subscribing households 4,000; 42 channels; 1 community access channel; 168 hours per week community access programming.

7474 WLAG-AM - 1240
304 Broome St., Box 1429 Phone: (706)882-5100
La Grange, GA 30241 Fax: (706)845-8642

Format: Talk. **Networks:** ABC; People's Network. **Owner:** Jim Vice, at above address. **Founded:** 1941. **Operating Hours:** Continuous. **ADI:** Atlanta (Athens & Rome), GA. **Key Personnel:** Jim Vice, General Mgr. **Wattage:** 1000. **Ad Rates:** $6 for 30 seconds; $12 for 60 seconds.

7475 WOAK-FM - 90.9
1921 Hamilton Rd. Phone: (706)884-2950
La Grange, GA 30241 Fax: (706)884-2930

Format: Religious. **Networks:** USA Radio. **Owner:** Oakside Christian School, at above address, (706)882-7729. **Founded:** 1984. **Operating Hours:** Continuous. **Key Personnel:** Steve Miller, Contact; Deena Brand, Program Dir. **Wattage:** 3400.

7476 WTRP-AM - 620
806 Franklin Rd. Phone: (706)884-8611
PO Box 1203 Fax: (706)884-8612
La Grange, GA 30241

Format: Adult Contemporary; Sports; News; Talk. **Networks:** Mutual Broadcasting System. **Owner:** Larry Thompson Broadcasting, Inc., 806 Franklin Rd., La Grange, GA 30240. **Founded:** 1953. **Operating Hours:** Continuous; 10% network, 90% local. **ADI:** Atlanta (Athens & Rome), GA. **Key Personnel:** Larry Thompson, Sr., Contact; Carolyn S. Thompson, Contact; Michael Thompson, Contact; Larry Thompson, Jr., Contact; Steve Reed, News Dir.; Ted Ronnebucger, Chief Engineer. **Wattage:** 1000 day; 500 night. **Ad Rates:** $5.40-8.60 for 30 seconds; $5.90-8.90 for 60 seconds.

LAKELAND†, pop. 2,647.

C. Ga. Lanier Co. 20 mi. NE of Valdosta. Agricultural market.

7477 Lanier County News
Cook Publishing Co.
335 W. Church St. Phone: (912)482-8230
Lakeland, GA 31635
General newspaper. **Founded:** 1920. **Freq:** Weekly. **Print Method:** Offset. **Cols./Page:** 6. **Key Personnel:** Sylvia C. Ragan, Editor. **Subscription Rates:** $15.90 individuals; $23.60 out of area. **Remarks:** Accepts advertising.
Ad Rates: PCI: $2.95 **Circ:** ‡1,200

LAWRENCEVILLE†, pop. 8,467.

NC GA. Gwinnett Co. 30 mi. NE of Atlanta. Industrial and research parks. Manufactures telephone cables, satellite components, missile systems, color video display terminals & television sets, insulated entry doors and windows, micro-measuring devices, garments, leather goods. Steel & aluminum fabrication. Farming.

7478 Gwinnett Daily Post
Gray Communications Systems
166 Buford Dr. Phone: (770)963-9205
Lawrenceville, GA 30045 Fax: (770)338-7353
Publication E-mail: gwinnpost@mindspring.com; gwinnpost@aol.com

Community newspaper. **Founded:** 1970. **Freq:** 6/week. **Print Method:** Offset. **Trim Size:** 13 x 21. **Cols./Page:** 6. **Col. Width:** 2 1/16 inches. **Col. Depth:** 21 inches. **Key Personnel:** Richard Rae, President; J.K. Murphy, Editor; Jim Brumbelow, Operations Dir.; Susan Colmar, Financial Dir.; Leo Pieri, Publisher; Michael Buavit, Advertising Dir.; Bill Herbert, Circulation Mgr. **ISSN:** 1086-0096. **Subscription Rates:** $48 individuals; $74.95 out of area. **Remarks:** Advertising accepted; rates available upon request. **Formerly:** Gwinnett Home Weekly; Gwinnett Post-Tribune.
Circ: Paid ♦**54,451**
Non-paid ♦**196**

7479 WPLO-AM - 610
PO Box 2063
Lawrenceville, GA 30246-2063

Format: Country; Sports; Talk. **Networks:** NBC. **Founded:** 1954. **Formerly:** WLAW-AM (1985). **Operating Hours:** 6 a.m.-midnight; 10% network, 90% local. **ADI:** Atlanta (Athens & Rome), GA. **Key Personnel:** Dennis Wayne, News Dir.; Jan Hill, Office Mgr.; Sally Russell, Program Dir.; Bobby Johnson, Sales Mgr.; Len Anthony, Station Mgr.; Sally Russell, Music Dir. **Wattage:** 1500. **Ad Rates:** $13-18 for 30 seconds; $16-22 for 60 seconds.

LEESBURG

7480 Lee County Ledger
124 4th St. Phone: (912)759-2413
PO Box 715 Fax: (912)759-6599
Leesburg, GA 31763
Community newspaper. **Founded:** 1977. **Freq:** Weekly (Thurs.). **Cols./Page:** 6. **Col. Width:** 2 1/16 inches. **Col. Depth:** 21 1/2 inches. **Key Personnel:** Charles Quinn, Editor; Derryl Quinn, Publisher; Jim Quinn, Associate Editor. **USPS:** 470-310. **Subscription Rates:** $9.50. **Remarks:** Accepts advertising.
Ad Rates: GLR: $2.60 **Circ:** Paid ‡1,942
BW: $290.25 Free ‡25
4C: $410
PCI: $2.25

LEXINGTON†, pop. 322.

NE GA. Oglethorpe Co. 15 mi. SE of Athens. Pine timber. Agriculture. Cotton, corn, cattle.

Oglethorpe Echo - See Oglethorpe

LILBURN, pop. 3,765.

NW GA. Gwinnett Co. 20 mi. NE of Atlanta. Residential.

7481 Coaching Women's Basketball
4646 B Lawrenceville Hwy. Phone: (770)279-8027
Lilburn, GA 30247 Fax: (770)279-8473
Publication E-mail: info@wbca.org

Magazine for women's basketball coaches. **Founded:** 1987. **Freq:** Bimonthly. **Trim Size:** 8 1/2 x 11. **Cols./Page:** 3 and 2. **Col. Width:** 2 and 3 1/8 inches. **Col. Depth:** 7 3/4 and 7 3/4 inches. **Key Personnel:** Nelson P. Holmberg, Editor. **ISSN:** 0894-4245. **Subscription Rates:** $20 individuals; $30 institutions; $5 single issue.
Ad Rates: BW: $500 **Circ:** Paid 4,400
4C: $1,200 Non-paid 200

7482 Cogeneration and Competitive Power Journal
Fairmont Press, Inc.
700 Indian Trail Phone: (770)925-9388
Lilburn, GA 30047 Fax: (770)381-9865

Journal designed to fill the needs of engineers and executives involved in the assessment, planning, implementation and management of cogeneration projects. **Freq:** Quarterly. **Print Method:** Offset. **Cols./Page:** 1. **Col. Width:** 52 nonpareils. **Col. Depth:** 98 agate lines. **Key Personnel:** William Payne, Editor; Richard Miller, Publisher. **Subscription Rates:** $115 U.S.; $115 Canada; $145 other countries; $210 two years

U.S.; $210 two years Canada; $270 two years other countries. **Remarks:** Accepts advertising.
Ad Rates: BW: $600 **Circ:** Paid 2,200

7483 Energy Engineering
Fairmont Press, Inc.
700 Indian Trail Phone: (770)925-9388
Lilburn, GA 30047 Fax: (770)381-9865

Engineering trade journal. **Founded:** 1904. **Freq:** Bimonthly. **Print Method:** Offset. **Cols./Page:** 1. **Col. Width:** 52 nonpareils. **Col. Depth:** 98 agate lines. **Key Personnel:** Anna Williams, Editor; Richard Miller, Publisher. **ISSN:** 0199-8595. **Subscription Rates:** $115 individuals U.S. and Canada; $210 two years U.S. and Canada; $270 two years Other Countries. **Remarks:** Accepts advertising.
Ad Rates: BW: $600 **Circ:** Paid 9,000

7484 Strategic Planning for Energy and the Environment
Fairmont Press, Inc.
700 Indian Trail Phone: (770)925-9388
Lilburn, GA 30047 Fax: (770)381-9865

Magazine on energy and environmental planning. **Freq:** Quarterly. **Print Method:** Offset. **Cols./Page:** 1. **Col. Width:** 52 nonpareils. **Col. Depth:** 98 agate lines. **Key Personnel:** William Payne, Editor; Richard Miller, Publisher. **ISSN:** 1048-5236. **Subscription Rates:** $115 U.S. and Canada; $145 other countries; $210 two years U.S. and Canada; $270 two years Other Countries. **Remarks:** Accepts advertising.
Ad Rates: BW: $600 **Circ:** Paid 8,600

LINCOLNTON

7485 Lincolnton Journal
PO Box 399 Phone: (706)359-3229
Lincolnton, GA 30817 Fax: (706)359-2884

Community newspaper. **Freq:** Weekly (Thurs.). **Cols./Page:** 6. **Col. Width:** 12.5 picas. **Col. Depth:** 21 inches. **Key Personnel:** James Drinkard, Editor and Publisher.
Circ: 2,300

LOUISVILLE†, pop. 2,823.

C. GA. Jefferson Co. 40 mi. SW of Augusta. Lumber, peanuts, cotton.

7486 News & Former & Wadley Herald/The Jefferson Reporter
Fall Line Publishing, Inc.
PO Box 487 Phone: (912)625-7722
Louisville, GA 30434 Fax: (912)625-8816

Local newspaper. **Founded:** Aug. 1843. **Freq:** Weekly. **Print Method:** Offset. **Trim Size:** 14 x 22 1/2. **Cols./Page:** 6. **Col. Width:** 12.3 picas. **Col. Depth:** 21 inches. **Key Personnel:** Joyce P. Drinkwater, Publisher; Jennifer W. Newton, Editor. **Subscription Rates:** $16 individuals; $18 out of area; $20 out of state. **Remarks:** Accepts advertising.
Ad Rates: PCI: $4.25 **Circ:** Paid ‡4,800
Free ‡65

7487 WPEH-AM - 1420
5442 Middleground Rd. Phone: (706)625-7248
PO Box 425 Fax: (912)625-7249
Louisville, GA 30434

Format: Country. **Simulcasts:** WPEH-FM. **Networks:** Mutual Broadcasting System. **Owner:** Peach Broadcasting Co., Inc., at above address. **Founded:** 1960. **Operating Hours:** 6 a.m.-midnight; 15% network, 85% local. **ADI:** Augusta, GA. **Key Personnel:** Ottis G. Stephens, General Mgr.; Wendell F. Stephens, Contact; John D. Reid, Music Dir. **Wattage:** 1000. **Ad Rates:** $5.00-7.00 for 30 seconds; $6.50-8.50 for 60 seconds.

7488 WPEH-FM - 92.1
5442 Middleground Rd. Phone: (706)625-7248
PO Box 425 Fax: (912)625-7249
Louisville, GA 30434

Format: Country. **Simulcasts:** WPEH-AM. **Networks:** Mutual Broadcasting System. **Founded:** 1971. **Operating Hours:** 6 a.m.-midnight; 15% network, 85% local. **ADI:** Augusta, GA. **Key Personnel:** Ottis G. Stephens, General Mgr.; Wendell F. Stephens, Contact; John D. Reid, Music Dir. **Wattage:** 3000. **Ad Rates:** $5.00-7.00 for 30 seconds; $6.50-8.50 for 60 seconds.

LYONS†, pop. 4,270.

NE GA. Toombs Co. 72 mi. W. of Savannah. Lumber and agriculture.

7489 WBBT-AM - 1340
901 N. Victory Dr. Phone: (912)526-8122
PO Box 111 Fax: (912)526-8123
Lyons, GA 30436-0111

Format: Oldies; Talk. **Networks:** NBC; Georgia Radio. **Owner:** Harry H. Thompson Jr., at above address, Fax: (912)526-9155. **Founded:** 1959. **Operating Hours:** 18 hours daily. **ADI:** Savannah, GA. **Key Personnel:** Ray Bilbrey, Contact; Tony Deloach, Contact; Heather Freeland, Contact; Tony Delosch, Sports Dir.; Earl Averett, Contact; Peggy Spikes, Contact. **Wattage:** 1000. **Ad Rates:** $2.75-4 for 30 seconds; $3.75-5 for 60 seconds.

7490 WLYU-FM - 100.9
901 N. Victory Dr. Phone: (912)526-8122
PO Box 111 Fax: (912)526-8123
Lyons, GA 30436-0111

Format: Contemporary Country. **Networks:** NBC. **Owner:** Harry H. Thompson Jr., at above address, Fax: (912)526-9155. **Founded:** 1989. **Operating Hours:** Continuous. **ADI:** Savannah, GA. **Key Personnel:** Ray Bilbrey, Contact; Tony DeLoach, Contact; Heather Freeland, Contact; Tony Deloach, Sports Dir.; Earl Averett, Contact; Peggy Spikes, Contact. **Wattage:** 3000. **Ad Rates:** $4.25-6.95 for 30 seconds; $5.25-6.50 for 60 seconds.

MABLETON

7491 WAWE-FM - 102.5
150 Eason Way
Mableton, GA 30126

Owner: Gonzales Broadcasting, Inc., at above address.

MACON†, pop. 116,044.

C. GA. Bibb Co. On Ocmulgee River, 92 mi. SE of Atlanta. Wesleyan College (women); Mercer University; Macon Junior College. Kaolin, fuller's earth mines; timber. Peach production center. Manufactures wood furniture, linens, cotton yarns, cigarettes, brick & cement block, processed poultry, boxes, container board.

7492 The Cluster
Mercer University
1400 Coleman Ave. Phone: (912)752-2715
Macon, GA 31207 Fax: (912)752-4124
Free: (800)837-2911

Newspaper featuring university contributors, alumni news, faculty news, and general information. **Founded:** 1889. **Freq:** Quarterly (during the academic year). **Cols./Page:** 2. **Col. Width:** 36 nonpareils. **Col. Depth:** 136 agate lines. **URL:** http://www.mercer.edu. **Formerly**: The Mercer Spirit.
Circ: Paid ‡30,000

7493 Georgia Cattleman
Georgia Cattleman's Association
PO Box 11307, 100 Cattlemen's Dr. Phone: (912)474-6560
Fax: (912)474-5732
Macon, GA 31212
Agriculture and cattle industry magazine. **Founded:** 1972. **Freq:** Monthly. **Print Method:** Web offset. **Trim Size:** 8 3/8 x 10 7/8. **Cols./Page:** 3. **Col. Width:** 27 nonpareils. **Col. Depth:** 140 agate lines. **Key Personnel:** Glenn Smith, Advertising Mgr. **Subscription Rates:** $10 individuals. **Remarks:** Accepts advertising.
Ad Rates: GLR: $.25 **Circ:** Paid 7,000
BW: $575 Non-paid 250
4C: $925

7494 Georgia Farm Bureau News
Georgia Farm Bureau Federation
PO Box 7068 Phone: (912)474-8411
1620 Bass Rd. Fax: (912)474-8750
Macon, GA 31298
Publication E-mail: jengfb@aol.com

Magazine featuring news of major Georgia commodities, government farm programs, legislation affecting farmers and rural residents, taxes, finances, and news of general interest to farm bureau members. **Founded:** 1938. **Freq:** Monthly. **Print Method:** Offset. **Trim Size:** 8 1/4 x 10 3/8. **Key Personnel:** Paul Beliveau, Publisher; Jennifer Whittaker, Editor/Publications Supervisor; Sara Hudson, Production & Advertising Mgr. **ISSN:** 0735-696X. **Subscription Rates:** $9 individuals. **Remarks:** Accepts advertising. **URL:** http://www.gfb.org.
Ad Rates: BW: $1,580 **Circ:** ‡66,312
4C: $2,180
PCI: $46

7495 Macon Magazine
Macon Magazine, Inc.
227 Orange St. Phone: (912)746-7779
Macon, GA 31201 Fax: (912)743-4608
Publication E-mail: maconmag@macon.mindspring.com

Consumer magazine covering local history, the arts, lifestyle, and cultural events. **Founded:** 1987. **Freq:** Bimonthly. **Print Method:** Web offset. **Trim Size:** 8 1/2 x 11. **Cols./Page:** 3. **Key Personnel:** Lynn Cass, Publisher; Joni Woolf, Editor. **Subscription Rates:** $11.95 individuals; $3 single issue. **Remarks:** Accepts advertising.
Circ: (Not Reported)

7496 The Macon Telegraph
Knight-Ridder, Inc.
120 Broadway Phone: (912)744-4200
Macon, GA 31201-3444 Fax: (912)744-4269

General newspaper. **Founded:** 1826. **Freq:** Mon.-Sun. (morn.). **Print Method:** Flexographic. **Cols./Page:** 6. **Col. Width:** 26 nonpareils. **Col. Depth:** 301 agate lines. **Key Personnel:** Edmund E. Olson, Publisher, phone (912)744-4290, fax (912)744-4469; Richard D. Thomas, Vice-President/Editor, phone (912)744-4340, fax (912)744-4385; Ron Woodgeard, General Mgr., phone (912)744-4319, fax (912)744-4385; Barbara Stinson, Managing Editor, Features, phone (912)744-4221, fax (912)744-4385; Bill Weaver, Assistant Managing Editor, News, phone (912)744-4330, fax (912)744-4385; Jane Self, Assistant Features Editor, phone (912)744-4225, fax (912)744-4385; Ella Haynes, Television Editor, phone (912)744-4418, fax (912)744-4385; Steve Bills, Business Editor, phone (912)744-4389, fax (912)744-4385; Oby Brown, Metro Editor, phone (912)744-4220, fax (912)744-4385; Kevin Proctor, Sports Editor, phone (912)744-4335, fax (912)744-4385; Sharese Shields, Education Editor, phone (912)744-4394, fax (912)744-4385; Paul Alexander, Book Editor, phone (912)744-4383, fax (912)744-4385; Jodi White, Medical Editor, phone (912)744-4384, fax (912)744-4385; Danny Gilleland, Chief of Photography, phone (912)744-4233, fax (912)744-4385. **Subscription Rates:** $121.16 individuals. **Remarks:** Accepts advertising. **URL:** http://www.macontelegraph.com. **Feature Editors:** Steve Bills, *Financial/Business, Real Estate, Rural Development*, phone (912)744-4200; Arlette Copeland, *Food*, phone (912)744-4200; Danny Gilleland, *Photo*, phone (912)744-4200; Ella Haynes, *TV*, phone (912)744-4200; Dan Maley, *Movie, Music, Radio*, phone (912)744-4200; James Palmer, *Consumer Affairs, Lifestyle, Living, Society, Women's*, phone (912)744-4345, fax (912)744-4385; Kevin Proctor, *Sports*, phone (912)744-4200; Jane Self, *Travel*, phone (912)744-4200; Bill Weaver, *Metro, News, Political, Science, Suburban*, phone (912)744-4200; Bill Weaverr, *Religion*, phone (912)744-4200; Jodi White, *Medical*, phone (912)744-4200.
Ad Rates: GLR: $2.43 **Circ:** Mon.-Thurs. ★**68,996**
BW: $6,406.06 Fri. ★**80,075**
4C: $7,096.06 Sat. ★**77,234**
SAU: $33.51 Sun. ★**96,828**
PCI: $43.85

7497 The Mercer Cluster
Mercer University Phone: (912)752-2871
Campus Box 72728 Fax: (912)752-5544
Macon, GA 31207
Publisher E-mail: cluster@acadmn.mercer.edu

Collegiate newspaper. **Founded:** 1920. **Freq:** Biweekly. **Print Method:** Offset. Uses mats. **Trim Size:** 11 1/4 x 15. **Cols./Page:** 5. **Col. Width:** 24 nonpareils. **Col. Depth:** 196 agate lines. **Key Personnel:** Jaime Helmer, Editor, helmer-jl@acadmn.mercer.edu; Jonathan Linnaman, Editor, linneman_jp@acadmn.mercer.edu. **Remarks:** Accepts advertising.
Ad Rates: BW: $500 **Circ:** Free ‡2,000
SAU: $3.50
PCI: $8

7498 The Pilot Log
Pilot International
244 College St. Phone: (912)743-7403
PO Box 4844 Fax: (912)743-2173
Macon, GA 31208-4844
Publication E-mail: pilot.hdqtrs@internetmci.com

Magazine for Pilot International, a civic service organization for executives and professionals. **Founded:** Sept. 1933. **Freq:** Bimonthly. **Print Method:** Web. **Trim Size:** 8 1/2 x 11. **Cols./Page:** 3. **Key Personnel:** Jan G. Brown, Editor. **USPS:** 433-020. **Subscription Rates:** $10 U.S.; $15 other countries. **Remarks:** Advertising not accepted.
Circ: Controlled ‡19,000

7499 WALJ-FM - 107.1
RR 006, Box 735 Phone: (912)743-9107
Macon, GA 31201-9580 Fax: (912)742-2293
E-mail: j107@accucomm.net

Format: Big Band/Nostalgia; Jazz. **Networks:** ABC; Georgia Radio. **Owner:** Griffith Communications, at above address,

(912)745-3301, (912)745-3302. **Founded:** 1985. **Formerly:** WQXM-FM (1992); WNEX-FM (1996); WMRW-FM. **Operating Hours:** Continuous; 100% local. **ADI:** Macon, GA. **Key Personnel:** Bob Davis, Program Dir. & Operations Mgr.; Howard Ebo, Sales Mgr.; Lisa Bacarro, Office and Traffic Mgr. **Wattage:** 6000. **Ad Rates:** $15-30 for 60 seconds.

7500 WAYS-FM - 99.1
1314 Gray Hwy. Phone: (912)752-9999
Macon, GA 31211 Fax: (912)752-1339
E-mail: balder@99ways.com

Format: Oldies. **Networks:** Mutual Broadcasting System. **Owner:** Ocmulgee Broadcasting Co., PO Box 4387, Macon, GA 31213, (912)752-1393. **Founded:** 1984. **Formerly:** WMAZ-FM. **Operating Hours:** Continuous. **ADI:** Macon, GA. **Key Personnel:** Jim McLendon, General Mgr.; Dorrie F. Sapp, Business Mgr., phone (912)752-1392. **Local Programs:** *Bill Elder Show*, David Nolin; *Brad Majors Show*, David Nolin; *David Nolin Show*, David Nolin. **Wattage:** 100,000.

7501 WBML-AM - 900
PO Box 6298 Phone: (912)743-5453
Macon, GA 31208 Fax: (912)743-9265

Format: Religious; Gospel. **Networks:** UPI. **Owner:** David Rodgers, PO Box 6298, Macon, GA 31208-6298. **Founded:** 1941. **Operating Hours:** 6 a.m.-11 p.m.; 25% network, 75% local. **ADI:** Macon, GA. **Key Personnel:** Orvil Nichols, Contact; Michael Mimbs, Contact. **Local Programs:** *Camps Meeting Time*, Michael Mimbs; *Gospel Jubilee*, Orvil Nichols. **Wattage:** 2000. **Ad Rates:** $5-9 for 30 seconds; $7-14 for 60 seconds.

7502 WBNM-AM - 1120
RR 006, Box 735 Phone: (912)745-1077
Macon, GA 31201-9580 Fax: (912)742-2293
E-mail: jion@jion.com

Format: News; Talk. **Networks:** Business Radio. **Owner:** Quality Broadcasting, Inc., at above address. **Operating Hours:** Continuous; 75% network, 25% local. **ADI:** Macon, GA. **Key Personnel:** Bob Davis, Prog. Dir./Operations Mgr.; Howard Ebo, Sales Mgr.; Lisa Bacarro, Office Mgr. **Wattage:** 10,000. **Ad Rates:** $19.50-25 for 60 seconds.

7503 WDDO-AM - 1240
544 Mulberry St. Phone: (912)746-6286
Macon, GA 31201 Fax: (912)742-8061

Format: Gospel. **Networks:** Mutual Broadcasting System. **Founded:** 1940. **Operating Hours:** Continuous; 1% network, 99% local. **ADI:** Macon, GA. **Key Personnel:** Oscar Leverette, Station Mgr.; Willie Ollins, Program Dir.; Laura Worth, News Dir. **Wattage:** 1000. **Ad Rates:** $15-30 for 30 seconds; $20-40 for 60 seconds.

7504 WDEN-AM - 1500
544 Mulberry, 7th Fl. Phone: (912)745-3383
Macon, GA 31202 Fax: (912)745-9693
E-mail: wden@mylink.net

Format: Country. **Networks:** NBC. **Owner:** U.S. Broadcasting Ltd. Partnership, Box 46, Macon, GA 31297. **Founded:** 1967. **Formerly:** WPTC-AM. **Operating Hours:** Sunrise-sunset. **ADI:** Macon, GA. **Key Personnel:** Doug Grimm, General Mgr.; Leigh Hurd, Sales Mgr.; Gerry Marshall, Program Dir., phone (912)741-8811, fax (912)741-8811. **Wattage:** 1000. **Ad Rates:** $10 for 30 seconds; $12 for 60 seconds.

7505 WDEN-FM - 105.3
544 Mulberry St., No. 700 Phone: (912)745-3383
Macon, GA 31201 Fax: (912)745-9693
E-mail: wden@mylink.net

Format: Contemporary Country. **Networks:** NBC. **Owner:** Box 46, Macon, GA 31202. **Founded:** 1968. **Operating Hours:** Continuous; 10% network, 90% local. **ADI:** Macon, GA. **Key Personnel:** Doug Grimm, General Mgr., fax (912)745-2078; Jim Jones, Sales Mgr., fax (912)745-9693; Gerry Marshall, Program Dir., fax (912)741-8811. **Wattage:** 100,000. **Ad Rates:** $45-130 per unit.

7506 WGNM-TV - 64
PO Box 2637 Phone: (912)746-6464
Macon, GA 31203 Fax: (912)745-2367

Format: Commercial TV. **Networks:** United Paramount Network. **Owner:** Macon Urban Ministries, Inc., at above address. **Founded:** Nov. 1990. **Operating Hours:** Continuous. **ADI:** Macon, GA. **Key Personnel:** David Wood, Station Mgr.; Don King, Program Dir.; Daniel Jaskula, Sales Mgr. **Ad Rates:** $20-100 for 30 seconds.

7507 WGXA-TV - 24
559 Martin Luther King Jr. Phone: (912)745-2424
Macon, GA 31201 Fax: (912)750-4347
Free: (800)592-4240

Format: Commercial TV. **Networks:** Fox. **Owner:** Gorom Communications, 7621 Little Ave., Ste. 506, Charlotte, NC 28226, (704)341-0944, Fax: (704)341-0945. **Founded:** 1982. **Operating Hours:** Continuous 25% network, 75% local. **ADI:** Macon, GA. **Key Personnel:** Mitchell Maund, General Mgr.; Karen Alston, General Sales Mgr.; Richard Blanton, Chief Engineer; Scott Park, Operations Mgr.; George Jobin, Station Mgr. **Wattage:** 1,290,000. **Ad Rates:** $20-1,200 per unit. **URL:** http://www.fox24.com. **Additional Contact Info: Mailing Address:** PO Box 340, Macon, GA 31297.

7508 WMAC-AM - 940
PO Box 900 Phone: (912)746-6286
Macon, GA 31202

Format: News; Talk; Sports. **Networks:** ABC. **Owner:** U. S. Broadcasting Limited Partnership, at above address. **Founded:** 1922. **Formerly:** WMAZ-AM; WMMR-AM. **Operating Hours:** Continuous. **ADI:** Macon, GA. **Key Personnel:** Don McCoy, President; Doug Grimm, Executive V. P.; Vicki Schnyder, Dir. of Sales; Ken Burgamy, Program Dir. **Wattage:** 50,000. **Ad Rates:** Advertising accepted; rates available upon request.

7509 WMAZ-AM - 940
PO Box 5008 Phone: (912)752-9494
Macon, GA 31297 Fax: (912)752-1339

Format: News; Talk; Sports. **Networks:** ABC. **Founded:** 1922. **Operating Hours:** Continuous. **ADI:** Macon, GA. **Key Personnel:** Jim McLendon, General Mgr., phone (912)752-1393; Dorrie F. Sapp, Business Mgr., phone (912)752-1392. **Local Programs:** *Morning Traffic Jam*, Hal Sutton. **Wattage:** 50,000 day; 10,000 night.

7510 WMAZ-TV - 13
1314 Gray Hwy. Phone: (912)752-1313
Macon, GA 31211 Fax: (912)752-1331

Format: Commercial TV. **Networks:** CBS. **Owner:** Multimedia, Inc., PO Box 1688, Greenville, SC 29602. **Founded:** 1953. **ADI:** Macon, GA. **Key Personnel:** Gostin Freeney, General Sales Mgr.; Dodie Cantrell, Chief Engineer; Tony Villasana, News Dir.; Tom Garner, Contact; Sydney Thum, Program Dir.; Ron Leppig, Contact; Jim Elrod, Contact; Don McGourick, Contact.

7511 WMGB-FM - 93.7
PO Box 900 Phone: (912)746-6286
Macon, GA 31202 Fax: (912)742-8061

Format: Contemporary Hit Radio (CHR). **Owner:** U. S. Broadcasting Co., L. P., at above address. **Operating Hours:** Continuous. **ADI:** Macon, GA. **Key Personnel:** Don McCoy, President; Doug Grimm, Executive V. P./General Mgr.; Victoria Schnyder, Dir. of Sales; James Gregory, Program Dir. **Wattage:** 50,000. **Ad Rates:** $50 per unit.

7512 WMGT-TV - 41
6525 Ocomulgee E Blvd. Phone: (912)745-4141
Macon, GA 31201 Fax: (912)742-2626

Format: Commercial TV. **Networks:** NBC. **Founded:** Dec. 19, 1968. **Operating Hours:** Continuous. Sun.-Thur.; 5 a.m.-3 a.m. Fri.-Sat. **ADI:** Macon, GA. **Key Personnel:** L.A. Sturdivant, General Mgr.; Deborah McDaniel, Program Dir. **Additional Contact Info: Mailing Address:** PO Box 4328, Macon, GA 31213.

7513 WPEZ-FM - 107.9
544 Mulberry St. Phone: (912)746-6286
Macon, GA 31201 Fax: (912)742-8061

Format: Adult Contemporary. **Networks:** Unistar. **Founded:** 1973. **Operating Hours:** Continuous. **ADI:** Macon, GA. **Key Personnel:** Oscar Leverette, Station Mgr.; Laura Worth, News Dir. **Wattage:** 100,000. **Ad Rates:** $45-105 for 30 seconds; $60-140 for 60 seconds.

7514 WQBZ-FM - 106.3
7080 Industrial Hwy. Phone: (912)781-1063
Macon, GA 31206-7538 Fax: (912)781-6711
E-mail: taylor@hom.net

Format: Album-Oriented Rock (AOR). **Founded:** 1981. **Operating Hours:** Continuous; 100% local. **ADI:** Macon, GA. **Key Personnel:** Rick Humphrey, General Mgr.; Vance Shepherd, Program Dir.; Robbie Brown, Local Sales. **Wattage:** 50,000. **Ad Rates:** $40-70 per unit. **URL:** http://www.q106online.com.

MADISON†, pop. 2,954.

NC GA. Morgan Co. 55 mi. E. of Atlanta. Residential. Lumber and plywood mills. Cordage mill. Manufactures furniture. Agriculture. Pine timber. Beef cattle. Dairying.

7515 WYTH-AM - 1250
1281 Eatonton Rd. Phone: (706)342-1250
PO Box 635 Fax: (706)342-1752
Madison, GA 30650

Format: Country; News; Talk. **Networks:** NBC; Georgia Radio; For The People. **Owner:** James F. Small and Annie Lee Small, at above address. **Founded:** 1955. **Formerly:** WMGE-AM (1958). **Operating Hours:** 6 a.m.-sunset; 35% network, 65% local. **Key Personnel:** James F. Small, Sr., President; Jim Small, Jr., Gen. Mgr./Operations Dir.; Christine Beaver, Office Mgr.; Preston Small, Sports Dir. **Wattage:** 1000. **Ad Rates:** $5.50-7.50 for 60 seconds.

MANCHESTER, pop. 4,796.

W. GA. Meriwether Co. 40 mi. NE of Columbus. Lumber mills. Pine, oak timber. Agriculture. Cattle, grains.

7516 Harris County Journal
PO Box 426 Phone: (404)846-3188
Manchester, GA 31816 Fax: (706)846-2206

Community newspaper. **Founded:** 1886. **Freq:** Weekly (Thurs.). **Print Method:** Offset. **Trim Size:** 11 1/2 x 14. **Cols./Page:** 6. **Col. Width:** 12 picas. **Col. Depth:** 21 1/2 inches. **Key Personnel:** Johnny Kuykendall, Publisher; Mike Hale, General Mgr. **USPS:** 235-960. **Subscription Rates:** $15.75; $23.63 out of area; $30 out of state. **Remarks:** Accepts advertising.
Ad Rates: GLR: $.30 **Circ:** 2,200
BW: $541.80
4C: $791.80
SAU: $4.20
PCI: $4.20

7517 WFDR-AM - 1370
PO Box 510 Phone: (706)846-3115
Manchester, GA 31816 Fax: (706)846-2425
E-mail: wvfj@aol.com

Networks: NBC. **Owner:** Provident Broadcasting Co., at above address. **Founded:** Mar. 1983. **Formerly:** WQCK-AM. **Operating Hours:** Daytime; 95% network, 5% local. **Key Personnel:** Rick Davison, General Mgr. **Wattage:** 1000. **Ad Rates:** $2-4 for 15 seconds; $3-6 for 30 seconds; $6-8 for 60 seconds.

7518 WVFJ-FM - 93.3
PO Box 510 Phone: (706)846-3115
Manchester, GA 31816 Fax: (706)846-2425
E-mail: wvfj@aol

Format: Adult Contemporary; Contemporary Christian. **Networks:** USA Radio. **Formerly:** WFDR-FM; WQCK-FM. **Operating Hours:** Continuous; 15% network, 85% local. **Key Personnel:** Rick Davison, General Mgr.; Wayne Hagan, Operations Mgr.; Steve Cox, Music Dir. **Wattage:** 100,000. **Ad Rates:** $12-17 for 15 seconds; $18-24 for 30 seconds; $22-30 for 60 seconds.

MARIETTA†, pop. 30,805.

NW GA. Cobb Co. 20 mi. NW of Atlanta. Southern Technical Institute, Kennesaw College. Aircraft plant. Manufactures textiles, furniture, chemicals, marble, plastics, paper products. Metal and food processing.

Acworth Neighbor - See Acworth

7519 Alabama Game and Fish
Game & Fish Publications, Inc.
2250 Newmarket Pkwy., Ste. 110
Marietta, GA 30067

Hunting and fishing magazine. **Founded:** 1980. **Freq:** Monthly. **Print Method:** Offset. **Cols./Page:** 3. **Col. Width:** 27 nonpareils. **Col. Depth:** 140 agate lines. **Key Personnel:** Jimmy Jacobs, Editor; Steven Vaughn, Publisher. **Subscription Rates:** $14.95 individuals. **Remarks:** Accepts advertising.
Ad Rates: BW: $529 **Circ:** ‡19,808
4C: $1,729

Austell Neighbor - See Austell

Chamblee De Kalb Neighbor - See Chamblee

Cherokee Plus - See Cherokee

7520 Circuits Assembly Asia
Miller Freeman, Inc.
2000 Powers Ferry Center, Ste. 450 Phone: (770)952-1303
Fax: (770)952-6461
Marietta, GA 30067
Publication E-mail: ca@mtl.com
Publisher E-mail: techlearning_ editors@mfi.com

Serves the PCB assembly marketplace in Asia. **Founded:** Nov. 1993. **Freq:** Bimonthly. **Print Method:** Offset. **Trim Size:** 8 x 10 3/4. **Cols./Page:** 3 and 2. **Col. Width:** 26 and 40 nonpareils. **Col. Depth:** 140 agate lines. **Key Personnel:** Ron Daniels, Editor and Publisher; Frances Stewart, Group Dir.; Sherri Gronli, Circulation Mgr. **ISSN:** 1070-4779. **Subscription Rates:** Free to qualified subscribers; $135 other countries. **Remarks:** Accepts advertising. **URL:** http://www.cassembly.com.
Ad Rates: BW: $3,325 **Circ:** Controlled 10,000
4C: $4,120
PCI: $190

7521 The Clayton Neighbor
Neighbor Newspapers, Inc.
580 Fairground St. Phone: (770)428-9411
PO Box 449 Fax: (770)428-7945
Marietta, GA 30060
Community newspaper. **Founded:** 1976. **Freq:** Weekly (Wed.). **Print Method:** Offset. **Cols./Page:** 6. **Col. Width:** 26 nonpareils. **Col. Depth:** 301 agate lines. **Key Personnel:** Otis A. Brumby, Jr., Publisher. **USPS:** 321-870. **Subscription Rates:** $12 individuals; $18 out of area; $24 out of state. **Remarks:** Accepts advertising.
Ad Rates: GLR: $1.40 **Circ:** Paid 22
BW: $2,973.45 Non-paid 38,287
4C: $3,298.45
SAU: $19.60
PCI: $23.05

Decatur De Kalb Neighbor - See Decatur

Doraville De Kalb Neighbor - See Doraville

7522 The Douglas Neighbor
Neighbor Newspapers, Inc.
580 Fairground St. Phone: (770)428-9411
PO Box 449 Fax: (770)428-7945
Marietta, GA 30060
Community newspaper. **Founded:** 1978. **Freq:** Weekly (Wed.). **Print Method:** Offset. **Cols./Page:** 6. **Col. Width:** 26 nonpareils. **Col. Depth:** 301 agate lines. **Key Personnel:** Otis A. Brumby, Jr., Publisher. **USPS:** 531-950. **Subscription Rates:** $12 individuals; $18 out of area; $24 out of state.
Ad Rates: GLR: $.88 **Circ:** Paid 15
BW: $1,586.70 Non-paid 18,762
4C: $1,876.70
SAU: $12.30

Dunwoody De Kalb Neighbor - See Dunwoody

The East Cobb Neighbor - See East Cobb

7523 Financial Product News
Enterprise Communications, Inc.
1165 North Chase Pky. NE, Ste. 350 Phone: (404)988-9558
Fax: (404)859-9166
Marietta, GA 30067
Professional magazine. **Founded:** 1985. **Freq:** Monthly.
Circ: Paid 486
Non-paid 48,384

7524 Game & Fish Magazine
Game & Fish Publications, Inc.
2250 Newmarket Pkwy., Ste. 110 Phone: (770)953-9222
Fax: (770)933-9510
PO Box 721
Marietta, GA 30061-0741
Magazine with specific state editions providing in-depth information on the wheres, whens, and hows of hunting and fishing in these states. **Founded:** 1980. **Freq:** Monthly. **Print Method:** Offset. **Trim Size:** 8 x 10 7/8. **Cols./Page:** 3. **Col. Width:** 27 nonpareils. **Col. Depth:** 140 agate lines. **Key Personnel:** David Morris, Editor; C.W. "Chuck" Larsen, Publisher; Curtis Richison, Advertising Mgr. **Subscription Rates:** $11.95 individuals; $1.95 single issue. **Remarks:** Accepts advertising.
Ad Rates: BW: $8,539 **Circ:** Paid ★576,580
4C: $11,889

7525 Georgia Sportsman
Game & Fish Publications, Inc.
2250 Newmarket Pkwy., Ste. 110 Phone: (770)953-9222
Fax: (770)933-9510
PO Box 721
Marietta, GA 30061-0741
Magazine for fishermen and hunters. **Founded:** 1976. **Freq:** Monthly. **Print Method:** Offset. **Cols./Page:** 3. **Col. Width:** 27 nonpareils. **Col. Depth:** 140 agate lines. **Key Personnel:** Jimmy Jacobs, Editor; Steven W. Vaughn, Publisher. **Subscription Rates:** $14.95 individuals. **Remarks:** Accepts advertising.
Ad Rates: BW: $989 **Circ:** 41,000
4C: $2,689

The Henry Neighbor - See Henry

Kennesaw Neighbor - See Kennesaw

7526 Mableton Neighbor
Neighbor Newspapers, Inc.
580 Fairground St. Phone: (770)428-9411
PO Box 449 Fax: (770)428-7945
Marietta, GA 30060
Community newspaper. **Founded:** 1974. **Freq:** Weekly (Thurs.). **Print Method:** Offset. **Cols./Page:** 6. **Col. Width:** 26 nonpareils. **Col. Depth:** 301 agate lines. **Key Personnel:** Otis A. Brumby, Jr., Publisher. **USPS:** 074-350. **Subscription Rates:** $12 individuals; $18 out of area; $24 out of state.
Ad Rates: GLR: $.88 **Circ:** Combined 21,474
BW: $1,586.70
4C: $1,876.70
SAU: $12.30

Michigan Sportsman - See Lansing, Michigan

Powder Springs Neighbor - See Powder Springs

7527 Printed Circuit Fabrication
Miller Freeman, Inc.
2000 Powers Ferry Ctr., No. 450
Marietta, GA 30067
Publisher E-mail: techlearning_ editors@mfi.com

Serves the PCB fabrication marketplace. **Founded:** 1978. **Freq:** Monthly. **Print Method:** Offset. **Trim Size:** 8 1/4 x 10 7/8. **Cols./Page:** 3. **Col. Width:** 28 nonpareils. **Col. Depth:** 136 agate lines. **Key Personnel:** Ron Daniels, Publisher; Frances Stewart, Publisher; Sherri Gronli, Circulation Mgr. **ISSN:** 1075-4350. **Subscription Rates:** $60. **Remarks:** Accepts advertising. **URL:** http://www.pcfab.com/pcfab. **Alt. Formats:** Microfilm, UMI.
Ad Rates: GLR: $19 **Circ:** 16,650
BW: $4,575
4C: $5,500

7528 Pulp and Paper
Pulp & Paper
2000 Powers Ferry Center, Ste. 450 Phone: (770)952-1303
Marietta, GA 30067
Magazine serving the pulp and paper industry. **Founded:** 1927. **Freq:** Monthly. **Print Method:** Offset. **Trim Size:** 8 1/8 x 10 7/8. **Cols./Page:** 3. **Col. Width:** 26 nonpareils. **Col. Depth:** 140 agate lines. **Key Personnel:** Kelly Ferguson, Editor; Cyndi Ratcliff, Publisher, phone (770)952-1303, fax (770)933-0666, cratcliff@mfi.com. **ISSN:** 0033-4081. **Subscription Rates:** Free to qualified subscribers; $135 individuals. **Remarks:** Accepts advertising. **URL:** http://www.pponline.com.
Ad Rates: BW: $5,650 **Circ:** Paid 2,000
4C: $8,300 Controlled 39,798

Rockdale Neighbor - See Rockdale

7529 Roswell Neighbor
Neighbor Newspapers, Inc.
580 Fairground St. Phone: (770)428-9411
PO Box 449 Fax: (770)428-7945
Marietta, GA 30060
Community newspaper. **Founded:** 1968. **Freq:** Weekly (Wed.). **Subscription Rates:** $12; $18 out of area; $24 out of state. **Remarks:** Combined advertising rates available with other Neighbor Newspapers.
Circ: Combined 41,496

7530 Sandy Springs Neighbor
Neighbor Newspapers, Inc.
580 Fairground St. Phone: (770)428-9411
PO Box 449 Fax: (770)428-7945
Marietta, GA 30060
Community newspaper. **Founded:** 1970. **Freq:** Weekly (Wed.). **Subscription Rates:** $12; $18 out of area; $24 out of state. **Remarks:** Combined advertising rates available with other Neighbor Newspapers.
Circ: Free 27,259
Paid 215

The Smyrna Neighbor - See Smyrna

South Carolina Game and Fish - See Columbia, South Carolina

7531 The South De Kalb Neighbor
Neighbor Newspapers, Inc.
580 Fairground St. Phone: (770)428-9411
PO Box 449 Fax: (770)428-7945
Marietta, GA 30060
Community newspaper. **Founded:** 1980. **Freq:** Weekly (Wed.). **Print Method:** Offset. **Cols./Page:** 6. **Col. Width:** 26 nonpareils. **Col. Depth:** 301 agate lines. **Key Personnel:** Otis A. Brumby, Jr., Publisher. **USPS:** 523-710. **Subscription Rates:** $12 individuals; $18 out of area; $24 out of state.
Ad Rates: GLR: $1.10 **Circ:** Non-paid 17,575
BW: $1,980.15
4C: $2,305.15
SAU: $15.35

7532 The South Fulton Neighbor
Neighbor Newspapers, Inc.
580 Fairground St. Phone: (770)428-9411
PO Box 449 Fax: (770)428-7945
Marietta, GA 30060
Community newspaper. **Founded:** 1968. **Freq:** Weekly (Thurs.). **Print Method:** Offset. **Cols./Page:** 6. **Col. Width:** 26 nonpareils. **Col. Depth:** 301 agate lines. **Key Personnel:** Otis Brumby, Jr., Publisher. **USPS:** 951-940. **Subscription Rates:** $12 individuals; $18 out of area; $24 out of state.
Ad Rates: GLR: $1.22 **Circ:** Paid 92
BW: $2,205.90 Non-paid 26,711
4C: $2,530.90
SAU: $17.10

7533 The Sting
Southern Polytechnic State University
110 S. Marietta Pkwy. Phone: (770)528-7310
Marietta, GA 30060-2855 Fax: (770)528-7303
Publication E-mail: vortex0007@mindspring.com

Collegiate newspaper. **Founded:** 1948. **Freq:** Semimonthly. **Print Method:** Offset. **Trim Size:** 11 1/4 x 16. **Cols./Page:** 5. **Col. Width:** 22 nonpareils. **Col. Depth:** 196 agate lines. **Key Personnel:** Bryan Garmon, Editor. **Subscription Rates:** Free. **Remarks:** Accepts advertising.
Ad Rates: BW: $300 **Circ:** Free ‡2,500
PCI: $5

The Stone Mountain De Kalb Neighbor - See Stone Mountain

7534 Today's Chiropractic
Life University
1269 Barclay Circle Phone: (770)499-9824
Marietta, GA 30060 Fax: (770)419-0568
Free: (800)543-3430

Professional chiropractic magazine. **Founded:** 1972. **Freq:** Bimonthly. **Print Method:** Web offset. **Trim Size:** 8 x 10 3/4. **Cols./Page:** 3. **Col. Width:** 2 1/4 inches. **Col. Depth:** 9 3/4 inches. **Key Personnel:** James Panter, Editor, jpanter@life.edu; Bob Duppenthaler, Adv. Mgr., duppenthaler@chiroworld.net; Pattie Stechschulte, Assoc. Editor, pattist@life.edu; Loyota Moss, Circ./Classified Ad. Coordinator, lmoss@life.edu; Bob Duppenthaler, Dir. of Communications, duppenthaler@chiroworld.net; Darlene Lanter, Customer Serv., phone (770)426-2887, dlanter@life.edu. **ISSN:** 0091-2360. **Subscription Rates:** $24. **Remarks:** Accepts advertising. **URL:** http://todayschiropractic-com.
Ad Rates: BW: $1,856 **Circ:** 60,000
4C: $2,006

7535 The Truth at Last
The Thunderbolt, Inc.
PO Box 1211
Marietta, GA 30061

Right-wing segregationist newspaper. **Subtitle:** News Suppressed by the Daily Press. **Founded:** Oct. 1958. **Freq:** Monthly. **Print Method:** Offset. **Cols./Page:** 5. **Col. Width:** 22 nonpareils. **Col. Depth:** 193 agate lines. **Key Personnel:** Edward R. Fields, Editor. **Subscription Rates:** $15 individuals. **Remarks:** Advertising not accepted.
Circ: Paid ‡30,000
Free ‡12,000

7536 Tucker De Kalb Neighbor
Neighbor Newspapers, Inc.
580 Fairground St. Phone: (770)428-9411
PO Box 449 Fax: (770)428-7945
Marietta, GA 30060
Community newspaper. **Founded:** 1970. **Freq:** Weekly (Wed.). **Subscription Rates:** $12; $18 out of area; $24 out of state. **Remarks:** Combined advertising rates available with other Neighbor Newspapers.
Circ: Combined 45,551

7537 Vinings Neighbor
Neighbor Newspapers, Inc.
580 Fairground St. Phone: (770)428-9411
PO Box 449 Fax: (770)428-7945
Marietta, GA 30060
Community newspaper. **Founded:** 1970. **Freq:** Weekly (Wed.). **Subscription Rates:** Free; $12; $18 out of area; $24 out of state. **Remarks:** Combined advertising rates available with other Neighbor Newspapers.
Circ: Combined 10,907

7538 Wood Technology
Miller Freeman, Inc.
2000 Powers Ferry Center, Ste. 450 Phone: (770)952-1303
Fax: (770)956-7938
Marietta, GA 30067
Publisher E-mail: techlearning_ editors@mfi.com

Wood products industry magazine. **Founded:** 1889. **Freq:** 10/year. **Print Method:** Offset. **Trim Size:** 8 x 10 3/4. **Cols./Page:** 3. **Col. Width:** 2 3/16 inches. **Col. Depth:** 10 inches. **Key Personnel:** Kathy Porter, Assoc. Publisher, phone (770)563-0124, kporter@mfi.com. **Subscription Rates:** Free to industry professionals. **Remarks:** Accepts advertising. **URL:** http://www.woodtechmag.com. **Formerly**: Forest Industries (1993).
Ad Rates: BW: $2,145 **Circ:** Paid 472
4C: $3,420 Controlled 24,200

7539 WFTD-AM - 1080
774 Roswell St. Phone: (404)424-9850
Marietta, GA 30060 Fax: (404)424-9853

Format: Contemporary Christian; Talk. **Networks:** USA Radio. **Founded:** 1987. **Operating Hours:** Daytime. **ADI:** Atlanta (Athens & Rome), GA. **Key Personnel:** Nelson L. Price, President; Rocky L. Payne, General Mgr. **Wattage:** 10,000.

7540 WGHR-FM - 100.7
1100 S. Marietta Pkwy. Phone: (770)528-7354
Marietta, GA 30060 Fax: (770)528-7409
E-mail: wghr@broadcast.net

Format: Eclectic. **Owner:** Southern Polytechnic State University, at above address. **Founded:** 1972. **Operating Hours:** Continuous. **ADI:** Atlanta (Athens & Rome), GA. **Key Personnel:** David Edwin Stone, General Mgr., dstone@spsu.edu; Jon Licata, Engineering Dir., jlicata@spsu.edu; Reggie Walton, Program Mgr., rwaltor@spsu.edu; Eric Corsten, Promotions Dir., ecarsten@spsu.edu. **URL:** http://www.wghr.net.

WNGM-TV - See Atlanta

7541 Wometco Cable TV of Georgia Inc.
1145 Powder Springs Rd. Phone: (404)427-0010
Marietta, GA 30064 Fax: (404)425-7524

Owner: Wometco Cable TV, Inc., 9400 S. Dadeland Blvd., Miami, FL 33156, (305)662-2205. **Key Personnel:** Greg Ownby, General Mgr. **Cities Served:** Cobb County: subscribing households 56,000; 45 channels.

7542 WTLK-TV - 14
200 N. Cobb Pkwy., Ste. 114 Phone: (404)528-1400
Marietta, GA 30062-3538 Fax: (404)528-1403

Format: Commercial TV. **Networks:** Independent. **Owner:** Paxson Communications of Atlanta, 200 N. Cobb Pkwy., Ste. 114, Marietta, GA 30062. **Founded:** 1988. **Formerly:** WAWA-TV (Nov. 1990). **Operating Hours:** Continuous. **ADI:** Atlanta (Athens & Rome), GA. **Key Personnel:** Jack Crumpier, General Mgr.; Stephanie Moore, Business Mgr. **Local Programs:** *Daybreak*, Bill Owens; *Pam & Buffy Show*, Pam Weeks; *Shoppers Showcase*, Joe Pedicino. **Ad Rates:** $50-200 per unit.

MARTINEZ, pop. 12,000.

E. GA. Columbia Co. 10 mi. NW of Augusta. Manufactures paint, fishing lures, textiles.

7543 Columbia County News Times
PO Box 204178 Phone: (706)863-6165
Martinez, GA 30907 Fax: (706)863-9080

Community newspaper. **Founded:** 1921. **Freq:** Semiweekly (Wed. and Fri.). **Print Method:** Offset. **Cols./Page:** 6. **Col. Width:** 12 picas. **Col. Depth:** 21 inches. **Key Personnel:** Bill Kirby, Editor and Publisher. **USPS:** 124-100. **Subscription Rates:** $32 individuals. **Remarks:** Accepts advertising. **Formerly**: Columbia News/Martinez-Evans Times.
Ad Rates: GLR: $.323 **Circ:** (Not Reported)
BW: $619.20

MCDONOUGH

7544 WKKP-AM - 1410
12 N. Cedar St. Phone: (770)957-0208
PO Box 351 Fax: (770)957-0279
McDonough, GA 30253

Format: Middle-of-the-Road (MOR); Adult Contemporary; Oldies; News. **Networks:** Independent. **Owner:** Henry Co.-Radio Co., Inc., at above address. **Founded:** 1979. **Formerly:** WZAL-AM (1991). **Operating Hours:** 6 a.m.-8:10 p.m.; 100% local. **ADI:** Atlanta (Athens & Rome), GA. **Key Personnel:** Don Earnhart, General Mgr.; Tom Lynde, Program Dir.; Susan Voyles, Sales Mgr. **Wattage:** 2500. **Ad Rates:** $5-6 for 30 seconds; $7-8 for 60 seconds.

MCRAE

7545 Telfair Enterprise
237 W. Oak St. Phone: (912)868-6015
PO Box 269 Fax: (912)868-5486
McRae, GA 31055
Free: (888)825-3441

Newspaper with Democratic orientation. **Founded:** Sept. 1887. **Freq:** Weekly (Wed.). **Print Method:** Offset. **Trim Size:** 7 1/4 x 11 1/2. **Cols./Page:** 6. **Col. Width:** 2 inches. **Col. Depth:** 21 inches. **Key Personnel:** Eric Denty, Publisher, phone (912)427-3757; Roger Naylor, Editor. **USPS:** 537-220. **Subscription Rates:** $19 individuals in county; $23 out of county; $25 out of state.
Ad Rates: GLR: $4 **Circ:** ‡3,400
BW: $548.25
4C: $768.25
SAU: $4.25
PCI: $3

7546 WYIS-AM - 1410
Hwy. 341 S. Phone: (912)868-5611
PO Box 247 Fax: (912)868-5611
McRae, GA 31055

Format: Southern Gospel. **Networks:** International Broadcasting. **Owner:** All Resource, Inc., at above address. **Founded:** 1957. **Formerly**: WDAX-AM (1992). **Operating Hours:** Sunrise-sunset. **Key Personnel:** Sherwin Bell, General Mgr.; Donna Bell, Program Dir. **Wattage:** 1000.

METTER†, pop. 3,531.

E. GA. Candler Co. 60 mi. NW of Savannah. Manufactures lumber, fertilizer manufactured. Cotton ginning; naval stores. Agriculture. Cotton, tobacco stock.

7547 The Metter Advertiser
Snell Publications, Inc.
15 S. Rountree Phone: (912)685-6566
Metter, GA 30439 Fax: (912)685-4901

Local newspaper. **Founded:** 1912. **Freq:** Weekly (Wed.). **Print Method:** Offset. **Cols./Page:** 6. **Col. Width:** 26 nonpareils. **Col. Depth:** 294 agate lines. **Key Personnel:** Carvy Snell, Editor and Publisher. **USPS:** 410-910. **Subscription Rates:** $15 individuals. **Remarks:** Advertising accepted; rates available upon request.
Circ: ‡2,966

7548 WBMZ-FM - 103.7
PO Box 238 Phone: (912)685-2136
Metter, GA 30439 Fax: (912)685-2137
E-mail: boom70s@frontiernet.net

Format: Oldies. **Simulcasts:** WHCG-AM. **Networks:** Georgia Radio; Westwood One Radio; Gannett News; NBC. **Founded:** 1971. **Formerly**: WQKK-FM; WHCG-FM. **Operating Hours:** Continuous. **Key Personnel:** Jimmy Page, General Mgr.; Jason Williams, Prog.Coord.; O. Lucille Page, Station Mgr. **Wattage:** 6000. **Ad Rates:** $6-8 for 30 seconds; $8-10 for 60 seconds. WHCG-FM, WMAC-AM.

7549 WHCG-AM -
PO Box 238 Phone: (912)685-2136
Metter, GA 30439 Fax: (912)685-2137
E-mail: boom705@frontiernet.net

Format: Classic Rock. **Networks:** Westwood One Radio. **Owner:** Radio Metter, Inc., at above address. **Founded:** 1961. **Former name**: WMAC-AM. **Operating Hours:** Continuous. **Key Personnel:** Steve Lawson, Operations Mgr.; Jason Williams, Programming. **Wattage:** 1000. **Ad Rates:** $6 for 30 seconds; $8 for 60 seconds.

MILLEDGEVILLE†, pop. 15,613.

C. GA. Baldwin Co. On Oconee River, 33 mi. NE of Macon. Georgia College at Milledgeville; Georgia Military College. Tile, clay products plants; lumber, knitting and spinning (yarn) mills; bottling works. Manufactures pharmaceuticals, mobile homes, airplane parts. Pine and hardwood timber. Dairy, truck, poultry farms.

7550 Georgia College Connection
Georgia College Alumni Association, Inc.
517 Hancock St. Phone: (912)453-5400
PO Box 98 Fax: (912)453-5744
Milledgeville, GA 31061
Collegiate newspaper (tabloid). **Founded:** 1973. **Freq:** Quarterly (during the academic year). **Print Method:** Offset. **Trim Size:** 11 1/2 x 15 1/2. **Cols./Page:** 4. **Col. Width:** 28 nonpareils. **Col. Depth:** 210 agate lines. **Key Personnel:** Edward Leonard, Editor; Edwin G. Speir, Jr., Publisher. **Subscription Rates:** Free to qualified subscribers. **Remarks:** Advertising not accepted.
Circ: Free ‡23,000

7551 The Union-Recorder
Community Newspaper Holdings, Inc.
1 U-Recorder Plz. Phone: (912)453-1450
PO Box 520 Fax: (912)453-1449
Milledgeville, GA 31061
Publication E-mail: union@accucomm.net

Local newspaper. **Subtitle:** The Union-Recorder. **Founded:** Feb. 1820. **Freq:** Tues.-Sat. (morn.). **Print Method:** Offset. **Trim Size:** 13 3/4 x 22 3/4. **Cols./Page:** 6. **Col. Width:** 2 1/16 inches. **Col. Depth:** 21 1/2 inches. **Key Personnel:** Susan L. Patterson, Publisher, phone (912)453-1450, spatterson@union-recorder.com; Don Schanche, Jr., Managing Editor, phone (912)453-1451, fax (912)453-1459; Percy Canon, Advertising Mgr., phone (912)453-1437, fax (912)453-1439. **Subscription Rates:** $79.30 individuals. **Remarks:** Accepts advertising.
Ad Rates: GLR: $1.75 **Circ:** 8,500
BW: $1,328.70
4C: $1,578.70
SAU: $11.25
PCI: $7.65

7552 Rigel Communications Inc.
70 Leah Hollow Rd. Phone: (203)354-9945
Sherman, CT 06784

Founded: 1986. **Formerly**: Gulf Cable TV; Haddock Cable TV; Oconee Cablevision; PV Cable; Twiggs Cablevision; Walker Cable; Wilkinson County Cablevision. **Key Personnel:** Wesley L. Owens, Contact; Brady Spires, Contact; Scott Long, Chief Engineer; Eric Rothenburg, Contact; Ed Bond, Contact; Gertrud Yampierre, Contact. **Cities Served:** subscribing households 9,929; 36 channels; 1 community access channel; 8 hours per week community access programming.

7553 WGUR-FM - 88.9
Box 3124 Phone: (912)445-4102
Milledgeville, GA 31061-1000 Fax: (912)454-1483
E-mail: wgur@rage.gcsu.edu

Format: Top 40; Alternative/New Music/Progressive. **Founded:** 1970. **Formerly**: WXGC-FM (1996). **Operating Hours:** 12 p.m.-midnight. **ADI:** Macon, GA. **Key Personnel:** Chris McAndrew, General Mgr., phone (912)445-0195, chrmca@rage.gcsu.edu; Stuart Crosby, News & Public Svc. Dir. **Wattage:** 10.

7554 WKGQ-AM - 1060
156 Lake Laurel Rd. NE Phone: (912)452-1838
PO Box 832 Fax: (912)452-2004
Milledgeville, GA 31061

Format: News; Talk. **Networks:** Unistar; Daynet. **Founded:** 1975. **Formerly**: WXLX-AM. **Operating Hours:** Sunrise-sunset; 80% network; 20% local. **Key Personnel:** John W. Ferguson, General Mgr. **Wattage:** 1000. **Ad Rates:** $5-6 for 30 seconds; $9-11 for 60 seconds.

7555 WKZR-FM - 102.3
1250 W. Charlton St. Phone: (912)452-0587
PO Box 519 Fax: (912)452-5886
Milledgeville, GA 31061
E-mail: wmvgwkzr@accucomm.net

Format: Country. **Networks:** ABC. **Owner:** WMVG, Inc., at above address. **Founded:** 1966. **Formerly**: WMVG-FM (1980). **Operating Hours:** Continuous; 10% network, 90% local. **Key Personnel:** Dale Van Cantfort, President/General Mgr.; Scott MacLeod, Operations Dir.; Ken Jones, News Dir. **Wattage:** 3300. **Ad Rates:** $10-17 for 30 seconds; $14-20 for 60 seconds. Combined advertising rates available with WMVG.

7556 WMVG-AM - 1450
1250 W. Charlton St. Phone: (912)452-0586
PO Box 519 Fax: (912)452-5886
Milledgeville, GA 31061
E-mail: wmvgwkzr@accuco.mm.net

Format: Contemporary Christian. **Networks:** ABC. **Owner:** WMVG, Inc., at above address. **Founded:** 1946. **Operating Hours:** Continuous; 10% network, 90% local. **Key Personnel:** Dale Van Cantfort, Pres./Gen. Mgr.; Scott MacLeod, Operations Dir.; Ken Jones, News Dir. **Wattage:** 1000. **Ad Rates:** Advertising accepted; rates available upon request. Combined advertising rates available with WKZR.

MILLEN†.

EC GA. Jenkins Co. 20 mi. E. of Herndon.

7557 Millen News
The Millen News
PO Box 909 Phone: (912)982-5460
Millen, GA 30442 Fax: (912)982-1785

Community newspaper. **Freq:** Weekly (Thurs.). **Print Method:**

Offset. **Cols./Page:** 6. **Col. Width:** 12.5 picas. **Col. Depth:** 21 1/2 inches. **Key Personnel:** Roy F. Chalker, Editor and Publisher, chalker@thetruecitizen.com. **Subscription Rates:** $15.90. **Remarks:** Accepts advertising.
Ad Rates: BW: $483.75 **Circ:** 2,000
4C: $823.75
PCI: $3.75

MONROE†, pop. 8,854.

NC GA. Walton Co. 45 mi. E. of Atlanta. Manufactures textiles, china products, plastic pipe, fertilizer, cottonseed oil. Poultry, egg processing plant. Agriculture. Cotton, corn, poultry, dairy and beef cattle.

7558 Walton Tribune/Advertiser
PO Box 808 Phone: (770)267-8371
Monroe, GA 30655-0808 Fax: (770)267-7780
Publisher E-mail: tribstaff@waltontribune.com

Community newspaper. **Founded:** 1900. **Freq:** Semiweekly (Wed. and Sun.). **Print Method:** Offset. **Cols./Page:** 6. **Col. Width:** 20 nonpareils. **Col. Depth:** 301 agate lines. **Key Personnel:** Robert Hale, Editor and Publisher; Wes Swietek, Managing Editor; Deana Hale, Advertising Mgr. **Subscription Rates:** $40 individuals. **Remarks:** Color advertising accepted; rates available upon request.
Ad Rates: SAU: $6.50 **Circ:** Paid 5,961
PCI: $6.30 Non-paid 15,000

7559 City of Monroe, Water, Light, & Gas Commission
215 N. Broad St. Phone: (770)267-3429
Box 725 Fax: (770)267-3698
Monroe, GA 30655
E-mail: wlgc@mindspring.com

Founded: Feb. 1972. **Key Personnel:** Mark S. Ennis, General Mgr., mennis@mwlgc.com. **Cities Served:** Good Hope, Monroe, GA: subscribing households 5,167; 64 channels; 1 community access channel; 168 hours per week community access programming.

7560 WKUN-AM - 1580
PO Box 649 Phone: (770)267-6558
Monroe, GA 30655 Fax: (770)267-0341

Format: Country. **Networks:** Satellite Music Network. **Owner:** B.R. Anderson Sr., at above address. **Founded:** 1971. **Operating Hours:** Sunrise-sunset. **Key Personnel:** Grace Morris, General Mgr. **Wattage:** 1000. **Ad Rates:** $5.5 for 30 seconds; $8 for 60 seconds.

MONTICELLO†, pop. 2,382.

NC GA. Jasper Co. 38 mi. N. of Macon. Manufactures forest products, plywood, feed, fertilizer. Pine timber. Agriculture. Poultry, dairy farms. Soybeans, corn, cattle.

7561 The Monticello News
237 Washington St. Phone: (706)468-6511
PO Box 30 Fax: (706)468-6576
Monticello, GA 31064-0030
Community newpaper. **Founded:** 1881. **Freq:** Weekly (Thurs.). **Print Method:** Offset. **Cols./Page:** 6. **Col. Width:** 12 picas. **Col. Depth:** 301 agate lines. **Key Personnel:** W.T. Hughes, Jr., Publisher; Kathy Pope, Editor/Gen. Mgr.; Jenny Phillips, Advertising Mgr. **USPS:** 361-640. **Subscription Rates:** $16.96 individuals; $21.20 out of county; $.50 single issue. **Remarks:** Accepts advertising.
Ad Rates: GLR: $4 **Circ:** ‡2,800
BW: $375
4C: $475
SAU: $3.70
PCI: $3.70

MORROW

Clayton Co.

7562 WSSA-AM - 1570
2424 Old Rex Morrow Rd. Phone: (404)361-8843
PO Box 831
Morrow, GA 30260-0831
E-mail: programming@wssa1570.com

Format: Religious; Southern Gospel. **Networks:** Family Stations Radio. **Owner:** Saints, Inc., PO Box 831, Morrow, GA 30260. **Founded:** 1959. **Operating Hours:** 24 hra. **ADI:** Atlanta (Athens & Rome), GA. **Key Personnel:** Tony St. Cyr, Contact, tony@wssa1570.com; Randy James, Program Dir., randy@wssa1570.com; Donnie St. Cyr, Office Mgr., donnie@wssa1570.com. **Wattage:** 5000. **Ad Rates:** $18-30 for 60 seconds.

MOULTRIE†, pop. 15,608.

S. GA. Colquitt Co. 65 mi. NE of Tallahassee, FL. Manufactures textiles, lumber, mobile homes, aluminum cans, cottonseed oil, fertilizer. Carpet yarn spinning; die casting; pork packing plant. Agriculture. Tobacco, peanuts, livestock, grains, vegetables.

7563 Moultrie Observer
PO Box 889 Phone: (912)985-4545
Moultrie, GA 31776-0889 Fax: (912)985-3569

General newspaper. **Founded:** 1905. **Freq:** Mon.-Sat. (morn.). **Print Method:** Offset. **Cols./Page:** 6. **Col. Width:** 24 nonpareils. **Col. Depth:** 301 agate lines. **Key Personnel:** Dwain Walden, Editor; Gary W. Boley, Publisher. **Subscription Rates:** $60.16 individuals. **Remarks:** Accepts advertising.
Ad Rates: SAU: $6.82 **Circ:** 7,306

7564 WMGA-AM - 580
Box 1380 Phone: (912)985-0580
Moultrie, GA 31776-1380 Fax: (912)890-8609

Format: Talk; News. **Networks:** CBS. **Founded:** 1939. **Operating Hours:** Continuous; 75% network, 25% local. **ADI:** Albany (Valdosta & Cordele), GA. **Key Personnel:** Jay Ussery, Contact; Jay Ussery, Station Mgr.; Jay Ussery, News Dir.; Jerry Crowe, Sales Mgr. **Wattage:** 1000. **Ad Rates:** Advertising accepted; rates available upon request.

7565 WMTM-AM - 1300
WMTM Rd. Phone: (912)985-1300
PO Box 788 Fax: (912)890-0905
Moultrie, GA 31776

Format: Middle-of-the-Road (MOR). **Networks:** ABC. **Owner:** Douglas J. Turner, at above address. **Founded:** 1953. **Operating Hours:** 6 a.m.-sunset. **Key Personnel:** Jim Turner, Contact; Jim Lane, Music Dir. **Wattage:** 5000. **Ad Rates:** $9 for 30 seconds.

7566 WMTM-FM - 93.9
WMTM Rd. Phone: (912)985-1300
PO Box 788 Fax: (912)890-0905
Moultrie, GA 31776

Format: Country; News. **Networks:** Mutual Broadcasting System. **Owner:** Douglas J. Turner, at above address. **Founded:** 1964. **Operating Hours:** 6 a.m.-midnight. **Key Personnel:** Douglas J. Turner, Contact; Lee Redmond, Music Dir. **Wattage:** 100,000. **Ad Rates:** $4-6.75 for 30 seconds; $5-8.00 for 60 seconds.

MOUNT BERRY

Campus Carrier - See Rome

MOUNTAIN CITY

7567 The Active Learner
The Foxfire Fund, Inc.
PO Box 541 Phone: (706)746-5828
Mountain City, GA 30562-0541 Fax: (706)746-5829
Publisher E-mail: foxfire@foxfire.org

Professional journal for teachers of grades K-12. **Subtitle:** A Foxfire Journal for Teachers. **Founded:** Aug. 1996. **Freq:** Triennial. **Print Method:** Offset. **Trim Size:** 9 1/4 x 12 1/4. **Cols./Page:** 2. **Key Personnel:** Sara Day Hatton, Editor. **Subscription Rates:** $20 individuals; $8 single issue. **Remarks:** Advertising not accepted. **Former name:** Hands On.
Circ: Combined 437

7568 The Foxfire Magazine
The Foxfire Fund, Inc.
PO Box 541 Phone: (706)746-5828
Mountain City, GA 30562-0541 Fax: (706)746-5829
Publication E-mail: foxfire@acme-brain.com
Publisher E-mail: foxfire@foxfire.org

Magazine focusing on the Appalachian culture, edited by Appalachian high school students. **Founded:** Mar. 1967. **Freq:** Semiannual. **Trim Size:** 10 1/2 x 7 3/4. **Cols./Page:** 2. **Col. Width:** 3 inches. **Col. Depth:** 8 inches. **Key Personnel:** Joyce Green, Advisor, phone (706)782-6355; Angela Cheek, Advisor, phone (706)782-6355. **ISSN:** 0015-9220. **Subscription Rates:** $12.95 individuals; $24.95 other countries; $7.50 single issue. **Remarks:** Advertising not accepted. **Formerly:** Foxfire.
Circ: 3,000

7569 WALH-AM - 1340
Box F Phone: (706)746-2256
Mountain City, GA 30562 Fax: (706)746-2259

Format: Gospel; Contemporary Country; Bluegrass. **Networks:** USA Radio. **Founded:** 1986. **Formerly:** New 1986.

Operating Hours: 6 a.m.-11 p.m. **Key Personnel:** W.L. Savage, General Manager/Sales and News Dir.; Lorraine Savage, Station/Sales Mgr.; W.P. Franklin, Music Dir. **Wattage:** 1000. **Ad Rates:** $4 for 30 seconds; $5 for 60 seconds.

NAHUNTA†, pop. 951.

SE GA. Brantley Co. 23 mi. E. of Waycross. Pine timber. Agriculture. Tobacco, cotton, corn.

7570 Brantley Enterprise
The Brantley Enterprise
PO Box 454 Phone: (912)462-6776
Nahunta, GA 31553 Fax: (912)462-6776
Publication E-mail: klbuck@aol.com

Community newspaper. **Founded:** 1920. **Freq:** Weekly (Thurs.). **Print Method:** Offset. **Cols./Page:** 6. **Col. Width:** 12.25 picas. **Col. Depth:** 126 picas. **Key Personnel:** Robert Page, Publisher. **Subscription Rates:** $15 individuals. **Remarks:** Accepts advertising.
Ad Rates: BW: $387 **Circ:** 2,300
4C: $487
SAU: $3.25

NASHVILLE†, pop. 4,831.

S. GA. Berrien Co. 117 mi. SE of Macon. Manufactures automotive parts, carpet backing, feed, boats. Textile mill. Tobacco warehouse. Screen printing. Pine timber. Agriculture. Corn, tobacco, peanuts, cotton.

7571 The Berrien Press
Box 455 Phone: (912)686-3523
Nashville, GA 31639 Fax: (912)686-7771

Community newspaper. **Founded:** June 1, 1959. **Freq:** Weekly (Wed.). **Print Method:** Offset. **Cols./Page:** 6. **Col. Width:** 12 picas. **Col. Depth:** 21 1/2 inches. **Key Personnel:** Donald Boyd, Editor and Publisher, dboyd@surfsouth.com. **Subscription Rates:** $15 individuals; $25 out of area; $30 out of state. **Remarks:** Accepts advertising.
Ad Rates: BW: $567 **Circ:** ‡4,200
4C: $627
SAU: $5

NEWNAN†, pop. 11,449.

W. GA. Coweta Co. 40 mi. SW of Atlanta. Manufactures safety goggles, textiles, aluminum products, concrete blocks, tanks, plastics, lumber. Agriculture. Cotton, dairy products, corn, peanuts.

7572 The Newnan Times-Herald
PO Box 1052 Phone: (770)253-1576
Newnan, GA 30264 Fax: (770)253-2538

Community newspaper. **Founded:** 1865. **Freq:** Semiweekly (Wed. and Sat.). **Print Method:** Offset. **Cols./Page:** 6. **Col. Width:** 24 nonpareils. **Col. Depth:** 301 agate lines. **Key Personnel:** Sam Jones, Publisher. **Subscription Rates:** $26.50 individuals. **Remarks:** Accepts advertising. **URL:** http://newnan.com. **Formerly:** Times-Herald.
Ad Rates: 4C: $90 **Circ:** 14,000
PCI: $5.95

7573 WCOH-AM - 1400
154 Boone Dr. Phone: (770)253-4636
Newnan, GA 30263 Fax: (770)251-8260

Format: Country. **Networks:** Mutual Broadcasting System. **Founded:** 1947. **Operating Hours:** 6 a.m.-midnight. **ADI:** Atlanta (Athens & Rome), GA. **Key Personnel:** Alvin Johnston, General Mgr.; Richard Mann, Production Dir. **Wattage:** 1000.

7574 WNEA-AM - 1300
PO Box 1213 Phone: (770)253-4711
Newnan, GA 30264 Fax: (770)254-1399

Format: Gospel. **Networks:** NBC; Georgia Radio. **Owner:** Harold Banks, at above address. **Founded:** 1962. **Operating Hours:** Mon-Sat 6am-sunset, Sun 6am-6pm; 20-30% network 70-80% local. **Key Personnel:** Harold Banks, Owner. **Wattage:** 1000. **Ad Rates:** $5.50-6.75 for 30 seconds; $5-8 for 60 seconds.

NORCROSS, pop. 3,317.

NC GA. Gwinnett Co. 15 mi. N. of Atlanta. Manufactures cables, plastic, fabricated metal products. Diversified farming. Cotton, corn, cattle.

7575 The Atlanta Small Business Monthly
6129 Oakbrook Pkwy Phone: (770)446-5434
Norcross, GA 30093 Fax: (770)446-3970
Publication E-mail: asbm@bellsouth.net

Magazine with information on how to run businesses better. **Subtitle:** For Small and Big Business. **Founded:** June 1987. **Freq:** Monthly. **Print Method:** Offset. **Trim Size:** 11 1/2 x 15. **Cols./Page:** 4. **Col. Width:** 27 nonpareils. **Col. Depth:** 180 agate lines. **Key Personnel:** Jennifer Farwell, Editor; Lisa Amspaugh, Publisher. **Subscription Rates:** Free to qualified subscribers; $15. $1.50 single issue. **Remarks:** Accepts advertising. **Formerly**: The Atlanta Small Business Journal (Nov. 1987).
Ad Rates: BW: $1,937 **Circ:** Paid ‡4,000
4C: $2,387 Controlled ‡24,000

7576 Better Crops with Plant Food
Potash and Phosphate Institute
655 Engineering Dr., Ste. 110 Phone: (770)447-0335
Norcross, GA 30092-2821 Fax: (770)448-0439

Agricultural magazine. **Founded:** 1923. **Freq:** Quarterly. **Print Method:** Offset. **Trim Size:** 6 x 9. **Cols./Page:** 1 and 2. **Col. Width:** 68 and 32 nonpareils. **Col. Depth:** 105 agate lines. **Key Personnel:** Donald L. Armstrong, Editor. **ISSN:** 0006-0089. **Subscription Rates:** $8 individuals. **Remarks:** Advertising not accepted. **Alt. Formats:** Microform.
Circ: Paid ‡50
Non-paid ‡16,000

7577 Construction Market Data, A/E/C Magazine
CMD Group
30 Technology Pkwy., No. 100 Phone: (770)417-4112
Norcross, GA 30092 Fax: (770)417-4138
Publisher E-mail: chris.caset@cmdg.com

Trade journal for local architects, engineers and contractors. **Founded:** May 1998. **Freq:** Monthly. **Trim Size:** 7 7/8 x 10 7/8. **Cols./Page:** 3. **Col. Width:** 2 inches. **Col. Depth:** 9 inches. **Key Personnel:** George Rekela, Editor; Bob Story, Advertising Mgr.; Jane Senem, Circulation Mgr. **Subscription Rates:** $35 individuals. **Remarks:** Accepts advertising. **URL:** http://www.cmdg.com.
Ad Rates: BW: $995 **Circ:** Combined 8,000
4C: $1,345

7578 Georgia Trend
Trend Publications LLC
5880 Live Oak Pkwy., Ste. 280
Norcross, GA 30093
Publication E-mail: gtrend@aol.com; gatrend@applied.net
Publisher E-mail: gatrend@applied.net

Business and politics magazine. **Founded:** Sept. 1985. **Freq:** Monthly. **Print Method:** Offset. **Trim Size:** 8 1/4 x 10 7/8. **Cols./Page:** 3. **Col. Width:** 27 nonpareils. **Col. Depth:** 140 agate lines. **Key Personnel:** Neely Young, Editor and Publisher; Amanda Patterson, Advertising Mgr. **ISSN:** 0882-5971. **Subscription Rates:** $18; $30 other countries; $33 two years; $2.95 single issue. **Remarks:** Accepts advertising. **Alt. Formats:** Microform.
Ad Rates: BW: $4,430 **Circ:** Paid 7,235
4C: $5,780 Non-paid 39,908

7579 Gwinnett Extra
The Atlanta Journal and Constitution
6455 Best Friend Rd. Phone: (404)263-3858
Norcross, GA 30071 Fax: (404)263-3011
Publication E-mail: gwinnette@ajc.com

Community newspaper. **Founded:** 1989. **Freq:** Semiweekly (Wed. and Sun.). **Key Personnel:** Susan Gast, Editor. **Subscription Rates:** Free. **Remarks:** Advertising accepted; rates available upon request.
Circ: Sun. 41,230
Wed. 48,758

7580 IIE Solutions
Institute of Industrial Engineers
25 Technology Park/Atlanta Phone: (770)449-0461
Norcross, GA 30092 Fax: (770)263-8532
Free: (800)494-0460
Publication E-mail: advertising@iienet.org
Publisher E-mail: cs@iienet.org

Magazine covering industrial engineering, facilities design, systems integration, production control, material handling, quality, productivity, management, and other industrial engineering topics. **Founded:** 1969. **Freq:** Monthly. **Print Method:** Offset. **Trim Size:** 8 1/8 x 10 7/8. **Cols./Page:** 3. **Col. Width:** 26 nonpareils. **Col. Depth:** 140 agate lines. **Key Personnel:** Heather Sutton, Advertising Admin.; Jane Gaboury, Editor, editor@iienet.org; Cliff Cary, Publisher. **ISSN:** 0019-8234. **Subscription Rates:** $60 individuals; $7 single issue. **Remarks:** Accepts advertising. **URL:** http://www.solutions.iienet.org. **Alt. Formats:** Microform. **Formerly**: Industrial Engineering.
Ad Rates: BW: $3,413 **Circ:** Paid 23,000
4C: $4,739 Non-paid 13,000

7581 NAC Focus
NAC International
655 Engineering Dr., Ste. 200 Phone: (770)447-1144
Norcross, GA 30092-2843 Fax: (770)447-1797
Publisher E-mail: msmith@nacintl.com

Trade magazine for the nuclear fuel industry. **Founded:** Aug. 1980. **Freq:** Quarterly. **Key Personnel:** Tim O'Shea, Editor. **Subscription Rates:** $4,000 individuals. **Remarks:** Advertising not accepted. **Former name**: Update—A Bimonthly Review of the Nuclear Industry.
Circ: (Not Reported)

7582 Site Selection Magazine
Conway Data, Inc.
35 Technology Pkwy., Ste. 150 Phone: (770)446-6996
Norcross, GA 30092 Fax: (770)263-8825
Publication E-mail: infomer@conway.com
Publisher E-mail: info.mgr@conway.com

Magazine containing information useful to corporate real estate executives and site selectors. **Founded:** 1954. **Freq:** Bimonthly. **Print Method:** Offset. **Trim Size:** 8 1/8 x 10 7/8. **Cols./Page:** 3. **Col. Width:** 26 nonpareils. **Col. Depth:** 140 agate lines. **Key Personnel:** Jack Lyne, Editor; H. McKinley Conway, Publisher; Jim Cummins, Advertising Mgr. **ISSN:** 1080-7799. **Subscription Rates:** $85 individuals; $125 other countries. **Remarks:** Accepts advertising. **URL:** http://www.sitenet.com. **Formerly**: Site Selection and Industrial Development Magazine.
Ad Rates: GLR: $6,855 **Circ:** Combined 45,000
BW: $6,875
4C: $2,230

7583 TOPS
Georgia Forestry Association, Inc.
500 Pinnacle Ct., Ste. 505 Phone: (770)416-7621
Norcross, GA 30071 Fax: (770)840-8961
Free: (800)9-GROWGA
Publisher E-mail: gfagrowga@aol.com

Forestry magazine. **Founded:** 1966. **Freq:** Annual. **Print Method:** Offset. **Trim Size:** 8 1/2 x 11. **Cols./Page:** 3. **Col. Width:** 30 nonpareils. **Col. Depth:** 134 agate lines. **Key Personnel:** Lance Compton, Editor. **ISSN:** 0563-9093. **Subscription Rates:** $10 individuals GFA Members Only. **Remarks:** Accepts advertising.
Ad Rates: BW: $700 **Circ:** Paid ‡4,800
4C: $1,295

7584 Trucker's Connection
Trucker's Connection, Inc.
5960 Crooked Creek Rd., Ste. 15 Phone: (770)416-0927
Fax: (770)416-1734
Norcross, GA 30092
Publication E-mail: 102400.573@compuserve.com

Trade magazine for over-the-road, long haul truck operators. **Founded:** 1987. **Freq:** Monthly. **Print Method:** Web. **Trim Size:** 5 5/16 x 8 1/4. **Key Personnel:** Megan Coleman, Editor-in-Chief, megan_coleman@compuserve.com; Wendell Adcock, Associate Publisher, wendell@truckersconnectioninc.com; Jon Grassi, Circulation Director. **Subscription Rates:** $26.95 individuals. **Remarks:** Accepts advertising.
Ad Rates: BW: $3,895 **Circ:** △201,000
4C: $5,695

7585 MediaOne, Inc.
2925 Courtyards Dr. Phone: (770)559-2710
Norcross, GA 30071-1555 Fax: (770)559-2134

Owner: Media One Group, 188 Iverness Drive West, Englewood, CO 80112, (303)858-3415, Free: (800)879-4357. **Founded:** Dec. 6, 1994. **Formerly**: Southern Multimedia; Wometco; GCTV; US West, Inc. **Key Personnel:** Ellen Filipiak, President, phone (770)559-2424; Mike Ricks, CFO; Reg Griffin, Dir. Of Communications. **Cities Served:** Atlanta Metro Area: subscribing households 520,000; 90 channels. **URL:** http://www.mediaone.com.

7586 WATC-TV - 57
1862 Enterprise Dr. Phone: (770)300-9828
Norcross, GA 30093 Fax: (770)300-9838

Format: Educational. **Owner:** Community Television, Inc., at above address. **Founded:** 1996. **Operating Hours:** Continuous. **ADI:** Atlanta (Athens & Rome), GA. **Key Personnel:** James Thompson, General Mgr., phone (864)244-1616; Greg West, Program Dir.; Pat Mathis, Office Mgr.; Vincent Thompson, Production Mgr. **Wattage:** 1,700,000. **Ad Rates:** Noncommercial.

7587 Wometco of Gwinnett
2925 Courtyards Dr. Phone: (404)921-0010
Norcross, GA 30071-1555 Fax: (404)979-0101

Founded: 1979. **Cities Served:** Gwinnett County, GA.

OCILLA†, pop. 3,436.

S. Ga. Irwin Co. 50 mi. N. of Valdosta. Manufactures cottonseed oil, lumber, turpentine. Meat curing plant. Pine timber. Stock, poultry farms. Cotton, corn, peanuts.

7588 Star
102 E. 4th St. Phone: (912)468-5433
PO Box 25 Fax: (912)468-5045
Ocilla, GA 31774
Newspaper with a Democratic orientation. **Founded:** 1903. **Freq:** Weekly (Wed.). **Print Method:** Offset. **Cols./Page:** 6. **Col. Width:** 21 1/2 nonpareils. **Col. Depth:** 298 agate lines. **Key Personnel:** Robert M. Williams, Jr., Publisher; Diane Pless, Sales & Advertising; Beverly Bradford, Gen. Mgr./Sec./Bookkeeper; Steve Carter, Sports Editor. **Subscription Rates:** $16 individuals. **Remarks:** Accepts advertising.
Ad Rates: BW: $483.75 **Circ:** 2,300
4C: $608.75
SAU: $3
PCI: $3

OGLETHORPE

7589 Oglethorpe Echo
PO Box 268 Phone: (404)743-5510
Lexington, GA 30648
Newspaper. **Founded:** 1874. **Freq:** Weekly (Thurs.). **Print Method:** Offset. **Cols./Page:** 6. **Col. Width:** 27 nonpareils. **Col. Depth:** 301 agate lines. **Key Personnel:** Ralph Maxwell, Jr., Editor and Publisher. **Subscription Rates:** $9.27 individuals. **Remarks:** Accepts advertising.
Ad Rates: GLR: $.15 **Circ:** (Not Reported)

PALMETTO

7590 Tipularia
Georgia Botanical Society
7575 Rico Rd. Phone: (770)463-4227
Palmetto, GA 30268
Journal magazine covering botany in Georgia. **Subtitle:** A botanical magazine. **Founded:** 1986. **Freq:** Annual. **Trim Size:** 6 x 9. **Cols./Page:** 2. **Col. Width:** 2 3/8 inches. **Col. Depth:** 7 7/8 inches. **Key Personnel:** David L. Emory, Chm., Editorial Board, dandsemory@aol.com. **ISSN:** 1090-1876. **Subscription Rates:** $10 individuals. **Remarks:** Advertising not accepted.
Circ: Paid 450

PARROTT

WACS-TV - See Dawson

PAULDING

7591 The Paulding Neighbor
Neighbor Newspapers, Inc.
208 Main St. Phone: (404)445-9401
Dallas, GA 30132 Fax: (404)445-3151

Community newspaper. **Founded:** 1978. **Freq:** Weekly (Thurs.). **Print Method:** Offset. **Cols./Page:** 6. **Col. Depth:** 301 agate lines. **Key Personnel:** Otis A. Brumby, Jr., Publisher. **USPS:** 406-910. **Subscription Rates:** $12 individuals; $18 out of area; $24 out of state.
Ad Rates: GLR: $.58 **Circ:** Paid 23
BW: $1,367.40 Non-paid 15,670
4C: $1,334.90
SAU: $9
PCI: $10.60

PEACHTREE CITY, pop. 6,411.

W. GA. Fayette Co. 25 mi. SW of Atlanta. Commercial and industrial areas. McIntosh Trail.

7592 Contemporary Impressions
American Print Alliance
302 Larkspur Turn Phone: (770)486-6680
Peachtree City, GA 30269
Journal of critical writings on prints, paperworks, and artists' books; includes one original print each year. **Subtitle:** The Journal of the American Print Alliance. **Founded:** 1993. **Freq:** Semiannual plus one annual original print per subscription. **Print Method:** Offset, duotone. **Trim Size:** 8 1/2 x 9 1/2. **Cols./Page:** 2. **Col. Width:** 2, 5 1/2 inches. **Col. Depth:** 8 1/4 inches. **Key Personnel:** Carol Pulin, PhD, Editor. **ISSN:** 1066-9434. **Subscription Rates:** $35 individuals; $50 institutions Add $3 to Canada, $8 other foreign; $53.00 institutions, Canada; $58.00 other countries. **Remarks:** Advertising ac-

cepted; rates available upon request. **URL:** http://www.thewww.com/printalliance.
Circ: (Not Reported)

7593 Intermedia
Box 2670 Phone: (404)487-5011
Peachtree City, GA 30269 Fax: (404)487-0773
Free: (800)282-8262

Owner: Inter Media Partners, 235 Montgomery St., Ste. 420, San Francisco, CA 94104, (415)397-4121. **Formerly**: Peach State Cablevision. **Key Personnel:** Joe Haight, General Mgr. **Cities Served:** Fulton, Fayette and Coweta Counties.: 65 channels.

7594 WMKJ-FM - 96.7
PO Box 2547 Phone: (404)577-4850
Peachtree City, GA 30269 Fax: (404)251-8260
E-mail: wmkjfm@aol.com

Format: Adult Contemporary. **Founded:** 1948. **Formerly**: WBUS-FM. **Operating Hours:** Continuous; 50% network, 50% local. **ADI:** Atlanta (Athens & Rome), GA. **Key Personnel:** Brad Myers, Music Dir.; Stephen Tarkenton, Vice President; Richard Mann, Program Dir.; Tom Corker, News Dir.; Mike Copeland, Sales Mgr. **Wattage:** 3000.

PEARSON†, pop. 1,827.

S. GA. Atkinson Co. 30 mi. NW of Waycross. Manufactures garments, mobile homes, wood products manufactured. Naval stores; sawmill. Agriculture. Cotton, corn, tobacco.

7595 Atkinson County Citizen
Atkinson County Citizen, Inc.
PO Box 398 Phone: (912)422-3824
Pearson, GA 31642 Fax: (912)422-6050

Community newspaper. **Founded:** Oct. 15, 1914. **Freq:** Weekly (Thurs.). **Print Method:** Offset. **Cols./Page:** 6. **Col. Width:** 21 nonpareils. **Col. Depth:** 294 agate lines. **Key Personnel:** Patsy W. Kirkland, Editor. **Subscription Rates:** $12.84 individuals; $19.26 out of area; $0.35 single issue. **Remarks:** Accepts advertising. **Formerly**: Pearson Tribune.
Ad Rates: BW: $378 **Circ:** Paid ‡1,400
SAU: $2 Free ‡53

PERRY

7596 Houston Times-Journal
807 Carroll St.
PO Drawer M
Perry, GA 31069

Community newspaper. **Founded:** 1870. **Freq:** Weekly. **Print Method:** Offset. **Cols./Page:** 6. **Col. Width:** 2 inches. **Col. Depth:** 21 1/2 inches. **Key Personnel:** J. Johnson, Editor and Publisher, jjedit@hom.net. **Subscription Rates:** $20; $.50 single issue. **Remarks:** Accepts advertising. **Formerly**: Houston Home Journal; The Perry Times.
Ad Rates: GLR: $4.75 **Circ:** 3,600
BW: $743.34
4C: $833.04
CNU: $4.75

7597 WPGA-AM - 980
PO Drawer 980 Phone: (912)987-2980
Perry, GA 31069-0980 Fax: (912)987-7595

Format: Country. **Networks:** Independent. **Founded:** 1955. **Operating Hours:** 6 a.m.-10 p.m. **Key Personnel:** Lowell Register, General Mgr.; Janice Register, Contact. **Wattage:** 5000.

7598 WPGA-FM - 100.9
PO Drawer 980 Phone: (912)987-2980
Perry, GA 31069-0980 Fax: (912)987-7595

Format: Urban Contemporary. **Networks:** ABC. **Founded:** 1966. **Operating Hours:** Continuous. **Key Personnel:** Lowell Register, General Mgr.; Janice Register, Contact; John Lynn, Station Mgr. **Wattage:** 3000.

POWDER SPRINGS

7599 Powder Springs Neighbor
Neighbor Newspapers, Inc.
580 Fairground St. Phone: (770)428-9411
PO Box 449 Fax: (770)428-7945
Marietta, GA 30060
Community newspaper. **Founded:** 1969. **Freq:** Weekly (Thurs.). **Subscription Rates:** $12; $18 out of area; $24 out of state. **Remarks:** Combined advertising rates available with other Neighbor Newspapers.
Circ: Combined 21,474

QUITMAN

7600 WSFB-AM - 1490
Box 632 Phone: (912)263-4373
Quitman, GA 31643-0632 Fax: (912)263-7693

Format: Contemporary Country; Soft Rock; Gospel; Easy Listening. **Networks:** Georgia Radio; NBC. **Owner:** Jim S. Chion, Rt. 2, Box 533, Tallahassee, FL 32311, (904)878-5746. **Founded:** 1957. **Operating Hours:** 13 hours Daily; 10% network, 15% local, 75% other. **Key Personnel:** Jim S. Chion, Contact; Gail H. Taylor, Program Mgr. **Wattage:** 1000. **Ad Rates:** $4.90 for 30 seconds; $4.60-6.95 for 60 seconds.

REIDSVILLE†, pop. 2,296.

SE GA. Tattnall Co. 60 mi. W. of Savannah. Naval stores; cotton ginning. Pine timber. Agriculture. Tobacco, cotton, sweet potatoes.

7601 Tattnall Journal
The Tattnall Journal
PO Box 278 Phone: (912)557-6761
149 Folson St. Fax: (912)557-4132
Reidsville, GA 30453
Publisher E-mail: tjournal@pineland.net

Newspaper with Democratic orientation. **Founded:** 1879. **Freq:** Weekly (Thurs.). **Print Method:** Offset. **Cols./Page:** 6. **Col. Width:** 21 nonpareils. **Col. Depth:** 294 agate lines. **Key Personnel:** Russell B. Rhoden, Editor and Publisher. **Subscription Rates:** $15.96 individuals; $24.38 others; $.50 single issue.
Ad Rates: GLR: $4.75 **Circ:** ‡3,900
BW: $500
4C: $50
PCI: $4.75

7602 Cablevision of Pembroke Inc.
Hwy. 280 W. Phone: (912)653-2668
Box 2069
Reidsville, GA 30453

Owner: J. Roger Kennedy, Jr., at above address, (912)557-4751. **Cities Served:** Ellabell, Pembroke, GA; Bryan County: subscribing households 1,083; 33 channels.

7603 Kennedy Cablevision, Inc.
Hwy. 280 W Phone: (912)557-6133
PO Box 2069 Fax: (912)557-4039
Reidsville, GA 30453

Owner: J. Roger Kennedy, Jr., at above address, (912)557-4751, Fax: (912)557-6545, Free: (800)673-7322. **Founded:** 1974. **Key Personnel:** J. Roger Kennedy, Jr., President; Donna McCumber, Office Mgr. **Cities Served:** Cobbtown, Reidsville, GA: subscribing households 1360; 41 channels.

7604 WRBX-FM - 104.1
125 Friar Tuck Cir. Phone: (912)557-3777
PO Box 69 Fax: (912)557-6956
Reidsville, GA 30453-0069
Free: (800)972-9104

Format: Southern Gospel. **Networks:** USA Radio; Ambassador Inspirational Radio. **Owner:** WRBX/WTNL, Inc., at above address. **Operating Hours:** Continuous. **Key Personnel:** Dan Brown, V. P./General Mgr.; Brenda Brown, Program Dir.; Elizabeth Hart, Account Exec. **Wattage:** 5,000.

7605 WTNL-AM - 1390
125 Friar Tuck Cir. Phone: (912)557-3777
PO Box 69 Fax: (912)557-6956
Reidsville, GA 30453-0069
Free: (800)972-9104
E-mail: wrbx@cybersouth.com

Format: Southern Gospel. **Networks:** USA Radio. **Owner:** WRBX/WTNL, Inc., at above address. **Founded:** 1976. **Operating Hours:** 6:00 a.m.-5:30 p.m. **Key Personnel:** Dan Brown, V. P./General Mgr.; Brenda Brown, Program Dir.; Elizabeth Hart, Account Exec. **Wattage:** 500.

RICHLAND, pop. 1,802.

SW GA. Stewart Co. 38 mi. SE of Columbus. Lumber mill; box factories. Pine, hardwood timber. Dairy, poultry, fruit farms. Pecans, peanuts, cotton, corn.

The Hogansville Herald - See Hogansville

7606 Manchester Star-Mercury
Rolin Press Group
PO Box 250 Phone: (912)887-3674
Richland, GA 31825 Fax: (912)887-2800

Community newspaper. **Founded:** 1911. **Freq:** Weekly (Wed.). **Print Method:** Offset. **Trim Size:** 11 1/2 x 14. **Cols./Page:** 6. **Col. Width:** 12 picas. **Col. Depth:** 21 1/2 inches. **Key Personnel:** Bob Tribble, Publisher; Mike Hale, General Mgr. **Subscription Rates:** $18 individuals; $25 out of area; $30 out of state; $0.50 single issue. **Remarks:** Accepts advertising.
Ad Rates: GLR: $.34 **Circ:** Paid ‡3,650
BW: $599.85 Free ‡26
PCI: $4.65

7607 Meriwether-Vindicator
Rolin Press Group
PO Box 250 Phone: (912)887-3674
Richland, GA 31825 Fax: (912)887-2800

Community newspaper. **Founded:** 1872. **Freq:** Weekly (Fri.). **Print Method:** Offset. **Trim Size:** 11 1/2 x 14. **Cols./Page:** 6. **Col. Width:** 12 picas. **Col. Depth:** 21 1/2 inches. **Key Personnel:** Micky D'Avy, Editor; Robert E. Tribble, Publisher; Mike Hale, General Mgr. **Subscription Rates:** $15.75 individuals; $23.63 out of area; $30 out of state; $0.35 single issue. **Remarks:** Accepts advertising.
Ad Rates: GLR: $.29 **Circ:** ‡1,700
BW: $509.55
4C: $664.40
SAU: $3.95
PCI: $3.95

Stewart-Webster Journal - See Stewart

RICHMOND HILL

7608 WRHQ-FM - 105.3
PO Box 1150 Phone: (912)234-1053
Richmond Hill, GA 31324 Fax: (912)756-4689
E-mail: qualityrockatwrhq.com

Format: Adult Contemporary. **Owner:** Thoroughbred Communications, Inc., at above address. **Founded:** 1991. **Operating Hours:** Continuous. **ADI:** Savannah, GA. **Key Personnel:** Jerry Rogers, General Mgr.; Bill Edwards; Verna Arkwood, Business Mgr. **Ad Rates:** $5-25 per unit. **URL:** http://www.wrhq.com.

RINCON

7609 The Effingham Herald
270 Coulumbia Ave. Phone: (912)826-5012
PO Box 799 Fax: (912)826-0381
Rincon, GA 31326
Publication E-mail: herald@premierweb.net

Newspaper. **Subtitle:** Effingham Herald. **Founded:** 1908. **Freq:** Weekly (Wed.). **Print Method:** Offset. **Trim Size:** 6 x 21 1/2. **Cols./Page:** 6. **Col. Width:** 26 nonpareils. **Col. Depth:** 294 agate lines. **Key Personnel:** Don Lowery, Editor; Gayle Boykin, Publisher. **Subscription Rates:** $20 individuals. **Alt. Formats:** CD-ROM. **Formerly**: Herald.
Ad Rates: GLR: $.28 **Circ:** 5,300
BW: $806.25
4C: $956.25
SAU: $6.25
PCI: $6.25

RINGGOLD

7610 Catoosa County News
7513 Nashville St. Phone: (404)935-2621
PO Box 40 Fax: (404)965-5934
Ringgold, GA 30736
Publication E-mail: ccnnews@aol.com

Community newspaper. **Founded:** 1949. **Freq:** Weekly (Wed.). **Print Method:** Offset. **Cols./Page:** 6. **Col. Width:** 2 inches. **Col. Depth:** 21 inches. **Key Personnel:** Richard L. Ball, Editor; Burgett Mooney III, Publisher. **Subscription Rates:** $14 individuals; $22 out of area; $.50 single issue.
Ad Rates: BW: $478.13 **Circ:** 4,700
4C: $803.13
SAU: $4.20
PCI: $6.00

ROBERTA, pop. 859.

C. GA. Crawford Co. 22 mi. WSW of Macon. Sawmills.

7611 The Georgia Post
PO Box 860 Phone: (912)836-3195
Roberta, GA 31078
Community newspaper. **Founded:** Feb. 6, 1921. **Freq:** Weekly. **Print Method:** Letterpress. **Trim Size:** 13 1/8 x 21 1/2. **Cols./Page:** 6. **Col. Width:** 2 inches. **Col. Depth:** 21.5 inches. **Key Personnel:** Floyd M. Buford, Jr., Publisher; Celia Martin, Office Mgr. **Subscription Rates:** $10.60 individuals; $15.90 out of area.
Ad Rates: BW: $322.50 **Circ:** Paid 1,850
PCI: $3.75 Free 3

ROCHELLE

7612 WMCG-FM - 104.9
Box 1060 Phone: (912)365-7788
Rochelle, GA 31079 Fax: (912)365-7799

Format: Country. **Networks:** ABC. **Owner:** Tel-Dodge Broadcasting Co., at above address. **Founded:** 1982. **Operating Hours:** Continuous; 90% local. **ADI:** Macon, GA. **Key Personnel:** Ted White, Gen. Mgr./Operations Dir. **Local Programs:** *MRN NASCAR Races*; *Paul Harvey*. **Wattage:** 50,000. **Ad Rates:** $3-8.50 for 30 seconds; $3.63-11.50 for 60 seconds.

ROCKDALE

7613 Rockdale Neighbor
Neighbor Newspapers, Inc.
580 Fairground St. Phone: (770)428-9411
PO Box 449 Fax: (770)428-7945
Marietta, GA 30060
Community newspaper. **Founded:** 1980. **Freq:** Weekly (Thurs.). **Print Method:** Offset. **Cols./Page:** 6. **Col. Width:** 26 nonpareils. **Col. Depth:** 301 agate lines. **Key Personnel:** Otis A. Brumby, Jr., Publisher. **USPS:** 525-510. **Subscription Rates:** $12 individuals; $18 out of area; $24 out of state.
Ad Rates: GLR: $.68 **Circ:** Non-paid 14,433
BW: $1,225.50
4C: $1,515.50
SAU: $9.50

ROCKMART

NW GA. Polk Co. 10 mi. E. of Cedartown.

7614 Rockmart Journal
News Publishing Co.
240 S. Piedmont Ave. Phone: (770)684-7811
Rockmart, GA 30153
Community newspaper. **Founded:** 1920. **Freq:** Weekly. **Print Method:** Offset. **Trim Size:** 13 3/4 x 21 1/4. **Cols./Page:** 6. **Col. Width:** 2 1/16 inches. **Col. Depth:** 21 1/4 inches. **Key Personnel:** J.A. Thaxton, Editor. **Subscription Rates:** $14 individuals; $22 out of county.
Ad Rates: GLR: $6.50 **Circ:** Paid ‡3,382
BW: $828.75
4C: $1,078.75
SAU: $4.50
PCI: $6.50

7615 WZOT-AM - 1220
Box 527 Phone: (770)684-7848
Rockmart, GA 30153-0527 Fax: (404)684-7848

Format: Gospel. **Networks:** NBC. **Owner:** Broadcast Investment Associates, Inc., at above address. **Formerly:** WPLK-AM (1990). **Operating Hours:** 6 a.m.-8 p.m.; 10% network, 90% local. **Key Personnel:** Ned Ingle, Manager. **Wattage:** 500. **Ad Rates:** $5.25-8 for 30 seconds; $6.75-10 for 60 seconds.

ROME†, pop. 29,654.

NW GA. Floyd Co. On Coosa River, 68 mi. NW of Atlanta. Museums, Berry Waterwheel. Shorter College; Floyd Junior College; Berry College. Pine, hardwood timber; stone quarry. Manufactures tiles, plastic products, cotton textiles, steel wire, furniture, woodwork, fertilizer, flour, valves, hand trucks, aluminum die casting, lumber, boxes, paper, paper products, transformers, carpets, carpet yarn. Agriculture.

7616 Campus Carrier
Berry College
520 Mt. Berry Sta. Phone: (706)236-2294
Mount Berry, GA 30149-0520 Fax: (706)236-2248
Publication E-mail: campus_ carrier@loki.berry.edu

Collegiate newspaper. **Founded:** 1913. **Freq:** Weekly. **Print Method:** Offset. **Trim Size:** 13 7/8 x 11 3/8. **Cols./Page:** 5. **Col. Width:** 11 1/2 picas. **Col. Depth:** 72 picas. **Key Personnel:** Kristen Hill, Editor, khill@lokiberry.edu; Julie Yamamoto, Advertising Mgr., jyamamoto@hotmail.com; Kevin Kleine, Adviser, phone (706)236-7871, kkleine@berry.edu. **Subscription Rates:** Free yearly; $20 by mail. **Remarks:** Accepts advertising.
Ad Rates: BW: $300 **Circ:** Paid 100
4C: $600 Free 1,900
PCI: $8.05

7617 Rome News-Tribune
News Publishing Co.
PO Box 1633 Phone: (706)290-5330
Rome, GA 30162-1633 Fax: (706)232-9632

General newspaper. **Founded:** 1843. **Freq:** Daily (eve.). **Print Method:** Offset. **Trim Size:** 13 3/4 x 22 3/4. **Cols./Page:** 6. **Col. Width:** 2 1/16 inches. **Col. Depth:** 21 1/4 inches. **Key Personnel:** B.H. Mooney III, Publisher, phone (706)290-5290; Gayle Touchstone, Advertising Dir., phone (706)290-5216. **USPS:** 470-320. **Subscription Rates:** $94.80 individuals. **Remarks:** Accepts advertising.
Ad Rates: GLR: $1.20 **Circ:** Mon.-Sat. ★**20,363**
BW: $2,139.45 Sun. ★**20,004**
4C: $2,464.45
SAU: $16.78
PCI: $19.33

7618 WKCX-FM - 97.7
710 Turner-McCall Blvd. Phone: (706)291-9766
Rome, GA 30161 Fax: (706)291-9706
E-mail: k98radio@aol.com

Format: Adult Contemporary. **Networks:** Mutual Broadcasting System. **Owner:** Briar Creek Broadcasting Corp., at above address. **Founded:** 1966. **Operating Hours:** Continuous. **ADI:** Atlanta (Athens & Rome), GA. **Key Personnel:** Mills Fitzner, General Mgr. **Wattage:** 25,000 ERP.

7619 WLAQ-AM - 1410
2 Mt. Alto Rd. Phone: (706)232-7767
Rome, GA 30165 Fax: (706)295-9225

Format: News; Talk; Sports. **Networks:** CBS. **Owner:** Cripple Creek Broadcasting Co., at above address. **Founded:** 1947. **Operating Hours:** 5 a.m.-1 a.m. Mon-Fri; 6 a.m.-midnight Sun. **ADI:** Atlanta (Athens & Rome), GA. **Key Personnel:** Randy Davis, General Mgr.; Sandy Davis, Vice President; Ina Carver, Contact; Jim Bojo, Sales Mgr.; Tony Lambert, Program Dir. **Wattage:** 1000. **Ad Rates:** $4.75-5.25 for 15 seconds; $7.50-12 for 30 seconds; $8.50-13 for 60 seconds.

7620 WQTU-FM - 102.3
Broadcast Center Phone: (706)295-1023
104 E. 6th Ave. Fax: (706)291-7155
PO Box 1187
Rome, GA 30162
E-mail: info@wqtu.ga.net

Format: Adult Contemporary. **Networks:** Independent. **Owner:** McDougald Broadcasting Corp., at above address. **Founded:** 1946. **Formerly:** WRGA-FM (1977). **Operating Hours:** Continuous; 100% local. **ADI:** Atlanta (Athens & Rome), GA. **Key Personnel:** Michael H. McDougald, GM/CEO; Randy Quick, Operations Dir. **Local Programs:** *Seventies Superset* 5 p.m.-6 p.m. Monday-Friday; *Shannon & Company Show* 6 a.m. - 10 a.m. Monday-Saturday. **Wattage:** 6000. **Ad Rates:** $16-18 for 30 seconds; $18-20 for 60 seconds. **URL:** http://www.com/centurion.

7621 WRGA-AM - 1470
Broadcast Center Phone: (706)291-9742
104 E. 6th Ave. Fax: (706)291-7155
PO Box 1187
Rome, GA 30162
E-mail: info@wrga.ga.net

Format: News; Talk. **Networks:** ABC; CNN Radio; AP. **Owner:** McDougald Broadcasting Corp., at above address. **Founded:** 1929. **Formerly:** WFDV-AM (1931). **Operating Hours:** Continuous; 5% network, 95% local. **ADI:** Atlanta (Athens & Rome), GA. **Key Personnel:** Michael H. McDougald, GM/CEO; Randy Quick, Operations Dir. **Wattage:** 5000. **Ad Rates:** $16-18 for 30 seconds; $18-20 for 60 seconds. **URL:** http://www.com/centurion.

7622 WROM-AM - 710
1105 Calhoun Ave. Phone: (706)234-7171
PO Box 5031 Fax: (706)234-8043
Rome, GA 30162-5031

Format: Religious; Southern Gospel. **Owner:** LGV Broadcasting, Inc., at above address. **Founded:** 1946. **Operating Hours:** Sunrise-sunset. **ADI:** Atlanta (Athens & Rome), GA. **Key Personnel:** Mark Lumpkin, General Mgr.; Robert Vines, Station Mgr.; Alton Stamey, Sales Mgr. **Local Programs:** *Morning Show*. **Wattage:** 1000. **Ad Rates:** $7.50-8 for 30 seconds; $9-10 for 60 seconds.

7623 WTSH-AM - 1360
PO Box 6008 Phone: (706)291-9496
Rome, GA 30162 Fax: (706)235-7107
E-mail: south107@aol.com

Format: Gospel. **Simulcasts:** WTSH-FM. **Networks:** NBC; Unistar. **Founded:** 1964. **Formerly:** WIYN-AM (1988). **Operating Hours:** 6 a.m.-6 p.m.; 20% network; 80% local. **ADI:** Atlanta (Athens & Rome), GA. **Key Personnel:** Kris Cantrell, General Mgr.; Cheryl Scott, Office Mgr. **Wattage:** 500. **Ad Rates:** $8 for 30 seconds; $10 for 60 seconds.

7624 WTSH-FM - 107.1
PO Box 6008 Phone: (706)291-9496
Rome, GA 30162 Fax: (706)235-7107
E-mail: south107@aol.com

Format: Country. **Networks:** Unistar. **Owner:** Broadcast Investment Associates, Inc., at above address, (706)291-9196, Fax: (706)235-7107. **Founded:** 1962. **Formerly:** WIYN-FM. **Operating Hours:** Continuous. **ADI:** Atlanta (Athens & Rome), GA. **Key Personnel:** Paul J. Stone, President; Kris Cantrell, General Mgr. **Wattage:** 50,000. **Ad Rates:** $25-60 for 30 seconds; $35-65 for 60 seconds.

ROSSVILLE

7625 WSDT-AM - 1240
215 W. Gordon Ave.
Rossville, GA 30741-1260

Format: Country; Contemporary Country. **Networks:** ABC. **Founded:** 1970. **Operating Hours:** 5:30 a.m.-10 p.m. **Key Personnel:** Roberta Davis, Contact; Darrell Clark, Contact. **Wattage:** 100,000.

ROSWELL

Alpharetta Neighbor - See Alpharetta

7626 The Atlanta Tribune
L & L Communications, Inc.
875 Old Roswell Rd., Ste. C-100 Phone: (770)587-0501
Fax: (770)642-6501
Roswell, GA 30076
Publication E-mail: tribune@mindspring.com

Minority business newsmagazine. **Founded:** 1986. **Freq:** Monthly. **Print Method:** Web offset. **Trim Size:** 9 13/16 x 13 7/8. **Cols./Page:** 4. **Col. Width:** 2 5/16 inches. **Col. Depth:** 13 inches. **Key Personnel:** Rick Sherrell, Managing Editor, rsherrell@mindspring.com; Patricia Lottier, Publisher, plottier@mindspring.com. **Subscription Rates:** $24 individuals. **Remarks:** Accepts advertising. **URL:** www:/atlantatribune.com; http://www.mindspring.com. **Alt. Formats:** Microform.
Ad Rates: GLR: $66 **Circ:** Paid ‡22,000
BW: $1922 Non-paid ‡10,000
4C: $2572
PCI: $66

7627 Over the Road
RAM Publishing Group
610 Colonial Park Dr. Phone: (404)587-0311
Roswell, GA 30075-3746 Fax: (404)642-8874
Free: (800)878-0311

Magazine for the trucking industry. **Founded:** 1981. **Freq:** Monthly. **Subscription Rates:** Free to qualified subscribers.
Circ: Paid 131
Non-paid 74,293

7628 Pondscapes Magazine
Happy Pondering
3933 Loch Highland Pass Phone: (770)643-0112
Roswell, GA 30075 Fax: (770)643-0712
Free: (800)742-4701
Publication E-mail: nps@pondscapes.com
Publisher E-mail: ponds@bellsouth.net

Consumer magazine. **Subtitle:** A Practical Guide To Successful Pond Keeping. **Founded:** 1989. **Freq:** 6/year. **Print Method:** Offset. **Trim Size:** 7 x 8 1/2. **Cols./Page:** 2. **Col. Width:** 3 inches. **Col. Depth:** 8 inches. **Key Personnel:** Alan Sperling, Editor and Publisher. **ISSN:** 1060-9644. **Subscription Rates:** $24 individuals. **Remarks:** Accepts advertising. **URL:** http://www.pondscapes.com. **Alt. Formats:** Fax on demand.
Ad Rates: BW: $5 **Circ:** Paid 8,000
4C: $1,225 Controlled 3,000
CNU: $850
PCI: $1,200

7629 Pro Trucker
Ramp Publishing Group
610 Colonial Park Dr. Phone: (404)587-0311
Roswell, GA 30075-3746 Fax: (404)642-8874

Trucking industry magazine. **Founded:** 1988. **Freq:** Monthly. **Print Method:** Web offset. **Trim Size:** 5 3/8 x 8 3/8. **Cols./Page:** 2. **Col. Width:** 2 1/4 inches. **Col. Depth:** 7 1/2 inches. **Key Personnel:** Carol Prins, Editor; Marvin Shefsky, Publisher; Gary L. Kelley, Advertising Mgr.; Lacic Turner, Circulation Mgr. **Subscription Rates:** $40. **Remarks:** Accepts advertising.
Ad Rates: BW: $3,495 **Circ:** Paid 126
4C: $3,595 Non-paid 74,222

ROYSTON, pop. 2,404.

NE GA. Franklin, Hart, and Madison Co. 9 mi. S. of Carnesville.

7630 The News Leader
PO Box 26 Phone: (706)245-7351
Royston, GA 30662-0006 Fax: (706)245-5991

Local newspaper. **Founded:** 1978. **Freq:** Weekly (Thurs.). **Print Method:** Offset. Uses mats. **Cols./Page:** 6. **Col. Width:** 25 nonpareils. **Col. Depth:** 298 agate lines. **Key Personnel:** Joe Edwards, Editor; Peggy Vickery, Publisher. **Subscription Rates:** $13 annually.
Ad Rates: BW: $439.89 **Circ:** ‡3,300
4C: $584.50
SAU: $3.41

7631 WBIC-AM - 810
259 Turner St. Phone: (706)245-6101
Royston, GA 30662 Fax: (706)245-9571
Free: (800)736-1039

Format: Religious; Southern Gospel. **Networks:** Georgia Radio; NBC. **Owner:** Southern Broadcasting of Athens, at above address, Free: (800)736-1037. **Founded:** 1970. **Formerly:** WBLW-AM (1990). **Operating Hours:** Sunrise-sunset; 25% network, 75% local. **Key Personnel:** Don Nestor, Program Dir./General Mgr.; Frank Mosley, Music Dir.; Darlene Nixon, Sales Mgr./News Dir.; Dan Davis, Chief Engineer. **Wattage:** 250. **Ad Rates:** $5 for 30 seconds; $7 for 60 seconds.

ST. MARYS

7632 Camden County Tribune & Georgian
Community Newspapers Inc.
707 Osborne St. Phone: (912)882-4927
Box 470 Fax: (912)882-6519
St. Marys, GA 31558
Publisher E-mail: ccnews@eagnet.com

Newspaper with no political orientation. **Founded:** 1950. **Freq:** Biweekly. **Print Method:** Offset. **Cols./Page:** 6. **Col. Width:** 12.5 picas. **Col. Depth:** 21 1/2 inches. **Key Personnel:** Linn Hudson, Publisher. **USPS:** 083-64. **Subscription Rates:** $20 local; $30 out of area state; $30 out of state. **Remarks:** Accepts advertising. **Formerly:** Camden County Tribune.
Ad Rates: GLR: $7.25 **Circ:** ‡7,500
BW: $935.25
4C: $1110.25
SAU: $7.25
PCI: $7.25

7633 WECC-AM - 1190
2101 Hwy. 40 E. Phone: (912)882-1190
PO Box 1190 Fax: (912)882-9322
St. Marys, GA 31558
Free: (800)577-9322
E-mail: wecc@weccradio.org

Format: Religious; Contemporary Christian. **Networks:** USA Radio. **Owner:** Lighthouse Christian Broadcasting Corp., at above address. **Founded:** 1985. **Operating Hours:** Sunrise-sunset. **ADI:** Jacksonville (Brunswick), FL. **Key Personnel:** Paul Hafer, General Mgr.; Vickie Hafer, General Mgr. **Wattage:** 2500. **URL:** www.gnatnet.net/@tldwecc1.

ST. SIMONS ISLAND, pop. 6,600.

E. GA. Glynn Co. Island off E. coast of Glynn Co.

7634 The Islander
PO Box 20539 Phone: (912)265-9654
St. Simons Island, GA 31522 Fax: (912)265-3699

Local newspaper (tabloid). **Founded:** Sept. 1972. **Freq:** Weekly. **Print Method:** Offset. **Trim Size:** 10 x 13. **Cols./Page:** 4. **Col. Width:** 2 inches. **Col. Depth:** 13 inches. **Key Personnel:** E.J. Permar, Publisher; M.J. Permar, Editor; P.P. Shierling, Assoc. Editor. **Subscription Rates:** $14.50 individuals; $16.50 out of area.
Ad Rates: BW: $285 **Circ:** 4,000
4C: $470
PCI: $5.91

SANDERSVILLE†.

EC GA. Washington Co. 45 mi. NE of Macon.

7635 Sandersville Progress
Unipress
118 E. Haynes St. Phone: (912)552-3161
PO Box 431 Fax: (912)552-5177
Sandersville, GA 31082-0431
Community newspaper. **Founded:** 1887. **Freq:** Weekly (Wed.). **Print Method:** Offset. **Trim Size:** 14 1/2 x 21 1/2. **Cols./Page:** 6. **Col. Width:** 10 1/2 picas. **Col. Depth:** 21 inches. **Key Personnel:** Robert Garrett, Editor; Bob Tribble, Publisher. **Subscription Rates:** $19.08; $26.50 out of area; $30 out of state. **Remarks:** Accepts advertising.
Ad Rates: BW: $516 **Circ:** 5,300
4C: $636
SAU: $4
PCI: $4

7636 The Wrightsville Headlight
The Sandersville Georgian, Inc.
PO Box 431 Phone: (912)552-3161
Sandersville, GA 31082 Fax: (912)552-5777

Community newspaper. **Founded:** 1880. **Freq:** Weekly (Thurs.). **Print Method:** Offset. **Cols./Page:** 6. **Col. Width:** 12 picas. **Col. Depth:** 280 agate lines. **Key Personnel:** Bobby Garrett, General Mgr. **Subscription Rates:** $15.90 individuals; $29.85 in state; $30 out of state. **Remarks:** Accepts advertising.
Ad Rates: GLR: $.14 **Circ:** ‡2,200
BW: $387
4C: $507
SAU: $3.75
PCI: $3.75

7637 WSNT-AM - 1490
PO Box 150 Phone: (912)552-5182
Sandersville, GA 31082 Fax: (912)553-0800
E-mail: waco100@accucomm.net

Format: Urban Contemporary. **Networks:** ABC. **Owner:** WSNT, Inc., at above address. **Founded:** 1956. **Operating Hours:** Continuous, 90% network, 10% local. **ADI:** Macon, GA. **Key Personnel:** Barry Stewart, Station Mgr.; Curtis Parsons, Sports Dir.; Curtis Parsons, News Dir.; Capers Brazzell, Sales Dir./Gen. Mgr.; Sunshine Anglin, Production/Public Service Dir. **Wattage:** 1000. **Ad Rates:** $5-10 for 30 seconds; $7.50-12.50 for 60 seconds. WSNT-FM.

7638 WSNT-FM - 99.9
PO Box 150 Phone: (912)552-5182
Sandersville, GA 31082 Fax: (912)553-0800
E-mail: waco100@accucomm.net

Format: Country. **Networks:** ABC. **Owner:** WSNT, Inc., at above address. **Founded:** 1975. **Operating Hours:** Continuous; 90% network, 10% local. **ADI:** Macon, GA. **Key Personnel:** Curt Parsons, News Dir.; Barry Stewart, Station Mgr.; Capers Brazzell, General Mgr.; Sunshine Anglin, Prod./Public Service Dir. **Wattage:** 6000. **Ad Rates:** $10-20 for 30 seconds; $15-25 for 60 seconds. CBR WSNT-AM.

SAVANNAH†, pop. 141,634.

SE GA. Chatham Co. On Savannah River, 18 mi. from Atlantic Ocean, 254 mi. SE of Atlanta. Port of entry. Armstrong State College; Savannah State College; Savannah College of Art and Design. Resort. Restored historic district. Shipyards. Fisheries. Timber. Cotton and naval stores market. Manufactures airplanes, injection molded plastics, plywood, sugar, table top conveyors, lumber, fertilizer, paper bags, cottonseed products, roofing metal, steel products, fuel oil, paint, rosin oils, burlap and bagging, asphalt, wire fencing, gypsum products.

7639 Contents
PO Box 8879
Savannah, GA 31412

Magazine covering art, design, literature and music. **Key Personnel:** Joseph Alfieris, Creative Dir. **Subscription Rates:** $20 annual.
Circ: (Not Reported)

7640 The Herald
1803 Barnard St. Phone: (912)232-4505
PO Box 486 Fax: (912)232-4079
Savannah, GA 31401-8022
Black community newspaper. **Founded:** 1945. **Freq:** Weekly (Wed.). **Print Method:** Offset. **Cols./Page:** 5. **Col. Width:** 11 picas. **Col. Depth:** 14 inches. **Key Personnel:** Floyd Adams, Editor and Publisher. **Subscription Rates:** $15.90 individuals. **Remarks:** Accepts advertising.
Ad Rates: GLR: $.40 **Circ:** 8,000
BW: $392
4C: $617
PCI: $7

7641 Rodale's SCUBA Diving
Rodale Books
6600 Abercorn St., Ste. 208 Phone: (912)351-0855
Savannah, GA 31405-5840 Fax: (912)351-0890
Publisher E-mail: ddonche1@rodalepress.com

Magazine on scuba diving. **Subtitle:** The Magazine Divers Trust. **Founded:** Apr. 1992. **Freq:** 9/year. **Print Method:** Offset. **Trim Size:** 8 1/8 x 10 7/8. **Cols./Page:** 3. **Key Personnel:** Dave McAfee, Publisher; Dane Farnum, Advertising Dir. **Remarks:** Accepts advertising. **Formerly:** California Diver (1988); Pacific Diver.
Circ: Paid ★145,481
Non-paid ★39,546

7642 Savannah Business Journal
6203 Abercorn St., Ste. 103E Phone: (912)233-5711
Savannah, GA 31405
Business journal. **Founded:** Mar. 1990. **Freq:** Monthly. **Print Method:** Web offset. **Trim Size:** 11 1/2 x 15. **Cols./Page:** 4. **Col. Width:** 2 3/8 inches. **Col. Depth:** 13 inches. **Key Personnel:** Donald R. Blum, Editor and Publisher, phone (912)354-5553, fax (912)354-5558. **Subscription Rates:** $15 individuals. **Remarks:** Accepts advertising. **URL:** http://www.biztrac.com/sbj.
Ad Rates: BW: $700 **Circ:** Paid ⊕100
4C: $1,300 Non-paid ⊕5,300

7643 Savannah Jewish News
Savannah Jewish Federation
PO Box 23527 Phone: (912)355-8111
Savannah, GA 31403-3527 Fax: (912)355-8116

Jewish newspaper covering local, national, and world news. **Founded:** Mar. 1949. **Freq:** 10/year. **Print Method:** Offset. **Trim Size:** 10 x 14. **Cols./Page:** 4. **Col. Width:** 14 picas. **Col. Depth:** 12 3/4 agate lines. **Key Personnel:** Midge Lasky Schildkraut, Editor, phone (912)692-2587, fax (912)692-2039. **Subscription Rates:** Free. **Remarks:** Accepts advertising.
Ad Rates: BW: $600 **Circ:** ‡1,700
SAU: $18

7644 Savannah Morning News
PO Box 1088 Phone: (912)236-9511
Savannah, GA 31402-1088 Fax: (912)234-6522
Free: (800)533-1150
Publication E-mail: letted@savannahnow.com

General newspaper. **Founded:** 1850. **Freq:** Mon.-Sun. (morn.). **Print Method:** Offset. **Cols./Page:** 6. **Col. Width:** 24 nonpareils. **Col. Depth:** 301 agate lines. **Key Personnel:** Frank Anderson, Publisher, phone (912)652-0265; Tom Barton, Editor, phone (912)652-0300, fax (912)234-6522; Donald Bailey, Advertising Dir., phone (912)652-0238, fax (912)652-0260. **Subscription Rates:** $148 individuals. **Remarks:** Accepts advertising. **URL:** http://www.savannahnow.com.
Ad Rates: PCI: $39.05 **Circ:** Mon.-Fri. ‡67,351
Sat. ‡70,594
Sun. ‡77,070

7645 Savannah Pennysaver
Morris Newspaper Corp.
PO Box 5100 Phone: (912)238-2040
Savannah, GA 31414-5100 Fax: (912)238-2141
Free: (800)643-1468

Shopper (tabloid), issued in three editions. **Founded:** Aug. 1984. **Freq:** Weekly (Wed.). **Print Method:** Offset. **Trim Size:** 10 1/4 x 13. **Cols./Page:** 6. **Col. Width:** 20 nonpareils. **Col. Depth:** 182 agate lines. **Key Personnel:** Steve Hartley, General Mgr. **Subscription Rates:** Free. **Remarks:** Accepts advertising. **URL:** http://www.savpennysaver.com.
Ad Rates: GLR: $.82 **Circ:** Free ‡81,500
BW: $1,092
4C: $1,259
PCI: $14

7646 The Savannah Tribune
Savannah Tribune, Inc.
916 Montgomery St. Phone: (912)233-6128
PO Box 2066 Fax: (912)233-6140
Savannah, GA 31402
Black community newspaper. **Founded:** 1875. **Freq:** Weekly (Wed.). **Print Method:** Offset. **Trim Size:** 13 x 21 1/2. **Cols./Page:** 6. **Col. Width:** 2 inches. **Col. Depth:** 21 1/2 inches. **Key Personnel:** Shirley B. James, Editor and Publisher. **ISSN:** 1086-2285. **Subscription Rates:** $28 individuals; $30 out of area. **Remarks:** Accepts advertising.
Ad Rates: GLR: $.86 **Circ:** Paid ‡8,000
PCI: $15 Free ‡8,000

7647 Jones Communications
5515 Abercorn St. Phone: (912)354-2813
Box 22907 Fax: (912)353-6045
Savannah, GA 31405

Owner: Jones Intercable, 9697 E. Mineral Ave., PO Box 3309, Englewood, CO 80155-3309, (303)792-3111. **Founded:** 1965. **Formerly:** Savannah TV Cable (1984); Cablevision of Savannah (1996). **Key Personnel:** Tom Autry, General Mgr.; Kurt Decker, Operations Mgr.; Sherry Walden, Marketing Mgr.; Mark Dunn, Business Mgr.; Tia Schoen, Advertising Sales Mgr.; Wayne Nix, Local Origination Mgr. **Cities Served:** Bloomingdale, Garden City, Midway, Pooler, Port Wentworth, Rincon, Springfield, Thunderbolt, Vernonburg, GA; Brunson, Varnville, SC; Bryan County, Chatham County, Effingham County, and Liberty C ounty, GA; and Hampton County, SC.: subscribing households 66,000; 46 channels.

7648 U.S. Cable Coastal Properties
416 Landings Way Phone: (912)598-1381
Savannah, GA 31411 Fax: (912)758-3701

Owner: US Cable Coastal Properties, 28 W. Grand Ave., Montvale, NJ 07645, (201)930-9000. **Founded:** 1978. **Formerly:** Skidaway Cable TV (1992); US Cable TV. **Key Personnel:** Randall S. Houser, Contact. **Cities Served:** subscribing households 2,185; 35 channels.

7649 WAEV-FM - 97.3
24 W. Henry St. Phone: (912)232-0097
Savannah, GA 31401 Fax: (912)232-6144

Format: Adult Contemporary. **Networks:** Unistar. **Owner:** Patterson/Capstar Broadcasting, at above address. **Operating Hours:** Continuous; 1% network, 99% local. **ADI:** Savannah, GA. **Key Personnel:** Dennis Jones, General and National Sales; Jerry Stevens, General Sales Mgr.; Walt Boston, Business Mgr.; Scotty Snipes, Program Dir./Operations Mgr. **Wattage:** 100,000. **Ad Rates:** $30-70 per unit.

7650 WBMQ-AM - 630
PO Box 876 Phone: (912)897-1529
Savannah, GA 31498-6901 Fax: (912)897-9795

Format: Talk; Sports; Oldies. **Networks:** CBS. **Founded:** 1939. **Formerly:** WKBX-AM. **Operating Hours:** Continuous. **ADI:** Savannah, GA. **Key Personnel:** John Ade, General Mgr.; Doc Washburn, Program Dir. **Local Programs:** *Open-Line Savannah*, Doc Washburn. **Wattage:** 5000. **Ad Rates:** $7-12 for 30 seconds; $9-16 for 60 seconds.

7651 WCHY-AM - 1290
PO Box 1247 Phone: (912)964-7794
Savannah, GA 31402-1247 Fax: (912)964-9414

Format: Contemporary Country. **Networks:** ABC. **Owner:** Roth Communications, 830 Main St., Melrose, MA 02176, (617)662-4800. **Founded:** 1929. **Operating Hours:** Continuous; 1% network, 99% local. **ADI:** Savannah, GA. **Key Personnel:** Dennis Jones, General Mgr.; Bill West, Sales Mgr.; Dean McNeil, Program Dir. **Wattage:** 5000.

7652 WCHY-FM - 94.1
PO Box 1247 Phone: (912)964-7794
Savannah, GA 31402-1247 Fax: (912)964-9414

Format: Contemporary Country. **Networks:** ABC. **Owner:** Roth Communications, Inc., 830 Main St., Melrose, MA 02176. **Founded:** 1946. **Operating Hours:** Continuous. **ADI:** Savannah, GA. **Key Personnel:** Dennis Jones, General Mgr.; Bill West, Sales Mgr.; Dean McNeil, Program Dir. **Wattage:** 100,000. **Ad Rates:** $18-53 for 30 seconds; $22-64 for 60 seconds.

7653 WEAS-AM - 900
2515 Abercorn St. Phone: (912)234-7264
Savannah, GA 31401 Fax: (912)233-7247
E-mail: thefan@weas.com

Format: Sports; Talk. **Networks:** CBS; ESPN Radio; ABC. **Founded:** 1950. **Operating Hours:** Continuous. **ADI:** Savannah, GA. **Key Personnel:** M.B. Rivers, President; Rick Whitson, General Mgr.; Ray Williams, OPS MGR. **Wattage:** 5000 day; 157 night. **Ad Rates:** $7-10 for 30 seconds; $9-12 for 60 seconds. **URL:** http://www.weas.com.

7654 WGCO-FM - 98.3
401 Mall Blvd., Ste. 201-F Phone: (912)351-9830
Savannah, GA 31406 Fax: (912)352-4821

Format: Oldies. **Founded:** 1973. **Formerly:** WSKS-FM (1974). **Operating Hours:** Continuous. **ADI:** Savannah, GA. **Key Personnel:** Jet Angel, General Mgr. **Wattage:** 100,000. **Ad Rates:** $30-50 for 30 seconds; $30-50 for 60 seconds.

7655 WHCJ-FM - 90.3
Box 20484 Phone: (912)356-2399
Savannah, GA 31402-9716 Fax: (912)356-2996

Format: Jazz; Gospel; Blues. **Founded:** 1975. **Operating Hours:** 8 a.m.-midnight Mon,Tu.,Th.,Sat.& Sun.; 8-1a.m. Wed.;8-2a.m.Fri. **ADI:** Savannah, GA. **Key Personnel:** Theron Cotter, General Mgr. **Wattage:** 6000.

7656 WIXV-FM - 95.5
PO Box 876 Phone: (912)897-1529
Savannah, GA 31498 Fax: (912)897-4047

Format: Album-Oriented Rock (AOR). **Networks:** Independent. **Owner:** Radio Southeast, at above address. **Founded:** 1972. **Formerly:** WSGF-FM. **Operating Hours:** Continuous; 100% local. **ADI:** Savannah, GA. **Key Personnel:** John Ade, General Mgr.; Mark Blake, Program Dir.; Jay Sinclair, Music Dir. **Wattage:** 100,000. **Ad Rates:** $40-55 per unit.

7657 WJCL-FM - 96.5
PO Box 60789 Phone: (912)921-0965
Savannah, GA 31420 Fax: (912)921-2218
Free: (800)365-0549
E-mail: kix96@wce.com

Format: Country; Hot Country. **Owner:** Cumulus Broadcasting, at above address. **Founded:** 1972. **Operating Hours:** Continuous. **ADI:** Savannah, GA. **Key Personnel:** Raleigh Neal, Station Mgr. **Wattage:** 100,000. **Ad Rates:** $16-50 for 30 seconds; $18-55 for 60 seconds. **URL:** http://www.kix965.com.

7658 WJCL-TV - 22
10001 Avacorn St. Phone: (912)925-0022
Savannah, GA 31406 Fax: (912)925-8621
Free: (800)365-0549

Format: Commercial TV. **Networks:** ABC. **Founded:** 1970. **Operating Hours:** 5 a.m.-2 a.m. **ADI:** Savannah, GA. **Key Personnel:** Fred Pierce, Contact.

7659 WNMT-AM - 1520
217 E. 65th St. Phone: (912)354-4601
Savannah, GA 31405-5308

Format: Country. **Networks:** Georgia Radio. **Owner:** Chris Watkins, at above address. **Founded:** 1968. **Operating Hours:** 14 hrs. Daily; 15% network, 85% local. **ADI:** Savannah, GA. **Wattage:** 1000. **Ad Rates:** $5-15 per unit.

7660 WSAV-TV - 3
1430 E. Victory Dr. Phone: (912)651-0300
PO Box 2429 Fax: (912)651-0304
Savannah, GA 31404
Free: (800)289-WSAV
E-mail: wsav@ix.netcom.com

Format: Commercial TV. **Networks:** NBC. **Owner:** Raycom Media, Inc., One Buckhead Plz., 3060 Peachtree Rd., Ste. 340, Atlanta, GA 30305, (404)240-0924, Fax: (404)240-0542. **Founded:** 1956. **Operating Hours:** Continuous. **ADI:** Savannah, GA. **Key Personnel:** Stan Crumley, Vice President; Ron Kelly, General Sales Mgr., fax (912)236-0712; David Stagnitto, Operations Mgr.; Dan Kurtz, Promotions Mgr.; Michael Sullivan, News Dir., fax (912)651-0320; Lucie Giles, Business Mgr., fax (912)236-0712. **URL:** http://www.wsav.com.

7661 WSOK-AM - 1230
PO Box 727 Phone: (912)232-3322
Savannah, GA 31402-0727 Fax: (912)232-6144

Format: Religious. **Networks:** American Urban Radio; American Urban Radio; ABC. **Owner:** Opus Media Group, 210 University Dr., Ste. 303, Coral Springs, FL 33071. **Operating Hours:** Continuous; 16% network, 84% local. **ADI:** Savannah, GA. **Key Personnel:** Daniel Gorby, General Mgr.; Jay Bryant, Operations Mgr.; Paige Grady, General Sales Mgr. **Wattage:** 1000. **Ad Rates:** $25-44 for 30 seconds.

7662 WTGS-TV - 28
214 Television Cir. Phone: (912)925-2287
Savannah, GA 31406 Fax: (912)925-7026

Format: Commercial TV. **Networks:** Fox; Independent. **Operating Hours:** Continuous. **ADI:** Savannah, GA. **Key Personnel:** Sherry Fowler, General Mgr.; Patrick Picone, Program Dir.

7663 WTOC-TV - 11
PO Box 8086 Phone: (912)234-1111
Savannah, GA 31412 Fax: (912)238-5133

Format: Commercial TV. **Networks:** CBS. **Founded:** 1954. **Operating Hours:** Continuous. **ADI:** Savannah, GA. **Key Personnel:** William Cathcart, General Mgr.; Tricia Thurman, Business Mgr.

SCOTTDALE

7664 WATB-AM - 1240
3589 N. Decatur Rd.
Scottdale, GA 30079

Owner: Freedom Network, at above address.

SMYRNA

7665 Georgia Food Connection
Georgia Food Industry Association
1260 Winchester Pkwy., Ste. 216 Phone: (770)438-7744
Smyrna, GA 30080 Fax: (770)438-7761
Trade magazine covering food industry issues for members. **Freq:** Annual. **Key Personnel:** Nancy Pruitt, Advertising. **Subscription Rates:** Free to qualified subscribers.

7666 The Smyrna Neighbor
Neighbor Newspapers, Inc.
580 Fairground St. Phone: (770)428-9411
PO Box 449 Fax: (770)428-7945
Marietta, GA 30060
Community newspaper. **Founded:** 1969. **Freq:** Weekly (Thurs.). **Print Method:** Offset. **Cols./Page:** 6. **Col. Width:** 26 nonpareils. **Col. Depth:** 301 agate lines. **Key Personnel:** Otis A. Brumby, Jr., Publisher. **USPS:** 925-860. **Subscription Rates:** $12 individuals; $18 out of area; $24 out of state.
Ad Rates: GLR: $.82 **Circ:** Combined 10,907
BW: $1,483.50
4C: $1,773.50
SAU: $11.50

7667 Smyrna Cable TV
PO Box 1587 Phone: (404)433-2338
Smyrna, GA 30081 Fax: (404)333-3430

Key Personnel: Wendell Dean, Vice President. **Cities Served:** subscribing households 3,075; 25 channels; 2 community access channels.

7668 WAZX-AM - 1550
2460 Atlanta Rd. Phone: (770)436-6171
Smyrna, GA 30080 Fax: (770)436-0100
E-mail: wazxamfm@bellsouth.net

Format: Hispanic. **Owner:** Ga-Mex Broadcasting, Inc., at above address. **Operating Hours:** Continuous. **ADI:** Atlanta (Athens & Rome), GA. **Wattage:** 50,000. **Ad Rates:** $40-60 for 30 seconds; $70-90 for 60 seconds. **URL:** http://www.enespanol.com.radio.exitos.

SOPERTON†, pop. 2,930.

SE GA. Treutlen Co. 70 mi. SE of Macon. Turpentine distillery; carpetbacking factory; cotton ginning; printing plants. Pine timber. Agriculture. Cotton, corn, tobacco.

7669 The Montgomery Monitor
Soperton News Building
PO Box 537 Phone: (912)529-6624
Soperton, GA 30457 Fax: (912)529-5399

Community newspaper. **Founded:** 1886. **Freq:** Weekly (Wed.). **Print Method:** Offset. **Cols./Page:** 6. **Col. Width:** 26 nonpareils. **Col. Depth:** 294 agate lines. **Key Personnel:** James T. Windsor, Editor. **Subscription Rates:** $15.75 local; $26.25 all others. **Remarks:** Accepts advertising.
Ad Rates: GLR: $.27 **Circ:** 2,100
BW: $485.10
4C: $745.10
SAU: $1.68
PCI: $3.78

7670 The Soperton News
Soperton News Building
PO Box 537 Phone: (912)529-6624
Soperton, GA 30457 Fax: (912)529-5399

Community newspaper. **Founded:** 1914. **Freq:** Weekly (Wed.). **Print Method:** Offset. **Cols./Page:** 6. **Col. Width:** 25 nonpareils. **Col. Depth:** 294 agate lines. **Key Personnel:** S. Du Bose Porter, Editor. **Subscription Rates:** $15.75 individuals; $26.25 out of area.
Ad Rates: GLR: $.27 **Circ:** 3,950
BW: $485.10
4C: $745.10
SAU: $1.68
PCI: $3.78

STATESBORO†, pop. 20,000.

E. GA. Bulloch Co. 50 mi. W. of Savannah. Georgia Southern College. Manufactures iron castings, textiles, shears, plastic products. Lumber mills. Cold storage; peanut and pecan plants. Agriculture. Soybeans, corn, peanuts, tobacco, livestock, forestry.

7671 The George-Anne
Georgia Southern University
PO Box Box 8001 Phone: (912)681-0069
Statesboro, GA 30460 Fax: (912)486-7113
Publication E-mail: stud_pub@gsaix2.cc.gasou.edu
Publisher E-mail: stud_pub@gsaix2.cc.gasou.edu; reflector@gsvms2.gasou.edu

Collegiate newspaper. **Founded:** 1927. **Freq:** Semiweekly (Tues. and Fri.; during the academic year). **Print Method:** Offset. **Trim Size:** 13 3/4 x 22 3/4. **Cols./Page:** 6. **Col. Width:** 12 picas. **Col. Depth:** 21 inches. **Key Personnel:** Kelley McGonnell, Editor; Stacey Wysong, Managing Editor; Bill Neville, General Mgr. **Subscription Rates:** $18 individuals.

Remarks: Accepts advertising. **Available Online. URL:** http://www.stp.gasou.edu.
Ad Rates: GLR: $.55 **Circ:** Free ‡7,000
BW: $624
4C: $759
SAU: $4.50
PCI: $7.75

7672 SECOLAS Annals
Southeastern Council on Latin American Studies
PO Box 8106 Phone: (912)681-5929
Georgia Southern University Fax: (912)681-0824
Statesboro, GA 30460-8106
Scholarly journal covering Latin American studies. **Founded:** 1968. **Freq:** Annual. **Trim Size:** 6 x 9. **Key Personnel:** Nancy W. Shumaker, Editor, shumaker@gsvms2.cc.gasou.edu. **ISSN:** 0081-2951. **Subscription Rates:** $4 individuals. **Remarks:** Advertising not accepted.
Circ: (Not Reported)

7673 Southeastern Political Review
Georgia Southern University
PO Box 8101 Phone: (912)681-5573
Statesboro, GA 30460-8101 Fax: (912)681-5348

Scholarly journal covering political science. **Founded:** 1973. **Freq:** Quarterly. **Print Method:** Offset. **Trim Size:** 6 x 9. **Key Personnel:** Dr. George Cox, Editor, gcox@gsvms1.cc.gasoce.edu; Dr. G. Lane Van Tassell, Managing Editor. **ISSN:** 0730-2177. **Subscription Rates:** $18 individuals; $35 institutions. **Remarks:** Accepts advertising.
Ad Rates: BW: $150 **Circ:** Paid 400

7674 Southern Reflector
Georgia Southern University
PO Box Box 8001 Phone: (912)681-0069
Statesboro, GA 30460 Fax: (912)486-7113
Publisher E-mail: stud_ pub@gsaix2.cc.gasou.edu; reflector@gsvms2.gasou.edu

Magazine about student life at GSU. **Founded:** 1927. **Freq:** Quarterly. **Print Method:** Web offset. **Trim Size:** 10 1/2 x 8. **Cols./Page:** 3. **Col. Width:** 2 inches. **Col. Depth:** 9 1/2 inches. **Key Personnel:** Kathy Jacobus, Art Dir.; Jennifer Gordon, Editor; Bill Nevillen, General Mgr., bneville@gasou.edu. **Subscription Rates:** $15 individuals. **Remarks:** Accepts advertising. **Available Online. URL:** http://www.stp.gasou.edu. **Formerly**: Reflector Yearbook.
Ad Rates: BW: $200 **Circ:** Paid 100
4C: $350 Controlled 4,500

7675 Northland Cable TV
32 E. Vine St. Phone: (912)489-8715
PO Box 407 Fax: (912)764-4870
Statesboro, GA 30458

Owner: Northland Communications, Inc., at above address, Fax: (912)489-5479. **Formerly**: Statesboro CATV Inc. **Key Personnel:** Rick Hutchison, Regional Mgr.; Tripp Sims, Sales Mgr., phone (912)764-0503. **Cities Served:** Brooklet, Statesboro, GA: subscribing households 8,500; 45 channels; 1 community access channel.

7676 WMCD-FM - 100.1
561 E. Olliff St. Phone: (912)764-5446
Statesboro, GA 30459 Fax: (912)764-8827
E-mail: wwnswmcd@frontiernet.net

Format: Adult Contemporary. **Networks:** Independent. **Founded:** 1967. **Operating Hours:** Continuous; 100% local. **ADI:** Savannah, GA. **Key Personnel:** Pat Hirsch, GM/VP, phone (912)764-6000, fax (912)769-8827; Buddy Horne, Operations Mgr./Program Dir., phone (912)264-6000; Ted Byrne, News Dir. **Wattage:** 50,000. **Ad Rates:** $12-14 per unit. Combined advertising rates available with WUNS-AM, WSYL-AM, WZBX-FM.

7677 WVGS-FM - 91.9
Georgia Southern University Phone: (912)681-0877
Box 8016 Fax: (912)871-1357
Statesboro, GA 30460

Format: Alternative/New Music/Progressive; Rap; Urban Contemporary. **Owner:** Board of Regents - University System of Georgia, at above address. **Founded:** 1974. **Operating Hours:** Continuous; 100% local. **Key Personnel:** Russ Dewey, Contact, phone (912)6815446, rdewey@gasou.edu; Chaz Pike, General Mgr.; Tracey Varnell, Music Dir., phone (912)681-5507; Ryan King, Operations Mgr. **Wattage:** 1000. **URL:** http://www.cs.gasou.edu/wvgs/index.html.

7678 WWNS-AM - 1240
PO Box 958 Phone: (912)764-5446
Statesboro, GA 30458 Fax: (912)764-8827
E-mail: wwnswmcd@frontiernet.net

Format: Talk. **Networks:** CBS. **Owner:** Radio Statesboro, Inc., at above address. **Founded:** 1946. **Operating Hours:** Continuous; 75% network, 25% local. **Key Personnel:** Pat Hirsch, VP/General Manager; Derek Smith, News Dir.; Buddy Horne, Program Dir. **Local Programs:** *Eagle Hotline GSU Sports*, Nate Hirsch. **Wattage:** 1000. **Ad Rates:** $8-10 per unit.

STEWART

7679 Stewart-Webster Journal
Rolin Press Group
PO Box 250 Phone: (912)887-3674
Richland, GA 31825 Fax: (912)887-2800

Community newspaper. **Subtitle:** Serving Georgia's Fastest Growing Tourist Area. **Founded:** 1850. **Freq:** Weekly (Thurs.). **Print Method:** Offset. **Trim Size:** 6 x 21 1/2. **Cols./Page:** 6. **Col. Width:** 20 nonpareils. **Col. Depth:** 21.5 agate lines. **Key Personnel:** Ron Provencher, Publisher; Linda Provencher, Editor, phone (912)887-3675. **Subscription Rates:** $18.50 individuals; $27 out of county; $36 out of state. **Remarks:** Accepts advertising.
Ad Rates: GLR: $.14 **Circ:** ‡1950
BW: $516
4C: $614.40
SAU: $4
PCI: $4

STOCKBRIDGE

7680 Charter Communications
PO Box 1470 Phone: (770)389-9999
Stockbridge, GA 30281 Fax: (770)389-0166

Owner: Charter Communications, at above address. **Founded:** Apr. 1990. **Formerly**: Bijo Cablevision Inc.; Billy R. Jones. **Key Personnel:** Ron Johnson, General Mgr., phone (770)389-0167; Mike Clark, State Engineer, phone (770)389-8907; Amy Adams, Customer Service Mgr., phone (770)389-8907. **Cities Served:** Stockbridge, GA; Henry county: subscribing households 28,000; 56 channels; 1 community access channel. **URL:** http://www.charter.com.

STONE MOUNTAIN

7681 Fencepost Magazine
Dempsey Management Services
5300 Memorial Dr. Phone: (404)299-5413
Ste. 116 Fax: (404)299-8927
Stone Mountain, GA 30083
Free: (800)822-4342
Publication E-mail: afa@mindspring.com

Magazine for the American Fence Association. **Subtitle:** The Magazine of Fence Industry Decision-Makers. **Founded:** 1972. **Freq:** Bimonthly. **Print Method:** Sheet fed. **Trim Size:** 8 1/2 x 11. **Cols./Page:** 3. **Col. Width:** 2 1/4 inches. **Col. Depth:** 9 3/4 inches. **Key Personnel:** Terry Dempsey, Publisher; Maura Jacob, Editor/Advertising Manager, maura.jacob@mindspring.com. **ISSN:** 1082-2062. **Subscription Rates:** $18 individuals; $42 other countries; $3 single issue. **Remarks:** Accepts advertising.
Ad Rates: BW: $1,420 **Circ:** Non-paid ⊕13,000
4C: $2,160
PCI: $80

7682 The Stone Mountain De Kalb Neighbor
Neighbor Newspapers, Inc.
580 Fairground St. Phone: (770)428-9411
PO Box 449 Fax: (770)428-7945
Marietta, GA 30060
Community newspaper. **Founded:** 1970. **Freq:** Weekly (Wed.). **Print Method:** Offset. **Cols./Page:** 6. **Col. Width:** 26 nonpareils. **Col. Depth:** 301 agate lines. **Key Personnel:** Otis A. Brumby, Jr., Publisher. **USPS:** 951-920. **Subscription Rates:** $12 individuals; $18 out of area; $24 out of state.
Ad Rates: GLR: $1.64 **Circ:** Combined 45,551
BW: $2,967
4C: $3,292
SAU: $23

SUMMERVILLE†, pop. 4,878.

NW GA. Chattoga Co. 9 mi. E. of Menlo. Residential.

7683 Chattooga Press
News Publishing Co.
PO Box 485 Phone: (706)857-5433
Summerville, GA 30747
Newspaper. **Founded:** 1982. **Freq:** Weekly. **Print Method:** Offset. **Cols./Page:** 6. **Col. Width:** 2 1/16 inches. **Col. Depth:** 21 1/4 inches. **Key Personnel:** B.H. Mooney III, Publisher. **Subscription Rates:** Free. **Remarks:** Accepts advertising.
Ad Rates: GLR: $4.65 **Circ:** Free 11,100
BW: $592.88
PCI: $6.50

7684 The Summerville News
ESPY Pub. Co.
PO Box 310 Phone: (706)857-2494
Summerville, GA 30747 Fax: (706)857-2393

Local newspaper. **Founded:** 1886. **Freq:** Weekly (Thurs.). **Print Method:** Offset. **Cols./Page:** 8. **Col. Width:** 21 nonpareils. **Col. Depth:** 301 agate lines. **Key Personnel:** Greg Espy, Production Mgr.; David T. Espy, General Mgr.; Winston E. Espy, Editor and Publisher; Bill Hudsputh, Advertising Dir. **Subscription Rates:** $10.60 individuals. **Remarks:** Accepts advertising.
Ad Rates: GLR: $.19 **Circ:** ‡7,850
BW: $516
PCI: $3

7685 Clear-Vu Cable Inc.
Box 368 Phone: (706)857-2551
Summerville, GA 30747 Fax: (706)857-2194

Owner: Boyce Dooley, at above address. **Key Personnel:** Boyce Dooley, General Mgr. **Cities Served:** Summerville, GA.

7686 WGTA-AM - 950
State Hwy. 100 Phone: (706)857-2466
PO Box 200 Fax: (706)857-3652
Summerville, GA 30747

Format: Country; Gospel. **Networks:** NBC; Georgia Radio; Westwood One Radio. **Owner:** TTA Broadcasting, Inc., at above address. **Founded:** 1950. **Operating Hours:** 6:00 a.m.-7:00 p.m.; 100% local. **ADI:** Atlanta (Athens & Rome), GA. **Key Personnel:** Earl S. Newton, General Mgr.; Anthony Giullano, Jr., News Dir.; Margaret Dillard, Program Dir. **Wattage:** 5000. **Ad Rates:** $5 for 15 seconds; $7-9 for 30 seconds; $8-10 for 60 seconds.

SWAINSBORO†, pop. 7,602.

E. GA. Emanuel Co. 65 mi. SW of Augusta. Manufactures lumber, lawn mowers, electrical equipment, feed, textiles. Pine timber. Agriculture. Cotton, corn, tobacco.

7687 The Blade
Forest-Blade Publishing Inc.
Box 938 Phone: (912)237-9971
Swainsboro, GA 30401 Fax: (912)237-9451
Publication E-mail: fprest@pineland.net
Publisher E-mail: news@forest-blade.com

Newspaper. **Founded:** 1859. **Freq:** Weekly. **Print Method:** Offset. **Cols./Page:** 6. **Col. Width:** 28 nonpareils. **Col. Depth:** 301 agate lines. **Key Personnel:** W.C. Rogers, C.E., Editor and Publisher; Rudy Fagler, News Editor. **Subscription Rates:** $24 in state; $34 out of state.
Ad Rates: GLR: $.27 **Circ:** Paid 6,000
BW: $538.02 Free 8,388
4C: $666.02
SAU: $3.92
PCI: $4.27

7688 WJAT-AM - 800
PO Box 289 Phone: (912)237-2011
Swainsboro, GA 30401 Fax: (912)237-0988
Free: (800)482-0389
E-mail: wjat@jazz.cybermedia.net

Format: Country. **Networks:** Georgia Radio. **Owner:** Box Broadcasting Corp., at above address. **Founded:** 1950. **Operating Hours:** Continuous; 2% network, 98% local. **ADI:** Augusta, GA. **Key Personnel:** Donald R. Box, President; Paul W. Box, V. Pres./Gen. Mgr.; Randall Johnson, News Dir. **Wattage:** 1000 day; 500 night. **Ad Rates:** $7-8 for 30 seconds; $9-10 for 60 seconds. Combined advertising rates available with WJAT-FM.

7689 WJAT-FM - 98.1
PO Box 289 Phone: (912)237-2011
Swainsboro, GA 30401 Fax: (912)237-0988
Free: (800)482-0389

Format: Country. **Networks:** Georgia Radio. **Owner:** Box Broadcasting Corp., at above address. **Founded:** 1966. **Formerly**: WGKS-FM (1988). **Operating Hours:** Continuous; 2% network, 98% local. **ADI:** Augusta, GA. **Key Personnel:** Paul W. Box, Music Dir.; Randall Johnson, News Dir.; Annie H. Box, Station Mgr. **Wattage:** 6000. **Ad Rates:** $7-8 for 30 seconds; $9-10 for 60 seconds. Combined advertising rates available with WJAT-AM.

7690 WXRS-AM - 1590
Box 1590 Phone: (912)237-1590
Swainsboro, GA 30401 Fax: (912)237-3559
E-mail: wxrsamfm@pineland.net

Format: Urban Contemporary; Gospel. **Networks:** ABC. **Owner:** Lacom Communications, Inc., at above address. **Founded:** 1978. **Operating Hours:** Continuous; 50% network, 50% local. **Key Personnel:** Bobby Gardner, Music Dir.; Dean Morgan, Sales Rep.; Jeff Wiggins, News Dir. **Wattage:** 2500 day; 23 night. **Ad Rates:** $7.50 for 30 seconds; $9.50 for 60 seconds.

7691 WXRS-FM - 100.5
Box 1590 Phone: (912)237-1590
Swainsboro, GA 30401 Fax: (912)237-3559
E-mail: wxrsamfm@pineland.net

Format: Contemporary Country. **Networks:** AP; ABC. **Owner:** LACOM Communications, Inc., at above address. **Founded:** 1982. **Operating Hours:** Continuous; 50% network, 50% local. **Key Personnel:** Owen L. Studstill, Contact; Dean Morgan, News Dir.; Jeff Wiggins, Contact; Melinda Studstill, Sales Mgr. **Wattage:** 3000. **Ad Rates:** $9.50-15.50 per unit.

SYLVANIA†, pop. 3,323.

E. GA. Screven Co. 60 mi. NW of Savannah. Manufactures synthetic yarn, textiles, lumber, industrial bearings, cottonseed oil, fertilizer. Pine timber. Agriculture. Soybeans, grain, stock.

7692 Sylvania Telephone
PO Box 10 Phone: (912)564-2045
Sylvania, GA 30467 Fax: (912)564-7085

Community newspaper. **Founded:** 1879. **Freq:** Weekly (Thurs.). **Print Method:** Offset. **Cols./Page:** 6. **Col. Width:** 24 nonpareils. **Col. Depth:** 2 1/2 inches. **Key Personnel:** Tom Ten Broeck, Publisher. **Subscription Rates:** $15.90 individuals; $23.33 out of state. **Remarks:** Accepts advertising.
Ad Rates: GLR: $4 **Circ:** 5,061
BW: $648.90
PCI: $5.15

SYLVESTER†, pop. 5,860.

S. GA. Worth Co. 20 mi. E. of Albany. Manufactures lumber, turpentine. Meat packing, peanut blanching, tobacco and textile plants. Pine timber. Diversified farming. Grains, peanuts, melons. Cattle.

7693 The Sylvester Local News
103 E. Kelly Phone: (912)776-7713
PO Box 387
Sylvester, GA 31791
Newspaper. **Founded:** Nov. 1884. **Freq:** Weekly (Wed.). **Print Method:** Offset. **Trim Size:** 14 1/2 x 22 3/4. **Cols./Page:** 6. **Col. Width:** 2 1/8 inches. **Col. Depth:** 21 inches. **Key Personnel:** Marian A. Sumner, Editor and Publisher; John.F. Porter, Advertising Mgr. **ISSN:** 8750-5312. **Subscription Rates:** $15 individuals; $19 state; $27 out of state. **Remarks:** Accepts advertising.
Ad Rates: BW: $378 **Circ:** ‡3,800
4C: $453
SAU: $3

TALBOTTON†, pop. 1,140.

W. GA. Talbot Co. 45 mi. W. of Macon. Residential.

7694 Talbotton New Era
PO Box 248 Phone: (404)846-3188
Talbotton, GA 31827 Fax: (706)846-2206

Community newspaper. **Freq:** Weekly (Thurs.). **Print Method:** Offset. **Cols./Page:** 6. **Col. Width:** 13 inches. **Col. Depth:** 21 1/2 inches. **Key Personnel:** Bob Tribble, Publisher; Mike Hale, General Mgr.; Billy Bryant, Editor. **USPS:** 532-000. **Subscription Rates:** $15; $30 out of area. **Remarks:** Accepts advertising.
Ad Rates: GLR: $.27 **Circ:** ‡1,000
BW: $483.75
4C: $683.75
SAU: $3.75
PCI: $3.75

TALLAPOOSA

NW GA. Haralson Co. 10 mi. S. of Buchanan.

7695 WKNG-AM - 1060
Box 626 Phone: (770)574-1060
Tallapoosa, GA 30176 Fax: (770)574-1062

Format: Country. **Networks:** ABC; Georgia Radio. **Owner:** Steven L. Gradick, at above address. **Founded:** 1976. **Operating Hours:** Sunrise-sunset. **Key Personnel:** Steven L. Gradick, Contact. **Wattage:** 5000.

THOMASTON†, pop. 9,682.

C. GA. Upson Co. 38 mi. W. of Macon. Textiles, lumber, fruit farms.

7696 Thomaston Times
Thomaston Publishing Co.
PO Box 430 Phone: (706)647-5414
Thomaston, GA 30286-0430 Fax: (706)647-2833

Community newspaper. **Founded:** 1869. **Freq:** Triweekly (Mon., Wed., Fri.). **Print Method:** Offset. **Trim Size:** 22 3/4 x 14. **Cols./Page:** 6. **Col. Width:** 11.6 picas. **Col. Depth:** 21 1/2 inches. **Key Personnel:** Chris Smith, Publisher; Kim Madlom, News Editor; Elmo Jackson, General Mgr. **Subscription Rates:** $34; $45 out of area; $55 out of state. **Remarks:** Accepts advertising.
Ad Rates: GLR: $2.08 **Circ:** 6,700
BW: $728.85
4C: $1,028.85
PCI: $5.65

7697 WSFT-AM - 1220
PO Box 689 Phone: (404)647-5421
Thomaston, GA 30286

Format: News. **Networks:** NBC; Georgia Radio. **Owner:** Upson Broadcasting Co., at above address, (706)647-5421. **Founded:** 1947. **Operating Hours:** 6 a.m.-sunset; 20% network, 80% local. **ADI:** Atlanta (Athens & Rome), GA. **Key Personnel:** Claude D. Thames, General Mgr.; John W. Thames, Contact. **Wattage:** 1000. **Ad Rates:** $4.50-5.50 for 30 seconds; $6-7 for 60 seconds.

THOMASVILLE†, pop. 20,000.

SW GA. Thomas Co. 35 mi. N. of Tallahassee, FL. Historic sites. Winter resort. Famous for its roses and annual Rose Festival. Manufactures meat products, mattresses, mobile homes, elastics, paint, carbide drill bits, jet engines blades, aluminum windows, furniture, plastics, rubber, fertilizers, pipe, thread. Sawmills; silica sand mining. Diversified farming. Tobacco, corn, soybeans, watermelon, peanuts, mixed vegetables, livestock.

7698 South Georgia Business Journal
South Georgia Business Journal, Inc.
PO Box 2036 Phone: (912)228-1299
Thomasville, GA 31799 Fax: (912)228-7033
Publication E-mail: sgcoc@surfsouth.com
Publisher E-mail: sgcoc@surfsouth.com

Periodical covering South Georgia business, financial, and educational news. **Founded:** July 1989. **Freq:** Quarterly. **Trim Size:** 11 1/2 x 15. **Cols./Page:** 4. **Col. Width:** 2 13/16 inches. **Col. Depth:** 14 inches. **Key Personnel:** Lloyd Eckberg, Editor and Publisher. **Subscription Rates:** Free to qualified subscribers; $24 individuals. **Remarks:** Accepts advertising.
Ad Rates: BW: $750 **Circ:** Paid ⊕**1,000**
4C: $1,050 Controlled ⊕**7,700**

7699 Times-Enterprise
PO Box 650 Phone: (912)226-2400
Thomasville, GA 31792 Fax: (912)228-5863

General newspaper. **Founded:** 1889. **Freq:** Daily (eve.) and Sat. (morn.). **Print Method:** Offset. **Cols./Page:** 6. **Col. Width:** 25 nonpareils. **Col. Depth:** 301 agate lines. **Key Personnel:** Den Dickerson, Publisher; Dan Sutton, Advertising Mgr. **Subscription Rates:** $59.50 individuals. **Remarks:** Accepts advertising.
Ad Rates: SAU: $8.33 **Circ:** Tues.-Fri. ★**10,064**
Sat. ★**10,064**
Sun. ★**10,220**

7700 WHGH-AM - 840
PO Box 2218 Phone: (912)228-4124
Thomasville, GA 31799 Fax: (912)225-9508

Format: Urban Contemporary. **Networks:** American Urban Radio. **Owner:** Gross Broadcasting Co., PO BOX 2218, Thomasville, GA 31799, Fax: (912)228-9508. **Founded:** 1986. **Operating Hours:** Sunrise-sunset; 9% network, 91% local. **ADI:** Tallahassee, FL-Thomasville (Bainbridge), GA. **Key Personnel:** Mosos L. Gross, General Mgr.; Lisa Webb, Office Mgr.; Raymond Johnson, Contact. **Wattage:** 10,000. **Ad Rates:** $8.50-9.50 for 30 seconds; $8-8.50 for 60 seconds.

7701 WJEP-AM - 1020
Hwy. 3 Phone: (912)228-5683
PO Box 90 Fax: (912)436-0544
Thomasville, GA 31799-0090

Format: Religious; Contemporary Christian. **Networks:** USA Radio. **Owner:** Lifeline Communications Corp., at above address. **Founded:** 1983. **Operating Hours:** 7:30 a.m.-5:30 p.m; 25% network, 75% local. **ADI:** Tallahassee, FL-Thomasville (Bainbridge), GA. **Key Personnel:** Jimmy Keyton, President. **Wattage:** 10,000. **Ad Rates:** $8-10 for 60 seconds.

7702 WPAX-AM - 1240
117 Remington Ave. Phone: (912)226-1240
Thomasville, GA 31792 Fax: (912)226-1361
E-mail: lenrob@rose.net

Format: News; Middle-of-the-Road (MOR); Big Band/Nostalgia; Easy Listening. **Networks:** CBS; Georgia Radio. **Owner:** Len Robinson, PO Box 129, Thomasville, GA 31799, Fax: (912)226-1240. **Founded:** 1922. **Operating Hours:** 24 hrs., 95% local. **ADI:** Tallahassee, FL-Thomasville (Bainbridge), GA. **Key Personnel:** Len Robinson, Contact, lenrob@rose.net; Mark Brannon, News Dir. **Wattage:** 1000. **Ad Rates:** $10.60 for 30 seconds; $12.50 for 60 seconds. Combined advertising rates available with WTVF-FM.

THOMSON†, pop. 7,001.

E. GA. McDuffie Co. 35 mi. W. of Augusta. Manufactures lumber, cottonseed oil, fertilizer, textiles. Pine, hardwood timber. Agriculture. Cotton, corn, potatoes.

7703 Dollar Saver
McDuffie Progress
101 Church St. Phone: (706)595-1601
PO Box 1090 Fax: (706)597-8974
Thomson, GA 30824
Shopper. **Founded:** 1984. **Freq:** Weekly (Wed.). **Print Method:** Offset. **Trim Size:** 13 x 21 1/2. **Cols./Page:** 6. **Col. Width:** 13 inches. **Col. Depth:** 21 1/2 inches. **Key Personnel:** Ted Delaney, Publisher. **Subscription Rates:** Free. **Remarks:** Accepts advertising.
Ad Rates: GLR: $.32 **Circ:** Free 13,550
BW: $85
4C: $180
SAU: $4
PCI: $4.50

7704 Gibson Record and Guide
Gibson Record & Guide
PO Box 370
Thomson, GA 30824

Community newspaper. **Founded:** Feb. 27, 1991. **Freq:** Weekly (Fri.). **Cols./Page:** 6. **Col. Width:** 9 1/2 picas. **Col. Depth:** 21 inches. **Key Personnel:** Ronda Phillips, Editor; Alva Haywood, Publisher. **Subscription Rates:** $4.15 annual newspaper rates.
Ad Rates: BW: $592 **Circ:** 5,100
4C: $808
PCI: $4.70

7705 McDuffie Progress
101 Church St. Phone: (706)595-1601
PO Box 1090 Fax: (706)597-8974
Thomson, GA 30824
Community newspaper. **Founded:** 1899. **Freq:** Semiweekly (Wed. and Sun.). **Print Method:** Offset. **Trim Size:** 13 x 21 1/2. **Cols./Page:** 6. **Col. Width:** 2 1/16 inches. **Col. Depth:** 21 1/2 inches. **Key Personnel:** Ted Delaney, Publisher. **USPS:** 335-140. **Subscription Rates:** $25. **Remarks:** Accepts advertising.
Ad Rates: GLR: $.33 **Circ:** 4,300
BW: $85
4C: $180
CNU: $4

7706 WTHO-FM - 101.7
PO Drawer 900 Phone: (706)595-5122
Thomson, GA 30824 Fax: (706)595-3021

Format: Country; News; Sports. **Networks:** NBC; Georgia Radio. **Founded:** 1971. **Operating Hours:** Continuous. **ADI:** Augusta, GA. **Key Personnel:** Mike Wall, General Mgr. **Wattage:** 6,000. **Ad Rates:** $4-12 for 30 seconds; $5.70-17.15 for 60 seconds.

7707 WTWA-AM - 1240
PO Drawer 900 Phone: (706)595-1561
Thomson, GA 30824 Fax: (706)595-3021

Format: Middle-of-the-Road (MOR). **Networks:** Mutual Broadcasting System; Georgia Radio. **Founded:** 1948. **Operating Hours:** Continuous. **ADI:** Augusta, GA. **Key Personnel:** Mike Wall, General Mgr. **Wattage:** 1000. **Ad Rates:** $3.60-9.15 for 30 seconds; $5.15-13.05 for 60 seconds.

TIFTON†, pop. 13,749.

S. GA. Tift Co. 40 mi. E. of Albany. Abraham Baldwin College. Coastal Plain Experiment Station. Manufactures lumber, aluminum products, refrigerator coils, textiles, plastics, concrete, and pipes. Cotton, saw, peanut mills; bottling, brick works; tobacco market. Tomato, cabbage plants shipped. Timber. Diversified farming. Tobacco, peanuts.

7708 Gazette Shopping Guide
PO Box 708 Phone: (912)382-4321
Tifton, GA 31793 Fax: (912)387-7322

Shopper. **Founded:** 1974. **Freq:** Weekly (Wed.). **Print Method:** Offset. **Cols./Page:** 6. **Col. Width:** 26 nonpareils. **Col. Depth:** 301 agate lines. **Key Personnel:** Anne Rice, Editor; Lee Browne, Publisher; Randy Blalock, Advertising Mgr. **Remarks:** Accepts advertising.
Ad Rates: GLR: $.27 **Circ:** Free ‡15,850

7709 The Peanut Grower
Vance Publishing
PO Box 83, 128 1st St., Ste. 223 Phone: (912)386-8591
Tifton, GA 31793 Fax: (912)386-9772
Publication E-mail: peanuts@sursouth.com

Magazine on peanut farming. Includes information on production, research, and marketing. **Founded:** 1989. **Freq:** 8/year (Jan.-July and Nov). **Print Method:** Web Offset. **Trim Size:** 8 x 10 3/4. **Cols./Page:** 3. **Col. Width:** 2 1/4 inches. **Key Personnel:** Catherine Andrews, Editor; Sonia Tighe, Publisher. **ISSN:** 1042-9379. **Subscription Rates:** $25 nonmembers; Free to qualified subscribers. **Remarks:** Accepts advertising.
Ad Rates: BW: $4,960 **Circ:** Controlled 22,500
4C: $6,785

7710 Southeastern Peanut Farmer
PO Box 706 Phone: (912)386-3470
Tifton, GA 31793 Fax: (912)386-3501

Newspaper (tabloid) distributed to peanut growers in Georgia, Florida, Alabama, and South Carolina. **Founded:** Mar. 1962. **Freq:** 10/year. **Print Method:** Offset. **Trim Size:** 11 1/2 x 16. **Cols./Page:** 4. **Col. Width:** 32 nonpareils. **Col. Depth:** 210 agate lines. **Key Personnel:** Joan Underwood, Advertising/Production Mgr. **ISSN:** 0038-3694. **Subscription Rates:** $5 individuals; $20 out of country. **Remarks:** Accepts advertising. **Alt. Formats:** Microform.
Ad Rates: BW: $1,544 **Circ:** ‡11,100
4C: $1,883
PCI: $19.69

7711 Tiftarea Shopper
147 Love Ave. Phone: (912)386-0472
Tifton, GA 31793 Fax: (912)386-0478

Shopper. **Founded:** 1973. **Freq:** Weekly (Tues.). **Print Method:** Offset. **Cols./Page:** 6. **Col. Width:** 19 nonpareils. **Col. Depth:** 224 agate lines. **Key Personnel:** Gene Bowers, Publisher. **Subscription Rates:** Free. **Remarks:** Accepts advertising.
Ad Rates: GLR: $1 **Circ:** Free 16,500
BW: $518.40
4C: $818.40
PCI: $6

7712 The Tifton Gazette
PO Box 708 Phone: (912)382-4321
Tifton, GA 31793-0708 Fax: (912)387-7322

General newspaper. **Founded:** 1888. **Freq:** Daily (eve.). **Print Method:** Offset. **Cols./Page:** 6. **Col. Width:** 26 nonpareils. **Col. Depth:** 301 agate lines. **Key Personnel:** Mike Jones, Managing Editor; Randy Blalock, Advertising Mgr. **Subscription Rates:** $72 individuals. **Remarks:** Accepts advertising.
Ad Rates: BW: $1,039.74 **Circ:** 9,880
4C: $1,244.75
SAU: $8.49

7713 WJYF-FM - 95.3
PO Box 968 Phone: (912)382-1340
Tifton, GA 31793-0968 Fax: (912)386-8658

Format: Adult Contemporary. **Networks:** Westwood One Radio. **Owner:** Tifton Broadcasting Corp., at above address. **Founded:** 1986. **Operating Hours:** Continuous; 100% local. **ADI:** Albany (Valdosta & Cordele), GA. **Key Personnel:** Ron Yontz, President; David Haire, Contact; Al Cohen, Contact. **Wattage:** 25,000. **Ad Rates:** $6 for 30 seconds; $10 for 60 seconds.

7714 WPLH-FM - 103.1
PO Box 36, ABAC Sta. Phone: (912)386-7158
Tifton, GA 31793 Fax: (912)386-7006
E-mail: wplh@mail.abac.peachnet.edu

Format: Classic Rock; Blues; Alternative/New Music/Progressive; Country. **Owner:** ABAC, at above address. **Founded:** 1988. **Formerly:** WABR-FM (1987). **Operating Hours:** Continuous. **Key Personnel:** Oren Hayes, Program Dir.; Andy Jones, Station Mgr., jonesa@mail.abac.peachnet.edu; Libby Campbell, Contact. **Wattage:** 250. **Ad Rates:** Noncommercial.

7715 WTIF-AM - 1340
PO Box 968 Phone: (912)382-1340
Tifton, GA 31794 Fax: (912)386-8658

Format: Country. **Networks:** CBS; Westwood One Radio. **Owner:** Tift Area Radio, Inc., at above address. **Founded:** 1957. **Operating Hours:** Continuous. **ADI:** Albany (Valdosta & Cordele), GA. **Key Personnel:** K.C. Edwards, Contact; David Haire, Contact; Ron Yontz, General Mgr. **Wattage:** 1000. **Ad Rates:** $4.20-6.50 for 15 seconds; $6.20-8.50 for 30 seconds; $7.20-9.50 for 60 seconds.

TOCCOA†, pop. 9,104.

NE GA. Stephens Co. 100 mi. NE of Atlanta. Toccoa Falls. Manufactures furniture, carpet yarn, textiles, caskets, foundry products, paints, plastics, small appliances. Metalworking. Agriculture. Poultry, livestock.

7716 Chieftain & Toccoa Record
Chieftain & Toccoa Record Co.
151 W. Doyle St. Phone: (706)886-9476
PO Drawer 1069 Fax: (706)886-2161
Toccoa, GA 30577
Newspaper. **Founded:** 1873. **Freq:** Twice weekly (Tues./Fri.). **Print Method:** Offset. **Cols./Page:** 6. **Col. Width:** 26 nonpareils. **Col. Depth:** 301 agate lines. **Key Personnel:** Patrick C. Neal, Editor and Publisher. **USPS:** 632-120. **Subscription Rates:** $18 individuals; $25 out of area; $30 out of state. **Remarks:** Advertising accepted; rates available upon request. **Formed by the merger of:** Toccoa Record (1995); Chieftain Record (1995).
Circ: Paid 8,000
Free 125

7717 WLET-AM - 1420
423 Prather Bridge Rd. Phone: (706)886-2191
Toccoa, GA 30577

Format: Talk; Information; Gospel. **Founded:** 1941. **Formerly:** WRLC-AM (1945). **Operating Hours:** Continuous. **ADI:** Greenville-Spartanburg, SC-Asheville, NC. **Key Personnel:** Gene Bollinger, Station Mgr.; Woody Bollinger, Operations Mgr. **Local Programs:** *Gene's Wake-up Machine*, Gene Bollinger; *Woody and Friends*, Woody Bollinger. **Wattage:** 5000 day, 73 night. **Ad Rates:** $5-6 for 30 seconds; $6-8 for 60 seconds.

7718 WNEG-AM - 630
121 W. Dole St. Phone: (706)886-3131
PO Box 907 Fax: (706)282-0189
Toccoa, GA 30577

Format: Middle-of-the-Road (MOR). **Networks:** AP. **Owner:** Lee Street Properties, at above address. **Founded:** 1956. **Operating Hours:** 6 a.m.-sunset; 15% network, 85% local. **ADI:** Greenville-Spartanburg, SC-Asheville, NC. **Key Personnel:** Elliott Caudell, General Mgr.; Ken Brady, Commerical Mgr.; John Durham, Program Dir.; Lamar Ramey, News Dir.; John Durham, Music Dir. **Local Programs:** *Connie Gaines Show*, Connie Gaines, (706)886-3132; *Soul Session*, Bill Rice, (706)886-3132; *Sunday Down South*, John Durham, (706)886-3132. **Wattage:** 500. **Ad Rates:** $8-9 for 15 seconds; $9-10 for 30 seconds; $11-12 for 60 seconds. Combined advertising rates available with WLET-AM.

7719 WNEG-TV - 32
100 Boulevard Phone: (706)886-0032
Box 907 Fax: (706)886-7033
Toccoa, GA 30577

Format: Commercial TV. **Networks:** CBS. **Owner:** Stephens County Broadcasting Co., at above address. **Founded:** 1984. **Operating Hours:** Continuous. **ADI:** Greenville-Spartanburg, SC-Asheville, NC. **Key Personnel:** Jimmy Sanders, General Mgr.; David Austin, General Sales Mgr.; Connie Gaines, Program Dir. **Wattage:** 647,000 visual/ 120,000 audio. **Ad Rates:** $20-75 for 30 seconds.

TOCCOA FALLS

Stephens Co.

7720 WRAF-FM - 90.9
Toccoa Falls College Phone: (706)886-1912
PO Box 780 Fax: (706)886-0690
Toccoa Falls, GA 30598
Free: (800)251-8326
E-mail: tfcrn@toccoalfalls.edu

Format: Religious. **Owner:** Toccoa Falls College, at above address, (706)886-6831, Fax: (706)886-0210, Free: (800)868-3257. **Founded:** 1980. **Operating Hours:** Continuous. **Key Personnel:** Bob Biermann, Chief Engineer; Lillian Cash, Office Mgr.; David Cornelius, Station Mgr. **Local Programs:** *The Nightwatchman*, Frank Nagle, (706)886-1912; *Prayer Time*, David Cornelius, (706)886-1912; *'Round the Country*, Lillian Cash, (706)886-1912. **Wattage:** 100,000.

TRENTON†, pop. 1,636.

NW GA. Dade Co. 15 mi. NW of Lafayette. Residential.

7721 The Dade County Sentinel
The Sentinel
385 West Church St. Phone: (706)657-6182
PO Box 277 Fax: (706)657-4970
Trenton, GA 30752
Community newspaper. **Founded:** 1965. **Freq:** Weekly (Wed.). **Print Method:** Offset. **Cols./Page:** 6. **Col. Width:** 23 nonpareils. **Col. Depth:** 301 agate lines. **Key Personnel:** William E. Gifford, Editor and Publisher, wegiff@aol.com. **Subscription Rates:** $15 individuals. **Remarks:** Accepts advertising. **Alt. Formats:** CD-ROM.
Ad Rates: GLR: $5.50 **Circ:** ‡3,850
BW: $709.50
4C: $959.50
PCI: $5.50

7722 WKWN-AM - 1420
Box 829 Phone: (706)657-7594
Trenton, GA 30752 Fax: (706)398-1658
E-mail: www.wkwn@aol.com

Format: Oldies; Religious. **Networks:** CNN Radio. **Owner:** Dade County Broadcasting, Inc., at above address, Fax: (706)657-6767. **Founded:** 1982. **Formerly:** WADX-AM (1995). **Operating Hours:** 24HRS. **Key Personnel:** Evan Stone, Owner. **Local Programs:** *Radio Classifieds*, June Pike, Office Mgr.; *Talkin' Sports*, Tom Scruggs, Mailing contact. **Wattage:** 2500. **Ad Rates:** $4-7 for 30 seconds.

TUCKER, pop. 12,500.

NW GA. De Kalb Co. 20 mi. N. of Atlanta. Residential.

7723 Applied Microwave & Wireless
Applied Microwave and Wireless
2245 Dillard St. Phone: (770)908-2320
Tucker, GA 30084-4824 Fax: (770)939-0157
Publication E-mail: jfwhite@amwireless.com; tlink@amwireless.com; amw@amwireless.com

Trade magazine serving the microwave and wireless OEM and user markets. **Founded:** May 1989. **Freq:** Bimonthly. **Trim Size:** 10 7/8 x 8 1/8. **Cols./Page:** 2. **Col. Width:** 3 3/8 inches. **Col. Depth:** 10 inches. **Key Personnel:** Gary A. Breed, Publisher. **ISSN:** 1075-0207. **Subscription Rates:** $30 individuals; $7 single issue. **Remarks:** Accepts advertising. **Formerly:** Applied Microwave Magazine.
Ad Rates: BW: $3,350 **Circ:** Paid 500
4C: $4,200 Non-paid 28,500

7724 GEORGIA Magazine
Georgia Electric Membership Corp.
PO Box 1707 Phone: (770)270-6950
Tucker, GA 30085 Fax: (770)270-6995
Free: (800)544-4362
Publication E-mail: magazine@georgiacmc.com

General interest magazine for and about Georgians. **Subtitle:** Official Publication of Georgia Electric Membership Corporation. **Founded:** July 1945. **Freq:** Monthly. **Print Method:** Offset. **Trim Size:** 8 3/8 x 10 7/8. **Cols./Page:** 3. **Col. Width:** 28 nonpareils. **Col. Depth:** 140 agate lines. **Key Personnel:** Laurel George, Advertising Mgr., laurel.george@georgiaemc.com; Ann Orowski, Editor. **ISSN:** 1061-5822. **Subscription Rates:** $9.95 individuals. **Remarks:** Advertising not accepted for alcoholic beverages, tobacco products and firearms.
Ad Rates: BW: $3,500 **Circ:** ‡250,000
4C: $4,300

7725 Performance Management Magazine
Performance Management Publications
3531 Habersham at Northlake Phone: (404)475-8740
Tucker, GA 30084 Fax: (404)493-5095

Magazine promoting improved productivity and performance through use of applied behavioral analysis. **Founded:** 1982. **Freq:** Quarterly. **Print Method:** Offset. **Trim Size:** 8 1/2 x 11. **Cols./Page:** 3. **Key Personnel:** Gail Snyder, Editor; Aubrey Daniels, Publisher; Sandy Stewart, Advertising Mgr. **ISSN:** 0734-029X. **Subscription Rates:** $24. $6.00 single issue. **Remarks:** Accepts advertising.
Ad Rates: BW: $400 **Circ:** 3,000
4C: $695

7726 WGUN-AM - 1010
2901 Mountain Industrial Blvd. Phone: (404)491-1010
Tucker, GA 30084-3073 Fax: (404)491-3019

Format: Information. **Networks:** Independent. **Founded:** 1947. **Operating Hours:** Continuous. **ADI:** Atlanta (Athens & Rome), GA. **Key Personnel:** Fred J. Webb, General Mgr.; Heather Flynt, Public Service Dir.; Chris Edmonds, Operations

Mgr. **Wattage:** 50,000. **Ad Rates:** $30-40 for 30 seconds; $40-60 for 60 seconds.

UNION CITY

7727 The Atlanta Metro
4405 Mall Blvd., No. 520 Phone: (770)969-7711
Union City, GA 30291 Fax: (770)969-7811

Magazine aimed at African-American Atlantans featuring articles on news, entertainment, travel, health, education, tax, and legal subjects. Includes calendar of events. **Subtitle:** The Magazine Dedicated to Affirming the Positive. **Freq:** Monthly. **Print Method:** Web offset. **Trim Size:** 10 1/8 x 14 1/4. **Cols./Page:** 4. **Col. Width:** 2 1/8 inches. **Col. Depth:** 13 inches. **Key Personnel:** Phillipe Smith, Advertising Mgr.; Lee Haven, Editor-in-Chief; Shantra Hill, Managing Editor. **Subscription Rates:** $12. **Remarks:** Accepts advertising.
Ad Rates: BW: $2,088 **Circ:** Controlled ‡29,000
4C: $2,488
PCI: $38.67

VALDOSTA†, pop. 37,596.

SE GA. Lowndes Co. 45 mi. E. of Thomasville. Valdosta State College. Manufactures boats, batteries, lumber, agricultural chemicals. Pecan shelling; food processing; paper mills; naval stores; concrete pipe, paperboard, garment and mobile homes factories. Pine, hardwood timber. Diversified farming. Tobacco, vegetables, watermelons, peanuts.

7728 Snake Nation Review
110 W. Force St., No. 2
Valdosta, GA 31601

Journal covering fiction, poetry and art. **Founded:** 1989. **Freq:** Quarterly. **Trim Size:** 6 x 9. **Key Personnel:** Roberta George, Editor; Nancy Phillips, Editor. **Subscription Rates:** $20 individuals; $6 single issue. **Remarks:** Accepts advertising.
Ad Rates: BW: $100 **Circ:** Controlled 700

7729 Spectator
Valdosta State University
Box 7052 Phone: (912)333-5686
Valdosta, GA 31698-0002 Fax: (912)249-2618

University newspaper. **Founded:** 1930. **Freq:** Weekly (Thurs.). **Print Method:** Offset. **Trim Size:** 13 x 21 1/2 in. **Cols./Page:** 6. **Col. Width:** 1.8 inches. **Col. Depth:** 11.5 inches. **Key Personnel:** Jason Miszck, Managing Editor; Dana Delaney, Editor; Wes Sewell, Advertising Mgr., hwsewell@valdosta.edu. **Subscription Rates:** $50 annual. **URL:** http://www.valdosta.edu/vsu/stuorg/spec.
Ad Rates: GLR: $5.55 **Circ:** Combined 5,000
BW: $572.76
4C: $747.76
PCI: $5.55

7730 The Valdosta Daily Times
Thomson Newspapers
PO Box 968 Phone: (912)244-1880
Valdosta, GA 31603 Fax: (912)244-2560

General newspaper. **Founded:** 1867. **Freq:** Mon.-Sun. (morn.). **Print Method:** Offset. **Cols./Page:** 6. **Col. Width:** 2 1/8 inches. **Col. Depth:** 21 1/2 inches. **Key Personnel:** Robert F. Morrell, Publisher; Frank Sayles, Jr., Editor. **Subscription Rates:** $86.40 individuals. **Remarks:** Accepts advertising.
Ad Rates: GLR: $.68 **Circ:** Mon.-Sat. ♦**19,740**
BW: $1,234.53 Sun. ♦**21,166**
4C: $1,584.53
PCI: $9.57

7731 Cable TV Fund IX-B
Box 2416 Phone: (912)247-9786
Valdosta, GA 31604 Fax: (912)242-1318

Owner: Falcon Cable Media, at above address. **Founded:** 1981. **Formerly:** Jones Intercable Fund IX-B. **Key Personnel:** Jerry C. Sheffield, Manager. **Cities Served:** subscribing households 3,600; 22 channels.

7732 WAAC-FM - 92.9
2973 US 84 Phone: (912)242-4513
Valdosta, GA 31601-0321 Fax: (912)247-7676

Format: Contemporary Country. **Networks:** ABC. **Founded:** 1966. **Formerly:** WGOV-FM (1984). **Operating Hours:** Continuous. **ADI:** Albany (Valdosta & Cordele), GA. **Key Personnel:** Jay Clark, General Mgr.; Tod Edwards, Promotions Dir.; Robert Whitt, Program Dir.; Shay Pierce, Business Mgr.; Ken Collins, News Dir. **Wattage:** 100,000. **Ad Rates:** $14-30 for 30 seconds; $19-35 for 60 seconds. **URL:** http://www.waac.datasys.net/c-93.

7733 WAFT-FM - 101.1
PO Box 338 Phone: (912)244-5180
Valdosta, GA 31603-0338 Fax: (912)242-8808
E-mail: f_tidwell@pm-systems.com

Format: Gospel. **Owner:** Christian Radio Fellowship, Inc., at above address. **Founded:** 1971. **Operating Hours:** Continuous. **ADI:** Albany (Valdosta & Cordele), GA. **Key Personnel:** Bill Tidwell, General Mgr. **Wattage:** 100,000. **Ad Rates:** $8-8.50 per unit.

7734 WFVR-AM - 910
4908-6 NW 34th St. Phone: (904)376-4442
Gainesville, FL 32605 Fax: (904)372-5338

Format: Country. **Networks:** NBC. **Founded:** 1951. **ADI:** Gainesville (Ocala), FL. **Key Personnel:** Alan Murray, General Mgr.; C.H. Fletcher, Contact. **Wattage:** 5000.

7735 WGOV-AM - 950
2973 U.S. 84 W. Phone: (912)242-4513
Valdosta, GA 31601 Fax: (912)247-7676

Format: Urban Contemporary. **Networks:** ABC. **Founded:** 1940. **Operating Hours:** Continuous; 100% local. **ADI:** Albany (Valdosta & Cordele), GA. **Key Personnel:** Harvey Moore, Music Dir.; Jay Clark, General Mgr.; Harvey Moore, Program Dir.; Robert Whitt, Traffic Dir.; Lamar Freeman, Contact. **Wattage:** 5000 day; 1000 night. **Ad Rates:** $8-14 for 30 seconds; $10-19 for 60 seconds. WAAC-FM.

7736 WGVP-TV - 44
1202B W. Gordon St. Phone: (912)253-9487
Valdosta, GA 31601-3009 Fax: (912)241-0432
E-mail: wgvp@wgup.com

Format: Commercial TV. **Networks:** United Paramount Network. **Owner:** Hutchens Communications, inc., at above address. **Founded:** 1980. **Formerly:** WVGA-TV. **Operating Hours:** Continuous. **ADI:** Tallahassee, FL-Thomasville (Bainbridge), GA. **Key Personnel:** Gary L. Hutchens, CEO/GM, ghutchens@wgup.com; Mary Ann Saliba, Business Mgr.; Gary L. Hutchens, Chief Engineer; Pamela Griffin, Business Mgr.; Brad Stromman, Chief Engineer. **Wattage:** 1.8 million.

7737 WJEM-AM - 1150
PO Box 368 Phone: (912)241-9797
Valdosta, GA 31603-0368 Fax: (912)253-0483

Format: Talk; News; Country. **Simulcasts:** with WVCM-FM. **Networks:** NBC. **Owner:** CDJ, Inc., at above address. **Founded:** 1955. **Formerly:** WVCM-FM. **Operating Hours:** 6 a.m.-8 p.m.; 8% network, 92% local. **ADI:** Albany (Valdosta & Cordele), GA. **Key Personnel:** J.C. Johnson, General Mgr.; Rebecca J. Damon, Promotions Mgr.; M.B. Roberts, Music Dir. **Wattage:** 5000. **Ad Rates:** $9-21.50 for 30 seconds; $11-26.50 for 60 seconds.

7738 WQPW-FM - 95.7
1001 W. Gordon St. Phone: (912)244-8642
PO Box 1327 Fax: (912)242-7620
Valdosta, GA 31603

Format: Adult Contemporary. **Networks:** Independent. **Owner:** Metro Media Broadcasting, at above address. **Founded:** 1977. **Formerly:** WLGA-FM (1980). **Operating Hours:** Continuous; 100% local. **ADI:** Albany (Valdosta & Cordele), GA. **Key Personnel:** Harrison Cooper, Contact; Jimmy Holmes, P.D. **Wattage:** 50,000. **Ad Rates:** $24-42 for 60 seconds.

7739 WSTI-FM - 105.3
614 Baytree Rd., Box 5286 Phone: (912)247-7568
Valdosta, GA 31602 Fax: (912)247-7617

Format: Adult Contemporary. **Owner:** ORB Communications, Inc., at above address. **Founded:** 1986. **Operating Hours:** Continuous. **ADI:** Albany (Valdosta & Cordele), GA. **Key Personnel:** Bob Harrison, President/GM. **Wattage:** 3000.

7740 WVVS-FM - 90.9
Box 142 Phone: (912)333-5661
Valdosta, GA 31698-0002 Fax: (912)333-7313

Format: Alternative/New Music/Progressive; Urban Contemporary. **Owner:** Valdosta State College, 1500 N. Patterson, Valdosta, GA 31698, (912)333-5600. **Founded:** 1971. **Operating Hours:** Continuous. **ADI:** Albany (Valdosta & Cordele), GA. **Key Personnel:** C.M. Fletcher, Engineer; Mitch Long, Traffic Dir.; Chris Waldrip, General Mgr.; Scott Ragan, Music Dir.; Alison Gought, Operations Mgr.; Katy Martin, Program Dir.; Heather Nowalski, Library Dir. **Wattage:** 5300. **Ad Rates:** Noncommercial.

7741 WWRQ-FM - 107.7
5A A1 Brooks Dr. Phone: (912)244-1009
Valdosta, GA 31601 Fax: (912)247-4722

Format: Album-Oriented Rock (AOR). **Networks:** ABC. **Owner:** Al Brooks, at above address. **Founded:** 1992. **Operating Hours:** Continuous. **ADI:** Albany (Valdosta & Cordele), GA. **Key Personnel:** Al Brooks, General Mgr.; Scott James, Program Dir. **Wattage:** 25,000. **Ad Rates:** $14-20 for 30 seconds; $16-25 for 60 seconds. $14-$20 for 30 seconds; $16-$25 for 60 seconds.

VIDALIA, pop. 10,393.

SE GA. Toombs Co. 82 mi. W. of Savannah. Residential.

7742 The Advance Progress
Advance Publishing Co., Inc.
PO Box 669 Phone: (912)537-3131
Vidalia, GA 30474 Fax: (912)537-4899

Local newspaper. **Subtitle:** Advance - Progress. **Founded:** 1903. **Freq:** Weekly (Wed.). **Print Method:** Offset. **Trim Size:** 14 1/4 x 21 1/2. **Cols./Page:** 6. **Col. Width:** 2 1/4 inches. **Col. Depth:** 21 inches. **Key Personnel:** William F. Ledford, Sr., Editor and Publisher; William F. Ledford, Jr., Advertising Mgr. **Subscription Rates:** $27.50 out of state; $41.00. **Remarks:** Accepts advertising.
Ad Rates: BW: $612.72 **Circ:** 6,500
4C: $912.76
PCI: $4.75

7743 The Advantage
Advance Publishing Co., Inc.
PO Box 669 Phone: (912)537-3131
Vidalia, GA 30474 Fax: (912)537-4899

Shopper. **Subtitle:** ADVANTAGE. **Founded:** 1980. **Freq:** Weekly (Mon.). **Print Method:** Offset. **Trim Size:** 10 1/2 x 14. **Cols./Page:** 6. **Col. Width:** 10 picas. **Col. Depth:** 13 inches. **Key Personnel:** William F. Ledford, Sr., Editor and Publisher; William F. Ledford, Jr., Advertising Mgr. **Remarks:** Accepts advertising.
Ad Rates: BW: $440.70 **Circ:** Free 20,400
4C: $740.70
PCI: $5.56

7744 WGPH-FM - 91.5
3213 Huxley Dr. Phone: (706)733-8201
Augusta, GA 30909-3128 Fax: (706)736-1269
E-mail: good_news_network@msn

Format: Religious. **Owner:** Augusta Radio Fellowship Institute Inc., at above address. **Founded:** 1989. **Operating Hours:** Continuous. **Key Personnel:** C.T. Barinowski, President; M.C. Barinowski, Vice President. **Wattage:** 50,000. **Ad Rates:** Noncommercial.

7745 WKTM-FM - 106.1
PO Box 900 Phone: (912)537-9202
Vidalia, GA 30475

Format: Country. **Networks:** Jones Satellite. **Owner:** Vidalia Communications Corp., at above address. **Operating Hours:** Continuous. **ADI:** Macon, GA. **Key Personnel:** John Ladson, President; Zack Fowler, General Mgr. **Wattage:** 6000. **Ad Rates:** $3.50-5.50 for 30 seconds; $5-7 for 60 seconds.

7746 WTCQ-FM - 97.7
1501 Mount Vernon Rd. Phone: (912)537-9202
PO Box 900 Fax: (912)537-4477
Vidalia, GA 30474

Format: Adult Contemporary. **Networks:** ABC. **Founded:** 1969. **Operating Hours:** Continuous. **ADI:** Savannah, GA. **Key Personnel:** John Ladsen, President; Zack Fowler, General Mgr.; Bill Boyd, Program Dir. **Local Programs:** *Morning Show* 6-9 a.m., Bill Boyd; *Noon Hour* 12 p.m. - 1 p.m., Bill Boyd. **Wattage:** 6000. **Ad Rates:** $3.50-5.50 for 30 seconds; $5-7 for 60 seconds.

7747 WVOP-AM - 970
PO Box 900 Phone: (912)537-9202
Vidalia, GA 30474 Fax: (912)537-4477

Format: Oldies. **Networks:** ABC. **Founded:** 1946. **Operating Hours:** Continuous. **ADI:** Savannah, GA. **Key Personnel:** John Ladson, President; Zack Fowler, General Mgr.; Maruin McIntyre, Program Dir. **Local Programs:** *Lunch Bunch* 12-1 p.m., Marvin McIntyre; *The Morning Show* 6-10 a.m., Marvin McIntyre; *Open Line Weekly*, Zack Fowler. **Wattage:** 5000. **Ad Rates:** $3.50-5.50 for 30 seconds; $5-7 for 60 seconds.

VIENNA†, pop. 2,900.

SC GA. Dooly Co. 40 mi. NE of Albany. Tobacco, peanuts, watermelons.

7748 The News Observer
Dooly Newspapers, Inc.
115 E. Union St. Phone: (912)268-2096
PO Box 186 Fax: (912)268-1924
Vienna, GA 31092
Community newspaper. **Founded:** 1875. **Freq:** Weekly. **Print**

Method: Offset. **Cols./Page:** 6. **Col. Width:** 2 1/8 inches. **Col. Depth:** 21 1/2 inches. **Key Personnel:** Peggy King, Editor; Robert Tribble, Publisher, phone (706)846-4336, fax (706)846-4418. **USPS:** 659-140. **Subscription Rates:** $17.50 individuals; $16.70 senior citizens; $26.50 out of area; $35 out of state. **Remarks:** Accepts advertising. **Formerly:** The Vienna News Observer.
Ad Rates: BW: $477.30 **Circ:** Paid 1,843
SAU: $5.20 Free 77
PCI: $3.95

VILLA RICA, pop. 3,420.

W. GA. Carroll and Douglas Co. 25 mi. W. of Atlanta. Residential.

7749 Villa Rican
PO Box 757 Phone: (404)459-5166
Villa Rica, GA 30180 Fax: (404)459-4804

Newspaper. **Founded:** 1935. **Freq:** Weekly (Thurs.). **Print Method:** Offset. **Cols./Page:** 6. **Col. Width:** 26 nonpareils. **Col. Depth:** 301 agate lines. **Key Personnel:** Frank X. Ellis, Editor; Dawn Weatherby, Publisher; Patricia Darbonne, Office Mgr.; Peggy Polland, Sales Rep. **Subscription Rates:** $20 individuals; $29 out of state; $18 seniors; $26.50 outside county. **Remarks:** Color advertising accepted; rates available upon request.
Ad Rates: GLR: $4.25 **Circ:** 2,500
BW: $503.10
4C: $40
SAU: $3.90
PCI: $3.90

WADLEY, pop. 2,363.

Jefferson Co. 42 mi. SE of Augusta. Manufactures forest equipment products, textiles. Sawmills. Corn, cotton, soybeans.

7750 Logger and Lumberman
S/K Publishing Group, Inc.
257 N. Main St. Phone: (912)252-5237
PO Box 489 Fax: (912)252-1140
Wadley, GA 30477-0489
Free: (800)634-1261
Publisher E-mail: loglumber@jeffersonenergy.com

Magazine for the forest products industry. **Founded:** 1952. **Freq:** Monthly. **Print Method:** Offset. **Trim Size:** 8 3/8 x 10 7/8. **Cols./Page:** 3. **Col. Width:** 26 nonpareils. **Col. Depth:** 133 agate lines. **Key Personnel:** Jack D. Smith, Editor and Publisher; Jane K. Smith, Advertising Mgr. **ISSN:** 0192-7124. **Subscription Rates:** $25 individuals. **Remarks:** Accepts advertising.
Ad Rates: GLR: $45 **Circ:** Non-paid 18,677
BW: $1,950
4C: $2,645

WARM SPRINGS

7751 WJSP-FM - 88.1
609 White House Pkwy. Phone: (706)655-2145
Warm Springs, GA 31830

Format: Classical; News; Public Radio. **Networks:** Peach State Public Radio; National Public Radio (NPR). **Founded:** 1985. **Operating Hours:** 6 a.m.-midnight. **Key Personnel:** Norman Bemelmans, Radio Dir.; James Argroves, Sr. Reporter; Al Korn, Engineering Dir.; John H. Davis, Chief Engineer. **Wattage:** 100,000 ERP. **Ad Rates:** Noncommercial. **URL:** http://www.gpb.org.

WARNER ROBINS, pop. 39,893.

C. GA. Houston Co. 17 mi. S. of Macon. Robin Air Force Base. Machine shop. Manufactures aircraft parts. Agriculture. Soybeans, peaches, peanuts.

7752 Citizen Airman
Air Force Reserve Command
HQ AFRC/PA Phone: (912)327-1773
Warner Robins, GA 31098-1635 Fax: (912)327-0878
Publication E-mail: citamn@tecnet2.jcte.jcs.mil

Subtitle: The Official Magazine of the Air Force Reserve. **Founded:** 1949. **Freq:** Bimonthly. **Print Method:** Offset. Uses mats. **Trim Size:** 8 1/8 x 10 7/8. **Cols./Page:** 3. **Col. Width:** 13.6 picas. **Col. Depth:** 9 3/4 inches. **Key Personnel:** Cliff Tyler, Editor, phone (912)327-1770, cliff.tyler@afres.af.mil. **ISSN:** 0887-9680. **Subscription Rates:** $9.50 individuals; $11.90 other countries. **Remarks:** Advertising not accepted. **URL:** http://www.afres.af.mil/hq/citamn/default.htm. **Formerly:** The Air Reservist.
Circ: Controlled 85,000

7753 The Daily Sun
PO Box 2768 Phone: (912)923-6432
Warner Robins, GA 31098-2768 Fax: (912)328-7682

General newspaper. **Founded:** Feb. 24, 1949. **Freq:** Daily (eve.), Sunday (morn.). **Print Method:** Offset. **Cols./Page:** 6. **Col. Width:** 25 nonpareils. **Col. Depth:** 301 agate lines. **Key Personnel:** Robin Booker, Editor; John Hall, General Mgr.; Debbie Lord, Advertising Mgr. **Subscription Rates:** $90 individuals. **Remarks:** Accepts advertising.
Ad Rates: BW: $1,073.28 **Circ:** Mon.-Fri. ‡9,214
4C: $1,263.28 Sun. ‡10,011
SAU: $9.41

7754 Robins Rev-Up
The Daily Sun
WR-ALC Office of Public Affairs Phone: (912)926-2137
215 Page Rd., Ste. 106 Fax: (912)926-9597
Warner Robins, GA 31098-1662
Military newspaper (tabloid). **Founded:** 1954. **Freq:** Weekly (Fri.). **Print Method:** Offset. **Trim Size:** 11 3/4 x 14. **Cols./Page:** 5. **Col. Width:** 2 1/16 inches. **Col. Depth:** 13 inches. **Key Personnel:** Bill Chiusano, Publisher. **Remarks:** Accepts advertising.
Ad Rates: BW: $1,609 **Circ:** Free ‡20,000
4C: $1,804
SAU: $12.43
PCI: $12.43

7755 The Robins Review
1764 Watson Blvd. Phone: (912)922-5758
PO Drawer 1969 Fax: (912)922-4559
Warner Robins, GA 31099
Official newspaper of American Federation of Government Employees, Local 987. **Founded:** Sept. 1973. **Freq:** Semimonthly. **Print Method:** Offset. **Trim Size:** 10 x 14. **Cols./Page:** 6. **Col. Width:** 9 1/2 picas. **Col. Depth:** 14 inches. **Key Personnel:** Jane Armstrong Newell, Editor and Publisher; Rod Newell, Advertising Mgr. **Subscription Rates:** Free. **Remarks:** Accepts advertising.
Ad Rates: GLR: $.38 **Circ:** Free ‡13,800
BW: $376.32
4C: $676.32
PCI: $5.32

7756 The Warner Robins Buyers Guide
The Warner Robins Buyers' Guide
1111 Leverette Rd. Phone: (912)929-2696
Warner Robins, GA 31088 Fax: (912)328-0977

Shopper. **Founded:** 1982. **Freq:** Weekly (Wed.). **Print Method:** Offset. **Key Personnel:** Jim DeRoy, Publisher; Michael Hall, Editor. **Remarks:** Accepts advertising.
Ad Rates: GLR: $.45 **Circ:** (Not Reported)

7757 WCOP-AM - 1350
PO Box 2127 Phone: (912)923-3416
Warner Robins, GA 31099-2127 Fax: (912)923-3416

Format: Religious. **Networks:** USA Radio. **Formerly:** WAVC-AM. **Operating Hours:** Continuous. **Key Personnel:** Bill Bruton, Station Mgr.; Bill Best, Sales Mgr.; Nelda Bruton, Office Mgr.; Paul Alford, President. **Wattage:** 5000. **Ad Rates:** $4.50-8.00 for 30 seconds; $7.00-11.00 for 60 seconds.

WARRENTON

7758 The Warrenton Clipper
407 Norwood Street Phone: (706)465-3395
PO Box 306 Fax: (706)465-3396
Warrenton, GA 30828-0306
Community newspaper. **Founded:** 1843. **Freq:** Weekly (Fri.). **Print Method:** Offset. **Cols./Page:** 8. **Col. Width:** 9 1/2 picas. **Col. Depth:** 21 inches. **Key Personnel:** Judy U. Johnson, Editor; Karl N. Haywood, General Mgr. **Subscription Rates:** $19.08 individuals; $22.26 out of area. **Remarks:** Accepts advertising.
Ad Rates: BW: $337 **Circ:** 3,300
4C: $524
PCI: $3.95

WASHINGTON†, pop. 4,662.

NE GA. Wilkes Co. 40 mi. S. of Athens. Historic sites, museums. Manufactures fibre glass fabrics, polyethylene film, textiles. Pine, hardwood timber. Agriculture. Dairy, beef, poultry, cornmeal.

7759 News-Reporter
116 W. Robert Toombs Ave. Phone: (404)678-2636
PO Box 340 Fax: (706)678-3857
Washington, GA 30673-0340
Local newspaper. **Founded:** 1912. **Freq:** Weekly (Thurs.). **Print Method:** Offset. **Cols./Page:** 6. **Col. Width:** 27 nonpareils. **Col. Depth:** 301 agate lines. **Key Personnel:** P. Smythe Newsome, Editor and Publisher. **Subscription Rates:** $10 individuals. **Remarks:** Accepts advertising.
Ad Rates: GLR: $.20 **Circ:** 4,900
BW: $245.10

7760 WLOV-AM - 1370
823 Berkshire Dr. Phone: (706)678-2125
Washington, GA 30673 Fax: (706)678-1925

Format: Oldies. **Networks:** Satellite Music Network; Gannett News. **Owner:** Ptak Broadcasting, Inc., Box 400, Washington, GA 30673, (404)367-9246. **Founded:** 1955. **Operating Hours:** 18 hours daily; 60% network, 40% local. **Key Personnel:** Rodney Holloway, Manager; Jan VanDiver, Contact. **Wattage:** 1000. **Ad Rates:** $5.50 for 30 seconds; $8 for 60 seconds.

7761 WLOV-FM - 100.1
823 Berkshire Dr. Phone: (706)678-2125
Washington, GA 30673 Fax: (706)678-1925

Format: Hot Country; Sports. **Networks:** Jones Satellite. **Owner:** P & T Broadcasting, Inc., at above address. **Founded:** 1970. **Operating Hours:** 6 a.m.-midnight; 60% network, 40% local. **ADI:** Augusta, GA. **Key Personnel:** Chip Hardin, General Mgr.; Wes Jerigan, Program Dir. **Wattage:** 3000. **Ad Rates:** $5.50 for 30 seconds; $8 for 60 seconds.

WATKINSVILLE

7762 Oconee Enterprise
PO Box 535 Phone: (404)769-5175
Watkinsville, GA 30677 Fax: (404)769-8532

Community newspaper. **Founded:** 1884. **Freq:** Weekly (Thurs.). **Print Method:** Offset. **Trim Size:** 6 x 21 1/2. **Cols./Page:** 6. **Col. Width:** 13 1/2 picas. **Col. Depth:** 21 1/2 inches. **Key Personnel:** Vinnie Williams, Publisher; Joe Feeney, Editor; Cathe Stein, Advertising Dir. **USPS:** 402-720. **Subscription Rates:** $14; $16 out of area; $18 out of state. **Remarks:** Accepts advertising.
Ad Rates: GLR: $6.90 **Circ:** Thurs. ★4,031
BW: $831.60
4C: $956.60
PCI: $6.60

WAYCROSS, pop. 19,302.

SE GA. Ware Co. 90 mi. SW of Savannah. Manufactures caskets, footwear, mobile homes, cigars, furniture, rubber products, textiles. Meat packing, cold storage plants; naval stores. Pine, cypress, gum timber. Diversified farming. Tobacco, corn.

7763 Waycross Journal Herald
Isabella St. Phone: (912)283-2244
PO Box 219 Fax: (912)283-2815
Waycross, GA 31502
Newspaper with Democratic orientation. **Founded:** 1876. **Freq:** Mon.-Sat. (eve.). **Print Method:** Offset. **Cols./Page:** 6. **Col. Width:** 24 nonpareils. **Col. Depth:** 301 agate lines. **Key Personnel:** Jack Williams III, Editor; Roger Williams, Publisher. **Subscription Rates:** $79.20 individuals. **Remarks:** Accepts advertising.
Ad Rates: GLR: $.85 **Circ:** Paid ‡13,435
PCI: $6.75

7764 WACL-AM - 570
528 Memorial Dr. Phone: (912)283-4660
PO Box 858 Fax: (912)283-4661
Waycross, GA 31502

Format: Religious. **Networks:** ABC. **Founded:** 1951. **Operating Hours:** 6 a.m.-midnight; 7% network, 93% local. **Key Personnel:** Jim Rivers, Manager; Bill Parker, Sales Mgr. **Wattage:** 5000. **Ad Rates:** $8 for 30 seconds; $10 for 60 seconds.

7765 Waycross Cable Co.
PO Box 37 Phone: (912)283-2332
Waycross, GA 31502 Fax: (912)285-9836

Key Personnel: John Harrison, General Mgr. **Cities Served:** Ware and Brantley counties.

7766 WKUB-FM - 105.1
Box 1472 Phone: (912)449-3391
Waycross, GA 31502 Fax: (912)449-6284
E-mail: wkub@almatel.net

Format: Country. **Networks:** ABC. **Owner:** Gentry Troy Mattox, at above address. **Founded:** 1979. **Operating Hours:** Continuous. **ADI:** Savannah, GA. **Key Personnel:** T. Mattox, Contact; James E. Miller, Sales Mgr.; Ray Williamson, Music Dir.; June Strickland, Traffic. **Local Programs:** *Brian Blount Morning Show* 6 a.m.-8 a.m. Monday-Friday; *High School Football* night Friday. **Wattage:** 25,000. **Ad Rates:** $10-14 for 30 seconds; $12-16 for 60 seconds.

7767 WWUF-FM - 97.7
701 Carserll Ave. Phone: (912)283-2229
Waycross, GA 31501 Fax: (912)285-9797

Format: Classic Rock. **Networks:** Independent. **Owner:** Joann Brehm, at above address. **Founded:** 1986. **Formerly:** WMUI-FM. **Operating Hours:** Continuous. **ADI:** Jacksonville (Brunswick), FL. **Key Personnel:** Tim Chisholm, President; Steve Summers, Program Dir.; Patty Hickox, Traffic Mgr. **Local Programs:** *Big Wolf Top 5 at 5*; *Bigger Better Birthday & Anniversary Bash*; *Laser Lunch Set.* **Wattage:** 6000. **Ad Rates:** $8 for 30 seconds; $10.30-12.60 for 60 seconds.

WAYNESBORO†, pop. 5,760.

E. GA. Burke Co. 30 mi. S. of Augusta. Cotton and lumber mills; garment, steel, and metal factories. Nuclear generating plant. Timber. Agriculture. Cotton, corn, soybeans, peanuts.

7768 The Signal
Citizen Newspapers
PO Box 948 Phone: (706)554-2111
Waynesboro, GA 30830 Fax: (706)554-2437
Publication E-mail: chalker@csranet.com

Military and community newspaper. **Freq:** Weekly (Fri.). **Print Method:** Offset. **Trim Size:** 14 x 21 1/2. **Cols./Page:** 6. **Col. Width:** 26 nonpareils. **Col. Depth:** 301 agate lines. **Key Personnel:** Bonnie K. Taylor, Administration/Gen. Mgr. **Subscription Rates:** $18 individuals. **Remarks:** Accepts advertising. **Alt. Formats:** CD-ROM. **Former name:** The Semaphore.
Ad Rates: GLR: $.32 **Circ:** ‡18,600
BW: $1,083.60
4C: $1,423.60
SAU: $8.40
PCI: $8.40

7769 The True Citizen
Citizen Newspapers
601 E. 6th St. Phone: (706)554-2111
PO Box 948 Fax: (706)554-2437
Waynesboro, GA 30830
Community newspaper. **Founded:** 1882. **Freq:** Weekly (Wed.). **Print Method:** Offset. **Trim Size:** 14 x 21 1/2. **Cols./Page:** 6. **Col. Width:** 26 nonpareils. **Col. Depth:** 301 agate lines. **Key Personnel:** Roy F. Chalker, Jr., Publisher, chalker@csranet.com; Bonnie K. Taylor, Administration/Gen. Mgr. **Subscription Rates:** $18 individuals. **Remarks:** Accepts advertising.
Ad Rates: GLR: $.33 **Circ:** ‡5,200
BW: $619.20
4C: $959.20
SAU: $4.80
PCI: $4.80

7770 WYFA-FM - 107.1
1388 Old Waynesboro Rd. Phone: (706)554-3942
Waynesboro, GA 30830-9684 Fax: (706)554-3942

Format: Religious. **Networks:** Bible Broadcasting. **Founded:** 1985. **Operating Hours:** Continuous; 99% network, 1% local. **Key Personnel:** George Quick, Station Mgr. **Wattage:** 25000.

WEST POINT

WC GA. Troup and Harris Co. 2 mi. E. of Lanett.

7771 WCJM-FM - 100.9
705 4th Ave. Phone: (706)645-1310
West Point, GA 31833 Fax: (706)645-2991

Format: Country; Contemporary Country; Gospel; News. **Networks:** CBS. **Owner:** Fuller Broadcasting of Valley, Inc., at above address, (706)645-2991, Fax: (706)645-3364. **Founded:** 1958. **Formerly:** WBMK-FM (1975). **Operating Hours:** 5 a.m.-10 p.m.; 3% network, 97% local. **Key Personnel:** John Kennedy, General Mgr.; Ernie Pearce, News Dir.; Audra Prather, Office Mgr.; Clint Stanton, PD. **Wattage:** 6000. **Ad Rates:** $6 for 15 seconds; $8 for 30 seconds; $12 for 60 seconds.

WINDER†, pop. 9,500.

NE GA. Barrow Co. 20 mi. W. of Athens. Manufactures furniture, textiles, fiberglass, railroad cars, rugs, fertilizer. Poultry processing, seed cleaning plants. Agriculture. Cotton, corn, vegetables, chickens and cattle.

7772 The Barrow County Shopper
The WinderNews
189 W. Athens St. Phone: (770)867-7557
PO Drawer C Fax: (770)867-1034
Winder, GA 30680
Publisher E-mail: windernews@mindspring.com

Shopper guide. **Founded:** 1984. **Freq:** Weekly (Wed.). **Print Method:** Photo offset. **Cols./Page:** 6. **Col. Width:** 13 inches. **Col. Depth:** 21 inches. **Key Personnel:** Debbie Burgamy, Publisher. **Subscription Rates:** Free. **Remarks:** Accepts advertising. **Former name:** The Advantage (Feb. 3, 1999).
Ad Rates: BW: $1,341.60 **Circ:** Free ‡11,700
PCI: $9.90

7773 The Winder News
The WinderNews
189 W. Athens St. Phone: (770)867-7557
PO Drawer C Fax: (770)867-1034
Winder, GA 30680
Publisher E-mail: windernews@mindspring.com

Local newspaper. **Founded:** 1893. **Freq:** Biweekly (Wed. & Sun.). **Print Method:** Offset. **Cols./Page:** 6. **Col. Width:** 25 nonpareils. **Col. Depth:** 294 agate lines. **Key Personnel:** Phil Hermann, Editor; Debbie Burgamy, Publisher; JoAnn Craven, Circulation Mgr. **Subscription Rates:** $20 individuals; $0.50 single issue. **Remarks:** Accepts advertising.
Ad Rates: GLR: $.70 **Circ:** Wed. ♦**5,752**
BW: $1,019.10 Sun. ♦**5,497**
SAU: $7.90

7774 WIMO-AM - 1300
Corinth Church Rd. Phone: (770)867-1300
PO Box 1300 Fax: (770)868-1962
Winder, GA 30680

Format: Top 40; Country; Sports; Gospel. **Networks:** ABC; Georgia Radio. **Owner:** WIMO-AM 1300, at above address. **Founded:** 1952. **Operating Hours:** 6 a.m.-9 p.m. 25% network; 75% local. **ADI:** Atlanta (Athens & Rome), GA. **Key Personnel:** Sid Griffin, Gen.Mgr./Sales/Production; Sid Griffin, News/Production/Sports Dir.; Barbara Hudson, Traffic/News/Production Dir. **Local Programs:** *Community Calendar* Mon. - Sun.; 9:30 am, 12:30 pm, 5:15 pm, Barbara Hudson. **Wattage:** 1000. **Ad Rates:** $4.00 for 15 seconds; $5.50 for 30 seconds; $7.50 for 60 seconds.

7775 WYFW-FM - 89.5
71 N. Broad St., Ste. 405 Phone: (770)867-8133
Winder, GA 30680 Fax: (770)867-8133
E-mail: wyfw@aol.com

Format: Middle-of-the-Road (MOR); Religious. **Networks:** Bible Broadcasting. **Founded:** 1987. **Formerly:** WBPS FM. **Operating Hours:** Continuous. **Key Personnel:** Paul D. Montgomery, Station Mgr. **Wattage:** 6,000. **Ad Rates:** Noncommercial.

WINTERVILLE

7776 KERP-FM - 91.9
730 Lem Edwards Rd.
Winterville, GA 30683-9554

Format: Religious. **Networks:** Moody Broadcasting. **Owner:** Colorado Broadcasting Foundation Inc., at above address. **Founded:** 1986. **Operating Hours:** Continuous. **Key Personnel:** Ralph Arnold, President; Merle Arnold, Contact. **Wattage:** 600.

WOODSTOCK, pop. 2,699.

NW GA. Cherokee Co. 33 mi. N. of Atlanta. Residential.

7777 News Shopper
News Shopper, Inc.
5 N. Main St. Phone: (404)926-4467
Woodstock, GA 30188 Fax: (404)591-8478

Shopping guide (tabloid). **Founded:** 1973. **Freq:** Weekly (Wed.). **Print Method:** Photo offset. **Cols./Page:** 4. **Col. Width:** 2 3/8 inches. **Col. Depth:** 14 inches. **Key Personnel:** Bill Godwin, Publisher, phone (770)926-4467; Jim McElreath, Publisher, phone (770)974-6495. **Subscription Rates:** Free. **Remarks:** Advertising accepted; rates available upon request.
Circ: Non-paid 20,542

YOUNG HARRIS

NE GA. Towns Co. 10 mi. W. of Hiawassee.

7778 WZCM-AM - 770
5301 Meadow Ln. Phone: (404)379-3168
PO Box 860 Fax: (404)379-3169
Young Harris, GA 30582
Free: (800)226-0771

Format: Religious. **Owner:** Young Harris Broadcasting, Inc., at above address, Free: (800)379-9770. **Founded:** 1984. **Formerly:** WZEL-AM (1993). **Operating Hours:** 100% satellite. **Key Personnel:** Mark Mote, Program Dir. **Wattage:** 750. **Ad Rates:** $3.50 for 30 seconds; $6 for 60 seconds.

ZEBULON†, pop. 995.

W. GA. Pike Co. 12 mi. S. of Griffin. Residential. Agricultural.

7779 Pike County Journal-Reporter
Hometown News Corp.
PO Box 789 Phone: (706)567-3446
Zebulon, GA 30295 Fax: (706)567-8814

Community newspaper. **Founded:** 1889. **Freq:** Weekly (Wed.). **Print Method:** Offset. **Cols./Page:** 6. **Col. Width:** 27 nonpareils. **Col. Depth:** 301 agate lines. **Key Personnel:** Rachel N. McClelland, Editor and Publisher. **Subscription Rates:** $12 individuals. **Remarks:** Accepts advertising.
Ad Rates: GLR: $.17 **Circ:** ‡2,300

HAWAII

State Capital, HONOLULU

The Hawaiian Islands are situated in the North Pacific Ocean about 2,000 nautical miles southwest of San Francisco. There are 20 islands. The combined area of the eight principal islands is 6,423 square miles (about half the size of Connecticut). The Island of Hawaii is the largest (4,038 square miles), but the concentration of population is on Oahu. The islands are mountainous and volcanic in origin. The average medium elevation of all of the islands is about 2,000 feet. Notable exceptions are Mauna Kea, the highest peak (13,796 feet-dormant), Mauna Loa (13,677 feet-active), Haleakala (10,023 feet-dormant). Mount Waialeale, Kauai Island, has more rain than any place in the world with a 28-year annual average of 489 inches. Hawaii, with its abundant rainfall and prevailing northeast trade winds, has mild, uniform climate with an annual average temperature of 77.2; highest on record, 100; lowest on record, 52. Honolulu, the capital city located on the island of Oahu, is the commercial center and seat of government in the island state. The University of Hawaii is located in Honolulu. Also situated in Honolulu is one of our largest army posts and the nation's largest naval base and shipyard installation (Pearl Harbor).

POPULATION: 1,160,000 (1992). Rank among the states, 40th.

AGRICULTURE: Number of farms: 5,000 (1992). Farm acreage: 2,000,000 (1992). Cash receipts from farm marketings: crops, $506,000,000 (1991); livestock and products, $91,000,000 (1991).

FISHERIES: Total catch: 28,000,000 lbs. (1991), $58,000,000 value. Principal fish: tuna, snapper, marlin.

FORESTS: Total forest land: less than 500,000 acres (1991).

MINERALS: Value of production: $141,000,000 (1991). Principal minerals: stone, cement, sand and gravel.

MANUFACTURES: Value added by manufacture: $1,383,000,000 (1991). Leading industry groups: food and related products.

LIST OF COUNTIES

Total number of counties 4

County, Location on Map, and County Seat	Pop.
Hawaii (SE), Hilo	120,317
Honolulu (SE), Honolulu	836,231
Kauai (SW), Lihue	51,177
Maui (E), Wailuku	100,374

STATISTICS

Newspapers

Period of Issue	
Daily	5
Evening Daily	4
Morning Daily	2
Daily with Sunday edition	4
Weekly	12
Biweekly	1
Bimonthly	4
Free or partly free	8
Total Newspapers	20

Periodicals

Period of Issue	
Weekly	4
Semimonthly	1
Monthly	11
Bimonthly	4
Quarterly	10
Total Periodicals	44

Total number of publications 64

Radio Stations

AM Stations	21
FM Stations	25
Total Radio Stations	46

TV Stations

Total TV Stations 7

Cable Stations

Total Cable Systems 8

Total number of broadcast listings 61

CAMP H M SMITH

7780 Asia-Pacific Defense Forum
U.S. Pacific Command
Box 64013 Phone: (808)477-2813
Camp H M Smith, HI 96861-4013 Fax: (808)477-0618
Publication E-mail: apdforum@hq.pacom.mil

Professional journal for members of the militaries of all nations in the Asia-Pacific region. **Freq:** Quarterly. **Trim Size:** 8 1/4 x 10 1/2. **Cols./Page:** 3. **Key Personnel:** Paul S. Stankiewicz, Editor-in-Chief, phone (808)477-0760, fax (808)477-1471, paul@poidog.pacom.mil. **Subscription Rates:** Free to qualified subscribers. **Remarks:** Advertising not accepted. **URL:** http://www.pacom.mil/forum/forum.htm.
Circ: Non-paid 27,000

ELEELE, pop. 580.

S HI. Kauai Co. S. coast of Kauai Island, E. of Hanapepe.

7781 KUAI-AM - 720
4469 Waialo Rd. Phone: (808)335-3171
PO Box 720 Fax: (808)335-3834
Eleele, HI 96705-0720

Format: Full Service; Ethnic. **Networks:** Mutual Broadcasting System. **Owner:** American Islands Broadcasting Corp., at above address. **Founded:** 1965. **Operating Hours:** 5 a.m.-midnight; 8% network, 92% local. **Key Personnel:** William G. Dahle, General Mgr.; J.S. Robertson, Contact; Reggie DeRoos, Contact. **Wattage:** 5000. **Ad Rates:** $18-25 for 30 seconds; $22-30 for 60 seconds.

HANALEI

7782 KAQA-FM - 91.9
PO Box 825 Phone: (808)826-7774
Hanalei, HI 96714 Fax: (808)826-7977
E-mail: kkcr@hawaiian.net

Format: Public Radio. **Networks:** Pacifica. **Owner:** Kekahu Foundation, Inc., at above address. **Founded:** 1993. **Operating Hours:** Continuous. **Key Personnel:** Jon Scott, Music Dir., bornarebel@aol.com; Mary Cunning, Station Mgr.; Jeff Shepard, Program Dir. **Wattage:** 1000. **Ad Rates:** Noncommercial; underwriting available. **URL:** http://www.kkcr.org.

7783 KKCR-FM - 90.9
PO Box 825 Phone: (808)826-7774
Hanalei, HI 96714 Fax: (808)876-7977
E-mail: kkcr@hawaiian.net

Format: Public Radio. **Owner:** Kekahu Foundation, Inc., at above address. **Founded:** 1993. **Operating Hours:** Continuous. **Key Personnel:** Jon Scott, Music Dir., bornarebel@aol.com; Mary Cunning, Station Mgr.; Jeff Shepard, Program Dir. **Wattage:** 1000. **Ad Rates:** Noncommercial; underwriting available. **URL:** http://www.kkcr.org.

HAWI

7784 Sun Cablevision
Box 174 Phone: (808)889-5868
Hawi, HI 96719

Formerly: Kamehameha Cablevision.

HILO†, pop. 37,017.

SE HI. Hawaii Co. On NE coast of the Island of Hawaii. Port of entry. Tourist resort. This is the most tropical of the islands and the only one with an active volcano. Agriculture. Sugar cane, coffee, vegetables, orchids, tropical flowers, papaya, macadamia nuts. Tuna, mullet fisheries.

7785 Hawaii Tribune-Herald
Donrey Media Group
777 Kilauea Ave. Phone: (808)935-6621
Hilo, HI 96720 Fax: (808)961-0098

General newspaper. **Founded:** 1895. **Freq:** Daily and Sunday (morn.). **Print Method:** Offset. **Cols./Page:** 6. **Col. Width:** 25 nonpareils. **Col. Depth:** 301 agate lines. **Key Personnel:** Eugene Tao, Editor; Jim Wilson, Publisher. **Subscription Rates:** $81 individuals.
Ad Rates: SAU: $13.75 **Circ:** Mon.-Fri. 19,140
Sun. 22,891

7786 Hawaiian Cablevision
1257 Kilauea Ave. Phone: (808)961-0443
Hilo, HI 96720-4205 Fax: (808)935-0148

Key Personnel: Jay R. Warkentin, Contact. **Cities Served:** subscribing households 17,000; 37 channels.

7787 KAHU-AM - 1060
PO Box 4727 Phone: (808)959-2056
Hilo, HI 96720 Fax: (808)959-4507

Format: Ethnic; Hawaiian. **Owner:** KANI Communications Inc., at above address. **Founded:** Oct. 1985. **Key Personnel:** Haunani Baker, Station Mgr. **Local Programs:** *Hawaiian Moon Calendar; Kahu's Island Showcase; Legends of Old Hawai'i.* **Wattage:** 1 kw.

7788 KCIF-FM - 90.3
PO Box 1060 Phone: (808)935-7434
Hilo, HI 96721 Fax: (808)961-6022

Format: Religious. **Networks:** SkyLight Satellite. **Owner:** Hilo Christian Broadcasting Corp., at above address. **Founded:** Sept. 1, 1995. **Operating Hours:** Continuous. **Key Personnel:** Dean Manley, President, phone (808)959-8257, kh6b@juno.com; Rev. Robert Daley, Vice President, phone (808)982-6688. **Wattage:** 850. **Ad Rates:** Noncommercial. **URL:** http://home1.gte.net/keif/index.htm.

7789 KHLO-AM - 850
913 Kanuelehua Phone: (808)935-1952
Hilo, HI 96720-5116 Fax: (808)935-0396

Format: Oldies. **Networks:** Independent. **Owner:** Li Hing Mui, Inc., at above address. **Founded:** 1950. **Operating Hours:** Continuous. **Key Personnel:** Dave R. Fransen, Station Mgr.; Terry Connor, Sales Mgr. **Wattage:** 5000. **Ad Rates:** $6-12 for 30 seconds; $10-16 for 60 seconds.

7790 KHWI-FM - 100.3
688 Kinoole St. Phone: (808)935-6858
Hilo, HI 96720 Fax: (808)969-7949

Format: Album-Oriented Rock (AOR). **Simulcasts:** KAOY-FM. **Owner:** Big Island Radio, L.P., at above address. **Founded:** 1988. **Formerly:** KIPA-FM. **Operating Hours:** Continuous. **Key Personnel:** Buddy Gordon, President/Gen. Mgr.; Danny Yamamoto, Operations Mgr. **Wattage:** 74,000. **Ad Rates:** Advertising accepted; rates available upon request. Combined advertising rates available with KIPA-AM, KLUA, KPVS, KKON, KAOY, KAOE.

7791 KIPA-AM - 620
688 Kinoole St. Phone: (808)935-6858
Hilo, HI 96720 Fax: (808)969-7949

Format: Middle-of-the-Road (MOR). **Networks:** NBC. **Owner:** Big Island Radio, L.P., at above address. **Founded:** 1947. **Operating Hours:** Continuous. **Key Personnel:** Buddy Gordon, President/Gen. Mgr.; Danny Yamamoto, Operations Mgr. **Wattage:** 10,000. **Ad Rates:** Advertising accepted; rates available upon request. Combined advertising rates available with KHWI-FM, KAAY, KLUA, KPVS, KKON, KAOE.

7792 KKBG-FM - 97.9
913 Kanoelehua Ave. Phone: (808)961-0651
Hilo, HI 96720 Fax: (808)935-0396

Format: Contemporary Hit Radio (CHR); Adult Contemporary. **Networks:** Independent. **Owner:** Brewer Broadcasting Hawaii, 913 Kanoellthun Ave, Hilo, HI 96720, (808)961-0657, Fax: (808)935-0396. **Founded:** 1979. **Operating Hours:** Continuous; 100% local. **Key Personnel:** Jeanine Atebara, Station Mgr.; Nelson Parker, Music Dir.; Rodney Pacheco, Contact; Nelson Parker, Program Dir. **Wattage:** 40,000. **Ad Rates:** $22-35 for 30 seconds; $19-25 for 60 seconds.

7793 KPUA-AM - 670
1145 Kilauea Ave. Phone: (808)935-5461
Hilo, HI 96720-4203 Fax: (808)935-7761
Free: (800)321-0670

Format: News; Talk; Sports. **Networks:** CBS. **Founded:** 1932. **Operating Hours:** Continuous. **Key Personnel:** Chris Leonard, Contact. **Wattage:** 10,000. **Ad Rates:** $11-15 for 30 seconds; $14-19 for 60 seconds. $11-$15 for 30 seconds; $14-$19 for 60 seconds. Combined advertising rates available with KWXX-FM.

7794 KWXX-FM - 94.7
1145 Kilauea Ave. Phone: (808)935-5461
Hilo, HI 96720-4203 Fax: (808)935-7761

Format: Adult Contemporary; Hawaiian. **Networks:** CBS. **Owner:** New West Broadcasting Corp., at above address. **Founded:** 1984. **Operating Hours:** Continuous. **Key Personnel:** John F. Leonard, Pres./Gen. Mgr.; Chris Leonard, General Sales Mgr.; Jacqueline (Skylark) Ota, Program Dir. **Wattage:** 100,000. **Ad Rates:** $18 for 30 seconds; $20 for 60 seconds. KPUA-AM.

HONOLULU†, pop. 365,048.

SC HI. Honolulu Co. On Oahu Island. University of Hawaii. State capital. Tourist resort. Principal port and business center of the islands. Major military installations. Oil refining. Wood carvings. Pineapple canneries; sugar industries; fish packing and canning. Manufactures fertilizer, cement, concrete products, steel bars, flour, soap, garments, awnings, tents, beverages.

7795 Asian Perspectives
University of Hawaii Press
346 Social Sciences Building Phone: (808)956-7500
Dept. of Anthropology Fax: (808)956-9541
Univ. of Hawaii
Honolulu, HI 96822
Publication E-mail: mgraves@hawaii.edu; lorilee@hawaii.edu
Publisher E-mail: uhpjourn@hawaii.edu

Journal centering on the archaeology and prehistory of Asia and the Pacific. **Subtitle:** The Journal of Archaeology for Asia and the Pacific. **Founded:** 1957. **Freq:** Semiannual. **Trim Size:** 7 x 10. **Cols./Page:** 1. **Key Personnel:** Michael W. Graves, Editor. **ISSN:** 0066-4835. **Subscription Rates:** $26 individuals; $33 institutions. **Remarks:** Accepts advertising. **Alt. Formats:** Microform.
Ad Rates: BW: $200 **Circ:** Paid 550
Controlled 25

7796 Asian Theater Journal
University of Hawaii Press
Journals Dept. Phone: (808)956-8833
2840 Kolowalu St. Fax: (808)988-6052
Honolulu, HI 96822
Free: (800)956-2840
Publisher E-mail: uhpjourn@hawaii.edu

Journal focusing on the modern and traditional forms of performing arts in Asia. **Founded:** 1984. **Freq:** Semimonthly. **Trim Size:** 7 x 10. **Key Personnel:** Samuel L. Leiter, Editor, phone (718)843-2799, fax (718)843-0946, sleiter@brooklyn.cuny.edu. **ISSN:** 0742-5457. **Subscription Rates:** $20 individuals; $40 institutions. **Remarks:** Accepts advertising. **Alt. Formats:** Microform.
Ad Rates: BW: $200 **Circ:** Paid 550
Controlled 40

7797 Bamboo Ridge
Bamboo Ridge Press
PO Box 61781 Phone: (808)626-1481
Honolulu, HI 96839-1781 Fax: (808)626-1481

Journal covering Hawaii's literary scene. **Subtitle:** A Hawaii Writers Journal. **Founded:** 1978. **Freq:** Semiannual. **Print Method:** Offset. **Trim Size:** 6 x 9. **Key Personnel:** Eric Chock, Editor and Publisher; Darrell Lum, Editor and Publisher. **ISSN:** 0733-0308. **Subscription Rates:** $20 individuals. **Remarks:** Accepts advertising.
Ad Rates: BW: $100 **Circ:** ‡500

7798 Biography
University of Hawaii Press
University of Hawaii Phone: (808)956-3774
Honolulu, HI 96822 Fax: (808)956-3774
Publication E-mail: biograph@hawaii.edu
Publisher E-mail: uhpjourn@hawaii.edu

Journal acting as a forum for learned articles dealing with life-writing. **Subtitle:** An Interdisciplinary Quarterly. **Founded:** Jan. 1978. **Freq:** Quarterly. **Print Method:** Offset. **Trim Size:** 6 x 9. **Cols./Page:** 1. **Col. Width:** 26 picas. **Col. Depth:** 46.5 picas. **Key Personnel:** Craig Howes, Editor, phone (808)956-3037, craighow@hawaii.edu. **ISSN:** 0162-4962. **Subscription Rates:** $28 individuals; $36 institutions. **Remarks:** Accepts advertising. **Alt. Formats:** Microform.
Ad Rates: BW: $200 **Circ:** Paid ‡450
Controlled ‡50

7799 Building Management Hawaii
Trade Publishing Co.
287 Mokauea St. Phone: (808)848-0711
Honolulu, HI 96819 Fax: (808)841-3053
Publisher E-mail: tradepub@lana.net

Magazine covering maintenance and building management. **Founded:** 1983. **Freq:** Bimonthly. **Cols./Page:** 3. **Col. Width:** 13 picas. **Col. Depth:** 57 picas. **Key Personnel:** John Black, Managing Editor; Terrence N.K. Sing, Managing Editor. **Subscription Rates:** $3 single issue.
Ad Rates: BW: $995 **Circ:** Non-paid 4,700
4C: $1,665

7800 China Review International
University of Hawaii Press
Journals Dept. Phone: (808)956-8833
2840 Kolowalu St. Fax: (808)988-6052
Honolulu, HI 96822
Free: (800)956-2840
Publication E-mail: china@hawaii.edu
Publisher E-mail: uhpjourn@hawaii.edu

Journal presenting reviews of important current publications

relating to China. **Subtitle:** A Journal of Reviews of Scholarly Literature in Chinese Studies. **Founded:** 1994. **Freq:** Semiannual. **Trim Size:** 7 x 10. **Cols./Page:** 1. **Col. Width:** 30 picas. **Col. Depth:** 48 picas. **Key Personnel:** Roger T. Ames, Editor, phone (808)956-7288, fax (808)956-9228, rthames@hawaii.edu; Daniel Cole, Managing Editor, danielc@hawaii.edu; Cynthia Ning, Managing Editor, cyndy@hawaii.edu. **ISSN:** 1069-5834. **Subscription Rates:** $30 individuals; $36 institutions. **Remarks:** Accepts advertising. **Alt. Formats:** Microform.
Ad Rates: BW: $200 **Circ:** Paid 600
Controlled 45

7801 The Contemporary Pacific
University of Hawaii Press
Moore 225 Phone: (808)943-7743
Center for Pacific Island Studies Fax: (808)956-7053
University of Hawaii at Maui
Honolulu, HI 96822
Publication E-mail: tenorio@hawaii.edu
Publisher E-mail: uhpjourn@hawaii.edu

Journal covering a wide range of current issues and events in the Pacific islands. **Subtitle:** A Journal of Island Affairs. **Founded:** 1989. **Freq:** Semiannual. **Trim Size:** 7 x 10. **Key Personnel:** Geoffrey M. White, Editor. **ISSN:** 1043-898X. **Subscription Rates:** $23 individuals; $35 other countries; $50 institutions other countries; $30 institutions Pacific countries. **Remarks:** Accepts advertising. **Alt. Formats:** Microform.
Ad Rates: BW: $200 **Circ:** Paid 560
Controlled 15

7802 Elepaio
Hawaii Audubon Society
850 Richards St., Ste. 505 Phone: (808)528-1432
Honolulu, HI 96813-4709 Fax: (808)537-5294

Magazine on birds and conservation. **Founded:** 1939. **Freq:** 9/year (combined issues June/July, Aug/Sept, Dec/Jan). **Print Method:** Offset. **Trim Size:** 8.5 x 11. **Cols./Page:** 3. **Col. Width:** 39 nonpareils. **Col. Depth:** 140 agate lines. **ISSN:** 0013-6069. **Subscription Rates:** $10 individuals /institutions. **Remarks:** Advertising not accepted.
Circ: ‡2,000

7803 Hawaii
Fancy Publications
1210 Auahi St., No. 231 Fax: (808)947-0924
Honolulu, HI 96814
Publication E-mail: hawaii@fancypubs.com

Magazine about Hawaii for both visitors and residents. **Founded:** 1985. **Freq:** Bimonthly. **Print Method:** Web offset. **Trim Size:** 8 3/8 x 10 7/8. **Key Personnel:** John Hollon, Editor, jhollon@fancypubs.com. **ISSN:** 0892-0990. **Subscription Rates:** $20; $3.95 single issue. **Remarks:** Advertising accepted; rates available upon request.
Circ: Paid ★85,752

7804 Hawaii Bar Journal
Grass Shack Productions
1136 Union Mall, PH-1 Phone: (808)537-1868
Honolulu, HI 96813 Fax: (808)521-7936

Legal journal containing Hawaii State Bar news and articles for Hawaii attorneys. **Founded:** 1968. **Freq:** Monthly. **Print Method:** Offset. **Trim Size:** 8 1/8 x 10 7/8. **Cols./Page:** 3. **Col. Width:** 2.5 inches. **Col. Depth:** 8 inches. **Key Personnel:** Nancy Arcayna, Managing Editor, phone (808)537-1868, fax (808)521-7936, narcayna@hsba.org; Carol K. Muranaka, Editor. **Subscription Rates:** $30; $60 other countries; $3 single issue. **Remarks:** Accepts advertising. **Formerly:** Hawaii Bar News.
Ad Rates: GLR: $6 **Circ:** Paid 5,400
BW: $695 Non-paid 500
4C: $1,045

7805 Hawaii Beverage Guide
PO Box 853
Honolulu, HI 96808

Magazine for the beverage industry; including brand index, local and national news, product and special events promotion, and government agency releases. **Founded:** 1949. **Freq:** Monthly. **Print Method:** Offset. **Trim Size:** 8 1/2 x 11. **Cols./Page:** 3. **Col. Width:** 28 nonpareils. **Col. Depth:** 140 agate lines. **Key Personnel:** Campbell Mansfield, Editor and Publisher; Lorraine Walters, Advertising Dir. **USPS:** 018-010. **Subscription Rates:** $32. **Remarks:** Accepts advertising.
Ad Rates: BW: $720 **Circ:** ‡2,000
4C: $1,364

7806 Hawaii Business
Hawaii Business Publishing Co.
PO Box 913 Phone: (808)537-9500
Honolulu, HI 96808 Fax: (808)537-6455
Publication E-mail: hawbus@pixi.com

Business magazine for management personnel in Hawaii. **Founded:** 1955. **Freq:** Monthly. **Print Method:** Offset. **Trim Size:** 8 1/8 x 10 7/8. **Cols./Page:** 3. **Col. Width:** 27 nonpareils. **Col. Depth:** 140 agate lines. **Key Personnel:** Floyd Takeuchi, Editor and Publisher. **ISSN:** 0440-5056. **Subscription Rates:** $24 individuals.
Ad Rates: BW: $1,990 **Circ:** Paid ★5,277
4C: $2,590

7807 Hawaii Catholic Herald
1184 Bishop St. Phone: (808)533-1791
Honolulu, HI 96813 Fax: (808)521-8428

Official newspaper (tabloid) of the Roman Catholic Diocese of Honolulu, HI. **Founded:** 1936. **Freq:** Biweekly. **Print Method:** Offset. **Trim Size:** 11 1/2 x 17. **Cols./Page:** 5. **Col. Width:** 1 7/8 inches. **Col. Depth:** 15 inches. **Key Personnel:** Patric Downes, Editor; Most Rev. Joseph A. Ferrario, D.D., Publisher; Donna Aquino, Circulation Mgr. **ISSN:** 1045-3636. **Subscription Rates:** $15; $17 out of state; $20 other countries. **Remarks:** Accepts advertising.
Ad Rates: GLR: $.35 **Circ:** Paid ‡7,000
Non-paid ‡500

7808 Hawaii CPA News
Hawaii Medical Journal
1345 S. Beretania St., No. 301
Honolulu, HI 96814-1821

Publication for accountants. **Founded:** 1966. **Freq:** Monthly. **Print Method:** Photo offset. **Trim Size:** 8 1/8 x 10 7/8. **Cols./Page:** 3. **Col. Width:** 2 1/4 inches. **Col. Depth:** 10 inches. **Key Personnel:** Stephen S. Lent, Publisher. **Subscription Rates:** Free to qualified subscribers. **Remarks:** Accepts advertising. **Formerly:** The Balance Sheet.
Ad Rates: GLR: $7.45 **Circ:** Paid 1,750
BW: $480
4C: $1,060

7809 Hawaii Crop Weather
Hawaii Agricultural Statistics Service
PO Box 22159 Phone: (808)973-9588
Honolulu, HI 96823-2159 Fax: (808)973-2909

Government Report. **Founded:** 1956. **Freq:** Weekly (Mon.). **Print Method:** Offset. **Cols./Page:** 1. **Col. Width:** 84 nonpareils. **Col. Depth:** 133 agate lines. **Key Personnel:** H.K. Rowley, Editor. **Subscription Rates:** $15 individuals. **Remarks:** Advertising not accepted.
Circ: (Not Reported)

7810 Hawaii Dental Journal
Hawaii Medical Journal
1345 S. Beretania St., No. 301
Honolulu, HI 96814-1821

Dental journal. **Founded:** 1967. **Freq:** Bimonthly. **Print Method:** Photo offset. **Trim Size:** 8 1/8 x 10 7/8. **Cols./Page:** 3. **Col. Width:** 2 1/4 inches. **Col. Depth:** 10 inches. **Key Personnel:** Stephen S. Lent, Publisher. **Remarks:** Accepts advertising.
Ad Rates: GLR: $7.45 **Circ:** Paid 1,100
BW: $480
4C: $1,060

7811 Hawaii Hospitality
Rainbow Pacific Publishing Co., Ltd.
1188 Bishop St., No. 1512 Phone: (808)521-8877
Honolulu, HI 96813 Fax: (808)521-8876

Hotel management newsmagazine in Hawaii, Guam, and Micronesia. **Founded:** 1984. **Freq:** Quarterly. **Print Method:** Offset. **Trim Size:** 8 1/8 x 10 7/8. **Key Personnel:** John M. Black, Editor and Publisher. **Subscription Rates:** $18 individuals. **Remarks:** Accepts advertising.
Ad Rates: BW: $1,070 **Circ:** Non-paid ‡2,800
4C: $1,495

7812 Hawaii Medical Journal
1345 S. Beretania St., No. 301
Honolulu, HI 96814-1821

Medical journal. **Founded:** 1941. **Freq:** Monthly. **Print Method:** Offset. **Trim Size:** 8 1/8 x 10 7/8. **Cols./Page:** 3. **Col. Width:** 27 nonpareils. **Col. Depth:** 140 agate lines. **Key Personnel:** Norman Goldstein, M.D., Editor. **Subscription Rates:** $25 individuals; $3 single issue. **Remarks:** Accepts advertising.
Ad Rates: GLR: $7.45 **Circ:** ‡1800
BW: $640
4C: $1375

7813 Hawaii Orchid Journal
Honolulu Orchid Society/Pacific Orchid Society
3335 Huelani Dr. Phone: (808)988-7229
Honolulu, HI 96822-1276 Fax: (808)988-4569

Botany journal covering orchid culture and breeding. **Subtitle:** Na Okika O Hawaii. **Founded:** 1972. **Freq:** Quarterly. **Print Method:** Letterpress and offset. **Trim Size:** 6 x 9. **Cols./Page:** 1. **Col. Width:** 54 nonpareils. **Col. Depth:** 102 agate lines. **Key Personnel:** Yoneo Sagawa, Editor. **ISSN:** 0099-8745. **Subscription Rates:** $20 individuals annually with membership. **Remarks:** Accepts advertising. **Foreign language name:** Na Okika O Hawaii.
Ad Rates: BW: $80 **Circ:** ‡750

7814 Hawaii Pacific Review
Hawaii Pacific University
1060 Bishop St. Phone: (808)544-1107
Honolulu, HI 96813 Fax: (808)544-0862
Publication E-mail: hpreview@hpu.edu

Literary magazine containing short stories, poetry, and personal essays. **Founded:** Sept. 1987. **Freq:** Annual. **Print Method:** Perfect bound. **Trim Size:** 6 x 9. **Key Personnel:** Patrice M. Wilson, Poetry Editor; Catherine Sustana, Fiction Editor. **ISSN:** 1047-4331. **Subscription Rates:** $7 individuals; $5 single issue back issues. **Remarks:** Advertising not accepted.
Circ: Non-paid 500

7815 Hawaiian Journal of History
Hawaiian Historical Society
560 Kawaiahao St.
Honolulu, HI 96813-5023

Journal covering Hawaiian and Pacific history. **Founded:** 1967. **Freq:** Annual. **Trim Size:** 6 x 9. **Cols./Page:** 1. **Col. Width:** 4 1/4 inches. **Col. Depth:** 7 inches. **Key Personnel:** Michael E. Macmillan, Editor. **ISSN:** 0440-5145. **Subscription Rates:** $20 institutions; $30 members. **Remarks:** Advertising not accepted.
Circ: Combined ⊕1,800

7816 The Honolulu Advertiser
News Bldg. Phone: (808)525-8090
605 Kapiolani Blvd. Fax: (808)525-8037
PO Box 3110
Honolulu, HI 96802
Metropolitan newspaper. **Founded:** Feb. 2, 1856. **Freq:** Mon.-Sun. (morn.). **Print Method:** Letterpress. **Trim Size:** 13 3/4 x 22 1/2. **Cols./Page:** 6. **Col. Width:** 29 agate lines. **Col. Depth:** 21 1/2 inches. **Key Personnel:** Jim Gatti, Editor, phone (808)525-8080, jgatti@aloha.net; Dick Adair, Cartoonist, phone (808)525-8067; Wanda Adams, Living Section Editor, phone (808)525-8034; Judi Erickson, Money Section Editor, phone (808)525-8063; Dennis Anderson, Sports Writer, phone (808)525-8067; Jerry Burris, Editorial Page Editor, phone (808)525-8090; Hugh Clark, Big Isle Bureau Chief; Bev Creamer, Staff Writer, phone (808)525-8013; Kevin Dayton, Government Bureau Writer, phone (808)525-8070; Wayne Harada, Entertainment Editor, phone (808)525-8034; Susan Hooper, Business Writer, phone (808)525-8090; Joan Clarke, Food Editor, phone (808)525-8069; Ed Tanji, Maui Bureau Chief; Dave Koga, Sports Editor, phone (808)525-8006; Andy Yamaguchi, Night City Editor, phone (808)525-8024; Stanley Yamashita, Wire Editor, phone (808)525-8058. **Remarks:** Accepts advertising. **Feature Editors:** Wayne Harada, *Drama*, phone (808)525-8067.
Ad Rates: BW: $7,048 **Circ:** Mon.-Sat. ★102,358
4C: $8,338 Sun. ★187,887
PCI: $52.45

7817 Honolulu Magazine
Honolulu Publishing Co. Ltd.
36 Merchant St. Phone: (808)524-7400
Honolulu, HI 96813 Fax: (808)531-2306
Free: (800)272-5245
Publisher E-mail: honpub@aloha.net

City magazine. **Founded:** Jan. 1888. **Freq:** Monthly. **Print Method:** Web offset. **Trim Size:** 8 x 10 7/8. **Cols./Page:** 3. **Col. Width:** 26 nonpareils. **Col. Depth:** 140 agate lines. **Key Personnel:** John Alves, Publisher, phone (808)524-7400; Elaine Evans, Advertising Dir., phone (808)524-7400, fax (808)531-2306; John Heckathorn, Editor, phone (808)524-7400, fax (808)531-2306, nonpub@aloha.net. **Subscription Rates:** $15 individuals; $2.95 single issue; $3.95 annual holiday issue (Nov.); $3.95 annual restaurant guide (Aug.). **Remarks:** Accepts advertising.
Ad Rates: BW: $3,370 **Circ:** Paid ★26,365
4C: $4,430

7818 Honolulu Star-Bulletin
Liberty Newspapers Limited Partnership
PO Box 3080 Phone: (808)525-8640
Honolulu, HI 96802-3080 Fax: (808)523-8509

General newspaper. **Founded:** 1882. **Freq:** Mon.-Sat. (eve.). **Print Method:** Letterpress. **Trim Size:** 78 picas x 129 picas. **Cols./Page:** 6. **Col. Width:** 12 picas. **Col. Depth:** 129 picas. **Key Personnel:** John M. Flanagan, Editor and Publisher; Dave Shapiro, Managing Editor; Rupert E. Phillips, CEO; Frank Bridgewater, Asst. Managing Editor; Michael Rovner, Asst. Managing Editor; Stirling Morita, Night Editor; Dan Woods, Graphics Editor; Carl Zimmerman, Sr. Asst. Editorial Page Editor. **USPS:** 249-460. **Subscription Rates:** $338 individuals; $720.20 out of state. **Remarks:** Accepts advertis-

ing, **Feature Editors:** Joe Edwards, *Sports*; Ed Lynch, *Financial/Business*; Cynthia Oi, *Features*; Steven Petranik, *News*; Lucy Young-Oda, *City*.
Ad Rates: BW: $6,199.74 **Circ:** Mon.-Sat. ★**67,533**
4C: $7,836.40
PCI: $52.41

7819 Honolulu Weekly
Honolulu Weekly, Inc.
1200 College Walk, Ste. 214 Phone: (808)528-1475
Honolulu, HI 96817
Community newspaper. **Freq:** Weekly (Wed.). **Subscription Rates:** Free.
Circ: Free ❑**41,987**
Paid ❑**57**

7820 Indo-Pacific Fishes
Bishop Museum Press
1525 Bernice St. Phone: (808)847-3511
Honolulu, HI 96817-2704 Fax: (808)841-8968
Publisher E-mail: museum@bishopmuseum.org

Scientific publication for ichthyologists. **Founded:** 1982. **Freq:** Irregular. **Trim Size:** 7 x 10. **Cols./Page:** 1. **Key Personnel:** John E. Randall, Editor, phone (808)848-4115, fax (808)847-8252, johne@bishopmuseum.org; Helen A. Randall, Managing Editor; Lori R. O'Hara, Circ. & Subscription, lorri-o@bishopmuseum.org. **ISSN:** 1736-0460. **Remarks:** Advertising not accepted.
Circ: (Not Reported)

7821 Island Business
Honolulu Publishing Co. Ltd.
36 Merchant St. Phone: (808)524-7400
Honolulu, HI 96813 Fax: (808)531-2306
Free: (800)272-5245
Publication E-mail: honpub@aloha.net
Publisher E-mail: honpub@aloha.net

Magazine focusing on small business. **Subtitle:** The Hawaii Report. **Founded:** 1984. **Freq:** Monthly. **Trim Size:** 8 1/8 x 10 7/8. **Key Personnel:** Lucy Jokiel, Editor; Mary V. Winpenny, Publisher; Brett Uprichard, Managing Editor. **ISSN:** 0745-7073. **Subscription Rates:** $15 individuals. **Remarks:** Accepts advertising. **Formerly:** Hawaii Investor.
Ad Rates: BW: $1,190 **Circ:** Paid ★**711**
4C: $2,595 Non-paid ★**12,747**

7822 Journal of Biochemistry, Molecular Biology and Biophysics
Harwood Academic Publishers
c/o Richard J. Guillory Phone: (808)956-7178
2314 Maile Way Fax: (808)956-9498
Honolulu, HI 96822
Journal covering biophysics, biochemistry and molecular biology with a focus on the Pacific Rim. **Founded:** Aug. 1, 1997. **Freq:** Quarterly. **Print Method:** Offset. **Trim Size:** 8 1/2 x 11. **Cols./Page:** 2. **Col. Width:** 3 inches. **Col. Depth:** 8 1/10 inches. **Key Personnel:** Ikuo Yamashina, Editor-in-Chief; Richard Guillory, Managing Editor, richardg@hawaii.edu. **ISSN:** 1025-8140. **Subscription Rates:** $90 single issue; $50 members. **Remarks:** Accepts advertising. **URL:** http://www.gbhap.com/. **Alt. Formats:** CD-ROM.
Ad Rates: 4C: $900 **Circ:** Combined 4,000

7823 Journal of World History
University of Hawaii Press
Sakamaki A-407 Phone: (808)956-8505
Dept. of History Fax: (808)956-9600
Univ. of Hawaii
Honolulu, HI 96822
Publication E-mail: lorilee@hawaii.edu
Publisher E-mail: uhpjourn@hawaii.edu

Journal centering on historical analysis from a global point of view. **Founded:** 1990. **Freq:** Semiannual. **Trim Size:** 6 x 9. **Key Personnel:** Jerry H. Bentley, Editor. **ISSN:** 1045-6007. **Subscription Rates:** $25 individuals; $35 institutions; $25 individuals other countries; $40 institutions other countries. **Remarks:** Accepts advertising. **Alt. Formats:** Microform.
Ad Rates: BW: $200 **Circ:** Paid 1,575
Controlled 50

7824 Kapio
Board of Student Publications
Kapiolani Community College Phone: (808)734-9120
4303 Diamond Head Rd. Fax: (808)734-9287
Honolulu, HI 96816
Publication E-mail: kapio@hawaii.edu

Collegiate newspaper. **Founded:** 1960. **Freq:** Weekly. **Print Method:** Offset. **Trim Size:** 11 x 16. **Cols./Page:** 5. **Col. Width:** 11 picas. **Col. Depth:** 210 agate lines. **Key Personnel:** Winifred Au, Advisor, winifred@hawaii.edu. **Subscription Rates:** $5 individuals; $5 agency. **Remarks:** Accepts advertising. **Available Online. URL:** http://www.naio.kcc.hawaii.edu/bosp.
Ad Rates: BW: $480 **Circ:** 3,000
PCI: $5

7825 Korean Studies
University of Hawaii Press
1881 East-West Rd. Phone: (808)956-6389
Center for Korean Studies Fax: (808)956-2213
Honolulu, HI 96822
Publication E-mail: lorilee@hawaii.edu
Publisher E-mail: uhpjourn@hawaii.edu

Journal addressing a broad range of topics through interdisciplinary and multicultural articles, book reviews and scholarly essays. **Founded:** 1977. **Freq:** Annual. **Trim Size:** 6 x 9. **Key Personnel:** Edward J. Shultz, Editor; Joel Bradshaw, Managing Editor, bradshaw@hawaii.edu. **ISSN:** 0145-840X. **Subscription Rates:** $15 individuals; $15 institutions. **Remarks:** Accepts advertising. **Alt. Formats:** Microform.
Ad Rates: BW: $200 **Circ:** Paid 160
Controlled 60

7826 Manoa
University of Hawaii Press
Dept. of English Phone: (808)956-3070
Univ. of Hawaii Fax: (808)956-7808
Honolulu, HI 96822
Publication E-mail: mjournal-l@hawaii.edu
Publisher E-mail: uhpjourn@hawaii.edu

Journal presenting U.S. and international fiction, poetry, essays, book reviews. **Subtitle:** A Pacific Journal of International Writing. **Founded:** 1989. **Freq:** Semiannual. **Print Method:** Offset. **Trim Size:** 7 x 10. **Key Personnel:** Frank Stewart, Editor, fstewwt@hawaii.edu. **ISSN:** 1045-7909. **Subscription Rates:** $22 individuals; $28 institutions. **Remarks:** Accepts advertising. **URL:** http://www2.hawaii.edu/mjournal. **Alt. Formats:** Microform.
Ad Rates: BW: $200 **Circ:** Paid 1,000
Controlled 65

7827 Marine Geodesy
Taylor & Francis
Holmes 383 Phone: (808)956-7338
2540 Dole St. Fax: (808)956-2580
University of Hawaii at Manoa
Honolulu, HI 96822
Publisher E-mail: info@taylorandfrancis.com

Ocean Mapping & Remove Sewing. **Subtitle:** An International Journal of Ocean Surveys, Mapping, and Sensing. **Founded:** 1977. **Freq:** Quarterly. **Print Method:** Offset. **Trim Size:** 7 x 10. **Cols./Page:** 1. **Col. Width:** 51 nonpareils. **Col. Depth:** 96 agate lines. **Key Personnel:** Narendra Saxena, Editor, saxena@wiliki.eng.hawaii.edu. **ISSN:** 0149-0419. **Subscription Rates:** $108; $220 institutions.
Ad Rates: BW: $550 **Circ:** (Not Reported)
4C: $1,450

7828 Marine Georesources and Geotechnology
Taylor & Francis
Marine Minerals Technology Center - Look Lab Phone: (808)522-5611 Fax: (808)522-5618
University of Hawaii at Manoa
811 Olomebani St.
Honolulu, HI 96813
Publisher E-mail: info@taylorandfrancis.com

Journal publishing research on scientific and engineering aspects of sea floor sediments and rocks, and marine minerals exploration. **Founded:** 1975. **Freq:** Quarterly. **Print Method:** Offset. **Trim Size:** 7 x 10. **Cols./Page:** 1. **Col. Width:** 51 nonpareils. **Col. Depth:** 96 agate lines. **Key Personnel:** Michael Cruikshank, Co-Editor; Ronald Chaney, Co-Editor. **ISSN:** 0360-8867. **Subscription Rates:** $90; $175 institutions full. **Absorbed:** Marine Geotechnology (1992); Marine Mining (1992).
Ad Rates: BW: $550 **Circ:** (Not Reported)
4C: $1,450

7829 Oceanic Linguistics
University of Hawaii Press
1890 East-West Rd. Phone: (808)956-8374
Dept. of Linguistics Fax: (808)956-9166
Univ. of Hawaii
Honolulu, HI 96822
Publication E-mail: oceanic@hawaii.edu
Publisher E-mail: uhpjourn@hawaii.edu

Journal focusing on the study of indigenous languages of the Oceanic area. **Founded:** 1962. **Freq:** Semiannual. **Trim Size:** 6 x 9. **Key Personnel:** Byron W. Bender, Editor, phone (808)956-8374, fax (808)956-9166, bender@hawaii.edu. **ISSN:** 0029-8115. **Subscription Rates:** $22 individuals; $28 institutions. **Remarks:** Accepts advertising. **Alt. Formats:** Microform.
Ad Rates: BW: $200 **Circ:** Paid 400
Controlled 30

7830 Pacific Business News
American City Business Journals
PO Box 833 Phone: (808)521-2021
Honolulu, HI 96808-0833 Fax: (808)528-2535

Business tabloid. **Founded:** Mar. 18, 1963. **Freq:** Weekly (Mon.). **Print Method:** Offset. **Trim Size:** 11 1/2 x 16. **Cols./Page:** 6. **Col. Width:** 19 nonpareils. **Col. Depth:** 207 agate lines. **Key Personnel:** Michelle Yanaguchi, Editor; Mike Kallay, Publisher. **USPS:** 417-340. **Subscription Rates:** $64 individuals; $128 three years; $114 mainland; $360 three years mainland; $2 single issue. **Remarks:** Accepts advertising. **URL:** http://www.amcity.com/pacific/.
Ad Rates: BW: $4,065 **Circ:** Paid ★**14,968**
4C: $4,415
PCI: $39.20

7831 Pacific Science
University of Hawaii Press
Department of Zoology Phone: (808)956-8620
Edmondson Hall 351 Fax: (808)956-9812
2538 The Mall
Honolulu, HI 96822
Publisher E-mail: uhpjourn@hawaii.edu

Journal Focusing on the Biological and Physical Sciences of the Pacific Region. **Subtitle:** A Quarterly Devoted to the Biological and Physical Sciences of the Pacific Region. **Founded:** 1947. **Freq:** Quarterly. **Print Method:** Offset. **Trim Size:** 7 x 10. **Cols./Page:** 2. **Col. Width:** 16 picas. **Col. Depth:** 46.5 picas. **Key Personnel:** E. Alison Kay, Editor, eakay@zoogate.zoo.hawaii.edu. **ISSN:** 0030-8870. **Subscription Rates:** $33 individuals; $50 institutions. **Remarks:** Accepts advertising. **Alt. Formats:** Microfiche.
Ad Rates: BW: $200 **Circ:** Paid ‡675
Controlled ‡30

7832 Pacific Telecommunications Review
Pacific Telecommunications Council
2454 S. Beretania St., Ste. 302 Phone: (808)941-3789
Honolulu, HI 96826-1596 Fax: (808)944-4874
Publisher E-mail: info@ptc.org

Trade magazine covering technical, management and policy issues in telecommunications, broadcasting, and informatics in the Pacific Hemisphere. **Founded:** 1978. **Freq:** Quarterly. **Key Personnel:** Richard Nickelson, Editor, richard@ptc.org; Puja Barries, Advertising, puja@ptc.org. **ISSN:** 1066-3894. **Subscription Rates:** $35 individuals; $50 out of country; $10 single issue. **Remarks:** Accepts advertising. **URL:** http://www.ptc.org.
Ad Rates: BW: $1,200 **Circ:** Controlled 2,500
4C: $1,750

7833 Philosophy East & West
University of Hawaii Press
2530 Dole St. Phone: (808)956-7288
Honolulu, HI 96822-2383 Fax: (808)956-9228
Publisher E-mail: uhpjourn@hawaii.edu

Journal on comparative philosophy. **Subtitle:** A Quarterly of Comparative Philosophy. **Founded:** 1951. **Freq:** Quarterly. **Print Method:** Offset. **Trim Size:** 7 x 10. **Cols./Page:** 1. **Col. Width:** 26.5 picas. **Col. Depth:** 46.5 picas. **Key Personnel:** Roger Ames, Editor, rtames@hawaii.edu. **ISSN:** 0031-8221. **Subscription Rates:** $31 individuals; $40 institutions. **Remarks:** Accepts advertising. **Alt. Formats:** Microform.
Ad Rates: BW: $200 **Circ:** Paid ‡1,550
Controlled ‡50

7834 Spirit of Aloha
Honolulu Publishing Co. Ltd.
36 Merchant St. Phone: (808)524-7400
Honolulu, HI 96813 Fax: (808)531-2306
Free: (800)272-5245
Publication E-mail: nflight@aloha.net
Publisher E-mail: honpub@aloha.net

Airline in-flight magazine. **Subtitle:** Aloha Airlines/Aloha Island Air Magazine. **Founded:** 1976. **Freq:** Monthly. **Print Method:** Offset. **Trim Size:** 8 x 10 7/8. **Cols./Page:** 3 and 2. **Col. Width:** 27 and 40 nonpareils. **Col. Depth:** 140 agate lines. **Key Personnel:** Janice Otaguro, Editor; Jim Myers, Publisher. **Subscription Rates:** Free. **Remarks:** Accepts advertising.
Ad Rates: BW: $3,680 **Circ:** Non-paid 65,000
4C: $4,245

7835 Spotlight Big Island
Spotlight Hawaii Publishing
532 Cummins St. Phone: (808)593-9404
Honolulu, HI 96814 Fax: (808)593-9494

Magazine serving as a visitor's guide to the island of Hawaii, the "Big Island.". **Founded:** 1991. **Freq:** Monthly. **Print Method:** Offset. **Trim Size:** 4 x 10 3/4. **Cols./Page:** 1. **Col. Width:** 3 1/2 inches. **Col. Depth:** 10 inches. **Key Personnel:** Ron Ihori, Editor; William R. Schoen, Publisher; Larry W. King,

Publisher; Larry W. King, Publisher. **Subscription Rates:** $3 single issue. **Remarks:** Accepts advertising.
Ad Rates: BW: $1,275 **Circ:** Non-paid 42,000
4C: $1,695

7836 Spotlight Kauai
Spotlight Hawaii Publishing
532 Cummins St. Phone: (808)593-9404
Honolulu, HI 96814 Fax: (808)593-9494

Magazine serving as a visitor's guide to Kauai. **Founded:** 1986. **Freq:** Monthly. **Print Method:** Offset. **Trim Size:** 4 x 10 3/4. **Cols./Page:** 1. **Col. Width:** 3 1/2 inches. **Col. Depth:** 10 inches. **Key Personnel:** Ron Ihori, Editor; William R. Schoen, Publisher; Joan Nozaki, Publisher; Joan Nozaki, Publisher. **Subscription Rates:** $3 single issue. **Remarks:** Accepts advertising.
Ad Rates: BW: $1,300 **Circ:** Non-paid 42,000
4C: $1,720

7837 Spotlight Oahu
Spotlight Hawaii Publishing
532 Cummins St. Phone: (808)593-9404
Honolulu, HI 96814 Fax: (808)593-9494

Magazine serving as a visitor's guide to Oahu, Kauai, Maui and Big Island. **Founded:** 1980. **Freq:** Weekly. **Print Method:** Web offset. **Trim Size:** 4 x 10 3/4. **Cols./Page:** 1. **Col. Width:** 3 1/2 inches. **Col. Depth:** 10 inches. **Key Personnel:** Ron Ihori, Editor; William R. Schoen, Publisher; Joan Nozaki, Assoc. Publisher; Joan Nozaki, Associate Publisher. **ISSN:** 0273-8422. **Subscription Rates:** $3 single issue. **Remarks:** Accepts advertising.
Ad Rates: BW: $710 **Circ:** Non-paid 35,000
4C: $855

7838 This Week Big Island
This Week Publications
274 Puuhale Rd., Ste. 200 Phone: (808)845-0572
Honolulu, HI 96819 Fax: (808)852-6350
Publication E-mail: twbi@ilhawaii.net; editor@thisweek.com
Publisher E-mail: editor@thisweek.com

Visitor magazine with maps, coupons, and tourist information. **Founded:** Jan. 1966. **Freq:** Weekly (Mon.). **Print Method:** Offset. **Trim Size:** 4 x 10 3/4. **Cols./Page:** 2. **Col. Width:** 22 nonpareils. **Key Personnel:** Ron Cruger, Publisher; Diane Rivas, Advertising Mgr. **Subscription Rates:** Free. **Remarks:** Accepts advertising. **URL:** http://www.thisweek.com.
Ad Rates: BW: $408 **Circ:** (Not Reported)
4C: $508

7839 This Week Kauai
This Week Publications
274 Puuhale Rd., Ste. 200 Phone: (808)845-0572
Honolulu, HI 96819 Fax: (808)852-6350
Publisher E-mail: editor@thisweek.com

Visitor magazine with maps, coupons, and tourist information. **Founded:** Jan. 1966. **Freq:** Monthly. **Print Method:** Offset. **Trim Size:** 4 x 10 3/4. **Cols./Page:** 2. **Col. Width:** 22 nonpareils. **Col. Depth:** 140 agate lines. **Key Personnel:** Keri Shepherd, Editor; Ron Cruger, Publisher. **Subscription Rates:** Free. **Remarks:** Accepts advertising. **URL:** http://www.thisweek.com.
Ad Rates: BW: $1233 **Circ:** Non-paid 480,000
4C: $1838

7840 This Week Oahu
This Week Publications
274 Puuhale Rd., Ste. 200 Phone: (808)845-0572
Honolulu, HI 96819 Fax: (808)852-6350
Publisher E-mail: editor@thisweek.com

Visitor magazine with maps, coupons, and visitor information. **Founded:** Jan. 1966. **Freq:** Weekly (Mon.). **Print Method:** Offset. **Trim Size:** 4 x 10 3/4. **Cols./Page:** 2. **Col. Width:** 22 nonpareils. **Col. Depth:** 140 agate lines. **Key Personnel:** Ron Cruger, Publisher; Madeline Kwok-Dodd, Controller; Keri Shepherd, Editor, editor@thisweek.com. **Subscription Rates:** Free. **Remarks:** Accepts advertising. **URL:** http://www.thisweek.com/.
Ad Rates: BW: $882 **Circ:** Non-paid ‡42,000
4C: $1,050

7841 The Voice of Hawai'i
University of Hawaii at Manoa
Ka Leo Bldg. Phone: (808)956-7043
1755 Pope Rd., Bldg. 31D Fax: (808)956-9962
Honolulu, HI 96822
Publication E-mail: ka-leo@hawaii.edu
Publisher E-mail: bop-l@hawaii.edu

Collegiate newspaper (tabloid). **Founded:** 1922. **Freq:** Mon. - Fri. (during the academic year). **Print Method:** Offset. **Trim Size:** 11 1/2 x 17. **Cols./Page:** 5. **Col. Width:** 22 nonpareils. **Col. Depth:** 224 agate lines. **Key Personnel:** Jim Reis, Coordinator; Derek Seu, Office Mgr. **Subscription Rates:** $54 individuals. **Remarks:** Accepts advertising. **Foreign language name:** Ka Leo O Hawai'i.
Ad Rates: GLR: $1.30 **Circ:** Mon.-Fri. ‡14,000
BW: $1,120
PCI: $14

7842 Waterbirds
Waterbird Society
Pacific Cooperative Study Unit Phone: (808)956-8369
Department of Botany Fax: (808)973-2936
University of Hawaii Manoa
3190 Maile Way
Honolulu, HI 96822
Publication E-mail: afdcd1@uaa.alaska.edu

Ornithology journal. **Founded:** 1977. **Freq:** 3/year. **Print Method:** Offset. **Cols./Page:** 2. **Col. Width:** 24 nonpareils. **Col. Depth:** 119 agate lines. **Key Personnel:** David Duffy, Editor, david_duffy@sprynet.com. **Subscription Rates:** $25; $45 individuals. **Remarks:** Advertising accepted; rates available upon request. **Former name:** Colonial Waterbirds.
Circ: ‡900

7843 Cable TV Services
PO Box 6481 Phone: (808)422-2711
Honolulu, HI 96818 Fax: (808)423-0990

Owner: Starstream Communications, PO Box 3129, 590 Kelly Ave., Half Moon Bay, CA 94019. **Founded:** 1985. **Formerly:** Clearview TV Cable of Hawaii Inc. (1990). **Key Personnel:** Helen Gibson, Manager; Robin Hollison, Contact. **Cities Served:** Hickam Air Force Base.: subscribing households 3075; 25 channels; 2 community access channels.

7844 KAIM-AM - 870
3555 Harding Ave. Phone: (808)735-2424
Honolulu, HI 96816 Fax: (808)735-2428
Free: (800)435-5246
E-mail: kaim@kaimradio.org

Format: Talk. **Networks:** Independent. **Founded:** 1953. **Operating Hours:** Continuous. **ADI:** Honolulu, HI. **Key Personnel:** Del Gibbs, General Mgr.; Jack Waters, Program Dir. **Wattage:** 50,000.

7845 KAIM-FM - 95.5
3555 Harding Ave. Phone: (808)735-2424
Honolulu, HI 96816-2444 Fax: (808)735-2428
E-mail: kaim@kaimradio.org

Format: Contemporary Christian. **Networks:** Independent. **Owner:** Christian Broadcasting Association, at above address. **Founded:** 1953. **Operating Hours:** Continuous; 100% local. **ADI:** Honolulu, HI. **Key Personnel:** Del Gibbs, General Mgr.; Michael Shishido, Program Dir. **Wattage:** 100,000 ERP.

7846 KBFD-TV - 32
1188 Bishop St. Phone: (808)521-8066
Penthouse 1 Fax: (808)521-5233
Honolulu, HI 96813
E-mail: kbfd@hits.net

Format: Commercial TV. **Networks:** Independent. **Owner:** The Allen Broadcasting Corp., at above address. **Founded:** 1986. **Operating Hours:** 9 a.m.- 12:30am. **ADI:** Honolulu, HI. **Key Personnel:** Kea S. Chung, President/CEO; Yun Hee Chung, Sales Dir.; Jeff Chung, Station Mgr. **Wattage:** 145 kw. **Ad Rates:** $305-125 for 30 seconds; $54-250 for 60 seconds.

7847 KCCN-AM - 1420
900 Fort St., Ste. 700 Phone: (808)536-2728
Honolulu, HI 96813

Format: Ethnic. **Owner:** KHWY Inc., at above address. **Founded:** 1966. **Formerly:** Diamond Head Radio Inc. **Operating Hours:** Continuous. **ADI:** Honolulu, HI. **Key Personnel:** Michael Kelly, General Sales Mgr./Pres., fax (808)536-1921; Rhoda-Ann Kihikihi, V. Pres., fax (808)536-2528; Leila James, Business Mgr., fax (808)536-2528. **Wattage:** 5000.

7848 KCCN-FM - 100.3
900 Fort St., Ste. 400 Phone: (808)536-2728
Honolulu, HI 96813 Fax: (808)536-2528
E-mail: kccn@kestrok.com

Format: Ethnic; Adult Contemporary; Eclectic; Reggae; Hawaiian. **Owner:** KHWY, Inc., 12381 Wilshire Blvd., Los Angeles, CA 90025, (310)820-4628, Fax: (310)826-7866. **Founded:** 1990. **Operating Hours:** Continuous. **ADI:** Honolulu, HI. **Key Personnel:** Michael Kelly, General Mgr., phone (x22)4; David Daniels, Program Dir., phone ( )Ext. 247; Leslie Keith, V. Pres. Marketing, phone ( )Ext. 222; Leila James, Business Mgr., phone (x22)7; Mona Diaz-Malasig, Promotions Dir. **Wattage:** 100,000. **Ad Rates:** $70 for 30 seconds; $84 for 60 seconds. **URL:** http://www.kestrok.com/~kccn.

7849 KDEO-FM - 102.7
711 Kapiolani Blvd., Ste. 1193 Phone: (808)591-9369
Honolulu, HI 96813 Fax: (808)591-9349

Format: Classic Rock. **Owner:** Caribou Broadcasting, at above address. **Founded:** 1988. **Operating Hours:** Continuous; 100% local. **Key Personnel:** Linda Yali, General Sales Mgr.; Brock Whaley, Program Dir.; Candace Loew, Promotions Dir.; Christopher Chang, Music Dir.; Bernie Armstrong, General Mgr. **Wattage:** 61,000. **Ad Rates:** $12-36 for 30 seconds; $17-47 for 60 seconds.

7850 KGMD-TV - 9
1534 Kapiolani Blvd. Phone: (808)973-5462
Honolulu, HI 96814 Fax: (808)944-5252

Format: Commercial TV. **Simulcasts:** KGMD-TV, Hilo, HI. **Networks:** CBS. **Formerly:** KGMB-TV. **ADI:** Honolulu, HI. **Key Personnel:** Rodney Shimabukuro, Chief Engineer.

7851 KGU-AM - 760
560 N. Nimitz Hwy, Ste. 114-13 Phone: (808)533-0065
Honolulu, HI 96817 Fax: (808)528-5467
E-mail: admin@kgu.com

Format: Sports. **Networks:** CBS; Westwood One Radio; ESPN Radio. **Founded:** 1922. **Operating Hours:** Continuous; 60% network, 40% local. **ADI:** Honolulu, HI. **Key Personnel:** Alan Zee, Vice Pres./General Mgr., alanzee@aloha.com. **Wattage:** 10,000. **URL:** http://www.kgu.com.

7852 KHET-TV - 11
2350 Dole St. Phone: (808)973-1000
Honolulu, HI 96822 Fax: (808)973-1090
E-mail: email@khet.pbs.org

Format: Public TV. **Networks:** Public Broadcasting Service (PBS). **Owner:** Hawaii Public Broadcasting Authority, at above address. **Founded:** 1972. **Operating Hours:** Continuous. **ADI:** Honolulu, HI. **Key Personnel:** Don Robbs, Exec. Dir./Gen. Mgr.; Kei Yamamoto, Business Mgr.; Cavlos Molina, Program Dir.; Jerri Chong, Developmental Dir. **Ad Rates:** Noncommercial. **URL:** http://www.khet.org.

7853 KHON-TV - 2
1116 Auahi St. Phone: (808)591-2222
Honolulu, HI 96814 Fax: (808)591-9085
E-mail: news@khon.com

Format: Commercial TV. **Networks:** Fox. **Owner:** Emmis Television Broadcasting, 40 Monumet Circle, Ste. 700, Indianapolis, IN, (317)266-0100, Fax: (317)631-3750. **Founded:** 1955. **Formerly:** KONA-TV. **Operating Hours:** 5 a.m.-2:30 a.m. **ADI:** Honolulu, HI. **Key Personnel:** Kent Baker, V.P./Gen. Mgr., phone (808)591-4224; Steve Hiramoto, Dir. of Sales, phone (808)591-4240, fax (818)593-2418; Jim Mccoy, News Dir., phone (808)591-4242; Lynne Mueller, Station Mgr./Gen. Sales Mgr., phone (808)591-4273. **Local Programs:** *Let's Go Fishing* 5:00 pm Sunday; *Let's Go Fishing*; *Hawaii's Kitchen* 5:30 pm. **Wattage:** 100,000.

7854 KHPR-FM - 88.1
738 Kaheka St. Phone: (808)955-8821
Honolulu, HI 96814 Fax: (808)942-5477
E-mail: hpr@lava.net

Format: Information; Classical. **Networks:** National Public Radio (NPR); Public Radio International (PRI); AP. **Owner:** Hawaii Public Radio, at above address, HI, Fax: (808)955-8821. **Founded:** 1981. **Operating Hours:** Continuous; 40% network, 60% local. **ADI:** Honolulu, HI. **Key Personnel:** Michael Titterton, General Mgr.; J.P. Muntal, News Dir.; Valerie Yee, Dir. Development/Marketing; Alan Bunin, Music Dir.; Mark Wagner, Operations Dir. **Wattage:** 27,000. **Ad Rates:** Noncommercial.

KIFO-AM - See Pearl City

7855 KIKI-AM - 990
345 Queen St., Ste. 601 Phone: (808)531-4602
Honolulu, HI 96813 Fax: (808)531-4606

Format: Contemporary Hit Radio (CHR). **Networks:** Independent; ABC. **Founded:** 1948. **Operating Hours:** Continuous. **ADI:** Honolulu, HI. **Key Personnel:** Bob Longwell, General and Sales Manager, phone (808)531-4602; Barbara Brill, Contact, phone (808)5314602; Alan Oda, Operations Mgr., phone (808)5375267; Jerry Varoujean, Chief Engineer; Chandra Furuto, Business Mgr.; Tamar Kauahi, Promotions Dir. **Wattage:** 10,000.

7856 KIKI-FM - 93.9
345 Queen St., Ste. 601 Phone: (808)531-4602
Honolulu, HI 96813-4715 Fax: (808)531-4606

Format: Contemporary Hit Radio (CHR). **Networks:** Independent. **Owner:** Patterson Honolulu Broadcasting Corp., at above address. **Founded:** 1978. **Formerly:** KMAI-FM (1989). **Operating Hours:** Continuous. **ADI:** Honolulu, HI. **Key Per-**

sonnel: Bob Longwell, General Mgr.; Barbara Dean Brill, Sales Mgr.; Alan Oda, Operations Mgr.; Jerry Varoujean, Chief Engineer; Chandra Furuto, Business Mgr.; Tamar Kauahi, Promotions Dir. **Wattage:** 100,000. **Ad Rates:** $90-$100 for 30 seconds; $100-$120 for 60 seconds. Combined advertising rates available with KIKI-AM.

7857 KIKU-TV - 20
197 Sand Island Access Rd., No. 2021 Phone: (808)847-2021
Honolulu, HI 96819-2224 Fax: (808)841-3326

Format: Commercial TV. **Networks:** Independent. **Owner:** International Media Group, 1990 S. Bundy Dr., Ste. 850, Los Angeles, CA 90025, (310)479-1818, Fax: (310)478-8118. **Founded:** 1983. **Formerly:** KHAI-TV (Apr. 9, 1993). **Operating Hours:** 6:30am-12:30a Mon.-Fri.; 8am-12:30am Sat.; 7am-midnight Sun. **ADI:** Honolulu, HI. **Key Personnel:** Joanne Ninomiya, Gen. Mgr./Dir. of Japanese Programming, phone (808)836-0361; Sharon Kanaley, Station Mgr., phone (808)847-2021; Hank Kaul, Dir of Engineering; Mika Tamaka Lee, Promotion/Publicity, phone (808)836-0361; Stan Emoto, Local Sales Mgr.; Phyllis Kehara, General Sales Mgr. **Ad Rates:** Advertising accepted; rates available upon request.

7858 KIPO-FM - 89.3
738 Kaheka St. Phone: (808)955-8821
Honolulu, HI 96814 Fax: (808)942-5477
E-mail: hpr@lpr@lava.net

Format: Classical; Information; Jazz. **Networks:** Public Radio International (PRI); National Public Radio (NPR). **Owner:** Hawaii Public Radio, at above address. **Founded:** 1989. **Operating Hours:** Continuous. **ADI:** Honolulu, HI. **Key Personnel:** Michael Titterton, General Mgr.; Alan Bunin, Music Dir.; J.P. Muntal, News Dir.; Valerie Yee, Dir. Development/Marketing; Mark Wagner, Operations Dir. **Wattage:** 3200.

7859 KISA-AM - 1540
904 Kohou St., Ste. 204 Phone: (808)841-4555
Honolulu, HI 96817 Fax: (808)841-4855

Format: Adult Contemporary; Ethnic. **Founded:** 1973. **Operating Hours:** Continuous. **ADI:** Honolulu, HI. **Key Personnel:** Rick Manayan, President. **Local Programs:** *Mr. Kupido* Monday; *Ms Sampaguita Show* 4-6 a.m. Monday-Friday, Ricky Manayan, General Sales Mgr.; *Your Health* 12:30 Wednesday. **Wattage:** 5,000.

7860 KITV-TV - 4
801 S. King St. Phone: (808)535-0400
Honolulu, HI 96813 Fax: (808)536-8777
E-mail: news4@kitv.com

Format: Commercial TV. **Networks:** ABC. **Owner:** Hearst-Argyle Television Inc., 888 Seventh Ave., New York, NY 10106, (212)887-6800, Fax: (212)887-6835. **Founded:** 1954. **Formerly:** KHVH-TV (1959). **Operating Hours:** 24 hrs. **ADI:** Honolulu, HI. **Key Personnel:** Michael Rosenberg, President, phone (808)535-0206; Bill Gaeth, General Sales Mgr., phone (808)535-0254; Wally Zimmermann, News Dir., phone (808)535-0469, fax (808)536-8993. **Local Programs:** *KITV4 News* 5 p.m., 6 p.m., 10 p.m., Wally Zimmermann, (808)535-0469; *Merrie Monarch Festival*, John Wray, (808)535-0229; *Mixed Plate*, Pamela Young, (808)535-0450, Fax (808)536-8993. **Ad Rates:** $30-1,500 for 15 seconds; $40-2,000 for 30 seconds; $80-4,000 for 60 seconds.

7861 KKUA-FM - 90.7
738 Kaheka St. Phone: (808)955-8821
Honolulu, HI 96814 Fax: (808)942-5477
E-mail: hpr@lava.net

Format: Public Radio; Classical; News. **Networks:** AP; National Public Radio (NPR); Public Radio International (PRI). **Owner:** Hawaii Public Radio Inc., at above address, Fax: (808)942-5547. **Founded:** 1988. **Operating Hours:** Continuous. **ADI:** Honolulu, HI. **Key Personnel:** Mark Wagner, Operations Dir.; Alan Bunin, Music Dir.; J.P. Muntal, News Dir.; Valerie Yee, Dir. Development/Marketing; Michael Titterton, General Mgr. **Local Programs:** *Morning Concert*, Alan Bunin; *News of Hawaii and the Pacific*, Scott Kim; *Price of Paradise*, Randy Roth. **Wattage:** 7000. **Ad Rates:** Noncommercial.

7862 KLHT-AM - 1040
1190 Nuuanu Ave. Phone: (808)524-1040
Honolulu, HI 96817 Fax: (808)524-0998
E-mail: klht@gte.net

Format: News; Contemporary Hit Radio (CHR); Religious. **Networks:** Ambassador Inspirational Radio. **Owner:** Calvary Chapel of Honolulu, at above address. **Founded:** 1985. **Formerly:** KIFH-AM. **Operating Hours:** Continuous. **ADI:** Honolulu, HI. **Key Personnel:** Jim Neuman, General Mgr. **Wattage:** 7,500. **Ad Rates:** $12-14 for 30 seconds; $15-17 for 60 seconds.

7863 KNDI-AM - 1270
1734 S. King St. Phone: (808)946-2844
Honolulu, HI 96826 Fax: (808)947-3531
Free: (800)649-5634

Format: Ethnic; Religious. **Networks:** Independent. **Owner:** KNDI Radio, at above address. **Founded:** 1960. **Operating Hours:** Continuous. **ADI:** Honolulu, HI. **Key Personnel:** Leona Jona, Owner/General Mgr.; Harvey Weinstein, Operations/Public Service/Music Dir. **Wattage:** 5000. **Ad Rates:** $20-25 for 30 seconds; $25-30 for 60 seconds.

7864 KPOI-FM - 97.5
771 Kapiolani Blvd., Ste. 1193 Phone: (808)591-9369
Honolulu, HI 96813 Fax: (808)591-9349

Format: Album-Oriented Rock (AOR). **Owner:** Caribou Broadcasting, at above address. **Founded:** 1964. **Operating Hours:** Continuous. **Key Personnel:** Bernie Armstrong, General Mgr.; Kerry Gray, Program Dir.; Teo Taylor, Music Dir.; Jamie Hartrett, Promotions Dir.; Mike Vassar, Sales Mgr. **Local Programs:** *Local Edge*, Larry Lieberman. **Wattage:** 83,000. **Ad Rates:** $50-100 per unit.

7865 KQMQ-AM - 690
711 Kapiolani Blvd., Ste. 1193 Phone: (808)591-9369
Honolulu, HI 96814 Fax: (808)591-9349

Format: Contemporary Hit Radio (CHR). **Simulcasts:** KQMQ-FM. **Owner:** Caribou Broadcasting, at above address. **Founded:** 1947. **Operating Hours:** Continuous. **ADI:** Honolulu, HI. **Key Personnel:** Bernie Armstrong, General Mgr.; Diane Ward, General Sales Mgr.; Jamie Hyatt, Program Dir.; Cary Ebesugawa, Business Mgr.; Maggie Gaston, Executive Asst.; Alan Yamamoto, National Sales Mgr.; Lynn Dunn, Traffic Dir.; Sherry Peterson, Promotions Mgr.; Darah York, Production Dir. **Wattage:** 10,000. **Ad Rates:** $30-85 for 30 seconds; $add 20% for 60 seconds.

7866 KQMQ-FM - 93.1
711 Kapiolani Blvd., Ste. 1193 Phone: (808)591-9369
Honolulu, HI 96814 Fax: (808)591-9349
E-mail: kqmqaatshula.net

Format: Contemporary Hit Radio (CHR). **Simulcasts:** KQMQ-AM. **Owner:** Caribou Broadcasting, at above address. **Founded:** 1967. **Operating Hours:** Continuous. **ADI:** Honolulu, HI. **Key Personnel:** Bernie Armstrong, General Mgr.; Diane Ward, General Sales Mgr.; Jamie Hyatt, Production Dir.; Cary Ebesugawa, Business Mgr. **Wattage:** 10,000. **Ad Rates:** Advertising accepted; rates available upon request.

7867 KSSK-AM - 590
1505 Dillingham Blvd., Ste. 208 Phone: (808)841-8300
Honolulu, HI 96817 Fax: (808)841-9259
E-mail: kssk@pixi.com

Format: Adult Contemporary. **Owner:** Patterson Broadcasting Co., at above address, (404)391-9525, Fax: (404)391-0260. **Founded:** 1929. **Formerly:** KGMB-AM. **Operating Hours:** Continuous. **ADI:** Honolulu, HI. **Key Personnel:** Ray Barnett, General Mgr.; Mimi Beans, General Sales Mgr.; Dick Wainwright, Director of Programming; Michael Shishido, Operations Mgr. **Wattage:** 7500. **Ad Rates:** $35-90 for 30 seconds; $40-105 for 60 seconds. $35-$90 for 30 seconds; $40-$105 for 60 seconds. Combined advertising rates available with KSSK-FM. **URL:** http://www.pixi.com/˜kssk/.

7868 KSSK-FM - 92.3
1505 Dillingham Blvd., Ste. 208 Phone: (808)841-8300
Honolulu, HI 96817 Fax: (808)841-9292
E-mail: kssk@pixi.com

Format: Adult Contemporary. **Owner:** Patterson Board, at above address, (404)391-9525, Fax: (404)391-0260. **Founded:** 1976. **Formerly:** KULA-FM (1987). **Operating Hours:** Continuous; 100% local. **ADI:** Honolulu, HI. **Key Personnel:** Ray Barnett, General Mgr.; Michael Shishido, Operations Mgr.; Scott Mackenzie, Promotions Dir.; Dick Wainwright, Director of Programming. **Wattage:** 100,000. **Ad Rates:** $30-230 per unit. **URL:** http://www.pixi/˜kssk/.

7869 KTUH-FM - 90.3
2445 Campus Rd., Ste. 202 Phone: (808)956-7431
Honolulu, HI 96822 Fax: (808)956-5271
E-mail: ktuh@hawaii.edu

Format: Full Service. **Networks:** Independent. **Founded:** 1968. **Operating Hours:** Continuous; 100% local. **ADI:** Honolulu, HI. **Wattage:** 3,000. **Ad Rates:** Noncommercial. **URL:** http://ktuh.hawaii.edu.

7870 KUMU-FM - 94.7
765 Amana St., Ste. 206 Phone: (808)531-4511
Honolulu, HI 96814-3248 Fax: (808)538-6425

Format: Easy Listening. **Owner:** John Weiser, Jr., at above address. **Founded:** 1963. **Formerly:** KFOA-FM. **Operating Hours:** Continuous. **ADI:** Honolulu, HI. **Key Personnel:** John Weiser, Jr., PRS/Owner; Jeff Coelho, VPR/Gen. Mgr.; George Rudolph, Station Mgr.; George Rudolph, Music Dir.; Gene Schiller, News Dir. **Wattage:** 100,000. **Ad Rates:** $30-85 for 30 seconds; $35-105 for 60 seconds.

7871 KWAI-AM - 1080
100 N Beretania St., Ste. 401 Phone: (808)523-3868
Honolulu, HI 96817-4712 Fax: (808)531-6532

Format: Talk; Sports. **Networks:** Independent. **Owner:** KWAI, at above address. **Founded:** 1988. **Formerly:** KZHI-AM. **Operating Hours:** Continuous; 10% network, 90% local. **ADI:** Honolulu, HI. **Key Personnel:** Sam Wagenvoord, Contact; Joe Maldonado, Sales Mgr.; Moana May, Contact. **Wattage:** 5000. **Ad Rates:** $29 for 30 seconds; $48 for 60 seconds.

7872 KWHE-TV - 14
1188 Bishop St., Ste. 502 Phone: (808)538-1414
Honolulu, HI 96813 Fax: (808)526-0326

Format: Commercial TV; Religious. **Networks:** Independent. **Owner:** Le Sea Broadcasting Corp., 1188 Bishop St., Ste. 502, Honolulu, HI 96813. **Founded:** 1986. **Operating Hours:** Continuous. **ADI:** Honolulu, HI. **Key Personnel:** Van Mylar, General Mgr.; George Playdon, Production Mgr.; Malia Elliott, Public Relations Mgr.

7873 KZOO-AM - 1210
250 Ward Ave., Ste. 209 Phone: (808)593-2880
Honolulu, HI 96814-4066 Fax: (808)596-0083
E-mail: kzoo@ia.com

Format: Talk; Ethnic; News; Eclectic; Religious; Big Band/Nostalgia; Easy Listening. **Owner:** Mr. and Mrs. Noboru Furuya, at above address. **Founded:** 1963. **Operating Hours:** 5:30 a.m.-midnight; 5% network, 95% local. **ADI:** Honolulu, HI. **Key Personnel:** David Furuya, Contact; David Furuya, General Mgr.; Robin Furuya, Contact; Maggie Tateishi, Contact. **Wattage:** 1000.

KAHULUI

7874 Shemp!
Larry Yoshida
593 Waikala St. Phone: (808)877-5198
Kahului, HI 96732-1736
Magazine containing reviews, criticism, and articles. **Subtitle:** The Lowlife Culture Magazine. **Founded:** 1993. **Freq:** Bimonthly. **Trim Size:** 6 1/2 x 4 1/4. **Key Personnel:** Lawrence K. Yoshida, Editor. **Subscription Rates:** $1 single issue.
Circ: Combined 400

7875 KMVI-AM - 550
311 Ano St. Phone: (808)877-5566
Kahului, HI 96732-1304 Fax: (808)877-2137

Format: Adult Contemporary; Ethnic; Religious. **Networks:** CNN Radio. **Owner:** Media, at above address. **Founded:** 1947. **Operating Hours:** Continuous. **Key Personnel:** Pamela Tsutsui, General Mgr.; Kathy Collins, Program Dir.; Paul Robinson, Sales Mgr.; Fred Guzman, News Dir.; Jeff Hunter, Operations Mgr.; Jack Sweeney, General Sales Mgr. **Wattage:** 5000. **Ad Rates:** $10-20 for 30 seconds; $14-22 for 60 seconds. Combined advertising rates available with KMVI-FM.

KMVI-FM - See Pukalani

7876 KNUI-AM - 900
311 Ano St. Phone: (808)877-5566
Kahului, HI 96732-1304 Fax: (808)871-0666

Format: Adult Contemporary; News; Sports. **Networks:** ABC. **Founded:** 1962. **Operating Hours:** Continuous; 25% network, 75% local. **Key Personnel:** Jeff Hunter, Operations Mgr.; Pamela Tsutsui, Station Mgr.; Fred Guzman, News Dir. **Wattage:** 5000. **Ad Rates:** $10-25 for 30 seconds; $12-27 for 60 seconds. $10-$25 for 30 seconds; $12-$27 for 60 seconds. Combined advertising rates available with KNUI-FM.

7877 KNUI-FM - 99.9
311 Ano St. Phone: (808)877-5566
Kahului, HI 96732-1304 Fax: (808)871-0666

Format: Adult Contemporary; Soft Rock. **Networks:** ABC. **Founded:** 1984. **Formerly:** KHUI-FM (1990). **Operating Hours:** Continuous; 100% local. **Key Personnel:** Pamela Tsutsui, Station Mgr.; Fred Guzman, News Dir. **Wattage:** 100,000. **Ad Rates:** $15-25 for 30 seconds; $17-27 for 60 seconds. $10-$25 for 30 seconds; $11-$27 for 60 seconds; Combined advertising rates available with KNUI-AM.

7878 TCI Hawaiian Islands
350 Hoohana Phone: (808)877-4425
Kahului, HI 96732 Fax: (808)877-3534

Owner: TCI, Corporate Headquarters, 5619 DTC Parkway, Englewood, CO 80111-3000, (303)267-5500. **Founded:** 1968.

Key Personnel: Ms. G.G. Sakamoto, General Mgr., phone (808)877-4425, fax (808)877-3534. **Cities Served:** Hawaii Kai (Honolulu), Ka'u District, Lanai, Maui, Molokai, HI: subscribing households 39,521.

KAILUA

NC HI. Honolulu Co. 40 mi. SE of Kaneohe.

7879 Aquatic Mammals
European Association for Aquatic Mammals
PO Box 1106 Phone: (808)236-4001
Kailua, HI 96734 Fax: (808)247-5831
Publication E-mail: nachtig@nosc.mil

Scientific journal covering the science of care, conservation, and medicine of aquatic mammals. **Founded:** 1973. **Freq:** 3/year. **Trim Size:** 7 x 10. **Cols./Page:** 2. **Col. Width:** 2 3/4 inches. **Col. Depth:** 8 inches. **Key Personnel:** P. E. Nachtigall, Editor, phone (808)247-5297, nachtig@nosc.mil. **ISSN:** 0167-5427. **Subscription Rates:** $95 individuals and institutions. **Remarks:** Advertising not accepted.
Circ: 250

7880 KLEI-AM - 1130
4120 Marina Dr.
Santa Barbara, CA 93110

Format: Easy Listening. **Owner:** Merit Media International, at above address. **Founded:** 1953. **ADI:** Santa Barbara-Santa Maria-San Luis Obispo,CA. **Key Personnel:** Carl Schuele, President; Lucille Cordeiro, General Mgr.; Dave Wiggins, Sports Dir. **Wattage:** 10,000.

7881 KRTR-FM - 96.3
Pali Palms Plaza Phone: (808)254-3596
970 N. Kalaheo, Ste. C-107 Fax: (808)254-3299
Kailua, HI 96734-1866

Format: Adult Contemporary. **Simulcasts:** KULA-AM. **Owner:** New Planet Radio, at above address. **Founded:** 1978. **Operating Hours:** Continuous; 100% local. **Key Personnel:** Sharon Billingsley, General Sales Mgr.; Carolyn Kam, Contact; Britt Hansen, Traffic Mgr.; Patrick Leonard, Promotions Dir.; Jane Pascual, News Dir. **Wattage:** 75,000. **Ad Rates:** $110-205 per unit. Combined advertising rates available with KGMZ-FM.

7882 KULA-AM - 1460
Pali Palms Plaza Phone: (808)254-3596
970 N. Kalaheo, Ste. C-107 Fax: (808)254-3299
Kailua, HI 96734

Format: Oldies. **Networks:** CNN Radio; Unistar. **Owner:** Mauna Kea Broadcasting, at above address. **Founded:** 1990. **Operating Hours:** Continuous. **Key Personnel:** Austin Vali, Contact; Linda Manown, General Sales Mgr.; Carolyn Kam, Contact; Britt Hansen, Traffic Mgr.; Patrick Leonard, Promotions Dir.; Jane Pascual, News Dir. **Wattage:** 5000.

KAILUA KONA

7883 West Hawaii Today
Donrey Media Group
PO Box 789 Phone: (808)329-9311
Kailua Kona, HI 96745-0789 Fax: (808)329-3659
Publication E-mail: wht@aloha.net

General newspaper. **Founded:** 1968. **Freq:** DLY, except Saturday. **Print Method:** Offset. **Cols./Page:** 5. **Col. Width:** 1 1/16 inches. **Col. Depth:** 15 13/16 inches. **Key Personnel:** Richard Asbach, Publisher. **USPS:** 744-459. **Subscription Rates:** $8.25 individuals per month; $9.50 out of area per month. **Remarks:** Accepts advertising.
Ad Rates: BW: $975.75 **Circ:** Mon.-Thurs. ★**10,332**
4C: $1,265.75 Fri. ★**11,856**
SAU: $13.01 Sun. ★**13,756**
PCI: $13.01

7884 Sun Cablevision
74-5605 Luhia St. Phone: (808)329-2418
Kailua Kona, HI 96740 Fax: (808)329-9459

Key Personnel: Uaha Gerard, General Mgr.; Dionne Aukai, Business Operations Manager; Wayne Iokepa, Plant Manager; Karen Statman, Mgr. of Marketing. **Cities Served:** 24 hours per week community access programming.

KANEOHE, pop. 35,600.

SC HI. Honolulu Co. On Oahu Island, 9 mi. NW of Honolulu. Windward Community College; Hawaii Loa College. Sea Life Park, Ulu Mau Village and fishpond Valley of Temples.

7885 Central Sun-Press
RFD Publications, Inc.
45-525 Luluku Rd. Phone: (808)235-5881
Kaneohe, HI 96744-1945 Fax: (808)247-7246

Community newspaper. **Founded:** 1959. **Freq:** Weekly (Thurs.). **Print Method:** Offset. **Trim Size:** 11 1/2 x 13 1/2. **Cols./Page:** 6. **Col. Width:** 26 nonpareils. **Col. Depth:** 294 agate lines. **Key Personnel:** Bill Stone, Editor; Ken Berry, Publisher; Chris McMahon, General Sales Mgr.; Dianne LoMonte, Advertising Dir. **Subscription Rates:** Free; $25 by mail. **Remarks:** Accepts advertising.
Ad Rates: GLR: $.81 **Circ:** Combined 12,286
BW: $1,461.57
4C: $1,907.57
PCI: $11.33

7886 Hawaii Army Weekly
RFD Publications, Inc.
45-525 Luluku Rd. Phone: (808)235-5881
Kaneohe, HI 96744-1945 Fax: (808)247-7246

Military newspaper. **Founded:** 1988. **Freq:** Weekly (Thurs.). **Print Method:** Offset. **Trim Size:** 11 1/2 x 13 1/2. **Cols./Page:** 6. **Key Personnel:** Bill Stone, Editor; Ken Berry, Publisher; Chris McMahon, Advertising Mgr.; Dianne LoMonte, Advertising Dir. **Subscription Rates:** Free. **Remarks:** Accepts advertising.
Ad Rates: GLR: $.85 **Circ:** Free 13,489
BW: $1,533.81
4C: $1,979.81
PCI: $11.89

7887 Hawaii Kai/East Oahu Sun Press
RFD Publications, Inc.
45-525 Luluku Rd. Phone: (808)235-5881
Kaneohe, HI 96744-1945 Fax: (808)247-7246

Community newspaper. **Founded:** 1969. **Freq:** Weekly (Thurs.). **Print Method:** Offset. **Trim Size:** 11 1/2 x 13 1/2. **Cols./Page:** 6. **Col. Width:** 26 nonpareils. **Col. Depth:** 294 agate lines. **Key Personnel:** Bill Stone, Editor; Ken Berry, Publisher; Chris McMahon, General Sales Mgr.; Dianne LoMonte, Advertising Dir. **Subscription Rates:** Free; $25 by mail. **Remarks:** Accepts advertising.
Ad Rates: GLR: $.82 **Circ:** Combined 7,193
BW: $1,475.76
4C: $1,921.76
PCI: $11.44

7888 Hawaii Marine
RFD Publications, Inc.
PO Box 63002 Phone: (808)257-5600
MCBH Fax: (808)257-2511
Kaneohe, HI 96744
Publication E-mail: millimanj@emh1.mfp.usmc.mil

Unofficial military newspaper for Marines serving in the Hawaiian Islands. **Founded:** 1973. **Freq:** Weekly (Thurs.). **Print Method:** Offset. **Cols./Page:** 6. **Col. Width:** 26 nonpareils. **Col. Depth:** 294 agate lines. **Key Personnel:** Donna Klapakis, Editor, klapakisd@mcbh.usmc.mil; Capt. John C. Milliman, Public Affairs Officer; Ken Berry, Publisher; Chris McMahon, General Sales Mgr.; Dianne LoMonte, Advertising Dir.; Sgt. Stephen Gude, Press Chief, gudes@mcbh.usmc.mil. **Subscription Rates:** Free; $25 by mail. **Remarks:** Accepts advertising. **URL:** http://www.mcbh@usmc.mil.
Ad Rates: GLR: $.71 **Circ:** Free 9,000
BW: $1,271.94
4C: $1,717.94
PCI: $9.86

7889 Hawaii Navy News
RFD Publications, Inc.
45-525 Luluku Rd. Phone: (808)235-5881
Kaneohe, HI 96744-1945 Fax: (808)247-7246

Military newspaper. **Subtitle:** Civilian Enterprise Newspaper. **Founded:** 1975. **Freq:** Weekly (Thurs.). **Print Method:** Offset. **Trim Size:** 11 1/2 x 13 1/2. **Cols./Page:** 6. **Col. Width:** 26 nonpareils. **Col. Depth:** 294 agate lines. **Key Personnel:** Bill Stone, Editor; Ken Berry, Publisher; Chris McMahon, Advertising Mgr. **Subscription Rates:** Free; $25 by mail. **Remarks:** Accepts advertising.
Ad Rates: GLR: $.74 **Circ:** Free 15,873
BW: $1,109.40
4C: $1,403.40
PCI: $10.39

7890 Hawaiian Falcon
RFD Publications, Inc.
45-525 Luluku Rd. Phone: (808)235-5881
Kaneohe, HI 96744-1945 Fax: (808)247-7246

Military newspaper. **Founded:** 1988. **Freq:** Weekly (Thurs.). **Print Method:** Offset. Uses mats. **Trim Size:** 6 3/4 x 11 1/2. **Cols./Page:** 5. **Col. Width:** 2 1/8 inches. **Col. Depth:** 21 1/2 inches. **Key Personnel:** Bill Stone, Editor; Ken Berry, Publisher; Chris McMahon, General Sales Mgr.; Dianne LoMonte, Advertising Dir. **Subscription Rates:** Free; $25 by mail. **Remarks:** Accepts advertising.
Ad Rates: GLR: $.80 **Circ:** Free 7,315
BW: $1,435.77
4C: $1,881.77
PCI: $11.13

7891 Military Sun Press
Sun Newspapers
45-525 Luluku Rd. Phone: (808)235-5881
Kaneohe, HI 96744 Fax: (808)247-7246

Military newspaper. **Founded:** 1988. **Freq:** Weekly (Thurs.). **Subscription Rates:** Free. **Formerly:** Central Military Sun Press (Feb. 25, 1988).
Circ: Free ‡7,374

7892 Windward Sun-Press
RFD Publications, Inc.
45-525 Luluku Rd. Phone: (808)235-5881
Kaneohe, HI 96744-1945 Fax: (808)247-7246

Suburban newspaper. **Founded:** 1969. **Freq:** Weekly (Thurs.). **Print Method:** Offset. **Trim Size:** 11 1/2 x 13 1/2. **Cols./Page:** 6. **Col. Width:** 26 nonpareils. **Col. Depth:** 294 agate lines. **Key Personnel:** Bill Stone, Editor; Ken Berry, Publisher; Chris McMahon, General Sales Mgr.; Dianne LoMonte, Advertising Dir. **Subscription Rates:** Free; $25 by mail. **Remarks:** Accepts advertising.
Ad Rates: GLR: $.92 **Circ:** Combined 23,030
BW: $1,648.62
4C: $2,094.62
PCI: $12.78

LAHAINA, pop. 10,284.

E HI. Maui Co. 15 mi. NE of Lanai.

7893 Hawaiian Cable Vision Co.
910 Honoapiilani Hwy., Ste. 6 Phone: (808)661-4607
Lahaina, HI 96761 Fax: (808)661-8865
E-mail: james@oceanic-maui.com

Founded: 1969. **Key Personnel:** Jim McBride, General Mgr., james@oceanic-maui.com; Mickie Sheets, Plant Manager; Nancy Chaplack, Commercial Development Manager; Kimberly Caywood, Advertising Account Executive; Gail Corrigan, Customer Service Manager. **Cities Served:** subscribing households 16,800; 54 channels; 3 community access channels.

7894 KPOA-FM - 93.5
505 Front St., No. 215 Phone: (808)667-9110
Lahaina, HI 96761-1231 Fax: (808)661-8850
E-mail: kpoa@maui.net

Format: Ethnic. **Owner:** Lahaina Broadcasting Co. Ltd., at above address. **Founded:** 1984. **Operating Hours:** Continuous. **Key Personnel:** Chuck Bergson, Contact; Debra H. Prost, Station Mgr.; Debra H. Prost, Contact; Bernard Clark, Chief Operating Officer. **Wattage:** 25,000. **Ad Rates:** $15-35 for 30 seconds; $18-45 for 60 seconds. Combined advertising rates available with KLHI-FM. **URL:** http://www.mauigateway.commm/kpoa.

LIHUE†, pop. 4,000.

W HI. Kauai Co. On Kauai Island, 100 mi. NW of Honolulu. Sugar mills; canneries. Resorts. Fisheries. Agriculture. Sugar cane, pineapples.

7895 The Garden Island
Kauai Publishing Co.
3137 Kuhio Hwy. Phone: (808)245-3681
PO Box 231 Fax: (808)245-5286
Lihue, HI 96766
General newspaper. **Subtitle:** Serving the people of Kauai since 1902. **Founded:** 1902. **Freq:** Mon.-Sat. (eve.). **Print Method:** Offset. **Cols./Page:** 6. **Col. Width:** 24 nonpareils. **Col. Depth:** 301 agate lines. **Key Personnel:** Rita DeSilva, Managing Editor; Roy Callaway, Publisher. **Subscription Rates:** $84 individuals. **Remarks:** Accepts advertising.
Ad Rates: 4C: $254 **Circ:** Mon.-Fri. ★**8,729**
SAU: $9.90 Sun. ★**9,336**

7896 Garden Isle Telecommunications
3022 Peleke St., Ste. 8 Phone: (808)245-7720
Lihue, HI 96766 Fax: (808)245-5221

Founded: 1970. **Formerly:** Kauai CableVision (1981); Garden Isle Cablevision (1987). **Key Personnel:** Bill Harkins, President, phone (808)246-9315; Ron Crown, System Engineer, phone (808)245-5086; Bill Wallace, Ad Sales, phone (808)245-1947. **Cities Served:** Barking Sands Naval Base, Kauai County, HI: subscribing households 17,500; 59 channels; 3 community access channels; 504 hours per week community access programming.

7897 KFMN-FM - 96.9
PO Box 1566 Phone: (808)246-1197
Lihue, HI 96766-5566 Fax: (808)246-9697

Format: Adult Contemporary. **Networks:** AP. **Owner:** FM 97 Associates, at above address. **Founded:** 1988. **Operating Hours:** Continuous. **Key Personnel:** Dianne Mikami, Sales Mgr.; John C. Wada, General Mgr. **Wattage:** 100,000. **Ad Rates:** $25 for 30 seconds; $30 for 60 seconds.

7898 KQNG-AM - 570
KONG Radio Bldg. Phone: (808)245-9527
4271 Halenani St. Fax: (808)245-3563
Lihue, HI 96766

Format: Oldies. **Networks:** AP. **Owner:** Sanchez Communications Corp., at above address. **Founded:** 1939. **Formerly:** KONG-AM. **Operating Hours:** Continuous. **Key Personnel:** Rodney T. Sanchez, Contact; Jimmy Davis, General Sales Mgr. **Wattage:** 1000. **Ad Rates:** $15-29 for 30 seconds; $18-34 for 60 seconds. Combined advertising rates available with KQNG-AM: $15-$29 for 30 seconds; $18-$34 for 60 seconds.

7899 KQNG-FM - 93.5
KONG Radio Bldg. Phone: (808)245-9527
4271 Halenani St. Fax: (808)245-3563
Lihue, HI 96766

Format: Contemporary Hit Radio (CHR). **Networks:** AP. **Owner:** Sanchez Communications Corp., at above address. **Founded:** 1983. **Formerly:** KONG-FM. **Operating Hours:** Continuous. **Key Personnel:** Rodney T. Sanchez, Contact; Jimmy Davis, General Sales Mgr. **Wattage:** 100,000. **Ad Rates:** $18-34 for 30 seconds; $22-42 for 60 seconds. Combined advertising rates available with KQNG-AM: $18-$34 for 30 seconds; $22-$42 for 60 seconds.

MAUNALOA

7900 The Dispatch
New Regime Press, Inc.
PO Box 96 Phone: (808)552-2781
Maunaloa, HI 96770 Fax: (808)552-2334
Publication E-mail: mkkdisp@aloha.net

Community newspaper of Molokai, Hawaii. **Founded:** Jan. 1984. **Freq:** Weekly. **Print Method:** Web. **Trim Size:** 10 1/4 x 14 3/4. **Cols./Page:** 4. **Col. Width:** 2 3/8 inches. **Col. Depth:** 14 3/4 inches. **Key Personnel:** Gerald M. Anderson, Editor and Publisher; Edith F. Anderson, Editor and Publisher. **Subscription Rates:** Free; $50 individuals out of area. **Remarks:** Accepts advertising. **Former name:** Molokai Dispatch.
Ad Rates: BW: $550 **Circ:** Controlled ⊕**5,150**
4C: $596
PCI: $15

MILILANI

7901 Oceanic Cablevision, Inc.
200 Akamainui St. Phone: (808)625-2100
Mililani, HI 96789 Fax: (808)625-5888

Founded: 1971. **Key Personnel:** Don Carroll, President; Kit Beuret, Contact, kbeurret@oceanic.com. **Cities Served:** Honolul, HI, & surrounding communities: subscribing households 245,000; 75 channels; 5 community access channels.

PEARL CITY

7902 KIFO-AM - 1380
738 Kaheka St. Phone: (808)955-8821
Honolulu, HI 96814 Fax: (808)942-5477
E-mail: lpr@lcva.net

Format: News; Information. **Networks:** Public Radio International (PRI); National Public Radio (NPR). **Owner:** Hawaii Public Radio, at above address. **Founded:** 1989. **Formerly:** KIPO-AM (1993). **Operating Hours:** Continuous. **ADI:** Honolulu, HI. **Key Personnel:** J.P. Muntal, News Dir.; Valerie Yee, Director, Development/Marketing; Alan Bunin, Music Dir.; Mark Wagner, Operations Dir.; Michael Titterton, General Mgr. **Wattage:** 6,200.

PUKALANI

7903 KMVI-FM - 98.3
311 Ano St. Phone: (808)877-5566
Kahului, HI 96732-1304 Fax: (808)877-2137

Format: Classic Rock. **Owner:** Obie Communications Inc. of Maui, at above address. **Founded:** 1984. **Operating Hours:** Continuous. **Key Personnel:** Pamela Tsutsui, General Mgr.; Jack Sweeney, General Sales Mgr.; Jeff Hunter, Operations Mgr.; Paul Robinson, Sales Mgr.; Kirk Hamilton, Program Dir.; Fred Guzman, News Dir. **Wattage:** 50,000. **Ad Rates:** $15-25 for 30 seconds; $17-27 for 60 seconds. Combined advertising rates available with KMVI-AM.

WAILUKU†, pop. 10,674.

E HI. Maui Co. On Maui Island, 90 mi. SE of Honolulu. Nearest port is three miles, Kahului. Tourist resort. Sugar factory. Agriculture. Sugar cane, pineapples.

7904 Maui News
Maui Publishing
100 Mahalani Phone: (808)244-3981
Wailuku, HI 96793 Fax: (808)242-6390
Free: (800)827-0347
Publication E-mail: mauinews@maui.net

General newspaper. **Subtitle:** The Maui News. **Founded:** 1900. **Freq:** Daily (eve.). **Print Method:** Offset. **Cols./Page:** 6. **Col. Width:** 25 nonpareils. **Col. Depth:** 301 agate lines. **Key Personnel:** Dave Hoff, Editor-in-Chief; Richard H. Cameron, Publisher; Patrick Saka, General Mgr. **Subscription Rates:** $48 individuals. **Remarks:** Accepts advertising. **URL:** http://www.mauinews.com.
Ad Rates: BW: $1,586.70 **Circ:** Mon.-Thurs. ★**16,447**
4C: $1,785.45 Fri. ★**18,672**
SAU: $14.60 Sun. ★**23,439**
PCI: $14.60

7905 KAOI-FM - 95.1
1900 Main St. Phone: (808)244-9145
Wailuku, HI 96793-1707

Format: Album-Oriented Rock (AOR); Contemporary Hit Radio (CHR). **Owner:** KA-OI Communications, Inc., at above address. **Founded:** 1974. **Operating Hours:** Continuous. **Key Personnel:** John Detz, President. **Wattage:** 100,000 ERP.

IDAHO

State Capital, BOISE

Idaho is bounded on the north by British Columbia, east by Montana and Wyoming, south by Utah and Nevada, and west by Oregon and Washington. Its length from north to south is about 480 miles, its width varies from 44 to 325 miles. The total land area is 82,751 square miles, and includes 47 square miles of Yellowstone Park; rank in area, tenth.. The state's surface is diversified, being mountainous in the northern and central portions and having arid plains in the south. Mt. Borah, 12,655 feet in the Lost River Range is the highest point in the state. In the southeast there is a volcanic region abounding in geysers and saline springs. The Snake River, which abounds in falls, forms part of the state's western boundary and flows through the southern part. The Salmon River, a tributary, flows through a lengthy canyon that is filled with game. The state has large mineral resources. The climate is dry and healthful, warm in the summer and cold in winter. The Weather Bureau at Boise gives the temperature (annual average) as 50.9; highest on record, 109; lowest on record, -13. Total annual precipitation is 12.11 inches. The University of Idaho is located at Moscow and Idaho State University in Pocatello. The volcanic field 130 miles southwest of Yellowstone Park, called Craters of the Moon, was set aside in 1924 as a national monument.

POPULATION: 1,067,000 (1992). Rank among the states, 42nd.

AGRICULTURE: Number of farms: 21,000 (1992). Farm acreage: 14,000,000 (1992). Cash receipts from farm marketings: crops, $1,543,000,000 (1991); livestock and products, $1,073,000,000 (1991).

FORESTS: Total forest land: 21,674,000 acres (1991). Principal woods: ponderosa pine, white pine, douglas fir, white fir, larch, western red cedar, englemann spruce, lodgepole pine, hemlock, cottonwood, aspen.

MINERALS: Value of production: $297,000,000 (1991). Principal minerals: phosphate rock, silver, molybdenum.

MANUFACTURES: Value added by manufacture: $3,895,000,000 (1991). Leading industry groups: food and related products, lumber and wood products.

LIST OF COUNTIES

Total number of counties 44

County, Location on Map, and County Seat	Pop.
Ada (SW), Boise	205,775
Adams (W), Council	3,254
Bannock (SE), Pocatello	66,026
Bear Lake (SE), Paris	6,084
Benewah (NW), St. Maries	7,937
Bingham (SE), Blackfoot	37,583
Blaine (S), Hailey	13,552
Boise (SW), Idaho City	3,509
Bonner (NW), Sandpoint	26,622
Bonneville (E), Idaho Falls	72,207
Boundary (NW), Bonners Ferry	8,332
Butte (S), Arco	2,918
Camas (S), Fairfield	727
Canyon (SW), Caldwell	90,076
Caribou (SE), Soda Springs	6,963
Cassia (S), Burley	19,532
Clark (E), Dubois	762
Clearwater (NW), Orofino	8,505
Custer (C), Challis	4,133
Elmore (SW), Mountain Home	21,205
Franklin (SE), Preston	9,232
Fremont (E), St. Anthony	10,937
Gem (W), Emmett	11,844
Gooding (C), Gooding	11,633
Idaho (C), Grangeville	13,783
Jerome (S), Jerome	15,138
Kootenai (NW), Coeur d'Alene	69,795
Latah (NW), Moscow	30,617
Lemhi (C), Salmon	6,899
Lewis (W), Nez Perce	3,516
Lincoln (S), Shoshone	3,308
Madison (E), Rexburg	23,674
Minidoka (S), Rupert	19,361
Nez Perce (W), Lewiston	33,754
Oneida (SE), Malad City	3,492
Owyhee (SW), Murphy	8,392
Payette (W), Payette	16,434
Power (SE), American Falls	7,086
Shoshone (NW), Wallace	13,931
Teton (E), Driggs	3,439
Twin Falls (S), Twin Falls	53,580
Valley (C), Cascade	6,109
Washington (W), Weiser	8,550

STATISTICS

Newspapers

Period of Issue	
Daily	10
Evening Daily	5
Morning Daily	5
Daily with Sunday edition	7
Semiweekly	4
Weekly	44
Bimonthly	1
Quarterly	1
Free or partly free	7
Shopper	1
Total Newspapers	63

Periodicals

Period of Issue	
Daily	1
Monthly	6
Bimonthly	4
Quarterly	5
Total Periodicals	30

Total number of publications 93

Radio Stations

AM Stations	39
FM Stations	49
Total Radio Stations	88

TV Stations

Total TV Stations 12

Cable Stations

Total Cable Systems 15

Total number of broadcast listings 115

ABERDEEN, pop. 1,528.

SE ID. Bingham Co. 25 mi. W. of Pocatello. Potato processing. Stock, dairy, poultry, grain farms. Potatoes, sugar beets, alfalfa seed.

7906 The Aberdeen Times
Aberdeen Publishing
Box X Phone: (208)397-4440
Aberdeen, ID 83210 Fax: (208)226-5295

Local newspaper. **Founded:** 1910. **Freq:** Weekly (Wed.). **Print Method:** Offset. **Cols./Page:** 7. **Col. Width:** 10 1/2 picas. **Col. Depth:** 21 inches. **Key Personnel:** Erma Crompton, Publisher; Vicki Gamble, Editor. **Subscription Rates:** $22 individuals; $21 senior citizens; $26 out of state; $25 out of state senior citizens. **Remarks:** Accepts advertising.
Ad Rates: GLR: $.44 **Circ:** Paid ⊕**1,200**
BW: $602 Free ⊕**18**
4C: $827
SAU: $5.85
PCI: $5.10

AMERICAN FALLS†, pop. 3,626.

SE ID. Power Co. 25 mi. SW of Pocatello. Hydroelectric power production. Potato processing. Grain elevator. Stock, dairy, poultry farms. Wheat, potatoes, hay.

7907 The Power County Press
Crompton Publishing
PO Box 547 Phone: (208)226-5294
American Falls, ID 83211 Fax: (208)226-5295
Publication E-mail: pcpress@ifirmci.net

Community newspaper. **Founded:** 1901. **Freq:** Weekly (Wed.). **Print Method:** Offset. **Cols./Page:** 7. **Col. Width:** 11 picas. **Col. Depth:** 21 inches. **Key Personnel:** Brett Crompton, Editor; Erma Crompton, Publisher; Debbie Crompton, Advertising Mgr. **USPS:** 440-940. **Subscription Rates:** $22 individuals; $26 out of state. **Remarks:** Accepts advertising.
Ad Rates: BW: $999.60 **Circ:** ‡2,090
4C: $1,320
SAU: $6.80
PCI: $5.85

ARCO†, pop. 1,241.

S. ID. Butte Co. 90 mi. NW of Pocatello. Silver, lead mines. Dairy, stock, grain farms. Hay, potatoes.

7908 The Arco Advertiser
PO Box 803 Phone: (208)527-3038
Arco, ID 83213-0803 Fax: (208)527-8210
Free: (800)927-3038

Community newspaper. **Founded:** Mar. 12, 1909. **Freq:** Weekly (Thurs.). **Print Method:** Offset. **Trim Size:** 14 x 22 1/2. **Cols./Page:** 6. **Col. Width:** 26 nonpareils. **Col. Depth:** 294 agate lines. **Key Personnel:** Charles L. Cammack, Editor; Donald L. Cammack, Publisher; Thomas D. Cammack, Advertising Mgr. **ISSN:** 0890-1511. **Subscription Rates:** $20 individuals local; $23 out of area. **Remarks:** Color advertising not accepted. **Available Online.**
Ad Rates: GLR: $.23 **Circ:** ‡2,185
BW: $504
PCI: $4

BLACKFOOT†, pop. 10,100.

C. ID. Bingham Co. 23 mi. N. of Pocatello. Farm machinery, sugar beets.

7909 The Morning News
American Publishing Co.
34 N. Ash Phone: (208)785-1100
PO Box 70 Fax: (208)785-4239
Blackfoot, ID 83221
Publication E-mail: mhoid@poky.srv.net

Local newspaper. **Subtitle:** The Morning News. **Founded:** 1904. **Freq:** Mon.-Sat. (morn.). **Print Method:** Web offset. **Trim Size:** 13 x 21 1/2. **Cols./Page:** 6. **Col. Width:** 12 1/2 picas. **Col. Depth:** 21 1/2 inches. **Key Personnel:** Brian Lee, Editor; Don Black, Publisher; Annette Cathey, Advertising Mgr. **ISSN:** 0745-712X. **Subscription Rates:** $8.50 carrier delivery; $9.40 motor route; $12.90 out of area. **Remarks:** Accepts advertising.
Ad Rates: 4C: $180 **Circ:** ‡5,000
SAU: $10.50
PCI: $8.50

7910 KECN-AM - 690
Hwy. 91, Box 699 Phone: (208)785-1400
Blackfoot, ID 83221 Fax: (208)785-0184

Format: Contemporary Country. **Owner:** Western Communications Inc., at above address. **Founded:** 1951. **Formerly:** KBLI-AM (1992). **Operating Hours:** 6 a.m.-midnight. **Key Personnel:** James T. Burgoyne, Contact; Keith A. Walker, Sales Mgr. **Wattage:** 1000 days; 42 nights.

7911 KTEE-AM - 1260
Box 192
Blackfoot, ID 83221

Format: Big Band/Nostalgia. **Founded:** 1960. **Key Personnel:** Arnold D. Hildreth, Contact; Brad Moss, Contact; Norris Ashment, Chief Engineer. **Wattage:** 5000 day; 64 night.

BOISE†, pop. 102,451.

SW ID. Ada Co. On the Boise River, 45 mi. E. of the Oregon border. The State Capital. Boise State University. The central city of the intermountain region. Manufacturing trade and service industries.

7912 The Arbiter
Hemingway Western Studies Series
1910 University Dr. Phone: (208)426-1999
Boise, ID 83725 Fax: (208)426-4373
Free: (800)992-TEXT
Publication E-mail: arbiter@claven.idbsu.edu

Collegiate newspaper. **Founded:** 1932. **Freq:** Weekly (Wed.). **Print Method:** Offset. **Cols./Page:** 5. **Col. Width:** 23 nonpareils. **Col. Depth:** 217 agate lines. **Key Personnel:** Kate Bell, Editor; Chris Adamsson, Business Mgr.; Matt Pottenger, Advertising Mgr. **Subscription Rates:** $20 individuals. **Remarks:** Accepts advertising. **URL:** http://www.idbsu.edu/arbiter/intro.html.
Ad Rates: BW: $564.20 **Circ:** Free ‡5,000
PCI: $6

7913 Boise Family Magazine
PO Box 3178 Phone: (208)853-2516
Boise, ID 83703 Fax: (208)853-2756
Publisher E-mail: boisefamily@family.com

Local consumer magazine covering parenting and family issues. **Founded:** Oct. 1993. **Freq:** Monthly. **Print Method:** Web. **Trim Size:** 8 x 10 3/4. **Cols./Page:** 3. **Col. Width:** 2 1/4 inches. **Col. Depth:** 9 1/2 inches. **Key Personnel:** Liz Buckingham, Editor. **Subscription Rates:** $12 individuals. **Remarks:** Accepts advertising.
Ad Rates: BW: $810 **Circ:** Controlled ‡17,000
4C: $1,020

7914 Boise Weekly
PO Box 1657 Phone: (208)344-2055
Boise, ID 83701
Community newspaper. **Freq:** Weekly (Thurs.). **Subscription Rates:** Free.
Circ: Non-paid 15,719

7915 The Chemical Educator
Springer-Verlag New York, Inc.
Boise State University Phone: (208)385-4491
1910 University Dr. Fax: (208)385-4493
Boise, ID 83725
Publisher E-mail: journals@springer-ny.com

Online journal for chemical educators. **Founded:** Mar. 1996. **Freq:** Bimonthly. **Key Personnel:** Clifford LeMaster, Editor-in-Chief. **ISSN:** 1430-4171. **Subscription Rates:** Free. **Remarks:** Accepts advertising. **URL:** http://journals.springer-ny.com/chedr.
Circ: (Not Reported)

7916 Genealogical Journal of Jefferson County, New York
The Family Tree
PO Box 4311 Phone: (208)939-9141
Boise, ID 83711
Publisher E-mail: familytre@aol.com

Journal of genealogical information. **Founded:** 1989. **Freq:** Annual. **Key Personnel:** Pat James, Contact, phone (208)382-3629, familytre@aol.com; Anna Nasman, Contact, anasman@juno.com. **ISSN:** 1045-8166. **Subscription Rates:** $17.50 individuals. **Remarks:** Advertising not accepted.
Circ: Paid ‡200

7917 Genealogical Journal of Oneida County, New York
The Family Tree
PO Box 4311 Phone: (208)939-9141
Boise, ID 83711
Publisher E-mail: familytre@aol.com

Genealogical journal of Oneida County, New York. **Founded:** Oct. 1997. **Freq:** Annual. **Key Personnel:** Patricia James, Contact; Anna Nasman, Contact. **Subscription Rates:** $17.50 individuals. **Remarks:** Advertising not accepted.
Circ: Paid 300

7918 Gunfighter
Graphic Art Publishing
5325 Kendall Phone: (208)375-1010
Boise, ID 83706 Fax: (208)376-0434

Newspaper (tabloid) distributed to personnel at Mountain Home Air Force Base. **Founded:** 1953. **Freq:** Weekly (Fri.). **Print Method:** Offset. **Trim Size:** 10 3/4 x 17. **Cols./Page:** 4. **Col. Width:** 28 nonpareils. **Col. Depth:** 224 agate lines. **Key Personnel:** Reed Hansen, Publisher; Ron Coffield, Advertising Mgr. **Remarks:** Accepts advertising.
Ad Rates: GLR: $.30 **Circ:** Free ‡5,400
PCI: $7.50

7919 The Idaho Business Review
PO Box 8866 Phone: (208)336-3768
Boise, ID 83707 Fax: (208)336-5534
Publication E-mail: ibr@cyberhighway.com
Publisher E-mail: ibr@cyberhighway.com

Business newspaper (tabloid). **Founded:** May 1984. **Freq:** Weekly. **Print Method:** Offset. **Trim Size:** 11 1/4 x 17 1/2. **Cols./Page:** 5. **Col. Width:** 12 picas. **Col. Depth:** 210 agate lines. **Key Personnel:** Brian Hunt, Publisher. **Subscription Rates:** $59 individuals.
Ad Rates: BW: $720 **Circ:** Paid 4,100
4C: $876 Free 450
SAU: $14
PCI: $14

7920 Idaho Catholic Register
303 Federal Way Phone: (208)342-1311
Boise, ID 83705 Fax: (208)342-0224
Publication E-mail: idcathreg@rcdb.org

Newspaper for the Catholic community. **Founded:** 1958. **Freq:** 2/month. **Print Method:** Offset. **Trim Size:** 11 x 14 1/2. **Cols./Page:** 5. **Col. Width:** 25 nonpareils. **Col. Depth:** 210 agate lines. **Key Personnel:** Colette Cowman, Editor; Bishop Michael Driscoll, Publisher; Leonard George, Advertising Mgr. **ISSN:** 0891-5792. **Subscription Rates:** $16 individuals. **Remarks:** Accepts advertising. **Formerly:** Idaho Register.
Ad Rates: GLR: $.70 **Circ:** ‡16,200
BW: $750
4C: $1,125
PCI: $10

7921 The Idaho Statesman
Gannett Co., Inc.
1200 N. Curtis Rd. Phone: (208)377-6200
PO Box 40 Fax: (208)377-6309
Boise, ID 83707
Free: (800)635-8934
Publication E-mail: news@idstates.com

General newspaper. **Founded:** July 26, 1864. **Freq:** Mon.-Sun. (morn.). **Print Method:** Offset. **Cols./Page:** 6. **Col. Width:** 2 inches. **Col. Depth:** 22 inches. **Key Personnel:** Margaret Buchanan, Publisher, phone (208)377-6301, fax (208)377-6303, mbuchana@boise.gannett.com; Steve Silberman, Managing Editor, phone (208)377-6406, ssilberm@boise.gannett.com; Robert Pedersen, Circulation Mgr., pbederse@boise.gannett.com. **ISSN:** 0093-1179. **Subscription Rates:** $156 individuals Monday-Friday; $174.20 out of area; $293.80 out of state. **Remarks:** Accepts advertising. **Online:** LEXIS-NEXIS; DataTimes Corporation; Dialog (The Dialog Corporation); CompuServe Information Service. **URL:** http://www.accessatlanta.com. **Alt. Formats:** CD-ROM. **Feature Editors:** Holly Anderson, *News*; Vickie Ashwell, *Family*; Alan Bauer, *Editorials*; Paul Beebe, *Financial/Business*; Michael Deeds, *Entertainment*; Andy Horan, *Metro*; Sara Kuhl, *City*; Camille Nichols, *Weekend*; Dan Popkey, *Columnist*; Jennifer Swindell, *Sports*.
Ad Rates: GLR: $5.60 **Circ:** Mon.-Sat. 65,975
BW: $5,236 Sun. 687,397
4C: $5,696
SAU: $23.80
PCI: $46.81

7922 Idaho Wildlife
Idaho Dept. of Fish and Game
600 S. Walnut St. Phone: (208)334-3746
Box 25 Fax: (208)334-2148
Boise, ID 83707-0025
Free: (800)IDA-WILD

Magazine on conservation and natural history. **Founded:** 1978. **Freq:** Bimonthly. **Print Method:** Offset. **Trim Size:** 8 1/8 x 10 7/8. **Cols./Page:** 3. **Col. Width:** 28 nonpareils. **Col. Depth:** 140 agate lines. **Key Personnel:** Diane M. Ronayne, Editor, dronayne@idfg.state.id.us. **ISSN:** 8755-2469. **Subscription Rates:** $12.95 individuals; $18 other countries per year; $2.50 single issue. **Remarks:** Advertising accepted; rates available upon request. **URL:** http://www.state.id.us/fishgame/fishgame.html.
Circ: Paid ‡6,741
Non-paid ‡1,000

7923 IEA Reporter
Idaho Education Association
PO Box 2638 Phone: (208)344-1732
Boise, ID 83701
Educational magazine (tabloid). **Founded:** 1946. **Freq:** 9/year. **Print Method:** Offset. **Trim Size:** 11 x 17. **Cols./Page:** 4. **Col. Width:** 2 1/4 inches. **Col. Depth:** 16 inches. **Key Personnel:** Gayle Moore, Editor/Administration. **USPS:** 782-760. **Subscription Rates:** $10 individuals. **Remarks:** Color advertising not accepted.
Ad Rates: BW: $300 **Circ:** Paid ‡9,700
PCI: $13.13 Non-paid ‡600

7924 The Line Rider
Idaho Cattle Association
PO Box 15397 Phone: (208)343-1615
Boise, ID 83715 Fax: (208)344-6695

Official magazine of the Idaho cattle industry. **Founded:** 1984. **Freq:** Bimonthly. **Trim Size:** 8 1/2 x 11. **Cols./Page:** 3. **Key Personnel:** Sharon Olsen, Editor. **Subscription Rates:** $25. **Remarks:** Accepts advertising.
Ad Rates: BW: $500 **Circ:** ‡1,500
4C: $900

7925 Miner's News
PO Box 5694 Phone: (208)345-7488
2504 Kootenai St. Fax: (208)345-7905
Boise, ID 83705
Free: (800)624-7212
Publication E-mail: minersnews@aol.com

Mining newspaper. **Founded:** 1985. **Freq:** Bimonthly. **Print Method:** Web offset. **Trim Size:** 11 x 16 1/2. **Cols./Page:** 5. **Col. Width:** 2 inches. **Col. Depth:** 14 1/2 inches. **Key Personnel:** Gary White, Publisher. **ISSN:** 0890-6157. **Subscription Rates:** $25; $30 Canada. **Remarks:** Accepts advertising.
Ad Rates: BW: $1,695 **Circ:** Paid ‡2,552
4C: $2,245 Non-paid ‡3,612

7926 Society for Commercial Archeology Journal
Society for Commercial Archeology
1136 River St.
Boise, ID 83702

Scholarly journal covering the commercial landscape and architecture of the U.S. **Founded:** 1978. **Freq:** Semiannual. **Key Personnel:** Mike Bedeau, Editor; Sara Amy Leach, Editor. **ISSN:** 0735-1399. **Subscription Rates:** $25 individuals; $40 institutions. **Remarks:** Advertising not accepted. **Former name:** SCA News Journal.
Circ: Controlled 1,100

7927 Consolidated Freightways
1755 Westkey Dr. Phone: (208)377-2941
Boise, ID 83704 Fax: (208)377-7500

Founded: 1979. **Formerly:** UAE. **Cities Served:** Ada County and Canyon County, Eagle, Garden City, Kuna, Meridian, and Nampa, ID.

7928 KAID-TV - 4
1455 N. Orchard Phone: (208)373-7220
Boise, ID 83706 Fax: (208)373-7245
Free: (800)543-6868

Format: Public TV. **Networks:** Public Broadcasting Service (PBS). **Founded:** 1971. **Operating Hours:** 7 a.m.-11 p.m.; 90% network, 10% local. **ADI:** Boise, ID. **Key Personnel:** Gail Richardson, Personnel Officer; Peter Morrill, General Mgr.; Joan Hill, Devel. Dir. **Ad Rates:** Noncommercial.

7929 KBOI-AM - 670
1419 W. Bannock Phone: (208)336-3670
Boise, ID 83702 Fax: (208)336-3734
Free: (800)649-3670

Format: Full Service; Adult Contemporary. **Networks:** ABC. **Owner:** Charles Wilson, at above address. **Founded:** 1947. **Operating Hours:** Continuous. **ADI:** Boise, ID. **Key Personnel:** Bill Scott, News Dir.; Larry Doss, Program Dir.; Paul J. Schneider, Sports Dir.; Drew Harold, Music Dir.; Bob Rosenthal, General Mgr. **Local Programs:** *Bosie State Football/Basketball*; *Inside on the Outdoors*. **Wattage:** 50,000.

KBSM-FM - See Mc Call

7930 KBSU-FM - 90.3
Boise State University Phone: (208)426-3663
1910 University Dr. Fax: (208)344-6631
Boise, ID 83725
E-mail: akbradio@idbsu.idbsu.edu

Format: Public Radio; Classical; News. **Networks:** National Public Radio (NPR); Public Radio International (PRI). **Owner:** BSU Radio Network, at above address. **Founded:** 1977. **Operating Hours:** Continuous; 70% network, 30% local. **ADI:** Boise, ID. **Key Personnel:** James Paluzzi, General Mgr. **Wattage:** 19,000. **Ad Rates:** Noncommercial.

KBSW-FM - See Twin Falls

7931 KBSY-FM - 88.5
1910 University Dr. Phone: (208)426-3663
Boise, ID 83725 Fax: (208)344-6631
E-mail: dwoods@bsu.idbsu.edu

Format: News; Information. **Networks:** National Public Radio (NPR). **Owner:** Idaho State Board of Education, at above address. **Founded:** Oct. 1998. **Operating Hours:** Continuous. **URL:** http://www.idbsu.edu/bsuradio.

7932 KBXL-FM - 94.1
1477 S. Five Mile Rd. Phone: (208)466-0110
Boise, ID 83709-1308 Fax: (208)377-3792

Format: Contemporary Christian; Talk. **Networks:** USA Radio. **Owner:** Lee Schafer, at above address. **Founded:** 1970. **Operating Hours:** Continuous; 50% local, 50% network. **ADI:** Boise, ID. **Key Personnel:** Lee Schafer, Contact; Beth Schafer, Contact. **Wattage:** 40,000. **Ad Rates:** $10 for 30 seconds; $12 for 60 seconds.

7933 KCID-FM - 107.1
5601 Cassia Phone: (208)344-3511
Boise, ID 83705 Fax: (208)336-3264

Networks: ABC. **Founded:** 1983. **Operating Hours:** Continuous. **ADI:** Boise, ID. **Key Personnel:** Vicki Swain, VP/Gen.Mgr., swain@journalbroadcastgroup.com; Carl Follick, Operations Dir. **Wattage:** 3000. **Ad Rates:** KQXR-FM.

7934 KCIX-FM - 105.9
5257 Fairview Ave., Ste. 250 Phone: (208)376-6666
Boise, ID 83706 Fax: (208)323-7918

Format: Adult Contemporary. **Networks:** Independent. **Owner:** Contemporary Media Corp., at above address. **Founded:** 1985. **Operating Hours:** Continuous; 100% local. **ADI:** Boise, ID. **Key Personnel:** Kip Guth, Owner; Vicki Mann, Actg. PD; Russ Novak, Contact; Melissa Dawn, News; Robin Grube, Promotions Mgr. **Wattage:** 50,000.

7935 KGEM-AM - 1140
5601 Cassia Phone: (208)344-3511
Boise, ID 83705 Fax: (208)336-3264

Format: Big Band/Nostalgia; Oldies. **Networks:** Westwood One Radio. **Founded:** 1945. **Operating Hours:** Continuous. **ADI:** Boise, ID. **Key Personnel:** Ken Koch, General Mgr. **Wattage:** 10,000.

7936 KIDO-AM - 630
Box 63 Phone: (208)344-6363
Boise, ID 83707-0063 Fax: (208)334-1134

Format: Talk; News. **Networks:** NBC; ABC; Mutual Broadcasting System. **Owner:** Sundance Broadcasting of Idaho, at above address. **Founded:** 1928. **Operating Hours:** Continuous; 60% network, 40% local. **ADI:** Boise, ID. **Key Personnel:** Dick Lumenello, Station Mgr.; Jon Duane, Program Dir.; Les Leland, News Dir. **Wattage:** 5000. **Ad Rates:** Advertising accepted; rates available upon request.

KIOV-AM - See Payette

7937 KIZN-FM - 92.3
7272 Potomac Dr. Phone: (208)378-9200
Boise, ID 83704-9149 Fax: (208)375-2707

Format: Contemporary Country. **Founded:** 1990. **Formerly:** KBBK-FM. **Operating Hours:** Continuous. **ADI:** Boise, ID. **Key Personnel:** Monty Ivey, General Mgr.; David Pedersen, Sales Mgr.; Alissa Puckett, Marketing Director; Chris Walton, Creative Services Director. **Wattage:** 88,000. **Ad Rates:** $50 for 30 seconds; $50 for 60 seconds.

7938 KJHY-FM - 101.9
PO Box 4489 Phone: (208)322-3437
Boise, ID 83711

Format: Jazz; Easy Listening. **Founded:** 1973. **ADI:** Boise, ID. **Key Personnel:** Bert S. Mitchell, Contact; Steve Zimmer, General Mgr. **Wattage:** 57 KW.

7939 KJOT-FM - 105.1
5601 Cassia Phone: (208)344-3511
Boise, ID 83705 Fax: (208)336-3264

Format: Classic Rock. **Founded:** 1979. **Operating Hours:** Continuous. **ADI:** Boise, ID. **Key Personnel:** Vicki Swain, General Mgr. **Wattage:** 43,000. **Ad Rates:** Advertising accepted; rates available upon request. **URL:** http://www.j105.com.

7940 KKIC-AM - 950
Box 4489 Phone: (208)322-3437
Boise, ID 83711

Format: Country; Agricultural. **Founded:** 1961. **ADI:** Boise, ID. **Key Personnel:** Steve Summer, Contact. **Wattage:** 5000 day; 35 night.

7941 KLCI-FM - 96.9
1419 W. Bannock Phone: (208)336-3670
Boise, ID 83702 Fax: (208)336-3734
Free: (800)649-3670

Format: Classic Rock. **Networks:** ABC; Satellite Music Network. **Owner:** Pacific NW Broadcasting Corp., at above address. **Founded:** 1987. **Operating Hours:** Continuous. **ADI:** Boise, ID. **Key Personnel:** Bob Rosenthal, General Mgr.; Paul Wilson, Program Dir.; Carl Scheider, Music Dir. **Wattage:** 44,000 ERP.

7942 KLTB-FM - 104.3
PO Box 63 Phone: (208)344-6363
Boise, ID 83707-0063 Fax: (208)385-9064

Format: Oldies. **Networks:** Independent. **Owner:** Sundance Broadcasting of Idaho, at above address. **Founded:** 1979. **Operating Hours:** Continuous; 100% local. **ADI:** Boise, ID. **Key Personnel:** Dick Lumenello, General Mgr.; Jack Armstong, Program Dir.; Les Leland, News Dir. **Wattage:** 52,000. **Ad Rates:** $11-30 per unit.

7943 KQFC-FM - 97.9
1419 W. Bannock Phone: (208)336-3670
Boise, ID 83702 Fax: (208)336-3734

Format: Contemporary Country. **Networks:** Independent. **Founded:** 1960. **Formerly:** KBOI-FM (1985). **Operating Hours:** Continuous; local. **ADI:** Boise, ID. **Key Personnel:** Bob Rosenthal, General Mgr.; Bill Scott, News Dir., phone (208)336-1821, fax (208)336-3735; Paul Wilson, Program Dir. **Wattage:** 47,000. **Ad Rates:** Combined advertising rates available with KBOL-AM; KKGL-FM.

7944 KSPD-AM - 790
1477 S. Five Mile Rd. Phone: (208)377-3790
Boise, ID 83709-1308 Fax: (208)377-3792

Format: Religious. **Networks:** Moody Broadcasting; USA Radio; International Broadcasting; Ambassador Inspirational Radio. **Founded:** 1959. **Operating Hours:** 6 a.m.-9 p.m. **ADI:** Boise, ID. **Key Personnel:** Lee Schafer, President/General Sales Mgr./Product. **Wattage:** 1000. **Ad Rates:** $8 for 30 seconds; $10 for 60 seconds.

7945 KTIK-AM - 1340
5257 Fairview Ave., Ste. 250 Phone: (208)376-6666
Boise, ID 83706 Fax: (208)375-9248
Free: (800)966-5845
E-mail: ktik@aol.com

Format: Sports. **Owner:** Diamond Broadcasting, 290 Bobwhitect, Boise, ID 83706. **Founded:** 1962. **Formerly:** KANR-AM (1994). **Operating Hours:** Continuous; 100% local. **ADI:** Boise, ID. **Key Personnel:** Jeff Caves, Contact. **Local Programs:** *Idaho Sports Talk*, Jeff Caves; *Sports Buffet*, Mike Responts. **Wattage:** 1000.

7946 KTVB-TV - 7
5407 Fairview Ave. Phone: (208)375-7277
PO Box 7 Fax: (208)378-1762
83707
Boise, ID 83706

Format: Commercial TV. **Networks:** NBC. **Founded:** 1953. **Formerly:** KIDO-TV. **Operating Hours:** Continuous. **ADI:** Boise, ID. **Key Personnel:** Douglas Armstrong, Pres./Gen. Mgr.; Lance Hankins, Dir. of Engineering; John Lewis, National Sales Mgr.; Rod Gramer, News Dir.; Kristi Edmunds, Dir. Sales & Marketing. **Ad Rates:** $50-1,000 for 30 seconds; $100-2,000 for 60 seconds.

7947 KWEI-FM - 99.5
PO Box 45234 Phone: (208)549-2241
Boise, ID 83704 Fax: (208)549-0112
E-mail: kwei@cyberhighway.net

Format: Hispanic. **Owner:** Treasure Valley Broadcasting, at above address. **Founded:** 1978. **Operating Hours:** Continuous. **ADI:** Boise, ID. **Key Personnel:** Randy Williamson, General Mgr.; Ricardo Quitantan, Station Mgr. **Wattage:** 50,000. **Ad Rates:** Combined advertising rates available with KWEI-AM.

7948 KZMG-FM - 93.1
7272 Potomac Dr. Phone: (208)375-9300
Boise, ID 83704-9149 Fax: (208)375-9305

Format: Contemporary Hit Radio (CHR). **Owner:** PTI Broadcasting, Inc., 557 Washington, Reno, NV 89503, (702)323-

0123. **Founded:** 1982. **Formerly:** KIZN-FM (1990). **Operating Hours:** Continuous. **ADI:** Boise, ID. **Key Personnel:** Bruce Wetten, General Mgr.; Mike Uasper, Program Dir.; Constance Magaw, Contact. **Wattage:** 50,000.

BONNERS FERRY†, pop. 1,900.

C. ID. Boundry Co. 75 mi. NNE of Coeur d'Alene. Sawmills, farming, and mining.

7949 Bonners Ferry Herald
PO Box 539 Phone: (208)267-5521
Bonners Ferry, ID 83805 Fax: (208)267-5523

Community newspaper. **Freq:** Semiweekly (Wed. and Fri.). **Cols./Page:** 6. **Col. Width:** 2 1/8 inches. **Col. Depth:** 21 1/2 inches. **Key Personnel:** David Keyes, Publisher. **Subscription Rates:** $25.50 individuals; $29.50 out of area. **Remarks:** Accepts advertising.
Ad Rates: BW: $600 **Circ:** ‡3,000
4C: $900
PCI: $7

BOVILL

Latah Co.

7950 Bovill TV Cable Co.
204 Main St. Phone: (208)826-3234
PO Box 707
Bovill, ID 83806

Owner: Lloyd L. Hall, at above address. **Founded:** 1947. **Key Personnel:** Dewayne Allert, Manager, phone (208)882-2710. **Cities Served:** Bovill, ID: subscribing households 90; 13 channels; 2 community access channels.

BUHL, pop. 3,629.

S. ID. Twin Falls Co. 16 mi. W. of Twin Falls. Manufactures dairy products. Corn cannery; trout hatchery and processing. Diversified farming. Beans, potatoes, sugar beets, sweet corn.

7951 Buhl Herald
Buhl Herald, Inc.
PO Box 312 Phone: (208)543-4335
Buhl, ID 83316-0312 Fax: (208)543-6834

Community newspaper. **Founded:** 1906. **Freq:** Weekly (Wed.). **Print Method:** Offset. **Trim Size:** 14 1/2 x 23. **Cols./Page:** 6. **Col. Width:** 13 picas. **Col. Depth:** 21 1/2 inches. **Key Personnel:** Robert M. Bailey, Publisher. **USPS:** 069-860. **Subscription Rates:** $13.65 individuals; $16.80 other countries; $19 out of state. **Remarks:** Accepts advertising.
Ad Rates: GLR: $.268 **Circ:** Paid ‡2,700
BW: $483.75 Free ‡45
SAU: $3.75

BURLEY†, pop. 8,525.

S. ID. Cassia Co. 42 mi. E. of Twin Falls. Sugar mill; canning and potato processing plants; bottling works; brickyard. Grain, stock, dairy, poultry farms. Potatoes, hay, sugar beets, beans.

7952 South Idaho Press
230 E. Main St. Phone: (208)678-2201
Burley, ID 83318 Fax: (208)678-0412
Publication E-mail: sip@safelink.net; http://www.safelink.net/sip

General newspaper. **Founded:** 1904. **Freq:** Daily (eve.) Sun. a.m. **Print Method:** Offset. **Cols./Page:** 6. **Col. Width:** 12 picas. **Col. Depth:** 301 agate lines. **Key Personnel:** Ken Otoole, Editor; Cliff Barborka, Advertising Mgr.; Jay Lenkersdorfer, Publisher. **Subscription Rates:** $89 individuals; $.50 single issue; $.75 single copy, Sunday. **Remarks:** Accepts advertising.
Ad Rates: GLR: $.48 **Circ:** Mon.-Fri. 5,028
BW: $922.35 Sun. 5,175
4C: $1,057.35
SAU: $8.75
CNU: $6.50
PCI: $7.15

7953 KBAR-AM - 1230
1841 W. Main Phone: (208)678-2244
Burley, ID 83318 Free: (800)225-0999

Format: Middle-of-the-Road (MOR). **Networks:** ABC. **Founded:** 1945. **Operating Hours:** 5 a.m.-midnight; 8% network, 92% local. **Key Personnel:** Richard Huizinga, General Mgr.; Gerald Thaxton, Contact. **Wattage:** 1000. **Ad Rates:** $9.00-11.00 for 30 seconds; $11.00-15.00 for 60 seconds.

7954 KZDX-FM - 99.9
1841 W. Main Phone: (208)678-2244
Burley, ID 83318 Free: (800)225-0999

Format: Top 40. **Networks:** ABC. **Founded:** 1974. **Operating Hours:** Continuous. **Key Personnel:** Richard Huizinga, General Mgr.; Gerald Thaxton, Asst. Mgr. **Wattage:** 100,000. **Ad Rates:** $9.00-11.00 for 30 seconds; $11.00-15.00 for 60 seconds.

CALDWELL†.

SW ID. Canyon Co. 30 mi. W. of Boise.

7955 La Voz de Idaho
Idaho Migrant Council, Inc.
104 N. Kimball Phone: (208)454-1652
PO Box 490 Fax: (208)459-0448
Caldwell, ID 83606-0490
Community newspaper. (English and Spanish). **Founded:** 1980. **Freq:** Quarterly (March, June, Sept., and Dec.). **Print Method:** Offset. **Trim Size:** 11 1/4 x 16 1/2. **Cols./Page:** 5. **Col. Width:** 11 picas. **Col. Depth:** 15 inches. **Key Personnel:** Maria Salazar, Editor. **Subscription Rates:** $6; $2.50 farmworkers; $5 ex-farmworkers; $10 supportive members. **Remarks:** Accepts advertising.
Ad Rates: BW: $450 **Circ:** ‡2,000
PCI: $6

7956 KBGN-AM - 1060
3303 E. Chicago Phone: (208)459-3635
Caldwell, ID 83605

Format: Religious. **Networks:** USA Radio. **Owner:** Nelson M. Wilson or Karen E. Wilson, at above address. **Founded:** 1960. **Operating Hours:** 6 a.m.-two hours past sunset; 10% network, 90% local. **ADI:** Boise, ID. **Key Personnel:** Nelson M. Wilson, Contact; Marnie Fillmore, News/Operations Dir. **Local Programs:** *Studio B*, Nelson Wilson. **Wattage:** 10,000. **Ad Rates:** Advertising accepted; rates available upon request.

7957 KCID-AM - 1490
PO Box 968 Phone: (208)459-3608
Caldwell, ID 83606-0968 Fax: (208)454-1490

Format: Adult Contemporary; Sports; Hispanic. **Networks:** AP. **Founded:** 1947. **Operating Hours:** 5:45 a.m.-10 p.m. **ADI:** Boise, ID. **Key Personnel:** Larry Hancock, Sales/Gen. Mgr.; Sam Bass, News Dir.; Carl Follick, Operations Dir.; Cheryl Wolf, Office Mgr. **Local Programs:** *Albertson College of Idaho Basketball*, Keith Radockvich. **Wattage:** 1000. **Ad Rates:** $10-15 for 30 seconds; $13-18 for 60 seconds. KCID-FM.

CAMBRIDGE, pop. 428.

W. ID. Washington Co. 70 mi. N. of Boise. Brownlee, Oxbow & Hells Canyon Dam. Diversified farming. Hay, grain, cattle.

7958 Upper Country News-Reporter
155 N. Superior Phone: (208)257-3515
PO Box 9
Cambridge, ID 83610
Local newspaper. **Founded:** 1889. **Freq:** Weekly (Thurs.). **Print Method:** Offset. **Cols./Page:** 7. **Col. Width:** 22 nonpareils. **Col. Depth:** 294 agate lines. **Key Personnel:** Stuart Dopf, Publisher. **USPS:** 653-180. **Subscription Rates:** $18 individuals. **Remarks:** Accepts advertising.
Circ: Paid ‡1,056
Free ‡50

CHALLIS†, pop. 758.

C. ID. Custer Co. 50 mi. SE of Salmon. Residential.

7959 The Challis Messenger
Custer Publishing, Inc.
PO Box 405 Phone: (208)879-4445
Challis, ID 83226 Fax: (208)879-5276
Publisher E-mail: cuspub@cyberhighway.net

Community newspaper. **Founded:** May 21, 1881. **Freq:** Weekly (Thurs.). **Print Method:** Offset. **Trim Size:** 11 1/2 x 17 1/2. **Cols./Page:** 5. **Col. Width:** 11 1/2 picas. **Col. Depth:** 16 inches. **Key Personnel:** Peggy Parks, Editor and Publisher. **USPS:** 099-660. **Subscription Rates:** $18.90 individuals in county; $25.20 out of country.
Ad Rates: GLR: $0.32 **Circ:** ‡1,950
BW: $360
SAU: $4.75
PCI: $4.75

CHUBBUCK

7960 KRCD-FM - 1490
PO Box Z Phone: (208)232-0010
Pocatello, ID 83206-1394

Format: Talk. **Networks:** People's Network. **Founded:** 1981. **Formerly:** KKLB-FM (1987). **ADI:** Idaho Falls-Pocatello, ID. **Key Personnel:** Thomas W. Mathis, General Mgr. **Wattage:** 1000.

COEUR D'ALENE†, pop. 20,054.

N. ID. Kootenai Co. On Coeur d'Alene Lake and Spokane River, 33 mi. E. of Spokane, WA. Boat connections. Ski Resorts. Vacation Area. Manufactures lumber, shingles, railroad ties, boats, electronic equipment, box shooks, flour, dairy products. Timber. Agriculture.

7961 Coeur d'Alene Press
201 N. 2nd St. Phone: (208)664-8176
Coeur d'Alene, ID 83814 Fax: (208)664-0212
Free: (800)374-5380

General newspaper. **Founded:** 1879. **Freq:** Mon.-Sat. (morn.). **Print Method:** Offset. **Cols./Page:** 6. **Col. Width:** 25 nonpareils. **Col. Depth:** 294 agate lines. **Key Personnel:** James A. Hail, Editor and Publisher; Joe Grimes, Advertising Mgr. **Subscription Rates:** $132 individuals. **Remarks:** Accepts advertising.
Ad Rates: GLR: $.75 **Circ:** Mon.-Sat. ‡14,500
BW: $1,450.59 Sun. ‡28,200
4C: $1,780.54

7962 NIC Sentinel
North Idaho College
1000 W. Garden Phone: (208)769-3228
Coeur d'Alene, ID 83814 Fax: (208)769-3431
Publication E-mail: sentinel@nic.edu

College newspaper. **Freq:** Semimonthly. **Key Personnel:** Nils Rosdahl, Advisor, nrosdahl@nic.edu. **Subscription Rates:** Free. **Remarks:** Advertising not accepted. **URL:** http://www.nic.edu/sentinel. **Former name:** NIJC Review (1960); Cardinal (1970).
Circ: Non-paid 3,300

7963 Blockstone Cable TV
1104 Ironwood Phone: (208)664-3370
Coeur d'Alene, ID 83814 Fax: (208)664-5888
Free: (800)641-0795

Owner: Premier Cable II, Ltd., at above address. **Formerly:** Premier Cable TV. **Key Personnel:** Ted Hughett, Contact. **Cities Served:** subscribing households 14,000.

7964 Century Communications
108 Indiana Ave. Phone: (208)664-5963
Coeur d'Alene, ID 83814 Fax: (208)667-4804

Founded: 1970. **Absorbed:** Impact Cable TV Ads. **Formerly:** Kootenai Cable Inc. **Key Personnel:** Peter E. Quam, phone (208)667-0882. **Cities Served:** subscribing households 34,000; 60 channels; 1 community access channel; 4 hours per week community access programming.

7965 KVNI-AM - 1080
101 Lakeside Ave. Phone: (208)664-9271
Box 308 Fax: (208)667-0945
Coeur d'Alene, ID 83814

Format: Adult Contemporary; News. **Networks:** NBC. **Owner:** North Idaho Broadcasting Co., at above address. **Founded:** 1946. **Operating Hours:** Continuous; 10% network, 90% local. **ADI:** Spokane, WA. **Key Personnel:** Bruce Deming, General Mgr.; Dick Haugen, News Dir.; Jeff McLean, Sports Dir. **Wattage:** 10,000. **Ad Rates:** Combined advertising rates available with KHTQ-FM.

COTTONWOOD, pop. 941.

C. ID. Idaho Co. 56 mi. S. of Lewiston. Logging; grain elevators. Pine timber. Grain, dairy, stock, poultry farms. Wheat, hogs.

7966 Cottonwood Chronicle
503 King St. Phone: (208)962-3851
Box 157 Fax: (208)962-7131
Cottonwood, ID 83522
Community newspaper. **Founded:** 1893. **Freq:** Weekly (Thurs.). **Print Method:** Offset. **Cols./Page:** 5. **Col. Width:** 26 nonpareils. **Col. Depth:** 182 agate lines. **Key Personnel:** Patricia Wherry, Publisher. **Subscription Rates:** $18 individuals. **Remarks:** Accepts advertising.
Ad Rates: GLR: $0.37 **Circ:** ‡1,150

COUNCIL†, pop. 917.

W. ID. Adams Co. 125 mi. N. of Boise. Residential. Logging; ranching. Timber. Agriculture.

7967 Adams County Leader
Box 23 Phone: (208)253-4311
Council, ID 83612
Community newspaper. **Founded:** 1902. **Freq:** Weekly (Thurs.). **Print Method:** Letterpress. Uses mats. **Cols./Page:** 5. **Col. Width:** 2 inches. **Col. Depth:** 280 agate lines. **Key Personnel:** Gary Rogers, Editor and Publisher. **Subscription Rates:** $12.50 individuals; $14 out of area. **Remarks:** Accepts advertising.
Ad Rates: PCI: $2.78 **Circ:** 800

DEARY

Latah Co.

7968 Deary Television Co-op Inc.
513 Wyoming Phone: (208)877-1582
PO Box 105
Deary, ID 83823-0105

Founded: 1953. **Key Personnel:** Barb Femreite, General Mgr. **Cities Served:** deary, ID: subscribing households 202; 19 channels.

DRIGGS†, pop. 727.

E. ID. Teton Co. 50 mi. NE of Idaho Falls. Ski Resort. Diversified farming. Wheat, barley, hay, seed potatoes.

7969 Teton Valley News
Box 49 Phone: (208)354-8101
Driggs, ID 83422-0049 Fax: (208)354-8621

Local newspaper. **Founded:** 1909. **Freq:** Weekly (Thurs.). **Print Method:** Offset. **Trim Size:** 11 3/8 x 17. **Cols./Page:** 6. **Col. Width:** 20 nonpareils. **Col. Depth:** 224 agate lines. **Key Personnel:** Tammie van Leerdam, Editor. **ISSN:** 0889-9851. **Subscription Rates:** $20 individuals; $25 out of area. **Remarks:** Color advertising not accepted.
Ad Rates: BW: $384 **Circ:** ‡2,300
4C: $518.40
SAU: $5.50
PCI: $6

EMMETT†, pop. 4,605.

W. ID. Gem Co. 20 mi. NE of Caldwell. Residential.

7970 Messenger Index
PO Box 577 Phone: (208)365-6066
Emmett, ID 83617 Fax: (208)365-6068

Newspaper. **Founded:** 1893. **Freq:** Weekly (Wed.). **Print Method:** Offset. **Cols./Page:** 6. **Col. Width:** 25 nonpareils. **Col. Depth:** 297 agate lines. **Key Personnel:** Kathy Steed, Advertising Mgr. **Subscription Rates:** $21 individuals; $34.50 by mail. **Remarks:** Accepts advertising.
Ad Rates: GLR: $.43 **Circ:** 7,000
BW: $909.45
4C: $1,159.45
SAU: $7.05

GARDEN VALLEY

7971 The Idaho World
World Publishing Co., Inc.
PO Box 99 Phone: (208)462-3487
Garden Valley, ID 83622 Fax: (208)462-3325

County newspaper. **Founded:** 1863. **Freq:** Weekly (Wed.). **Cols./Page:** 5. **Col. Width:** 12 picas. **Col. Depth:** 16 inches. **Key Personnel:** Wayne Hart, Publisher, whart@micron.net; Deanna Stevenson, Editor. **Subscription Rates:** $25 individuals. **Remarks:** Accepts advertising.
Ad Rates: PCI: $4.50 **Circ:** 1200

GRANGEVILLE†, pop. 3,666.

C. ID. Idaho Co. 80 mi. SE of Lewiston. White water rafting; fishing; camping; winter sports. Logging mills. Agriculture. Peas, barley, clover, wheat, hay. Beef, sheep, hog production.

7972 Idaho County Free Press
318 E. Main St. Phone: (208)983-1070
PO Box 690 Fax: (208)983-1336
Grangeville, ID 83530
Community newspaper. **Founded:** June 1886. **Freq:** Weekly (Wed.). **Print Method:** Offset. **Cols./Page:** 6. **Col. Width:** 12 picas. **Col. Depth:** 21 inches. **Key Personnel:** Andrew McNab, Publisher/Advertising Dir. **Subscription Rates:** $24 individuals; $32 out of area.
Ad Rates: SAU: $8.25 **Circ:** Paid ‡4,100
PCI: $8.25 Free ‡10,100

7973 KORT-AM - 1230
PO Box 510 Phone: (208)983-1230
Grangeville, ID 83530 Fax: (208)983-2744

Format: Hot Country. **Networks:** ABC. **Owner:** 4-K Radio, Box 936, Lewiston, ID 83501. **Operating Hours:** 19 hours Daily. Sun.-Thurs overnight Fri & Sat. **Key Personnel:** Melinda Fischer, Operations Mgr./Sales Mgr. **Wattage:** 1000. **Ad Rates:** Advertising accepted; rates available upon request. $9 for 30 seconds; $14 for 60 seconds.

7974 KORT-FM - 92.7
Box 510 Phone: (208)983-1230
Grangeville, ID 83530 Fax: (208)983-2744

Format: Full Service; Hot Country; Agricultural. **Networks:** ABC. **Owner:** 4-K Radio, Box 936, Lewiston, ID 83501. **Operating Hours:** 19 hours Daily. Sun.-Thurs. Overnight Fri. and Sat. **Key Personnel:** Melinda Fischer, Operations and Sales Mgr. **Wattage:** 460. **Ad Rates:** $9 for 30 seconds; $14 for 60 seconds.

HAILEY†, pop. 2,109.

S. ID. Blaine Co. 75 mi. W. of Twin Falls. Recreation. Mining. Agriculture.

7975 Wood River Journal
PO Box 988 Phone: (208)788-3444
11 E. Bullion Fax: (208)788-0083
Hailey, ID 83333
Publication E-mail: wrjidaho@micron.net

Community newspaper. **Founded:** 1881. **Freq:** Weekly (Wed.). **Print Method:** Web. **Cols./Page:** 5. **Col. Width:** 24 nonpareils. **Col. Depth:** 224 agate lines. **Key Personnel:** Dan Gorham, Editor; Wayne Adair, News Editor. **Subscription Rates:** Free; $26 by mail. **Remarks:** Accepts advertising. **URL:** http://www.wrjournal.com.
Ad Rates: PCI: $9.75 **Circ:** Free 10,310
Paid 2,000

7976 KSKI-FM - 103.7
PO Box 1340 Phone: (208)788-4504
Hailey, ID 83333 Fax: (208)788-4444
Free: (888)733-KSKI
E-mail: kski@sunvalley.net

Format: Alternative/New Music/Progressive. **Owner:** E-Da-Hoe, Inc., at above address. **Founded:** 1977. **Operating Hours:** Continuous; 15% network, 85% local. **Key Personnel:** Clint Stennett, President. **Wattage:** 53,000. **Ad Rates:** $5-20 per unit.

IDAHO CITY†, pop. 300.

C. ID. Boise Co.

7977 Idaho City Cable TV
PO Box 70 Phone: (208)392-4290
Idaho City, ID 83631 Fax: (208)392-4505

Owner: Don Campbell, at above address. **Founded:** 1984. **Key Personnel:** Don Campbell, Owner/Mgr. **Cities Served:** Idaho City, ID: subscribing households 200; 38 channels; 1 community access channel.

IDAHO FALLS†, pop. 39,590.

E. ID. Bonneville Co. 50 mi. NE of Pocatello. Potato, flour, dairy factories; bottling works; foundry; planing mill. Ships agriculture products. Agriculture. Potatoes, wheat, seed peas, dairy, sheep, cattle.

7978 Cable Scene
Pioneer Publications
PO Box 3838 Phone: (208)523-7777
Idaho Falls, ID 83403
TV listings. **Founded:** 1970. **Freq:** Weekly. **Print Method:** Offset. **Trim Size:** 10 1/8 x 16 1/2. **Cols./Page:** 5. **Col. Width:** 12 picas. **Col. Depth:** 16 1/2 inches. **Key Personnel:** Terry Carr, Publisher; Earlene Poole, Advertising Mgr.; Erv Smith, Advertising Saleman. **Subscription Rates:** $17.75 individuals; $.50 single issue. **Remarks:** Accepts advertising.
Ad Rates: BW: $320 **Circ:** Paid 1400
PCI: $6

7979 Houseboat Magazine
Harris Publishing, Inc.
520 Park Ave. Phone: (208)524-7000
Idaho Falls, ID 83402 Fax: (208)522-5241
Publication E-mail: hbmag@srv.net
Publisher E-mail: richard@potatogrower.com

Magazine for houseboating in America. **Subtitle:** The Family Magazine for American Houseboaters. **Founded:** 1990. **Freq:** Monthly 10/year. **Cols./Page:** 3. **Col. Width:** 13.5 picas. **Col. Depth:** 59 picas. **Key Personnel:** Mike Harris, Publisher/Ad Sales, mike@houseboating.net; Steve Smede, Editor, steve@houseboating.net. **Subscription Rates:** $24.95 to qualified subscribers; $5 single issue. **Remarks:** Accepts advertising.
Ad Rates: BW: $1,889 **Circ:** Paid △**8,000**
4C: $2,763 Non-paid △**9,000**
PCI: $100

7980 The Post-Register
POB 1800
Idaho Falls, ID 83403

General newspaper. **Founded:** 1880. **Freq:** Daily A.M. **Print Method:** Offset. **Cols./Page:** 6. **Col. Width:** 25 nonpareils. **Col. Depth:** 301 agate lines. **Key Personnel:** Jerry M. Brady, Editor and Publisher, jbrady@idahonews.com; Roger Plothow, General Mgr., rplothow@idahonews.com; Scott Stawski, Advertising Dir., sstawski@idahonews.com. **Subscription Rates:** $10.25 individuals per month. **Remarks:** Accepts advertising. **URL:** http://www.idahonews.com.
Ad Rates: GLR: $10.50 **Circ:** Mon.-Fri. 26,773
BW: $2,559 Sun. 28,076
4C: $2,959
PCI: $19.84

7981 Potato Grower
Harris Publishing, Inc.
520 Park Ave. Phone: (208)524-7000
Idaho Falls, ID 83402 Fax: (208)522-5241
Publication E-mail: potatogr@srr.net
Publisher E-mail: richard@potatogrower.com

Magazine serving the potato growing, shipping, and processing industries. **Founded:** 1972. **Freq:** Monthly. **Print Method:** Offset. **Trim Size:** 8 3/8 x 10 7/8. **Cols./Page:** 3. **Col. Width:** 27 nonpareils. **Col. Depth:** 140 agate lines. **Key Personnel:** Gary Rawlings, Editor-in-Chief, gary@potatogrower.com; Jason Harris, Publisher, jason@potatogrowth.com; Richard Holley, Advertising Dir., richard@potatogrower.com. **Subscription Rates:** $19 individuals. **Remarks:** Accepts advertising.
Ad Rates: BW: $2,727 **Circ:** Combined 16,000
4C: $4,172

7982 SnoWest
Harris Publishing, Inc.
520 Park Ave. Phone: (208)524-7000
Idaho Falls, ID 83402 Fax: (208)522-5241
Publication E-mail: info@snowest.com
Publisher E-mail: richard@potatogrower.com

Magazine for snowmobilers. **Founded:** 1974. **Freq:** 8/year. **Print Method:** Offset. **Trim Size:** 8 x 10 3/4. **Cols./Page:** 3. **Col. Width:** 2 1/4 nonpareils. **Col. Depth:** 10 agate lines. **Key Personnel:** Steve Janes, Publisher, janes@snowest.com; Greg Manwaring, Sales Mgr., greggm@snowest.com; Lane Lindstrom, Editor, lindstm@snowest.com. **Subscription Rates:** $15.97 individuals. **Remarks:** Accepts advertising.
Ad Rates: BW: $11,005 **Circ:** Paid 11,200
4C: $15,503 Non-paid 132,285

7983 The Sugar Producer
Harris Publishing, Inc.
520 Park Ave. Phone: (208)524-7000
Idaho Falls, ID 83402 Fax: (208)522-5241
Publication E-mail: sugarmag@srv.net
Publisher E-mail: richard@potatogrower.com

Magazine for sugar beet growers. **Founded:** 1975. **Freq:** 7/year. **Print Method:** Offset. **Trim Size:** 8 3/8 x 10 7/8. **Cols./Page:** 3. **Col. Width:** 28 nonpareils. **Col. Depth:** 140 agate lines. **Key Personnel:** Richard Holley, Advertising Mgr., richard@sugarproducer.com; Gary Rawlings, Editor-in-Chief, gary@sugarproducer.com; Jason Harris, Publisher, jason@sugarproducer.com. **Subscription Rates:** $14 individuals. **Remarks:** Accepts advertising.
Ad Rates: BW: $3,087 **Circ:** Controlled ‡16,000
4C: $4,723

7984 KFTZ-FM - 103.3
PO Box 1805 Phone: (208)523-3722
Idaho Falls, ID 83403-1805 Fax: (208)525-2575

Format: Contemporary Hit Radio (CHR). **Networks:** Independent. **Owner:** Al Lee, at above address. **Founded:** 1987. **Operating Hours:** Continuous; 100% local. **ADI:** Idaho Falls-Pocatello, ID. **Key Personnel:** Kim Allen Lee, General Mgr.; Jay Stevens, Program Dir.; Dana Page, Sales Mgr. **Wattage:** 52,000. **Ad Rates:** $6-20 for 30 seconds; $7-25 for 60 seconds.

7985 KID-AM - 590
1655 S. Woodruff Ave., Ste. A Phone: (208)524-5900
Idaho Falls, ID 83404 Fax: (208)522-9696
Free: (800)967-3585

Format: Full Service; News; Talk; Sports. **Networks:** CBS; Precision Racing. **Owner:** Jacor Communications, at above address. **Founded:** 1929. **Operating Hours:** Continuous; 65% network, 35% local. **ADI:** Idaho Falls-Pocatello, ID. **Key Personnel:** Mike Hudson, General Mgr.; Madeline Larsen, Business and Traffic Dir.; Jeff Evans, PD OM. **Local Programs:** *Let's Get Cooking*; *Public Pulse*, Bob Ziel. **Wattage:** 5000. **Ad Rates:** $7-18 per unit.

7986 KID-FM - 96.1
1655 S. Woodruff Ave., Ste. A Phone: (208)524-5900
Idaho Falls, ID 83404 Fax: (208)522-9696

Format: Hot Country. **Networks:** Independent. **Founded:** 1965. **Formerly:** KID-FM (1986). **Operating Hours:** Continuous; 100% local. **ADI:** Idaho Falls-Pocatello, ID. **Key Personnel:** Miki Hudson, Gen. Mgr./Sales Mgr.; Jeff Evans, Operations Mgr.; Madeline Larsen, Traffic Mgr. **Wattage:** 40,000 ERP. **Ad Rates:** $1-20 per unit.

7987 KIDK-TV - 3
1255 E. 17th St. Phone: (208)522-5100
Idaho Falls, ID 83404 Fax: (208)522-5103
E-mail: kidktv3@srv.net

Format: Commercial TV. **Networks:** CBS. **Operating Hours:** 8 a.m.-5:30 p.m. **ADI:** Idaho Falls-Pocatello, ID. **Key Personnel:** Jim D. Kunz, General Mgr., fax (208)535-0946, jimk@kidk.com.

7988 KIFI-TV - 8
1915 N. Yellowstone Hwy. Phone: (208)525-8888
Idaho Falls, ID 83401 Fax: (208)522-1930
E-mail: idaho8@abc.com

Format: Commercial TV. **Networks:** ABC. **Founded:** 1961. **Operating Hours:** Continuous. **ADI:** Idaho Falls-Pocatello, ID. **Key Personnel:** Rickie Orchin Brady, General Mgr.; Kathy Walden, Program Dir.; Rick Landon, National Sales Mgr.; Monte Young, General Sales Mgr.

7989 KLCE-FM - 97.3
765 S. Woodruff, Box 51097 Phone: (208)522-5523
Idaho Falls, ID 83405 Fax: (208)785-0184
E-mail: klce-jb@srv.net

Format: Adult Contemporary. **Owner:** Western Communications, Inc., at above address. **Founded:** 1975. **Operating Hours:** Continuous. **ADI:** Idaho Falls-Pocatello, ID. **Key Personnel:** James Burgoyne, Contact; Keith A. Walker, Sales Mgr.; Wayne Richards, Operations Mgr. **Wattage:** 100,000. **Ad Rates:** $18-30 for 30 seconds; $24-36 for 60 seconds.

7990 KUPI-AM - 980
854 Lindsay Blvd. Phone: (208)522-1101
Idaho Falls, ID 83401 Fax: (208)522-6110

Format: Big Band/Nostalgia; Sports. **Networks:** ABC; Unistar. **Owner:** KUPI, Inc., at above address. **Founded:** 1957. **Operating Hours:** Continuous. **ADI:** Idaho Falls-Pocatello, ID. **Key Personnel:** Ray Groth, President; Michael Groth, Vice President; James Garshow, General Mgr. **Wattage:** 5000 day; 1000 night. **Ad Rates:** $29-41 for 30 seconds; $39-52 for 60 seconds. Combined advertising rates available with KUPI-FM: $29-$41 for 30 seconds; $39-$52 for 60 seconds.

7991 KUPI-FM - 99.1
854 Lindsay Blvd. Phone: (208)522-1101
Idaho Falls, ID 83401 Fax: (208)522-6110

Format: Country. **Networks:** ABC. **Owner:** KUPI Broadcasting Co., at above address. **Founded:** 1975. **Operating Hours:** Continuous. **ADI:** Idaho Falls-Pocatello, ID. **Key Personnel:** Ray Groth, President; Michael Groth, Vice President; James C. Garshow, General Mgr. **Wattage:** 100,000 ERP. **Ad Rates:** $29-41 for 30 seconds; $39-52 for 60 seconds. Combined advertising rates available with KUPI-AM: $29-$41 for 30 seconds; $39-$52 for 60 seconds.

7992 TCI Cable
PO Box 1827 Phone: (208)523-4567
Idaho Falls, ID 83401 Fax: (208)524-9983

Owner: Tele-Communications, Inc. (TCI), 4643 S. Ulster St., Ste. 600, Denver, CO 80237, (303)987-9552. **Formerly:** Upper Valley Tele-Cable. **Key Personnel:** Dean Jones, General Mgr.; Frank Park, Contact. **Cities Served:** 36 channels.

JEROME†, pop. 6,891.

S. ID. Jerome Co. 105 mi. E. of Boise. Manufactures cinder block, plows, plastic moldings, business forms. Machine shop. Grain, truck, fruit, poultry farms. Beans, beets, potatoes, alfalfa, clover seed.

7993 North Side News
Magic Valley Publishing Co., Inc.
PO Box 468 Phone: (208)324-3391
Jerome, ID 83338 Fax: (208)324-3391
Publisher E-mail: mutrio@northrim.net

Newspaper. **Founded:** 1908. **Freq:** Weekly (Wed.). **Print Method:** Offset. **Cols./Page:** 5. **Col. Width:** 11.7 picas. **Col. Depth:** 16 inches. **Key Personnel:** P. Nance, Publisher. **Subscription Rates:** $21 individuals. **Remarks:** Accepts advertising.
Ad Rates: BW: $440 **Circ:** ‡1,500
4C: $615
SAU: $5.75
PCI: $5.75

7994 KART-AM - 1400
47 North 100 West Phone: (208)324-8181
Jerome, ID 83338 Fax: (208)324-7124

Networks: CBS. **Owner:** KART Broadcasting Co., at above address. **Founded:** 1964. **Operating Hours:** 5:00 a.m.-midnight, Mon-Fri; 6:00 a.m.-midnight, Sat-Sun. 10% local. **Key Personnel:** Kent Lee, Program Dir. **Wattage:** 1000. **Ad Rates:** $6-9 for 30 seconds; $8-11 for 60 seconds. Combined advertising rates available with KKMU-FM, KMUX-FM.

7995 KKMV-FM - 92.5
144 Seminole Cir. Phone: (208)436-4757
Jerome, ID 83338 Fax: (208)436-3050

Format: Contemporary Country. **Owner:** Tri-Market Radio Broadcasters, Inc., at above address. **Formerly:** KNAQ-FM. **Operating Hours:** Continuous. **Key Personnel:** Kim Lee, General Mgr.; Penne Mainwhite, Sales Mgr. **Wattage:** 100,000. **Ad Rates:** $18 for 30 seconds; $21 for 60 seconds.

7996 KMVX-FM - 102.9
47 North 100 West Phone: (208)324-8182
Jerome, ID 83338 Fax: (208)324-7124

Format: Adult Contemporary. **Founded:** 1970. **Formerly:** KFMA-FM (1991); KMVX-FM. **Operating Hours:** Continuous. **Key Personnel:** Lamont Summers, Contact. **Wattage:** 100,000. **Ad Rates:** $14-17 for 30 seconds; $17-20 for 60 seconds. $5-$14 for 30 seconds; $6-$16 for 60 seconds. Combined advertising rates available with KART-AM.

KAMIAH, pop. 1,478.

W. ID. Lewis Co. 50 mi. E. of Lewiston. Nezperce Indian Reservation. Tourist resort. Logging, sawmill. Grain, stock farms.

7997 The Clearwater Progress
Liberty Publications
417 Main St. Phone: (208)935-0838
PO Box 428 Fax: (208)935-0973
Kamiah, ID 83536-0428
Publisher E-mail: progress@cybrquest.com

Community newspaper. **Founded:** Nov. 24, 1905. **Freq:** Weekly (Wed.). **Print Method:** Offset. Uses mats. **Cols./Page:** 6. **Col. Width:** 26 nonpareils. **Col. Depth:** 294 agate lines. **Key Personnel:** Shirley Glenn, Publisher. **USPS:** 117-260. **Subscription Rates:** $18 individuals; $22 Idaho; $26 out of state. **Remarks:** Accepts advertising.
Ad Rates: GLR: $4.50 **Circ:** ‡1,775
BW: $567

KENDRICK, pop. 395.

NW ID. Latah Co. 20 mi. NW of Genesee. Residential.

7998 The Kendrick Gazette
Kendrick Gazette, Inc.
PO Box 177 Phone: (208)289-5731
Kendrick, ID 83537
Community newspaper. **Founded:** 1888. **Freq:** Weekly (Thurs.). **Print Method:** Letterpress. **Cols./Page:** 6. **Col. Width:** 26 nonpareils. **Col. Depth:** 280 agate lines. **Key Personnel:** Wm. A. Roth, Editor and Publisher. **USPS:** 001-133. **Subscription Rates:** $10.50 individuals. **Remarks:** Color advertising not accepted.
Ad Rates: BW: $240 **Circ:** Paid ‡860
PCI: $2 Free ‡50

KETCHUM, pop. 2,200.

S. ID. Blaine Co. Adjoining Sun Valley, 80 mi. N. of Twin Falls. Summer and winter resort.

7999 Idaho Mountain Express
Express Publishing, Inc.
PO Box 1013 Phone: (208)726-8060
Ketchum, ID 83340 Fax: (208)726-2329
Publisher E-mail: express@micron.net

Community newspaper (tabloid). **Founded:** Nov. 1974. **Freq:** Weekly (Wed.). **Print Method:** Offset. **Cols./Page:** 5. **Col. Width:** 2 inches. **Col. Depth:** 16 inches. **Key Personnel:** Pam Morris, Publisher; Mary Gibson, Advertising Mgr. **USPS:** 720-490. **Subscription Rates:** $41 out of area. **Remarks:** Accepts advertising. **URL:** http://www.mtexpress.com.
Ad Rates: GLR: $.34 **Circ:** Paid ‡2,200
BW: $824 Free ‡11,300
SAU: $7.78
PCI: $10.30

8000 KEZQ-FM - 92.9
PO Box 2158
Ketchum, ID 83340

Format: Soft Rock. **Networks:** CNN Radio. **Owner:** Alpine Broadcasting, Ltd., at above address. **Former name:** KWWF-FM (1998). **Operating Hours:** Continuous. **Key Personnel:** Rick Ward, Operations Mgr., phone (208)535-0704; Scott Parker, General Mgr.; Bob Thompson, Program Dir.; Sandy McManus, Business Mgr. **Wattage:** 46,000. **Ad Rates:** $14-20 per unit.

8001 KWYS-AM - 920
PO Box 2158 Phone: (208)646-7361
Ketchum, ID 83340

Format: Oldies. **Networks:** Westwood One Radio. **Owner:** Alpine Broadcasting, Ltd., at above address. **Operating Hours:** Sunrise-sunset. **Key Personnel:** Scott Parker, General Mgr.; Rick Ward, Operations Mgr. **Wattage:** 1,000. **Ad Rates:** Advertising accepted; rates available upon request.

LEWISTON†, pop. 27,986.

NW ID. Nez Perce Co. At head of Snake River, 110 mi. S. of Spokane, WA. Boat connections. Flour, lumber, veneer, pulp, paper mills; fruit, vegetable canning and freezing. Manufactures beverages, tents, awnings. White pine timber. Stock, fruit, grain farms.

8002 Lewiston Morning Tribune
Tribune Publishing
505 C St. Phone: (208)743-9411
Lewiston, ID 83501-1843 Fax: (208)746-7341
Free: (800)745-9411

General newspaper. **Founded:** 1892. **Freq:** Mon.-Sun. (morn.). **Print Method:** Offset. **Cols./Page:** 6. **Col. Width:** 24 nonpareils. **Col. Depth:** 294 agate lines. **Key Personnel:** A.L. Alford, Jr., Editor and Publisher, fax (208)746-1185, alajr@lmtribune.com; Robert J. Minervini, Advertising Dir., fax (208)746-1341, robm@lmtribune.com; Wayne Hollingshead, General Mgr., fax (208)746-1341, wh@lmtribune.com. **Subscription Rates:** $138 individuals. **Remarks:** Accepts advertising. **URL:** http://www.lmtribune.com.
Ad Rates: BW: $2,838 **Circ:** Mon.-Sat. ‡26,330
4C: $3,288 Sun. ‡27,608
SAU: $22

8003 Moneysaver (Lewiston)
Triad News Publishing, Inc.
PO Box 682 Phone: (208)746-0483
Lewiston, ID 83501 Fax: (208)746-8507
Free: (800)473-4158
Publication E-mail: ads@moneysav.com; msave@moneysav.com

Free shopper. **Founded:** Jan. 1973. **Freq:** Weekly (Thurs.). **Print Method:** Offset. **Trim Size:** 11 1/4 x 16. **Cols./Page:** 7. **Col. Width:** 8 picas. **Col. Depth:** 15 1/2 inches. **Key Personnel:** Judith McFadden, Publisher; Philip Shinn, General Mgr. **Subscription Rates:** Free; $52 out of area. **Remarks:** Accepts advertising. **URL:** http://www.moneysaver.com; http://www.iea.com.
Ad Rates: BW: $802.90 **Circ:** Free ❑**35,584**
PCI: $7.40

8004 KATW-FM - 101.5
403 C St. Phone: (208)743-6564
Lewiston, ID 83501 Fax: (208)746-6397

Format: Adult Contemporary. **Networks:** CBS. **Owner:** Woodcom, Inc., at above address. **Founded:** 1985. **Operating Hours:** Continuous; 10% network, 90% local. **ADI:** Spokane, WA. **Key Personnel:** Mark Bolland, President/Gen. Mgr., markbol@catfm.com; Brian Stauffer, News Dir., briansta@catfm.com; Justin Ralston, Business Mgr., justinral@catf.com; Ben Bonfield, Sales Mgr., benbon@catfm.com. **Local Programs:** *Lewiston High School Bengal Football*; *The 70's at 7*. **Wattage:** 100,000. **Ad Rates:** $20-25 per unit.

8005 KLEW-TV - 3
2626 17th St., Box 615 Phone: (208)746-2636
Lewiston, ID 83501 Fax: (208)746-4819

Format: Commercial TV. **Networks:** CBS. **Founded:** 1955. **Operating Hours:** 20 hrs.; 45% network, 55% local. **ADI:** Spokane, WA. **Key Personnel:** Noel Hardin, News Dir.; Greg Meyer, Production Mgr.; Marlin Jackson, Chief Engineer; Fred Fickenwirth, Station & General Sales Mgr., klewfred@valley-internet.net; Margo Aragon, Public Service Dir.; Lori Krause, Traffic Coord.; Greg Meyer, Promotions Dir. **Wattage:** 56,200 video, 12,300 audio. **Ad Rates:** $10-150 per unit.

8006 KLHS-FM - 88.9
1114 9th Ave. Phone: (208)743-5557
Lewiston, ID 83501-2659 Fax: (208)746-7724

Format: Album-Oriented Rock (AOR). **Networks:** Independent. **Founded:** 1967. **Operating Hours:** 8 a.m.-2:30 a.m. **Key Personnel:** Cheryl Flory, General Mgr. **Wattage:** 150.

8007 KMOK-FM - 106.9
805 Stewart Ave. Phone: (208)746-5056
Lewiston, ID 83501 Fax: (208)743-4440

Format: Hot Country. **Networks:** AP. **Owner:** IDAVEND Co., at above address, (208)743-1551. **Founded:** 1983. **Operating Hours:** Continuous. **Key Personnel:** Robert Prasil, General Mgr., phone (208)743-1551, rprasil@valley-internet.net; Melva Prasil, Station Mgr.; John Thomas, News Dir.; Jim Nelly, Program Dir.; Ben Bonfield, Sales Mgr. **Wattage:** 100,000. **Ad Rates:** $12-18 for 30 seconds; $15-23 for 60 seconds. $16-$22 for 30 seconds; $19-$25 for 60 seconds. Combined advertising rates available with KRLC-AM.

8008 KOZE-AM - 950
Box 936 Phone: (208)743-2502
Lewiston, ID 83501

Format: Oldies. **Networks:** ABC. **Owner:** 4-K Radio, Inc., at above address. **Founded:** 1955. **Operating Hours:** Continuous. **Key Personnel:** Mike Ripley, President. **Wattage:** 5000 days; 1000 nights. **Ad Rates:** $7-11 for 30 seconds; $10-14 for 60 seconds. $7-$11 for 30 seconds; $10-$14 for 60 seconds. Combined advertising rates available with KOZE-FM.

8009 KOZE-FM - 96.5
Box 936 Phone: (208)743-2502
Lewiston, ID 83501 Fax: (208)743-1995

Format: Album-Oriented Rock (AOR). **Networks:** ABC. **Owner:** 4-K Radio, Inc., at above address. **Founded:** 1961. **Operating Hours:** Continuous. **Key Personnel:** Mike Ripley, President. **Wattage:** 25,000 ERP. **Ad Rates:** $7-11 for 30 seconds; $10-14 for 60 seconds. $7-$11 for 30 seconds; $10-$14 for 60 seconds. Combined advertising rates available with KOZE-AM.

8010 KRLC-AM - 1350
805 Stewart Ave. Phone: (208)743-1551
Lewiston, ID 83501 Fax: (208)743-4440
E-mail: rprasil@valley-internet.net

Format: Country. **Networks:** AP. **Owner:** IDAVEND Co., at above address. **Founded:** 1935. **Operating Hours:** Continuous. **Key Personnel:** Robert Prasil, General Mgr., rprasil@valley.internet.net; Melva Prasil, Station Mgr.; John Thomas, News Dir.; Gene Deforest, Program Dir.; Ben Bonfield, Local Sales Mgr. **Wattage:** 5000. **Ad Rates:** $8-14 for 30 seconds; $11-17 for 60 seconds. 16-$22 for 30 seconds; $19-$25 for 60 seconds. Combined advertising rates available with KMOK-FM: $12-$23 for 30 seconds; $14-.

MALAD CITY†, pop. 1,900.

EC ID. Oneida Co.

8011 Malad City Idaho Enterprise
Idaho Enterprise
PO Box 205 Phone: (208)766-4773
Malad City, ID 83252 Fax: (208)766-4774

Community newspaper. **Founded:** June 1879. **Freq:** Weekly. **Print Method:** Offset. **Cols./Page:** 6. **Col. Width:** 13 picas. **Col. Depth:** 21 1/2 inches. **Key Personnel:** Kristine D. Smith, Editor and Publisher. **USPS:** 255-800. **Subscription Rates:** $16 individuals; $21 out of county. **Remarks:** Accepts advertising.
Ad Rates: SAU: $7 **Circ:** ‡1,500
PCI: $7

MC CALL

8012 The Star-News
Central Idaho Publishing
Box 985
Mc Call, ID 83638
Publication E-mail: strnews@aol.com

Community newspaper. **Founded:** 1915. **Freq:** Weekly (Thurs.). **Print Method:** Offset. **Cols./Page:** 6. **Col. Width:** 24 nonpareils. **Col. Depth:** 294 agate lines. **Key Personnel:** Tom Grote, Editor; A.L. Alford, Jr., Publisher; Tomi Grote, Advertising Mgr. **ISSN:** 0747-248X. **Subscription Rates:** $24 individuals. **Remarks:** Accepts advertising.
Ad Rates: BW: $976.50 **Circ:** ‡4,000
PCI: $7.75

8013 KBSM-FM - 91.7
c/o KBSU-FM Phone: (208)426-3663
Boise State University Fax: (208)344-6631
1910 University Dr.
Boise, ID 83725

Format: Public Radio; Classical; News. **Simulcasts:** KBSU-FM. **Networks:** National Public Radio (NPR); Public Radio International (PRI). **Owner:** BSU Radio Network, at above address. **Operating Hours:** Continuous; 70% network, 30% local. **ADI:** Boise, ID. **Key Personnel:** James Paluzzi, General Mgr. **Wattage:** 2000 ERP. **Ad Rates:** Noncommercial. **URL:** http://www.idbsu.edu/bsuradio/.

8014 KMCL-FM - 101.1
100 N. 3rd Phone: (208)634-4777
PO Box 813 Fax: (208)634-3059
Mc Call, ID 83638-0813

Format: Adult Contemporary. **Networks:** Satellite Music Network. **Founded:** 1994. **Operating Hours:** Continuous. **Key Personnel:** David Eaton, President. **Wattage:** 3900. **Ad Rates:** $8.50 for 30 seconds; $16 for 60 seconds.

MERIDIAN, pop. 6,658.

SW ID. Ada Co. 10 mi. W. of Boise. Feed mills; pre-built home factory; meat packing plant. Manufactures lumber, custom doors, furniture. Fruit, dairy, stock, grain, poultry farms.

8015 The Valley News
PO Box 299 Phone: (208)888-1941
Meridian, ID 83680-0299 Fax: (208)888-1097

Community newspaper. **Subtitle:** Serving Western Ada County from Meridian. **Founded:** 1903. **Freq:** Weekly (Wed.). **Print Method:** Offset. **Trim Size:** 17 x 11. **Cols./Page:** 5. **Col. Width:** 11 picas. **Col. Depth:** 294 agate lines. **Key Personnel:** Tere Foley, Publisher; Loren Roberts, Editor; Lezli Luneckas, Advertising Dir.; Peter Mundt, Advertising Rep. Reporter. **Subscription Rates:** $22; $13 seniors. **Remarks:** Accepts advertising. **Formerly:** Valley News-Times.
Ad Rates: BW: $345 **Circ:** ‡1,700
4C: $733
PCI: $15.50

8016 KFXD-AM - 580
455 W. Amity Phone: (208)888-4321
Meridian, ID 83642 Fax: (208)888-2841
E-mail: kfxd@micron.net

Format: News; Sports; Talk. **Networks:** CNN Radio; Mutual Broadcasting System; Westwood One Radio. **Owner:** Double DEE Broadcast Group Inc., 455 W. Amity, Meridian, ID 83642. **Founded:** 1920. **Operating Hours:** Continuous. **Key Personnel:** Rick Weight, General Mgr.; Rochelle Bell, Production Dir. **Wattage:** 5000. **Ad Rates:** Combined advertising rates available with KFXD-FM.

8017 KFXJ-FM - 94.9
455 W. Amity Phone: (208)888-4321
Meridian, ID 83642 Fax: (208)888-2841
E-mail: kfxj@micron.net

Format: Adult Album Alternative. **Owner:** DoubleDee Broadcast Group, Inc., at above address. **Founded:** 1974. **Formerly:** KFXD-FM. **Operating Hours:** Continuous. **Key Personnel:** Rick Weight, General Mgr.; Toni McKnee, Traffic; Kevin Welch, P.D. **Wattage:** 46,000 ERP. **Ad Rates:** $18-35 per unit.

8018 KFXJ-FM -
455 W. Amity Phone: (208)888-4321
Meridian, ID 83642 Fax: (208)888-2841
E-mail: kfxj@micron.met

Format: Adult Album Alternative. **Owner:** DoubleDee Broadcast Group, at above address. **Founded:** 1972. **Formerly:** KFXD-FM. **Key Personnel:** Rick Weight, General Mgr.; Scott Ruelos, General Sales Mgr.; Kevin Welch, Program Dir.; Rockwell Smith, Chief Engineer.

MONTPELIER, pop. 3,100.

C. ID. Bear Lake Co. 70 mi. Se of Pocatello. Manufactures gloves. Stone quarries.

8019 The Bear Laker
Citizen Publishing Co.
847 Washington Phone: (208)847-0552
PO Box 278 Fax: (208)847-0553
Montpelier, ID 83254
Tourism publication. **Freq:** 6 times during summer. **Print Method:** Offset. **Cols./Page:** 4. **Col. Width:** 14 picas. **Col. Depth:** 14 inches. **Key Personnel:** Rosa Moosman, Editor. **Subscription Rates:** Free. **Remarks:** Accepts advertising.
Ad Rates: BW: $230 **Circ:** ‡5,000
4C: $590
PCI: $5.43

8020 The News-Examiner
Citizen Publishing Co.
847 Washington Phone: (208)847-0552
PO Box 278 Fax: (208)847-0553
Montpelier, ID 83254
Publication E-mail: editor@news.examine.net

Community newspaper. **Founded:** 1895. **Freq:** Weekly. **Print Method:** Offset. **Trim Size:** 15 x 23. **Cols./Page:** 6. **Col. Width:** 2 inches. **Col. Depth:** 21 1/2 inches. **Key Personnel:** Rosa Moosman, Managing Editor. **Subscription Rates:** $15 individuals; $21.50 out of state.
Ad Rates: SAU: $4.93 **Circ:** Paid 1,975
Free 50

8021 KVSI-AM - 1450
24681 US 89, Box 340 Phone: (208)847-1450
Montpelier, ID 83254 Fax: (208)847-1451

Format: Country. **Networks:** ABC. **Owner:** Tri-State Broadcasting Co., Inc., at above address. **Founded:** 1965. **Operating Hours:** 6 a.m.-7 p.m. **Key Personnel:** Keith Martindale, Contact. **Wattage:** 1000. **Ad Rates:** $4-5.75 for 30 seconds; $5-6.75 for 60 seconds.

MOSCOW†, pop. 16,513.

NW ID. Latah Co. 85 mi. SE of Spokane, WA. University of Idaho. Manufactures bricks, clay products, flour, pea harvesters, lumber, creamery products. Split pea and seed pea plants. Timber; clay deposits. Dairy and grain farms. Wheat, peas, lentils, dairy products.

8022 Appaloosa Journal
Appaloosa Horse Club
5070 Hwy. 8 West Phone: (208)882-5578
Moscow, ID 83843 Fax: (208)882-8150
Publication E-mail: journal@appaloosa.com
Publisher E-mail: aphc@appaloosa.com

Magazine about Appaloosa horses and the people making an impact on the industry. **Subtitle:** Official Publication of the Appaloosa Horse Club. **Founded:** 1946. **Freq:** Monthly. **Print Method:** Web offset. **Trim Size:** 8 1/8 x 10 7/8. **Cols./Page:** 3. **Col. Width:** 13 picas. **Col. Depth:** 58 picas. **Key Personnel:** Robin Hirzel, Editor. **ISSN:** 0892-385X. **Subscription Rates:** $25 individuals; $35 other countries; $3 single issue plus shipping. **Remarks:** Accepts advertising. **Available Online.** **URL:** http://www.appaloosa.com. **Formerly:** Appaloosa News.
Ad Rates: BW: $580 **Circ:** 25,000
4C: $1,025

8023 Daily News
409 S. Jackson Phone: (208)882-5561
PO Box 8187 Fax: (208)883-8205
Moscow, ID 83843-2231
Free: (800)776-4137

Community newspaper. **Founded:** 1911. **Freq:** Daily (eve.). **Print Method:** Offset. **Cols./Page:** 6. **Col. Width:** 25 nonpareils. **Col. Depth:** 301 agate lines. **Key Personnel:** Mark N. Trahant, Editor and Publisher, editor@moscow.com; Randy Pressnall, Advertising Mgr. **Subscription Rates:** $65 individuals. **URL:** http://www.dnews.com.
Circ: ‡9,800

8024 Electronic Green Journal (EGJ)
University of Idaho Library
Moscow, ID 83844-2360 Phone: (208)885-6631
Fax: (208)885-6817

Electronic journal containing scholarly articles, bibliographies, reviews, announcements, and editorial comment on international environmental sources and topics. **Founded:** 1994. **Freq:** Irregular. **Key Personnel:** Maria A. Jankowska, Editor, majanko@uidaho.edu; Mike Pollastro, Managing Editor. **ISSN:** 1076-7975. **Subscription Rates:** Free. **Remarks:** Accepts advertising. **Available Online.** **URL:** http://

www.lib.uidaho.edu/70/docs/egj.html. **Formerly**: Green Library Journal.
Ad Rates: GLR: $75 **Circ:** Non-paid 2,000

8025 Focus on Renewable Natural Resources
University of Idaho
Moscow, ID 83844-1130 Phone: (208)885-6673 Fax: (208)885-6226

Report on natural resources, land management, conservation, environmental issues and related issues in the state of Idaho. Lists faculty researcher specialties, publications, and research projects. **Founded:** 1974. **Freq:** Annual. **Print Method:** 8 1/4 x 11. **Key Personnel:** Denise Ortiz, Editor, ortiz@uidaho.edu. **ISSN:** 0273-009X. **Subscription Rates:** Free to qualified subscribers. **Remarks:** Advertising not accepted. **URL:** http://www.uidaho.edu/cfwr. **Formerly**: Station Bulletin.
Circ: Controlled 2,000

8026 Focus on Security
115 N. Grant St. Phone: (208)883-0817
Moscow, ID 83843 Fax: (208)883-5353
Publication E-mail: focus@turbonet.com

Publication featuring practical articles and news in the areas of library, archive, and museum security. **Subtitle:** The Magazine of Library, Archive and Museum Security. **Founded:** Oct. 1993. **Freq:** Quarterly. **Trim Size:** 5 x 8. **Key Personnel:** Eileen Brady, Editor; Jon M. Gustafson, Publisher & Ad Mgr., jmgustafson@turbonet.com; J. Stephen Huntsberry, Exec.Dir. **ISSN:** 1071-9997. **Subscription Rates:** $70 individuals; $125 two years; $20 single issue. **Remarks:** Accepts advertising.
Ad Rates: BW: $75 **Circ:** Paid 100

8027 Idaho Argonaut
The Argonaut
Student Media Phone: (208)885-7825
301 Student Union Fax: (208)885-2222
Moscow, ID 83844-4271
Collegiate newspaper. **Founded:** 1898. **Freq:** Semiweekly (Tues. and Fri.). **Print Method:** Offset. **Trim Size:** 11 x 17. **Cols./Page:** 5. **Col. Width:** 26 nonpareils. **Col. Depth:** 220 agate lines. **Key Personnel:** Michelle Kalbeitzer, Editor; Ryan Donahue, Advertising Mgr. **ISSN:** 0896-1409. **Subscription Rates:** $25 semester; $35 academic year. **Remarks:** Accepts advertising.
Ad Rates: BW: $536 **Circ:** Paid 250
4C: $776 Free 8,250
PCI: $6.70

8028 Idaho Law Review
University of Idaho
Moscow, ID 83843

Journal of law review. **Founded:** Nov. 1998. **Freq:** 3/year. **Key Personnel:** Kevin E. Dinius, Editor-in-Chief; Jeremy P. Pisca, Business Editor. **ISSN:** 0019-1205. **Subscription Rates:** $33 individuals; $12 single issue. **Remarks:** Accepts advertising.
Ad Rates: GLR: $350 **Circ:** (Not Reported)

8029 Latah Legacy
Latah County Historical Society
327 E. Second Phone: (208)882-1004
Moscow, ID 83843 Fax: (208)882-0759
Publisher E-mail: lcha@moscow.com

Scholarly journal covering local history. **Founded:** Oct. 1972. **Freq:** Semiannual. **Key Personnel:** Mary Reed, Editor. **Subscription Rates:** $4 single issue. **Remarks:** Advertising not accepted.
Circ: (Not Reported)

8030 Mushroom, The Journal
861 Harold St. Phone: (208)882-8720
PO Box 3156
Moscow, ID 83843
Publisher E-mail: mushroom@moscow.com

Magazine featuring articles about wild mushroom hunting and the cultivation of exotic mushrooms. **Subtitle:** The Journal of Wild Mushrooming. **Founded:** 1983. **Freq:** Quarterly. **Print Method:** Offset. **Trim Size:** 8 1/2 x 11. **Cols./Page:** 3. **Col. Width:** 13.5 picas. **Col. Depth:** 9 1/2 inches. **Key Personnel:** Maggie Rogers, Editor; Don H. Coombs, Publisher, phone (208)882-8720. **ISSN:** 0740-8161. **Subscription Rates:** $16; $28 two years. **Remarks:** Accepts advertising.
Ad Rates: BW: $125 **Circ:** ‡2,000

8031 Northwest Anthropological Research Notes
625 N. Garfield Phone: (208)882-0413
Moscow, ID 83843-3624 Fax: (208)882-3393

Journal covering Pacific Northwest anthropology. **Founded:** 1967. **Freq:** Semiannual. **Print Method:** Web offset. **Trim Size:** 8 x 10 1/2. **Cols./Page:** 1. **Key Personnel:** Roderick Sprague, Editor, rsprague@uidaho.edu. **ISSN:** 0029-3296. **Subscription Rates:** $35 individuals; $55 institutions. **Remarks:** Advertising not accepted.
Circ: Paid 350

8032 Women in Natural Resources
University of Idaho
Bowers Laboratory Phone: (208)885-6754
Moscow, ID 83844-1114 Fax: (208)885-5878

Periodical for women in forestry, wildlife, range, fisheries, recreation, and related social sciences. **Founded:** 1979. **Freq:** Quarterly. **Trim Size:** 8 1/2 x 11. **Key Personnel:** Dr. Dixie L. Ehrenreich, Editor, dixie@uidaho.edu. **Subscription Rates:** $17 students; $23 individuals; $39 institutions. **URL:** http://www.ets.uidaho.edu/winr/.
Ad Rates: BW: $900 **Circ:** (Not Reported)

8033 KRPL-AM - 1400
1114 N. Almon Phone: (208)882-2551
Box 8849 Fax: (208)883-3571
Moscow, ID 83843

Format: Oldies; Adult Contemporary. **Networks:** ABC. **Owner:** KRPL, Inc., at above address. **Founded:** 1947. **Operating Hours:** Continuous. **Key Personnel:** Dennis Deccio, Contact. **Wattage:** 1000.

8034 KUOI-FM - 89.3
University of Idaho Phone: (208)885-6433
Student Union Bldg. Fax: (208)885-2222
Moscow, ID 83843
E-mail: kuoi@uidaho.edu

Format: Alternative/New Music/Progressive. **Networks:** Pacifica. **Founded:** 1945. **Operating Hours:** Continuous; 4% network, 96% local. **ADI:** Spokane, WA. **Key Personnel:** Dan Robertson, Station Mgr., phone (208)885-2218, danr@sub.uidaho.edu; Jeff Kimberling, Chief Engineer, phone (208)885-6947, jeff@sub.uidaho.edu; Leigh Robartes, News Dir., phone (208)885-2218, leigh@sub.uidaho.edu; Christina Carney, Music Dir., phone (208)8856433, cristina@sub.uidaho.edu. **Wattage:** 400. **Ad Rates:** Noncommercial. $5 per unit. **URL:** http://kuoi.com.

8035 KZFN-FM - 106.1
1114 N. Almon Phone: (208)882-2551
Box 8849 Fax: (208)883-3571
Moscow, ID 83843
E-mail: garyc@moscow.com

Format: Contemporary Hit Radio (CHR). **Networks:** ABC. **Owner:** KRPL, Inc., at above address. **Founded:** 1972. **Operating Hours:** Continuous. **ADI:** Spokane, WA. **Key Personnel:** Dennis Deccio, Contact. **Local Programs:** *Agri-Business PGM*, Dennis Deccio. **Wattage:** 62,100 ERP.

8036 Pullman TV Cable Co., Inc.
PO Box 8336 Phone: (208)882-2832
Moscow, ID 83843 Fax: (208)882-9106
Free: (800)643-6569

Owner: Rock Assoc., 5808 Lake Washington Blvd., Ste. 400, Kirkland, WA 98033. **Founded:** 1960. **Key Personnel:** Jim Uebelher, General Mgr.; Clare Perkins, Office Mgr.; Virginia Chidester, Contact; Tom Saylor, Contact; Ken Johnson, Contact. **Cities Served:** Genesse, Julietta, Kendrick, Onaway, Potlatch, ID; Albion, Colton, Moscow, Palouse, Pullman, Uniontown, WA: subscribing households 14,000; 39 channels; 1 community access channel.

MOUNTAIN HOME†, pop. 7,540.

SW ID. Elmore Co. 40 mi. SE of Boise. Sawmills; chick hatchery. Silver, gold, copper mines. Pine timber. Stock, sugar beets, potatoes, hay. Lava rock.

8037 Mountain Home News
U.S. Media Group
195 S. 3rd St. Phone: (208)587-3331
PO Box 1330 Fax: (208)587-9205
Mountain Home, ID 83647
Community newspaper. **Founded:** 1886. **Freq:** Weekly (Wed.). **Print Method:** Offset. Uses mats. **Cols./Page:** 6. **Col. Width:** 28 nonpareils. **Col. Depth:** 294 agate lines. **Key Personnel:** Kelly Everitt, Editor; Coleen Swenson, Publisher; Debra Shoemaker, Advertising Dir. **Subscription Rates:** $21 individuals. **Remarks:** Accepts advertising.
Ad Rates: BW: $767.55 **Circ:** ‡4,000
4C: $1,017.55
PCI: $5.95

8038 Pipeline
PO Box 1330 Phone: (208)587-3331
Mountain Home, ID 83647 Fax: (208)587-9205

Community newspaper. **Founded:** 1992. **Freq:** Weekly. **Cols./Page:** 4. **Col. Width:** 28 nonpareils. **Col. Depth:** 15 inches. **Key Personnel:** Kelly Everitt, Editor; Coleen W. Swenson, Publisher; Debra Shoemaker, Advertising Dir. **Subscription Rates:** $20 individuals. **Remarks:** Accepts advertising.
Ad Rates: BW: $356 **Circ:** Free 4,200
4C: $506
PCI: $4.45

8039 KLVJ-FM - 99.1
PO Box 704 Phone: (208)587-8424
Mountain Home, ID 83647 Fax: (208)587-8425

Format: Country. **Owner:** Jack Jensen, at above address. **Founded:** 1992. **Formerly**: KFLI-FM (1990); KJCY-FM. **Operating Hours:** Continuous. **Key Personnel:** Jack Jensen, Manager; Brian Mobley, Production Mgr.; Penni Jensen, Office Mgr. **Local Programs:** *Alvin Lee Power Sports Show*; *Brian Mobley Morning Drive Show.* **Wattage:** 100,000. **Ad Rates:** $8 for 30 seconds; $15 for 60 seconds.

MULLAN

NE ID. Shoshone Co. 10 mi. E. of Wallace.

8040 Mullan Television Co.
Box 615 Phone: (208)744-1223
Mullan, ID 83846

Founded: 1954. **Key Personnel:** John Erickson, President; Carl Scheel, Vice President. **Cities Served:** Mullan, ID: subscribing households 377; 17 channels.

NAMPA, pop. 25,112.

SW ID. Canyon Co. 16 mi. W. of Boise. Northwest Nazarene College. College of Idaho. Manufactures wood mouldings, corrugated cardboard containers, cheese, mobile homes, furniture, computer chips. Wineries. Agriculture. Seeds, fruit, livestock.

8041 Crusader
Northwest Nazarene College
623 Holly St. Phone: (208)467-8656
Nampa, ID 83686 Fax: (208)467-8469
Publication E-mail: crusader@student.nnc.edu

Collegiate newspaper. **Founded:** 1938. **Freq:** Weekly. **Print Method:** Offset. **Cols./Page:** 6. **Col. Width:** 18 nonpareils. **Col. Depth:** 182 agate lines. **Key Personnel:** John Fraley, Editor; Brenda Clough, Advertising Mgr., phone (208)467-8656. **Subscription Rates:** $20 individuals. **Remarks:** Accepts advertising. **URL:** http://science.nnc.edu/˜dazirsch/crusader/.
Ad Rates: BW: $90 **Circ:** Paid 100
4C: $180 Non-paid 1,400
PCI: $5

8042 Idaho Press Tribune
1618 N. Midland Blvd. Phone: (208)467-9251
PO Box 9399 Fax: (208)467-9562
Nampa, ID 83652-9399
Publication E-mail: newsroom@idahopress.com

General newspaper. **Founded:** 1919. **Freq:** Daily (eve.), Sat. and Sun. (morn.). **Print Method:** Offset. **Cols./Page:** 6. **Col. Width:** 24 nonpareils. **Col. Depth:** 301 agate lines. **Key Personnel:** James T. Barnes, Publisher; Vickie Holbrook, Managing Editor; Carolyn Sinnard, Advertising Dir. **Remarks:** Accepts advertising.
Ad Rates: SAU: $8.40 **Circ:** Mon.-Sat. 20,488
Sun. 20,653

8043 Signs of the Times
Pacific Press Publishing Association
PO Box 5353 Phone: (208)465-2500
Nampa, ID 83653-5353 Fax: (208)465-2531
Free: (800)447-7377

Religious magazine. **Founded:** June 4, 1874. **Freq:** Monthly. **Print Method:** Offset. **Trim Size:** 8 1/8 x 10 5/8. **Cols./Page:** 3. **Col. Width:** 26 nonpareils. **Col. Depth:** 139 agate lines. **Key Personnel:** Marvin Moore, Editor, mmoore@pacificpress.com. **USPS:** 496-480. **Subscription Rates:** $18.95 individuals; $21.95 other countries. **Remarks:** Advertising not accepted. **URL:** http://www.pacificpress.com/signs.
Circ: ‡230,000

8044 KIVI-TV - 6
1866 E. Chisholm Dr. Phone: (208)381-6600
Nampa, ID 83687 Fax: (208)381-6680

Format: Commercial TV. **Networks:** ABC. **Founded:** 1974. **Operating Hours:** Continuous Sun.-Thurs., midnight-12:30 a.m. Fri., 6 a.m.-2 a.m. Sat. **ADI:** Boise, ID. **Key Personnel:** Kelly Sugai, General Mgr.; Ken Ritchie, General Sales Mgr.; Lynn Hightower, News Dir.; James Roddey, Promotions Dir.

8045 KTRV-TV - 12
PO Box 1212 Phone: (208)888-1200
Nampa, ID 83653 Fax: (208)467-6958

Format: Commercial TV. **Networks:** Fox. **Owner:** Blade Communications, 541 Superior St., Toledo, OH 43660. **Founded:** 1981. **Operating Hours:** Continuous 7% network, 93% local. **ADI:** Boise, ID. **Key Personnel:** Diane Frisch, General Mgr., dfrisch@ktru.com; Ron Grisham, Contact; Rick Joseph, Contact. **Wattage:** 50,000. **Ad Rates:** $25-450 per unit. **URL:** http://www.ktrv.com.

NEZPERCE†, pop. 517.

W. ID. Lewis Co. 40 mi. SE of Lewiston. Grain elevators; seed processing plant. Stock, grain farms.

8046 Lewis County Herald
PO Box 159 Phone: (208)937-2671
Nezperce, ID 83543 Fax: (208)962-7131

Community newspaper. **Founded:** 1896. **Freq:** Weekly (Thurs.). **Print Method:** Offset. **Cols./Page:** 5. **Col. Width:** 26 nonpareils. **Col. Depth:** 182 agate lines. **Key Personnel:** Francie Hill, Editor; Robert Wherry, Publisher; Patricia Wherry, Publisher. **Subscription Rates:** $20 individuals; $23. **Remarks:** Accepts advertising.
Ad Rates: GLR: $.32 **Circ:** ‡1,050
SAU: $3.75

OLD TOWN

8047 KMJY-AM - 700
PO Box 1740 Phone: (208)437-5700
Old Town, ID 83822
E-mail: kmjy@povn.com

Format: Contemporary Country. **Networks:** CNN Radio. **Owner:** James & Helen Stargel, at above address. **Founded:** 1986. **Operating Hours:** 6 a.m.-10 p.m. **Key Personnel:** James Stargel, Owner/Mgr.; C. B. Franks, News Dir.; Patrick Scott, Music Dir. **Local Programs:** *Job Line Swap and Shop*, James Stargel. **Wattage:** 10,000. **Ad Rates:** $3-5 for 15 seconds; $5-7 for 30 seconds; $7-10 for 60 seconds.

8048 KMJY-FM - 104.9
PO Box 1740 Phone: (208)437-5700
Old Town, ID 83822
E-mail: kmjy@kmjy.com

Format: Contemporary Country. **Simulcasts:** KMJY-AM. **Networks:** CNN Radio. **Owner:** James & Helen Stargel, at above address. **Founded:** 1989. **Operating Hours:** 6 a.m.-10 p.m. **ADI:** Spokane, WA. **Key Personnel:** James Stargel, Manager; Patrick Scott, Music Dir.; C.B. Franks, News Dir. **Local Programs:** *Job Line Swap and Shop*, James Stargel. **Wattage:** 12,000. **Ad Rates:** $3-5 for 15 seconds; $5-7 for 30 seconds; $7-10 for 60 seconds.

OROFINO†, pop. 3,711.

NW ID. Clearwater Co. 44 mi. E. of Lewiston. Dworshak Dam. Hunting, skiing. Steelhead fishing. Boating saw and planing mills; machine shop; logging. White pine timber. Diversified farming. Hay, grain, dairy products, beef.

8049 Clearwater Tribune
161 Main St. Phone: (208)476-4571
PO Box 71 Fax: (208)476-0765
Orofino, ID 83544
Community newspaper. **Founded:** 1910. **Freq:** Weekly (Thurs.). **Print Method:** Offset. **Cols./Page:** 6. **Col. Width:** 25 nonpareils. **Col. Depth:** 294 agate lines. **Key Personnel:** Cloann Wilkins McNall, Editor and Publisher. **Subscription Rates:** $23 individuals; $31 out of area; $.50 single issue. **Remarks:** Accepts advertising.
Ad Rates: GLR: $.35 **Circ:** ‡3,600
BW: $434.70
4C: $594.70
SAU: $3.50
PCI: $3.60

8050 KLER-AM - 1300
Box 32 Phone: (208)476-5702
Orofino, ID 83544 Fax: (208)476-5703
E-mail: klerorofino@clearwater.net

Format: Country. **Networks:** ABC. **Owner:** Central Idaho Broadcasting, at above address. **Founded:** 1958. **Operating Hours:** 5 a.m.-midnight Mon.-Sat.; 6 a.m.-10 p.m. Sun. **Key Personnel:** Jeff Jones, General Sales Mgr.; Monica Jones, Music Dir.; Warren Stone, News Dir.; David Forsman, Chief Engineer. **Wattage:** 5000 day; 1000 night. **Ad Rates:** $4.50-5.50 for 30 seconds; $7.50-8.50 for 60 seconds. $4.50-$5.50 for 30 seconds; $7.50-$8.50 for 60 seconds. Combined advertising rates available with KLER-FM.

8051 KLER-FM - 95.3
Box 32 Phone: (208)476-5702
Orofino, ID 83544 Fax: (208)476-5703
E-mail: klerorofino@clearwater.net

Format: Adult Contemporary. **Networks:** Independent. **Owner:** Central Idaho Broadcasting, at above address. **Founded:** 1979. **Operating Hours:** 5 a.m.-midnight Mon.-Sat.; 6 a.m.-10 p.m. Sun. **Key Personnel:** Jeff Jones, Station Mgr.; Mike Benson, PSA Dir.; Monica Jones, Music Dir. **Wattage:** 2300. **Ad Rates:** $4.50-5.50 for 30 seconds; $7.50-8.50 for 60 seconds. $4.50-$5.50 for 30 seconds; $7.50-$8.50 for 60 seconds. Combined advertising rates available with KLER-AM.

OSBURN

NE ID. Shoshone Co. 5 mi. N. of Wallace.

8052 KWAL-AM - 620
PO Box U Phone: (208)752-1141
Osburn, ID 83849 Fax: (208)753-5111

Format: Country; Middle-of-the-Road (MOR). **Networks:** ABC. **Owner:** Silver Valley Broadcasters Inc., at above address. **Founded:** 1938. **Operating Hours:** 5:30 am-10 pm MXS; 7 am-10 pm Sun. **Key Personnel:** Paul E. Robinson, Owner; George White, Manager; Darren Warren, News Dir.; Larry Crigger, Production Dir.; John Davis, Music Dir. **Local Programs:** *This That and The Other*, John Davis. **Wattage:** 1000. **Ad Rates:** $3.20-4.75 for 15 seconds; $4.25-7.75 for 30 seconds; $5.75-10.50 for 60 seconds.

PARMA, pop. 1,820.

SW ID. Canyon Co. 44 mi. NW of Boise. Beef cattle. U.S. Agriculture Experimental Station. Seed production.

8053 Journal of Potato Production and Postharvest Handling
The Haworth Press, Inc.
Southern Idaho Agricultural Researchers Phone: (208)722-5585
Fax: (208)722-5586
27080 Pearl Rd
Parma, ID 83660
Publisher E-mail: getinfo@haworthpressinc.com

Journal on potato production and postharvesting handling. **Founded:** 1994. **Freq:** Quarterly. **Trim Size:** 6x8 1/2. **Key Personnel:** R. Gary Beaver, PHD, Editor; Bill Cohen, Publisher. **Subscription Rates:** $36; $60 industry; $75 libraries; 30% more for Canada;40% more for other countries. **Remarks:** Accepts advertising.
Ad Rates: BW: $300 **Circ:** (Not Reported)

8054 Three Rivers Chronicle
PO Box 540 Fax: (208)642-4140
Parma, ID 83660
Community newspaper. **Founded:** 1909. **Freq:** Weekly (Wed.). **Print Method:** Offset. **Cols./Page:** 5. **Col. Width:** 11 picas. **Col. Depth:** 15 inches. **Key Personnel:** Eric Ellis, Editor; David G. Landmann, Publisher; Shelby Hilliard, Advertising Mgr. **USPS:** 422-381. **Subscription Rates:** $18 individuals; $14 students and senior citizens; $20 other countries. **Remarks:** Accepts advertising.
Ad Rates: GLR: $.19 **Circ:** Paid ‡1,400
BW: $514.50 Free ‡35
4C: $614.50
PCI: $5.25

PAYETTE†, pop. 5,448.

W. ID. Payette Co. 67 mi. NW of Boise. Manufactures dairy, wood products, canned and dried fruits and vegetables, electrical fences, vinegar, cider, boxes. Fresh fruit and produce packing. Diversified farming.

8055 Independent-Enterprise
Wick Communications Co.
PO Box 520 Phone: (208)642-3357
Payette, ID 83661
Newspaper with an Idaho orientation. **Founded:** May 1891. **Freq:** Weekly (Wed.). **Print Method:** Offset. **Trim Size:** 13 x 21 1/2. **Cols./Page:** 6. **Col. Width:** 12 picas. **Col. Depth:** 21 1/2 inches. **Key Personnel:** Mrs. Marilyn Rhinehart, Office Mgr.; Eugene A. Rhinehart, Publisher; Linda Warren, Advertising Mgr. **Subscription Rates:** $22 individuals local; $29 out of area. **Remarks:** Accepts advertising.
Ad Rates: GLR: $0.45 **Circ:** Paid 1,852
BW: $812.70 Free 63
4C: $1,082.70
SAU: $6.30
PCI: $6.30

8056 KIOV-AM - 1450
401 S. 9th St. Phone: (208)881-1450
Boise, ID 83702-7004

Format: Top 40; Country. **Founded:** 1957. **ADI:** Boise, ID. **Key Personnel:** Stephen P. Kohl, President; Russell Strawn, Program Dir. **Wattage:** 1000 day; 250 night.

POCATELLO†, pop. 46,340.

SE ID. Bannock Co. 50 mi. SW of Idaho Falls. Idaho State University. Flour and feed mills; heavy mining equipment, phosphate fertilizer and chemical factories; cement plants. Electronics manufacturing. Diversified farming.

8057 ISU Bengal
Idaho State University
Campus Box 8009 Phone: (208)236-2246
Pocatello, ID 83209 Fax: (208)236-4600
Publication E-mail: bengal@isu.edu

Collegiate newspaper. **Founded:** 1977. **Freq:** Weekly (Thurs.). **Print Method:** Offset. **Trim Size:** 11 x 17. **Cols./Page:** 5. **Col. Width:** 22 nonpareils. **Col. Depth:** 224 agate lines. **Key Personnel:** Becky Thornton, Editor-in-Chief, phone (208)236-2247, thormany@isu.edu; Nichole Shell, Editor. **Subscription Rates:** Free. **Formerly:** Advocate.
Ad Rates: GLR: $4 **Circ:** Free ‡5,000
BW: $400
4C: $800
PCI: $4

8058 Rendezvous
Idaho State University Press
Box 8113
Pocatello, ID 83209-0009
Publication E-mail: cantdant@isu.edu

Scholarly literary journal. **Subtitle:** Journal of Arts and Letters. **Founded:** 1965. **Freq:** Semiannual. **Key Personnel:** Dante Cantrill, Editor, phone (208)236-4384. **ISSN:** 0034-4400. **Subscription Rates:** $7 individuals. **Remarks:** Advertising not accepted.
Circ: Paid 100

8059 KISU-TV - 10
Box 8111 Phone: (208)236-2857
Pocatello, ID 83209-0009 Fax: (208)236-2848

Format: Public TV. **Networks:** Public Broadcasting Service (PBS). **Owner:** Idaho State Board of Education, Len B. Jordan Bldg., State Capitol, Boise, ID 83707. **Founded:** 1971. **Formerly:** KBGL-TV (1981). **Operating Hours:** 6 a.m.-1 a.m. **ADI:** Idaho Falls-Pocatello, ID. **Key Personnel:** MarDee Porath, Public Info., mardee_ porath@idptv.pbs.org; Dave Turnmire, Chief Technical Officer, phone (208)236-3696, dave_ turnmire@idptv.pbs.org; Marcia Hosking, Development Dir., phone (208)236-3677, marciahosking@idptv.pbs.org; Pat Hunter, Membership Dir., phone (208)236-2471; Helen Humphries, Development Asst., phone (208)236-3619. **Local Programs:** *Health Care for Seniors*; *Idaho Reports* 8 p.m. Friday; *Outdoor Idaho*. **URL:** http://idptv.state.id.us.

8060 KMGI-FM - 102.5
544 N. Arthur Ave., Box 40 Fax: (208)234-0105
Pocatello, ID 83204

Format: Classic Rock. **Networks:** Westwood One Radio. **Owner:** Pacific Empire Communications, Inc., at above address, (208)233-2121, Fax: (208)234-7682. **Founded:** 1978. **Formerly:** KSEI-FM (1993); Conway Broadcasting. **Operating Hours:** Continuous. **ADI:** Idaho Falls-Pocatello, ID. **Key Personnel:** Neil Maberry, General Mgr., neilmab@catfm.com; Don Craig, P.D. **Wattage:** 100,000 ERP. **Ad Rates:** $27.75 for 30 seconds; $35.25 for 60 seconds. $8-$14 for 30 seconds; $10-$16 for 60 seconds. Combined advertising rates available with KSEI-AM.

8061 KPKY-FM - 94.9
PO Box 670 Phone: (208)233-1133
Pocatello, ID 83204-0670 Fax: (208)232-1240
Free: (800)967-3595

Format: Oldies; News. **Networks:** ABC. **Founded:** 1980. **Operating Hours:** Continuous; 1% network, 99% local. **ADI:** Idaho Falls-Pocatello, ID. **Key Personnel:** Steve Powers, Program Dir.; Greg Sigerson, Sales Mgr.; Wendy Kynaston, Traffic Mgr.; Pam Anderson, Accountant; Mike Hudson, General Mgr. **Wattage:** 100,000. **Ad Rates:** Advertising accepted; rates available upon request.

8062 KPVI-TV - 6
902 E. Sherman Phone: (208)232-6666
Pocatello, ID 83201 Fax: (208)233-6678
Free: (800)366-5784
E-mail: kpvinews6@aol.com

Format: Commercial TV. **Networks:** NBC. **Owner:** Oregon

Trail Broadcasting Co., at above address. **Founded:** 1974. **Operating Hours:** Continuous. 69% network, 31% local. **ADI:** Idaho Falls-Pocatello, ID. **Key Personnel:** Tonia Ellis, News Dir.; Nick Davidson, Chief Engineer; Rick Landon, Sales Mgr.; Bruce Franzen, General Mgr.; Jim Reed, Promotions Mgr.; Mark Watson, Production Mgr.; Dotie Diaz, Prog. Mgr. **Ad Rates:** Advertising accepted; rates available upon request.

8063 KRCD-AM - 1490
PO Box Z Phone: (208)234-1415
Pocatello, ID 83206-1394

Format: Talk; Sports. **Founded:** 1981. **Formerly:** KKLB-AM (1987). **Operating Hours:** Continuous. **ADI:** Idaho Falls-Pocatello, ID. **Key Personnel:** Tom Mathis, General Mgr. **Wattage:** 1000. **Ad Rates:** $8 for 30 seconds; $10 for 60 seconds.

KRCD-FM - See Chubbuck

8064 KSEI-AM - 930
544 N. Arthur Ave., Box 40 Phone: (208)233-2121
Pocatello, ID 83204 Fax: (208)234-0105
Free: (800)726-5734

Format: Sports; Talk. **Networks:** Mutual Broadcasting System; Westwood One Radio; ABC; CBS. **Owner:** Pacific Empire Communications, at above address, Fax: (208)234-7682. **Founded:** 1926. **Formerly:** Conway Broadcasting. **Operating Hours:** Continuous. **ADI:** Idaho Falls-Pocatello, ID. **Key Personnel:** Neil Maberry, General Mgr., neilmab@catfm.com; Don Craig, Program Dir. **Local Programs:** *One on One Sports*, Neil Maberry. **Wattage:** 5000. **Ad Rates:** $15 for 30 seconds; $18.50 for 60 seconds. $8-$14 for 30 seconds; $10-$16 for 60 seconds. Combined advertising rates available with KSEI-FM.

8065 KWIK-AM - 1240
PO Box 998 Phone: (208)233-1133
Pocatello, ID 83204-0998 Fax: (208)232-1240
Free: (800)582-1240

Format: News; Sports. **Networks:** ABC. **Owner:** Jacor Communications, at above address. **Founded:** 1946. **Operating Hours:** Continuous; 1% network, 99% local. **ADI:** Idaho Falls-Pocatello, ID. **Key Personnel:** Mike Hudson, General Mgr.; Wendy Kynaston, Traffic Mgr.; Gary Shockley, Program Dir.; Pam Anderson, Accountant. **Wattage:** 1000. **Ad Rates:** Advertising accepted; rates available upon request.

8066 KXTF-TV - 35
1061 Blue Lakes Blvd. N. Phone: (208)733-0035
Pocatello, ID 83201 Fax: (208)733-0160

Format: Commercial TV. **Networks:** Fox; United Paramount Network. **Owner:** Sunbelt Communications Co., 1500 Foremaster Ln., Las Vegas, NV 89101. **Founded:** Oct. 23, 1995. **Operating Hours:** 6 a.m.-2 a.m. **Key Personnel:** Ted Meairs, Station Mgr., tmeairs@kxtf.com; Tom Nelson, Sales Mgr., tnelson@magiclink.com. **Ad Rates:** Advertising accepted; rates available upon request.

8067 KZBQ-AM - 1290
436 N. Main, Box 97 Phone: (208)234-1290
Pocatello, ID 83204 Fax: (208)234-9451

Format: Contemporary Country. **Owner:** Idaho Wireless Corp., at above address. **Founded:** 1959. **Operating Hours:** Continuous. **ADI:** Idaho Falls-Pocatello, ID. **Key Personnel:** Paul E. Anderson, General Mgr. **Wattage:** 1000. **Ad Rates:** $5-7 for 30 seconds; $6-9 for 60 seconds.

8068 KZBQ-FM - 93.7
436 N. Main, Box 97 Phone: (208)234-1290
Pocatello, ID 83204 Fax: (208)234-9451

Format: Contemporary Country. **Owner:** Idaho Wireless Corp., at above address. **Founded:** 1969. **Operating Hours:** Continuous. **ADI:** Idaho Falls-Pocatello, ID. **Key Personnel:** Paul E. Anderson, General Mgr. **Wattage:** 100,000 ERP. **Ad Rates:** $13-35 for 30 seconds; $15-40 for 60 seconds.

8069 TCI Cablevision of Idaho
204 W. Alameda Rd. Phone: (208)232-1784
Pocatello, ID 83201 Fax: (208)234-4756

Founded: 1954. **Key Personnel:** Sue Parker, Manager; Jerry Ransbottom, Contact; Mike Waldron, Office Mgr. **Cities Served:** Bannock County, Chubbock, Pocatello, and Inkom, ID: 54 channels; 2 community access channel; 252 hours per week of community access programming.

PONDERAY

8070 Craft - Crafts
Box 441 Phone: (208)263-6885
Ponderay, ID 83852
Consumer magazine covering spirituality and associated crafts. **Founded:** 1994. **Freq:** Quarterly. **ISSN:** 1074-7996. **Subscription Rates:** $15 individuals; $4.50 single issue. **Remarks:** Accepts advertising.
Circ: Combined 480

POST FALLS, pop. 5,736.

NW ID. Kootenai Co. 6 mi. W. of Coeur d'Alene. Saw, veneer, plywood, grass seed, and fertilizer factories. Nurseries. Grain, fruit, stock farms.

8071 Post Falls Tribune
318 Spokane St. Phone: (208)773-7502
Post Falls, ID 83854 Fax: (208)773-7002

Community newspaper. **Founded:** 1896. **Freq:** Weekly (Thurs.). **Print Method:** Offset. **Cols./Page:** 6. **Col. Width:** 27 nonpareils. **Col. Depth:** 294 agate lines. **Key Personnel:** Lila Horvath, Editor and Publisher. **Subscription Rates:** $20 individuals. **Remarks:** Accepts advertising.
Ad Rates: GLR: $2 **Circ:** 1,200
BW: $813
4C: $1,198
PCI: $6.30

PRESTON†, pop. 3,759.

SE ID. Franklin Co. 28 mi. N. of Logan, UT. Meat packing plant; flour mill. Agriculture. Dairy products, stock, poultry.

8072 KACH-AM - 1340
1133 E. Glendale Rd. Phone: (208)852-1340
Preston, ID 83263 Fax: (208)852-1342

Format: Oldies. **Networks:** CNN Radio. **Owner:** Alan and Nelada White, at above address. **Founded:** 1948. **Formerly:** KPST-AM. **Operating Hours:** 6:00 a.m.-10:00p.m. **Key Personnel:** Alan White, General Mgr. **Ad Rates:** $5-7.50 for 30 seconds; $8-13.50 for 60 seconds.

PRIEST RIVER, pop. 1,639.

N. ID. Bonner Co. 45 mi. NE of Spokane, WA. Fishing. Logging, saw, shingle, grain mills. Pine timber. Dairy farms. Hay, alfalfa, potatoes.

8073 The Priest River Times
Box 10 Phone: (208)448-2431
Priest River, ID 83856 Fax: (208)448-2938

Local newspaper. **Founded:** 1914. **Freq:** Weekly (Wed.). **Print Method:** Offset. **Cols./Page:** 6. **Col. Width:** 2 inches. **Col. Depth:** 21 1/2 inches. **Key Personnel:** Linda Jordan, Publisher. **Subscription Rates:** $18 individuals; $26 out of area; $.50 single issue. **Remarks:** Color advertising accepted; rates available upon request. **Formerly:** The Times (1994).
Ad Rates: GLR: $.75 **Circ:** Free ‡6,800
BW: $903
4C: $375
SAU: $6.40

REXBURG†, pop. 11,559.

E. ID. Madison Co. 28 mi. Ne of Idaho Falls. Ricks College. Sugar, cheese, concrete block, dehydrated potato products factories; lumber mill. Agriculture. Sugar beets, wheat, cattle, sheep, potatoes, dairying, poultry.

8074 Rexburg Standard Journal
Box 10 Phone: (208)356-5441
Rexburg, ID 83440 Fax: (208)356-8312
Publisher E-mail: sjnews@srv.net

Local newspaper. **Founded:** 1911. **Freq:** 3/week Monday, Wednesday, and Friday. **Print Method:** Offset. **Cols./Page:** 6. **Col. Width:** 26 nonpareils. **Col. Depth:** 301 agate lines. **Key Personnel:** Roger O. Porter, Publisher, roporter@srv.net; Kristy Johansson, Assoc. Dir., kjo@srv.net. **USPS:** 464-460. **Subscription Rates:** $45 individuals. **Remarks:** Accepts advertising. **Alt. Formats:** CD-ROM.
Ad Rates: GLR: $8 **Circ:** ‡6200
BW: $1,032
4C: $1088.50
PCI: $6.50

8075 Snake River Echoes
Upper Snake River Valley Historical Society
PO Box 244 Phone: (208)356-7030
Rexburg, ID 83440
Publication E-mail: dhc@srv.net

Journal covering history of Idaho. **Founded:** 1971. **Freq:** Semiannual. **Cols./Page:** 2. **Col. Width:** 3 1/4 inches. **Col. Depth:** 9 inches. **Key Personnel:** Louis Clements, Editor. **ISSN:** 0882-374X. **Subscription Rates:** $10 individuals; $5 libraries. **Remarks:** Advertising not accepted.
Circ: Controlled 250

8076 KADQ-FM - 94.3
90 S. 1st W., Box 66 Phone: (208)356-7323
Rexburg, ID 83440 Fax: (208)356-7324

Format: Adult Contemporary; News; Sports. **Simulcasts:** KIGO-AM. **Networks:** USA Radio; Unistar. **Owner:** Ted W. Austin, at above address. **Founded:** 1975. **Operating Hours:** Continuous; 70% network, 30% local. **Key Personnel:** David Plourde, Contact. **Local Programs:** *Nightside*. **Wattage:** 30,001. **Ad Rates:** $5 for 30 seconds; $8 for 60 seconds.

8077 KRIC-FM - 100.5
Ricks College Phone: (208)356-2907
Rexburg, ID 83460-0115 Fax: (208)356-2911
Free: (800)554-KRIC
E-mail: kric@ricks.edu

Format: Full Service; Classical; Public Radio. **Networks:** National Public Radio (NPR). **Owner:** Ricks College, at above address. **Founded:** 1984. **Operating Hours:** Continuous. **Key Personnel:** Dale Hiller, Asst. Program Dir., phone (209)346-2909; LaMar Barrus, General Mgr., phone (208)356-2906, barrus@ricks.edu; Mark Bailey, News Dir., phone (208)356-2908. **Wattage:** 100,000. **Ad Rates:** Noncommercial.

RIGBY†, pop. 2,624.

E. ID. Jefferson Co. 14 mi. N. of Idaho Falls. Potato processing and meat packing plants. Diversified farming. Sugar beets, potatoes, seed peas, dairying.

8078 Jefferson Star
Pioneer Publishing
Box 37 Phone: (208)745-8701
Rigby, ID 83442 Fax: (208)745-8703

Community newspaper. **Founded:** 1903. **Freq:** Weekly (Wed.). **Print Method:** Offset. **Trim Size:** 17 x 23. **Cols./Page:** 5. **Col. Width:** 12 picas. **Col. Depth:** 215 agate lines. **Key Personnel:** Terry Carr, Editor and Publisher; Earlene Poole, Advertising Mgr. **Subscription Rates:** $21 individuals; $26.25 other countries; $32 out of state.
Ad Rates: PCI: $7.04 **Circ:** ‡2,200

RUPERT†, pop. 5,476.

S. ID. Minidoka Co. 40 mi. E. of Twin Falls. Manufactures cheese. Bean processing warehouses; frozen food plants. Potatoes shipped. Agriculture. Potatoes, beans, sugar beets, alfalfa, wheat, cattle, sheep.

8079 KBBK-AM - 970
120 South 300 West Phone: (208)436-4757
Rupert, ID 83350 Fax: (208)436-3050

Format: Country; Contemporary Country; Bluegrass; Hispanic; Agricultural. **Networks:** CBS; AP; USA Radio. **Founded:** 1955. **Formerly:** KAYT-AM (1984). **Operating Hours:** Continuous. **Key Personnel:** Frank White, Contact; Jim Lee, Contact, phone (208)670-4757; Denis Jeffs, Contact. **Wattage:** 2500 day, 900 night. **Ad Rates:** $8 for 30 seconds; $10 for 60 seconds. Combined advertising rates available with KKMV-FM, KZDX-FM, KBAR-AM.

8080 KKMV-FM - 92.5
120 South 300 West Phone: (208)436-4757
Rupert, ID 83350 Fax: (208)436-3050

Format: Country. **Founded:** 1978. **Formerly:** KNAP-FM. **Operating Hours:** Continuous. **Key Personnel:** Frank White, Contact; Jim Lee, Contact, phone (208)670-4757; Denis Jeffs, Contact. **Wattage:** 24,000 ERP. **Ad Rates:** $15 for 30 seconds; $18 for 60 seconds. Combined advertising rates available with KBBK-AM, KZDX-FM, KBAR-AM.

ST. ANTHONY

8081 Fremont County Herald-Chronicle
Standard Journal Newspapers
44 N. Bridge St. Phone: (208)624-4455
PO Box 568 Fax: (208)356-8312
St. Anthony, ID 83445-0568
Community newspaper. **Founded:** 1890. **Freq:** Semiweekly (Tues. and Thurs.). **Print Method:** Offset. Uses mats. **Cols./Page:** 6. **Col. Width:** 12.5 picas. **Col. Depth:** 21 1/2 inches. **Key Personnel:** Roger O. Porter, Publisher; John C. Porter, Publisher. **Subscription Rates:** $26 local; $31 out of area. **Remarks:** Accepts advertising.
Ad Rates: GLR: $.30 **Circ:** ‡8,547
SAU: $6.20
PCI: $6.20

ST. MARIES

8082 St. Marie's Gazette-Record
The Corp.
127 S. 7th St. Phone: (208)245-4538
St. Maries, ID 83861-1801 Fax: (208)245-4991

Community newspaper. **Founded:** Mar. 26, 1906. **Freq:** Weekly (Wed.). **Print Method:** Offset. **Trim Size:** 16 x 23. **Cols./Page:** 7. **Col. Width:** 24 nonpareils. **Col. Depth:** 294 agate lines. **Key Personnel:** Daniel A. Hammes, Publisher. **Subscription Rates:** $24 individuals. **Remarks:** Advertising not accepted for tobacco products.
Ad Rates: SAU: $4.24 **Circ:** ‡3,507

8083 KOFE-AM - 1240
PO Box 278 Phone: (208)245-1240
St. Maries, ID 83861 Fax: (208)245-6525
E-mail: koferadio@nidlink.com

Format: Country; Talk. **Networks:** ABC. **Owner:** Frank Janda, at above address. **Founded:** 1970. **Operating Hours:** Continuous. **Key Personnel:** Sherry Janda, Office Mgr. **Wattage:** 1000. **Ad Rates:** $6 for 30 seconds; $11.50 for 60 seconds.

SALMON

8084 The Recorder-Herald
519 Van Dreff St. Phone: (208)756-2221
PO Box 310 Fax: (208)756-2222
Salmon, ID 83467
Community newspaper. **Subtitle:** The Recorder Herald. **Founded:** 1886. **Freq:** Weekly (Thurs.). **Print Method:** Offset. **Trim Size:** 14 x 22 3/4. **Cols./Page:** 6. **Col. Width:** 12 picas. **Col. Depth:** 21 inches. **Key Personnel:** Ricky Hodges, Publisher; Sheila Hodges, Advertising Mgr. **USPS:** 458-060. **Subscription Rates:** $18 individuals; $22; $0.50 single issue. **Remarks:** Accepts advertising.
Ad Rates: GLR: $4.30 **Circ:** Paid 3,550
BW: $718.20 Non-paid 48
4C: $300
PCI: $5.95

8085 KSRA-AM - 960
315 Hwy. 93 N. Phone: (208)756-2218
Salmon, ID 83467 Fax: (208)756-2098

Format: Talk; Adult Contemporary; News; Top 40; Country. **Simulcasts:** KSRA-FM. **Networks:** ABC. **Owner:** Renee Smith, at above address. **Founded:** 1959. **Operating Hours:** 6 a.m.- sundown. **Key Personnel:** Leo Marshall, Sales Mgr.; Blair Smith, Program Dir.; Leslie Shumate, News Dir. **Wattage:** 1000. **Ad Rates:** $4.50 for 15 seconds; $4.50-6.00 for 30 seconds; $7.25 for 60 seconds.

8086 TCI Cable TV Inc.
PO Box 1716 Phone: (208)756-4111
Salmon, ID 83467 Fax: (208)756-4111

Owner: Tele-Comunications, Inc. (TCI), 4643 S. Ulster St., Ste. 600, Denver, CO 80237, (303)987-9552. **Key Personnel:** Bud Worth, Manager. **Cities Served:** Salmon, ID.

SANDPOINT

8087 Airways
Airways International, Inc.
Box 1109 Phone: (208)683-6009
Sandpoint, ID 83864-0872 Fax: (208)683-7063

Trade magazine covering commercial aviation and air travel. **Founded:** 1984. **Freq:** Monthly. **Print Method:** Web offset. **Trim Size:** 8 3/8 x 10 7/8. **Cols./Page:** 3. **Col. Width:** 2 5/8 inches. **Col. Depth:** 10 inches. **Key Personnel:** John Wegg, Editor-in-Chief. **ISSN:** 1074-4320. **Subscription Rates:** $36 individuals; $4.95 single issue. **Remarks:** Accepts advertising.
Ad Rates: BW: $2,700 **Circ:** Paid ⊕**30,000**
4C: $3,500

8088 The Bonner County Daily Bee
PO Box 159 Phone: (208)263-9534
Sandpoint, ID 83864-0159 Fax: (208)263-9091

Newspaper with a Democratic orientation. **Founded:** 1924. **Freq:** Weekly (Wed.). **Print Method:** Offset. **Cols./Page:** 6. **Col. Width:** 25 nonpareils. **Col. Depth:** 294 agate lines. **Key Personnel:** Chris Bessler, Editor; Pete Thompson, Publisher; Herb Offerman, Advertising Mgr. **Subscription Rates:** $10 individuals. **Remarks:** Accepts advertising.
Ad Rates: GLR: $.29 **Circ:** (Not Reported)

8089 The Daily Bee
310 Church St. Phone: (208)263-9534
PO Box 159 Fax: (208)263-9091
Sandpoint, ID 83864-0159
General newspaper. **Freq:** Daily (eve.). **Cols./Page:** 6. **Col. Width:** 2 1/16 inches. **Col. Depth:** 21 1/2 inches. **Key Personnel:** Kary Miller, Managing Editor; Joe Grimes, Publisher. **Remarks:** Accepts advertising.
Ad Rates: SAU: $5.20 **Circ:** (Not Reported)

8090 MultiLingual Computing & Technology
Multilingual Computing, Inc.
Sandpoint, ID 83864 Phone: (208)263-8178
Fax: (208)263-6310
Free: (800)748-9824
Publication E-mail: info@multilingual.com

Magazine for international business readers especially in the software development fields who need technology to do business, produce and market their products and materials in foreign languages. Features product reviews, announcements and press releases, user guidelines, and technology and innovation updates. **Founded:** 1987. **Freq:** Bimonthly. **Print Method:** Offset. **Trim Size:** 8 1/4 x 10 7/8. **Cols./Page:** 3. **Col. Width:** 2 1/4 inches. **Col. Depth:** 10 inches. **Key Personnel:** Seth Thomas Schneider, Publisher/Editor-in-Chief; Mike Bennett, Ed./Assoc. Pub., mike@multilingual.com. **ISSN:** 1523-0309. **Subscription Rates:** $39 individuals for 6 issues. **Remarks:** Accepts advertising. **Formerly:** Multilingual Computing; Multilingual Communications & Computing; Multilingual Communications & Technology.
Ad Rates: BW: $2,850 **Circ:** Combined 7,000
4C: $3,550

SHELLEY

8091 The Shelley Pioneer
Pioneer Publications
PO Box P Phone: (208)357-7661
Shelley, ID 83274 Fax: (208)357-3435

Community newspaper. **Founded:** 1905. **Freq:** Weekly (Thurs.). **Print Method:** Offset. **Cols./Page:** 5. **Col. Width:** 12 nonpareils. **Col. Depth:** 224 agate lines. **Key Personnel:** Terry Carr, Publisher; Crystal Foster, General Mgr. **Subscription Rates:** $17.85 in county; $27 out of state.
Ad Rates: GLR: $.24 **Circ:** ‡1,850
PCI: $4.50

SHOSHONE

8092 Lincoln County Journal
Magic Valley Publishing Co., Inc.
PO Box 704 Phone: (208)886-2740
Shoshone, ID 83352 Fax: (208)324-3391
Publisher E-mail: mutrio@northrim.net

Community newspaper. **Founded:** 1884. **Freq:** Weekly (Wed.). **Print Method:** Offset. **Trim Size:** 10 x 16. **Cols./Page:** 5. **Col. Width:** 11.5 picas. **Col. Depth:** 16 inches. **Key Personnel:** P. Nance, Publisher. **USPS:** 313-420. **Subscription Rates:** $21 individuals. **Remarks:** Accepts advertising.
Ad Rates: BW: $440 **Circ:** ‡1,100
4C: $120
PCI: $5.50

SODA SPRINGS

8093 Caribou County Sun
PO Box 815 Phone: (208)547-3260
Soda Springs, ID 83276
Community newspaper. **Founded:** 1931. **Freq:** Weekly (Thurs.). **Print Method:** Offset. **Cols./Page:** 6. **Col. Width:** 12 picas. **Col. Depth:** 300 agate lines. **Key Personnel:** Mark Steele, Publisher. **USPS:** 090-560. **Subscription Rates:** $16 individuals; $20 out of county. **Remarks:** Accepts advertising.
Ad Rates: GLR: $.28 **Circ:** ‡3,000
PCI: $5.60

8094 KBRV-AM - 790
PO Box 777 Phone: (208)547-4012
Soda Springs, ID 83276-0777 Fax: (208)547-3775

Format: Country; Talk; News; Sports. **Networks:** UPI. **Owner:** Doug Mathis, at above address. **Founded:** 1964. **Operating Hours:** Sunrise-sunset. **Key Personnel:** Doug Mathis, General Mgr.; Cindy Mathis, News and Product. **Wattage:** 5000. **Ad Rates:** $4.75-6.25 for 30 seconds; $6-7.50 for 60 seconds.

8095 KFIS-FM - 100.1
PO Box 777 Phone: (208)547-4012
Soda Springs, ID 83276-0777 Fax: (208)547-3775

Format: Country. **Networks:** UPI. **Owner:** Doug Mathis, at above address, Fax: (208)847-3725. **Founded:** 1982. **Operating Hours:** Continuous. **Key Personnel:** Doug Mathis, General Mgr.; Cindy Mathis, Production Dir.; Scott Taylor. **Local Programs:** *High School Sports*; *Local and Regional News*; *Road - In Winter Reports*. **Wattage:** 3000. **Ad Rates:** $5.25-7.25 for 30 seconds; $6-8.50 for 60 seconds.

8096 Premier Cable
Box 655 Phone: (208)547-4341
Soda Springs, ID 83276 Fax: (208)547-4833
Free: (800)451-3029
E-mail: blkstone@cyberhighay.net

Founded: 1988. **Key Personnel:** Marilyn Moore, Contact. **Cities Served:** subscribing households 14,000.

SUN VALLEY

8097 Environmental News Network
Box 1996 Phone: (208)726-3649
Sun Valley, ID 83353 Fax: (208)726-2476
Publisher E-mail: news@enn.com

Online magazine covering environmental and science topics. **Founded:** Jan. 1993. **Freq:** Daily. **Key Personnel:** Steven Schowengerdt, Editor-in-Chief; Hillary Mayell, Managing Editor; Tom Iselin, Business Development. **Remarks:** Accepts advertising. **URL:** http://www.enn.com.
Ad Rates: GLR: $15 **Circ:** Controlled 125,000

TROY

NE ID. Latah Co. 10 mi. E. of Moscow.

8098 Troy Television Cable Co. Inc.
Box 37 Phone: (208)835-4422
Troy, ID 83871-0037

Owner: Troy Television Co. Inc., at above address. **Founded:** 1953. **Key Personnel:** Raymond Soderstrom, Contact. **Cities Served:** Troy, ID: subscribing households 300; 19 channels.

TWIN FALLS†, pop. 26,209.

SW JID. Twin Falls Co. 140 mi. E. of Boise. Manufactures sugar, dried and canned fruit, flour, creamery and meat products, potato starch, tallow, vinegar, beverages, frozen potatoes, concrete pipe, bags, potato machinery. Extensive shipping of agricultural products. Beans, potatoes, sugar beets, stock.

8099 Times-News
Howard Publications, Inc.
132 3rd St. W. Phone: (208)733-0931
Box 548 Fax: (208)734-5538
Twin Falls, ID 83303
Free: (800)658-3883
Publication E-mail: twinad@micron.net

General newspaper. **Founded:** Oct. 28, 1904. **Freq:** Mon.-Sun. (morn.). **Print Method:** Offset. **Trim Size:** 13 3/4 x 22. **Cols./Page:** 6. **Col. Width:** 25 nonpareils. **Col. Depth:** 301 agate lines. **Key Personnel:** Clark Walworth, Managing Editor; Stephen Hartgen, Publisher; Peter York, Advertising Mgr. **Subscription Rates:** $200.20 individuals.
Ad Rates: GLR: $1.11 **Circ:** Mon.-Sat. 22,350
BW: $2193 Sun. 23,079
4C: $2548
SAU: $17

8100 KAWZ-FM - 89.9
241 Main Ave. W. Phone: (208)734-4357
PO Box 271 Fax: (208)736-1958
Twin Falls, ID 83303
Free: (800)357-4226
E-mail: csnmusic@calvarychapel.com

Format: Religious; Contemporary Christian. **Owner:** Calvary Chapel of Twin Falls, Inc., at above address. **Founded:** 1988. **Operating Hours:** Continuous; 100% local. **ADI:** Twin Falls, ID. **Key Personnel:** Mike Kestler, Station Mgr., mikekestler@calvarychapel.com; Don Mills, Program Dir., donmills@calvarychapel.com. **Local Programs:** *It's Time*, Don Mills; *Life Line*, Lois Mills. **Wattage:** 11,500. **Ad Rates:** Noncommercial.

8101 KBGH-TV - 19
PO Box 1238 Phone: (208)736-3046
Twin Falls, ID 83303 Fax: (208)736-2188
Free: (888)859-5279
E-mail: akblowther@orion1.csi.cc.id.us

Format: Educational. **Owner:** State of Idaho, Board of Education, at above address. **Key Personnel:** Ken Campbell, General Mgr.; Tom Lowther, Chief Engineer; Leo Malburg, Operations. **URL:** http://www.csi.cc.id.us.

8102 KBSW-FM - 91.7
c/o KBSU-FM Phone: (208)736-3046
Boise State University Fax: (208)736-2188
1910 University Dr.
Boise, ID 83725

Format: Public Radio; Classical; News. **Simulcasts:** KBSU-

FM Boise, ID. **Networks:** National Public Radio (NPR); American Public Radio (APR). **Owner:** BSU Radio Network, at above address. **Operating Hours:** Continuous; 70% network, 30% local. **ADI:** Boise, ID. **Key Personnel:** James Paluzzi, General Mgr.; Don Wimberly, Mgr., Network Production Center; Tom Lowther, KBSW Engineer. **Wattage:** 1950. **Ad Rates:** Noncommercial.

8103 KCIR-FM - 90.7
1446 Filer Ave. E. Phone: (208)734-5777
Twin Falls, ID 83301-4121 Fax: (208)734-0331

Format: Talk; Educational; Adult Contemporary; Religious. **Networks:** SOS Radio. **Owner:** Faith Communications Corp., 2201 S. 6th St., Las Vegas, NV 89104, (702)731-5452. **Founded:** 1982. **Operating Hours:** Continuous; 95% network, 5% local. **ADI:** Twin Falls, ID. **Key Personnel:** Duane Luchsinger, Station Mgr., phone (208)734-5777; Christine Staley, Program Dir.; Jay Goemmer, Contact. **Wattage:** 20,000 ERP. **Ad Rates:** Noncommercial.

8104 KEZJ-AM - 1450
415 Park Ave. Phone: (208)733-7512
PO Box 1259 Fax: (208)733-7525
Twin Falls, ID 83303-0346

Format: Talk; Contemporary Country. **Networks:** CBS; NBC. **Founded:** 1946. **Operating Hours:** 5 a.m.-midnight; 29% network, 71% local. **ADI:** Twin Falls, ID. **Key Personnel:** Sherry Kesler, Program Dir.; Terry Tario, General Mgr. **Wattage:** 1000. **Ad Rates:** Advertising accepted; rates available upon request.

8105 KEZJ-FM - 95.7
415 Park Ave. Phone: (208)733-7512
PO Box 1259 Fax: (208)733-7525
Twin Falls, ID 83301

Format: Country. **Networks:** ABC. **Owner:** B & B Broadcasting, at above address. **Founded:** 1976. **Operating Hours:** Continuous; 2% network, 98% local. **ADI:** Twin Falls, ID. **Key Personnel:** Terry C. Tario, General Mgr.; Brad Hollstrom, Program Dir.; Kelly Klaas, Contact; Connie Lively, Office Mgr. **Wattage:** 50,000. **Ad Rates:** Advertising accepted; rates available upon request.

8106 KLIX-AM - 1310
415 Park Ave. Phone: (208)733-7512
PO Box 1259 Fax: (208)733-7525
Twin Falls, ID 83303-1259

Format: Talk; News. **Networks:** ABC; Westwood One Radio; Canadian Broadcasting Corporation (CBC)/Societe Radio-Canada (SRC). **Founded:** 1946. **Operating Hours:** Continuous; 95% network, 5% local. **ADI:** Twin Falls, ID. **Key Personnel:** Terry Tario, General Mgr.; Logan Tusow, Sales Mgr. **Local Programs:** *The "Baron" Ron Heron* 6 a.m.-10 a.m. **Wattage:** 5000. **Ad Rates:** Advertising accepted; rates available upon request.

8107 KLIX-FM - 96.5
Box 1259 Phone: (208)733-1310
Twin Falls, ID 83303 Fax: (208)423-4622

Format: Oldies. **Networks:** ABC; Satellite Music Network. **Founded:** 1974. **Operating Hours:** Continuous. **ADI:** Twin Falls, ID. **Key Personnel:** Terry Tario, General Mgr.; Kelly Klaas, Chief Engineer; Brad Hollstrom, PD. **Wattage:** 100,000. **Ad Rates:** Advertising accepted; rates available upon request.

8108 KMVT-TV - 11
1100 Blue Lake Blvd. N. Phone: (208)733-1100
Twin Falls, ID 83301 Fax: (208)733-4649

Format: Commercial TV. **Networks:** CBS. **Owner:** KMUT Broadcasting, Inc., PO Box 2860, Daytona Beach, FL 32120, (904)258-1235. **Founded:** 1955. **Operating Hours:** 80% network, 20% local. **ADI:** Twin Falls, ID. **Key Personnel:** Lee P. Wagner, General Mgr.; Robert P. Thomas, General Sales Mgr.; George Brown, Program Dir.; Doug Maughan, News Dir.; Karen Lent, Contact; Tom Frank, Production Mgr.; Penne Main, Promotions Dir.; Denny Lowe, Chief Engineer. **Ad Rates:** $10-350 per unit.

8109 KTFI-AM - 1270
616 Blue Lakes Blvd. N, No. 1270 Phone: (208)733-1270
Twin Falls, ID 83301 Fax: (208)733-4196
E-mail: ktfi@impactradio.com

Format: Full Service; Adult Contemporary. **Networks:** ABC; Northern Agricultural. **Owner:** AM 1270 Co., at above address. **Founded:** 1928. **Operating Hours:** Continuous. **ADI:** Twin Falls, ID. **Key Personnel:** Larry Johnson, General Mgr.; Shannon Rinehart, Sales Mgr., shannonr@impactradio.com. **Local Programs:** *Community Forum*, Carol Stephens, (208)733-1270, Fax (208)733-4196; *Local & Gem State News*, Carol Stephens, (208)733-1270, Fax (208)733-4196. **Wattage:** 5000/1000. **Ad Rates:** $9-12 for 30 seconds; $11-14 for 60 seconds.

8110 TCI of Idaho, Inc.
261 Eastland Dr. Phone: (208)733-6230
Box 1946 Fax: (208)733-6296
Twin Falls, ID 83301
Free: (800)231-2502

Founded: 1977. **Formerly:** King Videocable (1995); Continental Cablevision (1997). **Key Personnel:** Vince Thompson, General Mgr.; Tim Williams, Tech. Mgr.; Russ Young, Mkt. Mgr. **Cities Served:** Aberdeen, American Falls, Fairfield, Filer, Gooding, Hansen, Jerome, Kimberly, Oakley, Twin Falls, Wendell, ID: subscribing households 16,350; 52 channels.

WEISER†, pop. 4,800.

SW ID. Washington Co. 62 mi. NW of Boise. Copper mines. Dairy products, potatoes, and sugarbeets.

8111 Weiser Signal American
Signal American Printers, Inc.
18 E. Idaho Phone: (208)549-1717
PO Box 709 Fax: (208)549-1718
Weiser, ID 83672
Community newspaper. **Founded:** 1882. **Freq:** Semiweekly. **Print Method:** Offset. **Cols./Page:** 6. **Col. Width:** 2 inches. **Col. Depth:** 21 inches. **Key Personnel:** James R. Simpson, Publisher. **Subscription Rates:** $29 individuals.
Ad Rates: BW: $919.80 **Circ:** Paid ‡2,500
SAU: $7.30 Free ‡500

8112 Falcon Video Communications
PO Box 71 Phone: (208)549-3040
Weiser, ID 83672 Fax: (208)549-3328
Free: (800)264-1572

Owner: Falcon Cable TV, 10866 Wilshire Blvd., Ste. 500, Los Angeles, CA 90024. **Formerly:** Snake River Valley Cablevision (1992). **Key Personnel:** John West, Contact; Carla Roberts, Office Mgr. **Cities Served:** subscribing households 5,020; 36 channels; 1 community access channel.

8113 KWEI-AM - 1260
556 Hwy. S. 95 Phone: (208)549-2241
Box 791 Fax: (208)549-0112
Weiser, ID 83672
E-mail: kwei@cyberhighway.net

Networks: Cadena Radio Centro (CRC). **Founded:** 1947. **Operating Hours:** Continuous; 6 a.m. to sunset. **ADI:** Boise, ID. **Key Personnel:** Randall Williamson, General Mgr.; Ricardo Quilantan, Station Mgr. **Wattage:** 1000. **Ad Rates:** $5-15 for 60 seconds. Combined advertising rates available with KWEI-FM.

ILLINOIS

State Capital, SPRINGFIELD

Illinois is bounded on the north by Wisconsin, northeast by Lake Michigan, east by Indiana, southeast and south by Kentucky, and west by Missouri and Iowa. Its extreme length north to south is 385 miles; extreme breadth 218 miles. Its total land area is 55,593 square miles. The surface is mostly level table-land inclining gently toward the south, with bluffs along the principal rivers. A small tract in the northwest, around Galena, is somewhat broken, and a low mountain ridge extends across the southern end from Grand Tower, on the Mississippi River, to Shawneetown, on the Ohio, about 850 feet above sea level. The prairies are sometimes level, but generally undulating. With the exception of Iowa, no other state has so large a portion of land susceptible to cultivation. There are over 275 streams in the state grouped into two river systems, one having the Mississippi as outlet, the other tributary to the Ohio River. The most important river is the Illinois which crosses the north central and western parts of the state, draining 24,726 square miles. The Chicago Drainage Canal is an important and unique artificial waterfall supplying drainage and transportation. The climate is noted for its extremes of heat and cold. The Weather Bureau at Chicago gives the temperature (annual average) as 49.0; highest on record, 105; lowest on record, -23. Total annual precipitation is 35.82 inches. Chicago is the center of immense business activity and a prodigious number of industries. Illinois is remarkably well-supplied with transportation facilities by rail, river, and lake, and is one of the leading states in export trade. Its many institutions of higher education include the University of Chicago, the University of Illinois, located at Urbana, and Northwestern University at Evanston.

POPULATION: 11,631,000 (1992). Rank among the states, 6th.

AGRICULTURE: Number of farms: 81,000 (1992). Farm acreage: 29,000,000 (1992). Cash receipts from farm marketings: crops, $5,165,000,000 (1991); livestock and products, $2,344,000,000 (1991).

FORESTS: Total forest land: 840,000 acres (1991). Principal woods: oak, cottonwood, aspen, elm, maple, sycamore, hickory, red and sap gum, ash, yellow poplar, walnut, beech, basswood.

MINERALS: Value of production: $673,000,000 (1991). Principal minerals: stone, cement, sand gravel. Value of petroleum production: $385,000,000 (1991).

MANUFACTURES: Value added by manufacture: $70,104,000,000 (1991). Leading industry groups: machinery (except electrical), food and related products, electrical machinery, fabricated metal products.

LIST OF COUNTIES

Total number of counties 102

County, Location on Map, and County Seat	Pop.
Adams (W), Quincy	66,090
Alexander (S), Cairo	10,626
Bond (S), Greenville	14,991
Boone (N), Belvidere	30,806
Brown (W), Mount Sterling	5,836
Bureau (NW), Princeton	35,688
Calhoun (W), Hardin	5,322
Carroll (NW), Mount Carroll	16,805
Cass (WC), Virginia	13,437
Champaign (E), Urbana	173,025
Christian (C), Taylorville	34,418
Clark (E), Marshall	15,921
Clay (SE), Louisville	14,460
Clinton (SW), Carlyle	33,944
Coles (E), Charleston	51,644
Cook (NE), Chicago	5,105,067
Crawford (SE), Robinson	19,464
Cumberland (E), Toledo	10,670
De Kalb (N), Sycamore	77,932
De Witt (C), Clinton	16,516
Douglas (E), Tuscola	19,464
Du Page (NE), Wheaton	781,666
Edgar (E), Paris	19,595
Edwards (SE), Albion	7,440
Effingham (S), Effingham	31,704
Fayette (SC), Vandalia	20,893
Frankling (S), Benton	40,319
Fulton (W), Lewiston	38,080
Gallatin (SE), Shawneetown	6,909
Greene (W), Carrollton	15,317
Grundy (NE), Morris	32,337
Hamilton (S), McLeansboro	8,499
Hancock (W), Carthage	21,373
Hardin (SE), Elizabethtown	5,189
Henderson (W), Oquawka	8,096
Henry (NW), Cambridge	51,159
Iroquois (E), Watseka	30,787
Jackson (SW), Murphysboro	61,067
Jasper (SE), Newton	20,539
Jefferson (S), Mount Vernon	37,020
Jersey (SW), Jerseyville	20,539
Jo Daviess (NW), Galena	21,821
Johnson (S), Vienna	11,347
Kane (NE), Geneva	317,471
Kankakee (E), Kankakee	96,255
Kendall (NE), Yorkville	39,413
Knox (NWC), Galesburg	56,393
Lake (NE), Waukegan	516,418
La Salle (N), Ottawa	106,913
Lawrence (SE), Lawrenceville	15,972
Lee (N), Dixon	34,392
Livingston (NEC), Pontiac	39,301
Logan (C), Lincoln	30,798
Macon (C), Decatur	117,206
Macoupin (SWC), Carlinville	47,679
Madison (SW), Edwardsville	249,238
Marion (S), Salem	41,561
Marshall (NC), Lacon	12,846
Mason (C), Havana	16,269
Massac (S), Metropolis	14,752
McDonough (W), Macomb	35,244
McHenry (NE), Woodstock	183,241
McLean (C), Bloomington	129,180
Menard (C), Petersburg	11,164
Mercer (NW), Aledo	17,290
Monroe (SW), Waterloo	22,422
Montgomery (SC), Hillsboro	30,728
Morgan (WC), Jacksonville	36,397
Moultrie (SEC), Sullivan	13,930
Ogle (N), Oregon	45,957
Peoria (NWC), Peoria	182,827
Perry (S), Pinckneyville	21,412
Piatt (EC), Monticello	15,548
Pike (W), Pittsfield	17,577
Pope (S), Golconda	4,373
Pulaski (S), Mound City	7,523
Putnam (NC), Hennepin	5,730
Randolph (SW), Chester	34,583
Richland (SE), Olney	16,545
Rock Island (NW), Rock Island	148,723
Saint Clair (SW), Belleville	262,852
Saline (S), Harrisburg	26,551
Sangamon (C), Springfield	178,386
Schuyler (W), Rushville	7,498
Scott (W), Winchester	5,644
Shelby (SC), Shelbyville	22,261
Stark (NWC), Toulon	6,534
Stephenson (N), Freeport	48,052

Tazewell (NC), Pekin 123,692
Union (S), Jonesboro 17,619
Vermillion (E), Danville 88,257
Wabash (SE), Mount Carmel 13,111
Warren (W), Monmouth 19,181
Washington (S), Nashville 14,965
Wayne (S), Fairfield 17,241
White (SE), Carmi 16,522
Whiteside (NW), Morrison 60,186
Will (NE), Joliet 357,313
Williamson (S), Marion 57,733
Winnebago (N), Rockford 252,913
Woodford (NC), Eureka 32,653

STATISTICS

Newspapers

Period of Issue
Daily 76
 Evening Daily 51
 Morning Daily 19
 Daily with Sunday edition 25
Semiweekly 41
Weekly 486
Biweekly 9
Semimonthly 9
Monthly 11
Bimonthly 2
Quarterly 2
Free or partly free 108
Shopper 25
 Total Newspapers 658

Periodicals

Period of Issue
Semiweekly 0
Weekly 16
Biweekly 8
Semimonthly 11
Monthly 260
Bimonthly 152
Quarterly 190
Variant 2
Free or partly free 1
 Total Periodicals 815

Total number of publications 1,473

Radio Stations

AM Stations 102
FM Stations 180
 Total Radio Stations 282

TV Stations

 Total TV Stations 46

Cable Stations

 Total Cable Systems 33

Total number of broadcast listings 361

ABINGDON

8114 Abingdon Argus
Eagle Publications
405 Western, Ste. 6 Phone: (309)426-2255
PO Box 32 Fax: (309)462-3221
Abingdon, IL 61410
Free: (800)500-1961
Publisher E-mail: eaglepub@macomb.com

Community newspaper. **Founded:** 1952. **Freq:** Weekly (Thurs.). **Print Method:** Offset. **Cols./Page:** 6. **Col. Width:** 9.6 picas. **Col. Depth:** 224 agate lines. **Key Personnel:** Tom Hutson, Publisher; Joyce Cannon, Editor. **Subscription Rates:** $17; $19 out of area; $22 out of state; $0.40 single issue. **Remarks:** Accepts advertising.
Ad Rates: BW: $230.40 **Circ:** Paid 2,000
4C: $570.40 Free 15
SAU: $3.55
CNU: $4.50
PCI: $2.40

8115 Roseville Independent
Eagle Publications
405 Western, Ste. 6 Phone: (309)426-2255
PO Box 32 Fax: (309)462-3221
Abingdon, IL 61410
Free: (800)500-1961
Publisher E-mail: eaglepub@macomb.com

Newspaper with a Republican orientation. **Founded:** 1956. **Freq:** Weekly (Thurs.). **Print Method:** Offset. **Cols./Page:** 6. **Col. Width:** 20 nonpareils. **Col. Depth:** 224 agate lines. **Key Personnel:** Phil Gerding, Editor; Tom Hutson, Publisher. **USPS:** 470-940. **Subscription Rates:** $17 individuals; $19 out of county; $22 out of state. **Remarks:** Accepts advertising.
Ad Rates: BW: $220.80 **Circ:** Paid ‡750
4C: $620.16 Free ‡25
SAU: $3.40
PCI: $2.30

ADDISON, pop. 28,836.

DuPage Co. (NE). 19 m W of Chicago. Manufactures metal works, mining machinery & equipment tool and dies. Dairy, poultry and truck farms.

8116 Aberdeen's Concrete Construction
The Aberdeen Group a division of Hanley-Wood, Inc.
426 S. Westgate St. Phone: (630)543-0870
Addison, IL 60101-4546 Fax: (630)543-3112
Free: (800)837-0870
Publication E-mail: aberdeen@wocnet.com
Publisher E-mail: aberdeen@wocnet.com

Trade magazine that reaches companies involved in the design, placement, repair, specification, and utilization of concrete in the construction industry. **Founded:** 1956. **Freq:** Monthly. **Print Method:** Web offset. **Trim Size:** 8 x 10 3/4. **Key Personnel:** Anne Balogh, Managing Editor, phone (630)705-2606, fax (630)543-3112, abalogh@wocnet.com; Patrick J. Carroll, Publisher, phone (630)705-2504, pcarroll@wocnet.com. **ISSN:** 1051-5526. **Subscription Rates:** $30 individuals; $39 Canada and Mexico; $93 other countries; $4 single issue. **Remarks:** Accepts advertising. **URL:** http://www.wocnet.com. **Formerly:** Concrete Construction.
Ad Rates: BW: $6,920 **Circ:** Paid △**7,124**
4C: $8,905 Non-paid △**73,580**

8117 Aberdeen's Magazine of Masonry Construction
The Aberdeen Group a division of Hanley-Wood, Inc.
426 S. Westgate St. Phone: (630)543-0870
Addison, IL 60101-4546 Fax: (630)543-3112
Free: (800)837-0870
Publisher E-mail: aberdeen@wocnet.com

Trade magazine. **Subtitle:** For contracts, architects, engineers and others involved in masonry construction. **Founded:** Apr. 1988. **Freq:** Monthly. **Print Method:** Offset. **Trim Size:** 8 x 10 3/4. **Cols./Page:** 3. **Col. Width:** 3 5/16 inches. **Col. Depth:** 10 inches. **Key Personnel:** William D. Palmer, Editorial Dir., phone (630)823-8284, wpalmer@wocent.com; Elizabeth Keating, Managing Editor, phone (630)705-2624, ekeating@wocnet.com; Patrick Carroll, Publisher, phone (630)705-2504, pcarroll@wocnet.com. **ISSN:** 0899-6088. **Subscription Rates:** $30. **Remarks:** Accepts advertising. **URL:** http://www.wocnet.com/mags/mc.htm.
Ad Rates: BW: $4,275 **Circ:** Paid 2,881
4C: $5,570 Non-paid 39,029

8118 The League-Sandara
Lithuanian National League of America, Inc.
208 W. Natoma Ave. Phone: (630)543-8198
PO Box 241 Fax: (630)543-8198
Addison, IL 60101
Fraternal magazine (English and Lithuanian). **Founded:** 1914. **Freq:** Bimonthly. **Print Method:** Offset. **Cols./Page:** 3. **Col. Width:** 36 nonpareils. **Col. Depth:** 178 agate lines. **Key Personnel:** G. J. Lazauskas, Editor. **ISSN:** 8750-2348. **Subscription Rates:** $10 nonmembers. **Foreign language name:** Sandara.
Circ: Paid ‡1,000

ALBION†, pop. 2,285.

Edwards Co. (SE). 40 m NW of Evansville, Ind. Filter manufacturing; dress factory. Oil production. Hog and beef production, dairy and fruit farms.

8119 Journal-Register
19 W. Main St. Phone: (618)445-2355
PO Box 10 Fax: (618)445-3459
Albion, IL 62806
Community newspaper. **Founded:** June 30, 1869. **Freq:** Weekly (Wed.). **Print Method:** Offset. **Cols./Page:** 8. **Col. Width:** 20 nonpareils. **Col. Depth:** 301 agate lines. **Key Personnel:** Katherine R. Greenfield, Editor and Publisher. **USPS:** 012-580. **Subscription Rates:** $28; $31 out of country. **Alt. Formats:** Mailing labels.
Ad Rates: GLR: $.26 **Circ:** ‡3,162
BW: $623
4C: $833
SAU: $.42
PCI: $4.60

ALEDO†, pop. 3,881.

Mercer Co. (NW). 30 m S of Rock Island. Feed mill. Stock, dairy, grain farms.

8120 The Gun Report
World Wide Gun Report, Inc.
110 S. College Phone: (309)582-5311
PO Box 38 Fax: (309)582-5555
Aledo, IL 61231
Publication E-mail: gunrprt@netins.net

Magazine on antique gun collecting. **Founded:** June 1955. **Freq:** Monthly. **Print Method:** Web. **Trim Size:** 8 1/2 x 11. **Cols./Page:** 3. **Col. Width:** 28 nonpareils. **Col. Depth:** 140 agate lines. **Key Personnel:** Kenneth W. Liggett, Emeritus, Editor and Publisher; Kandice Liggett-Dehle, Editor; Margaret Shipley, Production Mgr. **ISSN:** 0017-5617. **Subscription Rates:** $33 individuals; $5 single issue; $43 other countries. **Remarks:** Accepts advertising.
Ad Rates: BW: $499.57 **Circ:** ‡5,000
4C: $1,020.86
PCI: $32.35

8121 The Times-Record
113-115 S. College Ave. Phone: (309)582-5112
Aledo, IL 61231 Fax: (309)582-5319

Newspaper with a Report orientation. **Subtitle:** The Times Record; Town Crier Advertiser, The ridge, Target. **Founded:** 1857. **Freq:** Weekly (Wed.). **Print Method:** Offset. **Cols./Page:** 6. **Col. Width:** 28 nonpareils. **Col. Depth:** 301 agate lines. **Key Personnel:** Ray McGrew, Publisher; Teresa Larson, Advertising Mgr. **Subscription Rates:** $45 individuals. **Remarks:** Accepts advertising.
Ad Rates: GLR: $9.04 **Circ:** Paid 3,500
PCI: $9.04 Non-paid 8,600

8122 WRMJ-FM - 102.3
Box 187 Phone: (309)582-5666
Aledo, IL 61231 Fax: (309)582-5667
E-mail: wrmj@mcol.net

Format: Country. **Networks:** ABC. **Owner:** Western Illinois Broadcasting, Inc., at above address. **Founded:** 1979. **Operating Hours:** Continuous .10% network, 90% local. **Key Personnel:** John W. Hoscheidt, General Mgr.; Bee Daniels, Program Dir. **Local Programs:** *Focus* 9:20 am Wednesday, Jim Taylor, Mailing contact; *Sportsline*, Jim Taylor, Mailing contact. **Wattage:** 3000. **Ad Rates:** $4.35-8.00 for 30 seconds; $5.05-9.75 for 60 seconds.

ALGONQUIN

8123 Algonquin Countryside
Pioneer Press Newspapers
200 James St. Phone: (847)381-9200
Barrington, IL 60010 Fax: (847)381-5840

Community newspaper (tabloid). **Founded:** 1972. **Freq:** Weekly (Thurs.). **Print Method:** Offset. **Cols./Page:** 4. **Col. Width:** 13 3/5 picas. **Col. Depth:** 196 agate lines. **Key Personnel:** Paul Sassone, Managing Editor; Matt Aredo, Editor. **Subscription Rates:** $12.95 individuals; $19.95 out of county. **Remarks:** Advertising accepted; rates available upon request. **URL:** http://www.pioneerlocal.com.
Circ: Thurs. ★**2,839**

ALTAMONT, pop. 2,389.

Effingham Co. (S). 40 m SW of Mattoon. Panelized housing manufactured. Grain elevator. Grain, livestock, dairy, poultry farms.

8124 The Altamont News
Altamont
118 N. Main Phone: (618)483-6176
Altamont, IL 62411-0315 Fax: (618)483-5177

Community newspaper. **Founded:** Dec. 9, 1881. **Freq:** Weekly (Tues.). **Print Method:** Offset. **Key Personnel:** Omer W. Siebert, Editor and Publisher. **Subscription Rates:** $14 individuals; $17 out of area; $18 out of state. **Remarks:** Accepts advertising.
Ad Rates: GLR: $.19 **Circ:** ‡1,972
SAU: $3.27

ALTON, pop. 34,171.

Madison Co. (SW). On Mississippi River, 25 m N of St Louis. Lewis and Clark Community College, Principia College. Tourism. Boat connections. Coal mines. Limestone quarries. Oil refineries; foundries.

8125 The Telegraph
Journal Register Co.
111 E. Broadway Phone: (618)463-2563
PO Box 278
Alton, IL 62002-0278
General newspaper. **Founded:** Jan. 15, 1836. **Freq:** Mon.-Sun. (morn.). **Print Method:** Offset. **Trim Size:** 12 x 21 5/8. **Cols./Page:** 6. **Col. Width:** 1 7/8 inches. **Col. Depth:** 21 5/8 inches. **Key Personnel:** Dan Brannan, Editor, phone (618)463-2561; James Schrader, Publisher, phone (618)463-2580; Judy Symmonds-Hayden, Advertising Dir., phone (618)463-2543, fax (618)463-0951. **Subscription Rates:** $169 home delivery; $234 by mail. **Remarks:** Accepts advertising. **Formerly:** Alton Telegraph.
Ad Rates: BW: $3,250.55 **Circ:** Mon.-Sat. 28,058
4C: $3,665.55 Sun. 30,575
SAU: $26.02

8126 Today's Advantage
325 Belle St. Phone: (618)463-0612
PO Box 8003 Fax: (618)463-0733
Alton, IL 62002
Publication E-mail: eric@todaysadvantage.com

Community newspaper (tabloid). **Founded:** 1986. **Freq:** Weekly (Wed.). **Print Method:** Offset. **Cols./Page:** 5. **Col. Depth:** 16 1/2 inches. **Key Personnel:** James L. Seibold, Publisher; Sharon E. McRoy, Publisher. **Subscription Rates:** Free; $12 (mail). **Remarks:** Accepts advertising.
Ad Rates: BW: $1,485 **Circ:** Free ‡42,216
4C: $1,770
PCI: $18

8127 WBGZ-AM - 1570
227 Market St. Phone: (618)465-3535
PO Box 615 Fax: (618)465-3546
Alton, IL 62002
E-mail: wbgz@piasanet.com

Format: Talk; News; Sports. **Networks:** USA Radio; Westwood One Radio. **Owner:** Metroplex Communications, Inc., at above address. **Founded:** 1945. **Formerly:** WOKZ-AM (1984). **Operating Hours:** Continuous. **ADI:** St. Louis, MO (Mt. Vernon, IL). **Key Personnel:** Sam Stemm, General Mgr.; Mark Ellebracht, News Dir.; Brent Burklund, Sports Dir. **Wattage:** 1,000. **Ad Rates:** $16.75-22.65 for 30 seconds; $21-28.70 for 60 seconds.

AMBOY, pop. 2,377.

Lee Co. (N). 40 m SW of Rockford. Food processing, packaging plant. Dairy, grain farms,

8128 The Amboy News
219 E. Main St. Phone: (815)857-2311
PO Box 162 Fax: (815)857-2517
Amboy, IL 61310
Community newspaper. **Founded:** 1854. **Freq:** Weekly (Thurs.). **Print Method:** Offset. **Trim Size:** 11 1/4 x 17. **Cols./Page:** 4. **Col. Width:** 14 PCA nonpareils. **Col. Depth:** 16 INS agate lines. **Key Personnel:** John A. Koski, Editor and Publisher. **USPS:** 016-820. **Subscription Rates:** $18 individuals; $24 out of area. **Remarks:** Accepts advertising.
Ad Rates: GLR: $.25 **Circ:** 2,400
BW: $214.40
SAU: $3.87
PCI: $3.80

AMF OHARE

Scanning Microscopy - See Chicago

ANNA, pop. 5,408.

Union Co. (S). 30 m N of Cairo. Stone quarries. Manufactures shoes, truck trailers, mobile homes. Flour mill; fruit and vegetable packaging, marble and granite works. Agriculture. Fruits, vegetables, grain, soybeans, alfalfa, oats. Nursery stock production.

8129 Gazette-Democrat
Reppert Publications
PO Box 529 Phone: (618)833-2158
Anna, IL 62906 Fax: (618)833-5813

Newspaper. **Founded:** 1849. **Freq:** Weekly (Thurs.). **Print Method:** Offset. **Cols./Page:** 6. **Col. Width:** 16 nonpareils. **Col. Depth:** 294 agate lines. **Key Personnel:** Geof Skinner, Editor; Jerry L. Reppert, Publisher, reppert@midwest.net; Russell Mertz, Advertising Mgr.; James West, General Mgr. **Subscription Rates:** $21 individuals. **Remarks:** Color advertising not accepted.
Ad Rates: GLR: $.61 **Circ:** Thurs. ★4,570
BW: $768.40
SAU: $.53
PCI: $7.55

8130 Monday's Pub
Reppert Publications
PO Box 529 Phone: (618)833-2158
Anna, IL 62906 Fax: (618)833-5813

Free weekly. **Founded:** 1979. **Freq:** Weekly (Mon.). **Print Method:** Offset. **Cols./Page:** 6. **Col. Width:** 16 nonpareils. **Col. Depth:** 294 agate lines. **Key Personnel:** Geof Skinner, Editor; Jerry L. Reppert, Publisher, reppert@midwest.net; Russell Mertz, Advertising Mgr.; James West, General Mgr. **USPS:** 215-280. **Subscription Rates:** $21; $22. **Remarks:** Accepts advertising.
Ad Rates: GLR: $0.72 **Circ:** Free ‡12,000
4C: $300
PCI: $7.90

ANTIOCH, pop. 4,500.

Lake Co. (NE). 20 m NW of Waukegan. Hub of the Lake region. Arboretum tours. Industrial Park. Manufactures china.

8131 The Advertiser
Lakes Area Advertiser, Inc.
236 Rte. 173 Phone: (847)395-4444
Antioch, IL 60002 Fax: (847)395-8480

Shopper. **Founded:** 1938. **Freq:** Weekly (Wed.). **Print Method:** Offset. **Cols./Page:** 6. **Col. Width:** 22 nonpareils. **Col. Depth:** 217 agate lines. **Key Personnel:** Carol Anderson, Publisher; James D. Hyerdall, Advertising Mgr.; William Pringle, Circulation Mgr.; Mark Mehaffey, Operations. **Subscription Rates:** Free; $50 out of area. **Remarks:** Accepts advertising.
Circ: Paid ‡234
Free ‡200,000

8132 Antioch News Reporter
Lakeland Publishers, Inc.
30 S. Whitney St. Phone: (847)223-8161
PO Box 268 Fax: (847)223-8810
Grayslake, IL 60030-0268
Publication E-mail: edit@lnd.com

Community newspaper. **Founded:** 1886. **Freq:** Weekly (Thurs.). **Print Method:** Offset. **Trim Size:** 11 x 17. **Cols./Page:** 5. **Col. Width:** 2 inches. **Col. Depth:** 16 inches. **Key Personnel:** Wm. H. Schroeder, Publisher; Esther Hebbard, Advertising Mgr. **Subscription Rates:** $24.50 individuals; $35 out of area. **Remarks:** Accepts advertising.
Ad Rates: BW: $674.80 **Circ:** ‡3,714
4C: $1,023.40
SAU: $8.48

8133 Lakes Area Advertiser
Lakes Area Advertiser, Inc.
236 Rte. 173 Phone: (847)395-4444
Antioch, IL 60002 Fax: (847)395-8480

Newspaper. **Freq:** Weekly. **Key Personnel:** Carol Anderson, President. **Subscription Rates:** $80.
Circ: Free 170,975
Paid 149

ARCOLA, pop. 2,713.

Douglas Co. (E). 40 m SE of Decatur. Collegiate caps, gowns and brooms manufactured. Oil production. Grain farms. Broom corn.

8134 Arcola Record Herald
Rankin Publishing
118 E. Main St. Phone: (217)268-4959
PO Box 130
Aroola, IL 61910
Community newspaper. **Freq:** Weekly (Thurs.). **Cols./Page:** 8. **Col. Width:** 10.5 picas. **Col. Depth:** 21 inches. **Key Personnel:** Don Rankin, Editor and Publisher; Linda Rankin, Editor and Publisher.
Circ: 2,100

8135 Broom Brush and Mop
Rankin Publishing
118 E. Main St. Phone: (217)268-4959
PO Box 130
Arcola, IL 61910
Magazine for the broom, mop and brush trade. **Founded:** 1912. **Freq:** Monthly. **Print Method:** Offset. **Cols./Page:** 3. **Col. Width:** 28 nonpareils. **Col. Depth:** 131 agate lines. **Key Personnel:** Don Rankin, Editor and Publisher, drankin125@aol.com; Linda Rankin, Publisher, rankin@msnews.com. **Subscription Rates:** $25 individuals; $35 Canada and Mexico; $100 other countries (air mail). **Remarks:** Accepts advertising.
Ad Rates: BW: $392 **Circ:** (Not Reported)
4C: $859

ARLINGTON HEIGHTS, pop. 71,100.

Cook Co. (NE). 23 m NW of Chicago. Residential. Manufactures marking systems, folding doors, kitchen cabinets, machine metal parts, ornamental iron, patterns, minted coins, plateware, playground equipment, concrete products, precision castings, sewer pipe, silos, swim pools, textiles, tools and dies.

8136 Arbor Age
Adams/Green Publishing
2101 S. Arlington Hts., Road, Ste. 150 Phone: (847)427-9512
Fax: (847)427-2006
Arlington Heights, IL 60005
Magazine covering the tree care industry. **Founded:** 1981. **Freq:** Monthly. **Print Method:** Offset. **Trim Size:** 8 x 10 3/4. **Cols./Page:** 3. **Key Personnel:** Mark Adams, President; Colleen Murphy, Publisher; Nancy Sappington, Editor, nsappington@mail.aip.com. **ISSN:** 0279-0106. **Subscription Rates:** $40 individuals; Free to qualified subscribers. **Remarks:** Accepts advertising. **URL:** http://www.arborage.com.
Ad Rates: BW: $2,480 **Circ:** Paid 120
4C: $3,280 18,469

8137 Arlington Heights Post
Pioneer Press Newspapers
291 N. Dunton Ave. Phone: (847)797-5100
Arlington Heights, IL 60004 Fax: (847)797-5151

Community newspaper. **Founded:** Apr. 4, 1996. **Freq:** Weekly (Thurs.). **Key Personnel:** Paul Sassone, Managing Editor; Robert Loerzel, Editor. **Subscription Rates:** $18.95 individuals. **Remarks:** Accepts advertising. **Available Online. URL:** http://www.pioneerlocal.com.
Circ: Thurs. ★6,908

8138 AS/400 Systems Management
Adams Business Media
2101 South Arlington Heights Rd., Ste. 150 Phone: (847)427-9512
Fax: (847)427-2006
Arlington Heights, IL 60005
Publication E-mail: 73222.3344@compuserve.com

Management-oriented magazine for DP/MIS managers with an IBM AS/400 on site. **Subtitle:** Strategic Information for Managers of IBM Midrange Computers. **Founded:** 1973. **Freq:** Monthly. **Print Method:** Offset. **Trim Size:** 8 x 10 3/4. **Cols./Page:** 3. **Col. Width:** 26 nonpareils. **Col. Depth:** 140 agate lines. **Key Personnel:** Gary Moffat, Publisher; Mayu Mishina, Assoc. Editor, phone (847)427-2021, mmishina@mail.aip.com; Wayne Rhodes, Editor, phone (847)427-2026, wrhodes@mail.aip.com; Sue Garrison, Managing Editor, fax (847)247-2027, sgarrison@mail.a.p.com. **ISSN:** 1055-7768. **Subscription Rates:** $42 individuals. **Remarks:** Accepts advertising. **URL:** http://www.hotlink400.com. **Formerly:** Systems 3X/400.
Ad Rates: BW: $3,750 **Circ:** Controlled ‡45,000
4C: $4,795
PCI: $125

8139 Bear Report
Royal Publications Co., Inc.
PO Box 4205 Phone: (847)934-6363
Arlington Heights, IL 60006
Publication E-mail: bearviewpt@aol.com

Sports magazine for Chicago Bears and N.F.L. **Founded:** 1975. **Freq:** 26/year. **Print Method:** Offset. **Trim Size:** 11 3/8 x 15. **Cols./Page:** 4. **Col. Width:** 14 nonpareils. **Col. Depth:** 14 inches. **Key Personnel:** Larry Mayer, Managing Editor, lbearwritr@aol.com; John Weishar, Publisher. **ISSN:** 1056-4284. **Subscription Rates:** $34.95; $2 single issue. **Remarks:** Accepts advertising. **URL:** http://www.bear-rpt.com.
Circ: Paid ⊕17,500
Non-paid ⊕2,000

Buffalo Grove Countryside - See Buffalo Grove

8140 Daily Herald
Paddock Publications
PO Box 280 Phone: (847)427-4300
Arlington Heights, IL 60006 Fax: (847)427-1301

General newspaper. **Founded:** 1872. **Freq:** Mon.-Sun. (morn.). **Print Method:** Offset. **Trim Size:** 13 1/2 x 22. **Cols./Page:** 6. **Col. Width:** 26 nonpareils. **Col. Depth:** 294 agate lines. **Key Personnel:** Douglas Ray, Vice President; John Lampinen, Managing Editor; David Beery, Editorial Page Editor; Jim Slusher, Editor; Pamela DeFiglio, Writer; Colin O'Donnell, Metro Editor; Tom Quinlan, Sports Editor; Madeleine Doubek, Political Editor; Diane Dungey, Projects Editor; James Kane, Business Editor; Don Thompson, State Gov't Writer; Richard Klicki, News Editor; Theresa Schmedding, Asst. News Editor; Colleen Thomas, Metro News Editor; Jim Harvey, Copy Editor-Neighbor; Tom Jachimiec, Features Copy Desk Chief; Jeff Nordlund, National Editor; Jean Rudolph, Editor; Eileen Brown, Assistant Feature Editor; Ernie Schweit, Assistant Features Editor; Mike Seeling, Dir. of Photography; Dave Tonge, Chief Photographer; Bob Frisk, Editor; Don Friske, Editor; Marty Stengle, Prep Sports Coordinator; Scot Gregor, Sports Columnist; Mike Imrem, Sports Columnist; Bob Logan, Sports Columnist; Tim Sassone, Sports Columnist; Bob Finch, Sr. Graphics Editor; Dick Westgard, Editorial Artist; Mary Tomasello, Librarian; Jim Walsh, Vice President; Aaron Gabriel, Asst. Sports Editor; Ginny Lee Herrimann, Asst. City Editor; Carla Kemp, Asst. City Editor; Jim Davis, Editor; Aaron Gabriel, Asst. Sports Editor; Ginny Lee Herrmann, Asst. City Editor; Carla Kemp, Asst. City Editor; Scott Orton, Neighbor Editor; Robert Smith, Asst. City Editor; Scott Sanders, Asst. Dir. of Photography. **Subscription Rates:** $182 individuals. **URL:** http://www.dailyherald.com.
Ad Rates: GLR: $2.75 **Circ:** Mon.-Sat. 139,576
BW: $6,449 Sun. 136,391
4C: $7,109
SAU: $38.40
PCI: $38.50

Elk Grove Times - See Elk Grove Village

8141 Golf Course Turf & Irrigation
Adams/Green Publishing
2101 S. Arlington Hts., Road, Ste. 150 Phone: (847)427-9512
Fax: (847)427-2006
Arlington Heights, IL 60005
Trade magazine covering golf course management. **Founded:** 1992. **Freq:** Bimonthly. **Print Method:** Web offset. **Trim Size:** 8 x 10 3/4. **Cols./Page:** 3. **Key Personnel:** Mark Adams, President; Colleen Murphy, Publisher; Jerry Roche, Editor, jroche@mail.aip.com. **ISSN:** 1092-9649. **Subscription Rates:** $40 individuals; Free to qualified subscribers. **Remarks:** Accepts advertising. **URL:** http://www.golfcourseirrigation.com. **Former name:** Golf Course Irrigation.
Ad Rates: BW: $2,205 **Circ:** (Not Reported)
4C: $2,955

Hoffman Estates Review - See Hoffman Estates

8142 Irrigation Journal
Adams/Green Publishing
2101 S. Arlington Hts., Road, Ste. 150 Phone: (847)427-9512
Fax: (847)427-2006
Arlington Heights, IL 60005
Magazine about agricultural irrigation. **Founded:** 1951. **Freq:** 10/year. **Print Method:** Offset. **Trim Size:** 8 x 10 3/4. **Cols./Page:** 3. **Key Personnel:** Mark Adams, President; Colleen Murphy, Publisher; Jerry Roche, Editor, jroche@mail.aip.com. **ISSN:** 0047-1518. **Subscription Rates:** $40 individuals; Free to qualified subscribers. **Remarks:** Accepts advertising. **Available Online. URL:** http://www.irrigationjournal.com.
Ad Rates: BW: $2,290 **Circ:** Controlled ‡16,500
4C: $3,090

8143 Journal of the History of Dentistry
American Academy of the History of Dentistry
100 S. Vail Ave. Phone: (847)670-7561
Arlington Heights, IL 60005-1866
Trade journal covering the history of dentistry. **Founded:** 1952. **Freq:** 3/year. **Cols./Page:** 2. **Key Personnel:** Dr. H. T. Loevy, Editor; Aletha Kowitz, Circulation Mgr. **ISSN:** 0007-5132. **Subscription Rates:** $45 individuals; $15 single issue. **Remarks:** Accepts advertising. **Former name:** Bulletin of the History of Dentistry.
Circ: Paid 750

8144 Journal of Occupational and Environmental Medicine
Lippincott Williams & Wilkins
1114 N. Arlington Heights Rd. Phone: (847)818-1800
Arlington Heights, IL 60004
Occupational and environmental medicine journal. **Founded:** 1959. **Freq:** Monthly. **Print Method:** Web offset. **Trim Size:** 8 1/8 x 10 7/8. **Cols./Page:** 3. **Col. Width:** 30 nonpareils. **Col. Depth:** 133 agate lines. **Key Personnel:** Paul W. Brandt-Rauf, M.D., Editor; Elizabeth Popper, M.A., Managing Editor; Gary Walchli, Advertising Dir.; Marianne Dreger, M.A., Director of Publications, mdreger@acoem.org. **ISSN:** 0096-1736. **Subscription Rates:** $171 individuals; $221 institutions; $25 single issue; $226 other countries; $276 institutions, other countries; $25 single issue other countries. **Remarks:** Accepts advertising. **URL:** http://www.acoem.org. **Formerly**: Journal of Occupational Medicine.
Ad Rates: BW: $1,165 **Circ:** Paid 9,318
4C: $2,180 Non-paid 170

8145 Landscape Design
Adams/Green Publishing
2101 S. Arlington Hts., Road, Ste. 150 Phone: (847)427-9512 Fax: (847)427-2006
Arlington Heights, IL 60005
Magazine for licensed landscape architects. **Founded:** 1988. **Freq:** Quarterly. **Print Method:** Sheet-fed offset. **Trim Size:** 8 x 10 3/4. **Cols./Page:** 3. **Key Personnel:** Colleen Heraty, Editor, phone (847)427-2032, fax (847)427-2006, cheraty@mail.aip.com; Colleen Murphy, Publisher, cmurphy@mail.aip.com; Mark Adams, President, madams@mail.aip.com. **ISSN:** 1070-3853. **Subscription Rates:** Free to qualified subscribers. **Remarks:** Advertising accepted; rates available upon request. **Available Online. URL:** http://www.greenindustrynet.com.
Circ: ‡38,000

8146 Landscape & Irrigation
Adams/Green Publishing
2101 S. Arlington Hts., Road, Ste. 150 Phone: (847)427-9512 Fax: (847)427-2006
Arlington Heights, IL 60005
Magazine for the landscape and irrigation contracting industry. **Founded:** 1977. **Freq:** Monthly. **Print Method:** Offset. **Trim Size:** 8 x 10 3/4. **Cols./Page:** 3. **Key Personnel:** Mark Adams, President; Colleen Murphy, Publisher; Jerry Roche, Editor, jroche@mail.aip.com. **ISSN:** 0745-3795. **Subscription Rates:** Free to qualified subscribers; $40 individuals. **Remarks:** Accepts advertising. **Available Online. URL:** http://www.landscapeirrigation.com.
Ad Rates: BW: $4,050 **Circ:** Paid 63
4C: $4,900 Controlled 37,979

8147 Motor Service
Adams Business Media
2101 South Arlington Heights Rd., Ste. 150 Phone: (847)427-9512 Fax: (847)427-2006
Arlington Heights, IL 60005
Publication E-mail: autonet@mail.aip.com

Magazine for auto repair shops. **Subtitle:** The Journal for Professional Automotive Repair. **Founded:** 1921. **Freq:** Monthly. **Print Method:** Offset. **Trim Size:** 8 x 10 3/4. **Cols./Page:** 3 and 2. **Col. Width:** 26 and 40 nonpareils. **Col. Depth:** 140 agate lines. **Key Personnel:** Eric Schroder, Editor-in-Chief, phone (847)427-2089, fax (847)427-2006, eschroder@mail.aip.com; James Gillespie, Publisher, phone (847)427-2098, fax (847)427-2006, jgillespie@mail.aip.com; Gillian Babicz, Managing Editor, phone (847)427-2046, fax (847)427-2006, gbabicz@mail.aip.com. **ISSN:** 0027-1977. **Subscription Rates:** $38 individuals. **Remarks:** Accepts advertising. **URL:** http://www.autotruck.net.
Ad Rates: BW: $11,237 **Circ:** Controlled ‡175,000
4C: $14,612

8148 Outdoor Power Equipment
Adams/Green Publishing
2101 S. Arlington Hts., Road, Ste. 150 Phone: (847)427-9512 Fax: (847)427-2006
Arlington Heights, IL 60005
Publication E-mail: dirmktg@chilton.net

Outdoor power equipment magazine. **Founded:** 1959. **Freq:** Monthly. **Print Method:** Offset. **Trim Size:** 6 x 9. **Cols./Page:** 2. **Col. Width:** 28 nonpareils. **Col. Depth:** 114 agate lines. **Key Personnel:** Rick Carter, Managing Editor; Jan Brenny, Senior editor. **ISSN:** 0192-7558. **Subscription Rates:** Free to qualified subscribers; $16. $3 single issue. **Remarks:** Accepts advertising. **URL:** http://www.aip.com.
Ad Rates: BW: $1,400 **Circ:** Paid 1,089
4C: $2,090 Controlled 16,930

Palatine Countryside - See Palatine

8149 Recreation Resources
Adams Business Media
2101 South Arlington Heights Rd., Ste. 150 Phone: (847)427-9512 Fax: (847)427-2006
Arlington Heights, IL 60005
Tabloid for managers of parks, resorts, schools, and clubs. **Subtitle:** New Products, Services & Ideas for Planning Tomorrow's Facilities. **Founded:** Sept. 1981. **Freq:** 9/year. **Print Method:** Offset. **Trim Size:** 11 1/8 x 16. **Cols./Page:** 3. **Col. Width:** 20 picas. **Col. Depth:** 15 1/2 inches. **Key Personnel:** Miriam Wuensch, Associate Publisher, phone (847)427-2019, mwuensch@mail.aip.com; Sue Garrison, Managing Editor, phone (847)427-2027, fax (847)427-2079, sgarrison@mail.aip.com. **ISSN:** 0227-707X. **Subscription Rates:** Free to qualified subscribers; $24. $3 single issue. **URL:** http://www.aip.com. **Formerly**: Recreation, Sports & Leisure.
Ad Rates: BW: $7,330 **Circ:** Controlled 51,100
4C: $8,550

Rolling Meadows Review - See Rolling Meadows

Schaumburg Review - See Schaumburg

8150 Sportsturf
Adams/Green Publishing
2101 S. Arlington Hts., Road, Ste. 150 Phone: (847)427-9512 Fax: (847)427-2006
Arlington Heights, IL 60005
Magazine tracking the care of golf and athletic turf. **Founded:** Aug. 1985. **Freq:** Monthly. **Print Method:** Offset. **Trim Size:** 8 x 10 3/4. **Cols./Page:** 3. **Key Personnel:** Jim Williams, Editor, jwilliamsmainel.aip.com; Colleen Murphy, Publisher; Mark Adams, President. **ISSN:** 1061-687X. **Subscription Rates:** Free to qualified subscribers; $40 individuals. **Remarks:** Accepts advertising. **Available Online. URL:** http://www.sportsurfonline.com.
Ad Rates: BW: $2,770 **Circ:** Paid 157
4C: $3,620 Controlled 19,288

8151 The Standard
Baptist General Conference
2002 S. Arlington Heights Rd. Phone: (847)228-0200
Arlington Heights, IL 60005 Fax: (847)228-5376
Free: (800)323-4215

News magazine. **Subtitle:** The Newsmagazine of the Baptist General Conference. **Founded:** 1911. **Freq:** 10/year. **Print Method:** Offset. **Trim Size:** 8 1/4 x 11. **Cols./Page:** 3. **Col. Width:** 27 nonpareils. **Col. Depth:** 133 agate lines. **Key Personnel:** Gary Marsh, Director of Publishing, gmbgcstd@aol.com; Jodi Hanning, Managing Editor. **ISSN:** 0038-9382. **Subscription Rates:** $15.75 individuals. **Remarks:** Accepts advertising.
Ad Rates: GLR: $3.50 **Circ:** Paid 11,000
BW: $490 Non-paid 1,000
PCI: $25

Wheeling Countryside - See Wheeling

8152 WCBR-FM - 92.7
120 W. University Dr. Phone: (847)255-5800
Arlington Heights, IL 60004-1892 Fax: (847)255-0129

Format: Talk; Alternative/New Music/Progressive; Sports. **Founded:** 1960. **Operating Hours:** Continuous. **Key Personnel:** Darrel L. Peters, President; Alaine Peters, Station Mgr. **Wattage:** 3000.

ARTHUR

8153 Arthur Graphic Clarion
PO Box 19 Phone: (217)543-2151
Arthur, IL 61911 Fax: (217)543-2152

Newspaper of the Illinois Amish country. **Founded:** Nov. 5, 1905. **Freq:** Weekly (Thurs.). **Print Method:** Offset. **Cols./Page:** 8. **Col. Width:** 10.5 picas. **Col. Depth:** 21.5 picas. **Key Personnel:** Allen Mann, Editor and Publisher; Lowell Cutsinger, Publisher; Lila Hogan, Editor. **USPS:** 032-960. **Subscription Rates:** $19 individuals; $22 out of area.
Ad Rates: GLR: $.40 **Circ:** ‡3,100
BW: $378.50
SAU: $5.20
PCI: $2.75

ASHTON, pop. 1,140.

Lee Co. (N) 35 m S of Rockford. Cement vaults; ice cream stabilizers manufactured. Diversified farming.

8154 The Ashton Gazette
PO Box 287 Phone: (815)453-2551
Ashton, IL 61006 Fax: (815)453-2551

Community newspaper (tabloid). **Founded:** 1895. **Freq:** Weekly (Thurs.). **Print Method:** Offset. **Cols./Page:** 4. **Col. Width:** 14 picas. **Col. Depth:** 16 inches. **Key Personnel:** John Koski, Editor and Publisher. **Subscription Rates:** $15 individuals; $18 out of area. **Remarks:** Accepts advertising.
Ad Rates: BW: $212 **Circ:** Paid ‡900
4C: $272 Free ‡10
SAU: $3.90
PCI: $2.65

ASSUMPTION, pop. 1,283.

Christian Co. (C). 23 m SW of Decatur. Grain elevators. Grain farms. Corn, wheat, soybeans.

8155 Golden Prairie News
301 S. Chestnut Phone: (217)226-3721
Assumption, IL 62510 Fax: (217)226-3579

Community newspaper. **Founded:** 1884. **Freq:** Weekly (Thurs.). **Print Method:** Offset. **Cols./Page:** 6. **Col. Width:** 12 picas. **Col. Depth:** 21 inches. **Key Personnel:** Willard Raymond, Editor and Publisher. **Subscription Rates:** $20 individuals; $20 out of state.
Ad Rates: GLR: $.15 **Circ:** ‡2,200
BW: $400
SAU: $3
PCI: $3

ATWOOD, pop. 1,464.

Piatt Co. (EC). 25 m E of Decatur. Creamery. Diversified farming. Soybeans, corn, wheat.

8156 Atwood Herald
Tri-Village Publications
107 N. Main St. Phone: (217)578-3213
PO Box 589 Fax: (217)578-2833
Atwood, IL 61913
Newspaper. **Founded:** 1887. **Freq:** Weekly (Thurs.). **Print Method:** Offset. **Cols./Page:** 4. **Col. Width:** 29 nonpareils. **Col. Depth:** 210 agate lines. **Key Personnel:** Don Weaver, Publisher. **Subscription Rates:** $3 individuals. **Remarks:** Accepts advertising.
Ad Rates: BW: $160 **Circ:** ‡1,150
SAU: $4.41

AUBURN, pop. 3,616.

Sangamon Co. (C). 13 m SW of Springfield. Grain, dairy, stock, poultry farms. Corn, wheat, oats, soybeans.

8157 Auburn Citizen
110 N. 5th St. Phone: (217)438-6155
Auburn, IL 62615 Fax: (217)438-6156

Newspaper. **Founded:** Apr. 30, 1874. **Freq:** Weekly (Thurs.). **Print Method:** Offset. **Cols./Page:** 7. **Col. Width:** 24 nonpareils. **Col. Depth:** 301 agate lines. **Key Personnel:** Joseph Michelich, Jr., Editor and Publisher; Connie Michelich, Advertising Mgr. **Subscription Rates:** $20 individuals. **Remarks:** Accepts advertising.
Ad Rates: SAU: $3.50 **Circ:** ‡1,600
PCI: $3.00

8158 Chatham Clarion
South County Publications
110 N. 5th St. Phone: (217)483-2614
Auburn, IL 62615 Fax: (217)438-6155

Community newspaper. **Founded:** 1962. **Freq:** Weekly (Thurs.). **Print Method:** Offset. **Cols./Page:** 7. **Col. Width:** 24 nonpareils. **Col. Depth:** 301 agate lines. **Key Personnel:** Joseph Michelich, Jr., Editor and Publisher; Connie Michelich, Advertising Mgr. **Subscription Rates:** $20 individuals.
Ad Rates: SAU: $3.50 **Circ:** 1,850
PCI: $2.75

Divernon News - See Divernon

8159 Pawnee Post
South County Publications
110 N. 5th St. Phone: (217)483-2614
Auburn, IL 62615 Fax: (217)438-6155

Community newspaper. **Founded:** 1965. **Freq:** Weekly (Thurs.). **Print Method:** Offset. **Cols./Page:** 7. **Col. Width:** 25 nonpareils. **Col. Depth:** 301 agate lines. **Key Personnel:** Joseph Michelich, Jr., Editor; Connie Michelich, Advertising Mgr. **Subscription Rates:** $20 individuals.
Ad Rates: SAU: $3.50 **Circ:** ‡800
PCI: $2.75

AUGUSTA, pop. 764.

Hancock Co. (W). 42 m NE of Quincy. Coal mines. Stock, grain farms.

8160 The Augusta Eagle
Augusta Eagle
Box 257 Phone: (217)392-2715
Augusta, IL 62311
Newspaper. **Founded:** Oct. 30, 1884. **Freq:** Weekly (Wed.). **Print Method:** Offset. **Cols./Page:** 6. **Subscription Rates:** $15 individuals; $18 out of state. **Remarks:** Accepts advertising.
Ad Rates: PCI: $1.60 **Circ:** Paid ‡1,161

AURORA, pop. 81,293.

Kane Co. (NE). 38 m W of Chicago. Aurora University. Waubonsee. Community College. Illinois Mathematics and Science Academy. Sand, gravel pits. Manufactures rubber, plastics, furniture, paper and paper products, fabricated metal products, clothing, glass, chemicals, transportation equipment, farm and machinery, aluminum products.

8161 Advances in Wound Care
Spring House
434 W Downer Pl. Free: (800)950-0879
Aurora, IL 60506
Medical Journal. **Subtitle:** The Journal of Skin Ulcers. **Founded:** 1988. **Freq:** Quarterly. **Trim Size:** 8 x 10 7/8. **Cols./Page:** 3. **ISSN:** 0898-1655. **Subscription Rates:** $18. **Remarks:** Accepts advertising.
Ad Rates: BW: $760 **Circ:** Paid ‡4,500
4C: $1,455 Non-paid ‡2,000

8162 Aurora Borealis
Aurora University
347 S. Gladstone Ave. Phone: (630)844-7867
Aurora, IL 60506-4877 Fax: (630)844-5463

Campus newspaper. **Subtitle:** The Student Newspaper of Aurora University. **Founded:** 1934. **Freq:** Semimonthly (during academic year). **Print Method:** Web offset. **Trim Size:** 11 1/2 x 17. **Cols./Page:** 5. **Key Personnel:** Joye Granstrom, Editor; Liz Castillo,Business Manager. **Subscription Rates:** Free; $25 (mail). **Remarks:** Accepts advertising. **Formerly:** The Borealis.
Ad Rates: BW: $125 **Circ:** Free ‡2,000
4C: $725
PCI: $9

8163 The Beacon-News
Copley Newspapers/Fox Valley Press
101 S. River St.
Aurora, IL 60506

General newspaper. **Founded:** 1846. **Freq:** Mon.-Sun. (morn.). **Print Method:** Offset. **Trim Size:** 22 3/4 x 13 3/4. **Cols./Page:** 6. **Col. Width:** 17 nonpareils. **Col. Depth:** 21 1/2 inches. **Key Personnel:** Peggy Kirby, General Mgr., phone (630)844-5969, fax (630)844-5863; Mike Chapin, Managing Editor, phone (630)844-5881, fax (630)844-1043, mike.chapin@exchange.copleypress.com. **USPS:** 037-800. **Subscription Rates:** $156 individuals. **Remarks:** Accepts advertising. **URL:** http://www.copleynewspapers.com.
Circ: Mon.-Sat. ★30,182
Sun. ★32,757

8164 Nursing Management
Spring House
434 W Downer Pl. Free: (800)950-0879
Aurora, IL 60506
Magazine focusing on nursing management. **Founded:** 1970. **Freq:** Monthly. **Print Method:** Offset. **Trim Size:** 8 1/2 x 11. **Cols./Page:** 3. **Col. Width:** 26 nonpareils. **Col. Depth:** 134 agate lines. **Key Personnel:** Leah Curtin, Editor; John H. Harling, Publisher. **Subscription Rates:** $25 individuals. **Remarks:** Accepts advertising.
Ad Rates: GLR: $18 **Circ:** Paid 109,492
BW: $4,125 Controlled 19,337
4C: $5,500
PCI: $216

8165 WBIG-AM - 1280
620 Eola Rd. Phone: (630)851-5200
Aurora, IL 60504 Fax: (630)851-5286

Format: News; Talk. **Networks:** Mutual Broadcasting System; Westwood One Radio. **Owner:** Midwest Broadcasting of Chicago, at above address. **Founded:** 1938. **Formerly:** WMRO-AM (1992); WYSY-AM. **Operating Hours:** Continuous. **ADI:** Chicago (LaSalle), IL. **Key Personnel:** Steve Marten, General Mgr.; Kevin Scott, Production Dir.; Ron Newman, News Dir.; Bradley D. Bohler, Operations Mgr. **Wattage:** 1000. **Ad Rates:** Advertising accepted; rates available upon request.

8166 WKKD-AM - 1580
1884 Plain Ave. Phone: (708)898-1580
Aurora, IL 60505 Fax: (708)898-2463

Format: News; Sports; Classic Rock. **Networks:** USA Radio. **Owner:** Salter Broadcasting Company, PO Box C-1730, Aurora, IL 60507, (708)898-6668, Fax: (708)898-2463. **Founded:** 1961. **Operating Hours:** Continuous. **ADI:** Chicago (LaSalle), IL. **Key Personnel:** William H. Baker, Sports Dir.; Jeff Blanton, News Dir.; Bob Coyne, Interactive Sales; Annette Leck, General Mgr.; Claudia Biesterfield, Business Mgr.; Chuck Ingle, Chief Engineer. **Wattage:** 250. **Ad Rates:** $36 for 30 seconds; $42 for 60 seconds. $36 for 30 seconds; $39 for 60 seconds. Combined advertising rates available with WKKD-FM.

8167 WKKD-FM - 95.9
1884 Plain Ave. Phone: (708)898-1580
Aurora, IL 60505 Fax: (708)898-2463

Format: Oldies. **Networks:** USA Radio. **Owner:** Salter Broadcasting, PO Box C-1730, Aurora, IL 60507, (708)898-6668, Fax: (708)898-2463. **Founded:** 1960. **Operating Hours:** Continuous; 10% network, 90% local. **ADI:** Chicago (LaSalle), IL. **Key Personnel:** Bob Coyne, Interactive Sales; William H. Baker, Sports Dir.; Jeff Blanton, News Dir.; Chuck Ingle, Chief Engineer; Claudia Biesterfield, Office Mgr.; Dave Beckman, Contact; Rosa Saltijeral, Contact; Annette Leck, General Mgr. **Wattage:** 3000. **Ad Rates:** $36 for 30 seconds; $42 for 60 seconds. $36 for 30 seconds; $39 for 60 seconds. Combined advertising rates available with WKKD-AM.

AVA

Jackson Co. (SW). 5 m S of Campbell Hill.

8168 WXAN-FM - 103.9
9077 Ava Rd. Phone: (618)426-3308
Ava, IL 62907 Fax: (618)426-3310
E-mail: wxan@egyptian.net

Format: Gospel. **Networks:** USA Radio; Illinois News; Tribune Radio. **Owner:** Harold L. Lawder, 14081 Hwy. 149, Murphysboro, IL 62966, (618)684-4208. **Founded:** 1982. **Operating Hours:** Continuous; 30% network, 70% local. **Key Personnel:** Doug Apple, Contact; Ted Cunningham, Sports Dir. **Wattage:** 6000. **Ad Rates:** $7 for 30 seconds; $10 for 60 seconds.

AVON

8169 Avon Sentinel
Eagle Publications
107 S. Main Phone: (309)465-0020
PO Box 259 Fax: (309)462-3221
Avon, IL 61415
Free: (800)500-1961
Publisher E-mail: eaglepub@macomb.com

Community newspaper. **Founded:** 1879. **Freq:** Weekly (Thurs.). **Print Method:** Offset. **Cols./Page:** 6. **Col. Width:** 20 nonpareils. **Col. Depth:** 224 agate lines. **Key Personnel:** Kathleen Myers, Managing Editor; Tom Hutson, Publisher. **Subscription Rates:** $17 individuals; $19 out of area; $22 out of state; $.40 single issue. **Remarks:** Accepts advertising.
Ad Rates: BW: $201.60 **Circ:** Paid ‡950
4C: $541.60 Free ‡100
SAU: $3.10
CNU: $4
PCI: $2

BANNOCKBURN

8170 Pro Football Weekly
2525 Wauxegan Rd., Ste. 270 Phone: (847)940-1100
Bannockburn, IL 60015 Fax: (847)940-1108
Free: (800)331-7529

Tabloid newspaper on professional football. **Founded:** 1967. **Freq:** Weekly. **Print Method:** Offset. **Trim Size:** 10 x 13. **Cols./Page:** 4. **Col. Width:** 2 1/4 inches. **Col. Depth:** 12 3/4 inches. **Key Personnel:** Ron Pollack, Editor; Hub Arkush, Publisher; Gregg Mihallik, Business Mgr., greggm@pfwa.com. **ISSN:** 0032-9053. **Subscription Rates:** $79.95 individuals for 32 issues. **Remarks:** Accepts advertising.
Ad Rates: BW: $1,750 **Circ:** Paid ‡55,000
4C: $2,500 Non-paid ‡342
PCI: $95

BARRINGTON, pop. 9,029.

Lake Co. (NE). 12 m NE of Elgin. Sand, gravel pits. Coffee and tea packing; dresses, pressure canners and cookers, castings, machine tools, aircraft cameras and controls, electronic equipment, weather instruments manufactured. Mink, poultry, grain farms.

Algonquin Countryside - See Algonquin

8171 Barrington Courier-Review
Pioneer Press Newspapers
200 James St. Phone: (847)381-9200
Barrington, IL 60010 Fax: (847)381-5840

Community newspaper (tabloid). **Founded:** 1889. **Freq:** Weekly (Thurs.). **Print Method:** Offset. **Cols./Page:** 5. **Col. Width:** 13 3/5 picas. **Col. Depth:** 196 agate lines. **Key Personnel:** Paul Sassone, Managing Editor; Andy Robeznieks, Editor. **Subscription Rates:** $24.95 individuals; out of county. **URL:** http://www.pioneerlocal.com.
Circ: Thurs. ★7,674

Cary-Grove Countryside - See Cary

Lake Zurich Courier - See Lake Zurich

8172 Maintenance Technology
Applied Technolgy Publications
1300 S. Grove Ave., Ste. 205 Phone: (847)382-8100
Barrington, IL 60010 Fax: (847)304-8603
Publication E-mail: mainttech@aol.com

Magazine containing technical and business information for managers, engineers, and technicians responsible for facility upkeep. **Founded:** Jan. 1988. **Freq:** Monthly. **Print Method:** Web. **Trim Size:** 8 x 10 3/4. **Cols./Page:** 3. **Col. Width:** 27 nonpareils. **Col. Depth:** 140 agate lines. **Key Personnel:** Robert C. Baldwin, Editor; Art Rice, Publisher. **ISSN:** 0899-5729. **Subscription Rates:** Free to qualified subscribers; $95 individuals; $165 out of country. **Remarks:** Accepts advertising.
Ad Rates: BW: $5,470 **Circ:** Controlled 52,000
4C: $6,720
PCI: $150

BARRY, pop. 1,487.

Pike Co. (W). 18 m E of Hannibal, Mo. Glove factory. Agriculture. Livestock, corn, soybeans, wheat, apples.

8173 The Paper
725 Bainbridge St. Phone: (217)335-2112
Barry, IL 62312 Fax: (217)335-2112

Community newspaper. **Founded:** 1966. **Freq:** Weekly (Wed.). **Print Method:** Offset. **Trim Size:** 10 1/2 x 15 1/2. **Cols./Page:** 5. **Col. Width:** 1 3/4 inches. **Col. Depth:** 15 1/2 inches. **Key Personnel:** Debra J. Harshman, Editor and Publisher. **Subscription Rates:** $12 individuals; $18 out of state. **Remarks:** Accepts advertising.
Ad Rates: SAU: $3.20 **Circ:** ‡2,000

BARTLETT

8174 Bartlett Examiner
Examiner Publications
4N781 Gerber Rd. Phone: (630)830-4145
Bartlett, IL 60103
Publisher E-mail: staff@examinerpublications.com

Local newspaper. **Founded:** 1978. **Freq:** Weekly (Wed.). **Print Method:** Web offset. **Trim Size:** 11 x 17. **Cols./Page:** 4. **Col. Width:** 28 nonpareils. **Col. Depth:** 224 agate lines. **Key Personnel:** Randall E. Petrik, Editor and Publisher; Steve Eckelberry, Managing Editor. **USPS:** 625-680. **Subscription Rates:** $24. **Remarks:** Accepts advertising.
Ad Rates: BW: $448 **Circ:** 10,000
4C: $1008
SAU: $45

Hanover Park Examiner - See Hanover Park

BARTONVILLE, pop. 6,110.

Peoria Co. (NWC). 5 m SW of Peoria. Residential.

8175 Limestone Independent News
114 Roosevelt Phone: (309)697-1851
Bartonville, IL 61607
Newspaper. **Founded:** Dec. 1967. **Freq:** Weekly (Wed.). **Print Method:** Offset. **Cols./Page:** 5. **Col. Width:** 12 picas. **Col. Depth:** 118 agate lines. **Key Personnel:** Pat Johnson, Editor and Publisher; Barb Widener, Managing Editor. **USPS:** 082-330. **Subscription Rates:** $20 individuals. **Remarks:** Accepts advertising.
Ad Rates: GLR: $.59 **Circ:** Paid 2,300
BW: $375 Free 200
PCI: $5

BATAVIA, pop. 12,574.

Kane Co. (NE) 40 m W of Chicago. Manufactures cosmetics, toilet preparations, electric switches, automatic controlles. Accelerator laboratory for atom smasher.

8176 FloraCulture International Magazine
Ball Publishing
335 N. River St. Phone: (630)208-9080
Batavia, IL 60510 Fax: (630)208-9350

Trade magazine for professional growers of flowering plants worldwide. **Founded:** Nov. 1990. **Freq:** Monthly. **Print Method:** Offset. **Trim Size:** 8 1/8 x 10 7/8. **Cols./Page:** 3. **Col. Width:** 27 nonpareils. **Col. Depth:** 140 agate lines. **Key Personnel:** Charlie Olentine, Jr., Publisher, phone (815)734-4171, fax (815)734-4201; Ms. Mindy Laff, Editor, mlaff@growertalks.com; Diane Blazek, U.S. Sales, growertalks@aol.com; Dave Konsoer, Taiwanese Sales, growertalks@aol.com; Cynthia Stevens-Glawe, Central American Sales, growertalks@aol.com; Marta Pinzano de Marquez, South American Sales, phone (57)1 6218108, fax (57)1 6170730, hortitec@openway.com.co; Philip Staal, Isreali Sales, phone (972)6-6 270381, fax (972)6-6 270382, staal@sisanit.co.il. **ISSN:** 1051-9076. **Subscription Rates:** $22 U.S. and Canada; $4 single issue; $48 other countries. **Remarks:** Accepts advertising. **URL:** http://www.growertalks.com.
Ad Rates: GLR: $15 **Circ:** Combined 11,750
BW: $2,785
4C: $3,685
PCI: $90

8177 Green Profit Magazine
Ball Publishing
335 N. River St. Phone: (630)208-9080
Batavia, IL 60510 Fax: (630)208-9350

Trade magazine for flower and plant retailers. **Founded:** July 1997. **Freq:** Bimonthly. **Print Method:** Offset. **Trim Size:** 8 1/8 x 10 7/8. **Cols./Page:** 3. **Col. Width:** 27 nonpareils. **Col. Depth:** 140 agate lines. **Key Personnel:** Joli Shaw, Editor, shaw@growertalks.com; Diane Blazek, Assoc. Publisher, blazek@growtalks.com; Dave Konsoer, Advertising, konsoer@groweralks.com; Georgette Demos, Advertising, gdemos@growertalks.com. **ISSN:** 1094-0650. **Subscription Rates:** Free to qualified subscribers. **Remarks:** Accepts advertising. **URL:** http://www.greenprofit.com.
Ad Rates: GLR: $5.50 **Circ:** Non-paid 22,000
BW: $2,471
4C: $3,423
PCI: $92

BEARDSTOWN

8178 Star Gazette Extra
1210 Wall St. Phone: (217)323-1010
Beardstown, IL 62618 Fax: (217)323-5402
Publisher E-mail: stargaz@cityscape.net

Shopper. **Founded:** 1969. **Freq:** Weekly (Mon.). **Print Method:** Offset. **Cols./Page:** 8. **Col. Width:** 1 1/2 inches. **Col. Depth:** 21 inches. **Key Personnel:** William Mitchell, Publisher; Sally Lael, Editor. **Remarks:** Accepts advertising. **Formerly:** The Star Shopper.
Ad Rates: BW: $1,073.52 **Circ:** Free ‡8,700
4C: $1,333.52
SAU: $10.92
PCI: $7.75

BEECHER

Will Co. (NE). 20 m S of Chicago Heights.

8179 Beecher Herald
Russell Publications
PO Box 429 Phone: (708)258-3473
Peotone, IL 60468 Fax: (708)258-6295

Community newspaper. **Freq:** Weekly (Wed.). **Cols./Page:** 5. **Col. Width:** 2 inches. **Col. Depth:** 16 inches. **Key Personnel:** Gilbert L. Russell, Publisher; Gilbert L. Russell, Publisher. **Subscription Rates:** $16. **Remarks:** Accepts advertising.
Ad Rates: BW: $236 **Circ:** 1,700
PCI: $2.95

BEECHER CITY, pop. 492.

Effingham Co. (S). 50 m S of Decatur. Oil wells. Grain, dairy, hog, poultry farms. Corn, wheat, oats, alfalfa, beans.

8180 Beecher City Journal
PO Box 38 Phone: (618)487-5634
Beecher City, IL 62414
Community newspaper. **Founded:** 1915. **Freq:** Weekly (Mon.). **Print Method:** Offset. **Cols./Page:** 5. **Col. Width:** 11 picas. **Col. Depth:** 16 inches. **Key Personnel:** P.J. Ryan, Editor and Publisher. **USPS:** 047-900. **Subscription Rates:** $17 individuals; $20 out of area; $22 out of state.
Ad Rates: BW: $280 **Circ:** 1,600
SAU: $3.50
PCI: $3.50

BELLEVILLE†, pop. 45,200.

St Clair Co. (SW). 15 m SE of St Louis. Scott Air Force Base. Manufactures stoves, shoes, dresses, tacks, patterns, and dies, boilers, industrial furnaces, castings, drinking fountains, beer, stencil machines, bricks, concrete blocks, chemicals, shingle and brick tile, cutting and mining machinery, enameled ware, leather products, corrugated paper boxes, batteries, cryogenic equipment. Coal.

8181 Belleville News-Democrat
Knight-Ridder, Inc.
PO Box 427 Phone: (618)234-1000
120 S. Illinois St. Fax: (618)234-9597
Belleville, IL 62222-0427
Free: (800)642-3878

General newspaper. **Founded:** 1855. **Freq:** Mon.-Sun. (morn.). **Print Method:** Offset. **Cols./Page:** 6. **Col. Width:** 2 1/16 inches. **Col. Depth:** 21 1/2 inches. **Key Personnel:** Gary Berkley, Pres./Publisher, phone (618)239-2100; Greg Edwards, VP/Editor, phone (618)239-2551; Frank Duke, VP/Dir. of Mktg., phone (618)239-2103; Randy Atkisson, VP/CFO, phone (618)239-2552; Jay Tebbe, Circulation Mgr., phone (618)239-2521; David Baur, Advertising Dir., phone (618)239-2541; Tim Vizer, Chief Photographer, phone (618)239-2470. **Subscription Rates:** $169 individuals. **Remarks:** Accepts advertising. **Feature Editors:** Lori Browning, *Editorials*, phone (618)239-2472; Maureen Houston, *Sunday*, phone (618)239-2641; Joe Ostermeier, *Sports*, phone (618)239-2516.
Ad Rates: BW: $4,193.79 **Circ:** Mon.-Sat. ★**51,920**
4C: $4,743.79 Sun. ★**62,279**
PCI: $32.51

8182 County Journal
Suburban Journal
219 N. Illinois Phone: (618)277-7000
Belleville, IL 62220-1316 Fax: (618)277-7018

Newspaper. **Founded:** 1967. **Freq:** Weekly (Wed.). **Print Method:** Offset. **Cols./Page:** 6. **Col. Width:** 25 nonpareils. **Col. Depth:** 308 agate lines. **Key Personnel:** Mike Gothberg, Editor; Gene Gebhart, Publisher; Dave Krieger, Advertising Mgr. **Remarks:** Accepts advertising.
Ad Rates: SAU: $6.95 **Circ:** Free ‡11,915

8183 Fairview Heights/O'Fallon Journal
Suburban Journal
219 N. Illinois Phone: (618)277-7000
Belleville, IL 62220-1316 Fax: (618)277-7018

Newspaper. **Freq:** Weekly (Wed.). **Print Method:** Offset. **Cols./Page:** 6. **Col. Width:** 252 nonpareils. **Col. Depth:** 308 agate lines. **Key Personnel:** Mike Gothberg, Editor; Gene Gebhart, Publisher. **Remarks:** Accepts advertising.
Ad Rates: SAU: $9.75 **Circ:** Free ‡7,318

8184 Continental Cablevision
4336 E. Rt. 161 Phone: (618)566-2218
Belleville, IL 62221 Fax: (618)566-4624

Key Personnel: Audrey Simmons, Contact. **Cities Served:** subscribing households 7,423; 42 channels; 1 community access channel.

BELVIDERE†, pop. 14,500.

Boone Co. (N). 14 m E of Rockford. Manufactures plastic foam, silk screening, tools and dies, men's work clothes, wire products, rubber products, milk and milk products, beauty supplies, chemicals, tools boxes, paper, paper food containers. Automobile assembly. Canned and frozen food plants. Grain elevator. Grain, dairy farms. Hogs.

8185 Belvidere Daily Republican
401 Whitney Blvd. Phone: (815)544-9811
Belvidere, IL 61008 Fax: (815)544-6334
Publication E-mail: bdrnews1@aol.com

General newspaper. **Founded:** 1894. **Freq:** Mon.-Sat. (eve.). **Print Method:** Offset. **Trim Size:** 14 x 22 3/4. **Cols./Page:** 6. **Col. Width:** 2 1/16 inches. **Col. Depth:** 21 inches. **Key Personnel:** Nancy S. Mattison, Publisher; Patrick Mattison, Pres./Associate Publisher.
Ad Rates: SAU: $8.20 **Circ:** (Not Reported)

8186 Boone County Shopper, Inc.
Boone County Shopper Inc.
112 Leonard Ct. Phone: (815)544-2166
Belvidere, IL 61008 Fax: (815)544-5558

Shopper. **Founded:** 1947. **Freq:** Weekly (Thurs.). **Print Method:** Offset. **Cols./Page:** 6. **Col. Width:** 24 nonpareils. **Col. Depth:** 210 agate lines. **Key Personnel:** William H. Branom, Publisher, fax (815)547-4587. **Subscription Rates:** Free. **Remarks:** Accepts advertising. **URL:** http://www.boonecountyshopper.com.
Ad Rates: GLR: $.66 **Circ:** Paid ‡63
BW: $831.60 Free ‡15,793

BENTON†, pop. 7,693.

Franklin Co. (S). 8 m N of West Frankfort. Coal mine industry. Manufactures boats, boat trailers, rubber, mining equipment, hose, brass.

8187 News
Benton Evening News Co.
111 E. Church Phone: (618)438-5611
Benton, IL 62812-2238 Fax: (618)435-2413

General newspaper. **Founded:** 1921. **Freq:** Mon.-Sat. (eve.). **Print Method:** Offset. **Cols./Page:** 6. **Col. Width:** 24 nonpareils. **Col. Depth:** 301 agate lines. **Key Personnel:** Joe R. Browning, Editor and Publisher. **Subscription Rates:** $21 individuals. **Remarks:** Accepts advertising.
Ad Rates: PCI: $5.68 **Circ:** (Not Reported)

8188 WQRL-FM - 106.3
303 North Main St. Phone: (618)435-8100
PO Box 818 Fax: (618)435-8102
Benton, IL 62812
Free: (800)439-1063

Format: Oldies. **Networks:** Westwood One Radio. **Founded:** 1973. **Formerly:** WQRX-FM. **Operating Hours:** Continuous. **ADI:** Peoria-Bloomington, IL. **Key Personnel:** Dana Withers, President/General Manager; Alan Stockman, Sales Mgr.; Nancy Kayes, Program/PSD. **Local Programs:** *Sports*, Jim Muir. **Wattage:** 12,500. **Ad Rates:** $9.85 for 30 seconds.

BERKELEY

8189 WJJG-AM - 1530
5629 St. Charles Rd., No. 208 Phone: (708)493-1530
Berkeley, IL 60163

Format: Talk. **Networks:** Standard Broadcast News. **Owner:** Joseph J. Gentile, at above address. **Founded:** 1974. **Formerly:** WKDC-AM (1994). **Operating Hours:** Sunrise-sunset; 75% network 25% local. **ADI:** Chicago (LaSalle), IL. **Key Personnel:** Shane Ruff, General/Office/Gen. Sales Mgr.; Mike Baker, Program Dir.; Skip Kubicki, News/Public Service Dir. **Local Programs:** *Bob Cannella Show*, Bob Cannella, General Mgr. **Wattage:** 760. **Ad Rates:** $25 for 30 seconds; $35 for 60 seconds.

BERWYN, pop. 46,849.

Cook Co. (NE). 10 m SW of Chicago. Residential. Small business retail center.

8190 Cicero-Berwyn-Stickney Life
Life Newspapers
2601 S. Harlem Ave. Phone: (708)484-1234
Berwyn, IL 60402 Fax: (708)484-3348
Publication E-mail: bercic@life.mhs.compuserve.com

Community newspaper. **Founded:** 1927. **Freq:** 3/week. **Print Method:** Offset. **Trim Size:** 13 1/8 x 21 1/4. **Cols./Page:** 6. **Col. Width:** 2 inches. **Col. Depth:** 21 1/2 inches. **Key Personnel:** Robert Lifka, Editor, phone (708)795-9212, rdl@life.mhs.compuserve; Jack R. Kubik, Publisher, phone (708)795-9211; Dave Kuehl, Advertising Dir., phone (708)368-8845, fax (630)368-1188. **Subscription Rates:** $31.50 individuals. **Remarks:** Accepts advertising.
Ad Rates: BW: $2,492.28 **Circ:** Paid ❑**14,614**
4C: $2,892.28 Free ❑**3,899**
PCI: $19.32

BLANDINSVILLE

8191 Blandinsville Star Gazette
PO Box 79 Phone: (309)776-3700
Blandinsville, IL 61420
Publisher E-mail: coelho@netins.net

Community newspaper. **Freq:** Weekly (Mon.). **Print Method:** Web. **Cols./Page:** 5. **Col. Width:** 2 1/8 inches. **Col. Depth:** 13 inches. **Key Personnel:** Stacey Nicholas, Editor. **Subscription Rates:** $13.50 in McDonough County; $16 elsewhere. **Remarks:** Accepts advertising.
Ad Rates: GLR: $3 **Circ:** ‡300
BW: $195
PCI: $2

BLOOMINGTON†, pop. 44,189.

McLean Co. (C). 42 m SE of Peoria. Adjoins Normal. Illinois Wesleyan University. Illinois State Univ. Manufactures electric control switches, farm machinery, vacuum cleaners, air conditioning and ventilating equipment, feeds, electronic equipment, insulations, machine parts, candy, paper and dairy products, railroad equipment, institutional furniture, tires. Food processing plant.

8192 Accent on Living
Cheever Publishing, Inc.
PO Box 700 Phone: (309)378-2961
Bloomington, IL 61702 Fax: (309)378-4420
Free: (800)787-8444
Publication E-mail: acntlung.com.aol
Publisher E-mail: cheeverpub@aol.com

Magazine for people with physical disabilities, their families, and the professional and lay persons working with disabled people. Features motivational articles that emphasize success stories of handicapped people and contains new inventions and ideas for making daily living easier. **Founded:** 1956. **Freq:** Quarterly. **Print Method:** Offset. **Trim Size:** 5 x 7. **Cols./Page:** 2. **Col. Width:** 24 nonpareils. **Col. Depth:** 87 agate lines. **Key Personnel:** Betty Garee, Editor; Raymond C. Cheever, Publisher; Nancy Kiel, Advertising Mgr.; Julie Cheever-Starshak, Marketing Manager. **ISSN:** 0001-4508. **Subscription Rates:** $12 individuals annual subscription; $3.50 individuals. **Alt. Formats:** Microform. **Formerly**: Polio Living.
Ad Rates: GLR: $14.42 **Circ:** Paid ‡19,000
BW: $1,141.09 Controlled ‡300
4C: $1,825.71
PCI: $174.16

8193 Civil RICO Litigation Reporter
Andrews Publications
2702 Binghamton Ln. Phone: (309)827-4777
Bloomington, IL 61704 Fax: (309)828-1849
Publication E-mail: editor@andrewspub.com

National journal recording state and federal litigation under the Racketeer Influenced and Corrupt Organizations Act. **Founded:** Sept. 1984. **Freq:** Monthly. **Print Method:** Mimeograph. **Trim Size:** 8 1/2 x 11. **Cols./Page:** 1. **Col. Width:** 100 nonpareils. **Col. Depth:** 154 agate lines. **Key Personnel:** Gerry Matics, Editor, gmatics@aol.com; John E. Backe, Publisher. **ISSN:** 0887-7874. **Subscription Rates:** $800 individuals; $480 six months. **Remarks:** Accepts advertising. **Available Online**. **Formerly**: Racketeering Litigation Reporter (Mar. 1987).
Circ: (Not Reported)

8194 Clockwatch Review
Clockwatch Review Press
Dept. of English Phone: (309)556-3352
Illinois Wesleyan University Fax: (309)556-3411
Bloomington, IL 61702
Literary journal covering fine arts. **Subtitle:** (a journal of the arts). **Founded:** 1983. **Freq:** Annual. **Print Method:** Web offset. **Key Personnel:** James Plath, Editor, jplath@titan.iwu.edu; Zarwa Mullan Plath, Editor. **ISSN:** 0749-9311. **URL:** http://www.titan.iwu.edu/~jplath/clockwatch.html.
Circ: Combined 1,200

8195 FarmWeek
Illinois Agricultural Association
1701 Towanda Ave. Phone: (309)557-3140
Bloomington, IL 61701 Fax: (800)998-6090
Publication E-mail: lagoltz@aol.com

Agricultural publication (tabloid) for Illinois farmers. **Founded:** June 10, 1974. **Freq:** Weekly (Mon.). **Print Method:** Offset. **Trim Size:** 11 1/4 x 15 3/4. **Cols./Page:** 5. **Col. Width:** 11 picas. **Col. Depth:** 15 inches. **Key Personnel:** Dave McClelland, Editor, phone (309)557-3156, fax (800)640-1995; Richard Verdery, Advertising Mgr., rverdery@ilfb.org. **ISSN:** 0197-6680. **Subscription Rates:** Free with membership; $75 nonmembers. **Remarks:** Accepts advertising.
Ad Rates: GLR: $2.71 **Circ:** Paid ★**80,608**
BW: $1,950
4C: $2,300
PCI: $26

8196 The Historical Messenger
Historical Society, Illinois Great Rivers Conference, United Methodist Church
Box 515 Phone: (309)828-5092
Bloomington, IL 61702-0515 Fax: (309)829-4820

Religious and historical publication. **Founded:** 1968. **Freq:** Quarterly. **Print Method:** Offset. **Cols./Page:** 3. **Col. Width:** 14 picas. **Col. Depth:** 60 picas. **Key Personnel:** Vera Swantner, Editor. **Subscription Rates:** $10 individuals. **Remarks:** Advertising not accepted.
Circ: Paid ‡290
Non-paid ‡140

8197 The Pantagraph
Chronicle Publishing Co.
301 W. Washington St. Phone: (309)829-9411
Bloomington, IL 61701-3803 Fax: (309)829-9104
Free: (800)647-7323

General newspaper. **Founded:** 1837. **Freq:** Mon.-Sun. (morn.). **Print Method:** Offset. **Trim Size:** 13 3/4 x 22 5/8. **Cols./Page:** 6. **Col. Width:** 24 nonpareils. **Col. Depth:** 298 agate lines. **Key Personnel:** John R. Goldrick, Publisher. **Subscription Rates:** $127.40 individuals. **Remarks:** Accepts advertising. **Online:** DataTimes Corporation. **URL:** http://www.pantagraph.com. **Feature Editors:** Byran Bloodworth, *Sports*; Dan Craft, *Entertainment, Movie, Radio*; Stephan Gleason, *Book, Drama, Family, Fashion, Features, Garden/Home, Lifestyle, Music, Real Estate, Society, Sunday, Travel, Women's*; Nancy Gordon, *Food*; Karen Hansen, *Education*; James Keeran, *TV*; Mark Lewis, *Saturday*; Kathy McKinney, *Financial/Business*; Mark Pickering, *Metro, News, Religion*; David Proeber, *Photo*; Lenore Sobota, *Editorials*; Don Thompson, *Political*.
Ad Rates: BW: $1.93 **Circ:** Mon.-Sat. ★**49,618**
4C: $3,483 Sun. ★**53,679**
SAU: $27

8198 Partners
Illinois Farm Bureau
1701 Towanda Ave. Phone: (309)557-2238
Bloomington, IL 61701 Free: (800)640-1995
Publication E-mail: lagoltz@aol.com
Publisher E-mail: lgoltz@ilfb.org

Publication for members of the Illinois Farm Bureau Assoc. **Founded:** 1982. **Freq:** Quarterly. **Print Method:** Offset. **Trim Size:** 11 x 16. **Cols./Page:** 4. **Col. Width:** 14 1/2 inches. **Col. Depth:** 15 inches. **Key Personnel:** Dave McClelland, Editor, fweditor@ilfb.org. **ISSN:** 0725-5386. **Remarks:** Accepts advertising. **Formerly**: Illinois Farm Bureau Almanac.
Ad Rates: BW: $2,850 **Circ:** Paid 287,683
Non-paid 609

8199 The Twin City Community News
202 N. Center St. Phone: (309)827-8555
PO Box 1625 Fax: (309)829-6926
Bloomington, IL 61702
Weekly community newspaper. **Founded:** 1976. **Freq:** Weekly (Wed.). **Print Method:** Offset. **Cols./Page:** 5. **Col. Width:** 22 nonpareils. **Col. Depth:** 210 agate lines. **Key Personnel:** Gail Gaboda, Editorial and Creative Mgr.; J.C. Brown, General Mgr./Publisher. **Subscription Rates:** Free. **Remarks:** Accepts advertising. **Formerly**: McLean County Community News.
Ad Rates: GLR: $7.50 **Circ:** Free 30,000
BW: $1,105
PCI: $12.95

8200 WBNQ-FM - 101.5
PO Box 8 Phone: (309)829-1221
236 Greenwood Ave. Fax: (309)827-8071
Bloomington, IL 61702

Format: Adult Contemporary. **Networks:** Independent. **Founded:** 1947. **Operating Hours:** Continuous. **ADI:** Peoria-Bloomington, IL. **Key Personnel:** Richard Johnson, General Mgr.; Timothy O. Ives, Station Mgr., toives@wbnq.com. **Wattage:** 50,000. **Ad Rates:** $29-52 for 30 seconds; $33-65 for 60 seconds. **URL:** http://www.wbnq.com.

8201 WBWN-FM - 104.1
236 Greenwood Ave. Phone: (309)829-1221
Bloomington, IL 61704 Fax: (309)662-8598
Free: (800)552-0104
E-mail: wbwn@wbwn.com

Format: Hot Country. **Owner:** Twin Cities Radio, PO Box 8, Bloomington, IL 61702. **Founded:** 1990. **Formerly**: WMLA-FM (1991); WRXZ-FM. **Operating Hours:** Continuous. **ADI:** Peoria-Bloomington, IL. **Key Personnel:** Richard Johnson, General Mgr.; Dan Westhoff, Program Dir., danw@wbwn.com; Kevin Bessler, News Dir., kevinb@wbwn.com. **Wattage:** 25,000. **Ad Rates:** $50-75 per unit. **URL:** http://www.wbwn.com.

8202 WIHN-FM - 96.7
PO Box 610 Phone: (309)888-4496
Bloomington, IL 61702-0610 Fax: (309)452-9677

Format: Oldies. **Founded:** 1973. **Operating Hours:** Continuous. **ADI:** Peoria-Bloomington, IL. **Key Personnel:** Ed Neaves, General Mgr.; Pat Walston, Program Dir.; Christine Knight, Sales Mgr.; John Sparx, Promotions Dir.; Greg Sutter, Production Dir. **Wattage:** 6000. **Ad Rates:** $27 for 30 seconds; $30 for 60 seconds.

8203 WJBC-AM - 1230
PO Box 8 Phone: (309)829-1221
Bloomington, IL 61702-0008 Fax: (309)827-8071

Format: Full Service. **Networks:** ABC. **Owner:** Bloomington Broadcasting Corp., at above address. **Founded:** 1925. **Operating Hours:** Continuous. **ADI:** Peoria-Bloomington, IL. **Key Personnel:** Richard Johnson, General Mgr.; Wm. Pitcher, Station Mgr.; Duane Moss, News Dir.; James Cutler, Sales Mgr. **Local Programs:** *Don Munson Morning Show*, Don Munson, Mailing contact; *Ken Behrens Show*, Ken Behrens, Mailing contact; *Problems & Solutions*, Wm. Pitcher, Mailing contact. **Wattage:** 1000. **Ad Rates:** $15-75 for 30 seconds; $10-120 for 60 seconds.

8204 WYZZ-TV - 43
2714 E. Lincoln Phone: (309)662-4373
Bloomington, IL 61704 Fax: (309)663-6943

Format: Commercial TV. **Networks:** Fox; Independent. **Owner:** Bloomington Comco, Inc., at above address. **Founded:** 1982. **ADI:** Peoria-Bloomington, IL. **Key Personnel:** Mike Lennon, General Mgr.; Larry Halcomb, Contact; William Rogala, Contact. **Ad Rates:** Advertising accepted; rates available upon request.

BLUE ISLAND, pop. 21,855.

Cook Co. (NE). On Cal Sag Canal, 16 m S of Chicago. Manufactures brick, tile, steel specialty products, lumber, boiler compound, wire goods, barrels. Diversified farming.

8205 Aslip/Crestwood/Blue Island Star
Star Newspapers
6901 W 159th St. Phone: (708)802-8800
Tinley Park, IL 60477 Fax: (708)802-8899

Newspaper group serving 51 communities in Chicago's southern suburbs. **Founded:** 1890. **Freq:** Semiweekly (Thurs. and Sun.). **Print Method:** Offset. **Trim Size:** 13 3/4 x 23. **Cols./Page:** 6. **Col. Width:** 2 inches. **Col. Depth:** 21 1/2 inches. **Key Personnel:** Lester Sons, Editor; Norman Rosinski, Publisher; Jim Meidell, Advertising Mgr.; Jay Frederickson. **Remarks:** Accepts advertising.
Ad Rates: GLR: $56.76 **Circ:** Thurs. 64,637
Sun. 68,267

BLUE MOUND, pop. 1,338.

Macon Co. (C). 13 m. S.W. of Decatur.

8206 Blue Mound Leader
PO Box 318 Phone: (217)692-2323
Blue Mound, IL 62513-0318 Fax: (217)692-2323

Community newspaper. **Founded:** 1886. **Freq:** Weekly (Thurs.). **Print Method:** Web offset. **Trim Size:** 9 3/4 x 16. **Cols./Page:** 5. **Col. Width:** 11 picas. **Col. Depth:** 15 inches. **Key Personnel:** Cynthia L. Stuart, Editor and Publisher. **USPS:** 869-980. **Subscription Rates:** $10 individuals; $11.50 out of area; $13.50 out of state.
Ad Rates: SAU: $4.25 **Circ:** Paid 850
PCI: $2 Free 50

BLUFFS, pop. 821.

Scott Co. (W). 12 m N of Glasgow. Residential.

8207 Bluffs Times
Da'Laine Publishing
PO Box 320 Phone: (217)754-3369
Bluffs, IL 62621-0320 Fax: (217)754-3369

Local newspaper. **Founded:** 1889. **Freq:** Weekly (Wed.). **Print Method:** Offset. **Cols./Page:** 8. **Col. Width:** 16 inches. **Col. Depth:** 294 agate lines. **Key Personnel:** Dallas M. Warrum, Publisher. **Subscription Rates:** $22 individuals in county; $26 out of county. **Remarks:** Accepts advertising.
Ad Rates: GLR: $.28 **Circ:** ‡2,850
BW: $168
PCI: $3

8208 Meredosia Budget
Da'Laine Publishing
PO Box 320 Phone: (217)754-3369
Bluffs, IL 62621-0320 Fax: (217)754-3369

Local newspaper. **Founded:** 1905. **Freq:** Weekly (Wed.). **Print Method:** Offset. **Cols./Page:** 8. **Col. Width:** 16 inches. **Col. Depth:** 294 agate lines. **Key Personnel:** Dallas M. Warrum, Publisher. **Subscription Rates:** $22 individuals in county; $26 out of county. **Remarks:** Accepts advertising.
Ad Rates: GLR: $.28 **Circ:** ‡1,000
BW: $168
PCI: $3.40

8209 Triopia Tribune
Da'Laine Publishing
PO Box 320 Phone: (217)754-3369
Bluffs, IL 62621-0320 Fax: (217)754-3369

Local newspaper. **Founded:** 1982. **Freq:** Weekly (Wed.).

Print Method: Offset. **Cols./Page:** 8. **Col. Width:** 16 inches. **Col. Depth:** 294 agate lines. **Key Personnel:** Dallas M. Warrum, Publisher. **Subscription Rates:** $22 individuals; $26 out of area. **Remarks:** Accepts advertising.
Ad Rates: BW: $168 **Circ:** ‡1,000
PCI: $3.40

BOLINGBROOK

8210 Bolingbrook Metropolitan
Press Publication
223 Main St. Phone: (630)739-2300
Lemont, IL 60439 Fax: (630)257-5640

Community newspaper. **Founded:** June 1973. **Freq:** Weekly (Thurs.). **Cols./Page:** 4. **Col. Width:** 14 1/2 picas. **Col. Depth:** 16 inches. **Key Personnel:** Peggy Drey, Editor; Robert Norfleet, Publisher. **Subscription Rates:** $8 individuals.
Ad Rates: PCI: $10 **Circ:** 6,700

BOODY, pop. 350.

Macon Co. (C) 10 m S of Decatur. Residential.

8211 Full Cry
Gault Publications, Inc.
Box 10 Phone: (217)865-2332
Boody, IL 62514 Fax: (217)865-2334
Publication E-mail: fullcry@compuserve.com; heavytruck.com

Consumer magazine for trail and tree hound enthusiasts. **Founded:** Feb. 1939. **Freq:** Monthly. **Print Method:** Offset. **Trim Size:** 8 1/4 x 10 7/8. **Cols./Page:** 3. **Col. Width:** 28 nonpareils. **Col. Depth:** 10 inches. **Key Personnel:** Seth R. Gault, Editor. **ISSN:** 0016-2620. **Subscription Rates:** $20 individuals; $28 other countries; $1.95 single issue. **Remarks:** Color advertising not accepted.
Ad Rates: BW: $250 **Circ:** Paid ★**19,000**
PCI: $15

BOURBONNAIS, pop. 13,025.

Kankakee Co. (E). 50 m S.W. of Chicago.

8212 The Herald/Country Market
B & B Publishing Co.
500 Brown Blvd. Phone: (815)933-1131
Bourbonnais, IL 60914 Fax: (815)933-3785
Publication E-mail: theherald@keynet.net

Newspaper. **Founded:** May 8, 1975. **Freq:** Weekly (Tues.). **Print Method:** Offset. **Trim Size:** 10 x 16. **Cols./Page:** 5. **Col. Width:** 22 nonpareils. **Col. Depth:** 224 agate lines. **Key Personnel:** Toby Olszewski, Editor and Publisher; Jonathan Olszewski, General Mgr. **USPS:** 111-210. **Subscription Rates:** $22 individuals; $25 out of area. **Remarks:** Accepts advertising.
Ad Rates: 4C: $350 **Circ:** Paid ‡5,100
SAU: $11.67 Free ‡26,000
PCI: $10.58

BREESE, pop. 3,516.

Clinton Co. (SW) 38 m E of St. Louis, Mo. Agricultural center. Storage buildings, industry. Dairy, grain farms.

8213 Breese Journal
8060 Old Hwy. 50 Phone: (618)526-7211
PO Box 405 Fax: (618)526-2590
Breese, IL 62230
Newspaper. **Founded:** 1921. **Freq:** Weekly (Thurs.). **Print Method:** Offset. **Trim Size:** 15 1/4 x 21 1/2. **Cols./Page:** 7. **Col. Width:** 15 1/4 inches. **Col. Depth:** 21 1/2 inches. **Key Personnel:** Dave Mahlandt, Editor and Publisher. **USPS:** 063-780. **Subscription Rates:** $17.50 individuals; $21 out of area.
Ad Rates: GLR: $.17 **Circ:** 6,141
BW: $869
4C: $1,170
SAU: $5.90
PCI: $5.90

BRIGHTON, pop. 4,500.

Macoupin Co. (SW). 10 m N of Alton. Agricultural, coal mining.

8214 The Southwestern Journal
Bunker Hill Publications
PO Box 606 Phone: (618)372-8451
Brighton, IL 62012 Fax: (618)372-8451

Local newspaper serving Brighton, Shipman, Piasa, and Medora. **Founded:** Nov. 1971. **Freq:** Weekly. **Print Method:** Offset. **Trim Size:** 11 1/2 x 17. **Cols./Page:** 5. **Col. Width:** 2 1/16 inches. **Col. Depth:** 16 1/2 inches. **Key Personnel:** John Galer, Editor and Publisher; Julie Kramer, Advertising Mgr. **Subscription Rates:** $8.50 individuals; $10.50 out of area; $12.50 out of state.
Ad Rates: GLR: $0.40 **Circ:** 1,550
PCI: $3.90

8215 Southwestern Shoppers Guide
Bunker Hill Publications
PO Box 606 Phone: (618)372-8451
Brighton, IL 62012 Fax: (618)372-8451

Shopper. **Freq:** Weekly (Tues.). **Print Method:** Offset. **Key Personnel:** John Galer, Publisher; Donna Funk, Editor.
Circ: Free ‡3,579

BROUGHTON

8216 WCIL-FM - 101.5
PO Box 370 Phone: (618)985-4843
Broughton, IL 62817 Fax: (618)985-6529

Format: Contemporary Hit Radio (CHR). **Owner:** Zimmer Radio Group, Southern Illinois, at above address. **Founded:** 1968. **Operating Hours:** Continuous. **ADI:** Paducah,KY-Cape Girardeau,MO-Marion,IL. **Key Personnel:** Bruce Welker, General Mgr., bwelker@mvp.net; Steve Falat, Sales Mgr.; Chad Elliot, Program Dir., chad@mychoice.net; Joey Helleny, Engineer; Roz Whitlock, News Dir.; Wanda Evans, Sales Mgr.; Dave Wisnewski, Sales Dir. **Wattage:** 50,000 ERP. **Ad Rates:** $23-35 for 30 seconds; $28-38 for 60 seconds.

BUFFALO GROVE, pop. 27,060.

Lake Co. 25 m NW of Chicago.

8217 Buffalo Grove Countryside
Pioneer Press Newspapers
291 N. Dunton Ave. Phone: (847)797-5100
Arlington Heights, IL 60004 Fax: (847)797-5151

Newspaper covering Buffalo Grove, Wheeling, and North Arlington Heights in northwest Cook County. **Founded:** 1968. **Freq:** Weekly (Thurs.). **Print Method:** Offset. **Cols./Page:** 4. **Col. Width:** 28 nonpareils. **Col. Depth:** 184 agate lines. **Key Personnel:** Paul Sassone, Managing Editor; David Kirkpatrick, Editor. **Subscription Rates:** $14 individuals. **Formerly:** Countryside Reminder News.
Circ: Thurs. ★**5,624**

BUNKER HILL, pop. 1,700.

Macoupin Co. (SWC). 20 m NE of Alton. Small Industry. Farm service elevators.

8218 The Bunker Hill Gazette-News
Bunker Hill Publications
PO Box Z Phone: (618)585-4411
Bunker Hill, IL 62014 Fax: (618)585-3354

Community newspaper. **Founded:** 1866. **Freq:** Weekly (Thurs.). **Print Method:** Offset. **Cols./Page:** 5. **Col. Width:** 12 picas. **Col. Depth:** 16 1/2 inches. **Key Personnel:** John Galer, Publisher; Evelyn Pickerill, Advertising Mgr. **Subscription Rates:** $10.50 individuals; $12.50 state; $14.50 out of state. **Remarks:** Accepts advertising.
Ad Rates: GLR: $.40 **Circ:** ‡1,580
PCI: $2.80

BUSHNELL, pop. 3,800.

McDonough Co. (NE). 29 m S of Galesburg. Agricultural, stockyards, nurseries; manufactures garden tools.

8219 The McDonough Democrat
Spoon River Press
358 E. Main St. Phone: (309)772-2129
PO Box 269 Fax: (309)772-3994
Bushnell, IL 61422
Community newspaper. **Founded:** 1884. **Freq:** Weekly (Wed.). **Print Method:** Web press. **Trim Size:** 16 1/2 x 20. **Cols./Page:** 8. **Col. Width:** 11 picas. **Col. Depth:** 21 inches. **Key Personnel:** William B. Lorton, Editor and Publisher; Jean Russell, Advertising Mgr. **Subscription Rates:** $17 individuals; $21.75 out of state. **Remarks:** Accepts advertising.
Ad Rates: GLR: $0.40 **Circ:** ‡2,500
BW: $630
SAU: $5
PCI: $3.75

CAHOKIA, pop. 18,904.

St. Clair Co. (SW) .22 m N.W. of Belleville.

8220 The Herald
Knight-Ridder
713 Range Ln. Phone: (618)337-7300
PO Box 1638 Fax: (618)332-1348
Cahokia, IL 62206
Community newspaper. **Founded:** 1932. **Freq:** Weekly (Wed.). **Print Method:** Offset. **Cols./Page:** 6. **Col. Width:** 30 nonpareils. **Col. Depth:** 301 agate lines. **Key Personnel:** Mark Schmersahl, General Mgr. **Subscription Rates:** Free; $45 institutions. **Remarks:** Accepts advertising.
Ad Rates: GLR: $.59 **Circ:** Paid ‡100
BW: $1,068.12 Free ‡12,500
4C: $1,618.12
PCI: $10.17

CAIRO†, pop. 5,931.

Alexander Co. (S). 6 m S of Mounds. Residential.

8221 Herald Citizen
711 Washington Ave. Phone: (618)734-4242
PO Box 33 Fax: (618)734-4244
Cairo, IL 62914-0033
Community newspaper. **Freq:** Weekly. **Print Method:** Offset. **Cols./Page:** 8. **Col. Width:** 18 nonpareils. **Col. Depth:** 301 agate lines. **Key Personnel:** Bill L. Calvin, Editor and Publisher; Leeann Bellamy, Advertising Mgr. **Subscription Rates:** $39 individuals.

8222 WKRO-AM - 1490
Rte. 1, US-51 Phone: (618)734-0884
Box 311 Fax: (618)734-0884
Cairo, IL 62914
Free: (800)800-9576

Format: Country. **Owner:** Roger Price, at above address, (618)734-1490. **Founded:** 1942. **Operating Hours:** Continuous; 7% network; 93% local. **Key Personnel:** R.J. Price, Program/Sports Dir.; Roger Price, Sales Mgr. **Wattage:** 1000. **Ad Rates:** $5.25-9.25 for 30 seconds; $6.50-10.75 for 60 seconds.

CALUMET CITY

8223 Burnham/Calumet City Star
Star Newspapers
6901 W 159th St. Phone: (708)802-8800
Tinley Park, IL 60477 Fax: (708)802-8899

Newspaper group serving 51 communities in Chicago's southern suburbs. **Founded:** 1890. **Freq:** Semiweekly (Thurs. and Sun.). **Print Method:** Offset. **Trim Size:** 13 3/4 x 23. **Cols./Page:** 6. **Col. Width:** 2 inches. **Col. Depth:** 21 1/2 inches. **Key Personnel:** Lester Sons, Editor; Norman Rosinski, Publisher; Jim Meidell, Advertising Mgr.; Jay Frederickson; Jay Frederickson.
Ad Rates: GLR: $56.76 **Circ:** Thurs. 64,637
Sun. 68,267

8224 Private Varnish
American Association of Private Railroad Car Owners
PO Box 1244 Phone: (708)891-2030
Calumet City, IL 60409-1244 Fax: (708)891-2030
Publication E-mail: pvarnish@trainride.com

Magazine covering history, technical information, and news on historic railroad passenger cars. **Subtitle:** The Magazine of Privately Owned Railroad Cars. **Founded:** 1976. **Freq:** Bimonthly. **Print Method:** Offset. **Trim Size:** 8 1/2 x 11. **Cols./Page:** 3. **Key Personnel:** John Kuehl, Editor; Fred Seibold, Advertising Mgr., seibold@trainride.com. **ISSN:** 1047-9473. **Subscription Rates:** $22 individuals; $4 single issue. **Remarks:** Accepts advertising.
Circ: Controlled 2,500

CAMBRIDGE†, pop. 2,217.

Henry Co. (NW). 30 m N.E. of Galesburg. Agriculture. Hogs, beef cattle.

8225 Chronicle
119 W. Exchange Phone: (309)937-3303
Cambridge, IL 61238 Fax: (309)944-6161
Free: (800)837-7963

Newspaper with a Report orientation. **Founded:** 1858. **Freq:** Weekly (Thurs.). **Print Method:** Offset. **Cols./Page:** 8. **Col. Width:** 22 nonpareils. **Col. Depth:** 294 agate lines. **Key Personnel:** Lisa Walters, Editor, editor@terrynews.com; Thomas Terry, Publisher, phone (309)944-2119, fax (309)944-6161; Linda Venable, Advertising Mgr., phone (309)944-2119, fax (309)944-6161. **Subscription Rates:** $36 individuals in state; $38 out of state. **Remarks:** Accepts advertising. **Online:** Geneseo Telephone Co. **URL:** http://www.terrynews.com.
Ad Rates: GLR: $.80 **Circ:** Paid ‡1,350
BW: $6.50
SAU: $11.20

CAMP POINT

8226 Camp Point Journal
Elliott Publishing, Inc.
202 E. State Phone: (217)593-6515
Camp Point, IL 62320 Fax: (217)593-7720

Local newspaper. **Founded:** 1876. **Freq:** Weekly (Tues.). **Print Method:** Offset. **Trim Size:** 17 1/2 x 22 1/2. **Cols./Page:** 9. **Col. Width:** 1 5/8 inches. **Col. Depth:** 21 inches. **Key Personnel:** Marcia Elliott, Editor; James Elliott, Publisher/ Production Mgr. **Subscription Rates:** $10 individuals; $12 out of area; $15 out of state. **Remarks:** Accepts advertising.
Ad Rates: GLR: $2.75 **Circ:** 800
BW: $378
SAU: $3.40

Enterprise - See Clayton

Mendon Dispatch-Times - See Mendon

New Era - See Golden

CANTON, pop. 14,626.

Fulton Co. (W). 31 m SW of Peoria. Overall and implement factories. Millwork. Coal mines. Clay pits. Diversified farming.

8227 The Daily Ledger
American Publishing Co.
53 W. Elm St. Phone: (309)647-5100
PO Box 540 Fax: (309)647-4665
Canton, IL 61520
General newspaper. **Founded:** 1849. **Freq:** Daily (eve.) and Sat. (morn.). **Print Method:** Offset. **Cols./Page:** 8. **Col. Width:** 22 nonpareils. **Col. Depth:** 301 agate lines. **Key Personnel:** Ross Gardiner, Editor; Scott Koon, Publisher. **Subscription Rates:** $78 individuals. **Remarks:** Accepts advertising.
Ad Rates: GLR: $1.40 **Circ:** ‡7,183
BW: $817
4C: $1,017
SAU: $6.36
PCI: $4.75

8228 WBYS-AM - 1560
1000 E. Linn St. Phone: (309)647-1560
Box 600 Fax: (309)647-1563
Canton, IL 61520
Free: (800)860-1560

Format: Full Service; Agricultural; Eclectic. **Simulcasts:** 6a.m.-10a.m. WBYS-FM. **Networks:** ABC; Tribune Radio; Illinois Public Radio. **Founded:** 1947. **Operating Hours:** Sunrise-sunset. **Key Personnel:** Kevin Stephenson, Station Mgr.; Leon Groover, Program Dir.; Deb Fowlks, News Dir.; Michelle Myers, Traffic Dir. **Wattage:** 250. **Ad Rates:** Combined advertising rates available with WBYS-FM.

8229 WBYS-FM - 107.9
1000 E. Linn St. Phone: (309)647-1560
Box 600 Fax: (309)674-1563
Canton, IL 61520
Free: (800)860-1560

Simulcasts: 6a.m.-10a.m. WBYS-AM. **Networks:** ABC; Tribune Radio; Illinois Public Radio. **Founded:** 1968. **Operating Hours:** 5:30 a.m.-midnight weekdays; 5:30-11 Saturday and Sunday. **Key Personnel:** Kevin Stephenson, Station Mgr.; Leon Groover, Program Dir.; Deb Fowlks, News Dir.; Natalie Orwig, Traffic Dir. **Wattage:** 7800. **Ad Rates:** Combined advertising rates available with WBYS-AM.

CARBONDALE, pop. 27,194.

Jackson Co. (SW). 50 m S of Centraila. Southern Illinois University. Manufactures ladies fashions, tape, wildlife materials. Coal mines. Nursery. Grain, fruit, truck, poultry farms.

8230 Alumnus
Southern Illinois University at Carbondale
Communications Bldg. Phone: (618)536-3311
PO Box 6887 Fax: (618)453-3248
Carbondale, IL 62901
University alumni magazine. **Founded:** 1940. **Freq:** Quarterly. **Print Method:** Offset. Uses mats. **Trim Size:** 8 1/2 x 10 3/4. **Cols./Page:** 3. **Col. Width:** 29 nonpareils. **Col. Depth:** 140 agate lines. **Key Personnel:** Laraine J. Wright, Editor. **ISSN:** 8750-3360. **Subscription Rates:** $20 individuals. **Remarks:** Advertising not accepted.
Circ: 105,000

8231 American Journal of Semiotics
Semiotic Society of America
Speech Communication Dept. Phone: (618)453-1894
Southern Illinois University Fax: (618)453-2812
Carbondale, IL 62901-6605
Journal on the nature and role of sign and code processes. **Founded:** 1981. **Freq:** Quarterly. **Print Method:** Offset. Uses mats. **Cols./Page:** 1. **Col. Width:** 84 nonpareils. **Col. Depth:** 138 agate lines. **Key Personnel:** Richard L. Lanigan, Editor, rlanigan@siu.edu; Linda Rogers, Executive Dir., irogers@kent.edu. **ISSN:** 0277-7126. **Subscription Rates:** Included in membership. **Remarks:** Accepts advertising. **URL:** http://www.sla.purdue.edu/semiotics/.
Ad Rates: BW: $200 **Circ:** ‡600

8232 Daily Egyptian
Southern Illinois University at Carbondale
Communications Bldg. Phone: (618)536-3311
PO Box 6887 Fax: (618)453-3248
Carbondale, IL 62901
Collegiate newspaper (tabloid). **Founded:** Oct. 1916. **Freq:** Daily (morn.) (during the academic year). **Print Method:** Offset. **Trim Size:** 11 x 17. **Cols./Page:** 5. **Col. Width:** 11.5 picas. **Col. Depth:** 16 inches. **Key Personnel:** Robert Jaross, General Mgr.; Lance Speere, Managing Editor. **Subscription Rates:** Free on campus; $55 individuals; $140 other countries. **Remarks:** Accepts advertising. **Available Online. URL:** http://www.dailyegyptian.com.
Ad Rates: BW: $740 **Circ:** Free ‡22,500
4C: $940
PCI: $9.25

8233 French Review
American Association of Teachers of French
Southern Illinois University Phone: (618)453-5731
Mailcode 4510 Fax: (618)453-5733
Carbondale, IL 62901-4510
Publication E-mail: fmajatf@uiuc.edu
Publisher E-mail: abrate@siu.edu

Magazine for French teachers. **Founded:** 1927. **Freq:** Irregular. **Print Method:** Letterpress. **Trim Size:** 6 x 9. **Cols./Page:** 1. **Col. Width:** 27 nonpareils. **Col. Depth:** 98 agate lines. **Key Personnel:** Christopher Pinet, Editor, phone (406)994-6444, fax (406)994-6199, umlcp@montana.edu. **ISSN:** 0016-111X. **Subscription Rates:** $35 individuals; $38 other countries. **Remarks:** Color advertising not accepted. **Alt. Formats:** Microfiche; Microfilm; Mailing labels.
Ad Rates: BW: $250 **Circ:** 12,000

8234 Law Library Journal
American Association of Law Libraries
Southern Illinois University Phone: (618)453-8788
Mail Code 6803 Fax: (618)453-8728
Carbondale, IL 62901-6803
Publisher E-mail: aallhq@aall.org

Legal and library science journal. **Founded:** 1908. **Freq:** Quarterly. **Print Method:** Offset. **Cols./Page:** 1. **Col. Width:** 30 nonpareils. **Col. Depth:** 112 agate lines. **Key Personnel:** Frank Houdek, Editor; Peter Beck, Business Mgr. **Subscription Rates:** $50 individuals. **Remarks:** Accepts advertising.
Ad Rates: BW: $400 **Circ:** ‡5,200

8235 Sacred Dance Guild Journal
Sacred Dance Guild
201 Hewitt Phone: (618)457-8603
Carbondale, IL 62901
Scholarly journal covering liturgical dance. **Founded:** 1958. **Freq:** Triennial. **ISSN:** 1043-5328. **Subscription Rates:** $8 individuals; $5 single issue. **Remarks:** Accepts advertising.
Ad Rates: BW: $100 **Circ:** (Not Reported)

8236 The Sociological Quarterly
Midwest Sociological Society
Dept. of Sociology
Southern Illinois University
Carbondale, IL 62901

Subtitle: Official Journal of the Midwest Sociological Society. **Founded:** 1960. **Freq:** Quarterly. **Print Method:** Offset. **Trim Size:** 6 7/8 x 10. **Key Personnel:** Norman Denzin, Editor. **ISSN:** 0038-0253. **Subscription Rates:** $60; $125 institutions. **Remarks:** Accepts advertising.
Ad Rates: BW: $300 **Circ:** ‡2,800

8237 Southern Illinoisan
710 N. Illinois Phone: (618)529-5454
Carbondale, IL 62901 Fax: (618)457-2935
Free: (800)228-0429
Publication E-mail: sietpress@aol.com

General newspaper. **Founded:** 1877. **Freq:** Mon.-Sun. (morn.). **Print Method:** Offset. **Cols./Page:** 6. **Col. Width:** 24 nonpareils. **Col. Depth:** 301 agate lines. **Key Personnel:** Carl Rexroad, Editor; Richard R. Johnston, Publisher. **Subscription Rates:** $115.96 individuals. **Remarks:** Accepts advertising.
Ad Rates: SAU: $16.52 **Circ:** Mon.-Sat. ★26,310
Sun. ★34,320

8238 WDBX-FM - 91.1
100 E. Jackson St. Phone: (618)529-5900
Carbondale, IL 62901

Format: Eclectic. **Networks:** Pacifica. **Owner:** Heterodyne Broadcasting Co., at above address. **Operating Hours:** 7:00 a.m.-2:00 a.m. Mon-Sun. **Key Personnel:** Brian R. Powell, Station Mgr.; Marc Poole, Marketing Dir.; Devin Miller, Program Coor.; Bill Woelbeling, Special Events Coor. **Local Programs:** *Back to Bluegrass*, Tom Connelly; *The Beat Blender*, Beth Tyron; *Here's to the Women*, Faye Anderson. **Wattage:** 700. **URL:** http://www.wdbx.org.

8239 WOOZ-FM - 99.9
1025 E. Main Phone: (618)549-3243
Carbondale, IL 62901 Fax: (618)549-2455
Free: (800)455-3243
E-mail: z100fm@midwest.com

Format: Hot Country. **Networks:** Unistar. **Owner:** Zimmer Communications, at above address. **Founded:** 1947. **Formerly:** WEBQ-FM (1990). **Operating Hours:** Continuous. **Key Personnel:** Jerry R. Zimmer, President; Bruce Welker, General Mgr.; Julia Schartz, Sales Mgr. **Wattage:** 50,000. **Ad Rates:** Advertising accepted; rates available upon request.

8240 WSIU-FM - 91.9
Southern Illinois University Phone: (618)453-4343
Communications Bldg. Fax: (618)453-6246
Carbondale, IL 62901-6602

Format: Public Radio; News; Classical; Jazz. **Networks:** National Public Radio (NPR); American Public Radio (APR). **Founded:** 1958. **Operating Hours:** 5 a.m.- 1 a.m.; 50% network, 50% local. **Key Personnel:** Tom Godell, Station Mgr.; T. Lilley, News Dir.; E. Zelten, Operations Dir. **Wattage:** 50,000. **Ad Rates:** Noncommercial.

8241 WSIU-TV - 8
Southern Illinois University Phone: (618)453-4343
1048 Communications Bldg. Fax: (618)453-6186
Carbondale, IL 62901-6602

Format: Public TV. **Networks:** Public Broadcasting Service (PBS). **Founded:** 1961. **Operating Hours:** 6:00 a.m.-approximately 2.00 a.m. **ADI:** Paducah,KY-Cape Girardeau,MO-Marion,IL. **Key Personnel:** Jerry Parks, Business Mgr.; Robert Gerig, General Mgr., phone (618)453-4343, fax (618)453-6186, bob_ gerig@wsiu.pbs.org; Trina Mueth, Station Mgr.; David Kidd, Contact; Regina Smith, Program Mgr.; Robert Henderson Henderson, Production Mgr.

CARLINVILLE†, pop. 5,439.

Macoupin Co. (SWC). 45 m SW of Springfield. Blackburn College. Truck bodies, tubular steel, butter manufactured. Nursery; Creamery. Diversified farming. Corn, wheat, livestock, milk.

8242 Carlinville Democrat
118 N. West St. Phone: (217)854-2561
PO Box 470 Fax: (217)854-DEMO
Carlinville, IL 62626
Community newspaper. **Founded:** 1856. **Freq:** Weekly (Thurs.). **Print Method:** Offset. **Trim Size:** 8 1/2 x 11. **Cols./Page:** 8. **Col. Width:** 11.5 picas. **Col. Depth:** 21.5 picas. **Key Personnel:** Thomas E. Hatalla, Sr., Editor. **Subscription Rates:** $17 individuals; $19 out of area. **Remarks:** Accepts advertising.
Ad Rates: GLR: $.90 **Circ:** ‡2,800
BW: $498.80
SAU: $2.89
PCI: $2.90

8243 Enquirer Express
Macoupin County Enquirer
PO Box 200 Phone: (217)854-2534
Carlinville, IL 62626-0200 Fax: (217)854-2535

Shopper. **Founded:** 1985. **Freq:** Weekly (Mon.). **Print Method:** Offset. **Cols./Page:** 5. **Col. Width:** 2 inches. **Col. Depth:** 15 1/2 inches. **Key Personnel:** Chris Schmitt, Editor and Publisher; Bev Neighbors, Advertising Mgr. **Remarks:** Accepts advertising.
Ad Rates: GLR: $.75 **Circ:** Free 15,000
SAU: $5.00
PCI: $3

8244 Macoupin County Enquirer
PO Box 200 Phone: (217)854-2534
Carlinville, IL 62626-0200 Fax: (217)854-2535

Community newspaper. **Founded:** 1852. **Freq:** Weekly (Thurs.). **Print Method:** Offset. **Trim Size:** 8 1/4 x 11 1/2. **Cols./Page:** 7. **Col. Width:** 2 inches. **Col. Depth:** 21x1/2 inches. **Key Personnel:** Chris Schmitt, Editor and Publisher;

Bev Neighbors, Advertising Mgr. **Subscription Rates:** $17; $25 outside of county. **Remarks:** Accepts advertising.
Ad Rates: GLR: $.75 **Circ:** Paid 4,650
PCI: $3.50 Free 80

8245 WIBI-FM - 90.5
POB 140 Phone: (217)854-4800
Carlinville, IL 62626 Fax: (217)854-4810
Free: (800)707-9191

Format: Religious. **Owner:** Illinois Bible Institute, PO Box 140, Carlinville, IL 62626. **Founded:** 1975. **Operating Hours:** Continuous; 100% local. **ADI:** Springfield-Decatur-Champaign, IL. **Key Personnel:** Dick Whitworth, General Mgr.; Paul Anthony, Station Mgr.; Deena Browne, Underwriting Dir.; Colleen Weir, Public Relations Dir. **Local Programs:** *Perspective*, Alberta Thorpe. **Wattage:** 46,000. **Ad Rates:** Noncommercial; underwriting available.

CARLYLE†, pop. 3,386.

Clinton Co. (SW). 50 m E of East St. Louis. Large Lake attraction. Oil well. Manufactures placemats, infant's shoes, steel fabrication, plastic products. Diversified farming. Dairy production.

8246 Union Banner
PO Box 220 Phone: (618)594-3131
671 10th St. Fax: (618)594-3115
Carlyle, IL 62231
Community newspaper. **Founded:** June 11, 1863. **Freq:** Weekly (Wed.). **Print Method:** Offset. **Trim Size:** 8 1/2 x 11 1/2. **Cols./Page:** 7. **Col. Width:** 12 1/2 picas. **Col. Depth:** 21 1/2 inches. **Key Personnel:** Warren Dempsey, Editor, dempsey@unionbanner.com; Michael Langham, Advertising Mgr. **USPS:** 647-880. **Subscription Rates:** $17.50 individuals; $27.50 out of area. **Remarks:** Accepts advertising.
Ad Rates: GLR: $.30 **Circ:** Paid ‡4,931
BW: $630 Free ‡89
SAU: $5.18
PCI: $4

CARMI†.

White Co. (SE). 5 m E of Enfield.

8247 Angus Topics
Angus Topics, Inc.
PO Box 397 Phone: (618)382-8553
Carmi, IL 62821 Fax: (618)382-3436
Publication E-mail: angustopics@wworld.com

Magazine about Angus cattle. **Founded:** 1955. **Freq:** Monthly. **Trim Size:** 8 1/2 x 11. **Cols./Page:** 3. **Col. Width:** 2 1/4 inches. **Col. Depth:** 10 inches. **Key Personnel:** Ernest Bingman, Advertising Mgr.; Judy Bingman, Editor. **ISSN:** 0402-4265. **Subscription Rates:** $12. **Remarks:** Accepts advertising.
Ad Rates: BW: $550 **Circ:** ‡8,300
4C: $800
PCI: $35

8248 Carmi Times
American Publishing Co.
323-325 E. Main St. Phone: (618)382-4176
PO Box 190 Fax: (618)384-2163
Carmi, IL 62821-1810
General newspaper. **Founded:** 1950. **Freq:** Daily (eve.) and Sat. (morn.). **Print Method:** Offset. **Cols./Page:** 6. **Col. Width:** 2 inches. **Col. Depth:** 21 1/2 inches. **Key Personnel:** Barry Cleveland, Publisher; Barbara Childress, Advertising Mgr. **Subscription Rates:** $75 individuals. **Remarks:** Accepts advertising.
Ad Rates: GLR: $1.35 **Circ:** 3,350
BW: $496.65
4C: $796.65
SAU: $4.95

8249 WROY-AM - 1460
101 N. Church Phone: (618)382-4161
PO Box 400 Fax: (618)382-4162
Carmi, IL 62821

Format: Oldies; News; Sports. **Networks:** RFD Illinois; ABC. **Founded:** 1948. **Operating Hours:** Continuous; 10% network, 90% local. **Key Personnel:** Roger Swan, Contact; Irma O'Dell, Program Dir.; Scott Mareing, Music Dir.; Ray Mitchell, Contact. **Local Programs:** *Open Line*, Ray Mitchell, (618)382-4161; *Swap Shop*, Toby Brown; *Trivia*, Scott Mareing. **Wattage:** 1,000. **Ad Rates:** $10.50 for 30 seconds; $13.75 for 60 seconds.

8250 WRUL-FM - 97.3
101 N. Church Phone: (618)382-4161
PO Box 400 Fax: (618)382-4162
Carmi, IL 62821

Format: Country; News; Sports. **Networks:** ABC; UPI. **Founded:** 1951. **Formerly:** WROY-FM (1951). **Operating Hours:** Continuous; 95% network, 5% local. **ADI:** Evansville, IN (Madisonville, KY). **Key Personnel:** Roger Swan, General Mgr.; Irma O'Dell, Operations Dir.; Ray Mitchell, News Dir. **Wattage:** 50,000. **Ad Rates:** $10-13 for 30 seconds; $13-16 for 60 seconds.

CAROL STREAM

8251 Books and Culture
Christianity Today, Inc.
465 Gundersen Dr. Phone: (630)260-6200
Carol Stream, IL 60188 Fax: (630)260-0114
Publication E-mail: bcedit@aol.com

Analysis of the books and ideas that shape our society from an evangelical Protestant viewpoint. **Subtitle:** A Christian Review. **Founded:** Sept. 1, 1995. **Freq:** Bimonthly. **Trim Size:** 10 3/4 x 14 1/2. **Key Personnel:** John Wilson, Managing Editor, wilsonbks@aol.com; David Neff, Executive Editor, david.neff@aol.com; Michael Mauldin, Executive Editor, mg_maudlin@aol.com. **ISSN:** 1082-8931. **Subscription Rates:** $24.95 individuals; $3.95 single issue. **Remarks:** Accepts advertising. **Online:** America Online, Inc. **URL:** http://www.christianity.net/bc.
Ad Rates: BW: $1,284 **Circ:** Paid 17,800

8252 Campus Life
Christianity Today, Inc.
465 Gundersen Dr. Phone: (630)260-6200
Carol Stream, IL 60188 Fax: (630)260-0114

Magazine for high school and early college students espousing Christian-centered values and faith. **Founded:** 1944. **Freq:** 6/year. **Print Method:** Offset. **Trim Size:** 8 1/8 x 10 7/8. **Cols./Page:** 3. **Col. Width:** 27 nonpareils. **Col. Depth:** 140 agate lines. **Key Personnel:** Chris Lutes, Editor; Harold Smith, Exec. Editor, cledit@aol.com. **ISSN:** 0008-2438. **Subscription Rates:** $19.95 individuals; $3.95 single issue. **Remarks:** Accepts advertising. **URL:** htp://www.christianity.net/campuslife.
Ad Rates: BW: $3,826 **Circ:** Paid **95,392**
4C: $4,876 Non-paid **5,559**

8253 Carol Stream Press
Press Publications
112 S. York St. Phone: (630)834-0900
Elmhurst, IL 60126 Fax: (630)834-0910
Publisher E-mail: presspub@aol.com

Community newspaper. **Founded:** 1976. **Freq:** Weekly (Thurs.). **Print Method:** Offset. **Cols./Page:** 5. **Col. Width:** 24 nonpareils. **Col. Depth:** 224 agate lines. **Key Personnel:** Kathy Catrawbone, Editor; John Cruger, Publisher.
Ad Rates: PCI: $8.18 **Circ:** (Not Reported)

8254 Christian History Magazine
Christianity Today, Inc.
465 Gundersen Dr. Phone: (630)260-6200
Carol Stream, IL 60188 Fax: (630)260-0114
Publication E-mail: chedit@aol.com

Magazine on Christian history. **Founded:** 1983. **Freq:** Quarterly. **Print Method:** Offset. **Trim Size:** 8 x 10 3/4. **Cols./Page:** 2 and 3. **Col. Width:** 2 1/4 inches. **Col. Depth:** 140 agate lines. **Key Personnel:** Mark Galli, Editor; Linda Schambach, Advertising Mgr. **ISSN:** 0891-9666. **Subscription Rates:** $19.95. **Remarks:** Accepts advertising. **URL:** http://www.christianhistory.net. **Alt. Formats:** CD-ROM.
Ad Rates: BW: $2,867 **Circ:** ‡70,000
4C: $3,399

8255 Christian Reader
Christianity Today, Inc.
465 Gundersen Dr. Phone: (630)260-6200
Carol Stream, IL 60188 Fax: (630)260-0114

A digest magazine of the best in Christian reading. **Subtitle:** Stories of Faith, Hope, and God's Love. **Founded:** Oct. 1963. **Freq:** Bimonthly. **Print Method:** Offset. **Trim Size:** 5 1/8 x 7 1/4. **Cols./Page:** 2. **Col. Width:** 24 nonpareils. **Col. Depth:** 98 agate lines. **Key Personnel:** Bonne Steffen, Editor, creditoria@aol.com; Marshall Shelley, Exec. Editor. **USPS:** 560-280. **Subscription Rates:** $17.95 individuals; $2.95 single issue. **Remarks:** Accepts advertising. **Online:** America Online, Inc. **URL:** http://www.christianreader.net.
Ad Rates: BW: $3,315 **Circ:** Paid **204,150**
4C: $3,977 Non-paid **738**

8256 Christianity Today
Christianity Today, Inc.
465 Gundersen Dr. Phone: (630)260-6200
Carol Stream, IL 60188 Fax: (630)260-0114

Religious magazine. **Subtitle:** A Magazine of Evangelical Conviction. **Founded:** Oct. 15, 1956. **Freq:** 14/year. **Print Method:** Offset. **Trim Size:** 8 1/8 x 10 7/8. **Cols./Page:** 3. **Col. Width:** 2 1/4 inches. **Col. Depth:** 140 agate lines. **Key Personnel:** David Neff, Exec. Editor, ctedit@aol.com; Michael G. Maudlin, Managing Editor; Linda Schambach, Exec. Dir., Advertising. **ISSN:** 0009-5753. **Subscription Rates:** $24.95 individuals; $2.50 single issue. **Remarks:** Accepts advertising. **URL:** http://www.christianity.net/ct.
Ad Rates: BW: $5,359 **Circ:** Paid ‡171,161
4C: $6,133 Non-paid 2,241

8257 Cosmetics & Toiletries
Allured Publishing Corp.
362 S. Schmale Rd. Phone: (630)653-2155
Carol Stream, IL 60188-2787 Fax: (630)653-2192
Publication E-mail: cosmtoil@allured.com
Publisher E-mail: allured@allured.com

Trade magazine on cosmetic and toiletries manufacturing with an emphasis on product research and development issues. **Subtitle:** The international magazine of cosmetic technology. **Founded:** 1906. **Freq:** Monthly. **Print Method:** Offset. **Trim Size:** 8 1/4 x 11 1/4. **Cols./Page:** 3 and 2. **Col. Width:** 2 1/8 and 3 inches. **Col. Depth:** 10 inches. **Key Personnel:** Nancy Allured, President; Cynthia Champney Urbano, Group Publisher; Maria Tardi, National Advertising Mgr.; Sandie Mitchell, Advertising Production; Amy Knutson Strack, Editor; Jane Evison, Sales Rep. **ISSN:** 0361-4387. **Subscription Rates:** $85 individuals; $117 Canada; $168 other countries (air). **Remarks:** Accepts advertising.
Ad Rates: BW: $1,599 **Circ:** Paid ★**3,558**
4C: $2,589

8258 FFA New Horizons
The National FFA Organization
191 S. Gary Ave. Phone: (630)462-2342
Carol Stream, IL 60188 Fax: (630)462-2202

Youth magazine. **Subtitle:** The Magazine of the National FFA Organization. **Founded:** 1952. **Freq:** Bimonthly. **Print Method:** Web offset. **Trim Size:** 8 1/8 x 10 1/2. **Cols./Page:** 3. **Col. Width:** 27 nonpareils. **Col. Depth:** 143 agate lines. **Key Personnel:** Erich Gaukel, Editor, egaukel@chilton.net; Jack Keller, Advertising Mgr. **ISSN:** 0027-9315. **Subscription Rates:** $5. **Remarks:** Accepts advertising. **Formerly:** The National Future Farmer.
Ad Rates: BW: $7,420 **Circ:** Controlled ‡425,000
4C: $9,841
PCI: $300

8259 Journal of Orofacial Pain
Quintessence Publishing Co., Inc.
551 Kimberly Dr. Phone: (630)682-3223
Carol Stream, IL 60188-1881 Fax: (630)682-3288
Free: (800)621-0387
Publication E-mail: quinted@aol.com
Publisher E-mail: quintpub@aol.com

Professional publications covering facial pain, headaches, and occlusion for the dental industry. **Founded:** 1987. **Freq:** Quarterly. **Print Method:** Sheetfed offset. **Trim Size:** 8 1/8 x 10 7/8. **Key Personnel:** Dr. Barry Sessle, Editor; William Hartman, Advertising Mgr. **ISSN:** 1064-6655. **Subscription Rates:** $76 individuals; $24 single issue. **Remarks:** Accepts advertising.
Ad Rates: BW: $600 **Circ:** Paid ⊕**2,800**
4C: $1,100

8260 Leadership
Christianity Today, Inc.
465 Gundersen Dr. Phone: (630)260-6200
Carol Stream, IL 60188 Fax: (630)260-0114
Publication E-mail: leaderj@aol.com.

Subtitle: A Practical Journal for Church Leaders. **Founded:** 1980. **Freq:** Quarterly. **Print Method:** Offset. **Trim Size:** 8 1/2 x 11. **Cols./Page:** 3 and 2. **Col. Width:** 27 and 36 nonpareils. **Col. Depth:** 140 agate lines. **Key Personnel:** Marshall Shelley, Editor; Harold Myra, Publisher; Linda Schambach, Advertising Mgr. **ISSN:** 0199-7661. **Subscription Rates:** $22 individuals; $6 single issue. **Remarks:** Accepts advertising. **Online:** America Online, Inc. **URL:** http://www.leadershipjournal.net.
Ad Rates: BW: $2,952 **Circ:** Combined 73,000

8261 Marriage Partnership
Christianity Today, Inc.
465 Gundersen Dr. Phone: (630)260-6200
Carol Stream, IL 60188 Fax: (630)260-0114
Publication E-mail: mpedit@aol.com

Magazine on Christian marriage. **Founded:** Jan. 1984. **Freq:** Quarterly. **Print Method:** Web offset. **Trim Size:** 8 1/8 x 10 7/8. **Cols./Page:** 3. **Col. Width:** 2 1/4 inches. **Col. Depth:** 9 1/2 inches. **Key Personnel:** Ron Lee, Editor, mpedit@aol.com; Harold Myra, Publisher; Annette LaPlaca, Associate Editor; Louise Ferrebee, Assoc. Editor. **Subscription Rates:** $19.95. $5 single issue. **Remarks:** Accepts advertising. **Online:** America Online, Inc.; Christianity Online. **URL:** http://

www.marriagepartnership.net. **Formerly:** Partnership (Sept. 1987).
Ad Rates: BW: $1,589 **Circ:** Paid 59,000
4C: $2,231 Non-paid 2,000

8262 Metal Center News
Cahners Publishing
191 S. Gary Ave. Phone: (630)665-1000
Carol Stream, IL 60188-2086 Fax: (630)462-2225
Free: (800)826-6270

Trade magazine. **Founded:** 1961. **Freq:** 13/year.
Circ: Non-paid ‡13,542

8263 Perfumer and Flavorist
Allured Publishing Corp.
362 S. Schmale Rd. Phone: (630)653-2155
Carol Stream, IL 60188-2787 Fax: (630)653-2192
Publisher E-mail: allured@allured.com

Magazine for flavor and perfumer chemists. **Founded:** 1976. **Freq:** Bimonthly. **Print Method:** Offset. **Trim Size:** 8 1/4 x 11 1/4. **Cols./Page:** 2 and 3. **Col. Width:** 28 and 26 nonpareils. **Col. Depth:** 140 agate lines. **Key Personnel:** Stanley E. Allured, Publisher; Nancy Allured, Advertising Mgr. **ISSN:** 0272-2666. **Subscription Rates:** $110 individuals U.S. and Canada; $150 other countries. **Remarks:** Accepts advertising.
Ad Rates: BW: $1,480 **Circ:** ‡1,774
4C: $2,470

8264 QDT
Quintessence Publishing Co., Inc.
551 Kimberly Dr. Phone: (630)682-3223
Carol Stream, IL 60188-1881 Fax: (630)682-3288
Free: (800)621-0387
Publication E-mail: quinted@aol.com
Publisher E-mail: quintpub@aol.com

Professional magazine covering dental laboratory practice. **Founded:** 1976. **Freq:** Annual. **Print Method:** Sheetfed offset. **Trim Size:** 8 1/8 x 10 7/8. **Key Personnel:** Dr. John Sorensen, Editor; William Hartman, Advertising Mgr. **Subscription Rates:** $60 individuals. **Remarks:** Accepts advertising.
Ad Rates: BW: $1,395 **Circ:** Paid 3,000
4C: $2,245

8265 Skin Inc.
Allured Publishing Corp.
362 S. Schmale Rd. Phone: (630)653-2155
Carol Stream, IL 60188-2787 Fax: (630)653-2192
Publisher E-mail: allured@allured.com

The complete business guide for Face & Body care. **Subtitle:** Professional Skin Care. **Founded:** 1988. **Freq:** 8/year. **Print Method:** Sheet fed offset. **Trim Size:** 8 3/16 x 10 7/8. **Cols./Page:** 2 and 3. **Col. Width:** 3 1/4 and 2 inches. **Col. Depth:** 10 inches. **Key Personnel:** Marian S. Raney, Editor and Publisher; Mehrida Taschetta-Millane, Managing Editor. **ISSN:** 0898-6525. **Subscription Rates:** $46 individuals; $10 single issue. **Remarks:** Accepts advertising.
Ad Rates: PCI: $175 **Circ:** Paid ‡7,537
Controlled ‡5,463

Today's Christian Woman - See Wheaton

8266 Virtue
Christianity Today, Inc.
465 Gundersen Dr. Phone: (630)260-6200
Carol Stream, IL 60188 Fax: (630)260-0114
Publication E-mail: virtuemag@aol.com

Christian magazine for women. **Subtitle:** Helping Women Build Christ-like Character. **Founded:** 1978. **Freq:** Bimonthly. **Print Method:** Offset. **Trim Size:** 8 x 10 3/4. **Cols./Page:** 3. **Col. Width:** 28 nonpareils. **Col. Depth:** 140 agate lines. **Key Personnel:** Harold Smith, Publisher; Linda Schambach, VP, Sales/Advertising. **ISSN:** 0164-7288. **Subscription Rates:** $18.95 individuals. **Remarks:** Accepts advertising.
Ad Rates: BW: $3,867 **Circ:** Paid ‡100,000
4C: $4,640 Non-paid ‡10,000

8267 Your Church
Christianity Today, Inc.
465 Gundersen Dr. Phone: (630)260-6200
Carol Stream, IL 60188 Fax: (630)260-0114
Publication E-mail: yceditor@aol.com

Magazine about church business administration. **Subtitle:** Helping You with the Business of Ministry. **Founded:** 1955. **Freq:** Bimonthly. **Print Method:** Offset. **Trim Size:** 8 x 10 3/4. **Cols./Page:** 3. **Col. Width:** 13 picas. **Col. Depth:** 60 picas. **Key Personnel:** Phyllis Ten Elshof, Editor, yceditor@aol.com. **ISSN:** 0049-8394. **Subscription Rates:** $15 individuals; $19 other countries.
Ad Rates: BW: $6,026 **Circ:** Controlled 150,000
4C: $6,902

CARROLLTON†, pop. 2,816.

Greene Co. (W). 33 m NW of Alton. Grain elevator. Grain, stock, poultry, dairy farms.

8268 Gazette-Patriot
428 N. Main St. Phone: (217)942-3626
PO Box 231 Fax: (217)942-3699
Carrollton, IL 62016-0231
Publisher E-mail: gazette@midwest.net

Community newspaper with Democratic orientation. **Founded:** 1846. **Freq:** Weekly (Thurs.). **Print Method:** Offset. **Trim Size:** 8 1/2 x 11. **Cols./Page:** 7. **Col. Width:** 22 nonpareils. **Col. Depth:** 300 agate lines. **Key Personnel:** A.W. Scott III, Editor and Publisher. **USPS:** 091-780. **Subscription Rates:** $20 individuals; $25 out of area. **Remarks:** Accepts advertising. **Alt. Formats:** CD-ROM.
Ad Rates: GLR: $.70 **Circ:** Paid ⊕1,659
BW: $525 Free ⊕60
SAU: $3.75
PCI: $3.75

8269 Greene County Shopper
Carrollton Gazette Patriot, Inc.
PO Box 231 Phone: (217)942-3626
Carrollton, IL 62016 Fax: (217)942-3699
Publisher E-mail: gazette@midwest.net

Free shopper including classifieds. **Founded:** 1965. **Freq:** Weekly. **Print Method:** Offset. **Trim Size:** 8 1/2 x 11. **Cols./Page:** 5. **Col. Width:** 2 inches. **Col. Depth:** 16 inches. **Key Personnel:** Janelle Schnelten, Editor. **Subscription Rates:** Free. **Remarks:** Accepts advertising.
Ad Rates: GLR: $.75 **Circ:** Free 12,000
BW: $270
4C: $630
PCI: $5.18

8270 Jersey County Shopper
Carrollton Gazette Patriot, Inc.
PO Box 231 Phone: (217)942-3626
Carrollton, IL 62016 Fax: (217)942-3699
Publisher E-mail: gazette@midwest.net

Shopper with classifieds. **Founded:** 1965. **Freq:** Weekly. **Print Method:** Offset. **Trim Size:** 8 1/2 x 11. **Cols./Page:** 5. **Col. Width:** 2 inches. **Col. Depth:** 16 inches. **Key Personnel:** Cathy Williams, Editor. **Subscription Rates:** Free. **Remarks:** Accepts advertising.
Ad Rates: GLR: $.75 **Circ:** Free 13,050
BW: $270
4C: $670
PCI: $5.18

CARTERVILLE

Williamson Co. (SC). 10 m W of Marion.

KPOB-TV - See Poplar Bluff, Missouri

8271 WCIL-AM - 1020
PO Box 370 Phone: (618)985-4843
Carterville, IL 62918 Fax: (618)985-6529

Format: News. **Networks:** ABC; CNN Radio. **Founded:** 1946. **Operating Hours:** Sunrise-sunset. **ADI:** Paducah,KY-Cape Girardeau,MO-Marion,IL. **Key Personnel:** Dennis Lyle, General Mgr.; Joey Helleny, News Dir.; Rich Bird, Program Dir. **Local Programs:** *Focus 10/20*, Joey Helleny. **Wattage:** 1000. **Ad Rates:** $12 for 30 seconds; $19 for 60 seconds. $16.15-$28.99 for 30 seconds; $19.34-$31.79 for 60 seconds. Combined advertising rates available with WCIL-FM. **URL:** http://www.2100fm.com.

8272 WSIL-TV - 3
Rte. 13 Phone: (618)985-2333
Carterville, IL 62918 Fax: (618)985-3709

Format: Commercial TV. **Simulcasts:** KPOB-TV. **Networks:** ABC. **Owner:** WSIL, Inc., at above address. **Founded:** 1953. **ADI:** Paducah,KY-Cape Girardeau,MO-Marion,IL. **Key Personnel:** Steve Wheeler, General Mgr.; Dave Cisco, Sales Mgr.

CARTHAGE†, pop. 2,978.

Hancock Co. (W). 14 m E of Keokuk, Iowa. Agriculture. Livestock, corn.

8273 Hancock County Journal Pilot
31 N. Washington Phone: (217)357-2149
PO Box 478 Fax: (217)357-2177
Carthage, IL 62321
Community newspaper. **Founded:** Nov. 1887. **Freq:** Weekly (Wed.). **Print Method:** Offset. **Trim Size:** 13 x 21 1/2. **Cols./Page:** 8. **Col. Width:** 1 1/2 inches. **Col. Depth:** 21 1/2 inches. **Key Personnel:** Bill Ferguson, Publisher; Joy Swearingan, Editor. **USPS:** 234-220. **Subscription Rates:** $23 individuals in county. **Remarks:** Accepts advertising.
Ad Rates: GLR: $0.60 **Circ:** Paid ‡4,000
BW: $946
4C: $150
SAU: $8.80
PCI: $5.50

8274 WCAZ-AM - 990
84 S. Madison Phone: (217)357-3128
Carthage, IL 62321 Fax: (217)357-2014
E-mail: wcazam@adams.net

Format: News; Eclectic; Agricultural; Country. **Networks:** UPI; RFD Illinois. **Owner:** Rob Dunham, PO Box 498, Carthage, IL 62321. **Founded:** 1918. **Operating Hours:** Continuous; 25% network, 75% local. **Key Personnel:** Chuck Porter, Chief Engineer; Don Thurman, News Dir.; Keith Yex, General Mgr. **Wattage:** 1000. **Ad Rates:** Advertising accepted; rates available upon request.

CARY, pop. 6,640.

McHenry Co. (NW). 25 m SW of Waukegan. Manufactures tools and dies, coils, transformers, septic tanks, hampers, plastic products and valves. Grain, dairy farms.

8275 Cary-Grove Countryside
Pioneer Press Newspapers
200 James St. Phone: (847)381-9200
Barrington, IL 60010 Fax: (847)381-5840

Community newspaper (tabloid). **Founded:** 1972. **Freq:** Weekly (Thurs.). **Print Method:** Offset. **Cols./Page:** 4. **Col. Width:** 13 3/5 picas. **Col. Depth:** 196 agate lines. **Key Personnel:** Paul Sassone, Managing Editor; Matt Arado, Editor. **Subscription Rates:** $12.95 individuals; $19.95 out of county. **Remarks:** Advertising accepted; rates available upon request.
Circ: Thurs. ★2,918

8276 Outside Plant Magazine
Practical Communications, Inc.
PO Box 183 Phone: (847)639-2200
Cary, IL 60013-9986 Fax: (847)639-9542
Publisher E-mail: pcinc@mc.net

Telecommunications magazine. **Subtitle:** The Only Full-Time Outside Plant Telecommunications Publication. **Founded:** July 1983. **Freq:** Monthly. **Print Method:** Offset. **Trim Size:** 8 1/8 x 10 7/8. **Cols./Page:** 3. **Col. Width:** 27 nonpareils. **Col. Depth:** 140 agate lines. **Key Personnel:** Sharon Stober, Editor; Judy Chance, Publisher. **ISSN:** 0747-8763. **Subscription Rates:** $30 individuals. **Remarks:** Accepts advertising. **Alt. Formats:** Mailing labels.
Ad Rates: BW: $3,805 **Circ:** Paid 995
4C: $4,655 Controlled 18,211
PCI: $127

8277 Utility & Telephone Fleets
Practical Communications, Inc.
PO Box 183 Phone: (847)639-2200
Cary, IL 60013-9986 Fax: (847)639-9542
Publication E-mail: utfmag@utfmag.com
Publisher E-mail: pcinc@mc.net

Magazine for fleet managers, maintenance supervisors, and administrators at utility and sales, marketing and public works departments and related contractors. **Founded:** 1987. **Freq:** 8/year. **Print Method:** Offset. **Trim Size:** 8 1/8 x 10 7/8. **Cols./Page:** 3. **Col. Width:** 2 1/4 inches. **Col. Depth:** 10 inches. **Key Personnel:** Judy Chance, Publisher; James Queenan, Vice President. **ISSN:** 1058-9090. **Subscription Rates:** $22 individuals; $5 single issue. **Remarks:** Accepts advertising.
Ad Rates: BW: $2,350 **Circ:** Paid ‡259
4C: $2,995 Controlled ‡18,804
PCI: $80

CASEY, pop. 3,026.

Clark Co. (E). 35 m SW of Terre Haute, Ind. Oil well. Manufactures shoes, faucets, limestone products, radio, TV, auto parts. Poultry, dairy, grain farms.

8278 The Marketplace for Greenup & Toledo
Lincoln Trail Publishing
PO Box 158 Phone: (217)932-5211
Casey, IL 62420 Fax: (217)932-5214
Free: (800)252-3356

Shopper with community news. **Founded:** 1983. **Freq:** Weekly. **Print Method:** Offset - Tab. **Trim Size:** 11 1/2 x 13 1/2. **Cols./Page:** 5. **Col. Width:** 2 inches. **Col. Depth:** 13 inches. **Key Personnel:** Greg Gravemier, Editor; Ronald J. Isbell,

Publisher; Lynn Wilhoit, Advertising Mgr. **Subscription Rates:** Free. **Remarks:** Accepts advertising.
Ad Rates: BW: $195 **Circ:** Free ⊕3,300
4C: $395
SAU: $4.55
PCI: $3

8279 Reporter
Lincoln Trail Publishing
PO Box 158 Phone: (217)932-5211
Casey, IL 62420 Fax: (217)932-5214
Free: (800)252-3356

Community newspaper. **Founded:** 1938. **Freq:** Semiweekly (Mon. and Thurs.). **Print Method:** Offset. **Trim Size:** 13 3/4 x 22 3/4. **Cols./Page:** 6. **Col. Width:** 2 inches. **Col. Depth:** 21 inches. **Key Personnel:** Greg Gravemier, Editor; Ronald J. Isbell, Publisher. **Subscription Rates:** $35 individuals; $44 out of area; $52 out of state. **Remarks:** Accepts advertising.
Ad Rates: BW: $567 **Circ:** Paid ‡2,500
4C: $767
SAU: $6.33
PCI: $5.25

8280 WKZI-AM - 800
6 E. Colorado Alley Phone: (217)932-4051
PO Box 8
Casey, IL 62420-0008
E-mail: wkzi@rr1.net

Format: Contemporary Christian. **Networks:** Moody Broadcasting. **Owner:** Word Power, Inc., at above address. **Founded:** 1963. **Operating Hours:** Continuous. **Key Personnel:** Paul Dean Ford, President; Mark Stephen Ford, Vice President. **Wattage:** 250. **Ad Rates:** $7 for 30 seconds; $10 for 60 seconds. **URL:** http://www.rr1.net/users/wkzi/index.htm.

8281 WPFR-FM - 93.9
6 E. Colorado Ave. Phone: (217)932-4051
Casey, IL 62420

Format: Contemporary Christian. **Networks:** Moody Broadcasting. **Owner:** Word Power, Inc., at above address. **Operating Hours:** Continuous. **Wattage:** 2,000. **Ad Rates:** Noncommercial.

CENTRALIA, pop. 15,126.

Marion Co. (S). 65 m E of St. Louis, Mo. Manufactures plastics, fiberglass Laminates, pipe, casting, armatures, potato chips, candy, dresses. Meat packing. Fruit, dairy, poultry, grain farms.

8282 Centralia Sentinel
Centralia Press, Ltd.
232 E. Broadway Phone: (618)532-5604
PO Box 627 Fax: (618)533-1212
Centralia, IL 62801
Free: (800)371-9892

General newspaper. **Founded:** 1863. **Freq:** Daily (eve.). **Print Method:** Offset. **Cols./Page:** 7. **Col. Width:** 26 nonpareils. **Col. Depth:** 298 agate lines. **Key Personnel:** Randy Snyder, General Mgr.; Dan Nichols, General Mgr. **Subscription Rates:** $78 individuals. **Remarks:** Accepts advertising.
Ad Rates: GLR: $.42 **Circ:** Mon.-Fri. 16,134
BW: $855.31 Sun. 17,191
4C: $1,155.31
SAU: $5.75

CERRO GORDO, pop. 1,553.

Piatt Co. (EC). 14 m NE of Decatur. Ships grain. Diversified farming. Corn, wheat, soybeans.

8283 The News-Record
221 E. South Phone: (217)763-3541
PO Box 49 Fax: (217)578-2833
Cerro Gordo, IL 61818-0049
Community newspaper. **Founded:** Sept. 1908. **Freq:** Weekly. **Print Method:** Offset. **Cols./Page:** 6. **Col. Width:** 14.2 picas. **Key Personnel:** Joe Lenhart, Editor and Publisher; Shari Lenhart, Advertising Mgr. **USPS:** 099-140. **Subscription Rates:** $17 individuals annually.
Ad Rates: GLR: $4.85 **Circ:** ‡1,500
BW: $253.75
4C: $365
SAU: $4.85
PCI: $4.85

CHAMPAIGN, pop. 58,133.

Champaign Co. (E). 125 m SW of Chicago. University of Illinois is situated equally in Urbana and Champaign. Manufactures computer software, castings, drop forgings, paper cup products, road machinery, concrete culverts, butter, vegetable shortening, athletic equipment, railroad registers. Soybean oil processing. Agriculture. Corn.

8284 Adapted Physical Activity Quarterly
Human Kinetics Publishers, Inc.
1607 N. Market St. Phone: (217)351-5076
PO Box 5076 Fax: (217)351-2674
Champaign, IL 61825-5076
Free: (800)747-4457
Publisher E-mail: humank@hkusa.com

Journal on the study of physical activity for special populations. **Founded:** 1984. **Freq:** Quarterly. **Print Method:** Offset. **Trim Size:** 6 x 9. **Cols./Page:** 1. **Col. Width:** 65 nonpareils. **Col. Depth:** 108 agate lines. **Key Personnel:** Claudine Sherrill, PhD, Editor, phone (972)625-8771, fax (940)898-2581, f_ sherrill@twu.edu. **ISSN:** 0736-5829. **Subscription Rates:** $42 individuals; $100 institutions; $26 students. **Remarks:** Accepts advertising.
Ad Rates: BW: $300 **Circ:** Paid ‡977
‡26

8285 American Journal of Psychology
University of Illinois Press at Urbana-Champaign
Psychology Bldg. Phone: (217)333-5234
603 E. Daniel St. Fax: (217)244-5876
Champaign, IL 61820
Publication E-mail: ajp@s.psych.uiuc.edu

Journal dealing with experimental psychology and basic principles of psychology. **Founded:** 1887. **Freq:** Quarterly. **Print Method:** Offset. **Trim Size:** 6 x 9. **Cols./Page:** 1. **Col. Width:** 26 picas. **Col. Depth:** 43 picas. **Key Personnel:** Caroline Waldron, Advertising Mgr.; Donelson Dulany, Editor, phone (217)333-2971, ddulany@s.psych.uiuc.edu. **ISSN:** 0002-9556. **Subscription Rates:** $105 institutions; $112 foreign.
Ad Rates: BW: $275 **Circ:** ‡2108

8286 Arborist News Magazine
International Society of Arboriculture
PO Box 3129 Phone: (217)355-9411
Champaign, IL 61826-3129 Fax: (217)355-9516

Trade magazine covering tree care. **Founded:** Feb. 1992. **Freq:** Bimonthly. **Print Method:** Sheetfed offset. **Trim Size:** 8 1/4 x 10 7/8. **Cols./Page:** 3. **Key Personnel:** Derek Vannice, Managing Editor, dvannice@isa-arbor.com; Carole Abbott, Membership/Member Svcs. Mgr. **Remarks:** Accepts advertising. **URL:** http://www.ag.uiuc.edu/~isa.
Ad Rates: BW: $839 **Circ:** Controlled 11,500
4C: $1,272

8287 Athletic Therapy Today
Human Kinetics Publishers, Inc.
1607 N. Market St. Phone: (217)351-5076
PO Box 5076 Fax: (217)351-2674
Champaign, IL 61825-5076
Free: (800)747-4457
Publisher E-mail: humank@hkusa.com

Journal devoted to understanding sports-related behavior and social organization. **Founded:** 1996. **Freq:** Bimonthly. **Print Method:** Offset. **Trim Size:** 8 1/2 x 11. **Cols./Page:** 3. **Key Personnel:** Joseph J. Godek, Editor, phone (610)436-2515, fax (610)436-2803, jgodek@wcupa.edu. **ISSN:** 1078-7895. **Subscription Rates:** $30; $70 institutions; $20 students. **Remarks:** Accepts advertising.
Ad Rates: BW: $450 **Circ:** 918

8288 The Bulletin of the Center for Children's Books
University of Illinois Press at Urbana-Champaign
51 E. Armory Ave. Phone: (217)244-0324
Champaign, IL 61820-6601 Fax: (217)333-5603
Publication E-mail: bccb@alexia.lis.uiuc.edu

Journal containing concise summaries and critical evaluations of books for children. **Founded:** 1947. **Freq:** 11/year. **Print Method:** Offset. **Trim Size:** 6 x 9. **Cols./Page:** 1. **Col. Width:** 70 nonpareils. **Col. Depth:** 110 agate lines. **Key Personnel:** Patt Leonard, Advertising Mgr., phone (217)244-6496. **ISSN:** 0008-9036. **Subscription Rates:** $35 individuals; $40 institutions. **Remarks:** Accepts advertising. **URL:** http://www.edfu.lis.uiuc.edu/puboff/bccb.
Ad Rates: BW: $275 **Circ:** 5000

8289 Canadian Journal of Applied Physiology
Human Kinetics Publishers, Inc.
1607 N. Market St. Phone: (217)351-5076
PO Box 5076 Fax: (217)351-2674
Champaign, IL 61825-5076
Free: (800)747-4457
Publication E-mail: humank@hkusa.com
Publisher E-mail: humank@hkusa.com

Journal publishing original work in applied human biomechanics, physiology, and motor learning as well as the psychology and sociocultural aspects of sport and sports medicine. **Founded:** 1984. **Freq:** Bimonthly. **Print Method:** Offset. **Trim Size:** 6 x 9. **Cols./Page:** 1. **Col. Width:** 65 nonpareils. **Col. Depth:** 108 agate lines. **Key Personnel:** Phillip Gardner, Editor, phone (514)343-2176, fax (514)343-2181; Francois Perronet, Editor. **ISSN:** 1066-7814. **Subscription Rates:** $50 individuals; $120 institutions; $32 students. **Remarks:** Accepts advertising.
Ad Rates: BW: $300 **Circ:** Paid ‡879
Non-paid ‡37

8290 Comparative Labor Law & Policy Journal
University of Illinois
116 Law Bldg. Phone: (217)333-9852
504 E Pennsylvania Ave. Fax: (217)244-1478
Champaign, IL 61820
Publication E-mail: mfinkinlaw.uiuc.edu

Scholarly journal covering international comparison issues in labor law and employment policies. **Founded:** 1976. **Freq:** Quarterly. **Print Method:** Offset litho. **Trim Size:** 6 3/4 x 10. **Cols./Page:** 1. **Col. Width:** 28 picas. **Col. Depth:** 48 picas. **Key Personnel:** Prof. Matthew W., Finkin, Editor, phone (217)333-3884, mfinkin@law.uiuc.edu; Linda Payne, Managing Editor, lpayne@law.uiuc.edu. **ISSN:** 1095-6654. **Subscription Rates:** $30 individuals; $40 out of country. **Remarks:** Accepts advertising. **Online:** LEXIS-NEXIS; WESTLAW. **Former name:** Comparative Labor Law Journal.
Circ: Combined 800

8291 The Daily Illini
Illini Media Co.
57 E. Green St. Phone: (217)333-3733
Champaign, IL 61820 Fax: (217)244-6616
Publication E-mail: di@illinimedia.com

Collegiate newspaper. **Founded:** 1871. **Freq:** Daily (morn.) (during academic year). **Print Method:** Offset. **Cols./Page:** 5. **Col. Width:** 24 nonpareils. **Col. Depth:** 224 agate lines. **Key Personnel:** Jim McKellar, Publisher. **Subscription Rates:** $100 individuals. **URL:** http://www.illinimedia.com.
Ad Rates: GLR: $.18 **Circ:** ‡20,000
BW: $704
4C: $1204
PCI: $9.60

8292 Disc Golf Journal
PO Box 3577 Phone: (217)398-7880
Champaign, IL 61826-3577 Fax: (217)398-7881
Free: (800)651-DISC

Magazine for the sport of disc golf. **Subtitle:** "The World's Finest Disc Golf Publication". **Founded:** 1991. **Freq:** Bimonthly. **Print Method:** Offset. **Trim Size:** 8 1/2 x 11. **Cols./Page:** 3. **Col. Width:** 2 1/2 inches. **Col. Depth:** 9 1/2 inches. **Key Personnel:** Tom Schlueter, Publisher; Kathy Ignowski, Managing Editor, kathyig@aol.com. **ISSN:** 1055-4785. **Subscription Rates:** $17.97 individuals. **Remarks:** Accepts advertising.
Ad Rates: BW: $175 **Circ:** Paid ‡2,500
Free ‡600

8293 Exercise Immunology Review
Human Kinetics Publishers, Inc.
1607 N. Market St. Phone: (217)351-5076
PO Box 5076 Fax: (217)351-2674
Champaign, IL 61825-5076
Free: (800)747-4457
Publisher E-mail: humank@hkusa.com

Journal relating to all aspects of immunology, including sport, exercise, and regular physical activity. **Founded:** Mar. 1995. **Freq:** Annual. **Print Method:** Offset. **Trim Size:** 6 x 9. **Key Personnel:** Hinnek Northoff, Editor; Linda A. Bump, Journal Director; Rainer Martens, Publisher. **ISSN:** 1077-5552. **Subscription Rates:** $20 individuals; $40 institutions; $12 students.
Circ: Paid ‡170

8294 Human Dimensions of Wildlife
Sagamore Publishing Inc.
PO Box 647 Phone: (217)359-5940
Champaign, IL 61824-0647 Fax: (217)359-5975
Free: (800)327-5557
Publisher E-mail: books@sagamorepub.com

Journal covering wildlife, resource management and forestry. **Founded:** 1996. **Freq:** Quarterly. **Trim Size:** 6 x 9. **Cols./Page:** 1. **Col. Width:** 6 inches. **Col. Depth:** 9 inches. **Key Personnel:** Delia Barrett, Circulation Mgr., phone (717)632-3535, fax (717)632-8920. **ISSN:** 1087-1209. **Subscription Rates:** $50 individuals; $70 out of country; $15 single issue. **Remarks:** Advertising not accepted.
Circ: (Not Reported)

8295 Illinois Natural History Survey Bulletin
Illinois Natural History Survey
Natural Resources Bldg. Phone: (217)244-2115
607 E. Peabody Dr. Fax: (217)333-4949
Champaign, IL 61820
Bulletin presenting research related to the biological resources of Illinois. **Founded:** 1876. **Freq:** Periodic. **Print Method:** Letterpress and Offset. **Trim Size:** 6 3/4 x 10. **Cols./Page:** 2. **Col. Width:** 14 1/5 picas. **Col. Depth:** 111 agate lines. **Key Personnel:** Charles Warwick, Editor, cwarwick@mail.inhs.uiuc.edu. **ISSN:** 0073-4918. **Subscription Rates:** $10 single issue. **Remarks:** Advertising not accepted.
Circ: Paid ‡1,500
Non-paid ‡550

8296 Illinois Technograph
Illini Media Co.
57 E. Green St. Phone: (217)333-3733
Champaign, IL 61820 Fax: (217)244-6616

Magazine for students, faculty and affiliates of the College of Engineering at the University of Illinois. **Founded:** 1885. **Freq:** Quarterly (during the academic year). **Print Method:** Offset. **Trim Size:** 8 1/2 x 11. **Cols./Page:** 3. **Col. Width:** 27 nonpareils. **Col. Depth:** 140 agate lines. **Key Personnel:** Michael Moody, Editor; Jim McKellar, Publisher, phone (217)244-3434; George J. Thiruvathukal, Advertising Mgr. **USPS:** 258-760. **Subscription Rates:** $7.35 individuals. **Remarks:** Accepts advertising.
Ad Rates: BW: $550 **Circ:** Paid ‡800
4C: $1,025 Non-paid ‡5,200

8297 INFORM (International News on Fats, Oils and Related Materials)
AOCS Press (American Oil Chemists' Society)
PO Box 3489
Champaign, IL 61826-3489
Publication E-mail: publications@aocs.org
Publisher E-mail: publications@aocs.org

Magazine covering news about fats, oils, and related materials. **Founded:** 1990. **Freq:** Monthly. **Print Method:** Offset. **Trim Size:** 8 1/4 x 11. **Cols./Page:** 3 and 2. **Col. Width:** 2 1/8 and 3 3/16 inches. **Col. Depth:** 10 and 10 inches. **Key Personnel:** James B. Rattray, Editor. **ISSN:** 0097-8026. **Subscription Rates:** $110 individuals; $121 other countries. **Remarks:** Accepts advertising.
Ad Rates: BW: $1,160 **Circ:** 7,000
4C: $2,110

8298 The International Journal of Accounting
Elseiver
University of Illinois Phone: (217)333-4545
1206 S. 6th St. Fax: (217)244-6565
Champaign, IL 61820
Publication E-mail: 102062.2525@compuserve.com
Publisher E-mail: fcentres@gpu.stv.ualberta.ca

Scholarly journal covering global accounting issues. **Founded:** 1965. **Freq:** Quarterly. **Trim Size:** 7 x 10. **Cols./Page:** 1. **Col. Width:** 5 inches. **Col. Depth:** 8 inches. **Key Personnel:** Andrew D. Bailey, Jr., Editor. **ISSN:** 0020-7063. **Subscription Rates:** $75 individuals; $180 institutions. **Remarks:** Advertising accepted; rates available upon request.
Circ: (Not Reported)

8299 International Journal of Sport Nutrition
Human Kinetics Publishers, Inc.
1607 N. Market St. Phone: (217)351-5076
PO Box 5076 Fax: (217)351-2674
Champaign, IL 61825-5076
Free: (800)747-4457
Publisher E-mail: humank@hkusa.com

Journal advancing the understanding of nutritional aspects of human physical and athletic performance. **Founded:** 1991. **Freq:** Quarterly. **Print Method:** Offset. **Trim Size:** 6 x 9. **Cols./Page:** 1. **Col. Width:** 65 nonpareils. **Col. Depth:** 108 agate lines. **Key Personnel:** Priscilla M. Clarkson, PhD, Editor, phone (413)545-6069, fax (413)548-9574. **ISSN:** 1050-1606. **Subscription Rates:** $42 individuals; $100 institutions; $26 students. **Remarks:** Accepts advertising.
Ad Rates: BW: $375 **Circ:** Paid ‡1,372

8300 The Journal of Aesthetic Education
University of Illinois Press at Urbana-Champaign
University of Illinois at Urbana-Champaign Phone: (217)333-7211
Fax: (217)244-7064
361 Education Bldg.
1310 S. Sixth St.
Champaign, IL 61820
Journal exploring aspects of aesthetic and humanities education. **Founded:** 1966. **Freq:** Quarterly. **Print Method:** Offset. **Trim Size:** 6 x 9. **Cols./Page:** 1. **Col. Width:** 52 nonpareils. **Col. Depth:** 107 agate lines. **Key Personnel:** Ralph A. Smith, Editor, phone (217)359-7425, fax (217)244-7064, r-smith@uiuc.edu; Rick Canning, Advertising Mgr. **ISSN:** 0021-8510. **Subscription Rates:** $35 individuals; $14 single issue; $60 institutions, other countries; $57 out of country. **Remarks:** Accepts advertising.
Ad Rates: BW: $200 **Circ:** Paid 1,000
Non-paid 50

8301 Journal of Aging and Physical Activity
Human Kinetics Publishers, Inc.
1607 N. Market St. Phone: (217)351-5076
PO Box 5076 Fax: (217)351-2674
Champaign, IL 61825-5076
Free: (800)747-4457
Publisher E-mail: humank@hkusa.com

Journal examining the relationship between physical activity and the aging process. **Founded:** 1993. **Freq:** Quarterly. **Print Method:** Offset. **Trim Size:** 6 x 9. **Cols./Page:** 1. **Col. Width:** 65 nonpareils. **Col. Depth:** 108 agate lines. **Key Personnel:** Wojtek Chodzko-Zajko, PhD, Editor, phone (216)672-2857, fax (216)672-4106; Rainer Martens, Publisher, phone (217)351-5076; Linda Anne Bump, Director. **ISSN:** 1063-8652. **Subscription Rates:** $42 individuals; $100 institutions; $26 students. **Remarks:** Accepts advertising.
Ad Rates: BW: $375 **Circ:** Paid 745

8302 Journal of the American Oil Chemists' Society
American Oil Chemists' Society
PO Box 3489 Phone: (217)359-2344
Champaign, IL 61826-0489 Fax: (217)351-8091
Publication E-mail: publications@aocs.org
Publisher E-mail: general@aocs.org

Technical journal devoted to fundamental and practical research in the field of fats, oils, oleochemicals, proteins, surfactants, and detergents. **Founded:** 1922. **Freq:** Monthly. **Print Method:** Offset. **Trim Size:** 8 1/4 x 11. **Cols./Page:** 2. **Col. Width:** 20.5 picas. **Col. Depth:** 57 picas. **Key Personnel:** Dr. L.H. Princen, Editor; Mary Lane, Publisher. **ISSN:** 0003-021X. **Subscription Rates:** $145. **Remarks:** Advertising not accepted. **URL:** http://www.aocs.org.
Circ: Paid ‡3,500
Non-paid ‡50

8303 Journal of Applied Biomechanics
Human Kinetics Publishers, Inc.
1607 N. Market St. Phone: (217)351-5076
PO Box 5076 Fax: (217)351-2674
Champaign, IL 61825-5076
Free: (800)747-4457
Publisher E-mail: humank@hkusa.com

Journal covering the applied aspects of human biomechanics in sport, excercise, and rehabilitation. **Founded:** 1985. **Freq:** Quarterly. **Print Method:** Offset. **Trim Size:** 6 x 9. **Cols./Page:** 1. **Col. Width:** 65 nonpareils. **Col. Depth:** 108 agate lines. **Key Personnel:** Mark Grabiner, PhD, Editor. **ISSN:** 0740-2082. **Subscription Rates:** $42 individuals; $100 institutions; $26 students. **Remarks:** Accepts advertising.
Ad Rates: BW: $300 **Circ:** Paid ‡1,164
Non-paid ‡40

8304 Journal of the Philosophy of Sport
Human Kinetics Publishers, Inc.
1607 N. Market St. Phone: (217)351-5076
PO Box 5076 Fax: (217)351-2674
Champaign, IL 61825-5076
Free: (800)747-4457
Publisher E-mail: humank@hkusa.com

Journal focusing on philosophic thought as it applies to sport. **Founded:** 1975. **Freq:** 1/year. **Print Method:** Offset. **Trim Size:** 6 x 9. **Cols./Page:** 1. **Col. Width:** 65 nonpareils. **Col. Depth:** 108 agate lines. **Key Personnel:** William J. Morgan, Ph.D, Editor, phone (615)974-1273, fax (615)974-8981. **ISSN:** 0094-8705. **Subscription Rates:** $20 individuals; $32 institutions; $12 students.
Circ: Paid 590
Non-paid 30

8305 Journal of Sport & Exercise Psychology
Human Kinetics Publishers, Inc.
1607 N. Market St. Phone: (217)351-5076
PO Box 5076 Fax: (217)351-2674
Champaign, IL 61825-5076
Free: (800)747-4457
Publisher E-mail: humank@hkusa.com

Journal of research and theory in sport and exercise psychology. **Founded:** 1979. **Freq:** Quarterly. **Print Method:** Offset. **Trim Size:** 6 x 9. **Cols./Page:** 1. **Col. Width:** 65 nonpareils. **Col. Depth:** 108 agate lines. **Key Personnel:** Thelma Horn, PhD, Editor, phone (513)529-2723, fax (513)529-5006. **ISSN:** 0895-2779. **Subscription Rates:** $40 individuals; $100 institutions; $26 students. **Remarks:** Accepts advertising.
Ad Rates: BW: $300 **Circ:** Paid ‡1,891

8306 Journal of Sport Management
Human Kinetics Publishers, Inc.
1607 N. Market St. Phone: (217)351-5076
PO Box 5076 Fax: (217)351-2674
Champaign, IL 61825-5076
Free: (800)747-4457
Publisher E-mail: humank@hkusa.com

Journal focusing on the theory and application of management to sport, exercise, dance, and play. **Founded:** 1987. **Freq:** Quarterly. **Print Method:** Offset. **Trim Size:** 6 x 9. **Cols./Page:** 1. **Col. Width:** 65 nonpareils. **Col. Depth:** 108 agate lines. **Key Personnel:** Trevor Slack, Editor, tslack@dmu.ac.uk; Wendy Frisby, Co-editor, phone (604)822-6445, fax (604)822-5884, frisby@unixg.ubc.ca. **ISSN:** 0888-4773. **Subscription Rates:** $42 individuals; $100 Industry; $26 students. **Remarks:** Accepts advertising.
Ad Rates: BW: $300 **Circ:** Paid 1,126

8307 Journal of Sport Rehabilitation
Human Kinetics Publishers, Inc.
1607 N. Market St. Phone: (217)351-5076
PO Box 5076 Fax: (217)351-2674
Champaign, IL 61825-5076
Free: (800)747-4457
Publisher E-mail: humank@hkusa.com

Journal dedicated to research and practical articles concerning the rehabilitation of sport and exercise injuries. **Founded:** 1992. **Freq:** Quarterly. **Print Method:** Web offset. **Trim Size:** 6 x 9. **Cols./Page:** 1. **Col. Width:** 65 nonpareils. **Col. Depth:** 108 agate lines. **Key Personnel:** Scott Lephart, Ph.D., ATC, phone (412)648-8261. **ISSN:** 1056-6716. **Subscription Rates:** $42; $100 institutions; $26 students. **Remarks:** Accepts advertising.
Ad Rates: BW: $300 **Circ:** Paid ‡800
Non-paid ‡53

8308 Journal of Strength and Conditioning Research
Human Kinetics Publishers, Inc.
1607 N. Market St. Phone: (217)351-5076
PO Box 5076 Fax: (217)351-2674
Champaign, IL 61825-5076
Free: (800)747-4457
Publisher E-mail: humank@hkusa.com

Journal focusing on strength and conditioning in sport and exercise. **Founded:** 1987. **Freq:** Quarterly. **Print Method:** Offset. **Trim Size:** 8 1/2 x 11. **Cols./Page:** 2. **Key Personnel:** William Kraemer, PhD, Editor, phone (814)865-7109, fax (814)865-7077, wjk3@psu.edu. **ISSN:** 1064-8011. **Subscription Rates:** $80 institutions. **Remarks:** Advertising not accepted. **Formerly:** Journal of Applied Sport Science Research.
Circ: Paid 13,222

8309 Journal of Teaching in Physical Education
Human Kinetics Publishers, Inc.
1607 N. Market St. Phone: (217)351-5076
PO Box 5076 Fax: (217)351-2674
Champaign, IL 61825-5076
Free: (800)747-4457
Publisher E-mail: humank@hkusa.com

Journal on the teaching process and education in physical education. **Founded:** 1981. **Freq:** Quarterly. **Print Method:** Offset. **Trim Size:** 6 x 9. **Cols./Page:** 1. **Col. Width:** 65 nonpareils. **Col. Depth:** 108 agate lines. **Key Personnel:** Nell Faucette, Editor, phone (813)974-4658, fax (813)974-4676; Patt Dodds, Editor, phone (413)545-0529. **ISSN:** 0273-5024. **Subscription Rates:** $40 individuals; $100 institutions; $26 students. **Remarks:** Accepts advertising.
Ad Rates: BW: $375 **Circ:** Paid ‡1,078

8310 Library Trends
University of Illinois Graduate School of Library & Information Science
501 E. Daniel St. Phone: (217)333-1359
Champaign, IL 61820 Fax: (217)244-7329
Publication E-mail: puboff@alexia.lis.uiuc.edu

Library and information science Journal. **Founded:** 1952. **Freq:** Quarterly. **Print Method:** Letterpress and Offset. **Trim Size:** 6 x 9. **Cols./Page:** 1. **Col. Width:** 52 nonpareils. **Col. Depth:** 101 agate lines. **Key Personnel:** F.W. Lancaster, Editor; James S. Dowling, Managing Editor, phone (217)244-1412, dowling@alexia.lis.uiuc.edu. **ISSN:** 0024-2594. **Subscription Rates:** $75 individuals; $82 other countries. **Remarks:** Advertising not accepted. **Online:** Ebsco; UMI; Information Access.
Circ: 3,200

8311 Lipids
American Oil Chemists' Society
PO Box 3489 Phone: (217)359-2344
Champaign, IL 61826-0489 Fax: (217)351-8091
Publisher E-mail: general@aocs.org

Scientific journal containing original research on lipids, bio-

chemistry, and related biomedical subjects. **Founded:** Jan. 1967. **Freq:** Monthly. **Print Method:** Offset. **Trim Size:** 8 1/4 x 11. **Cols./Page:** 2. **Col. Width:** 20.5 picas. **Col. Depth:** 57 picas. **Key Personnel:** Howard R. Knapp, Editor, phone (319)353-7338, fax (319)353-7340; Mary Lane, Publisher. **ISSN:** 0024-4201. **Subscription Rates:** $215 industry. **Remarks:** Advertising not accepted. **URL:** http://www.aocs.org.
Circ: 1,750
Controlled 50

8312 Marathon and Beyond
Human Kinetics Publishers, Inc.
1607 N. Market St. Phone: (217)351-5076
PO Box 5076 Fax: (217)351-2674
Champaign, IL 61825-5076
Free: (800)747-4457
Publisher E-mail: humank@hkusa.com

Journal on training for marathoners. **Founded:** 1997. **Freq:** Bimonthly. **Print Method:** Offset. **Trim Size:** 6 x 9. **Key Personnel:** Richard Benyo, Editor. **ISSN:** 1088-6672. **Subscription Rates:** $29.95 individuals; $44.95 institutions. **Remarks:** Accepts advertising.
Ad Rates: BW: $500 **Circ:** Paid ‡1,609

8313 Motor Control
Human Kinetics Publishers, Inc.
1607 N. Market St. Phone: (217)351-5076
PO Box 5076 Fax: (217)351-2674
Champaign, IL 61825-5076
Free: (800)747-4457
Publisher E-mail: humank@hkusa.com

Journal devoted to the exchange of scientific information on the control of movement across the lifespan, including issues related to motor disorders. **Founded:** 1997. **Freq:** Quarterly. **Print Method:** Offset. **Trim Size:** 6 x 9. **Cols./Page:** 1. **Col. Width:** 65 nonpareils. **Col. Depth:** 108 agate lines. **Key Personnel:** Mark Latash, Editor, phone (814)863-5374, fax (814)865-2440. **ISSN:** 1087-1640. **Subscription Rates:** $40; $90 institutions; $24 students. **Remarks:** Accepts advertising.
Ad Rates: BW: $300 **Circ:** Paid ‡242

8314 The News-Gazette
Professional Impressions Media Group, Inc.
15 Main St. Phone: (217)351-5252
PO Box 677 Fax: (217)351-5291
Champaign, IL 61820
General newspaper. **Founded:** 1852. **Freq:** Daily (eve.), Sat. and Sun. (morn.). **Print Method:** Offset. **Cols./Page:** 6. **Col. Width:** 25 nonpareils. **Col. Depth:** 301 agate lines. **Key Personnel:** John R. Foreman, Editor; Marajen S. Chinigo, Publisher; Sue Trippiedi, Advertising Dir. **URL:** http// www.news-gazette.com. **Feature Editors:** John Beck, *News*, phone (217)351-5212; Anne Cook, *Farm*, phone (217)351-5217; Dan Corkery, *Religion, Saturday*, phone (217)351-5213; Don Dodson, *Aviation, Financial/Business, Real Estate*, phone (217)351-5223; Rosemary Garhart, *Editorials*, phone (217)351-5381; Darrell Hoemann, *Photo*, phone (217)351-5214; Mike Howie, *Radio*, phone (217)351-5368; Tom Kacich, *Book, Consumer Affairs, Entertainment, Family, Fashion, Features, Food, Garden/Home, Lifestyle, Living, Movie, Music, Society, TV, Travel, Women's*, phone (217)351-5221; Julie Kistler, *Drama*, phone (217)351-5368; Jean McDonald, *Sports*, phone (217)351-5231; Mary Sharp, *City, Education, Environmental, Metro, Political, Rural Development, Suburban*, phone (217)351-5211; Paul Wood, *Medical, Science*, phone (217)351-5222.
Ad Rates: BW: $2,988.93 **Circ:** Mon.-Fri. ★**43,843**
4C: $3,388.93 Sat. ★**45,913**
PCI: $23.17 Sun. ★**50,050**

8315 Oil and Gas
Illinois State Geological Survey
Natural Resources Bldg. Phone: (217)333-4747
615 E. Peabody Dr. Fax: (217)244-7004
Champaign, IL 61820
Publisher E-mail: isgs@isgs.uiuc.edu

Petroleum industry magazine. **Subtitle:** Monthly Report on Drilling in Illinois. **Founded:** Nov. 1936. **Freq:** Monthly. **Print Method:** Offset. **Trim Size:** 8 1/2 x 11. **Cols./Page:** 1. **Col. Width:** 90 nonpareils. **Col. Depth:** 130 agate lines. **Key Personnel:** Bryan G. Huff, Editor, phone (217)244-2509, huff@geoserv.isgs.uiuc.edu. **ISSN:** 0747-5306. **Subscription Rates:** $15 individuals. **Remarks:** Advertising not accepted.
Circ: Paid ‡200
Controlled ‡120

8316 Pediatric Exercise Science
Human Kinetics Publishers, Inc.
1607 N. Market St. Phone: (217)351-5076
PO Box 5076 Fax: (217)351-2674
Champaign, IL 61825-5076
Free: (800)747-4457
Publisher E-mail: humank@hkusa.com

Journal stimulating better understanding and greater awareness of the importance of childhood exercise to scientists, health-care providers, and physical educators. **Founded:** 1989. **Freq:** Quarterly. **Print Method:** Offset. **Trim Size:** 6 x 9. **Cols./Page:** 1. **Col. Width:** 65 nonpareils. **Col. Depth:** 108 agate lines. **Key Personnel:** Thomas W. Rowland, M.D., Editor, phone (413)784-4440, fax (413)784-5995. **ISSN:** 0899-8493. **Subscription Rates:** $45 individuals; $105 institutions; $26 students. **Remarks:** Accepts advertising.
Ad Rates: BW: $300 **Circ:** Paid ‡600
Non-paid ‡32

8317 Policy Studies Journal
Policy Studies Organization
711 Ashton Lane South Phone: (217)359-8541
Champaign, IL 61820 Fax: (217)352-3037

Journal devoted to political and social science and applications to important policy problems. **Founded:** Sept. 1972. **Freq:** Quarterly. **Print Method:** Offset. **Trim Size:** 6 x 9. **Cols./Page:** 1. **Col. Width:** 57 nonpareils. **Col. Depth:** 108 agate lines. **Key Personnel:** Mack Shelley, Co-editor, phone (515)294-4144, fax (515)294-1003, mshelley@iastate.edu; Uday Desai, Co-editor, phone (618)536-2371, fax (618)453-3253, udesai@siu.edu; Stuart Nagel, Advertising Mgr., s-nagel@uiuc.edu. **ISSN:** 0190-292X. **Subscription Rates:** $32 individuals; $178 libraries. **Remarks:** Accepts advertising.
Ad Rates: BW: $180 **Circ:** Paid ‡2,350
Non-paid ‡50

8318 The Quarterly Review of Economics and Finance
Elsevier
University of Illinois Phone: (217)333-2332
1206 S. 6th St. Fax: (217)333-7410
Champaign, IL 61820
Publication E-mail: qref@cba.uiuc.edu

Magazine on economics and finance. **Founded:** 1961. **Freq:** Quarterly. **Print Method:** Offset. **Trim Size:** 6 x 9. **Cols./Page:** 1. **Col. Width:** 28 picas. **Col. Depth:** 52 picas. **Key Personnel:** Richard J. Arnould, Editor, phone (217)333-0120, fax (217)333-7412, rarnould@uiuc.edu; Richard E. Finnerty, Editor, phone (217)333-2815, finnerty@uiuc.edu. **ISSN:** 0033-5797. **Subscription Rates:** $100 individuals; $230 institutions. **Formerly:** Quarterly Review of Economics & Business.
Ad Rates: BW: $200 **Circ:** 2,000

8319 Quest
Human Kinetics Publishers, Inc.
1607 N. Market St. Phone: (217)351-5076
PO Box 5076 Fax: (217)351-2674
Champaign, IL 61825-5076
Free: (800)747-4457
Publisher E-mail: humank@hkusa.com

Journal featuring articles on the physical education profession. **Founded:** 1949. **Freq:** Quarterly. **Print Method:** Offset. **Trim Size:** 6 x 9. **Cols./Page:** 1. **Col. Width:** 65 nonpareils. **Col. Depth:** 108 agate lines. **Key Personnel:** Karen DePauw, Editor, phone (509)335-5581, fax (312)413-3699. **ISSN:** 0033-6297. **Subscription Rates:** $40 individuals; $100 institutions; $26 students. **Remarks:** Accepts advertising.
Ad Rates: BW: $300 **Circ:** Paid 1,562
Non-paid 44

8320 Sociology of Sport Journal
Human Kinetics Publishers, Inc.
1607 N. Market St. Phone: (217)351-5076
PO Box 5076 Fax: (217)351-2674
Champaign, IL 61825-5076
Free: (800)747-4457
Publisher E-mail: humank@hkusa.com

Journal of research and theory on the sociology of sports issues. **Founded:** 1983. **Freq:** Quarterly. **Print Method:** Offset. **Trim Size:** 6 x 9. **Cols./Page:** 1. **Col. Width:** 65 nonpareils. **Col. Depth:** 108 agate lines. **Key Personnel:** Cynthia Hasbrook, Ph.D., Editor. **ISSN:** 0741-1235. **Subscription Rates:** $40 individuals; $90 institutions; $24 students. **Remarks:** Accepts advertising.
Circ: Paid ‡1,119

8321 Sport History Review
Human Kinetics Publishers, Inc.
1607 N. Market St. Phone: (217)351-5076
PO Box 5076 Fax: (217)351-2674
Champaign, IL 61825-5076
Free: (800)747-4457
Publisher E-mail: humank@hkusa.com

Journal on the history of sports. **Founded:** 1996. **Freq:** Semiannual. **Print Method:** Offset. **Trim Size:** 6 x 9. **Cols./Page:** 1. **Col. Width:** 65 nonpareils. **Col. Depth:** 108 agate lines. **Key Personnel:** Don Morrow, Ph.D., Editor. **ISSN:** 1087-1659. **Subscription Rates:** $24 individuals; $48 institutions; $18 students. **Remarks:** Advertising not accepted.
Circ: Paid ‡259

8322 The Sport Psychologist
Human Kinetics Publishers, Inc.
1607 N. Market St. Phone: (217)351-5076
PO Box 5076 Fax: (217)351-2674
Champaign, IL 61825-5076
Free: (800)747-4457
Publisher E-mail: humank@hkusa.com

Journal designed for educational and clinical sport psychologists. **Founded:** 1987. **Freq:** Quarterly. **Print Method:** Offset. **Trim Size:** 6 x 9. **Cols./Page:** 1. **Col. Width:** 65 nonpareils. **Col. Depth:** 108 agate lines. **Key Personnel:** Peter Crocker, Editor, phone (306)966-6510, fax (306)966-6502, tsp.journal@usask.ca. **ISSN:** 0888-4781. **Subscription Rates:** $40 individuals; $100 institutions; $26 students. **Remarks:** Accepts advertising.
Ad Rates: BW: $300 **Circ:** Paid ‡1,202
‡45

8323 Strength and Conditioning
Human Kinetics Publishers, Inc.
1607 N. Market St. Phone: (217)351-5076
PO Box 5076 Fax: (217)351-2674
Champaign, IL 61825-5076
Free: (800)747-4457
Publisher E-mail: humank@hkusa.com

Professional Journal focusing on the practical application of research and knowledge in strength and conditioning. **Founded:** 1979. **Freq:** Bimonthly. **Print Method:** Offset. **Trim Size:** 8 1/2 x 11. **Cols./Page:** 2. **Key Personnel:** Harvey Newton, Editor, phone (719)632-6722, fax (719)632-6367. **ISSN:** 1073-6840. **Subscription Rates:** $80 institutions. **Remarks:** Advertising not accepted.
Circ: Paid 11,600
Non-paid 1

8324 Teaching Elementary Physical Education
Human Kinetics Publishers, Inc.
1607 N. Market St. Phone: (217)351-5076
PO Box 5076 Fax: (217)351-2674
Champaign, IL 61825-5076
Free: (800)747-4457
Publisher E-mail: humank@hkusa.com

Journal providing elementary physical educators with news and information. **Founded:** 1990. **Freq:** 6/year. **Print Method:** Offset. **Trim Size:** 8 1/2 x 11. **Cols./Page:** 3. **Key Personnel:** Steve Sanders, Editor, phone (534)844-1471, sandesin@mail.auburn.edu; Rainer Martens, Publisher; Linda Bump, Dir., Journal Divisions. **ISSN:** 1045-4853. **Subscription Rates:** $24; $60 institutions; $16 students. **Remarks:** Accepts advertising.
Ad Rates: BW: $600 **Circ:** Paid ‡3,693
4C: $840

8325 University of Illinois Law Review
Christianson
University of Illinois Phone: (217)333-6756
504 E. Pennsylvania Ave. Fax: (217)244-1478
244 Law Bldg.
Champaign, IL 61820
Legal journal. **Founded:** 1949. **Freq:** Quarterly. **Print Method:** Letterpress. **Cols./Page:** 1. **Col. Width:** 55 nonpareils. **Col. Depth:** 108 agate lines. **Key Personnel:** Board of Editors Office, Editor, lreveds@law.uiuc.edu; Board of Trustees, Publisher. **Subscription Rates:** $30 U.S.; $38 out of country. **Remarks:** Accepts advertising.
Ad Rates: BW: $90 **Circ:** 900

8326 Visual Arts Research
University of Illinois at Urbana-Champaign
143 Art and Design Bldg. Phone: (217)351-2942
408 E. Peabody Dr. Fax: (217)244-6788
Champaign, IL 61820
Professional journal covering art education. **Founded:** 1973. **Freq:** Semiannual. **Trim Size:** 6 x 9. **Cols./Page:** 2. **Key Personnel:** Nancy C. Gardner, Editor, ngardner@wcl.cso.uiuc.edu; Christine Thompson, Assoc. Editor; Carle Smith, Subscription Database. **ISSN:** 0736-0770. **Subscription Rates:** $25 individuals. **Remarks:** Advertising not accepted.
Circ: Paid 500

WBCP-AM - See Urbana

8327 WBGL-FM - 91.7
2108 W. Springfield Phone: (217)359-8232
Champaign, IL 61821 Fax: (217)359-7374
Free: (800)475-9245
E-mail: wbgl@cis.compuserve.com

Format: Religious. **Networks:** USA Radio. **Founded:** 1982. **Operating Hours:** Continuous; 25% network, 75% local. **ADI:** Terre Haute, IN. **Key Personnel:** Michael Sadowski, Music Dir.; Joel Ruppert, Production Dir.; Meridith Foster, Promotions Dir. **Wattage:** 20,000. **Ad Rates:** Noncommercial.

WCFN-TV - See Springfield

8328 WCIA-TV - 3
509 S. Neil Phone: (217)356-8333
PO Box 20 Fax: (217)373-3648
Champaign, IL 61824-0020

Format: Commercial TV. **Networks:** CBS. **Founded:** 1953. **Operating Hours:** Continuous. **ADI:** Springfield-Decatur-Champaign, IL. **Key Personnel:** Robb Gray, Jr., General Mgr., phone (217)356-8333, fax (217)356-3648, vpgm@wcia.com.

8329 WDWS-AM - 1400
2301 S. Neil St. Rd. Phone: (217)351-5300
Box 3939 Fax: (217)351-5385
Champaign, IL 61826-3939
E-mail: wdws@prairienet.org

Format: Talk; News; Sports. **Networks:** CBS. **Owner:** DWS Inc, at above address, Fax: (217)317-5385. **Founded:** 1937. **Operating Hours:** Continuous; 3% network, 97% local. **ADI:** Springfield-Decatur-Champaign, IL. **Key Personnel:** James G. Turpin, Contact; Rick Atterberry, Contact; Eric Todd, News Dir.; Dave Loane, Sports Dir.; Dave Burns, Contact; Jan Jelly, Contact; Gene Bamert, Chief Engineer. **Wattage:** 1000. **Ad Rates:** Combined advertising rates available with WHMS-FM. **URL:** http://www.wdws.com.

8330 WEFT-FM - 90.1
113 N. Market St. Phone: (217)359-9338
Champaign, IL 61820-4004
E-mail: weft@prairienet.org

Format: Public Radio. **Networks:** Pacifica. **Founded:** 1981. **Operating Hours:** Continuous. **ADI:** Springfield-Decatur-Champaign, IL. **Key Personnel:** Mike Woolf, Station Mgr.; Don Bishop, Music Dir. **Wattage:** 10,000. **Ad Rates:** Noncommercial. **URL:** http://www.prairienet.org/weft.

8331 WHMS-FM - 97.5
2301 S. Neil St. Rd. Phone: (217)351-5300
Box 3939 Fax: (217)351-5385
Champaign, IL 61826-3939
E-mail: 975@whms.com

Format: Adult Contemporary. **Owner:** DWS Inc, at above address. **Founded:** 1949. **Formerly:** WDWS-FM (1988). **Operating Hours:** 100% Local. **ADI:** Springfield-Decatur-Champaign, IL. **Key Personnel:** James G. Turpin, Contact; Amy Morris, News Dir.; Dave Loane, Sports Dir.; Dave Burns, General Sales Mgr.; Jan Jelly, Contact; Gene Bamert, Chief Engineer; Paul Kraimer, Program Dir. **Wattage:** 50,000. **Ad Rates:** Combined advertising rates available with WDWS-AM. **URL:** http://www.whms.com.

8332 WICD-TV - 15
250 S. Country Fair Dr. Phone: (217)351-8500
Champaign, IL 61821 Fax: (217)351-6056

Format: Commercial TV. **Simulcasts:** WICS-TV. **Networks:** NBC. **Owner:** Guy Gannett Communications, One City Center, Portland, ME 04101, (207)828-8100, Fax: (207)828-8160. **Founded:** 1958. **Operating Hours:** 5:30 a.m.-1:30 a.m. **ADI:** Springfield-Decatur-Champaign, IL. **Key Personnel:** Les Vann, Vice Pres./Station Manager; Gary Hackler, Sales Mgr.; Grant Uitti, News Dir.; Doug Quick, Promotions Mgr.; Mark Statzer, Chief Engineer; Brian Stumph, Operations Mgr. **Wattage:** 358 visual; 35 aural. **Ad Rates:** $15-2,500 for 30 seconds. Combined advertising rates available with WICS-TV.

8333 WKIO-FM - 92.5
504 S. Neil St. Phone: (217)352-1040
Champaign, IL 61820 Fax: (217)356-3330
E-mail: wkio@wkio.com

Format: Oldies. **Networks:** CNN Radio. **Founded:** 1967. **Operating Hours:** Continuous. **ADI:** Springfield-Decatur-Champaign, IL. **Key Personnel:** Jeff Balding, General Mgr.; Thomas W. DiFilippo, General Sales Mgr.; Mike Haile, Program Dir. **Wattage:** 20,000 ERP. **Ad Rates:** $120 for 60 seconds.

8334 WLRW-FM - 94.5
2603 W. Bradley Ave. Phone: (217)352-4141
Champaign, IL 61821-1823 Fax: (217)352-1256

Format: Adult Contemporary; Contemporary Hit Radio (CHR). **Owner:** Saga Communications of Illinois, at above address. **Founded:** 1942. **Operating Hours:** Continuous. **ADI:** Springfield-Decatur-Champaign, IL. **Key Personnel:** Dale Weber, Contact; Mike Blakemore, Program Dir.; Karen Cochrane, Sales Mgr.; Sheila Crackel, Business Mgr. **Wattage:** 50,000. **Ad Rates:** Advertising accepted; rates available upon request.

8335 WPCD-FM - 88.7
2400 W. Bradley Ave. Phone: (217)351-2450
Champaign, IL 61821 Fax: (217)373-3899
E-mail: wpcd@eudoramail.com

Format: Classic Rock; Album-Oriented Rock (AOR); Urban Contemporary. **Networks:** AP. **Owner:** Parkland College, at above address. **Founded:** 1978. **Operating Hours:** 6 a.m.-10 p.m.; 10% network, 90% local. **ADI:** Springfield-Decatur-Champaign, IL. **Key Personnel:** Dan Hughes, General Mgr., dhughes@parkland.cc.il.us; Tom McDonnell, News Dir., phone (217)351-2230, tmcdonnell@parkland.cc.il.us; Rich Furr, Chief Engineer, phone (217)373-3719, rfurr@parkland.cc.il.us. **Wattage:** 3300. **Ad Rates:** Noncommercial.

8336 WPGU-FM - 107.1
24 E. Green St. Phone: (217)244-3000
Champaign, IL 61820 Fax: (217)244-3001
E-mail: wpgu@wpgu.com

Format: Alternative/New Music/Progressive. **Networks:** ABC. **Owner:** Illinois Media Co., S7 E. Green St., Champaign, IL 61820. **Founded:** 1967. **Operating Hours:** Continuous; 100% local. **ADI:** Springfield-Decatur-Champaign, IL. **Key Personnel:** Andy Worthington, General Mgr.; Pete Schiecke, Program Dir.; Liz Dvorachelc, News Dir.; Katie Brandt, Promotions Dir. **Wattage:** 3000.

CHARLESTON†, pop. 19,287.

Coles Co. (E). 50 m S. of Champaign-Urbana. Eastern Illinois University. Manufactures, truck trailers, urethane foam insulation, business forms, plastic packaging, pre fab modular home, agricultural and commercial building, gray castings, paper coating. Agriculture. Corn, soybeans, wheat, broom corn.

8337 Daily Eastern News
Eastern Illinois University
Eastern Illinois University Phone: (217)581-2812
600 Lincoln Ave. Fax: (217)581-2923
Charleston, IL 61920-3099
Publication E-mail: efjdr@eiu.edu

Collegiate newspaper. **Founded:** 1915. **Freq:** Daily (morn.) (during the academic year). **Print Method:** Offset. **Trim Size:** 11 x 17. **Cols./Page:** 5. **Col. Width:** 11 1/2 picas. **Col. Depth:** 16 inches. **Key Personnel:** John David Reed, Publisher. **ISSN:** 0894-1599. **Subscription Rates:** $64 individuals. **Remarks:** Accepts advertising.
Ad Rates: GLR: $.50 **Circ:** ‡9,400
4C: $360
PCI: $7

8338 Karamu
Karamu Association
Charleston, IL 61920

Literary journal. **Founded:** 1966. **Freq:** Annual. **Trim Size:** 5 x 8. **Key Personnel:** Olga Abella, Editor; Lauren Smith, Editor. **Subscription Rates:** $7.50 individuals. **Remarks:** Advertising not accepted.
Circ: Combined 750

8339 Times-Courier
Howard Publications
307 6th St. Phone: (217)345-7085
Box 650 Fax: (217)345-7090
Charleston, IL 61920
General newspaper. **Founded:** 1840. **Freq:** Mon.-Sat. (morn.). **Print Method:** Offset. **Cols./Page:** 6. **Col. Width:** 25 nonpareils. **Col. Depth:** 301 agate lines. **Key Personnel:** Betty H. Boyer, Editor and Publisher. **Subscription Rates:** $59.80 individuals. **Remarks:** Accepts advertising.
Ad Rates: SAU: $8.85 **Circ:** Mon.-Sat. 7,372

8340 WEIC-AM - 1270
RR. 2, Box 185B Phone: (217)345-2148
Charleston, IL 61920 Fax: (217)348-7036

Format: News; Gospel; Talk. **Founded:** 1954. **Operating Hours:** Continuous; 80% network, 20% local. **ADI:** Springfield-Decatur-Champaign, IL. **Key Personnel:** Gary Lee, General Mgr. **Wattage:** 1000. **Ad Rates:** $8-12 for 30 seconds; $12-16 for 60 seconds.

8341 WEIC-FM - 92.1
RR 2 Phone: (217)345-2148
Box 185A Fax: (217)348-7036
Charleston, IL 61920

Format: Adult Contemporary. **Networks:** Satellite Music Network. **Founded:** 1962. **Operating Hours:** Continuous; 90% network, 10% local. **ADI:** Springfield-Decatur-Champaign, IL. **Key Personnel:** Stephen H. Garman, President. **Wattage:** 3000. **Ad Rates:** $15 for 30 seconds; $24 for 60 seconds.

8342 WEIU-FM - 88.9
Eastern Illinois University Phone: (217)581-7370
Charleston, IL 61920 Fax: (217)581-6650
E-mail: cfjkh@eivedu

Format: Full Service. **Founded:** 1985. **Operating Hours:** 8 a.m.-midnight. **ADI:** Springfield-Decatur-Champaign, IL. **Key Personnel:** Joe Heumann, Station Mgr., cfjkh@eiu.edu; John Beabout, General Mgr., phone (217)581-5956, csjlb@eiv.edu; Ron Amyx, Chief Engineer, phone (217)581-7139, cszka@eiv.edu; Elaine Fine, Music Dir., phone (217)581-7211, csef@eiv.edu. **Wattage:** 4000.

8343 WEIU-TV - 51
Radio & TV Center Phone: (217)581-5956
Eastern Illinois University, 139 Buzzard Fax: (217)581-6650
Charleston, IL 61920
E-mail: csjlb@eiu.edu

Format: Public TV. **Networks:** Public Broadcasting Service (PBS). **Founded:** 1986. **Operating Hours:** 30% network, 10% local, 60% syndicated. **ADI:** Springfield-Decatur-Champaign, IL. **Key Personnel:** John Beabout, General Mgr., phone (217)581-6960, csjlb@eiu.edu; Audrey Bachelder, Promotions Mgr., phone (217)581-7193, csaab@eiu.edu; Ron Amyx, Chief Engineer, phone (217)581-7139, csrda@eiu.edu; Linda Kingery, Prog. Director, phone (217)581-7364, csllk@eiu.edu. **Local Programs:** *NewsScan 51* 9 p.m. Monday-Friday, John Eisenhour; *Panther Country* Monday. **Wattage:** 50,000.

CHESTER

8344 Randolph County Herald Tribune
Liberty Group Publishing
624 State St. Phone: (618)826-2385
PO Box 269 Fax: (618)826-5181
Chester, IL 62233
Community newspaper. **Founded:** 1863. **Freq:** Weekly (Thurs.). **Print Method:** Offset. **Cols./Page:** 6. **Col. Depth:** 21 inches. **Key Personnel:** Matthew Marcinkowski, Editor; Melody Rodgers, Publisher. **Subscription Rates:** $19.25; $22 outside county. $.50 single issue. **Remarks:** Accepts advertising.
Ad Rates: PCI: $5.05 **Circ:** 3,500

CHICAGO†, pop. 3,005,072.

Cook Co. (NE). On Lake Michigan and Chicago River. Two hundred twenty six colleges and universities; many medical, law, theological, music, art, commercial, technical, dental colleges and preparatory schools. Nations convention center. One of the great commercial centers of the United States. The livestock and grain market of the world and the largest mail order distributing center. Leads the United States in the production of telephone equipment, musical instruments, machinery, steel, diesel engines, office machines, radio and TV sets, auto accessories.

8345 AAII Journal
American Association of Individual Investors
625 N. Michigan Ave., Ste. 1900 Phone: (312)280-0170
Chicago, IL 60611 Fax: (312)280-1625
Free: (800)428-2244
Publication E-mail: journal@aaii.com

Journal containing practical information on personal finance and investment. **Founded:** 1979. **Freq:** Monthly. **Trim Size:** 8 1/2 x 11. **Cols./Page:** 2. **Key Personnel:** Maria Crawford Scott, Editor, mcs@aaii.com. **ISSN:** 0192-3315. **Subscription Rates:** $49 individuals; $6 single issue. **Remarks:** Advertising not accepted. **Online:** America Online. **URL:** http://www.aaii.com.
Circ: ‡170,000

8346 ABA Journal
American Bar Association
750 N. Lake Shore Dr. Phone: (312)988-5000
Chicago, IL 60611-4497 Fax: (312)988-5568
Free: (800)285-2221
Publication E-mail: abajournal@abanet.org

Legal publication. **Subtitle:** The Lawyer's Magazine. **Founded:** 1915. **Freq:** 12/year. **Print Method:** Offset. **Trim Size:** 8 3/16 x 10 3/4. **Cols./Page:** 3. **Col. Width:** 27 nonpareils. **Col. Depth:** 140 agate lines. **Key Personnel:** Gary Hengstler, Editor and Publisher, phone (312)988-5999, fax (312)988-6026, hengstler@staff.abanet.org; Robert A. Brouwer, Associate Publisher, phone (312)988-5993, fax (312)988-6014, brouwer@staff.abanet.org. **ISSN:** 0747-0088. **Subscription Rates:** $75 individuals. **Remarks:** Accepts advertising. **Online:** abanet.org. **Former name:** American Bar Association Journal.
Ad Rates: BW: $15,375 **Circ:** Paid ★322,547
4C: $20,000 Non-paid ★55,086
SAU: $400

8347 ADA News
ADA Publishing Co., Inc.
211 E. Chicago Ave. Phone: (312)440-2791
Chicago, IL 60611 Fax: (312)440-3538
Free: (800)621-8099
Publication E-mail: adanews@ada.org

Publisher E-mail: adapco@ada.org

Dental newspaper (tabloid). **Founded:** 1970. **Freq:** Biweekly (with single insurance in July & Dec.). **Print Method:** Offset. **Trim Size:** 11 x 14 3/4. **Cols./Page:** 4. **Col. Width:** 2 1/2 inches. **Col. Depth:** 13 1/4 inches. **Key Personnel:** Judy Jakush, Editor; Duane Billek, Advertising Sales Mgr. **ISSN:** 0895-2930. **Subscription Rates:** $50 individuals; $70 institutions; $69 other countries; $6 single issue; $89 institutions, other countries. **Remarks:** Accepts advertising.
Ad Rates: BW: $9,680 **Circ:** 140,000
4C: $1,550

8348 Advancing Philanthropy
National Society of Fund Raising Executives
303 E. Wacker Dr., Ste. 1030 Phone: (312)946-1900
Chicago, IL 60601 Fax: (312)946-1922
Publisher E-mail: nsfre@nsfre.org

Professional journal covering philanthropy. **Subtitle:** Journal of the National Society of Fund Raising Executives. **Freq:** Quarterly. **Key Personnel:** Marie A. Reed, Managing Editor; Robert M. Moore, Editorial Dir.; Jim Winters, Editor; Margaret Currie, Assoc. Editor. **ISSN:** 1056-2443. **Subscription Rates:** $50 individuals.

8349 Adventure Road
Amoco Enterprises, Inc.
200 E. Randolph Dr. Phone: (312)856-2583
Chicago, IL 60601 Fax: (312)856-2379

Travel magazine. **Subtitle:** Official Publication of the Amoco Motor Club. **Founded:** 1961. **Freq:** Quarterly. **Print Method:** Offset. **Trim Size:** 8 1/8 x 10 3/4. **Cols./Page:** 3. **Col. Width:** 27 nonpareils. **Col. Depth:** 140 agate lines. **Key Personnel:** M. Holstein, Editor; D.W. Larson, Publisher. **ISSN:** 0001-8805. **Subscription Rates:** $5 included in Amoco Motor Club; membership. **Remarks:** Accepts advertising.
Ad Rates: BW: $20,125 **Circ:** Paid 1,479,526
4C: $25,161 Controlled 250

8350 Advertising Age
Crain Communications, Inc.
740 N. Rush St. Phone: (312)649-5200
Chicago, IL 60611-2590 Fax: (312)649-5360

Advertising trade publication covering agency, media, and advertiser news and trends. **Subtitle:** Crain's International Newspaper of Marketing. **Founded:** Jan. 1930. **Freq:** Weekly (Mon.). **Print Method:** Offset. **Trim Size:** 11 x 14 1/2. **Cols./Page:** 5. **Col. Width:** 1 7/8 inches. **Col. Depth:** 14 inches. **Key Personnel:** David Klein, Editor; Joe Cappo, Senior VP; Ed Erhardt, Publisher. **ISSN:** 0001-8899. **Subscription Rates:** $99; $3 single issue. **Remarks:** Accepts advertising. **Online:** Apple Computer, Inc.; LEXIS-NEXIS; Dow Jones News-Retrieval; Prodigy Service Company.
Ad Rates: BW: $11,970 **Circ:** Paid 80,762
4C: $15,770
PCI: $150

8351 Advertising Age's Business Marketing
Crain Communications, Inc.
740 N. Rush St. Phone: (312)649-5200
Chicago, IL 60611-2590 Fax: (312)649-5360

Trade magazine on business-to-business marketing news, strategy, and tactics. **Founded:** 1916. **Freq:** Monthly. **Print Method:** Web. **Trim Size:** 11 x 14 1/2. **Cols./Page:** 5. **Col. Width:** 2 3/16 inches. **Col. Depth:** 14 inches. **Key Personnel:** Karen Egolf, Editor, phone (312)649-5239, fax (312)649-5462; Char Kosek, Managing Editor, phone (312)649-5326; Brian Reilly, Executive Editor, phone (312)649-5401. **ISSN:** 0745-5933. **Subscription Rates:** $59 individuals. **Online:** netb2b.com. **Also known as:** Business Marketing. **Formerly:** Industrial Marketing.
Ad Rates: BW: $6,160 **Circ:** Controlled 32,000
4C: $8,020

8352 Adweek/Midwest
BPI Communications, Inc.
936 Merchandise Mart Phone: (312)464-8500
Chicago, IL 60654 Fax: (312)464-8540

Periodical covering advertising, marketing, sales promotion, and merchandising. **Founded:** 1963. **Freq:** Weekly. **Print Method:** Offset. **Trim Size:** 8 3/8 x 10 7/8. **Cols./Page:** 3. **Col. Width:** 2 3/8 inches. **Col. Depth:** 10 inches. **Key Personnel:** Scott Hume, Editor, phone (312)464-8534, shume@adweek.com; Sherry Hollinger, Publisher, phone (312)464-8530. **Subscription Rates:** $105 individuals; $2.95 single issue. **Remarks:** Accepts advertising. **URL:** http://www.adweek.com.
Ad Rates: BW: $3,690 **Circ:** Combined 48,270
4C: $5,720

8353 AGD Impact
Academy of General Dentistry (AGD)
211 E. Chicago Ave. Phone: (312)440-4300
Chicago, IL 60611-2670 Fax: (312)440-0559
Free: (888)AGD-DENT
Publication E-mail: agdimpact@agd.org

Dental newsmagazine. **Subtitle:** Newsmagazine of the Academy of General Dentistry. **Founded:** 1973. **Freq:** 11/year. **Print Method:** Web offset. **Trim Size:** 8 3/8 x 10 7/8. **Cols./Page:** 2 and 3. **Key Personnel:** Roger Winland, DDS, Editor, phone (312)440-4348; Marilyn Mayes, Managing Editor, phone (312)440-4348; Jo-Ellyn Posselt, Dir. of Communications, phone (312)440-4307, jo-ellyn@aol.com; Todd Goldman, Advertising Mgr., phone (813)264-2772, fax (813)264-2343, todgoldman@aol.com. **ISSN:** 0194-729X. **Subscription Rates:** $25 individuals; $3 single issue; $40 institutions. **Alt. Formats:** Microform; Microform.
Ad Rates: BW: $2,005 **Circ:** ‡36,000
4C: $3,100

8354 Agnieszka's Dowry
A Small Garlic Press
5445 Sheridan Rd., No. 3003 Phone: (773)784-3844
Chicago, IL 60640-1941
Publication E-mail: asgp@enteract.com

Magazine that features poetry, arts, letters, and essays. **Founded:** 1996. **Trim Size:** 5 1/2 x 8. **Key Personnel:** Marek Lugowski, Editor, marek@enteract.com; Katrina Grace Conig, Editor, ketzle@aa.net. **ISSN:** 1088-4300. **Subscription Rates:** $3 single issue. **URL:** http://www.enteract.com/~asgp/agnieszka.html.

8355 AHA News
American Hospital Publishing, Inc.
1 N. Franklin Phone: (312)893-6800
Chicago, IL 60606 Fax: (312)422-4500
Free: (800)621-6902

Tabloid for healthcare industry professionals covering related business issues, legislative policies, and hospital management issues. **Subtitle:** American Hospital Association News. **Founded:** 1987. **Freq:** Weekly. **Print Method:** Offset. **Trim Size:** 11 5/16 x 15. **Cols./Page:** 4. **Col. Width:** 14 picas. **Col. Depth:** 14 1/2 inches. **Key Personnel:** Elizabeth Oplatka, Editor; John Sheehy, Publisher; Richard M. Dudley, Advertising Mgr. **ISSN:** 0891-6608. **Subscription Rates:** $45 members; $100 nonmembers. **Remarks:** Accepts advertising.
Circ: (Not Reported)

8356 AIDS Book Review Journal
University of Illinois at Chicago
Box 8198 Phone: (312)996-2730
Chicago, IL 60680-8198 Fax: (312)413-0424

Professional journal reviewing books and videos that cover AIDS and sexually transmitted diseases. **Founded:** Mar. 1993. **Freq:** Monthly. **Key Personnel:** H. Robert Malinowsky, Editor, hrm@uic.edu. **ISSN:** 1068-4174. **Subscription Rates:** Free. **Remarks:** Advertising not accepted. **URL:** http://www.uic.edu/depts/lib/aidsbkrv.
Circ: Non-paid 5,000

8357 Airports International
SKC Communication Services Ltd.
PO Box 31093 Phone: (847)884-1166
Chicago, IL 60631 Fax: (847)884-1262
Publication E-mail: 100574.1317@compuserv.com

Magazine covering the ground-based civil aviation industry worldwide. **Founded:** 1968. **Freq:** Monthly. **Print Method:** Offset, sheetfed. **Trim Size:** 8 1/4 x 11 1/4. **Cols./Page:** 3. **Key Personnel:** Tim Ornellas, Publisher; Mark Pilling, Editor; John C. Mallon, Sales Mgr., mmintl@starnetusa.com. **ISSN:** 0002-2853. **Subscription Rates:** $108 Free to qualified subscribers. **Remarks:** Accepts advertising.
Ad Rates: BW: $3,940 **Circ:** Controlled 10,721
4C: $5,540

8358 Alumni Report
University of Illinois at Chicago
College of Dentistry Phone: (312)996-8495
801 S. Paulina St. Fax: (312)413-2927
M/C 621
Chicago, IL 60612-7211
News for and about dentistry alumni. **Founded:** 1985. **Freq:** Semiannual. **Print Method:** Offset. **Trim Size:** 8 1/2 x 11. **Cols./Page:** 3. **Key Personnel:** William S. Bike, Editor, billbike@uic.edu. **ISSN:** 1088-9108. **Subscription Rates:** $6 individuals; $3 single issue. **Remarks:** Advertising not accepted.
Circ: Non-paid 5,500

8359 AMA Alliance Today
American Medical Association
515 N. State St. Phone: (312)464-5000
Chicago, IL 60610 Fax: (312)464-5830
Free: (800)621-8335
Publisher E-mail: amaa@ama-assn.org

Magazine for the families of physicians. **Founded:** 1965. **Freq:** Quarterly. **Print Method:** Offset. **Trim Size:** 7 15/16 x 10 3/4. **Cols./Page:** 3. **Col. Width:** 27 nonpareils. **Col. Depth:** 140 agate lines. **Key Personnel:** Susan G. Rubin, MPH, Editor; Hazel J. Lewis, Publisher. **ISSN:** 0163-0512. **Subscription Rates:** $7 individuals. **Remarks:** Advertising not accepted. **Formerly:** MD's Wife; Facets.
Circ: Controlled ‡70,000

8360 The American Archivist
Society of American Archivists
527 S. Wells St., 5th Fl. Phone: (312)922-0140
Chicago, IL 60617-3922 Fax: (312)347-1452
Publisher E-mail: info@archivists.org

Journal for the North American archival profession discussing trends in archival theory and practice and also featuring book reviews. **Founded:** 1938. **Freq:** Semiannual. **Print Method:** Offset. Uses mats. **Trim Size:** 6 3/4 x 10. **Cols./Page:** and 1. **Col. Depth:** 90 agate lines. **Key Personnel:** Philip B. Eppard, Editor, phone (518)442-5115; Teresa M. Brinati, Dir. Pub. **ISSN:** 0360-9081. **Subscription Rates:** $85 individuals; $100 out of country. **Remarks:** Accepts advertising. **Alt. Formats:** Microfilm.
Ad Rates: BW: $450 **Circ:** 4,634

8361 American Clean Car
American Trade Magazines
500 N. Dearborn St., Ste. 1100 Phone: (312)337-7700
Chicago, IL 60610 Fax: (312)337-8654

Magazine serving the car and truck washing and auto detailing industries. **Founded:** 1973. **Freq:** Bimonthly. **Print Method:** Offset. **Trim Size:** 8 1/8 x 10 7/8. **Cols./Page:** 3. **Col. Width:** 25 nonpareils. **Col. Depth:** 140 agate lines. **Key Personnel:** Larry Ebert, Editor; Ed Goldstein, Publisher. **ISSN:** 0095-1811. **Subscription Rates:** $35 individuals.
Ad Rates: BW: $2,045 **Circ:** ‡13,500
4C: $3,400

8362 American Coin-Op
American Trade Magazines
500 N. Dearborn St., Ste. 1100 Phone: (312)337-7700
Chicago, IL 60610 Fax: (312)337-8654

Trade magazine on coin-operated laundries and dry-cleaners. **Founded:** 1960. **Freq:** Monthly. **Print Method:** Web Offset. **Trim Size:** 8 1/8 x 10 7/8. **Cols./Page:** 3. **Col. Width:** 25 nonpareils. **Col. Depth:** 140 agate lines. **Key Personnel:** Paul Partyka, Editor; Ed Goldstein, Publisher. **USPS:** 964-740. **Subscription Rates:** $35 individuals.
Ad Rates: BW: $3,055 **Circ:** Controlled 18,800
4C: $4,505

8363 American Drycleaner
American Trade Magazines
500 N. Dearborn St., Ste. 1100 Phone: (312)337-7700
Chicago, IL 60610 Fax: (312)337-8654

Magazine on drycleaning. **Subtitle:** The Industry's Number One Magazine. **Founded:** 1934. **Freq:** Monthly. **Print Method:** Web Offset. **Trim Size:** 5 1/4 x 7 1/2. **Cols./Page:** 2. **Col. Width:** 26 nonpareils. **Col. Depth:** 90 agate lines. **Key Personnel:** Earl Fischer, Editor; Ed Goldstein, Publisher. **ISSN:** 0002-8258. **Subscription Rates:** $35 individuals; $6 single issue.
Ad Rates: BW: $2,760 **Circ:** Controlled ‡23,600
4C: $4,210

8364 American Field
542 S. Dearborn St. Phone: (312)372-1383
Chicago, IL 60605-1598 Fax: (312)663-5557

Journal featuring pure-bred sporting dogs. **Founded:** 1874. **Freq:** Weekly. **Print Method:** Offset. **Trim Size:** 10 3/4 x 13 3/4. **Cols./Page:** 4. **Col. Width:** 18 picas. **Col. Depth:** 72 picas. **Key Personnel:** B.J. Matthys, Publisher; Ron Betley, Advertising Mgr. **ISSN:** 0002-8452. **Subscription Rates:** $49 individuals. **Remarks:** Accepts advertising.
Ad Rates: BW: $672 **Circ:** Paid ‡10,000
PCI: $14 Non-paid ‡55

8365 American Laundry News
500 N. Dearborn St. Phone: (312)337-7700
Chicago, IL 60610 Fax: (312)337-8654

Institutional laundry magazine. **Subtitle:** The Newspaper of Record for Institutional Launderers. **Founded:** 1975. **Freq:** Monthly. **Print Method:** Web offset. **Trim Size:** 11 1/4 x 14 3/4. **Cols./Page:** 4. **Col. Width:** 28 nonpareils. **Col. Depth:** 195 agate lines. **Key Personnel:** Larry Ebort, Editor; Ed Goldstein, Publisher; Charles Thompson, Advertising Mgr. **ISSN:** 0164-

5765. **Subscription Rates:** $35; $6 single issue. **Remarks:** Accepts advertising. **Formerly:** Laundry News.
Ad Rates: BW: $3,010 **Circ:** ‡15,050
4C: $8,720

8366 American Libraries
American Library Association (ALA)
50 E. Huron St. Phone: (312)280-4216
Chicago, IL 60611 Fax: (312)440-0901
Free: (800)545-2433
Publication E-mail: americanlibraries@ala.org

Magazine including news and features of interest to library service professionals. **Founded:** 1907. **Freq:** 11/year. **Print Method:** Offset. **Trim Size:** 8 x 10 1/2. **Cols./Page:** 3. **Col. Width:** 27 nonpareils. **Col. Depth:** 136 agate lines. **Key Personnel:** Leonard Kniffel, Editor, phone (312)280-4215; Yolanda Washington, Advertising Traffic Coordinator, phone (312)280-5714. **ISSN:** 0002-9769. **Subscription Rates:** Free to qualified subscribers; $60 institutions; $70 other countries. **Online:** Data-Star; Dialog; LEXIS-NEXIS; Westlaw. **Alt. Formats:** Microform.
Ad Rates: GLR: $7.50 **Circ:** Combined ‡59,300
BW: $3,185
4C: $5,200

8367 American Medical News
American Medical Association
515 N. State St. Phone: (312)464-5000
Chicago, IL 60610 Fax: (312)464-5830
Free: (800)621-8335
Publisher E-mail: amaa@ama-assn.org

Socioeconomic trade publication. **Founded:** May 15, 1958. **Freq:** 48/year. **Print Method:** Offset. **Trim Size:** 11 1/16 x 15 1/8. **Cols./Page:** 4. **Col. Width:** 28 nonpareils. **Col. Depth:** 196 agate lines. **Key Personnel:** Robert L. Kennett, Publisher; Peter Murphy, Sales Mgr. **ISSN:** 0001-1843. **Subscription Rates:** $45 individuals. **Remarks:** Accepts advertising.
Ad Rates: GLR: $18.55 **Circ:** Paid 332,331
BW: $7,579 Non-paid 7,685
4C: $9,064

8368 American Nurseryman
American Nurseryman Publishing Co.
77 W. Washington St., Ste. 2100 Phone: (312)782-5505
Chicago, IL 60602-2904 Fax: (312)782-3232
Free: (800)621-5727
Publication E-mail: editors@amerinursery.com
Publisher E-mail: admin@amerinursery.com

Magazine containing information on horticulture and nursery, landscape and garden center management. **Subtitle:** Covering Commercial Horticulture Since 1904. **Founded:** Jan. 1, 1904. **Freq:** Semimonthly. **Print Method:** Offset. **Trim Size:** 8 x 10 7/8. **Cols./Page:** 6. **Col. Width:** 13 picas. **Col. Depth:** 10 inches. **Key Personnel:** Sally Benson, Editor; Allen W. Seidel, Publisher; Patricia Cleasby, Advertising Dir., advertising@amerinursey.com. **ISSN:** 0003-0198. **Subscription Rates:** $45 individuals; $75 other countries; $80.25 Canada; $5 single issue. **Remarks:** Accepts advertising.
Ad Rates: GLR: $4.50 **Circ:** Paid ★**13,005**
BW: $1,440
4C: $2,320

8369 American Planning Association Journal
American Planning Association
122 S. Michigan Ave., Ste. 1600 Phone: (312)786-6704
Chicago, IL 60603-6107 Fax: (312)431-9985
Publisher E-mail: jschwab@planning.org

Professional journal covering city planning. **Founded:** 1925. **Freq:** Quarterly. **Print Method:** Sheetfed offset. **Trim Size:** 8 1/2 X 11. **Key Personnel:** Donna Gamino, Advertising Mgr., phone (312)431-9100, dgamino@planning.org. **ISSN:** 0194-4363. **Subscription Rates:** $60 individuals; $85 out of country. **Remarks:** Accepts advertising. **Available Online.**
Ad Rates: BW: $840 **Circ:** Paid ⊕**11,400**

8370 American Printer
Intertec Publishing Co.
29 N. Wacker Dr. Phone: (312)726-2802
Chicago, IL 60606 Fax: (312)726-2574
Free: (800)621-9907

Magazine covering the printing and publishing market. **Subtitle:** The Graphic Arts Managers Magazine. **Founded:** 1883. **Freq:** Monthly. **Print Method:** Web offset. **Trim Size:** 8 1/8 x 10 7/8. **Cols./Page:** 3. **Col. Width:** 26 nonpareils. **Col. Depth:** 140 agate lines. **Key Personnel:** Jill Roth, Editorial Dir., phone (312)609-4232, fax (312)726-3091, jill_roth@intertec.com; Scott Bieda, Publisher, phone (312)609-4252, fax (312)726-3091, scott_bieda@intertec.com. **ISSN:** 0744-6616. **Subscription Rates:** $60 individuals. **Remarks:** Accepts advertising.
Ad Rates: GLR: $13 **Circ:** Controlled ‡89,755
BW: $8,500
4C: $10,800
PCI: $190

8371 American Zoologist
Society for Integrative and Comparative Biology
401 N. Michigan Ave. Phone: (312)527-6705
Chicago, IL 60611-4267 Fax: (312)321-3700
Free: (800)955-1236
Publisher E-mail: sicb@sba.com

Journal of zoological research. **Founded:** 1961. **Freq:** Bimonthly. **Print Method:** Offset. **Trim Size:** 6 7/8 x 10. **Cols./Page:** 2. **Col. Width:** 45 nonpareils. **Col. Depth:** 140 agate lines. **Key Personnel:** Jon Edwards, Editor. **ISSN:** 0003-1569. **Subscription Rates:** $245 individuals; $495 institutions; $260 Canada and Mexico; $510 institutions, Canada and Mexico; $275 other countries; $540 institutions, other countries. **Remarks:** Accepts advertising.
Ad Rates: BW: $550 **Circ:** Paid ‡3,200
4C: $1,620

8372 Anglican Advance
Diocese of Chicago
65 E. Huron St. Phone: (312)751-4207
Chicago, IL 60611 Fax: (312)787-4534

Episcopal newspaper. **Subtitle:** Official Publication of the Episcopal Diocese of Chicago. **Founded:** 1887. **Freq:** 7/year. **Print Method:** Offset. **Trim Size:** 11 x 17. **Cols./Page:** 4. **Col. Width:** 14 picas. **Col. Depth:** 11 picas. **Key Personnel:** David Skidmore, Editor, phone (312)751-4200, dskidmore@epischicago.com. **ISSN:** 1059-6763. **Subscription Rates:** $7 individuals. **Remarks:** Accepts advertising.
Ad Rates: BW: $1,000 **Circ:** 17,000

8373 Another Chicago Magazine
Left Field Press
3709 N. Kenmore
Chicago, IL 60613

Literary journal covering poetry and fiction. **Founded:** 1977. **Freq:** Annual. **Key Personnel:** Barry Silesky, Poetry Editor; Sharon Solwitz, Fiction Editor. **Subscription Rates:** $16 individuals; $8 single issue. **Remarks:** Advertising not accepted.
Circ: (Not Reported)

8374 Antiques & Collecting Magazine
Lightner Publishing Corp.
1006 S. Michigan Ave. Phone: (312)939-4767
Chicago, IL 60605 Fax: (312)939-0053
Free: (800)762-7576
Publisher E-mail: lightnerpb@aol.com

Magazine for antique and hobby collectors. **Founded:** 1931. **Freq:** Monthly. **Print Method:** Offset. **Trim Size:** 8 1/2 x 11. **Cols./Page:** 3. **Col. Width:** 2 3/16 inches. **Col. Depth:** 10 inches. **Key Personnel:** Frances L. Graham, Editor; Dale K. Graham, Publisher; Gregory K. Graham, Advertising Mgr. **ISSN:** 0884-6294. **Subscription Rates:** $28 individuals; $2.95 single issue. **Remarks:** Accepts advertising. **Alt. Formats:** Microfilm, UMI. **Formerly:** Antiques and Collecting Hobbies.
Ad Rates: BW: $598 **Circ:** Paid ‡10,000
4C: $910 Non-paid ‡6,000
PCI: $33

8375 The Appraisal Journal
Appraisal Institute
875 N. Michigan Ave., Ste. 2400 Phone: (312)335-4100
Chicago, IL 60611-1980 Fax: (312)335-4400

Real estate appraisal journal. **Founded:** Oct. 1932. **Freq:** Quarterly. **Print Method:** Offset. **Cols./Page:** 2. **Col. Width:** 16 picas. **Col. Depth:** 57 picas. **Key Personnel:** Donna O'Loughlin, Managing Editor, phone (312)335-4445. **ISSN:** 0003-7087. **Subscription Rates:** $35 individuals. **Remarks:** Advertising not accepted.
Circ: ‡24,200

8376 Archives of Dermatology
American Medical Association
515 N. State St. Phone: (312)464-5000
Chicago, IL 60610 Fax: (312)464-5830
Free: (800)621-8335
Publisher E-mail: amaa@ama-assn.org

Educational/clinical journal for dermatologists. **Founded:** 1882. **Freq:** Monthly. **Print Method:** Offset. **Trim Size:** 8 x 10 3/4. **Cols./Page:** 2. **Col. Width:** 41 nonpareils. **Col. Depth:** 140 agate lines. **Key Personnel:** Kenneth A. Arndt, M.D., Editor; Robert L. Kennett, Publisher; Michael D. Springer, Publisher. **ISSN:** 0003-987X. **Subscription Rates:** $120 individuals; $155 other countries; $12 single issue. **Remarks:** Accepts advertising. **Available Online.**
Ad Rates: BW: $1,300 **Circ:** Paid ‡6,477
4C: $2,415 Controlled ‡7,434

8377 Archives of General Psychiatry
AMA Center for Health Policy Research
515 N. State St. Phone: (312)464-5000
Chicago, IL 60610 Free: (800)621-8335
Publication E-mail: ahmcgreg@med.cornell.edu

Educational/clinical journal for psychiatrists. **Founded:** 1919. **Freq:** Monthly. **Print Method:** Offset. **Trim Size:** 8 x 10 3/4. **Cols./Page:** 2. **Col. Width:** 41 nonpareils. **Col. Depth:** 140 agate lines. **Key Personnel:** Jack D. Barchas, M.D., Editor; Robert Kennett, Publisher; Michael D. Springer, Publisher. **ISSN:** 0003-990X. **Subscription Rates:** $90 individuals annual subscription. **Remarks:** Accepts advertising. **Available Online. URL:** http://www.ama-assn.org. **Alt. Formats:** CD-ROM.
Ad Rates: BW: $1,610 **Circ:** Paid ‡6,434
4C: $2,650 Non-paid ‡26,967

8378 Archives of Internal Medicine
American Medical Association
515 N. State St. Phone: (312)464-5000
Chicago, IL 60610 Fax: (312)464-5830
Free: (800)621-8335
Publisher E-mail: amaa@ama-assn.org

Educational/clinical journal for internists, cardiologists, gastroenterologists, and other internal medicine subspecialists. **Founded:** 1908. **Freq:** Semimonthly. **Print Method:** Offset. **Trim Size:** 8 x 10 3/4. **Cols./Page:** 2. **Col. Width:** 41 nonpareils. **Col. Depth:** 140 agate lines. **Key Personnel:** James E. Dalen, M.D., Editor; Robert L. Kennett, Publisher; Michael D. Springer, Publisher. **ISSN:** 0003-9926. **Subscription Rates:** $110 individuals; $145 other countries; $12 single issue. **Remarks:** Accepts advertising. **Available Online.**
Ad Rates: BW: $3,435 **Circ:** Paid ‡6,529
4C: $4,915 Controlled ‡83,682

8379 Archives of Ophthalmology
American Medical Association
515 N. State St. Phone: (312)464-5000
Chicago, IL 60610 Fax: (312)464-5830
Free: (800)621-8335
Publisher E-mail: amaa@ama-assn.org

Educational/clinical journal for ophthalmologists. **Founded:** 1929. **Freq:** Monthly. **Print Method:** Offset. **Trim Size:** 8 x 10 3/4. **Cols./Page:** 3. **Col. Width:** 27 nonpareils. **Col. Depth:** 140 agate lines. **Key Personnel:** Daniel M. Albert, M.D., Editor; Robert Kennett, Publisher; Joseph Dennehy, Advertising Mgr. **ISSN:** 0003-9950. **Subscription Rates:** $65 individuals; $80 other countries; $10 single issue. **Remarks:** Accepts advertising.
Ad Rates: BW: $960 **Circ:** Paid ‡6,564
4C: $2,090 Non-paid ‡14,019

8380 Archives of Otolaryngology–Head & Neck Surgery
American Medical Association
515 N. State St. Phone: (312)464-5000
Chicago, IL 60610 Fax: (312)464-5830
Free: (800)621-8335
Publisher E-mail: amaa@ama-assn.org

Educational/clinical journal for otolaryngologists. **Founded:** 1925. **Freq:** Monthly. **Print Method:** Offset. **Trim Size:** 8 x 10 3/4. **Cols./Page:** 2. **Col. Width:** 41 nonpareils. **Col. Depth:** 140 agate lines. **Key Personnel:** Michael M.E. Johns, M.D., Editor; Robert L. Kennett, Publisher; Michael D. Springer, Publisher. **ISSN:** 0886-4470. **Subscription Rates:** $115 individuals; $150 other countries; $12 single issue. **Remarks:** Accepts advertising. **Available Online. URL:** http://www.ama-assn.org.
Ad Rates: BW: $720 **Circ:** Paid ‡4,763
4C: $1,680 Controlled ‡7,521

8381 Archives of Pathology & Laboratory Medicine
American Medical Association
515 N. State St. Phone: (312)464-5000
Chicago, IL 60610 Fax: (312)464-5830
Free: (800)621-8335
Publisher E-mail: amaa@ama-assn.org

Educational/clinical journal for pathologists. Published in cooperation with the College of American Pathologists. **Founded:** 1926. **Freq:** Monthly. **Print Method:** Offset. **Trim Size:** 8 x 10 3/4. **Cols./Page:** 2. **Col. Width:** 41 nonpareils. **Col. Depth:** 140 agate lines. **Key Personnel:** William W. McLendon, M.D., Editor; Robert L. Kennett, Publisher; Michael D. Springer, Publisher. **ISSN:** 0003-9985. **Remarks:** Accepts advertising. **Available Online. URL:** http://www.ama-assn.org.
Ad Rates: BW: $1,090 **Circ:** Paid ‡3,070
4C: $1,930 Controlled ‡13,274

8382 Archives of Pediatrics & Adolescent Medicine
American Medical Association
515 N. State St. Phone: (312)464-5000
Chicago, IL 60610 Fax: (312)464-5830
Free: (800)621-8335
Publisher E-mail: amaa@ama-assn.org

Educational/clinical journal for pediatricians. **Founded:** 1911. **Freq:** Monthly. **Print Method:** Offset. **Trim Size:** 8 x 10 3/4. **Cols./Page:** 2. **Col. Width:** 41 nonpareils. **Col. Depth:** 140 agate lines. **Key Personnel:** Catherine DeAngelis, Editor. **ISSN:** 0002-922X. **Subscription Rates:** $90 individuals; $125 other countries; $12 single issue. **Remarks:** Accepts advertising. **Available Online. Formerly:** AJDC: American Journal of Diseases of Children.
Ad Rates: BW: $1,825 **Circ:** Paid ‡5,494
4C: $2,950 Controlled ‡29,429

8383 Archives of Surgery
American Medical Association
515 N. State St. Phone: (312)464-5000
Chicago, IL 60610 Fax: (312)464-5830
Free: (800)621-8335
Publisher E-mail: amaa@ama-assn.org

Educational/clinical journal for general surgeons and surgical specialists. **Founded:** 1920. **Freq:** Monthly. **Print Method:** Offset. **Trim Size:** 8 x 10 3/4. **Cols./Page:** 2. **Col. Width:** 41 nonpareils. **Col. Depth:** 140 agate lines. **Key Personnel:** Claude H. Organ, Jr., Editor; Robert L. Kennett, Publisher; Michael D. Springer, Publisher. **ISSN:** 0004-0010. **Subscription Rates:** $90 individuals; $125 other countries; $12 single issue. **Remarks:** Accepts advertising. **Available Online.**
Ad Rates: BW: $2,445 **Circ:** (Not Reported)
4C: $3,770

8384 Art Institute of Chicago Museum Studies
Art Institute of Chicago
Graphic Design & Communications Services Phone: (312)443-3540
Fax: (312)443-1334
111 S. Michigan Ave.
Chicago, IL 60603-6110
Publisher E-mail: pubsmus@artic.edu

Professional journal covering art history and the collections of the Art Institute of Chicago. **Founded:** Apr. 1985. **Freq:** Semiannual. **Print Method:** Sheetfed. **Trim Size:** 8 3/8 x 10 1/4. **Cols./Page:** 2. **Col. Width:** 2 1/2 inches. **Col. Depth:** 8 1/4 inches. **Key Personnel:** Susan F. Rossen, Editor; Bryan Miller, Circulation Mgr., phone (312)857-7613. **ISSN:** 0069-3235. **Subscription Rates:** $25 individuals; $32 libraries; $35 out of country; $15 single issue. **Remarks:** Advertising not accepted.
Circ: Paid 1,500

8385 ASA News
ASA Communications, Inc.
222 Merchandise Mart Plz., Ste. 1360 Phone: (312)464-0090
Fax: (312)464-0091
Chicago, IL 60654
Publisher E-mail: asaemail@interserve.com

Magazine for Plumbing, PVF and Heating Distributors and Manufacturers. **Founded:** 1969. **Freq:** Bimonthly. **Trim Size:** 1/8. **Cols./Page:** 4. **Col. Width:** 2 inches. **Col. Depth:** 14 inches. **Key Personnel:** Mary Jo Martin, Editor-in-Chief, maryjomartin@earthlink.net; Molly-Frank Stewart, Advertising Dir., phone (708)386-3801, fax (708)386-3802; Matt Thomas, Assoc. Ed., mattthomas@earthlink.net. **Remarks:** Accepts advertising.
Circ: Controlled 22,500

8386 ASDA News
American Student Dental Association
211 E. Chicago Ave., Ste. 1160 Phone: (312)440-2795
Chicago, IL 60611 Fax: (312)440-2820
Free: (800)621-8099
Publisher E-mail: asda@asdaoffice.org

Newspaper (tabloid) for predoctoral dental students who are members of the ASDA. **Founded:** 1971. **Freq:** Monthly except July and August. **Print Method:** Offset. **Trim Size:** 11 x 17. **Cols./Page:** 4. **Col. Width:** 2 9/16 inches. **Col. Depth:** 14 inches. **Key Personnel:** Jennifer Doughty, Editor; Beth Winer, Adv. Coordinator. **ISSN:** 0277-3627. **Subscription Rates:** $24 individuals; $30 out of country. **Remarks:** Advertising accepted; rates available upon request.
Circ: 13,000

8387 At the Park
PO Box 597783 Phone: (773)465-4880
Chicago, IL 60659-7783 Fax: (773)465-0084
Publication E-mail: atthpark@mcs.com

Trade magazine covering the amusement and theme entertainment industry. **Founded:** Nov. 1989. **Freq:** Bimonthly. **Print Method:** Sheetfed offset. **Trim Size:** 8 1/2 x 10 7/8. **Key Personnel:** Allen Ambrosini, Editor and Publisher; Liucija Ambrosini, Publisher; Randy Geisler, Assoc. Editor. **ISSN:** 1048-9118. **Subscription Rates:** $39.95 individuals; $8 single issue. **Remarks:** Accepts advertising. **Former name:** DNA.
Circ: Controlled 9,000

8388 Automobile Red Book
National Market Reports
29 N. Wacker Dr. Phone: (312)726-2802
Chicago, IL 60606 Fax: (312)855-0137
Free: (800)621-9907

Auto guide. **Founded:** 1911. **Freq:** 8/year. **Key Personnel:** Patricia Arras, Publisher. **Subscription Rates:** $49.50 individuals; $19 single issue. **Remarks:** Advertising not accepted.
Circ: (Not Reported)

8389 Back of the Yards Journal
Back of the Yards Journal, Inc.
4642 S. Damen Phone: (312)927-7200
Chicago, IL 60609 Fax: (312)927-7940

Community newspaper serves the Back of the Yards and peripheral areas on the Southwest side of Chicago. Contains articles in English and Spanish languages. **Founded:** 1933. **Freq:** Weekly (Wed.). **Print Method:** Offset. **Trim Size:** 9 5/8 x 13. **Cols./Page:** 6. **Col. Width:** 1.5 inches. **Col. Depth:** 13 inches. **Key Personnel:** Susan Qualter, Editor, phone (773)927-7200, fax (773)927-7940; Patrick J. Salmon, Publisher, phone (773)523-4416, fax (773)254-3525; Susan Malone, General Mgr., phone (773)927-7203, fax (773)927-7940. **Subscription Rates:** $55 individuals. **Remarks:** Accepts advertising.
Ad Rates: SAU: $12 **Circ:** Combined 44,000
PCI: $8

8390 The Baffler Magazine
The Baffler
PO Box 378293 Phone: (773)493-0413
Chicago, IL 60637
Magazine concentrating on cultural criticism and discussing popular culture. **Subtitle:** The Journal That Blunts The Cutting Edge. **Founded:** 1988. **Freq:** 3/year. **Print Method:** perfect. **Trim Size:** 6 x 9. **Key Personnel:** Keith White, Director; Thomas Frank, Editor-in-Chief; Greg Lane, Publisher; Matt Weiland, Editor; Dave Mulcahey, Editor. **ISSN:** 1059-9789. **Subscription Rates:** $50 institutions. **Remarks:** Accepts advertising.
Ad Rates: BW: $1000 **Circ:** Paid 30,000

8391 The Bar Examiner
National Conference of Bar Examiners
333 N. Michigan Ave., Ste. 1025 Phone: (312)641-0963
Chicago, IL 60601-4001 Fax: (312)641-2052

Legal magazine. **Founded:** 1931. **Freq:** Quarterly. **Print Method:** Offset. **Cols./Page:** 2. **Col. Width:** 33 nonpareils. **Col. Depth:** 119 agate lines. **Key Personnel:** Ann Fisher, Editor. **ISSN:** 0005-5824. **Subscription Rates:** Free. **Remarks:** Advertising not accepted.
Circ: Non-paid ‡2,500

8392 The Beverly Review
TR Communications, Inc.
10546 S. Western Ave. Phone: (773)238-3366
Chicago, IL 60643 Fax: (773)238-1492

Community newspaper. **Founded:** 1905. **Freq:** Weekly (Wed.). **Print Method:** Offset. **Trim Size:** 11 x 16. **Cols./Page:** 5. **Col. Width:** 23 nonpareils. **Col. Depth:** 224 agate lines. **Key Personnel:** Robert M. Olszewski, Jr., Advertising Mgr.; Gerald Moore, Editor; Robert M. Olszewski, Sr., Publisher; Toby Olszewski, Publisher. **USPS:** 054-080. **Subscription Rates:** $18 individuals. **Remarks:** Accepts advertising.
Ad Rates: GLR: $.40 **Circ:** ‡6,000
BW: $672.50
PCI: $8.40

8393 The Bible Today
The Liturgical Press
Rev. Donald Senior Phone: (312)753-5345
Catholic Theological Union Fax: (312)324-4360
5401 S. Cornell Ave.
Chicago, IL 60615
Publisher E-mail: sales@litpress.org

Magazine promoting understanding and appreciation of Scripture, written especially for the nonspecialist reader, paraprofessional reader. **Subtitle:** Scripture for Life and Ministry. **Founded:** 1962. **Freq:** Bimonthly. **Print Method:** Offset. **Trim Size:** 6 x 9. **Cols./Page:** 1. **Col. Width:** 54 nonpareils. **Col. Depth:** 105 agate lines. **Key Personnel:** Michelle Verkuilen, Advertising Mgr., phone (612)363-2227; Brother Brad Vogt, Financial Mgr., phone (612)363-2538; Brother Robin Pierzina, Business Mgr., phone (612)363-3109. **ISSN:** 0006-0836. **Subscription Rates:** $22; $26 other countries. **Alt. Formats:** Audio tape.
Ad Rates: BW: $345 **Circ:** Paid 7,400
Non-paid 155

8394 Billiards Digest
Luby Publishing
122 S. Michigan Ave., Ste. 1506 Phone: (312)341-1110
Chicago, IL 60603 Fax: (312)341-1469
Publication E-mail: email@billiardsdigest.com
Publisher E-mail: lubyoub@aol.com

Billiards industry magazine. **Founded:** 1978. **Freq:** Monthly. **Print Method:** Offset. **Trim Size:** 8 1/2 x 11. **Cols./Page:** 2 and 3. **Col. Width:** 36 and 28 nonpareils. **Col. Depth:** 140 agate lines. **Key Personnel:** Michael E. Panozzo, Publisher; Keith Hamilton, President; Karl Lueders, Editor. **Subscription Rates:** $15 individuals. **Remarks:** Accepts advertising.
Ad Rates: BW: $730 **Circ:** 20,000
4C: $1,055

8395 Black Books Bulletin: Words Work
Third World Press
PO Box 19730 Phone: (773)651-0700
Chicago, IL 60619 Fax: (773)651-7286

Consumer magazine. **Freq:** Quarterly. **Subscription Rates:** $2.95 single issue. **Remarks:** Advertising accepted; rates available upon request.
Circ: (Not Reported)

8396 Black Music Research Journal
Columbia College Center for Black Music Research
600 S. Michigan Ave. Phone: (312)344-7559
Chicago, IL 60605 Fax: (312)344-8029
Publisher E-mail: cbmr@popmail.colum.edu

Magazine reporting on research in black music around the world. **Founded:** 1980. **Freq:** Semiannual. **Print Method:** Web. **Trim Size:** 6 x 9. **Cols./Page:** 1. **Col. Width:** 4 1/2 inches. **Col. Depth:** 7 inches. **Key Personnel:** Samuel A. Floyd, Jr., Editor, sfloyd@popmail.colum.edu. **ISSN:** 0276-3605. **Subscription Rates:** $35 individuals; $40 other countries; $17.50 single issue. **Remarks:** Accepts advertising.
Circ: (Not Reported)

8397 Book Links: Connecting Books, Libraries and Classrooms
American Library Association (ALA)
50 E. Huron St. Phone: (312)280-5038
Chicago, IL 60611 Fax: (312)280-5033
Free: (800)545-2433
Publication E-mail: BookLinks@ala.org

Magazine featuring themed bibliographies of children's books to support literature-based curriculum. **Founded:** 1991. **Freq:** Bimonthly. **Trim Size:** 8 3/8 x 10 7/8. **Key Personnel:** Judy O'Malley, Editor. **ISSN:** 1055-4742. **Subscription Rates:** $24.95 $5.00 single issue. **Remarks:** Accepts advertising. **URL:** http://www.ala.org/BookLinks.
Ad Rates: BW: $83,021 **Circ:** Paid 24,265
4C: $5,470 Non-paid 5,735

8398 Booklist
American Library Association (ALA)
50 E. Huron St. Phone: (312)280-5038
Chicago, IL 60611 Fax: (312)280-5033
Free: (800)545-2433

Guide to new books, audio visual, reference sources, and microcomputer software. Includes 7,000 reviews annually, plus 4,000 additional titles in subject bibliographies. **Subtitle:** Including Reference Books Bulletin. **Founded:** Jan. 1905. **Freq:** 22/year. **Print Method:** Offset. **Trim Size:** 8 3/8 x 10 7/8. **Cols./Page:** 3. **Col. Width:** 27 nonpareils. **Col. Depth:** 134 agate lines. **Key Personnel:** Bill Ott, Editor; Joanne Wilkinson, Circulation Mgr. **ISSN:** 0006-7385. **Subscription Rates:** $69.50 individuals; $85 other countries; $4.50 single issue. **Remarks:** Accepts advertising. **Alt. Formats:** CD-ROM.
Ad Rates: BW: $3,893 **Circ:** Paid ‡26,119
4C: $6,262 Non-paid ‡2,385

8399 Bowlers Journal
Luby Publishing
122 S. Michigan Ave., Ste. 1506 Phone: (312)341-1110
Chicago, IL 60603 Fax: (312)341-1469
Publisher E-mail: lubyoub@aol.com

Sports magazine. **Founded:** Nov. 1913. **Freq:** Monthly. **Print Method:** Offset. **Trim Size:** 8 1/4 x 10 7/8. **Cols./Page:** 3. **Col. Width:** 26 nonpareils. **Col. Depth:** 140 agate lines. **Key Personnel:** Mike Panozza; Keith Hamilton, President. **Subscription Rates:** $24 individuals. **Remarks:** Accepts advertising.
Ad Rates: BW: $1,830 **Circ:** 20,000
4C: $2,455

8400 Boxboard Containers
Intertec Publishing Co.
29 N. Wacker Dr. Phone: (312)726-2802
Chicago, IL 60606 Fax: (312)726-2574
Free: (800)621-9907
Publication E-mail: boxboard@intertec.com

Trade magazine for manufacturers of corrugated boxes, folding cartons, and rigid box converters. **Founded:** 1892. **Freq:** Monthly. **Print Method:** Offset. **Trim Size:** 8 1/8 x 10 7/8. **Cols./Page:** 4. **Col. Width:** 26 nonpareils. **Col. Depth:** 140 agate lines. **Key Personnel:** Robin Levine, Editor, robin_levineeintertec.com; Mike Walsh, Assoc. Pub., mike_walsheintertec.com. **ISSN:** 0006-8497. **Subscription Rates:** $30 individuals. **Remarks:** Accepts advertising.
Ad Rates: BW: $4,275 **Circ:** Paid ★2,582
4C: $5,845 Non-paid ★12,102
PCI: $95

8401 Bridgeport/Back of the Yards EXTRA
EXTRA Publications, Inc.
3918 W. North Ave. Phone: (312)252-3534
Chicago, IL 60647 Fax: (312)252-6031

Community newspaper. **Freq:** Weekly (Thurs.). **Key Personnel:** Mila Tellez, Publisher; Mary Montgomery, Editor; Miguel Alba, Managing Editor; Don Pringle, Editor.
Circ: ‡7,231

8402 Bridgeport News
3252 S. Halsted Phone: (312)842-5883
Chicago, IL 60608-6698 Fax: (312)842-5097

Community newspaper. **Founded:** 1938. **Freq:** Weekly (Wed.). **Print Method:** Offset. **Cols./Page:** 9. **Col. Width:** 19 nonpareils. **Col. Depth:** 301 agate lines. **Key Personnel:** Janice Racinowski, Editor; Joseph Feldman, Publisher. **Subscription Rates:** $75 individuals.
Ad Rates: GLR: $1.65 **Circ:** Combined ♦4,680
BW: $4,347
4C: $4,947
PCI: $23

8403 The Brief
American Bar Association
750 N. Lake Shore Dr. Phone: (312)988-5000
Chicago, IL 60611-4497 Fax: (312)988-5568
Free: (800)285-2221

Law magazine. **Founded:** 1970. **Freq:** Quarterly. **Print Method:** Offset. **Trim Size:** 8 3/8 x 10 7/8. **Cols./Page:** 3. **Col. Width:** 28 nonpareils. **Col. Depth:** 140 agate lines. **Key Personnel:** Anne Spencer, Editor, fax (312)988-6081, spencera@staff.abanet.org; John Elert, Advertising Mgr., phone (312)988-6115. **ISSN:** 0283-0995. **Subscription Rates:** $50 individuals. **Remarks:** Accepts advertising.
Ad Rates: BW: $1,580 **Circ:** Paid ‡32,000
4C: $2,680 Non-paid ‡1,741

8404 Brighton Park-McKinley Park Life
Litotype Publication
2949 W. Pope John Paul II Dr. Phone: (312)523-3663
Chicago, IL 60632 Fax: (312)523-3983

Community newspaper. **Founded:** Oct. 1933. **Freq:** Weekly (Thurs.). **Print Method:** Offset. **Cols./Page:** 8. **Col. Width:** 18 nonpareils. **Col. Depth:** 301 agate lines. **Key Personnel:** Albert H. Silinski, Editor. **Subscription Rates:** $60 individuals.
Ad Rates: GLR: $.63 **Circ:** Free ‡30,000
BW: $1102.50
SAU: $13
PCI: $8.75

8405 Bulletin of the Atomic Scientists
Educational Foundation for Nuclear Science, Inc.
6042 S. Kimbark Phone: (312)702-2555
Chicago, IL 60637 Fax: (312)702-0725
Publication E-mail: bulletin@bullatomsci.org
Publisher E-mail: bulletin@bullatomsci.org

Bulletin providing a forum for the debate of nuclear age issues. **Founded:** Dec. 10, 1945. **Freq:** Bimonthly. **Print Method:** Offset. **Trim Size:** 8 1/4 x 10 7/8. **Cols./Page:** 3. **Col. Width:** 13 picas. **Col. Depth:** 57 picas. **Key Personnel:** Steve Schwartz, Executive Dir., sschwartz@bullatomsci.org; Mike Moore, Editor, jmike@interaccess.com; Linda Rothstein, Managing Editor, lrio@interaccess.com; Brenden Matthews, Asst. Editor, brendan@interaccess.com; Mike Flynn, Associate Editor, mflynn@bullatomsci.org; Nora Wahlquist, Advertising/Promotions, noraw@interaccess.com; Hillary Metcalf, Business Mgr. **ISSN:** 0096-3402. **Subscription Rates:** $28 individuals; $6 single issue; $37.50 out of country. **Remarks:** Accepts advertising. **Available Online. URL:** http://www.bullatomsci.org. **Alt. Formats:** CD-ROM.
Ad Rates: BW: $995 **Circ:** ‡10,000
4C: $1,600

8406 Bulletin of the Medical Library Association
Medical Library Association
65 E. Wacker Dr., Ste. 1900 Phone: (312)419-9094
Chicago, IL 60601-7298 Fax: (312)419-8950
Publication E-mail: info@mlahq.org
Publisher E-mail: info@mlahq.org

Journal for library professionals in the health sciences. **Founded:** 1911. **Freq:** Quarterly. **Print Method:** Letterpress and offset. **Trim Size:** 8 1/2 x 11. **Cols./Page:** 2 and 3. **Col. Width:** 3 1/4 and 2 1/8 inches. **Col. Depth:** 8 5/8 and 8 1/4 inches. **Key Personnel:** J. Michael Homan, Editor. **ISSN:** 0025-7338. **Subscription Rates:** $136 individuals; $42.50 single issue; $174 other countries; $45 single issue other countries. **Remarks:** Accepts advertising. **URL:** www.kumc.edu/mla. **Alt. Formats:** Microform; Mailing labels.
Ad Rates: BW: $999 **Circ:** Non-paid ‡5685
4C: $1,898

8407 Business Insurance
Crain Communications, Inc.
740 N. Rush St. Phone: (312)649-5200
Chicago, IL 60611-2590 Fax: (312)649-5360

International newsweekly reporting on corporate risk, employee benefits, and managed health care news. **Founded:** 1967. **Freq:** Weekly. **Print Method:** Offset. **Trim Size:** 10 7/8 x 14 1/2. **Cols./Page:** 5. **Col. Width:** 11 1/2 picas. **Col. Depth:** 14 inches. **Key Personnel:** Paul Winston, Editor, phone (312)649-5442, pwinston@crain.com; Kathryn J. McIntyre, Publisher/Editorial Dir., phone (312)649-5286, kmcintyr@crain.com; Martin J. Ross, Assoc. Publisher/Advertising Dir., phone (212)210-0228, fax (212)210-0704, mross@crain.com. **ISSN:** 0007-6864. **Subscription Rates:** $87 individuals. **Remarks:** Accepts advertising. **Online:** Nexis; Dow Jones News Retrieval; Knight-Ridder Dialogue; Reuters Insurance Briefings. **URL:** http://www.businessinsurance.com.
Ad Rates: BW: $11,270 **Circ:** Paid 29,200
4C: $12,820 Controlled 23,011
PCI: $153

8408 Business Law Today
American Bar Association
750 N. Lake Shore Dr. Phone: (312)988-5000
Chicago, IL 60611-4497 Fax: (312)988-5568
Free: (800)285-2221

Magazine of the business law section, ABA. **Founded:** Mar. 1992. **Freq:** Bimonthly. **Print Method:** Offset. **Trim Size:** 8 3/8 x 10 7/8. **Cols./Page:** 3. **Col. Width:** 2 3/16 inches. **Col. Depth:** 10 inches. **Key Personnel:** Ray Delong, Editor; Nora Whitford, Advertising Mgr. **ISSN:** 1059-9436. **Remarks:** Accepts advertising.
Ad Rates: BW: $5,000 **Circ:** Paid 54,015
4C: $6,300 Non-paid 3,160

8409 The Business Lawyer
American Bar Association
750 N. Lake Shore Dr. Phone: (312)988-5000
Chicago, IL 60611-4497 Fax: (312)988-5568
Free: (800)285-2221

Law journal. **Founded:** 1946. **Freq:** Quarterly. **Print Method:** Offset. **Trim Size:** 6 x 9. **Cols./Page:** 1. **Col. Width:** 54 nonpareils. **Col. Depth:** 104 agate lines. **Key Personnel:** Nora C. Whitford, Advertising Mgr. **ISSN:** 0007-6899. **Subscription Rates:** $40 individuals. **Remarks:** Advertising not accepted.
Circ: Paid ‡56,011
Non-paid ‡5,064

8410 Catechumenate: A Journal of Christian Initiation
Liturgy Training Publications
1800 N. Hermitage Ave. Phone: (773)486-8970
Chicago, IL 60622-1101 Fax: (773)486-7094
Free: (800)933-1800
Publisher E-mail: marketing@ltp.org

Dedicated to the education and support of those engaged in the work of Christian initiation. **Founded:** 1978. **Freq:** Bimonthly. **Print Method:** Sheetfed. **Trim Size:** 6 x 9. **Cols./Page:** 1. **Col. Width:** 4 5/16 inches. **Col. Depth:** 6 7/8 inches. **Key Personnel:** Victoria Tufano, Editor, phone (773)486-8970, fax (773)486-7094, vtufano@ltp.org. **ISSN:** 1040-659X. **Subscription Rates:** $20; $25 other countries. $3 back issue. **Remarks:** Advertising not accepted. **Formerly**: The Chicago Catechumenate.
Circ: Paid 4,500
Non-paid 185

8411 CDS Review
Chicago Dental Society
401 N. Michigan Ave., Ste. 300 Phone: (312)836-7300
Chicago, IL 60611-4272 Fax: (312)836-7337
Publication E-mail: reviewvox@aol.com

Dental journal. **Founded:** 1921. **Freq:** 9/year. **Print Method:** Web offset. **Trim Size:** 8 1/2 x 10 5/8. **Cols./Page:** 3. **Col. Width:** 14.5 picas. **Col. Depth:** 126 agate lines. **Key Personnel:** Roger H. Scholle, DDS, Editor; Elizabeth Giangrego, Managing Editor. **Subscription Rates:** $25 individuals; $30 schools and industry; $45 other countries; $4 single issue; $6 November issue. **Remarks:** Accepts advertising. **Alt. Formats:** Microform.
Ad Rates: BW: $880 **Circ:** ‡8,500
4C: $1,880

8412 Chamber Way Germany/Midwest
German American Chamber of Commerce of the Midwest
401 N. Michigan Ave., Ste. 2525 Phone: (312)644-2662
Chicago, IL 60611-4212 Fax: (312)644-0738
Publisher E-mail: 106025.402@compuserve.com

Trade magazine covering international trade. **Founded:** Sept. 1982. **Freq:** Bimonthly. **Trim Size:** 8 1/2 x 11. **Cols./Page:** 2. **Col. Width:** 3.69 inches. **Col. Depth:** 8 1/2 inches. **Key Personnel:** Christian J. Roehr, Editor; Laurie L. Bowman, Asst. Editor; Diane Borker, Advertising Sales Rep. **Subscription Rates:** $25 individuals. **Remarks:** Accepts advertising. **Former name**: Focus Germany/Midwest; German American Business Journal Midwest.
Ad Rates: BW: $920 **Circ:** Controlled 6,000
4C: $1,820

8413 Chatham-Southeast Citizen
Citizen Newspapers
412 E. 87th St. Phone: (312)487-7700
Chicago, IL 60619 Fax: (312)487-7931

Newspaper serving Chicago's black community. **Subtitle:** A News Source You Can Trust. **Founded:** 1965. **Freq:** Weekly (Thurs.). **Print Method:** Offset. **Trim Size:** TABLOID. **Cols./Page:** 5. **Col. Width:** 25 nonpareils. **Col. Depth:** 196 agate lines. **Key Personnel:** William Garth, Publisher; Lisa Ely, Managing Editor. **Subscription Rates:** $25 individuals. **Online:** INTER ACCESS.
Ad Rates: BW: $1,799.70 **Circ:** Paid ‡20,597
PCI: $27.71 Free ‡9,365

8414 Chef
Talcott Communications Corp.
20 N. Wacker Dr., Ste. 1865 Phone: (312)849-2220
Chicago, IL 60606 Fax: (312)849-2174
Free: (800)229-1967
Publication E-mail: chefmag@aol.com
Publisher E-mail: talcottpub@aol.com

Food information for chefs. **Subtitle:** The Food Magazine for Professionals. **Founded:** 1956. **Freq:** 12/year. **Print Method:** Offset. **Trim Size:** 8 1/8 x 10 7/8. **Cols./Page:** 3. **Col. Width:** 24 nonpareils. **Col. Depth:** 140 agate lines. **Key Personnel:** Daniel Von Rabenau, Publisher; Brent T. Frei, Editor; Joseph Mooney, Managing Editor. **ISSN:** 1087-061X. **Subscription Rates:** $32 individuals; $2.95 per issue. **Remarks:** Accepts advertising. **Formerly**: Chef Institutional.
Ad Rates: BW: $3,775 **Circ:** Paid 1,500
4C: $4,995 Controlled 48,000

8415 Chicago
K-III Magazine Corp.
500 N. Dearborn, Ste. 1200
Chicago, IL 60610

Metropolitan magazine for the Chicago area. **Founded:** 1952. **Freq:** Monthly. **Print Method:** Offset. **Trim Size:** 8 x 10 3/4. **Cols./Page:** 3. **Col. Width:** 27 nonpareils. **Col. Depth:** 140 agate lines. **Key Personnel:** Richard Babcock, Editor; John Carroll, Publisher; George Gretser, Advertising Dir. **ISSN:** 0362-4595. **Subscription Rates:** $19.90 individuals; $2.95 single issue.
Ad Rates: BW: $9,310 **Circ:** Paid ★181,392
4C: $15,210
PCI: $290

8416 Chicago Apparel News
Apparel News Group
110 E. 9th St., Ste. A-777 Phone: (213)627-3737
Los Angeles, CA 90079-1777 Fax: (213)627-5707

Magazine covering the apparel industry; providing information about retail, fashion, textiles and accessories for women and children. **Founded:** 1979. **Freq:** 5/year. **Print Method:** Web press. **Trim Size:** 7 1/8 x 10. **Key Personnel:** Martin Wernicke, Publisher; Jack Maquette, Marketing Research. **ISSN:** 0195-0819. **Subscription Rates:** $20 individuals; $20 local; $4 single issue. **Remarks:** Accepts advertising.
Ad Rates: BW: $2,450 **Circ:** 10,764
4C: $3,250
PCI: $40

8417 Chicago Business
5801 S. Ellis Ave. Phone: (312)702-7422
Chicago, IL 60637-1404
Collegiate business school publication. **Founded:** 1977. **Freq:** Semimonthly. **Print Method:** Offset. **Trim Size:** 11 x 17. **Cols./Page:** 4. **Col. Width:** 24 nonpareils. **Col. Depth:** 224 agate lines. **Subscription Rates:** $15 individuals. **Remarks:** Accepts advertising.
Ad Rates: PCI: $12.50 **Circ:** Paid ‡300
Non-paid ‡2,500

8418 Chicago Catholic
New World Publications
1144 W. Jackson Blvd. Phone: (312)243-1300
Chicago, IL 60607-0181 Fax: (312)243-1526

Newspaper promoting education and evangelization in the Spanish community. **Founded:** 1985. **Freq:** Monthly. **Trim Size:** 11 1/2 x 16. **Cols./Page:** 5. **Col. Width:** 1 7/8 inches. **Col. Depth:** 14 3/4 inches. **Key Personnel:** Maria Del Carmen Macias, Editor. **Subscription Rates:** $13; $25 two years. **URL:** http://www.archdiocese-chgo.org.
Ad Rates: BW: $972 **Circ:** Paid 8,000
4C: $1,572 Non-paid 5,285
PCI: $21

8419 Chicago Chronicle
University of Chicago
University of Chicago Phone: (773)702-8353
5801 S. Ellis, Rm. 200 Fax: (773)702-8324
Chicago, IL 60637
Publication E-mail: chronicle@uchicago.edu

Collegiate newspaper. **Founded:** 1980. **Freq:** Semimonthly. **Print Method:** Offset. **Trim Size:** 11 1/2 x 17. **Cols./Page:** 4. **Col. Width:** 25 nonpareils. **Col. Depth:** 140 agate lines. **Key Personnel:** Colleen Newquist, Editor. **USPS:** 002-197. **Subscription Rates:** Free; $20 by mail. **Remarks:** Advertising not accepted. **URL:** http://www.globe.uchicago.edu/chronicle/current/titlepage.ht.
Circ: Paid 500
Free 13,500

8420 Chicago Citizen
Citizen Newspapers
412 E. 87th St. Phone: (312)487-7700
Chicago, IL 60619 Fax: (312)487-7931

Black community newspaper. **Founded:** 1965. **Freq:** Weekly (Thurs.). **Key Personnel:** Lisa Ely, Managing Editor; William A. Garth, Publisher. **Alt. Formats:** CD-ROM.

8421 The Chicago Computer Guide
Chicago Computer Guide, Inc.
954 W Washington, 5th Fl. Phone: (312)432-1662
Chicago, IL 60607 Fax: (312)432-0022
Publisher E-mail: ccg@ais.net

Technical, trade newspaper for business consumers making computer purchasing decisions. **Founded:** 1983. **Freq:** Monthly. **Key Personnel:** Scott L. Brown, Editor; George G. Scholemite, Publisher; Nick A. Scholomite, Marketing and Sales. **ISSN:** 1085-0767. **Subscription Rates:** $19.95 individuals. **Remarks:** Accepts advertising.
Ad Rates: BW: $1,800 **Circ:** Controlled 54,000
4C: $2,300

8422 Chicago Crusader
Crusader Newspapers
6429 S. Martin Luther King Dr. Phone: (773)752-2500
Chicago, IL 60637 Fax: (773)752-2817

Black community newspaper (tabloid). **Founded:** June 1940. **Freq:** Weekly (Sat.). **Print Method:** Offset. **Trim Size:** 10 x 14. **Cols./Page:** 5. **Col. Width:** 2 inches. **Col. Depth:** 14 inches. **Key Personnel:** Dorothy R. Leavell, Editor and Publisher; John Smith, Advertising Mgr. **USPS:** 596-080. **Subscription Rates:** $12 individuals. **Remarks:** Accepts advertising.
Ad Rates: BW: $793.10 **Circ:** Paid ‡57,000
4C: $1,002.20
PCI: $11.33

8423 Chicago Daily Law Bulletin
Law Bulletin Publishing Co.
415 N. State St. Phone: (312)644-7800
Chicago, IL 60610-4674 Fax: (312)644-1215

Legal and business newspaper. **Founded:** Oct. 1854. **Freq:** Daily. **Print Method:** Offset. **Trim Size:** 16 1/2 x 22 3/4. **Cols./Page:** 7. **Col. Width:** 25 nonpareils. **Col. Depth:** 294 agate lines. **Key Personnel:** Bernard Judge, Editor; Lanning MacFarland, Jr., Publisher; Sandy MacFarland, Advertising Mgr. **ISSN:** 0362-6148. **Subscription Rates:** $95 individuals. **Remarks:** Accepts advertising. **URL:** http://www.lawbulletin.com.
Ad Rates: BW: $1,543.50 **Circ:** ‡6,633

8424 Chicago Dental Society News
Chicago Dental Society
401 N. Michigan Ave., Ste. 300 Phone: (312)836-7300
Chicago, IL 60611-4272 Fax: (312)836-7337

Trade magazine covering dentistry in Chicago. **Founded:** 1901. **Freq:** 9/year. **Trim Size:** 8 3/8 x 10 7/8. **Cols./Page:** 3. **Col. Width:** 2 1/8 inches. **Col. Depth:** 9 inches. **Key Personnel:** Elizabeth Giangrego, Director of Publications; Karen Anderson, Asst. Managing Editor; Tom Long, Publications Asst. **USPS:** 573-520. **Subscription Rates:** Free to qualified subscribers; $25 individuals; $4 single issue. **Remarks:** Accepts advertising. **URL:** http://www.chicagodentalsociety.org. **Former name:** Fortnightly Review.
Ad Rates: BW: $880 **Circ:** Non-paid 8,000
4C: $1,880

8425 Chicago History
Chicago Historical Society
Clark St. at North Ave. Phone: (312)642-4600
Chicago, IL 60614 Fax: (312)266-2077

Magazine containing articles and photos about Chicago and American history. **Subtitle:** The Magazine of the Chicago Historical Society. **Founded:** 1945. **Freq:** 3/year. **Print Method:** Offset. **Trim Size:** 7 1/2 x 11 1/4. **Cols./Page:** 2. **Col. Width:** 17 picas. **Col. Depth:** 51 picas. **Key Personnel:** Rosemary K. Adams, Editor, adams@chicagohs.org. **ISSN:** 0272-8540. **Subscription Rates:** $30 individuals. **Remarks:** Advertising not accepted.
Circ: Paid 8,500
Non-paid 1,000

8426 Chicago Independent Bulletin
2037 W. 95th St. Phone: (312)783-1040
Chicago, IL 60643-1129
Black community newspaper. **Founded:** 1958. **Freq:** Weekly (Thurs.). **Key Personnel:** Hurley Green, Sr., Editor and Publisher.
Circ: 64,000

8427 Chicago Lawyer
Law Bulletin Publishing Co.
415 N. State St. Phone: (312)644-7800
Chicago, IL 60610-4674 Fax: (312)644-1215

Legal magazine. **Founded:** 1978. **Freq:** Monthly. **Print Method:** Offset. **Cols./Page:** 4. **Col. Width:** 30 nonpareils. **Col. Depth:** 182 agate lines. **Key Personnel:** Bernard Judge, Editor; Scott Anderson, Advertising Mgr., anderson@lbpc.com; Lisa Dede, Marketing Mgr., dede@lbpc.com. **Subscription Rates:** Free to qualified subscribers; $40 institutions. **Remarks:** Accepts advertising.
Ad Rates: BW: $1,320 **Circ:** Paid ★1,270
Non-paid ★9,016

8428 Chicago Life
1300 W. Belmont
Chicago, IL 60657
Publication E-mail: chgolife@mcs.com

Lifestyle magazine for Metropolitan Chicago residents. **Founded:** Dec. 1984. **Freq:** Bimonthly. **Print Method:** Offset. **Trim Size:** 8 3/8 x 10 7/8. **Cols./Page:** 3. **Col. Width:** 2 1/2 inches. **Col. Depth:** 9 5/8 inches. **Key Personnel:** Pam Berns, Press Editor. **Subscription Rates:** $30 individuals; $3 single issue. **Remarks:** Accepts advertising.
Ad Rates: BW: $3,325 **Circ:** Non-paid ★54,853
4C: $5,085

8429 The Chicago Maroon
1212 E. 59th St. Phone: (773)702-9555
Lower Level Fax: (773)702-3032
Chicago, IL 60637-1604
Community newspaper. **Founded:** 1892. **Freq:** Semiweekly (Tues. and Fri.; during the academic year). **Print Method:** Offset. Uses mats. **Trim Size:** 10 x 16. **Cols./Page:** 4. **Col. Width:** 29 nonpareils. **Col. Depth:** 210 agate lines. **Key Personnel:** Bryan Joiner, Editor-in-Chief, phone (773)702-1403, bnjoiner@midway.uchicago.edu; Judith Marciniak, Business Mgr., phone (773)702-9555, jmarcini@midway.uchicago.edu. **Subscription Rates:** $80 individuals; $150 out of country. **Remarks:** Accepts advertising. **URL:** http://www.chicagomaroon.com.
Ad Rates: BW: $375 **Circ:** ‡13,000
4C: $735
PCI: $9

8430 Chicago Medicine
Chicago Medical Society
The Medical Society of Cook County Phone: (312)670-2550
Fax: (312)670-3646
515 N. Dearborn St.
Chicago, IL 60610
Magazine for members of the Chicago Medical Society. Including features on practice management and medical and legal information. **Founded:** 1902. **Freq:** Semimonthly. **Print Method:** Letterpress and offset. **Trim Size:** 8 x 10 7/8. **Cols./Page:** 2 and 3. **Key Personnel:** Gary Baldwin, Editor. **ISSN:** 0009-3637. **Subscription Rates:** $30 individuals. **Remarks:** Accepts advertising.
Ad Rates: BW: $500 **Circ:** Paid 10,915
4C: $1,400

8431 Chicago Purchasor Magazine
Purchasing Management Association of Chicago
201 N. Wells St. Phone: (312)782-1940
Chicago, IL 60606 Fax: (312)782-9732

Magazine covering purchasing management. **Founded:** May 1922. **Freq:** Bimonthly. **Print Method:** Offset. **Trim Size:** 8 1/8 x 10 7/8. **Cols./Page:** 2. **Col. Width:** 42 nonpareils. **Col. Depth:** 139 agate lines. **Key Personnel:** John Pressley, Editor; Jackie Stinson, Advertising Mgr. **ISSN:** 0009-367X. **Subscription Rates:** $15 individuals; $2 single issue. **Remarks:** Accepts advertising.
Ad Rates: BW: $775 **Circ:** Paid ‡1,000
4C: $1,425 Controlled ‡4,600

8432 Chicago Reader
Chicago Reader, Inc.
11 E. Illinois Phone: (312)828-0350
Chicago, IL 60611 Fax: (312)828-0305
Publication E-mail: mail@chireader.com

Alternative newspaper covering urban issues and politics, arts and entertainment. **Subtitle:** Chicago's Free Weekly. **Founded:** 1971. **Freq:** Weekly (Fri.). **Print Method:** Offset. **Trim Size:** 11 x 17. **Cols./Page:** 5. **Col. Width:** 11.5 picas. **Col. Depth:** 16 inches. **Key Personnel:** Alison True, Editor; Jane Levine, Publisher; Don Humberton, Advertising Dir. **ISSN:** 1096-6919. **Subscription Rates:** $50 individuals; $100 Foreign. **Remarks:** Accepts advertising. **URL:** http://www.chicagoreader.com.
Ad Rates: BW: $2,370 **Circ:** Non-paid **★138,091**
4C: $3,795 Paid **★556**
PCI: $53.50

8433 The Chicago Reporter
Community Renewal Society
332 South Michigan Ave., Ste. 500 Phone: (312)427-4830
Fax: (312)427-6130
Chicago, IL 60604-9863
Publication E-mail: chgorptr@aol.com

Publication focusing on isues of race and poverty in the Chicago Metropolitan area. **Founded:** 1972. **Freq:** 11/year. **Key Personnel:** Laura Washington, Editor and Publisher, editor@chicagoreporter.com. **Subscription Rates:** $19 first-time subscription; $38 renewal. **Remarks:** Advertising not accepted.
Circ: Paid 1,500
Non-paid 4,000

8434 Chicago Review
University of Chicago
5801 S. Kenwood Phone: (773)702-0887
Chicago, IL 60637 Fax: (773)702-0887
Publication E-mail: chicago-review@uchicago.edu

Literary magazine presenting original poetry, short fiction, nonfiction, and art. **Founded:** 1946. **Freq:** Quarterly. **Print Method:** Offset. **Trim Size:** 6 x 9. **Cols./Page:** 1. **Col. Width:** 25 picas. **Col. Depth:** 44 picas. **Key Personnel:** Andrew Rathmann, Editor. **ISSN:** 0009-3696. **Subscription Rates:** $18 individuals; $35 institutions Add $5 for foreign postage; $6 single issue. **Remarks:** Accepts advertising. **Online:** EBSCO,WILSON. **URL:** www.uchicago.edu/humanities/review.
Ad Rates: BW: $150 **Circ:** Paid ‡2,700
Non-paid ‡100

8435 Chicago Shoreland News
AJA Enterprises
11740 S. Elizabeth Phone: (773)568-7091
Chicago, IL 60643 Fax: (773)928-6056

Black community newspaper. **Founded:** 1972. **Freq:** Weekly (Thurs.). **Print Method:** Offset. **Trim Size:** 9 3/4 x 14. **Cols./Page:** 5. **Col. Width:** 11.5 picas. **Col. Depth:** 14 inches. **Key Personnel:** Albert E. Johnson, Publisher; Michael A. Johnson, Editor; Andray Johnson, West Coast Editor; Theresa Delsoin, Entertainment Editor; Annette Johnson, General Mgr.; Marian Wright Edelman, Contributing Writer; Junious Richardo Stanton, Contributing Editor; Roy Hicks, Advertising Manager; Tony Conley, Circulation Mgr. **Subscription Rates:** $25 individuals.
Ad Rates: GLR: $15.50 **Circ:** 38,000
BW: $1,085 Paid 9,880
4C: $2,400
PCI: $200

8436 Chicago South Shore Scene
7426 S. Constance Phone: (773)363-0441
Chicago, IL 60649 Fax: (773)363-0441

Community newspaper (Black). **Founded:** 1959. **Freq:** Weekly (Thurs.). **Print Method:** Offset. **Trim Size:** 4 Cdumns. **Cols./Page:** 4. **Col. Width:** 18 nonpareils. **Col. Depth:** 224 agate lines. **Key Personnel:** Dr. Claudette McFarland, Editor and Publisher. **Subscription Rates:** $0 Free. **Remarks:** Accepts advertising.
Ad Rates: BW: $627 **Circ:** Paid ‡1,000
PCI: $18 Free ‡19,000

8437 Chicago Studies
1800 N. Hermitage Ave. Phone: (773)486-8970
Chicago, IL 60622-1101 Fax: (773)486-7094
Free: (800)933-4213
Publication E-mail: marketing@itp.org

Magazine for all who work in pastoral ministry. **Founded:** 1962. **Freq:** 3/year. **Trim Size:** 6 x 9. **Key Personnel:** Rev. George Dyer, Editor; John D. Wright, Marketing Dir. **Subscription Rates:** $17.50 individuals; $21.50 other countries; $6 back issues.
Ad Rates: BW: $500 **Circ:** Paid 3,000

8438 Chicago Sun-Times
Chicago Sun-Times Inc.
401 N. Wabash Ave. Phone: (312)321-3000
Chicago, IL 60611-3593 Fax: (312)321-3084

General newspaper. **Founded:** 1948. **Freq:** Mon.-Sun. (morn.). **Print Method:** Letterpress. **Trim Size:** 10 9/16 x 13 7/8. **Cols./Page:** 5. **Col. Width:** 26 nonpareils. **Col. Depth:** 196 agate lines. **Key Personnel:** F. David Radler, Publisher; Joe Sherman, Asst. Publisher; J. David Dodd, Executive VP; Nigel Wade, Editor-in-Chief; Larry Green, Exec. Editor. **Subscription Rates:** $156 individuals. **Remarks:** Accepts advertising. **Online:** DataTimes Corporation; LEXIS-NEXIS.
Ad Rates: GLR: $15.18 **Circ:** Mon.-Fri. ★**485,666**
BW: $10,305 Sat. ★**332,047**
4C: $13,205 Sun. ★**411,334**
PCI: $212.45

8439 Chicago Tribune
Tribune Publishing
435 N. Michigan Ave. Phone: (312)222-3232
Chicago, IL 60611-4022
General newspaper. **Founded:** 1847. **Freq:** Mon.-Sun. (morn.). **Print Method:** Offset. **Cols./Page:** 6. **Col. Width:** 25 nonpareils. **Col. Depth:** 21 inches. **Key Personnel:** Jac Fuller, V.P./Editor; John W. Madigan, Publisher. **Remarks:** Accepts advertising. **Online:** DataTimes Corporation; Dialog (The Dialog Corporation); CompuServe Information Service; LEXIS-NEXIS. **URL:** http://www.chicago.tribune.com. **Alt. Formats:** CD-ROM. **Feature Editors:** Al Borcover, *Travel*, phone (312)222-3589; Genevieve Buck, *Fashion*, phone (312)222-3521; Brenda Butler, *Garden/Home*, phone (312)222-4414; Dick Christiansen, *Drama, Entertainment*, phone (312)222-4281; Jack Corn, *Photo*, phone (312)222-4318; Colleen Dishon, *Features*, phone (312)222-4308; Dianne Donovan, *Book*, phone (312)222-4125; Bill Garrett, *City*, phone (312)222-3540; George Gunset, *Rural Development*, phone (312)222-3109; Carol Haddix, *Food*, phone (312)222-4533; Charles Hayes, *Real Estate*, phone (312)222-3459; Michael Hirsley, *Religion*, phone (312)222-3405; Dave Kehr, *Movie*, phone (312)222-3156; Charles Leroux, *Lifestyle*, phone (312)222-3577; Dick Leslie, *Sports*, phone (312)222-4133; Greg Lippert, *Sunday*, phone (312)222-4374; Charles Madigan, *Political*, phone (312)222-4226; Bill Neikirk, *Financial/Business*, phone (312)222-4523; Ellen Soeteber, *Metro*, phone (312)222-3432; Steve Swanson, *Environmental*, phone (312)222-3501; Cliff Terry, *TV & Radio*, phone (312)222-3428; Karen Thomas, *Education*, phone (312)222-3449; John Von Rhein, *Music*, phone (312)222-3570; Lois Wille, *Editorials*, phone (312)222-3431.
Ad Rates: SAU: $263 **Circ:** Mon.-Fri. ★**1,292,464**
Sat. ★**584,097**
Sun. ★**1,019,458**

8440 Chicago Tribune Magazine
Chicago Tribune
435 N. Michigan Ave. Phone: (312)222-3244
Chicago, IL 60611-4022 Fax: (312)222-3162

Magazine covering the people, places, and events throughout the greater Chicago area and the Midwest. **Freq:** Weekly (Sun.). **Print Method:** Rotogravure. **Trim Size:** 10 3/8 x 11 1/8. **Key Personnel:** Robert Reese, Editor. **Remarks:** Accepts advertising.
Ad Rates: BW: $19,166 **Circ:** (Not Reported)

8441 Chicago Weekend
Citizen Newspapers
412 E. 87th St. Phone: (312)487-7700
Chicago, IL 60619 Fax: (312)487-7931

Weekend newspaper serving Chicago's black community. **Subtitle:** A News Source You Can Trust. **Founded:** 1974. **Freq:** Weekly (Thurs.). **Print Method:** Offset. **Trim Size:** TABLOID. **Cols./Page:** 5. **Col. Width:** 25 nonpareils. **Col. Depth:** 196 agate lines. **Key Personnel:** William Garth, Publisher; Lisa Ely, Managing Editor. **Subscription Rates:** $25 individuals. **Online:** INTER-ACCESS. **Alt. Formats:** CD-ROM.
Ad Rates: BW: $1,799.70 **Circ:** Paid ‡22,583
PCI: $25.71 Free ‡2,053

8442 Chicago's Northwest Side Press
NADIG Newspapers, Inc.
4937 N. Milwaukee Ave. Phone: (773)286-6100
Chicago, IL 60630
Community newspaper. **Founded:** 1940. **Freq:** Weekly (Wed.). **Print Method:** Offset. **Cols./Page:** 8. **Col. Width:** 9.5 picas. **Col. Depth:** 294 agate lines. **Key Personnel:** Glenn Nadig, Publisher. **Subscription Rates:** Free; $85 individuals mail.
Ad Rates: BW: $2,016 **Circ:** Paid ‡9,000
PCI: $1,350 Free ‡40,000

8443 Children, Churches & Daddies
Scars Publications & Design
3625 W. Wrightwood, No. 2F Phone: (773)486-1174
Chicago, IL 60647
Publication E-mail: ccandd96@aol.com

Magazine containing poetry, short stories, art, and news. **Subtitle:** the unreligious, non-family-oriented literary & art magazine. **Founded:** June 1993. **Freq:** Monthly. **Trim Size:** 5 1/2 x 8 1/2. **Key Personnel:** Janet Kuypers, Publisher. **ISSN:** 1068-5154. **Subscription Rates:** $45; $4 single issue. **Remarks:** Advertising accepted; rates available upon request. **Online:** America Online, Inc. **URL:** http://www.gss-inc.net/scars/scars.html.
Circ: (Not Reported)

8444 Chip's Closet Cleaner
PO Box 11967
Chicago, IL 60611

Journal of popular culture and humor. **Founded:** 1989. **Freq:** Semiannual. **Print Method:** Offset. **Trim Size:** 8.5 x 11. **Cols./Page:** 3. **Key Personnel:** Chip Rowe, Publisher. **ISSN:** 1064-9719. **Subscription Rates:** $4 single issue. **Remarks:** Accepts advertising. **URL:** http://thetransom.com/chip. **Alt. Formats:** Diskette.
Ad Rates: BW: $200 **Circ:** Combined 1,000

8445 The Christian Century
The Christian Century Foundation
407 S. Dearborn St., Ste. 1405 Phone: (312)427-5380
Chicago, IL 60605-1150 Fax: (312)427-1302
Free: (800)208-4097
Publication E-mail: ccentury@aol.com

Religious magazine. **Founded:** Jan. 4, 1900. **Freq:** Weekly. **Print Method:** Web offset. **Trim Size:** 8 1/4 x 10 7/8. **Cols./Page:** 3 and 2. **Col. Width:** 27 and 43 nonpareils. **Col. Depth:** 140 agate lines. **Key Personnel:** Rev. James M. Wall, Editor; David Heim, Managing Editor; Heidi Baumgaertner, Advertising Mgr.; Lisa Tiede, Subscription Mgr. **ISSN:** 0009-5281. **Subscription Rates:** $40 individuals; $2 single issue. **Remarks:** Accepts advertising. **Alt. Formats:** Microform.
Ad Rates: BW: $1,210 **Circ:** ‡30,000
4C: $1,285
PCI: $50

8446 The Christian Ministry
The Christian Century Foundation
407 S. Dearborn St., Ste. 1405 Phone: (312)427-5380
Chicago, IL 60605-1150 Fax: (312)427-1302
Free: (800)208-4097
Publication E-mail: ccentadm@christiancentury.org

Religious magazine. **Founded:** 1969. **Freq:** Bimonthly. **Print Method:** Offset. **Trim Size:** 8 1/4 x 10 7/8. **Cols./Page:** 3 and 2. **Col. Width:** 13.5 and 20.5 picas. **Col. Depth:** 57 picas. **Key Personnel:** Rev. James M. Wall, Editor; Heidi Baumgaertner, Advertising Mgr.; Victoria Rebeck, Managing Editor. **ISSN:** 0033-4138. **Subscription Rates:** $17 individuals; $2.50 single issue. **Remarks:** Accepts advertising. **Formerly:** The Pulpit.
Ad Rates: BW: $550 **Circ:** Paid 5,506
PCI: $25 Non-paid 50

8447 Clear-Ridge Reporter
Vondrac Publishing
6225 S. Kedzie Ave. Phone: (312)476-4800
Chicago, IL 60629-3397 Fax: (312)475-7811

Shopper. **Freq:** Weekly (Wed.). **Cols./Page:** 6. **Col. Width:** 10 picas. **Col. Depth:** 16 inches. **Key Personnel:** James Vondrak, Publisher.
Circ: 22,900

8448 Coal Age
Intertec Publishing Co.
29 N. Wacker Dr. Phone: (312)726-2802
Chicago, IL 60606 Fax: (312)726-2574
Free: (800)621-9907

Coal production magazine. **Founded:** 1911. **Freq:** Monthly. **Print Method:** Offset. **Trim Size:** 8 1/8 x 10 7/8. **Cols./Page:** 3. **Col. Width:** 2 3/16 inches. **Col. Depth:** 10 inches. **Key Personnel:** Art Sanda, Editor, phone (304)252-6801, fax (304)252-8344; Robert E. Dimond, Publishing Dir. **ISSN:** 1040-7820. **Subscription Rates:** $62.50 Canada and U.S.; $100 other countries. **Remarks:** Accepts advertising. **Online:** LEXIS-NEXIS. **Formerly:** Coal.
Ad Rates: BW: $4,215 **Circ:** Controlled ‡19,609
4C: $5,710

8449 Collections and Credit Risk
Faulkner & Gray, Inc.
300 S. Wacker, 18th Fl. Phone: (312)913-1334
Chicago, IL 60606 Fax: (312)913-1365

Business publication tracking trends in the credit and collections industry. **Founded:** Jan. 1, 1997. **Freq:** Monthly. **Key Personnel:** John Stewart, Publisher; David E. Whiteside, Editor, phone (312)983-6130, david_whiteside@faulknergray.com. **Subscription Rates:** $95 individuals. **Remarks:** Accepts advertising. **URL:** http://ccr.faulknergray.com.
Circ: (Not Reported)

8450 College and Research Libraries News
Association of College and Research Libraries
50 E. Huron St. Phone: (312)280-2517
Chicago, IL 60611 Fax: (312)280-2520
Free: (800)545-2433
Publisher E-mail: acrl@ala.org

Magazine reporting news, trends, and research of interest to academic library professionals. **Founded:** 1966. **Freq:** 11/year. **Print Method:** Offset. **Trim Size:** 6 1/8 x 9 1/4. **Cols./Page:** 2. **Col. Width:** 29 nonpareils. **Col. Depth:** 109 agate lines. **Key Personnel:** Mary Ellen Davis, Editor, medavis@ala.org; Jack Helbig, Circulation Mgr., phone (312)280-2513, fax (312)280-7663, jhelbig@ala.org; Stu Foster, Advertising Mgr., phone (860)347-6933, fax (860)346-8586, sfoster@ala.org. **ISSN:** 0099-0086. **Subscription Rates:** $35 individuals. **Remarks:** Accepts advertising. **URL:** http://www.ala.org/acrl.html.
Ad Rates: GLR: $8.75 **Circ:** ‡12,000
BW: $935
4C: $1,710

8451 Commercial Investment Real Estate
Commercial Investment Real Estate Institute
430 N. Michigan Ave., Ste. 800 Phone: (312)321-4460
Chicago, IL 60611-4092 Fax: (312)321-4530
Publication E-mail: magazine@ccim.com

Professional development magazine for commercial investment professionals and allied fields. **Founded:** 1982. **Freq:** Bimonthly 6/year. **Print Method:** Web offset. **Trim Size:** 8 1/2 x 10 3/4. **Key Personnel:** Catherine A. Simpson, Publisher, csimpson@cirei.com; Barbara Stevenson, Editor, bstevenson@cirei.com. **ISSN:** 0887-4778. **Subscription Rates:** $38 individuals; $46 other countries. **Remarks:** Accepts advertising. **URL:** http://www.ccim.com/journal. **Alt. Formats:** Mailing labels. **Formerly:** Commercial Investment Real Estate Journal.
Ad Rates: BW: $1,895 **Circ:** Paid ‡600
4C: $2,650 Controlled ‡11,000

8452 Company
American Jesuits
3441 N. Ashland Ave. Phone: (312)281-1534
Chicago, IL 60657 Fax: (312)281-2667
Free: (800)955-5538
Publication E-mail: editor@companysj.com

Religious magazine for the American Society of Jesus (Jesuits) and those who work with them. **Subtitle:** A Magazine of the American Jesuits. **Founded:** Sept. 1983. **Freq:** Quarterly. **Print Method:** Offset. **Trim Size:** 8 3/8 x 10 7/8. **Cols./Page:** 3. **Col. Width:** 13 1/2 picas. **Col. Depth:** 120 agate lines. **Key Personnel:** Martin McHugh, Editor. **ISSN:** 0886-1293. **Subscription Rates:** Free. **Remarks:** Advertising not accepted. **Available Online. URL:** http://www.companysj.com. **Alt. Formats:** Audio tape.
Circ: Controlled ‡125,000

8453 The Compleat Lawyer
American Bar Association
750 N. Lake Shore Dr. Phone: (312)988-5000
Chicago, IL 60611-4497 Fax: (312)988-5568
Free: (800)285-2221

Legal magazine. **Founded:** 1984. **Freq:** Quarterly. **Print Method:** Offset. **Cols./Page:** 3. **Col. Width:** 26 nonpareils. **Col. Depth:** 135 agate lines. **Key Personnel:** Rachel Schick, Editor; Rita Novak, Advertising Mgr. **Subscription Rates:** $25 individuals. **Remarks:** Accepts advertising.
Ad Rates: BW: $750 **Circ:** Paid ‡17,698
4C: $1,300 Non-paid ‡1,877

8454 Complete Woman
Associated Publications, Inc.
875 N. Michigan Ave., Ste. 3434 Phone: (312)266-8680
Chicago, IL 60611-1901
Women's general interest. **Subtitle:** For All the Women You Are. **Founded:** 1980. **Freq:** Bimonthly. **Print Method:** Offset. **Cols./Page:** 3. **Col. Width:** 27 nonpareils. **Col. Depth:** 142

agate lines. **Key Personnel:** Bonnie L. Krueger, Editor; James L. Spurlock, Publisher. **Subscription Rates:** $17.50 individuals. **Remarks:** Accepts advertising.
Ad Rates: BW: $2,475 **Circ:** Paid 350,000
4C: $3,218 Non-paid 5,000

8455 Computerized Investing
American Association of Individual Investors
625 N. Michigan Ave., Ste. 1900 Phone: (312)280-0170
Chicago, IL 60611 Fax: (312)280-1625
Free: (800)428-2244

Magazine covering the use of computers for investment analysis. **Founded:** 1982. **Freq:** Bimonthly. **Cols./Page:** 3. **Key Personnel:** John Bajkowski, Managing Editor, johnb@aaii.com; Kenneth J. Michal, Asst. Ed., kmichal@aaii.com. **ISSN:** 0734-4597. **Subscription Rates:** $40 annually. **Remarks:** Advertising not accepted. **URL:** http://www.aaii.com.
Circ: ‡42,000

8456 Concrete Products
Intertec Publishing Co.
29 N. Wacker Dr. Phone: (312)726-2802
Chicago, IL 60606 Fax: (312)726-2574
Free: (800)621-9907

Magazine on concrete products and ready-mixed concrete. **Founded:** 1947. **Freq:** Monthly. **Print Method:** Offset. **Trim Size:** 8 1/8 x 10 7/8. **Cols./Page:** 3. **Col. Width:** 26 nonpareils. **Col. Depth:** 140 agate lines. **Key Personnel:** Don Marsh, Editor; Ken Hughes, Group Publisher. **USPS:** 128-180. **Subscription Rates:** $40 Canada and U.S.; $50 other countries. **Alt. Formats:** Microform.
Ad Rates: BW: $4,040 **Circ:** Non-paid ‡19,163
4C: $5,435

8457 Conscious Choice
Conscious Communications
920 N Franklin, No. 202 Phone: (312)440-4373
Chicago, IL 60610-3179 Fax: (312)751-3973
Publication E-mail: cc@consciouschoice.com

Consumer magazine covering health, nutrition and environmental issues. **Subtitle:** The Journal of Ecology & Natural Living. **Founded:** 1988. **Freq:** Bimonthly. **Print Method:** Web offset. **Trim Size:** 10 1/2 x 13. **Cols./Page:** 4. **Col. Width:** 2 1/4 inches. **Col. Depth:** 12 inches. **Key Personnel:** Ross Thompson, Managing Editor; Sheri Reda, Editor; Aliess Brady, Senior Editor; Sondra Brigandi, Advertising Dir. **Subscription Rates:** $18 individuals; $4 single issue. **Remarks:** Accepts advertising. **URL:** http://www.consciouschoice.com.
Ad Rates: BW: $1,520 **Circ:** Non-paid 50,000
4C: $1,990

8458 Cornerstone
Cornerstone Communications, Inc.
939 W. Wilson Ave. Phone: (773)561-2450
Chicago, IL 60640-5706 Fax: (773)989-2076

Issue-oriented magazine for contemporary evangelical Christians. **Founded:** May 1972. **Freq:** Periodic 3-4/year. **Print Method:** Web offset. **Trim Size:** 8 3/8 x 10 7/8. **Cols./Page:** 3. **Col. Width:** 2 1/4 inches. **Col. Depth:** 10 inches. **Key Personnel:** Dawn Mortimer, Editor-in-Chief, phone (312)561-2450, fax (312)561-2450, dawn@jpusa.pr.mcs.net. **ISSN:** 0275-2743. **Subscription Rates:** Free in U.S. **Remarks:** Accepts advertising. **URL:** http://www.cornerstonemag.com.
Ad Rates: GLR: $0.50 **Circ:** Controlled ‡37,000
BW: $1,300
4C: $1,730

8459 Corporate Legal Times
Legal Times Inc.
3 E. Huron St. Phone: (312)654-3500
Chicago, IL 60611 Fax: (312)654-3525
Publication E-mail: info@gsteps.com

Legal magazine. **Subtitle:** Managing In-House Law Departments and Outside Law Firms. **Founded:** 1991. **Freq:** Monthly. **Print Method:** Heatset. **Trim Size:** 10 7/8 x 15. **Cols./Page:** 4. **Col. Width:** 2 3/8 inches. **Col. Depth:** 13 1/2 inches. **Key Personnel:** Thomas L. Goodman, Publisher; Charles H. Carman, Gen. Counsel; Jennifer King, Managing Editor. **ISSN:** 1063-3006. **Subscription Rates:** $95 individuals; $15 single issue. **Remarks:** Accepts advertising. **Online:** LEXIS-NEXIS; Westlaw. **URL:** http://www/corporatelegaltimes.com.
Ad Rates: BW: $8,185 **Circ:** 40,000
4C: $9,361 5,000
PCI: $185

8460 The Covenant Companion
Covenant Publications
5101 N. Francisco Ave. Phone: (773)784-3000
Chicago, IL 60625 Fax: (773)784-4366
Publisher E-mail: covcom@compuserve.com

Religious magazine. **Subtitle:** The Official Publication of The Evangelical Covenant Church. **Founded:** 1911. **Freq:** Monthly. **Print Method:** Offset. **Trim Size:** 8 x 11. **Cols./Page:** 3. **Col. Width:** 26 nonpareils. **Col. Depth:** 133 agate lines. **Key Personnel:** Jane Swanson-Nystrom, Managing Editor; Steven Luce, Advertising Mgr. **ISSN:** 0011-0671. **Subscription Rates:** $29.95.
Ad Rates: GLR: $3.90 **Circ:** Paid 21,500
BW: $870 Non-paid 350
4C: $1,195
PCI: $32

8461 Crain's Chicago Business
Crain Communications, Inc.
740 N. Rush St. Phone: (312)649-5200
Chicago, IL 60611-2590 Fax: (312)649-5360

Newspaper covering news stories about various aspects of business and labor activity in the Chicago market. **Founded:** 1978. **Freq:** Weekly (Mon.). **Print Method:** Offset. **Trim Size:** 11 x 14 3/4. **Cols./Page:** 5. **Col. Width:** 22 nonpareils. **Col. Depth:** 196 agate lines. **Key Personnel:** David Snyder, Editor; Gloria Scoby, Publisher; Deborah Greif, Advertising Dir.; Robert Reed, Exec. Dir. **ISSN:** 0149-6956. **Subscription Rates:** $89 individuals. **Remarks:** Accepts advertising. **Online:** LEXIS-NEXIS. **URL:** http://www.crainchiagobusiness.com.
Ad Rates: BW: $10,290 **Circ:** Paid ★**47,281**
4C: $12,885 Non-paid ★**3,201**

8462 Criminal Justice Magazine
American Bar Association
750 N. Lake Shore Dr. Phone: (312)988-5000
Chicago, IL 60611-4497 Fax: (312)988-5568
Free: (800)285-2221

Magazine providing practical treatment of aspects of criminal law. **Founded:** 1986. **Freq:** Quarterly. **Print Method:** Web offset. **Trim Size:** 8 3/8 x 10 7/8. **Cols./Page:** 3. **Col. Width:** 2 3/16 inches. **Col. Depth:** 9 1/2 inches. **Key Personnel:** MaryAnn Dadisman, Editor, phone (312)988-6047, fax (312)988-6081; Rita Novak, Advertising Mgr., phone (312)988-6115, fax (312)988-6030. **ISSN:** 0887-7785. **Subscription Rates:** $38; $47 other countries; $10 single issue. **Remarks:** Accepts advertising.
Ad Rates: BW: $890 **Circ:** Paid 8,603
4C: $1,690 Non-paid 1,252

8463 Dawn
Slovenian Women's Union of America/Slovenska Zenska Zveza Ameriki
4851 S. Drexel Blvd. Phone: (312)548-8878
Chicago, IL 60615
Ethnic magazine. Reports on membership branches located in 14 states. **Subtitle:** Zarja - The Dawn. **Founded:** 1929. **Freq:** 8/year. **Print Method:** Offset. **Trim Size:** 8 x 11. **Cols./Page:** 3. **Col. Width:** 12 picas. **Col. Depth:** 60 picas. **Key Personnel:** Corinne Leskovar, Editor, phone (312)548-8878. **ISSN:** 0044-1848. **Subscription Rates:** $15 individuals; Free to members. **Remarks:** Color advertising not accepted. **Foreign language name:** Karja.
Ad Rates: BW: $150 **Circ:** Paid ‡5,800
PCI: $5 Controlled ‡25

8464 The Dental Assistant
American Dental Assistants Association
203 N. LaSalle St., Ste. 1320 Phone: (312)541-1550
Chicago, IL 60601-1225 Fax: (312)541-1496
Free: (800)733-2322
Publisher E-mail: adaa1@aol.com

Official journal of American Dental Assistants Association. **Subtitle:** Journal of the American Dental Assistants Association. **Founded:** 1931. **Freq:** 6/year. **Print Method:** Offset. **Trim Size:** 8 3/8 x 10 7/8. **Cols./Page:** 2. **Col. Depth:** 60 picas. **Key Personnel:** Doug McDonough, Editor. **ISSN:** 0011-8508. **Subscription Rates:** $20 individuals; $6 single issue; $25 foreign. **Remarks:** Accepts advertising. **Alt. Formats:** Microform.
Ad Rates: BW: $1,200 **Circ:** Paid ‡14,800
4C: $2,100
PCI: $100

8465 Dentistry
American Student Dental Association
211 E. Chicago Ave., Ste. 1160 Phone: (312)440-2795
Chicago, IL 60611 Fax: (312)440-2820
Free: (800)621-8099
Publisher E-mail: asda@asdaoffice.org

Magazine for dental students and new dentists. **Founded:** Dec. 1981. **Freq:** Quarterly. **Print Method:** Offset. **Trim Size:** 8 1/4 x 10 5/8. **Cols./Page:** 3. **Col. Width:** 28 nonpareils. **Col. Depth:** 127 agate lines. **Key Personnel:** Angela Green, Managing Editor, phone (312)440-2847; Beth Winer, Advertising Coord. **ISSN:** 0277-3635. **Subscription Rates:** $16 individuals U.S.; $24 Canada. **Remarks:** Advertising accepted; rates available upon request.
Circ: (Not Reported)

8466 The Diabetes Educator
American Association of Diabetes Educators
100 W. Monroe, 4th Fl. Phone: (312)424-2426
Chicago, IL 60603 Fax: (312)424-2427
Free: (800)338-3633

Journal featuring original literature from all disciplines regarding diabetes and diabetes patient education. **Subtitle:** The Journal of the American Association of Diabetes Educators. **Founded:** 1975. **Freq:** Bimonthly. **Print Method:** Offset. **Trim Size:** 8 3/8 x 11. **Cols./Page:** 3 and 2. **Col. Width:** 27 and 40 nonpareils. **Col. Depth:** 140 agate lines. **Key Personnel:** James A. Fain, Editor; Ellen Kosty, Advertising Sales Mgr. **Subscription Rates:** $45 individuals; $47 Canada; $52 other countries.
Ad Rates: BW: $840 **Circ:** Paid ‡11,000
4C: $2,015 Non-paid ‡100

8467 Disability Studies Quarterly
Center on Disability Studies
University of Illinois at Chicago
Dept. of Disability & Human Development
1640 Roosevelt Rd. No. 236
Chicago, IL 60608-6904
Publication E-mail: bar@uic.edu

Scholarly Journal containing articles on all aspects of disability. **Founded:** 1982. **Freq:** Quarterly. **Trim Size:** 9 x 6. **Key Personnel:** David Pfeiffer, Editor, phone (808)956-9202, pfeiffer@hawaii.edu; Prof. Carol Gill, Editor. **ISSN:** 1041-5718. **Subscription Rates:** $35 individuals; $45 institutions; add $15 outside the U.S. **Remarks:** Accepts advertising. **Alt. Formats:** Diskette; Large-print.
Ad Rates: BW: $300.00 **Circ:** Paid 500

8468 The DO
American Osteopathic Association
142 E. Ontario St. Phone: (312)202-8000
Chicago, IL 60611 Fax: (312)202-8200
Free: (800)621-1773
Publisher E-mail: info@aoa_net.org

Osteopathic medical magazine. **Founded:** 1960. **Freq:** Monthly. **Print Method:** Offset. **Trim Size:** 7 7/8 x 10 7/8. **Cols./Page:** 3. **Col. Width:** 26 nonpareils. **Col. Depth:** 127 agate lines. **Key Personnel:** Sandra Williamson, Exec. Editor/Publisher, phone (312)202-8150, swilliamson@aoa-net.org; Thomas W. Allen, D.O., Editor-in-Chief; Michael Fitzgerald, Assoc. Editor, phone (312)202-8157, mfitzgerald@aoa-net.org; Jeffrey Bouley, Managing Editor, phone (312)202-8158, jbouley@aoa-net.org; Julie Pagliai, Production Mgr., phone (312)202-8176, jpagliai@aoa-net.org. **ISSN:** 0011-5088. **Subscription Rates:** $55 by mail. **Remarks:** Accepts advertising.
Ad Rates: BW: $1,575 **Circ:** Non-paid ‡29,456
4C: $2,570

8469 Dodge Construction News (Illinois, Indiana, Wisconsin Edition)
The McGraw-Hill Companies
180 N. Stetson, No. 700 Phone: (312)616-3280
Chicago, IL 60601-0002 Fax: (312)616-3236

Construction newspaper covering building and engineering. **Subtitle:** Voice of the Construction Industry. **Founded:** 1946. **Freq:** Daily. **Print Method:** Offset. **Trim Size:** 8 1/4 x 11. **Cols./Page:** 3. **Col. Width:** 21 nonpareils. **Col. Depth:** 10 inches. **Key Personnel:** Paula Widholm, Editor, phone (312)616-3253, fax (312)616-3236, dcnchgo1@aol.com. **ISSN:** 0012-480X. **Subscription Rates:** $1,424 individuals. **Remarks:** Accepts advertising.
Ad Rates: GLR: $5.15 **Circ:** Paid ‡650
BW: $1,048
4C: $1,598

8470 Dog World
Primedia Special Interest Publications
29 N. Wacker Dr.
Chicago, IL 60606

Magazine serving breeders, exhibitors, hobbyists and professionals in kennel operations, groomers, veterinarians, animal hospitals/clinics and pet suppliers. **Founded:** 1916. **Freq:** Monthly. **Print Method:** Offset. **Trim Size:** 8 x 10 7/8. **Cols./Page:** 3. **Col. Width:** 26 nonpareils. **Col. Depth:** 140 agate lines. **Key Personnel:** Donna Marcel, Editor; Marty Gayle, Publisher; Kit G. Hatcher, Circulation Mgr. **ISSN:** 0012-4893. **Subscription Rates:** $28 individuals; $3.75 single issue. **Remarks:** Accepts advertising.
Ad Rates: BW: $3,960 **Circ:** Paid ★**60,100**
4C: $5,210
PCI: $120

8471 Ebony
Johnson Publishing Co., Inc.
820 S. Michigan Ave. Phone: (312)322-9200
Chicago, IL 60605-2191 Fax: (312)322-9375

General editorial magazine geared toward African-Americans. **Founded:** 1945. **Freq:** Monthly. **Print Method:** Offset. **Cols./Page:** 3. **Col. Width:** 30 nonpareils. **Col. Depth:** 140 agate lines. **Key Personnel:** John H. Johnson, Publisher. **Subscription Rates:** $16 individuals. **Remarks:** Accepts advertising.
Ad Rates: BW: $22,199 **Circ:** Paid ★**1,750,027**
4C: $29,990

8472 Edgebrook Reporter
NADIG Newspapers, Inc.
4937 N. Milwaukee Ave. Phone: (773)286-6100
Chicago, IL 60630
Community newspaper. **Founded:** 1964. **Freq:** Weekly. **Print Method:** Offset. **Cols./Page:** 6. **Col. Width:** 9.5 picas. **Col. Depth:** 224 agate lines. **Key Personnel:** Glenn Nadig, Publisher. **Subscription Rates:** Free; $85 individuals mail.
Ad Rates: BW: $1032 **Circ:** Free ‡12,800
PCI: $11.50

8473 Edison-Norwood Times Review
Pioneer Press Newspapers
130 S. Prospect Ave. Phone: (847)696-3133
Park Ridge, IL 60068 Fax: (847)696-3229

General newspaper covering the Edison-Norwood district of Chicago. **Founded:** 1936. **Freq:** Weekly (Thurs.). **Print Method:** Offset. **Key Personnel:** Paul Sassone, Managing Editor; Anne Lunde, Editor. **Subscription Rates:** Free; $18.95 by mail. **Remarks:** Advertising accepted; rates available upon request.
Circ: Thurs. ★**3,612**

8474 EDT
American Bar Association
750 N. Lake Shore Dr. Phone: (312)988-5000
Chicago, IL 60611-4497 Fax: (312)988-5568
Free: (800)285-2221

Legal and social magazine. **Founded:** Sept. 1972. **Freq:** 9/year. **Print Method:** Offset. **Trim Size:** 8 7/8 x 10 7/8. **Cols./Page:** 3. **Col. Width:** 25 nonpareils. **Col. Depth:** 140 agate lines. **Key Personnel:** Sarah Hoban, Editor; Miriam R. Krasno, Managing Editor; Rita Novack, Advertising Mgr. **Remarks:** Accepts advertising.
Ad Rates: BW: $1,685 **Circ:** Paid 28,557
4C: $1,870
PCI: $2,585

8475 El Imparcial
Santelices Communications, Inc.
3615 W. 26th St., 2nd Fl. Phone: (708)484-1188
Chicago, IL 60623 Fax: (708)484-0202

Community newspaper (Spanish). **Founded:** 1986. **Freq:** Weekly. **Print Method:** Offset. **Trim Size:** 10 5/16 x 13. **Cols./Page:** 6. **Key Personnel:** Alicia C. Santelices, Publisher. **Subscription Rates:** Free; $40 (mail). **Remarks:** Accepts advertising.
Ad Rates: GLR: $.80 **Circ:** Free 30,000
BW: $960
SAU: $12.50
PCI: $10

8476 El Manana News
El Manana
2700 S. Harding Phone: (312)521-9137
Chicago, IL 60623 Fax: (312)521-5351

General newspaper (Spanish). **Founded:** 1971. **Freq:** Daily (morn.). **Print Method:** Offset. **Cols./Page:** 9. **Col. Width:** 1 7/16 inches. **Col. Depth:** 194 agate lines. **Key Personnel:** Humberto Perales, Editor; Gorki Tellez, Publisher. **Remarks:** Accepts advertising.
Ad Rates: GLR: $1.815 **Circ:** (Not Reported)
PCI: $25.34

8477 Electrical Apparatus
Barks Publications, Inc.
400 N. Michigan Ave., Ste. 900 Phone: (312)321-9440
Chicago, IL 60611-4198 Fax: (312)321-1288
Publication E-mail: eamagazine@aol.com

Professional magazine focusing on the application and maintenance of electromechanical apparatus. **Subtitle:** The Magazine of Electromechanical and Electronic Application and Maintenance. **Founded:** 1948. **Freq:** Monthly. **Print Method:** Web offset. **Trim Size:** 8 x 10 3/4. **Cols./Page:** 2 and 3. **Col. Width:** 13 and 20 picas. **Col. Depth:** 10 inches. **Key Personnel:** Elsie Dickson, Associate Publisher; Lori Allison, Advertising Mgr.; Lucy Gregor, Circulation Mgr.; Horace B. Barks, Editor and Publisher. **ISSN:** 0190-1370. **Subscription Rates:** $40. $3.50 single issue. **Remarks:** Accepts advertising. **Formerly**: Volt/Age.
Ad Rates: GLR: $10 **Circ:** Paid 1,436
BW: $2,355 Controlled 17,099
4C: $3,360
PCI: $125

8478 Electronic Media
Crain Communications, Inc.
740 N. Rush St. Phone: (312)649-5200
Chicago, IL 60611-2590 Fax: (312)649-5360
Publication E-mail: emediachi@aol.com

Tabloid covering management, programing, syndication, cable and trends in the television, radio, and electronic media industry. **Founded:** Aug. 1982. **Freq:** Weekly (Mon.). **Print Method:** Heat-set web offset. **Trim Size:** 11 x 14 1/2. **Cols./Page:** 5. **Col. Width:** 1 7/8 inches. **Col. Depth:** 14 inches. **Key Personnel:** Ron Alridge, Publisher, phone (312)649-5293; P.J. Bednarski, Editor, phone (312)280-3105; Marc White, Assoc.Publisher, phone (212)210-0217, fax (212)210-0400; Priscilla Garston, Circulation Dir., phone (212)210-0286. **Subscription Rates:** $109 individuals. **Remarks:** Accepts advertising. **URL:** http://www.emonline.com.
Ad Rates: BW: $6,860 **Circ:** Paid ★**14,065**
4C: $9,320 Non-paid ★**13,332**
PCI: $72

8479 Eleven
WTTW/Chicago
5400 N. St. Louis Ave. Phone: (773)583-5000
Chicago, IL 60625-4623 Fax: (773)509-5305
Publication E-mail: hpp@wwnet.com
Publisher E-mail: 70550.143@compuserve.com

Magazine for WTTW, Chicago's public television station. **Founded:** 1987. **Freq:** 9/year. **Print Method:** Web offset. **Trim Size:** 8 1/8 x 10 7/8. **Cols./Page:** 4. **Key Personnel:** Carol Lezak, Editor, phone (847)205-3165, fax (847)564-8197; Denise Kowalski, Managing Editor, phone (773)509-5442, fax (773)509-5305; Shaunese Teamer, Advertising Mgr., phone (773)509-5441, fax (773)509-5305. **ISSN:** 0896-2502. **Subscription Rates:** $40. **Remarks:** Accepts advertising. **Available Online. URL:** http://www.wttw.com.
Ad Rates: BW: $4,180 **Circ:** ‡160,000
4C: $11,000

8480 The Elks Magazine
425 W. Diversey Pkwy. Phone: (773)528-4500
Chicago, IL 60614-6196
Publication E-mail: elksmag@elks.org

Fraternal magazine. **Founded:** 1922. **Freq:** 10/year. **Print Method:** Offset. **Trim Size:** 8 x 10 13/16. **Cols./Page:** 3. **Col. Width:** 27 nonpareils. **Col. Depth:** 140 agate lines. **Key Personnel:** Fred D. Oakes, Publisher. **ISSN:** 0013-6263. **Subscription Rates:** $5 individuals; $.50 single issue. **Remarks:** Accepts advertising. **URL:** http://www.elksmag.com.
Ad Rates: GLR: $25 **Circ:** Paid 1,250,475
BW: $8,986
4C: $13,435
PCI: $350

8481 EM: Ebony Man
Johnson Publishing Co., Inc.
820 S. Michigan Ave. Phone: (312)322-9200
Chicago, IL 60605-2191 Fax: (312)322-9375

Black men's magazine featuring regular columns on health, fashion, and sports. **Freq:** Monthly. **Key Personnel:** Ooloong J. Smith, Editor; John H. Johnson, Publisher; Errol Griffiths, Advertising Dir. **ISSN:** 0884-4879. **Subscription Rates:** $16. $2 single issue.
Circ: Paid 171,391

8482 Employee Benefit Plan Review
Charles D. Spencer & Associates, Inc.
250 S. Wacker Dr., Ste. 600 Phone: (312)993-7900
Chicago, IL 60606-5834 Fax: (312)993-7910
Free: (800)555-5490
Publisher E-mail: spencernet@mindspring.com

Magazine serving decision-makers who administer, design, install, and service employee benefit plans. **Founded:** 1946. **Freq:** Monthly. **Print Method:** Web Offset. **Trim Size:** 8 3/8 x 10 7/8. **Cols./Page:** 2 and 3. **Col. Width:** 2 5/8 and 2 1/4 inches. **Col. Depth:** 115 agate lines. **Key Personnel:** Bruce F. Spencer, Editor; Barbara Williams, Advertising Mgr.; Stephen A. Huth, Managing Editor; Seymour LaRock, Executive Editor; Sue Burzawa, Product Manager. **ISSN:** 0013-6808. **Subscription Rates:** $75 individuals. **Remarks:** Accepts advertising.
Ad Rates: BW: $2,300 **Circ:** Paid ★**2,755**
4C: $3,325 Non-paid ★**15,931**

8483 Engineering Journal
American Institute of Steel Construction, Inc.
1 E. Wacker Dr., Ste. 3100 Phone: (312)670-2400
Chicago, IL 60601-2001 Fax: (312)670-5403

Magazine devoted exclusively to the design of steel structures featuring papers of practical design value. Provides the latest information on steel design, research, and constuction to structural engineers, architects, and educators. **Founded:** 1964. **Freq:** Quarterly. **Print Method:** Offset. **Trim Size:** 8 1/2 x 11 7/8. **Cols./Page:** 2. **Col. Width:** 20 nonpareils. **Col. Depth:** 127 agate lines. **Key Personnel:** Jacqueline Joseffer, Dir. of Technical Publications; Cynthia J. Lanz, Technical Editor, lanz@aiscmail.com. **ISSN:** 0013-8029. **Subscription Rates:** $35 individuals 1 yr; $12 single issue; $75 three years. **Remarks:** Advertising not accepted. **URL:** http://www.aiscweb.com.
Circ: ‡10,500

8484 Environmental Solutions
Advanstar Communications
312 W. Randolph St., Ste. 600 Phone: (312)553-8900
Chicago, IL 60606-1721 Fax: (312)553-8926

Environmental magazine for industry. **Subtitle:** The Magazine for Environmental Management. **Founded:** 1988. **Freq:** Bimonthly. **Print Method:** Web offset. **Trim Size:** 8 x 10. **Key Personnel:** Cheryl L. McAdams, Editor-in-Chief, cmcadams@earthlink.net; Michael Wilson, Publisher. **ISSN:** 0898-5685. **Subscription Rates:** Free to qualified subscribers; $50 individuals. **Remarks:** Accepts advertising. **Formerly**: Hazmat World.
Ad Rates: BW: $4,574 **Circ:** Non-paid ‡45,000
4C: $5,719
PCI: $85

8485 Exito!
Chicago Tribune
820 N. Orleans St., Ste. 400 Phone: (312)654-3009
Chicago, IL 60610-3051 Fax: (312)654-3029
Publication E-mail: exitoed@aol.com

Spanish language tabloid. **Founded:** Sept. 1993. **Freq:** Weekly. **Cols./Page:** 5. **Col. Width:** 2.014 inches. **Col. Depth:** 14 inches. **Key Personnel:** Alejandro Escalona, Editor, phone (312)654-3016; Magdalena Garcia, Managing Editor, phone (312)654-3015, MGarcia@Tribune.com; Alvin Hysong, Advertising Dir., phone (312)654-3001, AHysong@Tribune.com; Lanette Cueto, Marketing and Promotions, phone (312)654-3002, LCueto@Tribune.com. **Remarks:** Accepts advertising.
Ad Rates: BW: $2,500 **Circ:** Controlled 70,000
4C: $2,950
PCI: $44.50

8486 Extension
Catholic Church Extension Society
150 S. Wacker Dr., No. 20th Phone: (312)236-7240
Chicago, IL 60606-4103 Fax: (312)236-5276

Magazine reporting on activities and issues of the American home missions. **Subtitle:** Magazine of Mission America. **Founded:** 1906. **Freq:** 12/year. **Print Method:** Offset. **Trim Size:** 8 x 10 7/8. **Cols./Page:** 3. **Col. Width:** 13 picas. **Col. Depth:** 57 picas. **Key Personnel:** Brad Collins, Editor; Mr. Richard A. Ritter, Publisher. **Subscription Rates:** Free. **Remarks:** Advertising not accepted.
Circ: Controlled ‡80,000

8487 Family Law Quarterly
American Bar Association
750 N. Lake Shore Dr. Phone: (312)988-5000
Chicago, IL 60611-4497 Fax: (312)988-5568
Free: (800)285-2221

Journal including regular coverage of judicial decisions, legislation, taxation, summaries of state and local bar association projects, and book reviews. **Founded:** 1967. **Freq:** Quarterly. **Trim Size:** 6x9. **Key Personnel:** Richard W. Bright, Managing Editor, phone (312)988-6083, fax (312)988-6081, rbright@staff.abanet.org. **ISSN:** 0014-729X. **Subscription Rates:** $49.95; $55.95 other countries; $14.95 single issue; Free to qualified subscribers. **Remarks:** Advertising not accepted.
Circ: (Not Reported)

8488 Fancy Food & Culinary Products
Talcott Communications Corp.
20 N. Wacker Dr., Ste. 1865 Phone: (312)849-2220
Chicago, IL 60606 Fax: (312)849-2174
Free: (800)229-1967
Publication E-mail: fancyfood@aol.com
Publisher E-mail: talcottpub@aol.com

Trade magazine for specialty food retailers. **Founded:** 1983. **Freq:** Monthly. **Print Method:** Offset. **Trim Size:** 8 1/8 x 10 7/8. **Cols./Page:** 3. **Col. Width:** 13 picas. **Col. Depth:** 135 agate lines. **Key Personnel:** Paddy Schwaar, Editorial Director. **Subscription Rates:** $34 individuals; Free to gourmet

retailers. **Remarks:** Accepts advertising. **URL:** http://www.talcott.com/fancyfood. **Formerly**: Fancy Food.
Ad Rates: BW: $3,075 **Circ:** Paid 3,060
4C: $3,960 Non-paid 22,000

8489 FEDA News and Views
Foodservice Equipment Distributors Association
223 W. Jackson Bldv., Ste. 620 Phone: (312)427-9605
Chicago, IL 60606 Fax: (312)427-9607
Publication E-mail: feda@earthlink.net

Magazine reporting association and industry news. **Founded:** 1933. **Freq:** Bimonthly. **Trim Size:** 8 1/2 x 11. **Key Personnel:** Ray Herrick, Editor and Publisher; Josephine Miller, Editor. **Subscription Rates:** $15 members; $25 nonmembers. **URL:** http://www.feda.com.
Circ: Controlled 1,600

8490 The Final Call
734 W. 79th St. Phone: (312)602-1230
Chicago, IL 60620 Fax: (312)602-1013

Newspaper serving the black community. **Founded:** 1979. **Freq:** Weekly. **Print Method:** Web offset. **Trim Size:** 11 3/8 x 13 3/4. **Cols./Page:** 5. **Col. Width:** 11.5 picas. **Col. Depth:** 12 1/2 inches. **Key Personnel:** James Muhammad, Editor-in-Chief; Richard Muhammed, Managing Editor; Fontaine Muhammed, General Mgr. **Subscription Rates:** $22. **Remarks:** Accepts advertising. **URL:** http://www.aol.org.
Ad Rates: BW: $1,000 **Circ:** 400,000
Free 2,000

8491 Fire Chief
Intertec Publishing Corp.
35 E. Wacker Dr., No. 700 Phone: (312)726-7277
Chicago, IL 60601 Fax: (312)726-0241
Publication E-mail: firechiefmag.com

Fire protection magazine. **Founded:** Sept. 1957. **Freq:** Monthly. **Print Method:** Offset. **Trim Size:** 8 1/8 x 10 7/8. **Cols./Page:** 3. **Col. Width:** 26 nonpareils. **Col. Depth:** 140 agate lines. **Key Personnel:** Scott Baltic, Editor, sbaltic@mindspring.com; Janet Wilmoth, Publisher, jwilmoth@mindspring.com. **ISSN:** 0015-2552. **Subscription Rates:** Free to qualified subscribers; $45 individuals. **Remarks:** Accepts advertising. **URL:** http://www.intertec.com.
Ad Rates: BW: $2,460 **Circ:** Paid 5,770
4C: $3,495 Non-paid 35,854

8492 Firewatch!
National Association of Fire Equipment Distributors
One E. Wacker Dr., No. 3600 Phone: (312)923-8500
Chicago, IL 60601 Fax: (312)923-8505
Publisher E-mail: nafed@sba.com

Trade magazine for fire protection professionals. **Freq:** Quarterly. **Key Personnel:** John Petrilli, Editor. **Remarks:** Accepts advertising.
Circ: (Not Reported)

8493 Floral Mass Marketing
Cenflo, Inc.
205 W. Wacker Drive, Ste. 1040 Phone: (312)739-5000
Chicago, IL 60606-3508 Fax: (312)739-0739
Free: (800)732-4581
Publisher E-mail: kbcenflo@aol.com

Magazine for volume buyers of floral products. **Founded:** 1982. **Freq:** Bimonthly. **Print Method:** Web offset. **Trim Size:** 11 1/4 x 16 1/4. **Cols./Page:** 5. **Col. Width:** 1 7/8 inches. **Col. Depth:** 15 3/4 inches. **Key Personnel:** Debbie M. Edwards, Editor; Kenneth Benjamin, Publisher. **Subscription Rates:** $15. **Remarks:** Accepts advertising.
Ad Rates: GLR: $4.25 **Circ:** ‡17,100
BW: $1,840
4C: $2,515
PCI: $37

8494 Flower News
Cenflo, Inc.
205 W. Wacker Drive, Ste. 1040 Phone: (312)739-5000
Chicago, IL 60606-3508 Fax: (312)739-0739
Free: (800)732-4581
Publisher E-mail: kbcenflo@aol.com

Trade newspaper for commercial, wholesale, and retail florists. **Founded:** 1947. **Freq:** Weekly. **Print Method:** Offset. **Trim Size:** 11 1/2 x 17. **Cols./Page:** 5. **Col. Width:** 23 nonpareils. **Col. Depth:** 221 agate lines. **Key Personnel:** Debbie M. Edwards, Editor; Kenneth M. Benjamin, Publisher. **Subscription Rates:** $20 individuals; $38 two years. **Remarks:** Accepts advertising.
Ad Rates: GLR: $4.10 **Circ:** Non-paid ‡11,188
BW: $1,822 Paid ‡5,941
4C: $2,935
PCI: $48

8495 Food Technology
Institute of Food Technologists
221 N. La Salle St., Ste. 300 Phone: (312)782-8424
Chicago, IL 60601 Fax: (312)782-8348
Publisher E-mail: info@ift.org

Food technology and science magazine. **Founded:** 1947. **Freq:** Monthly. **Print Method:** Offset. **Trim Size:** 8 1/8 x 10 7/8. **Cols./Page:** 3 and 2. **Col. Width:** 26 and 40 nonpareils. **Col. Depth:** 140 agate lines. **Key Personnel:** Fran Katz, Editor; Neil Mermelstein, Editor. **ISSN:** 0015-6639. **Subscription Rates:** $92 individuals; $102 other countries. **Remarks:** Accepts advertising. **Available Online**. **URL:** http://www.ift.org.
Ad Rates: BW: $2,995 **Circ:** Paid ★**25,364**
4C: $4,270 Non-paid ★**2,871**

8496 Form & Function
USG Corp.
125 S Franklin St. Phone: (312)606-4181
Chicago, IL 60606-4678 Fax: (312)606-5566

Professional magazine covering architectural construction. **Founded:** 1964. **Freq:** Quarterly. **Print Method:** Sheetfed offset. **Trim Size:** 8 1/2 x 11. **Cols./Page:** 3. **Col. Width:** 2 1/4 inches. **Col. Depth:** 7 inches. **Key Personnel:** William D. Leavitt, Editor, bleavitt@usg.com; Carolyn Hughes, Art Dir. **ISSN:** 0015-7686. **Subscription Rates:** Free to qualified subscribers. **Remarks:** Advertising not accepted.
Circ: Controlled 120,000

8497 The Friend
Lithuanian Catholic Press Society
4545 W. 63rd St. Phone: (773)585-9500
Chicago, IL 60629-5589 Fax: (773)585-8284
Publication E-mail: draugas@earthlink.com

Lithuanian Catholic daily newspaper. **Subtitle:** Draugas. **Founded:** 1909. **Freq:** Tues.-Sat. **Print Method:** Offset. **Cols./Page:** 7. **Col. Width:** 25 nonpareils. **Col. Depth:** 280 agate lines. **Key Personnel:** Ms. Danute Bindokas, Editor; Val Krumplis, General Mgr. **USPS:** 161-000. **Subscription Rates:** $95 individuals. **Remarks:** Accepts advertising. **Foreign language name:** Draugas.
Ad Rates: BW: $840.60 **Circ:** ‡6,200
PCI: $6

8498 Frontiers of Health Services Management
Health Administration Press
1 N. Franklin, Ste. 1700 Phone: (312)424-2800
Chicago, IL 60606-3491 Fax: (312)424-0014
Publisher E-mail: hap@ache.org

Journal presenting commissioned articles by leaders in health services administration on the future of the field, policy, and management issues. **Founded:** 1984. **Freq:** Quarterly. **Print Method:** Offset. **Trim Size:** 8 1/2 x 11. **Cols./Page:** 1 and 2. **Col. Width:** 29 and 19 inches. **Col. Depth:** 51 and 51 inches. **Key Personnel:** Mary E. Stefl, Ph.D, Editor. **ISSN:** 0748-8157. **Subscription Rates:** $65 individuals; $17 single issue. **Remarks:** Advertising not accepted. **Alt. Formats:** Microform.
Circ: ‡2,500

8499 Futures Magazine
250 S. Wacker Dr., Ste. 1150 Phone: (312)977-0999
Chicago, IL 60606 Fax: (312)977-1042
Free: (800)972-9316

Magazine covering news, analysis and strategies for futures, options and derivatives traders. **Founded:** Feb. 1972. **Freq:** Monthly. **Print Method:** Offset. **Trim Size:** 7 7/8 x 10 3/4. **Cols./Page:** 3. **Col. Width:** 27 nonpareils. **Col. Depth:** 138 agate lines. **Key Personnel:** Ginger Szala, Editor, gszala@futuresmag.com; Barbara Vogel, Publisher, bvogel@futuresmag.com; Bob Dorman, Director, Advertising Sales, bdorman@futuresmag.com. **ISSN:** 0746-2468. **Subscription Rates:** Free to qualified subscribers; $39 individuals. **Remarks:** Accepts advertising. **Online:** Internet. **URL:** http://www.futuresmag.com.
Ad Rates: BW: $9,500 **Circ:** Paid 18,077
4C: $11,750 Controlled 46,924

8500 Futures Magazine
Futures Communications Co., Inc.
250 S. Wacker, Ste. 1150 Phone: (312)977-0999
Chicago, IL 60606 Fax: (312)977-1042
Free: (800)635-3931

Professional magazine for futures traders. **Founded:** 1973. **Freq:** Monthly. **Print Method:** Web offset. **Trim Size:** 7 7/8 x 10 3/4. **Cols./Page:** 3. **Key Personnel:** Ginger Szala, Editor, gszala@futuresmag.com; Robert Dorman, Advertising Mgr.; Elizabeth Cicchetti, Circulation Mgr.; Dixie Ost, Promotions Mgr. **Subscription Rates:** $39 individuals; $4.50 single issue. **Remarks:** Accepts advertising. **URL:** http://www.futuresmag.com.
Ad Rates: BW: $9,500 **Circ:** Controlled ‡60,000
4C: $11,750

8501 Gab Magazine
3227 N. Sheffield Phone: (773)248-4542
Chicago, IL 60657 Fax: (773)477-6382
Publisher E-mail: gabmag@earthlink.net

Consumer lifestyle magazine covering gay interests. **Founded:** Apr. 1993. **Freq:** Weekly. **Print Method:** Web. **Trim Size:** 8 x 10. **Cols./Page:** 2. **Col. Width:** 3 3/8 inches. **Col. Depth:** 9 inches. **Key Personnel:** Jim Pickett, Editor. **Subscription Rates:** Free. **Remarks:** Accepts advertising. **Formerly**: Babble.
Ad Rates: BW: $450 **Circ:** Controlled 18,000

8502 Gay Chicago Magazine
Ultra Ink, Inc.
3121 N. Broadway St. Phone: (312)327-7271
Chicago, IL 60657-4522 Fax: (312)327-0112

Entertainment magazine for the gay community. **Founded:** 1976. **Freq:** Weekly. **Print Method:** Offset. **Trim Size:** 8 1/2 x 11. **Cols./Page:** 2. **Col. Width:** 13 picas. **Col. Depth:** 42 picas. **Key Personnel:** Ralph Paul Gernhardt, Publisher; Jerry Williams, General Mgr. **Subscription Rates:** Free; $80 institutions; $2 single issue. **Remarks:** Accepts advertising.
Ad Rates: GLR: $8.25 **Circ:** Paid ‡750
BW: $390 Free ‡20,000
4C: $850
PCI: $60

8503 General Dentistry
Academy of General Dentistry (AGD)
211 E. Chicago Ave. Phone: (312)440-4300
Chicago, IL 60611-2670 Fax: (312)440-0559
Free: (888)AGD-DENT
Publication E-mail: agdjournal@agd.org

Clinical dental journal. **Subtitle:** Journal of the Academy of General Dentistry. **Founded:** 1952. **Freq:** Bimonthly. **Print Method:** Offset. **Trim Size:** 8 3/8 x 10 7/8. **Cols./Page:** 3 and 2. **Key Personnel:** Roger Winland, DDS, Editor, phone (312)440-4344; Ellen Odehnal, Managing Editor, phone (312)440-4344; Todd Goldman, Advertising Mgr., phone (813)264-2772, todgoldman@aol.com; Jo-Ellyn Posselt, Dir. of Communications, phone (312)440-4307, jo-ellyn@agd.org. **ISSN:** 0363-6771. **Subscription Rates:** $30 individuals; $48 institutions; $6 single issue. **Alt. Formats:** Braille; Braille; Microform.
Ad Rates: BW: $2,985 **Circ:** Paid ‡38,000
4C: $4,160 Non-paid ‡25,000

8504 Giftware News
Talcott Communications Corp.
20 N. Wacker Dr., Ste. 1865 Phone: (312)849-2220
Chicago, IL 60606 Fax: (312)849-2174
Free: (800)229-1967
Publication E-mail: giftnews@aol.com
Publisher E-mail: talcottpub@aol.com

Magazine serving professionals in the gift, stationery, collectibles, tabletop, and home accessories industries. **Founded:** 1975. **Freq:** Monthly. **Print Method:** Offset. **Trim Size:** 10 5/8 x 14 3/8. **Cols./Page:** 4. **Col. Width:** 27 nonpareils. **Col. Depth:** 196 agate lines. **Key Personnel:** Anthony DeMasi, Editor, phone (609)227-0798, fax (609)227-6511; Daniel Von Rabenau, Publisher. **Subscription Rates:** $36 individuals. **Remarks:** Accepts advertising. **Available Online. URL:** http://www.giftwarenews.net.
Ad Rates: BW: $5,450 **Circ:** Paid 15,239
4C: $6,845 Non-paid 21,766

8505 Government Finance Review
Government Finance Officers Association
180 N. Michigan Ave., Ste. 800 Phone: (312)977-9700
Chicago, IL 60601-7401 Fax: (312)977-4806

Membership magazine covering finance and financial management for state and local governments. **Founded:** Apr. 1985. **Freq:** Bimonthly. **Print Method:** Offset. **Trim Size:** 8 1/2 x 11. **Cols./Page:** 3. **Col. Width:** 14 picas. **Col. Depth:** 116 agate lines. **Key Personnel:** Barbara Weiss, Editor; Sharon Fucone, Advertising Mgr.; Karen Utterback, Associate Editor. **USPS:** 368-120. **Subscription Rates:** $30 individuals.
Ad Rates: BW: $1,050 **Circ:** 14,000
4C: $3,075

8506 Grocery Headquarters
Trend Publishing
625 N. Michigan Ave., Ste. 1500 Phone: (312)654-2300
Chicago, IL 60611-3109 Fax: (312)654-2323

Magazine (tabloid) serving the supermarket industry. **Founded:** 1933. **Freq:** Monthly. **Print Method:** Offset. Uses mats. **Trim Size:** 10 1/2 x 13. **Cols./Page:** 4. **Col. Width:** 12.5 picas. **Col. Depth:** 150 agate lines. **Key Personnel:** Bill D'Alexander, Publisher; Jennifer Junitz, Advertising Mgr.; Bob Gatty, Editor; Leslie Beyer, Sr. Editor; Amy Hargrove, Managing Editor. **ISSN:** 0888-0360. **Subscription Rates:** Free to

qualified subscribers. **Remarks:** Accepts advertising. **Formerly**: Grocer's Spotlight; Grocery Marketing.
Ad Rates: BW: $6,800 **Circ:** Controlled ‡63,207
4C: $8,720

8507 Groom & Board
H.H. Backer Associates, Inc.
20 E. Jackson Blvd. Phone: (312)663-4040
Chicago, IL 60604 Fax: (312)663-5676

National trade magazine. **Subtitle:** Serving Pet-Care Professionals. **Founded:** 1980. **Freq:** 9/year. **Print Method:** Web fed. **Trim Size:** 8 1/4 x 10 7/8. **Cols./Page:** 3. **Col. Width:** 13 picas. **Col. Depth:** 60 picas. **Key Personnel:** Karen Long MacLeod, Editor; Ginger Norton, Publisher; Lou Carso, Advertising Dir. **ISSN:** 0199-8366. **Subscription Rates:** Free to qualified subscribers; $25 institutions; $35 other countries (surface mail); $2.50 single issue. **Remarks:** Accepts advertising.
Ad Rates: BW: $1,525 **Circ:** Controlled ‡16,431
4C: $2,290

8508 Harlem-Irving Times
Lerner Communications, Inc.
1115 W. Belmont Phone: (312)281-7500
Chicago, IL 60657 Fax: (312)281-0740
Publisher E-mail: lerner@enteract.com

Community newspaper. **Founded:** 1957. **Freq:** Weekly (Wed.). **Print Method:** Offset. **Trim Size:** 13 x 21 1/4. **Cols./Page:** 6. **Col. Width:** 25 nonpareils. **Col. Depth:** 297 agate lines. **Key Personnel:** Terry Levecke, Managing Editor; Joseph Ferstl, Exec. V.P. **Subscription Rates:** Free; $9.95 by mail. **URL:** http://www.intheloop.net.
Ad Rates: SAU: $54.90 **Circ:** Paid 2,945
Non-paid 489

8509 Headache Quarterly
Diamond Headache Clinic Research & Educational Foundation
467 W. Deming Place Phone: (773)388-6363
Suite 500 Fax: (773)477-9712
Chicago, IL 60614-1726
Free: (800)432-3224

Journal covering headaches. **Subtitle:** Current Treatment and Research. **Founded:** 1990. **Freq:** Quarterly. **Trim Size:** 8 1/4 x 10 3/4. **Cols./Page:** 2. **Key Personnel:** Seymour Diamond, Editor; Idell Applebaum, Advertising. **ISSN:** 1059-7565. **Subscription Rates:** $51.50; $96 out of country; $77.25 institutions Institutional, U.S.; $122 institutions, other countries Institutiona, other countries. **Remarks:** Accepts advertising.
Ad Rates: BW: $725 **Circ:** Paid ‡3,500
4C: $695

8510 Health Facilities Management
American Hospital Publishing, Inc.
1 N. Franklin Phone: (312)893-6800
Chicago, IL 60606 Fax: (312)422-4500
Free: (800)621-6902

Trade journal. **Founded:** 1988. **Freq:** Monthly. **Print Method:** Web offset. **Trim Size:** 8 1/8 x 10 7/8. **Cols./Page:** 3. **Key Personnel:** Michael Hemmes, Editor. **ISSN:** 0899-6210. **Subscription Rates:** $30; $50 Canada & other countries. $3 single issue. **Remarks:** Accepts advertising.
Ad Rates: GLR: $10 **Circ:** Paid 96
BW: $3,530 Controlled 37,328
4C: $4,630
PCI: $137

8511 Healthcare Executive
American College of Healthcare Executives
1 N. Franklin St. Ste. 1700 Phone: (312)424-2800
Chicago, IL 60606 Fax: (312)424-0023
Publication E-mail: geninfo@ache.org
Publisher E-mail: geninfo@ache.org

Health care management magazine examining trends, issues, and innovations. **Founded:** Nov. 1985. **Freq:** Bimonthly. **Print Method:** Offset. **Trim Size:** 8 1/8 x 10 7/8. **Cols./Page:** 3. **Col. Width:** 13 picas. **Col. Depth:** 60 picas. **Key Personnel:** Ann Bartling, Editor; Lynn Kahn, Publisher. **ISSN:** 0883-5381. **Subscription Rates:** $60 individuals; $75 other countries; $12 single issue.
Ad Rates: BW: $3,140 **Circ:** Paid 20,832
4C: $4,315 Non-paid 406

8512 Hlas Naroda (Voice of the Nation)
Czech-American Heritage Center
2340 S. 61st. Ave. Phone: (708)656-1050
Chicago, IL 60650-2608
Newspaper presenting religious, political, and other news of the church in the U.S. and in Czechoslovakia. **Founded:** 1976. **Freq:** Weekly. **Print Method:** Offset. **Cols./Page:** 5. **Col. Width:** 1 7/8 inches. **Col. Depth:** 12 3/4 inches. **Key Personnel:** Vojtech Vit, O.S.B., Editor. **Subscription Rates:** $30; $40 other countries. **Remarks:** Accepts advertising.
Ad Rates: PCI: $4 **Circ:** (Not Reported)

8513 Home & Away
AAA Chicago Motor Club
999 E. Touhy Ave. Phone: (708)390-9000
Des Plaines, IL 60018 Fax: (708)390-9112

Official publication for members of AAA-Chicago Motor Club. Features include travel stories and articles on motoring. **Founded:** 1980. **Freq:** Bimonthly. **Print Method:** Offset. **Trim Size:** 8 x 10 7/8. **Cols./Page:** 3. **Col. Width:** 13 1/2 picas. **Key Personnel:** Brian Nicol, Editor; Lionel Kramer, Publisher; Vern Cornish, Advertising Mgr. **Subscription Rates:** Free to qualified subscribers; $3 nonmembers; $1 single issue. **Remarks:** Accepts advertising.
Ad Rates: BW: $9100 **Circ:** 370,000
4C: $11765

8514 Horizon
National Religious Vocation Conference
5420 S Cornell Ave., No. 105 Phone: (773)363-5454
Chicago, IL 60615-5604 Fax: (773)363-5530
Publisher E-mail: nrvc@aol.com

Catholic publication. **Subtitle:** Journal of the National Religious Vocation Conference. **Founded:** 1975. **Freq:** Quarterly. **Print Method:** Offset. **Trim Size:** 8 1/2 x 11. **Cols./Page:** 2. **Col. Width:** 3 1/4 inches. **Key Personnel:** Carol Schuck Scheiber, Editor, phone (419)385-5746; Sr. Catherine Bertrand, SSND, Exec. Director. **ISSN:** 1042-8461. **Subscription Rates:** $17; $21 other countries. $6 single issue. **Remarks:** Advertising not accepted. **Formerly**: Call to Growth/Ministry.
Circ: Paid 2,089
Controlled 72

8515 Hyde Park Citizen
Citizen Newspapers
412 E. 87th St. Phone: (312)487-7700
Chicago, IL 60619 Fax: (312)487-7931

Newspaper serving Chicago's black community. **Subtitle:** A News Source You Can Trust. **Founded:** 1987. **Freq:** Weekly (Thurs.). **Print Method:** Offset. **Trim Size:** TABLOID. **Cols./Page:** 5. **Col. Width:** 25 nonpareils. **Col. Depth:** 196 agate lines. **Key Personnel:** William Garth, Publisher; Lisa Ely, Managing Editor. **Subscription Rates:** $25 individuals. **Online:** INTER ACCESS. **Alt. Formats:** CD-ROM.
Ad Rates: BW: $1,169 **Circ:** ‡17,000
SAU: $7
PCI: $16.70

8516 Hyde Park Herald
Southtown
5240 S. Harper Phone: (773)643-8533
Chicago, IL 60615 Fax: (773)643-8542
Publication E-mail: hpherald@aol.com

Newspaper. **Founded:** 1882. **Freq:** Weekly (Wed.). **Print Method:** Offset. **Cols./Page:** 6. **Col. Width:** 22 nonpareils. **Col. Depth:** 182 agate lines. **Key Personnel:** Susan J. Walker, General Mgr.; Bruce Sagan, Publisher; Kevin Knapp, Editor. **Subscription Rates:** $13 individuals. **Remarks:** Accepts classified advertising. **Online:** America Online, Inc. **Alt. Formats:** Microform.
Ad Rates: GLR: $4.87 **Circ:** Paid ‡9,000
BW: $2,838.69 Free ‡17,600
4C: $3,288.69
PCI: $35.34

8517 IBIS Review
Charles D. Spencer & Associates, Inc.
250 S. Wacker Dr. Phone: (312)993-7900
Chicago, IL 60606-5834 Fax: (312)993-7910
Publication E-mail: ibisret@mindspring.com
Publisher E-mail: spencernet@mindspring.com

News magazine for decision-makers who administer, design, install, and service international employee benefit plans. **Founded:** July 1986. **Freq:** Monthly. **Print Method:** Offset. **Trim Size:** 8 3/8 x 10 7/8. **Cols./Page:** 2. **Col. Width:** 2 3/4 inches. **Col. Depth:** 7 1/2 inches. **Key Personnel:** Bruce F. Spencer, Editor; Cathleen Reidy, Advertising Mgr. **Subscription Rates:** $100 U.S. and Canada; $125 out of country. **Remarks:** Accepts advertising.
Ad Rates: GLR: $361 **Circ:** Paid ‡673
BW: $1,360 Controlled ‡827
4C: $2,130

8518 IGA Grocergram
Pace Communications, Inc.
O'Hare Plaza Phone: (773)693-4520
8725 W. Higgins Rd. Fax: (773)693-7571
Chicago, IL 60631
Publication E-mail: igaggpc@aol.com

Retail grocery magazine. **Founded:** 1926. **Freq:** Monthly. **Print Method:** Offset. **Trim Size:** 8 1/8 x 10 7/8. **Cols./Page:** 3. **Col. Width:** 40 nonpareils. **Col. Depth:** 140 agate lines. **Key Personnel:** Wes Isley, Managing Editor; Bill Hayes, Assoc. editor & Editor-in-Chief. **ISSN:** 0018-9766. **Subscription Rates:** $40 individuals. **Remarks:** Accepts advertising.
Ad Rates: BW: $3,338 **Circ:** Paid ‡19,530
4C: $3,338 Non-paid ‡417

8519 Illinois Banker
Illinois Bankers Association (IBA)
111 N. Canal, Ste. 1111 Phone: (312)876-9900
Chicago, IL 60606 Fax: (312)876-3826
Free: (800)878-2265
Publication E-mail: illbankers@aol.com
Publisher E-mail: illbankers@aol.com

Magazine serving the Illinois professional trade association for banking. **Founded:** 1916. **Freq:** Monthly. **Print Method:** Offset. **Trim Size:** 8 3/8 x 10 7/8. **Cols./Page:** 3. **Col. Width:** 28 nonpareils. **Col. Depth:** 120 agate lines. **Key Personnel:** Kathleen Gill, Exec. Editor; William J. Hocter, Publisher; Cindy L. Altman, Advertising/Circulation. **Subscription Rates:** $60 individuals non-members; $5 single issue. **URL:** http://www.ilbanker.com.
Ad Rates: BW: $875 **Circ:** ‡2,504

8520 Illinois CPA Insight
Illinois CPA Society
222 S. Riverside Plaza, 16th Fl. Phone: (312)993-0393
Chicago, IL 60606 Fax: (312)993-7713

News magazine focusing on current professional issues for members of Illinois CPA Society. **Founded:** Aug. 1974. **Freq:** 10/year. **Print Method:** Offset. **Trim Size:** 8 3/8 x 10 7/8. **Cols./Page:** 3 and 2. **Col. Width:** 13 and 20 picas. **Col. Depth:** 61 picas. **Key Personnel:** Julia Winn, Editor and Publisher, phone (312)549-6072, fax (312)327-0365, jwinn@starnetinc.com; Martin H. Rosenberg, Production Dir., phone (312)993-0393, fax (312)993-9954; Ilene Zurla, Display Administration, phone (312)993-0393, fax (312)993-9954, izurla@aol.com. **ISSN:** 1043-7215. **Subscription Rates:** $25 individuals. **Remarks:** Accepts advertising. **URL:** http://www.icpas.org.
Ad Rates: BW: $995 **Circ:** ‡25,000
4C: $1,500

8521 Illinois Medicine
Illinois State Medical Society
20 N. Michigan Ave., No. 700 Phone: (312)782-1654
Chicago, IL 60602-4890 Fax: (312)782-2023

Tabloid presenting news and comment on health care issues and the professional concerns of Illinois physicians. **Founded:** 1989. **Freq:** Biweekly. **Print Method:** Offset. **Trim Size:** 11 x 15. **Cols./Page:** 4. **Col. Width:** 2 1/4 inches. **Col. Depth:** 10 1/2 inches. **Key Personnel:** Lynn Koslowsky, Editor. **ISSN:** 1044-6400. **Subscription Rates:** $12 individuals; $12.50 Canada; $19 other countries; $1.25 single issue. **Remarks:** Accepts advertising.
Ad Rates: BW: $1,420 **Circ:** Paid ‡18,499
4C: $900 Non-paid ‡2,338

8522 IMAGE
Sigma Theta Tau Intl.
845 S. Damen Ave. Phone: (312)996-0103
Chicago, IL 60612 Fax: (312)996-0680
Publisher E-mail: stti@stti-sun.iupui.com

Scholarly, peer-reviewed articles on nursing. **Subtitle:** Journal of Nursing Scholarship. **Founded:** 1967. **Freq:** Quarterly. **Print Method:** Web offset. **Trim Size:** 8 3/8 x 10 7/8. **Cols./Page:** 2. **Col. Width:** 21.5 nonpareils. **Col. Depth:** 58 picas. **Key Personnel:** Beverly Henry, R.N., Editor, phone (312)996-0103, fax (312)996-0680, imagebh@uic.edu; Nancy Dickenson-Hazard, R.N., Publisher. **ISSN:** 0743-5150. **Subscription Rates:** $32 individuals; $10 single issue; $42 out of country. **Remarks:** Color advertising not accepted.
Ad Rates: GLR: $20 **Circ:** ‡120,000
BW: $2,400

8523 In These Times
Institute for Public Affairs Inc.
2040 N. Milwaukee Ave., 2nd Fl. Phone: (773)772-0100
Chicago, IL 60647-4002 Fax: (773)772-4180
Free: (888)READ-ITT
Publication E-mail: itt@inthesetimes.com

National political newsmagazine. **Founded:** Nov. 1976. **Freq:** Biweekly. **Print Method:** Offset. **Trim Size:** 8 1/8 x 10 7/8. **Key Personnel:** James Weinstein, Editor; Patricia Gray, Advertising Mgr.; Joel Bleifuss, Managing Editor. **ISSN:** 0160-5992. **Subscription Rates:** $36.95 individuals. **Remarks:** Accepts advertising. **Feature Editors:** Kristin Kolb, *News.*
Ad Rates: GLR: $.95 **Circ:** ‡32,000
BW: $1,440
PCI: $45

8524 Independent Bulletin
Chicago Independent Bulletin
2037 W. 95th St. Phone: (312)783-1040
Chicago, IL 60643-1129
Community newspaper. **Founded:** 1972. **Freq:** Weekly (Thurs.). **Print Method:** Offset. **Trim Size:** 10 x 14. **Cols./Page:** 5. **Col. Width:** 2 inches. **Col. Depth:** 14 inches. **Key Personnel:** Hurley Green, Sr., Publisher. **Subscription Rates:** $20. **Remarks:** Accepts advertising.
Ad Rates: GLR: $5.70 **Circ:** 60,000
BW: $800
4C: $1,000
PCI: $11.43

8525 India Tribune
India Tribune Publications
3302 W. Peterson Ave. Phone: (773)588-5077
Chicago, IL 60659 Fax: (773)588-7011

Special interest newspaper (tabloid) featuring news of India for the Indian community in Chicago. **Freq:** Weekly (Sat.). **Trim Size:** 11 1/2 x 17. **Cols./Page:** 5. **Key Personnel:** Prashant Shah, Editor and Publisher. **USPS:** 380-230. **Subscription Rates:** $20; $35 two years.

8526 IndustrialnatioN
Moon Mystique
3420 N. Halsted Phone: (773)665-9016
Chicago, IL 60657 Fax: (773)665-9116
Publication E-mail: in@ripco.com
Publisher E-mail: moon@avalon.net

Magazine covering various genres of underground music, including industrial, gothic, and darkwave. Includes band interviews, album and 'zine reviews, and a "Networking" section designed to facilitate interaction between readers. **Freq:** Quarterly. **Key Personnel:** Paul A. Valerio, Editor; Sharon Maher, Assoc. Editor. **ISSN:** 1062-449X. **Subscription Rates:** $2.95 single issue. **Remarks:** Accepts advertising. **URL:** http://www.mozart.fin.depaul.edu/in.
Circ: (Not Reported)

8527 Information Technology and Libraries
Library and Information Technology Association (LITA)
50 E. Huron St. Phone: (312)280-4270
Chicago, IL 60611 Fax: (312)280-3257
Free: (800)545-2433
Publisher E-mail: lita@ala.org

Official publication of the Library and Information Technology Association. **Founded:** Mar. 1982. **Freq:** Quarterly. **Print Method:** Offset. **Trim Size:** 8 1/8 x 10 7/8. **Cols./Page:** 2 and 1. **Col. Width:** 42 and 20 picas. **Col. Depth:** 54 inches. **Key Personnel:** Dan Marmion, Editor, phone (616)387-5239, fax (616)387-5077, dan.marmion@wmich.edu; Bill Coffee, Advertising, phone (847)692-4695, fax (847)692-3877, bencof@aol.com. **ISSN:** 0730-9295. **Subscription Rates:** $50 individuals; $15 single issue; Free to qualified subscribers. **Alt. Formats:** Microfiche; Microfilm. **Formerly:** Journal of Library Automation.
Ad Rates: BW: $595 **Circ:** ‡7,192
4C: $1,500

8528 Inland Architect
Real Estate News Corp.
3525 W. Peterson, Ste. 103 Phone: (773)866-9900
Chicago, IL 60659 Fax: (773)866-9906

Subtitle: The Midwestern Building Arts Magazine. **Founded:** 1888. **Freq:** Bimonthly. **Print Method:** Offset. **Trim Size:** 8 3/4 x 11 1/2. **Cols./Page:** 3. **Col. Width:** 25 nonpareils. **Col. Depth:** 140 agate lines. **Key Personnel:** Richard Solomon, Editor; Timothy Hill, Gen. and Administration; Barbara Hower, Sr. Editor. **ISSN:** 0020-1472. **Subscription Rates:** $40. **Remarks:** Accepts advertising.
Ad Rates: BW: $1,500 **Circ:** Paid ‡6,000
4C: $1,950 Non-paid ‡500

8529 Insects are People Too
Puff 'N' Stuff Productions
Box 146486 Phone: (773)772-8686
Chicago, IL 60614
Poetry and literature magazine. **Founded:** 1994. **Freq:** Irregular. **Key Personnel:** H. R. Felgenhauer, Editor. **Subscription Rates:** $4 Issue 1; $5 Issue 2; $6 Issue 3. **Remarks:** Accepts advertising.
Circ: (Not Reported)

8530 Inside Gold Coast
Inside Publications
4710 N. Lincoln Ave. Phone: (773)878-7333
Chicago, IL 60625-2010 Fax: (773)878-0959
Publisher E-mail: inside@suba.com

Community newspaper. **Founded:** 1989. **Freq:** Weekly (Wed.). **Print Method:** Web offset. **Cols./Page:** 5. **Col. Width:** 2 inches. **Col. Depth:** 13 1/2 inches. **Key Personnel:** Nancy Amdur, Editor.
Ad Rates: GLR: $2.50 **Circ:** Free ‡48,600
BW: $1,450
4C: $2,050
PCI: $20

8531 Inside Lincoln Park
Inside Publications
4710 N. Lincoln Ave. Phone: (773)878-7333
Chicago, IL 60625-2010 Fax: (773)878-0959
Publication E-mail: inside@suba.com
Publisher E-mail: inside@suba.com

Community newspaper (tabloid) covering local news for Chicago's Northside. **Founded:** 1970. **Freq:** Weekly. **Print Method:** Offset. **Trim Size:** 10 x 13 1/2. **Cols./Page:** 5. **Col. Width:** 11 picas. **Col. Depth:** 189 agate lines. **Key Personnel:** Nancy Amdur, Editor; Ronald Roenigk, Publisher, phone (773)878-7333, fax (773)878-0959. **Subscription Rates:** Free to area households; $100 by mail. **Remarks:** Accepts advertising. **URL:** http://www.suba.com/~inside.
Ad Rates: BW: $1,450 **Circ:** Free ‡49,500
PCI: $21.48

8532 Inside Publications
4710 N. Lincoln Ave. Phone: (773)878-7333
Chicago, IL 60625-2010 Fax: (773)878-0959
Publication E-mail: inside@suba.com
Publisher E-mail: inside@suba.com

Community newspaper. **Founded:** 1968. **Freq:** Weekly (Wed.). **Print Method:** Web offset. **Cols./Page:** 5. **Col. Width:** 2 inches. **Col. Depth:** 13 1/2 inches. **Key Personnel:** Martin Northway, Editor. **URL:** http://www.suba.com/~inside. **Formerly:** Inside Lake View.
Ad Rates: GLR: $2.50 **Circ:** Free ‡48,600
BW: $1,450
4C: $2,050
PCI: $20

8533 Inside Ravenswood
Inside Publications
4710 N. Lincoln Ave. Phone: (773)878-7333
Chicago, IL 60625-2010 Fax: (773)878-0959
Publisher E-mail: inside@suba.com

Community newspaper. **Founded:** 1967. **Freq:** Weekly (Wed.). **Print Method:** Web offset. **Cols./Page:** 5. **Col. Width:** 2 inches. **Col. Depth:** 13 1/2 inches. **Key Personnel:** Larry Roenigk, Editor; Ronald C. Roenigk, Publisher; Martin Northway, Editor. **URL:** http://www.suba.com/~inside; http://www.inside@nine.com.
Ad Rates: GLR: $2.50 **Circ:** Free ‡8,382
BW: $1,450
4C: $2,050
PCI: $21.48

8534 Insight (Chicago)
Illinois CPA Society
222 S. Riverside Plaza, 16th Fl. Phone: (312)993-0393
Chicago, IL 60606 Fax: (312)993-7713

Professional journal for Certified Public Accountants in Chicago, IL. **Founded:** 1920. **Freq:** Monthly (Dec./Jan. and Feb./Mar. combined). **Print Method:** Sheetfed web. **Trim Size:** 8 3/8 x 10 7/8. **Cols./Page:** 2. **Key Personnel:** Julia Winn, Editor and Publisher; Ilene Zurla, Advertising Sales Mgr. **ISSN:** 1053-8542. **Subscription Rates:** $20 individuals. **Remarks:** Accepts advertising. **URL:** http://www.icpas.org.
Ad Rates: BW: $1,095 **Circ:** Controlled ⊕**27,000**
4C: $1,645

8535 Insights
The Chicago Center for Religion and Science
1100 East 55th St.
Chicago, IL 60615-5199

Magazine focusing on relating religious traditions with scientific theories to better understand life. **Subtitle:** The Magazine of the Chicago Center for Religion and Science. **Key Personnel:** Philip Hefner, Editor; Richard Busse, Editor.

8536 interface magazine
Stahl Haut Productions
PO Box 1209
Chicago, IL 60690-1209
Publication E-mail: intrface@ripco.com

Magazine focusing on electronic music, with an emphasis on the industrial genre. Includes interviews, record and magazine reviews, and electronic art. **Subtitle:** electronic music and art. **Freq:** Quarterly. **Key Personnel:** Andy Waggoner, Editor, catalyst@ripco.com; Eryn Dunn, Managing Editor. **ISSN:** 1081-8065. **Subscription Rates:** $10 individuals; $15 Canada and Mexico; $25 other countries. **Remarks:** Accepts advertising.
Circ: (Not Reported)

8537 Interior Landscape
American Nurseryman Publishing Co.
77 W. Washington St., Ste. 2100 Phone: (312)782-5505
Fax: (312)782-3232
Chicago, IL 60602-2904
Free: (800)621-5727
Publication E-mail: editors@amerinursery.com
Publisher E-mail: admin@amerinursery.com

Provides in-depth coverage of business and technical topics of importance to interior landscape professionals. **Subtitle:** Serving Professionals Who Bring Nature Indoors. **Founded:** Jan. 1984. **Freq:** Quarterly. **Print Method:** Offset. **Trim Size:** 8 1/8 x 10 7/8. **Cols./Page:** 3. **Col. Width:** 13 picas. **Col. Depth:** 10 inches. **Key Personnel:** Sarah McCollum, Managing Editor; Allen W. Seidel, Publisher; Wayne Larsen, Advertising Dir. **ISSN:** 1063-1607. **Subscription Rates:** $16 individuals; $24 other countries; $25.68 Canada; $5 single issue. **Remarks:** Accepts advertising.
Ad Rates: BW: $900 **Circ:** Paid 1,526
4C: $1,100 Non-paid 85
PCI: $45

8538 ISBA Bar News
Illinois State Bar Association
20 S. Clark St., Ste. 900 Phone: (312)726-8775
Chicago, IL 60603-1802 Fax: (312)726-1422

Legal newspaper for members. **Founded:** 1960. **Freq:** Semimonthly. **Print Method:** Offset. **Trim Size:** 17 1/2 X 11 3/8. **Key Personnel:** Stephen Anderson, Editor. **ISSN:** 1058-1863. **Subscription Rates:** $60 nonmembers; $9.50 members. **Remarks:** Advertising accepted; rates available upon request. **URL:** http://www.illinoisbar.org/publications.
Circ: Controlled ‡33,600

8539 ISIS
History of Science Society
University of Chicago Press Phone: (312)702-7600
Journals Division Fax: (312)702-0694
5720 S. Woodlawn Ave.
PO Box 37005
Chicago, IL 60637-1603
Publication E-mail: isis@cornell.edu

Journal on the history of science. **Subtitle:** An International Review Devoted to the History of Science and Its Cultural Influences. **Founded:** 1912. **Freq:** 5/year. **Print Method:** Offset. **Trim Size:** 6 3/4 x 10. **Cols./Page:** 2. **Col. Width:** 30 nonpareils. **Col. Depth:** 113 agate lines. **Key Personnel:** Margaret Rossiter, Editor; Tim Hill, Advertising Mgr. **ISSN:** 0021-1753. **Subscription Rates:** $57; $164 institutions. **Remarks:** Accepts advertising.
Ad Rates: BW: $375 **Circ:** ‡4,115

8540 Italian American Chamber of Commerce of Chicago Bulletin
Italian American Chamber of Commerce
30 S Michigan Ave., Ste. 504 Phone: (312)553-9137
Chicago, IL 60603 Fax: (312)533-9142
Publication E-mail: info.chicago@italchambers.net

Professional magazine covering trade with Italy. **Founded:** 1907. **Freq:** Bimonthly. **Trim Size:** 8 1/2 x 11. **Key Personnel:** Leonora ZiPuma, Editor. **Subscription Rates:** $50 individuals. **Remarks:** Accepts advertising.
Ad Rates: BW: $150 **Circ:** (Not Reported)
4C: $300

8541 Ivy Leaf
Alpha Kappa Alpha Sorority, Inc.
5656 S. Stony Island Ave. Phone: (312)684-1282
Chicago, IL 60637 Fax: (312)288-8251

Sorority publication for Black women. **Founded:** Dec. 1921. **Freq:** Quarterly. **Print Method:** Offset. **Trim Size:** 8 1/2 x 11. **Cols./Page:** 3. **Col. Width:** 14 picas. **Col. Depth:** 140 agate lines. **Key Personnel:** Alison A. Harris Alexander, Exec. Dir.; Vanessa Lovelace, Senior Ed. **ISSN:** 0021-3276. **Subscription Rates:** $12 individuals; $4 single issue. **URL:** http://www.aka1908.com.
Ad Rates: GLR: $.13 **Circ:** 40,000
BW: $1,250
4C: $1,500

8542 JAMA: Journal of the American Medical Association
American Medical Association
515 N. State St. Phone: (312)464-5000
Chicago, IL 60610 Fax: (312)464-5830
Free: (800)621-8335
Publisher E-mail: amaa@ama-assn.org

Scientific general medical journal. **Founded:** 1883. **Freq:** Weekly. **Print Method:** Offset. **Trim Size:** 8 x 10 3/4. **Cols./Page:** 3. **Col. Width:** 27 nonpareils. **Col. Depth:** 140 agate lines. **Key Personnel:** George D. Lundberg, M.D., Editor; Robert L. Kennett, V.P. Publishing; Joseph Dennehy, Publish-

er. **ISSN:** 0098-7484. **Subscription Rates:** $72 individuals. **Remarks:** Accepts advertising.
Ad Rates: BW: $6,825 4C: $8,860 **Circ:** ‡348,746

8543 Jet
Johnson Publishing Co., Inc.
820 S. Michigan Ave. Phone: (312)322-9200
Chicago, IL 60605-2191 Fax: (312)322-9375

Newsmagazine for the black community. **Founded:** 1951. **Freq:** Weekly (Mon.). **Print Method:** Offset. **Cols./Page:** 2. **Col. Width:** 30 nonpareils. **Col. Depth:** 90 agate lines. **Key Personnel:** John H. Johnson, Publisher. **Subscription Rates:** $36 individuals; $1.25 single issue. **Remarks:** Accepts advertising.
Ad Rates: BW: $9,905 4C: $13,810 **Circ:** Paid ★926,675

8544 JIAPAC (Journal of the International Association of Physicians in AIDS Care)
Journal of the International Association of Physicians in AIDS Care
225 W. Washington St., Ste. 2200 Phone: (312)419-7295
Chicago, IL 60606-3418 Fax: (312)419-7079
Publication E-mail: iapac@aol.com; iapac@iapac.org

Magazine featuring topics affecting the care of HIV-positive people. **Subtitle:** Int'l news/Clinical Presentations/Conference Reports/the Arts. **Founded:** Feb. 1995. **Freq:** Monthly. **Print Method:** 4-color press. **Trim Size:** 8 1/2x 11. **Cols./Page:** 3. **Key Personnel:** Gordon Nary, Editor and Publisher, phone (312)419-4652, fax (312)419-7160, gnary@iapac.orgg; Jose Zuniga, Associate/Political Ed., phone (312)419-7079, jzuniga@iapac.org. **ISSN:** 1081-454x. **Subscription Rates:** $60 individuals individual. **Remarks:** Accepts advertising. **URL:** http://www.iapac.org.
Ad Rates: BW: $3,000 4C: $3,000 **Circ:** Paid 5,575 Non-paid 2,900

8545 JMNR
E. J. Gossett Publishing, Inc.
7145 S. Maplewood Ave. Phone: (773)476-5978
Chicago, IL 60629-2045 Fax: (773)476-3259
Free: (800)779-JMNR

Journal covering nursing and medical research for military, veteran administration, and USPH professionals. **Subtitle:** Journal of Military Nursing and Research. **Founded:** Apr. 1995. **Freq:** Quarterly. **Print Method:** Offset. **Trim Size:** 7 1/8 x 9 3/4. **Key Personnel:** Evalyn J. Gossett, RN, Publisher, evalyng@aol.com; Carol Rogers Pitula, Ph.D., Editor; Patricia Johnson-Walker, Circulation Mgr. **ISSN:** 1070-4329. **Subscription Rates:** $29.95 individuals in U.S.; $49.95 institutions; $9 single issue; $69.95 individuals in other countries. **Remarks:** Accepts advertising.
Ad Rates: GLR: $10 BW: $500 4C: $3000 PCI: $35 **Circ:** Paid 900 Non-paid 1,500

8546 Journal
NADIG Newspapers, Inc.
4937 N. Milwaukee Ave. Phone: (773)286-6100
Chicago, IL 60630
Community newspaper. **Founded:** 1966. **Freq:** Saturday. **Print Method:** Offset. **Trim Size:** 11 1/2 x 17. **Cols./Page:** 6. **Col. Width:** 9.5 picas. **Col. Depth:** 16 inches. **Key Personnel:** Glenn Nadig, Editor. **Subscription Rates:** Free; $85 individuals.
Ad Rates: BW: $744 PCI: $10 **Circ:** Free ‡1,000

8547 Journal of Accounting Research
University of Chicago Graduate School of Business
1101 East 58th St. Phone: (773)702-7460
Chicago, IL 60637 Fax: (773)702-0458
Publication E-mail: jar@gsb.uchicago.edu

Trade journal covering all areas of accounting research. **Founded:** 1963. **Freq:** Semiannual. **Key Personnel:** Marjorie Holme, Managing Editor. **ISSN:** 0021-8456. **Subscription Rates:** $90 institutions; $45 single issue. **Remarks:** Advertising not accepted. **Alt. Formats:** Microform.
Circ: (Not Reported)

8548 Journal of AHIMA
American Health Information Management Association
919 N. Michigan Ave., Ste. 1400 Phone: (312)787-2672
Chicago, IL 60611 Fax: (312)787-9793
Publication E-mail: info@ahimo.org

A professional development tool for health information managers. Disseminates new knowledge, best practices, and industry news. **Founded:** Jan. 1929. **Freq:** Monthly 10/yr. **Print Method:** Offset. **Trim Size:** 8 1/2 x 11. **Key Personnel:** Anne Zender, Managing Editor; Jane Blumenthal, Assoc. Ed. **ISSN:** 1060-5487. **Subscription Rates:** $72 individuals. **URL:** http://www.ahima.org. **Formerly:** Journal of AMRA.
Ad Rates: BW: $1,670 4C: $2,860 **Circ:** Paid 38,000 Non-paid 500

8549 Journal of the American Dental Association
ADA Publishing Co., Inc.
211 E. Chicago Ave. Phone: (312)440-2791
Chicago, IL 60611 Fax: (312)440-3538
Free: (800)621-8099
Publisher E-mail: adapco@ada.org

Trade journal for the dental profession. **Founded:** 1913. **Freq:** Monthly. **Print Method:** Web. **Trim Size:** 2 1/8 x 10 7/8. **Cols./Page:** 3. **Col. Width:** 13 picas. **Col. Depth:** 10 inches. **Key Personnel:** Dr. Lawrence Meskin, Editor, phone (312)440-7475, fax (312)440-3538, meskinl@ada.org; Laura Kosden, CEO/Publisher, phone (312)440-2790, kosdenl@ada.org; James Berry, Associate Publisher, Editorial, phone (312)440-2786, berryj@ada.org; Gabriela Radulescu, Assoc. Publisher, Marketing & Operations, phone (312)440-2519, radulescug@ada.org. **ISSN:** 0002-8177. **Subscription Rates:** $85 individuals; $115 institutions, other countries and students; $11 single issue. **Remarks:** Advertising accepted; rates available upon request. **URL:** http://www.ada.org. **Alt. Formats:** CD-ROM.
Circ: Paid 110,298 Non-paid 32,932

8550 Journal of the American Dietetic Association
American Dietetic Association
216 W. Jackson Blvd. Phone: (312)899-0040
Chicago, IL 60606-6995 Fax: (312)899-4758
Free: (800)877-1600

Journal reporting original research on nutrition, diet therapy, education and administration. **Founded:** 1925. **Freq:** Monthly. **Print Method:** Offset. **Trim Size:** 8 1/8 x 10 7/8. **Cols./Page:** 3 and 2. **Col. Width:** 13 and 20 picas. **Col. Depth:** 55 picas. **Key Personnel:** Elaine R. Monsen, Editor; Elisabeth Crist, Managing Editor; Vicki Guinta, Advertising Dir., vguinta@eatright.org. **ISSN:** 0002-8223. **Subscription Rates:** $115 individuals; $140 Canada; $190 other countries; $9.75 single issue. **Remarks:** Accepts advertising.
Ad Rates: BW: $3,980 4C: $5,530 **Circ:** Paid 70,980 Non-paid 582

8551 Journal of the American Osteopathic Association
American Osteopathic Association
142 E. Ontario St. Phone: (312)202-8000
Chicago, IL 60611 Fax: (312)202-8200
Free: (800)621-1773
Publisher E-mail: info@aoa_ net.org

Osteopathic clinical journal. **Founded:** 1901. **Freq:** Monthly. **Print Method:** Offset. **Trim Size:** 8 x 10 7/8. **Cols./Page:** 3. **Key Personnel:** Gilbert E. D'Alonzo, D.O., Editor-in-Chief; Karen Stipp, Assistant Dir., kstipp@aoa-net.org. **ISSN:** 0098-6151. **Subscription Rates:** Free to qualified subscribers; $50 institutions. **Remarks:** Accepts advertising. **URL:** http://www.aoa-net.org. **Alt. Formats:** Microform.
Ad Rates: BW: $1,400 4C: $2,500 **Circ:** Controlled ‡36,615

8552 Journal of Correctional Health Care
National Commission on Correctional Health Care
1300 W. Belmont Ave. Phone: (773)880-1460
Chicago, IL 60657-3200 Fax: (773)880-2424
Publisher E-mail: ncchc@ncchc.org

Professional journal covering research in health care provided in prisons, jails, and juvenile confinement facilities. **Founded:** 1994. **Freq:** Semiannual. **Trim Size:** 6 x 9. **Key Personnel:** Paula Hancock, Contact, paulah@ncchc.org. **Subscription Rates:** $30 individuals; $20 single issue. **Remarks:** Advertising not accepted.
Circ: (Not Reported)

8553 Journal of Court Reporting
National Court Reporters Association
6166 N Sheridan Rd., Unit 10F Phone: (773)262-4464
Chicago, IL 60660 Fax: (773)262-1638
Publication E-mail: msic@ncrahq.org
Publisher E-mail: msic@ncrahq.org

Magazine. **Subtitle:** Official Publication of National Court Reporters Assn. **Founded:** 1905. **Freq:** 10/year. **Print Method:** Offset. **Trim Size:** 8 1/8 x 10 7/8. **Cols./Page:** 3. **Col. Width:** 27 nonpareils. **Col. Depth:** 139 agate lines. **Key Personnel:** Benjamin M. Rogner, Editor, phone (312)262-4464; Brian E. Cartier, Publisher; Annelie Glimka, Advertising Mgr., phone (703)556-6272; Marshall Jorpeland, Communications Dir., phone (703)556-6272. **ISSN:** 0274-5860. **Subscription Rates:** $49 individuals. **Formerly:** National Shorthand Reporter (1991).
Ad Rates: BW: $1,240 4C: $2,105 **Circ:** ‡34,000

8554 The Journal of Criminal Law and Criminology
Northwestern University School of Law Phone: (312)503-8547
357 E. Chicago Ave. Fax: (312)503-0132
Chicago, IL 60611-3008
Publication E-mail: jclclaw@nwu.edu

Legal journal. **Founded:** 1910. **Freq:** Quarterly. **Print Method:** Letterpress and offset. **Cols./Page:** 1. **Col. Width:** 65 nonpareils. **Col. Depth:** 119 agate lines. **Key Personnel:** Annaliese Flynn, Editor-in-Chief, a-flynn@nwu.edu. **Subscription Rates:** $40 individuals. **Remarks:** Advertising not accepted. **Online:** Lexis/Nexis; Westlaw. **Formerly:** Journal of Criminal Law, Criminology, & Political Science.
Circ: 3,000

8555 Journal of Dental Hygiene
American Dental Hygienists' Association
444 N. Michigan Ave., Ste. 3400 Phone: (312)440-8900
Chicago, IL 60611 Fax: (312)440-6780
Free: (800)243-ADHA
Publication E-mail: mail@adha.net

Professional journal on dental hygiene. **Founded:** 1923. **Freq:** 4x/year. **Print Method:** Offset. **Trim Size:** 8 1/8 x 10 7/8. **Cols./Page:** 2. **Col. Width:** 19 1/2 picas. **Col. Depth:** 59 1/2 picas. **Key Personnel:** Rosetta Gervasi, Editor; Mary-Alice Gaston, Director; Mark Berthdd, Sr. Ed., phone (312)440-8934, markb@adha.net. **ISSN:** 1043-254X. **Subscription Rates:** $60 other countries; $45 individuals; $7.50 single issue. **Remarks:** Accepts advertising.
Ad Rates: GLR: $18 BW: $1,905 4C: $3,300 PCI: $120 **Circ:** ‡36,000 Non-paid ‡308

8556 Journal of Dentistry for Children
American Society of Dentistry for Children
875 N. Michigan Ave., Ste. 4040 Phone: (312)943-1244
Chicago, IL 60611-1901 Fax: (312)943-5341
Free: (800)637-2732
Publisher E-mail: asdckids@aol.com

Magazine focusing on dentistry for children. **Founded:** 1933. **Freq:** Bimonthly. **Print Method:** Offset. **Cols./Page:** 2. **Col. Width:** 39 nonpareils. **Col. Depth:** 116 agate lines. **Key Personnel:** Dr. George W. Teuscher, Editor; Linda S. Sprouls, Managing Editor. **USPS:** 279-480. **Subscription Rates:** $100 individuals domestic; $120 institutions domestic; $120 other countries foreign individual; $150 institutions, other countries foreign. **Remarks:** Accepts advertising.
Ad Rates: BW: $1,650 4C: $2,650 **Circ:** Paid ‡4,265 Controlled ‡29

8557 Journal of Ethical Studies
International Association of Ethicists, Inc. (IAE International)
117 W. Harrison Bldg.
6th Fl., Ste. I-104
Chicago, IL 60605

Applied ethics journal. **Founded:** 1986. **Freq:** Quarterly. **Trim Size:** 5 1/2 x 8 1/2. **Key Personnel:** Dr. David A. Mrovka, Editor. **Subscription Rates:** $50. **Remarks:** Accepts advertising. **Alt. Formats:** Diskette.
Ad Rates: BW: $50 PCI: $11 **Circ:** (Not Reported)

8558 Journal of Graphoanalysis
International Graphoanalysis Society
111 N. Canal St. Phone: (312)930-9446
Ste. 399 Fax: (312)930-5903
Chicago, IL 60606
Publication E-mail: headquarters@igas.com
Publisher E-mail: headquarters@igas.com

Magazine on handwriting analysis. **Founded:** Jan. 1929. **Freq:** Monthly. **Print Method:** Offset. **Trim Size:** 8 1/2 x 11. **Cols./Page:** 3. **Col. Width:** 2 1/4 inches. **Col. Depth:** 10 inches. **Key Personnel:** K. Kusta, Publisher. **Subscription Rates:** $90. **Remarks:** Advertising not accepted.
Circ: (Not Reported)

8559 Journal of Health Care Marketing
American Marketing Association
311 S. Wacker Dr. Suite 5800 Phone: (312)648-0536
Chicago, IL 60606-5819 Fax: (312)993-7542
Free: (800)262-1150
Publisher E-mail: info@ama.org

Periodical that provides practitioners and academics with the latest research on techniques and applications. **Founded:** 1980. **Freq:** Quarterly. **Print Method:** Web offset. **Trim Size:** 8 1/2 x 11. **Cols./Page:** 2. **Col. Width:** 21 picas. **Col. Depth:** 141.75 agate lines. **Key Personnel:** Ron Keener, Publisher, phone (312)831-2794, fax (312)648-0103; Lynn Coleman, Managing Editor, phone (312)831-2756, fax (312)993-7540; Kathy Hays, Advertising Mgr. **ISSN:** 0737-3252. **Subscription**

Rates: $15 single issue; $45 AMA member; $70 nonmembers; $90 institutions. **Remarks:** Accepts advertising. **URL:** www.ama.org.
Ad Rates: BW: $700 **Circ:** Paid ‡3781
4C: $1600 Non-paid ‡179

8560 Journal of Healthcare Management
Health Administration Press
1 N. Franklin, Ste. 1700 Phone: (312)424-2800
Chicago, IL 60606-3491 Fax: (312)424-0014
Publisher E-mail: hap@ache.org

Professional journal focusing on healthcare management. **Founded:** 1956. **Freq:** Bimonthly. **Print Method:** Offset. **Trim Size:** 7 x 10. **Cols./Page:** 1. **Col. Width:** 32 picas. **Col. Depth:** 47 picas. **Key Personnel:** James A. Johnson, PhD., Editor; Helen-Joy Bechtle, Managing Editor. **ISSN:** 8750-3735. **Subscription Rates:** Free members of A.C.H.E.; $65 nonmembers; $75 nonmembers other countries; $14 single issue. **Remarks:** Advertising not accepted.
Circ: Paid ‡1,500
Controlled ‡27,000

8561 Journal of Healthcare Risk Management
American Hospital Association (AHA)
One N. Franklin Phone: (312)422-3366
Chicago, IL 60606 Fax: (312)422-4505

Professional journal covering risk management in healthcare. **Freq:** Quarterly. **Key Personnel:** Lynne Mangan, Editor, LMangan1@aha.org; Joy Roney, Ad Asst. **ISSN:** 1074-4797. **Subscription Rates:** $100 individuals. **Remarks:** Accepts advertising.
Ad Rates: BW: $500 **Circ:** (Not Reported)

8562 The Journal of Law and Economics
University of Chicago Press
5720 S. Woodlawn Ave. Phone: (773)702-7600
Chicago, IL 60637 Fax: (773)702-0172
Publication E-mail: m-callahan@uchicago.edu

Journal exploring the relationships between law and economics, focusing on the influence of regulation and legal institutions on the operation of economic systems. **Founded:** 1958. **Freq:** 2/year. **Print Method:** Offset. **Trim Size:** 6x9. **Cols./Page:** 1. **Key Personnel:** Dennis W. Carlton, Editor; Richard A. Epstein, Editor; Sam Peltzman, Editor; Alan O. Sykes, Editor; Cheryl Jones, Advertising Mgr., phone (773)702-7361. **ISSN:** 0022-2186. **Subscription Rates:** $30 individuals; $16 students; $21 students other countries; $22.12 students Canada; $35 other countries; $37.10 individuals Canada; $45 industry; $50 other countries industry; $53.15 Canada industry. **Remarks:** Accepts advertising.
Ad Rates: BW: $365 **Circ:** Paid ‡3,300

8563 The Journal of Legal Studies
University of Chicago Press
5720 S. Woodlawn Ave. Phone: (773)702-7600
Chicago, IL 60637 Fax: (773)702-0172

Interdisciplinary journal of theoretical and empirical research on law and legal institutions. **Founded:** 1972. **Freq:** 2/year. **Print Method:** Offset. **Trim Size:** 6x9. **Cols./Page:** 1. **Key Personnel:** J. Mark Ramseyer, Editor; Eric Posner, Editor; Tim Hill, Advertising Mgr., phone (773)702-8187. **ISSN:** 0047-2530. **Subscription Rates:** $30 individuals; $16 students; $21 students, other countries; $22.12 students, Canada; $35 individuals out of country; $37.10 individuals in Canada; $45 institutions; $50 institutions other countries; $53.15 institutions Canada. **Remarks:** Accepts advertising.
Ad Rates: BW: $365 **Circ:** Paid ‡1,600

8564 Journal of Marital & Family Therapy
American Association for Marriage and Family Therapy
University of Chicago Phone: (773)834-1213
969 E. 60th St. Fax: (773)702-0874
Chicago, IL 60637
Publication E-mail: jmft@ssasun.uchicago.edu

Journal for professional therapists. Covers clinical techniques, research, and theory of marital and family therapy. **Founded:** 1975. **Freq:** Quarterly. **Trim Size:** 7 x 10. **Cols./Page:** 1. **Col. Width:** 5 inches. **Col. Depth:** 8 inches. **Key Personnel:** Froma Walsh, PhD, Editor. **ISSN:** 0194-472X. **Subscription Rates:** $45 individuals; $75 two years; $140 institutions; $11.25 single issue.
Ad Rates: BW: $330 **Circ:** Paid 20,000
Non-paid 200

8565 Journal of Marketing
American Marketing Association
311 S. Wacker Dr. Suite 5800 Phone: (312)648-0536
Chicago, IL 60606-5819 Fax: (312)993-7542
Free: (800)262-1150
Publisher E-mail: info@ama.org

Scholarly journal covering marketing research studies. **Founded:** 1936. **Freq:** Quarterly. **Trim Size:** 8 1/2 x 11. **Cols./Page:** 2. **Col. Width:** 20 picas. **Col. Depth:** 140 agate lines. **Key Personnel:** Jack Hollaner, Publisher, jhollfelder@ama.org; Francesca VanGorp, Managing Editor, vfvangorp@ama.org; John Hubbard, Advertising Sales Manager, jhubbard@ama.org; Gloria Naurocki, Marketing Director, phone (312)831-2796, fax (312)648-0103. **ISSN:** 0022-2429. **Subscription Rates:** $20 single issue; $40 AMA members; $75 nonmembers; $150 institutions. **Remarks:** Accepts advertising.
Ad Rates: BW: $1000 **Circ:** Paid ‡9028
4C: $1300 Free 65

8566 Journal of Marketing Research
American Marketing Association
311 S. Wacker Dr. Suite 5800 Phone: (312)648-0536
Chicago, IL 60606-5819 Fax: (312)993-7542
Free: (800)262-1150
Publisher E-mail: Info@ama.org

Academic journal publishing scholarly research in the field of marketing. **Founded:** 1964. **Freq:** Quarterly. **Print Method:** Offset. **Trim Size:** 8 1/2 x 11. **Cols./Page:** 2. **Col. Width:** 40 nonpareils. **Col. Depth:** 140 agate lines. **Key Personnel:** Barton A. Weitz, Editor; Jeffrey Heilbrunn, Publisher; Kathy Hays, Advertising Mgr. **ISSN:** 0022-2437. **Subscription Rates:** $70 individuals; $40 members of AMA; $75 nonmembers; $150 institutions. **Remarks:** Accepts advertising.
Ad Rates: BW: $700 **Circ:** Paid ‡8,000

8567 Journal of Property Management
Institute of Real Estate Management
PO Box 109025 Phone: (312)329-6000
Chicago, IL 60610 Fax: (312)661-0217

Magazine serving real estate managers. **Founded:** 1934. **Freq:** Bimonthly. **Print Method:** Offset. **Trim Size:** 8 1/8 x 10 7/8. **Cols./Page:** 3. **Col. Width:** 26 nonpareils. **Col. Depth:** 138 agate lines. **Key Personnel:** Mariwyn Evans, Editor, phone (312)329-6058, fax (312)410-7958, mevans@irem.org. **ISSN:** 0022-3905. **Subscription Rates:** $43.95 individuals; $7.50 single issue. **Remarks:** Accepts advertising. **Available Online. URL:** http://www.irem.org. **Alt. Formats:** CD-ROM, Information Access.
Ad Rates: BW: $3,075 **Circ:** ‡23,400
4C: $4,275

8568 Journal of Public Policy & Marketing
American Marketing Association
311 S. Wacker Dr. Suite 5800 Phone: (312)648-0536
Chicago, IL 60606-5819 Fax: (312)993-7542
Free: (800)262-1150
Publisher E-mail: info@ama.org

Journal of marketing. **Founded:** 1982. **Freq:** 2/year. **Print Method:** Offset. **Trim Size:** 8 1/2 x 11. **Cols./Page:** 2. **Key Personnel:** J. Craig Andrews, Editor; Jack Hollander, Publisher. **ISSN:** 0743-9156. **Subscription Rates:** $55; $75 other countries. **Remarks:** Advertising accepted; rates available upon request.
Circ: Paid ‡472

8569 Journal of the Society of Architectural Historians (JSAH)
Society of Architectural Historians
1365 N. Astor St. Phone: (312)573-1365
Chicago, IL 60610-2144 Fax: (312)573-1141
Publisher E-mail: info@sah.org

Professional magazine devoted to architectural history. **Founded:** 1940. **Freq:** Quarterly. **Trim Size:** 8 1/2 x 11. **Cols./Page:** 3. **Col. Width:** 2 1/4 inches. **Col. Depth:** 9 1/2 inches. **Key Personnel:** Pauline Saliga, Contact; Pauline Saliga, psaliga@sah.org. **ISSN:** 0037-9808. **Subscription Rates:** $80 individuals. **Remarks:** Accepts advertising.
Ad Rates: BW: $400 **Circ:** Controlled ‡3,450

8570 Journal of Youth Services in Libraries
American Library Association (ALA)
50 E. Huron St. Phone: (312)280-5038
Chicago, IL 60611 Fax: (312)280-5033
Free: (800)545-2433
Publication E-mail: yalsa@ala.org

Magazine focusing on library services and materials for children and young adults. **Founded:** 1943. **Freq:** Quarterly. **Print Method:** Offset. **Trim Size:** 8 3/8 x 10 7/8. **Cols./Page:** 3. **Col. Width:** 30 nonpareils. **Col. Depth:** 105 agate lines. **Key Personnel:** Betty Carter, Co-Editor, phone (940)898-2616, f_carter@twu.edu; Keith Swigger, Co-Editor, phone (940)898-2602, a.swigger@twu.edu; William Coffee, Advertising Mgr., phone (847)692-4695, fax (847)692-3877, bencof@aol.com; Julie Walker, Business Mgr., phone (312)280-4388, fax (312)664-7459, jwalker@ala.org; Susan Roman, Business Mgr. **ISSN:** 0894-2498. **Subscription Rates:** $40 individuals; $50 other countries; $12 single issue. **Remarks:** Accepts advertising.
Ad Rates: GLR: $675 **Circ:** 6,427
BW: $675
4C: $750

8571 JUF News
Jewish Federation of Chicago
1 S. Franklin St., Rm. 701G Phone: (312)357-4848
Chicago, IL 60606 Fax: (312)855-2470

Jewish magazine. **Founded:** 1960. **Freq:** 12/year. **Print Method:** Offset. **Cols./Page:** 5. **Col. Width:** 29 agate lines. **Col. Depth:** 181 agate lines. **Key Personnel:** Aaron Cohen, Editor, aharon@interaccess.com; Janet Buzil, Advertising Mgr.; Sid Singer, Staff Writer; Abigail Pickus, Staff Writer; Kathleen Evans Mazur, Operations Mgr.; Michelle Mangold, Advertising Prod. Assistant. **Subscription Rates:** $10. **URL:** interaccess.
Ad Rates: GLR: $2.10 **Circ:** 55,000
BW: $1,389
4C: $2,029
PCI: $31.15

8572 Kane County Herald
Herald Co., Inc.
PO Box 10041 Phone: (312)232-9075
Chicago, IL 60610
Newspaper with Republican orientation. **Founded:** 1963. **Freq:** Weekly (Wed.). **Print Method:** Offset. **Cols./Page:** 6. **Col. Width:** 22 nonpareils. **Col. Depth:** 224 agate lines. **Key Personnel:** Roberta Campbell, Editor. **Subscription Rates:** $9 individuals. **Remarks:** Accepts advertising.
Circ: ‡10,000

8573 Keats-Shelley Journal
Coopers and Lybrand
Dept. of English
Crown Center 402
N. Sheridan Rd.
Chicago, IL 60626

Contains articles on John Keats, Percy Shelley, Mary Shelley, Lord Bryon, and Leigh Hunt, as well as news and notes, book reviews, and a bibliography. **Key Personnel:** Steven Jones, Editor, phone (773)508-2791, sjones1@puc.edu. **Subscription Rates:** $20. **Remarks:** Advertising not accepted. **URL:** http://www.luc.edu/publications/keats-shelley/ksjweb.htm.
Circ: (Not Reported)

8574 La Raza
Rossi Publications, Inc.
3909 N. Ashland Ave. Phone: (773)525-9400
Chicago, IL 60613 Fax: (773)525-5350
Publisher E-mail: adsales@laraza.com

Community newspaper (tabloid) (Spanish). **Founded:** 1972. **Freq:** Weekly Wed.& Thur. **Print Method:** Offset. **Cols./Page:** 5. **Col. Width:** 18 nonpareils. **Col. Depth:** 196 agate lines. **Key Personnel:** Jorge Oclander, Editor, phone (773)525-1763, fax (773)525-7747, joclander@laraza.com; Luis H. Rossi, Publisher, phone (773)327-6500, fax (773)327-3822, lrossi@laraza.com; Robert J. Armband, Publisher, phone (773)525-6285, fax (773)525-6449, armband@laraza.com. **Subscription Rates:** $35 individuals; $80 First Class mail. **Remarks:** Accepts advertising. **Available Online. URL:** http://www.laraza.com.
Ad Rates: BW: $3,865 **Circ:** Paid ♦**28,011**
4C: $4,600 Non-paid ♦**108,570**
PCI: $33

8575 Laboratory Medicine
American Society of Clinical Pathologists
2100 W. Harrison St. Phone: (312)738-1336
Chicago, IL 60612 Fax: (312)738-0101

Professional journal covering medical technology and pathology. **Subtitle:** An Official Publication of the American Society of Clinical Pathologists. **Founded:** 1970. **Freq:** Monthly. **Print Method:** Offset. **Trim Size:** 8 1/4 x 10 3/4. **Cols./Page:** 3. **Col. Width:** 26 nonpareils. **Col. Depth:** 140 agate lines. **Key Personnel:** Lynn Olson, Managing Editor; Joseph Dingee, Ad. Sales Asst. **ISSN:** 0007-5027. **Subscription Rates:** $50 individuals; $8 single issue. **Remarks:** Accepts advertising. **URL:** http://www.asep.org.
Ad Rates: GLR: $15 **Circ:** Paid 150,205
BW: $3,900 Non-paid 15,583
4C: $5,150

8576 LAMPlighter
American Bar Association
750 N. Lake Shore Dr. Phone: (312)988-5000
Chicago, IL 60611-4497 Fax: (312)988-5568
Free: (800)285-2221

Journal providing useful information to armed forces legal assistance officers and other interested parties. **Subtitle:** Legal Assistance for Military Personel (LAMP). **Founded:** 1988. **Freq:** Quarterly. **Trim Size:** 8 1/2 x 11. **Cols./Page:** 3. **Col. Width:** 2 1/4 inches. **Col. Depth:** 8 1/2 inches. **ISSN:** 1044-8756. **Subscription Rates:** Free.

8577 Law Practice Management
American Bar Association
750 N. Lake Shore Dr. Phone: (312)988-5000
Chicago, IL 60611-4497 Fax: (312)988-5568
Free: (800)285-2221

Magazine covering the economics of law practice and law office management. **Founded:** 1975. **Freq:** 8/year. **Print Method:** Web offset. **Trim Size:** 8 3/8 x 10 7/8. **Cols./Page:** 3. **Col. Width:** 28 nonpareils. **Col. Depth:** 138 agate lines. **Key Personnel:** Delmar L. Roberts, Editor; Rita Novak, Advertising Mgr. **ISSN:** 0360-1439. **Subscription Rates:** $48 individuals; $64 other countries. **Remarks:** Accepts advertising. **Formerly:** Legal Economics.
Ad Rates: BW: $2250 **Circ:** 22,005
4C: $3395

8578 Lenox Avenue
Columbia College Center for Black Music Research
600 S. Michigan Ave. Phone: (312)344-7559
Chicago, IL 60605 Fax: (312)344-8029
Publisher E-mail: cbmr@popmail.colum.edu

Journal exploring inter-relationships among the black expressive arts. **Subtitle:** A Journal of Interartistic Inquiry. **Founded:** 1995. **Freq:** Annual. **Print Method:** Web. **Trim Size:** 7 x 10. **Key Personnel:** Samuel A. Floyd, Jr., Editor, sfloyd@popmail.colum.edu. **ISSN:** 1080-0646. **Subscription Rates:** $35 individuals; $40 other countries. **Remarks:** Advertising not accepted.
Circ: (Not Reported)

8579 Libido
Box 146721 Phone: (773)275-0842
Chicago, IL 60614 Fax: (773)275-0752
Free: (800)495-1988
Publisher E-mail: rune@mcs.com

Consumer magazine covering sexuality and erotica for a gay, lesbian, and bisexual audience. **Subtitle:** The Journal of Sex and Sensibility. **Founded:** 1988. **Freq:** Quarterly. **Print Method:** Offset. **Trim Size:** 9 1/4 x 6 3/4. **Key Personnel:** Marianna Beck, Editor and Publisher; Jack Hafferkamp, Editor and Publisher; Jane Underwood, Sales Mgr., phone (415)550-1991, fax (415)550-1990, pjunder@sirius.com. **ISSN:** 0899-8272. **Subscription Rates:** $30 individuals; $10 single issue. **Remarks:** Accepts advertising. **URL:** http://www.sensualsource.com.
Ad Rates: BW: $500 **Circ:** Combined 10,100

8580 Library Administration & Management
American Library Association (ALA)
50 E. Huron St. Phone: (312)280-5038
Chicago, IL 60611 Fax: (312)280-5033
Free: (800)545-2433

Journal reporting on current administrative issues of concern to library managers and executives. **Founded:** Jan. 1987. **Freq:** Quarterly. **Print Method:** Offset. **Trim Size:** 8 1/2 x 11. **Cols./Page:** 3. **Col. Width:** 2 1/4 inches. **Col. Depth:** 9 5/8 inches. **Key Personnel:** William N. Coffee, Advertising Mgr., phone (847)692-4695, fax (847)692-3877, bencof@aol.com; Maria Otero-Boisvert, Editor. **ISSN:** 0888-4463. **Subscription Rates:** $50 individuals; $60 other countries; $14 single issue. **Remarks:** Accepts advertising. **URL:** http://www.ala.org/lama.
Ad Rates: BW: $490 **Circ:** Paid ‡6,100

8581 Library Resources & Technical Services
American Library Association (ALA)
50 E. Huron St. Phone: (312)280-5038
Chicago, IL 60611 Fax: (312)280-5033
Free: (800)545-2433

Magazine focusing on library cataloging, classification, acquisitions, and technical services operations, including the preservation and reproduction of library materials. **Founded:** 1957. **Freq:** Quarterly. **Print Method:** Offset. **Trim Size:** 6 x 9. **Cols./Page:** 1. **Col. Width:** 63 nonpareils. **Col. Depth:** 105 agate lines. **Key Personnel:** Jennifer Younger, Editor; Todd Goldman, Advertising Mgr.; Karen Muller, Business Mgr. **ISSN:** 0024-2527. **Subscription Rates:** $55 U.S., Canada and Mexico; $65 out of country; $14 single issue free with ALCTS membership. **Remarks:** Accepts advertising. **URL:** http://www.ala.org/alcts.
Ad Rates: BW: $490 **Circ:** ‡8,702

8582 Light
Box 7500 Phone: (847)853-1028
Chicago, IL 60680 Fax: (847)853-1102
Free: (800)285-4448

Journal featuring light verse. **Subtitle:** The Quarterly of Light Verse. **Founded:** Apr. 1992. **Freq:** Quarterly. **Print Method:** Offset. **Trim Size:** 6 x 9. **Cols./Page:** 2. **Key Personnel:** John Mella, Editor. **ISSN:** 1064-8186. **Subscription Rates:** $16 individuals; $5 single issue. **Remarks:** Advertising accepted; rates available upon request.
Circ: Combined ‡923

8583 Link
Yellow Pages Publishers Association
The Merchandise Mart, Ste. 2000 Phone: (312)527-7412
Fax: (312)527-7230
Chicago, IL 60654
Trade magazine. **Subtitle:** The Magazine for Yellow Pages and Directory Marketing. **Founded:** 1989. **Freq:** 10/year. **Print Method:** Offset. **Trim Size:** 8 x 10 7/8. **Cols./Page:** 3. **Col. Width:** 2 3/16 inches. **Col. Depth:** 11 1/8 inches. **Key Personnel:** James C. Logan, Jr., Publisher, phone (810)244-0707; Charles Laughlin, Editor-in-Chief. **ISSN:** 1045-9723. **Subscription Rates:** $60. $6 single issue. **Remarks:** Accepts advertising.
Ad Rates: BW: $1,705 **Circ:** Paid 2,022
4C: $3,040 Non-paid 9,971

8584 Literature and Medicine
Johns Hopkins University Press
Medical Humanities Program Phone: (312)996-7954
Dept. of Medical Education Fax: (312)413-2048
Univ. of Illinois at Chicago
808 S. Wood St.
Chicago, IL 60612
Publisher E-mail: jlinfo@jhupress.jhu.edu

Journal. **Founded:** 1982. **Freq:** Semiannual. **Print Method:** Offset. **Trim Size:** 6 x 9. **Cols./Page:** 1. **Col. Width:** 26 picas. **Col. Depth:** 7 inches. **Key Personnel:** Suzannedson Poirier, Editor, suzanne.poirier@uic.edu; Tara Dorai-Berry, Advertising Mgr., tdorai-berry@mail.press.jhu.edu. **ISSN:** 0278-9671. **Subscription Rates:** $29 individuals; $49 institutions. **Remarks:** Accepts advertising. **Available Online. URL:** http://www.press.jhu.edu/journals/literature_and_medicine/.
Ad Rates: BW: $225 **Circ:** 875

8585 Lithuanian Museum Review
Balzekas Museum of Lithuanian Culture
6500 S. Pulaski Rd. Phone: (312)582-6500
Chicago, IL 60629-5136 Fax: (312)582-5133

Magazine containing information on Lithuania and Lithuanians. **Founded:** 1966. **Freq:** Bimonthly. **Print Method:** Offset. **Cols./Page:** 3. **Col. Width:** 30 nonpareils. **Col. Depth:** 140 agate lines. **Key Personnel:** Loretta Visomirskyte, Editor. **Subscription Rates:** $25 individuals; $4 single issue.
Ad Rates: BW: $1000 **Circ:** Paid ‡3500
Controlled ‡8950

8586 Lituanus
Lituanus Foundation, Inc.
6621 S. Troy Phone: (773)434-0706
Chicago, IL 60629-2913 Fax: (773)476-5171

Journal on the arts and sciences of the Baltic states. **Founded:** Nov. 1954. **Freq:** Quarterly. **Print Method:** Offset. **Trim Size:** 5 1/2 x 8 1/2. **Cols./Page:** 1. **Col. Width:** 47 nonpareils. **Col. Depth:** 95 agate lines. **Key Personnel:** Dr. Ant. Klimas, Editor. **ISSN:** 0024-5089. **Subscription Rates:** $15 individuals; $3.75 single issue. **Remarks:** Advertising not accepted.
Circ: Paid 3,500

8587 Liturgy 90
Liturgy Training Publications
1800 N. Hermitage Ave. Phone: (773)486-8970
Chicago, IL 60622-1101 Fax: (773)486-7094
Free: (800)933-1800
Publisher E-mail: marketing@ltp.org

Articles and columns concerned with background and implementation of reforms in Catholic Worship. **Founded:** 1963. **Freq:** 8/year. **Print Method:** Sheetfed. **Trim Size:** 8 1/2 x 11. **Cols./Page:** 2. **Key Personnel:** David Philippart, Editor, phone (773)486-8970, fax (773)486-7094, dphilipp@ltp.org. **ISSN:** 1046-9990. **Subscription Rates:** $18; $25 other countries; $2 back issue. **Remarks:** Advertising not accepted. **Formerly:** Liturgy 80; Liturgy 70.
Circ: Paid ‡6,800
Non-paid ‡1,200

8588 Logan Square Extra
EXTRA Publications, Inc.
3918 W. North Ave. Phone: (312)252-3534
Chicago, IL 60647 Fax: (312)252-6031

Newspaper (Spanish & English). **Founded:** 1980. **Freq:** Weekly (Thurs.). **Print Method:** Offset. Uses mats. **Trim Size:** 11 x 14. **Cols./Page:** 4. **Col. Width:** 28 nonpareils. **Col. Depth:** 179 agate lines. **Key Personnel:** Mary Montgomery, Editor; Mila Tellez, Publisher; Adrio Baur, General Mgr. **Subscription Rates:** Free; $25 by mail. **Remarks:** Accepts advertising.
Ad Rates: GLR: $21.19 **Circ:** Free ‡16,000

8589 Loyola Magazine
Loyola University of Chicago
820 N. Michigan Ave., Lewis Towers, Ste. 1500 Phone: (312)915-6407
Fax: (312)915-6450
Chicago, IL 60611
Free: (800)424-1513

Collegiate magazine. **Subtitle:** The Magazine of Loyola University Chicago. **Founded:** 1971. **Freq:** 4/year. **Print Method:** Offset. **Trim Size:** 11 x 12. **Cols./Page:** 3. **Col. Width:** 26 nonpareils. **Col. Depth:** 140 agate lines. **Key Personnel:** Bill Noblitt, Editor-in-Chief. **ISSN:** 1054-7614. **Remarks:** Advertising not accepted.
Circ: Non-paid 120,000

8590 Loyola Phoenix
Loyola University of Chicago
6525 N. Sheridan Rd. Phone: (773)508-7110
Chicago, IL 60626 Fax: (773)508-7121
Publication E-mail: phoenix@luc.edu

Collegiate newspaper. **Founded:** 1969. **Freq:** Weekly. **Print Method:** Offset. **Trim Size:** 11 x 17. **Cols./Page:** 4. **Col. Width:** 2 5/16 inches. **Col. Depth:** 16 inches. **Key Personnel:** Steve Haro, Editor, sharo@orion.it.luc.edu; Bill McGuire, Business Mgr., phoenix@luc.edu. **Subscription Rates:** $20. **Remarks:** Accepts advertising. **Alt. Formats:** Microform.
Ad Rates: BW: $576 **Circ:** Free 7,000
4C: $976
PCI: $9

8591 Loyola University Chicago Law Journal
Loyola University-Chicago/School of Law
1 E. Pearson Phone: (312)915-7183
Chicago, IL 60611 Fax: (312)915-7201
Publication E-mail: law-journal@luc.edu

Law Journal. **Founded:** 1968. **Freq:** Quarterly. **Print Method:** Offset. **Trim Size:** 8 x 5. **Col. Width:** 26 nonpareils. **Col. Depth:** 140 agate lines. **Key Personnel:** Gina Chang, Managing Editor, phone (312)915-7183, fax (312)715-7201. **ISSN:** 0024-7081. **Subscription Rates:** $25 volume; $9 single issue. **Remarks:** Accepts advertising. **Online:** LEXIS-NEXIS; Westlaw. **Formerly:** Loyola University of Chicago Law Journal.
Ad Rates: BW: $100 **Circ:** Controlled ‡650

8592 Lumpen
Lumpen Media Group
PO Box 47050 Phone: (312)829-0022
Chicago, IL 60647
Publication E-mail: lumpen@lumpen.com
Publisher E-mail: lumpen@lumpen.com

Magazine investigating mainstream media, "exposing and resisting the degradation of our mental and physical environments". **Founded:** May 1, 1993. **Freq:** Monthly. **Print Method:** Web press. **Trim Size:** 8 1/4 x 11. **Cols./Page:** 3. **Col. Width:** 2 3/8 inches. **Col. Depth:** 9 7/8 inches. **Key Personnel:** Chris Molnar, Publisher; Ed Marczewski, Publisher; Leslie Stella, Managing Editor; Lothar Jones, Circulation Mgr. **ISSN:** 1092-3667. **Subscription Rates:** $25 individuals; $3 single issue; $10 for 4 issues. **Remarks:** Accepts advertising. **URL:** http://www.lumpen.com. **Formerly:** The Lumpen Times.
Ad Rates: BW: $725 **Circ:** Paid 30,000
4C: $1,055

8593 The Lutheran
Augsburg Fortress, Publishers
8765 W. Higgins Rd. Phone: (773)380-2540
Chicago, IL 60631-4183 Fax: (773)380-2751
Free: (800)638-3522
Publication E-mail: lutheran@elca.org
Publisher E-mail: afp_bookstore.topic@ecunet.org

Magazine of the Evangelical Lutheran Church in America. **Founded:** 1988. **Freq:** Monthly. **Print Method:** Offset. **Trim Size:** 8 1/8 x 10 1/2. **Cols./Page:** 3. **Col. Width:** 13 picas. **Col. Depth:** 133 agate lines. **Key Personnel:** Edgar R. Trexler, Editor, etrexler@elca.org; Roger R. Kahle, Managing Editor, rkahle@elca.org; David L. Miller, Sr., Sr. Editor, dmiller@elca.org; Sonia C. Solomonson, Sr. Editor, ssolomon@elca.org; Michael Watson, Art Dir., mwatson@elca.org; Brad Gray, Ad Sales, grayb@augsburg-fortress.org. **ISSN:** 0024-743X. **Subscription Rates:** $11.90 individuals; $1.50 single issue. **Remarks:** Accepts advertising. **URL:** http://www.thelutheran.org. **Alt. Formats:** Audio tape; Braille.
Ad Rates: BW: $13,813 **Circ:** ‡640,000
4C: $18,139
PCI: $833

8594 Lutheran Partners
Augsburg Fortress, Publishers
ELCA (DM) Phone: (773)380-2875
8765 W. Higgins Rd. Fax: (773)380-2829
Chicago, IL 60631
Free: (800)638-3522
Publication E-mail: lpartmag@elca.org; lutheran_partners.parti@ecunet.org

Publisher E-mail: afp_ bookstore.topic@ecunet.org

Magazine featuring those involved in the public ministry of the Evangelical Lutheran Church in America. **Founded:** Feb. 1979. **Freq:** Bimonthly. **Print Method:** Offset. **Trim Size:** 8 3/8 x 11. **Cols./Page:** 2 and 3. **Col. Width:** 14 and 21 picas. **Col. Depth:** 58 picas. **Key Personnel:** Carl E. Linder, Editor, phone (773)380-2875, fax (773)380-2829, clinder@elca.org; William A. Decker, Managing Editor, phone (773)380-2884, fax (773)380-2829, wdecker@elca.org; Ann Rezny, Designer, phone (773)380-2725, fax (773)380-2751, arezny@elca.org; Jeannette May, Advertising Rep., phone (847)823-4545, fax (847)823-4547, jmaymkt@earthlink.net. **ISSN:** 0885-9922. **Subscription Rates:** Free to rostered leaders of ELCA; $10; $15 other countries; $2 single issue. **Remarks:** Accepts advertising. **URL:** http://www.elca.org/dm/lp. **Alt. Formats:** Audio tape; Braille. **Formerly:** LCA Partners (1985).
Ad Rates: BW: $1,080 **Circ:** Paid 71
PCI: $65 Controlled 20,000

8595 Manufactured Home Merchandiser
RLD Group, Inc.
203 N. Wabash, Ste. 800 Phone: (312)236-3528
Chicago, IL 60601
Magazine on manufactured housing. **Founded:** Mar. 1952. **Freq:** Monthly. **Print Method:** Offset. **Trim Size:** 8 1/8 x 10 7/8. **Cols./Page:** 3 and 4. **Col. Width:** 27 nonpareils. **Col. Depth:** 140 agate lines. **Key Personnel:** Robert Overend, Editor; Herb Tieder, Publisher. **ISSN:** 0191-9768. **Subscription Rates:** $36 individuals.
Ad Rates: BW: $2,420 **Circ:** Controlled ‡15,500
4C: $3,335

8596 Marketing Management
American Marketing Association
311 S. Wacker Dr. Suite 5800 Phone: (312)648-0536
Chicago, IL 60606-5819 Fax: (312)993-7542
Free: (800)262-1150
Publisher E-mail: info@ama.org

Publication focusing on strategic marketing. **Subtitle:** Shaping the Profession of Marketing. **Founded:** 1992. **Freq:** Quarterly. **Cols./Page:** 2. **Col. Width:** 16.5 picas. **Col. Depth:** 136.5 agate lines. **Key Personnel:** Ronald Keener, Publisher, phone (312)831-2794, fax (312)648-0103; Lynn Coleman, Managing Editor, phone (312)831-2756, fax (312)648-0103; Gloria Naurocki, Marketing Director, phone (312)831-2796, fax (312)648-0103; Kathy Hays, Advertising Sales & Exhibit, phone (312)831-2729, fax (312)648-0103. **ISSN:** 1061-3846. **Subscription Rates:** $15 single issue; $45 AMA member; $70 nonmembers; $90 institutions. **Remarks:** Accepts advertising.
Ad Rates: BW: $1200 **Circ:** Paid ‡3118
4C: $2100 Non-paid ‡73

8597 Marketing News
American Marketing Association
311 S. Wacker Dr. Suite 5800 Phone: (312)648-0536
Chicago, IL 60606-5819 Fax: (312)993-7542
Free: (800)262-1150
Publication E-mail: 458-1615@mcimail.com
Publisher E-mail: info@ama.org

Business magazine focusing on current marketing trends. **Subtitle:** Reporting on the Marketing Profession. **Founded:** 1963. **Freq:** Biweekly. **Print Method:** Web offset. **Trim Size:** 11 x 15. **Cols./Page:** 5. **Col. Width:** 20 picas. **Col. Depth:** 14 inches. **Key Personnel:** Gregg Cebrzynski, Managing Editor; Kathy Hays, Interim Advertising Manager; Gloria Naurocki, Marketing Director. **ISSN:** 0025-3790. **Subscription Rates:** $30 AMA member; $75 nonmembers; $130 libraries and corporations; $3 single issue institutions. **Remarks:** Accepts advertising. **Available Online.**
Ad Rates: BW: $2615 **Circ:** Paid 24,322
4C: $3615 Non-paid 369
PCI: $90

8598 Marketing Research
American Marketing Association
311 S. Wacker Dr. Suite 5800 Phone: (312)648-0536
Chicago, IL 60606-5819 Fax: (312)993-7542
Free: (800)262-1150
Publisher E-mail: info@ama.org

For the professional whose primary interest is in marketing research. **Subtitle:** A Magazine of Management and Applications. **Founded:** 1989. **Freq:** Quarterly. **Print Method:** Web offset. **Trim Size:** 8 1/2 x 11. **Cols./Page:** 3. **Col. Width:** 14.5 picas. **Col. Depth:** 143.5 agate lines. **Key Personnel:** Ronald Kener, Publisher, phone (312)831-2794, fax (312)648-0103; Lynn Coleman, Editor, phone (312)831-2756, fax (312)993-7540; Kathy Hays, Advertising Mgr., phone (312)831-2729, fax (312)648-0103; Gloria Naurocki, Marketing Director, phone (312)831-2796, fax (312)648-0103. **ISSN:** 1040-8460. **Subscription Rates:** $20 single issue; $45 Annual for AMA members; $70 nonmembers; $120 institutions. **Remarks:** Accepts advertising. **URL:** http://www.ama.org.
Ad Rates: BW: $800 **Circ:** Paid ‡3305
4C: $1700 Non-paid ‡59

8599 Materials Management in Health Care
American Hospital Publishing, Inc.
1 N. Franklin Phone: (312)893-6800
Chicago, IL 60606 Fax: (312)422-4500
Free: (800)621-6902

Trade magazine for purchasers, managers, and manufacturers of health care equipment and supplies. **Founded:** 1992. **Freq:** Monthly. **Print Method:** Web offset. **Trim Size:** 8 1/8 x 10 7/8. **Cols./Page:** 3. **Key Personnel:** Laura Souhrada, Editor. **Subscription Rates:** $30; $50 other countries. $3 single issue. **Remarks:** Accepts advertising. **Available Online.**
Ad Rates: GLR: $14.60 **Circ:** Non-paid 24,534
BW: $2,455
4C: $3,455
PCI: $126

8600 Mathematical Finance
Blackwell Publishers
Department of Finance Phone: (312)996-7170
M/C 168 - University of Illinois Fax: (312)996-7170
601 S. Morgan Rm. 2431
Chicago, IL 60607-7124
Free: (800)835-6770
Publisher E-mail: subscript@blackwellpub.com

Journal. **Subtitle:** An International Journal of Mathematics, Statistics, and Financial Economics. **Founded:** 1991. **Freq:** Quarterly. **Trim Size:** 9 3/4 x 6 3/4. **Key Personnel:** Stanley R. Pliska, Editor, srpliska@uic.edu. **ISSN:** 0960-1627. **Subscription Rates:** $104 Individual in North America; $270 institutions. **Remarks:** Accepts advertising.
Ad Rates: BW: $260 **Circ:** ‡800

8601 Members
TruServ Corp.
8600 W. Bryn Mawr Ave. Phone: (773)695-5224
Chicago, IL 60631 Fax: (773)695-6785

Trade magazine covering hardware and hardware retailing. **Founded:** 1991. **Freq:** Monthly. **Print Method:** Heatset web. **Trim Size:** 8 1/4 x 10 7/8. **Cols./Page:** 3. **Col. Width:** 13 picas. **Key Personnel:** Bruce Bunschoten, Editor, bbunscho@truserv.com; Tom Delph, National Sales Mgr., phone (812)376-9299, fax (812)376-7395. **Subscription Rates:** Free to qualified subscribers. **Remarks:** Accepts advertising.
Ad Rates: 4C: $4,995 **Circ:** Non-paid 30,000

8602 Metmenys
A M & M Publications
Dept. of Slavic and Baltic
Languages & Literatures (m/c 306)
University of Illinois at Chicago
1610 University Hall
601 S. Morgan
Chicago, IL 60607-7112

Literary magazine covering writings of Lithuanian writers and poets. **Founded:** 1959. **Freq:** Semiannual. **Print Method:** Offset. **Trim Size:** 5 3/8 x 8. **Cols./Page:** 1. **Col. Width:** 3 3/4 inches. **Col. Depth:** 6 inches. **Key Personnel:** Violeta Kelertas, Editor; R. Silbajoris, Editor; Henrietta Vepstas, Technical Editor; Marija Paskevicius, Administrator. **ISSN:** 0543-615X. **Subscription Rates:** $15 individuals; $8 single issue. **Remarks:** Advertising not accepted.
Circ: Paid 700

8603 Metro Chicago Real Estate
Law Bulletin Publishing Co.
415 N. State St. Phone: (312)644-7800
Chicago, IL 60610-4674 Fax: (312)644-1215

Trade publication covering real estate development, investments, leasing, and mortgage lending activities. **Founded:** 1913. **Freq:** Bimonthly. **Print Method:** Offset. **Trim Size:** 8 1/2 x 11. **Cols./Page:** 3. **Col. Width:** 26 picas. **Col. Depth:** 140 agate lines. **Key Personnel:** Sandy Macfarland, Publisher; Linda Seggelke, Assoc. Publisher; Mark Menzies, Sales Mgr. **ISSN:** 0893-0775. **Subscription Rates:** $30 individuals. **Remarks:** Accepts advertising. **Formerly:** Real Estate Magazine; Chicagoland's Real Estate Advertiser.
Ad Rates: BW: $2,230 **Circ:** Controlled ‡8,582
4C: $2,990

8604 Metro EXTRA
EXTRA Publications, Inc.
3918 W. North Ave. Phone: (312)252-3534
Chicago, IL 60647 Fax: (312)252-6031

Community newspaper. **Freq:** Weekly (Thurs.). **Key Personnel:** Mila Tellez, Publisher; Mary Montgomery, Editor; Miguel Alba, Managing Editor; Don Pringle, Editor.
Circ: ‡4,709

8605 The Microscope
McCrone Research Institute
2820 S. Michigan Ave. Phone: (312)842-7100
Chicago, IL 60616-3292 Fax: (312)842-1078

Magazine outlining advances in light microscopy, instruments, and techniques. **Founded:** 1937. **Freq:** Quarterly. **Print Method:** Offset. **Trim Size:** 8 x 11. **Cols./Page:** 2. **Col. Width:** 54 nonpareils. **Col. Depth:** 154 agate lines. **Key Personnel:** David A. Stoney, Editor; Debra Gilliand, Production Mgr. **ISSN:** 0026-282X. **Subscription Rates:** $65 individuals. **Remarks:** Accepts advertising. **Alt. Formats:** Microfiche.
Ad Rates: BW: $250 **Circ:** Paid ‡900
4C: $900 Controlled ‡50

8606 Mid-America (Chicago)
Loyola University of Chicago
6525 Sheridan Rd.
Chicago, IL 60626

Historical journal. **Subtitle:** An Historical Review. **Freq:** Triennial. **Key Personnel:** Maryann Spiller, Copy Editor, phone (773)508-2217, midamjnl@luc.edu. **Subscription Rates:** $15 individuals; $16 out of country.

8607 Midwest Automotive & Autobody News
2900 W. Peterson Ave. Phone: (312)764-1640
Chicago, IL 60659
Automotive trade magazine. **Founded:** 1927. **Freq:** Monthly. **Print Method:** Offset. **Cols./Page:** 3. **Col. Width:** 27 nonpareils. **Col. Depth:** 140 agate lines. **Key Personnel:** Dale W. Daemicke, Editor; Warren B. Daemicke, Publisher; C.L. Anderson, Advertising Mgr. **Subscription Rates:** $10 individuals. **Remarks:** Accepts advertising.
Ad Rates: BW: $950 **Circ:** Controlled ‡10,500

8608 Midwest Engineer
Western Society of Engineers
53 W. Jackson Blvd., No. 1730 Phone: (312)913-1730
Chicago, IL 60604 Fax: (312)913-1731
Publisher E-mail: wse@wwa.com

Subtitle: News Magazine of the Western Society of Engineers. **Founded:** 1890. **Freq:** 5/year. **Print Method:** Offset. **Trim Size:** 8 3/4 x 10 7/8. **Cols./Page:** 3 and 2. **Col. Width:** 32 and 42 nonpareils. **Col. Depth:** 135 agate lines. **ISSN:** 0026-3370. **Subscription Rates:** $25 individuals.
Ad Rates: GLR: $.50 **Circ:** ‡1,000
BW: $610

8609 Midwest Real Estate News
Intertec Publishing Corp.
35 E. Wacker Dr., Ste. 700 Phone: (312)726-7277
Chicago, IL 60611 Fax: (312)726-0241

Trade magazine covering regional commercial real estate. **Founded:** 1985. **Freq:** Monthly. **Print Method:** Web offset. **Trim Size:** 11 x 14. **Cols./Page:** 4. **Col. Width:** 2 1/4 inches. **Col. Depth:** 13 1/2 inches. **Key Personnel:** Lauren Berg, Publisher; John Davis, Group Publisher; Matthew Valley, Editor; Michael McKinley, Assoc. Editor. **Subscription Rates:** $45 individuals; $71 two years; $65 out of country; $111 two years out of country. **Remarks:** Accepts advertising.
Ad Rates: BW: $2,215 **Circ:** (Not Reported)
4C: $3,305

8610 Modern Healthcare
Crain Communications, Inc.
740 N. Rush St. Phone: (312)649-5200
Chicago, IL 60611-2590 Fax: (312)649-5360

Weekly Business news magazine for Healthcare Management. **Subtitle:** The weekly healthcare business news magazine. **Founded:** 1974. **Freq:** Weekly. **Print Method:** Offset. **Trim Size:** 8 1/8 x 10 7/8. **Cols./Page:** 3. **Col. Width:** 26 nonpareils. **Col. Depth:** 130 agate lines. **Key Personnel:** Clark Bell, Editor, phone (312)649-5342, fax (312)280-3183, mhceditamerica online, inc.com; Charles S. Lauer, Publisher, phone (312)649-5297; Sheryl Bull, Advertising Dir. **ISSN:** 0160-7480. **Subscription Rates:** $125. **Remarks:** Accepts advertising. **Online:** Dow Jones News-Retrieval; LEXIS-NEXIS. **URL:** http://www.modernhealthcare.com.
Ad Rates: BW: $8,640 **Circ:** Paid 3,015
4C: $9,940 Non-paid 76,798

8611 Modern Metals
Trend Publishing
625 N. Michigan Ave., Ste. 1500 Phone: (312)654-2300
Chicago, IL 60611-3109 Fax: (312)654-2323

Metals fabrication magazine. **Founded:** 1945. **Freq:** Monthly. **Print Method:** Web offset. **Trim Size:** 7 1/8 x 10 3/4. **Cols./Page:** 3. **Col. Width:** 27 nonpareils. **Col. Depth:** 140 agate lines. **Key Personnel:** Karl D. Forth, Editor; John Kimler, Publisher; Jim D'Alexander, Reg. Mgr., phone (312)654-2300; Mike D'Alexander, Reg. Mgr. **USPS:** 357-640. **Subscription**

Rates: $85 individuals; $14 single issue. **Remarks:** Accepts advertising.
Ad Rates: BW: $4,100 **Circ:** Controlled ‡40,000
4C: $5,625
PCI: $190

8612 Modern Steel Construction
American Institute of Steel Construction, Inc.
1 E. Wacker Dr., Ste. 3100 Phone: (312)670-2400
Chicago, IL 60601-2001 Fax: (312)670-5403

Magazine covering fabricated structural steel design, application, and costs. For construction industry professionals including architects, engineers, and fabricators. **Founded:** 1960. **Freq:** Monthly. **Print Method:** Offset. **Trim Size:** 8 1/8 x 10 7/8. **Cols./Page:** 3. **Col. Width:** 28 nonpareils. **Col. Depth:** 114 agate lines. **Key Personnel:** Scott Melnick, Editor. **ISSN:** 0026-8445. **Subscription Rates:** $30 individuals; $36 other countries; $72 airmail. **URL:** http://www.aiscweb.com. **Alt. Formats:** Microfilm, UMI.
Ad Rates: BW: $3,275 **Circ:** Controlled ‡35,000
4C: $4,325

8613 Moody Magazine
Moody Bible Institute
820 N. LaSalle Blvd. Phone: (312)329-2164
Chicago, IL 60610 Fax: (312)329-2149
Publication E-mail: moodyltrs@moody.edu

Religious magazine. **Founded:** 1900. **Freq:** Bimonthly. **Print Method:** Offset. **Trim Size:** 8 x 10.5. **Cols./Page:** 3. **Col. Width:** 27 nonpareils. **Col. Depth:** 140 agate lines. **Key Personnel:** Bruce Anderson, General Mgr., phone (312)329-2157, banderso@moody.edu; Tim Willms, Operations Dir., phone (312)329-2147, twillms@moody.edu. **ISSN:** 1052-2271. **Subscription Rates:** $18.95 individuals; $3.95 single issue. **Remarks:** Accepts advertising. **Available Online. URL:** http://www.moody.edu/moodymag. **Alt. Formats:** Microform. **Formerly:** Moody Monthly.
Ad Rates: BW: $3,836 **Circ:** ‡115,000
4C: $4,436

8614 Mutual Funds
Morningstar Inc.
225 W. Wacker Dr., Ste. 400 Phone: (312)696-6000
Chicago, IL 60606 Fax: (312)696-6001
Free: (800)735-0700

Reference publication covering analysis and commentary on investments and mutual funds. **Freq:** Biweekly. **Key Personnel:** Valerie Leban, Advertising Mgr. **Remarks:** Advertising not accepted.
Circ: (Not Reported)

8615 N.A.M.A. Journal
National Account Management Association (NAMA)
150 N. Wacker Dr., Ste. 960 Phone: (312)251-3131
Chicago, IL 60606-1607 Fax: (312)251-3132

Trade magazine covering account management issues in the U.S. and worldwide. **Freq:** Quarterly. **Trim Size:** 8 1/2 x 11. **Cols./Page:** 3. **Key Personnel:** Lisa Napolitano, Editor; Maria T. Susano, Advertising Mgr. **Subscription Rates:** $100 individuals; Free to qualified subscribers. **Remarks:** Accepts advertising.
Ad Rates: BW: $1,600 **Circ:** Controlled 1,000

8616 Narod Polish
Polish Roman Catholic Union of America
984 N. Milwaukee Ave. Phone: (773)278-3210
Chicago, IL 60622-4101 Fax: (773)278-4595
Free: (800)772-8632

Catholic and Polish American newspaper (tabloid; English and Polish). **Founded:** 1886. **Freq:** Semimonthly. **Print Method:** Offset. **Trim Size:** 11 x 14 1/2. **Cols./Page:** 3. **Key Personnel:** Kathryn Rosypal, Exec. Editor, rosypal@prcua.org. **ISSN:** 0027-7894. **Subscription Rates:** Included in membership. **Remarks:** Advertising not accepted. **URL:** @prcua.orgv. **Also known as:** Polish Nation.
Circ: Non-paid ‡25,000

8617 National Security Law Report
American Bar Association
750 N. Lake Shore Dr. Phone: (312)988-5000
Chicago, IL 60611-4497 Fax: (312)988-5568
Free: (800)285-2221

Contains cases, articles, legislation, regulations, and other materials concerning national security. **Founded:** 1978. **Freq:** Monthly. **Print Method:** Offset. **Trim Size:** 8 1/2 x 11. **Cols./Page:** 2. **Col. Width:** 3 1/4 inches. **ISSN:** 0736-2773. **Subscription Rates:** Free.

8618 Near North News
Near North News, Inc.
222 W. Ontario St. Phone: (312)787-2677
Chicago, IL 60610-3695 Fax: (312)787-2680
Publication E-mail: nnnews@lbm.net

Community newspaper with Democratic orientation. **Founded:** May 1956. **Freq:** Weekly. **Print Method:** Offset. **Trim Size:** 10 3/4 x 16 1/2. **Cols./Page:** 6. **Col. Width:** 9.5 picas. **Col. Depth:** 224 agate lines. **Key Personnel:** Arnie Matanky, Editor and Publisher. **ISSN:** 0228-1788. **Subscription Rates:** $25 individuals; $30 out of country; $5 single issue.
Ad Rates: GLR: $0.90 **Circ:** Paid 7,265
BW: $967.68 Free 80
4C: $1,567.80
PCI: $12.60

8619 The Neighborhood Works
Center for Neighborhood Technology
2125 W. North Ave. Phone: (773)278-4800
Chicago, IL 60647 Fax: (773)278-3840
Publisher E-mail: tnwedi@cnt.org

Professional trade magazine. **Subtitle:** Building Alternative Visions for the City. **Founded:** 1978. **Freq:** Bimonthly. **Trim Size:** 8 1/2 x 11. **Cols./Page:** 3. **Key Personnel:** Christine McConville, Editor; Bridget Torres, Circulation Mgr.; Ed Finkel, Managing Editor. **ISSN:** 0193-719X. **Subscription Rates:** $30; $40 institutions; $3 single issue. **Remarks:** Accepts advertising. **URL:** http://www.cnt.org/tnw/.
Circ: Paid 2,500
Non-paid 500

8620 New Art Examiner
Chicago New Art Association
314 W. Institute Pl. Phone: (312)649-9900
Chicago, IL 60610 Fax: (312)649-9935
Publication E-mail: examiner@tezcat.com

Visual Arts Magazine. **Subtitle:** The Independent Voice of the Visual Arts. **Founded:** Oct. 1973. **Freq:** 10/year. **Print Method:** Offset. **Trim Size:** 8 3/8 x 10 7/8. **Key Personnel:** Kathryn Hixson, Editor; Joshua Rothkopf, Business/Circulation Mgr.; Mari Eastman, Advertising Dir. **ISSN:** 0886-8115. **Subscription Rates:** $35 individuals; $4.75 single issue; $68 foreign; $53 Canada. **Remarks:** Accepts advertising. **URL:** http://www.tezcat.com:80/~examiner.
Ad Rates: BW: $900 **Circ:** Paid ‡4,000
4C: $1,715 ‡10,000

8621 New City
New City Communications Inc.
770 N. Halsted Ste. 208 Phone: (312)243-8786
Chicago, IL 60622 Fax: (312)243-8802
Publisher E-mail: newcity@newcitynet.com

News and arts newspaper. **Founded:** Feb. 4, 1986. **Freq:** Weekly. **Print Method:** Web news print. **Cols./Page:** 5. **Col. Width:** 1 7/8 inches. **Col. Depth:** 14 inches. **Key Personnel:** Brian Hieggelke, Publisher, brian@newcitynet.com; Jan Hieggelke, Publisher, jan@newcitynet.com; Stephanie Sack, Advertising Dir., stephanie@newcitynet.com; Elaine Richardson, Managing Editor, elaine@newcitynet.com; Charles Willett, Jr., Circulation Mgr.; Alma Limprecht, Marketing, alma@newcitynet.com. **Subscription Rates:** $30 3rd class; $75 1st class. **Remarks:** Accepts advertising. **URL:** http.//www.newcitynet.com.
Ad Rates: BW: $1,520 **Circ:** Free 70,000
4C: $2,332 Paid 40
PCI: $38

8622 The New Electric Railway Journal
6305 N. Kenmore, No. 1 Phone: (773)764-5785
Chicago, IL 60660 Fax: (773)764-9551
Publication E-mail: cityrail@mcs.net

Industry magazine covering new light rail and heavy rail systems in cities throughout North America. Features articles on the "Return of the Trolley." Includes yearly directory. **Founded:** 1988. **Freq:** Quarterly. **Print Method:** Offset. **Trim Size:** 8 1/2 x 11. **Cols./Page:** 3. **Col. Width:** 13 picas. **Col. Depth:** 48 picas. **Key Personnel:** Richard R. Kunz, Editor. **ISSN:** 1048-3845. **Subscription Rates:** $27.50; $7.50 single issue. **Remarks:** Accepts advertising. **URL:** http://www.nethomes.com/cityrail.
Ad Rates: BW: $700 **Circ:** 5,000
4C: $1,100

8623 New Product News
444 N. Wells St., Ste. 204 Phone: (312)527-3555
Chicago, IL 60610 Fax: (312)527-3562
Publication E-mail: newproductnews@msn.com
Publisher E-mail: info@mintel-iis.com

Report on new supermarket food and nonfood product introductions. Aimed at retailers and food and drug manufacturers. Includes analyses of marketplace trends. **Founded:** 1964. **Freq:** Monthly. **Trim Size:** 8 1/2 x 11. **Cols./Page:** 2. **Col. Width:** 20.5 picas. **Col. Depth:** 55 picas. **Key Personnel:** Kim Charlet; Lynn Dornblaser. **ISSN:** 1048-020X. **Subscription Rates:** $695 individuals; $745 other countries. **Remarks:** Color advertising not accepted. **Alt. Formats:** CD-ROM. **Formerly:** Gorman's New Product News.
Ad Rates: BW: $1,075 **Circ:** Paid ‡800

8624 The New Star
St. Nicholas Diocesan Press
2208 W. Chicago Ave. Phone: (312)772-1919
Chicago, IL 60622
Newspaper of the Catholic Diocese of St. Nicholas for Ukrainians. **Founded:** 1965. **Freq:** Biweekly. **Key Personnel:** Iwanna Gorchynsky, Editor.
Circ: Paid 36,129
Controlled 2,035

8625 The New World
New World Publications
1144 W. Jackson Blvd. Phone: (312)243-1300
Chicago, IL 60607-0181 Fax: (312)243-1526
Publication E-mail: neworld201@aol.com

Catholic newspaper (tabloid). **Founded:** 1892. **Freq:** Weekly. **Print Method:** Offset. **Trim Size:** 11 1/8 x 14 1/2. **Cols./Page:** 5. **Col. Width:** 10 inches. **Col. Depth:** 13 1/2 inches. **Key Personnel:** Thomas H. Sheridan, Editor/GM, phone (312)243-4997, neworld201@aol.com. **ISSN:** 1043-3538. **Subscription Rates:** $25 individuals. **Remarks:** Accepts advertising. **Formerly:** The Chicago Catholic.
Ad Rates: GLR: $2.93 **Circ:** ‡35,000
BW: $2,138
4C: $2,738
PCI: $46.35

8626 News & Letters
59 E. Van Buren St., Ste. 707 Phone: (312)663-0839
Chicago, IL 60605 Fax: (312)663-9069
Publication E-mail: nandl@igc.apc.org
Publisher E-mail: nandl@igc.apc.org

Marxist-Humanist newspaper. **Founded:** 1955. **Freq:** 10/year. **Print Method:** Letterpress and offset. Uses mats. **Cols./Page:** 3. **Col. Width:** 39 nonpareils. **Col. Depth:** 196 agate lines. **Key Personnel:** Lou Turner, Managing Editor. **ISSN:** 0028-8969. **Subscription Rates:** $2.50 per year. **Remarks:** Advertising not accepted. **URL:** http://www.newsandletters.org. **Alt. Formats:** Audio tape.
Circ: ‡7,000

8627 Nightlines Weekly
Lambda Publications, Inc.
1115 W. Belmont Ave., Ste. 2-D Phone: (773)871-7610
Chicago, IL 60657 Fax: (773)871-7609

Community newspaper providing information on gay/lesbian events. **Subtitle:** Calendar, Clubs, Commentary, Sports, and More. **Founded:** 1991. **Freq:** Weekly. **Print Method:** Web offset. **Trim Size:** 5 x 8. **Cols./Page:** 4. **Col. Width:** 1 inches. **Key Personnel:** Tracy Baim, Publisher. **Subscription Rates:** $48 individuals. **Remarks:** Accepts advertising. **Online:** Suba Chicago. **URL:** http://www.suba.com/~outlines/.
Ad Rates: BW: $250 **Circ:** Non-paid 12,000

8628 Northwest Extra
EXTRA Publications, Inc.
3918 W. North Ave. Phone: (312)252-3534
Chicago, IL 60647 Fax: (312)252-6031

Newspaper (Spanish and English). **Founded:** 1980. **Freq:** Weekly. **Print Method:** Offset. Uses mats. **Cols./Page:** 4. **Col. Width:** 28 nonpareils. **Col. Depth:** 179 agate lines. **Key Personnel:** Janet Kownacki, Editor, email@editor.clrs.com; Mila Tellez, Publisher. **Subscription Rates:** Free; $25 by mail. **Remarks:** Accepts advertising.
Ad Rates: PCI: $33.85 **Circ:** Free 10,000

8629 Northwest Leader
Leader
6008 W. Belmont Ave. Phone: (773)283-7900
Chicago, IL 60634-5195 Fax: (773)283-7761

Community newspaper covering northwest area of Chicago. **Founded:** 1955. **Freq:** Weekly (Wed.). **Print Method:** Offset. **Cols./Page:** 6. **Col. Width:** 19 nonpareils. **Col. Depth:** 294 agate lines. **Key Personnel:** Ted Villaire, Editor; Ramona Diaz, Publisher. **Subscription Rates:** $19 individuals. **Absorbed:** Belmont Central Leader; Cragin Leader; The West Leader; Harlem-Irving Leader.
Ad Rates: GLR: $8 **Circ:** 25,000
PCI: $20

8630 Northwestern Journal of International Law & Business
Northwestern University School of Law
357 E. Chicago Ave. Phone: (312)503-8742
Chicago, IL 60611 Fax: (312)503-0132
Publication E-mail: jilblaw@nwu.edu

Journal covering business law issues worldwide. **Founded:**

1978. **Freq:** Triennial. **Print Method:** Offset. **Trim Size:** 6 3/4 x 10. **Cols./Page:** 1. **Col. Width:** 28 picas. **Col. Depth:** 50 picas. **Key Personnel:** Trevor Jefferson, Editor-in-Chief; Mark Plichta, Business Mgr. **ISSN:** 0196-3228. **Subscription Rates:** $25 individuals; $9 single issue. **Remarks:** Advertising not accepted. **Online:** LEXIS-NEXIS; Westlaw.
Circ: Combined 598

8631 Northwestern University Law Review
Northwestern University Law School
357 E. Chicago Ave.
Chicago, IL 60611-3008
Phone: (312)908-8467
Fax: (312)503-0132
Legal magazine. **Founded:** 1906. **Freq:** Quarterly. **Print Method:** Offset. **Cols./Page:** 1. **Col. Width:** 56 nonpareils. **Col. Depth:** 105 agate lines. **Key Personnel:** Juana Watkins, Contact. **Subscription Rates:** $30 individuals. **Remarks:** Advertising not accepted.
Circ: ‡1,500

8632 Numerical Heat Transfer, Part A: Applications
Taylor & Francis
Dept. of Mechanical Engineering
University of Illinois at Chicago
842 W. Taylor St.
Chicago, IL 60607-7022
Phone: (312)996-3467
Fax: (312)413-0447
Publisher E-mail: info@taylorandfrancis.com

Journal publishing research in the field of heat and mass transfer, and fluid flow. **Subtitle:** An International Journal of Computation and Methodology. **Founded:** 1978. **Freq:** 16/year. **Print Method:** Offset. Uses mats. **Trim Size:** 7 x 10. **Key Personnel:** W.J. Minkowycz, Editor, wjm@uic.edu. **ISSN:** 1040-7782. **Subscription Rates:** $1,610 institutions. **Remarks:** Advertising not accepted. **Formerly:** Numerical Heat Transfer: An International Journal of Computation and Metholdogy (1989).
Circ: ‡586

8633 Numerical Heat Transfer, Part B: Fundamentals
Taylor & Francis
Dept. of Mechanical Engineering
University of Illinois at Chicago
842 W. Taylor St.
Chicago, IL 60607-7022
Phone: (312)996-3467
Fax: (312)413-0447
Publisher E-mail: info@taylorandfrancis.com

Journal containing information on all aspects of the methodology for the numerical solution of problems in heat and mass transfer as well as fluid flow. **Subtitle:** An International Journal of Computation and Methodology. **Founded:** 1978. **Freq:** 8/year. **Print Method:** 7 x 10. **Key Personnel:** W.J. Minkowycz, Editor, wjm@uic.edu. **ISSN:** 1040-7790. **Subscription Rates:** $490 institutions. **Remarks:** Advertising not accepted.
Circ: (Not Reported)

8634 Nursery News
Cenflo, Inc.
205 W. Wacker Drive, Ste. 1040
Chicago, IL 60606-3508
Phone: (312)739-5000
Fax: (312)739-0739
Free: (800)732-4581
Publisher E-mail: kbcenflo@aol.com

Trade newspaper (tabloid) for nursery industry. **Founded:** 1986. **Freq:** Monthly. **Print Method:** Offset. **Trim Size:** 11 1/2 x 17. **Cols./Page:** 5. **Col. Width:** 23 nonpareils. **Col. Depth:** 221 agate lines. **Key Personnel:** Debbie M. Edwards, Editor; Peter C. Benjamin, Publisher, phone (505)867-3986, fax (505)867-4241, alex@swcp.com. **Subscription Rates:** $15; $28 two years. **Remarks:** Accepts advertising.
Ad Rates: GLR: $3.60; BW: $1,467; 4C: $2,466; PCI: $35
Circ: Paid ‡2,246; Non-paid ‡19,446

8635 Open Road USA
104 S. Michigan Ave., Ste. 1500
Chicago, IL 60603
Phone: (312)201-0101
Fax: (312)201-0214

Magazine for bicycle enthusiasts. **Subtitle:** Internationally-Edited, Ads-Free Alternative Bicycle Magazine. **Founded:** Jan. 1994. **Freq:** Quarterly. **Print Method:** WEB. **Key Personnel:** George Otto, Jr. **Subscription Rates:** $38 individuals annual; $9.50 single issue. **Remarks:** Advertising not accepted. **URL:** http://bikeculture.com/home/welcome.html.
Circ: Paid 6,000; Non-paid 500

8636 The Other Side of the Lake
Artistic Energy Group, Inc.
505 W. Locust St.
PO Box 303
Three Oaks, MI 49128
Phone: (616)756-2421
Fax: (616)756-7220
Journal for second homeowners and tourists. **Founded:** 1988. **Freq:** 9/year. **Print Method:** Web offset. **Trim Size:** 11 3/8 x 15. **Cols./Page:** 4. **Col. Width:** 2 7/16 inches. **Col. Depth:** 13 1/2 inches. **Key Personnel:** Michael Hojnacki, Publisher. **Subscription Rates:** $18 individuals. **Remarks:** Accepts advertising.
Ad Rates: BW: $840; 4C: $1,650; PCI: $10
Circ: 16,000

8637 Out! Resource Guide
Lambda Publications, Inc.
1115 W. Belmont Ave., Ste. 2-D
Chicago, IL 60657
Phone: (773)871-7610
Fax: (773)871-7609
Publication E-mail: outlines@suba.com

A business resource guide geared toward the gay and lesbian community. **Subtitle:** Guide to Gay and Lesbian Supportive Businesses and Organizations. **Founded:** 1990. **Freq:** Semi-annual. **Trim Size:** 4 x 9. **Cols./Page:** 1. **Col. Width:** 3 1/2 inches. **Col. Depth:** 8 1/2 inches. **Key Personnel:** Tracy Baim, Publisher. **Subscription Rates:** Free. **Remarks:** Accepts advertising.
Ad Rates: BW: $345
Circ: Non-paid 25,000

8638 Outlines
Lambda Publications, Inc.
1115 W. Belmont Ave., Ste. 2-D
Chicago, IL 60657
Phone: (773)871-7610
Fax: (773)871-7609

Gay and lesbian newspaper. **Subtitle:** The Voice of the Gay and Lesbian Community. **Founded:** 1987. **Freq:** Monthly. **Print Method:** Web offset. **Trim Size:** 10 1/2 x 13 1/2. **Cols./Page:** 4. **Col. Width:** 14 picas. **Col. Depth:** 13 inches. **Key Personnel:** Tracy Baim, Publisher. **Subscription Rates:** $32 individuals one-year subscription; $22 individuals six-month subscription. **Remarks:** Accepts advertising. **Available Online.**
Ad Rates: BW: $820
Circ: Paid 1,000; Non-paid 20,000

8639 Packaging World
Summit Publishing Co.
One IBM Plaza, Ste. 3131
330 Wabash Ave.
Chicago, IL 60611
Phone: (312)751-1616
Fax: (312)222-1310
Free: (800)355-5595
Publication E-mail: editorial@packworld.com

Packaging trade journal. **Founded:** Jan. 1, 1994. **Freq:** Monthly. **Print Method:** Web offset. **Trim Size:** 11 x 15 3/4. **Key Personnel:** Arnie Orloski, Jr, Editor; Joseph Angel, Publisher. **ISSN:** 1073-7367. **Subscription Rates:** $65. $8 single issue. **Remarks:** Accepts advertising. **Available Online. URL:** http://www.packworld.com.
Ad Rates: BW: $6,600; 4C: $8,500
Circ: Controlled 92,000

8640 Paper, Film & Foil Converter
Intertec Publishing Co.
29 N. Wacker Dr.
Chicago, IL 60606
Phone: (312)726-2802
Fax: (312)726-2574
Free: (800)621-9907

Magazine focusing on flexible packaging, paperboard, and film. **Founded:** 1927. **Freq:** Monthly. **Print Method:** Offset. **Trim Size:** 8 1/8 x 10 7 /8. **Cols./Page:** 3 and 2. **Col. Width:** 26 and 40 nonpareils. **Col. Depth:** 104 agate lines. **Key Personnel:** Yolanda Simonsis, Editor, yolanda_simonsis@intertec.com; Peter A. Rigney, Publisher. **ISSN:** 0031-1138. **Subscription Rates:** $62.50 individuals; $595 institutions. **Remarks:** Accepts advertising.
Ad Rates: GLR: $9; BW: $5,070; 4C: $6,805; PCI: $95
Circ: Non-paid ‡42,979

8641 PCI Journal
Precast/Prestressed Concrete Institute
175 W. Jackson Blvd., Ste. 1859
Chicago, IL 60604
Phone: (312)786-0300
Fax: (312)786-0353
Publication E-mail: info@pci.org
Publisher E-mail: info@pci.org

Concrete engineering journal. **Subtitle:** Journal of the Precast/Prestressed Concrete Institute. **Founded:** 1956. **Freq:** Bimonthly. **Print Method:** Offset. **Trim Size:** 8 1/8 x 10 7/8. **Cols./Page:** 3. **Col. Width:** 13 picas. **Col. Depth:** 140 agate lines. **Key Personnel:** George D. Nasser, Editor. **ISSN:** 0887-9672. **Subscription Rates:** $35 individuals; $83 three years. **Remarks:** Accepts advertising.
Ad Rates: BW: $990; 4C: $1,080; PCI: $55
Circ: Paid ‡5,495; Non-paid ‡1,310

8642 People's Tribune
PO Box 3524
Chicago, IL 60654-0524
Publication E-mail: pt@noc.org

Newspaper containing Political analysis of news. **Founded:** 1974. **Freq:** Monthly. **Print Method:** Offset. **Trim Size:** 11 x 14. **Cols./Page:** 4. **Col. Width:** 36 nonpareils. **Col. Depth:** 224 agate lines. **Key Personnel:** Laura Garcia, Editor. **ISSN:** 1081-4787. **Subscription Rates:** $25 individuals; $30 individuals by first-class mail; $35 institutions; $40 individuals outside U.S.; $80 institutions outside U.S. **Remarks:** Advertising not accepted. **Available Online. URL:** http://www.mcs.com/~jdav/league.html.
Circ: (Not Reported)

8643 Pet Age
H.H. Backer Associates, Inc.
20 E. Jackson Blvd.
Chicago, IL 60604
Phone: (312)663-4040
Fax: (312)663-5676
Publication E-mail: petage@aol.com

Trade magazine for pet supplies retailers. **Subtitle:** The Magazine for the Professional Retailer. **Founded:** July 1971. **Freq:** Monthly. **Print Method:** Web offset. **Trim Size:** 8 x 10 3/4. **Cols./Page:** 3. **Col. Width:** 13 picas. **Col. Depth:** 60 picas. **Key Personnel:** Karen Long MacLeod, Editor-in-Chief; Ginger Norton, Publisher; Lou Carso, National Sales Mgr. **ISSN:** 0098-5406. **Subscription Rates:** Free to qualified subscribers; $25 individuals; $50 other countries; $2.50 single issue. **Remarks:** Accepts advertising.
Ad Rates: BW: $1,650; 4C: $2,600
Circ: Controlled 22,037

8644 Philosophy Today
DePaul University
1150 W. Fullerton Ave.
Chicago, IL 60614-2204
Phone: (773)325-7267
Fax: (773)325-7268
Publication E-mail: phltoday@condor.depaul.edu

Magazine on contemporary philosophy and philosophers. **Founded:** 1957. **Freq:** Quarterly. **Print Method:** Offset. **Trim Size:** 7 x 10. **Cols./Page:** 2. **Col. Width:** 35 nonpareils. **Col. Depth:** 108 agate lines. **Key Personnel:** David Pellauer, Editor. **ISSN:** 0031-8256. **Subscription Rates:** $34. **Remarks:** Accepts advertising.
Ad Rates: BW: $100
Circ: Paid ‡1076; Non-paid ‡60

8645 Pilsen/Little Village/Cicero/Berwyn EXTRA
EXTRA Publications, Inc.
3918 W. North Ave.
Chicago, IL 60647
Phone: (312)252-3534
Fax: (312)252-6031

Community newspaper. **Freq:** Weekly (Thurs.). **Key Personnel:** Mila Telez, Publisher; Mary Montgomery, Editor; Miguel Alba, Managing Editor; Don Pringle, Editor. **Remarks:** Combined advertising rates available with Bridgeport/Back of the Yards EXTRA and Southwest EXTRA.
Ad Rates: SAU: $15
Circ: ‡13,297

8646 The Plastics Distributor & Fabricator Magazine
2701 N. Pulaski
Chicago, IL 60639
Phone: (773)235-3800
Fax: (773)235-7204

Magazine containing news for distributors and fabricators in the plastics industry. **Founded:** 1981. **Freq:** Bimonthly. **Print Method:** Offset. **Trim Size:** 8 1/2 x 11. **Cols./Page:** 2. **Col. Width:** 42 nonpareils. **Col. Depth:** 182 agate lines. **Key Personnel:** Brenda Kolar, Advertising Mgr.; Harry Greenwald, Editor and Publisher. **Subscription Rates:** $30 individuals Foreign; $37.50 libraries; $42.50 other countries.
Ad Rates: BW: $2,060; 4C: $2,460
Circ: Non-paid ‡25,000

8647 Playboy
680 N. Lake Shore Dr.
Chicago, IL 60611
Phone: (312)751-8000
Fax: (312)751-2818

Entertainment magazine for men. **Founded:** 1953. **Freq:** Monthly. **Print Method:** Offset, end rotogravure. **Trim Size:** 8 1/4 x 11 1/8. **Cols./Page:** 3. **Col. Width:** 13.5 picas. **Col. Depth:** 140 agate lines. **Key Personnel:** Arthur Kretchmer, Editorial Dir.; Richard Kinsler, Exec. VP & Publisher; Hugh M. Hefner, Editor-in-Chief. **ISSN:** 0032-1478. **Subscription Rates:** $29.97; $4.95 single issue. **Remarks:** Advertising not accepted for x-rated videos or phone sex. **Online:** LEXIS-NEXIS. **URL:** http://www.playboy.com. **Alt. Formats:** CD-ROM.
Ad Rates: BW: $57,740; 4C: $80,860; PCI: $4,280
Circ: Paid ★**3,336,213**

8648 The PMA
American Association of Medical Assistants
20 N. Wacker Dr., Ste. 1575
Chicago, IL 60606-2903
Phone: (312)899-1500
Fax: (312)899-1259

Professional health journal. **Subtitle:** Professional Medical Assistant. **Founded:** 1957. **Freq:** Bimonthly. **Print Method:** Offset. **Trim Size:** 8 1/4 x 10 7/8. **Cols./Page:** 2 and 3. **Col. Width:** 40 and 26 nonpareils. **Col. Depth:** 134 agate lines. **Key Personnel:** Jean M. Lynch, Editor; James Gillespie, Editorial Asst. **ISSN:** 0033-0140. **Subscription Rates:** Free to members; $30 nonmembers. **Remarks:** Accepts advertising.

Alt. Formats: Microfiche; Microfiche; Microfilm; Microfilm; Microform. **Formerly:** Professional Medical Assistant.
Ad Rates: BW: $940 **Circ:** 14,000
4C: $1,828

8649 Poetry
The Modern Poetry Association
60 W. Walton St. Phone: (312)255-3703
Chicago, IL 60610 Fax: (312)255-3702
Publication E-mail: poetry@poetrymagazine.org

Contemporary poetry magazine. **Founded:** Oct. 1912. **Freq:** Monthly. **Print Method:** Offset. **Trim Size:** 5 1/2 x 9. **Cols./Page:** 1. **Col. Width:** 45 nonpareils. **Col. Depth:** 98 agate lines. **Key Personnel:** Joseph Parisi, Editor; Helen Lothrop Klaviter, Managing Editor. **ISSN:** 0032-2032. **Subscription Rates:** $30 individuals; $3.50 single issue. **Remarks:** Accepts advertising. **Alt. Formats:** Braille; Microform.
Ad Rates: BW: $310 **Circ:** Paid ‡8,000
Non-paid ‡100

8650 Polish Daily News
Alliance Printers and Publishers, Inc.
5711 N. Milwaukee Phone: (773)763-3343
Chicago, IL 60646 Fax: (773)763-3825
Publication E-mail: polish@popmailinsnet.com

Polish newspaper (English and Polish). **Subtitle:** Polish Daily News. **Founded:** 1908. **Freq:** Daily (morn.). **Print Method:** Offset. **Trim Size:** 10 x 13. **Cols./Page:** 4. **Col. Width:** 2 5/16 inches. **Col. Depth:** 182 agate lines. **Key Personnel:** Wojciech Bialasiewicz, Editor; Emily Leszczynski, General Mgr. **USPS:** 163-400. **Subscription Rates:** $80 individuals. **Foreign language name:** Dziennik Zwiazkowy.
Ad Rates: GLR: $.80 **Circ:** Paid ‡10,847
4C: $600 Free ‡203
PCI: $10.50

8651 Poultry Magazine
Marketing & Technology Group
1415 N. Dayton St. Phone: (312)266-3311
Chicago, IL 60622 Fax: (312)266-3363
Publisher E-mail: mark@mtgplace.com

Trade magazine covering the poultry processing industry, markets, and technology. **Founded:** May 1993. **Freq:** Bimonthly. **Print Method:** Offset. **Trim Size:** 8 x 10 3/4. **Cols./Page:** 3. **Key Personnel:** Pam Bowers, Editor; Sara Snyder, Managing Editor, sara@mtgplace.com; Steve Gardberg, Circulation Mgr.; Jim Goldberg, Advertising. **ISSN:** 1096-3057. **Subscription Rates:** $40 individuals; $8 single issue. **Remarks:** Accepts advertising. **URL:** http://www.mtgplace.com. **Former name:** Poultry Marketing & Technology.
Ad Rates: BW: $2,431 **Circ:** Controlled ‡10,000
4C: $3,442.50

8652 Private Arts
PO Box 10936
Chicago, IL 60610

Magazine containing poems, art, fiction, and reviews. **Founded:** 1982. **Freq:** Annual. **Trim Size:** 5 1/2 x 8 1/2. **Key Personnel:** Dale Heiniger, Contact; Ken Saunders, Contact; Brooke Bergan, Contact; Steve Tomasula, Contact. **Subscription Rates:** $10 individuals. **Remarks:** Accepts advertising.
Circ: (Not Reported)

8653 Pro-Life Action News
Pro-Life Action League
6160 N. Cicero Ave. Phone: (773)777-2900
Chicago, IL 60646 Fax: (773)777-3061
Publisher E-mail: scheidl@ibm.net

Newspaper covering social issues. **Founded:** 1980. **Freq:** Quarterly. **Trim Size:** 10 x 16. **Cols./Page:** 4. **Subscription Rates:** Included in membership. **Remarks:** Accepts advertising.
Circ: (Not Reported)

8654 Probate and Property
American Bar Association
750 N. Lake Shore Dr. Phone: (312)988-5000
Chicago, IL 60611-4497 Fax: (312)988-5568
Free: (800)285-2221

Legal publication on real estate, wills, trusts, and financial planning. **Founded:** Jan. 1987. **Freq:** Bimonthly. **Print Method:** Offset. **Trim Size:** 8 3/8 x 10 7/8 in. **Cols./Page:** 3. **Col. Width:** 2 1/4 inches. **Col. Depth:** 9 11/16 inches. **Key Personnel:** Susan Talley, Editor; John Elert, Advertising Mgr., phone (312)988-6115, fax (312)988-6030; Mike Loquencio, Editor, phone (312)988-6114; Rick Bright, Contact, phone (312)988-6083, rbright@staff.abanet.org. **ISSN:** 0164-0372. **Subscription Rates:** Free to qualified subscribers; $40 nonmembers. **Remarks:** Accepts advertising.
Ad Rates: BW: $2,470 **Circ:** Paid 29,500
4C: $3,570 Controlled 1,391

8655 The Professional Lawyer
American Bar Association
541 N. Fairbanks Ct. Phone: (312)988-6210
Chicago, IL 60611-3314 Fax: (312)988-5368
Free: (800)285-2221

Magazine providing a forum for the exchange of views and ideas on professionalism and ethics issues for bar leaders, lawyers, law school educators, and others. **Founded:** 1989. **Freq:** Quarterly. **Trim Size:** 8 1/2 x 11. **Cols./Page:** 3. **Col. Width:** 2 1/4 inches. **Col. Depth:** 9 1/2 inches. **Key Personnel:** Jill Nicholson, Editor. **ISSN:** 1042-5675. **Subscription Rates:** $20; $15 ABA members. $5 single issue. **Remarks:** Advertising not accepted.
Circ: Paid 250
Non-paid 100

8656 Prosveta
Slovene National Benefit Society
247 W. Allegheny Rd. Phone: (724)695-1100
Imperial, PA 15126-9774 Fax: (724)695-1555
Free: (800)445-2693
Publisher E-mail: snpj@snpj.com

Fraternal newspaper (Slovene and English). **Subtitle:** Enlightenment. **Founded:** July 3, 1916. **Freq:** Weekly (Wed.). **Print Method:** Letterpress and offset. **Trim Size:** 14 x 22. **Cols./Page:** 8. **Col. Width:** 12.5 picas. **Col. Depth:** 21 inches. **Key Personnel:** Jay Sedmak, Editor; Kathy Yoders, Communications Coordinator. **USPS:** 448-080. **Subscription Rates:** $16 individuals; $24 other countries. **Remarks:** Accepts advertising. **Formerly:** Glas Svobode; Glasilo.
Ad Rates: PCI: $7 **Circ:** ‡21,000

8657 Public Contract Law Journal
American Bar Association
750 N. Lake Shore Dr. Phone: (312)988-5000
Chicago, IL 60611-4497 Fax: (312)988-5568
Free: (800)285-2221

Contains articles on all phases of federal, state, and local procurement and grant law. **Freq:** Quarterly. **Trim Size:** 6 x 9. **Cols./Page:** 1. **ISSN:** 0033-3341. **Subscription Rates:** $20. $5 single issue. **Remarks:** Advertising not accepted.
Circ: (Not Reported)

8658 Public Libraries
American Library Association (ALA)
50 E. Huron St. Phone: (312)280-5038
Chicago, IL 60611 Fax: (312)280-5033
Free: (800)545-2433

Professional journal covering librarianship. **Founded:** Jan. 1947. **Freq:** Bimonthly. **Trim Size:** 8 3/8 x 10 7/8. **Key Personnel:** Kathleen M. Hughes, Managing Editor, khughes@ala.org. **ISSN:** 0163-5506. **Subscription Rates:** $50 nonmembers; Free to qualified subscribers; $10 single issue. **Remarks:** Accepts advertising.
Ad Rates: BW: $675 **Circ:** Combined ‡8,304
4C: $1,375

8659 Railway Track & Structures
Simmons-Boardman Publishing Corp.
222 S. Riverside Plaza, Ste. 1870 Phone: (312)466-1870
Fax: (312)446-1055
Chicago, IL 60606
Publication E-mail: rtands@aol.com

Magazine focusing on railroad engineering and maintenance. **Founded:** 1884. **Freq:** Monthly. **Print Method:** Offset. **Trim Size:** 8 x 10 7/8. **Cols./Page:** 3. **Col. Width:** 26 nonpareils. **Col. Depth:** 140 agate lines. **Key Personnel:** Tom Judge, Editor, phone (312)466-1870, fax (312)466-1055, tomrail@ameritech.net; Bob DeMario, Publisher, phone (212)620-7200, fax (212)633-1165. **ISSN:** 0033-8915. **Subscription Rates:** $15. **Remarks:** Accepts advertising.
Ad Rates: BW: $3,170 **Circ:** Paid 46
4C: $4,730 Controlled 8,023

8660 Real Estate Business
Residential Sales Council
430 North Michigan Ave.
Ste. 300
Chicago, IL 60611

Trade magazine for real estate brokers and residential sales personnel. **Founded:** May 1981. **Freq:** Quarterly. **Print Method:** Offset. **Trim Size:** 8 x 10.75. **Cols./Page:** 3. **Col. Width:** 2 3/16 inches. **Col. Depth:** 8 inches. **ISSN:** 0744-642X. **Subscription Rates:** $20 members. **Remarks:** Accepts advertising.
Ad Rates: BW: $2,100 **Circ:** ‡40,000
4C: $3,035

8661 Real Estate Today
National Association of Realtors
430 N. Michigan Ave. Phone: (312)329-8458
Chicago, IL 60611-4087 Fax: (312)329-5978
Free: (800)374-6500

Applications-oriented magazine featuring how-to approach to aspects of residential real estate sales, brokerage management, and commercial real estate. **Subtitle:** Official Publication of the National Association of Realtors. **Founded:** 1968. **Freq:** 10/year (combined Jan/Feb and Nov/Dec issues). **Print Method:** Offset. **Trim Size:** 8 x 10 3/4. **Cols./Page:** 3. **Col. Width:** 2 3/16 inches. **Col. Depth:** 10 inches. **Key Personnel:** Maureen Glass, Publisher. **ISSN:** 0034-0804. **Subscription Rates:** $25 individuals; $2.50 single issue. **Remarks:** Accepts advertising.
Ad Rates: BW: $17,000 **Circ:** Paid 784,469
4C: $21,725 Controlled 1,182

8662 REALTORS Land Institute
National Association of Realtors
430 N. Michigan Ave. Phone: (312)329-8458
Chicago, IL 60611-4087 Fax: (312)329-5978
Free: (800)374-6500

Newsletter and journal. **Founded:** 1947. **Freq:** 6/year. **Print Method:** Offset. **Cols./Page:** 3. **Col. Width:** 28 nonpareils. **Col. Depth:** 140 agate lines. **Key Personnel:** Gina Speziale, Editor. **ISSN:** 0888-5427. **Subscription Rates:** $25 subscription included in; membership fee. **Remarks:** Accepts advertising. **URL:** http://www.rliland.com.
Ad Rates: BW: $500 **Circ:** Paid ‡1,600
4C: $1,000 Non-paid ‡500

8663 Realty and Building
Realty and Building Inc.
11 E. Hubbard St., Ste. 3A Phone: (312)467-1888
Chicago, IL 60611-3536 Fax: (312)467-0225

Magazine for executives in the real estate, construction, architectural, and mortgage financing fields in metropolitan Chicago. **Subtitle:** Metropolitan Chicago's Real Estate and Construction Biweekly. **Founded:** 1888. **Freq:** Biweekly Saturday. **Print Method:** Offset. **Trim Size:** 8 x 11. **Cols./Page:** 3. **Col. Width:** 13 picas. **Col. Depth:** 10 inches. **Key Personnel:** John C. Cutler, Editor and Publisher. **ISSN:** 0034-1045. **Subscription Rates:** $48 individuals; $3.00 single issue. **Remarks:** Accepts advertising.
Ad Rates: BW: $1,584 **Circ:** Paid ‡11,562
4C: $2,134 Controlled ‡920
PCI: $36

8664 The Revolutionary Worker
RCP Publications, Inc.
PO Box 3486 Phone: (312)327-1689
Chicago, IL 60654
Political newspaper (English and Spanish). **Founded:** 1979. **Freq:** Weekly. **Print Method:** Offset. **Trim Size:** 11 x 17. **Cols./Page:** 3. **Col. Width:** 26 nonpareils. **Col. Depth:** 140 agate lines.

8665 Rock Products
Intertec Publishing Co.
29 N. Wacker Dr. Phone: (312)726-2802
Chicago, IL 60606 Fax: (312)726-2574
Free: (800)621-9907

Trade magazine focusing on the sand, gravel, crushed stone, cement, lime and gypsum industries. **Founded:** 1896. **Freq:** Monthly. **Print Method:** Offset. **Trim Size:** 8 1/8 x 10 7/8. **Cols./Page:** 3 and 2. **Col. Width:** 26 and 40 nonpareils. **Col. Depth:** 140 agate lines. **Key Personnel:** Bob Drake, Editor; Ken Hughes, Group Publisher. **ISSN:** 0035-7464. **Subscription Rates:** $62.50 Canada and U.S.; $100 other countries. **Remarks:** Accepts advertising. **Alt. Formats:** Microform.
Ad Rates: BW: $4,885 **Circ:** Non-paid ‡22,425
4C: $6,515
PCI: $50

8666 Salome: A Journal for the Performing Arts
Ommation Press
5548 N. Sawyer Phone: (773)539-5745
Chicago, IL 60625
Professional magazine. **Founded:** 1976. **Freq:** Quarterly. **Print Method:** Offset. **Trim Size:** 8 1/2 x 11. **Cols./Page:** 3. **Col. Width:** 26 nonpareils. **Col. Depth:** 140 agate lines. **Key Personnel:** Effie Mihopoulos, Editor and Publisher. **Subscription Rates:** $12 individuals. **Remarks:** Accepts advertising.
Ad Rates: BW: $100 **Circ:** 1,000

8667 Scanning Microscopy
Scanning Microscopy International
PO Box 66507 Phone: (847)524-6677
AMF OHARE, IL 60666 Fax: (847)985-6698
Publication E-mail: 73211.647@compuserve.com
Publisher E-mail: 73211.647@compuserve.com

Publication covering scanning microscopes, techniques, and applications. **Subtitle:** Quarterly Journal of Scanning Electron

Microscopy, Other Scanning Microscopies, Related Techniques and Applications. **Founded:** Mar. 1987. **Freq:** Quarterly. **Print Method:** Offset. **Trim Size:** 8 1/4 x 11. **Cols./Page:** 2. **Col. Width:** 3 1/8 inches. **Col. Depth:** 8 7/8 inches. **Key Personnel:** Dr. Om Johari, Managing Editor; Godfried M. Roomans, Editor. **ISSN:** 0891-7035. **Subscription Rates:** $179 individuals; $209 other countries. **Remarks:** Advertising not accepted. **Formerly**: Scanning Electron Microscopy (1987).
Circ: ‡1,000

8668 School Library Media Quarterly
American Association of School Librarians
50 E. Huron St. Phone: (312)280-4383
Chicago, IL 60611 Fax: (312)664-7459
Free: (800)545-2433
Publisher E-mail: aasl@ala.org

Journal covering topics of interest to school library media specialists and educators at all levels. **Subtitle:** Journal of the American Association of School Librarians. **Founded:** 1951. **Freq:** Quarterly. **Print Method:** Offset. **Trim Size:** 8 1/8 x 10 7/8. **Cols./Page:** 3. **Col. Width:** 31 nonpareils. **Col. Depth:** 135 agate lines. **Key Personnel:** Mary K. Biagini, Editor. **ISSN:** 0278-4823. **Subscription Rates:** $40 individuals; $12 single issue. **Remarks:** Accepts advertising. **Alt. Formats:** CD-ROM, 1996 AASL Electronic Library. **Additional Contact Info: Advertising:** The Goldman Group, 10330 N. Dale Mabry Hwy., Ste. 226, Tampa, FL 33618, (813)264-2772, fax: (813)264-2343.
Ad Rates: BW: $630 **Circ:** Paid ‡8,850
4C: $1,500 Non-paid ‡311

8669 Screen Magazine
Screen Enterprises, Inc.
16 W. Erie St. Phone: (312)664-5236
Chicago, IL 60610 Fax: (312)664-8425
Publication E-mail: screen@screenmag.com
Publisher E-mail: screen@screenmag.com

Trade magazine presenting news of Chicago-originated motion picture, video, and audiovisual, multi media production. **Founded:** Jan. 1979. **Freq:** Weekly. **Print Method:** Sheet fed. **Trim Size:** 8 1/2 x 11. **Cols./Page:** 3. **Col. Width:** 13 picas. **Col. Depth:** 59 picas. **Key Personnel:** Ruth L. Ratny, Editor; Maureen Canny, Publisher; Wm. Clarke, CFO. **ISSN:** 0276-153X. **Subscription Rates:** $75 individuals; $3 single issue. **Remarks:** Accepts advertising. **URL:** http://www.screenmag.com.
Ad Rates: BW: $1,095 **Circ:** ‡15,000
4C: $1,445

8670 The Sentinel
Sentinel Publishing Co.
6 N. Michigan, Ste. 905
Chicago, IL 60602

Jewish interest newspaper. **Founded:** Feb. 11, 1911. **Freq:** Weekly (Thurs.). **Print Method:** Letterpress. **Trim Size:** 9 x 13. **Cols./Page:** 4. **Col. Width:** 27 nonpareils. **Col. Depth:** 168 agate lines. **Key Personnel:** Jack I. Fishbein, Editor and Publisher. **Subscription Rates:** $45 individuals; $1 single issue. **Remarks:** Accepts advertising.
Ad Rates: GLR: $.95 **Circ:** ‡46,000
BW: $840
4C: $1260
PCI: $13.30

8671 Services Marketing Today
American Marketing Association
311 S. Wacker Dr. Suite 5800 Phone: (312)648-0536
Chicago, IL 60606-5819 Fax: (312)993-7542
Free: (800)262-1150
Publisher E-mail: info@ama.org

Publication focusing on current issues that affect services marketing practitioners and educators. **Freq:** Bimonthly. **Trim Size:** 8 1/2 x 11. **Key Personnel:** Ann Pellegrini, Editor. **Subscription Rates:** $18; $15 AMA member; $30 Industry. **URL:** http://www.ama.org.

8672 Signs
University of Chicago Press
5720 S. Woodlawn Ave. Phone: (773)702-7600
Chicago, IL 60637 Fax: (773)702-0172
Publication E-mail: signs@u.washington.edu

Women's studies journal. **Subtitle:** Journal of Women in Culture and Society. **Founded:** 1975. **Freq:** Quarterly. **Print Method:** Offset. **Trim Size:** 6 x 9. **Cols./Page:** 1. **Col. Width:** 54 nonpareils. **Col. Depth:** 103 agate lines. **Key Personnel:** Carolyn Allen, Editor; Judith A. Howard, Editor; Jane M. Lichty, Managing Editor; Ruth Largay, Asst. Ed.; Gitana Garofalo, Program Asst. **ISSN:** 0097-9740. **Subscription Rates:** $38 individuals; $127 institutions; $44 individuals foreign; $133 institutions foreign. **Remarks:** Accepts advertising.
Ad Rates: BW: $385 **Circ:** ‡4,000

8673 South End Citizen
Citizen Newspapers
412 E. 87th St. Phone: (312)487-7700
Chicago, IL 60619 Fax: (312)487-7931

Newspaper serving Chicago's black community. **Subtitle:** A News Source You Can Trust. **Founded:** 1966. **Freq:** Weekly (Thurs.). **Print Method:** Offset. **Trim Size:** TABLOID. **Cols./Page:** 5. **Col. Width:** 25 nonpareils. **Col. Depth:** 196 agate lines. **Key Personnel:** William Garth, Publisher; Lisa Ely, Managing Editor. **Subscription Rates:** $25 individuals. **Online:** INTER ACCESS. **Alt. Formats:** CD-ROM.
Ad Rates: BW: $1,799.70 **Circ:** Free ‡19,586
SAU: $7 Paid ‡9,121
PCI: $27.71

8674 South Suburban Citizen
Citizen Newspapers
412 E. 87th St. Phone: (312)487-7700
Chicago, IL 60619 Fax: (312)487-7931

Newspaper serving Chicago's suburban black community. **Subtitle:** A News Source You Can Trust. **Founded:** 1983. **Freq:** Weekly (Thurs.). **Print Method:** Offset. **Trim Size:** TABLOID. **Cols./Page:** 5. **Col. Width:** 25 nonpareils. **Col. Depth:** 196 agate lines. **Key Personnel:** William Garth, Publisher; Lisa Ely, Managing Editor. **Subscription Rates:** $15 individuals. **Online:** INTER ACCESS. **Alt. Formats:** CD-ROM.
Ad Rates: BW: $1,169 **Circ:** Free ‡12,750
SAU: $7 Paid 8,750
PCI: $16.70

8675 Southwest EXTRA
EXTRA Publications, Inc.
3918 W. North Ave. Phone: (312)252-3534
Chicago, IL 60647 Fax: (312)252-6031

Community newspaper. **Freq:** Weekly (Thurs.). **Key Personnel:** Mila Tellez, Publisher; Mary Montgomery, Editor; Miguel Alba, Managing Editor; Don Pringle, Editor.
Circ: ‡4,926

8676 Southwest News-Herald
Vondrac Publishing
6225 S. Kedzie Ave. Phone: (312)476-4800
Chicago, IL 60629-3397 Fax: (312)475-7811

Community newspaper. **Founded:** 1924. **Freq:** Weekly (Thurs.). **Print Method:** Offset. **Cols./Page:** 9. **Col. Width:** 21 nonpareils. **Col. Depth:** 301 agate lines. **Key Personnel:** Joseph Boyle, Editor; James Vondrak, Publisher; Renee Lawrence, Advertising Mgr. **Subscription Rates:** $9 individuals.
Circ: ‡23,083

8677 Special Care in Dentistry
Federation of Special Care Organizations in Dentistry
211 E. Chicago Ave., 5th Fl. Phone: (312)440-2660
Chicago, IL 60611 Fax: (312)440-2824

Dental journal. **Founded:** 1981. **Freq:** Bimonthly. **Print Method:** Offset. **Cols./Page:** 3 and 2. **Col. Width:** 26 and 40 nonpareils. **Col. Depth:** 133 agate lines. **Key Personnel:** Dr. Ronald Ettinger, Editor; Dr. John S. Rutkauskas, Managing Editor; Bob Gillmeister, Publications mgr. **ISSN:** 1275-1879. **Subscription Rates:** $55 individuals; $92 institutions. **Remarks:** Accepts advertising. **Alt. Formats:** Microform.
Ad Rates: BW: $605 **Circ:** ‡2,500
4C: $1005

8678 Sport Literate
1623 W. Belmont, No. 6B
Chicago, IL 60657

Magazine of nonfiction, poetry, and interviews. **Freq:** 4/year. **Trim Size:** 5 1/2 x 8 1/2. **Key Personnel:** William Meiners, Editor; Jotham Burrello, Editor. **Subscription Rates:** $10 individuals; $3 single issue. **Remarks:** Advertising accepted; rates available upon request.
Circ: Paid 500

8679 Store Equipment & Design
SED Publishing
1700 W. Irving Park Rd. Phone: (312)281-4441
PO Box 578249 Fax: (312)281-8275
Chicago, IL 60657-6061
Publication E-mail: storeequip@aol.com

Trade magazine focusing on design trends, new equipment introductions, remodeling, engineering, and maintenance issues in supermarket planning and operations. **Founded:** Mar. 1992. **Freq:** 10/year. **Print Method:** Offset. **Trim Size:** 10 7/8 x 14 1/2. **Cols./Page:** 4. **Col. Width:** 2 1/4 inches. **Col. Depth:** 13 3/8 inches. **Key Personnel:** Bill Epmeier, Publisher; Craig Barrier, Associate Editor. **ISSN:** 1077-2348. **Subscription Rates:** $70 individuals. **Remarks:** Accepts advertising.
Ad Rates: BW: $4,800 **Circ:** Controlled 19,500
4C: $5,950

8680 Strategy & Leadership
Strategic Leadership Forum
435 N. Michigan Ave., Ste. 1717 Phone: (312)644-0829
Chicago, IL 60611 Fax: (312)644-8557
Free: (800)873-5995

Professional magazine focusing on corporate strategic management and planning. **Founded:** 1972. **Freq:** Bimonthly. **Print Method:** Offset. **Trim Size:** 8 1/2 x 11. **Cols./Page:** 2. **Col. Width:** 39 nonpareils. **Col. Depth:** 140 agate lines. **Key Personnel:** Gerard Soldner, Publisher, gsoldner@ulster.net. **ISSN:** 1087-8572. **Subscription Rates:** $115 US and Canada; $135 air mail. **Formerly**: Planning Review.
Ad Rates: BW: $1,722 **Circ:** Paid ‡2,000
4C: $2,442 Non-paid ‡4,000

8681 StreetWise
62 E 13th St. Phone: (312)554-0060
Chicago, IL 60605 Fax: (312)554-0770

Alternative street newspaper. **Subtitle:** Empowering People to Self-Sufficiency Through Employment. **Founded:** Apr. 1992. **Freq:** Semimonthly. **Key Personnel:** Lisa Ely, Editor. **Subscription Rates:** $40 individuals. **Remarks:** Accepts advertising. **URL:** http://www.streetwise.org.
Ad Rates: BW: $1,695 **Circ:** (Not Reported)
4C: $2,470

8682 Student Lawyer
American Bar Association
750 N. Lake Shore Dr. Phone: (312)988-5000
Chicago, IL 60611-4497 Fax: (312)988-5568
Free: (800)285-2221

Professional magazine covering legal education and other legal issues for members of the American Bar Association. **Founded:** 1972. **Freq:** 9/year. **Key Personnel:** Stephane Johnston, Editor; Michael Loquercio, National Sales Dir. **ISSN:** 0039-274X. **Subscription Rates:** $15 members individual/annual; $22 nonmembers individual/annual; $8 single issue. **Remarks:** Accepts advertising.
Ad Rates: BW: $1,820 **Circ:** (Not Reported)
4C: $2,755

8683 Suburban Leader
Leader
6008 W. Belmont Ave. Phone: (773)283-7900
Chicago, IL 60634-5195 Fax: (773)283-7761

Newspaper. **Founded:** 1949. **Freq:** Sunday. **Print Method:** Offset. **Cols./Page:** 6. **Col. Width:** 19 nonpareils. **Col. Depth:** 294 agate lines. **Key Personnel:** Ted Villaire, Editor; Ramona Diaz, Publisher. **Subscription Rates:** $40 individuals. **Remarks:** Accepts advertising. **Absorbed**: Jefferson Park Leader; The Mayfair Leader; Portage Park Leader.
Ad Rates: PCI: $20 **Circ:** 11,000

8684 Suburban Post
Leader
6008 W. Belmont Ave. Phone: (773)283-7900
Chicago, IL 60634-5195 Fax: (773)283-7761

Community newspaper serving the areas of Elmwood Park, Mont Clare, River Grove, Franklin Park, and Northlake. **Founded:** 1964. **Freq:** Weekly (Fri.). **Print Method:** Offset. **Cols./Page:** 6. **Col. Width:** 19 nonpareils. **Col. Depth:** 196 agate lines. **Key Personnel:** Ted Villaire, Editor; Ramona Diaz, Publisher. **Subscription Rates:** $40 individuals. **Remarks:** Accepts advertising. **Absorbed**: Elmwood Park Post; Mont Clare Post; River Grove Post; Franklin Park Post; Northlake Post.
Ad Rates: PCI: $20 **Circ:** 11,000

8685 Successful Black Parenting
2325 W. Ainslie, 2nd Fl. Phone: (773)769-8422
Chicago, IL 60625
Publication E-mail: blkparent@aol.com

Magazine for black parents and extended family. Designed to support the black family in raising children. **Founded:** Sept. 1995. **Freq:** Bimonthly. **Print Method:** Web offset. **Trim Size:** 8 x 10 1/2. **Cols./Page:** 3. **Col. Width:** 2 1/4 inches. **Col. Depth:** 9 1/4 inches. **Key Personnel:** Useni Eugene Perkins, Editor-in-Chief; Janice Robinson, Publisher; Marta Sanchez-Speer, Publisher, mspeer87@aol.com. **Subscription Rates:** $2.95 single issue. **Remarks:** Accepts advertising. **Online:** America Online, Inc. **URL:** http://www.netnoir.com/sbp/index.html. **Formerly**: Black Parenting.
Ad Rates: BW: $3,283 **Circ:** Paid ‡100,000
4C: $4,020 Non-paid ‡70,000

8686 Suicide and Life-Threatening Behavior
Guilford Publications, Inc.
Dept. of Psychiatry Phone: (773)702-9800
University of Chicago Fax: (773)702-2011
5737 S. University Ave.
Chicago, IL 60637-1507
Publisher E-mail: info@guilford.com

Journal devoted to new theoretical, research, and clinical approaches to suicide and other life-threatening behaviors. **Subtitle:** The Official Journal of the American Association of Suicidology. **Founded:** 1971. **Freq:** Quarterly. **Print Method:** Offset. **Trim Size:** 6 x 9. **Cols./Page:** 1. **Col. Width:** 72 nonpareils. **Col. Depth:** 126 agate lines. **Key Personnel:** Morton Silverman, M.D., Editor-in-Chief, msilverm@uhs.bsd.uchicago.edu. **ISSN:** 0363-0234. **Subscription Rates:** $40; $168 institutions. **Remarks:** Accepts advertising. **Alt. Formats:** Microfilm.
Ad Rates: BW: $350 **Circ:** 1,739

8687 The Surplus Record
Surplus Record, Inc.
20 N. Wacker Dr., No. 2500 Phone: (312)372-9077
Chicago, IL 60606 Fax: (312)372-6537
Publication E-mail: surplus@surplusrecord.com
Publisher E-mail: surplus@surplusrecord.com

Magazine focusing on used and surplus industrial equipment. **Subtitle:** Index of Available Machinery Equipment. **Founded:** 1924. **Freq:** Monthly. **Print Method:** Offset. **Trim Size:** 5 3/8 x 8 5/8. **Cols./Page:** 1. **Col. Width:** 54 nonpareils. **Col. Depth:** 108 agate lines. **Key Personnel:** T.C. Scanlan, Editor and Publisher. **ISSN:** 0039-615X. **Subscription Rates:** $30 individuals. **Remarks:** Accepts advertising. **Available Online. URL:** http://www.surplusrecord.com.
Ad Rates: BW: $395 **Circ:** Non-paid ‡70,500
Paid ‡1,950

8688 Swiss-American Historical Society
6440 N. Bosworth Phone: (773)262-9336
Chicago, IL 60626 Fax: (773)465-5292

Journal covering Swiss-American history. **Founded:** 1965. **Freq:** Triennial. **Key Personnel:** Prof. Leo Schelbert, Editor. **Subscription Rates:** $30 individuals. **Remarks:** Advertising not accepted.
Circ: Paid 400

8689 The Tax Lawyer
American Bar Association
750 N. Lake Shore Dr. Phone: (312)988-5000
Chicago, IL 60611-4497 Fax: (312)988-5568
Free: (800)285-2221

Tax law. **Founded:** 1947. **Freq:** Quarterly. **Print Method:** Offset. **Cols./Page:** 1. **Col. Width:** 54 nonpareils. **Col. Depth:** 104 agate lines. **Key Personnel:** Nora C. Whitford, Advertising Mgr. **Subscription Rates:** $53 individuals. **URL:** http://www.aba.net.org.
Circ: Paid 26,525
Non-paid 2,639

8690 Telephony
Intertec Publishing Corp.
1 IBM Plaza, Ste. 2300 Phone: (312)595-1080
Chicago, IL 60611 Fax: (312)595-0295

Magazine for executives and managers of telecommunications carriers, including wireline, wireless and new media. **Subtitle:** For Today's Competitive Public Network Market. **Founded:** 1901. **Freq:** Weekly. **Print Method:** Offset. **Trim Size:** 8 1/2 x 11. **Cols./Page:** 3. **Col. Width:** 30 nonpareils. **Col. Depth:** 140 agate lines. **Key Personnel:** Steven Titch, Editorial Dir.; Larry Lannon, Group Publisher; Mark Hickey, Publisher. **ISSN:** 0040-2656. **Subscription Rates:** Free to qualified subscribers; $79 individuals; $115 out of country. **Remarks:** Accepts advertising. **Online:** CompuServe Information Service.
Ad Rates: BW: $4924 **Circ:** Paid 13,445
4C: $6600 Non-paid 35,886

8691 Tempo
Chicago State University
Tempo SUB 230 Phone: (312)995-3699
95th at King Dr. Fax: (312)995-3593
Chicago, IL 60628-1598
Collegiate newspaper. **Founded:** 1894. **Freq:** Biweekly. **Print Method:** Letterpress. **Trim Size:** 11 1/2 x 13. **Cols./Page:** 5. **Col. Width:** 22 nonpareils. **Col. Depth:** 210 agate lines. **Key Personnel:** Sabrina Glover, Editor. **Remarks:** Accepts advertising.
Ad Rates: GLR: $7.60 **Circ:** Free 6,000
BW: $225

8692 32 Pages
Rain Crow Publishing
2127 W. Pierce Ave., Apt. 2B Phone: (773)276-9005
Chicago, IL 60622-1824
Publisher E-mail: rap@rai-crow-publishing.com

Magazine of poetry and prose. **Founded:** Jan. 1997. **Freq:** Quarterly. **Print Method:** Offset. **Trim Size:** 8 1/2 x 11. **Key Personnel:** Michael S. Manley, Editor and Publisher, manley@rain-crow-publishing.com. **ISSN:** 1091-6547. **Subscription Rates:** $10 individuals; $13 other countries; $2.50 single issue. **URL:** http://rain-crow-publishing.com/32pp/.
Ad Rates: BW: $50 **Circ:** Paid 1,000

8693 This Week in Chicago/Key Magazine
904 W. Blackhawk Phone: (312)993-0838
Chicago, IL 60622 Fax: (312)664-6113

Visitors' guide. **Founded:** 1920. **Freq:** Weekly. **Print Method:** Offset. **Trim Size:** 4.75 x 7.5. **Cols./Page:** 2. **Col. Width:** 26 nonpareils. **Col. Depth:** 105 agate lines. **Key Personnel:** Walter L. West, Jr., Publisher; Walter West III, Advertising Mgr.; Brad Klepac, Editor. **Subscription Rates:** $55 individuals. **Remarks:** Accepts advertising.
Ad Rates: BW: $1,000 **Circ:** Non-paid ‡20,000
4C: $1,400

8694 Tort & Insurance Law Journal
American Bar Association
750 N. Lake Shore Dr. Phone: (312)988-5000
Chicago, IL 60611-4497 Fax: (312)988-5568
Free: (800)285-2221

Scholarly journal on current or emerging issues of national scope in the fields of tort and insurance law. **Freq:** Quarterly. **Trim Size:** 6 x 9. **Cols./Page:** 1. **ISSN:** 0015-8356. **Subscription Rates:** $23; $28 other countries. $5 single issue. **Remarks:** Advertising not accepted. **Formerly:** The Forum.
Circ: (Not Reported)

8695 Townsfolk
919 N. Michigan Ave. Phone: (312)787-6579
Chicago, IL 60611
Magazine covering society, sports, travel, and fine arts in the Chicago area. **Founded:** 1929. **Freq:** Monthly. **Print Method:** Offset. **Trim Size:** 8 x 11. **Cols./Page:** 4. **Col. Width:** 24 nonpareils. **Col. Depth:** 154 agate lines. **Key Personnel:** A.M. Adams, Editor/Administration; J.P. Person, Publisher. **Subscription Rates:** $10 individuals; $2 single issue. **Remarks:** Accepts advertising.
Ad Rates: BW: $550 **Circ:** (Not Reported)
4C: $850
PCI: $25

8696 Truck Blue Book
National Market Reports
29 N. Wacker Dr. Phone: (312)726-2802
Chicago, IL 60606 Fax: (312)855-0137
Free: (800)621-9907

Book covering valuations on used trucks. **Subtitle:** Official Used Truck Valuations. **Founded:** 1917. **Freq:** Quarterly. **Print Method:** Offset. **Trim Size:** 4 1/2 x 7 1/2. **Cols./Page:** 1. **Col. Width:** 3 5/8 inches. **Col. Depth:** 6 5/8 inches. **Key Personnel:** Gary Dillow, Editor; George Stanton, Publisher. **ISSN:** 0273-9402. **Subscription Rates:** $120. **Remarks:** Advertising not accepted. **Alt. Formats:** CD-ROM, Electronic Truck Blue Book; Diskette.
Circ: Paid ‡10,588
Non-paid ‡335

8697 Truck Blue Book Residual Values
National Market Reports
29 N. Wacker Dr. Phone: (312)726-2802
Chicago, IL 60606 Fax: (312)855-0137
Free: (800)621-9907

Book covering residual value projections for medium and heavy-duty trucks. **Founded:** 1984. **Freq:** Quarterly. **Key Personnel:** George C. Stanton, Publisher. **Subscription Rates:** $65 individuals; $75 other countries; $30 single issue. **Remarks:** Advertising not accepted. **Formerly:** Truck Blue Book Lease Guide.
Circ: (Not Reported)

8698 Trustee
American Hospital Publishing, Inc.
1 N. Franklin Phone: (312)893-6800
Chicago, IL 60606 Fax: (312)422-4500
Free: (800)621-6902

Magazine for hospital and health care system governing board members containing information about events and issues affecting the health care industry. **Subtitle:** The Magazine for Hospital Governing Boards. **Founded:** 1947. **Freq:** Monthly. **Print Method:** Offset. **Trim Size:** 8 x 10 3/4. **Cols./Page:** 3. **Col. Width:** 32 nonpareils. **Col. Depth:** 115 agate lines. **Key Personnel:** Karen Gardner, Editor; Daniel S. Schechter, Publisher; Jim Dozois, Directory of Sales. **ISSN:** 0041-3674. **Subscription Rates:** $30 individuals. **Available Online.**
Ad Rates: BW: $4,980 **Circ:** ‡35,307
4C: $6,300

8699 Ukrainian Philatelist
Ukrainian Philatelic and Numismatic Society
PO Box 11184 Phone: (773)276-0355
Chicago, IL 60611-0184 Fax: (914)782-3048
Publisher E-mail: yurko@warwick.net

Trade journal covering philately and numismatics. **Founded:** 1952. **Freq:** Semiannual. **Trim Size:** 8 x 11. **Cols./Page:** 2. **Key Personnel:** Bohdan O. Pauk, Editor. **ISSN:** 0198-6252. **Subscription Rates:** $20 individuals; $10 single issue. **Remarks:** Accepts advertising. **Alt. Formats:** Microform.
Circ: Controlled 415

8700 U.S. Catholic
Claretian Publications
205 W. Monroe Phone: (312)236-7782
Chicago, IL 60606 Fax: (312)236-8207
Free: (800)328-6515
Publication E-mail: uscath@aol.com

Catholic magazine. **Founded:** 1935. **Freq:** Monthly. **Print Method:** Offset. **Cols./Page:** 3. **Col. Width:** 27 nonpareils. **Col. Depth:** 140 agate lines. **Key Personnel:** Rev. Mark Brummel, C.M.F., Editor. **Subscription Rates:** $22 individuals; $2 single issue. **Remarks:** Accepts advertising. **URL:** http://www.uscatholic.org.
Ad Rates: BW: $1,500 **Circ:** 52,000

8701 The University of Chicago Law Review
Darby Printers
1111 E. 60th St. Phone: (312)702-9832
University of Chicago Law School Fax: (312)702-0730
Chicago, IL 60637-2786
Legal magazine. **Founded:** 1933. **Freq:** Quarterly. **Print Method:** Offset. **Cols./Page:** 1. **Col. Width:** 54 nonpareils. **Col. Depth:** 102 agate lines. **Key Personnel:** Dale Carpenter, Editor. **Subscription Rates:** $26 individuals. **Remarks:** Accepts advertising.
Ad Rates: BW: $125 **Circ:** ‡2,600

8702 University of Chicago Magazine
1313 E. 60th St., Rm. 224 Phone: (773)702-2163
Chicago, IL 60637 Fax: (773)702-2166
Publication E-mail: uchicago-magazine@uchicago.edu

University alumni magazine. **Founded:** 1907. **Freq:** Bimonthly. **Print Method:** Offset. **Trim Size:** 8 1/8 x 10 7/8. **Cols./Page:** 3. **Col. Width:** 14.5 picas. **Col. Depth:** 58.25 picas. **Key Personnel:** Mary Ruth Yoe, Editor, phone (773)702-2164, ddog@midway.uchicago.edu. **ISSN:** 0041-9508. **Remarks:** Accepts advertising. **Available Online. URL:** http://www2.uchicago.edu/alumni/alumni.mag.
Ad Rates: BW: $1,500 **Circ:** Non-paid ‡110,000
4C: $2,500

8703 The Urban Lawyer
American Bar Association
750 N. Lake Shore Dr. Phone: (312)988-5000
Chicago, IL 60611-4497 Fax: (312)988-5568
Free: (800)285-2221

Articles on various areas of urban, state, and local government law. **Founded:** 1969. **Freq:** Quarterly. **Print Method:** Offset. **Trim Size:** 6 x 9. **Cols./Page:** 1. **Key Personnel:** Richard W. Bright, Managing Editor, phone (312)988-6083, fax (312)988-6081, rbright@staff.abanet.org. **ISSN:** 0042-0905. **Subscription Rates:** $64.95 individuals; $69.95 other countries; $12 single issue. **Remarks:** Advertising not accepted. **URL:** http://www.abanet.org.
Circ: Paid 6,200
Non-paid 300

8704 Utillaje
Utillaje, Inc.
20 N. Wacker Dr. Phone: (312)372-9077
Chicago, IL 60606 Fax: (312)372-6537
Publication E-mail: utillaje@mail.internet.com.mx
Publisher E-mail: utillaje@mail.internet.com.mx

Classified magazine listing over 10,000 pieces of industrial equipment (Spanish). **Subtitle:** Compendio de Maquinaria. **Founded:** 1993. **Freq:** Monthly. **Print Method:** Offset. **Trim Size:** 5 3/8 x 8 1/4. **Cols./Page:** 2. **Col. Width:** 2 1/4 inches. **Col. Depth:** 7 /12 inches. **Key Personnel:** Fabian Uribe, Editor; Thomas Scanlan, Publisher. **ISSN:** 1065-9862. **Subscription Rates:** $72 individuals; $6 single issue. **Remarks:** Color advertising not accepted. **Available Online. URL:** http://www.utillaje.com.
Ad Rates: GLR: $7 **Circ:** Paid 500
BW: $465 Controlled 30,250

8705 Van Conversion Blue Book
National Market Reports
29 N. Wacker Dr. Phone: (312)726-2802
Chicago, IL 60606 Fax: (312)855-0137
Free: (800)621-9907

Book covering valuations on used van conversions. **Founded:** 1982. **Freq:** Quarterly. **Key Personnel:** George C. Stanton, Publisher. **ISSN:** 0884-7231. **Subscription Rates:** $60 U.S.; $70 other countries; $30 single issue. **Remarks:** Advertising not accepted.
Circ: (Not Reported)

8706 Veery
Foxglove Company
1 North LaSalle, Ste. 2044 Phone: (773)804-0777
Chicago, IL 60602 Fax: (773)804-0777

Journal covering humanities and science. **Founded:** 1991. **Freq:** Semiannual. **Trim Size:** 8 1/2 x 11. **Key Personnel:** R. H. Crane, Editor; Steven Vita, Editor. **ISSN:** 1069-7144. **Subscription Rates:** $13 individuals; $26 institutions; $7 single issue. **Remarks:** Accepts advertising.
Ad Rates: BW: $250 **Circ:** Paid 1,200

8707 Visible Language
IIT Institute of Design Phone: (312)595-4921
350 N. LaSalle St. Fax: (312)595-4901
Chicago, IL 60610
Publisher E-mail: graphdes@risd.edu

Scholarly journal about written language. **Subtitle:** The Quarterly Concerned with All that is Involved in Our Being Literate. **Founded:** 1967. **Freq:** 3/year. **Print Method:** Offset. **Trim Size:** 6 x 9. **Cols./Page:** 1. **Col. Width:** 51 nonpareils. **Col. Depth:** 94 agate lines. **Key Personnel:** Sharon Helmer Poggenpohl, Editor, poggenpohl@id.iit.edu. **ISSN:** 0022-2224. **Subscription Rates:** $35 individuals; $65 institutions and libraries. **Remarks:** Advertising not accepted. **URL:** http://www.id.iit.edu/visiblelanguage. **Formerly:** The Journal of Typographic Research.
Circ: ‡1,300

8708 Waifs' Messenger
Mission of Our Lady of Mercy Inc.
1140 W. Jackson Phone: (312)738-7560
Chicago, IL 60607 Fax: (312)738-9250

Magazine reporting on activities of the young men and women of Mercy Home for Boys & Girls and seeking to inspire support. **Freq:** Quarterly. **Key Personnel:** John Riss, Editor, phone (312)738-7565. **Remarks:** Advertising not accepted.
Circ: 130,000

8709 The Wall Street Journal (Midwest Edition)
Dow Jones & Co., Inc.
1 S. Wacker Dr., Ste. 2100 Phone: (312)750-4000
Chicago, IL 60606 Fax: (312)750-4153

National business and finance newspaper. **Founded:** July 8, 1889. **Freq:** MXF (morn.). **Print Method:** Offset. **Cols./Page:** 6. **Col. Width:** 30 nonpareils. **Col. Depth:** 296 agate lines. **Key Personnel:** Joe Gurgone, Midwest Administration. **Subscription Rates:** $139 individuals.
Circ: Mon.-Fri. 492,514

8710 West Suburban Extra
EXTRA Publications, Inc.
3918 W. North Ave. Phone: (312)252-3534
Chicago, IL 60647 Fax: (312)252-6031

Community newspaper. **Founded:** 1980. **Freq:** Weekly. **Key Personnel:** Andrea Sharp, Editor. **Remarks:** Advertising accepted; rates available upon request.
Circ: (Not Reported)

8711 Wicker Park/West Town EXTRA
EXTRA Publications, Inc.
3918 W. North Ave. Phone: (312)252-3534
Chicago, IL 60647 Fax: (312)252-6031

Community newspaper (Spanish and English). **Freq:** Weekly (Thurs.). **Key Personnel:** Mila Tellez, Publisher. **Subscription Rates:** Free.

8712 Windy City Sports Magazine
Windy City Publishing, Inc.
1450 W. Randolph Phone: (312)421-1551
Chicago, IL 60607 Fax: (312)421-1454
Publisher E-mail: wcpublish@aol.com

Magazine covering amateur sports in the Chicago area. **Founded:** Apr. 1987. **Freq:** Monthly. **Print Method:** Offset. **Trim Size:** 10 x 13. **Cols./Page:** 4. **Col. Width:** 2 1/8 inches. **Col. Depth:** 12 1/4 inches. **Key Personnel:** Jeff Banowetz, Editor; Doug Kaplan, Publisher. **Subscription Rates:** $20 individuals; $3 single issue. **Remarks:** Accepts advertising. **Available Online. URL:** http://www.windycitysportsmag.com.
Ad Rates: BW: $5,067 **Circ:** Controlled ‡100,000
4C: $5,867

8713 Windy City Times
325 W. Huron, Ste. 510 Phone: (312)397-0020
Chicago, IL 60610 Fax: (312)397-0021
Publication E-mail: wct@wwa.com

Gay and lesbian community newspaper. **Founded:** Sept. 1985. **Freq:** Weekly. **Print Method:** Web. **Trim Size:** 11 x 17. **Cols./Page:** 4. **Col. Width:** 2 7/16 inches. **Col. Depth:** 10 inches. **Key Personnel:** Jeff McCourt, Publisher; Kelly Harmon, Business Mgr. **Subscription Rates:** $50 3rd class; $144 1st class. **Remarks:** Accepts advertising. **URL:** http://www.wctimes.com. **Feature Editors:** Louis Weisberg, *News.*
Ad Rates: BW: $850 **Circ:** Non-paid 1,800

8714 Womens's Music Plus
Empty Closet Enterprises, Inc.
5210 Wayne Ave. Phone: (312)769-9009
Chicago, IL 60640-2223 Fax: (312)728-7002

Annual directory listing contact information for approx. 6000 individuals and groups involved in feminist or lesbian culture. Includes performers, festivals, writers, publications, radio, film/video, craftswomen, cartoonists, photographers, bookstores, agents, etc. Women's music sampler CD may be included in the future editions. **Subtitle:** Directory of Resources in Women's Music and Culture. **Founded:** 1977. **Freq:** Annual. **Trim Size:** 8 1/2 x 11. **Cols./Page:** 3. **Col. Width:** 2.5 inches. **Col. Depth:** 9 inches. **Key Personnel:** Toni Armstrong, Jr., Editor, toniajr.@aol.com. **ISSN:** 0747-8887. **Subscription Rates:** $20. **Formerly:** We Shall Go Forth (1983).
Ad Rates: PCI: $11 **Circ:** Paid 2,000
Non-paid 10,000

8715 World Progress
Standard Educational Corp.
200 W. Madison St. Phone: (312)346-7440
Chicago, IL 60606 Fax: (312)580-7215

Current events magazine. **Founded:** 1928. **Freq:** Quarterly. **Print Method:** Offset. **Cols./Page:** 2. **Col. Width:** 28 nonpareils. **Col. Depth:** 98 agate lines. **Key Personnel:** Miriam Creeden, Editor. **ISSN:** 0043-8901. **Subscription Rates:** $18.95 individuals. **Remarks:** Advertising not accepted.
Circ: (Not Reported)

8716 Zacks Analyst Watch
Zacks Investment Research
155 N. Wacker Dr. Phone: (312)630-9880
Chicago, IL 60606 Fax: (312)630-9898

Journal providing brokerage research for major U.S. public companies. **Freq:** Bimonthly. **Subscription Rates:** $000 annual; $55 3 month trial. **URL:** http://www.zacks.com.

8717 Zacks Earnings Forecaster
Zacks Investment Research
155 N. Wacker Dr. Phone: (312)630-9880
Chicago, IL 60606 Fax: (312)630-9898

Journal providing earnings estimate data for U.S. public companies. **Freq:** Biweekly or monthly. **Subscription Rates:** $495 individuals; $195 quarterly; $375 monthly.

8718 Zacks EPS Calendar
Zacks Investment Research
155 N. Wacker Dr. Phone: (312)630-9880
Chicago, IL 60606 Fax: (312)630-9898

Journal providing expected earnings report dates for major U.S. companies. **Freq:** Monthly. **Subscription Rates:** $195 quarterly; $1500 weekly; $495 monthly.

8719 Zacks Profit Guide
Zacks Investment Research
155 N. Wacker Dr. Phone: (312)630-9880
Chicago, IL 60606 Fax: (312)630-9898

Journal providing total returns, projected stock prices, and stock performance measures for major U.S. public companies. **Freq:** Quarterly. **Subscription Rates:** $375 annual.

8720 Zontian
Zonta International
557 W. Randolph St. Phone: (312)930-5848
Chicago, IL 60661 Fax: (312)930-0951

Service club organization magazine of interest to executives and professionals concerned with the status of women. **Founded:** 1920. **Freq:** Quarterly. **Print Method:** Web press. **Trim Size:** 8 1/4 x 10 7/8. **Cols./Page:** 3. **Col. Width:** 26 nonpareils. **Col. Depth:** 115 agate lines. **ISSN:** 0279-3229. **Subscription Rates:** $7 individuals. **Remarks:** Advertising not accepted.
Circ: ‡36,000

8721 Chicago Cable TV
1931 W. Diversey Blvd. Phone: (312)880-9000
Chicago, IL 60614 Fax: (312)880-2257

Founded: 1986. **Cities Served:** Cook County, IL.

8722 KMLW-FM - 88.3
820 N. LaSalle Blvd. Free: (800)766-5624
Chicago, IL 60610
E-mail: kmbi@moody.edu

Format: Religious. **Owner:** Moody Bible Institute of Chicago, at above address. **Operating Hours:** Continuous. **Key Personnel:** D. Gray Leonard, Station Mgr.; Rich Monteith, Asst. Manager. **Wattage:** 4000. **Ad Rates:** Noncommercial. **URL:** http://www.kmbi@moody.edu.

8723 WBBM-AM - 780
630 N. McClurg Ct. Phone: (312)944-6000
Chicago, IL 60611 Fax: (312)951-3674

Format: News. **Networks:** CBS. **Founded:** 1923. **Operating Hours:** Continuous. **ADI:** Chicago (LaSalle), IL. **Key Personnel:** Steve Carver, General Mgr. **Wattage:** 50,000.

8724 WBBM-FM - 96.5
630 N. McClurg Ct. Phone: (312)944-6000
Chicago, IL 60611-3074 Fax: (312)951-3674

Format: Contemporary Hit Radio (CHR). **Networks:** CBS. **Founded:** 1941. **Operating Hours:** Continuous. **ADI:** Chicago (LaSalle), IL. **Key Personnel:** Tom Matheson, General Mgr. **Wattage:** 5000.

8725 WBBM-TV - 2
630 N. McClurg Ct. Phone: (312)944-6000
Chicago, IL 60611 Fax: (312)943-7193

Format: Commercial TV. **Networks:** CBS. **Operating Hours:** Continuous. **ADI:** Chicago (LaSalle), IL. **Key Personnel:** Bill Applegate, Contact.

WCEV-AM - See Cicero

8726 WCFC-TV - 38/51
38 S. Peoria Phone: (312)433-3838
Chicago, IL 60607 Fax: (312)433-3839

Format: Commercial TV. **Networks:** Independent. **Owner:** Christian Communications of Chicago, at above address. **Founded:** 1976. **Operating Hours:** Continuous; 67% network, 33% local. **ADI:** Chicago (LaSalle), IL. **Key Personnel:** Jerry K. Rose, President; David Oseland, Program and News Dir.; David Scott, VP/Gen. Mgr.; Kevin Sanhamel, Sales Mgr. **Wattage:** 5,000,000. **URL:** http://www.tv38.com.

8727 WCIU-TV - 26
26 N. Halsted Phone: (312)705-2600
Chicago, IL 60661 Fax: (312)705-2656

Format: Commercial TV. **Operating Hours:** 6:30 a.m.-3 a.m. **ADI:** Chicago (LaSalle), IL.

8728 WCKG-FM - 105.9
2 Prudential Plaza, Ste. 1059 Phone: (312)240-7900
Chicago, IL 60601 Fax: (312)565-3181

Format: Talk. **Networks:** Independent. **Operating Hours:** Continuous. **ADI:** Chicago (LaSalle), IL. **Key Personnel:** Michael G. Disney, GM/VP; Dave McBride, News Dir.; Gehrig Peterson, Marketing Dir. **Wattage:** 4200.

8729 WCRX-FM - 88.1
600 S. Michigan Phone: (312)663-1693
Chicago, IL 60605

Format: Alternative/New Music/Progressive. **ADI:** Chicago (LaSalle), IL. **Key Personnel:** Tom Joyce, Music Dir. **Ad Rates:** Noncommercial.

8730 WEDC-AM - 1240
5475 N. Milwaukee Ave. Phone: (312)631-0700
Chicago, IL 60630-1229

Format: Ethnic. **Networks:** Independent. **Owner:** Foreign Language Broadcasts, Inc., at above address. **Founded:** 1926. **Operating Hours:** midnight-6 am, 8:30-10 am, 3:30-5 pm, 7-8 pm, and 10-11 pm. **ADI:** Chicago (LaSalle), IL. **Key Personnel:** Jim Keithley, General Mgr.; Carmen Castro, Contact. **Wattage:** 1000.

8731 WEHS-TV - 60
100 S. Sangamon St., No. 300 Phone: (312)829-8860
Chicago, IL 60607 Fax: (312)829-1059

Format: Commercial TV. **Networks:** Independent. **Owner:** Silver King Communications, 2425 Olympic Blvd., Santa Monica, CA 90404, (310)247-7930. **Founded:** 1986. **Formerly:** WPWR-TV; WBBS-TV. **Operating Hours:** Continuous.

ADI: Chicago (LaSalle), IL. **Key Personnel:** Renee M. Genova, Operations Mgr.

8732 WEJM-FM - 106.3
800 S. Wells, Ste.250 Phone: (312)360-9000
Chicago, IL 60607 Fax: (312)306-9070

Format: Adult Contemporary; Urban Contemporary. **Simulcasts:** WJPC-AM. **Networks:** ABC. **Founded:** 1961. **Operating Hours:** Continuous. **ADI:** Chicago (LaSalle), IL. **Key Personnel:** Don More, General Mgr.; Cristina Wilson, Gen. Sales Mgr.; D.J. McLarin, Controller; Jay Alan, Program Dir. **Local Programs:** *Geto Boy Radio*, Pharris Thomas, (708)895-1400; *Yo! Show*, Pharris Thomas, (708)895-1400; *The Zone*, Cortney Hicks, (708)895-1400. **Wattage:** 3000.

WEMG-AM - See Knoxville, Tennessee

8733 WFLD-TV - 32
205 N. Michigan Ave. Phone: (312)565-5532
Chicago, IL 60601 Fax: (312)819-1332

Format: Commercial TV. **Networks:** Fox. **Owner:** Fox Broadcasting Corp., 5746 Sunset Blvd., Fernwood Bldg., Los Angeles, CA 90028, (213)462-7111. **Operating Hours:** Continuous. **ADI:** Chicago (LaSalle), IL. **Key Personnel:** Stuart B. Powell, Contact.

8734 WGBO-TV - 66
541 N. Fairbanks Cr., Ste. 1100 Phone: (312)670-1000
Chicago, IL 60611 Fax: (312)494-6492

Format: Commercial TV. **Networks:** Univision. **Founded:** 1981. **Formerly:** WFBN-TV (1985). **Operating Hours:** Continuous. **ADI:** Chicago (LaSalle), IL. **Key Personnel:** Jane Hepburn Fiore, Station Mgr., jfiore@univision.net; Jane Hepburn, General Sales Mgr., jfiore@univision.net; Shari Valentine, National Sales Manager, phone (312)494-2721, fax (312)494-6487, svalentine@univsion.net. **Wattage:** 5,000,000. **URL:** http://www.univision.net.

8735 WGCI-AM - 1390
332 S. Michigan Ave., Ste. 600 Phone: (312)427-4800
Chicago, IL 60604-4301 Fax: (312)987-4453

Format: Oldies; Blues. **Networks:** American Urban Radio. **Founded:** 1924. **Formerly:** WVON-AM. **Operating Hours:** Continuous. **ADI:** Chicago (LaSalle), IL. **Key Personnel:** Marv Dyson, General Mgr.; Sean Ross, Program Mgr. **Wattage:** 5000.

8736 WGCI-FM - 107.5
332 S. Michigan Ave., Ste. 600 Phone: (312)427-4700
Chicago, IL 60604 Fax: (312)427-7410

Format: Urban Contemporary. **Networks:** Independent. **Founded:** 1958. **Operating Hours:** Continuous. **ADI:** Chicago (LaSalle), IL. **Key Personnel:** Marv Dyson, President; Darryll J. Green, Vice President/General Manager; Muriel Funches, General Sales Mgr.; Elroy Smith, Operations Mgr. **Wattage:** 33,000.

8737 WGN-AM - 720
435 N. Michigan Ave. Phone: (312)222-4700
Chicago, IL 60611-4001 Fax: (312)222-5165
E-mail: wgnradio@tribune.com

Format: Full Service. **Networks:** ABC. **Founded:** 1922. **Formerly:** WDAP-AM (1924). **Operating Hours:** Continuous. **ADI:** Chicago (LaSalle), IL. **Key Personnel:** Wayne Vriesman, VP/General Mgr.; Tom Petersen, News Dir.; Dean Richards, Producer; Dave Eanet, Sports Dir.; Bob Kessler, Music Dir.; Robert Sparr, General Sales Mgr.; Mary June Rose, Program Dir.; Randy Eccles, Asst. Program Dir.; Jim Carollo, Chief Engineer. **Local Programs:** *The Bob Collins Show* 5 a.m. - 9 a.m.; *The Kathy & Judy Show* 9 a.m. - 2 p.m.; *The Spike O'Dell Radio Experiment* 2 p.m. - 6 p.m. **Wattage:** 50,000. **Ad Rates:** Advertising accepted; rates available upon request. **URL:** http://wgnradio.com.

8738 WGN-TV - 9
2501 Bradley Pl. Phone: (312)528-2311
Chicago, IL 60618 Fax: (312)528-6857

Format: Commercial TV. **Owner:** Tribune Broadcasting Co., 435 N. Michigan Ave., Chicago, IL 60611. **Founded:** Apr. 1948. **Operating Hours:** Continuous. **ADI:** Chicago (LaSalle), IL. **Key Personnel:** Peter Walker, V. Pres./Gen. Mgr., phone (773)883-3333, fax (773)528-6857; Jim Zerwekh, Station Mgr., phone (773)883-3450, fax (773)528-6857; Bob Ramsey, Program Dir., phone (773)883-3345, fax (773)472-0251; Steve Ramsey, Dir. of News, phone (773)883-3222, fax (773)528-6050; Marc Drazin, Dir. of Engineering, phone (773)883-3287, fax (773)528-9555; Mark Boe, Dir. of Sales, phone (773)883-3386, fax (773)248-2304; Jane Hayden, Dir. of Operations, phone (773)883-3401, fax (773)528-1357; Diana Dionisio, Publicity & Promotion Mgr., phone (773)883-3412, fax (773)477-4542. **Local Programs:** *The Bozo SHow*; *Chicago Cubs/Chicago White Sox/Chicago Bulls*; *News at Nine/News at Noon*. **Wattage:** 110 Kilowatts. **URL:** http://www.wgntv.com.

8739 WHPK-FM - 88.5
5706 S. University Ave. Phone: (773)702-8289
Chicago, IL 60637 Fax: (773)834-1488
E-mail: whpk@uchicago.edu

Format: Full Service; Eclectic. **Owner:** University of Chicago, 5801 S. Ellis Ave., Chicago, IL 60637, (312)702-1234. **Founded:** 1945. **Formerly:** WUCB-FM (1968). **Operating Hours:** Continuous. **ADI:** Chicago (LaSalle), IL. **Key Personnel:** Sandra Daindra, Station Mgr.; Ed Reno, Program Dir.; Ryan P. Jackson, Music Dir.; Sarah Mason, Promotions Dir.; Sam Leimer, Music Dir. **Wattage:** 100. **Ad Rates:** Noncommercial. **URL:** http://www.student.www.uchicago.edu/orgs/whpk-radio.

8740 WIND-AM - 560
625 N. Michigan Ave., Ste. 300 Phone: (312)751-5560
Chicago, IL 60611-3110 Fax: (312)664-2472

Format: Hispanic. **Owner:** Tichenor Media, 100 Crescent Ct., Dallas, TX 75201, (214)855-8882. **Founded:** 1927. **Operating Hours:** Continuous. **ADI:** Chicago (LaSalle), IL. **Key Personnel:** Lucy Diaz, Contact; Luis De Gonzalez, News Dir.; Luisa Torres, Program Dir.; Martha Muniz, Contact; Juan Montenegro, General Sales Mgr.; Chuck Brooks, General Mgr. **Wattage:** 5000. **Ad Rates:** $50-98 for 30 seconds; $62-118 for 60 seconds.

8741 WJCG-FM - 89
820 N. LaSalle Blvd. Phone: (312)329-4000
Chicago, IL 60610 Fax: (312)329-8980

Format: Religious. **Owner:** Moody Bible Institute, at above address. **Former name:** WMBY-FM. **Key Personnel:** Jeff Jacobsen, Station Mgr. **URL:** http://www.moody.edu.

8742 WJMK-FM - 104.3
180 N. Michigan Ave., Ste. 1200 Phone: (312)977-1800
Chicago, IL 60601 Fax: (312)855-1043
E-mail: wjmk.com

Format: Oldies. **Networks:** Unistar. **Founded:** 1961. **Formerly:** WJEZ-FM; WJJD-FM. **Operating Hours:** Continuous. **ADI:** Chicago (LaSalle), IL. **Key Personnel:** Harvey Pearlman, VP/Gen. Mgr.; Kevin Robinson, Program/Music Dir.; John Humi, Chief Engineer; Michelle Dirks, Promotions Dir.; Sheila Mulcahey, General Sales Mgr. **Local Programs:** *Big Mike Kelly* 10 a.m. - 3 p.m., Mike Kelly; *John Records Landecker Show* 5:30 a.m. - 10 a.m., Rick Kaempfer, Producer; *Scott Miller* 3 p.m. - 7 p.m., Scott Miller. **Wattage:** 4100 ERP. **URL:** http://wjark.com.

8743 WKKC-FM - 89.3
6800 S. Wentworth Ave. Phone: (773)602-5313
Chicago, IL 60621 Fax: (773)602-5532

Format: Full Service. **Networks:** Independent. **Owner:** Kennedy-King College, at above address, (312)962-3200. **Founded:** 1972. **Operating Hours:** 8 a.m.-midnight; 100% local. **ADI:** Chicago (LaSalle), IL. **Key Personnel:** Reggie Miles, phone (773)602-5537, rmilesWKKC@hotmail.com; Darryl Dennard, General Mgr., phone (773)602-5095. **Wattage:** 250. **Ad Rates:** $7.50 for 30 seconds; $15 for 60 seconds.

8744 WKQX-FM - 101.1
Merchandise Mart Plaza, Ste. 1700 Phone: (312)527-8348
Chicago, IL 60654 Fax: (312)245-0073

Format: Alternative/New Music/Progressive. **Networks:** Independent. **Founded:** 1948. **Operating Hours:** Continuous. **ADI:** Chicago (LaSalle), IL. **Key Personnel:** Chuck Hillier, General Mgr. **Wattage:** 8100.

8745 WLIT-FM - 93.9
150 N. Michigan Ave. Phone: (312)329-9002
Chicago, IL 60601 Fax: (312)346-2649

Format: Adult Contemporary. **Networks:** Independent. **Owner:** Viacom International Inc., 1515 Broadway, New York, NY 10036, (212)258-7120. **Founded:** 1956. **Formerly:** WLAK-FM (1989). **Operating Hours:** Continuous; 100% local. **ADI:** Chicago (LaSalle), IL. **Key Personnel:** Phil Redo, Vice President; Mark Edwards, Program Dir.; Kathleen Cahill, General Sales Mgr.; Julie Murphy, Contact; Terry O'Brien, Contact. **Wattage:** 4,600.

8746 WLS-AM - 890
190 N. State, 9th Fl. Phone: (312)984-0890
Chicago, IL 60601 Fax: (312)984-5305
E-mail: wlsam@aol.com

Format: News; Talk. **Networks:** ABC. **Owner:** Disney/ABC, Inc., at above address. **Founded:** 1924. **Operating Hours:** Continuous. **ADI:** Chicago (LaSalle), IL. **Key Personnel:** Zemira Jones, Contact. **Wattage:** 50,000. **Ad Rates:** WXCD-FM.

8747 WLS-TV - 7
190 N. State St. Phone: (312)750-7777
Chicago, IL 60601 Fax: (312)750-7557

Format: Commercial TV. **Networks:** ABC. **Owner:** Capitol Cities/ABC, Inc., 77 W. 66th St., New York, NY 10023, (212)456-7777. **Founded:** 1939. **Formerly:** WBKB-TV. **Operating Hours:** Continuous. **ADI:** Chicago (LaSalle), IL. **Key Personnel:** Emily L. Barr, Pres./General Mgr., phone (312)750-7000. **Wattage:** 55,000 visual; 11,200 audio. **URL:** http://www.abcnews.com/local/wls.

8748 WLUP-FM - 97.9
875 N. Michigan Ave., Ste. 3750 Phone: (312)440-5270
Chicago, IL 60611 Fax: (312)440-9896

Format: Album-Oriented Rock (AOR). **Networks:** Independent. **Formerly:** WSDM-FM. **Operating Hours:** Continuous. **ADI:** Chicago (LaSalle), IL. **Key Personnel:** Cristina Wilson-Ohr, Contact, phone (312)440-5270, fax (312)440-9377; Greg Solk, Program Dir. **Wattage:** 6000.

8749 WLUW-FM - 88.7
820 Michigan Ave. Phone: (312)915-6558
Chicago, IL 60611 Fax: (312)915-7095
E-mail: wluvradio@luc.edu

Format: Alternative/New Music/Progressive. **Networks:** ABC. **Owner:** Loyola University of Chicago, at above address. **Founded:** 1978. **Operating Hours:** Continuous. **ADI:** Chicago (LaSalle), IL. **Key Personnel:** Craig Kois, Station Mgr., phone (312)915-6557; Rob Creighton, Asst. Station Mgr./Program Dir., phone (312)915-6834; John Gleason, Sports Dir., phone (312)915-6558; Mati Johnson, Music Dir., phone (312)915-6559; Jennifer Lizak, Promotions Dir., phone (312)915-6831; Joy Austria, Director, phone (312)915-6558, fax (312)915-7095. **Wattage:** 100.

8750 WMAQ-AM - 670
455 Cityfront Plaza Phone: (312)670-6767
NBC Tower Fax: (312)245-6143
Chicago, IL 60611

Format: News. **Networks:** CNN Radio. **Owner:** Group W - Westinghouse Broadcasting, 888 7th Ave., New York, NY 10019, (212)307-3000. **Operating Hours:** Continuous. **ADI:** Chicago (LaSalle), IL. **Key Personnel:** Rick Starr, Contact; Weezie Kramer, V.P. & General Mgr.; Julie Roberts, Marketing Dir.; Jim Frank, News Dir.; Ron Suber, Controller; Julie Kirby, General Sales Mgr.; Greg Davis, Cheif Engineer; Chris Witting, Operations Mgr. **Wattage:** 50,000. **Ad Rates:** Advertising accepted; rates available upon request.

8751 WMAQ-TV - 5
NBC Tower Phone: (312)836-5555
454 N. Columbus Dr. Fax: (312)836-5520
Chicago, IL 60611-5555

Format: Commercial TV. **Networks:** NBC. **Operating Hours:** Continuous. **ADI:** Chicago (LaSalle), IL. **Key Personnel:** Robert Morse, Contact.

8752 WMBI-AM - 1110
820 N. LaSalle Dr. Phone: (312)329-4300
Chicago, IL 60610 Fax: (312)329-4468
Free: (800)356-6639
E-mail: wmbi@moody.edu

Format: Religious. **Networks:** Moody Broadcasting. **Owner:** Moody Bible Institute of Chicago, at above address. **Founded:** 1926. **Operating Hours:** Sunrise-sunset. **ADI:** Chicago (LaSalle), IL. **Key Personnel:** Bruce Everhart, Station Mgr., phone (312)329-4300, fax (312)329-4468, beverhar@moody.edu; Monte Larrick, News Dir., phone (312)329-8046, fax (312)329-4468. **Local Programs:** *Open Line*, Chris Fabry; *Prime Time America*, Jim Warren. **Wattage:** 5000. **Ad Rates:** Noncommercial.

8753 WMBI-FM - 90.1
820 N. LaSalle Blvd. Phone: (312)329-4300
Chicago, IL 60610 Fax: (312)329-4468
E-mail: wmbi@moody.edu

Format: Religious. **Networks:** Sun Radio; AP. **Owner:** Moody Bible Institute, at above address, Free: (800)356-6639. **Founded:** 1926. **Operating Hours:** Continuous. **ADI:** Chicago (LaSalle), IL. **Key Personnel:** Bruce Everhart, Station Mgr., phone (312)329-4300, fax (312)329-4468, beverhar@moody.edu; Monte Larrick, News Dir., phone (312)329-4468; Gerson Garcia, Hispanic Program Dir. **Local Programs:** *Midday Connection* 12:00 noon Monday-Friday, Beverly Upshaw, (312)329-4274, Fax (312)329-8016. **Wattage:** 100,000. **Ad Rates:** Noncommercial. **URL:** http://www.moody.edu.

8754 WMVP-AM - 1000
875 N. Michigan Ave., Ste. 3750 Phone: (312)440-5270
Chicago, IL 60611 Fax: (312)440-9896

Format: Sports; Talk. **Networks:** Independent. **Formerly:** WLUP-AM (1994); WCFL-AM. **Operating Hours:** Continuous. **ADI:** Chicago (LaSalle), IL. **Key Personnel:** Randy Friend, Contact; Mitch Rosen, Program Dir. **Wattage:** 50,000.

8755 WNIB-FM - 97.1
1140 W. Erie Phone: (312)633-9700
Chicago, IL 60622-5889 Fax: (312)633-9710

Format: Classical. **Founded:** 1955. **Operating Hours:** Continuous. **ADI:** Chicago (LaSalle), IL. **Key Personnel:** Sonia Florian, Manager; Ron Ray, Program Dir.; Steve Adler, Sales Mgr. **Wattage:** 8400.

8756 WNIZ-FM - 96.9
1140 W. Erie Phone: (312)633-9700
Chicago, IL 60622 Fax: (312)633-9710

Format: Classical. **Networks:** Independent. **Founded:** 1962. **Operating Hours:** 6 a.m.-midnight. **ADI:** Chicago (LaSalle), IL. **Key Personnel:** Sonia Florian, General Mgr. **Wattage:** 50,000.

8757 WNND-FM - 100.3
One Prudential Plz., Ste. 2780 Phone: (312)297-5100
Chicago, IL 60601 Fax: (312)297-5111

Format: Adult Contemporary. **Founded:** 1947. **Formerly:** WLOO-FM (1989); WPNT-FM (1997). **Operating Hours:** Continuous. **ADI:** Chicago (LaSalle), IL. **Key Personnel:** Chuck Williams, Vice Pres./General Mgr.; Mark Hamlin, Program Dir.; Sue Wekley, General Sales Mgr. **Wattage:** 50,000 ERP.

8758 WNUA-FM - 95.5
444 N. Michigan Ave., Ste. 300 Phone: (312)645-9550
Chicago, IL 60611 Fax: (312)645-9645

Format: Jazz. **Networks:** Independent. **Owner:** Pyramid Broadcasting, 99 Revere Beach Pkwy., Medford, MA 02155, (617)396-1430. **Founded:** 1959. **Formerly:** WDHF-FM (1986); WMET-FM; WRXR-FM. **Operating Hours:** Continuous; 100% local. **ADI:** Chicago (LaSalle), IL. **Key Personnel:** Ralph Sherman, Contact; Lee Hansen, Operations Mgr.; Suzyle Clair, Program Dir.; Bill Maylone, Chief Engineer; Charles Meyerson, News Dir.; Debbi Serrano, Office Mgr.; Charlie Meyerson, News Dir.; Debbi Serrano, Office Mgr. **Local Programs:** *City Voices* 8 a.m. Sunday; *Point of View* 8:30 a.m. Sunday; *Sunday Summit* 7 a.m. Sunday. **Wattage:** 8300.

8759 WOJO-FM - 105.1
625 N. Michigan Ave., 3rd Fl. Phone: (312)649-0105
Chicago, IL 60611-3110 Fax: (312)664-2472

Format: Hispanic. **Networks:** Independent. **Founded:** 1946. **Operating Hours:** Continuous. **ADI:** Chicago (LaSalle), IL. **Key Personnel:** Luis De Gonzalez, News Dir.; Chuck Brooks, General Mgr.; Jim Pagliai, General Sales Mgr.; Lucy Diaz, Contact; Martha Muniz, Contact; Alberto Augusto, Promotions Dir. **Wattage:** 6000. **Ad Rates:** $78-114 for 30 seconds; $97-142 for 60 seconds.

8760 WOUI-FM - 88.9
3300 S. Federal St. Phone: (312)567-3087
Chicago, IL 60616 Fax: (312)567-8930
E-mail: wov:@charlie.acc.iit.edu; woui@charlie.acc.iit.edu

Format: Alternative/New Music/Progressive; Urban Contemporary; Album-Oriented Rock (AOR). **Networks:** Independent. **Founded:** 1974. **Formerly:** WIIT-FM (1980). **Operating Hours:** 12 p.m-3 a.m.; 100% local. **ADI:** Chicago (LaSalle), IL. **Key Personnel:** Sam Shelton, Station Mgr.; Bryan Field, Program Dir.; Jason Annes, Music Dir.; Brian Kirby, Technical Dir. **Wattage:** 100. **Ad Rates:** Noncommercial. **URL:** http://www.iit.edu~ovi.

8761 WPWR-TV - 50
2151 N. Elston Ave. Phone: (312)276-5050
Chicago, IL 60614 Fax: (312)276-6477

Format: Commercial TV. **Networks:** United Paramount Network. **Owner:** Channel 50 TV Corp., at above address. **Founded:** 1982. **Operating Hours:** Continuous; 100% local. **ADI:** Chicago (LaSalle), IL. **Key Personnel:** Al Devaney, General Mgr.; Bob Minor, Chief Engineer; Tom Feie, Program Dir.; Sarah Horkavi, General Sales Mgr.

8762 WRCX-FM - 103.5
875 N. Michigan Ave., Ste. 4000 Phone: (312)861-8100
Chicago, IL 60611-1901 Fax: (312)440-9143

Format: Album-Oriented Rock (AOR). **Owner:** Evergreen Media Corp., at above address. **Founded:** 1994. **Formerly:** WRCX-FM. **Operating Hours:** Continuous. **ADI:** Chicago (LaSalle), IL. **Key Personnel:** Mike Fowler, Vice Pres./General Mgr.; Debbie Buckley, General Sales Mgr.; Lee Coleman, Local Sales Mgr.; Barbara Ficano, National Sales Mgr.; Kathy Holzman, NBD; Dave Richards, Program Dir.; Jo Robinson, Music Dir./Asst. Program Dir.; Natalie DiPietro, Promotions Dir.; Kate Darling, Marketing Dir.; Irma Blance, News Dir.; Bob Nowak, Traffic Dir.; Bob Fukuda, Chief Engineer; Johnetta Tyler, Controller. **Local Programs:** *Chris Payne's Chicago Rock*, Chris Payne, (312)8618100, Fax (312)4409143; *Lou Brutus Show*, Jim Gregg, (312)8618100, Fax (312)4409143. **Wattage:** 4300.

8763 WRZA-FM - 99.9
851 W. Grand Phone: (312)633-3800
Chicago, IL 60622 Fax: (312)733-2214

Format: Hispanic. **Founded:** 1962. **Formerly:** WBYG-FM (1984); WBUS-FM. **Operating Hours:** Continuous. **ADI:** Chicago (LaSalle), IL. **Key Personnel:** Joseph Antelo, Vice Pres./General Mgr. **Wattage:** 50,000. **Ad Rates:** $90 for 30 seconds; $150 for 60 seconds. WZCH-FM.

8764 WSBC-AM - 1240
4900 W. Belmont Ave. Phone: (773)282-WSBC
Chicago, IL 60641

Format: Gospel; Ethnic. **Owner:** Diamond Broadcasting, Inc., at above address. **Founded:** 1925. **Absorbed:** WCRW-AM (1996). **Operating Hours:** 6am-8:30am, 10am-3:30pm, 5pm-7pm, 8pm-10 pm, 11 pm-midnight. **ADI:** Chicago (LaSalle), IL. **Key Personnel:** Daniel R. Lee, President; Roy J. Bellavia, General Mgr.; Mark Nielsen, Chief Engineer. **Local Programs:** *Community Speaks*, Roy J. Bellavia, (312)282-WSBC. **Wattage:** 1000. **Ad Rates:** $12.80 for 30 seconds; $26 for 60 seconds.

8765 WSCR-AM - 1160
4949 W. Belmont Ave. Phone: (312)777-1700
Chicago, IL 60641 Fax: (312)777-5994

Format: Sports. **Networks:** CBS. **Owner:** Diamond Broadcasting, Inc., at above address. **Founded:** 1992. **Formerly:** WPNT-AM; WAIT-AM. **Operating Hours:** Continuous. **ADI:** Chicago (LaSalle), IL. **Key Personnel:** Harvey Wells, Vice President; Ron Gleason, Program/Sports Dir.; Jeffrey Schwartz, Operations Mgr.; Mike Alzamoran, Coordinating/Senior Producer. **Wattage:** 50,000 day, 5,000 night.

8766 WSNS-TV - 44
430 W. Grant Pl. Phone: (312)929-1200
Chicago, IL 60614 Fax: (312)929-8153

Format: Commercial TV. **Networks:** Telemundo. **Founded:** 1970. **Operating Hours:** 8 a.m.-1 a.m. **ADI:** Chicago (LaSalle), IL. **Key Personnel:** Jose Lamas, Station Mgr.

8767 WTAQ-AM - 1300
6012 S. Pulaski Rd. Phone: (312)284-8184
Chicago, IL 60629 Fax: (312)284-8134

Format: Hispanic. **Founded:** 1985. **Operating Hours:** Continuous. **ADI:** Chicago (LaSalle), IL. **Key Personnel:** Mary McEvilly-Hernandez, General Mgr.; Leon Martinez, News Dir.; Jose Alanis, Program Dir.; Maria Colunga, Promotions Mgr.; Nora Dominguez, Traffic Mgr. **Wattage:** 5,000. **Ad Rates:** $78 for 30 seconds; $92 for 60 seconds.

8768 WTTW-TV - 11
5400 N. St. Louis Ave. Phone: (773)583-5000
Chicago, IL 60625 Fax: (773)583-3046

Format: Public TV. **Networks:** Public Broadcasting Service (PBS). **Operating Hours:** 6 a.m.-2 a.m. **ADI:** Chicago (LaSalle), IL. **Key Personnel:** Bill McCarter, General Mgr. **URL:** http://www.wttw.com.

8769 WUSN-FM - 99.5
875 N. Michigan Ave., Ste. 1310 Phone: (312)649-0099
Chicago, IL 60611 Fax: (312)664-3999

Format: Country. **Networks:** Independent. **Founded:** 1940. **Operating Hours:** Continuous. **ADI:** Chicago (LaSalle), IL. **Key Personnel:** Steve Ennen, General Mgr.; Stephanie Bass, Contact. **Wattage:** 8,300.

8770 WVAZ-FM - 102.7
800 S. Wells, Ste. 250 Phone: (312)360-9000
Chicago, IL 60607 Fax: (312)360-9070

Format: Adult Contemporary; Urban Contemporary. **Networks:** ABC. **Owner:** Evergreen Media Corp, at above address, (312)951-7633, Fax: (312)951-7634. **Founded:** 1950. **Formerly:** WBMX-FM. **Operating Hours:** Continuous. **ADI:** Chicago (LaSalle), IL. **Key Personnel:** Don T. Moore, General Mgr.; Maxx Mynck, Program Dir.; Jamillah Muhammad, MD, Contact; Cris Wilson, General Sales Mgr. **Local Programs:** *Classic Chicago*, Herb Kent; *The Monds Squad* 3 - 7 p.m. Monday-Friday; *Nightmoods* 7 p.m. - midnight Monday-Friday, Mel Devonne. **Wattage:** 6000 ERP. **Ad Rates:** $500 per unit.

8771 WVMS-FM - 89.5
820 N. LaSalle Dr.
Chicago, IL 60610

Format: Religious. **Networks:** Moody Broadcasting; Sun Radio. **Owner:** Moody Bible Institute of Chicago, Inc., at above address. **Founded:** Nov. 23, 1958. **Operating Hours:** Continuous. **Key Personnel:** Dick Lee, Manager; Paul Carter, Asst. Manager; Gary Bittner, Music Dir. **Wattage:** 3000. **Ad Rates:** Noncommercial. **URL:** http://www.werf.mbn.org.

8772 WVON-AM - 1450
3350 S. Kedzie Ave. Phone: (773)247-6200
Chicago, IL 60623 Fax: (773)247-3343
E-mail: wvon@ix.netcom.com

Format: Talk; Religious. **Networks:** Mutual Broadcasting System; American Urban Radio; ABC. **Owner:** Midway Broadcasting Corp., at above address. **Founded:** 1979. **Formerly:** WXOL-AM (1984). **Operating Hours:** 10 p.m.-1 p.m. **ADI:** Chicago (LaSalle), IL. **Key Personnel:** Keshia Chavers, Program Mgr., keisha@wvon1450am.com; Toyia Baker, Producer, toyia@wvon1450am.com; Melody Spann, Gen.Mgr./President; Darryl Shelton, Sr. Acct. Exec., darryl@wvon1450am.com. **Local Programs:** *Cliff Kelley Show* 6:00 am - 10:00 am Monday-Friday, Keisha Chavers; *Mo In The Midday* 10:00 am - 1:00 pm Mon. thru Thurs., Toyia Baker; *On Target* 10:00 pm - 12:00 pm Monday-Friday, Lu Palmer. **Wattage:** 1000. **Ad Rates:** $75-85 per unit. **URL:** http://www.wvon1450am.com.

8773 WXAV-FM - 88.3
3700 W. 103rd St. Phone: (773)779-9858
Chicago, IL 60655 Fax: (312)779-9061

Format: Alternative/New Music/Progressive. **Owner:** Sisters of Mercy, 3700 W. 103rd St., Chicago, IL 60655, (773)298-3300. **Founded:** Oct. 1991. **Operating Hours:** 10 am-10 pm. **ADI:** Chicago (LaSalle), IL. **Key Personnel:** Don Pukala, General Mgr. **Wattage:** 150. **Ad Rates:** Noncommercial.

8774 WXCD-FM - 94.7
190 N State St. Phone: (312)984-9923
Chicago, IL 60601 Fax: (312)984-5357
E-mail: cd947@abc.com

Format: Classic Rock. **Networks:** ABC. **Founded:** May 1, 1997. **Formerly:** WKXK-FM (May 1, 1997); WLS-FM. **Operating Hours:** Continuous. **ADI:** Chicago (LaSalle), IL. **Key Personnel:** Zemira Jones, Pres./General Mgr., phone (312)984-5301; Bill Gamble, Program Dir.; Jeff Chardell, General Sales Mgr., phone (312)984-5289; Mark Campbell, Marketing and Promotion Dir.; Warren Shulz, Chief Engineer; Mark Cross, Business Mgr.; Vince Perez, National Sales Mgr. **Wattage:** 4400. **Ad Rates:** Advertising accepted; rates available upon request.

8775 WXRT-FM - 93.1
4949 W. Belmont Ave. Phone: (312)777-1700
Chicago, IL 60641 Fax: (312)777-5031
E-mail: comments@wxrt.com

Format: Album-Oriented Rock (AOR). **Networks:** Independent. **Owner:** Westinghouse/CBS Board, at above address. **Founded:** 1959. **Operating Hours:** Continuous. **ADI:** Chicago (LaSalle), IL. **Key Personnel:** Harvey Wells, Vice President; Norm Winer, Vice President; Patti Martin, Music Dir.; John Freberg, Engineer; Teri Gidwitz, Marketing Director; Marge Arnold, LSM; Sue Werley, LSM; Michael Damsky, General Sales Mgr.; Mark Neilsen, Chief Engineer. **Wattage:** 50,000. **URL:** www.wxrt.com.

8776 WYCC-TV - 20
7500 S. Pulaski Rd. Phone: (312)838-7880
Chicago, IL 60652 Fax: (312)581-2071

Format: Public TV. **Networks:** Public Broadcasting Service (PBS). **Founded:** 1983. **Operating Hours:** 6 a.m-midnight. **ADI:** Chicago (LaSalle), IL. **Key Personnel:** Eugene Williams, Station Mgr.; Gregory Slaughler, Business Mgr.; Don Rhodes, Chief Engineer. **Local Programs:** *Absolute Artistry*, Dale Sindt, Mailing contact; *Educate!*, Hanvind Rikaraj, Mailing contact; *First from Chicago*, Jan Thompson, Mailing contact.

8777 WYLL-FM - 106.7
Box 56889 Phone: (847)956-5030
Chicago, IL 60656 Fax: (847)956-5040

Format: Religious; Talk. **Owner:** Salem Media Corp., at above address. **Founded:** 1971. **Formerly:** WYEN-FM (1986). **Operating Hours:** Continuous. **ADI:** Chicago (LaSalle), IL. **Key Personnel:** John Timm, General Mgr., jtimm@wyll.com; Steve Bynum, Program Mgr.; Kelli Willis, Traffic Mgr.; Joyce Boudnek, Office Mgr., jboudnek@wyll.com. **Local Programs:** *Chicago Morning*, Ron Turner; *The Dick Staub Show*, Lori Solyom; *Sandy Rios Show*, Sandy Rios.

Wattage: 50,000. **Ad Rates:** $55-135 per unit. **URL:** http://www.wyll.com.

8778 WYSY-FM - 107.9
150 N. Michigan Ave., No. 1040 Phone: (312)920-9500
Chicago, IL 60601

Format: Adult Contemporary; Hispanic. **Networks:** Independent. **Operating Hours:** Continuous; 100% local. **ADI:** Chicago (LaSalle), IL. **Key Personnel:** Luis Diaz-Albortini, General Mgr.; Floria Alicea, Program Dir. **Wattage:** 50,000 ERP.

8779 WZRD-FM - 88.3
5500 North St. Louis Ave. Phone: (312)583-4780
Chicago, IL 60625 Fax: (312)794-6243
E-mail: wzrd@imagescape.com

Format: Eclectic. **Networks:** Pacifica. **Owner:** Northeastern Illinois University, at above address, (312)583-4050. **Founded:** 1972. **Operating Hours:** Variable. **ADI:** Chicago (LaSalle), IL. **Key Personnel:** Melissa Radja, Station Mgr.; Kimberly Hopp, Program Dir.; Phil McCracken, Music Dir. **Wattage:** 100. **URL:** http://www.imagescape.com/wzrd.

CHICAGO HEIGHTS, pop. 37,026.

Cook Co. (NE). 28 m S of Chicago. Manufactures steel, glass containers, railroad equipment, textiles, boxes, castings, school and steel furniture, tile accessories, asphalt products, road materials, chemicals, fertilizer; food processing plant; foundries. Truck farms.

8780 Chicago Standard News
Standard Newspapers
615 S. Halsted Phone: (708)755-5021
Chicago Heights, IL 60411 Fax: (708)755-5020
Publication E-mail: ssscn@usbol.com

Black community newspaper. **Subtitle:** Serving Chicago & South Suburbs. **Founded:** 1984. **Freq:** Weekly. **Print Method:** Offset. **Cols./Page:** 5. **Col. Width:** 11 picas. **Col. Depth:** 16 inches. **Key Personnel:** Lorenzo Martin, Editor and Publisher; Pat Rush Martin, Advertising Mgr. **Subscription Rates:** $30 individuals. **Remarks:** Accepts advertising. **URL:** http://standardnewspaper.com.
Ad Rates: BW: $873.60 **Circ:** 15,000
SAU: $21.84

8781 Journal of Irreproducible Results
JIR Publishers
PO Box 234 Phone: (708)758-3242
Chicago Heights, IL 60411 Fax: (708)758-3276
Publication E-mail: jir@interaccess.com

Journal of humor and satire. **Founded:** 1955. **Freq:** Bimonthly. **Print Method:** Offset. Uses mats. **Trim Size:** 8 1/2 x 11. **Cols./Page:** 2. **Col. Width:** 37 nonpareils. **Col. Depth:** 125 agate lines. **Key Personnel:** George H. Scherr, Editor; Jean Jacobs, Editorial Associate. **ISSN:** 0022-2038. **Subscription Rates:** $19.85 individuals; $32.00 institutions. **Remarks:** Accepts advertising.
Ad Rates: BW: $800 **Circ:** ‡5,000
4C: $1,750
PCI: $7

8782 Prairie State College Student Review
Prairie State College
202 S. Halsted St. Phone: (708)756-3110
Chicago Heights, IL 60411 Fax: (708)755-2587

Collegiate newspaper. **Founded:** 1958. **Freq:** Monthly. **Print Method:** Offset. **Cols./Page:** 4. **Col. Width:** 28 nonpareils. **Col. Depth:** 196 agate lines. **Key Personnel:** Glenn Moleferno, Editor; D.J. Ladwein, Advertising Mgr. **Remarks:** Accepts advertising.
Ad Rates: PCI: $13 **Circ:** (Not Reported)

8783 South Suburban Standard
Standard Newspapers
615 S. Halsted Phone: (708)755-5021
Chicago Heights, IL 60411 Fax: (708)755-5020
Publication E-mail: ssscsen@usbolcom

Black community newspaper. **Founded:** 1979. **Freq:** Weekly. **Print Method:** Offset. **Cols./Page:** 5. **Col. Width:** 11 picas. **Col. Depth:** 16 inches. **Key Personnel:** Lorenzo Martin, Publisher; Pat Rush Martin, Advertising Mgr. **Subscription Rates:** $30 individuals. **Remarks:** Accepts advertising. **URL:** http://www.standardnewspaper.com.
Ad Rates: GLR: $.56 **Circ:** 25,000
BW: $1,080
PCI: $13.50

CHILLICOTHE

Peoria Co. (NC). 5 m M of Rome.

8784 Chillicothe Bulletin
Times Newspapers, Inc.
1008 N. Fourth St. Phone: (309)274-2185
Chillicothe, IL 61523 Fax: (309)274-2741

Community newspaper. **Founded:** July 4, 1883. **Freq:** Weekly (Wed.). **Print Method:** Web offset. **Trim Size:** 21 1/2 x 12 5/8. **Cols./Page:** 6. **Col. Width:** 2 inches. **Col. Depth:** 21 1/2 inches. **Key Personnel:** Beth Gehrt, General Mgr./Editor; Heidi Whitman, Acct. Mgr.; Lisa Maricle, Office Mgr. **Subscription Rates:** $18.20 individuals; $20.80 out of area. **Remarks:** Accepts advertising.
Ad Rates: GLR: $12.05 **Circ:** Paid 2,700
BW: $850.11
PCI: $6.59

8785 Illinois Valley Advertiser
Times Newspapers, Inc.
1008 N. Fourth St. Phone: (309)274-2185
Chillicothe, IL 61523 Fax: (309)274-2741

Shopper. **Founded:** 1967. **Freq:** Weekly (Wed.). **Cols./Page:** 6. **Col. Width:** 2 inches. **Col. Depth:** 21 1/2 inches. **Key Personnel:** Beth Gehrt, General Mgr./Editor; Heidi Whitman, Acct. Mgr.; Lisa Maricle, Office Mgr. **Subscription Rates:** Free. **Remarks:** Accepts advertising.
Ad Rates: GLR: $0.30 **Circ:** Non-paid 4,252
BW: $788.19
4C: $1,048.19
PCI: $6.11

8786 Triax Cablevision
1102 N. 4th Fax: (309)274-3188
PO Box 334 Free: (800)443-1175
Chillicothe, IL 61523

Founded: 1982. **Key Personnel:** Gary Crosby, Contact. **Cities Served:** Various communities in Illinois and Wisconsin.: subscribing households 53,000.

CHRISTOPHER, pop. 3,100.

Franklin Co. (S). 12 m NW of West Frankfort. Coal mines. Agriculture.

8787 The Progress/Franklin Press
PO Box A Phone: (618)724-9423
Christopher, IL 62822 Fax: (618)724-9510

Community newspaper. **Founded:** 1904. **Freq:** Weekly (Thurs.). **Print Method:** Offset. **Cols./Page:** 6. **Col. Width:** 26 nonpareils. **Col. Depth:** 301 agate lines. **Key Personnel:** Danny Malkovich, Publisher, phone (618)438-5611. **Subscription Rates:** $21.95 individuals. **Remarks:** Accepts advertising. **Formerly**: The Progress. **Feature Editors:** Del Rea, *Saturday*, cstopher@intrnet.net.
Ad Rates: GLR: $5 **Circ:** ‡2,000
BW: $857.85
4C: $1107.85
SAU: $7

CICERO

Cook Co.

8788 Czechoslovak Herald
5906 W. 26th St. Phone: (708)863-1891
Cicero, IL 60804 Fax: (708)863-1893

General interest newspaper published in Czech, English, and Slovak. **Subtitle:** The Oldest Czechoslovak Newspaper in the World. **Founded:** May 1, 1891. **Freq:** Weekly. **Print Method:** Web offset. **Trim Size:** 10 3/16 x 16. **Cols./Page:** 4. **Col. Width:** 2 3/8 inches. **Col. Depth:** 16 inches. **Key Personnel:** Josef Kucera, Editor and Publisher; Rose Kucera, Advertising Mgr. **USPS:** 153-720. **Subscription Rates:** $75 by mail; $95 Canada; $115 other countries. **Remarks:** Color advertising not accepted. **Foreign language name**: Denni Hlasatel.
Ad Rates: GLR: $.46 **Circ:** Paid 10,000
BW: $400 Free 400
PCI: $10

8789 El Dia Newspaper
4818 W. 23rd Pl., Lower Level Phone: (708)652-6396
Cicero, IL 60650 Fax: (708)652-6653

Community newspaper (English, Spanish). **Founded:** 1984. **Freq:** Weekly (Fri.). **Print Method:** Broadsheet. **Trim Size:** 21 1/2 x 13. **Cols./Page:** 6. **Col. Width:** 2 inches. **Col. Depth:** 21 1/2 inches. **Key Personnel:** Jorge Arturo Montes De Oca, Publisher; Ana Maria Ugalde, Editor; Ana Maria Montes De Oca, Advertising Dir. **Subscription Rates:** $51 individuals.
Ad Rates: BW: $2,465.19 **Circ:** Paid 3,000
4C: $525 Free 27,000
SAU: $18.20
PCI: $19.11

8790 Mundo Hispano
2350 S. Cicero Ave. Phone: (708)780-8808
Cicero, IL 60804-2469 Fax: (708)780-8818

Spanish newspaper distributed in suburban Chicago. **Subtitle:** Mudno Hispano. **Founded:** Apr. 15, 1993. **Freq:** Weekly (Thurs.). **Print Method:** Web offset. **Trim Size:** 11 x 15. **Cols./Page:** 6. **Col. Width:** 1 5/8 inches. **Col. Depth:** 13 1/2 inches. **Key Personnel:** Elizabeth Quan Kiu Vazquez, Editor; Joseph A. Giarritano, Publisher. **Subscription Rates:** $45. **Remarks:** Accepts advertising.
Ad Rates: BW: $1200 **Circ:** Controlled 20,000
4C: $1,335
PCI: $17

8791 Nedelni Hlasatel
5906 W. 26th St. Phone: (708)863-1891
Cicero, IL 60804 Fax: (708)863-1893

Czech and Slovak language newspaper. **Subtitle:** Czechoslovak Daily Herald. **Founded:** 1891. **Freq:** Weekly. **Print Method:** Web offset. **Trim Size:** 10 3/16 x 16. **Cols./Page:** 4. **Col. Width:** 2 3/8 inches. **Col. Depth:** 16 inches. **Key Personnel:** Josef Kucera, Editor. **Subscription Rates:** $75. **Remarks:** Accepts advertising. **Also known as**: Denni Hlasatel.
Ad Rates: BW: $400 **Circ:** 10,000
PCI: $10

8792 Tele Guia de Chicago
Tele Guia Publications
3116 S. Austin Blvd. Phone: (708)656-6666
Cicero, IL 60804 Fax: (708)656-6679

Community newspaper (Spanish). **Founded:** July 1985. **Freq:** Weekly (Thurs.). **Print Method:** Web offset. **Trim Size:** 8 1/2 x 11. **Cols./Page:** 5. **Col. Width:** 1 1/2 inches. **Col. Depth:** 10 inches. **Key Personnel:** Maria Eugenia, Editor; Ezequiel Montes, Publisher. **Subscription Rates:** $65 individuals. **Remarks:** Accepts advertising.
Ad Rates: BW: $11,100 **Circ:** Paid 9,169
4C: $1,400 Non-paid 577

8793 WCEV-AM - 1450
5356 W. Belmont Ave. Phone: (773)282-6700
Chicago, IL 60641-4192 Fax: (773)282-0123

Format: Ethnic. **Networks:** Independent. **Owner:** Migala Communications Corp., at above address. **Founded:** 1979. **Operating Hours:** 1 pm-10 pm Mon.- Fri.; 1 pm-8:30 pm Sat.; 5 am-10 pm Sun. **ADI:** Chicago (LaSalle), IL. **Key Personnel:** Lucyna Migala, Program Dir.; Herman Rowe, Sales Mgr.; George Migala, Station Mgr. **Wattage:** 1000. **Ad Rates:** $40-55 for 30 seconds; $45-60 for 60 seconds.

CISSNA PARK, pop. 825.

Iroquois Co. (E). 40 m S of Kankakee. Silo, drain tile, building block factories; light industry. Grain, stock, dairy farms.

8794 News/Independent
119 W. Garfield Phone: (815)457-2245
Cissna Park, IL 60924-0008
Community newspaper. **Founded:** 1891. **Freq:** Weekly (Thurs.). **Print Method:** Offset. Uses mats. **Cols./Page:** 5. **Col. Width:** 23 nonpareils. **Col. Depth:** 224 agate lines. **Key Personnel:** Rick A. Baier, Editor and Publisher. **ISSN:** 0009-7543. **Subscription Rates:** $22. **Remarks:** Accepts advertising.
Ad Rates: GLR: $.75 **Circ:** ‡1,992
BW: $300
SAU: $4.50
PCI: $3.75

CLARENDON HILLS

8795 Airport Journal
PO Box 273 Phone: (847)318-6872
Clarendon Hills, IL 60514 Fax: (708)986-5010

Monthly newspaper serving the air transport industry in the Chicago area. **Founded:** 1980. **Freq:** Monthly. **Print Method:** Offset. **Trim Size:** 11 3/8 x 15 1/2. **Cols./Page:** 4. **Col. Width:** 2 3/8 inches. **Col. Depth:** 14 inches. **Key Personnel:** John Andrews, Editor and Publisher. **Subscription Rates:** $17. **Remarks:** Accepts advertising.
Ad Rates: PCI: $18 **Circ:** Paid ‡110
Non-paid ‡25,000

CLAYTON, pop. 889.

Adams Co. (W). 28 m NE of Quincy. Residential.

8796 Enterprise
Elliott Publishing, Inc.
202 E. State Phone: (217)593-6515
Camp Point, IL 62320 Fax: (217)593-7720

Newspaper. **Founded:** 1892. **Freq:** Weekly (Wed.). **Print Method:** Offset. **Cols./Page:** 5. **Col. Width:** 2 inches. **Col. Depth:** 16 inches. **Key Personnel:** Marcia Elliott, Editor; James Elliott, Publisher/Production Mgr. **Subscription Rates:** $12 individuals; $15 out of state. **Remarks:** Accepts advertising.
Ad Rates: GLR: $2.75 **Circ:** ‡293
BW: $378
SAU: $3.40

CLIFTON, pop. 1,390.

Iroquois Co. (E). 15 m S of Kankakee. Agriculture.

8797 Advocate
487 S. Main Phone: (815)694-2122
Clifton, IL 60927 Fax: (815)694-3770

Community newspaper. **Founded:** 1893. **Freq:** Weekly (Thurs.). **Print Method:** Offset. **Cols./Page:** 6. **Col. Width:** 19 nonpareils. **Col. Depth:** 224 agate lines. **Key Personnel:** Therese Simoneau, Editor and Publisher. **USPS:** 118-000. **Subscription Rates:** $12.95 individuals; $14.95 out of state. **Remarks:** Accepts advertising.
Ad Rates: GLR: $2 **Circ:** Paid ‡2,000
SAU: $3

CLINTON†, pop. 8,014.

De Witt Co. (C). 22 m N of Decatur. Nuclear power plant. Manufactures copper tubing, copper kitchen utensils, boxes, business forms, gasoline storage tanks, ceramic, lamps, metal buildings. Grain farms.

8798 Clinton Daily Journal
PO Box 615 Phone: (217)935-3171
Rte. 54 W. Fax: (217)935-6086
Clinton, IL 61727
General newspaper. **Founded:** 1908. **Freq:** Daily (eve.). **Print Method:** Offset. **Cols./Page:** 8. **Col. Width:** 9 picas. **Col. Depth:** 300 agate lines. **Key Personnel:** R. Michael Johnson, Editor; Terrie L. Baker, Publisher. **Subscription Rates:** $83 individuals. **Remarks:** Accepts advertising.
Ad Rates: PCI: $5.72 **Circ:** Paid ‡3,500
Non-paid ‡250

8799 Dewitt County Genealogical Society Quarterly
Dewitt County Genealogical Society
Box 632 Phone: (217)935-3493
Clinton, IL 61727-0632
Genealogical magazine. **Founded:** 1975. **Freq:** Quarterly. **Print Method:** Offset. **Trim Size:** 8 1/2 x 11. **Key Personnel:** Betty Adcock, Editor. **ISSN:** 0890-4456. **Subscription Rates:** $15 individuals; $4 single issue. **Remarks:** Advertising not accepted.
Circ: Controlled 200

8800 WHOW-AM - 1520
RR 2, Box 117M Phone: (217)935-2161
Clinton, IL 61727 Fax: (217)935-9600

Format: Country. **Owner:** Cornbelt Broadcasting Co., at above address. **Founded:** 1947. **Operating Hours:** Sunrise-sunset; 1% network, 99% local. **Key Personnel:** J.R. Livesay II, Contact; Betty Gross, Station Mgr.; Bill Ward, News Dir.; Betty Dellinger, Traffic Dir. **Local Programs:** *Coaches Corner*, Betty Gross, Mailing contact; *Press Box*, Betty Gross, Mailing contact; *Trad-e-o*, Betty Dellinger, Mailing contact. **Wattage:** 5000. **Ad Rates:** $9-12 for 30 seconds; $12-16.40 for 60 seconds. $6.75-$8 for 30 seconds; $9-$11 for 60 seconds; Combined advertising rates available with WHOW-FM.

8801 WHOW-FM - 95.9
RR 2, Box 117M Phone: (217)935-2161
Clinton, IL 61727 Fax: (217)935-9600

Format: Easy Listening. **Owner:** Cornbelt Broadcasting Co., at above address. **Founded:** 1947. **Operating Hours:** 6 a.m.-midnight; 1% network, 99% local. **Key Personnel:** Betty Dellinger, Traffic Dir.; J.R. Livesay II, PRS/Owner; Betty Gross, Station Mgr.; Betty Gross, Music Dir.; Bill Ward, News Dir. **Local Programs:** *High School Sports*, Betty Gross, Mailing contact; *Press Box*, Betty Gross, Mailing contact; *Trade-O*, Betty Dellinger, Mailing contact. **Wattage:** 3000. **Ad Rates:** $9-12 for 30 seconds; $12-16.40 for 60 seconds. $6.75-$8 for 30 seconds; $9-$11 for 60 seconds; Combined advertising rates available with WHOW-AM.

COAL CITY, pop. 3,028.

Grundy Co. (NE). 26 m SW of Joliet. Manufactures clothing, aerosol canned and chemical products, furniture. Coal mine and clay pits. Grain farms.

8802 The Braidwood Journal
The Free Press Newspapers
273 South Broadway Phone: (815)458-6246
PO Box 99 Fax: (815)634-2815
Coal City, IL 60416
Free: (800)750-0909
Publisher E-mail: wilfrepres@colint.com

Newspaper. **Founded:** 1959. **Freq:** Weekly (Wed.). **Print Method:** Offset. **Cols./Page:** 8. **Col. Width:** 21 nonpareils. **Col. Depth:** 294 agate lines. **Key Personnel:** Sheridan R. Bailey, Editor. **USPS:** 550-940. **Subscription Rates:** $18 individuals. **Remarks:** Accepts advertising.
Ad Rates: BW: $487.20 **Circ:** 1,125
SAU: $3.30
PCI: $2.90

8803 WYKT-FM - 105.5
195 Overton Rd. Phone: (815)458-2141
Coal City, IL 60416 Fax: (815)458-2154
Free: (888)528-1055

Format: Album-Oriented Rock (AOR). **Networks:** Independent. **Founded:** 1980. **Formerly:** WDND-FM. **Operating Hours:** Continuous. **Key Personnel:** Terry Marker, President; Ernest Cunnar, Vice Pres. & Gen. Mgr.; Michael Tomano, Music Dir.; David Bellah, Sales Marketing Mgr. **Wattage:** 3000. **Ad Rates:** $10-20 for 30 seconds; $12-25 for 60 seconds. **URL:** http://www.kat1055.com.

COLCHESTER, pop. 1,747.

McDonough Co. (W). 6 m W. of Macomb. State Park, recreation, camping area. Manufactures farm machinery. Grain and livestock farms. Hay.

8804 The Colchester Chronicle
118 E. Market St. Phone: (309)776-3700
PO Box 356
Colchester, IL 62326
Publisher E-mail: coelho@netins.net

Newspaper. **Founded:** 1951. **Freq:** Weekly (Wed.). **Print Method:** WEB. **Trim Size:** 11 1/2 x 13 1/2. **Cols./Page:** 5. **Col. Width:** 2 1/8 inches. **Col. Depth:** 13 inches. **Key Personnel:** Stacey Nicholas, Editor and Publisher, coelho@netins.net. **USPS:** 124-150. **Subscription Rates:** $13.50 individuals; $16 out of area. **Remarks:** Accepts advertising.
Ad Rates: BW: $178.75 **Circ:** 600
4C: $500
SAU: $3
PCI: $3

COLLINSVILLE, pop. 21,663.

Madison Co. (SW). 12 m NE of St. Louis, Mo. Race track, tourism. Cahokia mounds world heritage site. Manufactures food products, dresses and aprons. Agriculture.

8805 Collinsville Herald
Madison County Publications
113 E. Clay St. Phone: (618)344-0264
Collinsville, IL 62234 Fax: (618)344-3611

Community newspaper. **Founded:** 1879. **Freq:** Weekly (Thurs.). **Print Method:** Offset. **Cols./Page:** 6. **Col. Width:** 2 1/16 inches. **Col. Depth:** 21 1/2 inches. **Key Personnel:** Ed Gurney, News Editor; Marsha Dahm, General Mgr. **ISSN:** 0883-6574. **Subscription Rates:** $13 individuals; $15 in Illinois and Missouri; $21 other states. **Remarks:** Accepts advertising.
Ad Rates: BW: $1,074.48 **Circ:** ‡7,800
4C: $1,355.60
SAU: $8.32
PCI: $8.14

8806 Collinsville Herald-Journal
Madison County Publications
113 E. Clay St. Phone: (618)344-0264
Collinsville, IL 62234 Fax: (618)344-3611

Community newspaper. **Founded:** 1985. **Freq:** 3/week. **Print Method:** Offset. **Cols./Page:** 6. **Col. Width:** 26 nonpareils. **Col. Depth:** 308 agate lines. **Key Personnel:** Ed Gurney, News Editor; Marsha Dahm, General Mgr. **Subscription Rates:** Free. **Remarks:** Accepts advertising.
Ad Rates: GLR: $.58 **Circ:** Free ‡20,389
BW: $1,685.64
4C: $2,110.64
SAU: $13.06
PCI: $12.77

COLUMBIA, pop. 4,269.

Monroe Co. (SW). 14 m S of St Louis Mo. Stone quarries. Diversified farming.

8807 Monroe County Clarion Journal
Suburban Journal
212 W. Locust Phone: (618)281-4292
Columbia, IL 62236 Fax: (618)281-7693

Community newspaper. **Founded:** 1940. **Freq:** Weekly (Wed.). **Print Method:** Offset. **Cols./Page:** 6. **Col. Width:** 26 nonpareils. **Col. Depth:** 301 agate lines. **Key Personnel:** Craig Bonnett, Managing Editor. **Subscription Rates:** $17 individuals; $18 out of county. **Remarks:** Accepts advertising.
Ad Rates: GLR: $.25 **Circ:** Paid ‡316
BW: $706.20 Free ‡13,546
4C: $1,131.20
SAU: $5.35

COULTERVILLE

8808 Illinois Audubon
Illinois Audubon Society
PO Box 520
Coulterville, IL 62237

Magazine covering birds, wildlife, and conservation issues in Illinois for members. **Founded:** 1897. **Freq:** Quarterly. **Key Personnel:** Debbie Scott Newman, Editor. **ISSN:** 1061-9801. **Subscription Rates:** $20 individuals; $5 single issue. **Remarks:** Accepts advertising.
Circ: Combined 3,000

COUNTRY CLUB HILLS, pop. 14,676.

Cook Co. (NE). 3 m S of Oak Forest. Residential.

8809 Building Official and Code Administrator Magazine
BOCA International
4051 W. Flossmoor Rd. Phone: (708)799-2300
Country Club Hills, IL 60478 Fax: (708)799-4981
Publication E-mail: boca@bocai.org

Magazine on the building industry and construction code enforcement. **Founded:** 1952. **Freq:** Bimonthly. **Print Method:** Offset. **Trim Size:** 8 1/2 x 11. **Cols./Page:** 2 and 3. **Col. Width:** 42 and 27 nonpareils. **Col. Depth:** 140 agate lines. **Key Personnel:** Margaret M. Leddin, Managing Editor. **ISSN:** 0007-3547. **Subscription Rates:** $20 individuals. **Remarks:** Accepts advertising.
Ad Rates: BW: $1400 **Circ:** ‡14,000
4C: $2600

8810 Country Club Hills/Hazel Crest Star
Star Newspapers
6901 W 159th St. Phone: (708)802-8800
Tinley Park, IL 60477 Fax: (708)802-8899

Newspaper group serving 51 communities in Chicago's southern suburbs. **Founded:** 1890. **Freq:** Semiweekly (Thurs. and Sun.). **Print Method:** Offset. **Trim Size:** 13 3/4 x 23. **Cols./Page:** 6. **Col. Width:** 2 inches. **Col. Depth:** 21 1/2 inches. **Key Personnel:** Lester Sons, Editor; Norman Rosinski, Publisher; Jim Meidell, Advertising Mgr.; Jay Fredrickson; Jay Fredrickson. **Remarks:** Accepts advertising.
Ad Rates: GLR: $56.76 **Circ:** Thurs. 65,520
Sun. 68,788

CRETE

8811 Crete Record
Russell Publications
484 Cass St. Phone: (708)672-8843
Crete, IL 60417
Community newspaper. **Freq:** Weekly (Thurs.). **Cols./Page:** 5. **Col. Width:** 2 inches. **Col. Depth:** 16 inches. **Key Personnel:** Audrey DeMuth, Editor; Gilbert L. Russell, Publisher. **Remarks:** Accepts advertising.
Ad Rates: BW: $236 **Circ:** 2,100
PCI: $2.95

CREVE COEUR, pop. 6,230.

Tazewell Co. (NW).

8812 WHOI-TV - 19
500 N. Stewart St. Phone: (309)698-1919
Creve Coeur, IL 61611 Fax: (309)698-4819
Free: (800)568-4317
E-mail: whoi@aol.com

Format: Commercial TV. **Networks:** ABC. **Founded:** 1953. **Formerly:** WRAU-TV (1985). **Operating Hours:** 5 a.m. - 2 a.m. **ADI:** Peoria-Bloomington, IL. **Key Personnel:** John Hurley, General Mgr., phone (309)698-4819; Devoe Slisher, Program Mgr.; Otto Arcaute, Business Mgr. **URL:** http://www.whoi@aol.com.

CRYSTAL LAKE, pop. 18,590.

McHenry Co. (NE). 16 m N of Elgin. Manufactures twist drills, industrial laundry dryers, ceramic kelm, tools, concrete, switches, metal products, auto parts. Tool and dies; steel treating; engraving.

8813 Northwest Herald
Northwest Newspapers
7717 South Rt. 31
Crystal Lake, IL 60014

General newspaper. **Founded:** 1985. **Freq:** Mon.-Sun. (morn.). **Print Method:** Offset. **Trim Size:** 13 x 21. **Cols./Page:** 6. **Col. Width:** 2 1/8 inches. **Col. Depth:** 13 inches. **Key Personnel:** Mark Sweetwood, Editor; Robert A. Shaw, Publisher; Chris Golbeck, Advertising Mgr. **Subscription Rates:** $182 individuals. **Remarks:** Accepts advertising.
Ad Rates: BW: $2,918.16 **Circ:** Mon.-Sat. 33,572
4C: $4,044.16 Sun. 35,563
SAU: $23.16
PCI: $23.16

8814 Tartan
McHenry County College
8900 U.S. Highway 14 Phone: (815)455-3700
Crystal Lake, IL 60012-2761 Fax: (815)455-3999

Collegiate newspaper. **Founded:** 1968. **Freq:** Semimonthly. **Print Method:** Offset. **Trim Size:** 11 1/2 x 16. **Cols./Page:** 4. **Col. Width:** 14 picas. **Col. Depth:** 90 picas. **Key Personnel:** Patrick Connolly, Contact, phone (815)455-8570, fax (815)455-3762. **Subscription Rates:** Free. **Remarks:** Accepts advertising.
Ad Rates: BW: $100 **Circ:** Free ‡2,000
PCI: $5

8815 WAIT-AM - 850
8800 Rte. 14 Phone: (312)755-9248
Crystal Lake, IL 60012 Fax: (312)755-1059
Free: (888)755-9248

Format: Adult Contemporary. **Networks:** Independent. **Founded:** 1965. **Operating Hours:** Sunrise-sunset. **ADI:** Chicago (LaSalle), IL. **Key Personnel:** Rory Fraley, General Mgr.; Jim Hooker, Managing Partner; J.B. Hooker, Operations/Promotions Mgr.; Celeste Gerling, Traffic Mgr. **Wattage:** 2400.

8816 WZSR-FM - 105.5
8600 Rte. 14 Phone: (815)459-7000
Crystal Lake, IL 60012 Fax: (815)459-7027
E-mail: star105.com

Format: Adult Contemporary. **Networks:** Westwood One Radio. **Founded:** 1974. **Formerly:** WAIT-FM (1990). **Operating Hours:** Continuous. **ADI:** Chicago (LaSalle), IL. **Key Personnel:** J. B. Hooker, Operations Mgr.; Jim Hooker, General Mgr.; Celeste Gerling, Traffic Mgr. **Wattage:** 3000. **URL:** http://www.star105.com.

CUBA, pop. 1,648.

Fulton Co. (W). 38 m SW of Peoria. Coal mines. Stock and grain farms.

8817 Banner
Banner Publications, Inc.
111 S. 3rd St. Phone: (309)785-5058
PO Box 500 Fax: (309)785-5050
Cuba, IL 61427
Magazine covering sheep breeding programs. **Founded:** 1978. **Freq:** 9 issues per yer. **Trim Size:** 8 1/2 x 11. **Cols./Page:** 3. **Col. Width:** 14 picas. **Col. Depth:** 10 inches. **Key Personnel:** Greg Deakin, Editor and Publisher; Marilyn Carlson, Editor; Jan Bitner, Circulation Mgr. **ISSN:** 0194-7230. **Subscription Rates:** $18. **Remarks:** Accepts advertising.
Ad Rates: BW: $450 **Circ:** ‡3,500
4C: $850
PCI: $23

8818 Buyer's Guide Shopper
317 E. Jefferson Phone: (309)785-8500
PO Box 365 Fax: (309)785-4541
Cuba, IL 61427-0365
Publisher E-mail: advertiz@iconimaging.net

Shopper/weekly newspaper. **Founded:** 1947. **Freq:** Biweekly 2nd and 4th Tuesday. **Print Method:** Web. **Trim Size:** 11 x 17. **Cols./Page:** 5. **Col. Width:** 1 7/8 inches. **Col. Depth:** 16 inches. **Key Personnel:** David Reed, Editor and Publisher. **Remarks:** Accepts advertising.
Ad Rates: GLR: $.42 **Circ:** Paid ‡0
BW: $320 Free ‡4,838
SAU: $4
PCI: $4

DALLAS CITY, pop. 1,408.

Hancock Co. (W). On Mississippi River, 7 m E of Fort Madison, Iowa. Tourism. Manufactures moulding, modular homes; bee supplies, sand conditioning machines. Grain elevator. Commercial fisheries. Agriculture. Grain, cattle, tomatoes.

8819 Dallas City Enterprise
Box 455 Phone: (217)852-3511
Dallas City, IL 62330 Fax: (217)852-3528
Free: (888)432-NEWS
Publication E-mail: entrprse@netins.net

Community newspaper. **Founded:** Sept. 2, 1887. **Freq:** Weekly (Thurs.). **Print Method:** Web offset. **Cols./Page:** 7. **Col. Width:** 24 nonpareils. **Col. Depth:** 276 agate lines. **Key Personnel:** Susan Kempher, Editor and Publisher. **USPS:** 197-520. **Subscription Rates:** $19; $20 out of state. **Remarks:** Accepts advertising. **Formerly**: Dallas City Enterprise and Review.
Ad Rates: GLR: $.50 **Circ:** ‡1,600
BW: $329
4C: $479
SAU: $2.94
PCI: $2.94

DANVILLE†, pop. 38,985.

Vermilion Co. (E). 125 m S of Chicago. Manufactures artificial decorations, awnings, boxes, cartons, candy, canvas goods, casket hardware, castings, concrete blocks, fertilizer, fireworks, machine shop supplies, safety wearing apparel, uniforms, lift trucks, core binders, jackets, contract fillers, aerosol cans, cellulose casings, air conditioning equipment, diesel engine crank shaft forgings.

8820 Commercial-News
Gannett Co., Inc.
17 W. North St. Phone: (217)446-1000
Danville, IL 61833 Fax: (217)446-6648

General newspaper. **Founded:** 1866. **Freq:** Daily (eve.), Sat. and Sun. (morn.). **Print Method:** Offset. **Trim Size:** 13 1/2 x 22 3/4. **Cols./Page:** 6. **Col. Width:** 22 nonpareils. **Col. Depth:** 301 agate lines. **Key Personnel:** Denise Richter, Managing Editor; Charles E. Morris, Publisher; Carol Nichols, Advertising Dir.; Peg Pitchford, Circulation Dir.; Edison Amachree, Production Dir. **USPS:** 048-680. **Subscription Rates:** $135.20 individuals.
Ad Rates: GLR: $2.40 **Circ:** Mon.-Sat. ★**18,690**
BW: $5,353.50 Sun. ★**20,345**
4C: $5,687
SAU: $41.50

8821 Heritage of Vermilion County
Vermillion County Museum Society
116 N. Gilbert St. Phone: (217)442-2922
Danville, IL 61832
Journal covering local history in Illinois. **Founded:** 1965. **Freq:** Quarterly. **Print Method:** Offset. **Trim Size:** 8 1/2 x 11. **Key Personnel:** Donald G. Richter; Susan E. Richter. **ISSN:** 0018-0718. **Subscription Rates:** $10 individuals; $2.50 single issue. **Remarks:** Advertising not accepted.
Circ: Controlled ⊕**1,500**

8822 Danville Radio & TV
403 N. Logan Ave. Phone: (217)442-0751
Danville, IL 61832 Fax: (217)442-0866

Owner: Ken Bartlett, at above address. **Founded:** 1984. **Key Personnel:** Phillip R. Francis, Co-Owner; Kenneth W. Bartlett, Owner; Randall Raymer, Sales Mgr. **Cities Served:** Allerton, Longview, IL: subscribing households 155; 18 channels.

8823 Warner Cable of Danville
806 1/2 E. Main St., Ste. A Phone: (217)443-2941
Danville, IL 61832 Fax: (217)443-3907
Free: (800)367-4843

Key Personnel: Mary Ann Perkins, General Mgr.; Jennifer Munro, Office Mgr.; Stephen Schneider, Contact. **Cities Served:** subscribing households 16,000; 29 channels; 1 community access channel; 60 hours per week community access programming.

8824 WDAN-AM - 1490
1501 N. Washington Phone: (217)442-1700
Danville, IL 61832-2463 Fax: (217)431-1489

Format: Talk; News; Adult Contemporary; Sports. **Networks:** CBS. **Owner:** Newhoff Broadcasting, 3055 S. 4th St., Springfield, IL 62703, (217)528-3033. **Founded:** 1938. **Operating Hours:** Continuous; 30% network, 70% local. **ADI:** Springfield-Decatur-Champaign, IL. **Key Personnel:** Mike Hulvey, Station Mgr.; Bill Pickett, News Dir.; Scott Eisenhauer, Music Dir. **Wattage:** 1000. **Ad Rates:** $8 for 30 seconds; $15 for 60 seconds.

8825 WDNL-FM - 102.1
1501 N. Washington Phone: (217)442-1700
Danville, IL 61832 Fax: (217)431-1489
E-mail: carolw@soltec.net

Format: Adult Contemporary. **Networks:** Unistar; Westwood One Radio. **Owner:** Neuhoff Broadcasting, 3055 S. 4th St., Springfield, IL 62703, (217)528-3033, Fax: (217)787-9944. **Founded:** 1967. **Formerly**: WDAN-FM (1975). **Operating Hours:** Continuous; 5% Network, 95% Local. **ADI:** Springfield-Decatur-Champaign, IL. **Key Personnel:** Michael Hulvey, General Mgr., phone (217)442-1700, fax (217)431-1489; Carol Wade, Program Dir., carolw@soltec.net. **Wattage:** 50,000. **Ad Rates:** $12-20 for 30 seconds; $16-25 for 60 seconds. Combined advertising rates available with WDAN-AM, WRHK-FM. **URL:** http://www.wdnlfm.com.

8826 WIAI-FM - 99.1
PO Box 970 Phone: (217)443-5500
Danville, IL 61832 Fax: (217)443-6308

Format: Country. **Networks:** NBC. **Founded:** 1970. **Operating Hours:** Continuous. **ADI:** Springfield-Decatur-Champaign, IL. **Key Personnel:** Steven R. Keagle, Manager; Kathy Barnes, Office Mgr.; Mike Missledine, Program Dir.; Danny Ross, Farm Dir.; Pamela Ray, News Dir. **Wattage:** 50,000. **Ad Rates:** $21-45 per unit.

8827 WITY-AM - 980
PO Box 142 Phone: (217)446-1312
Danville, IL 61832 Fax: (217)446-1314

Format: Adult Contemporary. **Networks:** ABC. **Owner:** Vermilion Broadcasting Corp., at above address. **Founded:** 1953. **Operating Hours:** Continuous. **ADI:** Springfield-Decatur-Champaign, IL. **Key Personnel:** David Brown, General Mgr.; Bob Iverson, News Dir.; Linda Murphy, Sales Mgr.; Sheryll Jones, Office Mgr. **Wattage:** 1000. **Ad Rates:** $8-15 per unit.

DARIEN

8828 Darien Metropolitan
Press Publication
223 Main St. Phone: (630)739-2300
Lemont, IL 60439 Fax: (630)257-5640

Community newspaper. **Freq:** Weekly (Thurs.). **Cols./Page:** 4. **Col. Width:** 14.5 picas. **Col. Depth:** 16 inches. **Key Personnel:** Karen Walker, Editor; Robert Norfleet, Publisher. **Subscription Rates:** $8. **Remarks:** Advertising accepted; rates available upon request.
Circ: 4,400

8829 Editorial Pace
Derus Media Service, Inc.
7702 S. Cass Ave., Ste. 110 Phone: (630)960-4690
Darien, IL 60561-5080 Fax: (630)960-4695
Publication E-mail: derus@interaccess.com

Consumer advertising, marketing, and public relations and print media magazine (English and Spanish). **Founded:** 1955. **Freq:** Quarterly. **Trim Size:** 11 1/4 x 17. **Cols./Page:** 6. **Col. Width:** 20 nonpareils. **Col. Depth:** 224 agate lines. **Key Personnel:** Matt McGann, Editor/Administration. **Remarks:** Accepts advertising.
Ad Rates: GLR: $75 **Circ:** Controlled ‡10,000
BW: $3,000
4C: $7,500

DE KALB, pop. 33,099.

De Kalb Co. (N). 58 m W of Chicago. Northern Illinois University. Manufactures wire and wire products, pianos, bed springs, mattresses, women's cloth and fur trimmed coats, truck bodies, electric motors, road building equipment, canned food, tools, stoves. Hatchery. Dairy, stock, poultry, hybrid seed corn farms.

8830 Behavioral & Social Sciences Librarian
The Haworth Press, Inc.
University Library Phone: (815)753-9866
Northern Illinois Univ.
De Kalb, IL 60115
Publisher E-mail: getinfo@haworthpressinc.com

Journal focusing on all aspects of library information in the social and behavioral sciences. **Freq:** 2/year. **Trim Size:** 6x8 1/2. **Key Personnel:** David Lonergan, PhD, Editor; Bill Cohen,

PUB. **ISSN:** 0163-9269. **Subscription Rates:** $42 individuals; $90 institutions; $90 libraries. **Remarks:** Accepts advertising.
Ad Rates: BW: $300 **Circ:** 367

8831 Bulletin de la Societe Americaine de Philosophie de Langue Francaise
Societe Americaine de Philosophie de Langue Francaise
c/o Northern Illinois University Phone: (815)756-4639
635 Joanne Ln. Fax: (815)753-6302
De Kalb, IL 60115
Publisher E-mail: tc0cvmi@corn.cso.niu.edu

French language journal covering philosophy and literature. **Founded:** 1989. **Freq:** Semiannual. **Cols./Page:** 1. **Key Personnel:** C. Michael, Editor; R. Tourville, Treas. **Subscription Rates:** $18 individuals; $9 single issue. **Remarks:** Accepts advertising.
Ad Rates: BW: $100 **Circ:** (Not Reported)

8832 Crossroads
Southeast Asia Publications
Center for Southeastern Asian Studies Phone: (815)753-1981 Fax: (815)753-1776
Northern Illinois University
De Kalb, IL 60115
Free: (888)731-9599
Publisher E-mail: seap@niu.edu

Journal focusing on southeast Asian studies. **Subtitle:** An Interdisciplinary Journal of Southeast Asian Studies. **Founded:** 1983. **Freq:** Semiannual. **Trim Size:** 6 x 9. **Key Personnel:** Edwin Zehner, Editor, phone (815)753-5790. **ISSN:** 0741-2037. **Subscription Rates:** $20 individuals; $16 for agencies. **Remarks:** Accepts advertising.
Ad Rates: BW: $100 **Circ:** Paid 650

8833 The Daily Chronicle
Scripps League
2815 Barber Green Rd. Phone: (815)756-4841
PO Box 587 Fax: (815)756-2079
De Kalb, IL 60115
General newspaper. **Founded:** 1879. **Freq:** Daily (eve.), Sunday (morn.). **Print Method:** Offset. **Cols./Page:** 6. **Col. Width:** 22 nonpareils. **Col. Depth:** 301 agate lines. **Key Personnel:** Lloyd Pletsch, Editor; Roger N. Warkins, Publisher. **Subscription Rates:** $75 individuals. **Remarks:** Accepts advertising.
Ad Rates: GLR: $.90 **Circ:** Mon.-Fri. 10,616
BW: $1,440.93 Sun. 11,365
4C: $1,695.93
SAU: $12.55

8834 De Kalb Edition
For Formaulation Chemists-Only
216 W. State St.
Sycamore, IL 60178-1419

Community newspaper serving DeKalb County, IL. **Founded:** 1992. **Freq:** Weekly. **Cols./Page:** 6. **Col. Width:** 2 inches. **Col. Depth:** 2 inches. **Key Personnel:** Kim Kubiak, Editor. **Remarks:** Advertising accepted; rates available upon request.
Circ: Non-paid 22,000

8835 George Eliot—George Henry Lewes Studies
Northern Illinois University
De Kalb, IL 60115 Phone: (815)753-1857
Fax: (815)753-2003

Scholarly journal covering the works of George Eliot, G. H. Lewes and related writers. **Founded:** 1982. **Freq:** Semiannual. **Key Personnel:** Prof. W. Baker, Editor, wbaker@niu.edu; Prof. K. Wumack, Assoc. Editor, phone (814)949-5750, fax (814)949-5011, kaw16@psu.edu. **ISSN:** 0953-0754. **Subscription Rates:** $14 individuals. **Remarks:** Accepts advertising. **Former name**: George Eliot-G. H. Lewes Newsletter.
Circ: Combined 250

8836 Journal of Emotional and Behavioral Disorders
PRO-ED, Inc.
Dept. of Educational Psych., Counseling, & Special Education Phone: (815)753-8443
Northern Illinois University
Graham Hall
De Kalb, IL 60115-2854
Publisher E-mail: proedrd2@aol.com

Journal of special education. **Founded:** 1993. **Freq:** Quarterly. **Print Method:** Offset. **Trim Size:** 8 3/8 x 10 7/8. **Cols./Page:** 3. **Col. Width:** 2 2/8 inches. **Col. Depth:** 9 5/16 inches. **Key Personnel:** Michael Epstein, Editor; Douglas Cullinan, Editor; Donald Hammill, Publisher. **ISSN:** 1063-4266. **Subscription Rates:** $39; $110 other countries; $85 industry. **Remarks:** Accepts advertising. **Alt. Formats:** Microform.
Ad Rates: BW: $400 **Circ:** Paid ‡1,782
Non-paid ‡94

8837 The MidWeek
Siebrasse Publications, Inc.
PO Box 546 Phone: (815)758-0696
121 Industrial Dr.
De Kalb, IL 60115
Community newspaper. **Founded:** Apr. 5, 1967. **Freq:** Weekly (Wed.). **Print Method:** Offset. **Cols./Page:** 6. **Col. Width:** 9.5 picas. **Col. Depth:** 224 agate lines. **Key Personnel:** Charles Siebrasse, Publisher; Kathy Siebrasse, Pub./Ed. **Subscription Rates:** $78 individuals. **Remarks:** Accepts advertising.
Ad Rates: GLR: $.65 **Circ:** Free ‡30,000
BW: $1,440
4C: $1,784
SAU: $15
PCI: $15

8838 Music Reference Services Quarterly
The Haworth Press, Inc.
NIU Libraries Phone: (815)753-9856
De Kalb, IL 60115-2868 Fax: (815)753-2003
Publication E-mail: getinfo@haworth.com
Publisher E-mail: getinfo@haworthpressinc.com

Journal on music reference librarianship. **Founded:** 1992. **Freq:** Quarterly. **Trim Size:** 6x8 1/2. **Key Personnel:** William E. Studwell, Editor; H. Stephen Wright, Assoc. Editor, phone (815)753-9839. **ISSN:** 1058-8167. **Subscription Rates:** $32 individuals; $45 institutions; $75 libraries. **Remarks:** Accepts advertising.
Circ: 213

8839 Names
American Name Society
English Dept. Phone: (815)753-6627
Northern Illinois University Fax: (815)753-0606
De Kalb, IL 60115-2863
Language journal. **Subtitle:** A Journal of Onomastics. **Founded:** 1951. **Freq:** Quarterly. **Print Method:** Letterpress. **Trim Size:** 6 x 9. **Cols./Page:** 1. **Col. Width:** 48 nonpareils. **Col. Depth:** 110 agate lines. **Key Personnel:** Edward Callary, Editor, ecallary@niu.edu; Wayne H. Finke, Managing Editor, wayne_ finke@baruch.cuny.edu. **ISSN:** 0027-7738. **Subscription Rates:** $35 individuals; $40 institutions. **Remarks:** Advertising not accepted.
Circ: Paid 850

8840 The Northern Star
Northern Illinois University
Northern Illinois University Phone: (815)753-0101
Campus Life Bldg., Ste. 130 Fax: (815)753-0708
De Kalb, IL 60115
Publication E-mail: star@wpo.cso.niu.edu; star@wpo.cso.niu

Collegiate newspaper. **Founded:** 1899. **Freq:** Daily (morn.) (during the academic year). **Print Method:** Offset. **Trim Size:** 11 3/8 x 17. **Cols./Page:** 5. **Col. Width:** 2 inches. **Col. Depth:** 16 inches. **Key Personnel:** Kevin Wendt, Editor, phone (815)753-0105, kwendt@niu.edu; David Lipien, Advertising Mgr., phone (815)753-0107; Maria Krull, Advisor, phone (815)753-0707, mkrull@niu.edu; Jim Killam, Advisor, phone (815)753-4239, jkillam@niu.edu; Kara Pipitou, Editor, phone (815)753-9639. **Subscription Rates:** Free; $65 by mail. **URL:** http://www.star.niu.edu.
Ad Rates: PCI: $10.25 **Circ:** Free ‡16,000
Fri. 12,000

8841 Thresholds in Education
Thresholds in Education Foundation
LEPS/Foundation in Education Phone: (815)753-1561
427 Graham Hall Fax: (815)753-8750
De Kalb, IL 60115
Magazine covering future trends in education. **Founded:** Feb. 1975. **Freq:** Quarterly. **Print Method:** Offset. **Trim Size:** 8 1/2 x 11. **Cols./Page:** 3. **Key Personnel:** Byron F. Radebaugh, Exec. Editor. **ISSN:** 0196-9641. **Subscription Rates:** $20 individuals; $7.50 single issue. **Remarks:** Accepts advertising.
Ad Rates: BW: $200 **Circ:** ‡500

8842 WDEK-FM - 92.5
711 N. 1st St. Phone: (815)758-8686
De Kalb, IL 60115 Fax: (815)756-9723

Format: Contemporary Hit Radio (CHR); Top 40. **Networks:** Superadio. **Founded:** 1961. **Operating Hours:** Continuous. **Key Personnel:** Dianne Leifheit, General Mgr.; Keith Bansemer, Operations Mgr. **Wattage:** 20,000. **Ad Rates:** $35 for 60 seconds.

8843 WLBK-AM - 1360
711 N. 1st St. Phone: (815)758-8686
De Kalb, IL 60115 Fax: (815)756-9723
E-mail: mail@wlbk.com

Format: News; Talk. **Networks:** AP; Illinois Farm Bureau. **Founded:** 1947. **Operating Hours:** Continuous. **Key Personnel:** Dianne Leifheit, General Mgr.; Johnathan Stage, News Dir.; Jeff Palmero, Sports Dir. **Local Programs:** *Party Line* 8:35 am Monday-Friday, Katie Davis, Producer, (815)758-8686, Fax (815)756-9723. **Wattage:** 1000. **Ad Rates:** $35 for 60 seconds.

8844 WNIJ-FM - 90.5
NIU Broadcast Center Phone: (815)753-9000
801 N. 1st St. Fax: (815)753-9938
De Kalb, IL 60115-2854

Format: Public Radio; Jazz; News. **Networks:** National Public Radio (NPR). **Owner:** Northern Illinois University, at above address. **Founded:** 1991. **Operating Hours:** Continuous; 50% network; 50% local. **ADI:** Rockford, IL. **Key Personnel:** Michael Lazar, General Mgr.; John Hill, Music Dir.; Bill Drake, Operations Dir.; Robin Cross, Chief Engineer; Margaret Miller, Membership Dir.; Elaine Harrington, Development Dir. **Wattage:** 50,000. **Ad Rates:** Noncommercial.

8845 WNIU-FM - 89.5
NIU Broadcast Center Phone: (815)753-9000
801 N. 1st St. Fax: (815)753-9938
De Kalb, IL 60115-2854

Format: Public Radio; Classical. **Networks:** National Public Radio (NPR). **Owner:** Northern Illinois University, at above address. **Founded:** 1954. **Operating Hours:** Continuous; 25% network; 75% local. **ADI:** Rockford, IL. **Key Personnel:** Robin Cross, Chief Engineer; Bill Drake, Operations Dir.; Elaine Harrington, Development Dir.; Margaret Miller, Membership Director; Michael Lazar, General Mgr.; Eric Hradecky, Music Dir. **Wattage:** 50,000. **Ad Rates:** Noncommercial.

DECATUR†, pop. 94,081.

Macon Co. (C). On Lake Decatur, 38 m E of Springfield. Millikin University. Richland Community College. Manufactures earth moving tractors, tires, electronic equipment, plastics, carburetors, water and gas distribution systems, brass goods, steel tanks, rotary pumps, pressure valves, castings, women's garments. Corn, and soybean processing. Meat packing. Gasohol production.

8846 Decatur Voice of the Black Community
625 E. Wood St.
Decatur, IL 62523

Black community newspaper. **Founded:** 1968. **Freq:** Weekly. **Print Method:** Offset. **Trim Size:** 10 x 16. **Cols./Page:** 5. **Col. Width:** 2 inches. **Col. Depth:** 16 inches. **Key Personnel:** Horace G. Livingston, Jr., Publisher; Mildred Covington, Editor. **Subscription Rates:** $24. **Remarks:** Accepts advertising. **Formerly**: Decator Voice.
Ad Rates: BW: $400 **Circ:** Paid ‡16,000
4C: $800 Non-paid ‡3,000
PCI: $5

8847 Grain Journal
Grain Publications Inc.
2490 N. Water St. Phone: (217)877-9660
Decatur, IL 62526 Fax: (217)877-6647
Free: (800)728-7511

Trade magazine about grain elevators. **Subtitle:** The Voice of the Grain Industry. **Founded:** 1972. **Freq:** Bimonthly. **Print Method:** Offset. **Trim Size:** 8 1/4 x 10 7/8. **Cols./Page:** 3. **Col. Width:** 14 picas. **Col. Depth:** 10 inches. **Key Personnel:** Mark Avery, Publisher, mark@grainnet.com; Ed Zdrojewski, Editor, ed@grainnet.com; Deb Coontz, Sales Mgr., deb@grainnet.com. **ISSN:** 0274-7138. **Subscription Rates:** $40 individuals. **Remarks:** Accepts advertising. **URL:** http://www.grainnet.com.
Ad Rates: BW: $1,675 **Circ:** Paid 11,300
4C: $2,150

8848 Herald & Review
Herald & Review Newspapers
601 E. William St. Phone: (217)429-5151
PO Box 311 Fax: (217)421-6913
Decatur, IL 62525
Free: (800)453-3639
Publisher E-mail: hrnews@webmart.net

General newspaper. **Founded:** 1880. **Freq:** Mon.-Sun. (morn.). **Print Method:** Letterpress. **Cols./Page:** 6. **Col. Width:** 26 nonpareils. **Col. Depth:** 301 agate lines. **Key Personnel:** George Althoff, Editor; William K. Johnston, Publisher; Ken Elias, Retail Administration; Greg Sloan, Circulation Mgr.; Terre Engleton, Controller; Paul Rickman, Classified Mgr.; Terri Kuhle, Human Resources Mgr. **Subscription Rates:** $149.50 individuals. **Remarks:** Accepts advertising. **URL:** http://www.herald-review.com. **Feature Editors:** Carol Alexander, *Metro, News, Science, Suburban*; Steve Cahalan, *Consumer Affairs, Farm, Real Estate*; Damon Cain, *Photo*; Steve Cameron, *Sports*; Mike Carr, *Financial/Business, Real Estate, Rural Development*; Theresa Churchill, *Religion*; Burton Cole, *Education*; Bob Fallstrom, *Entertainment, Family, Fashion, Features, Food, Garden/Home, Lifestyle, Living, Movie, Music, Radio, Saturday, Society, TV, Travel, Women's*; Ron Ingram, *Automotive, Financial/Busi-*

ness, Rural Development; Dawn Morville, *Political*; Amy Ragsdale, *Environmental, Medical.*
Ad Rates: BW: $3,381.09 **Circ:** Mon.-Fri. ★**38,035**
4C: $3,878.09 Sat. ★**46,304**
SAU: $26.21 Sun. ★**46,947**

8849 Milling Journal
Country Journal Publishing Co., Inc.
3065 Pershing Ct. Phone: (217)877-9660
Decatur, IL 62526 Fax: (217)877-6647
Free: (800)728-7511

Trade magazine for the milling industry. **Founded:** 1992. **Freq:** Quarterly. **Print Method:** Sheetfed offset. **Trim Size:** 8 1/2 x 11. **Cols./Page:** 3. **Key Personnel:** Ed Zdrojewski, Editor, ed@grainnet.com; Deb Coontz, Advertising Mgr., deb@grainnet.com. **Subscription Rates:** $40 individuals. **Remarks:** Accepts advertising. **URL:** http://www.grainnet.com.
Ad Rates: BW: $450 **Circ:** Controlled 1,700
4C: $950

8850 Prairie Farmer
Farm Progress Companies
1301 E. Mound Rd. Phone: (217)877-9070
PO Box 3217 Fax: (217)877-9695
Decatur, IL 62524
Magazine covering commercial farming. **Founded:** 1841. **Freq:** 15/year. **Print Method:** Offset. **Trim Size:** 8 x 10 3/4. **Cols./Page:** 3. **Col. Width:** 2 1/8 inches. **Col. Depth:** 10 inches. **Key Personnel:** Thomas Budd, Publisher; Michael Wilson, Editor. **ISSN:** 0162-7104. **Subscription Rates:** $14 individuals.
Ad Rates: BW: $4,050 **Circ:** Paid 37,357
4C: $6,075 Non-paid 72,016
PCI: $160

8851 TCI
1275 N. Water St. Phone: (217)424-8455
Decatur, IL 62521 Fax: (217)429-0170

Founded: 1972. **Formerly**: UAE. **Cities Served:** Macon County, Forsyth, Long Creek, and Mount Zion, IL.

8852 WAND-TV - 17
904 Southside Dr. Phone: (217)424-2500
Decatur, IL 62525 Fax: (217)422-8203

Format: Commercial TV. **Networks:** ABC. **Owner:** LIN Broadcasting Corp., 1370 Ave. of Americas, New York, NY, (212)442-8203. **Formerly:** WTVP-TV (1966). **Operating Hours:** Continuous; 75% network, 25% local. **ADI:** Springfield-Decatur-Champaign, IL. **Key Personnel:** T. J. Vaughan, Pres./Gen. Mgr.; Lee Williams, News Dir.; Larry Katt, Vice Pres./Sales Dir.; Rod Whisenant, Local Sales; Mike Gross, National Sales; Jan Bell, Traffic Mgr.; Angie Rhodes, Business Mgr.; Pat Peters, Program Mgr.; Carol Thomas, Promotions Mgr. **URL:** http://www.wandtv.com.

8853 WDZ-AM - 1050
337 N. Water St. Phone: (217)423-9744
Decatur, IL 62523 Fax: (217)423-9764

Format: News; Talk; Sports. **Networks:** CNN Radio; Westwood One Radio. **Owner:** Prairieland Broadcasters, at above address. **Founded:** 1921. **Operating Hours:** Continuous. **ADI:** Springfield-Decatur-Champaign, IL. **Key Personnel:** Steve Bellinger, President; Brian Schimmel, General Mgr.; Jim Fleming, Program Dir. **Wattage:** 1000. **Ad Rates:** $13 for 30 seconds; $15 for 60 seconds.

8854 WDZQ-FM - 95.1
337 N. Water St. Phone: (217)429-9595
Decatur, IL 62523 Fax: (217)423-9764
E-mail: wdzq@midwest.net

Format: Contemporary Country. **Founded:** 1976. **Operating Hours:** Continuous. **ADI:** Springfield-Decatur-Champaign, IL. **Key Personnel:** Brian Schimmel, General Mgr. **Wattage:** 50,000. **Ad Rates:** $21 for 30 seconds; $26.25 for 60 seconds.

8855 WFHL-TV - 23
2510 Parkway Ct. Phone: (217)428-2323
Decatur, IL 62526 Fax: (217)428-6455
Free: (800)500-9345
E-mail: wfhl@midwest.net

Format: Commercial TV; Religious. **Networks:** Independent. **Owner:** Decatur Foursquare Broadcasting, Inc., at above address. **Founded:** 1984. **Operating Hours:** Continuous. **ADI:** Springfield-Decatur-Champaign, IL. **Key Personnel:** Mark Dreistadt, General Mgr.; Michael Jacobs, Traffic Mgr.; Jennifer Street, Promotions/Program Dir.; Leslie Kent, Development. **Local Programs:** *In Focus* 8:00 a.m.-10 p.m. Monday-Friday, Deanne Flaugher; *Touchpoint* Thursday, Dotty Fouse, Mailing contact. **Wattage:** 2 million. **Ad Rates:** $36 for 30 seconds; $72 for 60 seconds.

8856 WSOY-AM - 1340
1100 E. Pershing Rd. Phone: (217)877-5371
Decatur, IL 62526 Fax: (217)877-8777
Free: (800)500-WSOY
E-mail: y103@comcom.net

Format: Information; News; Talk. **Networks:** CBS. **Founded:** 1925. **Operating Hours:** Continuous; 90% local. **ADI:** Springfield-Decatur-Champaign, IL. **Key Personnel:** Carolyn Hilligoss, Contact; Jeff Daly, AM Program Director; Frank Konwinski, Engineer; Devan Robinette, FM Program Director; Craig Fata, News Dir.; Brian Schimmel, General Mgr.; Karl Cordes, FM Sales Manager. **Wattage:** 1000.

8857 WSOY-FM - 102.9
1100 E. Pershing Rd. Phone: (217)877-5371
Decatur, IL 62526 Fax: (217)877-8777
Free: (800)500-9769
E-mail: bigcordo@family-net.net

Format: Adult Contemporary. **Networks:** CBS; ABC. **Owner:** Pinnacle Broadcasting Co, 301 W. 57th St., Ste 43-C, New York, NY 10019, (212)247-1760, Fax: (212)459-0046. **Founded:** 1948. **Operating Hours:** Continuous. **ADI:** Springfield-Decatur-Champaign, IL. **Key Personnel:** Brian Schimmel, General Mgr.; Devan Robinette, Program Dir.; Karl Cordes, Sales Mgr. **Wattage:** 54,000. **Ad Rates:** $21-65 for 60 seconds. Combined advertising rates available with WSOY-AM, WDZQ-FM, WDZ-AM, WCZQ-FM.

DEERFIELD, pop. 17,430.

Lake Co. (NE). 25 m N of Chicago. Manufactures machinery, fabricated wire products, marking devices, metal doors, sash, semiconductor devices, dies, tools, musical instruments. Frozen food.

8858 Deerfield Review
Pioneer Press Newspapers
850 N. Milwaukee Ave. Phone: (847)680-6690
Vernon Hills, IL 60061 Fax: (847)573-2500

Community newspaper (tabloid). **Subtitle:** With News of Lincolnshire, Riverwoods, and Bannockburn. **Founded:** 1924. **Freq:** Weekly (Thurs.). **Print Method:** Offset. **Trim Size:** 11 x 14. **Cols./Page:** 5. **Col. Width:** 9 3/4 inches. **Col. Depth:** 12 3/4 inches. **Key Personnel:** Arnold Grahl, Editor; Paul Sassone, Managing Editor. **USPS:** 151-300. **Subscription Rates:** $32.95 individuals.
Circ: Thurs. ★**6,294**

8859 Law Office Economics & Management
Clark Boardman Callaghan
155 Pfingsten Rd. Phone: (708)948-7000
Deerfield, IL 60015 Fax: (708)948-9340
Free: (800)221-9428

Magazine covering law office economics and management topics for lawyers and legal administrators. **Founded:** 1960. **Freq:** Quarterly. **Key Personnel:** Paul S. Hoffman, Editor. **Remarks:** Advertising not accepted.
Circ: Paid 1,500

8860 Successful Dealer
Kona Communications, Inc.
707 Lake Cook Rd., Ste. 300 Phone: (847)498-3180
Deerfield, IL 60015 Fax: (847)498-3197
Free: (800)767-5662
Publication E-mail: truckbooks,@konacommunications.com

Trade magazine for dealers of heavy-duty truck and trailer dealers. **Founded:** 1978. **Freq:** Bimonthly. **Print Method:** Offset. **Trim Size:** 8 1/4 x 11. **Cols./Page:** 3. **Col. Width:** 13 picas. **Col. Depth:** 59 picas. **Key Personnel:** Denise Rondini, Editorial Dir./Assoc. Publisher, drondini@aol.com; James D. Moss, Publisher; John S. Dickson, National Sales Mgr. **ISSN:** 0161-6080. **Subscription Rates:** $50 individuals. **Remarks:** Accepts advertising.
Ad Rates: BW: $5,640 **Circ:** Controlled ‡19,134
4C: $8,465
PCI: $150

8861 Truck Parts & Service
Kona Communications, Inc.
707 Lake Cook Rd., Ste. 300 Phone: (847)498-3180
Deerfield, IL 60015 Fax: (847)498-3197
Free: (800)767-5662
Publication E-mail: truckbooks@konacommunications.com

Trade magazine for truck parts and service market. **Founded:** 1967. **Freq:** Monthly. **Print Method:** Offset. **Trim Size:** 8 1/4 x 11. **Cols./Page:** 3. **Col. Width:** 13 picas. **Col. Depth:** 59 picas. **Key Personnel:** David Zaritz, Editor; James D. Moss, Publisher; Denise L. Rondini, Managing Editor. **ISSN:** 0895-3856. **Subscription Rates:** $50 individuals. **Remarks:** Accepts advertising. **Formerly**: Heavy Duty Distribution.
Ad Rates: BW: $6,555 **Circ:** Controlled ‡24,578
4C: $9,695
PCI: $150

DELAVAN, pop. 1,973.

Tazewell Co. (NC). 18 m SE of Pekin. Manufactures feeds. Ready mix concrete. Tool and die works. Dairy, stock farms. Grain.

8862 The Delavan Times
314 Locust St. Phone: (309)244-7111
PO Box 199
Delavan, IL 61734
Community newspaper. **Founded:** Sept. 4, 1874. **Freq:** Weekly (Wed.). **Print Method:** Offset. **Cols./Page:** 6. **Col. Width:** 9.5 picas. **Col. Depth:** 224 agate lines. **Key Personnel:** Ruth Arnold Larimore, Editor and Publisher. **USPS:** 151-820. **Subscription Rates:** $16 individuals; $18 out of state. **Remarks:** Accepts advertising.
Ad Rates: BW: $153.60 **Circ:** ‡1,429
SAU: $5.11
PCI: $2

DES PLAINES, pop. 53,568.

Cook Co. (NE). 17 m NW of Chicago. Residential. Manufactures machine tools, steel strapping, fuses, cosmetics, electronics, photo copiers, chemicals, laundry equipment, cement blocks, nuclear instruments. Research Laboratories.

8863 AAA—Chicago Motor Club Home & Away
Home & Away Magazine
999 E. Touhy
Des Plaines, IL 60018-2798

Consumer magazine covering vacation and travel planning for members. **Freq:** Bimonthly. **Print Method:** Web offset. **Trim Size:** 7 7/8 x 10 7/8. **Remarks:** Advertising accepted; rates available upon request.
Circ: (Not Reported)

8864 Bridal Crafts
Clapper Publishing Co., Inc.
2400 Devon, Suite 375 Phone: (847)635-5800
Des Plaines, IL 60018-4618 Fax: (847)635-6311
Publication E-mail: 72567.1066@compuserve.com
Publisher E-mail: clappercom@compuserve.com

Craft magazine for bridal events. **Founded:** 1991. **Freq:** Annual. **Print Method:** Web offset. **Trim Size:** 8 x 10 1/2. **Cols./Page:** 3. **Col. Width:** 2 1/4 inches. **Col. Depth:** 10 inches. **Key Personnel:** Nona Piorkowski, Editor, npiorkowski@clapper.com; Stuart Hochwert, Advertising Mgr., shochwert@clapper.com; Toni Ballentine, Circulation Mgr., tballentine@clapper.com; Marie Clapper, Pres./Publisher, mclapper@clapper.com. **Subscription Rates:** $3.95 single issue. **Remarks:** Accepts advertising.
Ad Rates: BW: $1,407 **Circ:** Paid 52,066
4C: $1,754

8865 Building Design & Construction
Cahners Business Information
PO Box 5080 Phone: (847)635-8800
Des Plaines, IL 60017-5080 Fax: (847)390-2152
Publication E-mail: bkinross@cahners.com
Publisher E-mail: bkinross@cahners.com

Magazine on business and technology for the design and construction of commercial, institutional, and industrial buildings. **Subtitle:** The Magazine for the Building Team. **Founded:** 1950. **Freq:** Monthly. **Print Method:** Offset. **Trim Size:** 8 3/8 x 10 7/8. **Cols./Page:** 3 and 2. **Col. Width:** 27 and 40 nonpareils. **Col. Depth:** 140 agate lines. **Key Personnel:** Bill Kinross, Publisher, phone (847)390-2650, bkinross@cahners.com; John Gregerson, Editor-in-Chief, jgregerson@cahners.com. **ISSN:** 0007-3407. **Subscription Rates:** Free to qualified subscribers; $90 individuals. **Remarks:** Accepts advertising. **URL:** http://www.bdcmag.com.
Ad Rates: BW: $7,327 **Circ:** Non-paid ‡78,300
4C: $9,244

8866 Building Supply Home Centers
Cahners Business Information
1350 E. Touhy Ave. Phone: (847)635-8800
Des Plaines, IL 60018 Fax: (847)635-6856
Free: (800)446-6551
Publisher E-mail: bkinross@cahners.com

Magazine for owners, executives, and managers responsible for product selection and purchase, merchandising, marketing, and management within the building supply retail and home center market. **Subtitle:** The Magazine of Building Supply/Hardware Retailing. **Founded:** 1917. **Freq:** Monthly. **Print Method:** Offset. **Trim Size:** 8 x 10 3/4. **Cols./Page:** 2 and 4. **Col. Width:** 15 and 9.9 picas. **Key Personnel:** Craig A. Shutt,

Editor-in-Chief; Patricia Coleman, Publisher; Daniel E. Comiskey, Publisher. **ISSN:** 0890-9008. **Subscription Rates:** Free to qualified subscribers; $60 individuals. **Remarks:** Accepts advertising.
Ad Rates: BW: $5,625 **Circ:** Non-paid ‡51,305
4C: $7,025

8867 CabinetMaker
Chartwell Communications Inc.
380 E. Northwest Hwy. Phone: (847)390-6700
Des Plaines, IL 60016 Fax: (847)390-7100
Publication E-mail: http://www.cabinetmag.com

Trade magazine covering product design and production, including illustrations of kitchen cabinets and bath vanities. **Subtitle:** Indispensable Tool For The Cabinet Shop. **Founded:** 1987. **Freq:** 11/year. **Print Method:** Offset. **Trim Size:** 8 x 10 7/8. **Cols./Page:** 3 and 4. **Col. Width:** 13 and 8.5 picas. **Col. Depth:** 60 picas. **Key Personnel:** Bruce Plantz, Editor, phone (847)795-7699, bplantz@chartwell.com; S.L. Berliner, Publisher; Carole L. Widmayer, Advertising Mgr. **ISSN:** 1048-0196. **Subscription Rates:** Free to qualified subscribers; $40; $65 other countries. **Remarks:** Accepts advertising.
Ad Rates: BW: $2,395 **Circ:** Controlled 40,000
4C: $3,520

8868 Catholic Cemetery
National Catholic Cemetery Conference
710 N. River Rd. Phone: (847)824-8131
Des Plaines, IL 60016 Fax: (847)824-9608

Magazine on cemetery administration, maintenance, and equipment. **Founded:** 1949. **Freq:** Monthly. **Print Method:** Offset. **Trim Size:** 8 1/2 x 11. **Cols./Page:** 3 and 2. **Col. Width:** 26 and 40 nonpareils. **Col. Depth:** 133 agate lines. **Key Personnel:** Irene K. Pesce, Editor. **USPS:** 093-600. **Subscription Rates:** $35 individuals. **Remarks:** Accepts advertising.
Ad Rates: BW: $630 **Circ:** ‡2,060
4C: $680

8869 Construction Equipment
Cahners Business Information
1350 E. Touhy Ave. Phone: (847)635-8800
Des Plaines, IL 60018 Fax: (847)635-6856
Free: (800)446-6551
Publisher E-mail: bkinross@cahners.com

Magazine with information and ideas for managers of construction equipment and trucks. **Founded:** 1949. **Freq:** Monthly. **Print Method:** Offset. **Trim Size:** 7 7/8 x 10 1/2. **Cols./Page:** 3. **Col. Width:** 27 nonpareils. **Col. Depth:** 140 agate lines. **Key Personnel:** Kirk Landers, Editor, phone (847)390-2173, landers@cahners.com; Daniel Pels, pels@cahners.com. **Subscription Rates:** $80 Free to qualified subscribers; $10 single issue; $145 out of country. **Remarks:** Accepts advertising.
Ad Rates: BW: $7795 **Circ:** Controlled ‡80,021
4C: $9985

8870 Construction Products
Cahners Business Information
1350 E. Touhy Ave. Phone: (847)635-8800
Des Plaines, IL 60018 Fax: (847)635-6856
Free: (800)446-6551
Publisher E-mail: bkinross@cahners.com

Trade magazine for machinery, materials, and management tools. **Founded:** 1892. **Freq:** Bimonthly. **Print Method:** Offset. **Trim Size:** 10 7/8 x 14 3/4. **Cols./Page:** 3. **Col. Width:** 25 nonpareils. **Col. Depth:** 140 agate lines. **Key Personnel:** Michael J. Porcaro, Publisher; Tom Klemens, Editor. **Subscription Rates:** $34.95 individuals. **Remarks:** Accepts advertising.
Ad Rates: BW: $4,900 **Circ:** Non-paid 101,000
4C: $6,900

8871 Consulting-Specifying Engineer
Cahners Business Information
1350 E. Touhy Ave. Phone: (708)635-8800
Des Plaines, IL 60018 Fax: (708)635-9950
Publisher E-mail: bkinross@cahners.com

The integrated engineering magazine of the building construction industry. **Founded:** 1958. **Freq:** 13/year. **Print Method:** Offset. **Trim Size:** 7 7/8 x 10 1/2. **Cols./Page:** 3 and 2. **Col. Width:** 26 and 40 nonpareils. **Col. Depth:** 140 agate lines. **Key Personnel:** Paul E. Beck, Editor; Tim Kelly, V.P. & Publisher. **ISSN:** 0892-5046. **Subscription Rates:** $79.90 individuals. **Remarks:** Accepts advertising. **URL:** http://www.csemag.com. **Formed by the merger of:** Specifying Engineer; Consulting Engineer.
Ad Rates: GLR: $6,025 **Circ:** Controlled ‡47,508
BW: $5,580
4C: $7,300
PCI: $210

8872 Consumer Magazine Advertising Source
SRDS
1700 E. Higgins Rd., No. 500 Phone: (847)375-5000
Des Plaines, IL 60018 Fax: (847)375-5001
Free: (800)851-7737

Reference guide to current advertising rates and media information in consumer and agricultural magazines. **Founded:** 1919. **Freq:** Monthly. **Print Method:** Offset. **Trim Size:** 10 5/16 x 11. **Cols./Page:** 4. **Key Personnel:** Christopher M. Lehman, President and CEO; Kamy Rizzo, Publisher, krizz@srds.com. **ISSN:** 1071-4537. **Subscription Rates:** $587. **Remarks:** Accepts advertising. **Available Online. URL:** www.srds.com. **Alt. Formats:** CD-ROM. **Formerly:** SRDS Consumer Magazine and Agri-Media Rates and Data (1993); Consumer Magazine and Agri-Media Source.
Ad Rates: BW: $6,175 **Circ:** Paid 2,693
4C: $10,385

8873 Contractor Magazine
Cahners Business Information
PO Box 5080 Phone: (708)635-8800
Des Plaines, IL 60017-5080 Fax: (708)390-2690
Publisher E-mail: bkinross@cahners.com

Industry news and management how-to magazine for air conditioning, heating, plumbing and other mechanical specialties contracting firms. **Subtitle:** The Newsmagazine of Mechanical Contracting. **Founded:** 1954. **Freq:** Monthly. **Print Method:** Offset. **Trim Size:** 11 x 14 3/4. **Cols./Page:** 4. **Col. Width:** 24 nonpareils. **Col. Depth:** 196 agate lines. **Key Personnel:** Bob Miodonski, Editor; William F. Everham, Publisher. **ISSN:** 0897-7135. **Subscription Rates:** Free to qualified subscribers; $70 individuals. **Remarks:** Accepts advertising.
Ad Rates: BW: $5,590 **Circ:** Controlled 50,949
4C: $6,985

8874 Control Engineering
Cahners Business Information
1350 E. Touhy Ave. Phone: (847)635-8800
Des Plaines, IL 60018 Fax: (847)635-6856
Free: (800)446-6551
Publisher E-mail: bkinross@cahners.com

Magazine covering control and instrumentation systems. **Subtitle:** The Voice of the Control Industry. **Founded:** 1954. **Freq:** 15/year. **Print Method:** Offset. **Trim Size:** 8 x 10 3/4. **Cols./Page:** 3. **Col. Width:** 27 nonpareils. **Col. Depth:** 140 agate lines. **Key Personnel:** Michael Babb, Editor; Thomas H. Barry, Publisher; Susan Johnson, Production Mgr. **ISSN:** 0010-8049. **Subscription Rates:** Free to qualified subscribers; $75 institutions. **Remarks:** Accepts advertising.
Ad Rates: BW: $6,340 **Circ:** Controlled ‡100,095
4C: $7,940

8875 Converting Magazine
Cahners Business Information
1350 E. Touhy Ave. Phone: (847)635-8800
Des Plaines, IL 60018 Fax: (847)635-6856
Free: (800)446-6551
Publisher E-mail: bkinross@cahners.com

Magazine serving industries which convert paper, paperboard, plastic film and foil materials. **Founded:** 1983. **Freq:** Monthly. **Print Method:** Offset. **Trim Size:** 7 7/8 x 10 1/2. **Cols./Page:** 3. **Col. Width:** 26 nonpareils. **Col. Depth:** 140 agate lines. **Key Personnel:** Stephen D. Bowers, Publisher, phone (212)519-7220, sbowers@cahners.com; Mark Spaulding, Editor-in-Chief, phone (847)390-2337, m.spaulding@cahners.com. **ISSN:** 0746-7141. **Subscription Rates:** $82.90 individuals; $10 single issue. **Remarks:** Accepts advertising.
Ad Rates: GLR: $115 **Circ:** Controlled ‡44,414
BW: $4,825
4C: $6,530
PCI: $110

8876 Crafts 'N Things
Clapper Publishing Co., Inc.
2400 Devon, Ste. 375 Phone: (847)635-5800
Des Plaines, IL 60018-4618 Fax: (847)635-6311
Publication E-mail: 72567.1066@compuserve.com
Publisher E-mail: clappercom@compuserve.com

Craft magazine. **Founded:** 1975. **Freq:** 10/year. **Print Method:** Web offset. **Trim Size:** 8 x 10 1/2. **Key Personnel:** Nona Piorkowski, Editor, npiorkowski@clapper.com; Stuart Hochwert, Vice President, shochwert@clapper.com; Toni Ballentine, Circulation Mgr., tballentine@clapper.com; Marie Clapper, Publisher & President, mclapper@clapper.com. **ISSN:** 0146-6607. **Subscription Rates:** $19.97 individuals plus 2.00 postage & handling; $4.95 single issue. **Remarks:** Accepts advertising. **Available Online. URL:** http://www.craftnet.org/crafts-n-things.
Ad Rates: BW: $4,860 **Circ:** Paid ★274,052
4C: $7,335

8877 The Cross Stitcher
Clapper Publishing Co., Inc.
2400 Devon, Ste. 375 Phone: (847)635-5800
Des Plaines, IL 60018-4618 Fax: (847)635-6311
Publication E-mail: 72567.1066@compuserve.com
Publisher E-mail: clappercom@compuserve.com

Publication featuring cross stitch charts and designs. **Founded:** 1985. **Freq:** Bimonthly. **Print Method:** Web. **Trim Size:** 8 x 10 1/2. **Cols./Page:** 3. **Key Personnel:** B.J. McDonald, Editor, phone (512)251-3306, fax (521)251-3306, bjmcdonald@clapper.com; Stuart Hochwert, VP of Marketing & Sales, shochwert@clapper.com; Toni Ballentine, Circulation Mgr., tballentine@clapper.com; Marie Clapper, Publisher & President, mclapper@clapper.com. **ISSN:** 1055-2871. **Subscription Rates:** $14.97; $3.50 single issue. **Remarks:** Accepts advertising. **Available Online. URL:** http://www.craftnet.org/cross-stitcher.
Ad Rates: BW: $1,880 **Circ:** Paid 102,580
4C: $2,680

8878 Dairy Foods
Cahners Business Information
1350 E. Touhy Ave. Phone: (847)635-8800
Des Plaines, IL 60018 Fax: (847)635-6856
Free: (800)446-6551
Publisher E-mail: bkinross@cahners.com

Magazine featuring information on technologies, trends, and industry issues for dairy processors. **Founded:** Jan. 1899. **Freq:** Monthly. **Print Method:** Web offset. **Trim Size:** 7 7/8 x 10 3/4. **Key Personnel:** Dave Fusaro, Editor, phone (847)390-2417, fax (847)390-2445, dfusaro@cahners.com; Mike Flesch, Advertising Mgr., phone (847)390-2264. **ISSN:** 0888-0050. **Subscription Rates:** $99 individuals; $15 single issue. **Remarks:** Accepts advertising. **URL:** http://www.dairyfoods.com. **Formerly:** Dairy Record.
Ad Rates: BW: $5,060 **Circ:** Paid 656
4C: $6,990 Controlled 20,230

8879 Des Plaines Times
Pioneer Press Newspapers
130 S. Prospect Ave. Phone: (847)696-3133
Park Ridge, IL 60068 Fax: (847)696-3229

General newspaper. **Founded:** 1885. **Freq:** Weekly (Thurs.). **Print Method:** Offset. **Key Personnel:** Paul Sassone, Managing Editor; Craig Shaw, Editor. **Subscription Rates:** $18.95 by mail. **Remarks:** Advertising accepted; rates available upon request.
Circ: Thurs. ★3,594

8880 The DIAPASON
Scranton Gillette Communications, Inc.
380 E. Northwest Hwy., Ste. 200 Phone: (847)391-1000
Des Plaines, IL 60016-2282 Fax: (847)390-0408
Magazine devoted to pipe organ building, organ and church music performance, and repertoire. **Founded:** Dec. 1909. **Freq:** Monthly. **Print Method:** Offset. **Trim Size:** 9 3/4 x 14 1/4. **Cols./Page:** 4. **Col. Width:** 2 1/16 inches. **Col. Depth:** 13 inches. **Key Personnel:** Jerome Butera, Editor and Publisher, phone (847)391-1045; Wesley Vos, Assoc. Editor, phone (847)391-1044. **ISSN:** 0012-2378. **Subscription Rates:** $20 individuals; $6 single issue. **Remarks:** Color advertising not accepted.
Ad Rates: BW: $770 **Circ:** ‡5,100
PCI: $45

8881 Electronic Packaging & Production
Cahners Business Information
1350 E. Touhy Ave. Phone: (847)635-8800
Des Plaines, IL 60018 Fax: (847)635-6856
Free: (800)446-6551
Publisher E-mail: bkinross@cahners.com

Trade magazine. **Subtitle:** Manufacturing Innovations for Electronics.Worldwide. **Founded:** 1961. **Freq:** Monthly. **Print Method:** Offset. **Trim Size:** 7 7/8 x 10 1/2. **Cols./Page:** 3. **Col. Width:** 26 nonpareils. **Col. Depth:** 140 agate lines. **Key Personnel:** Donald E. Swanson, Editor; Randolph D. King, Publisher. **Subscription Rates:** Free to qualified subscribers. **Remarks:** Accepts advertising.
Ad Rates: BW: $4,780 **Circ:** Controlled ‡42,000
4C: $5,850
PCI: $165

8882 Energy User News
Cahners Business Information
1350 E. Touhy Ave. Phone: (847)635-8800
Des Plaines, IL 60018 Fax: (847)390-2618
Free: (800)446-6551

Magazine exreporting on the energy management market as it relates to commercial, industrial, and institutional facilites. **Founded:** 1976. **Freq:** Monthly. **Print Method:** Heat set web offset. **Trim Size:** 10 7/8 x 14 3/4. **Cols./Page:** 5. **Col. Width:** 1 7/8 inches. **Col. Depth:** 12 7/8 inches. **Key Personnel:** Chris Sullivan, Editor, phone (847)390-2183, fax (847)390-

2769; Tim Kelly, Publisher, phone (847)390-2730, fax (847)390-2769. **ISSN:** 0162-9131. **Subscription Rates:** $69.50. **Remarks:** Accepts advertising. **Online:** LEXIS-NEXIS. **URL:** http://energyusernews.com.
Ad Rates: BW: $4,200 **Circ:** Paid ★651
4C: $5,160 Non-paid ★40,321

8883 Financial Manager for the Media Professional
Broadcast Cable Financial Management Association
701 Lee St., No. 640 Phone: (847)296-0200
Des Plaines, IL 60016 Fax: (847)296-7510
Publication E-mail: mkuechel@bcfm.com
Publisher E-mail: info@bcfm.com

Trade magazine for professionals in the broadcast and cable industry. **Freq:** Bimonthly. **Trim Size:** 8 x 11. **Key Personnel:** Marie Kuechel, Editor. **Subscription Rates:** $49 individuals. **Remarks:** Accepts advertising. **Former name**: Broadcast Cable Financial Journal.
Ad Rates: BW: $985 **Circ:** Controlled 1,600
4C: $1,435

8884 Gas Abstracts Online
Institute of Gas Technology
1700 S. Mount Prospect Rd. Phone: (847)768-0673
Des Plaines, IL 60018
Publisher E-mail: publications@igt.org

Gas technology magazine reviewing U.S. and foreign journals and papers proceedings and conferences. **Founded:** 1945. **Freq:** Monthly. **Key Personnel:** P. Geith, Editor, geith@igt.org. **ISSN:** 0016-4844. **Subscription Rates:** $1100 five speciality databases; $650 extra password $350.00; $200 extra password $100.00; $295. **Remarks:** Advertising not accepted. **Online:** gasLine. **URL:** http://www.igt.org. **Alt. Formats:** Microform. **Former name**: Gas Abstracts.
Circ: (Not Reported)

Home & Away - See Chicago

8885 HOTELS
Cahners Business Information
1350 E. Touhy Ave. Phone: (847)635-8800
Des Plaines, IL 60018 Fax: (847)635-6856
Free: (800)446-6551
Publisher E-mail: bkinross@cahners.com

Magazine covering management and operations as well as foodservice and design in the hospitality industry. **Subtitle:** The Magazine of the Worldwide Hotel Industry. **Founded:** 1966. **Freq:** Monthly. **Print Method:** Offset. **Trim Size:** 8 3/8 x 10 7/8. **Cols./Page:** 4 and 3. **Col. Width:** 9.6 and 13 picas. **Key Personnel:** Jeff Weinstein, Editor, phone (847)390-2047, jweinstein@cahners.com; Tony Dela Cruz, Managing Editor, phone (847)390-2033; Dan Hogan, Publisher, phone (847)390-2977, dhogan@cahners.com. **ISSN:** 1047-2975. **Subscription Rates:** $93.90 individuals. **Remarks:** Accepts advertising.
Ad Rates: BW: $9,660 **Circ:** Non-paid 60,000
4C: $12,040

8886 Modern Baking
Donohue-Meehan Publishing Co.
2700 River Rd., Ste. 418 Phone: (847)299-4430
Des Plaines, IL 60018 Fax: (847)296-1968

Magazine on news, products, and trends of the baking industry. **Founded:** 1987. **Freq:** Monthly. **Print Method:** Offset. **Trim Size:** 8 x 10 7/8. **Key Personnel:** Ed Lee, Editor; Bill Donohue, Publisher. **ISSN:** 0897-6201. **Subscription Rates:** $60; Free to qualified subscribers. **Remarks:** Accepts advertising.
Ad Rates: BW: $3,750 **Circ:** Controlled ‡27,053
4C: $5,180

8887 Modern Casting Magazine
American Foundrymen's Society
505 State St. Phone: (847)847-0181
Des Plaines, IL 60016-8399 Fax: (847)824-7848
Free: (800)537-4237

Magazine on metal casting plants and pattern shops. **Founded:** 1938. **Freq:** Monthly. **Print Method:** Offset. **Trim Size:** 8 x 10 7/8. **Cols./Page:** 3. **Col. Width:** 26 nonpareils. **Col. Depth:** 140 agate lines. **Key Personnel:** David P. Kanicki, Publisher/CON; Dick Reynolds, Advertising Mgr.; Michael J. Lessiter, Editor; Rolf Petersen, Marketing Dir. **ISSN:** 0026-7562. **Subscription Rates:** $40 individuals; $5 single issue; $50 year; $75 by mail. **Remarks:** Accepts advertising.
Ad Rates: BW: $3,430 **Circ:** Paid 1,684
4C: $4,180 Controlled 24,806

8888 OCCurrence
Oakton Community College
1600 E. Golf Rd. Phone: (847)635-1678
Des Plaines, IL 60016-1256 Fax: (847)635-2610
Publication E-mail: reporter@oakton.edu

Collegiate newspaper. **Founded:** 1970. **Freq:** Bimonthly. **Print Method:** Offset. **Cols./Page:** 5. **Col. Width:** 26 nonpareils. **Key Personnel:** Scott Tharp, Editor-in-Chief; Steve Kacsmark, Production Editor. **Remarks:** Accepts advertising.
Ad Rates: BW: $375 **Circ:** Free ‡3,750
PCI: $8

8889 Pack-O-Fun
Clapper Publishing Co., Inc.
2400 Devon, Ste. 375 Phone: (847)635-5800
Des Plaines, IL 60018-4618 Fax: (847)635-6311
Publication E-mail: 72567.1066@compuserve.com
Publisher E-mail: clappercom@compuserve.com

Magazine devoted to family and group crafts and activities. **Subtitle:** Crafts, Games and Fun for Kids. **Founded:** 1951. **Freq:** Bimonthly. **Print Method:** Offset. **Trim Size:** 8 x 10 1/2. **Cols./Page:** 2. **Col. Width:** 27 nonpareils. **Col. Depth:** 102 agate lines. **Key Personnel:** Marie Clapper, President & Publisher, mclappercom@clapper.com; Billie Ciancio, Editor, bciancio@clapper.com; Stuart Hockwert, VP of Marketing & Sales, shockwert@clapper.com; Toni Ballentine, Circulation Mgr., tballentine@clapper.com. **ISSN:** 0030-901X. **Subscription Rates:** $14.97 individuals; $2.95 single issue. **Remarks:** Accepts advertising. **Available Online**. **URL:** http://www.craftnet.org/pack-o-fun. **Alt. Formats:** Microfiche; Microform.
Ad Rates: BW: $1,205 **Circ:** Paid ⊕120,717
4C: $1,735

8890 Packaging
Cahners Business Information
1350 E. Touhy Ave. Phone: (847)635-8800
Des Plaines, IL 60018 Fax: (847)635-6856
Free: (800)446-6551
Publisher E-mail: bkinross@cahners.com

Business trade magazine for the packaging field. **Subtitle:** For Buyers of Machinery, Materials, Supplies, Services. **Founded:** 1956. **Freq:** 13/year. **Print Method:** Web offset. **Trim Size:** 8 x 10 3/4. **Cols./Page:** 3. **Col. Width:** 13.4 picas. **Col. Depth:** 72 picas. **Key Personnel:** Greg Erickson, Editor; John Blatnik, Publisher. **ISSN:** 0746-3820. **Subscription Rates:** $84.95 individuals. **Remarks:** Accepts advertising.
Ad Rates: BW: $8,620 **Circ:** Paid 4,700
4C: $10,920 Controlled 111,600
PCI: $185

8891 Painting
Clapper Publishing Co., Inc.
2400 Devon, Suite 375 Phone: (847)635-5800
Des Plaines, IL 60018-4618 Fax: (847)635-6311
Publication E-mail: 72567.1066@compuserve.com
Publisher E-mail: clappercom@compuserve.com

Magazine for tole and decorative painters, featuring columns, and how-to and educational articles. **Founded:** 1985. **Freq:** Bimonthly. **Print Method:** Web. **Trim Size:** 8 x 10 1/2. **Cols./Page:** 2 and 3. **Col. Width:** 3 5/16 and 2 inches. **Col. Depth:** 10 inches. **Key Personnel:** Beth Browning, Editor, phone (407)870-2121, fax (407)932-1401, bbrowning@clapper.com; Marie Clapper, Publisher & President, mclapper@clapper.com; Stuart Hochwert, Vice President, shochwet@clapper.com. **ISSN:** 0888-076X. **Subscription Rates:** $19.95; $29.95 other countries. **Remarks:** Accepts advertising. **URL:** http://www.craftnet.org/painting. **Formerly**: Decorative Arts Digest (1992); Decorative Arts Painting.
Ad Rates: BW: $1,699 **Circ:** Paid ‡63,238
4C: $2,333

8892 Plant Engineering
Cahners Business Information
1350 E. Touhy Ave. Phone: (847)635-8800
Des Plaines, IL 60018 Fax: (847)635-6856
Free: (800)446-6551
Publisher E-mail: bkinross@cahners.com

Magazine focusing on engineering support and maintenance in industry. **Founded:** 1947. **Freq:** 13/year. **Print Method:** Offset. **Trim Size:** 8 x 10 3/4. **Cols./Page:** 3. **Col. Width:** 26 nonpareils. **Col. Depth:** 140 agate lines. **Key Personnel:** Richard Dunn, Editor, phone (847)390-2691, t.dunn@pe.cahners.com; Rick Schwer, Publisher, phone (847)390-2078. **ISSN:** 0032-082X. **Subscription Rates:** Free to qualified subscribers. **Remarks:** Accepts advertising.
Ad Rates: BW: $10,000 **Circ:** Controlled ‡116,700
4C: $11,000

8893 Pollution Engineering
Cahners Business Information
1350 E. Touhy Ave. Phone: (847)635-8800
Des Plaines, IL 60018 Fax: (847)635-6856
Free: (800)446-6551
Publisher E-mail: bkinross@cahners.com

Magazine focusing on pollution control, air, water, solid waste, and toxic/hazardous waste. **Subtitle:** The Magazine of Global Environmental Control. **Founded:** 1969. **Freq:** Semimonthly. **Print Method:** Offset. **Trim Size:** 8 x 10 7/8. **Cols./Page:** 3 and 2. **Col. Width:** 30 and 42 nonpareils. **Col. Depth:** 140 agate lines. **Key Personnel:** John Krukowski, Editor-in-Chief. **Subscription Rates:** $49.95 individuals. **Remarks:** Accepts advertising.
Ad Rates: BW: $4,710 **Circ:** Controlled ‡58,000
4C: $5,840
PCI: $90

8894 Process Heating
Business News Publishing Co., Inc.
3150 River Rd., No. 101 Phone: (847)297-3727
Des Plaines, IL 60018 Fax: (847)297-8371
Publication E-mail: processhtg@aol.com

Trade magazine covering industrial heat processing to 1000 degrees Fahrenheit. **Founded:** May 1994. **Freq:** 10/year. **Print Method:** Web offset. **Trim Size:** 8 1/8 x 10 7/8. **Cols./Page:** 3. **Col. Width:** 2 1/4 inches. **Key Personnel:** Anne Armel, Publisher; Linda Becker, Editor; Janice Saltz, Production Mgr., phone (847)297-3763, fax (847)297-3618. **ISSN:** 1077-5870. **Subscription Rates:** $39 individuals; $5 single issue. **Remarks:** Accepts advertising. **URL:** http://www.process-heating.com.
Ad Rates: BW: $3,895 **Circ:** Controlled 25,000
4C: $5,190
PCI: $100

8895 Professional Builder
Cahners Business Information
1350 E. Touhy Ave.
Des Plaines, IL 60018
Publisher E-mail: bkinross@cahners.com

Subtitle: The Magazine of the Housing and Light Construction Industry. **Founded:** 1936. **Freq:** Monthly. **Print Method:** Offset. **Trim Size:** 7 x 10. **Cols./Page:** 3. **Col. Width:** 39 picas. **Col. Depth:** 140 agate lines. **Key Personnel:** Jay McKenzie, Publisher, phone (847)390-2155, jmckenzie@cahners.com; Jim Carper, Editor, phone (847)390-2112. **ISSN:** 0885-8020. **Subscription Rates:** $10 single issue; $139.95 by mail. **Remarks:** Accepts advertising. **URL:** http://www.probuilder.com. **Alt. Formats:** CD-ROM, House Plans.
Ad Rates: BW: $6,870 **Circ:** 122,000
4C: $9,730 Controlled 140,018

8896 Professional Safety
American Society of Safety Engineers
1800 E. Oakton St. Phone: (847)699-2929
Des Plaines, IL 60018-2187 Fax: (847)296-3769
Free: (800)380-7101
Publisher E-mail: customerservice@asse.org

Magazine focusing on professional safety, risk management, and loss prevention. **Subtitle:** Journal of the American Society of Safety Engineers. **Founded:** 1956. **Freq:** Monthly. **Print Method:** Offset. Uses mats. **Trim Size:** 8 1/4 x 11 1/4. **Cols./Page:** 3. **Col. Width:** 26 nonpareils. **Col. Depth:** 140 agate lines. **Key Personnel:** Neal Lorenzi, Editor, nlorenzi@asse.org. **ISSN:** 0099-0027. **Subscription Rates:** $60 individuals; $5.50 single issue. **Remarks:** Accepts advertising. **Alt. Formats:** Microfiche.
Ad Rates: BW: $2,250 **Circ:** ‡32,000
4C: $3,685
PCI: $60

8897 R & D Magazine
Cahners Business Information
1350 E. Touhy Ave. Phone: (847)635-8800
Des Plaines, IL 60018 Fax: (847)390-2618
Free: (800)446-6551

Magazine serving research scientists, engineers, and technical managers. Reports significant advances, problems, and trends that affect the performance, funding, and adminstration of applied research and development. **Founded:** 1950. **Freq:** Monthly. **Print Method:** Offset. **Trim Size:** 7 7/8 x 10 1/2. **Cols./Page:** 3 and 2. **Col. Width:** 26 and 40 nonpareils. **Col. Depth:** 140 agate lines. **Key Personnel:** Tim Studt, Editor-in-Chief, phone (847)390-2623, t.studt@cahnrs.com; Robert Cassidy, Publisher, phone (847)380-2771, r.cassidy@cahners.com; Patricia Miller, Business Mgr. **ISSN:** 0746-9179. **Subscription Rates:** $79.90 individuals; $136.95 institutions, other countries; $10 single issue. **Remarks:** Accepts advertising. **URL:** http://www.rdmag.com. **Also known as**: Research & Development.
Ad Rates: BW: $9,430 **Circ:** Controlled 90,0230
4C: $11,415

8898 Restaurants & Institutions
Cahners Business Information
1350 E. Touhy Ave. Phone: (847)635-8800
Des Plaines, IL 60018 Fax: (847)635-6856
Free: (800)446-6551
Publication E-mail: riedit@cahners.com
Publisher E-mail: bkinross@cahners.com

Magazine focusing on foodservice and lodging management. **Subtitle:** Serving the total foodservice industry. **Founded:** 1937. **Freq:** Semimonthly. **Print Method:** Web offset. **Trim**

Size: 8 x 10 3/4. **Cols./Page:** 3 and 2. **Col. Width:** 26 and 58 nonpareils. **Col. Depth:** 140 agate lines. **Key Personnel:** Patricia Dailey, Editor-in-Chief, phone (847)390-2028, fax (847)390-2031, pdailey@cahners.com. **ISSN:** 0273-5520. **Subscription Rates:** $99.95 individuals. **Remarks:** Accepts advertising. **URL:** http://www.rimag.com.
Ad Rates: BW: $10,715 **Circ:** Non-paid ★**171,888**
4C: $12,605

8899 Roads & Bridges Magazine
Scranton Gillette Communications, Inc.
380 E. Northwest Hwy., Ste. 200 Phone: (847)391-1000
Fax: (847)390-0408
Des Plaines, IL 60016-2282
Publication E-mail: rdsnbrdgs@aol.com

Magazine containing information on highway, road, and bridge design, construction, and maintenance for government agencies, contractors, and consulting engineers. **Founded:** 1892. **Freq:** Monthly. **Print Method:** Offset. **Cols./Page:** 3. **Col. Width:** 26 nonpareils. **Col. Depth:** 140 agate lines. **Key Personnel:** Larry Flynn, Editor; Douglas B. Hebbard, Publisher. **Subscription Rates:** Free to qualified subscribers. **Remarks:** Advertising accepted; rates available upon request. **Formerly:** Rural and Urban Roads.
Circ: Controlled ‡71,000

8900 SECURITY
Cahners Business Information
1350 E. Touhy Ave. Phone: (847)635-8800
Des Plaines, IL 60018 Fax: (847)635-6856
Free: (800)446-6551
Publication E-mail: security@cahners.com
Publisher E-mail: bkinross@cahners.com

Magazine presenting news and technology for loss prevention and asset protection. **Subtitle:** For Buyers of Security Products, Systems, and Services. **Founded:** 1964. **Freq:** Monthly. **Print Method:** Offset. **Trim Size:** 8 3/8 x 10 7/8. **Cols./Page:** 3. **Col. Width:** 13.4 picas. **Col. Depth:** 66 agate lines. **Key Personnel:** Bill Zalud, Editorial Dir., phone (847)390-2371, bzalud@cahners.com; Steve Brackett, Publisher, phone (847)390-2978, sbrackett@cahners.com. **ISSN:** 0890-8826. **Subscription Rates:** $80 individuals; $10 single issue. **Remarks:** Accepts advertising. **URL:** http://www.secmag.com. **Formerly:** Security World.
Ad Rates: BW: $5,280 **Circ:** Controlled ‡38,836
4C: $6,805
PCI: $210

8901 Seed World
Scranton Gillette Communications, Inc.
380 E. Northwest Hwy, Ste. 200 Phone: (847)391-1034
Des Plaines, IL 60016-2282 Fax: (847)390-0408
Publication E-mail: gpnbeth@aol.com

Magazine for breeders, retailers, wholesalers, brokers, conditioners and growers of flower, vegetable, grain, forage and turf seeds. **Subtitle:** Serving the Seed Marketers of the World. **Founded:** 1915. **Freq:** Monthly. **Print Method:** Offset. **Trim Size:** 8 x 10 3/4. **Cols./Page:** 3 and 2. **Col. Width:** 2 1/8 and 3 inches. **Col. Depth:** 10 inches. **Key Personnel:** Ed Gillette, Publisher; Beth Meneghini, Editor, gpnbeth@aol.com. **ISSN:** 0037-0797. **Subscription Rates:** $25 individuals; $35 other countries. **URL:** www.seedworld.com. **Alt. Formats:** Microform.
Ad Rates: BW: $1,095 **Circ:** Paid 1,493
4C: $1,790 Non-paid 3,649
PCI: $40

8902 Semiconductor International
Cahners Business Information
1350 E. Touhy Ave. Phone: (847)635-8800
PO Box 5080 Fax: (847)390-2770
Des Plaines, IL 60017-5080
Publisher E-mail: bkinross@cahners.com

Magazine profiling semiconductor manufacturing issues. **Subtitle:** The Industry's Source Book for Processing, Assembly & Testing. **Founded:** 1978. **Freq:** Monthly. **Trim Size:** 8 x 10 3/4. **Cols./Page:** 3. **Key Personnel:** D.E. Swanson, Editorial Dir. **Subscription Rates:** Free to qualified subscribers. **Remarks:** Accepts advertising.
Ad Rates: BW: $5,805 **Circ:** Paid 1,015
4C: $7,255 Non-paid 45,541
PCI: $235

8903 Water Engineering & Management
Scranton Gillette Communications, Inc.
380 E. Northwest Hwy., Ste. 200 Phone: (847)391-1000
Fax: (847)390-0408
Des Plaines, IL 60016-2282
Publication E-mail: wem@mci.com

Trade magazine dedicated to the advancement of the state of the art and the transfer of technology in the field of municipal, county and regional water supply and water pollution control. Serves consulting sanitary engineers and managers of water/wastewater facilities who specify/buy products and services. **Founded:** 1882. **Freq:** Monthly. **Print Method:** Offset. **Trim Size:** 8 x 10 3/4. **Cols./Page:** 3. **Col. Width:** 26 nonpareils. **Col. Depth:** 140 agate lines. **Key Personnel:** Nanette Traetow, Publisher. **ISSN:** 0273-2238. **Subscription Rates:** $40 individuals; $6 single issue; $64 two years; $150 two years other countries. **Remarks:** Accepts advertising. **URL:** http://www.waterem.com.
Ad Rates: BW: $3850 **Circ:** Paid 3,648
4C: $4900 Non-paid 37,442

8904 Water & Wastes Digest
Scranton Gillette Communications, Inc.
380 E. Northwest Hwy., Ste. 200 Phone: (847)391-1000
Fax: (847)390-0408
Des Plaines, IL 60016-2282
Magazine (tabloid) featuring product news for decision makers in the municipal and industrial water and water pollution control industries. **Freq:** Bimonthly. **Print Method:** Offset. **Trim Size:** 11 x 16. **Cols./Page:** 3. **Col. Width:** 3 3/8 inches. **Col. Depth:** 15 inches. **Key Personnel:** Gail Hanczar, Editor; Ian Lisk, Exec. Editor; Wesley D. Shoup, Publisher; LaMay Eide, Advertising Mgr. **Subscription Rates:** $10 individuals; $13 other countries; $2 single issue.
Circ: Non-paid ‡100,332

DIVERNON, pop. 1,081.

Sangamon Co. (C). 18 m S of Springfield. Agriculture. Wheat, corn, oats and soybeans.

8905 Divernon News
South County Publications
110 N. 5th St. Phone: (217)483-2614
Auburn, IL 62615 Fax: (217)438-6155

Community newspaper. **Founded:** 1898. **Freq:** Weekly (Thurs.). **Print Method:** Offset. **Cols./Page:** 7. **Col. Width:** 23 nonpareils. **Col. Depth:** 301 agate lines. **Key Personnel:** Joseph Michelich, Jr., Editor; Connie Michelich, Advertising Mgr. **Subscription Rates:** $20 individuals.
Ad Rates: SAU: $3.50 **Circ:** 400
PCI: $2.75

DIXON†, pop. 16,000.

Lee Co. (N). 100 m W of Chicago. Manufactures cement, paper bags, automotive parts, plastic products, shoes, electronic parts, metal specialties, dairy products, cereals, stock feed, candy, cheese, condensed milk, garage doors. Sand, gravel pits. Hatcheries. Stock, poultry, grain farms.

8906 The Telegraph
Dixon Telegraph Inc.
113-115 S. Peoria Ave. Phone: (815)284-2222
Dixon, IL 61021 Fax: (815)284-2870

Newspaper with Report orientation. **Founded:** 1851. **Freq:** Daily and Sunday. **Print Method:** Offset. **Cols./Page:** 6. **Col. Width:** 26 nonpareils. **Col. Depth:** 301 agate lines. **Key Personnel:** Wm. E. Shaw, Publisher; J.W. Nelson, General Mgr. **USPS:** 158-860. **Subscription Rates:** $129.85 individuals. **Remarks:** Accepts advertising.
Ad Rates: BW: $1224.21 **Circ:** Mon.-Sat. 9,904
4C: $1414.21
SAU: $9.49

8907 WIXN-AM - 1460
1460 S. College Ave. Phone: (815)288-3341
Dixon, IL 61021 Fax: (815)284-1017

Format: Oldies. **Networks:** ABC. **Founded:** 1961. **Key Personnel:** Allan L. Knickrehm, Contact; Steve Marco, Program Dir. **Wattage:** 1000.

DONGOLA, pop. 1,000.

Union Co. (S).27 m N of Cairo. Meat processor. Livestock. Diversified farming. Peaches, sweet potatoes, tomatoes, melons. Grain.

8908 Dongola Tri-County Record
130 Front St. Phone: (618)827-4353
Box 189
Dongola, IL 62926
Newspaper. **Founded:** 1932. **Freq:** Weekly (Thurs.). **Print Method:** Offset. **Cols./Page:** 6. **Col. Depth:** 21 inches. **Key Personnel:** Burman P. Eddleman, Editor and Publisher. **USPS:** 159-820. **Subscription Rates:** $16 individuals; $18 out of area. **Remarks:** Accepts advertising.
Ad Rates: BW: $452.34 **Circ:** ‡1,040
SAU: $3.59
PCI: $3.08

DORSEY

8909 Weight Engineering
Society of Allied Weight Engineers, Inc.
c/o Robert W. Ridenour
4814 Loop Rd.
Dorsey, IL 62021
Publisher E-mail: saweedge@king.cts.com

Journal of the Society of Allied Weight Engineers, Inc. **Subtitle:** International Journal. **Founded:** 1941. **Freq:** Triennial. **Print Method:** Offset. **Trim Size:** 8 1/2 x 11. **Cols./Page:** 2. **Col. Width:** 3 1/4 inches. **Col. Depth:** 9 1/4 inches. **Key Personnel:** Robert W. Ridenour, Contact. **Subscription Rates:** Free to qualified subscribers; $30 individuals; $10 single issue. **Remarks:** Advertising accepted; rates available upon request. **Formerly:** Journal of Weight Engineering.
Circ: Controlled ‡1,000

DOWNERS GROVE, pop. 39,274.

Du Page Co. (NE). 21 m SW of Chicago. Residential. Manufactures spiral bevel gears, fabricated metal products, plastic molds and coils, condensers, bearings, chain conveyors, construction equipment, boiler feed systems. Nurseries. Dairy, poultry, truck farms.

8910 Clarendon Hills Progress
Reporter/Progress Newspapers
922 Warren Ave. Phone: (630)969-0188
Downers Grove, IL 60515 Fax: (630)969-0228

Suburban community newspaper (tabloid). **Founded:** 1969. **Freq:** Weekly (Thurs.). **Print Method:** Offset. **Trim Size:** 11 1/2 x 17. **Cols./Page:** 5. **Col. Width:** 22 nonpareils. **Col. Depth:** 16 inches. **Key Personnel:** C.J. Winter, Editor and Publisher; P.K. Winter, Publisher; Edward Rooney, Advertising Mgr. **Subscription Rates:** $19 individuals. **Remarks:** Accepts advertising.
Ad Rates: BW: $439.20 **Circ:** Thurs. ♦**826**
4C: $939.20
PCI: $5.49

8911 Darien DuPage Progress
Reporter/Progress Newspapers
922 Warren Ave. Phone: (630)969-0188
Downers Grove, IL 60515 Fax: (630)969-0228

Suburban community newspaper (tabloid). **Founded:** 1969. **Freq:** Weekly (Thurs.). **Print Method:** Offset. **Trim Size:** 11 1/2 x 17. **Cols./Page:** 5. **Col. Width:** 11 picas. **Col. Depth:** 16 inches. **Key Personnel:** C.J. Winter, Editor and Publisher; P.K. Winter, Publisher; Edward Rooney, Advertising Mgr. **Subscription Rates:** $19 individuals. **Remarks:** Accepts advertising.
Ad Rates: BW: $636.00 **Circ:** Thurs. ♦**9,097**
4C: $1,136.00
PCI: $7.95

8912 Downers Grove Reporter
Reporter/Progress Newspapers
922 Warren Ave. Phone: (630)969-0188
Downers Grove, IL 60515 Fax: (630)969-0228

Suburban community newspaper (tabloid). **Founded:** 1883. **Freq:** Semiweekly (Wed. and Fri.). **Print Method:** Offset. **Trim Size:** 11 1/2 x 17. **Cols./Page:** 5. **Col. Width:** 11 picas. **Col. Depth:** 16 inches. **Key Personnel:** C.J. Winter, Editor; Jack Winter, Publisher; Pat Winter, Publisher; Edward Rooney, Advertising Mgr. **Subscription Rates:** $25 individuals.
Ad Rates: GLR: $14.75 **Circ:** Wed. ♦**5,381**
BW: $1,239.20 Fri. ♦**23,554**
4C: $1,739.20
PCI: $15.49

8913 Florist
FTD Association
PO Box 7051 Free: (800)383-4383
Downers Grove, IL 60515
Publication E-mail: flormag@ix.netcom.com

Magazine for florists. **Founded:** 1967. **Freq:** Monthly. **Print Method:** Offset. **Trim Size:** 8 3/8 x 10 7/8. **Cols./Page:** 3 and 2. **Col. Width:** 14 and 21 1/2 picas. **Col. Depth:** 55 picas. **Key Personnel:** William P. Golden, Editor; Denise Mazzetti, Advertising Mgr.; Barbara Koch, Managing Editor. **Subscription Rates:** $39 individuals. **Remarks:** Accepts advertising.
Ad Rates: BW: $1,670 **Circ:** Paid ‡25,713
4C: $2,347

8914 Illinois Standardbred & Mid-America Harness News
Resource Development Press Ltd.
2235 Durand Dr. Phone: (630)963-0398
PO Box 399 Fax: (630)963-2625
Downers Grove, IL 60515
Racing news (standardbreds). **Founded:** 1979. **Freq:** Monthly. **Print Method:** Uses mats. Offset. **Trim Size:** 8 3/8 x 10 7/

8. **Cols./Page:** 3. **Col. Width:** 27 nonpareils. **Col. Depth:** 140 agate lines. **Key Personnel:** Sam Lilly, Publisher, slilly@idt.net. **Subscription Rates:** $24 individuals. **Remarks:** Accepts advertising. **URL:** http://www.harnessracing2.com. **Formerly:** Illinois Standardbred and Sulky News.
Ad Rates: BW: $457 **Circ:** 1,643
4C: $627
PCI: $25

8915 Journal of Christian Nursing
Nurses Christian Fellowship of InterVarsity Christian Fellowship
PO Box1650 Phone: (630)887-2500
Downers Grove, IL 60515-0780 Fax: (630)887-2520
Publication E-mail: jcn@ivpress.com

Nursing magazine. **Founded:** 1984. **Freq:** Quarterly. **Print Method:** Offset. Uses mats. **Trim Size:** 8 1/2 x 11. **Cols./Page:** 3. **Col. Width:** 30 nonpareils. **Col. Depth:** 133 agate lines. **Key Personnel:** Judith Allen Shelly, R.N., Senior Editor; Melodee Yohe, R.N., Managing Editor; Marian Hall, Business Mgr., mhall@ivcf.org. **ISSN:** 0743-2550. **Subscription Rates:** $19.95 individuals; $5.50 single issue. **Remarks:** Accepts advertising. **Alt. Formats:** Microform.
Ad Rates: BW: $500 **Circ:** Paid ‡10,000
4C: $750 Controlled ‡150

8916 Journal of the Coin Laundry and Drycleaning Industry
Coin Laundry Association
1315 Butterfield Rd., Ste. 212 Phone: (630)963-5547
Downers Grove, IL 60515 Fax: (630)963-5864
Publisher E-mail: info@coinlaundry.com

Trade magazine for coin laundry and drycleaning business owners. **Founded:** Oct. 1990. **Freq:** Monthly. **Print Method:** Web offset. **Trim Size:** 8 1/4 x 10 7/8. **Cols./Page:** 3. **Col. Width:** 3 3/8 inches. **Key Personnel:** Kathy Yolles, Editor; Kathy Sherman, Circulation Dir.; Laurie Moore, Ad Sales Mgr. **ISSN:** 1062-8008. **Subscription Rates:** Free to qualified subscribers. **Remarks:** Accepts advertising.
Ad Rates: BW: $2,906 **Circ:** Controlled 26,000
4C: $3,951
PCI: $99

8917 Matrimony
Worldwide Marriage Encounter
3943 W. End Rd.
Downers Grove, IL 60515

Magazine containing articles of encouragement for couples as well as messages on relationships, spirituality, and family. **Founded:** 1972. **Freq:** Quarterly. **Key Personnel:** Larry Eck, Editor; Mary Sue Eck, Advertising Mgr.; Rev. Don Skerry, S.V.D., Editor.

8918 Westmont Du Page Progress
Reporter/Progress Newspapers
922 Warren Ave. Phone: (630)969-0188
Downers Grove, IL 60515 Fax: (630)969-0228

Suburban community newspaper. **Founded:** 1959. **Freq:** Weekly (Thurs.). **Print Method:** Offset. **Trim Size:** 11 1/2 x 17. **Cols./Page:** 5. **Col. Width:** 22 nonpareils. **Col. Depth:** 16 inches. **Key Personnel:** C.J. Winter, Editor and Publisher; P.K. Winter, Publisher; Edward Rooney, Advertising Mgr. **Subscription Rates:** $19 individuals. **Remarks:** Accepts advertising.
Ad Rates: BW: $608.00 **Circ:** Thurs. ♦**7,040**
4C: $1,108.00
PCI: $7.60

8919 Woodridge Progress
Reporter/Progress Newspapers
922 Warren Ave. Phone: (630)969-0188
Downers Grove, IL 60515 Fax: (630)969-0228

Suburban community newspaper (tabloid). **Founded:** 1969. **Freq:** Weekly (Thurs.). **Print Method:** Offset. **Trim Size:** 11 1/2 x 17. **Cols./Page:** 5. **Col. Width:** 22 nonpareils. **Col. Depth:** 16 inches. **Key Personnel:** C.J. Winter, Editor and Publisher; P.K. Winter, Publisher; Edward Rooney, Advertising Mgr. **Subscription Rates:** $19 individuals. **Remarks:** Accepts advertising.
Ad Rates: BW: $674.40 **Circ:** Thurs. ♦**9,005**
4C: $1,174.40
PCI: $8.43

DU QUOIN

8920 WDQN-AM - 1580
PO Box 190 Phone: (618)542-3894
Du Quoin, IL 62832 Fax: (618)542-4514

Format: Adult Contemporary. **Networks:** ABC. **Founded:** 1951. **Operating Hours:** Continuous. **Key Personnel:** Gene Showalter, General Mgr.; Greg G. Showalter, Manager. **Wattage:** 250.

DWIGHT, pop. 4,146.

Livingston Co. (NEC). 31 m W of Kankakee. Light industry. Grain, stock farms.

8921 Dwight Star & Herald
Star Newspapers
204 E. Chippewa St. Phone: (815)584-3007
PO Box 159
Dwight, IL 60420-0159
Community newspaper. **Founded:** 1868. **Freq:** Weekly (Thurs.). **Print Method:** Offset. **Trim Size:** 7 1/2 x 11. **Cols./Page:** 8. **Col. Width:** 1 3/4 inches. **Col. Depth:** 301 agate lines. **Key Personnel:** Keith Gottschalk, Editor; Scott McGraw, Publisher. **USPS:** 518-980. **Subscription Rates:** $17.50 individuals; $19.50 out of area; $25 out of state. **Remarks:** Accepts advertising.
Ad Rates: GLR: $.19 **Circ:** Paid 2,384
BW: $245 Free 15
PCI: $2.60

Emington Joker - See Emington

Gardner Chronicle - See Gardner

Herscher Press - See Herscher

Odell Times - See Odell

Reddick-Essex Courier - See Reddick

EARLVILLE, pop. 1,382.

La Salle Co. (N). 20 m N of Ottawa. Stock, grain farms. Corn, soybeans, oats.

8922 The Earlville Leader
PO Box 606 Phone: (815)246-6911
Earlville, IL 60518 Fax: (815)246-6911

Newspaper. **Subtitle:** Experience the Heartland (monthly supplement). **Founded:** 1867. **Freq:** Weekly (Wed.). **Print Method:** Offset. **Trim Size:** 11 x 16. **Cols./Page:** 5. **Col. Width:** 25 nonpareils. **Col. Depth:** 210 agate lines. **Key Personnel:** Jean Albert, Editor and Publisher. **Subscription Rates:** $17 individuals; $21 out of area. **Remarks:** Accepts advertising.
Ad Rates: GLR: $.18 **Circ:** ‡1,300
BW: $210
SAU: $2.80
PCI: $2.50

EAST DUBUQUE, pop. 2,194.

Jo Daviess Co. (NW). On Mississippi River, opposite Dubuque, Iowa. Fishing and boating. Foundry. Ammonia, cement block plants. Stock, grain, hogs, dairy farms.

8923 Register
East Dubuque Register
141 Sinsinawa Ave. Phone: (815)747-3171
East Dubuque, IL 61025
Newspaper. **Founded:** 1894. **Freq:** Weekly (Fri.). **Print Method:** Offset. **Trim Size:** 12 x 18. **Cols./Page:** 5. **Col. Width:** 26 nonpareils. **Col. Depth:** 224 agate lines. **Key Personnel:** Carrie Werner, Editor. **Subscription Rates:** $2.75; $3.25. **Remarks:** Accepts advertising.
Ad Rates: GLR: $.14 **Circ:** ‡1,300
BW: $150
SAU: $3

EAST MOLINE

8924 WDLM-AM - 960
Box 149 Phone: (309)234-5111
East Moline, IL 61244

Format: Religious. **Networks:** Moody Broadcasting. **Founded:** 1960. **Operating Hours:** 5 a.m.-10 p.m. **ADI:** Davenport,IA-Rock Island, Moline,IL. **Key Personnel:** Lane Morgan, Station Mgr.; Dave Bergevin, Contact. **Wattage:** 1000 day; 102 night. **Ad Rates:** Noncommercial.

8925 WDLM-FM - 89.3
Box 149 Phone: (309)234-5111
East Moline, IL 61244

Format: Religious. **Networks:** Moody Broadcasting. **Founded:** 1980. **Operating Hours:** Continuous. **ADI:** Davenport,IA-Rock Island, Moline,IL. **Key Personnel:** Lane Morgan, Station Mgr.; Dave Bergevin, Contact. **Wattage:** 100,000. **Ad Rates:** Noncommercial.

EAST PEORIA

Tazewell Co. (NC). 5 m E of Peoria.

8926 Material Handling Network
Material Handling Network, Inc.
PO Box 2338 Phone: (309)699-4431
East Peoria, IL 61611 Fax: (309)698-0801
Free: (800)447-6901
Publication E-mail: mhnetwork@wcinet.com

Trade magazine for the materials handling industry. **Founded:** Jan. 1981. **Freq:** Monthly. **Print Method:** Web. **Trim Size:** 11 13 3/8. **Cols./Page:** 4. **Col. Width:** 2 3/8 inches. **Col. Depth:** 12 3/4 inches. **Key Personnel:** Mike Hawkins, General Mgr.; Tony Martin, Sales Mgr.; Nancy Gudat, Circulation Mgr.; Andra Stephens, Advertising Mgr. **Subscription Rates:** Free to qualified subscribers; $65 Canada and Mexico; $120 other countries. **Remarks:** Accepts advertising. **Available Online. URL:** http://www.mhnetwork.com.
Ad Rates: BW: $435 **Circ:** Paid 155
4C: $675 Non-paid 13,475

8927 WPEO-AM - 1020
1708 Highview Rd. Phone: (309)698-9736
East Peoria, IL 61611 Fax: (309)698-9740
Free: (800)728-1020
E-mail: wpeo@wpeo.com

Format: Religious. **Networks:** USA Radio; Ambassador Inspirational Radio. **Founded:** 1946. **Operating Hours:** Sunrise-sunset. **ADI:** Peoria-Bloomington, IL. **Key Personnel:** Robert Ulrich, General Mgr.; Linda Butler, Contact. **Local Programs:** *Straight Talk*, Linda Butler, Mailing contact. **Wattage:** 1000. **Ad Rates:** $9 for 15 seconds; $14 for 30 seconds; $18 for 60 seconds. **URL:** http://www.wpeo.com.

8928 WVEL-AM - 1140
PO Box 2370 Phone: (309)346-2134
East Peoria, IL 61611-0370 Fax: (309)644-2600

Format: Religious. **Networks:** Christian Broadcasting (CBN). **Founded:** 1948. **Formerly:** WSIV-AM. **Operating Hours:** 6 a.m.-8 p.m. **Key Personnel:** Gil Rosenwald, Managing Dir.; Robert Caruth, Station/Sales Mgr., phone (309)694-7578. **Wattage:** 5000. **Ad Rates:** $15 for 30 seconds; $20 for 60 seconds. Combined advertising rates available with WGLO-FM, WFRY-FM, WIXO-FM.

EAST ST. LOUIS

8929 East St. Louis Monitor
East St. Louis Monitor Publishing, Inc.
1501 State St. Phone: (618)271-0468
Box 2137 Fax: (618)271-0468
East St. Louis, IL 62205
Black community newspaper. **Founded:** 1963. **Freq:** Weekly. **Print Method:** Offset. **Trim Size:** 13 1/8 x 21 1/2. **Cols./Page:** 6. **Col. Width:** 2 inches. **Col. Depth:** 21 1/2 inches. **Key Personnel:** Thomas Gibson, Acting Editor; Anne E. Jordan, Publisher; George Laktzian, Advertising Mgr. **ISSN:** 3708-9565. **Subscription Rates:** $21.80 individuals. **Remarks:** Accepts advertising.
Ad Rates: GLR: $14.60 **Circ:** ‡22,500
SAU: $14.60
PCI: $14.60

8930 WESL-AM - 1490
149 S. 8th St. Phone: (618)271-7687
East St. Louis, IL 62201 Fax: (618)875-4315

Format: Blues. **Networks:** American Urban Radio; Unistar; Mutual Broadcasting System. **Founded:** 1934. **Operating Hours:** Continuous. **ADI:** Chicago (LaSalle), IL. **Key Personnel:** Robert Riggins, Contact; Doug Eason, Program Dir.; Betty Robinson, Office Mgr. **Wattage:** 1000 day; 250 night. **Ad Rates:** $25 for 15 seconds; $30 for 30 seconds; $35 for 60 seconds.

EDGEBROOK

8931 Edgebrook Times Review
Pioneer Press Newspapers
130 S. Prospect Ave. Phone: (847)696-3133
Park Ridge, IL 60068 Fax: (847)696-3229

General newspaper. **Founded:** 1985. **Freq:** Weekly (Thurs.). **Print Method:** Offset. **Key Personnel:** Paul Sassone, Managing Editor; Anne Lunde, Editor. **Subscription Rates:** Free; $18.95 by mail. **Remarks:** Advertising accepted; rates available upon request.
Circ: Thurs. ★**953**

EDINBURG, pop. 1,231.

Christian Co. (C). 18 m SE of Springfield. Grain, stock farms. Corn, wheat, soybeans.

8932 The Herald-Star
Herald-Star
PO Box 50 Phone: (217)623-5523
Edinburg, IL 62531-0050 Fax: (217)623-4216

Newspaper with a Democratic orientation. **Founded:** 1882. **Freq:** Weekly (Thurs.). **Print Method:** Letterpress. Uses mats. **Cols./Page:** 5. **Col. Width:** 2 inches. **Col. Depth:** 17 inches. **Key Personnel:** Glenn Luttrell, Editor and Publisher. **USPS:** 578-980. **Subscription Rates:** $14 individuals; $17 out of state; $0.35 single issue. **Remarks:** Accepts advertising.
Ad Rates: SAU: $3.12 **Circ:** Paid ‡666
PCI: $2 Free ‡28

EDWARDSVILLE†, pop. 12,460.

Madison Co. (SW). 21 m NE of St. Louis, Mo. Southern Illinois University, Edwardsville Campus. Brick plant. Nursery. Hatcheries. Diversified farming.

8933 Command Post
Edwardsville Publishing Co., Inc.
117 N. 2nd St. Phone: (618)656-4700
PO Box 70 Fax: (618)656-7618
Edwardsville, IL 62025-1938
Civilian newspaper published and distributed to military and civilian personnel at Scott Air Force Base. **Founded:** 1941. **Freq:** Weekly (Fri.). **Print Method:** Offset. **Trim Size:** 10 13/16 x 13 1/2. **Cols./Page:** 5. **Col. Width:** 2 1/16 inches. **Col. Depth:** 13 1/2 inches. **Key Personnel:** Nancy Schubert, General Mgr. **Subscription Rates:** $25 individuals. **Remarks:** Advertising not accepted.
Circ: ‡14,100

8934 Edwardsville Intelligencer
Edwardsville Publishing Co., Inc.
117 N. 2nd St. Phone: (618)656-4700
PO Box 70 Fax: (618)656-7618
Edwardsville, IL 62025-1938
Local newspaper. **Founded:** Nov. 13, 1862. **Freq:** Daily (eve.) and Sat. (morn.). **Print Method:** Offset. **Trim Size:** 13 3/4 x 22 3/4. **Cols./Page:** 6. **Col. Width:** 24 nonpareils. **Col. Depth:** 301 agate lines. **Key Personnel:** Bruce Coury, Publisher, bcoury@edwpub.com; Dan Heaton, Editor, dheaton@edwpub.com; Marge Smith, Advertising Dir., msmith@edwpub.com. **Subscription Rates:** $140 individuals year by mail; $111 year by carrier. **Remarks:** Accepts advertising. **Available Online. Alt. Formats:** CD-ROM.
Ad Rates: GLR: $1.18 **Circ:** Mon.-Sat. ★**6,453**
BW: $1362
4C: $1737
SAU: $10.56

8935 Papers on Language & Literature
Southern Illinois University at Edwardsville Phone: (618)650-2119
Fax: (618)650-3509
Edwardsville, IL 62026-1434
Publisher E-mail: pll@siue.edu

Literary history, theory, and interpretation. **Subtitle:** A Journal for Scholars and Critics of Language and Literature. **Founded:** 1965. **Freq:** Quarterly. **Print Method:** Offset. Uses mats. **Trim Size:** 6 x 9. **Cols./Page:** 1. **Col. Width:** 54 nonpareils. **Col. Depth:** 110 agate lines. **Key Personnel:** Brian Abel Ragen, Editor, phone (618)692-2119, fax (618)692-3509. **ISSN:** 0031-1294. **Subscription Rates:** $48 institutions locations outside USA $5 postage; $24 individuals locations outside USA $5 postage. **Alt. Formats:** Microform.
Ad Rates: BW: $60 **Circ:** Paid 706
Non-paid 54

8936 WSIE-FM - 88.7
Southern Illinois University Phone: (618)650-2228
Box 1773 Fax: (618)650-2233
Edwardsville, IL 62026
Free: (888)325-8870
E-mail: wsie@siue.edu

Format: Public Radio; Jazz; News. **Networks:** National Public Radio (NPR); American Public Radio (APR). **Owner:** Southern Illinois University, at above address. **Founded:** 1970. **Operating Hours:** Continuous; 10% network, 90% local. **ADI:** St. Louis, MO (Mt. Vernon, IL). **Key Personnel:** Frank Akers, General Mgr.; Tom Dehner, News/Public Affairs Dir.; Jay Harkey, Music Dir.; David Caires, Chief Engineer. **Local Programs:** *Jazz in the A.M.* 8:00 am - 1:00 am Monday-Friday, LaVerne Holliday, Fax (618)650-2228; *Late Night Jazz* 12:00 am - 5:00 am Monday-Friday, Leo Chears, Fax (618)692-2228; *Standard in Jazz* 1:00 pm - 6:00 pm Monday-Friday, Ross Gentile, Fax (618)650-2228. **Wattage:** 50,000. **Ad Rates:** Noncommercial.

EFFINGHAM†, pop. 11,270.

Effingham Co. (S). 60 m SE of Decatur. Manufactures clutch plates, air conditioning, feed, insecticides, printing ink, electrographics, hardwood lumber, gloves, wood blocks, laminated furniture components, oil, prefabricated homes. Milling.

8937 Effingham Daily News
201 N. Banker St. Phone: (217)347-7151
PO Box 370 Fax: (217)342-9315
Effingham, IL 62401-2304
Free: (800)526-7205

General newspaper. **Founded:** 1899. **Freq:** Daily (eve.) and Sat. (morn.). **Print Method:** Offset. **Cols./Page:** 6. **Col. Width:** 21 nonpareils. **Col. Depth:** 301 agate lines. **Key Personnel:** Paul E. Semple, Publisher; Carl H. Thoele, Advertising Mgr.; Susan Duncan, Managing Editor. **Subscription Rates:** $78. **Remarks:** Accepts advertising.
Ad Rates: GLR: $.52 **Circ:** Mon.-Sat. 13,175
BW: $1,173.90
4C: $1,450
SAU: $9.10

8938 WCBH-FM - 104.3
PO Box 568 Phone: (217)342-4141
Effingham, IL 62401 Fax: (217)342-4143

Format: Adult Contemporary. **Networks:** The Source. **Owner:** Discovery Group LLC, at above address. **Founded:** 1988. **Formerly:** Casey Broadcast Group. **Operating Hours:** Continuous. **ADI:** Terre Haute, IN. **Key Personnel:** Ken Brown, General Mgr.; Steve Bagley, Program Dir. **Wattage:** 25,000 ERP. **Ad Rates:** $12.50-19 for 30 seconds; $15-21 for 60 seconds. Combined advertising rates available with WCRC/WCRA.

8939 WCRA-AM - 1090
PO Box 568 Phone: (217)342-4141
Effingham, IL 62401 Fax: (217)342-4143

Format: Talk; News. **Networks:** Independent. **Founded:** 1947. **Operating Hours:** 12 hours Daily; 100% local. **Key Personnel:** Ed Howard, Contact; Mark Turner, News Dir. **Wattage:** 1000. **Ad Rates:** $10-25 per unit.

8940 WCRC-FM - 95.7
208 W. Jefferson Phone: (217)342-4141
PO Box 568 Fax: (217)342-4143
Effingham, IL 62401

Format: News; Country; Agricultural. **Networks:** Independent. **Founded:** 1963. **Formerly:** WCRA-FM (1972). **Operating Hours:** Continuous. **Key Personnel:** Mark Turner, News Dir.; Ed Howard, Contact. **Wattage:** 50,000. **Ad Rates:** $10-25 per unit.

ELBURN, pop. 1,124.

Kane Co. (NE). 45 m W of Chicago. Light manufacturing. Dairy, stock, poultry, grain farms.

8941 The Elburn Herald
Kaneland Publications, Inc.
123 N. Main St. Phone: (630)365-6446
Elburn, IL 60119 Fax: (630)365-2251
Publication E-mail: herald@elnet.com

Community newspaper. **Founded:** 1908. **Freq:** Weekly (Thurs.). **Print Method:** Offset. **Cols./Page:** 4. **Col. Width:** 2 1/2 inches. **Col. Depth:** 16 inches. **Key Personnel:** Kim M. Boyd, Manager; Richard L. Cooper, Publisher. **Subscription Rates:** $18 Kane County; $23 Illinois; $28 out of state. **Remarks:** Accepts advertising.
Ad Rates: BW: $640 **Circ:** 2,800
PCI: $10

ELGIN, pop. 63,798.

Kane Co (NE). On Fox River, 38 m NW of Chicago. Judson College. Manufactures food products, metal fasteners, street sweepers, steel kitchens, switchboards, electric appliances, paper boxes, novelties, filling machinery, oil seals, steel tube containers, diamond cutting tools and abrasives, flexible metal hose, furniture, paint, steel, iron, pottery, plastic cloth. Woodworking.

8942 Aeronautica & Air Label Collectors Club
Aeronautica and Air Label Collectors Club
PO Box 1239 Phone: (847)468-0840
Elgin, IL 60121-1239 Fax: (847)468-0840

Journal covering philately. **Subtitle:** Air Log. **Founded:** 1943. **Freq:** Quarterly. **Print Method:** Offset. **Subscription Rates:** $20 individuals; $5 single issue. **Remarks:** Accepts advertising. **Formerly:** Jack Knight Air Log.
Circ: Controlled 850

8943 The Courier News
Copley Newspapers/Copley Press
300 Lake St. Phone: (708)888-7800
Elgin, IL 60120 Fax: (708)888-7714

Daily newspaper. **Founded:** 1874. **Freq:** Daily (eve.), Sat. and Sun. (morn.). **Print Method:** Letterpress. **Trim Size:** 13 3/4 x 22 7/8. **Cols./Page:** 6. **Col. Width:** 12.2 picas. **Col. Depth:** 21 1/4 inches. **Key Personnel:** Paul P. Seveska, General Mgr. **Subscription Rates:** $102.90 individuals. **Remarks:** Accepts advertising.
Ad Rates: GLR: $2.04 **Circ:** Mon.-Sat. ★**19,322**
BW: $3,633.75 Sun. ★**20,064**
4C: $3,873.75
SAU: $28.50

8944 Illinois Racing News
Equine Market
1074 Woodhill Ct. Phone: (847)468-9355
Elgin, IL 60120
Racing news (thoroughbreds). **Founded:** 1972. **Freq:** Monthly. **Print Method:** Offset. **Trim Size:** 8 3/8 x 10 7/8. **Cols./Page:** 3. **Col. Width:** 27 nonpareils. **Col. Depth:** 140 agate lines. **Key Personnel:** Joan Colby, Editor; Eugene Laulunen, Publisher. **Subscription Rates:** $24 individuals. **Remarks:** Accepts advertising.
Ad Rates: BW: $520 **Circ:** ‡3,800
4C: $780
PCI: $35

8945 Messenger
Church of the Brethren General Board
1451 Dundee Ave. Phone: (847)742-5100
Elgin, IL 60120 Fax: (847)742-6103
Free: (800)323-8039
Publication E-mail: cobnews@aol.com

Religious magazine. **Founded:** Apr. 1851. **Freq:** Monthly. **Print Method:** Letterpress and offset. **Trim Size:** 8 1/2 x 11. **Cols./Page:** 2 and 3. **Col. Width:** 42 and 28 nonpareils. **Col. Depth:** 140 agate lines. **Key Personnel:** Nevin Dulabaum, Managing Editor; Wendy McFadden, Publisher. **ISSN:** 0026-0355. **Subscription Rates:** $16.50 individuals. **Alt. Formats:** Audio tape.
Ad Rates: BW: $850 **Circ:** ‡19,500
4C: $1075
PCI: $75

8946 Midwest Equine Market
Equine Market
1074 Woodhill Ct. Phone: (847)468-9355
Elgin, IL 60120
Magazine covering all breeds and events. **Subtitle:** and Horsemen's Review. **Founded:** 1971. **Freq:** Monthly. **Print Method:** Offset. **Cols./Page:** 4. **Col. Width:** 27 nonpareils. **Col. Depth:** 224 agate lines. **Key Personnel:** Midge Koonz, Editor/Administration; Sandrock Hill, Publisher. **Subscription Rates:** $12.95 individuals. **Remarks:** Accepts advertising.
Ad Rates: BW: $299 **Circ:** ‡2,000
PCI: $10

8947 MidWest Outdoors
Equine Market
1074 Woodhill Ct. Phone: (847)468-9355
Elgin, IL 60120
Outdoor sports tabloid. **Founded:** Nov. 1967. **Freq:** Monthly. **Print Method:** Offset. **Cols./Page:** 4. **Col. Width:** 27 nonpareils. **Col. Depth:** 224 agate lines. **Key Personnel:** Gene Laulunen, Editor and Publisher; Dan Ferris, Advertising Mgr. **Subscription Rates:** $12.95; $1.95 single issue. **Remarks:** Accepts advertising.
Ad Rates: BW: $1,387 **Circ:** Paid 41,104
4C: $2,114
PCI: $42

8948 KSHP-AM - 1400
14 Douglas Ave.
Elgin, IL 60120

Format: News; Talk. **Owner:** Las Vegas Radio Co., Inc., at above address. **Founded:** 1996. **Operating Hours:** Continuous. **ADI:** Las Vegas, NV. **Key Personnel:** Rick Jakle, President, phone (847)741-7700; Mike Lawrence, VP/General Mgr.; Brett Grant, General Sales Mgr.; Joe Sands, Chief Engineer. **Wattage:** 1000. **Ad Rates:** $32 for 30 seconds; $40 for 60 seconds. **URL:** http://www.kshp.com.

8949 WEPS-FM - 88.9
355 E. Chicago St. Phone: (847)888-5000
Elgin, IL 60120 Fax: (847)888-0272

Format: Eclectic; Educational. **Owner:** School District U-46, 355 E. Chicago St., Elgin, IL 60120, (708)888-5000. **Founded:** 1950. **Operating Hours:** 9:30 am - 4:00 pm, Mon - Fri. **Key Personnel:** Larry Ascough, Station Mgr., phone (847)888-5000; Carolyn Brandes, Program Dir. **Wattage:** 740.

8950 WJKL-FM - 94.3
14 Douglas Ave. Phone: (847)741-7700
Elgin, IL 60120 Fax: (847)888-4227

Format: Adult Contemporary. **Networks:** Satellite Music Network. **Founded:** 1960. **Formerly:** WRMN-FM (1973). **Operating Hours:** Continuous; 80% network, 20% local. **ADI:** Chicago (LaSalle), IL. **Key Personnel:** Richard Jakle, Pres./Gen. Mgr.; Brad Bohlen, Station Mgr.; Harold Cattron, Engineer; Mike Sullivan, News Dir. **Wattage:** 6000. **Ad Rates:** $40-60 for 60 seconds.

8951 WRMN-AM - 1410
14 Douglas Ave. Phone: (847)741-7700
Elgin, IL 60120 Fax: (847)888-4227

Format: Talk; News. **Networks:** NBC; Mutual Broadcasting System; Talknet. **Owner:** Elgin Broadcasting Company, Inc., at above address. **Founded:** 1949. **Operating Hours:** Continuous; 20% network, 80% local. **ADI:** Chicago (LaSalle), IL. **Key Personnel:** Mike Sullivan, News Dir.; Brad Bohlen, Station Mgr.; Richard Jakle, Contact. **Local Programs:** *People to People*, Brad Bohlen; *Problems and Solutions*, Dee Hubbard; *Your Turn*, Brad Bohlen. **Wattage:** 1000. **Ad Rates:** $22.50-37.50 per unit.

ELIZABETHTOWN†, pop. 478.

Hardin Co. (SE). On Ohio River, 30 m SE of Harrisburg. Tourist attractions. Flourspar, lead, zinc mines. Stock, dairy, poultry farms.

8952 Hardin County Independent
Box 328 Phone: (618)287-2361
Elizabethtown, IL 62931
Newspaper with Report orientation. **Founded:** 1871. **Freq:** Weekly (Thurs.). **Print Method:** Offset. **Trim Size:** 13 3/4 x 22 3/4. **Cols./Page:** 6. **Col. Width:** 22 nonpareils. **Col. Depth:** 301 agate lines. **Key Personnel:** Noel E. Hurford, Editor and Publisher. **USPS:** 235-140. **Subscription Rates:** $22.50 individuals. **Remarks:** Accepts advertising.
Ad Rates: GLR: $.30 **Circ:** ‡2,700
BW: $318.75
SAU: $3.80
PCI: $2.50

ELK GROVE VILLAGE, pop. 28,907.

Cook Co. (NW). NW of Chicago. Residential.

8953 Elk Grove Times
Pioneer Press Newspapers
291 N. Dunton Ave Phone: (847)797-5100
Arlington Heights, IL 60004 Fax: (847)797-5151

Community newspaper. **Founded:** 1987. **Freq:** Weekly (Thurs.). **Print Method:** Offset. **Trim Size:** 14 x 22 1/2. **Cols./Page:** 5. **Col. Width:** 1 7/8 inches. **Col. Depth:** 294 agate lines. **Key Personnel:** Paul Sassone, Managing Editor; Terri McHugh, Editor. **USPS:** 524-400. **Subscription Rates:** $12.95 by mail. **Remarks:** Advertising accepted; rates available upon request. **URL:** http://www.pioneerlocal.com.
Circ: Thurs. ★**2,410**

8954 Gear Technology
Randall Publishing Inc.
1425 Lunt Ave. Phone: (847)437-6604
Elk Grove Village, IL 60007 Fax: (847)437-6618
Publication E-mail: people@geartechnology.com

Magazine featuring design, testing, processing, and new technology for gears and gear manufacturing products, and equipment. **Subtitle:** The Journal of Gear Manufacturing. **Founded:** 1984. **Freq:** Bimonthly. **Print Method:** Web offset. **Trim Size:** 8 x 10 3/4. **Cols./Page:** 2 and 3. **Col. Width:** 20 and 13 nonpareils. **Col. Depth:** 150 agate lines. **Key Personnel:** Charles Cooper, Editor; Michael Goldstein, Pub./Editor-in-Chief; William R. Stott, Managing. **ISSN:** 0743-6858. **Subscription Rates:** Free to qualified subscribers; $40 individuals; $50 Canada; $55 other countries. **Remarks:** Accepts advertising. **Available Online. URL:** http://www.geartechnology.com.
Ad Rates: GLR: $35 **Circ:** Paid 500
BW: $4,100 Controlled 13,500
4C: $5,265

8955 Pediatrics
American Academy of Pediatrics
141 Northwest Point Blvd. Phone: (847)228-5005
Elk Grove Village, IL 60007 Fax: (847)228-5097
Free: (800)433-9016
Publication E-mail: journals@aap.org
Publisher E-mail: aapnews@aap.org

Medical journal reporting on pediatrics. **Founded:** 1948. **Freq:** Monthly. **Print Method:** Web offset. **Trim Size:** 8 1/8 x 10 7/8. **Cols./Page:** 2. **Key Personnel:** Jerold Lucey, M.D., Editor; Kent Anderson, Managing Editor, kanderson@aap.org; Gary Wachli, Advertising Mgr. **ISSN:** 0031-4005. **Subscription Rates:** $120 individuals; $190 other countries. **URL:** http://www.pediatrics.org. **Alt. Formats:** CD-ROM, CMC Research.
Ad Rates: BW: $2,535 **Circ:** Paid 57,000
4C: $1,765 Non-paid 4,000

ELMHURST, pop. 44,251.

Du Page Co. (NE). 16 m W of Chicago. Elmhurst College. Residential.

8956 Ad ExPress
Press Publications
112 S. York St. Phone: (630)834-0900
Elmhurst, IL 60126 Fax: (630)834-0910
Publisher E-mail: presspub@aol.com

Weekly direct-mail shopper. **Founded:** 1984. **Freq:** Weekly. **Print Method:** Offset. **Cols./Page:** 5. **Col. Width:** 2 inches. **Col. Depth:** 16 inches.
Ad Rates: PCI: $5.95 **Circ:** (Not Reported)

8957 Addison Press
Press Publications
112 S. York St. Phone: (630)834-0900
Elmhurst, IL 60126 Fax: (630)834-0910
Publisher E-mail: presspub@aol.com

Community newspaper. **Founded:** 1953. **Freq:** Semiweekly (Wed. and Fri.). **Print Method:** Offset. **Cols./Page:** 6. **Col. Width:** 2 inches. **Col. Depth:** 21 1/2 inches. **Key Personnel:** Jack Cruger, Publisher; Nick Pullia, Editor-in-Chief. **Subscription Rates:** Free; $39 by mail.
Circ: (Not Reported)

8958 Bartlett Press
Press Publications
112 S. York St. Phone: (630)834-0900
Elmhurst, IL 60126 Fax: (630)834-0910
Publisher E-mail: presspub@aol.com

Community newspaper. **Founded:** 1993. **Freq:** Weekly. **Print Method:** Offset. **Cols./Page:** 5. **Col. Width:** 2 inches. **Col. Depth:** 16 inches.
Ad Rates: PCI: $8.95 **Circ:** (Not Reported)

8959 Bensenville Press
Press Publications
112 S. York St. Phone: (630)834-0900
Elmhurst, IL 60126 Fax: (630)834-0910
Publisher E-mail: presspub@aol.com

Founded: 1993. **Freq:** Semiweekly. **Print Method:** Offset. **Cols./Page:** 5. **Col. Width:** 10 1/2 inches. **Col. Depth:** 16 inches.
Ad Rates: PCI: $7.55 **Circ:** (Not Reported)

Carol Stream Press - See Carol Stream

8960 Countryside Press
Press Publications
112 S. York St. Phone: (630)834-0900
Elmhurst, IL 60126 Fax: (630)834-0910
Publisher E-mail: presspub@aol.com

Community newspaper. **Founded:** 1993. **Freq:** Weekly. **Print Method:** Offset. **Cols./Page:** 5. **Col. Width:** 2 inches. **Col. Depth:** 16 inches.
Ad Rates: PCI: $7.55 **Circ:** Thurs. 2,544

8961 Down Beat
Maher Publications, Inc.
102 N. Haven Rd. Phone: (630)941-2030
Elmhurst, IL 60126 Fax: (630)941-3210
Free: (800)535-7496

Magazine edited for the learning musician. **Subtitle:** Jazz, Blues & Beyond. **Founded:** July 14, 1934. **Freq:** Monthly. **Print Method:** Offset. **Trim Size:** 8 1/8 x 10 7/8. **Cols./Page:** 3. **Col. Width:** 2 1/4 inches. **Col. Depth:** 9 7/8 inches. **Key Personnel:** John Ephland, Managing Editor; Kevin Maher, Publisher; Frank Alkyer, Publisher. **ISSN:** 0012-5768. **Subscription Rates:** $26 individuals; $2.50 single issue. **Remarks:** Accepts advertising.
Ad Rates: BW: $4,315 **Circ:** ‡93,797
4C: $5,215
PCI: $230

8962 The Elmhurst College Magazine
Elmhurst College
190 Prospect Phone: (630)617-3500
Elmhurst, IL 60126 Fax: (630)617-3657

Collegiate alumni magazine. **Founded:** 1967. **Freq:** Semiannual. **Print Method:** Web offset. **Trim Size:** 8 1/2 x 11. **Cols./Page:** 2. **Key Personnel:** James W. Winters, Editor, phone (630)617-3125, fax (630)617-3657, jimw@elmhurst.edu. **Remarks:** Advertising not accepted. **URL:** http://www.elmhurst.edu. **Former name:** Elmhurst College Magazine.
Circ: Controlled ‡37,000

8963 Elmhurst Press
Press Publications
112 S. York St. Phone: (630)834-0900
Elmhurst, IL 60126 Fax: (630)834-0910
Publisher E-mail: presspub@aol.com

Community newspaper. **Founded:** 1891. **Freq:** Semiweekly (Wed. and Fri.). **Print Method:** Offset. **Cols./Page:** 6. **Col. Width:** 2 inches. **Col. Depth:** 21 1/2 inches. **Key Personnel:** Nick Pullia, Editor; Jack Cruger, Publisher. **Subscription Rates:** Free; $39 by mail.
Ad Rates: SAU: $8.94 **Circ:** Paid 8,754
PCI: $10.53

Glen Ellyn Press - See Glen Ellyn

Glendale Heights Press - See Glendale Heights

8964 Itasca Press
Press Publications
112 S. York St. Phone: (630)834-0900
Elmhurst, IL 60126 Fax: (630)834-0910
Publisher E-mail: presspub@aol.com

Founded: 1993. **Freq:** Weekly. **Print Method:** Offset. **Cols./Page:** 5. **Col. Width:** 2 inches. **Col. Depth:** 16 inches. **Key Personnel:** Wendy Ann Riehm, phone (630)307-1101, fax (630)307-1190, presspub@aol.com.
Ad Rates: PCI: $7.55 **Circ:** (Not Reported)

8965 LaGrange Park Press
Press Publications
112 S. York St. Phone: (630)834-0900
Elmhurst, IL 60126 Fax: (630)834-0910
Publisher E-mail: presspub@aol.com

Founded: 1993. **Freq:** Weekly. **Print Method:** Offset. **Cols./Page:** 5. **Col. Width:** 2 1/2 inches. **Col. Depth:** 16 inches. **Key Personnel:** Nick Pullia, Editor.
Ad Rates: PCI: $7.55 **Circ:** (Not Reported)

8966 Lombard Spectator
Press Publications
112 S. York St. Phone: (630)834-0900
Elmhurst, IL 60126 Fax: (630)834-0910
Publisher E-mail: presspub@aol.com

Community newspaper. **Founded:** 1927. **Freq:** Semiweekly (Wed. and Fri.). **Print Method:** Offset. **Cols./Page:** 6. **Col. Width:** 2 inches. **Col. Depth:** 21 1/2 inches. **Key Personnel:** Jack Cruger, Publisher; Nick Pullia, Editor-in-Chief. **Subscription Rates:** Free; $39 by mail.
Circ: (Not Reported)

8967 Marquee
Theatre Historical Society of America
York Theatre Bldg., 2nd Fl. Phone: (630)782-1800
152 N. York St. Fax: (630)782-1802
Elmhurst, IL 60126-2806
Publisher E-mail: thrhistsoc@aol.com

Magazine devoted to historic theater information and theater architecture. **Founded:** 1969. **Freq:** Quarterly. **Print Method:** Offset. **Trim Size:** 8 1/2 x 11. **Cols./Page:** 2. **Col. Width:** 36 nonpareils. **Col. Depth:** 137 agate lines. **Key Personnel:** Richard J. Sklenar, Executive Dir. **ISSN:** 0025-3928. **Subscription Rates:** $40 individuals; $6 single issue. **Alt. Formats:** Microform.
Ad Rates: BW: $200 **Circ:** Controlled ‡1,000

8968 Music Inc.
Maher Publications, Inc.
102 N. Haven Rd. Phone: (630)941-2030
Elmhurst, IL 60126 Fax: (630)941-3210
Free: (800)535-7496
Publication E-mail: musicincupbeat@worldnet.att.net

Magazine serving retailers of music and sound products. **Founded:** 1978. **Freq:** 11/year. **Print Method:** Offset. **Trim Size:** 8 1/4 x 10 7/8. **Cols./Page:** 3. **Col. Width:** 27 nonpareils. **Col. Depth:** 140 agate lines. **Key Personnel:** Kevin Maher, Publisher; Frank Alkyer, Editorial Director; John Cahill, Adv. Sales Mgr. **Subscription Rates:** $16.50 individuals. **Remarks:** Accepts advertising.
Ad Rates: BW: $1,470 **Circ:** Controlled ‡8,900
4C: $2,095

Oak Brook Press - See Oak Brook

Oak Brook Terrace Press - See Oak Brook

8969 Roselle Press
Press Publications
112 S. York St. Phone: (630)834-0900
Elmhurst, IL 60126 Fax: (630)834-0910
Publisher E-mail: presspub@aol.com

Founded: 1993. **Freq:** Weekly. **Print Method:** Offset. **Cols./Page:** 5. **Col. Width:** 2 inches. **Col. Depth:** 16 inches.
Ad Rates: PCI: $7.55 **Circ:** (Not Reported)

8970 Up Beat Daily
Maher Publications, Inc.
102 N. Haven Rd. Phone: (630)941-2030
Elmhurst, IL 60126 Fax: (630)941-3210
Free: (800)535-7496
Publication E-mail: musicincupbeat@woldnet.att.net

Tabloid serving the National Association of Music Merchants (NAMM) trade shows. **Subtitle:** The Official NAMM Publication. **Founded:** 1953. **Freq:** Daily during the NAMM trade shows. **Print Method:** Offset. Uses mats. **Trim Size:** 10 7/8 x 14 1/2. **Cols./Page:** 4. **Col. Width:** 30 nonpareils. **Col. Depth:** 168 agate lines. **Key Personnel:** Ed Enright, Editor; Kevin Maher, Publisher; Frank Alkyer, Publisher. **Remarks:** Accepts advertising.
Ad Rates: BW: $2,090 **Circ:** Non-paid ‡10,000
4C: $2,840

8971 Villa Park Argus
Press Publications
112 S. York St. Phone: (630)834-0900
Elmhurst, IL 60126 Fax: (630)834-0910
Publisher E-mail: presspub@aol.com

Community newspaper. **Founded:** 1925. **Freq:** Semiweekly (Wed. and Fri.). **Print Method:** Offset. **Cols./Page:** 6. **Col. Width:** 2 inches. **Col. Depth:** 21 1/2 inches. **Key Personnel:** Jack Cruger, Publisher; Nick Pullia, Editor-in-Chief. **Subscription Rates:** $39 by mail.
Circ: (Not Reported)

8972 West Cook County Press
Press Publications
112 S. York St. Phone: (630)834-0900
Elmhurst, IL 60126 Fax: (630)834-0910
Publisher E-mail: presspub@aol.com

Community newspaper. **Founded:** 1955. **Freq:** Weekly (Thurs.). **Print Method:** Offset. **Cols./Page:** 5. **Col. Width:** 2 inches. **Col. Depth:** 16 inches. **Key Personnel:** Nick Pullia, Editor-in-Chief; Rosemarie T. Cruger, Publisher; William Hamon, Advertising Mgr. **Subscription Rates:** Free; $28 by mail.
Circ: (Not Reported)

8973 Westchester News
Press Publications
112 S. York St. Phone: (630)834-0900
Elmhurst, IL 60126 Fax: (630)834-0910
Publisher E-mail: presspub@aol.com

Founded: 1993. **Freq:** Weekly. **Print Method:** Offset. **Cols./Page:** 5. **Col. Width:** 2 inches. **Col. Depth:** 16 inches. **Key Personnel:** Nick Pullia, Editor.
Ad Rates: PCI: $7.55 **Circ:** (Not Reported)

Wheaton Press - See Wheaton

8974 Wood Dale Press
Press Publications
112 S. York St. Phone: (630)834-0900
Elmhurst, IL 60126 Fax: (630)834-0910
Publisher E-mail: presspub@aol.com

Founded: 1993. **Freq:** Weekly. **Print Method:** Offset. **Cols./Page:** 5. **Col. Width:** 2 inches. **Col. Depth:** 21 1/2 inches.
Ad Rates: PCI: $7.55 **Circ:** (Not Reported)

8975 Continental Cablevision
688 Industrial Dr. Phone: (708)470-0803
Elmhurst, IL 60126 Fax: (708)716-2424

Founded: 1979. **Key Personnel:** Andy Harris, General Mgr.; Amy Hanson, Office Mgr. **Cities Served:** Northern Cook County, IL.: subscribing households 18,500; 56 channels; 3 community access channels.

8976 MediaOne
688 Industrial Dr. Phone: (630)716-2300
Elmhurst, IL 60126 Fax: (630)716-2424

Founded: 1982. **Formerly:** Continental Cablevision. **Key Personnel:** Terrance Cantwell, Contact, phone (630)716-2408, fax (630)716-2696, tcantwell@mediaone.com; Mike Henderson, Production Supervisor. **Cities Served:** Elmhurst, Rolling Meadows, Romeoville, IL: subscribing households 365,000; 70 hours per week community access programming. **URL:** http://www.mediaone.com.

8977 WRSE-FM - 88.7
190 Prospect Ave. Phone: (630)617-3729
Elmhurst, IL 60126 Fax: (630)617-3313
E-mail: jonm@elmhunst.edu

Format: Jazz; Album-Oriented Rock (AOR); Alternative/New Music/Progressive. **Networks:** Independent. **Founded:** 1947. **Operating Hours:** 4 p.m.-1 a.m. Sun.-Fri. **ADI:** Chicago (LaSalle), IL. **Key Personnel:** Jon Morgan, Contact, phone (630)617-3498, jonm@elmhurst.edu. **Wattage:** 100. **Ad Rates:** Underwriting available.

ELMWOOD, pop. 2,117.

Peoria Co. (NWC). 10 m. NW of Bartonville. Residential.

8978 The Advertiser
116 S. Magnolia Phone: (309)742-2521
PO Box 289 Fax: (309)742-2511
Elmwood, IL 61529
Shopper. **Founded:** 1972. **Freq:** Weekly (Tues.). **Print Method:** Offset. **Cols./Page:** 6. **Col. Width:** 20 nonpareils. **Col. Depth:** 224 agate lines. **Key Personnel:** DeEllda Swindler, Publisher. **Subscription Rates:** Free.
Ad Rates: BW: $288 **Circ:** Free ‡5,500
PCI: $3.45

8979 Elmwood Gazette
Tri-County News Edition
116 S. Magnolia Phone: (309)742-2521
PO Box 289 Fax: (309)742-2511
Elmwood, IL 61529
Community newspaper. **Founded:** 1873. **Freq:** Weekly (Thurs.). **Print Method:** Offset. **Cols./Page:** 6. **Col. Width:** 20 nonpareils. **Col. Depth:** 224 agate lines. **Key Personnel:** DeEllda Swindler, Publisher. **Subscription Rates:** $16 individuals.
Ad Rates: GLR: $.79 **Circ:** ‡550
BW: $192
4C: $292
PCI: $2.50

Farmington Bugle - See Farmington

8980 Home Shopper
116 S. Magnolia Phone: (309)742-2511
Box 289 Fax: (309)742-2511
Elmwood, IL 61529
Shopper. **Founded:** 1956. **Freq:** Weekly (Tues.). **Print Method:** Offset. **Cols./Page:** 6. **Col. Width:** 20 nonpareils. **Col. Depth:** 224 agate lines. **Key Personnel:** Adrian C. Swindler, Editor; Deellda J. Swindler, Publisher. **Subscription Rates:** Free. **Remarks:** Accepts advertising.
Ad Rates: BW: $288 **Circ:** Free ‡7,635
PCI: $3.45

Williamsfield Times - See Williamsfield

Yates City Banner - See Yates City

ELSAH

8981 WTPC-FM - 105.3
1 Mayback Pl. Phone: (618)374-4391
Elsah, IL 62028 Fax: (618)374-5122
E-mail: wtpc@prin.edu

Format: Alternative/New Music/Progressive. **Owner:** Principia Communications Corp., at above address. **Operating Hours:** 4:00 p.m.-2:00 a.m. **Key Personnel:** George Cooke, General Mgr., phone (618)374-5117, gvc@prin.edu. **Local Programs:** *Science Discovery*, Paul Robinson; *Rock of Ages*, Phil Webster. **Wattage:** 10. **URL:** http://www.prin.edu.

EMINGTON, pop. 119.

Livingston Co. (NEC). 28 m SW of Kankakee. Grain, stock, dairy farms. Corn, oats, beans, hay.

8982 Emington Joker
Star Newspapers
204 E. Chippewa St. Phone: (815)584-3007
PO Box 159
Dwight, IL 60420-0159
Community newspaper. **Founded:** 1902. **Freq:** Weekly (Thurs.). **Print Method:** Offset. **Trim Size:** 8 x 11 1/4. **Cols./Page:** 8. **Col. Width:** 1 3/4 inches. **Col. Depth:** 301 agate lines. **Key Personnel:** Scott McGraw, Publisher. **USPS:** 175-040. **Subscription Rates:** $12 individuals; $17 out of state.
Ad Rates: GLR: $.16 **Circ:** Paid 415
BW: $161.25 Free 10
SAU: $2.64
PCI: $2.24

ERIE

Whiteside Co. (SW).

8983 The Review
WNS Publications
914 Albany St.
Erie, IL 61250

Community newspaper. **Founded:** 1857. **Freq:** Weekly (Wed.). **Print Method:** Offset. **Trim Size:** 15 1/2 x 21. **Cols./Page:** 8. **Col. Width:** 11 picas. **Col. Depth:** 21 inches. **Key Personnel:** Judy James, Editor; Tony Komlanc, Publisher; Beth Armstrong, Advertising. **Subscription Rates:** $23 individuals; $29 out of county; $41 out of state. **Remarks:** Color advertising not accepted.
Ad Rates: GLR: $6 **Circ:** 2,500
BW: $1,008
SAU: $6.95
PCI: $6

EUREKA†, pop. 4,306.

Woodford Co. (NC). 17 m E of Peoria. Eureka College. Manufactures automatic livestock feeding systems, road building machinery. Grain, stock farms.

The Le Roy Journal - See Le Roy

8984 Woodford County Journal
Illinois Valley Press
1926 S. Main St. Phone: (309)467-3314
PO Box 36 Fax: (309)467-4563
Eureka, IL 61530
Free: (800)747-7323
Publisher E-mail: journal@farmwagon.com

Community newspaper. **Founded:** 1867. **Freq:** Weekly (Thurs.). **Print Method:** Offset. **Cols./Page:** 6. **Col. Width:** 2 1/8 inches. **Col. Depth:** 21 1/2 inches. **Key Personnel:** Mark Barra, General Mgr.; J. W. Shults, Editor. **USPS:** 690-440. **Subscription Rates:** $27 individuals; $30 out of area; $35 out of state. **Remarks:** Accepts advertising.
Ad Rates: BW: $741.75 **Circ:** ‡1,810
4C: $876.75
SAU: $4.85
PCI: $5.75

8985 Woodford Star
Illinois Valley Press
1926 S. Main St. Phone: (309)467-3314
PO Box 36 Fax: (309)467-4563
Eureka, IL 61530
Free: (800)747-7323
Publisher E-mail: journal@farmwagon.com

Shopper. **Founded:** 1985. **Freq:** Weekly (Mon.). **Print Method:** Offset. **Cols./Page:** 6. **Col. Width:** 2 1/8 inches. **Col. Depth:** 21 1/2 inches. **Key Personnel:** Mark Barra, General Mgr. **Subscription Rates:** Free. **Remarks:** Accepts advertising.
Ad Rates: BW: $838.50 **Circ:** Free ‡8,925
4C: $973.50
PCI: $6.50

8986 Midwest Cablevision
1926 S. Main St.
Box 320
Eureka, IL 61530-0320

Owner: InterMedia Partners, 235 Montgomery St., Ste. 420, San Francisco, CA 94104. **Cities Served:** Woodford County: subscribing households 20,000; 36 channels.

EVANSTON, pop. 73,706.

Cook Co. (NE). On Lake Michigan, adjacent to Chicago. Primarily suburban residential. Northwestern University and two famed hospitals. Manufactures auto and truck accessories, baking and packaging machinery, candy, cosmetics, electronic equipment, fancy food products, film projection equipment, hospital supplies, household chemicals, laundry and dry cleaning equipment, paints, pharmaceuticals, photocopy equipment, pumps, margarine, rust preventer, sashes and screens, steel products, toys, containers, postal scales. Headquarters for more than forty national firms.

8987 Arsenal
Black Swan Press/Surrealist Editions
PO Box 6424 Phone: (773)465-7774
Evanston, IL 60204
Magazine on art and literature. **Founded:** 1970. **Freq:** Irregular. **Key Personnel:** Franklin Rosemont, Editor.

8988 Auto Racing Digest
Century Publishing Co.
990 Grove St. Phone: (847)491-6440
Evanston, IL 60201-4370 Fax: (847)491-0459
Publisher E-mail: century@wwa.com

Magazine covering auto racing. **Founded:** 1973. **Freq:** Bimonthly. **Print Method:** Web offset. **Trim Size:** 5 3/8 x 7 1/2.

Cols./Page: 2. **Col. Width:** 26 nonpareils. **Col. Depth:** 91 agate lines. **Key Personnel:** Norman Jacobs, Publisher; Jim O'Connor, Senior Editor; Dale Jacobs, Production Dir.; James O'Connor, Managing Editor. **ISSN:** 9909-8029. **Subscription Rates:** $23.94 individuals; $4.99 single issue. **Remarks:** Accepts advertising.
Ad Rates: BW: $670 **Circ:** Paid ‡50,201
PCI: $70

8989 Baseball Digest
Century Publishing Co.
990 Grove St. Phone: (847)491-6440
Evanston, IL 60201-4370 Fax: (847)491-0459
Publisher E-mail: century@wwa.com

Magazine featuring major league baseball. **Founded:** May 1942. **Freq:** Monthly. **Print Method:** Web offset. **Trim Size:** 5 3/8 x 7 1/2. **Cols./Page:** 2. **Col. Width:** 24 nonpareils. **Col. Depth:** 91 agate lines. **Key Personnel:** John Kuenster, Editor; Norman Jacobs, President/Publisher. **ISSN:** 0005-609X. **Subscription Rates:** $23.94 individuals; $4.99 single issue. **Remarks:** Accepts advertising.
Ad Rates: BW: $2,940 **Circ:** Paid ★**172,088**
PCI: $295

8990 Basketball Digest
Century Publishing Co.
990 Grove St. Phone: (847)491-6440
Evanston, IL 60201-4370 Fax: (847)491-0459
Publisher E-mail: century@wwa.com

Magazine covering pro basketball action. **Founded:** 1973. **Freq:** 8/year. **Print Method:** Web offset. **Trim Size:** 5 3/8 x 7 1/2. **Cols./Page:** 2. **Col. Width:** 24 nonpareils. **Col. Depth:** 91 agate lines. **Key Personnel:** Norman Jacobs, Publisher; Dale Jacobs, Production Dir. **ISSN:** 0098-5988. **Subscription Rates:** $23.94 individuals; $4.99 single issue. **Remarks:** Accepts advertising.
Ad Rates: BW: $1,260 **Circ:** Paid ‡103,313
PCI: $125

8991 Bowling Digest
Century Publishing Co.
990 Grove St. Phone: (847)491-6440
Evanston, IL 60201-4370 Fax: (847)491-0459
Publisher E-mail: century@wwa.com

Magazine featuring tips and information for bowlers and fans. **Founded:** 1983. **Freq:** Bimonthly. **Print Method:** Web offset. **Trim Size:** 8 x 10 1/2. **Cols./Page:** 3. **Col. Width:** 27 nonpareils. **Col. Depth:** 140 agate lines. **Key Personnel:** Norman Jacobs, Publisher; Dale Jacobs, Director; James O'Connor, Managing Editor. **Subscription Rates:** $19.94 individuals; $29 Canada and other countries; $4.99 single issue. **Remarks:** Accepts advertising.
Ad Rates: BW: $1,950 **Circ:** Paid ★**95,232**
4C: $2,725
PCI: $115

8992 Builder Magazine, Uniform Series Edition
Herald Press
2840 Sheridan Rd.
Evanston, IL 60201
Publisher E-mail: hp@mph.org

Professional religious magazine. **Subtitle:** An Educational Magazine for Congregational Leaders. **Founded:** 1951. **Freq:** Monthly. **Print Method:** Offset. **Trim Size:** 5 1/4 x 7 5/8. **Cols./Page:** 2. **Col. Width:** 12 1/2 picas. **Col. Depth:** 38 picas. **Key Personnel:** David Hiebert, Editor, hiebert%mph@mcimail.com. **ISSN:** 0745-1687. **Subscription Rates:** $30.60 individuals; $26.20 Bulk; $2.70 single issue. **Remarks:** Advertising not accepted.
Circ: 6,500

8993 Cruise Travel Magazine
World Publishing Co.
990 Grove St. Phone: (847)491-6440
Evanston, IL 60201-4370 Fax: (847)491-6462
Publisher E-mail: century@wwa.com

Magazine covering consumer-oriented cruise-ship vacations. **Subtitle:** The Worldwide Cruise Vacation Magazine. **Founded:** June 1979. **Freq:** Bimonthly. **Print Method:** Offset. **Trim Size:** 8 x 10 1/2. **Cols./Page:** 3. **Col. Width:** 13 1/2 picas. **Col. Depth:** 134 agate lines. **Key Personnel:** Robert Meyers, Editor; Norman Jacobs, Publisher; Charles Doherty, Managing Editor. **ISSN:** 0199-5111. **Subscription Rates:** $23.94 individuals; $4.99 single issue.
Ad Rates: BW: $5,880 **Circ:** Paid ★**171,351**
4C: $10,500
PCI: $190

8994 The Daily Northwestern
Northwestern University Students Publishing Co.
1999 Sheridan Rd., Norris Center Phone: (847)491-7206
Fax: (847)491-9905
Evanston, IL 60208
Publication E-mail: daily@merle.acns.nwu.edu

Collegiate. **Founded:** 1879. **Freq:** Daily (during academic year). **Print Method:** Offset. **Trim Size:** 10 3/8 x 15 7/8. **Cols./Page:** 4. **Col. Width:** 2 1/2 inches. **Col. Depth:** 2 1/2 inches. **Key Personnel:** Stacia Campbell, Publisher. **USPS:** 852-520. **Subscription Rates:** $48 individuals. **Remarks:** Accepts advertising.
Ad Rates: BW: $480 **Circ:** Paid ‡800
4C: $19.28 Free ‡7,700
SAU: $17
PCI: $21

8995 Eighteenth-Century Studies
Johns Hopkins University Press
Eighteenth Century Studies
Department of French & Italian
Northwestern University
Evanston, IL 60208-2204
Publisher E-mail: jlinfo@jhupress.jhu.edu

Magazine containing articles and reviews on eighteenth-century subjects, including a variety of languages and literatures, classics, drama, history, religion, philosophy, music, science, and political science. **Founded:** 1967. **Freq:** Quarterly. **Print Method:** Offset. **Trim Size:** 6 x 9. **Cols./Page:** 1. **Col. Width:** 52 nonpareils. **Col. Depth:** 93 agate lines. **Key Personnel:** Bernadette Fort, Editor, fax (847)491-3877, b_fort@nwu.edu. **ISSN:** 0013-2586. **Subscription Rates:** $59; $70.4 other countries. **Remarks:** Accepts advertising. **URL:** http://muse.jhu.edu/.
Ad Rates: BW: $250 **Circ:** ‡4400

8996 Electronics News for China
Trade Sources, Inc.
1020 Church St. Phone: (847)475-1900
Evanston, IL 60201 Fax: (847)475-2794

Magazine for executives in the electronics manufacturing industry (Chinese). **Founded:** 1985. **Freq:** Monthly. **Print Method:** Webfed press. **Trim Size:** 8 1/16 x 10 5/8. **Cols./Page:** 2. **Key Personnel:** Jonathon Bigelow, General Mgr., phone (562)946-6089, fax (562)944-9478; Dianne Corriero, Circulation Mgr., phone (562)906-2320, fax (562)906-2420. **Subscription Rates:** Free to qualified subscribers. **Remarks:** Advertising accepted; rates available upon request. **URL:** http://www.asiansources.com.
Circ: Controlled 20,178

8997 Evanston Review
Pioneer Press Newspapers
1601 Sherman Ave. Phone: (847)866-6501
Evanston, IL 60201 Fax: (847)866-0965

Community newspaper (tabloid). **Founded:** 1925. **Freq:** Weekly (Thurs.). **Print Method:** Offset. **Trim Size:** 11 x 14. **Cols./Page:** 5. **Col. Width:** 9 3/4 inches. **Col. Depth:** 123/4 inches. **Key Personnel:** Gary Taylor, Editor; Paul Sassone, Managing Editor. **ISSN:** 1044-7733. **Subscription Rates:** $27.95 individuals. **Remarks:** Advertising accepted; rates available upon request. **URL:** http://www.pioneerlocal.com.
Circ: Thurs. ★**13,658**

8998 Football Digest
Century Publishing Co.
990 Grove St. Phone: (847)491-6440
Evanston, IL 60201-4370 Fax: (847)491-0459
Publisher E-mail: century@wwa.com

Pro football magazine. **Founded:** 1971. **Freq:** 10/year. **Print Method:** Web offset. **Trim Size:** 5 3/8 x 7 1/2. **Cols./Page:** 2. **Col. Width:** 26 nonpareils. **Col. Depth:** 91 agate lines. **Key Personnel:** Norman Jacobs, Publisher; Dale Jacobs, Production Dir. **ISSN:** 0015-6760. **Subscription Rates:** $23.94 individuals; $3.50 single issue. **Remarks:** Accepts advertising. **Alt. Formats:** Microfilm.
Ad Rates: BW: $1,765 **Circ:** Paid 233,639
4C: $2,565
PCI: $175

8999 Harmony
Symphony Orchestra Institute
1618 Orrington Ave., Ste. 318 Phone: (847)475-5001
Evanston, IL 60201 Fax: (847)475-2460
Publisher E-mail: symphonyoi@worldnet.att.net

Professional journal covering issues in symphony orchestra organizations. **Subtitle:** Forum of the Symphony Orchestra Institute. **Founded:** Oct. 1995. **Freq:** Semiannual. **Trim Size:** 6 x 9. **Cols./Page:** 1. **Col. Width:** 5 inches. **Key Personnel:** Paul R. Judy, Publisher, pjudy@soi.org; Emily Melton, Editor, emelton@soi.org. **ISSN:** 1083-9836. **Subscription Rates:** $35 individuals; $175 institutions. **Remarks:** Advertising not accepted. **URL:** http://www.soi.org.
Circ: Combined 6,500

9000 Hockey Digest
Century Publishing Co.
990 Grove St. Phone: (847)491-6440
Evanston, IL 60201-4370 Fax: (847)491-0459
Publisher E-mail: century@wwa.com

Magazine covering professional hockey. **Founded:** 1972. **Freq:** 8/year (Nov.-June). **Print Method:** Web offset. **Trim Size:** 5 3/8 x 7 1/2. **Cols./Page:** 2. **Col. Width:** 26 nonpareils. **Col. Depth:** 91 agate lines. **Key Personnel:** Norman Jacobs, Publisher; Kenneth Leiker, Senior Editor; Dale Jacobs, Production Dir.; James O'Connor, Managing Editor. **ISSN:** 0046-7693. **Subscription Rates:** $23.94 individuals; $4.99 single issue. **Remarks:** Accepts advertising.
Ad Rates: BW: $1,260 **Circ:** Paid ‡103,003
PCI: $125

9001 Journal of Biological Rhythms
Sage Publications Inc.
Dept. of Neurobiology and Physiology Phone: (847)491-2865
Fax: (847)467-4065
Northwestern University
2153 N. Campus Dr.
Evanston, IL 60208-3520
Publication E-mail: order@sagepub.com
Publisher E-mail: info@sagepub.com

Journal focusing on experimental biological research. **Founded:** 1986. **Freq:** 6/year. **Print Method:** Offset. **Trim Size:** 8 1/2 x 11. **Cols./Page:** 1. **Col. Width:** 72 nonpareils. **Col. Depth:** 126 agate lines. **Key Personnel:** Susan Hanscom, Circulation Mgr. **ISSN:** 0748-7304. **Subscription Rates:** $93 individuals; $282 institutions. **Remarks:** Accepts advertising. **URL:** http://www.sagepub.com. **Alt. Formats:** Microfilm.
Ad Rates: BW: $300 **Circ:** Paid ‡478
Non-paid ‡77

9002 Journal of Economics and Management Strategy
The MIT Press
Kellogg GSM, Leverone Hall Phone: (847)467-1776
Northwestern University Fax: (847)467-1777
Evanston, IL 60208-2013
Publication E-mail: jems@nwu.edu
Publisher E-mail: webmistress@mitpress.mit.edu

Journal providing a forum for research and discussion on competitive strategies of managers and the organizational structure of firms. **Founded:** 1992. **Freq:** Quarterly. **Trim Size:** 6 x 9. **Key Personnel:** Daniel F. Spulber, Editor. **ISSN:** 1058-6407. **Subscription Rates:** $40 U.S. and Canada; $102 institutions; $25 students and retirees; $10 single issue; $56 other countries; $118 institutions, other countries. **Remarks:** Accepts advertising. **Online:** Dialog (The Dialog Corporation). **Alt. Formats:** CD-ROM.
Circ: (Not Reported)

9003 The Magazine of Sigma Chi
Sigma Chi Fraternity
1714 Hinman Ave. Phone: (847)869-3655
PO Box 469 Fax: (847)869-4906
Evanston, IL 60204-0469
College fraternity publication. **Founded:** 1881. **Freq:** Quarterly. **Print Method:** Web offset. **Cols./Page:** 3. **Col. Width:** 26 nonpareils. **Col. Depth:** 134 agate lines. **Key Personnel:** Walter Hutchens, Editor. **Subscription Rates:** $40 individuals. **Remarks:** Advertising accepted; rates available upon request.
Circ: ‡50,000

9004 Massage Therapy Journal
American Massage Therapy Association
820 Davis St., Ste. 100 Phone: (847)864-0123
Evanston, IL 60201-4444 Fax: (847)864-1178

Magazine focusing on professional massage therapy benefits, techniques, research, news, and practitioners. **Founded:** 1948. **Freq:** Quarterly. **Key Personnel:** Theodore Berland, Editor. **Subscription Rates:** $20 individuals. **Remarks:** Accepts advertising.
Ad Rates: BW: $1,050 **Circ:** Paid 36,000

Morton Grove Champion Review - See Morton Grove

9005 New Directions for Teaching and Learning
Jossey-Bass Inc., Publishers
2003 Sheridan Rd.
Evanston, IL 60201
Publisher E-mail: webperson@jbp.com

Journal offering the latest ideas and techniques for improving college teaching. **Founded:** 1980. **Freq:** Quarterly. **Print Method:** Sheetfed offset. **Trim Size:** 6 x 9. **Cols./Page:** 1. **Col. Width:** 27 picas. **Col. Depth:** 45 picas. **Key Personnel:** Robert J. Menges, Editor; Marilla D. Svinicki, Advertising Mgr.

ISSN: 0271-0633. **Subscription Rates:** $47 individuals; $62 institutions. **Remarks:** Advertising not accepted.
Circ: Paid 828
Non-paid 65

9006 Patient Care and Nursing Products
Card-Zine Communications, Inc.
8912 Ewing Ave.
Evanston, IL 60203

Journal for health-care professionals reporting products that serve the needs of limited mobility and immobilized patients. **Subtitle:** A Compendium of Patient Care, Products, Equipment, Supplies, Technology and Services. **Founded:** 1987. **Freq:** Quarterly. **Print Method:** Web offset. **Trim Size:** 6 x 10 7/8. **Key Personnel:** Ira Lieb, Publisher; Julie Euler, Editor. **Subscription Rates:** Free. **Remarks:** Accepts advertising. **Formerly:** Limited Mobility and Immobilized and Patient Products.
Ad Rates: BW: $5,385 **Circ:** Controlled ‡75,171
4C: $6,185

9007 The ROTARIAN
Rotary International
One Rotary Center Phone: (847)866-3000
1560 Sherman Ave. Fax: (847)866-9732
Evanston, IL 60201
Publication E-mail: 75457.3577@compuserve.com

General interest magazine on community service and international understanding. **Founded:** Jan. 1911. **Freq:** Monthly. **Print Method:** Offset. **Trim Size:** 8 1/8 x 10 13/16. **Cols./Page:** 3. **Col. Width:** 2 1/4 inches. **Col. Depth:** 140 agate lines. **Key Personnel:** Willmon L. White, Editor-in-Chief, phone (847)866-3046; Edward A. Schimmelpfennig, Advertising Mgr., phone (847)866-3195, schimme@riorc.mhs.compuserve.c; Charles W. Pratt, Editor, phone (847)866-3205, prattc@riotc.mhs.compuserve.com. **ISSN:** 0035-838X. **Subscription Rates:** $12 individuals; $1 single issue. **Remarks:** Accepts advertising.
Ad Rates: GLR: $30 **Circ:** Paid ★**513,057**
BW: $8,145
4C: $11,150
PCI: $420

Skokie Review - See Skokie

9008 Soccer Digest
Century Publishing Co.
990 Grove St. Phone: (847)491-6440
Evanston, IL 60201-4370 Fax: (847)491-0459
Publisher E-mail: century@wwa.com

Soccer magazine. **Founded:** 1978. **Freq:** Bimonthly. **Print Method:** Web offset. **Trim Size:** 5 3/8 x 7 1/2. **Cols./Page:** 2. **Col. Width:** 2 1/16 inches. **Col. Depth:** 6 1/2 inches. **Key Personnel:** Norman Jacobs, Publisher; Kenneth Leiker, Senior Editor; Mike Gallagher, Production Dir.; James O'Connor, Managing Editor. **ISSN:** 0149-2365. **Subscription Rates:** $23.94 individuals; $3.50 single issue. **Remarks:** Accepts advertising.
Ad Rates: BW: $630 **Circ:** ‡36,000
PCI: $50

9009 tomorrowsf
Unifont Co. Inc.
Box 6038 Phone: (847)864-3668
Evanston, IL 60204 Fax: (847)864-2840
Publisher E-mail: tomorrowsf.com

Consumer magazine covering fiction, reviews, cartoons, and poetry. **Founded:** 1993. **Freq:** Bimonthly. **Key Personnel:** Algis Budrys, Editor/Art Dir., abudrys@tomorrowsf.com; Kandis Elliot, Production Mgr. **ISSN:** 1092-4990. **Subscription Rates:** $10 individuals. **Remarks:** Accepts advertising. **URL:** http://www.tomorrowsf.com. **Former name:** Tomorrow Speculative Fiction.
Ad Rates: GLR: $.15 **Circ:** Paid 1,000
BW: $100
4C: $150

9010 TravelAmerica
World Publishing Co.
990 Grove St. Phone: (847)491-6440
Evanston, IL 60201-4370 Fax: (847)491-6462
Publisher E-mail: century@wwa.com

Consumer travel magazine. **Subtitle:** The No. 1 U.S. Vacation Magazine. **Founded:** 1985. **Freq:** Bimonthly. **Print Method:** Offset. **Trim Size:** 8 x 10 1/2. **Cols./Page:** 3. **Col. Width:** 27 nonpareils. **Col. Depth:** 140 agate lines. **Key Personnel:** Robert Meyers, Editor; Randy Mink, Managing Editor; Norman Jacobs, Publisher, fax (847)491-0459, normj@wwa.com. **ISSN:** 0890-2852. **Subscription Rates:** $23.94 individuals; $4.99 single issue. **Remarks:** Accepts advertising. **URL:** http://www.travelamerica.com.
Ad Rates: BW: $12,495 **Circ:** Paid ★**401,035**
4C: $16,995

9011 Triquarterly
Northwestern University Press
2020 Ridge Ave. Fax: (847)467-2096
Evanston, IL 60208-4302 Free: (800)832-3615
Publisher E-mail: nupress@nwu.edu

Scholarly journal covering writing, art, and culture. **Founded:** 1964. **Freq:** Quarterly. **Key Personnel:** Susan Hahn, Editor; Kimberly Maselli, Publisher; Kirstie Felland, Operations. **ISSN:** 0041-3097. **Subscription Rates:** $24 individuals; $36 institutions; $11.95 single issue. **Remarks:** Advertising accepted; rates available upon request.
Circ: (Not Reported)

9012 Union Signal
National Woman's Christian Temperance Union
1730 Chicago Ave. Phone: (847)864-1396
Evanston, IL 60201-4585 Fax: (847)864-9497
Free: (800)755-1321
Publisher E-mail: sarah@wctu.com

Magazine concerning alcohol, tobacco, and illegal drugs. **Subtitle:** A Journal of Social Welfare. **Founded:** 1883. **Freq:** Quarterly. **Print Method:** Offset. **Trim Size:** 5 1/2 x 8 1/2. **Cols./Page:** 2. **Col. Width:** 42 nonpareils. **Col. Depth:** 133 agate lines. **Key Personnel:** Sarah F. Ward, Editor, sarah@uctu.org. **ISSN:** 0041-7033. **Subscription Rates:** $8 individuals. **Remarks:** Advertising accepted; rates available upon request.
Circ: ‡2,000

9013 WKTA-AM - 1330
4320 Dundee Rd. Phone: (847)498-3350
Northbrook, IL 60062 Fax: (847)498-5743
E-mail: pclradio@techinter.com

Format: Ethnic. **Networks:** Independent Broadcasting. **Founded:** 1953. **Formerly:** WSSY-AM (1987). **Operating Hours:** Continuous; 100% local. **ADI:** Chicago (LaSalle), IL. **Key Personnel:** Kent Gustafson, Vice President/General Manager; Bill Wallace, Sales Mgr.; Sterling Hazen, Contact; Walter Kotaba, President. **Wattage:** 5000. **Ad Rates:** $40 for 30 seconds; $80 for 60 seconds. International Network. **URL:** http://www.pclradio.com.

9014 WNUR-FM - 89.3
1905 Sheridan Rd. Phone: (708)491-7101
Evanston, IL 60208-2260 Fax: (708)467-2058

Format: Alternative/New Music/Progressive. **Owner:** Northwestern University, at above address. **Founded:** 1950. **Operating Hours:** Continuous. **Key Personnel:** Todd Hyman, Music Dir.; Sieah Huang Grahm, Music Dir.; Michael Schneider, General Mgr.; Matt Walters, Program Dir.; Sean Claiborne, Operations Dir.; Dana Hirsch, Promotions Dir. **Local Programs:** *Airplay*, Matt Smith, (708)491-7102; *Public Affairs*, Katherine Trinidad, (708)491-7101; *Sports Voice*, Jeff Kasper, (708)491-2234. **Wattage:** 7200. **Ad Rates:** Noncommercial.

9015 WONX-AM - 1590
2100 Lee St. Phone: (847)475-1590
Evanston, IL 60202 Fax: (773)273-1590

Format: Hispanic; Ethnic. **Networks:** Independent. **Owner:** Kovas Communications, at above address. **Founded:** 1947. **Formerly:** WNMP-AM; WLTD-AM. **Operating Hours:** Continuous. **Key Personnel:** Ken Kovas, General Mgr.; Judy Selby, Sales Mgr. **Wattage:** 3500 day; 2500 night.

FAIRBURY, pop. 3,544.

Livingston Co. (NEC). 36 m NE of Bloomington. Limestone pits. Manufactures women's dresses, steel tubing, insulators, feed, prefabricated buildings; tool and dies. Grain, stock, poultry farms. Soybeans, livestock, corn, oats.

9016 Blade
Leader American Publishing
125 W. Locust St. Phone: (815)692-2366
Fairbury, IL 61739 Fax: (815)692-3782
Publication E-mail: dlfby@feg.net

Community newspaper. **Subtitle:** The Blade. **Founded:** 1868. **Freq:** Weekly (Thurs.). **Print Method:** Offset. **Cols./Page:** 6. **Col. Width:** 30 nonpareils. **Col. Depth:** 284 agate lines. **Key Personnel:** Judy Knauer, Editor; Jim Foster, Publisher. **USPS:** 183-280. **Subscription Rates:** $25 individuals; $30 out of county. **Remarks:** Accepts advertising.
Ad Rates: GLR: $.39 **Circ:** ‡3,500
SAU: $5.85

9017 Illinois Entertainer
Roberts Publishing, Inc.
319 W. Locust St. Phone: (312)922-9333
Fairbury, IL 61739
Music entertainment magazine. **Founded:** 1975. **Freq:** Monthly. **Print Method:** Offset. **Trim Size:** 10 7/8 x 12. **Cols./Page:** 6. **Col. Width:** 21 nonpareils. **Col. Depth:** 189 agate lines. **Key Personnel:** Michael C. Harris, Editor; Dave Roberts, Publisher; John Vernon, Advertising Mgr. **Subscription Rates:** $35 First Class; $26 Third Class; $5 single issue. **Remarks:** Advertising accepted; rates available upon request (708)298-7970. **Available Online.**
Ad Rates: BW: $2,100 **Circ:** Combined 74,606
4C: $3,100

FAIRFIELD†, pop. 5,954.

Wayne Co. (S). 32 m N.E. of Mt Vernon. Manufactures auto parts, doors, windows, children wear and uniforms, component parts. Oil wells Grain, dairy, poultry farms. Corn, soybeans.

9018 Wayne County Press
213 E. Main St. Phone: (618)842-2662
PO Box F Fax: (618)842-7912
Fairfield, IL 62837
Publication E-mail: wcpress@midwest.net

Community newspaper. **Founded:** 1866. **Freq:** Semiweekly (Mon. and Thurs.). **Print Method:** Offset. Uses mats. **Cols./Page:** 6. **Col. Width:** 26 nonpareils. **Col. Depth:** 294 agate lines. **Key Personnel:** Jack Vertrees, Editor; Tom Mathews, Jr., Editor and Publisher. **Subscription Rates:** $33. **Remarks:** Accepts advertising.
Ad Rates: GLR: $.60 **Circ:** ‡8,125
BW: $1,058.40
PCI: $8.12

9019 WFIW-AM - 1390
Box 310 Phone: (618)842-2159
Fairfield, IL 62837 Fax: (618)847-5907

Format: News; Talk. **Networks:** ABC. **Owner:** Wayne County Broadcasting Co., Inc., at above address. **Founded:** 1953. **Operating Hours:** Continuous. **ADI:** Evansville, IN (Madisonville, KY). **Key Personnel:** Tom Land, Chairman; David H. Land, President; Len Wells, News Dir.; Stan David, Sports Dir. **Wattage:** 710. **Ad Rates:** $11 for 30 seconds; $15 for 60 seconds. Combined advertising rates available with WFIW-FM, WOKZ-FM.

9020 WFIW-FM - 104.9
Box 310 Phone: (618)842-2159
Fairfield, IL 62837 Fax: (618)847-5907

Format: Oldies. **Networks:** ABC; Jones Satellite. **Owner:** Wayne County Broadcasting Co., Inc., at above address. **Founded:** 1965. **Operating Hours:** Continuous. **ADI:** Evansville, IN (Madisonville, KY). **Key Personnel:** Tom Land, Chairman; David H. Land, President; Len Wells, News Dir.; Stan David, Sports Dir. **Wattage:** 4900. **Ad Rates:** $11 for 30 seconds; $15 for 60 seconds. Combined advertising rates available with WFIW-AM & WAKZ-FM.

9021 WOKZ-FM - 105.9
Box 310 Phone: (618)842-2159
Fairfield, IL 62837 Fax: (618)847-5907

Format: Country. **Networks:** Jones Satellite. **Owner:** Wayne County Broadcasting Co., Inc., at above address. **Founded:** 1996. **Operating Hours:** Continuous. **ADI:** Evansville, IN (Madisonville, KY). **Key Personnel:** Thomas S. Land, Chm.; David H. Land, Pres./Gen. Mgr.; Len Wells, News Dir. **Wattage:** 6000. **Ad Rates:** $11 for 30 seconds; $15 for 60 seconds. Combined advertising rates available with WFIW-AM & WFIW-FM.

FARINA, pop. 594.

Fayette Co. (S). 100 m SW of Champaign. Egg freezing plant. Nursery. Grain and fruit farming.

9022 Farina News
Salem Times Commoner
PO Box H Phone: (618)245-6216
Farina, IL 62838 Fax: (618)245-6216

Newspaper. **Founded:** 1882. **Freq:** Weekly (Thurs.). **Print Method:** Offset. **Cols./Page:** 8. **Col. Width:** 21 nonpareils. **Col. Depth:** 301 agate lines. **Key Personnel:** Shirley Ann Quick, Editor and Publisher. **Subscription Rates:** $7 individuals.

FARMER CITY, pop. 2,252.

De Witt Co. (C). 18 m NE of Clinton.

9023 Farmer City Journal
Illinois Valley Press
221 S. Main Phone: (309)928-2193
PO Box 80 Fax: (309)928-0360
Farmer City, IL 61842
Publisher E-mail: journal@farmwagon.com

Community newspaper. **Founded:** 1872. **Freq:** Weekly (Wed.). **Print Method:** Offset. **Trim Size:** 11 1/4 x 13 3/4. **Cols./Page:** 5. **Col. Width:** 23 nonpareils. **Col. Depth:** 182 agate lines. **Key Personnel:** Steve Hoffman, Editor, shoff@farmwagon.com. **ISSN:** 1874-6000. **Subscription Rates:** $25 individuals. **Remarks:** Accepts advertising combination rates avaiable with the LeRoy and Mahomet Journals.
Ad Rates: BW: $373.75 **Circ:** Combined ‡1,700
PCI: $5.75

9024 WZRO-FM - 98.3
407 N. Main Phone: (309)928-9876
Farmer City, IL 61842

Format: Contemporary Country. **Networks:** Satellite Music Network; Motor Racing; Brownfield. **Owner:** Potomac Broadcasting, Inc., at above address, Leonardtown, MD 20650. **Founded:** 1983. **Operating Hours:** Continuous. **Key Personnel:** Robert E. Johnson, General Mgr.; Sharon C. Johnson, President. **Wattage:** 3000. **Ad Rates:** Advertising accepted; rates available upon request.

FARMINGTON

9025 Farmington Bugle
Tri-County News Edition
116 S. Magnolia Phone: (309)742-2521
PO Box 289 Fax: (309)742-2511
Elmwood, IL 61529
Community newspaper. **Founded:** 1881. **Freq:** Weekly (Thurs.). **Print Method:** Offset. **Cols./Page:** 6. **Col. Width:** 20 nonpareils. **Col. Depth:** 224 agate lines. **Key Personnel:** DeEllda Swindler, Publisher. **Subscription Rates:** $16 individuals.
Ad Rates: BW: $192 **Circ:** ‡375
4C: $292
PCI: $2.50

FISHER, pop. 1,572.

Champaign Co. (E). On Sangamon River, 40 m E of Bloomington. Agriculture. Corn, soybeans, oats.

9026 Fisher Reporter
118 S. 3rd St. Phone: (217)897-1525
PO Box 400
Fisher, IL 61843
Newspaper. **Founded:** 1889. **Freq:** Weekly (Wed.). **Trim Size:** 11 1/2 x 17 1/2. **Cols./Page:** 5. **Col. Width:** 2 inches. **Col. Depth:** 16 inches. **Key Personnel:** Susan Hanes Helle, Editor; Ed Pyne, Publisher. **Subscription Rates:** $12 individuals. **Remarks:** Advertising not accepted for liquor.
Ad Rates: GLR: $.80 **Circ:** ‡1,067
SAU: $3.60
PCI: $3.60

FLORA, pop. 5,379.

Clay Co. (SE). 100 m E of St. Louis, Mo. Manufactures shoes, wood stains, steel products, marine parts, rayon garments, automotive parts. Oil producers. Argiculture. Clover seed, soybeans, peas.

9027 Daily Clay County Advocate-Press
Clay County Advocate Press, Inc.
105 W. North Ave. Phone: (618)662-8392
PO Box 519 Fax: (618)662-2939
Flora, IL 62839-1613
General newspaper. **Founded:** 1886. **Freq:** Daily (eve.). **Print Method:** Offset. **Trim Size:** 14 x 23. **Cols./Page:** 6. **Col. Width:** 12 picas. **Col. Depth:** 21 1/2 inches. **Key Personnel:** Duane E. Crays, Publisher, phone (618)662-2108; Shirley Garrett, Advertising, phone (618)662-2108. **USPS:** 116-560. **Subscription Rates:** $70.50 individuals; $84.50 out of county. **Remarks:** Accepts advertising.
Ad Rates: GLR: $.30 **Circ:** Paid 3,750
SAU: $6.05 Free 50
PCI: $5.65

9028 WNOI-FM - 103.9
12th & N. Olive Phone: (618)662-8331
Flora, IL 62839 Fax: (618)662-2407

Format: Adult Contemporary; Oldies. **Networks:** Jones Satellite; RFD Illinois. **Owner:** H&R Communications, Inc., PO Box 368, Flora, IL 62839. **Founded:** 1971. **Operating Hours:** Continuous; 9% network, 91% local. **ADI:** Terre Haute, IN. **Key Personnel:** Brenda Miller, Sales Mgr.; Steve Lovellette, President; Randy Poole, General Mgr.; Bill Thompson, Contact. **Wattage:** 3300. **Ad Rates:** $6.90 for 30 seconds; $9.90 for 60 seconds.

FLOSSMOOR

9029 Adhesives & Sealants Industry
Business News Publishing Co., Inc.
PO Box 400 Phone: (708)922-0761
Flossmoor, IL 60422 Fax: (708)922-0762
Publication E-mail: edasi@worldnet.att.net

Trade magazine for manufacturers, formulators, and applicators of adhesives and sealants. **Founded:** Feb. 1994. **Freq:** 9/year. **Print Method:** Web offset. **Trim Size:** 8 1/8 x 10 7/8. **Key Personnel:** Karen Kramer, Editor; Donna Campbell, Assoc. Publisher, phone (610)650-4050, fax (610)650-4051, donnabnp@aol.com; Tracy Briggs, Circulation Dir., phone (248)244-6256, fax (248)362-4932, briggst@bnp.com. **ISSN:** 1070-9592. **Subscription Rates:** Free to qualified subscribers. **Remarks:** Accepts advertising.
Ad Rates: BW: $2,910 **Circ:** Controlled 16,500
4C: $4,295

9030 WHFH-FM - 88.5
999 Kedzie Ave. Phone: (708)798-9434
Flossmoor, IL 60422 Fax: (708)799-3142

Format: Album-Oriented Rock (AOR); Alternative/New Music/Progressive. **Networks:** Independent. **Owner:** Homewood Flossmoor High School District 233, at above address. **Founded:** 1965. **Operating Hours:** 7 a.m.-9 p.m., Mon.-Fri.; 100% local. **Key Personnel:** Robert Comstock, General Mgr.; Paul Boomer, Station Mgr.; Kevin Brow, Operations Dir.; Doug Hink, News Dir.; Megan Bromlette, Sports Dir.; Dan Abernathy, Business & P.R. **Wattage:** 1500. **Ad Rates:** Noncommercial.

FORD HEIGHTS

Cook Co.

9031 WCFJ-AM - 1470
1000 Lincoln Hwy. Phone: (708)758-8600
Ford Heights, IL 60411-2946 Fax: (708)737-7124

Format: Gospel; Contemporary Christian; Religious. **Networks:** Independent. **Founded:** 1963. **Formerly:** WMPP-AM (1989). **Operating Hours:** Continuous. **Key Personnel:** Darryl Chavers, General Mgr. **Wattage:** 1000. **Ad Rates:** $10 for 30 seconds; $20 for 60 seconds.

FOREST PARK, pop. 15,177.

Cook Co. (NE). 3 m S of Elmwood Park. Residential.

9032 S Gaugian
Heimburger House Publishing Co.
7236 W. Madison St. Phone: (708)366-1973
Forest Park, IL 60130 Fax: (708)366-1973

Magazine focusing on "S" scale (1:64 scale) model railroading. **Founded:** 1962. **Freq:** Bimonthly. **Print Method:** Offset. **Trim Size:** 8 1/2 x 11. **Cols./Page:** 3. **Col. Width:** 27 nonpareils. **Col. Depth:** 138 agate lines. **Key Personnel:** Donald J. Heimburger, Editor and Publisher; Susan O'Brien, Assoc. Ed. **ISSN:** 0273-6241. **Subscription Rates:** $29 individuals in USA; $6.25 single issue; $35 out of country.
Ad Rates: BW: $249 **Circ:** ‡6,000
4C: $399

9033 Sn3 Modeler
Heimburger House Publishing Co.
7236 W. Madison St. Phone: (708)366-1973
Forest Park, IL 60130
Consumer magazine covering model railroading. **Founded:** 1984. **Freq:** Semiannual. **Print Method:** Offset. **Key Personnel:** Don Heimburger, Editor; Susan O'Brien, Assoc. Editor. **Subscription Rates:** $12 individuals; $18 out of country; $4.75 single issue. **Remarks:** Accepts advertising.
Ad Rates: BW: $174 **Circ:** Paid 2,000
4C: $324

FORRESTON, pop. 1,384.

Ogle Co. (N). 14 m S of Freeport. Egg farms. Manufactures plastic, tile, roofing materials. Agriculture. Feed, oats, barley. Dairy, hogs, cattle.

9034 Journal
313 E. Main
Forreston, IL 61030

Newspaper with a Republican orientation. **Founded:** 1865. **Freq:** Weekly (Thurs.). **Print Method:** Offset. **Cols./Page:** 5. **Col. Width:** 23 nonpareils. **Col. Depth:** 238 agate lines. **Key Personnel:** Bruce Harrison, Reporter. **Subscription Rates:** $19.50 individuals. **Remarks:** Accepts advertising.
Ad Rates: GLR: $.19 **Circ:** 1,175
PCI: $4.30

FRANKLIN, pop. 645.

Morgan Co. (WC). 12 m SE of Jacksonville. Agriculture.

9035 The Franklin Times
Franklin Times Publishing
208 Main Phone: (217)675-2461
Franklin, IL 62638 Fax: (217)675-2461

Newspaper. **Founded:** 1867. **Freq:** Weekly (Thurs.). **Print Method:** Offset. **Trim Size:** 10 1/4 x 16. **Cols./Page:** 5. **Col. Width:** 24 nonpareils. **Col. Depth:** 218 agate lines. **Key Personnel:** Ira Lionts, Editor and Publisher, ijlionts@juno.com; Fred Greer, Sales Mgr. **USPS:** 208-520. **Subscription Rates:** $8 individuals; $12 out of area; $2.75 single issue. **Remarks:** Accepts advertising.
Ad Rates: BW: $180 **Circ:** ‡550
PCI: $2.75

FRANKLIN PARK

9036 Franklin Park Herald-Journal
Pioneer Press Newspapers
1148 Westgate Ave. Phone: (708)383-3200
Oak Park, IL 60301 Fax: (708)383-3678

Community newspaper (tabloid). **Founded:** 1970. **Freq:** Weekly (Wed.). **Print Method:** Offset. **Cols./Page:** 5. **Col. Width:** 10 inches. **Col. Depth:** 14 inches. **Key Personnel:** Rick Behren, Editor; Paul Sassone, Managing Editor. **Subscription Rates:** $13.95 individuals; $15.95 out of county.
Circ: Wed. ★3,593

FREEBURG, pop. 2,989.

St Clair Co. (SW). 7 m SE of Belleville. Manufactures brass and aluminum castings, electrical supplies, fire engines. Flour mills. Coal mines. White oak timber. Dairy, stock, truck, grain farms.

9037 The Freeburg Tribune
10 S. Monroe St. Phone: (618)539-3320
Box 98
Freeburg, IL 62243
Founded: 1897. **Freq:** Weekly (Thurs.). **Print Method:** Offset. **Cols./Page:** 6. **Col. Width:** 2 1/4 inches. **Col. Depth:** 301 agate lines. **Key Personnel:** Harold Carpenter, Editor. **Subscription Rates:** $15 St. Clair; $20 out of St. Clair. **Remarks:** Accepts advertising.
Ad Rates: SAU: $7.50 **Circ:** ‡2,700

FREEPORT†, pop. 26,406.

Stephenson Co. (N). 116 m NW of Chicago. Manufactures water coolers, batteries, patent medicines, dental processing, hardware, farm and woodworking machinery, plastics, precision screw products, construction vehicle components, metal plating, ultrasonic equipment barbecue grills, spices, cosmetics, brooms, boxes, potato chips, curtain rods, tires, plaques, switches, concrete vaults, Foundries. Grain, dairy farms. Corn, oats, soybeans. feed pellets.

9038 Freeport Journal-Standard
The Journal-Standard
27 S. State Ave. Phone: (815)232-1171
PO Box 330 Fax: (815)232-3601
Freeport, IL 61032
Free: (800)325-6397

General newspaper. **Founded:** 1847. **Freq:** Daily (eve.) and Sat. (morn.). **Print Method:** Offset. **Cols./Page:** 6. **Col. Width:** 26 nonpareils. **Col. Depth:** 300 agate lines. **Key Personnel:** Julie Taulman, Publisher. **Subscription Rates:** $126 individuals. **Remarks:** Accepts advertising. **Feature Editors:** Olga Carlisle, *Food*; Greg Douglas, *Medical*; Maisy Fernandez, *Entertainment*, *Travel*; Sara Greene, *Regional*; Laurel Rudd, *Garden/Home*.
Ad Rates: GLR: $.95 **Circ:** Mon.-Sat. ★16,003
BW: $1,677
4C: $2,031
SAU: $13
PCI: $9.01

9039 WFPS-FM - 92.1
Box 747 Phone: (815)235-7191
Freeport, IL 61032 Fax: (815)235-4318
E-mail: star921@aeroinc.net

Format: Adult Contemporary. **Networks:** NBC. **Owner:** Mayfair Communications, L.L.C., at above address. **Founded:** Nov. 1, 1970. **Formerly:** WACI-FM (1982). **Operating Hours:** Continuous. **ADI:** Rockford, IL. **Key Personnel:** Kim Grimes, General Mgr.; Brad Hart, News Dir.; Patrick Walstow, Oper. Mgr./Prog. Dir. **Wattage:** 6000. **Ad Rates:** $8.5-10 for 30 seconds. Combined advertising rates available with WFRL-AM.

9040 WFRL-AM - 1570
834 N Tower Rd. Phone: (815)235-7191
PO Box 747 Fax: (815)235-4318
Freeport, IL 61032-0747
E-mail: star921@aeroinc.net

Networks: ABC; Satellite Music Network. **Owner:** Mayfair Communications, L. L. C., at above address. **Founded:** Oct. 28, 1947. **Operating Hours:** Continuous. **ADI:** Rockford, IL. **Key Personnel:** Kim Grimes, General Mgr.; Patrick Walstow, Oper. Mgr./Prog. Dir. **Wattage:** 5000 day; 500 night. **Ad Rates:** $8-35 for 60 seconds. Combined advertising rates available with WFPS-FM.

FULTON, pop. 3,936.

Whiteside Co. (NW). On Mississippi River, across from Clinton, Ia. Grain shipping port. Manufactures household items, industrial chain, metal fabrications. Vegetable hothouses. Agriculture. Corn, wheat, soybeans.

9041 Fulton Press
The Fulton Press
PO Box 30 Phone: (815)589-2424
Fulton, IL 61252 Fax: (815)589-2568

Newspaper. **Founded:** 1854. **Freq:** Weekly (Wed.). **Print Method:** Offset. **Cols./Page:** 8. **Col. Width:** 21 nonpareils. **Col. Depth:** 252 agate lines. **Key Personnel:** Henry Kramer, Editor; Henry and Doris M. Kramer, Publisher. **Subscription Rates:** $32 individuals. **Remarks:** Accepts advertising.
Ad Rates: GLR: $5 **Circ:** Combined 5,500
PCI: $5

9042 Whiteside Shopper
The Fulton Press
PO Box 30 Phone: (815)589-2424
Fulton, IL 61252 Fax: (815)589-2568

Shopper. **Freq:** Weekly (Tues.). **Print Method:** Offset. **Cols./Page:** 8. **Col. Width:** 21 nonpareils. **Col. Depth:** 252 agate lines. **Key Personnel:** Henry Kramer, Publisher.
Circ: (Not Reported)

GALENA†, pop. 3,897.

Jo Daviess Co. (NW). On Galena River, 20 m SE of Dubuque, Ia. Foundries. Manufactures stoves, lubricating oil, mining machinery, neon signs, dairy products, batteries. Dairy farms.

9043 Galena Gazette and Advertiser
Galena Gazette Publications, Inc.
PO Box 319 Phone: (815)777-0019
Galena, IL 61036-0319 Fax: (815)777-2578
Free: (800)373-6397

Community newspaper. **Founded:** Nov. 15, 1834. **Freq:** Weekly (Wed.). **Print Method:** Offset. **Trim Size:** 10 x 16. **Cols./Page:** 4. **Col. Width:** 15 picas. **Col. Depth:** 16 inches. **Key Personnel:** P. Carter Newton, Publisher; Robin Buss, Advertising Mgr. **USPS:** 574-400. **Subscription Rates:** $23 individuals; $28 out of area; $35 out of state. **Remarks:** Accepts advertising. **Absorbed:** North Western Gazette; Elizabeth-Hanover Gazette.
Ad Rates: GLR: $.56 **Circ:** ‡5,500
BW: $630
4C: $750
SAU: $6.50

GALESBURG†, pop. 35,305.

Knox Co. (NWC). 53 m NW of Peoria. Knox College. Coal mines. Manufactures foundry products, refrigerators, steel stampings and enameling products, sanitary supplies, uniforms, marine accessories, prefabricated metal buildings, industrial hose, tanks, gates, ladders, garage doors, auto parts, paint, railway equipment, air conditioners, power mowers, bricks, overalls, dairy products.

9044 The Galesburg Post
80 S. Cherry St. Phone: (309)343-5617
Galesburg, IL 61401 Fax: (309)343-2518

Community newspaper. **Founded:** July 1928. **Freq:** Weekly (Thurs.). **Print Method:** Offset. **Trim Size:** 10 x 16. **Cols./Page:** 6. **Col. Width:** 1 5/8 inches. **Col. Depth:** 16 inches. **Subscription Rates:** $11.95 individuals; $21.95 out of area; $24.95 out of state. **Remarks:** Accepts advertising. **URL:** http://www.galesburg.post@misslink.net.
Ad Rates: GLR: $.10 **Circ:** Paid ‡2,033
BW: $75 Free ‡70
SAU: $2
PCI: $3

9045 Knox Student
Knox College
College Box 240 Phone: (309)341-7418
Galesburg, IL 61401 Fax: (309)343-4258
Publication E-mail: tks@knox.knox.edu

Collegiate newspaper. **Founded:** 1878. **Freq:** Biweekly. **Print Method:** Letterpress and offset. **Trim Size:** 11 x 17. **Cols./Page:** 5. **Col. Width:** 4 nonpareils. **Col. Depth:** 224 agate lines. **Key Personnel:** Brynn Seibert, Editor, mseibert@knox.edu. **Subscription Rates:** $25 individuals. **Remarks:** Accepts advertising. **Feature Editors:** Katie Holx, *Features*, kholx@knox.edu.
Ad Rates: GLR: $.41 **Circ:** ‡1,800
BW: $225
PCI: $3

9046 The Register-Mail
140 S. Prairie St. Phone: (309)343-7181
PO Box 310 Fax: (309)342-5171
Galesburg, IL 61402-0310
Free: (800)747-7181

General newspaper. **Founded:** 1870. **Freq:** Daily (eve.) and Sat. (morn.). **Print Method:** Offset. **Cols./Page:** 6. **Col. Width:** 25 nonpareils. **Col. Depth:** 301 agate lines. **Key Personnel:** Robert Harrison, Editor; Don Cooper, Publisher; Doris Medhurst, Advertising Mgr. **USPS:** 213-060. **Subscription Rates:** $98 in state; $147 out of state. **Remarks:** Accepts advertising.
Ad Rates: GLR: $1.04 **Circ:** Mon.-Sat. ★**16,960**
BW: $2,174.94 Sun. ★**15,834**
4C: $2,384.94
SAU: $16.86
PCI: $14.56

9047 Nova Cablevision Inc.
1345 No Seminary Phone: (309)342-9681
Box 1412 Fax: (309)342-4408
Galesburg, IL 61401

Founded: 1988. **Key Personnel:** Robert G. Fisher, Jr., President; Dave West, Technician; Robert G. Fisher, Jr. **Cities Served:** Cameron, Gladstone, Little York, Norris, Trivoli, IL: subscribing households 698; 23 channels.

9048 WAAG-FM - 94.9
154 E. Simmons Phone: (309)342-5131
Galesburg, IL 61401 Fax: (309)342-0840
E-mail: fm95@galesburg.net

Format: Contemporary Country. **Networks:** Mutual Broadcasting System. **Founded:** 1966. **Operating Hours:** Continuous; 100% local. **Key Personnel:** Roger Lundeen, General Mgr.; Brad Bennewitz, Sports Director; Brian Prescott, Program Dir.; Brian Prescott, Music Dir.; Shawn Harmsen, News Dir. **Wattage:** 50,000. **Ad Rates:** $18-36 for 30 seconds; $20-40 for 60 seconds.

9049 WAIK-AM - 1590
235 E. Main St. Phone: (309)342-3161
Galesburg, IL 61401 Fax: (309)342-0199

Format: Talk. **Networks:** ABC. **Owner:** WPW Broadcasting, 51 N. Prairie St., Galesburg, IL 61401. **Founded:** 1957. **Formerly:** WQUB-AM (1958). **Operating Hours:** Continuous. **Key Personnel:** David Klockenga, General Mgr.; Jon Raymond, Director; David Klockenga, News Dir. **Wattage:** 5000. **Ad Rates:** $10 for 30 seconds; $10 for 60 seconds. Combined advertising rates available with WBYS-AM/FM.

9050 WGIL-AM - 1400
154 E. Simmons Phone: (309)342-5131
Galesburg, IL 61401 Fax: (309)342-0840
E-mail: wgil@galesburg.net

Format: Sports; News; Talk. **Networks:** Mutual Broadcasting System; Illinois Public Radio. **Founded:** 1938. **Operating Hours:** Continuous; 20% network, 80% local. **Key Personnel:** Roger Lundeen, General Mgr.; Brian Prescott, Program Dir.; Brad Bennewitz, Sports Dir.; Terry Cavanaugh, Music Dir.; Shawn Harmsen, News Dir. **Wattage:** 1000. **Ad Rates:** $12-28 for 30 seconds; $16-32 for 60 seconds.

9051 WLSR-FM - 92.7
235 E. Main St. Phone: (309)342-3161
Galesburg, IL 61401 Fax: (309)342-0199

Format: Classic Rock. **Networks:** ABC. **Owner:** Northern Broadcast Group, Inc., 51 N. Prairie St., Galesburg, IL 61401. **Founded:** 1978. **Formerly:** WGBQ-FM. **Operating Hours:** Continuous; 1% network, 99% local. **Key Personnel:** Albert Berglund, General Mgr.; Rick Heath, Program Dir.; David Klockenga, News Dir.; David Lavendar, Music Dir. **Wattage:** 3000. **Ad Rates:** $5-25-11 for 30 seconds; $7.25-13 for 60 seconds.

GALVA, pop. 3,185.

Henry Co. (NW). 6 m SW of Kewanee. Residential.

9052 Galva News
Galesburg Printing and Publishing Co.
210 S. Exchange St. Phone: (309)923-2103
Galva, IL 61434 Fax: (309)932-3282

Community newspaper. **Founded:** Oct. 18, 1879. **Freq:** Weekly (Wed.). **Print Method:** Offset. **Trim Size:** 13 3/4 x 21. **Cols./Page:** 8. **Col. Width:** 9 3/5 picas. **Col. Depth:** 294 agate lines. **Key Personnel:** Brenda M. Ring, Editor; Donald Cooper, Publisher; Stacey Swanson, Advertising Mgr. **ISSN:** 0747-282X. **Subscription Rates:** $15 individuals; $17 out of state. **Remarks:** Accepts advertising.
Ad Rates: BW: $571.20 **Circ:** 2,314
SAU: $6.87
PCI: $3.40

9053 WGEN-AM - 1500
PO Box 222 Phone: (309)932-2288
Galva, IL 61434 Fax: (309)932-2248
Free: (888)944-4408
E-mail: hawk@inw.net

Format: Full Service; Agricultural; Sports; Adult Contemporary. **Simulcasts:** WHHK-FM. **Networks:** Brownfield; Tribune Radio; RFD Illinois; ABC. **Owner:** Coleman Broadcasting, at above address. **Founded:** 1963. **Operating Hours:** 16.5 hours daily; 75% network, 25% local. **ADI:** Davenport,IA-Rock Island, Moline,IL. **Key Personnel:** Roger Coleman, Contact; Sue Stackhouse, Contact; Brian Fritz, News Dir.; Rick Pierce, Contact. **Wattage:** 250. **Ad Rates:** $8.50-15 for 30 seconds; $12.50-20 for 60 seconds. Combined advertising rates available with WHHK-FM.

GARDNER, pop. 1,322.

Grundy Co. (NE). 30 m SW of Joliet. Electronic factory. Grain, dairy farms. Corn, oats, wheat.

9054 Gardner Chronicle
Star Newspapers
204 E. Chippewa St. Phone: (815)584-3007
PO Box 159
Dwight, IL 60420-0159
Community newspaper. **Founded:** 1895. **Freq:** Weekly (Thurs.). **Print Method:** Offset. **Trim Size:** 8 x 11 1/4. **Cols./Page:** 8. **Col. Width:** 1 3/4 inches. **Col. Depth:** 301 agate lines. **Key Personnel:** Scott McGraw, Editor and Publisher. **USPS:** 213-940. **Subscription Rates:** $12; $17 out of state. **Remarks:** Accepts advertising.
Ad Rates: GLR: $.16 **Circ:** Paid 779
BW: $161.25 Free 10
SAU: $2.64
PCI: $2.24

GENESEO, pop. 6,154.

Henry Co. (NW). 25 m E of Moline. Grain, stock, poultry farms. Hybrid seed corn. Cattle and hogs.

9055 Geneseo Republic
Terry Newspapers
108 W. 1st St. Phone: (309)944-2119
Geneseo, IL 61254-0209 Fax: (309)944-6161
Free: (888)837-7963
Publication E-mail: editor@terrynews.com

Founded: 1856. **Freq:** Weekly (Fri.). **Print Method:** Offset. **Cols./Page:** 6. **Col. Width:** 21 1/2 nonpareils. **Col. Depth:** 294 agate lines. **Key Personnel:** Thomas Terry, Publisher. **Subscription Rates:** $36 individuals; $38 out of state. **Remarks:** Accepts advertising. **URL:** http://www.terrynews.com.
Ad Rates: GLR: $.72 **Circ:** 3,821
4C: $150
SAU: $11.90
PCI: $10.08

9056 Shopper
Terry Newspapers
108 W. 1st St. Phone: (309)944-2119
Geneseo, IL 61254-0209 Fax: (309)944-6161
Free: (888)837-7963

Shopper. **Founded:** 1939. **Freq:** Weekly (Wed.). **Print Method:** Offset. **Cols./Page:** 8. **Col. Width:** 21-1/2 nonpareils. **Col. Depth:** 294 agate lines. **Key Personnel:** Thos Terry, Publisher, editor@terrynews.com. **Subscription Rates:** $10 individuals. **Remarks:** Accepts advertising.
Ad Rates: GLR: $.60 **Circ:** Free 15,106
4C: $150
PCI: $8.40

GENEVA†, pop. 9,881.

Kane Co. (NE). On Fox River, 10 m N of Aurora. Manufactures interval timers and time switches, metal filings, farm machinery, wire-cable products, electronics components, foundry products, auto parts, batteries. Greenhouses. Grain, dairy farms.

9057 Fox River Super Saver
Chronicle Newspapers, Inc.
1000 Randall Rd. Phone: (630)232-9222
Geneva, IL 60134 Fax: (630)232-4962
Publisher E-mail: chronedit@aol.com

Shopper. **Founded:** 1981. **Freq:** Weekly (Thurs.). **Print Method:** Offset. **Trim Size:** 11 1/2 x 14. **Cols./Page:** 5. **Col. Width:** 2 1/16 inches. **Col. Depth:** 13 inches. **Key Personnel:** Dave Heun, Editor; Roger F. Coleman, Publisher; Jim Holm, Director. **Remarks:** Accepts advertising. **Formerly:** Fox River Trader.
Ad Rates: PCI: $3.80 **Circ:** Free ‡17,400

9058 The Geneva Republican
Press-Republican Newspapers Inc.
6 James St. Phone: (630)232-2324
PO Box 708 Fax: (630)232-9974
Geneva, IL 60134
Publication E-mail: managing-editor@press-repb.com

Community newspaper. **Founded:** 1847. **Freq:** Weekly (Thurs.). **Print Method:** Offset. **Trim Size:** 10 1/4 x 15 7/8. **Cols./Page:** 4. **Col. Width:** 14 picas. **Col. Depth:** 16 inches. **Key Personnel:** Richard Nagel, Managing Editor; Wayne G. Woltman, Editor and Publisher; Dustin Hawkins, Advertising Mgr.
Ad Rates: BW: $640 **Circ:** ‡3,900
4C: $1,090

9059 Kane County Chronicle
Chronicle Newspapers, Inc.
1000 Randall Rd. Phone: (630)232-9222
Geneva, IL 60134 Fax: (630)232-4962
Publication E-mail: kcchron1@aol.com
Publisher E-mail: chronedit@aol.com

Community newspaper serving St. Charles, Geneva, Batavia, and Elburn, IL. **Founded:** 1881. **Freq:** 5/wk (Tues.-Sat.). **Print Method:** Offset. **Trim Size:** 13 1/2 x 22 3/4. **Cols./Page:** 6. **Col. Width:** 2 1/16 inches. **Col. Depth:** 21 inches. **Key Personnel:** Dave Heun, Editor; Roger F. Coleman, Publisher; Jim Holm, Sales Development Dir. **Subscription Rates:** $68.85 individuals. **Remarks:** Accepts advertising. **Formerly:** St. Charles Chronicle, Geneva Chronicle, Batavia Chronicle, and Elburn Chronicle.
Ad Rates: GLR: $1.10 **Circ:** Mon.-Sat. 14,440
BW: $2,501.10
4C: $2,851.10
PCI: $19.85

9060 Valleykids Parent News for Chicago's West Suburbs
227 N. 2nd St.
Geneva, IL 60134-1436
Publication E-mail: mbrown@starnetinc.com

Parenting newspaper. **Subtitle:** Parent News Chicago's West Suburbam Family Lifestyle Resource. **Founded:** June 1991. **Freq:** 12/year. **Print Method:** Web Offset. **Trim Size:** 11 1/4 x 13 1/2. **Cols./Page:** 8. **Col. Width:** 2 3/8 inches. **Col. Depth:** 4 3/4 inches. **Subscription Rates:** $15 individuals. **Remarks:** Accepts advertising. **Formerly:** Valleykids Newsmagazine for West Suburban Parents.
Ad Rates: BW: $1,040 **Circ:** Free ❑55,357
4C: $1,465 Paid ❑29

GIBSON CITY

9061 Target
East Central Communications, Inc.
310 N. Sangamon Phone: (217)784-4244
Gibson City, IL 60936 Fax: (217)784-4246

Community shopper. **Freq:** Weekly (Mon.). **Print Method:** Photo offset. **Key Personnel:** Dennis Kaster, Publisher. **Subscription Rates:** Free.
Circ: Non-paid ♦13,897

GILLESPIE, pop. 3,740.

Macoupin Co. (SWC). 28 m NE of Alton. Coal mines. Dress factory. Dairy, stock, grain farms.

9062 Gillespie Area News
112-16 W. Chestnut St. Phone: (217)839-2130
PO Box 209 Fax: (217)839-2139
Gillespie, IL 62033-0209
Publisher E-mail: intouch@ctnet.net

Community newspaper. **Founded:** Nov. 22, 1905. **Freq:** Weekly (Wed.). **Print Method:** Desktop and offset. **Trim Size:** 18 x 21 1/2. **Cols./Page:** 7. **Col. Width:** 24 nonpareils. **Col. Depth:** 301 agate lines. **Key Personnel:** Dave Ambrose, Editor and Publisher; Patty Ambrose, Editor and Publisher. **Subscription Rates:** $18 individuals; $20 out of county. **Remarks:** Accepts advertising. **Formerly:** Area News.
Ad Rates: BW: $426.30 **Circ:** ‡2,715
PCI: $3.20

GILMAN, pop. 1,891.

Iroquois Co. (E). 30 m SW of Kankakee. Dress factories. Hybrid seed corn, fertilizer plants. Stock, dairy, grain farms.

9063 Star
PO Box 7 Phone: (815)265-7332
Gilman, IL 60938 Fax: (815)265-7880

Newspaper. **Founded:** 1868. **Freq:** Weekly (Thurs.). **Print Method:** Offset. **Cols./Page:** 7. **Col. Width:** 12.5 nonpareils. **Col. Depth:** 301 agate lines. **Key Personnel:** John Elliott, Editor; George Elliott, Publisher. **Subscription Rates:** $19 individuals. **Remarks:** Accepts advertising.
Ad Rates: GLR: $.144 **Circ:** 2,800
BW: $320
SAU: $4.50
PCI: $2.80

GLASFORD, pop. 1,201.

Peoria Co. (NWC). 18 m SW of Peoria. Planing, feed mills. Grain, stock, dairy farms.

9064 The Glasford Gazette
402 E. Main St. Phone: (309)389-2811
Glasford, IL 61533-0260
Community newspaper. **Founded:** 1899. **Freq:** Weekly (Thurs.). **Print Method:** Offset. **Trim Size:** 9 x 11 1/2. **Cols./Page:** 5. **Col. Width:** 24 nonpareils. **Col. Depth:** 224 agate lines. **Key Personnel:** William Watkins, Editor and Publisher. **USPS:** 219-200. **Subscription Rates:** $20.50 individuals; $23 out of state.
Ad Rates: GLR: $.23 **Circ:** ‡1,100

GLEN ELLYN, pop. 23,649.

Du Page Co. (NE). 6 m N. of Woodridge. College of Dupage. Residential. Historical sites. Antique and specialty shops.

9065 Chicago Cigar Smoker Magazine
Jonathan Scott's Cigar Smoker Magazine
PO Box 2323 Phone: (630)790-3433
Glen Ellyn, IL 60138 Fax: (630)986-0369
Publication E-mail: ccsm1@aol.com

Men's lifestyle magazine featuring articles on cigar smoking, celebrities, fashion, food, and the media. **Founded:** Dec. 1995. **Freq:** Quarterly. **Print Method:** Web offset. **Trim Size:** 8 1/8 x 10 3/4. **Cols./Page:** 3. **Key Personnel:** Jonathan Scott, Publisher/CEO; Gregory S. Bayer, Technical Svcs. **Subscription Rates:** $12. **Remarks:** Accepts advertising. **URL:** http://www.chicagocigar.com.
Ad Rates: 4C: $3,500 **Circ:** Paid 5,000
Controlled 80,000

9066 Church Libraries
Evangelical Church Library Association
PO Box 353 Phone: (847)296-3964
Glen Ellyn, IL 60138-0353 Fax: (847)296-0754
Publication E-mail: eclalib@aol.com
Publisher E-mail: eclalib@aol.com

Magazine to assist church librarians in starting and maintaining library resource centers. **Founded:** Apr. 1970. **Freq:** Quarterly. **Print Method:** Offset. **Trim Size:** 8 1/2 x 11. **Cols./Page:** 3. **Col. Width:** 2 1/2 inches. **Col. Depth:** 168 agate lines. **Key Personnel:** Judi Turek, Secretary; Lin Johnson, Editor, linjohnson@compuserve.com. **ISSN:** 0739-0297. **Subscription Rates:** $25 individuals; $35 other countries; $9 single issue. **Remarks:** Accepts advertising. **Formerly:** Librarian's World.
Ad Rates: BW: $300 **Circ:** Paid ‡450
Controlled ‡100

9067 Courier
College of DuPage
425 22nd St. Phone: (630)942-2379
Glen Ellyn, IL 60137 Fax: (630)942-3747
Publication E-mail: stablein@cdnet.cod.edu

Collegiate newspaper. **Founded:** 1969. **Freq:** Weekly (Fri.). **Print Method:** Offset. **Cols./Page:** 4. **Col. Width:** 28 nonpareils. **Col. Depth:** 224 agate lines. **Key Personnel:** Catherine Stablein, Advisor, stablein@cdnet.cod.edu; Joanne Leone, Advertising Mgr. **Subscription Rates:** Free. **Remarks:** Accepts advertising.
Ad Rates: BW: $388 **Circ:** Free ‡7,000
PCI: $6.10

9068 Glen Ellyn News
Glen News Printing Co.
460 Pennsylvania Ave., No. 352 Phone: (708)469-0100
Glen Ellyn, IL 60137-4402 Fax: (708)469-4472

Community newspaper. **Founded:** 1927. **Freq:** Weekly. **Print Method:** Offset. **Trim Size:** 11 x 17. **Cols./Page:** 5. **Col. Width:** 2 inches. **Col. Depth:** 16 inches. **Key Personnel:** Patricia Schwarze, Editor; Virginia Stone, Publisher; Stuart Stone, Publisher. **Subscription Rates:** $20; $21 out of county; $24 out of state.

9069 Glen Ellyn Press
Press Publications
112 S. York St. Phone: (630)834-0900
Elmhurst, IL 60126 Fax: (630)834-0910
Publisher E-mail: presspub@aol.com

Community newspaper. **Founded:** 1976. **Freq:** Weekly (Thurs.). **Print Method:** Offset. **Cols./Page:** 5. **Col. Width:** 24 nonpareils. **Col. Depth:** 224 agate lines. **Key Personnel:** Dave Fornell, Editor, phone (630)307-1101, fax (630)307-1190; Rosemarie T. Cruger, Publisher; William Haman, Advertising Mgr. **Subscription Rates:** Free; $28 by mail. **Remarks:** Accepts advertising.
Ad Rates: SAU: $8.94 **Circ:** Paid ‡219
Free ‡4,252

9070 Law Enforcement Legal Defense Manual
Law Enforcement Legal Publications
421 Ridgewood Ave., Ste. 100 Phone: (630)858-6392
Glen Ellyn, IL 60137-4900 Fax: (630)858-6392
Publisher E-mail: lelp@xnet.com

Journal for the public and private safety sectors who have an interest in civil litigation involving state, county, and municipal public safety agencies and private security. **Founded:** 1973. **Freq:** Bimonthly. **Print Method:** Offset. **Trim Size:** 8 x 10. **Cols./Page:** 2. **Key Personnel:** James P. Manak, Editor and Publisher. **ISSN:** 0191-877X. **Subscription Rates:** $118 individuals. **Remarks:** Advertising not accepted.
Circ: Paid 1,000

9071 Nuclear Plant Journal
799 Roosevelt Rd., Bldg. 6, Ste. 208 Phone: (630)858-6161
Fax: (708)858-8787
Glen Ellyn, IL 60137
Publication E-mail: npj@goinfo.com; eqes@goinfo.com

Magazine focusing on nuclear power plants. **Subtitle:** An International Publication Published in the United States. **Founded:** Jan. 1983. **Freq:** 6/year. **Print Method:** Web offset. **Trim Size:** 8 1/4 x 10 7/8. **Cols./Page:** 3. **Col. Width:** 27 nonpareils. **Col. Depth:** 98 agate lines. **Key Personnel:** Newal K. Agnihotri, Editor and Publisher, newal@goinfo.com. **ISSN:** 0892-2055. **Subscription Rates:** $107 individuals; $20 single issue; $139 other countries. **Remarks:** Accepts advertising. **URL:** http://www.npj.goinfo.com.
Ad Rates: BW: $2,427 **Circ:** Controlled ‡20,000
4C: $3,207

9072 Presidents & Prime Ministers
President & Prime Ministers
799 Roosevelt Rd., Bldg. 6, Ste. 208 Phone: (630)858-6161
Fax: (630)858-8787
Glen Ellyn, IL 60137
Publication E-mail: eqes@goinfo.com; ppm@goinfo.com

Magazine includes speeches, statements and news items from leaders and governments worldwide. **Subtitle:** International Perspectives from World Leaders. **Founded:** Sept. 1992. **Freq:** Bimonthly. **Print Method:** Web offset. **Trim Size:** 8 1/4 x 10 7/8. **Cols./Page:** 3. **Col. Width:** 2 1/4 inches. **Col. Depth:** 9 4/5 inches. **Key Personnel:** Newal K. Agnihotri, Editor, newal@goinfo.com; Anu Agnihotri, Editor, anu@goinfo.com. **ISSN:** 1060-5088. **Subscription Rates:** $22.35; $41.35 out of country; $4.15 single issue. **Remarks:** Accepts advertising. **Online:** Prodigy. **URL:** http://www.goinfo.com. **Alt. Formats:** CD-ROM.
Ad Rates: BW: $975 **Circ:** Paid 270
4C: $1,755 Non-paid 5,200
PCI: $100

Wheaton Leader - See Wheaton

9073 WDCB-FM - 90.9
College of DuPage Phone: (630)942-4200
425 22nd St. Fax: (630)942-2788
Glen Ellyn, IL 60137

Format: Public Radio; Folk; Jazz; News. **Founded:** 1977. **Operating Hours:** Continuous. **Key Personnel:** Brian O'Keefe, News Coordinator, phone (630)942-3701; Sid Fryer, General Mgr., phone (630)942-3068; Scott Wager, Operations

Coordinator, phone (630)942-3706; Mary Pat LaRue, Programming Coordinator, phone (630)942-3702; Steve Edwards, Asst. News Coordinator, phone (630)942-3702; Ken Scott, Marketing Coordinator, phone (630)942-3716; Erv Jezek, Assistant Programming Coordinator, phone (630)942-3709. **Wattage:** 5000. **Ad Rates:** Noncommercial; underwriting available. $25-50 per unit. **URL:** http://www.cod.edu/wbcb; http://www.cod.edu/wdcb.

GLENDALE HEIGHTS

9074 Glendale Heights Press
Press Publications
112 S. York St. Phone: (630)834-0900
Elmhurst, IL 60126 Fax: (630)834-0910
Publisher E-mail: presspub@aol.com

Community newspaper. **Founded:** 1976. **Freq:** Weekly (Thurs.). **Print Method:** Offset. **Cols./Page:** 5. **Col. Width:** 24 nonpareils. **Col. Depth:** 224 agate lines. **Key Personnel:** John S. Davis, Editor; Rosemarie T. Cruger, Publisher; William Haman, Advertising Mgr. **Subscription Rates:** Free; $28 by mail. **Remarks:** Accepts advertising.
Ad Rates: SAU: $8.94 **Circ:** Paid ‡395
Free ‡4,469

GLENVIEW, pop. 30,842.

Cook Co. (NE). 16 m N of Chicago. Residential. Grove (national historic preserve). Commercial, industrial and manufacturing.

9075 Finishers' Management
Publication Management Inc.
4350 DiPaolo Center Phone: (847)699-1706
Glenview, IL 60025 Fax: (847)699-1703

Magazine on metal-finishing management. **Founded:** 1957. **Freq:** 10/year. **Print Method:** Offset. **Trim Size:** 8 1/8 x 10 7/8. **Cols./Page:** 3. **Col. Width:** 26 nonpareils. **Col. Depth:** 140 agate lines. **Key Personnel:** Hugh Morgan, Publisher. **ISSN:** 0015-2358. **Subscription Rates:** $35 individuals; Free to qualified subscribers. **Remarks:** Accepts advertising. **Alt. Formats:** Microfilm.
Ad Rates: BW: $2,205 **Circ:** Paid 422
4C: $3,535 Non-paid 10,466
PCI: $66

9076 Glencoe News
Pioneer Press Newspapers
3701 W. Lake Ave. Phone: (847)486-9200
Glenview, IL 60025 Fax: (847)486-7451

Community newspaper (tabloid). **Founded:** 1911. **Freq:** Weekly (Thurs.). **Print Method:** Offset. **Trim Size:** 11 x 14. **Cols./Page:** 5. **Col. Width:** 9 3/4 inches. **Col. Depth:** 12 3/4 inches. **Key Personnel:** Elaine Fandell, Editor; Paul Sassone, Managing Editor. **USPS:** 219-700. **Subscription Rates:** $32.95 individuals. **URL:** http://www.pioneerlocal.com.
Circ: Thurs. ★**2,323**

9077 Glenview Announcements
Pioneer Press Newspapers
3701 W. Lake Ave. Phone: (847)486-9200
Glenview, IL 60025 Fax: (847)486-7451

Community newspaper (tabloid). **Founded:** 1940. **Freq:** Weekly (Thurs.). **Print Method:** Offset. **Trim Size:** 11 x 14. **Cols./Page:** 5. **Col. Width:** 9 3/4 inches. **Col. Depth:** 12 3/4 inches. **Key Personnel:** Cathy Backer, Editor; Paul Sassone, Managing Editor. **Subscription Rates:** $32.95 individuals.
Circ: Thurs. ★**7,769**

9078 Glenview Weekend Voice
Lerner Communications, Inc.
7331 N. Lincoln Ave. Phone: (847)329-2000
Lincolnwood, IL 60646-1704 Fax: (847)329-2060
Publisher E-mail: lerner@enteract.com

Community newspaper. **Freq:** Weekly. **Trim Size:** 11 x 17. **Key Personnel:** Leah A. Zeldes, Managing Editor. **Subscription Rates:** Free. **URL:** http://www.intheloop.net. **Formerly:** Glenview Place.
Circ: Paid 86
Free 6,000

9079 Journal for Healthcare Quality
Healthcare Quality Corp.
4700 W. Lake Ave. Phone: (847)375-4720
Glenview, IL 60025 Fax: (847)375-4777
Free: (800)966-9392
Publication E-mail: jhq@nahq.org

Professional publication that explores safe, cost-effective, quality healthcare. **Subtitle:** The Official Journal of the National Association for Healthcare Quality. **Founded:** 1979. **Freq:** Bimonthly. **Print Method:** Sheetfed offset. **Trim Size:** 8 1/2 x 11. **Cols./Page:** 2. **Col. Width:** 2 5/16 inches. **Col. Depth:** 8 5/8 inches. **Key Personnel:** Luc R. Pelletier; Barbara Simmons, phone (847)375-4824, bsimmons@amctec.com; Pat Delaney, Sales Mgr., phone (847)375-4829, pdelaney@amctec.com. **ISSN:** 1062-2551. **Subscription Rates:** $125; $20 single issue. **Remarks:** Accepts advertising. **URL:** http://www.nahq.org/. **Formerly:** Journal of Quality Assurance.
Ad Rates: BW: $1,145 **Circ:** Paid 8,000
4C: $1,990 Controlled 500

9080 North Shore Magazine
Pioneer Press Newspapers
3701 W. Lake Ave. Phone: (847)486-9200
Glenview, IL 60025 Fax: (847)486-7451
Publication E-mail: nshorechgo@aol.com

Consumer lifestyle magazine for Chicago and its affluent suburbs. **Subtitle:** Serving Chicago's Finest Communities. **Founded:** 1978. **Freq:** Monthly. **Print Method:** Offset. **Trim Size:** 9 x 10 7/8. **Cols./Page:** 3. **Col. Width:** 2.5 inches. **Col. Depth:** 10 inches. **Key Personnel:** Ted Biedron, Publisher. **ISSN:** 0295-1653. **Subscription Rates:** $18.95 individuals; $3 single issue. **Remarks:** Accepts advertising.
Ad Rates: BW: $3,550 **Circ:** Paid ★**67,231**
4C: $5,290

9081 Northbrook Star
Pioneer Press Newspapers
3701 W. Lake Ave. Phone: (847)486-9200
Glenview, IL 60025 Fax: (847)486-7451

Community newspaper (tabloid). **Founded:** 1940. **Freq:** Weekly (Thurs.). **Print Method:** Offset. **Trim Size:** 10 x 14 in. **Cols./Page:** 5. **Col. Width:** 10 inches. **Col. Depth:** 14 inches. **Key Personnel:** Cathy Backer, Editor; Paul Sassone, Managing Editor. **ISSN:** 0774-9550. **Subscription Rates:** $32.95 individuals; $41.50 out of county.
Circ: Thurs. ★**7,533**

9082 Rehabilitation Nursing
4700 West Lake Ave. Phone: (847)375-4710
Glenview, IL 60025 Fax: (847)375-4777
Free: (800)229-7530
Publication E-mail: info@rehabnurse.org

Magazine focusing on rehabilitation nursing involving clinical practice, research, education, and administration. **Subtitle:** The Official Journal of the Association of Rehabilitation Nurses; Advancing the care of persons with chronic illness and disability across the continu. **Founded:** Nov. 1975. **Freq:** Bimonthly. **Print Method:** Offset. **Trim Size:** 8 1/2 x 11. **Cols./Page:** 2 and 3. **Col. Width:** 20.6 and 13.6 picas. **Col. Depth:** 52 picas. **Key Personnel:** Susan L. Dean-Baar, PhD, Editor; Sheila Lee, Sales Mgr. **ISSN:** 0278-4807. **Subscription Rates:** $50 individuals; $95 institutions; $110 other countries; $16 single issue; $95 Canada. **Remarks:** Accepts advertising.
Ad Rates: BW: $1,462 **Circ:** ‡11,500
4C: $2,357

9083 Wilmette Life
Pioneer Press Newspapers
3701 W. Lake Ave. Phone: (847)486-9200
Glenview, IL 60025 Fax: (847)486-7451

Community newspaper (tabloid). **Subtitle:** With News of Kenilworth. **Founded:** 1912. **Freq:** Weekly (Thurs.). **Print Method:** Offset. **Trim Size:** 11 x 14. **Cols./Page:** 5. **Col. Width:** 9 3/4 inches. **Col. Depth:** 12 3/4 inches. **Key Personnel:** Elaine Fandell, Editor; Paul Sassone, Managing Editor. **ISSN:** 0745-0044. **Subscription Rates:** $32.95 individuals. **Remarks:** Advertising accepted; rates available upon request.
Circ: Thurs. ★**7,484**

Winnetka Talk - See Winnetka

GODFREY

Madison Co.

9084 WLCA-FM - 89.9
5800 Godfrey Rd. Phone: (618)466-3411
Godfrey, IL 62035
E-mail: wlca@ezl.com

Networks: USA Radio. **Owner:** Lewis & Clark Community College, at above address. **Founded:** 1974. **Operating Hours:** Continuous; 5% network, 95% local. **ADI:** St. Louis, MO (Mt. Vernon, IL). **Key Personnel:** Michael Lemons, Station Mgr. **Wattage:** 1400. **Ad Rates:** $5 for 30 seconds; $8 for 60 seconds.

GOLCONDA†, pop. 960.

Pope Co. (S). On Ohio River, 45 m NE of Cairo. Fluorspar mines; timber for railroad ties. Flour mill. Diversified farming. Fruit.

9085 Herald-Enterprise
PO Box 400 Phone: (618)683-3531
Golconda, IL 62938 Fax: (618)683-3831

Community newspaper. **Founded:** May 6, 1858. **Freq:** Weekly (Thurs.). **Print Method:** Offset. **Cols./Page:** 6. **Col. Width:** 26 nonpareils. **Col. Depth:** 280 agate lines. **Key Personnel:** Sandra Cowsert, Editor and Publisher, sandra@shawneelink.com. **Subscription Rates:** $16 individuals; $18 out of area. **Remarks:** Accepts advertising.
Ad Rates: BW: $350 **Circ:** ‡2,000
SAU: $5
PCI: $3

GOLDEN, pop. 558.

Adams Co. (W). 30 m NE of Quincy. Grist mill. Grain, stock farms. Corn, wheat, beans.

9086 New Era
Elliott Publishing, Inc.
202 E. State Phone: (217)593-6515
Camp Point, IL 62320 Fax: (217)593-7720

Community newspaper. **Founded:** 1898. **Freq:** Weekly (Tues.). **Print Method:** Offset. **Trim Size:** 17 1/2 x 22 1/2. **Cols./Page:** 5. **Col. Width:** 2 inches. **Col. Depth:** 16 inches. **Key Personnel:** Marcia Elliott, Editor; James Elliott, Publisher/Production Mgr. **Subscription Rates:** $12 individuals; $15 out of state. **Remarks:** Accepts advertising.
Ad Rates: GLR: $2.75 **Circ:** 500
BW: $378
SAU: $3.40

9087 Adams Telcom Inc.
PO Box 248 Phone: (217)696-2701
Golden, IL 62339 Fax: (217)696-4811
Free: (800)696-2632
E-mail: adamstel@adams.net

Founded: July 11, 1983. **Key Personnel:** Walter Rowland, General Mgr. **Cities Served:** Bowen, Coatsburg, Fowler, Lima, Loraine, Marcelline, Mendon, Paloma, Plymouth, Ursa, IL: subscribing households 2,065; 18 channels; 1 community access channel; 168 hours per week community access programming.

GOREVILLE, pop. 978.

Johnson Co. (S). 15 m S. of Marion.

9088 Goreville Gazette
Hwy. 37 Phone: (618)995-9445
PO Box 70
Goreville, IL 62939
Local newspaper serving Goreville and Lake of Egypt. **Freq:** Weekly (Wed.). **Cols./Page:** 5. **Col. Width:** 2 inches. **Col. Depth:** 185 1/2 agate lines. **Key Personnel:** Don Sanders, Editor and Publisher; Sandy Lively, Advertising Mgr. **Subscription Rates:** $9.25 individuals. **Remarks:** Accepts advertising.
Ad Rates: SAU: $4.16 **Circ:** Paid 800
Free 100

GRANITE CITY, pop. 36,815.

Madison Co. (SW). 5 m E of St. Louis, Mo. Manufactures railway equipment, steel and steel castings, oxygen and nitrogen products, lubricants, corn syrup, earth pigment, chemicals, magnesium, coke, tar and creosoted products, fire brick, fertilizer, auto frames, soft drinks, roofing material, plastics. Meat packing.

9089 Granite City Journal
1815 Delmar Phone: (618)877-7700
Granite City, IL 62040 Fax: (618)876-4240

Newspaper. **Founded:** 1977. **Freq:** Weekly (Wed.). **Print Method:** Offset. **Cols./Page:** 6. **Col. Width:** 156 nonpareils. **Col. Depth:** 301 agate lines. **Key Personnel:** Rick Jarvis, Publisher; Leo Swift, Advertising Dir. **Subscription Rates:** Free; $137.80 by mail. **Remarks:** Accepts advertising.
Ad Rates: BW: $1,511.40 **Circ:** Free ‡22,475
4C: $2,151
SAU: $11.45

9090 Granite City Press Record
1815 Delmar Ave. Phone: (618)877-7700
Granite City, IL 62040 Fax: (618)876-4240

Community newspaper. **Founded:** 1901. **Freq:** Weekly (Thurs.). **Print Method:** Offset. **Cols./Page:** 6. **Col. Width:** 156 nonpareils. **Col. Depth:** 301 agate lines. **Key Personnel:** Dennis Grubaugh, Editor; Rick Jarvis, Publisher; Leo Swift,

Advertising Dir. **Subscription Rates:** $30 individuals. **Remarks:** Accepts advertising.
Ad Rates: BW: $1,511.40 **Circ:** ‡11,000
4C: $2,151
SAU: $11.45

9091 Sunday Home Journal
Granite City Journal
1815 Delmar Phone: (618)877-7700
Granite City, IL 62040 Fax: (618)876-4240

Newspaper. **Freq:** Weekly (Sun.). **Print Method:** Offset. **Cols./Page:** 6. **Col. Width:** 156 nonpareils. **Col. Depth:** 301 agate lines. **Key Personnel:** Rick Jarvis, Publisher; Leo Swift, Advertising Dir. **Subscription Rates:** Free; $137.80 by mail. **Remarks:** Accepts advertising.
Ad Rates: BW: $1,511.40 **Circ:** Free 23,000
4C: $2,151
SAU: $11.45

GRANT PARK

9092 Grant Park Gazette
Russell Publications
PO Box 429 Phone: (708)258-3473
Peotone, IL 60468 Fax: (708)258-6295

Community newspaper. **Freq:** Weekly (Thurs.). **Cols./Page:** 5. **Col. Width:** 2 inches. **Col. Depth:** 16 inches. **Key Personnel:** Gilbert L. Russell, Publisher; Gilbert L. Russell, Publisher. **Subscription Rates:** $16 individuals. **Remarks:** Accepts advertising.
Ad Rates: PCI: $2.95 **Circ:** 880

GRANVILLE

9093 Putnam County Record
Record Newspaper Inc.
318 S. McCoy Phone: (815)339-2321
PO Box 48
Granville, IL 61326
Community newspaper. **Freq:** Weekly (Wed.). **Cols./Page:** 5. **Col. Width:** 11 1/2 picas. **Col. Depth:** 15 inches. **Key Personnel:** Elin Arnold, Editor and Publisher, phone (815)339-6727, fax (815)339-6727. **Subscription Rates:** $18. **Remarks:** Accepts advertising.
Ad Rates: GLR: $.40 **Circ:** 3,200
BW: $262.50
PCI: $3.75

GRAYSLAKE, pop. 5,260.

Lake Co. (NE). 10 m W of Waukegan. Suburban area. Manufactures plastics, electrical appliances, electronic equipment. Dairy, grain farms. Corn, oats, wheat.

Antioch News Reporter - See Antioch

9094 The Chronicle
College of Lake County
19351 W. Washington St. Phone: (847)223-3634
Grayslake, IL 60030 Fax: (847)223-9266

Collegiate newspaper. **Founded:** 1969. **Freq:** Semimonthly. **Print Method:** Offset. **Trim Size:** 11 x 17. **Cols./Page:** 4. **Col. Width:** 2.5 inches. **Col. Depth:** 15 inches. **Key Personnel:** Sulyn Foust, Editor-in-Chief, phone (847)223-6601; Michael Rubin, Managing Editor, phone (847)223-6601; Connie S. Kindsvater, Advisor; Diane Summers, Advertising Coord. **Subscription Rates:** Free. **Remarks:** Accepts advertising.
Ad Rates: BW: $340 **Circ:** Free 4,000
PCI: $7

9095 Fox Lake Press
Lakeland Publishers, Inc.
30 S. Whitney St. Phone: (847)223-8161
PO Box 268 Fax: (847)223-8810
Grayslake, IL 60030-0268
Publication E-mail: edit@lnd.com

Community newspaper. **Subtitle:** Fox Lake Press. **Founded:** 1934. **Freq:** Weekly (Thurs.). **Print Method:** Offset. **Trim Size:** 11 x 17. **Cols./Page:** 5. **Col. Width:** 2 inches. **Col. Depth:** 16 inches. **Key Personnel:** W.H. Schroeder, Editor and Publisher; Jill A. DePasquale, Advertising Mgr. **Subscription Rates:** $24.50 individuals; $35 out of area. **Remarks:** Accepts advertising.
Ad Rates: BW: $674.80 **Circ:** ‡4,713
4C: $1,023.40
SAU: $8.48

9096 Grayslake Review
Pioneer Press Newspapers
850 N. Milwaukee Ave. Phone: (847)680-6690
Vernon Hills, IL 60061 Fax: (847)573-2500

Community newspaper (tabloid). **Founded:** 1989. **Freq:** Weekly (Thurs.). **Print Method:** Offset. **Cols./Page:** 5. **Col. Width:** 10 inches. **Col. Depth:** 14 inches. **Key Personnel:** Marah Shuman, Editor; Paul Sassone, Managing Editor. **Subscription Rates:** $5; $11.95 out of county. **Remarks:** Combined advertising rates available with other Pioneer Press Newspapers.
Circ: Thurs. ★3,261

9097 Grayslake Times
Lakeland Publishers, Inc.
30 S. Whitney St. Phone: (847)223-8161
PO Box 268 Fax: (847)223-8810
Grayslake, IL 60030-0268
Publication E-mail: edit@lnd.com

Community newspaper. **Founded:** 1905. **Freq:** Weekly (Thurs.). **Print Method:** Offset. **Trim Size:** 11 x 17. **Cols./Page:** 5. **Col. Width:** 1 3/4 inches. **Col. Depth:** 16 inches. **Key Personnel:** W.H. Schroeder, Publisher; Esther Decker Hebbard, Advertising Mgr.; Rhonda Burke, Editor. **Subscription Rates:** $24.50 individuals. **Remarks:** Accepts advertising.
Ad Rates: GLR: $.354 **Circ:** ‡4,800
BW: $476.16
4C: $751.16
SAU: $8.21
PCI: $4.96

Gurnee Press - See Gurnee

9098 Lake County Market Journal
Market Journal
PO Box 410 Phone: (847)223-3200
Grayslake, IL 60030-0410 Fax: (847)223-9390

Shopping guide (tabloid). **Founded:** 1974. **Freq:** Weekly (Wed.). **Print Method:** Offset. **Cols./Page:** 4. **Col. Width:** 3 1/8 inches. **Col. Depth:** 2 3/8 inches. **Subscription Rates:** Free. **Remarks:** Accepts advertising.
Ad Rates: GLR: $8 **Circ:** Free 101,808
BW: $2,117.61
PCI: $20.80

Lake Villa Record - See Lake Villa

Lake Zurich Enterprise - See Lake Zurich

Libertyville News - See Libertyville

Lindenhurst News - See Lindenhurst

9099 Mundelein News
Lakeland Publishers, Inc.
30 S. Whitney St. Phone: (847)223-8161
PO Box 268 Fax: (847)223-8810
Grayslake, IL 60030-0268
Publication E-mail: edit@lnd.com

Community newspaper. **Subtitle:** Mundelein News. **Founded:** 1942. **Freq:** Weekly (Thurs.). **Print Method:** Offset. **Trim Size:** 11 x 17. **Cols./Page:** 5. **Col. Width:** 2 inches. **Col. Depth:** 16 inches. **Key Personnel:** W.H. Schroeder, Publisher; Esther Hebbard, Advertising Mgr.; Rhonda Hetrick Burke, Editor. **Subscription Rates:** $24.50 individuals; $35 out of area. **Remarks:** Accepts advertising.
Ad Rates: BW: $674.80 **Circ:** ‡3,000
4C: $1,032.40
SAU: $8.48

Round Lake News - See Round Lake

Vernon Hills News - See Vernon

Wadesworth News - See Warren

Wauconda Leader - See Wauconda

GREENUP, pop. 1,655.

Cumberland Co. (E). 43 m SW of Terre Haute, Ind. Shoe and broom factories. Agriculture. Fruit.

9100 Greenup Press
104 E. Cumberland Phone: (217)923-3704
Box 127 Fax: (217)923-3704
Greenup, IL 62428
Community newspaper. **Founded:** 1889. **Freq:** Weekly (Thurs.). **Print Method:** Offset. **Cols./Page:** 6. **Col. Width:** 12 picas. **Col. Depth:** 21 inches. **Key Personnel:** W.J. McMorris, Editor and Publisher. **USPS:** 229-140. **Subscription Rates:** $18 individuals; $23 out of state.
Ad Rates: GLR: $.60 **Circ:** Paid 1,703
BW: $837 Paid 57
4C: $1,137
SAU: $8
PCI: $6

9101 Command Cable of Eastern Illinois
PO Box 306 Phone: (217)923-5126
Greenup, IL 62428 Fax: (217)923-5121
Free: (800)851-3868

Key Personnel: Douglas G. Pearson, Contact. **Cities Served:** Broadlands, Casey, Chrisman, Greenup, Homer, Marshall, Martinsville, Neoga, Newman, Ogden, Philco, Ridge Farm, St. Joseph, Sidney, and Toledo, IL.

GREENVILLE†, pop. 5,271.

Bond Co. (S). 44 m NE of St. Louis, Mo. Greenville College. Manufactures condensed milk, food flavoring, uniforms, steel products, rubber roofing, ball pitching machine, springs, electric scoreboards. Agriculture. Dairy products, grain, alfalfa.

9102 The Greenville Advocate
305 S. 2nd St. Phone: (618)664-3144
PO Box 9 Fax: (618)664-3277
Greenville, IL 62246-1726
County seat newspaper. **Founded:** Feb. 11, 1858. **Freq:** Semiweekly (Tues. and Thurs.). **Print Method:** Offset. **Trim Size:** 13 x 21 1/2. **Cols./Page:** 6. **Col. Width:** 12 picas. **Col. Depth:** 21 1/2 inches. **Key Personnel:** Duane L. Reeves, Editor and Publisher; Richards D. Reeves, Advertising Mgr., phone (618)664-3277. **USPS:** 229-180. **Subscription Rates:** $32 individuals. **Remarks:** Accepts advertising.
Ad Rates: GLR: $.40 **Circ:** ‡5,100
BW: $786.90
SAU: $6.10

9103 Papyrus
Greenville College
315 E. College Ave. Phone: (618)664-1840
PO Box 159 Fax: (618)664-1748
Greenville, IL 62246-1199
Collegiate Free-Methodist newspaper. **Subtitle:** The Student Newspaper of Greenville College. **Founded:** 1919. **Freq:** Semimonthly. **Print Method:** Offset. **Cols./Page:** 5. **Col. Width:** 2 inches. **Col. Depth:** 160 agate lines. **Subscription Rates:** $10 individuals. **Remarks:** Accepts advertising.
Ad Rates: PCI: $3 **Circ:** ‡1,100

9104 WGEL-FM - 101.7
309 W. Main Phone: (618)664-3300
PO Box 177 Fax: (618)664-3318
Greenville, IL 62246

Format: Contemporary Country. **Networks:** UPI. **Owner:** John T. Kennedy, at above address. **Founded:** 1984. **Operating Hours:** Continuous. **Key Personnel:** Melody McKenzie, News Dir.; Fred Baumberger, Farm Dir. **Wattage:** 3000. **Ad Rates:** $15 for 30 seconds; $19 for 60 seconds.

9105 WGRN-FM - 89.5
315 E. College Ave. Phone: (618)664-2800
Greenville, IL 62246 Fax: (618)664-1373

Format: Religious; Contemporary Christian. **Networks:** USA Radio. **Owner:** Greenville College Educational Broadcasting Foundation, Inc., at above address. **Founded:** 1953. **Operating Hours:** Continuous. **Key Personnel:** Dona Kerman, Manager; Jeff Jordan, Station Mgr.; Veronica Ross, Business Mgr.; Scott Whyte, Engineering Manager. **Wattage:** 300. **Ad Rates:** $8 per unit.

GURNEE, pop. 7,179.

Lake Co. (NE). 5 m W of Waukegan. Suburban area. Marriott's Great America Theme Park. Manufactures plastic glass and lumber products, electronic commponents. Horse, grain.

9106 Gurnee Press
Lakeland Publishers, Inc.
30 S. Whitney St. Phone: (847)223-8161
PO Box 268 Fax: (847)223-8810
Grayslake, IL 60030-0268
Publication E-mail: edit@lnd.com

Community newspaper. **Subtitle:** Gurnee Press. **Founded:** 1973. **Freq:** Weekly (Thurs.). **Print Method:** Offset. **Trim Size:** 11 x 17. **Cols./Page:** 5. **Col. Width:** 2 inches. **Col. Depth:** 16 inches. **Key Personnel:** W.H. Schroeder, Publisher; Esther Hebbard, Advertising Mgr. **Subscription Rates:** $24.50; $35 out of area. **Remarks:** Accepts advertising.
Ad Rates: BW: $674.80 **Circ:** ‡2,147
4C: $1,023.40
SAU: $8.48

9107 Gurnee Review
Pioneer Press Newspapers
850 N. Milwaukee Ave. Phone: (847)680-6690
Vernon Hills, IL 60061 Fax: (847)573-2500

Community newspaper (tabloid). **Founded:** 1989. **Freq:** Weekly (Thurs.). **Print Method:** Offset. **Cols./Page:** 4. **Col.**

Width: 13 3/5 picas. **Col. Depth:** 196 agate lines. **Key Personnel:** Paul Sassone, Managing Editor; Marah Shuman, Editor. **Subscription Rates:** $5; $11.95 out of county. **Remarks:** Combined advertising rates available with other Pioneer Press Newspapers.
Circ: Thurs. ★**4,280**

HAMILTON, pop. 3,509.

Hancock Co. (W). On Mississippi River, opposite Keokuk, Ia. with bridge connections. Stone quarry. Beekeepers' suppliers factory. Grain, stock farms. Corn, wheat, soybeans.

9108 American Bee Journal
Dadant & Sons, Inc.
51 S. 2nd St. Phone: (217)847-3324
Hamilton, IL 62341 Fax: (217)847-3660
Free: (800)637-7468
Publication E-mail: abj@dadant.com
Publisher E-mail: dadant@dadant.com

Magazine for hobbyist and professional beekeepers. Covers hive management, honey handling, disease control, honey markets, foreign beekeeping, beekeeping history, bee laws, honey plants, marketing, and government beekeeping research. **Founded:** Jan. 1861. **Freq:** Monthly. **Print Method:** Offset. **Trim Size:** 8 x 10 3/4 in. **Cols./Page:** 3. **Col. Width:** 26 nonpareils. **Col. Depth:** 136 agate lines. **Key Personnel:** Joe M. Graham, Editor; Marta Menn, Advertising Mgr. **ISSN:** 0002-7626. **Subscription Rates:** $19.25 individuals; $3.00 single issue. **Remarks:** Accepts advertising. **URL:** http://www.dadant.com. **Alt. Formats:** Microform.
Ad Rates: BW: $790 **Circ:** Paid ‡13,000
4C: $948
PCI: $40.50

HAMPSHIRE, pop. 1,735.

Kane Co. (N). 18 m N. of Elgin.

9109 Hampshire Register News
Kane/DeKalb News Weeklies
PO Box 337 Phone: (847)683-2627
Hampshire, IL 60140 Fax: (815)899-4329

Community newspaper. **Founded:** Mar. 5, 1884. **Freq:** Weekly (Wed.). **Print Method:** Offset. **Cols./Page:** 6. **Col. Width:** 26 nonpareils. **Col. Depth:** 295 agate lines. **Key Personnel:** Mike Crase, Editor; Roger Coleman, Publisher; Bernice Bieber, Advertising Mgr.; Gloria Ream, Circulation Mgr.; Bernice Bieber, Classified Advertising Mgr. **Subscription Rates:** $30 individuals; $42 out of area. **Remarks:** Accepts advertising. **Formerly:** Hampshire Register. **Feature Editors:** Mike Crase, *City*, phone (847)683-3426, thenews@pbcnet.com.
Ad Rates: BW: $1,436.40 **Circ:** Paid 1,654
4C: $365 Free 23
SAU: $11.40
PCI: $11.40

HANOVER PARK, pop. 28,850.

Cook & Du Page Co. (NE). 35 m W of Evanston. Residential.

9110 Hanover Park Examiner
Examiner Publications
4N781 Gerber Rd. Phone: (630)830-4145
Bartlett, IL 60103
Publisher E-mail: staff@examinerpublications.com

Local newspaper. **Founded:** 1978. **Freq:** Weekly (Wed.). **Print Method:** Web offset. **Trim Size:** 11 x 17. **Cols./Page:** 4. **Col. Width:** 28 nonpareils. **Col. Depth:** 224 agate lines. **Key Personnel:** Randall E. Petrik, Editor and Publisher.; Steve Eckelberry, Managing Editor. **USPS:** 625-680. **Subscription Rates:** $24. **Remarks:** Accepts advertising.
Ad Rates: BW: $448 **Circ:** 5,600
4C: $1,008
SAU: $45.00

HARDIN†, pop. 1,107.

Calhoun Co. (W). On Illinois River, 30 m NW of Alton. Resort. Ships apples. Fruit, grain farms. Apples, corn, wheat.

9111 Calhoun News-Herald
310 S. County Rd. Phone: (618)576-2345
PO Box 367 Fax: (618)576-2245
Hardin, IL 62047
Community newspaper. **Founded:** 1872. **Freq:** Weekly (Wed.). **Print Method:** Offset. **Cols./Page:** 6. **Col. Width:** 26 nonpareils. **Col. Depth:** 301 agate lines. **Key Personnel:** Bruce Campbell, Publisher. **Subscription Rates:** $18 individuals; $26 out of area. **Remarks:** Accepts advertising.
Ad Rates: SAU: $4.60 **Circ:** ‡4,000
PCI: $4.60

HARRISBURG†, pop. 9,322.

Saline Co. (S). 68 m NE of Cairo. Manufactures wood cabinets. Coal mines; timber. Diversified farming. Fruit, wheat, corn.

9112 The Daily Register
American Publishing
35 S. Vine St., No. 248 Phone: (618)253-7146
Harrisburg, IL 62946-1725 Fax: (618)252-0863

General newspaper. **Founded:** 1904. **Freq:** Mon.-Sat. (eve.). **Print Method:** Offset. **Cols./Page:** 6. **Col. Width:** 25 nonpareils. **Col. Depth:** 308 agate lines. **Key Personnel:** Lee Smith, Editor; George Wilson, Publisher, gwilson@ampub.com; Sally Wofford, Advertising Mgr. **Subscription Rates:** $69 individuals. **Remarks:** Accepts advertising. **URL:** www.dailyregister.com.
Ad Rates: SAU: $7 **Circ:** Combined 5,201

9113 WEBQ-AM - 1240
701 South Commercial St. Phone: (618)253-7282
Harrisburg, IL 62946 Fax: (618)252-2366

Format: Country; Agricultural; Agricultural. **Networks:** Florida Radio; Illinois News. **Owner:** Visher-Choate Broadcasting, at above address. **Founded:** 1923. **Operating Hours:** 5 a.m.-midnight; 20% network, 80% local. **ADI:** Paducah,KY-Cape Girardeau,MO-Marion,IL. **Key Personnel:** Dave Bard, General Mgr., phone (618)252-6309; Cathy Horton, Program Dir.; Bob Romonosky, Chief Engineer. **Wattage:** 1000. **Ad Rates:** $6.50-10 for 30 seconds; $9-12.50 for 60 seconds.

9114 WEBQ-FM - 102.3
701 S. Commercial Phone: (618)253-7812
Harrisburg, IL 62946 Fax: (618)252-2366
Free: (800)634-8193
E-mail: webq@midwest.net

Format: Adult Contemporary. **Networks:** ABC. **Owner:** Visher-Choate Broadcasting, at above address. **Founded:** 1971. **Former name:** WKSI-FM (1987). **Operating Hours:** Continuous. **Key Personnel:** Dave Bard, Station and Sales Mgr., phone (618)253-7282, webq@midwest.net; Cathy Horton, Program and Music Dir., djlady1240@hotmail.com; Bob Romonosy, Chief Engineer; Faye Bard, Traffic/Accounting. **Wattage:** 3000. **Ad Rates:** $2.50-8 for 30 seconds; $3.25-9.50 for 60 seconds.

HARVARD, pop. 5,126.

McHenry Co. (NE). 28 m NE of Rockford. Manufactures lawn and garden equipment, snow throwers, dairy equipment, refrigerator doors, aircraft hangers, aerospace components, plastic drainage tubing, transmission equipment for telephone lines.

9115 WMCW-AM - 1600
67 N. Ayer Phone: (815)943-3100
PO Box 786 Fax: (815)943-5120
Harvard, IL 60033

Format: Middle-of-the-Road (MOR). **Networks:** NBC. **Founded:** 1955. **Operating Hours:** 5 a.m.-10 p.m.; 5% network, 95% local. **Key Personnel:** Doug Cartland, Program Dir.; Mianne Nelson, General Mgr., rdolady@mc.net; Sybil Goodyear, News Dir.; Mike Bellamy, Sports Dir. **Wattage:** 500.

HARVEY

9116 Harvey/Markham Star
Star Newspapers
6901 W 159th St. Phone: (708)802-8800
Tinley Park, IL 60477 Fax: (708)802-8899

Newspaper group serving 51 communities in Chicago's southern suburbs. **Founded:** 1890. **Freq:** Semiweekly (Thurs. and Sun.). **Print Method:** Offset. **Trim Size:** 13 3/4 x 23. **Cols./Page:** 6. **Col. Width:** 2 inches. **Col. Depth:** 21 1/2 inches. **Key Personnel:** Lester Sons, Editor; Norman Rosinski, Publisher; Jim Meidell, Advertising Mgr.; Jay Fredrickson. **Remarks:** Accepts advertising.
Ad Rates: GLR: $56.76 **Circ:** Thurs. 65,520
Sun. 68,788

9117 WBEE-AM - 1570
15700 Campbell Ave. Phone: (708)331-7840
Harvey, IL 60426 Fax: (708)333-7840

Format: Jazz. **Networks:** Independent. **Founded:** 1955. **Operating Hours:** Continuous. **ADI:** Chicago (LaSalle), IL. **Key Personnel:** Charles Sherrell, President; Carl Farley, General Mgr. **Wattage:** 1000. **Ad Rates:** $30-85 for 30 seconds; $60-135 for 60 seconds.

HARWOOD HEIGHTS

9118 Norridge-Harwood Heights News
Pioneer Press Newspapers
130 S. Prospect Ave. Phone: (847)696-3133
Park Ridge, IL 60068 Fax: (847)696-3229

Community newspaper (tabloid). **Founded:** 1985. **Freq:** Weekly (Thurs.). **Print Method:** Offset. **Cols./Page:** 5. **Col. Width:** 11 picas. **Col. Depth:** 14 inches. **Key Personnel:** Paul Sassone, Managing Editor; Anne Lunde, Editor. **Subscription Rates:** $10.95; $11.95 out of county. **Remarks:** Combined advertising rates available with other Pioneer Press Newspapers. **URL:** http://www.pioneerlocal.com.
Circ: Thurs. ★**3,695**

HAVANA†, pop. 4,277.

Mason Co. (W). 38 m SW of Peoria. Flour, farm implements, and gasoline engines.

9119 Havana Mason County Democrat
Martin Publishing, Inc.
217 W. Market St. Phone: (309)543-3311
Havana, IL 62644 Fax: (309)543-6844

Local newspaper. **Founded:** 1849. **Freq:** Weekly. **Print Method:** Offset. **Cols./Page:** 6. **Col. Width:** 12 picas. **Col. Depth:** 21 1/2 inches. **Key Personnel:** W.J. Martin, Editor; Robert L. Martin, Jr., Publisher. **Subscription Rates:** $25 individuals. **Remarks:** Accepts advertising.
Ad Rates: SAU: $6 **Circ:** Combined 6,300

HAZEL CREST, pop. 13,973.

Cook Co. (NE). 5 m N of Chicago Heights. Residential.

9120 Muslim Journal
Muslim Journal Enterprises, Inc.
929 W. 171st. St. Phone: (708)647-9600
Hazel Crest, IL 60429-1901 Fax: (708)647-0754
Free: (800)837-8402
Publication E-mail: muslimjrnl@aol.com

International Islamic newspaper. **Founded:** 1975. **Freq:** Weekly (Fri.). **Print Method:** Offset. **Cols./Page:** 5. **Col. Width:** 22 nonpareils. **Col. Depth:** 208 agate lines. **Key Personnel:** Ayesha K. Mustafaa, Editor/Contact; Monte I Fateen, Circulation Mgr.; Rabbani Mubashshir, Advertising Dir. **ISSN:** 0883-816X. **Subscription Rates:** $45 individuals; $75 two years. **URL:** http://www.worldforum.com/muslimj. **Alt. Formats:** Microfiche.
Ad Rates: BW: $869.70 **Circ:** ‡16,000
4C: $1,043.64
SAU: $13.38
PCI: $13.38

HENRY, pop. 2,740.

Marshall Co. (NC). On Illinois River, 35 m NE of Peoria. Boat connections. Hunting, fishing resort. Oak timber. Nurseries. Hatcheries. Grain elevators. Creamery. Manufactures chemicals, farm equipment, hunting goods. Stock, poultry, fruit, grain farms.

9121 Henry News-Republican
Henry News-Republican, Inc.
709 3rd St., No. 190 Phone: (309)364-3250
Henry, IL 61537-1446 Fax: (309)364-3858

Newspaper with a Republican orientation. **Founded:** 1852. **Freq:** Weekly (Wed.). **Print Method:** Offset. **Trim Size:** 16 x 23 1/2. **Cols./Page:** 7. **Col. Width:** 24 nonpareils. **Col. Depth:** 294 agate lines. **Key Personnel:** Doug Ziegler, Editor and Publisher. **Subscription Rates:** $20 individuals; $24 out of area.
Ad Rates: GLR: $.31 **Circ:** 2,850
BW: $624
4C: $815.08
SAU: $3.90

9122 Wenona Index
PO Box 190 Phone: (309)364-3250
Henry, IL 61537 Fax: (309)364-3858

Newspaper. **Subtitle:** Community Newspaper. **Founded:** 1865. **Freq:** Weekly (Thurs.). **Print Method:** Offset. **Cols./Page:** 7. **Col. Width:** 24 nonpareils. **Col. Depth:** 294 agate lines. **Key Personnel:** Doug Ziegler, Editor and Publisher. **Subscription Rates:** $14 individuals. **Remarks:** Accepts advertising.
Ad Rates: BW: $257.25 **Circ:** 1,000
4C: $537.25
SAU: $2.66

HERRIN, pop. 10,040.

Williamson Co. (S). 5 m W. of Johnston City. Residential.

9123 The Spokesman
American Publishing Co.
216 N. Park Ave. Phone: (618)942-5000
PO Box 128 Fax: (618)942-4630
Herrin, IL 62948
Publication E-mail: herrun@ampub.com

Newspaper. **Founded:** 1957. **Freq:** Weekly (Thurs.). **Print Method:** Offset. **Cols./Page:** 6. **Col. Width:** 26 nonpareils. **Col. Depth:** 301 agate lines. **Key Personnel:** Nancy Sims, Publisher. **Subscription Rates:** Free; $21.95 individuals. **Remarks:** Accepts advertising.
Ad Rates: GLR: $.24 **Circ:** Paid ‡10,578
BW: $645
4C: $2,880
PCI: $5

9124 WJPF-AM - 1340
Box 550 Phone: (618)942-2181
Herrin, IL 62948 Fax: (618)988-8111

Format: Talk; News. **Networks:** Mutual Broadcasting System. **Owner:** Egyptian Broadcasting Co., at above address. **Founded:** 1940. **Operating Hours:** Continuous; 60% network, 40% local. **Key Personnel:** Mike Murphy, Contact; Robert A. Ferrari, Program Mgr.; John Chase, Contact. **Wattage:** 1000. **Ad Rates:** $4-6 for 15 seconds; $6-8 for 30 seconds; $8-10 for 60 seconds.

HERSCHER, pop. 1,247.

Kankakee Co. (E) 33 m S. of Joliet.

9125 Herscher Press
Star Newspapers
204 E. Chippewa St. Phone: (815)584-3007
PO Box 159
Dwight, IL 60420-0159
Community newspaper. **Founded:** 1971. **Freq:** Weekly (Thurs.). **Print Method:** Offset. **Trim Size:** 8 x 11 1/4. **Cols./Page:** 8. **Col. Width:** 1 3/4 inches. **Col. Depth:** 301 agate lines. **Key Personnel:** Brian Heiar, Editor; Scott McGraw, Publisher. **USPS:** 782-800. **Subscription Rates:** $11 individuals; $16 out of state.
Ad Rates: GLR: $.16 **Circ:** Paid 882
BW: $161.25 Free 10
SAU: $2.64
PCI: $2.24

HEYWORTH, pop. 1,598.

McLean Co. (C). 10 m s of Bloomington. Grain, stock, poultry, dairy farms. Corn, wheat, oats, soybeans.

9126 The Heyworth Star
Heyworth Star Inc.
105 S. Buchanan Phone: (309)473-2414
Heyworth, IL 61745-0367 Fax: (309)473-3610
Free: (800)288-2414

Community newspaper. **Founded:** 1889. **Freq:** Weekly (Thurs.). **Print Method:** Offset. **Cols./Page:** 6. **Col. Width:** 2 inches. **Col. Depth:** 21 1/4 inches. **Key Personnel:** James M. Beveridge, Editor and Publisher. **USPS:** 242-200. **Subscription Rates:** $15 individuals; $16.50 out of area. **Remarks:** Accepts advertising.
Ad Rates: GLR: $0.40 **Circ:** ‡1,095
PCI: $3.90

HICKORY HILLS

9127 Metrovision
7720 W 98th St. Phone: (708)430-4840
Hickory Hills, IL 60457-2300 Fax: (708)430-1870

Key Personnel: Ron Murray, Contact. **Cities Served:** Palos Hills, IL.

HIGHLAND, pop. 7,122.

Madison Co. (SW). 32 m E of St. Louis, Mo. Manufactures pipe organs, cellophane products, tools and dies, transformers, electronic equipment, feed, paint, boxboard, machine and screw products. Dairy, poultry, grain farms. Livestock. Wheat corn.

9128 Highland News Leader
PO Box 250 Phone: (618)654-2366
Highland, IL 62249
Newspaper with a Republican orientation. **Founded:** 1861. **Freq:** Semiweekly (Mon. and Thurs.). **Print Method:** Offset. **Cols./Page:** 9. **Col. Width:** 22 nonpareils. **Col. Depth:** 294 agate lines. **Key Personnel:** Stephen L. Holt, President; Kay Maue, Publisher; Gay Bentlage, Promotions Mgr. **Subscription Rates:** $28 individuals Madison, Clinton, Bond & St. Clair County; $.50 single issue. **Remarks:** Accepts advertising.
Ad Rates: SAU: $11.05 **Circ:** Paid 8,000
Free ‡7,800

9129 WINU-AM - 880
13063 Winu Dr. Phone: (618)654-7521
PO Box 303 Fax: (618)654-6333
Highland, IL 62249

Format: Talk; News; Agricultural; Full Service; Sports; Religious. **Networks:** CBS; UPI; Tribune Radio; Sun Radio; Westwood One Radio; RFD Illinois. **Owner:** New Life Evangelistic Center, at above address, Free: (800)242-3276. **Founded:** 1962. **Formerly:** Win You, Ltd. **Operating Hours:** Continuous; 6% network, 94% local. C.P. at 880 Khz. **ADI:** St. Louis, MO (Mt. Vernon, IL). **Key Personnel:** Dennis Harper, General Mgr. **Wattage:** 2500 day; 250 night. **Ad Rates:** $10-28 for 30 seconds; $20-38 for 60 seconds. Combined advertising rates available with WCBW-AM, KNLC-TV24.

HIGHLAND PARK, pop. 30,611.

Lake Co. (NE). On Lake Michigan, 23 m N of Chicago. Residential suburb of Chicago.

9130 December
December Press, Inc.
PO Box 302 Phone: (708)940-4122
Highland Park, IL 60035
Literary magazine covering fiction, poetry, essays, art and reviews. **Founded:** 1958. **Freq:** Irregular. **Print Method:** Offset. **Trim Size:** 6 x 9. **Cols./Page:** 1. **Col. Width:** 5 inches. **Col. Depth:** 8 inches. **Key Personnel:** Curt Johnson, Editor. **ISSN:** 0070-3141. **Subscription Rates:** $6 single issue. **Remarks:** Advertising not accepted.
Circ: Paid 1,000

9131 Highland Park News
Pioneer Press Newspapers
850 N. Milwaukee Ave. Phone: (847)680-6690
Vernon Hills, IL 60061 Fax: (847)573-2500

Community newspaper. **Founded:** 1971. **Freq:** Weekly (Thurs.). **Print Method:** Offset. **Cols./Page:** 4. **Col. Width:** 24 nonpareils. **Col. Depth:** 196 agate lines. **Key Personnel:** Kyle Leonard, Editor; Paul Sassone, Managing Editor. **Subscription Rates:** $8.50 individuals.
Circ: Thurs. 7,561

9132 Made to Measure
Halper Publishing Co.
600 Central Ave., Ste. 226 Phone: (847)433-1114
Highland Park, IL 60035 Fax: (847)433-6602
Publication E-mail: mtm@halper.com

Trade magazine for the uniform, career apparel, and allied trades. **Founded:** 1930. **Freq:** Semiannual. **Print Method:** Sheetfed offset. **Trim Size:** 6 3/4 x 9 3/4. **Key Personnel:** Rick Levine, Publisher. **Subscription Rates:** Free to qualified subscribers. **Remarks:** Accepts advertising. **URL:** http://www.halper.com/mtm.
Ad Rates: BW: $1,755 **Circ:** Controlled ⊕**25,000**
4C: $2,955

9133 WEEF-AM - 1430
210 Skokie Valley Rd. Phone: (708)831-5440
Highland Park, IL 60035

Format: Ethnic. **Networks:** Independent. **Founded:** 1963. **Operating Hours:** Sunrise-sunset. **Key Personnel:** Myra Winston, General Mgr.; Chris T. Bagat, Program Dir. **Wattage:** 1000.

9134 WVVX-FM - 103.1
210 Skokie Valley Rd. Phone: (847)831-5250
Highland Park, IL 60035 Fax: (847)831-5296

Format: Polka. **Networks:** Independent. **Founded:** 1963. **Formerly:** WEEF-FM (1973). **Operating Hours:** Continuous; 100% local. **ADI:** Chicago (LaSalle), IL. **Key Personnel:** Sara Fell, Jr., Business Mgr.; Tony Jacobs, Regional Mktg. Mgr.; Steve Bertok, Operations Dir. **Local Programs:** *Rebel Radio.* **Wattage:** 3000. **Ad Rates:** Advertising accepted; rates available upon request.

HILLSBORO†, pop. 4,408.

Montgomery Co. (SC). 50 m SE of Springfield. Glass beverage bottles manufactured. Coal mines. Agriculture. Zinc smelters. Electrical generating. Dairy and grain farms. Corn, wheat, hay, soybeans.

9135 M & M Journal
Hillsboro Journal, Inc.
PO Box 100 Phone: (217)532-3933
Hillsboro, IL 62049 Fax: (217)532-3632

Community newspaper. **Freq:** Weekly (Mon.). **Print Method:** Offset.
Circ: 21,238

9136 Montgomery County News
PO Box 250 Phone: (217)532-3929
Hillsboro, IL 62049-0250 Fax: (217)532-3522
Free: (800)529-6397

Newspaper with a Democratic orientation. **Founded:** 1869. **Freq:** Semiweekly (Mon. and Thurs.). **Print Method:** Offset. **Cols./Page:** 8. **Col. Width:** 22 nonpareils. **Col. Depth:** 301 agate lines. **Key Personnel:** Nancy Bliss, Editor; Richard Slepicka, Advertising Mgr.; Robert R. Bliss, Publisher. **Subscription Rates:** $15 individuals. **Remarks:** Accepts advertising.
Ad Rates: GLR: $.15 **Circ:** 6,700

HINSDALE, pop. 16,726.

Du Page Co. (NE). 17 m SW of Chicago. Residential. Commercial office center.

9137 Appliance
Dana Chase Publications, Inc.
1110 Jorie Blvd., Ste. 203 Phone: (630)990-3484
Hinsdale, IL 60522-9019 Fax: (630)990-0078

Trade magazine focusing on appliances: commercial, consumer, medical and business. **Subtitle:** Serving the Appliance Industry Worldwide. **Founded:** Jan. 1944. **Freq:** Monthly. **Print Method:** Offset. **Trim Size:** 8 x 10 7/8. **Cols./Page:** 3. **Col. Width:** 26 nonpareils. **Col. Depth:** 140 agate lines. **Key Personnel:** Scot M. Stevens, Publisher, scot@appliance.com; Dana Chase, Jr., President. **ISSN:** 0003-6781. **Subscription Rates:** $75 individuals individual; $10 single issue; $85 students, other countries add $12. **Remarks:** Accepts advertising. **URL:** http://appliance.com.
Ad Rates: BW: $3,840 **Circ:** Non-paid ‡33,600
4C: $5,310

9138 Business Communications Review
BCR Enterprises, Inc.
950 York Rd., Ste. 203 Phone: (630)986-1432
Hinsdale, IL 60521-2939 Fax: (630)323-5324
Free: (800)227-1234

Magazine covering telecommunications management, networking, and technology. **Founded:** 1971. **Freq:** Monthly. **Print Method:** Offset. **Trim Size:** 8 1/8 x 10 7/8. **Cols./Page:** 2 and 3. **Col. Width:** 20 and 13 picas. **Col. Depth:** 54 picas. **Key Personnel:** Fred Knight, Editor and Publisher; Eric Krapf, Managing Editor; Steve Maxey, Production Editor; Joanne Bonaminio, Marketing Mgr. **ISSN:** 0162-3885. **Subscription Rates:** $45 individuals; $5 single issue. **Remarks:** Accepts advertising. **URL:** http://www.bcr.com.
Ad Rates: BW: $3,145 **Circ:** Paid ★**11,348**
4C: $3,970 Non-paid ★**3,347**

9139 Doings
Doings Newspapers, Inc.
118 W. 1st St. Phone: (630)887-0600
PO Box 151 Fax: (630)887-9646
Hinsdale, IL 60522
Publisher E-mail: doingsnews@aol.com

Community newspaper. **Founded:** 1895. **Freq:** Semiweekly (Wed. and Fri.). **Print Method:** Offset. **Trim Size:** 10 1/8 x 15. **Cols./Page:** 4. **Col. Width:** 28 nonpareils. **Col. Depth:** 210 agate lines. **Key Personnel:** J. Peter Teschner, Editor and Publisher; Laurie Adams, Executive Editor; Jim Slonoff, General Mgr.; Pam Lannom, Managing Editor. **Subscription Rates:** $49.50 individuals; $0.75 single issue. **Remarks:** Accepts advertising. **URL:** http://www.thedoings.com. **Alt. Formats:** Microform. **Feature Editors:** Susan Ryan, *Society.*
Ad Rates: GLR: $1.37 **Circ:** 10,500
BW: $960
4C: $250
PCI: $16

9140 WHSD-FM - 88.5
55th and Grant Sts. Phone: (708)655-6119
Hinsdale, IL 60521

Format: Classic Rock. **Founded:** 1972. **Operating Hours:** 3 p.m.-10 p.m.; 100% local. **Key Personnel:** Terry Kohl, Contact. **Wattage:** 125. **Ad Rates:** Noncommercial.

HOFFMAN ESTATES, pop. 38,258.

Cook Co. (NE). 6 m W of Evanston. Residential.

9141 Danish Pioneer
Bertelsen Publishing Co.
1582 Glen Lake Rd. Phone: (708)882-2552
Hoffman Estates, IL 60195 Fax: (708)882-7082

Danish interest magazine. **Subtitle:** Den Danske Pioneer. **Founded:** 1872. **Freq:** Biweekly. **Print Method:** Offset. **Trim Size:** 10 x 13. **Cols./Page:** 5. **Col. Width:** 24 nonpareils. **Col. Depth:** 210 agate lines. **Key Personnel:** Chris Steffensen, Editor. **ISSN:** 0747-3869. **Subscription Rates:** $25 individuals; $31; $1 single issue. **Remarks:** Accepts advertising. **Foreign language name**: Danske Pioneer.
Ad Rates: BW: $360 **Circ:** Paid ‡3,000
PCI: $7 Non-paid ‡250

9142 Hoffman Estates Review
Pioneer Press Newspapers
291 N. Dunton Ave. Phone: (847)797-5100
Arlington Heights, IL 60004 Fax: (847)797-5151

Community newspaper (tabloid). **Founded:** 1989. **Freq:** Weekly (Thurs.). **Print Method:** Offset. **Cols./Page:** 5. **Col. Width:** 10 3/5 inches. **Col. Depth:** 14 inches. **Key Personnel:** Terri McHugh, Editor; Paul Sassone, Managing Editor. **Subscription Rates:** $12.95. **Remarks:** Combined advertising rates available with other Pioneer Press Newspapers. **URL:** http://www.pioneerlocal.com.
Circ: Thurs. ★2,682

HOMER TOWNSHIP

9143 Homer Township Star
Star Newspapers
6901 W 159th St. Phone: (708)802-8800
Tinley Park, IL 60477 Fax: (708)802-8899

Newspaper group serving 51 communities in Chicago's southern suburbs. **Founded:** 1890. **Freq:** Semiweekly (Thurs. and Sun.). **Print Method:** Offset. **Trim Size:** 13 3/4 x 23. **Cols./Page:** 6. **Col. Width:** 2 inches. **Col. Depth:** 21 1/2 inches. **Key Personnel:** Lester Sons, Editor; Norman Rosinski, Publisher; Jim Meidell, Advertising Mgr.; Jay Frederickson. **Remarks:** Accepts advertising.
Ad Rates: GLR: $56.76 **Circ:** Thurs. 64,637
Sun. 68,267

HOMEWOOD, pop. 19,724.

Cook Co. (NE). 22 m S of Chicago. Residential.

9144 Homewood/Flossmoor Star
Star Newspapers
6901 W 159th St. Phone: (708)802-8800
Tinley Park, IL 60477 Fax: (708)802-8899

Newspaper group serving 51 communities in Chicago's southern suburbs. **Founded:** 1890. **Freq:** Semiweekly (Thurs. and Sun.). **Print Method:** Offset. **Trim Size:** 13 3/4 x 23. **Cols./Page:** 6. **Col. Width:** 2 inches. **Col. Depth:** 21 1/2 inches. **Key Personnel:** Lester Sons, Editor; Norman Rosinski, Publisher; Jim Meidell, Advertising Mgr.; Jay Frederickson, Advertising Manager.
Ad Rates: GLR: $56.76 **Circ:** Thurs. 64,637

HOOPESTON, pop. 6,411.

Vermilion Co. (E). 25 m N of Danville. Manufactures battery charges, tin cans, canning machinery, canned vegetables, malleable castings. Agriculture.

9145 Chronicle
308 E. Main St. Phone: (217)283-5111
Hoopeston, IL 60942 Fax: (217)283-5846

Community newspaper. **Founded:** Jan. 11, 1872. **Freq:** Semiweekly (Tues. and Fri.). **Print Method:** Offset. **Trim Size:** 10 1/4 x 14. **Cols./Page:** 6. **Col. Width:** 9 1/2 picas. **Col. Depth:** 14 inches. **Key Personnel:** JoAnn Gocking, Editor; Bette D. Schmid, Publisher; Joy Neakomm, Advertising Mgr. **Subscription Rates:** $33 individuals; $46.50 out of area.
Ad Rates: BW: $310.80 **Circ:** 2,087
PCI: $3.70

9146 WHPO-FM - 100.9
627 N. Market Phone: (217)283-7744
Box 55 Fax: (217)283-6090
Hoopeston, IL 60942
Free: (800)245-4101
E-mail: whpo@main.cu-online.com

Networks: Jones Satellite. **Founded:** 1979. **Operating Hours:** Continuous: 70% network, 30% local. **Key Personnel:** Gary Voss, General Mgr.; Becky Buss, Program/Promoter; Tina Voss, Office Mgr. **Wattage:** 3000. **Ad Rates:** $10-12 for 30 seconds; $12-15 for 60 seconds.

HUNTLEY, pop. 1,432.

McHenry Co. (SC). 11 m NW of Elgin. Dairy.

9147 The Huntley Farmside
11801 Main St. Phone: (847)669-5621
PO Box 127 Fax: (847)669-5623
Huntley, IL 60142-0127
Community newspaper. **Founded:** Apr. 1960. **Freq:** Weekly (Thurs.). **Print Method:** Offset. **Trim Size:** 11 1/2 x 16. **Cols./Page:** 5. **Col. Width:** 2 1/8 inches. **Col. Depth:** 13 inches. **Key Personnel:** Suzanne L. Brown, Publisher. **USPS:** 580-360. **Subscription Rates:** $8 individuals; $15 two years. **Remarks:** Accepts advertising.
Ad Rates: BW: $285 **Circ:** Paid 1350
PCI: $6.50 Non-paid 150

ILLIOPOLIS, pop. 1,118.

Sangamon Co. (C). 18 m W of Decatur. Grain elevator; chemical factory. Diversified farming. Corn, wheat, oats, poultry.

9148 County Line Observer
Illiopolis Sentinel
PO Box 477 Phone: (217)486-7321
Illiopolis, IL 62539
Community newspaper. **Founded:** 1940. **Freq:** Weekly (Fri.). **Print Method:** Offset. **Cols./Page:** 5. **Col. Width:** 24 nonpareils. **Col. Depth:** 140 agate lines. **Key Personnel:** Frank J. Bell, Editor and Publisher. **Subscription Rates:** $12.50 individuals; $15 out of county. **Remarks:** Accepts advertising.
Ad Rates: GLR: $.40 **Circ:** ‡750
BW: $145
SAU: $2.84
PCI: $2.60

9149 Illiopolis Sentinel
PO Box 477 Phone: (217)486-7321
Illiopolis, IL 62539
Community newspaper. **Founded:** 1925. **Freq:** Weekly (Thurs.). **Print Method:** Offset. **Cols./Page:** 5. **Col. Width:** 24 nonpareils. **Col. Depth:** 280 agate lines. **Key Personnel:** Frank J. Bell, Editor and Publisher. **Subscription Rates:** $17.50 individuals. **Remarks:** Accepts advertising.
Ad Rates: GLR: $.40 **Circ:** Paid ‡840
BW: $145 Free ‡80
SAU: $2.84
PCI: $2.60

ITASCA, pop. 7,948.

DuPage Co. (NE). 6 m N of Glen Ellyn. Residential

9150 Chemical Processing
Putman Publishing Co.
555 W. Pierce Rd., Ste. 301 Phone: (630)467-1300
Itasca, IL 60143 Fax: (630)467-1123

Magazine for the chemical process industry. **Subtitle:** Solutions For Plant & Operating Management. **Founded:** 1938. **Freq:** Monthly. **Print Method:** Offset. **Trim Size:** 8 x 10 3/4. **Cols./Page:** 3. **Col. Width:** 26 nonpareils. **Col. Depth:** 140 agate lines. **Key Personnel:** Bob Strack, Editor; Larry Potter, Publisher; John Cappelletti, Advertising Mgr. **Subscription Rates:** $35 individuals. **Remarks:** Accepts advertising.
Ad Rates: BW: $5,540 **Circ:** Non-paid ‡80,030
4C: $7,535

9151 Control
Putman Publishing Co.
555 W. Pierce Rd., Ste. 301 Phone: (630)467-1300
Itasca, IL 60143 Fax: (630)467-1123

Magazine targeting instrumentation and control systems professionals in the process industries. **Subtitle:** For the Process Industries. **Founded:** Oct. 1988. **Freq:** 12/year. **Print Method:** Offset. **Trim Size:** 8 x 10 3/4. **Cols./Page:** 3. **Key Personnel:** Keith Larson, Publisher. **ISSN:** 1049-5541. **Subscription Rates:** $60 individuals; $12 single issue. **Remarks:** Accepts advertising. **Available Online. URL:** www.controlmagazine.com.
Ad Rates: BW: $6,715 **Circ:** Non-paid ‡72,217
4C: $8,335

9152 Control Ad-Lits
Putman Publishing Co.
555 W. Pierce Rd., Ste. 301 Phone: (630)467-1300
Itasca, IL 60143 Fax: (630)467-1123

Trade magazine for control and instrumentation professionals in the process industries. **Founded:** 1988. **Freq:** Monthly. **Key Personnel:** Joe Feeley, Editor; Paul Studebaker, Editor-in-Chief; Erin Inselberger, Circulation Mgr. **Remarks:** Accepts advertising. **URL:** http://www.controlmagazine.com.
Circ: (Not Reported)

9153 Control Isa Show Reporter
Putman Publishing Co.
555 W. Pierce Rd., Ste. 301 Phone: (630)467-1300
Itasca, IL 60143 Fax: (630)467-1123

Newspaper on America's tradeshows. **Subtitle:** Highlights From the ISA Convention Floor. **Founded:** 1991. **Freq:** DLY during tradeshow. **Key Personnel:** Peggy Smedley, Editor.

9154 Family Safety & Health
National Safety Council
1121 Spring Lake Dr. Phone: (630)775-2286
Itasca, IL 60143-3201 Fax: (630)775-2285
Free: (800)621-7615

Magazine aimed at preventing accidents at home and on the road and promoting health and fitness. **Founded:** 1961. **Freq:** Quarterly. **Print Method:** Offset. **Trim Size:** 8 1/4 x 10 3/4. **Cols./Page:** 3 and 2. **Key Personnel:** Laura Coyne, Editor, phone (630)775-2276; Sharon Lewis, Assoc. Editor; John Kennedy, Publisher. **ISSN:** 0749-310X. **Subscription Rates:** $15 members; $19 nonmembers; Quantity discounts available. **Remarks:** Accepts advertising. **URL:** http://www.nsc.org/pubs/fsh.htm.
Circ: ‡1,000,000

9155 Food Business
Putman Publishing Co.
555 W. Pierce Rd., Ste. 301 Phone: (630)467-1300
Itasca, IL 60143 Fax: (630)467-1123

Magazine devoted to coverage of the latest food industry, business and marketing developments in a unique news format. **Founded:** Oct. 1988. **Freq:** Semimonthly. **Print Method:** Web offset. **Trim Size:** 8 x 10 3/4. **Cols./Page:** 3 and 4. **Col. Width:** 13 and 9.6 picas. **Key Personnel:** Bob Messenger, Editor; Peggy Stath, Publisher. **ISSN:** 1049-5568. **Subscription Rates:** $53. $3 single issue. **Remarks:** Accepts advertising.
Ad Rates: BW: $5,100 **Circ:** Controlled ‡50,039
4C: $6,700

9156 Plant Services
Putman Publishing Co.
555 W. Pierce Rd., Ste. 301 Phone: (630)467-1300
Itasca, IL 60143 Fax: (630)467-1123
Publication E-mail: chuck.boyles@publishers.com

Magazine on plant maintenance professionals. **Founded:** 1980. **Freq:** Monthly. **Print Method:** Web offset. **Trim Size:** 8 1/8 x 10 7/8. **Cols./Page:** 2 and 3. **Key Personnel:** John Blatnik, Publisher, fax (630)467-1120, john.blatnik@publishers.com; Larry Howe, Assoc. Publisher; Chuck Boyles, Editor-in-Chief, chuck.boyles@publishers.com. **ISSN:** 0199-8013. **Subscription Rates:** $80 individuals; $120 other countries; $20 single issue. **Remarks:** Accepts advertising. **Available Online. URL:** http://www.plantservices.com.
Ad Rates: BW: $8,975 **Circ:** Controlled ‡110,000
4C: $10,475

9157 Processing
Putman Publishing Co.
555 W. Pierce Rd., Ste. 301 Phone: (630)467-1300
Itasca, IL 60143 Fax: (630)467-1123

Equipment selection guide. **Founded:** 1987. **Freq:** 12/yr. and special handbooks. **Trim Size:** 10 7/8 x 15 3/4. **Key Personnel:** Joan Leeney, Editor, jleeney@aol.com; Michael Wasson, Publisher, mlwasson@aol.com. **Remarks:** Accepts advertising.
Circ: Paid 105,000

9158 Safe Driver
National Safety Council
1121 Spring Lake Dr. Phone: (630)285-1121
Itasca, IL 60143-3201 Fax: (630)285-1315
Free: (800)539-7468

Trade magazine for professional car, bus and truck drivers. **Founded:** 1926. **Freq:** Monthly. **Key Personnel:** Laura Coyne, Editor, phone (446)30775-2276, fax (630)775-2285, coyne/@nsc.org; John H. Kennedy, Publisher, phone (630)775-2103, kennedyj@usc.org; Kathleen Misovic, Assoc. Ed., phone (630)775-2288, misovick@nsc.org. **Subscription Rates:** $15 members; $19 nonmembers. **Remarks:** Advertising not accepted.
Circ: Paid 140,000

9159 Safety & Health
National Safety Council
1121 Spring Lake Dr. Phone: (630)285-1121
Itasca, IL 60143-3201 Fax: (630)285-1315
Free: (800)539-7468

Publication focusing on safety and health issues. **Founded:** 1919. **Freq:** Monthly. **Print Method:** Offset. **Trim Size:** 8 1/8 x 10 7/8. **Cols./Page:** 3. **Col. Width:** 2 1/8 inches. **Col. Depth:** 10 inches. **Key Personnel:** John H. Kenngos, Publisher; Joel Wakitsch, Advertising Mgr.; Carrie Fearn, Editor. **ISSN:** 0891-

1797. **Subscription Rates:** $56. $5 single issue. **Remarks:** Accepts advertising. **URL:** http://p://www.nsc.org/pubs/sh.htm.
Ad Rates: BW: $3,100 **Circ:** Paid ‡40,000
4C: $4,050

9160 Safeworker
National Safety Council
1121 Spring Lake Dr. Phone: (630)285-1121
Itasca, IL 60143-3201 Fax: (630)285-1315
Free: (800)539-7468

Trade magazine covering safety tips to workers on various topics. **Founded:** 1926. **Freq:** Monthly. **Key Personnel:** Laura Coyne, Editor, phone (630)775-2276, fax (630)775-2285, coynel@nsc.org; Kathleen Misovic, Assoc. Editor, phone (630)775-2288, misovick@nsc.org; John Kennedy, Publisher, phone (630)775-2103, kennedyj@nsc.org. **Subscription Rates:** $15 members; $19 nonmembers. **Remarks:** Advertising not accepted.
Circ: Paid 140,000

9161 Today's Supervisor
National Safety Council
1121 Spring Lake Dr. Phone: (630)285-1121
Itasca, IL 60143-3201 Fax: (630)285-1315
Free: (800)539-7468

Magazine for the front-line supervisor containing articles related to safety and health. **Founded:** 1935. **Freq:** Monthly. **Print Method:** Offset. **Trim Size:** 5 1/2 x 8 1/2. **Cols./Page:** 2. **Col. Width:** 26 nonpareils. **Col. Depth:** 104 agate lines. **Key Personnel:** Laura Coyne, Editor, phone (630)775-2276, fax (630)775-2285, coynel@nsc.org; Kathleen Misovic, Assoc. Ed., phone (630)775-2288, fax (630)775-2285, misovic@nsc.org; John Kennedy, Publisher, phone (630)775-2103, fax (630)775-2285, kennedyj@nsc.org. **ISSN:** 0734-3302. **Subscription Rates:** $23 nonmembers; $18 members. **Remarks:** Advertising not accepted.
Circ: ‡100,000

9162 Traffic Safety
National Safety Council
1121 Spring Lake Dr. Phone: (630)285-1121
Itasca, IL 60143-3201 Fax: (630)285-1315
Free: (800)539-7468

Vehicle collision prevention magazine includes information on driver training, traffic and road engineering, and law enforcement. **Founded:** July 1957. **Freq:** Bimonthly. **Print Method:** Offset. **Trim Size:** 8 x 10 7/8. **Cols./Page:** 2 and 3. **Col. Width:** 20 and 13 picas. **Col. Depth:** 60 picas. **Key Personnel:** John H. Kennedy, Publisher, phone (603)775-2103, fax (630)775-2285; Kathy Henderson, Editor, hendersk@nsc.org. **ISSN:** 0041-0721. **Subscription Rates:** $24 members; $30 nonmembers; $4.25 single issue. **Remarks:** Accepts advertising.
Ad Rates: BW: $1,450 **Circ:** Paid ‡25,000
4C: $1,950 Non-paid ‡66

JACKSONVILLE†, pop. 20,284.

Morgan Co. (WC). 35 m SW of Springfield. Illinois College, MacMurray College. Manufactures and processors.

9163 The Daily Other
MacMurray College
447 E. College Ave. Phone: (217)479-7049
Box 1140 Fax: (217)245-0405
Jacksonville, IL 62650
Publication E-mail: daily@mac.edu

Collegiate newspaper. **Founded:** 1976. **Freq:** Daily (during the academic year). **Print Method:** Offset. **Cols./Page:** 3. **Col. Width:** 21 nonpareils. **Col. Depth:** 105 agate lines. **Key Personnel:** Adam Bennington, Editor, abenning@mac.edu; Dr. Allen Metcalf, Publisher.
Ad Rates: GLR: $.25 **Circ:** Non-paid ‡700
BW: $25

9164 Murrayville Gazette
909 N. Church St. Phone: (217)675-2461
Jacksonville, IL 62650-1327 Fax: (217)675-2470

Newspaper (tabloid). **Founded:** Apr. 1981. **Freq:** Weekly (Thurs.). **Print Method:** Offset. **Trim Size:** 11 x 16. **Cols./Page:** 5. **Col. Width:** 2 inches. **Col. Depth:** 16 inches. **Key Personnel:** Ira Lionts, Editor and Publisher, ijlionts@juno.com; Eleanor L. Ramsey, Advertising Mgr. **Subscription Rates:** Free; $10 by mail; $12 out of state. **Remarks:** Color advertising not accepted.
Ad Rates: GLR: $.15 **Circ:** Free 600
BW: $130
PCI: $2.25

9165 Marcus Cable
PO Box 607 Phone: (217)245-9686
Jacksonville, IL 62650-0607 Fax: (217)243-1136

Owner: Marcus Cable, 2911 Turtle Creek Blvd., Ste. 1300, Dallas, TX 75219, (214)521-7898, Fax: (214)526-2154. **Formerly:** Sammons Communications of Illinois Inc. **Key Personnel:** Jeffrey A. Marcus, CEO/Pres.; Louis A. Borrelli, COO/Executive Vice Pres.; Thomas P. McMillin, CFO. **Cities Served:** Jacksonville, South Jacksonville, IL: subscribing households 8,600; 78 channels; 1 community access channel; 168 hours per week community access programming.

9166 WEAI-FM - 107.1
E. Old State Rd. Phone: (217)243-2800
PO Box 1180
Jacksonville, IL 62650

Format: Oldies; Adult Contemporary. **Owner:** Jerdon Broadcasting Co., at above address, (217)245-7171. **Founded:** 1989. **Operating Hours:** 5:30 a.m.-midnight. **Key Personnel:** Jerry Symons, General Mgr.; Don Hamilton, General Sales Mgr.; Perry Brown, Program Dir. **Wattage:** 6000. **Ad Rates:** $22-30 for 30 seconds; $29-39 for 60 seconds. **URL:** http://www.csj.net/weai.

9167 WJIL-AM - 1550
E. Morton Rd. Phone: (217)245-5119
PO Box 1065 Fax: (217)245-1596
Jacksonville, IL 62651

Format: News; Talk. **Networks:** ABC; Tribune Radio; Westwood One Radio; Meadows Racing; USA Radio. **Owner:** Morgan County Broadcasting, at above address. **Founded:** 1961. **Operating Hours:** Continuous; 8% network, 92% local. **ADI:** Springfield-Decatur-Champaign, IL. **Key Personnel:** Sarah Letterly, General Sales Mgr.; Terry Melohn, News Dir. **Wattage:** 1000. **Ad Rates:** $13-16 for 30 seconds; $17-20 for 60 seconds.

9168 WJVO-FM - 105.5
E. Morton Rd. Phone: (217)245-5119
Box 1065 Fax: (217)245-1596
Jacksonville, IL 62651
E-mail: wjvofm@fgi.net

Format: Country. **Networks:** ABC; Westwood One Radio. **Owner:** Morgan County Broadcasting, at above address. **Founded:** 1986. **Operating Hours:** Continuous; 100% local. **ADI:** Springfield-Decatur-Champaign, IL. **Key Personnel:** Sarah Letterly, General Sales Mgr.; Larry Bostwick, Sports Dir.; Brian Wayne, P.D. **Wattage:** 6000. **Ad Rates:** $13-16 for 30 seconds; $17-20 for 60 seconds.

9169 WLDS-AM - 1180
E. Old State Rd. Phone: (217)245-7171
PO Box 1180
Jacksonville, IL 62651

Format: Talk; Adult Contemporary; News; Agricultural; Big Band/Nostalgia. **Networks:** CBS. **Owner:** Jerdon Broadcasting Co., at above address, (217)243-2800. **Founded:** 1941. **Operating Hours:** Sunrise-sunset; 10% network, 90% local. **Key Personnel:** Mike Adams, Farm Dir.; Perry Brown, Program Dir.; Jerry Symons, General Mgr.; Don Hamilton, Sales Mgr.; Gary Scott, News Dir.; Gary Ballard, Music Dir. **Local Programs:** *Whats on Your Mind*, Gary Scott. **Wattage:** 1000. **Ad Rates:** $20-28 for 30 seconds; $27-37 for 60 seconds. **URL:** http://www.csj.net/weai.

JERSEYVILLE†, pop. 7,506.

Jersey Co. (SW). 17 NW of Alton. Manufactures railroad utility machines, specialty vehicles, pedestal cranes, truck cranes and rail gear, spreading equipment, seed cleaners, concrete products, beverage.Ships apples fruit, poultry, stock farms.

9170 WJBM-AM - 1480
1010 Shipman Rd. Phone: (618)498-2185
Jerseyville, IL 62052-2826 Fax: (618)498-9830

Format: Country; Agricultural; Sports. **Networks:** ABC; Brownfield. **Owner:** Gateway Radio Partners Ltd. Partnership, at above address. **Founded:** 1959. **Operating Hours:** 6 a.m.-7 p.m.; 25% network, 75% local. **ADI:** St. Louis, MO (Mt. Vernon, IL). **Key Personnel:** Gary Brown, Contact; Craig Bhalman, Program Dir.; Alan Ringhausen, News Dir.; Shirley Scott, Office Mgr. **Wattage:** 500. **Ad Rates:** $9 for 30 seconds; $14 for 60 seconds.

JOLIET†, pop. 77,956.

Will Co. (NE). On Des Plaines River, with barge terminal on Lakes to Gulf Waterway, 37 m SW of Chicago. College of St. Francis, Lewis University, Joliet Junior College. Limestone quarries. Oil refineries. Manufactures wallpaper, wire, roofing, chemicals, fire brick, tanks, cartons, earth moving equipment, bakery machinery, packaging machines, barrels, dairy products, clothing.

9171 The Blazer
Joliet Junior College
1215 Houbolt Ave. Phone: (815)729-9020
Joliet, IL 60435-9352 Fax: (815)744-5507

Collegiate newspaper. **Founded:** 1929. **Freq:** Semimonthly. **Print Method:** Offset. **Cols./Page:** 4. **Col. Width:** 28 nonpareils. **Col. Depth:** 192 agate lines. **Key Personnel:** Janet Inman, Editor. **Subscription Rates:** Free. **Remarks:** Accepts advertising.
Ad Rates: BW: $180 **Circ:** Free ‡3,000
SAU: $3
PCI: $4

9172 The Encounter
College of St. Francis
500 Wilcox Phone: (815)740-3816
Joliet, IL 60435-6188 Fax: (815)740-4285

Collegiate newspaper (tabloid). **Founded:** 1976. **Freq:** 5/year (during the academic year). **Print Method:** Offset. **Trim Size:** 11 1/2 x 17. **Cols./Page:** 5. **Col. Width:** 22 nonpareils. **Col. Depth:** 224 agate lines. **Key Personnel:** Rita Travis, Advisor. **Remarks:** Accepts advertising.
Ad Rates: GLR: $.34 **Circ:** Free ‡1,200
BW: $320
PCI: $5

9173 Farmers' Weekly Review
100 Manhattan Rd. Phone: (815)727-4811
Joliet, IL 60433 Fax: (815)727-5570

Community newspaper. **Founded:** June 6, 1921. **Freq:** Weekly (Thurs.). **Print Method:** Offset. **Cols./Page:** 5. **Col. Width:** 23 nonpareils. **Col. Depth:** 224 agate lines. **Key Personnel:** P.J. Cleary, Publisher; Debbie Werner, Managing Editor. **USPS:** 187-680. **Subscription Rates:** $15 individuals. **Remarks:** Color advertising accepted; rates available upon request.
Ad Rates: GLR: $.44 **Circ:** 11,500
BW: $520
PCI: $7.90

9174 Glasilo KSKJ (Americanski Slovenec)
American Slovenian Catholic Union
2439 Glenwood Ave. Phone: (815)741-2001
Joliet, IL 60435 Fax: (815)741-2002

Religious newspaper (Slovenian). **Freq:** Biweekly. **Key Personnel:** Robert G. Gibbons, Editor.

9175 Herald-News
Copley Newspapers/Copley Press
300 Caterpillar Dr. Phone: (815)729-6161
Joliet, IL 60436 Fax: (815)729-6063

Newspaper with a conservative orientation. **Founded:** 1839. **Freq:** Mon.-Sun. (morn.). **Print Method:** Offset. **Cols./Page:** 6. **Col. Width:** 2 1/8 inches. **Col. Depth:** 21.5 inches. **Key Personnel:** Marx Gibson, General Mgr.; Cory Bollinger, Advertising Dir. **Subscription Rates:** $106.60 individuals; $130 out of area. **Remarks:** Accepts advertising. **URL:** copleypress.com.
Ad Rates: GLR: $2.16 **Circ:** Mon.-Sat. ★37,723
BW: $3,908.70 Sun. ★41,286
4C: $4,158.70
SAU: $30.30

KWHN-FM - See Haynesville, Louisiana

9176 WCCQ-FM - 98.3
1520 N. Rock Run Dr. Phone: (815)729-4400
Joliet, IL 60435 Fax: (815)729-4444
E-mail: fmwccq@aol.com

Format: Country; Contemporary Country. **Networks:** Satellite Music Network. **Owner:** Three Eagles Communications, at above address. **Founded:** 1976. **Operating Hours:** Continuous; 60% network, 40% local. **ADI:** Chicago (LaSalle), IL. **Key Personnel:** Robert A. Straczek, General Mgr.; Roy Gregory, Program Dir. **Local Programs:** *Chicagoland Country*, Roy Gregory; *Fishing & Outdoor Show*, Ray Ludkevica; *Q-Country Perspective*, Sharon Irvine. **Wattage:** 3000. **Ad Rates:** Advertising accepted; rates available upon request. **URL:** http://www.wccq.com.

9177 WJCH-FM - 91.9
13 Fairlane Dr. Phone: (815)725-1331
Joliet, IL 60435

Format: Religious. **Networks:** Family Stations Radio. **Founded:** 1986. **Operating Hours:** Continuous; 90% network, 10% local. **Key Personnel:** Harold Camping, Contact, phone (510)568-5600; Virginia Beehn, Station Mgr.; Craig Hulsebos, Program Dir., phone (510)568-5600. **Wattage:** 50,000. **Ad Rates:** Noncommercial.

9178 WJOL-AM - 1340
601 Walnut St. Phone: (815)726-4761
Joliet, IL 60432 Fax: (815)726-0357

Format: News; Information. **Networks:** ABC. **Owner:** Pride Communications, LLC, at above address. **Founded:** 1924. **Operating Hours:** Continuous. **ADI:** Chicago (LaSalle), IL. **Key Personnel:** Dennis Mockler, General Mgr.; Kevin Hegerty, News Dir.; Scott Slocam, Program Dir.; Scott Slocum, Sports Dir. **Local Programs:** *Art Hellyer Show* Saturday and Sunday, Art Hellyer, Mailing contact; *Frankly Speaking*, Frank O'Leary, Mailing contact. **Wattage:** 1000. **Ad Rates:** $20.00-40.00 for 30 seconds; $25.00-45.00 for 60 seconds. Combined advertising rates available with WJTW.

9179 WLLI-FM - 96.7
601 Walnut St. Phone: (815)726-4761
Joliet, IL 60432 Fax: (815)726-0357

Format: Classic Rock. **Networks:** Westwood One Radio. **Owner:** Pride Communications, LLC, at above address. **Founded:** 1960. **Operating Hours:** Continuous. **Key Personnel:** Lonny Tyler, Operations Mgr.; Dennis Mockler, General Mgr.; Andrea Darlas, News Dir. **Wattage:** 3000. **Ad Rates:** $25.00-45.00 for 30 seconds; $30.00-50.00 for 60 seconds. Combined advertising rates available with WBVS.

KANKAKEE, pop. 30,141.

Kankakee Co. (E). On Kankakee River, 57 m SW of Chicago. Kankakee Community College, Olivet Nazarene College. Manufactures furniture, stoves, work clothing, brick, tile, paint, asphalt products, iron castings, glass containers, concrete products, hydraulic tools, agricultural implements, water heaters, industrial batteries, chemicals, pharmaceuticals; steel fabricating; foundry; magnesium refinery; soybean and corn processing plants. Stone quarries.

9180 The Daily Journal
Small Newspaper Group
8 Dearborn Sq. Phone: (815)937-3300
Kankakee, IL 60901 Fax: (815)937-3301
Publication E-mail: edit@daily-journal.com

Newspaper. **Subtitle:** The Daily Journal. **Founded:** 1884. **Freq:** Daily (eve.), Sunday (morn.). **Print Method:** Offset. **Cols./Page:** 6. **Col. Width:** 25 nonpareils. **Col. Depth:** 301 agate lines. **Key Personnel:** Jean Alice Small, Editor and Publisher. **USPS:** 289-780. **Subscription Rates:** $96.20 individuals. **Remarks:** Accepts advertising.
Ad Rates: GLR: $1.09 **Circ:** Mon.-Fri. 29,038
BW: $1,786.65 Sun. 33,331
4C: $2,081.65
SAU: $13.85

9181 TCI of Illinois, Inc.
6 Dearborn Sq. Phone: (815)937-2700
Kankakee, IL 60901 Fax: (815)937-2714

Owner: Telecommunications Inc., Box 5630, Denver, CO 80217, (303)721-5500. **Formerly:** Cooke Cablevision Inc. (1990). **Key Personnel:** John Niebur, Contact. **Cities Served:** Areas in Kankakee and Iroquois counties.: subscribing households 21,000; 28 channels.

9182 WKAN-AM - 1320
2 Dearborn Sq. Phone: (815)935-9555
Kankakee, IL 60901 Fax: (815)935-9593
E-mail: wkan1320@aol.com

Format: Adult Contemporary. **Networks:** Independent. **Founded:** 1948. **Operating Hours:** Continuous; 100% local. **ADI:** Chicago (LaSalle), IL. **Key Personnel:** Gary Wright, General Mgr.; Larry Timpe, Operations Mgr.; Ed Munday, News Dir.; Bill Guertin, Sales Mgr. **Wattage:** 1000. **Ad Rates:** $12-33 for 30 seconds; $12-39 for 60 seconds. Combined advertising rates available with WLRT-FM.

9183 WLRT-FM - 92.7
2 Dearborn Sq. Phone: (815)935-9555
Kankakee, IL 60901-3933 Fax: (815)935-9593
E-mail: wlrt@aol.com

Format: Country. **Networks:** Independent. **Founded:** 1986. **Operating Hours:** Continuous; 100% local. **ADI:** Chicago (LaSalle), IL. **Key Personnel:** Gary Wright, General Mgr.; Larry Timpe, Operations Mgr.; Ed Munday, News Dir. **Wattage:** 3000. **Ad Rates:** $12-33 for 30 seconds; $12-39 for 60 seconds.

9184 WONU-FM - 89.7
Olivet Nazarene University Phone: (815)939-5330
Kankakee, IL 60901-0592 Fax: (815)939-5087
E-mail: wonu@olivet.edu

Format: Religious. **Networks:** CNN Radio. **Owner:** Olivet Nazarene University, at above address, (815)939-5011. **Founded:** 1967. **Formerly:** WKOC-FM. **Operating Hours:** Continuous. **ADI:** Chicago (LaSalle), IL. **Key Personnel:** Bill DeWees, General Mgr.; Eric Allen, Operations Mgr., eallen@olivet.edu; Beth Kaye, Marketing Dir. **Wattage:** 35,000. **Ad Rates:** Noncommercial. **URL:** http://www.wonu.org.

KEMPTON

9185 Nexus Magazine
The Back Office
PO Box 177 Phone: (815)253-6464
Kempton, IL 60946 Fax: (815)253-6454
Free: (888)909-7474
Publication E-mail: sergfx@earthlink.net

Contains news on alternative health, politics, science, and metaphysics. **Subtitle:** New Times. **Founded:** 1982. **Freq:** Semimonthly. **Print Method:** Web. **Key Personnel:** Duncan Roads, Editor. **Subscription Rates:** $25; $5 single issue; $35 institutions. **URL:** http://www.peg.apc.org/~nexus/.
Ad Rates: BW: $700 **Circ:** Paid 15,000
4C: $1300 Non-paid 2,000

KENILWORTH

9186 Arabian Horse Express
Goss Publications, Inc.
512 Green Bay Rd. Phone: (847)256-7111
Kenilworth, IL 60043-1073 Fax: (708)256-5898
Free: (800)533-9734

Magazine for national and international Arabian horse owners and enthusiasts. **Founded:** Jan. 1977. **Freq:** Monthly. **Print Method:** Offset. **Trim Size:** 11 1/2 x 15. **Cols./Page:** 3. **Col. Width:** 24 nonpareils. **Col. Depth:** 167 agate lines. **Key Personnel:** Frederick K. Goss, Publisher. **ISSN:** 0194-6803. **Subscription Rates:** $25 individuals; $33 other countries; $4 single issue. **Remarks:** Accepts advertising.
Ad Rates: BW: $425 **Circ:** Paid ‡1,000
4C: $745

KEWANEE, pop. 14,508.

Henry Co. (NW). 50 m SE of Rock Island. Manufactures boilers, window and door frames, leather goods, farm equipment, window guards, heavy construction equipment, truck and farm trailers. Agriculture.

9187 Atkinson-Annawan News
Kewanee Star Courier
E. Central Blvd. Phone: (309)936-7741
Kewanee, IL 61443 Fax: (309)936-7150

Community newspaper. **Founded:** 1916. **Freq:** Weekly (Thurs.). **Cols./Page:** 6. **Col. Width:** 13 picas. **Col. Depth:** 293 agate lines. **Key Personnel:** Sheryl Plumley, Editor. **Subscription Rates:** $25 in tri-county area; $29 out of area. **Remarks:** Accepts advertising.
Ad Rates: BW: $387 **Circ:** ‡475
4C: $550
SAU: $3

9188 Star-Courier
Lee Enterprises
105 E. Central Blvd. Phone: (309)852-2181
Kewanee, IL 61443-0836 Fax: (309)852-0010
Free: (800)397-7827
Publication E-mail: starcourier@star.com; strcuryr@starcourier.com

Community newspaper. **Founded:** 1876. **Freq:** Daily (eve.) 6 days. **Print Method:** Offset. **Trim Size:** 13 3/4 x 23. **Cols./Page:** 6. **Col. Width:** 26 nonpareils. **Col. Depth:** 301 agate lines. **Key Personnel:** Mike Berry, Editor; Anita Bird, Advertising Mgr.; Larry Greider, Advertising Mgr.; Joyce Wirth, Circulation Mgr.; Janice Nugent, Marketing Mgr. **Subscription Rates:** $108.7 individuals; $154 mailed; $.5 single issue. **Remarks:** Accepts advertising. **Available Online. URL:** http://www.starcourier.com.
Ad Rates: GLR: $.81 **Circ:** Mon.-Sat. ★**6,365**
BW: $1162.98
4C: $1337.98
SAU: $9.50

9189 WJRE-FM - 93.9
PO Box 266 Phone: (309)853-4471
Kewanee, IL 61443 Fax: (309)853-4474

Format: Soft Rock. **Founded:** 1966. **Operating Hours:** Continuous. **Key Personnel:** Gary Petersen, General Mgr.; Danielle Arch, Program Dir.; Dave Stone, News Dir. **Wattage:** 3100. **Ad Rates:** $8-13 for 30 seconds; $10-16 for 60 seconds.

9190 WKEI-AM - 1450
PO Box 266 Phone: (309)853-4471
Kewanee, IL 61443 Fax: (309)853-4474

Format: Talk; News. **Networks:** CBS. **Owner:** Virden Broadcasting, Corp, at above address, (309)853-4431, (309)853-4474, Free: (800)346-4473. **Founded:** 1952. **Operating Hours:** Continuous. **Key Personnel:** Gary Petersen, General Mgr.; Danielle Arch, Program Dir.; Dave Stone, News Dir. **Local Programs:** *POeople to People*, Dave Stone. **Wattage:** 500 day; 1000 night. **Ad Rates:** $8-13 for 30 seconds; $10-16 for 60 seconds.

KINGSTON MINES

9191 KMHC Inc.
205 Madison St. Phone: (309)389-4567
Kingston Mines, IL 61539

Founded: 1983. **Key Personnel:** Tom Hedge, Contact. **Cities Served:** Kingston Mines, IL: subscribing households 84; 17 channels; 1 community access channel.

KINMUNDY, pop. 945.

Marion Co. (S). 21 m NE of Centralia. Grain elevator. Diversified farming. Recreational. State Park.

9192 Kinmundy Express
PO Box 220 Phone: (618)547-3111
Kinmundy, IL 62854
Newspaper. **Founded:** 1883. **Freq:** Weekly (Thurs.). **Print Method:** Offset. **Cols./Page:** 7. **Col. Width:** 24 nonpareils. **Col. Depth:** 280 agate lines. **Key Personnel:** Rudolph Slane, Editor and Publisher. **Subscription Rates:** $5.50 individuals.

LA FAYETTE, pop. 281.

Stark Co. (NWC). 11 m W of Castleton. Residential.

9193 Prairie Shopper
McGirgan Productions
101 Jefferson Phone: (309)995-3877
PO Box 27 Fax: (309)995-3975
La Fayette, IL 61449-9927
Newspaper with shopping guide. **Founded:** 1981. **Freq:** Weekly (Wed.). **Print Method:** Offset. **Cols./Page:** 6. **Col. Width:** 19 nonpareils. **Col. Depth:** 224 agate lines. **Key Personnel:** Lowell E. McKirgan, Publisher. **Subscription Rates:** $20. **Remarks:** Accepts advertising.
Ad Rates: GLR: $.25 **Circ:** Free 5,900
BW: $268.80
SAU: $4.20
PCI: $2.80

9194 Prairie Times
McKirgan Productions
101 Jefferson Phone: (309)995-3877
Box 27
La Fayette, IL 61449-9927
Newspaper (tabloid) with shopping guide. **Founded:** 1986. **Freq:** Weekly (Thurs.). **Print Method:** Offset. **Cols./Page:** 6. **Col. Width:** 19 nonpareils. **Col. Depth:** 224 agate lines. **Key Personnel:** Lowell E. McKirgan, Editor and Publisher. **USPS:** 001-989. **Subscription Rates:** $18 individuals; $24 out of state. **Remarks:** Accepts advertising.
Ad Rates: GLR: $.25 **Circ:** Paid ‡1140
BW: $211.20
SAU: $3.30
PCI: $2.20

LA GRANGE, pop. 15,681.

Cook Co. (NE). Adjoins Brookfield. Residential. Limestone quarries. Manufactures diesel locomotives, aluminum utensils.

9195 Nuclear News
American Nuclear Society
555 N. Kensington Ave. Phone: (708)352-6611
La Grange, IL 60526 Fax: (708)352-6464
Publication E-mail: nuclear@ans.org
Publisher E-mail: nucleus@ans.org

Magazine focusing on applications of nuclear energy. **Founded:** 1959. **Freq:** Monthly. **Print Method:** Offset. **Trim Size:** 8 1/4 x 10 7/8. **Cols./Page:** 3. **Col. Width:** 27 nonpareils. **Col. Depth:** 140 agate lines. **Key Personnel:** Gregg M. Taylor, Editor; Jon Payne, Publisher. **ISSN:** 0029-5574. **Subscription Rates:** $218 individuals; $18 single issue. **Remarks:** Accepts advertising. **Online:** LEXIS-NEXIS. **URL:** http://www.ans.org.
Ad Rates: BW: $2,255 **Circ:** Paid 12,000
4C: $3,055 Controlled 1,610

9196 Nuclear Science and Engineering
American Nuclear Society
555 N. Kensington Ave. Phone: (708)579-8312
La Grange, IL 60526 Fax: (708)579-8313
Publication E-mail: melpayne@ans.org
Publisher E-mail: nucleus@ans.org

Scientific research journal. **Founded:** 1956. **Freq:** 9/year. **Print Method:** Offset. **Trim Size:** 8 1/2 x 11. **Cols./Page:** 2. **Col. Width:** 40 nonpareils. **Col. Depth:** 126 agate lines. **Key Personnel:** Dr. Dan G. Cacuci, Editor. **Subscription Rates:** $602 individuals. **Remarks:** Advertising not accepted.
Circ: 1,200

9197 Nuclear Technology
American Nuclear Society
555 N. Kensington Ave. Phone: (708)352-6611
La Grange, IL 60526 Fax: (708)352-6464
Publication E-mail: rczimer@ans.org
Publisher E-mail: nucleus@ans.org

Nuclear power; science and engineering. **Founded:** 1965. **Freq:** Monthly. **Print Method:** Offset. **Trim Size:** 8 1/2 x 11. **Cols./Page:** 2. **Col. Width:** 39 nonpareils. **Col. Depth:** 126 agate lines. **Key Personnel:** Dr. Nicholas Tsaulfandis, Editor, phone (708)579-8281. **ISSN:** 0029-5450. **Subscription Rates:** $595 individuals. **Remarks:** Advertising not accepted.
Circ: 1,300

9198 Pavement
Cygnus Publishing Inc.
PO Box 368 Phone: (708)354-7039
La Grange, IL 60525 Fax: (708)354-7268
Publication E-mail: pmedit@aol.com

Trade magazine covering asphalt and concrete maintenance and reconstruction. **Founded:** 1986. **Freq:** 8/year. **Print Method:** Offset. **Trim Size:** 7 7/8 x 10 3/4. **Key Personnel:** Brad Pett, Publisher, phone (800)547-7377, fax (920)563-1702, bpett@jhpress.com; Allan Heydorn, Assoc. Publisher/Editor, phone (708)354-7039, fax (708)354-7268, pmedit@aol.com; Toby Linzmeier, Assoc. Editor, phone (800)547-7377, fax (920)563-1702, tlinzmeier@jhpress.com; Sean Dunphy, Sales Rep., phone (800)547-7377, fax (920)563-1702, sdunphy@jhpress.com; Loretta Miles, National Sales Mgr., phone (630)369-5699, fax (630)369-5785; Scott Cravens, Circulation Dir., phone (800)547-7377, fax (920)563-1702, scravens@jhpress.com. **ISSN:** 1085-8520. **Subscription Rates:** Free to qualified subscribers; $18 individuals; $26 Canada and Mexico; $90 other countries. **Remarks:** Accepts advertising. **Formerly**: Pavement Maintenance; Pavement Maintenance and Reconstruction.
Ad Rates: BW: $2,675 **Circ:** Controlled 20,000
4C: $3,675

LA SALLE, pop. 10,347.

LaSalle Co. (N). On Illinois River 90 m W of Chicago. Chemicals, electronic components, cement, aluminum, zinc. Manufactures automotive transmissions. Agriculture.

9199 Illinois Agri-News
Agri-News Publications
420 2nd St. Phone: (815)223-2558
La Salle, IL 61301 Fax: (815)223-5997
Free: (800)426-9438
Publication E-mail: agrinews@theramp.net
Publisher E-mail: agrinews@theramp.net

Farm and rural community magazine. **Founded:** 1977. **Freq:** Weekly. **Print Method:** Offset. **Trim Size:** 14 5/8 x 22 3/4. **Cols./Page:** 9. **Col. Width:** 16 nonpareils. **Col. Depth:** 301 agate lines. **Key Personnel:** W. Pufahl, Managing Editor; Lynn Barker, Publisher. **Subscription Rates:** $20 individuals; $0.50 single issue. **Remarks:** Accepts advertising. **URL:** http://www.agrinews-pubs.com. **Alt. Formats:** Microform.
Ad Rates: GLR: $12 **Circ:** Paid ‡34,000
BW: $4,237.65
4C: $4,787.65
PCI: $21.90

9200 News-Tribune
News-Tribune Publication
426 2nd St. Phone: (815)223-3200
La Salle, IL 61301 Fax: (815)223-2543
Free: (800)892-6452
Publication E-mail: newsitib@ivnet.com

Local newspaper. **Founded:** 1891. **Freq:** Mon.-Sat. (eve.). **Print Method:** Offset. **Cols./Page:** 6. **Col. Width:** 25 nonpareils. **Col. Depth:** 301 agate lines. **Key Personnel:** Linda Kleczewski, Managing Editor; Peter Miller III, Publisher. **Subscription Rates:** $84 (carrier delivered). **Remarks:** Accepts advertising.
Ad Rates: SAU: $12 **Circ:** Mon.-Sat. ★18,855

9201 WAJK-FM - 99.3
PO Box 215 Phone: (815)223-3100
La Salle, IL 61301 Fax: (815)223-3095
E-mail: wajk@ivnet.com

Format: Adult Contemporary. **Networks:** Independent. **Owner:** La Salle County Broadcasting Corp., at above address. **Founded:** 1963. **Formerly**: WLPO-FM (1980). **Operating Hours:** Continuous; 100% local. **ADI:** Chicago (LaSalle), IL. **Key Personnel:** Joyce McCullough, Vice President; Peter Miller III, General Mgr.; Joseph Hogan, News/Operations Dir.; Lanny Slevin, Sports Dir.; John Spencer, Program Dir.; Dave Ebener, Sales Mgr.; Jenny Bagby, Promotions Mgr. **Wattage:** 11,000. **Ad Rates:** $5-13 for 15 seconds; $7-17 for 30 seconds; $9-22 for 60 seconds. $5-$14 Tennessee; $7-$19 for 30 seconds; $9-$24 for 60 seconds. Combined advertising rates available with WLPO-AM. **URL:** http://www.cybercitylasalle.com/wajk.html.

9202 WLPO-AM - 1220
PO Box 215 Phone: (815)223-3100
La Salle, IL 61301 Fax: (815)223-3095
E-mail: wlpo@ivnet.com

Format: Oldies. **Networks:** NBC. **Owner:** La Salle County Broadcasting Corp., at above address. **Founded:** 1947. **Operating Hours:** Continuous; 25% network, 75% local. **ADI:** Chicago (LaSalle), IL. **Key Personnel:** Joyce McCullough, Vice President; Peter Miller III, General Mgr.; Joseph Hogan, News/Program Dir.; Lanny Slevin, Sports Dir.; Dave Ebener, Sales Mgr.; Jenny Bagby, Promotions Mgr. **Wattage:** 1000 day, 500 night. **Ad Rates:** $7-15 for 15 seconds; $10-20 for 30 seconds; $12-25 for 60 seconds. Combined advertising rates available with WAJK-FM. **URL:** http://www.cybercitylasalle.com/wlpo.html.

LACON†, pop. 2,135.

Marshall Co. (NC). On Illinois River, 26 m N of Peoria. Bridge to Sparland. Manufactures gasket seals, decoys. Gravel pits; lumber mill. Stock and grain farms.

9203 Illinois Valley Peach
Marshall County Publishing Co.
204 S. Washington St. Phone: (309)246-2865
Lacon, IL 61540 Fax: (309)246-3214

Shopper. **Founded:** Mar. 1968. **Freq:** 16/year. **Print Method:** Offset. **Cols./Page:** 5. **Col. Width:** 12 picas. **Col. Depth:** 16 inches. **Key Personnel:** William H. Sondag, Editor and Publisher; A.J. Sondag, Advertising Mgr./Contact. **Subscription Rates:** Free.
Ad Rates: GLR: $.25 **Circ:** Free ‡9,400
BW: $292
4C: $250
SAU: $3.85
PCI: $3.85

9204 Lacon Home Journal
Marshall County Publishing Co.
204 S. Washington St. Phone: (309)246-2865
Lacon, IL 61540 Fax: (309)246-3214

Community newspaper. **Founded:** Jan. 1837. **Freq:** Weekly (Thurs.). **Print Method:** Offset. **Cols./Page:** 5. **Col. Width:** 12 picas. **Col. Depth:** 16 inches. **Key Personnel:** William H. Sondag, Editor and Publisher; A.J. Sondag, Advertising Mgr./Contact. **USPS:** 301-060. **Subscription Rates:** $25 individuals; $30 out of state; $0.45 single issue.
Ad Rates: GLR: $.26 **Circ:** ‡2,400
BW: $292
4C: $250
SAU: $3.85
PCI: $3.85

9205 Sunbeam
204 S. Washington St. Phone: (309)246-2865
Lacon, IL 61540 Fax: (309)246-3214

Newspaper. **Founded:** Apr. 1972. **Freq:** Monthly. **Print Method:** Offset. **Cols./Page:** 5. **Col. Width:** 11 1/2 picas. **Col. Depth:** 16 1/2 inches. **Key Personnel:** William H. Sondag, Editor and Publisher. **USPS:** 986-200. **Remarks:** Accepts advertising.
Ad Rates: GLR: $.16 **Circ:** ‡9,000
BW: $292
4C: $500
SAU: $3.65

LAKE FOREST, pop. 15,600.

Lake Co. (NE). On Lake Michigan, 8 m S of Waukegan. Barat College of the Sacred Heart (Cath. women); Lake Forest College. Suburban residential town.

9206 Chicago Home and Garden
Chicago Home & Garden
825 S. Waukegan Rd., No. A8-146
Lake Forest, IL 60045

Magazine covering home and garden style in the Chicago, IL, area. **Founded:** Sept. 1995. **Freq:** Quarterly. **Print Method:** Web offset. **Trim Size:** 8 1/8 x 10 7/8. **ISSN:** 1085-4363. **Subscription Rates:** $12. **Remarks:** Accepts advertising.
Ad Rates: BW: $2,970 **Circ:** Paid 30,000
4C: $3,445

9207 Lake Forester
Pioneer Press Newspapers
850 N. Milwaukee Ave. Phone: (847)680-6690
Vernon Hills, IL 60061 Fax: (847)573-2500
Publication E-mail: edito@pioneerlocal.com

Community newspaper (tabloid). **Subtitle:** Serving Lake Bluff. **Founded:** 1896. **Freq:** Weekly (Thurs.). **Print Method:** Offset. **Trim Size:** 11 x 14. **Cols./Page:** 5. **Col. Width:** 9 3/4 inches. **Col. Depth:** 12 3/4 inches. **Key Personnel:** Paul Sassone, Managing Editor; Kyle Leonard, Editor, leonard@pioneerlocal.com. **ISSN:** 0774-7973. **Subscription Rates:** $32.95 individuals.
Circ: Thurs. ★6,778

9208 Physicians and Computers
810 S. Waukegan Rd., Suite 200 Phone: (847)615-8333
Lake Forest, IL 60045
Journal containing information about computer application to medical practice, including office management. **Founded:** May 1983. **Freq:** Monthly. **Print Method:** Web offset. **Trim Size:** 8 1/8 x 10 3/4. **Cols./Page:** 3. **Key Personnel:** Tom Moorehead, Publisher; Rogers Piercy, Sr. Editor; Michael Moorhead, Production Mgr. **Subscription Rates:** $35 individuals; $40 Canada; $54 other countries; $4 single issue. **Remarks:** Accepts advertising.
Ad Rates: BW: $2,925 **Circ:** Controlled 89,583
4C: $3,640

9209 WOODALL's California RV Traveler
Woodall Publishing Co.
13975 W. Polo Trail Dr. Phone: (847)362-6700
Lake Forest, IL 60045-5000 Fax: (847)362-8776
Free: (800)323-9076
Publisher E-mail: emd@woodallpub.com

Magazine serving RVers in southern and central California. **Founded:** 1995. **Freq:** Monthly. **Print Method:** Web. **Cols./Page:** 4. **Col. Width:** 2 3/8 inches. **Col. Depth:** 13 inches. **Key Personnel:** Ann Emerson, Publisher; Brent Peterson, Editor; Jenny Marshall, Advertising Dir. **Subscription Rates:** $12 individuals; $2.50 single issue. **Remarks:** Accepts advertising.
Ad Rates: BW: $1,170 **Circ:** Controlled 25,000
4C: $1,695

9210 WOODALL'S Camp-orama
Woodall Publishing Co.
13975 W. Polo Trail Dr. Phone: (847)362-6700
Lake Forest, IL 60045-5000 Fax: (847)362-8776
Free: (800)323-9076
Publisher E-mail: emd@woodallpub.com

Magazine covering the RV industry and camping destinations. **Subtitle:** The RVers Guide to Camping and RVing. **Freq:** Monthly. **Cols./Page:** 4. **Col. Width:** 14 picas. **Col. Depth:** 84 picas. **Key Personnel:** Brent Peterson, Editor, phone (800)362-7989, bpeterson@woodallpub.com; Ann Emerson, President, phone (708)362-6700. **Subscription Rates:** $15. $2.50 single issue. **Remarks:** Accepts advertising. **URL:** http://www.woodalls.com. **Formerly**: Camp-orama.
Ad Rates: BW: $1,129 **Circ:** 35,000
4C: $1,654

9211 WOODALL'S Camperways
Woodall Publishing Co.
13975 W. Polo Trail Dr. Phone: (847)362-6700
Lake Forest, IL 60045-5000 Fax: (847)362-8776
Free: (800)323-9076
Publisher E-mail: emd@woodallpub.com

Magazine covering the RV industry and camping destinations. **Subtitle:** The Middle Atlantic RV Lifestyle source. **Founded:** 1979. **Freq:** Monthly. **Cols./Page:** 4. **Col. Width:** 14 picas. **Col. Depth:** 84 picas. **Key Personnel:** Brent Peterson, Editor, bpeterson@woodallpub.com. **Subscription Rates:** $15 individuals; $2.50 single issue. **Remarks:** Accepts advertising. **Formerly**: Camperways.
Ad Rates: BW: $1,129 **Circ:** 40,000
4C: $1.654

9212 WOODALL's Campground Management
Woodall Publishing Co.
13975 W. Polo Trail Dr. Phone: (847)362-6700
Lake Forest, IL 60045-5000 Fax: (847)362-8776
Free: (800)323-9076
Publisher E-mail: emd@woodallpub.com

Magazine focusing on operating and maintaining recreation vehicle parks. **Founded:** Mar. 1970. **Freq:** Monthly. **Print Method:** Offset. Uses mats. **Trim Size:** 11 3/8 x 14 15/16. **Cols./Page:** 4. **Col. Width:** 2 5/16 inches. **Col. Depth:** 13 inches. **Key Personnel:** Mike Byrnes, Editor, mbyrnes@woodallpub.com. **ISSN:** 0162-3796. **Subscription Rates:** $24.95 individuals; $34.95 Canada in Canada.
Ad Rates: BW: $2,770 **Circ:** Paid ‡90
4C: $3,220 Non-paid ‡10,000
PCI: $104

9213 WOODALL's Carolina RV Traveler
Woodall Publishing Co.
13975 W. Polo Trail Dr. Phone: (847)362-6700
Lake Forest, IL 60045-5000 Fax: (847)362-8776
Free: (800)323-9076
Publisher E-mail: emd@woodallpub.com

Magazine serving RVers in North and South Carolina. **Founded:** 1996. **Freq:** Monthly. **Print Method:** Web. **Cols./Page:** 4. **Col. Width:** 2 3/8 inches. **Col. Depth:** 13 inches. **Key Personnel:** Ann Emerson, Publisher; Brent Peterson, Editor; Jenny Marshall, Advertising Dir. **Subscription Rates:** $12 individuals; $2.50 single issue. **Remarks:** Accepts advertising.
Ad Rates: BW: $1,325 **Circ:** Controlled 22,000
4C: $1,850

9214 WOODALL's Discover RVing
Woodall Publishing Co.
13975 W. Polo Trail Dr. Phone: (847)362-6700
Lake Forest, IL 60045-5000 Fax: (847)362-8776
Free: (800)323-9076
Publisher E-mail: emd@woodallpub.com

Magazine for first-time RV buyers; covers the RV lifestyle. **Founded:** 1995. **Freq:** Annual. **Print Method:** Web. **Cols./Page:** 4. **Col. Width:** 2 3/8 inches. **Col. Depth:** 13 inches. **Key Personnel:** Ann Emerson, Publisher; Brent Peterson, Editor; Jenny Marshall, Advertising Dir. **Subscription Rates:** $2.50 single issue. **Remarks:** Accepts advertising.
Ad Rates: BW: $931 **Circ:** Controlled 50,000
4C: $1,456

9215 WOODALL's Northeast Outdoors
Woodall Publishing Co.
13975 W. Polo Trail Dr. Phone: (847)362-6700
Lake Forest, IL 60045-5000 Fax: (847)362-8776
Free: (800)323-9076
Publisher E-mail: emd@woodallpub.com

Magazine serving campers and RVers in the Northeast. **Founded:** 1968. **Freq:** Monthly. **Print Method:** Web. **Cols./Page:** 4. **Col. Width:** 2 3/8 inches. **Col. Depth:** 13 inches. **Key Personnel:** Ann Emerson, Publisher; Brent Peterson, Editor; Jenny Marshall, Advertising Dir. **ISSN:** 0199-8463. **Subscription Rates:** $12 individuals; $2.50 single issue. **Remarks:** Accepts advertising. **Formerly**: Northeast Outdoors.
Ad Rates: BW: $1,533 **Circ:** Paid 10,000
4C: $2,058 Non-paid 10,000

9216 WOODALL's Northeast Summers
Woodall Publishing Co.
13975 W. Polo Trail Dr. Phone: (847)362-6700
Lake Forest, IL 60045-5000 Fax: (847)362-8776
Free: (800)323-9076
Publisher E-mail: emd@woodallpub.com

Magazine covering summer RVing in the Northeast. **Founded:** 1994. **Freq:** Annual. **Print Method:** Web. **Cols./Page:** 4. **Col. Width:** 2 3/8 inches. **Col. Depth:** 13 inches. **Key Personnel:** Ann Emerson, Publisher; Brent Peterson, Editor; Jenny Marshall, Advertising Dir. **Subscription Rates:** $2.50 single issue. **Remarks:** Accepts advertising.
Ad Rates: BW: $1,709 **Circ:** Controlled 60,000
4C: $2,484

9217 WOODALL'S RV Traveler
Woodall Publishing Co.
13975 W. Polo Trail Dr. Phone: (847)362-6700
Lake Forest, IL 60045-5000 Fax: (847)362-8776
Free: (800)323-9076
Publisher E-mail: emd@woodallpub.com

Magazine covering the RV industry and camping destinations. **Subtitle:** The RV Guide to the Midwest. **Founded:** 1971. **Freq:** Monthly. **Cols./Page:** 4. **Col. Width:** 14 picas. **Col. Depth:** 84 picas. **Key Personnel:** Ann Emerson, Publisher; Brent Peterson, Editor, bpeterson@woodall.com. **Subscription Rates:** $15. $2.50 single issue. **Remarks:** Accepts advertising. **Formerly**: Trails-A-Way.
Ad Rates: BW: $1,455 **Circ:** 40,000
4C: $1,980

9218 WOODALL'S Southern RV
Woodall Publishing Co.
13975 W. Polo Trail Dr. Phone: (847)362-6700
Lake Forest, IL 60045-5000 Fax: (847)362-8776
Free: (800)323-9076
Publisher E-mail: emd@woodallpub.com

Magazine on recreational vehicles and campgrounds. **Subtitle:** The RVers Guide to Family Camping in the Southeast. **Founded:** 1976. **Freq:** Monthly. **Print Method:** Offset. **Trim Size:** 10 3/8 x 14 1/2. **Cols./Page:** 4. **Col. Width:** 33 agate lines. **Col. Depth:** 203 agate lines. **Key Personnel:** Ann Emerson, Publisher; Brent Peterson, Editor, bpeterson@woodallpub.com. **Subscription Rates:** $15 individuals.
Ad Rates: BW: $1,005 **Circ:** Paid 30,000
4C: $1,530

9219 WOODALL'S Sunny Destinations
Woodall Publishing Co.
13975 W. Polo Trail Dr. Phone: (847)362-6700
Lake Forest, IL 60045-5000 Fax: (847)362-8776
Free: (800)323-9076
Publisher E-mail: emd@woodallpub.com

Guide to camping in the sunbelt region, geared toward the northern population. **Founded:** 1993. **Freq:** Annual. **Print Method:** Web. **Cols./Page:** 4. **Col. Width:** 2 3/8 inches. **Col. Depth:** 13 inches. **Key Personnel:** Ann Emerson, Publisher; Brent Peterson, Editor; Jenny Marshall, Advertising Dir. **Subscription Rates:** $2.50 single issue. **Remarks:** Accepts advertising.
Ad Rates: BW: $1,048 **Circ:** Controlled 55,000
4C: $1,823

9220 WOODALL's Texas RV
Woodall Publishing Co.
13975 W. Polo Trail Dr. Phone: (847)362-6700
Lake Forest, IL 60045-5000 Fax: (847)362-8776
Free: (800)323-9076
Publisher E-mail: emd@woodallpub.com

Magazine serving RVers and campers in East Texas, both resident and winter Texans. **Founded:** 1994. **Freq:** Bimonthly. **Print Method:** Web. **Cols./Page:** 4. **Col. Width:** 2 3/8 inches. **Col. Depth:** 13 inches. **Key Personnel:** Ann Emerson, Publisher; Brent Peterson, Editor; Jenny Marshall, Advertising Dir. **Subscription Rates:** $6 individuals; $2.50 single issue. **Remarks:** Accepts advertising.
Ad Rates: BW: $1,170 **Circ:** Controlled 27,000
4C: $1,695

9221 WMXM-FM - 88.9
Lake Forest College Phone: (708)735-5350
555 North Sheridan Rd.
Lake Forest, IL 60045

Format: Eclectic. **Founded:** 1976. **Operating Hours:** 8 a.m.-2 a.m. **Key Personnel:** Brad Swanson, General Mgr.; Kate Evelyn, Program Dir.; Adam Yoffe, Music Dir. **Wattage:** 300. **Ad Rates:** Noncommercial.

LAKE VILLA, pop. 1,462.

Lake Co. (NE). 15 m W of Waukegan. Suburban residental area. Resort. Chain O'Lakes Area. Manufactures plastics. Tool and die works. Diversified farming.

9222 Lake Villa Record
Lakeland Publishers, Inc.
30 S. Whitney St. Phone: (847)223-8161
PO Box 268 Fax: (847)223-8810
Grayslake, IL 60030-0268
Publication E-mail: edit@ind.com

Community newspaper. **Founded:** 1955. **Freq:** Weekly (Thurs.). **Print Method:** Offset. **Trim Size:** 11 x 17. **Cols./Page:** 5. **Col. Width:** 2 inches. **Col. Depth:** 16 inches. **Key Personnel:** W. H. Schroeder, Contact; Jill De Pasquale, Advertising Mgr. **Subscription Rates:** $24.50 individuals; $35 out of area. **Remarks:** Accepts advertising.
Ad Rates: BW: $674.80 **Circ:** ‡1,874
4C: $1,023.40
SAU: $8.48

LAKE ZURICH, pop. 8,225.

Lake Co. (NE). 35 m NW of Chicago. Lake resort. Manufactures meat slicers, tools manufactured, plastic film, chemicals, and tool products.

9223 Lake Zurich Courier
Pioneer Press Newspapers
200 James St. Phone: (847)381-9200
Barrington, IL 60010 Fax: (847)381-5840

Community newspaper for Lake Co., IL. **Founded:** 1968. **Freq:** Weekly (Thurs.). **Print Method:** Offset. **Cols./Page:** 4. **Col. Width:** 28 nonpareils. **Col. Depth:** 184 agate lines. **Key Personnel:** Paul Sassone, Managing Editor; Matt Arado, Editor. **Subscription Rates:** $18.95 individuals. **Remarks:** Advertising accepted; rates available upon request. **URL:** http://www.pioneerlocal.com.
Circ: Thurs. ★**4,005**

9224 Lake Zurich Enterprise
Lakeland Publishers, Inc.
30 S. Whitney St. Phone: (847)223-8161
PO Box 268 Fax: (847)223-8810
Grayslake, IL 60030-0268
Publication E-mail: edit@lnd.com

Community newspaper. **Founded:** 1958. **Freq:** Weekly (Thurs.). **Print Method:** Offset. **Trim Size:** 11 x 17. **Cols./Page:** 5. **Col. Width:** 2 inches. **Col. Depth:** 16 inches. **Key Personnel:** W.H. Schroeder, Publisher; Esther Hebbard, Advertising Mgr.; Rhonda Hetrick Burke, Editor. **Subscription Rates:** $24.50; $35 out of area. **Remarks:** Accepts advertising.
Ad Rates: BW: $974.80 **Circ:** ‡4,255
4C: $1,023.40
SAU: $8.48

LANARK, pop. 1,483.

Carroll Co. (NW). 15 m E Savanna. Residential.

9225 Prairie Advocate
K-O Printing & Publishing Co.
446 S. Broad St. Phone: (815)493-2560
PO Box 84 Fax: (815)493-2561
Lanark, IL 61046
Free: (888)493-2560
Publication E-mail: pa@internetni.com

County community newspaper. **Subtitle:** News for Carroll County. **Founded:** Apr. 5, 1937. **Freq:** Weekly (Wed.). **Print Method:** Offset. **Trim Size:** 11 x 17. **Cols./Page:** 5. **Col. Width:** 12 picas. **Col. Depth:** 15 3/4 inches. **Key Personnel:** Lynn Kocal, Editor; Thomas Kocal, Publisher; Tammy Burkholder, Marketing; Elizabeth Sarber, Office Mgr., phone (815)273-2560, fax (815)273-2576. **Subscription Rates:** Free; $24 out of county. **Remarks:** Accepts advertising. **URL:** http://www.internetni.com/pa. **Formerly**: The Advertiser. **Feature Editors:** Caralee Aschenbrenner, *Features.*
Ad Rates: BW: $528 **Circ:** Free ‡9,748
4C: $678 Paid ‡3,072
PCI: $10.60

LANSING, pop. 29,039.

Cook Co. (NE). 15 m S of Chicago. Near suburban community.Light industries. Steel mills.Oil refineries.Truck farms.

9226 Daily South Town/News Marketer
Daily South Town
18127 Williams St. Phone: (708)895-3700
Lansing, IL 60438 Fax: (708)895-0344

Newspaper. **Founded:** 1906. **Freq:** Semiweekly (Wed. and Sun.). **Print Method:** Offset. **Cols./Page:** 6. **Col. Width:** 26 nonpareils. **Col. Depth:** 301 agate lines. **Key Personnel:** Kathy Wantuck, Editor; Bruce Sagan, Publisher; Terrance Boyle, Advertising Mgr. **Subscription Rates:** $10.20 individuals. **Remarks:** Accepts advertising. **Formerly**: South Town Economist.
Ad Rates: GLR: $.96 **Circ:** Paid 1,051
Free 513

9227 Lansing/Lynwood Star
Star Newspapers
6901 W 159th St. Phone: (708)802-8800
Tinley Park, IL 60477 Fax: (708)802-8899

Newspaper group serving 51 communities in Chicago's southern suburbs. **Founded:** 1890. **Freq:** Semiweekly (Thurs. and Sun.). **Print Method:** Offset. **Trim Size:** 13 3/4 x 23. **Cols./Page:** 6. **Col. Width:** 2 inches. **Col. Depth:** 21 1/2 inches. **Key Personnel:** Lester Sons, Editor; Norman Rosinski, Publisher; Jim Meidell, Advertising Mgr.; Jay Fredrickson. **Remarks:** Accepts advertising.
Ad Rates: GLR: $56.76 **Circ:** Thurs. 65,520
Sun. 68,788

LAWRENCEVILLE†, pop. 5,652.

Lawrence Co. (SE). 9 m W of Vincennes, Ind. Manufactures

telephone and oil well equipment, asphalt products, chemicals. Oil and gas wells. Stock, grains farms.

9228 Daily Record
1209 State St. Phone: (618)943-2331
PO Box 559 Fax: (618)943-3976
Lawrenceville, IL 62439
Free: (800)943-2331
Publisher E-mail: d.record@midwest.net

General newspaper. **Founded:** 1847. **Freq:** Daily (eve.). **Print Method:** Offset. **Cols./Page:** 6. **Col. Width:** 25 nonpareils. **Col. Depth:** 294 agate lines. **Key Personnel:** Larry H. Lewis, Editor; Byron Tracy, Managing Editor; Deborah Cashmore, Publisher; Don Shreve, Advertising Mgr. **Subscription Rates:** $59 individuals. **Remarks:** Accepts advertising.
Ad Rates: BW: $611.10 **Circ:** Paid 4,005
SAU: $4.85

9229 Lawrence County News
Daily Record
1209 State St. Phone: (618)943-2331
PO Box 559 Fax: (618)943-3976
Lawrenceville, IL 62439
Free: (800)943-2331
Publisher E-mail: d.record@midwest.net

Community newspaper. **Founded:** Dec. 1894. **Freq:** Weekly (Wed.). **Print Method:** Offset. **Cols./Page:** 6. **Col. Width:** 22 nonpareils. **Col. Depth:** 294 agate lines. **Key Personnel:** Bryon Tracy, Editor; Larry Lewis, Publisher; Deborah Cashmore, Publisher. **Subscription Rates:** $16 individuals. **Remarks:** Advertising not accepted.
Circ: Paid 401

9230 WAKO-AM - 910
Hwy. 250 E. Phone: (618)943-3354
PO Box 210 Fax: (618)943-4173
Lawrenceville, IL 62439

Format: Adult Contemporary. **Simulcasts:** WAKO-FM. **Networks:** Mutual Broadcasting System. **Owner:** Stuart K. Lankford, at above address. **Founded:** 1959. **Operating Hours:** 19 hrs. Daily; 9% network, 91% local. **Key Personnel:** Stuart K. Lankford, General Mgr.; S. Kent Lankford, Contact; David Dasch, Contact. **Wattage:** 500. **Ad Rates:** $6.50-12 for 30 seconds; $8.50-14 for 60 seconds.

9231 WAKO-FM - 103.1
Hwy. 250 E. Phone: (618)943-3354
PO Box 210 Fax: (618)943-4173
Lawrenceville, IL 62439

Format: Adult Contemporary. **Simulcasts:** WAKO-AM. **Networks:** Mutual Broadcasting System. **Owner:** Stuart K. Lankford, at above address. **Founded:** 1965. **Operating Hours:** 19 hrs. Daily; 9% network, 91% local. **Key Personnel:** S. Kent Lankford, Contact; David Dasch, Contact. **Wattage:** 6,000. **Ad Rates:** $6.50-12 for 30 seconds; $8.50-14 for 60 seconds.

LE ROY, pop. 2,870.

McLean Co. (C). 17 m SE of Bloomington. Manufactures prefabricated houses. Agriculture. Grain, soybeans, corn.

9232 The Le Roy Journal
Illinois Valley Press
1926 S. Main St. Phone: (309)467-3314
PO Box 36 Fax: (309)467-4563
Eureka, IL 61530
Free: (800)747-7323
Publisher E-mail: journal@farmwagon.com

Community newspaper. **Founded:** July 1887. **Freq:** Weekly (Wed.). **Print Method:** Offset. Uses mats. **Trim Size:** 10 1/4 x 13. **Cols./Page:** 5. **Col. Width:** 22 nonpareils. **Col. Depth:** 182 agate lines. **Key Personnel:** Sue Bratcher, Editor; Bruce Swartz, General Mgr.; Carol Cowgur, Advertising Mgr. **USPS:** 307-140. **Subscription Rates:** $23.25 individuals. **Remarks:** Accepts advertising.
Ad Rates: BW: $302.25 **Circ:** Paid ‡1,350
SAU: $6

LEBANON, pop. 3,245.

St Clair Co. (SW). 12 m NE of Belleville. Mckendree College. Grain farms. Corn, wheat.

9233 Advertiser
Lebanon Advertiser
309 W. St. Louis St. Phone: (618)537-4498
Box 126
Lebanon, IL 62254
Community newspaper. **Founded:** July 14, 1911. **Freq:** Weekly (Wed.). **Print Method:** Uses mats. Offset. **Cols./Page:** 8. **Col. Width:** 11 picas. **Col. Depth:** 294 agate lines. **Key Personnel:** Harrison Leon Church, Publisher. **Subscription Rates:** $9 individuals.
Circ: 1,750

LEMONT

Bolingbrook Metropolitan - See Bolingbrook

Darien Metropolitan - See Darien

9234 Lemont Metropolitan
Press Publication
223 Main St. Phone: (630)739-2300
Lemont, IL 60439 Fax: (630)257-5640

Community newspaper. **Freq:** Weekly (Thurs.). **Key Personnel:** Eric Kavanagh, Editor; Robert Norfleet, Publisher. **Subscription Rates:** $8. **Remarks:** Advertising accepted; rates available upon request.
Circ: 4,800

Romeoville Metropolitan - See Romeoville

LENA, pop. 2,295.

Stephenson Co. (N). 12 m NW of Freeport. State Park. Cheese factories. Diversified farming. Lumber.

9235 Northwestern Illinois Farmer
Box 536 Phone: (815)369-2811
Lena, IL 61048-0536 Fax: (815)369-2816

Local and agriculture newspaper. **Founded:** 1867. **Freq:** Weekly (Wed.). **Print Method:** Offset. **Trim Size:** 11 3/8 x 16. **Cols./Page:** 5. **Col. Width:** 25 nonpareils. **Col. Depth:** 210 agate lines. **Key Personnel:** Norman C. Templin, Publisher. **USPS:** 397-700. **Subscription Rates:** $18 individuals. **Remarks:** Accepts advertising.
Ad Rates: GLR: $.60 **Circ:** ‡9,850
BW: $472.50
PCI: $6.30

LEWISTOWN†, pop. 2,758.

Fulton Co. (W). 15 m SW of Canton. Coal mines. Grain, stock farms.

9236 Fulton Democrat
165 W. Lincoln Phone: (309)547-3055
PO Box 191 Fax: (309)543-6844
Lewistown, IL 61542
Community newspaper. **Freq:** Weekly (Wed.). **Cols./Page:** 8. **Col. Width:** 10 1/2 picas. **Col. Depth:** 21 1/2 inches. **Key Personnel:** Robert L. Martin, Publisher.
Circ: Free 4,800

LIBERTY, pop. 587.

Adams Co. (W). 10 m S of Clayton. Residential.

9237 Liberty Bee-Times
PO Box 198 Phone: (217)645-3033
Liberty, IL 62347 Fax: (217)645-3083
Free: (800)648-3033
Publication E-mail: libertyb@adams.net

Community newspaper. **Founded:** June 1875. **Freq:** Weekly (Wed.). **Print Method:** Offset. Uses mats. **Trim Size:** 10 1/4 x 16. **Cols./Page:** 5. **Col. Width:** 11.5 picas. **Col. Depth:** 16 inches. **Key Personnel:** Marcia L. Elliott, Editor/Administration; James W. Elliott, Publisher. **USPS:** 311-640. **Subscription Rates:** $10.50 individuals; $12.50 out of area. **Remarks:** Accepts advertising. **Alt. Formats:** CD-ROM.
Ad Rates: GLR: $1.05 **Circ:** ‡1,400
BW: $125
SAU: $2.28
PCI: $1.75

LIBERTYVILLE, pop. 16,520.

Lake Co. (NE). 12 m SW of Waukegan. Manufactures macaroni, medical supplies, kitchen cabinets, tractors, heavy machinery, flexible couplings, material handling equipment, upholstery fabrics.Lime and cement research. Agriculture. Grain.

9238 Advanced Packaging
IHS Publishing Group
17730 W. Peterson Rd. Phone: (847)362-8711
PO Box 159 Fax: (847)362-3484
Libertyville, IL 60048-0159
Publication E-mail: ap@ihspubs.com
Publisher E-mail: ihs@ihspubs.com

Trade journal serving designers, fabricators, assemblers and suppliers in leading-edge electronic packaging technologies. **Founded:** 1992. **Freq:** Monthly. **Print Method:** Web offset. **Trim Size:** 7 7/8 x 10 7/8. **Cols./Page:** 3. **Col. Width:** 2 1/8 inches. **Col. Depth:** 10 inches. **Key Personnel:** Marsha Robertson, VP and Publisher, marshar@ihspubs.com; Greg Reed, Editor, gregr@ihspubs.com; Theresa Grant-Wartham, Managing Editor, theresagw@ihspubs.com; Lauren Guthrie, Publisher. **ISSN:** 1065-0555. **Subscription Rates:** Free to qualified subscribers. **Remarks:** Accepts advertising.
Ad Rates: BW: $3,594 **Circ:** Controlled △26,523
4C: $4,644

9239 Compliance Magazine
IHS Publishing Group
17730 W. Peterson Rd. Phone: (847)362-8711
PO Box 159 Fax: (847)362-3484
Libertyville, IL 60048-0159
Publication E-mail: compliance@ihspubs.com
Publisher E-mail: ihs@ihspubs.com

Trade magazine covering workplace safety, health, and environment for professionals. **Founded:** Sept. 1994. **Freq:** 10/year. **Print Method:** Offset. **Trim Size:** 11 x 15 3/4. **Cols./Page:** 4. **Col. Width:** 2 3/8 inches. **Col. Depth:** 14 3/4 inches. **Key Personnel:** Marsha Robertson, Group Publisher, marshar@ihspubs.com; Elizabeth Hintch, Editor, bettyht@ihspubs.com; Lauren Guthrie, Publisher, laureng@ihspubs.com. **ISSN:** 1077-5889. **Subscription Rates:** Free to qualified subscribers; $55 individuals; $10 single issue. **Remarks:** Accepts advertising. **URL:** http://www.compliancemag.com.
Ad Rates: BW: $8,027 **Circ:** Non-paid △60,014
4C: $9,077

9240 Connector Specifier
IHS Publishing Group
17730 W. Peterson Rd. Phone: (847)362-8711
PO Box 159 Fax: (847)362-3484
Libertyville, IL 60048-0159
Publication E-mail: cs@ihspubs.com
Publisher E-mail: ihs@ihspubs.com

Magazine for electronic engineers on the use of connectors and interconnection products. **Founded:** 1985. **Freq:** 10/year. **Print Method:** Offset. **Trim Size:** 11 x 15 3/4. **Cols./Page:** 4 and 3. **Col. Width:** 2 3/8 and 3 1/4 inches. **Col. Depth:** 14 3/4 and 14 3/4 inches. **Key Personnel:** Marsha Robertson, V.P. & Group Publisher, marshar@ihspubs.com; Greg Reed, Editor, gregr@ihspubs.com; Susan Pfeil, Managing Editor, susanp@ihspubs.com; Lauren Guthrie, Assoc. Publisher, lauren@ihspubs.com. **ISSN:** 8756-4076. **Subscription Rates:** Free to qualified subscribers. **Remarks:** Accepts advertising. **Available Online. URL:** http://www.csmag.com. **Formerly**: InterConnection Technology (1994).
Ad Rates: BW: $7,112 **Circ:** Controlled △35,013
4C: $8,162
PCI: $180

9241 High Volume Printing
Innes Publishing Co.
28100 N. Ashley Phone: (847)816-7900
PO Box 7280 Fax: (847)247-8855
Libertyville, IL 60048-7280
Publisher E-mail: innespub@aol.com

Magazine for printers, trade binderies, and color tradehouses with more than 20 employees. **Founded:** 1925. **Freq:** Bimonthly. **Print Method:** Offset. **Trim Size:** 8 3/8 x 10 7/8. **Cols./Page:** 3. **Col. Width:** 27 nonpareils. **Col. Depth:** 140 agate lines. **Key Personnel:** Ray Roth, Ed./VP; Steve Austin, Publisher. **ISSN:** 0737-1020. **Subscription Rates:** $75 Free to qualified subscribers; $15 single issue. **Remarks:** Accepts advertising. **Formerly**: Book & Magazine Production.
Ad Rates: GLR: $15 **Circ:** Controlled ‡38,201
BW: $4,540
4C: $6,240
PCI: $250

9242 In-Plant Printer & Electronic Publisher
Innes Publishing Co.
28100 N. Ashley Phone: (847)816-7900
PO Box 7280 Fax: (847)247-8855
Libertyville, IL 60048-7280
Publisher E-mail: innespub@aol.com

Magazine serving printing, graphics, typesetting facilities, educational, government, and non-profit organizations. **Founded:** 1961. **Freq:** Bimonthly. **Print Method:** Offset. **Trim Size:** 8 1/8 x 10 7/8. **Cols./Page:** 3. **Col. Width:** 26 nonpareils. **Col. Depth:** 140 agate lines. **Key Personnel:** Ed Innes, Publisher; David Barista, Editor. **ISSN:** 0891-8996. **Subscription Rates:** $75 Free to qualified subscribers; $15 single issue. **Remarks:** Accepts advertising.
Ad Rates: BW: $4,335 **Circ:** Controlled ‡30,526
4C: $5,835

9243 Instant and Small Commercial Printer
Innes Publishing Co.
28100 N. Ashley Phone: (847)816-7900
PO Box 7280 Fax: (847)247-8855
Libertyville, IL 60048-7280
Publisher E-mail: innespub@aol.com

Magazine serving the field of instant/quick printers, copy shops, small commercial printers, combination printers, industry suppliers and others allied to the field, including typesetters and thermographers. **Founded:** 1982. **Freq:** Monthly 12/year. **Print Method:** Offset. **Trim Size:** 8 1/8 x 10 7/8. **Cols./Page:** 3. **Col. Width:** 27 nonpareils. **Col. Depth:** 140 agate lines. **Key Personnel:** Anne Marie Mohan, Editor; Dan Innes, Publisher. **ISSN:** 1044-3746. **Subscription Rates:** $85; Free to qualified subscribers; $15 single issue. **Remarks:** Accepts advertising.
Ad Rates: BW: $2,700 **Circ:** Controlled ‡50,953
4C: $3,700
PCI: $75

9244 Libertyville News
Lakeland Publishers, Inc.
30 S. Whitney St. Phone: (847)223-8161
PO Box 268 Fax: (847)223-8810
Grayslake, IL 60030-0268
Publication E-mail: edit@lnd.com

Community newspaper. **Subtitle:** Libertyville News. **Founded:** 1989. **Freq:** Weekly (Thurs.). **Print Method:** Offset. **Trim Size:** 11 x 17. **Cols./Page:** 5. **Col. Width:** 2 inches. **Col. Depth:** 16 inches. **Key Personnel:** W.H. Schroeder, Publisher; Esther Hebbard, Advertising Mgr.; Rhonda Hetrick Burke, Editor. **Subscription Rates:** $24.50; $35 out of area. **Remarks:** Accepts advertising.
Ad Rates: BW: $674.80 **Circ:** ‡3,225
4C: $1,023.40
SAU: $8.48

9245 Libertyville Review
Pioneer Press Newspapers
850 N. Milwaukee Ave. Phone: (847)680-6690
Vernon Hills, IL 60061 Fax: (847)573-2500

Community newspaper (tabloid). **Founded:** 1981. **Freq:** Weekly (Thurs.). **Print Method:** Offset. **Cols./Page:** 5. **Col. Width:** 10 inches. **Col. Depth:** 14 inches. **Key Personnel:** Sheila Richard, Editor; Paul Sassone, Managing Editor. **Subscription Rates:** $14.95 individuals; $16.50 out of county. **Remarks:** Advertising accepted; rates available upon request.
Circ: Thurs. ★**4,564**

9246 SMT
IHS Publishing Group
17730 W. Peterson Rd. Phone: (847)362-8711
PO Box 159 Fax: (847)362-3484
Libertyville, IL 60048-0159
Publication E-mail: smt@ihspubs.com
Publisher E-mail: ihs@ihspubs.com

Trade magazine for professional engineers involved in surface mount technology circuit design and board assembly. **Founded:** 1986. **Freq:** Monthly. **Print Method:** Web offset. **Trim Size:** 7 7/8 x 10 7/8. **Cols./Page:** 3. **Col. Width:** 2 1/8 inches. **Col. Depth:** 10 inches. **Key Personnel:** Marsha Robertson, VP & Group Publisher, marshar@ihspubs.com; Greg Reed, Editor, gregr@ihspubs.com; Sandy Ruroede, Managing Editor, sandyr@ihspubs.com; Lauren Guthrie, Assoc. Publisher, laureng@ihspubs.com. **ISSN:** 0893-3588. **Subscription Rates:** Free to qualified subscribers. **Remarks:** Accepts advertising. **Available Online. URL:** http://www.smtmag.com. **Formerly:** Surface Mount Technology.
Ad Rates: BW: $6,486 **Circ:** Controlled 46,017
4C: $7,536

LINCOLN†, pop. 16,327.

Logan Co. (C). 31 m NE of Springfield. Manufactures glass bottles, plate glass, store fixtures, paper boxes, cosmetics, electric controls. Dairy, stock, grain, poultry farms. Sand and gravel pits.

9247 Courier
Copley Corp.
601 Pulaski St. Phone: (217)732-2101
Lincoln, IL 62656-2825 Fax: (217)732-7039
Free: (800)397-8757

General newspaper. **Founded:** 1856. **Freq:** Daily (eve.). **Print Method:** Offset. **Cols./Page:** 6. **Col. Width:** 24 nonpareils. **Col. Depth:** 294 agate lines. **Key Personnel:** Jack Clarke, Publisher; Jeff Nelson, Managing Editor. **Subscription Rates:** $91 individuals. **Remarks:** Accepts advertising.
Ad Rates: GLR: $7.35 **Circ:** Mon.-Sat. ★**6,940**
BW: $937.13
4C: $1,097.13
SAU: $7.35

LINCOLNSHIRE

9248 CWB: Custom Woodworking Business
Vance Publishing Corp.
400 Knightsbridge Parkway Phone: (847)634-2600
Lincolnshire, IL 60069 Fax: (847)634-4379
Free: (800)343-2016

Magazine for professional custom woodworkers. **Founded:** 1990. **Freq:** Monthly. **Print Method:** Web offset. **Trim Size:** 8 x 10 3/4. **Key Personnel:** Helen Kuhl, Editor-in-Chief; Harry Urban, VP/Publishing Dir.; Laurel Didier, Assoc. Publisher. **Subscription Rates:** Free to qualified subscribers; $35; $100 other countries. $3 single issue. **Remarks:** Accepts advertising.
Ad Rates: BW: $4,830 **Circ:** Controlled ‡60,000
4C: $6,880

9249 Modern Salon
Vance Publishing Corp.
400 Knightsbridge Parkway Phone: (847)634-2600
Lincolnshire, IL 60069 Fax: (847)634-4379
Free: (800)343-2016
Publication E-mail: modernsalon.com

Magazine focusing on hairstyling salons for men and women. **Founded:** 1924. **Freq:** Monthly. **Print Method:** Web offset. **Trim Size:** 8 x 10 3/4. **Cols./Page:** 3 and 2. **Col. Width:** 26 and 40 nonpareils. **Col. Depth:** 140 agate lines. **Key Personnel:** Jackie Summers, Editor, fax (800)643-4342; Bob Bellew, Publisher, phone (847)634-4354, fax (800)643-4342; Sherry Fisher, Operations Mgr., phone (847)634-4338, fax (800)643-4342. **ISSN:** 0148-4001. **Subscription Rates:** $20 individuals; $4 single issue. **Remarks:** Accepts advertising.
Ad Rates: BW: $10,385 **Circ:** Paid ★**74,730**
4C: $12,180 Non-paid ★**50,552**

9250 Residential Lighting
Vance Publishing Corp.
400 Knightsbridge Parkway Phone: (847)634-2600
Lincolnshire, IL 60069 Fax: (847)634-4379
Free: (800)343-2016
Publication E-mail: decor.vance@interaccess.com

Magazine catering to lighting showroom dealers, manufacturers of lighting products, and related electrical distributors. **Founded:** Apr. 1, 1993. **Freq:** Monthly. **Trim Size:** 8 x 10 3/4. **Key Personnel:** Mark Gates, Publisher, phone (847)634-7896; Laura Bening, Editor, phone (847)634-7886. **ISSN:** 1072-1614. **Subscription Rates:** $5 single issue; $100 out of country; Free.
Ad Rates: 4C: $2,760 **Circ:** Non-paid ★**11,177**

9251 Salon Today Magazine
Vance Publishing Corp.
400 Knightsbridge Parkway Phone: (847)634-2600
Lincolnshire, IL 60069 Fax: (847)634-4379
Free: (800)343-2016

Management guide for beauty salon owners and managers. **Founded:** 1983. **Freq:** Monthly. **Print Method:** Web offset. **Trim Size:** 8 x 10 3/4. **Cols./Page:** 3. **Col. Width:** 13.5 picas. **Col. Depth:** 8.5 inches. **Key Personnel:** Michele Musgrove, Editor, phone (847)634-4890, fax (847)634-4342; Bob Bellew, Publisher, phone (847)634-4354, fax (847)634-4342; Sherry Fisher, Operations Mgr., phone (847)634-4338, fax (847)634-4342. **ISSN:** 0743-6394. **Subscription Rates:** $42 individuals; $10 single issue. **Remarks:** Accepts advertising.
Ad Rates: BW: $3,500 **Circ:** ‡30,000
4C: $4,120

9252 Wood & Wood Products
Vance Publishing Corp.
400 Knightsbridge Parkway Phone: (847)634-2600
Lincolnshire, IL 60069 Fax: (847)634-4379
Free: (800)343-2016

Magazine for furniture, cabinet, and woodworking industry. **Founded:** 1896. **Freq:** Monthly. **Print Method:** Web offset. **Trim Size:** 8 x 10 3/4. **Cols./Page:** 3. **Col. Width:** 26 nonpareils. **Col. Depth:** 140 agate lines. **Key Personnel:** Rich Christianson, Editor; Harry Urban, Publisher; Laurel Didier, Natl. Sales Manager. **Subscription Rates:** $30 individuals; $50 other countries; $3 single issue. **Remarks:** Accepts advertising.
Ad Rates: BW: $3,990 **Circ:** Non-paid ‡51,573
4C: $5,590

LINCOLNWOOD, pop. 11,921.

Cook Co (NE). 6 m SW of Evanston.

9253 The Booster
Lerner Communications, Inc.
7331 N. Lincoln Ave. Phone: (847)329-2000
Lincolnwood, IL 60646-1704 Fax: (847)329-2060
Publisher E-mail: lerner@enteract.com

Community newspaper. **Founded:** 1937. **Freq:** Weekly (Wed.). **Print Method:** Offset. **Trim Size:** 13 x 21 1/4. **Cols./Page:** 6. **Col. Width:** 25 nonpareils. **Col. Depth:** 297 agate lines. **Key Personnel:** William Santamour, Managing Editor; Joseph Ferstl, Exec. V.P. **USPS:** 060-980. **Subscription Rates:** Free; $14.50 by mail; $10.50 senior citizens; $31.50 out of state.
Ad Rates: SAU: $54.90 **Circ:** Paid 4,898
Non-paid 677

9254 Collectible Automobile
Publications International, Ltd.
7373 N. Cicero Phone: (847)676-3470
Lincolnwood, IL 60646 Fax: (847)676-3671

Magazine on collectible automobiles. **Founded:** 1984. **Freq:** Bimonthly. **Print Method:** Offset. **Trim Size:** 9 x 10 7/8. **Cols./Page:** 3. **Col. Width:** 28 nonpareils. **Col. Depth:** 140 agate lines. **Key Personnel:** John Biel, Editor; Frank Peiler, Publisher. **Subscription Rates:** $37.95; $6.95 single issue. **Remarks:** Advertising not accepted.
Circ: ‡90,000

9255 Consumer Guide
Publications International, Ltd.
7373 N. Cicero Phone: (847)676-3470
Lincolnwood, IL 60646 Fax: (847)676-3671

Consumer magazine featuring articles on products, sports, entertainment, and health and fitness. **Founded:** 1966. **Freq:** 34/year. **Print Method:** Offset. **Key Personnel:** Becky Bell, Exec. Editorial Dir.; Louis Weber, CEO; Frank Peiler, Publisher. **Remarks:** Advertising not accepted.
Circ: (Not Reported)

9256 Elmwood Park/River Grove Times
Chicago Lerner Newspapers
7331 N. Lincoln Ave. Phone: (847)329-2000
Lincolnwood, IL 60646 Fax: (847)329-2060
Publisher E-mail: lerner@aol.com

Community newspaper. **Founded:** 1965. **Freq:** Weekly (Thurs.). **Print Method:** Offset. **Trim Size:** 13 x 21 1/4. **Cols./Page:** 6. **Col. Width:** 25 nonpareils. **Col. Depth:** 297 agate lines. **Key Personnel:** Leigh Hanlon, Exec Editor; Brian Steele, Managing Editor; Chuck Geigas, V.P. Adv. **Subscription Rates:** Free; $9.95 by mail.
Ad Rates: SAU: $54.90 **Circ:** Paid 1,364
Non-paid 442

Glenview Weekend Voice - See Glenview

9257 Harlem-Foster Times
Lerner Communications, Inc.
7331 N. Lincoln Ave. Phone: (847)329-2000
Lincolnwood, IL 60646-1704 Fax: (847)329-2060
Publisher E-mail: lerner@enteract.com

Community newspaper. **Founded:** 1949. **Freq:** Weekly (Wed.). **Print Method:** Offset. **Cols./Page:** 6. **Col. Width:** 25 nonpareils. **Col. Depth:** 297 agate lines. **Key Personnel:** Terry Levecke, Managing Editor; Joseph Ferstl, Exec. V.P. **Subscription Rates:** Free; $9.95 by mail.
Ad Rates: SAU: $54.90 **Circ:** Paid 2,990
Non-paid 1,017

9258 Jefferson Park/Portage Park Times
Lerner Communications, Inc.
7331 N. Lincoln Ave. Phone: (847)329-2000
Lincolnwood, IL 60646-1704 Fax: (847)329-2060
Publisher E-mail: lerner@enteract.com

Community newspaper. **Founded:** 1928. **Freq:** Weekly (Thurs.). **Print Method:** Offset. **Trim Size:** 13 x 21 1/4. **Cols./Page:** 6. **Col. Width:** 25 nonpareils. **Col. Depth:** 297 agate lines. **Key Personnel:** Terry Levecke, Managing Editor; Joseph Ferstl, Exec. V.P. **USPS:** 007-953. **Subscription Rates:** Free; $9.95 by mail. **Remarks:** Accepts advertising.
Ad Rates: SAU: $54.90 **Circ:** Combined 4,388
Free 313

9259 Lincoln-Belmont Booster
Chicago Lerner Newspapers
7331 N. Lincoln Ave. Phone: (847)329-2000
Lincolnwood, IL 60646 Fax: (847)329-2060
Publisher E-mail: lerner@aol.com

Community newspaper. **Founded:** 1920. **Freq:** Weekly (Wed.). **Print Method:** Offset. **Trim Size:** 13 x 21 1/4. **Cols./Page:** 6. **Col. Width:** 25 nonpareils. **Col. Depth:** 297 agate lines. **Key Personnel:** William Santamour, Managing Editor; Joseph Ferstl, Exec. V.P. **Subscription Rates:** Free; $14.50 by mail; $10.50 senior citizens; $31.50 out of county.
Ad Rates: SAU: $54.90 **Circ:** Paid 1,188

9260 Lincolnwood Life
Lerner Communications, Inc.
7331 N. Lincoln Ave. Phone: (847)329-2000
Lincolnwood, IL 60646-1704 Fax: (847)329-2060
Publisher E-mail: lerner@enteract.com

Community newspaper. **Founded:** 1946. **Freq:** Weekly (Thurs.). **Print Method:** Offset. **Trim Size:** 13 x 21 1/4. **Cols./Page:** 6. **Col. Width:** 25 nonpareils. **Col. Depth:** 297 agate lines. **Key Personnel:** William Santamonr, Executive editor; Marcy Marzuki, Managing Editor; Chuck Gekas, V.P. of Advertising. **USPS:** 314-000. **Subscription Rates:** $16.50 individuals. **Remarks:** Accepts advertising.
Ad Rates: SAU: $35.28 **Circ:** Paid 1,161
Non-paid 240

9261 Morton Grove-Niles Life
Lerner Communications, Inc.
7331 N. Lincoln Ave. Phone: (847)329-2000
Lincolnwood, IL 60646-1704 Fax: (847)329-2060
Publication E-mail: lenwennew@aol.com
Publisher E-mail: lerner@enteract.com

Community newspaper. **Founded:** 1946. **Freq:** Weekly (Thurs.). **Print Method:** Offset. **Trim Size:** 13 x 21 1/4. **Cols./Page:** 6. **Col. Width:** 25 nonpareils. **Col. Depth:** 297 agate lines. **Key Personnel:** Pan Demetrakakes, Managing Editor; Joseph Ferstl, Exec. V.P. **Subscription Rates:** $11.95 individuals. **Remarks:** Accepts advertising.
Ad Rates: SAU: $25.81 **Circ:** Paid 2,152
Non-paid 1,221

9262 The Niles Bugle
Bugle Publications
7400 Waukekan Rd. Phone: (847)588-1900
Niles, IL 60714 Fax: (847)588-1911

Local community newspaper (tabloid). **Founded:** June 1957. **Freq:** Weekly (Thurs.). **Print Method:** Offset. **Trim Size:** 10 x 13. **Cols./Page:** 5. **Col. Width:** 1 7/8 inches. **Col. Depth:** 13 inches. **Key Personnel:** Robert Besser, Editor and Publisher; Diane Miller, Advertising Mgr. **Subscription Rates:** Free; $26 by mail; $26 out of area (mail). **Remarks:** Accepts advertising. **Formerly:** The Bugle.
Ad Rates: GLR: $2.50 **Circ:** Paid ‡2,500
BW: $1,250 Free ‡17,000
PCI: $35

9263 The Niles Life
Lerner Communications, Inc.
7331 N. Lincoln Ave. Phone: (847)329-2000
Lincolnwood, IL 60646-1704 Fax: (847)329-2060
Publisher E-mail: lerner@enteract.com

Community newspaper. **Founded:** 1946. **Freq:** Weekly (Thurs.). **Print Method:** Offset. **Trim Size:** 13 x 21 1/4. **Cols./Page:** 6. **Col. Width:** 25 nonpareils. **Col. Depth:** 297 agate lines. **Key Personnel:** Pan Demetrakakes, Managing Editor; Joseph Ferstl, Exec. V.P. **USPS:** 007-259. **Subscription Rates:** $14.50 year. **Remarks:** Accepts advertising.
Ad Rates: SAU: $35.28 **Circ:** Paid ‡650
Free ‡257

9264 Norridge Times
Lerner Communications, Inc.
7331 N. Lincoln Ave. Phone: (847)329-2000
Lincolnwood, IL 60646-1704 Fax: (847)329-2060
Publisher E-mail: lerner@enteract.com

Community newspaper. **Founded:** 1965. **Freq:** Weekly (Wed.). **Print Method:** Offset. **Trim Size:** 13 x 21 1/4. **Cols./Page:** 6. **Col. Width:** 25 nonpareils. **Col. Depth:** 297 agate lines. **Key Personnel:** Terry Levecke, Managing Editor; Joseph Ferstl, Exec. V.P. **Subscription Rates:** Free; $9.95 by mail.
Ad Rates: SAU: $54.90 **Circ:** Paid 3,652
Non-paid 970

9265 North Center-Irving Park Booster
Chicago Lerner Newspapers
7331 N. Lincoln Ave. Phone: (847)329-2000
Lincolnwood, IL 60646 Fax: (847)329-2060
Publisher E-mail: lerner@aol.com

Community newspaper. **Founded:** 1920. **Freq:** Weekly (Wed.). **Print Method:** Offset. **Trim Size:** 13 x 21 1/4. **Cols./Page:** 6. **Col. Width:** 25 nonpareils. **Col. Depth:** 297 agate lines. **Key Personnel:** William Santamour, Managing Editor; Joseph Ferstl, Exec. V.P. **Subscription Rates:** Free; $14.50 by mail; $10.50 senior citizens; $31.50 out of county. **URL:** http://www.intheloop.net.
Ad Rates: SAU: $54.90 **Circ:** Paid 396
Free 12,997

9266 North Town News-Star
Lerner Communications, Inc.
7331 N. Lincoln Ave.. Phone: (847)329-2000
Lincolnwood, IL 60646-1704 Fax: (847)329-2060
Publisher E-mail: lerner@enteract.com

Community newspaper. **Founded:** 1922. **Freq:** Weekly (Wed.). **Print Method:** Offset. **Trim Size:** 13 x 21 1/4. **Cols./Page:** 6. **Col. Width:** 25 nonpareils. **Col. Depth:** 297 agate lines. **Key Personnel:** Joel Schatz, Managing Editor; Joseph Ferstl, Exec. V.P. **USPS:** 395-000. **Subscription Rates:** $14.50 individuals. **Remarks:** Accepts advertising.
Ad Rates: SAU: $35.28 **Circ:** Paid ‡5,801
Free ‡537

Northbrook Weekend Voice - See Northbrook

9267 Rogers Park/Edgewater/Uptown News-Star
Lerner Communications, Inc.
7331 N. Lincoln Ave. Phone: (847)329-2000
Lincolnwood, IL 60646-1704 Fax: (847)329-2060
Publisher E-mail: lerner@enteract.com

Community newspaper. **Founded:** 1922. **Freq:** Weekly (Wed.). **Print Method:** Offset. **Cols./Page:** 6. **Col. Width:** 25 nonpareils. **Col. Depth:** 297 agate lines. **Key Personnel:** Joel Schatz, Managing Editor; Joseph Ferstl, Exec. V.P. **USPS:** 469-800. **Subscription Rates:** $14.50 individuals; $10.50 senior citizens; $31.50 out of county.
Ad Rates: SAU: $35.29 **Circ:** Combined 6,333

9268 Schiller Park
Lerner Communications, Inc.
7331 N. Lincoln Ave. Phone: (847)329-2000
Lincolnwood, IL 60646-1704 Fax: (847)329-2060
Publisher E-mail: lerner@enteract.com

Community newspaper. **Freq:** Weekly. **Subscription Rates:** Free. **Formerly:** Schiller Times.
Circ: Paid 341
Free 7,345

Skokie Life - See Skokie

9269 Skyline
Lerner Communications, Inc.
7331 N. Lincoln Ave. Phone: (847)329-2000
Lincolnwood, IL 60646-1704 Fax: (847)329-2060
Publisher E-mail: lerner@enteract.com

Community newspaper. **Founded:** 1965. **Freq:** Weekly (Thurs.). **Print Method:** Offset. **Trim Size:** 13 x 21 1/4. **Cols./Page:** 6. **Col. Width:** 25 nonpareils. **Col. Depth:** 297 agate lines. **Key Personnel:** Peter L. Strazz, Managing Editor, phone (847)329-2999. **Subscription Rates:** $9.95. **Remarks:** Accepts advertising. **URL:** http://www.intheloop.com.
Ad Rates: SAU: $54.90 **Circ:** Paid ‡222
Free ‡31,525

9270 Uptown News Star
Chicago Lerner Newspapers
7331 N. Lincoln Ave. Phone: (847)329-2000
Lincolnwood, IL 60646 Fax: (847)329-2060
Publication E-mail: lernernew@aol.com
Publisher E-mail: lerner@aol.com

Community newspaper. **Freq:** Weekly.
Circ: Paid 6,806
Free 1,641

LINDENHURST

9271 Lindenhurst News
Lakeland Publishers, Inc.
30 S. Whitney St. Phone: (847)223-8161
PO Box 268 Fax: (847)223-8810
Grayslake, IL 60030-0268
Publication E-mail: edit@lnd.com

Community newspaper. **Founded:** 1988. **Freq:** Weekly (Thurs.). **Print Method:** Offset. **Trim Size:** 11 x 17. **Cols./Page:** 5. **Col. Width:** 2 inches. **Col. Depth:** 16 inches. **Key Personnel:** W.H. Schroeder, Publisher; Esther Hebbard, Advertising Mgr.; Rhonda Hetrick Burke, Editor. **Subscription Rates:** $24.50; $35 out of area. **Remarks:** Accepts advertising.
Ad Rates: BW: $674.80 **Circ:** ‡1,961
4C: $1,023.40
SAU: $8.48

9272 The Review of Lake Villa/Lindenhurst
Pioneer Press Newspapers
850 N. Milwaukee Ave. Phone: (847)680-6690
Vernon Hills, IL 60061 Fax: (847)573-2500

Community newspaper (tabloid). **Founded:** 1989. **Freq:** Weekly (Thurs.). **Print Method:** Offset. **Cols./Page:** 5. **Col. Width:** 10 inches. **Col. Depth:** 14 inches. **Key Personnel:** Marah Shuman, Editor; Paul Sassone, Managing Editor. **Subscription Rates:** $5; $11.95 out of county. **Remarks:** Combined advertising rates available with other Pioneer Press Newspapers. **Formed by the merger of:** Lindenhurst Review (Dec. 1990); Lake Villa Review (Dec. 1990).
Circ: Thurs. ★2,300

LISLE, pop. 13,625.

Du Page Co. (NE). 28 m W of Chicago. Benedictine College.(Co-ed.) Suburban area. Light manufacturing.

9273 ABNF Journal
Tucker Publications, Inc.
PO Box 580 Phone: (630)969-3809
Lisle, IL 60532-0580 Fax: (630)969-3895

Professional journal covering health care related to minority clients, students, and faculty members. **Founded:** 1990. **Freq:** Bimonthly. **Trim Size:** 7 x 10. **Cols./Page:** 2. **Key Personnel:** Dr. Sallie Tucker-Allen, Editor, sallen@tuckerpub.com; Clay Allen, Advertising Mgr., callen@tuckerpub.com; Monique Allen, Circulation Mgr. **ISSN:** 1046-7041. **Subscription Rates:** $85 individuals; $150 institutions; $30 single issue. **Remarks:** Accepts advertising.
Ad Rates: GLR: $30 **Circ:** Combined 450
BW: $2,275
4C: $2,825

9274 Journal of Cultural Diversity
Tucker Publications, Inc.
PO Box 580 Phone: (630)969-3809
Lisle, IL 60532-0580 Fax: (630)969-3895

Scholarly journal covering cultural diversity for educators, researchers, and practitioners. **Subtitle:** An Interdisciplinary Journal. **Founded:** 1994. **Freq:** Quarterly. **Trim Size:** 7 x 10. **Key Personnel:** Charles Allen, Advertising Mgr., callen@tuckerpub.com; S. Monique Allen, Assoc. Publisher; Dr. Zaiga Kalnins, Editor, phone (217)410-4390, fax (217)410-4239; Dr. Joseph Hoff, Editor, phone (217)479-7103. **ISSN:** 1071-5568. **Subscription Rates:** $60 individuals; $165 institutions; $50 single issue. **Remarks:** Accepts advertising.
Ad Rates: GLR: $25 **Circ:** Combined 550
BW: $1,600
4C: $2,250

9275 Journal of Theory Construction Testing
Tucker Publications, Inc.
PO Box 580 Phone: (630)969-3809
Lisle, IL 60532-0580 Fax: (630)969-3895
Publication E-mail: sallen@tuckpub.com

Scholarly journal covering theory development. **Founded:** 1997. **Freq:** Semiannual. **Trim Size:** 7 x 10. **Cols./Page:** 2. **Key Personnel:** Dr. Margaret T. Beard, Editor, phone (940)387-9066, fax (940)898-2437; Clay Allen, Advertising Mgr., callen@tuckerpub.com; Monique N. Allen, Circulation Mgr. **ISSN:** 1086-4431. **Subscription Rates:** $30 individuals; $50 institutions. **Remarks:** Accepts advertising.
Ad Rates: GLR: $25 **Circ:** Combined 250
BW: $1,600
4C: $2,250

9276 Voices Magazine
Benedictine University
5700 College Rd. Phone: (630)829-6000
Lisle, IL 60532-0900 Fax: (630)960-1126

Collegiate magazine. **Founded:** Sept. 1971. **Freq:** Quarterly (during the academic year). **Print Method:** Offset. **Trim Size:** 8 1/2 x 11. **Cols./Page:** 3. **Col. Width:** 13 picas. **Col. Depth:** 60 picas. **Key Personnel:** Bob Tenczar, Editor. **Remarks:** Advertising not accepted. **Formerly:** Illinois Benedictine University.
Circ: Non-paid ‡16,000

LITCHFIELD, pop. 7,204.

Montgomery Co. (SC). 44 m S of Springfield. Manufactures shoes, milk, plastic products and plastic pipe paper and aluminum products, brake parts, soft drinks, steel specialties, farm equipment attachments, dresses, athletic equipment. Dairy farms. Corn, wheat, soybeans.

9277 Litchfield News-Herald
Litchfield News-Herald, Inc.
112 E. Ryder St. Phone: (217)324-2121
PO Box 160 Fax: (217)324-2122
Litchfield, IL 62056-2031
General newspaper. **Founded:** 1856. **Freq:** Daily (eve.). **Print Method:** Offset. **Trim Size:** 13 1/2 x 23. **Cols./Page:** 6. **Col. Width:** 12 picas. **Col. Depth:** 21 inches. **Key Personnel:** Micki Romanus, Editor; John C. Hanafin, Publisher; Fred W.

Jones, Advertising Mgr. **Subscription Rates:** $41.60 individuals. **Remarks:** Accepts advertising.
Ad Rates: GLR: $.16 **Circ:** ‡5,800
BW: $270.27
4C: $570.27
PCI: $2.38

9278 WSMI-AM - 1540
Box 10 Phone: (217)324-2345
Litchfield, IL 62056 Fax: (217)532-2431
E-mail: wsmi@cillnet.com

Format: Full Service; Agricultural; Country. **Networks:** Mutual Broadcasting System. **Founded:** 1950. **Operating Hours:** Sunrise-sunset. **Key Personnel:** Hayward L. Talley, President/Gen. Mgr.; Brian Talley, Vice President; Terry Todt, Program Dir. **Local Programs:** *Monday Morning Talk Show*, Rita Frazer, Mailing contact; *RFD with Rita Frazer*, Rita Frazer, Mailing contact; *WSMI Forum*, Jill Pyle, Mailing contact. **Wattage:** 1000. **Ad Rates:** Combined advertising rates available with WSMI-FM.

9279 WSMI-FM - 106.1
Box 10 Phone: (217)324-2345
Litchfield, IL 62056 Fax: (217)532-2431
E-mail: wsmi@cllnet.com

Format: Country; Agricultural. **Networks:** Mutual Broadcasting System. **Owner:** Talley Broadcasting Corp, at above address. **Founded:** 1960. **Operating Hours:** 20.5 hrs. Daily. **Key Personnel:** Hayward L. Talley, President/Gen. Mgr.; Brian Talley, Vice President; Terry Todt, Program Dir. **Local Programs:** *Forum*, Dan Hanson; *RFD with Rita Frazer*, Rita Frazer, Mailing contact; *TalkTime*, Ted Lay, Mailing contact. **Wattage:** 50,000. **Ad Rates:** Combined advertising rates available with WSMI.

LOMBARD, pop. 37,295.

Du Page Co. (NE). 22 m NW of Chicago. Chiropractic College. Engineering College. Printing. Manufactures boxes, packaging materials.

9280 Appliance Service News
Gamit Enterprises, Inc.
110 W. St. Charles Rd. Phone: (630)932-9550
PO Box 789 Fax: (630)932-9552
Lombard, IL 60148
Publication E-mail: asnews@cin.net

Magazine for appliance technicians. **Founded:** 1950. **Freq:** Bimonthly. **Print Method:** Offset. **Trim Size:** 8 1/2 x 11 in. **Cols./Page:** 4. **Col. Width:** 26 nonpareils. **Col. Depth:** 60 picas. **Key Personnel:** William Wingstedt, Editor and Publisher. **ISSN:** 0003-6803. **Subscription Rates:** $9.95 individuals. **Remarks:** Accepts advertising.
Ad Rates: BW: $2,480 **Circ:** Combined ‡32,000
4C: $3,620
PCI: $99

9281 EGM2
Ziff Davis Video Game Group
1920 Highland Ave., No. 222 Phone: (630)916-7222
Lombard, IL 60148 Fax: (630)916-7227

Consumer magazine covering video games. **Founded:** June 1994. **Freq:** Monthly. **Print Method:** Web offset. **Trim Size:** 7 7/8 x 10 1/2. **Key Personnel:** Joe Funk, Editorial Dir.; Howard Grossman, Editor-in-Chief; Joan McInerney, Circulation Director, jmcinern@zd.com; Jonathan Lane, Publisher. **ISSN:** 1077-338X. **Subscription Rates:** $24.97 individuals; $4.99 single issue. **Remarks:** Accepts advertising. **URL:** http://www.videogames.com.
Ad Rates: BW: $2,700 **Circ:** Paid 126,310
4C: $3,600

9282 Electronic Gaming Monthly
Ziff Davis Video Game Group
1920 Highland Ave., No. 222 Phone: (630)916-7222
Lombard, IL 60148 Fax: (630)916-7227
Publication E-mail: egm@zd.com

Consumer magazine covering video gaming. **Founded:** Apr. 1989. **Freq:** Monthly. **Print Method:** Web offset. **Trim Size:** 7 3/8 x 10 1/2. **Key Personnel:** Joe Funk, Editorial Dir.; Joan McInerney, Circulation Dir., jmcinern@zd.com; Jonathan Lane, Publisher; John Davison, Editor-in-Chief. **ISSN:** 1058-918X. **Subscription Rates:** $24.97 individuals; $4.99 single issue. **Remarks:** Accepts advertising. **URL:** http://www.videogames.com.
Ad Rates: BW: $7,495 **Circ:** Paid ★389,219
4C: $9,995

9283 The Landscape Contractor
Illinois Landscape Contractor Association
2200 S. Main, Ste. 304 Phone: (630)932-8443
Lombard, IL 60148 Fax: (630)932-8939
Publication E-mail: mptxzba@prodigy.com

Magazine for the landscape trade. **Subtitle:** Landscape Contracting. **Founded:** 1960. **Freq:** Monthly. **Print Method:** WEB. **Trim Size:** 8 1/2 x 11. **Cols./Page:** 3 and 2. **Col. Width:** 26 and 40 nonpareils. **Col. Depth:** 140 agate lines. **Key Personnel:** Joan C. King, Publisher; Esther Baricza, Advertising Mgr. **ISSN:** 0194-7257. **Subscription Rates:** $65 individuals. **Remarks:** Accepts advertising.
Ad Rates: BW: $575 **Circ:** Paid ‡2,000
4C: $1,075 Non-paid ‡760

9284 Lombardian
613 S. Main St. Phone: (630)627-7010
Lombard, IL 60148 Fax: (630)627-7027
Publisher E-mail: lombardian@aol.com

Newspaper with a Republican orientation. **Founded:** 1958. **Freq:** Weekly (Wed.). **Print Method:** Offset. **Cols./Page:** 5. **Col. Width:** 22 nonpareils. **Col. Depth:** 224 agate lines. **Key Personnel:** Bonnie MacKay, Editor; Scott D. MacKay, Publisher. **Subscription Rates:** $18 individuals. **Remarks:** Accepts advertising.
Ad Rates: GLR: $.44 **Circ:** ‡21,500
BW: $624
4C: $100
PCI: $7.80

9285 NARDA Independent Retailer
North American Retail Dealers Association
10 E. 22nd St., Ste. 310 Phone: (630)953-8950
Lombard, IL 60148 Fax: (630)953-8957
Publication E-mail: nardanews@aol.com

Magazine for appliance, consumer electronics, furniture, and computer dealers. **Subtitle:** Serving consumer electronics, appliance, and furniture businesses. **Founded:** 1943. **Freq:** Monthly. **Print Method:** Offset. **Trim Size:** 8 1/4 x 10 3/4. **Cols./Page:** 3. **Col. Width:** 2 1/4 inches. **Col. Depth:** 9 1/2 inches. **Key Personnel:** Russ Gager, Editor. **ISSN:** 1098-9717. **Subscription Rates:** $78. **Remarks:** Accepts advertising. **Formerly:** NARDA News.
Ad Rates: BW: $1,850 **Circ:** ‡4,000
4C: $2,525

9286 Official U.S. PlayStation Magazine
Ziff Davis Video Game Group
1920 Highland Ave., No. 222 Phone: (630)916-7222
Lombard, IL 60148 Fax: (630)916-7227

Consumer magazine covering video gaming for the Sony PlayStation. **Founded:** Oct. 1997. **Freq:** Monthly. **Print Method:** Web offset. **Trim Size:** 7 7/8 x 10 1/2. **Key Personnel:** Joe Funk, Editorial Dir.; Wataru Maruyama, Editor-in-Chief; Joan McInerney, Circulation Dir., jmcinern@zd.com; Jonathan Lane, Publisher. **ISSN:** 1094-6683. **Subscription Rates:** $49.97 individuals; $7.99 single issue. **Remarks:** Accepts advertising. **URL:** http://www.videogames.com. **Former name:** PSX.
Ad Rates: BW: $4,500 **Circ:** Paid ★179,472
4C: $5,995

9287 Villa Park Review/Lombardian
Lombardian
613 S. Main St. Phone: (630)627-7010
Lombard, IL 60148 Fax: (630)627-7027
Publisher E-mail: lombardian@aol.com

Newspaper with a Republican orientation. **Founded:** 1959. **Freq:** Weekly (Wed.). **Print Method:** Offset. Uses mats. **Cols./Page:** 5. **Col. Width:** 22 nonpareils. **Col. Depth:** 224 agate lines. **Key Personnel:** Scott D. MacKay, Publisher. **Subscription Rates:** $18 individuals. **Remarks:** Accepts advertising.
Ad Rates: GLR: $.50 **Circ:** ‡21,500
BW: $664 13,500
4C: $100
PCI: $8.30

LOUISVILLE†, pop. 1,166.

Clay Co. (C). Oil wells, diversified agriculture.

9288 Louisville Clay County Republican
Clay County Republican
165 Church St. Phone: (618)665-3135
PO Drawer B Fax: (618)665-3135
Louisville, IL 62858
Local newspaper. **Founded:** 1895. **Freq:** Weekly (Thurs.). **Print Method:** Offset. **Cols./Page:** 7. **Col. Width:** 12 picas. **Col. Depth:** 21 1/2 inches. **Key Personnel:** Danny E. Fender, Publisher. **Subscription Rates:** $14 individuals; $15 out of area. **Remarks:** Accepts advertising.
Ad Rates: PCI: $2.80 **Circ:** ‡2,250

LOVES PARK, pop. 14,250.

Winnebago Co. (EC). NE of Rockford.

9289 Journal
Rock Valley Community Press, Inc.
2124 Harlem Rd. Phone: (815)877-4044
PO Box 15340 Fax: (815)654-4857
Loves Park, IL 61132
Publication E-mail: rvcp01@aol.com
Publisher E-mail: rvcpress@lx.netcom.

Community newspaper. **Founded:** 1969. **Freq:** Weekly (Wed.). **Print Method:** Offset. **Cols./Page:** 5. **Col. Width:** 25 nonpareils. **Col. Depth:** 217 agate lines. **Key Personnel:** William R. Brennan, Pres./Pub., billy3X@aol.com; Cyndi Jensen, Controller; Debbie McDaniel, Editor, mcdaniel98@aol.com. **Subscription Rates:** $25. **Remarks:** Accepts advertising.
Ad Rates: GLR: $.96 **Circ:** Paid 43,000
BW: $1,080
4C: $1,230
SAU: $13.50

9290 News Gazette
Rock Valley Community Press, Inc.
2124 Harlem Rd. Phone: (815)877-4044
PO Box 15340 Fax: (815)654-4857
Loves Park, IL 61132
Publisher E-mail: rvcpress@lx.netcom.

Community newspaper. **Founded:** 1858. **Freq:** Weekly (Wed.). **Print Method:** Offset. **Trim Size:** 10 1/8 x16. **Cols./Page:** 4. **Col. Width:** 22 nonpareils. **Col. Depth:** 224 agate lines. **Key Personnel:** Randy Johnson, General Mgr. **Subscription Rates:** $23 individuals. **Remarks:** Accepts advertising.
Ad Rates: GLR: $.45 **Circ:** ‡7,400
PCI: $5.23

9291 Northern Ogle Tempo
Rock Valley Community Press, Inc.
2124 Harlem Rd. Phone: (815)877-4044
PO Box 15340 Fax: (815)654-4857
Loves Park, IL 61132
Publisher E-mail: rvcpress@lx.netcom.

Community newspaper. **Founded:** 1934. **Freq:** Weekly (Tues.). **Print Method:** Offset. **Trim Size:** 11 x 17. **Cols./Page:** 4. **Col. Width:** 22 nonpareils. **Col. Depth:** 224 agate lines. **Key Personnel:** Randall Johnson, General Mgr.; Ellen Smith, Editor. **Subscription Rates:** $26 individuals. **Remarks:** Accepts advertising.
Ad Rates: BW: $375 **Circ:** Paid 6,488
4C: $1,125 Free 71
PCI: $5.85

9292 The Park and Metro Rockford Journal
Rock Valley Community Press, Inc.
2124 Harlem Rd. Phone: (815)877-4044
PO Box 15340 Fax: (815)654-4857
Loves Park, IL 61132
Publisher E-mail: rvcpress@lx.netcom.

Community newspaper. **Founded:** 1947. **Freq:** Weekly. **Print Method:** Offset. **Trim Size:** 11 3/8 x 17. **Cols./Page:** 5. **Col. Width:** 2 1/4 inches. **Col. Depth:** 16 inches. **Key Personnel:** Janine Nunes, Editor; Randall Johnson, General Mgr. **Subscription Rates:** $23. **Remarks:** Accepts advertising. **Formerly:** The Loves Park Post-Machesney Park Pilot-Buyer's Guide; The Loves Park Post - Machesney Park Journal.
Ad Rates: BW: $512 **Circ:** ‡21,855
4C: $1,580
PCI: $21.09

9293 WGSL-FM - 91.1
5375 Pebble Creek Trail Phone: (815)654-1200
PO Box 2730 Fax: (815)282-7779
Loves Park, IL 61132

Format: Religious. **Networks:** Moody Broadcasting; USA Radio. **Owner:** Christian Life Center School, at above address. **Founded:** 1988. **Operating Hours:** Continuous. **ADI:** Rockford, IL. **Key Personnel:** Charles Alexander, General Mgr.; Ron Tietsort, Operations Mgr., ront@radio91.com; Joe Buchanan, Music Dir., joeb@radio91.com. **Wattage:** 4000. **Ad Rates:** Noncommercial.

9294 WQFL-FM - 100.9
5375 Pebble Creek Tr. Phone: (815)654-1200
Loves Park, IL 61111-4326 Fax: (815)282-7779
E-mail: positive@101qfl.com

Format: Religious; Contemporary Christian. **Networks:** Independent. **Founded:** 1974. **Operating Hours:** Continuous. **ADI:** Rockford, IL. **Key Personnel:** Charles Alexander, General Mgr.; Jim Beeler, Program Dir. **Wattage:** 3000. **Ad Rates:** $12-22.50 for 30 seconds; $16-30 for 60 seconds. Combined advertising rates available with WGSL-FM.

LOVINGTON

Moultrie Co. (SC). 20 m N of Sullivan.

9295 Moultrie Telecommunications, Inc.
111 State & Broadway Phone: (217)873-5215
Box 350 Fax: (217)873-4990
Lovington, IL 61937

Founded: 1981. **Key Personnel:** David A. Bowers, President, dbowers@moultrie.com; Francis E. Bowers, Contact; Stuart D. Bowers, Vice President; Steven G. Bowers, Contact. **Cities Served:** Lovington, IL: subscribing households 474; 36 channels; 1 community access channel; 168 hours per week community access programming.

MACOMB†, pop. 19,632.

McDonough Co. (W). 40 m SW of Galesburg. Western Illinois University.Spoon River College. Museum. State Park. Manufactures pottery, porcelain insulators, clay and steel products, metal furniture, industrial bearings, chicken incubators, agriculture equipment. Coal mines. Clay deposits. Agriculture. Corn, soybeans, hogs, cattle.

9296 The Journal of Developing Areas
Western Illinois University
Morgan Hall, Rm. 232 Phone: (309)298-1108
Macomb, IL 61455 Fax: (309)298-2865

Journal on economic, social, and political issues pertaining to developing nations. **Founded:** Oct. 1966. **Freq:** Quarterly. **Trim Size:** 6 x 9. **Cols./Page:** 1. **Col. Width:** 56 nonpareils. **Col. Depth:** 105 agate lines. **Key Personnel:** Nicholas C. Pano, Editor, nc-pano@wiu.edu; Spencer H. Brown, Assoc. Editor, sh_brown@wiu.edu. **ISSN:** 0022-037X. **Subscription Rates:** $29 individuals; $39 institutions.
Ad Rates: BW: $200 **Circ:** Paid ‡1,122
Non-paid ‡60

9297 The Journal of Socio-Economics
Elseiver
Dept. of Economics
Western Illinois University
Macomb, IL 61455
Publication E-mail: 102062-2525@compuserve.com
Publisher E-mail: fcentres@gpu.stv.ualberta.ca

Economics journal. **Founded:** 1972. **Freq:** Bimonthly. **Print Method:** Offset. **Trim Size:** 6 7/8 x 10. **Cols./Page:** 1. **Key Personnel:** Richard Hattwick, Editor, phone (309)298-1594, fax (309)298-1020, hattwick@macomb.com. **ISSN:** 1053-5359. **Subscription Rates:** $215 institutions; $245 institutions, other countries; $275 institutions, other countries airmail; $100 individuals; $130 other countries; $160 other countries airmail; $37.50 single issue; $42.50 single issue other couuntries; $47.50 single issue other countries airmail. **Remarks:** Accepts advertising. **Formerly:** The Journal of Behavioral Economics.
Ad Rates: BW: $300 **Circ:** (Not Reported)

9298 Macomb Journal
Community Newspaper Holdings, Inc.
128 N. Lafayette Phone: (309)833-2114
Box 597 Fax: (309)833-2346
Macomb, IL 61455-2226
Free: (800)237-6858
Publication E-mail: journal@macomb.com

Newspaper. **Founded:** 1855. **Freq:** Daily (eve.), Sunday (morn.). **Print Method:** Offset. **Cols./Page:** 6. **Col. Width:** 25 nonpareils. **Col. Depth:** 301 agate lines. **Key Personnel:** Randy Lohrenz, General Mgr.; Tom Martin, Managing Editor; Lisa Havens, Advertising Dir. **Subscription Rates:** $106 individuals. **Remarks:** Accepts advertising. **URL:** http://journal-web.com. **Alt. Formats:** Microform.
Ad Rates: GLR: $8.70 **Circ:** 7,122
BW: $1,122.30 Sun. 7,874
4C: $1,572.30
SAU: $9.19

9299 PALAESTRA
Challenge Publications, Ltd.
PO Box 508 Phone: (309)833-1902
Macomb, IL 61455-0508 Fax: (309)833-1902
Publication E-mail: challpub@macomb.com
Publisher E-mail: challpub@macomb.com

Journal focusing on sports, physical education, and recreation for persons with disabilities. **Subtitle:** Forum of Sport, Physical Education & Recreation for Those with Disabilities. **Founded:** 1984. **Freq:** Quarterly. **Print Method:** Sheet-fed offset. **Trim Size:** 8 3/8 x 10 7/8. **ISSN:** 8756-5811. **Subscription Rates:** $19 individuals; $25 institutions. **URL:** http://www.palaestra.com.
Ad Rates: BW: $1,270 **Circ:** Combined ‡5000
4C: $2,045-1x1975

9300 Western Courier
Western Illinois University
1 University Circle Phone: (309)298-1876
PO Box 6009 Fax: (309)298-2309
Macomb, IL 61455-1330
Collegiate newspaper. **Founded:** 1904. **Freq:** 3/week. **Print Method:** Offset. **Trim Size:** 10 3/4 x 16. **Cols./Page:** 5. **Col. Width:** 11.8 picas. **Col. Depth:** 1 inches. **Key Personnel:** Terry Lawhorn, Advisor, ta-lawhorn@wiu.edu. **Subscription Rates:** $30 individuals; $3 summer; $15 semester. **Remarks:** Accepts advertising. **URL:** http://courier.wiu.edu.
Ad Rates: BW: $549.50 **Circ:** Free ‡6,500
4C: $849.50
SAU: $7
PCI: $7.50

9301 WIUM-FM - 91.3
Western Illinois University Phone: (309)298-1873
1 University Circle Fax: (309)298-2133
Macomb, IL 61455
E-mail: publicradio@wiu.edu

Format: Public Radio; Folk; Jazz; News; Eclectic; Classical. **Networks:** National Public Radio (NPR); Illinois Public Radio; Public Radio International (PRI). **Owner:** Western Illinois University, at above address, (309)298-2424. **Founded:** 1956. **Operating Hours:** Continuous; 80% network, 20% local. **Key Personnel:** Sharon Fausty, Development Dir.; Dorothy Vallilo, Station Mgr.; Richard Egger, News Dir.; Kenneth Thermon, Operations Mgr.; Jeff Holtz, Music Dir. **Local Programs:** *Emphasis*, Tim Crowley, Mailing contact, (309)298-1873; *Ovation*, Jeff Holtz, Mailing contact, (309)298-1873. **Wattage:** 50,000. **Ad Rates:** Noncommercial.

9302 WLRB-AM - 1510
119 W. Carroll Phone: (309)833-5561
PO Box 250 Fax: (309)833-3460
Macomb, IL 61455

Format: News; Middle-of-the-Road (MOR); Agricultural; Easy Listening. **Networks:** ABC. **Owner:** Sharp Broadcasting, at above address. **Founded:** 1947. **Formerly:** WKAI-AM (1984). **Operating Hours:** 7 a.m.-5:00 p.m.; 10% network, 90% local. **Key Personnel:** Don Sharp, Contact; Rick Bulger, Operations Mgr. **Wattage:** 1000. **Ad Rates:** $4.75-12 for 30 seconds; $7.50-18 for 60 seconds.

9303 WMEC-TV - 22
c/o CONVOCOM Phone: (217)786-6647
PO Box 6248 Fax: (217)786-7267
Springfield, IL 62708
Free: (800)232-3605
E-mail: viewer@wvnec.pbs.org

Format: Public TV. **Networks:** Public Broadcasting Service (PBS). **Owner:** CONVOCOM, at above address. **Founded:** 1984. **Formerly:** WIUM-TV (1989). **Operating Hours:** 6:30 a.m.-12 a.m.; 75% network, 25% local. **ADI:** Springfield-Decatur-Champaign, IL. **Key Personnel:** Jerold Gruebel, Contact; Maureen Earley, Contact; Terry Kenny, Contact; Rich Plotkin, Contact.

MAHOMET, pop. 1,986.

Champaign Co (E). 14 m NW of Champaign. Museum. Antique stores.

9304 Mahomet Citizen
Illinois Valley Press
427 E. Main Phone: (217)586-2512
Mahomet, IL 61853 Fax: (217)586-4821
Publisher E-mail: journal@farmwagon.com

Community newspaper. **Founded:** 1975. **Freq:** Weekly (Wed.). **Print Method:** Offset. **Trim Size:** 11 1/4 x 13 3/4. **Cols./Page:** 5. **Col. Width:** 11 picas. **Col. Depth:** 13 inches. **Key Personnel:** Erik Anderson, Editor. **USPS:** 063-930. **Subscription Rates:** $24 individuals. **Remarks:** Accepts advertising.
Ad Rates: BW: $302.25 **Circ:** 2,400
4C: $402.25
PCI: $5.25

MANHATTAN

9305 Manhattan Cable TV Co.
Box 11 Phone: (815)478-4000
Manhattan, IL 60442

Founded: 1980. **Cities Served:** Manhattan, IL: 42 channels.

MANTENO, pop. 3,155.

Kankakee Co. (E). 10 m N of Kankakee. Grain, dairy, stock farms. Soybeans.

9306 The Manteno News
415 S. Locust Phone: (815)468-6397
Manteno, IL 60950 Fax: (815)468-7577

Community newspaper. **Founded:** 1886. **Freq:** Weekly (Thurs.). **Print Method:** Offset. **Cols./Page:** 5. **Col. Width:** 22 nonpareils. **Col. Depth:** 224 agate lines. **Key Personnel:** Gilbert Russell, Publisher; Betty Knauth, Assoc. Editor. **USPS:** 328-380. **Subscription Rates:** $18 individuals. **Remarks:** Accepts advertising.
Ad Rates: BW: $220 **Circ:** ‡2,000
PCI: $3.15

MARION†, pop. 14,031.

Williamson Co. (S). 55 m S of Centralia. Manufactures explosives, fiberglass boats. Coal mines. Fruit, grain and livestock farms.

9307 Chariton Courier
American Publishing Co.
606 N. Van Buren
Marion, IL 62959

Newspaper. **Founded:** 1869. **Freq:** Weekly (Thurs.). **Print Method:** Offset. **Cols./Page:** 6. **Col. Width:** 26 nonpareils. **Col. Depth:** 301 agate lines. **Key Personnel:** Melva Benett, Editor; Ivan R. Buckman, Publisher; Bill Evans, General Mgr. **Subscription Rates:** $28. **Remarks:** Accepts advertising.
Ad Rates: BW: $328.95 **Circ:** ‡550
SAU: $2.70

9308 Harrison Daily Times
American Publishing Co.
606 N. Van Buren
Marion, IL 62959

General newspaper. **Founded:** 1876. **Freq:** Daily (eve.). **Print Method:** Offset. **Cols./Page:** 6. **Col. Width:** 12 picas. **Col. Depth:** 129 picas. **Key Personnel:** J.E. Dunlap, Jr., Editor. **Subscription Rates:** $37 individuals. **Remarks:** Accepts advertising.
Ad Rates: BW: $567.60 **Circ:** Paid 11,011
4C: $732 Controlled 127
SAU: $5.55
PCI: $4.40

9309 Marion Daily Republican
American Publishing Company of Illinois
502 W. Jackson Phone: (618)993-2626
PO Box 490 Fax: (618)993-8326
Marion, IL 62959
General newspaper. **Founded:** 1908. **Freq:** Mon.-Sun. **Print Method:** Offset. **Cols./Page:** 6. **Col. Width:** 24 nonpareils. **Col. Depth:** 300 agate lines. **Key Personnel:** Sam Shelton, Publisher; Russell Darby, Editor; Michelle Bean, Marketing Dir.; Steve Shelton, Director Comp. Mgr. **Subscription Rates:** $56.50 by mail. **Remarks:** Accepts advertising.
Ad Rates: BW: $1,025.55 **Circ:** Paid 3,958
4C: $1,250.55
PCI: $7.95

9310 WBVN-FM - 104.5
PO Box 1126 Phone: (618)997-1500
Marion, IL 62959 Fax: (618)997-3194
E-mail: wbvn@midwest.net

Format: Adult Contemporary; Religious. **Owner:** Ken Anderson, at above address. **Founded:** 1990. **Operating Hours:** Continuous; 50% local; 50% network 24hrs. **ADI:** Paducah,KY-Cape Girardeau,MO-Marion,IL. **Key Personnel:** Ken Anderson, Contact, wbvn@midwest.net; Mark Miles, Program Mgr. **Wattage:** 6000. **Ad Rates:** Noncommercial. **URL:** http://www.wbvn.org.

9311 WDDD-AM - 810
1 Broadcast Center Phone: (618)997-8123
Marion, IL 62959-0127 Fax: (618)993-2319

Format: News; Sports; Talk. **Simulcasts:** WDDD-FM. **Founded:** 1979. **Formerly:** WDDW-AM (1983). **Operating Hours:** Continuous. **ADI:** Paducah,KY-Cape Girardeau,MO-Marion,IL. **Key Personnel:** Dutch Doelitzsch, General Mgr.; Jerry Crouse, Station Mgr.; Steve Land, News Dir. **Wattage:** 250. **Ad Rates:** Advertising accepted; rates available upon request.

9312 WDDD-FM - 107.3
1 Broadcast Center Phone: (618)997-8123
Marion, IL 62959 Fax: (618)993-2319
E-mail: wddd@midwest.net

Format: Country. **Founded:** 1970. **Operating Hours:** Continuous. **ADI:** Paducah,KY-Cape Girardeau,MO-Marion,IL. **Key Personnel:** Dutch Doelitzsch, General Mgr.; Jerry Crouse, Station Mgr.; Steve Land, News Dir.; Tracy McSherry, Music Dir.; Jon Prell, Program Dir. **Wattage:** 50,000. **Ad Rates:** Advertising accepted; rates available upon request.

9313 WGGH-AM - 1150
PO Box 340 Phone: (618)993-8102
Marion, IL 62959 Fax: (618)997-2307
E-mail: wggh@ldd.net

Format: Southern Gospel. **Networks:** USA Radio. **Owner:** Vine Broadcasting, Inc., at above address. **Founded:** 1949. **Operating Hours:** 6 a.m.-9 p.m. **ADI:** Paducah,KY-Cape Girardeau,MO-Marion,IL. **Key Personnel:** Johnny Gomez, Contact; Shannon Taylor, News Dir.; Elaine Gomez, Station Mgr.; Marcia Raubauch, Sales Mgr. **Wattage:** 5000. **Ad Rates:** $12.36-14.12 for 30 seconds; $14.71-16.48 for 60 seconds.

9314 WTCT-TV - 27
Rte. 37 N. Phone: (618)997-4700
PO Box 698 Fax: (618)993-9778
Marion, IL 62959
E-mail: wtct@tct-net.org

Format: Commercial TV; Religious. **Founded:** 1981. **Formerly:** WDDD-TV. **Operating Hours:** Continuous (except midnight-6 a.m. Mon.). **ADI:** Paducah,KY-Cape Girardeau,MO-Marion,IL. **Key Personnel:** Garth Coonce, President, phone (618)997-9333, fax (618)997-1859; Don Gladden, General Mgr., dog@tct-net.org; Bryan Minniegerode, Production Mgr.; Anna VanDeventer, Sales Mgr., phone (616)895-4154, fax (616)892-4401, avd@tct-net.org; Bryan Minniegerode, Production Mgr.; Fortune Brayfield, Manager, fmb@tct-net.org. **Local Programs:** *Ask the Pastor*, *Tri-State Alive*; *TCT Today*. **Wattage:** 3,000,000. **Ad Rates:** $40 for 30 seconds; $60 for 60 seconds. **URL:** http://www.tct-net.org.

MARISSA, pop. 2,568.

St. Clair Co. (SW). 41 m Edwardsville. Residential.

9315 Journal-Messenger
QUAD County Printing
615 E. Lyons Phone: (618)295-2812
Marissa, IL 62257 Fax: (618)295-3422

Community newspaper. **Founded:** 1915. **Freq:** Weekly (Thurs.). **Print Method:** Offset. **Cols./Page:** 6. **Col. Width:** 25 nonpareils. **Col. Depth:** 224 agate lines. **Key Personnel:** Robert Laws, Editor; Debbie Smith, Advertising Mgr. **Subscription Rates:** $20 individuals. **Remarks:** Accepts advertising. **Formerly**: Journal.
Ad Rates: GLR: $4.75 **Circ:** 2,600
4C: $4.75

MARYVILLE

9316 Charter Communications
210 W. Division St. Phone: (618)345-8121
Maryville, IL 62062 Fax: (618)345-6234
Free: (800)233-0119

Owner: Charter Communications, 12444 Powerscourt Dr., Ste. 100, St. Louis, MO 63131, (314)965-0555, Fax: (314)965-8793. **Founded:** 1986. **Formerly**: South-Western Cable TV, Ltd.; Cencom; Cencom Cable Associates; Crown Cable. **Key Personnel:** Darrel D. Gerbert, System Mgr.; Monica Foster, Office Mgr. **Cities Served:** Caseyville, Collinsville, Columbia, Dupo, Edwardsville, Glen Carbon, Granite City, Highland, Madison, Madison County, Marine, Maryville, Millstadt, Pontoon Beach, Saint Jacob, Troy, Venice, Waterloo, IL: subscribing households 49,000; 68 channels; 1 community access channel; 20 hours per week community access programming.

MASCOUTAH, pop. 4,962.

St Clair Co. (SW). 10 m SE of Belleville. Manufactures cooking ranges, foundry products, carpets. Coal mines. Grain, stock, farms.

9317 Fairview Heights Tribune
Herald Publications
314 E. Church St. Phone: (618)566-8282
PO Box C Fax: (618)566-8283
Mascoutah, IL 62258
Publisher E-mail: herald@accessus.net

Community newspaper. **Founded:** 1884. **Freq:** Weekly. **Key Personnel:** Gene Isbell, Managing Editor; Vicki Santel, Advertising Mgr. **Subscription Rates:** $20 individuals. **Remarks:** Advertising accepted; rates available upon request.
Circ: (Not Reported)

9318 Farm Impact
Drawer C Phone: (618)566-8282
Mascoutah, IL 62258 Fax: (618)566-8283
Publisher E-mail: herald@accessus.net

Local agriculture news. **Founded:** 1975. **Freq:** Monthly. **Print Method:** Offset. **Cols./Page:** 6. **Key Personnel:** Greg Hoskins, Publisher; Gene Isbell, Editor. **Subscription Rates:** $9 individuals. **Remarks:** Accepts advertising.
Ad Rates: BW: $325 **Circ:** Non-paid 40,000
PCI: $10

9319 Herald
Herald Publications
314 E. Church St. Phone: (618)566-8282
PO Box C Fax: (618)566-8283
Mascoutah, IL 62258
Publisher E-mail: herald@accessus.net

Newspaper. **Founded:** 1885. **Freq:** Weekly (Thurs.). **Print Method:** Offset. **Cols./Page:** 6. **Col. Width:** 2 inches. **Col. Depth:** 21-1/2 inches. **Key Personnel:** Greg Hoskins, Publisher; Gene Isbell, Editor. **Subscription Rates:** $20 individuals. **Remarks:** Accepts advertising.
Ad Rates: BW: $510.84 **Circ:** 2,450
4C: $710.84
PCI: $5

9320 Herald Scott Flyer
Herald Publications
314 E. Church St. Phone: (618)566-8282
PO Box C Fax: (618)566-8283
Mascoutah, IL 62258
Publisher E-mail: herald@accessus.net

Community newspaper. **Founded:** 1884. **Freq:** Weekly. **Key Personnel:** Gene Isbell, Managing Editor; Vicki Santel, Advertising Mgr. **Subscription Rates:** $20 individuals. **Remarks:** Accepts advertising.
Circ: (Not Reported)

9321 Lebanon Herald
Herald Publications
314 E. Church St. Phone: (618)566-8282
PO Box C Fax: (618)566-8283
Mascoutah, IL 62258
Publisher E-mail: herald@accessus.net

Community newspaper. **Founded:** 1884. **Freq:** Weekly. **Key Personnel:** Gene Isbell, Managing Editor; Vicki Santel, Advertising Mgr. **Subscription Rates:** $20 individuals. **Remarks:** Accepts advertising.
Circ: (Not Reported)

9322 Mascoutah Herald
Herald Publications
314 E. Church St. Phone: (618)566-8282
PO Box C Fax: (618)566-8283
Mascoutah, IL 62258
Publisher E-mail: herald@accessus.net

Community newspaper. **Founded:** 1884. **Freq:** Weekly. **Key Personnel:** Gene Isbell, Managing Editor; Michael King, Advertising Mgr. **Subscription Rates:** $20 individuals. **Remarks:** Advertising accepted; rates available upon request.
Circ: (Not Reported)

MASON CITY

9323 Manito Review
Banner Times Publications
PO Box 71 Phone: (217)482-3276
Mason City, IL 62664 Fax: (217)482-3277

Newspaper. **Founded:** 1967. **Freq:** Weekly (Tues.). **Print Method:** Offset. **Cols./Page:** 6. **Col. Width:** 21 nonpareils. **Col. Depth:** 301 agate lines. **Key Personnel:** Victor J. Rickard, Editor and Publisher. **Subscription Rates:** $22 out of area. **Remarks:** Accepts advertising. **Alt. Formats:** CD-ROM.
Ad Rates: GLR: $.33 **Circ:** Free 3,250
BW: $731
SAU: $7.80
PCI: $6

9324 Mason City Banner Times
126 N. Tonica St. Phone: (217)482-3276
PO Box 71 Fax: (217)482-3277
Mason City, IL 62664
Community newspaper. **Freq:** Weekly (Tues.). **Cols./Page:** 6. **Col. Width:** 9 1/2 picas. **Col. Depth:** 21 inches. **Key Personnel:** Victor J. Rickard, Editor and Publisher. **Subscription Rates:** $22; $27 out of area. **Remarks:** Accepts advertising.
Ad Rates: BW: $731 **Circ:** Paid 2,100
SAU: $7.80 Free 7,500
PCI: $6

MATTESON

9325 Matteson/Richton Star
Star Newspapers
6901 W 159th St. Phone: (708)802-8800
Tinley Park, IL 60477 Fax: (708)802-8899

Newspaper group serving 51 communities in Chicago's southern suburbs. **Founded:** 1890. **Freq:** Semiweekly (Thurs. and Sun.). **Print Method:** Offset. **Trim Size:** 13 3/4 x 23. **Cols./Page:** 6. **Col. Width:** 2 inches. **Col. Depth:** 21 1/2 inches. **Key Personnel:** Lester Sons, Editor; Norman Rosinski, Publisher; Jim Meidell, Advertising Mgr.; Jay Frederickson.
Ad Rates: GLR: $56.76 **Circ:** Thurs. 64,637
Sun. 68,267

MATTOON, pop. 19,787.

Coles Co. (E). 178 m S of Chicago. Manufactures heavy road machinery, radiators, quartz lighting, pet food, paper products, roofing, frozen food products, commercial printing, metal hose. Grain, stock, fruit, broom corn.

9326 Journal-Gazette
Mid-Illinois Newspapers, Inc.
100 Broadway Phone: (217)235-5656
Mattoon, IL 61938 Fax: (217)235-1925
Publication E-mail: journal@advant.com

Local newspaper. **Founded:** 1874. **Freq:** Mon.-Sat. (morn.). **Print Method:** Offset. **Cols./Page:** 6. **Col. Width:** 25 nonpareils. **Col. Depth:** 301 agate lines. **Key Personnel:** Harry Reynolds, Editor. **Subscription Rates:** $114.40 individuals. **Remarks:** Combined advertising rates available with Charleston Times-Courier.
Ad Rates: BW: $1,470.60 **Circ:** Mon.-Sat. 11,762
4C: $1,695.60
SAU: $11.40

9327 WLBH-AM - 1170
N. Rte. 45 Phone: (217)234-6464
PO Box 1848 Fax: (217)234-6019
Mattoon, IL 61938

Format: Adult Contemporary. **Networks:** ABC. **Owner:** Mattoon Broadcasting Co., at above address. **Founded:** 1946. **Operating Hours:** Sunrise-sunset. **ADI:** Springfield-Decatur-Champaign, IL. **Key Personnel:** Jim Livesay II, Contact. **Local Programs:** *Open Line* 9:45 a.m.-10:30 a.m. Monday-Friday; *Question and Answer* 1 p.m.-1:30 p.m. Monday-Friday. **Wattage:** 5000.

9328 WLBH-FM - 96.9
N. Rte. 45 Phone: (217)234-6464
PO Box 1848 Fax: (217)234-6019
Mattoon, IL 61938

Format: Adult Contemporary. **Networks:** ABC. **Owner:** Mattoon Broadcasting Co., at above address. **Founded:** 1949. **Operating Hours:** Continuous. **ADI:** Springfield-Decatur-Champaign, IL. **Key Personnel:** J.R. Livesay II, Contact; Mark Ridgeway, Contact. **Wattage:** 50,000 ERP.

9329 WLKL-FM - 89.9
Lake Land College Phone: (217)234-5271
5001 Lake Land Blvd. Fax: (217)258-6459
Mattoon, IL 61938
Free: (800)252-4121

Format: Adult Contemporary; Top 40; Alternative/New Music/Progressive. **Founded:** Jan. 20, 1975. **Operating Hours:** 7am-10 pm Mon.-Fri, 9am - midnight Sat., 9am -10 pm Sun. **ADI:** Springfield-Decatur-Champaign, IL. **Key Personnel:** Kenneth Beno, Station Mgr., kbeno@lakeland.cc.il.us. **Wattage:** 1300 ERP. **Ad Rates:** Underwriting available.

MAYWOOD

9330 Aim–America's Intercultural Magazine
Aim Publications
PO Box 1174
Maywood, IL 60153

Magazine promoting intercultural awareness and understanding in America. **Subtitle:** Aim Quarterly. **Founded:** 1974. **Freq:** Quarterly. **Trim Size:** 8 1/2 x 11. **Cols./Page:** 3. **Col. Width:** 2 1/4 inches. **Col. Depth:** 9 3/4 inches. **Key Personnel:** Myron Apilado, Managing Editor, phone (253)952-3930; Ruth Apilado, Editor and Publisher. **Subscription Rates:** $12 individuals. **Remarks:** Color advertising not accepted. **Online:** Ubiquity.
Ad Rates: GLR: $3 **Circ:** Paid ‡4,000
BW: $500 Controlled ‡3,000
4C: $300
PCI: $40

9331 Maywood Herald
Pioneer Press Newspapers
1148 Westgate Ave. Phone: (708)383-3200
Oak Park, IL 60301 Fax: (708)383-3678

Community newspaper (tabloid). **Founded:** 1970. **Freq:** Weekly (Wed.). **Print Method:** Offset. **Cols./Page:** 5. **Col. Width:** 10 inches. **Col. Depth:** 14 inches. **Key Personnel:**

Paul Sassone, Managing Editor; Kevin Beese, Editor. **Subscription Rates:** $13.95 individuals; $15.95 out of county.
Circ: Wed. ★3,251

9332 Maywood Star-Sentinel
Shannon Publications, Inc.
1440 W. North Ave., Ste. 210
Melrose Park, IL 60160

Community newspaper. **Freq:** Weekly (Wed.). **Print Method:** Offset. **Trim Size:** 11 x 14. **Cols./Page:** 6. **Col. Width:** 20 nonpareils. **Col. Depth:** 170 agate lines. **Key Personnel:** David Roberts, Publisher; David Jones, Editor. **Subscription Rates:** $12. **Remarks:** Accepts advertising.
Ad Rates: GLR: $.45 BW: $475 4C: $775 SAU: $4.75
Circ: Paid ‡500 Free ‡8,000

MC HENRY

9333 Lynn—Linn Lineage Quarterly
Phyllis J. Bauer, Editor and Publisher
3510 Turnberry Dr. Phone: (815)385-9626
Mc Henry, IL 60050-7557
Publisher E-mail: pjbauer@mc.net

Trade publication covering genealogy. **Founded:** 1987. **Freq:** Quarterly. **Trim Size:** 8 x 11. **Cols./Page:** 1. **Key Personnel:** Pyhllis J. Bauer, Editor and Publisher. **ISSN:** 0892-418X. **Subscription Rates:** $22 individuals.
Circ: Combined 130

9334 Northwest Herald
Shaw Publications
1111 N. Green St., No. 200 Phone: (815)385-0170
Mc Henry, IL 60050-5714 Fax: (815)385-0916

General newspaper. **Founded:** 1875. **Freq:** Mon.-Sun. (morn.). **Print Method:** Offset. **Cols./Page:** 6. **Col. Width:** 24 nonpareils. **Col. Depth:** 294 agate lines. **Key Personnel:** R.A. Shaw, Publisher; Sam R. Fisher, Advertising Mgr. **Subscription Rates:** $62.40 individuals.

9335 TCI of Illinois
2508 Rte. 120 Phone: (815)344-3150
Mc Henry, IL 60050 Fax: (815)344-5787

Founded: 1977. **Formerly:** Lakes Cablevision. **Key Personnel:** Brian Adams, Contact. **Cities Served:** subscribing households 21,000; 35 channels; 1 community access channel.

MCLEANSBORO

9336 WMCL-AM - 1060
Rte.1, Box 46A Phone: (618)643-2311
McLeansboro, IL 62859 Fax: (618)643-3299
Free: (888)MCL-1060
E-mail: wmcl@midwest.net

Format: Contemporary Country; Agricultural; News. **Networks:** CNN Radio; USA Radio. **Owner:** Four Star Radio, at above address. **Founded:** 1968. **Operating Hours:** Sunrise-sunset; 10% network, 90% local. **Key Personnel:** Danny Johnson, Gen. Mgr./Program Dir.; Rich Lane, News Dir.; Charlie Pendell, Sports Dir.; Jackie Johnson, Office Mgr.; Lee Crawford, Sales Mgr. **Wattage:** 2500. **Ad Rates:** $19 for 30 seconds; $22.00 for 60 seconds. **URL:** http://wmcl1060.com.

MCNABB

9337 McNabb Cablevision
302 W. Main St. Phone: (815)882-2202
PO Box 218 Fax: (815)882-2141
McNabb, IL 61335

Owner: Leslie Troyan, at above address. **Founded:** 1985. **Key Personnel:** Jackie Smith, General Mgr.; Pam Grasick, Secretary; Leslie Troyan, President. **Cities Served:** Cedar Point, Kickapoo/Edwards, Malden, McNabb, IL: subscribing households 425; 12 channels.

MELROSE PARK, pop. 20,735.

Cook Co. (NE). 12 m NW of Chicago. Manufactures plastic, cosmetic type products, screw machine, steel and rubber products, tractors, T.V. picture tubes, railroad supplies, paint, hydraulic presses, tools, dies, cement blocks.

Maywood Star-Sentinel - See Maywood

9338 Melrose Park Herald
Pioneer Press Newspapers
1148 Westgate Ave. Phone: (708)383-3200
Oak Park, IL 60301 Fax: (708)383-3678

Community newspaper (tabloid). **Founded:** 1970. **Freq:** Weekly (Wed.). **Print Method:** Offset. **Cols./Page:** 5. **Col. Width:** 10 inches. **Col. Depth:** 14 inches. **Key Personnel:** Paul Sassone, Managing Editor; Kevin Beese, Editor. **Subscription Rates:** $13.95 individuals; $15.95 out of county. **Remarks:** Advertising accepted; rates available upon request. **URL:** http://www.pioneerlocal.com.
Circ: Wed. ★2,155

9339 Northlake Star-Sentinel
Shannon Publications, Inc.
1440 W. North Ave., Ste. 210
Melrose Park, IL 60160

Community newspaper. **Founded:** 1961. **Freq:** Weekly (Wed.). **Print Method:** Offset. **Trim Size:** 11 x 14. **Cols./Page:** 6. **Col. Width:** 20 nonpareils. **Col. Depth:** 170 agate lines. **Key Personnel:** David Roberts, Publisher; David Jones, Advertising Mgr. **Subscription Rates:** $12 individuals. **Remarks:** Accepts advertising.
Ad Rates: GLR: $.45 BW: $475 4C: $775 SAU: $4.75
Circ: Paid ‡1,080 Free ‡1,119

9340 Proviso Star-Sentinel
Shannon Publications, Inc.
1440 W. North Ave., Ste. 210
Melrose Park, IL 60160

Community newspaper. **Founded:** 1924. **Freq:** Weekly (Wed.). **Print Method:** Offset. **Trim Size:** 11 x 14. **Cols./Page:** 6. **Col. Width:** 20 nonpareils. **Col. Depth:** 170 agate lines. **Key Personnel:** David Roberts, Publisher; David Jones, Advertising Mgr. **Subscription Rates:** $12 individuals. **Remarks:** Accepts advertising.
Ad Rates: GLR: $.45 BW: $475 4C: $775 SAU: $4.75
Circ: Paid ‡8,749 Free ‡9,537

MELVIN

9341 Ford County Press
115 W. Main Phone: (217)388-7721
PO Box 195 Fax: (217)388-2864
Melvin, IL 60952
Community newspaper. **Founded:** 1908. **Freq:** Weekly. **Print Method:** Offset. **Trim Size:** 14 1/2 x 22. **Cols./Page:** 6. **Col. Width:** 13 picas. **Col. Depth:** 21 inches. **Key Personnel:** Fred Thackeray, Editor and Publisher. **Subscription Rates:** $16; $17 out of state. **Remarks:** Accepts advertising.
Ad Rates: BW: $175 PCI: $2.25
Circ: Paid 983 Free 29

MENARD, pop. 9,685.

Randolph Co. (SW). 65 m SE of St. Louis, Mo. Diversified farming.

9342 The Menard Times
Menard Times Publishing
Box 711
Menard, IL 62259

Newspaper with prison-related news and features. **Founded:** 1934. **Freq:** Monthly. **Print Method:** Offset. **Trim Size:** 11 x 15. **Cols./Page:** 4. **Col. Width:** 14 picas. **Col. Depth:** 82 picas. **Key Personnel:** Leon F. Washington, Editor; Dick Crain, Graphics Arts Instructor. **USPS:** 339-000. **Subscription Rates:** $3 individuals. **Remarks:** Advertising not accepted.
Circ: Paid ‡850 Non-paid ‡4,000

MENDON, pop. 883.

Adams Co. (NC). 11 m NNE of Quincy. Agriculture.

9343 Mendon Dispatch-Times
Elliott Publishing, Inc.
202 E. State Phone: (217)593-6515
Camp Point, IL 62320 Fax: (217)593-7720

Local newspaper. **Founded:** 1869. **Freq:** Weekly. **Print Method:** Offset. **Trim Size:** 17 1/2 x 22 1/2. **Cols./Page:** 5. **Col. Width:** 2 inches. **Col. Depth:** 16 inches. **Key Personnel:** Marcia Elliott, Editor; James Elliott, Publisher/Production Mgr. **Subscription Rates:** $12 individuals; $15 out of state. **Remarks:** Accepts advertising.
Ad Rates: GLR: $2.75 BW: $378 SAU: $4
Circ: 1,000

MENDOTA, pop. 7,134.

La Salle Co. (N). 16 m N of La Salle. Manufactures woodworking machinery, farm implements, feed, concrete and building products, cranes, furnaces. Vegetable cannery. Grain, stock farms. Corn, hogs, cattle.

9344 Mendota Reporter
News Media Corp.
703 Illinois Ave. Phone: (815)539-9396
PO Box 300 Fax: (815)539-7862
Mendota, IL 61342
Publication E-mail: mendotareporter@softfarm.com

Local newspaper. **Founded:** 1878. **Freq:** Weekly (Wed.). **Print Method:** Offset. **Trim Size:** 13 3/4 x 22 1/2. **Cols./Page:** 6. **Col. Width:** 12 1/2 picas. **Col. Depth:** 301 agate lines. **Key Personnel:** Kip Cheek, Editor; Maria Elston, General Mgr. **USPS:** 339-100. **Subscription Rates:** $29.50 individuals. **URL:** http://www.softfarm.com/business/menrep.
Ad Rates: GLR: $.34 BW: $1077.15 4C: $1327.15 SAU: $8.55 PCI: $5.70
Circ: Paid ‡4,400 Free ‡8,000

9345 Mendota Shopping Guide
504 9th St. Phone: (815)539-7476
Mendota, IL 61342-1794 Fax: (815)539-7477
Publisher E-mail: msg1@tsf.net

Shopper. **Founded:** 1970. **Freq:** Weekly (Wed.). **Print Method:** Offset. **Cols./Page:** 6. **Col. Width:** 21 nonpareils. **Col. Depth:** 224 agate lines. **Key Personnel:** Thomas G. Merkel, Editor; Forrest G. Merkel, Publisher. **Subscription Rates:** $27.50 individuals. **Remarks:** Accepts advertising.
Ad Rates: GLR: $0.46 BW: $432 PCI: $6.44
Circ: Free ‡11,500

9346 WGLC-FM - 100.1
4162 3rd Rd. Phone: (815)539-6751
PO Box 88 Fax: (815)539-5956
Mendota, IL 61342
Free: (800)786-6751
E-mail: wglc@softfarm.com

Format: Country. **Simulcasts:** WGLC, WALS. **Networks:** ABC; Jones Satellite. **Owner:** Cole Studstill, at above address. **Founded:** 1965. **Operating Hours:** Continuous. **Key Personnel:** Cole Studstill, Manager; Judy Miller, Sales Mgr.; Chris Tornow, Program Dir., phone (815)224-2480, fax (815)224-2066. **Wattage:** 6000. **Ad Rates:** Advertising accepted; rates available upon request. WGLC-AM.

METAMORA, pop. 2,482.

Woodford Co. (NC). 18 m NE of Peoria. Furniture factory. Machine shop. Agriculture.

9347 Herald
214 E. Partridge Phone: (309)367-2335
Box 229 Fax: (309)367-4277
Metamora, IL 61548
Newspaper. **Founded:** 1862. **Freq:** Weekly (Thurs.). **Print Method:** Offset. **Cols./Page:** 4. **Col. Width:** 27 nonpareils. **Col. Depth:** 203 agate lines. **Key Personnel:** Scott Hubbell, Publisher. **Subscription Rates:** $11 individuals. **Remarks:** Accepts advertising.
Ad Rates: PCI: $21
Circ: 2,300

METROPOLIS†, pop. 7,171.

Massac Co. (S). On Ohio River, 12 m NW of Paducah, Ky. Chemicals, coat hangers, gloves, railroad ties, hardwood lumber, pearl buttons, implement woodwork manufactured. Timber. Diversified farming. Corn, hay, soybeans. Cattle, hogs.

9348 Metropolis Planet
Metropolis Media, Inc.
111 E. 5th St. Phone: (618)524-2141
Box 820 Fax: (618)524-4727
Metropolis, IL 62960-0820
Publication E-mail: planet@midwest.net

Local newspaper. **Founded:** 1865. **Freq:** Weekly (Wed.). **Print Method:** Offset. **Cols./Page:** 6. **Col. Width:** 24 nonpareils. **Col. Depth:** 294 agate lines. **Key Personnel:** Cly de Wills, Editor. **USPS:** 776-360. **Subscription Rates:** $23 individuals; $32 out of area. **Remarks:** Accepts advertising.
Ad Rates: GLR: $4.65 BW: $746 SAU: $6.50 PCI: $6.50
Circ: Paid 5,256 Free 106

9349 WIBH-AM - 1440
6120 Waldochurch Rd. Phone: (618)564-2171
Metropolis, IL 62960 Fax: (618)564-3202

Format: Country. **Networks:** ABC. **Owner:** Benjamin Stratemeyer, at above address. **Founded:** 1957. **Formerly:**

WRAJ-AM. **Operating Hours:** Continuous; 7.5% network, 92.5% local. **Key Personnel:** Benjamin Stratemeyer, President/Gen. Manager; Tim Meehan, News/Sports Dir. **Wattage:** 500. **Ad Rates:** $5.50 for 30 seconds; $8.25 for 60 seconds. WRAJ-FM.

9350 WKIB-FM - 96.5
6120 Waldochurch Rd. Phone: (618)564-2171
Metropolis, IL 62960 Fax: (618)564-3202

Format: Adult Contemporary. **Networks:** ABC. **Owner:** Benjamin Stratemeyer, at above address. **Founded:** 1957. **Formerly:** WRAJ-FM. **Operating Hours:** Continuous. **Key Personnel:** Benjamin Stratemeyer, President/General Manager; Tim Meehan, News/Sports Dir. **Wattage:** 50,000. **Ad Rates:** $10 for 30 seconds; $15 for 60 seconds. WRAJ-FM.

9351 WMOK-AM - 920
PO Box 720 Phone: (618)524-9209
Metropolis, IL 62960-0720 Fax: (618)524-3133

Format: Country. **Networks:** CBS. **Founded:** 1951. **Operating Hours:** Continuous; 8% network; 92% local. **ADI:** Paducah,KY-Cape Girardeau,MO-Marion,IL. **Key Personnel:** John Lowry, News Dir.; Steve Bunyard, Program Dir.; Michele Kidd, Station Mgr.; Gary Kidd, General Mgr. **Local Programs:** *Coffee Break* 8:05-8:30 a.m. Monday-Friday, Jim Young. **Wattage:** 1000. **Ad Rates:** Advertising accepted; rates available upon request.

MIDLOTHIAN, pop. 14,274.

Cook Co. (NE). 5 m S of Blue Island. Residential.

9352 Alsip Express
Southwest Messenger Press, Inc.
3840 W. 147th St. Phone: (708)388-2425
PO Box 548 Fax: (708)385-7811
Midlothian, IL 60445
Community newspaper. **Founded:** 1945. **Freq:** Weekly (Thurs.). **Print Method:** Offset. **Cols./Page:** 6. **Col. Width:** 1 3/4 inches. **Col. Depth:** 16 inches. **Key Personnel:** Walter H. Lysen, Publisher; Donald E. Talac, Advertising Mgr. **Subscription Rates:** $15 individuals; $18 out of area; $26 out of state.
Ad Rates: GLR: $.38 **Circ:** Paid ‡5,000
BW: $510.72 Free ‡1,000
4C: $300
SAU: $11.08

9353 Beverly News
Southwest Messenger Press, Inc.
3840 W. 147th St. Phone: (708)388-2425
PO Box 548 Fax: (708)385-7811
Midlothian, IL 60445
Newspaper. **Founded:** 1943. **Freq:** Weekly (Thurs.). **Print Method:** Offset. **Cols./Page:** 6. **Col. Width:** 1 3/4 inches. **Col. Depth:** 16 inches. **Key Personnel:** Walter H. Lysen, Publisher; Donald E. Talac, Advertising Mgr.
Ad Rates: GLR: $.38 **Circ:** Paid ‡4,080
BW: $510.72 Free ‡100
4C: $300
SAU: $11.08

9354 Bridgeview Independent
Southwest Messenger Press, Inc.
3840 W. 147th St. Phone: (708)388-2425
PO Box 548 Fax: (708)385-7811
Midlothian, IL 60445
Newspaper. **Founded:** 1962. **Freq:** Weekly (Wed.). **Print Method:** Offset. **Cols./Page:** 6. **Col. Width:** 1 3/4 inches. **Col. Depth:** 16 inches. **Key Personnel:** Tom Gavin III, Editor/Administration; Walter H. Lysen, Publisher. **Subscription Rates:** $45 individuals.
Ad Rates: GLR: $.38 **Circ:** Paid ‡2,600
BW: $510.72 Free ‡800
4C: $300
SAU: $11.08

9355 Burbank Stickney Independent
Southwest Messenger Press, Inc.
3840 W. 147th St. Phone: (708)388-2425
PO Box 548 Fax: (708)385-7811
Midlothian, IL 60445
Community newspaper. **Founded:** 1957. **Freq:** Weekly (Thurs.). **Print Method:** Offset. **Cols./Page:** 6. **Col. Width:** 1 3/4 inches. **Col. Depth:** 16 inches. **Key Personnel:** Walter H. Lysen, Editor and Publisher; Donald E. Talac, Advertising Mgr. **Subscription Rates:** $15 individuals; $18 out of area; $24 out of state.
Ad Rates: GLR: $.66 **Circ:** Paid ‡5,700
BW: $887.04 Free ‡200
4C: $300
SAU: $11.08
PCI: $9.24

9356 Chicago Ridge Citizen
Southwest Messenger Press, Inc.
3840 W. 147th St. Phone: (708)388-2425
PO Box 548 Fax: (708)385-7811
Midlothian, IL 60445
Community newspaper. **Founded:** 1962. **Freq:** Weekly (Thurs.). **Print Method:** Offset. **Cols./Page:** 6. **Col. Width:** 1 3/4 inches. **Col. Depth:** 16 inches. **Key Personnel:** Walter H. Lysen, Publisher; Thomas E. Gavin, Advertising Mgr. **Subscription Rates:** $15 individuals; $18 out of area; $28 out of state.
Ad Rates: GLR: $.38 **Circ:** Paid ‡3,600
BW: $510.72 Free ‡300
4C: $300
SAU: $11.08

9357 Evergreen Park Courier
Southwest Messenger Press, Inc.
3840 W. 147th St. Phone: (708)388-2425
PO Box 548 Fax: (708)385-7811
Midlothian, IL 60445
Community newspaper. **Founded:** 1930. **Freq:** Weekly (Thurs.). **Print Method:** Offset. **Cols./Page:** 6. **Col. Width:** 20 nonpareils. **Col. Depth:** 224 agate lines. **Key Personnel:** Walter H. Lysen, Publisher; Donald E. Talac, Advertising Mgr. **Subscription Rates:** $15 individuals; $18 out of area; $24 out of state.
Ad Rates: GLR: $.38 **Circ:** Paid ‡4,410
BW: $510.72 Free ‡500
4C: $300
SAU: $11.08

9358 Hickory Hills Citizen
Southwest Messenger Press, Inc.
3840 W. 147th St. Phone: (708)388-2425
PO Box 548 Fax: (708)385-7811
Midlothian, IL 60445
Community newspaper. **Founded:** 1958. **Freq:** Weekly (Thurs.). **Print Method:** Offset. **Cols./Page:** 6. **Col. Width:** 20 nonpareils. **Col. Depth:** 224 agate lines. **Key Personnel:** Walter H. Lysen, Publisher; Thomas E. Gavin, Advertising Mgr. **Subscription Rates:** $15 individuals; $18 out of area; $24 out of state.
Ad Rates: GLR: $.38 **Circ:** Paid ‡3,530
BW: $510.72 Free ‡400
4C: $300
SAU: $11.08

9359 Midlothian-Bremen Messenger
Southwest Messenger Press, Inc.
3840 W. 147th St. Phone: (708)388-2425
PO Box 548 Fax: (708)385-7811
Midlothian, IL 60445
Community newspaper. **Founded:** 1929. **Freq:** Weekly (Thurs.). **Print Method:** Offset. **Cols./Page:** 6. **Col. Width:** 20 nonpareils. **Col. Depth:** 224 agate lines. **Key Personnel:** Walter H. Lysen, Publisher. **Subscription Rates:** $13 individuals; $18 out of area; $24 out of state.
Ad Rates: GLR: $.38 **Circ:** Paid ‡10,200
BW: $510.72 Free ‡500
4C: $300
SAU: $11.08
PCI: $5.32

9360 Mount Greenwood Express
Southwest Messenger Press, Inc.
3840 W. 147th St. Phone: (708)388-2425
PO Box 548 Fax: (708)385-7811
Midlothian, IL 60445
Community newspaper. **Founded:** 1942. **Freq:** Weekly (Thurs.). **Print Method:** Offset. **Cols./Page:** 6. **Col. Width:** 18 nonpareils. **Col. Depth:** 224 agate lines. **Key Personnel:** Walter H. Lysen, Publisher. **Subscription Rates:** $15 individuals; $18 out of area; $24 out of state.
Ad Rates: GLR: $.38 **Circ:** Paid ‡7,471
BW: $510.72 Free ‡300
4C: $300
SAU: $11.08

9361 Oak Lawn Independent
Southwest Messenger Press, Inc.
3840 W. 147th St. Phone: (708)388-2425
PO Box 548 Fax: (708)385-7811
Midlothian, IL 60445
Community newspaper. **Founded:** 1929. **Freq:** Weekly (Thurs.). **Print Method:** Offset. **Cols./Page:** 6. **Col. Width:** 20 nonpareils. **Col. Depth:** 224 agate lines. **Key Personnel:** Walter H. Lysen, Publisher. **Subscription Rates:** $15; $24 out of state.
Ad Rates: GLR: $.38 **Circ:** Paid ‡12,000
BW: $510.72 Free ‡1,800
4C: $300
SAU: $11.08

9362 Orland Township Messenger
Southwest Messenger Press, Inc.
3840 W. 147th St. Phone: (708)388-2425
PO Box 548 Fax: (708)385-7811
Midlothian, IL 60445
Community newspaper. **Founded:** 1977. **Freq:** Weekly (Thurs.). **Print Method:** Offset. **Cols./Page:** 6. **Col. Width:** 18 nonpareils. **Col. Depth:** 224 agate lines. **Key Personnel:** Linnea Gavin, Editor; Walter H. Lysen, Publisher; Tom Gavin III, Advertising Mgr. **Subscription Rates:** $45 individuals.
Ad Rates: GLR: $.38 **Circ:** Paid ‡3,788
BW: $510.72 Free ‡200
4C: $300
SAU: $11.08
PCI: $5.32

9363 Palos Citizen
Southwest Messenger Press, Inc.
3840 W. 147th St. Phone: (708)388-2425
PO Box 548 Fax: (708)385-7811
Midlothian, IL 60445
Community newspaper. **Founded:** 1958. **Freq:** Weekly (Thurs.). **Print Method:** Offset. **Trim Size:** 11 1/2 x 17. **Cols./Page:** 6. **Col. Width:** 1 3/4 inches. **Col. Depth:** 16 inches. **Key Personnel:** Walter H. Lysen, Publisher; Tom Gavin, Advertising Mgr. **Subscription Rates:** $15 individuals; $18 out of area; $24 out of state.
Ad Rates: GLR: $.38 **Circ:** Paid ‡4,500
BW: $599 Free ‡500
4C: $300
SAU: $11.80
PCI: $5.32

9364 Scottsdale Ashburn Independent
Southwest Messenger Press, Inc.
3840 W. 147th St. Phone: (708)388-2425
PO Box 548 Fax: (708)385-7811
Midlothian, IL 60445
Community newspaper. **Founded:** 1955. **Freq:** Weekly (Thurs.). **Print Method:** Offset. **Cols./Page:** 6. **Col. Width:** 20 nonpareils. **Col. Depth:** 224 agate lines. **Key Personnel:** Walter H. Lysen, Publisher. **Subscription Rates:** $45.
Ad Rates: GLR: $.38 **Circ:** Free ‡5,800
BW: $510.72
4C: $300
SAU: $11.08

9365 Worth Citizen
Southwest Messenger Press, Inc.
3840 W. 147th St. Phone: (708)388-2425
PO Box 548 Fax: (708)385-7811
Midlothian, IL 60445
Community newspaper. **Founded:** 1930. **Freq:** Weekly (Thurs.). **Print Method:** Offset. **Cols./Page:** 6. **Col. Width:** 20 nonpareils. **Col. Depth:** 224 agate lines. **Key Personnel:** Linnea M. Gavin, Editor; Walter H. Lysen, Publisher; Thomas E. Gavin, Advertising Mgr. **Subscription Rates:** $15 individuals; $18 out of area; $24 out of state. **Remarks:** Accepts advertising.
Ad Rates: GLR: $.66 **Circ:** Paid ‡2,600
BW: $887.04 Free ‡300
4C: $300
SAU: $11.08

MILFORD, pop. 1,716.

Iroquois Co. (NE). 40 m N of Danville. Manufactures nuts, bolts, screws, electronic components and motors. Canning factory. Diversified farming. Hybrid seed corn, popcorn and bird seeds.

9366 Milford Herald-News
18 S. Axtel Ave. Phone: (815)889-4321
PO Box 200 Fax: (815)889-4321
Milford, IL 60953-0200
Community newspaper with Republican orientation. **Founded:** 1876. **Freq:** Weekly (Wed.). **Print Method:** Offset. **Cols./Page:** 7. **Col. Width:** 1 3/4 nonpareils. **Col. Depth:** 20 agate lines. **Key Personnel:** John Hallock, Sr., Publisher. **Subscription Rates:** $22 individuals; $27 out of county. **Remarks:** Accepts advertising.
Ad Rates: GLR: $2.50 **Circ:** ‡1,050
BW: $350
PCI: $2.50

MILLSTADT, pop. 2,736.

St. Clair Co. (SW). 5 m W of Columbia. Residential.

9367 Kansas City Commerce
Printing & Publishing, Inc.
109 W. Washington St. Phone: (618)476-7770
Millstadt, IL 62260 Fax: (618)476-1616
Free: (800)451-0914
Publication E-mail: bizmag@stlmo.com

Trade magazine covering manufacturing news in Western Missouri and Eastern Kansas. **Founded:** Jan. 1990. **Freq:**

Monthly. **Print Method:** Offset. **Trim Size:** 8 1/4 x 10 7/8. **Cols./Page:** 3. **Col. Width:** 2 1/4 inches. **Col. Depth:** 10 inches. **Key Personnel:** Paul Adrignola, Publisher; Paul Stoecklein, Editor; Janine Tate, Sales Mgr. **ISSN:** 1056-6015. **Subscription Rates:** $20 individuals; Free to qualified subscribers. **Remarks:** Accepts advertising.
Ad Rates: BW: $930 **Circ:** Controlled ⊕**8,170**
4C: $1,330

9368 Meat Business Magazine
Printing & Publishing, Inc.
109 W. Washington St. Phone: (618)476-7770
Millstadt, IL 62260 Fax: (618)476-1616
Free: (800)451-0914
Publication E-mail: bizmag@mo.net

Monthly publication for small to medium meat processors. **Founded:** 1939. **Freq:** Monthly. **Print Method:** Offset. **Trim Size:** 8 1/2 x 11. **Cols./Page:** 3. **Col. Width:** 26 nonpareils. **Col. Depth:** 140 agate lines. **Key Personnel:** Paul B. Stoecklein, Editor. **ISSN:** 1049-5908. **Subscription Rates:** $20. **Remarks:** Accepts advertising. **Formerly:** Meat Plant Magazine.
Ad Rates: BW: $878 **Circ:** Non-paid ‡6,300
4C: $1,278

MINIER, pop. 1,261.

Tazewell Co. (NC). 21 m SE Of Peoria. Residential.

9369 Olympia Review
Rickard Publishing Co.
PO Box 710 Phone: (309)392-2414
Minier, IL 61759 Fax: (309)392-2169

Local newspaper. **Founded:** 1969. **Freq:** Weekly (Tues.). **Print Method:** Offset. **Trim Size:** 13 3/4 x 22 3/4. **Cols./Page:** 6. **Col. Width:** 9 1/2 picas. **Col. Depth:** 21 inches. **Key Personnel:** Victor J. Rickard, Editor and Publisher. **Subscription Rates:** Free; $22 out of area. **Remarks:** Accepts advertising.
Ad Rates: BW: $731 **Circ:** Free ‡6,900
SAU: $7.80
PCI: $6

MINONK, pop. 2,039.

Woodford Co. (NC). 30 m N of Bloomington. Metal fabricating factory, grain elevator, dairy products, stock, poultry, grain farms.

9370 Minonk News-Dispatch
Illinois Valley Press
224 E. 5th St. Phone: (309)432-2505
PO Box 68 Fax: (309)432-2506
Minonk, IL 61760
Publisher E-mail: journal@farmwagon.com

Community newspaper. **Founded:** 1874. **Freq:** Weekly (Thurs.). **Print Method:** Offset. **Cols./Page:** 6. **Col. Width:** 26 nonpareils. **Col. Depth:** 301 agate lines. **Key Personnel:** Mark Barra, General Mgr.; Jenn L. Poe, Editor. **USPS:** 352-420. **Subscription Rates:** $27 individuals; $30 out of area; $33 out of state. **Remarks:** Accepts advertising.
Ad Rates: BW: $741.75 **Circ:** ‡672
4C: $876.75
PCI: $5.75

MOKENA

9371 Frankfort/Mokena Star
Star Newspapers
6901 W 159th St. Phone: (708)802-8800
Tinley Park, IL 60477 Fax: (708)802-8899

Newspaper group serving 54 communities in Chicago's southern suburbs. **Founded:** 1890. **Freq:** Semiweekly (Thurs. and Sun.). **Print Method:** Offset. **Trim Size:** 13 3/4 x 23. **Cols./Page:** 6. **Col. Width:** 2 inches. **Col. Depth:** 21 1/2 inches. **Key Personnel:** Lester Sons, Editor; Norman Rosinski, Publisher; Jim Meidell, Advertising Mgr.; Jay Frederickson. **Subscription Rates:** $25.20.
Ad Rates: BW: $3,977 **Circ:** (Not Reported)
4C: $4,677
SAU: $34.64

MOLINE, pop. 45,709.

Rock Island Co. (NW). On Mississippi River, opposite Davenport, Iowa., 168 m SW of Chicago. Blackhawk Community College. Manufactures agricultural implements, traffic signals, heating and ventilating equipment, paint, tools and dies, electric welding apparatus, candy; fabricated steel; forgings; elevators and escalators; iron foundry.

9372 The Chieftain
Black Hawk College
6600 34th Ave. Phone: (309)796-1311
Moline, IL 61265 Fax: (309)792-5976
Free: (800)334-1311

Collegiate newspaper. **Founded:** 1970. **Freq:** Weekly. **Print Method:** Offset. **Trim Size:** 13 1/2 x 21. **Cols./Page:** 5. **Col. Width:** 24 nonpareils. **Col. Depth:** 224 agate lines. **Key Personnel:** Carrie L. Browning, Contact. **Remarks:** Accepts advertising.
Ad Rates: PCI: $5 **Circ:** Free ‡2,000

9373 The Dispatch and the Rock Island Argus
Moline Dispatch Publishing Co.
1720 5th Ave. Phone: (309)764-4344
Moline, IL 61265 Fax: (309)786-7639
Publication E-mail: sysop@qconline.com; press@qconline.com

Newspaper with a Republican orientation. **Founded:** 1868. **Freq:** Daily and Sat. (morn.). **Print Method:** Offset. **Cols./Page:** 6. **Col. Width:** 25 nonpareils. **Col. Depth:** 21 1/2 inches. **Key Personnel:** Gerald Taylor, Editor and Publisher; Nick Norman, Marketing Dir. **Subscription Rates:** $135 individuals. **Remarks:** Accepts advertising. **URL:** http://www.qconline.com; www.qconline.com.
Ad Rates: BW: $4,033.83 **Circ:** Mon.-Sat. ‡41,203
4C: $4,378,83 Sun. 34,144
SAU: $31.27

9374 The Gold Book
Moline Dispatch Publishing Co.
1720 5th Ave. Phone: (309)764-4344
Moline, IL 61265 Fax: (309)786-7639

Magazine covering the Quad-cities. **Founded:** 1985. **Freq:** Monthly. **Print Method:** Offset. **Trim Size:** 6 x 9. **Cols./Page:** 4. **Key Personnel:** Jan Heintz, Editor, phone (309)757-4948. **Subscription Rates:** $12. **Remarks:** Advertising accepted; rates available upon request. **URL:** http://www.qconline.com.
Circ: (Not Reported)

9375 Rental Management
American Rental Association
1900 19th St. Phone: (309)764-2475
Moline, IL 61265 Fax: (309)764-1533
Free: (800)334-2177
Publisher E-mail: ara@ararental.org

Magazine for business owners who rent equipment to consumers, industries, institutions and commercial firms. **Subtitle:** Official Publication of the American Rental Association. **Founded:** 1970. **Freq:** Monthly. **Print Method:** Web offset. **Trim Size:** 8 1/4 x 10 7/8. **Cols./Page:** 3. **Col. Width:** 2 1/4 inches. **Col. Depth:** 10 inches. **Key Personnel:** Brian Alm, Editor, brian.alm@ararental.org; Frederick Anderson, Publisher, fred.anderson@ararental.org; Robert Kruhm, Advertising Mgr., phone (800)578-3216, fax (301)854-2464, rhkruhm@mindspring.com; Tammy Dawson, Associate Publisher, tammy.dawson@ararental.org; Jane Swanson, Assoc. Editor, jane.swanson@ararental.org; Erin Jorgensen, Asst. Editor, erin.jorgensen@ararental.org. **ISSN:** 0098-8529. **Subscription Rates:** $24 individuals. **Remarks:** Accepts advertising. **URL:** http://www.ararental.org/cmhome.html; http://www.ararental.org/rm/rmhome.html.
Ad Rates: BW: $1,965 **Circ:** Paid 5,414
4C: $3,010 Non-paid 10,368

9376 Cox Cable Quad Cities
3900 26th Ave. Phone: (309)797-2580
Moline, IL 61265 Fax: (309)797-2414

Founded: 1972. **Cities Served:** subscribing households 60,162.

9377 WQAD-TV - 8
3003 Park 16th St. Phone: (309)764-8888
Moline, IL 61265 Fax: (309)764-5763

Format: Commercial TV. **Networks:** ABC. **Founded:** 1963. **Operating Hours:** Continuous Daily; 60% network, 40% local. **ADI:** Davenport,IA-Rock Island, Moline,IL. **Key Personnel:** Marion Meginnis, General Mgr.; Trent Poindexter, General Sales Mgr.; Griff Potter, News Dir.; Lori Evans, Creative Service/Promotion Mgr.; Kristi Peterson, Director. **Ad Rates:** $20-2,000 per unit. **URL:** http://www.wqad.com.

9378 WQPT-TV - 24
Black Hawk College Phone: (309)796-2424
6600 34th Ave. Fax: (309)796-2484
Moline, IL 61265
E-mail: wqpt@bhc1.bhc.edu

Format: Public TV. **Networks:** Public Broadcasting Service (PBS). **Owner:** Black Hawk College, at above address, Fax: (309)792-5976. **Founded:** 1983. **Operating Hours:** 7:15 a.m.-midnight. **ADI:** Davenport,IA-Rock Island, Moline,IL. **Key Personnel:** Rick Best, General Mgr.; Steve Ellis, Chief Engineer; Jerry Myers, Program Mgr.; Susan McPeters, Public Affairs Dir.; Norma Adams, Business Mgr. **Local Programs:** *Perspective*; *Quad Cities Life and Times.* **Wattage:** 30,000.

MOMENCE, pop. 3,297.

Kankakee Co. (E). 14 m E of Kankakee. Stone quarries. Manufactures textiles, health and dog foods, venetian blinds, steel products, pharmaceuticals, truck bodies. Diversified farming. Milk condensery.

9379 Momence Progress-Reporter
PO Box 289 Phone: (815)472-2000
110 W. River St. Fax: (815)472-3877
Momence, IL 60954
Newspaper with a Republican orientation. **Founded:** 1901. **Freq:** Weekly (Wed.). **Print Method:** Offset. **Cols./Page:** 5. **Col. Width:** 22 nonpareils. **Col. Depth:** 224 agate lines. **Key Personnel:** M. Sue Lincoln, Editor; H. Gene Lincoln, Publisher. **Subscription Rates:** $11 individuals; $12 out of area; $15 out of state. **Remarks:** Accepts advertising.
Ad Rates: GLR: $.115 **Circ:** ‡2,500
BW: $168
SAU: $2.60
PCI: $2.10

MONEE

9380 Monee Monitor
Russell Publications
PO Box 429 Phone: (708)258-3473
Peotone, IL 60468 Fax: (708)258-6295

Community newspaper. **Freq:** Weekly (Thurs.). **Cols./Page:** 6. **Col. Width:** 2 inches. **Col. Depth:** 16 inches. **Key Personnel:** Gilbert L. Russell, Editor; Gilbert L. Russell, Publisher. **Subscription Rates:** $16. **Remarks:** Accepts advertising.
Ad Rates: BW: $236 **Circ:** 800
PCI: $2.95

MONMOUTH†, pop. 10,706.

Warren Co. (W). 16 m W of Galesburg. Monmouth College. Warren Achievement School and Center for Handicapped. Manufactures pottery, farm implements, boats, toys, feed. Diversified farming. Beef cattle, hogs, corn, soybeans.

9381 The Daily American
American Publishing Co.
PO Box 650 Phone: (309)734-3176
Monmouth, IL 61462
Community newspaper. **Founded:** 1916. **Freq:** Mon.-Sat. (eve.). **Print Method:** Offset. **Cols./Page:** 6. **Col. Width:** 26 nonpareils. **Col. Depth:** 301 agate lines. **Key Personnel:** Richard Charo, General Mgr.; Greg Hoskins, Publisher; Diann Walthes, Advertising Mgr. **Subscription Rates:** $80.60 individuals. **Remarks:** Accepts advertising.
Ad Rates: BW: $637.26 **Circ:** Combined 3,297
4C: $827.26
SAU: $5.34

9382 Daily Journal
American Publishing Co.
PO Box 650 Phone: (309)734-3176
Monmouth, IL 61462
General newspaper. **Founded:** 1911. **Freq:** Mon.-Sat. (eve.). **Print Method:** Offset. **Cols./Page:** 6. **Col. Width:** 24 nonpareils. **Col. Depth:** 301 agate lines. **Key Personnel:** Erin Brothers, Editor; Mike Brothers, Publisher. **Subscription Rates:** $57.50 individuals. **Remarks:** Accepts advertising.
Ad Rates: GLR: $3.80 **Circ:** Combined 1,159

9383 Daily Review Atlas
American Publishing
400 S. Main St. Phone: (309)734-3176
Monmouth, IL 61462 Fax: (309)734-7649

Local newspaper. **Founded:** 1846. **Freq:** Mon.-Sat. (eve.). **Print Method:** Offset. **Cols./Page:** 9. **Col. Width:** 19 nonpareils. **Col. Depth:** 301 agate lines. **Key Personnel:** Beverlee Kritz, Editor; Scott Champion, Publisher. **Remarks:** Accepts advertising.
Ad Rates: SAU: $7.95 **Circ:** ‡4,000
PCI: $5.04

9384 Murphysboro American
American Publishing Co.
PO Box 650 Phone: (309)734-3176
Monmouth, IL 61462
Community newspaper. **Founded:** 1982. **Freq:** Semiweekly (Mon. and Thurs.). **Trim Size:** 6 x 12. **Cols./Page:** 6. **Col. Width:** 12 picas. **Col. Depth:** 21 1/2 inches. **Key Personnel:** Pat Wiseman, Editor; Cleon Birkemyer, Publisher. **Subscription Rates:** $25; $30 out of county; $.35 single issue.
Circ: Combined 8,770

9385 The Oracle
Monmouth College
College Box 941 Phone: (309)457-3456
Monmouth, IL 61462
Collegiate newspaper. **Founded:** 1867. **Freq:** Weekly (Mon.). **Print Method:** Offset. **Trim Size:** 9.75 x 16. **Cols./Page:** 5. **Col. Width:** 11 picas. **Col. Depth:** 180 agate lines. **Key Personnel:** Thomas M. Withenbury, Dir., Student Publications. **Subscription Rates:** Free to students; $21 others. **Remarks:** Accepts advertising. **Formerly:** The Monmouth Oracle.
Ad Rates: GLR: $.393 **Circ:** Free 1,000
BW: $396
4C: $516
PCI: $6

9386 Pennysaver
American Publishing
400 S. Main St. Phone: (309)734-3176
Monmouth, IL 61462 Fax: (309)734-7649

Shopper. **Founded:** 1973. **Freq:** Weekly (Wed.). **Print Method:** Offset. **Cols./Page:** 6. **Col. Width:** 19 nonpareils. **Col. Depth:** 224 agate lines. **Key Personnel:** Scott Champion, Publisher. **Subscription Rates:** $15 newspaper. **Remarks:** Accepts advertising.
Ad Rates: PCI: $5.21 **Circ:** Free ‡14,019

9387 WMCR-CAFM - 88.9
Monmouth College Phone: (309)457-2107
Monmouth, IL 61462 Fax: (309)734-7500
E-mail: wmCr@lycosmail.com

Format: Alternative/New Music/Progressive. **Founded:** 1961. **Formerly:** WFS (1973); WMCR-AM. **Operating Hours:** 8am - 1am. **Key Personnel:** Cynthia Elder, Manager, phone (309)457-2107, fax (309)734-7500, wmcr@lycosmail.com; Ann Maksymowicz, Music Dir., phone (309)457-2107, fax (309)734-7500, wmcr@lycosmail.com. **Ad Rates:** Noncommercial.

9388 WMOI-FM - 97.7
55 Public Sq. Phone: (309)734-9452
PO Box 885 Fax: (309)734-3276
Monmouth, IL 61462

Format: Adult Contemporary; News; Agricultural; Sports. **Networks:** AP; CBS. **Owner:** KCD Enterprises, Inc., at above address. **Founded:** 1977. **Formerly:** WDRL-FM (1981). **Operating Hours:** Continuous Daily; 5% network, 95% local. **Key Personnel:** David T. Madison, CEO/Pres.; Aron Winskiletti, News Dir.; Kris Kinney, Admin. Dir.; Tom Peterson, Farm Dir.; Dan Nolan, Operations Dir. **Wattage:** 6000. **Ad Rates:** $11.15-16.50 for 30 seconds; $14.45-20.75 for 60 seconds.

9389 WRAM-AM - 1330
55 Public Sq. Phone: (309)734-9452
PO Box 885 Fax: (309)734-3276
Monmouth, IL 61462

Format: Talk; News; Country; Agricultural; Sports. **Networks:** AP; CBS. **Owner:** WPW Broadcasting, at above address. **Founded:** 1957. **Operating Hours:** 12 hours Daily; 90% local. **Key Personnel:** David Madison, CEO/Pres.; Aron Winski, Chief Engineer; Kris Kinney, Admin. Dir.; Tom Peterson, Farm Dir.; Herm Gerbert, Station Mgr. **Local Programs:** *The Morning Show*, Dan Nolan; *Trading Post*, Dan Nolan. **Wattage:** 1000. **Ad Rates:** $10.15-16.50 for 30 seconds; $12.45-20.75 for 60 seconds.

MONTICELLO†, pop. 4,753.

Piatt Co. (C). 25 m NE of Decatur. Agriculture.

9390 Piatt County Journal-Republican
East Central Communications, Inc.
118 E. Washington Phone: (217)762-2511
PO Box 110 Fax: (217)352-1722
Monticello, IL 61856
Community newspaper. **Founded:** 1856. **Freq:** Weekly. **Print Method:** Offset. **Trim Size:** 14 x 22 1/2. **Cols./Page:** 6. **Col. Width:** 2 1/16 inches. **Col. Depth:** 21 inches. **Key Personnel:** Maggie Schwarzentraub, Editor; Kim Parrish, Advertising; Dennis Kaster, Publisher; Janelle Jackson, Circulation Mgr. **Subscription Rates:** $20.20 individuals; $21.32 out of area. **Remarks:** Accepts advertising.
Ad Rates: GLR: $0.58 **Circ:** Paid 3,675
BW: $847.98
4C: $1,222.78
PCI: $6.73

9391 WCZQ-FM - 105.5
PO Box 105 Phone: (217)762-2588
Monticello, IL 61856 Fax: (217)762-2589
E-mail: wczq@piatt.com

Format: Country. **Founded:** 1972. **Formerly:** WVLJ-FM (1991). **Operating Hours:** Continuous; 100% local. **ADI:** Springfield-Decatur-Champaign, IL. **Key Personnel:** Frederick W. Seibold, Station Mgr. **Local Programs:** *Breakfast Club*, Frederick W. Seibold, Station Mgr. **Wattage:** 3000. **Ad Rates:** $12 for 30 seconds; $18-24 for 60 seconds.

MOOSEHEART, pop. 600.

Kane Co. (NE). 5 m N of Aurora. Residential.

9392 Moose Magazine
Moose International
Mooseheart, IL 60539 Phone: (708)859-2000
Fax: (708)859-6620

News for and about the 1.7 million men and women the Moose Fraternal Organization and its endeavors on behalf of children, seniors and communities. **Founded:** 1910. **Freq:** Bimonthly. **Print Method:** Offset. **Cols./Page:** 3. **Col. Width:** 13.5 picas. **Col. Depth:** 10 inches. **Key Personnel:** Kurt N. Wehrmeister, Managing Editor; Frank A. Sarnecki, Publisher. **ISSN:** 1063-6226. **Subscription Rates:** $2 included in membership dues. **Remarks:** Advertising not accepted.
Circ: Controlled ‡1,250,000

MORRIS†, pop. 8,833.

Grundy Co. (NE). On Illinois River and Lakes to Gulf Waterway, 23 m SW of Joliet. Synthetic natural gas. Manufactures aluminum sheet, rubber products, vending machines, fire bricks, explosives, industrial resins, paper board. Stock farms.

9393 Morris Daily Herald
Shaw Newspapers
1804 N. Division St. Phone: (815)942-3221
Morris, IL 60450-1127 Fax: (815)942-0988

General newspaper. **Subtitle:** Local county newspaper. **Founded:** 1854. **Freq:** Daily (eve.). **Print Method:** Offset. **Trim Size:** 22 3/4 x 27 1/2. **Cols./Page:** 6. **Col. Width:** 2 1/16 inches. **Col. Depth:** 21 1/2 inches. **Key Personnel:** Timothy West, Editor and Publisher; Jon Ringer, Advertising Mgr. **USPS:** 363-560. **Subscription Rates:** $65 individuals; $75 out of area. **Remarks:** Accepts advertising.
Ad Rates: BW: $1,096.50 **Circ:** ‡7,800
4C: $1,246.50
PCI: $9.20

9394 WCFL-FM - 104.7
1802 N. Division St., Ste.403 Phone: (815)942-4400
Morris, IL 60450 Fax: (815)942-4401
Free: (800)520-WCFL
E-mail: wcfl@aol.com

Format: Contemporary Christian. **Founded:** 1994. **Formerly:** WLLZ-FM (1990). **Operating Hours:** Continuous; 3% network, 97% local. **ADI:** Chicago (LaSalle), IL. **Key Personnel:** Jay Greener, Station Mgr. **Wattage:** 50,000.

MORRISON†, pop. 4,605.

Whiteside Co. (NW. 15 m W of Sterling. Automatic control devices, furniture, coils manufactured. Limestone quarries. Grain, dairy, stock farms. Hay.

9395 Whiteside News Sentinel
WNS Publications
100 E. Main St. Phone: (815)772-7244
Morrison, IL 61270 Fax: (815)772-4105
Free: (800)245-4927

Community newspaper. **Founded:** 1857. **Freq:** Weekly (Tues.). **Print Method:** Offset. **Cols./Page:** 8. **Col. Width:** 11 picas. **Col. Depth:** 21 inches. **Key Personnel:** Sarah Thorndike, Editor; Tony Komlanc, Jr., Publisher. **Subscription Rates:** $23 individuals.
Ad Rates: GLR: $7.25 **Circ:** ‡3,000
BW: $1,218
4C: $100
SAU: $7.85
PCI: $6.85

MORRISONVILLE, pop. 1,208.

Christian Co. (C). 38 m SE of Springfield. Manufactures soybean products. Grain, stock farms.

9396 Morrisonville Times
511 Carlin St. Phone: (217)526-3323
PO Box 16 Fax: (217)526-3323
Morrisonville, IL 62546
Community newspaper. **Founded:** 1875. **Freq:** Weekly (Wed.). **Print Method:** Offset. **Cols./Page:** 8. **Col. Width:** 22 nonpareils. **Col. Depth:** 294 agate lines. **Key Personnel:** Julia Lennon, Editor; John A. Lennon, Publisher. **Subscription Rates:** $11 individuals; $12.50 out of county. **Remarks:** Accepts advertising.
Ad Rates: PCI: $1.85 **Circ:** 1,000

MORTON GROVE

9397 Morton Grove Champion Review
Pioneer Press Newspapers
1601 Sherman Ave. Phone: (847)866-6501
Evanston, IL 60201 Fax: (847)866-0965

Community newspaper (tabloid). **Founded:** 1957. **Freq:** Weekly (Thurs.). **Print Method:** Offset. **Cols./Page:** 5. **Col. Width:** 10 inches. **Col. Depth:** 14 inches. **Key Personnel:** Dan Obermaier, Editor; Paul Sassone, Managing Editor. **Subscription Rates:** $11.95 individuals; $12.95 out of county. **Remarks:** Advertising accepted; rates available upon request.
Circ: Thurs. 3,474

9398 Continental Cablevision
8101 N. Austin Ave. Phone: (708)470-0803
Morton Grove, IL 60053 Fax: (708)470-0817

Owner: The Pilot House, Lewis Wharf, Boston, MA 02110, (617)742-9500. **Founded:** 1979. **Key Personnel:** Andy Harris, General Mgr.; Marty Rosenbaum, Operations Mgr.; Kevin Oates, Program Mgr. **Cities Served:** Morton Grove, Northfield, Wilmette, IL: subscribing households 20,000; 60 channels; 3 community access channels.

MOUNDS, pop. 1,669.

Pulaski Co. (S). 8 m NW of Cairo. Diversified farming. Corn, peaches, strawberries.

9399 The Pulaski Enterprise
315 1st St. Phone: (618)745-6267
PO Box 459
Mounds, IL 62964
Community newspaper. **Founded:** 1861. **Freq:** Weekly (Wed.). **Print Method:** Offset. **Trim Size:** 6 1/2 x 11. **Cols./Page:** 8. **Col. Width:** 18 nonpareils. **Col. Depth:** 304 agate lines. **Key Personnel:** Edward A. Taylor, Jr., Publisher. **USPS:** 605-040. **Subscription Rates:** $20.80 individuals. **Remarks:** Accepts advertising.
Ad Rates: GLR: $1.80 **Circ:** ‡3,865
BW: $2,476.80
4C: $2,956.80
SAU: $14.40
PCI: $10.80

MOUNT CARMEL†, pop. 8,908.

Wabash Co. (SE). On Wabash River, 25 m SW of Vincennes, Ind. Manufactures radio coils, tools, electronic components, women's dresses, flintkote roofing. Coal mines. Oil well. Agriculture. Corn, wheat, soybeans.

9400 Daily Republican Register
117 E. 4th St. Phone: (618)262-5144
PO Box 550 Fax: (618)263-4437
Mount Carmel, IL 62863
General newspaper. **Founded:** 1839. **Freq:** Daily (eve.). **Print Method:** Offset. **Trim Size:** 11 1/2 x 14. **Cols./Page:** 6. **Col. Width:** 25 nonpareils. **Col. Depth:** 294 agate lines. **Key Personnel:** Phillip L. Gower, Editor; Jack Rodgers, Publisher. **Subscription Rates:** $88.90 individuals. **Remarks:** Accepts advertising.
Ad Rates: BW: $957.60 **Circ:** Paid ⊕**4,094**
4C: $1,092.60 Free ⊕**63**
SAU: $7.60

9401 WRBT-FM - 94.9
PO Box 490 Phone: (618)263-6567
Mount Carmel, IL 62863 Fax: (618)263-3220

Format: Classic Rock. **Networks:** ABC. **Owner:** Old Northwest Broadcasting, Inc, PO Box 490, MT. Carmel, IL 62863. **Founded:** 1960. **Operating Hours:** Continuous. **ADI:** Evansville, IN (Madisonville, KY). **Key Personnel:** Scott J. Fenneman, Pres./Gen. Mgr. **Wattage:** 50,000.

9402 WVJC-FM - 89.1
2200 College Dr. Phone: (618)262-8989
Mount Carmel, IL 62863 Fax: (618)262-7317

Format: Alternative/New Music/Progressive. **Networks:** AP. **Founded:** 1973. **Operating Hours:** Continuous; 100% local. **ADI:** Evansville, IN (Madisonville, KY). **Key Personnel:** James L. Cox, General Mgr., coxj@iecc.ccil.us; Robert Effland, Chief Engineer; Glenda Raber, Contact. **Wattage:** 50,000. **Ad Rates:** Noncommercial.

9403 WVMC-AM - 1360
PO Box 490 Phone: (618)262-4102
Mount Carmel, IL 62863 Fax: (618)262-4102
E-mail: wsjd@midwest.net

Format: Middle-of-the-Road (MOR); Big Band/Nostalgia. **Networks:** NBC; ABC. **Owner:** Wabash Communications Inc., 606 Market St., Mount Carmel, IL 62863. **Founded:** 1949. **Formerly:** WYER-AM. **Operating Hours:** Continuous;. **ADI:**

Evansville, IN (Madisonville, KY). **Key Personnel:** Scott Allen, Pres./General Mgr.; Kevin Madden, General Sales Mgr. **Wattage:** 500. **Ad Rates:** Advertising accepted; rates available upon request. **URL:** http://www.wsjd.com.

MOUNT CARROLL†, pop. 1,936.

Carroll Co. (NW). 30 m SW of Freeport. Shimer College. Small automotive parts manufactured. Dairy, grain, stock, poultry farms.

9404 Carroll County Mirror-Democrat
Mirror-Democrat Publishing Co.
308 N. Main St. Phone: (815)244-2411
PO Box 191 Fax: (815)244-2965
Mount Carroll, IL 61053
Community newspaper. **Founded:** 1860. **Freq:** Weekly (Wed.). **Print Method:** Offset. **Cols./Page:** 6. **Col. Width:** 12 nonpareils. **Col. Depth:** 21 inches. **Key Personnel:** Robert W. Watson, Editor and Publisher. **Subscription Rates:** $18 individuals; $24 out of area.
Ad Rates: BW: $441 **Circ:** ‡2,000
SAU: $6

MOUNT MORRIS, pop. 2,989.

Ogle Co. (N). 26 m SW of Rockford. Printing and publishing houses. Diversified farming.

9405 Egg Industry
Watt Publishing Co.
122 S. Wesley Ave. Phone: (815)734-4201
Mount Morris, IL 61054-1497 Fax: (815)734-7727

Magazine serving those involved in the production, processing, and marketing of eggs. **Founded:** 1895. **Freq:** Bimonthly. **Print Method:** Offset. **Trim Size:** 8 x 10 3/4. **Cols./Page:** 3. **Col. Width:** 27 nonpareils. **Col. Depth:** 140 agate lines. **Key Personnel:** Charles Olentine, Jr., Editor and Publisher, olentine@wattmm.mhs.compuserve.com; Terry Janes, Advt. Business Mgr., fax (815)734-4220, janes@wattmm.mhs.compuserve.com. **Subscription Rates:** $24 individuals. **Remarks:** Advertising accepted; rates available upon request. **URL:** http://www.wattnet.com.
Circ: Controlled 1,500

9406 Feed International
Watt Publishing Co.
122 S. Wesley Ave. Phone: (815)734-4201
Mount Morris, IL 61054-1497 Fax: (815)734-7727

Magazine serving the international feed manufacturing industry. **Founded:** May 1980. **Freq:** Monthly. **Print Method:** Web offset. **Trim Size:** 8 x 10 3/4. **Cols./Page:** 2 and 3. **Col. Width:** 3 3/8 and 2 1/8 inches. **Col. Depth:** 10 and 10 inches. **Key Personnel:** Clayton Gill, Editorial Dir., gill@wattmm.mhs.compuserve.com; Clayton J. Schreiber, Publisher, schreibe@wattmm.mhs.compuserve.com; Terry Janes, Advertising Mgr., janes@wattmm.mhs.compuserve.com. **ISSN:** 0274-5771. **Subscription Rates:** $48 individuals; $8 single issue; $48 additional for airmail. **Remarks:** Accepts advertising. **URL:** http://www.wattnet.com. **Alt. Formats:** Microfilm.
Ad Rates: BW: $4,785 **Circ:** Paid 179
4C: $6,505 Non-paid 19,182

9407 Feed Management
Watt Publishing Co.
122 S. Wesley Ave. Phone: (815)734-4201
Mount Morris, IL 61054-1497 Fax: (815)734-7727

Magazine for feed manufacturers. **Founded:** 1950. **Freq:** Monthly. **Print Method:** Offset. **Trim Size:** 8 x 10 3/4. **Cols./Page:** 3 and 2. **Col. Width:** 2 1/8 and 3 3/8 inches. **Col. Depth:** 140 and 140 agate lines. **Key Personnel:** Phil Labo, Editor, labo@wattmm.mhs.compuserve.com; Clayton Schreiber, Publisher, schreibe@wattmm.mhs.compuserve.com; Marty Wittig, Sales Mgr., wittig@wattmm.mhs.compuserve.com. **ISSN:** 0014-956x. **Subscription Rates:** $48 individuals; $8 single issue. **Remarks:** Accepts advertising. **URL:** http://www.wattnet.com. **Alt. Formats:** Microfilm.
Ad Rates: BW: $4,100 **Circ:** Paid 229
4C: $5,410 Non-paid 20,271

9408 Industria Avicola
Watt Publishing Co.
122 S. Wesley Ave. Phone: (815)734-4201
Mount Morris, IL 61054-1497 Fax: (815)734-7727
Publication E-mail: wright@wattmm.mhs.compuserve.com

Magazine for all phases of the Latin American poultry industry. Printed in Spanish. **Founded:** 1952. **Freq:** Monthly. **Print Method:** Web offset. **Trim Size:** 8 x 10 3/4. **Cols./Page:** 2. **Col. Width:** 3 3/8 inches. **Col. Depth:** 10 inches. **Key Personnel:** Charles Olentine, Jr., Publisher; Christopher Wright, Editor, wright@wattmm.mhs.compuserve.com; Terry Janes, Adv. Bus. Mgr. **ISSN:** 0019-7467. **Subscription Rates:** $48 individuals; $6 single issue. **Remarks:** Accepts advertising. **URL:** http://www.wattnet.com.
Ad Rates: BW: $3,750 **Circ:** 15,160
4C: $4,775

9409 Industria Porcina
Watt Publishing Co.
122 S. Wesley Ave. Phone: (815)734-4201
Mount Morris, IL 61054-1497 Fax: (815)734-7727

Spanish-language magazine for the pork industry. Distributed in Latin America. **Founded:** 1981. **Freq:** Quarterly. **Print Method:** Web offset. **Trim Size:** 8 x 10 3/4. **Cols./Page:** 2 and 3. **Col. Width:** 3 3/8 and 2 1/8 inches. **Col. Depth:** 10 and 10 inches. **Key Personnel:** Clayton Gill, Editorial Dir., gill@wattmm.mhs.compuserve.com; Clay Schreiber, Publisher, schreibe@wattmm.mhs.compuserve.com; Peter Best, Editor, best@wattpe.mhs.compuserve.com. **ISSN:** 0279-771. **Subscription Rates:** Free to qualified subscribers; $25 individuals; $8 single issue. **Remarks:** Accepts advertising. **URL:** http://www.wattnet.com. **Alt. Formats:** Microfilm.
Ad Rates: BW: $3,140 **Circ:** Non-paid 9,305
4C: $4,270

9410 Meat Processing
Watt Publishing Co.
122 S. Wesley Ave. Phone: (815)734-4201
Mount Morris, IL 61054-1497 Fax: (815)734-7727

Magazine for managers of meat, poultry, and seafood processing operations. **Founded:** 1962. **Freq:** Monthly. **Print Method:** Web offset. **Trim Size:** 8 x 10 7/8. **Cols./Page:** 3 and 2. **Col. Width:** 27 and 40 nonpareils. **Key Personnel:** Greg Watt, Publisher, watt@wattmm.mhs.compuserve.com; Brent Langman, Editor, langman@wattmm.mhs.compuserve.com; Steve Bjerklie, Exec. Editor. **ISSN:** 0025-6390. **Subscription Rates:** $72 /year; $8 single issue. **URL:** http://www.wattnet.com.
Ad Rates: BW: $3,110 **Circ:** Paid 322
4C: $4,300 Non-paid 22,031

9411 Mt. Morris Times
Ogle County Newspapers
PO Box 8 Phone: (815)732-6166
Oregon, IL 61061-0008 Fax: (815)946-2501

Local newspaper. **Founded:** 1969. **Freq:** Weekly (Thurs.). **Print Method:** Offset. Uses mats. **Key Personnel:** Vin de Wells, Editor; Ruth Cody, Publisher. **Subscription Rates:** $17.50 individuals. **Remarks:** Advertising accepted; rates available upon request.
Circ: ‡1,945

9412 National Catholic Register
Circle Media
PO Box 373 Phone: (815)288-5600
Mount Morris, IL 61054 Fax: (815)288-5157
Free: (800)421-3230
Publisher E-mail: cmedia@pipeline.com

Religious newspaper. **Founded:** 1921. **Freq:** Weekly (Sun.). **Print Method:** Offset. **Cols./Page:** 6. **Col. Width:** 26 nonpareils. **Col. Depth:** 287 agate lines. **Key Personnel:** Lawrence Montali, Jr., Editor; Father Owen Kearns, Publisher; Michelle Kopfmann, Advertising Mgr. **ISSN:** 0027-8920. **Subscription Rates:** $49.95 individuals. **Remarks:** Accepts advertising alcoholic beverages and tobacco products.
Ad Rates: GLR: $2.36 **Circ:** Paid 15,000
BW: $1,890 Free 453
4C: $2,290
SAU: $33
PCI: $15

9413 Petfood Industry
Watt Publishing Co.
122 S. Wesley Ave. Phone: (815)734-4201
Mount Morris, IL 61054-1497 Fax: (815)734-7727

Magazine for pet food manufacturers. **Founded:** 1959. **Freq:** Bimonthly. **Print Method:** Web offset. **Trim Size:** 8 x 10 3/4. **Cols./Page:** 2 and 3. **Col. Width:** 3 3/8 and 2 1/8 inches. **Col. Depth:** 140 and 140 agate lines. **Key Personnel:** Tim Phillips, DVM, Editor, phillips@wattmm.mhs.compuserve.com; Clayton Schreiber, Publisher, schreibe@wattmm.mhs.compuserve.com. **ISSN:** 0031-6245. **Subscription Rates:** $42 individuals; $25 3rd Quarter Source Book; $8 single issue. **Remarks:** Accepts advertising. **URL:** http://www.attnet.com. **Alt. Formats:** Microfilm.
Ad Rates: BW: $2,475 **Circ:** Controlled ‡8,554
4C: $3,365

9414 Pig International
Watt Publishing Co.
122 S. Wesley Ave. Phone: (815)734-4201
Mount Morris, IL 61054-1497 Fax: (815)734-7727

Magazine focusing on pig production and marketing. **Founded:** 1971. **Freq:** Monthly. **Print Method:** Web offset. **Trim Size:** 8 x 10 3/4. **Cols./Page:** 2 and 2. **Col. Width:** 3 3/8 and 2 1/8 inches. **Col. Depth:** 140 and 140 agate lines. **Key Personnel:** Peter Best, Editor, best@wattpe.mhs.compuserve.com; Clay Schreiber, Publisher, schreibe@wattmm.mhs.compuserve.com. **ISSN:** 0191-8834. **Subscription Rates:** $48 individuals; $8 single issue. **Remarks:** Accepts advertising. **URL:** http://www.wattnet.com. **Alt. Formats:** Microfilm.
Ad Rates: BW: $4,525 **Circ:** Controlled 19,140
4C: $6,155

9415 Poultry International
Watt Publishing Co.
122 S. Wesley Ave. Phone: (815)734-4201
Mount Morris, IL 61054-1497 Fax: (815)734-7727

Magazine serving the poultry industry in Europe, Middle East/Africa, and Asia/Pacific. **Founded:** Jan. 1962. **Freq:** Monthly. **Print Method:** Web offset. **Trim Size:** 8 x 10 3/4. **Cols./Page:** 2 and 3. **Col. Width:** 2 3/8 and 2 inches. **Col. Depth:** 10 inches. **Key Personnel:** David Martin, Editor, martin@wattpe.mhs.compuserve.com; Charles Olentine, Jr., Publisher, olentine@wattmm.mhs.compuserve.com; Terry Janes, Advt. Business Mgr., fax (815)734-4220, janes@wattmm.mhs.compuserve.com. **ISSN:** 0032-5767. **Subscription Rates:** $63 individuals; $8 single issue. **Remarks:** Accepts advertising. **URL:** http://www.wattnet.com.
Ad Rates: BW: $4,550 **Circ:** Combined 23,346
4C: $5,800

9416 Turkey World
Watt Publishing Co.
122 S. Wesley Ave. Phone: (815)734-4201
Mount Morris, IL 61054-1497 Fax: (815)734-7727

Magazine focusing on turkey production, processing and marketing. **Founded:** 1926. **Freq:** 6/year. **Print Method:** Offset. **Trim Size:** 8 x 10 3/4. **Cols./Page:** 3. **Col. Width:** 27 nonpareils. **Col. Depth:** 140 agate lines. **Key Personnel:** Bernard E. Heffernan, Editor, fax (815)734-7727, heffernan@wattmm.mhs.compuserve.com; Charles Olentine, Jr., Publisher, fax (815)734-7727, olentine@wattmm.mhs.compuserve.com; Terry Janes, Adv. Bus. Mgr., fax (815)734-7727, janes@wattmm.mhs.compuserve.com. **Subscription Rates:** $27 individuals Annually; $8 single issue. **Remarks:** Accepts advertising. **URL:** http://www.wattnet.com.
Ad Rates: BW: $2,500 **Circ:** Combined 7,011
4C: $3,200

MOUNT OLIVE

9417 Mt. Olive Herald
PO Box 300 Phone: (217)999-3941
Mount Olive, IL 62069 Fax: (217)999-5105

Community newspaper. **Founded:** June 1880. **Freq:** Weekly (Thurs.). **Cols./Page:** 6. **Col. Width:** 9 1/2 picas. **Col. Depth:** 14 inches. **Key Personnel:** Linda Hasquin, Editor; Daniel Fischer, Publisher. **Remarks:** Advertising accepted; rates available upon request.
Circ: 1,500

MOUNT PROSPECT, pop. 52,634.

Cook Co. (NE). 24 m NW of Chicago. Industrial Park. Central business district. Shopping centers. Manufactures copying equipment, pharmaceutical products.

9418 The Frat
National Fraternal Society of the Deaf
1300 W. Northwest Hwy. Phone: (847)392-9282
Mount Prospect, IL 60056 Fax: (847)392-9298
Publication E-mail: jim-crook@utk.edu

Newsletter containing news items about fraternal activities and general information articles. **Founded:** Feb. 1904. **Freq:** Quarterly. **Print Method:** Offset. **Trim Size:** 8 1/2 x 11. **Cols./Page:** 3. **Col. Width:** 30 nonpareils. **Col. Depth:** 137 agate lines. **Key Personnel:** Al Van Nevel, Editor. **ISSN:** 0739-9243. **Subscription Rates:** $8 individuals.
Ad Rates: BW: $225 **Circ:** ‡8,166
PCI: $35

9419 Journal of The Institute of Environmental Sciences
Institute of Environmental Sciences and Technology
940 E. Northwest Hwy. Phone: (847)255-1561
Mount Prospect, IL 60056-2444 Fax: (847)255-1699
Publisher E-mail: iest@iest.org

Professional journal. **Founded:** 1958. **Freq:** Bimonthly. **Print Method:** Offset. **Trim Size:** 8 1/4 x 11. **Cols./Page:** 2. **Col. Width:** 42 nonpareils. **Col. Depth:** 140 agate lines. **Key Personnel:** Irma Komro, Advertising Mgr.; Julie Kendrick, Sr. Editor; Joan Harpham, Assoc. Dir., Educational Programs. **ISSN:** 0022-0906. **Subscription Rates:** $30 individuals; $50

other countries. **Remarks:** Accepts advertising. **Formerly:** Journal of Environmental Sciences; Journal of the IES.
Ad Rates: BW: $865 **Circ:** ‡6,000
4C: $1,640

9420 Mt. Prospect Times
Pioneer Press Newspapers
130 S. Prospect Ave. Phone: (847)696-3133
Park Ridge, IL 60068 Fax: (847)696-3229

General newspaper. **Founded:** 1980. **Freq:** Weekly (Thurs.). **Print Method:** Offset. **Cols./Page:** 6. **Key Personnel:** Paul Sassone, Managing Editor; Craig Shaw, Editor. **Subscription Rates:** $18.95 by mail. **Remarks:** Advertising accepted; rates available upon request.
Circ: Thurs. ★2,668

9421 NSGA Retail Focus
National Sporting Goods Association (NSGA)
1699 Wall St. Phone: (847)439-4000
Mount Prospect, IL 60056-5780 Fax: (847)439-0111
Publisher E-mail: nsga1699@aol.com

Trade magazine focusing on sporting goods retailing. **Founded:** Jan. 1947. **Freq:** 6/year. **Print Method:** Offset. **Trim Size:** 8 1/2 x 11. **Key Personnel:** Larry N. Weindruch, Editor and Publisher. **ISSN:** 1045-2087. **Subscription Rates:** $50 individuals. **Remarks:** Accepts advertising. **URL:** htpp://www.nsga.org.
Ad Rates: BW: $1,210 **Circ:** Paid ‡6,719
4C: $2,205 Non-paid ‡2,213

9422 PIMA's Papermaker Magazine
Paper Industry Management Association
1699 Wall St., No. 212 Phone: (847)956-0250
Mount Prospect, IL 60056-5782 Fax: (847)956-0520
Publication E-mail: pimastaf@wrldnet.net

Publication for the pulp and paper industry that deals with managerial issues. **Subtitle:** The Official Publication of the Paper Industry/Management Association. **Founded:** 1919. **Freq:** Monthly. **Print Method:** Offset. **Trim Size:** 8 1/8 x 10 7/8. **Cols./Page:** 3 and 2. **Col. Width:** 26 and 40 nonpareils. **Col. Depth:** 140 agate lines. **Key Personnel:** Alan Rooks, Editor, alan@pima-online.org; E. Lindsay Beddingfield, Publisher, phone (334)271-3318, fax (334)277-3536. **ISSN:** 1046-4352. **Subscription Rates:** $105 individuals. **Remarks:** Accepts advertising. **Alt. Formats:** CD-ROM; Microform. **Formerly:** American Papermaker; PIMA Magazine.
Ad Rates: BW: $5,995 **Circ:** Paid ‡5,000
4C: $8,290 Non-paid ‡37,000

9423 Signalman's Journal
Brotherhood of Railroad Signalmen
601 W. Golf Rd. Phone: (847)439-3732
PO Box U Fax: (847)439-3743
Mount Prospect, IL 60056
Union publication. **Subtitle:** Official Publication of the Brotherhood of Railroad Signalmen. **Founded:** 1920. **Freq:** Bimonthly. **Print Method:** Offset. **Trim Size:** 7 x 10. **Cols./Page:** 3. **Col. Width:** 13 picas. **Key Personnel:** T.J. DePaepe, Editor, tjd@netwave.net. **ISSN:** 0037-5020. **Subscription Rates:** $10. **Remarks:** Advertising accepted; rates available upon request.
Circ: ‡15,000

9424 TCI of Illinois, Inc.
411 Business Center Dr., Ste. 104 Phone: (847)699-7500
Fax: (847)299-8976
Mount Prospect, IL 60056

Founded: 1982. **Key Personnel:** Brian Sullivan, Vice President; John Higgins, Dir., Customer Sat.; John Harrision, Dir., Technical Operations; Paul Venturella, Dir., Customer Sat. **Cities Served:** 15 communities in Cook County,IL.: subscribing households 110,000; 62 channels; 8 community access channels; 75 hours per week community access programming.

MOUNT PULASKI, pop. 1,783.

Logan Co. (C). 11 m SE of Lincoln. Manufactures corn cob products, molasses, feed. Diversified farming. Corn, wheat, soybeans, hay.

9425 Mt. Pulaski Weekly News
311 S. Washington St. Phone: (217)792-5557
PO Box 114 Fax: (217)792-5482
Mount Pulaski, IL 62548
Publication E-mail: wklynews@frontiernet.net

Community newspaper. **Founded:** 1884. **Freq:** Weekly (Thurs.). **Print Method:** Offset. **Cols./Page:** 7. **Key Personnel:** Michael Lakin, Editor and Publisher. **USPS:** 441-400. **Subscription Rates:** $15 individuals; $.30 single issue. **Remarks:** Accepts advertising.
Ad Rates: SAU: $6 **Circ:** 1,743
PCI: $6

MOUNT STERLING, pop. 2,186.

Brown Co. (W). 39 m E of Quincy. Coal, oil, gas. Dairy, hogs, cattle, poultry. Corn, wheat, soybeans.

9426 The Democrat-Message
The Democrat-Message, Inc.
110 W. Main St. Phone: (217)773-3371
PO Box 71 Fax: (217)773-3369
Mount Sterling, IL 62353
Community and agricultural newspaper (tabloid). **Founded:** 1848. **Freq:** Weekly (Wed.). **Print Method:** Offset. **Trim Size:** 11 1/4 x 17 1/2. **Cols./Page:** 6. **Col. Width:** 9.5 picas. **Col. Depth:** 16 inches. **Key Personnel:** Suzanne Kassing, Editor; Pat Webel, Advertising Mgr. **Subscription Rates:** $15 individuals; $20 out of area. **Remarks:** Accepts advertising.
Ad Rates: GLR: $.16 **Circ:** Paid 2,900
BW: $408
SAU: $4.25

MOUNT VERNON†, pop. 16,995.

Jefferson Co. (S). 20 m SE of Centralia. Manufactures radial tires, auto radiators, power cores, transformers, dryers and evaporators, feed. Diversified farming. Fruits, poultry, corn, soybeans.

9427 Register-News
118 N. 9th St. Phone: (618)242-0113
PO Box 489 Fax: (618)242-8286
Mount Vernon, IL 62864
General newspaper. **Founded:** 1884. **Freq:** Mon.-Sat. (eve.). **Print Method:** Offset. **Cols./Page:** 6. **Col. Width:** 24 nonpareils. **Col. Depth:** 294 agate lines. **Key Personnel:** Charles E. Deitz, Publisher; Sarah Sledge, Advertising Mgr. **Subscription Rates:** $78 individuals. **Remarks:** Accepts advertising.
Ad Rates: BW: $1,464.15 **Circ:** Mon. 11,821
4C: $1,674.15 Tues.-Fri. 10,688
SAU: $11.35 Sat. 10,688

MOUNT ZION, pop. 4,563.

Macon Co. (C). 7 m SE of Decatur. Glass factory. Diversified farming.

9428 Region News
130 Wildwood Dr. Phone: (217)864-4212
Box 79 Fax: (217)578-2833
Mount Zion, IL 62549
Community newspaper. **Founded:** 1959. **Freq:** Weekly (Thurs.). **Print Method:** Offset. **Cols./Page:** 4. **Col. Width:** 29 nonpareils. **Col. Depth:** 196 agate lines. **Key Personnel:** Mike Brothers, Editor. **Subscription Rates:** $20 individuals. **Remarks:** Accepts advertising.
Ad Rates: GLR: $.48 **Circ:** ‡1,650
BW: $290
PCI: $5.50

9429 WXFM-FM - 99.3
120 Wildwood Phone: (217)864-4141
Mount Zion, IL 62549

Format: Adult Contemporary; Soft Rock. **Owner:** Technicom, Inc., at above address. **Founded:** 1984. **Operating Hours:** Continuous. **ADI:** Springfield-Decatur-Champaign, IL. **Key Personnel:** Mary Ellen Beirus, Contact; Linda Davis, Sales Mgr. **Wattage:** 3000 ERP. **Ad Rates:** $18.50-20.50 for 30 seconds; $25-27 for 60 seconds.

MUNDELEIN

9430 Art Therapy
1202 Allanson Rd. Phone: (847)949-6064
Mundelein, IL 60060-3808 Fax: (847)566-4580
Free: (888)290-0878
Publication E-mail: arttherapy@ntr.net

Journal for art therapists. **Subtitle:** Art Therapy: Journal of the American Art Therapy Association. **Founded:** Oct. 1983. **Freq:** Quarterly. **Trim Size:** 8 1/2" x 11". **Key Personnel:** Karen D. Savage, Contact, fax (847)566-4580, kdssaturn@aol.com. **ISSN:** 0742-1656. **Subscription Rates:** $50 individuals; $77 institutions; $74 individuals out of the country; $100 institutions out of the country. **Remarks:** Advertising accepted; rates available upon request.
Circ: 5,000

9431 Mundelein Review
Pioneer Press Newspapers
850 N. Milwaukee Ave. Phone: (847)680-6690
Vernon Hills, IL 60061 Fax: (847)573-2500

Community newspaper (tabloid). **Founded:** 1981. **Freq:** Weekly (Thurs.). **Print Method:** Offset. **Cols./Page:** 5. **Col. Width:** 10 inches. **Col. Depth:** 14 inches. **Key Personnel:** Paul Sassone, Managing Editor; Sheila Richard, Editor. **Subscription Rates:** $8.50 individuals; $14.95 out of county. **Remarks:** Advertising not accepted. **URL:** http://www.pioneerlogo.com.
Circ: Thurs. ★2,917

MURPHYSBORO

9432 WINI-AM - 1420
1677 Business Hwy. 13 Phone: (618)684-2128
Murphysboro, IL 62966-2923 Fax: (618)687-4318

Format: News; Talk. **Networks:** People's Network. **Founded:** 1954. **Operating Hours:** Continuous Mon.-Fri. **Key Personnel:** Dale W. Adkins, General Mgr.; Nancy Engel, Operations Mgr. **Wattage:** 420 day; 500 night. **Ad Rates:** $10.50 for 30 seconds; $12.50 for 60 seconds.

NAPERVILLE, pop. 42,330.

Du Page Co. (SW). 29 m W of Chicago. North Central College. Manufactures carbon, concrete products, machine tools, cotton and burlap bags, chewing gum, dietetic foods, cereal. Research and development center. Boiler works.

9433 The Bolingbrook/Romeoville Sun
Sun Publications
9 W. Jackson Phone: (630)355-0063
PO Box 269 Fax: (630)416-5163
Naperville, IL 60566-0269
Publisher E-mail: thesun@exchange.copleysun.com

Local newspaper. **Founded:** 1963. **Freq:** Weekly (Wed.). **Print Method:** Offset. **Trim Size:** 10 1/4 x 13. **Cols./Page:** 5. **Col. Width:** 2 1/4 inches. **Key Personnel:** Tim West, Editor, phone (630)416-5290, fax (630)416-5168; Greg Mellis, General Mgr., phone (630)416-5171, fax (630)416-5220; Rick Taden, Contact, phone (630)416-5120, fax (630)416-5147. **Subscription Rates:** $10 individuals.
Ad Rates: PCI: $7.95 **Circ:** Paid 8,000
Free 246

9434 Catholic Forester Magazine
Catholic Order of Foresters
355 Shuman Blvd. Phone: (630)983-3380
PO Box 3012 Fax: (630)983-3384
Naperville, IL 60566-7012
Free: (800)552-0145

Fraternal and general interest magazine. **Founded:** 1883. **Freq:** Bimonthly. **Print Method:** Offset. **Trim Size:** 8 1/4 x 10 3/4. **Cols./Page:** 2 and 3. **Col. Width:** 40 and 26 nonpareils. **Col. Depth:** 137 agate lines. **Key Personnel:** Dorothy Deer, Editor. **ISSN:** 0008-8048. **Subscription Rates:** free to policy holders. **Remarks:** Advertising not accepted.
Circ: Free ‡100,000

9435 The Lisle Sun
Sun Publications
9 W. Jackson Phone: (630)355-0063
PO Box 269 Fax: (630)416-5163
Naperville, IL 60566-0269
Publisher E-mail: thesun@exchange.copleysun.com

Community newspaper. **Founded:** 1938. **Freq:** Weekly (Thurs.). **Print Method:** Offset. **Cols./Page:** 5. **Col. Width:** 24 nonpareils. **Col. Depth:** 224 agate lines. **Key Personnel:** Dan Cassidy, Editor; James Tejak, General Mgr.; Cleo Keller, Advertising Dir. **USPS:** 314-800. **Subscription Rates:** $10.50 individuals; $16.35 out of county. **Remarks:** Accepts advertising.
Ad Rates: GLR: $.33 **Circ:** Paid 5,000
BW: $526 Free 400
4C: $871
PCI: $4.70

9436 The Naperville Sun
Sun Publications
9 W. Jackson Phone: (630)355-0063
PO Box 269 Fax: (630)416-5163
Naperville, IL 60566-0269
Publisher E-mail: thesun@exchange.copleysun.com

Community newspaper. **Founded:** July 1935. **Freq:** 3/week. **Print Method:** Offset. Uses mats. **Cols./Page:** 5. **Col. Width:** 2 1/16 inches. **Col. Depth:** 224 agate lines. **Key Personnel:** Tim West, Editor; James Tezak, General Mgr.; Rick Taden, Advertising Mgr. **Subscription Rates:** $40 individuals; $75 out of area. **Remarks:** Accepts advertising.
Ad Rates: BW: $698.75 **Circ:** Paid 22,600
4C: $948.75 Free 2,083
PCI: $10.75

The Romeoville Sun - See Romeoville

Wheaton Journal - See Wheaton

9437 WONC-FM - 89.1
30 N. Brainard St. Phone: (630)637-8989
PO Box 3063 Fax: (630)637-5900
Naperville, IL 60566-3063
E-mail: wonc@noctrl.edu

Format: Alternative/New Music/Progressive; Classic Rock. **Networks:** Independent. **Owner:** North Central College, at above address, (630)637-5100, Fax: (630)637-5121. **Founded:** 1968. **Operating Hours:** Continuous; 100% local. **Key Personnel:** John V. Madormo, Contact; Greg Burks, Station Mgr., phone (630)637-5960, fax (630)637-5967. **Local Programs:** *From the Upper Deck* 6:00 pm - 7:00 pm Sunday, Kevin Juday, (630)637-5968; *Mission Rock* 12:00 noon - 2:00 pm Sunday, Jeremy Gudeuskas; *C-Trends* 8:00 am Saturday, Judy Rudow, Operations Mgr. **Wattage:** 3900. **Ad Rates:** Noncommercial.

NASHVILLE†, pop. 3,186.

Washington Co. (S). 25 m SW of Centralia. Manufactures corrugated products, auto parts, feed. Diversified farming. Dairy, pork, beef Wheat, corn, soybeans.

9438 The Nashville News
Riccon, Inc.
211 W. St. Louis St. Phone: (618)327-3411
PO Box 47 Fax: (618)327-3299
Nashville, IL 62263-0047
General news. **Founded:** 1934. **Freq:** Weekly (Wed.). **Print Method:** Offset. **Trim Size:** 13 3/4 x 22 3/4. **Cols./Page:** 6. **Col. Width:** 29 nonpareils. **Col. Depth:** 300 agate lines. **Key Personnel:** Richard Tomaszewski, Editor and Publisher. **USPS:** 371-520. **Subscription Rates:** $20 in Washington, Perry, and Jefferson counties; $24 in other counties. **Remarks:** Accepts advertising.
Ad Rates: GLR: $.36 **Circ:** ‡5,500
BW: $548.25
4C: $783.75
SAU: $5.30
PCI: $5.20

NAUVOO

9439 The New Independent
Sonora Landing Enterprises Inc.
PO Box 415 Phone: (217)453-6771
Nauvoo, IL 62354 Fax: (217)453-2707

Community newspaper. **Founded:** 1990. **Freq:** Weekly (Wed.). **Print Method:** Web offset. **Cols./Page:** 5. **Col. Width:** 11 1/2 picas. **Col. Depth:** 16 inches. **Key Personnel:** Jane Langford, Publisher. **USPS:** 090-790. **Subscription Rates:** $30; $35 out of area. **Remarks:** Accepts advertising. **Alt. Formats:** Mailing labels. **Formerly:** Nauvoo Grapevine.
Ad Rates: BW: $400 **Circ:** ‡515
SAU: $5.32
PCI: $5

NEW BADEN, pop. 2,476.

Clinton Co. (SW). 19 m E of Belleville. Coal mines. Bottling works; electrical equipment factories. Dairy, poultry, grain farms.

9440 Clinton County News
Herald Publications
PO Box 226 Phone: (618)588-7720
New Baden, IL 62265 Fax: (618)566-8283

Community newspaper. **Founded:** 1938. **Freq:** Weekly (Thurs.). **Print Method:** Letterpress and offset. **Trim Size:** 10 1/4 x 16. **Cols./Page:** 6. **Key Personnel:** Greg Hoskins, Publisher. **USPS:** 377-600. **Subscription Rates:** $15 individuals. **Remarks:** Accepts advertising.
Ad Rates: BW: $354.75 **Circ:** ‡1,500
4C: $554.75
PCI: $3.43

NEW BERLIN, pop. 834.

Sangamon Co. (C). 15 m W of Springfield. Coal mine. Agriculture. Purebred stock breeding. Soybeans, corn, wheat.

9441 New Berlin Bee
Swettman Publications
Box 50 Phone: (217)626-1711
Pleasant Plains, IL 62677
Community newspaper. **Founded:** 1889. **Freq:** Weekly (Fri.). **Print Method:** Offset. **Trim Size:** 10 x 16. **Cols./Page:** 5. **Col. Width:** 22 nonpareils. **Col. Depth:** 215 agate lines. **Key Personnel:** Al Swettman, Jr., Publisher. **USPS:** 777-800. **Subscription Rates:** $10 individuals. **Remarks:** Accepts advertising.
Ad Rates: GLR: $.16 **Circ:** ‡600
PCI: $1.75

NEW LENOX

9442 New Lenox Community Reporter
Russell Publications
PO Box 429 Phone: (708)258-3473
Peotone, IL 60468 Fax: (708)258-6295

Community newspaper. **Freq:** Weekly (Wed.). **Cols./Page:** 5. **Col. Width:** 11 1/2 picas. **Col. Depth:** 16 inches. **Key Personnel:** Gilbert L. Russell, Publisher; Gilbert L. Russell, Publisher. **Remarks:** Advertising accepted; rates available upon request.
Circ: 950

NEWMAN

9443 Newman Independent
54 S. Broadway Phone: (217)837-2414
PO Box 417 Fax: (217)837-2130
Newman, IL 61942
Publication E-mail: newsi@cu-online.com

Community newspaper. **Freq:** Weekly (Thurs.). **Cols./Page:** 4. **Col. Width:** 14 1/2 picas. **Col. Depth:** 15 inches. **Key Personnel:** Laura Sarins, Editor and Publisher. **Subscription Rates:** $15; $25 out of state. **Remarks:** Accepts advertising. **URL:** http://newman.net.
Ad Rates: GLR: $3.15 **Circ:** 900
BW: $169

NEWTON†, pop. 3,186.

Jasper Co. (SE). 50 m SW of Terre Haute, Ind. Manufactures academic caps and gowns, choir and clergy robes, girls gym suits, brooms, handles, battery cables, automotive wiring hardness, beverages. Oil fields. Agriculture. Soybeans, corn, livestock, poultry.

9444 Newton Press-Mentor
101 South Jackson Phone: (618)783-2324
PO Box 151 Fax: (618)783-2325
Newton, IL 62448
Community newspaper. **Subtitle:** Newton Press. **Founded:** 1862. **Freq:** Semiweekly (Mon. and Thurs.). **Print Method:** Offset. **Trim Size:** 22 3/4. **Cols./Page:** 6. **Col. Width:** 24 nonpareils. **Col. Depth:** 294 agate lines. **Key Personnel:** Don Hecke, Publisher. **Subscription Rates:** $26 individuals. **Remarks:** Accepts advertising.
Ad Rates: GLR: $.23 **Circ:** ‡4,000
BW: $588
PCI: $5.60

9445 WIKK-FM - 103.5
Hwy 33 W. Phone: (618)783-8000
PO Box 304 Fax: (618)783-4040
Newton, IL 62448

Format: Adult Contemporary. **Networks:** Mutual Broadcasting System. **Founded:** 1992. **Operating Hours:** 5 a.m.-midnight; 9% network, 91% local. **ADI:** Terre Haute, IN. **Key Personnel:** S. Kent Lankford, Contact. **Wattage:** 25,000. **Ad Rates:** $8-10 for 30 seconds; $9-12 for 60 seconds. Combined advertising rates available with WAKO-AM/FM.

NILES, pop. 30,363.

Cook Co. (NE). 14 m NW of Chicago. Manufactures tools and dies, office machines, stationary supplies, video games, dental products, bus parts, gloves soft drinks, testing products, heating controls.

9446 Boat and Motor Dealer
Preston Publications
6600 W. Touhy Ave. Phone: (847)647-2900
PO Box 48312 Fax: (847)647-1155
Niles, IL 60714
Publisher E-mail: tpreston@prestonpub.com

Magazine for boat, motor, and accessory dealers. **Founded:** 1958. **Freq:** Monthly. **Trim Size:** 8 1/8 x 10 7/8. **Cols./Page:** 2 and 3. **Col. Width:** 20 and 13 picas. **Col. Depth:** 10 and 10 inches. **Key Personnel:** Diana Weaver, Editor; S. Tinsley Preston III, President; Sandra Ruroede, Assoc. Editor; Jerry Burns, Publisher. **ISSN:** 0006-5366. **Subscription Rates:** $30 individuals; $10 single issue. **Remarks:** Accepts advertising. **URL:** http://www.prestonpub.com.
Ad Rates: BW: $3,200 **Circ:** Paid 34
4C: $4,150 Controlled 31,706

9447 Contractors Guide
G & M Communications
6213 Howard St. Phone: (847)588-3333
Niles, IL 60714 Fax: (847)647-7055

Trade magazine on roofing and insulation. **Founded:** Jan. 1984. **Freq:** Monthly. **Print Method:** Offset. **Trim Size:** 8 3/8 x 11 1/4. **Cols./Page:** 3. **Col. Width:** 30 nonpareils. **Col. Depth:** 140 agate lines. **Key Personnel:** Greg Ettling, Editor, greg@constructiongroup.com; Philip Miller, Publisher; Megan Ettling, Advertising Mgr., megan@constructiongroup.com. **ISSN:** 0273-5954. **Subscription Rates:** Free to qualified subscribers; $25 individuals; $5 single issue. **Remarks:** Accepts advertising. **URL:** http://www.constructiongroup.com.
Ad Rates: BW: $3,665 **Circ:** Paid 148
4C: $5,460 Non-paid 23,434

9448 Gas & Liquid Chromatography Abstracts and Index
Preston Publications
6600 W. Touhy Ave. Phone: (847)647-2900
PO Box 48312 Fax: (847)647-1155
Niles, IL 60714-3426
Journal. **Subtitle:** Abstracts and Index. **Freq:** Bimonthly. **Trim Size:** 8 1/2 x 11. **Cols./Page:** 2. **Col. Width:** 3 1/2 inches. **Col. Depth:** 9 1/2 inches. **ISSN:** 1059-3160. **Subscription Rates:** $620 individuals; $558 institutions. **Remarks:** Advertising not accepted. **Alt. Formats:** CD-ROM.
Circ: Paid 20
Non-paid 20

9449 Journal of Analytical Toxicology
Preston Publications
6600 W. Touhy Ave. Phone: (847)647-2900
PO Box 48312 Fax: (847)647-1155
Niles, IL 60714
Publisher E-mail: tpreston@prestonpub.com

Journal for clinical and forensic toxicologists. **Founded:** 1977. **Freq:** 7/year. **Print Method:** Offset. **Trim Size:** 8 1/4 x 11. **Cols./Page:** 3. **Col. Width:** 2 1/8 inches. **Col. Depth:** 10 inches. **Key Personnel:** R.C. Baselt, Editor; Julie Weber-Roark, Managing Editor, jweber@jatox.com; S. Tinsley Preston III, Publisher. **ISSN:** 0146-4760. **Subscription Rates:** $305 individuals; $50 single issue. **Remarks:** Accepts advertising. **Alt. Formats:** Microfiche.
Ad Rates: BW: $370 **Circ:** Paid ‡1,250
4C: $1,050 Non-paid ‡64

9450 Journal of Chromatographic Science
Preston Publications
6600 W. Touhy Ave. Phone: (847)647-2900
PO Box 48312 Fax: (847)647-1155
Niles, IL 60714
Publisher E-mail: tpreston@prestonpub.com

Magazine focusing on chemical analysis. **Founded:** 1963. **Freq:** Monthly. **Print Method:** Offset. **Trim Size:** 8 1/4 x 11. **Cols./Page:** 3. **Col. Width:** 2 1/8 inches. **Col. Depth:** 10 inches. **Key Personnel:** J.Q. Walker, Editor; Bert M. Gordon, Advertising Mgr.; S. Tinsley Preston III, Publisher, tpreston@jatox.com. **ISSN:** 0021-9665. **Subscription Rates:** $240 individuals; $255 other countries; $25 single issue. **Remarks:** Accepts advertising. **Available Online. URL:** http://www.j-chrom-sci.com.
Ad Rates: BW: $1,100 **Circ:** Paid ‡2,619
4C: $1,800 Non-paid ‡78

9451 Journal of the Illinois Optometric Association
Illinois Optometric Association
8118 Milwaukee Ave. Phone: (847)825-6339
Niles, IL 60714-2836 Fax: (847)825-3407
Publication E-mail: ioapr@fgi.net

Professional journal containing clinical material, research reports, practice management articles, and material of interest to practicing optometrists who are members of the association. **Founded:** 1942. **Freq:** Quarterly. **Print Method:** Offset. Uses mats. **Trim Size:** 8 1/2 x 11. **Cols./Page:** 2. **Col. Width:** 38 nonpareils. **Col. Depth:** 12 agate lines. **Key Personnel:** Walter Zinn, O.D., Editor, wjzod@aol.com. **Subscription Rates:** $9 individuals; $18 nonmembers. **Remarks:** Accepts advertising.
Ad Rates: BW: $330 **Circ:** 1,200
4C: $930
PCI: $.30

9452 Marina/Dock Age
Preston Publications
6600 W. Touhy Ave. Phone: (847)647-2900
PO Box 48312 Fax: (847)647-1155
Niles, IL 60714
Publisher E-mail: tpreston@prestonpub.com

Magazine for marina and boat yard owners and managers. **Founded:** 1988. **Freq:** Bimonthly. **Print Method:** Web offset. **Trim Size:** 8 1/8 x 10 7/8. **Cols./Page:** 2. **Col. Width:** 20 picas. **Col. Depth:** 10 inches. **Key Personnel:** S. Tinsley Preston III, Publisher; Jerry P. Burns, Assoc. Publisher; Diana Levey Weaver, Editor, phone (919)468-9853, fax (919)465-1517, dianaweave@aol.com. **ISSN:** 1079-1930. **Subscription Rates:** $24; $10 single issue. **Remarks:** Accepts advertising. **URL:** http://www.prestonpub.com.
Ad Rates: BW: $1,595 **Circ:** Controlled ‡17,090
4C: $2,395

The Niles Bugle - See Lincolnwood

9453 Niles Herald-Spectator
Pioneer Press Newspapers
130 S. Prospect Ave. Phone: (847)696-3133
Park Ridge, IL 60068 Fax: (847)696-3229

Community newspaper (tabloid). **Founded:** 1950. **Freq:** Weekly (Thurs.). **Print Method:** Offset. **Cols./Page:** 5. **Col. Width:** 10 inches. **Col. Depth:** 14 inches. **Key Personnel:** Paul Sassone, Managing Editor; Gregg Canfield, Editor. **Subscription Rates:** $11.95 individuals; $12.95 out of county. **Remarks:** Advertising accepted; rates available upon request. **URL:** http://www.pioneerlocal.com. **Formed by the merger of:** Niles Spectator; Niles Herald.
Circ: Thurs. 2,571

9454 Photo Techniques
Preston Publications
6600 W. Touhy Ave. Phone: (847)647-2900
PO Box 48312 Fax: (847)647-1155
Niles, IL 60714
Publisher E-mail: tpreston@prestonpub.com

Consumer photography magazine. **Founded:** 1979. **Freq:** Bimonthly. **Print Method:** web offset. **Trim Size:** 8 1/8 x 10 7/8. **Cols./Page:** 3. **Col. Width:** 2 1/8 inches. **Col. Depth:** 10 inches. **Key Personnel:** S. Tinsley Preston III, Publisher; Mike Johnston, Jr., Editor, mjohnston@prestonpub.com; mjohnston@phototechmag.com; Bonnie Bomhack, Advertising Mgr. **ISSN:** 0195-3850. **Subscription Rates:** $21.95 individuals; $4.50 single issue. **Remarks:** Accepts advertising. **Formerly:** Darkroom & Creative Camera Techniques.
Ad Rates: BW: $2,670 **Circ:** Paid ★33,197
4C: $3,875

NOKOMIS, pop. 2,656.

Montgomery Co. (SC). 42 m SW of Decatur. Concrete block. Manufactures electronics, novelty stuffed toys. Rock quarries.

9455 Free Press-Progress
Free Press Inc.
112 W. State Phone: (217)563-2115
PO Box 130 Fax: (217)563-7464
Nokomis, IL 62075-0130
Community newspaper. **Founded:** 1868. **Freq:** Weekly (Wed.). **Print Method:** Offset. **Cols./Page:** 8. **Col. Width:** 22 nonpareils. **Col. Depth:** 301 agate lines. **Key Personnel:** Fred Christner, Editor. **Subscription Rates:** $19.50 individuals.
Ad Rates: GLR: $.40 **Circ:** ‡2,350
BW: $438.60
PCI: $2.65

NORMAL, pop. 35,672.

McLean Co. (C). Adjoins Bloomington. Illinois State University. Residential. Canning factories; nurseries. Dairy, stock farms. Corn, wheat, oats.

9456 The American Book Review
The Unit for Contemporary Literature
Illinois State Univ. Phone: (309)438-2127
Campus Box 4241 Fax: (309)438-3523
Normal, IL 61790-4241
Book review. **Founded:** 1977. **Freq:** Bimonthly. **Trim Size:** 11 1/2 x 16. **Cols./Page:** 3 and 4. **Col. Width:** 3 1/4 and 3 inches. **Col. Depth:** 13 3/4 inches. **Key Personnel:** Charles Harris, Publisher; Ronald Sukenick, Publisher; Rebecca Kaiser, Managing Editor, phone (309)438-3026, rakaise@ilstu.edu. **ISSN:** 0149-9408. **Subscription Rates:** $24 individuals; $4 single issue. **URL:** http://www.litline.org.
Ad Rates: BW: $850 **Circ:** Paid ‡1,200
Non-paid ‡1,000

9457 Daily Vidette
Illinois State University
Locust & University Phone: (309)438-7685
Campus Box 0890 Fax: (309)438-5211
Normal, IL 61761
Collegiate newspaper. **Founded:** Feb. 1888. **Freq:** Daily. **Print Method:** Offset. **Trim Size:** 11 3/8 x 16. **Cols./Page:** 5. **Col. Width:** 23 nonpareils. **Col. Depth:** 196 agate lines. **Key Personnel:** Scott Cooley, Editor; James Munz, Advertising Mgr. **Subscription Rates:** $20 mail delivery. **Remarks:** Accepts advertising. **URL:** http://www.ilstu.edu/depts/vidette.
Ad Rates: GLR: $.735 **Circ:** Paid ‡300
PCI: $5.35 Free ‡15,700

9458 Illinois State University Alumni Today
Illinois State University
University Communications Phone: (309)438-8404
Campus Box 3420 Fax: (309)438-8411
Normal, IL 61790
College alumni tabloid. **Founded:** 1968. **Freq:** Quarterly. **Print Method:** Offset. **Trim Size:** 11 1/2 x 13 1/2 in. **Cols./Page:** 4. **Key Personnel:** David Mathis, Editor, drmathis@ilstu.edu. **Remarks:** Advertising not accepted.
Circ: Non-paid ‡95,000

9459 International Journal of Historical Archaeology
Plenum Publishing Corp.
c/o Charles E. Orser Phone: (309)438-2271
Anthropology, Campus Box 4640 Fax: (309)438-7177
Illinois State University
Normal, IL 61790-4640
Publication E-mail: ceorser@ilstu.edu
Publisher E-mail: info@plenum.com

Scholarly journal covering historical archaeology. **Founded:** June 1997. **Freq:** Quarterly. **Trim Size:** 6 x 9. **Cols./Page:** 1. **Col. Width:** 27 picas. **Key Personnel:** Charles Orser, Editor, ceorser@ilstu.edu. **ISSN:** 1092-7697. **Subscription Rates:** $35 individuals. **Remarks:** Accepts advertising.
Circ: (Not Reported)

9460 Normal Normalite
Normalite
102 Parkinson St. Phone: (309)454-5476
Normal, IL 61761-3015 Fax: (309)454-5476

Local newspaper. **Founded:** Mar. 1900. **Freq:** Weekly (Thurs.). **Print Method:** Offset. **Trim Size:** 10 3/4 x 16. **Cols./Page:** 5. **Col. Width:** 11 1/2 picas. **Key Personnel:** Edward Pyne, Editor and Publisher. **USPS:** 391-720. **Subscription Rates:** $12.95 individuals; $14.95 out of area. **Remarks:** Accepts advertising.
Ad Rates: GLR: $.30 **Circ:** ‡1,817
BW: $240
4C: $500
SAU: $4.20

9461 Spoon River Poetry Review
c/o Dr. Lucia Getsi Phone: (309)438-7906
Illinois State University Fax: (309)438-5414
4240 English
Normal, IL 61790-4240
Literary magazine covering poetry. **Founded:** 1974. **Freq:** Semiannual. **Key Personnel:** Dr. Lucia C. Getsi, Editor. **ISSN:** 0738-8993. **Subscription Rates:** $14 individuals; $8 single issue. **Remarks:** Advertising not accepted. **Former name:** Spoon River Quarterly.
Circ: Combined 1,000

9462 Teaching Sociology
University of Arizona
Dept. of Sociology/Anthropology
Schroeder 338
Illinois State University
Normal, IL 61761
Publisher E-mail: edwards@asanet.org

Journal with research articles, teaching tips, and reports on teaching sociology. **Founded:** 1973. **Freq:** Quarterly. **Print Method:** Offset. **Trim Size:** 6 3/4 x 9 7/8. **Cols./Page:** 2. **Col. Width:** 27 nonpareils. **Col. Depth:** 112 agate lines. **Key Personnel:** Dean Dorn, Editor; Michele Walczak, Advertising Mgr. **ISSN:** 0092-055X. **Subscription Rates:** $20 members; $40 nonmembers; $80 institutions. **Remarks:** Color advertising not accepted.
Ad Rates: BW: $200 **Circ:** ‡2,000

9463 TCI of Bloomington/Normal, Inc.
1202 W. Division St. Phone: (309)454-3350
Normal, IL 61761 Fax: (309)452-6271

Founded: 1969. **Formerly:** TeleCable of Bloomington-Normal. **Cities Served:** McLean County, IL.

9464 WGLT-FM - 103.3
Campus PO Box 8910 Phone: (309)438-2255
Normal, IL 61761 Fax: (309)438-7870
E-mail: wglt@ilstu.edu

Format: Jazz; Blues; News. **Networks:** National Public Radio (NPR); AP. **Founded:** 1966. **Operating Hours:** Continuous; 20% network, 80% local. **Key Personnel:** Bruce Bergethon, General Mgr., phone (309)438-2393; Mike McCurdy, Program Dir., phone (309)438-2394; Willis Kern, News Dir., phone (309)438-5426, wekern@ilstu.edu; Marc Boon, Music Dir., phone (309)438-8955. **Wattage:** 25,000. **Ad Rates:** Noncommercial. **URL:** http://www.ilstu.edu/depts/wglt.

NORTHBROOK, pop. 30,735.

Cook Co. (NE). 6 m NW of Winnetka. Residential.

9465 AWHP's Worksite Health
Association for Worksite Health Promotion
60 Revere Dr., No. 500 Phone: (847)480-9574
Northbrook, IL 60062 Fax: (847)480-9282
Publisher E-mail: awhp@awhp.org

Professional journal for health promotion practitioners. **Founded:** 1995. **Freq:** Quarterly. **Print Method:** Sheetfed offset. **Trim Size:** 8 1/2 x 11. **Cols./Page:** 2. **Key Personnel:** Kristen Lambert s, Managing Editor; George Pfeiffer, Editor; Vicki Diffendal, Editor; Angie Leondedis, Advertising Mgr. **ISSN:** 1085-2174. **Subscription Rates:** $45 individuals. **Remarks:** Accepts advertising.
Circ: Controlled 2,900

9466 Candy Industry
Stagnito Communications Inc.
1935 Shermer Rd., No. 100 Phone: (847)205-5660
Northbrook, IL 60062-5354 Fax: (847)205-5680

Magazine serving candy industry management. **Subtitle:** The Global Magazine of Management and Technology. **Founded:** 1944. **Freq:** Monthly. **Print Method:** Offset. **Trim Size:** 8 x 10 3/4. **Cols./Page:** 3. **Col. Width:** 27 nonpareils. **Col. Depth:** 140 agate lines. **Key Personnel:** Susan Tiffany, Editor, editor@candyindustry.com; Patricia L. Magee, Publisher; Wendy Kimbrell, Group Publisher; Mike Kleeblatt, Senior Marketing Mgr. **ISSN:** 0745-1032. **Subscription Rates:** $39; $7 single issue. **URL:** http://www.candyindustry.com.
Ad Rates: BW: $3,710 **Circ:** Paid 1,848
4C: $5,110 Non-paid 4,855
PCI: $130

9467 Career World
Weekly Reader Corp.
900 Skokie Blvd. Phone: (847)205-3000
Northbrook, IL 60062-4028 Fax: (847)564-8197

Magazine serving as a guide to jobs and careers for students in grades 7-12. **Founded:** 1972. **Freq:** 7/year (during academic year). **Print Method:** Offset. **Trim Size:** 7 1/2 x 10 3/8. **Cols./Page:** 3. **Col. Width:** 25 nonpareils. **Col. Depth:** 133 agate lines. **Key Personnel:** Carole Rubenstein, Editor, phone (847)205-3000, fax (847)564-8197, ruben@glcomm.com; Richard LeBrasseur, President and Publisher; Eric Ecker, V.P. of Circulation and Marketing, phone (203)705-3500, fax (203)705-1662. **ISSN:** 0744-1002. **Subscription Rates:** $8.75 per subscription for 15 or more; $8.50 per sub for 15 or more 95-96 school year. **Remarks:** Advertising accepted; rates available upon request. **Formerly:** Career World/Real World.
Circ: Paid 87,000

9468 Current Health 1
Weekly Reader Corp.
900 Skokie Blvd. Phone: (847)205-3000
Northbrook, IL 60062-4028 Fax: (847)564-8197

Magazine for elementary school children. **Subtitle:** The Beginning Guide to Health Education. **Founded:** 1977. **Freq:** 8/year (monthly during the academic year). **Print Method:** Offset. **Trim Size:** 7 1/2 x 10 3/8. **Cols./Page:** 3. **Col. Width:** 25 nonpareils. **Col. Depth:** 133 agate lines. **Key Personnel:** Carole Rubenstein, Editor, phone (847)205-3141, ruben@glcomm.com; Peter E. Berger, Pres./CEO. **ISSN:** 0199-820X. **Subscription Rates:** $8.95 individuals (15 or more subscriptions); $17.90 (14 or fewer subscriptions). **Remarks:** Advertising not accepted. **Alt. Formats:** Microform.
Circ: Paid 165,793

9469 Current Health 2
Weekly Reader Corp.
900 Skokie Blvd., Ste. 200 Phone: (847)205-3000
Northbrook, IL 60062-4028 Fax: (847)564-8197

Magazine for middle and secondary school students. **Subtitle:** The Continuing Guide to Health Education. **Founded:** 1973. **Freq:** 8x/year (monthly during the academic year). **Print Method:** Offset. **Trim Size:** 7 1/2 x 10 3/8. **Cols./Page:** 3. **Col. Width:** 25 nonpareils. **Col. Depth:** 133 agate lines. **Key Personnel:** Carole Rubenstein, Editor, phone (847)205-3141, fax (847)564-8197, ruben@glcomm.com; Peter E. Bergen, Pres./CEO. **ISSN:** 0163-156X. **Subscription Rates:** $8.95 individuals 15 subscriptions; $17.90 (2-14 subscriptions). **Remarks:** Advertising not accepted. **Alt. Formats:** Microfilm, NewsBank.
Circ: Paid 229,274

9470 Draperies and Window Coverings
L.C. Clark Publishing
666 Dundee Rd., Ste.807 Phone: (847)498-9880
Northbrook, IL 60062 Fax: (847)498-9299
Publication E-mail: info@dwcdesigNET.com

Trade magazine. **Subtitle:** The Magazine for the Interior Fashion Professional. **Founded:** 1981. **Freq:** 13/year. **Print Method:** Offset. **Trim Size:** 8 1/4 x 11. **Cols./Page:** 3. **Col. Width:** 14 picas. **Col. Depth:** 60 picas. **Key Personnel:** Katie Sosnowchik, Editor, katie@dwcdesignnet.com; John A. Clark, Publisher; Carolyn Silberman, Assoc. Publisher. **ISSN:** 0279-4918. **Subscription Rates:** $33 individuals; $4.95 single issue; $50 Canada and Mexico; $100 other countries. **Re-**

marks: Accepts advertising. **URL:** http://www.dwcdesignnet.com.
Ad Rates: BW: $3,975 **Circ:** Paid 5,265
4C: $5,050 Non-paid 20,006

9471 Floral & Nursery Times
XXX Publishing Enterprises Ltd.
601 Skokie Blvd., Ste. 505 Phone: (847)562-9797
PO Box 8470 Fax: (847)562-9898
Northbrook, IL 60062
Floriculture industry tabloid. **Founded:** Dec. 17, 1979. **Freq:** Semimonthly. **Print Method:** Offset. **Trim Size:** 11 x 14 1/2. **Cols./Page:** 5. **Col. Width:** 22 nonpareils. **Col. Depth:** 193 agate lines. **Key Personnel:** Lila DiCanio, Managing Editor; Barbara Gilbert, Co.-Pub.; Thomas C. DiCanio, Publisher. **Subscription Rates:** $45 individuals; $7.50 single issue. **Remarks:** Accepts advertising.
Ad Rates: BW: $947 **Circ:** Paid ‡4,276
4C: $1190 Controlled ‡13,228
PCI: $28

9472 Food Product Design
Weeks Publishing Co.
3400 Dundee Rd., Ste. 100 Phone: (847)559-0385
Northbrook, IL 60062-2333 Fax: (847)559-0389
Publisher E-mail: weeksfpd@aol.com

Trade magazine for food product design and reformulation professionals in retail and foodservice markets internationally. **Founded:** Apr. 1991. **Freq:** Monthly. **Print Method:** Web offsite. **Trim Size:** 8 1/8 x 10 7/8. **Cols./Page:** 3. **Key Personnel:** Lynn A. Kuntz, Editor, lakfpd@aol.com; Kathy Colwell, Advertising Mgr., kathyfpd@aol.com; Robert F. Weeks, Publisher, weeksfpd@aol.com. **ISSN:** 1065-772X. **Subscription Rates:** $100 individuals; $175 out of country; $12 single issue. **Remarks:** Accepts advertising.
Ad Rates: BW: $3,930 **Circ:** Combined ‡26,195
4C: $5,180
PCI: $85

9473 In Motion
General Learning Communications
900 Skokie Blvd., Ste. 200 Phone: (847)205-3000
Northbrook, IL 60062 Fax: (847)564-8197

Driver education magazine. **Subtitle:** The Guide to Safe Driving. **Founded:** 1986. **Freq:** Annual. **Print Method:** Offset. **Trim Size:** 7 3/4 x 10 1/2. **Cols./Page:** 3. **Col. Width:** 25 nonpareils. **Col. Depth:** 133 agate lines. **Key Personnel:** Carole Rubenstein, Editor, phone (847)205-3141, ruben@glcomm.com; Julio Abreu, Publisher, jabreu@lcomm.com. **Subscription Rates:** Free to schools. **Remarks:** Advertising not accepted.
Circ: Non-paid 1,000,000

9474 Industria
Stagnito Communications Inc.
1935 Shermer Rd., No. 100 Phone: (847)205-5660
Northbrook, IL 60062-5354 Fax: (847)205-5680

Trade magazine for the Latin American food and beverage industry. **Founded:** Sept. 1990. **Freq:** Monthly. **Print Method:** Offset. **Trim Size:** 8 x 10. **Cols./Page:** 2. **Key Personnel:** Mario A. Schacher, Publisher; Elsa Rico-Torres, Editor. **Subscription Rates:** $110 individuals; $10 single issue. **Remarks:** Accepts advertising.
Circ: (Not Reported)

9475 Industria Alimenticia
Stagnito Communications Inc.
1935 Shermer Rd., No. 100 Phone: (847)205-5660
Northbrook, IL 60062-5354 Fax: (847)205-5680

Trade magazine for the Latin American food and beverage industry. **Founded:** Sept. 1990. **Freq:** Monthly. **Print Method:** Offset. **Trim Size:** 8 x 10 3/4. **Cols./Page:** 3. **Key Personnel:** Mario Schacher, Publisher; Elsa Rico-Torres, Editor. **Subscription Rates:** $120 individuals; $15 single issue. **Remarks:** Accepts advertising.
Ad Rates: BW: $3,080 **Circ:** (Not Reported)
4C: $4,430

9476 Journal of Nuclear Materials Management
Institute of Nuclear Materials Management
60 Revere Dr., Ste. 500 Phone: (847)480-9573
Northbrook, IL 60062 Fax: (847)480-9282
Publication E-mail: inmm@inmm.org

Scholarly/technical journal for professionals involved in nuclear materials management and safeguards. **Founded:** 1972. **Freq:** Quarterly. **Print Method:** Sheetfed offset. **Trim Size:** 8 1/8 x 10 7/8. **Key Personnel:** Greg Schultz, Managing Editor; Dennis Mangan, Editor, phone (505)845-8710, fax (505)844-6067, dlmanga@gasandia.gov; Angie Leondedis, Advertising Mgr.; Bill Kaprelian, Advertising Dir. **ISSN:** 0893-6188. **Subscription Rates:** $100 U.S., Canada, and Mexico; $135 other countries; $25 single issue. **Remarks:** Accepts advertising. **Formerly:** Nuclear Materials Management.
Ad Rates: BW: $912 **Circ:** Paid ‡8,000
4C: $1,512

9477 Norris City Banner
Liberty Group
3000 Dundee Rd., Ste. 203
Northbrook, IL 60062

Community newspaper. **Founded:** Sept. 4, 1974. **Freq:** Weekly (Wed.). **Print Method:** Offset. **Cols./Page:** 6. **Col. Width:** 24 nonpareils. **Col. Depth:** 294 agate lines. **Key Personnel:** Jeannie Gossett, Managing Editor & Advertising Mgr.; Scott Koon, Publisher, phone (309)647-5100, fax (309)647-4665. **USPS:** 058-950. **Subscription Rates:** $25 local; $30 out of area. **Remarks:** Accepts advertising.
Ad Rates: GLR: $.40 **Circ:** Paid ‡1,289
BW: $466.20 Free ‡15
SAU: $3.70
PCI: $5.90

9478 Northbrook Weekend Voice
Lerner Communications, Inc.
7331 N. Lincoln Ave. Phone: (847)329-2000
Lincolnwood, IL 60646-1704 Fax: (847)329-2060
Publisher E-mail: lerner@enteract.com

Community newspaper. **Freq:** Weekly. **Trim Size:** 11 x 17. **Key Personnel:** Leah A. Zeldes, Managing Editor. **Subscription Rates:** Free. **URL:** http://www.intheloop.com. **Formerly:** Northbrook Voice.
Circ: Paid 82
Free 6,000

9479 On the Mark
Corporate Communications
333 Pfingsten Rd. Phone: (847)272-8800
Northbrook, IL 60062 Fax: (847)509-6235
Publication E-mail: poilockr@ul.com
Publisher E-mail: northbrook@ul.com

Trade magazine covering business issues. **Founded:** Apr. 1995. **Freq:** Quarterly. **Print Method:** Offset. **Trim Size:** 8 1/2 x 11. **Cols./Page:** 4. **Key Personnel:** Carole Feil, Editor, feilc@ul.com; Michael Nissen, Editor, nissenm@ul.com. **Subscription Rates:** Free. **Remarks:** Advertising not accepted. **URL:** http://www.ul.com.
Circ: Non-paid 80,000

9480 Plumbing Engineer
TMB Publishing Inc.
1838 Techny Ct. Phone: (847)564-1127
Northbrook, IL 60062 Fax: (847)564-1264
Publisher E-mail: tmbpubs@earthlink.net

Trade journal for consulting engineering, mechanical engineering, architecture, and contracting professionals. **Founded:** 1973. **Freq:** 12/year. **Print Method:** Offset. **Trim Size:** 8 1/4 x 11. **Cols./Page:** 3. **Key Personnel:** Tom Brown, Publisher; Tom Klemens, Editor, tmbpubs@earthlink.net. **ISSN:** 0192-1711. **Subscription Rates:** Free to qualified subscribers; $50. **Remarks:** Accepts advertising. **Alt. Formats:** Microfilm.
Ad Rates: BW: $3,200 **Circ:** Free ‡25,600
4C: $4,350

9481 RadTech Report
RadTech International North America
60 Revere Dr., Ste. 500 Phone: (847)480-9576
Northbrook, IL 60062 Fax: (847)480-9282
Publisher E-mail: uveb@radtech.org

Contains articles on applications of ultraviolet and electron beam curing technology. **Founded:** 1987. **Freq:** Bimonthly. **Print Method:** Sheetfed. **Trim Size:** 8 1/4 x 10 7/8. **Cols./Page:** 3. **Key Personnel:** Kelly Xintaris, Editor, kxintaris@radtech.org; Don Wink, Advertising Mgr.; Christine Dionne, Executive Dir., cdionne@radtech.org. **ISSN:** 1056-0793. **Subscription Rates:** $7.50 single issue; $60 individuals; $95 foreign. **Remarks:** Accepts advertising. **URL:** http://www.radtech.com.
Ad Rates: BW: $610 **Circ:** Non-paid 1,750
4C: $1,330

9482 Writing!
Weekly Reader Corp.
900 Skokie Blvd., Ste. 200 Phone: (708)205-3000
Northbrook, IL 60062-4028 Fax: (708)564-8197

Magazine for students in grades 7-12. **Subtitle:** The Continuing Guide to Written Communication. **Founded:** 1979. **Freq:** 7/year (monthly during the academic year). **Print Method:** Offset. **Trim Size:** 7 1/2 x 10 1/2. **Cols./Page:** 3. **Col. Width:** 25 nonpareils. **Col. Depth:** 133 agate lines. **Key Personnel:** Alan Lenhoff, Editor, alenhoff@glcomm.com; Richard Le Brasseur, Publisher. **ISSN:** 0279-7208. **Subscription Rates:** $8.65 (15+ subscriptions). **Remarks:** Advertising not accepted.
Circ: (Not Reported)

WKTA-AM - See Evanston

9483 WNVR-AM - 1030
4320 Dundee Rd. Phone: (773)588-6300
Northbrook, IL 60062 Fax: (773)267-4913
E-mail: pclradio@techinter.com

Format: Ethnic. **Networks:** International Media Service. **Founded:** 1988. **Operating Hours:** Daytime. **ADI:** Chicago (LaSalle), IL. **Key Personnel:** Walter Kotaba, President; Kent Gustatson, Vice President; Zofia Oravec, Sales Mgr.; Sterling Hazen, Operations Mgr. **Local Programs:** *Czuma Radio*, Andrew Czuma; *Radio for You*, Stan Kedzia; *Studio A*, Jerzy Jurnak. **Wattage:** 4000. **Ad Rates:** $45-65 for 30 seconds; $80-120 for 60 seconds. International Network. **URL:** http://www.pclradio.com.

NORTHFIELD, pop. 5,807.

Cook Co. (NE). 17 m N of Chicago. Residential.

9484 CAP Today
College of American Pathologists
325 Waukegan Rd. Phone: (847)832-7000
Northfield, IL 60093-2750 Fax: (847)832-8150
Free: (800)323-4040
Publication E-mail: captoday@interaccess.com

Magazine covering advances in pathology tests and equipment, clinical lab management and operations trends, and related regulatory and legislative changes. **Founded:** 1987. **Freq:** Monthly. **Print Method:** Offset. **Trim Size:** 10 7/8 x 16. **Cols./Page:** 4. **Col. Width:** 26 nonpareils. **Col. Depth:** 296 agate lines. **Key Personnel:** Sherrie Rice, Editor, phone (847)832-7504, srice@cap.org; Bob McGonnagle, Publisher, phone (847)832-7476. **ISSN:** 0891-1525. **Subscription Rates:** $40 individuals U.S.; $60 Canada; $95 Foreign. **Remarks:** Accepts advertising. **URL:** http://www.cap.org.
Circ: Paid 10,000
Non-paid 40,000

9485 Clavier
Instrumentalist Co.
200 Northfield Rd. Phone: (847)446-5000
Northfield, IL 60093 Fax: (847)446-6263

Trade magazine for keyboard performers, teachers, and students. **Founded:** 1962. **Freq:** 10/year. **Print Method:** Offset. **Trim Size:** 8 1/4 x 11 1/4. **Cols./Page:** 3. **Col. Width:** 13 picas. **Col. Depth:** 10 inches. **Key Personnel:** Judy Nelson, Editor; James T. Rohner, Publisher; Will Garvey, Advertising Mgr. **ISSN:** 0009-854X. **Subscription Rates:** $18 individuals.
Ad Rates: BW: $1,374 **Circ:** ‡16,700
4C: $1,374
PCI: $76

9486 Dental Lab Products
MEDEC Dental Communications
2 Northfield Plaza No. 300 Phone: (847)441-3700
Northfield, IL 60093 Fax: (847)441-3702
Free: (800)323-3337

Professional tabloid for dental laboratory owners and managers. Covering new products, training seminars, conferences, and techniques. **Founded:** 1976. **Freq:** Bimonthly. **Print Method:** Offset. **Trim Size:** 11 x 14 3/4. **Cols./Page:** 3 and 4. **Col. Width:** 39 and 28 nonpareils. **Col. Depth:** 189 agate lines. **Key Personnel:** Roger Colahan, Publisher, phone (847)441-3707, roger.colahan@medec.com; Pamela Johnson, Editor, phone (847)771-3716, pam.johnson@medec.com. **ISSN:** 0146-9738. **Subscription Rates:** $27 individuals. **Remarks:** Accepts advertising. **Available Online. URL:** http://www.medec.com/dlp/.
Ad Rates: BW: $4,445 **Circ:** Non-paid 18,827
4C: $5,795

9487 Dental Products Report
MEDEC Dental Communications
2 Northfield Plaza No. 300 Phone: (847)441-3700
Northfield, IL 60093 Fax: (847)441-3702
Free: (800)323-3337
Publication E-mail: dpr@medec.com

Professional tabloid for dentists. Covering new products, new literature, conferences, technical exhibits, esthetic dentistry techniques, and infection-control procedures. **Subtitle:** Products and News for the Dental Profession. **Founded:** 1967. **Freq:** 12/year. **Print Method:** Offset. **Trim Size:** 11 x 14 3/4. **Cols./Page:** 4 and 3. **Col. Width:** 13.6 and 19 picas. **Col. Depth:** 183 agate lines. **Key Personnel:** Gail Weisman, Editor, phone (847)441-3722, gail.weisman@medec.com; Roger Colahan, Publisher, phone (847)441-3707, roger.calahan@medec.com. **ISSN:** 0011-8737. **Subscription**

Rates: $110. **Remarks:** Accepts advertising. **Available Online. URL:** http://www.medec.com/dpr/.
Ad Rates: BW: $11,300 **Circ:** Controlled 156,779
4C: $12,850

9488 Healthcare Purchasing News
McKnight Medical Communications
2 Northfield Plz., Ste. 300 Phone: (847)441-3700
Northfield, IL 60093 Fax: (847)441-3701
Free: (800)451-7838
Publication E-mail: hpn@medec.com

Magazine for healthcare material management, central service, operating room, and infection control professionals. **Subtitle:** Business News and Analysis for Purchasing Decision-Makers. **Founded:** 1977. **Freq:** Monthly. **Print Method:** Offset. **Trim Size:** 10 7/8 x 14. **Cols./Page:** 4. **Col. Width:** 28 nonpareils. **Col. Depth:** 140 agate lines. **Key Personnel:** Rick Dana Barlow, Editor; John Andrews, Sr. Assoc. Editor; Stephanie A. Ellis, National Sales Mgr.; Charlene Swanson, Classified Advertising; Cheryl Hackos, Eastern Account Mgr. **ISSN:** 0278-4799. **Subscription Rates:** $44.95 U.S.; $54.95 Canada; $59.95 foreign; $5 single issue; $9 single issue back issue. **Remarks:** Advertising accepted; rates available upon request. **URL:** http://www.medec.com/hpn/. **Formerly**: HPN; Hospital Purchasing News.
Circ: Paid 80
Non-paid 31,000

9489 The Instrumentalist
Instrumentalist Co.
200 Northfield Rd. Phone: (847)446-5000
Northfield, IL 60093 Fax: (847)446-6263

Magazine for school band and orchestra directors, professional instrumentalists, and students. **Founded:** 1946. **Freq:** Monthly. **Print Method:** Offset. **Trim Size:** 8 1/4 x 11 1/4. **Cols./Page:** 3. **Col. Width:** 26 nonpareils. **Col. Depth:** 140 agate lines. **Key Personnel:** Catherine Lenzini, Editor; James T. Rohner, Publisher; William H. Garvey, Advertising Mgr. **ISSN:** 0020-4331. **Subscription Rates:** $22 individuals. **Remarks:** Accepts advertising.
Ad Rates: BW: $1,809 **Circ:** ‡18,200
4C: $2,104
PCI: $100

9490 McKnight's Long-Term Care News
McKnight Medical Communications
2 Northfield Plz., Ste. 300 Phone: (847)441-3700
Northfield, IL 60093 Fax: (847)441-3701
Free: (800)451-7838
Publication E-mail: ltcnews@medec.com

Professional magazine. **Subtitle:** News/Ideas for Administrators & Patient Care Managers. **Founded:** 1980. **Freq:** Monthly. **Print Method:** Offset. **Trim Size:** 10 7/8 x 14. **Cols./Page:** 4. **Col. Width:** 28 nonpareils. **Col. Depth:** 140 agate lines. **Key Personnel:** Irene Oneito, Publisher; John O'Connor, Editor; Irene Oneito, National Sales Mgr.; Bob Santini, Eastern Sales Mgr.; Charlene Swanson, Inside Sales Mgr. **ISSN:** 1084-3314. **Subscription Rates:** Free to qualified subscribers in U.S.; $5 single issue; $9 single issue back issue; $54.95 Canada; $59.95 foreign. **Remarks:** Accepts advertising. **Formerly**: Today's Nursing Home.
Ad Rates: BW: $4,695 **Circ:** Paid 850
4C: $5,955 Controlled 46,025
PCI: $120

9491 Pharmaceutical Representative
McKnight Medical Communications
2 Northfield Plz., Ste. 300 Phone: (847)441-3700
Northfield, IL 60093 Fax: (847)441-3701
Free: (800)451-7838
Publication E-mail: pr@medec.com

Trade magazine. **Subtitle:** The only newsmagazine designed solely for the pharmaceutical representative. **Founded:** 1971. **Freq:** Monthly. **Print Method:** Offset. **Trim Size:** 10 7/8 x 14. **Cols./Page:** 4. **Col. Width:** 38 nonpareils. **Col. Depth:** 140 agate lines. **Key Personnel:** Kristen Mally, Editor, phone (708)441-3733, kristen_ mally@medec.com; Irene Onesto, Publisher, phone (708)441-3723. **ISSN:** 0161-8415. **Subscription Rates:** $39.95 individuals; $5 single issue; $41.95 Canada; $52.95 other countries. **Remarks:** Accepts advertising. **Available Online. URL:** http://www.pharmrep.com.
Ad Rates: BW: $1,995 **Circ:** 42,000
4C: $3,195

Wisconsin Beverage Journal - See Madison, Wisconsin

O FALLON

9492 The Legal Reporter
O'Fallon Progress
PO Box 970 Phone: (618)632-3643
612 E. State St. Fax: (618)632-6438
O Fallon, IL 62269-0970
Free: (888)234-3365

Court and legal newspaper (tabloid). **Subtitle:** Court information from St. Clair, Madison, and Monroe, counties, in IL. **Founded:** 1945. **Freq:** Weekly (Wed.). **Print Method:** Offset. **Cols./Page:** 6. **Col. Width:** 61 picas. **Col. Depth:** 96 picas. **Key Personnel:** Jennifer Gammage, Editor; Bud Ross, Publisher. **USPS:** 461-600. **Subscription Rates:** $42 individuals; $1 single issue. **Remarks:** Accepts advertising. **Formerly**: The Reporter.
Ad Rates: GLR: $1 **Circ:** Paid 1,000
SAU: $5.25 Free 10

9493 O'Fallon Progress
PO Box 970 Phone: (618)632-3643
612 E. State St. Fax: (618)632-6438
O Fallon, IL 62269-0970
Free: (888)234-3365
Publication E-mail: basenews@apci.net

Community newspaper. **Founded:** 1895. **Freq:** Weekly. **Print Method:** Offset. **Cols./Page:** 6. **Col. Width:** 12 picas. **Col. Depth:** 21 1/2 inches. **Key Personnel:** Jennifer Gammage, Managing Editor; Bud Ross, Publisher; Michael King, Advertising & Mktg. Dir. **USPS:** 464-000. **Subscription Rates:** $20 individuals; $.5 single issue.
Ad Rates: GLR: $3.30 **Circ:** 4,000
BW: $1,041
4C: $1,241
SAU: $11.55

OAK BROOK, pop. 6,641.

DuPage Co. (NE). 17 m SW of Chicago. Residential.

9494 Assembly
Cahners Business Information
2000 Clearwater Dr. Phone: (630)320-7000
Oak Brook, IL 60523
Magazine focusing on assembly of hard goods, including electronic and mechanical products. **Founded:** 1958. **Freq:** 12/year. **Print Method:** Web Offset. **Trim Size:** 8 x 10 3/4. **Cols./Page:** 3. **Col. Width:** 26 nonpareils. **Col. Depth:** 140 agate lines. **Key Personnel:** Donald E. Hegland, Editor; Ed McCallum, Publisher. **ISSN:** 0004-0563. **Subscription Rates:** $68 individuals. **Remarks:** Accepts advertising. **URL:** http://www.assemblymag.com. **Formerly**: Assembly Engineering.
Ad Rates: BW: $5,820 **Circ:** Controlled ‡60,000
4C: $7,370

9495 Business Ledger
Ledger Publishing Co.
600 Enterprise Dr., Ste. 100 Phone: (630)571-8911
Oak Brook, IL 60523 Fax: (630)571-4053
Publication E-mail: bizledger@aol.com

Regional business newspaper covering DuPage, Northwest Cook County and the Fox Valley. **Founded:** Apr. 1993. **Freq:** Biweekly. **Print Method:** Offset. **Trim Size:** 10 3/4 x 13 3/4. **Cols./Page:** 4. **Col. Width:** 2 1/4 inches. **Col. Depth:** 12 1/4 inches. **Key Personnel:** Don Kopriva, Editor; Joe Castelluccio, Advertising Dir.; James E. Elsener, Publisher. **ISSN:** 1082-8397. **Subscription Rates:** $25 individuals; $2 single issue. **URL:** http://www.thebusinessledger.com. **Formerly**: Northwest Business Ledger; DuPage Business Ledger.
Ad Rates: BW: $3,025 **Circ:** Controlled 17,000
4C: $3,625

9496 Construction Equipment Distribution
Associated Equipment Distributors
615 W. 22nd St. Phone: (630)574-0650
Oak Brook, IL 60523 Fax: (630)574-0132
Free: (800)388-0650
Publication E-mail: aedonline@aol.com
Publisher E-mail: info@aednet.org

Trade magazine for construction equipment distributors. **Founded:** 1936. **Freq:** Monthly. **Print Method:** Offset. **Trim Size:** 8 1/4 x 11. **Cols./Page:** 3 and 2. **Col. Width:** 27 and 40 nonpareils. **Col. Depth:** 140 agate lines. **Key Personnel:** Edward Salek, Editor. **ISSN:** 0010-6755. **Subscription Rates:** $25 individuals. **Remarks:** Accepts advertising. **URL:** http://www.asednet.org.
Ad Rates: BW: $900 **Circ:** ‡4,000
4C: $1,530

9497 CSA Journal
CSA Fraternal Life
122 W. 22nd St. Phone: (630)472-0500
Oak Brook, IL 60523 Fax: (630)472-1100
Free: (800)543-3272
Publisher E-mail: lifecsa@aol.com

Fraternal insurance magazine (English and Czech). **Founded:** 1891. **Freq:** Monthly. **Print Method:** Offset. **Cols./Page:** 3. **Col. Width:** 42 nonpareils. **Col. Depth:** 133 agate lines. **Key Personnel:** Karin Stritzke, Editor. **ISSN:** 0195-9050. **Subscription Rates:** $12. **Remarks:** Advertising not accepted.
Circ: (Not Reported)

9498 Employee Services Management
National Employee Services and Recreation Association
2211 York Rd., Ste. 207 Phone: (630)368-1280
Oak Brook, IL 60523-2371 Fax: (630)368-1286
Publisher E-mail: nesrahq@nesra.org

Trade magazine focusing on employee services, fitness, and recreation programming. **Founded:** 1958. **Freq:** 10/year. **Print Method:** Desktop system. **Trim Size:** 8 1/4 x 11 1/4. **Cols./Page:** 3. **Col. Width:** 26 nonpareils. **Col. Depth:** 140 agate lines. **Key Personnel:** Cynthia Helson, Editor; Patrick B. Stinson, Publisher; Charles A. Bashian, Advertising Mgr.; Chuck Bashian, Marketing, phone (800)335-7500. **ISSN:** 0744-3676. **Subscription Rates:** $42 individuals; $4.50 single issue. **Remarks:** Accepts advertising. **URL:** http://www.nesra.org.
Ad Rates: BW: $990 **Circ:** Paid ‡4,000
4C: $645 Non-paid ‡600

9499 Industrial Paint and Powder
Cahners Business Information
2000 Clearwater Dr. Phone: (630)320-7000
Oak Brook, IL 60523
Magazine focusing on the development and application of OEM coatings. **Founded:** 1924. **Freq:** Monthly. **Print Method:** Offset. **Cols./Page:** 2 and 3. **Col. Width:** 55 and 26 nonpareils. **Col. Depth:** 140 agate lines. **Key Personnel:** Ed McCallum, Publisher; Jane Bailey, Editor; Dan Davis, Senior Editor. **Subscription Rates:** Free to qualified subscribers; $60 by mail. **Remarks:** Accepts advertising. **URL:** http://www.ippmagazine.com. **Formerly**: Industrial Finishing.
Ad Rates: BW: $3,700 **Circ:** Controlled ‡38,300
4C: $5,290

9500 Lion En Espanol
Lions Clubs International
300 W. 22nd St. Phone: (630)571-5466
Oak Brook, IL 60523-8815 Fax: (630)571-8890

Magazine containing club news for business men, printed in Spanish. **Founded:** 1944. **Freq:** Bimonthly. **Print Method:** Offset. **Cols./Page:** 3. **Col. Width:** 26 nonpareils. **Col. Depth:** 140 agate lines. **Key Personnel:** Fernando Fernandez, Editor. **Subscription Rates:** $3.75 single issue.

9501 The Lion Magazine
Lions Clubs International
300 W. 22nd St. Phone: (630)571-5466
Oak Brook, IL 60523-8815 Fax: (630)571-8890

Magazine containing club news for service minded men and women. **Founded:** 1918. **Freq:** 10/year. **Print Method:** Offset. **Trim Size:** 8 1/4 x 10 7/8. **Cols./Page:** 3. **Col. Width:** 2 1/4 inches. **Col. Depth:** 140 agate lines. **Key Personnel:** Robert Kleinfelder, Editor, phone (630)571-5466; Mary Kay Rietz, Advertising & Production Manager, phone (630)571-5466. **ISSN:** 0024-4163. **Subscription Rates:** $6.00 individuals. **Alt. Formats:** Audio tape.
Ad Rates: BW: $4,660 **Circ:** Paid ★**543,580**
4C: $5,725

9502 Manufacturing Systems
Cahners Business Information
2000 Clearwater Dr. Phone: (630)320-7000
Oak Brook, IL 60523
Professional magazine covering information technology for manufacturing managers. **Founded:** 1984. **Freq:** Monthly. **Print Method:** Web offset. **Trim Size:** 7 7/8 x 10 1/2. **Key Personnel:** Kevin Parker, Editor, kparker@cahners.com. **Subscription Rates:** $70 individuals; $257 international. **Remarks:** Accepts advertising. **URL:** http://www.manufacturingsystems.com.
Ad Rates: BW: $11,325 **Circ:** Non-paid ‡106,600
4C: $12,175

9503 New Steel
Cahners Business Information
2000 Clearwater Dr. Phone: (630)320-7000
Oak Brook, IL 60523
Serves ferrous and non-ferrous metal-producing industries. **Subtitle:** Mini & Integrated mill management and technologies. **Founded:** 1855. **Freq:** Monthly. **Print Method:** Web offset. **Trim Size:** 7 7/8 x 10 3/4. **Key Personnel:** Adam Ritt, Executive Editor, phone (630)462-2286; Robert Higgins, Publisher, phone (630)462-2285; Bryan Berry, Editorial Director,

phone (630)4622282, bberry@chilton.net; Mike Greissel, Managing Editor, phone (630)462-2972; Jim Bagan, Director of Sales, phone (630)462-2290, fax (630)462-4862; Tom Bagsarian, Senior Associate Editor, phone (630)462-2236; Pamela Patel, Production Editor, phone (630)4322294, fax (630)4622862; Craig Woker, Associate Editor, phone (630)462-2221. **ISSN:** 0897-4365. **Subscription Rates:** Free to qualified subscribers. **Remarks:** Accepts advertising. **Online:** Nexus. **Alt. Formats:** Microform. **Formerly:** Iron Age.
Ad Rates: BW: $4,220 **Circ:** Controlled ‡19,586
4C: $5,480

9504 OAG Air Cargo Guide
Official Airline Guides
2000 Clearwater Dr. Phone: (630)574-6000
Oak Brook, IL 60523-8806 Fax: (630)574-6667
Free: (800)323-3537

Guide to shipping freight by air containing current domestic, international and combination passenger cargo flight schedules. **Founded:** 1957. **Freq:** Monthly. **Print Method:** Offset. **Trim Size:** 8 1/8 x 10 7/8. **Cols./Page:** 3. **Col. Width:** 27 nonpareils. **Col. Depth:** 140 agate lines. **Key Personnel:** Richard A. Nelson, Publisher; Alex Igyarto, Publisher; Gene E. Gander, Advertising Mgr. **ISSN:** 0191-152X. **Subscription Rates:** $183 individuals. **Remarks:** Accepts advertising.
Ad Rates: BW: $2,045 **Circ:** ‡6,029

9505 OAG Desktop Guide – Worldwide Edition
OAG Worldwide
2000 Clearwater Dr. Phone: (630)654-6000
Oak Brook, IL 60523 Fax: (630)574-6565
Free: (800)323-3537

Guide containing schedules of airlines operating throughout the world, published as a service for business travelers, travel agents, and airlines. **Founded:** 1962. **Freq:** Monthly. **Print Method:** Offset. **Trim Size:** 8 1/8 x 11. **Cols./Page:** 4. **Col. Width:** 1 3/4 inches. **Col. Depth:** 9 7/8 inches. **Key Personnel:** Richard A. Nelson, Publisher, phone (630)574-6113, fax (630)574-7500, rnelson@oag.com; Barbara Comiskey, phone (630)574-6514, fax (630)574-6449, bcomiskey@oag.com; Gene Glendinning, Advertising Mgr., phone (630)574-6195, fax (630)574-6050, gglendinning@oag.com. **ISSN:** 1057-0454. **Subscription Rates:** $399 individuals. **Remarks:** Accepts advertising. **Alt. Formats:** CD-ROM. **Formerly:** Official Airline Guide, Worldwide Edition (1992).
Ad Rates: BW: $2,000 **Circ:** Paid 12,984
Non-paid 1,042

9506 OAG Pocket Flight Guide - Europe/Africa/ Middle East Edition
Official Airline Guides
2000 Clearwater Dr. Phone: (630)574-6000
Oak Brook, IL 60523-8806 Fax: (630)574-6667
Free: (800)323-3537

Guide containing quick reference airline schedules for Europe, Africa and the Middle East, plus schedules between these areas and all other countries. **Founded:** 1978. **Freq:** Monthly. **Print Method:** Offset. **Trim Size:** 4 3/16 x 8 7/16. **Cols./Page:** 2. **Key Personnel:** Richard A. Nelson, Publisher, phone (630)574-6113, fax (630)574-7500, rnelson@oag.com; Barbara Comiskey, Editor, phone (630)574-6514, fax (630)574-6449, bcomiskey@oag.com; Gene Glendinning, Advertising Mgr., phone (630)574-6159, fax (630)574-6050, gglendinning@oag.com. **USPS:** 952-620. **Subscription Rates:** $96 individuals. **Remarks:** Color advertising accepted; rates available upon request.
Ad Rates: BW: $2,000 **Circ:** Paid ‡5,769
Non-paid ‡996

9507 OAG Pocket Flight Guide - Latin American/ Caribbean Edition
Official Airline Guides
2000 Clearwater Dr. Phone: (630)574-6000
Oak Brook, IL 60523-8806 Fax: (630)574-6667
Free: (800)323-3537

Guide containing quick reference schedules of direct flights within and between South America, Central America, Mexico, and the Caribbean, plus all scheduled direct flights between these areas and all other countries. **Founded:** 1988. **Freq:** Monthly. **Print Method:** Offset. **Trim Size:** 4 3/16 x 8 7/16. **Cols./Page:** 2. **Key Personnel:** Richard A. Nelson, Publisher, phone (630)574-6113, fax (630)574-7500, rnelson@oag.com; Barbara J. Comiskey, Editor, phone (630)574-6514, fax (630)574-6449, bcomiskey@oag.com; Gene Glendinning, Advertising Mgr., phone (630)574-6159, fax (630)574-6050, gglendinning@oag.com. **USPS:** 952-620. **Subscription Rates:** $96 individuals. **Remarks:** Color advertising accepted; rates available upon request.
Ad Rates: BW: $2,000 **Circ:** Paid ‡2,683
Non-paid ‡816

9508 OAG Pocket Flight Guide - North American Edition
Official Airline Guides
2000 Clearwater Dr. Phone: (630)574-6000
Oak Brook, IL 60523-8806 Fax: (630)574-6667
Free: (800)323-3537

Directory containing quick reference airline schedules of nonstop and multi-stop flights on the most frequently traveled routes throughout all 50 United States, Canada, Caribbean, and Mexico. **Founded:** 1970. **Freq:** Monthly. **Print Method:** Offset. **Trim Size:** 4 3/16 x 8 7/16. **Key Personnel:** Richard A. Nelson, Publisher; Barbara J. Comiskey, Editor; Paul B. Beatty, General Mgr. **USPS:** 952-620. **Subscription Rates:** $89 individuals. **Remarks:** Accepts advertising.
Ad Rates: BW: $16,555 **Circ:** ‡249,925

9509 OAG Pocket Flight Guide - Pacific Asia Edition
Official Airline Guides
2000 Clearwater Dr. Phone: (630)574-6000
Oak Brook, IL 60523-8806 Fax: (630)574-6667
Free: (800)323-3537

Guide containing quick reference airline schedules within and between all countries of the Pacific geographic area; plus all schedules between the area and North America, Europe, the Middle East, Africa, and Central/South America. **Founded:** 1982. **Freq:** Monthly. **Print Method:** Offset. **Trim Size:** 4 3/16 x 8 7/16. **Cols./Page:** 2. **Key Personnel:** Richard A. Nelson, Publisher, phone (630)574-6113, fax (630)574-7500, rnelson@oag.com; Barbara Comiskey, Editor, phone (630)574-6514, fax (630)574-6449, bcomiskey@oag.com; Gene Glendinning, Advertising Mgr., phone (630)574-6195, fax (630)574-6050, gglendinning@oag.com. **USPS:** 952-620. **Subscription Rates:** $96 individuals. **Remarks:** Accepts advertising.
Ad Rates: BW: $2,000 **Circ:** Paid ‡5,303
Non-paid ‡996

9510 Oak Brook Press
Press Publications
112 S. York St. Phone: (630)834-0900
Elmhurst, IL 60126 Fax: (630)834-0910
Publisher E-mail: presspub@aol.com

Community newspaper. **Founded:** 1960. **Freq:** Weekly (Fri.). **Print Method:** Offset. **Cols./Page:** 6. **Col. Width:** 24 nonpareils. **Col. Depth:** 301 agate lines. **Key Personnel:** Jack Cruger, Publisher; Nick Pullia, Editor-in-Chief. **Subscription Rates:** Free; $39 by mail.
Ad Rates: PCI: $10.53 **Circ:** Paid 417
Free 202

9511 Oak Brook Terrace Press
Press Publications
112 S. York St. Phone: (630)834-0900
Elmhurst, IL 60126 Fax: (630)834-0910
Publisher E-mail: presspub@aol.com

Community newspaper. **Founded:** 1985. **Freq:** Semiweekly (Wed. and Fri.). **Print Method:** Offset. **Cols./Page:** 6. **Col. Width:** 11.5 picas. **Col. Depth:** 301 agate lines. **Key Personnel:** Jack Cruger, Publisher; Nick Pullia, Editor. **Subscription Rates:** Free; $39 by mail. **Remarks:** Accepts advertising.
Ad Rates: SAU: $7.98 **Circ:** Paid 328
PCI: $9.36 Free 182

9512 Prime Times
Life Printing and Publishing Co., Inc.
709 Enterprise Dr. Phone: (630)368-8837
Oak Brook, IL 60521 Fax: (630)368-1220
Publication E-mail: subnews@lice.mhs.compuserv.com; lifenews@ix.netcom.com

Senior citizens' interests publication. **Founded:** 1988. **Freq:** Monthly. **Print Method:** Offset. **Cols./Page:** 5. **Col. Width:** 2 inches. **Col. Depth:** 12 inches. **Key Personnel:** Will Conkis, Editor; Allan Pollak, Publisher. **Subscription Rates:** Free; $15. **URL:** http://www.adone.con/lice. **Alt. Formats:** Large-print.
Ad Rates: BW: $750 **Circ:** Non-paid ‡62,000

9513 Radio Graphics
Radiological Society of North America
820 Jorie Blvd. Phone: (630)571-2670
Oak Brook, IL 60523-2251 Fax: (630)571-7837
Publication E-mail: arnold@rsna.org

Scientific publication for radiologists. **Subtitle:** The Journal of Continuing Education in Radiology. **Founded:** 1981. **Freq:** Bimonthly. **Print Method:** Offset. **Trim Size:** 8 1/4 x 11 1/4. **Cols./Page:** 2. **Col. Width:** 19 picas. **Col. Depth:** 55 picas. **Key Personnel:** William W. Olmsted, M.D., Editor, phone (202)659-4080; Jim Drew, Advertising Dir., phone (630)571-7819; Sue Harmon, Managing Editor, phone (630)571-7832. **ISSN:** 0271-5333. **Subscription Rates:** $110 individuals; $125 other countries. **Remarks:** Accepts advertising. **URL:** http://www.rsna.org.
Ad Rates: GLR: $.40 **Circ:** 29,000
BW: $1,625
4C: $2,715

9514 Springs
Spring Manufacturers Institute
2001 Midwest Rd., No. 106 Phone: (630)495-8588
Oak Brook, IL 60523 Fax: (630)495-8595
Publication E-mail: smieditor@aol.com

Trade magazine covering spring technology. **Subtitle:** The Magazine of Spring Technology. **Founded:** 1962. **Freq:** Quarterly. **Print Method:** Web offset. **Trim Size:** 8 1/8 x 10 7/8. **Cols./Page:** 2. **Key Personnel:** Ken Boyce, Publisher; Rita Schauer, Editor; Lynne Carr, Circulation Mgr./Advertising. **ISSN:** 0584-966. **Subscription Rates:** $50 air; $25 surface. **Remarks:** Accepts advertising.
Ad Rates: BW: $1,948 **Circ:** Non-paid 8,623
4C: $3,073

9515 Suburban Life
Life Newspapers
709 Enterprise Dr. Phone: (630)368-1100
Oak Brook, IL 60523-8814 Fax: (630)368-1199
Publication E-mail: subnews@life.mhs.compuserve.com

Community newspaper. **Founded:** 1976. **Freq:** Semiweekly (Wed. and Sat.). **Print Method:** Offset. **Trim Size:** 13 3/4 x 21 1/2. **Cols./Page:** 6. **Col. Width:** 2 inches. **Col. Depth:** 301 agate lines. **Key Personnel:** Joseph DeRosier, Editor; Jack R. Kubik, Publisher; Peter Manning, Advertising Mgr.; Trever Bricker, Circulation Mgr. **Subscription Rates:** $23 (carrier delivery). **Formerly:** Suburban Life Graphic.
Ad Rates: GLR: $1.53 **Circ:** Paid ❑7,811
BW: $2,871.54 Free ❑20,750
4C: $3,396.54
PCI: $16.80

OAK FOREST

9516 Oak Forest/Midlothian Star
Star Newspapers
6901 W 159th St. Phone: (708)802-8800
Tinley Park, IL 60477 Fax: (708)802-8899

Newspaper group serving 51 communities in Chicago's southern suburbs. **Founded:** 1890. **Freq:** Semiweekly (Thurs. and Sun.). **Print Method:** Offset. **Trim Size:** 13 3/4 x 23. **Cols./Page:** 6. **Col. Width:** 2 inches. **Col. Depth:** 21 1/2 inches. **Key Personnel:** Lester Sons, Editor; Norman Rosinski, Publisher; Jim Meidell, Advertising Mgr.; Jay Fredrickson. **Remarks:** Accepts advertising.
Ad Rates: GLR: $56.76 **Circ:** Thurs. 65,520
Sun. 68,788

OAK LAWN, pop. 60,590.

Cook Co. (NE). 10 m SW of Chicago. Residential, and Industrial. Nursery. Truck farms.

9517 Oak Lawn-Evergreen Park Reporter
Regional Publishing Corp.
12247 S. Harlem Ave. Phone: (708)448-6161
Palos Heights, IL 60463
Community newspaper. **Founded:** 1960. **Freq:** Weekly. **Print Method:** Offset. **Trim Size:** 14 1/2 x 22 3/4. **Cols./Page:** 6. **Col. Width:** 2 inches. **Col. Depth:** 21 1/2 inches. **Key Personnel:** Jack Murray, Editor; Charles Richards, Publisher; Carol McLaughlin, Advertising Mgr. **USPS:** 118-690. **Subscription Rates:** $26 individuals; $36 out of area. **Remarks:** Accepts advertising.
Ad Rates: GLR: $1.12 **Circ:** ‡17,868
BW: $1,000
4C: $1,240
SAU: $15.68

9518 Oak Lawn Star
Star Newspapers
6901 W 159th St. Phone: (708)802-8800
Tinley Park, IL 60477 Fax: (708)802-8899

Newspaper group serving 51 communities in Chicago's southern suburbs. **Founded:** 1890. **Freq:** Semiweekly (Thurs. and Sun.). **Print Method:** Offset. **Trim Size:** 13 3/4 x 23. **Cols./Page:** 6. **Col. Width:** 2 inches. **Col. Depth:** 21 1/2 inches. **Key Personnel:** Lester Sons, Editor; Norman Rosinski, Publisher; Jim Meidell, Advertising Mgr.; Jay Fredrickson.
Ad Rates: GLR: $56.76 **Circ:** Thurs. 64,637
Sun. 68,267

OAK PARK, pop. 54,887.

Cook Co. (NE). Adjoins Chicago on the west. Residential suburb. Manufactures food products, veneer machinery, tools and dies, transformers, candy.

9519 Chicago Parent Magazine
Wednesday Journal, Inc.
141 S. Oak Park Ave. Phone: (708)386-5555
Oak Park, IL 60302 Fax: (708)524-0447
Publication E-mail: chiparent@aol.com

Tabloid featuring child-related articles and comprehenseive calendar of events, programs, and activities for the greater Chicago area. **Subtitle:** Connecting with Families. **Founded:** Oct. 1984. **Freq:** Monthly. **Print Method:** Offset. **Trim Size:** 10 1/4 x 12 1/2. **Cols./Page:** 4. **Col. Width:** 2 1/4 inches. **Col. Depth:** 11 3/8 inches. **Key Personnel:** Sharon Bloyd-Peshkin, Editor; Kit Olah, Sales Mgr. **Subscription Rates:** $6.95 by mail. **Remarks:** Accepts advertising. **Online:** America Online, Inc.
Ad Rates: BW: $2,163 **Circ:** Free 78,985
4C: $2,713 Paid 1,399

9520 Cinefantastique
Box 270 Phone: (708)366-5566
Oak Park, IL 60303 Fax: (708)366-1441
Free: (800)798-6515
Publication E-mail: mail@cfq.com

Magazine devoted to motion pictures. **Subtitle:** The Magazine with a Sense of Wonder. **Founded:** Nov. 1970. **Freq:** Monthly. **Print Method:** Offset. **Trim Size:** 8 1/2 x 11. **Cols./Page:** 4. **Col. Width:** 21 nonpareils. **Col. Depth:** 140 agate lines. **Key Personnel:** Frederick S. Clarke, Editor and Publisher. **ISSN:** 0145-6032. **Subscription Rates:** $48 individuals; $8 single issue; $55 other countries. **Remarks:** Accepts advertising. **URL:** http://www.cfq.com.
Ad Rates: BW: $900 **Circ:** ‡30,000
4C: $1,700
PCI: $60

9521 Doody's Health Sciences Book Review Journal
Doody's Review Service
1100 W. Lake St., No. 306 Phone: (708)386-9500
Oak Park, IL 60301-9918 Fax: (708)386-0860
Free: (800)219-9500

Journal containing bibliographic citations, analyses and original reviews on newly published health sciences books. **Subtitle:** Doody's Journal–Health Sciences Book Review. **Founded:** Oct. 1994. **Freq:** Bimonthly. **Trim Size:** 8.5 x 11. **Key Personnel:** Megan M. Dunn, Contact, megan@doody.com. **ISSN:** 1071-7560. **Subscription Rates:** $250 U.S. and Canada; $280 other countries. **Remarks:** Accepts advertising. **URL:** http://wwww.doody.com.
Ad Rates: BW: $650 **Circ:** Paid 750
Non-paid 100

9522 Elm Leaves
Pioneer Press Newspapers
1148 Westgate Ave. Phone: (708)383-3200
Oak Park, IL 60301 Fax: (708)383-3678

Community newspaper (tabloid). **Founded:** 1970. **Freq:** Weekly (Wed.). **Print Method:** Offset. **Cols./Page:** 5. **Col. Width:** 10 inches. **Col. Depth:** 14 inches. **Key Personnel:** Rick Behren, Editor; Paul Sassone, Managing Editor. **Subscription Rates:** $13.95 individuals; $15.95 out of county.
Circ: Wed. 4,018

Forest Leaves - See River Forest

9523 Forest Park Review
Wednesday Journal, Inc.
141 S. Oak Park Ave. Phone: (708)386-5555
Oak Park, IL 60302 Fax: (708)524-0447

Community newspaper. **Founded:** 1917. **Freq:** Weekly (Wed.). **Print Method:** Offset. **Trim Size:** Tabloid. **Cols./Page:** 4. **Col. Width:** 14 1/2 picas. **Col. Depth:** 12 3/4 inches. **Key Personnel:** Paige Fuomo, Managing Editor. **Subscription Rates:** $12 individuals. **Remarks:** Accepts advertising. **URL:** http://www.wjinc.com.
Ad Rates: BW: $323 **Circ:** 2,900
4C: $548
PCI: $4.85

Franklin Park Herald-Journal - See Franklin Park

9524 Irish American News
503 S. Oak Park Ave., Ste. 205 Phone: (708)445-0700
Oak Park, IL 60304 Fax: (708)445-0784

Tabloid for Irish-Americans. **Founded:** 1976. **Freq:** Monthly. **Print Method:** Offset. **Trim Size:** 11 x 13. **Cols./Page:** 5. **Col. Width:** 2 inches. **Col. Depth:** 12 5/8 inches. **Key Personnel:** Cliff Carlson, Editor and Publisher; Merry Dailey, Sales. **USPS:** 013-454. **Subscription Rates:** $14 individuals; $20 two years. **Remarks:** Accepts advertising.
Ad Rates: BW: $750 **Circ:** Paid ‡5,240
4C: $1,100 Non-paid ‡4,760
PCI: $15.50

9525 Journal of General Orthodontics
International Association for Orthodontics
1100 Lake St., Ste. 240 Phone: (708)445-0320
Oak Park, IL 60301 Fax: (708)445-0321

Professional journal covering clinical and scientific articles on orthodontics. **Founded:** Mar. 1990. **Freq:** Quarterly. **Print Method:** Web offset. **Trim Size:** 8 1/2 x 11. **Cols./Page:** 2. **Col. Width:** 3 inches. **Col. Depth:** 7 1/4 inches. **Key Personnel:** Dr. Yash Jefferson, Editor; Dr. James McIlwain, Editor; Joanna Carey, Managing Editor. **ISSN:** 1048-1990. **Subscription Rates:** $40 individuals; $60 out of country; $10 single issue; $15 single issue out of country. **Remarks:** Accepts advertising. **URL:** http://www.iaowordheaquarters.com.
Ad Rates: BW: $525 **Circ:** Paid ⊕**4,100**
4C: $629

Maywood Herald - See Maywood

Melrose Park Herald - See Melrose Park

9526 Oak Leaves
Pioneer Press Newspapers
1148 Westgate Ave. Phone: (708)383-3200
Oak Park, IL 60301 Fax: (708)383-3678

Community newspaper (tabloid). **Founded:** 1877. **Freq:** Weekly (Wed.). **Print Method:** Offset. **Cols./Page:** 5. **Col. Width:** 10 inches. **Col. Depth:** 14 inches. **Key Personnel:** Rich Hibbert, Editor; Paul Sassone, Managing Editor. **Remarks:** Advertising accepted; rates available upon request.
Circ: Wed. ★**1,761**

River Grove Messenger - See River Grove

9527 Tri-City Journal
Tri-County Journal
7115 W. North Ave., No. 308 Phone: (312)346-8123
Oak Park, IL 60302-1002 Fax: (312)606-0860

Black community newspaper. **Founded:** 1978. **Freq:** Weekly (Thurs.). **Print Method:** Offset. **Trim Size:** 10 x 14 in. **Cols./Page:** 5. **Col. Width:** 11 1/2 inches. **Col. Depth:** 14 inches. **Key Personnel:** Ibn Sharrieff, Editor and Publisher. **Remarks:** Accepts advertising.
Ad Rates: SAU: $9.90 **Circ:** 50,000

9528 Vegetarian Times
Cowles Enthusiast Media
PO Box 570 Phone: (708)848-8100
Oak Park, IL 60303 Fax: (708)848-8175

Magazine devoted to vegetarian food and related topics such as health, fitness, and the environment. **Founded:** Nov. 1973. **Freq:** 12/year. **Print Method:** Offset. Uses mats. **Trim Size:** 8 1/4 x 10 1/2. **Cols./Page:** 3. **Col. Width:** 26 nonpareils. **Col. Depth:** 140 agate lines. **Key Personnel:** Susan Tauster, phone (708)848-8100, fax (708)848-8175, susant@cowles.com. **Subscription Rates:** $24.95 individuals. **Remarks:** Accepts advertising.
Ad Rates: BW: $10,370 **Circ:** Paid ★**325,044**
4C: $13,285

9529 Wednesday Journal of Oak Park & River Forest
Wednesday Journal, Inc.
141 S. Oak Park Ave. Phone: (708)386-5555
Oak Park, IL 60302 Fax: (708)524-0447
Publication E-mail: wjinc@aol.com

Community newspaper. **Founded:** July 30, 1980. **Freq:** Weekly (Wed.). **Print Method:** Offset. **Trim Size:** Tabloid. **Cols./Page:** 4. **Col. Width:** 14 1/2 picas. **Col. Depth:** 12 3/4 inches. **Key Personnel:** Dan Haley, General Mgr. **Subscription Rates:** $15. **Remarks:** Accepts advertising. **URL:** http://www.wjinc.com.
Ad Rates: BW: $1,030 **Circ:** Paid ❑**6,926**
4C: $1,255 Free ❑**5,940**
SAU: $29.32
PCI: $30.49

West Proviso Herald - See Proviso

Westchester Herald - See Westchester

9530 WPNA-AM - 1490
408 S. Oak Park Ave. Phone: (708)848-8980
Oak Park, IL 60302 Fax: (708)848-9220
Free: (708)898-8980
E-mail: wpna@radio.com

Networks: Independent. **Owner:** Polish National Alliance, 6100 N. Cicero, Chicago, IL 60646, (773)286-0500, Fax: (773)763-2835. **Founded:** 1987. **Formerly:** WOPA-AM. **Operating Hours:** Continuous; 100% local. **Key Personnel:** Emily Leczynski, Communications Dir., phone (773)763-3343, fax (773)763-2835; Jerry Obrecki, Sales Mgr., phone (708)848-8980, fax (708)848-9220; Len Petrulis, Contact, lenp2@aol.com. **Wattage:** 1000. **Ad Rates:** $25-28 for 30 seconds; $32-40 for 60 seconds.

OAKBROOK TERRACE

9531 The Joint Commission Journal on Quality Improvement
1 Renaissance Blvd. Phone: (630)792-5453
Oakbrook Terrace, IL 60181 Fax: (630)792-4453

Magazine directed to health care providers and administrators quality assurance/improvement managers and researchers concerned with the quality of health care; specifically quality improvement, CQI/TQM, and risk management. **Founded:** 1974. **Freq:** Monthly. **Print Method:** Offset. **Trim Size:** 8 1/2 x 11. **Cols./Page:** 2. **Col. Width:** 19 1/2 picas. **Col. Depth:** 53 picas. **Key Personnel:** Steven Berman, Editor, sberman@jcaho.org. **ISSN:** 1070-3241. **Subscription Rates:** $145; $165.85 Canada; $155 other countries. **Formerly:** Quality Review Bulletin.
Ad Rates: BW: $860 **Circ:** ‡5,300

OAKLAND

9532 The Oakland-Hindsboro Prairie Sun
Lincoln Trail Publishing
9 E. Main St. Phone: (217)346-2521
Oakland, IL 61943 Fax: (217)346-2522

Community newspaper. **Founded:** 1984. **Freq:** Weekly (Thurs.). **Print Method:** Offset. **Cols./Page:** 5. **Col. Width:** 12 nonpareils. **Col. Depth:** 182 agate lines. **Key Personnel:** Abby Hudson, Editor; Mary Leeks, Publisher. **Subscription Rates:** $17; $20 out of area; $24 out of state. **Remarks:** Accepts advertising.
Ad Rates: BW: $260 **Circ:** ‡1,300
4C: $395
SAU: $4
PCI: $3

ODELL, pop. 1,083.

Livingston Co. (NEC). 47 m S of Joliet. Grain farms. Corn, oats, beans, hay. Stock farms.

9533 Odell Times
Star Newspapers
204 E. Chippewa St. Phone: (815)584-3007
PO Box 159
Dwight, IL 60420-0159
Community newspaper. **Founded:** 1941. **Freq:** Weekly (Thurs.). **Print Method:** Offset. **Trim Size:** 15 x 21 1/2. **Cols./Page:** 8. **Col. Width:** 21 nonpareils. **Col. Depth:** 301 agate lines. **Key Personnel:** Scott McGraw, Publisher. **USPS:** 402-920. **Subscription Rates:** $11 in state. **Remarks:** Accepts advertising.
Ad Rates: GLR: $.16 **Circ:** Paid 421
BW: $161.25 Free 10
SAU: $2.64
PCI: $2.24

OGDEN

9534 Ogden Leader
The Leader
115 East Ave. Phone: (217)582-2373
PO Box 97 Fax: (217)582-2237
Ogden, IL 61859
Community newspaper. **Founded:** June 14, 1979. **Freq:** Weekly (Thurs.). **Cols./Page:** 7. **Col. Width:** 1 5/8 inches. **Col. Depth:** 21 1/2 inches. **Key Personnel:** Darlena Hunter, Editor; Scott Hunter, Publisher. **Remarks:** Accepts advertising. **Formerly:** Ogden Leader.
Ad Rates: GLR: $.54 **Circ:** Free 7,800
SAU: $9.50
PCI: $7.56

OKAWVILLE, pop. 1,976.

Washington Co. (S). 25 m SE of Belleville. Grain elevator. Mineral springs, health resort. Concrete mixing plant. Dairy, poultry, grain farms.

9535 Times
Okawville Times
PO Box 68 Phone: (618)243-5563
Okawville, IL 62271 Fax: (618)243-5563

Newspaper. **Founded:** 1893. **Freq:** Weekly (Thurs.). **Print Method:** Offset. **Cols./Page:** 9. **Col. Width:** 24 nonpareils. **Col. Depth:** 252 agate lines. **Key Personnel:** Debby Stricker, Editor; Gary W. Stricker, Publisher. **Subscription Rates:** $9 individuals.

OLNEY†, pop. 9,026.

Richland Co. (SE). 60 m NW of Evansville, Ind. Manufactures toys, vinegar, chain link fence and fence fittings, bicycle accessary, tire repairing equipment. Oil production. Oak, walnut timber. Machine shop. Diversified farming.

9536 Olney Daily Mail
American Publishing
206 Whittle Ave. Phone: (618)393-2931
PO Box 340 Fax: (618)392-2953
Olney, IL 62450
General newspaper. **Subtitle:** The Olney Daily Mail. **Founded:** 1898. **Freq:** Daily (eve.) and Sat. (morn.). **Print Method:** Offset. **Cols./Page:** 6. **Col. Width:** 25 nonpareils. **Col. Depth:** 301 agate lines. **Key Personnel:** Steve Raymond, Publisher. **Subscription Rates:** $80 individuals. **Remarks:** Accepts advertising.
Ad Rates: SAU: $6.50 **Circ:** (Not Reported)

9537 WVLN-AM - 740
Box L Phone: (618)393-2156
Radio Tower Rd. Fax: (618)392-4536
Olney, IL 62450

Format: News; Talk. **Networks:** RFD Illinois. **Owner:** Key Broadcasting, PO Box 1450, Corbin, KY 40701, (606)528-9600, Fax: (606)528-8487. **Founded:** 1947. **Operating Hours:** Continuous; 5% network; 17% local; 78% other. **ADI:** Terre Haute, IN. **Key Personnel:** Mike Lowe, General Mgr.; Mark Weiler, News Dir.; Jason Millman, Sports Dir.; Mike Shipman, Operations Mgr. **Wattage:** 250. **Ad Rates:** $8 for 30 seconds; $10 for 60 seconds.

OQUAWKA†, pop. 1,352.

Henderson Co. (NW).

9538 Oquawka Current
American Publish Co.
PO Box 606 Phone: (309)867-2515
Oquawka, IL 61469 Fax: (309)867-2515

Rural local newspaper. **Founded:** May 1978. **Freq:** Weekly. **Print Method:** Offset. **Trim Size:** 13 x 21 1/2. **Cols./Page:** 6. **Col. Width:** 12.5 picas. **Col. Depth:** 14 inches. **Key Personnel:** Sally Day, Editor; Scott Champion, Publisher. **USPS:** 444-050. **Subscription Rates:** $22 individuals; $29.50 out of area. **Remarks:** Accepts advertising.
Ad Rates: GLR: $.75 **Circ:** Paid 1,957
BW: $496.65 Free 48
4C: $546.65
SAU: $5.00
PCI: $4.32

OREGON†, pop. 3,559.

Ogle Co. (N). On Rock River, 100 m W of Chicago. Manufactures piano plates, tanks, street sprinklers, agricultural cutters; silica plant.; yard spinning. Agriculture. Corn, oats, hay.

Mt. Morris Times - See Mount Morris

9539 Republican-Reporter
121A South 4th Phone: (815)732-6166
PO Box 8 Fax: (815)732-4238
Oregon, IL 61061
Local newspaper. **Founded:** 1851. **Freq:** Weekly (Thurs.). **Print Method:** Offset. **Cols./Page:** 8. **Col. Width:** 24 nonpareils. **Col. Depth:** 315 agate lines. **Key Personnel:** Ruth Cody, Publisher; Leisa Reidy, Advertising Dir. **Subscription Rates:** $18.50 individuals. **Remarks:** Accepts advertising.
Ad Rates: BW: $445.05 **Circ:** Paid 1,300
4C: $610.05 Free 2,000
SAU: $3.45

ORLAND PARK, pop. 23,045.

Cook Co. (NE). 5 m S W of Blue Island.

9540 Orland Park Star
Star Newspapers
6901 W 159th St. Phone: (708)802-8800
Tinley Park, IL 60477 Fax: (708)802-8899

Newspaper group serving 51 communities in Chicago's southern suburbs. **Founded:** 1890. **Freq:** Semiweekly (Thurs. and Sun.). **Print Method:** Offset. **Trim Size:** 13 3/4 x 23. **Cols./Page:** 6. **Col. Width:** 2 inches. **Col. Depth:** 21 1/2 inches. **Key Personnel:** Lester Sons, Editor; Norman Rosinski, Publisher; Jim Meidell, Advertising Mgr.; Jay Frederickson.
Ad Rates: GLR: $56.76 **Circ:** Thurs. 64,637
Sun. 68,267

OSWEGO, pop. 3,021.

Kendall Co. (NE). 42 m W of Chicago.

9541 Ledger-Sentinel
Kendall County Record Inc.
64 Main St. Phone: (630)554-8565
PO Box 669 Fax: (630)554-8573
Oswego, IL 60543
Publication E-mail: 71540.1756@compuserve.com

Community newspaper serving Oswego, Boulder Hill, and Montgomery. **Founded:** 1980. **Freq:** Weekly (Thurs.). **Print Method:** Offset. **Cols./Page:** 6. **Col. Width:** 19 nonpareils. **Col. Depth:** 224 agate lines. **Key Personnel:** Roger A. Matile, Editor; Jeff Farren, Publisher; Kathy Farren, Publisher. **Subscription Rates:** $15 individuals; $18.50 out of area; $22.50 out of state. **Remarks:** Accepts advertising.
Ad Rates: GLR: $.29 **Circ:** ‡3,100
BW: $384
SAU: $5.20

OTTAWA†, pop. 18,166.

La Salle Co. (N). On Illinois and Fox Rivers and Lakes to Gulf Waterway, 16 m E of La Salle. Manufactures plates and safety glass, glass marbles, plastics, raw material and finished products, asphalt, indicating devices, dredge pumps, tools, auto parts. Silica sand pits. Diversified farming.

9542 The Daily Times
Ottawa Publishing Co.
110 W. Jefferson Phone: (815)433-2000
Ottawa, IL 61350 Fax: (815)433-1626
Publication E-mail: thetimes@theramp.net

Newspaper with Republican orientation. **Founded:** 1844. **Freq:** Mon.-Sat. (eve.). **Print Method:** Offset. **Cols./Page:** 6. **Col. Width:** 24 nonpareils. **Col. Depth:** 301 agate lines. **Key Personnel:** Joan Heyers, Asst. Gen. Mgr.; Jim Malley, General Mgr., fax (815)433-7393. **USPS:** 565-800. **Subscription Rates:** $88.20 individuals. **Remarks:** Accepts advertising.
Ad Rates: BW: $1,367.40 **Circ:** Mon.-Sat. 12,654
4C: $1,617.40
SAU: $10.60
PCI: $10.60

9543 Thrif-T-Nickel Weekly News-Tab
F.W. Gray & Associates Ltd.
Box 279 Phone: (815)433-5595
801 Canal St., No. 279 Fax: (815)433-5596
Ottawa, IL 61350-4901
Free: (800)527-4729

Community newspaper. **Founded:** July 1973. **Freq:** Weekly (Wed.). **Print Method:** Offset. **Trim Size:** 11 x 17. **Cols./Page:** 5. **Col. Width:** 2 1/16 inches. **Col. Depth:** 16 inches. **Key Personnel:** Judy Logsdon, Editor; Fred W. Gray, Publisher; Judy Standard, Advertising Mgr. **Subscription Rates:** $45 individuals. **Remarks:** Accepts advertising.
Ad Rates: GLR: $.48 **Circ:** Paid ‡12
BW: $553.60 Free ‡14,539
SAU: $6.72
PCI: $6.72

Town & Country - See Seneca

9544 WRKX-FM - 95.3
216 W. Lafayette St. Phone: (815)434-6050
Ottawa, IL 61350 Fax: (815)434-5311
E-mail: wcmyk953@ivnet.com

Owner: Virginia Broadcasting Corp., at above address. **Founded:** 1964. **Operating Hours:** Continuous. **Key Personnel:** Dan Parker, Contact; Robin Malpass, Contact. **Wattage:** 4300 ERP.

9545 WWTO-TV - 35
420 E. Stevenson Rd. Phone: (815)434-2700
Ottawa, IL 61350 Fax: (815)434-2458
E-mail: wwto35@theramp.net

Format: Commercial TV. **Founded:** 1986. **Operating Hours:** Continuous. **ADI:** Chicago (LaSalle), IL. **Key Personnel:** Roger Crawford, Station Mgr. **Wattage:** 5,000,000. **URL:** http://www.aatv.org.

PALATINE, pop. 32,166.

Cook Co. (NW). 28 m N.W. of Chicago. Residential. Commercial Manufactures safety glass and equipment, plastic molds, fuses, bulletin boards, signs, adhesives and coatings, electronic testing equipment, electrical equipment, bar BQ grills.

9546 Fleet Equipment
Maple Communications Co.
134 W. Slade St. Phone: (847)359-6100
Palatine, IL 60067-1696 Fax: (847)359-6420
Publication E-mail: femaple@aol.com; semaple@aol.com

Magazine for equipment managers of truck, trailer, and bus fleets. **Subtitle:** The Leading Information Resource for fleet equipment managers. **Founded:** 1974. **Freq:** Monthly. **Print Method:** Offset. **Trim Size:** 8 x 10 3/4. **Cols./Page:** 3. **Col. Width:** 26 nonpareils. **Col. Depth:** 140 agate lines. **Key Personnel:** Tom Gelinas, Editor, tgelinas@truklink.com; Bob Dorn, Publisher. **ISSN:** 0747-2544. **Subscription Rates:** $82 individuals. **Remarks:** Accepts advertising. **URL:** http://www.truklink.com.
Ad Rates: BW: $7,505 **Circ:** Controlled ‡63,000
4C: $9,180
PCI: $90

9547 Harbinger
William Rainey Harper College
1200 W. Algonquin Rd. Phone: (708)925-6460
Palatine, IL 60067 Fax: (708)925-6033

Collegiate newspaper. **Founded:** 1969. **Freq:** Weekly (Thurs.). **Print Method:** Offset. **Cols./Page:** 5. **Col. Width:** 24 nonpareils. **Col. Depth:** 224 agate lines. **Key Personnel:** Marc Balke, Advertising Mgr. **Remarks:** Advertising not accepted for alcoholic beverages and tobacco products.
Ad Rates: GLR: $4.50 **Circ:** Free ‡5,000
BW: $385
4C: $685
PCI: $5.50

9548 Palatine Countryside
Pioneer Press Newspapers
291 N. Dunton Ave. Phone: (847)797-5100
Arlington Heights, IL 60004 Fax: (847)797-5151

Community newspaper (tabloid). **Founded:** 1972. **Freq:** Weekly (Thurs.). **Print Method:** Offset. **Cols./Page:** 4. **Col. Width:** 13 3/5 picas. **Col. Depth:** 196 agate lines. **Key Personnel:** Paul Sassone, Managing Editor; Tom Scott, Editor. **Subscription Rates:** $18.95 individuals; $19.95 out of county. **URL:** http://www.pioneerlocal.com.
Circ: Thurs. ★6,849

9549 The Steam Automobile Bulletin
Steam Automobile Club of America, Inc.
150 S. Quentin Rd. Phone: (847)991-3911
Palatine, IL 60067
Publisher E-mail: 72202.2450@compuserve.com

Club magazine covering steam automobile history and development. **Founded:** 1958. **Freq:** Quarterly. **Print Method:** Offset. **Trim Size:** 8 1/2 x 11. **Cols./Page:** 2. **Col. Width:** 42 nonpareils. **Col. Depth:** 135 agate lines. **Key Personnel:** Scott Finegan, Editor. **Subscription Rates:** $15. **Formerly:** The Steam Automobile.
Ad Rates: GLR: $1 **Circ:** Paid 600
BW: $85
PCI: $1

PALOS HEIGHTS, pop. 11,096.

Cook Co. (NE). 18 m SW of Chicago.

Oak Lawn-Evergreen Park Reporter - See Oak Lawn

9550 Regional News
Regional Publishing Corp.
12243 S. Harlem Ave. Phone: (708)448-4000
Palos Heights, IL 60463-0932 Fax: (708)448-4012

Community newspaper. **Founded:** Oct. 21, 1941. **Freq:** Weekly (Thurs.). **Print Method:** Offset. **Trim Size:** 14 1/2 x 22 3/4. **Cols./Page:** 6. **Col. Width:** 2 1/4 inches. **Col. Depth:** 21 1/4 inches. **Key Personnel:** Charles Richards, Publisher; Marilyn Shaw, Advertising Mgr. **USPS:** 419-260. **Subscription Rates:** $32 individuals; $42 out of area. **Remarks:** Accepts advertising. **Formerly:** Palos Regional.
Ad Rates: GLR: $1.13 **Circ:** Paid ‡18,841
BW: $1,200 Free 100
4C: $1,400
SAU: $15.82
PCI: $15.82

The Reporter - See Palos Hills

PALOS HILLS

Cook Co. (NE). 5 m S of Oak Lawn.

9551 The Reporter
Regional Publishing Corp.
12243 S. Harlem Ave. Phone: (708)448-4000
Palos Heights, IL 60463-0932 Fax: (708)448-4012

Community newspaper. **Founded:** 1960. **Freq:** Weekly. **Print Method:** Offset. **Trim Size:** 14 1/2 x 22 3/4. **Cols./Page:** 6. **Col. Width:** 2 1/4 inches. **Col. Depth:** 21.5 inches. **Key Personnel:** Jack Murray, Editor, phone (708)448-6161; Charles Richards, Publisher, phone (708)448-6161; Carol McLaughlin, Advertising Mgr., phone (708)448-6161. **USPS:** 118-690. **Subscription Rates:** in state; $36 out of state. **Remarks:** Accepts advertising. **Formerly:** Worth-Palos Reporter; Palos Hills-Hickory Hills; Worth-Ridge Reporter.
Ad Rates: GLR: $1.13 **Circ:** Paid ‡18,044
BW: $1,600 Free ‡100
4C: $1,800
SAU: $15.82
PCI: $15.82

PANA, pop. 6,040.

Christian Co. (C). 30 m S Decatur. Manufactures wire, electronics. Creameries. Cultivation of roses and potted plants. Grain, dairy farms.

9552 WXKO-FM - 100.9
PO Box 465 Phone: (217)562-7000
Pana, IL 62557 Fax: (217)562-3945

Format: Country. **Networks:** CNN Radio. **Founded:** 1977. **Formerly:** WKXK-FM (1990). **Operating Hours:** Continuous; 10% network, 90% local. **Key Personnel:** Randal J. Miller, Pres./General Mgr. **Local Programs:** *Morning Show* 6:00 am - 10:00 am Monday-Friday. **Wattage:** 6000.

PARIS†, pop. 9,885.

Edgar Co. (E). 39 m S Danville. Grain milling. Manufacturing industrial machinery, truck bodies, wood furniture, wood milling, porcelain, steel fabrication, steel sinks, metal products, pet foods, farm seeds. Farming.

9553 Beacon-News
Beacon News Publishing
PO Box 100 Phone: (217)465-6424
Paris, IL 61944 Fax: (217)463-1232
Free: (800)587-5955

Newspaper with a Republican orientation. **Founded:** 1848. **Freq:** Mon.-Sat. (eve.). **Print Method:** Offset. **Cols./Page:** 6. **Col. Width:** 25 nonpareils. **Col. Depth:** 294 agate lines. **Key Personnel:** E.H. Jenison, Editor and Publisher. **Subscription Rates:** $98.80.
Ad Rates: BW: $819 **Circ:** 6,300
4C: $1,069
PCI: $6.50

9554 WACF-FM - 98.5
PO Box 277 Phone: (217)465-6336
Paris, IL 61944 Fax: (217)466-1408

Format: Country. **Networks:** NBC; ABC; Westwood One Radio. **Founded:** 1952. **Operating Hours:** Continuous; 10% network, 90% local. **ADI:** Terre Haute, IN. **Key Personnel:** Rebecca Dole, General Mgr.; John Clark, Sales Mgr.; Kent Walls, Traffic Mgr.; Johnny McCrory, News/Sports Dir. **Wattage:** 50,000. **Ad Rates:** $12.00-17.00 for 60 seconds.

9555 WPRS-AM - 1440
PO Box 367 Phone: (217)465-6336
Paris, IL 61944 Fax: (217)466-1408

Format: Middle-of-the-Road (MOR). **Networks:** NBC; Business Radio; Global Satellite. **Founded:** 1951. **Operating Hours:** 19 hours daily; 10% network, 90% local. **ADI:** Terre Haute, IN. **Key Personnel:** Kent Walls, Traffic Mgr.; Johnny McCrory, News & Sports Dir.; Rebecca Dole, General Mgr. **Wattage:** 1000 day; 250 night. **Ad Rates:** $12.20-17.15 for 60 seconds.

PARK FOREST, pop. 26,222.

Cook Co. (NE). 5 m SW of Chicago Heights. Residential.

9556 Park Forest Star
Star Newspapers
6901 W 159th St. Phone: (708)802-8800
Tinley Park, IL 60477 Fax: (708)802-8899

Newspaper group serving 51 communities in Chicago's southern suburbs. **Founded:** 1890. **Freq:** Semiweekly (Thurs. and Sun.). **Print Method:** Offset. **Trim Size:** 13 3/4 x 23. **Cols./Page:** 6. **Col. Width:** 2 inches. **Col. Depth:** 21 1/2 inches. **Key Personnel:** Lester Sons, Editor; Norman Rosinski, Publisher; Jim Meidell, Advertising Mgr.; Jay Frederickson. **Remarks:** Accepts advertising.
Ad Rates: GLR: $56.76 **Circ:** Thurs. 64,637
Sun. 68,262

PARK RIDGE, pop. 38,704.

Cook Co. (NE). 13 m NW of Chicago. Residential.

9557 AANA Journal
AANA Publishing, Inc.
222 S. Prospect Ave. Phone: (847)692-7050
Park Ridge, IL 60068 Fax: (847)692-6968

Nursing and anesthesia journal. **Subtitle:** Journal of the American Association of Nurse Anesthetists. **Founded:** 1933. **Freq:** Bimonthly. **Print Method:** Web offset. **Trim Size:** 8 1/2 x 11. **Cols./Page:** 2. **Col. Width:** 20 picas. **Col. Depth:** 55 picas. **Key Personnel:** Sally Aquino, Managing Editor; Wayne B. McCourt, Advertising Mgr., phone (609)848-1000, fax (609)848-6091. **ISSN:** 0094-6354. **Subscription Rates:** $24 individuals; $5 single issue. **Remarks:** Accepts advertising. **Alt. Formats:** Microform.
Ad Rates: BW: $2,690 **Circ:** Paid ‡25,872
4C: $4,485 Non-paid ‡700

9558 AMT Events
American Medical Technologists
710 Higgins Rd. Phone: (847)823-5169
Park Ridge, IL 60068-5765 Fax: (847)823-0458
Publisher E-mail: AMTMAIL@aol.com

Professional journal of the American Medical Technologists. **Founded:** 1939. **Freq:** Bimonthly. **Print Method:** Offset. **Trim Size:** 8 x 10 7/8. **Key Personnel:** Diane Powell, Editor. **Subscription Rates:** Included in membership; $35 nonmembers; $45 nonmembers out of country. **Remarks:** Accepts advertising.
Ad Rates: BW: $975 **Circ:** Controlled **26,000**
4C: $1,675

Des Plaines Times - See Des Plaines

Edgebrook Times Review - See Edgebrook

Edison-Norwood Times Review - See Chicago

9559 Greenhouse Business
McCormick Communications Group, Ltd.
PO Box 698 Phone: (847)823-5650
Park Ridge, IL 60068-0698 Fax: (847)696-3445

Trade magazine for commercial greenhouse growers. **Founded:** Jan. 1995. **Freq:** Monthly. **Print Method:** Web offset. **Trim Size:** 10 7/8 x 14 1/2. **Cols./Page:** 3. **Col. Depth:** 14 inches. **Key Personnel:** Gene H. McCormick, Editor and Publisher. **Subscription Rates:** $45 individuals; $90 out of country. **Remarks:** Accepts advertising. **URL:** http://www.greenhousebiz.com/.
Ad Rates: BW: $1,590 **Circ:** Non-paid ★**16,716**
4C: $2,335

9560 Locksmith Ledger International
Locksmith Publishing Corp.
850 Busse Hwy. Phone: (847)692-5940
Park Ridge, IL 60068 Fax: (847)692-4604
Publication E-mail: lledger@aol.com
Publisher E-mail: lledger@simon-net.com

Physical and electronic security. **Subtitle:** The Technical News Magazine for the Security Professional. **Founded:** 1939. **Freq:** Monthly. **Print Method:** Offset. **Trim Size:** 8 1/8 x 10 7/8. **Cols./Page:** 2. **Col. Width:** 13 picas. **Col. Depth:** 140 agate lines. **Key Personnel:** Steven Lasky, Publisher, slasky@worldnet.att.net; Gale Johnson, Editor. **ISSN:** 1050-2254. **Subscription Rates:** $38 individuals; $5 single issue. **Remarks:** Accepts advertising. **URL:** www.simon-net.com.
Ad Rates: GLR: $2,000 **Circ:** Paid ★**14,843**
4C: $2,925
PCI: $70

9561 Lubrication Engineering
Society of Tribologists and Lubrication Engineers
840 Busse Hwy. Phone: (708)825-5536
Park Ridge, IL 60068-2302 Fax: (708)825-1456

Magazine focusing on lubrication related research, theory, and practice. **Founded:** June 1, 1945. **Freq:** Monthly. **Print Method:** Offset. **Trim Size:** 8 1/4 x 11. **Cols./Page:** 3 and 2. **Col. Width:** 26 and 40 nonpareils. **Col. Depth:** 140 agate lines. **Key Personnel:** Jeanie Shearer McCoy, Editor; Karen J. VanderHeyden, Production and Administration. **ISSN:** 0024-7154. **Subscription Rates:** $56 individuals; $83 other countries. **Remarks:** Accepts advertising.
Ad Rates: BW: $1,009 **Circ:** Paid ‡6,020
4C: $1,704

Mt. Prospect Times - See Mount Prospect

9562 MPC Chronicle
Metal Packaging Consultants
PO Box 436
Park Ridge, IL 60068-0436

Trade magazine for the metal can and packaging industry. **Founded:** 1991. **Freq:** Monthly. **Trim Size:** 8 x 11. **Cols./Page:** 2. **Key Personnel:** Hugh W. Baxter, Editor. **Remarks:** Accepts advertising.
Circ: Controlled 1,800

Niles Herald-Spectator - See Niles

Norridge-Harwood Heights News - See Harwood Heights

9563 Park Ridge Herald-Advocate
Pioneer Press Newspapers
130 S. Prospect Ave. Phone: (847)696-3133
Park Ridge, IL 60068 Fax: (847)696-3229

Community newspaper (tabloid). **Founded:** 1933. **Freq:** Weekly (Thurs.). **Print Method:** Offset. **Cols./Page:** 5. **Col. Width:** 10 inches. **Col. Depth:** 14 inches. **Key Personnel:** Paul Sassone, Managing Editor; Gregg Canfield, Editor. **Subscription Rates:** $16.95 individuals. **Remarks:** Advertising accepted; rates available upon request. **URL:** http://www.pioneerlocal.com. **Formed by the merger of:** Park Ridge Herald; Park Ridge Advocate.
Circ: Thurs. ★**8,685**

9564 Round the Table
Million Dollar Round Table
325 Touhy Phone: (847)692-6378
Park Ridge, IL 60068 Fax: (847)518-8921

Trade magazine for an international association of top life insurance salespeople. **Freq:** Bimonthly. **Key Personnel:** Mary Kay Ams, Editor, mkams@mdrt.org. **Subscription Rates:** $10 individuals; $2 single issue. **Remarks:** Advertising not accepted.
Circ: (Not Reported)

9565 Security Technology & Design
Locksmith Publishing Corp.
850 Busse Hwy. Phone: (847)692-5940
Park Ridge, IL 60068 Fax: (847)692-4604
Publisher E-mail: lledger@simon-net.com

Trade magazine covering security systems and technology. **Subtitle:** The Publication for Integrated Systems. **Founded:** 1991. **Freq:** Monthly. **Print Method:** Web offset. **Trim Size:** 8 1/8 x 10 7/8. **Cols./Page:** 3. **Key Personnel:** Steven Lasky, Editor and Publisher, phone (770)886-0800, fax (770)889-7703, slasky@worldnet.att.net; David Crost, Advertising Mgr. **ISSN:** 1069-1804. **Subscription Rates:** $38 individuals; $5 single issue. **Remarks:** Accepts advertising. **URL:** http://www.simon-net.com.
Ad Rates: BW: $3,370 **Circ:** Controlled 31,000
4C: $4,520

9566 WMTH-FM - 90.5
2601 W. Dempster St. Phone: (708)692-8484
Park Ridge, IL 60068

Format: News; Eclectic. **Networks:** American Urban Radio. **Owner:** Board of Education, School District No. 207, 1131 S. Dee Rd., Park Ridge, IL 60068. **Founded:** 1959. **Operating Hours:** Various; 100% local. **Key Personnel:** William Mitchell, General Mgr. **Wattage:** 180. **Ad Rates:** Noncommercial.

PAXTON†, pop. 4,258.

Ford Co. (E). 25 m N of Champaign. Manufacturers brooms, electronic components, industrial air conditioners, air coils; corn processing. Agriculture. Corn, soybeans.

9567 Loda Times
Paxton Printing, Inc.
218 N. Market Phone: (217)379-2356
PO Box 73 Fax: (217)379-3104
Paxton, IL 60957
Community newspaper. **Founded:** 1891. **Freq:** Weekly (Wed.). **Print Method:** Offset. **Cols./Page:** 6. **Col. Width:** 27 nonpareils. **Col. Depth:** 294 agate lines. **Key Personnel:** Toni Swan, Advertising Mgr. **Subscription Rates:** $25 individuals; $30 outside of Ford and Iroquois Counties. **Remarks:** Accepts advertising.
Ad Rates: BW: $585.90 **Circ:** ‡350
SAU: $4.65
PCI: $4.65

9568 Paxton Daily Record
Paxton Printing, Inc.
218 N. Market Phone: (217)379-2356
PO Box 73 Fax: (217)379-3104
Paxton, IL 60957
General newspaper. **Founded:** 1898. **Freq:** Daily (eve.). **Print**

Method: Offset. **Cols./Page:** 6. **Col. Width:** 2 1/16 inches. **Col. Depth:** 21 inches. **Key Personnel:** Bob Maney, Editor; Toni Swan, Advertising Mgr. **Subscription Rates:** $55 individuals; $85 out of Ford County. **Remarks:** Accepts advertising.
Ad Rates: BW: $585.90 **Circ:** ‡1,280
SAU: $4.65
PCI: $4.65

9569 WPXN-FM - 104.9
361 N. Railroad Ave. Phone: (217)379-4333
Paxton, IL 60957 Fax: (217)379-4334

Format: Adult Contemporary. **Networks:** Brownfield. **Founded:** 1984. **Operating Hours:** Continuous. **Key Personnel:** Joel Cluver, Traffic Mgr., phone (217)379-9796; Dan Daugherity, General Sales Mgr., phone (217)379-9796; Steve Fast, Program Dir. **Wattage:** 3000. **Ad Rates:** $9-12 for 30 seconds; $11-13 for 60 seconds.

PECATONICA

9570 Clydesdale News
Clydesdale Breeders of the United States
17346 Kelly Rd. Phone: (815)247-8780
Pecatonica, IL 61063 Fax: (815)247-8337
Publisher E-mail: clydesusa@aol.com

Trade magazine covering Clydesdale horses for breeders. **Freq:** Annual. **Trim Size:** 8 1/2 x 11. **Key Personnel:** Betty Groves, Contact; Cathy Behn, Contact. **Subscription Rates:** $12 single issue. **Remarks:** Accepts advertising.
Ad Rates: BW: $150 **Circ:** (Not Reported)
4C: $465

PEKIN†, pop. 33,967.

Tazewell Co. (NC). On Illinois River, 10 m S of Peoria. Marine grain elevator on Illinois Waterways. Manufactures health products, corn products, liquors, alcohol, malt, cereal, wire and concrete products, burial vaults, chip board, tractor, automotive parts. Brass, copper, iron, aluminum castings. Non-ferrous metal processing. Coal mines. Agriculture.

9571 Pekin Daily Times
Howard Publications
20 S. 4th St. Phone: (309)346-1111
PO Box 430 Fax: (309)346-9815
Pekin, IL 61554
Free: (800)888-6397

General newspaper. **Founded:** 1853. **Freq:** Daily (eve.) and Sat. (morn.). **Print Method:** Offset. **Cols./Page:** 6. **Col. Width:** 2 1/16 inches. **Col. Depth:** 21 inches. **Key Personnel:** David C. Simpson, Publisher; Kent R. Davy, Editor; Eleanor Gibbons. **Subscription Rates:** $78 individuals; $90 out of state. **Remarks:** Accepts advertising.
Ad Rates: GLR: $8.35 **Circ:** Mon.-Sat. ★**14,116**
BW: $1,562.40
4C: $1,862.40
SAU: $10
PCI: $12.40

9572 WBNH-FM - 88.5
Box 1132 Phone: (309)347-8850
Pekin, IL 61555

Format: Religious. **Networks:** Moody Broadcasting. **Owner:** Central Illinois Radio Fellowship Inc., at above address. **Operating Hours:** Continuous. **Key Personnel:** Scott Krus, Station Mgr. **Wattage:** 7000.

9573 WCIC-FM - 91.5
3263 Court St. Phone: (309)353-9191
Pekin, IL 61554 Fax: (309)353-1141
E-mail: wcic@dpc.net

Format: Contemporary Christian. **Owner:** Illinois Bible Institute, PO Box 140, Carlinville, IL 62626. **Founded:** 1983. **Operating Hours:** Continuous. **Key Personnel:** Dave Brooks, Station Mgr.; Chuck Pryor, Program Dir. **Local Programs:** *Lifestyle with Dave Brooks*, Rachel Hedrick, Mailing contact, (309)353-9191, Fax (309)353-1141. **Wattage:** 45,000. **Ad Rates:** Noncommercial. **URL:** http://www.wcicfm.com.

PEORIA†, pop. 124,160.

Peoria Co. (NWC). On Illinois River, linked to the Gulf Waterway on the south and the St. Lawrence Seaway to the north. 160 m SW of Chicago. Bradley University. Illinois Central College Boat facilities. Manufactures of tractors, alcohol and solvents, brick, tile, caskets, castings, cordage, cotton goods, fencing and wire products, nails, feed, pharmaceuticals, steel, paper, household products, furnaces, oil burners, road machinery, heavy graders, strawboard, tools, dies, labels. Millwork.

9574 Catholic Post
409 N. Monroe Phone: (309)673-3603
Peoria, IL 61603 Fax: (309)673-0334
Free: (800)340-5630
Publication E-mail: cathpost@aol.com

Catholic newspaper. **Founded:** 1934. **Freq:** Weekly (Fri.). **Print Method:** Offset. **Trim Size:** 14 x 22 3/4. **Cols./Page:** 6. **Col. Width:** 2 inches. **Col. Depth:** 21 1/2 inches. **Key Personnel:** Tom Dermody, Editor; Bishop John J. Myers, Publisher. **USPS:** 557-000. **Subscription Rates:** $15 individuals; $16 out of state; $30 other countries. **Remarks:** Accepts advertising.
Ad Rates: BW: $1,083.50 **Circ:** 28,900
SAU: $1,312.62
PCI: $13.90

CATS - See Port Orange

9575 Crafts Magazine
Primedia Special Interest Publication
2 News Plaza Phone: (309)682-6626
PO Box 1790 Fax: (309)682-7394
Peoria, IL 61656-1790
Free: (800)521-2885
Publication E-mail: crafts@primediasi.com

Crafts is a how-to magazine which offers attractive projects in a variety in crafting techniques, such as painting, cross stitch, papercrafts, plastic canvas, polymer clay, fabric crafts, florals, dollmaking, crochet and others. Crafts provides full-size patterns, complete instructions and clear photos that show the projects' details. **Subtitle:** More Project-More Skills-More Fun. **Founded:** May 1978. **Freq:** 10/year. **Print Method:** Offset. **Trim Size:** 7 7/8 x 10 1/2. **Cols./Page:** 3. **Col. Width:** 13.5 picas. **Col. Depth:** 9 7/8 inches. **Key Personnel:** Miriam Olson, Editor; Steve Elzy, President; Mike Irish, Associate Publisher; Harry Sailer, VP/General Mgr. **ISSN:** 0148-9127. **Subscription Rates:** $21.98 individuals; $3.50 single issue.
Ad Rates: BW: $6,450 **Circ:** Paid 331,611
4C: $8,170

9576 The Daily Record
503 NE Madison, Ste. A Fax: (888)616-4285
Peoria, IL 61603 Free: (888)616-4205

Newspaper (tabloid) publishing court and commercial news. **Founded:** Mar. 1925. **Freq:** Tues.-Fri. (morn.). **Print Method:** Letterpress. **Trim Size:** 11 1/2 x 16 1/2. **Cols./Page:** 5. **Col. Width:** 12 picas. **Col. Depth:** 15 inches. **Key Personnel:** Fred Wing, Editor and Publisher. **USPS:** 427-720. **Subscription Rates:** $37.50 individuals. **Remarks:** Accepts advertising. **Formerly:** Peoria Daily Record.
Ad Rates: GLR: $1.20 **Circ:** Paid ‡400
BW: $200 Free ‡50
PCI: $2.50

9577 East Peoria Times-Courier
Times Newspapers, Inc.
PO Box 9426 Phone: (309)692-6600
Peoria, IL 61612 Fax: (309)692-6447

Community newspaper. **Founded:** 1927. **Freq:** Weekly (Wed.). **Print Method:** Offset. **Trim Size:** 22 3/4 x 13 1/2. **Cols./Page:** 6. **Col. Width:** 12 picas. **Col. Depth:** 21 1/2 inches. **Key Personnel:** Paula J. King, Managing Editor, pking@timestoday.com; Beth Gehrt, General Mgr., ggehrt@timestoday.com. **Subscription Rates:** Free; $15.60 by mail in county; $18.20 out of county (mail). **Remarks:** Accepts advertising. **URL:** http://www.timestoday.com. **Formerly:** East Peoria Courier.
Ad Rates: GLR: $.40 **Circ:** Paid 506
BW: $1,075.86 Free 10,061
4C: $1,335.86
SAU: $8.34

9578 HandGunning
Primedia Special Interest Publication
2 News Plaza Phone: (309)682-6626
PO Box 1790 Fax: (309)682-7394
Peoria, IL 61656-1790
Free: (800)521-2885

Magazine for handgunners; includes reports, techniques, and event coverage. **Founded:** 1987. **Freq:** Bimonthly. **Print Method:** Offset. **Trim Size:** 8 x 10 3/4. **Cols./Page:** 3. **Col. Width:** 27 nonpareils. **Col. Depth:** 140 agate lines. **Key Personnel:** John Crowley, Editor. **ISSN:** 1042-6108. **Subscription Rates:** $21.98 individuals. **Remarks:** Accepts advertising.
Ad Rates: BW: $1,310 **Circ:** ‡80,000
4C: $2,385

9579 Herbal Choice
3457 N. University, Ste. 120
Peoria, IL 61604-1322

Magazine highlighting herbal alternatives for women. **Founded:** 1995. **Freq:** 4/year. **Trim Size:** 8 1/2 x 11. **Key Personnel:** Uni M. Tiamat, Editor.

9580 Journal Star
The Peoria Journal Star, Inc.
1 News Plaza Phone: (309)686-3000
Peoria, IL 61643 Fax: (309)686-3296
Free: (800)225-5757

General newspaper. **Founded:** 1855. **Freq:** Mon.-Sun. (morn.). **Print Method:** Letterpress. **Trim Size:** 13 x 21 1/2. **Cols./Page:** 6. **Col. Width:** 2 1/16 inches. **Col. Depth:** 21 1/2 inches. **Key Personnel:** Barb Drake, Editorial Page Ed., phone (309)686-3133; Clare Howard, Business Reporter, phone (309)686-3250; Dennis Dmond, Ed. Systems Man., phone (309)686-3243; Eric Behrens, Photo/Graphics Ed., phone (309)686-3137; Mike Miller, Religion/TV Editor, phone (309)686-3120; Ken Kirchoefer, State Editor, phone (309)686-3041. **Subscription Rates:** $169; $241.80 by mail. **URL:** http://www.pjstar.com. **Feature Editors:** Eric Behrens, *Photo*, phone (309)686-3137; Dennis Dimond, *Lifestyle*, phone (309)686-3243; Ken Kirchoefer, *Rural Development*, phone (309)686-3041; Jerry McDowell, *Metro, News*, phone (309)686-3117; Mike Miller, *Religion, TV & Radio*, phone (309)686-3106; Gary Panetta, *Art, Movie, Music*, phone (309)686-3132; Kirk Wessler, *Sports*, phone (309)686-3216.
Ad Rates: GLR: $5.09 **Circ:** Mon.-Fri. ★**70,522**
BW: $8,108.94 Sat. ★**87,461**
4C: $8,843.94 Sun. ★**97,998**
SAU: $62.86
PCI: $62.86

9581 The Labor Paper
400 NE Jefferson, No. 400 Phone: (309)674-3148
Peoria, IL 61603-3756 Fax: (309)674-9714
Publication E-mail: theeditor5@aol.com

Labor tabloid. **Founded:** 1896. **Freq:** Semimonthly. **Print Method:** Offset. **Cols./Page:** 4. **Col. Width:** 28 nonpareils. **Col. Depth:** 182 agate lines. **Key Personnel:** Sharon K. Williams, Editor; Donald G. Noe, Publisher. **Subscription Rates:** $15 individuals. **Remarks:** Advertising not accepted for non-union advertisements.
Ad Rates: BW: $560 **Circ:** ‡10,500
4C: $875
SAU: $35

9582 Marketeer
1602 E. Glen Ave. Phone: (309)688-8106
Peoria, IL 61614
Magazine on new product merchandising for industries. **Founded:** 1952. **Freq:** Monthly. **Print Method:** Letterpress. **Cols./Page:** 3. **Col. Width:** 22 nonpareils. **Col. Depth:** 116 agate lines. **Key Personnel:** J. Cook, Editor and Publisher. **Subscription Rates:** $15 individuals. **Remarks:** Accepts advertising.
Ad Rates: BW: $300 **Circ:** Controlled ‡2,000

9583 Morton Times News
Times Newspapers
1616 W. Pioneer Pkwy. Phone: (309)692-4910
Peoria, IL 61615 Fax: (309)692-6447
Free: (888)42-TIMES

Community newspaper. **Founded:** 1888. **Freq:** Semiweekly (Wed. and Sat.). **Print Method:** Offset. **Trim Size:** 22 3/4 x 13 1/2. **Cols./Page:** 6. **Col. Width:** 24 nonpareils. **Col. Depth:** 301 agate lines. **Key Personnel:** Laura Lelm, Editor, phone (309)263-2211; Beth Gehrt, Exec. Editor. **Subscription Rates:** $23.40 in county; $35 out of county. **Remarks:** Accepts advertising.
Ad Rates: GLR: $.40 **Circ:** Paid 3,282
BW: $1,199.70 Free 6,157
4C: $1,427.70
SAU: $9.30

9584 Peoria Times Observer
Times Newspapers
1616 W. Pioneer Pkwy. Phone: (309)692-4910
Peoria, IL 61615 Fax: (309)692-6447
Free: (888)42-TIMES

Community newspaper. **Founded:** 1962. **Freq:** Weekly (Wed.). **Print Method:** Offset. **Trim Size:** 11 1/2 x 16. **Cols./Page:** 6. **Col. Width:** 12 picas. **Col. Depth:** 21 1/2 inches. **Key Personnel:** Rick Wade, Editor; Beth Gehrt, Exec. Editor; Chris Gullett, VP & Group Mgr. **Formerly:** Observer.
Ad Rates: BW: $1,809.87 **Circ:** ‡24,390
4C: $2,069.87
SAU: $14.03

9585 Shooting Times
Primedia Special Interest Publication
2 News Plaza Phone: (309)682-6626
PO Box 1790 Fax: (309)682-7394
Peoria, IL 61656-1790
Free: (800)521-2885

Magazine focusing on guns and shooting sports. **Founded:**

1960. **Freq:** Monthly. **Print Method:** Offset. **Trim Size:** 7 7/8 x 10 1/2. **Cols./Page:** 3. **Col. Width:** 27 nonpareils. **Col. Depth:** 140 agate lines. **Key Personnel:** Beth Nelson, Advertising Mgr.; Joel Hutchcroft, Editor, phone (309)679-5402. **Subscription Rates:** $23.98 individuals; $3.50 single issue. **Remarks:** Accepts advertising.
Ad Rates: BW: $6,950 **Circ:** Paid ★200,176
4C: $10,950
PCI: $385

9586 Shotgun News
Primedia Special Interest Publication
2 News Plaza Phone: (309)682-6626
PO Box 1790 Fax: (309)682-7394
Peoria, IL 61656-1790
Free: (800)521-2885
Publication E-mail: SGNewsamerica online, inc.com

Advertising magazine for gun collectors, dealers and hunters. **Subtitle:** The World's Largest Gun Sales Publication. **Founded:** 1946. **Freq:** 3/mo. **Print Method:** Web Offset. **Trim Size:** 10 7/8 x 13. **Cols./Page:** 5. **Col. Width:** 24 nonpareils. **Col. Depth:** 210 agate lines. **Key Personnel:** Robert W. Hunnicurt, General Mgr.; Chuck Boysen, Circulation Mgr.; Debi Fontaine, Class. Adv. **ISSN:** 0049-0415. **Subscription Rates:** $29 for 36 issues. **Remarks:** Accepts advertising.
Ad Rates: GLR: $.25 **Circ:** 135,000
BW: $1,200
4C: $4,200
PCI: $24

9587 Spotted News
National Spotted Swine Record, Inc.
PO Box 9758 Phone: (309)693-1804
Peoria, IL 61612-9756 Fax: (309)691-0168

Magazine covering swine raising. **Founded:** 1913. **Freq:** Monthly. **Print Method:** Offset. Uses mats. **Trim Size:** 8 3/8 x 11. **Cols./Page:** 3. **Col. Width:** 28 nonpareils. **Col. Depth:** 140 agate lines. **ISSN:** 0038-8432. **Subscription Rates:** Free to qualified subscribers; $10 individuals. **Remarks:** Accepts advertising.
Ad Rates: BW: $225 **Circ:** Paid ‡4,000
Non-paid ‡3,000

9588 Step-By-Step Graphics
Step by Step Graphics
6000 N. Forest Park Phone: (309)688-2300
Peoria, IL 61614 Fax: (309)688-8515
Free: (800)255-8800
Publisher E-mail: sbspub@dgusa.com

Magazine serving traditional and electronic visual communicators of all kinds, including graphic designers, art directors, and illustrators. **Subtitle:** The Inside View of the Design World. **Founded:** 1985. **Freq:** Bimonthly. **Print Method:** Offset. **Trim Size:** 8 3/8 x 10 7/8. **Cols./Page:** 3. **Col. Width:** 27 nonpareils. **Col. Depth:** 140 agate lines. **Key Personnel:** Michael Hammer, Publisher, hammer@dgusa.com. **ISSN:** 0886-7682. **Subscription Rates:** $42 individuals. **Remarks:** Accepts advertising. **Online:** CompuServe. **URL:** http://www.dgusa.com.
Ad Rates: BW: $2,225 **Circ:** ‡42,000
4C: $3,125

9589 Washington Times-Reporter
Times Newspapers, Inc.
PO Box 9426 Phone: (309)692-6600
Peoria, IL 61612 Fax: (309)692-6447
Publication E-mail: washington@timestoday.com

Community newspaper. **Founded:** 1840. **Freq:** Weekly (Wed.). **Print Method:** Offset. **Trim Size:** 22 3/4 x 13 1/2. **Cols./Page:** 6. **Col. Width:** 24 nonpareils. **Col. Depth:** 301 agate lines. **Key Personnel:** Beth Gehrt, Executive Editor, bgehrt@timestoday.com; Chris Gullett, Group Manager, cgullert@timestoday.com. **Subscription Rates:** Free; $0.50 single issue. **Remarks:** Advertising accepted; rates available upon request. **Formerly:** Washington Reporter.
Circ: Paid 225
Free 8,150

9590 TCI Cablevision of Central Illinois
3517 N. Dries Ln. Phone: (309)686-2600
Peoria, IL 61604 Fax: (309)688-9828

Founded: 1973. **Formerly:** United Artists Entertainment. **Key Personnel:** Jeanne Coleman, General Mgr.; MaryAnn Vaupel, Marketing Manager. **Cities Served:** subscribing households 55,383; 1 channel; 30 community access channels; 61 hours per week community access programming.

9591 WEEK-TV - 25
2907 Springfield Rd. Phone: (309)698-2525
Peoria, IL 61611 Fax: (309)698-9335

Format: Commercial TV. **Networks:** NBC. **Owner:** Granite Broadcasting Corp., 1 Dag Hammerslejold Plaza, New York, NY 10017. **Founded:** 1953. **Operating Hours:** Continuous; 60% network, 40% local. **ADI:** Peoria-Bloomington, IL. **Key Personnel:** John Deushane, President/Gen. Mgr.; Pete Russell, Sales Dir.; Phil Supple, News Dir. **Wattage:** ERP 1,410,000. **Ad Rates:** Advertising accepted; rates available upon request.

9592 WIRL-AM - 1290
PO Box 3335 Phone: (309)694-6262
Peoria, IL 61612 Fax: (309)694-2233

Format: Talk; News; Sports. **Networks:** ABC. **Owner:** WIRL/WSWT, at above address. **Founded:** 1947. **Operating Hours:** Continuous; 3% network, 97% local. **ADI:** Peoria-Bloomington, IL. **Key Personnel:** Jim Glassman, President; Henry Baltanz, Contact; Lee Malcolm, Program Dir. **Local Programs:** *Marc Truelove Show*, Lynn Marie. **Wattage:** 5000.

9593 WMBD-AM - 1470
3131 N. University St. Phone: (309)688-3131
Peoria, IL 61604 Fax: (309)686-8655

Format: Full Service. **Networks:** CBS. **Founded:** 1927. **Operating Hours:** Continuous. **ADI:** Peoria-Bloomington, IL. **Key Personnel:** Gene C. Robinson, Contact; Mike Wild, Station Mgr.; Dave Wisniewski, General Sales Mgr. **Local Programs:** *Ag Business with Colleen Callahan*; *Bradley University Basketball*, Dave Wisniewski, General Sales Mgr.; *Gary and Danny* 5-10a.m. **Wattage:** 5000.

9594 WMBD-TV - 31
3131 N. University St. Phone: (309)688-3131
Peoria, IL 61604 Fax: (309)686-8650
E-mail: wmbdtv@wmbd.com

Format: Commercial TV. **Networks:** CBS. **Founded:** Jan. 1, 1958. **Operating Hours:** continuous. **ADI:** Peoria-Bloomington, IL. **Key Personnel:** Bill Lamb, General Mgr., phone (309)686-9400, fax (309)686-8666, billlamb@wmbd.com; Duane Wallace, News Dir., phone (309)686-9446, fax (309)686-8658, duanew@wmbd.com; Don Locke, General Sales Mgr., phone (309)686-9431, fax (309)686-8666, rvsales@wmbd.com. **URL:** http://www.wmbd.com.

9595 WPBG-FM - 93.3
3131 N. University St. Phone: (309)688-3131
Peoria, IL 61604 Fax: (309)686-8655
E-mail: bigoldies@bigoldies933.com

Format: Oldies. **Networks:** Independent. **Founded:** 1947. **Formerly:** WKZW-AM (Apr. 1994); WMXP-FM (Apr. 1997). **Operating Hours:** Continuous. **ADI:** Peoria-Bloomington, IL. **Key Personnel:** Michael R. Wild, Station Mgr.; Rob Brown, Program Dir.; Rebecca Mandel, Promotions Mgr. **Wattage:** 41,000.

9596 WQEZ-FM - 94.3
335 E. High Point Rd. Fax: (309)688-9346
Peoria, IL 61614-3011 Free: (800)808-9430

Format: Adult Contemporary; Soft Rock. **Networks:** Satellite Music Network. **Founded:** 1977. **Formerly:** WTXR-FM; WBZM-FM; WKZW-FM. **Operating Hours:** Continuous. **ADI:** Peoria-Bloomington, IL. **Key Personnel:** Bill Bro, President. **Wattage:** 50,000. **Ad Rates:** $60 for 30 seconds; $70 for 60 seconds.

9597 WTAZ-FM - 102.3
P.O. Box 6255 Phone: (309)263-2915
Peoria, IL 61601-6255 Free: (800)948-0102
E-mail: talk@wtaz.com

Format: Talk. **Networks:** ABC; NBC; EFM; Westwood One Radio; CBS. **Founded:** 1976. **Operating Hours:** Continuous; 90% network, 10% local. **ADI:** Peoria-Bloomington, IL. **Key Personnel:** Jerry Scott, Station Mgr.; John Malone, Operations Mgr. **Wattage:** 6,000. **Ad Rates:** $28 for 30 seconds; $35 for 60 seconds.

9598 WTVP-TV - 47
1501 W. Bradley Ave. Phone: (309)677-4747
Peoria, IL 61625 Fax: (309)677-4730
Free: (800)837-4747
E-mail: wtvpmail@wtvp.pbs.org

Format: Public TV. **Networks:** Public Broadcasting Service (PBS). **Owner:** Illinois Valley Public Telecommunications Corp., at above address. **Founded:** 1971. **Operating Hours:** 7 a.m.-12 a.m. **ADI:** Peoria-Bloomington, IL. **Key Personnel:** Chet Tomczyk, General Mgr., phone (309)677-2789, chet_tomczyk@wtvp.pbs.org; Guy Serumgard, Production Mgr., phone (309)677-2790, guy_serumgard@wtvp.pbs.org; John Morris, Marketing Manager, phone (309)677-3525, john_morris@wtvp.pbs.org. **Wattage:** 55,000. **Ad Rates:** Noncommercial. **URL:** http://www.wtvp.com.

9599 WWCT-FM - 105.7
4701 North War Memorial Dr. Phone: (309)688-2000
Peoria, IL 61614 Fax: (309)688-2805
Free: (800)WWC-T106

Format: Classic Rock. **Networks:** Independent. **Founded:** 1976. **Operating Hours:** Continuous; 100% local. **ADI:** Peoria-Bloomington, IL. **Key Personnel:** Bruce Foster, Contact; Michael Rea, General Sales Mgr.; Rick Hirschmann, Program Dir. **Wattage:** 50,000. **URL:** http://www.rock106.com.

9600 WXCL-AM - 1350
PO Box 180 Phone: (309)685-5975
Peoria, IL 61650-0180 Fax: (309)685-7150

Format: Country. **Operating Hours:** Continuous. **ADI:** Peoria-Bloomington, IL. **Wattage:** 1000. **Ad Rates:** $4-40 for 15 seconds; $5-50 for 30 seconds; $10-60 for 60 seconds.

9601 WXCL-FM - 104.9
PO Box 180 Phone: (309)685-5975
Peoria, IL 61650-0810 Fax: (309)685-7150

Format: Country. **Networks:** Independent. **Founded:** 1973. **Formerly:** WKQA-FM (1990). **Operating Hours:** Continuous. **ADI:** Peoria-Bloomington, IL. **Key Personnel:** Bill Early, Contact. **Wattage:** 3000. **Ad Rates:** $4-40 for 15 seconds; $5-50 for 30 seconds; $10-60 for 60 seconds.

PEOTONE

Beecher Herald - See Beecher

Grant Park Gazette - See Grant Park

9602 Manhattan American
Russell Publications
PO Box 429 Phone: (708)258-3473
Peotone, IL 60468 Fax: (708)258-6295

Community newspaper. **Freq:** Weekly (Wed.). **Cols./Page:** 5. **Col. Width:** 11 1/2 picas. **Col. Depth:** 16 inches. **Key Personnel:** Barb Dougherty, Editor; Gilbert L. Russell, Publisher. **Remarks:** Advertising accepted; rates available upon request.
Circ: 1,000

Monee Monitor - See Monee

New Lenox Community Reporter - See New Lenox

9603 Peotone Vedette
Russell Publications
PO Box 429 Phone: (708)258-3473
Peotone, IL 60468 Fax: (708)258-6295

Community newspaper. **Freq:** Weekly (Wed.). **Cols./Page:** 5. **Col. Width:** 11 1/2 picas. **Col. Depth:** 16 inches. **Key Personnel:** Gilbert L. Russell, Publisher; Gilbert L. Russell, Publisher. **Subscription Rates:** $16. **Remarks:** Accepts advertising.
Ad Rates: BW: $236 **Circ:** 2600

PERCY, pop. 1,053.

Randolph Co. (SW). 11 m S of Coulterville. Residential.

9604 The County Journal
Willis Publishing Co.
PO Box 369 Phone: (618)497-8272
Percy, IL 62272 Fax: (618)497-2607

Local newspaper. **Founded:** Apr. 10, 1980. **Freq:** Weekly (Thurs.). **Print Method:** Offset. **Trim Size:** 13 1/2 x 21. **Cols./Page:** 6. **Col. Width:** 26 nonpareils. **Col. Depth:** 294 agate lines. **Key Personnel:** Larry R. Willis, Editor and Publisher; Jerry Willis, Editor and Publisher; Judy Willis, Advertising Mgr. **Subscription Rates:** $15.50 individuals; $17.50 out of area.
Ad Rates: BW: $724.50 **Circ:** 7,000
4C: $1,500
SAU: $6.75

PERU, pop. 10,886.

LaSalle Co. (WC). 15 m W of Ottawa.

9605 Babybug
The Cricket Magazine Group
315 5th St. Phone: (815)224-6656
Peru, IL 61354 Fax: (815)224-6615
Free: (800)588-8585

Magazine featuring children's literature. **Founded:** Jan. 1995. **Freq:** Monthly. **Trim Size:** 6 1/4 x 7. **Key Personnel:** Marianne Corus, Editor-in-Chief; Bob Harper, Publisher; Paula Morrow, Editor; John Toraason, General Mgr.; Karen Dauck, Production Mgr.; Jennifer Gross, Circulation and Mktg. Dir.

ISSN: 1077-1131. **Subscription Rates:** $32.97; $42.97 other countries and Canada. **Remarks:** Advertising not accepted.
Circ: 46,500

9606 Cricket Magazine
The Cricket Magazine Group
315 5th St. Phone: (815)224-6656
Peru, IL 61354 Fax: (815)224-6615
Free: (800)588-8585

Literary magazine for children, ages 9-14. **Founded:** Sept. 1973. **Freq:** Monthly. **Print Method:** Offset. **Trim Size:** 8 x 10. **Key Personnel:** Marianne Carus, Editor-in-Chief; Bob Harper, Publisher; John Toraason, General Mgr. **ISSN:** 0090-6034. **Subscription Rates:** $32.97 libraries and Schools; $27.97 institutions schools and libraries; $42.97 Canada; $42.97 other countries; $3.95 single issue. **Remarks:** Advertising not accepted. **Formerly:** Cricket, the Magazine for Children.
Circ: Paid ‡71,000

9607 Ladybug
The Cricket Magazine Group
315 5th St. Phone: (815)224-6656
Peru, IL 61354 Fax: (815)224-6615
Free: (800)588-8585

Magazine of ideas, adventures, and activities for children ages 2 to 6. **Subtitle:** The Magazine for Young Children. **Founded:** 1990. **Freq:** Monthly. **Print Method:** Offset. **Trim Size:** 8 x 10. **Key Personnel:** Marianne Carus, Editor-in-Chief; Bob Harper, Publisher; John Toraason, General Mgr. **ISSN:** 1051-4961. **Subscription Rates:** $32.97; $27.97 schools and libraries; $41.97 other countries; $42.97 Canada; $3.95 single issue. **Remarks:** Advertising not accepted.
Circ: Paid ‡130,000

9608 The Monist
The Hegeler Institute
315 Fifth St. Phone: (815)224-6651
Peru, IL 61354 Fax: (815)223-4486

Subtitle: An International Quarterly Journal of General Philosophical Inquiry. **Founded:** 1890. **Freq:** Quarterly. **Print Method:** Offset. **Trim Size:** 6 x 9. **Cols./Page:** 1. **Col. Width:** 54 nonpareils. **Col. Depth:** 98 agate lines. **Key Personnel:** Barry Smith, Editor, phismith@acu.buffalo.edu; Sherwood J.B. Sugden, Managing Editor. **ISSN:** 0026-9662. **Subscription Rates:** $25 individuals; $9 single issue; $48 institutions. **Remarks:** Accepts advertising. **Alt. Formats:** CD-ROM, Intelex.
Ad Rates: BW: $150 **Circ:** Paid ‡1,500
Non-paid ‡200

9609 Spider
Carus Publishing
315 5th St. Phone: (815)224-6656
Peru, IL 61354 Fax: (815)224-6615
Free: (800)588-8585

Magazine of stories, games, and projects for children ages 6 to 9. **Subtitle:** The Magazine for Children. **Founded:** 1993. **Freq:** Monthly. **Trim Size:** 8 x 10. **Key Personnel:** Marianne Carus, Editor-in-Chief; Bob Harper, Publisher; Laura Tillotson, Editor. **ISSN:** 1070-2911. **Subscription Rates:** $32.97; $27.97 institutions; $42.97 Canada; $42.97 other countries; $3.95 single issue. **Remarks:** Advertising not accepted.
Circ: Paid 82,000

9610 WAIV-FM - 103.3
3905 Progress Blvd. Phone: (815)224-2100
Peru, IL 61354 Fax: (815)224-2066
Free: (800)375-9657

Format: Adult Contemporary. **Networks:** ABC. **Owner:** Crest Broadcasting, at above address. **Founded:** 1995. **Operating Hours:** Continuous. **Key Personnel:** Lee Studstill, General Mgr., lstudsti@aol.com; Judy Miller, Sales Mgr.; Mary Politsch, Office Mgr.; Stuart Hall, Program Mgr. **Local Programs:** *Illinois Valley Newsmaker*, J. Burt; *Value Line Shopping Show*, Sue Parker. **Wattage:** 6000. **Ad Rates:** $8-15 for 30 seconds. Combined advertising rates available with WGLC-FM, WLRZ-FM, WALS-FM.

9611 WLRZ-FM - 100.9
3905 Progress Blvd. Phone: (815)224-2100
Peru, IL 61354 Fax: (815)224-2066
Free: (800)375-9257

Format: Classic Rock. **Networks:** Westwood One Radio. **Owner:** Valley Plus Broadcasting, at above address. **Operating Hours:** Continuous. **Key Personnel:** Owen Studstill, General Mgr.; Judy Miller, Sales Mgr.; Mary Politsch, Office Mgr.; Stuart Hall, Program Mgr. **Wattage:** 3000 ERP. **Ad Rates:** $16-22 for 60 seconds. Combined advertising rates available with WGLC-FM, WALS-FM, WAIV-FM.

PETERSBURG†, pop. 2,419.

Menard Co. (C). 23 m NW of Springfield. New Salem State Park (historical). Manufactures electrical connectors. Bottling works. Grain, stock farms.

9612 Ashland Sentinel
Petersburg Observer
116 N. Hardin
PO Box 418
Ashland, IL 62612-0418

Community newspaper. **Founded:** 1884. **Freq:** Weekly (Thurs.). **Print Method:** Offset. **Cols./Page:** 5. **Col. Width:** 11 1/2 picas. **Col. Depth:** 16 inches. **Key Personnel:** Barbara Hill Nowack, Publisher. **Remarks:** Accepts advertising.
Ad Rates: PCI: $4 **Circ:** ‡850

9613 The Petersburg Observer
Petersburg Observer
Petersburg, IL 62675 Phone: (217)476-3332
Fax: (217)476-3332

Community newspaper (broadsheet). **Founded:** 1874. **Freq:** Weekly (Thurs.). **Print Method:** Offset. **Cols./Page:** 8. **Col. Width:** 11 1/2 picas. **Col. Depth:** 21 inches. **Key Personnel:** Jane Cutright, Editor and Publisher. **Subscription Rates:** $18 in state; $20 out of state. **Remarks:** Accepts advertising.
Ad Rates: PCI: $4.90 **Circ:** ‡3,150

9614 WLUJ-FM - 97.7
Box 500 Phone: (217)632-2266
Petersburg, IL 62675

Format: Middle-of-the-Road (MOR); Religious; Easy Listening. **Networks:** Moody Broadcasting; USA Radio. **Owner:** Richard Van Zendt, 15 Walnut Hills, Springfield, IL 62707, (217)487-7711. **Founded:** 1986. **Operating Hours:** Continuous; 85% network, 15% local. **Key Personnel:** Richard Van Zandt, General Mgr.; Howard Fouks, Station Mgr. **Wattage:** 6000.

PITTSFIELD†, pop. 4,170.

Pike Co. (W). 40 m SE of Quincy. Feed mills. Cheese and garment factories; dried milk processing; meat packing. Agriculture. Corn, wheat, soybeans, livestock.

9615 Pike Press
Pike Press Pike County Publishing Co.
115 W. Jefferson Phone: (217)285-2345
Box 70 Fax: (217)285-5222
Pittsfield, IL 62363
Community newspaper. **Founded:** 1842. **Freq:** Weekly (Wed.). **Print Method:** Offset. **Trim Size:** 14 x 22 3/4. **Cols./Page:** 6. **Col. Width:** 2 1/16 inches. **Col. Depth:** 21 1/2 inches. **Key Personnel:** Julie Boren, Publisher. **USPS:** 602-540. **Subscription Rates:** $25 individuals; $35 out of area.
Ad Rates: SAU: $7.50 **Circ:** ‡7,900
PCI: $5.25

9616 WBBA-AM - 1580
PO Box 150 Phone: (217)285-2157
Pittsfield, IL 62363 Fax: (217)285-4006

Format: Talk; News. **Simulcasts:** WBBA-FM. **Networks:** Jones Satellite; Brownfield; Illinois Farm Bureau; People's Network; UPI. **Owner:** Brown Radio Group, Inc., at above address, (217)285-9750, Fax: (217)285-4006. **Founded:** 1954. **Operating Hours:** Continuous; 75% network, 25% local. **ADI:** Quincy, IL-Hannibal, MO. **Key Personnel:** David Fuhler, Gen. Mgr./Program, Music & Sports Dir.; Debi Conner, Sales Mgr. **Local Programs:** *Coffee Break*, Tammy Hanlin; *Farm Reports*, Wayne Ator; *News*, Tammy Hanlin. **Wattage:** 250. **Ad Rates:** $10 for 30 seconds; $13 for 60 seconds. Combined advertising rates available with WJBM, KDAM, WBBA-FM.

9617 WBBA-FM - 97.5
PO Box 150 Phone: (217)285-2157
Pittsfield, IL 62363 Fax: (217)285-4006

Format: Contemporary Country. **Networks:** Jones Satellite; Illinois Farm Bureau; Brownfield. **Owner:** Brown Radio Group, Inc., at above address, (217)285-9750, Fax: (217)285-4006. **Founded:** 1965. **Operating Hours:** Continuous; 50% network, 50% local. **ADI:** Quincy, IL-Hannibal, MO. **Key Personnel:** David Fuhler, Contact; David Fuhler, Music and Sports Dir.; Debi Conner, Sales Mgr. **Local Programs:** *Coffee Break*, Tammy Hanlin; *Farm Reports*, Wayne Ator; *News*, Tammy Hanlin. **Wattage:** 10,000. **Ad Rates:** $10 for 30 seconds; $13 for 60 seconds. Combined advertising rates available with WJBM-AM, KDAM-FM.

PLAINFIELD, pop. 4,485.

Will Co. (NE). 9 m NW of Joliet. Lake Renwick Bird Sanctuary. Small business. Industrial. Grain farms.

9618 The Enterprise
Box 127 Phone: (815)436-2431
519 Lockport St. Fax: (815)436-2592
Plainfield, IL 60544
Free: (800)997-9922
Publication E-mail: entrprse@aol.com; entrprse1@aol.com

Community newspaper. **Founded:** Aug. 1887. **Freq:** Weekly (Wed.). **Print Method:** Offset. **Cols./Page:** 5. **Col. Width:** 22 nonpareils. **Col. Depth:** 224 agate lines. **Key Personnel:** Beverly Perry, Publisher; Wayne Perry, Publisher. **Subscription Rates:** $15 Will and DuPage counties; $22 in state; $30 out of state. **Remarks:** Accepts advertising.
Ad Rates: PCI: $8.25 **Circ:** 6,200

PLANO, pop. 4,875.

Kendall Co. (NE). 18 m S.W. of Aurora. Birthplace of the harvesters.

9619 WSPY-FM - 107.1
1 Broadcast Center Phone: (708)552-1000
Plano, IL 60545 Fax: (708)552-9300

Format: Talk; Adult Contemporary; News. **Networks:** ABC. **Founded:** 1974. **Operating Hours:** Continuous. **ADI:** Chicago (LaSalle), IL. **Key Personnel:** Larry W. Nelson, President; Beth Abbott, Sales Mgr. **Wattage:** 3000. **Ad Rates:** $28 for 60 seconds.

PLEASANT PLAINS, pop. 688.

Sangamon Co. (C). 16 m NW of Springfield. Grain elevator. Grain, dairy, stock farms. Corn, wheat, soybeans.

New Berlin Bee - See New Berlin

9620 The Pleasant Press
Swettman Publications
Box 50 Phone: (217)626-1711
Pleasant Plains, IL 62677
Community newspaper. **Founded:** 1889. **Freq:** Weekly (Fri.). **Print Method:** Offset. **Trim Size:** 10 x 16. **Cols./Page:** 5. **Col. Width:** 22 nonpareils. **Col. Depth:** 215 agate lines. **Key Personnel:** Al Swettman, Jr., Publisher. **USPS:** 435-860. **Subscription Rates:** $10 individuals. **Remarks:** Accepts advertising.
Ad Rates: GLR: $.16 **Circ:** ‡510
PCI: $1.75

PLYMOUTH, pop. 740.

Hancock Co. (SE). 35 m NE of Quincy.

9621 Tri-County Scribe
KK Stevensons Pub.
PO Box N Phone: (217)392-2715
Plymouth, IL 62367
Community newspaper. **Founded:** 1889. **Freq:** Weekly. **Print Method:** Offset. **Cols./Page:** 6. **Col. Width:** 11 nonpareils. **Col. Depth:** 19 inches. **Key Personnel:** Lea A. Flack, Editor and Publisher; John T. Flack, Editor and Publisher. **USPS:** 639-380. **Subscription Rates:** $15 individuals; $18 out of area. **Remarks:** Accepts advertising.
Ad Rates: BW: $153.60 **Circ:** ‡552
SAU: $1.60
PCI: $1.60

POLO, pop. 2,643.

Ogle Co. (N). 12 m N of Dixon. Creamery; hatchery. Manufactures cheese, pre-fabricated buildings, refrigeration units, lawn tools, hair dryers. Livestock, dairy, poultry farms.

9622 Bus Tours Magazine
National Bus Trader, Inc.
9698 W. Judson Rd. Phone: (815)946-2341
Polo, IL 61064 Fax: (815)946-2347

Magazine for bus tour planners. **Subtitle:** The Magazine of Bus Tours and Long Distance Charters. **Founded:** 1979. **Freq:** Bimonthly. **Print Method:** Offset. **Trim Size:** 8 1/2 x 11. **Cols./Page:** 3. **Col. Width:** 14 picas. **Col. Depth:** 60 picas. **Key Personnel:** Larry Plachno, Editor. **ISSN:** 0199-6096. **Subscription Rates:** $10. **Remarks:** Accepts advertising.
Ad Rates: BW: $1,460 **Circ:** Controlled ‡7,200
4C: $2,060

9623 National Bus Trader
National Bus Trader, Inc.
9698 W. Judson Rd. Phone: (815)946-2341
Polo, IL 61064 Fax: (815)946-2347

Equipment magazine for intercity buses. **Subtitle:** The Magazine of Bus Equipment for the United States and Canada. **Founded:** 1977. **Freq:** Monthly. **Print Method:** Offset. **Trim Size:** 8 1/2 x 11. **Cols./Page:** 3. **Col. Width:** 14 picas. **Col.**

Depth: 60 picas. **Key Personnel:** Larry Plachno, Editor. **ISSN:** 0194-939X. **Remarks:** Accepts advertising.
Ad Rates: BW: $810 **Circ:** Paid ‡5,800
4C: $1,210

9624 Tri-County Press
PO Box 97 Phone: (815)946-2364
Polo, IL 61064 Fax: (815)732-4238

Local newspaper. **Founded:** 1857. **Freq:** Weekly (Thurs.). **Print Method:** Offset. **Cols./Page:** 6. **Col. Depth:** 21 1/2 inches. **Key Personnel:** Eurleen Hinton, Publisher, phone (815)732-6166; Missy Gruben, Advertising Mgr., phone (815)732-6166. **Subscription Rates:** $22 individuals; $27 out of state. **Remarks:** Accepts advertising.
Ad Rates: BW: $786.90 **Circ:** Combined 7,500
4C: $1086.90
PCI: $6.10

PONTIAC†, pop. 11,227.

Livingston Co. (NEC). 35 m NE of Bloomington. Publishing houses. Manufactures chairs, pallet racks, molded concrete products, gloves, hybrid seed, engineered products for metal industries, flexible conduit, lawn mowing equipment, diesel engine parts.

9625 The Flanagan Home Times
Liberty Group Publishing
318 N. Main St. Phone: (815)842-1153
Pontiac, IL 61764 Fax: (815)842-4388

Community newspaper. **Founded:** 1885. **Freq:** Weekly (Wed.). **Print Method:** Offset. **Cols./Page:** 6. **Col. Width:** 13 inches. **Col. Depth:** 21 1/2 inches. **Key Personnel:** John Faddoul, Editor; Richard Westerfield, Publisher. **USPS:** 249-160. **Subscription Rates:** $20 individuals. **Remarks:** Accepts advertising.
Ad Rates: PCI: $3.50 **Circ:** Paid ‡1,050
Free ‡50

9626 Leader
American Publishing
318 N. Main St. Phone: (815)842-1153
PO Box 170 Fax: (815)842-4388
Pontiac, IL 61764
Daily newspaper. **Founded:** 1880. **Freq:** Daily (eve.) and Sat. (morn.). **Print Method:** Offset. **Cols./Page:** 6. **Col. Width:** 25 nonpareils. **Col. Depth:** 301 agate lines. **Key Personnel:** Pat Graziano, Editor; R.A. Westerfield, Publisher/Contact. **Subscription Rates:** $106.60 individuals.
Ad Rates: SAU: $7.26 **Circ:** ‡6,800
PCI: $8.75

9627 WJEZ-FM - 93.7
315 North Mill St. Phone: (815)844-6101
Pontiac, IL 61764 Fax: (815)842-6515

Format: Adult Contemporary; Soft Rock. **Networks:** Westwood One Radio. **Owner:** Collins Miller, at above address. **Founded:** 1969. **Formerly**: WPOK-FM (1985). **Operating Hours:** Continuous; 40% network, 60% local. **Key Personnel:** Roy Frakenhoff, News Dir.; Marc Edwards, Contact. **Wattage:** 25,000. **Ad Rates:** Advertising accepted; rates available upon request.

PORT ORANGE

9628 CATS
PO Box 1790 Phone: (309)682-6626
Peoria, IL 61656 Fax: (309)679-5454
Publication E-mail: pjspubs15@aol.com
Publisher E-mail: info@catsmag.com

Magazine for the cat enthusiast. **Founded:** 1945. **Freq:** Monthly. **Print Method:** Web offset. **Trim Size:** 8 x 10 7/8. **Cols./Page:** 2 and 3. **Key Personnel:** Annette Gentry Bailey, Editor; Marty Gale, Publisher, phone (312)609-4302, fax (312)236-2413. **ISSN:** 0008-8544. **Subscription Rates:** $21.99 individuals; $2.95 single issue. **Remarks:** Accepts advertising. **URL:** http://www.catsmag.com. **Formerly**: CATS Magazine.
Ad Rates: BW; $5,245 **Circ:** Paid **★118,315**
4C: $6,745

PRINCETON†, pop. 7,342.

Bureau Co. (NW). 22 m W of La Salle. Nursery. Produce packing. Manufactures air compressors, gas jets, sealing wax, fertilizer. Stock, poultry, grain farms. Spots of historical interest.

9629 Bureau County Republican
316 S. Main St. Phone: (815)875-4461
PO Box 340 Fax: (815)875-1235
Princeton, IL 61356-2023
Free: (800)639-7237

Community newspaper. **Founded:** 1847. **Freq:** 3/week. **Print Method:** Offset. **Trim Size:** 13 x 21 1/2. **Cols./Page:** 6. **Col. Width:** 21 nonpareils. **Col. Depth:** 301 agate lines. **Key Personnel:** Sam Fisher, Publisher. **ISSN:** 0894-1181. **Subscription Rates:** $57.60 individuals; $68 out of area. **Remarks:** Accepts advertising. **Online:** America Online, Inc. **Alt. Formats:** Microform.
Ad Rates: GLR: $.50 **Circ:** 7,000
BW: $945
4C: $1,145
SAU: $7.90
PCI: $5.75

9630 WZOE-AM - 1490
Broadcast Center Phone: (815)875-8014
Rte. 5, Box 69
Princeton, IL 61356

Format: News; Talk. **Networks:** Mutual Broadcasting System. **Founded:** 1961. **Operating Hours:** Continuous; 9% network, 91% local. **Key Personnel:** Steve Samet, General Mgr.; Greg Halbleib, News Dir. **Wattage:** 1000.

9631 WZOE-FM - 98.1
Broadcast Center Phone: (815)875-8014
Rte. 5, Box 69
Princeton, IL 61356

Format: Oldies. **Founded:** 1980. **Operating Hours:** Continuous; 100% local. **Key Personnel:** Steve Samet, General Mgr.; Paul Bomleny, Program Dir. **Wattage:** 6000.

PRINCEVILLE

9632 Towing and Recovery Phootnotes
Phootnote Publishing Co.
11520 N. Princeville Jubilee Rd. Phone: (309)243-7900
Princeville, IL 61559 Fax: (309)243-7801
Publisher E-mail: pnotes@ix.netcom.com

Trade magazine covering business management for the towing industry. **Founded:** 1991. **Freq:** Monthly. **Trim Size:** 10 1/4 x 15. **Cols./Page:** 4. **Key Personnel:** Jon Lehman, Editor and Publisher. **Subscription Rates:** $45 individuals. **Remarks:** Accepts advertising.
Ad Rates: BW: $2,878 **Circ:** Controlled 46,075
4C: $3,253

PROPHETSTOWN, pop. 2,141.

Whiteside Co. (NW). On Rock River, 25 m SE of Clinton, Ia. Manufactures disposable surgical tools, precision made gears. Grain, stock, poultry, dairy farms.

9633 The Prophetstown Echo
Prophetstown Echo
342 Washington St. Phone: (815)537-5107
PO Box 7 Fax: (815)537-2658
Prophetstown, IL 61277
Newspaper. **Founded:** 1871. **Freq:** Weekly (Tues.). **Print Method:** Offset. **Trim Size:** 10 1/2 x 13 1/2. **Cols./Page:** 6. **Col. Width:** 20 nonpareils. **Col. Depth:** 224 agate lines. **Key Personnel:** Neil Robinson, Editor and Publisher. **USPS:** 447-900. **Subscription Rates:** $15 individuals; $20 out of county. **Remarks:** Accepts advertising.
Ad Rates: GLR: $.24 **Circ:** 2,300
BW: $150
SAU: $4.12
PCI: $2.75

PROSPECT HEIGHTS

9634 Night Roses
PO Box 393 Phone: (847)392-2435
Prospect Heights, IL 60070
Literary journal covering poetry and short stories. **Subtitle:** Friendship Rose Series. **Founded:** 1987. **Freq:** Semiannual. **Key Personnel:** Allen T. Billy; Sandra Taylor. **ISSN:** 1076-4259. **Subscription Rates:** $10 individuals; $5 single issue. **Remarks:** Advertising not accepted. **Former name**: Friendship Rose.
Circ: Controlled 300

PROVISO

9635 West Proviso Herald
Pioneer Press Newspapers
1148 Westgate Ave. Phone: (708)383-3200
Oak Park, IL 60301 Fax: (708)383-3678

Community newspaper (tabloid). **Founded:** 1970. **Freq:** Weekly (Wed.). **Print Method:** Offset. **Cols./Page:** 5. **Col. Width:** 10 inches. **Col. Depth:** 14 inches. **Key Personnel:** Paul Sassone, Managing Editor; Kevin Beese, Editor. **Subscription Rates:** $13.95 individuals; $15.96 out of county. **Remarks:** Advertising accepted; rates available upon request. **URL:** http://www.pioneerlocal.com.
Circ: Wed. **★2,479**

QUINCY†, pop. 42,352.

Adams Co. (W). On Mississippi River, 110 m N of St. Louis, Mo. Bridge to West Quincy, Mo. Quincy College. Manufactures pumps, elevators, stoves, store fixtures, poultry supplies, radio and television receivers and transmitters, broadcasting equipment, truck bodies, farms wagons, women's wear, shirts, overalls, air compressors, wallboard, stock food, air conditioning and heating units, stereo phonographs, limestone and fertilizer spreaders, industrial trailers, rock drills, electric signs, metal wheels, steel fabrication, paper board specialties, paper bags.

9636 ICUC: I See You See
Looking Glass Publications
Box 3604
Quincy, IL 62305

Consumer large print magazine for the visually impaired. **Subtitle:** Bringing the Joy of Reading to Those With Limited Vision. **Founded:** 1987. **Freq:** Quarterly. **Key Personnel:** Linda Ann Hughes, Editor. **ISSN:** 0899-5451. **Subscription Rates:** $20 individuals; $30 out of country; $6 single issue. **Remarks:** Advertising not accepted. **Alt. Formats:** Large-print.
Circ: Paid 300

9637 The Quincy Herald Whig
ABC Quincy Newspaper, Inc.
130 S. 5th St. Phone: (217)223-5100
PO Box 909 Fax: (217)223-9757
Quincy, IL 62306-0909
Free: (800)373-9444
Publication E-mail: whig@bcl.net

General newspaper. **Founded:** 1835. **Freq:** Daily (eve.), Sat. and Sun. (morn.). **Print Method:** Offset. **Cols./Page:** 6. **Col. Width:** 26 nonpareils. **Col. Depth:** 294 agate lines. **Key Personnel:** Joe Conover, Editor, phone (217)221-3395; T.A. Oakley, Publisher, phone (217)223-5019; James W. Collins, General Mgr.; Mel Evanoff, Advertising Dir., phone (217)221-3397. **Subscription Rates:** $128.05 individuals. **Remarks:** Accepts advertising. **URL:** http://www.bcl.net-whig/.
Ad Rates: GLR: $1.82 **Circ:** Mon.-Sat. **★23,688**
BW: $2,750.58 Sun. **★28,232**
4C: $3,375.58
SAU: $21.83

9638 KGRC-FM - 92.9
329 Maine Phone: (217)224-4102
PO Box 1205 Fax: (217)224-4133
Quincy, IL 62301
Free: (800)930-5472

Format: Adult Contemporary. **Networks:** ABC. **Owner:** Taylor Broadcast Corp., at above address. **Founded:** 1968. **Operating Hours:** Continuous; 5% network, 95% local. **ADI:** Quincy, IL-Hannibal, MO. **Key Personnel:** Pam Hunt, General Mgr. **Local Programs:** *Jazz Traxx*, Paul Ericson, (217)224-4102. **Wattage:** 100,000. **Ad Rates:** $19-37 for 30 seconds; $23-42 for 60 seconds.

9639 KHQA-TV - 7
301 S. 36th St. Phone: (217)222-6200
Quincy, IL 62301 Fax: (217)228-3164
Free: (800)929-3581
E-mail: khqa@khqa.com

Format: Commercial TV. **Networks:** CBS. **Owner:** Benedek Broadcasting Corp., 100 Park Ave., Rockford, IL 61101, (815)987-5350, Fax: (815)987-5335. **Founded:** Sept. 1953. **Operating Hours:** Continuous. **ADI:** Quincy, IL-Hannibal, MO. **Key Personnel:** Bob Romine, VP/General Mgr., bromine@khqa.com; Phil Alexander, General Sales Mgr., phone (217)224-4909, drewry@khqa.com; Carol Sowers, News Dir., phone (217)222-5078, news7@khqa.com; Mike Seaver, Chief Engineer, phone (217)222-5078, engineering@khqa.com; Tom Stemmler, Production Mgr., fax (217)222-5078, stemmler@khqa.com; Carol Rees, Business Mgr.

9640 WGCA-FM - 88.5
Ellington & Cannonball Rds. Phone: (217)223-7700
Box 467 Fax: (217)223-7738
Quincy, IL 62306
E-mail: wgca@rnet.com

Format: Religious. **Networks:** Christian Broadcasting (CBN); USA Radio. **Owner:** Great Commission Broadcasting Corp., 301 Oak St., Quincy, IL 62301, (217)224-9422, Fax: (217)228-5501. **Founded:** 1987. **Operating Hours:** Continuous. **ADI:**

Quincy, IL-Hannibal, MO. **Key Personnel:** Jim Taylor, Station Mgr.; Bruce Rice, Contact, phone (217)224-9422, fax (272)28-5501, br@minister.com. **Wattage:** 40,000. **Ad Rates:** Noncommercial.

9641 WGEM-AM - 1440
513 Hampshire St. Phone: (217)228-6600
Quincy, IL 62301 Fax: (217)228-6670
Free: (800)728-6600
E-mail: manager@wgem.com

Format: News; Sports; Information. **Networks:** ABC. **Owner:** Quincy Newspapers, Inc., at above address. **Founded:** 1948. **Operating Hours:** Continuous. **ADI:** Quincy, IL-Hannibal, MO. **Key Personnel:** Leo Henning, General Mgr., manager@wgem.com; Karen Kelly, General Sales Mgr., phone (217)228-6627, fax (217)228-6670, kkelly@wgem.com; Richard Cain, Operations Dir., phone (217)228-6634, fax (217)228-6670, richcain@wgem.com; Chris Brenneman, Promotions Dir., phone (217)228-6675. **Wattage:** 5000. **Ad Rates:** $6-31 for 30 seconds; $8.25-85 for 60 seconds. **URL:** http://www.wgemquincy.com.

9642 WGEM-FM - 105.1
513 Hampshire St. Phone: (217)228-6600
Quincy, IL 62301 Fax: (217)228-6670
Free: (800)728-6600
E-mail: radio@wgemquincy.com

Format: Country; Agricultural. **Networks:** ABC. **Owner:** Quincy Newspapers, Inc., at above address. **Founded:** 1947. **Formerly:** WQNI-FM. **Operating Hours:** Continuous. **ADI:** Quincy, IL-Hannibal, MO. **Key Personnel:** Leo Henning, General Mgr., manager@wgen.com; Karen Kelly, General Sales Mgr., phone (217)228-6627, kkelly@wgem.com; Richard Cain, Operations Dir., phone (217)228-6634, rcain@wgem.com; Chris Brenneman, Promotions Dir., phone (217)228-6675. **Wattage:** 27,500. **Ad Rates:** $8.25-47 for 30 seconds; $11.75-85 for 60 seconds. Combined advertising rates available with WGEM-AM. **URL:** http://www.wgemquincy.com.

9643 WGEM-TV - 10
513 Hampshire Phone: (217)228-6600
Box 80 Fax: (217)228-6670
Quincy, IL 62306
E-mail: manager@wgemquincy.com

Format: Commercial TV. **Networks:** NBC. **Owner:** Quincy Broadcasting Co., at above address. **Founded:** Sept. 3, 1953. **Operating Hours:** Continuous. **ADI:** Quincy, IL-Hannibal, MO. **Key Personnel:** L. Henning, Contact; Jim Lawrence, Operations Mgr. **Wattage:** 316,000. **URL:** http://www.wgemquincy.com.

9644 WQCY-FM - 99.5
Box 731 Phone: (217)228-2800
Quincy, IL 62306 Fax: (217)228-1031
E-mail: wqcy@bcl.net

Format: Adult Contemporary. **Networks:** ABC; Unistar. **Owner:** Tele-Media Broadcasting Co., at above address. **Founded:** 1948. **Operating Hours:** Continuous. **ADI:** Quincy, IL-Hannibal, MO. **Key Personnel:** Jeff Dorsey, General Mgr.; Steve Boll, Operations/Program Dir. **Wattage:** 50,000 ERP.

9645 WQEC-TV - 27
c/o CONVOCOM Phone: (217)786-6647
PO Box 6248 Fax: (217)786-7267
Springfield, IL 62708
Free: (800)232-3605
E-mail: viewer@wmec.pbs.org

Format: Public TV. **Networks:** Public Broadcasting Service (PBS). **Owner:** CONVOCOM, at above address. **Founded:** 1985. **Operating Hours:** 7:00 a.m.-12 midnight; 70% network, 30% local and other. **ADI:** Quincy, IL-Hannibal, MO. **Key Personnel:** Jerold Gruebel, Contact; Terry Kenny, Contact; Maureen Early, Contact; Rich Plotkin, Contact.

9646 WQUB-FM - 90.3
1800 College Ave. Phone: (217)228-5410
Quincy, IL 62301 Fax: (217)228-5616
E-mail: wqub@quincy.edu

Format: Public Radio; Eclectic; Alternative/New Music/Progressive; Classical; Jazz; Folk. **Networks:** National Public Radio (NPR); Public Radio International (PRI). **Owner:** Quincy University Corp., at above address, (217)222-8020. **Founded:** 1974. **Formerly:** WWQC-FM (1994). **Operating Hours:** 18 hours daily; 60% network, 40% local. **ADI:** Quincy, IL-Hannibal, MO. **Key Personnel:** Will Kinnally, Station Mgr., phone (217)228-5409; Mick Freeman, Music Dir.; Pixy Whitfield, Dir. of Development; Jim Lenz, Operations Dir., phone (217)228-5433. **Local Programs:** *Intermezzo* 11:00 am - 1:00 pm Monday-Friday, Mick Freeman; *Jazz Waves* 6:00 pm - 9:00 am Sunday, Mike Smith; *Conversations* 6:00 pm - 6:30 pm Monday, Jim Lenz. **Wattage:** 28,000 ERP. **Ad Rates:** Noncommercial. **URL:** http://www.quincy.edu/wqub.

9647 WTAD-AM - 930
Box 731 Phone: (217)228-2800
Quincy, IL 62306 Fax: (217)228-1031
Free: (800)228-9823

Format: News; Talk. **Networks:** CBS; Mutual Broadcasting System. **Owner:** Tele-Media Broadcasting Co., at above address. **Founded:** 1926. **Operating Hours:** Continuous. **ADI:** Quincy, IL-Hannibal, MO. **Key Personnel:** Jeff Dorsey, General Mgr.; Steve Boll, Operations Mgr. **Wattage:** 5000 day; 1000 night.

9648 WTJR-TV - 16
Old Cannonball Rd. Phone: (217)228-1275
RR 8, Box 1189
Quincy, IL 62306

Format: Commercial TV. **Networks:** Independent. **Operating Hours:** Continuous. **ADI:** Quincy, IL-Hannibal, MO. **Key Personnel:** Carl Geisendorfer, General Mgr.

RAMSEY, pop. 1,058.

Fayette Co. (S). 55 m SE of Springfield. Recreation. Ramsey Lake State Park. Lumber. Grain, stock, dairy. Livestock.

9649 Ramsey News-Journal
217 S. Superior St. Phone: (618)423-2411
PO Box 218 Fax: (618)423-2514
Ramsey, IL 62080-0218
Community newspaper. **Founded:** 1881. **Freq:** Weekly (Thurs.). **Print Method:** Offset. **Trim Size:** 11 1/2 x 17 1/2. **Cols./Page:** 5. **Col. Width:** 23 nonpareils. **Col. Depth:** 224 agate lines. **Key Personnel:** Robert J. Mueller, Jr., Editor; Robert J. Mueller, Sr., Publisher. **Subscription Rates:** $17 individuals; $21 in state; $25 out of state. **Remarks:** Advertising not accepted for alcoholic beverages.
Ad Rates: GLR: $.25 **Circ:** 1,856
BW: $370
4C: $610
SAU: $4.70

9650 Becks Cable Systems
Box 300A, RR2 Phone: (618)423-2844
Ramsey, IL 62080

Founded: 1980. **Cities Served:** Dix, Donnellson, Kell, Panama, IL: subscribing households 426; 22 channels.

RANTOUL, pop. 20,161.

Champaign Co. (E). 15 m N of Champaign. Technical Air Force training center. Light industry. Stock farms. Corn, oats, beans.

9651 Gibson City Courier
East Central Communications, Inc.
1332 Harmon Dr. E. Phone: (217)892-9613
PO Box 909 Fax: (217)892-9451
Rantoul, IL 61866
Free: (800)776-8555

Community newspaper. **Founded:** 1872. **Freq:** Weekly. **Print Method:** Offset. **Trim Size:** 14 x 22 1/2. **Cols./Page:** 6. **Col. Width:** 2 1/16 inches. **Col. Depth:** 21 inches. **Key Personnel:** Doris Benter, Editor; Jody Donaghy, Advertising Mgr.; Dennis Kaster, Publisher; Melinda Davis, Circulation Mgr. **Subscription Rates:** $16.50; $17.50 out of area. **Remarks:** Accepts advertising.
Ad Rates: GLR: $.58 **Circ:** Paid ♦**1,846**
BW: $798.84
4C: $1,098.84
SAU: $5.48
CNU: $6.34
PCI: $3.65

9652 Rantoul Press
East Central Communications, Inc.
1332 Harmon Dr. E. Phone: (217)892-9613
PO Box 909 Fax: (217)892-9451
Rantoul, IL 61866
Free: (800)776-8555

Community newspaper. **Founded:** 1874. **Freq:** Weekly (Wed.). **Print Method:** Offset. **Trim Size:** 14 x 22 7/8. **Cols./Page:** 6. **Col. Width:** 12 picas. **Col. Depth:** 21 inches. **Key Personnel:** Joseph Baker, Editor; Dennis C. Kaster, Publisher; Jody Donaghy, Advertising Mgr. **Subscription Rates:** $22 individuals. **Remarks:** Accepts advertising.
Ad Rates: GLR: $.64 **Circ:** Combined ♦**10,522**
BW: $1,456.56
4C: $1,756.56
SAU: $10.89
CNU: $11.56
PCI: $8.61

RAYMOND, pop. 957.

Montgomery Co. (SC). 30 m S of Springfield. Grain, dairy, stock farms.

9653 The Panhandle Press
Gold Nugget Publications, Inc.
PO Box 15 Phone: (217)229-4412
Raymond, IL 62560-0015
Community newspaper. **Founded:** 1964. **Freq:** Weekly (Wed.). **Print Method:** Offset. **Cols./Page:** 7. **Col. Width:** 28 nonpareils. **Col. Depth:** 300 agate lines. **Key Personnel:** Norris E. Jones, Editor, nj1655@aol.com; Charles E. Jones, Publisher; Dorothy Jones, Publisher; Nathan E. Jones, Advertising Mgr., nj1655@aol.com. **Subscription Rates:** $21 individuals; $0.50 single issue. **Remarks:** Accepts advertising.
Ad Rates: GLR: $.33 **Circ:** ‡1,200
BW: $500
SAU: $4
PCI: $4

9654 The Raymond News
PO Box 200 Phone: (217)532-2933
Raymond, IL 62560 Fax: (217)532-3632

Community newspaper. **Founded:** 1940. **Freq:** Weekly (Thurs.). **Print Method:** Offset. **Cols./Page:** 6. **Col. Width:** 12 picas. **Key Personnel:** Phillip Galer, Publisher; Nancy Galer, Publisher; Susan Galer, Editor. **USPS:** 455-980. **Subscription Rates:** $9 individuals. **Remarks:** Accepts advertising.
Ad Rates: GLR: $2.00 **Circ:** Paid 600
BW: $2.00 Non-paid 25
SAU: $2.00

REDDICK, pop. 243.

Kankakee Co. (E). 20 m W of Kankakee. Grain farms.

9655 Reddick-Essex Courier
Star Newspapers
204 E. Chippewa St. Phone: (815)584-3007
PO Box 159
Dwight, IL 60420-0159
Community newspaper. **Founded:** 1906. **Freq:** Weekly (Thurs.). **Print Method:** Offset. **Trim Size:** 8 x 11 1/4. **Cols./Page:** 8. **Col. Width:** 1 3/4 inches. **Col. Depth:** 301 agate lines. **Key Personnel:** Brian Heiar, Editor; Scott McGraw, Publisher. **USPS:** 458-500. **Subscription Rates:** $12 individuals; $17 out of state.
Ad Rates: GLR: $.16 **Circ:** Paid 401
BW: $161.25 Free 10
SAU: $2.64
PCI: $2.24

RIVER FOREST, pop. 12,392.

Cook Co. (NE) 25 m W. of Chicago. Residential.

9656 Forest Leaves
Pioneer Press Newspapers
1148 Westgate Ave. Phone: (708)383-3200
Oak Park, IL 60301 Fax: (708)383-3678

Community newspaper (tabloid). **Founded:** 1907. **Freq:** Weekly (Wed.). **Print Method:** Offset. **Cols./Page:** 5. **Col. Width:** 10 inches. **Col. Depth:** 14 inches. **Key Personnel:** Rick Hibbert, Editor; Paul Sassone, Managing Editor. **Subscription Rates:** $17.95 individuals; $19.95 out of county. **Remarks:** Advertising accepted; rates available upon request. **URL:** http://www.pioneerlocal.com.
Circ: Wed. ★**2,463**

9657 Lutheran Education
Concordia University Phone: (708)771-8300
7400 Augusta St. Fax: (708)209-3176
River Forest, IL 60305-1499
Publisher E-mail: lea@crf.cuis.edu

Magazine focusing on Lutheran education. **Founded:** Sept. 1865. **Freq:** 5/year. **Print Method:** Letterpress. **Trim Size:** 6 x 9. **Col. Width:** 28 nonpareils. **Col. Depth:** 103 agate lines. **Key Personnel:** Dr. Jonathan Barz, Editor, phone (708)209-3146, fax (708)209-3176; Jo Ann Kiefer, Ed. Asst. **ISSN:** 0024-7448. **Subscription Rates:** $10 individuals. **Remarks:** Accepts advertising.
Ad Rates: BW: $350 **Circ:** ‡4,200

9658 World Libraries
Dominican University Graduate School of Library and Information Science
7900 W. Division Phone: (708)366-2490
River Forest, IL 60305 Fax: (708)524-6657
Publication E-mail: roslitc@email.dom.edu

Professional journal covering library and information science. **Subtitle:** An International Journal Focusing on Libraries and Socio-Economic Development in Africa, Asia and Latin-America. **Trim Size:** 6 x 9. **Key Personnel:** Tze-chung Li, Editor.

ISSN: 1092-7441. **Subscription Rates:** $35 U.S. and Canada; $35 Australia, New Zealand, Europe and Japan; $50 elsewhere. **Remarks:** Advertising not accepted.
Circ: Controlled 450

RIVER GROVE, pop. 10,368.

Cook Co. (NE). 3 m N of Maywood. Residential.

9659 Fifth Avenue Journal
Triton College
2000 N. 5th Ave. Phone: (708)456-0300
River Grove, IL 60171-1995 Fax: (708)583-3121
Publication E-mail: 5thavenue@triton.cc.il.us

Collegiate newspaper including fiction, poetry, and drama has semi-annual food guide. **Founded:** 1964. **Freq:** Biweekly. **Print Method:** Offset. **Trim Size:** 11 x 17. **Cols./Page:** 4. **Col. Width:** 2 3/8 inches. **Col. Depth:** 14 inches. **Key Personnel:** Kelly McAuley, Editor-in-Chief; Summer Zandrew, Advertising Mgr.; Wendy Baxter, Arts Editor; Oliver Witte, Advisor. **Remarks:** Accepts advertising. **Formerly**: The Trident.
Ad Rates: BW: $350 **Circ:** Free ‡5,000
PCI: $11.18

9660 Illinois Truck News
Illinois Transportation Association
2000 5th Ave. Phone: (708)452-3500
River Grove, IL 60171 Fax: (708)452-3508

Magazine for trucking industry managers. **Founded:** 1954. **Freq:** Quarterly. **Print Method:** Offset. **Trim Size:** 8 1/4 x 11. **Key Personnel:** Julie McGown, Editor. **Subscription Rates:** $10. $2.50 single issue. **Remarks:** Accepts advertising.
Ad Rates: BW: $500 **Circ:** Controlled ‡7,500

9661 River Grove Messenger
Pioneer Press Newspapers
1148 Westgate Ave. Phone: (708)383-3200
Oak Park, IL 60301 Fax: (708)383-3678

Community newspaper (tabloid). **Founded:** 1951. **Freq:** Weekly (Thurs.). **Print Method:** Offset. **Cols./Page:** 5. **Col. Width:** 10 inches. **Col. Depth:** 14 inches. **Key Personnel:** Rich Behren, Editor; Paul Sassone, Managing Editor. **Subscription Rates:** $12.95 individuals; $14.95 out of county.
Circ: Wed. ★**1,309**

9662 WRRG-FM - 88.9
2000 5th Ave. Phone: (708)456-0300
River Grove, IL 60171 Fax: (708)583-3120
E-mail: wrrg@aol.com

Format: Alternative/New Music/Progressive. **Networks:** Independent. **Owner:** Triton College, at above address. **Founded:** 1975. **Operating Hours:** 8:30 a.m - 12 a.m; 100% Local. **ADI:** Chicago (LaSalle), IL. **Key Personnel:** Joe DeCeault, Program Dir./Chief Engineer; Jenne Van Eynde, Music Dir.; Randee Robinson, News Dir.; Tim McKinney, Sports Dir. **Local Programs:** *Jazzarena*, Tom MACek; *Metal Bible*, Dan Sullivan; *The Morning Shift* Monday-Friday. **Wattage:** 100.

RIVERTON, pop. 2,783.

Sangamon Co. (NC).

9663 Buffalo Tri City Register
Riverton Register Publishing
100 N. 6th St. Phone: (217)629-9247
Box 200
Riverton, IL 62561
Community newspaper. **Founded:** Mar. 1948. **Freq:** Weekly. **Print Method:** Offset. **Trim Size:** 10 x 13 1/2. **Cols./Page:** 5. **Col. Width:** 2 inches. **Col. Depth:** 13 1/2 inches. **Key Personnel:** Barbara J. Rhodes, Editor and Publisher. **Subscription Rates:** $10 individuals; $12 out of area out of county. **Remarks:** Accepts advertising.
Ad Rates: PCI: $2.06 **Circ:** (Not Reported)

9664 Williamsville Sun
Riverton Register Publishing
100 N. 6th St. Phone: (217)629-9247
Box 200
Riverton, IL 62561
Community newspaper. **Freq:** Weekly. **Print Method:** Offset. **Trim Size:** 10 x 13 1/2. **Cols./Page:** 5. **Col. Width:** 2 inches. **Col. Depth:** 13 1/2 inches. **Key Personnel:** Barbara Rhodes, Editor and Publisher. **Subscription Rates:** $8 individuals; $9 out of county. **Remarks:** Accepts advertising.
Ad Rates: PCI: $2.06 **Circ:** (Not Reported)

RIVERWOODS

9665 Bankruptcy Law Reports
CCH Inc.
2700 Lake Cook Rd. Phone: (847)267-7260
Riverwoods, IL 60015 Fax: (847)267-2945
Free: (800)449-6435

Loose leaf series devoted to bankruptcy law. **Founded:** 1933. **Freq:** Biweekly. **Print Method:** Offset. **Trim Size:** 6 x 9. **Cols./Page:** 2. **Col. Width:** 40 nonpareils. **Col. Depth:** 133 agate lines. **Key Personnel:** Andrew Turner, Managing Editor, turnera@cch.com. **ISSN:** 0005-5530. **Subscription Rates:** $1,099 individuals. **Remarks:** Advertising not accepted.
Circ: ‡900

9666 Common Market Reporter Doing Business in Europe
CCH Inc.
2700 Lake Cook Rd. Phone: (847)267-7000
Riverwoods, IL 60015 Fax: (847)224-8299
Free: (800)449-8114

Loose leaf series on international trade. **Founded:** 1962. **Freq:** Biweekly. **Print Method:** Offset. **Cols./Page:** 2. **Col. Width:** 40 nonpareils. **Col. Depth:** 133 agate lines. **Key Personnel:** Maureen Schwartz, Editor. **Subscription Rates:** $1,695 individuals. **Remarks:** Advertising not accepted.
Circ: ‡1,000

9667 Doing Business in Europe
CCH Inc.
2700 Lake Cook Rd. Phone: (847)267-7000
Riverwoods, IL 60015 Fax: (847)224-8299
Free: (800)449-8114

Loose leaf journal providing coverage of the legal aspects of operating in European Common Market and other European countries, as well as general information on doing business in any European country. **Founded:** 1972. **Freq:** Monthly. **Trim Size:** 6 x 9. **Cols./Page:** 1. **Key Personnel:** Daniel Newquist, Editor. **Subscription Rates:** $775; $1,410 two years. **Remarks:** Advertising not accepted. **URL:** http://www.cchinc.com.
Circ: Paid ‡125

9668 Federal Audit Guides
CCH Inc.
2700 Lake Cook Rd. Phone: (847)267-7000
Riverwoods, IL 60015 Fax: (847)224-8299
Free: (800)449-8114

Professional journal covering external audits of recipients of federally assisted grant programs. **Key Personnel:** Shelby Webb, Jr., Managing Editor. **Subscription Rates:** $611 individuals. **Remarks:** Advertising not accepted.
Circ: (Not Reported)

9669 Financial and Estate Planning
CCH Inc.
2700 Lake Cook Rd. Phone: (847)267-7000
Riverwoods, IL 60015 Fax: (847)224-8299
Free: (800)449-8114

Monthly plus the monthly Estate Planning Review; financial planning to build and preserve wealth; forms and planning aids; will and trust forms and clauses; investment plans; insurance and annuity forms; tax planning and administration for estates and trusts; in-depth articles offering new planning ideas; analysis of court decisions; new rulings and legislative developments; year begins first of any month. **Freq:** Monthly. **Key Personnel:** Karen Notaro, Managing Editor. **Subscription Rates:** $845 individuals. **Remarks:** Advertising not accepted. **Alt. Formats:** CD-ROM.
Circ: (Not Reported)

9670 Pension Plan Guide
CCH Inc.
2700 Lake Cook Rd. Phone: (847)267-7000
Riverwoods, IL 60015 Fax: (847)224-8299
Free: (800)449-8114

Loose leaf series on pension plans. **Founded:** 1953. **Freq:** Weekly. **Print Method:** Offset. **Trim Size:** 6 x 9. **Cols./Page:** 2. **Col. Width:** 40 nonpareils. **Col. Depth:** 133 agate lines. **Key Personnel:** Theodore Simons, Managing Editor, phone (847)267-2459, fax (847)267-2514. **Subscription Rates:** $1,077 individuals. **Remarks:** Advertising not accepted. **Online:** CCH Incorporated. **URL:** http://www.cch.com. **Alt. Formats:** CD-ROM, Pension & Welfare Benefits Library.
Circ: ‡6,800

9671 Tax Treaties
CCH Inc.
2700 Lake Cook Rd. Phone: (847)267-7000
Riverwoods, IL 60015 Fax: (847)224-8299
Free: (800)449-8114

Professional journal covering tax treaties between U.S. and foreign countries. **Freq:** Monthly. **Key Personnel:** Gregg Robbert, Managing Editor. **Subscription Rates:** $534 individuals. **Remarks:** Advertising not accepted.
Circ: (Not Reported)

9672 Taxes–The Tax Magazine
CCH Inc.
2700 Lake Cook Rd. Phone: (847)267-7000
Riverwoods, IL 60015 Fax: (847)224-8299
Free: (800)449-8114
Publication E-mail: taxes@cch.com

Magazine on tax laws and regulations. **Founded:** 1923. **Freq:** Monthly. **Trim Size:** 8 1/2 x 11. **Key Personnel:** Laura Lowe, Managing Editor, phone (847)267-2492; Mary Hamlin, Legal Editor, phone (847)267-7166; Kurt Diefenbach, Legal Editor. **ISSN:** 0040-0181. **Subscription Rates:** $186 individuals; $17 single issue. **Remarks:** Advertising not accepted.
Circ: Paid ‡10,745
Non-paid ‡500

ROANOKE, pop. 2,001.

Woodford Co. (NC). 28 m NE of Peoria. Manufactures concrete blocks, slats, and pumps; incinerators. Grain farms. Corn, oats, wheat.

9673 Roanoke Review
Illinois Valley Press
105 E. Broad Phone: (309)923-5841
PO Box 200
Roanoke, IL 61561
Publisher E-mail: journal@farmwagon.com

Community newspaper. **Founded:** 1913. **Freq:** Weekly (Thurs.). **Print Method:** Offset. **Cols./Page:** 6. **Col. Width:** 24 nonpareils. **Col. Depth:** 297 agate lines. **Key Personnel:** Cheryl Wolfe, Editor; Mark Barra, General Mgr. **USPS:** 467-320. **Subscription Rates:** $26 individuals; $29 out of area; $36 out of state. **Remarks:** Accepts advertising.
Ad Rates: BW: $741.75 **Circ:** Paid ‡998
4C: $876.75
PCI: $5.75

ROCHELLE, pop. 8,982.

Ogle Co. (N). 25 m S of Rockford. Manufactures canned vegetables, worsted yarn, sweaters, hauling machinery, furtilizers, plastics naphtha filters, pre-stressed concrete beans, electrical controls, milk. Meat packing plant. Cold storage warehouse. Agriculture.

9674 Farmer's Report
Leader
211 Hwy. 38E Phone: (815)562-4171
Rochelle, IL 61068 Fax: (815)562-2161

Agricultural publication. **Founded:** 1979. **Freq:** Monthly. **Print Method:** Offset. **Cols./Page:** 8. **Col. Width:** 14 nonpareils. **Col. Depth:** 210 agate lines. **Key Personnel:** Kip Cheek, Editor, phone (815)539-9396; Tom Cross, Publisher. **Subscription Rates:** $7.50 individuals. **Remarks:** Accepts advertising.
Ad Rates: SAU: $9.95 **Circ:** (Not Reported)

9675 News-Leader
211 Hwy. 38 E. Phone: (815)562-4171
Box 46 Fax: (815)562-2161
Rochelle, IL 61068
Community newspaper. **Founded:** 1921. **Freq:** 3/week (Sun., Tues., and Thurs.). **Print Method:** Offset. **Cols./Page:** 8. **Col. Width:** 21 nonpareils. **Col. Depth:** 301 agate lines. **Key Personnel:** Jeff Robertson, Editor; C. Thomas Cross, Publisher; Pat Duffy, Advertising Mgr. **Subscription Rates:** $68.25 individuals. **Remarks:** Accepts advertising. **Formed by the merger of:** News (Mar. 1, 1995); Leader (Mar. 1, 1995).
Ad Rates: GLR: $9.95 **Circ:** Paid ‡4,850
SAU: $8.27 Non-paid ‡150
PCI: $6.95

9676 Ogle County Life
401 N. Main St. Phone: (815)732-2156
Rochelle, IL 61068-1619 Fax: (815)732-6154

Newspaper. **Founded:** 1966. **Freq:** Weekly (Mon.). **Print Method:** Offset. **Trim Size:** 11 3/8 x 15 1/4. **Cols./Page:** 6. **Col. Width:** 1 5/8 inches. **Col. Depth:** 14 inches. **Key Personnel:** Doug Olsen, Editor; Tom Cross, Publisher; Bryant Vangsness, Advertising Mgr. **Subscription Rates:** $35 individuals. **Remarks:** Accepts advertising.
Ad Rates: GLR: $.51 **Circ:** Paid ‡1,324
BW: $331 Free ‡11,535
SAU: $5.39
PCI: $3.95

ROCK FALLS, pop. 10,624.

Whiteside Co. (N). 120 m W of Chicago. Manufactures fiberglass products, nuts, bolts, steel, iron, metal products, electric door devices. Communication equipment. Meat processing.

9677 TCI Cablevision Co.
PO Box 580 Phone: (815)625-5618
Rock Falls, IL 61071 Fax: (815)626-7415

Formerly: Rock River Cablevision Co. **Key Personnel:** Shelby Rowzie, Manager. **Cities Served:** Hopkins, Mont Morency, Rock Falls, and Sterling, IL.

ROCK ISLAND†, pop. 47,036.

Rock Island Co. (NE). On Mississippi River, opposite Davenport, Ia., 168 m SW of Chicago. Augustana College. Manufactures agricultural implements, government supplies and munitions, rubber footwear, clothing, oil burners, furnaces, machine tools, electrical appliances, paper containers. Foundries.

9678 Augustana College Magazine
Augustana College
639 38th St. Phone: (309)794-7000
Rock Island, IL 61201 Fax: (309)794-7422
Publication E-mail: apudb@augustana.edu

College alumni magazine. **Founded:** 1935. **Freq:** Semiannual. **Print Method:** Offset. **Trim Size:** 8 x 11 1/2. **Cols./Page:** 3. **Col. Width:** 2 1/2 inches. **Col. Depth:** 9 1/4 inches. **Key Personnel:** Debbie Blaylock, Editor, phone (309)794-7721, apudb@augustana.edu. **Remarks:** Advertising not accepted.
Circ: Controlled ‡26,500

9679 The Modern Woodmen Magazine
Modern Woodmen of America
1701 1st Ave. Phone: (309)786-6481
PO Box 2005 Fax: (309)786-5603
Rock Island, IL 61204-2005
Fraternal magazine. **Founded:** 1885. **Freq:** Quarterly. **Print Method:** Offset. **Cols./Page:** 3. **Col. Width:** 27 nonpareils. **Col. Depth:** 140 agate lines. **Key Personnel:** Gloria Bergh, Editor; Jill Lain Weaver, Editor, jweaver@modern-woodmen.org. **Subscription Rates:** Free to qualified subscribers. **Remarks:** Advertising not accepted.
Circ: ‡400,000

9680 The Observer
639 38th St. Phone: (309)794-7484
Rock Island, IL 61201 Fax: (309)794-7484

Collegiate newspaper. **Founded:** 1920. **Freq:** Weekly. **Print Method:** Offset. **Cols./Page:** 5. **Col. Width:** 11 picas. **Col. Depth:** 16 inches. **Key Personnel:** Alexis Didzerekis, Editor-in-Chief; Kelli Dietman, Advertising Mgr.; Clayton Guler, Business Mgr., phone (309)794-7485. **Subscription Rates:** $15 individuals. **Remarks:** Accepts advertising.
Ad Rates: PCI: $5.25 **Circ:** Paid 215
Free 2,200

9681 Rock Island Argus
Moline Dispatch Publishing Co.
1724 4th Ave. Phone: (309)786-6441
Rock Island, IL 61201-8713 Fax: (309)786-6441

General newspaper. **Founded:** 1851. **Freq:** Daily (eve.), Sat. and Sun. (morn.). **Print Method:** Offset. **Trim Size:** 13 x 21 1/2. **Cols./Page:** 6. **Col. Width:** 2 1/16 inches. **Col. Depth:** 21 1/2 inches. **Key Personnel:** Gerald J. Taylor, Editor and Publisher, phone (309)757-4924, fax (309)797-0311; Roger Ruthhart, Managing Editor, rogeruthart@qconline.com; Nick Norman, Advertising Dir., fax (309)797-0321, nsquared@qconine.com. **Subscription Rates:** $104 individuals. **Remarks:** Accepts advertising.
Ad Rates: GLR: $1.67 **Circ:** Mon.-Sat. ★**13,020**
BW: $3,199.20 Sun. ★**15,437**
4C: $3,674.20
SAU: $24.80

9682 The Royal Neighbor
Royal Neighbors of America
230 16th St. Phone: (309)788-4561
Rock Island, IL 61201 Fax: (309)788-9234
Free: (800)627-4762
Publication E-mail: rnafields@ix.netcom.com
Publisher E-mail: rnafield@ix.netcom.com

Fraternal magazine. **Founded:** 1900. **Freq:** Bimonthly. **Print Method:** Offset. **Trim Size:** 8 1/2 x 11. **Cols./Page:** 3. **Col. Width:** 27 nonpareils. **Col. Depth:** 140 agate lines. **Key Personnel:** Kathy Teel, APR, Sr. Mgr., Public Relations/Printing. **ISSN:** 0035-905X. **Subscription Rates:** Included in membership. **Remarks:** Advertising not accepted.
Circ: ‡190,000

9683 Tri-City Labor Review
Tri-City Review Publishing Co.
311 21st St. Phone: (309)786-6439
Rock Island, IL 61201 Fax: (309)786-6439

Magazine focusing on labor. **Founded:** 1919. **Freq:** Monthly. **Print Method:** Offset. **Cols./Page:** 5. **Col. Width:** 24 nonpareils. **Col. Depth:** 224 agate lines. **Key Personnel:** William R. Keith, Editor. **Subscription Rates:** $3 individuals. **Remarks:** Accepts advertising.
Ad Rates: PCI: $3 **Circ:** ‡4,700

9684 WHBF-TV - 4
231 18th St. Phone: (309)786-5441
Rock Island, IL 61201 Fax: (309)788-4975

Format: Commercial TV. **Networks:** CBS. **Operating Hours:** 6 a.m.-1 or 2 a.m. **ADI:** Davenport,IA-Rock Island, Moline,IL. **Key Personnel:** Ron Johnson, Vice Pres./Gen. Mgr.

9685 WVIK-FM - 90.3
Augustana College Phone: (309)794-7500
Rock Island, IL 61201 Fax: (309)794-1236
E-mail: wvik@augustana.edu

Format: Public Radio; Jazz; News; Classical. **Networks:** National Public Radio (NPR). **Founded:** 1980. **Operating Hours:** Continuous; 12% network, 88% local. **Key Personnel:** Don Wooten, General Mgr.; Lowell Dorman, Contact; Chris Downs, Chief Engineer; Dave Garner, Contact. **Wattage:** 31,000. **Ad Rates:** Noncommercial.

ROCKFORD†, pop. 139,712.

Winnebago Co. (N). On Rock River, 90 m NW of Chicago. Rockford College. Manufactures airplane and auto parts, air conditioning and heating equipment, castings, chewing gum, furniture, gears, governors, hardware, leather goods, machine tools, packaging equipment, paint, pet food, plastics, pumps, tin containers, farm machinery, wire goods, motors, scales, sports equipment, screw products and fasteners.

9686 Chronicles: A Magazine of American Culture
The Rockford Institute
928 N. Main St. Phone: (815)964-5054
Rockford, IL 61103 Fax: (815)964-9403
Publisher E-mail: rkfdinst@bossnt.com

Magazine containing book reviews, cultural criticism, and opinion. **Subtitle:** A Magazine of American Culture. **Founded:** Sept. 1977. **Freq:** Monthly. **Print Method:** Web offset. **Trim Size:** 8 1/2 x 11. **Cols./Page:** 2 and 3. **Key Personnel:** Thomas J. Fleming, Editor; Allan C. Carlson, Publisher; Ted Pappas, Managing Editor. **ISSN:** 0887-5731. **Subscription Rates:** $39 individuals; $51 other countries; $3.95 single issue. **Formerly**: Chronicles of Culture.
Ad Rates: BW: $400 **Circ:** ‡11,125
4C: $700

9687 The FABRICATOR
The Croydon Group, Ltd.
833 Featherstone Rd. Phone: (815)399-8700
Rockford, IL 61107-6302 Fax: (815)399-7279
Publisher E-mail: info@fmametalfab.org

Trade journal covering the metal-forming and fabricating industry. **Founded:** 1971. **Freq:** Monthly. **Print Method:** Offset. Heat-set Web. **Trim Size:** 10 3/4 x 14. **Cols./Page:** 4. **Col. Width:** 14 picas. **Col. Depth:** 11 picas. **Key Personnel:** Brad Benedict, Sales Dir.; Theresa Houck, Exec. Editor, theresah@aol.com; Kim Clothier, Circulation Mgr. **ISSN:** 0888-0301. **Subscription Rates:** Free to qualified subscribers; $30 individuals; $125 other countries. **Remarks:** Accepts advertising.
Ad Rates: BW: $4,795 **Circ:** Controlled 55,000
4C: $5,915
PCI: $55

9688 The Herald
Rock Valley Community Press, Inc.
PO Box 15340
Rockford, IL 61110
Publisher E-mail: rvcpress@lx.netcom.

Community newspaper for Rockford, Illinois, suburbs. **Founded:** 1875. **Freq:** Weekly (Wed.). **Print Method:** Web offset. **Trim Size:** 11 1/2 x 17. **Cols./Page:** 5. **Col. Width:** 2 1/2 inches. **Col. Depth:** 16 inches. **Key Personnel:** Bill Brennan, Publisher; Ken Frampton, Editor. **Subscription Rates:** Free; $25 mailed; $18.40 out of area. **Remarks:** Accepts advertising. **Formerly**: Rockton-Roscoe Herald; North Suburban Herald.
Ad Rates: BW: $692 **Circ:** Paid 3,000
4C: $842 Free 7,400
SAU: $8.65
PCI: $8.65

9689 Metal Fabricating News
W.A. Whitney Corp.
PO Box 1178 Phone: (815)965-4031
Rockford, IL 61105 Fax: (815)964-3175

Magazine focusing on sheet metal, plate, and structural fabricating. **Founded:** 1968. **Freq:** Quarterly. **Print Method:** Offset. **Cols./Page:** 4. **Col. Width:** 28 nonpareils. **Col. Depth:** 283 agate lines. **Key Personnel:** Ronald L. Fowler, Editor/Administration. **Subscription Rates:** $1.50 individuals. **Remarks:** Accepts advertising.
Ad Rates: BW: $1,858 **Circ:** ‡36,000

9690 The Observer
921 W. State St. Phone: (815)963-3471
Rockford, IL 61102 Fax: (815)968-2808
Free: (800)252-1775
Publication E-mail: observer@cathconnect.org

Catholic tabloid. **Founded:** 1935. **Freq:** Weekly except Semimonthly Summer months. **Print Method:** Offset. **Trim Size:** 10 1/4 x 14. **Cols./Page:** 6. **Col. Width:** 19 nonpareils. **Col. Depth:** 210 agate lines. **Key Personnel:** Owen C. Phelps, Jr., Editor; Most Rev. Thos G. Doran, Publisher. **ISSN:** 0029-7739. **Subscription Rates:** $24.95 individuals. **Remarks:** Accepts advertising.
Ad Rates: GLR: $.79 **Circ:** Paid ‡42,000
BW: $990 Non-paid ‡309
4C: $1,800
PCI: $13

9691 Practical Welding Today
The Croydon Group, Ltd.
833 Featherstone Rd. Phone: (815)399-8700
Rockford, IL 61107-6302 Fax: (815)399-7279
Publisher E-mail: info@fmametalfab.org

Trade magazine covering instructional and educational information on welding. **Founded:** July 1997. **Freq:** Bimonthly. **Trim Size:** 8 1/4 x 10 3/4. **Cols./Page:** 3. **Col. Width:** 14 picas. **Key Personnel:** Theresa Houck, Exec. Editor, theresah@aol.com; Brad Benedict, Sales Dir.; Kim Clothier, Circulation Mgr. **ISSN:** 1092-3942. **Subscription Rates:** Free to qualified subscribers. **Remarks:** Accepts advertising.
Ad Rates: BW: $2,730 **Circ:** Controlled ‡40,000
4C: $3,780

9692 The Rock River Times
128 N. Church St. Phone: (815)964-9767
Rockford, IL 61101 Fax: (815)964-9825
Publication E-mail: mail@trrt.com

Newspaper. **Subtitle:** The Voice of the Community. **Founded:** Jan. 1987. **Freq:** Weekly. **Print Method:** Web. **Trim Size:** 11 x 16. **Cols./Page:** 6. **Col. Width:** 1.5 inches. **Col. Depth:** 15.5 inches. **Key Personnel:** Frank Schier, Editor and Publisher; Joe Baker, Editor; Susan Johnson, Copy Editor. **Subscription Rates:** Free; $40 out of area. **Remarks:** Accepts advertising. **URL:** http://www.trrt.com.
Ad Rates: GLR: $1 **Circ:** Free ‡16,000
BW: $480
4C: $980
PCI: $7

9693 Rockford Register Star
Gannett Co., Inc.
99 E. State St. Phone: (815)987-1302
Rockford, IL 61104 Fax: (815)962-6578

General newspaper. **Founded:** 1855. **Freq:** Mon.-Sun. (morn.). **Print Method:** Letterpress. **Cols./Page:** 6. **Col. Width:** 24 nonpareils. **Col. Depth:** 301 agate lines. **Key Personnel:** Linda G. Cunningham, Exec. Editor; Mary P. Stier, Publisher. **Subscription Rates:** $169 individuals. **Remarks:** Accepts advertising. **URL:** http://www.gannett.com. **Feature Editors:** Gail Baruch, *Drama, Movie, Radio*, phone (815)987-1200; Mike Bradley, *Environmental, Medical*, phone (815)987-1200; Chad Brooks, *Editorials*, phone (815)987-1200; Brad Burt, *Photo*, phone (815)987-1200; Leona Carlson, *Fashion, Food, Society*, phone (815)987-1200; Mark Curnutte, *Entertainment, Music*, phone (815)987-1200; Wally Haas, *News*, phone (815)987-1200; Peggy Howe, *Religion*, phone (815)987-1200; Mary Kaull, *Rural Development*, phone (815)987-1200; Co Leber, *Book, Travel, Women's*, phone (815)987-1200; Geri Nikolai, *City*, phone (815)987-1200; Ben Rubendall, *Real Estate*, phone (815)987-1200; Nan Seelman, *Garden/Home*, phone (815)987-1200; Judith Selby, *Family, Features, Lifestyle*, phone (815)987-1200; Dave Shultz, *Sports*, phone (815)987-1200; Chuck Sweeny, *Political*, phone (815)987-1200; Mike Townsend, *Aviation, Financial/Business, Metro*, phone (815)987-1200; Cathy Ward, *Education*, phone (815)987-1200; Sherri Winans, *TV*, phone (815)987-1200.
Ad Rates: GLR: $4.45 **Circ:** Mon.-Sat. ★**72,434**
BW: $5,466.27 Sun. ★**84,241**
4C: $6,010.70
PCI: $53.89

📖 **9694 Rockford Review**
Rockford Writers' Guild
Box 858
Rockford, IL 61105

Literary magazine covering poetry, prose, drama and art. **Founded:** 1980. **Freq:** Monthly. **Print Method:** Offset. **Trim Size:** 5 1/2 x 8 1/2. **Key Personnel:** David Ross, Editor. **ISSN:** 1046-0985. **Subscription Rates:** $15 individuals; $5 single issue. **Remarks:** Advertising not accepted.
Circ: Paid 750

📖 **9695 Sales and Marketing Strategies & News**
Hughes Communications, Inc.
211 W. State St. Phone: (815)963-4000
PO Box 197 Fax: (815)963-7773
Rockford, IL 61105-0197
Free: (800)435-2937

Magazine on sales and marketing. **Subtitle:** The Nations's Comprehensive News Source for Successful Sales & Marketing Strategies. **Founded:** Sept. 1991. **Freq:** 9/year. **Print Method:** Web heatset. **Trim Size:** 10 1/16 x 13 1/2. **Cols./Page:** 4. **Col. Width:** 2 1/4 inches. **Col. Depth:** 12 inches. **Key Personnel:** Bill Hughes, CEO; Bruce Ericson, President. **ISSN:** 1066-5463. **Subscription Rates:** $49 individuals in U.S.; $54 individuals in Canada; $84 two years in U.S.; $94 two years in Canada; $98 other countries (surface mail); $150 other countries (air mail). **Remarks:** Accepts advertising.
Ad Rates: BW: $7,850 **Circ:** Controlled 62,000
4C: $9,550
PCI: $400

📖 **9696 Stamping Journal**
The Croydon Group, Ltd.
833 Featherstone Rd. Phone: (815)399-8700
Rockford, IL 61107-6302 Fax: (815)399-7279
Publisher E-mail: info@fmametalfab.org

Trade magazine covering metal stamping technology. **Founded:** 1989. **Freq:** Bimonthly. **Print Method:** 8 1/4 x 10 3/4. **Key Personnel:** Theresa Houck, Exec. Editor, theresah@aol.com; Brad Benedict, Sales Dir.; Kim Clothier, Circulation Mgr. **ISSN:** 1091-2460. **Subscription Rates:** Free to qualified subscribers. **Remarks:** Advertising accepted; rates available upon request. **Formerly:** Stamping Quarterly.
Circ: Controlled 35,000

📖 **9697 TPJ—The Tube & Pipe Journal**
The Croydon Group, Ltd.
833 Featherstone Rd. Phone: (815)399-8700
Rockford, IL 61107-6302 Fax: (815)399-7279
Publisher E-mail: info@fmametalfab.org

Trade magazine covering metal tube and pipe production and metal tube and pipe fabricating. **Founded:** 1990. **Freq:** Bimonthly. **Trim Size:** 8 1/4 x 10 3/4. **Cols./Page:** 3. **Col. Width:** 14 picas. **Key Personnel:** Theresa Houck, Exec. Editor, theresah@aol.com; Brad Benedict, Sales Director; Kim Clothier, Circulation Mgr. **ISSN:** 1091-2479. **Subscription Rates:** Free to qualified subscribers. **Remarks:** Accepts advertising. **Former name:** TPQ—The Tube & Pipe Quarterly.
Circ: Controlled ‡30,000

📖 **9698 Weighing & Measurement**
Key Markets Publishing Co.
PO Box 5867 Phone: (815)636-7739
Rockford, IL 61125 Fax: (815)636-7741

Industry magazine. **Founded:** 1914. **Freq:** Bimonthly. **Print Method:** Offset. **Trim Size:** 8 1/8 x 10 7/8. **Cols./Page:** 3 and 2. **Col. Width:** 26 and 40 nonpareils. **Col. Depth:** 140 agate lines. **Key Personnel:** David M. Mathieu, Editor and Publisher, dwam@inwave.com. **ISSN:** 0095-537X. **Subscription Rates:** $10 individuals.
Ad Rates: BW: $1,320 **Circ:** ‡15,000
4C: $1,870

🎙 **9699 Insight Comuunications**
227 N. Wyman St. Phone: (815)962-4400
Rockford, IL 61101 Fax: (815)962-9643

Founded: 1973. **Formerly:** A-R Cable Services, Inc. **Key Personnel:** K.C. McWilliams, General Mgr., fax (815)968-0030, mcwilliams.kc@insight-com.com; Jeff Cohen, Sales Mgr., cohen.j@insight-com.com; Steve Burger, Engineering Mgr., fax (815)398-5469, burger.s@insight-com.com. **Cities Served:** Cherry Valley, Loves Park, Machesney Park, New Milford, Rockford, IL: subscribing households 66,000; 100 channels; 3 community access channels; 15 hours per week community access programming. **URL:** http://www.insight-oom.com.

🎙 **9700 WIFR-TV - 23**
PO Box 123 Phone: (815)987-5300
2523 N. Meridian Rd. Fax: (815)965-0981
Rockford, IL 61101

Format: Commercial TV. **Networks:** CBS. **Owner:** Benedek Broadcasting of Illinois Inc., Box 123, Rockford, IL 61105. **Founded:** 1965. **Operating Hours:** Continuous (Sun.-Thurs.). **ADI:** Rockford, IL. **Key Personnel:** Bob Smith, General Mgr.; Rich McBride, Operations Dir.; Jim Glendenning, General Sales Mgr. **Local Programs:** *Action News*; *23 This Morning*. **Ad Rates:** $5-600 for 30 seconds; $10-1,200 for 60 seconds.

🎙 **9701 WKMQ-FM - 95.3**
PO Box 7180 Phone: (815)874-7861
Rockford, IL 61126 Fax: (815)874-2202

Format: Oldies. **Networks:** Independent. **Owner:** Segueway Broadcasting Corp., Box 253, Madison, WI 53701, (608)271-1743. **Founded:** 1970. **Operating Hours:** Continuous. **ADI:** Rockford, IL. **Key Personnel:** David W. McAley, General Mgr. **Wattage:** 3000.

🎙 **9702 WLUV-FM - 96.7**
2272 Elmwood Phone: (815)877-9588
Rockford, IL 61103 Fax: (815)877-9649

Format: Sports; Urban Contemporary. **Networks:** CBS; Satellite Music Network. **Owner:** Angelo Joseph Salvi, at above address. **Founded:** 1964. **Operating Hours:** Continuous. **ADI:** Rockford, IL. **Key Personnel:** Angelo Joseph Salvi, General Mgr.; Virgie Lameyer, Office Mgr. **Local Programs:** *Papa Joe Show* 6 a.m.-9 a.m. Monday-Friday. **Wattage:** 3000. **Ad Rates:** $7.75-13.50 for 10 seconds; $12.75-16 for 30 seconds; $15.25-21 for 60 seconds.

🎙 **9703 WQRF-TV - 39**
401 S. Main St. Phone: (815)987-3950
Rockford, IL 61101 Fax: (815)964-9974

Format: Commercial TV. **Networks:** Fox. **Owner:** Petracom, Inc., 1527 N. Dale Mabry Highway, Suite 105, Lutz, FL 33549, (813)933-0023. **Founded:** 1978. **Operating Hours:** 5:30 a.m.-3 a.m. **ADI:** Rockford, IL. **Key Personnel:** Greg Graber, Contact; Terry McHugh, General Sales Mgr.; Bill Zuckerman, Contact. **Local Programs:** *A Closer Look*. **Ad Rates:** $25-1500 for 30 seconds.

🎙 **9704 WREX-TV - 13**
10322 Auburn Rd. Phone: (815)335-2213
Rockford, IL 61103 Fax: (815)335-1002
E-mail: wrex@wrex.com

Format: Commercial TV. **Networks:** NBC. **Owner:** Quincy Newspapers, Inc., PO Box 909, Quincy, IL 62306, (217)223-5100, Fax: (217)221-3323, Free: (800)373-9444. **Founded:** 1953. **Operating Hours:** 24 hrs. **ADI:** Rockford, IL. **Key Personnel:** John Chadwick, General Mgr.; Kim Carney, Program Mgr.; Maggie Hradecky, News Dir., fax (815)335-2297. **URL:** http://www.wrex.com.

🎙 **9705 WROK-AM - 1440**
3901 Brendenwood Phone: (815)399-2233
Rockford, IL 61107 Fax: (815)399-8148

Format: News; Talk. **Networks:** ABC. **Owner:** Connoisseur Communications, PO Box 136, Westport, CT 06880, (203)227-1978, Fax: (203)227-2373. **Founded:** 1923. **Operating Hours:** Continuous. **ADI:** Rockford, IL. **Key Personnel:** David P. Bevins, General Mgr.; Phil Davidson, Sales Mgr.; Bruce Butler, PD. **Local Programs:** *Dr. Laura* 1 - 4P; *Pat Cunningham* 9 - 12N. **Wattage:** 5000. **Ad Rates:** $21-45 for 30 seconds; $29-52 for 60 seconds. $12-$60 for 30 seconds; $15-$74 for 60 seconds. Combined advertising rates available with WZOK-FM.

🎙 **9706 WTVO-TV - 17**
Box 470 Phone: (815)963-5413
Rockford, IL 61105 Fax: (815)963-0201

Format: Commercial TV. **Networks:** NBC. **Owner:** Young Broadcasting Inc., 3 E. 54th St., New York, NY 10022. **Founded:** 1953. **ADI:** Rockford, IL. **Key Personnel:** Michael Khouri, General Mgr.; Paul Freifeld, News Dir.; Wilma Hollis, Contact; Terry Kowalski, Contact.

🎙 **9707 WXRX-FM - 104.9**
2830 Sandy Hollow Rd. Phone: (815)874-7861
Rockford, IL 61109-2369 Fax: (815)874-2202

Format: Album-Oriented Rock (AOR). **Founded:** 1971. **Formerly:** WYBR-FM (1990). **Operating Hours:** Continuous; 100% local. **ADI:** Rockford, IL. **Key Personnel:** David W. McAley, General Mgr.; Keith Edwards, Program Dir.; Sky Drysdale, Promotions Dir. **Wattage;** 4000.

🎙 **9708 WZOK-FM - 97.5**
3901 Brendenwood Phone: (815)399-2233
Rockford, IL 61107 Fax: (815)399-8148

Format: Contemporary Hit Radio (CHR). **Owner:** Connoisseur Communications, 136 Main St., Westport, CT 06880, (203)227-1978, Fax: (203)227-2373. **Founded:** 1949. **Operating Hours:** Continuous. **ADI:** Rockford, IL. **Key Personnel:** David P. Bevins, General Mgr.; Roanna Petrie, Local SAL; Tom Garrett, Mktg. Dir. **Local Programs:** *Retro Mania*, Tom Garrett, Fax (815)399-8148; *Top 30 Countdown*, Tom Garrett, Fax (815)399-8148. **Wattage:** 50,000. **Ad Rates:** $27-65 for 30 seconds; $38-78 for 60 seconds.

ROCKTON

🎙 **9709 WRWC-FM - 103.1**
4570 Rockton Rd. Phone: (815)624-2603
PO Box 345 Fax: (815)624-7777
Rockton, IL 61072

Format: Adult Contemporary; Soft Rock. **Owner:** Salter Broadcasting Co., PO Box C 1730, Aurora, IL 60507, (708)898-6668. **Founded:** 1961. **Operating Hours:** Continuous. **ADI:** Rockford, IL. **Key Personnel:** Scott Maenner, Sales Mgr.; Jim Mackey, Program Dir. **Wattage:** 3000. **Ad Rates:** $35-40 for 30 seconds; $40-50 for 60 seconds.

ROLLING MEADOWS, pop. 20,167.

Cook Co. (NE). 4 m NW of Mt. Prospect. Residential. Commercial. Industrial.

📖 **9710 The National Dipper**
1841 Hicks Rd., Ste. C Phone: (847)202-4770
Rolling Meadows, IL 60008 Fax: (847)202-4791

Magazine for ice cream retail stores. **Founded:** Apr. 1985. **Freq:** 6/year. **Print Method:** Sheet fed offset. **Trim Size:** 8 1/2 x 11. **Cols./Page:** 3. **Col. Width:** 13 picas. **Col. Depth:** 10 inches. **Key Personnel:** Lynda Utterback, Editor and Publisher, lynda@nationaldipper.com. **ISSN:** 0895-9722. **Subscription Rates:** $55 individuals; $5 single issue. **Remarks:** Accepts advertising. **URL:** http://www.nationaldipper.com.
Ad Rates: BW: $2,380 **Circ:** Non-paid 20,000
4C: $3,130

📖 **9711 Rolling Meadows Review**
Pioneer Press Newspapers
291 N. Dunton Ave. Phone: (847)797-5100
Arlington Heights, IL 60004 Fax: (847)797-5151

Founded: 1989. **Freq:** Weekly (Thurs.). **Print Method:** Offset. **Cols./Page:** 4. **Col. Width:** 13 3/5 picas. **Col. Depth:** 196 agate lines. **Key Personnel:** Paul Sassone, Managing Editor; Tom Scott, Editor. **Subscription Rates:** $9.95; $15.95 out of county. **Remarks:** Combined advertising rates available with other Pioneer Press Newspapers.
Circ: Thurs. **★2,036**

📖 **9712 Turf News**
Turfgrass Producers International
1855 A Hicks Rd. Phone: (847)705-9898
Rolling Meadows, IL 60008-1215 Fax: (847)705-8347
Free: (800)405-8873
Publisher E-mail: turf-grass@msn.com

Trade magazine. **Founded:** Oct. 1977. **Freq:** Bimonthly. **Print Method:** Offset. **Trim Size:** 8 1/8 x 10 7/8. **Cols./Page:** 1. **Col. Width:** 3 1/4 inches. **Key Personnel:** Wendell Mathews, Editor and Production; Douglas Fender, Exec. Dir.; Terri Berkowitz, Advertising. **ISSN:** 0899-417X. **Subscription Rates:** Included in membership. **Remarks:** Accepts advertising.
Ad Rates: BW: $1010 **Circ:** ‡1,300
4C: $1,305
PCI: $70

ROMEOVILLE

📖 **9713 Catholic Explorer**
402 S. Independence Blvd. Phone: (815)838-6477
Romeoville, IL 60446 Fax: (815)834-4068
Publisher E-mail: newcathexp@aol.com

Official Catholic newspaper for the Diocese of Joliet. **Founded:** 1976. **Freq:** Weekly. **Print Method:** Offset. **Trim Size:** 13 x 21. **Cols./Page:** 6 and 4. **Col. Width:** 12.5 and 14.6 picas. **Col. Depth:** 21 and 13 inches. **Key Personnel:** Mary Breslin, Editor, phone (815)838-6475; Bishop Joseph L. Imesch, Publisher. **ISSN:** 1044-8322. **Subscription Rates:** $20 individuals; $35 two years; $50 three years. **Remarks:** Advertising not accepted for alcohol. **URL:** http://www.newcathexp.com. **Formerly:** New Catholic Explorer.
Ad Rates: GLR: $1 **Circ:** ‡22,500
BW: $1,764
4C: $2,264
PCI: $14

📖 **9714 Romeoville Metropolitan**
Press Publication
223 Main St. Phone: (630)739-2300
Lemont, IL 60439 Fax: (630)257-5640

Community newspaper. **Freq:** Weekly (Thurs.). **Cols./Page:** 5. **Col. Width:** 11.5 picas. **Col. Depth:** 16 inches. **Key**

Personnel: Peggy Drey, Editor; Robert Norfleet, Publisher. **Remarks:** Advertising accepted; rates available upon request. **Circ:** (Not Reported)

9715 The Romeoville Sun
Sun Publications
9 W. Jackson Phone: (630)355-0063
PO Box 269 Fax: (630)416-5163
Naperville, IL 60566-0269
Publisher E-mail: thesun@exchange.copleysun.com

Community newspaper. **Founded:** 1963. **Freq:** Weekly (Wed.). **Print Method:** Offset. **Trim Size:** 10 1/2 x 16. **Cols./Page:** 5. **Col. Width:** 24 nonpareils. **Col. Depth:** 224 agate lines. **Key Personnel:** Bob Vavra, Editor; Harold E. White, Publisher; Eva A. White, Publisher; Ken Guenther, Advertising Mgr. **Subscription Rates:** $10 individuals; $11.50 out of county. **Remarks:** Accepts advertising.
Ad Rates: GLR: $.34 **Circ:** Paid 1,467
BW: $386.40 Free 131
4C: $836.40
PCI: $4.83

9716 WLRA-FM - 88.1
Lewis University Phone: (815)838-0500
Rte. 53 Fax: (815)838-9149
Romeoville, IL 60441

Format: Public Radio; Eclectic. **Owner:** Lewis University, at above address. **Founded:** 1974. **Operating Hours:** Continuous. **Key Personnel:** Adam Schwake, General Mgr.; Bevin Oades, Program Dir.; Candice Foiles, Music Dir.; Peter Chinderle, News Dir.; Brian Berfino, Sports Dir.; Kathryn Kasper Lambert, Promotions Dir.; Michael Horn, Production Dir. **Wattage:** 250. **Ad Rates:** Noncommercial.

ROSEMONT, pop. 4,137.

Cook Co. (NE). 14 m N.W. of Chicago.

9717 Die Casting Engineer
North American Die Casting Association
9701 W. Higgins Rd., Ste. 880 Phone: (847)292-3600
Rosemont, IL 60018-4721 Fax: (847)292-3620
Publisher E-mail: dce@diecasting.org

Trade magazine serving the die casting industry. **Founded:** Mar. 1957. **Freq:** Bimonthly. **Print Method:** Offset. **Trim Size:** 8 1/4 x 11 1/4. **Cols./Page:** 3 and 2. **Col. Width:** 13 and 20 picas. **Col. Depth:** 10 and 10 inches. **Key Personnel:** Paul M. Bralower, Editor, bralower@diecasting.org; Ariana L. Busking, Asst. Editor, busking@diecasting.org. **ISSN:** 0012-253X. **Subscription Rates:** $55 U.S., Canada, and Mexico; $68 other countries; $10 single issue. **Remarks:** Accepts advertising. **Alt. Formats:** Microform.
Ad Rates: BW: $1,530 **Circ:** Paid ‡3,400
4C: $2,605 Non-paid ‡350
PCI: $70

9718 Plumbing & Mechanical
Horton Publishing Co., Inc.
1350 E. Touhy Ave., Ste. 100E
Rosemont, IL 60018-3331

Trade journal. **Founded:** 1984. **Freq:** Monthly.
Circ: Free ‡36,068

9719 Professional Roofing
National Roofing Contractors Association
10255 W. Higgins Rd., Ste. 600 Phone: (847)299-9070
Rosemont, IL 60018-5607 Fax: (847)299-1183
Free: (800)323-9545
Publisher E-mail: nrca@.net

Roofing industry magazine. **Founded:** 1968. **Freq:** Monthly. **Print Method:** Offset. **Trim Size:** 8 1/4 x 10 7/8. **Cols./Page:** 3. **Col. Width:** 13.5 picas. **Col. Depth:** 58.5 picas. **Key Personnel:** Ambika Puniani, Editor, apuniani@nrca.net; Joan Kriete, Advertising and Circulation Manager, jkriete@nrcanet; Mary E. Carravallah, Dir. of Advertising, mcarravallah@nrca.net; Marietta Dembski, Advertising Rep., phone (847)482-9115, mdembski@nrca.net. **ISSN:** 0896-5552. **Subscription Rates:** $30 individuals U.S. and Canada; $70 other countries. **Remarks:** Accepts advertising. **URL:** http://www.roofonline.org/proroofing/. **Formerly:** Roofing Spec (1987).
Ad Rates: GLR: $2 **Circ:** Paid 5,709
BW: $3,200 Controlled 13,788
4C: $5,025
PCI: $105

ROSSVILLE, pop. 1,363.

Vermillion Co. (E). 6 m E of Hoopeston. Residential.

9720 Illinois Wildlife
Illinois Wildlife Federation
112 E. Attica St. Phone: (217)748-6365
Rossville, IL 60963 Fax: (217)748-6304
Publication E-mail: wildlife@cu-online.com
Publisher E-mail: wildlife@verm.rurllnet.org

Tabloid focusing on conservation, hunting, fishing, camping, & outdoor recreation. **Founded:** 1945. **Freq:** Bimonthly. **Print Method:** Offset. **Trim Size:** 11 1/4 x 13 1/2. **Cols./Page:** 4. **Col. Width:** 28 nonpareils. **Col. Depth:** 182 agate lines. **Key Personnel:** Tom Mills, Editor. **ISSN:** 0019-2317. **Subscription Rates:** $10 individuals. **Remarks:** Accepts advertising.
Ad Rates: PCI: $7.50 **Circ:** ‡12,684

ROUND LAKE, pop. 2,644.

Lake Co. (NE). 14 m W of Waukegan. Suburban. Manufactures industrial ovens, electronic equipment machine tools, medicial equipment, commercial signs, printed circuits.

9721 Round Lake News
Lakeland Publishers, Inc.
30 S. Whitney St. Phone: (847)223-8161
PO Box 268 Fax: (847)223-8810
Grayslake, IL 60030-0268
Community newspaper. **Subtitle:** Round Lake News. **Founded:** 1938. **Freq:** Weekly (Thurs.). **Print Method:** Offset. **Trim Size:** 11 x 17. **Cols./Page:** 5. **Col. Width:** 2 inches. **Col. Depth:** 16 inches. **Key Personnel:** W.H. Schroeder, Publisher; Esther Hebbard, Advertising Mgr.; Rhonda Hetrick Burke, Editor. **Subscription Rates:** $24.50 individuals; $35 out of area. **Remarks:** Accepts advertising.
Ad Rates: BW: $674.80 **Circ:** ‡3,933
4C: $1,023.40
SAU: $8.48

RUSHVILLE†, pop. 3,348.

Schuyler Co. (W). 60 m SW of Peoria. Coal mines. Meat packing plants. Diversified farming.

9722 Times
PO Box 226 Phone: (217)322-3321
110 East Lafayette Fax: (217)322-2770
Rushville, IL 62681
Community newspaper. **Founded:** 1848. **Freq:** Weekly (Wed.). **Print Method:** Offset. **Cols./Page:** 8. **Col. Width:** 11 1/2 picas. **Col. Depth:** 21 inches. **Key Personnel:** Alan Icenogle, Editor; Wayne Perry and Beverly Perry, Publisher. **Subscription Rates:** $15 individuals; $24 out of state. **Remarks:** Color advertising accepted; rates available upon request.
Ad Rates: PCI: $4.90 **Circ:** Paid ‡3,325
Free ‡50

9723 WKXQ-FM - 92.5
123 N. Liberty Phone: (217)322-9200
Box 196 Fax: (217)322-4925
Rushville, IL 62681
Free: (888)704-9200

Format: Adult Contemporary. **Networks:** CNN Radio; Illinois News; RFD Illinois. **Founded:** 1985. **Operating Hours:** 15% network, 85% local. Continuous. **ADI:** Quincy, IL-Hannibal, MO. **Key Personnel:** L.K. Price, General Mgr., bprice@inx.net; Cathy M. Price, Sales Mgr.; Kevin B. Sager, Program Dir.; Bob Utter, Contact; Wanda Coy, Contact; Bill Lovecamp, Contact; Dwayne Davis, Contact. **Wattage:** 6,000. **Ad Rates:** $5.75-7.50 for 30 seconds; $7.75-9.75 for 60 seconds.

ST. ANNE

9724 Record
Record Press, Inc.
6980 S. Rt.1 Phone: (815)427-6734
St. Anne, IL 60964 Fax: (815)427-6751

Newspaper. **Founded:** 1892. **Freq:** Weekly (Thurs.). **Print Method:** Offset. **Trim Size:** 11 x 17. **Cols./Page:** 5. **Col. Width:** 11 1/2 inches. **Col. Depth:** 16 inches. **Key Personnel:** Wilfred J. Goreham, Jr., Editor. **USPS:** 475-580. **Subscription Rates:** $15 individuals; $18 out of area; $22 out of state; $10 St. Anne. **Remarks:** Accepts advertising.
Ad Rates: BW: $140 **Circ:** ‡670
SAU: $3
PCI: $1.75

ST. CHARLES

9725 Country Sampler
Sampler Publications, Inc.
707 Kautz Rd. Phone: (630)377-8000
St. Charles, IL 60174 Fax: (630)377-8914

Country arts, crafts, and interior design magazine. **Founded:** 1984. **Freq:** Bimonthly. **Print Method:** Web offset. **Trim Size:** 8 1/8 x 10 3/4. **Key Personnel:** Mark A. Nickel, CEO; Margaret Kernan, President; Robert Sexton, Circulation Mgr. **ISSN:** 1047-3955. **Subscription Rates:** $19.96; $33.98 U.S $23.97, $39.98 (2 Years) Canada 33.97, 59.98(2-Years). **Remarks:** Accepts advertising. **URL:** http://www.sampler.com.
Ad Rates: BW: $11,475 **Circ:** Paid ★462,780
4C: $13,500

9726 Country Sampler's Decorating Ideas
Sampler Publications, Inc.
707 Kautz Rd. Phone: (630)377-8000
St. Charles, IL 60174 Fax: (630)377-8914

Do-it-yourself decorating magazine. **Subtitle:** The Magazine That Shows You How. **Founded:** Jan. 5, 1993. **Freq:** Bimonthly. **Trim Size:** 8 1/7 x 10 3/4. **Key Personnel:** Ann Wilson, Editor; Dawn Wiggerman, Nat'l. Sales Mgr.; Robert Sexton, Circulation Mgr. **Subscription Rates:** $19.95 individuals; $3.95 single issue. **Remarks:** Accepts advertising.
Ad Rates: BW: $5,710 **Circ:** Paid ★221,247
4C: $9,975

9727 Crown Jewels of the Wire
PO Box 1003 Phone: (630)513-1544
St. Charles, IL 60174 Fax: (630)513-8278
Publication E-mail: editor@crownjewelsofthewire.com

Magazine of collecting, research, and humor. **Founded:** May 1969. **Freq:** Monthly. **Print Method:** Offset. **Trim Size:** 5 1/2 x 8 1/2. **Cols./Page:** 2. **Col. Width:** 2 inches. **Col. Depth:** 7 inches. **Key Personnel:** Carol M. McDougald, Editor. **ISSN:** 0884-7983. **Subscription Rates:** $23.50 individuals; $3 single issue. **Remarks:** Accepts advertising.
Ad Rates: BW: $40 **Circ:** Paid ⊕1,670
Non-paid ⊕15

9728 Dietary Manager Magazine
Dietary Managers Association (DMA)
406 Surrey Woods Dr. Phone: (630)587-6336
St. Charles, IL 60174 Fax: (630)587-6308
Free: (800)323-1908

Professional magazine focusing on nutrition and management issues encountered by dietary managers in healthcare facilities. **Subtitle:** The Magazine for Dietary Managers. **Founded:** 1992. **Freq:** 10/year. **Print Method:** Web offset. **Trim Size:** 8 1/8 x 10 7/8. **Key Personnel:** Diane Everett, Editor; Susan Wrona, Advertising Sales; Diane Everett. **ISSN:** 1062-1121. **Subscription Rates:** $35 individuals; $5 single issue.
Ad Rates: BW: $800 **Circ:** 17,000
4C: $1,300
PCI: $60

9729 Food & Drug Packaging
Independent Publishing Co.
210 S. 5th St., No. 202 Phone: (630)377-0100
St. Charles, IL 60174 Fax: (630)377-1678
Free: (800)346-6229
Publisher E-mail: publisher@fdp.com

Trade magazine for packaging professionals in food and pharmaceutical industries. **Founded:** Jan. 1, 1959. **Freq:** Monthly. **Print Method:** Web offset. **Trim Size:** 11 x 15 3/4. **Cols./Page:** 4. **Key Personnel:** Lisa Pierce, Editor-in-Chief, lpierce@fdp.com; Sharon Needham, Advertising Mgr., sneedham@fdp.com; Bob DePauw, General Mgr., bdepauw@independentpublishing.com. **ISSN:** 1085-2077. **Subscription Rates:** $65 individuals; $75 Canada; $140 other countries; $10 single issue. **Remarks:** Accepts advertising. **URL:** http://www.fdp.com. **Former name:** The New Food & Drug Packaging.
Ad Rates: BW: $7,330 **Circ:** Combined 74,878
4C: $9,200
PCI: $100

9730 Interior Construction
Ceilings and Interior Systems Construction Association
1500 Lincoln Hwy., No. 202 Phone: (630)584-1919
St. Charles, IL 60174 Fax: (630)584-2003
Publisher E-mail: cisca@juno.com

Magazine covering interior system construction. **Founded:** 1956. **Freq:** Bimonthly. **Print Method:** Offset. **Trim Size:** 8 x 10 7/8. **Cols./Page:** 3 and 2. **Col. Width:** 26 and 40 nonpareils. **Col. Depth:** 126 agate lines. **Key Personnel:** Jan Foxen, Publisher; John Sanger, Editor. **ISSN:** 0888-0387. **Subscription Rates:** $35 individuals. **Remarks:** Accepts advertising.
Ad Rates: BW: $1,255 **Circ:** Controlled ‡8,300
4C: $2,029
PCI: $50

9731 Romantic Homes
Sampler Publications, Inc.
707 Kautz Rd. Phone: (630)377-8000
St. Charles, IL 60174 Fax: (630)377-8914

Home and garden magazine. **Subtitle:** Romantic Decorating for Everyone!. **Founded:** 1988. **Freq:** Bimonthly. **Print Method:** Web Offset. **Trim Size:** 8 1/8 x 10 3/4. **Key Personnel:** Peg Short, Editor-in-Chief; Dawn Anderson, National Sales Mgr. **ISSN:** 1047-3947. **Subscription Rates:** $19.96; $29.96 Canada. **Remarks:** Accepts advertising. **Formerly:** Victorian Sampler.
Ad Rates: 4C: $3,575 **Circ:** Paid ★**134,187**

9732 St. Charles Republican
Republican Newspapers
1519 E. Main St. Phone: (630)513-5050
PO Box 3380 Fax: (630)513-6660
St. Charles, IL 60174
Publisher E-mail: press@press-repub.com

Community newspaper. **Founded:** 1989. **Freq:** Weekly. **Print Method:** Offset. **Cols./Page:** 4. **Col. Width:** 14 picas. **Col. Depth:** 16 inches. **Key Personnel:** Rick Nagel, Managing Editor; Wayne G. Woltman, Editor and Publisher; James Fry, News Ed. **Subscription Rates:** Free. **Remarks:** Accepts advertising. **URL:** http://www.press-repub.com.
Ad Rates: BW: $673 **Circ:** Free 15,000
4C: $976

9733 WFXW-AM - 1480
1215 E. Fern Ave. Phone: (630)232-6464
St. Charles, IL 60174 Fax: (630)513-1101
Free: (800)480-1480
E-mail: jonn@elmhurst.edu

Format: Oldies. **Networks:** ABC; Westwood One Radio. **Founded:** 1961. **Formerly:** WGSB-AM (1981). **Operating Hours:** Continuous; 5% net, 95% local. **ADI:** Chicago (LaSalle), IL. **Key Personnel:** Linda Girardi, News Dir.; Robinn Lange, General Mgr.; Jon Morgan, Program Dir.; Greg Springer, Sports Dir.; Joe Stutler, Public Service Director; Ken Misch, Production Dir. **Wattage:** 1000 day; 500 night. **Ad Rates:** $15.00 for 30 seconds; $20 for 60 seconds.

ST. ELMO

9734 Banner
407 N. Main St. Phone: (618)829-3246
PO Box 157 Fax: (618)483-6176
St. Elmo, IL 62458
Community newspaper. **Founded:** 1871. **Freq:** Weekly (Wed.). **Print Method:** Offset. **Trim Size:** 19 x 17. **Cols./Page:** 9. **Col. Width:** 9 1/2 picas. **Col. Depth:** 16 inches. **Key Personnel:** Gretchen Rudd, General Mgr. **USPS:** 475-90. **Subscription Rates:** $11 individuals; $15 out of area. **Remarks:** Accepts advertising.
Ad Rates: GLR: $.15 **Circ:** ‡1,300
PCI: $1.80

SALEM

9735 Salem Times-Commoner
120 S. Broadway Phone: (618)548-3330
PO Box 548 Fax: (618)548-3593
Salem, IL 62881
Community newspaper. **Founded:** 1860. **Freq:** 3/week. **Print Method:** Offset. **Trim Size:** 22 1/2 x 28. **Cols./Page:** 6. **Col. Width:** 2 1/16 inches. **Col. Depth:** 21 1/2 inches. **Key Personnel:** Lela Colclasure, Editor; Francis Rees, General and Administration. **USPS:** 115-190. **Subscription Rates:** $26.50 individuals; $28.75 out of state. **Remarks:** Accepts advertising.
Ad Rates: BW: $842.37 **Circ:** Paid 5,264
4C: $250 Free 123
SAU: $6.53
PCI: $5.64

9736 WJBD-AM - 1350
PO Box 70 Phone: (618)548-2000
Salem, IL 62881 Fax: (618)548-2079

Format: Adult Contemporary; Full Service. **Networks:** NBC; Illinois Farm Bureau; Illinois News. **Owner:** Virginia Broadcasting Corporation, 232 N. Kings Hwy., Ste. 205, St. Louis, MO 63108, (314)367-0232. **Founded:** 1956. **Operating Hours:** Continuous; 10% network, 90% local. **ADI:** Davenport,IA-Rock Island, Moline,IL. **Key Personnel:** Dick Fister, President; Bruce Kropp, Contact; Doris Baker, Contact. **Wattage:** 430 day; 60 night. **Ad Rates:** $10.50-18.75 for 30 seconds; $14-23 for 60 seconds.

9737 WJBD-FM - 100.1
PO Box 70 Phone: (618)548-2000
Salem, IL 62881 Fax: (618)548-2079

Format: Adult Contemporary; News; Sports. **Networks:** NBC; Illinois Farm Bureau; Illinois News. **Owner:** Virginia Broadcasting Corp., 232 N. Kings Hwy., Ste. 205, St. Louis, MO 63108, (314)367-0232. **Founded:** 1972. **Operating Hours:** Continuous; 10% network; 90% local. **ADI:** St. Louis, MO (Mt. Vernon, IL). **Key Personnel:** Dick Fister, President; Bruce Kropp, Contact; Doris Baker, Contact. **Wattage:** 1600. **Ad Rates:** $10.50-18.75 for 30 seconds; $14-23 for 60 seconds.

SAVANNA

9738 Northwestern Illinois Dispatch
Times-Journal
PO Box 218 Phone: (815)273-2277
Savanna, IL 61074 Fax: (815)273-2715

Community newspaper (tabloid). **Founded:** 1957. **Freq:** Weekly (Wed.). **Print Method:** Offset. **Cols./Page:** 4. **Col. Width:** 10 1/2 picas. **Col. Depth:** 16 inches. **Key Personnel:** Robert W. Watson, Publisher. **Remarks:** Accepts advertising.
Ad Rates: BW: $416 **Circ:** Free ‡10,000
4C: $741
SAU: $6.50
PCI: $6.50

9739 Times-Journal
PO Box 218 Phone: (815)273-2277
Savanna, IL 61074 Fax: (815)273-2715

Community newspaper (tabloid). **Founded:** 1875. **Freq:** Weekly. **Print Method:** Offset. **Cols./Page:** 4. **Col. Width:** 10.5 picas. **Col. Depth:** 16 inches. **Key Personnel:** Robert Watson, Editor and Publisher. **Subscription Rates:** $22 individuals; $27 out of area; $33 out of state.
Ad Rates: GLR: $.29 **Circ:** ‡2,100
BW: $336
4C: $636
SAU: $6
PCI: $6.50

9740 WCCI-FM - 100.3
316 Main St. Phone: (815)273-7757
PO Box 310 Fax: (815)273-2760
Savanna, IL 61074
E-mail: wcci@essex1.com

Format: Country; Sports. **Networks:** Brownfield; Illinois Farm Bureau; Jones Satellite. **Owner:** Carroll County Communications, Inc., at above address. **Founded:** 1971. **Operating Hours:** Continuous; 10% network, 90% local. **Key Personnel:** John L. Miller, Contact; Ann E. Murphy, Station Mgr.; Leslie Anne Smith, Program Dir.; Mark R. Schoening, Contact. **Local Programs:** *In Touch*, Mark R. Schoening. **Wattage:** 25,000. **Ad Rates:** $4.95-6 for 15 seconds; $5.95-7.00 for 30 seconds; $7.95-9.00 for 60 seconds.

SAVOY

9741 Journal of Dairy Science
American Dairy Science Association
1111 N. Dunlap Ave. Phone: (217)356-3182
Savoy, IL 61874 Fax: (217)398-4119
Publisher E-mail: adsa@assochq.org

Journal devoted to dairy science. **Founded:** 1917. **Freq:** Monthly. **Print Method:** Offset. **Trim Size:** 8 1/2 x 11. **Cols./Page:** 2. **Key Personnel:** Cheryl Nimz, Contact, phone (217)3563182, fax (217)3984119, cheryln@assochq.org. **ISSN:** 0022-0302. **Subscription Rates:** $90 individuals; $160 institutions. **Remarks:** Accepts advertising. **Available Online. URL:** http://www.adsa.uiuc.edu/. **Alt. Formats:** Microform.
Ad Rates: BW: $500 **Circ:** ‡5,062

SCHAUMBURG

9742 American Journal of Veterinary Research
American Veterinary Medical Association
1931 N. Meacham Rd, Ste. 100 Phone: (847)925-8070
Schaumburg, IL 60173-4360 Fax: (847)925-1329
Publisher E-mail: avmainfo@avma.org

Veterinary research journal reporting on nutrition and diseases of domestic, wild, and furbearing animals. **Founded:** 1940. **Freq:** Monthly. **Print Method:** Offset. **Trim Size:** 8 1/8 x 10 7/8 in. **Cols./Page:** 2. **Col. Width:** 45 nonpareils. **Col. Depth:** 60 picas. **Key Personnel:** Janis H. Audin, Editor-in-Chief; Bernadine Clune, Production Mgr. **ISSN:** 0002-9645. **Subscription Rates:** $150 individuals. **Remarks:** Advertising not accepted.
Circ: Paid 6,700
Non-paid 211

9743 Journal of the American Veterinary Medical Association
American Veterinary Medical Association
1931 N. Meacham Rd, Ste. 100 Phone: (847)925-8070
Schaumburg, IL 60173-4360 Fax: (847)925-1329
Publisher E-mail: avmainfo@avma.org

Trade journal for veterinary medical professionals. **Founded:** 1877. **Freq:** Semimonthly.
Circ: Paid 48,504
Non-paid 3,198

9744 Leaven
La Leche League International, Inc.
1400 N Meacham Rd. Phone: (847)519-7730
Schaumburg, IL 60173 Fax: (708)519-0035
Free: (800)525-3243
Publisher E-mail: lllhq@llli.org

Magazine for volunteer lactation specialists who help mothers breastfeed their infants. **Founded:** 1965. **Freq:** Bimonthly. **Print Method:** Offest. **Trim Size:** 8 x 11. **Cols./Page:** 3. **Col. Width:** 2 1/4 inches. **Col. Depth:** 10 inches. **Key Personnel:** Judy Torgus, Exec. Editor, jtorgus@llli.org; Dor Sachetti, Managing Editor; Maureen Schumar, Advertising Mgr.; Diana Grinvalds, Circulation Mgr. **ISSN:** 8750-2011. **Subscription Rates:** Included in membership. **Remarks:** Accepts advertising.
Ad Rates: BW: $1,105 **Circ:** Paid ⊕**6,849**
4C: $1,360 Controlled ⊕**225**

9745 Medical Electronics & Equipment News
Reilly Communications Group
16 E. Schaumburg Rd. Phone: (847)882-6336
Schaumburg, IL 60194 Fax: (847)519-0166
Publication E-mail: rcgroup@flash.net
Publisher E-mail: rcgroup@flash.net

Trade magazine (tabloid) serving physician specialists and hospital department supervisors who need medical product technology. **Founded:** Jan. 1961. **Freq:** Bimonthly. **Print Method:** Offset. **Trim Size:** 10 7/8 x 14 3/4. **Cols./Page:** 4. **Col. Width:** 2 3/8 inches. **Col. Depth:** 14 inches. **Key Personnel:** Andrea Donner, Editor, phone (847)882-6336, fax (847)519-0166, andread@flash.net; Sean P. Reilly, Publisher, seanr@flash.net; Cyndi Wiley, Production Mgr., prodmgr@flash.net; John Reilly, President. **ISSN:** 0361-4174. **Subscription Rates:** $50 individuals; $80 Canada; $80 other countries; $10 single issue. **Remarks:** Accepts advertising.
Ad Rates: BW: $4,460 **Circ:** Non-paid ‡48,000
4C: $5,660
PCI: $125

9746 MH/RV Builders News
716 Webley Ct.
Schaumburg, IL 60193

New product trade magazine (tabloid) serving builders of manufactured, mobile, modular, recreational homes, park models and marine homes. **Founded:** Sept. 1965. **Freq:** Bimonthly. **Print Method:** Offset. **Trim Size:** 9 5/8 x 12 5/8. **Cols./Page:** 4. **Col. Width:** 2 inches. **Col. Depth:** 11 1/2 inches. **Key Personnel:** Patrick Finn, Editor; Dan Kamrow, Publisher. **Subscription Rates:** $15 individuals; $20 Canada; $3 single issue. **Remarks:** Accepts advertising.
Ad Rates: BW: $2,405 **Circ:** Controlled 9,000
4C: $3,105

9747 New Beginnings
La Leche League International, Inc.
1400 N Meacham Rd. Phone: (847)519-7730
Schaumburg, IL 60173 Fax: (708)519-0035
Free: (800)525-3243
Publisher E-mail: lllhq@llli.org

Magazine offering education, information, and support to women who wish to breastfeed their infants. **Founded:** 1958. **Freq:** Bimonthly. **Print Method:** Offset. **Trim Size:** 8 x 10 3/4. **Cols./Page:** 3. **Col. Width:** 2 1/4 inches. **Col. Depth:** 9 3/8 inches. **Key Personnel:** Judy Torgus, Exec. Editor; Nancy Jo Bykowski, Managing Editor; Maureen Schumar, Advertising Mgr.; Diana Grinvalds, Circulation Mgr. **ISSN:** 8756-9981. **Subscription Rates:** Included in membership. **Remarks:** Accepts advertising.
Ad Rates: BW: $1,938 **Circ:** Paid ⊕**29,463**
4C: $2,100 Controlled ⊕**300**

9748 Outpatient Care Technology
Reilly Communications Group
16 E. Schaumburg Rd. Phone: (847)882-6336
Schaumburg, IL 60194 Fax: (847)519-0166
Publisher E-mail: rcgroup@flash.net

Trade magazine (tabloid) serving physician specialists, chief medical officers, administrators, business managers, and others concerned with product evaluation and procurement in freestanding ambulatory, diagnostic and surgical centers, group practices, HMOs, and PPOs. **Founded:** Jan. 1985. **Freq:** Bimonthly. **Print Method:** Offset. **Trim Size:** 10 7/8 x 14 3/4. **Cols./Page:** 4. **Col. Width:** 2 1/2 inches. **Col. Depth:** 14 inches. **Key Personnel:** Andrea Donner, Editor, andread@flash.net; John O'Neil, Publisher; John Reily, President, jsoneill@aol.com. **ISSN:** 0897-6198. **Subscription Rates:** $50 individuals; $80 Canada; $80 other countries; $10 single

issue. **Remarks:** Accepts advertising. **Formerly:** ICCN/Outpatient Care; Outpatient Care.
Ad Rates: BW: $3,775 **Circ:** △35,039
4C: $4,975
PCI: $125

9749 RSC (Refrigeration Service and Contracting)
Business News Publishing Co.
999 Plaza Dr. Phone: (847)413-1323
Ste. 675 Fax: (847)413-9030
Schaumburg, IL 60173
Publication E-mail: 103145.3653@compuserve.com
Publisher E-mail: beardenk@bnp.com

Reporting on service, repair, installation, and replacement articles. **Founded:** Jan. 1933. **Freq:** Monthly. **Print Method:** Offset. **Trim Size:** 8 x 10 3/4. **Cols./Page:** 3. **Col. Width:** 26 nonpareils. **Col. Depth:** 140 agate lines. **Key Personnel:** Peter Powell, Editor, phone (847)413-1323, fax (847)413-9030, 103145.3653@compuserve.com; Bonnie Kaye, Advertising Mgr., phone (612)462-2600, fax (612)462-4598. **ISSN:** 0148-382X. **Subscription Rates:** $36; $51 other countries. **Remarks:** Accepts advertising.
Ad Rates: BW: $3,750 **Circ:** Paid ★15,394
4C: $4,960 Non-paid ★3,127

9750 Schaumburg Review
Pioneer Press Newspapers
291 N. Dunton Ave. Phone: (847)797-5100
Arlington Heights, IL 60004 Fax: (847)797-5151

Community newspaper (tabloid). **Founded:** 1989. **Freq:** Weekly (Thurs.). **Print Method:** Offset. **Cols./Page:** 5. **Col. Width:** 13 3/5 picas. **Col. Depth:** 196 agate lines. **Key Personnel:** Paul Sassone, Managing Editor; Terri McHugh, Editor. **Subscription Rates:** $12.95 individuals. **Remarks:** Combined advertising rates available with other Pioneer Press Newspapers. **URL:** http//www.pioneerlocal.com; http://www.pioneerlocal.com.
Circ: Thurs. ★5,871

9751 VANTAGE
The Signature Group
200 N. Martingale Rd. Phone: (847)605-4601
Schaumburg, IL 60173 Fax: (847)605-4595

Magazine for active consumers over 55 years of age. **Subtitle:** Publication of the Montgomery Ward Y.E.S. Discount Club. **Founded:** 1985. **Freq:** Bimonthly. **Print Method:** Web offset. **Trim Size:** 7 3/4 x 10 3/4. **Cols./Page:** 3. **Col. Width:** 2.25 picas. **Col. Depth:** 10 inches. **Key Personnel:** Paul Misniak, Publisher; Joanie Davies, Associate Publisher, fax (847)605-4595. **Subscription Rates:** $17.50. $3 single issue. **Remarks:** Accepts advertising.
Ad Rates: BW: $7,260 **Circ:** ‡330,000
4C: $9,240

SCHILLER PARK

9752 AIM Liturgy Resources
J.S. Paluch Co., Inc.
3825 N. Willow Rd. Phone: (847)678-9300
PO Box 2703 Fax: (847)671-5715
Schiller Park, IL 60176
Free: (800)621-5197

Magazine on liturgy, pastoral planning, parish ministry, and church music. **Founded:** 1973. **Freq:** Quarterly. **Print Method:** Web offset. **Trim Size:** 8 1/4 x 10 1/4. **Key Personnel:** Alan J. Hommerding, Editor; Laura Kutscher-Dankler, Managing Editor. **ISSN:** 1079-459X. **Subscription Rates:** $12; $24 other countries. $8 single issue. **Formerly:** AIM: Aids in Ministry.
Circ: Paid 25,000

9753 Living The Word
J.S. Paluch Co., Inc.
3825 N. Willow Rd. Phone: (847)678-9300
PO Box 2703 Fax: (847)671-5715
Schiller Park, IL 60176
Free: (800)621-5197

Inspirational commentary and scripture readings. **Subtitle:** Not Only on Sunday. **Founded:** 1986. **Freq:** 7/year. **Print Method:** Web offset. **Trim Size:** 5 3/8 x 8 3/8. **Cols./Page:** 1 and 2. **Col. Width:** 26.5 and 12.5 picas. **Col. Depth:** 43 picas. **Key Personnel:** Laura Kutscher-Dankler, Managing Editor; J. Tyrrell Keller, Editor, kellert@jspaluch.com. **Subscription Rates:** $9.95 individuals. **Remarks:** Advertising not accepted.
Circ: ‡22,000

SENECA

9754 Town & Country
F.W. Gray & Associates Ltd.
Box 279 Phone: (815)433-5595
801 Canal St., No. 279 Fax: (815)433-5596
Ottawa, IL 61350-4901
Free: (800)527-4729

Community newspaper. **Founded:** 1981. **Freq:** Weekly (Wed.). **Print Method:** Offset. **Trim Size:** 11 x 17. **Cols./Page:** 5. **Col. Width:** 2 1/16 inches. **Col. Depth:** 16 inches. **Key Personnel:** Steven F. Gray, Publisher. **Subscription Rates:** $50 by mail. **Remarks:** Accepts advertising.
Ad Rates: GLR: $.40 **Circ:** Paid ‡29
BW: $458 Free ‡6,403
4C: $638
SAU: $8.25

SESSER

9755 American Cooner
CNH Publishing
116 E. Franklin Phone: (618)625-2711
Sesser, IL 62884 Fax: (618)625-6221

Hounds, coon, and bird hunting magazine. **Founded:** 1945. **Freq:** Monthly. **Print Method:** Offset. **Trim Size:** 8 1/2 x 11. **Cols./Page:** 3. **Col. Width:** 28 nonpareils. **Col. Depth:** 139 agate lines. **Key Personnel:** George O. Slankard, Editor. **Subscription Rates:** $17 individuals. **Remarks:** Accepts advertising.
Ad Rates: BW: $220 **Circ:** (Not Reported)
PCI: $13

9756 The Hunter's Horn
Hunter's Horn, Inc.
PO Box 777 Phone: (618)625-2711
Sesser, IL 62884 Fax: (618)625-6221

Magazine containing breed and competition information about the foxhound. **Founded:** 1921. **Freq:** Monthly. **Trim Size:** 8 1/2 x 11. **Cols./Page:** 3. **Key Personnel:** George Slankard, Editor and Publisher. **Subscription Rates:** $16 individuals. **Remarks:** Accepts advertising.
Ad Rates: BW: $120 **Circ:** ‡10,000
PCI: $5

SHELBYVILLE

9757 Union
Shelbyville Union Bay Inc.
100 W. Main St. Phone: (217)774-2161
PO Box 347
Shelbyville, IL 62565-1652
General newspaper. **Founded:** 1869. **Freq:** Daily (eve.). **Print Method:** Offset. **Cols./Page:** 6. **Col. Width:** 25 nonpareils. **Col. Depth:** 301 agate lines. **Key Personnel:** G.A. Frazier, Editor and Publisher; F.L. Frazier, Advertising Mgr. **Subscription Rates:** $32 individuals. **Remarks:** Accepts advertising.
Ad Rates: SAU: $2.70 **Circ:** (Not Reported)

9758 WRAN-FM - 98.3
111 W. Main Cross Phone: (217)774-3456
PO Box 169 Fax: (217)774-3640
Taylorville, IL 62568-0169

Format: Talk; News. **Networks:** CBS; Brownfield; Westwood One Radio; Hometown Illinois Radio. **Owner:** Virden Broadcasting Corp., at above address. **Founded:** Nov. 25, 1997. **Operating Hours:** Continuous. **ADI:** Springfield-Decatur-Champaign, IL. **Key Personnel:** Randal J. Miller, Pres./General Mgr.; Misty Kiser, Program Dir.; Kami Payne, Traffic Dir. **Ad Rates:** Advertising accepted; rates available upon request.

SIDELL

9759 Sidell Reporter
116 E. Market St. Phone: (217)288-9365
PO Box 475
Sidell, IL 61876
Community newspaper. **Founded:** 1888. **Freq:** Weekly (Thurs.). **Print Method:** Offset. **Cols./Page:** 6. **Col. Width:** 27 nonpareils. **Col. Depth:** 294 agate lines. **Key Personnel:** Rinda Maddox, Owner/Editor. **Subscription Rates:** $21 individuals; $24 out of state. **Remarks:** Accepts advertising. **Formerly:** Sidell Journal.
Ad Rates: BW: $400 **Circ:** ‡850
4C: $300
SAU: $3.50

SKOKIE

9760 Chicago's Amateur Athlete
7840 N. Lincoln Ave., Ste. 204 Phone: (847)675-0200
Skokie, IL 60077 Fax: (847)675-2903
Publication E-mail: chicagorun@aol.com

Magazine on running, cycling, and triathlon events. **Founded:** 1987. **Freq:** 7/year. **Print Method:** Web offset. **Trim Size:** 8 3/8 x 10 7/8. **Cols./Page:** 3. **Key Personnel:** Eliot Wineberg, Publisher. **Available Online. Formerly:** The Amateur Athlete.
Ad Rates: BW: $1,920 **Circ:** Paid 1,000
4C: $3,360 Controlled 54,000

9761 Computer Listing Service's Machinery & Equipment Guide
Wineberg Publications
7842 N. Lincoln Ave. Phone: (847)676-1900
Skokie, IL 60077 Fax: (847)676-0063
Free: (800)323-1818
Publication E-mail: imp@wwa.com

Trade magazine covering industrial machinery and equipment. **Founded:** Apr. 1969. **Freq:** Quarterly. **Print Method:** Offset. **Trim Size:** 8 x 10. **Cols./Page:** 3. **Col. Width:** 28 nonpareils. **Col. Depth:** 135 agate lines. **Key Personnel:** Joel Wineberg, Publisher. **Subscription Rates:** Free to qualified subscribers. **Remarks:** Advertising not accepted. **URL:** http://machinerylisting.com.
Circ: Non-paid ‡4,000

9762 CONSUMERS DIGEST
Consumers Digest Inc.
8001 N. Lincoln Ave. Phone: (847)763-9200
Skokie, IL 60077-3657 Fax: (847)763-0200
Free: (800)727-4438

Magazine featuring product and service evaluation, information, and advice. **Subtitle:** For People Who Demand Value. **Founded:** 1959. **Freq:** Bimonthly. **Print Method:** Offset. **Trim Size:** 8 x 10 7/8. **Cols./Page:** 3. **Col. Width:** 13.5 nonpareils. **Col. Depth:** 140 agate lines. **Key Personnel:** John Manos, Editor; Randy Weber, Publisher; Howard Plissner, VP/Dir. of Advertising, phone (212)685-9489, fax (212)685-9528; J. Raymond Quinn, Marketing Research Dir., phone (212)685-9489, fax (212)685-9528. **ISSN:** 0010-7182. **Subscription Rates:** $15.97 individuals. **Remarks:** Accepts advertising.
Ad Rates: BW: $27,640 **Circ:** Paid ★1,255,309
4C: $41,425

9763 Family Advocate
American Bar Association
8205 N. Laramie Phone: (847)675-2864
Skokie, IL 60077 Fax: (847)673-5514

Law journal. **Founded:** 1978. **Freq:** Quarterly. **Print Method:** Offset. **Trim Size:** 8 3/8 x 10 7/8. **Cols./Page:** 3. **Col. Width:** 13 picas. **Col. Depth:** 132 agate lines. **Key Personnel:** Deborah Eisel, Editor, eiseld@aol.com; Michael Loquercio, National Sales Dir., phone (312)588-6114. **Subscription Rates:** $39.50 Subscription. **Remarks:** Accepts advertising. **URL:** http://www.abanet.com/family/latest; http://www.abanet.org/family/advocate.
Ad Rates: BW: $1,315 **Circ:** Paid ‡11,517
4C: $2,305 Non-paid ‡1,387

9764 Harmony
Eintracht Inc.
9456 N. Lawler Ave. Phone: (847)677-9456
Skokie, IL 60077-1271 Fax: (847)677-9471

Newspaper (German and English). **Subtitle:** Serving a community of over 300,000 German-Americans. **Founded:** 1922. **Freq:** Weekly (Sat.). **Print Method:** Offset. **Cols./Page:** 7. **Col. Width:** 2 1/8 inches. **Col. Depth:** 20 1/2 inches. **Key Personnel:** Klaus Juengling, Editor and Publisher; Walter Juengling, Editor and Publisher; Annerose Goerge, Advertising Mgr.; Helga Blaumueller, Contact. **USPS:** 169-280. **Subscription Rates:** $30 individuals. **Foreign language name:** Eintracht.
Ad Rates: BW: $900 **Circ:** ‡25,000
PCI: $9.00

9765 Industrial Market Place
Wineberg Publications
7842 N. Lincoln Ave. Phone: (847)676-1900
Skokie, IL 60077 Fax: (847)676-0063
Free: (800)323-1818
Publication E-mail: imp@wwa.com

Trade magazine focusing on metal and metalworking machinery, and plant & factory equipment. **Founded:** Jan. 4, 1951. **Freq:** Biweekly. **Print Method:** Offset. **Trim Size:** 9 x 13. **Cols./Page:** 7. **Col. Width:** 18 nonpareils. **Col. Depth:** 196 agate lines. **Key Personnel:** Adrienne Gallender, Publish-

er. **Subscription Rates:** $175 individuals. **URL:** http://www.industrialmktpl.com.
Ad Rates: GLR: $5.50 **Circ:** Controlled ‡100,000
BW: $1,115
4C: $1,215
PCI: $13.27

9766 Insider Magazine
Michiana Ventures, Inc.
4124 Oakton St. Phone: (847)673-3703
Skokie, IL 60076 Fax: (847)329-0358
Publication E-mail: insidermag.com

Magazine focusing on entertainment, careers, and issues concerning 18-34 year olds. **Subtitle:** Careers, Issues and Entertainment for the Next Generation. **Founded:** 1983. **Freq:** 5/year. **Print Method:** Web offset. **Trim Size:** 8 3/8 x 10 7/8. **Cols./Page:** 3. **Col. Width:** 2 1/4 inches. **Key Personnel:** Mark Jansen, Publisher; Rita Cook, Editorial Dir.; Maxine Milks, Assoc. Publisher. **ISSN:** 1070-6534. **Subscription Rates:** $23. **Remarks:** Accepts advertising. **URL:** http://www.insideread@aol.com. **Formerly:** Collegiate Insider; T & B.
Ad Rates: BW: $29,910 **Circ:** Paid 1,000,000
4C: $36,910
PCI: $479

9767 School Social Work Journal
Illinois Association of School Social Workers
8401 Drake Phone: (847)676-3365
Skokie, IL 60076 Fax: (847)676-3358

Professional journal for school social workers. **Freq:** Semiannual. **Key Personnel:** Tamara Waskin, Editor, mtwaskin@aol.com. **ISSN:** 0161-5653. **Subscription Rates:** $12 individuals. **Remarks:** Advertising not accepted.
Circ: (Not Reported)

9768 Skokie Life
Lerner Communications, Inc.
7331 N. Lincoln Ave. Phone: (847)329-2000
Lincolnwood, IL 60646-1704 Fax: (847)329-2060
Publisher E-mail: lerner@enteract.com

Community newspaper. **Founded:** 1946. **Freq:** Weekly (Thurs.). **Print Method:** Offset. **Trim Size:** 13 x 21 1/4. **Cols./Page:** 6. **Col. Width:** 25 nonpareils. **Col. Depth:** 297 agate lines. **Key Personnel:** Pan Demetrakakes, Managing Editor; Joseph Ferstl, Exec. V.P. **USPS:** 498-220. **Remarks:** Accepts advertising. **URL:** http://www.intheloop.net.
Ad Rates: SAU: $35.28 **Circ:** Paid 3,400
Non-paid 1,903

9769 Skokie Review
Pioneer Press Newspapers
1601 Sherman Ave. Phone: (847)866-6501
Evanston, IL 60201
Community newspaper (tabloid). **Founded:** 1946. **Freq:** Weekly (Thurs.). **Print Method:** Letterpress and offset. **Cols./Page:** 5. **Col. Width:** 10 inches. **Col. Depth:** 14 inches. **Key Personnel:** Dan Obermaier, Editor; Paul Sassone, Managing Editor. **Subscription Rates:** $10.95 individuals; $12.95 out of county. **Remarks:** Advertising accepted; rates available upon request.
Circ: Thurs. **★7,724**

9770 Toxicology Pathology
Society of Toxicologic Pathologists
c/o Dr. Carl L. Alden, Ed. Phone: (847)982-7379
G.D. Searle & Co. Fax: (847)982-7374
4901 Searle Pkwy.
Skokie, IL 60077
Professional medical journal covering toxicology and pathology in animal, including human tissues and body fluids. **Founded:** 1972. **Freq:** Bimonthly. **Key Personnel:** Carl L. Alden, Editor; Jill Young, Asst. Editor; Eleanor Lohmann, Managing Editor. **ISSN:** 0192-6233. **Subscription Rates:** $160 members; $175 nonmembers; $40 single issue. **Remarks:** Accepts advertising.
Ad Rates: BW: $480 **Circ:** Combined 1,000
4C: $1,180

9771 Your Money
Consumers Digest Inc.
8001 N. Lincoln Ave. Phone: (847)763-9200
Skokie, IL 60077-3657 Fax: (847)763-0200
Free: (800)727-4438

Magazine containing personal finance and investment advice. **Subtitle:** A Consumers Digest Publication. **Founded:** 1979. **Freq:** Bimonthly. **Print Method:** Offset. **Trim Size:** 8 x 10 7/8. **Cols./Page:** 3 and 2. **Col. Width:** 27 and 40 nonpareils. **Col. Depth:** 137 agate lines. **Key Personnel:** Dennis Fertig, Editor; Randy Weber, Publisher; Howard S. Plissner, VP/Dir. of Advertising, phone (212)685-9489, fax (212)685-9528. **ISSN:** 0730-692X. **Subscription Rates:** $15.97 individuals. **Remarks:** Accepts advertising.
Ad Rates: BW: $10,985 **Circ:** Paid **★552,012**
4C: $16,465

SOUTH HOLLAND

9772 Courier
South Suburban College
15800 S. State St., Rm. 3234 Phone: (708)596-2000
South Holland, IL 60473 Fax: (708)210-5776

Collegiate newspaper. **Subtitle:** The Oldest Community Newspaper in the Country. **Founded:** 1927. **Freq:** Monthly (during the academic year). **Print Method:** Offset. **Cols./Page:** 5. **Col. Width:** 24 nonpareils. **Col. Depth:** 217 agate lines. **Key Personnel:** Charles E. Burke, Editor-in-Chief; Michael A. Kralj, Production Mgr.; Julie Ann Dertz, Advertising Mgr.; D. Frank Coffman, Faculty Advisor. **Remarks:** Color advertising not accepted.
Ad Rates: BW: $400 **Circ:** ‡3,500
PCI: $6

9773 Parish Liturgy
American Catholic Press
16565 S. State St. Phone: (708)331-5485
South Holland, IL 60473 Fax: (708)331-5484

Magazine for clergy, musicians, and others who plan the liturgy. **Founded:** 1977. **Freq:** Quarterly. **Print Method:** Sheetfed offset. **Trim Size:** 9 x 12. **Key Personnel:** Rev. Michael Gilligan, Ph.D., Editor. **ISSN:** 0164-6443. **Subscription Rates:** $20 two years; $5 single issue. **Remarks:** Advertising not accepted.
Circ: Paid 1,800
Non-paid 200

9774 The Prepress Bulletin
International Prepress Association
552 W. 167th St. Phone: (708)596-5110
South Holland, IL 60473 Fax: (708)596-5112
Publisher E-mail: info@ipa.org

Trade magazine on graphic arts news for the visual communications industry. **Founded:** 1911. **Freq:** Bimonthly. **Print Method:** Offset. **Trim Size:** 8 1/4 x 10 3/4. **Cols./Page:** 3. **Col. Width:** 2 1/8 inches. **Col. Depth:** 9 1/4 inches. **Key Personnel:** Bessie Halfacre, Editor, bessieipa@earthlink.com. **ISSN:** 8750-2224. **Subscription Rates:** $15 individuals; $17 other countries; $3 single issue. **Remarks:** Accepts advertising.
Ad Rates: BW: $480 **Circ:** ‡1,600
4C: $1,370

9775 South Holland/Dolton Star
Star Newspapers
6901 W 159th St. Phone: (708)802-8800
Tinley Park, IL 60477 Fax: (708)802-8899

Newspaper group serving 51 communities in Chicago's southern suburbs. **Founded:** 1890. **Freq:** Semiweekly (Thurs. and Sun.). **Print Method:** Offset. **Trim Size:** 13 3/4 x 23. **Cols./Page:** 6. **Col. Width:** 2 inches. **Col. Depth:** 21 1/2 inches. **Key Personnel:** Lester Sons, Editor; Norman Rosinski, Publisher; Jim Meidell, Advertising Mgr.; Jay Frederickson. **Remarks:** Accepts advertising.
Ad Rates: GLR: $56.76 **Circ:** Thurs. 64,637
Sun. 68,267

9776 Transport Fleet News
Transport Publishing Co.
15435 S. Park Ave. Phone: (708)596-8044
South Holland, IL 60473 Fax: (708)596-8410

Trucking magazine. **Founded:** Jan. 1980. **Freq:** Monthly. **Print Method:** Offset. **Trim Size:** 8 1/2 x 11. **Cols./Page:** 3. **Col. Width:** 14.4 picas. **Col. Depth:** 138 agate lines. **Key Personnel:** Liliana Rogala, Editor and Publisher. **Subscription Rates:** $15 individuals; $1.50 single issue. **Remarks:** Accepts advertising.
Ad Rates: BW: $643 **Circ:** Controlled ‡10,500
4C: $1,243

SPARTA

9777 WHCO-AM - 1230
Hwy. 154 W. Phone: (618)443-2121
PO Box 255 Fax: (618)443-2280
Sparta, IL 62286

Format: Talk; Sports; News; Religious. **Networks:** RFD Illinois; Brownfield; Interstate Radio. **Founded:** 1955. **Operating Hours:** Continuous; 20% network, 80% local. **Key Personnel:** J.L. Scheper, Pres./GM; Mike Arnold, News Dir.; Dan Schnoeker, Sports Dir.; Mike Hoefft, Contact; Barb Beck, Traffic Dir.; John Scheper, Contact; B.K. Joiner, Contact; Eric Stock, Music Dir. **Wattage:** 1000.

SPAULDING

9778 WMAY-AM - 970
502 S. Allen Phone: (217)629-7077
Spaulding, IL 62561 Fax: (217)629-7952
E-mail: wmay@fgi.net

Format: News. **Networks:** ABC. **Owner:** Long Nine, Inc., at above address. **Founded:** 1950. **Operating Hours:** Continuous. **Key Personnel:** Thomas M. Kushak, Contact; Marilyn Kushak, General Sales Mgr.; Chris Murphy, Contact. **Local Programs:** *Jim Leach*, Jim Leach; *One Eyed Jack*, Barb Ferguson. **Wattage:** 1000 day; 500 night. **Ad Rates:** $12-33 for 60 seconds. $12-$33 for 60 seconds. Combined advertising rates available with WNNS-FM.

SPRINGFIELD

9779 Illinois Beef
Illinois Beef Association
2060 West Iles Ave., Ste. B Phone: (217)787-4280
Springfield, IL 62704 Fax: (217)793-3605
Publication E-mail: ilbeef@aol.com

Magazine for Illinois beef producers. **Founded:** Mar. 1987. **Freq:** Bimonthly. **Trim Size:** 8 x 10 3/4. **Cols./Page:** 3 and 2. **Col. Width:** 24 1/8 and 34 1/3 inches. **Col. Depth:** 9.5 and 9.5 inches. **Key Personnel:** Maralee M. Johnson, Editor. **Subscription Rates:** Free to members. **Remarks:** Accepts advertising.
Ad Rates: BW: $450 **Circ:** Controlled ‡6,000
4C: $850
PCI: $30

9780 Illinois County & Township Official
Township Officials of Illinois
408 S. 5th St. Phone: (217)744-2212
Springfield, IL 62701 Fax: (217)744-7419
Free: (800)319-4204
Publisher E-mail: iltownships@cwix.mail.com

Magazine for county and township officials. **Founded:** 1945. **Freq:** Monthly (July/August combined). **Print Method:** Offset. **Cols./Page:** 3. **Col. Width:** 27 nonpareils. **Col. Depth:** 133 agate lines. **Key Personnel:** Bryan E. Smith, Editor, bryantoi@fgi.net'; Erin J. Brothers, Associate Editor, erintoi@fgi.net. **Subscription Rates:** $22 individuals. **Remarks:** Accepts advertising. **URL:** http://www.toi.org.
Ad Rates: BW: $500 **Circ:** Paid ‡12,000
4C: $575 Non-paid ‡200
PCI: $21

9781 Illinois Dental Journal
Illinois State Dental Society
1010 S. 2nd St. Phone: (217)525-1406
PO Box 376 Fax: (217)525-8872
Springfield, IL 62705
Publication E-mail: ildent@isds.org

Dental magazine. **Founded:** 1931. **Freq:** Monthly. **Print Method:** Offset. Uses mats. **Trim Size:** 11 x 16. **Cols./Page:** 4. **Col. Width:** 2 1/2 inches. **Col. Depth:** 14 inches. **Key Personnel:** D. Milton Salzer, DDS, Editor; Lee Winkleblack, Managing Editor, phone (217)525-1406, fax (217)525-8872, lwinkle@isds.org; Stefany Henson, Production Mgr., shenson@isds.org. **ISSN:** 1084-8282. **Subscription Rates:** $25 members; $35 nonmembers; $45 nonmembers other countries; $5 single issue. **Remarks:** Accepts advertising.
Ad Rates: BW: $950 **Circ:** Controlled ‡6,300

9782 Illinois Engineer
Illinois Society of Professional Engineers, Inc.
1304 S. Lowell Phone: (217)544-7424
Springfield, IL 62704
Engineering Association magazine. **Founded:** 1886. **Freq:** Bimonthly. **Print Method:** Offset. **Trim Size:** 8 1/2 x 11. **Cols./Page:** 3 and 2. **Col. Width:** 26 and 42 nonpareils. **Col. Depth:** 140 agate lines. **Key Personnel:** Chuck Stockus, Editor. **ISSN:** 0019-2015. **Subscription Rates:** $28 individuals; $34 out of country.
Ad Rates: BW: $580 **Circ:** Paid 3,200
4C: $1,030 Non-paid 100

9783 Illinois Guard Chronicle
Department of Military Affairs
Public Affairs Office Phone: (217)785-3569
1301 N. Mac Arthur Fax: (217)785-3527
Springfield, IL 62702-2399
National Guard periodical. **Founded:** 1985. **Freq:** Quarterly. **Print Method:** Offset. **Cols./Page:** 3. **Key Personnel:** Captain Rona L. Pierce, Dir., Public Affairs; Sgt. John Fundator, Managing Editor. **Subscription Rates:** Free to qualified members. **Remarks:** Advertising accepted; rates available upon request.
Circ: Controlled ‡15,000

9784 Illinois Insurance Broker
16921 E. Palisades Blvd., No. 109 Phone: (602)816-1400
Fax: (602)816-1292
Fountain Hills, AZ 85268
Free: (800)475-3565
Publication E-mail: brokerp@goodnet.com

Trade publication containing information on insurance issues for agents and brokers in Illinois. **Founded:** Jan. 1991. **Freq:** Quarterly. **Print Method:** Web offset. **Trim Size:** 11 x 17. **Cols./Page:** 4. **Col. Width:** 2 3/16 inches. **Col. Depth:** 10 inches. **Key Personnel:** Aaron Witsoe, Editor and Adv.Mgr. **Subscription Rates:** Free. **Remarks:** Accepts advertising.
Ad Rates: BW: $2,393 **Circ:** Controlled 60,000
4C: $2,743

9785 Illinois Issues
University of Illinois
Springfield, IL 62794-9243 Phone: (217)786-6084
Fax: (217)786-7257

Magazine focusing on public affairs and state and local government. **Founded:** 1975. **Freq:** Monthly. **Print Method:** Offset. **Trim Size:** 8 1/2 x 11. **Cols./Page:** 3. **Col. Width:** 14 picas. **Col. Depth:** 56.5 picas. **Key Personnel:** Peggy Boyer-Long, Editor; Ed Wojcicki, Publisher; Marvin Diamond, Advertising Representative; Elizabeth Curl, Circulation Mgr. **ISSN:** 0738-9663. **Subscription Rates:** $39.95 individuals; $72 two years; $3.95 single issue. **Remarks:** Accepts advertising.
Ad Rates: BW: $1,260 **Circ:** Paid ‡6,000
4C: $1,725 Non-paid ‡500

9786 Illinois Libraries
Illinois State Library
300 S. 2nd St. Phone: (217)785-0052
Springfield, IL 62701-1796 Fax: (217)782-8261
Free: (800)665-5576

Professional magazine covering various library issues. **Founded:** 1919. **Freq:** Quarterly. **Print Method:** Offset. **Trim Size:** 8 1/2 x 11. **Cols./Page:** 2. **Col. Width:** 42 nonpareils. **Col. Depth:** 133 agate lines. **Key Personnel:** Kathleen Bloomberg, Editor, kbloomb@library.sos.state.il.us; Kristie Metrow, Asst. Editor, phone (217)785-8232. **ISSN:** 0019-2104. **Subscription Rates:** Free to qualified subscribers. **Remarks:** Advertising not accepted. **Online:** Wilson.
Circ: Controlled ‡5,800

9787 The Illinois Manufacturers
The Illinois Manufacturers' Association
PO Box 2147 Phone: (217)522-1240
Springfield, IL 62705-2147 Fax: (217)522-8469

Journal focusing on the economic, social, environmental and governmental conditions affecting manufacturing in Illinois. **Subtitle:** The Official Magazine of the Illinois' Manufacturers Association. **Founded:** 1991. **Freq:** Bimonthly. **Trim Size:** 8 1/2 x 11. **Cols./Page:** 3. **Key Personnel:** Jane C. Frech, Editor, jfrech95@aol.com; Max Montgomery, Managing Editor. **Subscription Rates:** $30 individuals. **Available Online. URL:** http://www.ima-net.org.
Ad Rates: BW: $1,340 **Circ:** Paid 6,000
4C: $2,040

9788 Illinois Master Plumber
Illinois Association of Plumbing-Heating-Cooling Contractors
821 S. Grand Ave. W. Phone: (217)522-7219
Springfield, IL 62704 Fax: (217)522-4315
Free: (800)795-PHCC
Publisher E-mail: iaphcc@aol.com

Magazine containing news, product, and service information for PHC contractors. **Founded:** 1919. **Freq:** Monthly. **Print Method:** Offset. **Trim Size:** 8 1/2 x 11. **Cols./Page:** 3. **Col. Width:** 27 nonpareils. **Col. Depth:** 138 agate lines. **Key Personnel:** Chris J. Lechner, Editor. **Subscription Rates:** $60 individuals.
Ad Rates: BW: $350 **Circ:** ‡2,000
4C: $860
PCI: $60

9789 Illinois Music Educator
Illinois Music Educators Association
72 Marchelle Phone: (217)787-6323
Springfield, IL 62702 Fax: (217)787-3610
Publisher E-mail: stateoffice@ilmea.org

Scholarly journal of the Illinois Music Educators Association covering music and music research. **Freq:** 3/year. **Trim Size:** 8 1/2 x 11. **Cols./Page:** 3. **Col. Width:** 2 1/4 inches. **Col. Depth:** 10 inches. **Key Personnel:** Dr. Don Davis, dondavis.map@att.net. **Subscription Rates:** $10 individuals. **Remarks:** Accepts advertising.
Ad Rates: BW: $230 **Circ:** Controlled 2,775
4C: $750
PCI: $25

9790 Illinois Parks & Recreation Magazine
Illinois Association of Park Districts
211 E. Monroe St. Phone: (217)523-4554
Springfield, IL 62701-1186 Fax: (217)523-4273
Publisher E-mail: iapd@eosinc.com

Publication for park conservation, recreation, and forest preservation agencies. **Founded:** 1971. **Freq:** Bimonthly. **Print Method:** Offset. **Trim Size:** 8 1/2 x 11. **Cols./Page:** 2. **Col. Width:** 27 nonpareils. **Col. Depth:** 126 agate lines. **Key Personnel:** Ted Flickinger, Managing Editor; Ann Londrigan, Editor, phone (217)523-4554, fax (217)523-4273; Bill Bodine, Business Mgr. **ISSN:** 0019-2155. **Subscription Rates:** $25 individuals. **Remarks:** Accepts advertising.
Ad Rates: BW: $450 **Circ:** 5,500
4C: $790

9791 Illinois Pharmacist
Illinois Pharmacists Association
204 W. Cook Phone: (217)522-7300
Springfield, IL 62704 Fax: (217)522-7349

Magazine covering drugs and other areas of interest to pharmacists. **Founded:** 1937. **Freq:** Bimonthly. **Print Method:** Offset. **Trim Size:** 8 1/2 x 11. **Cols./Page:** 2. **Col. Width:** 40 nonpareils. **Col. Depth:** 210 agate lines. **Key Personnel:** Cathy Huffman, Managing Editor, cathyh@fgi.net. **ISSN:** 0195-2099. **Subscription Rates:** $36 individuals; $8 single issue; $54 out of country. **Remarks:** Accepts advertising.
Ad Rates: BW: $500 **Circ:** ‡2,610
4C: $1,100
PCI: $50

9792 Illinois Press Lines
Illinois Press Association
701 S. Grand Ave. W. Phone: (217)523-5092
Springfield, IL 62704 Fax: (217)523-5103
Publication E-mail: ronipa@aol.com; roaipa@aol.com

Magazine for editors and publishers, business, education, and government leaders. **Founded:** 1917. **Freq:** Bimonthly. **Print Method:** Offset. **Trim Size:** 10 x 16. **Cols./Page:** 5. **Col. Width:** 11.2 picas. **Col. Depth:** 15 inches. **Key Personnel:** Ron DeBtock, Editor. **Subscription Rates:** $25 individuals. **Remarks:** Accepts advertising. **Formerly:** Illinois Publisher.
Ad Rates: BW: $400 **Circ:** ‡2,000
4C: $700
PCI: $5

9793 Illinois Rural Electric News
Association of Illinois Electric Cooperatives
PO Box 3787 Phone: (217)529-5561
Springfield, IL 62708 Fax: (217)529-5810

Rural electric magazine. **Founded:** May 1943. **Freq:** Monthly. **Print Method:** Offset. **Trim Size:** 8 1/8 x 10 3/4. **Cols./Page:** 3. **Col. Width:** 13 picas. **Col. Depth:** 140 agate lines. **Key Personnel:** John Lourey, Editor. **USPS:** 258-420. **Subscription Rates:** $3.60 individuals; $5 nonmembers. **Remarks:** Accepts advertising.
Ad Rates: GLR: $7.70 **Circ:** ‡142,000
BW: $1,600.30
4C: $2,200.03
PCI: $107.80

9794 Illinois School Board Journal
Illinois Association of School Boards
430 E. Vine St. Phone: (217)528-9688
Springfield, IL 62703-2236 Fax: (217)528-2831

Magazine containing news, articles, and features providing information and advice for local boards of education. **Founded:** 1934. **Freq:** Bimonthly. **Print Method:** Offset. **Trim Size:** 8 1/4 x 11 1/4. **Cols./Page:** 3. **Col. Width:** 13 picas. **Col. Depth:** 10 inches. **Key Personnel:** Gerald R. Glaub, Exec. Editor; Jessica C. Billings, Managing Editor; Wayne L. Sampson, Publisher; Diane M. Cape, Advertising Mgr. **ISSN:** 0019-221X. **Subscription Rates:** $18 individuals; $3 single issue; $20 other countries. **Remarks:** Color advertising accepted; rates available upon request.
Ad Rates: BW: $450 **Circ:** Paid ‡7,737
4C: $750 Non-paid ‡690

9795 Illinois Times
PO Box 3524 Phone: (217)753-2226
Springfield, IL 62708 Fax: (217)753-2281

Local newspaper (tabloid). **Founded:** Sept. 1975. **Freq:** Weekly (Thurs.). **Print Method:** Offset. **Trim Size:** 10 1/4 x 12. **Cols./Page:** 4. **Col. Width:** 2.4 inches. **Col. Depth:** 12 inches. **Key Personnel:** Fletcher Farrar, Jr., Editor and Publisher; Simon Mulverhill, Advertising Mgr. **Subscription Rates:** $35 individuals. **Remarks:** Accepts advertising.
Ad Rates: BW: $1,130 **Circ:** Free 31,489
4C: $1,430 Paid 100
PCI: $27

9796 ILMDA Advantage
Illinois Lumber and Material Dealers Association, Inc.
932 S. Spring St. Phone: (217)544-5405
Springfield, IL 62704 Fax: (217)544-4206

Magazine for lumber and building material dealers. **Founded:** 1932. **Freq:** Monthly. **Print Method:** Offset. **Trim Size:** 8 1/4 x 11 1/4. **Cols./Page:** 3. **Col. Width:** 26 nonpareils. **Col. Depth:** 140 agate lines. **Key Personnel:** Larry Carroll, Editor. **Subscription Rates:** $10 individuals. **Remarks:** Advertising accepted; rates available upon request.
Circ: Combined ‡918

9797 Insurance Insight
Professional Independent Insurance Agents of Illinois
4360 Wabash Ave. Phone: (217)793-6660
Springfield, IL 62707 Fax: (217)793-6744

Trade magazine for the insurance industry. **Freq:** Monthly. **Trim Size:** 8 x 11. **Cols./Page:** 3. **Key Personnel:** Libby Shawgo, Editor, lshawgo@netscape.net; Cindy Marcy, Advertising & Art Dir., cmarcy@netscape.net. **Subscription Rates:** $50 individuals. **Remarks:** Accepts advertising. **URL:** http://www.piiai.org.
Ad Rates: BW: $766 **Circ:** Controlled 2,500
4C: $1,455

9798 Legislative Synopsis and Digest
Legislative Reference Bureau
Rm. 112, Statehouse
Springfield, IL 62706

Government publication covering a synopsis of each bill and resolution introduced and the action of those bills and resolutions in Illinois. **Freq:** Weekly. **Key Personnel:** Richard C. Edwards, Exec. Director. **Subscription Rates:** $55 individuals.

9799 The Living Museum
Illinois State Museum
Spring & Edwards Sts. Phone: (217)782-7386
Springfield, IL 62706-5000 Fax: (217)782-1254
Publisher E-mail: editor@museum.state.il.us

Magazine devoted to anthropology, art, natural history, and museum topics. **Founded:** 1939. **Freq:** Quarterly. **Print Method:** Offset. **Trim Size:** 8 1/2 x 11 in. **Cols./Page:** 3. **Col. Width:** 27 nonpareils. **Col. Depth:** 131 agate lines. **Key Personnel:** Amy Mitchell, Editorial Asst. and Designer, editor@museum.state.il.us; Kimberly Britton, Museum Ed., britton@museum.state.il.us. **ISSN:** 0024-5283. **Subscription Rates:** Free. **Remarks:** Advertising not accepted. **Alt. Formats:** Braille.
Circ: Non-paid ‡18,000

9800 Minnesota Pharmacist
204 W. Cook St.
Springfield, IL 62704-2526

Publication focusing on pharmaceutical issues. **Freq:** Monthly. **Print Method:** Offset. **Trim Size:** 8 1/2 x 11. **Subscription Rates:** Available with mambership in the State Pharmaceutical Editorial Association. **Remarks:** Accepts advertising.
Ad Rates: BW: $480 **Circ:** Paid 3,781
4C: $550

9801 The Oil Can
Illinois Petroleum Marketers Association/Illinois Association of Convenience Stores
112 W. Cook St. Phone: (217)544-4609
PO Box 12020 Fax: (217)789-0222
Springfield, IL 62791-2020
Publisher E-mail: ipma@fgi.net

Trade magazine focusing on petroleum/convenience stores. **Founded:** Oct. 1926. **Freq:** Bimonthly. **Print Method:** Offset. **Trim Size:** 8 1/2 x 11. **Cols./Page:** 3 and 2. **Col. Width:** 30 and 45 nonpareils. **Col. Depth:** 140 and 140 agate lines. **Key Personnel:** William Fleischli, Editor; Lori Mitchell, Managing Editor. **USPS:** 707-400. **Subscription Rates:** $8 individuals; $36 nonmembers. **Remarks:** Accepts advertising.
Ad Rates: BW: $400 **Circ:** Controlled ‡1,250
4C: $800
PCI: $8.90

9802 State Journal-Register
1 Copley Plaza Phone: (217)788-1300
PO Box 219 Fax: (217)788-1372
Springfield, IL 62701-1927
Free: (800)397-8757

General newspaper. **Founded:** 1831. **Freq:** Daily and Sunday (morn.). **Print Method:** Offset. **Trim Size:** 13 3/4 x 22 3/4. **Cols./Page:** 6. **Col. Width:** 26 nonpareils. **Col. Depth:** 297 agate lines. **Key Personnel:** J. Stephen Fagan, Editor; John P. Clarke, Publisher; Joe Fitzgerald, Natl. Administration. **USPS:** 614-200. **Subscription Rates:** $104 individuals. **Remarks:** Accepts advertising. **Feature Editors:** Tom Alesia, *Entertainment, TV*; Jim Betzold, *Travel*; Chris Dettro, *Finan-*

cial/Business; Charlyn Fargo, *Fashion, Food*; Sean Noble, *Education*; Paul Povse, *Features, Lifestyle, Movie, Music*; Jim Ruppert, *Sports*; Ted Wolf, *News, Sunday*.
Ad Rates: PCI: $29.84 **Circ:** Mon.-Sat. ★**62,132**
Sun. ★**71,137**

9803 Cox Communications
711 S. Dirksen Pkwy. Phone: (217)788-5656
Box 3066 Fax: (217)788-8093
Springfield, IL 62708

Founded: 1967. **Formerly**: Cox Communications & Times Mirror Cable TV of Sprinfield. **Key Personnel:** Mike Gianpietro, General Mgr., phone (217)788-5898, fax (217)788-8093; Libbie Stehn, Business Operations Mgr., phone (217)788-5898, fax (217)788-8093; Jan Miller, Customer Serv. Mgr., phone (217)788-5898, fax (217)788-8093; Kurt Suliger, Technical Operations Mgr., phone (217)788-5898, fax (217)788-8093. **Cities Served:** Ball Township, Bissell Township, Curran Township, Curran-Gardner Township, Gardner Township, Grandview, Jerome, Leland Grove, Rochester, Southern View, Spaulding, Springfield, Springfield Township, Woodside Township, IL; Sangamon County: subscribing households 47,905; 93 channels; 3 community access channels.

9804 WCFN-TV - 49
c/o WCIA-TV Phone: (217)525-2306
509 S. Neil St. Fax: (217)355-1120
PO Box 20
Champaign, IL 61824-0020

Format: Commercial TV. **Simulcasts:** WCIA-TV Champaign, IL. **Networks:** CBS. **ADI:** Springfield-Decatur-Champaign, IL.

9805 WFMB-AM - 1450
3055 S. 4th St. Phone: (217)528-3033
Springfield, IL 62708 Fax: (217)528-5348
E-mail: wfmbam@fgi.net

Format: Sports. **Networks:** ABC; ESPN Radio; Tribune Radio. **Owner:** Capstar Broadcasting Partners, Inc., at above address. **Founded:** 1927. **Formerly**: WCVS-AM (1993). **Operating Hours:** Continuous; 5% network, 95% local. **ADI:** Springfield-Decatur-Champaign, IL. **Key Personnel:** Kevin O'Dea, General Mgr.; Phil Voth, Sales Mgr.; John Price, Program Dir.; John Harris, News Dir. **Wattage:** 1000. **Ad Rates:** Advertising accepted; rates available upon request.

9806 WFMB-FM - 104.5
3055 S. 4th, Box 2989 Phone: (217)528-3033
Springfield, IL 62708 Fax: (217)528-5348
E-mail: wfmbfm@fgi.net

Format: Contemporary Country. **Owner:** Capstar Broadcasting Partners, Inc., at above address. **Founded:** 1965. **Operating Hours:** Continuous. **ADI:** Springfield-Decatur-Champaign, IL. **Key Personnel:** Kevin O'Dea, General Mgr.; Phil Voth, General Sales Mgr.; Mark Phillips, Program Dir. **Wattage:** 50,000 ERP. **Ad Rates:** Combined advertising rates available with WFMB-AM & WCVS-FM.

9807 WICS-TV - 20
2680 E. Cook St. Phone: (217)753-5620
Springfield, IL 62703 Fax: (217)753-8177

Format: Commercial TV. **Simulcasts:** WICD-TV. **Networks:** NBC. **Owner:** Guy Gannett Communications, 1 City Center, Portland, ME 04101, (207)828-8100, Fax: (207)828-8160. **Founded:** 1953. **Operating Hours:** 5:30 a.m.-2:30 a.m. **ADI:** Springfield-Decatur-Champaign, IL. **Key Personnel:** Jack Connors, General Mgr., phone (217)753-5808; Nancy Davis, General Sales Mgr.; Gary Spears, Program Dir., phone (217)522-6720; Jeff Schlindwein, Business Mgr.; Frank Lilley, Dir. of Technical Operations; Virginia Rush, National Sales Mgr., fax (217)753-5679; John Wamsley, Chief Engineer; Mark Wilson, Creative Services Dir.; Sue Stephens, News Dir., phone (217)753-5681. **Wattage:** 676 KW (video) 67.6 KW (audio). **URL:** http://www.fgi.netnews20.

9808 WLGM-FM - 89.7
600 W. Mason St. Phone: (217)528-2300
Springfield, IL 62702 Fax: (217)528-2400
E-mail: wlgm@aol.com

Format: Religious. **Networks:** SkyLight Satellite. **Owner:** Cornerstone Community Radio, Inc., at above address. **Founded:** 1995. **Operating Hours:** Continuous. **ADI:** Springfield, MO. **Key Personnel:** Richard Van Zandt, President; Rich Beaman, Station Mgr. **Wattage:** 10,000. **URL:** http://www.wlgm@org.

WMEC-TV - See Macomb

9809 WNNS-FM - 98.7
Box 460 Phone: (217)629-7077
Springfield, IL 62705 Fax: (217)629-7952
E-mail: wnns@fgi.net

Format: Adult Contemporary. **Networks:** Independent. **Owner:** Long Nine, Inc., 502 S. Allen St., Spaulding, IL 62561. **Founded:** 1979. **Operating Hours:** Continuous; 100% local. **ADI:** Springfield-Decatur-Champaign, IL. **Key Personnel:** Kellie Michaels, Program Dir., phone (217)698-6559, fax (217)629-6FAX, bandk@wnns.com; Marilyn Kushak, Sales Mgr., phone (217)629-7077; Tom Kushak, General Mgr. **Wattage:** 50,000. **Ad Rates:** $59.50 for 30 seconds; $100 for 60 seconds. $59.50 for 30 seconds; $100 for 60 seconds. Combined advertising rates available with WMAY-AM. **URL:** http://www.wnns.com.

WQEC-TV - See Quincy

9810 WQLZ-FM - 92.7
PO Box 460 Phone: (217)629-7077
Springfield, IL 62705 Fax: (217)629-7952
E-mail: wqlz@wqlz.com

Format: Album-Oriented Rock (AOR). **Networks:** Independent. **Owner:** Long Nine, Inc., at above address. **Founded:** Mar. 16, 1993. **Former name:** WTJY-FM. **Operating Hours:** Continuous. **ADI:** Springfield-Decatur-Champaign, IL. **Key Personnel:** Tom Kushak, President/General Mgr.; Marilyn Kushak, General Sales Mgr.; Dana Dame, Local Sales Mgr.; Jeff Braun, Program Dir. **Wattage:** 11,500. **Ad Rates:** Advertising accepted; rates available upon request. **URL:** http://www.wqlz.com.

9811 WQNA-FM - 88.3
2201 Toronto Rd. Phone: (217)529-5431
Springfield, IL 62707 Fax: (217)529-7861
E-mail: wqna@cavc.org

Format: Eclectic. **Networks:** ABC. **Owner:** Capital Area Career Center, at above address. **Founded:** 1979. **Operating Hours:** 8 a.m.-4 p.m.; 5% network, 95% local. **ADI:** Springfield-Decatur-Champaign, IL. **Key Personnel:** Jim Grimes, GM/Inst.; Jerry Schneider, Instr.; H. James Dunn, Chief Engineer. **Wattage:** 3000. **Ad Rates:** Noncommercial. **URL:** http://www.wqna.org.

9812 WRSP-TV - 55
3003 Old Rochester Rd. Phone: (217)523-8855
Springfield, IL 62703 Fax: (217)523-4410

Format: Commercial TV. **Networks:** Fox; Independent. **Founded:** June 1, 1979. **Operating Hours:** M-F 6:00 a.m.- 2 a.m., Sat 6:00 a.m.- 3 a.m. SUN.6 To 1 a.m. **ADI:** Springfield-Decatur-Champaign, IL. **Key Personnel:** Tom MacArthur, General Mgr.; Jennifer Smith, Program Coordinator; Vytas Paskus, General Sales Mgr. **Wattage:** 1.3.

9813 WSEC-TV - 14/65
c/o CONVOCOM Phone: (217)786-6647
PO Box 6248 Fax: (217)786-7267
Springfield, IL 62708
Free: (800)232-3605
E-mail: viewer@wmec.pbs.org

Format: Public TV. **Networks:** Public Broadcasting Service (PBS). **Owner:** CONVOCOM, at above address. **Founded:** 1984. **Formerly**: WJPT-TV (1990). **Operating Hours:** 7a.m.-12 p.m.; 75% network, 25% local. **ADI:** Springfield-Decatur-Champaign, IL. **Key Personnel:** Jerold Gruebel, Contact; Terry Kenny, Contact; Richard Plotkin, Contact; Maureen Earley, Contact.

9814 WTAX-AM - 1240
PO Box 2759 Phone: (217)753-5400
Springfield, IL 62708 Fax: (217)753-7902

Format: Full Service; Middle-of-the-Road (MOR); Agricultural. **Networks:** CBS. **Founded:** 1930. **Operating Hours:** Continuous; 15% network, 85% local. **ADI:** Springfield-Decatur-Champaign, IL. **Key Personnel:** Tim Huelsing, General Mgr.; Paul Brayfield, General Sales Mgr.; Steve Grzanich, News Dir.; Glenn Hopkins, Chief Engineer. **Wattage:** 1000. **Ad Rates:** $40 for 30 seconds; $60 for 60 seconds.

9815 WTJY-FM - 92.7
PO Box 460 Phone: (217)824-3395
Springfield, IL 62705-0460

Format: Album-Oriented Rock (AOR). **Networks:** CNN Radio. **Owner:** USA Radio Corp., at above address. **Founded:** 1967. **Formerly**: WEEE-FM. **Operating Hours:** 6 a.m.-2 a.m. **ADI:** Springfield-Decatur-Champaign, IL. **Key Personnel:** Todd Ellis, Operations Mgr.; Joe Swank, Music Dir.; Matt McLemore, Contact; Shawn Balint, News Dir. **Wattage:** 2700. **Ad Rates:** $6.25-9.75 for 30 seconds; $10.25-13.75 for 60 seconds.

9816 WUIS-FM - 91.9
University of Illinois at Springfield Phone: (217)786-6516
Springfield, IL 62794-9243 Fax: (217)786-6527
E-mail: wuis@uis.edu

Format: Public Radio; News; Classical. **Simulcasts:** WIPA-FM. **Networks:** National Public Radio (NPR); American Public Radio (APR). **Founded:** 1975. **Formerly**: WSSR-FM (1989); WSSU-FM (1995). **Operating Hours:** Continuous. **ADI:** Springfield-Decatur-Champaign, IL. **Key Personnel:** Brad Swanson, Program Dir., swanson@uis.edu; Rich Bradley, News Dir., rbradley@uis.edu; Karl Scroggins, Music Dir., scroggins@uis.edu; Sinta Seiber, Operations Dir., sseiber@uis.edu. **Wattage:** 50,000. **Ad Rates:** Noncommercial. **URL:** http://www.uis.edu/wuis.

9817 WVEM-FM - 101.9
2029 Cambridge Rd. Phone: (217)529-9500
Springfield, IL 62704-4129 Fax: (217)529-9500

Format: Adult Contemporary; Soft Rock. **Founded:** 1965. **Operating Hours:** 19 hrs. Daily; 5% network, 95% local. **ADI:** Springfield-Decatur-Champaign, IL. **Key Personnel:** Dan Menghini, Contact. **Wattage:** 50,000 ERP. **Ad Rates:** $11-20 for 30 seconds; $14-25 for 60 seconds.

9818 WYMG-FM - 100.5
1030 Dunkin Dr. Phone: (217)546-9000
Springfield, IL 62704 Fax: (217)546-4388

Format: Classic Rock. **Networks:** Independent. **Owner:** Saga Communications, 73 Kercheval Ave., Grosse Pointe Farms, MI 48236, (313)886-7070. **Founded:** 1948. **Formerly**: WEAI-FM (1986). **Operating Hours:** Continuous; 100% local. **ADI:** Springfield-Decatur-Champaign, IL. **Key Personnel:** Kevin Maskek, Vice President; Peter Stott, Program Dir.; Andrew Powaski, Sales Mgr.; Sheila Whetherall, Business Mgr. **Wattage:** 50,000. **Ad Rates:** Advertising accepted; rates available upon request.

9819 WYXY-FM - 93.9
3501 Sangamon Ave. Phone: (217)753-5400
Springfield, IL 62707 Fax: (217)753-7902

Format: Contemporary Country. **Owner:** Central States Network, L.P., at above address. **Founded:** Oct. 1994. **Operating Hours:** Continuous. **ADI:** Springfield-Decatur-Champaign, IL. **Key Personnel:** Jack Swart, General Mgr.; Joe Crain, Program Dir.; Andrew Powalski, Sales Mgr. **Wattage:** 25,000. **Ad Rates:** Advertising accepted; rates available upon request.

STAUNTON, pop. 4,744.

Macoupin Co. (SWC). 38 m NE of St Louis, Mo. Residential. Oil wells. Grain, dairy farms.

9820 Staunton Star-Times
Star-Times Publishing Co., Inc.
108 W. Main St. Phone: (618)635-2000
PO Box 180 Fax: (618)635-5281
Staunton, IL 62088
Publication E-mail: startime@midwest.net

Community newspaper. **Founded:** 1878. **Freq:** Weekly (Thurs.). **Print Method:** Offset. **Cols./Page:** 6. **Col. Width:** 12 picas. **Col. Depth:** 21 1/2 inches. **Key Personnel:** Walter F. Haase, Jr., Editor. **USPS:** 520-800. **Subscription Rates:** $15 individuals; $22 out of area annual.
Ad Rates: BW: $580.50 **Circ:** Paid ‡3,880
SAU: $5.85
PCI: $5.25

STEELEVILLE, pop. 2,240.

Randolph Co. (W). 50 m SE of St. Louis, Mo. Coal mines. Wheat, dairy, poultry farms.

9821 Steeleville Ledger
Webster Printing Co.
108 N. Sparta Phone: (618)965-3417
Steeleville, IL 62288 Fax: (618)965-3548

Newspaper. **Founded:** 1893. **Freq:** Weekly (Thurs.). **Print Method:** Offset. **Cols./Page:** 6. **Col. Width:** 21 inches. **Key Personnel:** Clent H. Webster, Editor. **Subscription Rates:** $7 individuals. **Remarks:** Accepts advertising.
Ad Rates: GLR: $2 **Circ:** Paid ‡1,758
BW: $409.50 Non-paid ‡202
4C: $509.50
SAU: $3.25

STERLING, pop. 16,273.

Whiteside Co. (NW). 38 m SW of Rockford. Manufactures builders' hardware, industrial fasteners, garage doors, garden tools, wire specialties, electrical appliances. Dairy, stock, truck, grain farms.

9822 The Daily Gazette
PO Box 498 Phone: (815)625-3600
Sterling, IL 61081-0498 Fax: (815)625-9390

General newspaper. **Founded:** 1854. **Freq:** Daily (eve.), Sat.

and Sun. (morn.). **Print Method:** Offset. **Trim Size:** 14 x 23. **Cols./Page:** 6. **Col. Width:** 24 nonpareils. **Col. Depth:** 301 agate lines. **Key Personnel:** Dennis W. Hall, Publisher; Dianna Johnson, Contact. **Subscription Rates:** $110 individuals.
Ad Rates: GLR: $.59 **Circ:** 14,639
BW: $1,058
4C: $1,298
PCI: $8.20

9823 WSDR-AM - 1240
3101 Freeport Rd. Phone: (815)625-3400
Sterling, IL 61081 Fax: (815)625-6940
E-mail: wsdr@essexl.com

Format: Talk; News; Sports; Agricultural. **Networks:** CBS. **Owner:** W.Thens Broadcasting Companies, 3501 Broadway, P.O. Box 1508, Mt. Vernon, IL 62864, (618)242-3500, Fax: (618)242-4090. **Founded:** 1949. **Operating Hours:** Continuous. **ADI:** Davenport,IA-Rock Island, Moline,IL. **Key Personnel:** Gary Brigitt, General Mgr.; Jay Pauley, Program Dir.; Jim Hardesty, News Dir. **Wattage:** 1000 day; 500 night. **Ad Rates:** $35-80 for 30 seconds. Combined advertising rates available with WSSQ-FM, WZZT-FM.

9824 WSSQ-FM - 94.3
3101 Freeport Rd. Phone: (815)625-3400
Sterling, IL 61081 Fax: (815)625-6940
E-mail: wsdr1240@aol.com

Format: Adult Contemporary; Top 40. **Networks:** Westwood One Radio. **Owner:** Withers Broadcasting Co., PO Box 1508, Mt. Vernon, IL 62864, (618)242-3500, Fax: (618)242-2490. **Founded:** 1966. **Formerly:** WJVM-FM (1988). **Operating Hours:** Continuous. **ADI:** Davenport,IA-Rock Island, Moline,IL. **Key Personnel:** Gary Bright, General Mgr.; Jim Hardesty, News Dir.; Jay Pauley, Program Dir. **Wattage:** 6000. **Ad Rates:** $20-28 for 30 seconds; $30-44 per unit. Combined advertising rates available with WSDR-AM.

9825 WZZT-FM - 95.1
3101 Freeport Rd. Phone: (815)625-3400
Sterling, IL 61081 Fax: (815)625-6940

Format: Classic Rock. **Owner:** Withers Broadcasting Co., at above address. **Founded:** 1992. **Operating Hours:** Continuous. **Key Personnel:** Gary Bright, General Mgr.; Sherry Smith, Business Mgr.; Jay Pauley, Program Dir.; Jim Hardesty, News Dir. **Wattage:** 3000. **Ad Rates:** $15 per unit.

STREAMWOOD, pop. 23,456.

Cook Co. (NE). 22 m W of Evanston. Residential. Commercial. Industrial.

9826 National Locksmith
National Publishing Co., Inc.
1533 Burgundy Pkwy. Phone: (630)837-2044
Streamwood, IL 60107 Fax: (630)837-1210
Publication E-mail: natlock@aol.com; natllock@aol.com

Magazine focusing on physical security and locksmithing. **Founded:** 1929. **Freq:** 13 times a year. **Print Method:** Web offset. **Trim Size:** 8 1/4 x 11. **Cols./Page:** 3. **Col. Width:** 27 nonpareils. **Col. Depth:** 140 agate lines. **Key Personnel:** Greg Mango, Managing Editor; Marc Goldberg, Editor and Publisher. **ISSN:** 0364-3719. **Subscription Rates:** $41 individuals; $5 single issue. **Remarks:** Accepts advertising. **URL:** http://www.thenationallocksmith.com.
Ad Rates: BW: $1,645 **Circ:** Paid ★**14,080**
4C: $2,420

STREATOR, pop. 14,769.

La Salle Co. (N). 98 m SW of Chicago. Manufactures bricks, sewer cleaning and street sweeping equipment, truck bodies, spreader, snow plows, glass containers, foam packing materials, steel tubing, carbonated beverages, syrups, peanut butter.

9827 Times-Press
Ottawa Daily Times
115 Oak St. Phone: (815)673-3771
Streator, IL 61364-2805 Fax: (815)672-9332

General newspaper. **Founded:** 1873. **Freq:** Mon.-Sat. (eve.). **Print Method:** Offset. **Cols./Page:** 6. **Col. Width:** 24 nonpareils. **Col. Depth:** 301 agate lines. **Key Personnel:** Stanton M. White, Publisher. **Subscription Rates:** $62 individuals. **Remarks:** Accepts advertising.
Ad Rates: GLR: $.70 **Circ:** Mon.-Sat. ★**8,290**
BW: $857.85
4C: $1,032.85
SAU: $7.84
PCI: $6.65

9828 WIZZ-AM - 1250
PO Box 377 Phone: (815)672-2947
Streator, IL 61364 Fax: (815)673-1833

Format: Full Service. **Networks:** ABC. **Owner:** Steven Bellinger, WDZ Radio, 337 N Water St., Decatur, IL 62523, (217)423-9744. **Founded:** 1953. **Operating Hours:** 6 a.m.-10 p.m.; 10% network, 90% local. **Key Personnel:** Robert Kersmarki, General Mgr.; Jacki Sims, Traffic; Al Hauessler, Contact; Chere Kersmarki, Sales Mgr. **Wattage:** 500. **Ad Rates:** $7.50-12 for 30 seconds; $10.50-15 for 60 seconds.

STRONGHURST, pop. 865.

Henderson Co. (W). 16 m SE of Burlington Ia. Ships stock. Dairy farms. Corn, cattle, hogs.

9829 Hancock County Quill
Hancock-Henderson Quill, Inc.
PO Box 149 Phone: (217)924-1871
Stronghurst, IL 61480 Fax: (309)924-1212

Newspaper. **Founded:** 1892. **Freq:** Weekly (Wed.). **Print Method:** Offset. **Cols./Page:** 6. **Col. Width:** 22 nonpareils. **Col. Depth:** 231 agate lines. **Key Personnel:** Dessa Rodeffer, Editor and Publisher; Lucille Rodeffer, Manager; Belva M. Bell, Publisher. **Subscription Rates:** $17 individuals; $18 out of state.
Ad Rates: GLR: $.45 **Circ:** ‡1,237
BW: $220
SAU: $6
PCI: $3.25

9830 The Henderson County Quill
Hancock-Henderson Quill, Inc.
PO Box 149 Phone: (217)924-1871
Stronghurst, IL 61480 Fax: (309)924-1212

Community newspaper. **Founded:** 1873. **Freq:** Weekly (Wed.). **Print Method:** Offset. **Trim Size:** 11 1/2 x 17 1/2. **Cols./Page:** 6. **Col. Width:** 22 nonpareils. **Col. Depth:** 231 agate lines. **Key Personnel:** Shirley Linder, Manager; Dessa Rodeffer, Publisher; Belva Bell, Publisher. **Subscription Rates:** $19 individuals; $20 out of state. **Remarks:** Accepts advertising. **Alt. Formats:** CD-ROM.
Ad Rates: GLR: $.50 **Circ:** ‡1,770
BW: $280
4C: $580
SAU: $7
PCI: $3.75

SULLIVAN†, pop. 4,526.

Moultrie Co. (SEC). 16 m NW of Mattoon. Impregrated apparatus for export, candy, steel sub-assembly, garage doors manufactured. Corn, soybeans, wheat.

9831 News Progress
PO Box 290 Phone: (217)728-7381
Sullivan, IL 61951-0290 Fax: (217)728-2020
Publication E-mail: newspro@cu-online.com
Publisher E-mail: newsprogress@sullivanil.com

Community newspaper. **Founded:** 1981. **Freq:** Weekly (Wed.). **Print Method:** Offset. **Cols./Page:** 6. **Col. Width:** 25 nonpareils. **Col. Depth:** 294 agate lines. **Key Personnel:** Barry Morgan, Advertising Mgr. **USPS:** 744-141. **Subscription Rates:** $20 in country; $25 out of area. **Remarks:** Color advertising accepted; rates available upon request.
Ad Rates: BW: $611.10 **Circ:** Paid ‡3,800
SAU: $5.65 Free ‡154

SUMMIT, pop. 10,110.

Cook Co. (NE). 11 m SW of Chicago. Residential.

9832 Des Plaines Valley News
PO Box 348 Phone: (708)594-9340
Summit, IL 60501 Fax: (708)594-9494

Newspaper. **Founded:** Oct. 18, 1913. **Freq:** Weekly (Thurs.). **Print Method:** Offset. Uses mats. **Trim Size:** 11 1/2 x 15. **Cols./Page:** 6. **Col. Width:** 9.5 picas. **Col. Depth:** 250 agate lines. **Key Personnel:** John C. Noonan, Editor and Publisher. **Subscription Rates:** $16 individuals. **Remarks:** Accepts advertising.
Ad Rates: GLR: $1 **Circ:** ‡8,000
BW: $756
SAU: $8
PCI: $9

9833 WARG-FM - 88.9
7329 W. 63rd St. Phone: (708)728-3222
Summit, IL 60501 Fax: (708)728-3155

Format: Eclectic. **Networks:** AP. **Founded:** 1975. **Operating Hours:** 6 a.m.-midnight. **Key Personnel:** Pamela J. Konkol, General Mgr. **Wattage:** 500. **Ad Rates:** Noncommercial.

SUMNER, pop. 1,238.

Lawrence Co. (SE). 18 m W of Vincennes, Ind. Oil and natural gas wells. Agriculture.

9834 The Sumner Press
The Sumner Press, Inc.
216 S. Christy Phone: (618)936-2212
PO Box 126 Fax: (618)936-2858
Sumner, IL 62466
Publisher E-mail: sumner.press@juno.com

Community newspaper. **Founded:** 1876. **Freq:** Weekly (Thurs.). **Print Method:** Offset. **Cols./Page:** 8. **Col. Width:** 18 nonpareils. **Col. Depth:** 294 agate lines. **Key Personnel:** Jo Ann Dowty, Editor. **Subscription Rates:** $15 individuals; $17 out of area; $0.35 single issue. **Remarks:** Accepts advertising.
Ad Rates: GLR: $.21 **Circ:** ‡2,505
BW: $420
4C: $620
SAU: $3

SYCAMORE†, pop. 9,219.

De Kalb Co. (N). 4 m N of Dekalb.

De Kalb Edition - See De Kalb

TAYLORVILLE†, pop. 11,386.

Christian Co. (C). 28 m SE of Springfield. Coal mines. Manufactures paper, feed, tools, steel products, stationery and greeting cards, dresses, cigars. Hatcheries; grain drying & soybean processing plant. Dairy, stock, poultry farms. Soybeans.

9835 Breeze-Courier
212 S. Main St. Phone: (217)824-2233
PO Box 440 Fax: (217)824-2026
Taylorville, IL 62568
Free: (800)200-6397

General newspaper. **Founded:** 1894. **Freq:** Mon.-Sat. (eve.) Mon.-Fri. eve., Sun. morn. **Print Method:** Offset. **Cols./Page:** 6. **Col. Width:** 25 nonpareils. **Col. Depth:** 294 agate lines. **Key Personnel:** James F. Cooper, Publisher. **Subscription Rates:** $84.50 individuals. **Remarks:** Accepts advertising.
Ad Rates: BW: $693 **Circ:** Mon.-Fri. ★**6,700**
4C: $973 Sun. ★**6,700**
SAU: $7.20
PCI: $5.50

9836 WMKR-FM - 94.3
PO Box 169 Phone: (217)824-3395
Taylorville, IL 62568 Fax: (217)824-3301

Format: Soft Rock. **Owner:** Randall J. Miller, at above address. **Founded:** July 12, 1996. **Operating Hours:** Continuous. **Key Personnel:** Randall J. Miller, General Mgr./Program Dir. **Wattage:** 6000.

WRAN-FM - See Shelbyville

9837 WTIM-FM - 97.3
PO Box 169 Phone: (217)824-3395
Taylorville, IL 62568 Fax: (217)824-3301

Format: News; Talk; Sports. **Networks:** Illinois Farm Bureau; CNN Radio. **Owner:** Randall J. Miller, at above address. **Founded:** 1952. **Formerly:** WTIM-AM (1997). **Operating Hours:** Continuous 5% network, 95% local. **Key Personnel:** Randall J. Miller, General Mgr.; Matt McLemore, Program Dir. **Wattage:** 6000.

TECHNY

9838 Divine Word Missionaries
PO Box 6099 Phone: (847)272-7600
Techny, IL 60082-6099 Fax: (847)272-8572

Magazine reporting on the Society's missionary activities. **Founded:** 1958. **Freq:** Quarterly. **Print Method:** Web offset. **Trim Size:** 8 1/4 x 10 3/4. **Cols./Page:** 2. **Col. Width:** 3 inches. **Col. Depth:** 9 inches. **Key Personnel:** Rev. Thomas A. Krosnicki, S.V.D., Editor. **Subscription Rates:** Free; $5 (mail). **Remarks:** Advertising not accepted.
Circ: Free 210,000

TEUTOPOLIS, pop. 1,414.

Effingham Co. (S). 30 m S of Mattoon. Flour mill. Grain, dairy farms. Wheat, oats, corn.

📖 **9839 Teutopolis Press and Dieterich Special Gazette**
Techopolis & Dieterich
PO Box 667 Phone: (217)857-3116
Teutopolis, IL 62467 Fax: (217)857-3623

Community newspaper. **Founded:** 1898. **Freq:** Weekly (Wed.). **Print Method:** Offset. **Cols./Page:** 6. **Col. Width:** 22 nonpareils. **Col. Depth:** 224 agate lines. **Key Personnel:** Joyce Probst, Editor; Don Hecke, Publisher. **Remarks:** Accepts advertising.
Ad Rates: GLR: $.18 **Circ:** ‡2,149
PCI: $3.50

THOMSON, pop. 917.

Carroll Co. (NW). On Mississippi River, 12 m NE of Clinton, Ia. Tourism. Industry. Dairy stock, grain farms. Melons, corn, soybeans, wheat.

📖 **9840 Carroll County Review**
Box 369 Phone: (815)259-2131
Thomson, IL 61285 Fax: (815)259-3226

Community newspaper. **Founded:** 1863. **Freq:** Weekly (Wed.). **Print Method:** Offset. **Trim Size:** 11 1/4 x 17. **Cols./Page:** 5. **Col. Width:** 2 1/16 inches. **Col. Depth:** 16 inches. **Key Personnel:** Jonathan K. Whitney, Publisher; Nancy Whitney, Advertising Mgr. **USPS:** 628-180. **Subscription Rates:** $20 individuals. **Remarks:** Accepts advertising.
Ad Rates: GLR: $0.43 **Circ:** ‡2,212
BW: $466.55
SAU: $6.02
PCI: $6.02

TINLEY PARK, pop. 26,171.

Cook Co. (NE). 23 m SW of Chicago.

Aslip/Crestwood/Blue Island Star - See Blue Island

Burnham/Calumet City Star - See Calumet City

📖 **9841 Chicago Heights Star**
Star Newspapers
6901 W 159th St. Phone: (708)802-8800
Tinley Park, IL 60477 Fax: (708)802-8899

Newspaper group serving 52 communities in Chicago's south and southwest suburbs. **Founded:** 1890. **Freq:** Semiweekly (Thurs. and Sun.). **Print Method:** Offset. **Trim Size:** 13 3/4 x 23. **Cols./Page:** 6. **Col. Width:** 2 inches. **Col. Depth:** 21 1/2 inches. **Key Personnel:** Lester Sons, Editor; Norman Rosinski, Publisher; Jim Meidell, General Mgr.; Mark Lacey, Advertising Mgr. **Subscription Rates:** $43.20 individuals.
Ad Rates: SAU: $36.35 **Circ:** Thurs. 60,413
PCI: $36.72 Sun. 63,384

Country Club Hills/Hazel Crest Star - See Country Club Hills

Crete/University Park Star - See University Park

📖 **9842 Daily Southtown**
Midwest Suburban Publishing
6901 W. 159th St. Phone: (708)633-6900
Tinley Park, IL 60477-1604 Fax: (708)633-6999

General newspaper. **Founded:** 1904. **Freq:** Mon.-Sun. (morn.). **Print Method:** Offset. **Cols./Page:** 6. **Col. Width:** 25 nonpareils. **Col. Depth:** 301 agate lines. **Key Personnel:** Doug Williams, Editor, dmwillns@interaccess.com; Ken DePaola, Publisher. **Subscription Rates:** $52 individuals. **Remarks:** Accepts advertising.
Ad Rates: GLR: $1.60 **Circ:** Mon.-Fri. ★**51,171**
SAU: $22.47 Sun. ★**60,257**
Sat. ★**41,579**

Frankfort/Mokena Star - See Mokena

Harvey/Markham Star - See Harvey

Homer Township Star - See Homer Township

Homewood/Flossmoor Star - See Homewood

Lansing/Lynwood Star - See Lansing

Matteson/Richton Star - See Matteson

Oak Forest/Midlothian Star - See Oak Forest

Oak Lawn Star - See Oak Lawn

Orland Park Star - See Orland Park

📖 **9843 Palos Area Star**
Star Newspapers
6901 W 159th St. Phone: (708)802-8800
Tinley Park, IL 60477 Fax: (708)802-8899

Newspaper group serving 52 communities in Chicago's south and southwest suburbs. **Founded:** 1901. **Freq:** Semiweekly (Thurs. and Sun.). **Print Method:** Offset. **Trim Size:** 13 3/4 x 23. **Cols./Page:** 6. **Col. Width:** 2 inches. **Col. Depth:** 21 1/2 inches. **Key Personnel:** Frank Shuftan, Editor; Norman Rosinski, Publisher; Jim Meidell, General Mgr.; Mark Lacey, Advertising Mgr.; Peter Neill, Editor-in-Chief; Jay Fredrickson. **Subscription Rates:** $25.20 individuals. **Remarks:** Accepts advertising.
Ad Rates: BW: $3,977 **Circ:** Thurs. 61,629
4C: $4,677 Sun. 64,601
SAU: $34.64

Park Forest Star - See Park Forest

📖 **9844 The Penny Saver**
Penny Saver Publications, Inc.
6901 W. 159th St. Phone: (708)633-6890
Tinley Park, IL 60477 Fax: (708)633-4919

Shopping guide (tabloid) printed in 22 zoned editions. **Founded:** 1964. **Freq:** Weekly (Tues.). **Print Method:** Offset. **Trim Size:** 10 13/16 x 12 1/2. **Cols./Page:** 5. **Col. Width:** 2 1/16 inches. **Col. Depth:** 12 1/2 inches. **Key Personnel:** Norman Rosinski, Editor and Publisher. **Remarks:** Accepts advertising.
Ad Rates: PCI: $12 **Circ:** 450,000

South Holland/Dolton Star - See South Holland

📖 **9845 Tinley Park Star**
Star Newspapers
6901 W 159th St. Phone: (708)802-8800
Tinley Park, IL 60477 Fax: (708)802-8899

Newspaper group serving 52 communities in Chicago's south and southwest suburbs. **Founded:** 1901. **Freq:** Semiweekly (Thurs. and Sun.). **Print Method:** Offset. **Trim Size:** 13 3/4 x 23. **Cols./Page:** 6. **Col. Width:** 2 inches. **Col. Depth:** 21 1/2 inches. **Key Personnel:** Frank Shuftan, Editor; Norman Rosinski, Publisher; Jim Meidell, General Mgr.; Mark Lacey, Advertising Mgr.; Peter Neill, Editor-in-Chief. **Remarks:** Advertising accepted; rates available upon request.
Circ: Thurs. ★**55,929**
Sun. ★**58,290**

📖 **9846 Worth/Chicago Ridge Star**
Star Newspapers
6901 W 159th St. Phone: (708)802-8800
Tinley Park, IL 60477 Fax: (708)802-8899

Newspaper group serving 52 communities in Chicago's south and southwest suburbs. **Founded:** 1901. **Freq:** Semiweekly (Thurs. and Sun.). **Print Method:** Offset. **Trim Size:** 13 3/4 x 23. **Cols./Page:** 6. **Col. Width:** 2 inches. **Col. Depth:** 21 1/2 inches. **Key Personnel:** Frank Shuftan, Editor; Norman Rosinski, Publisher; Jim Meidell, General Mgr.; Mark Lacey, Advertising Mgr.; Peter Neill, Editor-in-Chief. **Subscription Rates:** $25.20. **Remarks:** Accepts advertising.
Ad Rates: SAU: $34.64 **Circ:** Thurs. 61,629
Sun. 64,601

TOLEDO

📖 **9847 Toledo Democrat**
Olney Daily Mail
116 Courthouse Sq. Phone: (217)849-2000
PO Box 7 Fax: (217)849-3237
Toledo, IL 62468
Community newspaper. **Founded:** 1857. **Freq:** Weekly (Thurs.). **Print Method:** Offset. **Trim Size:** 13 x 21. **Cols./Page:** 6. **Col. Width:** 2 1/16 inches. **Col. Depth:** 21 inches. **Key Personnel:** Billie Chambers, Editor and Publisher. **USPS:** 632-820. **Subscription Rates:** $15.50; $17 out of area; $21 out of state. **Remarks:** Accepts advertising.
Ad Rates: GLR: $.30 **Circ:** 1,200
BW: $252
SAU: $2.94
PCI: $2.00

TOLONO, pop. 2,434.

Champaign Co. (E). 10 m S of Urbana. Stock, poultry, grain farms.

📖 **9848 County Star**
Professional Impressions Media Group, Inc.
Drawer N Phone: (217)485-4010
Tolono, IL 61880 Fax: (217)485-4010

Newspaper. **Founded:** 1957. **Freq:** Weekly (Thurs.). **Print Method:** Offset. **Cols./Page:** 5. **Col. Width:** 18 nonpareils. **Col. Depth:** 210 agate lines. **Key Personnel:** Steve Davis, General Mgr.; Christine Walsh, Managing Editor; Darlene Murdent, Production Asst. **USPS:** 504-020. **Subscription Rates:** $18 individuals; $21 out of county. **Remarks:** Accepts advertising.
Ad Rates: BW: $243.75 **Circ:** Paid ⊕**1,850**
4C: $443.75
PCI: $4.15

TONICA, pop. 695.

La Salle Co. (N). 52 m N of Bloomington. Manufacturing Area. Corn, bean farming. Cattle farms.

📖 **9849 The Tonica News**
Arnold Press
PO Box 67 Phone: (815)442-8419
Tonica, IL 61370 Fax: (815)339-6PCR

Community newspaper. **Founded:** Mar. 1874. **Freq:** Weekly (Fri.). **Print Method:** Offset. **Trim Size:** 10 1/2 x 15. **Cols./Page:** 5. **Col. Width:** 23 nonpareils. **Col. Depth:** 210 agate lines. **Key Personnel:** Elin A. Arnold, Editor and Publisher. **Subscription Rates:** $16; $18. **Remarks:** Accepts advertising.
Ad Rates: BW: $120 **Circ:** ‡1,000
SAU: $2.75

TRENTON, pop. 2,500.

Clinton Co. (SW). 20 m NE of Belleville. Grain, stock, dairy, poultry farms.

📖 **9850 Sun**
Sun Trenton Publishing
PO Box 118 Phone: (618)224-9422
Trenton, IL 62293-0118 Fax: (618)224-9422

Community newspaper. **Founded:** July 1, 1880. **Freq:** Weekly (Wed.). **Print Method:** Offset. **Trim Size:** 17 3/4 x 23. **Cols./Page:** 8. **Col. Width:** 11 picas. **Col. Depth:** 21 inches. **Key Personnel:** Michael L. Conley, Editor and Publisher. **USPS:** 638-200. **Subscription Rates:** $12 individuals. **Remarks:** Color advertising not accepted.
Ad Rates: GLR: $.50 **Circ:** Paid ‡1,450
BW: $294 Free ‡50
SAU: $3
PCI: $1.75

TUSCOLA†, pop. 3,839.

Douglas Co. (E). 22 m S of Champaign. Seed corn processing. Manufactures liquid petroleum gases, sulfuric acid, silicon dioxide, polyethyene, industrial alcohol. Grain, stock farms. Corn, wheat, soybeans.

📖 **9851 Review**
Tuscola Review, Inc.
PO Box 350 Phone: (217)253-2358
Tuscola, IL 61953
Publisher E-mail: reviews1@tuscola.net

Community newspaper. **Founded:** 1875. **Freq:** Weekly (Tues.). **Print Method:** Offset. **Cols./Page:** 8. **Col. Width:** 22 nonpareils. **Col. Depth:** 294 agate lines. **Key Personnel:** Randy Hastings, Publisher. **Subscription Rates:** $20 in county; $25 out of county. **Remarks:** Accepts advertising.
Ad Rates: GLR: $.26 **Circ:** ‡7,000
BW: $504
4C: $804
SAU: $5
PCI: $3.82

UNIVERSITY PARK

📖 **9852 Crete/University Park Star**
Star Newspapers
6901 W 159th St. Phone: (708)802-8800
Tinley Park, IL 60477 Fax: (708)802-8899

Newspaper group serving 51 communities in Chicago's southern suburbs. **Founded:** 1890. **Freq:** Semiweekly (Thurs. and Sun.). **Print Method:** Offset. **Trim Size:** 13 3/4 x 23. **Cols./Page:** 6. **Col. Width:** 2 inches. **Col. Depth:** 21 1/2 inches. **Key Personnel:** Lester Sons, Editor; Norman Rosinski, Publisher; Jim Meidell, Advertising Mgr.; Jay Frederickson.
Ad Rates: GLR: $56.76 **Circ:** ‡84,250

📖 **9853 The GSU Innovator**
Governors State University
Student Life Campus Center Phone: (708)534-4517
University Pkwy. Fax: (708)534-8953
University Park, IL 60466-3186
Collegiate newspaper (tabloid). **Founded:** 1972. **Freq:** Bimonthly. **Print Method:** Offset. **Cols./Page:** 5. **Col. Width:** 21 nonpareils. **Col. Depth:** 223 agate lines. **Key Personnel:**

Jennifer C. Kosco, Managing Editor. **ISSN:** 0888-8469. **Subscription Rates:** Free. **Remarks:** Accepts advertising.
Ad Rates: BW: $200 **Circ:** Free ‡3,000
4C: $350
PCI: $5.18

URBANA†, pop. 35,978.

Champaign Co. (E). 125 m SW of Chicago. University of Illinois. Manufactures scientific instruments, track and field equipment, paper cups, concrete products. Agriculture.

9854 Bulletin of the Council for Research in Music Education
School of Music Phone: (217)333-1027
University of Illinois Fax: (217)244-4585
1114 W. Nevada
Urbana, IL 61801
Publication E-mail: crme@uiuc.edu
Publisher E-mail: crme@utuc.edu

Music education journal. **Founded:** 1963. **Freq:** Quarterly. **Print Method:** Offset. **Trim Size:** 6 x 9. **Cols./Page:** 1. **Col. Width:** 72 nonpareils. **Col. Depth:** 126 agate lines. **Key Personnel:** Eunice Boardman, Editor; John Grashel, Co-Editor. **ISSN:** 0010-9894. **Subscription Rates:** $20 individuals; $28 institutions; $12 students; $5 single issue. **Remarks:** Advertising not accepted. **Alt. Formats:** Microform.
Circ: Paid ‡1,600
Non-paid ‡100

9855 Champaign County Genealogical Society Quarterly
Champaign County Genealogical Society
c/o Champaign County Historical Archives Phone: (217)367-4025
Fax: (217)367-4061
201 S. Race St.
Urbana, IL 61801-3283
Genealogical publication. **Founded:** 1979. **Freq:** Quarterly. **Print Method:** Offset. **Trim Size:** 8 1/2 x 11. **Key Personnel:** Joan Black Lund, Editor. **Subscription Rates:** $15 individuals; $3.50 single issue. **Remarks:** Advertising not accepted.
Circ: Controlled 250

9856 College Composition and Communication
National Council of Teachers of English (NCTE)
1111 W. Kenyon Rd. Phone: (217)328-3870
Urbana, IL 61801-1096 Fax: (217)328-0977
Free: (877)369-6283
Publisher E-mail: orders@ncte.org

Magazine providing forum for teachers of writing in two-and four-year colleges. Contributions discuss the theory and practice of teaching composition or communication, and relate them to the teaching of literature and language. **Founded:** 1950. **Freq:** Quarterly. **Print Method:** Offset. **Trim Size:** 6 x 9. **Cols./Page:** 1. **Col. Width:** 56 nonpareils. **Col. Depth:** 102 agate lines. **Key Personnel:** Joseph Harris, Editor; Carrie Stewart, Advertising Mgr., cstewart@ncte.org; Tom Tiller, Editing/Production, ttiller@ncte.org. **ISSN:** 0010-096X. **Subscription Rates:** $48 individuals. **Remarks:** Accepts advertising. **Alt. Formats:** Mailing labels.
Ad Rates: BW: $995 **Circ:** Paid 11,500

9857 College English
National Council of Teachers of English (NCTE)
1111 W. Kenyon Rd. Phone: (217)328-3870
Urbana, IL 61801-1096 Fax: (217)328-0977
Free: (877)369-6283
Publisher E-mail: orders@ncte.org

Magazine containing articles on the working concepts of criticism, the nature of critical and scholarly reasoning, pedagogy and educational theory, and issues of concern to college English teachers. Contemporary poetry, reviews of recent books, Comment and Response section. **Founded:** 1939. **Freq:** 6/year. **Print Method:** Offset. Uses mats. **Trim Size:** 6 3/4 x 9 1/4. **Cols./Page:** 2 and 1. **Col. Width:** 29 and 60 nonpareils. **Col. Depth:** 106 agate lines. **Key Personnel:** Louise Smith, Editor, phone (617)287-6733, fax (617)265-7173; Carrie Stewart, Advertising Mgr., cstewart@ncte.org; Tom Tiller, Editing/Production, ttiller@ncte.org. **ISSN:** 0010-0994. **Subscription Rates:** $50 individuals. **Remarks:** Accepts advertising. **Alt. Formats:** Mailing labels.
Ad Rates: BW: $1,050 **Circ:** Paid 16,000

9858 The Council Chronicle
National Council of Teachers of English (NCTE)
1111 W. Kenyon Rd. Phone: (217)328-3870
Urbana, IL 61801-1096 Fax: (217)328-0977
Free: (877)369-6283
Publisher E-mail: orders@ncte.org

Newspaper for teachers of English or language arts at all levels. **Founded:** 1991. **Freq:** 5/year. **Print Method:** Offset. **Trim Size:** 10 3/8 x 12 3/4. **Cols./Page:** 4. **Col. Width:** 14.5 picas. **Col. Depth:** 78 picas. **Key Personnel:** Felice Kaufman, Editor; Carrie Stewart, Advertising Mgr. **ISSN:** 1057-4190. **Subscription Rates:** $40 members. **Remarks:** Accepts advertising. **URL:** http://www.ncte.org.
Ad Rates: BW: $1,650 **Circ:** Paid 104,000
PCI: $72

9859 English Education
National Council of Teachers of English (NCTE)
1111 W. Kenyon Rd. Phone: (217)328-3870
Urbana, IL 61801-1096 Fax: (217)328-0977
Free: (877)369-6283
Publisher E-mail: orders@ncte.org

Magazine containing articles for instructors involved in teacher preparation and inservice education. **Subtitle:** Journal of the Conference on English Education (CEE). **Founded:** 1969. **Freq:** Quarterly. **Print Method:** Offset. **Trim Size:** 6 x 9. **Cols./Page:** 1. **Col. Width:** 54 nonpareils. **Col. Depth:** 97 agate lines. **Key Personnel:** Rona Smith, Editing/Production, rsmith@ncte.org; Carrie Stewart, Advertising Mgr., cstewart@ncte.org; Ruth Vinz, Editor; David Schaafsma, Editor. **ISSN:** 0007-8204. **Subscription Rates:** $45. **Remarks:** Accepts advertising. **Alt. Formats:** Mailing labels.
Ad Rates: BW: $500 **Circ:** Paid 4,000

9860 Fusion Technology
American Nuclear Society
University of Illinois Phone: (217)333-3772
Fusion Studies Laboratory Fax: (217)333-2906
103 S. Goodwin Ave.
Urbana, IL 61801
Publisher E-mail: nucleus@ans.org

Fusion energy research and technical engineering. **Founded:** 1981. **Freq:** 7/year. **Print Method:** Offset. **Trim Size:** 8 1/2 x 11. **Cols./Page:** 2. **Col. Width:** 39 nonpareils. **Col. Depth:** 126 agate lines. **Key Personnel:** George H. Miley, Editor, g-miley@uiuc.edu. **Subscription Rates:** $698 individuals. **Remarks:** Advertising not accepted.
Circ: 600

9861 Illinois Alumni
University of Illinois Alumni Association
227 Illini Union Phone: (217)333-1471
1401 W Green St. Fax: (217)333-7803
Urbana, IL 61801
Publication E-mail: illinoisalumni@uiuc.edu
Publisher E-mail: alumni@uiuc.edu

Alumni association magazine. **Subtitle:** The University of Illinois Alumni Association Magazine. **Founded:** 1989. **Freq:** Bimonthly. **Print Method:** Offset. **Trim Size:** 8 3/8 x 10 7/8. **Key Personnel:** Vanessa Faurie, Editor. **ISSN:** 1047-4536. **Remarks:** Accepts advertising. **Alt. Formats:** Audio tape; Braille; Large-print. **Formerly:** Illinois Quarterly.
Ad Rates: BW: $1,500 **Circ:** Paid ‡80,000
4C: $1,800

9862 Illinois Archaeology
University of Illinois
Center for American Archaeology Phone: (618)653-4688
PO Box 366 Fax: (618)653-4688
Kampsville, IL 62053
Professional journal covering archaeology of Illinois and surrounding regions. **Founded:** 1989. **Freq:** Semiannual. **Trim Size:** 7 x 10. **Cols./Page:** 1. **Col. Width:** 5.42 inches. **Col. Depth:** 7.67 inches. **Key Personnel:** Dr. Jodie O'Gorman, Editor, jogorman@caa-archeology.org. **ISSN:** 1050-8244. **Subscription Rates:** $20 individuals. **Remarks:** Advertising not accepted.
Circ: Controlled 200

9863 Illinois Classical Studies
Scholars Press
Department of Classics Phone: (217)333-1008
Foreign Languages Bldg.
707 s. Matthews Ave.
Urbana, IL 61801
Publication E-mail: dsansone@uiuc.edu
Publisher E-mail: scholars@emory.edu

Scholarly journal covering classical studies. **Founded:** 1976. **Freq:** Annual. **Print Method:** Offset. **Trim Size:** 6 x 9. **Cols./Page:** 1. **Col. Width:** 4 1/4 inches. **Col. Depth:** 7 inches. **Key Personnel:** David Sansone, Editor. **ISSN:** 0353-1923. **Subscription Rates:** $30 individuals; $35 out of country. **Remarks:** Advertising not accepted.
Circ: Controlled 260

9864 Illinois English Bulletin
University of Illinois at Urbana-Champaign
608 Wright St.
Urbana, IL 61801

Journal for members of the Illinois Association of Teachers of English. **Founded:** 1928. **Freq:** Quarterly. **Print Method:** Offset. **Trim Size:** 5 1/2 x 8 1/2. **Cols./Page:** 1. **Col. Width:** 4 1/2 inches. **Col. Depth:** 6 inches. **Key Personnel:** Michael Pemberton, Editor. **ISSN:** 0019-2023. **Subscription Rates:** $20 individuals; $5 single issue. **Remarks:** Advertising not accepted.
Circ: (Not Reported)

9865 Illinois Journal of Mathematics
University of Illinois Press at Urbana-Champaign
University of Illinois Phone: (217)333-3410
Math Dept. Fax: (217)333-9576
1409 W. Green St.
Urbana, IL 61801
Publication E-mail: ijm@math.uiuc.edu

Mathematics research journal. **Founded:** Mar. 1957. **Freq:** Quarterly. **Print Method:** Offset. **Trim Size:** 6 x 9. **Cols./Page:** 1. **Col. Width:** 56 nonpareils. **Col. Depth:** 106 agate lines. **Key Personnel:** H.J. Hildebrand, Managing Editor. **ISSN:** 0019-2082. **Subscription Rates:** $125 individuals. **Remarks:** Advertising not accepted. **Alt. Formats:** Microform.
Circ: Paid ‡1,200

9866 Illinois Research
University of Illinois College of Agriculture
1401 W. Green St. Phone: (217)333-2548
227 Illini Union Fax: (217)333-7803
Urbana, IL 61801
Agricultural magazine. **Founded:** 1959. **Freq:** Quarterly. **Print Method:** Offset. **Trim Size:** 8 1/2 x 11. **Cols./Page:** 3. **Col. Width:** 28 nonpareils. **Col. Depth:** 133 agate lines. **Key Personnel:** Nancy Nichols, Editor. **Subscription Rates:** Free. **Remarks:** Advertising not accepted.
Circ: Controlled ‡7,000

9867 International Journal of Expert Systems
Elseiver
Univ. of Illinois
1304 W. Springfield
3270 Digital Computer Lab
Urbana, IL 61801
Publication E-mail: 102062-2525@compuserve.com
Publisher E-mail: fcentres@gpu.stv.ualberta.ca

Subtitle: Research and Applications. **Founded:** 1988. **Freq:** Quarterly. **Print Method:** Offset. **Trim Size:** 6 7/8 x 10. **Cols./Page:** 1. **Key Personnel:** Mehdi Harandi, Editor; Kenneth Ford, Advertising Mgr. **ISSN:** 0894-9077. **Subscription Rates:** $240 institutions; $260 institutions, other countries; $280 institutions, other countries airmail; $110 individuals; $130 other countries; $150 other countries airmail; $62.50 single issue; $67.50 single issue other couuntries; $72.50 single issue other countries airmail. **Remarks:** Accepts advertising.
Ad Rates: BW: $300 **Circ:** (Not Reported)

9868 Journal of English and Germanic Philology
University of Illinois Press at Urbana-Champaign
109D English Bldg. Phone: (217)333-0426
University of Illinois Fax: (217)333-4321
Urbana, IL 61801
Publication E-mail: aguibbor@uicic.edu

Philology journal. **Founded:** 1897. **Freq:** Quarterly. **Print Method:** Offset. **Trim Size:** 6 x 9. **Cols./Page:** 1. **Col. Width:** 52 nonpareils. **Col. Depth:** 101 agate lines. **Key Personnel:** Prof. Achsah Guibbory, Editor; Marianne E. Kalinke, Editor; Ann Lowry, Journals Mgr. **ISSN:** 0363-6941. **Subscription Rates:** $30 individuals; $14 single issue; $37 other countries; $52 institutions; $57 institutions, other countries.
Ad Rates: BW: $200 **Circ:** ‡1,400
4C: $135

9869 The Journal of Symbolic Logic
Association for Symbolic Logic
University of Illinois Phone: (217)244-7902
Department of Mathematics Fax: (217)333-9576
1409 W. Green St.
Urbana, IL 61801
Publisher E-mail: asl@math.uiuc.edu

Scientific journal containing research on symbolic logic. **Founded:** 1936. **Freq:** Quarterly. **Print Method:** offset. **Trim Size:** 7 x 10. **Key Personnel:** Herbert B. Enderton, Editor. **ISSN:** 0022-4812. **Subscription Rates:** $310 institutions; $56 individuals. **Remarks:** Advertising not accepted.
Circ: ‡2,500

9870 Language Arts
National Council of Teachers of English (NCTE)
1111 W. Kenyon Rd. Phone: (217)328-3870
Urbana, IL 61801-1096 Fax: (217)328-0977
Free: (877)369-6283
Publisher E-mail: orders@ncte.org

Magazine containing practical, classroom-tested ideas for helping children (grades K-8) learn to read, write, and speak more effectively. Covers such topics as language development, ethnic studies, creativity, and uses of varied media. Regular features include new research findings, instructional materials, and current books for children. **Founded:** 1924. **Freq:** 6/year. **Print Method:** Offset. **Trim Size:** 8 1/2 x 11.

Cols./Page: 2 and 1. **Col. Width:** 18 picas. **Col. Depth:** 52 picas. **Key Personnel:** Sharon Murphy, Editor, phone (416)736-5002, la@edu.yorku.edu; Carrie Stewart, Advertising Mgr., cstewart@ncte.org; Carol Schanche, Editing/Production, carolschanche@ncte.org; Curt Dudley-Marling, Editor. **ISSN:** 0360-9170. **Subscription Rates:** $50 individuals. **Remarks:** Accepts advertising. **Alt. Formats:** Mailing labels.
Ad Rates: BW: $900 **Circ:** Paid 20,000
4C: $1,900

9871 NACTA Journal
National Association of Colleges and Teachers of Agriculture
608 W. Vermont Phone: (217)344-5738
Urbana, IL 61801
Journal on college-level teaching of agriculture. **Founded:** 1957. **Freq:** Quarterly. **Print Method:** Offset. **Trim Size:** 8 1/4 x 10 7/8. **Cols./Page:** 2. **Col. Width:** 20 nonpareils. **Col. Depth:** 137 agate lines. **Key Personnel:** Jack C. Everly, Editor. **ISSN:** 0149-4910. **Subscription Rates:** $25 individuals. **Remarks:** Accepts advertising.
Ad Rates: BW: $200 **Circ:** ‡1,400

9872 Policy Studies Review
Policy Studies Organizaion Phone: (217)359-8541
711 S. Ashton Lane Fax: (217)244-3037
Urbana, IL 61801
Political and social science journal. **Founded:** Aug. 1981. **Freq:** Quarterly. **Print Method:** Offset. **Trim Size:** 6 x 9. **Cols./Page:** 1. **Col. Width:** 57 nonpareils. **Col. Depth:** 108 agate lines. **Key Personnel:** David Feldman, Editor, phone (423)974-4251, fax (423)974-1838, feldman@utk.edu; Stuart Nagel, Advertising Mgr., phone (217)352-7700, fax (217)352-3037, s-nagel@uiuc.edu. **ISSN:** 0278-4416. **Subscription Rates:** $32 individuals; $178 libraries. **Remarks:** Accepts advertising.
Ad Rates: BW: $180 **Circ:** Paid ‡2,350
Non-paid ‡50

9873 Political Communication
Taylor & Francis
Department of Speech Communication
University of Illinois
Lincoln Hall
702 S. Wright St.
Urbana, IL 61801
Publisher E-mail: info@taylorandfrancis.com

Journal examining the roles of governmental, intergovernmental, and nongovernmental organizations as political communicators. **Founded:** 1980. **Freq:** Quarterly. **Print Method:** Offset. **Trim Size:** 7 x 10. **Cols./Page:** 1. **Col. Width:** 32 picas. **Col. Depth:** 51 picas. **Key Personnel:** David Swanson, Editor, phone (217)333-2633, fax (217)344-0575. **ISSN:** 1058-4609. **Subscription Rates:** $43 members; $87 individuals. **URL:** http://www.tkandf.co.uk. **Formerly:** Political Communication and Persuasion.
Ad Rates: BW: $500 **Circ:** 450
4C: $1,200

9874 Poodle Review
2003 E. Illini Airport Rd. Phone: (217)328-7375
Urbana, IL 61801-7561
Magazine containing poodle breeding and showing information. **Founded:** 1955. **Freq:** Bimonthly. **Print Method:** Offset. **Trim Size:** 6 x 9. **Cols./Page:** 2. **Col. Width:** 14 picas. **Col. Depth:** 112 agate lines. **Key Personnel:** Del Dahl, Editor and Administration; Sara Dahl, Co-Editor. **Subscription Rates:** $30 U.S., Canada, and Mexico; $35 other countries. **Remarks:** Accepts advertising.
Ad Rates: BW: $100 **Circ:** Paid 1,700
PCI: $18 Non-paid 300

9875 Primary Voices K-6
National Council of Teachers of English (NCTE)
1111 W. Kenyon Rd. Phone: (217)328-3870
Urbana, IL 61801-1096 Fax: (217)328-0977
Free: (877)369-6283
Publisher E-mail: orders@ncte.org

Magazine for elementary teachers describing innovative classroom practices. **Founded:** 1993. **Freq:** Quarterly. **Print Method:** Offset. **Trim Size:** 8 1/4 x 11. **Cols./Page:** 2. **Col. Width:** 17 picas. **Col. Depth:** 51.5 picas. **Key Personnel:** Kathy Meyer Reimer, Editor; Diane Stephens, Editor; Tom Tiller, Editing/Production, ttiller@ncte.org; Carrie Stewart, Advertising Mgr., cstewart@ncte.org; Jennifer Story, Editor. **ISSN:** 1068-073X. **Subscription Rates:** $45 individuals. **Remarks:** Accepts advertising.
Circ: Paid 8,500

9876 Research in the Teaching of English
National Council of Teachers of English (NCTE)
1111 W. Kenyon Rd. Phone: (217)328-3870
Urbana, IL 61801-1096 Fax: (217)328-0977
Free: (877)369-6283
Publisher E-mail: orders@ncte.org

Magazine on language teaching and learning. A forum for researchers, and a background source for teachers and curriculum planners at all levels. **Founded:** 1967. **Freq:** Quarterly. **Print Method:** Offset. **Trim Size:** 6 x 9. **Cols./Page:** 1. **Col. Width:** 56 nonpareils. **Col. Depth:** 102 agate lines. **Key Personnel:** Michael W. Smith, Editor; Carrie Stewart, Advertising Mgr., cstewart@ncte.org; Rona Smith, Editing/Production, rsmith@ncte.org; Peter Smagorinsky, Editor. **ISSN:** 0034-527X. **Subscription Rates:** $45 individuals. **Remarks:** Accepts advertising. **Alt. Formats:** Mailing labels.
Ad Rates: BW: $500 **Circ:** Paid 5,000

9877 Steward Anthropological Society Journal
University of Illinois
109 Davenport Hall Phone: (217)244-0183
607 S Matthews St. Fax: (217)244-3498
Urbana, IL 61801
Publication E-mail: stewardjournal@uiuc.edu

Scholarly journal of anthropological interest. **Founded:** 1969. **Freq:** Annual. **Print Method:** Web offset. **Trim Size:** 5 x 8. **Cols./Page:** 1. **Col. Width:** 4 inches. **Col. Depth:** 7 inches. **ISSN:** 0039-1344. **Subscription Rates:** $18 individuals; $25 institutions. **Remarks:** Advertising not accepted.
Circ: Paid 150

9878 Studies in the Linguistic Sciences
University of Illinois at Urbana-Champaign
707 S. Mathews, 4088 Foreign Language Bldg. Phone: (217)333-3563 Fax: (217)333-3466
Urbana, IL 61801
Publication E-mail: deptling@uiuc.edu

Academic journal covering linguistics. **Founded:** 1970. **Freq:** Semiannual. **Print Method:** Offset. **Trim Size:** 5 3/8 x 8 1/4. **Cols./Page:** 1. **Key Personnel:** Elmer H. Antonsen, Editor. **ISSN:** 0049-2388. **Subscription Rates:** $10 single issue. **Remarks:** Advertising not accepted.
Circ: Controlled 260

9879 Teaching English in the Two-Year College
National Council of Teachers of English (NCTE)
1111 W. Kenyon Rd. Phone: (217)328-3870
Urbana, IL 61801-1096 Fax: (217)328-0977
Free: (877)369-6283
Publisher E-mail: orders@ncte.org

Journal providing a national forum for English teachers to share and find professional ideas and information. **Founded:** 1974. **Freq:** Quarterly. **Print Method:** Offset. **Trim Size:** 6 x 9. **Cols./Page:** 2. **Col. Width:** 13.5 picas. **Col. Depth:** 45 picas. **Key Personnel:** Mark Reynolds, Editor; Carrie Stewart, Advertising Mgr., cstewart@ncte,org; Rona Smith, Editing/Production, rsmith@ncte.org. **ISSN:** 0098-6291. **Subscription Rates:** $45 individuals. **Remarks:** Accepts advertising. **Alt. Formats:** Mailing labels.
Ad Rates: BW: $595 **Circ:** Paid 5,000

9880 WBCP-AM - 1580
PO Box 1023 Phone: (217)359-1580
Champaign, IL 61820 Fax: (217)359-1583

Format: Urban Contemporary; Adult Contemporary. **Networks:** American Urban Radio; ABC. **Owner:** WBCP Inc., 904 N. 4th St. Unit D., Champaign, IL 61820. **Founded:** 1948. **Formerly:** WJTX-AM. **Operating Hours:** Continuous. **ADI:** Springfield-Decatur-Champaign, IL. **Key Personnel:** Lonnie Clark, President; Linda Randall, Program Dir.; Sandra Harris, Music Dir. Traffic Mgr. **Wattage:** 250. **Ad Rates:** $18 for 30 seconds; $21 for 60 seconds.

9881 WCCU-TV - 27
712 Killarney Phone: (217)367-8827
Urbana, IL 61801 Fax: (217)367-8839

Format: Commercial TV. **Networks:** Fox. **Founded:** Aug. 10, 1987. **Operating Hours:** Mon-Fri to 2 a.m., Sat. to 3 a.m., Sun. to 1 a.m. **ADI:** Springfield-Decatur-Champaign, IL. **Key Personnel:** Greg Thomas, LSM; Al Schmidt, Engineering. **Wattage:** 3.3. **Ad Rates:** $15-1200 per unit. Combined advertising rates available with WRSP-TV,. **URL:** http://www.wccutv.com.

9882 WILL-AM - 580
Campbell Hall Phone: (217)333-0850
300 N. Goodwin Fax: (217)333-7151
Urbana, IL 61801

Format: News; Talk; Agricultural. **Networks:** National Public Radio (NPR); American Public Radio (APR). **Owner:** University of Illinois Board of Trustees, at above address. **Founded:** 1922. **Formerly:** WRM-AM. **Operating Hours:** 5 a.m.-9 p.m. **Key Personnel:** Dan Simeone, Contact; Jay Pearce, News Dir.; Charles Lindy, Contact; Donald P. Mullally, General Mgr.; Dick Hertel, Contact; R. Edward West, Chief Engineer; Debbie Day, Contact; Tom Galer-Unti, Contact. **Wattage:** 5000. **Ad Rates:** Noncommercial. **URL:** http://www.will.uiuc.edu.

9883 WILL-TV - 12
Campbell Hall for Telecommunications Phone: (217)333-1070 Fax: (217)244-6386
300 N. Goodwin Ave.
Urbana, IL 61801
E-mail: will-tv@uiuc.edu

Format: Public TV. **Networks:** Public Broadcasting Service (PBS). **Owner:** University of Illinois, at above address. **Founded:** 1955. **Operating Hours:** 18 hrs. Daily; 99% network, 1% local. **ADI:** Springfield-Decatur-Champaign, IL. **Key Personnel:** Ellis Bromberg, Station Mgr.; David Thiel, Program Dir.; Larry Inman, Chief Engineer; Debbie Day, Development Director; Kate Dobrovolny, Marketing Director. **Local Programs:** *Illinois Gardener*, *Prairie Fire*, *Talking Point.* **URL:** http://www.will.uiuc.edu.

9884 WZNF-FM - 95.3
400 N. Broadway Ave. Phone: (217)367-1195
Urbana, IL 61801 Fax: (217)367-3291

Format: Album-Oriented Rock (AOR). **Owner:** Liberty Radio II, at above address. **Founded:** 1995. **Operating Hours:** Continuous. **ADI:** Springfield-Decatur-Champaign, IL. **Key Personnel:** Bruce Andre, Sales Mgr.; Chad Schubert, Program Dir.; Stacy Connor, Music Dir. **Wattage:** 3000. **Ad Rates:** Advertising accepted; rates available upon request. **URL:** http://www.wznf.com.

VANDALIA†, pop. 5,338.

Fayette Co. (S). 68 m NE of St. Louis Mo. Manufactures pencils, draperies, mechanical seals, concrete building products, feed, electric transformers, telephone booths, plastic bottles. Oil wells. Grain, dairy farms. Corn, wheat, beans.

9885 Vandalia Leader Union
Landmark Community Newspapers, Inc.
229 S. 5th St. Phone: (618)283-3374
Vandalia, IL 62471 Fax: (618)283-0977
Publication E-mail: leader@fgi.net

Community newspaper. **Founded:** 1864. **Freq:** Semiweekly (Wed. and Fri.). **Print Method:** Offset. **Cols./Page:** 6. **Col. Width:** 12 picas. **Col. Depth:** 301 agate lines. **Key Personnel:** David Bell, Publisher; Sheila Spaeth, Advertising Mgr. **Subscription Rates:** $29.95 individuals in county. **Remarks:** Accepts advertising.
Ad Rates: BW: $942 **Circ:** 5,300
4C: $1,173
SAU: $7

9886 WPMB-AM - 1500
232 S. 4th St. Phone: (618)283-2325
PO Box 100 Fax: (618)283-1503
Vandalia, IL 62471

Format: Middle-of-the-Road (MOR); Oldies. **Networks:** Agri-Voice; Tribune Radio. **Founded:** 1963. **Operating Hours:** 12 hrs. Daily; 5% network, 95% local. **Key Personnel:** Don Hecke, General Mgr.; Bernice Hinrichs, Office Mgr.; Dan Michel, Operations Mgr.; Darrell Isbell, Sales Mgr.; John Harris, Manager; Valerie Zuraw, News Dir. **Local Programs:** *Morning Show* 8-9 a.m., Bernice Hinrichs; *Swap Show* 11:08-11:30 a.m., Dan Michel. **Wattage:** 250. **Ad Rates:** $9-15.25 for 30 seconds; $11.25-18.25 for 60 seconds.

VERNON

9887 Vernon Hills News
Lakeland Publishers, Inc.
30 S. Whitney St. Phone: (847)223-8161
PO Box 268 Fax: (847)223-8810
Grayslake, IL 60030-0268
Publication E-mail: edit@lnd.com

Community newspaper. **Subtitle:** Vernon Hills News. **Founded:** 1958. **Freq:** Weekly (Thurs.). **Print Method:** Offset. **Trim Size:** 11 x 17. **Cols./Page:** 5. **Col. Width:** 2 inches. **Col. Depth:** 16 inches. **Key Personnel:** W.H. Schroeder, Publisher; Esther Hebbard, Advertising Mgr.; Rhonda Hetrick Burke, Editor. **Subscription Rates:** $24.50; $35 out of area. **Remarks:** Accepts advertising.
Ad Rates: BW: $674.80 **Circ:** ‡2,810
4C: $1,023.40
SAU: $8.48

VERNON HILLS, pop. 9,827.

Lake Co. (NE) 8 m N of Prairie View. Residential.

9888 ALA News
Association of Legal Administrators
175 E. Hawthorn Pkwy., Ste. 325 Phone: (847)816-1212 Fax: (847)816-1213
Vernon Hills, IL 60061-1428
Professional magazine covering legal management for mem-

bers. **Founded:** 1981. **Freq:** Bimonthly. **Trim Size:** 8 3/8 x 10 7/8. **Cols./Page:** 3. **Col. Width:** 2 1/4 inches. **Col. Depth:** 10 inches. **Key Personnel:** Kirstin Finneran, Editor, kfinneran@alanet.org; Rich Murowski, Advertising Mgr. **Subscription Rates:** $36 individuals. **Remarks:** Accepts advertising. **URL:** http://www.alanet.org.
Ad Rates: BW: $1,191 **Circ:** Controlled 8,550
4C: $1,400

Deerfield Review - See Deerfield

Grayslake Review - See Grayslake

Gurnee Review - See Gurnee

Highland Park News - See Highland Park

Lake Forester - See Lake Forest

9889 Legal Management
Association of Legal Administrators
175 E. Hawthorn Pkwy., Ste. 325 Phone: (847)816-1212
Vernon Hills, IL 60061-1428 Fax: (847)816-1213
Publication E-mail: editorial@alanet.org

Magazine covering aspects of law office management, including systems and technology, human resource management, finance, planning, and marketing. **Subtitle:** The Journal of the Association of Legal Administrators. **Founded:** 1982. **Freq:** Bimonthly. **Print Method:** Offset. **Trim Size:** 8 1/8 x 10 7/8. **Cols./Page:** 3 and 3. **Col. Width:** 40 inches and 26 nonpareils. **Col. Depth:** 126 agate lines. **Key Personnel:** Jay Strother, Editor, editorial@alanet.org; Rich Murowski, Ad Sales Representative, phone (630)980-6570. **ISSN:** 0745-0532. **Subscription Rates:** Free to qualified subscribers; $10 single issue. **Remarks:** Advertising accepted; rates available upon request. **Online:** Westlaw. **URL:** http://www.alanet.org. **Alt. Formats:** Microform; Mailing labels. **Former name**: Legal Administrator.
Circ: Controlled ‡25,200

Libertyville Review - See Libertyville

Mundelein Review - See Mundelein

The Review of Lake Villa/Lindenhurst - See Lindenhurst

9890 Vernon Hills Review
Pioneer Press Newspapers
850 N. Milwaukee Ave. Phone: (847)680-6690
Vernon Hills, IL 60061 Fax: (847)573-2500

Community newspaper (tabloid). **Founded:** 1972. **Freq:** Weekly (Thurs.). **Print Method:** Offset. **Cols./Page:** 5. **Col. Width:** 10 inches. **Col. Depth:** 14 inches. **Key Personnel:** Sheila Richard, Editor; Paul Sassone, Managing Editor. **Subscription Rates:** $14.95 individuals; $16.50 out of county. **Remarks:** Advertising accepted; rates available upon request.
Circ: Thurs. ★2,098

VIENNA†, pop. 1,420.

Johnson Co. (S). 34 m NW of Paducah, Ky. Nursery. Timber. Diversified farming. Corn, dairy products, beef cattle.

9891 The Vienna Times
PO Box 457 Phone: (618)658-4321
Vienna, IL 62995
Community newspaper. **Founded:** 1879. **Freq:** Weekly (Thurs.). **Print Method:** Offset. **Cols./Page:** 6. **Col. Width:** 24 nonpareils. **Col. Depth:** 294 agate lines. **Key Personnel:** Don Sanders, Editor and Publisher. **Subscription Rates:** $22 individuals; $26 out of area. **Remarks:** Accepts advertising.
Ad Rates: GLR: $.24 **Circ:** ‡2,800
BW: $526.32
SAU: $4.76

VILLA GROVE, pop. 2,707.

Douglas Co. (E). 23 m S of Champaign. Manufactures farm implements. Machine shop. Cannery. Grain elevator. Coal mining. Hybrid see growing. Diversified farming.

9892 Villa Grove News
Holmes Publications
PO Box 20 Phone: (217)832-4201
Villa Grove, IL 61956 Fax: (217)834-4001

Community newspaper. **Founded:** 1904. **Freq:** Weekly (Thurs.). **Print Method:** Offset. **Cols./Page:** 6. **Col. Width:** 29 nonpareils. **Col. Depth:** 294 agate lines. **Key Personnel:** Jeffrey W. Holmes, Editor and Publisher. **Subscription Rates:** $16 individuals. **Remarks:** Accepts advertising.
Ad Rates: SAU: $4.30 **Circ:** ‡1,750

VIRGINIA†, pop. 1,825.

Cass Co. (WC). 11 m SE of Beardstown. Residential.

9893 Cass County Star-Gazette
Beardstown Newspapers, Inc.
117 E Springfield St. Phone: (217)452-3513
Virginia, IL 62691 Fax: (217)452-3382
Publisher E-mail: stargaz@cityscape.net

Community newspaper. **Founded:** 1872. **Freq:** Weekly (Wed.). **Print Method:** Offset. **Cols./Page:** 8. **Col. Width:** 1.5 inches. **Col. Depth:** 21 inches. **Key Personnel:** William Mitchell; Publisher; Nikki Kaul, Editor. **Subscription Rates:** $24. **Remarks:** Accepts advertising. **Alt. Formats:** Microform. **Formed by the merger of**: Virginia Gazette; Illinoian Star. **Formerly**: Virginia Gazette of Cass County.
Ad Rates: BW: $871.92 **Circ:** Combined 3,300
4C: $1,171.92
SAU: $6.92

9894 Cass Cable TV Inc.
PO Box 200 Phone: (217)452-7725
Virginia, IL 62691 Fax: (217)452-7030

Founded: 1964. **Key Personnel:** Linda Hodges, Office Mgr.; Marvin Seward, Vice President; Donna Troutman, Marketing Manager. **Cities Served:** Ashland, Baylis, Chandlerville, Chatham, Divernon, Easton, Glenarm, Havana, Kampsville, Manito, Milton, Mt. Sterling, Pawnee, Pleasant Plains, Rushville, Tallula, Versailles, Virginia, IL; Palmyra, MO: subscribing households 16,521; 69 channels; 1 community access channel; 24 hours per week community access programming.

WALNUT, pop. 1,513.

Bureau Co. (NW). 20 m S of Sterling. Construction of gravel screening equipment & conveyors and cheese plants. Grain, dairy farms. Corn, wheat, oats.

9895 The Walnut Leader
110 Jackson St. Phone: (815)379-9290
PO Box 280 Fax: (815)379-2659
Walnut, IL 61376
Community newspaper. **Founded:** 1892. **Freq:** Weekly (Mon.). **Print Method:** Offset. **Cols./Page:** 6. **Col. Width:** 21 nonpareils. **Col. Depth:** 224 agate lines. **Key Personnel:** Gary Brooks, Editor and Publisher. **Subscription Rates:** $12 individuals. **Remarks:** Accepts advertising.
Ad Rates: 4C: $130.56 **Circ:** ‡2,300
SAU: $1.43

WARREN, pop. 1,595.

Jo Daviess Co. (NW). 26 m NW of Freeport. Micro switches, plastics and chesse factories. Dairy, grain, stock, poultry farms. Corn, oats, barley.

9896 Wadesworth News
Lakeland Publishers, Inc.
30 S. Whitney St. Phone: (847)223-8161
PO Box 268 Fax: (847)223-8810
Grayslake, IL 60030-0268
Publication E-mail: edit@lnd.com

Community newspaper. **Founded:** 1960. **Freq:** Weekly (Thurs.). **Print Method:** Offset. **Trim Size:** 11 x 17. **Cols./Page:** 5. **Col. Width:** 2 inches. **Col. Depth:** 16 inches. **Key Personnel:** W.H. Schroeder, Editor and Publisher; Jill A. DePasquale, Advertising Mgr. **Subscription Rates:** $24.50 individuals; $35 out of area. **Remarks:** Accepts advertising. **Formerly**: Warren Newport Press.
Ad Rates: BW: $674.80 **Circ:** ‡2,378
4C: $1,023.40
SAU: $8.48

WASHBURN, pop. 1,206.

Woodford Co. (NC). 25 m NE of Peoria. Cheese, feed, hog and poultry remedies manufactured. Dairy, poultry, grain farms. Corn, oats, wheat.

9897 Leader
PO Box 490 Phone: (309)248-7413
Washburn, IL 61570
Newspaper. **Founded:** 1890. **Freq:** Weekly (Thurs.). **Print Method:** Offset. **Cols./Page:** 4. **Col. Width:** 27 nonpareils. **Col. Depth:** 203 agate lines. **Key Personnel:** Scotte Hubbell, Publisher, phone (309)367-2335, fax (309)367-4271. **Subscription Rates:** $25 individuals. **Remarks:** Accepts advertising.
Ad Rates: PCI: $21 **Circ:** 1,000

WASHINGTON, pop. 10,364.

Tazewell Co. (NC). 12 m E of Peoria. Residential.

9898 Courier
100 Ford Ln. Phone: (309)444-3139
PO Box 349 Fax: (309)444-8505
Washington, IL 61571
Publication E-mail: hagelnews1@aol.com

Local newspaper. **Founded:** 1955. **Freq:** Weekly (Wed.). **Print Method:** Offset. **Trim Size:** 10 1/4 x 15. **Cols./Page:** 5. **Col. Width:** 2 inches. **Col. Depth:** 15 inches. **Key Personnel:** Roger Hagel, Publisher; Joi DeArmond, Editor. **Subscription Rates:** $19.50 individuals; $24.50 institutions. **Remarks:** Accepts advertising.
Ad Rates: BW: $637 **Circ:** Paid ‡500
4C: $1,495 Free ‡22,700
SAU: $12.95
PCI: $12.95

WATERLOO†, pop. 4,646.

Monroe Co. (SW). 24 m S of St Louis, Mo. Suburban. Retail trade center. Feed mill; grain elevators. Diversified farming.

9899 Republic Times
Republic Times Inc.
222 S. Main Phone: (618)939-3814
PO Box 147 Fax: (618)939-3815
Waterloo, IL 62298
Community newspaper. **Founded:** 1890. **Freq:** Weekly (Wed.). **Print Method:** Offset. **Trim Size:** 14 1/2 x 22 3/4. **Cols./Page:** 6. **Col. Width:** 2 1/16 inches. **Col. Depth:** 21 1/2 inches. **Key Personnel:** Mark Schmersahl, Publisher; Marvin Cortner, Managing Editor; Laurel Kelly, Advertising Mgr.; Tammy Clubbs, Office Mgr.; Frank Kohn, Sports Editor. **USPS:** 669-060. **Subscription Rates:** $18 individuals; 20 state; $23 out of state.
Ad Rates: GLR: $.6 **Circ:** ‡4128
4C: $75
PCI: $6.6

9900 Republic-Times Shopper
Republic Times Inc.
222 S. Main Phone: (618)939-3814
PO Box 147 Fax: (618)939-3815
Waterloo, IL 62298
Shopper. **Founded:** 1981. **Freq:** Weekly (Mon.). **Print Method:** Offset. **Trim Size:** 14 1/2 x 22 3/4. **Cols./Page:** 6. **Col. Width:** 25 nonpareils. **Col. Depth:** 297 agate lines. **Key Personnel:** Mark Schmersahl, Publisher; Marvin Cortner, Managing Editor; Laurel Kelly, Advertising Mgr.; Tammy Clubbs, Office Mgr.; Frank Kohn, Sports Editor. **Subscription Rates:** free. **Remarks:** Advertising accepted; rates available upon request.
Circ: Free ‡11,388

WATSEKA†, pop. 5,543.

Iroquois Co. (E). 25 m SE of Kankakee. Cheese, butter, radio condensers, business forms, transformers manufactured. Greenhouse. Hatchery. Stock, poultry, grain, dairy farms.

9901 Illinois Spirit Shopping Guide
PO Box 250 Phone: (815)432-5227
1492 E. Walnut Fax: (815)432-5159
Watseka, IL 60970
Shopper. **Founded:** 1966. **Freq:** Weekly (Tues.). **Print Method:** Offset. **Cols./Page:** 6. **Col. Width:** 9 1/2 picas. **Col. Depth:** 14 inches. **Key Personnel:** Kevin Lashbrook, Publisher; Carol Christy, Advertising Mgr. **USPS:** 669-520. **Online:** Quest Network 1-800-Free-List. **Formerly**: Times-Spirit Shopping Guide.
Ad Rates: BW: $441 **Circ:** Free ‡2,797
PCI: $5.25

9902 Iroquois County's Times-Republic
Twin States Publishing
1492 E. Walnut St. Phone: (815)432-5227
PO Box 250 Fax: (815)432-5159
Watseka, IL 60970
Local newspaper. **Founded:** 1870. **Freq:** Daily (eve.). **Print Method:** Offset. **Trim Size:** 11 1/4 x 15. **Cols./Page:** 6. **Col. Width:** 9 1/2 picas. **Col. Depth:** 14 inches. **Key Personnel:** Carla Waters, Editor; Kevin Lashbrook, Publisher; Carol Christy, General Mgr. **ISSN:** 6695-2000. **Subscription Rates:** $89 by mail; $99 out of area; $110 out of state. **Remarks:** Accepts advertising.
Ad Rates: BW: $357.80 **Circ:** 2,813
PCI: $4.25

9903 Midwest Cablevision
PO Box 425
Watseka, IL 60970

Formerly: Star Cablevision (1992). **Key Personnel:** Linda Wyndell, Manager. **Cities Served:** Momence, IN.

9904 WGFA-AM - 1360
1950 North Rd. Phone: (815)432-4955
Watseka, IL 60970 Fax: (815)432-4957
E-mail: 941fm@wgfaradio.com

Format: Big Band/Nostalgia; Easy Listening. **Networks:** ABC. **Founded:** 1960. **Operating Hours:** 6 a.m.-8 p.m. **Key Personnel:** R.A. Martin, President; Maggie Martin, Contact, mmartin@wgfaradio.com. **Wattage:** 1000. **Ad Rates:** $19-37 for 30 seconds; $25-46 for 60 seconds. Combined rates with WGFA-FM. **URL:** http://www.wgfaradio.com.

9905 WGFA-FM - 94.1
1950 North Rd. Phone: (815)432-4955
Watseka, IL 60970 Fax: (815)432-4957
E-mail: mmartin@wgfaradio.com

Format: Adult Contemporary. **Networks:** ABC. **Owner:** Iroquois County Broadcasting Co., at above address. **Founded:** 1961. **Operating Hours:** Continuous. **ADI:** Springfield-Decatur-Champaign, IL. **Key Personnel:** Ron Hunt, Contact, rhunt@wgfaradio.com. **Wattage:** 50,000. **Ad Rates:** $28-37 for 30 seconds; $35-46 for 60 seconds. Combined advertising rates available with WGFA-AM. **URL:** http://www.wgfaradio.com.

WAUCONDA, pop. 5,688.

Lake Co. (NE). 20 m SW of Waukegan. Suburban. Summer resort. Light Industry. Dairy Farms.

9906 The Classical Bulletin
Bolchazy-Carducci Publishers, Inc.
1000 Brown St., Unit 101 Phone: (847)526-4344
Wauconda, IL 60084 Fax: (847)526-2867
Free: (800)392-6453
Publication E-mail: cb@bolchazy.com
Publisher E-mail: latin@bolchazy.com

Magazine on classical languages, history, and literature. **Founded:** 1925. **Freq:** Semiannual. **Print Method:** Offset. **Trim Size:** 6 x 9. **Cols./Page:** 1. **Key Personnel:** Ladislaus J. Bolchazy, Editor, bolchazy@decphi.com. **ISSN:** 0009-8337. **Subscription Rates:** $25 individuals; $30 Canada; $35 other countries; $40 institutions. **Remarks:** Accepts advertising.
Ad Rates: BW: $250 **Circ:** Paid ‡520
Non-paid ‡480

9907 SuperAutomotive Service
Irving-Cloud Publishing Co.
379 Hollow Hill Dr. Phone: (847)487-7010
Wauconda, IL 60084 Fax: (847)487-5589

Trade magazine covering the technical aspects of normal service station/tire dealership/garage repair and service operations. **Subtitle:** An Irving-Cloud Publication Serving and Professional Aftermarket Technicians. **Founded:** June 1929. **Freq:** Monthly. **Print Method:** Offset. **Trim Size:** 8 x 10 3/4. **Cols./Page:** 3 and 2. **Col. Width:** 2 3/16 and 3 inches. **Col. Depth:** 140 agate lines. **Key Personnel:** Martin Schultz, Editor; Taylor L. Kennedy, Jr., Publisher; Charles S. Wilson IV, Sales and Mktg. Dir. **ISSN:** 0896-0437. **Subscription Rates:** $40 individuals; $50 other countries; $4 single issue. **Remarks:** Accepts advertising.
Ad Rates: BW: $6,950 **Circ:** Non-paid ‡104,121
4C: $9,210

9908 Wauconda Leader
Lakeland Publishers, Inc.
30 S. Whitney St. Phone: (847)223-8161
PO Box 268 Fax: (847)223-8810
Grayslake, IL 60030-0268
Publication E-mail: edit@lnd.com

Community newspaper. **Subtitle:** Wauconda Leader. **Founded:** 1888. **Freq:** Weekly (Thurs.). **Print Method:** Offset. **Trim Size:** 11 x 17. **Cols./Page:** 5. **Col. Width:** 2 inches. **Col. Depth:** 16 inches. **Key Personnel:** W.H. Schroeder, Publisher; Esther Hebbard, Advertising Mgr.; Rhonda Hetrick Burke, Editor. **Subscription Rates:** $24.50 individuals; $35 out of area. **Remarks:** Accepts advertising.
Ad Rates: BW: $674.80 **Circ:** ‡5,300
4C: $1,023.40
SAU: $8.48

WAUKEGAN†, pop. 67,653.

Lake Co. (NE). On Lake Michigan, 36 m N of Chicago. Good harbor. Fisheries. Manufactures asbestos and gypsum products, roofing, glass products, electronic components, pharmaceuticals, bakery goods, iron and brass castings, outboard motors, auto accessories, confectionery, envelopes, milling machines, lacquers, tools, dies. mink farms.

9909 The News Sun
Copley Newspapers/Copley Press
100 W. Madison St. Phone: (708)249-7200
Waukegan, IL 60085 Fax: (847)249-7202
Publication E-mail: nsdrive@aol.com

General newspaper. **Founded:** 1892. **Freq:** Daily (eve.) and Sat. (morn.). **Print Method:** offset. **Cols./Page:** 6 and 10. **Col. Width:** 2 1/16 and 1 1/4 inches. **Col. Depth:** 21 and 21 inches. **Key Personnel:** Arthur E. Wible, Publisher; William J. Todd, General Mgr.; William Brennan, Advertising Mgr.; Chris Adams, Managing Editor. **Subscription Rates:** $130 individuals. **Remarks:** Accepts advertising. **Absorbed:** South West News-Sun (1990).
Ad Rates: GLR: $1.29 **Circ:** Mon.-Fri. ★**24,585**
BW: $2,268 Sat. ★**28,350**
4C: $2,518
SAU: $20.97
PCI: $18

9910 U.S. Cable of Lake County
3233 W. Grand Ave. Phone: (708)336-7200
Waukegan, IL 60085 Fax: (708)336-6233

Owner: U.S. Cable Corp., 28 W. Grand Ave., Montvale, NJ 07645, (201)930-9000. **Founded:** 1980. **Key Personnel:** Paul Ashley, General Mgr.; Jim Emrick, Chief Engineer; Diane Schepis, Contact; Steve Tracy, Contact. **Cities Served:** Unincorporated Lake County, IL.: subscribing households 53,000; 53 channels; 1 community access channel.

9911 WKRS-AM - 1220
3250 Belvidere Rd. Phone: (847)336-7900
Waukegan, IL 60085 Fax: (847)336-1523

Format: News; Sports; Information. **Networks:** ABC; Illinois News. **Founded:** 1949. **Operating Hours:** 6 a.m.-10 p.m. **ADI:** Chicago (LaSalle), IL. **Key Personnel:** Mike Topoll, General Mgr., topollsr@xlc.com. **Wattage:** 1000. **Ad Rates:** $30-45 for 60 seconds.

9912 WXLC-FM - 102.3
3250 Belvidere Rd. Phone: (847)336-7900
Waukegan, IL 60085 Fax: (847)336-1523

Format: Top 40. **Networks:** Independent. **Operating Hours:** Continuous. **Key Personnel:** Mike Topoll, General Mgr. **Wattage:** 3000. **URL:** http://www.xlc.com.

WAVERLY, pop. 1,537.

Morgan Co. (WC). 25 M SW OF Springfield. Grain, stock farms. Corn, wheat, soybeans.

9913 Waverly Journal
130 S. Pearl Phone: (217)435-9221
PO Box 78 Fax: (217)435-4511
Waverly, IL 62692
Community newspaper. **Founded:** 1872. **Freq:** Weekly (Fri.). **Print Method:** Offset. **Cols./Page:** 5. **Col. Width:** 23 nonpareils. **Col. Depth:** 224 agate lines. **Key Personnel:** Nancy P. Springer, Publisher; Julie A. Springer, Editor. **USPS:** 776-420. **Subscription Rates:** $24 individuals; $28 out of state. **Remarks:** Accepts advertising.
Ad Rates: GLR: $.35 **Circ:** ‡1,350
BW: $160
SAU: $3.94
PCI: $2.00

WEST CHICAGO, pop. 12,550.

Du Page Co. (NE). 14 m NE of Aurora.

9914 The West Chicago Press
Press Newspapers
100 Arbor Ave. Phone: (630)231-0500
West Chicago, IL 60185 Fax: (630)231-6813

Community newspaper. **Founded:** 1907. **Freq:** Weekly (Thurs.). **Print Method:** Offset. **Trim Size:** 10 x 16. **Cols./Page:** 4. **Col. Width:** 29 nonpareils. **Col. Depth:** 224 agate lines. **Key Personnel:** Wayne G. Woltman, Editor and Publisher; Scott Hubbell, Advertising Mgr. **Subscription Rates:** $15 individuals. **Remarks:** Accepts advertising.
Ad Rates: GLR: $1.07 **Circ:** ‡5,000
BW: $561
4C: $1,029

Winfield Press - See Winfield

WEST LAFAYETTE

9915 Seedstock Edge
National Swine Registry
1769 US Highway 52 W. Phone: (765)463-3594
PO Box 2417 Fax: (765)497-2959
West Lafayette, IL 47996-2417
Publisher E-mail: nsr@nationalswine.com

Magazine containing general swine information. **Founded:** 1994. **Freq:** 9/year. **Print Method:** Offset. **Trim Size:** 7 7/8 x 10 3/4. **Cols./Page:** 3. **Col. Width:** 27 nonpareils. **Col. Depth:** 140 agate lines. **Key Personnel:** Elaine Hughes, Managing Editor; Dan Baker, Advertising Coord. **ISSN:** 1079-7963. **Subscription Rates:** $15 individuals. **Remarks:** Accepts advertising. **Formerly:** Hampshire Herdsman; Duroc News; Yorkshire Journal.
Ad Rates: BW: $450 **Circ:** Paid 4,900
4C: $700 Non-paid 250
PCI: $10

WEST SALEM, pop. 1,145.

Edwards Co. (E). 50 m NE of Mount Vernon. Manufactures oil filters, castings. Oil. Dairy, poultry, stock, grain farms. Corn, wheat, soybeans.

9916 Times Advocate
108 N. Albion St. Phone: (618)456-8808
West Salem, IL 62476 Fax: (618)456-8809

Community newspaper. **Founded:** Feb. 1, 1900. **Freq:** Semiweekly (Wed. and Fri.). **Print Method:** Offset. **Cols./Page:** 8. **Col. Width:** 9 1/2 picas. **Col. Depth:** 21 1/2 inches. **Key Personnel:** Harry Bradham, Editor and Publisher. **Subscription Rates:** $36 individuals.
Ad Rates: GLR: $.25 **Circ:** Paid 1,100
BW: $602 Free 7,400
4C: $802
SAU: $4.67
PCI: $3.50

WESTCHESTER, pop. 17,730.

Cook Co. (NE). 7 m SW of Oak Park.

9917 Westchester Herald
Pioneer Press Newspapers
1148 Westgate Ave. Phone: (708)383-3200
Oak Park, IL 60301 Fax: (708)383-3678

Community newspaper (tabloid). **Founded:** 1985. **Freq:** Weekly (Wed.). **Print Method:** Offset. **Cols./Page:** 5. **Col. Width:** 10 inches. **Col. Depth:** 14 inches. **Key Personnel:** Paul Sassone, Managing Editor; Kevin Beese, Editor. **Subscription Rates:** $9.95; $11.95 out of county. **Remarks:** Combined advertising rates available with other Pioneer Press Newspapers.
Circ: Wed. ★**1,289**

WHEATON†, pop. 43,043.

Du Page Co. (NE). 25 m W of Chicago. Wheaton College. Residential. Nurseries. Diversified farming.

9918 Evangelical Missions Quarterly
Evangelical Missions Information Service
PO Box 794 Phone: (630)752-7158
Wheaton, IL 60189 Fax: (630)752-7155
Publication E-mail: emqjournal@aol.com
Publisher E-mail: emis@wheaton.edu

Religious missionary journal. **Subtitle:** The Journal for Professional Missionaries. **Founded:** 1964. **Freq:** Quarterly. **Print Method:** Offset. **Trim Size:** 5 1/2 x 8 1/2. **Cols./Page:** 1. **Col. Width:** 42 nonpareils. **Col. Depth:** 105 agate lines. **Key Personnel:** Gary Corwin, Editor, 76065.2115@compuserve.com. **ISSN:** 014 -3359. **Subscription Rates:** $21.95 individuals; $6 single issue.
Ad Rates: BW: $600 **Circ:** ‡7,500
4C: $975

9919 Pioneer Clubs Perspective
Pioneer Clubs
PO Box 788 Phone: (630)293-1600
Wheaton, IL 60189-0788 Fax: (630)293-3053
Publication E-mail: pcgwall@enteract.com

Magazine for lay leaders of Pioneer Clubs in churches (clubs for boys and girls age 2 to grade 12). **Founded:** 1967. **Freq:** 3/year. **Print Method:** Offset. **Trim Size:** 8 1/2 x 11. **Cols./Page:** 3. **Col. Width:** 14 picas. **Col. Depth:** 60 picas. **Key Personnel:** Rebecca Powell Parat, Editor, bparat@yahoo.com; Marilyn Schneider, Asst. Editor. **Subscription Rates:** $6 individuals. **Remarks:** Advertising not accepted.
Circ: ‡24,000

9920 The Quest
Theosophical Society in America
PO Box 270 Phone: (630)668-1571
Wheaton, IL 60189-0270 Fax: (630)668-4976
Publication E-mail: questmag@theasophia.org

Journal focusing on a wholistic world view of philosophy, religion, science, and the arts. **Subtitle:** A Quarterly Journal of Philosophy, Science, Religion, and the Arts. **Founded:** 1988. **Freq:** Bimonthly. **Print Method:** Web offset. **Trim Size:** 8 1/4 x 10 3/4. **Cols./Page:** 2. **Col. Width:** 16 picas. **Col. Depth:** 7.25 picas. **Key Personnel:** John Algeo, Editor. **ISSN:** 1040-533X. **Subscription Rates:** $15.97. $3.95 single issue. **Remarks:** Accepts advertising.
Ad Rates: BW: $500 **Circ:** 20,000

9921 Today's Christian Woman
Christianity Today, Inc.
465 Gundersen Dr. Phone: (630)260-6200
Carol Stream, IL 60188 Fax: (630)260-0114
Publication E-mail: tcwedit@aol.com

Religious magazine for contemporary Christian women. **Founded:** 1978. **Freq:** Bimonthly. **Print Method:** Offset. **Trim Size:** 8 x 10 3/4. **Cols./Page:** 3. **Col. Width:** 2 1/4 inches. **Col. Depth:** 10 inches. **Key Personnel:** Ramona Cramer Tucker, Editor, tcwedit@aol.com; Jane J. Struckbrink, Sr. Ed.; Harold L. Myra, Publisher. **ISSN:** 0163-1799. **Subscription Rates:** $17.95 individuals; $3.95 single issue. **Remarks:** Accepts advertising. **Online:** America Online, Inc. **URL:** http://www.christianity.net/tcw.
Ad Rates: BW: $4,818.65 **Circ:** Paid ‡305,000
4C: $6,025.65 Non-paid ‡6,892
PCI: $330

9922 Wheaton Journal
Copley Newspapers/Copley Press
PO Box 269 Phone: (708)462-5349
Naperville, IL 60566 Fax: (708)355-2432

General newspaper. **Founded:** 1910. **Freq:** Daily (eve.), Sat. and Sun. (morn.). **Print Method:** Letterpress. **Cols./Page:** 6. **Col. Width:** 24 nonpareils. **Col. Depth:** 301 agate lines. **Key Personnel:** D. Ray Wilson, Publisher; Robert Propernick, General Mgr. **Subscription Rates:** $78 individuals. **Remarks:** Accepts advertising. **Formerly:** The Daily Journal (1992).
Ad Rates: BW: $1,549.13 **Circ:** ‡8,609
4C: $1,729.13
PCI: $12.15

9923 Wheaton Leader
Glen News Printing Co.
460 Pennsylvania Ave., No. 352 Phone: (708)469-0100
Glen Ellyn, IL 60137-4402 Fax: (708)469-4472

Community newspaper. **Freq:** Weekly. **Print Method:** Offset. **Cols./Page:** 5. **Col. Width:** 2 inches. **Col. Depth:** 16 inches. **Key Personnel:** Patricia Schwarze, Editor; Virginia Stone, Publisher; Stuart Stone, Publisher. **Subscription Rates:** $20 individuals.

9924 Wheaton Press
Press Publications
112 S. York St. Phone: (630)834-0900
Elmhurst, IL 60126 Fax: (630)834-0910
Publisher E-mail: presspub@aol.com

Community newspaper. **Founded:** 1923. **Freq:** Weekly (Thurs.). **Print Method:** Offset. **Cols./Page:** 5. **Col. Width:** 2 inches. **Col. Depth:** 16 inches. **Key Personnel:** Dave Fornell, Editor, phone (630)307-1101; Rosemarie T. Cruger, Publisher; William Haman, Advertising Mgr. **Subscription Rates:** Free; $28 by mail.
Circ: (Not Reported)

9925 WETN-FM - 88.1
Wheaton College Phone: (708)752-5074
501 E. College Ave. Fax: (708)752-5286
Wheaton, IL 60187
E-mail: wetn@wheaton.edu

Format: Religious; Contemporary Christian; Educational. **Owner:** Wheaton College Board of Trustees, at above address. **Founded:** 1962. **Operating Hours:** Continuous. **Key Personnel:** David Houk, Asst STA; John Rorvik, General Mgr. **Local Programs:** *Contate Domino*, John Fawcett; *Jazz Room*, Ron Henzel; *Staying on Course*, Bill Lothers. **Wattage:** 250. **Ad Rates:** Noncommercial.

WHEELING, pop. 23,266.

Cook Co. (NE). 23 m NW of Chicago. Manufactures office and data communications products, paint, paint shakers, insecticides, aluminum foil, tools and dies.

9926 Wheeling Countryside
Pioneer Press Newspapers
291 N. Dunton Ave. Phone: (847)797-5100
Arlington Heights, IL 60004 Fax: (847)797-5151

Community newspaper. **Freq:** Weekly (Thurs.). **Key Personnel:** Paul Sassone, Managing Editor; David Kirkpatrick, Editor. **Subscription Rates:** $18.95 Local Annual. **Remarks:** Accepts advertising. **URL:** http://www.pioneerlocal.com.
Circ: Thurs. ★2,089

WHITE HALL, pop. 2,935.

Greene Co. (W). 4 m SW of Roodhouse. Residential

9927 Greene Prairie Press
112 E. Sherman Phone: (217)742-3313
PO Box 261 Fax: (217)742-3596
White Hall, IL 62092
Community newspaper. **Founded:** 1898. **Freq:** Weekly (Thurs.). **Print Method:** Offset. **Cols./Page:** 5. **Col. Width:** 24 nonpareils. **Col. Depth:** 185 agate lines. **Key Personnel:** Elmer Fedder, Publisher. **USPS:** 459-780. **Subscription Rates:** $24 individuals; $29 out of country. **Remarks:** Accepts advertising.
Ad Rates: BW: $240 **Circ:** 2,900
PCI: $3.64

WILLIAMSFIELD

9928 Williamsfield Times
Tri-County News Edition
116 S. Magnolia Phone: (309)742-2521
PO Box 289 Fax: (309)742-2511
Elmwood, IL 61529
Community newspaper. **Founded:** 1871. **Freq:** Weekly (Thurs.). **Print Method:** Offset. **Cols./Page:** 6. **Col. Width:** 20 nonpareils. **Col. Depth:** 224 agate lines. **Key Personnel:** DeEllda Swindler, Publisher. **Subscription Rates:** $16 individuals.
Ad Rates: BW: $192 **Circ:** ‡625
4C: $292
PCI: $2.50

WILMETTE, pop. 28,229.

Cook Co. (NE). 14 m N of Chicago. Residential.

9929 The Informer
The Simon Foundation for Continence
PO Box 835 Phone: (847)864-3913
Wilmette, IL 60091 Fax: (847)864-9758
Free: (800)237-4666

Magazine for persons with bladder or bowel incontinence. **Freq:** Quarterly. **Subscription Rates:** $15 individuals. **Remarks:** Advertising not accepted. **URL:** http://www.simonfoundation.org.
Circ: Paid 150,000

9930 Law and Order
1000 Skokie Blvd. Phone: (847)256-8555
Wilmette, IL 60091 Fax: (847)256-8574
Publication E-mail: laworder@concentric.net

Law enforcement trade magazine. **Subtitle:** The Magazine for Police Management. **Founded:** 1953. **Freq:** Monthly. **Print Method:** Offset. **Trim Size:** 8 1/8 x 10 7/8. **Cols./Page:** 3. **Col. Width:** 26 nonpareils. **Col. Depth:** 140 agate lines. **Key Personnel:** Bruce Cameron, Editor; Scott Kingwill, Publisher. **USPS:** 079-430. **Subscription Rates:** $22 individuals.
Ad Rates: BW: $2,400 **Circ:** Paid 11,890
4C: $3,100 Controlled 19,888

9931 World Order
National Spiritual Assembly of the Baha'is of the United States
415 Linden Ave. Phone: (847)251-1854
Wilmette, IL 60091-2886 Fax: (847)251-3652
Publication E-mail: worldorder@usbnc.org

Religious magazine. **Founded:** 1966. **Freq:** Quarterly. **Print Method:** Offset. **Trim Size:** 7 x 10 in. **Cols./Page:** 3. **Col. Width:** 27 nonpareils. **Col. Depth:** 140 agate lines. **Key Personnel:** Dr. Betty J. Fisher, Editor. **ISSN:** 0043-8804. **Subscription Rates:** $19 individuals; $4.75 single issue. **Remarks:** Advertising not accepted.
Circ: ‡1,500

WILMINGTON, pop. 4,424.

Will Co. (NE). 16 m S of Joliet. Manufactures tissues, napkins, feminine hygiene products, felts, rooting materials. Agriculture.

9932 The Coal City Courant
The Free Press Newspapers
PO Box 327
Wilmington, IL 60481
Publisher E-mail: wilfrepres@collnt.com

Community newspaper. **Founded:** 1901. **Freq:** Weekly (Wed.). **Print Method:** Offset. **Cols./Page:** 6. **Col. Depth:** 21 nonpareils. **Key Personnel:** Eric Fisher, Editor. **USPS:** 120-060. **Subscription Rates:** $24 individuals; $32 out of state. **Remarks:** Accepts advertising.
Ad Rates: GLR: $.40 **Circ:** 21,900
BW: $1,386.75
SAU: $10
PCI: $2.90

WINCHESTER†, pop. 1,716.

Scott Co. (W). 18 m SW of Jacksonville. Agriculture. Corn, wheat, oats.

9933 The Winchester Times
Roodhouse Record Inc.
4 S. Hill St. Phone: (217)742-3313
Winchester, IL 62694 Fax: (217)742-3596

Community newspaper. **Founded:** 1865. **Freq:** Weekly (Thurs.). **Print Method:** Offset. **Trim Size:** 5 x 16. **Cols./Page:** 5. **Col. Width:** 24 nonpareils. **Col. Depth:** 294 agate lines. **Key Personnel:** Elmer Fedder, Editor. **USPS:** 686-060. **Subscription Rates:** $21 individuals. **Remarks:** Accepts advertising.
Ad Rates: GLR: $.17 **Circ:** ‡1,800
4C: $90
SAU: $3.25
PCI: $2.90

WINFIELD, pop. 4,422.

Du Page Co. (N.E.) 30 m W. of Chicago. Residential.

9934 Winfield Press
Press Newspapers
100 Arbor Ave. Phone: (630)231-0500
West Chicago, IL 60185 Fax: (630)231-6813

Community newspaper. **Founded:** 1980. **Freq:** Weekly (Thurs.). **Print Method:** Offset. **Trim Size:** 10 x 16. **Cols./Page:** 4. **Col. Width:** 29 nonpareils. **Col. Depth:** 224 agate lines. **Key Personnel:** Wayne G. Woltman, Publisher; Scott Hubbell, Advertising Mgr. **Subscription Rates:** $15 individuals. **Remarks:** Accepts advertising.
Ad Rates: BW: $561 **Circ:** ‡600
4C: $880

WINNETKA, pop. 12,772.

Cook Co. (NE). 19 m N of Chicago. Residential.

9935 The Highlander
560 Green Bay Rd., Ste. 204 Phone: (847)523-4141
Winnetka, IL 60093 Fax: (847)532-7474
Publication E-mail: hilander@gvi.net

Scottish history and culture, publication. **Subtitle:** The Magazine of Scottish Heritage. **Founded:** Mar. 1963. **Freq:** 7/year. **Print Method:** Offset. **Trim Size:** 8 1/2 x 11. **Cols./Page:** 3. **Col. Width:** 2 1/4 inches. **Col. Depth:** 10 inches. **Key Personnel:** David K. Ray, Publisher; Crennan M. Wade, Editor. **ISSN:** 0161-5378. **Subscription Rates:** $17.50 individuals; $4 single issue.
Ad Rates: BW: $700 **Circ:** 35,000
4C: $1,100

9936 Winnetka Talk
Pioneer Press Newspapers
3701 W. Lake Ave. Phone: (847)486-9200
Glenview, IL 60025 Fax: (847)486-7451

Community newspaper (tabloid). **Founded:** 1911. **Freq:** Weekly (Thurs.). **Print Method:** Offset. **Cols./Page:** 5. **Col. Width:** 10 inches. **Col. Depth:** 14 inches. **Key Personnel:** Paul Sassone, Managing Editor; Elaine Fandell, Editor. **USPS:** 686-780. **Subscription Rates:** $29.95 individuals; $31.50 out of county. **Remarks:** Advertising accepted; rates available upon request.
Circ: Thurs. ★5,398

9937 WNTH-FM - 88.1
385 Winnetka Ave. Phone: (847)446-7000
Winnetka, IL 60093 Fax: (847)501-6400
E-mail: wnth@radiolink.net

Format: Public Radio; Talk; News; Sports. **Owner:** New Trier High School, at above address. **Founded:** 1960. **Operating Hours:** 6:30 a.m.-10 p.m. **Key Personnel:** Alex Taft, Station Mgr.; Marisa Wegrzyn, Program Dir. **Local Programs:** *Night*

Talk 8:00 - 10:00 Tuesday, Ross Gianfortune, Public Affairs Director; *Sports Talk* 9:00 - 10:00 Monday, John Corwin, Sports Dir.; *WNTH News* 3:20 - 3:30 Monday-Friday, Andrew Fraerman, Public Affairs Director. **Wattage:** 100. **Ad Rates:** Noncommercial.

WONDER LAKE

9938 Die Casting Management
C-K Publishing, Inc.
3110 Pleasant Dr. Phone: (815)728-0912
Box 247
Wonder Lake, IL 60097
Magazine for the die casting industry. **Founded:** Aug. 1982. **Freq:** Bimonthly. **Print Method:** Offset. **Trim Size:** 8 3/8 x 11. **Cols./Page:** 3. **Col. Width:** 27 nonpareils. **Col. Depth:** 140 agate lines. **Key Personnel:** Robert Crofts, Publisher, editor@diecastmgmt.com. **ISSN:** 0745-449X. **Subscription Rates:** $35 U.S. and Canada; $84 other countries. **Remarks:** Accepts advertising.
Ad Rates: BW: $1,620 **Circ:** Paid ‡55
4C: $2,660 Non-paid ‡4,369
PCI: $50

WOODRIDGE

9939 Chicagoland Golf
Chicagoland Golf Publishing Co.
6825 Hobson Valley Dr., No. 204
Woodridge, IL 60517

Consumer golf magazine. **Founded:** 1989. **Freq:** 15/year. **Print Method:** Offset. **Trim Size:** 11 x 17. **Cols./Page:** 4. **Col. Width:** 14 picas. **Col. Depth:** 16 inches. **Key Personnel:** Phil Kosin, Publisher. **Subscription Rates:** $14. **Remarks:** Accepts advertising.
Ad Rates: BW: $2,045 **Circ:** Paid **1,450**
4C: $2,495 Controlled **41,250**

WORDEN

9940 Madison County Chronicle
Bunker Hill Publications
PO Box 490 Phone: (618)459-3655
Worden, IL 62097-0490 Fax: (618)459-3655

Community newspaper. **Founded:** 1976. **Freq:** Weekly (Thurs.). **Print Method:** Offset. **Cols./Page:** 5. **Col. Width:** 24 nonpareils. **Col. Depth:** 224 agate lines. **Key Personnel:** Vera Eckhardt, Editor; John M. Galer, Publisher. **Subscription Rates:** $10.50 out of area; $12.50 out of state; $14.50. **Remarks:** Accepts advertising. **Formerly**: Hamel and Worden News (Jan. 1987).
Ad Rates: PCI: $4.10 **Circ:** ‡1,100

YATES CITY

9941 Yates City Banner
Tri-County News Edition
116 S. Magnolia Phone: (309)742-2521
PO Box 289 Fax: (309)742-2511
Elmwood, IL 61529
Community newspaper. **Founded:** 1873. **Freq:** Weekly (Thurs.). **Print Method:** Offset. **Cols./Page:** 6. **Col. Width:** 20 nonpareils. **Col. Depth:** 224 agate lines. **Key Personnel:** DeEllda Swindler, Publisher. **Subscription Rates:** $16 individuals.
Ad Rates: BW: $192 **Circ:** ‡350
4C: $292
PCI: $2.50

YORKVILLE†, pop. 3,422.

Kendall Co. (NE). On Fox River, 12 m SW of Aurora. Grain elevator. Grain farms. Corn, oats, soybeans, cattle and hogs.

9942 Fox Valley Shopping News
PO Box 609 Phone: (708)553-7431
Yorkville, IL 60560-0609 Fax: (708)553-0310

Shopper. **Freq:** Weekly (Wed.). **Print Method:** Offset. **Trim Size:** 10 1/4 x 16. **Cols./Page:** 6. **Col. Width:** 20 nonpareils. **Col. Depth:** 224 agate lines. **Key Personnel:** James Stark, Publisher. **Remarks:** Accepts advertising.
Ad Rates: GLR: $.32 **Circ:** Paid 228
Free 21,773

9943 Kendall County Record
PO Box J Phone: (630)553-7034
222 Bridge St. Fax: (630)553-7085
Yorkville, IL 60560
Community newspaper. **Founded:** 1864. **Freq:** Weekly (Thurs.). **Print Method:** Offset. **Cols./Page:** 6. **Col. Width:** 20 nonpareils. **Col. Depth:** 224 agate lines. **Key Personnel:** Kathy Farren, Editor; Jeffery A. Farren, Publisher; Allen Verachtert, Advertising Mgr. **Subscription Rates:** $15 individuals.
Ad Rates: GLR: $.24 **Circ:** ‡3,600

9944 Tri County Today
c/o Fox Alley Shopping News Phone: (815)786-2125
PO Box 609 Fax: (815)553-0310
Yorkville, IL 60560
Newspaper. **Founded:** 1873. **Freq:** Weekly (Wed.). **Print Method:** Offset. **Cols./Page:** 6. **Col. Width:** 18 nonpareils. **Col. Depth:** 224 agate lines. **Key Personnel:** Patricia Stark, Publisher. **Subscription Rates:** $7 individuals. **Remarks:** Accepts advertising.
Ad Rates: GLR: $.22 **Circ:** 3,735

ZION, pop. 17,861.

Lake Co. (NE). 6 m N of Waukegan. Manufactures candy, bakery products, curtains, microfilm industrial coatings, carriers. Horse farms.

9945 The Bargaineer
Zion-Benton News
2719 Elisha Ave. Phone: (847)746-9000
Zion, IL 60099 Fax: (847)746-9150

Shopper. **Freq:** Weekly. **Print Method:** Offset. **Cols./Page:** 5 and 7. **Col. Width:** 2 1/16 and 1 5/16 inches. **Key Personnel:** Frank Misureli, Publisher, phone (414)657-1000, fax (414)657-5105. **Subscription Rates:** Free. **Remarks:** Accepts advertising.
Ad Rates: GLR: $1 **Circ:** Non-paid 35,000
PCI: $9.75

9946 Zion Benton News
2719 Elisa Ave. Phone: (847)746-9000
Zion, IL 60099 Fax: (847)746-9150
Publication E-mail: zion@keroshanews.com

Community newspaper. **Founded:** 1919. **Freq:** Weekly (Thurs.). **Print Method:** Offset. **Cols./Page:** 5. **Col. Width:** 20 nonpareils. **Col. Depth:** 182 agate lines. **Key Personnel:** Mona Shannon, Editor, mona@kenoshanews.com; Frank Misureli, Publisher, phone (414)657-5101. **Subscription Rates:** $20.95 Lake and Kenosha Counties; $22.95 elsewhere. **Remarks:** Accepts advertising.
Ad Rates: GLR: $1 **Circ:** ‡3,500
PCI: $6

INDIANA

State Capital, INDIANAPOLIS

Indiana is bounded on the north by Michigan and Lake Michigan, east by Ohio, south by Kentucky, from which it is separated by the Ohio River, and west by Illinois. The extreme length north and south is 276 miles; its average breadth is 140 miles. The total land area is 35,870 square miles. The greater part of the surface is undulating prairie land, with sand-hills in the north, and picturesque rocky hills, some 500 feet high, in the south along the Ohio River. In the northern part of the state are numerous lakes, and in the limestone regions of the south are many caves. Mineral springs are found throughout the south and south central parts. The Ohio and White River valleys are of sandstone and limestone formation. The soil for the greater part of the state is a loose calcareous loam of considerable depth. The Weather Bureau at Indianapolis gives the temperature (annual average) as 52.3; highest on record, 166; lowest on record, -35. Total annual precipitation is 39.94 inches. Indiana is exceedingly well-supplied with transportation facilities including interstate highways and railways; and fully half of its borders, or about 600 miles, are on navigable water. Enormous tonnage enters and leaves the Lake Michigan ports. Evansville, on the Ohio river, is a large hardwood market; Indianapolis is the largest city. Indiana University, located at Bloomington; Purdue University, at Lafayette; Notre Dame, at South Bend; and De Paul University, at Greenscastle, are notable among the state's institutions of higher education.

POPULATION: 5,662,000 (1992). Rank among the states, 14th.

AGRICULTURE: Number of farms: 65,000 (1992). Farm acreage: 16,000,000 (1992). Cash receipts from farm marketings: crops, $2,582,000,000 (1991); livestock and products, $1,893,000,000 (1991).

FORESTS: Total forest land: 644,000 acres (1991). Principal woods: oak, beech, maple, elm, yellow poplar, sycamore, cottonwood and aspen, hickory, red and sap gum, ash , basswood.

MINERALS: Value of products: $403,000,000 (1991). Principal minerals: stone, cement, sand and gravel. Value of petroleum production: $61,000,000 (1991).

MANUFACTURES: Value added by manufacture: $43,805,000,000 (1991). Leading industry groups: primary metal industries, electrical machinery, transportation equipment, machinery (except electrical).

LIST OF COUNTIES

Total number of counties 92

County, Location on Map, and County Seat	Pop.
Adams (NE), Decatur	31,095
Allen (NE), Fort Wayne	300,836
Bartholomew (SE), Columbus	63,657
Benton (NW), Fowler	9,441
Blackford (E), Hartford City	14,067
Boone (C), Lebanon	38,147
Brown (SC), Nashville	14,080
Carroll (NWC), Delphi	18,809
Cass (NC), Logansport	38,413
Clark (SE), Jeffersonville	87,777
Clay (W), Brazil	24,705
Clinton (C), Frankfort	30 974
Crawford (S), English	9,914
Daviess (SW), Washington	21,533
Dearborn (SE), Lawrenceburg	38,835
Decatur (SE), Greensburg	23,645
DeKalb (NE), Auburn	35,324
Delaware (E), Muncie	119,659
Dubois (SW), Jasper	36,616
Elkhart (N), Goshen	156,198
Fayette (E), Connersville	26,015
Floyd (S), New Albany	64,404
Fountain (W), Covington	17,808
Franklin (E), Brookville	19,580
Fulton (N), Rochester	18,840
Gibson (SW), Princeton	31,913
Grant (NEC), Marion	74,169
Greene (SW), Bloomfield	30,410
Hamilton (C), Noblesville	108,936
Hancock (EC), Greenfiled	45,527
Harrison (S), Corydon	29,890
Hendricks (C), Danville	75,717
Henry (E), New Castle	48,139
Howard (NC), Kokomo	80,827
Huntington (NE), Huntington	35,427
Jackson (S), Brownstown	37,730
Jasper (NW), Renssalaer	24,960
Jay (E), Portland	21,512
Jefferson (SE), Madison	29,797
Jennings (SE), Vernon	23,661
Johnson (SC), Franklin	88,109
Knox (SW), Vincennes	39,884
Kosciusko (N), Warsaw	65,294
Lagrange (NE), Lagrange	29,477
Lake (NW), Crown Point	475,594
La Porte (NW), La Porte	107,066
Lawrence (S), Bedford	42,836
Madison (EC), Anderson	130,669
Marion (C), Indianapolis	797,159
Marshall (N), Plymouth	42,182
Martin (SW), Shoals	10,369
Miami (NC), Peru	36,897
Monroe (SWC), Bloomington	108,978
Montgomery (WC), Crawfordsville	34,436
Morgan (C), Martinsville	55,920
Newton (NW), Kentland	13,551
Noble (NE), Albion	37,877
Ohio (SE), Rising Sun	5,315
Grange (S), Paoli	18,409
Owen (SWC), Spencer	17,281
Parke (W), Rockville	15,410
Perry (S), Cannelton	19,107
Pike (SW), Petersburg	12,509
Porter (NW), Valparaiso	128,932
Posey (SW), Mount Vernon	25,968
Pulaski (NW), Winamac	12,643
Putnam (WC), Greencastle	30,315
Randolph (E), Winchester	27,148
Ripley (SE), Versailles	24,616
Rush (SEC), Rushville	18,129
St. Joseph (N), South Bend	247,052
Scott (SE), Scottsburg	20,991
Shelby (SEC), Shelbyville	40,307
Spencer (SW), Rockport	19,490
Starke (NW), Knox	22,747
Steuben (NE), Angola	27,446
Sullivan (SW), Sullivan	18,993
Switzerland (SE), Vevay	7,738
Tippecanoe (NWC), Lafayette	130,598
Tipton (NC), Tipton	16,119
Union (SE), Liberty	6,976
Vanderburg (SW), Evansville	165,058
Vermillion (W), Newport	16,773
Vigo (W), Terre Haute	106,107
Wabash (NEC), Wabash	35,069
Warren (W), Williamsport	8,176
Warrick (SW), Booneville	44,920
Washington (S), Salem	23,717
Wayne (E), Richmond	71,951
Wells (NE), Bluffton	25,948
White (NW), Monticello	23,265
Whitley (NE), Columbia City	27,651

STATISTICS

Newspapers

Period of Issue

Daily	72
Evening Daily	51
Morning Daily	14
Daily with Sunday edition	21
Semiweekly	7
Weekly	199
Biweekly	2
Semimonthly	1
Monthly	4
Quarterly	2
Free or partly free	38
Shopper	30
Total Newspapers	292

Periodicals

Period of Issue

Weekly	9
Semimonthly	2
Monthly	58
Bimonthly	41
Quarterly	53
Total Periodicals	209

Total number of publications 501

Radio Stations

AM Stations	82
FM Stations	139
Total Radio Stations	221

TV Stations

Total TV Stations 36

Cable Stations

Total Cable Systems 43

Total number of broadcast listings 300

ALBION†, pop. 1,637.

Noble Co. (NE). 32 m NW of Fort Wayne. Manufactures cabinets, auto parts, mobile home parts, trailers, campers, electrical harness factories; hatchery; feed mills; poultry packing plant. Fruit, livestock farms.

9947 Albion New Era
All Printing & Publications Inc.
407 S. Orange St. Phone: (219)636-2727
PO Box 25 Fax: (219)636-2042
Albion, IN 46701
Free: (800)860-6776

Newspaper with a Republican orientation. **Founded:** 1872. **Freq:** Weekly (Wed.). **Print Method:** Offset. **Trim Size:** 11 x 17. **Cols./Page:** 6. **Col. Width:** 19 nonpareils. **Col. Depth:** 15.75 inches. **Key Personnel:** Joy Y. LeCount, Editor, jlecount@noble.cioe.com; Robert Allman, Publisher. **USPS:** 012-600. **Subscription Rates:** $20 individuals; $.50 single issue. **Remarks:** Accepts advertising.
Ad Rates: GLR: $3.50 **Circ:** ‡2,200
BW: $3.50
4C: $1,400
SAU: $3
PCI: $3.50

ALEXANDRIA, pop. 6,028.

Madison Co. (E). 10 m N of Anderson. Manufactures insulation, redwood outdoor furniture, cement mixers, gospel music printing and recording, plastics, boilers, tool and die fabrication, wire and metal products. Farming.

9948 Alexandria Times-Tribune
Elwood Publishing Co.
One Harrison Square Phone: (317)724-4469
PO Box 330
Alexandria, IN 46001
Community newspaper. **Founded:** Dec. 10, 1885. **Freq:** Weekly (Wed.). **Print Method:** Offset. **Cols./Page:** 6. **Col. Width:** 2 1/16 nonpareils. **Col. Depth:** 21 1/2 inches. **Key Personnel:** Neal Johnson, Editor-in-Chief, phone (765)675-2115; Linda Ferris, Managing Editor; Robert Nash, Publisher; Cindy Tyner, Advertising Mgr. **ISSN:** 1063-553X. **Subscription Rates:** $22 in country; $29 out of area.
Ad Rates: GLR: $.17 **Circ:** Paid 2,700
BW: $703.05
4C: $838.05
SAU: $5.45
PCI: $5.45

ANDERSON†, pop. 64,695.

Madison Co. (EC). 38 m NE of Indianapolis. Anderson College. Manufactures auto electrical equipment, paperboard products, studio couches, pumps, castings, tools, furniture springs, glass, brick, machinery, oil engines, playground equipment; meat packing.

9949 Anderson Herald-Bulletin
1133 Jackson St. Phone: (317)643-5371
Anderson, IN 46016-1466 Fax: (317)649-3271

General newspaper. **Founded:** 1868. **Freq:** Daily (morn.). **Print Method:** Offset. Broadsheet. **Cols./Page:** 6. **Col. Width:** 26 nonpareils. **Col. Depth:** 21 1/2 inches. **Key Personnel:** Elliot Tompkin, Editor; David C. Smith, Publisher; Steve Etkins, Mktg. Dir. **ISSN:** 0893-908X. **Subscription Rates:** $3 individuals Weekly. **Remarks:** Accepts advertising.
Ad Rates: GLR: $2.31 **Circ:** Mon.-Sat. ★**30,071**
BW: $4,186.05 Sun. ★**31,130**
4C: $4,466.05
PCI: $32.45

9950 Signatures
Anderson University
1100 E. 5th St. Phone: (765)649-9071
Anderson, IN 46012 Fax: (765)641-3851

Magazine for college alumni. **Subtitle:** The Alumni Quarterly of Anderson University. **Founded:** 1921. **Freq:** Quarterly. **Print Method:** Offset. Uses mats. **Trim Size:** 8 1/2 x 11. **Cols./Page:** 4. **Col. Depth:** 210 agate lines. **Key Personnel:** Jenine H. Nuwer, Editor, phone (317)641-4230, jnuwer@anderson.edu. **Remarks:** Advertising not accepted. **Formerly**: Anderson College News.
Circ: Free ‡27,000

9951 TCI of Central Indiana
633 Jackson St. Phone: (317)649-0407
Anderson, IN 46016 Fax: (317)649-1532

Founded: 1972. **Formerly**: UAE. **Key Personnel:** Kathy Norton, Office Mgr. **Cities Served:** Madison County, IN: subscribing households 28,000; 50 channels.

9952 WAXT-FM - 96.7
1106 Meridian St., Ste. 105 Phone: (765)644-7791
Anderson, IN 46016-1754 Fax: (765)641-2383
E-mail: waxt@astralite.com

Format: Adult Contemporary. **Networks:** Network Indiana; Meadows Racing; International Media Service; Jones Satellite. **Owner:** Triplett Broadcasting of Indiana, at above address. **Founded:** 1980. **Operating Hours:** Continuous; 100% local. **ADI:** Indianapolis (Marion), IN. **Key Personnel:** Diana Dunham, General Mgr., sidunham@metusa1.net; J. Wallace-Joyner, Program Dir.; Doug Edge, Sales Mgr. **Wattage:** 3000. **Ad Rates:** $18 for 30 seconds; $23 for 60 seconds.

9953 WHBU-AM - 1240
Union Bldg., Ste. 105 Phone: (765)644-7791
1106 Meridian Plaza Fax: (765)641-2383
Anderson, IN 46015
E-mail: whbu@astralite.com

Format: Talk; News; Sports. **Networks:** CBS; NBC. **Owner:** Anderson Communications Inc., at above address. **Founded:** 1923. **Operating Hours:** Continuous; 5% network, 95% local. **ADI:** Indianapolis (Marion), IN. **Key Personnel:** Tom Hayth, President; John Joyner, Program Dir.; Jeff Ingram, News Dir.; John Fox, Sports Dir.; Diana Dunham, General Mgr.; Dawn Ylngling, Sales Mgr.; Diana Dunham, General Mgr. **Local Programs:** *Green In the Morning*, Chet Green; *Mike Rence*; *Rush Limbaugh*. **Wattage:** 1000. **Ad Rates:** $9 for 30 seconds; $12 for 60 seconds.

9954 WQME-FM - 98.7
1100 E. 5th St. Phone: (765)641-4349
Anderson, IN 46012-3495

Format: Adult Contemporary; Contemporary Christian. **Networks:** CNN Radio. **Owner:** Anderson University, at above address. **Founded:** Nov. 30, 1989. **ADI:** Indianapolis (Marion), IN. **Key Personnel:** Donald Boggs, General Mgr.; Gary Brummitt, Station Mgr.; Michael Delon, Sales Mgr. **Wattage:** 4,500. **Ad Rates:** Underwriting available. $9.10-13.80 for 30 seconds; $11.90-18 for 60 seconds.

ANGOLA†, pop. 5,486.

Steuben Co. (NE). 42 m NE of Ft. Wayne. Tri-State University. Summer-Resort. Manufactures automobiles and trucks parts, wire, abrasive and honing equipment, gauges, die casting and metal spinning, air control cylinders, airplane parts, business forms. Grain and dairy farms.

9955 Daily Journal
Home News Enterprises
PO Box 180 Phone: (219)665-3117
Angola, IN 46703 Fax: (219)665-2322

General newspaper. **Founded:** 1963. **Freq:** Daily (eve.). **Print Method:** Offset. **Trim Size:** 13 x 21 1/2. **Cols./Page:** 6. **Key Personnel:** J. Fred Mattingly, Advertising Mgr. **USPS:** 565-520. **Subscription Rates:** $72 individuals. **Remarks:** Advertising not accepted for mail orders and work at home.
Ad Rates: BW: $1,315.80 **Circ:** Combined ♦**18,824**
4C: $1,570.80
PCI: $10.20

9956 Herald Republican
Home News Enterprises
PO Box 180 Phone: (219)665-3117
Angola, IN 46703 Fax: (219)665-2322

Community newspaper. **Founded:** 1857. **Freq:** Semiweekly (Wed. and Fri.). **Print Method:** Offset. **Trim Size:** 13 3/4 x 21 1/2. **Cols./Page:** 6. **Col. Width:** 12 1/2 picas. **Col. Depth:** 301 agate lines. **Key Personnel:** Colleen Anspaugh, Editor; Roger Huntzinger, Publisher; Jerry Kramer, Advertising Mgr.; Pat Martin, Special Publications Mgr. **Subscription Rates:** $24.75 individuals. **Remarks:** Accepts advertising.
Ad Rates: GLR: $6.10 **Circ:** ‡7,200
BW: $703.05
4C: $868.05
SAU: $6.95
PCI: $6.10

9957 WEAX-FM - 88.3
W. Park Ave. Phone: (219)665-7310
Stewart Hall Fax: (219)665-7310
Angola, IN 46703
E-mail: weax@tristate.edu

Format: Album-Oriented Rock (AOR); Classic Rock; Alternative/New Music/Progressive. **Networks:** Independent. **Founded:** 1975. **Formerly:** WTSC-FM. **Operating Hours:** Continuous. **Key Personnel:** Chad Gramling, General Mgr.; Chris Schuler, Music Dir.; Corey Pressler, Program Dir.; John Crumb, Sec./Treas.; Ryan Brown, Contact; Dan Mahan, Promotions; Lisa Jackson, Production; Travis Andrews, Engineer. **Local Programs:** *Wednesday Metal*, Michael Lynch. **Wattage:** 1000. **Ad Rates:** Underwriting available.

ATTICA, pop. 3,841.

Fountain Co. (W). On Wabash River, 21 m SW of Lafayette. Manufactures steel castings, electronic components, batteries. Grain, stock, dairy, poultry farms.

9958 Fountain County Neighbor
Twin States Publishing
1322 E. Main St. Phone: (317)762-2411
PO Box 30 Fax: (317)762-2163
Attica, IN 47918
Publication E-mail: editor@localline.com

Community newspaper. **Founded:** 1851. **Freq:** Semiweekly (Tues. and Fri.). **Print Method:** Offset. **Cols./Page:** 8. **Col. Width:** 19 nonpareils. **Col. Depth:** 196 agate lines. **Key Personnel:** Jeffery Stanton, Managing Editor; Howard W. Hewitt, Publisher. **Subscription Rates:** $40 individuals. **Formerly**: Star Tribune.
Ad Rates: GLR: $.25 **Circ:** Paid 1,740
BW: $647
PCI: $3.85

9959 The Messenger
Twin States Publishing
1322 E. Main St. Phone: (317)762-2411
PO Box 30 Fax: (317)762-2163
Attica, IN 47918
Publication E-mail: editor@localline.com

Shopper serving Fountain and Warren County. Companion to The Fountain County Neighbor, lis ted elsewhere. **Freq:** Weekly. **Print Method:** Offset. **Cols./Page:** 8. **Col. Width:** 19 nonpareils. **Col. Depth:** 294 agate lines. **Key Personnel:** Howard W. Hewitt, Publisher; James Hatfield, Advertising Mgr. **Subscription Rates:** Free.
Ad Rates: PCI: $6.95 **Circ:** Free ‡11,362

AUBURN†, pop. 8,122.

DeKalb Co. (NE) 25 m NE of Fort Wayne. Residential. Classic car museum.

9960 The Evening Star
Kendallville Publishing Co., Inc.
118 W. 9th St. Phone: (219)925-2611
PO Box 431 Fax: (219)925-2625
Auburn, IN 46706-2225
General newspaper. **Founded:** 1871. **Freq:** Daily (eve.). **Print Method:** Offset. **Cols./Page:** 6. **Col. Width:** 25 nonpareils. **Col. Depth:** 301 agate lines. **Key Personnel:** James Kroemer, Editor; George O. Witwer, Publisher; Martin Alexander, Advertising Mgr. **Subscription Rates:** $85 individuals; $110 by mail. **Remarks:** Accepts advertising.
Ad Rates: GLR: $7.25 **Circ:** ‡7,391
BW: $935.25
4C: $1,160.25
SAU: $7.25

9961 WGLL-AM - 1570
5446 CR 29 Phone: (219)925-1055
Auburn, IN 46706 Fax: (219)925-1345

Format: Talk. **Networks:** CNN Radio. **Owner:** Kovas Communications, 2000 Lower Huntington Rd., Fort Wayne, IN 46815, (219)747-1511, Fax: (219)747-3999. **Founded:** 1968. **Formerly:** WIFF-AM (1997). **Operating Hours:** Continuous; 95% network, 5% local. **ADI:** Fort Wayne (Angola), IN. **Key Personnel:** John Sloan, General Mgr. **Wattage:** 500 day; 151 night.

AURORA

Dearborn Co. (SE). 5 m S of Greendale.

9962 Fairbanks Cablevision
PO Box 445 Phone: (812)926-3694
Aurora, IN 47001 Fax: (812)926-1269

Key Personnel: Warren Evans, Manager. **Cities Served:** Aurora, Greendale, and Lawrenceburg, IN.

9963 WSCH-FM - 99.3
6857 Salem Ridge Phone: (812)438-2777
Aurora, IN 47001 Fax: (812)438-3495

Format: Contemporary Country. **Networks:** CNN Radio. **Owner:** John W. Schuler, at above address. **Founded:** 1970. **Operating Hours:** 6 a.m.-10 p.m. **Key Personnel:** John W. Schuler, Contact; Barbara Schuler, Office Mgr. **Wattage:** 3000.

BATESVILLE, pop. 4,152.

Franklin & Ripley Co. (SE). 49 m NW of Cincinnati, Oh. Manufactures furniture, caskets, hospital and metal equipment. Agriculture.

9964 The Herald-Tribune
Thomson Newspapers
PO Box 89 Phone: (812)934-4343
Batesville, IN 47006 Fax: (812)934-6406

Newspaper with a Democratic orientation. **Founded:** 1890. **Freq:** Semiweekly (Wed. and Sat.). **Print Method:** Offset. **Cols./Page:** 6. **Col. Width:** 22 nonpareils. **Col. Depth:** 294 agate lines. **Key Personnel:** Bryan Helvie, Publisher. **Subscription Rates:** $42 individuals.
Ad Rates: GLR: $.62 **Circ:** ‡4,500

9965 WRBI-FM - 103.9
133 S. Main St. Phone: (812)934-5111
PO Box 201 Fax: (812)934-2765
Batesville, IN 47006
E-mail: wrbi@venus.net

Format: Country. **Networks:** Mutual Broadcasting System. **Owner:** White River Broadcasting Co., at above address. **Founded:** 1977. **Operating Hours:** Continuous. 10% network, 90% local. **Key Personnel:** Ronald E. Green, Contact, wrbiem@vennus.nat; Tom Snape, News Dir. **Wattage:** 3000. **Ad Rates:** $10-13 for 30 seconds; $13-16 for 60 seconds.

BEDFORD†, pop. 14,410.

Lawrence Co. (S). 24 m S of Bloomington. Quarrying and fabricating building stone; foundry; saw and excelsior mills. Manufactures stoneworking machinery, saws, work shirts. Diversified farming.

9966 The Times-Mail
The Times News
813 16th St. Phone: (812)275-3355
Box 849 Fax: (812)275-4191
Bedford, IN 47421-3822
Publication E-mail: tmnews@tmnews.com

Newspaper. **Founded:** 1892. **Freq:** Daily (eve.), Sat. and Sun. (morn.). **Print Method:** Offset. **Trim Size:** 11 5/8 x 13 3/4. **Cols./Page:** 8. **Col. Width:** 19 nonpareils. **Col. Depth:** 294 agate lines. **Key Personnel:** Debbie Demitroulas, Editor, debbie@tmnews.com; Scott Schurz, Publisher. **Subscription Rates:** $100.80 individuals; $57.60 institutions, Canada. **Remarks:** Accepts advertising. **URL:** http://www.tmnews.com/.
Ad Rates: PCI: $7.81 **Circ:** Mon.-Sat. ★14,036

9967 WBIW-AM - 1340
424 Heltonville Rd. Phone: (812)275-7555
PO Box 1307 Fax: (812)279-8046
Bedford, IN 47421

Format: Oldies. **Networks:** ABC. **Owner:** Ad-Venture Media, Inc., PO Box 1307, Bedford, IN 47421. **Founded:** 1948. **Operating Hours:** Continuous; 10% network, 90% local. **ADI:** Louisville, KY. **Key Personnel:** Dean Spencer, General Mgr.; Laura Duncan, Program Dir.; Bill Silvers, News Dir.; Rebecca Godsey, Sales Mgr. **Wattage:** 1000.

9968 WQRK-FM - 105.5
424 Heltonville Rd. Phone: (812)279-5746
Bedford, IN 47421 Fax: (812)279-8046

Format: Classic Rock. **Networks:** ABC. **Owner:** Ad-Venture Media, Inc., at above address. **Founded:** 1975. **Formerly:** WBIF-FM (1986). **Operating Hours:** Continuous;. **Key Personnel:** Dean Spencer, General Mgr.; Laura Duncan, Program Dir.; Rebecca Godsey, Sales Mgr. **Wattage:** 3000.

BEECH GROVE, pop. 13,196.

Marion Co. (SC). 7 m SE of Indianapolis. Electrical equipment, dairy farms.

9969 The Perry Township Weekly
Reporter-Times, Inc.
PO Box 187 Phone: (317)787-3291
Beech Grove, IN 46107 Fax: (317)787-3325
Free: (800)873-7060

Community newspaper. **Founded:** 1928. **Freq:** Weekly (Thurs.). **Print Method:** Offset. **Cols./Page:** 6. **Col. Width:** 2 1/4 inches. **Col. Depth:** 21 1/2 inches. **Key Personnel:** Roger Huntzinger, Publisher; Amy Uhls, Editor. **Subscription Rates:** $9. **Remarks:** Accepts advertising.
Ad Rates: BW: $910 **Circ:** Free ‡22,500
4C: $1,280
PCI: $7

BERNE, pop. 3,300.

Adams Co. (NE). 33 m SE of Fort Wayne. Manufactures furniture, men's clothing, cedar chests, components, tubing, novelty boxes; electronics industry. Hatcheries. Diversified farming.

9970 Berne Tri-Weekly News
EP Graphics
PO Box 324 Phone: (219)589-2101
153 S. Jefferson St. Fax: (219)589-8614
Berne, IN 46711
Agricultural newspaper with a Republican orientation. **Founded:** 1896. **Freq:** 3/week. **Print Method:** Offset. **Cols./Page:** 6. **Col. Width:** 12 picas. **Col. Depth:** 21 inches. **Key Personnel:** R.P. Stimpson, Editor. **Subscription Rates:** $39.95 individuals. **Remarks:** Accepts advertising.
Ad Rates: GLR: $.18 **Circ:** 4,965
4C: $75
SAU: $4.50
PCI: $4.75

9971 Crochet Digest
House of White Birches
306 E. Parr Rd. Phone: (219)589-4000
Berne, IN 46711 Fax: (219)589-8093

Magazine containing crochet patterns for afghans, doilies, toys, clothing, holiday decorations, bazaar items, fashion, children, and home. **Founded:** 1981. **Freq:** Quarterly. **Print Method:** Offset. **Trim Size:** 5 3/8 x 7 1/2. **Cols./Page:** 2. **Col. Width:** 2 1/4 inches. **Col. Depth:** 6 1/4 inches. **Key Personnel:** Carl H. Muselman, Publisher; Arthur K. Muselman, Publisher; John Robinson, President; Vivian Rothe, Director; Laura Scott, Editor. **ISSN:** 0279-1978. **Subscription Rates:** $9.95 individuals; $14.95 Canada; $2.95 single issue. **Remarks:** Advertising accepted; rates available upon request.
Circ: ‡75,000

9972 Crochet World
House of White Birches
306 E. Parr Rd. Phone: (219)589-4000
Berne, IN 46711 Fax: (219)589-8093

Magazine containing crochet ideas and patterns, including toys, afghans, dolls, doilies, clothing, and household accessories. **Founded:** 1977. **Freq:** Bimonthly. **Print Method:** Offset. **Trim Size:** 8 x 10 3/4. **Cols./Page:** 3. **Col. Width:** 13 1/2 picas. **Col. Depth:** 58 picas. **Key Personnel:** Susan Hankins, Editor; George Hague, Advertising Mgr.; John Robinson, CEO; Vivian Rothe, Editorial Director; Scott Moss, Marketing Director. **ISSN:** 0164-7962. **Subscription Rates:** $14.97 individuals; $2.95 single issue. **Remarks:** Accepts advertising.
Circ: ‡78,769

9973 Doll World
House of White Birches
306 E. Parr Rd. Phone: (219)589-4000
Berne, IN 46711 Fax: (219)589-8093

Magazine on doll-making, history, costuming, restoration, and information on doll-identification services. **Founded:** 1977. **Freq:** Bimonthly. **Print Method:** Offset. **Trim Size:** 8 x 10 3/4. **Cols./Page:** 3. **Col. Width:** 13 1/2 picas. **Col. Depth:** 58 picas. **Key Personnel:** Carey Raesner, Editor; John Robinson, CEO; Vivian Rothe, Editorial Director; Scott Moss, Marketing Director; George Hague, Advertising Mgr. **USPS:** 001-430. **Subscription Rates:** $17.77 individuals; $2.95 single issue. **Remarks:** Accepts advertising.
Circ: ‡41,174

9974 Doll World Collector's Price Guide
House of White Birches
306 E. Parr Rd. Phone: (219)589-4000
Berne, IN 46711 Fax: (219)589-8093

Publication for collectors and investors in the doll market. Each issue includes sections on identifying and pricing dolls of all media, as well as auction and show reports and informative articles of interest to collectors. **Freq:** Quarterly. **Key Personnel:** Carl H. Muselman, Publisher; Arthur K. Muselman, Publisher; Cary Raesner, Editor; John Robinson, CEO; Tamara Hanes. **Subscription Rates:** $12.97. $2.95 single issue. **Remarks:** Advertising accepted; rates available upon request.
Circ: Paid 43,985

9975 Good Old Days
House of White Birches
306 E. Parr Rd. Phone: (219)589-4000
Berne, IN 46711 Fax: (219)589-8093

Magazine on the nostalgic past; including authentic photos, drawings, cartoons, memories, features, songs, poems, and advertising. **Founded:** 1964. **Freq:** Monthly. **Print Method:** Offset. **Trim Size:** 8 x 10 3/4. **Cols./Page:** 3. **Col. Width:** 13 1/2 picas. **Col. Depth:** 58 picas. **Key Personnel:** Ken Tate, Editor. **ISSN:** 0046-6158. **Subscription Rates:** $14.97 individuals; $1.95 single issue. **Remarks:** Accepts advertising.
Circ: ‡119,874

9976 Good Old Days Specials
House of White Birches
306 E. Parr Rd. Phone: (219)589-4000
Berne, IN 46711 Fax: (219)589-8093

Publication featuring recollections of yesterday and light-hearted anecdotes of days gone by. **Founded:** Jan. 1961. **Freq:** Bimonthly. **Trim Size:** 8 x 10 3/4. **Key Personnel:** Ken Tate, Editor. **ISSN:** 0046-6158. **Subscription Rates:** $12.97; $1.95 single issue. **Remarks:** Advertising accepted; rates available upon request.
Circ: Paid 30,845

9977 Home Cooking
House of White Birches
306 E. Parr Rd. Phone: (219)589-4000
Berne, IN 46711 Fax: (219)589-8093
Publication E-mail: home_ cooking@whitebirches.com

Magazine with approximately 100 recipes for home cooks who wish to make home-style foods with common ingredients. **Freq:** Monthly. **Key Personnel:** Carl H. Muselman, Publisher; Arthur K. Muselman, Publisher; Shelly Vaughan, Editor. **Subscription Rates:** $14.97 individuals; $1.95. **Remarks:** Accepts advertising.
Circ: ‡84,266

9978 Knitting Digest
House of White Birches
306 E. Parr Rd. Phone: (219)589-4000
Berne, IN 46711 Fax: (219)589-8093
Publication E-mail: knitting_ digest@whitebirches.com

Knitting magazine including patterns and tips. **Founded:** 1978. **Freq:** Bimonthly. **Print Method:** Offset. **Trim Size:** 5 3/8 x 7 1/2. **Cols./Page:** 2. **Col. Width:** 2 1/2 inches. **Col. Depth:** 6 1/4 inches. **Key Personnel:** Jeanne Staufter, Editor. **ISSN:** 0194-8083. **Subscription Rates:** $14.95 individuals; $3.95 single issue; $22.95 Canada. **Remarks:** Advertising accepted; rates available upon request. **Formerly**: Knitting World (1993).
Circ: ‡45,000

9979 Old-Time Crochet
House of White Birches
306 E. Parr Rd. Phone: (219)589-4000
Berne, IN 46711 Fax: (219)589-8093

Magazine containing crochet patterns dated from the past. **Founded:** 1978. **Freq:** Quarterly. **Print Method:** Offset. **Trim Size:** 8 x 10 3/4. **Cols./Page:** 3. **Key Personnel:** Marion L. Kelly, Co-Editor, phone (207)676-2786; Anne Morgan Jefferson, Co-Editor, phone (603)926-6047; John Robinson, CEO; Vivian Rothe, Editorial Director; Scott Moss, Marketing Director; George Hague, Ad Manager. **ISSN:** 1050-9518. **Subscription Rates:** $9.95 individuals. **Remarks:** Accepts advertising.
Circ: ‡73,475

9980 Plastic Canvas Crafts
House of White Birches
306 E. Parr Rd. Phone: (219)589-4000
Berne, IN 46711 Fax: (219)589-8093

Magazine, with a special theme each issue, that features plastic canvas designs. **Freq:** Bimonthly. **Key Personnel:** Carl H. Muselman, Publisher; Arthur K. Muselman, Publisher; Laura Scott, Editor; John Robinson, CEO; Vivian Rothe, Editorial Director; Scott Moss, Marketing Director; George Hague, Ad Manager. **Subscription Rates:** $14.97. **Remarks:** Accepts advertising. **Formerly**: Plastic Canvas and More.
Circ: ‡60,541

9981 Plastic Canvas World
House of White Birches
306 E. Parr Rd. Phone: (219)589-4000
Berne, IN 46711 Fax: (219)589-8093

Publication featuring photos, graphs, and patterns for plastic canvas projects. **Freq:** Bimonthly. **Key Personnel:** Marjorie Pearl, Editor. **Subscription Rates:** $14.97. **Remarks:** Accepts advertising.
Circ: ‡54,500

9982 Proven Home Plans For Today
HIS Publishing, Inc.
PO Box 213 Phone: (219)589-2145
Berne, IN 46711 Fax: (219)589-2810

Magazine containing home plans for sale. **Founded:** 1993. **Freq:** 3/year. **Print Method:** Offset. **Trim Size:** 8 x 10 3/4. **Cols./Page:** 3. **Key Personnel:** Roger Muselman, Publisher. **Subscription Rates:** $4.50 single issue. **Remarks:** Accepts advertising.
Ad Rates: BW: $1,960 **Circ:** Paid 60,000
4C: $3,500

9983 Quick & Easy Crafts
House of White Birches
306 E. Parr Rd. Phone: (219)589-4000
Berne, IN 46711 Fax: (219)589-8093

Magazine covering sewing, patchwork, knitting, embroidery, crochet, and cross-stitch. **Founded:** 1967. **Freq:** Bimonthly. **Print Method:** Offset. **Trim Size:** 8 x 10 3/4. **Cols./Page:** 3. **Col. Width:** 13 1/2 picas. **Col. Depth:** 58 picas. **Key**

Personnel: Beth Schwartz Wheeler, Editor; John Robinson, CEO; Vivian Rothe, Editorial Director; Scott Moss, Marketing Director; George Hague, Ad Manager. **ISSN:** 0892-8223. **Subscription Rates:** $14.97 individuals. **Remarks:** Accepts advertising.
Circ: ‡338,557

9984 Quick & Easy Quilting
House of White Birches
306 E. Parr Rd. Phone: (219)589-4000
Berne, IN 46711 Fax: (219)589-8093

Magazine containing quilt patterns for projects that can be completed in a short amount of time. **Founded:** 1978. **Freq:** Bimonthly. **Print Method:** Offset. **Trim Size:** 8 x 10 3/4. **Cols./Page:** 3. **Col. Width:** 2 1/4 inches. **Col. Depth:** 9 1/2 inches. **Key Personnel:** Sandra L. Hatch, Editor; John Robinson, CEO; Vivian Rothe, Editorial Director; Scott Moss, Marketing Director; George Hague, Ad Manager. **ISSN:** 1045-5965. **Subscription Rates:** $14.95 individuals; $2.95 single issue; $22.95 Canada. **Remarks:** Advertising accepted; rates available upon request.
Circ: ‡65,601

9985 Quilt World
House of White Birches
306 E. Parr Rd. Phone: (219)589-4000
Berne, IN 46711 Fax: (219)589-8093

Magazine about quilting including history, patterns, techniques, short stories, poems, and cartoons. **Founded:** Apr. 1975. **Freq:** Bimonthly. **Print Method:** Offset. **Trim Size:** 8 x 10 3/4. **Cols./Page:** 3. **Col. Width:** 13 1/2 picas. **Col. Depth:** 58 picas. **Key Personnel:** Sandra L. Hatch, Editor. **ISSN:** 0149-8045. **Subscription Rates:** $14.97 individuals. **Remarks:** Advertising accepted; rates available upon request.
Circ: ‡51,000

BLOOMFIELD†, pop. 2,705.

Greene Co. (SW) 24 m SW of Bloomington. Residential.

9986 The Bloomfield News
29 W. Main St. Phone: (812)384-3501
Bloomfield, IN 47424-0311 Fax: (812)384-3741

Newspaper with a Republican orientation. **Founded:** 1875. **Freq:** Daily. **Print Method:** Offset. **Cols./Page:** 6. **Col. Width:** 26 nonpareils. **Col. Depth:** 294 agate lines. **Key Personnel:** William G. Miles, Editor and Publisher; William H. Winfrey, Adv. Mgr. **Subscription Rates:** $33 individuals. **Remarks:** Accepts advertising. **Feature Editors:** Mark Downey, *Sports*.
Ad Rates: GLR: $.125 **Circ:** Paid ‡4,176
BW: $674
4C: $999
SAU: $3

9987 The Evening World
29 W. Main St. Phone: (812)384-3501
PO Box 311 Fax: (812)384-3741
Bloomfield, IN 47424
Newspaper. **Founded:** 1930. **Freq:** Daily (eve.). **Print Method:** Offset. **Cols./Page:** 6. **Col. Width:** 25 nonpareils. **Col. Depth:** 294 agate lines. **Key Personnel:** William C. Miles, Editor and Publisher. **Subscription Rates:** $69 individuals; $.35 single issue. **Remarks:** Accepts advertising.
Ad Rates: GLR: $.25 **Circ:** Paid 4,000
BW: $554.40 Free 125
4C: $804.40
SAU: $5.15

BLOOMINGTON†, pop. 51,646.

Monroe Co. (SWC). 50 m S of Indianapolis. Indiana University. Manufactures color TV receivers, refrigerators, capacitors, elevators, specialized medical instruments, semi-conductors, brake linings, paper speciality products, limestone quarrying & limestone products.

9988 The American Historical Review
American Historical Association
914 Atwater Ave. Phone: (812)855-7609
Bloomington, IN 47401 Fax: (812)855-5827
Publication E-mail: amhrev@indiana.edu
Publisher E-mail: aha@theaha.org

Scholarly journal. **Subtitle:** Journal of the American Historical Association. **Founded:** 1895. **Freq:** 5/year. **Print Method:** Offset. **Trim Size:** 7 1/4 x 10 1/4. **Cols./Page:** 2 and 1. **Col. Width:** 16 1/2 and 32 picas. **Col. Depth:** 52 and 52 picas. **Key Personnel:** Michael Grossberg, Editor. **ISSN:** 0002-8762. **Subscription Rates:** individuals sliding scale from $30-$120; $65 individuals average. **Remarks:** Accepts advertising.
Ad Rates: BW: $710 **Circ:** Controlled ‡18,000
4C: $1,610

9989 Black Renaissance/Renaissance Noire
Indiana University Press
601 N. Morton St. Phone: (812)855-4203
Bloomington, IN 47404 Fax: (812)855-8507
Free: (800)842-6796
Publisher E-mail: iupress@indiana.edu

Consumer magazine covering black art, fiction and poetry. **Freq:** Triennial. **Key Personnel:** Manthia Diawara, Editor-in-Chief. **ISSN:** 1089-3148. **Subscription Rates:** $27 individuals; $55 institutions; $12.95 single issue; $20 single issue institutions.

9990 Business Horizons
Elseiver
Kelley School of Business Phone: (812)855-6342
Indiana University Fax: (812)856-4971
Indiana Research Park, 501 N
Morton Ste. 110
Bloomington, IN 47405
Publication E-mail: 102062-2525@compuserve.com
Publisher E-mail: fcentres@gpu.stv.ualberta.ca

Business management magazine presented in non-technical language. **Founded:** 1958. **Freq:** Bimonthly. **Print Method:** Offset. **Trim Size:** 8 1/2 x 11. **Cols./Page:** 2. **Key Personnel:** Dennis W. Organ, Editor, phone (812)855-6342, fax (812)855-7332, organ@indiana.edu. **ISSN:** 0007-6813. **Subscription Rates:** $225 institutions; $245 institutions other countries, surface mail; $265 institutions, other countries airmail; $105 individuals; $125 other countries individuals, surface mail; $145 other countries individuals, airmail; $37.50 single issue; $42.50 single issue other couuntries; $47.50 single issue other countries airmail. **Remarks:** Advertising accepted; rates available upon request.
Circ: 3,300

9991 Camera Obscura
Indiana University Press
601 N. Morton St. Phone: (812)855-4203
Bloomington, IN 47404 Fax: (812)855-8507
Free: (800)842-6796
Publication E-mail: cameraob@humanitas.ucsb.edu
Publisher E-mail: iupress@indiana.edu

Subtitle: Feminism, Culture, and Media Studies. **Freq:** 3/year. **Trim Size:** 5 1/2 x 8 1/2. **Key Personnel:** Constance Penley, et al, Editor, phone (805)893-7069. **ISSN:** 0270-5346. **Subscription Rates:** $30; $65 industry; $75 out of country industry; $12.95 single issue. **Remarks:** Accepts advertising.
Ad Rates: BW: $200 **Circ:** 1,000

9992 Educational Horizons
Pi Lambda Theta
4101 E. 3rd St. Phone: (812)339-3411
PO Box 6626 Fax: (812)339-3462
Bloomington, IN 47407-6626
Free: (800)487-3411
Publisher E-mail: root@pilambda.org

Journal for professionals in education. **Founded:** 1921. **Freq:** Quarterly. **Trim Size:** 8 1/8 x 10 7/8. **Cols./Page:** 3. **Key Personnel:** Juli Knutson, Editor, juli@pilambda.org. **ISSN:** 0013-175X. **Subscription Rates:** $18; $25 other countries; $6.50 single issue. **Remarks:** Advertising not accepted. **Alt. Formats:** Microform.
Circ: Paid ⊕11,553

9993 Herald-Times
Herald-Times, Inc.
1900 S. Walnut St. Phone: (812)332-4401
PO Box 909 Fax: (812)331-4285
Bloomington, IN 47401-7720
Free: (800)489-5090

Newspaper with a Republican orientation. **Founded:** 1877. **Freq:** Mon.-Sat. (morn.). **Print Method:** Offset. **Cols./Page:** 6. **Col. Width:** 12 picas. **Col. Depth:** 21 inches. **Key Personnel:** Robert Zaltsberg, Editor; Scott C. Schurz, Publisher; Laura Inman, Advertising Mgr.; Natalie Hahn O'Flaherty, Marketing Mgr. **Subscription Rates:** $114 individuals. **Remarks:** Accepts advertising. **URL:** http://www.heraldt.com.
Ad Rates: BW: $2,858.94 **Circ:** Mon.-Sat. ★**28,886**
4C: $3,498.94 Sun. ★**41,846**
SAU: $22.69
PCI: $22.69

9994 History & Memory
Indiana University Press
601 N. Morton St. Phone: (812)855-4203
Bloomington, IN 47404 Fax: (812)855-8507
Free: (800)842-6796
Publisher E-mail: iupress@indiana.edu

Scholarly journal covering historical consciousness. **Subtitle:** Studies in Representation of the Past. **Freq:** Semiannual. **Key Personnel:** Saul Friedlander, Senior Editor. **ISSN:** 0935-560X. **Subscription Rates:** $20 individuals; $30 institutions; $12.95 single issue; $20 single issue institutions.

9995 Hypatia
Indiana University Press
601 N. Morton St. Phone: (812)855-4203
Bloomington, IN 47404 Fax: (812)855-8507
Free: (800)842-6796
Publisher E-mail: iupress@indiana.edu

Journal of feminist philosophy. **Subtitle:** A Journal of Feminist Philosophy. **Founded:** 1983. **Freq:** Quarterly. **Trim Size:** 6 x 9. **Key Personnel:** Nancy Tuana, Editor; Laurie Sharge, Editor. **ISSN:** 0887-5367. **Subscription Rates:** $35; $75 institutions.
Ad Rates: BW: $250 **Circ:** 1,600

9996 Indiana Alumni Magazine
Indiana University Alumni Association
1000 E. 17th St. Phone: (812)855-4822
Bloomington, IN 47408-1521 Fax: (812)855-4228
Free: (800)824-3044
Publisher E-mail: iualumni@indiana.edu

Magazine for college alumni. **Founded:** Sept. 1938. **Freq:** Bimonthly. **Print Method:** Web. **Trim Size:** 8 3/8 x 10 7/8. **Cols./Page:** 3. **Col. Width:** 28 nonpareils. **Col. Depth:** 131 agate lines. **Key Personnel:** Judith Schroeder, Editor, phone (812)855-5785, jschroed@indiana.edu; Andrea Crawford, Advertising Mgr., phone (812)855-5785, acrawfor@indiana.edu; Lauren Bryant, Managing Editor, phone (812)855-5785, labryant@indiana.edu. **Subscription Rates:** $40 individuals.
Ad Rates: BW: $1,180 **Circ:** ‡80,000
4C: $1,980

9997 Indiana Builder Magazine
Protec Publishing
PO Box 1494
Bloomington, IN 47402

Trade journal covering residential construction. **Founded:** 1989. **Freq:** Monthly. **Print Method:** Offset. **Trim Size:** 8 1/2 x 11. **Cols./Page:** 3. **Col. Depth:** 10 inches. **Key Personnel:** Dale Ross, Editor. **Subscription Rates:** Free to qualified subscribers; $24 individuals; $3 single issue. **Remarks:** Accepts advertising.
Circ: Non-paid 12,500

9998 Indiana Business Review
Indiana Business Research Center
Indiana University Phone: (812)855-5507
School of Business Fax: (812)855-7763
Bloomington, IN 47405
Magazine on Indiana business. **Founded:** 1926. **Freq:** 4 year. **Print Method:** Offset. **Trim Size:** 8 1/2 x 11. **Cols./Page:** 2. **Col. Width:** 33 nonpareils. **Col. Depth:** 210 agate lines. **Key Personnel:** Morton J. Marcus, Editor. **Subscription Rates:** Free to qualified subscribers. **Remarks:** Advertising not accepted.
Circ: Controlled 2,000

9999 Indiana Daily Student
Indiana University
Ernie Pyle Hall, Rm. 120 Phone: (812)855-0763
Bloomington, IN 47405 Fax: (812)855-8009

Collegiate newspaper. **Founded:** 1867. **Freq:** Daily (during academic year). **Print Method:** Offset. **Cols./Page:** 6. **Col. Width:** 24 nonpareils. **Col. Depth:** 294 agate lines. **Key Personnel:** Dave Adams, Publisher; Jennifer Hession, Advertising Mgr. **Remarks:** Accepts advertising.
Ad Rates: PCI: $7.62 **Circ:** ‡10,500

10000 Indiana Law Journal
Indiana University
211 S. Indiana Ave., Rm. 009 Phone: (812)855-5175
Bloomington, IN 47405 Fax: (812)855-0555

Professional journal covering law. **Founded:** 1926. **Freq:** Quarterly. **Key Personnel:** Byron B. Babb, Editor-in-Chief, phone (812)855-7497; Tami A. Earnhart, Sr. Managing Editor; Sandra L. Macklin, Exec. Articles Editor, phone (812)855-1898. **ISSN:** 0019-6665. **Subscription Rates:** $30 individuals; $9 single issue. **Remarks:** Accepts advertising. **Online:** LEXIS-NEXIS; Westlaw. **URL:** http://www.law.indiana.edu/ilj/ilj.html.
Ad Rates: BW: $150 **Circ:** Combined 750

10001 Indiana Libraries
Indiana Library Federation
c/o Judy Dye Phone: (812)855-7699
Indiana University Fax: (812)855-2576
Main Library, Rm. 170
Bloomington, IN 47405
Publisher E-mail: ilf@indy.net

Scholarly journal covering literature and libraries. **Freq:** Semiannual. **Print Method:** Web offset. **Trim Size:** 8 1/8 x 10 3/4. **Key Personnel:** Judy Dye, Editor, jdye@indiana.edu; Patty

Tallman, Advertising Mgr. **Subscription Rates:** $10 individuals; $5 single issue. **Remarks:** Accepts advertising.
Ad Rates: BW: $100 **Circ:** Controlled 3,500
4C: $150

10002 Indiana Magazine of History
Indiana University Press
Indiana University Phone: (812)855-4139
Ballantine 742 Fax: (812)855-3378
Bloomington, IN 47405
Publisher E-mail: iupress@indiana.edu

Journal featuring Indiana/and midwestern history. **Founded:** 1905. **Freq:** Quarterly. **Print Method:** Letterpress and offset. **Trim Size:** 4.25 x 7.5. **Cols./Page:** 1. **Col. Width:** 48 nonpareils. **Col. Depth:** 98 agate lines. **Key Personnel:** Bernard W. Sheehan, Editor, phone (812)855-6979. **ISSN:** 0019-6673. **Subscription Rates:** $15 individuals; $4 single issue. **Remarks:** Accepts advertising. **Alt. Formats:** Audio tape.
Ad Rates: BW: $300 **Circ:** 9,600
PCI: $3

10003 Indiana Review
1020 E. Lurkwood
Bloomington, IN 47405-7103

Literary magazine covering fiction, poetry, nonfiction and art. **Founded:** 1976. **Freq:** Semiannual. **Trim Size:** 6 x 9. **Key Personnel:** Brian Leung, Editor. **ISSN:** 0738-386X. **Subscription Rates:** $14 individuals; $8 single issue. **Remarks:** Accepts advertising.
Ad Rates: BW: $300 **Circ:** Combined 2,000

10004 Indiana University Mathematics Journal
Indiana University Phone: (812)855-2252
Rawles Hall 115 Fax: (812)855-0046
Bloomington, IN 47405
Publication E-mail: elena@beau.math.indiana.edu

Magazine on pure and applied mathematics. **Founded:** 1952. **Freq:** Quarterly. **Print Method:** Offset. **Cols./Page:** 1. **Col. Width:** 58 nonpareils. **Col. Depth:** 101 agate lines. **Key Personnel:** Hari Bercovici, Editor. **ISSN:** 0022-2518. **Subscription Rates:** $135 institutions; $140 institutions, other countries foreign. **Remarks:** Advertising not accepted.
Circ: (Not Reported)

10005 Israel Studies
Indiana University Press
601 N. Morton St. Phone: (812)855-4203
Bloomington, IN 47404 Fax: (812)855-8507
Free: (800)842-6796
Publisher E-mail: iupress@indiana.edu

Scholarly journal covering Israeli history, politics, society and culture. **Freq:** Semiannual. **Key Personnel:** S. Ilan, Trowen, Editor. **ISSN:** 1084-9513. **Subscription Rates:** $25 individuals; $50 institutions; $12.95 single issue; $20 institutions institutions.

10006 Jewish Social Studies
Indiana University Press
601 N. Morton St. Phone: (812)855-4203
Bloomington, IN 47404 Fax: (812)855-8507
Free: (800)842-6796
Publisher E-mail: iupress@indiana.edu

Magazine covering contemporary and historical aspects of Jewish life. **Founded:** 1939. **Freq:** Quarterly. **Print Method:** Offset. **Cols./Page:** 1. **Col. Width:** 60 nonpareils. **Col. Depth:** 112 agate lines. **ISSN:** 0021-6704. **Subscription Rates:** $40; $43 other countries.

10007 The Journal of American History
Organization of American Historians (OAH)
1125 E. Atwater Ave. Phone: (812)855-2816
Bloomington, IN 47401 Fax: (812)855-9939
Publisher E-mail: oah@oah.indiana.edu

History journal. **Founded:** 1914. **Freq:** Quarterly. **Print Method:** Web offset. **Trim Size:** 6 1/2 x 10. **Cols./Page:** 1. **Col. Width:** 75 nonpareils. **Col. Depth:** 140 agate lines. **Key Personnel:** Prof. David Thelen, Editor. **Remarks:** Accepts advertising.
Ad Rates: BW: $500 **Circ:** 12,000

10008 Journal of Modern Literature
Indiana University Press
601 N. Morton St. Phone: (812)855-4203
Bloomington, IN 47404 Fax: (812)855-8507
Free: (800)842-6796
Publisher E-mail: iupress@indiana.edu

Scholarly journal covering modern literature. **Freq:** Quarterly. **Key Personnel:** Morton P. Levitt, Editor. **ISSN:** 0022-281X. **Subscription Rates:** $25 individuals; $35 institutions; $12.95 single issue; $20 single issue institutions.

10009 The Journal of Women's History
Indiana University Press
601 N. Morton St. Phone: (812)855-4203
Bloomington, IN 47404 Fax: (812)855-8507
Free: (800)842-6796
Publication E-mail: jwh@osu.edu
Publisher E-mail: iupress@indiana.edu

Feminist journal on women's history. **Founded:** 1989. **Freq:** 4/year. **Trim Size:** 6 x 9. **Cols./Page:** 1. **Col. Width:** 4 1/2 inches. **Col. Depth:** 8 inches. **Key Personnel:** Leila J. Rupp, Editor, phone (614)688-3092, fax (614)292-2282. **ISSN:** 1042-7961. **Subscription Rates:** $35 individuals; $75 institutions; $12.95 single issue. **Remarks:** Accepts advertising.
Ad Rates: BW: $250 **Circ:** Paid ‡1,108
Non-paid ‡50

10010 Mongolian Studies
Mongolia Society Inc.
322 Goodbody Hall Phone: (812)855-4078
Indiana University Fax: (812)855-7500
Bloomington, IN 47405
Publisher E-mail: monsoc@indiana.edu

Scholarly journal covering Mongolian studies. **Founded:** 1974. **Freq:** Annual. **Trim Size:** 6 x 9. **Key Personnel:** Susie Drost, Manager. **Subscription Rates:** $20 individuals. **Remarks:** Accepts advertising.
Ad Rates: BW: $200 **Circ:** (Not Reported)

10011 NWSA Journal
Indiana University Press
601 N. Morton St. Phone: (812)855-4203
Bloomington, IN 47404 Fax: (812)855-8507
Free: (800)842-6796
Publisher E-mail: iupress@indiana.edu

Periodical containing feminist scholarship. **Subtitle:** A Publication of the National Women's Studies Association. **Founded:** 1988. **Freq:** 3/year. **Print Method:** Offset. **Cols./Page:** 1. **Col. Width:** 5 inches. **Col. Depth:** 8 inches. **Key Personnel:** Patrocinio Schweickart, Editor; Susan D. Franzosa, Advertising Mgr. **ISSN:** 1040-0656. **Subscription Rates:** $39.50; $24 member; $105 Industry. **Remarks:** Color advertising not accepted.
Ad Rates: BW: $200 **Circ:** ‡1,300

10012 Phi Delta Kappan
Phi Delta Kappa International
408 N. Union Phone: (812)339-1156
PO Box 789 Fax: (812)339-0018
Bloomington, IN 47402-0789
Free: (800)766-1156
Publication E-mail: kappan@pdkintl.org
Publisher E-mail: headquarters@pdkintl.org

Magazine for professional educators. **Subtitle:** Proffesional Journey for Education. **Founded:** 1915. **Freq:** 10/year(Sept.-June). **Print Method:** Offset. **Trim Size:** 8 x 10 7/8. **Cols./Page:** 3. **Col. Width:** 13.5 picas. **Col. Depth:** 54 picas. **Key Personnel:** Pauline B. Gough, Editor; Carol Bucheri, Advertising Dir. **ISSN:** 0031-7217. **Subscription Rates:** $39 individuals; $42.50 other countries; $46 libraries; $4.90 single issue. **URL:** http://www.kiva.net/˜pdicintl/. **Alt. Formats:** Microform.
Ad Rates: BW: $3,150 **Circ:** ‡130,000
4C: $4,400

10013 Philosophy of Music Education Review
Indiana University School of Music
Music Education Dept. Phone: (812)855-2051
1201 E. Third St. Fax: (812)855-4936
Bloomington, IN 47405-7006
Journal covering philosophical research in music education for music professionals and scholars. **Founded:** 1993. **Freq:** Semiannual. **Key Personnel:** Estelle R. Jorgensen, Editor; Karen Gast, Circulation Mgr., kgast@indiana.edu. **ISSN:** 1063-5734. **Subscription Rates:** $20 individuals; $40 institutions; $23 individuals other countries.; $45 institutions other countries.; $9 single issue. **Remarks:** Advertising not accepted. **URL:** http://www.music.indiana.edu.
Circ: Paid 255

10014 The Ryder
In The Dark Enterprises
117 E. 3rd St. Phone: (812)339-2001
Bloomington, IN 47401 Fax: (812)339-2002
Publication E-mail: ryder@bluemarvel.net; theryder@bluemarble.net

Magazine featuring arts and entertainment. **Founded:** 1979. **Freq:** Monthly. **Print Method:** Offset. **Cols./Page:** 3. **Col. Width:** 26 nonpareils. **Col. Depth:** 136 agate lines. **Key Personnel:** Peter Lopilato, Editor and Publisher. **Subscription Rates:** $12 individuals. **URL:** http://www.ryder.com; http://www.theryder.com.
Circ: Non-paid 19,000

10015 Technos Quarterly for Education and Technology
Agency for Instructional Technology (AIT)
1800 N. Stonelake Dr. Phone: (812)339-2203
POB A 47402 Fax: (812)333-4218
Bloomington, IN 47404
Free: (800)457-4509
Publication E-mail: http://www.technos.net
Publisher E-mail: info@ait.net

A forum on the use of technology in education with a focus on reform. **Subtitle:** The Journal of the Agency for Instructional Technology. **Founded:** 1992. **Freq:** Quarterly. **Trim Size:** 8 1/2 x 11. **Key Personnel:** Mardell Raney, Editor, mraney@ait.net; Michael Sullivan, Publisher. **ISSN:** 1060-5649. **Subscription Rates:** $28; $24 libraries; $32 out of country; $75 3 years. **Remarks:** Advertising not accepted. **Available Online. URL:** http://www.ait.net.
Circ: Paid 1,500
Controlled 5,000

10016 Victorian Studies
Indiana University Press
601 N. Morton St. Phone: (812)855-4203
Bloomington, IN 47404 Fax: (812)855-8507
Free: (800)842-6796
Publisher E-mail: iupress@indiana.edu

Scholarly journal covering English culture of the Victorian period. **Founded:** 1956. **Freq:** Quarterly. **Key Personnel:** Donald Gray, Editor; Andrew H. Miller, Editor; James Eli Adams, Editor. **ISSN:** 0042-5222. **Subscription Rates:** $30 individuals; $55 institutions; $12.95 single issue; $20 single issue institutions.

10017 TCI of Indiana, Inc.
Box 729 Phone: (812)332-9486
Bloomington, IN 47402 Fax: (812)330-0107

Founded: 1966. **Cities Served:** Bloomington County, IN.

10018 WBWB-FM - 96.7
PO Box 7797 Phone: (812)336-8000
304 State Rd. 446 Fax: (812)336-7000
Bloomington, IN 47407
E-mail: wbwb@wbwb.com

Format: Adult Contemporary. **Networks:** Independent. **Owner:** Artistic Media Partners, at above address, (317)594-0600, (317)594-9567. **Founded:** 1978. **Operating Hours:** Continuous. **ADI:** Indianapolis (Marion), IN. **Key Personnel:** Art Angotti, President, phone (317)594-0600, fax (317)594-0567; Bonnie Lavender, Station/Sales Mgr.; Kevin Osborne, Operations Dir. **Wattage:** 3000. **Ad Rates:** Advertising accepted; rates available upon request. Combined advertising rates available with WGCT-FM.

10019 WFIU-FM - 103.7
Radio-TV Center, Indiana University Phone: (812)855-1357
Fax: (812)855-5600
Bloomington, IN 47405

Format: Classical; Jazz; News. **Networks:** National Public Radio (NPR); Public Radio International (PRI). **Founded:** 1950. **Operating Hours:** Continuous. **Key Personnel:** Don Agostino, General Mgr., phone (812)855-8000, fax (812)855-0729, agostino@indiana.edu; Christina Kuzmych, Program Dir., phone (812)855-2088, ckutmych@indiana.edu; V.K. Metzger, Contact, phone (812)855-5801, fax (812)855-0729, vmetzger@indiana.edu. **Wattage:** 34,000. **URL:** http://www.indiana.edu/˜wfiu/wfiuhome.html.

10020 WGCL-AM - 1370
400 1 City Centre Phone: (812)332-3366
Bloomington, IN 47404 Fax: (812)331-4570
E-mail: am1370@bluemarble.net

Format: News; Talk. **Networks:** ABC; ESPN Radio. **Owner:** Sarkes Tarzian Inc., PO Box 62, Bloomington, IN 47401, (812)332-7251, Fax: (812)331-4575. **Founded:** 1949. **Formerly:** WTTS-AM; WGTC-AM. **Operating Hours:** Continuous. **ADI:** Indianapolis (Marion), IN. **Key Personnel:** Chris Doran, Program Dir. **Wattage:** 5000 day; 500 night.

10021 WIUS-AM - 1570
815 E. 8th St. Phone: (812)855-7862
Bloomington, IN 47408 Fax: (812)855-1073
E-mail: wius@indiana.edu

Format: Alternative/New Music/Progressive. **Networks:** CRN International. **Founded:** Oct. 1967. **Formerly:** WQAD-AM; WWIN-AM; WFQR-AM. **Operating Hours:** Continuous. **Key Personnel:** Lonyo Thompson, General Mgr.; Scott Caulfion, Sales Mgr.; Joe Kulszar, Program Dir.; Jason Depasqual, Music Dir.; Galen David, Public Relations; Ashley Shelby, News Dir., phone (812)855-6552; Sean Barter, Sports Dir., phone (812)855-6552. **Local Programs:** *Bloomington Vibes*, Kelly Sparks, (812)855-7862; *WIUS Top 35 College Picks*, Eric Weddle, (812)855-6552; *World Pass*, Tarsis Lopez,

(812)855-6552. **Wattage:** 20. **Ad Rates:** Noncommercial. $5 for 30 seconds. **URL:** http://www.indiana.edu/~wius/wius.html.

10022 WTIU-TV - 30
Indiana University Phone: (812)855-8000
Radio-TV Bldg. Fax: (812)855-0729
Bloomington, IN 47405
Free: (800)662-3311

Format: Public TV. **Networks:** Public Broadcasting Service (PBS). **Owner:** Trustees of Indiana University, Indiana University, Bryan Hall, Bloomington, IN 47405, (812)855-3762. **Founded:** 1969. **Operating Hours:** Continuous; 95% network, 5% local. **ADI:** Indianapolis (Marion), IN. **Key Personnel:** Don Agostino, General Mgr., phone (812)855-8000, fax (812)855-0729, agostino@indiana.edu; Nan Callaway, Station Mgr.; Suzann Owen, Contact; Virginia K. Metzger, Contact, vmetzger@indiana.edu. **Local Programs:** *Big Red Football* 10 p.m. (fall) Monday, Mickey Klein; *Business Perspectives* 10 p.m. Thursday, Mickey Klein; *Editors's Desk* 10 p.m. last Thursday of the month, Keith Klein. **Ad Rates:** Noncommercial. **URL:** http://www.indiana.edu/~radiotv/wtiu/.

10023 WTTS-FM - 92.3
400 1 City Centre Phone: (812)332-3366
Bloomington, IN 47404 Fax: (812)331-4570

Format: Blues; Alternative/New Music/Progressive; Classic Rock. **Owner:** Sarkes Tarzian Inc., PO Box 62, Bloomington, IN 47401, (812)332-7251. **Founded:** 1960. **Operating Hours:** Continuous. **ADI:** Indianapolis (Marion), IN. **Key Personnel:** Thomas Hunt, General Mgr.; Linda Clay, General Sales Mgr.; Rich Anton, Program Dir. **Wattage:** 37,000.

BLUFFTON†, pop. 8,705.

Wells Co. (NE). On Wabash River, 24 m S of Fort Wayne. Manufactures pumps, animal feeds and supplements, motors, machinery; agriculture feed systems. Limestone quarries. Agriculture.

10024 Bluffton News-Banner
News Banner Publications, Inc.
125 N. Johnson St. Phone: (219)824-0224
PO Box 436 Fax: (219)824-0700
Bluffton, IN 46714
Publisher E-mail: email@news-banner.com

Newspaper. **Founded:** 1892. **Freq:** Mon.-Sat. (eve.). **Print Method:** Web offset. **Cols./Page:** 6. **Col. Width:** 2 1/16 inches. **Col. Depth:** 21 1/2 inches. **Key Personnel:** Mark F. Miller, Publisher; Dianne Witwer, Mktg. Dir. **Subscription Rates:** $102 individuals; $135 out of state annually. **URL:** http://www.news-banner.com.
Ad Rates: BW: $1,070.70 **Circ:** Paid ‡5,675
4C: $1,310.70
SAU: $8.30

10025 The Echo
News Banner Publications, Inc.
125 N. Johnson St. Phone: (219)824-0224
PO Box 436 Fax: (219)824-0700
Bluffton, IN 46714
Publisher E-mail: email@news-banner.com

Shopper (with editorial). **Founded:** July 1, 1986. **Freq:** Weekly. **Cols./Page:** 6. **Col. Width:** 12 picas. **Col. Depth:** 126 picas. **Key Personnel:** Mark F. Miller, Editor and Publisher; Dianne Witwer, Mktg. Dir. **Subscription Rates:** Free. **Remarks:** Accepts advertising.
Ad Rates: BW: $412.80 **Circ:** Controlled ‡20,000
4C: $652.80
SAU: $5

10026 WNUY-FM - 100.1
118 S. Main Phone: (219)824-2804
PO Box 321 Fax: (219)824-2805
Bluffton, IN 46714

Format: Adult Contemporary. **Networks:** Tribune Radio. **Founded:** 1963. **Formerly:** WCRD-FM (1989). **Operating Hours:** 5am - 12 midnight. **ADI:** Fort Wayne (Angola), IN. **Key Personnel:** Joe Shanley, President. **Wattage:** 6000. **Ad Rates:** $10-14 per unit.

BOONVILLE†, pop. 6,300.

Warrick Co. (SW) 20 m NE of Evansville. Manufactures aluminum rods and billets, ammunition casing, machine shops, plastic custom molding. Coal mines. Agriculture. Fruit, tomatoes, grain, soybeans.

10027 Boonville Standard
Warrick Publishing Co.
204 W. Locust St. Phone: (812)897-2330
PO Box 71 Fax: (812)897-3703
Boonville, IN 47601
Publication E-mail: wpublish@comsource.net

Newspaper with a Republican orientation. **Founded:** 1875. **Freq:** Weekly (Wed.). **Print Method:** Offset. **Cols./Page:** 6. **Col. Width:** 12.4 picas. **Col. Depth:** 301 agate lines. **Key Personnel:** Jon Garrett, Editor; Myra Teal, Publisher. **Subscription Rates:** $26 individuals; $32 out of area; $50 out of state. **Remarks:** Accepts advertising.
Ad Rates: SAU: $9.89 **Circ:** Paid 4,219
CNU: $7.42
PCI: $5.76

10028 WBNL-AM - 1540
PO Box 270 Phone: (812)897-2080
Boonville, IN 47601 Fax: (812)897-2081

Format: Country. **Networks:** Network Indiana. **Owner:** Boonville Broadcasting Co. Inc., 2177 North Hwy. 61, Boonville, IN. **Founded:** 1950. **Operating Hours:** Sunrise-sunset; 15% network, 85% local. **Key Personnel:** Norman Hall, Contact; Gary Krick, Program Dir.; Carolyn Bryant, Traffic Dir.; Larry Schwiezer, News Dir. **Wattage:** 250. **Ad Rates:** $9.50-15 for 60 seconds.

BOSWELL, pop. 810.

Benton Co. (NW) of Lafayette. Diversified farming. Corn, wheat, hay.

10029 Boswell Enterprise
105 N. Clinton Phone: (765)869-5536
Box 614
Boswell, IN 47921
Newspaper with a Republican orientation. **Founded:** 1892. **Freq:** Weekly (Thurs.). **Print Method:** Uses mats. Letterpress. **Trim Size:** 19 x 13. **Cols./Page:** 6. **Col. Width:** 22 nonpareils. **Col. Depth:** 237 agate lines. **Key Personnel:** Cecil Krebs, Editor and Publisher. **Subscription Rates:** $14 individuals; $20 out of area. **Remarks:** Accepts advertising.
Ad Rates: PCI: $2.50 **Circ:** ‡425

BOURBON, pop. 1,522.

Marshall Co. (N). 32 m SE of South Bend. Manufactures orthopedic and surgical equipment, aluminum siding, truck bodies; printing; trucking; feed mills. Grain, stock, poultry farms. Corn, beans, wheat, hay.

10030 Bourbon News-Mirror
CNNI
116 E. Center St.
Bourbon, IN 46504

Newspaper with a Democratic orientation. **Founded:** 1870. **Freq:** Weekly (Thurs.). **Print Method:** Offset. **Cols./Page:** 6. **Col. Width:** 12.5 picas. **Col. Depth:** 301 agate lines. **Key Personnel:** Sheron L. Knepp, Editor. **ISSN:** 0618-6000. **Subscription Rates:** $15 individuals; $21 out of area. **Remarks:** Accepts advertising.
Ad Rates: GLR: $.14 **Circ:** ‡1,300
SAU: $2.11
PCI: $2.22

BRAZIL†, pop. 7,852.

Clay Co. (W). 16 m NE of Terre Haute. Manufactures clay products, extension cord assembly, jet engine components, mobile homes, semi trailers. Coal mines; clay pets. Agriculture. Corn, wheat, oats and soybeans.

10031 The Brazil Times
The Brazil Times Publishing Corp.
100 N. Meridian St. Phone: (812)446-2216
PO Box 429 Fax: (812)446-0938
Brazil, IN 47834
Free: (800)489-5090
Publication E-mail: btimes@intranix.com

Newspaper with a Republican orientation. **Founded:** 1888. **Freq:** Daily (eve.) and Sat. (morn.). **Print Method:** Offset. **Trim Size:** 22 3/4 x 13 3/4. **Cols./Page:** 6. **Col. Width:** 26 nonpareils. **Col. Depth:** 301 agate lines. **Key Personnel:** Cecil Davis, Editor; Earl Hutcheson, Publisher; William Harper, Advertising Dir.; Lynne Llwellyn. **Subscription Rates:** $78.50 individuals.
Ad Rates: GLR: $.47 **Circ:** Paid ‡5,242
BW: $787.50
4C: $987.50
SAU: $6.50
PCI: $6.50

10032 Times Advantage
The Brazil Times Publishing Corp.
100 N. Meridian St. Phone: (812)446-2216
PO Box 429 Fax: (812)446-0938
Brazil, IN 47834
Free: (800)489-5090
Publication E-mail: braziltimes.com

Shopper. **Subtitle:** Advantage. **Founded:** 1976. **Freq:** Weekly (Tues.). **Print Method:** Offset. Uses mats. **Trim Size:** 13 3/4 x 22 3/4. **Cols./Page:** 6. **Col. Width:** 2 1/16 inches. **Col. Depth:** 21.5 inches. **Key Personnel:** Cecil Davis, Editor; Earl Hutcheson, General Mgr.; Lynne Llewellyn, Advertising Dir., lynne@braziltimes.com. **Subscription Rates:** Free. **Remarks:** Accepts advertising. **URL:** http://www.braziltimes.com. **Alt. Formats:** Microform.
Ad Rates: BW: $258 **Circ:** Free ‡4,700
4C: $458
SAU: $2.00
PCI: $2.00

10033 Cable Brazil Inc.
604 E. National Ave. Phone: (812)448-8308
Box 485 Fax: (812)443-0808
Brazil, IN 47834-2696
Free: (800)886-5455
E-mail: cbiinc@indy.net

Owner: Omega Communications Inc., 29 E. Maryland, PO Box 1766, Indianapolis, IN 46206, (317)264-4010, Fax: (317)264-4020. **Founded:** 1972. **Key Personnel:** Robert E. Schloss, President, phone (317)264-4010, fax (317)264-4020, bob@omagac.com; Wanda Schraedley, System Mgr., phone (812)448-8308, fax (812)443-0808. **Cities Served:** Brazil, Carbon, Eastern Terre Haute, Harmony, Knightsville, Seelyville, Staunton, Vigo County, IN; Vigo County: subscribing households 7,502; 59 channels; 1 community access channel; 168 hours per week community access programming.

BREMEN

Marshall Co. (NC). 15 m NE of Plymouth.

10034 Bremen Enquirer
The Pilot Co.
126 E. Plymouth St. Phone: (219)546-2941
Bremen, IN 46506-0185 Fax: (219)546-3599

Community newspaper. **Subtitle:** The Bremen Enquirer. **Founded:** 1885. **Freq:** Weekly (Wed.). **Print Method:** Offset. **Cols./Page:** 6. **Col. Width:** 2 inches. **Col. Depth:** 21 1/2 inches. **Key Personnel:** Holly Fuchs, Editor; Jane Heckaman, Office Mgr.; Pat Norwick, Advertising Rep. **Subscription Rates:** $15 individuals; $21 out of area; $15 military; $15 students 9 mos. **Remarks:** Accepts advertising.
Ad Rates: PCI: $4.72 **Circ:** 1,600

BROOKVILLE†, pop. 2,874.

Franklin Co. (E). On Whitewater River, 40 m NW of Cincinnati, Ohio. Manufactures roofing, rubber, plastic products, feed, boys garments. Agriculture. Corn, wheat, tobacco.

10035 American
Whitewater Publications Inc.
PO Box 38 Phone: (317)647-4811
Brookville, IN 47012 Fax: (317)647-4811
Free: (888)227-6451
Publication E-mail: ww-puh@cnz.com

Newspaper with a Republican orientation. **Founded:** 1832. **Freq:** Weekly (Wed.). **Print Method:** Offset. **Trim Size:** 13 3/x x 22 3/4. **Cols./Page:** 6. **Col. Width:** 12 picas. **Col. Depth:** 21 inches. **Key Personnel:** Matt Koffenberger, Editor; Donald G. Sintz, Advertising Mgr.; Gary L. Wolf, President. **USPS:** 067-230. **Subscription Rates:** Free; $18 by mail; $23 out of area. **Remarks:** Accepts advertising. **Alt. Formats:** CD-ROM.
Ad Rates: BW: $472.50 **Circ:** Paid 1175
4C: $772.50
SAU: $4
PCI: $4

10036 Democrat
Whitewater Publications Inc.
531 Main St. Phone: (317)647-4221
Brookville, IN 47012 Fax: (317)647-4811
Free: (888)227-6451

Newspaper with a Democratic orientation. **Founded:** 1838. **Freq:** Weekly (Wed.). **Print Method:** Offset. **Trim Size:** 13.75 x 22.75. **Cols./Page:** 6. **Col. Width:** 12 picas. **Col. Depth:** 21 inches. **Key Personnel:** Donald G. Sintz, Advertising Mgr.; Gary L. Wolf, President. **USPS:** 067-260. **Subscription**

Rates: $18 individuals; $23 out of area. **Remarks:** Accepts advertising.
Ad Rates: BW: $472.50 **Circ:** ‡5,900
4C: $775
SAU: $4
PCI: $4

BROWNSTOWN†, pop. 2,704.

Jackson Co. (S). 10 m w of Seymour. Tourism. State and National Forests. Manufacturers floating radio sub warning devices. Paper flour, bricks, holloware, canned goods. Hatcheries. Agriculture. Melons, corn, wheat, soybeans.

10037 The Jackson County Banner
116 E. Cross St. Phone: (812)358-2111
PO Box G Fax: (812)358-5606
Brownstown, IN 47220
Publication E-mail: banner@hsonline.net

Community newspaper with Democratic orientation. **Founded:** Apr. 1, 1869. **Freq:** Semiweekly (Tues. and Thurs.). **Print Method:** Offset. **Cols./Page:** 6. **Col. Width:** 27 nonpareils. **Col. Depth:** 301 agate lines. **Key Personnel:** Joe Persinger, Managing Editor; Judy Persinger, Production/Administration. **USPS:** 067-920. **Subscription Rates:** $30 individuals; $35 in state; $41 out of state. **Remarks:** Accepts advertising.
Ad Rates: GLR: $.252 **Circ:** Paid 3,800
BW: $457.95 Free 5
4C: $757.95
SAU: $4.20

BUTLER, pop. 2,509.

De Kalb Co. (NE). 32 m NE of Fort Wayne. Manufactures automobile jacks, bicycle parts, shipping cartons, fertilizer, truck axles, aluminum billets. Dairy, stock, poultry farms. Corn, wheat, oats.

10038 The Butler Bulletin
108 E. Main St. Phone: (219)868-5501
Butler, IN 46721
Newspaper with a Democratic orientation. **Founded:** 1866. **Freq:** Weekly (Tues.). **Print Method:** Offset. **Cols./Page:** 8. **Col. Width:** 22 nonpareils. **Col. Depth:** 172 agate lines. **Key Personnel:** Joe Shelton, Editor and Publisher. **Subscription Rates:** $15 individuals. **Remarks:** Accepts advertising.
Ad Rates: SAU: $6.62 **Circ:** (Not Reported)
PCI: $5.25

10039 WINM-TV - 63
PO Box 159 Phone: (419)298-3703
Butler, IN 46721-0159 Fax: (419)298-3707
E-mail: winm@tct_ net.org

Format: Commercial TV; Religious. **Networks:** Independent. **Founded:** 1988. **Operating Hours:** Continuous. **ADI:** Fort Wayne (Angola), IN. **Key Personnel:** Rev. Joseph E. Robinson, Gen. Mgr./Programming and Sales, jer@tct_ net.org. **Local Programs:** *Benny Hinn*; *John Hagee*; *Praise the Lord*. **Wattage:** 1.5 million. **Ad Rates:** $40 for 30 seconds; $60 for 60 seconds.

CAMPBELLSBURG

10040 EQC Cable Inc.
PO Box 8 Phone: (812)755-4786
Campbellsburg, IN 47108

Owner: Engler Quality Construction, Inc., at above address. **Founded:** Jan. 1990. **Key Personnel:** Bert S. Engler, President; John K. Engler, Vice President. **Cities Served:** Campbellsburg, Medora, Saltillo, Vallonia, IN; Parts of Washington and Jackson counties.: subscribing households 698; 30 channels.

CARMEL, pop. 18,272.

Hamilton Co. (C). 15 m N of Indianapolis. Manufactures extension cords, seat belts, screw products; high-tech industry. Nurseries. Farming. Corn and soybeans.

The Good Life - See Geist

10041 Jones Intercable Corp.
516 E. Carmel Dr. Phone: (317)844-8877
Carmel, IN 46032 Fax: (317)843-2047

Owner: Jones Intercable Corp., at above address. **Founded:** 1988. **Key Personnel:** Todd Acker, General Mgr. **Cities Served:** Carmel, Fortyville, Zionsville, IN: subscribing households 15,564; 44 channels; 1 community access channel; 168 hours per week community access programming.

10042 WHJE-FM - 91.3
520 E. Main St. Phone: (317)846-7721
Carmel, IN 46032 Fax: (317)571-4066

Format: Alternative/New Music/Progressive; Classic Rock. **Networks:** AP. **Founded:** 1963. **Operating Hours:** Continuous; 100% local. **Key Personnel:** Thomas H. Shoeller, General Mgr.; Tom Allebrandi, Chief Engineer. **Wattage:** 400.

CAYUGA, pop. 1,258.

Vermillion Co. (W) 35 m N of Terre Haute. Residential

10043 Herald News
Box 158 Phone: (765)492-4401
Cayuga, IN 47928-0158
Newspaper with a Democratic orientation. **Founded:** 1892. **Freq:** Weekly (Wed.). **Print Method:** Offset. **Cols./Page:** 5. **Col. Width:** 18 nonpareils. **Col. Depth:** 196 agate lines. **Key Personnel:** Pat Dowers, Editor; C.W. Engelland, Publisher. **Subscription Rates:** $15 individuals; $18 out of area. **Remarks:** Accepts advertising. **Available Online.**
Ad Rates: GLR: $.22 **Circ:** ‡850
PCI: $3

CENTERVILLE, pop. 2,284.

Wayne Co. (E). 4 m W of Richmond. Historical Areas. Manufactured automatic tools and caskets.

10044 The Crusader
Spirit Media, Inc.
139 E. Main Phone: (765)825-2728
Centerville, IN 47330
Community newspaper. **Subtitle:** The Centerville Crusader. **Founded:** 1967. **Freq:** Weekly (Wed.). **Print Method:** Offset. **Trim Size:** 11 1/2 x 17. **Cols./Page:** 5. **Col. Width:** 2 1/16 inches. **Col. Depth:** 16 inches. **Key Personnel:** Tom & Annie Glen, phone (765)855-1005, fax (765)855-1141; Nancy Kinder, Publisher. **USPS:** 909-640. **Subscription Rates:** $13 individuals; $15 out of area. **Remarks:** Accepts advertising. **Alt. Formats:** Microform.
Ad Rates: GLR: $.21 **Circ:** Paid 1,127
BW: $240 Free 6
4C: $390
SAU: $3.50
PCI: $3.50

CHARLESTOWN, pop. 5,596.

Clark Co. (SE). NE of Jeffersonville. Chemicals.

10045 The Leader
Green Banner Publications, Inc.
382 Main Cross St. Phone: (812)967-3176
Charlestown, IN 47111 Fax: (812)256-3377
Free: (800)264-7336

Community newspaper. **Founded:** 1956. **Freq:** Weekly (Wed.). **Print Method:** Offset. **Trim Size:** 11 3/8 x 17. **Cols./Page:** 5. **Col. Width:** 25 nonpareils. **Col. Depth:** 224 agate lines. **Key Personnel:** Mark Grigsby, Editor; Joe Green, Publisher; John Roberts, Sales Mgr. **Subscription Rates:** $18.50 out of area to area households.
Ad Rates: GLR: $.38 **Circ:** Free 12,027
BW: $424 Paid 28
SAU: $5.30
PCI: $5.30

CHESTERTON, pop. 8,598.

Porter Co. (NC). 5 m S of Lake Michigan. Bronze castings.

10046 Chesterton Tribune
193 S. Calumet Rd. Phone: (219)926-1131
PO Box 919 Fax: (219)926-6389
Chesterton, IN 46304
Publication E-mail: chestertontrib@nila.net

General newspaper. **Freq:** Daily (eve.) Mon - Fri. **Print Method:** Offset. **Trim Size:** 13 3/4 x 22. **Key Personnel:** David Carnright, Managing Editor; Warren Canright, Publisher. **Subscription Rates:** $.50; $6 monthly; $85 yearly. **Remarks:** Accepts advertising.
Ad Rates: SAU: $5.80 **Circ:** ⊕5,000

10047 Guideposts for Kids
Guideposts
PO Box 638 Phone: (219)929-4429
Chesterton, IN 46304 Fax: (219)926-3839

Consumer magazine covering puzzles, games, and interfaith literature for children. **Founded:** Jan. 1990. **Freq:** Bimonthly. **Print Method:** Web offset. **Trim Size:** 8 1/4 x 10 3/4. **Cols./Page:** 3. **Col. Depth:** 9 1/4 inches. **Key Personnel:** Marylou Carney, Editor, mcarney@gp4k.org; Janine Scolpino, Circulation Dir. **ISSN:** 1068-9869. **Subscription Rates:** $15.95 individuals; $22.95 out of country; $2.95 single issue. **Remarks:** Advertising not accepted. **Former name:** Faith N Stuff.
Circ: Paid 180,000
Non-paid 45,000

10048 WDSO-FM - 88.3
651 W. Morgan Ave. Phone: (219)926-4700
Chesterton, IN 46304 Fax: (219)926-4387

Format: Album-Oriented Rock (AOR); Contemporary Hit Radio (CHR); Adult Contemporary; Oldies; Alternative/New Music/Progressive. **Owner:** Duneland School Corp., 700 W. Porter Ave., Chesterton, IN 46304, (219)926-1102, Fax: (219)926-7603. **Founded:** 1976. **Operating Hours:** 6 a.m.-7 p.m., Mon, Wed, Fri, Fri; 6 a.m.-5 p.m. Tues., Thur. **Key Personnel:** Michele Stipanovich, Operations Mgr., phone (219)926-4700, fax (219)926-4387; Brent Barber, Station Mgr., phone (219)926-4700, fax (219)926-4387. **Local Programs:** *Porter Co. Perspective* 4:30 pm Wednesday. **Wattage:** 413. **Ad Rates:** Noncommercial.

CHURUBUSCO, pop. 1,638.

Whitley Co. (NE). 15 m NW of Ft Wayne. Manufactures automotive gaskets and rubber products, oil seals, water conditioning equipment.

10049 Churubusco News
Churubusco News and Printing
123 N. Main St. Phone: (219)693-3949
PO Box 8 Fax: (219)693-6545
Churubusco, IN 46723
Publisher E-mail: chnews@fortwayne.infi.net

Community newspaper. **Founded:** Aug. 1, 1992. **Freq:** Weekly. **Print Method:** Offset. **Trim Size:** 11 x 17. **Cols./Page:** 6. **Col. Width:** 1 1/2 inches. **Col. Depth:** 15 3/4 inches. **Key Personnel:** Vivian Rosswurm, Editor. **USPS:** 009-385. **Subscription Rates:** $20. **Remarks:** Accepts advertising.
Ad Rates: GLR: $3.50 **Circ:** Paid ⊕1,766
BW: $3.50
PCI: $3.50

CLAY CITY, pop. 883.

Clay Co. (W). 24 m SE of Terre Haute. Pottery manufactured. Coal mines. Lumber mill. Grain, stock farms.

10050 The News
Spencer Evening World
717 Main St. Phone: (812)939-2163
Clay City, IN 47841-0038 Fax: (812)939-2286

Newspaper with a Democratic orientation. **Founded:** 1912. **Freq:** Weekly (Wed.). **Print Method:** Offset. **Cols./Page:** 7. **Col. Width:** 24 nonpareils. **Col. Depth:** 294 agate lines. **Key Personnel:** Rhonda G. Riggle, Editor. **Subscription Rates:** $16 individuals; $23 out of area. **Remarks:** Accepts advertising.
Ad Rates: PCI: $2.90 **Circ:** 2,000

CLINTON, pop. 5,267.

Vermillion Co. (W). On Wabash River, 16 m N of Terre Haute. Manufactures antibiotics, fertilizers, overalls, shirts. Meat packing Coal mine; gravel. Aluminum products. Grain farms.

10051 The Daily Clintonian
Clinton Color Crafters
422 S. Main St. Phone: (317)832-2443
PO Box 309
Clinton, IN 47842-0309
Newspaper with a Republican orientation. **Founded:** 1890. **Freq:** Daily (eve.). **Print Method:** Offset. **Trim Size:** 17 1/2 x 22 3/4. **Cols./Page:** 7. **Col. Width:** 12.5 picas. **Col. Depth:** 294 agate lines. **Key Personnel:** George L. Carey, Editor and Publisher; George B. Carey, Publisher. **ISSN:** 1423-0000. **Subscription Rates:** $68 individuals; $.50 single issue. **Remarks:** Accepts advertising.
Ad Rates: GLR: $.15 **Circ:** Paid ⊕5,481
BW: $441 Free ⊕35
SAU: $4.20

COLUMBIA CITY†, pop. 5,091.

Whitley Co. (NE). 20 m NW of Fort Wayne.

10052 The Post & Mail
Columbia City Publishing Co.
PO Box 128 Phone: (219)244-5753
Columbia City, IN 46725 Fax: (219)244-7598

General newspaper. **Founded:** 1854. **Freq:** Mon.-Sat. (eve.). **Print Method:** Offset. **Cols./Page:** 6. **Col. Depth:** 21 1/2 inches. **Key Personnel:** Rick Kreps, Editor/Administration;

Douglas C. Driscoll, Publisher. **ISSN:** 0746-9950. **Subscription Rates:** $91 individuals. **Remarks:** Accepts advertising.
Ad Rates: BW: $559 **Circ:** ‡4,867
4C: $709
SAU: $5.50
PCI: $3.85

10053 WJHS-FM - 91.5
600 N. Whitley St. Phone: (219)248-8915
Columbia City, IN 46725 Fax: (219)244-5610

Format: Alternative/New Music/Progressive; Sports. **Networks:** AP. **Owner:** Whitley County Consolidated Schools, 400 N. Whitley St., Columbia City, IN 46725. **Founded:** 1986. **Operating Hours:** 1% network, 99% local. **Key Personnel:** Tim Moriarty, Station Mgr., tim_ moriarty@wccs.k12.in.us. **Wattage:** 2650.

COLUMBUS†, pop. 30,292.

Bartholomew Co. (SE). 45 m S of Indianapolis. Manufactures auto parts, variable transmissions, diesel engines, metal furniture, metal, plastic products specialties, cement products, electric motors. Diversified farming.

10054 The Republic
333 2nd St. Phone: (812)372-7811
Columbus, IN 47201-6795 Fax: (812)379-5608

Newspaper with a Republican orientation. **Founded:** 1877. **Freq:** Daily (morn.). **Print Method:** Offset. **Cols./Page:** 6. **Col. Width:** 25 nonpareils. **Col. Depth:** 301 agate lines. **Key Personnel:** John Harmon, Editor; Don R. Bucknam, Publisher; Pamela Wells-Lego, Advertising Mgr. **Subscription Rates:** $123.50 individuals. **Remarks:** Accepts advertising. **Online:** ADSEND.
Ad Rates: GLR: $.98 **Circ:** Mon.-Sat. 21,874
BW: $1,902.75 Sun. 25,747
4C: $2,177.75
SAU: $14.75
PCI: $14.75

10055 WCSI-AM - 1010
3212 Washington St. Phone: (812)372-4448
Columbus, IN 47203

Format: News; Talk; Sports. **Networks:** Mutual Broadcasting System; ESPN Radio. **Founded:** 1957. **Operating Hours:** Continuous. **ADI:** Indianapolis (Marion), IN. **Key Personnel:** John Foster, Program Dir.; Tasha Kah, Station Mgr.; Wes Roy, News Dir.; Sam Simmermaker, Sports Dir. **Local Programs:** *A-M Columbus*, John Foster; *Computer Talk*, Dave Kleinschmidt; *Right At Home*, Nancy Kardl. **Wattage:** 500 day. 19 night. **Ad Rates:** $14 for 60 seconds. **URL:** http://www.columbusin/wcsi.com.

10056 WKKG-FM - 101.5
3212 Washington St., Box 709 Phone: (812)372-4448
Columbus, IN 47202

Format: Contemporary Country. **Networks:** Mutual Broadcasting System. **Owner:** Findlay Publishing Company, at above address. **Founded:** 1958. **Operating Hours:** Continuous. **Key Personnel:** Tasha Kah, General Mgr.; John Paul, Program Dir. **Wattage:** 50,000 ERP. **Ad Rates:** $42 for 60 seconds.

10057 WRZQ-FM - 107.3
825 Washington St. Phone: (812)379-1077
Columbus, IN 47201 Fax: (812)375-2555

Format: Adult Contemporary. **Networks:** CNN Radio. **Owner:** Keith Reising, at above address. **Founded:** 1968. **Formerly:** WTRE-FM (1983); WRZQ-FM; WRZQ-FM. **Operating Hours:** Continuous. **ADI:** Indianapolis (Marion), IN. **Key Personnel:** Keith Reising, Jr., President; Mary Monroe, Traffic and Business Mgr.; Mike King, Station Mgr.; Sue King, General Sales Mgr. **Local Programs:** *Face to Face*; *"In the Morning with Dave & Jennifer"*; *"Sunday Stretch" (Jazz)*. **Wattage:** 50,000 ERP. **Ad Rates:** $16.50-27 for 60 seconds. Combined advertising rates available with WTRE-AM. **URL:** http://www.qmix.com.

10058 WWWY-FM - 104.9
1333 Washington Phone: (812)372-9933
PO Box 487 Fax: (812)372-9935
Columbus, IN 47202

Format: Classic Rock. **Networks:** ABC. **Owner:** Mid-State Media, Inc., at above address. **Founded:** 1975. **Operating Hours:** 19 hours Daily; 9% network, 91% local. **ADI:** Indianapolis (Marion), IN. **Key Personnel:** Scott Goodwin, President; Mark Webber, News Dir.; Dennis Rediker, Operations Mgr. **Local Programs:** *Y-105's A.M. Addiction.* **Wattage:** 6000. **Ad Rates:** $10-18.20 for 30 seconds; $13-28.80 for 60 seconds.

CONNERSVILLE†, pop. 17,023.

Fayette Co. (E). On Whitewater River and canal, 60 m E of Indianapolis. Manufactures auto parts, rotary blowers, dishwashers, flour, metal and enamel products, tools, dies. Diversified farming.

10059 Connersville News-Examiner
406 Central Ave. Phone: (765)825-0585
PO Box 287 Fax: (765)825-4599
Connersville, IN 47331-0287
Free: (888)906-1700
Publisher E-mail: newsexaminer@newsexaminer.com

General newspaper. **Founded:** Oct. 19, 1887. **Freq:** Daily (eve.). **Print Method:** Web offset. **Cols./Page:** 6. **Col. Width:** 2 1/16 inches. **Col. Depth:** 21 inches. **Key Personnel:** Robert Powers, Editor; John Claxton, Publisher; Diane Howell, Advertising Mgr., dhowell@intranix.com; Kyle Sparks, Circulation Mgr. **Subscription Rates:** $96 city; $99 rural. **Remarks:** Accepts advertising. **URL:** http://www.nuxonnews.com/news_ex.
Ad Rates: GLR: $1.09 **Circ:** Paid 8,488
BW: $1,631.85
4C: $1,971.85
PCI: $14

10060 Poultry Press
PO Box 542 Phone: (765)827-0932
Connersville, IN 47331 Fax: (765)827-4186

Newspaper (tabloid) containing articles and features on poultry and poultry shows. **Founded:** 1914. **Freq:** Monthly. **Print Method:** Offset. **Trim Size:** 11 1/2 x 16. **Cols./Page:** 5. **Col. Width:** 1 3/4 inches. **Col. Depth:** 16 inches. **Key Personnel:** William F. Wulff, Editor and Publisher. **ISSN:** 0032-5783. **Subscription Rates:** $18 individuals; $35 two years; $2 single issue. **Remarks:** Accepts advertising.
Ad Rates: BW: $640 **Circ:** ‡5,800
4C: $700
PCI: $7

10061 Whitewater Valley Market Guide
Connersville News Examiner
406 Central Ave. Phone: (765)825-0585
PO Box 287 Fax: (765)825-4599
Connersville, IN 47331-0287
Free: (888)906-1700
Publisher E-mail: newsexaminer@newsexaminer.com

Shopper. **Subtitle:** Whitewater Valley Market Guide. **Founded:** 1976. **Freq:** Weekly (Mon.). **Print Method:** Web offset. **Cols./Page:** 6. **Col. Width:** 2 1/16 inches. **Col. Depth:** 21 inches. **Key Personnel:** Robert Powers, Editor, bpowers@connersvillein.com; John Claxton, Publisher; Diane Howell, Advertising Mgr., phone (765)825-2914, dhowell@newsexaminer.com; Kyle Sparks, Circulation Mgr. **Subscription Rates:** Free. **Remarks:** Combined advertising rates available with Connersville News Examiner. **Available Online. URL:** http://www.connersvillein.com/news-examiner.
Ad Rates: GLR: $1.09 **Circ:** Free 8,585
BW: $2,190.42
4C: $2,530.42
CNU: $7
PCI: $14

10062 WCNB-FM - 100.3
406 Central Ave. Phone: (317)825-6411
PO Box 619 Fax: (317)825-2411
Connersville, IN 47331

Format: Contemporary Country. **Simulcasts:** WIFE-AM. **Networks:** Satellite Music Network. **Owner:** Rodgers Broadcasting Corp., c/o WCBK, PO Box 1577, Martinsville, IN 46151, (317)342-3394. **Operating Hours:** 5 a.m.-11 p.m.; 50% network, 50% local. **Key Personnel:** John Trine, General Mgr.; Steve Frey, Sales Mgr.; Stephen Skinner, Operations Mgr.; John White, News Dir.; Mike Peacock, Contact. **Wattage:** 28,000. **Ad Rates:** $11.50-16 for 30 seconds; $13.50-19 for 60 seconds. Combined advertising rates available with WIFE-AM: $11.50-$16 for 30 seconds; $13.50-$19 for 60 seconds.

CORYDON†, pop. 2,724.

Harrison Co. (S) 25 m W of Louisville, Ky. Manufactures furniture, glass, cabinets. Battery separating plant. Poultry processing.

10063 The Clarion
Corydon Democrat
PO Box 220 Phone: (812)738-4552
Corydon, IN 47112 Fax: (812)738-1909

Newspaper. **Founded:** 1949. **Freq:** Weekly (Wed.). **Print Method:** Offset. **Cols./Page:** 8. **Col. Width:** 20 nonpareils. **Col. Depth:** 294 agate lines. **Key Personnel:** Mark Young, Editor; Dennis Huber, Publisher. **Subscription Rates:** $9 individuals. **Remarks:** Accepts advertising.
Ad Rates: GLR: $.18 **Circ:** Paid 12,569
Free 170

10064 The Corydon Democrat
O'Bannon Publishing Co., Inc.
PO Box 220 Phone: (812)738-2211
Corydon, IN 47112-0220 Fax: (812)738-1909

Newspaper with a Democratic orientation. **Founded:** 1856. **Freq:** Weekly (Wed.). **Print Method:** Letterpress and offset. **Cols./Page:** 6. **Col. Width:** 27 nonpareils. **Col. Depth:** 297 agate lines. **Key Personnel:** Randy West, Editor; Dennis Huber, Publisher; Fred Cromwell, Advertising Mgr. **Subscription Rates:** $18.95 individuals; $35 out of state. **Remarks:** Accepts advertising.
Ad Rates: GLR: $.32 **Circ:** 8,289
SAU: $6.06
PCI: $5.15

10065 WOCC-AM - 1550
211 N. Capitol Ave. Phone: (812)738-9622
PO Box 838 Fax: (812)738-1676
Corydon, IN 47112

Format: Oldies. **Networks:** USA Radio. **Owner:** Richard Brabandt, at above address. **Founded:** 1964. **Formerly:** WJDW-AM. **Operating Hours:** Sunrise-sunset. **Key Personnel:** R.L. Brabandt, General Mgr., phone (812)738-9622, fax (812)738-1676. **Local Programs:** *Local Sports*, R.L. Brabandt, Mailing contact. **Wattage:** 250. **Ad Rates:** $8.00 for 30 seconds; $12.00 for 60 seconds.

COVINGTON

10066 WFOF-FM - 90.3
610 3rd St. Phone: (765)793-4088
PO Box 227 Fax: (765)793-4039
Covington, IN 47932
E-mail: wfof-fm@juno.com

Format: Religious. **Networks:** Moody Broadcasting. **Founded:** 1984. **Operating Hours:** Continuous. **Key Personnel:** Ogle Snider, General Mgr. **Wattage:** 19,000.

10067 WKZS-FM - 103.1
at above address Phone: (765)793-4823
Covington, IN 47932 Fax: (765)793-4644
E-mail: kiss1031@aol.com

Format: Adult Contemporary; Soft Rock. **Networks:** Jones Satellite. **Owner:** Benton-Weatherford Broadcasting, Inc. of IN, PO Box 67, Covington, IN 47932. **Founded:** 1982. **Formerly:** WVWV-FM (1985); WCDV-FM (1998). **Operating Hours:** Continuous; 100% local. **Key Personnel:** Rhea Benton-Weatherford, General Mgr.; Greg Green, Station Mgr.; Larry Weatherford, President; Kimberly Haworth, Traffic Mgr. **Wattage:** 3000. **Ad Rates:** $18-34 for 30 seconds; $28-44 for 60 seconds.

CRAWFORDSVILLE†, pop. 13,325.

Montgomery Co. (W). 45 m NW of Indianapolis. Wabash College.

10068 Journal Review
Freedom Communications Inc.
119 N. Green St. Phone: (317)362-1200
PO Box 512 Fax: (317)364-5424
Crawfordsville, IN 47933
Free: (800)488-4414

General newspaper. **Founded:** 1841. **Freq:** Mon.-Sat. (morn.). **Print Method:** Offset. **Trim Size:** 13 3/4 x 22 3/4. **Cols./Page:** 6. **Col. Width:** 26 nonpareils. **Col. Depth:** 301 agate lines. **Key Personnel:** Gaildene Hamilton, Managing Editor; James McMillen, Publisher; Randy List, Advertising Mgr.; Rick Keller, Production Mgr.; Robert Catlett, Circulation Dir.; Brent Harris, Systems Mgr. **Subscription Rates:** $93 individuals; $126 out of area mailed; $1 out of state single copy, Mon.-Fri.; $1.50 single copy, Sat. **Remarks:** Accepts advertising.
Ad Rates: GLR: $.74 **Circ:** Mon.-Sat. 10,701
BW: $1341.60
4C: $1591.60
SAU: $10.40

10069 Marcus Cable
120 S. Washington St. Phone: (317)362-6161
Crawfordsville, IN 47933

Owner: Marcus Cable, 2911 Turtle Creek Blvd. Ste. 1300, Dallas, TX 75219. **Founded:** 1969. **Formerly:** Cardinal Communications (1993); Sammons Communications (1995). **Key Personnel:** LuAnne Rice, General Mgr. **Cities Served:** Covington, Crawfordsville, Veidersburg, IN: subscribing households 8,784; 60 channels.

10070 WCVL-AM - 1550
1880 N. Rd. 200 W. Phone: (765)362-8200
PO Box 603 Fax: (765)364-1550
Crawfordsville, IN 47933
E-mail: dmvnro@wico.net

Format: Oldies; Agricultural; Sports. **Networks:** ABC; Network Indiana. **Owner:** Key Broadcasting, PO Drawer 1450, Corbin, KY 40701. **Founded:** 1964. **Operating Hours:** 5 a.m.-midnight; 10% network, 90% local. **Key Personnel:** Dick Munro, General Mgr.; Ken Scott, Program Dir.; Joe Jarvis, Farm; Rob Lee, News Dir. **Local Programs:** *Community Focus*, Frank Phillips; *Farm World*, Joe Jarvis. **Wattage:** 250. **Ad Rates:** $5-23 for 30 seconds; $7-28 for 60 seconds.

10071 WIMC-FM - 103.9
1800 N. Rd. 200 W. Phone: (765)362-8200
PO Box 603 Fax: (765)364-1550
Crawfordsville, IN 47933

Format: Adult Contemporary. **Networks:** Network Indiana. **Owner:** Key Broadcasting, PO Box 1450, Corbin, KY 40701. **Founded:** 1974. **Formerly**: WLFQ-FM (1987). **Operating Hours:** 5 a.m.-midnight; 2% network, 98% local. **Key Personnel:** Dick Munro, General Mgr.; Ken Scott, Program Dir.; Joe Jarvis, Farm; Rob Lee, News Dir. **Local Programs:** *Coaches Corner*, Rob Lee; *Community Focus*, Frank Phillips. **Wattage:** 3000. **Ad Rates:** $8-23 for 30 seconds; $11-28 for 60 seconds.

CROTHERSVILLE

10072 Crothersville Times
510 Moore St., Ste. 100 Phone: (812)793-2188
PO Box 141 Fax: (812)793-2188
Crothersville, IN 47229
Publication E-mail: ctimes@hsonline.net

Community newspaper. **Founded:** Dec. 1980. **Freq:** Weekly (Wed.). **Print Method:** Offset. **Trim Size:** 10 1/4 x 13. **Cols./Page:** 6. **Col. Width:** 1 5/8 inches. **Col. Depth:** 13 inches. **Key Personnel:** Curt Kovener, Editor and Publisher. **USPS:** 586-710. **Subscription Rates:** $10 individuals; $15 two years; $15 out of area. **Remarks:** Accepts advertising.
Ad Rates: BW: $156 **Circ:** ‡2,800
4C: $309.20
PCI: $2.55

CROWN POINT†, pop. 16,455.

Lake Co. (NW). 16 m S of Gary. Manufactures machinery, wagon bodies, pulleys, golf balls, color film processing, cabinets. Agriculture. Corn, wheat, oats. soybeans.

10073 Cedar Lake-Lowell Star
15 N. Court St. Phone: (219)663-4212
PO Box 419 Fax: (219)663-0137
Crown Point, IN 46307
Newspaper with an independent slant. **Founded:** 1857. **Freq:** Weekly (Thurs.). **Print Method:** Offset. **Trim Size:** 10 1/2 x 12 1/2. **Cols./Page:** 5. **Col. Width:** 12 picas. **Col. Depth:** 175 agate lines. **Key Personnel:** Beth Monstwillo, Business Mgr.; Andrew Steele, Managing Editor; Anita Hilgeman, Advertising Mgr.; Karen Caffarini, Editor. **USPS:** 139-120. **Subscription Rates:** $37 individuals; $46 out of state. **Remarks:** Accepts advertising. **Formerly**: Crown Point Register.
Ad Rates: GLR: $0.57 **Circ:** ‡121
BW: $500
4C: $745
PCI: $8

10074 Crown Point Shopping News
111 Hack Ct. Phone: (219)663-5330
Crown Point, IN 46307 Fax: (219)663-2077
Publication E-mail: cpsn@mail.congrp.com

Shopping guide. **Founded:** 1965. **Freq:** Weekly (Wed.). **Cols./Page:** 6. **Col. Width:** 1 3/8 inches. **Col. Depth:** 1 inches. **Key Personnel:** Shari Struebig, General Mgr. **Subscription Rates:** Free. **Remarks:** Accepts advertising.
Ad Rates: GLR: $7.00 **Circ:** Free ♦21,110
BW: $565
4C: $2,000
PCI: $5.95

10075 Crown Point Star
15 N. Court St. Phone: (219)663-4212
PO Box 419 Fax: (219)663-0137
Crown Point, IN 46307
Newspaper with an independent slant. **Founded:** 1880. **Freq:** Weekly (Thurs.). **Print Method:** Offset. **Trim Size:** 10 1/2 x 12 1/2. **Cols./Page:** 5. **Col. Width:** 12 picas. **Col. Depth:** 175 agate lines. **Key Personnel:** Andrew Steele, Managing Editor; Anita Hilgeman, Advertising Mgr.; Beth Monstwillo, Business Mgr.; Karen Caffarini, Editor. **USPS:** 302-060. **Subscription Rates:** $37 individuals; $46 out of state. **Formerly**: Lake County Star.
Ad Rates: GLR: $0.57 **Circ:** 2,459
BW: $500
4C: $745
PCI: $8

10076 Southlake Register
The Lake County Star
15 N. Court St. Phone: (219)663-4212
PO Box 419 Fax: (219)663-0137
Crown Point, IN 46307
Shopper. **Founded:** 1951. **Freq:** Weekly (Sun.). **Print Method:** Offset. **Trim Size:** 10 1/14 x 16. **Cols./Page:** 5. **Col. Width:** 11.5 picas. **Col. Depth:** 224 agate lines. **Key Personnel:** Beth Monstwillo, General Mgr.; David Graves, Advertising Mgr. **Subscription Rates:** Free; $22 out of area; $27.25 out of state. **Remarks:** Accepts advertising. **Formerly**: Southlake and Cedar Lake Register.
Ad Rates: GLR: $0.54 **Circ:** Free ‡14,000
BW: $600
4C: $845
PCI: $7.50

CULVER

10077 Culver Citizen
Citizen Publications
107 S. Main St. Phone: (219)842-3229
PO Box 90 Fax: (219)935-0083
Culver, IN 46511
Publication E-mail: citizen@skyenet.net

Community newspaper. **Founded:** 1894. **Freq:** Weekly. **Print Method:** Offset. **Trim Size:** 14 x 22 1/2. **Cols./Page:** 6. **Col. Width:** 12 1/2 picas. **Col. Depth:** 21 inches. **Key Personnel:** Judith L. Karst, Editor; Frederick A. Karst, Publisher. **USPS:** 422-330. **Subscription Rates:** $18 individuals; $21 out of state. **Remarks:** Accepts advertising.
Ad Rates: BW: $564.48 **Circ:** Paid ⊕1,538
SAU: $5.17 Non-paid ⊕30
PCI: $4.48

DALE, pop. 1,693.

Spencer Co. (SW). 40 m NE of Evansville. Grist mills; Manufactures wood furniture, plastic furniture parts. Diversified farming.

10078 Spencer County Leader
Dubois Spencer Counties Publishing Co., Inc.
PO Box 38 Phone: (812)937-2100
Ferdinand, IN 47532
Publication E-mail: dalenews@psci.net

Newspaper with a Democratic orientation featuring local area and school news, and agricultural and religious issues. **Founded:** 1960. **Freq:** Weekly (Thurs.). **Print Method:** Offset. **Cols./Page:** 6. **Col. Width:** 24 nonpareils. **Col. Depth:** 224 agate lines. **Key Personnel:** Richard Tretter, Editor; Miriam Ash, General Mgr. **USPS:** 565-900. **Subscription Rates:** $20; $25 out of area; $30 out of state. **Remarks:** Accepts advertising. **URL:** http://www.dscp.com. **Formerly**: The Dale News.
Ad Rates: BW: $422.25 **Circ:** ‡2,000
PCI: $3.50

DANVILLE†, pop. 4,220.

Hendricks Co. (C). 19 m W of Indianapolis. Suburban Residential

10079 The Republican
Hendricks County Republican, Inc.
6 E. Main St. Phone: (317)745-2777
PO Box 149 Fax: (317)745-2777
Danville, IN 46122
Newspaper with a Republican orientation. **Founded:** 1847. **Freq:** Weekly (Thurs.). **Print Method:** Offset. **Cols./Page:** 7. **Col. Width:** 10 1/2 ems. **Col. Depth:** 21 inches. **Key Personnel:** Betty Jean Weesner, Editor. **USPS:** 462-200. **Subscription Rates:** $15 individuals. **Remarks:** Accepts advertising.
Ad Rates: BW: $438 **Circ:** ‡1,300
PCI: $3

DECATUR†, pop. 8,649.

Adams Co. (NE). 21 m SE of Fort Wayne. Manufactures small motors, soybean oil, modular homes, livestock feed, mobile homes, recreational vehicles, pipes, boats, cartons, boxes, castings, cement products. Ash, elm timber. Grain, dairy cattle farms. Soybeans.

10080 Decatur Daily Democrat
Decatur Publishing Co., Inc.
141 S. 2nd St. Phone: (219)724-2121
PO Box 1001 Fax: (219)724-7981
Decatur, IN 46733-5001
Publication E-mail: dailydemo@decaturnet.com

General newspaper. **Founded:** 1857. **Freq:** Daily (eve.) and Sat. (morn.). **Print Method:** Offset. **Trim Size:** 13 3/4 x 22 3/4. **Cols./Page:** 6. **Col. Width:** 2 1/16 inches. **Col. Depth:** 21 1/2 inches. **Key Personnel:** Robert Shraluka, Editor; Dick Stimpson, Advertising Mgr. **Subscription Rates:** $98 individuals; $106 out of area. **Remarks:** Accepts advertising.
Ad Rates: SAU: $7.70 **Circ:** ‡5,939
PCI: $7.70

DEMOTTE

10081 Action Plus Shopper
827 S. Halleck St. Phone: (219)987-5111
Box 110 Fax: (219)987-5119
DeMotte, IN 46310
Free: (888)809-5561
Publication E-mail: kvpostnews@nitco.com
Publisher E-mail: kvpost@netnitco.net

Shopper. **Founded:** 1975. **Freq:** Weekly (Mon.). **Print Method:** Offset. **Cols./Page:** 6. **Col. Width:** 24 nonpareils. **Col. Depth:** 301 agate lines. **Key Personnel:** Frank Copley, Publisher; Sally Snow, General Mgr. **Remarks:** Accepts advertising. **Feature Editors:** Carmen Cox, *Sports*.
Ad Rates: BW: $5 **Circ:** Free ‡14,750
4C: $400
SAU: $5
PCI: $5.36

ELKHART, pop. 41,305.

Elkhart Co. (N). On St Joseph River, 100 m E of Chicago. Manufacturers band instruments, brass, sheet metal and rubber products, ethical and proprietary medicine, railway, telephone, television controls, auto radio equipment, machinery, cardboard containers, castings, furniture, plastics, mobile homes, recreational vehicles and van conversion.

10082 The Paper (Elkhart Edition)
The Papers, Inc.
229 W. Marion Phone: (219)522-4111
Elkhart, IN 46516 Fax: (219)522-7448

Newspaper. **Founded:** 1976. **Freq:** Weekly (Tues.). **Print Method:** Offset. **Trim Size:** 11 3/8 x 16 3/4. **Cols./Page:** 5. **Col. Width:** 22 nonpareils. **Col. Depth:** 224 agate lines. **Key Personnel:** Jeri Seely, Editor; Della Baumgartner, Publisher. **Subscription Rates:** Free. **Remarks:** Accepts advertising.
Ad Rates: BW: $536 **Circ:** Free 27,022
PCI: $7.40

10083 RV Trade Digest
Continental Communications Co. of Indiana, Inc.
58025 C.R. No. 9 South Phone: (219)295-1962
PO Box 1805 Fax: (219)295-7574
Elkhart, IN 46517
Free: (800)380-2345
Publication E-mail: rvtd@aol.com

Magazine for the recreational vehicle industry. **Subtitle:** The Marketplace of the RV Industry. **Founded:** 1981. **Freq:** Monthly 13/year. **Print Method:** Web offset. **Trim Size:** 8 1/4 x 10 7/8. **Cols./Page:** 3. **Col. Width:** 2 1/4 inches. **Col. Depth:** 10 inches. **Key Personnel:** Doris Czoch, Publisher; Rosalie Corson, Editor/Gen. Manager; Kip Czoch, Vice President/Assoc. Publisher. **ISSN:** 0745-0389. **Subscription Rates:** $36; $55 Canada; $72 other countries; $3 single issue. **Remarks:** Accepts advertising.
Ad Rates: BW: $3,085 **Circ:** Paid △1
4C: $4,265 Controlled △16,085
PCI: $330

10084 Sports Truck Accessory Digest
Continental Communications Co. of Indiana, Inc.
58025 C.R. No. 9 South Phone: (219)295-1962
PO Box 1805 Fax: (219)295-7574
Elkhart, IN 46517
Free: (800)380-2345
Publication E-mail: rvtd@aol.com

Automotive magazine covering the light truck and sports utility market. **Subtitle:** Marketplace of the Sports Truck Accessory. **Founded:** July 1982. **Freq:** Bimonthly. **Print Method:** Offset. **Trim Size:** 8 3/8 x 10 7/8. **Cols./Page:** 3. **Col. Width:** 25 nonpareils. **Col. Depth:** 168 agate lines. **Key Personnel:** Rosalie Corson, Editor/Gen. Manager; Kip Czoch, Vice President/Assoc. Publisher; Doris Czoch, Publisher. **ISSN:** 1043-

4879. **Subscription Rates:** $40 individuals. **Remarks:** Accepts advertising. **Formerly:** Van and Truck Digest.
Ad Rates: BW: $2,685 **Circ:** Controlled 15,501
4C: $3,645
SAU: $100
PCI: $330

10085 Truth
Truth Publishing Co.
421 S. 2nd St. Phone: (219)294-1661
Box 487 Fax: (219)294-3895
Elkhart, IN 46516-3227
General newspaper. **Founded:** 1889. **Freq:** Daily (eve.), Sat. and Sun. (morn.). **Print Method:** Offset. **Cols./Page:** 6. **Col. Width:** 24 nonpareils. **Col. Depth:** 301 agate lines. **Key Personnel:** Anthony H. Biggs, Publisher. **Remarks:** Accepts advertising.
Ad Rates: SAU: $14.01 **Circ:** Mon.-Sat. 27,518
Sun. 31,620

10086 WFRN-AM - 1270
PO Box 307 Phone: (219)875-5166
Elkhart, IN 46515 Fax: (219)875-6662
Free: (800)933-0501

Format: Talk; Religious. **Networks:** SkyLight Satellite. **Owner:** Progressive Broadcasting System, Inc., at above address. **Founded:** 1956. **Formerly:** WCMR-AM (1993). **Operating Hours:** Continuous. **ADI:** South Bend-Elkhart, IN. **Key Personnel:** Edwin C. Moore, President; Steve Randolph, General Sales Mgr. **Wattage:** 5000 day; 1000 night. **Ad Rates:** $5-16 for 30 seconds; $7.50-24 for 60 seconds.

10087 WFRN-FM - 104.7
PO Box 307 Phone: (219)875-5166
Elkhart, IN 46515 Fax: (219)875-6662
Free: (800)933-0501

Format: Religious; Contemporary Christian. **Networks:** USA Radio. **Owner:** Progressive Broadcasting System, Inc., at above address. **Founded:** 1963. **Operating Hours:** Continuous. **ADI:** South Bend-Elkhart, IN. **Key Personnel:** Edwin C. Moore, President/Gen. Mgr.; Steve Randolph, General Sales Mgr. **Wattage:** 50,000 ERP. **Ad Rates:** $42 for 30 seconds; $47 for 60 seconds.

10088 WNIT-TV - 34
PO Box 3434, 2300 Charger Blvd. Phone: (219)674-5961
Fax: (219)262-8497
Elkhart, IN 46515
E-mail: viewers@wnit.pbs.org

Format: Public TV. **Networks:** Public Broadcasting Service (PBS). **Owner:** Michiana Public Broadcasting Corp., at above address. **Founded:** 1968. **Operating Hours:** 7 a.m.-11:30 p.m.; 98.5% network, 1.5% local. **ADI:** South Bend-Elkhart, IN. **Key Personnel:** Trina Cutter, President; Kenny Barnett, Chief Engineer; Laura Coyne, Meida & Comm. Relations Mgr.; Amy Cassidy, Chief Financial Officer; Gail Martin, Development Mgr. **Wattage:** 1.3 Million. **Ad Rates:** Noncommercial; underwriting available.

10089 WSJV-TV - 28
58096 County Rd. 7 S. Phone: (219)679-9758
Elkhart, IN 46517 Fax: (219)294-1324
E-mail: fox28@fox28.com

Format: Commercial TV. **Networks:** Fox. **Founded:** 1954. **Operating Hours:** Continuous. **ADI:** South Bend-Elkhart, IN. **Key Personnel:** Randy Ingram, Station Mgr., fax (219)294-1267, randi@fox28.com; Dick Frid, Sales Mgr., sales@fox28.com; Kevin Sargent, VP/General Mgr., fax (219)294-1267, gm@fox28.com; Scott Leiter, Creative Services Mgr., fax (219)294-1267. **Wattage:** 5,000,000.

10090 WTRC-AM - 1340
58096 C.R. 7 S. Phone: (219)293-5611
Elkhart, IN 46517 Fax: (219)295-2FAX

Format: Oldies; News; Sports. **Networks:** ABC; Westwood One Radio. **Owner:** Federated Media/Pathfinder Communications Corp., PO Box 487, Elkhart, IN 46516, (219)295-2500. **Founded:** 1931. **Formerly:** WJAK-AM. **Operating Hours:** Continuous; 70% network, 30% local. **ADI:** South Bend-Elkhart, IN. **Key Personnel:** Richard Rhodes, General Mgr.; Allen Strike, Program Dir.; Bob Henning, Chief Engineer. **Local Programs:** *Sound Off*, Allen Strike. **Wattage:** 1000. **Ad Rates:** $4-47 for 30 seconds; $5-56 for 60 seconds.

10091 WVPE-FM - 88.1
2424 California Rd. Phone: (219)262-5660
Elkhart, IN 46514 Fax: (219)262-5700
Free: (800)399-9873
E-mail: wvpe@wvpe.org

Format: Jazz; News; Public Radio; Folk. **Networks:** Public Radio International (PRI); National Public Radio (NPR). **Owner:** Elkhart Community School Corp., at above address, Fax: (219)262-5770. **Founded:** 1972. **Operating Hours:** 24 hrs.; 80% network, 20% local. **ADI:** South Bend-Elkhart, IN. **Key Personnel:** Tim Eby, Station Mgr., phone (219)262-5520, teby@wvpe.org; Bill Rice, News Dir., phone (219)262-5818, brice@wvpe.org; Joan Swanson, phone (219)2625774, jswanson@wvpe.org; Kim Macon, Contact, phone (219)2625699, kmacon@wvpe.org. **Wattage:** 10,500. **Ad Rates:** Noncommercial. **URL:** http://www.wvpe.org.

ELLETTSVILLE, pop. 3,328.

Monroe Co. (SWC). 7 m NW of Bloomington. Oolitic stone yards. Quarries; light industry; timber. Agriculture. Corn, wheat, oats.

10092 Journal
The Journal Publishing Co.
211 N. Sale St. Phone: (812)876-2254
PO Box 98 Fax: (812)876-2853
Ellettsville, IN 47429
Newspaper with a Democratic orientation. **Founded:** 1939. **Freq:** Weekly (Wed.). **Print Method:** Offset. **Cols./Page:** 7. **Col. Width:** 22 nonpareils. **Col. Depth:** 210 agate lines. **Key Personnel:** Maurice E. Endwright, Editor and Publisher; John T. Gillaspy, Publisher; Ranee Brown-Mounce, Advertising Mgr. **Subscription Rates:** $16 individuals local; $22 out of area other. **Remarks:** Accepts advertising.
Ad Rates: GLR: $.18 **Circ:** 2,500
BW: $441
PCI: $3.45

ELWOOD, pop. 10,900.

Madison Co. (NW). 25 m WNW of Muncie. Industrial center in tomato growing section.

10093 The Call-Leader
Elwood Publishing Co.
317 S. Anderson St.
PO Box 85
Elwood, IN 46036-2018

Local newspaper. **Founded:** 1894. **Freq:** Daily (eve.). **Print Method:** Offset. **Trim Size:** 14 x 22 3/4. **Cols./Page:** 6. **Col. Width:** 2 1/16 inches. **Col. Depth:** 21 1/2 inches. **Key Personnel:** Neil Johnson, Editor; Robert Nash, Publisher; Robert L. Nash, Advertising Mgr.; Sandy Burton, Managing Editor. **USPS:** 174-640. **Subscription Rates:** $80 individuals.
Ad Rates: BW: $748.20 **Circ:** Paid ‡4,000
4C: $135
SAU: $5.95

10094 WLHN-FM - 101.7
PO Box 17 Phone: (317)552-5043
Elwood, IN 46036-0017 Fax: (317)552-0506

Format: Adult Contemporary. **Networks:** Unistar. **Owner:** Joel Schneider Broadcasting, at above address. **Founded:** 1964. **Formerly:** WBMP-FM (1985). **Operating Hours:** Continuous. **Key Personnel:** Tony Chez, General Mgr.; Rick Stanger, Program Dir. **Wattage:** 3000. **Ad Rates:** $12-14 for 30 seconds; $16-18 for 60 seconds.

EVANSVILLE†, pop. 130,496.

Vanderburgh Co (SW). On Ohio River, 164 m S of Indianapolis. Bridges to Henderson, Ky. University of Evansville. University of Southern Indiana. Manufactures refrigerators, flour, beer, farm and garden implements, excavating machinery, aluminum, chemicals, furniture, plastics, mattresses, infant nutritionals, pottery, cigars, textiles. Meat, fruit, vegetable packing plants.

10095 The Evansville Courier
Evansville Courier Co., Inc.
300 Walnut St. Phone: (812)424-7711
Evansville, IN 47713 Fax: (812)422-8196
Free: (800)288-3200
Publication E-mail: vhue@evanville.net

General newspaper. **Founded:** 1845. **Freq:** Mon.-Sun. (morn.). **Print Method:** Flexographic. **Trim Size:** 13 1/6 x 22. **Cols./Page:** 6. **Col. Width:** 26 nonpareils. **Col. Depth:** 308 agate lines. **Key Personnel:** Thomas W. Tuley, Editor and Publisher; Robert K. Savage, Natl. Administration. **Subscription Rates:** $94.80 individuals; $67.20 Sunday. **Remarks:** Accepts advertising. **Online:** DataTimes Corporation. **URL:** http://www.evansville.net. **Feature Editors:** Marilou Berry, *Fashion, Society*, phone (812)424-7711; Mike Bucsko, *Medical*, phone (812)424-7711; Jim Bye, *Photo*, phone (812)424-7711; Rebecca Coudret, *Entertainment, TV & Radio*, phone (812)424-7711; Sherry Crawford, *Movie*, phone (812)424-7711; James Derk, *Rural Development*, phone (812)424-7711; Jim Derk, *Aviation*, phone (812)424-7711; Dave Johnson, *Sports*, phone (812)424-7711; Alan Julian, *City, Metro, News*, phone (812)424-7711; Mark Kroeger, *Financial/Business*, phone (812)424-7711; Chuck Leach, *Editorials*, phone (812)424-7711; Herb Marynell, *Education, Environmental*, phone (812)424-7711; Roger McBain, *Drama, Music*, phone (812)424-7711; James Michels, *Political*, phone (812)424-7711; Jim Michels, *Travel*, phone (812)424-7711; Linda Negro, *Religion*, phone (812)424-7711; John Reiter, *Book, Family, Features, Lifestyle, Women's*, phone (812)424-7711; Anne Schleper, *Food*, phone (812)424-7711; Fred Sievers, *Garden/Home*, phone (812)424-7711; Doug Sword, *Real Estate*, phone (812)424-7711.
Ad Rates: BW: $5,146.42 **Circ:** Mon.-Sat. ★**60,608**
4C: $6,111.42 Sun. ★**105,644**
PCI: $38.99

10096 The Evansville Press
Hartmann Publications
300 E. Walnut St. Phone: (812)464-7614
PO Box 454 Fax: (812)464-7614
Evansville, IN 47713
Free: (800)677-7737

General newspaper. **Founded:** 1845. **Freq:** Daily (eve.). **Print Method:** Letterpress. **Trim Size:** 13 1/6 x 22. **Cols./Page:** 6. **Col. Width:** 26 nonpareils. **Col. Depth:** 308 agate lines. **Key Personnel:** Bill Jackson, Editor; Bob Hartmann, Publisher. **Subscription Rates:** $90.60. **Remarks:** Accepts advertising.
Ad Rates: BW: $4,765 **Circ:** Mon.-Sat. ★**19,344**
4C: $5,656
PCI: $38.99

10097 The Formalist
320 Hunter Dr. Phone: (812)425-7684
Evansville, IN 47711
Consumer journal covering poetry. **Subtitle:** A Journal of Metrical Poetry. **Founded:** 1990. **Freq:** Semiannual. **Print Method:** Offset. **Trim Size:** 6 x 9. **Key Personnel:** William Baer, Editor. **ISSN:** 1046-7874. **Subscription Rates:** $12 individuals; $14 institutions; $6.50 single issue. **Remarks:** Advertising not accepted.
Circ: (Not Reported)

10098 Indiana Journal of Commerce & Industry
R & W Publishing, Inc.
PO Box 3275 Phone: (812)425-2210
Evansville, IN 47731 Fax: (812)464-7641
Free: (800)593-0350
Publication E-mail: ijournal@evansville.net; office@indianajournal.com

Publication featuring statewide business, commercial, and industrial news. **Subtitle:** Indiana Digest of Economic News. **Founded:** Feb. 1994. **Freq:** Monthly. **Trim Size:** 11 1/4 x 17. **Cols./Page:** 4. **Col. Width:** 2 inches. **Col. Depth:** 15 inches. **Key Personnel:** David Wou, President. **Subscription Rates:** $30 individuals. **Remarks:** Accepts advertising. **Formerly:** Indiana Industrial Journal.
Ad Rates: BW: $1,855 **Circ:** (Not Reported)

10099 The Message
PO Box 4169 Phone: (812)424-5536
Evansville, IN 47724-0169 Fax: (812)424-0972
Publication E-mail: message@diocese-evansville.org
Publisher E-mail: message@evansville-diocese.org

Catholic newspaper. **Founded:** Oct. 1, 1971. **Freq:** Weekly (Fri.). **Print Method:** Offset. **Trim Size:** 17 1/8 x 11 3/8. **Cols./Page:** 5. **Col. Width:** 22 nonpareils. **Col. Depth:** 224 agate lines. **Key Personnel:** Paul R. Leingang, Editor; Bishop Gerald A. Gettelfinger, Publisher; Paul A. Newland, Advertising Mgr. **Subscription Rates:** $18.50 individuals. **Remarks:** Accepts advertising.
Ad Rates: GLR: $.42 **Circ:** Controlled ‡8,100
BW: $400
4C: $300
PCI: $8.12

10100 Thrifty Nickel Want Ads
1301 E. Morgan Ave. Phone: (812)428-8484
Evansville, IN 47711 Fax: (812)428-8493
Free: (800)467-8480
Publication E-mail: tnickel@dynasty.com

Want ad newspaper. **Founded:** July 25, 1981. **Freq:** Weekly (Thurs.). **Print Method:** Offset. **Cols./Page:** 8. **Col. Width:** 7.1 picas. **Col. Depth:** 120 inches. **Key Personnel:** Jim Hall, Editor and Publisher. **Subscription Rates:** Free. **Remarks:** Accepts advertising. **Online:** Dynasty Online.
Ad Rates: GLR: $10 **Circ:** Free ‡40,500
BW: $803
4C: $1,080
PCI: $8

10101 TCL
1900 N. Fares Ave. Phone: (812)428-2462
Box 4658 Fax: (812)428-2427
Evansville, IN 47711

Founded: 1979. **Formerly:** UAE. **Cities Served:** Darmstadt, Evansville, Vanderburgh County, IN: 53 channels.

10102 WDKS-FM - 106.1
PO Box 78 Phone: (812)425-4226
Evansville, IN 47701-0078

Format: Adult Contemporary. **Owner:** Newburgh Broadcasting Corporation, at above address, (812)853-9422. **Founded:** 1991. **Formerly**: WJPS-FM (1996); WGAB-FM (1997). **Operating Hours:** Continuous. **ADI:** Evansville, IN (Madisonville, KY). **Key Personnel:** Don Davis, President, phone (812)853-9422; Don Griffin, General Mgr. **Local Programs:** *Les Shively Show*, Les Shively, (812)425-4555, Fax (812)464-1007; *Sports-on-Line*, Adam Alexander, (812)465-4565, Fax (812)465-4559. **Wattage:** 6000. **Ad Rates:** Advertising accepted; rates available upon request. WGAB, WGBF AM, WGBF-FM, WTRI-FM, WYNG-FM.

10103 WEHT-TV - 25
PO Box 25 Fax: (812)826-6823
Evansville, IN 47701 Free: (800)879-8542

Format: Commercial TV. **Networks:** ABC. **Owner:** Gilmore Broadcasting Corp., Box 25, Evansville, IN 47701, (800)879-8542. **Founded:** 1953. **Operating Hours:** Monday-Friday, Continuous, Saturday & Sunday 6am-2am. **ADI:** Evansville, IN (Madisonville, KY). **Key Personnel:** Douglas A. Padgett, Pres./General Mgr., phone (800)879-6522, fax (502)827-2605, dpadgett@abc25.com; Mike Riley, Station Mgr., phone (800)879-8541, mriley@abc2.com; John Sandwell, National Sakes Mgr, phone (800)879-6523, fax (562)827-2605, jsandwell@abc24.com; Ginny Powers, Program Dir., phone (800)879-6523, fax (502)827-2605, gpowers@abc2.cm; John Watson, Chief Engineer, phone (800)879-8557, jwatson@abc25.com. **Wattage:** 1,124,000.

10104 WEVV-TV - 44
44 Main St. Phone: (812)464-4444
Evansville, IN 47708 Fax: (812)465-4559

Format: Commercial TV. **Networks:** CBS. **Owner:** WEVV Inc., at above address, Fax: (812)465-9450. **Founded:** 1983. **Operating Hours:** 20 hrs. Daily; 75% network, 25% local. **ADI:** Evansville, IN (Madisonville, KY). **Key Personnel:** J.A. Simms, General Mgr.; Dick Schappa, General Sales Mgr.; Alice Lovell, Program Dir. **Ad Rates:** $10-400 for 30 seconds. Combined advertising rates available with WTSN-TV. **URL:** http://www.info@wevv.com.

10105 WFIE-TV - 14
1115 Mt. Auburn Rd. Phone: (812)426-1414
Evansville, IN 47720 Fax: (812)426-1945
E-mail: wfie@nbc14.com

Format: Commercial TV. **Networks:** NBC. **Owner:** Cosmos Broadcasting Corp., PO Box 19023, Greenville, SC 29602, (864)609-4366. **Founded:** 1953. **Operating Hours:** 6 a.m.-1:30 a.m.; 65% network, 35% local. **ADI:** Evansville, IN (Madisonville, KY). **Key Personnel:** Lucy Himstedt, Contact; Bob Freeman, News Dir.; Kirk Williams, Program Dir.; Bruce Villines, Promotions Mgr.; Sam Schaeffer, Business Mgr.; Linda Haddix, General Sales Mgr.; Gil Mazur, Marketing Dir. **Ad Rates:** $30-3,000 for 30 seconds.

10106 WGBF-AM - 1280
PO Box 78 Phone: (812)425-4226
Evansville, IN 47701 Fax: (812)421-0005

Format: News; Talk. **Simulcasts:** WGBF-FM. **Networks:** CNN Radio; Westwood One Radio; ESPN Radio. **Owner:** Connoisseur Communications of Evansville, L.P., at above address. **Founded:** 1923. **Formerly:** WWOK-AM (1996). **Operating Hours:** Continuous; 90% network, 10% local. **ADI:** Evansville, IN (Madisonville, KY). **Key Personnel:** Don Griffin, General Mgr.; Dan Egierski, News Dir.; John Story, Program Dir. **Wattage:** 5000. **Ad Rates:** $10-25 for 30 seconds; $12-30 for 60 seconds. Combined advertising rates available with WGBF-FM/WYNG-FM/WTRI-FM/WDUS-FM/WGAB-AM.

10107 WGBF-FM - 103.1
PO Box 78
Evansville, IN 47701

Format: Album-Oriented Rock (AOR). **Networks:** Westwood One Radio. **Owner:** Connoisseur Communications of Evansville, L.P., at above address. **Founded:** 1971. **Formerly**: WHKC-FM. **Operating Hours:** Continuous; 15% network, 85% local. **ADI:** Evansville, IN (Madisonville, KY). **Key Personnel:** Tom Hunt, General Mgr.; Mike Sanders, Program Dir.; Dan Egierski, News Dir.; Bob Smedley, Sales Mgr. **Local Programs:** *Julie Roberts Show*, Julie Roberts, Mailing contact; *Mike Sanders Show*, Mike Sanders, Mailing contact; *Turner Watson Show*, Turner Watson, Mailing contact. **Wattage:** 6000. **Ad Rates:** $25-80 for 30 seconds; $29-90 for 60 seconds.

10108 WIKY-FM - 104.1
1162 Mt. Auburn Rd.
PO Box 3848
Evansville, IN 47736

Format: Adult Contemporary. **Owner:** John D. Engelbrecht, at above address, (812)454-8284. **Founded:** 1948. **Operating Hours:** Continuous. **ADI:** Evansville, IN (Madisonville, KY). **Key Personnel:** Randy Wheeler, News Dir.; Rob Burton, General Mgr.; Mark Baker, Program Dir.; Rob Burton, General Sales Mgr.; Charlie Blake, Vice Pres. Agriculture. **Local Programs:** *Evansville in the Morning*, Charlie Blake. **Wattage:** 35,000. **Ad Rates:** $60-120 for 30 seconds; $70-140 for 60 seconds.

10109 WJPS-AM - 1400
1162 Mt. Auburn Rd.
PO Box 3848
Evansville, IN 47736

Format: Oldies. **Founded:** 1936. **Formerly**: WROZ-AM (1986). **Operating Hours:** Continuous; 100% local. **ADI:** Evansville, IN (Madisonville, KY). **Key Personnel:** Rob Burton, General Mgr.; Randy Wheeler, News Dir.; Johnny Michaels, Program Dir.; Rob Burton, General Sales Mgr. **Wattage:** 1,000. **Ad Rates:** $10-65 for 30 seconds; $13-75 for 60 seconds.

10110 WNIN-FM - 88.3
405 Carpenter St. Phone: (812)423-2974
Evansville, IN 47708 Fax: (812)428-7548

Format: Public Radio; Classical; Blues; News; Folk. **Networks:** Public Radio International (PRI); National Public Radio (NPR). **Founded:** 1982. **Operating Hours:** 24hrs 75% network, 25% local. **ADI:** Evansville, IN (Madisonville, KY). **Key Personnel:** David Dial, General Mgr., didial@wnin.org; Kent Teeters, Music Dir.; Jean Noyes, Station Mgr., jnoyes@wnin.org. **Wattage:** 45,000. **Ad Rates:** Noncommercial; underwriting available.

10111 WPSR-FM - 90.7
5400 1st Ave. Phone: (812)435-8241
Evansville, IN 47710 Fax: (812)435-8241
E-mail: wpsr@eusc.k12.in.us

Format: Full Service. **Networks:** UPI. **Owner:** Evansville-Vanderburgh School Corp., 1 S. 9th St., Evansville, IN 47708. **Founded:** 1957. **Operating Hours:** 7:00 a.m.-2:35 p.m. Mon.-Fri. (Aug.-June). **ADI:** Evansville, IN (Madisonville, KY). **Key Personnel:** Michael H. Reininga, General Mgr.; Sue Holland, Program Dir.; Frank Hertel, Chief Engineer. **Wattage:** 14,000.

10112 WSWI-AM - 820
Radio Center Phone: (812)464-1836
8600 University Blvd. Fax: (812)464-1960
Evansville, IN 47712

Format: Alternative/New Music/Progressive. **Networks:** AP. **Founded:** 1947. **Operating Hours:** Sunrise-sunset. **ADI:** Evansville, IN (Madisonville, KY). **Key Personnel:** Wayne Rinks, General Mgr. **Wattage:** 250. **Ad Rates:** Noncommercial.

10113 WTVW-TV - 7
PO Box 7 Phone: (812)424-7777
Evansville, IN 47701-0007 Fax: (812)421-4040
E-mail: question@wtvw.com

Format: Commercial TV. **Networks:** Fox. **Owner:** Petracom Inc, 1527 N. Dale Mabry Hwy., Ste 105, Lutz, FL 33549, (813)948-2554, Fax: (813)948-2557. **Founded:** 1956. **Operating Hours:** Continuous; 30% network, 70% local. **ADI:** Evansville, IN (Madisonville, KY). **Key Personnel:** Jerry Whitener, General Mgr., phone (812)424-7777, fax (812)421-7291, gm@wtvw.com; David Smith, News Dir., phone (812)421-4030, fax (812)421-7289; B. Briscoe, Promotions Mgr., brick@wtvw.com; Rich Miller, Sports Dir., phone (812)424-7777, fax (812)421-7289. **Wattage:** 316,000. **Ad Rates:** $20-800 per unit. **URL:** http://www.wtvw.com.

10114 WUEV-FM - 91.5
1800 Lincoln Ave. Phone: (812)479-2022
Evansville, IN 47722 Fax: (812)479-2320
E-mail: wuev@evansville.edu

Format: Full Service; Alternative/New Music/Progressive. **Networks:** Network Indiana. **Owner:** Board of Trustees of University of Evansville, at above address. **Founded:** 1951. **Formerly**: WEVC-FM (1977). **Operating Hours:** Continuous; 100% local. **ADI:** Evansville, IN (Madisonville, KY). **Key Personnel:** Leonard Clark, Station Mgr. **Local Programs:** *Heavy Metal Express*; *Inside Evansville*; *Party Lights*. **Wattage:** 6100. **Ad Rates:** Noncommercial. **URL:** http://www.evansville.edu/~wuevweb/index.html.

10115 WVHI-AM - 1330
10 NW 3rd Phone: (812)425-2221
Evansville, IN 47708 Fax: (812)425-2078

Format: Religious. **Networks:** Sun Radio. **Owner:** Geyer Broadcasting Co., Inc., at above address. **Founded:** 1964. **Operating Hours:** 5 a.m.-11 p.m. **ADI:** Evansville, IN (Madisonville, KY). **Key Personnel:** Sally Carr, Operations Mgr.; Jonathan Fosdick, Program Dir.; Steve Chapman, Music Dir.; Stan Hoffman, Sales Mgr. **Wattage:** 5000. **Ad Rates:** $10-12.50 for 30 seconds; $13-15.50 for 60 seconds.

10116 WYNG-FM - 105.3
PO Box 2777 Phone: (812)425-4226
Evansville, IN 47728 Fax: (812)421-0005

Format: Contemporary Country. **Networks:** CBS. **Owner:** Pinnacle Broadcasting, at above address, (817)649-0184. **Founded:** 1964. **Formerly**: WVHI-FM (1982). **Operating Hours:** Continuous; 5% network, 95% local. **ADI:** Evansville, IN (Madisonville, KY). **Key Personnel:** Joe Bell, General Mgr.; Pete Hanson, Promotions Dir. **Wattage:** 50,000. **Ad Rates:** $35-70 for 30 seconds. **URL:** http://www.wyng.com.

FAIRMOUNT, pop. 3,286.

Grant Co. (NEC). 8 m S of Marion. Manufactures liquid fertilizer, catsup, chili sauce. Agriculture.

10117 News-Sun
PO Box 25 Phone: (317)948-4164
Fairmount, IN 46928-0025
Newspaper with a Republican orientation. **Founded:** 1876. **Freq:** Weekly (Wed.). **Print Method:** Offset. **Cols./Page:** 5. **Col. Width:** 22 nonpareils. **Col. Depth:** 196 agate lines. **Key Personnel:** Jim Terhune, Publisher. **Subscription Rates:** $75 individuals. **Remarks:** Accepts advertising.
Ad Rates: GLR: $0.63 **Circ:** Mon.-Sat. 8,176
BW: $481.60
4C: $661.60
PCI: $6.88

FERDINAND, pop. 2,192.

Dubois Co. (SW). 50 m NE of Evansville. Manufactured furniture, kitchen cabinets, aluminum windows and doors. Oak timber. Grain farms. Corn, wheat, oats.

10118 The Ferdinand News
Dubois Spencer Counties Publishing Co., Inc.
PO Box 38 Phone: (812)937-2100
Ferdinand, IN 47532
Publication E-mail: ferdnews@psci.net

Newspaper with a Democratic orientation. **Founded:** May 1906. **Freq:** Weekly (Wed.). **Print Method:** Offset. **Cols./Page:** 6. **Col. Width:** 2 inches. **Col. Depth:** 21 1/2 inches. **Key Personnel:** Miriam Ash, General Mgr. **USPS:** 189-860. **Subscription Rates:** $17 individuals; $19 out of country; $23 out of state. **Remarks:** Accepts advertising.
Ad Rates: BW: $453.05 **Circ:** ‡3,500
PCI: $3.80

Spencer County Leader - See Dale

FISHERS

10119 The Daily Ledger
Topics Newspapers, Inc.
13095 Publisher's Dr. Phone: (317)598-6397
Fishers, IN 46038 Fax: (317)598-6340
Publisher E-mail: topics@inetdirect.net

Local newspaper. **Founded:** 1881. **Freq:** Mon.-Sat. **Print Method:** Offset. **Trim Size:** 22 3/4. **Cols./Page:** 6. **Col. Width:** 26 nonpareils. **Col. Depth:** 301 agate lines. **Key Personnel:** Tom Jekel, Editor, phone (317)598-6300; David Lewis, Publisher, phone (317)598-6300; Dennis Waldkoetter, Business Mgr., phone (317)598-6300; Jay Frederickson, Advertising Dir., phone (317)598-6300; Kevin Gossett, Production Mgr., phone (317)598-6300; Chip Gallagher, Circulation Dir., phone (317)598-6300. **Subscription Rates:** $15 individuals; $18 other countries.
Ad Rates: PCI: $12.48 **Circ:** Paid 11,963

10120 Fishers Sun-Herald
Topics Newspapers, Inc.
13095 Publisher's Dr. Phone: (317)598-6397
Fishers, IN 46038 Fax: (317)598-6340
Publisher E-mail: topics@inetdirect.net

Local newspaper. **Founded:** 1980. **Freq:** Weekly (Wed.). **Print Method:** Offset. **Trim Size:** 22 3/4. **Cols./Page:** 6. **Col. Width:** 26 nonpareils. **Col. Depth:** 301 agate lines. **Key Personnel:** David Lewis, Publisher; Tom Jekel, Editor; Dennis Waldkoetter, Business Mgr.; Scott Gause, Advertising Dir.; Kevin Gossett, Production Mgr.; Terry Coomer, Circulation

Director. **Subscription Rates:** Free; $15 individuals annual, voluntary pay - guaranteed delivery. **Remarks:** Accepts advertising.
Ad Rates: PCI: $11.58 **Circ:** Combined ♦**12,761**

Geist Gazette - See Geist

FLORA, pop. 1,877.

Carroll Co. (NWC) 20 m NE of Lafayette.

10121 Carroll County Comet
Carroll Papers, Inc.
14 E. Main Phone: (219)967-4135
Flora, IN 46929-0026 Fax: (219)967-4657
Publisher E-mail: comet@netusa1.net

Community newspaper. **Founded:** Feb. 6, 1974. **Freq:** Weekly (Wed.). **Print Method:** Offset. **Trim Size:** 14 x 22 3/4. **Cols./Page:** 6. **Col. Width:** 2 1/16 inches. **Col. Depth:** 21.5 inches. **Key Personnel:** Joseph Moss, Advertising Dir., fax (219)967-3384; Susan Scholl, Editor. **USPS:** 258-840. **Subscription Rates:** $24 by mail; $31 out of area. **Remarks:** Accepts advertising.
Ad Rates: GLR: $7.40 **Circ:** Paid ‡5,131
BW: $954.60 Free ‡35
4C: $989.60
SAU: $7.00
PCI: $7.40

FORT BRANCH, pop. 2,504.

Gibson Co. (SW). 20 m N of Evansville. Meat packing. Diversified farming.

10122 South Gibson Star-Times
PO Box 70 Phone: (812)753-3553
Fort Branch, IN 47648 Fax: (812)753-4251
Publisher E-mail: tpd@comsource.net

Community newspaper. **Founded:** 1898. **Freq:** Weekly. **Print Method:** Offset. **Trim Size:** 11 1/2 x 17 1/2. **Cols./Page:** 6. **Col. Width:** 1 1/2 inches. **Col. Depth:** 16 inches. **Key Personnel:** Frank Heuring, Publisher; Rachael Heuring, Publisher. **Subscription Rates:** $14 individuals; $22 out of area. **Remarks:** Accepts advertising. **Formerly:** Fort Branch Times; The Owensville Star-Echo.
Ad Rates: GLR: $.20 **Circ:** Paid ⊕**2,650**
BW: $216
4C: $471
SAU: $7.10
PCI: $4.75

FORT WAYNE†, pop. 172,196.

Allen Co. (NE). On Maumee, St Joseph and St Mary's Rivers, 105 m NE of Indianapolis. Indiana Institute of Technology, Concordia College (Luth. men), St. Francis College (Cath. co-ed), Fort Wayne Bible College (Missionary and co-ed), Indiana Purdue Fort Wayne Campus. Manufactures electric motors and supplies, trucks, tires, clothing, public speaking systems, television and electronic equipment, radios, valves, radio parts, copper wire, diamond wire dies, tools, trailers, aluminum pistons, gasoline pumps, liquid metering equipment, tanks and compressors, automotive axles, plastic, boats, feed, beer, paint, cranes and dredges, paper boxes, precision gears and counters, mobile homes.

10123 The American Chiropractor
Busch Publishing Co.
5005 Riviera Ct. Phone: (219)484-9600
Fort Wayne, IN 46825 Fax: (219)484-9604
Free: (800)837-4424
Publication E-mail: tac@centralnet.net

Journal covering chiropractic science and research. **Subtitle:** Magazine of the Chiropractic Profession. **Founded:** 1979. **Freq:** Bimonthly. **Print Method:** Offset. **Trim Size:** 7 7/8 x 10 7/8. **Cols./Page:** 3. **Col. Width:** 26 nonpareils. **Col. Depth:** 140 agate lines. **Key Personnel:** Paul F. Jaskoviak, D.C., Editor; Jaclyn Busch, Advertising Dir. **ISSN:** 0194-6536. **Subscription Rates:** $56 individuals; $10 single issue.
Ad Rates: BW: $1,838.55 **Circ:** Controlled ‡35,000
4C: $2,148.80
PCI: $90

10124 Business People Magazine
Michiana Business Publications, Inc.
205 Airport North Office Park Phone: (219)497-0433
Fort Wayne, IN 46825-6702 Fax: (219)497-0822

Consumer magazine covering business for Northeast Indiana. **Founded:** Feb. 1988. **Freq:** Monthly. **Print Method:** Sheetfed offset. **Cols./Page:** 3. **Key Personnel:** Stephen R. Harris, Editor. **Subscription Rates:** $16.95 individuals; $3 single issue; Free to qualified subscribers. **Remarks:** Accepts advertising.
Ad Rates: BW: $1,115 **Circ:** Controlled 8,000
4C: $1,540

10125 Concordia Theological Quarterly
Concordia Theological Seminary
6600 N. Clinton Phone: (219)452-2172
Fort Wayne, IN 46825 Fax: (219)452-2270
Publication E-mail: ctq@ctsfw.edu

Religion and theology journal. **Founded:** 1936. **Freq:** Quarterly. **Print Method:** Offset. **Cols./Page:** 1. **Col. Width:** 54 nonpareils. **Col. Depth:** 98 agate lines. **Key Personnel:** Heino O. Kadai, Th.D., Editor, kadai@ctsfw.edu; Douglas Judisch, Asst. Editor, judisch@ctsfw.edu; Lawrence Rast, Assoc. Editor, rast@ctsfw.edu. **ISSN:** 0038-8610. **Subscription Rates:** $15 individuals; $30 other countries; $20 Canada. **Remarks:** Accepts advertising. **Available Online. URL:** http://www.ctsfw.edu/cta/index.html. **Alt. Formats:** Microform.
Ad Rates: BW: $500 **Circ:** Paid 400
Non-paid 9,000

10126 The Family Digest
PO Box 40137
Fort Wayne, IN 46804

Catholic family and parish magazine. **Subtitle:** The Joy and Fulfillment of Catholic Family Life. **Founded:** 1945. **Freq:** Bimonthly. **Print Method:** Offset. **Trim Size:** 5 1/3 x 7 1/2. **Cols./Page:** 2. **Col. Width:** 26 nonpareils. **Col. Depth:** 93 agate lines. **Key Personnel:** Corine B. Erlandson, Editor; Clancy Mylan, President. **Subscription Rates:** subscription through Catholic parish. **Remarks:** Advertising accepted; rates available upon request. **Formerly:** Parish Family Digest.
Circ: Non-paid ‡150,000

10127 Frost Illustrated
Frost, Inc.
3121 S. Calhoun St. Phone: (219)745-0552
Fort Wayne, IN 46807-1901
Black community newspaper. **Founded:** Nov. 1968. **Freq:** Weekly (Wed.). **Print Method:** Offset. **Cols./Page:** 5. **Key Personnel:** Edna M. Smith, Editor; Edward N. Smith, Sr., Publisher; Edward N. Smith, Jr., Advertising Mgr. **Subscription Rates:** $12 individuals; $15 out of area. **Remarks:** Advertising not accepted for pornographic material.
Ad Rates: GLR: $.60 **Circ:** Paid ‡1,342
BW: $832 Free ‡32
4C: $1,032
PCI: $12.80

10128 Hunter & Sport Horse
Midwest Hunter Inc.
12204 Covington Rd. Phone: (219)625-4030
Fort Wayne, IN 46804-9720 Fax: (219)625-3480
Publisher E-mail: hshhorse@aol.com

Magazine about English riding sports. **Founded:** July 1989. **Freq:** 7/year. **Print Method:** Web offset. **Trim Size:** 8 1/8 x 10 7/8. **Key Personnel:** Laura Allen, Editor; Carol Craig, Advertising Dir. **ISSN:** 1057-8501. **Subscription Rates:** $21.95 individuals.
Ad Rates: BW: $1,260 **Circ:** Paid ⊕**7,597**
4C: $1,680 Controlled ⊕**22,657**

10129 The Journal Gazette
The Journal Gazette Co.
600 W. Main St. Phone: (219)461-8444
Fort Wayne, IN 46802 Fax: (219)461-8648
Publication E-mail: jgnews@jg.net

General newspaper. **Founded:** 1863. **Freq:** Mon.-Sun. (morn.). **Print Method:** Flexographic letterpress. **Trim Size:** 23 9/16. **Cols./Page:** 6. **Col. Width:** 12 picas. **Col. Depth:** 22 inches. **Key Personnel:** Craig Klugman, Editor, phone (219)461-8853, cklugman@jg.net; Julie Inskeep Walda, Publisher, phone (219)461-8490, jwalda@jg.net; Sherry Skufca, Managing Editor, phone (219)461-8201, sskufca@jg.net; Ed Breen, Graphics Editor, phone (219)461-8771, fax (219)461-8893, ebreen@jg.net; Tom Pellegrene, Jr., Mgr. of News Technologies, phone (219)461-8377, tpellegrene@jg.net; Tracy Warner, Metro Editor, phone (219)461-8428, twarner@jg.net; Jim Touvell, Sports Editor, phone (219)461-8260, jtouvell@jg.net; Valerie Vinyard Next, Editor, phone (219)461-8209, vvinyard@jg.net. **Subscription Rates:** $182 individuals. **Remarks:** Advertising not accepted for condoms. **URL:** http://www.jg.net/jg.
Ad Rates: GLR: $3.35 **Circ:** Mon.-Sat. ★**61,307**
BW: $8,076.16 Sun. ★**133,814**
4C: $8,570.01
SAU: $61.18
PCI: $61.18

10130 Macedonian Tribune
Macedonian Patriotic Organization
124 W. Wayne Phone: (219)422-5900
Fort Wayne, IN 46802 Fax: (219)422-1348
Publication E-mail: mtfw@macedonian.org

Ethnic newspaper (English, Bulgarian and Macedonian). **Founded:** Feb. 1927. **Freq:** Biweekly. **Print Method:** Offset. **Trim Size:** 11 x 17. **Cols./Page:** 4. **Col. Width:** 2 3/8 inches. **Col. Depth:** 15 inches. **Key Personnel:** A.A. Virginia N. Surso, Advertising Mgr. **ISSN:** 0024-9009. **Subscription Rates:** $25 individuals; $35 other countries; $75 other countries air mail. **Foreign language name:** Makedonska Tribuna.
Ad Rates: BW: $500 **Circ:** ‡1,600
4C: $550
PCI: $10

10131 The News-Sentinel
Knight-Ridder, Inc.
600 W. Main St. Phone: (219)461-8444
Fort Wayne, IN 46802 Fax: (219)461-8817

General newspaper. **Founded:** 1833. **Freq:** Mon.-Sat. (eve.). **Print Method:** Letterpress/Flexo. **Cols./Page:** 6. **Col. Width:** 26 nonpareils. **Col. Depth:** 308 agate lines. **Key Personnel:** Scott McGehee, Publisher, phone (219)461-8324; Joseph A. Weller, Exec. Editor, phone (219)461-8239; Richard Battin, Managing Editor, phone (219)461-8273. **Subscription Rates:** $75.40 individuals. **Remarks:** Advertising accepted; rates available upon request. **Online:** America Online, Inc.
Circ: Mon.-Sat. ★**46,327**

10132 Today's Catholic
PO Box 11169 Phone: (219)456-2824
Fort Wayne, IN 46856 Fax: (219)744-1473

Catholic. **Subtitle:** Newspaper of the Diocese of Fort Wayne-South Bend. **Founded:** 1926. **Freq:** Weekly (Sun.). **Print Method:** Offset. **Trim Size:** 11 3/8 x 15 1/2. **Cols./Page:** 5. **Col. Width:** 27 nonpareils. **Col. Depth:** 195 agate lines. **Key Personnel:** William Cone, Editor, phone (219)456-2909; Most Reverend John M. D'Arcy, Publisher. **ISSN:** 0891-1533. **Subscription Rates:** $17 individuals. **Remarks:** Accepts advertising. **Available Online. URL:** http://www.diocesefwsb.org.
Ad Rates: GLR: $.62 **Circ:** ‡16,500
BW: $638
4C: $782
SAU: $8.65
PCI: $8.40

10133 Waynedale News
2700 Lower Huntington Rd. Phone: (219)747-4535
Fort Wayne, IN 46809 Fax: (219)747-3282

Community newspaper. **Founded:** Sept. 1932. **Freq:** Semiweekly. **Print Method:** Offset. **Cols./Page:** 6. **Col. Width:** 20 nonpareils. **Col. Depth:** 196 agate lines. **Key Personnel:** David Perkins, Editor; Jim Imel, Publisher. **Subscription Rates:** $7.50 by mail. **Remarks:** Accepts advertising.
Ad Rates: GLR: $4 **Circ:** Free ‡6,000
BW: $312
PCI: $3.50

10134 Comcast Cablevision
720 Taylor St. Phone: (219)456-9000
Fort Wayne, IN 46802 Fax: (219)458-4138

Founded: 1979. **Cities Served:** Allen County, Huntington County, Noble County, Wells County, and Whitley County; Avilla, Canterbury Green, Huntertown, New Haven, and Roanoke, IN.

10135 WAJI-FM - 95.1
347 W. Berry St., Ste. 600 Phone: (219)423-3676
Fort Wayne, IN 46802 Fax: (219)422-5266
E-mail: @waji.com

Format: Adult Contemporary. **Networks:** Independent. **Owner:** Sarkes Tarzian, Inc., PO Box 62, Bloomington, IN 47402, (812)332-7251. **Founded:** 1959. **Formerly:** WPTH-FM (1985); WFWQ-FM. **Operating Hours:** Continuous. **ADI:** Fort Wayne (Angola), IN. **Key Personnel:** Candace A. Wendling, Pres./Gen. Mgr.; Daryl P. McIntire, General Sales Mgr.; Barb Richard, Program Dir. **Local Programs:** *Fort Wayne Feedback*, Carrie Wellman; *Sunday Side Up* 8:30 am - 9:00 am Sunday, Jeanette Rinard; *Sunny Side Up* 8:30 am - 9:00 am Sunday. **Wattage:** 39,000. **Ad Rates:** Advertising accepted; rates available upon request. Combined advertising rates available with WLDE-FM.

10136 WANE-TV - 15
2915 W. State Blvd. Phone: (219)424-1515
Box 1515 Fax: (219)424-1428
Fort Wayne, IN 46801

Format: Commercial TV. **Networks:** CBS. **Founded:** 1954. **Operating Hours:** 6 a.m.-2:30 a.m. **ADI:** Fort Wayne (Angola), IN. **Key Personnel:** Frank Moore, Contact.

10137 WBCL-FM - 90.3
1025 W. Rudisill Blvd. Phone: (219)745-0576
Fort Wayne, IN 46807 Fax: (219)745-2001

Format: Religious. **Simulcasts:** WBCJ-FM. **Networks:** AP. **Founded:** 1976. **Operating Hours:** Continuous. **ADI:** Fort Wayne (Angola), IN. **Key Personnel:** Char Binkley, General Mgr.; Lynne Ford, Contact; Tim Yazel, Operations Mgr.; Scott Tsuleff, Contact; Jim Stanley, News Dir.; Linda Richards, Contact; Marsha Bunker, Contact. **Wattage:** 50,000. **Ad Rates:** Noncommercial. **URL:** http://www.wbcl.org.

WBCY-FM - See Archbold, Ohio

10138 WBNI-FM - 89.1
3204 Clairmont Ct. Phone: (219)452-1189
Fort Wayne, IN 46808 Fax: (219)452-1188
E-mail: 76341.3303@compuserve.com

Format: Public Radio; News; Information; Classical; Jazz. **Networks:** National Public Radio (NPR); American Public Radio (APR); AP. **Founded:** 1978. **Formerly:** WIPU-FM (1982). **Operating Hours:** Continuous; 35% network, 65% local. **ADI:** Fort Wayne (Angola), IN. **Key Personnel:** Bruce R. Haines, Contact; Carol Ver Wiebe, Contact. **Wattage:** 34,000. **Ad Rates:** Noncommercial.

10139 WBTU-FM - 93.3
2100 Goshen Rd., Ste. 232 Phone: (219)482-9288
Fort Wayne, IN 46808 Fax: (219)482-8655
E-mail: wbtu@wbtu.com

Format: Contemporary Country. **Networks:** CNN Radio; ABC. **Owner:** Starboard Communications, at above address. **Founded:** 1948. **Operating Hours:** Continuous. **ADI:** Fort Wayne (Angola), IN. **Key Personnel:** T.J. Mckay, News Dir.; Richard J. Young, General Mgr.; Stormin Norman, Program Dir.; Dave Tarbet, Business Mgr. **Wattage:** 50,000. **Ad Rates:** $40-90 per unit. **URL:** http://www.wbtu.com.

10140 WBYR-FM - 98.9
PO Box 80397 Phone: (219)471-5100
Fort Wayne, IN 46898-0397 Fax: (219)471-5224

Format: Classic Rock; Album-Oriented Rock (AOR). **Owner:** Pathfinder Communications Corp., 421 S 2nd St., Elkhart, IN 46516, (219)294-1661. **Founded:** 1962. **Formerly:** WERT-FM (1987). **Operating Hours:** Continuous; 100% local. **ADI:** Fort Wayne (Angola), IN. **Key Personnel:** Bob Schutt, General Mgr., bschutt@fwi.com; Mark Osborn, General Sales Mgr., mosborn@fwi.com. **Local Programs:** *Allen County Magazine* 6:30 am Sunday, Jim Sack, Mailing contact, (219)744-1285. **Wattage:** 50,000. **Ad Rates:** $50-120 per unit. **URL:** wttp/wbyr.com; http://www.wbyr.com.

10141 WEJE-FM - 96.3
2000 Lower Huntington Rd. Phone: (219)747-1511
Fort Wayne, IN 46819 Fax: (219)747-3999

Format: Alternative/New Music/Progressive. **Owner:** Frank Kovas, at above address. **Founded:** 1995. **Operating Hours:** Continuous. **ADI:** Fort Wayne (Angola), IN. **Key Personnel:** Connie Kovas, General Mgr.; Scott Hecathorn, Operations Mgr./Program Dir.; Kyle Gudarian, Music Dir.; Brett Rump, General Sales Mgr. **Wattage:** 25,000.

10142 WFCV-AM - 1090
909 Coliseum Blvd. N. Phone: (219)423-2337
Fort Wayne, IN 46805 Fax: (219)423-6355

Format: Religious. **Networks:** Independent. **Owner:** Bott Broadcasting, at above address. **Founded:** 1980. **Operating Hours:** Daylight. **ADI:** Fort Wayne (Angola), IN. **Key Personnel:** Kathy McClish, Station Mgr.; Dale Gerke, Sales Mgr. **Wattage:** 1000. **Ad Rates:** $9-15 for 30 seconds; $15-22 for 60 seconds.

10143 WFFT-TV - 55
3707 Hillegas Rd. Phone: (219)471-5555
Fort Wayne, IN 46808 Fax: (219)484-4331

Format: Commercial TV. **Networks:** Fox. **Founded:** 1977. **Operating Hours:** Continuous. **ADI:** Fort Wayne (Angola), IN. **Key Personnel:** Steven Shine, News Dir.; Frank Hawkins, Contact; Steve Pozezanac, Contact; Jim Muhler, Production Mgr. **Ad Rates:** Advertising accepted; rates available upon request.

10144 WFWA-TV - 39
3632 Butter Rd. Phone: (219)484-8839
Fort Wayne, IN 46808 Fax: (219)482-3632
Free: (800)779-0839
E-mail: tv39@wfwa.pbs.org

Format: Public TV. **Networks:** Public Broadcasting Service (PBS). **Founded:** 1972. **Operating Hours:** Continuous. **ADI:** Fort Wayne (Angola), IN. **Key Personnel:** Richard Bienz, VP, Finance/Administration; Claudia Johnson, Production Mgr.; Bob Petts, Program Mgr.; Roger Rhodes, Pres./Gen. Mgr.; Tracy Brenneman, Acct. Executive. **Wattage:** 60,000. **Ad Rates:** Noncommercial; underwriting available.

10145 WGL-AM - 1250
2000 Lower Huntington Rd. Phone: (219)747-1511
Fort Wayne, IN 46819 Fax: (219)747-3999

Format: Talk. **Simulcasts:** WGLL-AM. **Networks:** CBS; Westwood One Radio; ESPN Radio. **Founded:** 1982. **Operating Hours:** Continuous. 90% network, 10% local. **ADI:** Fort Wayne (Angola), IN. **Key Personnel:** Frank Kovas, Owner; Connie Kovas, Vice President. **Wattage:** 2500 day; 1400 night. **Ad Rates:** $25-50 for 60 seconds.

10146 WGL-FM - 102
2000 Lower Hungtington Rd. Phone: (219)747-1511
Fort Wayne, IN 46819 Fax: (219)747-3999

Format: Adult Contemporary. **Owner:** Frank Kovas, at above address. **Founded:** 1997. **Operating Hours:** Continuous. **ADI:** Fort Wayne (Angola), IN. **Key Personnel:** Connie Kovas, General Mgr.; Kris Underwood, Program and Music Dir.; Brett Rump, General Sales Mgr.; Scott Hecathorn, Operations Mgr. **Wattage:** 6000.

10147 WKJG-TV - 33
2633 W. State Blvd. Phone: (219)422-7474
Fort Wayne, IN 46808 Fax: (219)422-9648
E-mail: nbc33@nbc33.com

Format: Commercial TV. **Networks:** NBC. **Founded:** 1953. **Operating Hours:** Continuous. **ADI:** Fort Wayne (Angola), IN. **Key Personnel:** Robert A. Klingle, Vice Pres./General Mgr.; Marvin Gottlieb, General & National Sales Mgr., fax (219)422-7523, sales@nbc33.com; Kay Atkin, Local Sales Mgr., fax (219)422-7523, sales@nbc.33.com; Rick Granger, Marketing/Promotions Dir., pro-mark@nbc33.com; Matt Kyle, Dir. of Engineering, engineering@nbc33.com; Stephen Buyze, Operations Mgr., ops@nbc33.com; Jim Bailey, Interim News Dir., phone (219)422-3333, news@nbc33.com; Elly Price, Public Affairs Dir.; Bob Lucas, Controller. **URL:** http://www.nbc33.com.

10148 WLAB-FM - 88.3
6600 N. Clinton St. Phone: (219)483-8236
Fort Wayne, IN 46825 Fax: (219)482-7707
Free: (800)359-8816

Format: Religious; Contemporary Christian. **Networks:** USA Radio. **Owner:** Indiana District Lutheran Church, 1145 S. Barr St., Fort Wayne, IN 46802, (219)423-1511. **Founded:** 1970. **Formerly:** WGHI-FM (1984). **Operating Hours:** Continuous; 5% network, 95% local. **ADI:** Fort Wayne (Angola), IN. **Key Personnel:** Jim Zix, General Mgr.; Melissa Etnyre, Music Dir.; Andrew Clark, Public Service Coordinator; Tim Dawson, News Mgr. **Local Programs:** *Conversations*, Melissa Etnyre. **Wattage:** 7000. **Ad Rates:** .

10149 WMEE-FM - 97.3
2915 Maples Rd. Phone: (219)447-5511
Fort Wayne, IN 46816 Fax: (219)447-7546

Format: Contemporary Hit Radio (CHR). **Networks:** Independent. **Owner:** Pathfinder Communications, at above address. **Founded:** 1947. **Formerly:** WKJG-FM (1971). **Operating Hours:** Continuous. **ADI:** Fort Wayne (Angola), IN. **Key Personnel:** Tony Richards, General Mgr.; Doug Wagner, General Sales Mgr.; Dean McNeil, Program Dir. **Wattage:** 48,000 ERP.

10150 WOWO-AM - 1190
2915 Maples Rd. Phone: (219)447-5511
Fort Wayne, IN 46816 Fax: (219)447-7546
Free: (800)333-1190

Format: News; Talk. **Networks:** ABC. **Owner:** Pathfinder Communications Corp., 421 S. 2nd St., Elkhart, IN 46516, (219)295-2500, Fax: (219)294-4014. **Founded:** 1925. **Operating Hours:** Continuous; 5% network, 95% local. **ADI:** Fort Wayne (Angola), IN. **Key Personnel:** Tony Richards, General Mgr.; Mark DePrez, General Sales Mgr.; Tommy Allen, Operations Mgr. **Wattage:** 50,000. **Ad Rates:** Advertising accepted; rates available upon request. **URL:** http://www.wowo.com.

10151 WPTA-TV - 21
3401 Butler Rd. Phone: (219)483-0584
Box 2121 Fax: (219)484-8240
Fort Wayne, IN 46801
E-mail: wpta@wpta.com

Format: Commercial TV. **Networks:** ABC. **Owner:** Granite Broadcasting Corp., 767 3rd Ave., 34th Fl., New York, NY 10017, (212)826-2530, Fax: (212)826-2858. **Founded:** 1957. **Operating Hours:** Continuous. **ADI:** Fort Wayne (Angola), IN. **Key Personnel:** Tim Gilbert, General Mgr., phone (219)483-0588, fax (219)483-1835, timg@wpta.com; Jan D'italia, Program Dir., phone (219)483-4468, fax (219)482-8750, jand@wpta.com; Dean Pantazi, Sports Dir., phone (219)471-7419, fax (219)484-8240, deanp@wpta.com; Bill Schneider, Contact, phone (219)482-5505, fax (219)483-1835, bills@wpta.com; Tom Long, General Sales Mgr., phone (219)471-9814, fax (219)483-2568, toml@wpta.com; Debbie Sand, Business Mgr., phone (219)482-6454, fax (219)483-0585, debbies@wpta.com; Don Bradley, News Dir., phone (219)484-4989, fax (219)484-8240, donb@wpta.com. **Wattage:** 30,000 transmitter; erp 490 kw visual; 49 kw aural. **Ad Rates:** Advertising accepted; rates available upon request. **URL:** http://www.wpta.com.

10152 WQHK-AM - 1380
2915 Maples Rd. Phone: (219)447-5511
Fort Wayne, IN 46816 Fax: (219)447-7546

Format: Country. **Networks:** ABC; Satellite Music Network. **Owner:** Pathfinder Communications Corp., at above address. **Founded:** 1947. **Formerly:** WKJG-AM (1971). **Operating Hours:** Continuous; 5% network, 95% local. **ADI:** Fort Wayne (Angola), IN. **Key Personnel:** Tony Richards, General Mgr.; Kevin Meek, General Sales Mgr.; Scott Miller, Program Dir. **Wattage:** 5000.

10153 WXKE-FM - 103.9
2541 Goshen Rd. Phone: (219)484-0580
Fort Wayne, IN 46808
E-mail: http://www.rock1039.com

Format: Album-Oriented Rock (AOR); Classic Rock; Alternative/New Music/Progressive. **Simulcasts:** 102.9 WEXI-Huntington. **Networks:** Independent. **Owner:** Robert B. Taylor, at above address. **Founded:** 1976. **Operating Hours:** Continuous; 100% local. **ADI:** Fort Wayne (Angola), IN. **Key Personnel:** David Riethmiller, General Mgr.; Rick West, Program Dir.; Dawn Sweet, Office Mgr.; Buzz Maxwell, Contact; Bonnie Ell, General Sales Mgr. **Local Programs:** *Blues Power Hour* 8:00 pm Sunday, David Riethmiller, General Mgr., (219)484-0580, Fax (219)482-5151. **Wattage:** 3000. **Ad Rates:** $45-80 per unit.

10154 WYSR-FM - 94.1
2000 Lower Hungtington Rd. Phone: (219)747-1511
Fort Wayne, IN 46819 Fax: (219)747-3999

Format: Adult Contemporary. **Owner:** Frank Kovas, at above address. **Founded:** 1997. **Operating Hours:** Continuous. **ADI:** Fort Wayne (Angola), IN. **Key Personnel:** Connie Kovas, General Mgr.; Kris Underwood, Program and Music Dir.; Brett Rump, General Sales Mgr.; Scott Hecathorn, Operations Mgr. **Wattage:** 6000.

FOWLER†, pop. 2,319.

Benton Co. (NW). 30 m NW of Lafayette. Manufactures food bags, fertilizers, printed products. Grain, stock, corn, soybeans, wheat.

10155 Benton Review
The Supermarket Gourmet
102 E. 5th St. Phone: (765)884-1902
PO Box 527 Fax: (765)884-8110
Fowler, IN 47944
Free: (888)805-5821
Publisher E-mail: sgourmet@aclass.com

Community newspaper. **Founded:** 1875. **Freq:** Weekly (Wed.). **Print Method:** Macintosh/Printed Offset Broadsheet. **Trim Size:** 14 x 23. **Cols./Page:** 6. **Col. Width:** 12.2 picas. **Col. Depth:** 21 inches. **Key Personnel:** Karen Hall Moyars, Publisher. **Subscription Rates:** $17.50 individuals; $21 out of area. **Remarks:** Accepts advertising.
Ad Rates: GLR: $1 **Circ:** Paid ‡2,859
BW: $378 Free ‡76
PCI: $2.50

10156 The Supermarket Gourmet
102 E. 5th St. Phone: (765)884-1902
PO Box 527 Fax: (765)884-8110
Fowler, IN 47944
Free: (888)805-5821
Publication E-mail: sgourmet@aclass.com
Publisher E-mail: sgourmet@aclass.com

Broadsheet newspaper featuring food news, recipes, pictures and columns on health, travel, and philosophy. **Founded:** 1996. **Freq:** Monthly plus holiday special section in November. **Print Method:** Offset. **Trim Size:** 14 x 23. **Cols./Page:** 6. **Col. Width:** 12 picas. **Col. Depth:** 21 inches. **Key Personnel:** Karen Hall Moyars, Publisher. **Subscription Rates:** $15. **Remarks:** Advertising not accepted.
Circ: Paid ‡200
Free ‡450

FRANCESVILLE, pop. 944.

Pulaski Co. (NW). 40 m N of Lafayette. Grain elevators; machine shop. Ships grain, milk. Grain, dairy, stock, poultry farms.

10157 Francesville Tribune
PO Box 458 Phone: (219)567-2221
Francesville, IN 47946
Newspaper with a Report orientation. **Founded:** 1897. **Freq:** Weekly (Thurs.). **Print Method:** Offset. **Trim Size:** 17 x 22. **Cols./Page:** 5. **Col. Width:** 11.5 picas. **Col. Depth:** 16 inches. **Key Personnel:** Darlene J. Ames, Editor and Publisher. **USPS:** 207-720. **Subscription Rates:** $9.50 individuals; $13 out of area. **Remarks:** Accepts advertising.
Ad Rates: GLR: $1.96 **Circ:** 900
BW: $4.25
PCI: $4.25

FRANKFORT†, pop. 15,168.

Clinton Co. (NC). 45 m NW of Indianapolis. Park, recreation and historical sites.

10158 Times
Frankfort Times, Inc.
251 E. Clinton St., No. 9 Phone: (317)659-4622
Frankfort, IN 46041-1906 Fax: (317)654-7031
Free: (800)467-4622
Publication E-mail: times@accs.net

General newspaper. **Founded:** 1894. **Freq:** Daily (eve.) and Sat. (morn.). **Print Method:** Offset. **Cols./Page:** 6. **Col. Width:** 26 nonpareils. **Col. Depth:** 301 agate lines. **Key Personnel:** J. Mark Ingels, Publisher. **USPS:** 208-000. **Subscription Rates:** $102 individuals. **Remarks:** Accepts advertising. **URL:** http://www.ftimes.com.
Ad Rates: GLR: $.22 **Circ:** Paid 7,351
PCI: $11.50

10159 Frankfort Cable Communications, Inc.
Box 9 Phone: (317)659-4678
Frankfort, IN 46041 Fax: (317)654-7031

Owner: Nixon Newspapers, Inc., 35 W. 3rd St., PO Box 1149, Peru, IN 46970, (317)473-3091. **Key Personnel:** Ron Emrick, Contact; Robert Vance, Contact; Terri Bowles, Office Mgr. **Cities Served:** subscribing households 5,033; 1 community access channel.

10160 KFAV-FM - 99.9
PO Box 545
Frankfort, IN 46041
E-mail: kwrekfav@kasparradio.com

Format: Hot Country. **Networks:** USA Radio. **Owner:** Kaspar B/Casting Company of Missouri, at above address. **Founded:** Dec. 6, 1991. **Operating Hours:** Continuous. **ADI:** St. Louis, MO (Mt. Vernon, IL). **Key Personnel:** Mark Becker, General Sales Mgr.; Mike Thomas, Program Coord.; Bev Wideman, Continuity Dir.; Lori Eggering, Traffic Dir.; Steve Kaspar, Sales Mgr.; Jay Murry, Sports Dir. **Wattage:** 25,000. **Ad Rates:** $36 for 60 seconds. **URL:** http://www.kfav.com.

10161 WILO-AM - 1570
1401-10 W. Barner St., Box 545 Phone: (317)659-3339
Frankfort, IN 46041

Format: Country; Agricultural; Sports. **Owner:** Kaspar Broadcasting Co., Inc., at above address. **Founded:** 1953. **Operating Hours:** 5:15 a.m.-11 p.m. **Key Personnel:** Vern Kaspar, Contact; Jim Riggs, Contact; Russell Kasper, General Sales Mgr. **Wattage:** 250.

10162 WSHW-FM - 99.7
1401-03 W. Barner St., Box 545 Phone: (317)659-3339
Frankfort, IN 46041 Fax: (317)659-3339

Format: Adult Contemporary; Agricultural. **Networks:** AP. **Owner:** Kaspar Broadcasting Co., Inc., at above address. **Founded:** 1962. **Operating Hours:** Continuous. **Key Personnel:** Vern Kaspar, Contact; Russell Kaspar, General Sales Mgr.; Jim Riggs, Contact. **Wattage:** 50,000 ERP.

FRANKLIN†, pop. 11,563.

Johnson Co. (SC). 20 m S of Indianapolis. Franklin College.

10163 Franklin Challenger
Challenger Newspapers
PO Box 73 Phone: (317)888-3376
Franklin, IN 46131 Fax: (317)888-3377
Publisher E-mail: challenger@netdirect.net

Community newspaper. **Founded:** May 24, 1984. **Freq:** Weekly (Thurs.). **Print Method:** Offset. **Trim Size:** 12 x 18. **Cols./Page:** 5. **Col. Width:** 12 picas. **Col. Depth:** 16 3/4 inches. **Key Personnel:** Don Guerrettaz, Editor and Publisher. **ISSN:** 8750-7390. **Subscription Rates:** $15 individuals; $.50 single issue. **Remarks:** Accepts advertising. **Alt. Formats:** CD-ROM.
Ad Rates: GLR: $2 **Circ:** Paid ‡300
BW: $160
4C: $385
SAU: $3.00
PCI: $3

10164 WFCI-FM - 89.5
Franklin College of Indiana Phone: (317)738-8205
Shirk Hall Fax: (317)738-8233
Franklin, IN 46131

Format: Album-Oriented Rock (AOR); Alternative/New Music/Progressive. **Founded:** 1960. **Operating Hours:** 3 a.m.-2 a.m. **ADI:** Indianapolis (Marion), IN. **Key Personnel:** Kim Jana, General Mgr.; Jake Rigney, Program Dir., rigneyj@franklincoll.edu; Jeff Carroll, Music Dir.; Joel Pollock, Sports Dir. **Wattage:** 1,150. **Ad Rates:** Noncommercial.

FRENCH LICK, pop. 2,265.

Orange Co. (S). 50 m N of Louisville, Ky. Health resort. Mineral springs. Stone quarry. Timber. Bottling works. Furniture factory. Agriculture. Stock, fruit, poultry.

10165 Springs Valley Herald
PO Box 311 Phone: (812)936-9630
French Lick, IN 47432
Newspaper with a Democratic orientation. **Founded:** 1903. **Freq:** Weekly (Wed.). **Print Method:** Offset. **Trim Size:** 17 1/2 x 23. **Cols./Page:** 8. **Col. Width:** 24 nonpareils. **Col. Depth:** 273 agate lines. **Key Personnel:** Ruth Marshall, Editor; D.G. Ballard, Publisher. **Subscription Rates:** $16.95 individuals.
Ad Rates: PCI: $4.75 **Circ:** ‡3,000

10166 WFLQ-FM - 100.1
PO Box 100 Phone: (812)936-9100
French Lick, IN 47432 Fax: (812)936-9495

Format: Country; Sports. **Networks:** Satellite Music Network. **Owner:** Willtronics Broadcasting, at above address. **Founded:** 1983. **Operating Hours:** 6 a.m.-midnight; 93% network, 7% local. **ADI:** Louisville, KY. **Key Personnel:** Wm. Gerald Willis, Contact; Catherine Willis, Contact; Jim Ingalls, Music Dir. **Wattage:** 6000. **Ad Rates:** $4.50 for 10 seconds; $5.50 for 15 seconds; $6.00-8.50 for 30 seconds; $7.50-10.00 for 60 seconds.

FRIENDSHIP, pop. 125.

Ripley Co. (SE). 22 m S of Batesville. Agriculture. Corn, wheat, hay.

10167 Muzzle Blasts
National Muzzle Loading Rifle Association
PO Box 67 Phone: (812)667-5131
Friendship, IN 47021 Fax: (812)667-5137
Publication E-mail: mblastmag@sridata.com
Publisher E-mail: nmlra@nmlra.org

Historical and modern muzzle loading firearms magazine. **Subtitle:** Historical and Modern Muzzleloading Arms Magazine. **Founded:** Sept. 1939. **Freq:** Monthly. **Print Method:** Web offset. **Trim Size:** 8 1/2 x 11. **Cols./Page:** 3. **Col. Width:** 2 1/8 inches. **Col. Depth:** 9 1/2 inches. **Key Personnel:** Terri Trowbridge, Dir. of Publications; Denise Goodpaster, Advertising Mgr. **ISSN:** 0027-5360. **Subscription Rates:** $35 individuals; $4 single issue. **URL:** http://www/mnlra.org; http://www.muzzleblasts.com.
Ad Rates: BW: $725 **Circ:** ‡23,000
4C: $1,535
PCI: $33

GARRETT, pop. 4,874.

De Kalb Co. (NE). 20 m N of Fort Wayne. Manufactures wood specialities, hospital furniture, electric motors, plastics, molded rubber products, machine shop. Agriculture. Corn, wheat, oats.

10168 The Garrett Clipper
106 S. Randolph St. Phone: (219)357-4123
PO Box 59 Fax: (219)357-4124
Garrett, IN 46738
Newspaper with a Democratic orientation. **Founded:** 1885. **Freq:** Semiweekly (Mon. and Thurs.). **Print Method:** Offset. **Cols./Page:** 7. **Col. Width:** 10 1/2 picas. **Col. Depth:** 21 inches. **Key Personnel:** Patricia A. Bartels, Editor; Raymond W. Bartels, Publisher. **USPS:** 214-260. **Subscription Rates:** $20 individuals; $23 out of area. **Remarks:** Accepts advertising.
Ad Rates: PCI: $2.80 **Circ:** ‡2,300

GARY, pop. 151,953.

Lake Co. (NW). On Lake Michigan 31 m SE of Chicago, Ill. Indiana Dunes State Park and National Park; Campus of Indiana University Northwest; Extensive iron, steel, sheet and tin plate, rail and cement plants. Car wheels, axles, structural shapes, alloys, coke, ammonium sulphate, tar, bridges, steel seamless tubes, steel springs, plastics, auto bodies, auto accessories, screws, jet engines, bolts, rivets, women's men's and children's wear, hosiery, lighting fixtures, bricks manufactured.

10169 Gary American
PO Box 1199 Phone: (219)883-4903
Gary, IN 46407-0199
Black community newspaper. **Founded:** 1927. **Freq:** Weekly (Fri.). **Print Method:** Offset. **Cols./Page:** 5. **Col. Width:** 27 nonpareils. **Col. Depth:** 224 agate lines. **Key Personnel:** Fred Harris, Editor and Publisher. **Subscription Rates:** $12 individuals; $16 out of state. **Remarks:** Color advertising accepted; rates available upon request.
Ad Rates: 4C: $90 **Circ:** Paid 10,000
PCI: $6 Free 1,000

10170 Gary New Crusader
1549 Broadway Phone: (219)885-4357
Gary, IN 46407-2240 Fax: (219)885-4359

Black community newspaper. **Founded:** 1961. **Freq:** Weekly (Thurs.). **Cols./Page:** 5. **Col. Width:** 2 inches. **Col. Depth:** 1 inches. **Key Personnel:** Dorothy R. Leavell, Editor and Publisher. **USPS:** 214-400. **Subscription Rates:** $15. **Remarks:** Accepts advertising.
Ad Rates: PCI: $7.13 **Circ:** ‡27,000

10171 Info
Info Printing & Publishing, Inc.
PO Box M 587
Gary, IN 46401

Black newspaper with a Democratic orientation. **Subtitle:** Northwest Indiana's Leading Weekly. **Founded:** 1963. **Freq:** Weekly (Thurs.). **Print Method:** Offset. **Trim Size:** 10 1/2 x 14 1/2. **Cols./Page:** 6. **Col. Width:** 1 5/8 inches. **Col. Depth:** 14 inches. **Key Personnel:** Imogene Harris, Editor and Publisher; Huston Pugh, Advertising Mgr. **Subscription Rates:** $12 individuals; $24 out of area. **Remarks:** Accepts advertising. **Formerly:** Info.
Ad Rates: GLR: $1 **Circ:** Paid ‡18,640
PCI: $13.91 Free ‡2,415

10172 The Northwest Phoenix
Indiana University Northwest
3400 Broadway, Moraine 110 Phone: (219)980-6795
Gary, IN 46408 Fax: (219)981-4233
Publication E-mail: phoenix@iunlabl.iun.indiana.edu

College newspaper. **Founded:** 1959. **Freq:** Semimonthly. **Print Method:** Offset. **Trim Size:** 11 x 14. **Cols./Page:** 8. **Col. Width:** 21 nonpareils. **Col. Depth:** 224 agate lines. **Key Personnel:** Shelia Turner, Business Mgr., stur7098@iunlab1.iun.indiana.edu; Margaret Holland, Editor-in-Chief. **Subscription Rates:** Free. **Remarks:** Accepts advertising. **URL:** http://stu.iun.indiana.edu/STUDGRUP/phoenix/phoenix.htm.
Ad Rates: GLR: $5 **Circ:** Free ‡2,500
BW: $420
4C: $377.36
PCI: $6

10173 Post-Tribune
Knight-Ridder, Inc.
1065 Broadway Phone: (219)881-3000
Gary, IN 46402-2907 Fax: (219)881-3232

General newspaper. **Founded:** 1907. **Freq:** Mon.-Sun. (morn.). **Print Method:** Offset. **Cols./Page:** 6. **Col. Width:** 24 nonpareils. **Col. Depth:** 301 agate lines. **Key Personnel:** Scott Bosley, Publisher; Mark Lett, Editor; Kay Mannino, Managing Editor. **USPS:** 440-000. **Subscription Rates:** $135.20 individuals; $210 out of area; $234.60 out of state. **Online:** America Online, Inc. **Feature Editors:** Matt Donney, *Sports*; Ron Recinto, *Lifestyle*; Ken Ross, *Financial/Business*; Virginia Thrower, *Editorials*.
Circ: Mon.-Sat. ★**60,675**
Sun. ★**67,016**

10174 Cablevision Associates of Gary
925 Kentucky Phone: (219)882-9700
Box M 869 Fax: (219)882-6946
Gary, IN 46402

Owner: Tele-Communications, Inc., 5619 DTC Parkway, Englewood, CO 80111, (303)267-5500, Fax: (303)779-1228. **Founded:** 1981. **Key Personnel:** Kerry Hogan, General Mgr.; Todd Franklin, Program Mgr.; Victor Mann, Chief Engineer. **Cities Served:** subscribing households 18,000; 37 channels; 2 community access channels; 40 hours per week community access programming.

10175 WGVE-FM - 88.7
1800 E. 35th Ave. Phone: (219)962-7571
Gary, IN 46409 Fax: (219)962-6269

Format: Educational. **Founded:** 1954. **Key Personnel:** Lawrence Ventura, General Mgr. **Wattage:** 2100.

10176 WLTH-AM - 1370
3669 Broadway Phone: (219)884-9409
Gary, IN 46409 Fax: (219)980-0483

Format: News; Talk. **Networks:** Independent. **Founded:** 1950. **Operating Hours:** 6 a.m.-2 a.m. **Key Personnel:** Pluria Marshall, General Mgr. **Wattage:** 1000 day; 500 night.

GAS CITY, pop. 6,370.

Grant Co. (NEC). 6 m SE of Marion. Glassware, concrete vaults, cement tile, barrels, manufactured. Cannery. Dairy, stock, poultry, grain farms. Wheat, corn, hogs.

10177 Twin City Journal-Reporter
Community Publishing Co.
238 E. Main St. Phone: (765)674-0070
Gas City, IN 46933
Community newspaper. **Founded:** 1887. **Freq:** Weekly (Wed.). **Print Method:** Offset. **Cols./Page:** 6. **Col. Width:** 24 nonpareils. **Col. Depth:** 301 agate lines. **Key Personnel:** Danny K Careins, Managing Editor. **Subscription Rates:** $18 in county; $27.50 out of state.
Ad Rates: BW: $483.75 **Circ:** ‡2,200
4C: $683.75
SAU: $4.00
PCI: $4.00

GEIST

10178 Geist Gazette
Topics Newspapers, Inc.
13095 Publisher's Dr. Phone: (317)598-6397
Fishers, IN 46038 Fax: (317)598-6340
Publisher E-mail: topics@inetdirect.net

Local newspaper. **Founded:** May 18, 1988. **Freq:** Weekly (Wed.). **Print Method:** Offset. **Trim Size:** 22 3/4. **Cols./Page:** 6. **Col. Width:** 26 nonpareils. **Col. Depth:** 301 agate lines. **Key Personnel:** David Lewis, Publisher; Tom Jekel, Editor; Dennis Waldkoetter, Business Mgr.; Jay Fredrickson, Advertising Dir.; Keven Gossett, Production Mgr.; Terry Coomer, Circulation Director. **Subscription Rates:** $15 Free annual voluntary pay (guaranteed delivery). **Remarks:** Accepts advertising.
Ad Rates: PCI: $7.04 **Circ:** Combined ♦5,965

10179 The Good Life
Publications Unlimited, Inc.
622 S. Rangeline Rd. Phone: (317)843-2993
Carmel, IN 46032 Fax: (317)843-2993

Regional lifestyle and entertainment magazine for Geist, Morse, and Eagle Creek, IN. **Founded:** 1989. **Freq:** Bimonthly. **Trim Size:** 8 3/8 x 10 7/8. **Cols./Page:** 3. **Col. Width:** 2 1/4 inches. **Key Personnel:** Joel Erwin, Publisher. **Subscription Rates:** Free.
Ad Rates: BW: $525 **Circ:** Controlled 10,000
4C: $780

GOODLAND

Newton Co. (NW). 10 m E of Kentland.

10180 Cable TV Services
301 W. Jasper Hwy. 24 W. Phone: (219)474-6332
PO Box 420 Fax: (219)474-6332
Goodland, IN 47948
Free: (800)693-2121

Founded: 1967. **Key Personnel:** Steven Mailloux, General Mgr.; Scott Mailloux, Contact; Diane Mailloux, Office Mgr.; Richard Mailloux, Vice President; Joanne Mailloux, President. **Cities Served:** Sheldon, IL; Boswell, Brook, Goodland, Kentland, IN: subscribing households 2,100; 44 channels.

GOSHEN†, pop. 19,665.

Elkhart Co. (N). 10 m SE of Elkhart. Goshen College (Menno.). Manufactures rubber goods, furniture, condensed milk, hydraulic presses, ladders, electric controls, batteries, sashes, doors, tanks, steel, glass and aluminum boats, trailers, plastics, lightning rods. Hardwood timber. Farming.

10181 Goshen College Bulletin
Goshen College
1700 S. Main St. Phone: (219)535-7568
Goshen, IN 46526
Publication E-mail: myrnack@goshen.edu

College alumni magazine. **Founded:** 1907. **Freq:** Quarterly (during the academic year). **Print Method:** Offset. **Trim Size:** 8 1/2 x 11. **Cols./Page:** 2 and 3. **Col. Width:** 42 and 28 nonpareils. **Col. Depth:** 116 agate lines. **ISSN:** 0017-2308. **Remarks:** Advertising not accepted.
Circ: ‡26,000

10182 The Goshen News
PO Box 569 Phone: (219)533-2151
Goshen, IN 46526-0569 Fax: (219)533-0839
Free: (800)487-2151

Independent newspaper with a Report orientation. **Founded:** 1837. **Freq:** Mon.-Sat. (eve.). **Print Method:** Offset. **Cols./Page:** 6. **Col. Width:** 24 nonpareils. **Col. Depth:** 301 agate lines. **Key Personnel:** Gerald R. Hertzler, Editor; James Young, Advertising Mgr.; John Gemmer, Publisher. **Subscription Rates:** $101 individuals. **Remarks:** Accepts advertising.
Ad Rates: BW: $1,403.52 **Circ:** Mon.-Sat. ★17,208
4C: $1,615.52
SAU: $10.88

10183 The Mennonite Quarterly Review
Mennonite Historical Society
1700 S. Main St. Fax: (219)535-7438
Goshen, IN 46526
Publication E-mail: mqr@goshen.edu

Journal covering Anabaptist, Mennonite, Amish, and Hutterite current events, history, and theology. **Founded:** Jan. 1927. **Freq:** Quarterly. **Print Method:** Offset. **Trim Size:** 6 x 9. **Cols./Page:** 1. **Col. Width:** 54 nonpareils. **Col. Depth:** 105 agate lines. **Key Personnel:** John D. Roth, Editor. **ISSN:** 0025-9373. **Subscription Rates:** $30 individuals; $7.50 single issue. **Remarks:** Advertising not accepted.
Circ: Paid ‡820
Controlled ‡180

10184 The Paper (Goshen Edition)
The Papers, Inc.
134 S. Main St. Phone: (219)534-2591
Goshen, IN 46526 Fax: (219)533-4280

Free newspaper. **Founded:** 1972. **Freq:** Weekly (Tues.). **Print Method:** Offset. **Trim Size:** 11 3/8 x 16 3/4. **Cols./Page:** 5. **Col. Width:** 22 nonpareils. **Col. Depth:** 224 agate lines. **Key Personnel:** Jeri Seely, Editor, jseely@the-papers.com; Della Baumgartner, Publisher; Kip Schumm, Advertising Mgr., kschumm@the-papers.com; Ron Baumgartner, President, rbaum@the-papers.com. **Subscription Rates:** Free.
Ad Rates: BW: $496 **Circ:** Free ♦29,759
4C: $744
PCI: $7.85

10185 WGCS-FM - 91.1
Goshen College Phone: (219)535-7488
1700 S. Main St. Fax: (219)535-7234
Goshen, IN 46526
Free: (888)912-7488
E-mail: wgcs@goshen.edu

Format: Classical; Folk. **Networks:** Public Radio International (PRI). **Owner:** Goshen College Broadcasting Corp., at above address, (219)535-7688. **Founded:** 1958. **Operating Hours:** Daily. **Key Personnel:** Jon Kauffmann-Kennel, General Mgr., phone (219)535-7688. **Local Programs:** *Crossings* 7:00 pm - 11:00 pm Monday-Friday, Jon Kauffmann-Kennel; *Momento de Gozo*, Tito Guedea; *A Women's Circle*, Wilma Harder. **Wattage:** 6000. **Ad Rates:** Noncommercial. **URL:** http://www.goshen.edu/wgcs.

10186 WKAM-AM - 1460
PO Box 497 Phone: (219)533-1460
Goshen, IN 46526 Fax: (219)534-3698
E-mail: wkam@wkam.com

Format: Adult Contemporary; Sports; Talk. **Networks:** USA Radio; Network Indiana; Tribune Radio. **Owner:** Northern Indiana Broadcasters, Inc., at above address. **Founded:** 1947. **Operating Hours:** Continuous. **ADI:** South Bend-Elkhart, IN. **Key Personnel:** Dan Eckelbarger, Operations Mgr.; Ernie Ferland, News Dir.; Brent Randall, Sales Mgr. **Wattage:** 2500 day; 500 night. **Ad Rates:** $10.60-12.95 for 30 seconds; $12.95-15.30 for 60 seconds. Combined advertising rates available with WZOW-FM.

10187 WZOW-FM - 97.7
PO Box 497 Phone: (219)533-5537
Goshen, IN 46526 Fax: (219)534-3698
E-mail: rocker@theclassic.com

Format: Classic Rock. **Founded:** 1976. **Operating Hours:** Continuous; 100%. **ADI:** South Bend-Elkhart, IN. **Key Personnel:** Doug Hawkes, General Mgr.; Kent Fulmer, Director. **Wattage:** 6000. **Ad Rates:** $15-27 for 30 seconds; $19-31 for 60 seconds. Combined advertising rates available with WKAM-AM.

GOSPORT

10188 Owen County History & Genealogy
Owen County Historical and Genealogical Society
c/o Vivian Zollinger Phone: (812)829-4466
RR 2, Box 49
Gosport, IN 47433
Journal covering history and genealogy of Owen County, Indiana. **Founded:** 1992. **Freq:** Quarterly. **Print Method:** Offset. **Key Personnel:** Vivian Zollinger, Editor, jzolling@ccrtc.com; Roger Peterson, Publications. **ISSN:** 2063-7400. **Subscription Rates:** $10 individuals; $2.50 single issue. **Remarks:** Advertising not accepted.
Circ: Paid 380

GRABILL, pop. 658.

Allen Co. (NE). 15 m NE of Fort Wayne. Manufactures furniture ornamental iron, plastic auto parts, steering wheels, wooden cabinets. Trucking. Grain, dairy, poultry farms.

10189 East Allen Courier
Box 77 Phone: (219)627-2728
Grabill, IN 46741-0077 Fax: (219)627-2519

Newspaper. **Subtitle:** East Allen Courier. **Founded:** 1949. **Freq:** Weekly. **Print Method:** Offset. **Cols./Page:** 6. **Col. Width:** 9.5 picas. **Col. Depth:** 224 agate lines. **Key Personnel:** Waldo P. Dick, Editor and Publisher. **Subscription Rates:** $0.25 single issue. **Remarks:** Accepts advertising.
Ad Rates: GLR: $.25 **Circ:** Paid ‡500
PCI: $3.50 Free ‡5,500

GREENCASTLE†, pop. 8,403.

Putnam Co. (WC). 40 m SW of Indianapolis. De Pauw University. Manufactures office products, cement, crushed stone. Lumber mill. Limestone quarries. Timber, stock, dairy farms.

10190 Banner-Graphic
Truth Publishing Co.
100 N. Jackson St. Phone: (317)653-5151
Greencastle, IN 46135-1240 Fax: (317)653-2063

General newspaper. **Founded:** 1850. **Freq:** Mon.-Sat. (eve.). **Print Method:** Offset. **Trim Size:** 14 x 23. **Cols./Page:** 6. **Col. Width:** 28 nonpareils. **Col. Depth:** 294 agate lines. **Key Personnel:** Eric Bernsee, Editor; Steve Hendershot, General Mgr. **Subscription Rates:** $72.80 individuals. **Remarks:** Accepts advertising.
Ad Rates: BW: $878.22 **Circ:** 6,181

10191 The De Pauw
De Pauw University
Center for Comtemporary Media Phone: (317)658-5972
609 S. Locust Fax: (317)658-5991
Greencastle, IN 46135
Collegiate newspaper. **Subtitle:** Indiana's Oldest College Newspaper. **Founded:** 1852. **Freq:** Biweekly (Tues. and Fri.; during the academic year). **Print Method:** Offset. **Trim Size:** Tabloid. **Cols./Page:** 5. **Col. Width:** 22 nonpareils. **Col. Depth:** 179 agate lines. **Key Personnel:** Brian Fisher, Editor, bjfisher@depauw.edu. **USPS:** 150-120. **Subscription Rates:** Free; $14 by mail. **Remarks:** Accepts advertising.
Ad Rates: GLR: $4.50 **Circ:** Paid 300
BW: $295 Free 2,500
PCI: $5.25

10192 Quill
Society of Professional Journalists
16 S. Jackson St. Phone: (317)653-3333
Greencastle, IN 46135-1514 Fax: (317)653-4631

Magazine for professional journalists and students of journalism. **Founded:** 1912. **Freq:** Monthly (Jan. /Feb., July/Aug. and Nov./Dec. issues combined). **Print Method:** Offset. **Trim Size:** 8 1/4 x 10 3/4. **Cols./Page:** 3. **Col. Width:** 2 1/4 inches. **Col. Depth:** 10 inches. **Key Personnel:** Peggy Verebone, Editor, peggyv@aol.com. **ISSN:** 0033-6475. **Subscription Rates:** $29 individuals Per year; $51 two years; $71 3 year; $3 single issue. **Remarks:** Accepts advertising. **Alt. Formats:** CD-ROM.
Ad Rates: GLR: $2 **Circ:** ‡16,000
BW: $2,970
4C: $3,950

10193 Science-Fiction Studies
SF-TH, Inc.
DePauw University Phone: (765)658-4758
Greencastle, IN 46135-0037 Fax: (765)658-4764

Scholarly journal covering the study of science fiction and utopian fiction. **Founded:** 1973. **Freq:** Triennial. **Trim Size:** 6 x 9. **Key Personnel:** Prof. Arthur B. Evans, Editor, aevans@depauw.edu. **ISSN:** 0091-7729. **Subscription Rates:**

$20 individuals; $9.50 single issue. **Remarks:** Accepts advertising.
Ad Rates: BW: $100 **Circ:** Controlled 1,150

10194 Heritage Lake Cable
602 N. Jackson St. Phone: (317)653-5541
Greencastle, IN 46135 Fax: (317)653-8262
Free: (800)288-3824
E-mail: eta@indy.tdsnet.com

Owner: Glass Antenna Systems, Inc., at above address. **Founded:** 1990. **Key Personnel:** Dick Glass, President; Larry Glass, Chief Engineer; Josh Brewer, Crew Chief. **Cities Served:** Heritage Lake Community, Putnam County,IN.: subscribing households 360; 28 channels; 0 community access channels; 0 hours per week community access programming.

10195 WGRE-FM - 91.5
Depauw University Phone: (765)658-4642
609 S. Locust St. Fax: (765)658-4639
Greencastle, IN 46135
E-mail: dbernsee@depauw.edu

Format: Alternative/New Music/Progressive. **Networks:** AP. **Founded:** 1949. **Operating Hours:** Continuous; 5% network, 95% local. **Key Personnel:** Jeff McCall, General Mgr., phone (765)658-4495, fax (765)658-4693, jeffmccall@depauw.edu; Bill Froehlich, Station Mgr., phone (765)658-4643, wfroehlich@depauw.edu; David Wormser, Program Dir., phone (765)658-4643, dwormser@depauw.edu; Craig Ericksonin, News Dir., cedrickson@depauw.edu. **Wattage:** 800. **Ad Rates:** Noncommercial. **URL:** http://www.depauw.edu/wgre/index.htm.

GREENFIELD†, pop. 11,439.

Hancock Co. (EC). 20 m E of Indianapolis. Manufactures prepainted metals, wire products, tool boxes, drugs, lock washers, knitwear. Farming. Wheat, corn, soybeans.

10196 Ad News
Indy Suburban Newspapers
119 W. North St. Phone: (317)462-7368
PO Box 602 Fax: (317)462-7779
Greenfield, IN 46140
Publication E-mail: tt3@spitfire.net

Community newspaper (tabloid). **Founded:** 1979. **Freq:** Weekly (Wed.). **Print Method:** Offset. **Trim Size:** 13 x 17. **Cols./Page:** 6. **Col. Width:** 10 picas. **Col. Depth:** 16 inches. **Key Personnel:** Jim Thomas, Publisher. **Subscription Rates:** $52 individuals. **Remarks:** Accepts advertising.
Ad Rates: BW: $325 **Circ:** ‡17,000
PCI: $4.90

10197 The Advertiser
Daily Reporter
22 W. New Rd. Phone: (317)462-5528
PO Box 279 Fax: (317)467-6009
Greenfield, IN 46140
Weekly shopper. **Founded:** 1970. **Freq:** Weekly (Mon.). **Print Method:** Offset. **Cols./Page:** 6. **Col. Width:** 2 1/16 inches. **Col. Depth:** 21 1/2 inches. **Key Personnel:** Randall D. Shields, Publisher; Dave Scott, Editor; Dave McCammon, Advertising Mgr. **Subscription Rates:** Free. **Remarks:** Accepts advertising. **Formerly:** The Daily Reporter Advertiser.
Ad Rates: GLR: $.50 **Circ:** Non-paid ‡18,000
BW: $812.70
4C: $962.70
SAU: $6.30

10198 Daily Reporter
22 W. New Rd. Phone: (317)462-5528
PO Box 279 Fax: (317)467-6009
Greenfield, IN 46140
General newspaper. **Founded:** 1908. **Freq:** Daily (eve.). **Print Method:** Offset. **Trim Size:** 13 3/4 x 22 3/4. **Cols./Page:** 6. **Col. Width:** 2 1/16 inches. **Col. Depth:** 21 1/2 inches. **Key Personnel:** Dave Scott, Editor; Randall Shields, Publisher; Dave McCammon, Advertising Dir. **USPS:** 228-720. **Subscription Rates:** $90 individuals. **Remarks:** Accepts advertising.
Ad Rates: BW: $1,006.20 **Circ:** Mon.-Sat. 9,500
4C: $1,156.20
SAU: $7.80

10199 Indy Suburban Newspapers
119 W. North St. Phone: (317)462-7368
PO Box 602 Fax: (317)462-7779
Greenfield, IN 46140
Publication E-mail: tt3@spitfire.net

Community newspapers (tabloid). **Founded:** 1976. **Freq:** Weekly (Wed.). **Print Method:** Offset. **Trim Size:** 13 x 17. **Cols./Page:** 6. **Col. Width:** 10 picas. **Col. Depth:** 16 inches. **Key Personnel:** Jim Thomas, Publisher; Ty Thomas, Advertising Mgr. **Subscription Rates:** $52. **Remarks:** Accepts advertising. **URL:** ifpa.com. **Formerly:** Ad News - Indy East - Westside Enterprise.
Ad Rates: BW: $591 **Circ:** Free ‡49,000
4C: $800
PCI: $8.25

10200 Westside Enterprise
Indy Suburban Newspapers
119 W. North St. Phone: (317)462-7368
PO Box 602 Fax: (317)462-7779
Greenfield, IN 46140
Publication E-mail: tt3@spitfire.net

Community newspaper (tabloid). **Founded:** Jan. 1926. **Freq:** Weekly (Wed.). **Print Method:** Offset. **Trim Size:** 13 x 17. **Cols./Page:** 6. **Col. Width:** 10 picas. **Col. Depth:** 16 inches. **Key Personnel:** Jim Thomas, Publisher. **Subscription Rates:** $52 individuals local. **Remarks:** Accepts advertising. **Alt. Formats:** CD-ROM, MAC. **Formerly:** West Side.
Ad Rates: GLR: $.50 **Circ:** Non-paid 12,000
PCI: $4.75

GREENSBURG†, pop. 9,254.

Decatur Co. (SE). 30 m NE of Columbus.

10201 The Greensburg Daily News
Greensburg Daily News, Inc.
135 S. Franklin St. Phone: (812)663-3111
PO Box 106 Fax: (812)663-2985
Greensburg, IN 47240-2023
General newspaper. **Founded:** 1894. **Freq:** Mon.-Sat. (eve.). **Print Method:** Offset. Uses slicks and veloxes. **Cols./Page:** 6. **Col. Width:** 26 nonpareils. **Col. Depth:** 301 agate lines. **Key Personnel:** Phillip Hart, Publisher; Jeff Emsweller, Editor. **ISSN:** 2289-8000. **Subscription Rates:** $104 individuals. **Remarks:** Accepts advertising.
Ad Rates: GLR: $1.85 **Circ:** ‡6,750
BW: $872.04
4C: $1,072.04
SAU: $7.95
PCI: $7.95

10202 Greensburg Times
American Publishing Co. of Indiana
135 S. Franklin St.
PO Box 106
Greensburg, IN 47240

Newspaper. **Founded:** 1910. **Freq:** Weekly (Fri.). **Print Method:** Offset. **Cols./Page:** 6. **Col. Width:** 26 nonpareils. **Col. Depth:** 301 agate lines. **Key Personnel:** Jeff Emsweller, Editor; Phillip Hart, Publisher. **Subscription Rates:** $30 individuals. **Remarks:** Advertising accepted; rates available upon request.
Circ: ‡446

10203 WTRE-AM - 1330
1217 West Park Rd. Phone: (812)663-3000
Box 487 Fax: (812)663-8355
Greensburg, IN 47240
E-mail: wtree00@gpbx.net

Format: Contemporary Country. **Networks:** Network Indiana. **Founded:** 1968. **Operating Hours:** Continuous 6 a.m.-10 p.m.; 5% network, 95% local. **Key Personnel:** Dave Gibson, phone ( )Dir. of Operations; Sandy Biddinger, Station Mgr. **Wattage:** 500. **Ad Rates:** $7.10-10 for 30 seconds; $8.90-12 for 60 seconds.

GREENWOOD, pop. 19,327.

Johnson Co. (SC) 11 m S of Indianapolis. Auto accessories, canned goods, stock remedies, mineral feeds manufactured. Dairy, stock, grain farms. Corn, wheat, oats, tomatoes.

10204 The Greenwood and Southside Challenger
PO Box 708 Phone: (317)888-3376
Greenwood, IN 46142 Fax: (317)888-3377
Publication E-mail: challenger@netdirect.net

Local newspaper (tabloid). **Founded:** Sept. 1972. **Freq:** Weekly (Wed.). **Print Method:** Offset. **Trim Size:** 12 x 18. **Cols./Page:** 5. **Col. Width:** 12 picas. **Col. Depth:** 16 3/4 inches. **Key Personnel:** Don Guerrettaz, Editor and Publisher; Judy Guerrettaz, Circulation Mgr. **USPS:** 369-770. **Subscription Rates:** $15 individuals. **Remarks:** Accepts advertising. **Alt. Formats:** CD-ROM; Mailing labels. **Formerly:** Southside Challenger.
Ad Rates: GLR: $2 **Circ:** ‡1,300
BW: $320
4C: $545
SAU: $6
PCI: $6

10205 MW-1 Cablesystems Inc.
PO Box 130 Phone: (317)865-2400
Greenwood, IN 46142-0130 Fax: (317)865-2426

Owner: Regional Cablesystems USA, at above address. **Formerly:** MW1; MN-1; SE-1; U.S.A. Cablesystems. **Key Personnel:** Paul Scott, General Mgr.; Rudy Pawlawski, Dir. of Finance; Dave Beasley, Dir. of Marketing; Gary Heimstead, Dir. of Technical Operations. **Cities Served:** Over 300 cities served throughout 12 states.: subscribing households 22,500; 22 channels.

10206 WCLJ-TV - 42
2528 U.S. 31 Hwy. S. Phone: (317)535-5542
Greenwood, IN 46143 Fax: (317)535-8584

Format: Commercial TV. **Founded:** 1987. **Operating Hours:** Continuous. **ADI:** Indianapolis (Marion), IN. **Key Personnel:** Mark Crouch, General Mgr.; Brian Renollet, Chief Engineer; Rick Bryant, Public Affairs; Diana Lohr, Contact. **Wattage:** 5,000,000 ERP. **Ad Rates:** $75 for 30 seconds; $100 for 60 seconds.

HAGERSTOWN, pop. 1,950.

Wayne Co. (E). 11 m E of Newcastle. Auto piston rings, gyroscopes manufactured. Agriculture. Stock, grain, dairy, farms. Corn, hogs, wheat.

10207 The Hagerstown Exponent
99 S. Perry St. Phone: (765)489-4035
Hagerstown, IN 47346-1521
Publication E-mail: hagersexpo@aol.com

Newspaper with a Report orientation. **Founded:** 1875. **Freq:** Weekly (Tues.). **Print Method:** Broadsheet. **Trim Size:** 13 x 21 1/2. **Cols./Page:** 6. **Col. Width:** 2.06 inches. **Col. Depth:** 21.5 inches. **Key Personnel:** Bob Hansen, Publisher. **USPS:** 232-196. **Subscription Rates:** $26.50 out of county. **Remarks:** Accepts advertising.
Ad Rates: BW: $472.50 **Circ:** ‡2,500
4C: $772.50
SAU: $6.35
PCI: $6.35

HAMILTON, pop. 587.

DeKalb and Steuben Co. (NE). 13 m NE of Auburn. Residential.

10208 The Hamilton News
Hamilton News, Inc.
1360 Ln. 201 Ball Lk.
Hamilton, IN 46742-9317

Newspaper with a Democratic orientation. **Freq:** Weekly (Tues.). **Print Method:** Offset. **Cols./Page:** 8. **Col. Width:** 19 nonpareils. **Col. Depth:** 224 agate lines. **Key Personnel:** Margo E. Teegardin, Editor. **Subscription Rates:** $12 individuals. **Remarks:** Accepts advertising.
Ad Rates: SAU: $2.25 **Circ:** ‡1,050

HAMMOND, pop. 93,714.

Lake Co. (NW). 20 m SE of Chicago, Ill. Oil refineries. Aluminum reprocessing; basic steel and fabrications. Manufactures soap products, oleomargarine, railway steel forgings, chemical products, locomotive superheaters, valves, castings, corn starch, candies, pulp products and plastics.

10209 Dow Theory Forecasts
Horizon Publishing Company LLC
7412 Calumet Ave. Fax: (219)931-6487
Hammond, IN 46324-2692
Financial magazine. **Founded:** 1946. **Freq:** Weekly. **Print Method:** Offset. **Key Personnel:** Richard Moroney, Editor. **ISSN:** 0300-7324. **Subscription Rates:** $233 individuals. **Remarks:** Advertising not accepted.
Circ: Paid 16,000

10210 Journal of Family Psychotherapy
The Haworth Press, Inc.
Purdue University Calumet
Family Studies Center
Hammond, IN 46323
Publisher E-mail: getinfo@haworthpressinc.com

Journal includes case studies, treatment reports, and strategies in clinical practice for psychotherapists. **Subtitle:** The Quarterly Journal of Case Studies, Treatment Reports, and Strategies in Clinical Practice. **Founded:** 1990. **Freq:** Quarterly. **Trim Size:** 6 x 8 1/2. **Cols./Page:** 1. **Col. Width:** 4 3/8 inches. **Col. Depth:** 7 1/8 inches. **Key Personnel:** Terry Trepper, PhD, Editor; Bill Cohen, Publisher. **ISSN:** 0897-5353. **Subscription Rates:** $34 individuals USA; $75 institutions USA; $175 libraries USA; $44.20 individuals CAN; $97.50 institutions CAN; $227.50 libraries CAN; $47.60 individuals

other countries; $105 institutions other countries; $245 libraries other countries. **Remarks:** Accepts advertising. **URL:** http://www.haworth.com. **Alt. Formats:** Microform. **Formerly:** Journal of Psychotherapy and the Family.
Ad Rates: BW: $300 **Circ:** 479

10211 The Times
Howard Publications
601 45th St. Phone: (219)933-3327
Munster, IN 46321 Fax: (219)933-3249

General newspaper. **Founded:** 1906. **Freq:** Daily (eve.), Sat. and Sun. (morn.). **Print Method:** Offset. **Cols./Page:** 9. **Col. Width:** 13 nonpareils. **Col. Depth:** 294 agate lines. **Key Personnel:** Wm. Nangle, Exec. Editor; Wm. Howard, Publisher; Don Caldwell, Advertising Dir. **Subscription Rates:** $119.60 individuals. **Remarks:** Accepts advertising. **URL:** http://www.thetimesonline.com. **Feature Editors:** Phil Britt, *Financial/Business*, phone (219)933-3399; Ron Brow, *Sports*, phone (219)933-3232; Lane Brown, *Fashion, Food, Garden/Home, Lifestyle, TV & Radio, Travel*, phone (219)933-3246; Nancy Pieters, *Real Estate*, phone (219)933-3216.
Ad Rates: GLR: $2.20 **Circ:** Mon.-Sat. 85,506
BW: $2,809.80 Sun. 93,201
4C: $3,309.80
SAU: $22.30

10212 TCI
844 169th St. Phone: (219)932-4711
Hammond, IN 46324 Fax: (219)931-4827

Founded: 1980. **Formerly:** UAE. **Cities Served:** Lake County, IN.

10213 WABT-FM - 103.9
6405 Olcott St.
Hammond, IN 46320-2835

Format: Album-Oriented Rock (AOR). **Networks:** ABC. **Owner:** Atlantic Morris Broadcasting, Inc., 28 W. Grand Ave., Montvale, NJ 07645, (201)307-0662. **Founded:** 1989. **Formerly:** WCRM-FM. **Operating Hours:** Continuous. **ADI:** Chicago (LaSalle), IL. **Key Personnel:** Sue Schmitz, General Mgr.; Cara Stern, Program Dir.; Tony Brinati, Sales Mgr. **Wattage:** 3000. **Ad Rates:** $40 for 30 seconds; $60 for 60 seconds.

10214 WJOB-AM - 1230
Radio Center Phone: (219)844-1230
Hammond, IN 46320 Fax: (219)844-6190

Format: Talk. **Networks:** Independent. **Founded:** 1924. **Operating Hours:** Continuous; 100% local. **Key Personnel:** Julian Colby, Contact; Judith Grambo, President; Mike Fray, Sales Mgr. **Wattage:** 1000. **Ad Rates:** $40-61 for 60 seconds.

10215 WWJY-FM - 103.9
6405 Olcott St.
Hammond, IN 46320-2835

Format: Adult Contemporary. **Owner:** M & M Broadcasting, at above address. **Founded:** 1972. **Formerly:** WFLM-FM (1981). **Operating Hours:** Continuous; 100% local. **ADI:** Chicago (LaSalle), IL. **Key Personnel:** Marty Wielgos, Vice President; Craig Hayden, Program Dir.; Tula Kalaris, Sales Mgr. **Wattage:** 3000. **Ad Rates:** $22.50 for 30 seconds; $32.50 for 60 seconds.

10216 WYCA-FM - 92.3
6336 Calumet Ave. Phone: (219)933-4455
Hammond, IN 46324

Format: Religious. **Owner:** Donald Crawford, PO Box 3003, Blue Bell, PA 19422, (215)628-3500. **Founded:** 1959. **Operating Hours:** Continuous. **ADI:** Chicago (LaSalle), IL. **Key Personnel:** Taft Harris, Station Mgr.; Tracie Reynolds, Program Dir. **Local Programs:** *The Spirit of Love*, Tracie Reynolds, Prog. Dir., (773)734-4455. **Wattage:** 50,000. **Ad Rates:** Advertising accepted; rates available upon request.

HARTFORD CITY†, pop. 7,622.

Blackford Co. (NE). 18 m N of Muncie. Manufactures paper, plastic - injection molded products, glass, hardware, garage doors. Food packing plants. Agriculture. Corn, wheat, oats.

10217 Hartford City News Times
American Publishing Co.
123 S. Jefferson St. Phone: (317)348-0110
Hartford City, IN 47348 Fax: (317)348-0112
Publication E-mail: hcnews@netusa1.net

General newspaper. **Founded:** 1886. **Freq:** Mon.-Sat. (eve.). **Print Method:** Offset. **Cols./Page:** 6. **Col. Width:** 12 picas. **Col. Depth:** 21 1/2 inches. **Key Personnel:** Beverly Everhart, General Mgr.; Chris Landis, Managing Editor; Connie Murray, Advertising Mgr. **ISSN:** 2362-6000. **Subscription Rates:** $125 individuals. **Remarks:** Accepts advertising.
Ad Rates: GLR: $5.06 **Circ:** ‡2,800
BW: $652.74
4C: $752.74
SAU: $5.06

HAUBSTADT

10218 WBGW-FM - 101.5
Rte. 2 Box 67 Phone: (812)768-5550
Haubstadt, IN 47639 Fax: (812)768-5552

Format: Religious. **Networks:** SkyLight Satellite. **Founded:** 1990. **Operating Hours:** Continuous; 95% network, 5% local. **Key Personnel:** Floyd E. Turner, Contact. **Wattage:** 1000. **Ad Rates:** Noncommercial.

HIGHLAND, pop. 25,935.

Lake Co. (NW). 5 m SE of Hammond. Manufactures machinery, concrete blocks, metal products. Truck farms.

10219 The Calumet Press
8411 Kennedy Ave. Phone: (219)838-0717
Highland, IN 46322 Fax: (219)838-1338

Community newspaper. **Founded:** 1959. **Freq:** Weekly (Wed.). **Print Method:** Offset. **Trim Size:** 17 x 22 1/2. **Cols./Page:** 6. **Col. Width:** 20 nonpareils. **Col. Depth:** 224 agate lines. **Key Personnel:** Jeanne Larsen, Editor; Wayne Kletzing, Publisher; William Palmateer, Sales Mgr. **Subscription Rates:** $8 individuals. **Remarks:** Accepts advertising. **Alt. Formats:** CD-ROM.
Ad Rates: BW: $350 **Circ:** Free ♦**40,340**

10220 The Midwest BEAT Magazine
Lounges Publications
2613 41st St. Phone: (219)972-9131
Highland, IN 46322 Fax: (219)972-9131
Publication E-mail: beatboss@aol.com

Magazine covering music, pop culture, film, and video. **Founded:** 1977. **Freq:** Monthly. **Print Method:** Letterpress. **Cols./Page:** 4. **Col. Width:** 28 nonpareils. **Col. Depth:** 168 agate lines. **Key Personnel:** Thomas E. Lounges, Exec. Editor & Publisher. **Subscription Rates:** $25 /year (for 1st class postage). **Remarks:** Accepts advertising. **URL:** http://www.htnc.com/thebeat/thebeat.htm. **Formerly:** The Beat; Night Rock News.
Ad Rates: BW: $600 **Circ:** Non-paid ‡30,000
4C: $1,000
PCI: $15

HOBART, pop. 22,987.

Lake Co. (NW). 8 m SE of Gary. Residential.

10221 Hobart Gazette
Herald News Group
3161 E. 84th St. Phone: (219)942-0521
Merrillville, IN 46410 Fax: (219)942-0820

Community newspaper. **Founded:** 1889. **Freq:** Weekly (Wed.). **Print Method:** Offset. **Trim Size:** 10 1/4 x 16. **Cols./Page:** 6. **Col. Width:** 1 9/16 inches. **Col. Depth:** 16 inches. **Key Personnel:** Steve Euvino, Editor; Diane Kemp, Advertising Dir.; Greg Lemburg, General Mgr. **Subscription Rates:** $15 individuals; $20 out of area. **Remarks:** Accepts advertising.
Ad Rates: GLR: $6.60 **Circ:** 6,814
BW: $380
PCI: $5.55

10222 Our Hope
Croatian Catholic Union of U.S.A. and Canada
1 E. Old Ridge Rd. Phone: (219)942-1191
Hobart, IN 46342 Fax: (219)942-8808

Catholic fraternal newspaper (Croatian). **Founded:** 1921. **Freq:** Monthly. **Print Method:** Offset. **Trim Size:** 11 x 16. **Cols./Page:** 5. **Col. Width:** 24 nonpareils. **Col. Depth:** 224 agate lines. **Key Personnel:** Melchior Masina, Managing Editor. **Subscription Rates:** $5 individuals. **Foreign language name:** Nasa Nada.
Circ: Paid ‡50
Free ‡3,500

HOPE, pop. 2,185.

Bartholomew Co. (SE). 40 m SE of Indianapolis. Agricultural community. Corn, beans.

10223 The Star-Journal
PO Box 65 Phone: (812)546-6113
Hope, IN 47246 Fax: (812)546-6114

Newspaper with a Democratic orientation. **Founded:** 1912. **Freq:** Weekly (Thurs.). **Print Method:** Offset. Broad sheet. **Cols./Page:** 6. **Col. Width:** 2 inches. **Col. Depth:** 21 1/2 inches. **Key Personnel:** Charles T. Biggs, Publisher; Jean Elliott, Manager. **USPS:** 519-480. **Subscription Rates:** $16 individuals.
Ad Rates: BW: $387 **Circ:** Paid 1,312
4C: $577 Free 102
SAU: $3

HUNTINGTON†, pop. 16,202.

Huntington Co. (NE). 25 m SW of Fort Wayne. Huntington College (U. Brethren).

10224 The Catholic Answer
Our Sunday Visitor Publishing
200 Noll Plaza Phone: (219)356-8400
Huntington, IN 46750 Fax: (219)356-8472
Free: (800)348-2440
Publisher E-mail: osvinc@osv.com

Magazine exploring and explaining Catholic beliefs, traditions, and history. **Founded:** 1987. **Freq:** Bimonthly. **Print Method:** Offset. **Trim Size:** 5 1/4 x 8 1/4. **Cols./Page:** 2. **Col. Width:** 2 1/4 inches. **Col. Depth:** 7 1/4 inches. **Key Personnel:** Rev. Peter Stravinskas, Editor; Peter Schownir, Advertising Mgr.; Robert P. Lockwood, Editor. **USPS:** 007-379. **Subscription Rates:** $15; $17 other countries. **Remarks:** Accepts advertising.
Ad Rates: BW: $950 **Circ:** Paid 43,863
4C: $1,250 Non-paid 923

10225 Catholic Parent
Our Sunday Visitor Publishing
200 Noll Plaza Phone: (219)356-8400
Huntington, IN 46750 Fax: (219)356-8472
Free: (800)348-2440
Publisher E-mail: osvinc@osv.com

Magazine featuring tips for Catholic parents raising children. **Founded:** 1993. **Freq:** Bimonthly. **Key Personnel:** Woodeen Koening-Bricker, Editor; Mary Achterhoff, Editor; Richard G. Beemer, Managing Editor; Greg Erlandson, Editor; Robert P. Lockwood, Publisher. **ISSN:** 1875-1956. **Subscription Rates:** $18; $24 other countries. $3 single issue.
Circ: Paid 20,000

10226 Herald-Press
Huntington Newspapers, Inc.
7 N. Jefferson St. Phone: (219)356-6700
PO Box 860 Fax: (219)356-9026
Huntington, IN 46750-0860
Publication E-mail: hpnews@h-ponline.com

Community newspaper. **Founded:** 1848. **Freq:** Daily (eve.). **Print Method:** Offset. **Cols./Page:** 6. **Col. Width:** 26 nonpareils. **Col. Depth:** 294 agate lines. **Key Personnel:** Michael Perkins, Editor; Steven Kimmel, Operations Dir., hpadmin@h-ponline.com. **Subscription Rates:** $93.60 individuals. **Remarks:** Accepts advertising. **URL:** http://www.h-ponline.com. **Alt. Formats:** Mailing lists; Microform.
Ad Rates: GLR: $.47 **Circ:** Mon.-Fri. ‡7,200
BW: $1128.96 Sun. ‡8,300
4C: $1238.96
PCI: $8.96

10227 My Daily Visitor
Our Sunday Visitor Publishing
200 Noll Plaza Phone: (219)356-8400
Huntington, IN 46750 Fax: (219)356-8472
Free: (800)348-2440
Publisher E-mail: osvinc@osv.com

Magazine containing meditations and daily readings from scripture. **Founded:** Feb. 1957. **Freq:** Bimonthly. **Print Method:** Letterpress and offset. **Trim Size:** 3 3/4 x 5 1/2. **Cols./Page:** 1. **Col. Width:** 34 nonpareils. **Col. Depth:** 64 agate lines. **Key Personnel:** Catherine M. Odell, Editor; William Odell, Editor. **USPS:** 369-360. **Subscription Rates:** $9 individuals; $2 single issue. **Remarks:** Advertising not accepted.
Circ: ‡29,277

10228 New Covenant
Our Sunday Visitor Publishing
200 Noll Plaza Phone: (219)356-8400
Huntington, IN 46750 Fax: (219)356-8472
Free: (800)348-2440
Publication E-mail: newcov@aol.com; 76440.3571@cis
Publisher E-mail: osvinc@osv.com

Magazine of Catholic spirituality. **Founded:** June 1971. **Freq:** Monthly. **Print Method:** Offset. **Trim Size:** 8 3/8 x 10 7/8.

Cols./Page: 3. **Col. Width:** 42 nonpareils. **Col. Depth:** 139 agate lines. **Key Personnel:** Mike Aquilina, Editor; Bob Lockwood, Publisher; Peter Schownir, Advertising Mgr. **ISSN:** 0744-8589. **Subscription Rates:** $18 individuals; $24 other countries; $1 single issue.
Ad Rates: BW: $1,000 **Circ:** ‡25,000
4C: $1,250
PCI: $58

10229 Our Sunday Visitor
Our Sunday Visitor Publishing
200 Noll Plaza Phone: (219)356-8400
Huntington, IN 46750 Fax: (219)356-8472
Free: (800)348-2440
Publication E-mail: oursunvis@osv.com
Publisher E-mail: osvinc@osv.com

Roman Catholic weekly newspaper. **Founded:** May 5, 1912. **Freq:** Weekly (Sun.). **Print Method:** Offset. **Trim Size:** 10 1/4 x 13 1/4. **Cols./Page:** 5. **Col. Width:** 24 nonpareils. **Col. Depth:** 185 agate lines. **Key Personnel:** Greg Erlandson, Editor-in-Chief; Robert P. Lockwood, Publisher; Peter Schownir, Advertising Dir. **ISSN:** 0030-6967. **Subscription Rates:** $30 individuals; $40 other countries. **Remarks:** Accepts advertising.
Ad Rates: BW: $2,900 **Circ:** 100,000
4C: $3,625
PCI: $80

10230 The Pope Speaks: The Church Documents Bimonthly
Our Sunday Visitor Publishing
200 Noll Plaza Phone: (219)356-8400
Huntington, IN 46750 Fax: (219)356-8472
Free: (800)348-2440
Publication E-mail: tpspeaks@osv.com
Publisher E-mail: osvinc@osv.com

Magazine providing an accurate record of selected papal speeches, letters, and other documents. **Subtitle:** The Church Documents Bimonthly. **Founded:** 1954. **Freq:** Bimonthly. **Print Method:** Offset. **Trim Size:** 6 x 9. **Cols./Page:** 2. **Col. Width:** 14 picas. **Col. Depth:** 43 picas. **Key Personnel:** Russell Shaw, Editor; Robert P. Lockwood, Publisher. **ISSN:** 0032-4353. **Subscription Rates:** $19.95. **Remarks:** Advertising not accepted. **Alt. Formats:** Microform, UMI.
Circ: Combined 4,900

10231 The Priest
Our Sunday Visitor Publishing
200 Noll Plaza Phone: (219)356-8400
Huntington, IN 46750 Fax: (219)356-8472
Free: (800)348-2440
Publication E-mail: tpriest@osv.com
Publisher E-mail: osvinc@osv.com

Magazine for Catholic clergy, seminarians, and permanent deacons. **Founded:** 1945. **Freq:** Monthly. **Print Method:** Offset. **Trim Size:** 8 1/4 x 11. **Cols./Page:** 3. **Col. Width:** 13 1/2 picas. **Col. Depth:** 132 agate lines. **Key Personnel:** Owen F. Campion, Editor; George P. Foster, Assoc. Editor. **ISSN:** 0032-8200. **Subscription Rates:** $35.97 individuals; $42.97 other countries; $4 single issue; $25.97 seminarians for 1 year. **Remarks:** Accepts advertising. **Alt. Formats:** Microform.
Ad Rates: BW: $895 **Circ:** 7,800
4C: $1,805
PCI: $41

10232 U.S. Catholic Historian
U.S. Catholic Historical Society
c/o Our Sunday Visitor Fax: (219)359-9117
200 Noll Pl. Free: (800)348-2440
Huntington, IN 46750
Publisher E-mail: uschistorian@osv.com

Magazine promoting interest in American Catholic heritage. **Founded:** 1980. **Freq:** Quarterly. **Key Personnel:** Christopher J. Kauffman, Editor.

10233 WPDJ-AM - 1300
1600 E. Taylor St. Phone: (219)358-0718
PO Box 367
Huntington, IN 46750-0367

Format: Full Service; Eclectic. **Founded:** 1957. **Formerly:** WCER-AM (1989). **Operating Hours:** Continuous. **Key Personnel:** William Dinkins, General Mgr.; Ruby Thompson, Station Mgr. **Wattage:** 500. **Ad Rates:** $8 for 30 seconds; $10 for 60 seconds.

INDIANAPOLIS†, pop. 700,807.

Marion Co. (C). The State Capital. On White River in center of State. Butler University, Indiana University, Purdue University at Indianapolis, University of Indianapolis. Colleges, private schools and many state institutions. Children's Museum (largest in the world), Indianapolis Museum of Art. Site of the "500 Mile Race". Home of the U.S. Clay Courts Sports Center (tennis stadium). Indianapolis Symphony Orchestra. Trucking and insurance center. Major producers of food and automotive products. Electrical equipment, heavy machinery, pharmaceuticals manufactured.

10234 Alcoholism: Clinical and Experimental Research
Lippincott Williams & Wilkins
545 Barnhill Dr., Emerson 421 Phone: (317)274-8495
Indianapolis, IN 46202-5124 Fax: (317)274-4311

Publishing original clinical and research studies on alcoholism and alcohol-induced organ damage. **Subtitle:** Official Journal of the Research Society on Alcoholism and International Society for Biomedical Research on Alcoholism. **Founded:** 1977. **Freq:** Monthly. **Print Method:** Offset. **Trim Size:** 8 1/8 x 10 7/8. **Cols./Page:** 2. **Col. Width:** 32 nonpareils. **Col. Depth:** 119 agate lines. **Key Personnel:** Ting-Kai Li, M.D., Editor, tkli@iupui.edu. **ISSN:** 0145-6008. **Subscription Rates:** $200 individuals; $380 institutions In-training 95. **Remarks:** Accepts advertising. **Alt. Formats:** Mailing labels.
Ad Rates: BW: $425 **Circ:** Paid ‡1,500
4C: $1,180 Non-paid ‡240

10235 American Legion Auxiliary's National News
American Legion Auxiliary's National News
777 N. Meridian, St., 3rd Fl. Phone: (317)635-6291
Indianapolis, IN 46204-1189 Fax: (317)636-5590
Publisher E-mail: alahq@iquest.net

Magazine for Auxiliary members. **Founded:** 1921. **Freq:** Bimonthly. **Print Method:** Web offset. **Trim Size:** 8 1/8 x 10 7/8. **Cols./Page:** 3. **Col. Width:** 13.5 picas. **Col. Depth:** 46 picas. **Key Personnel:** Lauralyn T. Mohr, Editor; Thomas G. Bowman, Advertising Mgr. **Subscription Rates:** $7 individuals. **Remarks:** Accepts advertising.
Ad Rates: BW: $6,833 **Circ:** Paid 776,415
4C: $9,699
PCI: $373

10236 American Legion Magazine
American Legion National Headquarters
PO Box 1055 Phone: (317)630-1212
Indianapolis, IN 46206 Fax: (317)630-1369
Publication E-mail: tal@legion.org

General interest magazine for veterans. **Founded:** 1919. **Freq:** Monthly. **Print Method:** Offset. **Trim Size:** 8 1/8 x 10 7/8. **Cols./Page:** 3. **Col. Width:** 25 nonpareils. **Col. Depth:** 136 agate lines. **Key Personnel:** Dick McNally, Publisher, phone (317)630-1289. **Subscription Rates:** $15 individuals; $2.50 single issue; $21 other countries. **Remarks:** Accepts advertising. **Available Online. URL:** http://www.legion.org. **Alt. Formats:** Audio tape.
Ad Rates: BW: $32,610 **Circ:** Paid ★**2,711,501**
4C: $44,250
PCI: $728

10237 American Trucker—Badger Edition
Southam, Inc.
PO Box 603 Phone: (317)297-5500
Indianapolis, IN 46206 Fax: (317)299-1356
Free: (800)827-7468
Publication E-mail: amtruck@trucker.com

Truck trader magazine. Part of the Allied Network. **Subtitle:** Serving Upper Peninsula of Michigan, Wisconsin. **Founded:** Jan. 1994. **Freq:** Monthly. **Print Method:** Offset. **Trim Size:** 7 1/2 x 10 1/16. **Cols./Page:** 3. **Col. Width:** 2 5/16 inches. **Col. Depth:** 9 3/4 inches. **Key Personnel:** James Bellin, President, jim@trucker.com; Lara Haag, Mailing contact, lhaag@trucker. **ISSN:** 1090-9648. **Subscription Rates:** $21 individuals. **Remarks:** Accepts advertising. **Formerly:** Badger Trucker.
Ad Rates: BW: $780 **Circ:** Combined 21,627
4C: $1,282

10238 American Trucker—Buckeye Edition
Southam, Inc.
PO Box 603 Phone: (317)297-5500
Indianapolis, IN 46206 Fax: (317)299-1356
Free: (800)827-7468
Publication E-mail: amtruck@trucker.com

Trade magazine covering motor trucks and accessories. **Subtitle:** Serving Ohio. **Founded:** Jan. 1994. **Freq:** Monthly. **Print Method:** Offset. **Trim Size:** 7 1/2 x 10 1/16. **Cols./Page:** 3. **Col. Width:** 28 nonpareils. **Col. Depth:** 140 agate lines. **Key Personnel:** James Bellin, President, jim@trucker.com; Lara Haag, Mailing contact, lhaag@trucker.com. **ISSN:** 1090-9656. **Subscription Rates:** $21 individuals. **Remarks:** Accepts advertising. **Formerly:** Buckeye Trucker.
Ad Rates: BW: $780 **Circ:** Combined 28,719
4C: $1,282

10239 American Trucker—California Edition
Southam, Inc.
PO Box 603 Phone: (317)297-5500
Indianapolis, IN 46206 Fax: (317)299-1356
Free: (800)827-7468
Publication E-mail: amtruck@trucker.com

Truck trader magazine. **Subtitle:** Serving California, Hawaii. **Founded:** Jan. 1994. **Freq:** Monthly. **Print Method:** Offset. **Trim Size:** 7 1/2 x 10 1/16. **Cols./Page:** 3. **Col. Width:** 2 5/16 inches. **Col. Depth:** 9 3/4 inches. **Key Personnel:** James Bellin, President, jim@trucker.com; Lara Haag, Mailing contact, lhaag@trucker.com. **ISSN:** 1090-9664. **Subscription Rates:** $21 individuals. **Remarks:** Accepts advertising. **Formerly:** California Trucker.
Ad Rates: BW: $885 **Circ:** Combined 42,000
4C: $1,406

10240 American Trucker—Cascade Edition
Southam, Inc.
PO Box 603 Phone: (317)297-5500
Indianapolis, IN 46206 Fax: (317)299-1356
Free: (800)827-7468
Publication E-mail: amtruck@trucker.com

Truck trader magazine. **Subtitle:** Serving Alaska, Idaho, Oregon, Washington. **Founded:** Jan. 1994. **Freq:** Monthly. **Print Method:** Offset. **Trim Size:** 7 1/2 x 10 1/16. **Cols./Page:** 3. **Col. Width:** 2 5/16 inches. **Col. Depth:** 9 3/4 inches. **Key Personnel:** James Bellin, Publisher, jim@trucker.com. **ISSN:** 1090-9672. **Subscription Rates:** $21 individuals. **Remarks:** Accepts advertising.
Ad Rates: BW: $885 **Circ:** Combined 24,008
4C: $1,406

10241 American Trucker—Central States Edition
Southam, Inc.
PO Box 603 Phone: (317)297-5500
Indianapolis, IN 46206 Fax: (317)299-1356
Free: (800)827-7468
Publication E-mail: amtruck@trucker.com

Truck trader magazine. **Subtitle:** Serving Iowa, Kansas, Nebraska, Western Missouri. **Founded:** Jan. 1994. **Freq:** Monthly. **Print Method:** Offset. **Trim Size:** 7 1/2 x 10 1/16. **Cols./Page:** 3. **Col. Width:** 2 5/16 inches. **Col. Depth:** 9 3/4 inches. **Key Personnel:** James Bellin, President, jim@trucker.com; Lara Haag, Mailing contact, lhaag@trucker.com. **ISSN:** 1090-9680. **Subscription Rates:** $21 individuals. **Remarks:** Accepts advertising. **Formerly:** Central States Trucker.
Ad Rates: BW: $780 **Circ:** Combined 25,729
4C: $1,282

10242 American Trucker—Florida Edition
Southam, Inc.
PO Box 603 Phone: (317)297-5500
Indianapolis, IN 46206 Fax: (317)299-1356
Free: (800)827-7468
Publication E-mail: amtruck@trucker.com

Truck trader magazine. **Subtitle:** Serving Florida. **Freq:** Monthly. **Print Method:** Offset. **Trim Size:** 7 1/2 x 10 1/16. **Cols./Page:** 3. **Col. Width:** 2 5/16 inches. **Col. Depth:** 9 3/4 inches. **Key Personnel:** James Bellin, Publisher, jim@trucker.com. **Subscription Rates:** $21 individuals. **Remarks:** Accepts advertising.
Ad Rates: BW: $635 **Circ:** Combined 28,375
4C: $1,100

10243 American Trucker—Illinois Edition
Southam, Inc.
PO Box 603 Phone: (317)297-5500
Indianapolis, IN 46206 Fax: (317)299-1356
Free: (800)827-7468
Publication E-mail: amtruck@trucker.com

Motor trucks and accessories trade magazine. **Subtitle:** Serving Eastern Missouri, Illinois. **Founded:** Jan. 1994. **Freq:** Monthly. **Print Method:** Offset. **Trim Size:** 7 1/2 x 10 1/16. **Cols./Page:** 3. **Col. Width:** 28 nonpareils. **Col. Depth:** 140 agate lines. **Key Personnel:** James Bellin, President, jim@trucker.com; Lara Haag, Mailing contact, lhaag@trucker.com. **ISSN:** 1090-9702. **Subscription Rates:** $21 individuals. **Remarks:** Accepts advertising. **Formerly:** Illinois Trucker.
Ad Rates: BW: $780 **Circ:** Combined 26,072
4C: $1,282

10244 American Trucker—Indiana Edition
Southam, Inc.
PO Box 603 Phone: (317)297-5500
Indianapolis, IN 46206 Fax: (317)299-1356
Free: (800)827-7468
Publication E-mail: amtruck@trucker.com

Trade magazine on trucks and accessories. **Subtitle:** Serving Indiana. **Founded:** Jan. 1994. **Freq:** Monthly. **Print Method:** Offset. **Trim Size:** 7 1/2 x 10 1/16. **Cols./Page:** 3. **Col. Width:**

28 nonpareils. **Col. Depth:** 140 agate lines. **Key Personnel:** James Bellin, President, jim@trucker.com; Lara Haag, Mailing contact, lhaag@trucker.com. **ISSN:** 1090-9710. **Subscription Rates:** $21 individuals. **Remarks:** Accepts advertising. **Formerly**: Indiana Trucker.
Ad Rates: BW: $780 **Circ:** Controlled 22,815
4C: $1,282

10245 American Trucker—Kentucky/Tennessee Edition
Southam, Inc.
PO Box 603 Phone: (317)297-5500
Indianapolis, IN 46206 Fax: (317)299-1356
Free: (800)827-7468
Publication E-mail: amtruck@trucker.com

Truck trader magazine. **Subtitle:** Serving Kentucky and Tennessee. **Freq:** Monthly. **Print Method:** Offset. **Trim Size:** 7 1/2 x 10 1/16. **Cols./Page:** 3. **Col. Width:** 2 5/16 inches. **Col. Depth:** 9 3/4 inches. **Key Personnel:** James Bellin, Publisher, jim@trucker.com. **Subscription Rates:** $21 individuals. **Remarks:** Accepts advertising.
Ad Rates: BW: $745 **Circ:** Combined 36,414
4C: $1,224

10246 American Trucker—Metro East Edition
Southam, Inc.
PO Box 603 Phone: (317)297-5500
Indianapolis, IN 46206 Fax: (317)299-1356
Free: (800)827-7468
Publication E-mail: amtruck@trucker.com

Truck trader magazine. **Subtitle:** Serving Metro New York, New Jersey, Eastern Pennsylvania. **Founded:** Jan. 1994. **Freq:** Monthly. **Print Method:** Offset. **Trim Size:** 8 x 10 3/4. **Cols./Page:** 3. **Col. Width:** 2 5/16 inches. **Col. Depth:** 9 3/4 inches. **Key Personnel:** James Bellin, President, jim@trucker.com; Lara Haag, Mailing contact, lhaag@trucker.com. **ISSN:** 1090-9737. **Subscription Rates:** $21 individuals. **Remarks:** Accepts advertising. **Formerly**: Keystone/Jersey Trucker.
Ad Rates: BW: $885 **Circ:** Combined 23,750
4C: $1,406

10247 American Trucker—Michigan Edition
Southam, Inc.
PO Box 603 Phone: (317)297-5500
Indianapolis, IN 46206 Fax: (317)299-1356
Free: (800)827-7468
Publication E-mail: amtruck@trucker.com

Truck trader magazine. **Subtitle:** Serving Michigan. **Founded:** Jan. 1994. **Freq:** Monthly. **Print Method:** Offset. **Trim Size:** 7 1/2 x 10 1/16. **Cols./Page:** 3. **Col. Width:** 2 5/16 inches. **Col. Depth:** 9 3/4 inches. **Key Personnel:** James Bellin, President, jim@trucker.com; Lara Haag, Mailing contact, lhaag@trucker.com. **ISSN:** 1090-9745. **Subscription Rates:** $21 individuals. **Remarks:** Accepts advertising. **Formerly**: Michigan Truck Exchange.
Ad Rates: BW: $580 **Circ:** Combined 26,282
4C: $1,029

10248 American Trucker—Mid-Atlantic Edition
Southam, Inc.
PO Box 603 Phone: (317)297-5500
Indianapolis, IN 46206 Fax: (317)299-1356
Free: (800)827-7468
Publication E-mail: amtruck@trucker.com

Truck trader magazine. **Subtitle:** Serving Delaware, Maryland, North & South Carolina, Virginia & West Virginia. **Founded:** Jan. 1994. **Freq:** Monthly. **Print Method:** Offset. **Trim Size:** 7 1/2 x 10 1/16. **Cols./Page:** 3. **Col. Width:** 2 5/16 inches. **Col. Depth:** 9 3/4 inches. **Key Personnel:** James Bellin, President, jim@trucker.com; Lara Haag, Mailing contact, lhaag@trucker.com. **ISSN:** 1090-9753. **Subscription Rates:** $21 individuals. **Remarks:** Accepts advertising. **Formerly**: Allegheny Trucker; Carolina Trucker.
Ad Rates: BW: $910 **Circ:** Non-paid 45,230
4C: $1,418

10249 American Trucker Minn/Dakota Truck Edition
Southam, Inc.
PO Box 603 Phone: (317)297-5500
Indianapolis, IN 46206 Fax: (317)299-1356
Free: (800)827-7468
Publication E-mail: trucker@.com

Truck trader magazine. **Freq:** Monthly. **Print Method:** Offset. **Trim Size:** 7 1/2 x 10 1/16. **Cols./Page:** 3. **Col. Width:** 2 5/16 inches. **Col. Depth:** 9 3/4 inches. **Key Personnel:** James Bellin, Publisher, jim@trucker.com. **Subscription Rates:** $21 individuals. **Remarks:** Accepts advertising.
Ad Rates: BW: $780 **Circ:** Paid 21,217
4C: $1,282

10250 American Trucker—Mountain America Edition
Southam, Inc.
PO Box 603 Phone: (317)297-5500
Indianapolis, IN 46206 Fax: (317)299-1356
Free: (800)827-7468
Publication E-mail: amtruck@trucker.com

Truck trader magazine. **Subtitle:** Serving Arizona, Colorado, Montana, Nevada, New Mexico, Utah, Wyoming. **Founded:** Jan. 1994. **Freq:** Monthly. **Print Method:** Offset. **Trim Size:** 7 1/2 x 10 1/16. **Cols./Page:** 3. **Col. Width:** 2 5/16 inches. **Col. Depth:** 9 3/4 inches. **Key Personnel:** James Bellin, President, jim@trucker.com; Lara Haag, Mailing contact, lhaag@trucker.com. **ISSN:** 1090-977X. **Subscription Rates:** $21 individuals. **Remarks:** Accepts advertising. **Formerly**: Mountain America Truck Trader.
Ad Rates: BW: $885 **Circ:** Combined 21,389
4C: $1,406

10251 American Trucker—New England Edition
Southam, Inc.
PO Box 603 Phone: (317)297-5500
Indianapolis, IN 46206 Fax: (317)299-1356
Free: (800)827-7468
Publication E-mail: amtruck@trucker.com

Truck trader magazine. **Subtitle:** Serving Connecticut, Maine, Massachusetts, New Hampshire, Rhode Island, Vermont. **Founded:** Jan. 1994. **Freq:** Monthly. **Print Method:** Offset. **Trim Size:** 7 1/2 x 10 1/16. **Cols./Page:** 3. **Col. Width:** 2 5/16 inches. **Col. Depth:** 9 3/4 inches. **Key Personnel:** James Bellin, President, jim@trucker.com; Lara Haag, Mailing contact, lhaag@trucker.com. **ISSN:** 1090-9788. **Subscription Rates:** $21 individuals. **Remarks:** Accepts advertising. **Formerly**: New England Truck Exchange.
Ad Rates: BW: $885 **Circ:** Combined 27,015
4C: $1,406

10252 American Trucker—New York/Pennsylvania Edition
Southam, Inc.
PO Box 603 Phone: (317)297-5500
Indianapolis, IN 46206 Fax: (317)299-1356
Free: (800)827-7468
Publication E-mail: amtruck@trucker.com

Truck trader magazine. **Subtitle:** Serving Western Pennsylvania, Upstate and Western New York. **Founded:** Jan. 1994. **Freq:** Monthly. **Print Method:** Offset. **Trim Size:** 7 1/2 x 10 1/16. **Cols./Page:** 3. **Col. Width:** 2 5/16 inches. **Col. Depth:** 9 3/4 inches. **Key Personnel:** James Bellin, President, jim@trucker.com; Lara Haag, Mailing contact, lhaag@trucker.com. **ISSN:** 1090-9796. **Subscription Rates:** $21 individuals. **Remarks:** Accepts advertising. **Formerly**: New York Truck Exchange.
Ad Rates: BW: $885 **Circ:** Combined 25,480
4C: $1,406

10253 American Trucker—South Central Edition
Southam, Inc.
PO Box 603 Phone: (317)297-5500
Indianapolis, IN 46206 Fax: (317)299-1356
Free: (800)827-7468
Publication E-mail: amtruck@trucker.com

Trade magazine featuring motor trucks and accessories. **Subtitle:** Serving Arkansas, Louisiana, Oklahoma, Texas. **Founded:** Jan. 1994. **Freq:** Monthly. **Print Method:** Offset. **Trim Size:** 7 1/2 x 10 1/16. **Cols./Page:** 3. **Col. Width:** 28 nonpareils. **Col. Depth:** 140 agate lines. **Key Personnel:** James Bellin, President, jim@trucker.com; Lara Haagan, Mailing contact, lhaag@trucker.com. **ISSN:** 1090-980X. **Subscription Rates:** $21 individuals. **Remarks:** Accepts advertising. **Formerly**: Texas/Louisiana Trucker.
Ad Rates: BW: $910 **Circ:** Controlled 59,000
4C: $1,418

10254 American Trucker—Southern Edition
Southam, Inc.
PO Box 603 Phone: (317)297-5500
Indianapolis, IN 46206 Fax: (317)299-1356
Free: (800)827-7468
Publication E-mail: amtruck@trucker.com

Truck trader magazine. **Subtitle:** Serving Alabama, Georgia, Mississippi. **Freq:** Monthly. **Print Method:** Offset. **Trim Size:** 7 1/2 x 10 1/16. **Cols./Page:** 3. **Col. Width:** 2 5/16 inches. **Col. Depth:** 9 3/4 inches. **Key Personnel:** James Bellin, Publisher, jim@trucker.com. **Subscription Rates:** $21 individuals. **Remarks:** Accepts advertising.
Ad Rates: BW: $840 **Circ:** Combined 39,550
4C: $1,335

10255 Arts Indiana Magazine
Arts Indiana, Inc.
47 S. Pennsylvania
Ste. 701
Indianapolis, IN 46204-3622
Publication E-mail: artsmag@1quest.net

Magazine covering visual, literary, and performing arts in Indiana. **Founded:** Feb. 1979. **Freq:** Bimonthly. **Print Method:** Sheetfed. **Trim Size:** 8 x 10 7/8. **Cols./Page:** 3 and 4. **Col. Width:** 14 and 19 picas. **Col. Depth:** 77 picas. **Key Personnel:** Orval Schierholz, Contact; Kay Ivcevich, Advertising Publisher; Julie Pratt McQuiston, Editor. **ISSN:** 0897-859X. **Subscription Rates:** $18 individuals; $15 students and senior citizens; $35 two years. **Remarks:** Accepts advertising. **Formerly**: Arts Insight.
Ad Rates: BW: $985 **Circ:** ‡12,000
4C: $1,235

10256 Branches Magazine
Apple Press, Inc.
PO Box 30348 Phone: (317)255-5594
Indianapolis, IN 46230 Fax: (317)254-0330
Free: (800)352-2817
Publication E-mail: editor@branches.com

Consumer magazine covering spirituality, health care and the environment, focusing on Indiana. **Subtitle:** Whole Life Living for Indiana. **Founded:** 1988. **Freq:** Bimonthly. **Print Method:** Web offset. **Trim Size:** 11 3/8 x 13 3/4. **Key Personnel:** Elsa F. Kramer, Editor; Thomas P. Healy, Publisher. **Subscription Rates:** $18 individuals. **Remarks:** Accepts advertising.
Circ: Combined 25,000

10257 Child Life
Children's Better Health Institute
1100 Waterway Blvd. Phone: (317)636-8881
PO Box 567 Fax: (317)684-8094
Indianapolis, IN 46202-2156
Free: (800)558-2376
Publisher E-mail: cbhiseif@tcon.net

Consumer magazine covering health, sports, and fitness for children ages 9-11. **Founded:** 1921. **Freq:** 8/year. **Print Method:** 7 5/8 x 10 1/8. **Key Personnel:** Lise Hoffman, Editor; Ron Keown, Advertising, phone (312)787-7900. **ISSN:** 0009-3971. **Subscription Rates:** $16.95 individuals Annual.
Ad Rates: BW: $1,368 **Circ:** Paid 47,330
4C: $1,800

10258 Children's Digest
Children's Better Health Institute
PO Box 567
Indianapolis, IN 46206
Publisher E-mail: cbhiseif@tcon.net

Magazine on children's health, exercise, nutrition, and safety for ages 9-12. **Founded:** 1950. **Freq:** 8/year. **Print Method:** Offset. **Trim Size:** 7 5/8 x 10 1/8. **Cols./Page:** 2. **Col. Width:** 31 nonpareils. **Col. Depth:** 112 agate lines. **Key Personnel:** Danny Lee, Editor. **ISSN:** 0272-7145. **Subscription Rates:** $17.95 individuals. **Remarks:** Accepts advertising.
Ad Rates: BW: $1,938 **Circ:** Paid 91,165
4C: $2,550

10259 Children's Playmate Magazine
Children's Better Health Institute
1100 Waterway Blvd. Phone: (317)636-8881
PO Box 567 Fax: (317)684-8094
Indianapolis, IN 46202-2156
Free: (800)558-2376
Publisher E-mail: cbhiseif@tcon.net

Magazine on children's health, exercise, nutrition, and safety for ages 6-8. **Founded:** 1929. **Freq:** 8/year. **Print Method:** Offset. **Trim Size:** 7 5/8 x 10 1/8. **Cols./Page:** 1. **Col. Width:** 54 nonpareils. **Col. Depth:** 100 agate lines. **Key Personnel:** Terry Harshman, Editor. **ISSN:** 0009-4161. **Subscription Rates:** $17.95 individuals. **Remarks:** Accepts advertising.
Ad Rates: BW: $1,672 **Circ:** Paid 85,155
4C: $2,200

10260 The Columbian
The Columbia Club
121 Monument Circle Phone: (317)767-1361
Indianapolis, IN 46204 Fax: (317)638-3137
Free: (800)635-1361
Publisher E-mail: htp.columbiaclub.club.org

Magazine covering club affairs. **Founded:** Jan. 1906. **Freq:** Monthly. **Print Method:** Offset. **Trim Size:** 8 1/2 x 11. **Cols./Page:** 3. **Col. Width:** 13 picas. **Col. Depth:** 116 agate lines. **Key Personnel:** Beverly Chalfant-Szili, Editor, phone (317)761-7525, fax (317)261-1375. **USPS:** 562-640. **Subscription Rates:** $36 individuals. **Remarks:** Accepts advertising.
Ad Rates: BW: $400 **Circ:** ‡4,000
4C: $625

10261 Construction Digest
5804 W. 74th St. Phone: (317)293-6860
Indianapolis, IN 46278 Fax: (317)293-7840
Free: (888)893-6860

Magazine for the public works and construction engineering industries. **Founded:** 1926. **Freq:** Semimonthly. **Print Method:** Offset. **Trim Size:** 8 1/8 x 10 7/8. **Cols./Page:** 3. **Col. Width:** 28 nonpareils. **Col. Depth:** 140 agate lines. **Key Personnel:** Tom Hale, Editor, tom.hale@cmdg.com. **USPS:** 130-100. **Subscription Rates:** $3 single issue. **Remarks:** Accepts advertising.
Ad Rates: BW: $1,579 **Circ:** Paid 496
4C: $2,104 Non-paid 12,576

10262 Court & Commercial Record
41 E. Washington St. Phone: (317)636-0200
Indianapolis, IN 46204 Fax: (317)263-5259

Newspaper of legal record. **Founded:** 1895. **Freq:** 3/week. **Trim Size:** 10 x 16. **Cols./Page:** 4. **Col. Width:** 2 inches. **Key Personnel:** Glenda J. Russell, Publisher, grussell@ibj.com; Scott Olson, Editor, solson@ibj.com. **Subscription Rates:** $89 individuals. **Remarks:** Accepts advertising. **Former name:** The Indianapolis Commercial.
Circ: Controlled ⊕**759**

10263 The Criterion
1400 N. Meridian St. Phone: (317)236-1570
PO Box 1717 Fax: (317)236-1434
Indianapolis, IN 46206-1717
Free: (800)382-9836
Publication E-mail: archindy@iglou.com

Official weekly church newspaper of the Roman Catholic Archdiocese of Indianapolis. **Founded:** 1960. **Freq:** Weekly. **Print Method:** Offset. **Trim Size:** 17 1/2 x 11 1/4. **Cols./Page:** 6. **Col. Width:** 1 5/8 inches. **Col. Depth:** 224 agate lines. **Key Personnel:** John F. Fink, Editor; Dan Conway, Assoc. Publisher; Donald Bramlage, Advertising Dir.; W. Ronald Hunt, Circulation Mgr.; Most. Rev. Daniel M. Buechlein, O.S.B., Publisher. **Subscription Rates:** $20. **Remarks:** Accepts advertising. **URL:** http://w1.iglou.com.criterion.
Ad Rates: GLR: $1.07 **Circ:** Combined 72,000
BW: $1,353
4C: $1,653
PCI: $26

10264 Cumberland Courier
Cumberland Courier/The Lawrence Township Journal
7962 Pendleton Pike Phone: (317)542-8149
Indianapolis, IN 46226 Fax: (317)542-1137

Community newspaper. **Founded:** 1983. **Freq:** Weekly Tues. **Print Method:** Offset. **Cols./Page:** 6. **Col. Width:** 20 nonpareils. **Col. Depth:** 224 agate lines. **Key Personnel:** J.E. Zainey, Publisher; Shelly Zainey. **Subscription Rates:** Free. **Remarks:** Accepts advertising. **Formerly:** Indianapolis Ad-Courier.
Ad Rates: PCI: $5 **Circ:** Non-paid 15,200

10265 The Disciple
Christian Board of Publication
130 E. Washington St. Phone: (317)635-3100
Indianapolis, IN 46204 Fax: (317)635-3700
Publication E-mail: TheDisciple@disciples.org

Religious magazine. **Subtitle:** Journal of the Christian Church (Disciples of Christ). **Founded:** 1863. **Freq:** Monthly (except February and August). **Print Method:** Web Offset. **Trim Size:** 7 3/4" x 10 1/2". **Cols./Page:** 3. **Col. Width:** 25 nonpareils. **Col. Depth:** 136 agate lines. **Key Personnel:** Patricia R. Case, Editor, pcase@cbp21.com; Angela K. Herrmann, Assoc. Editor, aherrmann@cbp21.com. **ISSN:** 0092-8372. **Subscription Rates:** $20. **Remarks:** Accepts advertising. **URL:** http://www.thedisciple.com.
Ad Rates: BW: $1,160 **Circ:** ‡25,500
4C: $1,800
PCI: $60

10266 The East Side Herald
East Side Suburban Newspapers
4309 E. Michigan St., No 11042 Phone: (317)356-2487
Indianapolis, IN 46201-3652
Community newspaper. **Founded:** 1938. **Freq:** Weekly (Thurs.). **Print Method:** Offset. **Cols./Page:** 8. **Col. Width:** 1 5/8 inches. **Col. Depth:** 21 inches. **Key Personnel:** William K. Thoele, Publisher; Carl Thoele, Advertising Mgr. **Subscription Rates:** Free; $20 by mail. **Remarks:** Accepts advertising.
Ad Rates: BW: $750 **Circ:** Paid ‡50
4C: $800 Free ‡14,000
PCI: $7

10267 Electric Consumer
Indiana Statewide Rural Electric Cooperative
PO Box 24517 Phone: (317)487-2220
Indianapolis, IN 46224 Fax: (317)247-5220
Free: (800)340-7362
Publication E-mail: ec@indremcs.org

Rural electric cooperative magazine. **Founded:** July 1951. **Freq:** Monthly. **Print Method:** Offset. **Trim Size:** 10 x 12 1/4. **Cols./Page:** 4. **Col. Width:** 7 1/2 picas. **Col. Depth:** 154 agate lines. **Key Personnel:** Emily Born Schilling, Editor, phone (317)487-2241, eschilli@indremcs.org; Richard G. Biever, Senior Editor, phone (317)487-2242, rbiever@indremcs.org. **ISSN:** 0745-4651. **Subscription Rates:** $10 individuals. **Remarks:** Advertising not accepted.
Circ: Paid 240,000
Non-paid 172

10268 The Employment Source Indianapolis
Key Art Publishing
8383 Craig St., Ste. 290 Phone: (317)570-1099
Indianapolis, IN 46250 Fax: (317)845-7569

Magazine featuring employment opportunities and information for Indianapolis residents. **Founded:** June 1996. **Freq:** Weekly. **Print Method:** Web offset. **Trim Size:** 8 1/2 x 10 3/4. **Cols./Page:** 5. **Col. Width:** 1 1/4 inches. **Col. Depth:** 9 1/2 inches. **Key Personnel:** Daniel S. Johnson, President; Kimberly Jones, Production Mgr. **Remarks:** Accepts advertising.
Ad Rates: BW: $450 **Circ:** (Not Reported)
4C: $660
PCI: $45

10269 Encounter
Christian Theological Seminary
1000 W. 42nd St. Phone: (317)924-1331
Indianapolis, IN 46208 Fax: (317)923-1961

Religious journal. **Subtitle:** Creative Theological Scholarship. **Founded:** Jan. 1940. **Freq:** Quarterly. **Print Method:** Offset. **Trim Size:** 6 3/4 x 10. **Cols./Page:** 1. **Col. Width:** 54 nonpareils. **Col. Depth:** 112 agate lines. **Key Personnel:** Ronald J. Allen, Editor, phone (317)931-2339. **ISSN:** 0013-7081. **Subscription Rates:** $18 individuals; $4.50 single issue. **Remarks:** Color advertising not accepted.
Ad Rates: BW: $60 **Circ:** Paid ‡568
Non-paid ‡58

10270 Endless Vacation
Resort Condominiums International, Inc.
3502 Woodview Trace Phone: (317)876-1692
Indianapolis, IN 46268 Fax: (317)871-9507
Publication E-mail: evletters@rci.com

Travel magazine. **Founded:** 1975. **Freq:** Bimonthly. **Print Method:** Offset. **Trim Size:** 8 1/8 x 10 7/8. **Cols./Page:** 3. **Col. Width:** 2 1/4 inches. **Col. Depth:** 10 1/4 inches. **Key Personnel:** Laurie Borman, Editor-in-Chief; Tom Heine, Art Dir.; Glenn Tourville, Advertising Mgr.; Bob Shenberger, Man., Prod. & Circ. **ISSN:** 0279-4853. **Subscription Rates:** $84 individuals. **Remarks:** Accepts advertising.
Ad Rates: BW: $22,000 **Circ:** Paid ★**1,151,193**
4C: $27,500
PCI: $350

10271 FFA Advisors Making a Difference
The National FFA Organization
6060 FFA Dr. Phone: (317)802-6060
PO Box 68960 Fax: (317)802-6061
Indianapolis, IN 46268-0960
Professional journal for agricultural educators. **Founded:** 1992. **Freq:** Monthly. **Trim Size:** 8 1/4 x 10 3/4. **Cols./Page:** 10. **Key Personnel:** Becky Meyer, Editor, bmeyer@ffa.org. **Subscription Rates:** $5 individuals; Free to qualified subscribers. **Remarks:** Advertising not accepted. **URL:** http://www.ffa.org. **Former name:** Between Issues.
Circ: Combined 11,100

10272 Fueling Indiana
Indiana Petroleum Marketers and Convenience Store Association (IPCA)
101 W. Washington St., Ste. 1338 E Phone: (317)633-4662
Indianapolis, IN 46204-3413 Fax: (317)630-1827
Free: (800)732-1423

Petroleum industry magazine. **Founded:** 1935. **Freq:** Quarterly. **Print Method:** Offset. **Trim Size:** 8 .25 x 10.75. **Cols./Page:** 3. **Col. Width:** 33 nonpareils. **Col. Depth:** 154 agate lines. **Subscription Rates:** Free to qualified subscribers. **Remarks:** Accepts advertising. **Formerly:** The Hoosier Independent.
Ad Rates: BW: $430 **Circ:** Controlled 1,000
4C: $930

10273 Heartland
Susquehanna Radio Corp.
8120 Knue Rd. Phone: (317)842-9550
Indianapolis, IN 46250 Fax: (317)577-3361

Country music magazine. **Freq:** Bimonthly. **Print Method:** Web press. **Trim Size:** 11 3/8 x 16 3/4. **Key Personnel:** Kay Reeney Caito, Editor. **Remarks:** Accepts advertising.
Ad Rates: 4C: $5,000 **Circ:** (Not Reported)

10274 Home & Away (Hoosier Edition)
Midwest Magazine Network
PO Box 88505 Phone: (317)923-1500
Indianapolis, IN 46208 Fax: (317)924-4669

Magazine for AAA Hoosier Motor Club members in Central Indiana. **Founded:** 1911. **Freq:** Bimonthly. **Print Method:** Offset. **Trim Size:** 8 x 10 7/8. **Cols./Page:** 3. **Col. Width:** 28 nonpareils. **Col. Depth:** 133 agate lines. **Key Personnel:** Stephanie Hinds, Regional Editor, phone (317)923-1500; Terry Farias, Publisher, phone (317)923-1500; Brian Nicol, Editor and Publisher, phone (412)390-1000; Vern Cornish, Advertising Mgr., phone (412)390-1000. **USPS:** 250-000. **Subscription Rates:** $6 nonmembers. **Remarks:** Accepts advertising.
Ad Rates: BW: $750 **Circ:** ‡198,000
4C: $865

10275 Hoosier Banker
Indiana Bankers Association
3135 N. Meridian St. Phone: (317)921-3135
Indianapolis, IN 46208-4717 Fax: (317)921-3131
Publication E-mail: iba@iquest.net

Magazine for bankers providing in-depth analysis of Indiana banking developments. **Subtitle:** The magazine of the Indiana Bankers Association. **Founded:** Jan. 1916. **Freq:** Monthly. **Print Method:** Offset. **Trim Size:** 8 1/2 x 11. **Cols./Page:** 3. **Col. Width:** 14 picas. **Col. Depth:** 57 picas. **Key Personnel:** Laura Wilson, Editor; William H. King, Publisher; Peggy D. Trieloff, Advertising Consultant. **ISSN:** 0018-473X. **Subscription Rates:** $27 individuals; $2.50 single issue. **Remarks:** Accepts advertising.
Ad Rates: BW: $552 **Circ:** ‡2,500
4C: $1,052

10276 The Hoosier Farmer
Indiana Farm Bureau, Inc.
225 South East St. Phone: (317)692-7822
PO Box 1290 Fax: (317)692-7854
Indianapolis, IN 46206
Publisher E-mail: infbinfo@farmbureau.com

Agricultural magazine. **Founded:** 1919. **Freq:** Bimonthly. **Print Method:** Offset. **Trim Size:** 8 1/4 x 10 7/8. **Cols./Page:** 3. **Key Personnel:** Tom Asher, Editor; Paul Miner, Managing Editor, phone (317)692-7822. **ISSN:** 0018-4748. **Subscription Rates:** $10 individuals. **Remarks:** Accepts advertising.
Ad Rates: BW: $3,150 **Circ:** 250,000
4C: $3,900

10277 The Hoosier Legionnaire
The American Legion, Indiana Dept.
777 N. Meridian St. Phone: (317)630-1391
Indianapolis, IN 46204 Fax: (317)237-9891
Free: (888)723-7999

Newspaper (tabloid) for members of the American Legion in Indiana. **Founded:** 1923. **Freq:** Quarterly. **Print Method:** Web press. **Trim Size:** 11 1/2 x 16 1/2. **Cols./Page:** 4. **Col. Width:** 15 picas. **Key Personnel:** K. Michael Ayers, Publisher, phone (317)630-1263; Maria Gottlieb, Managing Editor, maria4pu@aol.com. **ISSN:** 0018-4772. **Subscription Rates:** Free to members. **Remarks:** Advertising accepted; rates available upon request.
Circ: Free ‡133,000

10278 Hoosier Outdoors
Recreation Vehicle Indiana Council (RVIC)
3210 Rand Rd. Phone: (317)247-6258
Indianapolis, IN 46241 Fax: (317)243-9174
Free: (800)837-7842
Publisher E-mail: imharvic@ix.netcom.com

Recreation vehicle lifestyle magazine and Indiana campground directory. **Founded:** 1968. **Freq:** Annual. **Print Method:** Offset. **Trim Size:** 8 1/2 x 11. **Cols./Page:** 3. **Col. Width:** 27 nonpareils. **Col. Depth:** 140 agate lines. **ISSN:** 0018-4780. **Subscription Rates:** complimentary. **Remarks:** Accepts advertising. **Formerly:** Hoosier Camper.
Ad Rates: BW: $1,175 **Circ:** Non-paid ‡120,000

10279 Humpty Dumpty's Magazine
Children's Better Health Institute
PO Box 567 Phone: (317)636-8881
Indianapolis, IN 46206 Fax: (317)684-8094
Publisher E-mail: cbhiseif@tcon.net

Health, exercise, nutrition, and safety magazine for children

ages four to six. **Founded:** 1952. **Freq:** 8/year. **Print Method:** Web Offset. **Trim Size:** 7 5/8 x 10 1/8. **Cols./Page:** 1. **Key Personnel:** Nancy S. Axelrad, Editor. **ISSN:** 0273-7590. **Subscription Rates:** $17.95 individuals. **Remarks:** Accepts advertising. **Alt. Formats:** Braille.
Ad Rates: BW: $3,496 **Circ:** Paid 193,923
4C: $4,600

10280 Indac Magazine
Indianapolis Athletic Club
350 N. Meridian St. Phone: (317)634-4331
Indianapolis, IN 46204-1709 Fax: (317)686-4155

Magazine containing athletic club news. **Founded:** 1921. **Freq:** 6/year. **Print Method:** Offset. **Trim Size:** 8 1/2 x 11. **Cols./Page:** 2 and 3. **Col. Width:** 26 and 40 nonpareils. **Col. Depth:** 140 agate lines. **Key Personnel:** Aimee Helton, Editor. **ISSN:** 0019-3569. **Subscription Rates:** $20 individuals. **Remarks:** Advertising accepted; rates available upon request.
Circ: ‡3,200

10281 Indiana Agri-News
Agri-News Publications
2575 E. 55th Pl., Ste. A Phone: (317)726-5391
Indianapolis, IN 46220 Fax: (317)726-5390
Free: (800)772-9354
Publisher E-mail: agrinews@theramp.net

Farm and rural community magazine. **Founded:** 1982. **Freq:** Weekly. **Print Method:** Offset. **Trim Size:** 14 5/8 x 22 3/4. **Cols./Page:** 9. **Col. Width:** 16 nonpareils. **Col. Depth:** 301 agate lines. **Key Personnel:** Warren T. Pufahl, Managing Editor; James Henry, Editor; Mr. Lynn Baker, Publisher. **Subscription Rates:** $15 individuals; $.50 single issue. **Remarks:** Accepts advertising. **URL:** http://www.agrinews-pubs.com. **Alt. Formats:** Microform.
Ad Rates: GLR: $9 **Circ:** Paid ‡8,000
BW: $3,279.83 Controlled ‡21,000
4C: $3,829.83
PCI: $16.95

10282 Indiana Audubon Quarterly
Indiana Audubon Society, Inc.
2505 E. Maynard Dr. Phone: (317)786-5822
Indianapolis, IN 46227
Publication E-mail: cesak68@yuno.com

Scientific journal covering birds. **Founded:** 1950. **Freq:** Quarterly. **Print Method:** Offset. **Trim Size:** 5 x 8. **Cols./Page:** 1. **Col. Width:** 4 inches. **Col. Depth:** 7 inches. **Key Personnel:** Charles E. Keller, Editor, phone (317)786-5872. **ISSN:** 0019-6525. **Subscription Rates:** Included in membership; $4.25 single issue. **Remarks:** Advertising not accepted.
Circ: Combined 556

10283 Indiana Beef
Indiana Beef Cattle Association
8770 Guion Rd. Ste. A Phone: (317)872-2333
Indianapolis, IN 46268 Fax: (317)872-2364

Magazine for Indiana beef cattle industry and related industries. **Founded:** 1981. **Freq:** Bimonthly. **Print Method:** Offset. **Trim Size:** 8 1/2 x 11. **Cols./Page:** 3. **Col. Width:** 2 1/4 inches. **Col. Depth:** 9 15/16 inches. **Key Personnel:** Debbie Shoufler, Editor. **Subscription Rates:** Free to qualified subscribers. **Remarks:** Accepts advertising.
Ad Rates: BW: $495 **Circ:** ‡8,300

10284 Indiana Business Magazine
1000 Waterway Blvd. Phone: (317)692-1200
Indianapolis, IN 46202 Fax: (317)692-4250
Publication E-mail: curtismag@iquest.net
Publisher E-mail: info@curtismagazines.com

Business magazine. **Founded:** 1957. **Freq:** Monthly. **Print Method:** Uses mats. Offset. **Trim Size:** 10 7/8. **Cols./Page:** 3. **Col. Width:** 26 nonpareils. **Col. Depth:** 125 agate lines. **Key Personnel:** Eric Servaas, Publisher; Amy Krieg, Advertising Mgr.; Steve Kaelble, Editor. **ISSN:** 0273-7930. **Subscription Rates:** $19.95 individuals; $2.50 single issue.
Ad Rates: BW: $2,350 **Circ:** Controlled 3,175
4C: $2,850 Non-paid 26,622
2,619

10285 Indiana Contractor
Indiana Association of Plumbing Heating Cooling Contractors, Inc.
PO Box 40963 Phone: (317)575-9292
Indianapolis, IN 46240 Fax: (317)575-9378

Official publication of the Indiana Association of Plumbing, Heating, Cooling Contractors, Inc. **Subtitle:** Air Conditioning, Heating, Plumbing, Refrigeration, Sheet Metal. **Founded:** 1957. **Freq:** Bimonthly. **Print Method:** Offset. **Trim Size:** 8 1/2 x 11. **Cols./Page:** 3. **Col. Width:** 2 1/4 inches. **Col. Depth:** 7 inches. **Key Personnel:** Melissa Gibson, Editor; Philip G. Amodeo, Publisher. **Remarks:** Accepts advertising.
Ad Rates: BW: $680 **Circ:** Controlled ‡5,579
4C: $1,375

10286 Indiana Herald
2170 N. Illinois St. Phone: (317)923-8291
Indianapolis, IN 46202 Fax: (317)923-8292

Community newspaper. **Founded:** 1959. **Freq:** Weekly (Thurs.). **Key Personnel:** Mary Tandy, Editor and Publisher. **Subscription Rates:** $11 individuals. **Remarks:** Accepts advertising.
Ad Rates: PCI: $11.85 **Circ:** (Not Reported)

10287 Indiana Law Review
Indianapolis School of Law
Indiana University Phone: (317)274-4440
735 W. New York St. Fax: (317)274-8825
Indianapolis, IN 46202
Student-run law review. **Freq:** Quarterly. **Key Personnel:** Chris Paynter, Editorial Asst., cpaynter@iupui.edu. **Subscription Rates:** $25 individuals; $28 out of country; $5 single issue. **Remarks:** Accepts advertising.
Ad Rates: BW: $90 **Circ:** Combined 900

10288 Indiana Pharmacist
Indiana Pharmacists Association
729 North Penn Phone: (317)634-4968
Indianapolis, IN 46204 Fax: (317)632-1219
Publication E-mail: ipapeg@aol.com

Magazine for pharmacists. **Founded:** 1886. **Freq:** Quarterly. **Print Method:** Offset. **Trim Size:** 8 1/2 x 11. **Cols./Page:** 3. **Col. Width:** 27 nonpareils. **Col. Depth:** 140 agate lines. **Key Personnel:** Lawrence J. Sage, Editor, phone (317)634-4968. **Subscription Rates:** $15 individuals. **Remarks:** Accepts advertising.
Ad Rates: BW: $375 **Circ:** ‡1,500
4C: $875

10289 Indiana Prairie Farmer
Farm Progress Companies
2346 S. Lynhurst Dr. Phone: (317)248-0681
Ste. 304 Fax: (317)248-0828
Box 421309
Indianapolis, IN 46242-1309
Farm production and management magazine for Indiana farmers. **Founded:** 1841. **Freq:** Semimonthly Jan. - Mar., Monthly Apr. - Dec. **Print Method:** Offset. **Trim Size:** 8 x 10. **Cols./Page:** 3. **Col. Width:** 33 nonpareils. **Col. Depth:** 175 agate lines. **Key Personnel:** Allan R. Johnson, President, phone (708)462-2860; Sara Wyant, Vice President, phone (708)462-2892, swyant@farmprogress.com; Paul Queck, Editor, phone (317)248-0681, pqueck@farmprogress.com; Tom J. Bechman, Associate Editor, phone (317)248-0681, tbechman@farmprogress.com; Charles P. Roth, Vice President, phone (708)462-2874; Steve Joss, Vice President, phone (708)462-2890. **ISSN:** 0162-7104. **Subscription Rates:** $21.95 individuals; $30 out of area; $2 single issue. **Remarks:** Accepts advertising.
Ad Rates: BW: $4,250 **Circ:** ‡35,000
4C: $5,950

10290 Indianapolis Business Journal
IBJ Corp.
431 N. Pennsylvania St. Phone: (317)634-6200
Indianapolis, IN 46204 Fax: (317)263-5060
Publisher E-mail: info-ibj@ibj.com

Business journal. **Founded:** May 19, 1980. **Freq:** Weekly (Mon.). **Print Method:** Offset. **Trim Size:** 11 1/2 x 15. **Cols./Page:** 4. **Col. Width:** 2 5/16 inches. **Col. Depth:** 13 13/16 inches. **Key Personnel:** Tom Harton, Editor, ibjedit@aol.com; Christopher Katterjohn, Publisher; Greg Morris, Advertising Mgr. **ISSN:** 0274-4929. **Subscription Rates:** $64 individuals. **Remarks:** Accepts advertising. **Available Online. URL:** http://www.ibj.com.
Ad Rates: BW: $3,450 **Circ:** Paid ★15,547
4C: $3,950
PCI: $91

10291 Indianapolis Monthly
Emmis Publishing Corp.
40 Monument Circle, No. 100 Phone: (317)237-9288
Indianapolis, IN 46204-3908 Fax: (317)684-8356
Free: (800)876-5133
Publication E-mail: im-input@iquest.net

Consumer magazine covering Indianapolis lifestyle for a general audience. **Founded:** Jan. 1977. **Print Method:** Web offset. **Trim Size:** 8 x 10 7/8. **Cols./Page:** 3. **Col. Width:** 2 1/4 inches. **Col. Depth:** 9 7/8 inches. **Key Personnel:** Jack Marsella, Publisher, jack@indymonthly.emmis.com; Deborah Paul, Publisher/Editor-in-Chief, debbie@indymonthly.emmis.com; Sam Stall, Editor, sam@indymonthly.emmis.com; Keith Phillips, Advertising Dir., keith@indymonthly.emmis.com; Jody McMahel, Circulation Mgr. **Subscription Rates:** $19.95 individuals; $3.50 single issue. **Remarks:** Accepts advertising.
Ad Rates: BW: $4,330 **Circ:** Paid ★45,532
4C: $6,060
PCI: $100

10292 The Indianapolis News
Indianapolis Newspapers, Inc.
307 N. Pennsylvania St. Phone: (317)633-1240
Indianapolis, IN 46204-1811 Fax: (317)633-1038
Free: (800)669-7827

General newspaper. **Founded:** 1869. **Freq:** Mon.-Sat. (eve.). **Print Method:** Offset. **Cols./Page:** 6. **Col. Width:** 26 nonpareils. **Col. Depth:** 318 agate lines. **Key Personnel:** Frank Caperton, Exec. Editor, phone (317)633-9169; Nancy Comiskey, Managing Editor, Features/Photo/Graphics, phone (317)633-9104; Ted Daniels, Managing Editor, News, phone (317)633-9266; Chip Maury, Art Dir., phone (317)633-9279; Tom Peyton, Art Dir., phone (317)633-9853; Alex Waddell, A.M. News Editor, phone (317)633-9277; Tom Swenson, P.M. News Editor, phone (317)656-1397; Mark Rochester, Projects Editor, phone (317)633-9288. **Subscription Rates:** $52 individuals. **Remarks:** Advertising accepted; rates available upon request. **Feature Editors:** Liz Brown, *Suburban*, phone (317)633-9417; Patti Denton, *Food*, phone (317)633-9132; Zach Dunkin, *Art, Entertainment*, phone (317)633-9079; Steve Hall, *TV & Radio*, phone (317)633-9270; Ruth Holladay, *Lifestyle*, phone (317)633-9405; David Mannweiler, *Book, Travel*, phone (317)633-9084; John Schwantes, *City*, phone (317)633-9087.
Circ: Mon.-Sat. ★35,602

10293 The Indianapolis Recorder
The George P. Stewart Printing, Inc.
2901 N. Tacoma Ave. Phone: (317)924-5143
PO Box 18499 Fax: (317)924-5148
Indianapolis, IN 46218-2700
Black community newspaper. **Founded:** 1895. **Freq:** Weekly (Thurs.). **Print Method:** Offset. **Cols./Page:** 6. **Col. Width:** 13 picas. **Col. Depth:** 298 agate lines. **Key Personnel:** Bill Mays, Publisher; Charles Blain, President; Connie Caines Hayes, Managing Editor; Mike Handen, Advertising. **USPS:** 262-660. **Subscription Rates:** $23 individuals; $20 out of area. **Remarks:** Accepts advertising.
Ad Rates: PCI: $14.01 **Circ:** ‡10,281

10294 The Indianapolis Star
Indianapolis Newspapers, Inc.
307 N. Pennsylvania St. Phone: (317)633-1240
Indianapolis, IN 46204-1811 Fax: (317)633-1038
Free: (800)669-7827

General newspaper. **Founded:** 1903. **Freq:** Mon.-Sun. (morn.). **Print Method:** Letterpress. **Cols./Page:** 6. **Col. Width:** 2 1/16 inches. **Col. Depth:** 22 inches. **Key Personnel:** Frank Caperton, Exec. Editor, phone (317)633-9169; Nancy Comiskey, Managing Editor, Features/Photo/Graphics, phone (317)633-9104; Ted Daniels, Managing Editor, News, phone (317)633-9266; Chip Maury, Dir. of Photography, phone (317)633-9279; Tom Peyton, Art Dir., phone (317)633-9853; Mark Rochester, Projects Editor, phone (317)633-9288; Alex Wadell, A.M. News Editor, phone (317)633-9277; Tom Swenson, P.M. News Editor, phone (317)656-1397; John H. Lyst, Editor, phone (317)633-9172; Eugene S. Pulliam, Publisher, phone (317)633-1298. **Subscription Rates:** $62.40 daily; $44.20 sunday. **Remarks:** Accepts advertising. **Feature Editors:** Liz Brown, *Suburban*, phone (317)633-9417; Patti Denton, *Food*, phone (317)633-9132; Zach Dunkin, *Art, Entertainment*, phone (317)633-9079; Steve Hall, *TV & Radio*, phone (317)633-9270; Ruth Holladay, *Lifestyle*, phone (317)633-9405; David Mannweiler, *Book, Travel*, phone (317)638-9084; Jon Schwantes, *City*, phone (317)633-9087.
Ad Rates: SAU: $86.55 **Circ:** Mon.-Sat. ★230,223
Sun. ★391,496

10295 Indy's Child
Indy's Child, Inc.
836 E. 64th St. Phone: (317)722-8500
Indianapolis, IN 46220 Fax: (317)722-8510
Publication E-mail: inchild@netdirect.net

Magazine covering parenting news. **Founded:** 1984. **Freq:** Monthly. **Print Method:** Web press. **Trim Size:** 11 x 13 1/2. **Cols./Page:** 4. **Col. Width:** 2 3/8 inches. **Col. Depth:** 12 1/2 inches. **Key Personnel:** Gregory P. Wynne, Editor and Publisher; Anne-Marie Damler, Sales Mgr. **Subscription Rates:** $18. **Remarks:** Accepts advertising. **URL:** http://www.family.com.
Ad Rates: BW: $2,040 **Circ:** Free 60,000
4C: $2,440 Paid 100
PCI: $39.25

10296 ISBA Journal
Indiana School Boards Association
One N. Capitol, Ste. 1215 Phone: (317)639-0330
Indianapolis, IN 46204 Fax: (317)639-3591
Publication E-mail: dvalentine@iqvest.net

Trade magazine covering education for school board members and superintendents. **Founded:** Dec. 1954. **Freq:** Quarterly. **Trim Size:** 8 1/2 x 11. **Key Personnel:** Darci L. Valentine, Editor, dvalentine@iquest.net. **Subscription Rates:** $25 individuals; Free to qualified subscribers. **Remarks:** Accepts advertising.
Ad Rates: BW: $340 **Circ:** Paid ‡3,000
4C: $825

10297 ISTA Advocate
Indiana State Teachers Association
150 W. Market St., Ste. 900 Phone: (317)634-1515
Indianapolis, IN 46204-2875 Fax: (317)631-8715

Trade magazine (tabloid) covering education issues and employees. **Freq:** 5/year. **Print Method:** Offset. **Trim Size:** 11 x 15. **Cols./Page:** 3. **Col. Width:** 18 picas. **Col. Depth:** 14 inches. **Key Personnel:** Kathleen A. Berry, Asst. Editor/ Administration. **Subscription Rates:** members only. **Remarks:** Accepts advertising.
Ad Rates: BW: $1,346 **Circ:** Controlled ‡50,000
PCI: $48

10298 Jack And Jill
Children's Better Health Institute
1100 Waterway Blvd. Phone: (317)636-8881
PO Box 567 Fax: (317)684-8094
Indianapolis, IN 46202-2156
Free: (800)558-2376
Publisher E-mail: cbhiseif@tcon.net

General magazine for children ages 7-10. **Founded:** 1938. **Freq:** 8/year. **Print Method:** Offset. **Trim Size:** 7 5/8 x 10 1/8. **Key Personnel:** Daniel Lee, Editor. **ISSN:** 0021-3829. **Subscription Rates:** $17.95 individuals. **Remarks:** Accepts advertising. **Alt. Formats:** Braille.
Ad Rates: BW: $4,788 **Circ:** Paid 199,572
4C: $6,300

10299 JOM
Midwest Alliance in Nursing
6910 N. Shadeland Ave., Ste. 206 Phone: (317)541-3600
Fax: (317)541-3609
Indianapolis, IN 46220-4274
Publication E-mail: jom@tms.org
Publisher E-mail: main-org@inetdirect.net

Journal containing technical articles about metallurgy and materials science. **Founded:** 1949. **Freq:** Monthly. **Print Method:** Offset. **Trim Size:** 8 1/8 x 10 7/8. **Cols./Page:** 3. **Col. Width:** 2 1/8 inches. **Col. Depth:** 10 inches. **Key Personnel:** James J. Robinson, Editor; Alexander Scott, Publisher. **ISSN:** 0148-6608. **Subscription Rates:** $65 individuals; $127 Industry. **Remarks:** Accepts advertising. **URL:** http://www.tms.org/pubs/jounals/jom/jom.html. **Formerly:** Journal of Metals.
Ad Rates: GLR: $11.07 **Circ:** Paid ‡7979
BW: $1,365 Non-paid ‡4321
4C: $1,865
PCI: $80

10300 The Journal of Cognitive Rehabilitation
NeuroScience Publishers
6555 Carrollton Ave. Phone: (317)257-9672
Indianapolis, IN 46220 Fax: (317)257-9674
Publisher E-mail: nsp@neuroscience.cnter.com

Magazine for therapists, patients, and families; providing information relevant to the rehabilitation of brain-injured individuals. **Founded:** 1983. **Freq:** Bimonthly. **Print Method:** Offset. **Trim Size:** 8 1/2 x 11. **Cols./Page:** 2. **Col. Width:** 42 nonpareils. **Col. Depth:** 140 agate lines. **Key Personnel:** Odie L. Bracy, Editor, obracy@inetdirect.net; Nancy Bracy, Advertising Mgr. **ISSN:** 1062-2969. **Subscription Rates:** $40 individuals U.S.A.; $80 institutions other; $85 Canada; $95 other countries. **Remarks:** Accepts advertising.
Ad Rates: BW: $1,000 **Circ:** 1,500
4C: $4,000
PCI: $15

10301 Journal of Electronic Materials
Midwest Alliance in Nursing
6910 N. Shadeland Ave., Ste. 206 Phone: (317)541-3600
Fax: (317)541-3609
Indianapolis, IN 46220-4274
Publication E-mail: csc@tms.org
Publisher E-mail: main-org@inetdirect.net

Electronics journal. **Founded:** 1972. **Freq:** Monthly. **Print Method:** Web offset. **Key Personnel:** T.C. Harman, Editor. **ISSN:** 0361-5235. **Subscription Rates:** $114 individuals; $269 institutions. **Remarks:** Advertising not accepted. **URL:** http://www.tms.org/pubs/journals/jem/jem.html.
Circ: 1,400

10302 Journal of Pediatric Surgery
W.B. Saunders Co.
J.W. Riley Hospital for Children Phone: (317)274-5716
702 Barnhill Dr., Suite 2500 Fax: (317)274-5777
Indianapolis, IN 46202-5200
Medical journal. **Subtitle:** Official Journal of the Surgical Section of the American Academy of Pediatrics, and the British Association of Pediatric Surgeons. **Founded:** 1966. **Freq:** Monthly. **Print Method:** Offset. **Trim Size:** 8 1/4 x 11. **Cols./Page:** 1. **Col. Width:** 66 nonpareils. **Col. Depth:** 119 agate lines. **Key Personnel:** Jay L. Grosfeld, MD, Editor; Joan W. Blumberg, Publisher; Charles Cunningham, Advertising Mgr. **ISSN:** 0022-3468. **Subscription Rates:** $174 individuals; $239 institutions; $268 other countries; $135 students; $26 single issue. **Remarks:** Accepts advertising.
Ad Rates: BW: $800 **Circ:** ‡4,797
4C: $1,650

10303 Kappa Delta Pi Record
Kappa Delta Pi
3707 Woodview Trace Phone: (317)871-4900
Indianapolis, IN 46268-1158 Fax: (317)704-2323
Free: (800)284-3167
Publisher E-mail: pubs@kdp.org

Trade magazine covering education for teachers. **Founded:** 1964. **Freq:** Quarterly. **Print Method:** Web offset. **Cols./Page:** 2. **Key Personnel:** Nicholas Drake, Dir. of Publications Oper./Managing Ed., nick@kdp.org; Grant E. Mabie, Dir. of Publications Development. **ISSN:** 0022-8958. **Subscription Rates:** $18 individuals; $4 single issue. **Remarks:** Accepts advertising.
Ad Rates: BW: $1,300 **Circ:** Paid 60,000
4C: $2,900

10304 Keynoter
3636 Woodview Trace Phone: (317)875-8755
Indianapolis, IN 46268-3196
Publication E-mail: keynoter@kiwanis.org

Magazine of the high school service organization Key Club International. **Founded:** 1946. **Freq:** Bimonthly. **Key Personnel:** Julie A. Carson, Editor-in-Chief. **USPS:** 584-680. **Subscription Rates:** Included in membership; $4 nonmembers; $.60 single issue. **Remarks:** Accepts advertising.
Circ: Paid 190,000

10305 Kiwanis Magazine
Kiwanis International
3636 Woodview Trace Free: (800)549-2647
Indianapolis, IN 46268
Publication E-mail: kiwanismail@kiwanis.org

Magazine covering business, professional, and topics of general interest to Kiwanis. **Subtitle:** A magazine for community leaders. **Founded:** Feb. 1917. **Freq:** 10/year. **Print Method:** Offset. **Trim Size:** 8 x 10 7/8. **Cols./Page:** 3. **Col. Width:** 2 1/8 inches. **Col. Depth:** 10 inches. **Key Personnel:** Charles M. Jonak, Managing Editor, cjonak@kiwanis.org; Patrick A. Hatcher, Advertising Dir., phatcher@kiwanis.org. **ISSN:** 0162-5276. **Subscription Rates:** $7.50 members; $.75 single issue; $.75 single issue. **Remarks:** Accepts advertising.
Ad Rates: GLR: $20 **Circ:** Paid 258,674
BW: $5,775
4C: $8,230
PCI: $250

10306 Lawrence Township Journal
Cumberland Courier/The Lawrence Township Journal
7962 Pendleton Pike Phone: (317)542-8149
Indianapolis, IN 46226 Fax: (317)542-1137

Newspaper with a Republican orientation. **Founded:** 1944. **Freq:** Weekly (Wed.). **Print Method:** Offset. **Cols./Page:** 6. **Col. Width:** 20 nonpareils. **Col. Depth:** 224 agate lines. **Key Personnel:** J.E. Zainey, Publisher; Shelly Zainey, Contact. **Subscription Rates:** $20 individuals. **Remarks:** Accepts advertising.
Ad Rates: SAU: $5 **Circ:** Paid 10,500

10307 Light and Life
Free Methodist Church of North America
PO Box 535002 Phone: (317)244-3660
Indianapolis, IN 46253-5002 Fax: (317)248-9055
Free: (800)342-5531
Publication E-mail: llmads@aol.com
Publisher E-mail: llcomm1@aol.com

Church magazine. **Subtitle:** An Interactive Magazine for Earnest Christians. **Founded:** 1868. **Freq:** Monthly. **Print Method:** Offset web. **Trim Size:** 8 3/8 x 10 7/8. **Cols./Page:** 3. **Col. Width:** 27 nonpareils. **Col. Depth:** 120 agate lines. **Key Personnel:** Douglas M. Newton, Editor, LLMEditor@aol.com; Denise Chaney, Operations Mgr. **ISSN:** 0024-3299. **Subscription Rates:** $16 individuals.
Ad Rates: BW: $850 **Circ:** Paid ‡22,000
4C: $950 Controlled ‡200

10308 The Link
Synod of Lincoln Trails
1100 W. 42nd St. Phone: (317)577-9698
Indianapolis, IN 46208
Presbyterian newsletter. **Founded:** 1971. **Freq:** 6/year. **Print Method:** Offset. **Trim Size:** 8 1/2 x 11. **Cols./Page:** 4. **Col. Width:** 14 picas. **Col. Depth:** 12 1/2 inches. **Key Personnel:** David Crittenden, Editor. **Remarks:** Advertising not accepted. **Formerly:** The Trailmarker.
Circ: Non-paid 10,000

10309 The Lion of Alpha Epsilon Pi
Alpha Epsilon Pi Fraternity
8815 Wesleyan Rd. Phone: (317)876-1913
Indianapolis, IN 46268-1171 Fax: (317)876-1057
Publisher E-mail: aepihq@indy.net

Fraternity magazine. **Founded:** 1920. **Freq:** Quarterly. **Print Method:** Web offset. **Trim Size:** 8 1/2 x 11. **Cols./Page:** 3 and 2. **Col. Width:** 26 and 48 nonpareils. **Col. Depth:** 130 agate lines. **Key Personnel:** Sidney N. Dunn, Editor. **ISSN:** 1041-6935. **Subscription Rates:** $7.50 individuals; $74 life. **Remarks:** Accepts advertising.
Ad Rates: GLR: $20 **Circ:** 25,000
BW: $1,000

10310 Metallurgical and Materials Transactions A
Midwest Alliance in Nursing
6910 N. Shadeland Ave., Ste. 206 Phone: (317)541-3600
Fax: (317)541-3609
Indianapolis, IN 46220-4274
Publication E-mail: csc@tms.org
Publisher E-mail: main-org@inetdirect.net

Technical journal on metals research. **Founded:** 1969. **Freq:** Monthly. **Print Method:** Offset. **Trim Size:** 8 1/2 x 11. **Cols./Page:** 2. **Col. Width:** 40 nonpareils. **Col. Depth:** 137 agate lines. **Key Personnel:** D. Laughlin, Editor; Linda L. Gibb, Advertising Mgr. **ISSN:** 0360-2133. **Subscription Rates:** $50 members; $995 institutions. **Remarks:** Accepts advertising. **URL:** http://www.tm.org/pubs/journals/mt/mt.html. **Formerly:** Mettallurgical Transactions A.
Ad Rates: BW: $795 **Circ:** ‡2,500

10311 Metallurgical and Materials Transactions B
Midwest Alliance in Nursing
6910 N. Shadeland Ave., Ste. 206 Phone: (317)541-3600
Fax: (317)541-3609
Indianapolis, IN 46220-4274
Publication E-mail: csc@tms.org
Publisher E-mail: main-org@inetdirect.net

Technical journal on metals research. **Founded:** 1969. **Freq:** Bimonthly. **Print Method:** Offset. **Trim Size:** 8 1/2 x 11. **Cols./Page:** 2. **Col. Width:** 40 nonpareils. **Col. Depth:** 137 agate lines. **Key Personnel:** D. Laughlin, Editor; Linda Gibb, Advertising Mgr. **ISSN:** 0360-2141. **Subscription Rates:** $36 members; $715 institutions. **Remarks:** Accepts advertising. **URL:** http://www.tms.org/pubs/journals/mt/mt.html. **Formerly:** Metallurgical Transactions B.
Ad Rates: BW: $795 **Circ:** ‡1560

10312 Mine & Quarry Trader
7355 Woodland Dr. Phone: (317)297-5500
Indianapolis, IN 46278-1737 Fax: (317)299-1356
Free: (800)827-7468
Publication E-mail: amtrucker@trucker.com

Trade magazine featuring mining and aggregate equipment, supplies, and services. **Founded:** 1976. **Freq:** Monthly. **Print Method:** Web. **Trim Size:** 7 1/2 x 10 1/16. **Cols./Page:** 2 and 3. **Col. Width:** 2 5/16 and 3 inches. **Col. Depth:** 140 agate lines. **Key Personnel:** Kyle Eggert, Sales Mgr., kyle@trucker.com; Gina Kelly, Sales Rep., sales@trucker.com; Glenda Davis, Sales Rep. **ISSN:** 1049-1805. **Subscription Rates:** Free. **Remarks:** Accepts advertising.
Ad Rates: BW: $750 **Circ:** Non-paid 22,226
4C: $1,150
PCI: $75

10313 The National Jewish Post and Opinion
238 S. Meridian Phone: (317)972-7800
Indianapolis, IN 46202 Fax: (317)972-7807

National Jewish newspaper. **Founded:** 1932. **Freq:** Weekly. **Print Method:** Web offset. **Trim Size:** 11 1/2 x 15. **Cols./Page:** 5. **Col. Width:** 11 1/2 picas. **Col. Depth:** 14 inches. **Key Personnel:** Gabriel Cohen, Publisher. **USPS:** 275-580. **Subscription Rates:** $36 individuals. **Remarks:** Color advertising not accepted.
Ad Rates: BW: $1,120 **Circ:** (Not Reported)
PCI: $16.80

10314 The Northeast Reporter
East Side Suburban Newspapers
4309 E. Michigan St., No 11042 Phone: (317)356-2487
Indianapolis, IN 46201-3652
Local newspaper. **Founded:** 1935. **Freq:** Weekly (Thurs.).

Print Method: Offset. **Cols./Page:** 8. **Col. Width:** 1 5/8 inches. **Col. Depth:** 21 inches. **Key Personnel:** Ruth Thoele, Editor; William K. Thoele, Publisher. **Subscription Rates:** Free; $35 by mail. **Remarks:** Accepts advertising.
Ad Rates: BW: $750 **Circ:** Paid 50
4C: $800 Free 10,250
PCI: $7

10315 Our Paper
Grain Dealers Mutual Insurance Co.
1752 N. Meridian St., Box 1747 Phone: (800)428-7081
Indianapolis, IN 46206 Fax: (800)828-4124

Trade magazine covering loss control and safety for the grain elevator trade. **Founded:** 1913. **Freq:** Quarterly. **Key Personnel:** Scott North, Editor. **Subscription Rates:** Free to qualified subscribers. **Remarks:** Advertising not accepted.
Circ: (Not Reported)

10316 Paws & Claws
1508 E. 86th St., Ste. 135 Phone: (317)574-0181
Indianapolis, IN 46240 Fax: (317)574-0181
Publication E-mail: pawsandclaws@mailexcite.com

Magazine for pet owners. Covers health, diet, training, and care for all types of pets, including dogs, cats, birds, fish, reptiles, rabbits, and hamsters. **Founded:** Oct. 1993. **Freq:** Monthly. **Print Method:** Web offset. **Trim Size:** 10 1/4 x 13. **Cols./Page:** 4. **Col. Width:** 2 3/8 inches. **Col. Depth:** 9 5/8 inches. **Key Personnel:** Anthony Quattrocchi, Publisher; Adrian Quattrocchi, Circulation Mgr.; Amanda Quattrocchi, Editor. **Subscription Rates:** $15 individuals. **Remarks:** Accepts advertising.
Circ: Paid 1,000
Non-paid 40,000

10317 POA
Pony of Americas Club, Inc.
5240 Elmwood Ave. Phone: (317)788-0107
Indianapolis, IN 46203 Fax: (317)788-8974
Publisher E-mail: poac@iquest.net

Trade magazine. **Subtitle:** Pony of the Americas. **Founded:** 1960. **Freq:** Monthly. **Print Method:** Offset. **Trim Size:** 8 1/2 x 11. **Cols./Page:** 3. **Col. Width:** 14 picas. **Col. Depth:** 135 agate lines. **Key Personnel:** Paulette Baker, Editor; Jean Donley, Exec. Sec. **ISSN:** 0882-9624. **Subscription Rates:** $27 individuals; $2 single issue. **Remarks:** Accepts advertising.
Ad Rates: BW: $150 **Circ:** ‡1,600
4C: $1,200

10318 Previews
Indianapolis Museum of Art
1200 W. 38th St. Phone: (317)923-1331
Indianapolis, IN 46208-4196 Fax: (317)931-1978
Publisher E-mail: ima@ima-art.org

Publication covering exhibitions and programming. **Subtitle:** News and Events for Museum Members. **Founded:** 1906. **Freq:** Bimonthly. **Print Method:** Offset. **Trim Size:** 8 1/2 x 11. **Cols./Page:** 4. **Col. Width:** 1.725 inches. **Col. Depth:** 127 agate lines. **Key Personnel:** Anne Robinson, Editor. **Subscription Rates:** included with membership. **Remarks:** Advertising not accepted. **Formerly:** IMA Calendar/Previews.
Circ: Controlled ‡12,000

10319 RCI Premier
Resort Condominiums International, Inc.
3502 Woodview Trace Phone: (317)876-1692
Indianapolis, IN 46268 Fax: (317)871-9507

Magazine reporting on events and trends in the resort-condominium development, vacation-ownership/exchange, and travel industries. **Founded:** 1985. **Freq:** Bimonthly. **Print Method:** Sheetfed offset. **Trim Size:** 8 1/2 x 12. **Cols./Page:** 2 and 3. **Key Personnel:** Alyssa Chase, Editor, phone (317)871-9641, fax (317)871-9507, alyssa.chase@rci.com; Lynn Alderman, Sales Mgr., phone (317)871-9473, fax (317)871-9507, alyssa.chase@rci.com. **Remarks:** Accepts advertising. **Former name:** Perspective.
Ad Rates: BW: $1,800 **Circ:** Controlled 9,000
4C: $2,400

10320 Res Gestaie
Indiana State Bar Association
230 E. Ohio St. Phone: (317)639-5465
Indianapolis, IN 46204 Fax: (317)266-2588

Professional journal covering law for members. **Founded:** Nov. 1956. **Freq:** Monthly. **Print Method:** Sheetfed offset. **Key Personnel:** Susan J. Ferrer, Editor, ferrers@inbar.org. **USPS:** 462-500. **Subscription Rates:** Free to qualified subscribers. **Remarks:** Accepts advertising. **URL:** http://www.ai.org/isba/.
Ad Rates: BW: $547 **Circ:** Non-paid 10,500
4C: $842

10321 The Sagamore
Indiana University-Purdue University at Indianapolis
425 University Blvd. Phone: (317)274-5934
Indianapolis, IN 46202 Fax: (317)274-2953

Collegiate newspaper. **Subtitle:** The Weekly Newspaper of IUPUI. **Founded:** 1969. **Freq:** Weekly. **Print Method:** Offset. **Trim Size:** 13.75 x 21.625. **Cols./Page:** 6. **Col. Width:** 2.0275 inches. **Col. Depth:** 20.7 inches. **Key Personnel:** Patrick McKeand, Publisher. **Subscription Rates:** Free; $8.80 by mail; $13.90 other countries. **Remarks:** Accepts advertising. **Available Online. URL:** http://www.sagamore.iupui.edu.
Ad Rates: GLR: $1.35 **Circ:** Free ‡13,000
SAU: $19.80

10322 The Saturday Evening Post
The Saturday Evening Post Society
1100 Waterway Blvd. Phone: (317)636-8881
Indianapolis, IN 46202 Fax: (317)637-0126
Publication E-mail: silverbob@juno.com

General interest magazine. **Founded:** 1728. **Freq:** Bimonthly. **Print Method:** Offset. **Trim Size:** 8 1/8 x 10 13/16. **Cols./Page:** 3. **Col. Width:** 27 nonpareils. **Col. Depth:** 140 agate lines. **Key Personnel:** Dr. Cory J. SerVaas, Editor. **Subscription Rates:** $13.97 individuals; $20.97 other countries; $2.50 single issue. **Remarks:** Advertising not accepted for alcoholic beverages and tobacco products. **URL:** http://www.satevepost.org.
Ad Rates: GLR: $31.45 **Circ:** Paid ★**430,074**
BW: $10,897
4C: $14,259
PCI: $440.30

10323 Speedway Town Press
Speedway-Northwest Press, Inc.
1564 Main St. Phone: (317)241-4345
Indianapolis, IN 46224-6527
Local newspaper. **Founded:** 1956. **Freq:** Weekly (Wed.). **Print Method:** Offset. **Trim Size:** 11 1/2 x 17. **Cols./Page:** 7. **Col. Width:** 1 3/8 inches. **Col. Depth:** 16 inches. **Key Personnel:** Beth Sullivan, Publisher. **Subscription Rates:** free; $27 by mail. **Formerly:** Speedway West Wayne Press; Speedway-Northwest Press.
Ad Rates: GLR: $8 **Circ:** Free 7,000
BW: $672
SAU: $9.75
PCI: $6

10324 The Spotlight
4217 S. Meridian St. Phone: (317)788-4554
Indianapolis, IN 46217-3313
Suburban community newspaper. **Founded:** Feb. 16, 1939. **Freq:** Weekly (Wed.). **Print Method:** Offset. **Cols./Page:** 6. **Col. Width:** 2 1/16 inches. **Col. Depth:** 21 1/4 inches. **Key Personnel:** Jerry L. Cosby, Editor and Publisher; Ron Douglas, Sales Mgr. **Subscription Rates:** $45 individuals. **Remarks:** Accepts advertising.
Ad Rates: GLR: $8 **Circ:** Wed. ♦**24,609**
BW: $867
4C: $70
PCI: $8

10325 This is Indianapolis
Indianapolis Convention and Visitors Association
One RCA Dome, Ste. 100 Phone: (317)639-4282
Indianapolis, IN 46225 Fax: (317)684-2590
Free: (800)323-INDY
Publisher E-mail: icva@indianapolis.org

Hotel inroom Indianapolis visitors guide. **Founded:** 1990. **Freq:** 2/year. **Print Method:** Web offset. **Trim Size:** 8 3/8 x 10 7/8. **Cols./Page:** 3. **Col. Width:** 2 1/4 inches. **Col. Depth:** 10 inches. **Key Personnel:** William R. Hendrickson, Manager, bhendrickson@indianapolis.org; Mary K. Huggard, Vice President, mhuggard@indianapolis.org. **Subscription Rates:** Free. **Remarks:** Accepts advertising.
Ad Rates: BW: $10,800 **Circ:** Controlled 300,000
4C: $13,600

10326 Traces of Indiana and Midwestern History
Indiana Historical Society
315 W. Ohio St. Phone: (317)232-1882
Indianapolis, IN 46202-3299 Fax: (317)233-3109
Free: (800)447-1830
Publication E-mail: mmckee@statelib.lib.in.us

Illustrated history magazine. **Founded:** 1989. **Freq:** Quarterly. **Print Method:** Offset. **Trim Size:** 8 1/2 x 11. **Key Personnel:** Tom Mason, Executive Editor; Ray E. Boomhower, Managing Editor, phone (317)232-1877, rboomhower@indianahistory.org. **ISSN:** 1040-788X. **Subscription Rates:** $30 individuals; $5.25 single issue. **Remarks:** Advertising not accepted. **URL:** http://www.indianahistory.org/traces.htm.
Circ: 11,000

10327 Trap & Field
Curtis Publishing Co.
1000 Waterway Blvd. Phone: (317)633-8800
Indianapolis, IN 46202 Fax: (317)633-8813
Publication E-mail: trap_ field@iquest.net

Magazine for the amateur trapshooter. **Founded:** 1890. **Freq:** Monthly. **Print Method:** Offset. **Trim Size:** 8 3/8 x 10 7/8. **Cols./Page:** 3. **Col. Width:** 2 1/4 inches. **Col. Depth:** 10 inches. **Key Personnel:** Bonnie Nash, Editor and Publisher; Tracy Price, Advertising Mgr. **ISSN:** 0041-1760. **Subscription Rates:** $25 individuals. **Remarks:** Accepts advertising.
Ad Rates: BW: $1,200 **Circ:** Paid ‡15,500
4C: $1,650 Non-paid ‡500
PCI: $60

10328 Turtle Magazine for Preschool Kids
Children's Better Health Institute
1100 Waterway Blvd. Phone: (317)636-8881
PO Box 567 Fax: (317)684-8094
Indianapolis, IN 46202-2156
Free: (800)558-2376
Publication E-mail: cbhiseif@trader.com
Publisher E-mail: cbhiseif@tcon.net

Magazine for children (ages 2-5 years) with an emphasis on health, fitness and exercise. **Founded:** 1979. **Freq:** 8/year. **Trim Size:** 7 5/8 x 10 1/8. **Key Personnel:** Terry Harshman, Editor; Bart Rivers, Art Director; Cory SerVaas, M.D., Editorial Director; Greg Joray, Executive Publisher. **Subscription Rates:** $17.95 individuals. **Remarks:** Accepts advertising. **Formerly:** Turtle.
Ad Rates: BW: $5,320 **Circ:** Paid 343,923
4C: $7,000

10329 U.S.A. Gymnastics
USA Gymnastics
201 S. Capitol, Ste. 300 Phone: (317)237-5050
Indianapolis, IN 46225 Fax: (317)237-5069

Magazine covering major gymnastics competitions; promotes health, fitness, and safety. **Founded:** 1964. **Freq:** Bimonthly. **Print Method:** Web offset. **Trim Size:** 8 1/2 x 11. **Key Personnel:** Luan Peszek, Editor and Administration, lpeszek@usa-gymnastics.org. **ISSN:** 0748-6006. **Subscription Rates:** $20 individuals; $32 other countries. **Remarks:** Accepts advertising. **URL:** http://www.usa-gymnastics.org.
Ad Rates: BW: $1,465 **Circ:** ‡65,000
4C: $1,990

10330 U.S. Kids
Children's Better Health Institute
1100 Waterway Blvd. Phone: (317)636-8881
PO Box 567 Fax: (317)684-8094
Indianapolis, IN 46202-2156
Free: (800)558-2376
Publisher E-mail: cbhiseif@tcon.net

Magazine featuring stories and activities geared for children. **Founded:** 1987. **Freq:** 8/year. **Print Method:** Web Offset. **Trim Size:** 8 1/8 x 10 7/8. **Key Personnel:** Nancy Axelrad, Editor. **Subscription Rates:** $21.95 individuals. **Remarks:** Accepts advertising.
Ad Rates: BW: $4,522 **Circ:** Paid ‡225,000
4C: $5,950 Non-paid ‡2,000

10331 USRowing
The U.S. Rowing Association
201 S. Capitol Ave., Ste. 400 Phone: (317)237-5656
Indianapolis, IN 46225-1054 Fax: (317)237-5646
Free: (800)314-4769
Publisher E-mail: members@usrowing.org

Rowing magazine. **Founded:** 1968. **Freq:** Bimonthly. **Print Method:** Offset. **Trim Size:** 8 1/2 x 11. **Cols./Page:** 3. **Col. Width:** 28 nonpareils. **Col. Depth:** 140 agate lines. **Key Personnel:** Brett Johnson, Managing Editor, phone (317)237-5645, brett@usrowing.org. **ISSN:** 1094-1231. **Subscription Rates:** $55 out of country; $45 members 27 yrs. and older; $30 members 26 yrs. and younger. **Formerly:** The Oarsman; Rowing U.S.A.; American Rowing.
Ad Rates: BW: $850 **Circ:** 16,500
4C: $1,275

10332 The Voice
Metropolitan Indianapolis Board of Realtors, Inc.
1912 N. Meridian St. Phone: (317)956-1912
Indianapolis, IN 46202 Fax: (317)956-5050
Publication E-mail: voice@mibor.net

Magazine covering metropolitan real estate. **Subtitle:** The Voice for Real Estate in Central Indiana. **Founded:** 1920. **Freq:** Monthly. **Print Method:** Offset. **Trim Size:** 8 1/2 x 11. **Cols./Page:** 8. **Col. Depth:** 140 agate lines. **Key Personnel:** Leslie Haney, Editor; Stephen J. Sullivan, Publisher. **ISSN:** 1092-9886. **Subscription Rates:** $16 individuals. **Remarks:** Accepts advertising. **Formerly:** The Realtor Voice.
Ad Rates: BW: $650 **Circ:** Paid 5,000

10333 The Wesleyan Advocate
The Wesleyan Publishing House
PO Box 50434 Phone: (317)576-1313
Indianapolis, IN 46250-0434 Fax: (317)842-9188

Magazine. **Subtitle:** The Official Publication of the Wesleyan Church. **Founded:** Nov. 8, 1842. **Freq:** Monthly. **Print Method:** Offset. **Trim Size:** 8 1/2 x 11. **Cols./Page:** 3. **Col. Width:** 27 nonpareils. **Col. Depth:** 133 agate lines. **Key Personnel:** Jerry Brecheisen, Managing Editor; Nathan Birky, Publisher. **ISSN:** 0043-289X. **Subscription Rates:** $12.50 individuals; $15 out of country; $2 single issue. **Remarks:** Accepts advertising.
Ad Rates: GLR: $40 **Circ:** Paid ‡18,000
BW: $500 Controlled ‡500
4C: $750
PCI: $40

10334 West Side Messenger
Speedway-Northwest Press, Inc.
1564 Main St. Phone: (317)241-4345
Indianapolis, IN 46224-6527
Community newspaper. **Founded:** 1915. **Freq:** Weekly (Wed.). **Print Method:** Offset. **Trim Size:** 11 1/2 x 17. **Cols./Page:** 7. **Col. Width:** 1 3/8 inches. **Col. Depth:** 16 inches. **Key Personnel:** Beth Sullivan, Editor and Publisher. **Subscription Rates:** Free; $25 by mail.
Ad Rates: GLR: $8 **Circ:** Combined ‡15,000
BW: $726
SAU: $9.75
PCI: $6

10335 Comcast Cablevision of Indiana
5330 E. 65th St. Phone: (317)353-2225
Indianapolis, IN 46220 Fax: (317)842-5143

Founded: 1979. **Cities Served:** Hamilton County, Hancock County, Hendricks County, Marion County, Morgan County, and Shelby County; Beech Grove, Clemont, Crows Nest, Cumberland, Homecroft, Lawrence, Meridian Hills, Mooresville, North Crows Nest, Plainfield, Ravenswood, Southport, Speedway, Warren Park, Williams Creek, and Wynnedale, IN.

10336 Omega Communications Inc.
29 E. Maryland St. Phone: (317)264-4010
PO Box 1766 Fax: (317)264-4020
Indianapolis, IN 46206

Key Personnel: Merle Frey, Manager. **Cities Served:** Indianapolis, IN.

10337 Time Warner Cable
3030 Roosevelt Ave. Phone: (317)632-2288
Indianapolis, IN 46218 Fax: (317)632-5311

Owner: at above address. **Founded:** 1981. **Key Personnel:** Jay Satterfield, President. **Cities Served:** subscribing households 128,000; 78 channels.

10338 WAV-TV - 53
6264 Lapas Tr. Phone: (317)293-9600
Indianapolis, IN 46202-2304 Fax: (317)328-3870

Format: Commercial TV. **Owner:** IBL L.L.C., at above address. **Founded:** 1993. **Operating Hours:** Continuous. **ADI:** Indianapolis (Marion), IN. **Key Personnel:** Bill Shirk, General Mgr.; Doug Housemeyer, Sales Mgr.; Dan McNeal, Program Dir.

10339 WBDG-FM - 90.9
1200 N. Girls School Rd. Phone: (317)244-9234
Indianapolis, IN 46214

Format: Talk. **Owner:** Metropolitan School District of Wayne Township, at above address. **Founded:** 1965. **Operating Hours:** 6a.m.-8p.m. **ADI:** Indianapolis (Marion), IN. **Key Personnel:** Paul Mendenhall, General Mgr. **Wattage:** 400.

10340 WBRI-AM - 1500
4802 E. 62nd St. Phone: (317)255-5484
Indianapolis, IN 46220 Fax: (317)255-4452

Format: Talk; News; Contemporary Christian; Information. **Networks:** Independent. **Founded:** 1964. **Operating Hours:** Daytime. **ADI:** Indianapolis (Marion), IN. **Key Personnel:** Steve White, General Mgr./Morning Dir.; Debbie Coughenour, Office Mgr./Bookkeeper; Dick Sickels, General Sales Mgr.; Theresa Ross, Music Dir.; Keith Smiles, News Dir.; Jill Brewer, Office Operation. **Local Programs:** *Indiana Family Forum*, Bill Smith, (317)582-0300. **Wattage:** 5000.

10341 WCBW-FM - 104.9
8203 Indy Ct. Phone: (317)487-1006
Indianapolis, IN 46214-2300 Fax: (317)487-4148
Free: (800)8789229

Format: Religious; Contemporary Christian. **Networks:** Independent. **Owner:** Continental Broadcast Group, Inc., 8203 Indy Court, Indianapolis, IN 46214. **Founded:** 1964. **Operating Hours:** Continuous; 100% local. **ADI:** St. Louis, MO (Mt. Vernon, IL). **Key Personnel:** Marvin Kosofsky, Owner; Greg Lhamon, General Mgr.; Greg Cassidy, Program Dir.; Sandi Brown, Operations Mgr.; Phil Lewis, General Sales Mgr. **Wattage:** 7800.

10342 WCKN-AM - 1430
6161 Fall Creek Rd. Phone: (317)257-7565
Indianapolis, IN 46220 Fax: (317)253-6501

Format: Country. **Networks:** ABC. **Owner:** Broadcast Alchemy L.P., at above address. **Founded:** 1925. **Formerly:** WKVV-AM; WIRE-AM; WXTZ-AM. **Operating Hours:** Continuous; 100% local. **ADI:** Indianapolis (Marion), IN. **Key Personnel:** Chris Wheat, President/Gen Mgr.; Lee Anne Brooks, General Sales Mgr. **Wattage:** 5000.

10343 WEDM-FM - 91.1
Walker Career Ctr. Phone: (317)532-6301
9651 E. 21st St. Fax: (317)532-6199
Indianapolis, IN 46229

Format: Contemporary Hit Radio (CHR). **Networks:** Network Indiana. **Owner:** Metropolitan School District of Warren Township, 9301 E. 18th St., Indianapolis, IN 46229. **Founded:** 1970. **Operating Hours:** Continuous; 1% network, 99% local. **ADI:** Indianapolis (Marion), IN. **Key Personnel:** Daniel J. Henn, Station Mgr. **Wattage:** 180. **Ad Rates:** Noncommercial.

10344 WENS-FM - 97.1
950 N. Meridian, Ste. 1297 Phone: (317)266-9700
Indianapolis, IN 46204 Fax: (317)634-1618

Format: Adult Contemporary. **Networks:** Independent. **Owner:** Emmis Broadcasting, at above address. **Founded:** 1986. **Formerly:** WSUL-FM. **Operating Hours:** Continuous. **ADI:** Indianapolis (Marion), IN. **Key Personnel:** Christine Woodward-Duncan, General Mgr.; Donna Dwyer-Pitz, Contact; Lori Ballard, Contact. **Wattage:** 23,000. **Ad Rates:** $40-165 per unit.

10345 WFMS-FM - 95.5
8120 Knue Rd. Phone: (317)842-9550
Indianapolis, IN 46250 Fax: (317)577-3361
E-mail: person@wfms.com

Format: Country. **Networks:** Independent. **Founded:** 1957. **Operating Hours:** Continuous. **ADI:** Indianapolis (Marion), IN. **Key Personnel:** Monte-Maupin Gerard, VP/General Mgr.; Jennifer Skodt, Marketing Mgr.; Max Turner, Engineering Mgr. **Wattage:** 50,000.

10346 WFYI-FM - 90.1
1401 N. Meridian St. Phone: (317)636-2020
Indianapolis, IN 46202 Fax: (317)633-7418
E-mail: wfyi@wfyi.org

Format: Public Radio; Talk; Classical; News. **Networks:** National Public Radio (NPR); Public Radio International (PRI). **Owner:** Metropolitan Indianapolis Public Broadcasting, Inc., at above address, Fax: (317)633-7433. **Founded:** 1954. **Formerly:** WIAN-FM (1988). **Operating Hours:** Continuous; 50% network, 50% local. **ADI:** Indianapolis (Marion), IN. **Key Personnel:** Jed Duvall, Station Mgr., jduvall@wfyi.org; Lloyd Wright, General Mgr., lwright@wfyi.org; Jeanelle Adamak, Vice Pres. of Marketing & PR, jadamak@wfyi.org. **Local Programs:** *Classical Music with Dick Rick*, Dick Rice; *Indianapolis Symphony Orchestra*, Doug Dillon; *Nothing But the Blues*, Jay Zochowski. **Wattage:** 10,000. **Ad Rates:** Noncommercial. Combined advertising rates available with WFYI-TV.

10347 WFYI-TV - 20
1401 N. Meridian Phone: (317)636-2020
Indianapolis, IN 46202 Fax: (317)633-7418

Format: Public TV. **Networks:** Public Broadcasting Service (PBS). **Owner:** Metropolitan Indianapolis Public Broadcasting, Inc., at above address. **Founded:** 1970. **Operating Hours:** Continuous. **ADI:** Indianapolis (Marion), IN. **Key Personnel:** Lloyd Wright, President; Alan Cloe, Sr. Vice Pres.; Jerry Hughers, CFO; Jeanelle Adamak, VP of Marketing & PR. **Wattage:** 60 KW. **Ad Rates:** $28-175 for 15 seconds. **URL:** http://www.wfyi.org.

10348 WGLD-FM - 104.5
8120 Knue Rd. Phone: (317)842-9550
Indianapolis, IN 46250 Fax: (317)577-3361

Format: Oldies. **Founded:** 1993. **Formerly:** WGRL-FM. **ADI:** Indianapolis (Marion), IN. **Key Personnel:** Charlie Morgan, Vice Pres./Gen. Mgr.; Tim Burns, Sales Mgr.; Max Turner, Engineering Mgr. **Wattage:** 50,000. **Ad Rates:** $50 for 60 seconds.

10349 WHHH-FM - 96.3
6264 LaPas Trail Phone: (317)239-9696
Indianapolis, IN 46268 Fax: (317)328-3870

Format: Contemporary Hit Radio (CHR). **Founded:** 1991. **Operating Hours:** Continuous. **ADI:** Indianapolis (Marion), IN. **Key Personnel:** Bill Shirk, General Mgr.; Scott Wheeler, Program Dir. **Wattage:** 3000.

10350 WHUT-AM - 1470
36 S. Pennsylvania St., Ste. 200 Phone: (765)644-1255
Indianapolis, IN 46204-3627 Fax: (765)644-1775
Free: (800)452-9997

Format: Big Band/Nostalgia. **Networks:** ABC; Satellite Music Network. **Owner:** Anderson Radio, G.P., at above address. **Founded:** 1982. **Operating Hours:** Continuous; 80% network, 20% local. **ADI:** Indianapolis (Marion), IN. **Key Personnel:** Steve Brown, General Mgr.; Robin Chester, Sales Mgr. **Local Programs:** *WHVT Morning Show*, Mike Kase. **Wattage:** 1000 day; 35 night. **Ad Rates:** $17 for 60 seconds.

10351 WIBC-AM - 1070
9292 N. Meridian St. Phone: (317)844-7200
Indianapolis, IN 46260 Fax: (317)846-1081
E-mail: wibc.com

Format: Talk; News; Sports. **Networks:** ABC. **Owner:** Emmis Broadcasting, 950 Meridan, Indianapolis, IN 46204, (317)266-0100. **Founded:** 1938. **Operating Hours:** Continuous. **ADI:** Indianapolis (Marion), IN. **Key Personnel:** Tom Severino, General Mgr.; Jon Quick, Program Dir.; Lori Ballard, General Sales Mgr.; Morry Smulevitz, Mktng/PRDD; Sara Ritter, Business Mgr. **Local Programs:** *Dave Wilson Show* 4-7 pm, Dave Wilson, (317)582-4375; *Nightshift with Dave Elswick* 9-12M, Dave Elswick, (317)582-4312. **Wattage:** 50,000. **URL:** http://www.wibc.com.

10352 WICR-FM - 88.7
1400 E. Hanna Ave. Phone: (317)788-3280
Indianapolis, IN 46227 Fax: (317)788-3490
E-mail: wicr@uindy.edu

Format: News; Classical; Jazz; Alternative/New Music/Progressive; Jazz. **Networks:** Network Indiana; BBC World Service; Public Radio International (PRI); UPI. **Owner:** University of Indianapolis, at above address, (317)788-3314. **Founded:** 1962. **Operating Hours:** Continuous. **ADI:** Indianapolis (Marion), IN. **Key Personnel:** Edward W. Roehling, General Mgr., phone (317)788-3319, roehling@uindy.ed; Susi Benge, Secretary, phone (317)788-3280, sbenge@uindy.edu. **Local Programs:** *Conversations* 9:30 a.m. - 10 a.m. Friday, Susette Surprenant, (317)788-3280, Fax (317)788-3490; *Indiana Today* 10 - 11 a.m. Monday-Friday, Paul Irwin, (317)788-3280, Fax (317)788-3490; *Visions* 12:15 p.m. - 4 p.m. Monday-Friday, Ed Roehling, (317)788-3319, Fax (317)788-3490. **Wattage:** 30,000. **Ad Rates:** Noncommercial. **URL:** http://www.uindy.edu.

10353 WIRE-FM - 100.9
PO Box 68920 Phone: (317)482-4427
Indianapolis, IN 46268-0920

Format: Country. **Networks:** ABC. **Owner:** Boone County Broadcasters, Inc., at above address. **Founded:** 1967. **Formerly:** WNON-FM (1985). **Operating Hours:** 5:30 a.m.-midnight; 10% network, 90% local. **ADI:** Indianapolis (Marion), IN. **Key Personnel:** John R. Dotas, Contact; Paul R. Raymonds, Program Dir. **Local Programs:** *Coach's Corner*, Paul Raymonds, (312)482-4427; *Morning Magazine*, Helen Dotas, (312)482-4427. **Wattage:** 3000. **Ad Rates:** $6-9.50 for 30 seconds; $8-14 for 60 seconds.

10354 WISH-TV - 8
PO Box 7088 Phone: (317)923-8888
Indianapolis, IN 46207 Fax: (317)926-1144
E-mail: wishmail@wish-tv.com

Format: Commercial TV. **Networks:** CBS. **Operating Hours:** Continuous. **ADI:** Indianapolis (Marion), IN. **Key Personnel:** Scott Hainey, Promotions Mgr.; Lee Giles, News Dir.; Jeff White, General Sales Mgr.; John Dawson, President/General Mgr.; Denise Daniels, Local Sales; Mike Johnston, Marketing Mgr.; Rick Thedwall, Program Mgr.

10355 WNAP-FM - 93.1
One Emmis Plaza Phone: (317)236-9300
40 Monument Circle, Suite 600 Fax: (317)684-2024
Indianapolis, IN 46204

Format: Classic Rock. **Networks:** AP. **Owner:** Emmis Communications, at above address, Indianapolis, IN, (317)266-0100, Fax: (317)631-3750. **Founded:** 1968. **Formerly:** WKLR-FM (1994). **Operating Hours:** 24 hours. **ADI:** Indianapolis (Marion), IN. **Key Personnel:** Chris Woodward-Duncan, General Mgr.; Donna Dwyer Pitz, Sales Mgr. **Local Programs:** *Dual Airbags (Public Affairs)*, JoAnn Klooz, (317)266-9700, Fax (317)634-1618. **Wattage:** 50,000. **Ad Rates:** Advertising accepted; rates available upon request. $150 for 60 seconds. $150 for 60 seconds.

10356 WNDE-AM - 1260
6161 Fall Creek Rd. Phone: (317)257-7565
Indianapolis, IN 46220 Fax: (317)254-9619
E-mail: rlower@wnde.com

Format: Sports; Talk. **Networks:** Mutual Broadcasting System; ESPN Radio. **Founded:** 1924. **Operating Hours:** Continuous. **ADI:** Indianapolis (Marion), IN. **Key Personnel:** Chris Wheat, Contact. **Wattage:** 5000.

10357 WNDY-TV - 23
500 Brickyard Plaza Phone: (317)241-2388
4551 W. 16th St. Fax: (317)381-6975
Indianapolis, IN 46222
E-mail: bstar@paramant.com

Format: Commercial TV. **Networks:** United Paramount Network. **Owner:** Paramant Station Group, at above address. **Founded:** 1987. **Operating Hours:** Continuous. **ADI:** Indianapolis (Marion), IN. **Key Personnel:** Kathryn Bridgman, General Mgr.; Dave Ware, General Sales Mgr.; Mike Ruggiero, Local Sales Mgr.; Mary Jo Perry, Traffic Mgr.; Jim Brandenburg, Production Dir.; Byron King, Program Dir.; Bruce Stone, Creative Services Dir.; Eric Randles, Research; Bob Engle, Business Mgr. **Local Programs:** *Community Calendar* 3 times a day Monday-Friday, Jeff Degler; *The Jim Clark Show* 10 a.m. Saturday. **Wattage:** 5,000,000. **URL:** http://www.upn23.com.

10358 WNTS-AM - 1590
4800 E. Raymond St. Phone: (317)359-5591
Indianapolis, IN 46203

Format: Religious. **Networks:** USA Radio. **Owner:** S & M Broadcasting Co, Inc, at above address. **Founded:** 1974. **Formerly:** WGEE-AM; WNIR-AM. **Operating Hours:** 5:00 a.m.-midnight. **ADI:** Indianapolis (Marion), IN. **Key Personnel:** Jim Wilson, General Mgr. **Wattage:** 5000 day; 500 night.

10359 WPZZ-FM - 95.9
2021 E. 52nd St. No. 200 Phone: (317)736-4040
Indianapolis, IN 46205-1405 Fax: (317)736-7998

Format: Urban Contemporary. **Networks:** Southern Broadcasting. **Owner:** Willis Broadcast Co., 645 Church St., No. 400, Norfolk, VA 23510, (800)873-4600. **Founded:** 1988. **Formerly:** WGAQ-FM. **Operating Hours:** Continuous; 10% network, 90% local. **ADI:** Indianapolis (Marion), IN. **Key Personnel:** Eric Blakey, Program Dir.; John C. Asher, Operations Dir.; Kevin Simmons, Sales Mgr.; Pam Coomer, Contact. **Wattage:** 3000. **Ad Rates:** $18 for 30 seconds; $35 for 60 seconds.

10360 WRFT-FM - 91.5
6141 S. Franklin Rd. Phone: (317)862-6696
Indianapolis, IN 46259 Fax: (317)862-7262

Format: Eclectic. **Owner:** Franklin Twp. Comm. School Corp., at above address. **Founded:** 1978. **ADI:** Indianapolis (Marion), IN. **Key Personnel:** E.B. Carver, Superintendent, phone (317)862-2411; Jon Easter, General Mgr., phone (317)862-6649. **Wattage:** 130 ERP. **Ad Rates:** Noncommercial.

10361 WRTV-TV - 6
1330 N. Meridian St. Phone: (317)635-9788
Indianapolis, IN 46202 Fax: (317)269-1400

Format: Commercial TV. **Networks:** ABC. **Owner:** McGraw-Hill Broadcasting Co., Inc., 1221 Avenue of the Americas, New York, NY 10020, (212)512-2000. **Founded:** 1949. **Formerly:** WFBM-TV (1972). **Operating Hours:** 5:30 am-2:30 am. **ADI:** Indianapolis (Marion), IN. **Key Personnel:** C. Christian Schmidt, Vice Pres./Gen. Mgr., fax (317)269-1406; Marc Dunlap, General Sales Mgr.; Eric Hulnick, News Dir.; Judith Waugh, Public Affairs Dir.; Richard Pratt, Contact; Paul Montgomery, Contact; Martin L. Siddall, Dir. of Business Affairs, fax (317)269-1406.

10362 WRZX-FM - 103.3
6161 Fall Creek Rd. Phone: (317)257-7565
Indianapolis, IN 46220 Fax: (317)253-6501

Format: Alternative/New Music/Progressive. **Networks:** The Source. **Owner:** Broadcast Alchemy L.P., at above address. **Founded:** 1964. **Formerly:** WMJC-FM (1992); WFXF-FM. **Operating Hours:** Continuous. **ADI:** Indianapolis (Marion), IN. **Key Personnel:** Frank Wood, President; Chris Wheat, General Mgr.; Lee Anne Brooks, General Sales Mgr. **Wattage:** 18,000 ERP.

10363 WSYW-AM - 810
8203 Indy Ct. Phone: (317)271-1111
Indianapolis, IN 46214-2300 Fax: (317)273-1507

Format: Classical; Urban Contemporary. **Networks:** UPI; ABC. **Founded:** 1963. **Formerly:** WATI-AM (1991); WGRT-AM. **Operating Hours:** Daytime. **ADI:** Indianapolis (Marion), IN. **Key Personnel:** Rob Petit, General Mgr.; Rick Smith, Sales Mgr.; Dan Jensen, Program Dir. **Local Programs:** *AAHSLAND Show.* **Wattage:** 250.

10364 WSYW-FM - 107.1
8203 Indy Ct. Phone: (317)271-9799
Indianapolis, IN 46214-2300 Fax: (317)273-1507

Format: Classical. **Networks:** ABC. **Owner:** Universal Broadcasting Corp., at above address. **Founded:** 1975. **Formerly:** WGRT-FM (1984). **Operating Hours:** Continuous. **ADI:** Indianapolis (Marion), IN. **Key Personnel:** Martha Miller, General Mgr.; Krik D. Fields, Operations Mgr.; Marcia York, Sales Mgr. **Wattage:** 3000. **Ad Rates:** $25-40 for 30 seconds; $25-50 for 60 seconds.

10365 WTBU-TV - 69
2835 N. Illinois St. Phone: (317)940-9828
Indianapolis, IN 46208 Fax: (317)940-5971
E-mail: wtbu@butler.edu

Format: Public TV. **Founded:** 1992. **Formerly:** WTBO-TV. **Operating Hours:** 7 a.m. - 12 p.m. **ADI:** Indianapolis (Marion), IN. **Key Personnel:** Dr. Kenneth Creech, General Mgr., phone (317)940-5975; Richard Miles, Program Dir., phone (317)940-5972; Mark Harris, Operations, phone (317)940-5977; Marco Dominguez, Production, phone (317)940-5979; Allen Deck, Development, phone (317)940-5976; David Fort, Engineering, phone (317)940-5964. **Wattage:** 10,000. **Ad Rates:** Noncommercial. **URL:** http://www.butler.edu.

10366 WTHR-TV - 13
1000 N. Meridian St. Phone: (317)636-1313
Indianapolis, IN 46204 Fax: (317)636-3717
E-mail: wthrl3@aol.com; wmills@wthr.com

Format: Commercial TV. **Networks:** NBC. **Founded:** 1957. **Formerly:** WLWI-TV (1974). **Operating Hours:** Continuous Sun.- Thurs.; 6am - 3am Fri.- Sat. **ADI:** Indianapolis (Marion), IN. **Key Personnel:** Richard Pegram, VP/Gen. Mgr; Jacques Natz, News Dir.; Rod Porter, Program Mgr.; Lis Daily, Dir. of Community Affairs. **Local Programs:** *Eyewitness News 11 p.m.*, Leah Severson, Night Exec. Producer, (317)655-5782, Fax (317)632-6720; *Eyewitness News 6 p.m.*, Mike Wilhite, Producer, (317)655-5771, Fax (317)632-6720; *Eyewitness News Sunrise*, Terri Scott, Producer, (317)655-5774, Fax (317)632-6720. **Wattage:** 316,000 visual, 69,500 aural. **URL:** http://www.wthr.com.

10367 WTLC-FM - 105.7
2126 N. Meridan St. Phone: (317)923-1456
Indianapolis, IN 46202 Fax: (317)924-9684
E-mail: wtlc@aol.com

Format: Urban Contemporary. **Networks:** CBS. **Owner:** Panache Broadcasting, at above address. **Founded:** 1968. **Operating Hours:** Continuous. **ADI:** Indianapolis (Marion), IN. **Key Personnel:** Paul C. Major, General Mgr., pmajor@iquest.net; John Emerson, Operations Mgr., jemerson@iquest.net; Noreen Grace, Sales Mgr. **Wattage:** 50,000. **Ad Rates:** Advertising accepted; rates available upon request. Combined advertising rates available with WTLC-AM. **URL:** http://www.wtlc.com.

WTTK-TV - See Kokomo

10368 WTTV-TV - 4
3490 Bluff Rd. Phone: (317)782-4444
Indianapolis, IN 46217 Fax: (317)780-5464
E-mail: wb4@wb4.com

Format: Commercial TV. **Owner:** Sinclair Broadcsting Group, 2000 W. 41st St., Baltimore, MD 21211, (410)662-4700, Fax: (410)662-4278. **Founded:** 1949. **Operating Hours:** Continuous. **ADI:** Indianapolis (Marion), IN. **Wattage:** 55kw ERP. **URL:** http://www.wb4.com.

10369 WXIN-TV - 59
1440 N. Meridian St. Phone: (317)632-5900
Indianapolis, IN 46202 Fax: (317)687-6534
E-mail: wxinews@mail.wxin.com

Format: Commercial TV. **Networks:** Independent; Fox. **Owner:** Tribune Television Co., at above address, Fax: (317)687-6534. **Founded:** 1984. **Formerly:** WPDS-TV (1986). **Operating Hours:** Sun.-Thur.; Continuous Sun Sign off 2:30am to 5:00am. **ADI:** Indianapolis (Marion), IN. **Key Personnel:** Linda Gray, General Mgr., phone (317)687-6500; Jerry Harbin, General Sales Mgr., phone (317)687-6590, fax (317)687-6531; Jamie Berns, Production Mgr., phone (317)687-6520, fax (317)687-6532; Roger Bishop, Dir. of Engineering, phone (317)687-6566, fax (317)687-6532; Wendy Logsdon, Program Dir., phone (317)687-6560, fax (317)687-6532; Judy Paluso, Promotions Dir., phone (317)687-6570, fax (317)687-6532; Kevin Nunn, News Dir., phone (317)687-6540, fax (316)687-6556. **Wattage:** 5,000,000. **Ad Rates:** $100-16,000 for 30 seconds. **URL:** http://www.wxin.com.

10370 WXIR-FM - 98.3
4802 E. 62nd St. Phone: (317)255-5484
Indianapolis, IN 46220 Fax: (317)255-4452

Networks: Independent. **Founded:** 1964. **Operating Hours:** Continuous. **ADI:** Indianapolis (Marion), IN. **Key Personnel:** Steve White, General Mgr./Morning Dd.; Debbie Coughenour, Office Mgr. & Bookkeeper; Dick Siokels, General Sales Mgr.; Theresa Ross, Program and Music Dir.; Keith Smiley, News Dir.; Jill Brewer, Office Operations; David White, Promotions/ Church Development; Andrew Whitesel, Asst. to Sales Mgr.; Gary Sallee, Account Executive; Tom Stuckey, Account Executive; Daniel White, Traffic Dir. **Wattage:** 3000. **URL:** http://www.gtu/love98.

10371 WXTZ-FM - 93.9
9000 Keystone Crossing, Ste. 939
Indianapolis, IN 46240

Format: Easy Listening. **Founded:** 1993. **ADI:** Indianapolis (Marion), IN. **Key Personnel:** Mary Weiss, General Mgr.; John Coleman, Sales Mgr. **Wattage:** 6,000. **Ad Rates:** $40 for 60 seconds. $40 for 60 seconds.

10372 WXXP-FM - 97.9
36 S. Pennsylvania St., Ste. 200 Phone: (765)644-1255
Indianapolis, IN 46204-3627 Fax: (765)644-1775
Free: (800)452-9997
E-mail: wxxp@aol.com

Format: Adult Contemporary. **Owner:** Anderson Radio, G.P., at above address. **Founded:** 1973. **Formerly:** WLHN-FM. **Operating Hours:** Continuous;. **ADI:** Indianapolis (Marion), IN. **Key Personnel:** Kevin Spencer, Prog./Music Dir.; Robin Chester, Sales Mgr.; Steve Brown, General Mgr. **Wattage:** 50,000. **Ad Rates:** $37 for 60 seconds.

JASONVILLE, pop. 2,497.

Greene Co. (SW). 31 m SE of Terre Haute. Machine shop. Coal mines; hardwood timber. Light manufacturing. Agriculture. Corn, wheat, fruit.

10373 Jasonville Leader
603 W. Main St. Phone: (812)665-3145
PO Box 125 Fax: (812)665-3145
Jasonville, IN 47438
Local newspaper with a Democratic orientation. **Subtitle:** Jasonville Leader. **Founded:** 1899. **Freq:** Weekly (Thurs.). **Print Method:** Offset. **Trim Size:** 13 x 21 1/2. **Cols./Page:** 6. **Col. Width:** 2 inches. **Col. Depth:** 210 agate lines. **Key Personnel:** Nancy A. Enstrom, Editor and Publisher. **USPS:** 273-020. **Subscription Rates:** $17 individuals; $21 out of area; $.50 single issue. **Remarks:** Color advertising not accepted.
Ad Rates: GLR: $3 **Circ:** Paid ‡840
BW: $300 Free ‡20
PCI: $3

JASPER†, pop. 9,097.

Dubois Co. (SW). 50 m N of Evansville.

10374 The Herald
PO Box 31 Phone: (812)482-2424
Jasper, IN 47547-0031 Fax: (812)482-4104

Newspaper with a Democratic orientation. **Founded:** 1895. **Freq:** Mon.-Sat. (eve.). **Print Method:** Offset. **Cols./Page:** 5. **Col. Width:** 24 nonpareils. **Col. Depth:** 224 agate lines. **Key Personnel:** John A. Rumbach, Editor; Don Shreve, Advertising Mgr. **Subscription Rates:** $51 individuals. **Remarks:** Accepts advertising.
Ad Rates: BW: $720 **Circ:** Paid ‡12,865
PCI: $9

10375 WBDC-FM - 100.9
PO Box 1009 Phone: (812)683-4144
Jasper, IN 47547-1009 Fax: (812)683-5891
Free: (800)683-1033
E-mail: wbdc@psci.net

Format: Country. **Networks:** Mutual Broadcasting System. **Owner:** Paul Knies, at above address, (812)482-2727, Fax: (812)482-3696. **Founded:** 1975. **Operating Hours:** Continuous. **ADI:** Evansville, IN (Madisonville, KY). **Key Personnel:** Paul Knies, Contact; Joe Hamilton, Program Dir.; Dave Gerard, News Dir. **Wattage:** 25,000 ERP. **Ad Rates:** $10-15 for 30 seconds; $12-18 for 60 seconds. Combined advertising rates available with WAXL-FM & WRZR-FM.

10376 WITZ-AM - 990
Old U.S. 231 S. Phone: (812)482-2131
Box 167 Fax: (812)482-9609
Jasper, IN 47546
E-mail: witzamfm@psci.net

Format: Adult Contemporary; Top 40; Easy Listening. **Simulcasts:** WITZ-FM. **Networks:** Network Indiana; AgriAmerica; ABC. **Owner:** G. Earl Metzger, at above address. **Founded:** 1948. **Operating Hours:** Sunrise-sunset. **Key Personnel:** G. Earl Metzger, Contact; Bob Boyles, Sales Mgr.; James Baugh, News Dir.; Walt Ferber, Program Dir.; Jeri Weisheit, Business Mgr. **Wattage:** 1000. **Ad Rates:** $15-26.50 for 30 seconds; $19.65-33.35 for 60 seconds.

10377 WITZ-FM - 104.7
Old U.S. 231 S. Phone: (812)482-2131
Box 167 Fax: (812)482-9609
Jasper, IN 47546
E-mail: witzamfm@psci.net

Format: Adult Contemporary; Top 40; Easy Listening. **Simulcasts:** WITZ-AM. **Networks:** AP; AgriAmerica; ABC. **Owner:** G. Earl Metzger, at above address. **Founded:** 1948. **Operating Hours:** 5 a.m.-midnight. **Key Personnel:** G. Earl Metzger, Contact; Bob Boyles, Sales Mgr.; James Baugh, News Dir.; Jeri Weisheit, Business Mgr.; Walt Ferber, Program Dir. **Wattage:** 50,000. **Ad Rates:** $15-26.50 for 30 seconds; $19.65-33.35 for 60 seconds.

10378 WQKZ-FM - 98.5
1978 S. Witz Rd. Phone: (812)367-1884
Jasper, IN 47546 Fax: (812)482-9609
Free: (800)206-6605
E-mail: wqkz@psci.net

Format: Hot Country. **Networks:** Jones Satellite. **Owner:** Gem Communications, at above address. **Founded:** Nov. 1, 1991. **Operating Hours:** Continuous. **ADI:** Evansville, IN (Madisonville, KY). **Key Personnel:** Gene Kuntz, General Mgr.; Gary Lee, Program Dir. **Wattage:** 6000. **Ad Rates:** $11.75-12.40 for 30 seconds; $14.80-15.60 for 60 seconds.

JEFFERSONVILLE†, pop. 21,220.

Clark Co. (SE). On Ohio River, opposite Louisville, Ky.

10379 Clark County Journal
The Evening News
221 Spring St., Ste. 867 Phone: (812)283-6636
Jeffersonville, IN 47130 Fax: (812)284-7080
Publisher E-mail: enews@mis.net

Newspaper with a Republican orientation. **Founded:** 1854. **Freq:** Weekly (Wed.). **Print Method:** Offset. **Cols./Page:** 6. **Col. Width:** 27 nonpareils. **Col. Depth:** 297 agate lines. **Key Personnel:** Thomas J. Lindley III, Editor and Publisher. **Subscription Rates:** $25 individuals; $0.50 single issue. **Remarks:** Accepts advertising.
Ad Rates: GLR: $.36 **Circ:** 12,500
BW: $645
4C: $945
PCI: $5

10380 The Evening News
221 Spring St., Ste. 867 Phone: (812)283-6636
Jeffersonville, IN 47130 Fax: (812)284-7080
Publisher E-mail: enews@mis.net

Newspaper with a Democratic orientation. **Founded:** 1872. **Freq:** Mon.-Sat. (eve.). **Print Method:** Offset. **Cols./Page:** 6. **Col. Width:** 25 nonpareils. **Col. Depth:** 297 agate lines. **Key Personnel:** Thomas J. Lindley III, Editor and Publisher; Susan Miller, Advertising Mgr. **Subscription Rates:** $96 individuals. **Remarks:** Accepts advertising.
Ad Rates: GLR: $.58 **Circ:** Paid 10,500
BW: $883.65
4C: $1,183.65
PCI: $7.10

10381 Insight Communications
3408 Industrial Pkwy. Phone: (812)288-6471
Jeffersonville, IN 47130 Fax: (812)288-7818

Founded: 1986. **Formerly:** Insight Cablevision. **Key Personnel:** Bob Lillie, General Mgr., phone (812)218-6000, fax (812)288-2818. **Cities Served:** Crestwood, La Grange, KY; Oldham County, KY.: subscribing households 28,000; 48 channels.

10382 WAVG-AM - 1450
213 Magnolia Ave. Phone: (812)283-3577
PO Box 726 Fax: (812)285-5060
Jeffersonville, IN 47130

Format: Oldies; Big Band/Nostalgia; Music of Your Life. **Networks:** ABC. **Owner:** Sunnyside Communications, Inc., PO Box 1897, Louisville, KY 40201. **Founded:** 1961. **Former name:** WXVW-AM (June 17, 1997). **Operating Hours:** Continuous. **ADI:** Louisville, KY. **Key Personnel:** Blair Trask, President; Ron Chilton, Operations Dir.; Bob McIntosh, News Dir.; Betty Kelley, Contact; Katy Frank, Contact; Dorothy Clark, Contact; Claude Wayne, Production Dir. **Wattage:** 1000. **Ad Rates:** $44 per unit.

KENDALLVILLE, pop. 7,299.

Noble Co. (NE). 26 m N of Fort Wayne.

10383 Evening Star Plus
Kendallville Publishing Co.
PO Box 39 Phone: (219)347-0400
Kendallville, IN 46755 Fax: (219)347-2693
Publication E-mail: thestar@locl.net
Publisher E-mail: kpc@noblecan.org

Shopper. **Founded:** 1958. **Freq:** Weekly (Tues.). **Print Method:** Offset. **Trim Size:** 11 1/2 x 14. **Cols./Page:** 6. **Col. Width:** 2 1/16 inches. **Col. Depth:** 21 1/2 inches. **Key Personnel:** James D. Kroemer, Editor and Publisher, phone (219)925-2611, jimkroemer@kpcnews.net; Susan Carpenter, Advertising Mgr., phone (219)925-2611. **Subscription Rates:** $78. **Remarks:** Accepts advertising. **Formerly:** DeKalb County Advertiser.
Ad Rates: GLR: $1.75 **Circ:** Free ‡10,500
BW: $1161.00
4C: $1461.00
SAU: $9
PCI: $9

10384 News-Sun
102 N. Main St. Phone: (219)347-0400
PO Box 39 Fax: (219)347-2693
Kendallville, IN 46755
Publication E-mail: kpc@kpcnews.net

General newspaper. **Founded:** 1911. **Freq:** Daily (eve.) and Sat. (morn.). **Print Method:** Offset. **Trim Size:** 11 1/2 x 14. **Cols./Page:** 6. **Col. Width:** 12 1/2 picas. **Col. Depth:** 21 1/4 inches. **Key Personnel:** James D. Kroemer, Editor and Publisher, fax (219)347-7281, jimkroemer@kpcnews.net; LeAnn Robinson, Advertising Mgr., fax (219)347-7282, advertising@kpcnews.net. **Subscription Rates:** $119.60 individuals; $133.95 out of area. **Remarks:** Accepts advertising. **URL:** http://news-sun.kpcnews.net.
Ad Rates: GLR: $3.25 **Circ:** Mon.-Sat. 8,096
BW: $1,199.70
4C: $1,499.70
SAU: $9.50
PCI: $9.30

10385 WAWK-AM - 1140
931 East Ave. Phone: (219)347-2400
Kendallville, IN 46755 Fax: (219)347-2524

Format: Oldies. **Networks:** Brownfield; ABC. **Owner:** Don Moore-Wauk, at above address. **Founded:** 1957. **Operating Hours:** Sunrise-sunset; 100% local. **Key Personnel:** Don Moore, President; Mike Shultz, News Dir.; Bradon Baker, Program Dir. **Wattage:** 250. **Ad Rates:** $10-15 for 30 seconds; $12.50-18.75 for 60 seconds.

KENTLAND†, pop. 1,936.

Newton Co. (NW). 35 m W of Monticello. Residential.

10386 Indiana Spirit Shopping Guide
Twin States Publishing
PO Box 107 Phone: (219)474-5531
Kentland, IN 47951 Fax: (219)474-5354

Shopper. **Founded:** 1966. **Freq:** Weekly (Tues.). **Print Method:** Offset. **Cols./Page:** 6. **Col. Width:** 9 1/2 picas. **Col. Depth:** 14 inches. **Key Personnel:** Carla A. Waters, Editor; Bette Schmid, Publisher; Robin Hughes, Advertising Rep. **Subscription Rates:** $45 individuals. **Remarks:** Accepts advertising.
Ad Rates: GLR: $.33 **Circ:** Free ‡6,409
BW: $234
SAU: $4.62
PCI: $3.40

10387 Newton County Enterprise
Twin States Publishing
PO Box 107 Phone: (219)474-5532
Kentland, IN 47951 Fax: (219)474-5354

Newspaper with a Report orientation. **Founded:** 1865. **Freq:** Weekly (Wed.). **Print Method:** Offset. **Cols./Page:** 6. **Col. Width:** 9 1/2 picas. **Col. Depth:** 14 inches. **Key Personnel:** Carla A. Waters, Editor; Bette Schmid, Publisher; Robin Hughes, Advertising Rep. **USPS:** 390-060. **Subscription Rates:** $25 individuals; $35 out of area. **Remarks:** Accepts advertising.
Ad Rates: BW: $264.60 **Circ:** Paid 1,730
SAU: $5.76
PCI: $3.15

KEWANNA, pop. 711.

Fulton Co. (N). 10 m SW of Rochester. Manufactures wire forms, feed, coil springs. Grain, stock, poultry farms.

10388 The Observer
Box 307 Phone: (219)653-2101
Kewanna, IN 46939 Fax: (219)653-3418

Newspaper with a Republican orientation. **Founded:** 1946. **Freq:** Weekly (Thurs.). **Print Method:** Offset. **Trim Size:** 17 1/2 x 22 1/2. **Cols./Page:** 5. **Col. Width:** 23 nonpareils. **Col. Depth:** 224 agate lines. **Key Personnel:** Karen Good, Editor; Larry Joe Good, Publisher. **USPS:** 401-840. **Subscription Rates:** $12 individuals; $13 out of state. **Remarks:** Accepts advertising.
Ad Rates: BW: $144 **Circ:** ‡700
PCI: $2.00

KNIGHTSTOWN, pop. 2,325.

Henry Co. (E). 17 m SW of New Castle. Manufactures furniture, funeral car bodies, caskets and accessories. Stock, grain farms. Corn, wheat, hogs.

10389 AntiqueWeek (Eastern Edition)
Mayhill Publications
27 N. Jefferson St. Phone: (317)345-5133
PO Box 90 Fax: (800)695-8153
Knightstown, IN 46148
Free: (800)876-5133
Publication E-mail: antiqueweek@aol.com

Periodical covering antiques auctions and shows in Connecticut, Delaware, Washington, D.C., Maryland, New Jersey, New York, North Carolina, eastern Pennsylvania, Rhode Island, South Carolina, Virginia, and West Virginia. **Founded:** 1986. **Freq:** Weekly (Mon.). **Cols./Page:** 4. **Col. Width:** 15 picas. **Col. Depth:** 16 inches. **Key Personnel:** Connie Swaim, Editor. **Subscription Rates:** $28.45 individuals. **Remarks:** Accepts advertising. **Formerly:** Tri-State Trader.
Ad Rates: GLR: $1.14 **Circ:** 64,959
BW: $590.08
PCI: $14.38

10390 AntiqueWeek (Mid-Central Edition)
Mayhill Publications
27 N. Jefferson St. Phone: (317)345-5133
PO Box 90 Fax: (800)695-8153
Knightstown, IN 46148
Free: (800)876-5133
Publication E-mail: antiqueweek@aol.com

Periodical covering antiques and collectibles as well as auctions and shows in Illinois, Indiana, Iowa, Kentucky, Michigan, Minnesota, Missouri, Ohio, western Pennsylvania, Tennessee, and Wisconsin. **Founded:** 1968. **Freq:** Weekly (Mon.). **Trim Size:** 11 1/2 x 17. **Cols./Page:** 4. **Col. Width:** 15 picas. **Col. Depth:** 16 inches. **Key Personnel:** Tom Hoepf, Editor. **Subscription Rates:** $28.45 individuals. **Remarks:** Accepts advertising. **Formerly:** Tri-State Trader.
Ad Rates: GLR: $1.48 **Circ:** 64,959
BW: $856.30
PCI: $17.30

10391 Farmweek
Mayhill Publications
27 N. Jefferson St. Phone: (317)345-5133
PO Box 90 Fax: (800)695-8153
Knightstown, IN 46148
Free: (800)876-5133
Publication E-mail: mayhill@comsys.net

Newspaper covering agriculture in Indiana, Ohio, and Kentucky. **Founded:** Feb. 1955. **Freq:** Weekly (Wed.). **Print Method:** Letterpress. **Trim Size:** 11 1/2 x 7. **Cols./Page:** 4. **Col. Width:** 29 nonpareils. **Col. Depth:** 224 agate lines. **Key Personnel:** Nancy Searfoss, Editor; Tom Mayhill, Publisher; Freda Dudley, Advertising Dir. **Subscription Rates:** $21.95 individuals. **Remarks:** Accepts advertising.
Ad Rates: GLR: $1.10 **Circ:** Paid 35,141
BW: $960
PCI: $15

10392 Tri-County Banner
Tyswincher Publishing Co.
16 N. Washington Phone: (317)345-2111
PO Box 116 Fax: (317)345-2186
Knightstown, IN 46148
Community newspaper with a Report orientation. **Founded:** 1867. **Freq:** Weekly (Wed.). **Print Method:** Offset. **Cols./Page:** 5. **Col. Width:** 24 nonpareils. **Col. Depth:** 294 agate lines. **Key Personnel:** Janet Helms, Editor; Ronald J. Isbell, Publisher; Rhoda Hamblin, Advertising Mgr. **Subscription Rates:** $12.50 individuals. **Remarks:** Accepts advertising.
Ad Rates: BW: $210.40 **Circ:** ‡2,800
4C: $450.40
PCI: $3.40

10393 WKPW-FM - 90.7
10892 N. State Rd., Ste. 140 Phone: (765)345-9070
Knightstown, IN 46148 Fax: (765)345-7039
E-mail: wkpw@comsys.net

Format: Country. **Owner:** Indiana Soldiers & Sailors Children's Home, at above address. **Operating Hours:** Continuous. **Key Personnel:** Paul Wilkinson, General Mgr.; Dr. John Wittkamper, President; Mike York, Program Dir. **Wattage:** 4400.

KNOX†, pop. 3,674.

Starke Co. (NW). 45 m SW of South Bend. Manufactures electrical appliances, pickles, hydraulic cylinders, aluminum containers, cabinets. Poultry, truck, grain farms.

10394 The Leader
4 S. Main St. Phone: (219)772-2101
PO Box 38 Fax: (219)772-7041
Knox, IN 46534
Free: (888)772-2101

Shopper. **Subtitle:** The Review. **Founded:** 1862. **Freq:** Weekly (Wed.). **Print Method:** Offset. **Cols./Page:** 6. **Col. Width:** 11.5 picas. **Col. Depth:** 21 inches. **Key Personnel:** Frank Alan, Publisher; Eliene S. Alan, Advertising Mgr.; Melissa Andrade, Editor. **Subscription Rates:** $16 individuals; $18 out of area; $21 out of state. **Remarks:** Accepts advertising. **Alt. Formats:** CD-ROM.
Ad Rates: BW: $495 **Circ:** ‡4,237
PCI: $4.25

10395 WKVI-AM - 1520
400 W. Culver Rd. Phone: (219)772-6241
PO Box 10 Fax: (219)772-5920
Knox, IN 46534

Format: Oldies. **Founded:** 1969. **Key Personnel:** Ted Hayes, General Mgr.; Tim Price, Program Dir. **Wattage:** 250.

KOKOMO†, pop. 47,808.

Howard Co. (NC). 54 m N of Indianapolis. Manufactures aluminum products, alarm systems, hydraulic equipment, glass products, asphalt paving material, gloves, breakfast bars, dairy products, steel, wire, fencing, nails, abrasive and corrosive alloys, radio, auto transmission, plumbing supplies, tools, auto parts, castings, stamped metal, springs, electric signs, pottery; meat packing plant; canning factory.

10396 DOMESTIQUE
PenWorks
917 S. Waugh St.
Kokomo, IN 46901

Consumer Christian magazine covering women's interests, fiction, nonfiction and poetry. **Founded:** Feb. 1, 1996. **Freq:** Bimonthly. **Trim Size:** 8 1/2 x 11. **Key Personnel:** Penny E. Stone, Editor and Publisher. **ISSN:** 1086-3923. **Subscription Rates:** $22.50 U.S.; $25 Canada; $28 elsewhere. **URL:** http://www.freeyellow.com/members/domestique.

10397 Kokomo Perspective
209 N. Main St. Phone: (317)452-0055
Kokomo, IN 46901 Fax: (317)457-7209

Community newspaper. **Founded:** Aug. 1989. **Freq:** Weekly. **Cols./Page:** 6. **Col. Width:** 12 picas. **Col. Depth:** 21 1/2 inches. **Key Personnel:** Don Wilson, Publisher; Bill Eldridge, Sales; Curt Alexander, Editor.
Ad Rates: BW: $1,670.55 **Circ:** (Not Reported)
4C: $2,065.55
PCI: $14.95

10398 Kokomo Tribune
300 N. Union St. Phone: (317)459-3121
Kokomo, IN 46901 Fax: (317)456-3815
Free: (800)382-0695
Publication E-mail: ktonline@aol.com

General newspaper. **Founded:** 1850. **Freq:** Daily (eve.), Sat. and Sun. (morn.). **Print Method:** Offset. **Trim Size:** 13 7/8 x 22 5/8. **Cols./Page:** 6. **Col. Width:** 25 nonpareils. **Col. Depth:** 300 agate lines. **Key Personnel:** John C. Wiles, Editor; Arden A. Draeger, Publisher; Karen Spurlock, Production Mgr. **Subscription Rates:** $18.75 individuals. **Remarks:** Accepts advertising.
Ad Rates: BW: $23.05 **Circ:** Mon.-Sat. ★23,323
SAU: $16.17 Sun. ★25,885
PCI: $23.05

10399 WIOU-AM - 1350
PO Box 2208 Phone: (317)453-1212
Kokomo, IN 46904-2208 Fax: (317)455-3882

Format: Sports; Oldies. **Networks:** CBS. **Owner:** Mid-America Radio Group, at above address. **Founded:** 1948. **Operating Hours:** Continuous. **ADI:** Indianapolis (Marion), IN. **Key Personnel:** Rick Shaw, General Mgr. **Wattage:** 5000. **Ad Rates:** $24 for 30 seconds; $25 for 60 seconds.

10400 WTTK-TV - 29
c/o WTTV-TV Phone: (317)782-4444
3490 Bluff Rd. Fax: (317)780-5464
Indianapolis, IN 46217

Format: Commercial TV. **Owner:** Sinclair Broadcast Group, 2000 W. 41st St., Baltimore, MD 21211, (410)662-4700, (410)662-4278. **Operating Hours:** Continuous. **ADI:** Indianapolis (Marion), IN. **Key Personnel:** John Long, General Mgr., phone (317)780-5438; Phil Paligraf, General Sales Mgr., phone (317)780-5469, fax (317)780-5466; Jeff Sauerteig, Local Sales Manager, phone (317)780-5469, fax (317)780-5466; Gary Blitzer, National Sales Manager, phone (317)780-5418, fax (317)780-5466; Mike McClure, Director Of Sports Marketing, phone (317)780-5407, fax (317)780-5407; Jim Procelli, Business Mgr., phone (317)780-5440, fax (317)780-5465; Peggy McClelland, Operations Mgr., phone (317)780-5417; Harold Ridener, Chief Engineer, phone (317)780-5446; Cutch Armstrong, Promotions Mgr., phone (317)780-5447. **Wattage:** 55kw ERP. **URL:** http://www.wb4.com.

10401 WWKI-FM - 100.5
519 N. Main St. Phone: (765)459-4191
Kokomo, IN 46901-4619 Fax: (765)456-1111
Free: (800)456-1106

Format: Country. **Networks:** ABC. **Founded:** 1962. **Formerly:** WFKO-FM (1968). **Operating Hours:** Continuous; 5% network, 95% local. **Key Personnel:** Mike Christopher, Contact; Jim Stonecipher, General Sales Mgr.; Dave Broman, Program Dir.; Jim Schroeder, Chief Engineer. **Wattage:** 50,000. **Ad Rates:** $40-57 per unit. **URL:** http://www.wwki.com.

10402 WZWZ-FM - 92.5
PO Box 2208 Phone: (317)453-1212
Kokomo, IN 46904-2208 Fax: (317)455-3882

Format: Adult Contemporary. **Owner:** Mid-America Radio Group, at above address. **Founded:** 1964. **Operating Hours:** Continuous. **ADI:** Indianapolis (Marion), IN. **Key Personnel:** Rick Shaw, General Mgr. **Local Programs:** *A.K. in the A.M.*, Alan Kaye; *Rob Rupe Show*, Rob Rupe. **Wattage:** 6000 ERP. **Ad Rates:** $34 for 30 seconds; $36 for 60 seconds. Combined advertising rates available with WIOU-AM: $14-$36 for 30 seconds; $16-$43 for 60 seconds.

LA CROSSE, pop. 713.

La Porte Co. (NW). 42 m SW of South Bend. Diversified farming. Corn, wheat, soybeans.

10403 Regional News
PO Box 358 Phone: (219)754-2432
La Crosse, IN 46348
Newspaper with a Democratic orientation. **Founded:** 1915. **Freq:** Weekly (Thurs.). **Print Method:** Offset. **Cols./Page:** 6. **Col. Width:** 2 1/16 inches. **Col. Depth:** 21 1/2 inches. **Key Personnel:** Richard N. Slater, Editor and Publisher. **Subscription Rates:** $20 individuals; $24 out of area. **Remarks:** Accepts advertising.
Ad Rates: GLR: $.35 **Circ:** Paid ‡2,318
BW: $617.40 Free ‡342
SAU: $4.96

LA GRANGE†, pop. 2,164.

LaGrange Co. (C). 40 m SE of South Bend. Livestock and dairy farming.

10404 La Grange Countian
La Grange Publishing Co.
State Rd. 9 S. Phone: (219)463-2166
PO Box 148 Fax: (219)463-2734
La Grange, IN 46761
Publication E-mail: daypubco@kuntrynet.com
Publisher E-mail: lagpubco@kuntrynet.com

Community newspaper. **Founded:** 1966. **Freq:** Weekly (Wed.). **Print Method:** Offset. **Cols./Page:** 6. **Col. Width:** 9.6 picas. **Col. Depth:** 15 1/4 inches. **Key Personnel:** Rebecca Ramer, Editor; William Connelly, Publisher. **Subscription Rates:** Free. **Remarks:** Accepts advertising.
Ad Rates: GLR: $.59 **Circ:** ‡4,700
SAU: $8.26
PCI: $8.19

10405 La Grange News
La Grange Publishing Co.
State Rd. 9 S. Phone: (219)463-2166
PO Box 148 Fax: (219)463-2734
La Grange, IN 46761
Publication E-mail: dagpubco@kuntrynet.com
Publisher E-mail: lagpubco@kuntrynet.com

Community newspaper. **Founded:** 1856. **Freq:** Weekly (Fri.). **Print Method:** Offset. **Cols./Page:** 7. **Col. Width:** 12 2/5 picas. **Col. Depth:** 21 1/2 inches. **Key Personnel:** Monty J. Glick, Editor; William Connelly, Publisher. **Subscription Rates:** $25; $38 out of area. **Remarks:** Accepts advertising.
Ad Rates: GLR: $.59 **Circ:** ‡4,710
SAU: $8.26

10406 La Grange Standard
La Grange Publishing Co.
State Rd. 9 S. Phone: (219)463-2166
PO Box 148 Fax: (219)463-2734
La Grange, IN 46761
Publication E-mail: dagpubco@kuntrynet.com
Publisher E-mail: lagpubco@kuntrynet.com

Community newspaper. **Founded:** 1856. **Freq:** Weekly. **Print Method:** Offset. Broadsheet. **Trim Size:** 16 1/2 x 23. **Cols./Page:** 7. **Col. Width:** 12.75 picas. **Col. Depth:** 301 agate lines. **Subscription Rates:** $25 individuals; $38 out of area. **Remarks:** Color advertising not accepted.
Ad Rates: GLR: $.59 **Circ:** ‡5,706
SAU: $8.26
PCI: $7.70

10407 WTHD-FM - 105.5
206 S. High St. Phone: (219)463-8500
La Grange, IN 46761 Fax: (219)463-8580

Format: Country. **Networks:** ABC; Jones Satellite. **Owner:** Lake Cities Broadcasting Corp., at above address. **Operating Hours:** Continuous. **Key Personnel:** Tim Murray, News Dir.; Carter Snider, General Mgr.

LA PORTE†, pop. 21,796.

La Porte Co. (NW). 65 m SE of Chicago, Ill. Lake resort.

10408 La Porte Herald-Argus
701 State St. Phone: (219)362-2161
La Porte, IN 46350 Fax: (219)362-2166

General newspaper. **Founded:** Feb. 5, 1880. **Freq:** Mon.-Sat. (eve.). **Print Method:** Offset. **Cols./Page:** 6. **Col. Width:** 2 1/16 inches. **Col. Depth:** 21 1/2 inches. **Key Personnel:** C.T. Otolski, Publisher; Carol J. Kuta, Advertising Mgr. **Subscription Rates:** $75.40 individuals; $82 out of state. **Remarks:** Accepts advertising.
Ad Rates: GLR: $7.65 **Circ:** Mon.-Sat. ★12,374
BW: $793.35
4C: $993.35
PCI: $6.68

10409 Town Crier
Towndan Enterprises, Inc.
PO Box 576 Phone: (219)362-8519
La Porte, IN 46352 Fax: (219)325-0677

Shopper. **Founded:** May 13, 1933. **Freq:** Weekly (Mon.). **Print Method:** Offset. **Cols./Page:** 6. **Col. Width:** 24 nonpareils. **Col. Depth:** 231 agate lines. **Key Personnel:** Gregory L. Jones, President. **Remarks:** Advertising accepted; rates available upon request.
Circ: Free 97,224

10410 WCOE-FM - 96.7
1700 Lincolnway, Ste. 8 Phone: (219)362-5290
La Porte, IN 46350-3198 Fax: (219)324-7418
E-mail: wcoe@csinet.net

Format: Contemporary Country. **Networks:** ABC. **Owner:** La Porte County Broadcasting Co., Inc., at above address. **Founded:** 1964. **Operating Hours:** Continuous. **Key Personnel:** Kenneth S. Coe, President; Norma Sabie, Sales Coordinator; DeEtta Coe, Business Manager. **Wattage:** 3000 ERP. **Ad Rates:** $22.50 for 30 seconds; $23.50-23.50 for 60 seconds.

10411 WGTC-FM - 102.3
16455 Fox Cross Dr. Phone: (219)271-9482
La Porte, IN 46350-6616 Fax: (219)271-0494

Format: Contemporary Country. **Networks:** ABC. **Owner:** Summit Radio, Inc., at above address. **Founded:** 1989. **Operating Hours:** Continuous. **ADI:** South Bend-Elkhart, IN. **Key Personnel:** Jim Leep, General Mgr.; Peggy Neer, General Sales Mgr.; Doug Montgomery, Contact. **Wattage:** 12,000 ERP. **Ad Rates:** Advertising accepted; rates available upon request.

10412 WLOI-AM - 1540
Broadcast Center Phone: (219)362-6144
1700 Lincolnway Place, Ste. 8 Fax: (219)324-2418
La Porte, IN 46350
E-mail: wcoe@csinet.net

Format: Big Band/Nostalgia. **Networks:** ABC; Satellite Music Network. **Owner:** La Porte County Broadcasting Co., Inc., at above address, Fax: (219)324-7418. **Founded:** 1948. **Operating Hours:** Sunrise-sunset; 8% network, 92% local. **Key Personnel:** Ken Coe, President; Dennis Siddall, Program Dir.; DeEtta Coe, Business Mgr.; Norma Sabie, Asst. Sales Manager/Co-op Advertising Dir.; Rob Carpenter, Music Dir.; Harold Snure, Chief Engineer. **Wattage:** 250. **Ad Rates:** $19 for 30 seconds; $19-22 for 60 seconds.

LAFAYETTE†, pop. 43,011.

Tippecanoe Co. (NWC). On Wabash River, 63 m NW of Indianapolis. Purdue University. Computer software, toys.

10413 The Catholic Moment
The Times
PO Box 1603 Phone: (765)742-2050
Lafayette, IN 47902-1603 Fax: (765)742-7513
Publication E-mail: moment@dioceseoflafayette.org

Official newspaper (tabloid) of the Catholic Diocese of Lafayette, IN. **Founded:** 1945. **Freq:** Weekly. **Print Method:** Offset. **Trim Size:** 14 7/8 x 11 1/4. **Cols./Page:** 5. **Col. Width:** 1 7/8 inches. **Col. Depth:** 13 1/2 inches. **Key Personnel:** Thomas A. Russell, Editor, trussell@dioceseoflafayette.org; Most Rev. William L. Higi, Publisher. **ISSN:** 1087-2604. **Subscription Rates:** $20. **Remarks:** Accepts advertising. **Formerly:** The Sunday Visitor; Lafayette Sunday Visitor.
Ad Rates: BW: $810 **Circ:** ‡27,037
4C: $1,210
PCI: $12

10414 Journal and Courier
217 N. 6th St. Phone: (317)423-5511
Lafayette, IN 47901 Fax: (317)742-5633
Free: (800)456-3223
Publication E-mail: postmaster@jandc.mdn.com

General newspaper. **Founded:** 1829. **Freq:** Mon.-Sun. (morn.). **Print Method:** Letterpress. **Cols./Page:** 6. **Col. Width:** 25 nonpareils. **Col. Depth:** 298 agate lines. **Key Personnel:** George Benge, Editor; Dick Holtz, Publisher. **Subscription Rates:** $169 individuals. **Remarks:** Accepts advertising. **Available Online. URL:** http.//www.jconline.com.
Ad Rates: GLR: $3.59 **Circ:** Mon.-Sat. ★**37,030**
BW: $4,570.88 Sun. ★**44,164**
4C: $4,970.88
SAU: $35.85

10415 Lafayette Business Digest
Kapp Crowell Communications
Box 587 Phone: (765)742-6918
Lafayette, IN 47902 Fax: (765)423-8133

Newspaper covering local business. **Founded:** 1982. **Freq:** Weekly. **Print Method:** Web offset. **Trim Size:** 11 3/8 x 16/3/14. **Cols./Page:** 3. **Col. Width:** 3 1/4 inches. **Key Personnel:** Jennifer Kapp. **ISSN:** 1048-2822. **Subscription Rates:** $43.50 individuals. **Remarks:** Accepts advertising.
Ad Rates: GLR: $2.75 **Circ:** Controlled 1,500
BW: $810
PCI: $12.50

10416 The Lafayette Leader
Dunn & Hargitt, Inc.
22 N. 2nd St. Phone: (765)423-2624
Lafayette, IN 47902 Fax: (765)742-5156
Publication E-mail: lafleader@aol.com

Newspaper (tabloid) with a Democratic orientation. **Founded:** 1873. **Freq:** Weekly (Thurs.). **Print Method:** Offset. **Trim Size:** 11 1/2 x 15. **Cols./Page:** 4. **Col. Width:** 14.5 picas. **Col. Depth:** 14 inches. **Key Personnel:** Steve Georgeoff, Editor; Dennis Dunn, Publisher; Curtis Mullen, Advertising Mgr. **USPS:** 301-400. **Subscription Rates:** $48 individuals. **Remarks:** Accepts advertising.
Ad Rates: GLR: $.11 **Circ:** ‡4,000
BW: $350
4C: $550

10417 Insight Media Advertising
325 S. Creasy Ln. Phone: (317)447-7738
Box 4609 Fax: (317)447-7622
Lafayette, IN 47903

Founded: 1963. **Formerly:** Dimension Cable Services. **Cities Served:** Battle Ground, Dayton, Lafayette, Mullberry, Shadeland, West Lafayette, IN: subscribing households 39,000; 52 channels; 1 community access channel.

10418 WAZY-FM - 96.5
S. 18th St. Phone: (317)474-1410
Lafayette, IN 47905 Fax: (317)474-3442

Format: Adult Contemporary. **Networks:** ABC. **Owner:** University Broadcasting Co., 2380 1st Indiana Plaza, 135 N. Pennsylvania St., Indianapolis, IN 46204, (317)635-5696, Fax: (317)635-5699. **Founded:** 1964. **Operating Hours:** Continuous. **ADI:** Lafayette, IN. **Key Personnel:** Roger Bauer, General Mgr.; John Flint, Program Dir. **Local Programs:** *In Touch*, Tracy St. George; *Purdue Coaches Call-In Shows*; *Purdue University Football & Basketball.* **Wattage:** 50,000. **Ad Rates:** $12-16 per unit.

10419 WCFY-AM - 1410
108 Beck Ln. Phone: (317)474-4436
Lafayette, IN 47905 Fax: (317)474-5845

Format: Religious; Contemporary Christian. **Owner:** First Assembly of God, at above address, (317)474-1432. **Founded:** 1984. **Formerly:** WAZY-AM; WFTE-AM. **Operating Hours:** Continuous; 5% network; 95% local. **ADI:** Lafayette, IN. **Key Personnel:** Stevan Speheger, Chief Engineer; Parris Foxworthy, Gen. Mgr./Program/Music Dir.; Jeffrey Chase, Marketing Consultant; Christine Vollmer, PSA. **Wattage:** 1000. **Ad Rates:** $10 per unit. for Theater spot run 24 times per week.

10420 WJEF-FM - 91.9
1801 S. 18th St. Phone: (765)449-3400
Lafayette, IN 47905 Fax: (765)449-3413

Format: Oldies. **Networks:** Independent. **Owner:** Lafayette School Corp., 2300 Cason St., Lafayette, IN 47904, (765)449-3200. **Founded:** 1972. **Formerly:** WJJE-FM (1974). **Operating Hours:** 7:15 a.m.-4:00 p.m.; Mon.-Fri. **ADI:** Lafayette, IN. **Key Personnel:** Randall J. Brist, Radio/TV Director, rbrist@lsc.k12.in.us; Tina Hilt, Operations Asst. **Wattage:** 250. **Ad Rates:** Noncommercial. **URL:** http://www.lsc.k12.in.us/jeffrtv.

10421 WKHY-FM - 93.5
711 N. Earl Ave. Phone: (765)448-1566
PO Box 7093 Fax: (765)448-1348
Lafayette, IN 47904
E-mail: postmaster@wkhy.com

Format: Classic Rock; Album-Oriented Rock (AOR). **Networks:** AP. **Founded:** 1970. **Formerly:** WXUS-FM (1987). **Operating Hours:** Continuous. **ADI:** Lafayette, IN. **Key Personnel:** Eric F. McCart, General Mgr.; Ski Anderson, Promotions Dir.; Margot Walker, News Anchor; Beau Clark, Sales Mgr.; Gail Lewis, Music Dir.; Jane Cordell, Business Mgr. **Wattage:** 6,000. **URL:** http://www.wkhy.com.

10422 WKOA-FM - 105.3
PO Box 7880 Phone: (317)447-2186
Lafayette, IN 47903-7880 Fax: (317)448-4452

Format: Country. **Networks:** ABC. **Owner:** WASK, Inc./Schurz Communications Inc., at above address. **Founded:** 1964. **Formerly:** WASK-FM (1994). **Operating Hours:** Continuous. **ADI:** Lafayette, IN. **Key Personnel:** Hal Youart, Contact; John Trent, Contact. **Wattage:** 50,000. **Ad Rates:** $12-31.20 for 30 seconds; $15-39 for 60 seconds.

LAWRENCEBURG†, pop. 4,403.

Dearborn Co. (SE). On Ohio River, 25 m W of Cincinnati, Ohio. Manufactures feed, veneer, caskets, lumber, grain aerating machinery. Glass Bottles, rock crushing. Distilleries. Agriculture. Stock, dairy, grain farms.

10423 Dearborn County Register
Register Publications
126 W. High St. Phone: (812)537-0063
PO Box 328 Fax: (812)537-5576
Lawrenceburg, IN 47025
Newspaper with a Democratic orientation. **Founded:** 1825. **Freq:** Weekly (Thurs.). **Print Method:** Offset. **Trim Size:** 14 1/2 x 22 3/4. **Cols./Page:** 6. **Col. Width:** 13 millimeters. **Col. Depth:** 21 inches. **Key Personnel:** Joe Awad, Managing Editor; John Reiniger, Publisher; Janet Essert, Advertising Mgr.; Chase Barber, Production Mgr. **USPS:** 150-580. **Subscription Rates:** $36 individuals with Journal Press. **Remarks:** Accepts advertising.
Ad Rates: BW: $8.83 **Circ:** Paid ‡8,275
PCI: $8.53 Free ‡32

10424 The Journal Press
Register Publications
126 W. High St. Phone: (812)537-0063
PO Box 328 Fax: (812)537-5576
Lawrenceburg, IN 47025
Newspaper with a Republican orientation. **Founded:** 1858. **Freq:** Weekly (Tues.). **Print Method:** Offset. **Trim Size:** 14 1/2 x 22 3/4. **Cols./Page:** 6. **Col. Width:** 13 millimeters. **Col. Depth:** 21 inches. **Key Personnel:** Joe Awad, Editor; John Reiniger, Publisher; Janet Essert, Advertising Mgr.; Chase Barber, Production Mgr. **ISSN:** 0378-8800. **Subscription Rates:** $36 individuals with Register. **Remarks:** Accepts advertising.
Ad Rates: SAU: $5.75 **Circ:** Paid 6,446
PCI: $8.24 Free 35

LEBANON†, pop. 11,456.

Boone Co. (C). 24 m NW of Indianapolis.

10425 Reed Organ Society Quarterly
Dr. Edward A. Peterson
101 Ulen Blvd. Free: (800)841-4030
Country Club Park
Lebanon, IN 46052-3202
Publication E-mail: peterson@rosnet.com

Professional journal covering music and musical instruments. **Key Personnel:** Dr. Edward Peterson, Editor; Len Levasseur, Publisher. **Subscription Rates:** $17.50 individuals; $5 single issue. **Remarks:** Accepts advertising.
Circ: Paid 600

10426 The Reporter
Lebanon Newspapers, Inc.
117 E. Washington St. Phone: (765)482-5400
Lebanon, IN 46052 Fax: (765)482-4652
Free: (800)482-5400

Newspaper with a Report orientation. **Subtitle:** The Reporter. **Founded:** Sept. 29, 1891. **Freq:** Mon.-Sat. (eve.). **Print Method:** Offset. **Trim Size:** 14 x 22 3/4. **Cols./Page:** 6. **Col. Width:** 26 nonpareils. **Col. Depth:** 294 agate lines. **Key Personnel:** Micheal D. Mossman, General Mgr. **Subscription Rates:** $93.60 individuals. **Remarks:** Accepts advertising.
Ad Rates: GLR: $5.72 **Circ:** 7,200
BW: $756
4C: $981
SAU: $6
PCI: $5.72

LIBERTY†, pop. 1,844.

Union Co. (SE). 11 m E of Connersville. Fireproof doors, roof paint manufactured. Dairy, stock, grain farms. Hogs, corn, wheat.

10427 Liberty Herald
10-12 N. Market St. Phone: (317)458-5114
PO Box 30 Fax: (317)458-5115
Liberty, IN 47353-0030
Newspaper with a Republican orientation. **Founded:** 1851. **Freq:** Weekly (Thurs.). **Print Method:** Offset. **Trim Size:** 13.75x22.75. **Cols./Page:** 6. **Col. Width:** 12 picas. **Col. Depth:** 21 inches. **Key Personnel:** Vivian Risch, Editor. **USPS:** 311-720. **Subscription Rates:** $11 individuals; $13 out of state. **Remarks:** Accepts advertising.
Ad Rates: GLR: $.33 **Circ:** ‡2,400
BW: $441
4C: $750
SAU: $4
PCI: $4

LIGONIER, pop. 3,134).

Noble Co. (NE). 8 m SE Goshen. Manufactures plastic bottles, material & wallpaper sample books, culverts, flour. Stock, grain farms. Corn, wheat, oats.

10428 Advance Leader
Advance News
PO Box 30 Phone: (219)894-3102
Ligonier, IN 46767 Fax: (219)894-3104

Newspaper. **Founded:** 1880. **Freq:** Weekly (Thurs.). **Print Method:** Offset. **Cols./Page:** 6. **Col. Width:** 12 1/2 picas. **Col. Depth:** 21 1/2 inches. **Key Personnel:** Bob Buttgen, Editor; James Kroemer, Publisher. **Subscription Rates:** $20 individuals. **Remarks:** Accepts advertising.
Ad Rates: PCI: $4.15 **Circ:** ‡1,081

10429 The Monday Leader
Advance News
PO Box 30 Phone: (219)894-3102
Ligonier, IN 46767 Fax: (219)894-3104

Shopper. **Founded:** 1975. **Freq:** Monthly. **Print Method:** Offset. **Cols./Page:** 5. **Col. Width:** 12.3 picas. **Col. Depth:** 301 agate lines. **Key Personnel:** James Kroemer, Publisher; Bob Buttgen, Editor; Carol Arnold, Advertising Mgr. **Remarks:** Accepts advertising.
Ad Rates: BW: $477 **Circ:** Free 14,900
4C: $700
PCI: $5.80

LINTON

Greene Co. (SW). 10 m S of Worthington.

10430 WBTO-AM - 1600
Broadcast Park Phone: (812)847-4474
Linton, IN 47441

Format: News; Talk. **Owner:** Greene County Broadcasting Corp., at above address. **Founded:** 1953. **Operating Hours:** 24hrs. **ADI:** Terre Haute, IN. **Key Personnel:** Mike McDaniel, Owner. **Wattage:** 500 Watts. **Ad Rates:** Advertising accepted; rates available upon request.

LOGANSPORT†, pop. 19,255.

Cass Co. (NC). On Wabash and Eel Rivers, 70 m NW of Indianapolis.

10431 Pharos-Tribune
Thomson Newspapers
517 E. Broadway Phone: (219)722-5000
PO Box 210 Fax: (219)732-5070
Logansport, IN 46947
Free: (800)676-4125
Publication E-mail: loganpt@netusal.net

General newspaper. **Founded:** 1844. **Freq:** Daily (eve.), Sunday (morn.). **Print Method:** Offset. Uses mats. **Trim Size:** 13 x 21 1/2. **Cols./Page:** 6. **Col. Width:** 2 1/16 inches. **Col. Depth:** 21 1/2 inches. **Key Personnel:** Dollie Turpin, Publisher/Exec. Editor, dollie@indol.com. **Subscription Rates:** $10.60 4 weeks; $21.20 8 weeks; $34.45 13 weeks; $137.80 / year. **Remarks:** Accepts advertising.
Ad Rates: GLR: $.88 **Circ:** Mon.-Fri. ★**12,589**
4C: $355 Sun. ★**13,629**
PCI: $11.77

10432 WLHM-FM - 102.3
619 E. Main St., Box 719 Phone: (219)722-4000
Logansport, IN 46947

Format: Adult Contemporary. **Owner:** Logansport Radio Corp., at above address. **Founded:** 1965. **Formerly:** WSAL-FM (1965). **Operating Hours:** Continuous. **Key Personnel:** Andy Eubank, General Mgr.; Lynne Ness, Sales Mgr.; Joe Ulery, Programming. **Wattage:** 3000 ERP. **Ad Rates:** Combined advertising rates available with WSAL-AM.

10433 WSAL-AM - 1230
PO Box 719 Phone: (219)722-4000
Logansport, IN 46947 Fax: (219)722-4010
E-mail: wsal@wsal.com

Format: Full Service. **Networks:** ABC. **Founded:** 1949. **Operating Hours:** Continuous. **ADI:** Indianapolis (Marion), IN. **Key Personnel:** Andrew Eubank, General Mgr.; Dale Lowe, Operations Mgr.; Dick Prescott, News Dir.; Mike Montgomery, Sports Dir.; Lynne Ness, Sales Mgr. **Local Programs:** *Locally Speaking*, Dick Prescott; *Talk Line*, Dale Lowe. **Wattage:** 1000. **Ad Rates:** Combined advertising rates available with WLHM-FM.

LOOGOOTEE

Martin Co. (SW). 10 m NW of Shoals.

10434 Loogootee Tribune
PO Box 277 Phone: (812)295-2500
Loogootee, IN 47553 Fax: (812)295-5221

Community newspaper. **Freq:** Weekly (Thurs.). **Cols./Page:** 6. **Col. Width:** 12 3/10 picas. **Col. Depth:** 21 inches. **Key Personnel:** Harold Green, Editor and Publisher. **Subscription Rates:** $15 local; $17 in state; $20 out of state.
Ad Rates: GLR: $2 **Circ:** 3,300
PCI: $2.50

LOWELL, pop. 5,827.

Lake Co. (NW). 45 m SE of Chicago, Il. Manufactures asphalt felts and coatings, concrete blocks, septic tanks, electronic components. Sand and gravel pits. Hatchery; nursery. Agriculture. Dairy products.

10435 Cedar Lake Journal
Pilcher Publishing Co. Inc.
116-18 Clark St. Phone: (219)696-7711
PO Box 248 Fax: (219)696-7713
Lowell, IN 46356
Newspaper with a Report orientation. **Founded:** 1967. **Freq:** Weekly (Tues.). **Print Method:** Offset. **Cols./Page:** 8. **Col. Width:** 21 nonpareils. **Col. Depth:** 294 agate lines. **Key Personnel:** Mary Jeanette Pilcher, Publisher; Peggy Gonsiorowski, Office Mgr. **Subscription Rates:** Free; $24 out of area. **Remarks:** Accepts advertising.
Ad Rates: BW: $1,058.40 **Circ:** Free ‡5,400
4C: $400
PCI: $6.30

10436 Lowell Tribune
Pilcher Publishing Co. Inc.
116-18 Clark St. Phone: (219)696-7711
PO Box 248 Fax: (219)696-7713
Lowell, IN 46356
Newspaper with a Report orientation. **Founded:** 1885. **Freq:** Weekly (Tues.). **Print Method:** Offset. **Cols./Page:** 8. **Col. Width:** 10 1/2 picas. **Col. Depth:** 21 inches. **Key Personnel:** Mary Jeanette Pilcher, Publisher; Peggy Gonsiorowski, Office Mgr. **Subscription Rates:** $18 individuals; $24 out of area. **Remarks:** Accepts advertising.
Ad Rates: BW: $1,058.40 **Circ:** ‡3,942
4C: $400
PCI: $6.30

10437 The Northern Star
PO Box 248 Phone: (219)696-7711
Lowell, IN 46356 Fax: (219)696-7713

Newspaper with a Democratic orientation. **Founded:** 1955. **Freq:** Weekly (Wed.). **Print Method:** Offset. **Cols./Page:** 8. **Col. Width:** 21 nonpareils. **Col. Depth:** 280 agate lines. **Key Personnel:** Mary Jeanette Pilcher, Publisher; Peggy Gonsiorgwski, Office Mgr. **Subscription Rates:** $15 individuals; $21 out of area. **Remarks:** Accepts advertising.
Ad Rates: BW: $588 **Circ:** ‡2,300
4C: $400
PCI: $3.50

10438 South Lake Advertiser
Pilcher Publishing Co. Inc.
116-18 Clark St. Phone: (219)696-7711
PO Box 248 Fax: (219)696-7713
Lowell, IN 46356
Shopper. **Founded:** 1963. **Freq:** Weekly (Tues.). **Print Method:** Offset. **Cols./Page:** 8. **Col. Width:** 21 nonpareils. **Col. Depth:** 294 agate lines. **Key Personnel:** Mary Jeanette Pilcher, Publisher; Peggy Gonsiorlowski, Office Mgr. **Subscription Rates:** Free; $24 out of area. **Remarks:** Accepts advertising.
Ad Rates: GLR: $.35 **Circ:** Free ‡3,609
BW: $1,058.40
4C: $400
PCI: $6.30

MADISON†, pop. 13,081.

Jefferson Co. (SE). On Ohio River, 50 m NE of Louisville, Ky.

10439 The Madison Courier
310 Courier Sq. Phone: (812)265-3641
Madison, IN 47250 Fax: (812)273-6903

Newspaper. **Founded:** 1837. **Freq:** Daily (eve.) and Sat. (morn.). **Print Method:** Offset. **Trim Size:** 13 3/4 x 22 3/4. **Cols./Page:** 6. **Col. Width:** 2 1/16 inches. **Col. Depth:** 21 1/2 inches. **Key Personnel:** Elliot Thompkin, Editor; Jane Jacobs, Publisher; Doug Patrick, Circulation Mgr.; Phil Hatzel, Advertising Dir. **ISSN:** 3250-0000. **Subscription Rates:** $67.10 individuals; $88 out of area. **Remarks:** Accepts advertising.
Ad Rates: GLR: $.67 **Circ:** Paid 9,596
BW: $1,210.02 Free 56
4C: $1,530.02
PCI: $9.38

10440 The Weekly Herald
The Madison Courier
310 Courier Sq. Phone: (812)265-3641
Madison, IN 47250 Fax: (812)273-6903

Community newspaper. **Founded:** 1837. **Freq:** Weekly (Fri.). **Print Method:** Offset. **Trim Size:** 13 3/4 x 22 3/4. **Cols./Page:** 6. **Col. Width:** 2 1/16 inches. **Col. Depth:** 21 1/2 inches. **Key Personnel:** Jane Jacobs, Publisher. **Subscription Rates:** $17.25 Indiana and Kentucky; $21.75 elsewhere. **Remarks:** Advertising not accepted.
Circ: ‡386

10441 American Cable Entertainment
108 E. 2nd St. Phone: (812)265-4922
Madison, IN 47250 Fax: (812)265-6095
Free: (800)765-5152

Founded: 1962. **Formerly:** Ohio Valley Cable (1980); Simmons Cable TV of Kentucky/Indiana. **Key Personnel:** Joan Taylor, Office Mgr.; Bonnie Burkhardt, Contact. **Cities Served:** subscribing households 75,100; 35 channels; 1 community access channel.

10442 WIKI-FM - 95.3
WIKI Bldg. Phone: (812)273-CTRY
102 E. Main St. Fax: (812)265-4536
Madison, IN 47250-3411
Free: (800)953-WIKI

Format: Contemporary Country. **Networks:** CNN Radio; Jones Satellite. **Founded:** 1968. **Formerly:** WVCM-FM (1979). **Operating Hours:** Continuous; 85% network, 15% local. **ADI:** Louisville, KY. **Key Personnel:** Marty Pieratt, Owner/GM; Tom Cull, Station Mgr.; Ralph Hewitt, Production Mgr.; Larry Duke, News/Sports; Scarlet Feltner, Traffic Mgr.; Mary Franklin, Traffic Mgr. **Local Programs:** *Dick Witty's Madison Notebook*; *Ken Trimble in the Morning.* **Wattage:** 3000. **Ad Rates:** $7.50-18.25 for 30 seconds; $9.50-21.75 for 60 seconds.

10443 WORX-FM - 96.7
Telegraph Hill Phone: (812)265-WORX
PO Box 95 Fax: (812)273-5509
Madison, IN 47250-0095
Free: (800)660-9679

Format: Adult Contemporary; News; Sports. **Networks:** Independent; USA Radio; AP. **Owner:** Dubois County Broadcasting Inc., PO Box 1009, Jasper, IN 47546, (812)683-4144. **Founded:** 1950. **Operating Hours:** 24 hours; 100% local. **Key Personnel:** William C. Potter, Station Mgr.; Scott Davidson, Contact. **Local Programs:** *Monday Night Blues* 8:00 pm - 10:00 pm Monday, Bill Potter, Manager, (812)265-3322. **Wattage:** 3000. **Ad Rates:** $8.25-16 for 30 seconds; $11.25-19 for 60 seconds. Combined advertising rates available with WXGO-AM.

10444 WXGO-AM - 1270
Telegraph Hill Phone: (812)265-WORX
PO Box 95 Free: (800)660-9679
Madison, IN 47250

Format: Oldies; News; Sports. **Networks:** Independent; USA Radio; AP. **Owner:** Dubois County Broadcasting Inc., PO Box 1009, Jasper, IN 47546, (812)683-4144. **Founded:** 1956. **Formerly:** WORX-AM (1995). **Operating Hours:** 24 hours; 100% local. **Key Personnel:** William C. Potter, Station Mgr.; Scott Davidson, Contact. **Wattage:** 1000. **Ad Rates:** $5.25-13 for 30 seconds; $7.25-15 for 60 seconds. Combined advertising rates available with WORX-FM.

MARION†, pop. 35,874.

Grant Co. (NEC). 60 m NE of Indianapolis. Marion College (Wes. Meth.); Taylor University.

10445 Chronicle-Tribune
Gannett Co., Inc.
610 S. Adams Phone: (765)664-5111
Marion, IN 46953 Fax: (765)664-6292
Free: (800)955-7888

General newspaper. **Founded:** 1867. **Freq:** Mon.-Sun. (morn.). **Print Method:** Offset. **Cols./Page:** 6. **Col. Width:** 25 nonpareils. **Col. Depth:** 300 agate lines. **Key Personnel:** Randy Brandt, Managing Editor, cteditor@comteck.com; Vic Hussey, Publisher; Mike Casuscelli, Advertising Mgr. **Subscription Rates:** $194 individuals. **Remarks:** Accepts advertising. Monday-Saturday: GLR: $4.38; BW: $2,236.86; 4C: $408; PCI: $17.34; Sunday: GLR: $4.85; BW: $2,395.85; 4C: $408.
Circ: Mon.-Sat. ★**19,839**
Sun. ★**22,518**

10446 Time Warner Cable
2923 S. Western Ave. Phone: (317)662-0071
Marion, IN 46953-3569

Owner: Time Warner Cable, at above address. **Founded:** 1966. **Formerly:** Marion Cable TV (1992); Cablevision. **Key Personnel:** Cal Blumhorst, General Mgr.; Chuck Yarrington, Chief Engineer; Inge Harte-North, Program Mgr.; Petrea Caldwell, Customer Service Mgr. **Cities Served:** Gas City, Jonesboro, Marion, IN: subscribing households 16,100; 65 channels; 1 community access channel; 30 hours per week community access programming.

10447 WBAT-AM - 1400
120 N. Miller Ave. Phone: (765)664-6239
Box 839 Fax: (765)662-0730
Marion, IN 46952
E-mail: wbat@comteck.com

Format: Oldies. **Networks:** CBS; ESPN Radio. **Founded:** 1947. **Operating Hours:** Continuous. **ADI:** Indianapolis (Marion), IN. **Key Personnel:** Carolyn Bush, Office Mgr.; Jim Brunner, Sales Mgr.; Mark Nicholls, Program Dir.; Randy McPike, News Dir.; David Poehler, General Mgr. **Wattage:** 1000. **Ad Rates:** $19.50-20.25 for 30 seconds; $24-24.75 for 60 seconds. Combined advertising rates available with WCYC-FM.

10448 WCJC-FM - 99.3
120 N. Miller Ave. Phone: (765)664-6239
Box 839 Fax: (765)662-0730
Marion, IN 46952
E-mail: wbat@comteck.com

Format: Contemporary Country. **Networks:** Satellite Radio; ABC. **Founded:** 1989. **Operating Hours:** Continuous. **ADI:**

Indianapolis (Marion), IN. **Key Personnel:** David Poehler, General Mgr.; Jim Brunner, Sales Mgr.; Mark Metzner, Program Dir.; Tim Rush, News Dir.; Carolyn Bush, Office Mgr. **Local Programs:** *Classic Country Jamboree*, Walt Riddle. **Wattage:** 3000. **Ad Rates:** $13-15.75 for 30 seconds; $16.75-19.50 for 60 seconds. Combined advertising rates available with WBAT.

10449 WGOM-AM - 860
820 S. Pennsylvania St. Phone: (317)664-9466
PO Box 1538 Fax: (317)668-6767
Marion, IN 46952
E-mail: wmri@holli.com

Format: Talk; News; Sports. **Networks:** Network Indiana. **Owner:** Bomar Broadcasting, Inc., at above address. **Founded:** 1955. **Operating Hours:** Continuous; 50% network, 50% local. **ADI:** Indianapolis (Marion), IN. **Key Personnel:** Mike Day, President; Rich Coolman, Operations Mgr.; Maria Rocco, News Dir.; Paul Dixon, Chief Engineer. **Wattage:** 1000.

10450 WMRI-FM - 106.9
820 S. Pennsylvania St., Box 1538 Phone: (317)664-7396
Fax: (317)668-6767
Marion, IN 46952
E-mail: wmri@holli.com

Format: Easy Listening. **Simulcasts:** WLEZ-FM; WEZV-FM. **Networks:** ABC; CNN Radio. **Owner:** Bomar Broadcasting Co., at above address. **Founded:** 1948. **Operating Hours:** Continuous. **ADI:** Indianapolis (Marion), IN. **Key Personnel:** Michael Day, President; Rich Coolman, Operations Mgr.; Paul Dixon, Chief Engineer. **Wattage:** 50,000 ERP. **Ad Rates:** WLEZ-FM.

MARTINSVILLE†, pop. 11,311.

Morgan Co. (C). 30 m SW of Indianapolis. Manufactures, electronic equipment, industrial gratings, motorcycle farings, formed packaging, aircraft components; goldfish hatcheries; timber. Grain farms. Wheat, corn, oats, soybeans.

10451 Camping Magazine
American Camping Association
5000 State Rd. 67 N. Phone: (765)342-8456
Martinsville, IN 46151 Fax: (765)342-2065
Free: (800)428-CAMP
Publication E-mail: magazine@aca-camps.org
Publisher E-mail: bookstore@aca-camps.org

Magazine on organized camp management. **Founded:** Feb. 1926. **Freq:** Bimonthly. **Print Method:** Offset. **Trim Size:** 8 1/2 x 10 7/8. **Cols./Page:** 3. **Col. Width:** 13 picas. **Col. Depth:** 9 1/4 inches. **Key Personnel:** Sandy Cameron, Managing Editor, scameron@aca-camps.org; Ruth Lister, Dir. Communications, rlister@aca-camps.org; Bill Willems, Advertising Mgr., bwillems@aca-camps.org. **USPS:** 074-041. **Subscription Rates:** $24.95 individuals; $32.50 institutions inc. Guide to Accredited Camps; $4.50 single issue. **Alt. Formats:** CD-ROM; Microform.
Ad Rates: BW: $1375 **Circ:** Paid ‡6,550
4C: $1970 Non-paid ‡350

10452 Martinsville Daily Reporter
Reporter-Times, Inc.
60 S. Jefferson St. Phone: (765)342-3311
PO Box 1636 Fax: (765)342-1446
Martinsville, IN 46151
Community newspaper and Low Power TV Station. **Founded:** 1889. **Freq:** Mon.-Sat. (eve.). **Print Method:** Offset. **Cols./Page:** 6. **Col. Width:** 13.5 picas. **Col. Depth:** 301 agate lines. **Key Personnel:** Robert S. Kendall, Editor; R.K. Selch, Publisher; Hank Crockett, Circulation Mgr.; Eric Meyer, Station Mgr. **Subscription Rates:** $78 individuals. **URL:** http://www.sc/can.net/reporter/reporter/pages/reporter.html.
Ad Rates: BW: $402.95 **Circ:** Paid 8,293
4C: $65
PCI: $8.75

10453 WCBK-FM - 102.3
PO Box 1577 Phone: (317)342-3394
Martinsville, IN 46151 Fax: (317)342-5020

Format: Country. **Simulcasts:** WMCB-AM. **Networks:** USA Radio. **Founded:** 1968. **Operating Hours:** 4:58 a.m.-12 midnight. **ADI:** Indianapolis (Marion), IN. **Key Personnel:** David Rodgers, General Mgr. **Wattage:** 3000. **URL:** http://www.scican.net/~wcbk/.

10454 White River Cablevision
7847 Waverly Rd. Phone: (317)422-8600
Martinsville, IN 46151 Fax: (317)422-5075

Owner: Leonard Communications Inc., 13780 E. Rice Pl., Aurora, CO 80015, (303)693-0900, Fax: (303)690-4192. **Key Personnel:** James Ran, Manager.

10455 WMCB-AM - 1540
1639 Burton Ln. Phone: (317)342-3394
Martinsville, IN 46151

Format: Country. **Simulcasts:** WCBK-FM. **Networks:** USA Radio. **Founded:** 1967. **Operating Hours:** Sunrise-sunset. **Key Personnel:** David Rodgers, General Mgr. **Wattage:** 500.

MERRILLVILLE, pop. 27,677.

Lake Co. (NW). 10 m S of Gary. Residential.

10456 Griffith News
Herald News Group
3161 E. 84th St. Phone: (219)942-0521
Merrillville, IN 46410 Fax: (219)942-0820

Newspaper. **Founded:** 1940. **Freq:** Weekly (Wed.). **Print Method:** Offset. **Cols./Page:** 6. **Col. Width:** 1 9/16 inches. **Col. Depth:** 16 inches. **Key Personnel:** David Hendrix, Editor; Jim Hillman, Publisher, phone (219)942-0521, fax (219)942-0820. **Subscription Rates:** $3 individuals. **Remarks:** Accepts advertising. **Formerly:** Griffith Shopper.
Ad Rates: BW: $325 **Circ:** Free 9,780
PCI: $3.35

10457 Highland News
Herald News Group
3161 E. 84th St. Phone: (219)942-0521
Merrillville, IN 46410 Fax: (219)942-0820

Newspaper. **Founded:** 1984. **Freq:** Weekly (Wed.). **Print Method:** Offset. **Cols./Page:** 6. **Col. Width:** 1 9/16 inches. **Col. Depth:** 16 inches. **Key Personnel:** David Hendrix, Editor; Jim Hillman, Publisher, phone (219)942-0521, fax (219)942-0820. **Subscription Rates:** $3 individuals. **Remarks:** Accepts advertising. **Formerly:** Highland Shopper.
Ad Rates: BW: $325 **Circ:** Free 9,453
PCI: $3.35

Hobart Gazette - See Hobart

10458 Northwest Indiana Catholic
9292 Broadway Phone: (219)769-9292
Merrillville, IN 46410 Fax: (219)738-9034
Publication E-mail: nwic@dcgary.org

Official newspaper of the Diocese of Gary. **Founded:** 1987. **Freq:** Weekly. **Print Method:** Offset. **Cols./Page:** 6. **Col. Width:** 1 1/2 inches. **Col. Depth:** 224 agate lines. **Key Personnel:** Brian T. Olszewski, Editor, bolszews@dcgary.org; Most Rev. Dale J. Melczek, Publisher; Carol Macinga, Circulation Mgr. **USPS:** 403-670. **Subscription Rates:** $18 individuals. **Remarks:** Accepts advertising. **Alt. Formats:** Audio tape; Large-print.
Ad Rates: BW: $800 **Circ:** Paid ‡20,200
4C: $1,200
PCI: $9.75

10459 Portage Journal-Press
Herald News Group
3161 E. 84th St. Phone: (219)942-0521
Merrillville, IN 46410 Fax: (219)942-0820

Community newspaper (tabloid). **Founded:** 1970. **Freq:** Weekly (Thurs.). **Print Method:** Offset. **Trim Size:** 10 1/4 x 16. **Cols./Page:** 6. **Col. Width:** 1 9/16 inches. **Col. Depth:** 16 inches. **Key Personnel:** Jim Masters, Editor; Rory Holscher, Advertising Mgr.; Dave Trewin, Publisher; Don Caldwell, Editor. **ISSN:** 0746-8776. **Subscription Rates:** $16 county; $16 other. **Remarks:** Accepts advertising.
Ad Rates: GLR: $.20 **Circ:** ‡8,200
BW: $335
4C: $450
PCI: $5.25

Schererville News - See Schererville

10460 TCI Lake Area Cable
6161 Cleveland St. Phone: (219)887-6008
Merrillville, IN 46410 Fax: (219)887-3070

Founded: 1981. **Formerly:** U.S. Cable of Northern Indiana. **Key Personnel:** Jackie Swike, News Dir., phone (219)887-3031, fax (219)887-3070; Chris Chiappetta, Sports Dir., phone (219)887-3031, fax (219)887-3070; Mike Zimmer, General Mgr. **Cities Served:** Lake County, Porter County, IN: subscribing households 90,000; 62 channels; 2 community access channels.

10461 WYIN-TV - 56
8625 Indiana Pl. Phone: (219)736-5656
Merrillville, IN 46410 Fax: (219)755-4312
Free: (800)276-5656

Format: Public TV. **Networks:** Public Broadcasting Service (PBS). **Founded:** 1987. **Operating Hours:** 7:00 a.m.-12 a.m. **ADI:** Chicago (LaSalle), IL. **Wattage:** 1,350,000. **Ad Rates:** Noncommercial.

10462 WZVN-FM - 107.1
8105 Georgia St. Phone: (219)738-1071
Merrillville, IN 46410-6224 Fax: (219)736-6411

Format: Adult Contemporary; News. **Networks:** Satellite Music Network. **Owner:** M&M Broadcasting, 6405 Olcott, Hammond, IN 46323. **Founded:** 1972. **Formerly:** WLCL-FM (1981). **Operating Hours:** Continuous. **ADI:** Chicago (LaSalle), IL. **Key Personnel:** Marty Wielgos, VP. & General Mgr., phone (219)844-1230, fax (219)844-6190; Cheryl Varga, General Sales Mgr. **Wattage:** 3000. **Ad Rates:** $30-35 for 30 seconds; $38-43 for 60 seconds. **URL:** www.calunet.com/biz/wzvw.

MICHIGAN CITY, pop. 36,850.

La Porte Co. (NW). On Lake Michigan, 50 m SE of Chicago, Ill. Beach resort. Fisheries. Indiana State Prison. Lake commerce.

10463 The Beacher
911 Franklin St. Phone: (219)879-0088
Michigan City, IN 46360 Fax: (219)879-8070
Publication E-mail: beacher@adnet.com

Newspaper covering news and events in southwestern Michigan and northern Indiana. **URL:** http://www.adsnet.com/beacher.

10464 WEFM-FM - 95.9
1903 Springland Ave. Phone: (219)879-8201
Michigan City, IN 46360 Fax: (219)879-8202

Format: Adult Contemporary; Oldies. **Networks:** Network Indiana. **Founded:** 1966. **Formerly:** WMCB-FM (1982). **Operating Hours:** Continuous; 2% network, 98% local. **Key Personnel:** Bob Thomas Burns, General Mgr.; Ronald M. Miller, Station Mgr. **Local Programs:** *Community Focus* 8:10 a.m.-8:30 a.m. Monday-Friday, Ron Miller. **Wattage:** 3000. **Ad Rates:** Advertising accepted; rates available upon request.

10465 WIMS-AM - 1420
685 E. County Rd., 1675 N. Phone: (219)874-9467
Michigan City, IN 46360 Fax: (219)874-2464

Format: Full Service; Talk; Sports. **Networks:** Mutual Broadcasting System. **Founded:** 1947. **Operating Hours:** Continuous. **ADI:** South Bend-Elkhart, IN. **Key Personnel:** Marty Wielgos, VP/Gen. Mgr.; Cheryl Vargan, General Sales Mgr.; Elizabeth Sobkowiak, Office Mgr.; Mike Bonoventura, Program Dir. **Local Programs:** *At Your Service*, Tod Allen; *Public Forum*, Tod Allen; *Sunday News Magazine*, Kraig Hayden. **Wattage:** 5000. **Ad Rates:** $9-20 for 30 seconds; $10-25 for 60 seconds.

MIDDLEBURY, pop. 1,665.

Elkhart Co. (N). 12 m E of Elkart.

10466 Middlebury Independent
Largrange Publishing Co., Inc.
PO Box 68 Phone: (219)825-9112
Middlebury, IN 46540 Fax: (219)463-2734

Newspaper with a Democratic orientation. **Founded:** 1887. **Freq:** Weekly (Wed.). **Print Method:** Offset. **Cols./Page:** 6. **Col. Width:** 19 nonpareils. **Col. Depth:** 203 agate lines. **Key Personnel:** William F. Connelly, Editor and Publisher; Lu Martin, Advertising Mgr. **Subscription Rates:** $8.50 individuals.
Ad Rates: GLR: $.20 **Circ:** 780
SAU: $2.35
PCI: $2.25

MIDDLETOWN, pop. 2,978.

Henry Co. (E). 10 m SE of Anderson. Manufactures tools, gauges, dies, plastics; wool mills. Stock, grain, truck farms. Corn, wheat, tomatoes.

10467 Middletown News
469 E. Locust Phone: (765)354-2221
PO Box 96 Fax: (765)354-2221
Middletown, IN 47356
Newspaper (tabloid) with a Republican orientation. **Founded:** 1885. **Freq:** Weekly (Thurs.). **Print Method:** Offset. **Trim Size:** 11 x 15. **Cols./Page:** 5. **Col. Width:** 1 7/8 inches. **Col. Depth:** 14 inches. **Key Personnel:** Cheryl L. Hines, Editor; Jack N. White, Publisher. **Subscription Rates:** $18.75 out of state. **Remarks:** Accepts advertising.
Ad Rates: GLR: $0.35 **Circ:** ‡1,787
BW: $341.60
SAU: $5.25

MILFORD, pop. 1,153.

Kosciusko Co. (N). 13 m S of Goshen. Lake resort.–Manufactures trailers, feedbins, poultry equipment. Diversified farming. Corn, wheat, oats.

10468 The Mail-Journal
The Papers, Inc.
206 S. Main St. Phone: (219)658-4111
PO Box 188 Fax: (219)658-4701
Milford, IN 46542-0188
Free: (800)733-4111

Community newspaper with a Democratic orientation. **Founded:** 1888. **Freq:** Weekly (Wed.). **Print Method:** Offset. **Trim Size:** 15 x 22 3/4. **Cols./Page:** 7. **Col. Width:** 11 picas. **Col. Depth:** 21 1/2 inches. **Key Personnel:** Jeri Seely, Editor; Della Baumgartner, Publisher; Kip Schumm, Advertising Mgr.; Ron Baumgartner, General Mgr. & President. **USPS:** 325-840. **Subscription Rates:** $26 individuals; $31 out of county.
Ad Rates: BW: $615 **Circ:** Paid 3,800
4C: $922.50 Free 40
PCI: $4.90

10469 Senior Life (Allen County Edition)
The Papers, Inc.
206 S. Main St. Phone: (219)658-4111
PO Box 188 Fax: (219)658-4701
Milford, IN 46542-0188
Free: (800)733-4111

News magazine serving adults 50 and older in Fort Wayne and surrounding communities. **Founded:** 1988. **Freq:** Monthly. **Print Method:** Offset. **Trim Size:** 11 3/8 x 16 3/4. **Cols./Page:** 5. **Col. Width:** 11 picas. **Col. Depth:** 16 inches. **Key Personnel:** Jeri Seely, Editor; Della Baumgartner, Publisher; Jane Means, Advertising Mgr.; Ron Baumgartner, President and General Manager. **Subscription Rates:** $12 individuals; $20.50 two years. **Remarks:** Accepts advertising.
Ad Rates: BW: $1,040 **Circ:** Paid 224
4C: $1,280.00 Free 27,950
PCI: $16.70

10470 Senior Life (Elko Edition)
The Papers, Inc.
206 S. Main St. Phone: (219)658-4111
PO Box 188 Fax: (219)658-4701
Milford, IN 46542-0188
Free: (800)733-4111

Newsmagazine serving adults 50 and older in Elkhart, Kosciusko, Noble and Lagrange Counties. **Founded:** 1988. **Freq:** Monthly. **Print Method:** Offset. **Trim Size:** 11 3/8 x 16 3/4. **Cols./Page:** 5. **Col. Width:** 11 picas. **Col. Depth:** 16 inches. **Key Personnel:** Jeri Seely, Editor; Della Baumgartner, Publisher; Jane Means, Advertising Mgr.; Ron Baumgartner, President/General Manager. **Subscription Rates:** $12; $20.50 two years.
Ad Rates: BW: $632 **Circ:** Paid 11
4C: $872 Free 16,800
PCI: $12.45

10471 Senior Life (Northwest Edition)
The Papers, Inc.
206 S. Main St. Phone: (219)658-4111
PO Box 188 Fax: (219)658-4701
Milford, IN 46542-0188
Free: (800)733-4111

Newsmagazine serving adults 50 and older throughout Lake County, IN. **Freq:** Monthly. **Print Method:** Offset. **Trim Size:** 11 3/8 x 16 3/4. **Cols./Page:** 5. **Col. Width:** 11 picas. **Col. Depth:** 16 inches. **Key Personnel:** Jeri Seely, Editor; Della Baumgartner, Publisher; Jane Means, Advertising Mgr.; Ron Baumgartner, President and Gen. Mgr. **Subscription Rates:** $12 individuals; $20.50 two years. **Remarks:** Accepts advertising. **Formerly:** Senior Life (Saint Joseph County Edition).
Ad Rates: BW: $1,040 **Circ:** Free 28,100
4C: $1,280
PCI: $16.70

MISHAWAKA, pop. 40,224.

St. Joseph Co. (N). On St. Joseph River, at head of navigation adjacent to South Bend. Manufactures guided missiles, rubberized canvas, woolen and leather footwear, foam rubber cushions and mattresses, raincoats, foundry supplies, military vehicles, and equipment, concrete sewer and drain pipes.

10472 TCI of Michiana
815 W. Edison Rd. Phone: (219)259-8015
Mishawaka, IN 46545 Fax: (219)255-2423
Free: (800)968-5100

Owner: Tele-Communications, Inc., 5619 DTC Parkway, Englewood, CO 80111, (303)267-5500, Fax: (303)779-1228. **Founded:** 1968. **Formerly:** Valley Cable (1976); Indiana Cablevision (1983); Heritage Cablevision (1991). **Key Personnel:** Jim Peterson, General Mgr.; Tom White, Plant Mgr.; Karl Smith, Customer Serv. Mgr. **Cities Served:** Elkhart, Goshen, Mishawaka, Osceola, Plymouth, Rochester, South Bend, IN; Edwardsburg, MI: subscribing households 80,000; 42 channels; 1 community access channel; 39 hours per week community access programming.

10473 WBYT-FM - 100.7
1 Edison Ctr., Ste. 200 Phone: (219)258-5483
237 Edison Rd. Fax: (219)258-0930
Mishawaka, IN 46545

Format: Country. **Networks:** ABC. **Owner:** Pathfinders Communication Corp., at above address. **Founded:** 1947. **Formerly:** WYEZ-FM (1991); WLTA-FM (1996). **Operating Hours:** Continuous. **ADI:** South Bend-Elkhart, IN. **Key Personnel:** John Dille III, President; Steve Kline, General Mgr.; Gene Walker, Operations Dir. **Wattage:** 50,000 ERP.

10474 WRBR-FM - 103.9
237 W. Edison Rd., Ste.200 Phone: (219)258-5483
Mishawaka, IN 46545 Fax: (219)258-0930
E-mail: wrbr@wrbr.com

Format: Classic Rock. **Networks:** Independent. **Founded:** 1964. **Formerly:** WZZP-FM. **Operating Hours:** Continuous; 100% local. **Key Personnel:** Joe Turner, P.D.; Steve Kline, General Mgr. **Wattage:** 3000. **Ad Rates:** $40-52 per unit.

MITCHELL, pop. 4,641.

Lawrence Co. (S). 10 m S of Bedford. Brass, cement, bus body, precision tools; fruit processing and gypsum processing plants. Limestone quarries. Diversified farming. Apples, peaches, corn, wheat.

10475 The Mitchell Tribune
Box 378 Phone: (812)849-2075
Mitchell, IN 47446 Fax: (812)849-2911

Newspaper with a Republican orientation. **Founded:** 1898. **Freq:** Weekly (Wed.). **Print Method:** Offset. **Trim Size:** 6 x 21. **Cols./Page:** 6. **Col. Width:** 24 nonpareils. **Col. Depth:** 287 agate lines. **Key Personnel:** Norman and Becky Grissom, Publisher. **Subscription Rates:** $12 individuals; $14 out of area; $19 out of state. **Remarks:** Accepts advertising.
Ad Rates: GLR: $.12 **Circ:** Paid ‡3,000
BW: $252
SAU: $2.40
PCI: $2.40

MONON

10476 The Monon News
The News & Review
PO Box 98 Phone: (219)253-6234
Monon, IN 47959 Fax: (219)253-6234

Local newspaper. **Founded:** 1888. **Freq:** Weekly (Wed.). **Print Method:** Offset. **Trim Size:** 11 1/2 x 13. **Cols./Page:** 5. **Col. Width:** 11 1/2 centimeters. **Col. Depth:** 12 1/2 inches. **Key Personnel:** Pam Hughes, Publisher; Michael Allton, Editor. **ISSN:** 0704-2846. **Subscription Rates:** $20 individuals; $25 out of state. **Remarks:** Color advertising not accepted.
Ad Rates: GLR: $.20 **Circ:** Paid ‡1,740
BW: $235 Free ‡10
PCI: $4

MONTICELLO†, pop. 5,162.

White Co. (EC). 25 m NNE of Lafayette. Resort.

10477 Monticello Herald Journal
114 S. Main St. Phone: (219)583-5121
PO Box 409 Fax: (219)583-4241
Monticello, IN 47960-2328
Local newspaper. **Founded:** Feb. 14, 1862. **Freq:** Mon.-Sat. (morn.). **Print Method:** Offset. **Trim Size:** 13 x 21 1/2. **Cols./Page:** 6. **Col. Width:** 2 1/16 inches. **Col. Depth:** 21 1/2 inches. **Key Personnel:** David R. Maroney, Editor; Roger J. Huntzinger, Publisher; Don L. Hurd, Advertising Mgr. **Subscription Rates:** $60 individuals. **Remarks:** Accepts advertising.
Ad Rates: SAU: $5.05 **Circ:** (Not Reported)

10478 WNJY-FM - 102.9
PO Box 500 Phone: (317)564-2569
Monticello, IN 47960 Fax: (219)583-8363
Free: (888)367-9659
E-mail: oldies103@broadcast.net

Format: Oldies. **Networks:** Mutual Broadcasting System; Tribune Radio. **Owner:** LChance Inc. -LMA, PO Box 500, Monticello, IN 47960, (219)583-2569. **Founded:** 1984. **Operating Hours:** Continuous; 80% network, 20% local. **Key Personnel:** William M. Deibel, Contact; Mel Monnett, Contact; Rich Anthony, Operations Mgr. **Local Programs:** *Locker Room.* **Wattage:** 6,000. **Ad Rates:** $6.75-8.80 for 15 seconds; $7.10-12.70 for 30 seconds; $10.40-17.70 for 60 seconds. **URL:** http://www.wnjyoldies103.com.

MONTPELIER, pop. 1,995.

Blackford Co. (NE). 40 m S of Fort Wayne. Manufactures corrugated boxes and crates, lock nuts, rubber fittings, plastic drain tile, boxes, gloves. Stone quarries. Agriculture.

10479 The Montpelier Herald
Laymon Publishing Corp.
107 E. High St. Phone: (765)728-5322
Montpelier, IN 47359
Community newspaper. **Founded:** 1891. **Freq:** Weekly (Thurs.). **Print Method:** Letterpress. Uses mats. **Cols./Page:** 5. **Col. Width:** 2 inches. **Col. Depth:** 16 inches. **Key Personnel:** Thomas L. Laymon, Editor and Publisher. **USPS:** 361-740. **Subscription Rates:** $12 in county; $18 other countries. **Remarks:** Accepts advertising.
Ad Rates: GLR: $.42 **Circ:** Paid 414
SAU: $5.88 Free 6
PCI: $5.88

MOORESVILLE, pop. 5,349.

Morgan Co. (C). 15 m SW of Indianapolis. Manufactures face brick, paints, gravel and sand, paints, cement blocks, testing machines; machine shops. Grain, dairy, fruit farms. Corn, wheat, hay.

10480 The Times
Reporter-Times, Inc.
PO Box 308 Phone: (317)831-0280
Mooresville, IN 46158 Fax: (317)831-7068

Community newspaper with a Democratic orientation. **Founded:** 1869. **Freq:** Weekly (Wed.). **Print Method:** Offset. **Trim Size:** 13 x 21. **Cols./Page:** 6. **Col. Width:** 27 nonpareils. **Col. Depth:** 301 agate lines. **Key Personnel:** Scott Daravanla, Editor; Scott Schurz, Publisher, phone (812)331-4250, shurz@heraldt.com. **USPS:** 362-360. **Subscription Rates:** $20 individuals; $25 out of area senior citizens. **Remarks:** Accepts advertising.
Ad Rates: BW: $922.35 **Circ:** Paid ⊕**7,635**
4C: $1,092.35
SAU: $9.66
PCI: $7.80

MOROCCO, pop. 1,348.

Newton Co. (NW). 45 m N of Lafayette. Electronics factory; elevators. Grain stock farms. Corn, oats, wheat, soybeans.

10481 Morocco Courier
PO Box 138 Phone: (219)866-5111
Morocco, IN 47963 Fax: (219)866-3775

Local newspaper. **Founded:** 1877. **Freq:** Weekly (Tues.). **Print Method:** Offset. **Trim Size:** 14 x 22 3/4. **Cols./Page:** 6. **Col. Width:** 2 picas. **Col. Depth:** 21 inches. **Key Personnel:** William Kaye, Editor; Douglas Caldwell, Publisher; Sally Snow, Advertising Dir. **Subscription Rates:** $26. **Remarks:** Accepts advertising.
Ad Rates: PCI: $2.95 **Circ:** Paid ‡1,455
Free ‡23

MOUNT VERNON†, pop. 7,656.

Posey Co. (SW). On Ohio River, 20 m W of Evansville. Manufactures polycarbonates, hospital & industrial gases, roofing products, handles, flour, machinery, corn products, petroleum terminal and refinery. Agriculture. wheat, corn, hay.

10482 Democrat
News Publishing Co.
PO Box 767 Phone: (812)838-4811
Mount Vernon, IN 47620 Fax: (812)838-3696

Newspaper with a Democratic orientation. **Founded:** 1867. **Freq:** Weekly (Wed.). **Print Method:** Offset. **Cols./Page:** 6. **Col. Width:** 24 nonpareils. **Col. Depth:** 287 agate lines. **Key Personnel:** Tim A. Rutherford, Editor and Publisher. **Subscription Rates:** $19.95 individuals. **Remarks:** Accepts advertising.
Ad Rates: PCI: $5.02 **Circ:** Paid 3,746
Free 285

10483 WPCO-AM - 1590
601 Upton Rd. Phone: (812)838-4484
Mount Vernon, IN 47620 Fax: (812)838-6434

Format: Middle-of-the-Road (MOR). **Networks:** ABC; Sun Radio. **Owner:** Posey County Broadcasting, at above address. **Founded:** 1955. **Operating Hours:** Continuous; 55% network, 45% local. **ADI:** Evansville, IN (Madisonville, KY).

Key Personnel: Ann Nussel, General Mgr.; Dick Grogg, Station Mgr.; Darrin Smith, News Dir.; Mike Warren, Sports Dir. **Wattage:** 500. **Ad Rates:** $3.50-10 for 30 seconds; $4.50-12 for 60 seconds.

MUNCIE†, pop. 77,216.

Delaware Co. (NE). On White River, 54 m NE of Indianapolis. Ball State University. Manufactures auto parts and accessories, fencing, bottles, malleable castings, auto batteries, wire structural steel, electrical goods, lawn mowers, metal furniture, screw machine, industrial transformer products, auto transmissions, jet engine parts.

10484 The Advertiser
125 S. High St. Phone: (317)284-2528
Muncie, IN 47305-2811 Fax: (765)747-5727

Shopper. **Founded:** May 1980. **Freq:** Weekly Saturday. **Trim Size:** 13 x 21 1/2. **Cols./Page:** 6. **Col. Width:** 2 inches. **Col. Depth:** 21 1/2 inches. **Subscription Rates:** Free. **Remarks:** Accepts advertising.
Ad Rates: BW: $1,709.40 **Circ:** Controlled 48,200
4C: $1,829.40

10485 Ball State Daily News
Ball State University Daily News
2000 W. University Ave. Phone: (765)285-8218
Muncie, IN 47306 Fax: (765)285-8248

Collegiate newspaper. **Founded:** Mar. 30, 1922. **Freq:** Daily (morn.). **Print Method:** Offset. **Trim Size:** 13 x 21 1/2. **Cols./Page:** 6. **Col. Width:** 25 nonpareils. **Col. Depth:** 301 agate lines. **Key Personnel:** Brenda Burke, Advertising Dir., phone (765)285-8256. **USPS:** 144-360. **Subscription Rates:** $30 individuals. **Remarks:** Accepts advertising. **URL:** htttp://www.dailynews.bsu.edu.
Ad Rates: SAU: $8.50 **Circ:** 14,000
PCI: $8.50

10486 Indiana Musicator
Indiana Music Educators Association
Ball State University Phone: (765)285-5496
School of Music Fax: (765)285-1139
Muncie, IN 47306
Publisher E-mail: IND2MEA@aol.com

Professional journal covering music education. **Founded:** 1946. **Freq:** Quarterly. **Print Method:** Offset. **Trim Size:** 8 1/2 x 11. **Cols./Page:** 2. **Col. Width:** 2 1/4 inches. **Col. Depth:** 9 1/2 inches. **Key Personnel:** JoDea Marshall, Editor/Advertising Mgr. **ISSN:** 0273-9933. **Subscription Rates:** $20 individuals. **Remarks:** Accepts advertising.
Ad Rates: BW: $250 **Circ:** Paid 2,000
4C: $425
PCI: $25

10487 Mid-American Journal of Business
Bureau of Business Research
Ball State University Phone: (765)285-5926
Muncie, IN 47306 Fax: (317)285-8024

Journal informing business professionals about recent research developments and their practical implications. **Founded:** 1985. **Freq:** Semiannual. **Print Method:** 8 1/2 x 11. **Trim Size:** 3 3/8. **Cols./Page:** 2. **Col. Width:** 3 3/8 inches. **Col. Depth:** 9 1/8 inches. **Key Personnel:** Dr. W. Rocky Newman, Editor, phone (513)529-4219, fax (513)529-6992, newmanw@muohio.edu; Judy A. Lane, Managing Editor, jlane@bsu.edu. **ISSN:** 0895-1772. **Subscription Rates:** $12 U.S., Canada, and Mexico; $17 other countries. **Remarks:** Accepts advertising. **Online:** ANBAR.
Ad Rates: BW: $250 **Circ:** Paid 400
Non-paid 1,400

10488 The Star Press
Muncie Newspapers
PO Box 2408 Phone: (765)747-5700
Muncie, IN 47307-0408 Fax: (765)747-5727
Free: (800)783-7827
Publication E-mail: news@thestarpress.com

General newspaper. **Founded:** 1899. **Freq:** Mon.-Sun. (morn.). **Print Method:** Letterpress. **Cols./Page:** 6. **Col. Width:** 2 1/16 inches. **Col. Depth:** 22 inches. **Key Personnel:** Henry Bird, Publisher, phone (765)747-5749; Larry Lough, Editor, phone (765)747-5750, fax (765)747-5748, llough@thestarpress.com. **Subscription Rates:** $130 individuals. **Remarks:** Accepts advertising. **URL:** http://www.thestarpress.com. **Formerly:** The Muncie Star; The Muncie Evening Press.
Ad Rates: BW: $2,772 **Circ:** Mon.-Sat. 36,454
4C: $3,122 Sun. 40,310
SAU: $21

10489 The Teacher Educator
Ball State University
Teachers College 1008 Phone: (765)285-5453
Muncie, IN 47306 Fax: (765)285-5455
Publisher E-mail: lsiler@bsu.edu

Scholarly journal covering education of teachers and related issues. **Freq:** Quarterly. **Key Personnel:** David Feldman, Editor; Phyllis Gordon, Editor. **ISSN:** 0887-8730. **Subscription Rates:** $20 individuals; $25 institutions; $30 elsewhere; $40 two years US/individual; $50 two years US/institutional; $60 two years elsewhere. **Remarks:** Advertising not accepted.
Circ: Combined 740

10490 WBST-FM - 92.1
Ball State University Phone: (317)285-5888
BC 204 Fax: (317)285-1516
Muncie, IN 47306

Format: Public Radio; News; Classical. **Networks:** National Public Radio (NPR). **Owner:** Ball State University, at above address. **Founded:** 1960. **Operating Hours:** Continuous; 40% network, 60% local. **Key Personnel:** Stewart Vanderwilt, Contact; Steven Turpin, Program Mgr. **Wattage:** 3000. **Ad Rates:** Noncommercial.

10491 WCRD-AM - 540
Ball State University Phone: (317)285-1467
BC 132 Fax: (317)285-9278
Muncie, IN 47306

Format: Eclectic. **Founded:** Mar. 13, 1988. **Operating Hours:** Mon.-Fri., 3:00 pm-8:00 am; Sat.-Sun., Continuous. **Key Personnel:** David Riley, General Mgr., 00dcriley@bsu.edu; Sam Andrzejewski, Program Dir., samanthony@hotmail.com; Paul Briggs, Promotions Dir., godrawk@hotmail.com; Brian Lock, Sales Mgr., 00balock@bsu.edu; Jennie Jones, Music Dir., hystericalbender@yahoo.com. **Wattage:** 250.

10492 WERK-AM - 990
8510 S. State Rd. 3 Phone: (765)289-9375
Muncie, IN 47302-8710 Fax: (765)286-3493
Free: (888)289-9375
E-mail: wade@netusa1.net

Simulcasts: WERK-FM. **Networks:** Independent. **Owner:** Dream Weaver Broadcasting, Inc., PO Box 17, Elwood, IN 46036, (765)552-1017, Fax: (765)552-0506, Free: (800)456-5203. **Founded:** 1965. **Operating Hours:** 6 a.m. - 7 p.m. 100% local. **Key Personnel:** Walter Weaver, Contact; Phil Dashler, News Dir.; Mandy Adams, Business Mgr. **Ad Rates:** Combined advertising rates available with WLHN. **URL:** http://www.werkfm.com.

10493 WERK-FM - 104.9
8510 S. State Rd. 3 Phone: (765)289-9375
Muncie, IN 47302-8787 Fax: (765)286-3493
Free: (888)289-9375

Format: Oldies. **Networks:** Jones Satellite. **Founded:** 1986. **Formerly:** WOKZ-FM (1991). **Operating Hours:** Continuous; 100% local. **Key Personnel:** Wade Weaver, President; Walter Weaver, General Mgr.; Mandy Adams, Business Mgr.; Phil Dashler, News Dir. **Wattage:** 6000. **Ad Rates:** $8-18 for 30 seconds; $10-20 for 60 seconds. Combined advertising rates available with WLHN. **URL:** http://www.werkfm.com.

10494 WIPB-TV - 49
Edmund F. Ball Bldg. Phone: (765)285-1249
Ball State University Fax: (765)285-5548
Muncie, IN 47306
Free: (800)252-9472

Format: Public TV. **Networks:** Public Broadcasting Service (PBS). **Owner:** Ball State University, at above address, Muncie, IN 47306. **Founded:** 1971. **Operating Hours:** Continuous. **ADI:** Indianapolis (Marion), IN. **Key Personnel:** Robert R. Smith, Station Mgr., bsmith@teleplex.bsu.edu; Jerry Cole, Production Mgr., jcole@teleplex.bsu.edu; James E. Miller, Chief Engineer, jmiller@teleplex.bsu.edu; Alice Cheney, General Mgr., acheney@teleplex.bsu.edu; Thomas R. Beatty, Program Dir., tbeatty@teleplex.bsu.edu; Lori George, Promotions/Mktg., lgeorgi@tlelplex.bsu.edu. **Local Programs:** *Ball State Basketball*; *Country Hit Videos*; *Elmer & Friends*, Robert R. Smith. **Wattage:** 678 kw.

10495 WLBC-FM - 104.1
800 E. 29th St. Phone: (317)288-4403
Muncie, IN 47302 Fax: (317)288-0429
E-mail: info@wlbc.com

Format: Adult Contemporary. **Networks:** ABC. **Owner:** Sabre Communications Inc., at above address. **Founded:** 1947. **Formerly:** DRMS Communications, Inc. **Operating Hours:** Continuous. **ADI:** Indianapolis (Marion), IN. **Key Personnel:** Jeff Weller, General Mgr., generalmanager@wlbc.com; Steve Lindell, Program Dir., programdirector@wlbc.com; Elaine Meritt, Sales Mgr., sales@wlbc.com; Tom Hammond, News Dir., news@wlbc.com. **Local Programs:** *WLBC Morning Show*, Steve Lindell. **Wattage:** 50,000. **Ad Rates:** $21 for 30 seconds; $26 for 60 seconds.

10496 WWWO-FM - 93.5
5216 Bradburn Dr. Phone: (765)289-9500
Muncie, IN 47304 Fax: (765)289-9640
E-mail: wwwo@iquest.net

Format: Classic Rock. **Networks:** Westwood One Radio. **Owner:** Viking Communications Inc., at above address. **Founded:** 1965. **Formerly:** WWHC-FM (1985). **Operating Hours:** Continuous; 10% network, 90% local. **ADI:** Indianapolis (Marion), IN. **Key Personnel:** Judy Kvale, Pres./General Mgr.; Sean Mattlingly, Operations Mgr.; Rick Stephens, Sales Mgr. **Wattage:** 6000. **Ad Rates:** $13-34 for 30 seconds; $17-40 for 60 seconds. **URL:** http://www.wwwo.com.

10497 WXFN-AM - 1340
800 E. 29th St. Phone: (317)288-4403
Muncie, IN 47302 Fax: (317)288-0429
E-mail: wxfn@ecicnet.org

Format: Sports. **Networks:** ABC. **Owner:** DRMS Communications, Inc., at above address. **Founded:** 1926. **Formerly:** WLBC-AM. **Operating Hours:** Continuous. **ADI:** Indianapolis (Marion), IN. **Key Personnel:** Jeff Weller, General Mgr.; Steve Lindell, Program Dir.; Elaine Meritt, Sales Mgr.; Deborah Ross, News Dir.; Dave Preston, Morning Host. **Local Programs:** *WXFN Morning Sports Rush*, Dave Preston. **Wattage:** 1000. **Ad Rates:** $16 for 30 seconds; $21 for 60 seconds.

MUNSTER

The Times - See Hammond

NAPPANEE, pop. 4,694.

Elkhart & Kosciusko Co. (N). 19 m S of Elkhart. Manufactures electric automobile harnesses. Mobile homes, kitchen cabinets, recreational vehicles, sectional housing. Agriculture. Corn, soybeans oats, wheat.

10498 Farm and Home News
The Pilot Co., Inc.
158 W. Market St. Phone: (219)773-3127
PO Box 230 Fax: (219)936-3844
Nappanee, IN 46550
Shopper. **Founded:** 1954. **Freq:** Weekly (Wed.). **Print Method:** Offset. **Trim Size:** 18 x 22 1/2. **Cols./Page:** 6. **Col. Width:** 24 nonpareils. **Col. Depth:** 301 agate lines. **Key Personnel:** Barbara Keiser, Editor; Keith Isley, Advertising Mgr. **Subscription Rates:** Free; $5 by mail. **Remarks:** Accepts advertising.
Ad Rates: BW: $554.70 **Circ:** Free 18,500
4C: $894.70
SAU: $4.84

10499 Nappanee Advance-News
The Pilot Co., Inc.
158 W. Market St. Phone: (219)773-3127
PO Box 230 Fax: (219)936-3844
Nappanee, IN 46550
Local newspaper. **Founded:** 1879. **Freq:** Weekly (Wed.). **Print Method:** Offset. **Trim Size:** 18 x 22 1/2. **Cols./Page:** 6. **Col. Width:** 24 nonpareils. **Col. Depth:** 301 agate lines. **Key Personnel:** Barbara Keiser, Editor; Keith Isley, Advertising Mgr. **Subscription Rates:** $18 individuals; $25 out of area. **Remarks:** Accepts advertising.
Ad Rates: GLR: $.25 **Circ:** Paid 2,750
BW: $361.20 Free 150
4C: $561.20
SAU: $3.35

NASHVILLE†, pop. 705.

Brown Co. (SC). 40 m S of Indianapolis. Tourist center. Hardwood timber. Diversified farming. Apples, peaches, stock.

10500 Brown County Democrat
Heartland Communications, Inc.
136 N. Van Buren St. Phone: (812)988-2221
PO Box 277 Fax: (812)988-1570
Nashville, IN 47448-0277
Community newspaper. **Founded:** 1870. **Freq:** Weekly (Wed.). **Print Method:** Offset. **Trim Size:** 13 x 21. **Cols./Page:** 6. **Col. Width:** 2 1/16 inches. **Col. Depth:** 21 inches. **Key Personnel:** Mike Lewis, Editor; Bruce Gregory Temple, Publisher; Keith Fleener, Advertising Mgr. **USPS:** 067-640. **Subscription Rates:** $24 individuals; $34 out of country. **Remarks:** Accepts advertising.
Ad Rates: BW: $396 **Circ:** ‡4,406
4C: $496
SAU: $3.95

NEW ALBANY†, pop. 38,402.

Floyd Co. (S). On Ohio River, 7 m NW of downtown Louisville,

Ky., connected by bridge. Cultural centers. Manufactures apparel, food, lumber and plywood, veneer, chemicals, leather goods, electronic components, concrete products and award plaques.

10501 Pizza Today
ProTech Publishing and Communications, Inc.
137 E. Market St. Phone: (812)949-0909
New Albany, IN 47150 Fax: (812)941-9711

Pizza industry magazine published by the National Association of Pizza Operators. **Founded:** 1983. **Freq:** Monthly. **Print Method:** Offset. **Trim Size:** 8 1/8 x 10 7/8. **Cols./Page:** 3. **Col. Width:** 27 nonpareils. **Col. Depth:** 126 agate lines. **Key Personnel:** Gerry Durnell, Editor and Publisher. **ISSN:** 0743-3115. **Subscription Rates:** $24 individuals. **Remarks:** Accepts advertising.
Ad Rates: GLR: $244 **Circ:** Non-paid 42,912
BW: $4,795 Paid 7,026
4C: $6,190
PCI: $119.95

10502 The Tribune
The Albany Tribune
PO Box 997 Phone: (812)944-6481
New Albany, IN 47150 Fax: (812)949-6585

General newspaper. **Founded:** 1851. **Freq:** Weekly (Sun.). **Print Method:** Offset. **Cols./Page:** 6. **Col. Width:** 25 nonpareils. **Col. Depth:** 294 agate lines. **Key Personnel:** Marilyn Young, Editor; Greg Oxley, Publisher; Margarette Chasteen, Advertising Dir. **Subscription Rates:** $82 individuals. **Remarks:** Accepts advertising.
Ad Rates: SAU: $8.61 **Circ:** Mon.-Fri. 11,919

10503 Marcus Cable
3306 Plaza Dr., Ste. 150 Phone: (812)944-0430
New Albany, IN 47150 Fax: (812)948-7854
Free: (800)932-7388

Formerly: Cardinal Communications. **Key Personnel:** Mike Pattison, Manager. **Cities Served:** New Albany, IN.

10504 WXLM-FM - 105.7
PO Box 655
New Albany, IN 47151

Format: Contemporary Christian. **Networks:** USA Radio. **Owner:** Cross Country Communications, Inc., at above address. **Founded:** 1988. **Formerly:** WKXF-FM (1992); WXLN-FM. **Operating Hours:** Continuous; 100% local. **ADI:** Louisville, KY. **Key Personnel:** George Zarris, President; Olympus Zarris, Sales Mgr.; Don Schmitt, Production Dir. **Local Programs:** *Cross Country Crossfire*, George Zarris; *Professional Forum*, Richard Johnson. **Wattage:** 3000. **Ad Rates:** $20-40 for 60 seconds.

10505 WXLN-AM - 1570
PO Box 655 Phone: (812)941-1570
New Albany, IN 47151 Fax: (812)944-7782

Format: Southern Gospel. **Networks:** USA Radio. **Owner:** Cross Country Communications, Inc., at above address. **Founded:** 1949. **Formerly:** WZCC-AM. **Operating Hours:** Continuous; 100% local. **ADI:** Louisville, KY. **Key Personnel:** George Zarris, President/General Manager; Olympus Zarris, Sales Mgr.; Don Schitt, Production Dir. **Local Programs:** *Cross Country Crossfire*, George Zarris. **Wattage:** 1,500. **Ad Rates:** $20-40 for 60 seconds.

NEW CASTLE†, pop. 20,056.

Henry Co. (E). 18 m S of Muncie. Manufactures auto parts, folding partitions, heavy castings, structural steel, rolled steel products. Greenhouses. Stock, poultry farms. Corn, wheat, tomatoes.

10506 Courier-Times
201 S. 14th St. Phone: (317)529-1111
New Castle, IN 47362-3328 Fax: (317)529-1731

General newspaper. **Founded:** 1841. **Freq:** Mon.-Sat. (eve.). **Print Method:** Offset press. **Cols./Page:** 6. **Col. Width:** 28 nonpareils. **Col. Depth:** 301 agate lines. **Key Personnel:** John Wesley Rowe, Jr., Publisher. **Subscription Rates:** $88.40 individuals. **Remarks:** Accepts advertising.
Ad Rates: GLR: $.30 **Circ:** 12,000

10507 TCI of Indiana
Box 610 Phone: (317)529-8009
New Castle, IN 47362 Fax: (317)521-8654

Founded: 1971. **Key Personnel:** George M. Callaway, Manager. **Cities Served:** Henry County.: subscribing households 7,250; 35 channels.

10508 WMDH-AM - 1550
Box 690 Phone: (765)529-2600
New Castle, IN 47362 Fax: (765)529-1688
E-mail: wmdh.com

Format: Talk; Sports. **Networks:** Westwood One Radio; NBC; Talknet. **Owner:** Wicks Broadcast Group, at above address. **Founded:** 1960. **Formerly:** WCTW-AM (1990). **Operating Hours:** Continuous. **Key Personnel:** Don Hodges, General Mgr.; Mike Lees, Program Dir.; Beth Stone, Public Service Dir. **Local Programs:** *Morning Interview*, Don Ross, (317)529-2600, Fax (317)529-1688; *Sports Beat*, Dan Ross, (317)529-2600, Fax (317)529-1688. **Wattage:** 250. **Ad Rates:** Advertising accepted; rates available upon request.

10509 WMDH-FM - 102.5
PO Box 690 Phone: (765)282-7539
New Castle, IN 47362 Fax: (765)529-1688

Format: Country. **Networks:** NBC. **Owner:** at above address, (765)529-2600. **Founded:** 1947. **Operating Hours:** Continuous; 100% local. **ADI:** Indianapolis (Marion), IN. **Key Personnel:** Donald P. Hodges, General Mgr.; Paulette Lees, Sales Mgr.; Mike Lees, Program Dir.; Dan Russell, Public Service Dir. **Local Programs:** *Saturday Morning Memories*, Randy Lawson, Mailing contact; *Week-End Round-Up*, Mike Lees, Mailing contact. **Wattage:** 50,000. **Ad Rates:** Advertising accepted; rates available upon request.

NEW PARIS, pop. 1,300.

Elkhart Co. (N). 6 m S of Goshen. Boats, campers, cabinets, dairy and feed grain products manufactured. Agriculture. Corn, wheat, soybeans, dairy, livestock.

10510 Farmer's Exchange
Exchange Publishing Corp.
POB 45 Phone: (219)831-2138
New Paris, IN 46553 Fax: (219)831-2131

Agricultural newspaper. **Founded:** 1926. **Freq:** Weekly (Fri.). **Print Method:** Offset. **Cols./Page:** 6. **Col. Width:** 19 nonpareils. **Col. Depth:** 224 agate lines. **Key Personnel:** Paul Hershberger, Editor; Steve Yeater, Publisher. **Subscription Rates:** $20. **Remarks:** Advertising not accepted for alcoholic beverages and tobacco products.
Ad Rates: GLR: $.39 **Circ:** Paid ‡13,800
BW: $485 Free ‡800
PCI: $5.46

10511 New Paris Telephone Quality Cablevision
PO Box 7 Phone: (219)831-2225
New Paris, IN 46553 Fax: (219)831-7125
E-mail: qualcabl@npcc.net

Owner: New Paris Telephone Co., at above address. **Founded:** 1986. **Key Personnel:** Mark Grady, General Mgr.; Janet Johnson, Office Mgr.; Lisa Sweet, Account Executive. **Cities Served:** Goshen, Millersburg, New Paris, IN: subscribing households 1,511; 40 channels. **URL:** http://npcc.net˜qualcabl.

NEWBURGH, pop. 2,302.

Warrick Co. (SW). On Ohio River, 10 m E of Evansville. Light manufacturing. Aluminum smelters; coal; antique gift shops. Agriculture. Corn, wheat, tobacco.

10512 Newburgh Chandler Register
Warrick Publishing Co.
PO Box 535 Phone: (812)853-3366
Newburgh, IN 47629 Fax: (812)853-8685

Local newspaper. **Founded:** 1885. **Freq:** Weekly (Wed.). **Print Method:** Offset. **Cols./Page:** 6. **Col. Width:** 12.4 picas. **Col. Depth:** 301 agate lines. **Key Personnel:** Rick Davis, Editor; Myra Teal, Publisher. **Subscription Rates:** $26 individuals. **Remarks:** Accepts advertising. **Formed by the merger of:** Newburgh Register; Chandler Post.
Ad Rates: SAU: $10.19 **Circ:** ‡2,638
PCI: $10.19

10513 Western Kentucky Journal
Brenda Joyce Jerome
PO Box 325 Phone: (812)853-8092
Newburgh, IN 47629-0325
Genealogical publication. **Founded:** 1994. **Freq:** Quarterly. **Trim Size:** 8 1/2 x 11. **Key Personnel:** Brenda Joyce Jerome, Editor and Publisher, bjjerome@comsource.net. **ISSN:** 1072-6756. **Subscription Rates:** $22 individuals. **Remarks:** Advertising not accepted.
Circ: Paid 400

10514 Century Communications Corp.
PO Box 305 Phone: (812)853-2935
Newburgh, IN 47629-0305 Fax: (812)853-3299

Founded: 1980. **Formerly:** Century Cable. **Key Personnel:** Ron Page, Office Mgr.; Ronald N. Page, Contact. **Cities Served:** Surrounding Warrick County communities.: subscribing households 6,250; 34 channels; 1 community access channel.

10515 WGAB-AM - 1180
1180 Maple Ln. Phone: (812)853-9422
Newburgh, IN 47630

Format: Adult Album Alternative. **Owner:** Newburgh Broadcasting Corp., at above address. **Founded:** Mar. 5, 1984. **Formerly:** WJJN-AM (1990). **Operating Hours:** Daytime only; 90% network, 10% local. **ADI:** Evansville, IN (Madisonville, KY). **Key Personnel:** Don Davis, General Mgr.; Linda Davis, Program Dir.; Larry & Dave Wright, Public Affairs; Dr. Russ Vail, Sports Dir.; Nick Davis, News Dir.; Steve Smith, Public Service Dir. **Wattage:** 670. **Ad Rates:** Advertising accepted; rates available upon request. Combined advertising rates available with WDKS/WGBF-AM/WGBF-FM/WYNG/WTRI-FM.

NOBLESVILLE†, pop. 12,056.

Hamilton Co. (C). 24 m N of Indianapolis. Manufactures industrial rubber products, truck bodies, electronic components, furniture, castings. Stock grain farms. Wheat, corn, oats.

10516 Carmel News Tribune
Topics Newspapers, Inc.
PO BOX 1478 Phone: (317)598-6397
Noblesville, IN 46060
Publisher E-mail: topics@inetdirect.net

Local newspaper. **Founded:** 1969. **Freq:** Weekly (Wed.). **Print Method:** Offset. **Trim Size:** 22 3/4. **Cols./Page:** 6. **Col. Width:** 26 nonpareils. **Col. Depth:** 301 agate lines. **Key Personnel:** David Lewis, Publisher; Tom Jekel, Editor; Dennis Waldkoetter, Business Mgr.; Scott Gause, Advertising Dir.; Kevin Gossett, Production Mgr.; Terry Coomer, Circulation Director. **Subscription Rates:** Free; $15 voluntary pay - guaranteed delivery.
Ad Rates: SAU: $7.30 **Circ:** Combined ♦**19,173**
PCI: $12.75

10517 Castleton Banner
Topics Newspapers, Inc.
PO Box 1478 Phone: (317)598-6397
Noblesville, IN 46060 Fax: (317)598-6340
Publisher E-mail: topics@inetdirect.net

Local newspaper. **Founded:** 1966. **Freq:** Weekly (Wed.). **Print Method:** Offset. **Trim Size:** 22 3/4. **Cols./Page:** 6. **Col. Width:** 26 nonpareils. **Col. Depth:** 301 agate lines. **Key Personnel:** David Lewis, Publisher; Tom Jekel, Editor; Dennis Waldkoetter, Business Mgr.; Scott Gause, Advertising Dir.; Kevin Gossett, Production Mgr.; Terry Coomer, Circulation Director. **Subscription Rates:** free; $15 individuals voluntary pay guaranteed delivery.
Ad Rates: PCI: $13.20 **Circ:** Non-paid 8,438
Paid 199

10518 Heights Herald
Topics Newspapers, Inc.
PO Box 1478 Fax: (317)598-6360
Noblesville, IN 46061
Publisher E-mail: topics@inetdirect.net

Local newspaper. **Founded:** 1981. **Freq:** Weekly (Thurs.). **Print Method:** Offset. **Trim Size:** 22 3/4. **Cols./Page:** 6. **Col. Width:** 26 nonpareils. **Col. Depth:** 301 agate lines. **Key Personnel:** David Lewis, Publisher; Tom Jekel, Editor; Dennis Waldkoetter, Business Mgr.; Jay Fredrickson, Advertising Dir.; Kevin Gossett, Production Mgr.; Terry Coomer, Circulation Director. **Subscription Rates:** Free; $15 individuals annual voluntary pay. **Remarks:** Accepts advertising.
Ad Rates: PCI: $5.77 **Circ:** Paid 38
Non-paid 3,355

10519 Lawrence Times
Topics Newspapers, Inc.
PO Box 1478 Phone: (317)598-6397
Noblesville, IN 46060 Fax: (317)598-6360
Publisher E-mail: topics@inetdirect.net

Local newspaper. **Founded:** 1970. **Freq:** Weekly (Wed.). **Print Method:** Offset. **Trim Size:** 22 3/4 INS. **Cols./Page:** 6. **Col. Width:** 26 nonpareils. **Col. Depth:** 301 agate lines. **Key Personnel:** David Lewis, Publisher; Tom Jekel, Editor; Dennis Waldkoetter, Business Mgr.; Jay Fredrickson, Advertising Dir.; Kevin Gossett, Production Mgr.; Terry Coomer, Circulation Director. **Subscription Rates:** $15 Annual Voluntary Pay (Guaranteed Delivery).
Ad Rates: SAU: $2 1/16 INS **Circ:** Non-paid 7,560
PCI: $12.15 Paid 143

10520 Noblesville Times
PO Box 100 Phone: (317)773-3972
Noblesville, IN 46060 Fax: (317)773-3970

Community newspaper. **Freq:** Weekly (Thurs.). **Cols./Page:** 5. **Col. Width:** 11 picas. **Col. Depth:** 16 inches. **Key Personnel:** Marsha Jackson, Editor; Martha Hudler, Publisher.
Circ: 350

10521 Nora News Dispatch
Topics Newspapers, Inc.
PO Box 1478 Phone: (317)598-6397
Noblesville, IN 46061 Fax: (317)598-6360
Publisher E-mail: topics@inetdirect.net

Local newspaper. **Founded:** 1961. **Freq:** Weekly (Wed.). **Print Method:** Offset. **Trim Size:** 22 3/4 INS. **Cols./Page:** 6. **Col. Width:** 26 nonpareils. **Col. Depth:** 301 agate lines. **Key Personnel:** David Lewis, Publisher; Tom Jekel, Editor; Dennis Waldkoetter, Business Mgr.; Jay Fredrickson, Advertising Dir.; Kevin Gossett, Production Mgr.; Terry Coomer, Circulation Director. **Subscription Rates:** Free; $15 Annual Voluntary Pay (Guaranteed Delivery). **Remarks:** Accepts advertising.
Ad Rates: SAU: $2 1/16 INS **Circ:** Paid 192
PCI: $13.09 Non-paid 7,513

10522 North Meridian Observer
Topics Newspapers, Inc.
PO Box 1478 Phone: (317)598-6397
Noblesville, IN 46061 Fax: (317)598-6360
Publisher E-mail: topics@inetdirect.net

Local newspaper. **Founded:** 1961. **Freq:** Weekly (Wed.). **Print Method:** Offset. **Trim Size:** 22 3/4 INS. **Cols./Page:** 6. **Col. Width:** 26 picas. **Col. Depth:** 301 agate lines. **Key Personnel:** David Lewis, Publisher; Tom Jekel, Editor, fax (317)598-6360; Dennis Waldkoetter, Business Mgr.; Terry Coomer, Circulation Manager. **Subscription Rates:** Free; $15 Annual Voluntary Pay (Guaranteed Delivery).
Ad Rates: SAU: $2 1/16 INS **Circ:** Paid 134
PCI: $12.01 Non-paid 6,882

10523 Northside Topics
Topics Newspapers, Inc.
PO Box 1478 Phone: (317)598-6397
Noblesville, IN 46061 Fax: (317)598-6360
Publisher E-mail: topics@inetdirect.net

Local newspaper. **Founded:** 1922. **Freq:** Weekly (Wed.). **Print Method:** Offset. **Trim Size:** 22 3/4. **Cols./Page:** 6. **Col. Width:** 26 nonpareils. **Col. Depth:** 301 agate lines. **Key Personnel:** David Lewis, Publisher; Tom Jekel, Editor; Jay Frederickson, Advertising Dir.; Kevin Gossett, Production Mgr.; Terry Commer, Circulation Mgr.; Dennis Waldkoetter, Business Mgr. **Subscription Rates:** Free; $15 guaranteed delivery. **Remarks:** Accepts advertising. **Formerly:** Broadn Ripple-Glendale Northside Topics.
Ad Rates: PCI: $8.63 **Circ:** Combined ♦**6,511**

10524 Pike Register
Topics Newspapers, Inc.
PO Box 1478
Noblesville, IN 46061
Publisher E-mail: topics@inetdirect.net

Local newspaper. **Founded:** 1972. **Freq:** Weekly (Wed.). **Print Method:** Offset. **Cols./Page:** 6. **Col. Width:** 26 nonpareils. **Col. Depth:** 301 agate lines. **Key Personnel:** David Lewis, Publisher; Tom Jekel, Editor; Dennis Waldkoetter, Business Mgr.; Jay Fredrickson, Advertising Dir.; Kevin Gossett, Production Mgr.; Terry Coomer, Circulation Mgr. **Subscription Rates:** Free.
Ad Rates: GLR: $.55 **Circ:** Combined ♦**9,004**
BW: $620
4C: $920
SAU: $7.65
PCI: $13.20

10525 Sheridan News
PO Box 1478
Noblesville, IN 46061-1478

Local newspaper. **Founded:** 1882. **Freq:** Weekly (Thurs.). **Print Method:** Offset. **Cols./Page:** 6. **Col. Width:** 26 nonpareils. **Col. Depth:** 301 agate lines. **Key Personnel:** David Lewis, General Mgr.; Tom Jekel, Editor; Dennis Waldkoetter, Business Mgr.; Jay Fredrickson, Advertising Dir.; Kevin Gosset, Production Mgr.; Terry Coomer, Circulation Mgr. **Subscription Rates:** $12 individuals; $14 out of state.
Ad Rates: BW: $482.37 **Circ:** Paid 1,183
4C: $920.46 Non-paid 41
SAU: $6.47
PCI: $5.50

10526 Insight Communications, Inc.
15229 Stoney Creek Way Phone: (317)776-0660
Noblesville, IN 46060 Fax: (317)773-5439
Free: (800)439-9006

Owner: Insight Communications Corp., 126 E. 56th Ave., New York, NY 10022, (212)371-2266, Fax: (212)935-2575. **Founded:** May 1986. **Formerly:** Insight Cable. **Key Personnel:** David Servies, General Mgr., davidservies@insight-com.com; Dale Lambert, Plant Mgr.; Laura Hagerson, Marketing Mgr.; Jane Hawkins, Office Mgr.; Tony Holmes, Construction Mgr.; Al Orpurt, Rebuild Mgr.; Mary Hoffman, Installation Mgr. **Cities Served:** 1 channel; 24 community access channels.

10527 WHMB-TV - 40
10511 Greenfield Ave. Phone: (317)773-5050
Noblesville, IN 46060 Fax: (317)776-4051
E-mail: sales40@lesea.com

Format: Contemporary Christian. **Networks:** Independent. **Owner:** LeSea Broadcasting, Inc., Box 12, South Bend, IN 46624, (219)291-8200, Fax: (219)291-9043. **Founded:** 1972. **Operating Hours:** Continuous. **ADI:** Indianapolis (Marion), IN. **Key Personnel:** Keith Passon, General Mgr./Program Dir., kpasson@lesea.com; Dave Gooding, Chief Engineer, dgooding@lesea.com; Jeff Elliott, Promotions Mgr., jelliott@lesea.com. **Local Programs:** *High School Game* 10 p.m. Friday; *Inside Indy* 6:30 a.m. Thursday; *Lifeline* 11:30 p.m. Thursday. **Wattage:** 2.1 million. **Ad Rates:** Advertising accepted; rates available upon request.

NORTH MANCHESTER, pop. 5,998.

Wabash Co. (NE). 15 m N of Wabash. Residential.

10528 The News Journal
Weller Family Publishing
112 W. Main St. Phone: (219)982-6476
PO Box 324 Fax: (219)982-8233
North Manchester, IN 46962
Free: (888)982-6383

Newspaper with a Republican orientation. **Founded:** 1873. **Freq:** Weekly (Wed.). **Print Method:** Offset. **Cols./Page:** 5. **Col. Width:** 1 15/16 inches. **Col. Depth:** 15 1/2 inches. **Key Personnel:** Worth Weller, Editor and Publisher, whweller@ctlnet.com; Ric Rogers, General Mgr. **USPS:** 396-760. **Subscription Rates:** $34 individuals; $43 out of area. **Remarks:** Accepts advertising. **URL:** http://www.communist.org/News_ Journal.
Ad Rates: GLR: $2.50 **Circ:** Paid ‡2,395
SAU: $7.70
PCI: $6.64

10529 WBKE-FM - 89.5
Manchester College Phone: (219)982-5272
Box 88 Fax: (219)982-6868
North Manchester, IN 46962

Format: Educational. **Networks:** Network Indiana; UPI. **Founded:** 1968. **Operating Hours:** Continuous. **Key Personnel:** Dan Schnolis, Station Mgr.; Matt Baker, Program Dir.; Josh Brewster, Music Dir.; Chris Lake, Sports Dir.; Betsy Nottoli, News Dir.; Betsy Nottoli, News Dir. **Wattage:** 3000.

NORTH VERNON, pop. 5,768.

Jennings Co. (SE). 60 m S of Indianapolis. Manufactures plastics, gas filter tubes, injection molds, area rugs, plastic injection products, sausage. Hot and cold forgings. Metal work.

10530 North Vernon Plain Dealer
Plain Dealer & Sun
528 E. O&M Ave. Phone: (812)346-3973
PO Box 410 Fax: (812)346-8368
North Vernon, IN 47265
Community newspapers. **Founded:** 1862. **Freq:** Weekly (Thurs.). **Print Method:** Offset. **Cols./Page:** 6. **Col. Width:** 24 nonpareils. **Col. Depth:** 294 agate lines. **Key Personnel:** Barbara King, Publisher; Bryce Moyer, Editor. **Subscription Rates:** $30 /year for both papers; $0.50 single issue.
Ad Rates: BW: $412.80 **Circ:** **6,657**
PCI: $4.40

10531 North Vernon Sun
Plain Dealer & Sun
528 E. O&M Ave. Phone: (812)346-3973
PO Box 410 Fax: (812)346-8368
North Vernon, IN 47265
Publication E-mail: jcnews@seidata

Local newspaper with a Democratic orientation. **Founded:** 1872. **Freq:** Weekly (Tues.). **Print Method:** Offset. **Cols./Page:** 6. **Col. Width:** 24 nonpareils. **Col. Depth:** 294 agate lines. **Key Personnel:** Bryce Mayer, Editor; Josh Taylor, Advertising Mgr. **USPS:** 395-080. **Subscription Rates:** $26 individuals. **Remarks:** Accepts advertising.
Ad Rates: GLR: $5 **Circ:** 6,000
BW: $645
PCI: $4.60

10532 WNVI-AM - 1460
PO Box 46 Phone: (812)392-2710
North Vernon, IN 47265 Fax: (812)372-1061
Free: (888)262-1061

Format: News; Talk. **Networks:** Mutual Broadcasting System; AgriAmerica. **Owner:** White RNER Broadcasting, PO Box 1789, Columbus, IN 47202, (812)372-4448, Fax: (812)372-1061, Free: (888)262-1061. **Founded:** 1955. **Formerly:** WOCH-AM (1983). **Operating Hours:** Continuous; 80% network, 20% local. **Key Personnel:** Tasha Kay, General Mgr., phone (812)372-4448, fax (812)372-1061, tasha@wcsiradio.com; John Foster, Program Dir., phone (812)372-4448, fax (812)372-1061; Wes Roy, News Dir., phone (812)376-4770, fax (812)372-1061, wesroy@wcsiradio.com; Stan Gujas, Sales Mgr., fax (812)392-2605; Judy Watkins, Traffic Mgr., phone (812)372-4448, fax (812)372-1061, jwatkins@wcsiradio.com. **Local Programs:** *Daybreak* 6:00 am - 9:00 am Monday-Friday, Jamle Clack, News Editor. **Wattage:** 1000 day; 92 night. **Ad Rates:** $4-10 for 30 seconds; $6-12 for 60 seconds.

NOTRE DAME, pop. 10,700.

St. Joseph Co. (N). 3 m N of South Bend. University of Notre Dame. St Mary's College (Cath. Women).

10533 American Midland Naturalist
University of Notre Dame, PO Box 369 Phone: (219)631-7481
Fax: (219)631-7413
Notre Dame, IN 46556
Publication E-mail: ammidnat.l@nd.edu

Primary journal covering basic research in biology; including animal and plant ecology, systematics and physiology, entomology, mammalogy, ichthyology, parasitology, invertebrate zoology, and limnology. **Founded:** Apr. 1909. **Freq:** Quarterly. **Print Method:** Offset. **Trim Size:** 6 x 9. **Cols./Page:** 1. **Col. Width:** 50 nonpareils. **Col. Depth:** 98 agate lines. **Key Personnel:** Dr. Robert P. McIntosh, Editor. **ISSN:** 0003-0031. **Subscription Rates:** $85 North and South America; $90 elsewhere. **Remarks:** Advertising not accepted. **Online:** Information Access. **Alt. Formats:** Microform.
Circ: Paid ‡1,137
Controlled ‡54

10534 American Musicology Society Journal
American Musicological Society
c/o Paula Higgins, Editor Phone: (219)631-5139
University of Notre Dame Fax: (219)631-8609
Dept. Of Music
Notre Dame, IN 46556
Publication E-mail: subscriptions@journals.uchicago.edu

Scholarly journal covering academic musicology and music history. **Founded:** 1948. **Freq:** 3/year. **Print Method:** Offset. **Trim Size:** 6 x 9 1/4. **Cols./Page:** 1. **Col. Width:** 4 inches. **Col. Depth:** 7 1/4 inches. **Key Personnel:** Paula Higgins, Editor, higgins.l@nd.edu; Michael Tusa, Review Editor; Timothy Hill, Advertising Mgr.; Patricia Scarry, Assoc. Journals Mktg. Dir. **ISSN:** 0003-0139. **Subscription Rates:** $15 single issue. **Remarks:** Accepts advertising.
Ad Rates: BW: $225 **Circ:** Combined 4,800

10535 Applied and Preventive Psychology
Cambridge University Press
Univ Notre Dame
118 Haggar Hall
Notre Dame, IN
Publication E-mail: journals_ marketing@cup.org

Journal focusing on the treatment of psychological problems. **Subtitle:** The Journal of the American Association for Applied and Preventive Psychology. **Founded:** 1992. **Freq:** Quarterly. **Key Personnel:** David A. Smith, Editor, osipow@osu.edu. **ISSN:** 0962-1849. **Subscription Rates:** $105 institutions; $50 individuals; $28 single issue. **Remarks:** Accepts advertising.
Ad Rates: BW: $500 **Circ:** Paid ‡1,373
Non-paid ‡33

10536 Blue & Gold Illustrated—Notre Dame Football
Blue & Gold Illustrated
PO Box 1007 Phone: (219)255-9800
Notre Dame, IN 46556
Magazine covering Notre Dame Fighting Irish football. **URL:** http://www.bluegold.com.

10537 Gerontology & Geriatrics Education
The Haworth Press, Inc.
Univ. of Notre Dame Phone: (219)631-5289
Gerontology & Geriatrics Fax: (219)631-8700
Education Office
447 Flanner Hall
Notre Dame, IN 46556
Publisher E-mail: getinfo@haworthpressinc.com

Journal presenting practical curriculum information for educators, trainers, and supervisors in the aging field. **Founded:** 1980. **Freq:** Quarterly. **Print Method:** Offset. **Trim Size:** 6x8 1/2. **Cols./Page:** 1. **Col. Width:** 51 nonpareils. **Col. Depth:** 95 agate lines. **Key Personnel:** Grace D. Dawson, Ph. D., Editor, grace.d.dawson.2@nd.edu; Bill Cohen, Publisher. **ISSN:** 0270-1960. **Subscription Rates:** $45 individuals; $140 institutions; $200 libraries. **Remarks:** Accepts advertising.
Ad Rates: BW: $300 **Circ:** ‡407

10538 Journal of College and University Law
National Association of College & University Attorneys (NACUA)
c/o William P. Hoye, Faculty Editor
General Counsel Office
107 Huntley Bldg.
Notre Dame, IN 46556

Legal journal covering law and education. **Founded:** 1973. **Freq:** Quarterly. **Trim Size:** 6 3/4 x 10. **Cols./Page:** 1. **Col. Width:** 4 5/8 inches. **Col. Depth:** 8 inches. **Key Personnel:** William P. Hoye, Faculty Editor. **ISSN:** 0093-8688. **Subscription Rates:** $52.50 individuals; $13.50 single issue. **Remarks:** Advertising not accepted.
Circ: Paid 248

10539 Journal of Legislation
University of Notre Dame
Notre Dame, IN 46556 Phone: (219)631-5918
Fax: (219)631-6371

Professional legal journal covering legislation and public policy issues. **Freq:** Semiannual. **Key Personnel:** Jeffrey C. Montura, Editor-in-Chief; HaKung Wong, Managing Editor. **ISSN:** 0146-9584. **Subscription Rates:** $20 individuals; $22 out of country; $10 single issue. **Remarks:** Advertising accepted; rates available upon request. **Online:** LEXIS-NEXIS; WestLaw. **Former name**: New Dimensions in Legislation.
Circ: (Not Reported)

10540 Journal of Management
Elseiver
Dept. of Management
University of Notre Dame
Notre Dame, IN 46556
Publication E-mail: 102062.2525@compuserve.com
Publisher E-mail: fcentres@gpu.stv.ualberta.ca

Scholarly journal. **Subtitle:** Official Journal of the Southern Management Association. **Freq:** Bimonthly. **Key Personnel:** Robert P. Vecchio, Editor. **ISSN:** 0149-2063. **Subscription Rates:** $100 individuals; $225 institutions.

10541 Notre Dame Journal of Law, Ethics & Public Policy
University of Notre Dame
Rm. 341 Phone: (219)631-4888
Notre Dame, IN 46556
Journal covering ethics of federal, state and local government policy. **Founded:** 1986. **Freq:** Semiannual. **Cols./Page:** 1. **Col. Width:** 6 inches. **Col. Depth:** 8 inches. **ISSN:** 0883-3648. **Subscription Rates:** $20 individuals; $10 single issue. **Remarks:** Accepts advertising.
Ad Rates: BW: $100 **Circ:** Controlled 490

10542 Notre Dame Law Review
Notre Dame Law School
University of Notre Dame Phone: (219)239-7097
PO Box 988 Fax: (219)239-6371
Notre Dame, IN 46556
Law journal. **Founded:** 1925. **Freq:** Weekly (Wed.) 5/year. **Print Method:** Offset. **Cols./Page:** 1. **Col. Width:** 72 nonpareils. **Col. Depth:** 130 agate lines. **Key Personnel:** Jim Sweeny; Steve McClain. **ISSN:** 0745-3515. **Subscription Rates:** $28 individuals; $52 two years. **Remarks:** Accepts advertising. **Online:** Westlaw, Lexis. **Formerly**: Port Townsend Leader (Oct. 1, 1987).
Ad Rates: BW: $50 **Circ:** ‡1,500

10543 Notre Dame Magazine
University of Notre Dame
415 Administration Bldg. Phone: (219)631-5000
Notre Dame, IN 46556 Fax: (219)239-6947

Magazine for university alumni and friends. **Founded:** 1972. **Freq:** Quarterly. **Print Method:** Offset. **Trim Size:** 9 x 12. **Cols./Page:** 3. **Col. Width:** 30 nonpareils. **Col. Depth:** 150 agate lines. **Key Personnel:** Walton R. Collins, Editor. **ISSN:** 0161-987X. **Subscription Rates:** $15 individuals; $3.75 single issue. **Remarks:** Advertising not accepted. **URL:** http://www.nd.ndu.
Circ: Controlled ‡112,000

10544 Notre Dame Technical Review
University of Notre Dame Phone: (219)283-1122
College of Engineering Fax: (219)239-8007
Notre Dame, IN 46556
Magazine for engineering students. **Founded:** 1949. **Freq:** Quarterly. **Print Method:** Offset. **Cols./Page:** 3. **Col. Depth:** 10 inches. **Key Personnel:** Diane Peters, Editor. **ISSN:** 0029-4543. **Subscription Rates:** $15. **Remarks:** Accepts advertising.
Ad Rates: 4C: $340 **Circ:** 1,700
PCI: $11.11

10545 The Observer
University of Notre Dame
PO Box Q Phone: (219)631-5303
Notre Dame, IN 46556 Fax: (219)239-6927

Newspaper. **Subtitle:** The Independent Newspaper Serving Notre Dame and Saint Mary's. **Founded:** 1966. **Freq:** Daily (during the academic year). **Print Method:** Offset. **Trim Size:** 10 x 16. **Cols./Page:** 5. **Col. Width:** 22 nonpareils. **Col. Depth:** 224 agate lines. **Key Personnel:** Liz Forzn, Editor-in-Chief; Ellen Ryan, Advertising Mgr. **ISSN:** 5992-4000. **Subscription Rates:** $70 individuals. **Remarks:** Accepts advertising.
Ad Rates: BW: $440 **Circ:** 12,500
4C: $810
PCI: $5.50

10546 Religion and Literature
University of Notre Dame
Notre Dame, IN 46556 Phone: (219)631-5725
Fax: (219)631-8609
Publication E-mail: English.RandL.1@nd.edu

Scholarly journal covering the intersection between literature and religious belief. **Founded:** 1968. **Freq:** Triennial. **Key Personnel:** James Dougherty, Editor; Tom Werge, Editor. **ISSN:** 0029-4500. **Subscription Rates:** $25 individuals; $40 two years; $31 institutions; $52 two years institutions; $36 out of country institution; $60 out of country two years institutions. **Remarks:** Accepts advertising. **URL:** http://www.nd.edu/~RandL. **Alt. Formats:** Microfilm. **Former name**: NDEJ: A Journal of Religion in Literature.
Ad Rates: BW: $100 **Circ:** Paid 450

10547 Rethinking Marxism
Guilford Publications, Inc.
Dept. of Economics Phone: (219)631-6434
University of Notre Dame Fax: (219)631-8809
Notre Dame, IN
Publication E-mail: remarx.1@nd.edu
Publisher E-mail: info@guilford.com

Marxist journal containing interviews, articles, art, and poetry. **Subtitle:** A Journal of Economics, Culture and Society. **Founded:** 1988. **Freq:** Quarterly. **Trim Size:** 6 x 9. **Key Personnel:** Stephen Cullenberg, Editor; David Ruccio, Editor; Jacquelyn Southern, Managing Editor. **ISSN:** 0893-5696. **Subscription Rates:** $30; $35 students; $105 institutions. **Remarks:** Accepts advertising. **Alt. Formats:** Microfilm.
Ad Rates: BW: $200 **Circ:** Paid ‡900
Non-paid ‡105

10548 Review of Politics
PO Box B Phone: (219)631-6623
Notre Dame, IN 46556-0762 Fax: (219)631-3103
Publication E-mail: rop.editor.1@nd.edu

Journal covering political science, philosophy, and foreign affairs. **Founded:** 1939. **Freq:** Quarterly. **Print Method:** Letterpress and offset. **Trim Size:** 6 x 9. **Cols./Page:** 1. **Col. Width:** 48 nonpareils. **Col. Depth:** 128 agate lines. **Key Personnel:** Walter Nicgorski, Editor; Dennis William Moran, Managing Editor/Editor. **ISSN:** 0034-6705. **Subscription Rates:** $25 individuals; $40 other countries; $48 institutions; $52 institutions, other countries. **Remarks:** Accepts advertising. **URL:** http://www.nd.edu/~rop/. **Alt. Formats:** CD-ROM, UMI.
Ad Rates: BW: $200 **Circ:** 1,700

10549 Scholastic Magazine
University of Notre Dame - Ave Maria Press
555 Broadway Fax: (212)343-6620
New York, NY 10012-3999
Collegiate magazine. **Founded:** 1867. **Freq:** Weekly (during the academic year). **Print Method:** Uses mats. Letterpress. **Trim Size:** 8 1/4 x 10 3/4. **Cols./Page:** 3. **Col. Width:** 25 nonpareils. **Col. Depth:** 140 agate lines. **Key Personnel:** Steve Myers, Editor-in-Chief; Jenny Stachowiak, Advertising Mgr. **Subscription Rates:** $30 individuals. **Remarks:** Accepts advertising.
Ad Rates: BW: $175 **Circ:** 8,000

OAKLAND CITY, pop. 3,301.

Gibson Co. (SW). 12 m W of Princeton. Residential.

10550 Oakland City Journal
Princeton Publishing Inc.
222 N. Main St. Phone: (812)749-3913
PO Box 187
Oakland City, IN 47660
Community newspaper. **Founded:** 1893. **Freq:** Weekly (Wed.). **Print Method:** Offset. **Cols./Page:** 6. **Col. Width:** 2 1/16 inches. **Col. Depth:** 21 inches. **Key Personnel:** Peggy Whetstone, Editor; Gary Blackburn, Publisher; Phil Summers, General Mgr. **Subscription Rates:** $15 - $29 annually.
Ad Rates: BW: $883.26 **Circ:** Wed. ‡1,823
4C: $1,043.26
SAU: $7.01

10551 Oakland City Journal Dollar Saver
Princeton Publishing Inc.
222 N. Main St. Phone: (812)749-3913
PO Box 187
Oakland City, IN 47660
Shopping guide with features. **Founded:** 1975. **Freq:** Weekly (Wed.). **Print Method:** Offset. **Cols./Page:** 8. **Col. Width:** 21 nonpareils. **Col. Depth:** 194 agate lines. **Key Personnel:** Phil Summers, General Mgr.; Gary Blackburn, Publisher. **Subscription Rates:** Free. **Remarks:** Accepts advertising.
Ad Rates: SAU: $5.93 **Circ:** Free ‡3,850

ODON, pop. 1,463.

Daviess Co. (SW). 50 m SE of Terre Haute. Manufactures burial vaults, livestock litter. Flour, sawmills; creamery. Diversified farming. Corn, wheat, oats.

10552 Journal
Odon Journal
102 1/2 W. Main St. Phone: (812)636-7350
Odon, IN 47562 Fax: (812)636-7359

Newspaper with a Republican orientation. **Founded:** 1873. **Freq:** Weekly (Wed.). **Print Method:** Offset. **Cols./Page:** 6. **Col. Depth:** 21 1/4 inches. **Key Personnel:** John L. Myers, Editor and Publisher. **USPS:** 403-040. **Subscription Rates:** $12 individuals. **Remarks:** Accepts advertising.
Ad Rates: GLR: $.13 **Circ:** 2,782
SAU: $2.95
PCI: $2.95

ORLEANS, pop. 2,161.

Orange Co. (S). 16 m S of Bedford. Lumber, feed mills. Automotive electrical parts manufactured.

10553 Progress-Examiner
233 S. 2nd St. Phone: (812)865-3242
PO Box 225 Fax: (812)865-3242
Orleans, IN 47452
Community newspaper. **Founded:** 1879. **Freq:** Weekly (Wed.). **Print Method:** Offset. **Cols./Page:** 6. **Col. Width:** 12 millimeters. **Col. Depth:** 294 agate lines. **Key Personnel:** John F. Noblitt, Editor. **USPS:** 447-020. **Subscription Rates:** $12 individuals mail. **Remarks:** Accepts advertising.
Ad Rates: GLR: $0.15 **Circ:** ‡2,000
BW: $283.50
4C: $343.50
PCI: $2.25

OSSIAN, pop. 1,945.

Wells Co. (NE). 14 m S of Fort Wayne. Manufactures tools and dies, auto parts. Feed mills; meat packing plant. Agriculture.

10554 The Ossian Journal
News Banner Publications, Inc.
105 N. Jefferson Phone: (219)622-4108
PO Box 365 Fax: (219)622-4108
Ossian, IN 46777
Publisher E-mail: email@news-banner.com

Newspaper. **Founded:** 1914. **Freq:** Weekly (Thurs.). **Print Method:** Web offset. **Cols./Page:** 6. **Col. Width:** 2 1/16 inches. **Col. Depth:** 21 1/2 inches. **Key Personnel:** Jim Barbieri, Editor and Publisher; Nila Dafforn, Advertising and Sales Mgr. **Subscription Rates:** $15.50 individuals; $17 out of area. **Remarks:** Accepts advertising.
Ad Rates: GLR: $5.20 **Circ:** Paid ‡600
BW: $516
SAU: $4
PCI: $4

10555 The Sunriser News
News Banner Publications, Inc.
105 N. Jefferson Phone: (219)622-4108
PO Box 365 Fax: (219)622-4108
Ossian, IN 46777
Publisher E-mail: email@news-banner.com

Shopping guide with local news (tabloid). **Founded:** 1978. **Freq:** Weekly (Tues.). **Print Method:** Web offset. **Cols./Page:** 5. **Col. Width:** 12 1/2 picas. **Col. Depth:** 13 inches. **Key Personnel:** Jim Barbieri, Editor and Publisher; Nila Dafforn, Advertising and Sales Mgr. **Subscription Rates:** Free. **Remarks:** Accepts advertising.
Ad Rates: GLR: $5.80 **Circ:** Controlled ‡12,242
BW: $275.60
SAU: $5.40

PAOLI†, pop. 3,637.

Orange Co. (S). 24 m S of Bedford. Manufactures wood dimension parts, shoes, handles, furniture, chairs, electronics; lumber kilm drying; hardwood timber. Agriculture. Corn, wheat, hay.

10556 News
Orange County Publishing Co. Inc.
PO Box 190 Phone: (812)723-2572
Paoli, IN 47454 Fax: (812)723-2592

Newspaper with a Democratic orientation. **Founded:** 1872. **Freq:** Weekly (Thurs.). **Print Method:** Offset. **Cols./Page:** 6. **Col. Width:** 25 nonpareils. **Col. Depth:** 294 agate lines. **Key Personnel:** Jeanie Hampton, Editor; Mr. & Mrs. Arthur Hampton, Publishers. **Subscription Rates:** $21 individuals. **Remarks:** Accepts advertising.
Ad Rates: GLR: $.19 **Circ:** 3,150
PCI: $2.85

10557 Orange Countian
Orange County Publishing Co. Inc.
PO Box 190 Phone: (812)723-2572
Paoli, IN 47454 Fax: (812)723-2592

Shopper with news features. **Founded:** 1981. **Freq:** Weekly. **Print Method:** Offset. **Cols./Page:** 6. **Col. Width:** 2 1/16 inches. **Col. Depth:** 21 1/2 inches. **Key Personnel:** Arthur Hampton, Contact. **Remarks:** Accepts advertising.
Ad Rates: PCI: $4.75 **Circ:** Free 9,450

10558 Republican
Orange County Publishing Co. Inc.
PO Box 190 Phone: (812)723-2572
Paoli, IN 47454 Fax: (812)723-2592

Newspaper with a Republican orientation. **Founded:** 1875. **Freq:** Weekly (Tues.). **Print Method:** Offset. **Cols./Page:** 6. **Col. Width:** 25 nonpareils. **Col. Depth:** 294 agate lines. **Key Personnel:** Arthur Hampton, Editor; Mr. & Mrs. Arthur Hampton, Publishers. **Subscription Rates:** $21 individuals. **Remarks:** Accepts advertising.
Ad Rates: GLR: $.19 **Circ:** 3,150
SAU: $3
PCI: $3

10559 WSEZ-AM - 1560
PO Box 26 Phone: (812)723-4484
Paoli, IN 47454-0026 Fax: (812)723-4966
E-mail: wume@blueriver.net

Format: Oldies. **Networks:** Independent. **Owner:** Imojean Apple, at above address. **Founded:** 1960. **Formerly:** WVAK-AM (1978). **Operating Hours:** 6 a.m.-6 p.m.; 100% local. **Key Personnel:** Imojean Apple, General/Sales Mgr.; Dave Dedrick, Contact; Todd Edwards, Production Mgr. **Wattage:** 250. **Ad Rates:** $6-12 for 30 seconds; $8-14 for 60 seconds.

10560 WUME-FM - 95.3
192 S. Court St. Phone: (812)723-4484
PO Box 26 Fax: (812)723-4966
Paoli, IN 47454
E-mail: wume@blueriver.net

Format: Adult Contemporary. **Networks:** ABC. **Owner:** Ironic Broadcasting, Inc., at above address. **Founded:** 1972. **Former name:** WVAK-FM (1978). **Operating Hours:** Continuous. **Key Personnel:** Imojean Apple, General Sales and General Manager; Todd Edwards, Programming/Engineering, phone (812)723-9863; David Dedrick, News and Sports Dir., phone (812)723-4474; Joanne Feiock, Accounting Mgr. **Ad Rates:** $7-12 for 30 seconds; $8-15 for 60 seconds.

PEKIN, pop. 1,125.

(corporate name New Pekin); Washington Co. (S). 25 m NW of New Albany. Poultry processing plant. Ships berries. Diversified farming. Berries, poultry and dairy products.

10561 Austin Chronicle
Green Banner Publications, Inc.
PO Box 38 Phone: (812)967-3176
Pekin, IN 47165-0038 Fax: (812)967-3194
Free: (800)264-7336

Newspaper with a Republican orientation. **Founded:** 1880. **Freq:** Weekly. **Print Method:** Offset. **Cols./Page:** 6. **Col. Width:** 2 1/16 inches. **Col. Depth:** 21 inches. **Key Personnel:** Marcus Amos, Editor, phone (812)752-3171, fax (812)752-6486; Joe Green, Publisher; John C. Roberts, Advertising Mgr. **Subscription Rates:** $8.75 individuals; $14.75 out of area; $19.75 out of state. **Remarks:** Color advertising accepted; rates available upon request.
Ad Rates: GLR: $.36 **Circ:** 5,000
BW: $630
SAU: $5
PCI: $5

10562 The Banner-Gazette
Green Banner Publications, Inc.
PO Box 38 Phone: (812)967-3176
Pekin, IN 47165-0038 Fax: (812)967-3194
Free: (800)264-7336

Community newspaper. **Founded:** 1919. **Freq:** Weekly (Wed.). **Print Method:** Offset. **Trim Size:** 11 3/8 x 17. **Cols./Page:** 5. **Col. Width:** 25 nonpareils. **Col. Depth:** 224 agate lines. **Key Personnel:** Mark Grigsbey, Editor; Joe Green, Publisher; John Roberts, Sales Mgr. **Subscription Rates:** $18.50 individuals.
Ad Rates: GLR: $.57 **Circ:** Free 16,319
BW: $631.20 Paid 86
SAU: $7.89
PCI: $7.89

PENDLETON, pop. 2,130.

Madison Co. (EC). 30 m NE of Indianapolis. Residential.

10563 WEEM-FM - 91.7
1 Arabian Dr. Phone: (765)778-2161
Pendleton, IN 46064 Fax: (765)778-8207

Format: Oldies. **Networks:** Longhorn Radio. **Founded:** 1971. **Operating Hours:** 6:30am-5:30pm Mon-Fri; 8 am-5 pm Sat; 50% network; 50% local. **Key Personnel:** Jeff Purdy, Program Dir.; Jon Stoner, Sports Dir.; Steve Cherry, General Mgr. **Wattage:** 1200. **Ad Rates:** Noncommercial.

PERU†, pop. 13,764.

Miami Co. (NC). On Wabash River, 65 m N of Indianapolis. Manufacturing. Meat packing plants. Grain farms.

10564 The Good Times
Nixon Newspapers, Inc.
26 W. 3rd St. Phone: (317)473-6641
PO Box 87 Fax: (317)472-4438
Peru, IN 46970-2155
Shopper. **Founded:** Apr. 16, 1921. **Freq:** Weekly (Mon.). **Print Method:** Offset. Uses mats. **Cols./Page:** 6. **Col. Width:** 26 nonpareils. **Col. Depth:** 301 agate lines. **Key Personnel:** Alan Blanchard, Editor; Jack Howey, Publisher; Steve Leininger, Advertising Mgr. **Remarks:** Accepts advertising. **URL:** http://www.nixonnews.com/ptrib.
Ad Rates: BW: $1,154.55 **Circ:** Free 15,500

10565 Peru Daily Tribune
Nixon Newspapers, Inc.
26 W. 3rd St. Phone: (317)473-6641
PO Box 87 Fax: (317)472-4438
Peru, IN 46970-2155
General newspaper. **Founded:** Apr. 16, 1921. **Freq:** Daily (eve.) and Sat. (morn.). **Print Method:** Offset. **Cols./Page:** 6. **Col. Width:** 26 nonpareils. **Col. Depth:** 301 agate lines. **Key Personnel:** Alan Blanchard, Editor; Jack Howey, Publisher; Steve Leininger, Advertising Mgr. **Subscription Rates:** $78 individuals. **Remarks:** Accepts advertising.
Ad Rates: GLR: $8.68 **Circ:** ‡8,646
BW: $941.70
4C: $1,166.70
SAU: $8.95

10566 The Shopper News
Nixon Newspapers, Inc.
26A W. Main St. Phone: (317)473-4473
Peru, IN 46970 Fax: (317)473-5055

Shopping guide. **Founded:** 1969. **Freq:** Weekly (Wed.). **Trim Size:** 11 3/8 x 16 3/4. **Cols./Page:** 6. **Col. Width:** 9 picas. **Col. Depth:** 16 inches. **Key Personnel:** Ron Storey, Manager. **Subscription Rates:** Free. **Remarks:** Color advertising accepted; rates available upon request.
Ad Rates: BW: $432 **Circ:** Free ‡14,577
SAU: $4.50

10567 Marcus Cable
434 Chili Ave. Phone: (765)473-6633
Peru, IN 46970 Fax: (317)473-7077

Key Personnel: Glenn Russell, District Mgr.; Jack Ozminkowski, Operations Mgr.; Sara Lee Beller, Mktg. Mgr.; Kris Meyer, Plant Mgr.; Guy Hickle, Plant Mgr. **Cities Served:** Indianapolis, IN.

10568 WARU-AM - 1600
Box 1010 Phone: (317)473-4448
Peru, IN 46970 Fax: (317)473-4449

Format: Classic Rock. **Simulcasts:** WARU-FM. **Networks:** CNN Radio; Tribune Radio. **Owner:** Miami County B-Casting, at above address. **Founded:** 1954. **Operating Hours:** 5:00 a.m.-12 a.m. **Key Personnel:** Jerry Willis, General/General Sales Mgr.; Rae Ervin, Program Dir.; Mark Ramsey, Sports Dir.; Debby Mullikin, News Dir. **Wattage:** 900. **Ad Rates:** $5.25-11.55 for 60 seconds.

10569 WARU-FM - 98.3
PO Box 1010 Phone: (317)473-4448
Peru, IN 46970 Fax: (317)473-4449

Format: Classic Rock. **Networks:** CNN Radio; Tribune Radio. **Owner:** Miami County Broadcasting, at above address. **Founded:** 1954. **Operating Hours:** 5 a.m.-midnight. **Key Personnel:** Jerry Willis, General Mgr.; Rae Ervin, Program Dir.; Mark Ramsey, Sports Dir.; Jerry Willis, General Sales Mgr.; Debby Mullikin, News Dir. **Wattage:** 6,000.

PETERSBURG†, pop. 2,987.

Pike Co. (SW). 20 m SE of Vincennes. Wood tools and structural steel manufactured. Generating plants. Coal mines. Oil wells. Diversified farming.

10570 The Press-Dispatch
PO Box 68 Phone: (812)354-8500
Petersburg, IN 47567 Fax: (812)354-2014

Community newspaper. **Founded:** 1885. **Freq:** Weekly (Thurs.). **Print Method:** Offset. **Cols./Page:** 6. **Col. Width:** 2 1/2 inches. **Col. Depth:** 21 inches. **Key Personnel:** Frank Heuring, Publisher; John Heuring, Advertising Mgr.; Andy Heuring, News Editor. **USPS:** 604-340. **Subscription Rates:** $15 individuals. **Remarks:** Advertising not accepted for alcoholic beverages and tobacco products. **Formerly:** The Pike County Dispatch; The Petersburg Press.
Ad Rates: GLR: $.25 **Circ:** 5,472
BW: $390.60
4C: $635.60
PCI: $3.95

10571 WFPC-FM - 102.3
Hwy. 57 S. Phone: (812)354-9923
PO Box 538 Fax: (812)354-6601
Petersburg, IN 47567-0538
Free: (800)844-9372
E-mail: wfpc@comsource.com

Format: Country. **Networks:** Independent. **Owner:** Pike Broadcasting Corp., at above address. **Founded:** 1984. **Operating Hours:** Continuous; 85% network, 15% local. **Key Personnel:** Linda Padgett, Office Mgr.; Mike Voyles, Chief Engineer; Randy Harris, General Mgr.; Jerry Rauscher, Sports Dir.; Matt Sturgeon, News Dir. **Wattage:** 3000. **Ad Rates:** $6-11.05 for 30 seconds; $8.15-13.80 for 60 seconds.

PLAINFIELD, pop. 9,191.

Hendricks Co. (C). 14 m SW of Indianapolis. Residential. Agriculture. Corn, wheat, oats, soybeans.

10572 Hendricks County Flyer
McCarthy Media, Inc.
PO Box 6 Phone: (317)839-5129
Plainfield, IN 46168 Fax: (317)839-6546
Publication E-mail: flyergrp@iquest.net
Publisher E-mail: flyer@flyergroup.com

Community newspaper. **Founded:** 1965. **Freq:** Weekly (Mon.). **Print Method:** Offset. **Cols./Page:** 6. **Col. Width:** 21 1/2 nonpareils. **Col. Depth:** 224 agate lines. **Key Personnel:** W. Jack McCarthy, Publisher; Candy Wilson, Advertising Dir.; Derek Clay, Editor. **Subscription Rates:** $60 individuals; $70 out of state. **Remarks:** Accepts advertising. **URL:** http://www.flyergroup.com.
Ad Rates: GLR: $3 **Circ:** Combined ♦**31,781**
BW: $19.12
4C: $349
PCI: $15.65

10573 The Weekend Flyer
McCarthy Media, Inc.
PO Box 6 Phone: (317)839-5129
Plainfield, IN 46168 Fax: (317)839-6546
Publisher E-mail: flyer@flyergroup.com

Newspaper with a Democratic orientation. **Founded:** 1866. **Freq:** Weekly (Thurs.). **Print Method:** Offset. **Cols./Page:** 6. **Col. Width:** 21 1/2 nonpareils. **Col. Depth:** 297 agate lines. **Key Personnel:** Jennifer Northern, Editor; W. Jack McCarthy, Publisher; Candy Wilson, Advertising Mgr. **Subscription Rates:** $18 individuals. **Remarks:** Color advertising accepted; rates available upon request. **URL:** http://www.flyergroup.com.
Ad Rates: BW: $17.06 **Circ:** Combined ♦**21,148**
4C: $309
SAU: $2.95
PCI: $14.13

10574 Westside Flyer
McCarthy Media, Inc.
PO Box 6 Phone: (317)839-5129
Plainfield, IN 46168 Fax: (317)839-6546
Publication E-mail: flyergrp@iquest.net
Publisher E-mail: flyer@flyergroup.com

Newspaper with a Republican orientation. **Founded:** 1993. **Freq:** Weekly (Mon.). **Print Method:** Offset. **Cols./Page:** 6. **Col. Width:** 21.5 nonpareils. **Col. Depth:** 224 agate lines. **Key Personnel:** Candy Wilson, Advertising Dir.; Gus Pearcy, Editor; Jason Cornwell, Circulation Mgr.; W. Jack McCarthy, Publisher. **Subscription Rates:** Free. **URL:** http://www.flyergroup.com.
Ad Rates: BW: $12.35 **Circ:** Free ♦**10,329**
4C: $269
PCI: $10.25

PLYMOUTH†, pop. 7,693.

Marshall Co. (N). 10 m NW of Bourbon. Industrial area.

10575 The Pilot-News
The Pilot Co., Inc.
217 N. Center Phone: (219)936-3101
PO Box 220 Fax: (219)936-3844
Plymouth, IN 46563
General newspaper. **Founded:** 1851. **Freq:** Daily (eve.) and Sat. (morn.). **Print Method:** Offset. **Trim Size:** 13 3/4 x 23. **Cols./Page:** 6. **Col. Width:** 24 nonpareils. **Col. Depth:** 301 agate lines. **Key Personnel:** Robert Noren, General Mgr.; Terri Shirk, Advertising Mgr.; Bill Johnson, Production Mgr.; Bill Johnson, Production Mgr. **Subscription Rates:** $102 by mail. **Remarks:** Accepts advertising. **URL:** http://www.skynet.net/~pilot.com.
Ad Rates: BW: $986.85 **Circ:** Paid ‡7,492
4C: $1,176.85
SAU: $7.65
PCI: $7.65

10576 WNZE-FM - 94.3
112 W. Washington St. Phone: (219)936-4096
Plymouth, IN 46563

Format: Country. **Owner:** Community Service Broadcasters, Inc., at above address. **Founded:** 1966. **Formerly**: WTCA-FM. **Operating Hours:** 16 hours Daily; 5% network, 95% local. **Key Personnel:** James C. Kunze, News Dir.; Kenneth E. Kunze, Contact; Jim Botorff, Sales Mgr. **Wattage:** 3000. **Ad Rates:** $4.34-8.77 for 15 seconds; $6.52-13.16 for 30 seconds; $8.69-17.54 for 60 seconds.

10577 WTCA-AM - 1050
112 W. Washington St. Phone: (219)936-4096
Plymouth, IN 46563 Fax: (219)936-6776
Free: (888)943-6539

Format: Oldies. **Networks:** Independent; CNN Radio. **Owner:** Community Service Broadcasters, Inc., at above address. **Founded:** 1964. **Operating Hours:** Continuous. **Key Personnel:** Kenneth E. Kunze, Owner; Kathy Bottorff, Station Mgr.; Andy Banas, Program Dir.; James Kunze, Chief Engineer. **Wattage:** 250. **Ad Rates:** $5.43-10.97 for 15 seconds; $8.15-16.45 for 30 seconds; $10.86-21.93 for 60 seconds.

PORTAGE

10578 WNDZ-AM - 750
2576 Portage Mall Phone: (219)763-2750
Portage, IN 46368-3006 Fax: (219)762-0539

Format: Ethnic; Religious; News. **Founded:** 1987. **Operating Hours:** Sunrise-sunset. **Key Personnel:** Tony Jacobs, General Mgr.; Sarah Fell, Operations Mgr.; Steve Bertok, Contact. **Local Programs:** *Lesbibay*; *Sami Swdi*. **Wattage:** 5000. **Ad Rates:** Advertising accepted; rates available upon request.

PORTLAND†, pop. 7,074.

Jay Co. (NE). 27 m NE of Muncie. Manufacturing. Meat packing plant, molded & extruded plastic products. Agriculture. Corn, wheat, oats, soybeans.

10579 The Commercial Review
309 W. Main Phone: (219)726-8141
PO Box 1049 Fax: (219)726-8143
Portland, IN 47371
Newspaper with a Republican orientation. **Founded:** 1871. **Freq:** Daily (eve.) and Sat. (morn.). **Print Method:** Offset. **Cols./Page:** 6. **Col. Width:** 21 nonpareils. **Col. Depth:** 294 agate lines. **Key Personnel:** John C. Ronald, Editor and Publisher; Don Gillespie, Advertising Mgr. **USPS:** 125-820. **Subscription Rates:** $75 individuals. **Remarks:** Accepts advertising.
Ad Rates: PCI: $6.20 **Circ:** 5,922

10580 Dunkirk News & Sun
The Graphic Printing Co., Inc.
PO Box 1049 Phone: (317)768-6022
Portland, IN 47371 Fax: (219)726-8143

Jay County Democratic newspaper. **Founded:** May 8, 1952. **Freq:** Weekly. **Print Method:** Offset. **Cols./Page:** 6. **Col. Width:** 2 1/16 inches. **Col. Depth:** 21 inches. **Key Personnel:** Bob Banser, Editor; John C. Ronald, Publisher; Marlene Dornberger, Advertising Mgr. **USPS:** 385-540. **Subscription Rates:** $10.50 individuals; $11.50 out of area. **Remarks:** Accepts advertising.
Ad Rates: BW: $333.90 **Circ:** ‡1,547
4C: $513.90
SAU: $2.65

10581 WPGW-AM - 1440
PO Box 1440 Phone: (219)726-8780
Portland, IN 47371 Fax: (219)726-4311

Format: Adult Contemporary. **Networks:** Mutual Broadcasting System. **Founded:** 1951. **Operating Hours:** 6 a.m.-10 p.m. **Key Personnel:** Robert A. Weaver, General Mgr. **Wattage:** 500 day; 45 night. **Ad Rates:** $5-8.90 for 30 seconds; $7-12.85 for 60 seconds. $7.15-$8.90 for 30 seconds; $11.00-$12.85 for 60 seconds. Combined advertising rates available with WPGW-FM.

10582 WPGW-FM - 100.9
PO Box 1440 Phone: (219)726-8780
Portland, IN 47371 Fax: (219)726-4311

Format: Country. **Networks:** Mutual Broadcasting System. **Founded:** 1975. **Operating Hours:** 6 a.m.-10 p.m. **Key Personnel:** Robert A. Weaver, General Mgr. **Wattage:** 3000. **Ad Rates:** $5-8.90 for 30 seconds; $7-12.85 for 60 seconds. $7.15-$8.90 for 30 seconds; $11.50-$12.85 for 60 seconds. Combined advertising rates available with WPGW-AM.

POSEYVILLE, pop. 1,247.

Posey Co. (SW). 20 m W of Evansville. Fertilizer factory. Agriculture. Watermelons, grain, cattle.

10583 Posey County News
PO Box 250 Phone: (812)985-7989
Poseyville, IN 47633 Fax: (812)874-6397

Newspaper with a Republican orientation. **Subtitle:** Weekly Newspaper. **Founded:** 1882. **Freq:** Weekly (Tues.). **Print Method:** Offset. **Cols./Page:** 6. **Col. Width:** 26 nonpareils. **Col. Depth:** 294 agate lines. **Key Personnel:** James A. Kohlmeyer, Editor and Publisher. **Subscription Rates:** $21 individuals in county; $25 out of area. **Remarks:** Accepts advertising. **Formerly**: Poseyville News; New Harmony Times.
Ad Rates: BW: $858 **Circ:** ‡4,800
4C: $1,018
PCI: $6.50

PRINCETON†, pop. 8,976.

Gibson Co. (SW). 28 m N of Evansville. Electric clocks, relays, oil well supplies manufactured. Hatcheries. Coal mines; gas and oil wells. Farming. Wheat, corn, melons, soybeans, livestock.

10584 Gibson County Today
Princeton Publishing Inc.
100 N. Gibson Phone: (812)385-2525
PO Box 321 Fax: (812)386-6199
Princeton, IN 47670
Free: (800)467-5130

Shopping guide with features. **Founded:** 1975. **Freq:** Weekly (Mon.). **Print Method:** Offset. **Cols./Page:** 6. **Col. Width:** 21 nonpareils. **Col. Depth:** 194 agate lines. **Key Personnel:** Gary Blackburn, Publisher, gblack@comsource.net; Phil Summers, General Mgr., psummers@pdclarion.com. **Subscription Rates:** Free. **Remarks:** Accepts advertising. **URL:** http://www.pdclarion.com. **Formerly**: Gibson Dollar Saver.
Ad Rates: BW: $1,513.26 **Circ:** Free ‡5,300
4C: $1,673.26
SAU: $12.01

10585 Princeton Daily Clarion
Princeton Publishing Inc.
100 N. Gibson Phone: (812)385-2525
PO Box 321 Fax: (812)386-6199
Princeton, IN 47670
Free: (800)467-5130

General newspaper. **Founded:** 1846. **Freq:** Daily (morn.). **Print Method:** Offset. **Cols./Page:** 6. **Col. Width:** 2 1/16 inches. **Col. Depth:** 21 inches. **Key Personnel:** Gary Blackburn, Publisher; Phil Summers, General Mgr. **USPS:** 444-920. **Subscription Rates:** $66 individuals. **URL:** http://www.pdclarion.com.
Ad Rates: BW: $1,141.56 **Circ:** ‡6,623
4C: $1,301.56
SAU: $9.06

10586 WRAY-AM - 1250
PO Box 8 Phone: (812)386-1250
Princeton, IN 47670 Fax: (812)386-6249

Format: Hot Country. **Simulcasts:** WRAY-FM. **Networks:** AP. **Founded:** 1950. **Operating Hours:** Continuous; 5% network, 95% local. **ADI:** Evansville, IN (Madisonville, KY). **Key Personnel:** Stephen R. Lankford, General Mgr.; Mark Lathom, News Dir.; Charlene Garrison, Traffic Dir.; Jeff Lankford, Sports Dir. **Local Programs:** *Mystery Voice Program* 8:15 am - 8:30 am Monday-Friday, Roger Beard, (812)386-1250, Fax (812)386-6249; *Roots of Country Music* 9:00 am - 12:00 noon Saturday, Rodger Beard. **Wattage:** 1000. **Ad Rates:** $20-25 for 30 seconds; $25-30 for 60 seconds.

10587 WRAY-FM - 98.1
PO Box 8 Phone: (812)386-1250
Princeton, IN 47670 Fax: (812)386-6249

Format: Hot Country. **Simulcasts:** WRAY-AM. **Networks:** AP. **Founded:** 1960. **Operating Hours:** Continuous; 5% network, 95% local. **ADI:** Evansville, IN (Madisonville, KY). **Key Personnel:** Stephen R. Lankford, General Mgr.; Mark Lathom, News Dir.; Charlene Garrison, Traffic Dir.; Lynn Davis, Sales Mgr.; Jeff Lankford, Sports Dir. **Local Programs:** *Mystery Voice Program* 8:15 am - 8:30 am Monday-Friday, Roger Beard, (812)386-1250, Fax (812)386-6249; *Roots of Country Music* 9:00 am - 12:00 noon Saturday, Rodger Beard. **Wattage:** 50,000. **Ad Rates:** $20-25 for 30 seconds; $25-30 for 60 seconds.

REMINGTON, pop. 1,268.

Jasper Co. (NW). 12 m S of Rensselaer. Residential.

10588 Remington Press
PO Box 129 Phone: (219)261-3577
Remington, IN 47977 Fax: (219)866-3775

Newspaper with a Republican orientation. **Founded:** 1873. **Freq:** Weekly (Thurs.). **Print Method:** Offset. **Cols./Page:** 6. **Col. Width:** 24 nonpareils. **Col. Depth:** 301 agate lines. **Key Personnel:** William F. Kaye, Editor, phone (219)866-5111; Douglas Caldwell, Publisher; Sally Snow, Advertising Mgr. **Subscription Rates:** $26 individuals. **Remarks:** Accepts advertising.
Ad Rates: GLR: $.16 **Circ:** ‡1,010

RENSSELAER†, pop. 4,944.

Jasper Co. (NW). 40 m N of Lafayette. Manufactures cushion springs, trailers, fertilizer, toy trains. Grain and beef farms. Corn, oats, wheat.

10589 Kankakee Valley Post News
Kankakee Valley Publishing Co.
117 N. Van Rensselaer St. Phone: (219)866-5111
Rensselaer, IN 47978 Fax: (219)866-3775
Free: (888)809-5561
Publisher E-mail: kvpost@netnitco.net

Newspaper with a Democratic orientation. **Founded:** 1932. **Freq:** Weekly (Thurs.). **Print Method:** Offset. **Cols./Page:** 6. **Col. Width:** 24 nonpareils. **Col. Depth:** 301 agate lines. **Key Personnel:** Sally Snow, General Mgr.; Frank Copley, Publisher. **Subscription Rates:** $43 individuals. **Remarks:** Accepts advertising. **Feature Editors:** Carmen Cox, *Sports*.
Ad Rates: GLR: $.61 **Circ:** ‡3,192
4C: $200
PCI: $5.74

10590 Rensselaer Republican
Kankakee Valley Publishing Co.
117 N. Van Rensselaer St. Phone: (219)866-5111
Rensselaer, IN 47978 Fax: (219)866-3775
Free: (888)809-5561
Publication E-mail: daily@renssrep.com
Publisher E-mail: kvpost@netnitco.net

Newspaper with a Republican orientation. **Founded:** 1865. **Freq:** Mon.-Sat. (eve.). **Print Method:** Offset. **Cols./Page:** 6. **Col. Width:** 24 nonpareils. **Col. Depth:** 301 agate lines. **Key Personnel:** Frank Copley, Publisher; William F. Kaye, Editor; Lisa Myers, Business Mgr., ljmyers@renssrep.com; Marcia Mathew, Production Mgr.; Regina Warfel, Circulation Mgr. **Subscription Rates:** $88.60 individuals. **Remarks:** Accepts advertising.
Ad Rates: GLR: $0.48 **Circ:** ‡3,600

10591 Shoppers News
Kankakee Valley Publishing Co.
117 N. Van Rensselaer St. Phone: (219)866-5111
Rensselaer, IN 47978 Fax: (219)866-3775
Free: (888)809-5561
Publication E-mail: daily@renssrep.com
Publisher E-mail: kvpost@netnitco.net

Shopper. **Freq:** Weekly (Mon.). **Print Method:** Offset. **Cols./Page:** 6. **Col. Width:** 24 nonpareils. **Col. Depth:** 301 agate lines. **Key Personnel:** Frank Copley, Publisher; William F. Kaye, Editor; Lisa Myers, Business Mgr., ljmyers@renssrep.com; Marcia Mathew, Production Mgr.; Regina Warfel, Circulation Mgr. **Remarks:** Accepts advertising.
Ad Rates: GLR: $0.48 **Circ:** Free ‡13,500

10592 TV Cable
PO Box 319 Phone: (219)866-7101
Rensselaer, IN 47978 Fax: (219)866-5785
Free: (800)621-2344

Owner: Theodore W. Filson, at above address. **Founded:** 1966. **Key Personnel:** Steven T. Filson, President. **Cities Served:** Morocco, Rensselaer, IN: subscribing households 2,712; 47 channels.

10593 TV Cable of Rensselaer Inc.
215 W. Kellner Phone: (219)866-7101
Rensselaer, IN 47978 Fax: (219)866-5785
Free: (800)621-2344

Owner: Theodore W. Filson, at above address. **Founded:** 1966. **Key Personnel:** Steve Filson, President; Russell Scripter, Chief Technician. **Cities Served:** Rensselaer, IN: subscribing households 2,730; 48 channels.

10594 TV Cable of Winamac Inc.
215 W. Kellner Phone: (219)866-7101
Box 319 Fax: (219)866-5785
Rensselaer, IN 47978
Free: (800)621-2344

Owner: Theodore W. Filson, at above address, (219)946-3813, Fax: (219)946-3813. **Key Personnel:** Steve Filson, President; Eric Galbreath, Manager, phone (219)946-3813, fax (219)946-3813. **Cities Served:** Kewanna, Lake Bruce, Winamac, IN: subscribing households 1,540; 44 channels.

10595 WPUM-FM - 90.5
St. Joseph's College Phone: (219)866-6211
PO Box 651 Fax: (219)866-6100
Rensselaer, IN 47978
E-mail: wpum@saintjoe.edu

Format: Album-Oriented Rock (AOR). **Networks:** Independent. **Founded:** 1970. **Formerly:** WOWI-FM (1977). **Operating Hours:** 6 a.m.-3 a.m.; 100% local. **Key Personnel:** Peter Haze Haring, General Mgr. **Wattage:** 10. **Ad Rates:** Advertising accepted; rates available upon request.

10596 WRIN-AM - 1560
PO Box D Phone: (219)866-5105
Rensselaer, IN 47978 Fax: (219)866-5106

Format: Oldies. **Networks:** ABC; AgriAmerica; Tribune Radio. **Owner:** Brothers Broadcasting Corp., at above address, (219)866-4104. **Founded:** 1963. **Operating Hours:** Sunrise-sunset. **Key Personnel:** John Balvich, General Mgr.; Bob Burt, Program Dir. **Wattage:** 1000. **Ad Rates:** $8 for 30 seconds; $10 for 60 seconds. $2-$8 for 30 seconds; $4-$10 for 60 seconds. Combined advertising rates available with WLQI-AM: $9-$12 for 30 seconds; $12-$16.

RICHMOND†, pop. 41,349.

Wayne Co. (E). 68 m E of Indianapolis. Earlham College. Rose growing. Manufacturing.

10597 Palladium-Item
Palladium Publishing
1175 N. A St. Phone: (765)962-1575
PO Box 308 Fax: (765)973-4570
Richmond, IN 47374-3226
Free: (800)686-1330
Publication E-mail: palitem@richmond.gannett.com

General newspaper. **Founded:** 1831. **Freq:** Daily (eve.), Sat. and Sun. (morn.). **Print Method:** Offset. **Cols./Page:** 6. **Col. Width:** 2 1/16 inches. **Col. Depth:** 21 inches. **Key Personnel:** Bill Church, Editor, fax (317)966-6377; Emmett Smelser, Publisher; Nancy Walton, Advertising Dir. **Subscription Rates:** $156 individuals per year. **Remarks:** Accepts advertising.
Ad Rates: PCI: $13.91 **Circ:** Mon.-Sat. ★19,556
Sun. ★23,634

10598 Quaker Life
Friends United Meeting
101 Quaker Hill Dr. Phone: (317)962-7573
Richmond, IN 47374-1980 Fax: (317)966-1293
Publication E-mail: quakerlife@xc.org
Publisher E-mail: fuminfo@xc.org

Religious magazine. **Subtitle:** Informing and Equipping Friends. **Founded:** 1960. **Freq:** 10/year. **Print Method:** Offset. **Trim Size:** 8 1/2 x 11. **Cols./Page:** 3. **Col. Width:** 26 nonpareils. **Col. Depth:** 134 agate lines. **Key Personnel:** Johan Maurer, Editor; Ben Richmond, Managing Editor. **ISSN:** 0033-5061. **Subscription Rates:** $20 individuals; $2 single issue; $12 individuals every home plan; $54 Canada and Mexico three years; $32 other countries; $65 other countries three years. **URL:** http://www.fum.org/ql/ql/-index.htm.
Ad Rates: GLR: $3 **Circ:** 8,200
BW: $475
4C: $575
PCI: $30

10599 WECI-FM - 91.5
Earlham College Phone: (317)962-3541
Richmond, IN 47374 Fax: (317)983-1304

Format: Eclectic. **Networks:** AP. **Founded:** 1964. **Formerly:** WVOE-FM (1963). **Operating Hours:** 21 hours daily. **ADI:** Dayton, OH (Richmond, IN). **Key Personnel:** Cat Rayburn, Station Mgr.; Ritch Duncan, Program Dir.; Mike Milles, Operations Dir.; Bailey Anderson, Contact; Bekah Cole, Contact; Drew Williams, Production Mgr.; Owiso Ofera, Contact. **Local Programs:** *Freefall*, David Bell; *Morning Ramble*, Ed Brockman; *The Oldies Show*, Don Allen. **Wattage:** 400.

10600 WFMG-FM - 101.3
2301 W. Main St. Phone: (765)962-6533
PO Box 1646 Fax: (765)966-1499
Richmond, IN 47374
E-mail: hits1013@infocom.com

Networks: ABC; CBS; Talknet. **Founded:** 1926. **Operating Hours:** Continuous. **ADI:** Dayton, OH (Richmond, IN). **Key Personnel:** John Trine, General Mgr.; Rick Duncan, Program Dir. **Wattage:** 50,000. **Ad Rates:** $10-20 for 30 seconds; $15-23 for 60 seconds. Combined advertising rates available with WKBV-AM.

10601 WHON-AM - 930
Box 1647 Phone: (317)962-1595
Richmond, IN 47375 Fax: (317)966-4824

Format: News; Talk. **Networks:** Mutual Broadcasting System. **Operating Hours:** Continuous. **ADI:** Dayton, OH (Richmond, IN). **Key Personnel:** Dave Strycker, General Mgr.; Dan Mills, Program Dir.; Bill O'Hara, News Dir. **Wattage:** 500. **Ad Rates:** $10.00 for 30 seconds; $16 for 60 seconds.

10602 WKBV-AM - 1490
2301 W. Main St., Box 1646 Phone: (765)962-6533
Richmond, IN 47374 Fax: (765)966-1499
Free: (800)935-5155
E-mail: sports@infocom.com

Format: News; Talk. **Networks:** NBC; ABC. **Owner:** Whitewater Broadcasting, at above address. **Founded:** 1926. **Operating Hours:** Continuous. **ADI:** Dayton, OH (Richmond, IN). **Key Personnel:** Dave Rogers, President; John Traine, General Mgr.; Troy Derengowski, Program Dir. **Wattage:** 1000. **Ad Rates:** $15 for 60 seconds.

10603 WKOI-TV - 43
PO Box 1057 Phone: (317)935-2390
Richmond, IN 47375-1057 Fax: (317)935-5367

Format: Commercial TV; Religious. **Owner:** Trinity Broadcasting Network, 2442 Michelle Dr., Tustin, CA 92680, (714)832-2950. **Founded:** 1982. **Operating Hours:** Continuous; 95% network, 5% local. **ADI:** Dayton, OH (Richmond, IN). **Key Personnel:** Mary Laird, Station Mgr. **Wattage:** 1,410,000 ERP.

10604 WQLK-FM - 96.1
Box 1647 Phone: (317)962-1595
Richmond, IN 47375 Fax: (317)966-4824

Format: Hot Country. **Formerly:** WGLM-FM. **Operating Hours:** Continuous; 2% network, 98% local. **ADI:** Dayton, OH (Richmond, IN). **Key Personnel:** Dave Strycker, General Mgr.; Buzz Cannon, Program Dir.; Dan Mills, Sports Dir.; Bill O'hara, News Dir. **Wattage:** 50,000. **Ad Rates:** $20 for 30 seconds; $25 for 60 seconds.

RISING SUN†, pop. 2,478.

Ohio Co. (SE). On Ohio River, 22 m SW of Cincinnati, Ohio. Tourism. Feed mill. Agriculture. Tobacco, wheat, corn.

10605 Ohio County News
John Reiniger
235 Main St. Phone: (812)438-2011
PO Box 128 Fax: (812)438-3228
Rising Sun, IN 47040-0128
Community newspaper. **Founded:** 1879. **Freq:** Weekly (Thurs.). **Print Method:** Offset. **Trim Size:** 14 1/2 x 24 1/2. **Cols./Page:** 6. **Col. Width:** 12 picas. **Col. Depth:** 194 agate lines. **Key Personnel:** Tim Hillman, Editor; John Reiniger, Publisher; Janet Essert, Advertising Mgr. **ISSN:** 4044-0000. **Subscription Rates:** $18 individuals. **Remarks:** Accepts advertising.
Ad Rates: BW: $5 **Circ:** Paid ‡647
PCI: $5 Free ‡8

10606 Rising Sun Recorder
John Reiniger
235 Main St. Phone: (812)438-2011
PO Box 128 Fax: (812)438-3228
Rising Sun, IN 47040-0128
Community newspaper. **Founded:** 1833. **Freq:** Weekly (Thurs.). **Print Method:** Offset. **Trim Size:** 14 1/2 x 24 1/2. **Cols./Page:** 6. **Col. Width:** 12 6/10 picas. **Col. Depth:** 294 agate lines. **Key Personnel:** Tim Hillman, Editor; John Reiniger, Publisher; Janet Essert, Advertising Mgr. **ISSN:** 4665-2000. **Subscription Rates:** $18 individuals. **Remarks:** Accepts advertising.
Ad Rates: BW: $5 **Circ:** Paid 1,785
PCI: $5 Free 15

ROCHESTER†, pop. 5,050.

Fulton Co. (N). 44 m S of South Bend. Manufacturing. Summer resort. Dairy, stock, grain farms.

10607 Fulton County Images
Fulton County Historical Society, Inc.
37 East 375 North Phone: (219)223-4436
Rochester, IN 46975-8384
Journal covering local history. **Founded:** 1991. **Freq:** Annual. **Print Method:** Offset. **Trim Size:** 8 1/2 x 11. **Cols./Page:** 2. **Col. Width:** 3 3/4 inches. **Col. Depth:** 10 inches. **Key Personnel:** Shirley Willard, Editor, wwillard@rtcol.com. **ISSN:** 1070-7735. **Subscription Rates:** $15 individuals; $25 family or group. **Remarks:** Accepts advertising. **Former name:** Fulton County Historical Society Quarterly.
Ad Rates: BW: $200 **Circ:** Controlled 700

10608 Shopping Guide News
PO Box 229 Phone: (219)223-5417
Rochester, IN 46975 Fax: (219)223-8330

Shopping guide. **Freq:** Weekly (Wed.). **Print Method:** Web offset. **Trim Size:** 10 1/4 x 15. **Cols./Page:** 6. **Col. Width:** 9 1/2 picas. **Col. Depth:** 15 inches. **Key Personnel:** Don Towle, Publisher; Betty Foster, Editor. **Subscription Rates:** Free. **Remarks:** Accepts advertising.
Ad Rates: BW: $382.50 **Circ:** Free ♦**8,682**
PCI: $4.50 Paid ♦**37**

ROCKPORT†, pop. 2,565.

Spencer Co. (SW). On Ohio River, 32 m E of Evansville. Parks. Tourism. National trucking terminal operation. Manufacturing. Diversified farming. Wheat, corn, soybeans tobacco. Cattle, pigs.

10609 The Spencer County Journal-Democrat
Landmark Community Newspapers, Inc.
PO Box 6 Phone: (812)649-9196
Rockport, IN 47635 Fax: (812)649-9197

Community newspaper. **Founded:** 1855. **Freq:** Weekly. **Print Method:** Offset. **Cols./Page:** 6. **Col. Width:** 12 picas. **Col. Depth:** 21 1/2 inches. **Key Personnel:** Thomas Guengerich, Editor and Gen. Mgr. **Subscription Rates:** $21.50 individuals;

$28 out of area; $36.50 out of state. **Remarks:** Accepts advertising.
Ad Rates: GLR: $3.60 **Circ:** 5,625
BW: $621.78
4C: $921.78
SAU: $5.07
PCI: $5.07

ROCKVILLE†, pop. 2,785.

Parke Co. (W). 25 m NE of Terre Haute. State Parks. Historical area. Feed mill. Coal mines. Appliance industries. Timber Agriculture. Livestock.

10610 Parke County Sentinel
Torch Newspapers
PO Box 187 Phone: (317)569-2033
Rockville, IN 47872 Fax: (317)569-1424

Newspaper. **Founded:** 1833. **Freq:** Weekly (Wed.). **Print Method:** Offset. **Cols./Page:** 7. **Col. Width:** 20 nonpareils. **Col. Depth:** 294 agate lines. **Key Personnel:** Larry Bemis, Editor; Richard E. Harney, Publisher. **ISSN:** 1044-7822. **Subscription Rates:** $23 individuals; $25. **Remarks:** Accepts advertising.
Ad Rates: GLR: $.21 **Circ:** ‡4,500
BW: $432.18
SAU: $2.94

10611 WAXI-FM - 104.9
PO Box 20 Phone: (317)569-2026
Rockville, IN 47872 Fax: (317)569-2027

Format: Middle-of-the-Road (MOR); Agricultural. **Networks:** NBC; Satellite Music Network. **Owner:** Robert Rouse, at above address. **Founded:** 1974. **Operating Hours:** 6 a.m.-midnight; 85% network, 15% local. **ADI:** Terre Haute, IN. **Key Personnel:** Bill Cook, General Mgr. **Local Programs:** *High School Sports*, Bill Cook; *Saturday Side-Lines*, Bill Cook; *Wabash Valley Gospel Sing*, Bill Cook. **Wattage:** 1200. **Ad Rates:** $6-9 for 30 seconds; $8-11 for 60 seconds.

ROYAL CENTER, pop. 908.

Cass Co. (NC). 12 m NW of Logansport. Light manufacturing. Dairy, grain farms.

10612 Royal Center Record
PO Box 638 Phone: (219)643-3165
Royal Center, IN 46978 Fax: (219)643-9440
Publication E-mail: record@cqc.com

Tabloid newspaper with a Democratic orientation. **Founded:** 1889. **Freq:** Weekly (Thurs.). **Print Method:** Offset. **Trim Size:** 11 x 17. **Cols./Page:** 5. **Col. Width:** 12.5 ems. **Col. Depth:** 13 inches. **Key Personnel:** Jeffrey C. Funk, Editor and Publisher, jfunk@cqc.com. **USPS:** 472-320. **Subscription Rates:** $18; $20 out of state. **Remarks:** Accepts advertising. **URL:** http://www.cqc.com/~record.
Ad Rates: PCI: $3.25 **Circ:** ‡1,200

RUSHVILLE†, pop. 6,113.

Rush Co. (SEC). 39 m SE of Indianapolis. Manufacturing. Meat packing; vibration eliminators for heavy equipment; bottling works. Stone quarry. Agriculture. Cattle, hogs.

10613 Rushville Republican
Rushville Newspapers, Inc.
PO Box 189 Phone: (317)932-2222
Rushville, IN 46173-0189 Fax: (317)932-4358

Newspaper with a Republican orientation. **Founded:** 1840. **Freq:** Daily (eve.). **Print Method:** Offset. **Cols./Page:** 6. **Col. Width:** 25 nonpareils. **Col. Depth:** 301 agate lines. **Key Personnel:** Don Krause, Editor; Jeff Ensweller, Publisher. **Subscription Rates:** $42 individuals. **Remarks:** Accepts advertising.
Ad Rates: SAU: $5.88 **Circ:** ‡3,983

10614 WRCR-FM - 94.3
102 N. Perkins St. Phone: (317)932-3983
Rushville, IN 46173 Fax: (317)938-1916

Format: Full Service; Oldies; Agricultural; News; Sports. **Networks:** ABC; Brownfield. **Owner:** Quantum Broadcasting Corp., at above address. **Founded:** 1971. **Operating Hours:** 5 a.m.-10:30 p.m.; 20% network, 80% local. **Key Personnel:** Louis Uhl Disinger, Contact; Sharon K. Disinger, Contact; Kevin Stone, Sales Mgr.; Kevin Green, News Dir. **Wattage:** 2,050. **Ad Rates:** $8.70-12.50 for 30 seconds; $10.25-14.75 for 60 seconds.

SALEM†, pop. 5,290.

Washington Co. (S). 35 m NW of New Albany. Manufacturing. Hardwood timber. Rock quarries. Largest cattle producing county in the state. Diversified farming. Corn, wheat, oats.

10615 The Salem Democrat
Leader Publishing Co. of Salem, Inc.
117-119 E. Walnut St. Phone: (812)883-3281
PO Box 509 Fax: (812)883-4446
Salem, IN 47167
Newspaper with a Democratic orientation. **Founded:** 1827. **Freq:** Weekly (Thurs.). **Print Method:** Offset. **Cols./Page:** 6. **Col. Width:** 2 1/32 inches. **Col. Depth:** 21.5 picas. **Key Personnel:** Cecil J. Smith, Editor; Rodger J. Grossman, Publisher; Nancy G. Thomas, General Mgr.; Pat Robertson, Sales Mgr. **USPS:** 477-560. **Subscription Rates:** $24 in-country; $31.50 out of area; $37.50 out of state. **Remarks:** Accepts advertising.
Ad Rates: GLR: $.33 **Circ:** Paid 6,100
BW: $522.45 Free 176
4C: $762.45
SAU: $4.62
PCI: $4.75

10616 The Salem Leader
Leader Publishing Co. of Salem, Inc.
117-119 E. Walnut St. Phone: (812)883-3281
PO Box 509 Fax: (812)883-4446
Salem, IN 47167
Newspaper with a Republican orientation. **Founded:** 1878. **Freq:** Weekly (Tues.). **Print Method:** Offset. **Cols./Page:** 6. **Col. Width:** 2 1/32 inches. **Col. Depth:** 21.5 picas. **Key Personnel:** Cecil J. Smith, Editor; Rodger J. Grossman, Publisher; Nancy G. Thomas, General Mgr.; Pat Robertson, Sales Mgr. **USPS:** 008-980. **Subscription Rates:** $24 in-country; $31.50 out of area; $37.50 out of state.
Ad Rates: GLR: $.33 **Circ:** Paid 6,100
BW: $522.45 Free 176
4C: $762.42
SAU: $4.48
PCI: $4.75

10617 The Washington County Edition
Green Banner Publications, Inc.
105 East Walnut Phone: (812)883-5555
Salem, IN 47167 Fax: (812)883-3658

Community newspaper. **Founded:** 1982. **Freq:** Weekly (Wed.). **Print Method:** Offset. **Trim Size:** 11 3/8 x 17. **Cols./Page:** 5. **Col. Width:** 25 nonpareils. **Col. Depth:** 224 agate lines. **Key Personnel:** Mark Grigsby, Editor; Joe Green, Publisher; John Roberts, Sales Mgr. **Subscription Rates:** $18.50 individuals. **Remarks:** Accepts advertising.
Ad Rates: GLR: $.37 **Circ:** Free 10,315
BW: $414.40
SAU: $5.18
CNU: $5.18
PCI: $5.18

10618 WSLM-AM - 1220
Radio Ridge Phone: (812)883-5750
Hwy. 56 E. Fax: (812)883-2797
PO Box 385
Salem, IN 47167
E-mail: wslm@blueriver.net

Format: Contemporary Country; Agricultural. **Networks:** Independent. **Founded:** 1953. **Operating Hours:** 6 a.m.-midnight; 100% local. **ADI:** Louisville, KY. **Key Personnel:** Don H. Martin, General Mgr.; Rick Martin, News Dir.; Becky Lynn Coomer, Program Dir.; John Wood, Sports Dir.; Elmo Brough, Contact. **Local Programs:** *Coffee Club*, Norma Smedley; *Farm Family*, Don Martin; *Swap Shop*. **Wattage:** 5000. **Ad Rates:** $15-20 for 30 seconds; $20-25 for 60 seconds. $10-$20 for 30 seconds; $15-$25 for 60 seconds. Combined advertising rates available with WSLM-FM.

10619 WSLM-FM - 97.9
1308 E. Hackberry Phone: (812)883-5750
PO Box 385 Fax: (812)883-2797
Salem, IN 47167
Free: (800)230-3401
E-mail: wslm@blueriver.net

Format: Gospel; Sports; Talk; Agricultural; Talk. **Simulcasts:** WSIM-AM 1220. **Networks:** Independent. **Owner:** Rebecca L. White, at above address. **Founded:** 1962. **Formerly:** WDHM-FM (1993). **Operating Hours:** 6 a.m.-midnight; 100% local. **ADI:** Louisville, KY. **Key Personnel:** Don H. Martin, Contact; J.P. Martin, News Dir.; Becky Lynn Coomer, Program Dir.; John Wood, Sports Dir.; Elmo Brough, Contact. **Local Programs:** *Broomsige Ballet*, Don Martin; *Gospel Music Show*, Rebecca Coomer. **Wattage:** 5,000. **Ad Rates:** $15-20 for 30 seconds; $20-25 for 60 seconds. $10-$20 for 30 seconds; $15-$25 for 60 seconds. Combined advertising rates available with WSLM-AM.

SCHERERVILLE

10620 Schererville News
Herald News Group
3161 E. 84th St. Phone: (219)942-0521
Merrillville, IN 46410 Fax: (219)942-0820

Newspaper. **Founded:** 1940. **Freq:** Weekly (Wed.). **Print Method:** Offset. **Cols./Page:** 6. **Col. Width:** 1 9/16 inches. **Col. Depth:** 16 inches. **Key Personnel:** David Kemp, Advertising Dir.; Greg Lenburg, Operations Mgr. **Subscription Rates:** $3 individuals. **Remarks:** Accepts advertising.
Ad Rates: BW: $345 **Circ:** Free 5,663
PCI: $4.05

SCOTTSBURG†, pop. 5,068.

Scott Co. (SE). 31 m N of Louisville, Ky. Unfinished furniture, canning factories. Limestone quarries; hardwood timber. Agriculture. Tomatoes, corn, wheat.

10621 The Giveaway
Green Banner Publications, Inc.
183 East McClain St. Phone: (812)752-3171
Scottsburg, IN 47170 Fax: (812)752-6486

Community newspaper. **Founded:** 1937. **Freq:** Weekly (Wed.). **Print Method:** Offset. **Trim Size:** 11 3/8 x 17. **Cols./Page:** 5. **Col. Width:** 25 nonpareils. **Col. Depth:** 224 agate lines. **Key Personnel:** Mark Grigsby, Editor; Joe Green, Publisher; John Roberts, Sales Mgr. **Subscription Rates:** $18.50 out of area. **Remarks:** Accepts advertising.
Ad Rates: GLR: $.61 **Circ:** Free 16,873
BW: $679.20 Paid 90
SAU: $8.49
PCI: $8.49

10622 Scott County Journal
Green Banner Publications, Inc.
PO Box 159 Phone: (812)967-3176
Scottsburg, IN 47170 Fax: (812)752-2611
Free: (800)264-7336

Newspaper with a Republican orientation. **Founded:** 1882. **Freq:** Weekly. **Print Method:** Offset. **Cols./Page:** 6. **Col. Width:** 2 1/16 inches. **Col. Depth:** 21 inches. **Key Personnel:** Marcus Amos, Managing Editor, phone (812)752-3171, fax (812)752-6486; Joe Green, Publisher; John C. Roberts, Advertising Mgr. **Subscription Rates:** $8.75 individuals; $14.75 out of area; $19.70 out of state; $25 other countries. **Remarks:** Accepts advertising.
Ad Rates: GLR: $0.34 **Circ:** 5000
BW: $607.32
SAU: $4.82
PCI: $4.82

10623 WMPI-FM - 105.3
Box 270 Phone: (812)752-3688
Scottsburg, IN 47170 Fax: (812)752-2345
Free: (800)441-1053
E-mail: wmpi@scottsburg.com

Format: Contemporary Country. **Networks:** ABC. **Founded:** 1966. **Operating Hours:** Continuous; 5% network, 95% local. **ADI:** Louisville, KY. **Key Personnel:** Donald R. Rice, Contact; Raymond Rice, General Mgr.; John Ross, Program Dir. **Wattage:** 6,000. **Ad Rates:** $10.35-44.00 for 60 seconds. **URL:** http://www.wmpi.com.

SELMA

10624 Barnwood
Barnwood Press
PO Box 146 Phone: (765)288-0145
Selma, IN 47383
Poetry review. **Subtitle:** A Gathering of Poems. **Founded:** 1980. **Freq:** 3/year. **Print Method:** Offset. **Trim Size:** 8 1/2 x 7 1/2. **Key Personnel:** Tom Koontz, Editor, tkoontz@gw.bsu.edu. **ISSN:** 1063-0929. **Subscription Rates:** $6. $2 single issue. **Remarks:** Accepts advertising.
Ad Rates: GLR: $10 **Circ:** Paid ‡300
PCI: $25 Controlled ‡100

SEYMOUR, pop. 15,050.

Jackson Co. (S). 59 m S of Indianapolis. Manufacturing. Hardwood timber. Diversified farming.

10625 Seymour Daily Tribune
The Tribune
1215 E. Tipton St. Phone: (812)522-4871
PO Box 447 Fax: (812)522-7691
Seymour, IN 47274
Free: (800)800-8212

General newspaper. **Founded:** 1879. **Freq:** Mon.-Sat. **Print Method:** Offset. **Cols./Page:** 6. **Col. Width:** 12.2 picas. **Col.**

Depth: 301 agate lines. **Key Personnel:** Dan Davis, Editor; Tim Timmons, Publisher; Jeanne Piersall, Advertising Dir. **Subscription Rates:** $107.50 individuals. **Remarks:** Accepts advertising.
Ad Rates: BW: $1,115.85 **Circ:** Mon.-Sat. 9,158
4C: $1,475.85
PCI: $8.65

10626 Sammons Communications
998 N. O'Brien St. Phone: (812)522-8791
Seymour, IN 47274-1859 Fax: (812)522-8828
Free: (800)844-7722

Owner: Cardinal Communications, 1800 N Meridian St., Indianapolis, IN 46202, (317)923-2355. **Formerly**: Cardinal Communications. **Key Personnel:** Russ Smith, General Mgr.; Don Rogers, Contact. **Cities Served:** subscribing households 2,500; 35 channels.

10627 WQKC-FM - 93.7
1534 Ewing St. Phone: (812)522-1390
PO Box 806 Fax: (812)522-9541
Seymour, IN 47274

Format: Country. **Networks:** Jones Satellite. **Owner:** SCI, Inc., at above address. **Founded:** 1960. **Formerly**: WJCD-FM (1990). **Operating Hours:** Continuous. **Key Personnel:** Robert Shippee, Contact; Greg Scott Fisher, Program Dir.; Pam Hasty, Office Mgr.; Blair Trask, General Mgr. **Wattage:** 25,000. **Ad Rates:** $8-14 for 30 seconds; $11-20 for 60 seconds.

10628 WZZB-AM - 1390
1534 Ewing St. Phone: (812)522-1390
PO Box 806 Fax: (812)522-9541
Seymour, IN 47274

Format: News; Adult Contemporary; Oldies. **Networks:** Jones Satellite. **Owner:** SCI, Inc., at above address. **Founded:** 1949. **Formerly**: WJCD-AM (1990). **Operating Hours:** Continuous. **Key Personnel:** Robert Shippee, Contact; Greg Scott Fisher, Program Dir.; Beth Farris, Office Mgr.; Blair Trask, General Mgr. **Wattage:** 1000. **Ad Rates:** $8-14 for 30 seconds; $11-20 for 60 seconds.

SHELBYVILLE†, pop. 14,989.

Shelby Co. (SEC). 28 m SE of Indianapolis. Manufactures magnetic wire, precision aluminum die castings, molded rubber products, phonograph records, custom steel fabrication, business forms. Grain, stock, dairy farms.

10629 The Indiana Runner
PO Box 478 Phone: (317)392-1195
Shelbyville, IN 46176 Fax: (317)398-0194
Free: (800)362-0114
Publication E-mail: irunner@aol.com

Tabloid featuring information and articles about running. **Freq:** Monthly (except Jan.). **Print Method:** Offset. **Trim Size:** 13 3/4 x 11 1/2. **Cols./Page:** 4. **Col. Width:** 2 1/2 inches. **Col. Depth:** 12 1/2 inches. **Key Personnel:** John C. DePrez, Publisher; Jodi Bowman, General and Ad Mgr.; Bill Craig, Editor. **Subscription Rates:** $15 individuals. **Remarks:** Accepts advertising.
Ad Rates: BW: $526 **Circ:** Paid 1,000
4C: $721 Non-paid 9,000

10630 The Shelbyville News
Shelbyville Newspapers, Inc.
123 E. Washington St. Phone: (317)398-6631
PO Box 750 Fax: (317)398-0194
Shelbyville, IN 46176
Free: (800)362-0114
Publication E-mail: shelbynews@shelbynews.com

General newspaper. **Founded:** Dec. 2, 1947. **Freq:** Mon.-Sat. (eve.). **Print Method:** Offset. **Trim Size:** 13 3/4 x 22 3/4. **Cols./Page:** 6. **Col. Width:** 2 1/16 inches. **Col. Depth:** 301 agate lines. **Key Personnel:** Scarlett Syse, Editor, syse@shelbynews.com; Dee Bonner, Advertising Dir. **Remarks:** Accepts advertising.
Ad Rates: GLR: $8.06 **Circ:** Mon.-Sat. ★**10,716**
BW: $1,257.75
4C: $1,507.75
PCI: $9.75

10631 WOOO-AM - 1520
PO Box 338 Phone: (317)398-9757
Shelbyville, IN 46176 Fax: (317)392-3297

Format: Oldies. **Networks:** CNN Radio. **Owner:** ARS Broadcasting, PO Box 15435, Cincinnati, OH 45215, (513)821-7221, Fax: (513)821-7815. **Founded:** 1961. **Formerly**: WSVL-AM (1991). **Operating Hours:** Continuous. **ADI:** Indianapolis (Marion), IN. **Key Personnel:** Tom Hession, General Mgr., fax (317)382-3292; Alan Schriber, President; Wayne Thomas, News Dir., fax (317)392-3292; Pam Taylor, Sales Mgr. **Wattage:** 1000. **Ad Rates:** $8.50-12.95 for 30 seconds; $10.20-16.95 for 60 seconds.

SHERIDAN

10632 Concept Cablevision
106 Main St. Phone: (317)758-4475
Box 71 Free: (800)622-4871
Sheridan, IN 46069

Owner: Helen P. Belisle, PO Box 1203, Coraopolis, PA 15108. **Formerly**: Quality Cable (1985). **Key Personnel:** Randall L. Warrick, Manager. **Cities Served:** subscribing households 4,649; 22 channels.

SOUTH BEND†, pop. 109,727.

St. Joseph Co. (N). On St. Joseph River, adjacent to Mishawaka and 96 m SE of Chicago, Ill. University of Notre Dame, Indiana University at South Bend. St. Mary's College.

10633 Culture Wars
Ultramontane Associates, Inc.
206 Marquette Ave. Phone: (219)289-9786
South Bend, IN 46617 Fax: (219)289-1461

Magazine exploring social and family issues from the point of view of the Catholic Church. **Founded:** 1981. **Freq:** Monthly. **Key Personnel:** E. Michael Jones, Editor. **Subscription Rates:** $25; $25 institutions; $2.50 single issue. **Remarks:** Accepts advertising. **Formerly**: Fidelity Magazine.
Ad Rates: BW: $400 **Circ:** Paid ‡10,000

10634 Hometown News
225 W. Colfax Ave. Phone: (219)235-6161
South Bend, IN 46626 Fax: (219)235-1765

Newspaper. **Freq:** Daily. **Key Personnel:** Mike Siroky, Editor. **USPS:** 501-980. **Subscription Rates:** $120. **Remarks:** Advertising accepted; rates available upon request.
Circ: (Not Reported)

10635 South Bend Tribune
Schurz Communications Inc./South Bend Tribune
225 W. Colfax Ave. Phone: (219)235-6474
South Bend, IN 46626 Fax: (219)239-2646

General newspaper. **Founded:** 1872. **Freq:** Daily (eve.), Sat. and Sun. (morn.). **Print Method:** Letterpress. **Cols./Page:** 6. **Col. Width:** 24 nonpareils. **Col. Depth:** 308 agate lines. **Key Personnel:** John J. McGann, Editor and Publisher. **Subscription Rates:** $120 individuals. **Remarks:** Accepts advertising. **Feature Editors:** Kathy Borlik, *Religion*, phone (219)235-3434; Chris Bowman, *Education*, phone (219)235-3434; Jack Colwell, *Political*, phone (219)235-3434; Dan Cooreman, *Family, Movie, Society, Women's*, phone (219)235-3434; Paul Ditlinger, *Sunday*, phone (219)235-3434; Paul Dodson, *Financial/Business, Real Estate*, phone (219)235-3434; Wayne Falda, *Environmental, Rural Development*, phone (219)235-3434; Deanna Francis, *Features, Food*, phone (219)235-3434; Nancy J. Sulok, *Metro*, phone (219)235-3434; Tyna Landgrebe, *Garden/Home*, phone (219)235-3434; Linda McManus, *Book*, phone (219)235-3434; Bill Moor, *Sports*, phone (219)235-3434; Ed Perkins, *Editorials*, phone (219)235-3434; Kathy Sechowski, *Fashion*, phone (219)235-3434; Mark Stryker, *Music, TV & Radio*, phone (219)235-3434; Mark Styker, *Drama*, phone (219)235-3434.
Ad Rates: PCI: $35.56 **Circ:** Mon.-Sat. ★**75,255**
Sun. ★**107,890**

10636 Tri-County News
PO Box 6666 Phone: (219)287-0285
South Bend, IN 46660-6666 Fax: (219)282-1716

Legal advertising newspaper. **Founded:** 1923. **Freq:** Weekly (Fri.). **Print Method:** Letterpress. Uses mats. **Trim Size:** 10 1/4 x 16. **Cols./Page:** 6. **Col. Width:** 24 nonpareils. **Col. Depth:** 224 agate lines. **Key Personnel:** Cherie Jolly, Managing Editor. **Subscription Rates:** $12 in St. Joseph County; $20 two years in St. Joseph County; $17 out of area; $30 two years out of area. **Remarks:** Accepts advertising.
Ad Rates: BW: $260 **Circ:** ‡1,000
4C: $350
SAU: $4
PCI: $4

10637 Tribune Business Weekly
Schurz Communications Inc./South Bend Tribune
225 W. Colfax Ave. Phone: (219)235-6474
South Bend, IN 46626 Fax: (219)239-2646
Publication E-mail: tbw@sbt.sbtinfo.com

Regional business newspaper. **Founded:** 1990. **Freq:** Weekly. **Print Method:** Offset. **Trim Size:** 11 1/4 x 16 3/4. **Cols./Page:** 5. **Col. Width:** 2 inches. **Col. Depth:** 15 1/2 inches. **Key Personnel:** Philip A. Vitale, Editor. **ISSN:** 1051-7367. **Subscription Rates:** Free; $26 (mail). **Remarks:** Accepts advertising.
Ad Rates: BW: $995.10 **Circ:** Paid ‡2,600
4C: $1,345.10 Non-paid ‡6,383
PCI: $12.84

10638 WETL-FM - 91.7
635 S. Main St. Phone: (219)282-4076
South Bend, IN 46601 Fax: (219)282-4122

Format: Talk; Information; Eclectic. **Networks:** Longhorn Radio. **Owner:** South Bend Community School Corp., at above address, (219)283-8076, Fax: (219)283-8122. **Founded:** 1958. **Operating Hours:** 8 hrs. Daily; 10% network, 90% local. **ADI:** South Bend-Elkhart, IN. **Key Personnel:** Joanne Bendall, Station Mgr.; Jerry V. Limbert, Program Dir.; Al Wujcik, Chief Engineer. **Wattage:** 3000.

10639 WHLY-AM - 1620
2010 S. Michigan Fax: (219)280-5343
South Bend, IN 46613
E-mail: whly@aol.com

Format: Middle-of-the-Road (MOR). **Networks:** ABC. **Owner:** Times Communications, Inc., at above address, (219)251-1620. **Founded:** 1947. **Formerly**: WJVA-AM (1981); WAMJ-AM (1993). **Operating Hours:** Continuous; 65% network, 35% local. **ADI:** South Bend-Elkhart, IN. **Key Personnel:** Michael Shannon, Operations Mgr., whly@aol.com; Larry Humphrey, Chief Engineer; Deb Millard, Sales Mgr. **Local Programs:** *Friday Night Oldies Party*, Mike Shannon, Mailing contact; *Shannon In The Morning*, Mike Shannon, Mailing contact. **Wattage:** 10,000 day; 1000 night. **Ad Rates:** $12.50 for 30 seconds; $15.00 for 60 seconds. Combined advertising rates available with WJVA-AM.

10640 WHME-FM - 103.1
61300 S. Ironwood Rd. Phone: (219)291-8200
South Bend, IN 46614 Fax: (219)291-9043

Format: Religious; Contemporary Christian. **Networks:** Independent. **Founded:** 1968. **Operating Hours:** Continuous. **ADI:** South Bend-Elkhart, IN. **Key Personnel:** Pete Sumrall, General Mgr.; Tom Lewis, Contact. **Wattage:** 3000.

10641 WNDU-AM - 1490
Box 1616 Phone: (219)631-1616
South Bend, IN 46634 Fax: (219)631-1600

Format: Oldies; Sports; Talk. **Networks:** Westwood One Radio. **Owner:** Michiana Telecasting Corp., 54516 Business, US 31 North, South Bend, IN 46637. **Founded:** 1944. **Operating Hours:** Continuous;. **ADI:** South Bend-Elkhart, IN. **Key Personnel:** Lou Pierce, Promotions Dir.; Bill Mitchell, Contact; Debra Miles, News Dir. **Local Programs:** *Notre Dame Sports Talk*, Bill Mitchell, Mailing contact, (219)631-1616; *Pulse of Michiana*, Debra Miles, Mailing contact, (219)631-1616. **Wattage:** 1000. **Ad Rates:** $5-43 for 30 seconds; $5-50 for 60 seconds. $14 $25 for 30 seconds; $5-$30 for 60 seconds. Combined advertising rates available with WNDU-FM.

10642 WNDU-FM - 92.9
Box 1616 Phone: (219)631-1616
South Bend, IN 46634 Fax: (219)631-1600
E-mail: u93@u93.com

Format: Contemporary Hit Radio (CHR). **Networks:** Independent. **Owner:** Michiana Telecasting Corp., 54516 Business, US 31 North, South Bend, IN 46637. **Founded:** 1962. **Operating Hours:** Continuous; 100% local. **ADI:** South Bend-Elkhart, IN. **Key Personnel:** Bill Mitchell, Contact; Jim Behling, President; Lou Pierce, Promotions Dir.; Bill Mitchell, Program/Music Dir.; Debra Miles, News Dir. **Wattage:** 12,500. **Ad Rates:** $16-75 for 30 seconds; $20-90 for 60 seconds. $10-$75 for 30 seconds; $12-$90 for 60 seconds. Combined advertising rates available with WNDU-AM.

10643 WNDU-TV - 16
PO Box 1616 Phone: (219)631-1616
South Bend, IN 46634 Fax: (219)631-1600

Format: Commercial TV. **Networks:** Fox. **Owner:** Petra Corn Inc., 1527 N. Dale Mabry Hwy., Ste. 105, Lutz, FL 33549, (813)948-2554, Fax: (813)948-2557. **Founded:** 1955. **Operating Hours:** Continuous. **ADI:** South Bend-Elkhart, IN. **Key Personnel:** Jim Behling, Contact; Gregory J. Giczi, Contact; Mike Leyes, Sales Mgr.; Ellen Crooke, News Dir.; Melissa Collins, Promotions/Program Dir.; George Molnar, Chief Engineer. **Ad Rates:** $45-1000 per unit.

10644 WNSN-FM - 101.5
300 W. Jefferson Blvd.
South Bend, IN 46601

Format: Adult Contemporary. **Networks:** Independent. **Founded:** 1962. **Operating Hours:** Continuous. **ADI:** South Bend-Elkhart, IN. **Key Personnel:** Jim Freeman, General Mgr.; Sally Brown, Station Mgr., sally@wsbt.com; Phil Britain,

Program Dir. **Wattage:** 13,000. **Ad Rates:** Combined advertising rates available with WSBT, WZOL. **URL:** http://www.wsbt.com.

10645 WSBT-AM - 960
300 W. Jefferson Blvd.
South Bend, IN 46601

Format: News; Talk. **Networks:** CBS. **Founded:** 1922. **Operating Hours:** Continuous. **ADI:** South Bend-Elkhart, IN. **Key Personnel:** Sally Brown, Station Mgr.; Jim Freeman, General Mgr.; Bob Montgomery, Program Dir. **Local Programs:** *Week Day Sports Beat*, Tom Dennin, (219)233-3141, Fax (219)289-7382. **Wattage:** 5000. **URL:** http://www.wsbt.com.

10646 WSBT-TV - 22
300 W. Jefferson Blvd. Phone: (219)233-3141
South Bend, IN 46601 Fax: (219)288-6630
Free: (800)442-3141
E-mail: wsbtnews@wsbt.com

Format: Commercial TV. **Networks:** CBS. **Owner:** Schurz Communications, 225 W. Colfax Ave, South Bend, IN 46601, (219)287-1001. **Founded:** 1952. **Operating Hours:** Continuous 60% network, 40% local. **ADI:** South Bend-Elkhart, IN. **Key Personnel:** James D. Freeman, Pres./Gen. Mgr.; Roland Adeszko, Asst. Gen. Mgr/General Sales Mgr.; Julius DeCocq, Program Dir.; Meg Saver, News Dir.; Paula Carlson, Community Affairs Dir.; Bob Johnson, Operations Mgr.; Charlie Adams, Sports Dir.; Paul Stage, Chief Engineer. **Local Programs:** *22 In Touch*, Mary Simko, Producer. **Wattage:** 4790 kw. **URL:** http://www.wsbt.com.

SOUTH WHITLEY, pop. 1,575.

Whitley Co. (NE). 27 m W of Fort Wayne. Grip nut, trailer coach factories; small wire assemblies; grain elevators. Grain, stock farms. Corn, wheat, oats.

10647 Tribune News
Tranter Publishing Co.
113 S. State St. Phone: (219)723-4771
South Whitley, IN 46787 Fax: (219)723-4771

Newspaper with a Republican orientation. **Founded:** 1883. **Freq:** Weekly (Wed.). **Print Method:** Offset. **Cols./Page:** 6. **Col. Width:** 30 nonpareils. **Col. Depth:** 225 agate lines. **Key Personnel:** David Tranter, Editor and Publisher. **Subscription Rates:** $20 individuals; $0.60 single issue. **Remarks:** Accepts advertising.
Ad Rates: GLR: $.163 **Circ:** ‡2,145

SPENCER†, pop. 2,732.

Owen Co. (SWC). 53 m SW of Indianapolis. Manufacturing. Printing. Coal mines; limestone quarries. Agriculture. Corn, livestock, soybeans, apples.

10648 Spencer Owen Leader
114 E. Franklin St. Phone: (812)829-3936
PO Box 22 Fax: (812)829-4666
Spencer, IN 47460-0022
Community newspaper. **Founded:** 1913. **Freq:** Weekly (Wed.). **Print Method:** Offset. **Cols./Page:** 7. **Col. Width:** 12 1/2 picas. **Col. Depth:** 21 inches. **Key Personnel:** John T. Gillaspy, Editor and Publisher. **USPS:** 416-240. **Subscription Rates:** $10; $15 out of area. **Remarks:** Accepts advertising.
Ad Rates: GLR: $2 **Circ:** Paid 549
PCI: $2.75 Free 25

10649 World
Spencer Evening World
114 E. Franklin St. Phone: (812)829-2255
Spencer, IN 47460 Fax: (812)829-4666

Newspaper with a Democratic orientation. **Founded:** 1927. **Freq:** Daily (eve.). **Print Method:** Offset. **Cols./Page:** 7. **Col. Width:** 25 nonpareils. **Col. Depth:** 294 agate lines. **Key Personnel:** Thomas L. Douglas, Editor; John T. Gillespy, Publisher. **Subscription Rates:** $48 individuals. **Remarks:** Accepts advertising. **Online:** American Online, Inc.
Ad Rates: SAU: $4.45 **Circ:** Paid ‡3,550

10650 WSKT-FM - 92.7
PO Box 388 Phone: (812)829-9393
Spencer, IN 47460 Fax: (812)829-9747

Format: Country. **Networks:** Independent. **Owner:** Old Northwest Broadcasting, Inc, at above address. **Founded:** 1984. **Formerly:** WLSO-FM (1988). **Operating Hours:** Continuous; 100% local. **ADI:** Indianapolis (Marion), IN. **Key Personnel:** Dave Crooks, General/Sales Manager; Tony Kale, Program Dir. **Wattage:** 3000. **Ad Rates:** Advertising accepted; rates available upon request.

SULLIVAN†, pop. 4,774.

Sullivan Co. (SW). 27 m S of Terre Haute. Machine shops. Coal mines; oil and natural gas wells; timber. Dairy, poultry, grain farms.

10651 Daily Times
Daily News
PO Box 130 Phone: (812)268-6356
Sullivan, IN 47882-0130 Fax: (812)268-3110
Free: (800)264-6356

Newspaper with a Democratic orientation. **Founded:** 1897. **Freq:** Daily. **Print Method:** Offset. **Cols./Page:** 6. **Col. Width:** 2 1/16 inches. **Col. Depth:** 21 inches. **Key Personnel:** Nancy P. Gettinger, Publisher; Tom P. Gettinger, General Mgr. **Subscription Rates:** 525-200. **Remarks:** Accepts advertising.
Ad Rates: BW: $409.50 **Circ:** ‡4,700
SAU: $4.10
PCI: $3.50

10652 WNDI-AM - 1550
RR. 5, PO Box 19B Phone: (812)268-6322
Sullivan, IN 47882-9805 Fax: (812)266-6652

Format: Contemporary Country. **Networks:** CNN Radio. **Founded:** 1963. **Operating Hours:** 6a.m.-11p.m. M-Sat;7a.m. -11p.m. Sun; 10% local, 90% network. **Key Personnel:** John Montgomery, General Mgr.; Brian Ketterer, Prog. Dir/News Dir. **Local Programs:** *Community Perspective*, Brian Ketterer; *Local News*, Brian Ketterer; *WNDI Football & Basketball Games*, John Montgomery. **Wattage:** 250. **Ad Rates:** $5 for 30 seconds; $9 for 60 seconds.

10653 WNDI-FM - 95.3
RR 5, 19 B Phone: (812)268-6322
Sullivan, IN 47882-9805 Fax: (812)268-6652

Format: Contemporary Country. **Networks:** CNN Radio. **Owner:** John & Teresa Montgomery, at above address. **Founded:** 1963. **Operating Hours:** Continuous; 75% network, 25% local. **ADI:** Terre Haute, IN. **Key Personnel:** John Montgomery, General Mgr.; Brian Ketterer, Program and News Dir. **Local Programs:** *Partyline*, John Montgomery, Mailing contact; *Sullivan High Sports*, John Montgomery, Mailing contact. **Wattage:** 3000. **Ad Rates:** $5 for 30 seconds; $9 for 60 seconds.

SUNMAN

10654 Sunman Telecommunications Corp.
Box 145 Phone: (812)623-2123
Sunman, IN 47041 Fax: (812)623-4159
Free: (800)353-2123

Founded: May 1984. **Formerly**: Sunman Cablevision Co. **Key Personnel:** Robert Miles, Jr., President; Timothy Miles, Accountant; Brian Appleton, Systems Eng.; Mike Fledderman, Systems Manager; Terry Bivens, Mrktg. Dir. **Cities Served:** Napolean, New Point, St. Leon, Sunman, IN: subscribing households 625; 33 channels. **URL:** http://www.seidata.com/~stc.

SWAYZEE, pop. 1,073.

Grant Co. (WC). 9 m WSW of Marion.

10655 Oak Hill Times
Oak Hill Times, Inc.
PO Box 640 Phone: (317)922-7961
Swayzee, IN 46986 Fax: (317)674-0071

Local newspaper. **Founded:** 1979. **Freq:** Weekly (Thurs.). **Print Method:** Offset. **Trim Size:** 11 1/2 x 15. **Cols./Page:** 5. **Col. Width:** 22 1/2 nonpareils. **Col. Depth:** 182 agate lines. **Key Personnel:** Karen Owen, Editor; Cynthia Payne, Publisher. **Subscription Rates:** $15 individuals; $22.50 out of state. **Remarks:** Accepts advertising.
Ad Rates: GLR: $.25 **Circ:** ‡1,700
BW: $240
SAU: $3.53

SYRACUSE

10656 WAWC-FM - 103.5
10129 N. 800 E. Phone: (219)457-8181
Syracuse, IN 46567 Fax: (219)457-4488
Free: (800)779-1094
E-mail: wawasee@wawasee103.com

Format: Classic Rock. **Networks:** UPI. **Owner:** William Andrew Dixon, at above address. **Operating Hours:** Continuous. **ADI:** South Bend-Elkhart, IN. **Key Personnel:** William Dixon, General Mgr.; Splash Lucas, Program Dir.; Jason Samuel, Sports Dir. **Wattage:** 3,000. **Ad Rates:** $1.50-4 for 10 seconds; $3-8.25 for 30 seconds; $4.50-12.50 for 60 seconds. **URL:** http://www.wawasee103.com.

TELL CITY, pop. 8,704.

Perry Co. (S). On Ohio River, 45 m E of Evansville. Boat connections. Manufactures furniture, petrochemical filters, electric motors, boats, barges; foundry; flour, planing mills; bottling works; oil refinery; meat packing plants. Coal mines; hardwood timber. Dairy, stock, poultry farms.

10657 Lincolnland Shopping Guide
News Publishing Co.
PO Box 309 Phone: (812)547-3424
Tell City, IN 47586 Fax: (812)547-2847

Shopper. **Founded:** 1977. **Freq:** Weekly (Wed.). **Print Method:** Offset. **Cols./Page:** 6. **Col. Width:** 24 nonpareils. **Col. Depth:** 301 agate lines. **Key Personnel:** Ron Filkins, Publisher. **Subscription Rates:** Free.
Ad Rates: GLR: $5.77 **Circ:** Non-paid 7,759
BW: $917.19
4C: $1,277.19
SAU: $7.11
PCI: $7.11

10658 The Perry County News
News Publishing Co.
PO Box 309 Phone: (812)547-3424
Tell City, IN 47586 Fax: (812)547-2847
Publication E-mail: pcnews@psci.net

Community newspaper. **Founded:** 1891. **Freq:** Semiweekly (Mon. and Thurs.). **Print Method:** Offset. **Cols./Page:** 6. **Col. Width:** 24 nonpareils. **Col. Depth:** 301 agate lines. **Key Personnel:** Ron Filkins, Publisher; Tina Kunkler-Laake, Managing Editor; Cindy Dauby, Advertising Dir.; Bob Arnold, Plant Mgr. **Subscription Rates:** $35 individuals.
Ad Rates: GLR: $5.77 **Circ:** 7,490
BW: $1,039.74
4C: $1,304.55
SAU: $8.06
PCI: $8.06

10659 WTCJ-AM - 1230
Hwy. 66 Phone: (812)547-2345
PO Box 397 Fax: (812)547-2346
Tell City, IN 47586

Format: News; Talk. **Networks:** Westwood One Radio. **Owner:** Brewer Broadcasting Corp., 409 Chestnut St., Ste. A-154, Chattanooga, TN 37402, (423)265-9432, Fax: (423)266-2335. **Founded:** 1948. **Operating Hours:** Continuous; 15% network, 85% local. **ADI:** Evansville, IN (Madisonville, KY). **Key Personnel:** Jackie Colucci, News Dir., phone (812)547-2345, fax (812)547-2346; Jay Brewer, General Mgr.; Brenda Bryant, Office Mgr. **Wattage:** 1000. **Ad Rates:** $4-6 for 30 seconds; $4.45-8.10 for 60 seconds.

TERRE HAUTE†, pop. 61,125.

Vigo Co. (W). On Wabash River, 72 m SW of Indianapolis. Indiana State University, Rose Hulman Institute of Technology. Coal mines; shale and clay deposits; oil field. Manufacturing.

10660 African American Review
Dept. of English Phone: (812)237-2968
Indiana State University Fax: (812)237-3156
Terre Haute, IN 47809
Publication E-mail: ascleco@amber.indstate.edu

Journal presenting essays on African American literature and culture. Contains interviews, poems, ficton, and book reviews. **Founded:** 1967. **Freq:** Quarterly. **Print Method:** Offset. **Trim Size:** 7 x 10. **Cols./Page:** 2. **Col. Width:** 14 picas. **Col. Depth:** 54 picas. **Key Personnel:** Joe Weixlmann, Editor, phone (812)237-2788, ascweix@amber.indstate.edu; Connie LeComte, Managing Editor, phone (812)237-3267. **ISSN:** 1062-4783. **Subscription Rates:** $27 individuals; $54 institutions; $34 other countries; $61 institutions, other countries. **Formerly**: Negro American Literature Forum; Black American Literature Forum.
Ad Rates: BW: $200 **Circ:** Paid 4,200
Non-paid 167

10661 Automotive Contact
PO Box 517
Terre Haute, IN 47808

Automotive magazine. **Founded:** 1940. **Freq:** Monthly. **Print Method:** Offset. **Cols./Page:** 2. **Col. Width:** 27 nonpareils. **Col. Depth:** 105 agate lines. **Key Personnel:** Tom Spelman, Publisher. **Remarks:** Accepts advertising.
Ad Rates: BW: $180 **Circ:** Non-paid 4,000

10662 Classical and Modern Literature
CML, Inc.
PO Box 629 Phone: (812)237-2362
Terre Haute, IN 47808-0629 Fax: (812)237-2567

Literary journal. **Subtitle:** A Quarterly. **Founded:** 1980. **Freq:** Quarterly. **Print Method:** Offset. **Trim Size:** 6 x 9. **Key Personnel:** Virginia Leon DeVivero, Editor. **ISSN:** 0197-2227. **Subscription Rates:** $22 individuals; $6.50 single issue; $26 institutions.
Ad Rates: BW: $75 **Circ:** 500

10663 Contemporary Education
Indiana State University Phone: (812)237-2970
School of Education Fax: (812)237-4348
Terre Haute, IN 47809
Education journal. **Founded:** 1929. **Freq:** Quarterly. **Print Method:** Offset. **Trim Size:** 7 1/2 x 10 1/4. **Cols./Page:** 2. **Col. Width:** 40 nonpareils. **Col. Depth:** 120 agate lines. **Key Personnel:** Todd Whitaker, Editor; J. Adamson Hughes, Managing Editor, phone (812)237-2969; Sandra Shields, Circulation Mgr., soeshiel@befac.indstate.edu; Beth Whitaker, Editor, phone (812)237-2904. **ISSN:** 0010-7476. **Subscription Rates:** $12 individuals; $16 institutions; $15 other countries; $19 institutions, other countries; $4 single issue. **Remarks:** Advertising not accepted. **Online:** EBSCO.
Circ: 1,500

10664 Echoes
Rose-Hulman Institute of Technology
5500 Wabash Ave. Phone: (812)877-8258
Terre Haute, IN 47803 Fax: (812)877-8362

Newspaper (tabloid) for college alumni, parents, and friends. **Freq:** Quarterly (during the academic year). **Print Method:** Offset. **Trim Size:** 11 x 17. **Cols./Page:** 4. **Col. Width:** 28 nonpareils. **Col. Depth:** 217 agate lines. **Key Personnel:** Bryan Taylor, Editor, bryan.taylor@rose-hulman.edu. **USPS:** 470-700. **Remarks:** Advertising not accepted. **URL:** www.rose-hulman.edu/publications.html.
Circ: Free ‡15,378

10665 Global Business and Finance Review
Indiana State University
School of Business Phone: (812)237-2117
Terre Haute, IN 47809 Fax: (812)237-4820

The GBFR is a referred journal specializing in global business and finance. **Founded:** 1996. **Freq:** Semiannual. **Key Personnel:** Dr. David J. Kim, Editor, mtkim@befac.indstate.edu. **ISSN:** 1088-6931. **Subscription Rates:** $30 individuals; $80 institutions. **Remarks:** Accepts advertising.
Ad Rates: BW: $150 **Circ:** Paid 400
Non-paid 150

10666 The Indiana Statesman
Indiana State University
HMSU No. 719 Phone: (812)237-3025
Terre Haute, IN 47809 Fax: (812)237-7629
Publication E-mail: saseditr@scifac.indstate.edu

Collegiate newspaper. **Founded:** 1895. **Freq:** 3/week. **Print Method:** Offset. **Cols./Page:** 6. **Col. Width:** 2 inches. **Col. Depth:** 21.5 inches. **Key Personnel:** Merv Hendricks, Contact, sashendr@scifac.indstate.edu. **Subscription Rates:** $48 individuals. **Remarks:** Accepts advertising. **URL:** http://www.indstate.edu/statesman.
Ad Rates: GLR: $8.60 **Circ:** Free ‡7,000
BW: $1,109.40
4C: $1,259.40
PCI: $8.60

10667 Issues in Law & Medicine
National Legal Center for the Medically Dependent & Disabled, Inc.
3 South 6th St. Phone: (812)232-0103
Terre Haute, IN 47807-3510 Fax: (812)232-0103

Journal covering legal and ethical issues in the delivery of medical care. **Founded:** 1985. **Freq:** Quarterly. **Print Method:** Offset lithography. **Trim Size:** 6 3/4 x 9 1/2. **Cols./Page:** 1. **Col. Width:** 4 7/8 inches. **Col. Depth:** 7 5/8 inches. **Key Personnel:** James Bopp Jr., J.D., Editor-in-Chief, phone (812)232-2434, fax (812)235-3685; Larry G. Ligget, Managing Editor, phone (812)232-2434; Barry Bostrom, Editor, phone (812)232-2434. **ISSN:** 8756-8160. **Subscription Rates:** $59 individuals; $74 Canada; $79 other countries; $100 U.S. two years; $79 institutions; $140 institutions two years. **Remarks:** Advertising not accepted. **Online:** LEXIS-NEXIS; Westlaw. **URL:** http://www.ellbrary.com. **Alt. Formats:** Microform.
Circ: Paid 1,000
Controlled 2,000

10668 Poet's Roundtable
826 Center St.
Terre Haute, IN 47807

Magazine covering poetry. **Freq:** Bimonthly. **Key Personnel:** Esther Alman, Editor. **Subscription Rates:** $10 individuals. **Remarks:** Advertising not accepted.
Circ: Controlled 1,000

10669 The Rose Thorn
Rose-Hulman Institute of Technology
5500 Wabash Ave. Phone: (812)877-8258
Terre Haute, IN 47803 Fax: (812)877-8362
Publication E-mail: thorn@rose-hulman.edu

Collegiate newspaper covering local and national issues of interest to the Rose-Hulman Community. **Founded:** 1965. **Freq:** Weekly. **Print Method:** Offset. **Cols./Page:** 5. **Col. Width:** 22 nonpareils. **Col. Depth:** 224 agate lines. **Key Personnel:** Matt Gumbel, Business Mgr. **Subscription Rates:** Free. **Remarks:** Color advertising not accepted. **URL:** http://www.rose-hulman.edu/users/groups/thorn/html/index.htm.
Ad Rates: BW: $380 **Circ:** Free ‡1,500
PCI: $8

10670 Tribune-Star
PO Box 149 Phone: (812)231-4200
Terre Haute, IN 47808-0149 Fax: (812)231-4234
Free: (800)783-8742
Publication E-mail: dcox@mail.tribstar.com

Independent. **Founded:** 1903. **Freq:** Mon.-Sun. (morn.). **Print Method:** Offset. **Trim Size:** 22 3/4 x 27 1/4. **Cols./Page:** 6. **Col. Width:** 24 nonpareils. **Col. Depth:** 301 agate lines. **Key Personnel:** Jack Meany, Publisher, phone (812)231-4252, fax (812)231-4347, jmeany@mail.tribstar.com; Melony Baker, CFO, phone (812)231-4270, fax (812)231-4347, mbaker@mail.tribstar.com; David Cox, Editor, phone (812)231-4258, dcox@mail.tribstar.com. **Subscription Rates:** $169 individuals. **Remarks:** Accepts advertising. **Available Online. URL:** http://www.tribstar.com.
Ad Rates: GLR: $1.70 **Circ:** Mon.-Fri. ★**34,286**
BW: $2,777.37 Sat. ★**39,688**
4C: $3,150.87 Sun. ★**44,669**
SAU: $25.40

10671 Clinton Cable TV Co. Inc.
Box 665 Phone: (812)235-8174
Terre Haute, IN 47808 Fax: (812)232-3519

Owner: Nichols Family, at above address. **Founded:** 1965. **Key Personnel:** John E. Nichols, President; William F. George, Sec./Treas. and GM. **Cities Served:** Clinton, Fairview, Parke, Rosedale, Universal, Vermillion, Vigo, IN: subscribing households 4,530; 40 channels.

10672 Time Warner Cable
1605 Wabash Ave. Phone: (812)232-5013
Terre Haute, IN 47807-3701 Fax: (812)232-7453

Founded: 1966. **Key Personnel:** Mary Ann Perkins, General Mgr., phone (812)232-5808, fax (812)232-7453; Al Winn, Technical Manager; Sharon Brockmeier, Business/Customer Service. **Cities Served:** subscribing households 29,000; 71 channels.

10673 WBAK-TV - 38
138 Poplar St. Phone: (812)238-3838
Terre Haute, IN 47807 Fax: (812)235-3854

Format: Commercial TV. **Networks:** Fox. **Founded:** 1973. **Formerly:** WIIL-TV. **Operating Hours:** 6 a.m.-1 a.m. **ADI:** Terre Haute, IN. **Key Personnel:** Larry Manne, General Mgr.; Carla Peters, Operations Mgr. **Ad Rates:** $25-600 per unit. **URL:** http://www.fox38-wbak.com.

10674 WBOW-AM - 640
Box 35 Phone: (812)232-5034
Terre Haute, IN 47808 Fax: (812)234-4383
E-mail: w22Q1075@aol.com

Format: Full Service. **Networks:** CBS; Unistar. **Founded:** 1927. **Operating Hours:** Continuous. **ADI:** Terre Haute, IN. **Key Personnel:** John McDaniel, General Mgr., fm1075@aol.com. **Local Programs:** *Open Line*, Angel Stephenson; *Saturday Garage Sale*, Angel Stephenson. **Wattage:** 250. **Ad Rates:** $12-14 for 30 seconds; $15-17 for 60 seconds. Combined advertising rates available with W22Q.

10675 WISU-FM - 89.7
Indiana State University Phone: (812)237-3248
217 N. 6th St. Fax: (812)237-3241
Terre Haute, IN 47809
E-mail: cmwisu@ruby.indstate.edu

Format: Jazz; Blues. **Networks:** AP. **Owner:** Indiana State University, at above address. **Founded:** 1964. **Operating Hours:** 1 p.m.-midnight; 5% network, 95% local. **ADI:** Terre Haute, IN. **Key Personnel:** Dave Sabaini, Contact, cmsabain@ruby.indstate.edu; Lance Cope, Production/Promotions Dir., phone (812)237-3240; Rich Lidstrom, Sports Dir., phone (812)237-3255. **Local Programs:** *Small Business Insights*, Bill Minis, (812)237-3232; *Sport Scope*, Chris Miller, (812)237-3255. **Wattage:** 13,500. **Ad Rates:** Noncommercial.

10676 WJSH-AM - 1300
1215 Wabash Ave. Phone: (812)234-9770
Terre Haute, IN 47807 Fax: (812)238-1576
E-mail: wsdm@wsdm.com

Format: Southern Gospel. **Simulcasts:** WSDM-AM. **Owner:** Crossroads Communications, Inc., at above address. **Formerly:** WYTL-AM (1992). **Operating Hours:** Continuous. **ADI:** Terre Haute, IN. **Key Personnel:** Mike Peterson, General Mgr., mpeter@wsdm.com; Jimmy Beasley, Sports Dir.; Gretl Plessinger, News Dir./Operations Mgr., phone (812)234-0770, fax (812)238-1576, newsroom@wsdm.com. **Wattage:** 500. **Ad Rates:** $4-16 per unit. Combined advertising rates available with WSDM-FM, WAXI-FM.

10677 WMGI-FM - 100.7
824 S. 3rd St.
Terre Haute, IN 47807-4609

Format: Adult Contemporary. **Networks:** CBS. **Owner:** Bright Tower Communications, Inc., at above address, (812)232-4161, Fax: (812)234-9999. **Founded:** 1960. **Operating Hours:** Continuous. **ADI:** Terre Haute, IN. **Key Personnel:** Robert D. Swanson, General Mgr.; Kathleen Walker, General Sales Mgr.; Rich O'Brien, Program Dir. **Wattage:** 50,000 ERP. **Ad Rates:** $40-50 for 60 seconds.

10678 WSDM-AM - 1130
1215 Wabash Ave. Phone: (812)234-9770
Terre Haute, IN 47807 Fax: (812)238-1576
E-mail: wsdm@wsdm.com

Format: Southern Gospel; Talk. **Simulcasts:** WJSH-AM. **Networks:** Network Indiana. **Owner:** Crossroads Communications, Inc., at above address. **Founded:** 1959. **Formerly:** WWCM-AM (1972); WBZL-AM; WITE-AM. **Operating Hours:** 6 a.m.-2 hours past sunset. **ADI:** Terre Haute, IN. **Key Personnel:** Mike Peterson, General Mgr., mpeter@wsdm.com; Jim Beasley, Sports Dir.; Gretl Plessinger, News Dir./Operations Mgr., newsroom@wsdm.com. **Wattage:** 500. **Ad Rates:** $4-16 per unit. Combined advertising rates available with WSDM-FM, WAXI-FM. **URL:** http://www.indiana.net/wsdm.

10679 WSDM-FM - 97.7
1215 Wabash Ave. Phone: (812)234-9770
Terre Haute, IN 47807 Fax: (812)238-1576
E-mail: wsdn@wsdm.com; wsdm@indiana.net

Format: Oldies. **Networks:** ABC. **Owner:** Crossroads Communications, Inc., at above address. **Founded:** 1972. **Formerly:** WWCM-FM; WBDJ-FM. **Operating Hours:** Continuous. **ADI:** Terre Haute, IN. **Key Personnel:** Mike Petersen, General Mgr., mpeter@wsdm.com; Jim Beasley, Sports Dir.; Gretl Plessinger, News Dir., newsroom@wsdm.com. **Local Programs:** *High School Sports*, Jim Beasley. **Wattage:** 6000. **Ad Rates:** $16-24 per unit. Combined rates with WSDM-AM/WJSH-AM. **URL:** http://www.wsdm,com.

10680 WTHI-AM - 1480
PO Box 1486 Phone: (812)232-9481
Terre Haute, IN 47808 Fax: (812)234-0089
E-mail: wthi@iquest.net

Format: News; Talk. **Networks:** ABC. **Owner:** Wabash Valley Broadcasting Corp., at above address. **Founded:** 1948. **Operating Hours:** Continuous. **ADI:** Terre Haute, IN. **Key Personnel:** David L. Bailey, Senior VP/Gen. Mgr.; Frank Rush, Program Mgr.; James Conner, General Sales Mgr. **Wattage:** 5000 day; 1000 night.

10681 WTHI-FM - 99.9
PO Box 1486 Phone: (812)232-9481
Terre Haute, IN 47807 Fax: (812)234-0089
E-mail: wthi@iquest.net

Format: Contemporary Country. **Networks:** ABC. **Owner:** Wabash Valley Broadcasting Corp., at above address. **Founded:** 1948. **Operating Hours:** Continuous. **ADI:** Terre Haute, IN. **Key Personnel:** David L. Bailey, Senior VP/Gen. Mgr.; James Conner, General Sales Mgr.; Barry Kent, Operations Dir. **Wattage:** 50,000 ERP.

10682 WTHI-TV - 10
PO Box 1486 Phone: (812)232-9481
Terre Haute, IN 47808-1486 Fax: (812)232-8953

Format: Commercial TV. **Networks:** CBS. **Founded:** 1954. **Formerly:** Wabash Valley Broadcasting Corp. **Operating Hours:** Continuous. **ADI:** Terre Haute, IN. **Key Personnel:** David Bailey, Contact, dbailey@wthi.emmis.com; Phil Johnson, Contact, pjohnson@wthi.emmis.com; Rod Garvin, Contact, rgarvin@wthi.emmis.com. **Ad Rates:** $20-500 for 30 seconds.

10683 WTWO-TV - 2
PO Box 299 Phone: (812)696-2121
Terre Haute, IN 47808 Fax: (812)696-2755
E-mail: wtwotv2@indy.net

Format: Commercial TV. **Networks:** NBC. **Owner:** Nexstar Broadcasting of the Midwest, Inc., at above address. **Founded:** Sept. 1965. **Operating Hours:** Continuous. **ADI:** Terre Haute, IN. **Key Personnel:** Duane Lammers, General Mgr. **Local Programs:** *Religious Heritage*, Andy Alderton.

TIPTON†, pop. 5,044.

Tipton Co. (NC). 40 m N of Indianapolis. Manufacturing. Agriculture. Corn, soybean, wheat, hogs, cattle.

10684 Tipton Tribune
Elwood Publishing Co.
110 W. Madison Phone: (317)675-2115
PO Box 248 Fax: (317)675-4147
Tipton, IN 46072
General newspaper. **Founded:** 1895. **Freq:** Mon.-Sat. (eve.). **Print Method:** Offset. **Cols./Page:** 6. **Col. Width:** 25 nonpareils. **Col. Depth:** 301 agate lines. **Key Personnel:** Neil Johnson, Editor; Jack L. Barnes, Publisher; Rhonda Wolff, Advertising Mgr. **ISSN:** 0746-0619. **Subscription Rates:** $64.80 individuals. **Remarks:** Accepts advertising.
Ad Rates: GLR: $.31 **Circ:** Paid ⊕2,761
BW: $561.15 Free ⊕128
4C: $651.15
SAU: $4.35

TRAFALGAR

Johnson Co. (C). 7 m SW of Franklin.

10685 WIIB-TV - 63
2327 St. Rd. 252 West Phone: (317)878-5407
Trafalgar, IN 46181 Fax: (317)878-4458
E-mail: wiib@iquest.net

Format: Commercial TV. **Networks:** NTV Network. **Owner:** Channel 63, Inc., 2000 W. 41st St., Baltimore, MD 21211, (410)467-4545. **Founded:** 1988. **Operating Hours:** Continuous. **ADI:** Indianapolis (Marion), IN. **Key Personnel:** Barbara Kerr, Contact; Scott Burgett, Chief Engineer. **Ad Rates:** $10 per unit.

UNION CITY

10686 WOEI-FM - 88.9
PO Box 889 Phone: (540)961-2377
Blacksburg, VA 24063

Owner: Positive Alternative Radio, Inc., at above address. **Operating Hours:** Continuous. **Key Personnel:** Dan Franks, General Mgr., phone (937)968-3322; Vernon H. Baker. **Wattage:** 4,100. **Ad Rates:** Underwriting available.

VALPARAISO†, pop. 22,247.

Porter Co. (NW). 30 m SE of Chicago, Ill. Valparaiso University; Valparaiso Technical School. Residential. Lakes. Summer and Winter outside sports. Manufacturing.

10687 The Cresset
Valparaiso University Phone: (219)464-5274
Valparaiso, IN 46383 Fax: (219)464-5511

An Academic Review, opinion, letters generally - no fiction. **Subtitle:** A Review of Literature, the Arts, and Public Affairs. **Founded:** Nov. 1937. **Freq:** 7/year. **Print Method:** Offset. **Trim Size:** 8 1/2 x 11. **Cols./Page:** 3 and 2. **Col. Width:** 26 and 40 nonpareils. **Col. Depth:** 135 agate lines. **Key Personnel:** Gail McGrew Eifrig, Editor; Alan F. Harre, Publisher. **ISSN:** 0011-1198. **Subscription Rates:** $8.50 individuals; $14.75 two years; $4 students. **Remarks:** Advertising not accepted.
Circ: ‡4,700

10688 CSSR Bulletin
Council of Societies for the Study of Religion
CSSR Executive Office Phone: (219)464-5515
Valparaiso University Fax: (219)464-6714
Valparaiso, IN 46383-6493
Free: (888)422-2777
Publisher E-mail: cssr@valpo.edu

Religious publication. **Freq:** Quarterly. **Print Method:** Offset. **Trim Size:** 8 1/2 x 11. **Key Personnel:** Russell McCutcheon, Contact, phone (417)836-5514, fax (417)836-4757, rum628f@nic.smsu.edu; John T. Strong, Contact, jos226f@nic.smsu.edu. **ISSN:** 1060-1635.
Ad Rates: BW: $425 **Circ:** ‡6,500

10689 Religious Studies Review
Council of Societies for the Study of Religion
CSSR Executive Office Phone: (219)464-5515
Valparaiso University Fax: (219)464-6714
Valparaiso, IN 46383-6493
Free: (888)422-2777
Publisher E-mail: cssr@valpo.edu

Religious studies journal. **Subtitle:** A Quarterly Review of Publications in the Field of Religion and Related Disciplines. **Founded:** Sept. 1975. **Freq:** Quarterly. **Print Method:** Offset. **Trim Size:** 8 1/2 x 11. **Cols./Page:** 2 and 3. **Col. Width:** 21.5 and 14 picas. **Col. Depth:** 54.5 picas. **Key Personnel:** David G. Truemper, Managing Editor, david.truemper@valpo.edu. **ISSN:** 0319-485X. **Subscription Rates:** $40 individuals; $25 students; $35 members; $55 institutions. **Remarks:** Color advertising not accepted.
Ad Rates: BW: $410 **Circ:** ‡3,500

10690 Vidette-Times
1111 Glendale Blvd. Phone: (219)462-5151
Valparaiso, IN 46383-3799 Fax: (219)465-7298

General newspaper. **Founded:** 1866. **Freq:** Daily (eve.), Sat. and Sun. (morn.). **Print Method:** Offset. **Cols./Page:** 6. **Col. Width:** 27 nonpareils. **Col. Depth:** 301 agate lines. **Key Personnel:** Pasquale A. Rocchio, Editor; Richard B. Esposito, Publisher; Daniel R. Harrington, Advertising Mgr. **Subscription Rates:** $105.60 individuals; $100 by mail. **Remarks:** Accepts advertising. **Formerly**: Vidette-Messenger.
Ad Rates: GLR: $.80 **Circ:** Mon.-Fri. 15,795
BW: $1,448.67 Sun. 15,079
4C: $1,688.80
PCI: $11.23

10691 T. C. I.
17 N. Washington St. Phone: (219)464-2288
Valparaiso, IN 46383 Fax: (219)462-2413

Founded: 1981. **Formerly**: Lake Shore Cablevision; Multimedia Cablevision. **Key Personnel:** Anita Temple, Bus. Oper. Mgr. **Cities Served:** La Porte County.: subscribing households 22,200; 36 channels; 1 community access channel; 16 hours per week community access programming.

10692 WAKE-AM - 1500
2755 Sager Rd. Phone: (219)462-6111
Valparaiso, IN 46383 Fax: (219)462-4880

Format: Music of Your Life. **Networks:** ABC. **Owner:** Leigh Ellis, at above address. **Founded:** 1964. **Operating Hours:** Sunrise-sunset; 5% network, 95% local. **Key Personnel:** Leigh Ellis, Contact; Carl Fletcher, Contact; Gary Looper, Operations Mgr. **Wattage:** 1000. **Ad Rates:** $23 for 30 seconds; $27 for 60 seconds.

10693 WLJE-FM - 105.5
2755 Sager Rd. Phone: (219)462-8125
Valparaiso, IN 46383 Fax: (219)462-4880

Format: Country. **Networks:** ABC. **Founded:** 1967. **Formerly**: WAKE-FM (1974). **Operating Hours:** Continuous; 1% network, 99% local. **Key Personnel:** Leigh Ellis, President; Steve O'Brien, Operations Mgr.; Carl Fletcher, Contact. **Wattage:** 3000.

10694 WNWI-AM - 1080
1 Center St. Phone: (219)462-2158
PO Box 1130
Valparaiso, IN 46384

Format: Talk; Adult Contemporary; News; Oldies. **Networks:** AP. **Founded:** 1965. **Operating Hours:** 6 a.m.-sunset. **Key Personnel:** Mickey Hershman, Station Mgr.; Rande Dawson, News Dir.; Marvin Walther, Program Mgr.; Jason Cannon, Sports Dir.; Bruce Stombaugh, Contact. **Wattage:** 250. **Ad Rates:** $2.35-7.30 for 15 seconds; $3.30-13.15 for 30 seconds; $5.20-16.25 for 60 seconds.

VERSAILLES†, pop. 1,560.

Ripley Co. (SE). 50 m W of Cincinnati, Ohio. Manufactures shoes, metal fasteners, furniture, veneer. Poultry processing plant. Limestone quarries. Dairy, poultry farms. Livestock, grain.

10695 Osgood Journal
The Ripley Publishing Co.
115 S. Washington St. Phone: (812)689-6364
PO Box 158 Fax: (812)689-6508
Versailles, IN 47042
Publisher E-mail: ripleynews@seidata.com

Community newspaper. **Founded:** 1865. **Freq:** Weekly (Tues.). **Print Method:** Offset. **Cols./Page:** 6. **Col. Width:** 24 nonpareils. **Col. Depth:** 294 agate lines. **Key Personnel:** Gene Demaree, President; Linda Chandler, Publisher, lchande@seidata.com. **Subscription Rates:** $32 individuals; $35 out of area; $38 out of state. **Remarks:** Accepts advertising.
Ad Rates: SAU: $4.75 **Circ:** Paid ‡4,900
PCI: $4.75 Free ‡39

10696 Spotlight - Advertiser
The Ripley Publishing Co.
115 S. Washington St. Phone: (812)689-6364
PO Box 158 Fax: (812)689-6508
Versailles, IN 47042
Publisher E-mail: ripleynews@seidata.com

Weekly shopper. **Founded:** 1983. **Freq:** Weekly. **Print Method:** Offset. **Cols./Page:** 6. **Col. Width:** 12 picas. **Col. Depth:** 21 inches. **Key Personnel:** Linda Chandler, Publisher, lchande@seidata.com. **Subscription Rates:** Free.
Ad Rates: SAU: $4.75 **Circ:** Combined 13,000
PCI: $4.75

10697 The Versailles Republican
The Ripley Publishing Co.
115 S. Washington St. Phone: (812)689-6364
PO Box 158 Fax: (812)689-6508
Versailles, IN 47042
Publisher E-mail: ripleynews@seidata.com

Community newspaper. **Founded:** 1856. **Freq:** Weekly (Thurs.). **Print Method:** Offset. **Cols./Page:** 6. **Col. Width:** 24 nonpareils. **Col. Depth:** 294 agate lines. **Key Personnel:** Gene Demaree, President; Linda Chandler, Publisher, lchande@seidata.com. **Subscription Rates:** $32; $35 out of area; $38 out of state. **Remarks:** Accepts advertising.
Ad Rates: SAU: $4.75 **Circ:** ‡5,200
PCI: $4.75

VEVAY†, pop. 1,343.

Switzerland Co. (SE). On Ohio River, 40 m SW of Cincinnati, Ohio. Boats to river ports. Tourism. Flour mills; shoe factory. Diversified farming. Corn, wheat, tobacco and soybeans.

10698 The Switzerland Democrat
Vevay Newspapers, Inc.
111 W. Market St. Phone: (812)427-2311
PO Box 157 Fax: (812)427-2793
Vevay, IN 47043
Publisher E-mail: vevnews@venus.net

Newspaper. **Founded:** 1868. **Freq:** Weekly (Thurs.). **Print Method:** Offset. **Cols./Page:** 6. **Col. Width:** 26 nonpareils. **Col. Depth:** 301 agate lines. **Key Personnel:** Don R. Wallis, Publisher; Virginia Leap, Office Mgr. **USPS:** 531-060. **Subscription Rates:** $25 individuals; $30 out of area; $35 out of state. **Remarks:** Accepts advertising.
Circ: ‡800

10699 Vevay Reveille-Enterprise
Vevay Newspapers, Inc.
111 W. Market St. Phone: (812)427-2311
PO Box 157 Fax: (812)427-2793
Vevay, IN 47043
Publisher E-mail: vevnews@venus.net

Newspaper. **Founded:** 1816. **Freq:** Weekly (Thurs.). **Print Method:** Offset. **Trim Size:** 13 1/2 x 22 3/4. **Cols./Page:** 6. **Col. Width:** 26 nonpareils. **Col. Depth:** 301 agate lines. **Key Personnel:** Don R. Wallis, Publisher; Virginia Leap, Office Mgr. **USPS:** 658-620. **Subscription Rates:** $25 individuals; $30 out of area; $35 out of state. **Remarks:** Accepts advertising. **Alt. Formats:** Microform.
Ad Rates: BW: $667.50 **Circ:** ‡2,842
4C: $987.58
PCI: $7.66

VINCENNES†, pop. 20,857.

Knox Co. (SW). On Wabash River, 50 m N of Evansville. Vincennes University. George Rogers Clark National Historical Park, Fort Knox II, Sonotabac Prehistoric Indian Mound.

10700 Northwest Trail Tracer
Northwest Territory Genealogical Society
Vincennes, IN 47591 Phone: (812)888-4330

Journal covering genealogy. **Founded:** 1980. **Freq:** Quarterly. **Key Personnel:** Donna Beeson, Editor. **ISSN:** 0740-4999. **Subscription Rates:** $12 individuals.

10701 Vincennes Sun-Commercial
Central Newspaper Inc.
702 Main St. Phone: (812)886-9955
PO Box 396 Fax: (812)885-2235
Vincennes, IN 47591-2910
Free: (800)876-9955
Publication E-mail: currents@abcs.com

Daily newspaper. **Founded:** 1804. **Freq:** Daily (eve.), Sunday (morn.). **Print Method:** Offset. **Trim Size:** 14 x 23. **Cols./**

Page: 6. **Col. Width:** 24 nonpareils. **Col. Depth:** 294 agate lines. **Key Personnel:** Lloyd Pletsch, Managing Editor; Michael E. Quayle, Publisher, suncom1@abcs.com; Vickie Palmer, Retail Adv. Manager, vkpalmer@abcs.com; Darin Cornwell, Circulation Mgr.; Sarah Carie, Classified Adv. Manager. **Subscription Rates:** $90.00 individuals. **Remarks:** Accepts advertising. **URL:** http://www.adquest.com. **Alt. Formats:** Microform. **Feature Editors:** Jane Hall, *Food*; Bernie Schmitt, *Entertainment*.
Ad Rates: GLR: $1.33 BW: $1,491.84 4C: $1,726.84 SAU: $8.25 PCI: $11.84
Circ: Mon.-Fri. ★**12,588** Sun. ★**14,891**

10702 Cablevision Communications
PO Box 557 Phone: (812)882-8501
Vincennes, IN 47591 Fax: (812)886-5916
Free: (800)333-8501
E-mail: indcable@bestonline.net

Founded: 1987. **Formerly:** Full TU TV (1987); Wabash Cablevision. **Key Personnel:** Mitch Piskur, General Mgr., phone (812)882-8924, fax (812)886-5916, mpiskur@bestonline.net; Chuck Pfohl, Sales Mgr., phone (812)882-8924, adsales@bestonline.net. **Cities Served:** Bridgeport, Lawrenceville, IL; Bicknell, Bruceville, Edwardsport, Freelandville, Vincennes, Washington, IN: subscribing households 17,100; 42 channels; 1 community access channel; 20 hours per week community access programming.

10703 WAOV-AM - 1450
Box 2000 Phone: (812)882-6060
Vincennes, IN 47591 Fax: (812)885-2604
E-mail: wzdm@abcs.com

Format: News; Talk; Sports. **Networks:** CBS; CNN Radio; Brownfield; Motor Racing. **Owner:** Old Northwest Broadcasting, Inc., at above address. **Founded:** 1940. **Operating Hours:** Continuous; 5% network, 95% local. **ADI:** Terre Haute, IN. **Key Personnel:** Mark Lange, General Mgr.; Dave Crooks, Sales Mgr.; Wendell Hudson, News Dir. **Wattage:** 1000.

10704 WVUT-TV - 22
1200 N. 2nd St. Phone: (812)885-5326
Vincennes, IN 47591 Fax: (812)882-2237

Format: Public TV. **Networks:** Public Broadcasting Service (PBS). **Founded:** 1968. **Operating Hours:** 7 a.m.-midnight; 85% network, 15% local. **ADI:** Terre Haute, IN. **Key Personnel:** Al Rerko, General Mgr.; Sharon Kiefer, Program Dir.; Jim Ballinger, Production Mgr.

10705 WZDM-FM - 92.1
1 Executive Blvd., 6th Fl. Phone: (812)882-6060
PO Box 242 Fax: (812)885-2604
Vincennes, IN 47591
E-mail: wzdm@abcs.com

Format: Adult Contemporary. **Owner:** Original Co., Inc., 1309 Old Orchard Rd., Vincennes, IN 47591. **Founded:** 1988. **Operating Hours:** Continuous;. **ADI:** Terre Haute, IN. **Key Personnel:** Mark R. Lange, President; Dave Young, Operations Dir.; Wendell Hudson, News Dir.; Dave Crooks, Sales Mgr. **Wattage:** 4100. **Ad Rates:** Advertising accepted; rates available upon request.

WABASH†, pop. 12,985.

Wabash Co. (NEC). On Wabash River, 20 m N of Marion. Manufacturing. Agriculture. Corn, soybeans. Dairy. Hogs, cattle. Duck, squab, veal.

10706 The Paper
Highways 24 & 13 N Phone: (219)563-8326
PO Box 603 Fax: (219)563-2863
Wabash, IN 46992
Free: (800)766-6333
Publisher E-mail: thepaper@ctlnct.com

Community newspaper. **Founded:** 1977. **Freq:** Weekly (Wed.). **Print Method:** Offset. **Cols./Page:** 7. **Col. Width:** 16 nonpareils. **Col. Depth:** 224 agate lines. **Key Personnel:** Wayne W. Rees, Publisher; Julie Frieden, Advertising Mgr. **Subscription Rates:** $35 individuals.
Ad Rates: GLR: $.40 BW: $537.60 4C: $725.20 SAU: $9.00 PCI: $5.45
Circ: Wed. 16,225

10707 Plain Dealer
Nixon Publishing
123 W. Canal St. Phone: (219)563-2131
Box 379 Fax: (219)563-0816
Wabash, IN 46992
Free: (800)659-6321
Publication E-mail: wapd@holli.com; plaindealer@ctinet.com

General newspaper. **Founded:** 1859. **Freq:** Daily (eve.). **Print Method:** Offset. **Trim Size:** 13 1/2x22 3/4. **Cols./Page:** 6. **Col. Width:** 12 picas. **Col. Depth:** 21 1/2 inches. **Key Personnel:** Joseph Slacian, Managing Editor; James L. Widner, Publisher; Richard B. Welch, Adv. Mgr. **USPS:** 663-940. **Subscription Rates:** $.50 single issue. **Remarks:** Accepts advertising. **URL:** http://www.communinet.org/nixon-news.
Ad Rates: GLR: $4.90 BW: $1,296.45 4C: $1,521.45 SAU: $10.05
Circ: 7,450

10708 The $hopper
Wabash Plain-Dealer
123 W. Canal St. Phone: (219)563-2131
PO Box 379 Fax: (219)563-0816
Wabash, IN 46992
Publication E-mail: plaindealer@ctlnet.com

Subtitle: Extended Market Coverage. **Founded:** June 1995. **Freq:** Weekly (Tues.). **Key Personnel:** James L. Widner, Publisher; Richard B. Welch, Advertising Mgr. **Remarks:** Accepts advertising.
Ad Rates: BW: $643.71 4C: $868.71 SAU: $4.99 PCI: $4.75
Circ: 9,000

10709 WJOT-AM - 1510
1360 S. Wabash St. Phone: (219)563-1161
Wabash, IN 46992 Fax: (219)563-0883
E-mail: wjot@comteck.com

Format: Oldies. **Simulcasts:** WJOT-FM. **Networks:** ABC. **Owner:** MidAmerica Radio of Wabash, Inc., at above address. **Founded:** 1998. **Formerly:** WAYT-FM (1998). **Operating Hours:** Sunrise-sunset. **Key Personnel:** James F. Brunner, General Mgr. **Local Programs:** *Swap Shop* 9:00 am Monday-Friday, James Brunner, General Mgr.; *Wabash Talks* 8:30 am Friday. **Wattage:** 250. **Ad Rates:** $8.05-9.78 for 30 seconds.

WAKARUSA, pop. 1,281.

Elkhart Co. (N). 15 m SW of Goshen. Residential.

10710 Wakarusa Tribune
Ecom Publishing
PO Box 507 Phone: (219)862-2179
Wakarusa, IN 46573 Fax: (219)293-3705

Newspaper with a Democratic orientation. **Founded:** 1892. **Freq:** Weekly (Wed.). **Print Method:** Offset. Uses mats. **Cols./Page:** 4. **Col. Width:** 24 nonpareils. **Col. Depth:** 224 agate lines. **Key Personnel:** Mary Grantner, Publisher; Bill Nich, Editor, editorwaka@aol.com. **Subscription Rates:** $18.20 individuals.
Ad Rates: BW: $288 SAU: $4 PCI: $4.60
Circ: Paid ‡1,400 Free ‡90

WALKERTON, pop. 2,051.

St. Joseph Co. (N). 18 m SW of South Bend. Residential.

10711 The Independent-News
601-03 Roosevelt Rd. Phone: (219)586-3139
Walkerton, IN 46574 Fax: (219)586-3139

Community newspaper. **Subtitle:** The Independent-News. **Founded:** June 1884. **Freq:** Weekly (Thurs.). **Print Method:** Offset. **Cols./Page:** 5. **Col. Width:** 24 nonpareils. **Col. Depth:** 224 agate lines. **Key Personnel:** Robert E. Urbin, Editor and Publisher. **Subscription Rates:** $11 individuals; $13 out of state.
Ad Rates: GLR: $.14 BW: $145.20 PCI: $1.75
Circ: ‡2,400

WARREN

Huntington Co. (NE). 5 m S of Plum Tree.

10712 WarrenCable
426 N. Wayne Phone: (219)375-2111
PO Box 533 Fax: (219)375-2244
Warren, IN 46792

Founded: 1985. **Key Personnel:** Gordon Laymon, Contact, phone (219)375-2111, fax (219)375-2244, gelaymon@citznet.com. **Cities Served:** Warren, IN: subscribing households 677; 32 channels.

WARSAW†, pop. 10,647.

Kosciusko Co. (N). 45 m NW of Fort Wayne. Manufacturing. Lake resort. Farming.

10713 The Paper—Kosciusko Edition
The Papers, Inc.
114 W. Market St.
Warsaw, IN 46580

Newspaper. **Founded:** 1971. **Freq:** Weekly (Wed.). **Print Method:** Offset. **Trim Size:** 11 3/8 x 16 3/4. **Cols./Page:** 5. **Col. Width:** 22 nonpareils. **Col. Depth:** 224 agate lines. **Key Personnel:** Jeri Seely, Editor; Della Baumgartner, Publisher; Kip Schumm, Advertising Mgr.; Ron Baumgartner, President. **Remarks:** Accepts advertising.
Ad Rates: BW: $476 4C: $611 PCI: $5.95
Circ: Free 22,100

10714 Times-Union
Reub Williams and Sons, Inc.
PO Box 1448 Phone: (219)267-3111
Warsaw, IN 46581-1448 Fax: (219)267-7784
Publication E-mail: news@timeswrsw.com

General newspaper. **Founded:** 1856. **Freq:** Daily (eve.) and Sat. (morn.). **Print Method:** Offset. **Trim Size:** 13 3/4 x 22 1/2. **Cols./Page:** 6. **Col. Width:** 2 1/16 inches. **Col. Depth:** 21 inches. **Key Personnel:** Norman L. Hagg, Editor, normh@timeswrsw.com; M.R. Williams, Publisher; William Hays, Advertising Mgr. **USPS:** 666-680. **Subscription Rates:** $97.20 one year motor route; $108 local; $119 by mail out of area; $.50 single issue. **Remarks:** Accepts advertising. **URL:** http://www.timeswrsw.com.
Ad Rates: BW: $1,039.50 4C: $1,194.50 SAU: $8.25 PCI: $10
Circ: Mon.-Sat. ★**12,743**

10715 Warner Cable
919 E. Winona Ave., Ste. 1 Phone: (219)269-1681
Warsaw, IN 46580 Fax: (219)269-9750

Key Personnel: Tom Flora, General Mgr. **Cities Served:** Warsaw and Winoana Lake, IN.

10716 WRSW-AM - 1480
Box 1448, Times Bldg. Phone: (219)267-3115
Market and Indiana Sts. Fax: (219)267-7784
Warsaw, IN 46581-1448
E-mail: aofz@timeswrsw.com

Format: Classic Rock; Full Service. **Simulcasts:** WRSW-FM. **Networks:** CNN Radio; Westwood One Radio. **Founded:** 1951. **Operating Hours:** Continuous. **Key Personnel:** C.R. Williams, General Mgr.; Ladonna Odell, Program Dir. **Wattage:** 1000 day; 500 night. **Ad Rates:** $10.30-21 for 60 seconds. Combined advertising rates available with WRSW-FM.

WASHINGTON†, pop. 11,325.

Daviess Co. (SW). 20 m W of Vincennes. Manufacturing. Processed turkey products. Petroleum measuring and flexible packaging systems. Coal mines; oil and gas wells. Diversified farming. Corn, wheat, apples.

10717 Tri-County News
Daviess County Publishing Co.
PO Box 517 Phone: (812)254-7322
Washington, IN 47501 Fax: (812)254-7837

Newspaper with a Democratic orientation. **Founded:** 1981. **Freq:** Weekly (Thurs.). **Print Method:** Offset. **Cols./Page:** 6. **Col. Width:** 26 nonpareils. **Col. Depth:** 294 agate lines. **Key Personnel:** Michael E. Crosley, Editor and Publisher. **Subscription Rates:** $15 individuals. **Remarks:** Accepts advertising.
Ad Rates: BW: $359.10 4C: $409.10 PCI: $2.85
Circ: ‡3,000

10718 Washington Times-Herald
Donrey Media Group
102 E. Van Trees St. Phone: (812)254-0480
PO Box 471 Fax: (812)254-7517
Washington, IN 47501-4701
Free: (800)235-4113

General newspaper. **Founded:** 1867. **Freq:** Daily (eve.) and Sat. (morn.). **Print Method:** Offset. **Cols./Page:** 6. **Col. Width:** 26 nonpareils. **Col. Depth:** 301 agate lines. **Key Personnel:** Melody Maust, Editor, mmausf@dmtrc.net; Lars Purdue, Publisher; Don J. Brown, Advertising Mgr. **Subscription Rates:** $60 individuals. **Remarks:** Accepts advertising. **Ad Rates:** SAU: $6.22 **Circ:** Mon.-Sat. ★9,520
PCI: $5.35

10719 WAMW-AM - 1580
104 E. Main St. Phone: (812)254-6761
Washington, IN 47501 Fax: (812)254-6761

Format: Gospel. **Networks:** USA Radio. **Owner:** William A. Greene, at above address, (812)254-1116. **Founded:** 1955. **Operating Hours:** Sunrise-sunset. **Key Personnel:** William A. Greene, Contact; Zane Rudnik, Contact; James Ritterskamp, Sales Mgr.; Karen Killion, Contact. **Wattage:** 500. **Ad Rates:** $5.75-9.25 for 30 seconds; $7.50-11 for 60 seconds.

10720 WAMW-FM - 107.9
102 E. Main St. Phone: (812)254-6761
Washington, IN 47501 Fax: (812)254-6761

Format: Adult Contemporary; Agricultural. **Networks:** AgriAmerica; NBC. **Owner:** William A. Greene, 104 E. Main St., Washington, IN 47501. **Founded:** 1989. **Operating Hours:** Continuous. **Key Personnel:** William A. Greene, Contact; Zane Rudnik, Contact; James Ritterskamp, Sales Mgr.; Karen Killion, Contact. **Wattage:** 3000. **Ad Rates:** $5.75-8.25 for 30 seconds; $7.50-10 for 60 seconds.

10721 WWBL-FM - 106.5
PO Box 616 Phone: (812)254-4300
Washington, IN 47501 Fax: (812)886-1468
Free: (800)387-3358
E-mail: wwblfm@dmrtc.net

Format: Country. **Networks:** Brownfield; Mutual Broadcasting System. **Owner:** Old Northwest Broadcasting, Inc, at above address. **Founded:** 1948. **Formerly:** WRTB-FM. **Operating Hours:** Continuous. **ADI:** Terre Haute, IN. **Key Personnel:** Dave Crooks, General Mgr.; Brad Deetz, Operations Mgr. **Local Programs:** *Blue Grass Show*, Dave Foster; *Bullet Buster Trivia*, Brad Deetz; *Real Country Live*, Dave Foster. **Wattage:** 50,000. **Ad Rates:** Advertising accepted; rates available upon request.

WEST BADEN SPRINGS

10722 WBHQ-FM - 101.1
Rte. 2, Box 344
West Baden Springs, IN 47469

Format: Contemporary Country. **Networks:** Satellite Music Network. **Owner:** Wm. Gerald Willis, at above address. **Founded:** 1991. **Key Personnel:** Wm. Gerald Willis, General Mgr.; Catherine Willis, Contact. **Wattage:** 3000.

WEST LAFAYETTE, pop. 21,247.

Tippecanoe Co. (NW). 5 m W of Lafayette. Residential.

10723 Engineering Design Graphics Journal
American Society for Engineering Education
1419 Knoy Hall Phone: (765)494-7312
Purdue University
West Lafayette, IN 47907-1419
Professional journal covering the fundamentals of engineering graphics education and graphics technology. **Founded:** 1936. **Freq:** Triennial. **Print Method:** Offset. **Trim Size:** 8 1/2 x 11. **Cols./Page:** 2. **Key Personnel:** Judy A. Birchman, Editor, j.a.birchman@tech.purdue.edu; Mark W. Bannatyne, Advertising Mgr.; Clyde Kearns, Circulation Mgr. **ISSN:** 0046-2012. **Subscription Rates:** $20 nonmembers. **Remarks:** Accepts advertising.
Ad Rates: BW: $185 **Circ:** Controlled 575

10724 French Historical Studies
Duke University Press
Department of History Phone: (317)494-9437
Purdue University Fax: (317)743-3575
1358 University Hall
West Lafayette, IN 47907
Publisher E-mail: dukepress@duke.edu

Scholarly journal covering French history. **Freq:** Quarterly. **Key Personnel:** James Farri, Editor; John Contreni, Editor; Amy Hartzler, Advertising. **Subscription Rates:** $30 individuals; $12 single issue. **Remarks:** Accepts advertising.
Ad Rates: BW: $200 **Circ:** Paid 1,800

10725 The Journal of the Astronautical Sciences
American Astronautical Society
Purdue University Phone: (317)494-5786
Grissom 331 Fax: (317)494-0307
West Lafayette, IN 47907
Publisher E-mail: aas@astronautical.org

Archival journal on the sciences and technology of astronautics. **Freq:** Quarterly. **Print Method:** Offset. **Trim Size:** 6 3/4 x 9 1/2. **Cols./Page:** 1. **Key Personnel:** Kathleen Howell, Editor, howell@ecn.purdue.edu. **USPS:** 283-960. **Subscription Rates:** $140 domestic; $155 other countries. **Remarks:** Advertising not accepted.
Circ: ‡1,800

10726 Journal of the Early Republic
Society for Historians of the Early American Republic
1358 University Hall Phone: (765)494-4135
Department of History Fax: (765)496-1755
Purdue University
West Lafayette, IN 47907-1358
Publication E-mail: jer@sla.purdue.edu

Journal covering history of the Early American Republic for members. **Founded:** 1981. **Freq:** Quarterly. **Trim Size:** 7 x 10. **Key Personnel:** John L. Larson, Editor; Michael A. Morrison, Editor. **Subscription Rates:** Free to qualified subscribers. **Remarks:** Accepts advertising.
Ad Rates: BW: $90 **Circ:** Combined 1,450

10727 Modern Fiction Studies
Purdue University
West Lafayette, IN 47907-1389 Phone: (765)494-3758
Fax: (765)494-3780

Literary journal devoted to criticism and scholarship of 20th century fiction. **Founded:** 1955. **Freq:** Quarterly. **Print Method:** Offset. Uses mats. **Trim Size:** 6 x 9. **Cols./Page:** 1. **Col. Width:** 51 nonpareils. **Col. Depth:** 104 agate lines. **Key Personnel:** W. J. Palmer, Editor, phone (765)494-3758, wjpalmer@purdue.edu; Tara Dorai-Berry, Advertising Coord. **ISSN:** 0026-7724. **Subscription Rates:** $25 individuals; $45 institutions; $45 libraries; $34 out of country. **Remarks:** Accepts advertising.
Ad Rates: BW: $200 **Circ:** 3,000

10728 Purdue Alumnus
Purdue Alumni Association, Inc.
101 N. Grant St.
PMU 160
West Lafayette, IN 47906-6212

University alumni magazine. **Founded:** 1912. **Freq:** 6/year. **Print Method:** Offset. Uses mats. **Trim Size:** 8 1/8 x 10 7/8. **Cols./Page:** 3. **Col. Width:** 13 picas. **Col. Depth:** 57 picas. **Key Personnel:** Tim Newton, Editor; Sharon Martin, Advertising Dir. **Subscription Rates:** $30 individuals. **Remarks:** Accepts advertising.
Ad Rates: BW: $1,200 **Circ:** 55,000
4C: $1,900

10729 Purdue Exponent
Purdue University Student Foundation
PO Box 2506 Phone: (317)743-1111
West Lafayette, IN 47906 Fax: (317)743-6087
Publication E-mail: eonline@case.cioe.com

Collegiate newspaper. **Founded:** 1889. **Freq:** Daily (morn.) (during academic year). **Print Method:** Offset. **Cols./Page:** 6. **Col. Width:** 9.5 picas. **Col. Depth:** 224 agate lines. **Key Personnel:** Pat Kuhnle, Publisher. **Subscription Rates:** Free; $40 by mail. **Remarks:** Accepts advertising. **URL:** http://www.purdueexponent.org.
Ad Rates: GLR: $.65 **Circ:** Free 20,000
BW: $873.60
4C: $1,113.60
PCI: $9.10

10730 Social Cognition
Guilford Publications, Inc.
Dept. of Psychological Sciences Phone: (317)494-6889
Purdue Univ. Fax: (317)496-1264
West Lafayette, IN 47907
Publisher E-mail: info@guilford.com

Subtitle: A Journal of Social, Personality, and Developmental Psychology. **Founded:** 1982. **Freq:** Quarterly. **Print Method:** Offset. **Trim Size:** 6 x 9. **Cols./Page:** 1. **Col. Width:** 72 nonpareils. **Col. Depth:** 126 agate lines. **Key Personnel:** Donal Carlston, Ph.D., Editor. **ISSN:** 0278-016X. **Subscription Rates:** $40 individuals; $135 institutions. **Remarks:** Accepts advertising. **Alt. Formats:** Microfilm.
Ad Rates: BW: $200 **Circ:** 756

10731 Sycamore Review
Purdue University
West Lafayette, IN 47907-1389 Phone: (765)494-3758
Fax: (765)494-3780
Publication E-mail: sycamore@expert.cc.purdue.edu

Literary journal. **Founded:** 1989. **Freq:** Semiannual. **Key Personnel:** Sarah Griffiths, Editor-in-Chief; Emily Koehn, Managing Editor. **Subscription Rates:** $12 individuals; $14 out of country; $7 single issue. **Remarks:** Accepts advertising. **URL:** http://www.sla.purdue.edu/academic/engl/sycamore.
Circ: (Not Reported)

10732 Voices in Italian Americana
Bordighera, Inc.
Department of Foreign Phone: (765)494-3839
Languages and Literatures Fax: (765)496-1700
1359 Stanley Coulter Hall
Purdue University
West Lafayette, IN 47907-1359
Literary journal covering the contributions of Italian Americans in the culture and art of North America. **Founded:** 1990. **Freq:** Semiannual. **Trim Size:** 5 1/2 x 8 1/2. **Key Personnel:** Fred L. Gardaphe, Editor, phone (516)632-1215, fax (516)632-9612, fgar@aol.com; Anthony Julian Tamburri, Editor, tamburri@purdue.edu; Paolo Giordano, Editor. **ISSN:** 1048-292X. **Subscription Rates:** $20 individuals; $25 institutions; $30 out of country; $15 senior citizens. **Remarks:** Accepts advertising.
Ad Rates: BW: $100 **Circ:** Combined 300

10733 The Woman Conductor
Women Band Directors International
345 Overlook Dr. Phone: (765)463-1738
West Lafayette, IN 47906-1249 Fax: (765)463-1738
Publisher E-mail: agwright@gte.net

Journal reporting on career improvement, conducting techniques, and association news. **Subtitle:** Music Journal for Woman Band Conductors. **Founded:** 1984. **Freq:** 3/year. **Print Method:** Desktop. **Trim Size:** 8 1/2 x 11. **Cols./Page:** 2. **Key Personnel:** Gladys Wright, Editor. **Subscription Rates:** Included in membership. **Remarks:** Advertising not accepted.
Circ: (Not Reported)

10734 WBAA-AM & FM - 920 & 101.3
1740 Elliott Hall of Music Phone: (317)494-5920
West Lafayette, IN 47907-1740 Fax: (317)496-1542
Free: (888)WBAA-101
E-mail: wbaa@ellt-01.wbaa.purdue.edu

Format: Public Radio; Talk; Jazz; News; Eclectic; Classical. **Networks:** Public Radio International (PRI); National Public Radio (NPR). **Founded:** 1922. **Operating Hours:** Continuous; 60% network, 40% local. **Key Personnel:** Dan Skinner, Manager; David Bunte, Program Dir.; David Naylor, News Dir.; Jeff Lemon, Marketing Dir.; Caryl Matthews, FM Program Dir. **Local Programs:** *Local Talk Program*, David Naylor, News Dir. **Wattage:** 5000. **Ad Rates:** Noncommercial. **URL:** http://www.wbaa.purdue.edu/wbaa/.

10735 WBAA-FM - 101.3
17110 Elliott Hall of Music Phone: (765)494-5920
West Lafayette, IN 47907 Fax: (765)496-1542
E-mail: wbaa@wbaa.purdue.edu

Format: Classical. **Networks:** National Public Radio (NPR). **Owner:** Purdue University, at above address. **Founded:** Feb. 1, 1993. **Operating Hours:** Continuous. **Key Personnel:** Dan Skinner, Manager; Caryl Matthews, Program Dir. **Wattage:** 5000. **URL:** http://www.wbaa.purdue.edu/wbaa.

10736 WEZV-FM - 95.3
PO Box 2771 Phone: (317)497-9530
West Lafayette, IN 47906-0771 Fax: (317)497-9495
Free: (800)755-3489

Format: Easy Listening. **Networks:** Network Indiana. **Founded:** 1967. **Formerly:** WLZR-FM (1993); WWET-FM; WKJM-FM. **Operating Hours:** Continuous; 100% local. **ADI:** Lafayette, IN. **Key Personnel:** Doug Kern, Station Mgr.; Bob Miller, Music Dir. **Wattage:** 6000. **Ad Rates:** $14 for 30 seconds; $16 for 60 seconds.

10737 WLFI-TV - 18
2605 Yeager Rd., Box 2618 Phone: (317)463-1800
West Lafayette, IN 47906 Fax: (317)463-7979
E-mail: wlfitv18@holli.com

Format: Commercial TV. **Networks:** CBS. **Owner:** Blade Communications, Inc., at above address. **Founded:** 1953. **Operating Hours:** 6 a.m.-1:30 a.m. **ADI:** Lafayette, IN. **Key Personnel:** Robert A. Ford, General Mgr.; Tom Combs, General Sales Mgr.; David Bingham, Chief Engineer; Mike Piggot, News Dir.; Tina Parker, Operations Mgr. **URL:** http://www.wlfitv18.com.

WEST TERRE HAUTE

Vigo Co. (SW). 5 m W of Terre Haute.

10738 WWVR-FM - 105.5
3438 W. Larimer Dr. Phone: (812)533-1663
PO Box 207 Fax: (812)533-1663
West Terre Haute, IN 47885-0207

Format: Southern Gospel; Religious; Talk. **Networks:** USA Radio. **Owner:** United Broadcasting Co., Inc., at above address. **Founded:** 1966. **Operating Hours:** 6 a.m.-1 a.m.; 75% network, 25% local. **Key Personnel:** Betty Huey, General Mgr. **Wattage:** 3300. **Ad Rates:** $1 for 30 seconds; $2 for 60 seconds.

WESTVILLE, pop. 2,887.

La Porte Co. (NW). 12 m W of La Porte. Oil refinery. Grain elevators. Agriculture. Corn, wheat, soybeans.

10739 Westville Indicator
Box 828 Phone: (219)785-2234
Westville, IN 46391 Fax: (219)785-2242

Newspaper with a Republican orientation. **Founded:** 1882. **Freq:** Weekly (Thurs.). **Print Method:** Offset. **Cols./Page:** 6. **Col. Width:** 2 1/16 inches. **Col. Depth:** 21 1/2 inches. **Key Personnel:** Dean Henricksen, Contact. **Subscription Rates:** $20 individuals; $24 out of area. **Remarks:** Accepts advertising. **Available Online**. **Alt. Formats:** Microform; Mailing labels.
Ad Rates: GLR: $.34 **Circ:** ‡5,200
BW: $626.94
4C: $926.94
PCI: $4.86

WILLIAMSPORT†, pop. 1,747.

Warren Co. (NW). On Wabash River, 25 m SW of La Fayette. Diversified farming. Grain.

10740 The Review-Republican
Mary Ann Publishers, Inc.
38 N. Monroe Phone: (317)762-3322
Box 216
Williamsport, IN 47993
Community newspaper. **Founded:** 1854. **Freq:** Weekly (Thurs.). **Print Method:** Offset. **Cols./Page:** 8. **Col. Width:** 9 picas. **Col. Depth:** 21 inches. **Key Personnel:** Lee Anne Akers, Editor; Mary Ann Akers, Publisher. **USPS:** 463-860. **Subscription Rates:** $6 individuals; $30 out of state. **Remarks:** Advertising accepted; rates available upon request excluding alcoholic beverages.
Ad Rates: BW: $462 **Circ:** ‡3,650
4C: $742
PCI: $2.75

WINAMAC†, pop. 2,370.

Pulaski Co. (NW). 24 m NW of Logansport. Manufacturing. Grain elevators; sawmill; hatcheries. Dairy, stock, grain farms. Alfalfa, corn, soybeans.

10741 Pulaski County Journal
PO Box 19 Phone: (219)946-6628
Winamac, IN 46996 Fax: (219)946-7471

Community newspaper (tabloid). **Founded:** 1877. **Freq:** Weekly (Wed.). **Print Method:** Offset. **Cols./Page:** 6. **Col. Width:** 19 nonpareils. **Col. Depth:** 224 agate lines. **Key Personnel:** Douglas F. Haley, Publisher; Bev Powers, Editor; Valerie Powers, Advertising Mgr. **USPS:** 450-160. **Subscription Rates:** $20 individuals; $30 out of area other. **Remarks:** Accepts advertising.
Ad Rates: GLR: $.24 **Circ:** 3600
BW: $268.80
4C: $650
PCI: $3.45

WINCHESTER†, pop. 5,659.

Randolph Co. (E). 23 m E of Muncie. Glass factory. Machine shop. Grain, dairy, poultry farms. Wheat, corn, oats.

10742 News & Advertiser
The News Gazette
Box 429 Phone: (317)584-4501
Winchester, IN 47394 Fax: (317)584-3066

Local newspaper. **Freq:** Weekly. **Print Method:** Offset. **Cols./Page:** 6. **Col. Width:** 24 nonpareils. **Col. Depth:** 294 agate lines. **Key Personnel:** Mark Conover, Editor; Richard E. Wise, Publisher; Linda De Haven, Advertising Mgr. **Remarks:** Accepts advertising.
Ad Rates: SAU: $4.85 **Circ:** ‡18,688

10743 The News Gazette
American Publishing Co.
PO Box 429 Phone: (317)584-4501
Winchester, IN 47394-0429 Fax: (317)584-3066

General newspaper. **Founded:** 1860. **Freq:** Mon.-Sat. (eve.). **Print Method:** Offset. **Cols./Page:** 6. **Col. Width:** 24 nonpareils. **Col. Depth:** 294 agate lines. **Key Personnel:** Mark A. Conover, Editor; Roy H. Park, Publisher. **Remarks:** Accepts advertising.
Ad Rates: SAU: $4.43 **Circ:** Paid 4,906

WOLCOTT, pop. 923.

White Co. (NW). 10 m NW of Monticello. Residential.

10744 The New Wolcott Enterprise
125 W. Market St. Phone: (219)279-2167
PO Box 78 Fax: (219)279-2167
Wolcott, IN 47995
Newspaper with a Democratic orientation. **Founded:** 1967. **Freq:** Weekly (Thurs.). **Print Method:** Offset. **Cols./Page:** 5. **Col. Width:** 24 nonpareils. **Col. Depth:** 224 agate lines. **Key Personnel:** Barbara Lawson, Editor and Publisher; Deb Anker, Advertising Mgr. **USPS:** 596-760. **Subscription Rates:** $18 individuals; $20 out of state.
Ad Rates: GLR: $3 **Circ:** Paid ‡701
BW: $225 Free ‡39
PCI: $3

WORTHINGTON

10745 Worthington Times
12 S. Lessie St. Phone: (812)875-2141
Worthington, IN 47471-1513 Fax: (812)875-3815

Community newspaper. **Founded:** 1853. **Freq:** Weekly. **Print Method:** Offset. **Cols./Page:** 6. **Col. Width:** 12.3 picas. **Col. Depth:** 21 inches. **Key Personnel:** Anna Rochelle, Editor and Publisher. **USPS:** 693-220. **Subscription Rates:** $20 individuals; $25 out of area. **Remarks:** Accepts advertising.
Ad Rates: SAU: $2.50 **Circ:** ‡1,000
PCI: $3

ZIONSVILLE, pop. 3,948.

Boone Co. (C). 15 m NW of Indianapolis. Residential. Restored colonial village. Refinery. Manufactures drugs. Dairy, stock farms.

10746 Zionsville Times Sentinel
PO Box 838 Phone: (317)873-6397
Zionsville, IN 46077 Fax: (317)873-6253

Newspaper with a Republican orientation. **Founded:** 1860. **Freq:** Weekly (Wed.). **Print Method:** Offset. **Cols./Page:** 6. **Col. Width:** 25 nonpareils. **Col. Depth:** 301 agate lines. **Key Personnel:** Paula J. Endress, Editor and Publisher; Jay W. Endress, Publisher; Sherry Cornett-Baker, Advertising Sales Mgr. **Subscription Rates:** $23 individuals. **Remarks:** Accepts advertising.
Ad Rates: GLR: $.38 **Circ:** ‡3,800
BW: $674
4C: $814
SAU: $4.55

IOWA

State Capital, DES MOINES

Iowa is bounded on the north by Minnesota, east by the Mississippi River which separates it from Wisconsin and Illinois, south by Missouri, and west by the Missouri and Little Sioux Rivers which separate it from Nebraska and South Dakota. Its extreme length from north to south is 300 miles; its breadth 300 miles; total land area 55,875 miles. The distinguishing feature of Iowa is the fertile prairies. Nearly all parts of the state are gently rolling, without mountains or very high hills, but with frequent bluffs along the streams. The valleys of the Red Cedar, Iowa, and Des Moines Rivers are particularly productive. Transportation is highly developed with numerous railways and a large volume of traffic on the Mississippi and Missouri. The climate is one of extremes of heat and cold and dry winters and wet summers. The Weather Bureau at Des Moines gives the temperature (annual average) at 49.9: highest on record, 110; lowest on record, -30. Total annual precipitation is 49.9 inches. Some of Iowa's many colleges are University of Iowa (Iowa City), University of Northern Iowa (Cedar Falls), and Iowa State University (Ames), which is noted for its scientific investigation and original research.

POPULATION: 2,812,000 (1992). Rank among the states, 30th.

AGRICULTURE: Number of farms: 102,000 (1992). Farm acreage: 33,000,000 (1992). Cash receipts from farm marketings: crops, $4,458,000,000 (1991); livestock and products, $5,721,000,000 (1991).

FORESTS: Total forest land: 1,562,000 acres (1987).

MINERALS: Value of production: $344,000,000 (1991). Principal minerals: cement, stone, sand and gravel.

MANUFACTURES: Value added by manufacture: $19,062,000,000 (1991). Leading industry groups: food and related products, machinery (except electrical), electrical machinery.

LIST OF COUNTIES

Total number of counties 99

County, Location on Map, and County Seat	Pop.
Adair (SW), Greenfield	8,409
Adams (SW), Corning	4,866
Allamakke (NE), Waukon	13,855
Appanoose (S), Centerville	13,743
Audubon (SWC), Audubon	7,334
Benton (EC), Vinton	22,429
Black Hawk (NEC), Waterloo	123,798
Boone (C), Boone	25,186
Bremer (NE), Waverly	22,813
Buchanan (NEC), Independence	20,844
Buena Vista (NW), Storm Lake	19,965
Butler (NC), Allison	15,731
Calhoun (NWC), Rockwell City	11,508
Carroll (WC), Carroll	21,423
Cass (SW), Atlantic	15,128
Cedar (E), Tipton	17,381
Cerro Gordo (N), Mason City	46,733
Cherokee (N), Cherokee	14,098
Chickasaw (NE), New Hampton	13,295
Clarke (S), Osceola	8,267
Clay (NW), Spencer	17,585
Clayton (NE), Elkader	19,054
Clinton (E), Clinton	51,040
Crawford (W), Denison	16,775
Dallas (SWC), Adel	29,775
Davis (SE), Bloomfield	8,312
Decatur (E), Leon	8,338
Delaware (E), Manchester	18,035
Des Moines (SE), Burlington	42,614
Dickinson (NW), Spirit Lake	14,909
Dubuque (E), Dubuque	86,043
Emmet (NW), Estherville	11,569
Fayette (NE), West Union	21,843
Floyd (N), Charles City	17,058
Franklin (NC), Hampton	11,364
Fremont (SW), Sidney	8,226
Greene (WC), Jefferson	10,045
Grundy (WC), Grundy Center	12,029
Guthrie (SWC), Guthrie Center	10,935
Hamilton (C), Webster City	16,071
Hancock (N), Garner	12,638
Hardin (C), Eldora	19,094
Harrison (W), Logan	14,730
Henry (W), Mount Pleasant	19,226
Howard (NE), Cresco	9,809
Humboldt (NWC), Dakota City	10,756
Ida (W), Ida Grove	8,365
Jackson (E), Maquoketa	19,950
Jasper (SC), Newton	34,795
Jefferson (SE), Fairfield	16,310
Johnson (E), Iowa City	96,119
Jones (E), Anamosa	19,444
Keokuk (SE), Sigourney	11,624
Kossuth (N), Algona	18,591
Lee (SE), Fort Madison and Keokuk	38,687
Louisa (SE), Wapello	11,592
Lucas (S), Chariton	9,070
Lyon (NW), Rock Rapids	11,952
Madison (SWC), Winterset	12,483
Mahaska (SEC), Oskaloosa	21,522
Marion (SC), Knoxville	30,001
Marshall (C), Marshalltown	38,276
Mills (SW), Glenwood	13,202
Mitchell (N), Osage	10,928
Monona (W), Onawa	10,034
Monroe (S), Albia	8,114
Montgomery (SW), Red Oak	12,076
Muscatine (SE), Muscatine	39,907
O'Brien (NW), Primghar	15,444
Osceola (NW), Sibley	7,267
Page (SW), Clarinda	16,870
Pal Alto (NW), Emmetsburg	10,669
Plymouth (NW), Le Mars	23,338
Pocahontas (NW), Pocahontas	9,525
Polk (C), Des Moines	327,140
Pottawattamie (SW), Council Bluffs	82,628
Poweshiek (SEC), Montezuma	19,033
Ringgold (S), Mount Ayr	5,420
Sac (W), Sac City	12,324
Scott (E), Davenport	150,979
Shelby (W), Harlan	13,230
Sioux (NW), Orange City	29,903
Story (C), Nevada	74,252
Tama (EC), Toledo	17,419
Taylor (SW), Bedford	7,114
Union (S), Creston	12,750
Van Buren (SE), Keosauqua	7,676
Wapello (SE), Ottumwa	35,687
Warren (SC), Indianola	36,033
Washington (SE), Washington	19,612
Wayne (S), Corydon	7,067
Webster (NWC), Fort Dodge	40,342
Winnebago (N), Forest City	12,122
Winneshiek (NE), Decorah	20,847
Woodbury (NW), Sioux City	98,276
Worth (N), Northwood	7,991
Wright (N), Clarion	14,269

STATISTICS

Newspapers

Period of Issue	
Daily	34
Evening Daily	25
Morning Daily	9
Daily with Sunday edition	9

Semiweekly 12
Weekly 309
Biweekly 1
Semimonthly 2
Monthly 2
Bimonthly 1
Quarterly 1
Free or partly free 17
Shopper 48
Total Newspapers 371

Periodicals

Period of Issue
Weekly 5
Monthly 34
Bimonthly 32
Quarterly 28
Total Periodicals 132

Total number of publications 503

Radio Stations

AM Stations 82
FM Stations 126
Total Radio Stations 208

TV Stations

Total TV Stations 21

Cable Stations

Total Cable Systems 40

Total number of broadcast listings 269

ACKLEY, pop. 1,900.

SE IA. Franklin Co. 38 mi. W. of Waterloo.

10747 World Journal
Ackley Publishing Co., Inc.
617 Main St. Phone: (515)847-2623
Ackley, IA 50601
Community newspaper. **Founded:** 1895. **Freq:** Weekly. **Print Method:** Offset. **Trim Size:** 15 x 22. **Cols./Page:** 8. **Col. Width:** 9.5 picas. **Col. Depth:** 301 agate lines. **Key Personnel:** Jim Daggs, Editor and Publisher; Ritta Kurth, Advertising Mgr. **USPS:** 004-100. **Subscription Rates:** Free; $18 by mail; $21 out of area. **Remarks:** Accepts advertising.
Ad Rates: BW: $302.40 **Circ:** Paid 2,570
SAU: $3.80 Free 1,800

ADAIR, pop. 883.

SW IA. Adair Co. 60 mi. W. of Des Moines. Manufactures concrete. Grain, stock farms.

10748 The Adair News
403 Audubon St. Phone: (515)742-3241
PO Box 8 Fax: (515)742-3489
Adair, IA 50002-0008
Publication E-mail: adrnews@mddc.rom

Community newspaper for Adair and Casey, IA. **Founded:** Mar. 15, 1882. **Freq:** Weekly (Thurs.). **Print Method:** Offset. **Trim Size:** 15 1/2 x 23. **Cols./Page:** 8. **Col. Width:** 21 nonpareils. **Col. Depth:** 301 agate lines. **Key Personnel:** W.E. Littler, Editor and Publisher. **USPS:** 005-000. **Subscription Rates:** $17 individuals; $22 out of state. **Remarks:** Accepts advertising.
Ad Rates: SAU: $4.60 **Circ:** Paid ‡1,427
PCI: $3.90

ADEL, pop. 2,846.

SW IA. Dallas Co. 15 mi. W. of Urbandale. Residential. Manufactures brick and tile.

10749 Dallas County News
Box 156 Phone: (515)993-4233
Adel, IA 50003 Fax: (515)993-4235

Newspaper with a Democratic orientation. **Founded:** 1873. **Freq:** Weekly (Thurs.). **Print Method:** Offset. **Cols./Page:** 7. **Col. Width:** 24 nonpareils. **Col. Depth:** 287 agate lines. **Key Personnel:** Beth Dalbey, Editor; J. Burl Tiedemann, Publisher; L. Huggins, Advertising Mgr. **Subscription Rates:** $19 individuals. **Remarks:** Accepts advertising.
Ad Rates: GLR: $.20 **Circ:** 3,700
BW: $490
SAU: $3.60
PCI: $3.50

10750 Dallas County Round-up
Partnership Press
203 S. 8th Phone: (515)993-4233
Box 156 Fax: (515)993-4235
Adel, IA 50003
Shopper. **Founded:** 1970. **Freq:** Weekly (Wed.). **Print Method:** Offset. **Cols./Page:** 5. **Col. Width:** 24 nonpareils. **Col. Depth:** 192 agate lines. **Key Personnel:** Beth Dalbey, Editor; J. Burl Tiedemann, Publisher; L. Huggins, Advertising Mgr. **Subscription Rates:** Free; $18 by mail; $20 surrounding counties; $25 out of state.
Ad Rates: GLR: $.25 **Circ:** Free 9,700
BW: $315
4C: $395
SAU: $4.25
PCI: $4.10

AFTON, pop. 985.

S IA. Union Co. 60 mi. SW of Des Moines. Ships livestock. Stock, grain farms. Corn, oats, soybeans.

10751 Afton Star-Enterprise
Box 128 Phone: (515)347-8721
Afton, IA 50830
Community newspaper. **Founded:** 1880. **Freq:** Weekly (Thurs.). **Print Method:** Offset. **Cols./Page:** 5. **Col. Width:** 12 nonpareils. **Col. Depth:** 13 1/2 inches. **Key Personnel:** David A. Pugh, Editor. **Subscription Rates:** $19 individuals; $24 out of state; $.50 single issue. **Remarks:** Accepts advertising.
Ad Rates: GLR: $.15 **Circ:** ‡1185
BW: $195
SAU: $3

AKRON, pop. 1,517.

NW IA. Plymouth Co. 20 mi. W. of LeMars. Residential.

10752 Akron Register-Tribune
Good News Inc.
131 Reed Phone: (712)568-2551
Box 407 Fax: (712)568-3171
Akron, IA 51001
Local newspaper. **Founded:** 1890. **Freq:** Weekly. **Print Method:** Offset. **Trim Size:** 13 5/8 x 21 1/2. **Cols./Page:** 6. **Col. Width:** 12 picas. **Col. Depth:** 21 1/2 inches. **Key Personnel:** Bruce Odson, Publisher. **USPS:** 010-840. **Subscription Rates:** $24 individuals; $30 out of area; $.50 single issue. **Remarks:** Accepts advertising.
Ad Rates: GLR: $.21 **Circ:** Paid 1,400
BW: $645 Free 1,450
4C: $906
SAU: $5
PCI: $5

ALBIA†, pop. 4,184.

S IA. Monroe Co. 68 mi. SE of Des Moines. Coal mines; timber. Diversified farming.

10753 Monroe County News
Albia Newspapers Inc.
PO Box 338 Phone: (515)932-7121
Albia, IA 52531 Fax: (515)932-2822

Newspaper with a Democratic orientation. **Founded:** 1891. **Freq:** Weekly (Tues.). **Print Method:** Offset. **Cols./Page:** 5. **Col. Width:** 12 picas. **Col. Depth:** 13 1/2 inches. **Key Personnel:** David A. Paxton, General Mgr.; Marianne Crall, Advertising Mgr. **Subscription Rates:** $23.95 individuals. **Remarks:** Accepts advertising.
Ad Rates: PCI: $3.65 **Circ:** Paid 3,500
Free 300

10754 Union Republican
Albia Newspapers Inc.
PO Box 338 Phone: (515)932-7121
Albia, IA 52531 Fax: (515)932-2822

Newspaper with a Republican orientation. **Founded:** 1862. **Freq:** Weekly (Thurs.). **Print Method:** Offset. **Cols./Page:** 6. **Col. Width:** 12 picas. **Col. Depth:** 21 1/2 inches. **Key Personnel:** David A. Paxton, General Mgr.; Marianne Crall, Advertising Mgr. **Subscription Rates:** $23.95 individuals. **Remarks:** Accepts advertising.
Ad Rates: PCI: $3.65 **Circ:** Paid 3,500
Free 300

10755 KLBA-AM - 1370
10 N. Clinton Phone: (515)932-2112
Albia, IA 52531 Fax: (515)932-2113
Free: (888)732-9670
E-mail: cruizincountry@hotmail.com

Format: Country; Oldies. **Networks:** Brownfield; ABC; Radio Iowa. **Owner:** H & H Broadcasting Corp., 10 N. Clinton, Albia, IA 52531. **Founded:** 1979. **Operating Hours:** 6 a.m.-7:30 p.m. **Key Personnel:** Larry L. Mikesell, GM/Sales Manager; Sue Mikesell, Program Dir.; Joann McDonald, News Dir. **Wattage:** 500 day; 128 night. **Ad Rates:** $6 for 15 seconds; $10 for 30 seconds; $12 for 60 seconds.

10756 KLBA-FM - 96.7
10 N. Clinton Phone: (515)932-2112
Albia, IA 52531 Fax: (515)932-2113
Free: (888)732-9670
E-mail: cruzincountry@hotmail.com

Format: Country; Oldies. **Networks:** ABC; Brownfield; Radio Iowa. **Owner:** Larry Mikesell, at above address. **Founded:** 1995. **Operating Hours:** Continuous. **Key Personnel:** Larry Mikesell, Sales Mgr.; Sue Mikesell, Program Dir.; Joann McDonald, News and Music Dir. **Local Programs:** *Coaches Corner*, Larry Mikesell. **Wattage:** 25,000. **Ad Rates:** $6.00 for 15 seconds; $10.00 for 30 seconds; $12.00 for 60 seconds.

ALGONA†, pop. 6,289.

N IA. Kossuth Co. On Des Moines River, 42 mi. N. of Fort Dodge. Creameries; hatcheries; fertilizer, motor and aviation testing equipment, motor rebuilding, machine tools, bottled gas, feed manufactured. Seed corn processing plant. Grain farms. Corn, oats, hay, cattle and hogs.

10757 The Algona Upper Des Moines
Algona Publishing Co.
14 E. Nebraska Phone: (515)295-3535
PO Box 400 Fax: (515)295-7217
Algona, IA 50511
Free: (800)444-1957
Publisher E-mail: apc@ncn.net

Newspaper. **Founded:** 1866. **Freq:** Weekly (Thurs.). **Print Method:** Offset. **Cols./Page:** 6. **Col. Width:** 12 picas. **Col. Depth:** 21 1/2 inches. **Key Personnel:** Kent Thompson, Editor; Dick Plum, Publisher; Nancy Steburg, Advertising Mgr. **USPS:** 013-220. **Subscription Rates:** $39 individuals. **Remarks:** Accepts advertising.
Ad Rates: BW: $654.02 **Circ:** ‡4,950
4C: $864.07
SAU: $5.07
PCI: $5.37

10758 The Reminder
Algona Publishing Co.
14 E. Nebraska Phone: (515)295-3535
PO Box 400 Fax: (515)295-7217
Algona, IA 50511
Free: (800)444-1957
Publisher E-mail: apc@ncn.net

Shopper. **Founded:** 1976. **Freq:** Weekly (Tues.). **Print Method:** Offset. **Cols./Page:** 6. **Col. Width:** 12 picas. **Col. Depth:** 21.5 inches. **Key Personnel:** Carol Andersen, Editor; Dick Plum, Publisher; Nancy Steburg, Advertising Mgr. **Subscription Rates:** Free. **Remarks:** Accepts advertising.
Ad Rates: BW: $806.26 **Circ:** Free ‡13,100
4C: $1064.07
SAU: $6.25

10759 The Weekend Express
Algona Publishing Co.
14 E. Nebraska Phone: (515)295-3535
PO Box 400 Fax: (515)295-7217
Algona, IA 50511
Free: (800)444-1957
Publisher E-mail: apc@ncn.net

Shopper. **Founded:** 1990. **Freq:** Weekly (Sat.). **Print Method:** Offset. **Cols./Page:** 6. **Col. Width:** 12 picas. **Col. Depth:** 21.5 agate lines. **Key Personnel:** Carol Andersen, Editor; Dick Plum, Publisher; Nancy Steburg, Advertising Mgr. **Subscription Rates:** Free. **Remarks:** Accepts advertising.
Ad Rates: BW: $806.26 **Circ:** Non-paid ‡13,100
4C: $1016.26
SAU: $6.25

10760 KLGA-AM - 1600
2102 80th Ave. Phone: (515)295-2475
PO Box 160 Fax: (515)295-3851
Algona, IA 50511

Format: Adult Contemporary. **Networks:** ABC; Radio Iowa. **Owner:** KLGA Inc., at above address. **Founded:** 1956. **Operating Hours:** Continuous. **Key Personnel:** Bob Ketchum, General Mgr.; Al Lauck, Farm Dir. **Wattage:** 5000 day; 500 night. **Ad Rates:** $50 for 60 seconds. Combined advertising rates available with KLGA-FM.

10761 KLGA-FM - 92.7
2102 80th Ave. Phone: (515)295-2475
PO Box 160 Fax: (515)245-5138
Algona, IA 50511

Format: Adult Contemporary. **Networks:** ABC; Radio Iowa. **Owner:** KLGA Inc., at above address. **Founded:** 1970. **Operating Hours:** Continuous. **Key Personnel:** Bob Ketchum, General Mgr.; Al Lauck, Farm Dir. **Wattage:** 800. **Ad Rates:** $50 for 60 seconds. Combined advertising rates available with KLGA-AM.

ALLISON†, pop. 1,132.

NC IA. Butler Co. 38 mi. NW of Waterloo. Dairy products, poultry, stock farms.

10762 Butler County Tribune Journal
The Star Co.
PO Box 8 Phone: (319)267-2731
Allison, IA 50602 Fax: (319)267-2731

Newspaper. **Founded:** 1974. **Freq:** Weekly (Thurs.). **Print Method:** Offset. **Cols./Page:** 5. **Col. Width:** 24 nonpareils. **Col. Depth:** 238 agate lines. **Key Personnel:** Jerry Platter, Editor; F.C. Grawe, Publisher. **Subscription Rates:** $10.50 individuals. **Remarks:** Accepts advertising.
Ad Rates: GLR: $.16 **Circ:** ‡1,545

ALTA, pop. 1,722.

SW IA. Buena Vista Co. 13 mi. ESE of Cherokee. Dairy products.

10763 Alta Advertiser
Edwards Publishing
212 1/2 Main St. Phone: (712)284-2300
Alta, IA 51002 Fax: (712)732-3152

Community newspaper. **Founded:** 1877. **Freq:** Weekly (Wed.). **Print Method:** Offset. **Cols./Page:** 6. **Col. Width:** 11.5 and 9 picas. **Col. Depth:** 21 1/2 inches. **Key Personnel:**

Ken Larson, Editor; Dee Ober, Publisher/Advertising Mgr. **Subscription Rates:** $12 individuals; $14 out of state.
Ad Rates: SAU: $3.77 **Circ:** ‡900
PCI: $2.50

ALTOONA, pop. 5,764.

C IA. Polk Co. 4 mi. E. of Des Moines. Grain, stock farms.

10764 Altoona Herald-Mitchellville Index
809 8th St. SW, Ste C Phone: (515)967-4224
PO Box 427 Fax: (515)967-0553
Altoona, IA 50009
Community newspaper. **Founded:** 1888. **Freq:** Weekly (Thurs.). **Print Method:** Offset. **Trim Size:** 12 picas. **Cols./Page:** 6. **Col. Width:** 12 picas. **Col. Depth:** 21 inches. **Key Personnel:** Dave Dear, Publisher; Beth Meyer, Advertising Mgr.; Greg Gill, Commercial Printing Mgr. **Subscription Rates:** $21 individuals. **Remarks:** Accepts advertising.
Ad Rates: GLR: $5.25 **Circ:** ‡3,000
BW: $504
SAU: $4.71
PCI: $4

AMES, pop. 45,775.

C IA. Story Co. 32 mi. N. of Des Moines. Iowa State University of Science and Technology. Agriculture Experiment Station.Manufactures stock and poultry feeds, jackets, hydrostatic transmission, milk-products, toys, electronic equipment, abrasives, water filters, drawing instruments. Agriculture. Corn, hogs, cattle.

10765 The Advertiser
Van Drie Enterprises, Inc.
301 Fifth St. Phone: (515)233-1251
PO Box 904 Fax: (515)233-1244
Ames, IA 50010
Free: (800)873-1870
Publication E-mail: advertiser@ames.net

Shopper. **Founded:** 1958. **Freq:** Weekly (Wed.). **Print Method:** Offset. **Cols./Page:** 8. **Col. Width:** 21 nonpareils. **Col. Depth:** 224 agate lines. **Key Personnel:** Klynn Lynn, General Mgr. **Subscription Rates:** Free. **Remarks:** Accepts advertising.
Ad Rates: GLR: $1.50 **Circ:** Free ‡28,400
PCI: $10.25

10766 Aeon
Aeon: A Journal of Myth and Science
601 Hayward Ave. Phone: (515)292-6565
Ames, IA 50014-7366 Fax: (515)292-2603

Journal exploring archaeo-astronomical traditions and analysis of common patterns in ancient myths from around the world. **Subtitle:** A Journal of Myth and Science. **Founded:** Jan. 1988. **Freq:** 3/year. **Trim Size:** 8 x 11. **Cols./Page:** 2. **Key Personnel:** Ev Cochrane, Editor, phone (515)292-4562, ev.cochrane@ames.net. **ISSN:** 1066-5145. **Subscription Rates:** $45; $80 two years. **Remarks:** Accepts advertising. **URL:** http://www.ames.net/aeon/.
Ad Rates: BW: $80 **Circ:** Paid 500
Non-paid 100

10767 American Journal of Agricultural Economics
American Agricultural Economics Association
415 S. Duff, Ste. C Phone: (515)233-3202
Ames, IA 50010-6600 Fax: (515)233-3101
Publication E-mail: ajae@aaea.org
Publisher E-mail: membership@aaea.org

Journal of agricultural and resource economics. **Founded:** 1919. **Freq:** 5/year. **Print Method:** Offset. **Trim Size:** 7 x 10. **Cols./Page:** 2. **Col. Width:** 33 nonpareils. **Col. Depth:** 112 agate lines. **Key Personnel:** Spiro Stefanou, Editor, phone (814)863-8635, fax (814)865-3746, ttc@psu.edu; Sandra Clarke, Technical Editor, sandy@aaea.org. **ISSN:** 0002-9092. **Subscription Rates:** $98 individuals. **Remarks:** Accepts advertising. **Formerly:** Journal of Farm Economics.
Ad Rates: BW: $500 **Circ:** 4,700

10768 Choices
American Agricultural Economics Association
415 S. Duff, Ste. C Phone: (515)233-3202
Ames, IA 50010-6600 Fax: (515)233-3101
Publication E-mail: choices@aaea.org
Publisher E-mail: membership@aaea.org

Trade magazine covering food, farm, and resource issues, primarily from an economic view. **Subtitle:** The Magazine of Food, Farm and Resource Issues. **Founded:** 1986. **Freq:** Quarterly. **Print Method:** Web offset. **Trim Size:** 8 3/8 x 10 7/8. **Cols./Page:** 2. **Key Personnel:** Harry Ayer, Editor, phone (520)621-6257, fax (520)621-6250, ayer@ag.arizona.edu; Sandy Clarke, Managing Editor, sandy@aaea.org. **ISSN:** 0886-5558. **Subscription Rates:** $20 individuals; $5 single issue. **Remarks:** Accepts advertising.
Ad Rates: BW: $1,100 **Circ:** Combined 6,100
4C: $1,850

10769 The Daily Tribune
317 5th St. Phone: (515)232-2160
Ames, IA 50010 Fax: (515)232-2364
Publication E-mail: tribune@big12.metrobbs.com

General newspaper. **Founded:** 1867. **Freq:** Daily (eve.) and Sat. (morn.). **Print Method:** Offset. **Cols./Page:** 6. **Col. Width:** 25 nonpareils. **Col. Depth:** 301 agate lines. **Key Personnel:** J.M. Flansburg, Editor; Gary G. Gerlach, Publisher; Allen B. Weber, General Mgr. **Subscription Rates:** $59.80 individuals 26 Weeks. **Remarks:** Accepts advertising.
Ad Rates: BW: $1,083.60 **Circ:** ‡9,851
SAU: $8.40

10770 Favorite Brand Name Recipes Magazine
Publications International, Ltd.
3681 Carver Hall
Ames, IA 50011

Recipe magazine. **Founded:** 1985. **Freq:** 3/mo. **Print Method:** Web offset. **Trim Size:** 6 x 9. **Key Personnel:** Ivy Lester, Publisher. **Subscription Rates:** $2.50 single issue. **Remarks:** Advertising not accepted. **Formerly:** Campbell's Creative Cooking With Soup; New Joys of Jello; Favorite Recipes Magazine.
Circ: ‡300,000

10771 Iowa Bird Life
Iowa Ornithologists' Union
4024 Arkansas Dr. Phone: (515)292-3152
Ames, IA 50014
Publication E-mail: oldcoot@iastate.edu; oldoct@iastate.edu

Ornithology journal. **Founded:** Mar. 1931. **Freq:** Quarterly. **Print Method:** Offset. Uses mats. **Trim Size:** 6 1/8 x 9 1/4. **Cols./Page:** 1. **Col. Width:** 55 nonpareils. **Col. Depth:** 105 agate lines. **Key Personnel:** James J. Dinsmore, Editor. **ISSN:** 0021-0455. **Subscription Rates:** $15 individuals. **Remarks:** Advertising not accepted.
Circ: ‡550

10772 Iowa State Daily
Iowa State Daily Publication Board
108 Hamilton Hall, ISU Phone: (515)294-4120
Ames, IA 50011 Fax: (515)294-4119
Publisher E-mail: aforbes@iastate.edu

Collegiate newspaper. **Founded:** 1871. **Freq:** Daily (morn.) (during the academic year). **Print Method:** Offset. **Trim Size:** 14 x 22 3/4. **Cols./Page:** 6. **Col. Width:** 2 1/16 inches. **Col. Depth:** 21 inches. **Key Personnel:** Annette Forbes, General Mgr., phone (515)294-2609, aforbes@iastate.edu; Tara Deering, Editor-in-Chief, phone (515)294-5688, tweetyd@iastate.edu. **Subscription Rates:** $62 individuals. **Remarks:** Accepts advertising.
Ad Rates: GLR: $8.25 **Circ:** 14,000
BW: $1058.40
4C: $1283.40
PCI: $8.40

10773 The Iowa Stater
Iowa State University
105 Communications Bldg. Phone: (515)294-3129
Ames, IA 50011-0001 Fax: (515)294-9748
Publication E-mail: stater@iastate.edu

Magazine for university alumni. **Founded:** 1974. **Freq:** Semi-annual. **Print Method:** Offset. **Trim Size:** 11 1/2 x 16. **Cols./Page:** 4. **Col. Width:** 15 picas. **Col. Depth:** 15-1/2 inches. **Key Personnel:** Linda Charles, Managing Editor, lacharl@iastate.edu. **ISSN:** 0746-2204. **Subscription Rates:** Free to alumni and friends. **Remarks:** Advertising not accepted. **URL:** http://www.iastate.edu/lastater/tisindex.html.
Circ: Controlled 140,000

10774 Modern Logic: International Journal for the History of Mathematical Logic, Set Theory, and Foundation of Mathematics
Modern Logic Publishing
2408 1/2 Lincoln Way, Upper Level Phone: (515)292-1819
Ames, IA 50010
Journal covering historical studies of 19th- and 20th-century mathematical logic. **Founded:** 1990. **Freq:** Quarterly. **Print Method:** Offset. **Trim Size:** 6 x 9. **Cols./Page:** 1. **Key Personnel:** Irving H. Anellis, Editor and Publisher. **ISSN:** 1047-5982. **Subscription Rates:** $110. **Remarks:** Accepts advertising.
Ad Rates: BW: $200 **Circ:** Paid 125
Non-paid 20

10775 Needlework Retailer
Yarn Tree Design, Inc.
117 Alexander Ave. Phone: (515)232-3121
Ames, IA 50010 Fax: (515)232-0789
Publisher E-mail: info@yarntree.com

Trade magazine for the needlework industry, especially small, independent needlework retailers. **Founded:** Apr. 1992. **Freq:** Bimonthly. **Key Personnel:** Pamela B. Chaplin, Editor. **Remarks:** Accepts advertising.
Circ: (Not Reported)

10776 New Directions for Student Services
Jossey-Bass Inc., Publishers
Professional Studies in Education Phone: (515)294-6393
N247E Lagomarcino Hall
Iowa State University
Ames, IA 50011
Publisher E-mail: webperson@jbp.com

Journal for student services professionals offering guidelines and programs for aiding student intellectual, emotional, social, and physical development. **Founded:** 1978. **Freq:** Quarterly. **Print Method:** Sheetfed offset. **Trim Size:** 6 x 9. **Cols./Page:** 1. **Col. Width:** 27 picas. **Col. Depth:** 45 picas. **Key Personnel:** John H. Schlih, Editor-in-Chief; Elizabeth Whitt, Assoc Editor. **ISSN:** 0164-7970. **Subscription Rates:** $56 individuals; $99 institutions. **Remarks:** Advertising not accepted. **Online:** OCLC. **URL:** http://www.josseybass.com.
Circ: Paid 1,200
Controlled 95

10777 KASI-AM - 1430
415 Main St. Phone: (515)232-1430
Box 728 Fax: (515)232-1439
Ames, IA 50010

Format: Talk; Full Service. **Networks:** ABC; Radio Iowa. **Owner:** Betty A. Baudler, at above address. **Founded:** 1948. **Operating Hours:** 20 hrs. Daily; 5% network, 95% local. **Key Personnel:** Betty A. Baudler, Pres./Owner/Gen. Mgr.; Trent Rice, News/Sports Dir.; Mark Pitz, Operations Mgr.; Jeff Seaton, Sales Mgr. **Local Programs:** *AM Ames*, Dar Danielson. **Wattage:** 1000. **Ad Rates:** $11-20 for 30 seconds; $14-24 for 60 seconds.

10778 KCCQ-FM - 105.1
415 Main St. Phone: (515)232-1430
Box 728 Fax: (515)232-1439
Ames, IA 50010

Format: Top 40. **Networks:** Independent. **Owner:** Betty A. Baudler, at above address. **Founded:** 1968. **Operating Hours:** Continuous; 100% local. **Key Personnel:** Betty A. Baudler, Contact; Trent Rice, News/Sports Dir.; Mark Pitz, Operations Mgr.; Jeff Seaton, Sales Mgr. **Wattage:** 25,000. **Ad Rates:** $11-20 for 30 seconds; $14-24 for 60 seconds. Combined advertising rates available with KASI-AM.

10779 KUKE-FM - 88.5
Iowa State University Phone: (515)294-4332
1199 Friley Hall Fax: (515)294-8093
Ames, IA 50012
E-mail: kure@iastate.edu

Format: Alternative/New Music/Progressive; Eclectic. **Owner:** Iowa State University, at above address. **Founded:** Sept. 17, 1949. **Formerly:** KMRA-FM; KPGY-FM; KISU-FM; KUSR-FM. **Operating Hours:** Continuous. **Key Personnel:** Lewis Henderson, General Mgr., dtyrt@iastate.edu; Shane Ross, Marketing Dir., sross@iastate.edu; Andrew Seietz, Music Dir., phone (515)292-2258, lactose@iostate.edu; Justin Ihle, Sports Dir., u2fan@iastate.edu. **Local Programs:** *Against the Grain*, Ali Motameni; *Metal Works*, John Baldwin. **Wattage:** 250. **Ad Rates:** Underwriting available. $15 for 30 seconds. **URL:** http://www.public.iastate.edu/stu_ org/kure; http://www.webradio.com.

10780 KURE-FM - 88.5
1199 Friley Hall Phone: (515)294-4332
Ames, IA 50012 Fax: (515)294-8093
E-mail: kure@iastate.edu

Format: Alternative/New Music/Progressive. **Owner:** Iowa State University, at above address. **Founded:** July 1996. **Former name:** KUSR (1996). **Operating Hours:** Continuous. **Key Personnel:** Matthew Baker, General Mgr., phone (515)663-2961, dogmai1@iastate.edu; Eric McAndrew, Asst. General Mgr., phone (515)663-2985, plagued@iastate.edu; Matthew Borene, Chief Engineer, phone (515)663-2968, mborene@iastate.edu; Melissa McCall, Treasurer, phone (515)663-2982, emaleth@iastate.edu; Andrew Seitz, Music Dir., phone (515)663-2965, lactose@aistate.edu. **Wattage:** 250. **Ad Rates:** Noncommercial. **URL:** http://www.public.iastate.edu/˜stu_ org/kure.

10781 TCI of Central Iowa
225 S. Dayton Ave. Phone: (515)233-4646
Ames, IA 50010 Fax: (515)233-1422
Free: (800)262-3843

Owner: T.C.I., at above address. **Founded:** 1978. **Formerly:** Heritage Cablevision (1992). **Key Personnel:** Cyndi Pannkuk, Office Mgr.; Tim Adreon, Technical Operations Mgr. **Cities Served:** Ames, Boone, Granger, Guthrie Center, Huxley, Jefferson, Madrid, Nevada, Perry, Polk City, Randall, Sheldahl, Slater, Story City, Woodward, IA; Sheldahl, Slater, Story City, Woodward IA: subscribing households 20,171; 35 channels; 1 community access channel.

10782 WOI-AM - 640
Iowa State University Phone: (515)294-2025
Communications Bldg. Fax: (515)294-1544
Ames, IA 50011
E-mail: woi@iastate.edu

Format: Public Radio; News. **Networks:** National Public Radio (NPR); Public Radio International (PRI). **Owner:** Iowa State University of Science and Technology, at above address. **Founded:** 1921. **Operating Hours:** Continuous; 85% network, 15% local. **ADI:** Des Moines, IA. **Key Personnel:** E. Douglas Brown, Program Dir.; David Knippel, Chief Engineer; Donald Wirth, Business Mgr.; Bill McGinley, General Mgr. **Local Programs:** *Noon Report*, Todd Mundt; *Talk of Iowa*, Don Forsling. **Wattage:** 5000. **Ad Rates:** Noncommercial.

10783 WOI-FM - 90.1
Iowa State University Phone: (515)294-2025
Communications Bldg. Fax: (515)294-1544
Ames, IA 50011
E-mail: woi@iastate.edu

Format: Public Radio; Classical. **Networks:** National Public Radio (NPR); Public Radio International (PRI). **Owner:** Iowa State University of Science and Technology, at above address. **Founded:** 1949. **Operating Hours:** Continuous; 50% network, 50% local. **ADI:** Des Moines, IA. **Key Personnel:** E. Douglas Brown, Program Dir.; David Knippel, Chief Engineer; Donald Wirth, Business Mgr.; Cate Clark, Traffic Mgr.; Bill McGinley, General Mgr. **Wattage:** 100,000. **Ad Rates:** Noncommercial.

ANAMOSA†, pop. 4,958.

E IA. Jones Co. 20 mi. NE of Cedar Rapids. Iowa State reformatory. Manufactures electric motors, banking equipment, lumber products. Limestone quarries. Grain, stock farms. Seed corn, hogs, cattle.

10784 Anamosa Journal-Eureka
Anamosa Publications
208 W. Main Phone: (319)462-3511
Box 108 Fax: (319)462-4540
Anamosa, IA 52205
Newspaper. **Subtitle:** Anamosa Journal-Eureka. **Founded:** 1856. **Freq:** Weekly (Thurs.). **Print Method:** Offset. **Trim Size:** 11 1/2 x 17. **Cols./Page:** 6. **Col. Width:** 9 picas. **Col. Depth:** 16 inches. **Key Personnel:** Jennifer Hughes, News Editor; Daryl Schepanski, Sports Editor; Cindy Wollum, Sales Executive. **Subscription Rates:** $23 individuals; $27 out of area; $29 out of state.
Ad Rates: BW: $355.20 **Circ:** Paid 2,600
PCI: $3.70

10785 Wapsipinicon Almanac
Route 3 Press
19948 Shooting Star Rd.
Anamosa, IA 52205

Magazine containing regional essays, fiction, and reviews. **Founded:** 1988. **Freq:** Annual. **Print Method:** Letterpress. **Trim Size:** 6 5/8 x 9 3/4. **Cols./Page:** 2. **Col. Width:** 15 picas. **Col. Depth:** 50 picas. **Key Personnel:** Timothy Fay, Editor and Publisher. **Subscription Rates:** $6 single issue. **Remarks:** Accepts advertising.
Ad Rates: BW: $125 **Circ:** Non-paid 2,000

ANITA, pop. 1,153.

SW IA. Cass Co. 68 mi. W. of Des Moines. Stock, grain, poultry, dairy farms. Cattle, hogs, corn.

10786 Anita Tribune
850 Main St. Phone: (712)762-4188
PO Box 216 Fax: (712)762-4189
Anita, IA 50020-0216
Community newspaper. **Founded:** Dec. 28, 1883. **Freq:** Weekly (Thurs.). **Print Method:** Offset. **Cols./Page:** 7. **Col. Width:** 20 nonpareils. **Col. Depth:** 300 agate lines. **Key Personnel:** Gene Andrews, Editor and Publisher. **ISSN:** 0259-4000. **Subscription Rates:** $20 individuals; $24 out of state; $0.50 single issue. **Remarks:** Accepts advertising.
Ad Rates: GLR: $.20 **Circ:** ‡1,700
BW: $566
4C: $800
SAU: $4.56
PCI: $3.70

10787 Tradition Magazine
National Traditional Country Music Association
PO Box 492 Phone: (712)784-3001
Anita, IA 50020
Publication E-mail: anitapl@nwidt.com

Magazine promoting the preservation of all forms of acoustic traditional music. **Founded:** July 4, 1976. **Freq:** Bimonthly (during academic year; periodic during winter months). **Print Method:** Offset. **Trim Size:** 8 x 10. **Cols./Page:** 2. **Col. Width:** 26 nonpareils. **Col. Depth:** 110 agate lines. **Key Personnel:** Bob Everhart, Editor and Publisher. **Subscription Rates:** $15 individuals. **Remarks:** Accepts advertising.
Ad Rates: BW: $300 **Circ:** Paid ‡2,500
Controlled ‡2,500

ANKENY, pop. 15,429.

C IA. Polk Co. 6 mi. N. of Des Moines. Manufactures transmissions, farm equipment, prepared feeds, generator sets, fabricated parts, machines. Grain, stock, dairy farms.

10788 Journal of Soil and Water Conservation
Soil and Water Conservation Society
7515 NE Ankeny Rd. Phone: (515)289-2331
Ankeny, IA 50021 Fax: (515)289-1227
Free: (800)843-7645
Publisher E-mail: swcsjswc@netins.net

Magazine featuring land and water conservation news; including general interest features, applied research reports, viewpoints, commentary, book reviews, and current events. **Founded:** 1946. **Freq:** Bimonthly. **Print Method:** Offset. **Trim Size:** 8 1/2 x 11. **Cols./Page:** 3. **Col. Width:** 28 nonpareils. **Col. Depth:** 140 agate lines. **Key Personnel:** Sue Ballantine, Editor; Doug Snyder, Asst. Editor. **ISSN:** 0022-4561. **Subscription Rates:** $42 individuals; $52 other countries; $7.50 single issue. **Remarks:** Accepts advertising.
Ad Rates: BW: $460 **Circ:** 11,445
4C: $910

ANTHON

10789 Anthon Herald
Concord Publishing House, Inc.
PO Box 299
Anthon, IA 51004-0299

Community newspaper. **Founded:** 1901. **Freq:** Weekly (Wed.). **Print Method:** Offset. **Trim Size:** 15 x 30. **Cols./Page:** 6. **Col. Width:** 13 picas. **Col. Depth:** 20 inches. **Key Personnel:** Tom Stangl, Editor, phone (712)546-7031, fax (712)546-7035, sentinel@pionet.net. **USPS:** 026-860. **Subscription Rates:** $18.75; $22.50 out of area. **Remarks:** Accepts advertising.
Ad Rates: GLR: $2.50 **Circ:** ‡900
PCI: $1.95

ARMSTRONG, pop. 1,153.

NW IA. Emmet Co. 70 mi. NW of Mason City. Manufactures agricultural implements, wheel rims, fireplaces, pallets, feed; cement mixer plant. Grain farms. Corn, soybeans, oats.

10790 The Armstrong Journal
Community Publications
520 6th St. Phone: (712)864-3460
PO Box 285 Fax: (712)864-3028
Armstrong, IA 50514
Newspaper with a Democratic orientation. **Founded:** 1893. **Freq:** Weekly (Wed.). **Print Method:** Offset. **Cols./Page:** 5. **Col. Width:** 24 nonpareils. **Col. Depth:** 224 agate lines. **Key Personnel:** Jerry Wiseman, Editor and Publisher. **Subscription Rates:** $15 individuals; $20 out of area. **Remarks:** Accepts advertising.
Ad Rates: GLR: $.19 **Circ:** 915
SAU: $3.35

10791 The Ringsted Dispatch
Community Publications
520 6th St. Phone: (712)864-3460
PO Box 285 Fax: (712)864-3028
Armstrong, IA 50514
Newspaper. **Founded:** 1901. **Freq:** Weekly (Wed.). **Print Method:** Offset. **Cols./Page:** 5. **Col. Width:** 11.5 picas. **Col. Depth:** 15 inches. **Key Personnel:** Jerry D. Wiseman, Editor and Publisher. **Subscription Rates:** $15 individuals. **Remarks:** Accepts advertising.
Ad Rates: BW: $251.25 **Circ:** Paid 600
SAU: $3.35 Free 50

10792 Heck's TV & Cable
Box 517 Phone: (712)864-3431
Armstrong, IA 50514

Owner: Steven R. Heck, at above address. **Founded:** Oct. 1, 1984. **Formerly:** Heck's Cable TV. **Key Personnel:** Steve Heck, Owner. **Cities Served:** Crystal Lake, Lakota, Renwick, Woden, IA; Emmons, MN; subscribing households 550; 29 channels.

ATLANTIC†, pop. 7,789.

SW IA. Cass Co. 45 mi. E. of Council Bluffs. Livestock feed, lamps and lampshades, hatcheries; elevators; steel buildings. Manufactures diesel & automotive bearings, steel boxes, soft drinks. Agriculture. Corn, soybeans. Hogs, cattle.

10793 Atlantic News-Telegraph
PO Box 230 Phone: (712)243-2624
Atlantic, IA 50022-0230 Fax: (712)243-4988

Newspaper with a Report orientation. **Founded:** 1871. **Freq:** Daily (eve.) and Sat. (morn.). **Print Method:** Offset. **Cols./Page:** 6. **Col. Width:** 25 nonpareils. **Col. Depth:** 294 agate lines. **Key Personnel:** Mark D. Griggs. **Subscription Rates:** $39 individuals. **Remarks:** Accepts advertising.
Ad Rates: GLR: $.15 **Circ:** Paid 6,154
BW: $711 Free 18,800
4C: $820
SAU: $6.75
PCI: $5.65

10794 KJAN-AM - 1220
N. Olive St. Phone: (712)243-3920
Atlantic, IA 50022 Fax: (712)243-3937
Free: (800)283-5526

Format: News; Middle-of-the-Road (MOR). **Networks:** ABC; Radio Iowa. **Owner:** Wireless Communications Corp., PO Box 389, Atlantic, IA 50022. **Founded:** 1950. **Operating Hours:** 5:30 a.m.-11 p.m. **Key Personnel:** Jim Field, General Mgr./News Dir.; Merlyn Christensen, Sales Mgr. **Local Programs:** *Heartbeat Today*. **Wattage:** 250 day; 89 night. **Ad Rates:** $7.50-17.00 for 30 seconds; $9-22.00 for 60 seconds.

10795 KXKT-FM - 103.7
5010 Underwood Ave. Phone: (402)561-2000
Omaha, NE 68132 Fax: (402)556-8937

Format: Contemporary Hit Radio (CHR). **Networks:** AP. **Owner:** Ovation Broadcasting, at above address. **Founded:** 1966. **ADI:** Omaha, NE. **Key Personnel:** Colleen Hitz, General Sales Mgr.; Roger Olson, News Dir.; Donn Seidholz, General Mgr.; Jeanette DiMaur, Bus./Office Mgr. **Wattage:** 100,000.

AUBURN, pop. 320.

W IA. Sac Co. 75 mi. W. of Des Moines. Agriculture. Livestock, grain.

10796 Tri-County Special
Box E Phone: (712)688-2216
Auburn, IA 51433 Fax: (712)688-2216

Shopping guide. **Founded:** 1948. **Freq:** Weekly (Tues.). **Print Method:** Offset. **Trim Size:** 10 1/4 x 16. **Cols./Page:** 5. **Col. Width:** 2 inches. **Col. Depth:** 224 agate lines. **Key Personnel:** Delbert C. Morenz, Editor and Publisher. **Remarks:** Accepts advertising.
Ad Rates: BW: $220 **Circ:** Free 7,800
4C: $260
PCI: $2.75

AUDUBON†, pop. 2,841.

SWC IA. Audubon Co. 75 mi. W. of Des Moines. Farm equipment, feed, fertilizer, chemicals; alfalfa mill; nursery; produce packing house. Agriculture. Corn, hogs, cattle.

10797 Audubon County Advocate Journal
Audubon County Newspapers
301 Broadway Phone: (712)563-2661
PO Box 247 Fax: (712)563-3118
Audubon, IA 50025-0247
Free: (800)798-2635
Publisher E-mail: acnnews@aol.com

Community newspaper. **Founded:** 1878. **Freq:** Weekly (Fri.). **Print Method:** Offset. **Cols./Page:** 8. **Col. Width:** 10 1/2 picas. **Col. Depth:** 21 1/2 inches. **Key Personnel:** Judy Lauridsen, Managing Editor; Keith McGlade, Publisher.

USPS: 037-060. **Subscription Rates:** $.75 single issue. **Remarks:** Accepts advertising. **Formerly:** Audubon News Advocate.
Ad Rates: SAU: $5.50 **Circ:** Paid 2503
PCI: $4

AURELIA, pop. 1,148.

NW IA. Cherokee Co. 65 mi. NE of Sioux City. Stock, grain farms. Corn, oats, barley.

10798 The Aurelia Sentinel
PO Box 428 Phone: (712)434-2312
Aurelia, IA 51005 Fax: (712)434-2363

Newspaper. **Founded:** 1884. **Freq:** Weekly (Wed.). **Print Method:** Offset. **Cols./Page:** 5. **Col. Width:** 23 nonpareils. **Col. Depth:** 13 inches. **Key Personnel:** Marci Brown, Publisher, phone (712)225-5111. **USPS:** 037-700. **Subscription Rates:** $10 individuals. **Remarks:** Accepts advertising.
Ad Rates: GLR: $2.25 **Circ:** Paid 877
BW: $2.25 Non-paid 50
4C: $100
SAU: $3.78

AVOCA

10799 Avoca Journal-Herald
Nelson Publishing
PO Box 308 Phone: (712)343-2154
Avoca, IA 51521 Fax: (712)343-2262

Community newspaper. **Founded:** 1900. **Freq:** Weekly (Thurs.). **Print Method:** Offset. **Cols./Page:** 8. **Col. Width:** 10 1/2 picas. **Col. Depth:** 21 1/2 inches. **Key Personnel:** Donald L. Neilson, Editor and Publisher. **USPS:** 277-780. **Subscription Rates:** $14; $28 out of state. **Remarks:** Accepts advertising.
Ad Rates: SAU: $3 **Circ:** 1,750
PCI: $2.50

BANCROFT, pop. 1,082.

N IA. Kossuth Co. 60 mi. NW of Mason City. Feed. Creamery. Agriculture. Corn, oats, soybeans, hay.

10800 The Bancroft Register
Bancroft Publishing Co.
PO Box 175 Phone: (515)885-2531
Bancroft, IA 50517-0038 Fax: (515)885-2692

Community newspaper. **Founded:** 1881. **Freq:** Weekly (Wed.). **Print Method:** Offset. **Cols./Page:** 7. **Col. Width:** 2 1/16 inches. **Col. Depth:** 21.5 inches. **Key Personnel:** Cyndy Hutchinson, Staff Writer/News Editor, fax (515)885-2771; Rebecca Howard, Advertising. **USPS:** 040-960. **Subscription Rates:** $17 individuals; $22 out of country. **Remarks:** Accepts advertising.
Ad Rates: GLR: $.75 **Circ:** Paid ‡1,104
BW: $495 Free ‡30
SAU: $2.25
PCI: $4.40

BAYARD, pop. 637.

SWC IA. Guthrie Co. 60 mi. NW of Des Moines. Fertilizer plant; elevator. Grain, stock farms. Oats, corn, hogs. Poultry and eggs.

10801 News Gazette
Central Iowa Publishing, Inc.
PO Box 130 Phone: (712)651-2321
Bayard, IA 50029 Fax: (712)651-2599
Free: (800)962-2485
Publisher E-mail: ciapub@pionet.net

Official county newspaper. **Founded:** 1880. **Freq:** Weekly (Thurs.). **Print Method:** Offset. **Trim Size:** 16 1/2 x 23. **Cols./Page:** 8. **Col. Width:** 10 1/2 picas. **Col. Depth:** 21 1/2 inches. **Key Personnel:** Kenneth Robinson, Editor; Luann Waldo, Publisher. **Subscription Rates:** $18 individuals local; $22 out of area; $27 out of state. **Remarks:** Accepts advertising.
Ad Rates: PCI: $2.50 **Circ:** ‡2600

10802 Scranton Journal
Central Iowa Publishing, Inc.
PO Box 130 Phone: (712)651-2321
Bayard, IA 50029 Fax: (712)651-2599
Free: (800)962-2485
Publisher E-mail: ciapub@pionet.net

County newspaper. **Founded:** 1884. **Freq:** Weekly (Wed.). **Print Method:** Offset. **Trim Size:** 16 1/2 x 23. **Cols./Page:** 8. **Col. Width:** 10 1/2 picas. **Col. Depth:** 21 1/2 inches. **Key Personnel:** Luann Waldo, Publisher; Ken Robinson, Editor. **Subscription Rates:** $18 individuals; $22 out of state; $27 out of state. **Remarks:** Accepts advertising.
Ad Rates: PCI: $2.20 **Circ:** ‡1,100

BELLEVUE, pop. 2,450.

E IA. Jackson Co. On Mississippi River, 22 mi. SE of Dubuque. Washing machine, plastic bag, coil transformer factories. Fisheries. Tourist center. Dairy, stock, poultry farms.

10803 Herald-Leader
118 S. 2nd St. Phone: (319)872-4159
Bellevue, IA 52031 Fax: (319)872-4298
Publication E-mail: mspchief@aol.com

Newspaper. **Founded:** 1870. **Freq:** Weekly (Thurs.). **Print Method:** Offset. **Trim Size:** 10.5 x 16. **Cols./Page:** 6. **Col. Width:** 20 nonpareils. **Col. Depth:** 224 agate lines. **Key Personnel:** Lowell Carlson, Editor; Doug Melvold, Publisher, phone (319)652-2141, fax (319)632-6094; Lynne Hager, Advertising Mgr. **USPS:** 049-300. **Subscription Rates:** $28 individuals; $34 out of state. **Remarks:** Accepts advertising.
Ad Rates: GLR: $450 **Circ:** ‡2,800
BW: $255
4C: $493
SAU: $5.89
PCI: $4.45

BELMOND, pop. 2,505.

NC IA. Wright Co. On Iowa River, 32 mi. SW of Mason City. Hybrid seed corn, soybean processing, fertilizer and grain drying plants; horse, stock, grain trailers, engine valves, elevators. Farm machinery factory. Agrichemicals. Gravel pits. Stock, grain farms. Corn, hogs, cattle.

10804 Belmond Independent
215 E. Main St. Phone: (515)444-3333
Box 126
Belmond, IA 50421
Community newspaper. **Founded:** 1863. **Freq:** Weekly (Thurs.). **Print Method:** Offset. **Cols./Page:** 8. **Col. Width:** 22 nonpareils. **Col. Depth:** 294 agate lines. **Key Personnel:** Dirk Van Der Linden, Publisher. **USPS:** 049-660. **Subscription Rates:** $28 individuals.
Ad Rates: BW: $445 **Circ:** ‡2,200
SAU: $5.44

BETTENDORF

EC IA. Scott Co. 5 mi. E. of Davenport.

10805 Bettendorf News
1704 State St. Phone: (319)355-2644
PO Box L Fax: (319)355-0956
Bettendorf, IA 52722
Community newspaper for Iowa east of Interstate 74. **Subtitle:** The Community Newspaper for Bettendorf, LeClaire, Pleasant Valley, Riverdale and Panorama Park. **Founded:** 1927. **Freq:** Weekly (Thurs.). **Print Method:** Offset. **Cols./Page:** 5. **Col. Width:** 12 picas. **Col. Depth:** 13 inches. **Key Personnel:** Carly Otter, Editor. **USPS:** 053-420. **Subscription Rates:** $22; $25 out of county; $32 out of state. **Remarks:** Accepts advertising.
Ad Rates: BW: $455 **Circ:** ‡2,800
4C: $655
SAU: $7
PCI: $7.50

10806 Home & Away (Minnesota Edition)
AAA Minnesota/Iowa
2900 AAA Ct. Phone: (319)332-3316
Bettendorf, IA 52722 Fax: (319)332-1098

Travel and motoring magazine. **Founded:** Jan. 15, 1980. **Freq:** Bimonthly. **Print Method:** Web Offset. **Trim Size:** 8 x 10 7/8. **Cols./Page:** 3. **Col. Width:** 2.25 picas. **Key Personnel:** Sherry K. Freese, Editor/Advertising Mgr., phone (319)332-3361, sherry.freese@mn-ia.aa.com. **USPS:** 351-320. **Subscription Rates:** $12 individuals. **Remarks:** Accepts advertising.
Ad Rates: BW: $5,830 **Circ:** Paid 225,000
4C: $6,585 Controlled 400
PCI: $1,425

BLOOMFIELD†, pop. 2,849.

SE IA. Davis Co. 20 mi. S. of Ottumwa. Manufactures steel, metal, plastics, truck equipment, feed. Agriculture. Sheep, cattle, hogs, corn, soybeans.

10807 The Bloomfield Democrat
Bloomfield Democrat
PO Box 10
Bloomfield, IA 52537
Publication E-mail: gspurg@netins.net

Community newspaper serving Bloomfield and Davis counties in Iowa. **Freq:** Daily. **URL:** http://www.netins.net/showcase/bdemo/.

10808 KXOF-FM - 106.3
PO Box 186 Phone: (515)664-3721
Bloomfield, IA 52537 Fax: (515)664-3721

Format: Country; Top 40. **Networks:** USA Radio; Radio Iowa; Brownfield. **Owner:** Doug Smiley, at above address. **Founded:** 1982. **Operating Hours:** Continuous;. **Key Personnel:** Doug Smiley, President; Linda Hamilton, General Mgr.; Mark McVey, DJ, Production; Sheryl Husar, Sports & News. **Wattage:** 25,000.

BOONE†, pop. 12,602.

C IA. Boone Co. 14 mi. W. of Ames. Manufactures wire, iron and dairy products, refrigerators, cookies, envelopes, hydraulic and automotive equipment. Nurseries; machine shops; meat processing plant. Agriculture. Corn, soybeans, livestock.

10809 Boone County Shopping News
Partnership Press, Inc.
2126 Mamie Eisenhower Phone: (515)432-6153
Boone, IA 50036
Publication E-mail: boon2day@tdsi.net

Newspaper. **Founded:** Apr. 1987. **Freq:** Weekly. **Cols./Page:** 9. **Col. Width:** 9 picas. **Col. Depth:** 13 inches. **Subscription Rates:** free. **Remarks:** Accepts advertising. **Available Online. Alt. Formats:** CD-ROM.
Ad Rates: PCI: $6.85 **Circ:** Free 11,408

10810 Boone News-Republican
Schaub Publishing Inc.
Box 100 Phone: (515)432-1234
Boone, IA 50036 Fax: (515)432-7811
Free: (800)759-7811

General newspaper. **Founded:** 1865. **Freq:** Daily (eve.). **Print Method:** Offset. **Trim Size:** 14 x 22 3/4. **Cols./Page:** 6. **Col. Width:** 2 1/16 inches. **Col. Depth:** 21 1/2 inches. **Key Personnel:** James A. Bachtell, Managing Editor; R.C. Schaub, Publisher; Susan E. Tolan, Advertising Mgr. **USPS:** 060-800. **Subscription Rates:** $68 individuals; $125 out of area. **Remarks:** Accepts advertising.
Ad Rates: GLR: $.43 **Circ:** ‡3,834
BW: $838.50
4C: $936
SAU: $6.50

10811 Boone Today
2136 Mamie Eisenhower Phone: (515)432-6694
PO Box 375 Fax: (515)232-8395
Boone, IA 50036
Free: (888)270-0090
Publication E-mail: boon2day@tdsi.net

Newspaper broadsheet including agricultural, entertainment, fashion, automotive, and real estate sections. **Founded:** 1987. **Freq:** Semiweekly (Tues. and Sat.). **Print Method:** Letterpress. **Trim Size:** 11 1/2 x 17. **Cols./Page:** 6. **Col. Width:** 19.5 nonpareils. **Col. Depth:** 224 agate lines. **Key Personnel:** Rich Paulsen, General Mgr. **Subscription Rates:** Free. **Remarks:** Accepts advertising.
Ad Rates: GLR: $1.50 **Circ:** Free 11,238
BW: $504
4C: $789
PCI: $8.80

10812 KFGQ-AM - 1260
924 W. 2nd St. Phone: (515)432-6805
Boone, IA 50036

Format: Religious. **Networks:** Independent. **Owner:** Boone Biblical Ministries, Inc., at above address. **Founded:** 1927. **Operating Hours:** Sunrise-sunset; 100% local. **Key Personnel:** Denis R. James, Vice President; Mike Myers, Operations Dir.; Jolene James, Program Dir. **Wattage:** 5000. **Ad Rates:** Noncommercial.

10813 KFGQ-FM - 99.3
924 W. 2nd St. Phone: (515)432-6805
Boone, IA 50036

Format: Religious. **Networks:** Independent. **Owner:** Boone Biblical Ministries, Inc., at above address. **Founded:** 1951. **Operating Hours:** 16 hours daily; 100% local. **Key Personnel:** Denis R. James, Vice President; Mike Myers, Operations Dir.; Jolene James, Program Dir. **Wattage:** 3000. **Ad Rates:** Noncommercial.

10814 KWBG-AM - 1590
724 Story St., 2nd Fl. Phone: (515)432-2046
Boone, IA 50036 Fax: (515)432-1448
E-mail: kwbg@tdsi

Format: Information. **Networks:** ABC; ESPN Radio; Meadows Racing. **Owner:** G.O. Radio Boone Inc., at above address. **Founded:** 1950. **Operating Hours:** 17 hrs. Daily; 5% network, 95% local. **ADI:** Des Moines, IA. **Key Personnel:** Jamie Myers, Station Mgr.; Nate Claybern, Program Dir.; Jim Turbes, News Dir. **Wattage:** 1000. **Ad Rates:** $10.60-20 for 60 seconds.

BREDA

10815 Breda News
PO Box 183 Phone: (712)673-2318
Breda, IA 51436-0183 Fax: (712)673-4246

Community newspaper. **Freq:** Weekly (Wed.). **Cols./Page:** 5. **Col. Width:** 12 1/5 picas. **Col. Depth:** 21 1/2 inches. **Key Personnel:** Diane Lucas, Managing Editor. **USPS:** 063-760. **Subscription Rates:** $18; $21 out of area. **Remarks:** Accepts advertising.
Ad Rates: SAU: $3.15 **Circ:** 600
PCI: $3

BRITT, pop. 2,185.

N IA. Hancock Co. 30 mi W. of Mason City. Feeding equipment, dry milk, cleaning chemicals, sausage, concrete manufactured; seed corn processing; creamery. Ships grain. Corn, oats, soybeans.

10816 The Britt News-Tribune
Delete Prefin, Inc.
38 Center St. W., No. 42 Phone: (515)843-3851
Britt, IA 50423-1655
Local newspaper. **Founded:** 1893. **Freq:** Weekly (Wed.). **Print Method:** Offset. **Cols./Page:** 6. **Col. Width:** 2 1/8 inches. **Col. Depth:** 294 agate lines. **Key Personnel:** Joe Fokken, Editor; Jerry Wiseman, Publisher; Carol Kline, Advertising Mgr. **Subscription Rates:** $15 individuals; $17 out of area; $19 out of state. **Remarks:** Accepts advertising.
Ad Rates: PCI: $3.60 **Circ:** ‡2,000

10817 Town & County Advertiser
Delete Prefin, Inc.
38 Center St. W., No. 42 Phone: (515)843-3851
Britt, IA 50423-1655
Shopper. **Freq:** Weekly. **Print Method:** Offset. **Trim Size:** 14 x 21. **Cols./Page:** 6. **Col. Width:** 25 1/2 nonpareils. **Col. Depth:** 294 agate lines. **Key Personnel:** Joe Fokken, Managing Editor; Carol L. Kline, Advertising Mgr. **Remarks:** Accepts advertising.
Ad Rates: PCI: $3.20 **Circ:** Free ‡4,500

BROOKLYN, pop. 1,509.

SEC IA. Poweshiek Co. 12 mi. SE of Grinnell. Residential.

10818 Brooklyn Chronicle
Box 533 Phone: (515)522-7155
Brooklyn, IA 52211 Fax: (515)522-7909

Local newspaper. **Founded:** Apr. 29, 1981. **Freq:** Weekly (Wed.). **Print Method:** Offset. **Cols./Page:** 6. **Col. Width:** 28 nonpareils. **Col. Depth:** 294 agate lines. **Key Personnel:** Brian Cook, Editor; Dan DeBettignies, Publisher. **Subscription Rates:** $18 individuals; $20 out of area. **Remarks:** Color advertising not accepted.
Ad Rates: BW: $400 **Circ:** Paid ‡1,900
SAU: $3.19 Free ‡22
PCI: $3.85

10819 KSKB-FM - 99.1
108 Jackson Phone: (515)522-7202
PO Box 440
Brooklyn, IA 52211

Format: Religious. **Owner:** Florida Public Radio Inc., at above address. **Founded:** 1988. **Key Personnel:** Edie Kuntz, General Mgr. **Wattage:** 3000.

BUFFALO CENTER, pop. 1,233.

N IA. Winnebago Co. 60 mi. NW of Mason City. Manufactures cellulose insulation. Feedmill. Dairy, stock, poultry, grain farms. Corn, soybeans, oats, vegetables.

10820 Tribune
124 N. Main St. Phone: (515)562-2606
Box 367
Buffalo Center, IA 50424
Community newspaper. **Founded:** 1892. **Freq:** Weekly (Thurs.). **Print Method:** Offset. **Trim Size:** 8 x 1/8 x 11 1/2. **Cols./Page:** 6. **Col. Width:** 28 nonpareils. **Col. Depth:** 294 agate lines. **Key Personnel:** Merlyn R. Elman, Editor and Publisher. **USPS:** 069-400. **Subscription Rates:** $21 individuals; $23 out of area; $25 out of state. **Remarks:** Accepts advertising.
Ad Rates: BW: $370.44 **Circ:** Paid ‡1,625
SAU: $2.94
PCI: $3.08

BURLINGTON†, pop. 29,529.

SE IA. Des Moines Co. On Mississippi River, 60 mi. S. of Davenport. Barge connections. Limestone quarries. Manufactures soap, furniture, desks, mattresses, farm equipment, turbines, plastics, T.V. antennas, statellite dishes, electrical equipment, radio parts, fertilizers, insecticides, germicides, commercial chemicals, safety paper, bread, biscuits, paint, monuments, baskets, cartons, spark plugs. Ordnance works; electric switchgear, storage tanks, storage batteries.

10821 Ad Trends
National Research Bureau
320 Valley Phone: (319)752-5415
Burlington, IA 52601-5513 Fax: (319)752-3421

Looseleaf information service presenting advertising and merchandising ideas. **Founded:** 1933. **Freq:** Monthly. **Trim Size:** 8 1/2 x 11. **Key Personnel:** Teresa Levinson, Editor; Michael Darnall, Publisher. **Remarks:** Advertising not accepted.
Circ: (Not Reported)

10822 American Salesman
National Research Bureau
320 Valley Phone: (319)752-5415
Burlington, IA 52601-5513 Fax: (319)752-3421

Salesmanship magazine. **Founded:** 1955. **Freq:** Monthly. **Print Method:** Offset. **Trim Size:** 5 x 7. **Cols./Page:** 2. **Col. Width:** 24 nonpareils. **Col. Depth:** 81 agate lines. **Key Personnel:** Barbara Boeding, Editor. **ISSN:** 0003-0902. **Subscription Rates:** $48.65 individuals per year; $6.50 single issue. **Remarks:** Advertising not accepted. **Alt. Formats:** Microfilm.
Circ: ‡1,500

10823 Hawk Eye
Harris Enterprizes
PO Box 10 Phone: (319)754-6824
Burlington, IA 52601 Fax: (319)754-6824
Free: (800)397-1708

General newspaper. **Founded:** 1837. **Freq:** Daily (morn.). **Print Method:** Offset. **Cols./Page:** 6. **Col. Width:** 24 nonpareils. **Col. Depth:** 301 agate lines. **Key Personnel:** Bill Mertens, Publisher; Nelson H. Showalter, Advertising Mgr. **Subscription Rates:** $117 individuals. **Remarks:** Accepts advertising.
Ad Rates: PCI: $9.55 **Circ:** Mon.-Sat. ★**19,007**
Sun. ★**21,136**

10824 Radio Campaigns
National Research Bureau
320 Valley Phone: (319)752-5415
Burlington, IA 52601-5513 Fax: (319)752-3421

Looseleaf information service for radio station personnel. **Founded:** 1936. **Freq:** Monthly. **Trim Size:** 8 1/2 x 11. **Key Personnel:** Teresa Levinson, Editor; Michael Darnell, Publisher. **Remarks:** Advertising not accepted.
Circ: (Not Reported)

10825 Supervision
National Research Bureau
320 Valley Phone: (319)752-5415
Burlington, IA 52601-5513 Fax: (319)752-3421

Magazine for first-line foremen, supervisors, and office managers. **Founded:** 1939. **Freq:** Monthly. **Print Method:** Offset. **Trim Size:** 8 1/2 x 11. **Cols./Page:** 3. **Col. Width:** 26 nonpareils. **Col. Depth:** 122 agate lines. **Key Personnel:** Barbara Boeding, Editor. **ISSN:** 0039-5854. **Subscription Rates:** $48.85 individuals; $7 single issue. **Remarks:** Advertising not accepted.
Circ: ‡2,600

10826 KBUR-AM - 1490
1411 N. Roosevelt Ave. Phone: (319)752-2701
Burlington, IA 52601 Fax: (319)752-5287

Format: Adult Contemporary; Full Service. **Networks:** ABC. **Owner:** LWM, Inc., at above address, Fax: (319)752-5283. **Founded:** 1941. **Operating Hours:** Continuous; 5% network, 95% local. **ADI:** Davenport,IA-Rock Island, Moline,IL. **Key Personnel:** J.K. Martin, News Dir.; Steve Hexom, Program Dir.; Don Brandt, Sports Dir.; Steve Staebell, General Mgr.; John Weir, Contact. **Wattage:** 1000. **Ad Rates:** $18.00-39.00 for 30 seconds; $22.00-50.0 for 60 seconds. Combined advertising rates available with KGRS-FM.

10827 KCPS-AM - 1150
208 Jefferson St. Phone: (319)754-6698
PO Box 946
Burlington, IA 52601
E-mail: kcps@aol.com

Format: News; Talk; Sports. **Networks:** CBS; Mutual Broadcasting System; Tribune Radio; Westwood One Radio. **Owner:** John Giannettino, at above address. **Founded:** 1965. **Formerly:** KYED-AM (1967). **Operating Hours:** Continuous; 50% network, 50% local. **ADI:** Davenport,IA-Rock Island, Moline,IL. **Key Personnel:** Chip Giannettino, Contact; Joe Loffler, Sales; Roger Williams, Sales Mgr.; Kevin Francis, Music Dir.; Marybeth Bissig, Producer; Betty Morlan, Sales. **Local Programs:** *Big Show Inc.* 6:00 am - 9:00 am Monday-Friday, Marybeth Bissig, Producer. **Wattage:** 500. **Ad Rates:** $8.50 for 30 seconds. **URL:** http://www.listen.to/kcps.

10828 KDMG-FM - 103.1
2850 Mt. Pleasant St. Phone: (319)752-5402
Burlington, IA 52601 Fax: (319)752-4715

Format: Country. **Owner:** Pritchard Broadcasting Co., at above address. **Founded:** 1993. **Operating Hours:** Continuous. **ADI:** Davenport,IA-Rock Island, Moline,IL. **Key Personnel:** John Pritchard, General Mgr.; Chet Young, Sales Mgr.; Kathy Vance, Operations Mgr.; Bill Collins, Production Mgr. **Wattage:** 25,000. **Ad Rates:** $21 for 30 seconds; $25 for 60 seconds. Combined advertising rates available with KKMI-FM.

10829 KGRS-FM - 107.3
1411 N. Roosevelt Ave. Phone: (319)752-2701
Burlington, IA 52601 Fax: (319)752-5287

Format: Adult Contemporary. **Networks:** ABC. **Owner:** LWM, Inc., at above address. **Founded:** 1946. **Formerly:** KBUR-FM (1975). **Operating Hours:** Continuous; 1% network, 99% local. **ADI:** Davenport,IA-Rock Island, Moline,IL. **Key Personnel:** Steve Staebell, General Mgr.; Cosmo Leone, Program Dir. **Wattage:** 100,000. **Ad Rates:** $18.00-25.00 for 30 seconds; $22.00-31.00 for 60 seconds. Combined advertising rates available with KBUR-AM.

10830 KKMI-FM - 93.5
2850 Mt. Pleasant St. Phone: (319)752-5402
PO Box 832 Fax: (319)752-4715
Burlington, IA 52601

Format: Adult Contemporary; Oldies. **Owner:** Pritchard Broadcasting Co., at above address. **Founded:** 1981. **Formerly:** KDWD-FM (1991). **Operating Hours:** Continuous. **ADI:** Davenport,IA-Rock Island, Moline,IL. **Key Personnel:** John Pritchard, General Mgr.; Kathy Vance, Operations Mgr.; Bill Collins, Production Mgr.; Chet Young, Sales Mgr. **Local Programs:** *Kathy J. Vance.* **Wattage:** 6000 ERP. **Ad Rates:** $10 for 30 seconds; $12 for 60 seconds. Combined advertising rates available with KDMG-FM.

10831 TCI of Eastern Iowa
Box 519 Phone: (319)753-6571
Burlington, IA 52601-6571 Fax: (319)752-7109

Founded: 1979. **Formerly:** WestMarc Cable. **Cities Served:** Des Moines County, IA.

CALMAR

10832 Calmar Courier
PO Box 507 Phone: (319)562-3329
Calmar, IA 52132 Fax: (319)562-3940

Community newspaper. **Founded:** 1976. **Freq:** Weekly (Wed.). **Print Method:** Offset. **Cols./Page:** 4. **Col. Width:** 12.5 picas. **Col. Depth:** 15 inches. **Key Personnel:** Dan Driscoll, Editor, driscoll@calmar.polaritel.net. **Subscription Rates:** $12; $16 trade area; $22 out of area. **Remarks:** Accepts advertising.
Ad Rates: GLR: $.24 **Circ:** 2,000
BW: $150
4C: $230
PCI: $5

CARLISLE, pop. 3,073.

SC IA. Warren Co. 10 mi. SE of Des Moines. Agriculture. Corn, oats, wheat, cattle, hogs, soybeans.

10833 The Carlisle Citizen
PO Box 370 Phone: (515)989-0525
Carlisle, IA 50047
Local newspaper. **Founded:** 1926. **Freq:** Weekly (Thurs.). **Print Method:** Letterpress and offset. **Trim Size:** 11 x 17. **Cols./Page:** 6. **Col. Width:** 22 nonpareils. **Col. Depth:** 224 agate lines. **Key Personnel:** Steve Klein, Publisher. **USPS:**

090-740. **Subscription Rates:** $12 individuals; $15 out of area.
Ad Rates: GLR: $.18 **Circ:** ‡1,550
BW: $265
SAU: $3.58
PCI: $2.77

10834 Marion County News
Photo Printing
210 S. 1st St. Phone: (515)989-3251
Carlisle, IA 50047 Fax: (515)989-0743

Community newspaper. **Founded:** 1880. **Freq:** Weekly (Thurs.). **Cols./Page:** 6. **Col. Width:** 9.5 picas. **Col. Depth:** 16 inches. **Key Personnel:** Robert Klein, Publisher; Woody Fogle, Advertising Mgr.; Angela Ingle, Editor. **Subscription Rates:** $12; $10 senior citizens. **Remarks:** Accepts advertising.
Ad Rates: SAU: $3.81 **Circ:** 1,300
PCI: $3

CARROLL†, pop. 9,705.

WC IA. Carroll Co. 100 mi. NW of Des Moines. Cattle, hogs, poultry, grain farms. Corn, oats, beans.

10835 Carroll Today
Carroll Today Newspaper
526 N. Carroll St. Phone: (712)792-2179
Carroll, IA 51401 Fax: (712)792-2309

Community newspaper. **Founded:** 1983. **Freq:** Semiweekly (Tues. and Sat.). **Print Method:** Offset. **Cols./Page:** 6. **Col. Width:** 12 picas. **Col. Depth:** 21 1/2 inches. **Key Personnel:** Duane Winn, Editor; Greg Drees, Manager. **Subscription Rates:** $24; $37.50 out of state. **Remarks:** Accepts advertising.
Ad Rates: BW: $300 **Circ:** 2,000
SAU: $4

10836 The Times Herald
Herald Publishing
508 N. Court St. Phone: (712)792-3573
Carroll, IA 51401 Fax: (712)792-5218
Free: (800)262-5495

General newspaper. **Founded:** 1868. **Freq:** Daily (eve.). **Print Method:** Offset. **Cols./Page:** 6. **Col. Width:** 26 nonpareils. **Col. Depth:** 294 agate lines. **Key Personnel:** James B. Wilson, Publisher; Jim Hauer, Advertising Mgr. **Subscription Rates:** $55 individuals. **Remarks:** Accepts advertising.
Ad Rates: BW: $743.40 **Circ:** Paid ‡6,051
SAU: $5.90 Free ‡22,320

10837 KCIM-AM - 1380
1119 E. Plaza Dr. Phone: (712)792-4321
Carroll, IA 51401 Fax: (712)792-6667

Format: Country; Agricultural; Full Service. **Networks:** CBS. **Owner:** Carroll Broadcasting Co., at above address. **Founded:** 1950. **Operating Hours:** 5 a.m. - 12 midnight Mon.-Sat., 6 a.m. - 11 p.m. Sun. **Key Personnel:** Neil Trobak, General Mgr.; John Ryan, Program Dir.; Kevin Monson, Sport/News Dir. **Local Programs:** *Agriculture News Blocks*, Linda Thelin; *High School Sports*, Linda Thelin; *Local and Regional News Blocks*, Linda Thelin. **Wattage:** 1000.

10838 KKRL-FM - 93.7
1119 E. Plaza Dr. Phone: (712)792-4321
PO Box 886 Fax: (712)792-6667
Carroll, IA 51401

Format: Adult Contemporary. **Networks:** Westwood One Radio. **Owner:** Carroll Broadcasting Co., at above address. **Founded:** 1967. **Operating Hours:** 5am - Midnight. **Key Personnel:** Neil Trobak, General Mgr.; John Ryan, Program Dir.; Kim Hackett, Sales Mgr.; Joel Fox, Engineer; Rhonda Olerich, Office Mgr.; Kevin Monson, Sports & News Dir. **Wattage:** 100,000. **Ad Rates:** $7.50-28 for 30 seconds; $9.00-35 for 60 seconds.

CASCADE, pop. 1,912.

E IA. Dubuque Co. 24 mi. SW of Dubuque. Concrete block, recreational vehicles, metal products, tool and die companies. Agriculture. Corn, hay, oats.

10839 Pioneer Advertiser
Cascade Planner
PO Box 9 Phone: (319)852-3217
Cascade, IA 52033 Fax: (319)852-7188

Community newspaper. **Founded:** 1877. **Freq:** Weekly (Thurs.). **Print Method:** Offset. **Cols./Page:** 6. **Col. Width:** 21 nonpareils. **Key Personnel:** John Gross, Manager. **Subscription Rates:** $24 individuals; $40 out of state. **Remarks:** Accepts advertising. **Formerly:** Cascade Pioneer Advertiser.
Ad Rates: BW: $403 **Circ:** ‡2,400
SAU: $5.98
PCI: $4.60

CEDAR FALLS, pop. 36,322.

NEC IA. Black Hawk Co. On Cedar River, 5 mi. NW of Waterloo. University of Northern Iowa. Manufactures rotary pumps, farm equipment, golf equipment, corrugated boxes, steel products, garbage trucks, lightweight paving equipment, hoists, truck loading equipment, tools and dies; nurseries. Diversified farming.

10840 Hometowner, Inc.
Box 726 Phone: (319)277-3300
Cedar Falls, IA 50613 Fax: (319)277-3308
Publisher E-mail: hometowner@cfu-cybernet.net

Shopper. **Founded:** 1975. **Freq:** Weekly (Wed.). **Print Method:** Offset. **Cols./Page:** 5. **Col. Width:** 11.5 picas. **Col. Depth:** 13 inches. **Key Personnel:** Jayne A.T. Hall, General Mgr. **Subscription Rates:** Free. **Remarks:** Accepts advertising. **Formerly:** The HomeTowner.
Ad Rates: BW: $1,547 **Circ:** Free ‡61,650
4C: $1,857
PCI: $23.80

10841 Implement & Tractor
Freiberg Publishing
2302 W. 1st St. Phone: (319)277-3599
Cedar Falls, IA 50613 Fax: (319)277-3783

Magazine on farm and industrial machinery, trends and technology. **Founded:** 1886. **Freq:** Bimonthly and annual. **Print Method:** Web. **Trim Size:** 8 1/8 x 10 7/8. **Cols./Page:** 3. **Col. Width:** 2 1/8 inches. **Col. Depth:** 10 inches. **Key Personnel:** Bill Freiberg, Publisher; Mary Shepherd, Editor, mshepherd@cfu-cybernet.net. **ISSN:** 0019-2953. **Subscription Rates:** $25. **Remarks:** Accepts advertising.
Ad Rates: BW: $1,890 **Circ:** Paid ‡4,500
4C: $2,690 Non-paid ‡8,000

10842 Literary Magazine Review
The University of Northern Iowa
English Dept. Phone: (319)273-2821
115 Baker Hall Fax: (319)273-5807
Cedar Falls, IA 50614-0502
Journal providing critical appraisals of literary magazines' content for readers, writers, scholars, and librarians. **Founded:** Jan. 1, 1982. **Freq:** Quarterly. **Print Method:** Offset. **Trim Size:** 5 1/2 x 8 1/2. **Cols./Page:** 1. **Key Personnel:** Grant Tracey, Editor, phone (319)273-3782, fax (319)233-5688, grant.tracey@uni.edu; Karen Tracey, Assoc. Ed., phone (319)273-7193, fax (319)233-5688; Vince Gotera, Assoc. Ed., phone (319)266-3347; G.W. Clift, Contributing Ed., phone (913)776-6214. **ISSN:** 0732-6637. **Subscription Rates:** $13.50 individuals; $19.50 other countries; $4 single issue. **Remarks:** Advertising not accepted.
Circ: Paid ‡265
Non-paid ‡40

10843 The North American Review
University of Northern Iowa
Cedar Falls, IA 50614-0516 Phone: (319)273-6455
Fax: (319)273-6455
Publication E-mail: nar@uni.edu

Literary journal including fiction, poetry, essays, and commentary on current national and international affairs. **Founded:** Mar. 1815. **Freq:** Bimonthly. **Print Method:** Offset. **Trim Size:** 8 1/8 x 10 7/8. **Cols./Page:** 3. **Col. Width:** 27 nonpareils. **Col. Depth:** 140 agate lines. **Key Personnel:** Robley Wilson, Editor. **ISSN:** 0029-2397. **Subscription Rates:** $22 individuals; $4.95 single issue. **Remarks:** Accepts advertising. **Online:** EBSCO. **URL:** http://www.webdelsol/northamrev/nar. **Alt. Formats:** Microform.
Ad Rates: BW: $500 **Circ:** ‡4,000
4C: $950
PCI: $25

10844 Northern Iowa Today
University of Northern Iowa
Office of Public Relations Phone: (319)273-2761
127 Gilchrist Hall Fax: (319)273-2888
Cedar Falls, IA 50614-0017
Subtitle: The University of Northern Iowa Magazine. **Founded:** 1915. **Freq:** Quarterly. **Print Method:** Web press. **Trim Size:** 8 1/2 x 11. **Key Personnel:** Donavan Honnold, Managing Editor, donavan.honnold@uni.edu; Susan Chilcott, Exec. Editor. **Subscription Rates:** Free. **Remarks:** Advertising not accepted.
Circ: ‡73,000

10845 Northern Iowan
University of Northern Iowa
112 Maucker Union Phone: (319)273-2157
Cedar Falls, IA 50614-0001 Fax: (319)273-5931

Collegiate newspaper (tabloid). **Founded:** 1878. **Freq:** Semiweekly (Tues. and Fri.; during the academic year). **Print Method:** Offset. **Trim Size:** 11 1/2 x 17. **Cols./Page:** 5. **Col. Width:** 22 nonpareils. **Col. Depth:** 210 agate lines. **Key Personnel:** Jennifer Hengstenberg, Exec. Editor, phone (319)273-2157, fax (319)273-5931, hengstj2031@uni.edu; Dan Bonert, Advertising Mgr., bonertd4064@uni.edu; Michele Smith, Business Mgr., michele.smith@uni.edu. **ISSN:** 1217-2000. **Subscription Rates:** $17.50 out of area; $20 out of state. **Remarks:** Accepts advertising.
Ad Rates: BW: $393.75 **Circ:** ‡9,000
PCI: $3.70

10846 Seed & Crops Digest
Freiberg Publishing
PO Box 7 Phone: (319)277-3599
Cedar Falls, IA 50613 Fax: (319)277-3783
Free: (800)959-3276

Trade magazine covering seed management, technology, and biotechnology. **Founded:** 1950. **Freq:** 10/year. **Print Method:** Web. **Trim Size:** 8 1/8 x 10 7/8. **Cols./Page:** 3 and 2. **Col. Width:** 26 and 40 nonpareils. **Col. Depth:** 140 agate lines. **Key Personnel:** Bill Freiberg, Publisher, bfreiberg@cfu-cybernet.com. **ISSN:** 1088-4580. **Subscription Rates:** $35 individuals; $40 other countries surface mail; $65 other countries air mail. **Remarks:** Accepts advertising. **Available Online. URL:** http://ag-business.com. **Formerly**: Seed Industry Journal; Seedsman's Digest; Seed & Crops Industry.
Ad Rates: BW: $1,050 **Circ:** Paid 2,000
4C: $1,700 Controlled 4,000
PCI: $75

10847 KCNZ-AM - 1250
721 Shirley St. Phone: (319)277-1918
PO Box 248 Fax: (319)277-5202
Cedar Falls, IA 50613
Free: (800)913-9479
E-mail: kcnz@cedarnet.org

Format: News; Talk; Sports. **Networks:** ABC; ESPN Radio; Westwood One Radio; USA Radio. **Owner:** Fife Communications Co. L.C., at above address. **Founded:** 1995. **Formerly:** KCFI-FM (1995). **Operating Hours:** Continuous. **ADI:** Cedar Rapids-Waterloo-Dubuque, IA. **Key Personnel:** Jim Coloff, General Mgr.; Greg Alan, Program Dir.; Tracey Williams, Sports; Scott Fenzloff, News; Vicki Smith, Contact; Amy Monahan, Business Mgr. **Local Programs:** *Eastern Iowa's Morning News*, Jim Coloff; *Eastern Iowa's Morning News*, Jim Coloff; *The Morning Buzz*, Greg Alan; *The Morning Buzz*, Greg Alan; *Saturdays with Sid*, Sid Morris. **Wattage:** 500. **Ad Rates:** $15 for 30 seconds; $24 for 60 seconds. Combined advertising rates available with KCVM-FM. **URL:** http://cedarnet.org.kcnz.

10848 KHKE-FM - 89.5
University of Northern Iowa Phone: (319)273-6400
Cedar Falls, IA 50614-0359 Fax: (319)273-2682
Free: (800)772-2440
E-mail: kuni@uni.edu

Format: Public Radio; Jazz; Classical. **Networks:** Public Radio International (PRI). **Founded:** 1974. **Operating Hours:** 6:00 a.m.-1:00 a.m. 67% network, 33% local. **ADI:** Cedar Rapids-Waterloo-Dubuque, IA. **Key Personnel:** Doug Vernier, Station Mgr., phone (319)273-6446, doug.vernier@uni.edu; Carl Jenkins, Program Dir., phone (319)273-6464, carl.jenkins@uni.edu; Wayne Jarvis, Contact, phone (319)273-6484, wayne.jarvis@uni.edu; Jons Olsson, Contact, phone (319)273-6406, jons.olsson@uni.edu; Dave Hays, Contact, phone (319)273-6405, david.hays@uni.edu; Steve Schoon, Chief Engineer, phone (319)273-6465, steve.schoon@uni.edu; Al Schares, Music Dir., phone (319)273-6489, allen.schares@uni.edu; Greg Shanley, News Dir., phone (319)273-6408, gregory.shanley@uni.edu. **Wattage:** 10,000. **Ad Rates:** Noncommercial. **URL:** http://www.uni.edu/kuni.

KRNI-AM - See Mason City

10849 KUNI-FM - 90.9
University of Northern Iowa Phone: (319)273-6400
Cedar Falls, IA 50614-0359 Fax: (319)273-2682
Free: (800)772-2440
E-mail: kuni@.uni.edu

Format: Public Radio; Adult Contemporary; Ethnic; Eclectic; Urban Contemporary; Classical. **Networks:** Public Radio International (PRI); National Public Radio (NPR). **Founded:** 1960. **Formerly:** KTCF-FM (1972). **Operating Hours:** Continuous; 46% network, 54% local. **ADI:** Cedar Rapids-Waterloo-Dubuque, IA. **Key Personnel:** Doug Vernier, Station Mgr., phone (319)273-6446, doug.vernier@uni.edu; Carl Jenkins, Program Dir., phone (319)273-6464, carl.jenkins@uni.edu;

Wayne Jarvis, Contact, phone (319)273-6484, wayne.jarvis@uni.edu; Jons Olsson, Contact, phone (319)273-6406, jons.olsson@uni.edu; Dave Hays, Contact, phone (319)273-6405, david.hays@uni.edu; Steve Schoon, Chief Engineer, phone (319)273-6465, steven.schoon@uni.edu; Al Schares, Music Dir., phone (319)273-6489, allen.schares@uni.edu; Greg Shanley, News Dir., phone (319)273-6408, gregory.shanley@uni.edu. **Local Programs:** *Live from Studio One*, Karen Impola. **Wattage:** 100,000. **Ad Rates:** Noncommercial. **URL:** http://www.uni.edu/kuni.

KUNY-FM - See Mason City

CEDAR RAPIDS†, pop. 110,243.

E IA. Linn Co. On Cedar River, 110 mi. NE of Des Moines. Coe College, Mt. Mercy College, Kirkwood College. Manufactures cereal, meat products, electronic equipment, mining machinery, syrup, sugar, automotive tools and machinery, oil burners, furniture, pumps, gravel crushers, cranes, snow plows, trailer parts, candy, office and drainage equipment, rubber goods, plastic bags, medical and chemical products, plumbing supplies, furnaces, livestock feed, structural steel, compressed gas. Meat packing; foundries; rendering plant; building supplies.

10850 Buildings
Stamats Communications, Inc.
427 6th Ave. SE Phone: (319)364-6167
Cedar Rapids, IA 52401 Fax: (319)365-5421
Free: (800)553-8878
Publication E-mail: scott-edmunds@stamats.com

The facilities construction and management magazine covering news, concepts and technologies related to commercial building ownership and facilities management. **Subtitle:** The Facilities Construction and Management Magazine. **Founded:** 1906. **Freq:** Monthly. **Print Method:** Offset. **Trim Size:** 7 7/8 x 10 7/8. **Cols./Page:** 3. **Col. Width:** 26 nonpareils. **Col. Depth:** 140 agate lines. **Key Personnel:** Linda Monroe, Editor, lindamonroe@stamats.com; Neil Mahoney, Publisher. **ISSN:** 0007-3725. **Subscription Rates:** $70 individuals; $85 Canada; $6 single issue. **Remarks:** Accepts advertising. **Online:** Information Access Company; UMI; EBSCO. **URL:** http://www.buildingsmag.com. **Alt. Formats:** CD-ROM; Mailing labels.
Ad Rates: BW: $6,095 **Circ:** Non-paid ★**57,018**
4C: $7,645

10851 Coe Review
Coe College Student Senate
1220 1st Ave. NE Phone: (319)399-8539
Cedar Rapids, IA 52402
Publisher E-mail: caukema@coe.edu

Literary magazine covering poetry and fiction. **Founded:** 1971. **Freq:** Annual. **Key Personnel:** Shana Fried, Editor. **Subscription Rates:** $4 single issue. **Remarks:** Advertising not accepted.
Circ: Controlled 1,500

10852 Communique
Kirkwood Community College
6301 Kirkwood Blvd. SW Bldg. Phone: (319)398-5411
PO Box 2068
Cedar Rapids, IA 52404-5260
Collegiate newspaper (tabloid). **Subtitle:** The Student Voice of Kirkwood Community College. **Founded:** 1967. **Freq:** Semimonthly. **Print Method:** Offset. **Trim Size:** 11 1/4 x 17. **Cols./Page:** 4. **Col. Width:** 28 nonpareils. **Col. Depth:** 210 agate lines. **Key Personnel:** Karen Klinkefus, Advisor. **Subscription Rates:** $10 individuals; $4 single issue. **Remarks:** Accepts advertising.
Ad Rates: BW: $175 **Circ:** Free ‡4,000
PCI: $3.50

10853 Construction Equipment Operation and Maintenance
Construction Publications, Inc.
PO Box 1689
Cedar Rapids, IA 52406

Construction magazine sponsored by construction equipment dealers. **Founded:** Jan. 1949. **Freq:** Bimonthly. **Print Method:** Offset. **Trim Size:** 8 1/4 x 11. **Cols./Page:** 3. **Col. Width:** 28 nonpareils. **Col. Depth:** 138 agate lines. **Key Personnel:** Clark K. Parks, Publisher; Duane Anton, Advertising Mgr.; Gavin McComps, Editor. **Subscription Rates:** $7.50 individuals; $12 two years. **Remarks:** Accepts advertising.
Ad Rates: BW: $6,600 **Circ:** Controlled ‡63,487
4C: $8,280

10854 Fraternal Herald
Western Fraternal Life Association (WFLA)
1900 1st Ave. NE Phone: (319)363-2653
Cedar Rapids, IA 52402 Fax: (319)363-8806

Fraternal insurance benefit society magazine. **Founded:** 1897. **Freq:** Monthly. **Print Method:** Offset. **Trim Size:** 8 1/2 x 11. **Cols./Page:** 2 and 3. **Col. Width:** 21 3/5 and 14 picas. **Col. Depth:** 680 nonpareils. **Key Personnel:** Cathy M. Langer, Publications Coord.; Linda Grove, Publications Coord.; Sherry Bowers, Fraternal Mgr. **ISSN:** 0006-9256. **Subscription Rates:** $10 single issue. **Remarks:** Advertising not accepted. **Foreign language name:** Bratrsky Vestnik.
Circ: Non-paid ‡24,400

10855 Harlem News
3803 Blue Mound Dr. N. E.
Cedar Rapids, IA 52402-1734

Community newspaper. **Founded:** 1901. **Freq:** Weekly (Wed.). **Print Method:** Offset. **Cols./Page:** 6. **Col. Width:** 24 nonpareils. **Col. Depth:** 21.5 inches. **Key Personnel:** Mike Perry, Publisher. **Subscription Rates:** $13; $17 out of area; $21 out of state. **Remarks:** Accepts advertising.
Ad Rates: BW: $341.85 **Circ:** 1,400
4C: $850
SAU: $2.80
PCI: $2.65

10856 Iowa Farmer Today
501 2nd Ave. SE, 3rd Fl. Phone: (319)398-8461
PO Box 5279 Fax: (319)398-8482
Cedar Rapids, IA 52406
Free: (800)475-6655
Publication E-mail: ift@fyiowa.infi.net
Publisher E-mail: ift@fyiowa.infi.net

Agricultural newspaper containing production and agribusiness information. **Founded:** Sept. 8, 1984. **Freq:** Weekly. **Print Method:** Offset. **Trim Size:** 11 3/8 x 13 3/4. **Cols./Page:** 5. **Col. Width:** 12 picas. **Col. Depth:** 13 inches. **Key Personnel:** Lori Leonard Shellady, Editor; Steve DeWitt, Publisher, dewitt@fyiowa.com.infi.net; Terry Reilly, Advertising Mgr.; Bob Davis, Managing Editor. **USPS:** 002-141. **Subscription Rates:** $28 individuals. **URL:** http://www.fyiowa.com/ift/.
Ad Rates: BW: $3,900 **Circ:** Controlled ‡69,400
4C: $4,850
PCI: $70.60

10857 Iowa Pork Today
Iowa Farmer Today
501 2nd Ave. SE, 3rd Fl. Phone: (319)398-8461
PO Box 5279 Fax: (319)398-8482
Cedar Rapids, IA 52406
Free: (800)475-6655
Publisher E-mail: ift@fyiowa.infi.net

Magazine for Iowa's hog farmers. **Founded:** Jan. 1987. **Freq:** 10/year. **Print Method:** Web offset. **Trim Size:** 11 3/8 x 13 3/4. **Cols./Page:** 5. **Col. Width:** 2 1/16 inches. **Col. Depth:** 13 inches. **Key Personnel:** Lori Leonard, Advertising Mgr.; Stephen L. DeWitt, Publisher; Kevin Blind, Managing Editor; Terry Reilly, Advertising Sales Manager. **USPS:** 002-141. **Subscription Rates:** $16; $18 Canada and Mexico. **Remarks:** Accepts advertising. **URL:** http:/www.fyiowa.com/ift/.
Ad Rates: BW: $3058.25 **Circ:** Non-paid ‡30,313
4C: $3858.25
PCI: $47.05

10858 Penny Saver
Publications, Inc.
621 4th Ave. SE Phone: (319)399-5900
Cedar Rapids, IA 52401 Fax: (319)399-5918

Shopping guide. **Founded:** 1968. **Freq:** Weekly (Wed.). **Print Method:** Offset. **Trim Size:** 11 1/2 x 17. **Cols./Page:** 6. **Col. Width:** 1 9/16 inches. **Col. Depth:** 16 inches. **Key Personnel:** Steven H. Hunter, Publisher; Lisa Fisher, Admin. Asst./Adv. Services. **Subscription Rates:** Free. **Remarks:** Accepts advertising.
Ad Rates: BW: $1,881.60 **Circ:** Free 78,081
4C: $2,241.60
PCI: $19.60

10859 Russell's Official National Motor Coach Guide
Russells Guides, Inc.
PO Box 278 Phone: (319)364-6138
Cedar Rapids, IA 52406 Fax: (319)364-4853

Magazine containing national bus schedules. **Subtitle:** The Official Bus Guide. **Founded:** 1926. **Freq:** Monthly. **Print Method:** Offset. **Trim Size:** 8 1/2 x 9 1/2. **Cols./Page:** 2. **Col. Width:** 45 nonpareils. **Col. Depth:** 123 agate lines. **Key Personnel:** Charlotte Bonar, Editor; Karen Flint, Circulation Mgr. **ISSN:** 0036-0171. **Subscription Rates:** $101.55 individuals includes postage to US; $14.45 single issue. **Remarks:** Advertising accepted; rates available upon request.
Circ: ‡14,100

10860 KCCK-FM - 88.3
6301 Kirkwood Blvd. SW Phone: (319)398-5446
Cedar Rapids, IA 52406 Fax: (319)398-5492
Free: (800)373-5225
E-mail: kcck@inav.net

Format: Jazz; Blues; Information. **Networks:** Public Radio International (PRI); AP. **Owner:** Kirkwood Community College, at above address. **Founded:** 1972. **Operating Hours:** 5am-1am Mon-Fri, Continuous Sat. and Sun.; 16% network, 84% local. **ADI:** Cedar Rapids-Waterloo-Dubuque, IA. **Key Personnel:** George Dorman, News Dir., gdorman@kirkwood.cc.ia.us; Diane Allender, Program Dir., dallen@kirkwood.cc.ia.us; Lou Rapier, Development Dir., lrapier@kirkwood.cc.ia.us. **Local Programs:** *Da Blues*, Bob DeForest; *Sunday Brunch*, Nancy York. **Wattage:** 10,000. **Ad Rates:** Advertising accepted; rates available upon request. **URL:** http://www.kcck.org.

10861 KCRG-AM - 1600
2nd Ave. at 5th St. SE Phone: (319)395-9999
Box 816 Fax: (319)398-8378
Cedar Rapids, IA 52401
E-mail: 9online@kcrg.com

Format: News. **Networks:** ABC; AP. **Founded:** 1947. **Operating Hours:** Continuous. **ADI:** Cedar Rapids-Waterloo-Dubuque, IA. **Key Personnel:** Wally Pasbrig, Sales/Program Dir., phone (319)398-8388; Bob Allen, General Mgr.; Bob Smith, News Dir. **Wattage:** 5000. **Ad Rates:** $10-27 for 30 seconds; $12-32 for 60 seconds. **URL:** http://www.kcrg.com.

10862 KCRG-TV - 9
2nd Ave. at 5th St. SE Phone: (319)395-9999
Cedar Rapids, IA 52401 Fax: (319)398-8378
E-mail: 9online@kcrg.com

Format: Commercial TV. **Networks:** ABC. **Founded:** 1954. **Operating Hours:** Continuous. **ADI:** Cedar Rapids-Waterloo-Dubuque, IA. **Key Personnel:** Robert Allen, General Mgr. **Ad Rates:** $50-2,500 per unit. **URL:** http://www.kcrg.com. **Additional Contact Info: Mailing Address:** PO Box 816, Cedar Rapids, IA 52406-0816.

10863 KGAN-TV - 2
600-2 Old Marion Rd. NE Phone: (319)395-9060
Cedar Rapids, IA 52402 Fax: (319)395-0987

Format: Commercial TV. **Networks:** CBS. **Founded:** 1953. **Formerly:** WMT-TV (1981). **Operating Hours:** Continuous. **ADI:** Cedar Rapids-Waterloo-Dubuque, IA. **Key Personnel:** Mike Moran, President; Dan Olson, General Sales Mgr.; Dan Kuempel, LSM; Sharon Falduto, Traffic Mgr.; Kevin Schrader, Dir. of Technical Operations; Melissa Hubbard, Program Dir.; Randy Schildmeyer, Chief Engineer. **Wattage:** 100,000. **URL:** http://www.kgan.com.

10864 KHAK-FM - 98.1
425 2nd St. SE, Ste. 450 Phone: (319)365-9431
Cedar Rapids, IA 52401 Fax: (319)363-8062
Free: (800)798-5425

Format: Country. **Networks:** ABC. **Owner:** Quass Broadcasting Co., at above address. **Founded:** 1961. **Operating Hours:** Continuous; 5% network, 95% local. **ADI:** Cedar Rapids-Waterloo-Dubuque, IA. **Key Personnel:** Mary Quass, President; Britta Lee, News Dir.; Jeff Winfield, Program Dir.; Bob Brooks, Sports Dir.; Jennifer Patridge, Promotions Dir.; Dawn Johnson, Music Dir.; Dianne Harms, General Sales Mgr.; Stacy Jones, Contact; Tami Gillmore, Business Mgr. **Wattage:** 100,000. **Ad Rates:** Advertising accepted; rates available upon request.

10865 KMRY-AM - 1450
1957 Blairsferry Rd. NE Phone: (319)393-1450
Cedar Rapids, IA 52402 Fax: (319)393-1407
E-mail: kmry@inav.net

Format: Easy Listening. **Networks:** Satellite Music Network; CBS. **Owner:** Sellers Broadcasting, at above address. **Founded:** 1948. **Formerly:** KWCR-AM (1952); KPIG-AM (1962); KLWW-AM (1979); KCDR-AM (1988). **Operating Hours:** Continuous; 60% network, 40% local. **ADI:** Cedar Rapids-Waterloo-Dubuque, IA. **Key Personnel:** Rick Sellers, General Mgr./Pres., phone (319)393-1450, fax (319)393-1407; Rick Sampson, Operations Dir., phone (319)393-6397. **Local Programs:** *Remember When* 7:00 pm - 8:00 pm Saturday, Rick Sellers, President. **Wattage:** 1000. **Ad Rates:** Advertising accepted; rates available upon request.

10866 TCI of Iowa
6300 Council St., NE, Ste. A Phone: (319)395-9699
Cedar Rapids, IA 52402 Fax: (319)393-7017

Owner: TCI, 5619 DTC Pkwy., Englewood, CO 80111,

(303)267-5500. **Founded:** 1979. **Formerly:** Cox Cable Cedar Rapids Inc. (Jan. 1, 1997). **Key Personnel:** Denis Martel, Contact, phone (319)395-7801, fax (319)393-7017; Arlene Heck, Contact, phone (319)395-7801. **Cities Served:** Bertram, Cedar Rapids, Fairfax, Hiawatha, Marion, Toddville, IA; Linn County, IA: subscribing households 48,000; 72 channels; 4 community access channels; 114 hours per week community access programming.

10867 WMT-AM - 600
600 Old Marion Rd. NE Phone: (319)395-0530
Cedar Rapids, IA 52406 Fax: (319)393-0918
Free: (800)933-7767
E-mail: wmt@wmtradio.com

Format: Talk; News; Middle-of-the-Road (MOR); Agricultural. **Networks:** CBS. **Founded:** 1922. **Operating Hours:** Continuous; 20% network, 80% local. **ADI:** Cedar Rapids-Waterloo-Dubuque, IA. **Key Personnel:** Rick Sellers, General Mgr.; Vic McGill, General Sales Mgr.; Jim Boyd, News Dir.; Dawn Jaeger, Business Mgr.; Jim Davies, Chief Engineer; Ron Gonder, Sports Dir.; Rich Balvanz, Farm Dir.; Wayne Johnson, Music Dir.; Randy Lee, Program Dir. **Wattage:** 5000. **URL:** http://www.wmtradio.com.

10868 WMT-FM - 96.5
600 Old Marion Rd. NE Phone: (319)395-0530
Cedar Rapids, IA 52406 Fax: (319)393-0918
Free: (800)933-7767
E-mail: wmt@wmtradio.com

Format: Adult Contemporary; Oldies. **Networks:** CBS. **Founded:** 1963. **Operating Hours:** Continuous; 5% network, 95% local. **ADI:** Cedar Rapids-Waterloo-Dubuque, IA. **Key Personnel:** Rick Sellers, General Mgr.; Simon Will, Program and Music Dir.; Vic McGill, General Sales Mgr.; Dawn Jaeger, Business Mgr.; Jim Davies, Chief Engineer; Jim Boyd, News Dir. **Local Programs:** *Airtime*, Randy Lee. **Wattage:** 100,000 ERP. **URL:** http://www.wmtradio.com.

CENTERVILLE†, pop. 6,558.

S IA. Appanoose Co. 45 mi. SW of Ottumwa. Rathbun Fish Hatchery. Manufactures plastic bags, aluminum castings, heavy duty radiators, metal fabrication, heat transfer products, canvas and nylon products, ready mix concrete, Coal mines; rock quarry; timber. Agriculture. Corn, soybeans, alfalfa. Livestock.

10869 Ad Express
Box 610 Phone: (515)856-6336
Centerville, IA 52544
Shopper. **Founded:** 1973. **Freq:** Weekly (Wed.). **Print Method:** Offset. **Cols./Page:** 8. **Col. Width:** 21 nonpareils. **Col. Depth:** 294 agate lines. **Key Personnel:** John E. Arnold, Publisher; Bill Hayes, Advertising Mgr. **Remarks:** Accepts advertising.
Ad Rates: BW: $735.30 **Circ:** Free 10,200
SAU: $5.70

10870 Iowegian
105 N. Main St. Phone: (515)856-6336
Centerville, IA 52544 Fax: (515)856-8118

Newspaper with a Republican orientation. **Subtitle:** The Newspaper That Cares About Appanoose County. **Founded:** 1864. **Freq:** Daily (morn.). **Print Method:** Offset. **Cols./Page:** 6. **Col. Width:** 24 nonpareils. **Col. Depth:** 294 agate lines. **Key Personnel:** Steve Dunn, Editor; John Arnold, Publisher; Bill Hayes, Advertising Mgr. **Subscription Rates:** $49 individuals.
Ad Rates: PCI: $5.60 **Circ:** Paid 3,197
Non-paid 17

10871 KCOG-AM - 1400
402 N. 12th St. Phone: (515)437-4242
Centerville, IA 52544

Format: Adult Contemporary. **Networks:** USA Radio; Brownfield. **Owner:** KCOG Inc., at above address. **Founded:** 1949. **Operating Hours:** 5 a.m.-midnight. **Key Personnel:** Fred Jenkins, General Mgr.; Carolyn Jenkins, Sales Mgr. **Wattage:** 500 day; 1000 night.

10872 KMGO-FM - 98.7
402 N. 12th St. Phone: (515)856-3996
Centerville, IA 52544
E-mail: kmgofm@lisco.net

Format: Country. **Networks:** USA Radio. **Owner:** KMGO Inc., at above address. **Founded:** 1974. **Operating Hours:** Continuous. **Key Personnel:** Fred Jenkins, General Mgr.; Carolyn Jenkins, Sales Mgr. **Wattage:** 100,000.

CENTRAL CITY, pop. 1,067.

E IA. Linn Co. 20 mi. NE of Cedar Rapids. Conservation area. Agriculture. Dairy, corn, hogs.

10873 Linn News-Letter
Fourth Publishing Co.
Box A Phone: (319)438-1313
Central City, IA 52214
Community newspaper. **Founded:** 1888. **Freq:** Weekly (Tues.). **Print Method:** Offset. **Trim Size:** 11 1/2 x 17. **Cols./Page:** 6. **Col. Width:** 9 nonpareils. **Col. Depth:** 231 agate lines. **Key Personnel:** Vern J. McShane, Editor and Publisher. **Subscription Rates:** $17 individuals. **Remarks:** Accepts advertising.
Ad Rates: GLR: $.105 **Circ:** ‡2,450
BW: $225.60
4C: $725.60
PCI: $2.75

CHARITON†, pop. 4,987.

S IA. Lucas Co. 52 mi. SE of Des Moines. Clothing, cable layers, steel fabricating manufactured. Agriculture. Corn, hogs, cattle.

10874 Herald-Patriot
Chariton Newspapers
PO Box 651
Chariton, IA 50049
Publication E-mail: charnews@city.net

Community newspaper. **Founded:** 1856. **Freq:** Weekly (Thurs.). **Print Method:** Offset. **Cols./Page:** 6. **Col. Width:** 2 1/16 inches. **Col. Depth:** 21 1/2 inches. **Key Personnel:** Karen Wilker, Editor. **USPS:** 100-440. **Subscription Rates:** $29 individuals; $39 out of state. **Remarks:** Accepts advertising.
Ad Rates: SAU: $5 **Circ:** ‡3,650
PCI: $5.40

10875 Leader
Chariton Newspapers
817 Braden Ave. Phone: (515)774-2137
Chariton, IA 50049 Fax: (515)774-2139

Community newspaper. **Founded:** 1871. **Freq:** Weekly (Tues.). **Print Method:** Offset. **Cols./Page:** 6. **Col. Width:** 2 1/16 inches. **Col. Depth:** 21 1/2 inches. **Key Personnel:** Karen Wilker, Editor. **USPS:** 100-420. **Subscription Rates:** $30 individuals; $40 out of state. **Remarks:** Accepts advertising.
Ad Rates: SAU: $5 **Circ:** ‡3,650
PCI: $5.60

10876 KELR-FM - 105.5
927 1/2 Braden Ave. Phone: (515)774-8494
PO Box 693 Fax: (515)774-8495
Chariton, IA 50049
E-mail: kelr@lisco.net

Format: Adult Contemporary. **Networks:** NBC; Radio Iowa. **Founded:** 1985. **Formerly:** KYRS-FM. **Operating Hours:** Continuous; 3% network, 97% local. **Key Personnel:** Dave Russell, General Mgr.; Bill Bishop, News Dir.; Jackie Wilson, Sales Director. **Wattage:** 2100. **Ad Rates:** $4.20-6 for 15 seconds; $7-10 for 30 seconds; $8.40-12 for 60 seconds.

CHARLES CITY†, pop. 8,778.

N IA. Floyd Co. On Cedar River, 30 mi. E. of Mason City. Manufactures fertilizer feed, farm equipment, poultry remedies. Machine shops. Poultry processing. Stock, dairy, poultry farms.

10877 Charles City Press
801 Riverside Phone: (515)228-3211
PO Box 397 Fax: (515)228-2641
Charles City, IA 50616-0397
Publisher E-mail: ccpress@fiai.net

General newspaper. **Founded:** 1896. **Freq:** Tues.-Sat. (eve.). **Print Method:** Offset. **Trim Size:** 14 x 21 5/8. **Cols./Page:** 6. **Col. Width:** 12 picas. **Col. Depth:** 21 1/2 inches. **Key Personnel:** Mark Wicks, Editor; Gene A. Hall, Publisher; Richard Gifford, General Mgr. **USPS:** 100-480. **Subscription Rates:** $73.50 individuals. **Remarks:** Accepts advertising.
Ad Rates: GLR: $.57 **Circ:** ‡2,940
BW: $785.61
4C: $1,075.61
SAU: $7.98

10878 KCHA-AM - 1580
207 N. Main St. Phone: (515)228-1000
Charles City, IA 50616 Fax: (515)228-1200

Format: Adult Contemporary. **Networks:** NBC. **Founded:** 1948. **Operating Hours:** 18 hours daily; 10% network, 90% local. **Key Personnel:** Jim Hebel, Contact; Debra Lowe, Operations Mgr.; Jim Bernard, Program Dir.; Ed Redmond, Music Dir.; Mike Lyman, News Dir.; Randy Streneler, Contact; J.J. Nelson, Production Dir.; Stan McHenry, Sales Mgr.; Tim Cook, Chief Engineer. **Wattage:** 500. **Ad Rates:** $13.20 for 30 seconds; $16.24 for 60 seconds.

10879 KCHA-FM - 95.9
207 N. Main St. Phone: (515)228-1000
Charles City, IA 50616 Fax: (515)228-1200

Format: Adult Contemporary. **Founded:** 1971. **Operating Hours:** Continuous. **ADI:** Rochester, NY. **Key Personnel:** Theron Hayse, General Mgr., theron@willowtree.com; John Swinton, Operations Mgr.; Al Schwickerath, Music/News/Sports Director; Patricia Hayse, Business Mgr.; Steve Hoeft, Program Dir.; Dick Tector, Engineer. **Wattage:** 3000. **Ad Rates:** $15 for 30 seconds; $19 for 60 seconds.

10880 KCZE-FM - 95.1
207 N. Main St. Phone: (515)228-1000
Charles City, IA 50616 Fax: (515)228-1200

Format: Adult Contemporary. **Networks:** NBC. **Founded:** 1993. **Operating Hours:** 18 hours Daily. **Key Personnel:** Jim Hebel, Pres./Gen. Mgr.; Debra Lowe, Operations Mgr.; Jim Bernard, Program Dir.; Ed R. Redmond, Music Dir.; Mike Lyman, News Dir.; Randy Strevelgr, Farm Dir.; Stan McHenry, Production Dir.; Jim Hebel, Sales Mgr.; Dick Tector, Chief Engineer. **Wattage:** 5500.

CHEROKEE†, pop. 7,004.

NW IA. Cherokee Co. 50 mi. NE of Sioux City. Manufactures farm equipment, picnic tables, truck bodies, concrete blocks, feeds. Food chain warehouse. Meat packing and processing. Diversified farming.

10881 Cherokee Daily Times
Edwards Publications, Inc.
111 S. 2nd St. Phone: (712)225-5111
PO Box 281 Fax: (712)225-2910
Cherokee, IA 51012
Free: (800)747-5111
Publication E-mail: ckedt@ncn.net

General newspaper. **Founded:** 1871. **Freq:** Tues.-Sat. (morn.). **Print Method:** Offset. **Trim Size:** 13 1/2 x 23. **Cols./Page:** 6. **Col. Width:** 25 nonpareils. **Col. Depth:** 301 agate lines. **Key Personnel:** John P. Kern, Publisher; Deb Reynolds, Advertising Mgr.; Mike Palecek, Editor. **ISSN:** 0747-4776. **Subscription Rates:** $65 individuals. **Alt. Formats:** Microform.
Ad Rates: GLR: $0.53 **Circ:** Paid 3,100
BW: $967.50 Free 25
PCI: $8.20

10882 KCHE-AM - 1440
PO Box 141 Phone: (712)225-2511
Cherokee, IA 51012 Fax: (712)225-3782

Format: Middle-of-the-Road (MOR). **Key Personnel:** John M. O'Connor, Contact; Scott Hagerty, Program Dir.; Dave Lund, News Dir. **Wattage:** 500.

CLARINDA†, pop. 5,458.

SW IA. Page Co. 70 mi. SE of Council Bluffs. Manufactures neon signs, concrete, ball bearings, meat products, automotive tools. Sawmill. Seed houses. Agriculture.

10883 The Herald-Journal
Southwest Iowa Newsgroup
205 E. Main Phone: (712)542-2181
PO Box 278 Fax: (712)542-5424
Clarinda, IA 51632
Publication E-mail: hjournal@clarinda.heartland.net

Newspaper. **Founded:** 1859. **Freq:** Weekly (Wed.). **Print Method:** Offset. **Trim Size:** 8 1/2 x 11. **Cols./Page:** 6. **Col. Width:** 11 picas. **Col. Depth:** 21.5 inches. **Key Personnel:** Mark Anderson, Editor and Publisher. **Subscription Rates:** $25 individuals; $42 out of state. **Remarks:** Accepts advertising.
Ad Rates: GLR: $.27 **Circ:** Paid ‡3,900
BW: $638.12 Free ‡250
SAU: $5.64
PCI: $4.50

10884 KKBZ-FM - 99.3
209 N. Elm Phone: (712)246-5270
PO Box 960 Fax: (712)246-5275
Shenandoah, IA 51601
Free: (800)234-5622
E-mail: kma@shenessex.heartland.net

Format: Oldies. **Networks:** Westwood One Radio. **Owner:** May Broadcasting Co., at above address. **Founded:** 1990. **Formerly:** KMA-FM. **Operating Hours:** 5 a.m.-12 a.m. Mon-Sat., 6 a.m.-12a.m. Sun. **Key Personnel:** Edward W. May, President; Don Hansen, Station Mgr. **Wattage:** 50,000.

CLARION†, pop. 3,060.

NC IA. Wright Co. 30 mi. NE of Fort Dodge. Machine shops; hybrid seed corn plants; hatcheries. Ships cattle. Stock, grain, poultry farms. Corn, cattle, oats.

10885 Wright County Monitor
PO Box 153 Phone: (515)532-2871
Clarion, IA 50525
Newspaper. **Founded:** 1869. **Freq:** Weekly (Thurs.). **Print Method:** Offset. **Cols./Page:** 8. **Col. Width:** 22 nonpareils. **Col. Depth:** 301 agate lines. **Key Personnel:** Edward Dorsey, Co-Publisher; Barbara Dorsey, Co-Publisher. **Subscription Rates:** $28 individuals.
Ad Rates: GLR: $.29 **Circ:** ⊕**2,000**
SAU: $4.26
PCI: $2.75

CLARKSVILLE, pop. 1,424.

NC IA. Butler Co. 35 mi. NW of Waterloo. Light industry. Agriculture. Corn, oats, soybeans.

10886 Clarksville Star
The Star Co.
PO Box 788 Phone: (319)278-4641
Clarksville, IA 50619
Publication E-mail: wsn@mmi.net

Newspaper with a Republican orientation. **Founded:** 1866. **Freq:** Weekly (Thurs.). **Print Method:** Letterpress and offset. **Cols./Page:** 5. **Col. Width:** 24 nonpareils. **Col. Depth:** 238 agate lines. **Key Personnel:** Jerry A. Platter, Editor. **Subscription Rates:** $10.50 individuals.
Circ: 1,200

CLEAR LAKE, pop. 7,458.

NC IA. Cerro Gordo Co. 10 mi. W. of Mason City. Tourism. Residential.

10887 Clear Lake Reporter
Prefin, Inc.
12 N. 4th St. Phone: (515)357-2131
Clear Lake, IA 50428 Fax: (515)357-2133

Local newspaper. **Founded:** 1869. **Freq:** Weekly (Wed.). **Print Method:** Offset. **Trim Size:** 14 x 21. **Cols./Page:** 6. **Col. Width:** 13.3 picas. **Col. Depth:** 21.5 inches. **Key Personnel:** Marianne Morf, Editor; Michael Finnegan, Publisher. **Subscription Rates:** $37.50 U.S. and other countries; $43 out of country local; $55 out of state.
Ad Rates: GLR: $.32 **Circ:** ‡2,200
BW: $520
4C: $645
PCI: $5.23

10888 The Clear Lake Reporter/Advertiser
Prefin, Inc.
12 N. 4th St. Phone: (515)357-2131
Clear Lake, IA 50428 Fax: (515)357-2133

Shopper (tabloid). **Freq:** Weekly (Wed.). **Print Method:** Offset. **Trim Size:** 10 x 14. **Cols./Page:** 6. **Col. Width:** 18 nonpareils. **Col. Depth:** 196 agate lines. **Key Personnel:** Marianne Morf, Editor; Michael Finnegan, Publisher. **Subscription Rates:** Free.
Ad Rates: GLR: $.03 **Circ:** Free ‡2,500
BW: $520
4C: $645

CLEARFIELD, pop. 433.

SW IA. Ringgold & Taylor Co. 12 mi. N. of Bedford. Residential.

10889 Chronicle
PO Box 171 Phone: (515)333-2810
Clearfield, IA 50840-0155
Local newspaper. **Founded:** 1959. **Freq:** Weekly (Wed.). **Print Method:** Offset. **Cols./Page:** 5. **Col. Width:** 30 nonpareils. **Col. Depth:** 168 agate lines. **Key Personnel:** Lucille Bailey, Editor; George Bailey, Sr., Publisher. **Subscription Rates:** $8 individuals. **Remarks:** Accepts advertising.
Ad Rates: GLR: $.23 **Circ:** Paid 684
SAU: $1.40 Free 15

CLINTON†, pop. 32,828.

E IA. Clinton Co. On the Mississippi River, 30 mi. NE of Davenport. Bridges to Fulton and East Clinton, IL. Trade/industrial center. Manufactures corn syrup, sugars, salad oils, house dresses, culvert pipes, dog and cat food, paper cartons, ironworks.

10890 Clinton Herald
Donrey Media Group
221 6th Ave. S Phone: (319)242-7101
Clinton, IA 52732-4305 Fax: (319)242-3854

General newspaper. **Founded:** 1856. **Freq:** Daily (eve.) and Sat. (morn.). **Print Method:** Offset. **Trim Size:** 13 3/4 x 22 3/4. **Cols./Page:** 6. **Col. Width:** 24 nonpareils. **Col. Depth:** 301 agate lines. **Key Personnel:** William C. Baker, Editor; John J. Dermody, Publisher; Chris Allen, Advertising Dir. **USPS:** 111-680. **Subscription Rates:** $52.80 individuals. **Remarks:** Accepts advertising.
Ad Rates: GLR: $.90 **Circ:** Mon.-Sat. ★**15,023**
BW: $1,625.40
4C: $1,840.40
SAU: $12.60

10891 The Gallery
Clinton Community College
1000 Lincoln Blvd. Phone: (319)244-7001
Clinton, IA 52732 Fax: (319)244-7107
Free: (800)637-0559

Collegiate newspaper. **Founded:** 1964. **Freq:** Monthly. **Print Method:** Offset. **Trim Size:** 14 x 17. **Cols./Page:** 6. **Col. Width:** 1 5/8 inches. **Col. Depth:** 238 agate lines. **Key Personnel:** Kelly Gerlach, Editor; Dustin Freyer, Advertising Mgr.; Beth Hefner, Advisor. **Subscription Rates:** Free. **Remarks:** Accepts advertising.
Ad Rates: BW: $150 **Circ:** Paid ‡1,000
PCI: $5 Controlled ‡1,000

10892 KCLN-FM - 97.7
1853 442nd Ave. Phone: (319)243-1390
Clinton, IA 52732 Fax: (319)242-4567
E-mail: kcln@clinton.net

Format: Adult Contemporary. **Networks:** ABC. **Owner:** K&K Broadcasting, Inc., at above address. **Formerly:** KLNT-FM. **Operating Hours:** 5 a.m.-midnight. **Key Personnel:** Gene Kauffman, General Mgr., gkauffma@clinton.net; Justin Gill, Sales Mgr.; Heather Hilgendorf, News Dir.; Rob Reed, Program Dir. **Local Programs:** *Minor League Baseball*, Gene Kauffman. **Wattage:** 3000. **Ad Rates:** $9-15 for 30 seconds; $14-23 for 60 seconds. $7-$15 for 30 seconds; $11-$19 for 60 seconds. Combined advertising rates available with KLNT-AM. **URL:** http://kcln.clinton.net.

10893 KLNT-AM - 1390
1853 442nd Ave. Phone: (319)243-1390
Clinton, IA 52732

Format: Big Band/Nostalgia; Oldies; Agricultural. **Networks:** ABC. **Owner:** K&K Broadcasting, Inc., at above address, Fax: (319)242-4567. **Founded:** 1956. **Formerly:** KCLN-AM. **Operating Hours:** 5 a.m.-midnight. **Key Personnel:** Gene Kauffman, General Mgr., gkauffma@clinton.net; Justine Gill, Sales Mgr.; Heather Hilgendorf, News Dir.; Rob Reed, Program Dir. **Wattage:** 1000. **Ad Rates:** $9-15 for 30 seconds; $14-23 for 60 seconds. $7-$15 for 30 seconds; $11-$19 for 60 seconds. Combined advertising rates available with KCLN-FM. **URL:** http://kcln.clinton.net.

10894 KROS-AM - 1340
PO Box 0518 Phone: (319)242-1252
Clinton, IA 52733-0518 Fax: (319)242-4825
E-mail: kros@clinton.net

Format: News; Talk; Sports; Agricultural; Full Service. **Networks:** Mutual Broadcasting System. **Owner:** KROS Broadcasting Inc., at above address. **Founded:** 1941. **Operating Hours:** 5:30 a.m.-midnight; 13% network, 77% local. **Key Personnel:** Don Schneider, General Mgr.; Lauren Hyde, Sales Mgr.; Dave Vickers, News Dir.; Gary Determan, Sports Dir.; Valerie Hayes, Music Dir.; Paul Clark, Program Dir.; Brad Parker, Chief Engineer. **Local Programs:** *Homespun Lane*, Ellen Ketelsen, Mailing contact. **Wattage:** 1000. **Ad Rates:** $5.25 for 10 seconds; $10.50 for 30 seconds; $13 for 60 seconds.

10895 TCI of Eastern Iowa
112 N. 2nd. St Phone: (319)243-6350
Clinton, IA 52732-4115 Fax: (319)243-7146

Founded: 1974. **Cities Served:** Clinton, Jackson, and Scott counties, IA and Carroll and Whiteside counties, IL.

CLIVE

10896 Iowa Pork Producer
Iowa Pork Producers Association
Box 71009 Phone: (515)225-7675
Clive, IA 50325 Fax: (515)225-0563
Free: (800)372-7675
Publication E-mail: iapork@ngtins.net

Livestock magazine/Association newsmagazine (monthly). **Founded:** 1971. **Freq:** Monthly. **Print Method:** Offset (Web). **Trim Size:** 8 x 10 3/4. **Cols./Page:** 3. **Col. Width:** 13 picas. **Col. Depth:** 9 3/4 inches. **Key Personnel:** Peter Theodore, IPPA, Editor and Publisher. **Remarks:** Accepts advertising.
Ad Rates: BW: $1,400 **Circ:** Non-paid ‡25,000
4C: $2,150

COLFAX

10897 Jasper County Tribune
13 E. Front Phone: (515)674-3591
Box 7 Fax: (515)674-3591
Colfax, IA 50054
Free: (800)299-3591

Community newspaper. **Freq:** Weekly (Thurs.) Offset. **Cols./Page:** 6. **Col. Width:** 12 picas. **Col. Depth:** 21 inches. **Key Personnel:** Allen Arthur, Editor and Publisher. **Subscription Rates:** $17 individuals; $20 out of state. **Remarks:** Accepts advertising. **Formerly:** Colfax Tribune.
Ad Rates: SAU: $3.25 **Circ:** 2,000

COLUMBUS JUNCTION, pop. 1,429.

SE IA. Louisa Co. On Iowa River, 23 mi. W. of Muscatine. Manufactures social stationery, concrete. Meat packing plant. Limestone and sand quarries. Agriculture. Corn, soybeans, melons. Livestock.

10898 The Columbus Gazette
209 Main St. Phone: (319)728-2413
Box 267 Fax: (319)728-3272
Columbus Junction, IA 52738
Publication E-mail: cjgaz@lisco.net

Community newspaper covering local news, agriculture, and Hispanic interests. **Founded:** May 1887. **Freq:** Weekly (Wed.). **Print Method:** Offset. **Trim Size:** 28 x 22 3/4. **Cols./Page:** 6. **Col. Width:** 12.3 picas. **Col. Depth:** 21 1/2 inches. **Key Personnel:** Darwin K. Sherman, Publisher, phone (319)653-2191, fax (319)653-7524; John Carpenter, General Mgr. **ISSN:** 0747-2889. **Subscription Rates:** $20 local annual; newspaper rate; $.50 single issue magazine rate.
Ad Rates: BW: $601.14 **Circ:** ‡1,600
4C: $881.14
SAU: $4.66

CONRAD, pop. 1,133.

C IA. Grunly Co. 15 mi. N. of Marshalltown. Residential.

10899 The Record
PO Box 190 Phone: (515)366-2020
Conrad, IA 50621 Fax: (515)366-2020
Free: (888)851-2020
Publisher E-mail: therecord@marshallnet.com

Newspaper. **Subtitle:** Serving the Communities of Beaman, Conrad, Liscomb, Union and Whitten. **Founded:** 1880. **Freq:** Weekly (Thurs.). **Print Method:** Offset. **Trim Size:** 10 x 12 1/2. **Cols./Page:** 5. **Col. Width:** 22 nonpareils. **Col. Depth:** 203 agate lines. **Key Personnel:** Helen Kopsa, Editor and Publisher. **Subscription Rates:** $22.50 individuals; $26 out of state; $24 Snowbird. **Remarks:** Accepts advertising. **Formerly:** Conrad Record.
Ad Rates: GLR: $.16 **Circ:** ‡1,250
BW: $217.50
4C: $257.25
SAU: $4.37
CNU: $253.75
PCI: $3.15

COON RAPIDS

WC IA. Carroll Co. 5 mi. S. of Dedham.

10900 Coon Rapids Enterprise
504 Main St. Phone: (712)684-2821
Coon Rapids, IA 50058 Fax: (712)684-7783

Community newspaper. **Freq:** Weekly (Thurs.). **Cols./Page:** 5. **Col. Width:** 11 1/2 picas. **Col. Depth:** 15 inches. **Key Personnel:** Charles Nixon, Editor and Publisher.
Circ: 1,500

10901 Coon Rapids Municipal Cable
123 3rd Ave. Phone: (712)684-2225
PO Box 207 Fax: (712)684-5148
Coon Rapids, IA 50058

Founded: 1982. **Key Personnel:** Bradley A. Honold, General Mgr. **Cities Served:** Coon Rapids, IA: subscribing households 454; 24 channels; 2 community access channels; 1 hour per week community access programming.

CORNING

10902 Adams County Free Press
J-D Publishing Co.
800 Davis Ave. Phone: (515)322-3161
PO Box 46 Fax: (515)322-3162
Corning, IA 50841
Local newspaper. **Founded:** 1882. **Freq:** Weekly. **Print Method:** Offset. **Trim Size:** 13 x 21 1/2. **Cols./Page:** 6. **Col. Width:** 12.12 picas. **Col. Depth:** 21.5 picas. **Key Personnel:** Dan Field, Editor and Publisher. **USPS:** 005-100. **Subscription Rates:** $18 individuals; $23 out of area. **Remarks:** Accepts advertising.
Ad Rates: GLR: $.22 **Circ:** Paid 2,645
BW: $344 Free 66
4C: $510
SAU: $4.25
PCI: $3.10

CORRECTIONVILLE

10903 Correctionville News
Stangl Pub.
313 5th St. Phone: (712)372-4747
Correctionville, IA 51016
Community newspaper. **Freq:** Weekly (Wed.). **Cols./Page:** 6. **Col. Width:** 13 picas. **Col. Depth:** 20 inches. **Key Personnel:** Tom Stangl, Editor; Virgil Dorweiler, Publisher.
Circ: 600

CORYDON†, pop. 1,818.

S IA. Wayne Co. 61 mi. SE of Des Moines. Automobile batteries, zipper and plastic bags, soap, road machinery, concrete, bug deflectors manufactured. Hatchery. Dairy, stock, poultry farms.

10904 Times-Republican
PO Box 258 Phone: (515)872-1234
Corydon, IA 50060 Fax: (515)872-1965

Newspaper. **Founded:** 1870. **Freq:** Weekly (Tues.). **Print Method:** Offset. **Cols./Page:** 6. **Col. Width:** 24 nonpareils. **Col. Depth:** 294 agate lines. **Key Personnel:** James D. Lancaster, Owner; Rhonda Bennett, Publisher; Tammy Couter, Editor; Peggy Roberts, Owner. **Subscription Rates:** $18 individuals. **Remarks:** Accepts advertising.
Ad Rates: GLR: $4.00 **Circ:** ‡3,320
BW: $516
SAU: $2
PCI: $4.00

COUNCIL BLUFFS†, pop. 56,449.

SW IA. Pottawattamie Co. On Missouri River, E. of Omaha, NE. Four bridges to Omaha, NE. Iowa School for Deaf. Iowa Western Community College. Manufactures radio crystals and holders, cereals, powdered eggs, canned chickens, bee supplies, freight and passenger elevators, animal foods, remedies and serums, meat packing, foam plastic, oils and greases, steel pipes, plastics, farm machinery, playground equipment and pipe pushers, truck bodies, furniture. Roundhouses. Many grain elevators.

10905 The Council Bluffs Bulletin
Council Bluffs Shoppers Bulletin
152 Vine St. Phone: (712)323-1898
Council Bluffs, IA 51503 Fax: (712)323-8834

Free weekly tab. local news. **Founded:** Aug. 12, 1970. **Freq:** Weekly (Wed.). **Print Method:** Offset. **Trim Size:** 11 1/4 x 17. **Cols./Page:** 6. **Col. Width:** 10 picas. **Col. Depth:** 15.5 inches. **Key Personnel:** Dan Rutledge, Contact. **Remarks:** Accepts advertising. **Formerly:** Shopper's Bulletin.
Ad Rates: BW: $465 **Circ:** Free ‡29,087
4C: $765
PCI: $7

10906 Daily Devotions for the Deaf
Deaf Missions
21199 Greenview Rd. Phone: (712)322-5493
Council Bluffs, IA 51503 Fax: (712)322-7792

Religious publication for the deaf. **Founded:** Jan. 1990. **Freq:** Quarterly. **Print Method:** Offset. **Trim Size:** 6 x 8 1/2. **Cols./Page:** 2. **Col. Width:** 2 3/8 inches. **Col. Depth:** 7 1/4 inches. **Key Personnel:** Duane King, Editor. **ISSN:** 0744-9100. **Remarks:** Advertising not accepted. **URL:** http://www.deafmissions.com. **Alt. Formats:** Braille; Large-print.
Circ: Non-paid 23,000

10907 The Daily Nonpareil
117 Pearl St. Phone: (712)328-1811
Council Bluffs, IA 51503-0824 Fax: (712)328-1597

General newspaper. **Founded:** 1857. **Freq:** Daily (eve.), Sat. and Sun. (morn.). **Print Method:** Offset. **Cols./Page:** 6. **Col. Width:** 26 nonpareils. **Col. Depth:** 301 agate lines. **Key Personnel:** Charles Gates, Editor; M. Joseph Craig, Publisher; Dennis Koenders, Advertising Mgr. **ISSN:** 1046-1833. **Subscription Rates:** $110 individuals. **Remarks:** Accepts advertising. **Alt. Formats:** CD-ROM.
Ad Rates: GLR: $1.03 **Circ:** Mon.-Sat. 17,012
BW: $1,860.18 Sun. 18,704
4C: $2,235.18
PCI: $14.42

10908 KIWR-FM - 89.7
1700 College Rd. Phone: (712)325-3254
Council Bluffs, IA 51503 Fax: (712)325-3391
E-mail: theriver897@hotmail.com

Format: Public Radio; Alternative/New Music/Progressive. **Networks:** AP. **Owner:** Iowa Western Community College, 2700 College Rd., Box 4-C, Council Bluffs, IA 51502, (712)325-3200. **Founded:** 1981. **Operating Hours:** Continuous; 1% network, 99% local. **ADI:** Omaha, NE. **Key Personnel:** Vickie Ratliff, General Mgr.; Bill Stewart, Program Mgr.; Connie Kellie, Promotions Mgr.; Dave Ludwig, Chief Engineer; Chris Urly, Production Dir.; Gregg Daniels, Sports Dir.; Chris Fisher, Development Dir.; John Jeffries, News Dir.; William Salnk, Program Dir. **Local Programs:** *Retro River Rapids*, Gregory Brothers; *River Currents*, John Jeffries; *River Unplugged*, Chris Fisher. **Wattage:** 100,000. **Ad Rates:** Noncommercial; underwriting available. $13-30 per unit.

10909 KLNG-AM - 1560
120 S. 35th St., Ste. 2 Phone: (712)323-8100
Council Bluffs, IA 51501-8114 Fax: (712)323-0022

Format: Religious; Talk. **Networks:** Christian Broadcasting (CBN); USA Radio. **Founded:** 1947. **Operating Hours:** 6 a.m.-9 p.m. **Key Personnel:** Norman L. Brown, General Mgr., phone (712)323-0100. **Wattage:** 1000. **Ad Rates:** $10 for 30 seconds; $15 for 60 seconds.

10910 TCI of Council Bluffs
1729 McPherson Ave. Phone: (712)328-7207
Council Bluffs, IA 51503 Fax: (712)323-0754

Founded: 1975. **Formerly:** American Heritage Cablevision. **Key Personnel:** Dennis Jadlot, General Mgr.; Merrill Johnson, Operations Dir.; Steven K. Johnson, Contact; Lynette Langer Keagle, Contact. **Cities Served:** 1 community access channel.

CRESCO†, pop. 3,860.

NE IA. Howard Co. 65 mi. S. of Rochester, MN. Manufactures automobile parts, steel, aluminum horse and livestock trailers, cement blocks, drainage tile, fuel, industrial airfilter. Tool and die shops; creameries; nursery. Dairy, stock, poultry farms.

10911 Times-Plain Dealer
Front Page Communications, Inc.
214 N. Elm Phone: (319)547-3601
PO Box 350 Fax: (319)547-4602
Cresco, IA 52136
Publication E-mail: times-extra@pitnet.net

Agricultural newspaper. **Founded:** Jan. 4, 1867. **Freq:** Weekly (Wed.). **Print Method:** Offset. **Trim Size:** 14 3/4 x 21 1/2. **Cols./Page:** 7. **Col. Width:** 12.5 picas. **Col. Depth:** 294 agate lines. **Key Personnel:** John K. Hall, Editor and Publisher. **USPS:** 617-800. **Subscription Rates:** $27 individuals; $35 out of area; $49 out of state. **Remarks:** Accepts advertising.
Ad Rates: GLR: $.43 **Circ:** Paid ‡3,450
BW: $687.78 Free ‡7,650
4C: $912.78
SAU: $6.07
PCI: $6.07

10912 KCZQ-FM - 102.3
116 1st Ave. West Phone: (319)547-1000
Cresco, IA 52136 Fax: (319)547-2200

Format: Adult Contemporary. **Networks:** Superadio; Radio Iowa. **Owner:** Mega Media Ltd., at above address. **Founded:** 1991. **Operating Hours:** 18 hours Daily. **ADI:** Rochester, MN-Mason City, IA-Austin, MN. **Key Personnel:** James Hebel, Pres./Gen. Mgr.; Debra Lowe, Operations Mgr.; Jim Bernard, Program Dir.; Ed Redmond, Music Dir.; Phil Werts, News Dir.; Dean Lickteig, Farm Dir.; Stan McHenry, Production Dir.; Jim Hebel, Sales Mgr.; J. Hebel, Chief Engineer. **Wattage:** 3000.

CRESTON†, pop. 8,429.

S IA. Union Co. 73 mi. SW of Des Moines. Southwestern Community College. Manufactures lubricating devices, coffee makers. Plastic tile, planing mill; aluminum and magnesium foundry castings; food processing; stock yards, anhydrous ammonia plants. Ships livestock, grain. Gravel pits. Agriculture. Hogs, cattle, corn, soybeans.

10913 Creston News Advertiser
Creston Publishing Co.
Box 126 Phone: (515)782-2141
503 W. Adams St. Fax: (515)782-6628
Creston, IA 50801
Publication E-mail: cna@creston.heartland.net

General newspaper. **Founded:** 1879. **Freq:** Daily (eve.) Monday-Friday. **Print Method:** Offset. **Trim Size:** 13 3/4 x 22 3/4. **Cols./Page:** 6. **Col. Width:** 12 1/2 picas. **Col. Depth:** 21 1/2 inches. **Key Personnel:** Jeff Young, Editor, cnaed@creston.heartland.net; Arvid E. Huisman, Publisher, cnapub@creston.heartland.net; Roger Lanning, Advertising Dir. **USPS:** 137-820. **Subscription Rates:** $75 individuals; $122.50 out of area. **Absorbed:** Creston Shopper.
Ad Rates: GLR: $.54 **Circ:** ‡5,496
BW: $973.95
4C: $1,168.95
SAU: $7.55
PCI: $7.55

10914 KITR-FM - 101.3
Hwy. 34 W. Phone: (515)782-2155
Box 426 Fax: (515)782-6963
Creston, IA 50801

Format: Country; Big Band/Nostalgia. **Networks:** ABC. **Owner:** G.O. Radio Ltd., at above address. **Founded:** 1975. **Operating Hours:** 6 a.m.-11 p.m.; 10% network, 50% local, 40% other. **Key Personnel:** David Rieck, Contact; Mike Peterson, News Dir.; David W. Passehl, Contact; Charlie Maley, Contact; Eric Mains, Contact; Gary Bucklin, Sports Dir. **Wattage:** 25,000. **Ad Rates:** $5-8 for 30 seconds; $5.50-10.50 for 60 seconds.

10915 KSIB-AM - 1520
Hwy. 34 W. Phone: (515)782-2155
Box 426 Fax: (515)782-6963
Creston, IA 50801

Format: Country; Big Band/Nostalgia. **Networks:** ABC. **Owner:** G.O. Radio Ltd., Box 550, Webster City, IA 50595, (515)832-1570. **Founded:** 1947. **Operating Hours:** 6 a.m.-11 p.m.; 10% network, 45% local; 45% other. **Key Personnel:** David Rieck, Contact; Mike Peterson, News Dir.; David W. Passehl, Contact; Charlie Maley, Contact; Eric Mains, Contact; Gary Bucklin, Sports Dir. **Wattage:** 1000. **Ad Rates:** $5-8 for 30 seconds; $5.50-10.50 for 60 seconds.

DAVENPORT†, pop. 103,264.

E IA. Scott Co. On Mississippi River, 182 mi. W. of Chicago and opposite Rock Island, IL. Bridges to Rock Island and Moline, IL. St. Ambrose College, Marycrest College, and Palmer College of Chiropractic Medicine. Manufactures sheet aluminum, agricultural implements, construction machinery tractors, military equipment, cement and foundry products, cookies, crackers, meat products. Ships grain, limestone and cement.

10916 The Catholic Messenger
736 Federal St. Phone: (319)323-9959
PO Box 460 Fax: (319)323-6612
Davenport, IA 52805-0460
Publication E-mail: cathmess@sau.edu

Newspaper covering local, national, and international Catholic news. **Founded:** 1882. **Freq:** Weekly (Thurs.). **Print Method:** Offset. **Trim Size:** 15 x 21. **Cols./Page:** 6. **Col. Width:** 24 nonpareils. **Col. Depth:** 301 agate lines. **Key Personnel:** Fr. Francis C. Henricksen, Editor. **ISSN:** 0008-8234. **Subscription Rates:** $22 individuals 50 weeks. **Remarks:** Accepts advertising. **Alt. Formats:** Microform.
Ad Rates: GLR: $.50 **Circ:** Paid 21,879
BW: $642.60 Free 195
SAU: $7.30
PCI: $7.03

10917 The Leader
Moline Dispatch Publishing Co.
423 E. 32nd St., Ste. 1 Phone: (319)326-5848
Davenport, IA 52803
Community newspaper. **Founded:** 1986. **Freq:** Weekly. **Print Method:** Offset. **Cols./Page:** 6. **Col. Width:** 2 1/16 inches. **Col. Depth:** 21 1/2 inches. **Key Personnel:** Mike Romkey, Editor; Ted Lawrence, Advertising Mgr.; Arnold Norman, Circulation Mgr.; Phil Roberts, Assoc. Editor. **Subscription Rates:** Free Home delivery; $0.50 single issue In racks. **Formerly:** The Shopper (1986).
Ad Rates: BW: $2,064 **Circ:** Free 51,625
4C: $2,339
PCI: $16

10918 Operations Research/Management Science
Executive Sciences Institute
1005 Mississippi Ave.
Davenport, IA 52803

Operations research and management science journal. **Founded:** Jan. 1960. **Freq:** Bimonthly. **Print Method:** Offset. **Trim Size:** 6 x 9. **Cols./Page:** 1. **Key Personnel:** Bruce Brocka, Editor. **ISSN:** 0030-3658. **Subscription Rates:** $165 U.S.; $199 other countries; $25 single issue. **Remarks:** Advertising not accepted.
Circ: (Not Reported)

10919 Quad-City Times
500 E. 3rd St. Phone: (319)383-2200
PO Box 3828 Fax: (319)383-2433
Davenport, IA 52801-1708
Free: (800)437-4641
Publication E-mail: qctimes@aol.com

General newspaper. **Founded:** 1855. **Freq:** Mon.-Sun. (morn.). **Print Method:** Offset. **Cols./Page:** 6. **Col. Width:** 24 nonpareils. **Col. Depth:** 255 agate lines. **Key Personnel:** Dave Foselier, Publisher; Beth Clark, Publisher; Mark Ridolfi, General Mgr./Managing Editor, phone (319)383-2450; Jim Thompson, Circulation Mgr.; Roy Booker, Librarian, phone (319)383-2293. **Subscription Rates:** $166.40 individuals. **Remarks:** Accepts advertising. **URL:** http://www.qctimes.com. **Feature Editors:** Deborah Brasier, *Editorials*, phone (319)383-2452; Craig Chandler, *Photo*, phone (319)383-2361.
Ad Rates: BW: $3,401.70 **Circ:** Mon.-Fri. ★**53,467**
4C: $3,986.70 Sat. ★**67,566**
SAU: $26.86 Sun. ★**76,943**

10920 Quality Control and Applied Statistics
Executive Sciences Institute
1005 Mississippi Ave.
Davenport, IA 52803

International journal reporting quality control, reliability, and statistical methods information. **Founded:** Jan. 1956. **Freq:** Monthly. **Print Method:** Offset. **Trim Size:** 6 x 9. **Key Personnel:** Bruce Brocka, Editor; Suzanne Brocka, Publisher; Greta A. Lane, Advertising Mgr. **ISSN:** 0033-5207. **Subscription Rates:** $165 U.S.; $199 other countries; $25 single issue. **Remarks:** Advertising not accepted.
Circ: (Not Reported)

10921 KALA-FM - 88.5
518 W. Locust St. Phone: (319)333-6219
Davenport, IA 52803-2898 Fax: (319)333-6218
Free: (800)728-2586

Format: Jazz; Urban Contemporary; Alternative/New Music/Progressive. **Networks:** Longhorn Radio. **Owner:** St. Ambrose University, at above address. **Founded:** 1967. **Operating Hours:** 20 hours weekdays, Continuous Sat. and Sun. **ADI:** Davenport,IA-Rock Island, Moline,IL. **Key Personnel:** David Baker, General Mgr., dbaker@saunix.sau.edu; Alan Sivell, News Dir. **Local Programs:** *Jazz Images*, David Baker; *Jazz Perspectives*, David Baker; *Mad Flava Morning Show*, David Baker. **Wattage:** 100. **Ad Rates:** Noncommercial. **URL:** http://cs.sau.edu/~kala/.

10922 KBOB-FM - 99.7
1229 Brady St. Phone: (319)326-2541
Davenport, IA 52803-4616 Fax: (319)326-1819
Free: (800)319-5262

Format: Country. **Owner:** Connoisseur Communications, at above address. **Founded:** 1949. **Formerly:** KFMH-FM. **Operating Hours:** Continuous. **ADI:** Davenport,IA-Rock Island, Moline,IL. **Key Personnel:** Steve Watt, General Mgr.; Bill Grunder, Sales Mgr.; Tom McGuire, Program Dir. **Wattage:** 100,000 ERP.

10923 KJOC-AM - 1170
1229 Brady St. Phone: (319)326-2541
Davenport, IA 52803 Fax: (319)326-1819

Format: Sports. **Networks:** ESPN Radio; CBS. **Owner:** Connoisseur Communications, 136 Main St., Westport, CT 06880, (203)227-1978, Fax: (203)227-2373. **Founded:** 1946. **Formerly:** KKZX-AM (1987); KSTT-AM (1994). **Operating Hours:** Continuous; 75% network, 50% local. **ADI:** Davenport,IA-Rock Island, Moline,IL. **Key Personnel:** Steve Watt, General Mgr.; Bill Grunder, Sales Mgr.; Dan Burich, Program Dir. **Local Programs:** *Wild World of Sports*, Dan Burich. **Wattage:** 1000. **Ad Rates:** Advertising accepted; rates available upon request.

10924 KLJB-TV - 18
937 E. 53rd St., Ste. D Phone: (319)386-1818
Davenport, IA 52807 Fax: (319)386-8543

Format: Commercial TV. **Networks:** Fox. **Owner:** Quad Cities Television Acquisition Corp., at above address. **Founded:** 1985. **Operating Hours:** Continuous. **ADI:** Davenport,IA-Rock Island, Moline,IL. **Key Personnel:** John Bain, Program Mgr.; Randy Stone, General Sales Mgr.; Jane Scheckel, Traffic Mgr.; Don Bargmann, Chief Engineer; Brad Ruggles, Production Mgr. **Ad Rates:** Advertising accepted; rates available upon request. **URL:** http://www.kljb.com.

10925 KMXG-FM - 96.1
3535 E. Kimberly Rd. Phone: (319)344-7000
Davenport, IA 52807 Fax: (319)344-7065
Free: (800)397-0496
E-mail: mix96@conline.com

Format: Adult Contemporary. **Founded:** 1986. **Formerly:** KSAY-FM; KLIO-FM; KMJC-FM. **Operating Hours:** Continuous; 100% local. **ADI:** Davenport,IA-Rock Island, Moline,IL. **Key Personnel:** Larry Rosmilso, General Mgr.; Scott Bitting, General Sales Mgr., phone (319)344-7061, fax (319)344-7006; Matt Williams, Program Dir., phone (319)344-7048. **Wattage:** 100,000. **Ad Rates:** $25-40 for 30 seconds; $45-50 for 60 seconds.

10926 KUUL-FM - 103.7
3535 E. Kimberly Rd. Phone: (319)344-7000
Davenport, IA 52807 Fax: (319)344-7065
E-mail: kuul@qconline.com

Format: Oldies. **Networks:** Unistar; CBS. **Founded:** 1948. **Formerly:** WOC-FM (1972). **Operating Hours:** Continuous. **ADI:** Davenport,IA-Rock Island, Moline,IL. **Key Personnel:** Randall Odeneal, President; Steve Guenzler, Sales Mgr., phone (319)344-7027; Larry Rosmilso, General Mgr.; Chuck O'Brien, Program Dir., phone (319)344-7145. **Wattage:** 100,000. **Ad Rates:** $13-61 for 30 seconds; $15-72 for 60 seconds.

10927 KWQC-TV - 6
805 Brady St. Phone: (319)383-7000
Davenport, IA 52803 Fax: (319)383-7131
Free: (800)927-6397

Format: Commercial TV. **Networks:** NBC. **Owner:** Young Broadcasting of Davenport, Inc, 805 Brady St., Davenport, IA 52803. **Founded:** 1949. **Formerly:** WOC-TV (1986). **Operating Hours:** 5:30 a.m.-2 a.m.; 80% network, 20% local. **ADI:** Davenport,IA-Rock Island, Moline,IL. **Key Personnel:** Jim Graham, General Mgr./VP; Cathie Whiteside, Station Manager; Doug Retherford, News Dir.; John Hegeman, Operations Mgr.; Jeff Bilyeu, Program & Promotion Mgr.; Trish Tague, Marketing & Research Dir. **Wattage:** 100,000. **Ad Rates:** $60-2,500 per unit. **URL:** http://www.kwqc.com.

10928 WHTS-FM - 98.9
3535 E. Kimberly Rd. Phone: (319)344-9487
Davenport, IA 52807 Fax: (319)344-7037
E-mail: whts@qconline.com

Format: Contemporary Hit Radio (CHR). **Founded:** 1947. **Formerly:** WPXR-FM. **Operating Hours:** Continuous. **ADI:** Davenport,IA-Rock Island, Moline,IL. **Key Personnel:** Mary Swanson, Station Mgr.; Tony Waitekus, Program Dir.; Dave Seran, Sales Mgr. **Wattage:** 39,000. **Ad Rates:** $25-75 per unit. **URL:** http://www.qconline.com/whts.

10929 WKBF-AM - 1270
3535 E. Kimberly Rd. Phone: (319)344-7000
Davenport, IA 52807 Fax: (319)344-7087

Networks: Westwood One Radio. **Owner:** Segue Communications, at above address. **Founded:** 1925. **Formerly:** WHBF-AM. **Operating Hours:** Continuous; 95% network, 5 local. **ADI:** Davenport,IA-Rock Island, Moline,IL. **Key Personnel:** Bill Dudley, General Mgr.; Kevin Walker, Operations Mgr., phone (319)344-7070. **Wattage:** 5000; 5400. **Ad Rates:** $12 for 30 seconds; $15 for 60 seconds.

10930 WLLR-AM - 1230
3535 E. Kimberly Rd. Phone: (319)355-5331
Davenport, IA 52807 Fax: (319)359-8524

Format: Country; Sports. **Simulcasts:** WLLR-FM. **Networks:** Independent. **Owner:** Sconnix Broadcasting Co., Tyson International Plaza, 1921 Gallows Rd., Vienna, VA 22182, (703)356-6000. **Founded:** 1946. **Formerly:** WQUA-AM (1983). **Operating Hours:** Continuous; 80% network, 20% local. **ADI:** Davenport,IA-Rock Island, Moline,IL. **Key Personnel:** Larry P. Rosmilso, Contact, phone (319)344-7000; Jim O'Hara, Program Dir., phone (319)344-7114; Steve Watt, Sales Mgr., phone (319)344-7061; Mike Cocquit, Sports Dir. **Local Programs:** *Moline Football*, Mike Cocquit; *Quad City Thunder CBA Basketball*, Mike Cocquit; *Short Trackin*, Mike Cocquit, (319)344-7000. **Wattage:** 1000. **Ad Rates:** $30-73 for 30 seconds; $39-90 for 60 seconds.

10931 WLLR-FM - 103.7-FM
3535 E. Kimberly Rd. Phone: (319)355-5331
Davenport, IA 52807 Fax: (319)359-8524

Format: Contemporary Country. **Networks:** Independent. **Owner:** Sconnix Broadcasting Co., Tyson International Plaza, 1921 Gallows Rd., Vienna, VA 22182, (703)356-6000. **Founded:** 1975. **Formerly:** WEMO-FM (1980); WZZC-FM (1983). **Operating Hours:** Continuous; 100% local. **ADI:** Davenport,IA-Rock Island, Moline,IL. **Key Personnel:** Larry P. Rosmilso, Vice President; Jim O'Hara, Program Dir.; Steve Watt, Sales Mgr. **Local Programs:** *Jay Scott & Danielle*, Jay Scott, (319)344-7000; *Pat Leuck*, Pat Leuck, (319)344-7000. **Wattage:** 50,000. **Ad Rates:** $30-73 for 30 seconds; $39-90 for 60 seconds.

10932 WOC-AM - 1420
3535 E. Kimberly Rd. Phone: (319)344-7000
Davenport, IA 52807 Fax: (319)344-7007
E-mail: woc@qconline.com

Format: Talk; News. **Networks:** NBC; CNN Radio; Mutual Broadcasting System; Radio Iowa; Illinois News; ABC. **Founded:** 1926. **Operating Hours:** Continuous; 45% network, 55% local. **ADI:** Davenport,IA-Rock Island, Moline,IL. **Key Personnel:** Randall Odeneal, President; Tim Stinson, General Sales Mgr., phone (719)344-7128, fax (719)344-7065; Jon Book, Chief Engineer, phone (719)344-7135; Dan Kennedy, Program Dir., phone (719)344-7043; Larry Rosmilso, General Mgr. **Wattage:** 5000. **Ad Rates:** $12-36 for 30 seconds; $15-42 for 60 seconds.

10933 WXLP-FM - 96.9
1229 Brady St. Phone: (319)326-2541
Davenport, IA 52803 Fax: (319)326-1819
E-mail: wxlp97x@aol.com

Format: Album-Oriented Rock (AOR). **Networks:** Westwood One Radio. **Owner:** Connoisseur Communications, 136 Main St., Westport, CT 06880, (203)227-1978, Fax: (203)227-2373. **Founded:** 1978. **Formerly:** WHTT-FM (1978). **Operating Hours:** Continuous. **ADI:** Davenport,IA-Rock Island, Moline,IL. **Key Personnel:** Steve Watt, General Mgr.; Tony Wilkins, General Sales Mgr.; Steve Gunner, Operations Dir.; Dan Burich, Sports Dir.; Guy Perry, Program Dir. **Local Programs:** *Matt & Homey Mornings*, Dewey Berg. **Wattage:** 50,000. **Ad Rates:** Advertising accepted; rates available upon request.

DAYTON, pop. 941.

NWC IA. Webster Co. 23 mi. SE of Fort Dodge. Camps. Concrete, farm equipment factories. Grain elevator. Stock, poultry, grain farms. Corn, oats, soybeans.

10934 Dayton Review
24 E. Skillet Phone: (515)547-2811
Box 6 Fax: (515)547-2337
Dayton, IA 50530
Agricultural newspaper. **Founded:** 1879. **Freq:** Weekly (Wed.). **Print Method:** Offset. **Trim Size:** 11 1/2 x 17. **Cols./Page:** 6. **Col. Width:** 25 nonpareils. **Col. Depth:** 224 agate lines. **Key Personnel:** James A. Diehl, Editor and Publisher. **USPS:** 149-740. **Subscription Rates:** $19 individuals; $21 out of state. **Remarks:** Accepts advertising.
Ad Rates: GLR: $.25 **Circ:** ‡875
BW: $240
SAU: $4.23
PCI: $3.50

10935 Dayton Cable TV
202 1st Ave. SW Phone: (515)547-2711
Box 45 Fax: (515)547-2709
Dayton, IA 50530

Owner: City of Dayton, IA, at above address. **Founded:** 1987. **Formerly:** Cable TV Corp. of Dayton. **Key Personnel:** Ken Sanders, Chair, phone (515)547-2706; Randy Danielson, Manager, phone (515)547-2711. **Cities Served:** Dayton, IA: subscribing households 275; 31 channels; 1 community access channel; 168 hours per week community access programming.

DE WITT, pop. 4,512.

E IA. Clinton Co. 20 mi. W. of Clinton. Mattress insulator pads, bleach, business forms manufactured. Ships livestock. Agriculture. Hogs, corn, cattle soybeans.

10936 The Observer
The DeWitt Observer Publishing Co., Inc.
512 7th St. Phone: (319)659-3121
PO Box 118 Fax: (319)659-3778
De Witt, IA 52742
Publication E-mail: observer@netins.net

Community newspaper. **Founded:** July 15, 1864. **Freq:** Semiweekly (Wed. and Sat.). **Print Method:** Offset. **Trim Size:** 11 x 17. **Cols./Page:** 4. **Col. Width:** 15 picas. **Col. Depth:** 16 inches. **Key Personnel:** Mary Rueter, Editor/Gen. Mgr.; Jean Bormann, Advertising Mgr. **USPS:** 150-400. **Sub-**

scription Rates: $34 individuals; $40 out of area; $47 out of state; $57 West Coast states. **Remarks:** Accepts advertising.
Ad Rates: GLR: $1.16 **Circ:** Paid ‡4,445
BW: $308 Free ‡2,100
4C: $533
SAU: $6.68
PCI: $8.10

DECORAH†, pop. 7,991.

NE IA. Winneshiek Co. 65 mi. SW of La Crosse, WI. Luther College. Tourism. Creamery; automotive and computer parts, zinc casting, meat packing plants; feed mill; bottling works; machine shops. Grain, dairy, poultry farms. Corn, alfalfa, barley.

10937 Journal
Decorah Newspapers
Box 350 Phone: (319)382-4221
107 E. Water St. Fax: (319)382-5949
Decorah, IA 52101
Community newspaper. **Founded:** 1864. **Freq:** Weekly (Thurs.). **Print Method:** Offset. **Cols./Page:** 6. **Col. Width:** 30 nonpareils. **Col. Depth:** 301 agate lines. **Key Personnel:** Richard Fromm, Publisher; Julie Ude, Advertising Mgr. **Subscription Rates:** $30 individuals; $33 out of area; $41 out of state. **Remarks:** Accepts advertising.
Ad Rates: BW: $580.50 **Circ:** ‡6,400
4C: $780.50
SAU: $4.65

10938 Luther Alumni Magazine
Luther College
700 College Dr. Phone: (319)387-1350
Decorah, IA 52101-1045 Fax: (319)387-1075
Publication E-mail: magazine@luther.edu

College alumni magazine. **Freq:** 3/year. **Print Method:** Offset. **Trim Size:** 8 3/8 x 10 7/8. **Key Personnel:** Greg Vanney, Editor; Sara Friedl-Putnam, Asst. Editor. **Subscription Rates:** Free to qualified subscribers. **Remarks:** Advertising not accepted. **Former name:** Luther Alumni Quarterly.
Circ: Non-paid 30,000

10939 Public Opinion
Decorah Newspapers
Box 350 Phone: (319)382-4221
107 E. Water St. Fax: (319)382-5949
Decorah, IA 52101
Publication E-mail: decnews@oneota.net

Community newspaper. **Founded:** 1895. **Freq:** Tuesday and Thursday. **Print Method:** Offset. **Cols./Page:** 6. **Col. Width:** 30 nonpareils. **Col. Depth:** 301 agate lines. **Key Personnel:** Richard Fromm, Publisher; Julie Ude, Advertising Mgr. **Subscription Rates:** $30 individuals; $33 out of area; $41 out of state. **Remarks:** Accepts advertising.
Ad Rates: BW: $657.90 **Circ:** ‡6,330
4C: $857.90
SAU: $4.65

10940 KDEC-AM - 1240
110 Highland Dr. Phone: (319)382-4252
PO Box 27 Fax: (319)382-9540
Decorah, IA 52101

Format: News. **Networks:** ABC; Westwood One Radio. **Owner:** Decorah Broadcasting, at above address. **Founded:** 1948. **Operating Hours:** 17 hrs.; 50% network, 50% local. **ADI:** Cedar Rapids-Waterloo-Dubuque, IA. **Key Personnel:** Bob Holtan, Owner, phone (319)382-4251; Colleen Holtan, Owner, phone (319)382-4251; Barb Cuthbertson, Sales Mgr., phone (319)382-4251. **Wattage:** 1000. **Ad Rates:** $6-10 for 30 seconds; $8-13.23 for 60 seconds. KDEC-FM; Continuous, 30,000 watts.

10941 KDEC-FM - 100.5
110 Highland Dr. Phone: (319)382-4251
PO Box 27 Fax: (319)382-9540
Decorah, IA 52101

Format: Adult Contemporary. **Networks:** ABC. **Owner:** Decorah Broadcasting Inc., at above address. **Founded:** 1986. **Formerly:** KRDI-FM (1994). **Operating Hours:** Continuous; 6% network, 94% local. **ADI:** Cedar Rapids-Waterloo-Dubuque, IA. **Key Personnel:** Bob Holtan, Owner and General Manager; Barb Cuthbertson, General Sales Mgr.; Colleen Holtan, Owner and Business Manager; Cori Peterson, Music Dir.; Bob Holten, Program Dir. **Wattage:** 30,000. **Ad Rates:** $12-20 for 30 seconds; $16-26.46 for 60 seconds. Combined advertising rates available with KDEC-AM.

10942 KLSE-FM - 91.7
206 S. Broadway Ste. 735 Phone: (507)282-0910
Rochester, MN 55904 Fax: (507)282-2107

Format: Public Radio; Classical. **Owner:** Minnesota Public Radio Inc., at above address. **Founded:** 1977. **ADI:** La Crosse-Eau Claire, WI. **Key Personnel:** Roger Gomoll, Station Mgr., rgomoll@mpr.org. **Wattage:** 100. **Ad Rates:** Noncommercial. **URL:** http://www.mpr.org.

10943 KWLC-AM - 1240
700 College Dr. Phone: (319)387-1240
Decorah, IA 52101 Fax: (319)387-2158
E-mail: kwlcam@martin.luther.edu

Format: Jazz; Classical; Alternative/New Music/Progressive; Bluegrass; Folk; Information; Religious; Religious. **Networks:** Independent. **Owner:** Luther College, at above address. **Founded:** 1926. **Operating Hours:** 10 p.m.-12:30 a.m. weekdays, 7 a.m.- midnight weekends. **Key Personnel:** Emily Helin, Station Mgr.; Arika Anderson, News Dir.; Bonnie Thorson, Promotions Dir.; Bob Danz, Music Dir., phone (319)387-1571; Thatcher Vagts, Music Dir., phone (319)387-1571. **Wattage:** 1000. **Ad Rates:** Noncommercial.

10944 Telnet of Decorah
PO Box 226 Phone: (319)382-3560
Decorah, IA 52101-0226 Fax: (319)387-0436

Founded: 1957. **Formerly:** J & E Cable (1981); Teleview Systems Corp. **Key Personnel:** Ken Thompson, General Mgr., phone (515)276-3174, fax (515)270-9181; Chip Piper, Chief Technician, phone (319)382-3560, fax (319)387-0436. **Cities Served:** Decorah, IA: subscribing households 3,252; 48 channels; 1 community access channel; 168 hours per week community access programming.

DENISON†, pop. 6,675.

W IA. Crawford Co. 65 mi. NE of Council Bluffs. Stock waterer manufacturers. Seed houses; machine shops; meat processing plants. Dairy, stock, grain farms. Corn, soybeans, oats, wheat, hogs, poultry, beef.

10945 Ad-Visor
The Denison Bulletin/Review
PO Box 550 Phone: (712)263-2122
Denison, IA 51442
Shopper. **Subtitle:** Crawford County's Shopping Guide since 1934. **Founded:** Jan. 4, 1934. **Freq:** Weekly (Wed.). **Print Method:** Offset. **Trim Size:** 13 1/2 x 23. **Cols./Page:** 7. **Col. Width:** 12.375 picas. **Col. Depth:** 21.5 inches. **Key Personnel:** Mearl T. Luvaas, Advertising Mgr. **Subscription Rates:** Free; $8 by mail. **Remarks:** Accepts advertising.
Ad Rates: BW: $495 **Circ:** Free ‡8,500
4C: $675
SAU: $5.50
PCI: $5.50

10946 Bulletin
The Denison Bulletin/Review
PO Box 550 Phone: (712)263-2122
Denison, IA 51442 Fax: (712)263-2125

Community newspaper. **Founded:** 1873. **Freq:** Weekly (Tues.). **Print Method:** Offset. **Trim Size:** 13 1/2 x 23. **Cols./Page:** 6. **Col. Width:** 12.375 picas. **Col. Depth:** 21.5 inches. **Key Personnel:** Chuck Signs, Editor. **Subscription Rates:** $49. **Remarks:** Accepts advertising. **Formerly:** Denison Newspapers, Inc.
Ad Rates: BW: $595 **Circ:** Paid ‡4,383
4C: $720 Free ‡4,352
SAU: $8.35
CNU: $7
PCI: $8.35

10947 Review
The Denison Bulletin/Review
PO Box 550 Phone: (712)263-2122
Denison, IA 51442 Fax: (712)263-2125
Free: (800)657-5889

Community newspaper with a Republican orientation. **Founded:** 1866. **Freq:** Weekly. **Print Method:** Offset. **Trim Size:** 13 1/2 x 23. **Cols./Page:** 6. **Col. Width:** 12.375 picas. **Col. Depth:** 21.5 inches. **Key Personnel:** Greg Wehle, Publisher. **Subscription Rates:** $49. **Remarks:** Accepts advertising. **Formerly:** Denison Newspapers, Inc.
Ad Rates: BW: $595 **Circ:** Paid ‡4,286
4C: $720 Free ‡4,261
SAU: $8.35
CNU: $7
PCI: $8.35

10948 U.S. Farm News
U.S. Farmers Association
1407 2nd Ave. S. Phone: (712)263-2679
Denison, IA 51442-2017
Farmers union magazine. **Founded:** 1952. **Freq:** Quarterly. **Print Method:** Offset. **Cols./Page:** 3. **Col. Width:** 3 1/3 inches. **Col. Depth:** 224 agate lines. **Key Personnel:** Wm. Gudex, Editor and Publisher, phone (920)533-8020; Betty Lownes, Sec./Treas. **Subscription Rates:** $5 individuals. **Remarks:** Advertising not accepted.
Circ: ‡1,500

10949 KDSN-AM - 1530
1530 Ridge Rd.
PO Box 670
Denison, IA 51442
E-mail: kdsn@pionet.net

Format: Country. **Networks:** ABC. **Owner:** M&J Radio Corporation, at above address. **Founded:** 1956. **Operating Hours:** 6 a.m.-10 p.m.; 2% network, 98% local. **ADI:** Omaha, NE. **Key Personnel:** Jeff Fuller, General Mgr.; Michael Dudding, Sales Mgr.; Marilyn Hintz, Office Mgr., mhintz3@yahoo.com; Bernie Peoppe, News Dir., bernadettem@yahoo.com; Randy Grossman, Sports Dir.; Tom Hamilton, Music Dir., hamtom@yahoo.com; Brian Schmid, Farm Dir., bos_ farm@yahoo.com; Robin Buchanan, Promotions Dir., robin8r@yahoo.com; Kathy Dudding, Traffic Dir. **Local Programs:** *Market Reports*, Brian Schmid; *Mike & Jeff Talk Show*, Michael Dudding; *Polka Party*, Tom Hamilton. **Wattage:** 500. **Ad Rates:** $7.50-14 for 15 seconds; $9.50-16 for 30 seconds; $11-20 for 60 seconds. Combined advertising rates available with KOSN-FM.

10950 KDSN-FM - 107.1
1530 Ridge Rd. Phone: (712)263-3141
PO Box 670 Fax: (712)263-2088
Denison, IA 51442
E-mail: kdsn@pionet.net

Format: Adult Contemporary. **Networks:** ABC. **Owner:** M&J Corporation, at above address. **Founded:** 1967. **Operating Hours:** 19 hrs. daily; 5:00am-midnight, 1% network, 99% local. **ADI:** Omaha, NE. **Key Personnel:** Jeff Fuller, General Mgr.; Michael Dudding, Sales Mgr.; Marilyn Hintz, Office Mgr., mhintz@yahoo.com; Bernadette Peoppe, News Dir., bernadette@yahoo.com; Randy Grossman, Sports Dir.; Tom Hamilton, Music Dir., hamtom@yahoo.com; Brian Schmid, Farm Dir., bds_ farm@yahoo.com; Robin Buchanan, Promotions Dir., robin8r@yahoo.com. **Local Programs:** *All Request Oldies Show With Rockin' Robin*, Robin Buchanan; *High School Sports*, Randy Grossman; *Mike & Jeff Talk Show*, Michael Dudding. **Wattage:** 6000. **Ad Rates:** $7-14 for 15 seconds; $8-17 for 30 seconds; $11-20 for 60 seconds. Combined advertising rates available with KDSN-AM.

DES MOINES†, pop. 191,003.

C IA. Polk Co. On Des Moines and Raccoon Rivers, 340 mi. W. of Chicago. The State Capital. Grand View College; College of Osteopathic Medicine and Surgery; Drake University; College of Law; Pharmacy; Publishing and Trade Centers. Manufactures flour, cosmetics, furnaces, stove and furnace parts, agricultural implements, automotive and creamery equipment, leather products, medicine, brick, tires, clothing, refrigerators, dairy products, cement, crackers, biscuits, vegetable oils, paint, electric switches and elevators. Meat packing plants.

10951 American Patchwork and Quilting
Mennonite Central Committee
1912 Grand Ave. Phone: (515)284-2681
Des Moines, IA 50309-3379 Fax: (515)284-3884
Publisher E-mail: mailbox@mcc.org

Magazine which instructs and inspires quilters in all aspects of the art of quilt-making. **Founded:** Apr. 1993. **Freq:** Bimonthly. **Key Personnel:** William Reed, Publisher; Bev Rivers, Editor-in-Chief. **Subscription Rates:** $29.95; $4.95 single issue. **Remarks:** Advertising accepted; rates available upon request.
Circ: Combined 200,000

10952 Ankeny Press Citizen
Ogden Newspapers of Iowa, Inc.
2221 E. Ovid Phone: (515)262-1190
Des Moines, IA 50313 Fax: (515)262-2267

Community newspaper. **Founded:** 1970. **Freq:** Weekly (Wed.). **Print Method:** Offset. **Cols./Page:** 7. **Col. Width:** 16 nonpareils. **Col. Depth:** 224 agate lines. **Key Personnel:** Roger Smed, Publisher; Ron Wallace, Advertising Dir. **Subscription Rates:** Free. **Remarks:** Accepts advertising.
Ad Rates: GLR: $.34 **Circ:** Free ❑**16,847**
BW: $533.12
4C: $764.12
SAU: $7.14
PCI: $4.76

10953 Better Homes and Gardens Building Ideas
Meredith Corp.
1716 Locust St. Phone: (515)284-3000
Des Moines, IA 50309-3023 Fax: (515)284-3697
Free: (800)678-2674

Magazine offering ideas for designing and building single-family custom homes. **Founded:** 1937. **Freq:** Quarterly. **Print**

Method: Offset. **Key Personnel:** Linda Kast, Editor, phone (515)284-2892, fax (515)284-3697, lkast@mdp.com; Jerry Ward, Publisher, phone (515)284-2532, fax (515)284-3264; Pat Tomlinson, Advertising Mgr., phone (212)551-7043, fax (212)551-7192. **Remarks:** Accepts advertising.
Circ: Paid ‡450,000

10954 Better Homes and Gardens Do It Yourself
Meredith Corp.
1716 Locust St. Phone: (515)284-3000
Des Moines, IA 50309-3023 Fax: (515)284-3697
Free: (800)678-2674
Publication E-mail: creative@mdp.com

Consumer magazine covering do-it-yourself topics. **Subtitle:** Ideas for Your Home & Garden. **Founded:** 1982. **Freq:** Quarterly. **Key Personnel:** Kathy Barnes, Editor, phone (515)284-2976, fax (515)284-3697, kbarnes@mdp.com; Cathy Staub, Assoc. Editor, phone (515)284-2721, fax (515)284-3697, cstaub@mdp.com.

10955 Better Homes and Gardens: Garden, Deck and Landscape
Meredith Corp.
1716 Locust St. Phone: (515)284-3000
Des Moines, IA 50309-3023 Fax: (515)284-3697
Free: (800)678-2674

Consumer magazine covering gardening and landscaping. **Founded:** 1992. **Freq:** Quarterly. **Key Personnel:** Glenn DiNella, Editor; Stephen Levinson, Publisher; Pat Tomlinson, Advertising Dir. **ISSN:** 1092-5376. **Subscription Rates:** $16 individuals; $3.99 single issue. **Remarks:** Accepts advertising. **Former name:** Garden, Deck & Landscape Planner.
Circ: Controlled 459,000

10956 Better Homes and Gardens: Garden Ideas & Outdoor Living
Meredith Corp.
1716 Locust St. Phone: (515)284-3000
Des Moines, IA 50309-3023 Fax: (515)284-3697
Free: (800)678-2674

Consumer magazine covering gardening in the U.S. and Canada. **Freq:** Semiannual. **Key Personnel:** Kate Carter Frederick, Editor; Pat Tomlinson, Advertising Dir.; Jerry Ward, VP/Publishing Director. **ISSN:** 0733-0340. **Remarks:** Accepts advertising.
Circ: Controlled 500,000

10957 Better Homes and Gardens: Home Plan Ideas
Meredith Corp.
1716 Locust St. Phone: (515)284-3000
Des Moines, IA 50309-3023 Fax: (515)284-3697
Free: (800)678-2674

Consumer magazine covering plans for custom built homes. **Founded:** 1973. **Freq:** Quarterly. **Key Personnel:** Robert Wilson, Editor, phone (515)284-2173. **Subscription Rates:** $14 individuals; $7 single issue.

10958 Better Homes and Gardens Kitchen Plans
Better Homes and Gardens Home Plan Ideas
1716 Locust St. Phone: (515)284-2584
Des Moines, IA 50309-3023 Fax: (515)284-3697

Consumer magazine covering home kitchen plans. **Founded:** 1993. **Freq:** Annual. **Key Personnel:** Molly Sinnett, Editor.

10959 Better Homes and Gardens Special Interest Publications Low Calorie/Low Fat Recipes
Meredith Corp.
1716 Locust St. Phone: (515)284-3000
Des Moines, IA 50309-3023 Fax: (515)284-3697
Free: (800)678-2674
Publication E-mail: acolvill@mdp.com

Consumer magazine covering healthy recipes. **Founded:** 1987. **Freq:** Triennial. **Print Method:** Offset. **Trim Size:** 8 x 10 1/2. **Cols./Page:** 3. **Key Personnel:** Steve Levinson, Publisher, slevinson@nyc.mdp.com; Patrick Tomlinson, Advertising Dir.; Peggy Leib, Advertising Service Mgr. **ISSN:** 1088-2987. **Remarks:** Accepts advertising.
Ad Rates: BW: $17,940 **Circ:** Paid ★**144,000**
4C: $24,485

10960 Better Homes and Gardens WOOD
Mennonite Central Committee
1912 Grand Ave. Phone: (515)284-3785
Des Moines, IA 50309-3379 Fax: (515)284-3343
Publisher E-mail: mailbox@mcc.org

Subtitle: The World's Leading Woodworking Magazine. **Founded:** Sept. 1984. **Freq:** 9/year. **Print Method:** Offset. **Trim Size:** 8 x 10 1/2. **Cols./Page:** 3. **Key Personnel:** Larry Clayton, Editor, phone (515)284-2143; William Reed, Publisher, phone (212)551-7130; Jim Harrold, Managing Editor. **Subscription Rates:** $25; $4.95 single issue. **Remarks:** Accepts advertising.
Ad Rates: BW: $26,150 **Circ:** Paid 600,000
4C: $37,200

10961 The Catholic Mirror
601 Grand Ave. Phone: (515)244-6234
PO Box 10372 Fax: (515)237-5070
Des Moines, IA 50306
Publication E-mail: cathdiodm@aol.com

Official newspaper of the Diocese of Des Moines. **Founded:** 1936. **Freq:** 12/year. **Print Method:** Offset. **Cols./Page:** 5. **Col. Width:** 11 picas. **Col. Depth:** 15 3/4 inches. **Key Personnel:** Tom Chapman, Editor; Most Rev. Joseph Charron, Publisher. **ISSN:** 0896-6869. **Subscription Rates:** $10. **Remarks:** Accepts advertising. **URL:** http://members.aol.com/cathdiodm.
Ad Rates: SAU: $13.50 **Circ:** ‡31,000
PCI: $12

10962 Central Shopper
Ogden Newspapers of Iowa, Inc.
2221 E. Ovid Phone: (515)262-1190
Des Moines, IA 50313 Fax: (515)262-2267

Shopper. **Founded:** 1967. **Freq:** Weekly (Wed.). **Print Method:** Offset. **Cols./Page:** 7. **Col. Width:** 16 nonpareils. **Col. Depth:** 224 agate lines. **Key Personnel:** Roger Smed, Publisher; Ron Wallace, Advertising Dir. **Subscription Rates:** Free. **Remarks:** Accepts advertising.
Ad Rates: GLR: $.39 **Circ:** Free ❑**11,137**
BW: $611.52
4C: $842.52
SAU: $8.26
PCI: $5.46

10963 The Christian News
Christian Church in the Upper Midwest
3300 University Ave. Phone: (515)255-3168
Box 41217 Fax: (515)255-2625
Des Moines, IA 50311-0504
Publisher E-mail: ccum@ecunet.org

Newspaper for members of the Christian Church (Disciples of Christ) in Iowa, Minnesota, North and South Dakota. **Founded:** 1922. **Freq:** Quarterly. **Print Method:** Letterpress and offset. **Cols./Page:** 4. **Col. Width:** 27 nonpareils. **Col. Depth:** 182 agate lines. **Key Personnel:** Alan A. Mace, Editor. **Subscription Rates:** Free. **Remarks:** Advertising not accepted.
Circ: ‡18,000

10964 Country America
Meredith Corp.
1716 Locust St. Phone: (515)284-3000
Des Moines, IA 50309-3023 Fax: (515)284-3697
Free: (800)678-2674

Country America reflects and upholds the values, traditions, activities, and interests of country people who love country music. **Founded:** Oct. 1989. **Freq:** 6/year. **Trim Size:** 8 x 10 1/2. **Cols./Page:** 3. **Col. Width:** 2 1/4 inches. **Col. Depth:** 10 inches. **Key Personnel:** Richard Krumme, Editor-in-Chief, fax (515)284-3035; Bill Eftink, Managing Editor, fax (515)284-3035. **Subscription Rates:** $16.97; $2.99 single issue. **Remarks:** Accepts advertising.
Ad Rates: BW: $27,265 **Circ:** Paid 903,304
4C: $38,795

10965 Country Home
Meredith Corp.
1716 Locust St. Phone: (515)284-2015
Des Moines, IA 50309-3023 Fax: (515)284-2552
Publication E-mail: countryh@asm.mdp.com

Magazine furnishing information on American interior design, architecture, antiques and collectibles, gardening, art, and culinary endeavor. **Founded:** Oct. 1979. **Freq:** Bimonthly. **Print Method:** Offset. **Trim Size:** 8 x 10 1/2. **Cols./Page:** 3. **Col. Width:** 2 1/4 inches. **Col. Depth:** 10 inches. **Key Personnel:** Carol Sheehan, Editor, phone (515)284-2015, fax (515)284-2552; Joe Lagani, Publisher, phone (212)551-7117, fax (212)551-6918. **Subscription Rates:** $19.97 individuals; $3.95 single issue. **Remarks:** Accepts advertising.
Ad Rates: BW: $53,900 **Circ:** Paid ★**1,056,780**
4C: $72,200

10966 Country Home Country Gardens
Meredith Corp.
1716 Locust St. Phone: (515)284-3515
Des Moines, IA 50309-3023 Fax: (515)284-2552

Consumer magazine covering gardening. **Founded:** 1992. **Freq:** Bimonthly. **Key Personnel:** LuAnn Brandsen, Editor; Sue Katzen, Advertising Mgr.; David Ball, Circulation Mgr. **Subscription Rates:** $16 individuals. **Remarks:** Accepts advertising.
Ad Rates: 4C: $26,220 **Circ:** Paid ★**326,613**

10967 Decorative Woodcrafts
Mennonite Central Committee
1912 Grand Ave. Phone: (515)284-2509
Des Moines, IA 50304-3379 Fax: (515)284-3884
Publisher E-mail: mailbox@mcc.org

Instructional magazine for decorative painters and woodcraft enthusiasts. **Founded:** Oct. 1991. **Print Method:** Web offset. **Trim Size:** 8 x 10 1/2. **Cols./Page:** 3. **Key Personnel:** William Reed, Publisher; Jon Book, National Sales Mgr.; Beverly Rivers, Editor-in-Chief; Mary Bendgen, Art Dir.; Maureen Ruth, Marketing and Ancillary Sales Dir.; Marjon Schaefer, Managing Editor; Maureen Miller, Assoc. Art Dir.; Susan Sidler, Circulation Mgr.; Rick Pallister, Marketing Mgr. **ISSN:** 1056-716X. **Subscription Rates:** $29.97; $4.95 single issue. **Remarks:** Accepts advertising.
Ad Rates: BW: $4,725 **Circ:** Paid 250,000
4C: $6,750

10968 Des Moines Business Record
Business Publications Corp.
The Depot at Fourth Phone: (515)288-3336
100 4th St. Fax: (515)288-0309
Des Moines, IA 50309
Publisher E-mail: bpc@mail.common.link.com

Newspaper covering local business news. **Founded:** 1983. **Freq:** Weekly (Mon.). **Print Method:** Offset. **Trim Size:** 11 5/8 x 14 5/8. **Cols./Page:** 4. **Col. Width:** 14 picas. **Col. Depth:** 75 picas. **Key Personnel:** Bill Day, Editor; Connie Wimer, Publisher; Peter Kotz, Executive Ed.; Loretta J. Sieman, Community Relations & Promotions Dir. **USPS:** 154-740. **Subscription Rates:** $59.95 individuals. **Remarks:** Accepts advertising. **Formerly:** Business Record.
Ad Rates: BW: $1,595 **Circ:** Paid ‡3,932
4C: $2,170
SAU: $25.68
PCI: $29.06

10969 The Des Moines Register
Gannett Co., Inc.
PO Box 957 Phone: (515)284-8000
Des Moines, IA 50304 Fax: (515)286-2511

General newspaper. **Founded:** 1849. **Freq:** Mon.-Sun. (morn.). **Print Method:** DiLitho. **Cols./Page:** 7. **Col. Width:** 24. nonpareils. **Col. Depth:** 313 agate lines. **Key Personnel:** Dennis Ryerson, Vice President & Editor, phone (515)284-8502, fax (515)286-2511, dryerson@dmreg.com; Randy Brubaker, Sr. Asst. Mng. Editor, phone (515)284-8564, fax (515)286-2804, brubakerr@news.dmreg.com; Randy Essex, Iowa Editor, phone (515)284-8065, essexr@news.dmreg.com; Diane Graham, Managing Editor, phone (515)284-8530, dgraham@news.dmreg.com; Nancy Clark, Suburban Editor, phone (515)284-8039, clarkn@news.dmreg.com. **Subscription Rates:** $143 individuals. **Remarks:** Accepts advertising. **Online:** DataTimes Corporation. **Alt. Formats:** CD-ROM, NewsBank, Inc. **Feature Editors:** Jeanne Abbott, *Sports*, abbottj@news.dmreg.com; Joan Bunke, *Art*, phone (515)284-8535, bunkej@news.dmreg.com; Rick Tapscott, *Metro*, phone (515)284-8461, tapscottr@news.dmreg.com.
Ad Rates: PCI: $106.15 **Circ:** Mon.-Sat. ★**163,292**
Sun. ★**263,662**

10970 Drake Law Review
Drake Unviersity
Cartwright Hall Phone: (515)271-2930
Des Moines, IA 50311 Fax: (515)271-4926

Law review journal. **Founded:** 1951. **Freq:** Quarterly. **Key Personnel:** Todd McGuire, Editor-in-Chief; Bill Kelly, Managing Editor. **Subscription Rates:** $25 individuals; $8.50 single issue. **Remarks:** Advertising not accepted. **Online:** LEXIS-NEXIS; Westlaw.
Circ: (Not Reported)

10971 Drake Update
Drake University
316 Old Main Phone: (515)271-2169
Des Moines, IA 50311 Fax: (515)271-3798
Publication E-mail: barbara.boose@drake.edu

College newspaper. **Founded:** 1988. **Freq:** Triennial. **Subscription Rates:** Free to qualified subscribers. **Remarks:** Advertising not accepted. **URL:** http://www.drake.edu.
Circ: Controlled 52,000

10972 Entree
Iowa Hospitality Association
8525 Douglas Ave., Ste. 47 Phone: (515)276-1454
Des Moines, IA 50322 Fax: (515)276-3660

Industry magazine on restaurants, beverages, and volume-feeding. **Founded:** 1932. **Freq:** 3/year. **Print Method:** Offset. **Trim Size:** 8 1/2 x 11. **Cols./Page:** 3. **Col. Width:** 26 nonpareils. **Col. Depth:** 133 agate lines. **Key Personnel:** Erika Wilkins, Contact. **USPS:** 545-600. **Subscription Rates:**

$20 members. **Remarks:** Accepts advertising. **Formerly:** The Iowa Appetizer.
Circ: Non-paid ‡650

10973 Fishing Facts Magazine
Stover Publishing Co., Inc.
1901 Bell Ave., Ste. 4 Phone: (515)243-2472
PO Box 35098 Fax: (515)243-0233
Des Moines, IA 50315
Free: (800)767-4868
Publisher E-mail: stovpub@dwx.com

Magazine on freshwater sport fishing. **Subtitle:** Written by Fisherman, for Fisherman. **Founded:** 1963. **Freq:** Bimonthly. **Print Method:** Offset. **Trim Size:** 8 1/16 x 10 7/8. **Cols./Page:** 3. **Col. Width:** 26 nonpareils. **Col. Depth:** 140 agate lines. **Key Personnel:** Roger Sparks, Editor; Mary Stearns, Advertising Dir.; Dennis Nordell, Publisher. **USPS:** 199-260. **Subscription Rates:** $23.95 per year. **Remarks:** Accepts advertising.
Ad Rates: BW: $1,438 **Circ:** △29,494
4C: $2,091
PCI: $63

10974 The Gambler Magazine
27013 Pacific Highway South,
No. 333
Des Moines, IA 98198

Magazine offering information on recreational gambling in Nevada, Washington, California, Oregon, and British Columbia. **Founded:** 1984. **Freq:** Bimonthly. **Print Method:** Web offset. **Cols./Page:** 4. **Col. Width:** 2 3/8 inches. **Col. Depth:** 10 1/4 inches. **Key Personnel:** Lydic A. Pollak, Publisher. **Subscription Rates:** Free to qualified subscribers; $28 individuals. **Remarks:** Accepts advertising.
Ad Rates: BW: $1,544 **Circ:** Paid 1,500
4C: $1,800 Controlled 40,000

10975 Gun Dog
Stover Publishing Co., Inc.
1901 Bell Ave., Ste. 4 Phone: (515)243-2472
PO Box 35098 Fax: (515)243-0233
Des Moines, IA 50315
Free: (800)767-4868
Publisher E-mail: stovpub@dwx.com

Subtitle: The magazine of upland bird and waterfowl dogs. **Founded:** Sept. 1981. **Freq:** Bimonthly. **Print Method:** Offset. **Trim Size:** 8 1/4 x 10 7/8. **Cols./Page:** 2 and 3. **Col. Width:** 3.5 inches. **Col. Depth:** 2.25 inches. **Key Personnel:** Rick VanEtten, Editor; Dennis Nordell, Publisher; Mary Stearns, Dir., Ad. **ISSN:** 0279-5086. **Subscription Rates:** $24.97 individuals; $29.97 Canada; $4 single issue.
Ad Rates: BW: $2,268 **Circ:** Paid ★49,495
4C: $3,062
PCI: $100

10976 Hawkeye Heritage
Iowa Genealogical Society
Box 7735 Phone: (515)276-0287
Des Moines, IA 50322-7735
Publisher E-mail: igs@digiserve.com

Journal covering genealogy in Iowa. **Founded:** 1966. **Freq:** Quarterly. **Print Method:** Offset. **Trim Size:** 8 1/2 x 11. **Key Personnel:** Rhonda Q. Riordan, Exec.Dir. **ISSN:** 0440-5234. **Subscription Rates:** $25 members; $5 single issue. **Remarks:** Accepts advertising.
Ad Rates: BW: $100 **Circ:** Controlled 3,000

10977 Iowa Conservationist
Iowa Dept. of Natural Resources
Iowa Dept. of Natural Resources Phone: (515)281-6159
Wallace State Office Bldg. Fax: (515)281-8895
Des Moines, IA 50319-0034
Magazine discussing conservation and environmental issues. **Founded:** Feb. 1942. **Freq:** Bimonthly. **Print Method:** Offset. **Trim Size:** 8 1/2 x 10 3/4. **Cols./Page:** 3. **Col. Width:** 13.5 picas. **Col. Depth:** 56.5 picas. **Key Personnel:** Julia Sparks, Editor. **ISSN:** 0021-0471. **Subscription Rates:** $9.97 individuals; $14.97 two years. **Remarks:** Advertising not accepted.
Circ: Paid 50,000
Controlled 4,000

10978 Iowa Grocer
Iowa Grocery Industry Association
2540 106th St., Ste. 102 Phone: (515)270-2628
Des Moines, IA 50322-3771 Fax: (515)270-0316
Publication E-mail: info@iowagrocers.com

Magazine for grocery industry - retail and supply. **Founded:** 1932. **Freq:** Bimonthly. **Print Method:** Offset. **Trim Size:** 8 1/2 x 11. **Cols./Page:** 3 and 2. **Col. Width:** 26 and 42 nonpareils. **Col. Depth:** 140 agate lines. **Key Personnel:** Chris Killough, Editor, ckillough@iowagrocers.com; Jerry Fleagle, Publisher, jfleagle@iowagrovers.com. **Subscription Rates:** $25 individuals. **Remarks:** Accepts advertising. **Formerly:** Iowa Food Dealer.
Ad Rates: BW: $540 **Circ:** ‡2,500
4C: $1,110

10979 The Iowa Lawyer
Iowa State Bar Association
521 E. Locust, 3rd. Fl. Phone: (515)243-3179
Des Moines, IA 50309 Fax: (515)243-2511

Professional magazine covering law. **Founded:** 1940. **Freq:** Monthly. **Print Method:** Web offset. **Trim Size:** 8 1/2 x 11. **Cols./Page:** 3. **Key Personnel:** Charles A. Corcoran, Managing Editor, ccorcoran@iabar.org. **Subscription Rates:** $30 individuals. **Remarks:** Accepts advertising.
Ad Rates: BW: $735 **Circ:** Controlled 8,250
4C: $1,135

10980 Iowa Legionnaire
Iowa American Legion
720 Lyon St. Phone: (515)282-5068
Des Moines, IA 50309-5417 Fax: (515)282-7583
Free: (800)365-8387

American Legion magazine. **Founded:** 1921. **Freq:** Bimonthly. **Print Method:** Offset. **Cols./Page:** 5. **Col. Width:** 24 nonpareils. **Col. Depth:** 180 agate lines. **Key Personnel:** James E. Demarest, Editor. **Subscription Rates:** $2 individuals. **Remarks:** Accepts advertising.
Ad Rates: BW: $400 **Circ:** ‡78,000

10981 Iowa Parent & Family
Age Wave Communications
8350 Hickman Rd., Ste. 200 Phone: (515)272-7675
Des Moines, IA 50325 Fax: (515)253-2650
Publisher E-mail: iowaparent@family.com

Parenting newspaper for Central Iowa and Des Moines. **Founded:** June 1989. **Freq:** Monthly. **Print Method:** Web offset. **Key Personnel:** Deb Chalik, Editor; Pat Klopf, Advertising Mgr. **Subscription Rates:** $15 individuals. **Remarks:** Accepts advertising. **URL:** http://www.iowaparent.com. **Former name:** Iowa Parent.
Ad Rates: BW: $1,110 **Circ:** Controlled 25,000
4C: $1,510

10982 The Iowa School Board Dialogue
Iowa Association of School Boards
700 2nd Ave., Ste. 100 Phone: (515)288-1991
Des Moines, IA 50309-1731 Fax: (515)243-4992

Professional magazine for school board members. **Founded:** Jan. 1951. **Freq:** Bimonthly. **Print Method:** Offset. **Trim Size:** 8 1/2 x 11. **Cols./Page:** 2. **Col. Width:** 20 nonpareils. **Col. Depth:** 133 agate lines. **Key Personnel:** Lisa Bartusek, Editor and Administration. **ISSN:** 0021-0668. **Subscription Rates:** $1 individuals; $2 nonmembers. **Remarks:** Accepts advertising.
Ad Rates: BW: $385 **Circ:** Paid 4,086
Non-paid 682

10983 Iowa Smoke-Eater
Smoke-Eater Publications
PO Box 129 Phone: (402)329-4665
Pierce, NE 68767-0129 Fax: (402)329-6224

Magazine serving volunteer firemen. **Founded:** 1955. **Freq:** Monthly. **Print Method:** Offset. **Cols./Page:** 5. **Col. Width:** 22 nonpareils. **Col. Depth:** 217 agate lines. **Key Personnel:** Robert Zimmer, Publisher. **Subscription Rates:** $10. **Remarks:** Color advertising not accepted.
Ad Rates: BW: $310 **Circ:** ‡10,000
PCI: $4

10984 The Iowa Trucking Lifeliner
Iowa Motor Truck Association
Capital Center One Phone: (515)244-5193
600 East Court Fax: (515)244-2204
Des Moines, IA 50309
Magazine serving the trucking industry. **Founded:** 1943. **Freq:** Monthly. **Print Method:** Offset. **Cols./Page:** 3. **Col. Width:** 26 nonpareils. **Col. Depth:** 140 agate lines. **Key Personnel:** Peggy L. Blackford, Editor; Gary W. Shaw, Advertising Mgr. **Subscription Rates:** $4 individuals; $.40 single issue. **Remarks:** Accepts advertising.
Ad Rates: BW: $475 **Circ:** 3,000
4C: $920

10985 The Iowan
The Gazette Co.
504 E. Locust St. Phone: (515)282-8220
Des Moines, IA 50309 Fax: (515)282-0125
Publication E-mail: iowan@iowan.com

Regional general interest magazine with an emphasis on in-state travel. **Founded:** 1952. **Freq:** Bimonthly. **Print Method:** Offset. **Trim Size:** 8 1/2 x 11 1/2. **Cols./Page:** 3 and 2. **Col. Width:** 28 and 43 nonpareils. **Col. Depth:** 144 agate lines. **Key Personnel:** Dale Larson, Publisher; Jay Wagner, Editor; Carolyn Tenney, Account Manager; Kelly Roberson, Managing Editor. **ISSN:** 0021-0722. **Subscription Rates:** $24.50 individuals; $4.50 single issue.
Ad Rates: BW: $1,592 **Circ:** Paid ‡37,000
4C: $2,076 Non-paid ‡3,000

10986 The Journal
Iowa Pharmacy Association
Omega Pl., Ste. 16 Phone: (515)270-0713
8515 Douglas Ave. Fax: (515)270-2979
Des Moines, IA 50322
Publication E-mail: ipa@iarx.org
Publisher E-mail: ipa@netins.net

Pharmacy journal. **Founded:** 1946. **Freq:** Bimonthly. **Print Method:** Offset. **Trim Size:** 8 1/2 x 11. **Cols./Page:** 3. **Col. Width:** 26 nonpareils. **Col. Depth:** 140 agate lines. **Key Personnel:** Thomas Temple, Editor, ttemple@iarx.org; Kristen Dearden, Managing Editor, kdearden@iarx.org. **ISSN:** 0889-7735. **Subscription Rates:** Included in membership included in membership dues; $60 nonmembers; $120 nonmembers outside North America; $20 single issue. **Remarks:** Accepts advertising.
Ad Rates: BW: $400 **Circ:** Paid 1,300
4C: $1,010 Non-paid 50

10987 Journal of Feminist Family Therapy
The Haworth Press, Inc.
3833 Woods Dr.
Des Moines, IA 50312
Publisher E-mail: getinfo@haworthpressinc.com

Journal exploring the relationship between feminist theory and family therapy practice and theory. **Founded:** 1989. **Freq:** Quarterly. **Key Personnel:** Lois Braverman, ACSW, Editor; Bill Cohen, Publisher. **ISSN:** 0895-2833. **Subscription Rates:** $24; $40 Industry; $105 libraries. **Remarks:** Accepts advertising.
Ad Rates: BW: $300 **Circ:** (Not Reported)

10988 Journal of Food Protection
IAMFES, Inc.
6200 Aurora Ave., Ste. 200W Phone: (515)276-3344
Des Moines, IA 50322 Fax: (515)276-8655
Free: (800)369-6337
Publisher E-mail: iamfes@iamfes.org

Scientific journal reporting research in food microbiology for food safety. **Founded:** 1937. **Freq:** Monthly. **Print Method:** Offset. **Trim Size:** 8 1/2 x 11. **Cols./Page:** 2. **Col. Width:** 40 nonpareils. **Col. Depth:** 129 agate lines. **Key Personnel:** Bev Corron, Pub. Assist., bcorron@iamfes.org. **ISSN:** 0362-028X. **Subscription Rates:** $260 individuals. **Remarks:** Accepts advertising. **URL:** http://apt.allenpress.comlegi-bin/omisapi.dll/apt?request. **Alt. Formats:** Microform; Mailing labels. **Formerly:** Journal of Milk Technology; Journal of Food and Milk Technology.
Ad Rates: BW: $674 **Circ:** ‡3,100
4C: $1174

10989 Journal of Teacher Education
American Association of Colleges for Teacher Education
Drake University Phone: (515)271-2085
School of Education
Des Moines, IA 50311
Publisher E-mail: dmu@aacte.org

Magazine of interest to educators. **Founded:** 1950. **Freq:** 5/year. **Print Method:** Offset. **Trim Size:** 8 1/2 x 11. **Cols./Page:** 2. **Col. Width:** 36 nonpareils. **Col. Depth:** 125 agate lines. **Key Personnel:** Mary Ducharme, Editor; Gail Ostermann, Co-publisher; Jim Baumgart, Advertising Dir. **ISSN:** 0022-4871. **Subscription Rates:** $30.99 students; $35.99 out of state; $28.99 individuals senior citizens; $75 institutions; $85 institutions, other countries. **Remarks:** Accepts advertising.
Ad Rates: GLR: $7.26 **Circ:** Paid 3,000
BW: $558 Controlled 5,200
SAU: $8 Non-paid 86
PCI: $6.20

10990 Jukebox Collector
Jukebox Collector Magazine
2545 SE 60th Ct. Phone: (515)265-8324
Des Moines, IA 50317-5099 Fax: (515)265-1980

Magazine for jukebox collectors. **Founded:** Sept. 1977. **Freq:** Monthly. **Print Method:** Offset. **Trim Size:** 8 1/2 x 11. **Cols./Page:** 1. **Col. Width:** 96 nonpareils. **Col. Depth:** 142 agate lines. **Key Personnel:** Ricky J. Botts, Editor and Publisher. **ISSN:** 0882-4908. **Subscription Rates:** $30 individuals; $5 single issue. **Remarks:** Accepts advertising.
Ad Rates: BW: $120 **Circ:** ‡2,500
4C: $300

10991 Leetown Shopper
Ogden Newspapers of Iowa, Inc.
2221 E. Ovid Phone: (515)262-1190
Des Moines, IA 50313 Fax: (515)262-2267

Shopper. **Founded:** 1953. **Freq:** Weekly (Wed.). **Print Method:** Offset. **Cols./Page:** 7. **Col. Width:** 16 nonpareils. **Col. Depth:** 224 agate lines. **Key Personnel:** Roger Smed, Publisher; Ron Wallace, Advertising Dir. **Subscription Rates:** Free. **Remarks:** Accepts advertising.
Ad Rates: GLR: $.34 **Circ:** Free ❑**14,045**
BW: $533.12
4C: $764.12
SAU: $7.14
PCI: $4.76

10992 Midwest Living Magazine
Meredith Corp.
1716 Locust St. Phone: (515)284-3000
Des Moines, IA 50309-3023 Fax: (515)284-3697
Free: (800)678-2674

Midwest regional lifestyle magazine featuring travel, food, home, and garden. **Subtitle:** The Magazine of America's Heartland. **Founded:** Apr. 1987. **Freq:** Bimonthly. **Print Method:** Offset. **Trim Size:** 8 x 10 1/2. **Key Personnel:** Dan Kaercher, Editor; Tom E. Benson, Publisher; Lyle C.R. Landon, Advertising Mgr. **ISSN:** 0889-8138. **Subscription Rates:** $15.97. $3.50 single issue. **Remarks:** Accepts advertising.
Ad Rates: BW: $15,200 **Circ:** Paid ★**816,860**
4C: $21,800

10993 National Pork Report
Pork Publications, Inc.
PO Box 10383 Phone: (515)223-2600
Des Moines, IA 50306 Fax: (515)223-2646

Official magazine of the National Pork Producers Council, presenting industry news. **Founded:** 1982. **Freq:** Bimonthly 9/year. **Print Method:** Offset. **Trim Size:** 8 1/2 x 10 15/16. **Cols./Page:** 3 and 4. **Key Personnel:** Jan Tayloe, Editor; Don Frankson, Advertising Mgr. **Subscription Rates:** Free to members. **Remarks:** Accepts advertising.
Ad Rates: BW: $3,895 **Circ:** Non-paid ‡109,350
4C: $4,995
PCI: $90

10994 Northcentral Shopper
Ogden Newspapers of Iowa, Inc.
2221 E. Ovid Phone: (515)262-1190
Des Moines, IA 50313 Fax: (515)262-2267

Shopper. **Freq:** Weekly. **Print Method:** Offset. **Cols./Page:** 7. **Col. Width:** 16 nonpareils. **Col. Depth:** 224 agate lines. **Key Personnel:** Roger Smed, Publisher; Ron Wallace, Advertising Dir. **Subscription Rates:** Free. **Remarks:** Accepts advertising.
Ad Rates: GLR: $.37 **Circ:** Free ❑**17,045**
BW: $580.16
4C: $811.16
SAU: $7.84
PCI: $5.18

10995 Northeast Shopper
Ogden Newspapers of Iowa, Inc.
2221 E. Ovid Phone: (515)262-1190
Des Moines, IA 50313 Fax: (515)262-2267

Shopper. **Founded:** 1950. **Freq:** Weekly (Wed.). **Print Method:** Offset. **Cols./Page:** 7. **Col. Width:** 16 nonpareils. **Col. Depth:** 224 agate lines. **Key Personnel:** Roger Smed, Publisher; Ron Wallace, Advertising Dir. **Remarks:** Accepts advertising.
Ad Rates: GLR: $.32 **Circ:** Free ❑**14,440**
BW: $501.76
4C: $732.76
SAU: $6.72
PCI: $4.48

10996 Southside Shopper
Ogden Newspapers of Iowa, Inc.
2221 E. Ovid Phone: (515)262-1190
Des Moines, IA 50313 Fax: (515)262-2267

Shopper. **Founded:** 1945. **Freq:** Weekly (Wed.). **Print Method:** Offset. **Cols./Page:** 7. **Col. Width:** 16 nonpareils. **Col. Depth:** 224 agate lines. **Key Personnel:** Henry Phillips, Publisher; Greg Kytola, Advertising Dir. **Subscription Rates:** Free. **Remarks:** Accepts advertising.
Ad Rates: GLR: $.36 **Circ:** Free ❑**19,635**
BW: $564.48
4C: $795.48
SAU: $7.56
PCI: $5.04

10997 The Times-Delphic
Drake University/Board of Student Communications
124 N. Meredith Phone: (515)271-2805
Des Moines, IA 50311 Fax: (515)271-4110
Publication E-mail: delphic@acad.drake.edu

Collegiate newspaper. **Founded:** 1881. **Freq:** Semiweekly (Tues. and Fri.; during the academic year). **Print Method:** Offset. **Trim Size:** 11 x 17. **Cols./Page:** 5. **Col. Width:** 27 nonpareils. **Col. Depth:** 205 agate lines. **Key Personnel:** Mike DeCaire, Editor, phone (515)271-2020. **Subscription Rates:** Free; $20 by mail. **Online:** Internet.
Ad Rates: PCI: $6 **Circ:** Free 3,500

10998 Unclassified
Association of National Security Alumni
1909 M.L. King Jr. Pkwy. Phone: (515)283-2115
Des Moines, IA 50314 Fax: (515)278-4023
Publication E-mail: 73623.2551@compuserve.com

Journal tracking the Central Intelligence Agency's covert operations, budgeting process, campus activity, and foreign involvement, particularly relating to legal and constitutional issues. **Founded:** 1989. **Freq:** Quarterly. **Print Method:** Web offset. **Trim Size:** 8 x 10 3/4. **Cols./Page:** 3. **Col. Width:** 11 picas. **Col. Depth:** 55 picas. **Key Personnel:** Verne Lyon, Editor. **ISSN:** 1062-3450. **Subscription Rates:** $20; $25 other countries. **Remarks:** Color advertising not accepted. **URL:** http://ourworld.compuserve.com/homepages/verne_ lyon.
Ad Rates: GLR: $8 **Circ:** 2,000
BW: $350
PCI: $20

10999 Valley Shopper
Ogden Newspapers of Iowa, Inc.
2221 E. Ovid Phone: (515)262-1190
Des Moines, IA 50313 Fax: (515)262-2267

Shopper. **Founded:** 1967. **Freq:** Weekly (Wed.). **Print Method:** Offset. **Cols./Page:** 7. **Col. Width:** 16 nonpareils. **Col. Depth:** 224 agate lines. **Key Personnel:** Roger Smed, Publisher; Ron Wallace, Advertising Dir. **Subscription Rates:** Free. **Remarks:** Accepts advertising.
Ad Rates: GLR: $.47 **Circ:** Free ❑**21,380**
BW: $736.96
4C: $967.96
SAU: $9.94
PCI: $6.58

11000 Wallaces Farmer
Farm Progress Companies
6200 Aurora Ave. Phone: (515)278-6693
Ste. 609E Fax: (515)278-7797
Urbandale, IA 50322-2838
Magazine on commercial farming. **Founded:** 1855. **Freq:** 15/year. **Print Method:** Offset. **Trim Size:** 8 x 10 3/4. **Cols./Page:** 3. **Col. Width:** 2 1/8 inches. **Col. Depth:** 10 inches. **Key Personnel:** Allan Johnson, Publisher; Chuck Roth, Advertising Dir.; Frank Holdmeyer, Editor; Chuck Roth, Advertising Dir.; Monte Sesker, Editor. **ISSN:** 1048-5783. **Subscription Rates:** $19.98.
Ad Rates: BW: $4,900 **Circ:** Paid 12,289
4C: $6,860 Non-paid 55,513

11001 Wildfowl
Stover Publishing Co., Inc.
1901 Bell Ave., Ste. 4 Phone: (515)243-2472
PO Box 35098 Fax: (515)243-0233
Des Moines, IA 50315
Free: (800)767-4868
Publisher E-mail: stovpub@dwx.com

Subtitle: The Magazine for Duck & Goose Hunters. **Founded:** Aug. 1985. **Freq:** Bimonthly. **Print Method:** Offset. **Trim Size:** 8 1/4 x 10 7/8. **Cols./Page:** 2 and 3. **Col. Width:** 3.5 inches. **Col. Depth:** 2.25 inches. **Key Personnel:** Roger Sparks, Editor; Dennis Nordell, Publisher; Mary Stearns, Ad. Dir. **ISSN:** 0886-0637. **Subscription Rates:** $24.97 individuals; $26.97 Canada; $37.97 other countries; $40.97 other countries; $4.50 single issue.
Ad Rates: BW: $1,627 **Circ:** Paid ★**42,268**
4C: $2,366
PCI: $70

11002 Wing & Shot
Stover Publishing Co., Inc.
1901 Bell Ave., Ste. 4 Phone: (515)243-2472
PO Box 35098 Fax: (515)243-0233
Des Moines, IA 50315
Free: (800)767-4868
Publisher E-mail: stovpub@dwx.com

Subtitle: The Magazine for Upland Bird Hunters. **Founded:** Sept. 1986. **Freq:** Bimonthly. **Print Method:** Offset. **Trim Size:** 8 1/4 x 10 7/8. **Cols./Page:** 2 and 3. **Col. Width:** 2.25 inches. **Col. Depth:** 3.5 inches. **Key Personnel:** Rick VanEtten, Editor; Dennis Nordell, Publisher; Mary Stearns, Advertising Dir. **ISSN:** 0892-1849. **Subscription Rates:** $24.97 individuals; $29.97 Canada; $4.50 single issue.
Ad Rates: BW: $1,306 **Circ:** Paid ★**15,960**
4C: $1,898
PCI: $63

11003 WOOD
Mennonite Central Committee
1912 Grand Ave. Phone: (515)284-2235
Des Moines, IA 50309-3379 Fax: (515)284-3343
Publisher E-mail: mailbox@mcc.org

Magazine for people who enjoy woodworking. **Founded:** 1984. **Key Personnel:** William Reed, Publisher; Larry Clayton, Editor; Rick Pallister, Marketing Mgr/Media Contact. **Subscription Rates:** $25; $4.95 single issue. **Remarks:** Accepts advertising. **URL:** http://woodmagazine.com.
Circ: Paid ★**620,626**

11004 Woodsmith
August Home Publishing
2200 Grand Ave. Phone: (515)282-7000
Des Moines, IA 50312 Fax: (515)283-0447
Free: (800)311-3991

Magazine for woodworking hobbyists. **Founded:** 1979. **Freq:** Bimonthly. **Print Method:** Web offset. **Trim Size:** 10 7/8 x 8 3/8. **Key Personnel:** Donald Peschke, Publisher; Terry J. Strohman, Contact. **ISSN:** 0164-4114. **Subscription Rates:** $17.95; $3.95 single issue. **Remarks:** Advertising not accepted.
Circ: Paid 375,000

11005 Workbench
August Home Publishing
2200 Grand Ave. Phone: (515)282-7000
Des Moines, IA 50312 Fax: (515)283-0447
Free: (800)311-3991
Publication E-mail: workbench@workbenchmag.com

Home improvement, woodworking, and remodeling magazine. **Subtitle:** The Original Home Woodworking and Improvement Magazine. **Founded:** 1959. **Freq:** Bimonthly. **Print Method:** Offset. **Trim Size:** 7 7/8 x 10 3/4. **Cols./Page:** 3. **Col. Width:** 11.9 picas. **Col. Depth:** 57 picas. **Key Personnel:** Christopher A. Inman, Editor; Donald B. Peschke, Publisher; John Macarthy, VP Finance/Circulation; George Clark, Advertising Sales Mgr., fax (515)283-2003; George Chmielarz, Production Dir. **ISSN:** 0043-8057. **Subscription Rates:** $15.95 individuals; $3.95 single issue. **Remarks:** Accepts advertising. **URL:** http://www.augusthome.com.
Ad Rates: BW: $9,800 **Circ:** Paid ★**364,784**
4C: $14,000

11006 Yellowback Library
Yellowback Press
PO Box 36172 Phone: (515)287-0404
Des Moines, IA 50315
Magazine for enthusiasts of series literature and dime novels. **Founded:** Jan. 1981. **Freq:** Monthly. **Print Method:** Offset. **Trim Size:** 5 1/2 x 8 1/2. **Key Personnel:** Gil O'Gara, Editor. **Subscription Rates:** $30 individuals; $3 single issue. **Remarks:** Accepts advertising.
Ad Rates: BW: $30 **Circ:** ‡650

11007 KBGG - 1390
5161 Maple Dr. Phone: (515)261-6100
Des Moines, IA 50317-8454 Fax: (515)261-6192

Networks: UPI. **Owner:** Barnstable Broadcasting, at above address. **Founded:** 1947. **Formerly:** KKSO-AM. **Operating Hours:** Continuous. **ADI:** Des Moines, IA. **Key Personnel:** Al Kaneb, President; Eldon L. Schlenker, Chief Engineer; Andy Graham, General Mgr.; Ernie Caldemore, Sales Mgr. **Wattage:** 1000.

11008 KCCI-TV - 8
888 9th St. Phone: (515)247-8888
Des Moines, IA 50309 Fax: (515)243-4931
E-mail: kcci@kcci.com

Format: Commercial TV. **Networks:** CBS. **Founded:** 1955. **Formerly:** KRNT (1974). **Operating Hours:** Continuous. **ADI:** Des Moines, IA. **Key Personnel:** Paul Frederickson, General Mgr.; Dave Busiek, News Dir. **URL:** http://www.kcci.com.

11009 KDFR-FM - 91.3
PO Box 57023 Phone: (515)262-0449
Des Moines, IA 50317
E-mail: larryleev@juno.com

Format: Religious. **Networks:** Family Stations Radio. **Owner:** Family Stations, Inc., 290 Hegenberger Rd., Oakland, CA 94621, (510)568-6200. **Founded:** 1988. **Operating Hours:** Continuous; 98% network, 2% local. **ADI:** Des Moines, IA. **Key Personnel:** Larry Vavroch, Operations Mgr.; Mike Destefano, Regional Mgr., phone (712)246-5151, fax (712)246-5152. **Local Programs:** *KDFR Reports* Monday-Friday, Larry

Vavroch, Host/Producer. **Wattage:** 4000. **Ad Rates:** Noncommercial. **URL:** http://www.familyradio.com.

11010 KDIN-TV - 11
Iowa Public Television Phone: (515)242-3100
PO Box 6450
Johnston, IA 50131

Format: Public TV. **Networks:** Public Broadcasting Service (PBS). **Founded:** 1959. **Operating Hours:** 6:30 a.m.-midnight Sat.-Sun.; Continuous Mon.-Fri. **ADI:** Des Moines, IA. **Key Personnel:** Dennis Malloy, Dir. of Dev.; David Bolender, Exec. Dir.; Daniel K. Miller, Program Dir.; Pam Johnson, Dir. of Educ. Telecomm.; John Leiendecker, Production Mgr.; Don Saveraid, Dir. of Eng.; Sid Sprecher, Public Affairs.

11011 KDMI-AM - 1460
2907 Merle Hay Rd. Phone: (515)274-4968
Des Moines, IA 50310 Fax: (515)274-4967

Format: Religious; Sports; Eclectic. **Networks:** Independent. **Founded:** 1961. **Formerly:** FDMI-FM. **Operating Hours:** 18 hours daily. **ADI:** Des Moines, IA. **Key Personnel:** Ralph E. Duckworth, President; Maxine Brunekool, Manager; Jerry L. Slegh, Program Dir. **Wattage:** 5,000.

11012 KDPS-FM - 88.1
1800 Grand Ave. Phone: (515)242-7723
Des Moines, IA 50307 Fax: (515)242-7598

Format: Eclectic. **Networks:** Independent. **Owner:** Des Moines School District, at above address. **Founded:** 1956. **Operating Hours:** 8 a.m.-7:00 p.m.; 100% local. **ADI:** Des Moines, IA. **Key Personnel:** Bill Springer, Manager; Glen McLean, Chief Engineer. **Wattage:** 5200 ERP. **Ad Rates:** Noncommercial.

11013 KDSM-TV - 17
4023 Fleur Dr. Phone: (515)287-1717
Des Moines, IA 50321 Fax: (515)287-0064

Format: Commercial TV. **Networks:** Fox. **Owner:** Sinclair Broadcast Group, 2000 W. 41st St., Baltimore, MD 21211, (410)662-4700, Fax: (410)662-4778. **Founded:** 1983. **Operating Hours:** Approx. 24 hrs. Daily; 25% network, 75% local. **ADI:** Des Moines, IA. **Key Personnel:** Ted Stephens, General Mgr.; Dan Cohen, General Sales Mgr.; Marty Mohrfeld, Chief Engineer; Wendy Lyons, Promotions Mgr. **Local Programs:** *Fox 17 Kids Club*, Michele Brown.

KFMG-FM - See Pella

11014 KGGO-FM - 94.9
3900 NE Broadway Phone: (515)265-6181
Des Moines, IA 50317-8942 Fax: (515)265-9005

Format: Album-Oriented Rock (AOR). **Networks:** The Source. **Founded:** 1921. **Formerly:** KSO-AM (1989); KGGO-AM. **Operating Hours:** Continuous. **ADI:** Des Moines, IA. **Key Personnel:** Phil Wilson, Program Dir.; Peter McLane, General Mgr.; Dan Abbuehl, Sales Mgr. **Wattage:** 5000.

11015 KIIN-TV - 12
Iowa Public Television Phone: (515)242-3100
PO Box 6450
Johnston, IA 50131

Format: Public TV. **Simulcasts:** KDIN-TV Des Moines, IA. **Networks:** Public Broadcasting Service (PBS). **Founded:** 1970. **ADI:** Cedar Rapids-Waterloo-Dubuque, IA. **Key Personnel:** David Bolender, Exec. Dir.; Dennis Malloy, Dir. of Dev.; Daniel K. Miller, Program Dir.; Don Saveraid, Dir. of Eng.; Pam Johnson, Dir. of Educ. Telecomm.; John Leiendecker, Production Mgr.; Sid Sprecher, Public Affairs.

11016 KIOA-FM - 93.3
1416 Locust St. Phone: (515)280-1350
Des Moines, IA 50309-3014 Fax: (515)280-3011

Format: Oldies. **Owner:** Saga Communications, Inc., 73 Kercheval Ave., No. 201, Grosse Pointe Farms, MI 48236, (313)886-7070, Fax: (313)886-7150. **Founded:** 1972. **Formerly:** KMGK-FM (1971). **Operating Hours:** Continuous. **ADI:** Des Moines, IA. **Key Personnel:** Phil Hoover, President; Polly Carver-Kimm, News Dir.; Stephanie Spencer, Promotions Dir.; Rich Gilman, Sales Mgr.; Tim Fox, Program Dir. **Local Programs:** *Dic Youngs Saturday Nite Oldies Show*, Dic Young. **Wattage:** 100,000. **Ad Rates:** Advertising accepted; rates available upon request.

11017 KLTI-FM - 104.1
1416 Locust St. Phone: (515)280-1350
Des Moines, IA 50309 Fax: (515)280-3011
Free: (800)333-1041

Format: Adult Contemporary. **Networks:** Independent. **Owner:** Saga Communications of Iowa, at above address. **Founded:** Jan. 1, 1987. **Formerly:** KLFM-FM; KEZT-FM. **Operating Hours:** Continuous. **ADI:** Des Moines, IA. **Key Personnel:** Bill Wells, General Mgr.; Sharon Beninato, Business Mgr.; Paul Bunce, Sales Mgr. **Wattage:** 100,000.

11018 KLYF-FM - 100.3
1801 Grand Ave. Phone: (515)242-3500
Des Moines, IA 50309-3362 Fax: (515)242-3798

Format: Adult Contemporary. **Networks:** AP. **Founded:** 1948. **Operating Hours:** Continuous. **ADI:** Des Moines, IA. **Key Personnel:** Matt Gillan, Sales Mgr.; Kenn McCloud, Program Dir.; Rob Olson, News Dir.; Mark Halverson, General Mgr. **Wattage:** 100,000. **Ad Rates:** Advertising accepted; rates available upon request.

11019 KRKQ-FM - 98.3
5161 Maple Dr. Phone: (515)261-6100
Des Moines, IA 50317 Fax: (515)261-6192
Free: (800)545-5788
E-mail: 98rock@dwx.com

Format: Classic Rock. **Founded:** 1973. **Formerly:** KZBA-FM (1991); KWBG-FM; KRUU-FM; Radio Ingstad Iowa; KIAB-FM. **Operating Hours:** Continuous. **ADI:** Des Moines, IA. **Key Personnel:** Andy Graham, General Mgr. **Wattage:** 50,000.

11020 KRNT-AM - 1350
1416 Locust Phone: (515)280-1350
Des Moines, IA 50309 Fax: (515)280-3011

Format: Big Band/Nostalgia; Sports. **Networks:** CBS; Mutual Broadcasting System; Unistar. **Owner:** Saga Communications, Inc., 73 Kercheval Ave. No.201, Grosse Pointe Farms, MI 48236, (313)886-7070, Fax: (313)886-7150. **Founded:** 1935. **Operating Hours:** Continuous. **ADI:** Des Moines, IA. **Key Personnel:** Bill Wells, Contact; Polly Carver-Kimm, News Dir.; Steve Gibbons, Program Dir.; Matt Gillon, Sales Mgr. **Wattage:** 5,000. **Ad Rates:** Advertising accepted; rates available upon request.

11021 KSTZ-FM - 102.5
1416 Locust St. Phone: (515)280-1350
Des Moines, IA 50309 Fax: (515)280-3011
E-mail: kstz1025@aol.com

Format: Adult Contemporary. **Owner:** Saga Communications Inc., 73 Kercheval Ave., No. 201, Grosse Pointe Farms, MI 48236, (313)886-7070, Fax: (313)886-7150. **Founded:** 1970. **Formerly:** KRNQ-FM/Q-102 (1993). **Operating Hours:** Continuous. **ADI:** Des Moines, IA. **Key Personnel:** Bill Wells, General Mgr.; Jim Schaefer, Operations Mgr.; Carol Vann, Music Dir.; Scott Allen, Promotions Dir.; Mick Trier, Sports Dir.; Polly Carver-Kimm, News Dir.; Paul Bunce, Sales Mgr. **Wattage:** 100,000. **Ad Rates:** $60-85 for 30 seconds. Combined advertising rates available with KLTI-FM. **URL:** http://www.star1025.com.

11022 KUCB-FM - 89.3
1404-6th Ave. Phone: (515)246-1588
Des Moines, IA 50314 Fax: (515)246-0480
Free: (888)830-5318

Format: Eclectic; Urban Contemporary. **Owner:** Center for the Study and Applications of Black Economic Development, at above address. **Founded:** 1981. **Operating Hours:** 24Hrs. a day 7 days a week. **ADI:** Des Moines, IA. **Key Personnel:** Sekou Mtayari, General Mgr., phone (515)284-0739; Richard Fowler, Program Dir., phone (515)246-0025. **Wattage:** 10,000. **Ad Rates:** $17.50-24.50 for 30 seconds.

11023 KWKY-AM - 1150
PO Box 662 Phone: (515)981-0981
Des Moines, IA 50303 Fax: (515)981-0840

Format: Talk; Religious; Sports. **Networks:** USA Radio. **Owner:** Putbrese Communications LTD., at above address., Des Moines, IA 50303. **Founded:** 1947. **Formerly:** Norseman Broadcasting Corp. **Operating Hours:** 5 a.m.-1 a.m. **ADI:** Des Moines, IA. **Key Personnel:** Charles E. Putbrese, General Mgr.; Theresa Buchanan, Operations Mgr.; Dennis Ray, Program Dir.; John Putbrese, Sales Mgr.; Dick Fowler, Chief Engineer. **Local Programs:** *Breakfast at KWKY*, Maxine Sieleman; *Don Thompson Radio Shiow*, Chuck Putbrese; *Friendship*, Tom VandeBerg. **Wattage:** 1000. **Ad Rates:** $7.50-15.50 for 30 seconds; $11.50-20 for 60 seconds.

11024 KXTK-AM - 940
1416 Locust St. Phone: (515)280-1350
Des Moines, IA 50309 Fax: (515)280-3011

Format: Talk. **Networks:** ABC. **Owner:** Saga Communications, 73 Kercheval Ave., Ste. 201, Grosse Pointe Farms, MI 48236. **Founded:** 1945. **Operating Hours:** Continuous. **Key Personnel:** Phil Hoover, VP, Marketing; Bill Wells, Sales Mgr.

11025 KXTX-AM - 940
1416 Locust St. Phone: (515)280-1350
Des Moines, IA 50309-3014 Fax: (515)280-3011

Format: Oldies. **Networks:** ABC; Westwood One Radio. **Owner:** Saga Communications, Inc., 73 Kercheval Ave., No. 201, Grosse Pointe Farms, MI 48236, (313)886-7070, Fax: (313)886-7150. **Founded:** 1948. **Formerly:** KIOA-AM. **Operating Hours:** Continuous. **ADI:** Des Moines, IA. **Key Personnel:** Matt Gillon, Sales Mgr.; Scott Allen, Promotions Dir.; Bill Wells, Pres./General Mgr.; Sharon Beninato, Business Mgr.; Steve Gibbons, Program Dir. **Wattage:** 10,000 day; 5000 night. **Ad Rates:** Advertising accepted; rates available upon request.

11026 TCI
2205 Ingersoll Ave. Phone: (515)246-1555
Des Moines, IA 50312-5289 Fax: (515)246-2211

Founded: 1974. **Formerly:** Heritage Communications, Inc. **Cities Served:** Polk County, Warren County, Altoona, Ankeny, Bondurant, Carlisle, Clive, Grimes, Johnston, Lakewood, Norwalk, Pleasant Hill, Saylorville, Urbandale, West Des Moines, and Windsor Heights, IA.

11027 WHO-AM - 1040
1801 Grand Ave. Phone: (515)242-3500
Des Moines, IA 50309 Fax: (515)242-3798

Format: News; Talk; Sports. **Networks:** ABC. **Owner:** Jacor Broadcasting of Iowa, at above address. **Founded:** 1924. **Operating Hours:** Continuous. **ADI:** Des Moines, IA. **Key Personnel:** Matt Gillon, General Sales Mgr.; V. Harden, Program Dir.; J. Zabel, Sports Dir.; Mark Halverson, General Mgr.; Bob Quinn, News Dir.; Cheryl Pannier, Operations Supervisor. **Wattage:** 50,000.

11028 WHO-TV - 13
1801 Grand Ave. Phone: (515)242-3500
Des Moines, IA 50309 Fax: (515)242-3797

Format: Commercial TV. **Networks:** NBC. **Owner:** The New York Times Company Broadcast Group, 800 Channel 3 Dr., Memphis, TN 38103, (901)543-2135, Fax: (901)543-2384. **Founded:** 1954. **Operating Hours:** Continuous. **ADI:** Des Moines, IA. **Key Personnel:** Jerry Giesler, Program Dir.; Cheryl Semerad, Contact; Chuck Hensley, Sales Mgr.; Al Setka, News Dir., fax (515)242-3796; Brad Olk, Chief Engineer. **URL:** http://www.whooncall.com.

DIAGONAL, pop. 362.

S IA. Ringgold Co. 8 mi. NW of Mount Ayer. Printers museum. Fiberglass burial vault plant.

11029 The Diagonal Progress
PO Box 77
Diagonal, IA 50845-0077

Community newspaper. **Founded:** July 25, 1979. **Freq:** Weekly (Thurs.). **Print Method:** Offset. **Cols./Page:** 6. **Col. Width:** 22 nonpareils. **Col. Depth:** 210 agate lines. **Key Personnel:** David A. Pugh, Editor and Publisher. **Subscription Rates:** $8 individuals; $9 out of area. **Remarks:** Advertising not accepted for sexually oriented material.
Ad Rates: GLR: $.25 **Circ:** Paid 465
BW: $85.05
4C: $225.05
SAU: $1.40

DOON, pop. 537.

NW IA. Lyon Co. On Rock River, 55 mi. N. of Sioux City. Concrete, brick works. Stock, grain, poultry farms.

11030 Doon Press
Doon, IA 51235 Phone: (712)726-3313
Fax: (712)726-3334

Newspaper with a Republican orientation. **Founded:** Sept. 2, 1872. **Freq:** Weekly (Thurs.). **Print Method:** Offset. **Trim Size:** 11 x 17. **Cols./Page:** 5. **Col. Width:** 2 inches. **Col. Depth:** 16 inches. **Key Personnel:** Harold Aardema, Editor and Publisher. **Subscription Rates:** $14.70 individuals; $17.50 out of state. **Remarks:** Color advertising not accepted.
Ad Rates: GLR: $.21 **Circ:** ‡3,300

DOWS

11031 Dows Advocate
104 W. Ellsworth St. Phone: (515)852-3640
PO Box 139 Fax: (515)852-3571
Dows, IA 50071
Community newspaper. **Freq:** Weekly (Thurs.). **Cols./Page:** 5. **Col. Width:** 2 inches. **Col. Depth:** 15 inches. **Key Personnel:** Sharon J. Walbaum, Editor and Publisher. **USPS:** 455-930. **Subscription Rates:** $16 individuals; $22 out of area. **Remarks:** Accepts advertising.
Ad Rates: BW: $168.75 **Circ:** 900
4C: $220
SAU: $2.60
PCI: $2.25

DUBUQUE†, pop. 62,321.

E IA. Dubuque Co. On Mississippi River, 183 mi. NW of Chicago, IL. Bridges to East Dubuque, IL, and Wisconsin. University of Dubuque, Clarke College, Loras College, Wartburg Seminary (Lutheran), Univ. of Dubuque Seminary. Lead and zinc mines. Manufactures sashes and doors, pumps, farm implements, kitchen cabinets, metal products, processed meats, clothing, beer, furniture, batteries, snow plows, pipes, boilers, caskets, disinfectants, biscuits, plumbing, magnetic stirrers, plastics. Boat yards; packing plants; foundries. Boilers.

11032 Antique Trader Weekly
Antique Trader Publications
100 Bryant St. Phone: (319)588-2073
Dubuque, IA 52003-7405 Fax: (319)588-0888
Free: (800)364-5593
Publisher E-mail: traderpubs@aol.com

Magazine featuring stories, auction and show listings, and classified and display advertising for antiques and collectibles. **Founded:** 1957. **Freq:** Weekly (Wed.). **Print Method:** Offset. **Trim Size:** 11 x 14. **Cols./Page:** 6. **Col. Width:** 19 nonpareils. **Col. Depth:** 196 agate lines. **Key Personnel:** Kyle Husfloen, Editor; Ted Jones, Publisher; Karen Ruden, Advertising Mgr. **Subscription Rates:** $35 individuals. **Remarks:** Accepts advertising. **URL:** http://www.csmonline.com/atwpage.html.
Ad Rates: GLR: $1.75 **Circ:** ‡65,000
BW: $756
4C: $1,235
PCI: $15.50

11033 Clarke Courier
Clarke College
Dubuque, IA 52001-3198 Phone: (319)588-6300
Fax: (319)588-6789

Collegiate newspaper. **Founded:** 1930. **Freq:** Weekly (Fri.). **Print Method:** Offset. **Trim Size:** 11 x 17. **Cols./Page:** 4. **Col. Width:** 28 nonpareils. **Col. Depth:** 216 agate lines. **Key Personnel:** Mike Acton, Advisor. **Subscription Rates:** Free. **Remarks:** Accepts advertising.
Ad Rates: GLR: $5 **Circ:** Free 1,000

11034 Collector Magazine & Price Guide
Antique Trader Publications
100 Bryant St. Phone: (319)588-2073
Dubuque, IA 52003-7405 Fax: (319)588-0888
Free: (800)364-5593
Publication E-mail: collector@mwci.net
Publisher E-mail: traderpubs@aol.com

Collector magazine and price guide. **Founded:** 1970. **Freq:** Monthly. **Print Method:** Offset. **Trim Size:** 8 1/2 x 11. **Cols./Page:** 4. **Col. Width:** 27 nonpareils. **Col. Depth:** 140 agate lines. **Key Personnel:** Jan Nierling, Editor; Pat Cline, Advertising Mgr., phone (800)480-0134, fax (800)531-0880; Ted Jones, General Mgr. **ISSN:** 1077-2774. **Subscription Rates:** $19.95 individuals; $2.95 single issue. **Remarks:** Accepts advertising. **URL:** http://www.collect.com/collectormag. **Formerly:** The Antique Trader Price Guide to Antiques and Collectors' Items.
Ad Rates: BW: $515 **Circ:** ‡17,924
4C: $775

11035 The Dubuque Advertiser
The Dubuque Advertiser, Inc.
PO Box 782 Phone: (319)588-0162
Dubuque, IA 52004 Fax: (319)582-0335
Publisher E-mail: dbqadvertiser@mwci.net

Community shopping guide (tabloid). **Founded:** 1963. **Freq:** Weekly (Wed.). **Print Method:** Offset. **Trim Size:** 8 1/2 x 11 1/2. **Cols./Page:** 6. **Col. Width:** 10 picas. **Col. Depth:** 16 inches. **Key Personnel:** Greg Birkett, General Mgr. **Subscription Rates:** $15 individuals. **Remarks:** Accepts advertising.
Ad Rates: BW: $696 **Circ:** Free ‡36,500
4C: $270
PCI: $7.50

11036 Julien's Journal
PO Box 801 Phone: (319)557-1914
Dubuque, IA 52004-0801 Fax: (319)557-9635

Feature Magazine. **Subtitle:** The Dubuque Area Magazine. **Founded:** Feb. 1976. **Freq:** Monthly. **Trim Size:** 8 1/2 x 11. **Cols./Page:** 3. **Col. Width:** 2 1/4 inches. **Col. Depth:** 9 1/2 inches. **Key Personnel:** David Wm. Rusk, Publisher & Editor-in-Chief. **Subscription Rates:** $19; $2.25 single issue. **Remarks:** Advertising accepted; rates available upon request.
Circ: (Not Reported)

11037 Postcard Collector
Antique Trader Publications
100 Bryant St. Phone: (319)588-2073
Dubuque, IA 52003-7405 Fax: (319)588-0888
Free: (800)364-5593
Publisher E-mail: traderpubs@aol.com

Magazine for collectors of antique or modern postcards. **Founded:** 1983. **Freq:** Monthly. **Print Method:** Web offset. **Trim Size:** 8 x 11. **Cols./Page:** 3. **Col. Width:** 13 1/2 picas. **Col. Depth:** 10 inches. **Key Personnel:** Juli Kernall, Editor; Ted Jones, Publisher. **ISSN:** 0746-6102. **Subscription Rates:** $23.95; $35 other countries; $2.95 single issue. **Remarks:** Accepts advertising. **URL:** http://www.csmonline.com.
Ad Rates: BW: $198.41 **Circ:** Paid ‡5,866
Non-paid ‡233

11038 Telegraph Herald
Woodward Communications
801 Bluff St., Box 688 Phone: (319)588-5611
Dubuque, IA 52004-0688 Fax: (319)588-5739
Free: (800)553-4801
Publication E-mail: thonline@wcinet.com

General newspaper. **Founded:** 1836. **Freq:** Daily (morn.). **Print Method:** Offset. **Trim Size:** 14 1/2 x 22 1/4. **Cols./Page:** 6. **Col. Width:** 12 3/10 picas. **Col. Depth:** 21 3/4 inches. **Key Personnel:** Brian Cooper, Exec. Editor, bcooper@wcinet.com; Tom Yunt, Publisher, tyunt@wcinet.com. **Subscription Rates:** $176.80 individuals. **Remarks:** Accepts advertising. **URL:** http://www.thonline.com.
Ad Rates: BW: $3,506.53 **Circ:** Mon.-Sat. ★**28,964**
4C: $3,981.53 Sun. ★**34,657**
SAU: $26.87

11039 The Witness
Witness Publishing Co.
1229 Mt. Loretta Ave. Phone: (319)588-0556
PO Box 917 Fax: (319)556-5464
Dubuque, IA 52004-5200
Catholic newspaper. **Subtitle:** Archdiocese of Dubuque. **Founded:** Feb. 24, 1921. **Freq:** Weekly (Sun.). **Print Method:** Offset. **Trim Size:** 21 1/2 x 13 1/16. **Cols./Page:** 8. **Col. Width:** 20 nonpareils. **Col. Depth:** 301 agate lines. **Key Personnel:** Monsignor Thomas J. Ralph, Editor. **ISSN:** 0745-0427. **Subscription Rates:** $15 individuals; $.30 single issue; $.45 by mail. **Remarks:** Advertising accepted; rates available upon request.
Circ: Paid ‡18,880
Free 100

11040 KATF-FM - 92.9
PO Box 659 Phone: (319)588-5678
Dubuque, IA 52004-0659 Fax: (319)588-5688
Free: (800)324-2836
E-mail: katf@wcinet.com

Format: Adult Contemporary. **Networks:** ABC. **Founded:** 1967. **Operating Hours:** Continuous. **ADI:** Cedar Rapids-Waterloo-Dubuque, IA. **Key Personnel:** Perry Mason, Sales Mgr., phone (319)588-5777, pmason@wcinet.com; Tim Dillon, Program Dir., phone (319)588-5760; Cindy Campton, Local Sales Mgr., phone (319)588-5763. **Wattage:** 100,000. **Ad Rates:** Advertising accepted; rates available upon request.

11041 KDTH-AM - 1370
PO Box 659 Phone: (319)588-5691
Dubuque, IA 52004-0659 Fax: (319)588-5688
Free: (800)422-5384
E-mail: kdth@wcinet.com

Format: Talk; Adult Contemporary; News; Agricultural. **Networks:** CBS. **Owner:** Woodward Communications, Inc., at above address. **Founded:** 1941. **Operating Hours:** Continuous; 30% network, 70% local. **ADI:** Cedar Rapids-Waterloo-Dubuque, IA. **Key Personnel:** Perry Mason, Station Mgr., phone (319)588-5777, pmason@wcinet.com; Michael Kaye, Program Dir., phone (319)588-5699; Mary Beth Theis, Sales Mgr., phone (319)588-5763; John Everly, Contact, phone (319)588-5761. **Wattage:** 5000. **Ad Rates:** Advertising accepted; rates available upon request.

11042 KFXB-TV - 40
744 Main St. Phone: (319)556-4040
PO Box 1090 Fax: (319)557-7101
Dubuque, IA 52001

Format: Commercial TV. **Networks:** Fox. **Owner:** Dubuque TV Limited Partnership, at above address. **Founded:** 1975. **Formerly:** KDUB-TV (1995). **Operating Hours:** 6 am-1 am weekdays; 6:30 am-1 am Sat.; 7 am-12:30 am Sun. **ADI:** Cedar Rapids-Waterloo-Dubuque, IA. **Key Personnel:** Thomas Bond, General Mgr. **Wattage:** 630,000. **Ad Rates:** $10-150 for 30 seconds.

11043 KGGY-FM - 102.3
PO Box 1280 Phone: (319)557-8888
Dubuque, IA 52004-1280 Fax: (319)557-7424
Free: (800)790-1023

Format: Classic Rock. **Founded:** 1980. **Formerly:** KXKX-FM (1992); KDFX-FM. **Operating Hours:** Continuous. **ADI:** Cedar Rapids-Waterloo-Dubuque, IA. **Key Personnel:** Kevin Kelly, VP/GM; Ken Pieffer, Operations Mgr.; Scott Meyer, General Sales Mgr.; Wes Davis, Program Dir. **Wattage:** 3000. **URL:** http://www.kggy.com.

11044 KLCR-FM - 96.9
Loras College Phone: (319)588-7172
1450 Arta Visa Rd. Fax: (319)588-7292
Box 244
Dubuque, IA 52004-0178

Format: Alternative/New Music/Progressive; Rap; Heavy Metal; Classical. **Founded:** 1960. **Formerly:** KLOR-FM (1987). **Operating Hours:** 8 a.m.-12 a.m. **ADI:** Cedar Rapids-Waterloo-Dubuque, IA. **Key Personnel:** Mike Ferrin, General Mgr., phone (319)588-7123; Brad Koch (Cook), Music Dir., phone (319)588-7919, kochbt@lcoc3.loras.edu. **Ad Rates:** Noncommercial.

11045 KLYV-FM - 105.3
5490 Saratoga Phone: (319)557-1040
PO Box 1280 Fax: (319)583-4535
Dubuque, IA 52004-1280

Format: Top 40; Adult Contemporary. **Networks:** ABC. **Owner:** Communications Properties Inc., at above address. **Founded:** 1965. **Operating Hours:** Continuous. **ADI:** Cedar Rapids-Waterloo-Dubuque, IA. **Key Personnel:** Kevin Kelly, General Mgr. **Wattage:** 50,000. **Ad Rates:** Noncommercial.

11046 TCI of Iowa
Box 119 Phone: (319)557-8020
Dubuque, IA 52004-0119 Fax: (319)557-7413

Founded: 1954. **Cities Served:** Dubuque County, IA.

11047 WDBQ-AM - 1490
5490 Saratoga Rd. Phone: (319)583-6471
PO Box 1280 Fax: (319)583-4535
Dubuque, IA 52004-1280

Format: News; Talk. **Networks:** ABC. **Owner:** Communications Properties Inc., at above address. **Founded:** 1933. **Operating Hours:** Continuous. **ADI:** Cedar Rapids-Waterloo-Dubuque, IA. **Key Personnel:** Kevin Kelly, General Mgr. **Wattage:** 1000. **Ad Rates:** Noncommercial.

11048 WJOD-FM - 107.5
5490 Saratoga Rd. Phone: (319)557-1040
Dubuque, IA 52002 Fax: (319)583-4535
E-mail: kpieffer@wjod.com

Format: Contemporary Country. **Networks:** CNN Radio. **Owner:** Communications Properties, Inc., at above address, (319)557-8888, Fax: (319)557-7424. **Founded:** 1988. **Operating Hours:** Continuous. **ADI:** Cedar Rapids-Waterloo-Dubuque, IA. **Key Personnel:** Kevin Kelly, Vice-President/Gen.Manager. **Wattage:** 6000 ERP. **Ad Rates:** $15-25 for 60 seconds. Combined advertising rates available with KLYU, KXGE, KIKR, WDBX.

DUMONT

11049 Dumont Cablevision
506 Pine St. Phone: (515)857-3213
Dumont, IA 50625 Fax: (515)857-3300
E-mail: dumontel@netins.net

Founded: 1983. **Key Personnel:** Roger Kregel, Manager, phone (515)857-3211; Carryl Uhlenhopp, Office Mgr.; Stacy Miller, Technician. **Cities Served:** Bristow, Dumont, Geneva, IA: subscribing households 425; 33 channels; 1 community access channel.

DUNLAP, pop. 1,374.

W IA. Harrison Co. 18 mi. NE of Logan. Residential.

11050 The Dunlap Reporter
Dunlap Reporter
114 Iowa Ave. Phone: (712)643-5380
Dunlap, IA 51529 Fax: (712)643-2173

Newspaper. **Founded:** 1872. **Freq:** Weekly (Thurs.). **Print Method:** Offset. **Trim Size:** 16 x 22. **Cols./Page:** 8. **Col. Width:** 20 nonpareils. **Col. Depth:** 294 agate lines. **Key Personnel:** Charles Walker, Editor; Dianne Walker, Publisher & Advertising Mgr.; Agnes Morris, Advertising Mgr. **Subscription Rates:** $17 individuals.
Ad Rates: SAU: $2.95 **Circ:** ‡1,400
PCI: $3.65

DURANT

11051 Wilton-Durant Advocate News
North Scott Press, Inc.
101 W. 4th St. Phone: (319)732-2029
PO Box 415 Fax: (319)732-3144
Wilton, IA 52778
Community newspaper. **Founded:** 1894. **Freq:** Weekly (Thurs.). **Print Method:** Offset. **Trim Size:** 10 1/2 x 16. **Cols./Page:** 4. **Col. Width:** 15 picas. **Col. Depth:** 16 inches. **Key Personnel:** Craig A. Ducker, Editor. **USPS:** 685-760. **Subscription Rates:** $21 individuals; $23 out of area; $25 out of state. **Remarks:** Accepts advertising.
Ad Rates: BW: $210 **Circ:** Paid 2,628
SAU: $5.25 Free 32
PCI: $5.10

DYERSVILLE, pop. 3,825.

E IA. Dubuque Co. 26 mi. W. of Dubuque. Manufactures scale model farm toys, folding doors and partitions, modular homes. Ships livestock, corn, oats, dairy products.

11052 Dyersville Commercial
Northeast Iowa Publishers, Inc.
PO Box 128 Phone: (319)875-7131
Dyersville, IA 52040-0128 Fax: (319)875-2279

Community newspaper. **Founded:** 1873. **Freq:** Weekly (Wed.). **Print Method:** Offset. **Trim Size:** 21 1/2. **Cols./Page:** 6. **Col. Width:** 13 picas. **Col. Depth:** 21 inches. **Key Personnel:** Robert LeMay, Editor and Publisher; Theresa Neuhaus, Advertising Mgr. and Associate Publisher. **USPS:** 163-300. **Subscription Rates:** $25 individuals; $41 out of area. **Remarks:** Accepts advertising.
Ad Rates: BW: $604.80 **Circ:** Paid 3,941
4C: $754.80 Free 135
SAU: $7.75
PCI: $4.95

11053 KDST-FM - 99.3
1931 20th Ave SE Phone: (319)875-8193
Dyersville, IA 52040 Fax: (319)875-6001
Free: (800)905-5378
E-mail: 993kdst@mwci.net

Format: Country; News. **Networks:** Satellite Music Network; ABC. **Owner:** Design Homes Inc., PO Box 239, Prairie Du Chien, WI 53821-9990, (608)326-6041. **Founded:** 1988. **Formerly**: KDMG-FM (1984). **Operating Hours:** Continuous. **Key Personnel:** John Lightfoot, General Mgr.; Doug Langston, Operations Mgr. **Local Programs:** *Morning Motivation with Kit.* **Wattage:** 3000. **Ad Rates:** $11.50-15 for 30 seconds; $15.50-19 for 60 seconds. Combined advertising rates available with KCTN-FM, KADR-AM.

DYSART, pop. 1,355.

EC IA. Tama Co. 24 mi. So. of Waterloo. City Park. Fairgrounds. Agriculture. Corn, soybeans. Hogs, cattle, sheep.

11054 The Dysart Reporter
PO Box 70 Phone: (319)476-3550
Dysart, IA 52224 Fax: (319)476-2813
Publisher E-mail: dysrtrpt@netins.net

Community newspaper. **Founded:** 1878. **Freq:** Weekly (Thurs.). **Print Method:** Offset. **Cols./Page:** 6. **Col. Width:** 2 inches. **Col. Depth:** 301 agate lines. **Key Personnel:** Jody Stover, Editor; Michael Schlesinger, Publisher. **USPS:** 63–340. **Subscription Rates:** $22 individuals; $28 out of area. **Remarks:** Accepts advertising.
Ad Rates: BW: $378.40 **Circ:** ‡800
4C: $498.40
SAU: $6.36
PCI: $3.31

EAGLE GROVE, pop. 4,324.

NC IA. Wright Co. 28 mi. NE of Fort Dodge. Maufactures textiles, soybean oil, meal, fertilizer; poultry and livestock remedies. Trucking. Ships hogs. Stock, dairy, poultry, grain farms.

11055 Eagle Grove Eagle
314 W. Broadway Phone: (515)448-4745
PO Box 6 Fax: (515)448-3182
Eagle Grove, IA 50533-0006
Publisher E-mail: eagle@adquest.com

Community newspaper. **Founded:** 1889. **Freq:** Weekly (Wed.). **Print Method:** Offset. **Cols./Page:** 6. **Col. Width:** 26 nonpareils. **Col. Depth:** 301 agate lines. **Key Personnel:** Amy Meyer, Editor, phone (515)448-4747, fax (515)448-3182; Gary L. Milks, Publisher. **Subscription Rates:** $37 individuals. **Remarks:** Accepts advertising.
Ad Rates: GLR: $.38 **Circ:** ‡2,700
BW: $475
SAU: $5.30

11056 Wright County Shopper's Guide
Eagle Grove Eagle
314 W. Broadway Phone: (515)448-4745
PO Box 6 Fax: (515)448-3182
Eagle Grove, IA 50533-0006
Publisher E-mail: eagle@adquest.com

Shopper. **Founded:** 1980. **Freq:** Weekly. **Print Method:** Offset. **Cols./Page:** 6. **Col. Width:** 2 1/8 inches. **Col. Depth:** 21 inches. **Key Personnel:** Gary L. Milks, Publisher. **Subscription Rates:** Free. **Remarks:** Accepts advertising.
Ad Rates: SAU: $5.40 **Circ:** Free ‡2,800

EDDYVILLE

11057 Eddyville Tribune
Ottumwa Courier
PO Box 228 Phone: (515)969-4846
Walnut St. Fax: (515)933-4341
Eddyville, IA 52553
Community newspaper. **Founded:** 1886. **Freq:** Weekly (Thurs.). **Print Method:** Offset. **Cols./Page:** 6. **Col. Width:** 9 picas. **Col. Depth:** 13 inches. **Key Personnel:** Brien Fleck, Publisher. **Subscription Rates:** $15 in county. **Remarks:** Accepts advertising.
Ad Rates: BW: $160 **Circ:** 500
SAU: $3.74
PCI: $2.50

11058 KKSI-FM - 101.5
416 E. Main Phone: (515)684-5563
Ottumwa, IA 52501 Fax: (515)684-5832
Free: (800)794-6869
E-mail: kksi_ krkn@pcsia.com

Format: Classic Rock. **Networks:** AP. **Owner:** "O" Town Communications Inc., at above address. **Founded:** 1990. **Operating Hours:** Continuous. **ADI:** Des Moines, IA. **Key Personnel:** Don Linder, President, phone (507)345-4537; Greg List, Vice President; Mark McVey, Vice President. **Local Programs:** *Midnight Madness* 12 a.m. - 1 a.m. Sunday, Greg List, Vice President; *10 Great Songs, 1 Great Year* 5 p.m. - 6 p.m. Monday-Friday, Greg List, Vice President. **Wattage:** 50,000. **Ad Rates:** $12.50 for 30 seconds; $18.75 for 60 seconds. Combined advertising rates available with KRKN-FM.

EDGEWOOD, pop. 900.

E IA. Clayton Co. 15 mi. NE of Elkader. Residential.

11059 Edgewood Reminder
Skattum Publications
Box 458 Phone: (319)928-6876
Edgewood, IA 52042
Publication E-mail: reminder@mwci.net

Community newspaper. **Founded:** 1971. **Freq:** Weekly (Tues.). **Print Method:** Offset. **Cols./Page:** 6. **Col. Width:** 19 nonpareils. **Col. Depth:** 196 agate lines. **Key Personnel:** Roger Skattum, Publisher. **USPS:** 928-700. **Subscription Rates:** $18 individuals; $22 out of area; $0.50 single issue. **Remarks:** Accepts advertising.
Ad Rates: BW: $210 **Circ:** ‡1,500
PCI: $2.50

ELDON, pop. 1,255.

SE IA. Wapello Co. On Des Moines River, 13 mi. SE of Ottumwa. Coal mines. Agriculture. Wheat, corn, soybeans.

11060 Batavia Beacon
Big Grove Publications
PO Box 427 Phone: (515)652-7612
Eldon, IA 52554
Newspaper. **Founded:** 1891. **Freq:** Weekly (Wed.). **Print Method:** Offset. **Cols./Page:** 6. **Col. Width:** 27 nonpareils. **Col. Depth:** 294 agate lines. **Key Personnel:** Virginia Hindsley, Editor; Nancy Annis, Publisher. **Subscription Rates:** $11 individuals.

11061 Forum
Big Grove Publications
PO Box 427 Phone: (515)652-7612
Eldon, IA 52554
Newspaper. **Founded:** 1891. **Freq:** Weekly (Wed.). **Print Method:** Offset. **Cols./Page:** 6. **Col. Width:** 27 nonpareils. **Col. Depth:** 294 agate lines. **Key Personnel:** Virginia Hindsley, Editor. **Subscription Rates:** $11 individuals.

ELDORA†, pop. 3,063.

C IA. Hardin Co. 30 mi. NW of Marshalltown. Manufactures anhydrous ammonia, furniture, rust removers, concrete, clothes, fabricated metal; machine shop; creameries; hatcheries. Lake resort. Agriculture. Corn, hogs, dairy products.

11062 Hardin County Index
W. Edgington Ave. Phone: (515)858-5051
Eldora, IA 50627 Fax: (515)858-5541

Newspaper with a Republican orientation. **Founded:** 1932. **Freq:** Weekly (Fri.). **Print Method:** Offset. **Cols./Page:** 6. **Col. Width:** 28 nonpareils. **Col. Depth:** 301 agate lines. **Key Personnel:** Allyn Schafer, Publisher; David Namanny, Editor. **USPS:** 235-160. **Subscription Rates:** $31 individuals. **Remarks:** Accepts advertising. **Alt. Formats:** Microform.
Ad Rates: GLR: $.55 **Circ:** ‡3,020

11063 Herald-Ledger
PO Box 471 Phone: (515)858-5051
Eldora, IA 50627 Fax: (515)858-5541

Newspaper. **Founded:** 1865. **Freq:** Weekly (Tues.). **Print Method:** Offset. **Cols./Page:** 6. **Col. Width:** 28 nonpareils. **Col. Depth:** 301 agate lines. **Key Personnel:** Allyn Schafer, Publisher; Dave Namanny, Editor. **USPS:** 171-240. **Subscription Rates:** $31 individuals. **Remarks:** Accepts advertising. **Alt. Formats:** Microform.
Ad Rates: GLR: $.55 **Circ:** ‡3,020

ELDRIDGE, pop. 3,279.

E IA. Scott Co. 10 mi. N. of Davenport. Suburban. Agricultural.

11064 The North Scott Press
PO Box 200 Phone: (319)285-8111
Eldridge, IA 52748
Community newspaper. **Founded:** Jan. 1968. **Freq:** Weekly (Wed.). **Print Method:** Offset. **Cols./Page:** 4. **Col. Width:** 15 picas. **Col. Depth:** 16 inches. **Key Personnel:** Scott Campbell, Editor; William F. Tubbs, Publisher. **USPS:** 598-420. **Subscription Rates:** $28 individuals. **Remarks:** Accepts advertising.
Ad Rates: SAU: $8.50 **Circ:** Paid ‡5,700
PCI: $7.50 Free ‡1,900

ELGIN, pop. 702.

NE IA. Fayette Co. 60 mi. NE of Waterloo. Medical clinic, ethyl alcohol plant. Veterinarian clinic. Feed mill. Agriculture. Hogs, cattle, poultry.

11065 The Elgin Echo
Great Midwestern Publishing Co.
Box 97 Phone: (319)426-5591
Elgin, IA 52141-0097
Business and farming newspaper. **Founded:** 1891. **Freq:** Weekly (Wed.). **Print Method:** Offset. **Cols./Page:** 6. **Col. Width:** 28 nonpareils. **Col. Depth:** 301 agate lines. **Key Personnel:** Janell M. Bradley, Editor. **ISSN:** 1727-8000. **Subscription Rates:** $18 individuals. **Remarks:** Accepts advertising. **Alt. Formats:** CD-ROM.
Ad Rates: BW: $387 **Circ:** 1,700
4C: $547
PCI: $3

11066 Hawkeye Booster
247 Center St. Phone: (319)426-5591
PO Box 97
Elgin, IA 52141
General newspaper. **Founded:** 1946. **Freq:** Weekly (Wed.). **Print Method:** Offset. **Cols./Page:** 5. **Col. Depth:** 14 inches. **Key Personnel:** Janell Bradley, Publisher. **USPS:** 116-690. **Subscription Rates:** $11.50 individuals; $13.50 out of area; $16.50 out of state. **Remarks:** Accepts advertising.
Ad Rates: BW: $245 **Circ:** Paid ‡660
4C: $400 Free ‡5
SAU: $3.50
PCI: $3.50

ELK HORN, pop. 746.

W IA. Shelby Co. 48 mi. NE of Council Bluffs. Agriculture. Corn, oats, alfalfa.

11067 The Danish Villages Voice
PO Box 469 Phone: (712)764-4800
Elk Horn, IA 51531-0469
Newspaper. **Founded:** 1925. **Freq:** Weekly (Thurs.). **Print Method:** Offset. **Cols./Page:** 5. **Col. Width:** 22 nonpareils. **Col. Depth:** 248 agate lines. **Key Personnel:** M. Joan Breining, Publisher; Beth Loukaitis, Editor. **Subscription**

Rates: $18.50 individuals. **Remarks:** Accepts advertising. **Former name:** Elk Horn-Kimballton Review (Oct. 17, 1997).
Ad Rates: GLR: $1.96 **Circ:** 1,250
BW: $217
4C: $40
SAU: $3.94
PCI: $3.50

ELKADER†, pop. 1,688.

NE IA. Clayton Co. 45 mi. NW of Dubuque. Cabinet, wire display, sash and door factories; saw and feed mills. Ships livestock. Agriculture. Dairy, hogs, cattle.

11068 The Clayton County Register
Griffith Press, Inc.
PO Box 130 Phone: (319)245-1311
Elkader, IA 52043-0130 Fax: (319)245-1312
Publisher E-mail: ccregstr@netins.net

Newspaper with a Republican orientation. **Subtitle:** The Clayton County Register. **Founded:** 1878. **Freq:** Weekly (Wed.). **Print Method:** Offset. **Trim Size:** 11 1/4 x 16. **Cols./Page:** 4. **Col. Width:** 30 nonpareils. **Col. Depth:** 210 agate lines. **Key Personnel:** Bob Andersen, Editor; Robert P. Griffith, Publisher. **Subscription Rates:** $24 individuals. **Remarks:** Accepts advertising.
Ad Rates: GLR: $.37 **Circ:** Paid ‡2,350
BW: $315 Free ‡102
4C: $480
SAU: $4.35
PCI: $5.25

11069 KADR-AM - 1400
Rt. 1, Box 86 Phone: (319)245-1400
Elkader, IA 52043-9720 Fax: (319)245-1402

Format: Adult Contemporary. **Networks:** Satellite Music Network. **Founded:** 1983. **Operating Hours:** 12 hours Daily; 80% network, 20% local. **Key Personnel:** Troy Thein, Production Mgr.; John Lightfoot, Contact; Dan Berns, Contact. **Wattage:** 1000. **Ad Rates:** $6.50-10.50 for 30 seconds; $7.80-13.20 for 60 seconds.

11070 KCTN-FM - 100.1
Rte. 1, Box 86 Phone: (319)245-1400
Elkader, IA 52043-9720 Fax: (319)245-1402

Format: Country. **Networks:** Satellite Music Network. **Founded:** 1982. **Operating Hours:** Continuous; 95% network, 5% local. **Key Personnel:** Troy Thein, Production Mgr.; John Lightfoot, Gen. Mgr./V.P./Sales Mgr.; Dan Berns, News Dir. **Wattage:** 3000. **Ad Rates:** $9-14 for 30 seconds; $13-18 for 60 seconds.

EMMETSBURG†, pop. 4,621.

NW IA. Palo Alto Co. On Five Island Lake, 50 mi. NW of Fort Dodge. Iowa Lakes Community College. Lake resort. Manufactures dura-lifts, transmitters. Printing and publishing; Feed mill; rendering works. Seed house. Mill-working.

11071 Democrat
Emmetsburg Publishing Co.
Box 73 Phone: (712)852-2323
Emmetsburg, IA 50536 Fax: (712)852-3184

Community newspaper. **Founded:** 1877. **Freq:** Weekly (Thurs.). **Print Method:** Offset web. **Trim Size:** 7 x 11 1/2. **Cols./Page:** 6. **Col. Width:** 12 1/2 picas. **Col. Depth:** 21 1/2 inches. **Key Personnel:** Jane Whitmore, Editor; John Schmidt, Publisher; Dan McCain, Advertising Mgr. **Subscription Rates:** $26.50 individuals.
Ad Rates: GLR: $.53 **Circ:** ‡2,279
BW: $954.60
4C: $1,054.60
SAU: $7.84

11072 Reporter
Emmetsburg Publishing Co.
Box 73 Phone: (712)852-2323
Emmetsburg, IA 50536 Fax: (712)852-3184

Community newspaper. **Founded:** 1877. **Freq:** Weekly (Tues.). **Print Method:** Offset. **Cols./Page:** 6. **Col. Width:** 12 1/2 picas. **Col. Depth:** 21 1/2 inches. **Key Personnel:** Jane Whitmore, Editor; R. Scott Koon, Publisher; Dan McCain, Advertising Mgr. **Subscription Rates:** $26.50 individuals.
Ad Rates: GLR: $.53 **Circ:** ‡2,286
BW: $954.60
4C: $1,054.60
SAU: $7.84

11073 KEMB-FM - 100.1
2215 Main St. Phone: (712)852-4551
Box 390 Fax: (712)852-2088
Emmetsburg, IA 50536
E-mail: kemb@ncn.net

Format: Information; News; Talk; Sports; Adult Contemporary. **Networks:** ABC. **Owner:** Eisert Enterprises Inc., at above address, (712)852-4551. **Founded:** 1977. **Operating Hours:** 24Hrs. **Key Personnel:** John Eisert, President/General Mgr.; James Shaman, Program Dir.; Erik Peters, News Dir.; Mark Simpson, Sports Dir.; Sara Eisert, Vice President. **Local Programs:** *Open House Party*; *All Nite Cafe*. **Wattage:** 5000. **Ad Rates:** $12 for 30 seconds; $16 for 60 seconds.

ESSEX, pop. 1,001.

SW IA. Page Co. 6 mi. NE of Shenandoah. Residential.

11074 The Essex Independent
Media News Group
Box 59 Phone: (712)379-3313
Essex, IA 51638-0059
Community newspaper. **Founded:** 1895. **Freq:** Weekly (Thurs.). **Print Method:** Offset. **Trim Size:** 14 1/2 x 22 3/4. **Cols./Page:** 6. **Col. Width:** 12 picas. **Col. Depth:** 21 inches. **Key Personnel:** Robert D. Jackson, Editor; James R. Gray, Publisher. **USPS:** 178-940. **Subscription Rates:** $20 individuals; $26 out of area; $.50 single issue. **Remarks:** Accepts advertising.
Ad Rates: GLR: $.33 **Circ:** ‡550
BW: $579.60
SAU: $4.60
PCI: $4.60

ESTHERVILLE

11075 KILR-AM - 1070
Hwy. 4 N. Phone: (712)362-2644
PO Box 453 Fax: (712)362-5951
Estherville, IA 51334
Free: (800)316-4149
E-mail: jbcbroadcast@ncn.net

Format: News; Talk; Oldies. **Networks:** ABC. **Owner:** Jacobson Broadcasting Co., Inc., at above address. **Founded:** 1967. **Operating Hours:** 6 a.m.-6 p.m.; 60% network, 40% local. **Key Personnel:** Roger Jacobson, General Mgr.; Dave VanRockel, Sports Dir.; Matt Schedler, Program Dir.; Brent Palm, News Dir.; Peggy Zahrt, Traffic Dir. **Local Programs:** *Sports Spotlight*, Roger J. Jacobson; *Steve Weisman Outdoor Corner*, Roger J. Jacobson. **Wattage:** 250. **Ad Rates:** $11.50-15.50 for 30 seconds; $14.50-18.50 for 60 seconds.

11076 KILR-FM - 95.9
Hwy. 4 N. Phone: (712)362-2644
PO Box 453 Fax: (712)362-5951
Estherville, IA 51334
Free: (800)316-4149

Format: Country. **Networks:** ABC. **Owner:** Jacobson Broadcasting Co., Inc., at above address. **Founded:** 1969. **Operating Hours:** Continuous. **Key Personnel:** Matt Schedler, Program Dir.; Dave Van Rockel, Sports Dir.; Brent Palm, News Dir.; Peggy Zahr, Traffic Dir. **Local Programs:** *Steve Weisman Outdoor Corner*, Roger J. Jacobson. **Wattage:** 6000. **Ad Rates:** $11.50-18.50 for 30 seconds; $14.50-21 for 60 seconds.

EVERLY, pop. 796.

NW IA. Clay Co. 9 mi. W. of Spencer. Feed milling.

11077 Everly-Royal News
Hartley Sentinel, Inc.
71 1st St. SE Phone: (712)728-2223
Hartley, IA 51346 Fax: (712)728-2223

Rural newspaper. **Founded:** 1884. **Freq:** Weekly (Thurs.). **Print Method:** Offset. **Cols./Page:** 7. **Col. Width:** 24 nonpareils. **Col. Depth:** 301 agate lines. **Key Personnel:** Will Robinson, Editor; Ed Robinson, Publisher. **Subscription Rates:** $16.50 individuals; $26 out of area. **Remarks:** Accepts advertising.
Ad Rates: SAU: $4.18 **Circ:** Paid 859
Free 30

FAIRFIELD†, pop. 9,428.

SE IA. Jefferson Co. 23 mi. E. of Ottumwa. Maharishi International University. Manufactures cranes, washing machines, gloves, aluminum castings, textile, plastic, concrete, automotive, dairy products, feed. Foundries.

11078 The Fairfield Ledger
112 E. Broadway Ave. Phone: (515)472-4129
Box 171 Fax: (515)472-1916
Fairfield, IA 52556-3202
Local newspaper. **Founded:** 1849. **Freq:** Daily (eve.). **Print Method:** Offset. **Trim Size:** 14 x 22 3/4 in. **Cols./Page:** 6. **Col. Width:** 2 inches. **Col. Depth:** 21.5 inches. **Key Personnel:** Jeff Wilson, General Mgr.; Byron F. Kimble, Publisher; Gene Luedtke, Advertising Mgr. **USPS:** 184-200. **Subscription Rates:** $60 individuals; $70 out of area; $90 out of state. **Remarks:** Accepts advertising.
Ad Rates: BW: $632.10 **Circ:** ‡4,910
4C: $842.10
PCI: $4.90

11079 The HP Palmtop Paper
Thaddeus Computing, Inc.
110 North Court Phone: (515)472-6330
PO Box 869 Fax: (515)472-1879
Fairfield, IA 52556
Free: (800)373-6114
Publisher E-mail: orders@thaddeus.com

Trade magazine covering usages and products for HP 100/2002X handheld computers. **Founded:** 1991. **Freq:** Bimonthly. **Trim Size:** 9 x 11. **Key Personnel:** Hal Goldstein, Exec. Editor; Ed Keefe, Editor; Ralph C. Turner, Managing Editor. **ISSN:** 1065-6189. **Subscription Rates:** $39 individuals; $7.95 single issue. **Remarks:** Accepts advertising. **Alt. Formats:** Diskette.
Ad Rates: BW: $2,400 **Circ:** Paid 4,000
4C: $3,150 Non-paid 15,100

11080 KHOE-FM - 90.5
1000 N. 4th St. Phone: (515)469-5463
Fairfield, IA 52557
E-mail: khoe@mum.edu

Format: World Beat. **Owner:** Fairfield Educational Radio Station, MUM Box 1017, Fairfield, IA 52557. **Operating Hours:** Continuous. **Key Personnel:** Stan Stansberry, Station Mgr.; Julie Beaufort, News Dir.; Adrienne Fonte, Music Dir. **Wattage:** 100. **Ad Rates:** $5 per unit.

11081 KIIK-FM - 95.9
57 1/2 S. Court Phone: (515)472-4191
Fairfield, IA 52556 Fax: (515)472-2071

Format: Oldies. **Networks:** ABC. **Owner:** Fairfield Media Group, Inc., at above address. **Founded:** 1977. **Operating Hours:** Continuous. **ADI:** Ottumwa, IA-Kirksville, MO (Wapello, IA). **Key Personnel:** Jay Mitchell, President, jay@kmcdkick96.com. **Wattage:** 6000. **Ad Rates:** $6.25-15 for 30 seconds; $8.25-20 for 60 seconds. $6.25-$8 for 30 seconds; $8.25-$10 for 60 seconds. Combined advertising rates available with KMCD-AM. **URL:** http://www.kmcdkick96.com.

11082 KMCD-AM - 1570
57 1/2 S. Court Phone: (515)472-4191
Fairfield, IA 52556 Fax: (515)472-2071
Free: (888)337-2346
E-mail: kmcdkick@ffradio.com

Format: Country. **Networks:** ABC. **Owner:** Fairfield Media Group Inc., at above address. **Founded:** 1958. **Operating Hours:** 24 hours. **Key Personnel:** Jay Mitchell, President, jay@kmcdkick96.com; Bob Harvey, Sales Mgr., bob@kmcdkick96.com; Steve Smith, Director, steve@kmcdkick86.com; Mark Denney, News Director, mark@kmcdkick96.com; Lee Muntz, Sports Director, lee@kmcdkick96.com; Marie Kiefer, Office Manager, marie@kmcdkick96.com. **Local Programs:** *Hotline*, Rich Brown; *Spotlight*, Lee Muntz. **Wattage:** 250 day; 108 night. **Ad Rates:** $6.25-8 for 30 seconds; $8.25-10 for 60 seconds. $6.25-$8 for 30 seconds; $8.25-$10 for 60 seconds. Combined advertising rates available with KIIK-FM. **URL:** http://www.kmcdkick96.com.

FARMINGTON

11083 Van Buren County Leader-Record
102 Elm St. Phone: (319)878-4111
PO Box 155 Fax: (319)878-4111
Farmington, IA 52626
Community newspaper. **Founded:** 1855. **Freq:** Weekly. **Print Method:** Offset. **Trim Size:** 13 3/4 x 22 3/4. **Cols./Page:** 7. **Col. Width:** 10.5 picas. **Col. Depth:** 294 agate lines. **Key Personnel:** Steve Shriver, Editor. **USPS:** 373-530. **Subscription Rates:** $17 individuals. **Remarks:** Accepts advertising.
Ad Rates: GLR: $.15 **Circ:** ‡1784
BW: $330.75
SAU: $3.89
PCI: $3

FAYETTE, pop. 1,515.

NE IA. Fayette Co. 35 mi. NE of Waterloo. Upper Iowa College. Creamery; feed mill; hatchery. Dairy, poultry farms.

11084 Collegian
Upper Iowa University
PO Box 1857 Phone: (319)425-5273
Fayette, IA 52142 Fax: (319)425-5271

Collegiate newspaper. **Founded:** 1883. **Freq:** Weekly. **Print Method:** Offset. **Cols./Page:** 4. **Col. Width:** 24 nonpareils. **Col. Depth:** 210 agate lines. **Subscription Rates:** $10 individuals. **Remarks:** Accepts advertising.
Ad Rates: GLR: $2 **Circ:** 650
PCI: $5

11085 Fayette Leader
PO Box 220 Phone: (319)425-4162
Fayette, IA 52142
Community newspaper. **Founded:** 1910. **Freq:** Weekly (Wed.). **Print Method:** Offset. **Cols./Page:** 4. **Col. Width:** 14 picas. **Col. Depth:** 15 inches. **Key Personnel:** Janell Bradley, Publisher. **Subscription Rates:** $16; $16.50 out of country. **Remarks:** Accepts advertising.
Ad Rates: PCI: $3.09 **Circ:** ‡2,000

FONTANELLE, pop. 805.

SW IA. Adair Co. 50 mi. SW of Des Moines. Residential.

11086 Fontanelle Observer
PO Box 248 Phone: (515)745-3161
Fontanelle, IA 50846-0248 Fax: (515)745-1201

Community newspaper. **Founded:** 1879. **Freq:** Weekly (Wed.). **Print Method:** Offset. **Cols./Page:** 7. **Key Personnel:** Gary W. Pederson, Publisher. **Subscription Rates:** $17 individuals; $21 out of state. **Remarks:** Accepts advertising.
Ad Rates: BW: $250 **Circ:** ‡1,100
SAU: $3.50
PCI: $3.50

FOREST CITY†, pop. 3,920.

N IA. Winnebago Co. 34 mi. NW of Mason City. Manufactures recreational vehicles, motor homes, travel trailers, concrete, pesticides, sporting goods, upholstery filling, fertilizer. Agriculture. Dairying, livestock.

11087 Forest City Summit
Forest City Publishing Co.
PO Box 350 Phone: (515)582-2112
Forest City, IA 50436-0350 Fax: (515)582-4442

Community newspaper. **Founded:** Jan. 1867. **Freq:** Weekly (Wed.). **Print Method:** Offset. **Trim Size:** 14 x 22 3/4. **Cols./Page:** 6. **Col. Width:** 2 1/16 inches. **Col. Depth:** 21 1/2 inches. **Key Personnel:** Kristie Saatmann, Editor; Martin Bunge, Publisher; Dennis Burkholder, Advertising Mgr. **Subscription Rates:** $26 individuals; $32 out of area; $37 out of state. **Remarks:** Accepts advertising.
Ad Rates: GLR: $.28 **Circ:** Paid ‡3,573
BW: $652 Free ‡7,564
PCI: $5.95

11088 KIOW-FM - 107.3
18643 360th St. Phone: (515)582-3121
Box 308 Fax: (515)582-2990
Forest City, IA 50436

Format: Contemporary Country; Adult Contemporary; Full Service. **Networks:** NBC; Radio Iowa. **Owner:** Pilot Knob Broadcasting, Inc., at above address. **Founded:** 1978. **Operating Hours:** Continuous; 5% network, 95% local. **ADI:** Rochester, MN-Mason City, IA-Austin, MN. **Key Personnel:** Anthony G. Coloff, General Mgr.; Sue Coloff, Contact; Orin Harris, Sports Dir.; Melody Schlake, Sales Mgr. **Wattage:** 25,000. **Ad Rates:** $7.71-10.75 for 30 seconds; $11.18-14.63 for 60 seconds.

11089 KZOW-FM - 91.9
106 S. Sixth St. Phone: (515)582-8196
Forest City, IA 50436 Fax: (515)582-8194
E-mail: kzow@waldorf.edu

Format: Alternative/New Music/Progressive. **Owner:** Waldorf College, at above address. **Operating Hours:** Continuous. **Key Personnel:** Mark Newcom, Advisor, phone (515)582-8224, newcomm@waldorf.edu; Kelli Linn, Station Mgr., linnk@waldorf.edu; Tali Salberg, Station Mgr., salbergt@waldorf.edu. **Wattage:** 100. **Ad Rates:** Noncommercial. **URL:** http://www.waldorf.edu.

FORT DODGE†, pop. 29,423.

NWC IA. Webster Co. On Des Moines River, 90 mi. NW of Des Moines. Coal, gypsum mines. Manufactures gypsum and lime products, animal serum, sewer pipes, bricks, tile, building material, electronic components, culverts, plaster, chemicals, farm machinery. Farm feeds; meat packing plants; soybean processing mill; clay works.

11090 Aviators Hot Line
Heartland Communications Group, Inc.
1003 Central Ave. Phone: (515)574-2264
PO Box 1115 Fax: (515)574-2161
Fort Dodge, IA 50501
Free: (888)247-2000

Subtitle: Total Market Coverage For Active Buyers and Sellers of Corporate and General Aircraft, Parts, and Services. **Founded:** 1978. **Freq:** Monthly. **Print Method:** Offset. **Trim Size:** 7 5/8 x 10 3/4. **Cols./Page:** 4. **Col. Width:** 1 5/8 inches. **Key Personnel:** Linda Belew-Conaway, Editor. **Subscription Rates:** $21.95; $69 other countries. $2 single issue. **Remarks:** Accepts advertising.
Ad Rates: BW: $570 **Circ:** Paid ‡3,100
4C: $1,000 Non-paid ‡40,000
PCI: $30

11091 Business Air Today
Heartland Communications Group, Inc.
1003 Central Ave. Phone: (515)574-2264
PO Box 1115 Fax: (515)574-2161
Fort Dodge, IA 50501
Free: (888)247-2000

Subtitle: The Premiere Source For Corporate Aviation Acquisitions. **Founded:** 1992. **Freq:** Bimonthly. **Print Method:** Offset. **Trim Size:** 7 3/4 x 10 3/4. **Key Personnel:** Marty Anderson, Editor. **Subscription Rates:** $21.95; $69 other countries. $2 single issue. **Remarks:** Accepts advertising.
Ad Rates: 4C: $1,200 **Circ:** Non-paid ‡23,000

11092 Contractors Hot Line
Heartland Communications Group, Inc.
1003 Central Ave. Phone: (515)574-2264
PO Box 1115 Fax: (515)574-2161
Fort Dodge, IA 50501
Free: (888)247-2000

Buy-sell-trade catalog serving the heavy construction market. **Founded:** 1966. **Freq:** Weekly. **Print Method:** Offset. **Trim Size:** 7 7/8 x 10 3/4. **Cols./Page:** 4. **Col. Depth:** 10 inches. **Key Personnel:** Christina Baker, Publisher, fax (515)955-6636. **ISSN:** 0192-6330. **Subscription Rates:** $109 first class; $54 third class. **Remarks:** Accepts advertising. **URL:** http://www.contractorshotline.com.
Ad Rates: BW: $694 **Circ:** Paid ‡3,658
4C: $798.10 Non-paid ‡36,342

11093 Contractors Hot Line Monthly Equipment Guide
Heartland Communications Group, Inc.
1003 Central Ave. Phone: (515)574-2264
PO Box 1115 Fax: (515)574-2161
Fort Dodge, IA 50501
Free: (888)247-2000

Buy, sell, trade publication for the heavy contruction industry. **Subtitle:** The One-Of-A-Kind Locating and Pricing Guide for Construction Equipment. **Founded:** 1988. **Freq:** Monthly. **Print Method:** Offset. **Trim Size:** 7 7/8 x 10 3/4. **Cols./Page:** 4. **Col, Width:** 1 5/8 inches. **Col. Depth:** 10 inches. **Key Personnel:** Pamela Utley, Publisher, phone (515)574-2341, pam@hlipublishing.com. **Subscription Rates:** $79.95 individuals; $10 single issue. **Remarks:** Advertising accepted; rates available upon request. **URL:** http://www.contractorhotline.com; http://www.contractorshotline.com.
Circ: (Not Reported)

11094 The Equine Image
1003 Central Ave. Phone: (515)955-1600
PO Box 916 Fax: (515)574-2213
Fort Dodge, IA 50501
Free: (800)247-2000
Publication E-mail: hli1@dodgenet.com

Magazine of equestrian art and lifestyle. **Subtitle:** Reflections of the Equestrian Lifestyle. **Founded:** 1986. **Freq:** Bimonthly. **Print Method:** Web offset. **Trim Size:** 8 1/4 x 10 7/8. **Cols./Page:** 3. **Key Personnel:** Steve Scanlan, Publisher; Amelia Presler, Assoc. Publisher. **ISSN:** 1044-0224. **Subscription Rates:** $29.95; $49 two years; $6.95 single issue. **Remarks:** Accepts advertising. **Formerly:** Equine Images.
Ad Rates: BW: $1,515 **Circ:** Paid 8,000
4C: $1,895

11095 Farm Equipment Guide
Heartland Communications Group, Inc.
1003 Central Ave. Phone: (515)574-2264
PO Box 1115 Fax: (515)574-2161
Fort Dodge, IA 50501
Free: (888)247-2000
Publication E-mail: feg@farmequipmentguide.com

Publication with farm machinery prices and locating information. **Founded:** 1981. **Freq:** Monthly. **Trim Size:** 7 5/8 x 10 3/4. **Cols./Page:** 4. **Col. Width:** 39.6 picas. **Col. Depth:** 59 picas. **Key Personnel:** Nathan Roe, Publisher, phone (515)574-2181, fax (515)574-2182, nathan@farmequipmentguide.com. **ISSN:** 1047-725X. **Subscription Rates:** $50. **Remarks:** Accepts advertising. **URL:** http://www.farmequipmentguide.com.
Ad Rates: GLR: $20 **Circ:** Paid ‡9,294
BW: $500 Non-paid ‡7,506
PCI: $12.50

11096 Farmers Hot Line
Heartland Communications Group, Inc.
1003 Central Ave. Phone: (515)574-2264
PO Box 1115 Fax: (515)574-2161
Fort Dodge, IA 50501
Free: (888)247-2000

Trade magazine. **Subtitle:** Your Guide to the Newest and Latest Farm Products. **Founded:** 1975. **Freq:** 60/year. **Print Method:** Saddle stitched. **Trim Size:** 7 5/8 x 10 3/4. **Cols./Page:** 4. **Col. Width:** 42 picas. **Col. Depth:** 59 picas. **Key Personnel:** Sandra J. Simonson, Publisher, phone (800)674-4763, fhl@farmershotline. **ISSN:** 0192-6322. **Subscription Rates:** $24 individuals All edition 3rd class; $9.95 single issue Manufacturer's edition; $52.80 All edition 1st class. **Remarks:** Accepts advertising.
Ad Rates: BW: $600 **Circ:** Non-paid ‡47,540
4C: $1,100 Paid ‡1,660
PCI: $30

11097 Industrial Machine Trader
Heartland Communications Group, Inc.
1003 Central Ave. Phone: (515)574-2264
PO Box 1115 Fax: (515)574-2161
Fort Dodge, IA 50501
Free: (888)247-2000

Magazine reporting supply and demand of equipment in machine tool industry. **Subtitle:** The Only Weekly Nationwide Publication That Links Active Buyers And Sellers Of New And Used Industrial Machinery. **Founded:** 1983. **Freq:** Weekly. **Print Method:** Offset. **Trim Size:** 7 5/8 x 10 3/4. **Cols./Page:** 4. **Col. Width:** 1 5/8 inches. **Key Personnel:** Theresa Reisenberg, Publisher. **ISSN:** 1047-4374. **Subscription Rates:** $79 individuals First class; $39 individuals Third class. **Remarks:** Accepts advertising. **URL:** http://www.industrialgroup.com.
Ad Rates: BW: $560 **Circ:** Combined ‡12,000
4C: $630
PCI: $19

11098 Land and Water
Land & Water
918B 1st Ave. S. Phone: (515)576-3191
Fort Dodge, IA 50501 Fax: (515)576-2606
Publication E-mail: landandwater@dodgenet.com

Magazine on natural resource management and restoration. **Founded:** 1959. **Freq:** Bimonthly. **Print Method:** Offset. **Trim Size:** 8 1/4 x 10 7/8. **Cols./Page:** 3. **Col. Width:** 28 nonpareils. **Col. Depth:** 140 agate lines. **Key Personnel:** Teresa Doyle, Editor; Amy Dencklau, Publisher; Ann Crouse, Operations Mgr. **ISSN:** 0192-9453. **Subscription Rates:** $20 individuals; $32 other countries; $4 single issue. **Remarks:** Accepts advertising.
Ad Rates: BW: $2070 **Circ:** Paid 2,000
4C: $2620 Non-paid 18,000

11099 The Messenger
Odgen Newspaper
PO Box 659 Phone: (515)573-2141
Fort Dodge, IA 50501 Fax: (515)573-2148
Free: (800)622-6613
Publication E-mail: messenger@dodgenet.com

Newspaper with Republican orientation. **Founded:** 1856. **Freq:** Mon.-Sun. (morn.). **Print Method:** Letterpress. **Cols./Page:** 6. **Col. Width:** 25 nonpareils. **Col. Depth:** 301 agate lines. **Key Personnel:** Larry Johnson, Editor; Thomas C. Briley, Advertising Mgr.; Carolyn Lunn, Advertising Mgr. **Subscription Rates:** $96.20 individuals. **Remarks:** Accepts advertising. **URL:** http://www.oweb.com/messenger.
Ad Rates: SAU: $16.10 **Circ:** Mon.-Sat. 19,162
Sun. 21,483

11100 Mid-America Weekly Trucking
Heartland Communications Group, Inc.
1003 Central Ave. Phone: (515)574-2264
PO Box 1115 Fax: (515)574-2161
Fort Dodge, IA 50501
Free: (888)247-2000

Magazine serving all segments of America's largest regional trucking market. **Founded:** 1972. **Freq:** Weekly. **Trim Size:** 8 x 10 3/4. **Cols./Page:** 4. **Col. Width:** 1 13/16 inches. **Col. Depth:** 10 inches. **Key Personnel:** Beth Buehlar, Editor; Denise McLellan, Publisher; Cindy Youngquist, Advertising Mgr. **ISSN:** 1047-4366. **Subscription Rates:** $59. **Remarks:** Accepts advertising. **Formerly:** National Truck Trader; Midwest Truck Trader.
Ad Rates: BW: $400 **Circ:** Non-paid 100,000
4C: $600
PCI: $30

11101 Musicians Hotline
Heartland Communications Group, Inc.
1003 Central Ave. Phone: (515)574-2264
PO Box 1115 Fax: (515)574-2161
Fort Dodge, IA 50501
Free: (888)247-2000

Consumer magazine covering equipment, services, and supplies for professional, performing musicians. **Founded:** June 1995. **Freq:** Monthly. **Print Method:** Web offset. **Trim Size:** 7 5/8 x 10 3/4. **Cols./Page:** 4. **Col. Width:** 1 5/8 inches. **Col. Depth:** 1 7/8 inches. **Key Personnel:** Trent Salter, Publisher, phone (888)247-2009, fax (515)574-2217, trent@musicianshotline.com. **Subscription Rates:** $14.95 individuals; $1.50 single issue. **Remarks:** Accepts advertising. **URL:** http://www.musicianshotline.com. **Former name:** Midwest Musicians Hotline.
Ad Rates: BW: $320 **Circ:** Controlled 13,000
4C: $480
PCI: $7

11102 Packaging and Converting Hot Line
Heartland Industrial Group
1003 Central Ave. Phone: (515)955-1600
Fort Dodge, IA 50501 Fax: (515)574-2237
Free: (888)247-2007
Publication E-mail: igproduction@industrialgroup.com
Publisher E-mail: hli@hlipublishing.com

Contains information on packaging and converting equipment for sale, materials, business, and employment opportunities. **Subtitle:** The Nations Marketplace Serving Buyers and Converting Equipment, Mate rials, Services, and Supplies. **Founded:** 1996. **Freq:** Monthly. **Print Method:** Offset. **Trim Size:** 7 5/8 x 10 3/4. **Cols./Page:** 4. **Col. Width:** 1 5/8 inches. **Key Personnel:** Steve Scanlan, President; Denise McLellan, Publisher. **Subscription Rates:** $39 individuals first class; $29 individuals third class; $49 Canada; $59 Mexico; $89 other countries. **Remarks:** Accepts advertising. **URL:** http://www.industrialgroup.com. **Formerly:** Packaging Hotline.
Ad Rates: BW: $500 **Circ:** Combined 10,000
4C: $670

11103 Plastics Hot Line
Heartland Industrial Group
1003 Central Ave. Phone: (515)955-1600
Fort Dodge, IA 50501 Fax: (515)574-2237
Free: (888)247-2007
Publication E-mail: hli13@dodgenet.com
Publisher E-mail: hli@hlipublishing.com

Trade magazine. **Subtitle:** The Nation's Marketplace for Plastics Processing Equipment & Materials, Business and Employment Opportunities. **Founded:** 1990. **Freq:** Weekly. **Print Method:** Offset. **Trim Size:** 7 5/8 x 10 3/4. **Cols./Page:** 4. **Col. Width:** 1 5/8 inches. **Col. Depth:** 1 inches. **Key Personnel:** Steve Scanlan, President; Denise McLellan, Publisher. **Subscription Rates:** $69 by mail first class; $49 by mail third class; $89 Canada; $99 Mexico; $109 other countries. **Remarks:** Accepts advertising. **URL:** http://www.industrialgroup.com.
Ad Rates: BW: $580 **Circ:** Controlled ‡6,000
4C: $700
PCI: $20

11104 KIAQ-FM - 96.9
1014 Central Ave. Phone: (515)573-5748
Fort Dodge, IA 50501 Fax: (515)573-3376
Free: (800)239-9179

Format: Country; Hot Country. **Networks:** AP; NBC. **Founded:** 1964. **Formerly:** KRIT-FM. **Operating Hours:** Continuous; 100% local. **ADI:** Des Moines, IA. **Key Personnel:** Nancy Matzner, General Mgr. **Wattage:** 100,000. **Ad Rates:** $16 for 30 seconds; $22 for 60 seconds. Combined advertising rates available with KTLB-FM.

11105 KICB-FM - 88.1
330 Avenue M Phone: (515)995-5877
Fort Dodge, IA 50501-5734 Fax: (515)576-7206

Format: Classic Rock; Alternative/New Music/Progressive. **Founded:** 1971. **Operating Hours:** 15.5 hrs. Daily; 100% local. **Key Personnel:** Robert W. Wood, Contact. **Wattage:** 200.

11106 KKEZ-FM - 94.5
Box 578 Phone: (515)955-4100
Fort Dodge, IA 50501 Fax: (515)955-4250
Free: (800)552-9454
E-mail: kwmtkkez@frontiercomm.net

Format: Album-Oriented Rock (AOR). **Networks:** Independent. **Owner:** Jon Jenkins, 540 A St., Fort Dodge, IA 50501, (515)576-7333, Fax: (515)955-4250. **Founded:** 1955. **Operating Hours:** Continuous; 100% local. **ADI:** Des Moines, IA. **Key Personnel:** Jon Jenkins, General Mgr.; Jerry Sheeder, News Dir.; Linda Kaye, Program Mgr., phone (515)576-7333, webmaster@kkez.com. **Wattage:** 100,000. **Ad Rates:** $28 for 30 seconds; $43 for 60 seconds.

11107 KTIN-TV - 21
Iowa Public Television Phone: (515)242-3100
PO Box 6450
Johnston, IA 50131

Format: Public TV. **Simulcasts:** KDIN-TV Des Moines, IA. **Networks:** Public Broadcasting Service (PBS). **Founded:** 1977. **ADI:** Des Moines, IA. **Key Personnel:** David Bolender, Exec. Dir.; Dennis Malloy, Dir. of Development; Daniel K. Miller, Program Dir.; Don Saveraid, Dir. of Engineering; Pam Johnson, Dir. of Educational Telecommunications; John Leiendecker, Production Mgr.; Sid Sprecher, Public Affairs.

11108 KTPR-FM - 91.1
330 Ave. M Phone: (515)955-5877
Fort Dodge, IA 50501 Fax: (515)576-5656
E-mail: ktpr@duke.iccc.cc.ia.us

Format: Jazz; Classical; News. **Networks:** National Public Radio (NPR); Public Radio International (PRI). **Owner:** Iowa Central Community College, at above address. **Founded:** 1980. **Operating Hours:** 19 hours Daily; 50% network, 50% local. **Key Personnel:** Katherine Perkins, Program Dir., perkins-k@duke.iccc.cc.ia.us; Bob Wood, Broadcasting Dir., wood@duke.iccc.cc.ia.us; John Pemble, Operations Mgr., pemble@duke.iccc.cc.ia.us. **Wattage:** 100,000. **Ad Rates:** Noncommercial.

11109 KUEL-FM - 92.1
200 N. 10th St. Phone: (515)955-5656
PO Box Y Fax: (515)955-5844
Fort Dodge, IA 50501-0458

Format: Adult Contemporary. **Founded:** 1975. **Formerly:** KSMX-FM (1991); KFTX-FM; KFDC-FM. **Operating Hours:** Continuous. **Key Personnel:** Bill Grady, General Mgr. **Wattage:** 6000. **Ad Rates:** $10.40-20.80 per unit.

11110 KVFD-AM - 1400
PO Box Y Phone: (515)955-1400
Fort Dodge, IA 50501-0458 Fax: (515)955-5844

Format: Middle-of-the-Road (MOR). **Networks:** CBS. **Founded:** 1939. **Operating Hours:** Continuous; 5% network, 95% local. **Key Personnel:** Bill Grady, General Mgr. **Wattage:** 1000. **Ad Rates:** $8-17 for 30 seconds; $9.10-19.50 for 60 seconds.

11111 KWMT-AM - 540
PO Box 578. Phone: (515)576-7333
Fort Dodge, IA 50501-0578 Fax: (515)955-4250
E-mail: kwmt@frontiernet.net

Format: Country. **Networks:** ABC. **Founded:** 1956. **Operating Hours:** Continuous; 5% network, 95% local. **ADI:** Des Moines, IA. **Key Personnel:** Jon Jenkins, General Mgr.; Carl Lemon, Contact; Dale Eichor, Contact; Joe Zimmerman, Contact. **Wattage:** 5000. **Ad Rates:** Combined advertising rates available with KKEZ-FM.

FORT MADISON†, pop. 13,520.

SE IA. Lee Co. On Mississippi River, 19 mi. SW of Burlington. Bridge to Niota, IL. Manufactures truck trailers, fountain pens, pencils, aluminum cans, paper and paper products, ink, wire brushes, paints, electric transmission towers, bread wrappers, fertilizer, cement, rubber stamps, wood, synthetic products. Dairy, fruit, truck, poultry farms.

11112 Ft. Madison Daily Democrat
Brehm Comm.
1226 Avenue H Phone: (319)372-6421
Fort Madison, IA 52627-4544 Fax: (319)372-3867
Free: (800)798-8819
Publication E-mail: democrat@interl.net

General newspaper. **Founded:** July 5, 1868. **Freq:** Daily (eve.). **Print Method:** Offset. **Trim Size:** 13 1/2 x 21 3/4. **Cols./Page:** 8. **Col. Width:** 18 nonpareils. **Col. Depth:** 301 agate lines. **Key Personnel:** Robin Delaney, Editor; John Lowman, Publisher; Danna Campbell, Advertising Mgr. **Subscription Rates:** $65 individuals. **Remarks:** Accepts advertising. **Online:** AD SEND.
Ad Rates: GLR: $.52 **Circ:** ‡7,148
BW: $1,135.20
4C: $1,285.20
SAU: $8.80
PCI: $7.50

11113 KBKB-AM - 1360
2060 HWY 61 Phone: (319)372-1241
PO Box 369 Fax: (319)372-5254
Fort Madison, IA 52627

Format: Adult Contemporary. **Networks:** ABC. **Owner:** Talley Broadcasting Co., at above address. **Founded:** 1948. **Formerly:** KXGI-AM (1977). **Operating Hours:** 6 a.m.-midnight; 10% network, 90% local. **Key Personnel:** John R. Peters, Contact; Robert D. Clark, Jr., Contact; Mike Steenberg, News Dir.; Mardie Smith, Sales Director. **Wattage:** 1000. **Ad Rates:** $5.70-10 for 30 seconds.

11114 KBKB-FM - 101.7
2060 HWY 61 N. Phone: (319)372-1241
PO Box 369 Fax: (319)372-5254
Fort Madison, IA 52627

Format: Adult Contemporary. **Networks:** ABC. **Owner:** Talley Broadcasting Co., at above address. **Founded:** 1973. **Formerly:** KXGI-FM (1977). **Operating Hours:** Continuous; 10% network, 90% local. **Key Personnel:** John R. Peters, Contact; Robert D. Clark, Jr., Contact; Mike Steenberg, News Dir.; Mardie Smith, Sales Mgr. **Wattage:** 50,000. **Ad Rates:** $5.70-10 for 30 seconds.

GARNER†, pop. 2,908.

NC IA. Hancock Co. 12 mi. SE of Forest City. Residential.

11115 Garner Leader and Signal
365 State St. Phone: (515)923-2684
Garner, IA 50438 Fax: (515)923-2685

Community newspaper. **Freq:** Weekly (Wed.). **Print Method:** Offset. **Cols./Page:** 7. **Col. Width:** 12 picas. **Col. Depth:** 21 inches. **Key Personnel:** William F. Schrader, Editor and Publisher. **Subscription Rates:** Free; $18 by mail; $20 out of area by mail; $25 out of state by mail. **Remarks:** Accepts advertising.
Ad Rates: GLR: $.21 **Circ:** Paid ‡2,250
PCI: $3.50 Free ‡5,600

GEORGE, pop. 1,241.

NW IA. Lyon Co. 45 mi. SE of Sioux Falls, SD. Manufactures feed boxes, tank heaters, washers, farm equipment and machinery, cement blocks. Grain elevator. Stock, grain farms. Corn, oats, soybeans.

11116 Lyon County News
Box 68 Phone: (712)475-3351
George, IA 51237 Fax: (712)475-3353

Community newspaper. **Founded:** 1901. **Freq:** Weekly (Thurs.). **Print Method:** Offset. **Cols./Page:** 7. **Col. Width:** 28 nonpareils. **Col. Depth:** 300 agate lines. **Subscription Rates:** $16.50 individuals; $18.50 out of area. **Remarks:** Accepts advertising.
Ad Rates: GLR: $.26 **Circ:** 1,100
BW: $451.50
SAU: $4.50
PCI: $3.00

11117 Siebring Cable
301 S. Main St. Phone: (712)475-3747
PO Box 36 Fax: (712)475-2517
George, IA 51237-0036
E-mail: gary@siebring.com

Founded: 1981. **Key Personnel:** Gary Siebring, Contact. **Cities Served:** George, IA: subscribing households 400; 39 channels; 1 community access channel.

GLADBROOK, pop. 970.

EC IA. Tama Co. 20 mi. NE of Marshalltown. Brick, tile, blast meter, mustard factories; soybean processing mill; hatchery. Agriculture. Corn, oats, hogs.

11118 Northern Sun Print
423 2nd St. Phone: (515)473-2102
PO Box 340 Fax: (515)473-2102
Gladbrook, IA 50635-0340
Community newspaper. **Founded:** 1881. **Freq:** Weekly (Fri.). **Print Method:** Offset. **Cols./Page:** 5. **Col. Width:** 11 1/2 picas. **Col. Depth:** 14 1/2 inches. **Key Personnel:** Gregg A. Moser, Editor, phone (319)345-2031, fax (319)345-6767; Jeanne Paustian, Advertising Mgr.; Leroy A. Moser, Publisher. **Subscription Rates:** $22.50; $26 out of state. **Remarks:** Accepts advertising.
Ad Rates: GLR: $.30 **Circ:** 1,209
BW: $304.50
4C: $409.50
SAU: $4.52
PCI: $4.20

GLENWOOD†, pop. 5,503.

WC IA. Mills Co. 18 mi. SSE of Council Bluffs. Grain farms.

11119 Glenwood Opinion Tribune
PO Box 191 Phone: (712)527-3191
Glenwood, IA 51534 Fax: (712)527-3193

Rural newspaper covering Mills County. **Founded:** 1865. **Freq:** Weekly. **Print Method:** Offset. **Trim Size:** 13 x 21 1/2. **Cols./Page:** 6. **Col. Width:** 2 1/16 inches. **Col. Depth:** 21.5 inches. **Key Personnel:** Joe Foreman, Editor; Lois Helms, Publisher. **Subscription Rates:** Free to qualified subscribers; $24 Mills & Sur. Counties; $32 out of area; $42 out of state. **Remarks:** Accepts advertising.
Ad Rates: GLR: $4.22 **Circ:** Paid 3,800
BW: $65 Free 6500
SAU: $4.84
PCI: $3.95

GLIDDEN, pop. 1,076.

WC IA. Carroll Co. 75 mi. NW of Des Moines. Egg processing plant; feed mill; grain elevator. Agriculture. Corn, oats, soybeans, hogs, cattle.

11120 Glidden Graphic
PO Box 607 Phone: (712)659-3144
Glidden, IA 51443 Fax: (712)659-3143

Newspaper with Republican orientation. **Founded:** 1890. **Freq:** Weekly (Thurs.). **Print Method:** Offset. **Cols./Page:** 7. **Col. Width:** 12.5 picas. **Col. Depth:** 126 picas. **Key Personnel:** Cynthia S. Kerkhoff, Editor; Rick Morain, Publisher. **Subscription Rates:** $17 individuals; $24 out of state. **Remarks:** Accepts advertising.
Ad Rates: BW: $441 **Circ:** 1,054
PCI: $2.50

GOLDFIELD

11121 Goldfield Communication Services Corp.
PO Box 67 Phone: (515)825-3888
Goldfield, IA 50542 Fax: (515)825-3801
E-mail: gold@netins.net

Owner: Darrell L. Seaba, 6 Brassfield Dr., Goldfield, IA 50542, (515)825-3790. **Founded:** 1983. **Key Personnel:** Darrell L. Seaba, General Mgr. **Cities Served:** Badger, Goldfield, Woolstock, IA: subscribing households 477; 23 channels; 1 community access channel; 40 hours per week community access programming.

GOOSE LAKE, pop. 274.

E IA. Clinton Co. 14 mi. W. of Clinton. Recreational and Historical.

11122 Wildlife Harvest
Wildlife Harvest Publications
PO Box 96 Phone: (319)242-3046
Goose Lake, IA 52750 Fax: (319)242-7793
Publication E-mail: harvest@sanasys.com
Publisher E-mail: harvest@sanafyf.com

Magazine for hunting resorts, sportsmen's clubs, gun clubs, dog kennels, and commercial gamebird producers. **Founded:** 1973. **Freq:** Monthly. **Print Method:** Offset. **Cols./Page:** 2. **Col. Width:** 28 nonpareils. **Col. Depth:** 109 agate lines. **Key Personnel:** John M. Mullin, Editor and Publisher; Peggy Boehmer, Managing Editor. **USPS:** 403-910. **Subscription Rates:** Free to qualified subscribers; $30 individuals; $3 single issue. **Remarks:** Accepts advertising.
Ad Rates: BW: $210 **Circ:** Paid ‡2,349
PCI: $35 Non-paid ‡200

GOWRIE, pop. 1,089.

NWC IA. Webster Co. 22 mi. S. of Fort Dodge. Diversified farming. Corn, oats, soybeans, hay.

11123 The Gowrie News
Gowrie News
Box 473 Phone: (515)352-3325
Gowrie, IA 50543 Fax: (515)352-3309
Publisher E-mail: gnews@netins.net

Community newspaper. **Founded:** 1889. **Freq:** Weekly (Wed.). **Print Method:** Offset. **Cols./Page:** 7. **Col. Width:** 22 nonpareils. **Col. Depth:** 294 agate lines. **Key Personnel:** Robert Patton, Co-owner; Nancy Vogt, Co-owner. **Subscription Rates:** $17 individuals; $20 out of state. **Remarks:** Accepts advertising.
Ad Rates: GLR: $.50 **Circ:** ‡1,400
BW: $300
SAU: $4.00
PCI: $3

GRAETTINGER, pop. 907.

NC IA. Palo Alto Co. 10 mi. NNW of Emmetsburg.

11124 The Graettinger Times
102 E. Robbins Ave. Phone: (712)859-3780
PO Box 118
Graettinger, IA 51342
Community newspaper. **Founded:** 1893. **Freq:** Weekly (Wed.). **Cols./Page:** 5. **Col. Width:** 2 inches. **Col. Depth:** 15 inches. **Key Personnel:** Pete Olson, Editor and Publisher; Rhonda Henderson, Office Specialist; Joyce Bergmann, Reporter. **USPS:** 225-140. **Subscription Rates:** $18 individuals; $22 out of area; $25 out of state. **Remarks:** Accepts advertising.
Ad Rates: GLR: $3.50 **Circ:** Paid ‡741
BW: $250 Free ‡100
SAU: $3.50

GRAND JUNCTION

11125 Grand Junction Globe Free Press
Grand Junction Press
PO Box 110 Phone: (515)738-5041
Grand Junction, IA 50107 Fax: (515)738-2215

Community newspaper. **Freq:** Weekly (Thurs.). **Cols./Page:** 6. **Col. Width:** 10 picas. **Col. Depth:** 16 inches. **Key Personnel:** Bruce Hoening, Publisher. **Subscription Rates:** $3.50 local; $84.65 individuals. **Remarks:** Accepts advertising.
Ad Rates: GLR: $3.65 **Circ:** 1,100
BW: $190
SAU: $2.70
CNU: $2.70

GREENE, pop. 1,332.

NC IA. Butler Co. 35 mi. SE of Mason City. Butler Co. (NC). 35 m SE of Mason City. Feed mills; plastic injection moulding. Dairy, stock, poultry, grain farms.

11126 The Greene Recorder
219 N. 2nd St. Phone: (515)823-4525
Box 370 Fax: (515)823-4525
Greene, IA 50636
Community newspaper. **Founded:** 1884. **Freq:** Weekly (Wed.). **Print Method:** Offset. **Trim Size:** 14 x 21 1/4. **Cols./Page:** 7. **Col. Width:** 10 1/2 nonpareils. **Col. Depth:** 301 agate lines. **Key Personnel:** Sylvia J. Hawker, Editor; Fred J. Hawker, Publisher. **USPS:** 228-680. **Subscription Rates:** $22 Butler and Floyd Counties; $24 Iowa and Minnesota; $26 elsewhere. **Remarks:** Accepts advertising. **Alt. Formats:** Microform.
Ad Rates: GLR: $.225 **Circ:** 1,300
BW: $342.19
4C: $40
SAU: $3.15
PCI: $2.75

GREENFIELD†, pop. 2,243.

SW IA. Adair Co. 61 mi. SW of Des Moines. Light manufacturing. Stock, poultry, grain farms. Corn, hogs, cattle.

11127 Adair County Free Press
108 E. Iowa St. Phone: (515)743-6121
Box 148 Fax: (515)743-6122
Greenfield, IA 50849
Community newspaper. **Founded:** 1889. **Freq:** Weekly (Wed.). **Print Method:** Offset. **Cols./Page:** 7. **Col. Width:** 12 picas. **Col. Depth:** 21.5 inches. **Key Personnel:** Ken Sidey, Editor and Publisher. **Subscription Rates:** $21 individuals; $30 out of state. **Remarks:** Advertising not accepted for alcoholic beverages.
Ad Rates: BW: $495 **Circ:** ‡3,000
SAU: $4

GRINNELL, pop. 8,868.

SE IA. Poweshiek Co. 50 mi. NE of Des Moines. Grinnell College. Manufactures playground equipment, feed, farm equipment, gloves, jackets, aluminum, fiberglass, mufflers, windows, polyvinyl, chloride, pipe, stadium seating. Hybrid seed corn, alfalfa dehydrating plants. Agriculture. Grain, livestock.

11128 Grinnell Herald-Register
Herald-Register Publishing Co.
813 5th Ave. Phone: (515)236-3113
PO Box 360 Fax: (515)236-5135
Grinnell, IA 50112-1653
Community newspaper. **Founded:** 1868. **Freq:** Semiweekly (Mon. and Thurs.). **Print Method:** Offset. **Cols./Page:** 8. **Col. Width:** 21.5 nonpareils. **Col. Depth:** 301 agate lines. **Key Personnel:** A.J. Pinder, Editor and Publisher. **USPS:** 230-080. **Subscription Rates:** $36.50 individuals; $42 out of area. **Remarks:** Accepts advertising.
Ad Rates: GLR: $.33 **Circ:** Paid 3,693
BW: $387 Free 355
4C: $627
SAU: $6.26
PCI: $5.55

11129 KDIC-FM - 88.5
Grinnell College Phone: (515)269-3335
Grinnell, IA 50112

Format: Full Service. **Networks:** Independent. **Founded:** 1968. **Operating Hours:** 7 a.m.-2 a.m. **Wattage:** 130. **Ad Rates:** Noncommercial.

11130 KGRN-AM - 1410
Box 660 Phone: (515)236-6106
Grinnell, IA 50112 Fax: (515)236-8896
E-mail: kgrn@pcpartner.com

Format: Full Service; Middle-of-the-Road (MOR); Country; Adult Contemporary. **Networks:** ABC; Brownfield; Radio Iowa. **Founded:** 1957. **Operating Hours:** 6 a.m.-10 p.m. **ADI:** Des Moines, IA. **Key Personnel:** Russ Crawford, President/CEO; Chris Juni, Contact; Don Bradley, News Dir.; John Martenson, Sports Dir.; Jeff Bayer, Farm Markets. **Local Programs:** *Cooking in Iowa*, Chef Deb White; *On the Marcum Show*, Jack Marcum. **Wattage:** 500. **Ad Rates:** $14.25-18.20 for 30 seconds.

GRISWOLD

11131 Griswold American
PO Box 430 Phone: (712)778-4337
Griswold, IA 51535 Fax: (712)778-4350

Community newspaper. **Founded:** 1880. **Freq:** Weekly (Wed.). **Cols./Page:** 6. **Col. Width:** 12 1/2 inches. **Col. Depth:** 21 1/2 inches. **Key Personnel:** Gary Pederson, Editor and Publisher.
Circ: 1,722

GRUNDY CENTER†, pop. 2,880.

NEC IA. Grundy Co. 30 mi. SW of Waterloo. Manufactures plastic molded parts, wood veneer, chillers, salad dressing. Diversified farming. Corn, oats, soybeans.

11132 Collectors News & the Antique Reporter
506 2nd St. Phone: (319)824-6981
PO Box 156 Fax: (319)824-3414
Grundy Center, IA 50638
Free: (800)352-8039

Newsprint magazine covering antiques and collecting for pleasure and profit. **Founded:** May 1959. **Freq:** Monthly. **Print Method:** Offset. **Trim Size:** 8 x 11. **Cols./Page:** 4. **Col. Width:** 1 5/8 inches. **Col. Depth:** 10 inches. **Key Personnel:** Linda Kruger, Editor; Cheryl Souhrada, Publisher. **ISSN:** 0162-1033. **Subscription Rates:** $36 individuals; $4 single issue; $54 out of country. **Remarks:** Accepts advertising.
Ad Rates: BW: $388.00 **Circ:** ‡14,000
4C: $778.00
PCI: $11.41

11133 The Grundy Register
Register Printing Co.
601 G Ave. Phone: (319)824-6958
Grundy Center, IA 50638-1549 Fax: (319)824-6288

Community newspaper. **Founded:** 1868. **Freq:** Weekly (Thurs.). **Print Method:** Offset. **Trim Size:** 15 1/2 x 22. **Cols./Page:** 8. **Col. Width:** 10.6 picas. **Col. Depth:** 21 1/2 inches.

Key Personnel: Marlene J. Kothenbeutel, President; Ralph Kothenbeutel, Editor and Publisher. **Subscription Rates:** $27 individuals. **Remarks:** Accepts advertising. **Feature Editors:** Deb Werkman, *News*.
Ad Rates: SAU: $5.80 **Circ:** 3,200
PCI: $4.70

GUTHRIE CENTER†, pop. 1,713.

SWC IA. Guthrie Co. 50 mi. W. of Des Moines. Lake resort. Manufactures doors, windows, flour, dairy products. Agriculture. Cattle, hogs, corn.

11134 Guthrie Center Times
PO Box 217
Guthrie Center, IA 50115

Local newspaper. **Founded:** 1882. **Freq:** Weekly (Wed.). **Print Method:** Offset. **Trim Size:** 8 1/2 x 11. **Cols./Page:** 8. **Col. Width:** 10 1/2 inches. **Col. Depth:** 21 1/2 inches. **Key Personnel:** Charles P. Gonzales, Publisher. **USPS:** 232-280. **Subscription Rates:** $18 individuals; $20 out of area; $25 out of state. **Remarks:** Accepts advertising.
Ad Rates: GLR: $.10 **Circ:** Paid 2,022
BW: $381.20 Non-paid 17
4C: $486.20
SAU: $4.20
PCI: $3.26

GUTTENBERG, pop. 2,428.

NE IA. Clayton Co. On Mississippi River, 40 mi. NW of Dubuque. Tourism. Tool, toys, electronic assembly, extruded plastic components. Timber. Agriculture. Corn, hogs, beef.

11135 The Guttenberg Press
Guttenberg Publishing
Box 937 Phone: (319)252-2421
Guttenberg, IA 52052 Fax: (319)252-1275

Community newspaper. **Freq:** Weekly. **Print Method:** Offset. **Cols./Page:** 4. **Col. Width:** 15 picas. **Col. Depth:** 16 inches. **Key Personnel:** Diane Feldman, Editor; Robert LeMay, Publisher, phone (319)875-7131, fax (319)875-2279. **Subscription Rates:** $24; $32 out of area. **Remarks:** Advertising accepted; rates available upon request.
Circ: Paid 2,543
Non-paid 18

HAMPTON†, pop. 4,630.

NC IA. Franklin Co. 28 mi. S. of Mason City. Beedslake State Park. Manufactures hydraulic cylinders, truck trailers, steel tools, concrete culverts and tile, recreational vehicles, fiberglass, medical supplies. Nursery; cannery. Stock, poultry, grain farms. Corn, hogs.

11136 Conservative Chronicle
Hampton Publishing Co.
9 2nd St. NW Phone: (515)456-2585
PO Box 29 Fax: (515)456-2587
Hampton, IA 50441
Free: (800)558-1244

Tabloid reprinting newspaper columns of leading U.S. conservative commentators. **Founded:** 1985. **Freq:** Weekly. **Print Method:** Offset. **Trim Size:** 7 1/2 x 11 1/4. **Cols./Page:** 4. **Col. Width:** 12 picas. **Col. Depth:** 10 inches. **Key Personnel:** Joseph P. Roth, Publisher. **ISSN:** 0888-1359. **Subscription Rates:** $42. $1.50 single issue. **Remarks:** Advertising not accepted.
Circ: Paid ⊕**57,960**
Free 30

11137 Hampton Chronicle & Times
Hampton Publishing Co.
9 2nd St. NW Phone: (515)456-2585
PO Box 29 Fax: (515)456-2587
Hampton, IA 50441
Free: (800)558-1244

General newspaper. **Founded:** 1876. **Freq:** Semiweekly. **Print Method:** 15 x 22 3/4. Offset. **Cols./Page:** 8. **Col. Width:** 1 3/4 inches. **Col. Depth:** 21 inches. **Key Personnel:** Joseph P. Roth, Editor and Publisher; Brad Hicks, Advertising Mgr. **Subscription Rates:** $30 Local; $35 out of area; $41 out of state.
Ad Rates: GLR: $.19 **Circ:** Paid 3,820
BW: $579.60 Free ⊕**3,200**
4C: $678.40
SAU: $4.80
PCI: $3.00

11138 KLMJ-FM - 104.9
1509 4th St. NE Phone: (515)456-5656
PO Box 495 Fax: (515)456-5655
Hampton, IA 50441
E-mail: klmj@klmj.com

Format: Adult Contemporary; Contemporary Country; News; Sports. **Networks:** ABC; Brownfield. **Owner:** C.D. Broadcasting, at above address. **Founded:** 1983. **Formerly:** KWGG-FM (1993). **Operating Hours:** Continuous 10% network, 90% local. **Key Personnel:** Craig Donnelly, Owner/Gen. Mgr./Sales Mgr.; Pat Palmer, Operations; Duane Carstens, Sports Dir.; Mike Betten, Music Dir.; Paul Lundgren, News Dir.; Janis Hicks, Office Mgr. **Local Programs:** *The Good News*, Pat Palmer, Program Dir. **Wattage:** 6000. **Ad Rates:** $7-12 for 30 seconds; $9-14 for 60 seconds. **URL:** http://www.klmj.com.

HARLAN†, pop. 5,357.

W IA. Shelby Co. 40 mi. NE of Council Bluffs. Manufactures feeds, cement, farm implements, mill grinders. Agriculture. Corn, cattle, hogs.

11139 News-Advertiser
Tribune Newspapers, Inc.
1114 7th St. Phone: (712)755-3111
PO Box 721 Fax: (712)755-3324
Harlan, IA 51537-0721
Free: (800)909-6397
Publication E-mail: tribnews@fmctc.com

Community newspaper. **Founded:** 1870. **Freq:** Weekly (Fri.). **Print Method:** Offset. **Trim Size:** 15 1/2 x 22 3/4. **Cols./Page:** 6. **Col. Width:** 14 picas. **Col. Depth:** 21 1/2 inches. **Key Personnel:** Steve Mores, Publisher; Alan Mores, Publisher; Mike Kolbe, Advertising Mgr. **USPS:** 235-520. **Subscription Rates:** $36 individuals; $.75 single issue.
Ad Rates: BW: $690.15 **Circ:** ‡5,100
4C: $930.15
SAU: $5.35
PCI: $5.35

11140 PennySaver
Tribune Newspapers, Inc.
1114 7th St. Phone: (712)755-3111
PO Box 721 Fax: (712)755-3324
Harlan, IA 51537-0721
Free: (800)909-6397
Publication E-mail: tribnews@fmctc.com

Shopper. **Founded:** 1970. **Freq:** Weekly (Wed.). **Print Method:** Offset. **Cols./Page:** 6. **Col. Width:** 14 picas. **Col. Depth:** 21.5 inches. **Key Personnel:** Steve Mores, Editor and Publisher. **Subscription Rates:** Free.
Ad Rates: BW: $690.15 **Circ:** Free ‡11,000
4C: $930.15
SAU: $5.35
PCI: $5.35

11141 Rocket Common Supplement Shopper
Tribune Newspapers, Inc.
1114 7th St. Phone: (712)755-3111
PO Box 721 Fax: (712)755-3324
Harlan, IA 51537-0721
Free: (800)909-6397
Publisher E-mail: tribnews@fmctc.com

Common supplement of these publications: Harlan PennySaver, Manilla Times, Schleswig Leader, Odebolt/Early Chronicle, Avoca Journal Herald, Coon Rapids Enterprise, Manning Monitor, Mapleton Press, Dunlap Reporter/ Earling News, Mo. Valley Times, Mo. Valley Merchandiser, Charter Oak-Use NEWSpaper, Carroll Times Herald Weekly and Oakland Herald. **Founded:** 1960. **Freq:** Weekly. **Print Method:** Offset. **Trim Size:** 15 1/2 x 11 1/2. **Cols./Page:** 6. **Col. Width:** 10 picas. **Col. Depth:** 14 3/4 inches. **Key Personnel:** Steve Mores, Publisher. **Subscription Rates:** Free.
Ad Rates: BW: $531 **Circ:** Free 33,500
4C: $771
SAU: $6
PCI: $6

11142 Tribune
Tribune Newspapers, Inc.
1114 7th St. Phone: (712)755-3111
PO Box 721 Fax: (712)755-3324
Harlan, IA 51537-0721
Free: (800)909-6397
Publication E-mail: tribnews@fmctc.com

Community newspaper. **Founded:** 1879. **Freq:** Weekly (Tues.). **Print Method:** Offset. **Trim Size:** 15 1/2 x 22 3/4. **Cols./Page:** 6. **Col. Width:** 14 picas. **Col. Depth:** 21 1/2 inches. **Key Personnel:** Steve Mores, Publisher; Alan Mores, Publisher; Mike Kolbe, Advertising Mgr. **USPS:** 235-540. **Subscription Rates:** $36 individuals; $.75 single issue.
Ad Rates: BW: $690.15 **Circ:** ‡5,100
4C: $930.15
SAU: $5.35
PCI: $5.35

11143 Farmers Mutual Cooperative
PO Box 311 Phone: (712)744-3131
Harlan, IA 51537 Fax: (712)744-3100

Key Personnel: Thomas Convy, General Mgr.

11144 KNOD-FM - 105.3
902 Chatburn Ave. Phone: (712)755-3883
PO Box 723 Fax: (712)755-7511
Harlan, IA 51537-0723
E-mail: knod@fmctc.com

Format: Oldies. **Networks:** ABC; Brownfield; Jones Satellite. **Owner:** John Talbott, at above address. **Founded:** 1979. **Operating Hours:** Continuous. **Key Personnel:** John Talbott, Chief Engineer; Ron Novotny, Gen. Sales Mgr./Promotions Mgr. **Local Programs:** *Close-Up*, Pam Remmick; *Fair Coverage*, Pam Remmick; *Sports Wrap*, Ron Novotry. **Wattage:** 25,000. **Ad Rates:** $4.65 for 15 seconds; $5.25-7.70 for 30 seconds; $6.60-9.90 for 60 seconds.

HARTLEY, pop. 1,700.

NE IA. O'Brien Co. 70 mi. NE of Sioux City. Electric supply. Fertilizer plant. Feed mills. Meat processing plant. Grain terminal. Agriculture. Soybeans, corn, cattle, hogs.

Everly-Royal News - See Everly

11145 Hartley Sentinel
Hartley Sentinel, Inc.
71 1st St. SE Phone: (712)728-2223
Hartley, IA 51346 Fax: (712)728-2223

Newspaper with Republican orientation. **Founded:** 1912. **Freq:** Weekly (Thurs.). **Print Method:** Offset. **Cols./Page:** 7. **Col. Width:** 24 nonpareils. **Col. Depth:** 301 agate lines. **Key Personnel:** W.R. Vezina, Jr., Editor; E. Robinson, Publisher. **Subscription Rates:** $18.50 individuals; $26 out of area. **Remarks:** Accepts advertising.
Ad Rates: SAU: $4.57 **Circ:** Paid 1,433
Free 45

11146 Hartley Municipal Cable TV
11 S. Central Ave. Phone: (712)728-2240
Hartley, IA 51346 Fax: (712)728-2878

Founded: Mar. 1983. **Key Personnel:** Bryan Gerritson, Director; Rodney Roth, Technician; Berlou White, Office Mgr. **Cities Served:** Hartley, IA: subscribing households 704; 24 channels; 1 community access channel.

HAWARDEN, pop. 2,722.

SW IA. Sioux Co. 35 mi. N. of Sioux City. Sioux Empire College. Livestock, shipping.

11147 The Independent
PO Box 31 Phone: (712)552-1051
Hawarden, IA 51023 Fax: (712)552-2503

General newspaper. **Founded:** 1881. **Freq:** Weekly. **Print Method:** Offset. **Trim Size:** 11 1/2 x 17. **Cols./Page:** 4. **Col. Width:** 14 picas. **Col. Depth:** 224 agate lines. **Key Personnel:** Larry U. Meints, Editor and Publisher. **Subscription Rates:** $11 individuals; $13.50 out of area. **Remarks:** Color advertising accepted; rates available upon request.
Ad Rates: GLR: $2.50 **Circ:** 1,400
BW: $160

HOLSTEIN

11148 The Advance
Advance Publications, Inc.
116 N. Main Phone: (712)368-4368
PO Box 550
Holstein, IA 51025
Community newspaper. **Founded:** 1886. **Freq:** Weekly (Thurs.). **Print Method:** Offset. **Cols./Page:** 6. **Col. Width:** 12.9 picas. **Col. Depth:** 21.5 inches. **Key Personnel:** Mari Bauer, Publisher. **Subscription Rates:** $15 individuals; $16 out of country; $17 out of state. **Remarks:** Accepts advertising. **Formerly:** Holstein Advance.
Ad Rates: BW: $741.45 **Circ:** ‡1,300
4C: $806.75
SAU: $5.75

HOSPERS, pop. 646.

EC IA. Sioux Co. 9 mi. SSW of Sheldon. Livestock.

11149 Siouxland Press
PO Box 278 Phone: (712)752-8401
Hospers, IA 51238 Fax: (712)752-8405

Community newspaper. **Founded:** Apr. 1969. **Freq:** Weekly. **Print Method:** Offset. **Trim Size:** 11 x 16. **Cols./Page:** 6. **Col. Width:** 9 picas. **Col. Depth:** 15 inches. **Key Personnel:** Harlan Rouse, Editor and Publisher; Katie Rouse, Advertising Mgr. **Subscription Rates:** $12 individuals; $14 out of area; $16 out of state. **Remarks:** Accepts advertising.
Ad Rates: GLR: $2.25 **Circ:** Paid ‡1,785
BW: $180 Free ‡50
4C: $375
PCI: $2.74

HUBBARD, pop. 852.

C IA. Hardin Co. 15 mi. SW of Eldora. Residential.

11150 South Hardin Signal-Review
Box 457 Phone: (515)864-2288
Hubbard, IA 50122
Local newspaper. **Founded:** 1883. **Freq:** Weekly (Thurs.). **Print Method:** Offset. **Cols./Page:** 5. **Col. Width:** 24 nonpareils. **Col. Depth:** 196 agate lines. **Key Personnel:** Charles C. Mellows, Editor and Publisher; David Mellows, Advertising Mgr.; Laura L. Mellows, Editor and Publisher. **Subscription Rates:** $13 individuals; $15 local; $16 out of state. **Remarks:** Accepts advertising.
Ad Rates: GLR: $.28 **Circ:** Paid ‡1,361
4C: $176 Free ‡31
SAU: $2.21
PCI: $1.96

HUDSON, pop. 2,267.

NEC IA. Black Hawk Co. 9 mi. SW of Waterloo. Manufactures conveyor equipment; hybrid seed processing. Dairy, stock, grain farms.

11151 Hudson Herald
Box 210 Phone: (319)988-3855
Hudson, IA 50643-0210 Fax: (319)988-3855

Community newspaper. **Founded:** 1911. **Freq:** Weekly (Thurs.). **Print Method:** Offset. **Cols./Page:** 6. **Col. Width:** 13.5 picas. **Col. Depth:** 21.5 inches. **Key Personnel:** Clifford Murray, Editor and Publisher. **Subscription Rates:** $20 individuals; $22 out of area. **Remarks:** Accepts advertising.
Ad Rates: BW: $336 **Circ:** ‡1,250
PCI: $3.50

HULL, pop. 1,714.

NW IA. Sioux Co. 55 mi. N. of Sioux City. Elevators. Dairy, stock, poultry farms.

11152 Sioux County Index-Reporter
Lyon County Reporter
PO Box 420 Phone: (712)439-1075
Hull, IA 51239-0420 Fax: (712)439-1076

Tabloid. **Founded:** 1879. **Freq:** Weekly (Wed.). **Print Method:** Offset. **Cols./Page:** 5. **Col. Width:** 2 inches. **Col. Depth:** 15 inches. **Key Personnel:** David Enersen, Publisher. **USPS:** 497-320. **Subscription Rates:** $18 individuals; $27 out of state. **Remarks:** Accepts advertising.
Ad Rates: GLR: $2.90 **Circ:** ‡1,200
BW: $300
4C: $600
SAU: $4

HUMBOLDT, pop. 4,794.

NWC IA. Humboldt Co. On Des Moines River, 16 mi. N. of Fort Dodge. Manufactures concrete products, high pressure cleaning equipment, truck cover, aluminum awnings, fertilizer, church furniture, farm equipment, hydraulic parts, trailers, motor homes, conveyors, plastic products, truck parts, sporting goods, flashing mobile signs. Hatcheries. Limestone quarries. Agriculture.

11153 Humboldt Independent
Gargano Communications, Inc.
PO Box 157 Phone: (515)332-2514
Humboldt, IA 50548
Community newspaper. **Founded:** 1900. **Freq:** Weekly. **Print Method:** Offset. **Trim Size:** 13 x 21. **Cols./Page:** 8. **Col. Width:** 9.5 picas. **Col. Depth:** 21 inches. **Key Personnel:** Jeff Gargano, Editor; James Gargano, Publisher. **Subscription Rates:** $30 individuals; $40 elsewhere. **Remarks:** Accepts advertising.
Ad Rates: BW: $940.80 **Circ:** ‡5,000
PCI: $5.60

11154 Humboldt Reminder
Humboldt Reminder, Inc.
512 Sumner Ave. Phone: (515)332-3425
PO Box 549
Humboldt, IA 50548
Shopper. **Founded:** Nov. 1931. **Freq:** Weekly (Wed.). **Print Method:** Offset. **Cols./Page:** 6. **Col. Width:** 1 5/8 inches. **Col. Depth:** 224 agate lines. **Key Personnel:** James Gargano, Editor and Publisher. **Subscription Rates:** Free in area. **Remarks:** Accepts advertising.
Ad Rates: BW: $470.40 **Circ:** Free 13,017
PCI: $4.90

11155 KHBT-FM - 97.7
2196 Montana Ave. Phone: (515)332-4100
PO Box 217
Humboldt, IA 50548
E-mail: khbt@aol

Format: Soft Rock. **Networks:** AP; CNN Radio. **Owner:** Signature Communications, Inc., at above address. **Founded:** 1970. **Operating Hours:** Continuous. **ADI:** Des Moines, IA. **Key Personnel:** Frank Hayer, General Mgr.; Paulette Lundberg, General Sales Mgr. **Wattage:** 5800.

HUMESTON

11156 The Humeston New Era
Box 377 Phone: (515)877-3811
Humeston, IA 50123 Fax: (515)872-1965

Community newspaper. **Founded:** 1880. **Freq:** Weekly (Tues.). **Print Method:** Offset. **Cols./Page:** 5. **Col. Width:** 11 picas. **Col. Depth:** 12 1/2 inches. **Key Personnel:** Rhonda Bennett, Publisher, phone (515)872-1234; Virginia Sponsler, Contact, phone (515)877-3811. **Subscription Rates:** $13 in four county area; $15 out of area. **Remarks:** Accepts advertising.
Ad Rates: PCI: $2 **Circ:** ‡1,000

IDA GROVE†, pop. 2,285.

W IA. Ida Co. 50 mi. SE of Sioux City. Manufactures bolster, marine lines and boat hoists, farm equipment, paving finishing machines, feed, neon signs. Agriculture. Corn, beans, hogs, cattle.

11157 Ida County Courier-Reminder
Ida County Courier-Reminder Inc.
PO Box 249 Phone: (712)364-3131
Ida Grove, IA 51445 Fax: (712)364-3010
Publication E-mail: courier@pionet.net

Newspaper. **Founded:** 1975. **Freq:** Weekly (Wed.). **Print Method:** Offset. **Cols./Page:** 6. **Col. Width:** 26 nonpareils. **Col. Depth:** 301 agate lines. **Key Personnel:** Beth Wolterman, Editor; Roger Rector, Publisher; Kathy Leonard, Office Mgr. **Subscription Rates:** $24. **Remarks:** Accepts advertising. **URL:** http://www.idacountycourier.com. **Alt. Formats:** CD-ROM, Apple Compatible.
Ad Rates: BW: $345 **Circ:** 3,200
SAU: $3.35

11158 KIDA-FM - 92.9
513E W. 2nd St. Fax: (712)364-2559
Ida Grove, IA 51445 Free: (800)771-0036
E-mail: kida@pionet.net

Format: Country. **Networks:** ABC; Brownfield; Radio Iowa; Westwood One Radio. **Founded:** 1981. **Operating Hours:** Continuous. **ADI:** Sioux City, IA. **Key Personnel:** Charlie Roth, Manager, phone (712)364-2121. **Wattage:** 25,000. **Ad Rates:** $8 for 30 seconds; $12 for 60 seconds.

INDEPENDENCE

11159 KQMG-AM - 1220
231 1st St. E. Phone: (319)334-3300
Independence, IA 50644 Fax: (319)334-6158

Format: Adult Contemporary. **Networks:** ABC. **Owner:** Keene of Iowa, Inc., at above address. **Founded:** 1959. **Formerly:** KOUR-AM. **Key Personnel:** Don Morehead, General Mgr. **Wattage:** 250 day; 166 night. **Ad Rates:** Combined advertising rates available with KQMG-FM.

11160 KQMG-FM - 95.3
231 1st St. E Phone: (319)334-3300
Independence, IA 50644 Fax: (319)334-6158

Format: Adult Contemporary. **Networks:** ABC. **Owner:** Keene of Iowa, Inc., at above address. **Founded:** 1972. **Formerly:** KOUR-FM. **Key Personnel:** Don Morehead, General Mgr. **Wattage:** 6000. **Ad Rates:** Combined advertising rates available with KQMG-AM.

INDIANOLA†, pop. 10,843.

SC IA. Warren Co. 16 mi. S. of Des Moines. Simpson College (Meth.). Balloon museum. Grain elevators. Agriculture. Corn, oats, wheat.

11161 EXTRA
Record-Herald
1801 W. 2nd Ave., Ste. 2 Phone: (515)961-2511
PO Box 259 Fax: (515)961-4833
Indianola, IA 50125-0259
Shopper. **Founded:** 1972. **Freq:** Weekly (Tues.). **Print Method:** Offset. **Cols./Page:** 6. **Col. Width:** 2 inches. **Col. Depth:** 21 inches. **Key Personnel:** David Dear, Jr., Editor and Publisher; Daryl Barnard, Advertising Mgr. **Subscription Rates:** Free. **Remarks:** Accepts advertising.
Ad Rates: BW: $1,008 **Circ:** Free 11,500
4C: $1,208

11162 Record-Herald and Indianola Tribune
Record-Herald
1801 W. 2nd Ave., Ste. 2 Phone: (515)961-2511
PO Box 259 Fax: (515)961-4833
Indianola, IA 50125-0259
Community newspaper. **Founded:** 1855. **Freq:** Weekly (Wed.). **Print Method:** Offset. **Cols./Page:** 6. **Col. Width:** 24 nonpareils. **Col. Depth:** 21 inches. **Key Personnel:** David Dear, Jr., Editor and Publisher; Mike Rolands, Managing Editor. **ISSN:** 0895-3287. **Subscription Rates:** Free; $29 carrier; $35 out of area by mail. **Remarks:** Accepts advertising.
Ad Rates: BW: $1,023.12 **Circ:** Paid ‡5,056
4C: $1,223.12 Free ‡154
PCI: $8.12

11163 The Simpsonian
Simpson College
8 McNeil Hall Phone: (515)961-1738
Simpson College Fax: (515)961-1498
Indianola, IA 50125
Publication E-mail: thesimp@storm.simpson.edu

Collegiate newspaper (tabloid). **Founded:** Oct. 1, 1870. **Freq:** Weekly (Thurs.). **Print Method:** Letterpress and offset. **Trim Size:** 11 1/4 x 13 3/4. **Cols./Page:** 4. **Col. Width:** 2 3/8 inches. **Col. Depth:** 12 1/4 inches. **Key Personnel:** Cori Keeton, Editor; Allison Kelch, Business Mgr. **Subscription Rates:** $25 individuals. **Remarks:** Accepts advertising. **URL:** http://www.simpson.edu/~thesimp.
Ad Rates: BW: $156 **Circ:** ‡1,400
PCI: $3.25

11164 KJJC-FM - 107.1
PO Box 556 Phone: (515)961-9804
Indianola, IA 50125-0556 Fax: (515)961-3354
E-mail: sedwards@dwx.com

Format: Sports. **Networks:** ABC; ESPN Radio. **Founded:** 1982. **Operating Hours:** Continuous; 5% network, 95% local. **ADI:** Des Moines, IA. **Key Personnel:** Marty Tirrell, General Mgr.; Scott Pierce, Program Dir., spierce@kjjc.com; Ken Thompson, Asst. Program Dir. **Wattage:** 50,000. **Ad Rates:** $15-65 per unit. **URL:** http://www.kjjc.com.

INWOOD, pop. 755.

NW IA. Lyon Co. 32 mi. SE of Sioux Falls, SD. Meat processing plant; hatchery. Agriculture. Stock, grain and mink farms.

11165 West Lyon Herald
Lyon County Reporter
PO Box 340 Phone: (712)753-2258
Inwood, IA 51240 Fax: (712)753-4864

Community newspaper. **Founded:** Nov. 1900. **Freq:** Weekly (Wed.). **Print Method:** Offset. **Trim Size:** 11 1/2 x 16. **Cols./Page:** 5. **Col. Width:** 12.2 nonpareils. **Col. Depth:** 210 agate lines. **Key Personnel:** Jim Houck, Editor and Publisher; Pam Dykstra, Advertising Mgr. **Subscription Rates:** $20 in Lyon County; $22 in Iowa, S. Dakota, Minnesota; $27 elswhere in U.S. **Remarks:** Accepts advertising.
Ad Rates: BW: $315 **Circ:** Paid ‡1,700
4C: $545 Free ‡3,450
SAU: $4.10

IOWA CITY†, pop. 50,508.

E IA. Johnson Co. On Iowa River, 28 mi. S. of Cedar Rapids. University of Iowa. Manufactures adhesive paper, tooth brushes, toothpaste tubes, toiletries, foam rubber, feed, iron and sheet metal products, gravel and rock products. Bottling works; hatcheries; alfalfa drying. Stone quarries. Diversified farming, cattle feeding. Corn, oats, hay.

11166 The Advertiser
Publications, Inc.
PO Box 2597 Phone: (319)339-3114
Iowa City, IA 52244
Community newspaper and shopper. **Subtitle:** Community News Advertiser. **Founded:** 1981. **Freq:** Weekly (Wed.). **Print Method:** Offset. **Cols./Page:** 6. **Col. Width:** 9.5 picas. **Col. Depth:** 224 agate lines. **Key Personnel:** Scott Swenson, General Mgr.; Elaine Rayner, Sales Mgr. **Subscription Rates:** Free. **Remarks:** Accepts advertising.
Ad Rates: GLR: $.69 **Circ:** Free 35,638
BW: $926
4C: $1156
PCI: $9.65

11167 Annals of Iowa
State Historical Society of Iowa
402 Iowa Ave. Phone: (319)335-3931
Iowa City, IA 52240 Fax: (319)335-3935

State historical journal. **Founded:** 1863. **Freq:** Quarterly. **Print Method:** Offset. **Trim Size:** 6 x 9. **Cols./Page:** 1. **Col. Width:** 50 nonpareils. **Col. Depth:** 98 agate lines. **Key Personnel:** Marvin Bergman, Editor, phone (319)335-3931, mbergman@blue.weeg.uiowa.edu. **ISSN:** 0003-4827. **Subscription Rates:** $20 individuals; $6 single issue.
Ad Rates: BW: $150 **Circ:** ‡1,000

11168 Arteriosclerosis, Thrombosis, and Vascular Biology
American Heart Association
University of Iowa Phone: (319)353-5764
200 Hawkins Dr. Fax: (319)353-5766
609 MRC
Iowa City, IA 52242-1182
Publication E-mail: ATVB@uiowa.edu
Publisher E-mail: pubcust@amhrt.org

Journal featuring original research and reviews on the biology, prevention, and impact of vascular diseases. **Founded:** Jan. 1981. **Freq:** Monthly. **Print Method:** Offset. **Trim Size:** 8 1/8 x 10 7/8. **Cols./Page:** 2. **Col. Width:** 19 picas. **Col. Depth:** 57 picas. **Key Personnel:** Donald D. Heistad, Editor; Julie Eisele, Managing Editor. **ISSN:** 1079-5642. **Subscription Rates:** $196; $148 members; $228 institutions other countries. **Remarks:** Accepts advertising. **Alt. Formats:** CD-ROM. **Formerly:** Arteriosclerosis and Thrombosis: A Journal of Vascular Biology.
Ad Rates: BW: $685 **Circ:** ‡3,242
4C: $2,010

11169 Chord and Discord
Bruckner Society of America, Inc.
2150 Dubuque Rd. Phone: (319)351-5758
Iowa City, IA 52240-9632
Music journal covering the composers Anton Burckner and Gustav Mahler. **Founded:** 1993. **Freq:** Irregular. **Subscription Rates:** Free. **Remarks:** Advertising not accepted.
Circ: Non-paid 200

11170 Common Lives/Lesbian Lives
1802 7th Ave. Ct. Phone: (319)353-6265
Iowa City, IA 52240-6436
Magazine focusing on the lives of lesbians. Includes lesbian history, biography, correspondence, journal entries, fiction, poetry, and visual art. **Freq:** Quarterly.

11171 The Daily Iowan
Student Publications, Inc.
201 Communications Dept. Phone: (319)335-6063
Iowa City, IA 52242 Fax: (319)335-6297
Publication E-mail: daily-iowan@uiowa.edu

General newspaper. **Founded:** 1901. **Freq:** Daily (morn.) M - F. **Print Method:** Offset. **Trim Size:** 12 3/8 x 21. **Cols./Page:** 6. **Col. Width:** 2 1/16 inches. **Col. Depth:** 21 inches. **Key Personnel:** Brad Hahn, Editor; William B. Casey, Publisher; James Leonard, Advertising Mgr. **Subscription Rates:** $75 individuals. **Remarks:** Accepts advertising. **URL:** http://www.uiowa.edu/~dlyiowan.
Ad Rates: BW: $1,669.50 **Circ:** ‡20,500
4C: $300.75
SAU: $13.25
PCI: $13.25

11172 Iowa City Magazine
111 Wright St. Phone: (319)354-7738
Iowa City, IA 52240 Fax: (319)354-7738

Magazine for residents of and visitors to eastern Iowa. **Founded:** Sept. 1989. **Freq:** Monthly. **Print Method:** Web. **Trim Size:** 8 3/8 x 10 7/8. **Cols./Page:** 3. **Col. Width:** 2 1/2 inches. **Col. Depth:** 10 inches. **Key Personnel:** Christopher C. Green, Editor and Publisher. **Subscription Rates:** $19.70 annual; $2.50 single issue. **Remarks:** Accepts advertising. **Available Online. URL:** http://www.wcci.com/icmag.
Ad Rates: BW: $1,650 **Circ:** 20,000
4C: $1,900

11173 Iowa City Press Citizen
Gannett Co., Inc.
1725 N. Dodge St. Phone: (319)337-3181
Iowa City, IA 52245 Fax: (319)339-7342
Publication E-mail: icpc@inav.net

General newspaper. **Founded:** 1841. **Freq:** Daily (eve.) and Sat. (morn.). **Print Method:** Offset. **Trim Size:** 13 1/2 x 22 3/4. **Cols./Page:** 6. **Col. Width:** 2 inches. **Col. Depth:** 21.25 inches. **Key Personnel:** Charles T. Wanninger, Publisher, cwanninger@iowacity.gannett.com; Dave Parsons, Advertising Dir., dparsons@iowacity.gannett.com; Michael Beck, Managing Editor, mbeck@iowacity.gannett.com; Dan Brown, Market Development Dir., dbrown@iowacity.gannett.com. **Subscription Rates:** $130 individuals. **Remarks:** Saturday: BW: $2,538.53; 4C: $2,838.53; PCI: $19.91. **Feature Editors:** Chuck Gysi, *Art, Entertainment.*
Ad Rates: GLR: $2.44 **Circ:** Mon.-Fri. ★**15,472**
BW: $2,348.55 Sat. ★**18,573**
4C: $2,648.55
PCI: $18.42

11174 Iowa Heritage Illustrated
State Historical Society of Iowa
402 Iowa Ave. Phone: (319)335-3912
Iowa City, IA 52240 Fax: (319)335-3935

State history magazine. **Founded:** July 1920. **Freq:** Quarterly. **Print Method:** Offset. **Trim Size:** 8 1/2 x 11. **Cols./Page:** 2 and 3. **Col. Width:** 36 nonpareils. **Col. Depth:** 102 agate lines. **Key Personnel:** Ginalie Swaim, Editor, gswaim@blue.weeg.uiowa.edu. **ISSN:** 1088-5943. **Subscription Rates:** $19.95 individuals; $6 single issue. **Remarks:** Advertising not accepted. **Formerly:** The Palimpsest, Palimpsest.
Circ: ‡3,300

11175 Iowa Law Review
University of Iowa
Boyd Law Bldg., Rm. 188
Melrose & Byington
Iowa City, IA 52242
Publication E-mail: ilr@blue.weeg.uiowa.edu

Law journal. **Founded:** 1915. **Freq:** 5/year. **Print Method:** Letterpress. **Cols./Page:** 1. **Col. Width:** 56 nonpareils. **Col. Depth:** 112 agate lines. **ISSN:** 0021-0552. **Subscription Rates:** $36 individuals; $39 other countries; $10 single issue. **Remarks:** Accepts advertising. **Online:** Westlaw; LEXIS-NEXIS.
Ad Rates: BW: $50 **Circ:** 1,700

11176 Iowa Review
University of Iowa
308 EPB Phone: (319)335-0462
Iowa City, IA 52242
Publication E-mail: iowa-review@uiowa.edu

Literary journal. **Founded:** 1970. **Freq:** Triennial. **Print Method:** Offset. **Trim Size:** 6 x 9. **Key Personnel:** David Hamilton, Editor; Mary Hussmann, Editor. **ISSN:** 0021-065X. **Subscription Rates:** $18 individuals; $6.95 single issue. **Remarks:** Accepts advertising.
Ad Rates: BW: $200 **Circ:** Combined 2,700

11177 Journal of Clinical Immunoassay
Clinical Ligand Assay Society
200 Hawkins Dr. Phone: (319)356-1805
Iowa City, IA 52242 Fax: (319)356-8470
Publisher E-mail: clas@rust.net

Journal for pathologists, clinical chemists, and medical technologists. Focuses on ligand binding assays. **Founded:** 1978. **Freq:** Quarterly. **Print Method:** Offset. **Trim Size:** 8 1/4 x 11. **Cols./Page:** 2. **Col. Width:** 40 nonpareils. **Col. Depth:** 126 agate lines. **Key Personnel:** David Kellner, Ph.D., Publisher; Dr. George Johnson, PhD, Editor. **ISSN:** 0736-4393. **Subscription Rates:** $75 individuals; $80 Canada; $84 other countries. **Remarks:** Accepts advertising. **Formerly:** Ligand Quarterly (1983).
Ad Rates: BW: $760 **Circ:** ‡1,500
4C: $1,740

11178 Journal of Corporation Law
University of Iowa, College of Law
190 Boyd Law Bldg. Phone: (319)335-9061
Iowa City, IA 52242-1113 Fax: (319)335-9019
Publication E-mail: jcl@uiowa.edu

Law journal. **Founded:** 1975. **Freq:** Quarterly. **Key Personnel:** Chris Novak, Contact, phone (319)335-9065; Kendra Ball, Contact. **ISSN:** 0360-795X. **Subscription Rates:** $36 Domestic; $38 Foreign. **Remarks:** Accepts advertising. **Available Online.**
Ad Rates: BW: $50 **Circ:** Paid 800
Non-paid 200

11179 Journal of Lipid Research
609 MRC Phone: (319)353-5764
200 Hawkins Dr. Fax: (319)353-5767
Iowa City, IA 52242
Publication E-mail: jlipidres@uiowa.edu

Journal on Lipid Research. **Founded:** 1960. **Freq:** Monthly. **Print Method:** Offset. **Trim Size:** 8 1/2 x 11. **Cols./Page:** 2. **Col. Width:** 40 nonpareils. **Col. Depth:** 126 agate lines. **Key Personnel:** Dr. Lewis I. Gidez, Contact, phone (301)530-7100, fax (305)324-5665; Dr. Arthur A. Spector, Editor-in-Chief. **ISSN:** 0022-2275. **Subscription Rates:** $88 individuals; $262 institutions; $120 other countries industry; $252 other countries Industry; $292 single issue other countries Industry; $22 single issue. **Remarks:** Accepts advertising.
Ad Rates: BW: $494 **Circ:** Paid ‡2,029
4C: $955

11180 Journal of Paleontology Subscriptions
Allen Press
Department of Geology Fax: (319)535-1821
121 Trowbridge Hall
University of Iowa
Iowa City, IA 52242
Publication E-mail: fossils@hercules.geology.uiuc.edu

Scientific journal. **Founded:** 1927. **Freq:** Bimonthly. **Print Method:** Offset. **Trim Size:** 8 1/2 x 11. **Cols./Page:** 2. **Col. Width:** 30 nonpareils. **Col. Depth:** 105 agate lines. **Key Personnel:** A.F. Budd, Managing Editor; B.J. Witzke, Managing Editor; J. Golden, Managing Editor; T.J. Hazen, Assoc. Editor. **ISSN:** 0022-3360. **Subscription Rates:** $99. **Formerly:** Journal of Paleontology (1992).
Ad Rates: BW: $400 **Circ:** ‡2,500

11181 Journal of Personal and Interpersonal Loss
Taylor & Francis
Dept. of Psychology Phone: (319)335-2473
11 Seashore Hall E Fax: (319)335-2799
University of Iowa
Iowa City, IA 52242-1407
Publisher E-mail: info@taylorandfrancis.com

Journal focusing on personal losses relating to family, health, and aging issues and interpersonal losses surrounding such topics as marriage and divorce. **Founded:** 1996. **Freq:** Quarterly. **Print Method:** Offset. **Key Personnel:** John H. Harvey, Editor, john_harvey@uiowa.edu. **ISSN:** 1081-1443. **Subscription Rates:** $54 individuals; $139 institutions. **Remarks:** Accepts advertising.
Ad Rates: BW: $550 **Circ:** (Not Reported)
4C: $1,450

11182 Journal of Philosophical Research
Philosophy Documentation Center
c/o Professor Panayot Phone: (319)335-0495
Butcharov, Editor Fax: (319)353-2322
University of Iowa
Department of Philosophy
Iowa City, IA 52242-1488
Publication E-mail: poiesis@mailserver.bgsu.edu
Publisher E-mail: phildoc@opie.bgsu.edu

Scholarly journal covering philosophy. **Founded:** 1975. **Freq:** Annual. **Trim Size:** 6 x 9. **Key Personnel:** Prof. Panayot Butcharov, Editor, phone (319)335-0028, panayot_butcharov@uiowa.ed; Maurene Morgan, Editorial Asst., maurene_morgan@uiowa.edu. **ISSN:** 0153-8363. **Subscription Rates:** $32 individuals; $65 institutions. **Remarks:** Accepts advertising.
Circ: (Not Reported)

11183 Legislative Studies Quarterly
Comparative Legislative Research Center
University of Iowa Phone: (319)335-2361
334 Schaeffer Hall Fax: (319)335-3211
Iowa City, IA 52242
Publication E-mail: lsq@uiowa.edu

Political science journal. **Founded:** 1976. **Freq:** Quarterly. **Print Method:** Offset. **Trim Size:** 6 x 9. **Cols./Page:** 1. **Col. Width:** 51 nonpareils. **Col. Depth:** 98 agate lines. **Key Personnel:** Michelle L. Wiegand, Managing Editor; Gerhard Loewenberg, Contact/Co-Editor. **ISSN:** 0362-9805. **Subscription Rates:** $38 individuals; $19 students Add $10 for foreign address; $85 institutions. **Remarks:** Accepts advertising.
Ad Rates: BW: $100 **Circ:** Paid ‡1100
Non-paid ‡40

11184 Midwest Modern Language Association Journal
Midwest Modern Language Association
302 English-Philosophy Bldg. Phone: (319)335-0331
University of Iowa Fax: (319)335-3123
Iowa City, IA 52242-1408
Publisher E-mail: mmla@uiowa.edu

Scholarly journal covering book reviews and other academic

writing. **Founded:** 1968. **Freq:** Triennial. **Trim Size:** 6 x 9. **Key Personnel:** Thomas E. Lewis, Editor; Keli Eldridge, Managing Editor. **ISSN:** 0742-5562. **Subscription Rates:** $15 individuals; $20 Canada; $25 other countries; $7.50 single issue. **Remarks:** Accepts advertising. **Former name**: Bulletin of the Midwest Modern Language Association.
Ad Rates: BW: $225 **Circ:** Paid 2,000

11185 100 Words
International Writing Program
University of Iowa Phone: (319)335-0541
476 EPB Fax: (319)335-3843
Iowa City, IA 52242
Publication E-mail: carolyn-b-brown@uiowa.edu

Literary journal containing poetry and prose focused on a particular theme. **Founded:** Oct. 1993. **Freq:** 6/year. **Trim Size:** 4 3/4 x 8 1/4. **Subscription Rates:** $20 individuals; $3 single issue. **Remarks:** Advertising not accepted. **URL:** http://www.uiowa.edu/~100words.
Circ: 400

11186 Prairie News
Blooming Prairie Warehouse
2340 Heinz Rd. Phone: (319)337-6448
Iowa City, IA 52240 Fax: (319)337-4592

Food cooperatives magazine (tabloid). **Founded:** 1976. **Freq:** Bimonthly. **Print Method:** Offset. **Cols./Page:** 4. **Col. Width:** 26 nonpareils. **Col. Depth:** 226 agate lines. **Key Personnel:** Jodi DeMeulenaere, Editor/Administration. **Subscription Rates:** Free to qualified subscribers; $7.50 individuals. **Remarks:** Color advertising not accepted.
Ad Rates: BW: $350 **Circ:** Paid ‡200
Controlled ‡22,000

11187 Quill & Scroll
Quill and Scroll Society
University of Iowa Phone: (319)335-5795
School of Journalism & Mass Communication W312 55H Fax: (319)335-5210
Iowa City, IA 52242-1528
Publisher E-mail: quill-scroll@uiowa.edu

High school honorary journalism magazine. **Founded:** Oct. 1926. **Freq:** Quarterly. **Print Method:** Offset. **Trim Size:** 8 1/4 x 11. **Cols./Page:** 3. **Col. Width:** 13 picas. **Col. Depth:** 9 1/4 inches. **Key Personnel:** Richard P. Johns, Editor, richard-johns@uiowa.edu. **ISSN:** 0033-6505. **Subscription Rates:** $13 individuals; $3.75 single issue. **Available Online.**
Ad Rates: BW: $790 **Circ:** Paid ‡11,500
PCI: $200 Non-paid ‡152

11188 Special Recreation Digest
John A. Nesbitt
362 Koser Ave. Phone: (319)337-7578
Iowa City, IA 52246-3038
Magazine offering information on recreation needs of people with disabilities. **Subtitle:** Special Recreation for disABLED. **Freq:** Quarterly. **Subscription Rates:** $39.95 individuals. **Remarks:** Advertising not accepted.
Circ: (Not Reported)

11189 Syllecta Classica
University of Iowa
202 Schaeffer Hall
Iowa City, IA 52242
Publication E-mail: Syllecta@blue.weeg.uiowa.edu

Professional journal covering classical studies. **Founded:** 1989. **Freq:** Annual. **Cols./Page:** 1. **Key Personnel:** Helena Dettmer, Editor. **ISSN:** 1040-3612. **Subscription Rates:** $15 individuals; $30 institutions. **Remarks:** Accepts advertising.
Circ: Combined 120

11190 Walt Whitman Quarterly Review
University of Iowa
308 EPB Phone: (319)335-0592
Iowa City, IA 52242-1492 Fax: (319)335-2535

Academic journal featuring works about Walt Whitman. **Founded:** June 1983. **Freq:** Quarterly. **Print Method:** Offset. **Trim Size:** 6 x 9. **Cols./Page:** 1. **Col. Width:** 54 nonpareils. **Col. Depth:** 98 agate lines. **Key Personnel:** Edwin Folsom, Editor, ed-folsom@uiowa.edu. **ISSN:** 0737-0679. **Subscription Rates:** $15 individuals; $20 institutions; $4 single issue. **Remarks:** Accepts advertising. **URL:** http://www.wwqr.uiowa.edu.
Ad Rates: BW: $100 **Circ:** Paid 500
Non-paid 250

11191 KCJJ-AM - 1560
Box 2118 Phone: (319)354-1242
Iowa City, IA 52244 Fax: (319)354-1921

Format: Adult Contemporary; News; Sports. **Networks:** Jones Satellite; CNN Radio. **Owner:** River City Radio, at above address. **Founded:** 1977. **Operating Hours:** Continuous; 100% local. **ADI:** Cedar Rapids-Waterloo-Dubuque, IA. **Key Personnel:** Steve Bridges, Owner; Anthony Weller, News Dir.; Andy Andresen, Chief Engineer. **Wattage:** 1000. **Ad Rates:** $18 for 30 seconds; $21 for 60 seconds.

11192 KKRQ-FM - 100.7
PO Box 2388 Phone: (319)354-9500
Iowa City, IA 52244

Format: Top 40. **Networks:** ABC. **Owner:** Heartland Media Inc., at above address. **Founded:** 1966. **Key Personnel:** Ted Jacobsen, Program Dir.; Jerry Kintz, News Dir.; Steve Winkey, General Mgr. **Wattage:** 100,000.

11193 KRNA-FM - 94.1
2105 ACT Circle Phone: (319)362-0393
Iowa City, IA 52245-9636 Fax: (319)351-4943
E-mail: krna@krna.com

Format: Album-Oriented Rock (AOR). **Networks:** Independent. **Owner:** KRNA, Inc., at above address, (319)351-9300. **Founded:** 1974. **Operating Hours:** Continuous; 100% local. **ADI:** Cedar Rapids-Waterloo-Dubuque, IA. **Key Personnel:** Eliot A. Keller, PRS/Gen. Mgr., ekeller@krna.com; Robert K. Norton, Jr., EVP/Operations Mgr., rob@krna.com; Kellie J. Lala, Sales Mgr.; Chris Donahue, Office Mgr.; Joe Nugent, Program Dir.; Maureen Bradley, Production Director. **Wattage:** 100,000. **Ad Rates:** $36-60 for 30 seconds; $40-70 for 60 seconds. Combined advertising rates available with KXMX-FM.

11194 KRUI-FM - 89.7
129 Grand Ave. Ct. Phone: (319)335-9525
Iowa City, IA 52242 Fax: (319)335-9526
E-mail: krui@uiowa.edu

Format: Urban Contemporary; Alternative/New Music/Progressive. **Networks:** AP. **Owner:** Student Broadcasters, Inc., at above address. **Founded:** 1984. **Operating Hours:** Continuous; 100% local. **Key Personnel:** Matthew Walsh, General Mgr., mjwalsh@blue.weeg.uiowa.edu; Jennifer DeMarah, Program Dir., jdemarah@blue.weeg.uiowa.edu; Nick Schaub, Chief Engineer, schaub@blue.weeg.uiowa.edu. **Wattage:** 100. **URL:** http://www.uiowa.edu/~krui.

11195 KSUI-FM - 91.7
3300 Engineering Bldg. Phone: (319)335-5730
University of Iowa Fax: (319)335-6116
Iowa City, IA 52242

Format: Public Radio; Classical. **Networks:** National Public Radio (NPR). **Owner:** Iowa State Board of Regents, at above address. **Founded:** 1948. **Operating Hours:** Continuous. **Key Personnel:** John Fisher, Program Dir. **Wattage:** 100,000. **Ad Rates:** Noncommercial.

11196 KXIC-AM - 800
PO Box 2388 Phone: (319)354-9500
Iowa City, IA 52244-2388 Fax: (319)354-9504

Format: News. **Networks:** CNN Radio. **Owner:** Iowa City Broadcasting, at above address. **Founded:** 1948. **Operating Hours:** Continuous; 90% network, 10% local. **Key Personnel:** Steve Winkey, General Mgr.; Jerry Kintz, Contact; Roy Justis, Program Dir. **Wattage:** 5000. **Ad Rates:** $8-24 for 30 seconds.

11197 PEC Cable
Eastdale Plaza Phone: (319)351-2297
1700 1st Ave., No. 1 Fax: (319)358-5810
Iowa City, IA 52240

Owner: Professional Engineering Consultants, Inc., at above address. **Founded:** 1989. **Key Personnel:** Jim Peterson, President, phone (319)351-2297, fax (319)358-5810; Joe Peterson, Vice President, joepeter@aol.com. **Cities Served:** Nichols, IA: subscribing households 95; 22 channels.

11198 TCI of Eastern Iowa
Box 4500 Phone: (319)351-3984
Iowa City, IA 52244 Fax: (319)351-3839

Founded: 1980. **Formerly**: Heritage Cablevision. **Key Personnel:** Arlene Heck, General Mgr., phone (319)351-3984, fax (319)351-3839; Stacey Tillery, Office Mgr.; Denis Martel, Technical Operations Manager. **Cities Served:** Coralville, Johnston County, University Heights, IA: subscribing households 24,000; 37 channels; 5 community access channels; 840 hours per week community access programming.

11199 WSUI-AM - 910
710 CLSB, Univ. of Iowa Phone: (319)335-5730
Iowa City, IA 52242 Fax: (319)335-6116

Format: Public Radio; Talk; News. **Networks:** National Public Radio (NPR). **Owner:** University of Iowa, at above address. **Founded:** 1919. **Operating Hours:** Continuous; 70% network, 30% local. **ADI:** Cedar Rapids-Waterloo-Dubuque, IA. **Key Personnel:** John Monick, General Mgr., john-monick@uiowa.edu; Dennis Reese, Program Dir., dennis-reese@uiowa.edu; Terry Edmonds, Chief Engineer. **Wattage:** 5000. **Ad Rates:** Noncommercial.

IOWA FALLS, pop. 6,174.

C IA. Hardin Co. On Iowa River, 50 mi. W. of Waterloo. Manufactures luggage, pre-stressed concrete beams, plastic injection molded containers, portable grain aerators, steel mandrels. Agriculture. Dairy, stock, grain farms. Corn, soybeans, oats, rye.

11200 The Advertiser
406 Stevens Phone: (515)648-2521
Box 640 Fax: (515)648-4765
Iowa Falls, IA 50126
Free: (800)373-1719
Publication E-mail: linonline@aol.com

Advertiser broadsheet. **Freq:** Weekly. **Print Method:** Offset. **Cols./Page:** 6. **Col. Width:** 2 1/6 inches. **Col. Depth:** 21 inches. **Key Personnel:** Mark H. Hamilton, Publisher; Jo Martin, General Mgr.; Kent Osborn, Advertising Mgr. **Subscription Rates:** Free. **Remarks:** Accepts advertising. **Formerly**: The Citizen Shopper.
Ad Rates: BW: $610.79 **Circ:** Free 9,000
4C: $835.79
SAU: $6.55
PCI: $6.55

11201 Spokesman
Iowa Farm Bureau Federation
406 Stevens Phone: (515)648-2521
Iowa Falls, IA 50126 Fax: (515)648-4606
Free: (800)442-3276

Agricultural newspaper. **Founded:** 1934. **Freq:** Weekly. **Print Method:** Offset. **Trim Size:** 11 1/4 x 17. **Cols./Page:** 5. **Col. Width:** 1.9 inches. **Col. Depth:** 15 1/2 inches. **Key Personnel:** Darryl Jahn, Editor, phone (515)225-5413, fax (515)225-5419; Mark Hamilton, Publisher; Jo E. Martin, General Mgr.; Don Dauterive, National Account Mgr.; Larry Tucker, Co-op Account Manager. **Subscription Rates:** $7 individuals. **Remarks:** Accepts advertising.
Ad Rates: BW: $5,037.50 **Circ:** Paid 105,294
4C: $5,588
PCI: $60

11202 Times-Citizen
Times-Citizen Co.
406 Stevens Phone: (515)648-2521
PO Box 640 Fax: (515)648-4765
Iowa Falls, IA 50126-0640
Publication E-mail: linonline@aol.com
Publisher E-mail: tcc@iafalls.com

Community newspaper. **Founded:** Aug. 28, 1891. **Freq:** Semiweekly (Wed. and Sat.). **Print Method:** Offset. **Trim Size:** 15 x 22 1/2. **Cols./Page:** 6. **Col. Width:** 12 1/2 picas. **Col. Depth:** 21 inches. **Key Personnel:** Elaine Loring, Editor; Mark H. Hamilton, Publisher; Kent Osborn, Advertising Mgr.; Jo Martin, General Mgr. **ISSN:** 2351-8000. **Subscription Rates:** $28 individuals; $36 out of area; $40 out of state. **Online:** America Online, Inc. **Absorbed**: Iowa Falls Citizen. **Formerly**: Hardin County Times (1992).
Ad Rates: GLR: $.30 **Circ:** Paid ‡4,200
BW: $610.79 Free ‡9,000
4C: $881.70
SAU: $6.55
PCI: $5.51

11203 KIFG-AM - 95.3
410 Washington Phone: (515)648-4281
Iowa Falls, IA 50126 Fax: (515)648-2433

Format: Country. **Simulcasts:** KIFG-FM. **Networks:** Independent. **Owner:** PBW Broadcasting Corp., at above address. **Founded:** 1962. **Operating Hours:** 17 hrs daily; 100% local. **Key Personnel:** James W. Starr, Manager, phone (515)648-9528; John P. Whitesell, President, phone (515)648-4646. **Local Programs:** *Daily Diary*, Jim Starr; *Trading Post*, Pat Dunn; *Worry Bird*, Jim Starr. **Wattage:** 6000 FM. **Ad Rates:** $5.50-8.00 for 30 seconds; $6.50-9 for 60 seconds.

11204 KIFG-FM - 95.3
308 1/2 Stevens St. Phone: (515)648-4281
PO Box 307 Fax: (515)648-2433
Iowa Falls, IA 50126

Format: Country. **Simulcasts:** KIFG-AM. **Networks:** Independent. **Owner:** John P. Whitesell, at above address. **Founded:** 1964. **Operating Hours:** 17 hours Daily; 100% local. **Key Personnel:** James W. Starr, Manager; John P. Whitesell, President. **Local Programs:** *Worry Bird*, Jim Starr, Mailing contact. **Wattage:** 6000. **Ad Rates:** $4.45-7.25 for 30 seconds; $5.25-8 for 60 seconds.

IRETON, pop. 588.

NW IA. Sioux Co. 15 mi. W. of Alton. Residential.

11205 Ireton Examiner
Ireton Printing
Box 218 Phone: (712)278-2092
Ireton, IA 51027 Fax: (712)278-2926

Newspaper. **Founded:** 1954. **Freq:** Weekly (Wed.). **Print Method:** Offset. **Trim Size:** 12.5 x 16.5 picas. **Cols./Page:** 5. **Col. Width:** 27 nonpareils. **Col. Depth:** 189 agate lines. **Key Personnel:** Sharla Gradert, Editor, phone (712)278-2198, fax (712)722-2670. **Subscription Rates:** $15 individuals. **Remarks:** Accepts advertising.
Ad Rates: BW: $255.75 **Circ:** ‡640
SAU: $3.10

JEFFERSON†, pop. 4,854.

W IA. Greene Co. 40 mi. W. of Ames. Manufactures electric appliance parts, sporting goods, rivets, feed, farm equipment, washing machine transmission. Agriculture.

11206 The Bee
Bee and Herald Publishing Co., Inc.
214 N. Wilson Ave. Phone: (515)386-4161
PO Box 440 Fax: (515)386-4162
Jefferson, IA 50129
Community newspaper. **Founded:** 1866. **Freq:** Weekly (Tues.). **Print Method:** Offset. **Trim Size:** 16 3/4 x 22 3/4. **Cols./Page:** 7. **Col. Width:** 25 nonpareils. **Col. Depth:** 294 agate lines. **Key Personnel:** Frederick G. Morain, Editor and Publisher. **Subscription Rates:** Free to qualified subscribers; $26 individuals; $34.50 out of state. **Remarks:** Accepts advertising.
Ad Rates: GLR: $0.40 **Circ:** Paid 200
BW: $823.20 Free 7,100
SAU: $5.60

11207 The Jefferson Herald
Bee and Herald Publishing Co., Inc.
214 N. Wilson Ave. Phone: (515)386-4161
PO Box 440 Fax: (515)386-4162
Jefferson, IA 50129
Community newspaper. **Founded:** 1895. **Freq:** Weekly (Thurs.). **Print Method:** Offset. **Trim Size:** 16 3/4 x 22 3/4. **Cols./Page:** 7. **Col. Width:** 25 nonpareils. **Col. Depth:** 294 agate lines. **Key Personnel:** Frederick G. Morain, Editor and Publisher. **USPS:** 273-840. **Subscription Rates:** $26 individuals; $34.50 out of state. **Remarks:** Advertising not accepted for liquor and tobacco products.
Ad Rates: GLR: $0.31 **Circ:** 2,948
BW: $639.45
SAU: $4.35

11208 KGRA-FM - 98.9
116 E. State Phone: (515)386-2222
Jefferson, IA 50129 Fax: (515)386-2215
E-mail: kg98@netins.net

Format: News; Country; Talk; Oldies. **Networks:** ABC. **Founded:** 1994. **Formerly:** KLSN-FM (1993). **Operating Hours:** Continuous. **ADI:** Des Moines, IA. **Key Personnel:** Jim McBride, Owner; Pat Delaney, Owner; Gary Blair, Station & Sales Mgr. **Wattage:** 25,000. **Ad Rates:** $6.75-8.25 for 15 seconds; $9-11 for 30 seconds; $12-14.50 for 60 seconds. Combined advertising rates available with KKRF.

JESUP, pop. 2,343.

NEC IA. Buchanan Co. 9 mi. W. of Independence. Residential.

11209 Citizen Herald
Horizon Publishing Co.
930 6th St. Phone: (319)827-1128
Box 545 Fax: (319)827-1125
Jesup, IA 50648-0545
Publication E-mail: jesupch@aol.com

Local newspaper. **Founded:** 1901. **Freq:** Weekly (Wed.). **Print Method:** Offset. **Trim Size:** 7 1/4 x 11 1/4. **Cols./Page:** 6. **Col. Width:** 12.5 picas. **Col. Depth:** 21 1/2 inches. **Key Personnel:** Kim Edwards Adams, Editor and Publisher. **USPS:** 113-980. **Subscription Rates:** $20.00 individuals; $26.00.
Ad Rates: BW: $541.80 **Circ:** Paid ‡1,192
SAU: $4.20
PCI: $4.20

JEWELL, pop. 1,145.

C IA. Hamilton Co. 14 mi. SE of Webster City. Residential.

11210 South Hamilton Record News
PO Box 130 Phone: (515)827-5931
Jewell, IA 50130 Fax: (515)827-5760

Local and agriculture business newspaper. **Founded:** 1881. **Freq:** Weekly (Thurs.). **Print Method:** Offset. **Cols./Page:** 6. **Col. Width:** 24 nonpareils. **Col. Depth:** 301 agate lines. **Key Personnel:** Scott Ervin, Editor and Publisher. **Subscription Rates:** $25 individuals. **Remarks:** Accepts advertising.
Ad Rates: SAU: $3.65 **Circ:** 950
PCI: $2.50

JOHNSTON, pop. 2,617.

C IA. Polk Co. 5 mi. N. of Des Moines. Near Saylorville Lake. Residential.

KDIN-TV - See Des Moines

KHIN-TV - See Red Oak

KIIN-TV - See Des Moines

11211 KRIN-TV - 32
Iowa Public Television Phone: (515)242-3100
PO Box 6450
Johnston, IA 50131

Format: Public TV. **Simulcasts:** KDIN-TV Des Moines, IA. **Networks:** Public Broadcasting Service (PBS). **Founded:** 1974. **ADI:** Cedar Rapids-Waterloo-Dubuque, IA. **Key Personnel:** David Bolender, Exec. Dir.; Dennis Malloy, Dir. of Dev.; Daniel K. Miller, Program Dir.; Don Saveraid, Dir. of Eng.; John Leiendecker, Production Mgr.; Pam Johnson, Dir. of Educ. Telecomm.; Sid Sprecher, Public Affairs.

KSIN-TV - See Sioux City

KTIN-TV - See Fort Dodge

KYIN-TV - See Mason City

KALONA, pop. 1,862.

SE IA. Washington Co. 18 mi. SW of Iowa City. Creamery; elevator. Grain farms. Corn, oats, wheat.

11212 The Kalona News
419 B Ave. Phone: (319)656-2273
PO Box 430 Fax: (319)656-2299
Kalona, IA 52247-0430
Publication E-mail: knews@kctc.news

Community newspaper. **Founded:** 1891. **Freq:** Weekly (Thurs.). **Print Method:** Offset. **Cols./Page:** 6. **Col. Width:** 12 picas. **Col. Depth:** 21 1/2 inches. **Key Personnel:** Ronald C. Slechtra, Publisher. **USPS:** 289-560. **Subscription Rates:** $25 individuals; $28 out of area; $32 out of state. **Remarks:** Accepts advertising. **Online:** Kalona Cooperative Telephone Co. **URL:** http://www./ketc.net/knews. **Alt. Formats:** CD-ROM.
Ad Rates: BW: $500 **Circ:** 3,200
4C: $550
SAU: $5.25
PCI: $5.25

KANAWHA, pop. 756.

N IA. Hancock Co. 40 mi. NE of Fort Dodge. Northern Iowa Research Station for Iowa State University. Manufactures horse trailers, sportswear. Grain elevators. Agriculture. Corn, soybeans.

11213 The Kanawha Reporter
101 N. Main St. Phone: (515)762-3994
PO Box 190 Fax: (515)762-3994
Kanawha, IA 50447
Community newspaper. **Subtitle:** Legal Newspaper for Kanawha & Klemme and West Hancock School District. **Founded:** July 1899. **Freq:** Weekly (Thurs.). **Print Method:** Offset. **Trim Size:** 12 1/2 x 21. **Cols./Page:** 6. **Col. Width:** 2 inches. **Col. Depth:** 21 inches. **Key Personnel:** Rodger Tveiten, Editor and Publisher. **USPS:** 289-620. **Subscription Rates:** $22 individuals local; $25 other Iowa; $28 out of state. **Remarks:** Accepts advertising.
Ad Rates: BW: $200 **Circ:** Paid 800
SAU: $2.50 Free 100
PCI: $2.26

11214 Norway Cablevision Inc.
105 S. Main Phone: (515)762-3772
PO Box 20 Fax: (515)762-8201
Kanawha, IA 50447
Free: (800)469-3772

Owner: Norway Cablevision Inc., at above address. **Founded:** 1983. **Key Personnel:** Randy Yeakel, Contact; Randy Yeaket, Manager. **Cities Served:** subscribing households 371; 18 channels; 1 community access channel; 168 hours per week community access programming.

KEOKUK†, pop. 13,536.

SE IA. Lee Co. On Mississippi River at mouth of Des Moines River, 18 mi. S. of Fort Madison. Bridge to Hamilton, IL. Boat connections. Hydro-electric power plant. Sawmill. Manufactures starch, corn, dairy products, ferro-alloys, shipping cases, cereals, canned goods, fibre boxes, calcium-carbide, rubber products, steel and aluminum die castings, railroad wheels. Limestone quarries. Diversified farming.

11215 Daily Gate City
Brehm Communications, Inc.
c/o Daily Gate City Phone: (319)524-8300
1016 Main St. Fax: (319)524-4363
PO Box 430
Keokuk, IA 52632
Free: (800)779-8819
Publication E-mail: gatecity@interl.net; dailygate@interl.com

General newspaper. **Founded:** 1847. **Freq:** Daily (eve.). **Print Method:** Offset. **Cols./Page:** 8. **Col. Width:** 18 nonpareils. **Col. Depth:** 301 agate lines. **Key Personnel:** Jeff Hanan, Managing Editor; P. Wesley Grooms, Advertising Mgr.; Bill DeLost, Publisher. **Subscription Rates:** $83.20 individuals. **Online:** AP - AdSend. **URL:** http://www.dailygate.com.
Ad Rates: GLR: $7.90 **Circ:** Combined 23,300
PCI: $11.96

11216 KOKX-AM - 1310
PO Box 427 Phone: (319)524-5410
Keokuk, IA 52632-0427 Fax: (319)524-7275

Format: News; Talk. **Networks:** Mutual Broadcasting System. **Owner:** W. Russell Withers, Jr., PO Box 1508, Mount Vernon, IL 62864, (618)242-3500. **Founded:** 1947. **Operating Hours:** Continuous. **Key Personnel:** Tim Hawkin, Program Dir.; Jim Worrell, News Dir.; James K. Withers, General Mgr. **Local Programs:** *Tri-State This Week* 8:30 am - 9:00 am Saturday, Jim Worrell. **Wattage:** 1000. **Ad Rates:** Combined advertising rates available with KOKX-FM.

11217 KOKX-FM - 95.3
108 Washington Phone: (319)524-5410
PO Box 427 Fax: (319)524-7275
Keokuk, IA 52632

Format: Country. **Networks:** Mutual Broadcasting System. **Owner:** Russ Withers, at above address. **Founded:** 1973. **Operating Hours:** Continuous. **Key Personnel:** Jim Worrell, News Dir.; Tim Hawkins, Program Dir.; James K. Withers, General Mgr. **Wattage:** 3000. **Ad Rates:** Combined advertising rates available with KOKX-AM.

KEOSAUQUA†, pop. 1,003.

SE IA. Van Buren Co. 35 mi. W. of Fort Madison. State park. Historical. Residential.

11218 Van Buren County Register
Louisa Publishing Co., Ltd.
106 Van Buren St. Phone: (319)293-3197
PO Box 477
Keosauqua, IA 52565
Publisher E-mail: lpc@lisco.net

Community newspaper with Report orientation. **Freq:** Weekly (Thurs.). **Print Method:** Offset. Uses mats. **Cols./Page:** 8. **Col. Width:** 22 nonpareils. **Col. Depth:** 294 agate lines. **Key Personnel:** James L. Hodges, Publisher. **Subscription Rates:** $14 individuals; $17 out of area. **Remarks:** Accepts advertising.
Ad Rates: GLR: $.17 **Circ:** ‡2,987
PCI: $2.52

KEOTA, pop. 1,034.

SE IA. Keokuk Co. 35 mi. SW of Iowa City. Farm equipment, egg producing factories. Dairy, stock, grain farms. Corn, hogs, cattle.

11219 The Keota Eagle
Box 18 Phone: (515)636-2309
Keota, IA 52248 Fax: (515)622-2766

Newspaper. **Founded:** Dec. 25, 1875. **Freq:** Weekly (Wed.). **Print Method:** Offset. **Trim Size:** 7 x 11 1/2. **Cols./Page:** 6. **Col. Width:** 11.6 picas. **Col. Depth:** 21. inches. **Key Personnel:** Kenneth Chaney, Publisher; Angie Carr, Editor. **USPS:**

293-620. **Subscription Rates:** $14 individuals; $16 out of area. **Remarks:** Accepts advertising.
Ad Rates: BW: $382.50 **Circ:** ‡1,350
SAU: $2.40
PCI: $2.55

KEYSTONE

11220 South Benton Cablevision, Inc.
86 Main St. Phone: (319)442-3243
Keystone, IA 52249-0277 Fax: (319)442-3210

Owner: Keystone Farmers Cooperative Telephone Co., at above address. **Key Personnel:** John C. Brady, Manager. **Cities Served:** subscribing households 363; 23 channels; 1 community access channel; 168 hours per week community access programming.

KNOXVILLE†, pop. 8,143.

SC IA. Marion Co. 38 mi. SE of Des Moines. Ships coal, livestock. Coal mines. Stock, poultry, dairy farms.

11221 Journal-Express
Journal/Express Inc.
Journal/Express Inc. Phone: (515)842-2155
122 E. Robinson Fax: (515)842-2929
PO Box 458
Knoxville, IA 50138
Community newspaper. **Founded:** 1855. **Freq:** Weekly (Fri.). **Print Method:** Offset. **Cols./Page:** 6. **Col. Width:** 39 nonpareils. **Col. Depth:** 6 x 21 1 inches. **Key Personnel:** Jack Crook, Publisher. **USPS:** 297-440. **Subscription Rates:** $27 individuals. **Remarks:** Accepts advertising.
Ad Rates: BW: $743.35 **Circ:** 3500
4C: $1,048.85
SAU: $6.40

11222 The Reminder
Journal/Express Inc.
Journal/Express Inc. Phone: (515)842-2155
122 E. Robinson Fax: (515)842-2929
PO Box 458
Knoxville, IA 50138
Shopper. **Founded:** 1940. **Freq:** Weekly (Tues.). **Print Method:** Offset. **Cols./Page:** 6. **Col. Width:** 12 picas. **Col. Depth:** 294 agate lines. **Key Personnel:** Jack Crook, Publisher; Don Abrams, Advertising Mgr. **Remarks:** Accepts advertising.
Ad Rates: PCI: $6.75 **Circ:** Free 12,600

11223 KNIA-AM - 1320
1610 N. Lincoln Phone: (515)842-3161
P.O.Box 31 Fax: (515)842-5606
Knoxville, IA 50138

Networks: USA Radio. **Owner:** Mel Suhr / M and H Broadcastisng Inc., at above address. **Founded:** 1983. **Operating Hours:** 5 a.m.-11 p.m.; 2% network, 98% local. **Key Personnel:** Mel Suhr, Owner; Mike Sherman, Sports Dir.; Trevor Castle, News Dir.; Jim Butler, General Mgr.; J.B. Conoley, News & Sports Director, phone (515)628-9494. **Wattage:** 500 day; 250 night. **Ad Rates:** Combined advertising rates available with KRLS-FM.

LA PORTE CITY, pop. 2,324.

NEC IA. Black Hawk Co. 15 mi. SE of Waterloo. Feed mill. Agriculture. Corn, oats, soy beans.

11224 Progress Review
313 Main St. Phone: (319)342-2429
La Porte City, IA 50651 Fax: (319)342-2433

Newspaper. **Founded:** 1868. **Freq:** Weekly (Wed.). **Print Method:** Offset. **Trim Size:** 8 1/2 x 11. **Cols./Page:** 6. **Col. Width:** 10 inches. **Col. Depth:** 16 inches. **Key Personnel:** Robert Wagner, Publisher; Diane Roberts, Editor. **Subscription Rates:** $22 local; $25 out of state. **Remarks:** Accepts advertising.
Ad Rates: GLR: $.41 **Circ:** Paid 1,400
BW: $302.12 1,500
SAU: $4.80
PCI: $3.22

LAKE CITY

11225 Lake City Graphic
103 N. Center St. Phone: (712)464-3188
PO Box 121 Fax: (712)464-3188
Lake City, IA 51449
Community newspaper. **Founded:** 1892. **Freq:** Weekly (Wed.). **Print Method:** Offset. **Trim Size:** 17 x 21 1/2. **Cols./Page:** 8. **Col. Width:** 10 1/2 picas. **Col. Depth:** 21.5 picas. **Key Personnel:** Daniel Jackson, Publisher. **Subscription Rates:** $19; $22 out of area. **Remarks:** Accepts advertising.
Ad Rates: BW: $500 **Circ:** ‡1,800
4C: $1,000
SAU: $5.04
PCI: $3.40

LAKE MILLS, pop. 2,281.

N IA. Winnebago Co. 25 mi. NW of Mason City. Manufactures plastics, doors, windows, auto filters; creamery. Dairy, grain, stock farms.

11226 Graphic
Lake Mills Graphic
204 N. Mill St. Phone: (515)592-4222
Box 127 Fax: (515)592-6397
Lake Mills, IA 50450
Newspaper with a Republican orientation. **Founded:** 1872. **Freq:** Weekly (Wed.). **Print Method:** Offset. **Cols./Page:** 6. **Col. Width:** 28 nonpareils. **Col. Depth:** 301 agate lines. **Key Personnel:** Harris D. Honsey, Editor and Publisher. **Subscription Rates:** $18 individuals. **Remarks:** Accepts advertising.
Ad Rates: GLR: $.16 **Circ:** 2,990

11227 Winnebago Co-op Cablevision
704 E. Main St. Phone: (515)592-1000
Lake Mills, IA 50450 Fax: (515)592-6102
E-mail: wcta@wctatel.com

Founded: 1980. **Formerly:** Lake Mills Cablevision (1982). **Key Personnel:** Terry Wegener, General Mgr. **Cities Served:** Buffalo Center, Lake Mills, Thompson, IA: subscribing households 1,300; 24 channels; 1 community access channel; 24 hours per week community access programming.

LAKE VIEW, pop. 1,291.

W IA. Sac Co. 50 mi. SW of Fort Dodge. Lake resort. Gravel, cement block, tile plants. Agriculture. Corn, oats, popcorn.

11228 Lake View Resort and Green Saver
PO Box 470 Phone: (712)657-8588
Lake View, IA 51450 Fax: (712)657-2495

Newspaper. **Founded:** 1889. **Freq:** Weekly (Wed.). **Print Method:** Offset. **Cols./Page:** 6. **Col. Width:** 19 nonpareils. **Col. Depth:** 135 agate lines. **Key Personnel:** Penny Garrels, phone (712)657-2495; Marcia Haakenson, Editor, phone (712)657-2495. **Subscription Rates:** $17.50 individuals; $21 out of area.
Ad Rates: GLR: $.41 **Circ:** ‡1,650
SAU: $5.21
PCI: $4.50

LAMONI, pop. 2,705.

S IA. Decatur Co. 70 mi. S. of Des Moines. Graceland College. Meat processing plant. Ships livestock. Dairy products. Agriculture. Corn, soybeans, alfalfa.

11229 Chronicle
PO Box 40 Phone: (515)784-6397
Lamoni, IA 50140-0040 Fax: (515)784-7669

Newspaper. **Founded:** 1894. **Freq:** Weekly (Wed.). **Print Method:** Offset. **Cols./Page:** 4. **Col. Width:** 29 nonpareils. **Col. Depth:** 210 agate lines. **Key Personnel:** David O. Allen, Editor and Publisher. **Subscription Rates:** $10 individuals.

11230 Dean's Cablevision Inc.
115 S. Linden Phone: (515)784-6764
Lamoni, IA 50140 Fax: (515)784-7327
Free: (800)798-5488

Founded: 1978. **Key Personnel:** Robert D. Pierce, Owner/Pres.; Darren G. Hamilton, Chief Technician; Janice L. Bowers, Office Mgr. **Cities Served:** subscribing households 988; 20 channels.

LANSING, pop. 1,181.

NE IA. Allamakee Co. On Mississippi River, 36 mi. S. of La Crosse, WI. Park and recreational areas. Timber; fisheries. Agriculture. Cattle, hogs, corn.

11231 Barr's Post Card News
70 S. 6th St. Phone: (319)538-4500
Lansing, IA 52151 Fax: (319)538-4038
Free: (800)397-0145
Publisher E-mail: bpcn@salamander.com

Newspaper (tabloid) promoting the collecting of picture post cards. **Subtitle:** The World's Largest Deltiology Newspaper. **Founded:** Aug. 1974. **Freq:** Weekly. **Print Method:** Offset. **Trim Size:** 11 1/2 x 16. **Cols./Page:** 5. **Col. Width:** 1 7/8 inches. **Col. Depth:** 14.5 picas. **Key Personnel:** Bill Cote, Editor; Candy Cote, Advertising Mgr. **ISSN:** 0744-4540. **Subscription Rates:** $36 individuals; $46 Canada; $150 other countries. **Remarks:** Accepts advertising.
Circ: Paid ‡6,500
Non-paid ‡650

LAURENS, pop. 1,606.

NW IA. Pocahontas Co. 40 mi. NW of Fort Dodge. Food distribution center. Magazine printing plant. Hydraulic lifting devices and services. Manufactures hydraulic cylinders, robotics, tools & dies Grist mill. Ships grain. Livestock. Diversified farming.

11232 The Laurens Reminder
The Laurens Sun
119 S. 3rd St. Phone: (712)845-4541
PO Box 125 Fax: (712)845-4542
Laurens, IA 50554-0125
Shopper. **Founded:** 1940. **Freq:** Weekly (Wed.). **Print Method:** Offset. **Trim Size:** 15 x 23. **Cols./Page:** 8. **Col. Width:** 9.5 picas. **Col. Depth:** 300 agate lines. **Key Personnel:** Dar Chaffee, Editor; William Chaffee, Publisher. **Remarks:** Accepts advertising.
Ad Rates: GLR: $.27 **Circ:** Free 5,600
BW: $653.6
4C: $853.6
SAU: $4.3
PCI: $3.8

11233 The Laurens Sun
119 S. 3rd St. Phone: (712)845-4541
PO Box 125 Fax: (712)845-4542
Laurens, IA 50554-0125
Community newspaper. **Founded:** 1885. **Freq:** Weekly (Thurs.). **Print Method:** Offset. **Trim Size:** 15 x 23. **Cols./Page:** 8. **Col. Width:** 9.5 picas. **Col. Depth:** 300 agate lines. **Key Personnel:** Dar Chaffee, Editor; William Chaffee, Publisher. **USPS:** 306-040. **Subscription Rates:** $20 individuals; $22 out of area; $25 out of state. **Remarks:** Accepts advertising.
Ad Rates: GLR: $.21 **Circ:** ‡1,450
BW: $533
4C: $733
SAU: $3.6
PCI: $3

LE MARS†, pop. 8,276.

NW IA. Plymouth Co. 25 mi. NE of Sioux City. Westmar College. Foundry. Manufactures jeans and outerwear; cleaning chemicals processing. District utility headquarters, fertilizer, feed mills; meat processing, beef packing, dairy plants. Ships grain, livestock. Agriculture.

11234 The Daily Sentinel
La Mars Daily Sentinel
PO Box 930 Phone: (712)546-7031
Le Mars, IA 51031 Fax: (712)546-7035

Independent newspaper. **Founded:** 1870. **Freq:** Daily (eve.). **Print Method:** Offset. **Cols./Page:** 6. **Col. Width:** 27 nonpareils. **Col. Depth:** 301 agate lines. **Key Personnel:** John Buntsma, Editor; Alan C. Portner, Publisher. **Subscription Rates:** $79 individuals. **Remarks:** Accepts advertising.
Ad Rates: GLR: $.397 **Circ:** ‡4,025
BW: $699.30
4C: $869.30
PCI: $5.55

11235 KKMA-FM - 99.5
PO Box 1410 Phone: (712)546-4123
Le Mars, IA 51031-1410 Fax: (712)546-9672

Format: Adult Contemporary. **Networks:** Westwood One Radio. **Owner:** Paul W. Olson, at above address. **Formerly:** KZZL-FM. **Operating Hours:** Continuous; 95% network, 5% local. **ADI:** Sioux City, IA. **Key Personnel:** Roger Miller, General Sales Mgr.; Dave Ruden, Program Dir.; Larry Schmitz, News Dir. **Wattage:** 100,000. **Ad Rates:** $14 for 30 seconds; $20 for 60 seconds.

11236 KLEM-AM - 1410
PO Box 1410 Phone: (712)546-4121
Le Mars, IA 51031-1410 Fax: (712)546-9672
E-mail: klem@pionet.net

Format: Middle-of-the-Road (MOR). **Networks:** AP. **Owner:** Paul W. Olson, at above address. **Founded:** Oct. 12, 1954. **Operating Hours:** 10% network, 90% local. **ADI:** Sioux City, IA. **Key Personnel:** Roger Miller, General Sales Mgr.; Dave Ruden, Program Dir.; Larry Schmitz, News Dir. **Local Programs:** *Opinionaire*, Larry Schmitz; *What Now Show*, Paul Olson. **Wattage:** 1000. **Ad Rates:** $12 for 30 seconds; $14 for 60 seconds.

LENOX, pop. 1,338.

SW IA. Adam & Taylor Co. 30 mi. SE of Red Oak. Residential.

11237 Time Table
Last Time Table
101 1/2 East Temple Phone: (515)333-2810
Lenox, IA 50851
Local newspaper. **Founded:** 1874. **Freq:** Weekly (Wed.). **Print Method:** Offset. **Cols./Page:** 6. **Col. Width:** 24 nonpareils. **Col. Depth:** 294 agate lines. **Key Personnel:** Vickie S. Sprague, Editor; James Taylor, Publisher. **Subscription Rates:** $12 individuals; $15 out of area; $20 out of state. **Remarks:** Accepts advertising.
Ad Rates: BW: $232.20 **Circ:** Paid 1,000
SAU: $2.20 Free 15

11238 Lenox Municipal Cablevision
PO Box 96 Phone: (515)333-2550
Lenox, IA 50851-0096

Key Personnel: David Ferris, General Mgr. **Cities Served:** subscribing households 540; 22 channels; 1 community access channel.

LEON†, pop. 2,094.

S IA. Decatur Co. 65 mi. S. of Des Moines. Manufacturing, trucking. machine shops. Ships cattle, dairy products. Agriculture.

11239 Journal-Reporter
110 N. Main St. Phone: (515)446-4151
Leon, IA 50144
Newspaper with a Report orientation. **Founded:** 1861. **Freq:** Weekly (Wed.). **Print Method:** Offset. **Cols./Page:** 8. **Col. Width:** 22 nonpareils. **Col. Depth:** 294 agate lines. **Key Personnel:** Mary Ellen Stanley, Editor; W.R. Lindsey, Publisher; Gary Lindsey, Publisher. **USPS:** 310-410. **Subscription Rates:** $25 individuals; $28 out of area. **Remarks:** Accepts advertising.
Ad Rates: BW: $369.60 **Circ:** ‡2,300
SAU: $3.45
PCI: $3.10

LIME SPRINGS, pop. 476.

NE IA. Howard Co. 44 mi. SW of Rochester, MN. Home of restored Lidtke Mill. State conservation area. Food locker. Egg packing plant. Grain elevators. Beef, dairy, grain farms.

11240 Lime Springs Herald
PO Box 187 Phone: (319)566-2687
Lime Springs, IA 52155
Newspaper with a Report orientation. **Founded:** 1882. **Freq:** Weekly (Thurs.). **Print Method:** Offset. **Cols./Page:** 6. **Col. Width:** 2 1/4 inches. **Col. Depth:** 21 1/2 inches. **Key Personnel:** Sara G. Casebolt, Publisher. **USPS:** 313-300. **Subscription Rates:** $21.50 individuals; $25 out of state. **Remarks:** Accepts advertising.
Ad Rates: BW: $352.80 **Circ:** ‡850
4C: $377.80
SAU: $2.80
PCI: $2.80

LOGAN†, pop. 1,540.

W IA. Harrison Co. 30 mi. N. of Council Bluffs. School and office supplies manufactured. Stone quarries. Diversified farming.

11241 Logan Herald-Observer
Bloom Publishing Co.
112 S. 4th Ave. Phone: (712)644-2705
PO Box 148 Fax: (712)644-2788
Logan, IA 51546-0148
Local newspaper. **Founded:** 1884. **Freq:** Weekly (Wed.). **Print Method:** Offset. **Trim Size:** 16 x 23. **Cols./Page:** 6. **Col. Width:** 28 nonpareils. **Col. Depth:** 301 agate lines. **Key Personnel:** Gerald D. Bloom, Editor; Karen J. Bloom, Publisher, kjbloom@pionet.net. **USPS:** 317-740. **Subscription Rates:** $18.50 individuals; $23 Iowa and Nebraska; $24.50 Elsewhere.
Ad Rates: GLR: $.29 **Circ:** Paid 2,095
BW: $516 Free 35
4C: $666
SAU: $4.60
PCI: $4

LONE TREE, pop. 1,014.

SE IA. Johnson Co. 20 mi. W. of Muscatine. Residential.

11242 Lone Tree Reporter
Box 235 Phone: (319)629-5207
Lone Tree, IA 52755 Fax: (319)629-4203

Newspaper. **Founded:** 1879. **Freq:** Weekly (Thurs.). **Print Method:** Offset. **Cols./Page:** 5. **Col. Width:** 11 picas. **Col. Depth:** 16 inches. **Key Personnel:** Cate Spears, Editor; Ron Slechta, Publisher, phone (319)656-2273, fax (319)656-2299; Helen Slechl, Publisher. **Subscription Rates:** $18 individuals. **Remarks:** Accepts advertising. **Alt. Formats:** CD-ROM.
Ad Rates: GLR: $.22 **Circ:** ‡1,100
BW: $225
4C: $500
SAU: $5
PCI: $3

LOWDEN, pop. 717.

E IA. Cedar Co. 40 mi. SE of Cedar Rapids. Historical center. Limestone quarries. Diversified farming.

11243 Sun-News
518 Main St. Phone: (319)944-5387
Lowden, IA 52255 Fax: (319)886-6644

Community newspaper. **Founded:** 1976. **Freq:** Weekly (Thurs.). **Print Method:** Offset. **Cols./Page:** 6. **Col. Width:** 20 nonpareils. **Col. Depth:** 224 agate lines. **Key Personnel:** Pat Kroemer, Editor/Advertising, phone (319)886-2131, fax (319)886-6466; Stuart Clark, Publisher, stuartc108@aol.com; Mel Alloway, Advertising. **USPS:** 321-140. **Subscription Rates:** $18 individuals; $23 out of state; $35 out of country. **Remarks:** Accepts advertising.
Ad Rates: SAU: $4.40 **Circ:** ‡1,190
PCI: $3.15

MADRID

11244 Madrid Register-News
Medrid Register
102 S. Main Phone: (515)795-2730
Madrid, IA 50156 Fax: (515)795-2012

Community newspaper. **Freq:** Weekly (Thurs.). **Cols./Page:** 7. **Col. Width:** 2 inches. **Col. Depth:** 21 1/2 inches. **Key Personnel:** Irene Wilcox, Editor; Dennis Wilcox, Publisher.
Circ: 1,400

MALVERN, pop. 1,244.

SW IA. Mills Co. 10 mi. W. of Emerson. Residential.

11245 The Leader
The Malvern Leader
Box 129 Phone: (712)624-8512
Malvern, IA 51551 Fax: (712)624-9041

Newspaper with a Report orientation. **Founded:** 1875. **Freq:** Weekly (Thurs.). **Print Method:** Offset. **Cols./Page:** 6. **Col. Width:** 22 nonpareils. **Col. Depth:** 301 agate lines. **Key Personnel:** Julia Dinville, Editor; Mark A. Siekman, Editor and Publisher. **Subscription Rates:** $14 individuals. **Remarks:** Accepts advertising.
Ad Rates: PCI: $2.25 **Circ:** Paid ‡1,200
Free ‡50

MANCHESTER†, pop. 4,942.

E IA. Delaware Co. 43 mi. W. of Dubuque. State trout hatchery. Manufactures gates, batteries, polyethylene film packaging, playground equipment, aluminum and brass castings, feed truck bodies, molded fiberglass containers. Corn, oats, livestock, hogs, poultry, dairy farms.

11246 The Manchester Press
Manchester Publishing Co.
109 E. Delaware St. Phone: (319)927-2020
PO Box C Fax: (319)927-4945
Manchester, IA 52057-0703
Community newspaper. **Founded:** 1871. **Freq:** Weekly (Tues.). **Print Method:** Offset. **Cols./Page:** 8. **Col. Width:** 20 nonpareils. **Col. Depth:** 294 agate lines. **Key Personnel:** Larry K. Woellert, Editor and Publisher. **Subscription Rates:** $30 individuals. **Remarks:** Accepts advertising.
Ad Rates: GLR: $.26 **Circ:** ‡5,188
BW: $596.40
SAU: $6.20
PCI: $4.70

MANILLA, pop. 1,020.

W IA. Crawford Co. 25 mi. SW of Carroll. Residential.

11247 The Manilla Times
Manilla Printing Co.
Box 365 Phone: (712)654-2911
Manilla, IA 51454
Local newspaper. **Founded:** 1899. **Freq:** Weekly. **Print Method:** Offset. **Cols./Page:** 6. **Col. Width:** 18 nonpareils. **Col. Depth:** 210 agate lines. **Key Personnel:** Ronald A. Colling, Editor and Publisher; Joleen R. Sievertsen, Advertising Mgr. **Subscription Rates:** $20 individuals local; $25 out of area; $30 out of state.
Ad Rates: SAU: $3.57 **Circ:** ‡1,200

MANLY, pop. 1,496.

N IA. Worth Co. 10 mi. N. of Mason City. Agriculture. Stock, grain farms. Corn, oats, sugar beets.

11248 Signal
PO Box 250 Phone: (515)454-2216
Manly, IA 50456 Fax: (515)454-2216
Publisher E-mail: manlysig@netins.net

Community newspaper. **Founded:** 1921. **Freq:** Weekly (Thurs.). **Print Method:** Letterpress and offset. **Cols./Page:** 6. **Col. Depth:** 21 inches. **Key Personnel:** Scott Keil, Editor and Publisher; Susan Beckel, Advertising Mgr. **Subscription Rates:** $16.50 individuals; $19.50 out of area. **Remarks:** Accepts advertising.
Ad Rates: GLR: $.10 **Circ:** ‡1,000
SAU: $3
PCI: $2.85

MANNING, pop. 1,609.

WC IA. Carroll Co. 65 mi. NE of Council Bluffs. Manufactures grain, gravity box, transport augers, grain gates, chutes, feed handling systems. Automotive assembly. Alfalfa drying and moulding plastics plants. Agriculture. Soybean.

11249 The Manning Monitor
L & V Publishing Co., Inc.
411 Main Phone: (712)653-3854
Manning, IA 51455 Fax: (712)653-9430

Newspaper with Report orientation. **Founded:** 1881. **Freq:** Weekly (Thurs.). **Print Method:** Offset. **Cols./Page:** 7. **Col. Width:** 12 nonpareils. **Col. Depth:** 301 agate lines. **Key Personnel:** Ronald Colling, Editor. **USPS:** 328-160. **Subscription Rates:** $20 individuals; $30 out of area. **Remarks:** Accepts advertising.
Ad Rates: BW: $489.13 **Circ:** ‡1,700
4C: $549.13
SAU: $4
PCI: $5.50

MANSON, pop. 1,924.

NWC IA. Calhoun Co. 18 mi. W. of Fort Dodge. Manufactures calendars, golf and tote bags, fertilizer. Agriculture. Corn, oats, barley, soybeans, turkeys.

11250 Journal
Journal Publishing Co.
PO Box 40 Phone: (712)469-3381
Manson, IA 50563 Fax: (712)469-2648
Publication E-mail: journal@stewardnet.com

Newspaper. **Founded:** 1874. **Freq:** Weekly (Thurs.). **Print Method:** Offset. **Cols./Page:** 8. **Col. Width:** 22 nonpareils. **Col. Depth:** 294 agate lines. **Key Personnel:** Lloyd E. Ones, Editor. **Subscription Rates:** $11.50 individuals. **Remarks:** Accepts advertising.
Ad Rates: GLR: $.14 **Circ:** 2,085

MAPLETON

11251 Mapleton Press
Lyon Publishing, Inc.
504 Main St. Phone: (712)882-1101
Mapleton, IA 51034 Fax: (712)882-1330

Local newspaper. **Founded:** 1880. **Freq:** Weekly. **Print Method:** Offset. **Key Personnel:** Edward M. Lyon, Publisher. **Subscription Rates:** $17.50 by mail; $21.50 out of area. **Remarks:** Accepts advertising.
Ad Rates: SAU: $3.95 **Circ:** Paid 2,338
Free 75

11252 Schleswig Leader
Lyon Publishing, Inc.
504 Main St. Phone: (712)882-1101
Mapleton, IA 51034 Fax: (712)882-1330

Newspaper. **Founded:** 1899. **Freq:** Weekly (Thurs.). **Print Method:** Offset. **Cols./Page:** 7. **Col. Width:** 24 nonpareils. **Col. Depth:** 127 agate lines. **Key Personnel:** Edward M.

Lyon, Editor and Publisher. **Subscription Rates:** $14 individuals. **Remarks:** Accepts advertising.
Ad Rates: GLR: $.17 **Circ:** 1,175
SAU: $2.55

11253 Mapleton Municipal CATV
513 Main St. Phone: (712)882-1351
Mapleton, IA 51034 Fax: (712)882-2726

Owner: City of Mapleton, at above address. **Founded:** 1983. **Formerly:** Mapleton Communications. **Key Personnel:** Tom LeFebvre, Contact; Mavis Skow, Contact; Karla Uhl, Secretary to the Board. **Cities Served:** Mapleton, IA: subscribing households 466; 12 channels; 1 community access channel.

MAQUOKETA†, pop. 6,313.

E IA. Jackson Co. 32 mi. S. of Dubuque. Manufactures woven wood shades, oil filters, steel paving reinforcements, tractor cooling systems, dairy products, boat trailers. Ships livestock. Limestone quarries. Agriculture. Corn, alfalfa, dairy products.

11254 Maquoketa Sentinel-Press
PO Box 1150 Phone: (319)652-2441
108 W. Quarry Fax: (319)652-6094
Maquoketa, IA 52060-1150
Local newspaper. **Founded:** 1854. **Freq:** Semiweekly (Wed. and Sat.). **Print Method:** Offset. **Cols./Page:** 9. **Col. Width:** 10 picas. **Col. Depth:** 301 agate lines. **Key Personnel:** Sheri Melvold, Editor; Douglas Melvold, Publisher; Rosie Morehead, Advertising Mgr. **USPS:** 589-540. **Subscription Rates:** $28 individuals; $35 out of area; $40 out of state. **Remarks:** Accepts advertising.
Ad Rates: GLR: $.21 **Circ:** ‡5,500
BW: $280
SAU: $4.33
PCI: $3

11255 KMAQ-AM - 1320
129 N. Main St. Phone: (319)652-2426
Maquoketa, IA 52060-0940 Fax: (319)652-6210
Free: (800)747-0057
E-mail: kmaq@kmaq.com

Format: Country. **Networks:** USA Radio; Brownfield. **Owner:** Dennis W. Voy, at above address. **Founded:** 1958. **Operating Hours:** 6 a.m.-10 p.m.; 5% network, 95% local. **Key Personnel:** Dennis W. Voy, Contact; Leighton Hepker, Station Mgr. **Wattage:** 500 day; 167 night. **Ad Rates:** $4.50-8.90 for 30 seconds; $6.00-9.95 for 60 seconds.

11256 KMAQ-FM - 95.3
129 N. Main St. Phone: (319)652-2426
Maquoketa, IA 52060-0940 Fax: (319)652-6210
E-mail: kmaq@caves.net

Format: Adult Contemporary. **Networks:** USA Radio. **Owner:** Dennis W. Voy, at above address. **Founded:** 1958. **Operating Hours:** 6 a.m.-10 p.m.; 5% network, 95% local. **Key Personnel:** Dennis W. Voy, Contact; Leighton Hepker, Station Mgr. **Wattage:** 3000 ERP.

MARCUS

11257 Marcus News
PO Box 445 Phone: (712)376-4712
Marcus, IA 51035 Fax: (712)376-4712

Community newspaper. **Freq:** Weekly (Thurs.). **Cols./Page:** 6. **Col. Width:** 13 picas. **Col. Depth:** 21 1/2 inches. **Key Personnel:** George Koth, Editor and Publisher; Glenice Koth, Editor. **Remarks:** Accepts advertising.
Ad Rates: PCI: $3 **Circ:** 1,600

MARENGO†, pop. 2,308.

SEC IA. Iowa Co. On Iowa River, 32 mi. SW of Cedar Rapids. Manufactures stock feeds, seed corn, modular homes, wood by-products. Dairy, stock, grain, truck, poultry farms.

11258 The Belle Plaine Union
MPC Publishing Co.
100 W. Main St. Phone: (319)444-2520
Marengo, IA 52301-1412 Fax: (319)642-5509

Newspaper. **Freq:** Weekly (Wed.). **Print Method:** Offset. **Cols./Page:** 9. **Col. Width:** 18 nonpareils. **Col. Depth:** 301 agate lines. **Key Personnel:** Don E. Magdefrau, Publisher; Jim Magdefrau, Editor. **Subscription Rates:** $26 individuals. **Remarks:** Accepts advertising.
Ad Rates: GLR: $.31 **Circ:** 3,465
BW: $870.75
4C: $1,005.75
SAU: $6.75
PCI: $4.50

11259 The 4-County Market
Pioneer Republican
PO Box 208 Phone: (319)642-5506
Marengo, IA 52301 Fax: (319)642-5509
Free: (800)414-5506

Shopper. **Founded:** 1905. **Freq:** Weekly (Wed.). **Print Method:** Offset. **Trim Size:** 11 3/8 x 15. **Cols./Page:** 6. **Col. Depth:** 14 inches. **Key Personnel:** Don Magdefrau, Publisher, phone (319)444-2520; Donna Greenlee, Advertising Mgr., phone (319)444-2520. **Subscription Rates:** $23 individuals.
Ad Rates: GLR: $.32 **Circ:** Free ‡7350
BW: $378
4C: $515.40
SAU: $6.75
PCI: $4.50

11260 Iowa County Farmer
100 W. Main St. Phone: (319)642-5506
PO Box 208 Fax: (319)642-5509
Marengo, IA 52301
Free: (800)414-5506

Magazine on agriculture. **Founded:** 1950. **Freq:** Monthly. **Print Method:** Offset. Uses mats. **Trim Size:** 11 3/8 x 15. **Cols./Page:** 6. **Col. Width:** 20 nonpareils. **Col. Depth:** 196 agate lines. **Key Personnel:** Michael Simmons, Publisher; Paul Thompson, General Mgr.; G. Alan Sieve, Editor. **Subscription Rates:** $26 individuals; $33 out of state.
Ad Rates: GLR: $.32 **Circ:** Paid ‡10,140
BW: $575.40
4C: $725.40
SAU: $10.28
PCI: $6.85

11261 Journal-Tribune
PO Box 208 Phone: (319)642-5506
Marengo, IA 52301 Fax: (319)642-5509

Community newspaper. **Founded:** 1915. **Freq:** Weekly (Thurs.). **Print Method:** Offset. **Cols./Page:** 9. **Col. Width:** 18 nonpareils. **Col. Depth:** 301 agate lines. **Key Personnel:** Michael Simmons, Publisher; Karin Winwood, Advertising Mgr.; Todd Kimm, Editor. **Subscription Rates:** $4.35 individuals. **Remarks:** Accepts advertising.
Ad Rates: GLR: $.32 **Circ:** 4,800
BW: $870.75
4C: $1,005.75
SAU: $6.75
PCI: $4.50

11262 Pioneer Republican
PO Box 208 Phone: (319)642-5506
Marengo, IA 52301 Fax: (319)642-5509
Free: (800)414-5506

Community newspaper. **Subtitle:** Newspapers of Iowa County. **Founded:** 1854. **Freq:** Weekly (Thurs.). **Print Method:** Offset. **Trim Size:** 15 x 22 3/4. **Cols./Page:** 9. **Col. Width:** 10 nonpareils. **Col. Depth:** 21 1/2 inches. **Key Personnel:** G. Alan Sieve, Editor; Michael T. Simmons, Publisher; Daniel J. DeBettignies, General Mgr. **Subscription Rates:** $26 individuals. **Remarks:** Accepts advertising.
Ad Rates: GLR: $.32 **Circ:** ‡2,400
BW: $870.75
4C: $1,005.75
SAU: $6.75
PCI: $4.50

11263 South Benton Star-Press
MPC Publishing Co.
100 W. Main St. Phone: (319)444-2520
Marengo, IA 52301-1412 Fax: (319)642-5509

Newspaper. **Freq:** Weekly (Wed.). **Print Method:** Offset. **Cols./Page:** 9. **Col. Width:** 18 nonpareils. **Col. Depth:** 301 agate lines. **Key Personnel:** James E. Magdefrau, Editor; Don E. Magdefrau, Publisher. **Subscription Rates:** $26 individuals. **Remarks:** Accepts advertising.
Ad Rates: GLR: $.32 **Circ:** 2,500
BW: $870.75
4C: $1,005.75
SAU: $6.75
PCI: $4.50

MARSHALLTOWN†, pop. 26,938.

C IA. Marshall Co. 50 mi. NE of Des Moines. Manufactures furnaces, air conditioners, warm air registers; steam specialties, trowels, pressure gauges, farm machinery, auto accessories, surgical dressings, paper boxes. Iron, brass, aluminum foundries. Stone quarries. Agriculture.

11264 Pennysaver
507 E. Anson Phone: (515)752-6630
Box 246 Fax: (515)752-7073
Marshalltown, IA 50158
Shopper. **Founded:** 1973. **Freq:** Semiweekly (Wed. and Sat.). **Print Method:** Offset. **Cols./Page:** 7. **Col. Width:** 16 nonpareils. **Col. Depth:** 224 agate lines. **Key Personnel:** Jerry Lukan, Editor and Publisher. **Remarks:** Accepts advertising.
Ad Rates: BW: $812.00 **Circ:** Free ‡22,213
4C: $957.00
PCI: $8.40

11265 Times-Republican
Marshalltown Newspaper, Inc.
135 W. Main St. Phone: (515)753-6611
Marshalltown, IA 50158 Fax: (515)753-7221
Publication E-mail: trpub@marshallnet.com; tradv@marshallnet.com
Publisher E-mail: timesr@marshallnet.com

Independent newspaper. **Founded:** 1856. **Freq:** Daily (eve.), Sat. and Sun. (morn.). **Print Method:** Offset. **Trim Size:** 13 1/2 x 22 3/4. **Cols./Page:** 6. **Col. Width:** 12.5 picas. **Col. Depth:** 21.5 inches. **Key Personnel:** Jim Stern, Editor; D. Michael Schlesinger, Publisher; Max Nelson, Advertising Mgr. **USPS:** 331-060. **Subscription Rates:** $91 by carrier; $98 by mail; $114 out of state. **Remarks:** Accepts advertising. **URL:** http://www.oweb.com/times-republican.
Ad Rates: BW: $2,329.74 **Circ:** Mon.-Sat. ★**10,601**
4C: $2,509.74 Sun. ★**10,906**
SAU: $18.06
PCI: $18.06

11266 KDAO-AM - 1190
1930 N. Center St. Phone: (515)752-4122
Box 538 Fax: (515)752-5121
Marshalltown, IA 50158

Networks: ABC. **Owner:** MTN Broadcasting, Inc., at above address. **Founded:** 1978. **Operating Hours:** 2hrs before sunrise to 2hrs after sunset. **Key Personnel:** Mark Osmundson, General Mgr. **Wattage:** 250.

11267 KFJB-AM - 1230
123 W. Main St. Phone: (515)753-3361
Marshalltown, IA 50158 Fax: (515)752-7201

Format: Oldies. **Networks:** ABC. **Owner:** Marshalltown Broadcasting, Inc., at above address. **Founded:** 1923. **Operating Hours:** 5 a.m.-midnight. **ADI:** Des Moines, IA. **Key Personnel:** John Reardon, Contact; Kevin Pink, Contact; Jim Dalton, Program Dir. **Wattage:** 1000. **Ad Rates:** $9-11 for 30 seconds; $11-24 for 60 seconds. $6.90-$15.45 for 30 seconds; $9-$19.30 for 60 seconds. Combined advertising rates available with KXIA-FM.

11268 KXIA-FM - 101.1
123 W. Main St. Phone: (515)753-3361
Marshalltown, IA 50158 Fax: (515)752-7201

Format: Contemporary Country; Sports. **Networks:** ABC. **Owner:** Marshalltown Broadcasting, Inc., at above address. **Founded:** 1968. **Operating Hours:** Continuous. **ADI:** Des Moines, IA. **Key Personnel:** John Reardon, Contact; Scott Turner, Program/Music Dir.; Kevin Pink, Sports/News Dir. **Wattage:** 100,000. **Ad Rates:** $14-25 for 30 seconds; $16-30 for 60 seconds.

MASON CITY†, pop. 30,144.

N IA. Cerro Gordo Co. 85 mi. NW of Waterloo. Manufactures ice machines, envelopes, computers, leather goods, cement, foundry products, feed, fertilizer, sand and gravel, wire, metal window and door frames. Meat packing plant. Dairy, stock farms.

11269 The Business Journal
Lee Enterprises, Inc.
208 1st St., NW Phone: (515)424-0818
PO Box 1506 Fax: (515)424-6786
Mason City, IA 50401
Local business editorial. **Subtitle:** Monthly Business Magazine. **Founded:** 1992. **Freq:** Monthly. **Print Method:** Offset. **Trim Size:** 10 1/4 x 13. **Cols./Page:** 4. **Col. Width:** 29 nonpareils. **Col. Depth:** 224 agate lines. **Key Personnel:** Jim Murphy, General Mgr.; Martha Taylor, Editor. **Subscription Rates:** Free; $10 mail.
Ad Rates: BW: $647 **Circ:** Non-paid 2,362
4C: $847
PCI: $11.55

11270 Globe-Gazette
Howard Query
300 N. Washington Ave. Phone: (515)421-0500
PO Box 271 Fax: (515)421-0516
Mason City, IA 50401-3222
Free: (800)421-0524

General newspaper. **Founded:** 1861. **Freq:** Mon.-Sun. (morn.). **Print Method:** Flexographic. **Cols./Page:** 6. **Col. Width:** 24 nonpareils. **Col. Depth:** 301 agate lines. **Key Personnel:** John Smalley, Editor; Howard Query, Publisher,

hquery@globegazette.com. **Subscription Rates:** $70.20 individuals. **Remarks:** Accepts advertising.
Ad Rates: SAU: $13.48 **Circ:** Mon.-Sat. ★20,799
Sun. ★24,975

11271 Logos
North Iowa Area Community College
500 College Dr. Phone: (515)423-1264
Mason City, IA 50401-7213
Collegiate newspaper. **Founded:** 1968. **Freq:** Semiweekly during the academic year. **Trim Size:** 10 1/4 x 13. **Cols./Page:** 5. **Col. Width:** 20 nonpareils. **Col. Depth:** 187 agate lines. **Key Personnel:** Paul Peterson, Adviser, phone (515)422-4304. **Subscription Rates:** Free. **Remarks:** Accepts advertising.
Ad Rates: BW: $200 **Circ:** Non-paid 3,000
PCI: $5.50

11272 The Mason City Shopper
Lee Enterprises, Inc.
208 1st St. NW Phone: (515)424-3044
PO Box 1506 Fax: (515)424-6786
Mason City, IA 50401
Publication E-mail: shopper@mach3ww.com

Shopper (tabloid) with community editorial. **Founded:** 1969. **Freq:** Weekly (Tues.). **Print Method:** Offset. **Trim Size:** 10 1/4 x 16. **Cols./Page:** 5. **Key Personnel:** Jim Murphy, General Mgr.; Jim Hentges, Sales Mgr. **Subscription Rates:** Free; $15 by mail. **Remarks:** Accepts advertising.
Ad Rates: GLR: $11.68 **Circ:** Free 30,889
BW: $755
4C: $1,090
PCI: $12.95

11273 KCMR-FM - 97.9
PO Box 979 Phone: (515)424-9301
Mason City, IA 50402-0979 Fax: (515)423-2221

Format: Easy Listening; Religious. **Networks:** Independent. **Owner:** KCMR Radio, at above address, (515)424-9300. **Founded:** 1979. **Operating Hours:** Continuous. **ADI:** Rochester, MN-Mason City, IA-Austin, MN. **Key Personnel:** Mark Feustel, President, phone (515)424-8200; Bill Schickel, General Mgr., phone (515)424-9300. **Wattage:** 6000. **Ad Rates:** Noncommercial.

11274 KGLO-AM - 1300
PO Box 1300 Phone: (515)423-1300
Mason City, IA 50402-1300 Fax: (515)423-2906
Free: (800)747-2346
E-mail: bj@netms.net

Format: Adult Contemporary; News; Full Service. **Networks:** CBS. **Founded:** 1938. **Operating Hours:** Continuous; 30% network, 70% local. **ADI:** Rochester, MN-Mason City, IA-Austin, MN. **Key Personnel:** Kevin Lein, General Mgr.; Scott Bretey, General Sales Mgr.; Tim Fleming, Operations Dir.; Tim Renshaw, News Dir.; Greg Gaffney, Chief Engineer. **Wattage:** 5000. **Ad Rates:** $20-40 for 60 seconds. **URL:** http://www.netms.net/showcase/kgkifx.

11275 KIA-FM - 93.9
341 Yorktown Pike, Box 1300 Phone: (515)423-1300
Mason City, IA 50401 Fax: (515)423-2906
Free: (800)747-2346
E-mail: bj@netins.net

Format: Country. **Founded:** 1986. **Formerly:** KNIQ-FM (1992). **Operating Hours:** Continuous. **ADI:** Rochester, MN-Mason City, IA-Austin, MN. **Key Personnel:** Kevin Lein, General Mgr.; Stanton D. Ross, General Sales Mgr., stanross@netins.net. **Wattage:** 100,000. **Ad Rates:** $22 for 30 seconds; $33 for 60 seconds. **URL:** http://www.netins.net/showcase/kgkifx.

11276 KIMT-TV - 3
112 N. Pennsyvania Ave. Phone: (515)423-2540
PO Box 620 Fax: (515)423-9309
Mason City, IA 50401
E-mail: kimt@willowtree.com.

Format: Commercial TV. **Networks:** CBS. **Owner:** Spartan Radiocasting Co., PO Box 1717, Spartanburg, SC 29304, (803)576-7777. **Founded:** 1954. **Formerly:** KGLO-TV (1977). **Operating Hours:** Continuous. **ADI:** Rochester, MN-Mason City, IA-Austin, MN. **Key Personnel:** John Shine, General Mgr.; Dick Aune, General Sales Mgr.; Bart Curran, Program Dir.; John Deyo, Production Mgr.; Mary Ellen Schultz, Promotions Dir.; Larry Huegli, News Dir.; Dale Byre, Chief Engineer. **Ad Rates:** $20-500 for 30 seconds.

11277 KRNI-AM - 1010
c/o KUNI-FM Phone: (319)273-6400
University of Northern Iowa Fax: (319)273-2682
Cedar Falls, IA 50614-0359
Free: (800)772-2440
E-mail: kuni@uni.edu

Format: Public Radio; Eclectic. **Simulcasts:** KUNI-FM. **Networks:** National Public Radio (NPR); Public Radio International (PRI). **Owner:** University of Northern Iowa, at above address. **Founded:** 1948. **Formerly:** KLSS-AM. **Operating Hours:** 5:30 a.m.-midnight. **ADI:** Rochester, MN-Mason City, IA-Austin, MN. **Key Personnel:** Doug Vernier, General Mgr., phone (319)273-6446, doug.vernier@uni.edu; Carl Jenkins, Program Dir., phone (319)273-6464, carl.jenkins@uni.edu; Greg Shanley, News Dir., phone (319)273-6408, gregory.shanley@uni.edu; Al Schares, Music Dir., phone (319)273-6489, allen.schares@uni.edu; Steve Schoon, Chief Engineer, phone (310)273-6465, steven.schoon@uni.edu. **Wattage:** 1000 day; 15.8 night. **Ad Rates:** Noncommercial. **URL:** http://www.uni.edu/kuni.

11278 KUNY-FM - 91.5
c/o KUNI Phone: (319)273-6400
University of Northern Iowa Fax: (319)273-2682
Cedar Falls, IA 50614-0359
Free: (800)772-2440
E-mail: kuni@uni.edu

Format: Public Radio; Eclectic. **Simulcasts:** KUNI-FM. **Networks:** National Public Radio (NPR); Public Radio International (PRI). **Owner:** University of Northern Iowa, at above address. **Founded:** 1987. **Operating Hours:** Continuous. **ADI:** Rochester, MN-Mason City, IA-Austin, MN. **Key Personnel:** Doug Vernier, General Mgr., phone (319)273-6446, doug.vernier@uni.edu; Carl Jenkins, Program Dir., phone (319)273-6464, carl.jenkins@uni.edu; Greg Shanley, News Dir., phone (319)273-6408, gregory.shanley@uni.edu; Al Schares, Music Dir., phone (319)273-6489, allen.schares@uni.edu; Steve Schoon, Chief Engineer, phone (319)273-6465, steven.schoon@uni.edu. **Wattage:** 8000. **Ad Rates:** Noncommercial. **URL:** http://www.uni.edu/kuni.

11279 KYIN-TV - 24
Iowa Public Television Phone: (515)242-3100
PO Box 6450
Johnston, IA 50131

Format: Public TV. **Simulcasts:** KDIN-TV Des Moines, IA. **Networks:** Public Broadcasting Service (PBS). **Founded:** 1977. **ADI:** Rochester, MN-Mason City, IA-Austin, MN. **Key Personnel:** David Bolender, Exec. Dir.; Dennis Malloy, Dir. of Development; Daniel K. Miller, Program Dir.; Don Saveraid, Dir. of Engineering; Pam Johnson, Dir. of Educational Telecommunications; John Leiendecker, Production Mgr.; Sid Sprecher, Public Affairs.

MECHANICSVILLE, pop. 1,166.

E IA. Cedar Co. 22 mi. SE of Cedar Rapids. Residential.

11280 Mechanicsville Telephone Co.
107 N. John Phone: (319)432-7221
Mechanicsville, IA 52306 Fax: (319)432-7721

Founded: 1983. **Key Personnel:** Joe E. Paidar, General Mgr. **Cities Served:** Mechanicsville, IA: subscribing households 415; 48 channels; 1 community access channel.

MEDIAPOLIS, pop. 1,685.

SE IA. Des Moines Co. 13 mi. N. of Burlington. Industry. Concrete products, grain belt equipment, metal works, fiberglass. Diversified farming. Corn, beans, wheat, oats.

11281 Mediapolis News
Box 548 Phone: (319)394-3174
616 Main Fax: (319)394-3134
Mediapolis, IA 52637
Free: (800)949-3175

Community newspaper. **Founded:** 1875. **Freq:** Weekly (Thurs.). **Print Method:** Offset. **Cols./Page:** 8. **Col. Width:** 21 nonpareils. **Col. Depth:** 294 agate lines. **Key Personnel:** Kendra Jahn, Publisher; William Jahn, Jr., Asst. Pub; Joyce Swafford, Office Mgr. **ISSN:** 0747-3591. **Subscription Rates:** $23 individuals; $26 out of country. **Remarks:** Accepts advertising.
Ad Rates: BW: $591.36 **Circ:** 1,600
SAU: $4.84
PCI: $3.52

11282 Mediapolis Cablevision Co.
652 Main St. Phone: (319)394-3996
PO Box 398 Fax: (319)394-9155
Mediapolis, IA 52637

Key Personnel: William Malcom, General Mgr. **Cities Served:** subscribing households 450; 25 channels.

MISSOURI VALLEY, pop. 3,107.

W IA. Harrison Co. 22 mi. N. of Council Bluffs. Manufactures sewage treatment parts. Agriculture. Wheat, corn, soybeans, apples, livestock.

11283 Missouri Valley Merchandiser
Missouri Valley Merchandiser Missouri Valley Times-News
501 E. Erie Phone: (712)642-2791
PO Box 159 Fax: (712)642-2595
Missouri Valley, IA 51555
Shopper. **Subtitle:** Harrison County Merchandiser. **Founded:** 1912. **Freq:** Weekly (Wed.). **Print Method:** Offset. **Cols./Page:** 7. **Col. Width:** 2 1/16 inches. **Col. Depth:** 301 agate lines. **Key Personnel:** Jason Render, Editor; Mark A. Rhoades, Publisher; Charles Hickman, Advertising Mgr.; Chris Hinkel, General Mgr. **Remarks:** Accepts advertising.
Ad Rates: SAU: $6.50 **Circ:** (Not Reported)

11284 Missouri Valley Times News
501 E. Erie St. Phone: (712)642-2791
PO Box 159 Fax: (712)642-2595
Missouri Valley, IA 51555
Community newspaper. **Founded:** 1893. **Freq:** Semiweekly (Wed. and Fri.). **Print Method:** Offset. **Cols./Page:** 7. **Col. Width:** 24 nonpareils. **Col. Depth:** 294 agate lines. **Key Personnel:** Jesse Render, Editor; Charles Hickman, Advertising Mgr.; Chris Hinkel, General Mgr. **Subscription Rates:** $27 individuals. **Remarks:** Accepts advertising.
Ad Rates: GLR: $.39 **Circ:** 2,100
SAU: $5.70

MONONA

NE IA. Clayton Co. 10 mi. W. of Marquette.

11285 Monona Billboard
200 S. Main St. Phone: (319)539-4300
PO Box 628
Monona, IA 52159
Community newspaper. **Founded:** 1958. **Freq:** Weekly (Wed.). **Print Method:** Offset. **Cols./Page:** 5. **Col. Width:** 11 picas. **Col. Depth:** 16 inches. **Key Personnel:** Marcia Carroll, Editor; Gerald Carroll, Publisher. **Subscription Rates:** $12; $14 out of area. **Remarks:** Accepts advertising.
Ad Rates: BW: $192 **Circ:** ‡2,400
PCI: $2.40

11286 Northeast Iowa Telephone Co./CATV
113 N. Page Phone: (319)539-2122
PO Box 835 Fax: (319)539-2003
Monona, IA 52159

Owner: Northeast Iowa Telephone Co., at above address. **Founded:** 1903. **Key Personnel:** Ronald Kroesche, General Mgr. **Cities Served:** Farmersburg, Luana, Monona, St. Olaf, IA: subscribing households 850; 22 channels; 1 community access channel; 168 hours per week community access programming.

MONROE, pop. 1,875.

C IA. Jasper Co. 30 mi. SE of Des Moines. Plastic bottles, earth anchors, fencing, chemicals, fertilizers, printing. Agriculture. Corn, small grains.

11287 Monroe Legacy
KAB Enterprises, Inc.
PO Box 340 Phone: (515)259-2708
Monroe, IA 50170
Newspaper with a Report orientation. **Founded:** 1873. **Freq:** Weekly (Thurs.). **Print Method:** Offset. **Trim Size:** 11 1/2 x 18. **Cols./Page:** 5. **Col. Width:** 11 nonpareils. **Col. Depth:** 224 agate lines. **Key Personnel:** Kathleen Darrach, Editor and Publisher. **USPS:** 359-560. **Subscription Rates:** $15.50 individuals; $17.50 out of area. **Remarks:** Accepts advertising. **Formerly:** Monroe Mirror (1994).
Ad Rates: GLR: $.23 **Circ:** 760
BW: $192
PCI: $2.40

MONTEZUMA, pop. 1,485.

SEC IA. Poweshiek Co. 60 mi. E. of Des Moines. Manufactures-model airplane products, burial vaults, automotive trim parts. Stock, grain-farms, corn, oats, hogs.

11288 Montezuma Republican
406 E. Main St. Phone: (515)623-5116
PO Box 100 Fax: (515)623-5580
Montezuma, IA 50171
Free: (800)414-5506
Publisher E-mail: mtzanews@netins.net

Newspaper. **Founded:** 1856. **Freq:** Weekly (Wed.). **Print Method:** Offset. **Cols./Page:** 9. **Col. Width:** 20 nonpareils. **Col. Depth:** 301 agate lines. **Key Personnel:** Dennis Jacobs,

Editor; Dan Debettignies, Publisher. **Subscription Rates:** $20 individuals. **Remarks:** Accepts advertising.
Ad Rates: BW: $745 **Circ:** 2,175
4C: $995
SAU: $6.75
PCI: $3.85

MONTICELLO, pop. 3,641.

E IA. Jones Co. 35 mi. SW of Dubuque. Manufactures steel building, plastic products, hydraulic motors, pumps, garden tools, road graders, corrugated containers, utility baskets, barn, dairy equipment, livestock feeds, metal castings. Agriculture. Corn, beef cattle, hogs.

11289 The Monticello Express
111 E. Grand Phone: (319)465-3555
PO Box 191 Fax: (319)465-4611
Monticello, IA 52310-0191
Publication E-mail: mexpress@n-connect.net

Community newspaper. **Founded:** 1865. **Freq:** Weekly (Wed.). **Print Method:** Offset. **Cols./Page:** 6. **Col. Width:** 1 1/2 inches. **Col. Depth:** 16 inches. **Key Personnel:** Ryan Suchomel, Editor; Robert Goodyear, Publisher; Mark Spensley, Advertising Mgr. **USPS:** 361-580. **Subscription Rates:** $24; $26 out of area; $28 out of state. **Remarks:** Accepts advertising.
Ad Rates: BW: $293 **Circ:** ‡5,200
4C: $638
SAU: $5.14
PCI: $3.90

MORAVIA, pop. 706.

S IA. Appanoose Co. 8 mi. NE of Lake Rathbun. Residential.

11290 Moravia Union
PO Box 468 Phone: (515)724-3224
Moravia, IA 52571
Community newspaper. **Founded:** 1901. **Freq:** Weekly (Wed.). **Print Method:** Offset. **Cols./Page:** 6. **Col. Width:** 26 nonpareils. **Col. Depth:** 294 agate lines. **Key Personnel:** Richard Harl, Editor and Publisher. **Subscription Rates:** $14 individuals; $16 out of state.
Ad Rates: BW: $325 **Circ:** ‡1,000
PCI: $3.60

11291 Moulton Tribune
Moravia Union
PO Box 468 Phone: (515)724-3224
Moravia, IA 52571
Community newspaper. **Founded:** 1855. **Freq:** Weekly (Wed.). **Print Method:** Offset. **Cols./Page:** 6. **Col. Width:** 26 nonpareils. **Col. Depth:** 294 agate lines. **Key Personnel:** Patty Brown, Publisher. **Subscription Rates:** $14 individuals; $16 out of state. **Remarks:** Accepts advertising.
Ad Rates: BW: $325 **Circ:** ‡900
PCI: $3.60

MORNING SUN, pop. 959.

SE IA. Louisa Co. 20 mi. N. of Burlington. Large agricultural area.

11292 Morning Sun News-Herald
Louisa Publishing Co., Ltd.
Division St. Phone: (319)868-7509
PO Box 67
Morning Sun, IA 52640
Publisher E-mail: lpc@lisco.net

Newspaper with a Report orientation. **Founded:** 1890. **Freq:** Weekly (Thurs.). **Print Method:** Offset. **Trim Size:** 11 1/4 x 16. **Cols./Page:** 5. **Col. Width:** 22 nonpareils. **Col. Depth:** 210 agate lines. **Key Personnel:** Michael A. Hodges, Editor. **USPS:** 363-360. **Subscription Rates:** $15 individuals; $19 out of area; $22 out of state. **Remarks:** Accepts advertising.
Ad Rates: SAU: $3.27 **Circ:** ‡796
PCI: $2.77

MOUNT AYR†, pop. 1,938.

S IA. Ringgold Co. 75 mi. SW of Des Moines. Manufactures caps, non ferrous washers, furnaces, recreational equipment. Hatchery. Agriculture. Corn, soybeans, oats. Cattle, hogs.

11293 Mt. Ayr Record-News
Paragon Publications, Inc.
122 W. Madison Phone: (515)464-2440
PO Box 346 Fax: (515)464-2229
Mount Ayr, IA 50854
Publication E-mail: recnews@mtayr.heartland.net

Community newspaper. **Founded:** 1865. **Freq:** Weekly (Thurs.). **Print Method:** Offset. **Trim Size:** 17 x 22 1/2. **Cols./Page:** 7. **Col. Width:** 25 nonpareils. **Col. Depth:** 301 agate lines. **Key Personnel:** H. Alan Smith, Editor and Publisher. **USPS:** 365-120. **Subscription Rates:** $19 individuals in county & surrounding counties.
Ad Rates: BW: $465 **Circ:** ‡2,618
4C: $785
SAU: $3.10
PCI: $3.10

MOUNT PLEASANT†, pop. 7,322.

SE IA. Henry Co. 28 mi. SE of Cedar Rapids. Iowa Wesleyan College. Manufactures bus bodies, metal fabrication, electronic controls, pennants and badges. Agriculture. Corn, beans, oats.

11294 Mt. Pleasant News
Mount Pleasant News
215 W. Monroe St. Phone: (319)385-3131
PO Box 240
Mount Pleasant, IA 52641-0240
Publication E-mail: citypapers.com

General newspaper. **Founded:** 1878. **Freq:** Daily (eve.). **Print Method:** Offset. **Cols./Page:** 6. **Col. Width:** 25 nonpareils. **Col. Depth:** 301 agate lines. **Key Personnel:** Emery Styron, Publisher; Jim Hekel, News Editor. **Subscription Rates:** $81 individuals. **Remarks:** Accepts advertising.
Ad Rates: SAU: $7.20 **Circ:** Paid ‡3,200

11295 KILJ-AM - 1130
1816 Oakland Mills Rd. Phone: (319)385-8728
Mount Pleasant, IA 52641 Fax: (319)385-4517

Format: Oldies. **Networks:** ABC. **Owner:** Media Comm., at above address. **Founded:** 1974. **Operating Hours:** Sunrise-sunset. **Key Personnel:** John Kuhens, General Mgr. **Wattage:** 250. **Ad Rates:** $4 for 30 seconds; $8 for 60 seconds.

MOUNT VERNON, pop. 3,325.

E IA. Linn Co. 17 mi. SE of Cedar Rapids. Cornell College. Manufactures metal name plates, concrete. Produce packed. Stock, grain farms.

11296 The Cornellian
Cornell College
810 Commons Circle Phone: (319)895-4430
Mount Vernon, IA 52314 Fax: (319)895-5264

Collegiate newspaper. **Founded:** 1880. **Freq:** Weekly. **Print Method:** Offset. Uses mats. **Cols./Page:** 5. **Col. Width:** 32 nonpareils. **Col. Depth:** 210 agate lines. **Key Personnel:** Nick Adamson, Editor; David Evans, Advisor; Joel Pendergrass, Co. Editors; Bryan Moore, Advertising Mgr. **USPS:** 132-900. **Subscription Rates:** $17 individuals; $30 institutions. **Remarks:** Accepts advertising.
Ad Rates: BW: $240 **Circ:** Paid 200
PCI: $4 Free 1,100

11297 The Hillsboro Star-Journal
Wedel Publishing, LLC
113 1st St. W. Phone: (319)895-6216
PO Box 129 Fax: (319)895-6217
Mount Vernon, IA 52314-0129
Publication E-mail: starj@southwind.net
Publisher E-mail: mvlsun@cedarrapids.net; mvlsun@earthlink.net

Community newspaper. **Founded:** May 2, 1924. **Freq:** Weekly (Wed.). **Print Method:** Offset. **Trim Size:** 13 3/4 x 22 3/4. **Cols./Page:** 6. **Col. Width:** 2 1/16 inches. **Col. Depth:** 21 1/2 inches. **Subscription Rates:** $33 individuals; $39 out of area; $45 out of state. **Remarks:** Accepts advertising.
Ad Rates: SAU: $5.00 **Circ:** Paid ‡2,757
Free ‡150

11298 The Sun
Wedel Publishing, LLC
113 1st St. W. Phone: (319)895-6216
PO Box 129 Fax: (319)895-6217
Mount Vernon, IA 52314-0129
Publication E-mail: sunletter@aol.com
Publisher E-mail: mvlsun@cedarrapids.net; mvlsun@earthlink.net

Community newspaper. **Founded:** Jan. 29, 1869. **Freq:** Weekly (Thurs.). **Print Method:** Offset. **Trim Size:** 12 1/2 x 21 1/2. **Cols./Page:** 6. **Col. Width:** 2 1/16 inches. **Col. Depth:** 21 inches. **Key Personnel:** Kip A. Wedel, Editor and Publisher; LeAnn Pisarik, Advertising Mgr.; Julie Fisher, Business Mgr. **USPS:** 367-520. **Subscription Rates:** $21 individuals; $29 out of area; $35 out of state. **Formerly:** Mount Vernon Hawkeye.
Ad Rates: BW: $580.50 **Circ:** ‡2,203
PCI: $4.50

11299 The SUNlight
Wedel Publishing, LLC
113 1st St. W. Phone: (319)895-6216
PO Box 129 Fax: (319)895-6217
Mount Vernon, IA 52314-0129
Publication E-mail: sunletter@aol.com
Publisher E-mail: mvlsun@cedarrapids.net; mvlsun@earthlink.net

Shopping guide (tabloid). **Subtitle:** A Shopping Guide. **Founded:** 1976. **Freq:** Weekly (Tues.). **Print Method:** Offset. **Trim Size:** 9 3/4 x 16. **Cols./Page:** 4. **Col. Width:** 2 1/16 inches. **Col. Depth:** 14 1/2 inches. **Key Personnel:** Dennis F. Herrick, Editor and Publisher; LeAnn Pisarik, Advertising Mgr.; Julie Fisher, Business Mgr. **Remarks:** Accepts advertising.
Ad Rates: BW: $393.60 **Circ:** Free ‡4,000
SAU: $6.15

11300 KRNL-FM - 89.7
Cornell College Phone: (319)895-4431
810 Commons Circle Fax: (319)895-5188
Mount Vernon, IA 52314
E-mail: krnl@cornell-iowa.edu

Format: Eclectic. **Owner:** Cornell College, at above address. **Founded:** 1948. **Operating Hours:** 7 a.m.-3 a.m. **Key Personnel:** Will Dennison, General Mgr.; Dave McGuire, Station Mgr.; Kirk Andrew, Music Dir.; Matt Winegardner, Music Dir. **Wattage:** 36. **Ad Rates:** Noncommercial.

MOVILLE, pop. 1,198.

NC IA. Woodbury Co. 17 mi. E. of Sioux City.

11301 Moville Record
PO Box AE Phone: (712)873-3141
Moville, IA 51039
Community newspaper. **Founded:** June 1943. **Freq:** Weekly. **Print Method:** Offset. **Trim Size:** 14 1/2 x 22 1/2. **Cols./Page:** 6. **Col. Width:** 12.5 picas. **Col. Depth:** 21 1/2 inches. **Key Personnel:** Bedford Robinson, Editor and Publisher. **USPS:** 366-960. **Subscription Rates:** $19 individuals; $23 out of area. **Remarks:** Accepts advertising.
Ad Rates: SAU: $3.94 **Circ:** ‡1,475
PCI: $3.25

MUSCATINE†, pop. 23,467.

SE IA. Muscatine Co. On Mississippi River, 30 mi. SW of Davenport. Boat connections. Manufactures fertilizers, buttons, ladders, machinery, herbicides, sand & gravel, cement blocks. Steel dies, plastics, food processing, concrete culverts. Centrifugal pumps. Commercial fishing, soybean, feed and grain mills. Agriculture. Melons, sweet potatoes, corn, truck crops.

11302 Classic Images
Muscatine Journal
301 E. 3rd St. Phone: (319)263-2331
PO Box 809 Fax: (319)262-8042
Muscatine, IA 52761
Free: (800)383-3198
Publication E-mail: classicimages@classicimages.com

Magazine (tabloid) covering classic motion pictures for movie buffs and collectors; including film and video tape reviews, biographies, historical articles, obituaries, classified advertising, and coverage of conventions and festivals. **Founded:** June 1962. **Freq:** Monthly. **Print Method:** Offset. **Trim Size:** 11 x 14. **Cols./Page:** 6. **Col. Width:** 18 nonpareils. **Col. Depth:** 182 agate lines. **Key Personnel:** Bob King, Editor. **ISSN:** 0275-8423. **Subscription Rates:** $32 individuals; $42 out of country. **Remarks:** Accepts advertising. **URL:** http://www.classicimages.com. **Alt. Formats:** Microform.
Ad Rates: BW: $168 **Circ:** Paid 4,200
4C: $393 Non-paid 500
PCI: $3

11303 The Post
Lee Enterprises, Inc.
PO Box 438 Phone: (319)263-2169
Muscatine, IA 52761 Fax: (319)263-7240
Free: (800)588-7237
Publication E-mail: thepost@muscanet.com

Shopper. **Founded:** 1969. **Freq:** Weekly (Tues.). **Print Method:** Offset. **Cols./Page:** 7. **Col. Width:** 6.5 picas. **Col. Depth:** 16 inches. **Key Personnel:** Glenda Verdick, General Mgr. **Subscription Rates:** Free. **Formerly:** Muskie Trading Post.
Ad Rates: GLR: $7.50 **Circ:** Free 20,850
BW: $784
4C: $1,039
PCI: $7

11304 KWCC-FM - 93.1
3218 Mulberry Ave. Phone: (319)263-2442
Muscatine, IA 52761 Fax: (319)263-9206

Format: Country. **Networks:** AP; USA Radio. **Owner:** John and Darlene Schwandke, at above address. **Founded:** 1996. **Operating Hours:** Continuous. **Key Personnel:** John A. Schwandke, Contact; Darlene M. Schwandke, Contact; Tim Scott, Contact. **Local Programs:** *Buy, Sell or Trade*, John Schwandke; *Coffee Club Talk Show* 8:30 am Friday, John Schwandke; *F.Y.I*, Kristin McHugh. **Wattage:** 6,000. **Ad Rates:** $17 for 30 seconds; $20.50 for 60 seconds. Combined advertising rates available with KWPC-AM.

11305 KWPC-AM - 860
3218 Mulberry Ave. Phone: (319)263-2442
Muscatine, IA 52761

Format: Adult Contemporary; News. **Networks:** USA Radio; AP. **Owner:** Muscatine Communications, Inc., at above address. **Founded:** 1947. **Operating Hours:** 5:30 a.m.-12 p.m. **Key Personnel:** John Schwandke, President; Tim Scott, Chief Engineer; Kristin McHugh, News Dir.; Sonya Taylor, Traffic Mgr. **Wattage:** 250. **Ad Rates:** $13-17 for 30 seconds; $16.50-20.50 for 60 seconds.

NASHUA†, pop. 1,846.

N IA. Chickasaw Co. 8 mi. SE of Ionia. Residential.

11306 Nashua Reporter and Weekly Post
216 Main St. Phone: (515)435-4151
PO Box 67
Nashua, IA 50658
Community newspaper. **Founded:** 1875. **Freq:** Weekly (Wed.). **Print Method:** Offset. **Trim Size:** 21 x 13. **Cols./Page:** 6. **Col. Width:** 2 inches. **Col. Depth:** 21.5 picas. **Key Personnel:** Carmen Conklin, Contact; Wanda Orric, Contact. **Subscription Rates:** $19 individuals; $21 out of area. **Remarks:** Accepts advertising.
Ad Rates: GLR: $2.70 **Circ:** Paid ‡1,200
BW: $300 Free ‡20
PCI: $2.70

NEOLA, pop. 839.

SW IA. Pottawattamie Co. 20 mi. NE of Council Bluffs. Manufactures mill hammers, camper tops, recap tires. Agriculture. Corn, wheat, livestock.

Gazette - See Shelby

NEVADA†, pop. 5,912.

C IA. Story Co. 9 mi. E. of Ames. Manufactures brick, tile, poultry feeds, fertilizer. Poultry packing, hybrid corn processing plants. Ships livestock. Agriculture. Corn, oats, wheat.

11307 Money Saver
Nevada Journal
1210 6th St. Phone: (515)382-2161
PO Box 89 Fax: (515)382-4299
Nevada, IA 50201
Publisher E-mail: journal@nevia.net

Shopping guide. **Subtitle:** Shopper. **Founded:** 1980. **Freq:** Weekly (Wed.). **Print Method:** Offset. **Cols./Page:** 6. **Col. Width:** 2 inches. **Col. Depth:** 21 1/2 inches. **Key Personnel:** Roger Will, General Mgr. **Remarks:** Accepts advertising. **Formerly:** Money Miser.
Ad Rates: BW: $632.10 **Circ:** Free 7,448
SAU: $5.60
PCI: $5.60

11308 Nevada Journal
1210 6th St. Phone: (515)382-2161
PO Box 89 Fax: (515)382-4299
Nevada, IA 50201
Publication E-mail: nevjournal@aol.com
Publisher E-mail: journal@nevia.net

Community newspaper. **Founded:** 1895. **Freq:** Weekly (Thurs.). **Print Method:** Offset. **Cols./Page:** 6. **Col. Width:** 25 nonpareils. **Col. Depth:** 294 agate lines. **Key Personnel:** Marlys Barker, Editor; Shane Goodman, General Mgr. **Subscription Rates:** $25 individuals; $35 out of county. **Remarks:** Accepts advertising.
Ad Rates: SAU: $5.60 **Circ:** ‡3,200
PCI: $5.60

NEW HAMPTON†, pop. 3,940.

NE IA. Chickasaw Co. 40 mi. N. of Waterloo. Food, egg, and feed processing plant; tool manufactured; hatchery. Agriculture. Corn, oats, hogs.

11309 New Hampton Economist
New Hampton Publishing Co.
10 N. Chestnut Ave. Phone: (515)394-2111
PO Box 380 Fax: (515)394-2113
New Hampton, IA 50659
Community newspaper. **Freq:** Weekly (Tues.). **Cols./Page:** 9. **Col. Width:** 9 1/2 picas. **Col. Depth:** 21 1/2 inches. **Key Personnel:** Daniel Feuling, Editor and Publisher.
Circ: Free 3,500

NEW LONDON, pop. 2,043.

SE IA. Henry Co. 18 mi. NW of Burlington. Tourism. Manufactures gloves, lapidary equipment. Grain elevators. Ships livestock, grain. Dairy, stock, poultry, grain farms.

11310 The New London Journal
Louisa Publishing Co., Ltd.
138 W. Main Phone: (319)367-2366
New London, IA 52645
Publisher E-mail: lpc@lisco.net

Newspaper with a Republican orientation. **Subtitle:** Your Hometown Newspaper. **Founded:** 1876. **Freq:** Weekly (Thurs.). **Print Method:** Offset. **Cols./Page:** 8. **Col. Width:** 21 nonpareils. **Col. Depth:** 294 agate lines. **Key Personnel:** Michael A. Hodges, Publisher. **Subscription Rates:** $15 individuals; $18 out of area; $21 out of state. **Remarks:** Accepts advertising.
Ad Rates: GLR: $.11 **Circ:** 1,092
PCI: $2.94

NEW SHARON, pop. 1,225.

SEC IA. Mahaska Co. 12 mi. N. of Oskaloosa. Hatchery, elevators. Grain farms. Corn, wheat, oats.

11311 New Sharon
Mother Wit Publishing Co.
Box 90 Phone: (515)637-2632
New Sharon, IA 50207
Newspaper. **Founded:** 1860. **Freq:** Weekly (Thurs.). **Print Method:** Offset. **Cols./Page:** 6. **Col. Width:** 28 nonpareils. **Col. Depth:** 294 agate lines. **Key Personnel:** Chris Arnold, Publisher. **Subscription Rates:** $21 individuals. **Remarks:** Accepts advertising. **Formerly:** Star (1992).
Ad Rates: BW: $190 **Circ:** Paid 633
SAU: $3.74
PCI: $2.75

NEWELL, pop. 913.

NW IA. Buena Vista Co. 49 mi. W. of Fort Dodge. Elevators. Ships stock, grain. Agriculture. Corn, oats, hogs, cattle.

11312 Buena Vista County Journal
Pilot Tribune
PO Box 666-A Phone: (712)272-4417
Newell, IA 50568
Community newspaper. **Founded:** 1871. **Freq:** Weekly (Wed.). **Print Method:** Offset. **Key Personnel:** Martin G. Oakman, Editor; Dorothy Oakman, Publisher; Virgil Oakman, Publisher. **Subscription Rates:** $13 individuals. **Remarks:** Accepts advertising.
Ad Rates: PCI: $4.04 **Circ:** Paid ‡1,071
Free ‡63

NEWTON†, pop. 15,292.

SC IA. Jasper Co. 33 mi. E. of Des Moines. Manufactures washing machines, potato diggers, metal stampings, electric units, advertising specialties, dairy products. Foundry. Diversified farming.

11313 The Newton Daily News
Newton Printing Co.
200 1st Ave. E. Phone: (515)792-3121
Newton, IA 50208 Fax: (515)792-5505

Newspaper. **Founded:** 1902. **Freq:** Daily (eve.). **Cols./Page:** 6. **Col. Width:** 12 picas. **Col. Depth:** 21 1/2 inches. **Key Personnel:** Peter Hussmann, Editor; Joan McDermott, Publisher; David Stanley, Advertising Mgr. **Subscription Rates:** $74 individuals. **Remarks:** Accepts advertising.
Ad Rates: BW: $1,093.92 **Circ:** 7,200
SAU: $8.48

11314 KCOB-AM - 1280
PO Box 66 Phone: (515)792-5262
Newton, IA 50208-0066 Fax: (515)792-8403

Format: Country. **Simulcasts:** KCOB-FM. **Networks:** CNN Radio. **Founded:** 1957. **Operating Hours:** 14.5 hrs. Daily; 1% network, 99% local. **ADI:** Des Moines, IA. **Key Personnel:** Frank Liebl, Contact; Randy Van, News Dir.; Terry Walter, Contact. **Wattage:** 1000. **Ad Rates:** $7-27 for 30 seconds; $10-32 for 60 seconds. Combined advertising rates available with KRTI-FM.

11315 KCOB-FM - 95.9
PO Box 66 Phone: (515)792-5262
Newton, IA 50208-0066 Fax: (515)792-8403

Format: Country. **Networks:** CNN Radio. **Founded:** 1969. **Formerly:** KLVN-FM (1992). **Operating Hours:** Continuous. **ADI:** Des Moines, IA. **Key Personnel:** Frank Liebl, Station/Sales Mgr.; Randy Van, News Dir.; Terry Walter, Operations/Sports Mgr. **Wattage:** 6,000. **Ad Rates:** $7-27 for 30 seconds; $10-32 for 60 seconds.

NORTH ENGLISH, pop. 990.

SE IA. Iowa Co. 30 mi. SW of Iowa City. Butter, feeds, portable harrows manufactured. Stock, poultry, grain farms.

11316 The North English Record
Marengo Publishing Corp.
PO Box 155 Phone: (319)642-5506
North English, IA 52316 Fax: (319)642-5509
Free: (800)414-5506

Community newspaper. **Founded:** 1887. **Freq:** Weekly (Thurs.). **Print Method:** Offset. **Trim Size:** 14 1/2 x 21 1/2. **Cols./Page:** 6. **Col. Width:** 14 picas. **Col. Depth:** 196 agate lines. **Key Personnel:** Craig Cronbaugh, News Editor, phone (319)664-3237; Michael Simmons, Publisher. **Subscription Rates:** $22 individuals; $24 out of area; $29 out of state. **Remarks:** Accepts advertising.
Ad Rates: GLR: $.32 **Circ:** ‡900
BW: $870.75
4C: $1,005.75
SAU: $6.75
PCI: $4.50

NORWALK

SC IA. Warren Co. 5 mi. N. of Sommerset.

11317 North Warren Town and County News
North Warren Twon and Country News
PO Box 325 Phone: (515)981-0406
Norwalk, IA 50211
Suburban community newspaper. **Founded:** 1968. **Freq:** Weekly. **Print Method:** Offset. **Trim Size:** 11 1/2 x 17. **Cols./Page:** 6. **Col. Width:** 9 1/2 picas. **Col. Depth:** 16 inches. **Key Personnel:** Sally M. Huntoon, Editor; Steve Klein, Publisher. **USPS:** 395-120. **Subscription Rates:** $12; $14 out of area. **Remarks:** Color advertising not accepted.
Ad Rates: SAU: $3.28 **Circ:** Combined 1,445
PCI: $2.52

OAKLAND, pop. 1,552.

SW IA. Pottawattamie Co. 26 mi. E. of Council Bluffs. Stock, poultry, grain farms. Corn, wheat, oats.

11318 The Herald
PO Box 556
Oakland, IA 51560

Community newspaper. **Founded:** Oct. 1881. **Freq:** Weekly (Wed.). **Print Method:** Offset. **Cols./Page:** 6. **Col. Width:** 9 picas. **Col. Depth:** 14 1/2 inches. **Key Personnel:** Rich Price, Editor; Don Nielson, Publisher. **USPS:** 401-120. **Subscription Rates:** $18 individuals; $30 out of state. **Remarks:** Accepts advertising. **Formerly:** Acorn Times.
Ad Rates: BW: $217.50 **Circ:** Paid ‡1,814
SAU: $4.95 Free ‡22
PCI: $2.50

OCHEYEDAN, pop. 599.

NW IA. Osceola Co. On Ocheyedan River. Elevator. Agriculture. Corn, soybeans, cattle, hogs.

11319 Ocheyedan Press and Melvin News
The Press, Inc.
Box 456 Phone: (712)758-3140
Ocheyedan, IA 51354 Fax: (712)758-3186

Newspaper. **Founded:** 1891. **Freq:** Weekly (Wed.). **Print Method:** Web press. **Cols./Page:** 7. **Col. Width:** 24 nonpareils. **Col. Depth:** 301 agate lines. **Key Personnel:** Jan Reiste Pedley, Editor and Publisher; Arlyn Pedley, Advertising Mgr./Publisher. **USPS:** 402-680. **Subscription Rates:** $19 individuals; $22.50 out of area; $27.50 out of state. **Remarks:** Accepts advertising.
Ad Rates: GLR: $0.23 **Circ:** ‡1,524
BW: $2.84
SAU: $3.25

ODEBOLT

11320 The Chronicle
216 Main St. Phone: (712)668-2253
PO Box 485 Fax: (712)668-4364
Odebolt, IA 51458
Community newspaper. **Founded:** 1887. **Freq:** Weekly (Thurs.). **Cols./Page:** 5. **Col. Width:** 11 picas. **Col. Depth:** 14 1/2 inches. **Key Personnel:** Randy Flink, Editor; Robert Miller, Publisher. **Subscription Rates:** $17.50; $21.50 out of state. **Remarks:** Accepts advertising. **Formerly**: Odebolt Chronicle.
Ad Rates: PCI: $2.10 **Circ:** ‡3,000

OELWEIN, pop. 7,564.

NE IA. Fayette Co. 40 mi. NE of Waterloo. Corn cribs, chemicals, sprayers, sausage, mineral feed manufactured; planing mill; nursery. Ships livestock. Stock, dairy, grain, poultry farms.

11321 Register
Oelwein Publishing Co.
PO Box 511 Phone: (319)283-2144
25 1st St. SE Fax: (319)283-3268
Oelwein, IA 50662-2306
Free: (800)283-6371

Newspaper with a Report orientation. **Founded:** 1880. **Freq:** Mon.-Sat. (eve.). **Print Method:** Offset. **Cols./Page:** 6. **Col. Width:** 24 nonpareils. **Col. Depth:** 301 agate lines. **Key Personnel:** Cathy Martin, Advertising Mgr. **Subscription Rates:** $55 individuals.
Circ: 6,067

11322 KOEL-AM - 950
City Park Rd. Phone: (319)283-1234
PO Box 391 Fax: (319)283-3615
Oelwein, IA 50662
Free: (800)695-5635

Format: News. **Networks:** ABC. **Owner:** Connoisseur Communications, at above address. **Founded:** 1950. **Operating Hours:** Continuous; 10% network, 90% local. **ADI:** Cedar Rapids-Waterloo-Dubuque, IA. **Key Personnel:** Debbie Raborn, Contact; Pam Obrt, News Dir.; Phil Pannier, Operations Mgr. **Wattage:** 5000. **Ad Rates:** $11-52 for 30 seconds; $14-57 for 60 seconds.

OGDEN

11323 Ogden Reporter
The Ogden
PO Box R Phone: (515)275-4101
Ogden, IA 50212 Fax: (515)275-2844

Community newspaper. **Freq:** Weekly (Wed.). **Cols./Page:** 7. **Col. Width:** 12 3/10 picas. **Col. Depth:** 21 inches. **Key Personnel:** Gary Alban, Publisher.
Circ: 2,000

ONAWA†, pop. 3,283.

W IA. Morona Co. 37 mi. SE of Sioux City. Manufactures machinery, steel culverts. Stock, grain farms.

11324 Onawa Democrat
Wonder and Son Publishing
720 Iowa Ave. Phone: (712)423-2411
PO Box 418 Fax: (712)423-2411
Onawa, IA 51040-0418
Publisher E-mail: democrat@willinet.net

Community newspaper. **Founded:** Feb. 6, 1890. **Freq:** Weekly (Thurs.). **Print Method:** Offset. **Cols./Page:** 6. **Col. Width:** 2 inches. **Col. Depth:** 129 inches. **Key Personnel:** Fredrick Wonder, Publisher; William Wonder, Publisher. **ISSN:** 0899-6520. **Subscription Rates:** $20 individuals; $.50 single issue. **Remarks:** Accepts advertising. **Alt. Formats:** CD-ROM.
Ad Rates: BW: $504 **Circ:** Paid ⊕2,787
4C: $729
SAU: $4

11325 Sentinel
PO Box 208 Phone: (712)423-2021
Onawa, IA 51040-0208 Fax: (712)423-3038
Free: (800)603-2021

Newspaper with a Republican orientation. **Founded:** 1885. **Freq:** Weekly (Thurs.). **Print Method:** Offset. **Cols./Page:** 7. **Col. Width:** 12 nonpareils. **Col. Depth:** 301 agate lines. **Key Personnel:** Verlee Sawyer, Editor and Publisher; Larry Sawyer, Advertising Mgr., lsawyer@willinet.net. **Subscription Rates:** $19 individuals. **Remarks:** Accepts advertising.
Ad Rates: SAU: $3.50 **Circ:** 2,400

ORANGE CITY†, pop. 4,588.

NW IA. Sioux Co. 45 mi. NE of Sioux City. Steel fabrication, ready mix concrete, sport caps, paint, aircraft, bullets, steel arrowheads, farm equipment manufactured. Dairy, stock, poultry farms.

11326 Ad-Visor
Pluim Publishing, Inc.
113 Central Ave. SE Phone: (712)737-4266
Orange City, IA 51041-1738 Fax: (712)737-3896
Free: (800)747-5846

Shopper. **Subtitle:** Ad-Visor. **Founded:** Mar. 1955. **Freq:** Weekly (Tues.). **Print Method:** Web press. **Cols./Page:** 8. **Col. Width:** 19 nonpareils. **Col. Depth:** 301 agate lines. **Key Personnel:** Bob Hulstein, Editor and Publisher; Dennis Den Hartog, Advertising Mgr. **Remarks:** Accepts advertising.
Ad Rates: GLR: $4 **Circ:** Free 7,200
BW: $688
SAU: $3.45
PCI: $3.50

11327 Cattle-Log
Pluim Publishing, Inc.
113 Central Ave. SE Phone: (712)737-4266
Orange City, IA 51041-1738 Fax: (712)737-3896
Free: (800)747-5846

Farm newspaper. **Freq:** Bimonthly. **Remarks:** Advertising accepted; rates available upon request.
Circ: (Not Reported)

11328 Sioux County Capital-Democrat
Pluim Publishing, Inc.
113 Central Ave. SE Phone: (712)737-4266
Orange City, IA 51041-1738 Fax: (712)737-3896
Free: (800)747-5846

Newspaper. **Founded:** 1882. **Freq:** Weekly (Wed.). **Print Method:** Offset. Uses mats. **Trim Size:** 14 1/2 x 22 3/4. **Cols./Page:** 6. **Col. Width:** 27 nonpareils. **Col. Depth:** 301 agate lines. **Key Personnel:** Doug Marks, Editor; Dale Pluim, Publisher; Dennis Den Hartog, Advertising Mgr. **Subscription Rates:** $27 individuals. **Remarks:** Color advertising not accepted.
Ad Rates: GLR: $4.25 **Circ:** Paid ‡2,400
SAU: $4.03 Free ‡50
PCI: $3.50

OSAGE†, pop. 3,718.

N IA. Mitchell Co. 30 mi. NE of Mason City. Commercial drying of farming products. Manufactuers windows, socks, gloves, mittens, feed, business forms. Limestone quarries. Agriculture. Corn, hogs, cattle.

11329 Mitchell County Press-News
PO Box 60 Phone: (515)732-3721
112 N. 6th St. Fax: (515)732-5689
Osage, IA 50461
Publication E-mail: mcpress@osage.net

Community newspaper. **Founded:** 1865. **Freq:** Weekly (Wed.). **Print Method:** Offset. **Trim Size:** 15 x 21 3/4. **Cols./Page:** 6. **Col. Width:** 2.25 inches. **Col. Depth:** 21.5 inches. **Key Personnel:** Paul Bunge, Owner; David Stanley, General Mgr. **Subscription Rates:** $27 individuals; $.75 single issue.
Ad Rates: SAU: $5.89 **Circ:** Paid 3,496
PCI: $5.89 Free 61

11330 KWMM-FM - 98.7
200 N. 7th St. Phone: (515)228-1000
Osage, IA 50461 Fax: (515)228-1200

Format: Adult Contemporary. **Networks:** NBC; Westwood One Radio. **Owner:** Cumulus Broadcasting, 207 Main St., Charles City, IA 50616. **Founded:** 1980. **Formerly:** KOSG-FM (1989); KCZY-FM; Mega Media Ltd. **Operating Hours:** Continuous.; 10% network, 90% local. **Key Personnel:** C. North, Manager; Bob Williams, Program Dir. **Wattage:** 3000.

OSKALOOSA†, pop. 10,629.

SEC IA. Mahaska Co. 55 mi. SE of Des Moines. Residential.

11331 The Oskaloosa Herald
Donrey Media Group
1901 A Ave. W. Phone: (515)672-2581
Oskaloosa, IA 52577 Fax: (515)672-2994

General newspaper. **Founded:** 1850. **Freq:** Daily (eve.) and Sat. (morn.). **Print Method:** Offset. **Cols./Page:** 6. **Col. Width:** 25 nonpareils. **Col. Depth:** 301 agate lines. **Key Personnel:** Donald W. Reynolds, Publisher. **Remarks:** Accepts advertising.
Ad Rates: SAU: $5.70 **Circ:** (Not Reported)

11332 Oskaloosa Shopper
1901 A Avenue W. Phone: (515)672-2581
Box 530 Fax: (515)672-2294
Oskaloosa, IA 52577-0530
Shopping guide. **Freq:** Weekly (Wed.). **Print Method:** Offset. **Cols./Page:** 6. **Col. Width:** 26 nonpareils. **Col. Depth:** 301 agate lines. **Key Personnel:** Keith Ponder, Contact. **Subscription Rates:** Free; $18.75 by mail. **Remarks:** Accepts advertising.
Ad Rates: GLR: $.39 **Circ:** Free 20,500
BW: $664.35
4C: $1,024.35
SAU: $5.35

11333 KBOE-AM - 740
2172 230th St. Phone: (515)673-3493
Hwy. 63 N. Fax: (515)673-3495
PO Box 380
Oskaloosa, IA 52577-0380
E-mail: kboe@lisco.com

Format: Contemporary Country. **Simulcasts:** KBOE-FM. **Networks:** ABC. **Owner:** Jomast Corp., at above address. **Founded:** 1950. **Operating Hours:** Continuous. **ADI:** Des Moines, IA. **Key Personnel:** Scott Ewing, General Sales Mgr.; Lance Renaud, News Dir.; Lance Renaud, Sports Dir.; Steve Shettler, Program Dir.; Karla Allen, Office Mgr. **Wattage:** 250. **Ad Rates:** $7.30-12.20 for 30 seconds; $10.95-18.30 for 60 seconds. Combined advertising rates available with KBOE-FM. **URL:** http://www.lisco.com/kboe.

11334 KBOE-FM - 104.9
Hwy. 63 N. Phone: (515)673-3493
PO Box 380 Fax: (515)673-3495
Oskaloosa, IA 52577

Format: Country. **Networks:** ABC; Radio Iowa; Brownfield. **Owner:** Jomast Corp., at above address. **Founded:** 1964. **Formerly:** KOSK-FM (1992). **Operating Hours:** Continuous. **Key Personnel:** Scott Ewing, General Mgr.; Steve Shettler, Program Dir.; Karla Hawk, Office Mgr.; Lance Renand, News Dir. **Wattage:** 50,000. **URL:** http://www.lisco.com/kboe.

11335 KIGC-FM - 88.7
William Penn College Phone: (515)673-1095
201 Trueblood Ave.
Oskaloosa, IA 52577
E-mail: kigc@wmpenn.edu

Format: Contemporary Hit Radio (CHR); Alternative/New Music/Progressive; Urban Contemporary; Heavy Metal. **Networks:** Independent. **Owner:** William Penn College, at above address, (515)673-1092. **Founded:** 1965. **Formerly**: KFHL-AM. **Operating Hours:** 12 p.m.-midnight; 100% local. **Key Personnel:** Laura Bestler, Faculty Adviser; Flint Davis, Manager; Will Plummer, Music Dir. **Wattage:** 230. **Ad Rates:** Noncommercial.

OSSIAN, pop. 829.

NE IA. Winneshiek Co. 75 mi. E. of Mason City. Fertilizer, feed mixing plants. Grain elevator. Agriculture. Corn, oats, hay, livestock.

11336 The Ossian Bee
Ossain Bee
107 W. Main Phone: (319)532-9113
PO Box 96 Fax: (319)532-9081
Ossian, IA 52161-0096
Newspaper with a Democratic orientation. **Founded:** 1874. **Freq:** Weekly (Thurs.). **Print Method:** Offset. **Cols./Page:** 6. **Col. Width:** 28 nonpareils. **Col. Depth:** 301 agate lines. **Key Personnel:** Dirk Amundsen, Editor and Publisher. **Subscription Rates:** $15 individuals.
Ad Rates: GLR: $.19 **Circ:** ‡1,230
BW: $291.06
4C: $343.06
SAU: $2.35
PCI: $2.66

OTTUMWA†, pop. 27,381.

SE IA. Wapello Co. 90 mi. SE of Des Moines. Indian Hills Community College. Manufactures agricultural machinery, automobile parts, tile, brick, fiberglass bathtubs and shower stalls. Poultry, food processing. Photo finishing. Meat packing. Agriculture. Livestock, feed.

11337 The Ottumwa Courier
Lee Enterprises, Inc.
213 E. 2nd St. Phone: (515)684-4611
Ottumwa, IA 52501 Fax: (515)684-7834

General newspaper. **Founded:** 1848. **Freq:** Mon.-Sat. (morn.). **Print Method:** Offset. **Cols./Page:** 6. **Col. Width:** 12 1/2 picas. **Col. Depth:** 21 3/4 inches. **Key Personnel:** David Kraemer, Editor, editor@ottumwacourier.com; Martha Wells, Publisher. **Subscription Rates:** $124.50 individuals; $154.88

mail within 70 miles; $208.50 mail outside 70 miles. **Remarks:** Accepts advertising. **Formerly:** News Editor.
Ad Rates: GLR: $9.25 **Circ:** Mon.-Sat. ★18,034
BW: $1,305.48
4C: $1,530.48
SAU: $16.29
PCI: $11.90

11338 KBIZ-AM - 1240
Broadcast Center Phone: (515)682-4535
209 S. Market Fax: (515)684-5892
Ottumwa, IA 52501

Format: News; Sports; Oldies; Agricultural; Big Band/Nostalgia. **Networks:** CBS. **Founded:** 1941. **Operating Hours:** Continuous; 10% network, 90% local. **ADI:** Ottumwa, IA-Kirksville, MO (Wapello, IA). **Key Personnel:** Mel Moyer, Station Mgr.; Mike Buchanan, News/Farm Dir.; Tom Rodgers, Operations Mgr. **Wattage:** 1000. **Ad Rates:** $9 for 30 seconds; $13.5 for 60 seconds.

KKSI-FM - See Eddyville

11339 KLEE-AM - 1480
601 W. 2nd St. Phone: (515)682-8711
Ottumwa, IA 52501 Fax: (515)682-8482
E-mail: kleeam@adl.com

Format: Country; Talk. **Networks:** NBC; Mutual Broadcasting System; Westwood One Radio; Brownfield; Talknet. **Owner:** FMC Broadcasting, Inc, at above address. **Founded:** 1954. **Operating Hours:** Continuous; 40% network, 60% local. **ADI:** Ottumwa, IA-Kirksville, MO (Wapello, IA). **Key Personnel:** Thomas A. Palen, General Mgr.; Bill Bishop, News Dir.; Fred Jenkins, Chief Engineer; Steve Austin, Program Dir.; Jill Green, Sales Mgr. **Local Programs:** *Dialogue (Community Issues)*, Bob Craig, (515)682-8711. **Wattage:** 500. **Ad Rates:** $9.24 for 30 seconds; $11.59 for 60 seconds.

11340 KOTM-FM - 47.7
601 W. 2nd St. Phone: (515)682-8711
Ottumwa, IA 52501 Fax: (515)682-8482

Format: Contemporary Hit Radio (CHR). **Founded:** 1976. **Formerly:** KLEE-FM (1987). **Operating Hours:** Continuous; 5% network, 95% local. **ADI:** Ottumwa, IA-Kirksville, MO (Wapello, IA). **Key Personnel:** Thomas A. Palen, General Mgr.; Bill Bishop, News Dir.; Marci Barnes, Program Dir.; Fred Jenkins, Chief Engineer; Jill Green, Sales Mgr. **Local Programs:** *Eighties Lunch*, Marci Barnes, Mailing contact, (515)682-8711; *Goin' Home Show aka Quittin' Time.* **Wattage:** 6000. **Ad Rates:** $9.24 for 30 seconds; $11.59 for 60 seconds.

11341 KRKN-FM - 104.3
413 E. Main St. Phone: (515)684-5563
Ottumwa, IA 52501 Fax: (515)684-5832
Free: (800)794-6869
E-mail: kksi_ krkn@kissclassicrock.com

Format: Contemporary Country. **Networks:** ABC; Jones Satellite. **Owner:** Otown Communications Inc., at above address. **Founded:** Aug. 1996. **Operating Hours:** Continuous. **ADI:** Des Moines, IA. **Key Personnel:** Don Linder, President; Greg List, Vice President, glist@kissclassicrock.com; Mark McVey, Vice President, mcvey@kissclassicrock.com. **Wattage:** 25,000. **Ad Rates:** $12.50 for 30 seconds; $18.75 for 60 seconds. Combined advertising rates available with KKSI.

11342 KTWA-FM - 92.7
Broadcast Center Phone: (515)682-4535
PO Box 190 Fax: (515)684-5892
Ottumwa, IA 52501

Format: Adult Contemporary. **Networks:** Satellite Music Network. **Owner:** Gillbro Communications, 209 S. Market, Ottumwa, IA 52501. **Founded:** 1985. **Operating Hours:** Continuous; 90% network, 10% local. **ADI:** Ottumwa, IA-Kirksville, MO (Wapello, IA). **Key Personnel:** Mel Moyer, General Mgr. **Wattage:** 3000. **Ad Rates:** $9 for 30 seconds; $13.50 for 60 seconds.

11343 KYOU-TV - 15
820 W. 2nd St. Phone: (515)684-5415
Ottumwa, IA 52501 Fax: (515)682-5173
Free: (800)363-6915

Format: Commercial TV. **Networks:** Fox; Independent; United Paramount Network. **Owner:** Public Interest Broadcast Group, Inc., at above address. **Founded:** 1987. **Formerly:** KOIA-TV (1992). **Operating Hours:** Continuous; 98% network; 2% local. **ADI:** Ottumwa, IA-Kirksville, MO (Wapello, IA). **Key Personnel:** Dirk R. Engstrom, Gen. Mgr./Program Dir./President; Dianne Little, General Sales Mgr./Promotions Dir. **Wattage:** 2213 kw visual, 221 kw aural. **Ad Rates:** Advertising accepted; rates available upon request.

PANORA

11344 Guthrie County Vedette
111 E. Main Phone: (515)755-2115
PO Box 38 Fax: (515)755-2425
Panora, IA 50216
Community newspaper. **Freq:** Weekly (Thurs.). **Cols./Page:** 8. **Col. Width:** 10 1/2 picas. **Col. Depth:** 21 1/2 inches. **Key Personnel:** Scott Gonzales, Publisher. **Subscription Rates:** $15 individuals; $20 out of state. **Remarks:** Accepts advertising.
Circ: 1,400

11345 Panora Cooperative Cablevision Assoc. Inc.
114 E. Main Phone: (515)755-2200
PO Box 217 Fax: (515)755-2425
Panora, IA 50216
E-mail: panora@netins.net

Founded: 1981. **Key Personnel:** Bill Dorsett, Asst. Mgr.; Cheryl Castile, Commerical Mgr. **Cities Served:** Linden, Panora, Yale, IA: subscribing households 1,091; 33 channels; 1 community access channel; 168 hours per week community access programming.

PARKERSBURG, pop. 1,968.

NC IA. Butler Co. 9 mi. W. of New Hartford. Residential.

11346 Eclipse-News-Review
503 Coates St. Phone: (319)346-1461
Parkersburg, IA 50665
Local newspaper serving three towns. **Founded:** 1873. **Freq:** Weekly. **Print Method:** Offset. **Trim Size:** 16 x 21. **Cols./Page:** 8. **Col. Width:** 10.5 picas. **Col. Depth:** 21 inches. **Key Personnel:** Leon M. Thorne, Editor and Publisher. **USPS:** 167-260. **Subscription Rates:** $22 individuals; $24 out of state; $0.50 single issue.
Ad Rates: GLR: $.21 **Circ:** Paid ‡2,335
BW: $421.40 Free ‡52
4C: $511
SAU: $5.15
PCI: $4.55

PAULLINA, pop. 1,224.

NW IA. O'Brien Co. 50 mi. NE of Sioux City. Stock, grain farms. Corn, oats, soybeans. Lamb processing.

11347 The Paullina Times
O'Shillal Enterprises, Inc.
114 E. Broadway Phone: (712)448-3622
PO Box 637 Fax: (712)448-2622
Paullina, IA 51046
Newspaper with a Report orientation. **Founded:** 1883. **Freq:** Weekly (Thurs.). **Print Method:** Offset. **Cols./Page:** 6. **Col. Width:** 23 nonpareils. **Col. Depth:** 301 agate lines. **Key Personnel:** Mike Otto, Publisher. **USPS:** 423-660. **Subscription Rates:** $18 individuals; $22 other countries. **Remarks:** Accepts advertising.
Ad Rates: GLR: $4.50 **Circ:** Paid 1,250
SAU: $4 Free 15
PCI: $4

PELLA, pop. 8,349.

SC IA. Marion Co. 40 mi. SE of Des Moines. Residential.

11348 The Chronicle
Edwards Publications, Inc.
739 Franklin St.
PO Box 126
Pella, IA 50219

Community newspaper. **Founded:** 1864. **Freq:** Weekly (Fri.). **Print Method:** Offset. **Trim Size:** 13 x 21.5. **Cols./Page:** 6. **Col. Width:** 12 picas. **Col. Depth:** 21.25 inches. **Key Personnel:** Barry Johnson, Editor; Jack Crook, Publisher; Carol Rowland, Advertising Mgr.; Pat Reeves, Office Mgr. **Subscription Rates:** $24 individuals per year; $27 other/per year. **Remarks:** Accepts advertising. **Formerly:** Pella Chronicle.
Ad Rates: PCI: $5 **Circ:** ‡3,350

11349 Theatre History Studies
Mid-America Theatre Association
Central College Phone: (515)263-0110
Pella, IA 50219 Fax: (515)263-1161

Scholarly journal covering theatre history. **Founded:** 1980. **Freq:** Annual. **Key Personnel:** Robert A. Schanke, Editor, schanker@aol.com. **ISSN:** 0733-2033. **Subscription Rates:** $12 individuals. **Remarks:** Accepts advertising.
Ad Rates: BW: $150 **Circ:** Paid 1,000

11350 KCUI-FM - 89.1
Central College Phone: (515)628-5263
Pella, IA 50219 Fax: (515)628-5316
E-mail: kcui@central.edu

Format: Alternative/New Music/Progressive. **Owner:** Central University of Iowa, at above address, (515)628-9000, Free: (800)458-5503. **Founded:** 1961. **Operating Hours:** 11 a.m.-1 a.m. **Key Personnel:** Jennifer Stoepke, General Mgr.; Leah Reilly, News Dir.; Jennifer Raschke, Program Dir.; Gayle Nordyke, Music Dir. **Wattage:** 10. **Ad Rates:** Noncommercial.

11351 KFMG-FM - 103.3
PO Box 41143 Phone: (515)282-1033
Des Moines, IA 50311-0503 Fax: (515)282-1062

Format: Album-Oriented Rock (AOR). **Founded:** 1976. **Formerly:** KFMD-FM; KXJX-FM; KDMG-FM. **Operating Hours:** Continuous. **ADI:** Des Moines, IA. **Key Personnel:** Ron Sorenson, General Mgr.; J.D. Stites, General Sales Mgr. **Wattage:** 100,000 ERP.

PERRY, pop. 7,053.

SWC IA. Dallas Co. 28 mi. SW of Boone. Manufactures ice cream mix, cultivator shovels, plow welding products, fertilizer. Meat, poultry packing, hybrid seed corn plants; granite works; nursery. Agriculture. Corn, oats, hay, cattle. Hogs, soybeans.

11352 Chiefland Shopper
Chief Printing Co.
1323 2nd St. Phone: (515)465-4666
PO Box 98 Fax: (515)465-3087
Perry, IA 50220
Shopper. **Founded:** 1975. **Freq:** Weekly (Tues.). **Print Method:** Offset. **Trim Size:** 17 x 22 1/2. **Cols./Page:** 8. **Col. Width:** 11 picas. **Col. Depth:** 21 inches. **Key Personnel:** Linda Schumacher, Advertising Mgr.; Steve Whitehead, General Mgr. **Remarks:** Accepts advertising.
Ad Rates: SAU: $8.02 **Circ:** Free 17,400
PCI: $7.13

11353 Perry Chief
Chief Printing Co.
1323 2nd St. Phone: (515)465-4666
PO Box 98 Fax: (515)465-3087
Perry, IA 50220
Newspaper with a Report orientation. **Founded:** 1874. **Freq:** Weekly (Thurs.). **Print Method:** Offset. **Trim Size:** 17 x 22 1/2. **Cols./Page:** 8. **Col. Width:** 11 picas. **Col. Depth:** 21 inches. **Key Personnel:** Phillip Delaney, Editor; Linda Schumacher, Advertising Mgr. **USPS:** 428-260. **Subscription Rates:** $27 individuals; $30 out of area. **Remarks:** Accepts advertising.
Ad Rates: SAU: $5.80 **Circ:** Paid 2,722
PCI: $5.16 Free 36

11354 KDLS-AM - 1310
Box 548 Phone: (515)465-5357
Perry, IA 50220 Fax: (515)465-3952
Free: (800)532-1189

Format: Country; Contemporary Country. **Simulcasts:** KDLS-FM, KCCI TV8 NEWS@6PM. **Networks:** Mutual Broadcasting System. **Owner:** Tom Quinlan, at above address. **Founded:** 1961. **Operating Hours:** 6:00 a.m.-10:00 p.m. **Key Personnel:** Patrick Graney, General Mgr.; John Patrick, Operations Dir.; Patrick Graney, Sales Mgr.; Marcia Murphy, Station Mgr.; Les Fish, Engineer. **Local Programs:** *Chamber Report*, Patrick Graney; *Keeping in Touch*, John Patrick; *Market Report* 6:30, Patrick Graney. **Wattage:** 500. **Ad Rates:** $7-11 for 30 seconds; $9-13 for 60 seconds. Combined advertising rates available with KDLS-FM.

11355 KDLS-FM - 105.5
Box 548 Phone: (515)465-5357
Perry, IA 50220 Fax: (515)465-3952
Free: (800)532-1189

Format: Country. **Simulcasts:** KDLS-AM, KCCI TV 6:00 NEWS. **Networks:** Mutual Broadcasting System. **Owner:** Tom Quinlan, at above address. **Founded:** 1971. **Operating Hours:** 6:00 a.m.-midnight. **Key Personnel:** Patrick Graney, General Mgr.; John Patrick, Operations Dir.; Marcia Murphy, Station Mgr.; Les Fish, Engineer. **Wattage:** 6000. **Ad Rates:** $7-11 for 30 seconds; $9-13 for 60 seconds. Combined advertising rates available with KDLS-AM.

PETERSON, pop. 470.

NW IA. Clay Co. On Little Sioux River, 65 mi. NW of Fort Dodge. Grain elevator. Grain, stock, farms.

11356 Peterson Patriot
Peterson Patriot
PO Box 126 Phone: (712)295-7711
Peterson, IA 51047
Community newspaper covering agricultural news. **Founded:**

1883. **Freq:** Weekly (Thurs.). **Print Method:** Offset. **Cols./Page:** 6. **Col. Width:** 22 nonpareils. **Col. Depth:** 182 agate lines. **Key Personnel:** Jane Stoner, Editor; Roger Stoner, Publisher. **USPS:** 429-220. **Subscription Rates:** $16 individuals; $20 out of area. **Remarks:** Accepts advertising.
Ad Rates: GLR: $.19 **Circ:** ‡580
BW: $241.02
SAU: $3.09
PCI: $2.75

POCAHONTAS†, pop. 2,352.

NW IA. Pocahontas Co. 30 mi. NW of Fort Dodge. Residential.

11357 Pocahontas County Advertiser
Community Publications
218 N. Main Phone: (712)335-3553
Pocahontas, IA 50574 Fax: (712)335-3856
Free: (800)657-4355

Shopper. **Founded:** 1981. **Freq:** Weekly (Tues.). **Print Method:** Offset. **Trim Size:** 15 x 21 1/2. **Cols./Page:** 7. **Col. Width:** 10 picas. **Col. Depth:** 21 1/2 inches. **Key Personnel:** Chris Godredsen, Publisher. **Subscription Rates:** Free. **Remarks:** Accepts advertising.
Ad Rates: BW: $639.63 **Circ:** Free 4,700
SAU: $6.25
PCI: $4.25

11358 Pocahontas Record Democrat
Community Publications
218 N. Main Phone: (712)335-3553
Pocahontas, IA 50574 Fax: (712)335-3856
Free: (800)657-4355

Local newspaper. **Founded:** 1885. **Freq:** Weekly (Tues.). **Print Method:** Offset. **Trim Size:** 15 x 21 1/2. **Cols./Page:** 7. **Col. Width:** 10 picas. **Col. Depth:** 21 1/2 inches. **Key Personnel:** Chris Godfredsen, Editor and Publisher. **Subscription Rates:** $22 individuals; $26.50 out of area; $28.50 out of state.
Ad Rates: BW: $639.63 **Circ:** 1,950
PCI: $4.25

POMEROY, pop. 895.

NWC IA. Calhoun Co. 30 mi. W. of Fort Dodge. Feed, fertilizer, steel crates, hog pens manufactured. Agriculture. Corn, oats, soybeans.

11359 Journal Herald
Dudley Printing
PO Box 279 Phone: (712)468-2266
204 W. 1st St. Fax: (712)468-2266
Pomeroy, IA 50575
Newspaper. **Founded:** 1888. **Freq:** Weekly (Thurs.). **Print Method:** Offset. **Cols./Page:** 7. **Col. Width:** 22 nonpareils. **Col. Depth:** 301 agate lines. **Key Personnel:** John C. Heilman, Editor and Publisher. **Subscription Rates:** $10.50 individuals. **Remarks:** Accepts advertising. **Formerly:** Herald.
Ad Rates: GLR: $.12 **Circ:** 1,400

POSTVILLE, pop. 1,475.

NE IA. Allamakee Co. 60 mi. NE of Waterloo. Meat and turkey processing plants; laminated plastics, seed house; feed mill. Grain, stock, dairy, poultry farms.

11360 The Postville Herald-Leader
News Publishing Inc.
PO Box 100 Phone: (319)864-3333
Postville, IA 52162 Fax: (319)864-3400

Community newspaper. **Founded:** 1912. **Freq:** Weekly (Wed.). **Print Method:** Offset. **Trim Size:** 16 x 22 1/2. **Cols./Page:** 7. **Col. Width:** 28 nonpareils. **Col. Depth:** 301 agate lines. **Key Personnel:** Dan Witte, Publisher; Tom Johnson, General Mgr. **Subscription Rates:** $18 individuals; $24 out of area. **Remarks:** Accepts advertising.
Ad Rates: BW: $445.48 **Circ:** Paid 1,800
SAU: $2.96 Free 14

PRAIRIE CITY, pop. 1,278.

SC IA. Jasper Co. 20 mi. E. of Des Moines. Farm equipment and concrete products manufactured. Stock, poultry, fruit, grain farms.

11361 Prairie City News
Prairie City News, Inc.
108 E. Jefferson Phone: (515)994-2349
Box 249 Fax: (515)994-3169
Prairie City, IA 50228
Community newspaper. **Founded:** 1875. **Freq:** Weekly (Thurs.). **Print Method:** Offset. **Cols./Page:** 4. **Col. Width:** 20 nonpareils. **Col. Depth:** 222 agate lines. **Key Personnel:** Orian Woods, Editor and Publisher. **USPS:** 441-260. **Subscription Rates:** $16 individuals; $19 out of state. **Remarks:** Accepts advertising.
Ad Rates: BW: $229.76 **Circ:** Paid 1,105
SAU: $3.90 Free 22
PCI: $3.59

PRESTON

11362 Preston Times
Webb Printing
4 N. Stevens Phone: (319)689-3841
PO Box 9
Preston, IA 52069
Community newspaper. **Founded:** 1890. **Freq:** Weekly (Tues.). **Print Method:** Offset. **Cols./Page:** 6. **Col. Width:** 10 picas. **Col. Depth:** 15 inches. **Key Personnel:** Jerry Mertens, Editor; Terry Martin, Publisher. **Subscription Rates:** $14; $22 out of area. $.40 single issue. **Remarks:** Accepts advertising. **Formerly:** Preston Times Newspaper.
Ad Rates: PCI: $2.50 **Circ:** 1,000

PRIMGHAR†, pop. 1,050.

NW IA. O'Brien Co. 65 mi. NE of Sioux City. Burial vault factory; hatchery. Grain elevator. Stock, poultry farms. Corn, soybeans, oats, barley.

11363 O'Brien County Bell
O'Bren County Bell
Box 478 Phone: (712)757-4055
Primghar, IA 51245 Fax: (712)757-4055

Newspaper with a Democratic orientation. **Founded:** 1884. **Freq:** Weekly (Thurs.). **Print Method:** Offset. **Cols./Page:** 5. **Col. Width:** 22 nonpareils. **Col. Depth:** 210 agate lines. **Key Personnel:** Deborah Sue Fisch, Editor and Publisher. **Subscription Rates:** $16 individuals; $22 out of state. **Remarks:** Accepts advertising.
Ad Rates: GLR: $.21 **Circ:** ‡1,042
BW: $280
SAU: $3.94
PCI: $2.55

READLYN

11364 Readlyn Telephone Co.
121 Main St. Phone: (319)279-3375
Readlyn, IA 50668 Fax: (319)279-7575

Founded: 1983. **Key Personnel:** Sharon Huck, Manager; Larry Ganske, Plant Supervisor. **Cities Served:** Readlyn, IA: subscribing households 282; 18 channels.

RED OAK†, pop. 6,810.

SW IA. Montgomery Co. 50 mi. E. of Council Bluffs. Manufactures art calendars, batteries, automotive seat frames, advertising specialties, hydraulic hoses, machine shops, livestock equipment. Agriculture. Corn, livestock feed, soybeans.

11365 The Red Oak Express
2012 Commerce Dr. Phone: (712)623-2566
Red Oak, IA 51566-1010 Fax: (712)623-2568

Community newspaper. **Founded:** 1868. **Freq:** Weekly (Tues.). **Print Method:** Offset. **Cols./Page:** 6. **Col. Width:** 12 1/2 picas. **Col. Depth:** 21 1/2 inches. **Key Personnel:** Jan Castle Renander, Ed./General Mgr. **Subscription Rates:** $25 individuals.
Ad Rates: GLR: $6.70 **Circ:** 4,950
SAU: $5.53
PCI: $4.90

11366 KCSI-FM - 95.3
Rural Rte., No. 3 Phone: (712)623-2584
PO Box 465 Fax: (712)623-2583
Red Oak, IA 51566
Free: (800)766-5274

Format: Contemporary Country; News; Sports. **Networks:** ABC; Radio Iowa; Brownfield. **Owner:** Hawkeye Communications, Inc., at above address. **Founded:** 1979. **Formerly:** KOAK-FM. **Operating Hours:** Continuous. **Key Personnel:** Jerry V. Dietz, Owner/Mgr. **Wattage:** 25,000.

11367 KHIN-TV - 36
Iowa Public Television Phone: (515)242-3100
PO Box 6450
Johnston, IA 50131

Format: Public TV. **Simulcasts:** KDIN-TV Des Moines, IA. **Networks:** Public Broadcasting Service (PBS). **Founded:** 1975. **ADI:** Omaha, NE. **Key Personnel:** David Bolender, Exec. Dir; Dennis Malloy, Dir. of Div.; Daniel K. Miller, Program Dir.; Don Saveraid, Dir. of Eng.; Pam Johnson, Dir. of Educ. Telecomm; John Leiendecker, Production Mgr.; Sid Sprecher, Public Affairs.

11368 KOAK-AM - 1080
Rural Rte., No. 3 Phone: (712)623-2584
PO Box 465 Fax: (712)623-2583
Red Oak, IA 51566
Free: (800)766-5274

Format: News; Sports; Contemporary Country. **Simulcasts:** KCSI-FM. **Networks:** ABC; Radio Iowa; Brownfield. **Owner:** Hawkeye Communications, Inc., at above address. **Founded:** 1968. **Operating Hours:** Sunrise-sunset. **Key Personnel:** Jerry V. Dietz, Owner/MGR. **Wattage:** 250.

REINBECK, pop. 1,808.

NEC IA. Grundy Co. 20 mi. SW of Waterloo. Fertilizer lab, highway construction, landfill services. Poultry and produce packing plant. Agriculture. Corn, hogs, cattle.

11369 Courier
406 Grundy Ave. Phone: (319)345-2031
Reinbeck, IA 50669 Fax: (319)345-6767

Newspaper with a Report orientation. **Founded:** 1878. **Freq:** Weekly (Thurs.). **Print Method:** Offset. **Cols./Page:** 6. **Col. Width:** 26 nonpareils. **Col. Depth:** 301 agate lines. **Key Personnel:** Gregg A. Moser, Editor; Leroy A. Moser, Publisher. **USPS:** 460-120. **Subscription Rates:** $26.50 individuals; $30 out of state. **Remarks:** Accepts advertising.
Ad Rates: GLR: $0.31 **Circ:** Paid ‡1,850
BW: $429
4C: $534
SAU: $3.97
PCI: $3.50

REMSEN, pop. 1,592.

NW IA. Plymouth Co. 35 mi. NE of Sioux City. Stock, grain farms. Corn, oats, soybeans.

11370 Remsen Bell-Enterprise
Box 209 Phone: (712)786-1196
257 Washington St. Fax: (712)786-5566
Remsen, IA 51050
Local newspaper. **Founded:** Dec. 1887. **Freq:** Weekly (Thurs.). **Print Method:** Offset. **Trim Size:** 7 1/4 x 11 1/2. **Cols./Page:** 6. **Col. Width:** 12 picas. **Col. Depth:** 21 inches. **Key Personnel:** Noel N. Ahmann, Editor and Publisher. **USPS:** 048-760. **Subscription Rates:** $15 individuals; $17 out of state. **Remarks:** Accepts advertising.
Ad Rates: GLR: $.13 **Circ:** ‡1,300
BW: $226.80
SAU: $2.57
PCI: $3.50

RICEVILLE

11371 Riceville Recorder
Lock Box A Phone: (515)985-2142
Riceville, IA 50466 Fax: (515)985-4185

Community newspaper. **Founded:** 1886. **Freq:** Weekly (Thurs.). **Trim Size:** Offset. **Cols./Page:** 6. **Col. Width:** 12 3/10 picas. **Col. Depth:** 21 1/2 inches. **Key Personnel:** Gordon M. Fales, Editor and Publisher. **USPS:** 465-100. **Subscription Rates:** $20 individuals. **Remarks:** Accepts advertising.
Ad Rates: PCI: $4.32 **Circ:** ‡1,250

RICHLAND, pop. 600.

S IA. Keokuk Co. 90 mi. SE of Des Moines. Stock, grain farms. Corn, soybeans, wheat, livestock.

11372 Plainsman-Clarion
Louisa Publishing Co., Ltd.
PO Box 188 Phone: (319)456-6641
Richland, IA 52585
Publisher E-mail: lpc@lisco.net

Newspaper with a Report orientation. **Founded:** 1881. **Freq:** Weekly (Thurs.). **Print Method:** Offset. **Cols./Page:** 8. **Col. Width:** 21 nonpareils. **Col. Depth:** 294 agate lines. **Key Personnel:** Michael A. Hodges, Editor. **Subscription Rates:** $16 individuals; $19 out of area; $23 out of state. **Remarks:** Accepts advertising.
Ad Rates: GLR: $.22 **Circ:** ‡1,656
SAU: $3.63
PCI: $3.08

RIVERSIDE

11373 Riverside Current
31 E. 1st St. Phone: (319)648-2542
PO Box H Fax: (319)648-5923
MF 8-5 CST
Riverside, IA 52327
Community newspaper. **Founded:** 1978. **Freq:** Weekly (Fri.).

Cols./Page: 5. **Col. Width:** 10 1/2 picas. **Col. Depth:** 13 inches. **Key Personnel:** Joan Bex, Editor; James Bex, Publisher. **Subscription Rates:** $11; $14 out of state. **Remarks:** Accepts advertising.
Ad Rates: GLR: $.375 **Circ:** ‡620
BW: $275
SAU: $3.75
PCI: $3.75

ROCK RAPIDS†, pop. 2,693.

NW IA. Lyon Co. On Rock River, 35 mi. E. of Sioux Falls, SD. Manufactures caps and jackets, farm implements, sheet metal. Feed mill. Grain, stock, poultry farms. Corn, cattle, hogs.

11374 Lyon County Reporter
Lyon-Sioux Newspaper Publishing
310 1st Ave. W. Phone: (712)472-2525
Rock Rapids, IA 51246 Fax: (712)472-3414

Community newspaper. **Founded:** 1881. **Freq:** Weekly (Wed.). **Print Method:** Offset. **Trim Size:** 15 x 21 1/2. **Cols./Page:** 7. **Col. Width:** 12 picas. **Col. Depth:** 301 agate lines. **Key Personnel:** Frank Starr, General Mgr. **USPS:** 323-300. **Subscription Rates:** $24 individuals; $38 out of country. **Remarks:** Accepts advertising.
Ad Rates: GLR: $.34 **Circ:** Paid ‡2,542
BW: $716.38 Free ‡50
4C: $966.38
SAU: $4.76

11375 Modern Communications
115 1st Ave.-West Phone: (712)472-3816
Rock Rapids, IA 51246-1501 Fax: (712)472-3604

Owner: Modern Communications, at above address, (712)472-2941, Fax: (712)472-3296. **Founded:** 1982. **Key Personnel:** Carl DeJargh, Owner/Technician, phone (712)472-2941. **Cities Served:** Rock Rapids, IA: subscribing households 965; 34 channels; 1 community access channel; 1 hour per week community access programming.

ROCK VALLEY, pop. 2,706.

NW IA. Sioux Co. 14 mi. W. of Boyden. Residential.

11376 The Rock Valley Bee
1442 Main St. Phone: (712)476-2795
Rock Valley, IA 51247 Fax: (712)476-2796

Newspaper with a Report orientation. **Founded:** 1884. **Freq:** Weekly (Tues.). **Print Method:** Offset. **Cols./Page:** 6. **Col. Width:** 18 nonpareils. **Col. Depth:** 224 agate lines. **Key Personnel:** Donald L. Johnson, Editor and Publisher. **Subscription Rates:** Free; $18 by mail; $21 outside of 50 mile radius. **Remarks:** Accepts advertising.
Ad Rates: GLR: $5.80 **Circ:** Paid ‡1,600
BW: $556.80 Free ‡4,750

ROCKFORD, pop. 1,012.

N IA. Floyd Co. 14 mi. W. of Charles City. Residential.

11377 Advertiser-Register
The Advertiser
110 W. Main Phone: (515)756-3625
Rockford, IA 50468
Community newspaper. **Founded:** 1881. **Freq:** Weekly. **Print Method:** Offset. **Cols./Page:** 6. **Col. Width:** 14 picas. **Col. Depth:** 21 inches. **Key Personnel:** Fran Schmitt, Editor; Dan Cutler, Publisher. **USPS:** 468-500. **Subscription Rates:** $12; $17 out of state. **Remarks:** Accepts advertising.
Ad Rates: BW: $327.60 **Circ:** 1,900
PCI: $2.60

11378 The American Revenuer
American Revenue Association
PO Box 56 Phone: (515)756-3542
Rockford, IA 50468
Publication E-mail: hogman@netins.net

Magazine on collecting revenue and cinderella stamps. **Founded:** Aug. 1947. **Freq:** 10/year. **Print Method:** Offset. **Trim Size:** 8 1/2 x 11. **Cols./Page:** 2. **Col. Width:** 40. nonpareils. **Col. Depth:** 129 agate lines. **Key Personnel:** Kenneth Trettin, Editor. **ISSN:** 0163-1608. **Subscription Rates:** $20 with membership. **Remarks:** Accepts advertising.
Ad Rates: BW: $120 **Circ:** Paid 1,500
4C: $400 Non-paid 10

ROCKWELL CITY†, pop. 2,276.

NWC IA. Calhoun Co. 25 mi. SW of Fort Dodge. Hatchery; grain elevator. Agriculture. Corn, beans, grain.

11379 Calhoun County Advocate
Remma Inc.
328 Court St. Phone: (712)297-7544
PO Box 31 Fax: (712)297-7544
Rockwell City, IA 50579-9998
Community newspaper. **Founded:** 1878. **Freq:** Weekly (Wed.). **Print Method:** Offset. **Cols./Page:** 8. **Col. Width:** 21 nonpareils. **Col. Depth:** 301 agate lines. **Key Personnel:** Lisa Hedman, Editor; Dan Jackson, Publisher. **USPS:** 468-840. **Subscription Rates:** $19 individuals. **Remarks:** Accepts advertising.
Ad Rates: GLR: $.42 **Circ:** ‡2,187
PCI: $3.25

11380 Calhoun County Reminder
Dudley Printing Inc.
515 4th St. Phone: (712)297-8931
Rockwell City, IA 50579 Fax: (712)297-7193

Shopper. **Founded:** 1959. **Freq:** Weekly (Tues.). **Print Method:** Offset. **Cols./Page:** 6. **Col. Width:** 19 nonpareils. **Col. Depth:** 224 agate lines. **Key Personnel:** Gary D. Dudley, Publisher. **Subscription Rates:** Free; $12.50 by mail. **Remarks:** Accepts advertising.
Ad Rates: GLR: $.30 **Circ:** Free ‡7,200
BW: $403.20
4C: $900
PCI: $4.20

11381 KTLB-FM - 105.9
PO Box 105 Phone: (712)297-7588
Rockwell City, IA 50579-0105

Format: News; Information; Sports; Country; Adult Contemporary. **Networks:** ABC; Radio Iowa; Brownfield. **Owner:** Twin Lakes Broadcasting, Inc., 269 North Twin Lakes Rd., Rockwell City, IA 50579, (712)297-7586. **Founded:** 1975. **Operating Hours:** 5:30 a.m.-11 p.m.; 20% network, 80% local. **Key Personnel:** Duane Carstens, Sports Dir.; Lauri Struve, News Dir.; Pat Palmer, Contact; Sheila Phipps, Music Dir.; LaVonne Wood, Office Mgr. **Wattage:** 25,000. **Ad Rates:** $6-8 for 30 seconds; $8-12 for 60 seconds.

SAC CITY†, pop. 3,000.

NW IA. Sac Co. 10 mi. S. of Early.

11382 Sac City Reminder
Central Sun Media, Inc.
1405 W. Main St. Phone: (712)662-7161
PO Box 426 Fax: (712)662-4198
Sac City, IA 50583-0426
Shopper. **Subtitle:** Sac City Reminder (Shopper). **Founded:** 1932. **Freq:** Weekly (Tues.). **Print Method:** Offset. **Cols./Page:** 6. **Col. Width:** 18 nonpareils. **Col. Depth:** 13 inches. **Key Personnel:** Tessie McKinney, General Mgr. **Subscription Rates:** $17.50 individuals; $35 out of state. **Remarks:** Accepts advertising.
Ad Rates: GLR: $.19 **Circ:** Free 6,500
BW: $245
4C: $500
SAU: $4.50
PCI: $3.25

11383 Sac Sun
Central Sun Media, Inc.
1405 W. Main St. Phone: (712)662-7161
PO Box 426 Fax: (712)662-4198
Sac City, IA 50583-0426
Local newspaper. **Subtitle:** Central Sun Media, Inc. **Founded:** 1871. **Freq:** Weekly (Tues.). **Print Method:** Offset. **Cols./Page:** 6. **Col. Width:** 12 picas. **Col. Depth:** 21 1/2 inches. **Key Personnel:** Tessie McKinney, General Mgr. **Subscription Rates:** $19.50 individuals. **Remarks:** Accepts advertising.
Ad Rates: GLR: $.24 **Circ:** ‡1,900
BW: $350
4C: $1,200
SAU: $4.50
PCI: $3.10

SANBORN, pop. 1,398.

NW IA. O'Brien Co. 70 mi. NE of Sioux City. Fertilizer factory; creamery; cheese plant; grain elevator. Agriculture. Corn, beans, hogs, beef, dairy products.

11384 Sanborn Pioneer
Sanborn Publishing Co.
Box 280 Phone: (712)729-3201
Sanborn, IA 51248
Community newspaper. **Founded:** 1871. **Freq:** Weekly (Thurs.). **Print Method:** Offset. **Cols./Page:** 6. **Col. Width:** 14 picas. **Col. Depth:** 21.5 inches. **Key Personnel:** Dorothy Chrisman, Editor and Publisher. **Subscription Rates:** $19 individuals. **Remarks:** Accepts advertising.
Ad Rates: SAU: $3 **Circ:** Paid 900
PCI: $3

SCHALLER

11385 Schaller Herald
203 S. Main Phone: (712)275-4229
PO Box 129
Schaller, IA 51053
Community newspaper. **Freq:** Weekly (Wed.). **Cols./Page:** 8. **Col. Width:** 10 picas. **Col. Depth:** 21 1/2 inches. **Key Personnel:** Betty Bailey, Editor. **Subscription Rates:** $15 individuals; $18 out of area; $20 out of state. **Remarks:** Accepts advertising.
Ad Rates: SAU: $4.50 **Circ:** 850

SCRANTON, pop. 751.

C IA. Greene Co. 33 mi. W. of Boone.

11386 Scranton Community Antenna Television
1200 Main St. Phone: (712)652-3355
Box 8 Fax: (712)652-3777
Scranton, IA 51462

Owner: Scranton Telephone Co., at above address. **Founded:** Sept. 1983. **Key Personnel:** Sam Fengel, Manager. **Cities Served:** Scranton, IA: subscribing households 235; 35 channels; 1 community access channel; 168 hours per week community access programming.

SEYMOUR, pop. 1,036.

S IA. Wayne Co. 45 mi. SW of Ottumwa. Feed mill; fertilizer plant; machines shops. Agriculture. Corn, oats, poultry, livestock.

11387 The Seymour Herald
116 N. 4th St. Phone: (515)898-7554
PO Box 125 Fax: (515)898-7554
Seymour, IA 52590
Publisher E-mail: naaa@aol.com

Newspaper. **Founded:** 1883. **Freq:** Weekly (Wed.). **Print Method:** Offset. **Cols./Page:** 8. **Col. Width:** 24 nonpareils. **Col. Depth:** 280 agate lines. **Key Personnel:** Karen Young, Editor and Publisher; Ken Banks, Publisher. **Subscription Rates:** $18 individuals; $20. **Remarks:** Accepts advertising.
Ad Rates: SAU: $2.75 **Circ:** 1,600
PCI: $2

SHELBY

11388 Gazette
Box 7 Phone: (712)485-2276
Neola, IA 51559-0007 Fax: (712)485-2277

Community newspaper. **Founded:** 1889. **Freq:** Weekly (Thurs.). **Print Method:** Offset. **Cols./Page:** 6. **Col. Width:** 26 nonpareils. **Col. Depth:** 294 agate lines. **Key Personnel:** Maureen R. Olsen, Editor and Publisher. **USPS:** 377-080. **Subscription Rates:** $18 individuals; $25 out of area. **Remarks:** Accepts advertising.
Ad Rates: GLR: $.15 **Circ:** ‡1,850
BW: $338.63
SAU: $3.50
PCI: $3.50

SHELDON, pop. 5,003.

NW IA. O'Brien Co. 60 mi. N. of Sioux City. Medical equipment, tool and die, truck box fabrication, fiberglass tanks, rendering equipment, working clothes, feed manufactured. Soybean processing mill. Agriculture. Corn, oats, soybeans, livestock.

11389 Golden Shopper
Iowa Information, Inc.
227 9th St. Phone: (712)324-5347
PO Box 160 Fax: (712)324-2345
Sheldon, IA 51201
Free: (800)247-0186
Publisher E-mail: iowainformation.com

Shopping guide. **Founded:** Oct. 2, 1962. **Freq:** Weekly (Mon.). **Print Method:** Offset. **Trim Size:** 12 1/2 x 21 1/2. **Cols./Page:** 6. **Col. Width:** 18 nonpareils. **Col. Depth:** 301 agate lines. **Key Personnel:** Peter Wagner, Publisher, pww@iowainformation.com; Jeff Wagner, General Mgr.; Connie Wagner, Creative Dir. **Remarks:** Accepts advertising.
Ad Rates: BW: $666.93 **Circ:** Free ‡21,242
4C: $896.93
PCI: $7.98

11390 N'West Iowa Review
Iowa Information, Inc.
227 9th St. Phone: (712)324-5347
PO Box 160 Fax: (712)324-2345
Sheldon, IA 51201
Free: (800)247-0186
Publisher E-mail: iowainformation.com

Regional newspaper covering four counties. **Founded:** July 3, 1972. **Freq:** Weekly (Sat.). **Print Method:** Offset. **Cols./Page:** 6. **Col. Width:** 18 nonpareils. **Col. Depth:** 301 agate lines. **Key Personnel:** Jeff Grant, Editor, jeffgrant@iowainformation.com; Peter W. Wagner, Publisher; Jeff Wagner, General Mgr. **Subscription Rates:** $28 individuals in county; $36.50 out of state. **Remarks:** Accepts advertising.
Ad Rates: BW: $559.86 **Circ:** Paid ⊕4,491
4C: $789.86 Non-paid ⊕100
PCI: $6.93

11391 Sheldon Mail-Sun
Iowa Information, Inc.
227 9th St. Phone: (712)324-5347
PO Box 160 Fax: (712)324-2345
Sheldon, IA 51201
Free: (800)247-0186
Publisher E-mail: iowainformation.com

Community newspaper. **Founded:** Jan. 1, 1873. **Freq:** Weekly (Wed.). **Print Method:** Offset. **Cols./Page:** 6. **Col. Width:** 18 nonpareils. **Col. Depth:** 301 agate lines. **Key Personnel:** Jeff Grant, Editor, jeffgrant@iowainformation.com; Jeff Wagner, General Mgr.; Peter W. Wagner, Publisher; Jen Duke, Managing Editor. **Subscription Rates:** $22 individuals in county; $30 out of county. **Remarks:** Accepts advertising.
Ad Rates: BW: $575.19 **Circ:** Paid ⊕2,011
4C: $760.19 Free ⊕17
PCI: $6.93

11392 KIWA-AM - 1550
411 9th St. Phone: (712)324-2597
Sheldon, IA 51201 Fax: (712)324-2340
E-mail: frank@ncn.net

Format: Country; Talk. **Simulcasts:** KIWA-FM. **Networks:** ABC. **Owner:** Sheldon Broadcasting Co. Inc., at above address. **Founded:** 1961. **Operating Hours:** 5:30 a.m.-midnight; 20% network, 80% local. **ADI:** Sioux City, IA. **Key Personnel:** Frank Luepke, General Mgr.; Karen Mitchell, News Dir.; Mike Byker, Sports Dir.; Tom Traughber, Music Dir. **Wattage:** 500.

11393 KIWA-FM - 105.3
411 9th St. Phone: (712)324-2597
Sheldon, IA 51201 Fax: (712)324-2340
E-mail: kiwa@ncn.net

Format: Country; Talk. **Simulcasts:** KIWA-AM. **Networks:** ABC. **Owner:** Sheldon Broadcasting Co., Inc., at above address. **Founded:** 1971. **Operating Hours:** 5:30 a.m.-midnight; 20% network, 80% local. **ADI:** Sioux City, IA. **Key Personnel:** Frank Luepke, General Mgr.; Karen Mitchell, News Dir.; Mike Byker, Sports Dir.; Tom Tranghber, Music Dir. **Wattage:** 50,000.

SHELLSBURG

EC IA. Benton Co. 10 mi. SE of Vinton.

11394 Shellsburg Cablevision Corp.
124 Main St. Phone: (319)436-2224
PO Box 390 Fax: (319)436-2228
Shellsburg, IA 52332

Founded: 1984. **Key Personnel:** Charles Eldred, General Mgr. **Cities Served:** subscribing households 2,546; 35 channels; 1 community access channel; 168 hours per week community access programming.

SHENANDOAH, pop. 6,274.

SW IA. Page Co. 52 mi. SE of Omaha, NE. Manufactures aluminum gates, beverages, food flavoring extracts, truck transmissions. Nurseries; seed houses. Poultry and grain farms.

11395 Valley News Today
Valley Publications
702 W. Sheridan Ave.
Shenandoah, IA 51601

General newspaper. **Founded:** 1882. **Freq:** Daily (eve.). **Print Method:** Offset. **Trim Size:** 14 x 22 1/2. **Cols./Page:** 6. **Col. Width:** 26 nonpareils. **Col. Depth:** 301 agate lines. **Key Personnel:** Gregg K. Knowles, Publisher. **USPS:** 181-260. **Subscription Rates:** $82; $88 out of area. **Remarks:** Accepts advertising. **Formerly:** Evening Sentinel (1989).
Ad Rates: GLR: $0.52 **Circ:** ‡3,598
BW: $939.12
4C: $1,059.12
PCI: $7.28

KKBZ-FM - See Clarinda

11396 KMA-AM - 960
209 N. Elm Phone: (712)246-5270
PO Box 960 Fax: (712)246-5275
Shenandoah, IA 51601
Free: (800)234-5622
E-mail: kma@shenessex.heartland.net

Format: Contemporary Country; Agricultural; News. **Networks:** ABC; Radio Iowa. **Owner:** May Broadcasting Co., at above address. **Founded:** 1925. **Operating Hours:** 5 a.m.-12 midnight M-Sat; 6 a.m.-12 midnight Sunday. **Key Personnel:** Edward W. May, President; Don Hansen, Station Mgr. **Wattage:** 5000.

11397 KYFR-AM - 920
PO Box 286 Phone: (712)246-5151
Shenandoah, IA 51601

Format: Religious. **Owner:** Family Stations Inc., at above address. **Founded:** 1924. **Formerly:** KFNF-AM. **Operating Hours:** Continuous. **Key Personnel:** Harold Camping, President; Michael E. DeStefano, Contact. **Wattage:** 5000 day; 2.5 night.

SIBLEY†, pop. 3,051.

NW IA. Osceola Co. 58 mi. E. of Sioux Falls, SD. Manufactures bags, (multi wall feed and seed); concrete products; printing; dairy processing. Stock, beef, swine, grain farms.

11398 Osceola County Gazette-Tribune
Sibley Printing and Publishing Co.
201 9th St. Phone: (712)754-2551
Sibley, IA 51249-1827
Community newspaper. **Founded:** 1872. **Freq:** Weekly (Thurs.). **Print Method:** Offset. **Cols./Page:** 7. **Col. Width:** 24 nonpareils. **Col. Depth:** 301 agate lines. **Key Personnel:** Jay Mohr, Publisher. **Subscription Rates:** $25 individuals. **Remarks:** Accepts advertising.
Ad Rates: GLR: $.21 **Circ:** ‡1,800
SAU: $4.62

SIDNEY†, pop. 1,308.

SW IA. Fremont Co. 40 mi. SE of Omaha, NE. Continuous outdoor rodeo. Stock, grain farms. Corn, wheat, soybeans, hay.

11399 The Sidney Argus-Herald
PO Box 190 Phone: (712)374-2251
Sidney, IA 51652
Local newspaper. **Subtitle:** Fremont County's Leading Newspaper. **Founded:** 1916. **Freq:** Weekly (Thurs.). **Print Method:** Offset. **Trim Size:** 7 x 11. **Cols./Page:** 6. **Col. Width:** 12.5 picas. **Col. Depth:** 21 inches. **Key Personnel:** Dave West, Editor; Ellen West Longman, Publisher. **USPS:** 496-700. **Subscription Rates:** $25 individuals. **Remarks:** Accepts advertising.
Ad Rates: GLR: $.30 **Circ:** Paid ‡1,600
BW: $497.70
4C: $607.70
SAU: $3.95
PCI: $3.95

SIGOURNEY†, pop. 2,330.

SE IA. Keokuk Co. 30 mi. NE of Ottumwa. Manufactures turkey products. Feed mills. Corn, soybean, hog, cattle farming.

11400 Sigourney News-Review
114 E. Washington Phone: (515)622-3110
Sigourney, IA 52591 Fax: (515)622-2766
Free: (800)550-4237
Publication E-mail: signr@lisco.com; signr@se-iowa.net
Publisher E-mail: signr@se-iowa.net

Community newspaper. **Founded:** Jan. 1880. **Freq:** Weekly (Wed.). **Print Method:** Offset. **Trim Size:** 11 1/2 x 14 1/4. **Cols./Page:** 7. **Col. Width:** 11.5 picas. **Col. Depth:** 21 picas. **Key Personnel:** Kenneth Chaney, Owner and Publisher; Sharlene Bos, Editor; Ken Chaney, Advertising Mgr. **USPS:** 009-140. **Subscription Rates:** $26 individuals; $.75 single issue. **Remarks:** Accepts advertising. **URL:** http://www.sigourneynews-review.com. **Alt. Formats:** CD-ROM.
Ad Rates: GLR: $0.38 **Circ:** Paid ‡3,000
BW: $4.35 Free ‡48
PCI: $4.10

SIOUX CENTER, pop. 4,588.

NW IA. Sioux Co. 45 mi. N. of Sioux City. Dordt College. Manufactures electric motor components, truck frames. Egg processing; hog processing. Ships hogs. Grain, cattle, stock, dairy farms.

11401 Diamond
Dordt College
DC116 Phone: (712)722-6431
Sioux Center, IA 51250
Collegiate newspaper. **Founded:** 1957. **Freq:** Biweekly (during the academic year). **Print Method:** Offset. **Cols./Page:** 5. **Col. Width:** 24 nonpareils. **Col. Depth:** 226 agate lines. **Key Personnel:** Kate Dekker, Editor, phone (712)722-6627. **Subscription Rates:** $5.
Ad Rates: PCI: $2.50 **Circ:** ‡1,100

11402 PRO REGE
Dordt College
498 4th Ave. NE Phone: (712)722-3771
Sioux Center, IA 51250-1697 Fax: (712)722-1185
Publication E-mail: prorege@dordt.edu

Christian magazine in the Reformed tradition by the faculty at Dordt College. **Founded:** 1972. **Freq:** Quarterly. **Print Method:** Offset. **Trim Size:** 7 1/4 x 10 1/4. **Cols./Page:** 2. **Col. Width:** 2 3/4 inches. **Col. Depth:** 8 inches. **Key Personnel:** Hubert Krygsman, Editor, phone (712)722-6308, krygsman@dordt.edu. **ISSN:** 0276-4830. **Subscription Rates:** Free. **Remarks:** Advertising not accepted. **URL:** http://www.dordt.edu.
Circ: Non-paid ‡3,100

11403 The Sioux Center News
PO Box 198 Phone: (712)722-0741
Sioux Center, IA 51250 Fax: (712)722-0744
Publication E-mail: sctrnews@mtcnet.net

CNP. **Founded:** Mar. 16, 1892. **Freq:** Weekly (Tues.). **Print Method:** Offset. **Trim Size:** 15 x 21.5. **Cols./Page:** 9. **Col. Width:** 1 5/8 inches. **Col. Depth:** 21.5 inches. **Key Personnel:** Warren Overlie, Editor and Publisher; B.J. Overlie, Editor and Publisher. **USPS:** 497-220. **Subscription Rates:** $24 individuals; $28.50 out of area. **Remarks:** Advertising not accepted for alcohol and tobacco products.
Ad Rates: GLR: $.35 **Circ:** Paid 2,473
BW: $948.15 Free 71
4C: $1,047.13
SAU: $5.81
PCI: $4.90

11404 Sioux Center Shopper
67 3rd St. NE Phone: (712)722-0511
Sioux Center, IA 51250 Fax: (712)722-0507

Shopper. **Founded:** 1936. **Freq:** Weekly (Wed.). **Print Method:** Offset. **Trim Size:** 11 x 17. **Cols./Page:** 6. **Col. Width:** 24 nonpareils. **Col. Depth:** 226 agate lines. **Key Personnel:** Scott Beernink, Editor and Publisher. **Remarks:** Accepts advertising.
Ad Rates: GLR: $0.27 **Circ:** Free ‡12,500
BW: $436.80
4C: $800
PCI: $4.55

11405 KDCR-FM - 88.5
Dordt College Campus Phone: (712)722-0885
Sioux Center, IA 51250 Fax: (712)722-6244

Format: News; Eclectic; Sports; Religious; Agricultural. **Networks:** USA Radio. **Founded:** 1968. **Operating Hours:** 6 a.m.-12 a.m. **Key Personnel:** Denny DeWaard, Manager; Tim Vos, News Dir.; Jim Bolkema, Music Dir. **Wattage:** 100,000.

11406 KSOU-AM - 1090
PO Box 298 Phone: (712)722-1090
Sioux Center, IA 51250-0298 Fax: (712)722-1102

Format: Adult Contemporary. **Networks:** ABC. **Founded:** 1969. **Formerly:** KVDB-AM. **Operating Hours:** Sunrise-sunset. **ADI:** Sioux City, IA. **Key Personnel:** Craig Aukes, General Mgr. **Wattage:** 500. **Ad Rates:** $8.50-14 for 30 seconds; $10.00-16.00 for 60 seconds.

11407 KSOU-FM - 93.9
PO Box 298 Phone: (712)722-1090
Sioux Center, IA 51250-0288 Fax: (712)722-1102

Format: Adult Contemporary. **Networks:** ABC. **Owner:** SIOUX COUNTY BROADCASTING, at above address. **Founded:** 1974. **Formerly:** KVDB-FM. **Operating Hours:** 24 HRS. **ADI:** Sioux City, IA. **Key Personnel:** Craig Aukes, General Mgr. **Wattage:** 50,000. **Ad Rates:** $8.50-14 for 30 seconds; $10-16 for 60 seconds.

SIOUX CITY†, pop. 82,003.

W IA. Woodbury Co. On Missouri River, 100 mi. NW of Council Bluffs. Morningside College, Briar Cliff College. Livestock market and meat packing center. Manufactures auto accessories, fishing tackle, tools, truck bodies and trailers, farm implements, popcorn, dairy, lumber, food products, chemical fertilizers, structural steel, stock feeds, radios, fork lifts, hydraulic cylinders, paper boxes, metal awnings, doors, windows, culverts. Produce packing; foundries; machine shops.

11408 Collegian Reporter
Morningside College Phone: (712)274-5801
Box 1514 Fax: (712)274-5101
Sioux City, IA 51106
Free: (800)831-0806
Publication E-mail: colchief@alpha.morningside.edu

Collegiate newspaper. **Founded:** Sept. 1897. **Freq:** Weekly (Thurs.) (during the academic year). **Print Method:** Offset. **Trim Size:** 11 1/4 x 17. **Cols./Page:** 5. **Col. Width:** 11 picas. **Col. Depth:** 205 agate lines. **Key Personnel:** Rich Trippler, Editor. **Subscription Rates:** $12 Free. **Formerly:** Collegian Chief.
Ad Rates: BW: $300 **Circ:** Free ‡1,000
PCI: $4.50

11409 Sioux City Journal
Hagadone Corp.
515 Pavonia St. Phone: (712)279-5026
Sioux City, IA 51102 Fax: (712)279-5059
Free: (800)397-3530
Publication E-mail: scjournal@pronet.net

General newspaper. **Founded:** 1864. **Freq:** Daily (morn.). **Print Method:** Offset. **Cols./Page:** 6. **Col. Width:** 26 nonpareils. **Col. Depth:** 301 agate lines. **Key Personnel:** Larry Myhre, Editor; Tom Kurdy, Publisher; Steve Griffith, Advertising Mgr.; Glenn Olson, City Editor, phone (712)279-5072. **Subscription Rates:** $147 individuals. **Remarks:** Accepts advertising. **URL:** http://www.ltrib.com/scjournal. **Feature Editors:** Bruce Miller, *TV & Radio*, phone (712)279-5075; Larry Myhre, *Travel*, phone (712)279-5070; Marcia Poole, *Book, Women's*, phone (712)279-5070.
Ad Rates: GLR: $1.98 **Circ:** Mon.-Fri. 47,475
BW: $3,599.10 Sat. 47,047
4C: $3,899.10 Sun. 47,775
SAU: $27.90
PCI: $24.75

11410 CableONE
900 Steuben St. Phone: (712)233-2000
Sioux City, IA 51101 Fax: (712)233-2235
E-mail: jolson8925@aol.com

Owner: Cable One, Inc., 4742 N. 24th St., No. 270, Phoenix, AZ 85016, (602)468-1177, Fax: (602)468-9216. **Founded:** 1979. **Formerly:** Sooland Cablecom Corp. (May 31, 1997). **Key Personnel:** Jeffrey L. Olson, General Mgr., phone (712)233-2846, fax (712)233-2235, jolson8925@aol.com; Claudia Killinger, Ad. Sales Mgr., phone (712)233-1511, fax (712)233-2926. **Cities Served:** Sergeant Bluff, Sioux City, IA; North Sioux City, ND: subscribing households 26,000; 78 channels; 1 community access channel; 20 hours per week community access programming.

11411 KGLI-FM - 95.5
1113 Nebraska St. Phone: (712)258-5595
Sioux City, IA 51105 Fax: (712)252-2430

Format: Adult Contemporary. **Networks:** ABC. **Owner:** Cardinal Communications, at above address. **Founded:** 1974. **Formerly:** KBCM-FM. **Operating Hours:** Continuous. **ADI:** Sioux City, IA. **Key Personnel:** Ted Mann, General Mgr.; Rich Schorg, General Sales Mgr. **Wattage:** 100,000.

11412 KKSC-AM - 1470
1113 Nebraska St. Phone: (712)255-1470
Sioux City, IA 51105 Fax: (712)252-2430

Format: News; Talk. **Networks:** CNN Radio; Precision Racing; International Broadcasting; Sunstar. **Owner:** Cardinal Communications, at above address. **Founded:** 1938. **Formerly:** KWSL-AM. **Operating Hours:** Continuous. **ADI:** Sioux City, IA. **Key Personnel:** Ted Mann, General Mgr.; Rich Sching, General Sales Mgr.; Bob Bakken, Promotions Dir. **Wattage:** 5000.

11413 KMEG-TV - 14
7th & Floyd Blvd. Phone: (712)277-3554
PO Box 657 Fax: (712)277-4732
Sioux City, IA 51102
Free: (800)779-6364
E-mail: kmeg@kmeg.com

Format: Commercial TV. **Networks:** CBS. **Owner:** Waitt Broadcasting, Inc., 13906 Gold Circle, Ste. 201, Omaha, NE, (402)330-2520, Fax: (402)330-2445, Free: (888)656-0634. **Founded:** 1967. **Operating Hours:** 6 a.m.-10:00 a.m.; 55% network, 45% local. **ADI:** Sioux City, IA. **Key Personnel:** Rob Dean, General Mgr.; Janice Jessen, Sales Mgr.; Greg Funk, Business Mgr.; Fritz Miller, Station Mgr., kmeg@kmeg.com; Dick Herr, Dir. Eng.; Myra Baker, Traffic Dir. **Local Programs:** *Kids Club* 3 p.m. - 5 p.m. Monday-Friday. **Wattage:** 1,000,000. **URL:** http://www.kmeg.com.

11414 KMSC-FM - 88.3
1501 Morningside Ave. Phone: (712)274-5331
Sioux City, IA 51106 Fax: (712)274-5664
E-mail: fusion@alpha.morningside.edu

Networks: Independent. **Founded:** 1978. **Operating Hours:** Continuous. **ADI:** Sioux City, IA. **Key Personnel:** Matt Ohman, General Mgr., mjo@alpha.morningside.edu; Justine Stokes, Operations; Kevin Peterson, Program Dir.; Melissa Hamersma, News Dir. **Wattage:** 10. **Ad Rates:** Advertising accepted; rates available upon request.

11415 KSCJ-AM - 1360
2000 Indian Hills Dr. Phone: (712)239-2100
Sioux City, IA 51104 Fax: (712)239-3346

Format: Talk; News; Sports. **Networks:** ABC; NBC. **Owner:** Powell Broadcasting, at above address. **Founded:** 1927. **Operating Hours:** Continuous. **ADI:** Sioux City, IA. **Key Personnel:** Tom Spies, General Mgr.; Dennis Bullock, General Sales Mgr.; Gary Erickson, Program Dir. **Local Programs:** *Open Line*, Randy Renshaw, Mailing contact, (712)239-2100, Fax (712)239-3346; *Sports Line*, Chris Varney, Mailing contact, (712)239-2100, Fax (712)239-3346. **Wattage:** 5000. **Ad Rates:** Advertising accepted; rates available upon request. Combined advertising rates available with KSUX-FM.

11416 KSEZ-FM - 97.9
901 Steuben St. Phone: (712)258-6740
PO Box 177 Fax: (712)277-3299
Sioux City, IA 51102

Format: Album-Oriented Rock (AOR). **Networks:** ABC; NBC. **Owner:** Lelend Communications, at above address. **Founded:** 1960. **Operating Hours:** Continuous. **ADI:** Sioux City, IA. **Key Personnel:** George Pelletier, General Mgr.; Bev King, Contact. **Wattage:** 100,000 ERP.

11417 KSIN-TV - 27
Iowa Public Television Phone: (515)242-3100
PO Box 6450
Johnston, IA 50131

Format: Public TV. **Simulcasts:** KDIN-TV Des Moines, IA. **Networks:** Public Broadcasting Service (PBS). **Founded:** 1975. **ADI:** Sioux City, IA. **Key Personnel:** David Bolender, Exec. Dir.; Dennis Malloy, Dir. of Development; Daniel K. Miller, Program Dir.; Don Saveraid, Dir. of Engineering; Pam Johnson, Dir. of Educational Telecommunications; Sid Sprecher, Public Affairs.

11418 KSUX-FM - 105.7
2000 Indian Hills Dr. Phone: (712)239-2100
Sioux City, IA 51104-1699 Fax: (712)239-3346

Format: Country. **Founded:** 1991. **Formerly:** KBCM-FM (1992). **Operating Hours:** 24 hrs. **ADI:** Sioux City, IA. **Key Personnel:** Tom Spies, General Mgr.; Dennis Bullock, General Sales Mgr.; Jeff Miller, Program Dir. **Wattage:** 50,000. **Ad Rates:** Combined advertising rates available with KSCS-AM.

11419 KTFC-FM - 103.3
1534 Buchanan Ave. Phone: (712)252-4621
Sioux City, IA 51106 Fax: (712)255-6300

Format: Gospel. **Networks:** Satellite Radio. **Founded:** 1965. **Operating Hours:** Continuous. **ADI:** Sioux City, IA. **Key Personnel:** Don Swanson, Contact. **Wattage:** 100,000.

11420 KTIV-TV - 4
3135 Floyd Blvd. Phone: (712)239-4100
Sioux City, IA 51108 Fax: (712)239-2621
E-mail: ktiv4@ktiv.com; ktivnews@ktiv.com; ktiv4@ktiv.com

Format: Commercial TV. **Networks:** NBC. **Founded:** 1954. **Operating Hours:** Continuous; 90% network & syndicated, 10% local. **ADI:** Sioux City, IA. **Key Personnel:** James L. DeSchepper, Vice President; Dave Madsen, Program Dir.; Dave Nixon, Jr., News Dir.; Adrian Wisner, General Sales Mgr.; Scot Krayenhagen, Chief Engineer; Dave Washburn, Creative Svcs. Dir. **Ad Rates:** Advertising accepted; rates available upon request. **URL:** http://www.ktiv.com.

11421 KWIT-FM - 90.3
4647 Stone Ave. Phone: (712)274-6406
Sioux City, IA 51106 Fax: (712)274-6411

Format: Public Radio; Jazz; News; Classical; Hispanic. **Networks:** Public Radio International (PRI); National Public Radio (NPR). **Owner:** Western Iowa Tech Community College, at above address. **Founded:** 1978. **Operating Hours:** Continuous; 60% network, 40% local. **ADI:** Sioux City, IA. **Key Personnel:** Gretchen Gondek, General Mgr., gondek@switcc.cc.ia.us; Steve Smith, Operations Mgr., smiths@witcc.cc.ia.us; Duane Kraayenbrink, News, kraayed@witcc.cc.ia.us. **Wattage:** 100,000. **Ad Rates:** Noncommercial.

SIOUX RAPIDS, pop. 897.

NW IA. Buena Vista Co. 70 mi. NW of Fort Dodge. Manufactures fertilizer loading equipment, plastic waterers, hydraulic lifts, hardware specialties. Timber. Diversified farming. Corn, oats, beans.

11422 Sioux Rapids Bulletin-Press
Bulletin Press
PO Box 477 Phone: (712)283-2500
Sioux Rapids, IA 50585 Fax: (712)283-2500

Community newspaper. **Founded:** 1885. **Freq:** Weekly (Wed.). **Print Method:** Offset. **Cols./Page:** 8. **Col. Width:** 22 nonpareils. **Col. Depth:** 294 agate lines. **Key Personnel:** Jerry Edwards, Editor and Publisher. **Subscription Rates:** $18 individuals; $20 out of country. **Remarks:** Accepts advertising.
Ad Rates: SAU: $4.50 **Circ:** ‡1,200
PCI: $1.85

SLATER, pop. 1,312.

C IA. Story Co. 29 mi. N. of Des Moines. Creamery. Grain, dairy, stock farms.

11423 Tri County Times
Rood Printing
Box 237 Phone: (515)685-3412
Slater, IA 50244-0237 Fax: (515)685-3668

Newspaper. **Subtitle:** Serving 11 Cities in Official Capacity-3 Districts and 1 County. **Founded:** 1889. **Freq:** Weekly (Thurs.). **Print Method:** Offset. **Trim Size:** 15 x 21 1/2. **Cols./Page:** 7. **Col. Width:** 20 nonpareils. **Col. Depth:** 301 agate lines. **Key Personnel:** Edwin W. Rood, Editor and Publisher. **Subscription Rates:** $16 individuals.
Ad Rates: GLR: $.18 **Circ:** 4,500

SOLON, pop. 969.

E IA. Johnson Co. 10 mi. N. of Iowa City. Feed, flour mills. Agriculture. Corn, oats, hay.

11424 Solon Economist
Box 249 Phone: (319)644-2233
Solon, IA 52333 Fax: (319)644-1356

Newspaper. **Founded:** 1896. **Freq:** Weekly (Tues.). **Print Method:** Offset. **Cols./Page:** 6. **Col. Width:** 20 nonpareils. **Col. Depth:** 196 agate lines. **Key Personnel:** Brian Fleck, Editor and Publisher. **Subscription Rates:** $25 individuals. **Remarks:** Accepts advertising.
Ad Rates: GLR: $.15 **Circ:** (Not Reported)

SPENCER†, pop. 11,726.

NW IA. Clay Co. 80 mi. NE of Sioux City. Manufactures hydrostatic transmissions, lifts, garments, machinery, cement blocks, lubricating equipment, rendering works; grain elevator; meat packing. Stock. Agriculture. Livestock, grain farms. Corn, oats, barley.

11425 The Daily Reporter
Edwards Publications, Inc.
310 E. Milwaukee Phone: (712)262-6610
Spencer, IA 51301 Fax: (712)262-3044

General newspaper. **Founded:** 1876. **Freq:** Tues.-Sat. (morn.). **Print Method:** Offset. **Cols./Page:** 6. **Col. Width:** 24 nonpareils. **Col. Depth:** 294 agate lines. **Key Personnel:** Joni Weerheim, Publisher; Michael Kuehn, General Mgr. **Subscription Rates:** $65 individuals.
Ad Rates: GLR: $.33 **Circ:** ‡4,000

11426 Northwest Iowa Shopper
Edwards Publications, Inc.
310 E. Milwaukee Phone: (712)262-6610
Spencer, IA 51301 Fax: (712)262-3044

Shopper. **Founded:** 1963. **Freq:** Semiweekly (Wed. and Sat.). **Print Method:** Offset. **Cols./Page:** 6. **Col. Width:** 21 nonpareils. **Col. Depth:** 301 agate lines. **Key Personnel:** Joni Weerheim, Publisher; Chris Swanson, Advertising Mgr. **Remarks:** Accepts advertising.
Ad Rates: GLR: $.70 **Circ:** Free ‡25,500
SAU: $9.75

11427 KICD-AM - 1240
PO Box 260 Phone: (712)262-1240
Spencer, IA 51301 Fax: (712)262-2076

Format: Full Service; Adult Contemporary. **Networks:** ESPN Radio; Westwood One Radio; CBS. **Owner:** Iowa Great Lakes Broadcasting Co., Inc., at above address. **Founded:** Dec. 1942. **Operating Hours:** Continuous. **Key Personnel:** William R. Sanders, CEO/Pres.; Bill Campbell, Operations Mgr.; John F. Wirkler, General Mgr.; Joe Schloss, Chief Engineer; Mark Bruggom, News Dir. **Wattage:** 1000.

11428 KICD-FM - 107.7
2600 Highway Blvd., Box 260 Phone: (712)262-1240
Spencer, IA 51301 Fax: (712)262-2076
Free: (800)232-1240

Format: Contemporary Country. **Simulcasts:** KICD-AM. **Networks:** CBS. **Owner:** William R. Sanders, at above address. **Founded:** 1965. **Operating Hours:** 5 a.m.-midnight Mon.; Continuous Tues. - Sun. **ADI:** Sioux City, IA. **Key Personnel:** W.R. Sanders, President; Al Grigg, Farm Dir.; Valerie Cain, Traffic Dir.; John Wirkler, General Mgr.; Rhonda Wedeking, Program Dir. **Local Programs:** *Rhonda Wedeking Show*, Rhonda Wedeking. **Wattage:** 100,000 ERP. **Ad Rates:** Advertising accepted; rates available upon request.

11429 KIGL-FM - 104.9
PO Box 260 Phone: (712)262-3300
Spencer, IA 51301 Fax: (712)262-2076

Format: Adult Contemporary. **Networks:** Jones Satellite. **Owner:** Iowa Great Lakes Broadcasting Co., Inc., at above address. **Founded:** Feb. 1979. **Former name:** KJJG-FM. **Operating Hours:** Continuous. **Key Personnel:** William R. Sanders, CEO/Pres.; Bill Campbell, Operations Mgr.; Joel Endres, Music Dir.; Joe Schloss, Chief Engineer. **Wattage:** 25,000.

SPIRIT LAKE†, pop. 3,976.

NW IA. Dickinson Co. 100 mi. E. of Sioux Falls, SD. Lake resort. Industrial wire, air condition equipment, boats, fishing equipment, fiberglass products manufactured. Bottling works. Diversified farming. Corn, hay.

11430 The Beacon
Edwards Publications, Inc.
PO Box AE Phone: (712)336-1211
Spirit Lake, IA 51360 Fax: (712)336-1219
Publication E-mail: beacon@ncn.net

Community newspaper. **Founded:** 1870. **Freq:** Weekly (Thurs.). **Print Method:** Web. **Cols./Page:** 6. **Col. Width:** 12 picas. **Col. Depth:** 21 1/2 inches. **Key Personnel:** Michael Kuehn, Publisher; Frank Jaquith, Editor. **Subscription Rates:** $26 local; $28 in state; $30 out of state. **Remarks:** Accepts advertising.
Ad Rates: PCI: $5.42 **Circ:** Paid ‡3,458
Free ‡10

11431 Milford Mail and Terril Record
Spirit Lake Publishing Co.
P.O. Box AE Phone: (712)338-4712
Spirit Lake, IA 51360
Local newspaper. **Founded:** 1883. **Freq:** Weekly (Thurs.). **Print Method:** Offset. **Cols./Page:** 6. **Col. Width:** 24 nonpareils. **Col. Depth:** 294 agate lines. **Key Personnel:** Michael Kuehn, Publisher; Doris Welle, Editor. **USPS:** 348-920. **Subscription Rates:** $17 individuals.
Ad Rates: SAU: $4.62 **Circ:** Paid 1,148
PCI: $3.54 Free 25

11432 News
Spirit Lake Publishing Co.
PO Box AE
Spirit Lake, IA 51360

Local newspaper. **Founded:** 1890. **Freq:** Weekly. **Print Method:** Offset. **Cols./Page:** 6. **Col. Width:** 24 nonpareils. **Col. Depth:** 294 agate lines. **Key Personnel:** Michael Kuehn, Publisher; Bobbie McBride, Editor. **Subscription Rates:** $16 individuals. **Remarks:** Accepts advertising.
Ad Rates: BW: $322.50 **Circ:** 660
SAU: $2.50
PCI: $2.94

11433 KUOO-FM - 103.9
Box 528 Phone: (712)336-5800
Hwy. 9 W. Fax: (712)336-1634
Spirit Lake, IA 51360

Format: Adult Contemporary. **Networks:** ABC. **Owner:** Hedberg Broadcasting Group, at above address. **Founded:** 1985. **Operating Hours:** Continuous. **ADI:** Sioux City, IA. **Key Personnel:** Paul Keffake, General Mgr.; Joey Elbert, Program Dir. **Wattage:** 50,000. **Ad Rates:** $7-9.50 for 15 seconds; $10-12.50 for 30 seconds; $14-16.50 for 60 seconds.

11434 Spirit Lake Cable TV
Box 267 Phone: (712)336-5151
Spirit Lake, IA 51360 Fax: (712)336-5687
Free: (800)331-3569

Owner: Lakes Cable Systems, at above address. **Key Personnel:** Jerry Kittelson, General Mgr. **Cities Served:** Arnold Park, Montgomery, Okoboji, Orleans, Spirit Lake, Wapheton, and West Okoboji, IA.

STACYVILLE, pop. 538.

N IA. Mitchell Co. 40 mi. NE of Mason City. Creamery; fertilizer factory; grain elevator. Agriculture. Corn, oats, hay.

11435 The Monitor Review
PO Box 276 Phone: (515)737-2119
Stacyville, IA 50476 Fax: (515)737-2119

Community newspaper. **Founded:** 1909. **Freq:** Weekly (Thurs.). **Print Method:** Offset. **Cols./Page:** 6. **Col. Width:** 14 5/16 inches. **Col. Depth:** 21 1/2 inches. **Key Personnel:** Angela Schmitz, phone (515)582-3542. **Subscription Rates:** $19 individuals.
Ad Rates: GLR: $.16 **Circ:** ‡1,475
BW: $443.76
SAU: $3.44

STATE CENTER

11436 Enterprise-Record
Mid-Iowa Publishing Co.
130 W. Main Phone: (515)483-2120
PO Box 634 Fax: (515)483-2938
State Center, IA 50247
Community newspaper. **Founded:** 1871. **Freq:** Weekly (Wed.). **Print Method:** Offset. **Cols./Page:** 6. **Col. Width:** 12 3/10 picas. **Col. Depth:** 21 1/2 inches. **Key Personnel:** John C. Strawn II, Publisher. **USPS:** 519-880. **Subscription Rates:** $22 individuals; $26 out of area. **Remarks:** Accepts advertising.
Ad Rates: BW: $410 **Circ:** ‡1,200
SAU: $4.03
PCI: $4.03

STORM LAKE†, pop. 8,814.

NW IA. Buena Vista Co. 60 mi. W. of Fort Dodge. Buena Vista College. Manufactures jeans, valve hydrants. Pork and turkey packing plants; hog and poultry houses. Seed corn plants. Agriculture. Livestock, corn, oats, soybeans.

11437 Buena Vista Today
Buena Vista University
610 W. Fourth St. Phone: (712)749-1221
Storm Lake, IA 50588-1798 Fax: (712)749-1459
Free: (800)383-2821
Publication E-mail: bvunews@bvu.edu

Collegiate alumni magazine. **Founded:** 1895. **Freq:** 3/year. **Print Method:** Web press. **Trim Size:** 8 1/2 x 11. **Cols./Page:** 3. **Col. Width:** 24 nonpareils. **Col. Depth:** 136 agate lines. **Key Personnel:** Tim Seydel, Editor, phone (712)749-2120, seydelt@bru.edu; Angela Chaplin, Managing Editor, phone (712)749-2120, chaplina@bvu.edu. **USPS:** 069-260. **Subscription Rates:** Free to qualified subscribers. **Remarks:** Advertising not accepted.
Circ: Controlled ‡18,000

11438 The Pilot-Tribune
Press Web
111 W. 7th Phone: (712)732-3130
Storm Lake, IA 50588-1824 Fax: (712)732-3152
Publisher E-mail: sledt@ncn.net

Community newspaper. **Founded:** 1890. **Freq:** Weekly (Tuesday-Saturday) daily. **Print Method:** Web press. **Trim Size:** 15 1/4 x 22 1/2. **Cols./Page:** 6. **Col. Width:** 24 nonpareils. **Col. Depth:** 301 agate lines. **Key Personnel:** Mr. Dana Larsen, Editor and Publisher; Mrs. Reta Hoeking, Advertising Mgr. **Subscription Rates:** $50. **Remarks:** Accepts advertising.
Ad Rates: BW: $862.40 **Circ:** ‡3,950
SAU: $7.35

11439 The Tack
Buena Vista University
610 W. Fourth St. Phone: (712)749-1221
Storm Lake, IA 50588-1798 Fax: (712)749-1459
Free: (800)383-2821
Publication E-mail: tack@bvu.edu

Collegiate newspaper. **Founded:** 1895. **Freq:** 22/year. **Print Method:** Offset. **Cols./Page:** 4. **Col. Width:** 28 nonpareils. **Col. Depth:** 203 agate lines. **Key Personnel:** Buena Vista College, Publisher. **Subscription Rates:** Free. **Remarks:** Accepts advertising. **URL:** http://www.bvu.edu/~tack.
Ad Rates: BW: $200 **Circ:** Non-paid 1,200
4C: $250

11440 KAYL-AM - 990
604 1/2 Lake Ave. Phone: (712)732-3520
Storm Lake, IA 50588 Fax: (712)732-1746

Format: Big Band/Nostalgia. **Networks:** ABC. **Owner:** Hedberg Broadcasting Group, PO Box 528, Spirit Lake, IA 51360, (712)336-5800. **Founded:** 1948. **Operating Hours:** Sunrise-sunset; 5% network, 95% local. **ADI:** Sioux City, IA. **Key Personnel:** Mike Puetz, Station Mgr. **Wattage:** 250. **Ad Rates:** Advertising accepted; rates available upon request.

11441 KAYL-FM - 101.7
604 1/2 Lake Ave. Phone: (712)732-3520
Storm Lake, IA 50588 Fax: (712)732-1746

Format: Adult Contemporary. **Networks:** ABC. **Owner:** Hedberg Broadcasting Group, at above address. **Founded:** 1949. **Operating Hours:** Continuous. **Key Personnel:** Paul C. Hedberg, President; Mike Puetz, General Mgr. **Wattage:** 100,000 ERP.

11442 KBVU-FM - 97.5
610 W. Fort St. Phone: (712)749-1215
Storm Lake, IA 50588

Format: Alternative/New Music/Progressive. **Owner:** Buena Vista University, at above address. **Operating Hours:** Continuous. **Key Personnel:** Susanne Gubanc, General Mgr. **Ad Rates:** Noncommercial. **URL:** http://www.edge.bvu.edu.

STORY CITY, pop. 2,762.

C IA. Story Co. 12 mi. N. of Ames. Residential. Light Industry.

11443 The Story City Herald
423 Broad St. Phone: (515)733-4318
Story City, IA 50248 Fax: (515)733-4319
Publisher E-mail: scherald@timberidge.com

Newspapers. **Founded:** 1880. **Freq:** Weekly (Wed.). **Print Method:** Offset. **Cols./Page:** 6. **Col. Width:** 12 picas. **Col. Depth:** 21.5 inches. **Key Personnel:** Todd Thorson, Editor and Publisher; Laura Urbanek, Editor and Publisher. **USPS:** 522-720. **Subscription Rates:** $22 individuals; $26 out of area.
Ad Rates: BW: $612.75 **Circ:** Paid ‡2,300
4C: $892.75
SAU: $5.46
PCI: $4.75

11444 The Story City Reminder
The Story City Herald
423 Broad St. Phone: (515)733-4318
Story City, IA 50248 Fax: (515)733-4319
Publisher E-mail: scherald@timberidge.com

Shopping guide. **Founded:** 1957. **Freq:** Weekly. **Print Method:** Offset. **Cols./Page:** 6. **Col. Width:** 12 picas. **Col. Depth:** 21.5 inches. **Key Personnel:** Todd Thorson, Editor and Publisher; Laura Urbanek, Editor and Publisher. **USPS:** 522-720. **Subscription Rates:** Free. **Formerly:** Reminder.
Ad Rates: BW: $612.75 **Circ:** Free ‡2,000
4C: $892.75
SAU: $5.46
PCI: $4.75

STRAWBERRY POINT, pop. 1,463.

NE IA. Clayton Co. 18 mi. N. of Manchester. Residential.

11445 Press Journal
PO Box 70 Phone: (319)933-4370
Strawberry Point, IA 52076 Fax: (319)933-4370

Newspaper with a Democratic orientation. **Founded:** 1876. **Freq:** Weekly (Wed.). **Print Method:** Offset. **Cols./Page:** 6. **Col. Width:** 19 nonpareils. **Col. Depth:** 196 agate lines. **Key Personnel:** Harry L. Nolda, Publisher. **Subscription Rates:** $15 individuals. **Remarks:** Accepts advertising.
Ad Rates: SAU: $2.10 **Circ:** 1,876

STUART, pop. 1,650.

SW IA. Adair & Guthrie Co. 35 mi. W. of Des Moines. Residential.

11446 The 5 x 80 Bulletin
The Stuart Herald
Box 608 Phone: (515)523-1010
Stuart, IA 50250 Fax: (515)523-2825
Free: (800)622-1010
Publisher E-mail: 73652.3441@compuserve.com

Shopping guide. **Founded:** 1972. **Freq:** Semimonthly. **Print Method:** Offset. **Cols./Page:** 8. **Col. Width:** 21 nonpareils. **Col. Depth:** 301 agate lines. **Key Personnel:** Vicki Taylor, Editor; Alan Taylor, Publisher; Norma Thurman, Advertising Mgr. **USPS:** ECR-WSS. **Subscription Rates:** Free. **Remarks:** Combined advertising rates available with The Stuart Herald.
Ad Rates: SAU: $7.01 **Circ:** Free ‡9,023
PCI: $6.65

11447 The Stuart Herald
Box 608 Phone: (515)523-1010
Stuart, IA 50250 Fax: (515)523-2825
Free: (800)622-1010
Publication E-mail: 73652.3441@compuserve
Publisher E-mail: 73652.3441@compuserve.com

Community newspaper. **Founded:** 1870. **Freq:** Weekly (Thurs.). **Print Method:** Offset. **Cols./Page:** 8. **Col. Width:** 21 nonpareils. **Col. Depth:** 301 agate lines. **Key Personnel:** Vicki Taylor, Editor; Alan Taylor, Publisher; Norma Thurman, Advertising Mgr. **Subscription Rates:** $19.50 individuals; $23.50 out of state. **Remarks:** Accepts advertising.
Ad Rates: SAU: $5.80 **Circ:** Paid ‡1,350
PCI: $5.07 Free ‡50

SULLY, pop. 828.

SC IA. Jasper Co. 50 mi. E. of Des Moines. Residential.

11448 Diamond Trail News
301 7th Ave., Ste. 101 Phone: (515)594-4488
Box 186 Fax: (515)594-4498
Sully, IA 50251
Community newspaper (tabloid). **Founded:** Sept. 1975. **Freq:** Weekly (Wed.). **Print Method:** Offset. **Cols./Page:** 5. **Col. Width:** 24 nonpareils. **Col. Depth:** 16 inches. **Key Personnel:** Brenda De Nooy, General Mgr.; Mark Davitt, Editor and Publisher. **USPS:** 106-310. **Subscription Rates:** $20 individuals; $25 out of state. **Remarks:** Accepts advertising.
Ad Rates: BW: $280 **Circ:** Paid 1,730
SAU: $3.50 Free 18
PCI: $3.50

SUMNER, pop. 2,335.

NE IA. Bremer Co. 28 mi. NE of Waterloo. Manufactures cement blocks, chemicals. Dairy, poultry, stock, grain farms.

11449 Sumner Gazette
106 E. 1st St. Phone: (319)578-3351
Box 208
Sumner, IA 50674
Newspaper with a Republican orientation. **Founded:** Jan. 1, 1881. **Freq:** Weekly (Thurs.). **Print Method:** Offset. **Cols./Page:** 6. **Col. Width:** 26 nonpareils. **Col. Depth:** 301 agate lines. **Key Personnel:** C. Milnes, Publisher; K. Milnes, Publisher. **USPS:** 525-800. **Subscription Rates:** $20.50 by mail; $29.50 out of state. **Remarks:** Accepts advertising.
Ad Rates: GLR: $.80 **Circ:** Paid 1808
BW: $677 Free 65
4C: $877
PCI: $5.25

SUTHERLAND, pop. 897.

NW IA. O'Brien Co. 70 mi. NE of Sioux City. Mill Creek Indian Village Site. Dairy, stock, grain farms.

11450 Courier
PO Box 160 Phone: (712)446-3450
Sutherland, IA 51058 Fax: (712)446-3450

Newspaper. **Founded:** 1882. **Freq:** Weekly (Thurs.). **Print Method:** Offset. **Cols./Page:** 6. **Col. Width:** 23 nonpareils. **Col. Depth:** 301 agate lines. **Key Personnel:** Mike Otto, Publisher; Neilla Banse, Editor. **Subscription Rates:** $18 individuals; $22 out of area. **Remarks:** Accepts advertising.
Ad Rates: SAU: $4.50 **Circ:** Paid ‡764
PCI: $4 Free ‡30

SWEA CITY, pop. 813.

N IA. Kossuth Co. 60 mi. N. of Fort Dodge. Agriculture. Corn, oats, barley.

11451 Swea City Herald-Press
PO Box 428 Phone: (515)272-4660
Swea City, IA 50590
Tabloid newspaper. **Founded:** 1895. **Freq:** Weekly (Wed.). **Print Method:** Offset. **Cols./Page:** 5. **Col. Width:** 23 nonpareils. **Col. Depth:** 224 agate lines. **Key Personnel:** Pam Jerry, Wisema, Editor; Lupe Kollasch, Advertising Mgr. **Subscription Rates:** $16.50 individuals; $21.50 out of area. **Remarks:** Accepts advertising.
Ad Rates: GLR: $.19 **Circ:** ‡837
PCI: $3.50

TABOR, pop. 967.

SW IA. Fremont Co. 33 mi. S. of Council Bluffs. Agriculture. Corn, hogs, cattle.

11452 Fremont-Mills Beacon Enterprise
Freemont-Mills Beacon
PO Box 299 Phone: (712)629-2255
Tabor, IA 51653 Fax: (712)629-7405

Newspaper. **Founded:** 1881. **Freq:** Weekly (Wed.). **Print Method:** Offset. **Cols./Page:** 6. **Col. Width:** 21 nonpareils. **Col. Depth:** 301 agate lines. **Key Personnel:** Dale Hampton and Don Stanley, Editor and Publisher. **Subscription Rates:** $16 individuals. **Remarks:** Accepts advertising.
Ad Rates: GLR: $.09 **Circ:** (Not Reported)
SAU: $2.40
PCI: $2.40

TAMA, pop. 2,968.

EC IA. Tama Co. 48 mi. W. of Cedar Rapids. Manufactures egg case fillers, paper box board, asphalt products; beef processing plant. Ships hogs, eggs. Diversified farming.

11453 Tama County Shopper-Advisor
Tama County Publishing, Inc.
220 W. 3rd St. Phone: (515)484-2841
PO Box 118 Fax: (515)484-5705
Tama, IA 52339
Publication E-mail: trpub@marshallnet.com
Publisher E-mail: tcp@pcpartner.net

Shopper. **Freq:** Weekly (Wed.). **Print Method:** Offset. **Cols./Page:** 6. **Col. Width:** 1 1/4 inches. **Col. Depth:** 14 1/2 inches. **Key Personnel:** Mike Schlesinger, Publisher, phone (515)753-6611, fax (575)753-7221; Nancy Dostal, General Mgr. **Subscription Rates:** Free; $40 out of area mail. **Remarks:** Accepts advertising.
Ad Rates: BW: $802.10 **Circ:** Free ‡13,500
4C: $982.10
SAU: $12.34
PCI: $7.32

11454 The Tama News-Herald
Tama County Publishing, Inc.
220 W. 3rd St. Phone: (515)484-2841
PO Box 118 Fax: (515)484-5705
Tama, IA 52339
Publisher E-mail: tcp@pcpartner.net

Community newspaper. **Founded:** 1916. **Freq:** Weekly (Thurs.). **Print Method:** Offset. **Cols./Page:** 6. **Col. Width:** 12.5 picas. **Col. Depth:** 21 inches. **Key Personnel:** Nancy Dostal, Editor/General Manager; Mike Schlesinger, Publisher, phone (515)753-6611, fax (515)753-7221, trpub@marshallnet.com. **Subscription Rates:** $32 individuals; $38.50 out of area; $46 out of state. **Remarks:** Accepts advertising.
Ad Rates: BW: $1,261.62 **Circ:** Paid 3,200
4C: $1,441.62
SAU: $9.78
PCI: $9.78

Toledo Chronicle - See Toledo

TEMPLETON

11455 Templeton Telephone Co.
115 Main Phone: (712)669-3311
Box 77 Fax: (712)669-3312
Templeton, IA 51463
E-mail: temptel@netins.net

Founded: Nov. 1988. **Key Personnel:** Patricia Snyder, Manager; Loretta Friedman, President. **Cities Served:** Templeton, IA: subscribing households 135; 23 channels; 1 community access channel; 168 hours per week community access programming.

THOMPSON, pop. 668.

N IA. Winnebago Co. 45 mi. NW of Mason City. Grain and stock farms.

11456 The Thompson Courier-Rake Register
Forest City Summit
PO Box 350 Phone: (515)582-2112
Thompson, IA 50478-0350 Fax: (515)582-4442

Newspaper. **Founded:** 1892. **Freq:** Weekly (Thurs.). **Print Method:** Offset. **Cols./Page:** 5. **Col. Width:** 2 1/16 inches. **Key Personnel:** Cynthia Carter, Editor; Kim Norstrud, Managing Editor; Martin Bunge, Publisher. **Subscription Rates:** $19 individuals; $25 out of state. **Remarks:** Accepts advertising.
Ad Rates: BW: $161.25 **Circ:** Paid ‡900
SAU: $2.50 Free ‡20

TIPTON†, pop. 3,055.

E IA. Cedar Co. 30 mi. E. of Iowa City. Manufactures electronics, small parts; feed processing. Grain, livestock.

11457 Clarence-Lowden Sun News
Conservative Publishing Co.
Box 271 Phone: (319)886-2131
Tipton, IA 52772 Fax: (319)886-6466

Rural newspaper. **Subtitle:** Community newspaper. **Founded:** 1879. **Freq:** Weekly. **Print Method:** Offset. **Cols./Page:** 6. **Col. Width:** 10 picas. **Col. Depth:** 16 inches. **Key Personnel:** Pat Kroemer, Editor; Stuart Clark, Publisher. **Subscription Rates:** $16; $20 out of area. **Remarks:** Accepts advertising.
Ad Rates: GLR: $.20 **Circ:** ‡1,250
BW: $242
4C: $362
SAU: $3.84
PCI: $2.80

11458 The Tipton Conservative and Advertiser
Conservative Publishing Co.
Box 271 Phone: (319)886-2131
Tipton, IA 52772 Fax: (319)886-6466

Community newspaper. **Subtitle:** Rural Newspaper. **Founded:** 1853. **Freq:** Weekly (Wed.). **Print Method:** Offset. **Cols./Page:** 9. **Col. Width:** 20 nonpareils. **Col. Depth:** 300 agate lines. **Key Personnel:** Stuart Clark, Editor and Publisher, stuartc108@aol.com; Pat Kroemer, Advertising Mgr. **USPS:** 631-520. **Subscription Rates:** $25 individuals; $33 out of area. **Remarks:** Accepts advertising.
Ad Rates: GLR: $.28 **Circ:** ‡4,700
BW: $714
4C: $835
SAU: $5.65
PCI: $4.18

TITONKA, pop. 607.

N IA. Kossuth Co. 50 mi. W. of Mason City. Grain elevator. Agriculture. Corn, oats, beans, stock.

11459 Titonka Topic
Box 329 Phone: (515)928-2723
Titonka, IA 50480 Fax: (515)928-2506
Publication E-mail: titppic@netnis.net

Community newspaper. **Founded:** 1898. **Freq:** Weekly (Thurs.). **Print Method:** Offset. **Cols./Page:** 6. **Col. Width:** 25 nonpareils. **Col. Depth:** 294 agate lines. **Key Personnel:** Lanita Kardoes, Publisher. **Subscription Rates:** $18 individuals. **Remarks:** Accepts advertising.
Ad Rates: GLR: $.40 **Circ:** (Not Reported)
PCI: $2.20

11460 Titonka CATV
247 Main Phone: (515)928-2120
PO Box 321 Fax: (515)928-2897
Titonka, IA 50480
E-mail: tyketel@netins.net

Founded: 1983. **Key Personnel:** James Mayland, General Mgr. **Cities Served:** Titonka, IA: subscribing households 245; 19 channels; 1 community access channel.

TOLEDO

11461 Toledo Chronicle
Tama County Publishing, Inc.
220 W. 3rd St. Phone: (515)484-2841
PO Box 118 Fax: (515)484-5705
Tama, IA 52339
Publication E-mail: trpub@marshallnet.com
Publisher E-mail: tcp@pcpartner.net

Community newspaper. **Founded:** 1856. **Freq:** Weekly (Tues.). **Print Method:** Offset. **Cols./Page:** 6. **Col. Width:** 12.5 picas. **Col. Depth:** 21 inches. **Key Personnel:** Nancy Dostal, Editor; Mike Schlesinger, Publisher, phone (515)753-6611, fax (515)753-7221; Nancy Dostal, General Mgr. **Sub-**

scription Rates: $32; $38.50 out of area; $46 out of state. **Remarks:** Accepts advertising.
Ad Rates: BW: $1,261.62 **Circ:** ‡3200
4C: $1,441.62
SAU: $9.78
PCI: $9.78

TRAER, pop. 1,703.

EC IA. Tama Co. 24 mi. S. of Waterloo. Manufactures caskets, metal stampings. Seed corn processing plant. Grain, stock farms. Corn, oats, soybeans, hay.

11462 Star-Clipper
Marshalltown Newspaper Inc.
625 2nd St. Phone: (319)478-2323
PO Box 156 Fax: (319)478-2818
Traer, IA 50675
Newspaper. **Founded:** 1874. **Freq:** Weekly (Thurs.). **Print Method:** Offset. **Cols./Page:** 6. **Col. Width:** 21 1/2 ems. **Col. Depth:** 301 agate lines. **Key Personnel:** Ellen Young, Editor; Mike Schlesinger, Publisher. **Subscription Rates:** $21 individuals; $27 out of state.
Ad Rates: GLR: $.16 **Circ:** 2,300
PCI: $3.25

TRIPOLI, pop. 1,280.

NE IA. Bremer Co. 25 mi. NE of Waterloo. Manufactures recreational trailers. Agriculture. Corn, oats.

11463 Tripoli Leader
Leader
PO Box 39 Phone: (319)882-4207
Tripoli, IA 50676 Fax: (319)882-4200

Newspaper with a Republican orientation. **Founded:** 1894. **Freq:** Weekly (Wed.). **Print Method:** Offset. **Cols./Page:** 6. **Col. Width:** 20 nonpareils. **Col. Depth:** 300 agate lines. **Key Personnel:** Ken Schmith, Publisher/Editor; Rosalie Schmith, Publisher. **Remarks:** Accepts advertising.
Ad Rates: GLR: $.175 **Circ:** 1,512

URBANDALE, pop. 17,869.

SC IA. Polk Co. 10 mi. NW of Des Moines. Living history farms. U.S. Bulk Mail Center.

11464 The Hog Producer
Farm Progress Companies, Inc.
6200 Aurora Ave., No. 609E
Urbandale, IA 50322-2838

Trade publication for U.S. pork producers. **Founded:** 1980. **Freq:** Monthly. **Key Personnel:** JoAnn Alumbaugh, Editor, jalumbaugh@farmprogress.com; Steve Keppy, Advertising Mgr.; Steve Jones, Circulation Mgr. **Subscription Rates:** $21.95 individuals. **Remarks:** Accepts advertising.
Circ: (Not Reported)

11465 Iowa REC News
Iowa Association of Electric Cooperatives
8525 Douglas, No. 48 Phone: (515)276-5350
Urbandale, IA 50322 Fax: (515)276-7946

Magazine for members of rural electric cooperatives. **Founded:** 1948. **Freq:** Monthly. **Print Method:** Offset. **Trim Size:** 8 1/8 x 10 3/4. **Cols./Page:** 3. **Col. Width:** 14 picas. **Col. Depth:** 133 agate lines. **Key Personnel:** Robert A. Dikelman, Editor. **ISSN:** 0162-2412. **Subscription Rates:** $8 nonmembers. **Remarks:** Accepts advertising insurance and alcoholic beverages.
Ad Rates: GLR: $.60 **Circ:** Combined ‡93,000
BW: $1,152
4C: $2,400
PCI: $57

11466 Urbandale News
Rapid Printing, Inc.
3805 69th St. Phone: (515)276-0265
PO Box 3616 Fax: (515)276-5004
Urbandale, IA 50322
Local newspaper. **Founded:** Aug. 1954. **Freq:** Weekly (Thurs.). **Print Method:** Offset. **Trim Size:** 11 1/2 x 17 1/4. **Cols./Page:** 5. **Col. Width:** 19 nonpareils. **Col. Depth:** 224 agate lines. **Key Personnel:** Emery Bubany, Editor; Kevin Brown, Publisher; Mary Curtis, Advertising Mgr. **Subscription Rates:** $22 individuals; $27 out of area. **Remarks:** Color advertising accepted; rates available upon request.
Ad Rates: GLR: $6 **Circ:** Paid ‡4,100
BW: $240 Free ‡200

Wallaces Farmer - See Des Moines

VAIL

11467 The Observer
Miller Publishing Co.
PO Box 188 Phone: (712)677-2438
Vail, IA 51465 Fax: (712)677-2402

Community newspaper. **Founded:** 1878. **Freq:** Weekly (Thurs.). **Cols./Page:** 5. **Col. Width:** 11 picas. **Col. Depth:** 14 1/2 inches. **Key Personnel:** Cleone Podey, Editor; Robert Miller, Publisher, phone (712)668-2253. **Subscription Rates:** $19.50 in state; $21.50 out of state. **Remarks:** Accepts advertising.
Ad Rates: BW: $100 **Circ:** ‡1,114
SAU: $3.15
PCI: $2.10

VAN HORNE

EC IA. Benton Co. 30 mi. S. of Vinton.

11468 Van Horne Cablevision
204 Main St. Phone: (319)228-8791
Box 96 Fax: (319)228-8784
Van Horne, IA 52346
Free: (800)926-1341

Founded: 1983. **Key Personnel:** Donald Whipple, General Mgr. **Cities Served:** Van Horne, IA: subscribing households 248; 36 channels; 1 community access channel; 168 hours per week community access programming.

VINTON†, pop. 5,040.

EC IA. Benton Co. 32 mi. NW of Cedar Rapids. Concrete vault auto hubs, farm implements, fertilizer spreader, saline feeders. Ships farm products. Agriculture, poultry.

11469 Cedar Valley Times
Mid America Publishing
108 E. 5th St. Phone: (319)472-2311
PO Box 468 Fax: (319)472-4811
Vinton, IA 52349
Free: (800)388-9335

General newspaper. **Founded:** 1886. **Freq:** Daily (eve.). **Print Method:** Offset. **Cols./Page:** 6. **Col. Width:** 26 nonpareils. **Col. Depth:** 294 agate lines. **Key Personnel:** Doug Lindner, Publisher; Kathy Mahr, Advertising Mgr.; Dan Adix, Advertising Mgr. **Subscription Rates:** $54 individuals. **Remarks:** Accepts advertising.
Ad Rates: GLR: $.25 **Circ:** ‡3,099

11470 Vinton Livewire
110 E. 5th St. Phone: (319)472-3303
Vinton, IA 52349 Fax: (319)472-5478

Shopper. **Founded:** 1957. **Freq:** Weekly (Wed.). **Print Method:** Offset. **Cols./Page:** 5. **Col. Width:** 24 nonpareils. **Col. Depth:** 224 agate lines. **Key Personnel:** Mona Garwood, Publisher; Michelle Bruce, Office Mgr. **Remarks:** Accepts advertising.
Ad Rates: PCI: $3.40 **Circ:** Free ‡10,350

WALL LAKE

11471 Wall Lake Cable TV System
209 W. 2nd St. Phone: (712)664-2216
Wall Lake, IA 51466

Founded: Feb. 1984. **Key Personnel:** H. F. Schroeder, Mayor; Lynn Vilhauer, Maintenance. **Cities Served:** Wall Lake, IA: subscribing households 265; 17 channels.

WAPELLO†, pop. 2,011.

SE IA. Louisa Co. On Iowa River, 21 mi. S. of Muscatine. Wood pallets, furniture, feed, rubber cement dispensers manufactured. Stock, grain, poultry farms.

11472 The Wapello Republican
Louisa Publishing Co., Ltd.
301 James L. Hodges Ave. So. Phone: (319)523-4631
PO Box 306 Fax: (319)523-8167
Wapello, IA 52653-0306
Publisher E-mail: lpc@lisco.net

Newspaper with a Republican orientation. **Founded:** 1851. **Freq:** Weekly (Thurs.). **Print Method:** Offset. **Cols./Page:** 8. **Col. Width:** 21 nonpareils. **Col. Depth:** 294 agate lines. **Key Personnel:** Michael A. Hodges, Publisher; James L. Hodges, Publisher. **Subscription Rates:** $20 in county; $26 out of area; $30 out of state. **Remarks:** Accepts advertising.
Ad Rates: SAU: $5.03 **Circ:** ‡2,450
PCI: $4.27

WASHINGTON†, pop. 6,584.

SE IA. Washington Co. 34 mi. S. of Iowa City. Manufactures industrial wire products, valves, concrete, calendars, steel tanks, farm implement, beverages. Soybean, poultry processing plants. Agriculture. Corn, oats, hogs, poultry, soybeans. Cattle feeding.

11473 The Washington Evening Journal
PO Box 471 Phone: (319)653-2191
Washington, IA 52353 Fax: (319)653-7524

General newspaper. **Founded:** Feb. 15, 1893. **Freq:** Daily (eve.) Mon. thru Fri. **Print Method:** Offset. **Trim Size:** 14 x 22 3/4. **Cols./Page:** 6. **Col. Width:** 2 1/16 inches. **Col. Depth:** 21 1/2 inches. **Key Personnel:** Darwin K. Sherman, Editor and Publisher, darwink@e-iowa.net. **Subscription Rates:** $64 individuals; $67 by mail in county; $78 out of county; $94 out of state. **Remarks:** Accepts advertising.
Ad Rates: BW: $963.63 **Circ:** ‡4,591
4C: $1,283.63
PCI: $5.79

11474 KCII-AM - 1380
110 E. Main St. Phone: (319)653-2113
PO Box 524 Fax: (319)653-3500
Washington, IA 52353

Format: Adult Contemporary; Sports. **Simulcasts:** KCII-FM. **Networks:** ABC. **Owner:** Leighton Enterprises, PO Box 1458, St. Cloud, MN 56301, (612)251-1450. **Founded:** 1961. **Operating Hours:** 5:30 a.m.-11 p.m.; 10% network, 90% local. **ADI:** Cedar Rapids-Waterloo-Dubuque, IA. **Key Personnel:** Brian Sines, Contact; Loretta Barnhart, Office Mgr.; Lisa Boomershine, Program Dir.; Jon Grussing, News Dir.; Jim Mowen, Sports Dir.; Mark McVey, Engineer; Lisa Boomershine, Contact. **Wattage:** 500. **Ad Rates:** $9-12 for 30 seconds; $13-16 for 60 seconds.

11475 KCII-FM - 95.3
110 E. Main St. Phone: (319)653-2113
PO Box 524 Fax: (319)653-3500
Washington, IA 52353

Format: Adult Contemporary; Sports. **Simulcasts:** KCII-AM. **Networks:** ABC. **Owner:** Leighton Enterprises, PO Box 1458, St. Cloud, MN 56301, (612)251-1450. **Founded:** 1971. **Operating Hours:** 5:30 a.m.-11 p.m.; 10% network, 90% local. **ADI:** Cedar Rapids-Waterloo-Dubuque, IA. **Key Personnel:** Brian Sines, Vice President; Loretta Barnhart, Office Mgr.; Lisa Boomershine, PSA & Program Director; Jon Grussing, News Dir.; Jim Mowen, Sports Dir.; Mark McVey, Engineering. **Wattage:** 3000. **Ad Rates:** $9-12 for 30 seconds; $13-16 for 60 seconds.

WATERLOO†, pop. 75,985.

NEC IA. Black Hawk Co. On Cedar River, 93 mi. NE of Des Moines. Manufactures farm tractors, refrigerator shelves, truck mixers, livestock equipment, iron castings, printing systems, athletic uniforms, spreaders, overhead doors, corrugated boxes, feed, sulkies, tool and dies, fertilizers, silos.

11476 TeleProfessional Magazine
Advanstar Communications
209 W. 5th St., Ste. N Phone: (319)235-4473
Waterloo, IA 50701 Fax: (319)235-9850
Free: (800)338-8307

Magazine. **Subtitle:** The Forum for Call Center Information. **Founded:** 1989. **Freq:** 11/year. **Print Method:** Web offset. **Trim Size:** 8 1/4 x 10 7/8. **Cols./Page:** 3. **Col. Width:** 2 1/8 inches. **Col. Depth:** 10 inches. **Key Personnel:** Robert E. Van Voorhis, Jr., Editor-in-Chief, bobvv@telepro.com; Ross M. Scovotti, Publisher, rmscovotti@telepro.com; Wendy J. Jorgensen, Dir. of Operations, wendy@telepro.com; Angela Karr, Managing Editor, akarr@telepro.com. **ISSN:** 0886-9642. **Subscription Rates:** $39. **Remarks:** Accepts advertising.
Ad Rates: BW: $6,700 **Circ:** Paid 673
4C: $7,900 Controlled 40,425
PCI: $80

11477 Waterloo-Cedar Falls Courier
Howard Publications
501 Commercial St. Phone: (319)291-1400
Box 540 Fax: (319)234-6405
Waterloo, IA 50701-5413
Free: (800)798-1717
Publication E-mail: wcscareer@aol.com

General newspaper. **Founded:** 1854. **Freq:** Daily (eve.), Sunday (morn.). **Print Method:** Offset. **Cols./Page:** 6. **Col. Width:** 25 nonpareils. **Col. Depth:** 315 agate lines. **Key Personnel:** Saul Shapiro, Editor; James W. Lewis, Publisher; David E. Tansey, Publisher. **ISSN:** 8750-0868. **Subscription Rates:** $127.40 individuals. **Remarks:** Accepts advertising. **URL:** http://www.wcscareer.com. **Feature Editors:** Carolyn Cole, *Fashion, Features, Food, Lifestyle, Living, Travel*, phone

(319)291-1467; Kevin Evans, *Sports*, phone (319)291-1469; Amy Gades, *Religion, Rural Development*, phone (319)291-1454; Curt Glenn, *TV*, phone (319)291-1481; Pat Kinney, *Aviation, Financial/Business, Real Estate*, phone (319)291-1481; Dan Nierling, *Photo*, phone (319)291-1476; Melody Parker, *Drama, Entertainment, Garden/Home, Movie, Music*, phone (319)291-1462; Anne Phillips, *Education*, phone (319)291-1481; Nancy Raffensperger, *City, Consumer Affairs, Metro, Suburban*, phone (319)291-1481; Nancy Raffensperger, *News*, phone (319)291-1481; George Saucer, *Editorials*, phone (319)291-1458; Phyllis Singer, *Book, Family, Radio, Society, Women's*, phone (319)291-1461; William Slakey, *Environmental, Farm*, phone (319)291-1481; Eric Woolson, *Political*, phone (319)291-1481; Jackie Young, *Medical*, phone (319)291-1481.
Ad Rates: BW: $3,467.52 4C: $3,909.52 SAU: $26.88 **Circ:** Mon.-Fri. ★**46,788** Sun. ★**53,960**

11478 KBBG-FM - 88.1
918 Newell St. Phone: (319)234-1441
Waterloo, IA 50703 Fax: (319)234-6182
E-mail: kbbg@cedarnet.org

Format: Blues; Gospel; Jazz. **Networks:** Southern Broadcasting. **Owner:** African American Community Broadcasting, Inc., at above address. **Founded:** 1978. **Operating Hours:** 5:30am-midnight Mon-Thur, Sat; 5:30am-2am Fri; 6am-midnight Sun. **ADI:** Cedar Rapids-Waterloo-Dubuque, IA. **Key Personnel:** Jimmie Porter, Founder/CEO, phone (319)235-1515; Louise "Lou" Porter, President/Development Director, phone (319)235-1515; Bennie Walker, Jr., Station Mgr.; Marhson Glover, Music Dir.; Edyce Porter-Biggles, Contact. **Local Programs:** *In Business Tomorrow*; *Jimmie Porter Show*; *Mayor's Update*. **Wattage:** 10,000. **Ad Rates:** Advertising accepted; rates available upon request.

11479 KCRR-FM - 97.7
501 Sycamore St. Suite 300 Phone: (319)833-4800
PO Box 720 Fax: (319)833-4866
Waterloo, IA 50703
E-mail: kcrr@kcrr.com

Format: Classic Rock. **Founded:** 1983. **Operating Hours:** Continuous. **ADI:** Cedar Rapids-Waterloo-Dubuque, IA. **Key Personnel:** Dick Taylor, General Mgr.; Wes Davis, Engineer; Paul Velardi, Program Dir. **Wattage:** 25,000. **Ad Rates:** $35-50 per unit. Combined advertising rates available with KKCV-FM, KOEL-AM, KOEL-FM. **URL:** http://www.kcrr.com.

11480 KFMW-FM - 107.9
514 Jefferson St. Phone: (319)234-2200
Waterloo, IA 50701 Fax: (319)233-4946

Format: Album-Oriented Rock (AOR); Classic Rock; Contemporary Hit Radio (CHR). **Networks:** CNN Radio. **Founded:** 1968. **Formerly:** KWWL-FM. **Operating Hours:** Continuous. **ADI:** Cedar Rapids-Waterloo-Dubuque, IA. **Key Personnel:** Tim Mathews, General Mgr.; Fred Hendrickson, Sales Mgr.; Mark Hansen, Program Dir.; Kathy Flynn, News Dir.; Dolly Fortier, Contact. **Local Programs:** *At Issue*, Kathy Flynn. **Wattage:** 100,000.

11481 KNWS-AM - 1090
4880 Texas Phone: (319)296-1975
Waterloo, IA 50702-4742 Fax: (319)296-1977

Format: Religious. **Networks:** UPI. **Owner:** Northwestern College, 3003 N. Snelling, Roseville, MN 55113, (612)631-5100. **Founded:** 1953. **Operating Hours:** Sunrise-sunset; 15% network, 85% local. **ADI:** Cedar Rapids-Waterloo-Dubuque, IA. **Key Personnel:** Jeff Seeley, Manager; Dave Dobes, Chief Engineer. **Local Programs:** *Carousel* Monday-Friday, Lori Barrons, (319)296-1975; *Clockwatch*, Jeff Seeley, (319)296-1975; *Let's Sing*, Lyle Kreuger, (319)296-1975. **Wattage:** 1000. **Ad Rates:** Noncommercial.

11482 KNWS-FM - 101.9
4880 Texas Phone: (319)296-1975
Waterloo, IA 50702-4742 Fax: (319)296-1977

Format: Religious. **Networks:** UPI. **Owner:** Northwestern College, 3003 N. Snelling, Roseville, MN 55113, (612)631-5100. **Founded:** 1965. **Operating Hours:** Continuous; 15% network, 85% local. **ADI:** Cedar Rapids-Waterloo-Dubuque, IA. **Key Personnel:** Jeff Seeley, Manager; Dave Dobes, Chief Engineer. **Local Programs:** *Carousel*, Lori Barrons, (319)296-1975; *Clockwatch*, Jeff Seeler, (319)296-1975; *Let's Sing*, Lyle Krueger, (319)296-1975. **Wattage:** 100,000. **Ad Rates:** Noncommercial.

11483 KOEL-FM - 92.3
501 Sycamore St. Suite 300 Phone: (319)833-4800
pob 720 Fax: (319)833-4866
Waterloo, IA 50703
E-mail: koel@koel.com

Format: Country. **Networks:** AP. **Founded:** 1971. **Operating Hours:** Continuous. **ADI:** Cedar Rapids-Waterloo-Dubuque, IA. **Key Personnel:** Dick Taylor, General Mgr.; Austin James, Program Dir., ajames@sbt.net; Wes Davis, Chief Engineer. **Wattage:** 100,000. **Ad Rates:** $45-80 per unit. Combined advertising rates available with KKCV-FM, KCRR-FM, KOEL-AM. **URL:** http://www.koel.com.

11484 KOKZ-FM - 105.7
Box 1540 Phone: (319)233-3371
Waterloo, IA 50704 Fax: (319)233-7430

Format: Contemporary Hit Radio (CHR). **Owner:** KXEL Broadcasting Co., Inc., at above address. **Founded:** 1962. **Operating Hours:** Continuous. **ADI:** Cedar Rapids-Waterloo-Dubuque, IA. **Key Personnel:** Cy N. Bahakel, President; Tim Mathews, General Mgr.; Fred Hendrickson, Sales Mgr.; Laura Porter, Promotions Dir.; Dane McCormick, Program & Music Dir. **Wattage:** 100,000 ERP.

11485 KTOF-AM - 1360
3232 Osage Rd. Phone: (319)378-4400
Waterloo, IA 50703 Fax: (319)236-8777
Free: (800)329-8996
E-mail: kwof@pitnet.net

Format: Religious; Contemporary Christian. **Simulcasts:** KWOF. **Networks:** Moody Broadcasting; Sun Radio. **Founded:** 1995. **Formerly:** KTOF-FM (1995). **Operating Hours:** Continuous. **ADI:** Cedar Rapids-Waterloo-Dubuque, IA. **Key Personnel:** Bob Gougler, General Mgr.; Mike Kapler, Program Dir. **Local Programs:** *Body Builders*, J.D. Spencer, Mailing contact; *Share Time*, J.D. Spencer; *Sunshine Line*, Steve Pickering. **Wattage:** 1000.

11486 KWLO-AM - 1330
PO Box 1540 Phone: (319)234-2200
Waterloo, IA 50704 Fax: (319)234-9999
E-mail: kwlonews@aol.com

Format: Big Band/Nostalgia. **Networks:** NBC. **Owner:** Bahakel Communications, Ltd., at above address, Fax: (319)233-4946. **Founded:** 1947. **Formerly:** KWWL-AM (1981). **Operating Hours:** Continuous; 20% network, 80% local. **ADI:** Cedar Rapids-Waterloo-Dubuque, IA. **Key Personnel:** Kathy Flynn, News Dir.; Dave McCormick, Program Dir.; Ed Anderson, Sports Dir.; Fred Hendrickson, Sales Mgr.; Tim Mathews, General Mgr. **Wattage:** 5000.

11487 KWOF-AM - 850
3232 Osage Rd. Phone: (319)236-5700
Waterloo, IA 50703 Fax: (319)236-8777
Free: (800)774-5963
E-mail: kwof@pitnet.net

Format: Religious; Contemporary Christian. **Simulcasts:** KTOF-CEDAR RAPIDS. **Founded:** 1973. **Formerly:** KLEU-AM (1985). **Operating Hours:** Daytime. **ADI:** Cedar Rapids-Waterloo-Dubuque, IA. **Key Personnel:** Bob Gougler, General Mgr.; Mike Kapler, Program Dir. **Wattage:** 500. **Ad Rates:** $10 per unit. **URL:** http://www.friendshipconnection.com.

11488 KWWL-TV - 7
500 E. 4th St. Phone: (319)291-1200
Waterloo, IA 50703 Fax: (319)291-1233
E-mail: kwwl@kwwl.com

Format: Commercial TV. **Networks:** NBC; CNN Radio. **Founded:** Nov. 1953. **Operating Hours:** Continuous. **ADI:** Cedar Rapids-Waterloo-Dubuque, IA. **Key Personnel:** Jim Waterbury, General Mgr., fax (319)291-1255, jwaterbu-ryp.raycommedia.com. **Ad Rates:** Advertising accepted; rates available upon request.

11489 KXEL-AM - 1540
514 Jefferson St. Phone: (319)233-3371
Box 1540 Fax: (319)233-7430
Waterloo, IA 50704

Format: News; Talk. **Networks:** ABC. **Owner:** KXEL Broadcasting Co., Inc., at above address. **Founded:** 1942. **Operating Hours:** Continuous. **ADI:** Cedar Rapids-Waterloo-Dubuque, IA. **Key Personnel:** Cy N. Bahakel, President; Tim Mathews, General Mgr.; Fred Hendrickson, Sales Mgr.; Laura Porter, Promotions Dir.; Denis Cowe, Program Dir. **Wattage:** 50,000.

11490 TCI
Box 2457 Phone: (319)232-8800
Waterloo, IA 50704 Fax: (319)232-7841

Founded: 1979. **Formerly:** WestMarc Cable TV. **Cities Served:** Black Hawk County, IA.

WAUKON†, pop. 3,983.

NE IA. Allamakee Co. 90 mi. NW of Dubuque. Museums. Recreational. Creamery; truck body factory. Ships livestock, lumber. Agriculture. Cattle, hogs, corn, oats.

11491 Waukon Standard
News Publishing Co. Inc.
PO Box 286 Phone: (319)568-3431
Waukon, IA 52172 Fax: (319)568-4242

Newspaper. **Founded:** 1871. **Freq:** Weekly (Tues.). **Print Method:** Offset. **Cols./Page:** 9. **Col. Width:** 20 nonpareils. **Col. Depth:** 301 agate lines. **Key Personnel:** Richard Schilling, Editor; Tom Johnson, Publisher. **Subscription Rates:** $10.50 individuals.

11492 KNEI-AM - 1140
PO Box 492 Phone: (319)568-3476
Waukon, IA 52172 Fax: (319)568-3391
Free: (888)568-3476

Format: Contemporary Country. **Networks:** CBS; ABC. **Owner:** Marathon Media, 980 N. Michigan Ave., Ste. 1880, Chicago, IL 60611. **Founded:** 1967. **Operating Hours:** 18 hours daily; 80% local. **Key Personnel:** Chuck Allan, Sports Dir. **Wattage:** 1000. **Ad Rates:** $8 for 15 seconds; $10 for 30 seconds; $12.50 for 60 seconds.

11493 KNEI-FM - 103.5
Hwy. 9 N.
PO Box 492
Waukon, IA 52172

Format: Country. **Networks:** Jones Satellite; CBS; Radio Iowa. **Owner:** David H. Hogendorn, at above address, (319)568-3476, Fax: (319)568-3391. **Founded:** 1968. **Operating Hours:** Continuous. **Key Personnel:** David H. Hogendorn, Contact; Chuck Allen, Program Dir.; Chuck Bloxham, Operations Mgr. **Wattage:** 9.25Kw.

WAVERLY†, pop. 8,444.

NE IA. Bremer Co. On Cedar River, 22 mi. NW of Waterloo. Wartburg College. Instant dairy products processed. Manufactures cranes and excavator machines, remote control equipment, snow plows, fixtures, gauges. Soybeans, corn. Cattle. Pork. Dairying.

11494 Bremer County Independent
Waverly Newspapers
311 W. Bremer Phone: (319)352-3334
PO Box 858 Fax: (319)352-5135
Waverly, IA 50677
Free: (800)369-2226

Local newspaper. **Founded:** 1856. **Freq:** Weekly (Tues.). **Print Method:** Offset. **Cols./Page:** 8. **Col. Width:** 9 1/2 picas. **Col. Depth:** 22 inches. **Key Personnel:** Terri Lambert, Editor; Martin VanEe, Publisher; Cannie Glauerholtz, Advertising Mgr. **Subscription Rates:** $39 individuals; $59 out of area. **Remarks:** Accepts advertising.
Ad Rates: BW: $897.60 SAU: $7.63 PCI: $5.10 **Circ:** 6,350

11495 The Draft Horse Journal
Box 670 Phone: (319)352-4046
Waverly, IA 50677 Fax: (319)352-2232

Magazine on the heavy horse and mule trade. **Founded:** May 1964. **Freq:** Quarterly. **Print Method:** Offset. **Trim Size:** 8 1/2 x 11. **Cols./Page:** 3. **Col. Width:** 14 picas. **Col. Depth:** 57 picas. **Key Personnel:** Lynn Telleen, Editor. **ISSN:** 0012-5865. **Subscription Rates:** $25 /year; $30 other countries; $6.50 single issue. **Remarks:** Accepts advertising.
Ad Rates: BW: $500 4C: $850 **Circ:** Paid 22,000 Non-paid 125

11496 Wartburg Trumpet
Wartburg College
c/o McElroy Communication Arts Center Phone: (319)352-8289
Fax: (319)352-8610
Waverly, IA 50677
Free: (800)772-2085
Publication E-mail: trumpet@wartburg.edu

Collegiate newspaper. **Founded:** 1906. **Freq:** Weekly (Mon.). **Print Method:** Offset. **Cols./Page:** 5. **Col. Width:** 22 nonpareils. **Col. Depth:** 224 agate lines. **Key Personnel:** Dr. Lil Junas, Advisor, junas@wartburg.edu; Sara Baker, Editor, bakers@wartburg.edu. **ISSN:** 6667-4000. **Subscription Rates:** $18 individuals. **Remarks:** Accepts advertising alcoholic beverages, tobacco products, and term papers.
Ad Rates: GLR: $1.50 BW: $100 PCI: $8.10 **Circ:** Paid 1,850 Free 350

11497 Waverly Democrat
Waverly Newspapers
311 W. Bremer — Phone: (319)352-3334
PO Box 858 — Fax: (319)352-5135
Waverly, IA 50677
Free: (800)369-2226

Local newspaper. **Founded:** 1880. **Freq:** Weekly (Thurs.). **Print Method:** Offset. **Cols./Page:** 8. **Col. Width:** 9 1/2 picas. **Col. Depth:** 22 inches. **Key Personnel:** Terry Lamberts, Editor; Martin VanEe, Publisher; Connie Grauerholz, Advertising Mgr. **Subscription Rates:** $39 individuals; $59 out of area. **Remarks:** Accepts advertising.
Ad Rates: BW: $897.60 — **Circ:** 6,326
SAU: $7.63
PCI: $5.10

11498 KWAR-FM - 89.1
Wartburg College — Phone: (319)352-8209
Waverly, IA 50677 — Fax: (319)352-8610
Free: (800)772-2085
E-mail: kwar@ns.wartburg.edu

Format: Alternative/New Music/Progressive. **Owner:** Wartburg College, at above address. **Founded:** 1951. **Operating Hours:** 7 a.m.-2 a.m. weekdays, 9-midnight Sat.-Sun. **Key Personnel:** Liz Matthis, Contact. **Local Programs:** *Bitter Coffee*, Paul Yeager; *Fireside Chat*, Tim Stockman; *Talking Heads*, Justin DeVore. **Wattage:** 40. **Ad Rates:** Noncommercial. **URL:** http://www.wartburg.edu.

11499 KWAY-AM - 1470
PO Box 307 — Phone: (319)352-3550
Waverly, IA 50677 — Fax: (319)352-3601

Networks: AP. **Owner:** Cedar Valley Broadcasting Co., at above address. **Founded:** 1958. **Operating Hours:** 5:00 am until 12:00 midnight. **Key Personnel:** Ael Suhr, Contact. **Wattage:** 1000 day; 61 night. **Ad Rates:** $6-8 for 30 seconds; $12-23 for 60 seconds.

11500 KWAY-FM - 99.3
PO Box 307 — Phone: (319)352-3550
Waverly, IA 50677

Format: Adult Contemporary. **Owner:** Cedar Valley Broadcasting Co., at above address. **Founded:** 1971. **Operating Hours:** 5:00 am - 12:00 midnight. **Key Personnel:** Ael Sutton, phone (319)352-3550. **Wattage:** 3000. **Ad Rates:** $8-9 for 30 seconds; $23-27 for 60 seconds.

WEBSTER CITY†, pop. 8,572.

C IA. Hamilton Co. 20 mi. E. of Fort Dodge. Manufactures washing machines, aluminum castings, boats, scooters, concrete products, tile spades, hog feeders and waterers, electric scoreboards, metal grain bins, feed. Hatcheries. Ships hogs, cattle. Grain, stock, poultry farms.

11501 Daily Freeman-Journal
7 22nd St. — Phone: (515)832-4350
PO Box 490 — Fax: (515)832-2314
Webster City, IA 50595
General newspaper. **Founded:** 1857. **Freq:** Daily (eve.). **Print Method:** Offset. **Cols./Page:** 6. **Col. Width:** 29 nonpareils. **Col. Depth:** 300 agate lines. **Key Personnel:** Mike Fertig, Gen. Mgr./Pub.; Dan Corrow, Publisher; Lori Nilles, Editor. **USPS:** 142-940. **Subscription Rates:** $59.80 individuals. **Remarks:** Accepts advertising.
Ad Rates: GLR: $.45 — **Circ:** 3,908
BW: $812.70
SAU: $6.30
PCI: $6.30

11502 KQWC-AM - 1570
Box 550 — Phone: (515)832-1570
Webster City, IA 50595 — Fax: (515)832-2079
E-mail: flyteman@ncn.net

Format: Talk; Agricultural; News; Agricultural. **Simulcasts:** KQWC-FM. **Networks:** Mutual Broadcasting System. **Owner:** Glen Olson, at above address. **Founded:** 1950. **Formerly:** KJFJ-AM (1972). **Operating Hours:** 18 hours daily; 5% network, 95% local. **ADI:** Des Moines, IA. **Key Personnel:** Larry M. Schultz, General Mgr.; Andy Anderson, Sports Dir.; Carolyn Schultz, Program Dir. **Wattage:** 250. **Ad Rates:** $10.50-15.50 for 30 seconds; $14-21.50 for 60 seconds. $10.50-$15.50 for 30 seconds; $14-$21.50 for 60 seconds. Combined advertising rates available with KQWC-FM.

11503 KQWC-FM - 95.7
1020 E. 2nd St. — Phone: (515)832-1570
PO Box 550 — Fax: (515)832-2079
Webster City, IA 50595
E-mail: flyteman@ncn.net

Format: Talk; News; News. **Networks:** Mutual Broadcasting System. **Owner:** Glenn R. Olson, at above address. **Founded:** 1950. **Operating Hours:** 18 hours daily; 30% network, 70% local. **ADI:** Des Moines, IA. **Key Personnel:** Pat Powers, News Dir.; Andy Anderson, Sports Dir.; Carolyn Schultz, Program Dir.; Larry M. Schultz, General Mgr. **Wattage:** 25,000. **Ad Rates:** $10.50-15.50 for 30 seconds; $14-21.50 for 60 seconds. $10.50-$15.50 for 30 seconds; $14-$21.50 for 60 seconds. Combined advertising rates available with KQWC-AM.

WELLMAN

11504 Wellman Advance
PO Drawer I — Phone: (319)646-2712
Wellman, IA 52356 — Fax: (319)646-2712

Community newspaper. **Freq:** Weekly (Thurs.). **Cols./Page:** 8. **Col. Width:** 10 picas. **Col. Depth:** 21 inches. **Key Personnel:** Mike Hodges, Publisher; Mary Hodges, Publisher; Ranee Fladung, Co.-Editor. **Subscription Rates:** $16 individuals; $.50 single issue. **Remarks:** Accepts advertising.
Ad Rates: SAU: $3.64 — **Circ:** 1,300
PCI: $3.09

WEST BRANCH, pop. 1,867.

E IA. Cedar Co. 10 mi. E. of Iowa City. Herbert Hoover birthplace. Presidential library. Alfalfa dehydrating plant; feed mill. Printing plant. Foam manufacturing plant. Agriculture. Corn, hogs, cattle.

11505 West Branch Times
PO Box 368 — Phone: (319)643-2131
West Branch, IA 52358 — Fax: (319)643-2848

Community newspaper. **Founded:** 1886. **Freq:** Weekly (Thurs.). **Print Method:** Offset. **Cols./Page:** 4. **Col. Width:** 14 picas. **Col. Depth:** 16 inches. **Key Personnel:** David J. Johnson, Editor. **USPS:** 630-140. **Subscription Rates:** $22 individuals; $27 out of state. **Remarks:** Accepts advertising.
Ad Rates: BW: $249.60 — **Circ:** ‡1,450
SAU: $4.50

WEST BURLINGTON, pop. 3,371.

SE IA. Des Moines Co. 5 mi. NW of Burlington. Manufactures fertilizer, industrial switchgear, antenna, mat or truck line terminals.

11506 Des Moines County News
Louisa Publishing Co., Ltd.
204 Broadway — Phone: (319)752-8328
PO Box 177
West Burlington, IA 52655
Publisher E-mail: lpc@lisco.net

Community newspaper. **Founded:** 1954. **Freq:** Weekly (Fri.). **Print Method:** Offset. **Cols./Page:** 5. **Col. Width:** 22 nonpareils. **Col. Depth:** 210 agate lines. **Key Personnel:** Ramona Nahorny, Editor; Mike Campbell, Advertising Mgr. **Subscription Rates:** $16 individuals. **Remarks:** Accepts advertising.
Ad Rates: GLR: $.24 — **Circ:** 1,800
SAU: $4.37
PCI: $3.71

WEST DES MOINES, pop. 21,894.

C IA. Polk Co. 5 mi. W. of Des Moines. Manufactures silos, electric supplies, cement products. Foundry. Stone quarries. Data-processing. Industrial. Agriculture. Corn, wheat, hay.

11507 Business & Industry
Business Magazine, Inc.
1720 28th St., Ste. B — Phone: (515)225-2545
West Des Moines, IA 50266-1400 — Fax: (515)225-2318
Magazine for top level and purchasing management, manufacturing and design engineers, and quality control personnel. **Founded:** Oct. 1946. **Freq:** Monthly. **Print Method:** Offset. **Trim Size:** 8 3/8 x 10 7/8. **Cols./Page:** 3 and 2. **Col. Width:** 27 and 42 nonpareils. **Col. Depth:** 140 agate lines. **Key Personnel:** James V. Snyder, Editor; Robert J. Wagner, Advertising Mgr., rwagner289@aol.com. **ISSN:** 0021-0463. **Subscription Rates:** Free to qualified subscribers; $24 individuals. **Remarks:** Accepts advertising.
Ad Rates: BW: $977 — **Circ:** Controlled ‡12,100
4C: $1,377

11508 Iowa Medicine
Iowa Medical Society
1001 Grand Ave. — Phone: (515)223-1401
West Des Moines, IA 50265 — Fax: (515)223-8420
Free: (800)747-3070
Publication E-mail: kstoner@iowamedicalsociety.org
Publisher E-mail: tstoner@iowamedicalsociety.org

Medical journal. **Subtitle:** Journal of the Iowa Medical Society. **Founded:** 1910. **Freq:** 6/year. **Print Method:** Offset. Uses mats. **Trim Size:** 8 1/4 x 10 7/8. **Cols./Page:** 3. **Col. Width:** 1.676 inches. **Key Personnel:** Chris McMahon, Managing Editor; Tina Stoner, Production Coordinator. **ISSN:** 0746-8709. **Subscription Rates:** $25 individuals. **Remarks:** Accepts advertising.
Ad Rates: GLR: $2 — **Circ:** Paid 4,297
BW: $295 — Non-paid 150
4C: $895

11509 Iowa Oil Spout
Iowa Oil Jobber Services
1303 50th St.
West Des Moines, IA 50266-1705

Oil industry magazine. **Freq:** 10/year. **Key Personnel:** E. A. Kistenmacher, Editor.
Circ: 1,000

11510 KWDM-FM - 88.7
1140 35th St. — Phone: (515)226-2660
West Des Moines, IA 50266 — Fax: (515)226-2609
E-mail: kwdm@wdm.k12.ia.us

Format: Alternative/New Music/Progressive. **Owner:** West Des Moines Community School District, at above address, (515)226-2600. **Founded:** 1975. **Operating Hours:** 17 hrs. Sun. - Fri. **ADI:** Des Moines, IA. **Key Personnel:** Brian Christensen, Contact, christb@wdm.k12.ia.us. **Local Programs:** *Layla in the Afternoon* 3:00 pm - 6:00 pm Monday-Friday, Layla Hilton, (515)226-2660, Fax (515)226-2609; *Morning Show* 6:30 am - 8:00 am Monday-Friday, Justin Schoen, (515)226-2660, Fax (515)226-2609. **Wattage:** 100. **Ad Rates:** Noncommercial.

11511 WOI-TV - 5
3903 Westown Parkway — Phone: (515)457-9645
West Des Moines, IA 50266 — Fax: (515)457-1034
Free: (800)858-5555
E-mail: woitv@ecity.net

Format: Commercial TV. **Networks:** ABC. **Owner:** Capital Communications Company, Inc., at above address. **Founded:** 1951. **Operating Hours:** Continuous. **ADI:** Des Moines, IA. **Key Personnel:** Raymond H. Cole, Exec. VP & COO, phone (515)457-1033; Elaine Honold, Business Mgr.; Robert Richardson, National Sales Mgr.; Randy Shelton, Dir. of Broadcast Operations; Bill Bradley, General Mgr.; Bruce Howie, Sales Mgr.; Sean Murray, Promotions Mgr.; Jime Parker, News Dir., phone (515)457-1026, fax (515)457-1025; Scott Richardson, Assignment Editor; Brad Edwards, Chief Meteorologist; John Walters, Sports Dir./Traffic Mgr.; Zoe Ann Goedicke, Traffic Mgr. **URL:** http://www.woi-tr.com; http://www.woi-tv.com.

WEST LIBERTY, pop. 2,723.

E IA. Muscatine Co. 35 mi. W. of Davenport. Residential.

11512 West Liberty Index
Slechta Communications, Inc.
PO Box 96 — Phone: (319)627-2814
West Liberty, IA 52776-0096 — Fax: (319)627-2110
Free: (800)817-8729
Publication E-mail: index@netins.net

Local newspaper. **Founded:** 1868. **Freq:** Weekly. **Print Method:** Offset. **Trim Size:** 12 x 18. **Cols./Page:** 5. **Col. Width:** 11 1/2 picas. **Col. Depth:** 16 inches. **Key Personnel:** Chuck Gysi, Editor; Ronald Slechta, Publisher. **USPS:** 675-520. **Subscription Rates:** $22 individuals; $24 out of area; $26 out of state. **URL:** http://www.westlibertindex.com.
Ad Rates: PCI: $4.50 — **Circ:** ‡2,000

WEST POINT

11513 Donnellson Star
Ray Fullenkamp
PO Box 66 — Phone: (319)837-6722
West Point, IA 52656 — Fax: (319)372-3867

Local newspaper. **Freq:** Weekly (Thurs.). **Print Method:** Offset. **Cols./Page:** 3. **Col. Width:** 18 nonpareils. **Col. Depth:** 224 agate lines. **Key Personnel:** Ray Fullenkamp, Publisher. **Subscription Rates:** $14.50 individuals. **Remarks:** Accepts advertising.
Ad Rates: GLR: $.326 — **Circ:** (Not Reported)
BW: $218.88
PCI: $2.95

11514 West Point Bee
Ray Fullenkamp
PO Box 66 — Phone: (319)837-6722
West Point, IA 52656 — Fax: (319)372-3867

Local newspaper. **Freq:** Weekly (Thurs.). **Print Method:** Offset. **Cols./Page:** 3. **Col. Width:** 18 nonpareils. **Col. Depth:** 224 agate lines. **Key Personnel:** Ray Fullenkamp, Publisher.

Subscription Rates: $14.50 individuals. **Remarks:** Accepts advertising.
Ad Rates: GLR: $.326 **Circ:** (Not Reported)
BW: $218.88
PCI: $2.95

WEST UNION†, pop. 2,783.

NE IA. Fayette Co. 45 mi. NE of Waterloo. Manufactures pharmaceuticals, luggage, auto parts. Egg and meat processing plants; feed mill. Agriculture. Corn, hogs, dairy products.

11515 Fayette County Union
Fayette County Union, Inc.
Box 153 Phone: (319)422-3888
West Union, IA 52175-0153 Fax: (319)422-5557

Newspaper. **Founded:** 1866. **Freq:** Weekly (Thurs.). **Print Method:** Offset. **Cols./Page:** 6. **Col. Width:** 28 nonpareils. **Col. Depth:** 301 agate lines. **Key Personnel:** Gerald H. Blue, Editor. **Subscription Rates:** $19 individuals. **Remarks:** Accepts advertising.
Ad Rates: GLR: $.25 **Circ:** (Not Reported)
BW: $455
4C: $555

WHAT CHEER, pop. 803.

SE IA. Keokuk Co. 60 mi. SE of Des Moines. Residential.

11516 What Cheer Paper
What Cheer
PO Box 414 Phone: (515)634-2092
What Cheer, IA 50268 Fax: (515)522-9288

Community newspaper. **Founded:** 1879. **Freq:** Weekly (Thurs.). **Print Method:** Offset. **Cols./Page:** 6. **Col. Width:** 13 picas. **Col. Depth:** 20 1/2 inches. **Key Personnel:** Chas V. Dunham, Editor and Publisher. **USPS:** 681-440. **Subscription Rates:** $20 individuals. **Remarks:** Accepts advertising. **Formerly:** Patriot-Chronicle.
Ad Rates: GLR: $3.54 **Circ:** ‡1,400
BW: $344
SAU: $3.50
PCI: $3.50

WILTON, pop. 2,493.

SE IA. Muscatine Co. 25 mi. NW of Davenport. Feed mill; grain dryers; concrete; agricultural lime; steel bars; printing; computer services. Stock.

Wilton-Durant Advocate News - See Durant

WINFIELD, pop. 1,042.

SE IA. Henry Co. 35 mi. NW of Burlington. Residential. Tourism. Agriculture, rock quarries.

11517 Winfield Beacon & Wayland News
107 E. Elm Phone: (319)257-6813
Box F Fax: (319)257-6902
Winfield, IA 52659
Community newspaper. **Founded:** 1881. **Freq:** Weekly (Thurs.). **Print Method:** Offset. **Cols./Page:** 7. **Col. Width:** 12 1/2 picas. **Col. Depth:** 21 1/2 inches. **Key Personnel:** Cathy Lauderdale, Publisher. **ISSN:** 1042-1211. **Subscription Rates:** $21 individuals; $26 out of area.
Ad Rates: BW: $477.75 **Circ:** ‡1,850
SAU: $4
PCI: $3.20

WINTHROP, pop. 767.

NEC IA. Buchanan Co. 10 mi. E. of Aurora. Residential.

11518 The Winthrop News
Box A Phone: (319)935-3027
Winthrop, IA 50682 Fax: (319)935-3082
Publisher E-mail: winnews@netins.net

Local newspaper. **Founded:** 1890. **Freq:** Weekly (Thurs.). **Print Method:** Offset. **Cols./Page:** 6. **Col. Width:** 9.5 picas. **Col. Depth:** 14 inches. **Key Personnel:** Janet Jentz, Manager; Nancy Werner, Receptionist-Sec.; Jeanine Timp, Advertising; June Bonefas, News Dir.; Lorice Snyder, News Dir. **Subscription Rates:** $19; $21 out of area; $22 out of state. **Remarks:** Accepts advertising.
Ad Rates: BW: $318 **Circ:** ‡2,000
SAU: $6.07
PCI: $3.78

11519 East Buchanan Telephone Cooperative
214 3rd St. N. Phone: (319)935-3011
Winthrop, IA 50682 Fax: (319)935-3010

Key Personnel: Jay Hagge, General Mgr. **Cities Served:** Winthrop and Quafqueton, Iowa.

WYOMING, pop. 702.

E IA. Jones Co. 25 mi. E. of Cedar Rapids. Residential.

11520 Midland Times
Light Publishing Co.
Box 87 Phone: (319)488-2281
Wyoming, IA 52362
Local newspaper. **Freq:** Weekly (Fri.). **Print Method:** Offset. **Trim Size:** 10 1/4 x 16. **Cols./Page:** 6. **Col. Width:** 9 picas. **Col. Depth:** 16 inches. **Key Personnel:** Shirley Jones, Editor and Publisher. **USPS:** 997-780. **Subscription Rates:** $16 individuals; $19 out of area; $22 out of state. **Remarks:** Accepts advertising.
Ad Rates: BW: $192 **Circ:** Paid ‡1,000
PCI: $2.50 Free ‡20

KANSAS

State Capital, TOPEKA

Kansas in bounded on the north by Nebraska, east by Missouri, south by Oklahoma, and west by Colorado and is in almost the exact geographical center of the United States mainland. Its breadth from east to west is 410 miles, and from north to south 207 miles. Its total area is 81,823 square miles. Topography of Kansas is widely varied, ranging from 686 feet above sea level to 4,135 feet near the Colorado border in a combination of hills, valleys, and plains. The Flint Hills area and the Smoky Hills Upland are two of the finest grazing areas in the United States. There are about 50,000 streams large enough to be named and about 90 man-made reservoirs and lakes ranging up to 6,600 acres in size. The climate is warm in summer and severe in winter. The extremes are constantly modified by the winds. The Weather Bureau at Wichita gives the temperature (annual average) as 56.2; highest on record, 114; lowest on record, -22. Total annual precipitation is 29.33 inches. The livestock market and meat-packing industry at Kansas City, Kansas, is one of the largest in the country. Kansas is one of the greatest cattle producing states in the union, and nearly half the cattle received at its stockyards come from the state. There are 46 colleges, including two state universities: University of Kansas at Lawrence and Kansas State University at Manhattan.

POPULATION: 2,523,000 (1992). Rank among the states: 32nd.

AGRICULTURE: Number of farms: 67,000 (1992). Farm acreage: 48,000,000 (1992). Cash receipts from farm marketings: crops, $2,133,000,000 (1991); livestock and products, $4,802,000,000 (1991).

FORESTS: Total forest land: 116,000 acres (1991).

MINERALS: Value of production: $366,000,000 (1991). Principal minerals: salt, stone, and cement. Value of petroleum production: $1,139,000,000 (1991).

MANUFACTURES: Value added by manufacture $14,573,000,000 (1991). Leading industry groups: transportation equipment, food and related products, chemicals and allied products.

LIST OF COUNTIES

Total number of counties 105

County, Location on Map, and County Seat	Pop.
Allen (SE), Iola	14,638
Anderson (E), Garnett	7,803
Atchison (NE), Atchinson	16,932
Barber (S), Medicine Lodge	5,874
Barton (WC), Great Bend	29,382
Bourbon (SE), Fort Scott	14,966
Brown (NE), Hiawatha	11,128
Butler (SE), El Dorado	50 580
Chase (S), Cottonwood Falls	3,021
Chautauqua (SE), Sedan	4,407
Cherokee (SE), Columbus	21,374
Cheyenne (NW), St. Francis	3,243
Clark (S), Ashland	2,418
Clay (NEC), Clay Center	9,158
Cloud (N), Concordia	11,023
Coffey (SE), Burlington	8,404
Comanche (S), Coldwater	2,313
Cowley (SE), Winfield	36,915
Crawford (SE), Girard	35,568
Decatur (NW), Oberlin	4,021
Dickinson (NEC), Abilene	18,958
Doniphan (NE), Troy	8,134
Douglas (E), Lawrence	81,798
Edwards (SWC), Kinsley	3,787
Elk (SE), Howard	3,327
Ellis (SE), Hays	26,004
Ellsworth (C), Ellsworth	6,586
Finney (SW), Garden City	33,070
Ford (SW), Dodge City	27,463
Franklin (E), Ottawa	21,994
Geary (EC), Junction City	30,453
Gove (W), Gove	3,231
Graham (NW), Hill City	3,543
Grant (SW), Ulysses	7,159
Gray (SW), Cimarron	5,396
Greeley (W), Tribune	1,774
Greenwood (SE), Eureka	7,847
Hamilton (W), Syracuse	2,388
Harper (S), Anthony	7,124
Harvey (SC), Newton	31,028
Haskell (SW), Sublette	3,886
Hodgeman (SWC), Jetmore	2,177
Jackson (NE), Holton	11,525
Jefferson (N), Oskaloosa	15,905
Jewell (N), Mankato	4,251
Johnson (E), Olathe	355,054
Kearny (SW), Lakin	4,027
Kingman (S), Kingman	8,292
Kiowa (SW), Geensburg	3,660
Labette (SE), Oswego	23,693
Lane (WC), Dighton	2,375
Leavenworth (NE), Leavenworth	64,371
Lincoln (C), Lincoln	3,653
Linn (E), Mound City	8,254
Logan (W), Russell Springs	3,081
Lyon (EC), Emporia	34,732
Marion (SEC), Marion	12,888
Marshall (NE), Marysville	11,705
McPherson (C), McPherson	27,268
Meade (SW), Meade	4,247
Miami (E) Paola	23,466
Mitchell (NC), Beloit	7,203
Montgomery (SE), Independence	38,816
Morris (EC), Council Grove	6,198
Morton (SW), Richfield	3,480
Nemaha (NE), Seneca	10,446
Neosho (SE), Erie	17,035
Ness (WC), Ness City	4,033
Norton (NW), Norton	5,947
Osage (E), Lyndon	15,248
Osborne (N), Osborne	4,867
Ottawa (NC), Minneapolis	5,634
Pawnee (SWC), Larned	7,555
Phillips (N), Phillipsburg	6,590
Pottawatomie (NE), Westmoreland	16,128
Pratt (S), Pratt	4,702
Rawlins (NW), Atwood	3,404
Reno (C), Hutchinson	62,389
Republic (N), Belleville	6,482
Rice (C), Lyons	10,610
Riley (NEC), Manhattan	67,139
Rooks (NWC), Stockton	6,039
Rush (WC), La Crosse	3,842
Russell (NC), Russell	7,835
Saline (C), Salina	49,301
Scott (W), Scott City	5,289
Sedgwick (S), Wichita	403,662
Seward (SW), Liberal	18,743
Shawnee (E), Topeka	160,976
Sheridan (NW), Hoxie	3,043
Sherman (NW), Goodland	6,926
Smith (N), Smith Center	5,078
Stafford (SC), St. John	5,365
Stanton (SW), Johnson	2,333
Stevens (SW), Hugoton	5,048
Sumner (S), Wellington	25,841
Thomas (NW), Colby	8,258
Trego (NW), Wakeeney	3,694
Wabaunsee (NE), Alma	6,603
Wallace (W), Sharon Springs	1,821

Washington (N), Washington 7,073
Wichita (W), Leoti 2,758
Wilson (SE), Fredonia 10,289
Woodson (SE), Yates Center 4,116
Wyandotte (NE), Kansas City 161,993

STATISTICS

Newspapers

Period of Issue
Daily 42
Evening Daily 36
Morning Daily 8
Daily with Sunday edition 17
Semiweekly 20
Weekly 177
Biweekly 1
Semimonthly 5
Bimonthly 2
Monthly 4
Free or partly free 24
Shopper 15
Total Newspapers 258

Periodicals

Period of Issue
Weekly 5
Biweekly 2
Semimonthly 1
Monthly 42
Bimonthly 13
Quarterly 32
Total Periodicals 123

Total number of publications 381

Radio Stations

AM Stations 51
FM Stations 79
Total Radio Stations 130

TV Stations

Total TV Stations 21

Cable Stations

Total Cable Systems 34

Total number of broadcast listings 185

ABILENE†, pop. 6,572.

NEC KS. Dickinson Co. On the Smoky Hill River, 83 mi. SW of Topeka. Warehousing and distribution center for cattle, grain, and dairy products.

11521 Abilene Reflector Chronicle
Reflector Chronicle Publishing Corp.
303 N. Broadway Phone: (913)263-1000
PO Box 8 Fax: (913)263-1645
Abilene, KS 67410
Community Newspaper. **Founded:** 1887. **Freq:** Daily (eve.) and Sat. (morn.). **Print Method:** Offset. Uses mats. **Cols./Page:** 6. **Col. Width:** 26 nonpareils. **Col. Depth:** 301 agate lines. **Key Personnel:** Vivien L. Sadowski, Editor and Publisher; Janelle J. Gantenbein, Advertising Mgr. **Subscription Rates:** $78 individuals. **Remarks:** Accepts advertising.
Ad Rates: GLR: $.49 **Circ:** Paid 4,435
PCI: $6.86 Free 175

11522 Central Marketplace
Reflector Chronicle Publishing Corp.
303 N. Broadway Phone: (913)263-1000
PO Box 8 Fax: (913)263-1645
Abilene, KS 67410
Shopping guide. **Freq:** Weekly (Wed.). **Print Method:** Offset. Uses mats. **Cols./Page:** 6. **Col. Width:** 26 nonpareils. **Col. Depth:** 301 agate lines. **Key Personnel:** Vivien L. Sadowski, Editor and Publisher; Janelle J. Gantenbein, Editor.

11523 The Greyhound Review
National Greyhound Association
PO Box 543 Phone: (785)263-4660
Abilene, KS 67410-0543 Fax: (785)263-4689
Publisher E-mail: nga@jc.net

Magazine about Greyhound dog racing. **Founded:** 1973. **Freq:** Monthly. **Print Method:** Letterpress and offset. **Cols./Page:** 3. **Col. Width:** 26 nonpareils. **Col. Depth:** 133 agate lines. **Key Personnel:** Gary Guccione, Editor. **Subscription Rates:** $30 individuals. **Remarks:** Accepts advertising.
Ad Rates: BW: $320 **Circ:** ‡4,200
4C: $455

11524 KABI-AM - 1560
200 N. Broadway Phone: (785)263-1560
Abilene, KS 67410 Fax: (785)263-0166

Format: News; Sports; Adult Contemporary. **Networks:** ABC. **Owner:** EBC, Inc., at above address. **Founded:** 1963. **Operating Hours:** Continuous; 18% network, 82% local. **Key Personnel:** Billy Hansen, Program Dir., bhansen@informatics.net; John Anderson, News Dir., andnew@informatics.net; Larry Avery, General Mgr., lavery@informatics.net. **Wattage:** 250.

11525 KBLS-FM - 102.5
PO Box 69 Phone: (785)823-1111
Abilene, KS 67410

Format: Adult Contemporary. **Networks:** Jones Satellite. **Owner:** E.B.C., Inc., at above address. **Founded:** Jan. 1, 1993. **Operating Hours:** Continuous. **Key Personnel:** John Anderson, Program Dir.; Mitch Dress, Sales Mgr. **Wattage:** 100,000. **URL:** http://www.ebcinc.com.

ALLEN

11526 American Beef Cattleman
Walker
Box 1046, Hwy. 56 Phone: (316)528-3556
Allen, KS 66833
Newspaper (tabloid) for beef-cow/calf producers including test stations research reports. **Subtitle:** The National Beef Cattle Information Publication. **Founded:** 1987. **Freq:** Monthly. **Print Method:** Offset. **Trim Size:** 11 x 17. **Cols./Page:** 3. **Col. Width:** 3 inches. **Key Personnel:** Hayes Walker, Editor and Publisher; Phyllis Walker, Editor and Publisher. **Subscription Rates:** $15 two years. **Remarks:** Accepts advertising.
Ad Rates: BW: $1,000 **Circ:** ‡20,000
PCI: $25

ALMA†, pop. 925.

NE KS. Wabaunsee Co. 30 mi. SW of Topeka. Grain, stock, poultry farms.

11527 The Signal-Enterprise
323 Missouri Phone: (785)765-3327
Alma, KS 66401 Fax: (785)765-3384
Publisher E-mail: espsbsms@kansas.net

Newspaper. **Founded:** 1884. **Freq:** Weekly (Thurs.). **Print Method:** Offset. **Cols./Page:** 5. **Col. Width:** 24 nonpareils. **Col. Depth:** 224 agate lines. **Key Personnel:** Er van D. Stuewe, Editor and Publisher; Pamela K. Stuewe, Editor and Publisher. **USPS:** 496-340. **Subscription Rates:** $23.50 individuals; $25.50 out of state. **Remarks:** Accepts advertising.
Ad Rates: BW: $168 **Circ:** Paid ‡1,800
PCI: $3 Free ‡50

ANDOVER, pop. 2,801.

SE KS. Butler Co. 10 mi. E. of Wichita.

11528 The Andover Journal Advocate
The Andover Journal Publishing, Inc.
202 E. Rhondda Ave. C Phone: (316)733-2002
Andover, KS 67002 Fax: (316)733-4221
Publication E-mail: ajapaper@feist.com

Local newspaper. **Founded:** 1971. **Freq:** Weekly (Thurs.). **Print Method:** Offset. **Cols./Page:** 5. **Col. Width:** 10 3/16 inches. **Col. Depth:** 16 inches. **Key Personnel:** Kay L. Palmer, Publisher. **USPS:** 943-760. **Subscription Rates:** $25 individuals; $30 out of state. **Remarks:** Accepts advertising. **URL:** http://www.andovernet.com.
Ad Rates: GLR: $7 **Circ:** Paid ‡2,153
BW: $640 Free ‡18
4C: $850
PCI: $7

ANTHONY†, pop. 2,661.

SC KS. Harper Co. 58 mi. SW of Wichita. Wheat, cattle, hogs, sheep.

11529 The Anthony Republican
Dunn Enterprises, Inc.
121 E. Main Phone: (316)842-5129
Anthony, KS 67003-0031
Community newspaper. **Founded:** 1879. **Freq:** Weekly (Wed.). **Print Method:** Offset. **Trim Size:** 8 x 10 3/4. **Cols./Page:** 7. **Col. Width:** 12 picas. **Col. Depth:** 301 agate lines. **Key Personnel:** James W. Dunn, Editor and Publisher. **USPS:** 026-120. **Subscription Rates:** $20 individuals; $25 out of area. **Remarks:** Accepts advertising.
Ad Rates: GLR: $0.29 **Circ:** Paid 2,900
BW: $526.75 Free 30
PCI: $4

ARKANSAS CITY, pop. 13,201.

SE KS. Cowley Co. Located at juncture of Arkansas and Walnut rivers, 47 mi. SE of Wichita. Cowley County Community College. Oil refineries; flour mills; meat packing plants. Dairy and grain farms.

11530 The Press
Cowley County Community College
125 S. 2nd Phone: (316)441-5287
Arkansas City, KS 67005 Fax: (316)441-5350
Free: (800)593-2222
Publisher E-mail: bostwick@cowley.cc.ks.us

Collegiate newspaper. **Subtitle:** The Cowley Press. **Founded:** 1922. **Freq:** Semimonthly. **Print Method:** Offset. **Trim Size:** 11 x 14. **Cols./Page:** 4. **Col. Width:** 14 picas. **Col. Depth:** 165 agate lines. **Key Personnel:** David Bostwick, Advisor, bostwick@cowley.cc.ks.us. **Subscription Rates:** Free. **URL:** http://www.cowley.cc.ks.us. **Formerly:** The Cycle.
Ad Rates: BW: $120 **Circ:** Free 850
PCI: $3 Free ‡850

11531 Traveler
Staffer Communications
200 E. 5th Ave. Phone: (316)442-4200
Box 988 Fax: (316)442-7483
Arkansas City, KS 67005-2606
General newspaper. **Founded:** 1870. **Freq:** Daily (eve.) and Sat. (morn.). **Print Method:** Offset. **Cols./Page:** 6. **Col. Width:** 25 nonpareils. **Col. Depth:** 301 agate lines. **Key Personnel:** Kim Benedilt, Editor and Publisher. **USPS:** 031-360. **Subscription Rates:** $55.45 individuals. **Remarks:** Accepts advertising. **Online:** American Online, Inc.
Ad Rates: BW: $648.87 **Circ:** ‡6,300
4C: $818.28
SAU: $5.67

11532 Multimedia Cablevision, Inc.
PO Box 898
Arkansas City, KS 67005-0898

Owner: Gannett, 1100 Wilson Blvd., Arlington, VA 22234, (703)284-6000. **Founded:** 1969. **Key Personnel:** L. Allen Goff, District Mgr., phone (316)442-2280. **Cities Served:** Arkansas City, Newkirk, Oklahoma, Winfield, KS; Cowley County: 28 channels; 2 community access channels; 168 hours per week community access programming.

ASHLAND†, pop. 1,096.

SW KS. Clark Co. 52 mi. SE of Dodge City. Oil and gas wells. Grain and stock farms.

11533 Clark County Clipper
Box 457 Phone: (316)635-2312
Ashland, KS 67831 Fax: (316)635-2643

Newspaper. **Founded:** 1884. **Freq:** Weekly (Thurs.). **Print Method:** Offset. **Cols./Page:** 6. **Col. Width:** 24 nonpareils. **Col. Depth:** 294 agate lines. **Key Personnel:** Amber Woodruff, Editor. **Subscription Rates:** $15 individuals. **Remarks:** Accepts advertising.
Ad Rates: GLR: $.14 **Circ:** 1,345

ATCHISON†, pop. 11,407.

NE KS. Atchison Co. On Missouri river, 20 mi. N. of Leavenworth. St. Benedict's College; Mount St. Scholastica College. Limestone quarry; foundry. Manufactures locomotive parts, leather goods, industrial alcohol, flour. Diversified farming.

11534 Atchison Daily Globe
1015-25 Main St. Phone: (913)367-0583
PO Box 247 Fax: (913)367-7531
Atchison, KS 66002
Free: (800)748-7615
Publication E-mail: aglobe@journey.com

General newspaper. **Founded:** 1877. **Freq:** Daily (eve.) and Sat. (morn.). **Print Method:** Offset. **Cols./Page:** 6. **Col. Width:** 24 nonpareils. **Col. Depth:** 301 agate lines. **Key Personnel:** Stan Wilson, Publisher. **Subscription Rates:** $96 individuals; $110.40 out of area. **Remarks:** Accepts advertising.
Ad Rates: BW: $1,180.35 **Circ:** Mon.-Fri. 5,126
SAU: $9.15 Sun. 5,282
PCI: $9.15

11535 KAIR-FM - 93.7
Box G Phone: (913)367-1470
Atchison, KS 66002 Fax: (913)367-7021
Free: (800)655-0937

Simulcasts: KAIR-AM. **Networks:** UPI. **Owner:** KNZA Inc., PO Box 104, Hiawatha, KS, (913)547-3461, Fax: (913)547-9900. **Founded:** 1939. **Formerly:** KARE. **Operating Hours:** Continuous 10% network, 90% local. **ADI:** Kansas City, MO (Lawrence, KS). **Key Personnel:** Jason Drake, Program Dir.; James Ervin, Sales Mgr.; Greg Buser, General Mgr. **Wattage:** 25,000. **Ad Rates:** $5-10.50 for 30 seconds; $7-15 for 60 seconds. Combined advertising rates available with KAIR-AM.

ATTICA

11536 Attica Independent
115 N. Main Phone: (316)254-7968
Attica, KS 67009
Community newspaper. **Freq:** Weekly (Fri.). **Cols./Page:** 8. **Col. Width:** 10 1/2 picas. **Col. Depth:** 21 inches. **Key Personnel:** Raymond D. Howell, Editor and Publisher.
Circ: 800

ATWOOD†, pop. 1,665.

NW KS. Rawlins Co. 150 mi. NW of Great Bend. Oil wells; cheese factory; alfalfa pelleting mill. Dairy and grain farms.

11537 Atwood Cable Systems Inc.
423 State St. Phone: (785)626-3261
Atwood, KS 67730 Fax: (785)626-9005
E-mail: dunkertv@ruraltel.net

Owner: Harold J. Dunker, at above address. **Founded:** 1981. **Key Personnel:** Harold J. Dunker, President; Robert J. Dunker, Vice President, bobd@ruraltel.net. **Cities Served:** Atwood, KS: subscribing households 531; 32 channels; 1 community access channel; 6 hours per week community access programming.

AUGUSTA, pop. 6,968.

SE KS. Butler Co. 20 mi. E. of Wichita. Oil wells. Grain, stock, poultry, and dairy farms.

11538 Augusta Daily Gazette
204 E. 5th St. Phone: (316)775-2218
PO Box 9 Fax: (316)775-3220
Augusta, KS 67010-1012
General newspaper. **Founded:** 1892. **Freq:** Daily (eve.). **Print Method:** Offset. **Trim Size:** 14 x 22 3/4. **Cols./Page:** 6. **Col. Width:** 12 3/5 picas. **Col. Depth:** 21 1/2 inches. **Key Personnel:** Mike McDerrmott, Editor; Carter S. Verbe, Publisher; Paula Blake, Advertising Mgr. **USPS:** 037-420. **Sub-**

scription Rates: $72.45 individuals; $122.26 out of area. **Remarks:** Accepts advertising.
Ad Rates: GLR: $.45 **Circ:** ‡2,972
BW: $602
SAU: $5.33

BALDWIN CITY, pop. 2,829.

E KS. 17 mi. SW of Lawrence. Baker University. Historical sites. Small oil and gas wells. Diversified farming.

11539 KNBU-FM - 89.7
7th & Dearborn Sts. Phone: (913)594-6451
Baldwin City, KS 66006 Fax: (913)594-3570
E-mail: knbu@harvey.bakeru.edu

Format: Top 40; Album-Oriented Rock (AOR); Classic Rock; Alternative/New Music/Progressive. **Owner:** Baker University, at above address. **Founded:** 1965. **Operating Hours:** 16 hours Daily. **Key Personnel:** Richard Bayha, General Mgr.; Angie Brown, Station Mgr. **Wattage:** 100. **Ad Rates:** Noncommercial.

BAXTER SPRINGS

11540 Baxter Springs Citizen
Nichols Communications, Inc.
PO Box 290 Phone: (316)856-2115
Baxter Springs, KS 66713-0290 Fax: (316)856-3162
Publication E-mail: kansasnews@aol.com

Community newspaper. **Founded:** 1872. **Freq:** Semiweekly (Tues. and Fri.). **Print Method:** Offset. **Cols./Page:** 6. **Col. Width:** 2 inches. **Col. Depth:** 21 1/2 inches. **Key Personnel:** Brent Fisher, Editor; Jeffrey Nichols, Publisher. **ISSN:** 0455-6000. **Subscription Rates:** $30 individuals; $37 out of state. **Remarks:** Accepts advertising. **URL:** http://www.baxtercitizen.com.
Ad Rates: BW: $645 **Circ:** ‡2,500
4C: $825
SAU: $5.25
PCI: $5.25

11541 City of Baxter Springs
City Hall Phone: (316)856-2114
PO Box 577 Fax: (316)856-2460
Baxter Springs, KS 66713

Founded: 1980. **Key Personnel:** Darla Snook, City Clerk. **Cities Served:** Baxter Springs, KS: subscribing households 1,682; 35 channels; 1 community access channel; 168 hours per week community access programming.

BELLE PLAINE, pop. 1,791.

S KS. Sumner Co. 23 mi. S. of Wichita. Aircraft manufacturer; feed processing; oil wells. Diversified farming.

11542 The Belle Plaine News
431 N. Merchant Phone: (316)488-2234
PO Box 128 Fax: (316)488-3241
Belle Plaine, KS 67013
Publisher E-mail: bpnews@horizon.hit.net

Community newspaper. **Founded:** 1879. **Freq:** Weekly (Thurs.). **Print Method:** Offset. **Trim Size:** 11 1/2 x 15. **Cols./Page:** 5. **Col. Width:** 1 7/8 inches. **Col. Depth:** 294 agate lines. **Key Personnel:** Brett Bohannan, Editor; William Sam Clester, Publisher; Lona M. Trullinger, Advertising Mgr. **USPS:** 048-960. **Subscription Rates:** $21.50 individuals; $37.50 out of state; $37.50 two years in area. **Remarks:** Accepts advertising.
Ad Rates: BW: $309.23 **Circ:** Paid ‡1,030
SAU: $4.42 Free ‡150
PCI: $4.12

11543 The Cheney Sentinel
Clester Communications
Box 128 Phone: (316)488-2234
Belle Plaine, KS 67013 Fax: (316)488-3241

Newspaper. **Founded:** 1891. **Freq:** Weekly (Wed.). **Print Method:** Offset. **Cols./Page:** 5. **Col. Width:** 21 nonpareils. **Col. Depth:** 294 agate lines. **Key Personnel:** William Sam Clester, Publisher. **USPS:** 102-260. **Subscription Rates:** $20 individuals. **Remarks:** Accepts advertising.
Ad Rates: GLR: $.165 **Circ:** 1,200
BW: $245
PCI: $3.50

11544 The Oxford Register
The Belle Plaine News
431 N. Merchant Phone: (316)488-2234
PO Box 128 Fax: (316)488-3241
Belle Plaine, KS 67013
Publisher E-mail: bpnews@horizon.hit.net

Local newspaper. **Founded:** 1888. **Freq:** Weekly (Thurs.). **Print Method:** Offset. **Trim Size:** 11 1/2 x 15. **Cols./Page:** 5. **Col. Width:** 1 7/8 inches. **Col. Depth:** 294 agate lines. **Key Personnel:** Brett Bohannan, Editor; William Sam Clester, Publisher; Lona M. Trullinger, Advertising Mgr. **USPS:** 459-620. **Subscription Rates:** $21.50 individuals; $37.50 out of state. **Remarks:** Accepts advertising.
Ad Rates: BW: $288.40 **Circ:** Paid 400
PCI: $4.12 Free 150

11545 The Times Sentinel
Clester Communications
Box 128 Phone: (316)488-2234
Belle Plaine, KS 67013 Fax: (316)488-3241

Community newspaper. **Founded:** 1969. **Freq:** Weekly (Wed.). **Print Method:** Offset. **Cols./Page:** 5. **Col. Width:** 14 inches. **Key Personnel:** William Sam Clester, Publisher; Suzanne Foster, Advertising Mgr. **USPS:** 708-480. **Subscription Rates:** $20 individuals; $32 out of state; $35 two years in area. **Remarks:** Accepts advertising.
Ad Rates: BW: $288.40 **Circ:** Paid ‡1,035
SAU: $4.12 Free ‡35

BELLEVILLE†, pop. 2,805.

NC KS. Republic Co. 68 mi. N. of Salina. Pawnee Indian Village. Manufactures hospital supplies, sand, gravel, and concrete. Diversified agriculture.

11546 Belleville Telescope
Telescope Pub. Co.
1817 E. U.S. 81, Frontage Rd. Phone: (913)527-2224
Belleville, KS 66935 Fax: (913)527-2225

Community newspaper. **Founded:** 1870. **Freq:** Weekly (Thurs.). **Print Method:** Offset. **Cols./Page:** 6. **Col. Width:** 28 nonpareils. **Col. Depth:** 294 agate lines. **Key Personnel:** Mark L. Miller, Editor; Merle M. Miller, Publisher; Paul Haase, Advertising Mgr. **Subscription Rates:** $20 individuals. **Remarks:** Accepts advertising.
Ad Rates: GLR: $.41 **Circ:** ‡4,669
BW: $723.24
4C: $903.24
PCI: $5.74

11547 Farmer Stockman of the Midwest
Telescope Pub. Co.
1817 E. U.S. 81, Frontage Rd. Phone: (913)527-2224
Belleville, KS 66935 Fax: (913)527-2225

Farm magazine. **Founded:** 1960. **Freq:** Weekly (Mon.). **Print Method:** Offset. **Cols./Page:** 5. **Col. Width:** 22 nonpareils. **Col. Depth:** 210 agate lines. **Key Personnel:** Mark L. Miller, Editor; Merle M. Miller, Sr., Publisher; Robert Deterding, Advertising Mgr. **ISSN:** 0739-9235. **Subscription Rates:** $18 individuals; $22 outside Kansas and Nebraska.
Ad Rates: GLR: $0.78 **Circ:** ‡15,057
BW: $819
PCI: $10.92

11548 Scandia Journal
1710 M St. Phone: (913)527-5182
Belleville, KS 66935 Fax: (913)527-2159

Newspaper with a Republican orientation. **Founded:** 1872. **Freq:** Weekly (Thurs.). **Print Method:** Offset. **Cols./Page:** 6. **Col. Width:** 26 nonpareils. **Col. Depth:** 294 agate lines. **Key Personnel:** Carl Larson, Editor; Harold Blazek, Publisher. **Subscription Rates:** $13.77 in Kansas; $15.50 out of Kansas. **Remarks:** Accepts advertising.
Ad Rates: PCI: $2 **Circ:** Paid 650
Free 15

11549 Belleville Cable TV
1809 N. St. Phone: (913)527-2226
Belleville, KS 66935 Fax: (913)527-5820

Cities Served: Hebron, NE.

11550 KREP-FM - 92.1
2307 W. Frontage Rd. Phone: (913)527-2266
Belleville, KS 66935 Fax: (913)527-5919
E-mail: kr-92@nckcn.com

Format: Country. **Networks:** ABC; Mid-America Ag. **Founded:** 1984. **Operating Hours:** Continuous; 10% network, 90% local. **Key Personnel:** Deborah M. Hoeflicker, Pres./Gen. Mgr.; Christine Strutt, Traffic Dir.; Cody Moyer, Program Dir. **Wattage:** 14,500. **Ad Rates:** $17 for 30 seconds; $22 for 60 seconds.

BELOIT†, pop. 4,367.

NC KS. Mitchell Co. On Solomon river, 51 mi. NW of Salina. Agricultural and trade center.

11551 Beloit Daily Call
Beloit Newspapers
122 E. Court Phone: (913)738-3537
PO Box 366 Fax: (913)738-6442
Beloit, KS 67420
Daily newspaper. **Founded:** 1879. **Freq:** Mon.-Fri. **Print Method:** Offset. **Trim Size:** 13x21. **Cols./Page:** 6. **Col. Width:** 11.5 picas. **Col. Depth:** 21 inches. **Key Personnel:** Larry Hiatt, Editor and Publisher; Bob Milburne, Advertising Mgr. **Subscription Rates:** $.50 single issue. **Remarks:** Accepts advertising. **Alt. Formats:** CD-ROM. **Formerly:** N.C.K. Market Guide. **Merged with:** Solomon Valley Post.
Ad Rates: BW: $308.75 **Circ:** (Not Reported)
SAU: $4.75

BIRD CITY

11552 Bird City Times
PO Box 167 Phone: (913)734-2621
Bird City, KS 67731 Fax: (913)332-3001

Newspaper. **Founded:** 1925. **Freq:** Weekly (Thurs.). **Print Method:** Offset. **Col. Width:** 12 picas. **Col. Depth:** 21 inches. **Key Personnel:** Debbie Miller, Editor; Steven Haynes, Publisher. **Subscription Rates:** $21 individuals; $24 out of state.
Ad Rates: BW: $384 **Circ:** 628

BONNER SPRINGS, pop. 6,266.

NE KS. Wyandotte Co. 12 mi. SW of Kansas City. Agricultural Hall of Fame. Diversified farming.

11553 Chieftain
Chieftan
PO Box 256 Phone: (913)724-1887
128 Oak Fax: (913)422-4233
Bonner Springs, KS 66012
Newspaper with a Republican orientation. **Founded:** 1896. **Freq:** Weekly (Thurs.). **Print Method:** Offset. **Cols./Page:** 6. **Col. Width:** 25 nonpareils. **Col. Depth:** 301 agate lines. **Key Personnel:** Clausie Smith, Publisher; Jean Smith, Publisher. **Subscription Rates:** $12.75 individuals.
Ad Rates: SAU: $4.50 **Circ:** Paid ‡5,200
Non-paid ‡7,800

11554 Chieftain Shopper
Chieftan
PO Box 256 Phone: (913)724-1887
128 Oak Fax: (913)422-4233
Bonner Springs, KS 66012
Shopper. **Freq:** Weekly. **Print Method:** Offset. **Cols./Page:** 6. **Col. Width:** 25 nonpareils. **Col. Depth:** 301 agate lines. **Remarks:** Accepts advertising.
Ad Rates: SAU: $4.50 **Circ:** Paid ‡5,200
Non-paid ‡7,800

11555 Sentinel
Chieftan
PO Box 256 Phone: (913)724-1887
128 Oak Fax: (913)422-4233
Bonner Springs, KS 66012
Newspaper. **Founded:** 1969. **Freq:** Weekly (Thurs.). **Print Method:** Offset. **Cols./Page:** 6. **Col. Width:** 25 nonpareils. **Col. Depth:** 301 agate lines. **Key Personnel:** Jewell Wilthite, Editor; Clausie and Jean Smith, Publisher. **Subscription Rates:** $12.75 individuals.
Circ: Paid ‡5,200
Non-paid ‡7,800

BUNKER HILL

C. KS. Russell Co. 5 mi. N. of Russell.

11556 KOOD-TV - 9
Box 9 Phone: (913)483-6990
Bunker Hill, KS 67626 Fax: (913)483-4605

Format: Public TV. **Networks:** Public Broadcasting Service (PBS). **Founded:** 1978. **Operating Hours:** 16 hrs. Daily; 77% network, 1% local, 22% other. **ADI:** Wichita-Hutchinson, KS. **Key Personnel:** David M. Wilson, CEO/Gen. Mgr.; Lloyd Mintzmyer, Dir. of Engineering; Barbara Baldwin, Contact; Les Kinderknecht, Production Mgr.; Sherri Unrein, Public Information Dir.; Mary Pat Waymaster, Traffic Dir.; Linda Trowbridge, Dir. of Broadcasting; Debra Creamer, Dir. of Administration and Finance. **Local Programs:** *Gardening in the Great Plains*; *Kansas Arts Today*; *The Kansas Legislature*. **Ad Rates:** Noncommercial.

KSWK-TV - See Lakin

BURDEN, pop. 518.

SE KS. Cowley Co. 18 mi. NE of Winfield. Oil wells. Grain and stock farms.

11557 The Cowley County Reporter
H and H Publications
PO Box 97 Phone: (316)438-2370
414 Main St. Fax: (913)438-2370
Burden, KS 67019
Community newspaper. **Founded:** 1907. **Freq:** Weekly (Thurs.). **Print Method:** Offset. **Cols./Page:** 6. **Col. Width:** 2 1/16 inches. **Col. Depth:** 21 1/2 inches. **Key Personnel:** Ann Alexander, Managing Editor; Martin Hellar, Publisher. **Subscription Rates:** $20 individuals; $32 out of state. **Remarks:** Advertising not accepted for alcohol beverages. **Formerly:** The Burden Times.
Ad Rates: SAU: $2.35 **Circ:** Paid ‡465
Free ‡20

BURLINGAME, pop. 1,239.

E KS. Osage Co. 30 mi. SW of Topeka. Manufactures clothing, cleaning products and ice cream. Petroleum bulk storage. Stock, poultry. Corn, alfalfa, clover, wheat soybeans.

11558 Osage County Chronicle
107 E. Santa Fe Phone: (785)654-3621
Burlingame, KS 66413 Fax: (785)654-3438

Newspaper (local news). **Founded:** Sept. 1863. **Freq:** Weekly (Thurs.). **Print Method:** Offset. **Cols./Page:** 6. **Col. Width:** 26 nonpareils. **Col. Depth:** 301 agate lines. **Key Personnel:** K. Kurt Kessinger, Editor and Publisher, durt@aol.com; Kathleen M. Kessinger, Editor and Publisher. **Subscription Rates:** $25 individuals; $29. **Remarks:** Accepts advertising. **Formerly:** Osage City Journal Free-Press; Lyndon News Herald; Burlingame Enterprise-Chronicle; Overbrook Citizen-Times.
Ad Rates: GLR: $.24 **Circ:** 5,100
BW: $612.75
4C: $180
SAU: $5.15
PCI: $4.75

BURLINGTON†, pop. 2,901.

SE KS. Coffey Co. 65 mi. S. of Topeka. Diversified farming. Timber.

11559 Coffey County Republican
Braden Publications, Inc.
324 Hudson Phone: (316)364-5325
PO Drawer A Fax: (316)364-2607
Burlington, KS 66839
Publisher E-mail: ccrepub@kans.com

County newspaper with Report orientation. **Founded:** 1856. **Freq:** Semiweekly. **Print Method:** Offset. **Trim Size:** 14 x 22. **Cols./Page:** 6. **Col. Width:** 12 1/2 picas. **Col. Depth:** 21 inches. **Key Personnel:** Mark Petterson, Managing Editor, markpet@kans.com; Randall Braden, Publisher, phone (316)625-2181; Lou Braden, Advertising Mgr. **USPS:** 145-700. **Subscription Rates:** $42 individuals; $46 out of state. **Remarks:** Accepts advertising. **Formed by the merger of:** Coffey County Today; This Week.
Ad Rates: GLR: $.35 **Circ:** Paid 3,318
BW: $630 Free 41
4C: $880
PCI: $5

11560 KSNP-FM - 95.3
PO Box 233 Phone: (316)364-8807
Burlington, KS 66839 Fax: (316)364-2573

Format: Adult Contemporary; Country; Oldies. **Networks:** Independent. **Owner:** Coffey County Broadcasting Co., at above address. **Founded:** June 1990. **Operating Hours:** 6 a.m.-12 p.m. **Key Personnel:** W. R. Lawrence, General Mgr. **Wattage:** 6000.

CALDWELL, pop. 1,401.

SC KS. Sumner Co. 50 mi. SW of Wichita.

11561 The Caldwell Messenger
PO Box 313 Phone: (316)845-2320
Caldwell, KS 67022 Fax: (316)845-6461

Community newspaper. **Founded:** 1892. **Freq:** Weekly (Wed.). **Print Method:** Offset. **Trim Size:** 14 x 23. **Cols./Page:** 6. **Col. Width:** 2 inches. **Col. Depth:** 21 1/2 inches. **Key Personnel:** Damon F. Weber, Publisher. **Subscription Rates:** $16.50 individuale; $19 out of state. **Remarks:** Accepts advertising.
Ad Rates: BW: $434.70 **Circ:** Paid ‡1,498
PCI: $3.45 Free ‡30

CANEY, pop. 2,284.

SE KS. Montgomery Co. 19 mi. W. of Coffeyville. Oil, and gas wells. Corn, wheat, oats.

11562 Good News
Kirk Clinkscales
PO Box 96 Phone: (316)879-5460
Caney, KS 67333 Fax: (316)879-2264
Free: (800)942-6397

Shopper. **Founded:** July 10, 1978. **Freq:** Weekly (Wed.). **Print Method:** Offset. **Trim Size:** 11 1/2 x 15. **Cols./Page:** 6. **Col. Width:** 20 nonpareils. **Col. Depth:** 84 picas. **Key Personnel:** Kink Clinkscale, Editor and Publisher; Penny Coy, Advertising Mgr. **Subscription Rates:** Free. **Remarks:** Accepts advertising. **URL:** http://www.info.apple.com.
Ad Rates: GLR: $1.14 **Circ:** Free ‡47,100
BW: $1,149.12
PCI: $15.96

11563 Montgomery County Chronicle
202 W. 4th St. Phone: (316)879-2156
PO Box 186 Fax: (316)879-2855
Caney, KS 67333
Publication E-mail: caneychron@terraworld.net

Newspaper with Report orientation. **Founded:** 1885. **Freq:** Weekly (Wed.). **Print Method:** Offset. **Trim Size:** 12 x 18. **Cols./Page:** 5. **Col. Width:** 11 1/2 picas. **Col. Depth:** 336 agate lines. **Key Personnel:** Rudy M. Taylor, Editor/Administration. **USPS:** 088-340. **Subscription Rates:** $22 individuals; $39 out of area. **Remarks:** Accepts advertising. **Formerly:** Caney Chronicle.
Ad Rates: GLR: $.26 **Circ:** 3,100
BW: $240
PCI: $4.75

CANTON, pop. 926.

C KS. McPherson Co. 25 mi. N. of Newton. Oil wells. Grain, stock, and poultry farms.

11564 The Canton Pilot
PO Box 495
112 N. Main St.
Canton, KS 67428

Community newspaper. **Founded:** 1881. **Freq:** Weekly (Thurs.). **Print Method:** Offset. **Cols./Page:** 6. **Col. Width:** 24 nonpareils. **Col. Depth:** 301 agate lines. **Key Personnel:** D.S. Webster, Managing Editor. **Subscription Rates:** $12 individuals; $15 out of area. **Remarks:** Accepts advertising.
Ad Rates: BW: $387 **Circ:** ‡700
PCI: $3

CAWKER CITY, pop. 640.

NC KS. Mitchell Co. 65 mi. NW of Salina. Manufactures furniture. Grain and stock farms.

11565 Cawker City Ledger
PO Box 7 Phone: (785)781-4831
Cawker City, KS 67430 Fax: (785)781-4831

Newspaper. **Subtitle:** Cawheu City Ledger. **Founded:** 1912. **Freq:** Weekly (Thurs.). **Print Method:** Offset. **Cols./Page:** 8. **Col. Width:** 21 nonpareils. **Col. Depth:** 294 agate lines. **Key Personnel:** Darrel E. Miller, Publisher; R.C. Miller, Publisher Manager. **Subscription Rates:** $13.77 individuals; $15.89 out of area; $16 out of state. **Remarks:** Accepts advertising.
Ad Rates: GLR: $2.35 **Circ:** ‡1,200
BW: $172
SAU: $2.35
PCI: $1.50

11566 City of Cawker Cable TV
804 Locust St. Phone: (913)781-4713
PO Box 2 Fax: (913)781-4436
Cawker City, KS 67430

Owner: City of Cawker City, at above address. **Founded:** 1977. **Key Personnel:** Wayne Musgrove, Contact; Bennie Schmidt, Contact. **Cities Served:** Cawker City, KS; subscribing households 267; 38 channels; 1 community access channel.

CHANUTE, pop. 10,506.

SE KS. Neosho Co. 45 mi. WSW of Fort Scott. Neosho County Community College. Oil and gas wells; cement works. Diversified farming.

11567 The Chanute Tribune
Chanute Publishing Co.
15 N. Evergreen Phone: (316)431-4100
PO Box 559 Fax: (316)431-2635
Chanute, KS 66720
General newspaper. **Founded:** Apr. 9, 1892. **Freq:** Mon.-Sat. (eve.). **Print Method:** Offset. **Cols./Page:** 6. **Col. Width:** 25 nonpareils. **Col. Depth:** 301 agate lines. **Key Personnel:** Duane Schrag, Editor and Publisher; Stu Butcher, Managing Editor; Joanne D. Johnson, Advertising Dir.; Brenda Peck, Circulation Mgr. **USPS:** 100-140. **Subscription Rates:** $97.20 individuals. **Remarks:** Accepts advertising. **Alt. Formats:** CD-ROM, DailyNews.Net.
Ad Rates: BW: $804.96 **Circ:** Paid 4,644
4C: $954.96 Free 26
SAU: $6.24
PCI: $6.24

11568 KKOY-AM - 1460
Box 788 Phone: (316)431-3700
Chanute, KS 66720 Fax: (316)431-4643
Free: (800)954-8255

Format: Talk; News. **Networks:** ABC. **Founded:** 1952. **Operating Hours:** 6 a.m.-midnight. **Key Personnel:** Dale W. McCoy, Jr., Operations Mgr.; Mike Parnell, Traffic Dir.; Dan Johnson, News Dir.; Ann Ferguson, Office Mgr.; Cheryl Lyons, Sales Mgr. **Wattage:** 1000 day; 57 night. **Ad Rates:** $6.75-7.25 for 15 seconds; $10-12.25 for 30 seconds; $12.25-17.25 for 60 seconds.

11569 KKOY-FM - 105.5
Box 788 Phone: (316)431-3700
Chanute, KS 66720 Fax: (316)431-4643

Format: Country. **Networks:** ABC; Kansas Information. **Owner:** Neosho County Broadcasting Inc., at above address. **Founded:** 1971. **Operating Hours:** Continuous. **Key Personnel:** Phil McComb, VP/General Mgr. **Wattage:** 5700.

CHAPMAN, pop. 1,255.

NEC KS. Dickinson Co. 38 mi. E. of Salina. Flour mill. Grain, stock, and dairy farms.

11570 The Chapman Advertiser & Enterprise Journal
PO Box E Phone: (785)922-6856
Chapman, KS 67431 Fax: (785)922-6856
Publication E-mail: editor@02-online.net

Community newspaper. **Founded:** 1887. **Freq:** Weekly (Thurs.). **Print Method:** Offset. **Cols./Page:** 6. **Col. Width:** 26 nonpareils. **Col. Depth:** 301 agate lines. **Key Personnel:** Shawni Sheets, Ed./Pub./Photographer. **Subscription Rates:** $25 individuals; $30 out of state. **Remarks:** Accepts advertising.
Ad Rates: BW: $450.21 **Circ:** Paid ‡1,075
4C: $615.96
PCI: $4.10

CHETOPA

11571 The Chetopa Advance
Crowell, Inc.
PO Box 207 Phone: (316)236-7591
Chetopa, KS 67336 Fax: (316)795-2128

Community newspaper. **Freq:** Weekly (Thurs.). **Cols./Page:** 6. **Col. Width:** 13.5 picas. **Col. Depth:** 21 inches. **Key Personnel:** Charles Crowell, Editor and Publisher. **Subscription Rates:** $2.25 individuals; $.25 single issue.
Circ: 1,300

CIMARRON†, pop. 1,491.

SW KS. Gray Co. 18 mi. NW of Dodge City.

11572 Bucklin Banner
Golden Plains Publications
PO Box 528 Phone: (316)855-3902
Cimarron, KS 67835 Fax: (316)655-2489
Free: (800)658-3755

Community newspaper. **Freq:** Weekly (Wed.). **Cols./Page:** 5. **Col. Width:** 2 inches. **Col. Depth:** 12 inches. **Key Personnel:** Edna Ringwald, Editor; Jerry Anderson, Publisher.
Circ: 1,100

11573 Haskell County Monitor-Chief
Golden Plains Publications
PO Box 528 Phone: (316)855-3902
Cimarron, KS 67835 Fax: (316)655-2489
Free: (800)658-3755

Newspaper. **Founded:** 1885. **Freq:** Weekly (Wed.). **Print Method:** Offset. **Cols./Page:** 6. **Col. Width:** 12 picas. **Col. Depth:** 21 inches. **Key Personnel:** Charity Horinek, Editor; Bonnie Suffield, Publisher; Dorothy Birney, Advertising. **USPS:** 237-020. **Subscription Rates:** $16.94 individuals; $19.06 out of country. **Remarks:** Accepts advertising.
Ad Rates: PCI: $4.5 **Circ:** Paid ‡1,600
Free ‡10

11574 Jacksonian
Jerry Anderson
Box 528 · Phone: (316)855-3902
Cimarron, KS 67835 · Fax: (316)855-2489

Community newspaper. **Freq:** Weekly (Wed.). **Print Method:** Offset. **Cols./Page:** 6. **Col. Width:** 24 nonpareils. **Col. Depth:** 301 agate lines. **Key Personnel:** Delores Eberle, Editor/Administration; Jerry Anderson, Publisher. **Subscription Rates:** $14.04 individuals. **Remarks:** Accepts advertising.
Ad Rates: BW: $399.99 · **Circ:** 1,250
SAU: $3.10

CLAY CENTER†, pop. 4,948.

NEC KS. Clay Co. On Republican river, 82 mi. NW of Topeka. Diversified farming. Manufactures feed and farm equipment.

11575 KCLY-FM - 100.9
Box 16 · Phone: (785)632-5661
Clay Center, KS 67432 · Fax: (785)632-5662
Free: (800)652-5661
E-mail: taycom@kansas.net

Format: Country; Adult Contemporary; Contemporary Christian. **Networks:** ABC; Westwood One Radio. **Owner:** Kyle Bauer and Kent Lips, at above address. **Founded:** 1978. **Operating Hours:** Continuous. **Key Personnel:** Kyle Bauer, Contact; Travis Murphy, News Dir.; Rocky Downing, Sports Dir.; Joyce Beck, Sales Mgr.; Erica Craig, Traffic Dir.; Angie Komar, Production Mgr.; Jamie Bloom, Program Dir. **Local Programs:** *Up Close* 4:00 pm - 8:00 am Fri./Sat., Rocky Downing, Sports Dir. **Wattage:** 6000. **Ad Rates:** $8 for 30 seconds; $11 for 60 seconds. Combined advertising rates available with KFRM-AM.

CLYDE†, pop. 909.

NC KS. Cloud Co. 15 mi. E. of Belleville.

11576 Clyde Republican
305 Washington · Phone: (785)446-2201
PO Box 397
Clyde, KS 66938-0397
Community newspaper. **Subtitle:** Owner. **Founded:** 1877. **Freq:** Weekly (Thurs.). **Print Method:** Offset. **Cols./Page:** 6. **Col. Width:** 24 nonpareils. **Col. Depth:** 294 agate lines. **Key Personnel:** Margene Cash, Editor and Publisher. **Subscription Rates:** $14.16 individuals; $14.69 out of area; $15 out of state. **Remarks:** Color advertising not accepted.
Ad Rates: BW: $378 · **Circ:** ‡1,000
SAU: $3
PCI: $3

COFFEYVILLE, pop. 15,185.

SE KS. Montgomery Co. 69 mi. W. of Joplin, MO. Coffeyville Community College. Manufactures chemicals, structural steel. Oil refineries.

11577 Coffeyville Journal
Hometown Communication
Eight & Elm Sts. · Phone: (316)251-3300
PO Box 847 · Fax: (316)251-1905
Coffeyville, KS 67337
General newspaper. **Founded:** 1875. **Freq:** Daily (eve.), Sunday (morn.). **Print Method:** Offset. **Cols./Page:** 6. **Col. Width:** 24 nonpareils. **Col. Depth:** 301 agate lines. **Key Personnel:** Tim Flowers, Editor; Michael A. Lind, Publisher; David Perkins, Publisher. **Subscription Rates:** $72 individuals. **Remarks:** Accepts advertising.
Ad Rates: GLR: $.63 · **Circ:** Mon.-Fri. 6,983
BW: $1,124.88 · Sun. 8,105
4C: $1,304.88
SAU: $8.72

11578 The Collegian
Coffeyville Community College
400 West 11th St. · Phone: (316)251-7700
Coffeyville, KS 67337 · Fax: (316)251-7098

Collegiate magazine. **Freq:** Quarterly (during the academic year). **Print Method:** Offset. **Trim Size:** 8 1/2 x 11. **Cols./Page:** 3. **Col. Width:** 13 picas. **Key Personnel:** Marguerite Crump, Journalism Advisor. **Remarks:** Accepts advertising.
Ad Rates: SAU: $6 · **Circ:** ‡1,000

COLBY†, pop. 5,544.

NW KS. Thomas Co. 200 mi. NW of Salina. Colby Community Junior College. Diversified farming.

11579 Colby Free Press
155 W. 5th St. · Phone: (913)462-3963
Box 806 · Fax: (913)462-7749
Colby, KS 67701-2312
General newspaper. **Founded:** 1888. **Freq:** Mon.-Thurs. eve.; Sat.(morn.). **Print Method:** Offset. **Cols./Page:** 6. **Col. Width:** 26 nonpareils. **Col. Depth:** 301 agate lines. **Key Personnel:** Steve Walker, Publisher; Patty Decker, Publisher. **USPS:** 120-920. **Subscription Rates:** $35 individuals. **Remarks:** Accepts advertising.
Ad Rates: GLR: $.30 · **Circ:** 3,300
BW: $552.12
SAU: $4.28

11580 Cablevision Industries Inc.
158 W. 4th St. · Phone: (785)462-7523
Box 587 · Fax: (785)462-3570
Colby, KS 67701

Owner: Time Warner Cable, Box 6929, Englewood, CO 80155-6929, (303)799-9599, Fax: (303)649-8090, Free: (800)727-1855. **Founded:** 1967. **Formerly:** Manasett; Cablevision Industries. **Key Personnel:** Eugene K. Tennant, General Mgr., phone (785)462-7523; Kim Heilman, Sr. Office Clerk, phone (785)462-7523. **Cities Served:** Colby, KS; Trenton, NE: subscribing households 2,092; 35 channels; 1 community access channel; 168 hours per week community access programming.

11581 Community CATV of Oakley
Box 587 · Phone: (785)462-7523
Colby, KS 67701 · Fax: (785)462-3570
Free: (800)794-3048

Owner: Time Warner Cable, Box 6929, Englewood, CO 80155-6929, (303)799-9599, Fax: (303)649-8090, Free: (800)727-1855. **Founded:** 1976. **Formerly:** Great Plains Cable (1976). **Key Personnel:** Eugene K. Tennant, General Mgr., phone (785)462-7523, fax (785)462-3570; Kim Heilman, Sr. Office Clerk, phone (785)462-7523, fax (785)462-3570. **Cities Served:** Oakley, KS: subscribing households 798; 35 channels; 1 community access channel; 168 hours per week community access programming.

11582 KLBY-TV - 4
990 S. Range · Phone: (913)462-8644
Colby, KS 67701 · Fax: (913)462-3522
Free: (800)844-5529

Format: Commercial TV. **Networks:** ABC. **Owner:** Chronicle Broadcasting, at above address. **Founded:** 1984. **Operating Hours:** 6 a.m.-1 a.m. **ADI:** Wichita-Hutchinson, KS. **Key Personnel:** Steve South, General Mgr., phone (316)943-4221, fax (316)943-5493; Rich Epp, Station Mgr. **Wattage:** 100,000. **Ad Rates:** $15-120 for 30 seconds. Combined advertising rates available with KUPK, KAXE.

11583 KTCC-FM - 91.9
1255 S. Range · Phone: (913)462-4662
Colby, KS 67701 · Fax: (913)462-4600

Format: Contemporary Hit Radio (CHR). **Networks:** CNN Radio. **Owner:** Colby Community College, at above address, (913)462-3984. **Founded:** 1969. **Operating Hours:** Continuous; 10% network, 90% local. **Key Personnel:** Jon Burlew, General Mgr.; Carrie Jones, Station Mgr.; Roy Baum, Chief Engineer. **Wattage:** 3500.

11584 KXXX-AM - 790
1065 South Range · Phone: (913)462-3305
Colby, KS 67701 · Fax: (913)462-3307

Format: Contemporary Country. **Networks:** ABC. **Owner:** Goodstar Broadcasting, 1660 N Tyler Rd., Wichita, KS 67212, (316)729-8011, Fax: (316)729-9914. **Founded:** 1947. **Operating Hours:** Continuous. **ADI:** Wichita-Hutchinson, KS. **Key Personnel:** Mike Starr, President; Joe Munsell, Vice Pres./Gen. Mgr., phone (785)462-3305, fax (785)462-3307. **Wattage:** 5000. **Ad Rates:** Combined advertising rates available with KQLS-FM.

COLDWATER†, pop. 990.

SC KS. Comanche Co. 115 mi. SW of Wichita. Oil and gas wells. Diversified farming.

11585 The Western Star
113 S. Central · Phone: (316)582-2101
PO Box 518
Coldwater, KS 67029
Publication E-mail: weststar@rh.net

Community newspaper (tabloid). **Founded:** Aug. 16, 1884. **Freq:** Weekly (Thurs.). **Print Method:** Offset. **Trim Size:** 11 x 16. **Cols./Page:** 5. **Col. Width:** 21 nonpareils. **Col. Depth:** 203 agate lines. **Key Personnel:** Dennies D. Andersen, Editor. **ISSN:** 6796-6000. **Subscription Rates:** $18 individuals; $20. **Remarks:** Accepts advertising.
Ad Rates: GLR: $.27 · **Circ:** ‡1,250
BW: $271.88
PCI: $3.75

COLUMBUS†, pop. 3,426.

SE KS. Cherokee Co. 23 mi. SW of Pittsburg. Manufactures auto parts, fertilizer. Coal mines. Grain and dairy farms.

11586 Columbus Daily Advocate
Columbus Communications, Inc.
215 S. Kansas · Phone: (316)429-2773
PO Box 231 · Fax: (316)429-3223
Columbus, KS 66725
General newspaper. **Founded:** 1874. **Freq:** Daily (eve.). **Print Method:** Offset. **Trim Size:** 15 x 22 3/4. **Cols./Page:** 6. **Col. Width:** 26 nonpareils. **Col. Depth:** 294 agate lines. **Key Personnel:** Al Storey, Editor; Jay M. Lacy, General Mgr. **USPS:** 124-480. **Subscription Rates:** $38.48 individuals. **Remarks:** Accepts advertising.
Ad Rates: BW: $567.60 · **Circ:** Paid ⊕2,460
PCI: $4.40 · Free ⊕38

CONCORDIA, pop. 6,847.

NC KS. Cloud Co. On Republican River, 50 mi. N. of Salina. Manufactures plastic and bricks. Grain, poultry, dairy, and stock farms.

11587 Advertiser
PO Box 309 · Phone: (913)243-2424
Concordia, KS 66901-0309
Shopper. **Founded:** 1980. **Freq:** Weekly. **Print Method:** Offset. **Trim Size:** 22 1/2. **Cols./Page:** 6. **Col. Width:** 25 nonpareils. **Col. Depth:** 294 agate lines. **Key Personnel:** Brad Lowell, Editor; Art Lowell, Publisher. **Remarks:** Accepts advertising.
Ad Rates: BW: $378.00 · **Circ:** Free 11,804
SAU: $4.00

11588 Classic Cable, Inc.
407 W. 6th · Phone: (913)243-1776
PO Box 638 · Fax: (913)243-6051
Concordia, KS 66901

Owner: 605 NW 3rd, Plainville, KS 67663, Free: (800)732-7620. **Founded:** 1959. **Formerly:** Vumore (1959); Cablecom of Concordia; Cable ONE. **Key Personnel:** Gail Engle, Manager; Annette Gallagher, Office Mgr. **Cities Served:** Concordia, KS: subscribing households 2400; 57 channels.

11589 KCKS-FM - 95.3
Rte. 1, W. 11th St. · Phone: (913)243-1414
Box 629
Concordia, KS 66901

Format: Oldies. **Networks:** Satellite Music Network. **Owner:** KNCK Inc., at above address. **Founded:** 1978. **Operating Hours:** Continuous. **Key Personnel:** Joseph E. Jindra, Contact. **Wattage:** 6000.

11590 KNCK-AM - 1390
Rte. 1 W. 11th St. · Phone: (913)243-1414
Box 629
Concordia, KS 66901

Format: Information; Country; Sports. **Networks:** Satellite Music Network. **Founded:** 1954. **Operating Hours:** Continuous. **Key Personnel:** Joe Jindra, General Mgr.; Brian Strait, Operations Mgr. **Local Programs:** *Coaches Show*, Jerry Jones, Mailing contact; *Coffeetime*, Roger Nelson, Mailing contact, (913)243-1414. **Wattage:** 500.

CONWAY SPRINGS

11591 Conway Springs Star and the Argonia Argosy
Springs Star
214 W. Spring Ave. · Phone: (316)456-2473
PO Box 158 · Fax: (316)456-2472
Conway Springs, KS 67031
Community newspaper. **Freq:** Weekly (Thurs.). **Cols./Page:** 6. **Col. Width:** 13 picas. **Col. Depth:** 21 inches. **Key Personnel:** Raymond J. Cline, Editor and Publisher.
Circ: 1,600

11592 The South Haven New Era
A.J.'s Printing
309 W. Spring Ave. · Phone: (316)456-2232
Conway Springs, KS 67031
Community newspaper. **Founded:** Feb. 20, 1886. **Freq:** Weekly (Wed.). **Print Method:** Offset. **Trim Size:** 11 x 17. **Cols./Page:** 5. **Col. Width:** 24 nonpareils. **Col. Depth:** 210 agate lines. **Key Personnel:** Nina Barker, Editor; A.J. Bozarth, Publisher. **USPS:** 379-080. **Subscription Rates:** $9.50 individuals; $10.50 out of area. **Remarks:** Color advertising not accepted.
Ad Rates: GLR: $2.88 · **Circ:** ‡500
BW: $2.88
PCI: $2.88

COTTONWOOD FALLS†, pop. 954.

EC KS. Chase Co. 20 mi. SW of Emporia.

11593 Chase County Leader-News
PO Box K Phone: (316)273-6391
Cottonwood Falls, KS 66845-0436 Fax: (316)273-8674
Community newspaper. **Founded:** 1871. **Freq:** Weekly (Thurs.). **Print Method:** Offset. **Cols./Page:** 6. **Col. Width:** 12p inches. **Col. Depth:** 21 inches. **Key Personnel:** Jerry Schwilling, Editor and Publisher. **ISSN:** 1079-8188. **Subscription Rates:** $24 individuals; $27 out of county; $27 out of state; $40 out of country. **Remarks:** Accepts advertising.
Ad Rates: GLR: $.40 **Circ:** 1700
BW: $354.38
4C: $754.38
SAU: $3.75
PCI: $3.75

COUNCIL GROVE†, pop. 2,381.

EC KS. Morris Co. 24 mi. NW of Emporia. Manufactures plastic and metal products, cleaning equipment, and butter. Dairy, grain, poultry, and stock farms.

11594 Beef Today
Farm Journal, Inc.
RR 1 Phone: (316)767-7041
Box 51 Fax: (316)767-7028
Council Grove, KS 66846
Magazine for farmers and ranchers raising beef cows, feeders, and backgrounder cattle. **Subtitle:** The Magazine of American Beef Producers. **Founded:** 1985. **Freq:** 10/year. **Print Method:** Offset. **Trim Size:** 8 x 10 1/2. **Cols./Page:** 3. **Col. Width:** 2 1/4 inches. **Col. Depth:** 140 agate lines. **Key Personnel:** Dale E. Smith, President; Roger D. Randall, Publisher; Bill Miller, Editor. **ISSN:** 1056-1390. **Subscription Rates:** Controlled. **Remarks:** Accepts advertising. **Formerly:** Beef Extra (June 1987).
Ad Rates: BW: $7,800 **Circ:** Controlled 187,656
4C: $9,300

11595 Council Grove Republican
208 W. Main Phone: (316)767-5123
PO Box 237 Fax: (316)767-5124
Council Grove, KS 66846
Newspaper with a small town, rural orientation. **Founded:** 1872. **Freq:** Daily Monday-Friday. **Print Method:** Offset. **Trim Size:** 16 1/2 x 22 3/4. **Cols./Page:** 7. **Col. Width:** 12.5 picas. **Col. Depth:** 21.5 inches. **Key Personnel:** Craig A. McNeal, Editor and Publisher; Don A. McNeal, Advertising Mgr. **USPS:** 134-340. **Subscription Rates:** $43.98; $65.98 out of area; $75.98 out of state. **Remarks:** Accepts advertising. **Alt. Formats:** Microfilm.
Ad Rates: BW: $589.96 **Circ:** Paid 2,384
PCI: $3.92 Free 19

COURTLAND, pop. 377.

NC KS. Republic Co. 130 mi. NW of Topeka. Agriculture.

11596 Courtland Journal-Empire
Box 318 Phone: (913)374-4428
Courtland, KS 66939 Fax: (913)374-4209

Local newspaper. **Founded:** 1910. **Freq:** Weekly (Thurs.). **Print Method:** Offset. **Cols./Page:** 7. **Col. Width:** 23 nonpareils. **Col. Depth:** 280 agate lines. **Key Personnel:** Colleen Mainquist, Editor and Publisher. **Subscription Rates:** $12.71 individuals; $17 out of state. **Remarks:** Accepts advertising.
Ad Rates: PCI: $2.00 **Circ:** 800

DERBY

11597 The American Oil and Gas Reporter
National Publishers Group
PO Box 343 Phone: (316)788-6271
Derby, KS 67037-0343 Fax: (316)788-7568
Free: (800)847-8301
Publication E-mail: reporter@wichita.fn.net
Publisher E-mail: reporter@feist.com

Magazine for the independent oil and gas exploration and production industry. **Founded:** 1958. **Freq:** Monthly. **Print Method:** Offset. **Trim Size:** 8 1/4 x 10 3/4. **Cols./Page:** 3. **Col. Width:** 27 nonpareils. **Col. Depth:** 140 agate lines. **Key Personnel:** Bill Campbell, Editor; Charles W. Cookson, V.P. Finance; Charlie Cookson, Publisher. **Subscription Rates:** $50 individuals; $125 Canada; $250 other countries; $15 single issue. **Remarks:** Accepts advertising.
Ad Rates: BW: $2,370 **Circ:** ‡13,540
4C: $3,350

11598 The Daily Reporter
Liberty Group Publishing Co.
PO Box 190 Phone: (316)788-2835
Derby, KS 67037 Fax: (316)788-0854
Publication E-mail: dailyrep@Swbell.com
Publisher E-mail: dailyrep@Swbell.com

Community newspaper. **Founded:** 1961. **Freq:** Daily (eve.). **Print Method:** Offset. **Trim Size:** 14 x 22 3/4. **Cols./Page:** 6. **Col. Width:** 2 1/16 inches. **Col. Depth:** 21 inches. **Key Personnel:** Shane Farley, Editor; Jim Stephenson, Publisher; Jon Brake, Advertising Mgr.; Tim Mello, Circulation Mgr. **Subscription Rates:** $84 individuals. **Remarks:** Accepts advertising.
Ad Rates: BW: $831.60 **Circ:** Paid ‡2,000
4C: $1,041.60
SAU: $6.60
PCI: $6.60

11599 The Record
Liberty Group Publishing Co.
PO Box 190 Phone: (316)788-2835
Derby, KS 67037 Fax: (316)788-0854
Publication E-mail: dailyrep@swbell.com
Publisher E-mail: dailyrep@Swbell.com

General newspaper. **Founded:** 1883. **Freq:** Weekly. **Print Method:** Offset. **Cols./Page:** 5. **Col. Width:** 12.5 picas. **Col. Depth:** 13 inches. **Key Personnel:** Renee Browning, Editor; Jim Stephenson, Publisher; Tim Mello, Circulation Mgr.; Jon Brake, Advertising Mgr. **Subscription Rates:** $31.50 individuals. **Remarks:** Accepts advertising.
Ad Rates: GLR: $.50 **Circ:** 375
BW: $403.20
4C: $613.20
SAU: $6.40
PCI: $6.40

11600 The Weekly Shopper
Liberty Group Publishing Co.
PO Box 190 Phone: (316)788-2835
Derby, KS 67037 Fax: (316)788-0854
Publisher E-mail: dailyrep@Swbell.com

Shopper. **Founded:** 1989. **Freq:** Weekly (Wed.). **Print Method:** Offset. **Trim Size:** 11 1/2 x 14 1/4. **Cols./Page:** 5. **Col. Width:** 2 1/16 inches. **Col. Depth:** 13 inches. **Key Personnel:** Kim Moses-Stevens, Advertising Dir. **Subscription Rates:** Free. **Remarks:** Accepts advertising.
Ad Rates: BW: $403.20 **Circ:** Non-paid ‡14,100
4C: $613.20
PCI: $6.40

11601 Wichita Journal
Liberty Group Publishing Co.
PO Box 190
Derby, KS 67037
Publication E-mail: dailyrep@swbell.com
Publisher E-mail: dailyrep@Swbell.com

Community newspaper. **Founded:** 1888. **Freq:** Weekly (Thurs.). **Print Method:** Offset. **Trim Size:** 11 1/2 x 14. **Cols./Page:** 5. **Col. Width:** 14.5 picas. **Col. Depth:** 182 agate lines. **Key Personnel:** Renee Browning, Editor; Jim Stephenson, Publisher; Tim Mello, Circulation Mgr.; Jon Brake, Advertising Mgr. **USPS:** 878-860. **Subscription Rates:** $31.50 individuals. **Remarks:** Accepts advertising.
Ad Rates: GLR: $.50 **Circ:** 350
BW: $403.20
4C: $613.20
SAU: $6.40
PCI: $6.40

11602 KYFW-FM - 88.3
239 Harral St. Phone: (316)788-7883
Derby, KS 67037-2628 Fax: (316)788-7883
E-mail: kyfw@aol.com

Format: Religious. **Networks:** USA Radio. **Founded:** 1988. **Formerly:** KCEV-FM (1990). **Operating Hours:** Continuous. **Key Personnel:** Matt Johnson, Station Mgr. **Local Programs:** *Insight*, Matt Johnson. **Wattage:** 17,000. **URL:** http://www.amen.net/bbn.

DIGHTON†, pop. 1,390.

WC KS. Lane Co. 143 mi. NW of Hutchinson. Oil wells. Stock, poultry, and grain farms.

11603 The Dighton Herald
113 E. Long Phone: (316)397-5347
PO Box 637 Fax: (316)397-2618
Dighton, KS 67839-0637
Community newspaper. **Founded:** 1885. **Freq:** Weekly (Wed.). **Print Method:** offset. **Trim Size:** 22 1/2 x 13 1/2. **Cols./Page:** 6. **Col. Width:** 2 inches. **Col. Depth:** 21 inches. **Key Personnel:** Jim Gardner, Editor and Publisher; Barbara Gardner, Advertising Mgr. **USPS:** 157-040. **Subscription Rates:** $15.89 individuals; $16.94 out of area; $19 out of state. **Remarks:** Accepts advertising.
Ad Rates: BW: $346.50 **Circ:** 1303
CNU: $2.75

11604 Feed-Lot
Feed-Lot Magazine
Box 850 Phone: (316)397-2838
Dighton, KS 67839-0850 Fax: (316)397-2839

Trade magazine covering feedlot and cattle feeder information. **Founded:** Jan. 1992. **Freq:** Bimonthly. **Trim Size:** 8 x 10 3/4. **Cols./Page:** 3. **Key Personnel:** Robert Strong, Editor, rstrong@midusa.net; Gregory Strong, National Sales Mgr., phone (316)397-5394, fax (316)397-5395, bigguy@midusa.net. **Subscription Rates:** $15 individuals; $2.50 single issue; Free to qualified subscribers. **Remarks:** Accepts advertising.
Ad Rates: BW: $2,272 **Circ:** Controlled ‡10,454
4C: $2,742
PCI: $126

DODGE CITY†, pop. 18,001.

SW KS. Ford Co. On Arkansas River, 120 mi. SW of Hutchinson. Flour and grain products mills; beef processing plants.

11605 Dodge City Daily Globe
Stauffer Communications, Inc.
705 2nd Phone: (316)225-4151
Dodge City, KS 67801 Fax: (316)225-4154
Free: (800)279-8795

General newspaper. **Founded:** 1911. **Freq:** Mon.-Sat. (morn.). **Print Method:** Offset. **Cols./Page:** 6. **Col. Width:** 2 inches. **Col. Depth:** 21 1/2 inches. **Key Personnel:** Terry Cochran III, Editor and Publisher. **Subscription Rates:** $82.20 individuals. **Remarks:** Accepts advertising.
Ad Rates: BW: $870.75 **Circ:** ‡9,185
4C: $1,017.75
PCI: $6.75

11606 High Plains Journal
High Plains Publishers, Inc.
1500 E. Wyatt Earp Phone: (316)227-7171
PO Box 760 Fax: (316)227-7173
Dodge City, KS 67801
Free: (800)452-7171
Publication E-mail: hpj@pld.com

Agricultural magazine. **Founded:** 1881. **Freq:** Weekly. **Print Method:** Offset. **Trim Size:** 11 x 15. **Cols./Page:** 5. **Col. Width:** 11 1/2 picas. **Col. Depth:** 196 agate lines. **Key Personnel:** Galen Hubbs, Editor, ghubbs@pld.com; Duane Ross, Publisher; Tom Taylor, Advertising Mgr., ttaylor@.pld.com. **ISSN:** 0018-1471. **Subscription Rates:** $56 individuals; $2 single issue. **Remarks:** Accepts advertising. **URL:** http://www.hpj.com.
Ad Rates: BW: $8,271.20 **Circ:** Paid ★**53,473**
4C: $9,921
PCI: $109.62

11607 KBSD-TV - 6
Box 157 Phone: (316)227-3121
Dodge City, KS 67801 Fax: (316)225-1675
Free: (800)279-2271

Format: Commercial TV. **Networks:** CBS; Kansas Broadcasting System. **Founded:** 1957. **Formerly:** KTVC-TV (1989). **Operating Hours:** Continuous except Friday 5 a.m. - 2 a.m.; 95% network, 5% local. **ADI:** Wichita-Hutchinson, KS. **Key Personnel:** Kerri Baker, General Mgr. **Local Programs:** *Cong Talk* 10:30 a.m. - 11 a.m. Saturday, K. Baker, Mailing contact; *Health Chat* 12:15 p.m. - 12:27 p.m. Tuesday, K. Baker, Mailing contact. **Ad Rates:** $9-60 for 10 seconds; $10.50-70 for 15 seconds; $15-150 for 30 seconds.

11608 KGNO-AM - 1370
908 W. Frontview Phone: (316)225-8080
Dodge City, KS 67801 Fax: (316)225-6655

Format: Full Service; Oldies. **Networks:** ABC; Mid-America Ag. **Owner:** Goodstar Broadcasting L.L.C., 1660 N. Tyler, Wichita, KS 67212, (316)729-8011, Fax: (316)729-9914. **Founded:** 1930. **Operating Hours:** Continuous. **ADI:** Wichita-Hutchinson, KS. **Key Personnel:** Alan Goodman, President, phone (316)729-8011, fax (316)729-9914; Eric Carl, Program Dir., phone (316)225-8080, fax (316)225-6655; Bonita McClure, General Mgr./Sales Mgr. **Wattage:** 5000 day, 250 night. **Ad Rates:** Advertising accepted; rates available upon request.

11609 KOLS-FM - 95.5
980 W. Frontview Phone: (316)225-8080
Dodge City, KS 67801 Fax: (316)225-6655

Format: Adult Contemporary. **Networks:** ABC; Mid-America

Ag. **Owner:** Goodstar Broadcasting L.L.C., 1660 N. Tyler Rd., Wichita, KS 67212, (316)729-8011, Fax: (316)729-9914. **Founded:** 1966. **Formerly:** KDCK-FM (1994); KGNO-FM. **Operating Hours:** Continuous. **ADI:** Wichita-Hutchinson, KS. **Key Personnel:** Alan Goodman, President; Bonita McClure, General Mgr.; Phil Padilla, Program Dir. **Wattage:** 100,000. **Ad Rates:** Advertising accepted; rates available upon request.

11610 KONQ-FM - 91.9
Dodge City Community College Phone: (316)225-6720
3004 N. 14th Ave. Fax: (316)225-0918
Dodge City, KS 67801

Format: Contemporary Hit Radio (CHR); Religious; Oldies; Blues; Alternative/New Music/Progressive. **Networks:** Independent. **Owner:** Dodge City Community College, at above address, (316)227-9306. **Founded:** 1976. **Formerly:** KINF-FM (1994). **Operating Hours:** 9 a.m.-11 p.m.; 100% local. **Key Personnel:** John Ewy, Operations Mgr.; John Mulhern, Engineer. **Wattage:** 860. **Ad Rates:** Noncommercial.

DOWNS, pop. 1,324.

NC KS. Osborne Co. On Solomon River, 70 mi. NW of Salina. Meat packing; grain elevators. Diversified farming.

11611 Downs News and Times
PO Box 157 Phone: (913)454-3514
Downs, KS 67437 Fax: (785)454-3866

Newspaper. **Founded:** 1880. **Freq:** Weekly (Thurs.). **Print Method:** Offset. **Cols./Page:** 8. **Col. Width:** 21 nonpareils. **Col. Depth:** 280 agate lines. **Key Personnel:** Darrel Miller, Editor and Publisher. **Subscription Rates:** $13.70 individuals; $15.81 out of area; $16 out of state. **Remarks:** Accepts advertising.
Ad Rates: PCI: $2.30 **Circ:** Paid ‡1,250

EL DORADO†, pop. 11,300.

SE KS. Butler Co. 28 mi. NE of Wichita. Butler County Community Junior College. Oil refineries. Diversified farming.

11612 El Dorado Times
The American Publishing Company Inc.
PO Box 694 Phone: (316)321-1120
El Dorado, KS 67042 Fax: (316)321-7722

Newspaper. **Founded:** 1870. **Freq:** Mon.-Sat. (eve.). **Print Method:** Offset. **Cols./Page:** 6. **Col. Width:** 27 nonpareils. **Col. Depth:** 294 agate lines. **Key Personnel:** Mike Boucher, Editor; Guy P. Russell, Publisher; Bill Walton, Advertising Mgr. **Subscription Rates:** $65 individuals. **Remarks:** Accepts advertising.
Ad Rates: SAU: $9 **Circ:** ‡4,768

ELKHART, pop. 2,500.

SW KS. Morton Co.

11613 Elkhart Tri-State News
PO Box 777 Phone: (316)697-4716
Elkhart, KS 67950
Community newspaper. **Founded:** 1880. **Freq:** Weekly. **Print Method:** Offset. **Cols./Page:** 8. **Col. Width:** 9 picas. **Col. Depth:** 21 inches. **Key Personnel:** Rita Hondyshell, Editor; Edward Brady, Publisher. **Subscription Rates:** $10.45 individuals; $12.54 out of country. **Remarks:** Accepts advertising.
Ad Rates: PCI: $2 **Circ:** Paid 1,525
Free 50

11614 Elkhart TV Cable Co.
610 S. Cosmos Phone: (316)697-4466
Elkhart, KS 67950 Fax: (316)697-9997
Free: (800)554-4250

Founded: 1959. **Key Personnel:** Bob Boaldin, Contact; Dian Boaldin, Contact. **Cities Served:** Elkhart, Rolla, KS; Keyes, OK: subscribing households 1,290.

ELLINWOOD, pop. 3,224.

C KS. Barton Co. On Arkansas River, 42 mi. NW of Hutchinson. Oil wells and related equipment. Grain farms.

11615 The Ellinwood Leader
The Leader, Inc.
PO Box 487 Phone: (316)564-3116
Ellinwood, KS 67526
Community newspaper. **Founded:** 1894. **Freq:** Weekly (Thurs.). **Print Method:** Offset. **Cols./Page:** 6. **Col. Width:** 28 nonpareils. **Col. Depth:** 294 agate lines. **Key Personnel:** Chris Mohn, Editor. **Subscription Rates:** $15.95 individuals; $20 out of area; $19 out of state. **Remarks:** Accepts advertising.
Ad Rates: GLR: $.20 **Circ:** ‡1,400
BW: $345
PCI: $3.40

ELLIS, pop. 2,062.

WC KS. Ellis Co. 110 mi. W. of Salina. Oil wells. Diversified agriculture.

11616 The Ellis Review
Box 227 Phone: (785)726-4583
1018 Washington Fax: (785)726-3821
Ellis, KS 67637
Newspaper. **Founded:** 1883. **Freq:** Weekly (Thurs.). **Print Method:** Offset. **Cols./Page:** 6. **Col. Width:** 12 picas. **Col. Depth:** 21 inches. **Key Personnel:** Bill Gasper, Publisher; Joleen Fisher, Advertising Mgr., phone (913)726-4583; Connie Fox, Circulation Mgr. **Subscription Rates:** $17 individuals; $18 out of area; $19 out of state. **Alt. Formats:** Mailing labels.
Ad Rates: GLR: $2.50 **Circ:** Paid 1,244
BW: $2.40 Free 42
4C: $80
PCI: $2.40

ELLSWORTH†, pop. 2,465.

C KS. Ellsworth Co. On Smoky Hill River, 34 mi. SW of Salina. Oil and oil products. Grain.

11617 The Ellsworth Reporter
PO Box 7 Phone: (913)472-3103
Ellsworth, KS 67439 Fax: (913)472-3268

Community newspaper. **Founded:** 1871. **Freq:** Weekly (Thurs.). **Print Method:** Offset. **Cols./Page:** 6. **Col. Width:** 28 nonpareils. **Col. Depth:** 294 agate lines. **Key Personnel:** Karl K. Gaston, Publisher. **Subscription Rates:** $24.48 individuals; $27.66 out of area; $30.00 out of state. **Remarks:** Accepts advertising.
Ad Rates: GLR: $.28 **Circ:** ‡3,050
BW: $399
PCI: $3.80

11618 Kanhistique
The Ellsworth Reporter
PO Box 7 Phone: (913)472-3103
Ellsworth, KS 67439 Fax: (913)472-3268

Subtitle: Kansas History & Antique Monthly. **Founded:** 1975. **Freq:** Monthly. **Print Method:** Web offset. **Trim Size:** 11 x 16. **Cols./Page:** 4. **Col. Width:** 14 picas. **Col. Depth:** 15 inches. **Key Personnel:** Edna M. Lee, Editor; Karl K. Gaston, Publisher. **Subscription Rates:** $18 individuals; $2.50 single issue.
Ad Rates: GLR: $4.62 **Circ:** ‡5,215
BW: $249.50

11619 Marquette Tribune
The Ellsworth Reporter
PO Box 7 Phone: (913)472-3103
Ellsworth, KS 67439 Fax: (913)472-3268

Community newspaper. **Founded:** 1880. **Freq:** Weekly. **Print Method:** Web offset. **Trim Size:** 14 x 21. **Cols./Page:** 6. **Col. Width:** 12 picas. **Col. Depth:** 21 inches. **Key Personnel:** Nyla Rawson, Editor; Karl K. Gaston, Publisher. **Subscription Rates:** $16 individuals; $18 out of area.
Ad Rates: PCI: $3.36 **Circ:** ‡659

EMPORIA†, pop. 25,287.

EC KS. Lyon Co. On Neosho and Cottonwood Rivers, 50 mi. SW of Topeka. Way College of Emporia; Emporia State University. Manufactures printing equipment, cheese, flour. Meat packing plant; soybean processing plant.

11620 The Emporia Gazette
Emporia Gazette
517 Merchant St. Phone: (316)342-4800
Emporia, KS 66801 Fax: (316)342-8108
Publication E-mail: gazette@emporia.com

Newspaper. **Founded:** 1890. **Freq:** Mon.-Sat. (eve.). **Print Method:** Offset. **Cols./Page:** 6. **Col. Width:** 12 picas. **Col. Depth:** 21 inches. **Key Personnel:** Barbara White Walker, Editor; David Walker, Publisher; R. Bruce Knaak, Advertising Mgr., phone (316)342-4803. **USPS:** 175-800. **Subscription Rates:** $72 individuals. **Remarks:** Accepts advertising. **URL:** http://www.emporiagazette.com.
Ad Rates: BW: $943 **Circ:** Mon.-Sat. ★9,136
4C: $1,153
SAU: $8.19
PCI: $8.19

11621 Kansas Biology Teacher
Emporia State University Press
1200 Commercial
Emporia, KS 66801-5087

Professional journal for biology teachers at all levels. **Freq:** Irregular. **Trim Size:** 6 x 9. **Cols./Page:** 2. **Key Personnel:** John Richard Schrock, Editor; John Wachholz, Circulation Mgr. **ISSN:** 1064-105X. **Subscription Rates:** $10 individuals; $5 single issue. **Remarks:** Advertising not accepted.
Circ: Combined 300

11622 The Pentagon
Emporia State University
Emporia, KS 66801 Phone: (316)341-5633
Fax: (316)341-6055

Journal covering mathematics for undergraduates. **Founded:** 1941. **Freq:** Semiannual December & May. **Key Personnel:** C. Bryan Dawson, Contact, bdawson@buster.uu.edu; Larry Scott, Contact, scottlar@esumail.emporia.edu. **ISSN:** 0031-4870. **Subscription Rates:** $5 individuals; $10 libraries; $10 two years; $20 libraries two years; $5 single issue. **Remarks:** Advertising not accepted. **Alt. Formats:** Microfilm, UMI.
Circ: Paid 3,000

11623 KANS-FM - 92.9
1811 W. 6th Ave. Phone: (316)343-9393
Emporia, KS 66801 Fax: (316)342-7617
Free: (800)356-KANS
E-mail: kans@ksradio.com

Format: Oldies. **Networks:** Jones Satellite; USA Radio. **Owner:** C & C Consulting, Inc., at above address. **Operating Hours:** Continuous. **Key Personnel:** Marty Hill, General Mgr.; Tom Johnson, News/PSA Broadcaster. **Local Programs:** *Sharing with Ron Scott*, Ron Scott; *Y2K Talk*, Jeff Abney; *Lutheran Church Service*, Rev. Tegtmeier. **Wattage:** 50,000. **Ad Rates:** $2.35-11.76 for 15 seconds; $3.52-17.64 for 30 seconds; $5.88-23.53 for 60 seconds. **URL:** http://www.ksradio.com.

11624 KNGM-FM - 91.9
815 Graham St. Phone: (316)343-9292
Emporia, KS 66801 Free: (888)808-8034
E-mail: kngm@freeyellow.com

Format: Religious; Contemporary Christian. **Networks:** Independent. **Owner:** Christian Action Team, Inc., at above address. **Founded:** 1987. **Operating Hours:** Continuous; 100% local. **Key Personnel:** Steve Pearson, General Mgr.; Scott Pearson, Program Dir. **Wattage:** 3000. **URL:** http://www.freeyellow.com/members/kngm.

11625 KRWV-FM - 99.5
1811 W. 6th Ave. Phone: (316)343-9393
Emporia, KS 66801 Fax: (316)342-7617
Free: (800)356-5267
E-mail: krwv@ksradio.com

Format: Adult Contemporary. **Owner:** C & C Consulting, Inc., at above address. **Operating Hours:** Continuous. **Key Personnel:** Marty Hill, General Mgr.; Tom Johnson, News Dir. **Wattage:** 6,000. **Ad Rates:** $1.17-9.41 for 15 seconds; $2.35-14.11 for 30 seconds; $3.52-17.64 for 60 seconds. **URL:** http://www.ksradio.com.

11626 KVOE-FM - 101.7
PO Box 968 Phone: (316)342-1400
Emporia, KS 66801-0968 Fax: (316)342-0804

Format: Country. **Simulcasts:** KVOE-AM. **Networks:** ABC; Mid-America Ag. **Founded:** 1985. **Operating Hours:** Continuous. **Key Personnel:** Lea Firestone, General Mgr., phone (316)342-1400; Michael Scott, Program Dir. **Wattage:** 3000. **Ad Rates:** Advertising accepted; rates available upon request. **URL:** http://www.kvoe@kvoe.com.

ERIE†, pop. 1,415.

SE KS. Neosho Co. 18 mi. N. of Parsons. Oil and gas wells. Grain, stock, poultry, and dairy farms.

11627 The Erie Record
317 South Main Phone: (316)244-3371
PO Box 159 Fax: (316)244-3371
Erie, KS 66733
Newspaper with Republican orientation. **Founded:** 1876. **Freq:** Weekly (Thurs.). **Print Method:** Offset. **Trim Size:** 13 3/4 x 22 1/2. **Cols./Page:** 6. **Col. Width:** 25 nonpareils. **Col. Depth:** 301 agate lines. **Key Personnel:** Leah Kensinger, Editor and Publisher. **Subscription Rates:** $13.70 individuals; $18 out of area. **Remarks:** Accepts advertising.
Ad Rates: GLR: $.13 **Circ:** ‡1,375
BW: $407.64
4C: $567.64
PCI: $3.16

ESKRIDGE

11628 Flint Hills Independent
121 S. Main St. Phone: (913)449-7272
PO Box 27 Fax: (913)449-2411
Eskridge, KS 66423
Community newspaper. **Founded:** 1900. **Freq:** Weekly (Thurs.). **Print Method:** Web offset. **Cols./Page:** 5. **Col. Width:** 11 picas. **Col. Depth:** 15 inches. **Key Personnel:** Sam Elliott, Editor and Publisher. **Subscription Rates:** $21.50; $25 out of state. **Remarks:** Accepts advertising. **Formerly:** The Independent.
Ad Rates: GLR: $8 **Circ:** ‡3,143
BW: $375
4C: $575

EUREKA

11629 Eureka Herald
Greenwood County Publishing Co.
106 W. 2nd St. Phone: (316)583-5721
PO Box 590
Eureka, KS 67045-0590
Community newspaper. **Freq:** Weekly (Thurs.). **Cols./Page:** 7. **Col. Width:** 2 inches. **Col. Depth:** 21 inches. **Key Personnel:** Richard W. Clasen, Editor and Publisher.
Circ: 3,600

11630 KOTE-FM - 93.5
PO Box 331 Phone: (316)583-7414
Eureka, KS 67045 Fax: (316)583-7233
Free: (800)398-5684
E-mail: kote@fox-net.net

Format: Country. **Owner:** Newwood Productions, L. P., at above address. **Founded:** 1988. **Operating Hours:** 5:00 a.m.-12:00 a.m. **Wattage:** 3,000. **Ad Rates:** $4-10 for 30 seconds; $6-15 for 60 seconds.

FAIRVIEW

11631 Fairview Enterprise
PO Box 98 Phone: (913)467-3461
Fairview, KS 66425
Community newspaper. **Founded:** Mar. 26, 1888. **Freq:** Weekly (Thurs.). **Cols./Page:** 5. **Col. Width:** 13 picas. **Col. Depth:** 17 inches. **Key Personnel:** Louise Fanning, Editor and Publisher. **Subscription Rates:** $14 individuals; $15 out of state. **Remarks:** Accepts advertising.
Ad Rates: PCI: $2 **Circ:** 600

FORT LEAVENWORTH, pop. 10,731.

NE KS. Leavenworth Co. 22 mi. NW of Kansas City. Military outpost; state penitentiary.

11632 Military Review
USACGSC
290 Grant Ave., Bldg. 77 Phone: (913)684-9327
Fort Leavenworth, KS 66027-1254 Fax: (913)684-9328
Publication E-mail: milreve@leav-emh1.army.mil

Professional military journal (English, Spanish and Portuguese). **Subtitle:** The Professional Journal of the United States Army. **Founded:** 1922. **Freq:** Bimonthly (English); bimonthly (Spanish); quarterly (Portuguese). **Print Method:** Film. **Trim Size:** 8 x 10 5/8. **Cols./Page:** 2. **Col. Width:** 35 nonpareils. **Col. Depth:** 92 agate lines. **Key Personnel:** Lt.Col. Mike Roddin, Managing Editor. **Subscription Rates:** $20 individuals; $8 single issue. **Remarks:** Advertising not accepted. **URL:** http://www-cgsc.army.mil.milrev/.
Circ: Paid ‡5,000
Controlled ‡20,000

11633 Phylaxis Magazine
The Phylaxis Society
PO Box 3151 Phone: (913)651-4584
Fort Leavenworth, KS 66027
Magazine covering Masonic interests. **Founded:** 1974. **Freq:** Quarterly. **Print Method:** Offset. **Cols./Page:** 3. **Col. Width:** 27 nonpareils. **Col. Depth:** 140 agate lines. **Key Personnel:** Joseph A. Walkes, Jr., Editor. **Subscription Rates:** $20. **Remarks:** Advertising not accepted.
Circ: 3,000

FORT SCOTT†, pop. 8,893.

SE KS. Bourbon Co. 143 mi. ENE of Wichita. Fort Scott Community College.

11634 The Ft. Scott Tribune
Tribune-Monitor, Co.
6 E. Wall St. Phone: (316)223-1460
PO Box 150 Fax: (316)223-1469
Fort Scott, KS 66701
General newspaper. **Founded:** 1884. **Freq:** Daily (eve.) and Sat. (morn.). **Print Method:** Offset. **Trim Size:** 13 3/4 x 22 3/4. **Cols./Page:** 6. **Col. Width:** 2 inches. **Col. Depth:** 294 agate lines. **Key Personnel:** Tom Epling, Managing Editor; Frank Emery, Publisher; Melissa Grant, Advertising Dir. **ISSN:** 8755-3171. **Subscription Rates:** $68.50 by mail; $78.55 out of area mail; $73.35 out of area carrier. **Remarks:** Accepts advertising. **Alt. Formats:** Microform. **Feature Editors:** Scott Nuzum, *Sports*.
Ad Rates: GLR: $4.95 **Circ:** Paid ⊕**4,071**
BW: $623.70 Free ⊕**153**
4C: $803.70
SAU: $4.95

11635 KMDO-AM - 1600
2 N National Phone: (316)223-4500
Fort Scott, KS 66701 Fax: (316)223-5662

Format: Full Service. **Networks:** Kansas Agriculture. **Owner:** Timothy James McKenney, Rte. 5, Box A-1, Fort Scott, KS 66701, (316)223-3405. **Founded:** 1954. **Operating Hours:** 6 a.m.-1 a.m.; 5% network, 95% local. **Key Personnel:** Tim J. McKenney, Manager; Janiece Toms, Office Mgr. **Local Programs:** *Party Line*; *Radio Auction*; *Trading Post*. **Wattage:** 1000. **Ad Rates:** $8.95 for 30 seconds; $10.95 for 60 seconds. Combined advertising rates available with KOMB-FM.

11636 KOMB-FM - 103.9
2 N. National Phone: (316)223-4500
PO Box 72 Fax: (316)223-5662
Fort Scott, KS 66701-0072

Format: Contemporary Hit Radio (CHR); Album-Oriented Rock (AOR); Soft Rock; Classic Rock. **Owner:** Tim J. McKenney, at above address, (316)223-3405. **Founded:** 1981. **Operating Hours:** 6 a.m.-1 a.m.; 100% local. **Key Personnel:** Tim J. McKenney, Manager; Bill Hurst, News Dir.; Russ Warren, Sports Dir. **Wattage:** 3000. **Ad Rates:** $8.95 for 30 seconds; $10.95 for 60 seconds.

FREDONIA†, pop. 3,047.

SE KS. Wilson Co. 80 mi. SE of Wichita. Gas; oil. Diversified farming.

11637 Wilson County Citizen
Box 330 Phone: (316)378-4415
Fredonia, KS 66736 Fax: (316)378-4688

Newspaper with Report orientation. **Founded:** Apr. 14, 1870. **Freq:** Semiweekly (Mon. and Thurs.). **Print Method:** Offset. **Trim Size:** 7 1/2 x 11. **Cols./Page:** 6. **Col. Width:** 21.5 nonpareils. **Col. Depth:** 301 agate lines. **Key Personnel:** Mina S. DeBerry, Editor; Joseph S. Relph, Publisher. **USPS:** 685-640. **Subscription Rates:** $22.67 individuals; $27.30 out of area. **Remarks:** Accepts advertising.
Ad Rates: GLR: $0.25 **Circ:** Paid ‡3,990
BW: $483.75 Free ‡40
SAU: $4
PCI: $4

GALENA

11638 Galena Sentinel-Times
Galena Times
511 Main St. Phone: (316)783-5034
Galena, KS 66739 Fax: (316)783-1388

Community newspaper. **Freq:** Weekly (Wed.). **Cols./Page:** 6. **Col. Width:** 2 inches. **Col. Depth:** 21 inches. **Key Personnel:** David F. Nelson, Editor and Publisher. **Subscription Rates:** $11.82; $19.84 out of county; $19.95 out of state. **Remarks:** Accepts advertising.
Ad Rates: GLR: $2.83 **Circ:** 1,200

GARDEN CITY†, pop. 18,256.

SW KS. Finney Co. On Arkansas River, 50 mi. NW of Dodge City. Garden City Community Junior College. Manufactures cattle feeding equipment, alfalfa meal. Diversified farming.

11639 The Garden City Telegram
Telegram Publishing Co.
PO Box 958 Phone: (316)275-8500
Garden City, KS 67846 Fax: (316)275-5165
Free: (800)475-8600
Publication E-mail: gctelegram@gcnet.com

General newspaper. **Founded:** 1929. **Freq:** Mon.-Sat. **Print Method:** Offset. **Cols./Page:** 6. **Col. Width:** 24 nonpareils. **Col. Depth:** 301 agate lines. **Key Personnel:** Steve Delaney, Editor and Publisher, phone (316)276-6862, delaney@gctelegram.com. **USPS:** 213-600. **Subscription Rates:** $83.65 individuals; $90 motor route; $102.88 by mail. **Remarks:** Accepts advertising. **Alt. Formats:** Microfilm.
Ad Rates: GLR: $1.018 **Circ:** Mon.-Sat. ★**10,908**
BW: $1,051.35
4C: $1,291.35
PCI: $8.15

11640 KBUF-AM - 1030
1402 E. Kansas Phone: (316)276-2366
PO Box 759 Fax: (316)276-3568
Garden City, KS 67846
Free: (800)999-5283
E-mail: opman@adsgc.net

Format: Country; Agricultural; Talk. **Networks:** ABC; NBC; Kansas Agriculture. **Owner:** KBUF Partnership, at above address. **Founded:** 1948. **Operating Hours:** Continuous. **ADI:** Wichita-Hutchinson, KS. **Key Personnel:** Doug Harder, General Mgr.; Kay Leiker, Sales Mgr.; Sherri Iszler, Program Dir.; Hap Larson, Farm Dir. **Wattage:** 1,000 day; 1000 night. **Ad Rates:** $10-21 for 30 seconds.

11641 KIUL-AM - 1240
308 N. 7th St. Phone: (316)276-3251
PO Box 878 Fax: (316)276-3649
Garden City, KS 67846

Format: Full Service; Middle-of-the-Road (MOR). **Networks:** CBS; Kansas Information; Kansas Agriculture. **Owner:** Threjay, Inc., at above address. **Founded:** 1935. **Operating Hours:** 5:00 a.m.-1 a.m. **Key Personnel:** Ronald C. Isham, General Mgr.; Doug Wagner, Sales Mgr.; Scott Roberts, Program Dir.; Rob Houston, News Dir.; Kevin Shaffer, Sports Dir. **Wattage:** 1000. **Ad Rates:** $6-20 for 30 seconds; $9-21 for 60 seconds. Combined advertising rates available with KWKR-FM: $6-$20 for 30 seconds; $9-$21 for 60 seconds.

11642 KKJQ-FM - 97.3
1309 E. Fulton St. Phone: (316)276-2366
Garden City, KS 67846-6132 Fax: (316)276-3568
Free: (800)999-5283

Format: Country; Adult Contemporary. **Networks:** ABC. **Owner:** KBUF Partnership, at above address. **Founded:** 1962. **Operating Hours:** Continuous. **Key Personnel:** Cindy Landgraf, General Sales Mgr.; Bobby G, Program Dir.; Scott Smith, Manager. **Wattage:** 100,000.

11643 KSKZ-FM - 99.9
308 N. 7th St. Phone: (316)276-3251
PO Box 878 Fax: (316)276-3649
Garden City, KS 67846

Format: Adult Contemporary. **Networks:** Unistar. **Owner:** Threjay, Inc., at above address. **Founded:** 1983. **Formerly:** KWKR-FM (1995). **Operating Hours:** 5 a.m.-1 a.m. **Key Personnel:** Ronald C. Isham, President; Judith Isham, Vice President; Cindy Landgraff, Sales Mgr.; Doug Harder, Operations Mgr.; Charlie Hale, Chief Engineer. **Wattage:** 99,000. **Ad Rates:** $6-27 for 30 seconds; $9-40.50 for 60 seconds. Combined advertising rates available with KIUL-AM.

11644 KSNG-TV - 11
204 Fulton Terr. Phone: (316)276-2311
Garden City, KS 67846 Fax: (316)275-0576

Format: Commercial TV. **Networks:** NBC. **Founded:** 1958. **Formerly:** KGLD-TV. **Operating Hours:** 5:45 a.m.-2 a.m. **ADI:** Wichita-Hutchinson, KS. **Key Personnel:** Sharolyn Mayfield, General Mgr.; Joann Smith, Program Dir. **Ad Rates:** $3-125 per unit.

GARDNER

11645 Gardner News
Tri-County Newspapers
PO Box 303 Phone: (913)856-7615
Gardner, KS 66030 Fax: (913)856-6707
Publisher E-mail: triconews@aol.com

Community newspaper. **Founded:** 1940. **Freq:** Weekly (Wed.). **Cols./Page:** 6. **Col. Width:** 12 1/2 picas. **Col. Depth:** 21 inches. **Key Personnel:** Mark Taylor, Editor. **Subscription Rates:** $25 in-state; $30 out of state. **Remarks:** Accepts advertising.
Ad Rates: BW: $620 **Circ:** 2,000
PCI: $9

11646 The Spring Hill New Era
Tri-County Newspapers
PO Box 303 Phone: (913)856-7615
Gardner, KS 66030 Fax: (913)856-6707
Publisher E-mail: triconews@aol.com

Newspaper. **Founded:** 1893. **Freq:** Weekly. **Cols./Page:** 6. **Col. Width:** 2 1/2 inches. **Col. Depth:** 21 1/2 inches. **Key**

Personnel: Mark Taylor, Editor. **Subscription Rates:** $25; $30 out of state.
Ad Rates: PCI: $7.50 **Circ:** Paid 1,000
Free 3,000

GARNETT†, pop. 3,310.

EC KS. Anderson Co. 50 mi. SE of Emporia. Oil wells. Grain, poultry, stock, and dairy farms.

11647 Eastern Kansas Senior Star
Garnett Publishing, Inc.
PO Box 409 Phone: (913)448-3121
Garnett, KS 66032 Fax: (913)448-6253

Free magazine for Kansans, ages 55 and older. **Founded:** 1993. **Freq:** Bimonthly. **Print Method:** Offset. **Cols./Page:** 6. **Col. Width:** 24 nonpareils. **Col. Depth:** 294 agate lines. **Key Personnel:** Garold Dane Hicks, Publisher. **USPS:** 010-638. **Subscription Rates:** $12 individuals. **Remarks:** Advertising accepted; rates available upon request.
Circ: 8,521

11648 Review
Garnett Publishing, Inc.
PO Box 409 Phone: (913)448-3121
Garnett, KS 66032 Fax: (913)448-6253

Newspaper. **Founded:** 1865. **Freq:** Weekly (Mon.). **Print Method:** Offset. **Cols./Page:** 6. **Col. Width:** 24 nonpareils. **Col. Depth:** 294 agate lines. **Key Personnel:** Max H. Evans, Editor. **Subscription Rates:** $12 individuals. **Remarks:** Accepts advertising.
Ad Rates: GLR: $.195 **Circ:** 4,074

GIRARD†, pop. 2,888.

C. KS. Crawford Co. 10 mi. NW of Pittsburg. Grain farms.

11649 The Girard Press
Professional Resource Publishing, Inc.
PO Box 126 Phone: (316)724-4426
Girard, KS 66743 Fax: (316)724-4493
Publication E-mail: girardpress@ckt.net

Community newspaper. **Founded:** 1869. **Freq:** Weekly. **Print Method:** Offset. **Trim Size:** 14 x 21 1/2. **Cols./Page:** 6. **Col. Width:** 13 picas. **Col. Depth:** 21 1/2 inches. **Key Personnel:** Ed McKechnie, Editor and Publisher; Janet Beene, Managing Editor; Jim Perona, General Mgr. **USPS:** 218-800. **Subscription Rates:** $19.25; $24.75 out of county. **Remarks:** Accepts advertising.
Ad Rates: BW: $374.10 **Circ:** Paid 2,300
PCI: $3.50

GLASCO, pop. 709.

NC KS. Cloud Co. On Solomon River, 50 mi. NW of Salina. Grain farms.

11650 The Delphos Republican
Royann Tatro
213 E. Main Phone: (913)568-2565
PO Box 457
Glasco, KS 67445-0457
Community newspaper. **Founded:** 1888. **Freq:** Weekly (Thurs.). **Print Method:** Offset. **Cols./Page:** 7. **Col. Width:** 21 nonpareils. **Col. Depth:** 294 agate lines. **Key Personnel:** Royanne Tatro, Editor. **USPS:** 462-220. **Subscription Rates:** $14.83 individuals; $16.94 out of area; $16 out of state. **Remarks:** Accepts advertising.
Ad Rates: GLR: $.30 **Circ:** 384
BW: $220.50
SAU: $2.25
PCI: $1.75

11651 The Glasco Sun
Royann Tatro
213 E. Main Phone: (913)568-2565
PO Box 457
Glasco, KS 67445-0457
Community newspaper. **Founded:** Jan. 20, 1883. **Freq:** Weekly (Thurs.). **Print Method:** Offset. **Cols./Page:** 7. **Col. Width:** 21 nonpareils. **Col. Depth:** 294 agate lines. **Key Personnel:** Royanne Tatro, Editor. **USPS:** 279-180. **Subscription Rates:** $16 individuals; $18 out of area. **Remarks:** Accepts advertising.
Ad Rates: GLR: $.30 **Circ:** 870
BW: $257.25
SAU: $2.25
PCI: $2

GLEN ELDER

11652 KFRM-AM - 550
PO Box 88 Phone: (913)527-7118
Glen Elder, KS 67446-0088 Free: (800)876-0012

Format: Country. **Founded:** 1947. **Formerly:** KNNN-AM, KICT-AM. **Operating Hours:** 18 hours daily. **Key Personnel:** Herb Hoeflicker, Contact. **Wattage:** 5000 day; 110 night. **Ad Rates:** Advertising accepted; rates available upon request.

GOODLAND†, pop. 5,709.

NW KS. Sherman Co. 200 mi. E. of Denver, CO. Grain and livestock farms.

11653 Country Advocate
NorWest Newspapers
1205 Main St. Phone: (785)899-2338
Goodland, KS 67735-2946 Fax: (785)899-6186

Shopping guide. **Founded:** 1986. **Freq:** Weekly (Wed.). **Print Method:** Offset. **Trim Size:** 11 x 14. **Cols./Page:** 5. **Col. Width:** 2 inches. **Col. Depth:** 13 1/2 inches. **Key Personnel:** Tom Betz, Editor; Steve Haynes, Publisher. **Subscription Rates:** Free in area; $20 out of area.
Ad Rates: GLR: $8.95 **Circ:** Free ‡16,000
BW: $581.75
PCI: $8.95

11654 The Goodland Daily News
NorWest Newspapers
1205 Main St. Phone: (785)899-2338
Goodland, KS 67735-2946 Fax: (785)899-6186
Publication E-mail: daily@nwkansas.com

General newspaper. **Founded:** 1932. **Freq:** Daily. **Print Method:** Offset. **Trim Size:** 13 x 23. **Cols./Page:** 6. **Col. Width:** 2 1/16 inches. **Col. Depth:** 21.5 inches. **Key Personnel:** Tom Betz, Editor; Steve Haynes, Publisher. **Subscription Rates:** $65 individuals; $75 out of state. **Remarks:** Color advertising not accepted. **URL:** http://www.nwkansas.com.
Ad Rates: BW: $696.60 **Circ:** Paid ‡1,690
SAU: $5.40 Free ‡50

11655 KBSL-TV - 10
3023 W. 31st Phone: (785)899-2321
Goodland, KS 67735 Fax: (785)899-3138

Format: Commercial TV. **Networks:** CBS. **Founded:** 1960. **Formerly:** KLOE-TV (1989). **Operating Hours:** 6 a.m.-midnight; 85% network, 15% local. **ADI:** Wichita-Hutchinson, KS. **Key Personnel:** Wayne E. Roberts, Station Mgr., phone (785)625-5277; Kim Newell, Production Dir.; Terry Stover, Sales Mgr.; Don Newell, Acct. Rep; Dave Lamb, Ag. Dir. **Local Programs:** *Ag Markets/Reports*, Dave Lamb. **Ad Rates:** $10-50 for 30 seconds. **Additional Contact Info: Mailing Address:** Box 569, Broadcast Plaza, Goodland, KS 67735.

11656 KGCR-FM - 107.7
PO Box 948 Phone: (913)694-2877
Goodland, KS 67735 Fax: (913)694-2875
E-mail: kgcr@juno.com

Format: Religious; News; Agricultural. **Networks:** Moody Broadcasting; USA Radio; Ambassador Inspirational Radio. **Owner:** Grace Communications Inc., at above address, (913)694-2497. **Founded:** 1988. **Operating Hours:** Continuous; 15% network, 85% local. **Key Personnel:** Allen Quenzer, General Mgr.; James Claassen, Station Mgr.; Doug Bell, News Dir. **Wattage:** 100,000. **Ad Rates:** $2.50-5 for 30 seconds; $4-6.50 for 60 seconds.

11657 KKCI-FM - 102.5
Box 569 Phone: (913)899-2309
Broadcast Plaza Fax: (913)899-3062
Goodland, KS 67735
E-mail: kloe@goodland.ixks.com

Format: Adult Contemporary. **Networks:** Satellite Music Network; Westwood One Radio. **Owner:** Melia Communications, at above address. **Founded:** 1990. **Operating Hours:** Continuous. **ADI:** Wichita-Hutchinson, KS. **Key Personnel:** Martin Melia, Pres./General Mgr.; Jan Elliot, General Sales Mgr.; Curtis Duncan, PD; Ron Rempe, Music Dir. **Local Programs:** *Good Neighbor Hour* 6 a.m.-7 a.m.; *The Happy Hour* 4 p.m.-5 p.m.; *The Morning Show with Marty* 7 a.m.-8 a.m. **Wattage:** 100,000. **Ad Rates:** $11-14 for 30 seconds; $14-17 for 60 seconds. Combined advertising rates available with KLOE-AM. **URL:** kloe.com.

11658 KLOE-AM - 730
Box 569 Phone: (913)899-3062
Broadcast Plaza Fax: (913)899-3062
Goodland, KS 67735
E-mail: kloe@goodland.ixks.com

Format: Full Service; News; Country; Talk. **Networks:** CBS; Kansas Agriculture. **Owner:** Melia Communications, at above address. **Founded:** 1947. **Formerly:** KWGB-AM (1955); KBLR-AM (1961). **Operating Hours:** 5:30 a.m.-9 p.m. **ADI:** Wichita-Hutchinson, KS. **Key Personnel:** Martin Melia, Pres./General Mgr.; Jan Elliot, General Sales Mgr.; Curtis Duncan, PD. **Local Programs:** *Good Neighbor Hour* 6 a.m.-7 a.m.; *Midday Report* 12 p.m.-1 p.m.; *Morning Report* 7 a.m.-8 a.m. **Wattage:** 1000 day; 20 night. **Ad Rates:** $11-14 for 30 seconds; $14-17 for 60 seconds. **URL:** http://www.kloe.com.

GREAT BEND†, pop. 17,600.

C KS. Barton Co. On Arkansas River, 50 mi. WNW of Hutchinson. Barton County Community College. Oil and gas wells. Grain farms.

11659 Great Bend Tribune
Tribune
2012 Forest Ave. Phone: (316)792-1211
Box 228 Fax: (316)792-3441
Great Bend, KS 67530
Publication E-mail: tribune@midusd.net

General newspaper. **Founded:** 1876. **Freq:** Daily (eve.), Sunday (morn.). **Print Method:** Offset. **Cols./Page:** 6. **Col. Width:** 24 nonpareils. **Col. Depth:** 301 agate lines. **Key Personnel:** Daren Watkins, Managing Editor; Chuck Smith, Editor; Tom Lorimer, Publisher; Debbie Dietz, Advertising Mgr. **USPS:** 227-260. **Subscription Rates:** $91.80 individuals.
Ad Rates: GLR: $0.57 **Circ:** Mon.-Fri. ★7,620
BW: $1,185.85 Sun. ★8,093
4C: $1,195.85
PCI: $8.65

11660 KHOK-FM - 100.7
5501 10th St. Phone: (316)792-3647
Box 48 Fax: (316)792-3649
Great Bend, KS 67530

Format: Hot Country. **Networks:** ABC. **Owner:** Eagle Radio, Inc., PO Box 817, Hays, KS 67601, (913)625-2578. **Founded:** 1979. **Operating Hours:** Continuous; 2% network, 98% local. **ADI:** Wichita-Hutchinson, KS. **Key Personnel:** Rick Nulton, General Mgr.; Scott Donovan, Program Dir. **Wattage:** 100,000. **Ad Rates:** $10.59 for 30 seconds; $13.82 for 60 seconds.

11661 KSNC-TV - 2
RR 5, Box 262 Phone: (316)793-7868
Great Bend, KS 67530 Fax: (316)793-3079

Format: Commercial TV. **Networks:** NBC. **Founded:** 1954. **Operating Hours:** Continuous Mon.-Fri.; 6 a.m.-1:30 a.m. Sat.-Sun. **ADI:** Wichita-Hutchinson, KS. **Key Personnel:** Dan Bayes, General Mgr.

11662 KVGB-AM - 1590
PO Box 609 Phone: (316)792-3647
Great Bend, KS 67530 Fax: (316)792-3649
Free: (888)782-3647

Format: News; Talk; Sports. **Networks:** ABC. **Founded:** Mar. 1, 1937. **Operating Hours:** 6 a.m.-midnight. **ADI:** Wichita-Hutchinson, KS. **Key Personnel:** Rick Nulton, General Mgr.; Randy Goering, Sales Mgr. **Wattage:** 5000. **Ad Rates:** $7-12 for 30 seconds.

11663 KVGB-FM - 104.3
PO Box 609 Phone: (316)792-3647
Great Bend, KS 67530 Fax: (316)792-3649
Free: (888)792-3647

Format: Adult Contemporary. **Networks:** ABC. **Founded:** 1977. **Operating Hours:** Continuous. **ADI:** Wichita-Hutchinson, KS. **Key Personnel:** Rick Nulton, General Mgr.; Randy Goering, Sales Mgr. **Wattage:** 100,000. **Ad Rates:** $7-12 for 30 seconds.

GREENSBURG†, pop. 1,885.

SC KS. Kiowa Co. 80 mi. SW of Hutchinson. Livestock and grain farms.

11664 Kiowa County Signal
Tribune Newspaper Co.
120 N. Main St. Phone: (316)723-2115
PO Box 368
Greensburg, KS 67054
Community newspaper. **Founded:** June 1, 1885. **Freq:** Weekly (Wed.). **Print Method:** Offset. **Trim Size:** 13 x 21 1/2. **Cols./Page:** 6. **Col. Width:** 26 nonpareils. **Col. Depth:** 301 agate lines. **Key Personnel:** Abigail St. John, Editor; J.K. Phillips, Publisher; Lanissa Hammond, Advertising Mgr.

USPS: 295-960. **Subscription Rates:** $22 individuals; $0.50 single issue.
Ad Rates: GLR: $0.20 BW: $4 PCI: $3.90 **Circ:** Paid 1,600 Free 50

GYPSUM, pop. 423.

C KS. Saline Co. 20 mi. SE of Salina.

11665 Gypsum Advocate
Montgomery Communications, Inc.
PO Box 31 Phone: (913)227-3348
Lindsborg, KS 67456
Publication E-mail: dailynews@jc.net

Community newspaper. **Founded:** 1886. **Freq:** Weekly (Thurs.). **Print Method:** Offset. **Trim Size:** 13 x 21. **Cols./Page:** 6. **Col. Width:** 25 nonpareils. **Col. Depth:** 297 agate lines. **Key Personnel:** Sherry Swanson, Editor, phone (785)536-4258, fax (785)227-3740; John G. Montgomery, Publisher. **ISSN:** 3141-6000. **Subscription Rates:** $22 individuals; $24 out of state.
Ad Rates: GLR: $4.50 BW: $242 **Circ:** Paid ‡2,940 Non-paid ‡107

HALSTEAD, pop. 2,000.

SWC KS. Harvey Co. 23 mi. NNW of Wichita. Wheat.

11666 U.S. Water News
U.S. Water News, Inc.
230 Main St. Phone: (316)835-2222
Halstead, KS 67056-9983 Fax: (316)835-2223
Free: (800)251-0046
Publication E-mail: uswatrnews@aol.com

Water industry magazine (tabloid) covering water supply, water quality, government policy, legislation, litigation and water rights, conservation, finances, and markets. **Founded:** July 1984. **Freq:** Monthly. **Print Method:** Offset. **Trim Size:** 11 1/2 x 17. **Cols./Page:** 4. **Col. Width:** 2 1/4 inches. **Col. Depth:** 15 1/2 inches. **Key Personnel:** Thomas C. Bell, Publisher. **ISSN:** 0749-1980. **Subscription Rates:** $54 individuals; $98 two years. **Remarks:** Accepts advertising. **URL:** http://www.uswaternews.com.
Ad Rates: BW: $2,150 4C: $2,300 **Circ:** Paid ‡3,300 Controlled ‡16,700

HARPER

11667 Harper Advocate
Advocate
PO Box 36 Phone: (316)896-7311
Harper, KS 67058 Fax: (316)896-2754

Community newspaper. **Founded:** 1891. **Freq:** Weekly (Thurs.). **Print Method:** Offset. **Cols./Page:** 8. **Col. Width:** 10 1/2 picas. **Col. Depth:** 20 1/2 inches. **Key Personnel:** Ken Leu, Editor and Publisher. **Subscription Rates:** $22.50. **Remarks:** Accepts advertising.
Ad Rates: GLR: $5.29 PCI: $5.39 **Circ:** 1,910

HAYS†, pop. 18,100.

WC KS. Ellis Co. 100 mi. W. of Salina. Fort Hays State University. Oil well; large dryland farming experiment station.

11668 Ellis County Star
708 Main St. Phone: (913)625-7358
Hays, KS 67601 Fax: (913)625-7359

Newspaper. **Founded:** 1949. **Freq:** Weekly (Thurs.). **Print Method:** Offset. **Cols./Page:** 6. **Col. Width:** 25 nonpareils. **Col. Depth:** 294 agate lines. **Key Personnel:** Kim Billinger, Publisher; Tammy Schultz, Editor; Kim Billinger, Advertising Mgr. **Subscription Rates:** $16 individuals. **Remarks:** Accepts advertising.
Ad Rates: BW: $252 PCI: $3 **Circ:** ‡2,000

11669 The Hays Daily News
News Publishing Co.
507 Main St. Phone: (785)628-1081
PO Box 857 Fax: (785)628-8186
Hays, KS 67601-4228
Free: (800)657-6017

General newspaper. **Founded:** Nov. 11, 1929. **Freq:** Daily (eve.), Sunday (morn.). **Print Method:** Offset. **Trim Size:** 13 3/4 x 22 3/4. **Cols./Page:** 6. **Col. Width:** 2 1/16 inches. **Col. Depth:** 21 1/2 inches. **Key Personnel:** Jim Hitch, Editor and Publisher, hitch@dailynews.net; Michael H. Haas, Advertising Mgr. **Subscription Rates:** $85.10 individuals; $93.90 out of state. **Remarks:** Accepts advertising. **URL:** http://www.dailynews.net/hays/. **Formerly:** The Ellis County News.
Ad Rates: GLR: $10.20 BW: $1,315.80 4C: $1,570.80 PCI: $8 **Circ:** Mon.-Fri. ★**12,249** Sun. ★**13,255**

11670 The University Leader
Fort Hays State University
Picken Hall 104 Phone: (785)628-5301
600 Park St. Fax: (785)628-4004
Hays, KS 67601
Publication E-mail: ldjh@fhsuvm.fhsu.edu
Publisher E-mail: leader@scatcat.fhsu.edu

Collegiate newspaper. **Founded:** 1908. **Freq:** Semiweekly (Tues. and Fri.; during the academic year, Thurs. during summer.). **Print Method:** Offset. **Trim Size:** Broadsheet. **Cols./Page:** 6. **Col. Width:** 24 nonpareils. **Col. Depth:** 301 agate lines. **Key Personnel:** Jessica Smith, Editor; Nick Schwien, Advertising Mgr., phone (785)628-5884; Jody Hall, Business Mgr., phone (785)628-5889. **Subscription Rates:** $25 individuals. **Remarks:** Accepts advertising. **URL:** http://www.fhsu.edi/leader.
Ad Rates: BW: $650 4C: $950 PCI: $6.50 **Circ:** Free ‡4,800

11671 Hays Cable TV Co.
2300 Hall St. Phone: (913)625-5910
Hays, KS 67601 Fax: (913)625-8030

Owner: Eagle Communications, Inc., at above address. **Founded:** 1965. **Key Personnel:** Pete Collins, General Mgr., phone (913)625-4000; Larry Braun, Chief Engineer, phone (913)625-5910; Lila Krainbill, Division Office Mgr., phone (913)483-2534. **Cities Served:** Ellis, Goodland, Hays, Hoxie, Russell, Wakeeney, KS: subscribing households 13,000; 52 channels.

11672 KAYS-AM - 1400
2300 Hall St. Phone: (913)625-2578
PO Box 6 Fax: (913)625-3632
Hays, KS 67601
Free: (800)569-0144
E-mail: kays@eaglecom.net

Format: Full Service; Sports. **Networks:** ABC; ESPN Radio. **Founded:** 1948. **Operating Hours:** 5:00 a.m.-midnight. **Key Personnel:** Joe Engel, General Mgr.; Mike Cooper, Program Dir. **Wattage:** 1000. **Ad Rates:** $6 for 15 seconds; $8 for 30 seconds; $12 for 60 seconds.

11673 KBSH-TV - 7
2300 Hall St. Phone: (913)625-5277
Hays, KS 67601 Fax: (913)625-1161

Format: Commercial TV. **Networks:** CBS. **Founded:** 1958. **Formerly:** KAYS-TV (1989). **Operating Hours:** 6:45 a.m.-1 a.m.; 90% network, 10% local. **ADI:** Wichita-Hutchinson, KS. **Key Personnel:** Wayne Roberts, Station Mgr.; Dennis Massier, Chief Engineer. **Ad Rates:** $10-90 for 30 seconds.

11674 KHAZ-FM - 99.5
2300 Hall St. Phone: (785)625-2578
PO Box 6 Fax: (785)625-3632
Hays, KS 67601-0006
Free: (800)569-0144
E-mail: khaz@eaglecom.net

Format: Country. **Networks:** ABC. **Founded:** 1984. **Operating Hours:** Continuous. **ADI:** Wichita-Hutchinson, KS. **Key Personnel:** Mark Hinca, Contact; Joe Engel, General Mgr. **Wattage:** 100,000. **Ad Rates:** $9 for 30 seconds; $15 for 60 seconds.

11675 KJLS-FM - 103.3
107 W. 13th Phone: (785)628-1064
Box 597 Fax: (785)628-1822
Hays, KS 67601
Free: (800)681-9102

Format: Adult Contemporary. **Networks:** ABC. **Founded:** 1974. **Operating Hours:** Continuous. **Key Personnel:** Rick Kuehl, President; Robert Bunting, Vice President; Ken Billinger, Operations Mgr.; Cameron Perry, Program Dir.; Steve Klitzke, Sales Mgr. **Wattage:** 100,000. **Ad Rates:** KKQY-FM. **URL:** http://www.mix103fm.com.

11676 KPRD-FM - 88.9
301 W. 13th, No. 409 Phone: (785)628-6300
Hays, KS 67601 Fax: (785)628-6389
E-mail: kprd@dailynews.net

Format: Religious. **Networks:** Moody Broadcasting; Sun Radio. **Owner:** The Praise Network, Inc., Box 8, Aurora, NE 68818, (308)946-2656. **Operating Hours:** Continuous. **Key Personnel:** David Breeden, Asst. Mgr. **Wattage:** 83,000. **Ad Rates:** Noncommercial.

HERINGTON, pop. 2,930.

NEC KS. Dickinson Co. 30 mi. SE of Abilene. Oil wells. Grain farms.

11677 The Herington Times
7 N. Broadway Phone: (785)258-2211
PO Box 310 Fax: (785)258-2400
Herington, KS 67449
Community newspaper. **Founded:** July 1889. **Freq:** Weekly (Thurs.). **Print Method:** Offset. **Cols./Page:** 6. **Col. Width:** 25 nonpareils. **Col. Depth:** 294 agate lines. **Key Personnel:** Larry L. Byers, Editor and Publisher. **USPS:** 242-100. **Subscription Rates:** $36 individuals; $39 out of area; $41 out of state. **Remarks:** Accepts advertising.
Ad Rates: GLR: $.33 BW: $472.50 4C: $652.50 SAU: $5.25 PCI: $5.65 **Circ:** Paid 2,512 Free 27

11678 KDMM-FM - 105.7
PO Box 150 Phone: (785)258-2660
Herington, KS 67449 Fax: (785)258-2777

Format: Country. **Networks:** USA Radio; Kansas Information; Kansas Agriculture. **Owner:** Tri-County Broadcasting, Inc., at above address. **Operating Hours:** Continuous. **Key Personnel:** C. Kay Hutchinson, General Mgr.; Donald D. Willis, Chief Engineer. **Wattage:** 12,500. **Ad Rates:** Advertising accepted; rates available upon request.

HESSTON, pop. 3,008.

SC KS. Harvey Co. 30 mi. NNW of Wichita. Hesston College. Manufactures commercial turf and mowing equipment. Diversified farming.

11679 The Hesston Record
109 N. Main Phone: (316)327-4831
PO Box 340 Fax: (316)327-4830
Hesston, KS 67062-0340
Newspaper. **Founded:** 1916. **Freq:** Weekly (Thurs.). **Print Method:** Offset. **Trim Size:** 11 1/2 x 14. **Cols./Page:** 5. **Col. Width:** 24 nonpareils. **Col. Depth:** 182 agate lines. **Key Personnel:** Robert L. Latta, Editor and Publisher. **Subscription Rates:** $29 individuals; $30 out of area; $35 out of state. **Remarks:** Accepts advertising.
Ad Rates: GLR: $0.28 BW: $237.25 PCI: $3.85 **Circ:** Paid ‡1,000

HIAWATHA†, pop. 3,884.

NE KS. Brown Co. 54 mi. NNE of Topeka. Diversified farming.

11680 Everest World
607 Utah St. Phone: (913)742-2111
Hiawatha, KS 66434 Fax: (913)742-2276

Community newspaper (tabloid) with a Republican orientation. **Founded:** 1963. **Freq:** Weekly (Thurs.). **Print Method:** Offset. **Cols./Page:** 5. **Col. Width:** 25 nonpareils. **Col. Depth:** 182 agate lines. **Key Personnel:** Barry Stokes, Publisher; Virginia Regier, Editor. **Subscription Rates:** $18 individuals. **Remarks:** Accepts advertising.
Ad Rates: SAU: $3.08 PCI: $1.90 **Circ:** Paid 204 Non-paid 11

11681 Hiawatha Daily World
Cleveland Newspapers Inc.
607 Utah St. Phone: (785)742-2111
Hiawatha, KS 66434 Fax: (785)742-2276

General newspaper. **Founded:** 1908. **Freq:** Daily (eve.). **Print Method:** Offset. **Cols./Page:** 6. **Col. Width:** 26 nonpareils. **Col. Depth:** 294 agate lines. **Key Personnel:** Barry A. Stokes, Editor and Publisher; Bobi Dozier, Advertising Mgr.; Deb Rosenberger, Managing Editor. **USPS:** 243-100. **Subscription Rates:** $70 by mail out of state; $51.45 carrier; $63.09 by mail in state. **Remarks:** Accepts advertising. **Alt. Formats:** CD-ROM.
Ad Rates: BW: $541.80 4C: $691.80 SAU: $4.95 PCI: $4.95 **Circ:** Paid 2,185 Free 46

11682 Penny Press 4
Maverick Media, Inc.
PO Box 153 Phone: (913)742-7505
Hiawatha, KS 66434 Fax: (913)742-7540

Shopper (tabloid). **Freq:** Weekly (Tues.). **Print Method:** Offset. **Trim Size:** 11 1/2 x 16. **Cols./Page:** 6. **Col. Width:** 9

1/2 picas. **Col. Depth:** 15 inches. **Key Personnel:** William Welsh, President. **Subscription Rates:** Free; $24 by mail.
Ad Rates: GLR: $0.56 **Circ:** Free ‡14,350
BW: $831.60
4C: $1,111.60
SAU: $10.35
PCI: $7.85

11683 KNZA-FM - 103.9
Box 104 Phone: (913)547-3461
Hiawatha, KS 66434-0104 Fax: (913)547-9900

Format: News; Sports; Country; Agricultural. **Networks:** ABC. **Owner:** KNZA, Inc., at above address. **Founded:** 1977. **Operating Hours:** Continuous; 12% network, 88% local. **Key Personnel:** Gregory Buser, General Sales Mgr.; Robert Hilton, Operations Mgr.; L.J. Trant, Program Dir. **Wattage:** 50,000. **Ad Rates:** $6-14 for 30 seconds; $10-24 for 60 seconds. Combined advertising rates available with KAIR-AM/FM.

HIGHLAND, pop. 954.

NE KS. Doniphan Co. 50 mi. N. of Lawrence. Grain, stock, poultry, and fruit farms.

11684 The Highland Vidette
PO Box 98 Phone: (913)442-3791
Highland, KS 66035-0098 Fax: (913)442-3260

Community newspaper. **Founded:** 1892. **Freq:** Weekly (Thurs.). **Print Method:** Offset. **Cols./Page:** 6. **Col. Width:** 24 nonpareils. **Col. Depth:** 294 agate lines. **Key Personnel:** Deborah Hunsaker, Editor; Charles M. Parker, Publisher; Robert L. Corder, Publisher; William N. Noll, Publisher. **USPS:** 244-360. **Subscription Rates:** $12.70 individuals; $13 out of state. **Remarks:** Accepts advertising.
Ad Rates: GLR: $.25 **Circ:** ‡900
BW: $250
PCI: $2.50

HILL CITY†, pop. 2,028.

NW KS. Graham Co. 120 mi. N. of Dodge City. Oil wells. Stock and grain farms.

11685 The Hill City Times
110 N. Pomeroy Phone: (785)421-5700
Hill City, KS 67642 Fax: (785)421-5712
Publication E-mail: times@ruraltel.net

Community newspaper. **Founded:** May 1879. **Freq:** Weekly (Wed.). **Print Method:** Offset. **Trim Size:** 13 1/2 x 21 1/2. **Cols./Page:** 6. **Col. Width:** 2 1/4 inches. **Col. Depth:** 21 1/2 inches. **Key Personnel:** Robert A. Boyd, Publisher; James Logback, Editor/Administration; Diane Boyd, Assoc. Editor. **USPS:** 245-180. **Subscription Rates:** $17 individuals in area; $20 in state; $22 out of state. **Remarks:** Accepts advertising.
Ad Rates: GLR: $.24 **Circ:** Paid 2,600
BW: $413.28 Free 50
SAU: $3.36
PCI: $3.36

HOLTON†, pop. 3,132.

NE KS. Jackson Co. 30 mi. N. of Topeka. Manufactures farm machinery. Diversified farming.

11686 The Holton Recorder
109 W. 4th Phone: (913)364-3141
Box 311 Fax: (913)364-3422
Holton, KS 66436-0311
Community newspaper. **Founded:** 1867. **Freq:** Semiweekly (Mon. and Thurs.). **Print Method:** Offset. **Trim Size:** 13 3/4 x 22 7/8. **Cols./Page:** 6. **Col. Width:** 25 nonpareils. **Col. Depth:** 294 agate lines. **Key Personnel:** David M. Powls, Editor. **Subscription Rates:** $20 individuals. **Remarks:** Accepts advertising.
Ad Rates: GLR: $.22 **Circ:** ‡4,900
BW: $415.80
4C: $640.80
PCI: $3.30

HORTON, pop. 2,130.

NE KS. Brown Co. 28 mi. NW of Atchison. Manufactures fabricated steel, cattle feed. Grain, dairy, and stock farms.

11687 Horton Headlight
133 W. 8th St. Phone: (913)486-2512
PO Box 269 Fax: (913)486-2512
Horton, KS 66439
Community newspaper. **Founded:** Oct. 1886. **Freq:** Weekly (Thurs.). **Print Method:** Offset. **Cols./Page:** 6. **Col. Width:** 13 picas. **Col. Depth:** 294 agate lines. **Key Personnel:** Ethel Foley, Publisher. **Subscription Rates:** $14.97 individuals. **Remarks:** Accepts advertising.
Ad Rates: GLR: $0.34 **Circ:** 2,200
BW: $378
4C: $428
SAU: $2.40
PCI: $2.25

HOXIE†, pop. 1,462.

NW KS. Sheridan Co. 160 mi. W. of Salina. Grain farms. Livestock.

11688 The Hoxie Sentinel
Box 78 Phone: (785)675-3321
Hoxie, KS 67740 Fax: (785)675-3421

Community newspaper. **Founded:** 1885. **Freq:** Weekly (Thurs.). **Print Method:** Offset. **Cols./Page:** 6. **Col. Width:** 12 inches. **Col. Depth:** 21 1/2 inches. **Key Personnel:** Bill Gasper, Publisher; Pam Gasper, Publisher. **ISSN:** 1041-2921. **Subscription Rates:** $19.50 individuals; $21.50 out of area; $24.00 out of state. **Remarks:** Accepts advertising.
Ad Rates: GLR: $.14 **Circ:** ‡1,800
BW: $378
PCI: $3

HUGOTON†, pop. 3,160.

SW KS. Stevens Co. 95 mi. SW of Dodge City. Ships wheat. Gas wells. Stock, irrigation, grain farms.

11689 The Hugoton Hermes
Goering Publishing Co., Inc.
522 S. Main Phone: (316)544-4321
PO Box 849 Fax: (316)544-7321
Hugoton, KS 67951
Community newspaper. **Subtitle:** The Hugoton Hermes. **Founded:** Aug. 4, 1887. **Freq:** Weekly (Thurs.). **Print Method:** Offset. **Cols./Page:** 6. **Col. Width:** 25 nonpareils. **Col. Depth:** 294 agate lines. **Key Personnel:** Sherrill Goering, Editor; Donald S. Goering, Publisher. **ISSN:** 2538-2000. **Subscription Rates:** $24 individuals out of state; $20 local. **Remarks:** Accepts advertising.
Ad Rates: BW: $600 **Circ:** Paid 2,350
SAU: $5 Free 50
PCI: $5

HUTCHINSON†, pop. 40,284.

C KS. Reno Co. On Arkansas River, 45 mi. NW of Wichita. Hutchinson Community College. Wheat storage; flour mills; salt and oil refineries; meat packing plants.

11690 Hutchinson Collegian
Hutchinson Community College
1300 N. Plum Phone: (316)665-3415
Hutchinson, KS 67501 Fax: (316)665-3310

Collegiate newspaper. **Founded:** 1926. **Freq:** Weekly (during the academic year). **Print Method:** Offset. **Trim Size:** 12 x 18 in. **Cols./Page:** 5. **Col. Width:** 2 inches. **Col. Depth:** 15 1/2 inches. **Key Personnel:** Janet Hallford, Adviser. **Subscription Rates:** Free; $2 by mail one semester.
Ad Rates: PCI: $4.50 **Circ:** Free ‡1,200

11691 The Hutchinson News
Hutchinson Publishing Co.
PO Box 190 Phone: (316)694-5740
300 W. 2nd St Fax: (316)694-5767
Hutchinson, KS 67504-0190
Free: (800)766-5740

General newspaper. **Subtitle:** The Hutchinson News. **Founded:** July 4, 1872. **Freq:** Mon.-Sun. (morn.). **Print Method:** Offset. **Trim Size:** 13 x 21 1/2. **Cols./Page:** 6. **Col. Width:** 26 nonpareils. **Col. Depth:** 301 agate lines. **Key Personnel:** Jim Bloom, Editor and Publisher, phone (316)694-5757, fax (316)694-5857, jbloom@hutchnews.com; Greg Halling, Advertising Mgr., phone (316)694-5746, halling@hutchnews.com; Mike Distelhorst, Advertising Dir., phone (316)694-5726, fax (316)662-4186, miked@hutchnews; Jay Gillispie, Circulation Dir., phone (316)694-5777, jay%HUTCH.UCCP@HAYS.dailynews.net; Rex Christner, Business Mgr., phone (316)694-5776, rac061%HUTCH.UUCP@HAYS.dailynews.net; Kathy Beshears, HR Dir., phone (316)694-5791, ksb025%HUTCH.UUCP@hays.dailynews.net; Larry Probst, Pressroom Mgr., phone (316)694-5780; Greg Beals, Postpress Mgr., phone (316)694-5781, gab070%HUTCH.UUCP@hays.dailynews.net. **Subscription Rates:** $167.40 individuals; $.50 daily; $1.25 Sunday. **Remarks:** Accepts advertising. **Online:** AOL http://members.aol.com/hutchnews/hutch.htm. **Alt. Formats:** Microform. **Feature Editors:** Karen Martinez, *Lifestyle*, phone (316)694-5741, martinez@hutchnews.com; Greg Nucifora, *News*, phone (316)694-5750, nucifora@hutchnews.com; Mary Rintoul, *City*, phone (313)694-5769, ms@southwind.net.
Ad Rates: GLR: $0.85 **Circ:** Mon.-Sat. ★**37,581**
BW: $1,759.56 Sun. ★**42,365**
4C: $2,333.56
PCI: $13.64

11692 KCVW-FM - 94.3
100 N. Main St., Ste. 402 Phone: (316)663-0943
Hutchinson, KS 67501 Fax: (316)529-0943
Free: (888)681-0943

Format: Religious. **Networks:** Business Radio; Sun Radio. **Owner:** Bott Radio Network, 10550 Barkley, Ste. 108, Overland Park, KS 66212. **Founded:** 1998. **Operating Hours:** Continuous. **ADI:** Wichita-Hutchinson, KS. **Key Personnel:** Richard P. Bott II, Vice President; Charles A. Lambert, Dir., Network Pgrm. Svcs. **Wattage:** 50,000.

KDGB-FM - See Pratt

11693 KGGG-FM - 94.7
106 N. Main Phone: (316)665-5758
Hutchinson, KS 67501 Fax: (316)665-6655
Free: (800)662-5758
E-mail: kskukggg@mindspring.com

Format: Oldies. **Networks:** ABC. **Owner:** Ad Astra Per Aspera Broadcasting Inc., at above address. **Founded:** 1995. **Operating Hours:** Continuous; 100% local. **ADI:** Wichita-Hutchinson, KS. **Key Personnel:** J.J. Jeffries, News Dir.; Alisa Blattner, Office Mgr.; Cliff C. Shank, President/General Mgr.; Greg Smith, Program Dir.; Vicki Shank, Promotions Mgr.; Mike Hill, Sales Mgr.; J.J. Jeffries, Production Mgr. **Wattage:** 20,000. **Ad Rates:** $32 for 30 seconds; $36 for 60 seconds. Combined advertising rates available with KSKU.

11694 KHCC-FM - 90.1
815 N. Walnut, Ste. 300 Phone: (316)665-3555
Hutchinson, KS 67501-6217
E-mail: webmaster@radioks.org

Format: Public Radio; News; Classical; New Age. **Networks:** National Public Radio (NPR). **Founded:** 1979. **Operating Hours:** Continuous. **ADI:** Wichita-Hutchinson, KS. **Key Personnel:** Dave Horning, General Mgr.; Patsy Terrell, Promotions Dir.; Ken Baker, Program Dir. **Wattage:** 100,000. **Ad Rates:** Noncommercial. **URL:** http://www.radioks.org.

KHCD-FM - See Salina

11695 KHUT-FM - 102.9
17th & Harding St., Box 1036 Phone: (316)662-4486
Hutchinson, KS 67504-1036 Fax: (316)662-5357

Format: Country. **Owner:** Kays Inc., at above address. **Founded:** 1972. **Operating Hours:** Continuous. **ADI:** Wichita-Hutchinson, KS. **Key Personnel:** Mark Trotman, Manager. **Wattage:** 100,000 ERP.

11696 KSKU-FM - 106.1
106 N. Main Phone: (316)665-5758
Hutchinson, KS 67501 Fax: (316)665-6655
Free: (800)662-5758
E-mail: kskukggg@mindspring.com

Format: Adult Contemporary; Top 40; Alternative/New Music/Progressive. **Networks:** Independent. **Owner:** Ad Astra per Aspera Broadcasting, Inc., at above address. **Founded:** 1968. **Formerly:** KLFQ-FM (1986). **Operating Hours:** Continuous; 100% local. **ADI:** Wichita-Hutchinson, KS. **Key Personnel:** J.J. Jeffries, News Dir.; Alisa Blattner, Office Mgr.; Cliff C. Shank, President/General Mgr.; Greg Smith, Program Dir.; Cheryl Dinwiddie, Promotions Mgr.; Mike Hill, Sales Mgr.; J.J. Jeffries, Production Mgr. **Wattage:** 100,000. **Ad Rates:** $32 for 30 seconds; $36 for 60 seconds. Combined advertising rates available with KGGG-FM.

11697 KWBW-AM - 1450
PO Box 1036 Phone: (316)662-4486
Hutchinson, KS 67504-1036 Fax: (316)662-5357

Format: Talk; Information; Sports. **Networks:** NBC; Mutual Broadcasting System. **Founded:** 1935. **Formerly:** KWBG-AM (1941). **Operating Hours:** 4 a.m.-1 a.m.; 70% network, 30% local. **ADI:** Wichita-Hutchinson, KS. **Key Personnel:** Dan Deming, Station Mgr.; Doug Moore, Sales Mgr.; Jerry Kershaw, Sports Dir. **Wattage:** 1000. **Ad Rates:** $1.75-9 for 15 seconds; $2.50-13.95 for 30 seconds; $3.50-17.95 for 60 seconds.

INDEPENDENCE†, pop. 10,598.

SE KS. Montgomery Co. 86 mi. SE of Wichita. Independence Community College. Manufactures cement, corn, wheat. Oil and gas wells.

11698 Independence Daily Reporter
320 N. 6th St. Phone: (316)331-3550
PO Box 869 Fax: (316)331-3550
Independence, KS 67301
General newspaper. **Founded:** 1881. **Freq:** Daily (eve.), Sunday (morn.). **Print Method:** Offset. **Trim Size:** 14 x 21 3/4. **Cols./Page:** 6. **Col. Width:** 2 1/16 inches. **Col. Depth:** 21 inches. **Key Personnel:** H.A. Meyer III, Editor and Publisher; Steve McBride, Advertising Mgr. **Subscription Rates:** $73.95 individuals. **Remarks:** Accepts advertising.
Ad Rates: GLR: $4.50 **Circ:** Mon.-Fri. 8,854
BW: $802.62 Sun. 9,922
4C: $997.62
PCI: $6.37

11699 The Independence News
210 W. Main Phone: (316)331-4950
Independence, KS 67301 Fax: (316)251-1905

Community newspaper. **Founded:** 1948. **Freq:** Weekly. **Print Method:** Offset. **Cols./Page:** 6. **Col. Width:** 26 nonpareils. **Col. Depth:** 294 agate lines. **Key Personnel:** John F. Vermillion, Editor and Publisher. **USPS:** 580-920. **Subscription Rates:** $25 individuals. **Remarks:** Accepts advertising.
Ad Rates: GLR: $.30 **Circ:** Paid ‡650
BW: $200 Free ‡350
4C: $400
PCI: $5

11700 KIND-AM - 1010
PO Drawer A Phone: (316)331-3000
Independence, KS 67301

Format: Full Service. **Networks:** Mutual Broadcasting System. **Owner:** Central Broadcasting, Inc., at above address. **Founded:** 1947. **Operating Hours:** 6am-10pm Mon-Fri, 7am-10pm Sat, 7 am-6pm Sun. **Key Personnel:** Nelson Rupard, Manager. **Local Programs:** *Independence High School and City Rec Sports*; *Soundtrack of Your Memories*, Ron Lee. **Wattage:** 250. **Ad Rates:** $2.85-4.05 for 30 seconds; $4.70-6.75 for 60 seconds.

11701 KIND-FM - 101.7
PO Drawer A Phone: (316)331-3000
Independence, KS 67301

Format: Full Service. **Simulcasts:** KIND-AM. **Networks:** Mutual Broadcasting System. **Owner:** Central Broadcasting, Inc., at above address. **Founded:** 1951. **Operating Hours:** 6 am-10 p.m. Mon.-Fri., 7 am-10 pm Sat., 7 am-6 pm Sun. **Key Personnel:** Nelson Rupard, Manager. **Local Programs:** *Independence High School and City Rec Sports*; *Soundtrack of Your Memories*, Ron Lee. **Wattage:** 1800. **Ad Rates:** $2.85-4.05 for 30 seconds; $4.70-6.75 for 60 seconds.

IOLA†, pop. 6,938.

SE KS. Allen Co. 100 mi. S. of Kansas City. Allen County Community College. Cement works.

11702 The Iola Register
Iola Register
302 S. Washington Phone: (316)365-2111
PO Box 767 Fax: (316)365-6289
Iola, KS 66749
Free: (800)365-1901
Publication E-mail: register@midusa.net

General newspaper. **Founded:** 1867. **Freq:** Daily (eve.). **Print Method:** Offset. **Cols./Page:** 6. **Col. Width:** 24 nonpareils. **Col. Depth:** 301 agate lines. **Key Personnel:** Emerson E. Lynn, Jr., Editor and Publisher; Mark Hastings, Advertising Dir. **Subscription Rates:** $74.08 individuals in trade by mail; $99.95 out of area; $93.50 out of state.
Ad Rates: BW: $683.70 **Circ:** Paid 4,200
PCI: $5.80 Free 85

11703 KALN-AM - 1370
PO Box 710 Phone: (316)365-3151
Iola, KS 66749

Format: Country. **Networks:** Satellite Music Network; Satellite Network News. **Founded:** 1961. **Formerly:** KIKS-AM. **Operating Hours:** Continuous. **Key Personnel:** Mike Russell, General Mgr. **Wattage:** 500. **Ad Rates:** $6 for 30 seconds; $9 for 60 seconds. $6 for 30 seconds; $9 for 60 seconds. Combined advertising rates available with KIKS-FM.

11704 KIKS-FM - 99.3
PO Box 710 Phone: (316)365-3151
Iola, KS 66749

Format: Adult Contemporary. **Networks:** Satellite Network News. **Founded:** 1977. **Operating Hours:** 6 a.m.-12 midnight. **Key Personnel:** Mike Russell, General Mgr. **Wattage:** 3000. **Ad Rates:** $4 for 15 seconds; $6 for 30 seconds; $9 for 60 seconds. $4 for 15 seconds; $6 for 30 seconds; $9 for 60 seconds. Combined advertising rates available with KALN-AM.

JETMORE†, pop. 862.

C KS. Hodgeman Co. Livestock raising, rye.

11705 The Jetmore Republican
PO Box 337 Phone: (316)357-8316
Jetmore, KS 67854 Fax: (316)357-8464

Community newspaper. **Founded:** 1878. **Freq:** Weekly (Wed.). **Print Method:** Offset. **Trim Size:** 13 x 21 1/2. **Cols./Page:** 6. **Col. Width:** 24 nonpareils. **Col. Depth:** 21 1/2 inches. **Key Personnel:** Jerry Buxton, Editor. **Subscription Rates:** $18.88 individuals; $20 out of state. **Remarks:** Accepts advertising.
Ad Rates: GLR: $0.49 **Circ:** Paid ‡1,110
BW: $374.10 Free ‡20
SAU: $2.90
PCI: $2.90

JOHNSON

11706 The Johnson Pioneer
103 N. Main Phone: (316)492-6244
PO Box 10
Johnson, KS 67855
Community newspaper. **Freq:** Weekly (Thurs.). **Print Method:** Offset. **Cols./Page:** 8. **Col. Width:** 9 picas. **Col. Depth:** 20 1/2 inches. **Key Personnel:** Ronda Ford, Editor and Publisher. **Subscription Rates:** $16.94 individuals; $19.06 out of area. **Remarks:** Accepts advertising.
Ad Rates: BW: $588 **Circ:** ‡1,100
PCI: $3.50

JUNCTION CITY†, pop. 19,305.

EC KS. Geary Co. On Kansas River, 62 mi. W. of Topeka. Fort Riley (military post). Feed mills; foundry. Grain, stock, and dairy farms.

11707 Daily Union
Montgomery Communications, Inc.
222 W. 6th St. Phone: (785)762-5000
Junction City, KS 66441 Fax: (785)762-4584
Free: (800)657-6096
Publication E-mail: dailyu@jc.net

General newspaper. **Founded:** Sept. 12, 1861. **Freq:** Daily (eve.), Sunday (morn.). **Print Method:** Offset. **Cols./Page:** 6. **Col. Width:** 26 nonpareils. **Col. Depth:** 301 agate lines. **Key Personnel:** John G. Montgomery, Editor and Publisher; Patrick Keefe, Advertising Mgr. **ISSN:** 0745-743X. **Subscription Rates:** $126 individuals. **Remarks:** Accepts advertising.
Ad Rates: BW: $1,264.20 **Circ:** Mon.-Fri. 6,455
4C: $1,654.20 Sun. 7,099
PCI: $9.80

11708 Daily Union Plus
Montgomery Communications, Inc.
PO Box 129
Junction City, KS 66441
Publication E-mail: dailyu@jc.net

Shopper. **Founded:** 1861. **Freq:** Weekly (Wed.). **Print Method:** Offset. **Cols./Page:** 6. **Col. Width:** 26 nonpareils. **Col. Depth:** 301 agate lines. **Key Personnel:** John G. Montgomery, Editor and Publisher; Patrick Keefe, Advertising Mgr. **Subscription Rates:** Free.
Ad Rates: BW: $761.10 **Circ:** Free ‡7,803
4C: $1,151.10
PCI: $5.90

11709 Ft. Riley Post
Montgomery Communications, Inc.
222 W. 6th St. Phone: (785)762-5000
Junction City, KS 66441 Fax: (785)762-4584
Free: (800)657-6096
Publication E-mail: dailyu@jc.net

Military community newspaper. **Founded:** 1959. **Freq:** Weekly (Fri.). **Print Method:** Offset. **Cols./Page:** 6. **Col. Width:** 26 nonpareils. **Col. Depth:** 301 agate lines. **Key Personnel:** John Montgomery, Editor and Publisher; Patrick Keefe, Advertising Mgr. **Subscription Rates:** $20 individuals.
Ad Rates: BW: $1,831.80 **Circ:** Paid ‡250
4C: $2,256.80 Free ‡7,391
PCI: $14.20

11710 KJCK-AM - 1420
Box 789 Phone: (913)762-5525
Junction City, KS 66441 Fax: (913)762-5387
E-mail: radio@jc.net

Format: Contemporary Country. **Networks:** ABC. **Founded:** 1949. **Operating Hours:** Continuous; 10% network, 90% local. **ADI:** Topeka, KS. **Key Personnel:** Daryl W. Gatza, General Mgr.; Mark Ediger, Operations Mgr.; Darryl Gatza, Sales Mgr. **Wattage:** 1000. **Ad Rates:** $13.20 for 30 seconds; $19.80 for 60 seconds.

11711 KJCK-FM - 94.5
Box 789 Phone: (785)762-5525
Junction City, KS 66441 Fax: (785)762-5387
E-mail: kjck@flinthills.com

Format: Contemporary Hit Radio (CHR). **Founded:** 1965. **Operating Hours:** Continuous; 10% network, 90% local. **ADI:** Topeka, KS. **Key Personnel:** Daryl W. Gatza, Contact; Mark Ediger, Operations Dir.; J.J. Davis, Program Dir. **Wattage:** 100,000. **Ad Rates:** $11.88 for 15 seconds; $6-15.84 for 30 seconds; $7.50-19.80 for 60 seconds. Combined advertising rates available with KJCK-AM, KQLA-FM.

11712 KQLA-FM - 103.5
PO Box 789 Phone: (913)238-1035
Junction City, KS 66441-0789 Fax: (913)537-0110
E-mail: kqla@kansas.net

Format: Adult Contemporary; Classical. **Networks:** CBS. **Owner:** Kaw Valley Broadcasting Co., at above address, (913)587-0103, Fax: (913)776-0110. **Founded:** 1986. **Operating Hours:** Continuous; 5% network, 95% local. **ADI:** Topeka, KS. **Key Personnel:** Jeff Wichman, News Dir.; J.J. Davis, Program Dir.; Ed Klimek, General Mgr.; Betty Rader, Business Mgr. **Wattage:** 50,000. **Ad Rates:** $6-10 for 15 seconds; $9-19 for 30 seconds; $10-22 for 30 seconds.

KANSAS CITY†, pop. 161,087.

NW KS. Wyandotte Co. At junction of Missouri and Kansas Rivers, adjacent to Kansas City, MO. Central Baptist Theological Seminary; School of Medicine of University of Kansas. Manufactures fiberglass, cement, paper products, chemicals, brick, tile. Auto assembly plant; oil refining; canning; flour and grain milling. Livestock markets and meat packing plants. Ships corn, wheat, sorghum, and oats.

11713 The Advocate
Kansas City Kansas Community College
7250 State Ave. Phone: (913)334-1100
Kansas City, KS 66112-3003 Fax: (913)596-9606

Collegiate newspaper (tabloid). **Founded:** 1969. **Freq:** Semimonthly. **Print Method:** Offset. **Trim Size:** 11 x 13. **Cols./Page:** 4. **Col. Width:** 2 5/16 inches. **Col. Depth:** 16 inches. **Key Personnel:** Jamie Zimmerman, Editor; Kim Einhellig, Advertising Mgr.; CJ Janovy, Advisor. **Subscription Rates:** Free. **Remarks:** Color advertising not accepted.
Ad Rates: GLR: $.30 **Circ:** Free ‡2,000
BW: $135
PCI: $5

11714 Boilermaker Reporter
International Brotherhood of Boilermakers, Iron Shipbuilders, Blacksmiths, Forgers, and Helpers
753 State Ave., No. 570 Phone: (913)371-2640
Kansas City, KS 66101-2511
Newspaper covering trade and union membership news. **Founded:** 1961. **Freq:** Bimonthly. **Print Method:** Web offset. **Trim Size:** 11 x 17. **Cols./Page:** 4. **Col. Width:** 14 picas. **Col. Depth:** 89 picas. **Key Personnel:** Donald Caswell, Managing Editor. **Subscription Rates:** Free to qualified subscribers. **Remarks:** Advertising not accepted.
Circ: Non-paid 85,000

11715 Focus on Autism and Other Developmental Disabilities
PRO-ED, Inc.
Dept. of Special Ed. Phone: (913)588-5955
University of Kansas Medical School Fax: (913)588-5942
39th & Rainbow Blvd.
Kansas City, KS 66160-7335
Publisher E-mail: proedrd2@aol.com

Journal provides practical management, treatment, and planning strategies for professionals working with people with autism and developmental disabilities. **Founded:** 1995. **Freq:** Quarterly. **Print Method:** Offset. **Trim Size:** 8 3/8 x 10 7/8. **Cols./Page:** 3. **Col. Width:** 2 1/4 inches. **Col. Depth:** 9 1/4 inches. **Key Personnel:** Richard Simpson, Editor, rsimpson@kumc.edu; Donald D. Hammill, Publisher; Judith K. Voress, Director. **ISSN:** 0887-1566. **Subscription Rates:** $39 individuals; $85 institutions; $95 other countries. **Remarks:** Accepts advertising. **Formerly:** Focus on Autistic Behavior.
Ad Rates: BW: $400 **Circ:** Paid ‡1600

11716 Journal of Pharmacology & Experimental Therapeutics
American Society for Pharmacology and Experimental Therapeutics
KUMC Dept. of Pharm., Tox. & Ther. Phone: (913)588-7533
3901 Rainbow Blvd. Fax: (913)588-7373
Kansas City, KS 66106-7424
Publisher E-mail: aspetinfo@faseb.org

Medical and pharmaceutical journal. **Founded:** 1909. **Freq:** Monthly. **Print Method:** Offset. **Trim Size:** 8 3/8 x 10 7/8. **Cols./Page:** 2. **Col. Width:** 32 nonpareils. **Col. Depth:** 119 agate lines. **Key Personnel:** S.J. Enna, Ph.D., Editor; Frances Yates, Advertising Coord. **Subscription Rates:** $220 individuals; $315 individuals other countries; $505 institutions; $600 institutions, other countries. **Remarks:** Accepts advertising. **URL:** http://www.jpet.org. **Alt. Formats:** Mailing labels.
Ad Rates: BW: $675 **Circ:** Paid ‡2,320
4C: $1,415 Non-paid ‡221

11717 Kansas City Kansan
901 N. 8th St. Phone: (913)371-4300
Kansas City, KS 66101 Fax: (913)342-8620

General newspaper. **Founded:** 1921. **Freq:** Tues.-Fri. (eve.); Sun. (morn.). **Print Method:** Offset. **Cols./Page:** 6. **Col. Width:** 24 nonpareils. **Col. Depth:** 301 agate lines. **Key Personnel:** William Epperheimer, Publisher; Patrick Lowry, Advertising Mgr. **USPS:** 290-160. **Subscription Rates:** $62.50 individuals. **Remarks:** Accepts advertising.
Ad Rates: SAU: $11.25 **Circ:** Mon.-Fri. ‡11,027
Sun. ‡12,100

11718 Kansas City Wyandotte Echo
PO Box 2305
Kansas City, KS 66110

Community newspaper. **Freq:** Weekly (Tues.). **Cols./Page:** 5. **Col. Width:** 2 inches. **Col. Depth:** 18 inches. **Key Personnel:** Linda Schye, Editor; Roberta Peterson, Publisher.
Circ: 1,600

11719 The Leaven
12615 Parallel Pkwy. Phone: (913)721-1570
Kansas City, KS 66109 Fax: (913)721-5276
Publication E-mail: leaven@sky.net

Catholic newspaper. **Subtitle:** Official newspaper of the Catholic Archidiocese of Kansas City in Kansas. **Founded:** 1939. **Freq:** Weekly. **Print Method:** Offset. **Cols./Page:** 4. **Col. Width:** 2 1/4 inches. **Key Personnel:** Archbishop James P. Keleher, Publisher; Father Mark Goldasich, Editor; Buffy DeWolf, Advertising Mgr.; Anita McSorley, Associate Editor; Joe Bollig, Senior Reporter; Todd Habiger, Production Mgr. **ISSN:** 0194-9799. **Subscription Rates:** $12 individuals. **Remarks:** Accepts advertising. **Formerly:** Eastern Kansas Register.
Ad Rates: GLR: $8 **Circ:** Paid ‡47,453
BW: $640 Non-paid ‡384
PCI: $13

11720 The Record
The Record Publications
3414 Strong Ave. Phone: (913)362-1988
Kansas City, KS 66106 Fax: (913)362-1989

Newspaper (tabloid). **Founded:** 1887. **Freq:** Weekly (Wed.). **Print Method:** Web offset. Uses mats. **Trim Size:** 11 x 17. **Cols./Page:** 5. **Col. Width:** 22 nonpareils. **Col. Depth:** 224 agate lines. **Key Personnel:** Jon A. Males, Editor and Publisher, ejon123@aol.com. **Subscription Rates:** $10.55 by mail. **Remarks:** Accepts advertising.
Ad Rates: SAU: $6.50 **Circ:** ‡1,100

11721 Suburban Advertiser
Wyandotte West Communications, Inc.
7735 Washington Ave. Phone: (913)788-5565
Kansas City, KS 66112 Fax: (913)788-9812
Publisher E-mail: wyest@toto.net

Shopping guide. **Founded:** Sept. 28, 1978. **Freq:** Weekly (Wed.). **Print Method:** Offset. **Trim Size:** 11 x 17. **Cols./Page:** 4. **Col. Width:** 13.6 picas. **Col. Depth:** 16 inches. **Key Personnel:** Murrel W. Bland, Publisher; Barbara Imhoof, Advertising Mgr. **Subscription Rates:** Free. **Remarks:** Accepts advertising.
Ad Rates: GLR: $.76 **Circ:** Free **12,300**
BW: $680.96
4C: $1,080.96
SAU: $10.64
PCI: $10.64

11722 Topics in Early Childhood Special Education
PRO-ED, Inc.
Juniper Gardens Children's Project Phone: (913)321-3143
650 Minnesota Fax: (913)371-8522
Kansas City, KS 66101
Publisher E-mail: proedrd2@aol.com

Magazine for special education professionals. Provides information on research and teaching practices for young children with disabilities and their families. **Founded:** 1981. **Freq:** Quarterly. **Print Method:** Offset. **Trim Size:** 8 3/8 x 10 7/8. **Cols./Page:** 2. **Col. Width:** 3 3/8 inches. **Col. Depth:** 9 1/8 inches. **Key Personnel:** Judith J. Carta, Editor, carta@kuhub.cc.ukans.edu; Donald D. Hammill, Publisher; Judith K. Voress, Director. **ISSN:** 0271-1214. **Subscription Rates:** $39; $95 industry; $95 other countries. **Remarks:** Accepts advertising. **Online:** EBSCO. **Alt. Formats:** Microform.
Ad Rates: BW: $100 **Circ:** Paid 2,263
Non-paid 132

11723 Wyandotte County Shopper
Kansas City Kansan
901 N. 8th St. Phone: (913)371-4300
Kansas City, KS 66101 Fax: (913)342-8620

Shopper. **Founded:** Mar. 1934. **Freq:** Weekly (Wed.). **Print Method:** Offset. **Cols./Page:** 9. **Col. Width:** 1 1/4 inches. **Col. Depth:** 21 1/2 inches. **Key Personnel:** William Epperheimer, Publisher; Joie Mellenbrach, Advertising Dir. **Subscription Rates:** Free; $8.40 by mail. **Remarks:** Accepts advertising.
Ad Rates: GLR: $1.35 **Circ:** Free ‡46,000
BW: $1,444.80
4C: $1,744.80
PCI: $12

11724 Wyandotte West
Wyandotte West Communications, Inc.
7735 Washington Ave. Phone: (913)788-5565
Kansas City, KS 66112 Fax: (913)788-9812
Publisher E-mail: wyest@toto.net

Community newspaper. **Founded:** 1968. **Freq:** Weekly (Thurs.). **Print Method:** Offset. **Trim Size:** 11 x 17. **Cols./Page:** 4. **Col. Width:** 13.6 picas. **Col. Depth:** 16 inches. **Key Personnel:** Murrel W. Bland, Editor and Publisher; Barbara Imhoof, Advertising Mgr. **USPS:** 693-720. **Subscription Rates:** $19.49 individuals. **Alt. Formats:** Microform.
Ad Rates: GLR: $.76 **Circ: 2,547**
BW: $680.96
4C: $1,080.96
SAU: $10.64
PCI: $10.64

11725 KCNW-AM - 1380
4535 Metropolitan Phone: (913)236-5269
Kansas City, KS 66106 Fax: (913)236-9583
Free: (888)229-8530

Format: Talk; News. **Owner:** Catholic Radio Network, 8910 University Center Lane Ste. 130, San Diego, CA 92122-1085, (619)784-6900, Fax: (619)338-4318. **Founded:** Nov. 1998. **Formerly:** KUDL-AM; Children's Broadcasting Corporation. **Operating Hours:** 6 a.m.-midnight. **ADI:** Kansas City, MO (Lawrence, KS). **Key Personnel:** Jeff Bowles, General Mgr.; Shelley Hikson, Business Mgr. **Wattage:** 2500. **Ad Rates:** $25 for 30 seconds; $30 for 60 seconds.

11726 KFEZ-AM - 1340
4121 Minnesota Ave. Phone: (913)342-1600
Kansas City, KS 66102 Fax: (913)342-1351

Format: Music of Your Life. **Networks:** Jones Satellite. **Owner:** Bill Johnson, at above address. **Founded:** 1925. **Formerly:** KCKN-AM; KNHN-AM. **Operating Hours:** Continuous. **ADI:** Kansas City, MO (Lawrence, KS). **Key Personnel:** William R. Johnson, General Mgr.; Ed Treese, Chief Engineer; Greg Funk, Program Dir. **Local Programs:** *Civil Right*, Ron Freeman, (913)5243733; *Civil Rights*, Ron Freeman, (816)524-3733; *Fogel and Shanin*, Judy Harper; *KC Law*, Steve Mirakian, (913)342-1600. **Wattage:** 1000.

11727 KPHN-AM - 1190
4121 Minnesota Ave. Phone: (913)342-1600
Kansas City, KS 66102 Fax: (913)342-1351
Free: (800)266-1190

Format: News; Talk. **Networks:** CNN Radio; Westwood One Radio; Mutual Broadcasting System. **Founded:** 1970. **Formerly:** KAYQ-AM (1979); KJLA-AM (1992); KFEZ-AM. **Operating Hours:** Continuous. **ADI:** Kansas City, MO (Lawrence, KS). **Key Personnel:** Bill Johnson, General Mgr.; Teresa Sparkman, Sales Mgr.; Paul Knauer, Operations Mgr.; Carol Fraiser, Traffic Dir. **Wattage:** 5000 day; 250 night. **Ad Rates:** $30 for 60 seconds.

11728 KSMO-TV - 62
10 E. Cambridge Circle Dr., Ste. 300 Phone: (913)621-6262
Kansas City, KS 66103-1342 Fax: (913)621-4703

Format: Commercial TV. **Founded:** 1983. **Formerly:** KEKR-TV (1986); KZKC-TV. **Operating Hours:** Continuous. **ADI:** Kansas City, MO (Lawrence, KS). **Key Personnel:** Gloria Rudd, General Sales Mgr.; Joel Minsker, Nat'l Sales Mgr.; Melissa Gaines, General Mgr.; Matt Rankin, Program Dir.; Rick Borkowski, Promotions Mgr., rborkows@ksmo.sbgnet.com. **Wattage:** Video 2,183,000w; Audio 218,000w.

KINGMAN

11729 Kingman Journal
Courier/Journal, Inc.
140 N. Main Phone: (316)532-3151
PO Box 353 Fax: (316)532-3152
Kingman, KS 67068
Community newspaper. **Freq:** Weekly (Tues.). **Cols./Page:** 6. **Col. Width:** 14 picas. **Col. Depth:** 21 1/2 inches. **Key Personnel:** Robert McQuin, Editor and Publisher.
Circ: 3,700

11730 Kingman Leader-Courier
Courier/Journal, Inc.
140 N. Main Phone: (316)532-3151
PO Box 353 Fax: (316)532-3152
Kingman, KS 67068
Community newspaper. **Freq:** Weekly (Fri.). **Cols./Page:** 6. **Col. Width:** 14 picas. **Col. Depth:** 21 1/2 inches. **Key Personnel:** Robert McQuin, Editor and Publisher.
Circ: 3,700

KINSLEY†, pop. 2,000.

NW KS. Edwards Co. 38 mi. ENE of Dodge City. Flour mills, grain, and stock farming.

11731 Kline's TV and Two Way
110 E. 10th St. Phone: (316)659-3527
Kinsley, KS 67547

Owner: Don Kline, at above address. **Key Personnel:** Richard Kline, Contact. **Cities Served:** Offerle and Lewis, KS.

KIOWA, pop. 1,409.

S KS. Barber Co. 90 mi. SW of Wichita. Manufactures farm implements. Grain, stock, and poultry farms.

11732 News
Kiowa News
614 Main St. Phone: (316)825-4229
Kiowa, KS 67070 Fax: (316)825-4229

Newspaper. **Founded:** 1889. **Freq:** Weekly (Thurs.). **Print Method:** Offset. **Cols./Page:** 8. **Col. Width:** 21 nonpareils. **Col. Depth:** 301 agate lines. **Key Personnel:** Rex Zimmerman, Editor; Kenneth Leu, Publisher. **Subscription Rates:** $12 individuals. **Remarks:** Accepts advertising.
Ad Rates: GLR: $.17 **Circ:** 1,650

LA CROSSE†, pop. 1,618.

WC KS. Rush Co. 90 mi. NW of Hutchinson. Oil and gas wells. Diversified agriculture.

11733 The Rush County News
112 W. 8th Phone: (785)222-2555
Box 60 Fax: (785)222-2557
La Crosse, KS 67548
Weekly newspaper. **Founded:** 1897. **Freq:** Weekly (Thurs.). **Print Method:** Offset. Uses slicks. **Trim Size:** 13 3/4 x 22 3/4. **Cols./Page:** 6. **Col. Width:** 12 1/2 picas. **Col. Depth:** 21 1/2 inches. **Key Personnel:** Mary Engel, Publisher; Tim Engel, Editor. **Subscription Rates:** $21.50 individuals; $26.50 out of state; $.50 single issue. **Remarks:** Accepts advertising.
Ad Rates: GLR: $.24 **Circ:** Paid ‡2,100
BW: $535.35 Free ‡200
4C: $835.35
SAU: $3.95
PCI: $3.95

LAKE QUIVERA

11734 Leawood Sun, Blue Valley Edition
Sun Publications, Inc.
7373 W. 107th St. Phone: (913)648-4620
Overland Park, KS 66212-2547 Fax: (913)381-1402

Newspaper. **Founded:** Jan. 1, 1950. **Freq:** Semiweekly (Wed. and Fri.). **Print Method:** Offset. **Cols./Page:** 8. **Col. Width:** 21 nonpareils. **Col. Depth:** 292 agate lines. **Key Personnel:**

Jack Lovelace, Editor; Steve Rose, Publisher; Jo Stapleton, Advertising Manager. **Subscription Rates:** Free. **Remarks:** Accepts advertising.
Ad Rates: SAU: $24.75 **Circ:** Combined ‡112,441
PCI: $34.35

LAKIN†, pop. 1,827.

SW KS. Kearny Co. On Arkansas River, 70 mi. NW of Dodge City. Gas and oil wells.

11735 Independent
PO Box 45 Phone: (316)355-6162
Lakin, KS 67860-0045
Local newspaper. **Founded:** 1885. **Freq:** Weekly (Thurs.). **Print Method:** Offset. **Cols./Page:** 6. **Col. Width:** 12 picas. **Col. Depth:** 21 inches. **Key Personnel:** Monte E. Canfield, Editor and Publisher. **USPS:** 303-380. **Subscription Rates:** $18.40 individuals. **Remarks:** Accepts advertising.
Ad Rates: GLR: $.26 **Circ:** ‡1,705
PCI: $3.64

11736 KSWK-TV - 3
Box 9, 6th & Elm St. Phone: (913)483-6990
Bunker Hill, KS 67626 Fax: (913)483-4605
E-mail: shptv@pbs.org

Format: Public TV. **Networks:** Public Broadcasting Service (PBS). **Founded:** 1982. **Operating Hours:** 7a.m.-midnight. **ADI:** Wichita-Hutchinson, KS. **Key Personnel:** David M. Wilson, CEO/Gen. Mgr.; Lloyd Mintzmyer, Dir. of Engineering; Mary Pat Waymaster, Dir. of Broadcasting; Kristy Nyp, Public Info. Dir.; Malinda Walker, Membership Dir. **Local Programs:** *High Plains Outdoors*, Grace Blehm; *Kansas Arts Today*, Les Kinderknecht; *The KS Legistlature*, Grace Blehm. **Wattage:** 100,000. **Ad Rates:** Noncommercial; underwriting available. **URL:** http://www.pbs.org/shptv.

LARNED

11737 KGTR-FM - 96.7
121 1/2 W. 5th Phone: (316)285-2127
Larned, KS 67550 Fax: (316)285-2102

Format: Oldies. **Networks:** Kansas Information; Kansas Agriculture; Satellite Music Network. **Owner:** Good Star Broadcasting LLC, 1660 W. Tyler Rd., Hutchinson, KS 67501, (316)729-8011, Fax: (316)729-9914. **Founded:** 1965. **Formerly**: KQDF-FM (1995). **Operating Hours:** Continuous. **ADI:** Wichita-Hutchinson, KS. **Key Personnel:** Danny Cormack, Operations Mgr.; Greg Schmidt, General Mgr.; Sharon Williams, Traffic/Sales. **Wattage:** 3000. **Ad Rates:** $15 per unit. KNNS-AM.

11738 KNNS-AM - 1510
121 1/2 W. 5th Phone: (316)285-2127
Larned, KS 67550 Fax: (316)285-2102

Format: Middle-of-the-Road (MOR). **Networks:** Satellite Network News; Music of Your Life/Fairwest. **Owner:** Goodstar Broadcasting LLC, 1660 N. Tyler Rd., Hutchinson, KS 67501, (316)729-8011, Fax: (316)729-9914. **Founded:** 1963. **Formerly**: KANS-AM. **Operating Hours:** Continuous. **ADI:** Wichita-Hutchinson, KS. **Key Personnel:** Greg Schmidt, General Mgr.; Danny Cormack, Program Dir.; Sharon Williams, Traffic/Sales. **Wattage:** 1000. **Ad Rates:** $15 per unit.

LAWRENCE†, pop. 52,738.

E KS. Douglas Co. On Kansas River, 26 mi. SE of Topeka. University of Kansas; Haskell Institute (Indian). Manufactures railroad and truck air brakes, paper shipping cartons, fertilizers, chemicals, explosives, precision instruments, mobile homes, electronics equipment. Pharmaceutical research. Diversified farming.

11739 American Journal of Cosmetic Surgery
Allen Marketing and Management
PO Box 1897 Phone: (913)843-1235
Lawrence, KS 66044 Fax: (913)843-1274
Free: (800)627-0629
Publication E-mail: aacs@sba.com

Journal for professionals in cosmetic surgery. **Founded:** 1984. **Freq:** Quarterly. **Trim Size:** 8 1/2 x 11. **Key Personnel:** Melvin Shiffman, Editor-in-Chief; Jeffrey Knezovich, Executive Dir., phone (312)527-6713, fax (312)644-1815, jknezovich@sba.com; Onkar Sandal, Advertising. **ISSN:** 0748-8068. **Subscription Rates:** $100; $120 other countries; $18 back issues. **Remarks:** Accepts advertising. **Online:** Allen Press. **URL:** http://www.cosmeticsurgery.org.
Ad Rates: BW: $675 **Circ:** ‡3,000
4C: $1,500

11740 The Baldwin Ledger
The Lawrence Business Ledger
2951 Four Wheel Dr. Phone: (785)749-0006
Lawrence, KS 66047-3145 Fax: (785)749-0065
Publication E-mail: info@lbizl.com

Community newspaper. **Founded:** 1883. **Freq:** Weekly (Thurs.). **Print Method:** Offset. **Cols./Page:** 4. **Col. Width:** 2.45 inches. **Col. Depth:** 224 agate lines. **Key Personnel:** Chad Lawhorn, Publisher, chad@lbizl.com. **USPS:** 040-540. **Subscription Rates:** $35.13 individuals; $40.21 out of state. **Remarks:** Advertising not accepted for alcohol and tobacco products. **Alt. Formats:** CD-ROM. **Formerly**: Tele Graphics.
Ad Rates: GLR: $.47 **Circ:** Paid ‡3,500
BW: $896
4C: $400
SAU: $12.50
PCI: $14

11741 The Bulletin of Historical Research in Music Education
University of Kansas
311 Baily Hall Phone: (785)864-9638
Lawrence, KS 66045-2344 Fax: (785)864-5076

Scholarly journal covering music education history. **Founded:** July 1980. **Freq:** 3/year. **Print Method:** xerox. **Trim Size:** 7 x 8 1/2. **Cols./Page:** 1. **Col. Width:** 5 inches. **Col. Depth:** 6 1/4 inches. **Key Personnel:** George N. Heller, Editor, gnhkumus@falcon.cc.ukans.edu. **ISSN:** 0739-5639. **Subscription Rates:** $20 individuals. **Remarks:** Advertising not accepted.
Circ: Combined 227

11742 Chemical Times & Trends
Allen Press
PO Box 1897 Phone: (785)843-1221
Lawrence, KS 66044 Fax: (785)843-1274
Free: (800)627-0629

Journal serving chemists. **Founded:** 1977. **Freq:** Quarterly. **Print Method:** Offset. **Trim Size:** 8 1/2 x 11. **Cols./Page:** 3. **Col. Width:** 27 nonpareils. **Col. Depth:** 140 agate lines. **Key Personnel:** Connie Neuman, Editor; Ralph Engel, Publisher. **ISSN:** 0149-2381. **Subscription Rates:** $24 U.S. and Canada; $36 other countries. **Remarks:** Accepts advertising.
Ad Rates: BW: $985 **Circ:** ‡7,500
4C: $1,810

11743 Evolution
Allen Press
PO Box 1897 Phone: (785)843-1221
Lawrence, KS 66044 Fax: (785)843-1274
Free: (800)627-0629

Scholarly journal addressing all aspects of evolution, selection, and fitness. **Founded:** 1947. **Freq:** 6/year. **Print Method:** Offset. **Trim Size:** 8 1/2 x 11. **Cols./Page:** 2. **Col. Width:** 33 nonpareils. **Key Personnel:** Therese Markow, Editor; Sharon Kindall, Customer Svc. Rep.; Robert Kerley, Association Mgr., rkerley@allenpress.com. **ISSN:** 0014-3820. **Subscription Rates:** $170 U.S.; $180 other countries. **Remarks:** Color advertising not accepted. **URL:** http://www.lsvl.la.asu.edu/evolution/.
Ad Rates: BW: $350 **Circ:** (Not Reported)

11744 First Intensity
PO Box 665 Phone: (785)749-1501
Lawrence, KS 66044
Publication E-mail: leechapman@aol.com

Magazine containing poetry and literature. **Subtitle:** A Magazine of New Writing. **Founded:** Oct. 1993. **Freq:** Semiannual. **Print Method:** Offset. **Trim Size:** 6 x 9. **Cols./Page:** 1. **Col. Width:** 4 1/4 inches. **Col. Depth:** 7 1/2 inches. **Key Personnel:** Lee Chapman, Editor. **Subscription Rates:** $17 individuals; $9 single issue. **Remarks:** Accepts advertising.
Ad Rates: BW: $150 **Circ:** Paid ‡250

11745 Journal of Dramatic Theory and Criticism
Hall Center for the Humanities
211 Watkins Home Phone: (913)864-4798
Lawrence, KS 66045 Fax: (913)864-3884

Academic theatre journal. **Founded:** 1984. **Freq:** Semiannual. **Key Personnel:** John Gronbeck-Tedesco, Editor. **Subscription Rates:** $15 individuals; $25 institutions; $10 students.

11746 Journal of Social and Clinical Psychology
Guilford Publications, Inc.
Dept. of Psychology Phone: (785)864-9839
University of Kansas Fax: (785)864-5696
Fraser Hall
Lawrence, KS 66045
Publication E-mail: staff@guilford.com
Publisher E-mail: info@guilford.com

Journal featuring experimental social and clinical research. **Founded:** 1982. **Freq:** Quarterly. **Print Method:** Offset. **Trim Size:** 6 x 9. **Cols./Page:** 1. **Col. Width:** 72 nonpareils. **Col. Depth:** 126 agate lines. **Key Personnel:** C.R. Snyder, Editor, phone (913)864-4121, crsynder@kuhub.cc.unkans.edu. **ISSN:** 0736-7236. **Subscription Rates:** $45 individuals; $67 other countries; $165 institutions; $187 institutions, other countries; $10 single issue. **Remarks:** Accepts advertising.
Ad Rates: BW: $212 **Circ:** 700

11747 Journal of the Torrey Botanical Society
Torrey Botanical Club
Attn: Dana Floria Free: (800)627-0629
PO Box 1897
Lawrence, KS 66044
Publisher E-mail: dforio@allenpress.com

Scientific journal presenting original research papers in all fields of classical and experimental botany. **Founded:** 1870. **Freq:** Quarterly. **Print Method:** Offset. **Trim Size:** 6 3/4 x 10. **Cols./Page:** 2. **Col. Width:** 32 nonpareils. **Col. Depth:** 100 agate lines. **ISSN:** 0040-9618. **Subscription Rates:** $45; $50 other countries. **Former name**: Bulletin of the Torrey Botanical Club.
Ad Rates: BW: $350 **Circ:** Combined ‡1,483

11748 Journal-World
609 New Hampshire St. Phone: (913)843-1000
PO Box 888 Fax: (913)832-7207
Lawrence, KS 66044-0888
Free: (800)578-8748
Publication E-mail: webmaster@ljworld.com; news@ljworld.com

General newspaper. **Founded:** 1857. **Freq:** Daily mornings. **Print Method:** Offset. **Trim Size:** 13 3/8 x 22. **Cols./Page:** 6. **Col. Width:** 26 nonpareils. **Col. Depth:** 301 agate lines. **Key Personnel:** Dolph C. Simons, Jr., Editor and Publisher, fax (913)8327207. **Subscription Rates:** $157 individuals; $107.25 out of area. **Remarks:** Accepts advertising. **URL:** http://www.ljworld.com. **Alt. Formats:** Microform.
Ad Rates: BW: $1,921.50 **Circ:** Mon.-Sat. ★**19,202**
4C: $2,171.50 Sun. ★**20,307**
PCI: $15.25

11749 Kansas Alumni
University of Kansas Alumni Association
1266 Oread Ave. Phone: (913)864-4760
Lawrence, KS 66044-3100 Fax: (913)864-5397

University alumni magazine (tabloid). **Founded:** 1902. **Freq:** 8/year (during the academic year). **Print Method:** Offset. **Trim Size:** 11 1/2 x 16. **Cols./Page:** 4. **Col. Width:** 28 nonpareils. **Col. Depth:** 171 agate lines. **Key Personnel:** Jennifer Jackson Sanner, Editor; Fred B. Williams, Publisher. **ISSN:** 0745-3345. **Subscription Rates:** $25 individuals.
Circ: Paid ‡30,000
Non-paid ‡1,500

11750 Latin American Theatre Review
University of Kansas
107 Lippincott Hall Phone: (785)864-4213
Lawrence, KS 66045 Fax: (785)864-3800
Publisher E-mail: latamst@kuhub.cc.ukans.edu

Journal covering Spanish and Portuguese theatre in the U.S. **Founded:** 1967. **Freq:** Semiannual. **Key Personnel:** George Woodyard, Editor, phone (785)864-3851, woodyard@lark.cc.ukans.edu. **ISSN:** 0023-8813. **Subscription Rates:** $20 individuals; $40 institutions; $10 single issue; $20 single issue institutions. **Remarks:** Accepts advertising.
Circ: Paid 1,100

11751 Model for Process in the Soil
Catena Verlag
PO Box 1897 Phone: (913)843-1221
Lawrence, KS 66044-8897 Fax: (913)843-1274

Journal concerning the modelling of the micro- and macro-scale processes in the systems of the geo-biosphere. **Founded:** 1991. **Freq:** Quarterly. **Key Personnel:** Y. Mualem, Editor. **ISSN:** 0938-9563. **Subscription Rates:** $132. **Formerly**: Modelling of Geo-Biosphere Processes.

11752 Mycologia
Mycological Society of America
PO Box 1897
Lawrence, KS 66044-8897

Official journal of the Mycological Society of America. Features primary research and review articles on fungi and lichens (English and Latin). **Founded:** 1909. **Freq:** Bimonthly. **Print Method:** Offset. **Trim Size:** 8.5 x 11. **Cols./Page:** 21. **Col. Width:** 16 nonpareils. **Col. Depth:** 112 agate lines. **Key Personnel:** Dr. David Griffin, Editor-in-Chief, phone (315)470-6744, fax (315)470-6794, mycology@mailbox.syr.edu. **ISSN:** 0027-5514. **Subscription Rates:** $128; $139 other countries.
Ad Rates: BW: $600 **Circ:** ‡2,100

11753 Sys Admin
Miller Freeman, Inc.
1601 W. 23rd St., Ste. 200 Phone: (913)841-1631
Lawrence, KS 66046 Fax: (913)841-2624
Publication E-mail: saletter@mfi.com

Magazine for UNIX Systems administrators. **Founded:** May 1991. **Freq:** Monthly. **Print Method:** Web. **Trim Size:** 8 x 10 7/8. **Cols./Page:** 2. **Key Personnel:** Ralph Barker, Senior Editor, rbarker@mfi.com; Amber Ankerholz, Managing Editor, aankerholz@mfi.com; Edwin Rothrock, Publisher. **ISSN:** 1061-2688. **Subscription Rates:** $39 individuals; $4.95 single issue. **Remarks:** Accepts advertising. **Alt. Formats:** CD-ROM, Sys Admin CD-ROM.
Ad Rates: BW: $1,515 **Circ:** Paid ‡21,138
4C: $1,750

11754 The University Daily Kansan
University of Kansas
119 Stauffer-Flint Hall Phone: (785)864-4358
Lawrence, KS 66045 Fax: (785)864-5261
Publication E-mail: news@kansan.com

College newspaper. **Founded:** 1889. **Freq:** Daily (morn.). **Print Method:** Offset. **Cols./Page:** 6. **Col. Width:** 12 picas. **Col. Depth:** 20.5 inches. **Key Personnel:** Tom Eblen, General Mgr., phone (913)864-7667, teblen@kansan.com. **USPS:** 650-640. **Subscription Rates:** $120 individuals per year. **URL:** http://www.kansan.com.
Ad Rates: 4C: $200 **Circ:** Free 200
PCI: $7.80 Paid 12,300

11755 University of Kansas Law Review
Kansas Law Review, Inc.
University of Kansas Phone: (785)864-3463
Green Hall, Rm. 510 Fax: (785)864-3680
Lawrence, KS 66045
Law journal. **Founded:** 1952. **Freq:** Quarterly. **Print Method:** Offset. **Cols./Page:** 1. **Col. Width:** 60 nonpareils. **Col. Depth:** 119 agate lines. **Key Personnel:** Eric Madden, Editor-in-Chief. **ISSN:** 0083-4025. **Subscription Rates:** $31 individuals. **Remarks:** Accepts advertising.
Ad Rates: BW: $170 **Circ:** 1,000

11756 KJHK-FM - 90.7
2051 A Dole Center Phone: (913)864-4745
Lawrence, KS 66045 Fax: (913)864-0614
E-mail: kjhk@ukanaix.cc.ukans.edu

Format: Alternative/New Music/Progressive; Jazz. **Networks:** ABC. **Founded:** 1975. **Operating Hours:** Continuous; 100% local. **ADI:** Topeka, KS. **Key Personnel:** Gary Hawke, General Mgr., phone (913)864-0603; Christie Humphries, Station Mgr.; Ranita Wilks, Development Dir.; Sam Fisk, Program Dir., phone (913)864-4745. **Local Programs:** *Dinner Hour Album Playback*, Erin Kate Curtis, (913)864-LIVE; *Jazz in the Morning*, Chris McGee, (913)864-LIVE; *Plow the Fields*, Tom Humphrey, (913)864-LIVE. **Wattage:** 100. **Ad Rates:** Noncommercial. **URL:** http://www.cc.ukans.edu/~kjhknet.

11757 KLWN-AM - 1320
3125 W. 6th St. Phone: (913)843-1320
Lawrence, KS 66049-3101 Fax: (913)841-1320
E-mail: klwn@lazer.com

Format: Adult Contemporary; News; Talk. **Networks:** AP. **Owner:** Lawrence Broadcasters, Inc., at above address. **Founded:** 1951. **Operating Hours:** 5:30 a.m.-11 p.m. **ADI:** Kansas City, MO (Lawrence, KS). **Key Personnel:** Arden Booth, President; Hank Booth, General Mgr.; Bob Newton, Station Mgr.; John Flood, Program Dir.; Bob Newton, Chief Engineer; Warner Lewis, Sales Mgr.; Lorraine Bodin, Business Mgr. **Local Programs:** *According to the Record*, Hank Booth; *Comment on Current Affairs*, Barb Quinn; *David Lawrence Sports Talk*, John Flood. **Wattage:** 500 day; 250 night. **Ad Rates:** $10-22 for 30 seconds; $13-29 for 60 seconds.

11758 KLZR-FM - 105.9
3125 W. 6th St. Phone: (913)843-1320
Lawrence, KS 66049-3101 Fax: (913)841-1320
E-mail: 1059@lazer.com

Format: Classic Rock. **Founded:** 1963. **Formerly:** KLWN-FM (1979). **Operating Hours:** Continuous. **ADI:** Kansas City, MO (Lawrence, KS). **Key Personnel:** Hawk Booth, General Mgr.; Bob Newton, Station Mgr.; Warner Bewb, Sales Mgr.; Lorraine Bodon, Business Mgr.; Roger T. Dodger, Program Dir. **Wattage:** 100,000. **Ad Rates:** Advertising accepted; rates available upon request. **URL:** http:www.lazer.com.

11759 KMCI-TV - 38
2951 Four Wheel Dr. Phone: (913)749-3388
Lawrence, KS 66047-3145 Fax: (913)749-3377
E-mail: info@lbizl.com.

Format: Commercial TV. **Networks:** Independent. **Owner:** Miller Broadcasting, Inc., at above address. **Founded:** 1988. **Operating Hours:** Continuous. **ADI:** Kansas City, MO (Lawrence, KS). **Key Personnel:** Monte Miller, Pres./General Mgr.; Doris Miller, Operations Mgr.; Christopher Miller, Sales Mgr.; Quinn Miller, Production Mgr. **Local Programs:** *Fullspread*, Quinn Miller. **Wattage:** 5,000,000. **Ad Rates:** $30-50 per unit.

11760 Sunflower Cablevision
644 New Hampshire Phone: (785)841-2100
PO Box 808 Fax: (785)832-6363
Lawrence, KS 66044-0808

Owner: The World Co., 609 New Hampshire, Lawrence, KS 66044, (785)843-1000. **Founded:** 1971. **Key Personnel:** S. Holeman, phone (785)832-6321, fax (785)832-6363, sholeman@sunflower.com; Mike Kitzsteiner, Contact, phone (785)841-1123, fax (785)832-6364, kite@sunflower.com; D. McGough, General Mgr., phone (785)830-1204, fax (785)830-1140, dmcgough@sunflower.com; Judy Eldgridge, Contact, phone (785)832-8303, fax (785)830-1203, judye@sunflower.com; James Risner, Chief Technician, phone (785)832-6330, fax (785)832-6363, jrisner@sunflower.com. **Cities Served:** Eudora, Lawrence, KS; Douglas County: subscribing households 29,084; 56 channels; 2 community access channels.

LEAVENWORTH†, pop. 33,656.

NE KS. Leavenworth Co. On Missouri River, 33 mi. NW of Kansas City, MO. U.S. Army Command & General Staff College. Saint Mary College. Federal and state institutions. Manufactures mill and milling machinery, bridge and structural steel, furniture, feed products, auto batteries, marine products and equipment. Grain elevators, machine shops, flour mills. Diversified farming.

11761 The Chronicle Shopper
Chronicle Shopper
505 Cherokee Phone: (913)682-1334
Leavenworth, KS 66048 Fax: (913)682-1089
Free: (800)521-1447
Publication E-mail: advertise@chronicleshopper.com
Publisher E-mail: lushopper@aol.com

Free circulation shopping guide. **Founded:** 1903. **Freq:** Weekly (Wed.). **Print Method:** Offset. **Trim Size:** 10 1/2 x 16 1/4. **Cols./Page:** 4. **Col. Width:** 2 1/2 inches. **Col. Depth:** 1 inches. **Key Personnel:** David L. Thompson, Publisher; Troy Hayden, Circulation Mgr. **Subscription Rates:** Free. **Remarks:** Accepts advertising. **URL:** http://www.chronicleshopper.com. **Formerly:** The Leavenworth Chronicle.
Ad Rates: BW: $560 **Circ:** Non-paid 22,946
4C: $1,000
CNU: $8.75
PCI: $8.75

11762 Lansing Chronicle
Chronicle Shopper
505 Cherokee Phone: (913)682-1334
Leavenworth, KS 66048 Fax: (913)682-1089
Free: (800)521-1447
Publisher E-mail: lushopper@aol.com

Community newspaper. **Founded:** Mar. 6, 1996. **Freq:** Weekly. **Print Method:** Offset. **Trim Size:** 10 x 16. **Cols./Page:** 6. **Key Personnel:** Michelle Cain, Editor. **Subscription Rates:** Free. **Remarks:** Accepts advertising.
Ad Rates: BW: $216 **Circ:** Non-paid **3,800**
4C: $516
PCI: $4

11763 Leavenworth Times
PO Box 144
Leavenworth, KS 66048

General newspaper. **Founded:** Mar. 7, 1857. **Freq:** Daily (eve.), Sunday (morn.). **Print Method:** Offset. **Cols./Page:** 6. **Col. Width:** 24 nonpareils. **Col. Depth:** 294 agate lines. **Key Personnel:** Tom Throne III, Publisher; Ron Piche', Editor; Tim Larson, Advertising Mgr. **Subscription Rates:** $9.03 individuals a month. **Remarks:** Accepts advertising.
Ad Rates: GLR: $.51 **Circ:** Mon.-Fri. ★6,741
BW: $922.35 Sun. ★7,499
SAU: $7.15

11764 South County Chronicle
Chronicle Shopper
505 Cherokee Phone: (913)682-1334
Leavenworth, KS 66048 Fax: (913)682-1089
Free: (800)521-1447
Publisher E-mail: lushopper@aol.com

Community newspaper. **Founded:** June 4, 1997. **Freq:** Weekly. **Print Method:** Offset. **Trim Size:** 10 x 16. **Cols./Page:** 6. **Remarks:** Accepts advertising. **Former name:** Tonganoxie Chronicle.
Ad Rates: PCI: $4 **Circ:** Non-paid 2,750

11765 American Cablevision
541 McDonald Rd. Phone: (913)682-2113
PO Box 577 Fax: (913)682-8705
Leavenworth, KS 66048

Key Personnel: Gina Maddox, Contact. **Cities Served:** Fort Leavenworth B.V.A., Lansing, Leavenworth, Platte City, Tracy, Weston, KS: subscribing households 14,000; 38 channels; 2 community access channels.

11766 KKLO-AM - 1410
481 Muncie Rd. Phone: (913)724-2020
Leavenworth, KS 66048-4947 Fax: (913)727-2137

Format: Religious; Contemporary Christian. **Networks:** Independent. **Owner:** Wodlinger Broadcasting, at above address. **Founded:** 1948. **Formerly:** KCLO-AM (1988). **Operating Hours:** Continuous; 100% local. **Key Personnel:** Dave Barnett, Chief Engineer; Todd Chase, Contact; Tammy Cross, Station Mgr.; Bee Fender, Contact; Andrew Logue, Contact. **Wattage:** 5000. **Ad Rates:** $4-18 for 30 seconds; $9-23 for 60 seconds.

LEAWOOD

11767 The IAPD Magazine
International Association of Plastics Distributors
4707 College Blvd., Ste. 105 Phone: (913)345-1005
Leawood, KS 66211-1667 Fax: (913)345-1006
Publisher E-mail: iapd@iapd.org

Trade association magazine covering plastics. **Founded:** 1956. **Freq:** Bimonthly. **Print Method:** Offset. **Key Personnel:** Deborah Hamlin, Editor-in-Chief. **Subscription Rates:** $70 individuals. **Remarks:** Accepts advertising.
Ad Rates: BW: $2,750 **Circ:** (Not Reported)
4C: $3,400
SAU: $J

11768 Leawood Sun
Sun Publications, Inc.
7373 W. 107th St. Phone: (913)648-4620
Overland Park, KS 66212-2547 Fax: (913)381-1402

Newspaper. **Freq:** Semiweekly (Wed. and Fri.). **Print Method:** Offset. **Cols./Page:** 8. **Col. Width:** 21 nonpareils. **Col. Depth:** 292 agate lines. **Key Personnel:** Jack Lovelace, Editor; Steve Rose, Publisher; Jo Stapleton, Advertising Mgr. **Subscription Rates:** Free. **Remarks:** Accepts advertising.
Ad Rates: SAU: $24.75 **Circ:** Combined 112,441
PCI: $34.35

LEBANON, pop. 450.

N KS. Smith Co. 60 mi. S. of Hastings, NE. Stock, poultry, and grain farms.

11769 The Lebanon Times
PO Box 158 Phone: (785)389-6631
Lebanon, KS 66952-0158 Fax: (785)454-3866

Community newspaper. **Founded:** 1887. **Freq:** Weekly (Thurs.). **Print Method:** Offset. **Cols./Page:** 6. **Col. Width:** 21 1/2 nonpareils. **Key Personnel:** Phyllis Bell, Editor, phone (785)454-3514; Darrel E. Miller, Publisher, phone (785)454-3514, fax (785)282-3371. **Subscription Rates:** $12.06 individuals; $13.11 out of area; $13.50 out of state. **Remarks:** Advertising not accepted for alcoholic beverages.
Ad Rates: BW: $332 **Circ:** ‡650
SAU: $2.65

LECOMPTON, pop. 576.

E KS. Douglas Co. 8 mi. NW of Lawrence.

11770 Christmas Trees
Tree Publishers, Inc.
Box 107 Phone: (785)887-6324
Lecompton, KS 66050 Fax: (785)887-6734

Magazine covering the Christmas tree industry. **Subtitle:** World's Leading Christmas Tree Magazine. **Founded:** Apr. 1973. **Freq:** Quarterly. **Print Method:** Offset. **Trim Size:** 8 1/2 x 11. **Cols./Page:** 3. **Col. Width:** 14 picas. **Col. Depth:** 10 inches. **Key Personnel:** Charles (Chuck) W. Wright, Editor; Alice C. Wright, Advertising Mgr. **ISSN:** 0199-0217. **Subscription Rates:** $12 individuals; $20 two years; $3.00 single issue. **Remarks:** Accepts advertising.
Ad Rates: BW: $620 **Circ:** Paid ‡4,750
4C: $1,470 Controlled ‡41

LENEXA, pop. 18,639.

NE KS. Johnson Co. 5 mi. S. of Prairie Village.

11771 Drovers
Vance Publishing Corp.
10901 W. 84th Terrace Phone: (913)438-8700
Lenexa, KS 66214 Fax: (913)438-0765
Free: (800)255-5113
Publication E-mail: ghenderson@drovers.com

Trade magazine on beef cattle production and marketing. **Founded:** 1873. **Freq:** 12/year. **Print Method:** Offset. **Trim Size:** 8 x 10 3/4. **Cols./Page:** 3. **Col. Width:** 13 nonpareils. **Col. Depth:** 140 agate lines. **Key Personnel:** Greg Henderson, Assoc. Pub./Editor; Warren E. Morse, Publisher. **ISSN:** 0012-6454. **Subscription Rates:** Free to qualified subscribers; $20 institutions. **Remarks:** Accepts advertising. **Former name**: Drovers Journal.
Ad Rates: BW: $7,181 **Circ:** Paid 869
4C: $8,581 Controlled 98,000
PCI: $107

11772 The Grower
Vance Publishing Corp.
10901 W. 84th Terrace Phone: (913)438-8700
Lenexa, KS 66214 Fax: (913)438-0765
Free: (800)255-5113
Publication E-mail: 102234.1756@compuserve.com

Magazine providing management information for the commercial fruit and vegetable producer with emphasis on management, industry trends, effective marketing, chemicals, and legislative and regulatory environments. **Subtitle:** Serving the Needs of Commercial Fruit and Vegetable Growers. **Founded:** Apr. 1966. **Freq:** Monthly. **Print Method:** Web offset. **Trim Size:** 8 1/8 x 10 7/8. **Cols./Page:** 3. **Col. Width:** 13 picas. **Col. Depth:** 60 picas. **Key Personnel:** Steve Buckner, Editor; Sonia Tighe, Publisher. **ISSN:** 0745-1784. **Subscription Rates:** $20 individuals; $35 other countries. **Remarks:** Accepts advertising.
Ad Rates: GLR: $0.85 **Circ:** Controlled ‡27,742
BW: $2,900
4C: $4,425
PCI: $110

11773 The Packer
Vance Publishing Corp.
10901 W. 84th Terrace Phone: (913)438-8700
Lenexa, KS 66214 Fax: (913)438-0765
Free: (800)255-5113
Publication E-mail: 76207.2051@compuserve.com

Newspaper on produce marketing. **Subtitle:** The Business Newspaper of the Produce Industry. **Founded:** 1893. **Freq:** Weekly. **Print Method:** Offset. **Trim Size:** 14 1/8 x 21 1/2. **Cols./Page:** 6. **Col. Width:** 20 nonpareils. **Col. Depth:** 301 agate lines. **Key Personnel:** Bill O'Neill, Vice President/Publishing Dir.; Robb Bertels, Sales Mgr. **ISSN:** 0030-9168. **Subscription Rates:** $55 individuals; $3 single issue; $180 out of country.
Ad Rates: BW: $5,625 **Circ:** Paid ★**13,432**
4C: $7,410
PCI: $67.53

11774 Pork
Vance Publishing Corp.
10901 W. 84th Terrace Phone: (913)438-8700
Lenexa, KS 66214 Fax: (913)438-0765
Free: (800)255-5113
Publication E-mail: porkmag@aol.com

Magazine on pork production and marketing. **Founded:** Jan. 15, 1981. **Freq:** Monthly. **Print Method:** Offset. **Trim Size:** 8 x 10 3/4. **Cols./Page:** 3. **Col. Width:** 26 nonpareils. **Col. Depth:** 140 agate lines. **Key Personnel:** Marlys Miller, Editor, mmpork@aol.com; Bill Newham, Publisher, bnpork@aol.com. **ISSN:** 0745-3787. **Subscription Rates:** Free to qualified subscribers; $25 individuals; $4.95 single issue. **Remarks:** Accepts advertising.
Ad Rates: BW: $7,193 **Circ:** Controlled ‡75,261
4C: $8,593

11775 Produce Merchandising
Vance Publishing Corp.
10901 W. 84th Terrace Phone: (913)438-8700
Lenexa, KS 66214 Fax: (913)438-0765
Free: (800)255-5113
Publication E-mail:
producemerchandising@compuserv.com

Magazine covering the retail produce industry. **Founded:** 1988. **Freq:** Monthly. **Print Method:** Offset. **Trim Size:** 8 x 10 3/4. **Cols./Page:** 3. **Col. Width:** 13 picas. **Col. Depth:** 8 inches. **Key Personnel:** Elaine Symanski, Editor-in-Chief, phone (913)438-0783; Allison Myers, Sales Mgr., phone (913)438-0750; Janice L. McCall, Managing Editor. **Subscription Rates:** $25 individuals; Free to qualified subscribers. **Remarks:** Accepts advertising.
Ad Rates: BW: $3,840 **Circ:** 12,057
4C: $5,690

11776 Super Floral
Vance Publishing Corp.
10901 W. 84th Terrace Phone: (913)438-8700
Lenexa, KS 66214 Fax: (913)438-0765
Free: (800)255-5113
Publication E-mail: superflorl@aol.com

Magazine for managers and buyers in the high volume retail floral industry. **Subtitle:** Profitable strategies for the high-volume floral & garden industry. **Founded:** 1988. **Freq:** Monthly. **Print Method:** Web offset. **Trim Size:** 8 x 10 3/4. **Cols./Page:** 3. **Col. Width:** 2 1/4 inches. **Col. Depth:** 10 inches. **Key Personnel:** Amanda McManigal, Managing Editor, phone (913)438-0710, mcmanigal@superfloral.com; Monte Mace, Publisher, phone (913)438-0711, mace@superfloral.com. **ISSN:** 1058-4803. **Subscription Rates:** $35 individuals; $50 out of country; $80 airmail. **Remarks:** Accepts advertising. **URL:** http://www.superfloral.com. **Formerly**: Supermarket Floral.
Ad Rates: BW: $2,190 **Circ:** Controlled ‡15,000
4C: $3,265

11777 Swine Practitioner
Vance Publishing Corp.
10901 W. 84th Terrace Phone: (913)438-8700
Lenexa, KS 66214 Fax: (913)438-0765
Free: (800)255-5113

Professional magazine providing information on improving business and service opportunities for vets serving pork producers. **Founded:** 1988. **Freq:** 8/year. **Print Method:** Web offset. **Trim Size:** 8 x 10 3/4. **Cols./Page:** 3. **Col. Width:** 13 nonpareils. **Col. Depth:** 140 agate lines. **Key Personnel:** Jim Carlton, Editor, jcarlton@pigvet.com. **ISSN:** 0745-3787. **Subscription Rates:** $12. **Remarks:** Accepts advertising.
Ad Rates: BW: $2,715 **Circ:** ‡4,312
4C: $3,780

LENORA

11778 Vision Plus Inc.
PO Box 158
Lenora, KS 67645

Founded: 1969. **Formerly**: Osborne Cable Television Inc. (Aug. 1995). **Key Personnel:** Ken Kendall, Supervisor, phone (785)567-9226, fax (785)567-4401; Larry E. Sevier, General Mgr.; Rhonda Goddard, Controller. **Cities Served:** Osborne, KS: subscribing households 714; 46 channels.

LEOTI†, pop. 1,869.

W KS. Wichita Co. 205 mi. W. of Salina.

11779 Leoti Standard
The Leoti
114 S. 4th St. Phone: (316)375-2631
PO Box N Fax: (316)375-2184
Leoti, KS 67861
Community newspaper. **Founded:** 1885. **Freq:** Weekly (Wed.). **Print Method:** Offset. **Cols./Page:** 6. **Col. Width:** 2 inches. **Col. Depth:** 21 inches. **Key Personnel:** Linda Geyer, Editor/Administration; Jerry Anderson, Publisher. **Subscription Rates:** $24.08 individuals; $25.22 out of area. **Remarks:** Color advertising not accepted.
Ad Rates: GLR: $.75 **Circ:** ‡1,650
BW: $401.94
SAU: $3.19
PCI: $2.90

LEWIS

11780 The Edwards County Sentinel
The Lewis Press, Inc.
PO Box 68 Phone: (316)659-2080
Lewis, KS 67552 Fax: (316)324-5879

Community newspaper. **Freq:** Weekly. **Print Method:** Offset. **Cols./Page:** 7. **Col. Width:** 12 picas. **Col. Depth:** 21.5 inches. **Key Personnel:** David L. Kazmaier, Editor and Publisher; Cathy Woolard, Editor and Publisher. **Subscription Rates:** $25 in county; $30 in state; $35 out of state. **Remarks:** Accepts advertising. **Formerly**: The Kinsley Mercury; The Lewis Press.
Ad Rates: SAU: $3.23 **Circ:** ‡1,958
PCI: $4

11781 Lewis Press
The Lewis Press, Inc.
PO Box 68 Phone: (316)659-2080
Lewis, KS 67552 Fax: (316)324-5879

Community newspaper. **Freq:** Weekly (Thurs.). **Cols./Page:** 5. **Col. Width:** 11 1/2 picas. **Col. Depth:** 16 inches. **Key Personnel:** David L. Kazmaier, Editor and Publisher.
Circ: 400

LIBERAL†, pop. 14,870.

SW KS. Seward Co. 75 mi. SW of Dodge City. Manufactures material handling equipment, truck bodies. Beef packing plant. Grain milling. Oil and gas fields. Ships agricultural products. Grain and livestock farms.

11782 The Crusader
Seward County Community College
Box 1137 Phone: (316)629-2691
Liberal, KS 67905-1137 Fax: (316)629-2691
Publisher E-mail: earl@swdtimes.com

Collegiate newspaper. **Founded:** 1969. **Freq:** 14/year (during the academic year). **Print Method:** Offset. **Trim Size:** 10 3/4 x 13 1/2. **Cols./Page:** 5. **Col. Width:** 18 nonpareils. **Col. Depth:** 182 agate lines. **Key Personnel:** Anita Reed, Contact, phone (316)624-2541, reed@swdtimes.com. **Remarks:** Accepts advertising.
Ad Rates: PCI: $3 **Circ:** Free ‡2,000

11783 Leisure Times
Box 889 Phone: (316)624-2541
Liberal, KS 67905 Fax: (316)624-0735

Entertainment. **Founded:** 1973. **Freq:** Weekly. **Print Method:** Offset. **Cols./Page:** 6. **Col. Width:** 21 nonpareils. **Col. Depth:** 294 agate lines. **Key Personnel:** James S. Head, Editor and Publisher; Sherry Helmke, Advertising Mgr. **Remarks:** Accepts advertising.
Ad Rates: GLR: $.45 **Circ:** (Not Reported)

11784 Southwest Daily Times
Liberal Newspapers, Inc.
16 S. Kansas Ave.
Liberal, KS 67901-3732

General newspaper. **Founded:** Apr. 15, 1886. **Freq:** Daily (eve.), Sunday (morn.). **Print Method:** Offset. **Cols./Page:** 8. **Col. Width:** 18 nonpareils. **Col. Depth:** 294 agate lines. **Key Personnel:** Jeffery A. Burkhead, Editor and Publisher. **Subscription Rates:** $99 individuals. **Remarks:** Accepts advertising.
Ad Rates: GLR: $.82 **Circ:** Paid 6,829
BW: $982 Non-paid 328
4C: $1,132
SAU: $7.80
PCI: $7.80

11785 KSCB-AM - 1270
PO Box 3125 Phone: (316)624-3891
Liberal, KS 67905-3125 Fax: (316)624-9472

Format: Full Service; Contemporary Country. **Networks:** ABC. **Owner:** Seward County Broadcasting Co., Inc., at above address. **Founded:** 1948. **Operating Hours:** Continuous; 3% network, 97% local. **ADI:** Wichita-Hutchinson, KS. **Key Personnel:** Stuart Melchert, General Mgr.; Don Drees, Contact; Mark David, Program Dir. **Wattage:** 1000. **Ad Rates:** $6.80-12 for 30 seconds; $8.20-13.60 for 60 seconds. $6.80-$12 for 30 seconds; $8.20-$13.60 for 60 seconds. Combined advertising rates available with KSCB-FM.

11786 KSCB-FM - 107.5
PO Box 3125 Phone: (316)624-3891
Liberal, KS 67905-3125 Fax: (316)624-9472
Free: (800)373-3891

Format: Adult Contemporary. **Networks:** ABC. **Owner:** Seward County Broadcasting Co., Inc., at above address. **Founded:** 1978. **Operating Hours:** Continuous. **ADI:** Wichita-Hutchinson, KS. **Key Personnel:** Stuart Melchert, General Mgr.; Sharon Hannon, News Dir.; Mark David, Program Dir.; Tracy Utz, Sports Dir.; Beth Harris, Operations Dir. **Wattage:** 100,000. **Ad Rates:** $6.80-12 for 30 seconds; $8.20-13.60 for 60 seconds. $6.80-$12 for 30 seconds; $8.20-$13.60 for 60 seconds. Combined advertising rates available with KSCB-AM.

11787 KSLS-FM - 101.5
RR 2, Box 431 Phone: (316)624-8156
Liberal, KS 67901 Fax: (316)624-4606

Format: Contemporary Country. **Networks:** Mutual Broadcasting System; Mid-America Ag. **Owner:** Goodstar Broadcasting, 1660 N. Tyler, Wichita, KS 67202, (316)267-0293. **Founded:** 1978. **Operating Hours:** Continuous. **ADI:** Wichita-Hutchinson, KS. **Key Personnel:** Mark Moeder, Program Dir.; Larry Howell, General Mgr.; S.M. Williams, AG Dir.; Lucky Kidd, News Dir. **Wattage:** 100,000. **Ad Rates:** $12 for 30 seconds; $15 for 60 seconds. Combined advertising rates available with KYUU-AM.

11788 KYUU-AM - 1470
RR 2, Box 431 Phone: (316)624-8156
Liberal, KS 67901 Fax: (316)624-4606

Networks: Mutual Broadcasting System. **Owner:** Gordstar Broadcasting, 1660 N. Tyler, Wichita, KS 67202. **Founded:**

1960. **Formerly:** KILS-AM; KLIB-AM. **Operating Hours:** Continuous. **ADI:** Wichita-Hutchinson, KS. **Key Personnel:** Larry Howell, General Mgr.; Steve Williams, Contact; Rob Sprangler, Program Dir.; Lucky Kidd, News Dir. **Wattage:** 1000. **Ad Rates:** $8 for 30 seconds; $12 for 60 seconds.

LINCOLN†, pop. 1,599.

C KS. Lincoln Co. 42 mi. NW of Salina. Rock crushing plant. Grain, stock, poultry, and dairy farms.

11789 Lincoln Sentinel-Republican
Box 67 Phone: (913)524-4200
Lincoln, KS 67455
Newspaper with a Republican orientation. **Founded:** 1888. **Freq:** Weekly (Wed.). **Print Method:** Offset. **Trim Size:** 14 x 22 3/4. **Cols./Page:** 6. **Col. Width:** 21 nonpareils. **Col. Depth:** 294 agate lines. **Key Personnel:** Ray Rasmussen, Publisher. **Subscription Rates:** $19 individuals.
Ad Rates: GLR: $0.22 **Circ:** Paid ‡2,100
SAU: $3.05 Free ‡30
PCI: $3.05

LINDSBORG, pop. 3,155.

C KS. Mc Pherson Co. 20 mi. S. of Salina. Bethany College. Light manufacturing. Diversified farming.

11790 Bethany Magazine
College Relations
Presser Hall Phone: (913)227-3311
421 N. 1st St. Fax: (913)227-2004
Lindsborg, KS 67456-1897
College alumni magazine. **Founded:** 1904. **Freq:** Quarterly (during academic year). **Print Method:** Offset. **Trim Size:** 8 1/2 x 11. **Cols./Page:** 3. **Col. Width:** 30 nonpareils. **Col. Depth:** 137 agate lines. **Key Personnel:** Harold Rothgeb, Editor and Publisher, rothgebb@bethany.bethanylb.edu. **USPS:** 052-440. **Subscription Rates:** Free (to alumni and friends). **Remarks:** Advertising not accepted.
Circ: Controlled ‡7,500

11791 Bethany Messenger
Bethany College Press
Student Publications Phone: (913)227-3311
Union Box 181 Fax: (917)227-2004
421 N. 1st St.
Lindsborg, KS 67456-1897
Collegiate newspaper. **Founded:** 1892. **Freq:** Weekly (Fri.). **Print Method:** Offset. **Cols./Page:** 5. **Col. Width:** 24 nonpareils. **Col. Depth:** 190 agate lines. **Key Personnel:** Peter Kim, Editor; John Pearson, Advisor. **Subscription Rates:** $18 individuals. **Remarks:** Accepts advertising.
Ad Rates: GLR: $2 **Circ:** 1,000

Gypsum Advocate - See Gypsum

11792 Lindsborg News-Record
Montgomery Communications, Inc.
114 S. Main St. Phone: (913)227-3348
PO Box 31 Fax: (913)227-3740
Lindsborg, KS 67456
Newspaper. **Founded:** 1886. **Freq:** Weekly (Thurs.). **Print Method:** Offset. Uses mats. **Trim Size:** 13 x 21. **Cols./Page:** 6. **Col. Width:** 25 nonpareils. **Col. Depth:** 301 agate lines. **Key Personnel:** Marty Hardy, Editor; John G. Montgomery, Publisher; Carol Pearson, Advertising Mgr. **ISSN:** 3141-6000. **Subscription Rates:** $22 individuals; $24 out of state. **Remarks:** Accepts advertising.
Ad Rates: GLR: $4.05 **Circ:** ‡3,100
BW: $441
4C: $690
PCI: $4.75

LOGAN, pop. 771.

N KS. Phillips Co. 120 mi. NW of Salina. Oil. Grain and stock farms.

11793 The Logan Republican
Logan Republican
101 E. Main St. Phone: (913)689-4339
Box 97 Fax: (913)689-7492
Logan, KS 67646-0097
Community newspaper. **Founded:** 1880. **Freq:** Weekly (Thurs.). **Print Method:** Offset. **Trim Size:** 14 1/2 x 20 3/8. **Cols./Page:** 6. **Col. Width:** 27 nonpareils. **Col. Depth:** 287 agate lines. **Key Personnel:** Clyde M. Atkinson, Editor and Publisher; Laura M. Atkinson, Publisher. **Subscription Rates:** $13.50 individuals; $15.50 out of four-county area; $17.50 out of state. **Remarks:** Accepts advertising.
Ad Rates: GLR: $.19 **Circ:** ‡912
PCI: $2.68

LONGTON, pop. 394.

SE KS. Elk Co. 28 mi. NW of Independence. Oil and gas. Stock, and grain farms.

11794 The Elk County Citizen-Advance News
H & H Publications
226 E. Main Phone: (316)725-3176
PO Box 417 Fax: (316)725-3272
Sedan, KS 67361
Community newspaper. **Founded:** 1888. **Freq:** Weekly (Wed.). **Print Method:** Offset. **Cols./Page:** 6. **Col. Width:** 26 nonpareils. **Col. Depth:** 294 agate lines. **Key Personnel:** Martin Heller Hays, Publisher. **Subscription Rates:** $17.45 individuals. **Remarks:** Accepts advertising.
Ad Rates: GLR: $.24 **Circ:** Paid 1,550
BW: $290 Free 200
PCI: $2.55

LOUISBURG

11795 Louisburg Herald
15 S. Broadway Phone: (913)837-4321
Box 99 Fax: (913)837-4322
Louisburg, KS 66053-0099
Community newspaper. **Freq:** Weekly (Wed.). **Print Method:** Offset. **Cols./Page:** 6. **Col. Width:** 2 inches. **Col. Depth:** 21 inches. **Key Personnel:** Phil McLaughlin, Publisher. **Subscription Rates:** $24.50 local; $28.50 out of area; $35 out of state. **Remarks:** Accepts advertising.
Ad Rates: GLR: $3.20 **Circ:** 1,800
BW: $403.20
4C: $593.20
PCI: $3.20

LUCAS, pop. 524.

NC KS. Russell Co. 56 mi. NW of Salina. Grain, dairy, stock, and poultry farms.

11796 Lucas-Sylvan News
Lucas Publishing Co.
PO Box 337 Phone: (913)525-6355
Lucas, KS 67648 Fax: (913)525-6356

Community newspaper. **Founded:** 1899. **Freq:** Weekly (Thurs.). **Print Method:** Offset. **Trim Size:** 17 1/2 x 22 1/2. **Cols./Page:** 4. **Col. Width:** 14 picas. **Col. Depth:** 16 inches. **Key Personnel:** Carolyn Schultz, Editor; Craig D. Langdon, Publisher. **USPS:** 321-680. **Subscription Rates:** $17.49 individuals; $19.25 out of state.
Ad Rates: GLR: $.50 **Circ:** ‡890
BW: $166.40
PCI: $2.60

LYONS†, pop. 4,152.

C KS. Rice Co. 33 mi. NW of Hutchinson. Manufactures precision machine parts, transmissions, salt products. Salt mines. Gas & oil products. Wheat, corn, oats, alfalfa.

11797 Lyons Daily News
Lyons Publishing Co., Inc.
210 W. Commercial Phone: (316)257-2368
PO Box 560 Fax: (316)259-2369
Lyons, KS 67554-2716
Publication E-mail: ldnews@midusa.net

General newspaper. **Founded:** 1906. **Freq:** Daily (eve.). **Print Method:** Offset. **Cols./Page:** 6. **Col. Width:** 29 nonpareils. **Col. Depth:** 294 agate lines. **Key Personnel:** John Sayler, Editor; Paul E. Jones, Publisher. **USPS:** 323-320. **Subscription Rates:** $38 individuals. **Remarks:** Accepts advertising.
Ad Rates: GLR: $.30 **Circ:** ‡2,452
BW: $622.44
SAU: $5.20
PCI: $5.20

11798 Lyons CATV Inc.
112 East Ave. N Phone: (316)257-3411
Box 584 Fax: (316)257-3663
Lyons, KS 67554

Owner: Multimedia Cablevision Inc., 701 E. Douglas, PO Box 3027, Wichita, KS 67201, (316)262-4270, Fax: (316)262-2309. **Founded:** July 1973. **Key Personnel:** Roger Swenson, System Mgr. **Cities Served:** Lyons, KS: subscribing households 1,200; 33 channels; 1 community access channel; 168 hours per week community access programming.

MADISON, pop. 1,099.

SE KS. Greenwood Co. 20 mi. S. of Emporia. Oil wells. Agriculture. Livestock, hay, corn.

11799 The Madison News
118 S. 3rd St. Phone: (316)437-2433
Box 217 Fax: (316)437-2433
Madison, KS 66860
Publisher E-mail: madnews@midusa.net

Community newspaper. **Founded:** 1878. **Freq:** Weekly (Thurs.). **Print Method:** Offset. **Trim Size:** 7 1/4 x 11. **Cols./Page:** 6. **Col. Width:** 12 picas. **Col. Depth:** 21 inches. **Key Personnel:** Jola Casey, Editor & Publisher, phone (316)437-2029; Chris Murphy, Publisher, phone (316)437-2029; Patsy Murphy, Publisher, phone (316)437-2396. **USPS:** 325-160. **Subscription Rates:** $25.88 individuals; $27 out of area. **Remarks:** Advertising not accepted for tobacco products. **Formerly:** The Madisonian; Madison Livestock Belt; Madison Spirit.
Ad Rates: GLR: $0.37 **Circ:** Paid ‡740
BW: $370.44 Free ‡25
4C: $619
PCI: $3.24

MANHATTAN†, pop. 32,644.

NEC KS. Riley Co. On Kansas River, 56 mi. NW of Topeka. Kansas State University of Agricultural and Applied Science. Fort Riley (Military Post). Manufactures cut stones, patterns, mobile homes. Poultry packing and seed houses; bottling works. Stock, poultry, and truck farms.

11800 American Institute of Baking, Technical Bulletin
American Institute of Baking
1213 Bakers Way
PO Box 3999
Manhattan, KS 66505-3999

Professional journal covering baking. **Founded:** Nov. 1979. **Freq:** Monthly. **Subscription Rates:** $35 individuals; $49 out of country; $3 single issue; $4 single issue out of country. **Remarks:** Advertising not accepted.
Circ: (Not Reported)

11801 Grass & Grain
Ag Press, Inc.
1531 Yuma Phone: (913)539-7558
Box 1009 Fax: (913)539-2679
Manhattan, KS 66502-0037
Agricultural tabloid. **Founded:** Mar. 1, 1955. **Freq:** Weekly (Tues.). **Print Method:** Letterpress and offset. **Trim Size:** 10 1/2 x 16. **Cols./Page:** 6. **Col. Width:** 23 nonpareils. **Col. Depth:** 232 agate lines. **Key Personnel:** Steve Suther, Editor. **USPS:** 937-880. **Subscription Rates:** $19 individuals. **Remarks:** Accepts advertising.
Ad Rates: GLR: $.714 **Circ:** ‡16,500
BW: $1,000
4C: $1,300

11802 Jazz Educators Journal
International Association of Jazz Educators
PO Box 724 Phone: (785)776-8744
Manhattan, KS 66505 Fax: (785)776-6190
Publisher E-mail: iaje@ksu.edu

Professional journal for jazz music educators. **Founded:** 1972. **Freq:** Bimonthly. **Print Method:** Offset. **Trim Size:** 8 1/2 x 11. **Cols./Page:** 3. **Col. Width:** 42 nonpareils. **Col. Depth:** 134 agate lines. **Key Personnel:** William F. McFarlin, Contact, bill@iaje.org. **Subscription Rates:** $50 members. **Remarks:** Accepts advertising.
Ad Rates: BW: $690 **Circ:** Paid 7,500
4C: $1,782 Non-paid 300

11803 Journal of Research on Computing in Education
International Society for Technology in Education (ISTE)
363 Bluemont Hall Phone: (785)532-7686
Kansas State University Fax: (785)532-7304
Manhattan, KS 66506
Publisher E-mail: iste@oregon.uoregon.edu

Professional journal research in educational computing. **Founded:** 1982. **Freq:** Quarterly. **Print Method:** Offset. **Trim Size:** 6 x 9. **Cols./Page:** 1. **Col. Width:** 26 picas. **Col. Depth:** 7 inches. **Key Personnel:** William C. Bozeman, Editor; Diane McGrath, Editor, dmcgrath@coe.educ.ksu.edu. **ISSN:** 0888-6504. **Subscription Rates:** $78 nonmembers; $88 out of country; $18.50 single issue; $58 members in USA. **Remarks:** Color advertising not accepted. **URL:** http://www2.educ.ksu.edu/projects/jrce/v28-5/v28-5.htm. **Formerly:** AEDS Bulletin; International Association for Computing in Education Newsletter; AEDS Monitor.
Ad Rates: BW: $270 **Circ:** 2,500

11804 Journal of Social Studies Research
Kansas State University
Bluemont Hall
Manhattan, KS 66506-5301
Phone: (785)532-6158
Fax: (785)532-7304

Scholarly journal covering social studies research. **Freq:** Semiannual. **Key Personnel:** Ben Smith, Editor, bsmith@ksu.edu. **ISSN:** 0885-985X. **Subscription Rates:** $25 individuals; $30 out of country.

11805 Journal of the West
1531 Yuma
Manhattan, KS 66502
Free: (800)258-1232
Phone: (785)539-1888
Fax: (785)539-2233

Illustrated journal of western history and culture. **Founded:** 1962. **Freq:** Quarterly. **Print Method:** Offset. **Trim Size:** 8 1/2 x 11. **Cols./Page:** 2. **Col. Width:** 40 nonpareils. **Col. Depth:** 137 agate lines. **Key Personnel:** Robin Higham, Editor; Carol A. Williams, Publisher. **ISSN:** 0022-5169. **Subscription Rates:** $42 individuals; $54 institutions; $12 single issue; $15 single issue institution. **Remarks:** Accepts advertising. **URL:** http://www.sunflower-univ-press.org.
Ad Rates: BW: $375 **Circ:** 4,500
4C: $600
PCI: $15

11806 Kansas 4-H Journal
Kansas 4-H Foundation Inc.
Kansas State University
116 Umberger Hall
Manhattan, KS 66506-3417
Phone: (913)532-5881
Fax: (913)539-6963
Agriculture magazine for 4-H club youth. **Founded:** 1955. **Freq:** 10/year. **Print Method:** Offset. **Trim Size:** 8 1/2 x 11. **Cols./Page:** 3. **Col. Width:** 28 nonpareils. **Col. Depth:** 140 agate lines. **Key Personnel:** Rhonda Wessel Atkinson, Editor/Administration, ratkinso@ksu.edu. **Subscription Rates:** $6 individuals. **Remarks:** Color advertising not accepted.
Ad Rates: BW: $480 **Circ:** ‡13,500

11807 Kansas Living
Kansas Farm Bureau
2627 KFB Plaza
Manhattan, KS 66502
Phone: (913)587-6000
Fax: (913)587-6914

Farm news magazine. **Founded:** 1989. **Freq:** Quarterly. **Print Method:** Offset. **Trim Size:** 8 x 10 3/4. **Cols./Page:** 3. **Key Personnel:** Steve Logback, Editor; John Schlageck, Managing Editor; Debbie Hargrave, Business Mgr. **Subscription Rates:** Free to qualified subscribers. **Remarks:** Accepts advertising.
Ad Rates: BW: $2,100 **Circ:** Controlled ‡140,000
4C: $2,700
PCI: $200

11808 Kansas State Collegian
Kansas State University Student Publications, Inc.
Kedzie Hall 103
Manhattan, KS 66506-7167
Phone: (913)532-6555
Fax: (913)532-6456

Collegiate newspaper. **Founded:** Apr. 1914. **Freq:** Daily (during academic year). **Print Method:** Offset. Broadsheet. **Cols./Page:** 6. **Col. Width:** 2 1/16 inches. **Col. Depth:** 21 inches. **Key Personnel:** Ronald E. Johnson, Director; Gloria Freeland, Advertising Dir. **Subscription Rates:** $70 individuals. **Remarks:** Accepts advertising. **Available Online. URL:** http://www.fpub.ksu.edu.
Ad Rates: BW: $730.80 **Circ:** Paid ‡312
4C: $1,030.80 Free ‡14,260
SAU: $5.80
PCI: $5.80

11809 Kansas State Engineer
Kansas State University
College of Engineering
133 Ward Hall
Manhattan, KS 66506
Phone: (785)532-6026
Fax: (785)532-6952
Publication E-mail: kse@ksu.edu

Collegiate magazine for students, faculty, and alumni written by engineering students. **Founded:** 1915. **Freq:** Triennial (during academic year). **Print Method:** Offset. **Trim Size:** 8 1/2 x 11. **Cols./Page:** 3. **Col. Width:** 13 picas. **Col. Depth:** 9.75 inches. **Key Personnel:** Evan Dean, Editor, evld@ksu.edu; Michael Dorcey, Faculty Advisor, mdorcey@ksu.edu; Sherri Auld, Advertising Mgr., phone (785)532-4996. **ISSN:** 0047-3189. **Subscription Rates:** $8 individuals. **Remarks:** Accepts advertising.
Ad Rates: 4C: $540 **Circ:** Paid ‡100
PCI: $10 Non-paid ‡3,000

11810 Mercury
Mercury Inc.
PO Box 787
Manhattan, KS 66502
Phone: (785)776-8805
Fax: (785)776-8807

General newspaper. **Founded:** 1909. **Freq:** Daily (eve.), Sunday (morn.). **Print Method:** Offset. **Cols./Page:** 6. **Col. Width:** 12.4 picas. **Col. Depth:** 301 agate lines. **Key Personnel:** Edward Seaton, Editor and Publisher. **Subscription Rates:** $77.25 individuals. **Remarks:** Accepts advertising.
Ad Rates: SAU: $7.43 **Circ:** Mon.-Fri. ★**10,591**
Sun. ★**12,062**

11811 Veterinary and Human Toxicology
Comparative Toxicology Laboratories
Kansas State University
Manhattan, KS 66506
Phone: (785)532-4334
Fax: (785)532-4481

Professional journal containing refereed scientific articles, news, and reports from the field of toxicology. Includes reports of past meetings, announcements of forthcoming meetings, book reviews, job opportunities, membership, and other news from the several organizations in toxicology that sponsor this publi cation. **Subtitle:** The Journal of Comparative Toxiology. **Founded:** 1959. **Freq:** Bimonthly. **Print Method:** Letterpress and offset. **Trim Size:** 8 1/2 x 11. **Cols./Page:** 2. **Col. Width:** 40 nonpareils. **Col. Depth:** 136 agate lines. **Key Personnel:** Frederick W. Oehme, Editor and Publisher, oehme@vet.ksu.edu. **ISSN:** 0145-6296. **Subscription Rates:** $60 individuals; $70 Canada; $80 other countries. **Remarks:** Accepts advertising. **Alt. Formats:** Mailing labels. **Formerly:** Veterinary Toxicology.
Ad Rates: BW: $800 **Circ:** Paid ‡1,800
PCI: $50 Controlled ‡25

11812 KHCA-FM - 95.3
103 N. 3rd
Manhattan, KS 66502
Phone: (785)537-9595
Fax: (785)537-2955
E-mail: angel95@kansas.net

Format: Contemporary Christian. **Networks:** Sun Radio. **Founded:** 1986. **Formerly:** KAWQ-FM (1986); KSKT-FM (1990). **Operating Hours:** 6a.m.- midnight Mon-Fri; 7a.m.-1a.m. Sat-Sun. **Key Personnel:** Jerry Hutchinson, Contact; Kevin Block, Chief Engineer; Jerry Hutchinson, News Dir.; Alicia Williams, Traffic Dir.; Hal Keller, Music Dir.; James Felver, Music Dir. **Wattage:** 6000. **Ad Rates:** $8.25-3.75 for 30 seconds; $10-6 for 60 seconds; $sss-7.50 for 60 seconds. **URL:** http://www.tfsksu.net/~angel95/.

11813 KKSU-AM - 580
McCain Auditorium, Rm. 20
Kansas State University
Manhattan, KS 66506-4701
Phone: (785)532-5851
Fax: (785)532-5709
E-mail: kksu@oznet.ksu.edu

Format: News; Educational; Talk. **Networks:** Public Radio International (PRI). **Founded:** 1924. **Formerly:** KSAC-AM (1984). **Operating Hours:** 12:30 p.m.-5:30 p.m., Mon-Fri. **Key Personnel:** Larry Jackson, General Mgr., ljackson@oz.oznet.ksu.edu; Richard Baker, News Dir.; Duane Magedorn, Chief Engineer. **Wattage:** 5000. **Ad Rates:** Noncommercial. **URL:** http://www.oznet.ksu.edu/kksu.

11814 KMAN-AM - 1350
2414 Casement Rd.
PO Box 1350
Manhattan, KS 66502-0011
Phone: (913)776-4851
Fax: (913)539-1000

Format: Talk; Adult Contemporary. **Networks:** Mutual Broadcasting System. **Owner:** Manhattan Broadcasting Co., at above address. **Founded:** 1950. **Operating Hours:** Continuous; 2% network, 98% local. **Key Personnel:** Richard Wartell, General Mgr.; Ken Scott, News Dir.; Dave Lewis, Program Dir.; Al Linton, Sales Mgr. **Wattage:** 500. **Ad Rates:** $10-16 for 30 seconds; $12-20 for 60 seconds.

11815 KMKF-FM - 101.5
2414 Casement Rd.
PO Box 1350
Manhattan, KS 66502-0011
Free: (800)559-1350
Phone: (785)776-1350
Fax: (785)539-1000

Format: Album-Oriented Rock (AOR). **Networks:** Westwood One Radio. **Owner:** Manhattan Broadcasting Co., at above address. **Founded:** 1972. **Operating Hours:** Continuous; 1% network, 99% local. **ADI:** Topeka, KS. **Key Personnel:** Richard T. Wartell, General Mgr.; Ken Scott, News Dir.; Raubin Pierce, Program Dir.; Jason Schlitz, Sales Mgr. **Wattage:** 50,000. **Ad Rates:** $10-22 for 30 seconds; $13-25 for 60 seconds. **URL:** http://www.purerock.com.

11816 TCI of Kansas, Inc.
519 Richards Dr
Manhattan, KS 66502-6083
Phone: (913)776-9239
Fax: (913)539-0285

Founded: 1961. **Cities Served:** subscribing households 16,000; 40 channels.

MANKATO†, pop. 1,205.

N KS. Jewell Co. 75 mi. SE of Hastings, NE. Packing plant. Grain, dairy, poultry, stock farms.

11817 Jewell County News
Superior Publishing Co.
109 E. Main
PO Box 305
Mankato, KS 66956
Free: (800)359-2120
Phone: (913)378-3705
Fax: (913)378-3705
Publication E-mail: bblauvelt@navix.net

Community newspaper. **Subtitle:** The Superior Express. **Founded:** Jan. 1900. **Freq:** Weekly (Thurs.). **Print Method:** Offset. **Trim Size:** 16 x 22 3/4. **Cols./Page:** 8. **Col. Width:** 21 nonpareils. **Col. Depth:** 294 agate lines. **Key Personnel:** W.A. Blauvelt, Publisher, bblauvelt@navix.net. **ISSN:** 0740-0969. **Subscription Rates:** $16. **Remarks:** Accepts advertising. **Also known as:** The Superior Express.
Ad Rates: GLR: $.18 **Circ:** ‡4,068
BW: $423.36
SAU: $4
PCI: $3.78

11818 Jewell County Record
Superior Publishing Co., Inc.
111 E. Main
PO Box 305
Mankato, KS 66956
Free: (800)359-2120
Phone: (913)378-3191
Fax: (913)378-5437

Community newspaper. **Founded:** 1890. **Freq:** Weekly (Wed.). **Print Method:** Offset. **Trim Size:** 16 x 22 3/4. **Cols./Page:** 8. **Col. Width:** 10.5 picas. **Col. Depth:** 21 inches. **Key Personnel:** Bill Blauvelt, Publisher, phone (402)879-3291, bblauvelt@navix.net. **Subscription Rates:** $19.06 individuals; $22.24 out of area; $24.50 out of state. **Remarks:** Advertising accepted; rates available upon request tobacco and liquor products. **URL:** http://www.superiorne.com. **Alt. Formats:** CD-ROM. **Formerly:** Jewell County Post.
Ad Rates: GLR: $.18 **Circ:** Paid ‡1,095
BW: $423.50 Free ‡50
PCI: $3.78

MARYSVILLE†, pop. 3,670.

NE KS. Marshall Co. 95 mi. W. of St. Joseph, MO. Manufactures farm machinery, aircraft deicers, paper enveopes. Feed grains, wheat, alfalfa, soybeans, dairy, stock farms.

11819 The Marysville Advocate
107 S. 9th
Box 271
Marysville, KS 66508-0271

Newspaper. **Founded:** 1885. **Freq:** Weekly (Thurs.). **Print Method:** Offset. **Cols./Page:** 6. **Col. Width:** 24 nonpareils. **Col. Depth:** 294 agate lines. **Key Personnel:** Howard Kessinger, Editor and Publisher; Sharon Kessinger, Publisher; Darren Werth, Advertising Mgr.; Jon Smith, Circulation Mgr.; J.B. Coufal, Shop Superintendent. **USPS:** 332-260. **Subscription Rates:** $26.23 individuals in area; $36 out of area. **Remarks:** Accepts advertising.
Ad Rates: BW: $630 **Circ:** Paid 5,028
4C: $883 Free 61
SAU: $5
PCI: $5

11820 KNDY-AM - 1570
RR 3
Marysville, KS 66508-9803
Phone: (913)562-2361

Format: Country. **Networks:** ABC. **Owner:** Dierking Communications, Inc., at above address. **Founded:** 1956. **Operating Hours:** 6 a.m.-midnight; 5% network, 95% local. **Key Personnel:** Bruce Dierking, Contact; Paul Geston, News Dir.; Paul Lowell, Music Dir. **Wattage:** 250.

11821 KNDY-FM - 103.1
PO Box 1C
Rte. 3
Marysville, KS 66508-9803
Phone: (913)562-2361
Fax: (913)562-2188

Format: Contemporary Country. **Networks:** ABC. **Owner:** Dierking Communications, Inc., at above address. **Founded:** 1974. **Operating Hours:** 6 a.m.-midnight; 5% network, 95% local. **Key Personnel:** Bruce Dierking, Contact; Paul Geston, News Dir.; Paul Lowell, Music Dir. **Wattage:** 9000.

MCPHERSON†, pop. 11,800.

C. KS. McPherson Co. 50 mi. N. of Wichita. McPherson College (Ch. of Breth). Central College. Manufactures drugs, mobile homes and accessories, concrete products, fibre glass and plastic pipes. Flour mill. Refinery. Grain, dairy, poultry.

11822 McPherson Sentinel
301 S. Main
McPherson, KS 67460
Phone: (316)241-2422
Fax: (316)241-2425
Publisher E-mail: mepsent@southwind.net

Newspaper. **Founded:** 1885. **Freq:** Daily (eve.). **Print Meth-**

od: Offset. **Cols./Page:** 6. **Col. Width:** 25 nonpareils. **Col. Depth:** 301 agate lines. **Key Personnel:** Gary Mehl, Publisher. **Subscription Rates:** $92 individuals. **Remarks:** Accepts advertising.
Ad Rates: GLR: $.62 **Circ:** Paid ‡5,700
BW: $825 Free ‡6,400
4C: $1,035
SAU: $8.70
PCI: $8.70

11823 KBBE-FM - 96.7
Box 1069 Phone: (316)241-1504
McPherson, KS 67460 Fax: (316)241-3078

Format: Full Service. **Simulcasts:** KNGL-AM. **Networks:** ABC; Kansas Agriculture; Kansas Information. **Founded:** 1974. **Formerly:** KNEX-FM. **Operating Hours:** 4 a.m.- midnight. **Key Personnel:** Bill Olner, Manager; Wanda Morris, Office Mgr. **Wattage:** 6000. **Ad Rates:** $6-18 per unit. Combined advertising rates available with KNGC-AM.

11824 KNGL-AM - 1540
Box 1069 Phone: (316)241-1504
McPherson, KS 67460

Format: Full Service. **Simulcasts:** KBBE-FM. **Networks:** AP; Kansas Information; Kansas Agriculture. **Founded:** 1949. **Formerly:** KNEX-AM (1982). **Operating Hours:** 6 a.m.-midnight. **Key Personnel:** Bill Olner, Manager; Shawn White, Chief Engineer. **Wattage:** 250. **Ad Rates:** $5-6.75 for 30 seconds; $7.85-9.25 for 60 seconds. Combined advertising rates available with KBBE-FM.

11825 Multimedia Cablevision of McPherson
322 N. Main Phone: (316)241-6880
Box 887 Fax: (316)241-3187
McPherson, KS 67460

Owner: Multimedia Cablevision, Inc., at above address. **Founded:** 1981. **Formerly:** McPherson Cablevision. **Key Personnel:** Donna Cummings, Office Mgr.; Mark Smith, Contact. **Cities Served:** McPherson, KS: subscribing households 3,960; 46 channels; 1 community access channel; 24 hours per week community access programming.

MEADE†, pop. 1,700.

C. KS. Meade Co. 37 mi. SSW of Dodge City. Agriculture and natural gas-related industries, silica mines, livestock.

11826 Meade County News
Meade News
PO Box 310 Phone: (316)873-2118
Meade, KS 67864 Fax: (316)873-5456

Community newspaper. **Freq:** Weekly. **Cols./Page:** 6. **Col. Width:** 2 inches. **Col. Depth:** 21 1/2 inches. **Key Personnel:** Thomas Kuhns, Editor; Denice Kuhns, Advertising Mgr. **Subscription Rates:** $15.27 individuals; $17.32 out of county. **Remarks:** Color advertising not accepted.
Ad Rates: PCI: $3.19 **Circ:** ‡1,900

11827 KHYM-FM - 103.9
PO Box 991 Phone: (316)873-2991
Meade, KS 67864 Fax: (316)873-2755
E-mail: kjil@kjil.com

Format: Gospel. **Networks:** USA Radio; Ambassador Inspirational Radio. **Owner:** Great Plains Christian Radio, Inc., at above address. **Founded:** Dec. 23, 1997. **Operating Hours:** Continuous. **Key Personnel:** Don Hughes, General Mgr., don@kjil.com; Doug Wekekind, Operations Dir.; David Hayes, Music Dir. **Wattage:** 1,000,000. **Ad Rates:** Noncommercial. **URL:** http://www.kjil.com.

11828 KJIL-FM - 99.1
PO Box 991 Phone: (316)873-2991
Meade, KS 67864 Fax: (316)873-2755
E-mail: kjil@kjil.com

Format: Contemporary Christian. **Networks:** USA Radio; Ambassador Inspirational Radio. **Owner:** Great Plains Christian Radio, Inc., at above address. **Founded:** Sept. 5, 1992. **Operating Hours:** Continuous. **Key Personnel:** Don Hughes, General Mgr., don@kjil.com; Michael Luskey, Operations Dir.; Keith Sanderson, Production Dir. **Wattage:** 100,000. **Ad Rates:** Noncommercial. **URL:** http://www.kjil.com.

MEDICINE LODGE†, pop. 2,384.

N. KS. Barber Co. 75 mi. SW of Wichita. Scenic gypsum hills. Gypsum cement factory. Oil and gas wells. Gypsum mines. Refinery. Cattle rancher. Grain.

11829 Barber County Index
PO Box 349 Phone: (316)886-5617
Medicine Lodge, KS 67104
Newspaper. **Founded:** 1879. **Freq:** Weekly (Wed.). **Print Method:** Offset. **Cols./Page:** 6. **Col. Width:** 14 nonpareils. **Col. Depth:** 301 agate lines. **Key Personnel:** Jim Phillips, Publisher; Wayne White, Editor. **Subscription Rates:** $26 individuals; $36 out of state. **Remarks:** Accepts advertising.
Ad Rates: BW: $399.9 **Circ:** Paid 2,350
PCI: $3.1 Display
PCI: $3.6 Classified

11830 Multimedia Cablevision of Medicine Lodge
103 E. Washington St. Phone: (316)886-3731
Box 176 Free: (800)362-1053
Medicine Lodge, KS 67104

Owner: Multimedia Cablevision, Inc., PO Box 3027, Wichita, KS 67201, (316)262-4270. **Founded:** 1965. **Formerly:** Medicine Lodge CATV. **Key Personnel:** Riley Gamber, Contact, phone (316)886-3731; Robyn Tritt, Office Mgr. **Cities Served:** Harper, Medicine Lodge, Sharon, KS: subscribing households 1,600; 35 channels; 1 community access channel.

MERRIAM, pop. 12,020.

NE KS. Johnson Co. Suburb SSW of Kansas City.

11831 Northeast Johnson County Sun
Sun Publications, Inc.
7373 W. 107th St. Phone: (913)648-4620
Overland Park, KS 66212-2547 Fax: (913)381-1402

Newspaper. **Founded:** Jan. 1, 1950. **Freq:** Semiweekly (Wed. and Fri.). **Print Method:** Offset. **Cols./Page:** 8. **Col. Width:** 21 nonpareils. **Col. Depth:** 292 agate lines. **Key Personnel:** Jack Lovelace, Editor; Steve Rose, Publisher; Jo Stapleton, Advertising Manager. **Subscription Rates:** Free. **Remarks:** Accepts advertising. **Formerly:** Merriam Sun.
Ad Rates: SAU: $24.75 **Circ:** Combined ‡112,441
PCI: $34.35

MILTONVALE, pop. 588.

N. KS. Cloud Co. 40 mi. NE of Salina. Grain, stock, poultry, dairy farms. Wheat, livestock.

11832 Record
12 Spruce Phone: (785)427-2680
Miltonvale, KS 67466-0414 Fax: (785)427-2680

Newspaper with a Republican orientation. **Founded:** 1902. **Freq:** Weekly (Thurs.). **Print Method:** Offset. **Trim Size:** 22 1/2 x 30. **Cols./Page:** 6. **Col. Width:** 26 nonpareils. **Col. Depth:** 294 agate lines. **Key Personnel:** Richard R. Phelps, Publisher. **USPS:** 350-200. **Subscription Rates:** $16 individuals; $18 out of area. **Remarks:** Accepts advertising.
Ad Rates: GLR: $.30 **Circ:** Paid 700
BW: $252 Free 40
SAU: $2.25
PCI: $2.25

11833 Twin Valley Communications Inc.
PO Box 368 Phone: (913)427-2288
Miltonvale, KS 67466 Fax: (913)427-2216

MINNEAPOLIS†, pop. 2,075.

NC KS. Ottawa Co. 26 mi. N. of Salina. Elevators; camper coach and motor home factories. Dairy, stock, poultry, grain farms. Wheat, corn, alfalfa.

11834 The Minneapolis Messenger
Messenger
PO Box 249 Phone: (913)392-2129
Minneapolis, KS 67467 Fax: (913)392-2026

Community newspaper. **Founded:** 1875. **Freq:** Weekly (Thurs.). **Print Method:** Offset. **Cols./Page:** 6. **Col. Width:** 2 1/16 inches. **Col. Depth:** 300 agate lines. **Key Personnel:** John Wilson, Editor and Publisher. **Remarks:** Color advertising not accepted.
Ad Rates: GLR: $.19 **Circ:** Paid ‡2,543
BW: $327 Free ‡60
PCI: $3

MINNEOLA, pop. 712.

SW KS. Clark Co. 20 mi. S. of Dodge City. Residential. Farming and Ranching.

11835 The Minneola Record
Box 456 Phone: (316)885-4584
Minneola, KS 67865 Fax: (316)635-2643

Newspaper. **Founded:** 1976. **Freq:** Weekly (Thurs.). **Print Method:** Offset. **Cols./Page:** 5. **Col. Width:** 24 nonpareils. **Col. Depth:** 144 agate lines. **Key Personnel:** Amber Woodruff, Editor and Publisher, phone (316)635-2312; Jane Unruh, Bookkeeper/Adv., phone (316)885-4710. **Subscription Rates:** $18.89 individuals; $19.50 out of area.
Ad Rates: GLR: $.55 **Circ:** 558
PCI: $4

MISSION

11836 Mission Sun
Sun Publications, Inc.
7373 W. 107th St. Phone: (913)648-4620
Overland Park, KS 66212-2547 Fax: (913)381-1402

Newspaper. **Founded:** 1950. **Freq:** Semiweekly (Wed. and Fri.). **Print Method:** Offset. **Cols./Page:** 8. **Col. Width:** 21 nonpareils. **Col. Depth:** 292 agate lines. **Key Personnel:** Jack Lovelace, Editor; Steve Rose, Publisher; Joseph Mickelson, Vice Pres. of Sales & Marketing. **Subscription Rates:** Free. **Remarks:** Accepts advertising.
Ad Rates: BW: $5,096.70 **Circ:** Combined 137,000
4C: $5,396.70
SAU: $40.45
PCI: $21

11837 KXTR-FM - 96.5
5800 Foxridge Dr., 6th Fl. Phone: (913)432-1480
Mission, KS 66202-2333 Fax: (913)287-5209

Format: Classical. **Founded:** 1959. **Operating Hours:** Continuous. **Key Personnel:** Doyle Peterson, General Mgr.; Don Crawley, Program Dir.; Patrick Neas, Music Dir.; Stacey Hodges, Traffic Dir.; Charlan Wells, Public Service Dir. **Local Programs:** *Sounding Board*, Robert P. Ingram. **Wattage:** 100,000. **Ad Rates:** $55-90 for 30 seconds; $55-90 for 60 seconds.

MONTEZUMA

11838 Montezuma Press
Jean Loewen
208 Aztec Phone: (316)846-2312
PO Box 188 Fax: (316)846-2312
Montezuma, KS 67867
Community newspaper. **Founded:** 1914. **Freq:** Weekly (Thurs.). **Print Method:** Webb offset. **Cols./Page:** 6. **Col. Width:** 2 inches. **Col. Depth:** 21 1/2 inches. **Key Personnel:** Rudy Loewen and Jeanne Loewen, Publisher.
Circ: 1,100

MOUNDRIDGE, pop. 1,485.

C. KS. Mc Pherson Co. 28 mi. NE of Hutchinson. Manufactured cheese, grain drying equipment, riding mowers, farm equipment, roll forming machines. Feed mills. Oil, gas wells. Agriculture. Chicken, turkey hatcheries. Corn, oats, wheat.

11839 The Ledger
Davies Communications, Inc.
135 S. Christian Phone: (316)345-6343
PO Box 720 Fax: (316)345-2170
Moundridge, KS 67107
Free: (800)378-2117

Conservative newspaper (tabloid). **Founded:** Mar. 1887. **Freq:** Weekly (Thurs.). **Print Method:** Offset. **Trim Size:** 11 x 17. **Cols./Page:** 5. **Col. Width:** 12 picas. **Col. Depth:** 16 inches. **Key Personnel:** Mary Ann Musselwhite, Editor/Gen. Mgr./Administration. **USPS:** 277-360. **Subscription Rates:** $21.75 individuals; $28.75 out of state. **Remarks:** Accepts advertising.
Ad Rates: GLR: $.30 **Circ:** 1,800
BW: $308
4C: $900
SAU: $3.85
PCI: $3.85

11840 Mid-Kansas Cable Services, Inc.
109 N. Christian Phone: (316)345-2832
Moundridge, KS 67107 Fax: (316)345-6106

Founded: 1980. **Key Personnel:** Carl Krehbiel, Contact; Delonna Barnett, Office Mgr. **Cities Served:** subscribing households 465; 22 channels.

MOUNT HOPE

11841 The Mount Hope Clarion
Sole Proprietorship
101 S. Ohio Phone: (316)667-2697
PO Box 337 Fax: (316)667-2406
Mount Hope, KS 67108
Free: (800)794-3606

Community newspaper. **Founded:** 1885. **Freq:** Weekly (Thurs.). **Print Method:** Offset. **Trim Size:** 17 x 11 1/2. **Cols./Page:** 4. **Col. Width:** 14 picas. **Col. Depth:** 16 inches. **Key Personnel:** Delores Weve, Editor; Bill Chance, Publisher.

Subscription Rates: $19.50; $22 out of state. **Remarks:** Accepts advertising.
Ad Rates: GLR: $.414 **Circ:** 1,600
BW: $224
4C: $440
PCI: $5

MULLINVILLE

SC KS. Kiowa Co. 20 mi. W. of Greensburg. Kiowa Co. (SC). 20 m W of Greensburg.

11842 Mullinville Development Association
PO Box 92 Phone: (316)548-2528
Mullinville, KS 67109 Fax: (316)548-2232

Owner: Mullinville Development Assn., at above address. **Founded:** 1972. **Key Personnel:** Ron Freeman, President; Paul Kendall, Vice President. **Cities Served:** Mullinville, KS: subscribing households 110; 14 channels; 1 community access channel.

MULVANE, pop. 4,242.

S. KS. Sumner Co. 14 mi. SE of Wichita. Industrial Park. Sand and gravel plant. Grain, dairy, truck, stock farms.

11843 Bandwagon
Mulvane News
204 W. Main St. Phone: (316)777-4233
PO Box 157
Mulvane, KS 67110
Shopper. **Founded:** 1979. **Freq:** Weekly (Tues.). **Print Method:** Offset. **Cols./Page:** 6. **Col. Width:** 26 nonpareils. **Col. Depth:** 301 agate lines. **Key Personnel:** Mike Robinson, Editor and Publisher; Tracy Spencer, Advertising Mgr. **Remarks:** Accepts advertising.
Ad Rates: GLR: $8.60 **Circ:** Free 5,300

11844 The Mulvane News
Mulvane News
204 W. Main St. Phone: (316)777-4233
PO Box 157
Mulvane, KS 67110
Local newspaper. **Founded:** 1883. **Freq:** Weekly (Thurs.). **Print Method:** Offset. **Cols./Page:** 6. **Col. Width:** 26 nonpareils. **Col. Depth:** 301 agate lines. **Key Personnel:** Mike Robinson, Editor and Publisher; Tracy Spencer, Advertising Mgr. **Subscription Rates:** $24 individuals. **Remarks:** Accepts advertising.
Ad Rates: GLR: $8.60 **Circ:** 1,750

NATOMA, pop. 515.

N. KS. Osborne Co. 92 mi. NW of Salina. Oil wells. Diversified farming. Livestock, wheat.

11845 Independent Record
Natoma Publishing Co.
PO Box 160 Phone: (785)885-4582
Natoma, KS 67651-0160 Fax: (785)885-4582

Community newspaper. **Founded:** Feb. 1909. **Freq:** Weekly (Thurs.). **Print Method:** Offset. **Cols./Page:** 6. **Col. Width:** 29 nonpareils. **Col. Depth:** 300 agate lines. **Key Personnel:** Della Richmond, Editor. **Subscription Rates:** $26.88 individuals; $27.93 out of area; $30 out of state. **Remarks:** Accepts advertising.
Ad Rates: GLR: $2.20 **Circ:** ‡1,750
BW: $336.60
PCI: $2.02

NEODESHA, pop. 3,414.

SE KS. Wilson Co. 15 mi. N. of Independence. Alfalfa dehydrating plant; plows, boats, steel fabrication, aerosol products, plastics, insecticide, carpenter tools, cabinet products, dairy products manufactured; foundry. Oil wells. Grain, dairy, poultry, stock farms. Wheat, corn, oats.

11846 Neodesh Derrick
Neodesha Derrick
502 Main Phone: (316)325-3000
PO Box 356 Fax: (316)352-2880
Neodesha, KS 66757
Community newspaper. **Founded:** 1883. **Freq:** Weekly (Thurs.). **Print Method:** Offset. **Cols./Page:** 6. **Col. Width:** 12.5 picas. **Col. Depth:** 301 agate lines. **Key Personnel:** J. Hartley Harper, Editor; Judy Micus, Advertising Mgr. **Subscription Rates:** $25 individuals in county; $27 out of state out of county; $30 out of state. **Remarks:** Accepts advertising. **Formerly:** Neodesh Sun-Register.
Ad Rates: BW: $441 **Circ:** ‡1,800
SAU: $3.50
PCI: $3.50

NESS CITY†, pop. 1,776.

WC KS. Ness Co. 56 mi. N. of Dodge City. Oil wells. Grain, dairy, poultry, livestock farms. Wheat, corn, milo, alfalfa.

11847 Ness County News
PO Box C Phone: (785)798-2213
Ness City, KS 67560 Fax: (785)798-2214
Publisher E-mail: nessnews@ruraltel.net

Community newspaper. **Founded:** 1884. **Freq:** Weekly (Thurs.). **Print Method:** Offset. **Cols./Page:** 6. **Col. Width:** 24 nonpareils. **Col. Depth:** 294 agate lines. **Key Personnel:** John Clarke, Publisher; Jerry Clarke, Editor. **USPS:** 377-200. **Subscription Rates:** $18.50 individuals; $22.50 out of area; $.40 single issue. **Remarks:** Accepts advertising.
Ad Rates: GLR: $.16 **Circ:** ‡2,425
SAU: $2.80
PCI: $2.80

NEWTON†, pop. 16,332.

SC KS. Harvey Co. 25 mi. N. of Wichita. Bethel College (Mennon). Mobile homes manufactured Flour mills. Dairy, stock, grain farms.

11848 Mennonite Weekly Review
Mennonite Weekly Review, Inc.
Box 568 Phone: (316)283-3670
Newton, KS 67114 Fax: (316)283-6502
Free: (800)424-0718
Publication E-mail: menwkrv@southwind.net

Tabloid newspaper containing news and commentary regarding churches and institutions of the Mennonite denomination. **Founded:** Aug. 9, 1923. **Freq:** Weekly (Thurs.). **Print Method:** Offset. **Cols./Page:** 5. **Col. Width:** 24 nonpareils. **Col. Depth:** 224 agate lines. **Key Personnel:** Robert M. Schrag, Publisher; Paul R. Schrag, Editor; Laurie L. Oswald, Asst. Editor. **ISSN:** 0889-2156. **Subscription Rates:** $31 individuals; $40 other countries.
Ad Rates: PCI: $15 **Circ:** Paid ‡10,200
Free ‡840

11849 Newton Kansan
Morris Communications Corp.
121 W. 6th St. Phone: (316)283-1500
PO Box 268 Fax: (316)283-2471
Newton, KS 67114
General newspaper. **Founded:** 1872. **Freq:** Daily (eve.) and Sat. (morn.). **Print Method:** Offset. **Trim Size:** 11 3/4 x 14. **Cols./Page:** 6. **Col. Width:** 12.2 picas. **Col. Depth:** 21 1/2 inches. **Key Personnel:** Douglas J. Anstaett, Editor and Publisher, danstaet@thekansan.com; Dennis Garrison, Advertising Mgr. **Subscription Rates:** $94 individuals. **URL:** nknews@thekansan.com.
Ad Rates: BW: $941.70 **Circ:** Paid 7,517
4C: $1,091.70
SAU: $8.20
PCI: $8.20

11850 Prairie Advisor
Kansan
121-125 W. 6th St. Phone: (316)283-1500
Newton, KS 67114 Fax: (316)283-2471

Shopping guide. **Freq:** Weekly (Tues.). **Print Method:** Offset. **Trim Size:** 11 3/4 x 14. **Cols./Page:** 6. **Col. Width:** 12.2 picas. **Key Personnel:** Douglas J. Anstaett, Editor and Publisher; Dennis Garrison, Advertising Mgr. **Remarks:** Accepts advertising.
Ad Rates: BW: $838.50 **Circ:** Free 8,000
4C: $998.50
SAU: $7.30
PCI: $8.50

11851 With
Faith & Life Press
718 Main St. Phone: (316)283-5100
PO Box 347 Fax: (316)283-0454
Newton, KS 67114-0347
Free: (800)743-2484
Publication E-mail: deliag@gcmc.com
Publisher E-mail: flp@gcmc.org

Religious magazine promoting Christianity to high school youths. **Subtitle:** The Magazine for Radical Christian Youth. **Founded:** 1968. **Freq:** 8/year. **Print Method:** Offset. **Trim Size:** 8 1/2 x 11. **Key Personnel:** Carol Duerksen, Editor. **Subscription Rates:** $18.95 individuals.
Ad Rates: BW: $650 **Circ:** 6,000

11852 KJRG-AM - 950
209 N. Meridian Rd. Phone: (316)283-5150
Box 567 Fax: (316)284-2684
Newton, KS 67114-0567

Format: Religious. **Networks:** USA Radio. **Founded:** 1953. **Operating Hours:** 6 a.m.-11 p.m. **Key Personnel:** Gordon Anderson, General Mgr. **Wattage:** 500.

11853 KOEZ-FM - 92.3
209 Meridian Rd. Phone: (316)283-5150
Box 567 Fax: (316)284-2684
Newton, KS 67114-0567

Format: Easy Listening. **Networks:** CNN Radio; Wall Street Journal Radio. **Founded:** 1959. **Operating Hours:** Continuous. **Key Personnel:** Gordon Anderson, General Mgr. **Wattage:** 100,000.

11854 Multi Media Inc.
PO Box 684 Phone: (316)283-7270
Newton, KS 67114-0684 Fax: (316)283-7622

Owner: Tele-Communications Inc., PO Box 5630, Denver, CO 80217, (303)267-5500. **Founded:** 1976. **Formerly:** Crest Communications (1980); Newton Cable TV (1986); TCI of Kansas Inc. **Key Personnel:** Ray Hubbard, General Mgr.; Lowell Stone, Technical Operations Mgr.; Marilyn Lundblade, Office Mgr. **Cities Served:** Newton, North Newton, KS: 34 channels; 1 community access channel; 168 hours per week community access programming.

11855 Multimedia Cablevision, Inc.
206 W. 6th St. Phone: (316)283-7270
Box 684 Fax: (316)283-7622
Newton, KS 67114
Free: (800)765-4824

Owner: Multimedia Cablevision, Inc., at above address. **Founded:** 1976. **Formerly:** Newton Cable TV; Crest Communications. **Cities Served:** 33 channels; 1 community access channel; 168 hours per week community access programming.

NORTH NEWTON

11856 Bethel College Bulletin
Bethel College
300 E. 27th St. Phone: (316)283-2500
North Newton, KS 67117 Fax: (316)284-5286

Alumni magazine. **Founded:** 1914. **Freq:** Quarterly (during the academic year). **Print Method:** Offset. **Remarks:** Advertising not accepted.
Circ: Free ‡12,000

11857 KBCU-FM - 88.1
300 E. 27th St. Phone: (316)284-5368
North Newton, KS 67117 Fax: (316)284-5286
E-mail: kbcu@bethelks.edu

Format: Alternative/New Music/Progressive; Folk; Bluegrass. **Networks:** AP. **Founded:** 1989. **Operating Hours:** 10 a.m.-midnight; 100% local. **Key Personnel:** Bryan Reber, General Mgr., phone (316)284-5396; Tammy Unruh, Station Mgr., phone (316)284-5368; Rob Thieszen, Contact, phone (316)284-5214; Kelly Mick, Program Dir., phone (316)284-5368; Jen Janzen, Music Dir., phone (316)284-5368; Brandon Russell, News Dir., phone (316)284-5368; Aaron Sauyers, Marketing, phone (316)284-5368; Chris Grassez, Sports Dir., phone (316)284-5368; Cory Lamb, PSAs, phone (316)284-5368. **Local Programs:** *Radio Diferencia*, Mona Jimenez, (316)284-5368. **Wattage:** 149. **Ad Rates:** Noncommercial; underwriting available. $20 per unit. **URL:** http://www.bethelks.edu.

NORTON†, pop. 3,400.

NW KS. Norton Co. 200 mi. NW of Salina. State Hospital for Mentally Retarded.

11858 Norton Daily Telegram
215 S. Kansas Phone: (913)877-3361
Box 320
Norton, KS 67654-0320
General newspaper. **Founded:** 1907. **Freq:** Monday-Friday. **Print Method:** Offset. **Cols./Page:** 6. **Col. Width:** 20 nonpareils. **Col. Depth:** 294 agate lines. **Key Personnel:** Richard D. Boyd, Editor and Publisher. **Subscription Rates:** $52.70 local annual; $65 U.S.; $60.08 elsewhere in Kansas. **Remarks:** Advertising not accepted for alcohol and tobacco products.
Ad Rates: GLR: $.85 **Circ:** Free 2,008
BW: $370
SAU: $4.20
PCI: $4.20

11859 KQNK-AM - 1530
Box 220 Phone: (913)877-3378
Norton, KS 67654

Format: Middle-of-the-Road (MOR). **Networks:** Mutual Broadcasting System. **Founded:** 1963. **Key Personnel:** Larry Black, Contact. **Wattage:** 1000.

OAKLEY, pop. 2,268.

W. KS. Logan Co. 120 mi. NW of Dodge City. Elevator. Oil Grain farms. Wheat, corn, sunflowers, sorghum, cattle.

11860 The Oakley Graphic
118 Center Phone: (913)672-3228
Oakley, KS 67748-0545 Fax: (913)672-3229

Community newspaper. **Founded:** Nov. 22, 1889. **Freq:** Weekly (Wed.). **Print Method:** Offset. Uses mats. **Cols./Page:** 6. **Col. Width:** 2 inches. **Col. Depth:** 21 inches. **Key Personnel:** Barbara Glover, Editor; Jerry Anderson, Publisher. **Subscription Rates:** $20.65 individuals; $21.71 out of area. **Remarks:** Accepts advertising.
Ad Rates: GLR: $.22 **Circ:** Paid ‡1500
BW: $397.32 Free ‡30
SAU: $3.08

OBERLIN†, pop. 2,387.

NW KS. Decatur Co. 170 mi. NW of Salina. Oil wells. Grain, poultry, stock farms. Wheat, corn, alfalfa.

11861 The Oberlin Herald
Nor'West Newspapers Inc.
170 S. Penn Ave. Phone: (913)475-2206
Oberlin, KS 67749 Fax: (913)475-2800
Publication E-mail: obherald@nwkansas.com

Community newspaper. **Founded:** June 1879. **Freq:** Weekly (Wed.). **Print Method:** Offset. **Cols./Page:** 6. **Col. Width:** 2 1/16 inches. **Col. Depth:** 21 inches. **Key Personnel:** Steve Haynes, Publisher; Cynthia Haynes, Publisher; Brodie Farguhar, Managing Editor; Pat Cozad, Circulation Mgr. **USPS:** 401-600. **Subscription Rates:** $25 individuals; $29 out of area; $32 out of state. **Remarks:** Accepts advertising. **URL:** http://www.nwkansas.com.
Ad Rates: GLR: $4.45 **Circ:** Paid ‡2,716
BW: $574.05
SAU: $4.65
PCI: $4.45

11862 KSNK-TV - 8
West Hwy. 36 Phone: (913)475-2248
PO Box 238 Fax: (913)475-3944
Oberlin, KS 67749

Format: Commercial TV. **Simulcasts:** KSNW-TV. **Networks:** NBC. **Owner:** Kansas State Network, PO Box 333, Wichita, KS 67201, (316)265-3333. **Founded:** 1959. **Formerly:** KOMC-TV. **Operating Hours:** Continuous. **ADI:** Wichita-Hutchinson, KS. **Key Personnel:** Gloria Becker, Contact; Rhonda Manning, Traffic Mgr.; David Baker, Production Mgr. **Ad Rates:** $20-100 per unit.

OLATHE†, pop. 37,500.

E. KS. Johnson Co. 20 mi. SW of Kansas City. State School for the Deaf, Mid-America College. Manufactures batteries, radio and electronic parts for airplanes, X-Ray equipment, air-conditioning cooling towers, drilling machinery, grease, oil, cowboy boots, shoes. Stock, dairy farms.

11863 The Olathe Daily News
Keltatim Publishing Co., Inc.
Box 130 Phone: (913)764-2211
Olathe, KS 66051 Fax: (913)764-3672
Publication E-mail: adn@joconews.com

General newspaper. **Founded:** 1857. **Freq:** Mon.-Sat. (morn.). **Print Method:** Offset. **Cols./Page:** 6. **Col. Width:** 26 nonpareils. **Col. Depth:** 21 1/2 inches. **Key Personnel:** Timothy P. O'Donnell, Publisher; Scott Smith, General Mgr.; Rick Brown, Advertising Dir.; Chuck Kurtz, Managing Editor. **ISSN:** 0886-9871. **Subscription Rates:** $76.20 individuals; $86.60 out of area; $152 out of state. **Remarks:** Accepts advertising.
Ad Rates: SAU: $10.50 **Circ:** Mon.-Fri. ★7,962
PCI: $10.50 Sat. ★7,978

11864 Olathe Sun
Sun Publications, Inc.
7373 W. 107th St. Phone: (913)648-4620
Overland Park, KS 66212-2547 Fax: (913)381-1402

Newspaper. **Freq:** Semiweekly (Wed. and Fri.). **Print Method:** Offset. **Cols./Page:** 8. **Col. Width:** 21 nonpareils. **Col. Depth:** 292 agate lines. **Key Personnel:** Jack Lovelace, Editor; Steve Rose, Publisher; Jo Stapleton, Advertising Mgr. **Subscription Rates:** Free. **Remarks:** Accepts advertising.
Ad Rates: SAU: $24.75 **Circ:** Combined 112,441
PCI: $34.35

ONAGA, pop. 761.

NE KS. Pottawatomie Co. 40 mi. NW of Topeka.

11865 Onaga Herald
PO Box 309 Phone: (913)889-4681
Onaga, KS 66521 Fax: (913)889-4610

Community newspaper. **Founded:** Apr. 1890. **Freq:** Weekly. **Print Method:** Offset. **Trim Size:** 22 1/2 x 14. **Cols./Page:** 6. **Col. Width:** 12.2 nonpareils. **Col. Depth:** 21 inches. **Key Personnel:** William F. Harder, Editor and Publisher; Joe D. Harder, Advertising Mgr. **USPS:** 408-500. **Subscription Rates:** $20 individuals; $22 out of state. **Remarks:** Accepts advertising.
Ad Rates: BW: $378 **Circ:** ‡1,100
PCI: $3

OSBORNE†, pop. 2,120.

NC KS. Osborne Co. 70 mi. NW of Salina. Residential.

11866 Osborne County Farmer
Osborne Publishing Co., Inc.
PO Box 130 Phone: (785)346-5424
Osborne, KS 67473 Fax: (785)346-5400
Publisher E-mail: ospubco@ruraltel.net

Local newspaper. **Founded:** 1876. **Freq:** Weekly (Thurs.). **Print Method:** Offset. **Cols./Page:** 6. **Col. Width:** 26 nonpareils. **Col. Depth:** 287 agate lines. **Key Personnel:** Dale Worley, Publisher. **ISSN:** 1040-9033. **Subscription Rates:** $24.58 individuals. **Online:** Internet.
Ad Rates: GLR: $.20 **Circ:** ‡2,755
SAU: $3.35
PCI: $3.35

OSKALOOSA†, pop. 1,092.

NE KS. Jefferson Co. 22 mi. N. of Lawrence. Grain, stock, dairy farms. Wheat, corn.

11867 The Oskaloosa Independent
Wilson-Davis Publications, Inc.
PO Box 278 Phone: (913)863-2520
Oskaloosa, KS 66066 Fax: (913)863-2730

Community newspaper. **Founded:** 1896. **Freq:** Weekly (Thurs.). **Print Method:** Offset. **Cols./Page:** 7. **Col. Width:** 12 picas. **Col. Depth:** 21 inches. **Key Personnel:** John D. Montgomery, Editor and Publisher; Tom Love, Advertising Mgr. **Subscription Rates:** $15.79 individuals. **Remarks:** Color advertising not accepted.
Ad Rates: GLR: $.20 **Circ:** Paid 5,900
SAU: $1.37

OSWEGO

11868 Oswego Independent-Observer
Independent Observer
PO Box 269 Phone: (316)795-4712
Oswego, KS 67356
Community newspaper. **Freq:** Weekly (Wed.). **Cols./Page:** 6. **Col. Width:** 13 1/2 picas. **Col. Depth:** 21 inches. **Key Personnel:** Robert O. Crowell, Editor.
Circ: 1,500

OTTAWA†, pop. 11,016.

E. KS. Franklin Co. 26 mi. S. of Lawrence. Ottawa University. Manufactures milk, steel foundry products, TV antennas, cement, mobile homes, rural advertising signs, yard tractors. Mill work. Rock quarries. Diversified farming. Beef. Corn, wheat, alfalfa.

11869 Ottawa Herald
104 S. Cedar Phone: (913)242-4700
Ottawa, KS 66067 Fax: (913)242-9420
Free: (800)467-8383
Publication E-mail: letters@ottawaherald.com

General newspaper. **Founded:** 1869. **Freq:** Daily (eve.). **Print Method:** Offset. **Cols./Page:** 6. **Col. Width:** 11.5 picas. **Col. Depth:** 21.5 inches. **Key Personnel:** John D. Montgomery, Editor and Publisher; Jay Bemis, Managing Editor; Vernon J. Brown, Advertising Dir.; Gene Kelsey, Circulation Mgr.; Kathy Miller, Office Mgr. **Subscription Rates:** $90.88 in ottawa; $134.40 out of state. **Remarks:** Accepts advertising. **URL:** http://www.ottawaherald.com. **Alt. Formats:** Microfilm.
Ad Rates: BW: $1,012.65 **Circ:** Paid ‡6,322
4C: $1,162.65 Non-paid ‡7,583
PCI: $7.85

11870 The Ottawa Times
401 S. Main St., Ste. 1 Phone: (913)242-9200
PO Box 246 Fax: (913)242-9595
Ottawa, KS 66067
Publication E-mail: otimes@computer-services.com

Weekly community newspaper. **Founded:** 1932. **Freq:** Weekly (Thurs.). **Print Method:** Offset. **Trim Size:** 11 1/4 x 17. **Cols./Page:** 6. **Col. Width:** 10 picas. **Col. Depth:** 16 inches. **Key Personnel:** Bill Gray, Editor; Kent Ramsey, General Mgr. **USPS:** 413-660. **Subscription Rates:** $31 individuals. **Remarks:** Color advertising accepted; rates available upon request. **Alt. Formats:** CD-ROM.
Ad Rates: GLR: $.10 **Circ:** Paid 1,200
BW: $696
4C: $975
SAU: $4.75
PCI: $7.25

11871 Tauy Talk
Ottawa University
1001 S. Cedar Phone: (785)242-5200
Box 16 Fax: (785)242-7429
Ottawa, KS 66067-3399
Free: (800)755-5200

University alumni and friends magazine. **Founded:** 1928. **Freq:** Quarterly. **Print Method:** Offset. **Trim Size:** 8 1/2 x 11. **Cols./Page:** 3. **Col. Width:** 14 picas. **Col. Depth:** 59 picas. **Key Personnel:** Tracy Campbell, Editor and Publisher, campbell@ott.edu. **USPS:** 534-220. **Remarks:** Advertising not accepted.
Circ: Controlled ‡7,500

11872 KOFO-AM - 1220
PO Box 16 Phone: (913)242-1220
Ottawa, KS 66067 Fax: (913)242-1442
E-mail: kofo@ott.net

Format: Country. **Networks:** ABC; Kansas Information; Jones Satellite. **Owner:** Brandy Communications Inc., at above address, (785)242-1220, Fax: (785)242-1442. **Founded:** 1949. **Operating Hours:** Continuous. **Key Personnel:** Brad Howard, Contact; Kathy Niehoff, General Sales Mgr.; Karen Niehoff, Office Mgr. **Wattage:** 250. **Ad Rates:** $6.00-8 for 30 seconds; $8-10 for 60 seconds.

11873 KRBW-FM - 90.5
PO Box 22 Phone: (785)242-9050
Ottawa, KS 66067

Format: Contemporary Christian. **Owner:** Ottawa Christian Radio, Inc., at above address. **Operating Hours:** Continuous. **Key Personnel:** Rev. Fred Schaeffer, Station Coor., phone (785)242-2746, schaeff@ott.net; Pete Lounge, Public Affairs, phone (785)242-1906. **Local Programs:** *Sunday Morning Praise*, Ron Hughes, Fred Schaeffer. **Wattage:** 430. **Ad Rates:** Noncommercial. **URL:** http://www.christianradio.com/krbw/.

11874 KTJO-FM - 88.9
Ottawa University Phone: (913)242-5200
1001 S. Cedar Fax: (913)242-7429
PO Box 10
Ottawa, KS 66067-3399

Format: Contemporary Hit Radio (CHR). **Founded:** 1942. **Operating Hours:** 7 a.m.-11 p.m. Mon- Sat. **Key Personnel:** Barry King, Faculty Advisor. **Wattage:** 145. **Ad Rates:** Noncommercial.

OVERLAND PARK, pop. 81,784.

E. KS. Johnson Co. 12 mi. SW of Kansas City.

11875 American School & University
Intertec Publishing Corp.
9800 Metcalf Ave. Phone: (913)967-1854
Overland Park, KS 66212 Fax: (913)967-1898
Free: (800)262-1954
Publication E-mail: 75402.1726@compuserve.com

Trade magazine. **Subtitle:** Facilities, Purchasing and Business Administration. **Founded:** 1928. **Freq:** Monthly. **Print Method:** Offset. **Trim Size:** 8 1/8 x 10 7/8. **Cols./Page:** 3. **Col. Width:** 28 nonpareils. **Col. Depth:** 140 agate lines. **Key Personnel:** Joseph Agron, Editor, phone (610)566-7080, fax (610)566-6105, asuagron@compuserve.com; Brian Agnes, Group Publisher, phone (913)967-1854, fax (913)967-1898, brian_agnes@intertec.com; Susan Knuffman, Managing Editor. **ISSN:** 0003-0945. **Subscription Rates:** $50 individuals. **Remarks:** Accepts advertising. **URL:** http://www.intertec.com; http://www.asumag.com.
Ad Rates: BW: $7,900 **Circ:** Controlled 63,000
4C: $9,200

11876 The Auctioneer
National Auctioneers Association
8880 Ballentine Phone: (913)541-8084
Overland Park, KS 66214 Fax: (913)894-5281
Publisher E-mail: naahq@aol.com

Trade magazine for auctioneers. **Founded:** 1949. **Freq:** Monthly. **Trim Size:** 51 x 65 PCs. **Key Personnel:** Holly M. Neuman, Publications Dir., naahqholly@aol.com; Shawn

Bruce, Publications Asst., naahanshawn@aol.com. **ISSN:** 1070-0137. **Remarks:** Accepts advertising.
Ad Rates: BW: $460 **Circ:** (Not Reported)
4C: $1,060

11877 Broadcast Engineering
Intertec Publishing Corp.
9800 Metcalf Ave. Phone: (913)967-1854
Overland Park, KS 66212 Fax: (913)967-1898
Free: (800)262-1954

Magazine on television broadcast cable, telco, satellite equipment, products & technology. **Subtitle:** Journal of Digital Television. **Founded:** 1959. **Freq:** 13/year. **Print Method:** Offset. **Trim Size:** 8 x 10 7/8. **Cols./Page:** 3. **Col. Width:** 2 1/4 inches. **Col. Depth:** 10 inches. **Key Personnel:** Brad Dick, Editor, brad_dick@intertec.com; Dennis Triola, Publisher; Tom Brick, Marketing Director. **ISSN:** 0007-1794. **Subscription Rates:** $50 individuals; $5 single issue; $60 other countries; $110 by mail. **URL:** http://www.broadcastengineering.com.
Ad Rates: BW: $4,945 **Circ:** Controlled ‡32,000
4C: $5,845
PCI: $285

11878 Broker World
Insurance Publications, Inc.
PO Box 1131 Phone: (913)383-9191
Overland Park, KS 66207 Fax: (913)383-1247

Trade magazine on life and health insurance brokering. **Founded:** 1980. **Freq:** Monthly. **Print Method:** Offset. **Trim Size:** 8 x 10 7/8. **Cols./Page:** 3. **Col. Width:** 14 picas. **Col. Depth:** 140 agate lines. **Key Personnel:** Sharon A. Chace, Editor; William S. Howard, Publisher. **ISSN:** 0273-6551. **Subscription Rates:** $9 individuals. **Remarks:** Accepts advertising.
Ad Rates: GLR: $2,250 **Circ:** Paid ‡25,552
BW: $2,145 Non-paid ‡1902
4C: $3090

11879 California-Arizona Farm Press
Intertec Publishing Corp.
9800 Metcalf Ave. Phone: (913)967-1854
Overland Park, KS 66212 Fax: (913)967-1898
Free: (800)262-1954

Agriculture news tabloid. **Founded:** Jan. 9, 1979. **Freq:** Weekly. **Print Method:** Offset. **Trim Size:** 11 3/8 x 15 1/2. **Cols./Page:** 5. **Col. Width:** 21 nonpareils. **Col. Depth:** 203 agate lines. **Key Personnel:** Dan Bryant, Editor; Tommy L. Keith, Publisher. **Subscription Rates:** $12.50.

11880 Campus Ledger
Johnson Co.
Johnson Community College Phone: (913)469-8500
12345 College Blvd. Fax: (913)469-4409
Overland Park, KS 66210
Publication E-mail: ledger@jccc.net

Collegiate newspaper. **Founded:** 1978. **Freq:** Semimonthly (during the academic year). **Print Method:** Offset. **Trim Size:** 11 x 16. **Cols./Page:** 5. **Col. Width:** 11.5 picas. **Col. Depth:** 224 agate lines. **Key Personnel:** Danny Phillips, Editor; Greg Harrell, Faculty Advisor, gharrell@jcc.net. **Subscription Rates:** Free. **Remarks:** Accepts advertising. **URL:** http://www.johnco.cc.ks.us. **Feature Editors:** Brian Jones, *Art*, phone (913)469-2577.
Ad Rates: BW: $864 **Circ:** Free 6,000
PCI: $9

11881 CEE News
Intertec Publishing Corp.
9800 Metcalf Ave. Phone: (913)967-1854
Overland Park, KS 66212 Fax: (913)967-1898
Free: (800)262-1954

Electrical construction industry magazine. **Founded:** 1949. **Freq:** Monthly. **Print Method:** Offset. **Trim Size:** 10 7/8 x 15 7/8. **Cols./Page:** 3. **Col. Width:** 40 nonpareils. **Col. Depth:** 212 agate lines. **Key Personnel:** Stuart M. Lewis, Editor; Richard A. Hathaway, Publisher; Bob MacArthur, Assoc. Publisher. **ISSN:** 1045-2710. **Subscription Rates:** $52; $92 other countries; Free to qualified subscribers. **Remarks:** Accepts advertising. **Formerly:** Electrical Construction Technology.
Ad Rates: BW: $5,115 **Circ:** Controlled ‡105,221
4C: $6,340

11882 College Boulevard News
Sun Publications, Inc.
7373 W. 107th St. Phone: (913)648-4620
Overland Park, KS 66212-2547 Fax: (913)381-1402

Newspaper (tabloid) for the College Boulevard office work force in Overland Park, Kansas. **Founded:** Mar. 6, 1984. **Freq:** Weekly. **Print Method:** Offset. **Trim Size:** 10 3/8 x 13 1/2. **Cols./Page:** 6. **Col. Width:** 9.3 picas. **Col. Depth:** 13.5 inches. **Key Personnel:** Liz Irwin, Editor; Steve Rose, Publisher; Brad Caplan, Advertising Mgr.; Susan Karol, V.P. of Sales; John Yates, V.P. of Operations; Vicki Farris, General Mgr. **Subscription Rates:** Free; $40 by mail. **Remarks:** Accepts advertising.
Ad Rates: BW: $1,438 **Circ:** Paid ‡100
4C: $1,738 Free ‡30,000
PCI: $17.75

11883 Delta Farm Press
Intertec Publishing Corp.
9800 Metcalf Ave. Phone: (913)967-1854
Overland Park, KS 66212 Fax: (913)967-1898
Free: (800)262-1954

Agriculture tabloid. **Founded:** 1942. **Freq:** Weekly (Fri.). **Print Method:** Offset. **Trim Size:** 11 x 14 1/2. **Cols./Page:** 4. **Col. Width:** 2 1/4 inches. **Col. Depth:** 13 1/2 inches. **Key Personnel:** Ben Pryor, Editor; John Montandon, Publisher. **ISSN:** 0011-8036. **Subscription Rates:** $25. **Remarks:** Accepts advertising. **URL:** http://www.intertec.com.
Ad Rates: BW: $4,621 **Circ:** Paid 23,224
4C: $5,955 Non-paid 7,977
PCI: $93

11884 Electrical Construction and Maintenance (EC&M)
Intertec Publishing Corp.
9800 Metcalf Ave. Phone: (913)967-1854
Overland Park, KS 66212 Fax: (913)967-1898
Free: (800)262-1954

Magazine focusing on electrical engineering, construction, and maintenance. **Founded:** 1901. **Freq:** Monthly. **Print Method:** Offset. **Trim Size:** 8 x 10 3/4. **Cols./Page:** 3 and 2. **Col. Width:** 13 and 20 picas. **Col. Depth:** 10 inches. **Key Personnel:** John DeDad, Editor; Rich Hathaway, Group Publisher; Bob MacArthur, Publisher. **Remarks:** Accepts advertising.
Ad Rates: BW: $9,590 **Circ:** Controlled 102,521
4C: $11,985 Paid 1,214

11885 Electrical Wholesaling
Intertec Publishing Corp.
9800 Metcalf Ave. Phone: (913)967-1854
Overland Park, KS 66212 Fax: (913)967-1898
Free: (800)262-1954

Magazine focusing on electrical wholesaling. **Founded:** 1920. **Freq:** Monthly. **Print Method:** Offset. **Cols./Page:** 3. **Col. Width:** 27 nonpareils. **Col. Depth:** 136 agate lines. **Key Personnel:** A.J. Herbert, Editor; Richard Hathaway, Publisher; Bob MacArthur, Assoc. Publisher. **Subscription Rates:** $20 individuals. **Remarks:** Accepts advertising.
Ad Rates: BW: $2,600 **Circ:** Paid ★**12,707**
4C: $4,280 Non-paid ★**11,527**

11886 Engineering and Mining Journal
Intertec Publishing Corp.
9800 Metcalf Ave. Phone: (913)967-1854
Overland Park, KS 66212 Fax: (913)967-1898
Free: (800)262-1954

Magazine focusing on metal and non-metallic mining. **Founded:** 1866. **Freq:** Monthly. **Print Method:** Offset. **Trim Size:** 8 1/8 x 10 7/8. **Cols./Page:** 2 and 3. **Col. Width:** 45 and 26 nonpareils. **Col. Depth:** 140 agate lines. **Key Personnel:** Robert Wyllie, Editor; Robert Dimond, Publisher. **ISSN:** 0095-8948. **Subscription Rates:** $60 Canada and U.S.; $90 other countries. **Remarks:** Accepts advertising.
Ad Rates: BW: $4,990 **Circ:** Non-paid 24,721
4C: $6,640

11887 Expansion Management
New Hope Communications
9500 Nall Ave., Ste. 400 Phone: (913)381-4800
Overland Park, KS 66207 Fax: (913)381-8858
Free: (800)539-7263
Publisher E-mail: sales@newhope.com

Magazine assisting executives and managers worldwide in planning and overseeing their companies' facilities development and other expansion and relocation activities. **Founded:** Mar. 1985. **Freq:** Bimonthly. **Print Method:** Web offset. **Trim Size:** 8 x 10 1/2. **Cols./Page:** 3. **Key Personnel:** Gorton Wood, Publisher, phone (732)530-8801, fax (732)747-5530, gwood@newhope.com; Bill King, Editor, fax (913)381-8858, bking@newhope.com; Roy Harryman, Managing Editor, rharryman@newhope.com; Marla Fischer, Circulation Dir., phone (303)938-9354, fax (303)473-0519, mfischer@newhope.com. **ISSN:** 1073-8355. **Subscription Rates:** $40 individuals; $75 other countries; $50 Canada; Free to qualified subscribers. **URL:** http://www.expandman.com.
Ad Rates: BW: $5,225 **Circ:** Paid 499
4C: $67.20 Non-paid 40,500

11888 Expo
EXPO Magazine, Inc.
11600 College Blvd. Phone: (913)469-1185
Overland Park, KS 66210 Fax: (913)469-0806
Free: (800)444-4388

Trade magazine for those in the exposition industry. **Subtitle:** The Magazine for Exposition Management. **Founded:** 1989. **Freq:** 10/year. **Print Method:** Web Press. **Trim Size:** 8 x 10 3/4. **Key Personnel:** Danica O'Donnell Vasos, Editor, phone (913)469-1185, fax (913)469-0806; Kathy Hungerford, Sales/Mktg. Dir., phone (913)469-1185, fax (913)469-0806, khungerford@expoweb.com. **ISSN:** 1046-3925. **Subscription Rates:** $48 Free to qualified subscribers; $48 single issue; $6 single issue. **Remarks:** Accepts advertising. **URL:** http://www.expoweb.com.
Ad Rates: BW: $3,020 **Circ:** Controlled 7,500
4C: $3,955
PCI: $50

11889 Fleet Owner
Intertec Publishing Corp.
9800 Metcalf Ave. Phone: (913)967-1854
Overland Park, KS 66212 Fax: (913)967-1898
Free: (800)262-1954

Magazine for managers of commercial motor fleets. **Founded:** 1928. **Freq:** Monthly. **Print Method:** Offset. **Trim Size:** 7 7/8 x 10 3/4. **Cols./Page:** 2 and 3. **Col. Width:** 40 and 26 nonpareils. **Col. Depth:** 140 agate lines. **Key Personnel:** Thomas L. Moore, Editor, fax (914)682-0922, tmoore@fleetowner.com; Thomas W. Duncan, Publisher, phone (914)287-6710, tduncan@fleetowner.com. **ISSN:** 0731-9622. **Subscription Rates:** $45. **Remarks:** Accepts advertising. **URL:** http://www.fleetowner.com. **Formed by the merger of:** Fleet Owner—Big Fleet Edition (1989); Fleet Owner—Small Fleet Owner (1989).
Ad Rates: BW: $10,335 **Circ:** Non-paid ‡101,240
4C: $13,615
PCI: $110

11890 Grounds Maintenance
Intertec Publishing Corp.
9800 Metcalf Ave. Phone: (913)967-1854
Overland Park, KS 66212 Fax: (913)967-1898
Free: (800)262-1954
Publication E-mail: gm_editorial@intertec.com

Trade magazine on landscape design, maintenance, and installation. **Founded:** 1966. **Freq:** Monthly. **Print Method:** Offset. **Trim Size:** 8 x 10 7/8. **Cols./Page:** 3 and 2. **Col. Width:** 26 and 39 nonpareils. **Col. Depth:** 140 agate lines. **Key Personnel:** Dr Mark Welterlen, Editor, phone (913)967-1758, mark-welterlen@intertec.com; Brian J. Agnes, Publisher, phone (913)967-1854, brian-agnes@intertec.com. **Subscription Rates:** Free to qualified subscribers; $36; $10 single issue; $10 back issues (plus postage). **Remarks:** Accepts advertising. **URL:** http://www.grounds-mag.com.
Ad Rates: BW: $5895 **Circ:** Non-paid ‡51,536
4C: $7422

11891 International Construction
Intertec Publishing Corp.
9800 Metcalf Ave. Phone: (913)967-1854
Overland Park, KS 66212 Fax: (913)967-1898
Free: (800)262-1954

Trade magazine. **Founded:** 1962. **Freq:** Monthly. **Print Method:** Web offset. **Trim Size:** 210 x 276 mm. **Cols./Page:** 2 and 3. **Col. Width:** 42 and 50 millimeters. **Col. Depth:** 242 millimeters. **Key Personnel:** Alan Peterson, Editor. **ISSN:** 0020-6415. **Subscription Rates:** $85. **Remarks:** Accepts advertising. **URL:** http://www.intertec.com. **Formerly:** Construction Industry International (1992).
Ad Rates: BW: $4,080 **Circ:** 32,000
4C: $5,405

11892 Johnson County Sun
Sun Publications, Inc.
7373 W. 107th St. Phone: (913)648-4620
Overland Park, KS 66212-2547 Fax: (913)381-1402

Newspaper. **Founded:** 1950. **Freq:** Semiweekly (Wed. and Fri.). **Print Method:** Offset. **Cols./Page:** 8. **Col. Width:** 9.3 picas. **Col. Depth:** 21 inches. **Key Personnel:** Jack Lovelace, Editor; John Yates, V.P. of Operations; Steve Rose, Publisher; Jo Stapleton, Advertising Mgr. **Remarks:** Accepts advertising.
Ad Rates: SAU: $29.95 **Circ:** Combined 112,441
PCI: $34.35

11893 Kansas City Jewish Chronicle
Sun Publications, Inc.
7373 W. 107th St. Phone: (913)648-4620
Overland Park, KS 66212-2547 Fax: (913)381-1402
Publication E-mail: chronicle@unpublications.com

Newspaper (tabloid) for Jewish community. **Founded:** 1920. **Freq:** Weekly (Fri.). **Print Method:** Offset. **Trim Size:** 8.5 x 14.5. **Cols./Page:** 6. **Col. Width:** 1 1/2 inches. **Col. Depth:**

13.5 inches. **Key Personnel:** Steve Rose, Editor and Publisher; Ruth Berger, Advertising Mgr.; Rick Hellman, Managing Ed.; John Yates, Vice President. **ISSN:** 0022-8524. **Subscription Rates:** $38.71; $47.42 out of state. **Feature Editors:** Chris Goldman, *Book*.
Ad Rates: BW: $1,644.30 **Circ:** (Not Reported)
4C: $1,894.30
PCI: $20.30

11894 KC Computer User
Computer Reporter
PO Box 7810 Phone: (913)341-6881
Overland Park, KS 66207
Consumer magazine covering computers. **Subtitle:** Business Technology, Professional Development, The Internet. **Freq:** Monthly. **Key Personnel:** Ron Goertzen, Publisher; Amanda Jensen, Asst. Publisher; Jim Pullen, Marketing Dir. **Subscription Rates:** $12 individuals; Free to qualified subscribers. **Remarks:** Accepts advertising. **URL:** http://www.kccomputeruser.com.
Ad Rates: BW: $1,735 **Circ:** Paid 60,000

11895 Learning Disability Quarterly
Council for Learning Disabilities
PO Box 40303 Phone: (913)492-8755
Overland Park, KS 66204 Fax: (913)492-2546

Magazine containing research on various aspects of learning disabilities. **Founded:** 1978. **Freq:** Quarterly. **ISSN:** 0731-9487. **Subscription Rates:** $50 individuals. **Remarks:** Accepts advertising.
Circ: (Not Reported)

Leawood Sun - See Leawood

Leawood Sun, Blue Valley Edition - See Lake Quivera

11896 Lenexa Sun
Sun Publications, Inc.
7373 W. 107th St. Phone: (913)648-4620
Overland Park, KS 66212-2547 Fax: (913)381-1402
Publication E-mail: sunnews@sunpublications.com

Newspaper. **Founded:** 1950. **Freq:** Semiweekly (Wed. and Fri.). **Print Method:** Offset. **Cols./Page:** 8. **Col. Width:** 21 nonpareils. **Col. Depth:** 292 agate lines. **Key Personnel:** Jack Lovelace, Editor; Steve Rose, Publisher. **Subscription Rates:** Free. **Remarks:** Accepts advertising.
Ad Rates: SAU: $24.75 **Circ:** Combined 112,441
PCI: $34.35

11897 Millimeter Magazine
Intertec Publishing Corp.
9800 Metcalf Ave. Phone: (913)967-1854
Overland Park, KS 66212 Fax: (913)967-1898
Free: (800)262-1954

Magazine focusing on the process of motion picture and television production. **Founded:** 1973. **Freq:** Monthly. **Print Method:** Offset. **Trim Size:** 8 1/8 x 10 7/8. **Cols./Page:** 3 and 2. **Col. Width:** 27 and 42 nonpareils. **Col. Depth:** 140 agate lines. **Key Personnel:** Bruce Stockler, Editor, phone (212)613-9739, bruce_ stockler@intertec.com; Sam Kintzer, Publisher, phone (212)613-9703. **Subscription Rates:** $45. $7 single issue. **Remarks:** Accepts advertising.
Ad Rates: BW: $3,175 **Circ:** Paid 207
4C: $3,940 Paid 30,201

Mission Sun - See Mission

11898 Mobile Radio Technology
Intertec Publishing Corp.
9800 Metcalf Ave. Phone: (913)967-1854
Overland Park, KS 66212 Fax: (913)967-1898
Free: (800)262-1954
Publication E-mail: mrt@intertec.com

Technical magazine for the mobile communications industry. **Subtitle:** Technical Information for Paging, Trunking and Private Wireless Networks. **Founded:** Jan. 1983. **Freq:** Monthly. **Print Method:** Offset. **Trim Size:** 8 x 10 7/8. **Cols./Page:** 3. **Col. Width:** 2 1/4 inches. **Col. Depth:** 10 inches. **Key Personnel:** Don Bishop, Editor, phone (913)967-1741, don_ bishop@intertec.com; Mercy Contreras, Publisher, phone (720)489-3199, fax (720)489-3253, mercy_ contreras@intertec.com. **ISSN:** 0745-7626. **Subscription Rates:** $3 single issue; $2 single issue. **Remarks:** Accepts advertising. **Alt. Formats:** Microform.
Ad Rates: BW: $4,207 **Circ:** ‡25,002
4C: $4,942

Northeast Johnson County Sun - See Merriam

Olathe Sun - See Olathe

11899 Overland Park Sun
Sun Publications, Inc.
7373 W. 107th St. Phone: (913)648-4620
Overland Park, KS 66212-2547 Fax: (913)381-1402

Newspaper. **Founded:** 1950. **Freq:** Semiweekly (Wed. and Fri.). **Print Method:** Offset. **Cols./Page:** 8. **Col. Width:** 21 nonpareils. **Col. Depth:** 292 agate lines. **Key Personnel:** Jack Lovelace, Editor; Jo Stapleton, Advertising Mgr.; Steve Rose, Publisher. **Subscription Rates:** Free. **Remarks:** Accepts advertising.
Ad Rates: SAU: $24.75 **Circ:** Combined 112,441
PCI: $34.35

11900 Overland Park Sun, Blue Valley Edition
Sun Publications, Inc.
7373 W. 107th St. Phone: (913)648-4620
Overland Park, KS 66212-2547 Fax: (913)381-1402

Newspaper. **Founded:** Jan. 1, 1950. **Freq:** Semiweekly (Wed. and Fri.). **Print Method:** Offset. **Cols./Page:** 8. **Col. Width:** 21 nonpareils. **Col. Depth:** 292 agate lines. **Key Personnel:** Jack Lovelace, Editor; Steve Rose, Publisher; Jo Stapleton, Advertising Manager. **Subscription Rates:** Free. **Remarks:** Accepts advertising.
Ad Rates: SAU: $24.75 **Circ:** Combined 112,441
PCI: $34.35

Prairie Village Sun - See Prairie Village

11901 Retail Store Image
Intertec Publishing Corp.
9800 Metcalf Ave. Phone: (913)967-1854
Overland Park, KS 66212 Fax: (913)967-1898
Free: (800)262-1954

Magazine for retail industry professionals concerned with the visual dynamics of the retail store. **Founded:** 1990. **Freq:** Bimonthly. **Print Method:** Web offset. **Trim Size:** 8 1/8 x 10 7/8. **Cols./Page:** 2 and 3. **Col. Width:** 20 and 13 picas. **Col. Depth:** 59.5 picas. **Key Personnel:** Lise Slaviero, Publisher. **ISSN:** 1047-8841. **Subscription Rates:** $32; $8 single issue. **Remarks:** Accepts advertising. **URL:** http://www.intertec.com.
Ad Rates: BW: $3,195 **Circ:** Controlled 25,000
4C: $860

Roeland Park Sun - See Roeland Park

Shawnee-Merriam Sun - See Shawnee

11902 Sound & Video Contractor
Intertec Publishing Corp.
9800 Metcalf Ave. Phone: (913)967-1854
Overland Park, KS 66212 Fax: (913)967-1898
Free: (800)262-1954
Publication E-mail: s&vc@intertec.com

Magazine covering management and technical topics for the systems contracting industry. **Subtitle:** The International Management & Engineering Journal for Systems Contractors & Consultants. **Founded:** Sept. 1983. **Freq:** Monthly. **Print Method:** Offset. **Trim Size:** 8 x 10 7/8. **Cols./Page:** 3. **Col. Width:** 2 1/4 inches. **Col. Depth:** 10 inches. **Key Personnel:** Maria Arnone, Publisher, maria_ arnone@intertec.com; Nat Hecht, Editor, nat_ hecht@intertec.com. **ISSN:** 0741-1715. **Subscription Rates:** $27 individuals; $5 single issue. **Remarks:** Accepts advertising.
Ad Rates: BW: $3,724 **Circ:** Controlled ‡20,536
4C: $4,574

11903 Southwest Farm Press
Intertec Publishing Corp.
9800 Metcalf Ave. Phone: (913)967-1854
Overland Park, KS 66212 Fax: (913)967-1898
Free: (800)262-1954

Agriculture tabloid. **Founded:** Jan. 10, 1974. **Freq:** Semimonthly. **Print Method:** Offset. **Trim Size:** 11 3/8 x 15 1/2. **Cols./Page:** 4. **Col. Width:** 2 1/4 inches. **Col. Depth:** 14 1/2 inches. **Key Personnel:** James Calvin Pigg, Editor; Tommy L. Keith, Publisher. **Subscription Rates:** $12.50. **Remarks:** Accepts advertising.
Ad Rates: BW: $4,401 **Circ:** Paid 25,009
4C: $5,671 Non-paid 21,666
PCI: $89

Sun Newspaper - See Stillwell

11904 Transmission and Distribution Worldwide
Intertec Publishing Corp.
9800 Metcalf Ave. Phone: (913)967-1854
Overland Park, KS 66212 Fax: (913)967-1898
Free: (800)262-1954

Magazine about powerline construction, transmission, and distribution. **Founded:** 1949. **Freq:** Monthly. **Print Method:** Offset. **Trim Size:** 8 x 10 3/4. **Cols./Page:** 3. **Col. Width:** 2 1/8 inches. **Col. Depth:** 141 agate lines. **Key Personnel:** Rick Bush, Editor-in-Chief; Barry LeCerf, Publisher. **ISSN:** 0041-1280. **Subscription Rates:** Free to qualified subscribers; $32. $6 single issue. **Remarks:** Accepts advertising. **Formed by the merger of:** Transmission and Distribution; Transmission and Distribution International.
Ad Rates: BW: $5,710 **Circ:** Controlled ‡34,750
4C: $7,375
PCI: $125

11905 Trusts and Estates
Intertec Publishing Corp.
9800 Metcalf Ave. Phone: (913)967-1854
Overland Park, KS 66212 Fax: (913)967-1898
Free: (800)262-1954
Publication E-mail: trusts-estates@intertec.com

Financial, estate planning, and investment magazine. **Founded:** 1904. **Freq:** 13/year. **Print Method:** Offset. **Trim Size:** 7 7/8 x 10 7/8. **Cols./Page:** 3. **Col. Width:** 28 nonpareils. **Col. Depth:** 140 agate lines. **Key Personnel:** Michael S. Klim, Editor; David Premo, Publisher, phone (770)618-0168, davidpremo@intertec.com. **ISSN:** 0041-3682. **Subscription Rates:** $99 individuals. **Remarks:** Accepts advertising.
Ad Rates: BW: $2,905 **Circ:** Paid 10,850
4C: $4,375 Non-paid 4,250

11906 Video Systems
Intertec Publishing Corp.
9800 Metcalf Ave. Phone: (913)967-1854
Overland Park, KS 66212 Fax: (913)967-1898
Free: (800)262-1954
Publication E-mail: vs@intertec.com

Magazine for users of professional video equipment. **Founded:** 1975. **Freq:** Monthly. **Print Method:** Offset. **Trim Size:** 8 x 10 7/8. **Cols./Page:** 4. **Col. Width:** 27 nonpareils. **Col. Depth:** 140 agate lines. **Key Personnel:** Stephen Porter, Editor, phone (603)421-1922, fax (603)421-1933, stephen_ porter@intertec.com; Jud Alford, Publisher, phone (913)967-1834, fax (913)967-1988, jud_ alford@intertec.com. **ISSN:** 0361-0942. **Subscription Rates:** $60 individuals; $10 single issue; other countries; $135 by mail. **URL:** http://www.videosystems.com.
Ad Rates: BW: $5,000 **Circ:** Controlled ‡52,000
4C: $5,900
PCI: $285

11907 Wireless Review
Intertec Publishing Corp.
9800 Metcalf Ave. Phone: (913)967-1854
Overland Park, KS 66212 Fax: (913)967-1898
Free: (800)262-1954

Magazine serving the cellular and PCS communications industry. **Subtitle:** Intelligence for Competitive Providers. **Founded:** 1998. **Freq:** Semimonthly. **Print Method:** Offset. **Trim Size:** 8 x 10 7/8. **Cols./Page:** 3. **Col. Width:** 2 1/4 inches. **Col. Depth:** 10 inches. **Key Personnel:** Rhonda Wickham, Editor, phone (913)967-1742, fax (913)967-1905, rhonda_ wickham@omtertec.com; Darren Sextro, Publisher, phone (913)967-1836, darren_ sextro@intertec.com; Marcia Martinek, Managing Editor, phone (913)967-1968, fax (913)967-1905, marcia_ martinek@intertec.com. **ISSN:** 1097-3893. **Subscription Rates:** $3.50 single issue. **Remarks:** Accepts advertising. **URL:** http://www.wirelesreview.com. **Former name:** Cellular Business & Wireless World.
Ad Rates: BW: $5,095 **Circ:** Paid 1,797
4C: $5,939 Controlled 30,028

11908 World Broadcast News
Intertec Publishing Corp.
9800 Metcalf Ave. Phone: (913)341-1300
Overland Park, KS 66212 Fax: (913)967-1905
Publication E-mail: 74757.277@compuserve.com

International cable and television news trade magazine. **Founded:** 1979. **Freq:** Monthly 10/year. **Trim Size:** 8 x 10 7/8. **Key Personnel:** Gerald M. Walker, Editor-in-Chief, phone (516)288-4516, fax (516)288-7071; Dennis Triola, Publisher, phone (913)341-1300, fax (913)967-1900; Tom Cook, Senior Managing Editor, phone (913)341-1300, fax (913)967-1905; Carrie Poland, Senior Associate Editor; Jennifer Lowe, Editorial Asst. **ISSN:** 1050-012X. **Subscription Rates:** $50; $60 out of country. **Remarks:** Accepts advertising. **Online:** Individual Inc. **URL:** http://www.intertec.com. **Alt. Formats:** Microfilm.
Ad Rates: BW: $4,045 **Circ:** Non-paid ‡12,665
4C: $4,895

11909 KCCV-AM - 760
10550 Barkley Phone: (913)642-7600
Overland Park, KS 66212 Fax: (913)642-2424
Free: (800)758-1962

Format: Religious; News; Information. **Founded:** 1962. **Operating Hours:** Sunrise-sunset. **ADI:** Kansas City, MO (Lawrence, KS). **Key Personnel:** Richard Bott, President. **Wattage:** 6,000.

11910 KCCV-FM - 92.3
10550 Barkley, Ste. 108 Phone: (913)642-7600
Overland Park, KS 66212 Fax: (913)642-2424

Format: Religious; Talk. **Networks:** Sun Radio. **Owner:** Bott Radio Network, at above address. **Founded:** Dec. 1, 1993. **Operating Hours:** Continuous. **Key Personnel:** Richard P. Bott II, Vice President; Charles Lambert, Dir., Network Prgm. Svcs. **Wattage:** 25,000.

KQCV-FM - See Overland Park, Oklahoma

11911 TCI of Overland Park, Inc.
8221 W. 119th St. Phone: (913)451-5858
PO Box 25567 Fax: (913)345-8852
Overland Park, KS 66213

Founded: 1971. **Formerly:** TeleCable of Overland Park, Inc. **Key Personnel:** Woody Wood, Contact. **Cities Served:** subscribing households 93,450; 83 channels; 2 community access channels.

OVERLAND PASS

11912 KCHZ-FM - 95.7
11900 College Blvd., Ste. 320 Phone: (913)696-3700
Overland Pass, KS 66210

Format: Contemporary Hit Radio (CHR). **Owner:** Radio 2000, Inc., at above address. **Founded:** Jan. 16, 1997. **Operating Hours:** Continuous. **Key Personnel:** Frank Copsides, President; Dave Alexander, Vice President; Janel Thiesen, V.P./General Mgr. **Wattage:** 19,000. **URL:** http://www.channelz95.com.

PAOLA†, pop. 4,967.

E. KS. Miami Co. 48 mi. SW of Kansas City. Oil and natural gas production. Manufactures corrugated steel culverts, heavy steel pressure vessels, steel fabricating avionics, concrete products, cabinets, light commercial trailer. General farming.

11913 Miami County Republic
Miami County Publishing Co.
121 S. Pearl St. Phone: (913)294-2311
PO Box 389 Fax: (913)294-5318
Paola, KS 66071
Community newspaper. **Founded:** 1866. **Freq:** Semiweekly (Mon. & Wed.). **Print Method:** Offset. **Cols./Page:** 6. **Col. Width:** 2 1/6 inches. **Col. Depth:** 21 inches. **Key Personnel:** Phil McLaughlin, Editor and Publisher; Marla Youk, Advertising Mgr. **Subscription Rates:** $36.50 local; $47.50 out of area; $58 out of state. **Remarks:** Accepts advertising.
Ad Rates: BW: $630 **Circ:** Paid 6,000
4C: $820
PCI: $5.00

11914 Osawatomie Graphic
Miami County Publishing Co.
121 S. Pearl St. Phone: (913)294-2311
PO Box 389 Fax: (913)294-5318
Paola, KS 66071
Newspaper covering Miami, Linn, Anderson, and Franklin counties, Kansas. **Founded:** Mar. 23, 1888. **Freq:** Weekly (Wed.). **Print Method:** Offset. **Cols./Page:** 6. **Col. Width:** 2 1/16 inches. **Col. Depth:** 21 inches. **Key Personnel:** Phil McLaughlin, Owner; Kurt Gaston, Publisher; Carol Chitwood, Editor; Paul L. Branson, Advertising Mgr. **USPS:** 412-660. **Subscription Rates:** $28 individuals; $36 out of area; $42 out of state. **Remarks:** Accepts advertising.
Ad Rates: BW: $535.50 **Circ:** 4,800
4C: $725.50 Combined 7000
SAU: $5
PCI: $4.25

PARSONS, pop. 12,898.

NE KS. Labette Co. 28 mi. NE of Independence. Manufactures steel tanks, furnace burners, steel building accessories, garments, furniture, wood products, chemicals, paper boxes, ammunition. Diversified farming. Wheat, corn, hay.

11915 Farm Talk
Farm Talk Publishing
1801 S. Hwy. 59 Phone: (316)421-9450
PO Box 601 Fax: (316)421-9473
Parsons, KS 67357
Free: (800)356-8255
Publication E-mail: fteditor@terrworld.net
Publisher E-mail: farmtalk@terraworld.net

Agricultural newspaper (tabloid) serving 70 counties in eastern Kansas, western Missouri, northeast Oklahoma, and northwest Arkansas. **Founded:** Feb. 5, 1974. **Freq:** Weekly (Wed.). **Print Method:** Offset. **Trim Size:** 10 x 14. **Cols./Page:** 6. **Col. Width:** 18 nonpareils. **Col. Depth:** 196 agate lines. **Key Personnel:** Mark Parker, Publisher; Ted Gum, Publisher. **Subscription Rates:** $30 individuals. **Remarks:** Accepts advertising.
Ad Rates: BW: $441 **Circ:** ‡9,985
PCI: $6.75

11916 The Parsons News
Parsons News
1930 Clark Phone: (316)421-2990
Box 937 Fax: (316)421-1392
Parsons, KS 67357
Publication E-mail: parsonews@aol.com

Community newspaper. **Founded:** 1947. **Freq:** Weekly (Thurs.). **Print Method:** Offset. **Trim Size:** 11 1/2 x 15. **Cols./Page:** 5. **Col. Width:** 26 nonpareils. **Col. Depth:** 195 agate lines. **Key Personnel:** Riley Rosenstiel, Editor; Tracey L. Tippet, Publisher. **USPS:** 422-440. **Subscription Rates:** $18.95 individuals; $28.95 out of state. **Remarks:** Accepts advertising. **Available Online.**
Ad Rates: GLR: $5.00 **Circ:** Paid 1,800
GLR: $4.20 Free 620
BW: $280
4C: $7
SAU: $5.80
PCI: $5.80

11917 Parsons Sun
Parsons Publishing Co.
220 S. 18th Phone: (316)421-2000
PO Box 836 Fax: (316)421-2217
Parsons, KS 67357
Free: (800)530-5723

General newspaper. **Founded:** June 1871. **Freq:** Daily (eve.). **Print Method:** Offset. **Trim Size:** 13 3/4 x 22 3/4. **Cols./Page:** 6. **Col. Width:** 25 nonpareils. **Col. Depth:** 294 agate lines. **Key Personnel:** Ann K. Charles, Editor and Publisher, ann%parsons@hays.dailynews.net. **USPS:** 422-480. **Subscription Rates:** $64.91 individuals; $67.97 out of area; $101.20 out of state. **Remarks:** Accepts advertising. **URL:** http://www.parsonssun.com.
Ad Rates: BW: $1,016.82 **Circ:** 7,189
4C: $1,156.82
SAU: $7.69
PCI: $8.07

11918 KLKC-AM - 1540
RR 4 Phone: (316)421-6400
PO Box 853
Parsons, KS 67357

Format: Talk; Adult Contemporary; Oldies. **Networks:** Independent. **Founded:** 1951. **Operating Hours:** Sunrise-sunset; 100% local. **ADI:** Joplin, MO-Pittsburg, KS. **Key Personnel:** Gary Cantrell, General Mgr.; Steve Lardy, Sports Dir.; Ann Gentry, News Dir. **Local Programs:** *Let's Talk* 8:30 a.m.-9 a.m. Monday-Friday; *Parsons High School & Labertte Community College Sports Play by Play.* **Wattage:** 250. **Ad Rates:** $7.60-14.85 for 30 seconds; $10.20-17.40 for 60 seconds.

11919 KLKC-FM - 93.5
RR 4 Phone: (316)421-6400
PO Box 853 Fax: (316)421-5570
Parsons, KS 67357

Format: Talk; Adult Contemporary; Oldies. **Networks:** Independent. **Founded:** 1978. **Operating Hours:** 6 a.m.-11 p.m.; 100% local. **ADI:** Wichita-Hutchinson, KS. **Key Personnel:** Gary Cantrell, General Mgr., phone (316)421-5654; Steve Lardy, Sports Dir., phone (316)421-5552; Ann Gentry, News Dir., phone (316)421-5652. **Local Programs:** *Let's Talk* 8:30 a.m.-9 a.m.; *Parsons High School & Labette Committee College Sports Play by Play.* **Wattage:** 3000. **Ad Rates:** $7.60-14.85 for 30 seconds; $10.20-17.40 for 60 seconds.

PEABODY

11920 Peabody Gazette-Bulletin
118 N. Walnut Phone: (316)983-2185
PO Box 129 Fax: (316)983-2700
Peabody, KS 66866
Community newspaper. **Founded:** 1873. **Freq:** Weekly (Thurs.). **Print Method:** Offset. **Trim Size:** 22 3/4 x 14 1/4. **Cols./Page:** 6. **Col. Width:** 13 1/2 picas. **Col. Depth:** 21 inches. **Key Personnel:** Gary Bowlin, Editor and Publisher; Lou Ann Bowlin, Editor and Publisher; Emeline Bowlin, Editor and Publisher. **Subscription Rates:** $18 individuals; $22 out of area. **Remarks:** Accepts advertising. **Formerly:** Gazette-Herald.
Ad Rates: BW: $378 **Circ:** 1,400
4C: $648
PCI: $3.50

PHILLIPSBURG†, pop. 3,229.

N. KS. Phillips Co. 60 mi. N. of Hays. Pheasant hunting area. Zeolite asphalt roofing manufactured. Long line trucking. Oil refinery. Grain, stock farms. Cattle, hogs, milo, wheat.

11921 Phillips County Review
LST Publishing, Inc.
Box 446 Phone: (913)543-5242
Phillipsburg, KS 67661 Fax: (913)543-5243

Community newspaper. **Founded:** 1907. **Freq:** Weekly (Thurs.). **Print Method:** Offset. **Cols./Page:** 6. **Col. Width:** 27 nonpareils. **Col. Depth:** 290 agate lines. **Key Personnel:** Perry Hansen, Editor; Ron Lower, Publisher. **Subscription Rates:** $20 individuals; $23.65 out of area; $25 out of state. **Remarks:** Accepts advertising.
Ad Rates: PCI: $3.45 **Circ:** Paid ‡2,950

11922 KKAN-AM - 1490
693 3rd St. Phone: (785)543-2151
Phillipsburg, KS 67661 Fax: (785)543-2152

Format: Full Service; Eclectic; Hot Country; Adult Contemporary. **Networks:** AP; NBC; Kansas Information. **Owner:** Walter C. Seidel, at above address. **Founded:** 1959. **Operating Hours:** 18 hrs. daily; 20% network, 80% local. **ADI:** Lincoln-Hastings-Kearney, NE. **Key Personnel:** Tad Felts, Sports/News Dir.; Bob Yates, General Mgr.; Theresa Hageman, Office Mgr.; Sam Quanz, Sales Mgr. **Wattage:** 1000. **Ad Rates:** $9 for 30 seconds; $15 for 60 seconds. Combined advertising rates available with KQMA-FM.

11923 KQMA-FM - 92.5
Box 548 Phone: (785)543-2151
Phillipsburg, KS 67661 Fax: (785)543-2152

Format: Eclectic; Hot Country; Adult Contemporary. **Simulcasts:** KKAN-AM. **Networks:** AP; NBC; Kansas Information. **Owner:** Walter C. Seidel, 693 3rd St., Phillipsburg, KS 67661. **Founded:** 1985. **Operating Hours:** 18 hrs. Daily; 20% network, 80% local. **ADI:** Lincoln-Hastings-Kearney, NE. **Key Personnel:** Tad Felts, News/Sports Dir.; Walter C. Seidel, Owner; Bob Yates, General Mgr.; Sam Quanz, Sales Mgr.; Theresa Hageman, Office Mgr. **Wattage:** 100,000. **Ad Rates:** $9 for 30 seconds; $15 for 60 seconds. Combined advertising rates available with KKAN-AM.

PITTSBURG, pop. 18,770.

SE KS. Crawford Co. 30 mi. NW of Joplin, MO. State University. Manufactures ice cream products, mining machinery, coal by-products, metal thermal doors, plastic pipe, flexible packaging, cad-cam systems, sportswear, plastic bags, synthetic sports turf, lawn and garden fertilizer, wood cabinets. Limestone and coal mines. Clay, foundry and machine shop. Diversified farming.

11924 Collegio
Pittsburg State University
1701 S. Broadway Phone: (316)235-4809
Pittsburg, KS 66762 Fax: (316)235-4817

Collegiate newspaper. **Founded:** Sept. 1910. **Freq:** Weekly (Thurs.). **Print Method:** Offset. **Trim Size:** 13 x 21 1/2. **Cols./Page:** 6. **Col. Width:** 12 picas. **Key Personnel:** Laurie Sisk, Editor; Jan Hall, Business Mgr. **Subscription Rates:** $30 individuals. **Remarks:** Accepts advertising. **URL:** http://www.pittstate.edu/collegio.
Ad Rates: BW: $598.50 **Circ:** Free ‡6,000
SAU: $6
PCI: $6

11925 Journal of Managerial Issues
Pittsburg State University
Dept. of Economics, Finance & Banking Phone: (316)235-4547
Fax: (316)235-4572
Pittsburg, KS 66762
Scholarly refereed journal for business managers and business educators. **Subtitle:** JMI. **Founded:** 1989. **Freq:** Quarterly. **Trim Size:** 6 x 9. **Cols./Page:** 2. **Col. Width:** 13 1/2 picas. **Col. Depth:** 45 picas. **Key Personnel:** Charles C. Fischer, Editor, phone (316)235-4546, chuck@pittstate.edu. **ISSN:** 1045-3695. **Subscription Rates:** $35 individuals; $45 institutions industry; $65 other countries. **Remarks:** Advertising not accepted. **URL:** http://www.elibrary.com. **Alt. Formats:** CD-ROM, UMI; Microform.
Circ: Controlled 1,000

11926 The Midwest Quarterly
Pittsburg State University Phone: (316)235-4369
Pittsburg, KS 66762
Scholarly journal. **Subtitle:** A Journal of Contemporary Thought. **Founded:** 1959. **Freq:** Quarterly. **Print Method:** Offset. **Trim Size:** 6 x 9. **Cols./Page:** 1. **Col. Width:** 49 nonpareils. **Col. Depth:** 105 agate lines. **Key Personnel:** Dr. James B.M. Schick, Editor, phone (316)235-4317, fax (316)232-7515, jschick@pittstate.edu. **ISSN:** 0026-3451. **Subscription Rates:** $12 individuals; $17 other countries; $4 single issue. **Remarks:** Advertising not accepted. **Online:** University Microfilm, Inc. **Alt. Formats:** CD-ROM.
Circ: Paid ‡800
Non-paid ‡150

11927 Morning Sun
Pittsburg Publishing
PO Drawer H Phone: (316)231-2600
Pittsburg, KS 66762 Fax: (316)231-0645
Free: (800)794-6536

General newspaper. **Founded:** 1887. **Freq:** Mon.-Sun. (morn.). **Print Method:** Offset. **Cols./Page:** 6. **Col. Width:** 24 nonpareils. **Col. Depth:** 301 agate lines. **Key Personnel:** Thomas H. Collinson, Editor and Publisher. **Subscription Rates:** $93 individuals. **Remarks:** Accepts advertising.
Ad Rates: BW: $838.50 **Circ:** Paid 11,300
4C: $1,023.50 Free 242
SAU: $8.60

11928 KKOW-AM - 860
1162 E. Hwy 126 Phone: (316)231-7200
Pittsburg, KS 66762 Fax: (316)231-3321
E-mail: kkow@sunnetworks.net

Format: Country; Agricultural. **Networks:** CBS; Interstate Radio. **Founded:** 1937. **Formerly:** KOAM-AM (1981). **Operating Hours:** Continuous; 10% network, 90% local. **ADI:** Joplin, MO-Pittsburg, KS. **Key Personnel:** Lance L. Sayler, General Mgr./General Sales Mgr.; Tom Van Hoy, Sports Dir.; Chris Kelly, News Dir.; Steve Passeri, Program Dir.; Suzanne Hubbard, Farm Dir.; Dee Dee York, Promotions Mgr.; Judy Niegsch, Business Mgr.; Debbie Smith, Traffic Dir. **Wattage:** 10,000. **Ad Rates:** $70 for 30 seconds; $90 for 60 seconds.

11929 KKOW-FM - 96.9
1162 E. Hwy. 126 Phone: (316)231-7200
Pittsburg, KS 66762 Fax: (316)231-3321

Format: Contemporary Country. **Founded:** 1975. **Operating Hours:** Continuous. **ADI:** Joplin, MO-Pittsburg, KS. **Key Personnel:** Thom Watts, Program Dir.; Bob Burk, Music Dir.; Lance Sayler, General Mgr.; Chris Kelly, News Dir.; Judy Niegsch, Business Mgr.; Debbie Smith, Traffic Dir. **Wattage:** 100,000.

11930 KOAM-TV - 7
Box 659, Hwy. 69 & Lawton Rd. Phone: (316)231-0400
Pittsburg, KS 66762 Fax: (316)624-3115

Format: Commercial TV. **Networks:** CBS. **Founded:** 1953. **Operating Hours:** 24 hours. **ADI:** Joplin, MO-Pittsburg, KS. **Key Personnel:** Danny Thomas, Pres./Gen. Mgr.; Mark LaCrue, General Sales Mgr.; Shirley Beer, News Dir. **Local Programs:** *Chuck Broyles Coaches Show*; *Friday Night High School Football*.

11931 KSEK-AM - 1340
1604 E. Quincy Phone: (316)232-1340
Pittsburg, KS 66762 Fax: (316)232-5550
Free: (800)215-3853

Networks: Jones Satellite. **Founded:** 1948. **Operating Hours:** Continuous. **ADI:** Joplin, MO-Pittsburg, KS. **Key Personnel:** Rob Strand, General Mgr.; Rob Strand, Operations Mgr.; Jack Leotzinger, Chief Engineer. **Wattage:** 1000. **Ad Rates:** $12 per unit.

PLAINVILLE, pop. 2,458.

NWC KS. Rooks Co. 120 mi. W. of Salina. Oil wells. Manufactures campers, mobile homes. Ships grain, livestock. Grain, dairy, poultry farms. Wheat, corn.

11932 Plainville Times
400 W. Mill St. Phone: (913)434-4525
Plainville, KS 67663
Community newspaper. **Founded:** Dec. 1, 1904. **Freq:** Weekly (Thurs.). **Print Method:** Offset. **Trim Size:** 13 3/4 x 22 3/4. **Cols./Page:** 6. **Col. Width:** 25 nonpareils. **Col. Depth:** 294 agate lines. **Key Personnel:** Carol E. Van Dyke, Editor. **USPS:** 434-920. **Subscription Rates:** $20 individuals; $22.50 out of area; $25 out of state. **Remarks:** Accepts advertising.
Ad Rates: GLR: $.18 **Circ:** Paid ‡2,450
BW: $300 Free ‡40
SAU: $2.66

11933 Classic Cable
PO Box 429 Phone: (913)434-7620
Plainville, KS 67663-0429 Fax: (913)434-2614
Free: (800)999-8876

Absorbed: Mission Cable L.P. (1996). **Key Personnel:** Nita Basgall, Regional Mgr.; Jennifer Tremblay, Marketing Mgr. **Cities Served:** Hooker, OK: subscribing households 633; 33 channels; 1 community access channel.

PLEASANTON

11934 Linn County News
808 Main St. Phone: (913)352-6235
PO Box 478 Fax: (913)352-6607
Pleasanton, KS 66075
Community newspaper. **Freq:** Weekly (Thurs.). **Print Method:** Offset. **Cols./Page:** 6. **Col. Width:** 2 inches. **Col. Depth:** 21 inches. **Key Personnel:** Mike Crawford, Publisher, phone (417)646-2211, fax (417)646-8015. **USPS:** 439-950. **Subscription Rates:** $21.70 Linn county; $28.59 outside Linn county; $33.75 outside Kansas. **Remarks:** Accepts advertising.
Ad Rates: SAU: $4.50 **Circ:** 3,000
PCI: $3.50

PRAIRIE VILLAGE, pop. 24,657.

E. KS. Johnson Co. 18 mi. NW of Olathe.

11935 Cicindela
4637 W 69th Terrace Phone: (913)236-4043
Prairie Village, KS 66208-2547
Scholarly journal covering entomology. **Founded:** Mar. 1969. **Freq:** Quarterly. **Print Method:** Offset. **Trim Size:** 5 3/8 x 8 1/2. **Key Personnel:** Ronald L. Huber, Editor. **ISSN:** 0590-6334. **Subscription Rates:** $7 individuals; $2.50 single issue. **Remarks:** Advertising not accepted.
Circ: Controlled 160

11936 Kansas City Homes & Gardens
Showcase Publishing Inc.
5301 W. 75th Phone: (913)648-5757
Prairie Village, KS 66208 Fax: (913)648-5783

Magazine showcasing homes, gardens, and lifestyles of the Kansas City area. **Founded:** 1987. **Freq:** Bimonthly. **Print Method:** Web offset. **Trim Size:** 8 3/8 x 10 7/8. **Cols./Page:** 3. **Col. Width:** 2 1/4 inches. **Col. Depth:** 10 inches. **Key Personnel:** David Leathers, Editor and Publisher. **Subscription Rates:** $29 individuals; $39 two years. **Remarks:** Accepts advertising.
Ad Rates: BW: $2,090 **Circ:** Paid ‡13,000
4C: $2,490 Non-paid ‡2,800

11937 Prairie Village Sun
Sun Publications, Inc.
7373 W. 107th St. Phone: (913)648-4620
Overland Park, KS 66212-2547 Fax: (913)381-1402

Newspaper. **Freq:** Semiweekly (Wed. and Fri.). **Print Method:** Offset. **Cols./Page:** 8. **Col. Width:** 21 nonpareils. **Col. Depth:** 292 agate lines. **Key Personnel:** Jack Lovelace, Editor; Steve Rose, Publisher; Jo Stapleton, Advertising Mgr. **Subscription Rates:** Free. **Remarks:** Accepts advertising.
Ad Rates: PCI: $34.35 **Circ:** Combined 112,441

PRATT†, pop. 6,885.

S. KS. Pratt Co. 80 mi. W. of Wichita. Lawn furniture, hydraulic couplings; farm machinery factory; flour, feed mills; hatchery. Agriculture. Wheat, corn, alfalfa.

11938 The Pratt Tribune
320 S. Main Phone: (316)672-5511
Pratt, KS 67124 Fax: (316)672-5514

General newspaper. **Founded:** 1917. **Freq:** Daily (eve.). **Print Method:** Offset. **Key Personnel:** Conrad Easterday, Editor; J.K. Phillips, Publisher. **USPS:** 441-500. **Subscription Rates:** $80 individuals; $91 out of state. **Remarks:** Accepts advertising.
Ad Rates: GLR: $.45 **Circ:** ‡3,000
BW: $812.70
4C: $1,052.70
PCI: $6.30

11939 KDGB-FM - 93.1
1120 N. Halstead Phone: (316)662-5900
Hutchinson, KS 67501 Fax: (316)662-5797
E-mail: kdab@ourtownusa.net

Format: Classic Rock. **Owner:** Goodstar broadcasting LLL, 1660 N. Tyler, Wichita, KS 67212, (316)729-8011, Fax: (316)721-8276. **Founded:** 1965. **Formerly:** KGLS-FM (1997). **Operating Hours:** Continuous. **ADI:** Wichita-Hutchinson, KS. **Key Personnel:** Mike Starr Jr., General Mgr.; Scott Carlisle, Program Dir. **Wattage:** 100,000. **Ad Rates:** $8-20 for 30 seconds; $10-30 for 60 seconds.

11940 KWLS-AM - 1290-AM
PO Box 486 Phone: (316)672-5581
Pratt, KS 67124 Fax: (316)672-5583
Free: (877)672-1290
E-mail: kwls@pratt.net

Format: Country; News; Agricultural; Sports. **Networks:** Mid-America Ag; ABC. **Owner:** Goodstar Broadcasting, PO Box 486, Pratt, KS 67124. **Founded:** 1962. **Formerly:** KWNS-AM. **Operating Hours:** Continuous; 10% network, 90% local. **Key Personnel:** Carl R. Raida, Program Dir., kwls@pratt.net; Dana Hermanson, General Mgr.; Eric Strobel, Sales Mgr. **Wattage:** 5000 day; 500 night. **Ad Rates:** $10 for 30 seconds; $12 for 60 seconds. Combined advertising rates available with KDGB, KZLS, KILS, KOLS, KSLS, KFNF, KQLS, KGTR, KNNS.

PRETTY PRAIRIE

11941 Ninnescah Valley News
Valley News
201 Maple Phone: (316)459-6322
PO Box 327 Fax: (316)459-6729
Pretty Prairie, KS 67570
Community newspaper. **Founded:** 1910. **Freq:** Weekly (Thurs.). **Cols./Page:** 5. **Col. Width:** 11 1/2 picas. **Col. Depth:** 14 inches. **Key Personnel:** Tim Stucky, Editor and Publisher. **Subscription Rates:** $12.50; $14 out of county. **Remarks:** Accepts advertising.
Ad Rates: BW: $140 **Circ:** ‡750
PCI: $2.24

QUINTER

11942 Gove County Advocate
PO Box 365 Phone: (913)754-3651
Quinter, KS 67752 Fax: (913)754-3878

Community newspaper. **Freq:** Weekly (Wed.). **Print Method:** Offset. **Cols./Page:** 5. **Col. Width:** 11.5 picas. **Col. Depth:** 13 inches. **Key Personnel:** Tom Broeckelman, Editor and Publisher; Roxanne Broeckelman, Editor and Publisher. **Subscription Rates:** $14.75; $18.68 out of county; $19 out of state. $.30 single issue. **Remarks:** Accepts advertising.
Ad Rates: PCI: $2.50 **Circ:** 1,900

RILEY

11943 The Riley Countian
Countian
PO Box 333 Phone: (913)485-2290
Riley, KS 66531
Community newspaper. **Founded:** 1883. **Freq:** Weekly (Thurs.). **Cols./Page:** 6. **Col. Width:** 2 inches. **Col. Depth:** 21 inches. **Key Personnel:** Romelle Van Sickle, Editor; Wayne Van Sickle, Publisher. **USPS:** 466-100. **Subscription Rates:** $14; $16 out of area. **Remarks:** Accepts advertising.
Ad Rates: SAU: $2.96 **Circ:** 1,200

ROELAND PARK

11944 Roeland Park Sun
Sun Publications, Inc.
7373 W. 107th St. Phone: (913)648-4620
Overland Park, KS 66212-2547 Fax: (913)381-1402

Newspaper. **Freq:** Semiweekly (Wed. and Fri.). **Print Method:** Offset. **Cols./Page:** 8. **Col. Width:** 21 nonpareils. **Col. Depth:** 292 agate lines. **Key Personnel:** Jack Lovelace, Editor; Stan Rose, Publisher; Shirley Rose, Publisher; Steve Rose, Publisher; Mike Lomario, Editor. **Subscription Rates:** Free.
Circ: Combined 103,679

ROSE HILL, pop. 1,557.

SE KS. Butler Co. 24 mi. SW of El Dorado.

11945 The Rose Hill Reporter
110 N. Rose Hill Rd. Phone: (316)776-0097
PO Box 16
Rose Hill, KS 67133
Shopper. **Founded:** 1975. **Freq:** Thursday. **Print Method:** Offset. **Cols./Page:** 6. **Col. Width:** 13 1/2 picas. **Col. Depth:** 21 1/2 inches. **Key Personnel:** Sally Rathburn, Managing Editor, phone (316)776-0097; Michael Robinson, Publisher. **Subscription Rates:** $22 individuals; $29 out of state. **Remarks:** Accepts advertising.
Ad Rates: PCI: $2.85 **Circ:** (Not Reported)

RUSSELL†, pop. 5,427.

NC KS. Russell Co. 76 mi. W. of Salina. Manufactures oil, wire products, mobile homes. Grain, feed.

11946 Russell Daily News
802 N. Maple St. Phone: (913)483-2116
PO Box 513 Fax: (913)483-4012
Russell, KS 67665-1937
Free: (800)737-3023

Newspaper. **Founded:** 1930. **Freq:** Mon.-Sat. (eve.). **Print Method:** Offset. **Cols./Page:** 8. **Col. Width:** 22 nonpareils. **Col. Depth:** 301 agate lines. **Key Personnel:** Dan Holder,

Editor; Russell T. Townsley, Publisher; Allan D. Evans, Advertising Mgr. **Subscription Rates:** $42 individuals.

11947 The Russell Record
802 N. Maple St., No. 393 Phone: (913)483-2111
Russell, KS 67665-1937 Fax: (913)483-4012

Newspaper. **Founded:** 1872. **Freq:** Semiweekly (Mon. and Thurs.). **Print Method:** Offset. **Cols./Page:** 8. **Col. Width:** 22 nonpareils. **Col. Depth:** 301 agate lines. **Key Personnel:** Pauline Sturgeon, Editor; Russell T. Tounsley, Publisher; Allan D. Evans, Advertising Mgr. **Subscription Rates:** $12.36 individuals. **Remarks:** Accepts advertising.
Ad Rates: BW: $653.60 SAU: $3.80 **Circ:** (Not Reported)

11948 KRSL-AM - 990
Box 666 Phone: (913)483-3121
Russell, KS 67665 Fax: (913)483-6511
E-mail: krsl@media-net.net

Format: Adult Contemporary. **Simulcasts:** KCAY-FM. **Networks:** Satellite Music Network; Kansas Information. **Owner:** West Central Radio Inc., at above address. **Founded:** 1956. **Operating Hours:** 6 a.m.-10 p.m. **Key Personnel:** Wayne Grabbe, Contact; Gordon Gorton, Contact. **Wattage:** 250 day; 30 night. **Ad Rates:** $7.50-9.50 for 30 seconds; $11-13.50 for 60 seconds. Combined advertising rates available with KCAY-FM. **URL:** http://www.krsl.com.

11949 Russell Cable TV Co.
724 N. Main Phone: (785)483-3244
Russell, KS 67665 Fax: (785)483-2569

Owner: Eagle Communications Inc., 2703 Hall, Hays, KS 67601, (785)625-4000, Fax: (785)625-8030. **Formerly:** Falcon Cablevision (1990). **Key Personnel:** Pete Collins, General Mgr., phone (785)625-4000, fax (785)625-8030; Larry Braun, Tech. Mgr., phone (785)625-5910, fax (785)625-3465; Lila Krainbill, Office Mgr., phone (785)483-2534, fax (785)625-2569; Terry Elam, Technician, phone (785)483-2534. **Cities Served:** Russell, KS: subscribing households 1,800; 57 channels; 1 community access channel.

SABETHA, pop. 2,286.

NE KS. Nemaha Co. 60 mi. N. of Topeka. Historical Society and site. World wide food distribution food mixers. Creamery. Dairy, stock, poultry, grain farms. Alfalfa, clover.

11950 The Sabetha Herald
1024 Main Phone: (913)284-2177
PO Box 208 Fax: (913)284-2320
Sabetha, KS 66534-0208
Community newspaper. **Founded:** 1876. **Freq:** Weekly (Wed.). **Print Method:** Offset. **Cols./Page:** 6. **Col. Width:** 12 picas. **Col. Depth:** 21 inches. **Key Personnel:** Bryan McDaniel, Publisher; Linda Mishler, Editor. **Subscription Rates:** $16 individuals; $19 out of state. **Remarks:** Accepts advertising.
Ad Rates: GLR: $.273 BW: $413.28 PCI: $3.28 **Circ:** Paid ‡2,850 Free ‡25

ST. JOHN

11951 Chiron Review
Chiron Review Press
702 N. Prairie Phone: (316)549-6156
St. John, KS 67576-1516
Publisher E-mail: chironreview@hotmail.com

Literary journal covering fiction, nonfiction, art, and poetry. **Founded:** Feb. 19, 1982. **Freq:** Quarterly. **Print Method:** Offset. **Trim Size:** 10 x 13. **Key Personnel:** Michael Hathaway, Editor; Jane Hathoway, Asst. Editor; Gerald Locklin, Contributing Editor; Ray Zepeda, Contributing Editor. **ISSN:** 1046-8897. **Subscription Rates:** $12 individuals; $28 institutions; $24 out of country; $4 single issue. **Remarks:** Accepts advertising. **Former name:** The Kindred Spirit (1989).
Ad Rates: BW: $130 **Circ:** Combined 1,000

11952 St. John News
The Pratt Tribune
PO Box 488 Phone: (316)549-3201
St. John, KS 67576
Community newspaper. **Founded:** 1884. **Freq:** Weekly. **Print Method:** Offset. **Trim Size:** 14 3/4 x 21. **Cols./Page:** 6. **Col. Width:** 13 picas. **Col. Depth:** 21 1/2 inches. **Key Personnel:** Pam Martin, Editor; James K. Phillips, Publisher. **USPS:** 476-120. **Subscription Rates:** $24 individuals; $36 out of area. **Remarks:** Accepts advertising.
Ad Rates: BW: $316 PCI: $3.30 **Circ:** ‡1,350

ST. MARYS

11953 St. Marys Star
517 W. Bertrand Phone: (785)437-2935
PO Box 190 Fax: (785)437-2095
St. Marys, KS 66536-0190
Free: (800)334-9912

Community newspaper. **Founded:** Mar. 13, 1884. **Freq:** Weekly (Tues.). **Print Method:** Offset. **Trim Size:** 11 x 17. **Cols./Page:** 5. **Col. Width:** 11 1/2 picas. **Col. Depth:** 16 inches. **Key Personnel:** Anita H. Janssen, Editor and Publisher. **USPS:** 516-340. **Subscription Rates:** $29.65 individuals; $32 out of state. **Remarks:** Advertising not accepted for alcohol beverages.
Ad Rates: BW: $212 PCI: $2.90 **Circ:** Paid ‡1,900 Free ‡65

SALINA

11954 The Buyer's Guide
1118 W. Cloud Phone: (785)823-3209
Salina, KS 67401-0134 Fax: (785)823-3176

Shopper (tabloid). **Founded:** 1971. **Freq:** Weekly (Wed.). **Print Method:** Offset. **Cols./Page:** 6. **Col. Width:** 24 nonpareils. **Col. Depth:** 301 agate lines. **Key Personnel:** Harold Maring, Publisher. **Subscription Rates:** $11 by mail. **Remarks:** Accepts advertising. **URL:** http://www.guide@midusa.net.
Ad Rates: BW: $624 4C: $1,872 PCI: $8.50 **Circ:** Free 25,800

11955 Country Roads
The Buyer's Guide
1118 W. Cloud Phone: (785)823-3209
Salina, KS 67401-0134 Fax: (785)823-3176

Shopper (tabloid). **Founded:** Apr. 1996. **Freq:** Weekly (Wed.). **Print Method:** Offset. **Cols./Page:** 6. **Col. Width:** 24 nonpareils. **Col. Depth:** 301 agate lines. **Key Personnel:** Harold Maring, Publisher. **Subscription Rates:** Free; $11 by mail. **Remarks:** Accepts advertising. **URL:** http://www.guide@midusa.net.
Ad Rates: BW: $624 4C: $1,872 PCI: $8.50 **Circ:** (Not Reported)

11956 Northwestern Kansas Register
Abilene Reflector-Chronicle
PO Box 1038 Phone: (785)827-8746
Salina, KS 67402-1038 Fax: (785)827-6133

Official newspaper of the Catholic Diocese of Salina. **Founded:** 1937. **Freq:** Weekly. **Print Method:** Offset. **Cols./Page:** 6. **Col. Width:** 2 1/8 inches. **Col. Depth:** 21 1/2 inches. **Key Personnel:** Msgr. R.M. Menard, Editor; Mary Ann Huffman, Advertising/Circulation Mgr. **USPS:** 397-740. **Subscription Rates:** $16 individuals. **Remarks:** Accepts advertising.
Ad Rates: BW: $500 PCI: $5 **Circ:** Paid 7,870 Non-paid 40

11957 The Salina Journal
333 S. 4th St. Phone: (785)823-6363
PO Box 740 Fax: (785)823-3207
Salina, KS 67402-6740
Free: (800)827-6363
Publication E-mail: sjnews@saljournal.com

General newspaper. **Founded:** 1871. **Freq:** Mon.-Sun. (morn.). **Print Method:** Offset. **Trim Size:** 13 1/2 x 22 3/4. **Cols./Page:** 6. **Col. Width:** 24 3/4 nonpareils. **Col. Depth:** 297 1/2 agate lines. **Key Personnel:** George B. Pyle, Editoral page editor, gpyle@saljournal.com; Harris Rayl, Publisher, hrayl@saljournal.com; Scott Seirer, Executive editor, sseirer@saljournal.com; Jeanny Sharp, Advertising Dir., jsharp@saljournal.com; Bryan Sandmeier, Circulation Mgr., bsandmei@saljournal.com; David Martin, Business Mgr., dmartin@saljournal.com; David Atkinson, Production Mgr., datkinso@saljournal.com. **USPS:** 478-060. **Subscription Rates:** $152 individuals. **URL:** http://www.dailynews.net/salina/.
Ad Rates: GLR: $1.47 BW: $2,945.25 4C: $3,633.25 SAU: $23.10 PCI: $23.10 **Circ:** Mon.-Sat. ★**30,627** Sun. ★**32,089**

11958 KAAS-TV - 18
316 N. West St. Phone: (316)942-2424
Wichita, KS 67203 Fax: (316)942-8927

Format: Commercial TV. **Simulcasts:** KSAS-TV Wichita. **Networks:** Fox. **Owner:** Clear Channel Television Broadcasting, Inc., 7710 Jones Maltsberger Rd., No. 600, San Antonio, TX 78216, (210)822-2828, Fax: (210)822-2299. **Founded:** 1988. **Operating Hours:** Continuous; 3% network, 97% local. **ADI:** Wichita-Hutchinson, KS. **Key Personnel:** Diane Wilkin, General Mgr.; Virginia Edwards, Business Mgr.; Michael Hochman, Program Dir.; Ken Whitney, Production Mgr.; Tom Gateway, Promotions Dir.; Linda Madzey, Public Service Dir.; Lynn Kingsley, Traffic Mgr.

11959 KHCD-FM - 89.5
815 N. Walnut, Ste. 300 Phone: (316)665-3555
Hutchinson, KS 67501-6217
E-mail: webmaster@radioks.org

Format: Public Radio; News; Classical; New Age. **Networks:** National Public Radio (NPR). **Founded:** 1987. **Operating Hours:** Continuous. **ADI:** Wichita-Hutchinson, KS. **Key Personnel:** Dave Horning, General Mgr.; Ken Baker, Program Dir.; Patsy Terrell, Promotions Dir. **Wattage:** 100,000. **Ad Rates:** Noncommercial. **URL:** http://www.radioks.org.

11960 KQNS-FM - 95.5
1321 W. Crawford Phone: (913)826-9636
Salina, KS 67401 Fax: (913)826-9789
E-mail: kqns@midkan.com

Format: Contemporary Hit Radio (CHR). **Networks:** Westwood One Radio; USA Radio. **Owner:** B-B Broadcasting, Inc., at above address. **Founded:** 1985. **Operating Hours:** Continuous. **ADI:** Wichita-Hutchinson, KS. **Key Personnel:** Beth Chalmers, Gen. Mgr.; Gena Riley, Program Dir.; Bart Jones, Chief Engineer. **Wattage:** 25,000. **Ad Rates:** $12 for 30 seconds; $16 for 60 seconds. **URL:** http://www.mid-kan.com/star95.

11961 KSAJ-FM - 98.5
PO Box 80 Phone: (785)263-7111
Salina, KS 67402 Fax: (785)263-0166

Format: Oldies. **Networks:** ABC. **Owner:** EBC, Inc., at above address. **Founded:** 1985. **Operating Hours:** Continuous. **Key Personnel:** Jerry Hinrikus, General Mgr., jhinrikus@informatics.net; Larry Avery, General Sales Mgr., lavery@informatics.net; Billy Hansen, Program Dir., bhansen@informatics.net; Charlie Allen, Operations Mgr., callen@informatics.net; John Anderson, News Dir., andnew@informatics.net. **Wattage:** 100,000. **URL:** http://www.ebcinc.com.

11962 KSAL-AM - 1150
PO Box 80 Phone: (785)823-1111
Salina, KS 67402-0080 Fax: (785)823-2034
Free: (800)608-1150
E-mail: csanders@informatics.net

Format: Talk; News; Agricultural; Sports. **Networks:** ABC. **Owner:** EBC, Inc., PO Box 80, Salina, KS 67402-0080, (785)823-2034, Free: (800)608-1150. **Founded:** 1937. **Operating Hours:** Continuous; 60% network, 40% local. **ADI:** Wichita-Hutchinson, KS. **Key Personnel:** Jerry Hinrikus, General Mgr., phone (785)823-1111, fax (785)823-2034, jhinrikus@informatics.net; Clarke Sanders, Operations Mgr., csanders@informatics.net; Bob Protzman, Sales Mgr., bprotzman@informatics.net; Bruce Stienbrock, Sports Dir., bsteinbrock@informatics.net. **Local Programs:** *Kansas Live* 8:15 am - 9:00 am Monday-Friday, Steve Forman, (785)823-1111, Fax (785)823-2034. **Wattage:** 5000. **Ad Rates:** $18-27 for 60 seconds. Combined advertising rates available with KYEZ, KZBZ, KABI, KSAJ, KBLS. **URL:** http://www.ebcinc.com.

11963 KSKG-FM - 99.9
1825 South Ohio Phone: (913)825-4631
Salina, KS 67401 Fax: (913)825-4600

Format: Country. **Networks:** ABC. **Owner:** Eagle Communications, Inc., PO Box 817, Hays, KS 67601, (913)825-4000, Fax: (913)625-8030. **Founded:** 1960. **Operating Hours:** Continuous. **ADI:** Wichita-Hutchinson, KS. **Key Personnel:** Larry Riggins, General Mgr. **Local Programs:** *All Request Evenings* 6 p.m. - 10 p.m., Brian Karavan, Mailing contact; *Country Classic* Saturday, Randy McKay, Mailing contact. **Wattage:** 100,000. **Ad Rates:** $10-21 for 30 seconds; $13-27 for 60 seconds.

11964 KYEZ-FM - 93.7
131 N. Santa Fe Phone: (785)823-1111
Box 0080 Fax: (785)823-2034
Salina, KS 67402-0080
E-mail: ebcinc@informatics.net

Format: Contemporary Country. **Owner:** EBC, Inc., at above address. **Founded:** 1975. **Operating Hours:** Continuous. **ADI:** Wichita-Hutchinson, KS. **Key Personnel:** Jerry Hinrikus, Contact, jhinrikus@informatics.net; Steve Crawford, P.D., scrawford@informatics. **Wattage:** 100,000 ERP.

11965 TCI of Kansas, Inc.
Box 1577 Phone: (913)825-7151
Salina, KS 67402 Fax: (913)825-2162

Founded: 1962. **Cities Served:** Saline County, KS.

11966 Tristar Cable, Inc.
PO Box 2687 Phone: (913)238-3099
Salina, KS 67402-2687 Fax: (913)238-7190
Free: (800)888-4788
E-mail: tristar@fliphills.com

Cities Served: subscribing households 3,100.

SCOTT CITY

11967 News Chronicle
News Chronicle Printing Co., Inc.
PO Box 218 Phone: (316)872-2114
Scott City, KS 67871 Fax: (316)872-3572

Agricultural-hometown newspaper. **Founded:** Mar. 1886. **Freq:** Weekly (Wed.). **Print Method:** Offset. **Trim Size:** 7 1/2 x 11 1/2. **Cols./Page:** 6. **Key Personnel:** Bill Boyer, Editor and Publisher; Glenda Gough, Advertising Mgr. **ISSN:** 1040-5348. **Subscription Rates:** $18.20 individuals. **Remarks:** Accepts advertising.
Ad Rates: GLR: $.23 **Circ:** Paid 2,850
BW: $396.90 Free 25
PCI: $3.22

11968 KFLA-AM - 1310
Rte. 1, Box 14 Phone: (316)872-5345
Scott City, KS 67871 Fax: (316)872-5422

Format: Religious. **Owner:** Ingstad Broadcasters, Box 907, Valley City, ND 58072, Fax: (701)845-2903, Free: (800)999-5283. **Founded:** 1962. **Operating Hours:** 7 a.m.-11 a.m. **Key Personnel:** Kay Leiker, Contact; Scott Smith, General Mgr. **Wattage:** 500 day. **Ad Rates:** $5.25 for 30 seconds; $6.30 for 60 seconds.

SEDAN

The Elk County Citizen-Advance News - See Longton

11969 Messenger
Times Star
PO Box 417 Phone: (316)725-3176
Sedan, KS 67361 Fax: (316)725-3272

Newspaper. **Founded:** 1887. **Freq:** Weekly (Thurs.). **Print Method:** Offset. **Cols./Page:** 6. **Col. Width:** 26 nonpareils. **Col. Depth:** 294 agate lines. **Key Personnel:** Pat Jones, Editor; Sam Shade, Publisher; Mary Shade, Publisher. **Subscription Rates:** $9 individuals.

11970 Sedan Times-Star
H & H Publications
226 E. Main Phone: (316)725-3176
PO Box 417 Fax: (316)725-3272
Sedan, KS 67361
Newspaper. **Founded:** 1873. **Freq:** Weekly (Wed.). **Print Method:** Letterpress and offset. **Trim Size:** Broadsheet. **Cols./Page:** 6. **Col. Width:** 26 nonpareils. **Col. Depth:** 294 agate lines. **Key Personnel:** Paula Richards, General Mgr., phone (516)7253176, fax (516)7253272; Martin Heller, Publisher; Sheila Mill, Office Mgr. **Subscription Rates:** $19.10 individuals.
Ad Rates: BW: $350 **Circ:** Paid 2,100
PCI: $3

SHARON SPRINGS

11971 Western Times
Walker Publishing Inc.
PO Box 279 Phone: (913)852-4900
Sharon Springs, KS 67758 Fax: (913)852-4804
Free: (800)989-8969

Community newspaper. **Founded:** 1874. **Freq:** Weekly (Thurs.). **Print Method:** Offset. **Cols./Page:** 6. **Col. Width:** 12 picas. **Col. Depth:** 21 1/2 inches. **Key Personnel:** Barry and Jackie Walker, Owner. **Subscription Rates:** $18.88 individuals; $20.98 out of county; $23 out of state. **Remarks:** Accepts advertising.
Circ: ‡1,353

SHAWNEE

11972 Government Video
Miller Freeman PSN Inc.
10701 W. 54th St. Phone: (913)268-5973
Shawnee, KS 66203 Fax: (913)268-0461
Publication E-mail: gv@psn.com

Trade magazine for government video professionals. **Founded:** Dec. 1989. **Freq:** Monthly. **Print Method:** Offset. **Trim Size:** 8 1/8 x 10 7/8. **Cols./Page:** 3. **Col. Width:** 2 1/8 inches. **Col. Depth:** 7 inches. **Key Personnel:** Ron Merrell, Editor; Paul Gallo, Publisher; Joe Polombo, Dir., Sales (Video Division). **ISSN:** 1067-3407. **Subscription Rates:** $30; $36 institutions; $5 single issue. **Remarks:** Accepts advertising. **Formerly:** GMV Government & Military Video.
Ad Rates: BW: $2,490 **Circ:** Non-paid 15,000
4C: $3,190

11973 Shawnee-Merriam Sun
Sun Publications, Inc.
7373 W. 107th St. Phone: (913)648-4620
Overland Park, KS 66212-2547 Fax: (913)381-1402

Newspaper. **Founded:** Jan. 1, 1950. **Freq:** Semiweekly (Wed. and Fri.). **Print Method:** Offset. **Cols./Page:** 8. **Col. Width:** 21 nonpareils. **Col. Depth:** 292 agate lines. **Key Personnel:** Jack Lovelace, Editor; Jo Stapleton, Advertising Manager; Steve Rose, Publisher. **Subscription Rates:** Free. **Remarks:** Accepts advertising. **Formerly:** Shawnee Sun.
Ad Rates: SAU: $24.75 **Circ:** Combined ‡112,441
PCI: $34.35

SHAWNEE MISSION

11974 Electronic Servicing & Technology
CQ Communications
PO Box 12487 Phone: (913)492-4857
Shawnee Mission, KS 66282-2487 Fax: (913)492-4857
Publication E-mail: cpersedit@aol.com

Consumer electronics servicing magazine. **Subtitle:** The Professional Magazine for Electronics and Computer Servicing. **Founded:** 1951. **Freq:** Monthly. **Print Method:** Offset. **Trim Size:** 8 x 10 7/8. **Cols./Page:** 3. **Col. Width:** 2 1/4 inches. **Col. Depth:** 10 inches. **Key Personnel:** Conrad Persson, Editor, phone (913)492-4857, cpersedit@aol.com; Richard A. Ross, Publisher, phone (516)681-2922, fax (516)681-2926; Alycia Nicholsen, Assoc. Publisher, phone (516)681-2922, fax (516)681-2926, alyciaest@aol.com. **ISSN:** 0278-9922. **Subscription Rates:** $24 individuals. **Remarks:** Accepts advertising.
Ad Rates: BW: $4,292 **Circ:** 30,000
4C: $5,792
PCI: $235

11975 Kansas Food Dealers Bulletin
Kansas Food Dealers Association, Inc.
2809 W. 47th St. Phone: (913)384-3838
Shawnee Mission, KS 66207 Fax: (913)384-3868

Food industry trade magazine. **Founded:** 1927. **Freq:** Monthly. **Print Method:** Offset. **Cols./Page:** 2. **Col. Width:** 40 nonpareils. **Col. Depth:** 140 agate lines. **Key Personnel:** J.G. Sheehan, Editor. **Subscription Rates:** $5 individuals. **Remarks:** Advertising accepted; rates available upon request.
Circ: (Not Reported)

11976 Splash
World Waterpark Association
PO Box 14276
Shawnee Mission, KS 66285-4276
Publication E-mail: splash@waterparks.com; wwa@waterparks.com

Trade magazine involved in the water leisure industry. Targets owners, managers, suppliers, and developers of private and community owned water leisure facilities. **Founded:** July 1981. **Freq:** 9/year. **Print Method:** Offset. **Trim Size:** 8 1/2 x 10 7/8. **Cols./Page:** 3. **Key Personnel:** Al Turner, Publisher, phone (913)390-0800, fax (913)768-4204, al@waterparks.com; Jess Shockley, Managing Editor; Marilyn Turner, Editor, turnermj@swbell.net; Patty Miller, Advertising Dir., phone (913)381-8922, fax (913)381-6722, patty@waterparks.com. **Subscription Rates:** $45 U.S. and Canada; $75 out of country. **Remarks:** Advertising accepted; rates available upon request. **URL:** http://www.splashmagazine.com.
Circ: (Not Reported)

SMITH CENTER

11977 Smith County Pioneer
PO Box 266 Phone: (913)282-3371
Smith Center, KS 66967 Fax: (913)282-6383

Community newspaper. **Founded:** 1873. **Freq:** Weekly (Thurs.). **Print Method:** Offset. **Cols./Page:** 6. **Col. Width:** 12 nonpareils. **Col. Depth:** 20.5 agate lines. **Key Personnel:** Darrel Miller, Editor and Publisher; A. Clark, Publisher. **ISSN:** 4990-60. **Subscription Rates:** $19 individuals. **Remarks:** Accepts advertising.
Ad Rates: PCI: $3.10 **Circ:** 3,989

SPEARVILLE

11978 The Spearville News
Spearville News
400 Main St. Phone: (316)385-2200
PO Box 127 Fax: (316)385-2610
Spearville, KS 67876
Newspaper with a Republican orientation. **Founded:** 1897. **Freq:** Weekly (Thurs.). **Print Method:** offset. **Trim Size:** 11 1/4 x 16. **Cols./Page:** 5. **Col. Width:** 24 nonpareils. **Col. Depth:** 224 agate lines. **Key Personnel:** Lawrence A. Vierthaler, Publisher. **USPS:** 509-680. **Subscription Rates:** $16 individuals; $17 out of state. **Remarks:** Accepts advertising.
Ad Rates: GLR: $1 **Circ:** Paid 975
PCI: $1.47

STAFFORD, pop. 1,425.

SE KS. Stafford Co. 44 mi. W. of Hutchinson. Oil wells. Elevators. Light manufacturing. Stock and grain farms.

11979 The Stafford Courier
114 E. Bdwy Phone: (316)234-5241
PO Box 276
Stafford, KS 67578
Community newspaper. **Founded:** 1903. **Freq:** Weekly (Wed.). **Print Method:** Offset. **Cols./Page:** 6. **Col. Width:** 12 picas. **Col. Depth:** 21.5 picas. **Key Personnel:** Frank Smiley, Editor and Publisher. **USPS:** 517-240. **Subscription Rates:** $23 individuals; $25 institutions in state; $30.05 out of state. **Remarks:** Color advertising not accepted. **Online:** I.T.P.A. **Alt. Formats:** CD-ROM.
Ad Rates: PCI: $2.60 **Circ:** ‡1,750

STERLING

11980 Sterling Bulletin
PO Box 97 Phone: (316)278-2114
Sterling, KS 67579 Fax: (316)278-2330
Publication E-mail: bullet@sterlingks.net

Community newspaper. **Founded:** 1876. **Freq:** Weekly (Thurs.). **Print Method:** Offset. **Cols./Page:** 6. **Col. Width:** 12 picas. **Col. Depth:** 21 inches. **Key Personnel:** Ben Marshall, Publisher, phone (316)278-2114, fax (316)278-2330; Betty Childs, Editor. **USPS:** 521-460. **Subscription Rates:** $25.42 city; $27.53 county; $35.37 state; $33.00 out of state. **Remarks:** Accepts advertising.
Ad Rates: GLR: $3.95 **Circ:** Paid 1,200
BW: $497.70
PCI: $3.95

STILLWELL

11981 Sun Newspaper
Sun Publications, Inc.
7373 W. 107th St. Phone: (913)648-4620
Overland Park, KS 66212-2547 Fax: (913)381-1402

Newspaper. **Freq:** Semiweekly (Wed. and Fri.). **Print Method:** Offset. **Cols./Page:** 8. **Col. Width:** 21 nonpareils. **Col. Depth:** 292 agate lines. **Key Personnel:** Jack Lovelace, Editor; Stan Rose, Publisher; Shirley Rose, Publisher; Steve Rose, Publisher; Mike Lomario, Editor. **Formerly:** Stillwell Sun.
Circ: Combined 103,679

SYRACUSE

11982 Southwest Kansas Senior Beacon
PO Box 1137 Phone: (316)384-5640
Syracuse, KS 67878 Fax: (316)384-5228

Newspaper (tabloid) for seniors. **Founded:** Sept. 1984. **Freq:** Monthly. **Print Method:** Offset. **Trim Size:** 11 1/2 x 16. **Cols./Page:** 5. **Col. Width:** 12 picas. **Col. Depth:** 15 inches. **Key Personnel:** Linda Frantz, Editor; Jim Frantz, Publisher, jimf@pld.com. **Subscription Rates:** Free. **Remarks:** Accepts advertising.
Ad Rates: GLR: $.60 **Circ:** Free ‡8,500
BW: $402
SAU: $6

11983 Syracuse Journal
50 E. Hwy. 50 Phone: (316)384-5640
PO Box 1137 Fax: (316)384-5228
Syracuse, KS 67878
Community newspaper. **Founded:** Feb. 1885. **Freq:** Weekly (Wed.). **Print Method:** Web offset. **Cols./Page:** 6. **Col. Width:** 12 picas. **Col. Depth:** 21 inches. **Key Personnel:** Jim Frantz, Publisher, jimf@pld.com. **Subscription Rates:** $24.45 out of area; $26 out of state. **Remarks:** Accepts advertising.
Ad Rates: BW: $360 **Circ:** Paid 1,600
SAU: $3
PCI: $3

TONGANOXIE, pop. 1,717.

SW KS. Leavenworth Co. 24 mi. W. of Kansas City.

11984 Tonganoxie Mirror
613 E. 4th St. Phone: (913)845-2222
PO Box 920 Fax: (913)845-5491
Tonganoxie, KS 66086
Community newspaper. **Founded:** 1881. **Freq:** Weekly (Wed.). **Print Method:** Offset. **Cols./Page:** 6. **Col. Width:** 2 inches. **Col. Depth:** 21 inches. **Key Personnel:** Susan Waterman, Editor; Brian Waterman, Advertising Mgr.; Don Waterman, Publisher; Mary Waterman, Publisher. **Subscription Rates:** $23.39 individuals; $35 out of state. **Remarks:** Color advertising not accepted.
Ad Rates: PCI: $5 **Circ:** 2,500

TOPEKA†, pop. 115,266.

E. KS. Shawnee Co. On Kansas River, 65 mi. W. of Kansas City. The State Capital. , Washburn University, State institutions. Flour mills; printing and publishing; meat, poultry and egg packing plants; foundry and iron works. Manufactures creamery, pet foods, cellulose products, tires, tents, awnings, serum, steel fixtures, culverts, tanks, medicines, steel jetties.

11985 Animal Keepers' Forum
American Association of Zoo Keepers, Inc.
635 S.W. Gage Blvd. Phone: (785)273-1980
Topeka, KS 66606-2066 Fax: (785)273-1980
Free: (800)242-4519

Professional journal of the American Association of Zoo Keepers, Inc. **Founded:** Nov. 1974. **Freq:** Monthly. **Print Method:** Offset. **Trim Size:** 5 1/2 x 8 1/2. **Cols./Page:** 1. **Key Personnel:** Susan D. Chan, Managing Editor, 76761.720@compuserve.com. **ISSN:** 0164-9531. **Subscription Rates:** $35 individuals; $3 single issue. **Remarks:** Accepts advertising.
Ad Rates: BW: $210 **Circ:** Controlled 2,850

11986 Bulletin of the Menninger Clinic
Guilford Publications, Inc.
PO Box 829 Phone: (785)350-5856
Topeka, KS 66601-0829 Fax: (785)273-0797
Publication E-mail: jfalco@guilford.com
Publisher E-mail: info@guilford.com

Scholarly journal covering psychiatry, psychology, psychoanalysis, neuropsychology, and clinical research. **Subtitle:** A Journal for the Mental Health Professions. **Founded:** Sept. 1936. **Freq:** Quarterly. **Print Method:** Sheetfed offset. **Trim Size:** 6 x 9. **Cols./Page:** 1. **Col. Width:** 25 picas. **Col. Depth:** 43 picas. **Key Personnel:** Kathryn J. Zerbe, M.D., Editor, phone (785)350-5391, fax (785)272-9577, kjzerbe@menninger.edu; Philip R. Beard, M.A., Managing Editor, beardpr@menninger.edu. **ISSN:** 0025-9284. **Subscription Rates:** $60 individuals.
Ad Rates: BW: $500 **Circ:** Combined ‡1,220

11987 Capper's
1503 SW 42nd St. Phone: (785)274-4300
Topeka, KS 66609-1265 Fax: (785)274-4305
Free: (800)678-5779
Publication E-mail: cappers@kspress.com

Human interest magazine (tabloid). **Founded:** July 1879. **Freq:** Biweekly. **Print Method:** Offset. **Trim Size:** 10 3/4 x 12. **Cols./Page:** 5. **Col. Width:** 11 picas. **Col. Depth:** 150 agate lines. **Key Personnel:** Ann Crahan, Editor, phone (785)274-4346; Bryan Welch, Publisher, phone (785)274-4305; Keith Chartier, Advertising Mgr., phone (785)274-4330. **ISSN:** 0892-1148. **Subscription Rates:** $23 individuals; $1.50 single issue. **Remarks:** Accepts advertising. **Alt. Formats:** Audio tape. **Formerly:** Capper's Weekly.
Ad Rates: GLR: $10 **Circ:** Paid ★**230,030**
BW: $7,000
4C: $9,000
PCI: $140

11988 Florists' Review Magazine
Florist's Review Enterprises, Inc.
3641 SW Plass Ave. Phone: (785)266-0888
Topeka, KS 66611-2588 Fax: (785)266-0333
Free: (800)367-4708
Publication E-mail: florev@aol.com

Retail florist and wholesalers trade magazine. **Founded:** 1897. **Freq:** Monthly. **Print Method:** Offset. **Trim Size:** 8 1/8 x 10 7/8. **Cols./Page:** 3. **Col. Width:** 26 nonpareils. **Col. Depth:** 140 agate lines. **Key Personnel:** Doug Barrington, Editor; Debbi Simon, Publisher; Don Appel, Publisher; Rachel Kurtz, Advertising Account Coord.; David Coake, Editor; Frances Dudley, Publisher. **Subscription Rates:** $39 individuals; $4.50 single issue; $49 other countries; $30 students. **Remarks:** Accepts advertising.
Ad Rates: BW: $1,490 **Circ:** Combined ‡30,000
4C: $2,145

11989 Grit
Ogden Publications
1503 SW 42nd St. Phone: (913)274-4300
Topeka, KS 66609-1265 Fax: (913)274-4305
Publication E-mail: grit@kspress.com

Family oriented tabloid. **Subtitle:** American Life and Traditions. **Founded:** 1882. **Freq:** Biweekly. **Print Method:** Offset. **Trim Size:** 10 3/4 x 13. **Cols./Page:** 5. **Col. Width:** 23 nonpareils. **Col. Depth:** 170 agate lines. **Key Personnel:** Donna Doyle, Editor-in-Chief; Bryan Welch, Publisher; Keith Chartier, Advertising Mgr. **ISSN:** 0017-4289. **Subscription Rates:** $33 individuals; $1.50 single issue. **Remarks:** Advertising accepted; rates available upon request. **URL:** http://www.grit.com.
Circ: Paid ★**117,453**

11990 Hi-Tech Home
BBS Press Service Inc.
5610 SW 10th Ave. Phone: (785)271-0932
Topeka, KS 66604 Fax: (785)271-0192
Publication E-mail: sysop-news@worldnet.att.net

Professional operators of online services, web site designers, etc. **Founded:** Jan. 18, 1985. **Freq:** 1-3 times weekly. **Print Method:** On-line. **Key Personnel:** Alan R. Bechtold, Editor, phone (785)271-0932, fax (785)271-0192, sysop-news@worldnet.att.net. **Subscription Rates:** Free. **Remarks:** Advertising not accepted. **URL:** http://www.sysop.com.
Circ: Controlled ‡45,000

11991 Journal of Kansas Pharmacy
Kansas Pharmacists Association
1308 S.W. 10th Ave. Phone: (913)232-0439
Topeka, KS 66604-1206 Fax: (913)232-3764

Pharmacy journal. **Founded:** 1927. **Freq:** Quarterly. **Print Method:** Offset. **Trim Size:** 8 1/2 x 11. **Cols./Page:** 2 and 3. **Col. Width:** 21 nonpareils and 7 3/8 inches. **Col. Depth:** 135 agate lines and 9.25 inches. **Key Personnel:** Jenith Hoover, Editor; Martin Graham, Managing Editor. **ISSN:** 0194-5106. **Subscription Rates:** $18 (includes monthly updates).
Ad Rates: BW: $480 **Circ:** Paid 1,250
4C: $800 Controlled 147

11992 Kansas!
Department of Commerce and Housing
700 SW Harrison, Ste. 1300 Phone: (785)296-2009
Topeka, KS 66603-3712 Fax: (785)296-6988
Publisher E-mail: travtour@ink.org

Consumer magazine covering travel in Kansas. **Founded:** 1945. **Freq:** Quarterly. **Print Method:** Offset. **Key Personnel:** Andrea Glenn, Editor, phone (785)478-3268, fax (785)478-3415; Lisa Weigt, Tourism Marketing Mgr., lweigt@koch.state.ks.us. **ISSN:** 0022-8435. **Subscription Rates:** $15 individuals; $4 single issue. **Remarks:** Advertising not accepted.
Circ: Combined 48,250

11993 The Kansas Anthropologist
Kansas Anthropological Association
6425 SW 6th Ave. Phone: (785)272-8681
Topeka, KS 66615-1099 Fax: (785)272-8682

Professional journal covering archaeology, ethnohistory and ethnology in Kansas. **Founded:** 1989. **Freq:** Annual. **Trim Size:** 8 1/2 x 11. **Key Personnel:** Virginia A. Wulfkuhle, Editor, vwulfkuhle@kshs.org. **ISSN:** 1069-0379. **Subscription Rates:** $22 individuals; $6 single issue. **Remarks:** Advertising not accepted.
Circ: Paid 300

11994 The Kansas Banker
Kansas Bankers Association
1500 Merchant National Bank Phone: (913)232-3444
Topeka, KS 66612-1265 Fax: (913)232-3484

Kansas banking industry information magazine. **Subtitle:** The Magazine of the Kansas Bankers Association. **Founded:** 1911. **Freq:** Monthly. **Print Method:** Offset. **Trim Size:** 8 1/4 x 11 1/4. **Cols./Page:** 3. **Col. Width:** 2 1/8 inches. **Col. Depth:** 10 inches. **Key Personnel:** Kara Woodham, Editor; Linda Shinu, Advertising Mgr. **ISSN:** 0022-8478. **Subscription Rates:** $10 individuals; $2.50 single issue. **Remarks:** Accepts advertising.
Ad Rates: BW: $253 **Circ:** ‡1,100
4C: $715
PCI: $22

11995 Kansas Country Living
Kansas Electric Cooperative, Inc.
PO Box 4267 Phone: (913)478-4554
Gage Center Sta. Fax: (913)478-4852
Topeka, KS 66604-0267
Magazine for members of Kansas' electric cooperatives that promotes the uses of electrical energy around the farm and home. **Founded:** 1952. **Freq:** Monthly. **Print Method:** Offset. **Trim Size:** 7 7/8 x 10 3/4. **Cols./Page:** 3. **Col. Width:** 26 nonpareils. **Col. Depth:** 135 agate lines. **Key Personnel:** Larry Freeze, Editor. **ISSN:** 0091-9586. **Subscription Rates:** $8.40 individuals. **Remarks:** Advertising not accepted.
Circ: ‡80,957

11996 Kansas Farmer
Farm Progress Companies
2714 NW Topeka Blvd. Phone: (913)232-3276
Topeka, KS 66617 Fax: (913)232-3124
Publication E-mail: kfarmer@kspress.com

Agricultural magazine. **Founded:** 1863. **Freq:** 15/year, Semi-Monthly Jan-Mar, Monthly Apr-Dec. **Print Method:** Offset. **Trim Size:** 8 x 10 3/4. **Cols./Page:** 3. **Col. Width:** 25 nonpareils. **Col. Depth:** 140 agate lines. **Key Personnel:** Sara Wyant, Editorial Vice President; Allan Johnson, President; Charles Roth, Vice President of Advertising; Hank Ernst, Editor. **ISSN:** 0022-8583. **Subscription Rates:** $21.95 individuals. **Remarks:** Accepts advertising.
Circ: Paid 12,656
Non-paid 21,141

11997 Kansas Government Journal
League of Kansas Municipalities
300 SW 8th St. Phone: (785)354-9565
Topeka, KS 66603 Fax: (785)354-4186

Magazine covering Kansas' state and local government activities. **Founded:** 1914. **Freq:** Monthly. **Print Method:** Offset. **Trim Size:** 8 1/2 x 11. **Cols./Page:** 3. **Col. Width:** 27 nonpareils. **Col. Depth:** 140 agate lines. **Key Personnel:** Kim Gulley, Managing Editor, kgulley@ink.org. **Subscription Rates:** $28 individuals; $6 single issue. **Remarks:** Accepts advertising.
Ad Rates: GLR: $2 **Circ:** ‡6,000
BW: $325
4C: $600

11998 Kansas Insurance Agent and Broker
Kansas Association of Insurance Agents
815 SW Topeka Phone: (785)232-0561
Topeka, KS 66612 Fax: (785)232-6817
Publication E-mail: bigiks@aol.com

Insurance trade magazine. **Founded:** Mar. 1979. **Freq:** Bimonthly. **Print Method:** Offset. **Trim Size:** 8 1/2 x 11. **Cols./Page:** 3. **Col. Width:** 14 picas. **Col. Depth:** 58 picas. **Key Personnel:** Stephanie Parmenter, Dir. of Communications, stephanie@kaia.com. **ISSN:** 0194-634X. **Subscription Rates:** $30 individuals. **Formerly:** Kansas Insurance.
Ad Rates: BW: $450 **Circ:** Paid ‡934
4C: $800 Non-paid ‡106

11999 Kansas Nurse
Kansas State Nurses' Association
700 SW Jackson St., No. 601 Phone: (913)233-8638
Topeka, KS 66603-3731 Fax: (913)233-5222

Nursing journal. **Subtitle:** The Kansas Nurse. **Founded:** 1927. **Freq:** Monthly 10/year. **Print Method:** Offset. **Trim Size:** 8 1/2 x 11. **Cols./Page:** 3. **Key Personnel:** Dawn Reid, Editor. **Subscription Rates:** $24. **Remarks:** Accepts advertising.
Ad Rates: BW: $225 **Circ:** Paid ‡1,700
Non-paid ‡100

12000 Kansas Professional Engineer
Kansas Engineering Society, Inc.
627 S. Topeka Phone: (913)233-1867
PO Box 477 Fax: (913)357-4153
Topeka, KS 66601
Magazine for engineering society members. **Freq:** Monthly. **Print Method:** Offset. **Trim Size:** 8 1/2 x 11. **Cols./Page:** 3. **Col. Width:** 2 5/16 inches. **Col. Depth:** 9 11/16 inches. **Key Personnel:** Christine Stanek, Editor. **Remarks:** Accepts advertising.
Ad Rates: BW: $570 **Circ:** Non-paid 1,300
PCI: $20

12001 Kansas Stockman
Kansas Livestock Association
6031 SW 37th Phone: (913)273-5115
Topeka, KS 66614 Fax: (913)273-3399

Magazine for cattle producers and operators of commercial feedlots. **Founded:** 1916. **Freq:** 10/annually-combined May-June & Nov.-Dec. issues. **Print Method:** Offset. **Trim Size:** 8 1/2 x 11. **Cols./Page:** 3. **Col. Width:** 28 nonpareils. **Col. Depth:** 140 agate lines. **Key Personnel:** Todd Domer, Editor; Tammy Houk, Advertising Mgr. **Subscription Rates:** $100 individuals. **Remarks:** Accepts advertising.
Ad Rates: BW: $735 **Circ:** Paid ‡7,025
4C: $1,050 Non-paid ‡410
PCI: $20

12002 Lefthander Magazine
Lefthanders Intl.
POB 8249 Phone: (913)234-2177
Topeka, KS 66608 Fax: (913)232-3999

Magazine dealing with problems left-handed people experience; featuring articles on famous lefties and research on handedness; containing a catalog of special products for left-handed people. **Founded:** 1975. **Freq:** Bimonthly. **Print Method:** Offset. **Trim Size:** 8 1/4 x 10 3/4. **Cols./Page:** 3. **Col. Width:** 13 picas. **Col. Depth:** 8 inches. **Key Personnel:** Kim Kipers, Editor; Dean R. Campbell, Publisher; Carol Riddle, Advertising Dir. **Subscription Rates:** $15 individuals; $2 single issue. **Remarks:** Accepts advertising.
Ad Rates: BW: $1,200 **Circ:** 35,000
4C: $1,800

12003 Menninger Perspective
Menninger Foundation
PO Box 829 Phone: (913)350-5000
Topeka, KS 66601-0829 Fax: (913)271-9723
Free: (800)288-3950

Magazine for laymen covering psychiatry and work at The Menninger Foundation. **Founded:** 1961. **Freq:** Quarterly. **Print Method:** Offset. **Trim Size:** 8 1/2 x 11. **Cols./Page:** 3. **Col. Width:** 13 1/2 picas. **Col. Depth:** 55 picas. **Key Personnel:** Judith L. Craig, Editor; W. Walter Menninger, M.D., Publisher. **ISSN:** 0025-9292. **Subscription Rates:** $35 contribution for membership. **Remarks:** Advertising not accepted.
Circ: ‡66,000

12004 Mid-America Commerce and Industry
M.A.C.I., Inc.
1824 Cheyenne Phone: (785)272-5280
Topeka, KS 66604
Magazine on industrial purchasing. **Founded:** Sept. 1973. **Freq:** Monthly. **Print Method:** Offset. **Trim Size:** 8 1/2 x 11. **Cols./Page:** 3. **Col. Width:** 13 picas. **Col. Depth:** 10 inches. **Key Personnel:** N. Ray Lippe, Editor and Publisher. **Subscription Rates:** $18 individuals; $3 single issue. **Remarks:** Accepts advertising.
Ad Rates: BW: $1,070 **Circ:** Controlled ‡9,050
4C: $1,610
PCI: $45

12005 Mid-America Transporter
Kansas Motor Carriers Association
2900 S. Topeka Blvd. Phone: (785)267-1641
PO Box 1673 Fax: (785)266-6551
Topeka, KS 66601
Publication E-mail: mat@kmca.org

Industry magazine for regional motor carriers. **Founded:** 1946. **Freq:** 6/year. **Print Method:** Offset. **Trim Size:** 8 3/8 x 10 7/8. **Cols./Page:** 3. **Col. Width:** 31 nonpareils. **Col. Depth:** 140 agate lines. **Key Personnel:** Christi Wright, Editor; Carl Hill, Publisher. **Subscription Rates:** $12 individuals. **URL:** http://www.kmca.org. **Formerly:** Kansas Transporter.
Ad Rates: PCI: $15 **Circ:** Paid 3,758
Non-paid 352

12006 MOUTH
MOUTH: Voice of the Disability Nation
4201 SW 30th St.
Topeka, KS 66614

Magazine covering news and policy issues that affect disabled persons. **Subtitle:** The Voice of Disability Rights. **Founded:** May 1, 1989. **Freq:** 6/year. **Print Method:** Web Offset. **Trim Size:** 8 x 10 1/2. **ISSN:** 1071-5657. **Subscription Rates:** $16 individuals; $48 institutions. **Remarks:** Advertising not accepted. **Alt. Formats:** Audio tape; Large-print.
Circ: Paid 6,540

12007 Perspectives in Psychiatric Care
Nursecom, Inc.
1521 SW 24th St. Phone: (913)273-5899
Topeka, KS 66611-1328
Journal covering psychiatric care and nursing. **Founded:** 1963. **Freq:** Quarterly. **Print Method:** Offset, sheetfed. **Trim Size:** 10 1/4 x 10 3/4. **Cols./Page:** 2. **Col. Width:** 36 nonpareils. **Col. Depth:** 100 agate lines. **Key Personnel:** Margo Neal, R.N., Publisher. **ISSN:** 0031-5990. **Subscription Rates:** $40; $52 industry subscribers; $16 single issue. **Remarks:** Accepts advertising.
Ad Rates: GLR: $5 **Circ:** Paid ‡2,500
BW: $875
4C: $1,975

12008 The Social Science Journal
Elseiver
Department of Political Science Phone: (785)231-1010
Washburn University Fax: (785)232-5744
Topeka, KS 66621
Publication E-mail: 102062-2525@compuserve.com
Publisher E-mail: fcentres@gpu.stv.ualberta.ca

Scholarly journal covering the advancement and study of the social sciences. **Subtitle:** Official Journal of the Western Social Science Association. **Founded:** 1964. **Freq:** Quarterly 5/year. **Print Method:** type set. **Trim Size:** 6 7/8 x 10. **Key Personnel:** David A. Freeman, Editor, phone (785)231-1010, fax (785)232-5744, zzfree@washburn.edu. **ISSN:** 0302-3319. **Subscription Rates:** $205 institutions; $230 institutions, other countries; $255 institutions, other countries airmail; $90 individuals; $115 other countries; $140 other countries airmail; $42.50 single issue; $47.50 single issue other couuntries; $52.50 single issue other countries airmail. **Remarks:** Accepts advertising.
Ad Rates: BW: $300 **Circ:** ‡1,400

12009 The Topeka Capital-Journal
616 SE Jefferson St. Phone: (913)295-1111
Topeka, KS 66607-1120 Fax: (913)295-1230
Free: (800)777-7171
Publication E-mail: state@cjnetworks.com

General newspaper. **Founded:** 1879. **Freq:** Mon.-Sun. (morn.). **Print Method:** Offset. **Cols./Page:** 6. **Col. Width:** 26 nonpareils. **Col. Depth:** 22 inches. **Key Personnel:** John D. Goossen, Publisher, phone (785)-2951299, fax (785)295-5614, jgoossen@cjnetworks.com; Mark E. Nusbaum, Exec. Editor, phone (785)295-1191, mnusnaum@cjnetworks.com; H. Randall Magee, Division Controller, phone (785)295-1237, rmagee@cjnetworks.com; Gary Loftus, Advertising Dir., phone (785)295-1142, fax (785)295-1261, gloftus@cjnetworks; Garran M. Allison, Circulation Mgr., phone (785)295-1131, gallison@cjnetworks.com; Nancy Burkhardt, Marketing Dir., phone (785)295-1176, nburkhardt@cjnetworks.com; Larry E. Rogers, Production Dir., phone (785)295-1160, lrogers@cjnetworks.com. **Subscription Rates:** $225 by mail. **Remarks:** Accepts advertising. **URL:** http://www.cjnetworks.com. **Feature Editors:** Karen Sipes, *Features*, phone (785)295-1283, ksipes@cjnetworks.com.
Ad Rates: GLR: $2.50 **Circ:** Mon.-Sat. ★**59,858**
BW: $4,969.80 Sun. ★**66,813**
4C: $7,088.40
PCI: $37.65

12010 Topeka Genealogical Society Quarterly
Topeka Genealogical Society, Inc.
PO Box 4048 Phone: (785)233-5762
Topeka, KS 66604-0048
Publisher E-mail: tgs@networksplus.net

Journal covering local genealogy. **Founded:** 1970. **Freq:** Quarterly. **Print Method:** Photo offset. **Trim Size:** 8 1/2 x 11. **Key Personnel:** Marsha Neiswender, Editor; Helen L. King, Editor. **ISSN:** 0734-8495. **Subscription Rates:** $15 individuals; $20 other countries. **Remarks:** Accepts advertising. **Alt. Formats:** Microfilm.
Circ: Controlled 1,095

12011 The Topeka Sentinel
Content Communications
724 1/2 S. Kansas Ave. Free: (800)533-0241
Topeka, KS 66607
Publication E-mail: setnel@ksnows.com
Publisher E-mail: sentinel@networksplus.net

Newspaper featuring issues of interest to minorities and highlighting positive role models. **Subtitle:** The News in All its Colors. **Founded:** Oct. 1, 1994. **Freq:** Biweekly. **Print Method:** offset. **Trim Size:** 11 x 17. **Cols./Page:** 4. **Col. Width:** 13 picas. **Col. Depth:** 15 inches. **Key Personnel:** Jacalyn Mindell, Editor and Publisher. **ISSN:** 1079-1965. **Subscription Rates:** $15. **Remarks:** Accepts display advertising.
Ad Rates: BW: $110 **Circ:** Paid ‡500
4C: $300 Non-paid ‡500
PCI: $12.50

12012 KJTY-FM - 88.1
1005 SW 10th St. Phone: (913)357-8888
Topeka, KS 66604-1103 Fax: (913)357-0100
E-mail: joy88@wnetworks.com

Format: Religious; Educational. **Networks:** Moody Broadcasting; Voice of Christian Youth America; USA Radio. **Founded:** 1985. **Operating Hours:** Continuous; 20% network, 80% local. **ADI:** Topeka, KS. **Key Personnel:** Warren Wilson, General Mgr. **Wattage:** 100,000. **Ad Rates:** Noncommercial.

12013 KMAJ-AM - 1440
Box 4407 Phone: (913)272-2122
Topeka, KS 66604 Fax: (913)272-6219

Format: Talk. **Founded:** 1947. **ADI:** Topeka, KS. **Key Personnel:** Fritz Reynolds, President; Bill Reed, General Mgr.; Dave Waters, Program Dir.; Mike Manns, News Dir. **Wattage:** 5000 day; 1000 night.

12014 KMAJ-FM - 107.7
Box 4407 Phone: (913)272-2122
Topeka, KS 66604 Fax: (913)272-6219

Format: Adult Contemporary. **Owner:** Frederick P. Reynolds, Jr., 5315 W. 7th., Topeka, KS 66606. **Founded:** 1971. **Operating Hours:** Continuous. **ADI:** Topeka, KS. **Key Personnel:** Bill Reed, General Sales Mgr.; Pam Anderson, Business Mgr.; Dave Waters, Program Dir.; Kimberly Gerlach, Promotions Dir. **Wattage:** 100,000.

12015 KSNT-TV - 27
6835 NW Hwy. 24 Phone: (913)582-4000
Topeka, KS 66618 Fax: (913)582-5283
E-mail: 27news@ksnt.com

Format: Commercial TV. **Networks:** NBC. **Founded:** 1967. **Formerly:** KTSB-TV. **Operating Hours:** 6 a.m.-1 a.m. weekdays; 7 a.m.-midnight Sat.-Sun. **ADI:** Topeka, KS. **Key Personnel:** Gary McNair, Station Mgr., phone (913)582-4783.

12016 KTKA-TV - 49
PO Box 2229 Phone: (785)273-4949
Topeka, KS 66601 Fax: (785)273-7811
E-mail: 49email@newssource49.com

Format: Commercial TV. **Networks:** ABC. **Founded:** 1983. **Formerly:** KLDH-TV (1986). **Operating Hours:** 24 hrs. **ADI:** Topeka, KS. **Key Personnel:** Kent Cornish, General Mgr., 49gm@newssource49.com; Linda Hardesky, Program Dir., hardesky@newssource49.com; Bob Fulmer, General Sales Mgr., 49sales@newssource49.com. **Ad Rates:** $15-500 for 30 seconds.

12017 KTPK-FM - 106.9
2121 SW Chelsea Phone: (785)273-1069
Topeka, KS 66614 Free: (888)297-1069
E-mail: twister1069@twister1069.com

Format: Country. **Owner:** Kansas Capital Broadcasting, Inc., at above address. **Founded:** 1974. **Operating Hours:** Continuous. **ADI:** Topeka, KS. **Key Personnel:** Terry Weinacht, General Mgr., tweinacht@twister1069.com; Lee Kent, Program Dir.; Jim Allan, Sales Mgr.; Gloria Fellman, Office Mgr. **Local Programs:** *Marlena*, Lee O'Day, Program Dir.; *Sports*, Chuck Joslin, Sports Dir. **Wattage:** 100,000. **Ad Rates:** $32 for 30 seconds; $38 for 60 seconds.

12018 KTWU-TV - 11
1700 College Blvd Phone: (785)231-1111
Topeka, KS 66621-1100 Fax: (785)231-1112

Format: Public TV. **Networks:** Public Broadcasting Service (PBS). **Owner:** Washburn University of Topeka, at above address. **Founded:** 1965. **Operating Hours:** Continuous. **ADI:** Topeka, KS. **Key Personnel:** Eugene Williams, General Mgr.; Robert B. Fidler, Operations Dir., zzfidl@ktwu.washburn.edu; Cindy Barry, Devel. Dir., zzbarry@ktwu.washburn.edu; Brandy Schaefer, Promotions Dir., zzschaef@ktwu.washburn.edu; Duane Loyd, Chief Engineer, zzloyd@ktwu.washburn.edu. **Local Programs:** *Vintage Years* 5:30 p.m. Sunday, Rich O'Brien. **URL:** http://www.ktwu.washburn.edu.

12019 WIBW-AM - 580
PO Box 1818 Phone: (913)272-3456
Topeka, KS 66601 Fax: (913)272-3536

Format: News; Sports; Talk; Agricultural. **Networks:** CBS. **Owner:** Topeka Radio Trust, at above address. **Founded:** 1927. **Operating Hours:** 5:30 pm-12:30 pm weekdays; Continuous Sat-Sun; 25% network, 75% local. **ADI:** Topeka, KS. **Key Personnel:** Ben Bauman, News Dir.; Ed O'Donnell, Contact; Craig Colboch, Sales Mgr.; Al Lobeck, Vice President. **Local Programs:** *Let's Talk*, Sam Elliot, Mailing contact; *Sports Talk*, Len Lehmann, Mailing contact. **Wattage:** 5000.

12020 WIBW-FM - 97.3
PO Box 1818 Phone: (913)272-3456
Topeka, KS 66601 Fax: (913)272-3536

Format: Contemporary Country. **Owner:** Stauffer Topeka Radio Trust, at above address. **Founded:** 1961. **Operating Hours:** Continuous. **ADI:** Topeka, KS. **Key Personnel:** Al Lobeck, General Mgr.; Craig Colboch, General Sales Mgr.; Kevin Wagner, Program Dir. **Local Programs:** *Morning Show*, Bob Bowens. **Wattage:** 100,000 ERP.

TRIBUNE†, pop. 929.

W. KS. Greeley Co. 105 mi. NW of Dodge City. Grain, stock farms. Wheat, milo maize, sheep, cattle.

12021 Greeley County Republican
507 Broadway Phone: (316)376-4264
Box 610 Fax: (316)376-2433
Tribune, KS 67879
Community newspaper. **Founded:** 1886. **Freq:** Weekly

(Wed.). **Print Method:** Offset. **Cols./Page:** 6. **Col. Width:** 12 picas. **Col. Depth:** 21.5 inches. **Key Personnel:** Dan Epp, Editor and Publisher; Janalie Epp, Editor and Publisher. **USPS:** 228-020. **Subscription Rates:** $21.18 individuals; $25 out of area. **Remarks:** Advertising not accepted for alcohol and tobacco products.
Ad Rates: BW: $378 **Circ:** Paid 1,500
Free 16

TROY†, pop. 1,233.

NE KS. Doniphan Co. 14 mi. W. of St. Joseph, MO. Agriculture. Apples, corn, wheat, oats.

12022 Green Acres
113 S. Main Phone: (913)985-2560
PO Box 157 Fax: (913)985-3841
Troy, KS 66087
Farm newspaper. **Founded:** 1962. **Freq:** Semimonthly. **Print Method:** Offset. **Cols./Page:** 6. **Col. Width:** 1.6 inches. **Col. Depth:** 16 inches. **Key Personnel:** Steve C. Tetlow, Editor and Publisher; Glenn Sutherland, Production Mgr. **Subscription Rates:** Free; $12 by mail. **Remarks:** Accepts advertising.
Ad Rates: BW: $672 **Circ:** Paid 2,800
PCI: $9 Free 43,500

12023 Kansas Chief
Green Acres
113 S. Main Phone: (913)985-2560
PO Box 157 Fax: (913)985-3841
Troy, KS 66087
Publication E-mail: chief@midusa.net

Newspaper with a Republican orientation. **Founded:** 1857. **Freq:** Weekly (Thurs.). **Print Method:** Offset. **Cols./Page:** 6. **Col. Width:** 24 nonpareils. **Col. Depth:** 294 agate lines. **Key Personnel:** Steve C. Tetlow, Editor and Publisher. **USPS:** 290-040. **Subscription Rates:** $14.85 individuals. **Remarks:** Accepts advertising.
Ad Rates: BW: $368.68 **Circ:** Paid 1,495
SAU: $3.25 Free 39,000
PCI: $3.25

TURON

12024 The Record
Larry Green
PO Box 38 Phone: (316)497-6448
Turon, KS 67583-0038 Fax: (316)497-6435

Community newspaper. **Founded:** 1922. **Freq:** Weekly (Thurs.). **Print Method:** Offset. **Cols./Page:** 5. **Col. Width:** 11 1/2 picas. **Col. Depth:** 12 1/2 inches. **Key Personnel:** Joan Green, Editor; Larry Green, Publisher. **USPS:** 254-840. **Subscription Rates:** $3 individuals; $8.50 out of area; $10.50 out of state. **Remarks:** Accepts advertising.
Ad Rates: GLR: $.18 **Circ:** ‡800
BW: $130
PCI: $2.10

UDALL

12025 Wheat State Telecable Inc.
106 W. 1st St. Phone: (316)782-3341
Box 609 Fax: (316)782-3302
Udall, KS 67146
Free: (800)442-6835

Founded: 1982. **Key Personnel:** Arturo G. Macias, General Mgr. **Cities Served:** Udall, KS: subscribing households 240; 17 channels.

ULYSSES†, pop. 4,653.

SW KS. Grant Co. 70 mi. SW of Dodge City. Liquid petroleum products, carbon black, irrigation pipe manufactured. Grain farms. Wheat, corn, sorghum.

12026 The Ulysses News
Southwest Kansas Publications, Inc.
Box 706 Phone: (316)356-1201
Ulysses, KS 67880 Fax: (316)356-4610

Community newspaper. **Founded:** 1892. **Freq:** Weekly (Wed.). **Print Method:** Offset. **Cols./Page:** 6. **Col. Width:** 24 nonpareils. **Col. Depth:** 294 agate lines. **Key Personnel:** Michael A. Pace, Editor and Publisher; Karla Waechter, Marketing Dir. **USPS:** 647-280. **Subscription Rates:** $22.5 individuals; $28 out of county. **Remarks:** Accepts advertising. **Alt. Formats:** CD-ROM.
Ad Rates: BW: $579.6 **Circ:** ‡2600
4C: $829.6
SAU: $4.6
PCI: $4.6

12027 KFXX-FM - 106.7
2917 S. Colorado Phone: (316)356-1067
Ulysses, KS 67880 Fax: (316)356-3635

Format: Adult Contemporary. **Networks:** ABC; Westwood One Radio. **Owner:** KBUF Partnership, at above address. **Founded:** 1964. **Formerly:** KHUQ-FM (1990). **Operating Hours:** Continuous. **Key Personnel:** Jeffrey Dyer, General Mgr., phone (316)356-1420; Bob Dale, Program Dir., phone (316)356-1420. **Wattage:** 35,000. **Ad Rates:** $14-16 for 30 seconds; $21-24 for 60 seconds. Combined advertising rates available with KULY-AM.

12028 KULY-AM - 1420
2917 S. Colorado Phone: (316)356-1420
Ulysses, KS 67880 Fax: (316)356-3635

Format: Contemporary Country. **Networks:** ABC; Westwood One Radio. **Owner:** KBUF Partnership, at above address. **Founded:** 1964. **Operating Hours:** Continuous; 20% network, 80% local. **Key Personnel:** Jeffrey Dyer, General and Station Mgr.; Bob Dale, Operations Mgr. **Wattage:** 1000 day; 500 night. **Ad Rates:** $13-15 for 30 seconds; $20-23 for 60 seconds.

VALLEY CENTER, pop. 3,300.

S. KS. Sedgwick Co. 12 mi. N. of Wichita. Oil, gas wells. Elevator. Agriculture. Wheat, alfalfa, hogs.

12029 Ark Valley News
210 W. Main Phone: (316)755-0821
PO Box 218 Fax: (316)755-0644
Valley Center, KS 67147
Publication E-mail: avn@arkvalleynews.com

Community newspaper. **Founded:** 1896. **Freq:** Weekly (Thurs.). **Print Method:** Offset. **Cols./Page:** 4. **Col. Width:** 14 1/2 picas. **Col. Depth:** 16 inches. **Key Personnel:** Nancy and Les Anderson, Publisher. **Subscription Rates:** $28.00 individuals; $40 out of state. **Remarks:** Accepts advertising.
Ad Rates: PCI: $4.75 **Circ:** ‡2,100

VALLEY FALLS, pop. 1,189.

NE KS. Jefferson Co. 31 mi. NE of Topeka. Truck bodies manufactured. Walnut timber. Grain, stock, poultry, dairy farms. Corn, wheat, alfalfa.

12030 Valley Falls Vindicator
Davis Publications, Inc.
PO Box 187 Phone: (785)945-3257
Valley Falls, KS 66088 Fax: (785)995-3444
Publication E-mail: vindicator@grasshoppernet.com

Community newspaper. **Founded:** 1863. **Freq:** Weekly (Thurs.). **Print Method:** Offset. **Cols./Page:** 7. **Col. Width:** 25 nonpareils. **Col. Depth:** 294 agate lines. **Key Personnel:** Clarke Davis, Editor; Marveta Davis, Advertising Mgr. **USPS:** 655-520. **Subscription Rates:** $18 individuals. **Remarks:** Accepts advertising.
Ad Rates: GLR: $.225 **Circ:** ‡2,738
SAU: $1.39
PCI: $4

WA KEENEY†, pop. 2,388.

NW KS. Trego Co. 130 mi. W. of Salina. Oil wells. Stock, grain farms. Wheat, corn.

12031 Western Kansas World
PO Box 218 Phone: (913)743-2155
205 Main St. Fax: (913)743-5340
Wa Keeney, KS 67672
Community newspaper. **Founded:** Mar. 1, 1879. **Freq:** Weekly (Thurs.). **Print Method:** Offset. **Cols./Page:** 6. **Col. Width:** 24 nonpareils. **Col. Depth:** 294 agate lines. **Key Personnel:** Jerry Millard, Editor. **ISSN:** 678 -580. **Subscription Rates:** $21.71 individuals; $26 out of area. **Remarks:** Accepts advertising.
Ad Rates: GLR: $0.17 **Circ:** 2,150
BW: $327
SAU: $1.30
PCI: $2.60

12032 Wakeeney Cable TV Co.
529 Russell Phone: (913)743-5616
Box 426 Fax: (913)625-8030
Wa Keeney, KS 67672

Owner: Eagle Communications Inc., 2703 Hall, Hays, KS 67601, (913)625-4000, Fax: (913)625-8030. **Key Personnel:** Pete Collins, General Mgr.; Larry Braun, Tech. Mgr., phone (913)625-5910; Lila Krainbill, Office Mgr., phone (913)483-2534; Leroy Flax, Technician. **Cities Served:** Wakeeney, KS: subscribing households 900; 51 channels; 1 community access channel.

WAMEGO, pop. 3,157.

NE KS. Pottawatomie Co. On Kansas River, 37 mi. NW of Topeka. Manufactures snow plows, bull dozers, cheese, fertilizer, feeds. Grain, stock farms. Wheat, corn, alfalfa, soybeans.

12033 The Smoke Signal
Montgomery Communications, Inc.
PO Box 267 Phone: (913)456-2602
Wamego, KS 66547 Fax: (913)456-8400

Community newspaper with coverage of two counties. **Founded:** 1974. **Freq:** Weekly (Wed.). **Print Method:** Offset. **Trim Size:** 14 x 22 3/4. **Cols./Page:** 6. **Col. Width:** 30 nonpareils. **Col. Depth:** 301 agate lines. **Key Personnel:** Jim Gibbons, General Mgr.; John G. Montgomery, Publisher. **Subscription Rates:** $17 individuals; $21 out of state. **Remarks:** Accepts advertising. **Formerly:** Wamego Smoke Signal (1987).
Ad Rates: BW: $503.10 **Circ:** Free ‡10,700
4C: $703.10
SAU: $4.10
PCI: $4.75

12034 Wamego Times
Wamego
Box 247 Phone: (913)456-7838
Wamego, KS 66547 Fax: (913)456-9668

Newspaper. **Founded:** 1887. **Freq:** Weekly (Thurs.). **Print Method:** Offset. **Cols./Page:** 6. **Col. Width:** 28 nonpareils. **Col. Depth:** 294 agate lines. **Key Personnel:** Mark Portell, Editor and Publisher. **Subscription Rates:** $10 individuals. **Remarks:** Accepts advertising.
Ad Rates: GLR: $.18 **Circ:** 2,200
BW: $327.60

WASHINGTON†, pop. 1,488.

N. KS. Washington Co. 65 mi. N. of Manhattan. Grain, stock, dairy, farms. Wheat, milo, corn, cattle, hogs, alfalfa.

12035 Washington County News
211 C. St., Box 316 Fax: (913)325-3255
Washington, KS 66968
Publication E-mail: washnews@aol.com

Community newspaper. **Founded:** 1869. **Freq:** Weekly (Thurs.). **Print Method:** Offset. **Cols./Page:** 6. **Col. Width:** 24 nonpareils. **Col. Depth:** 294 agate lines. **Key Personnel:** William M. Hays, Editor and Publisher; Denise Powell, Advertising Mgr. **USPS:** 667-400. **Subscription Rates:** $20 individuals; $23 out of area; $25 out of state. **Remarks:** Accepts advertising. **Online:** Kansas Press Association; America Online, Inc. **Alt. Formats:** CD-ROM.
Ad Rates: PCI: $4.00 **Circ:** Paid ‡3,050

WATERVILLE, pop. 694.

NE KS. Marshall Co. 90 mi. NW of Topeka. Grain and feed elevators, grain storage. Dairy, stock, poultry, grain farms.

12036 Waterville Cable TV
123 W. Lincoln St. Phone: (913)363-2646
Box 424
Waterville, KS 66548

Owner: Ken and Sue Hula, at above address. **Founded:** Aug. 1, 1987. **Key Personnel:** Ken Hula, Owner. **Cities Served:** Waterville, KS: subscribing households 245; 26 channels.

WATHENA, pop. 1,418.

NE KS. Doniphan Co. 5 mi. W. of Saint Joseph. Residential.

12037 The Wathena Times
Box 368 Phone: (913)989-4415
Wathena, KS 66090-0368
Community newspaper. **Founded:** 1884. **Freq:** Weekly (Thurs.). **Print Method:** Offset. **Cols./Page:** 6. **Col. Width:** 13 picas. **Col. Depth:** 21 inches. **Key Personnel:** Mr. Dana Foley, Editor/Administration; Ethel Mae Foley, Publisher. **USPS:** 669-400. **Subscription Rates:** $15 individuals; $17 out of area. **Remarks:** Accepts advertising.
Ad Rates: GLR: $41 **Circ:** ‡1,800
BW: $386.40
SAU: $3.40
PCI: $3.50

WELLINGTON†, pop. 8,212.

SC KS. Sumner Co. 30 mi. S. of Wichita. Residential.

12038 Wellington Daily News
113 W. Harvey Ave. Phone: (316)326-3326
PO Box 368 Fax: (316)326-3290
Wellington, KS 67152-3840
Newspaper with a Republican orientation. **Founded:** 1901. **Freq:** Daily (eve.). **Print Method:** Offset. **Cols./Page:** 6. **Col. Width:** 26 nonpareils. **Col. Depth:** 294 agate lines. **Key Personnel:** Jackson Mitchell, Publisher, jmitch@idir.net; Bill Newland, Advertising Mgr. **Subscription Rates:** $51 individuals.
Ad Rates: BW: $743.40 **Circ:** Paid 3,800
PCI: $5.75

12039 KKLE-AM - 1550
338 S. Kley Dr. Phone: (316)221-3341
Wellington, KS 67152 Fax: (316)221-3342

Format: News; Sports. **Owner:** Johnson Enterprises Inc., at above address. **Formerly:** KVFW-AM. **Operating Hours:** Continuous. **Key Personnel:** Gordon Johnson, fax (P). **Wattage:** 250. **Ad Rates:** $7 for 30 seconds; $10 for 60 seconds.

12040 KLEY-AM - 1130
338 S. Kley Dr. Phone: (316)326-3341
Wellington, KS 67152-0707 Fax: (316)326-8512

Format: Talk. **Owner:** Johnson Enterprises, Inc., at above address. **Founded:** 1966. **Operating Hours:** 24 hours. **Key Personnel:** Gordon Johnson, Contact. **Wattage:** 250. **Ad Rates:** $3.10-4.40 for 10 seconds; $4.70-6.60, for 30 seconds; $6.30-9 for 60 seconds. Combined advertising rates available with KKLE/KWME.

12041 KWME-FM - 93.5
338 S. Kley Dr. Phone: (316)326-3341
Wellington, KS 67152 Fax: (316)326-8512

Format: Oldies. **Owner:** Johnson Enterprises, Inc., at above address. **Founded:** 1979. **Former name:** KZED-FM. **Operating Hours:** Continuous. **Key Personnel:** Gordon Johnson, President. **Wattage:** 6000. **Ad Rates:** $10.35 for 30 seconds; $17.25 for 60 seconds.

12042 Sumner Cable TV, Inc.
117 W. Harvey Phone: (316)326-8989
Wellington, KS 67152 Fax: (316)326-5332
E-mail: sumnertv@idir.net

Founded: 1978. **Key Personnel:** Philip Brown, General Mgr. **Cities Served:** Wellington, KS: subscribing households 3,225; 54 channels; 1 community access channel.

WESTMORELAND†, pop. 598.

NE KS. Pottawatomie Co. 50 mi. NW of Topeka. Agriculture. Milo, wheat, cattle.

12043 Westmoreland Recorder
Box 128 Phone: (913)457-3411
Westmoreland, KS 66549-0128 Fax: (913)457-3411
Publication E-mail: newsnose@kansas.net

Official county newspaper. **Founded:** 1882. **Freq:** Weekly (Thurs.). **Print Method:** Offset. Uses mats. **Cols./Page:** 6. **Col. Width:** 25 nonpareils. **Col. Depth:** 301 agate lines. **Key Personnel:** James I. Travis, Editor and Publisher. **Subscription Rates:** $18.07 individuals /year. **Remarks:** Accepts advertising.
Ad Rates: GLR: $.15 **Circ:** ‡1,000
BW: $193.50
4C: $513.50
SAU: $1.85

WESTWOOD

12044 KMBZ-AM - 980
4935 Belinder Rd. Phone: (913)677-8998
Westwood, KS 66205-1937 Fax: (913)677-8935

Format: News; Talk; Sports. **Owner:** Bonneville International Corp., Broadcast House, Salt Lake City, UT 84145-1160. **Founded:** 1921. **Formerly:** KMBC-AM (1967). **Operating Hours:** Continuous. **Key Personnel:** Ron Carter, General Mgr.; Bob Davis, Sports Dir.; Rich Myers, Chief Engineer. **Wattage:** 5000. **Ad Rates:** Advertising accepted; rates available upon request.

WHITE CITY

12045 Prairie Post
PO Box 326 Phone: (785)349-5516
White City, KS 66872-0326 Fax: (785)349-5516
Free: (800)593-5516

Weekly community newspaper. **Founded:** 1993. **Freq:** Weekly. **Print Method:** Offset. **Trim Size:** 11 1/2 x 15. **Cols./Page:** 5. **Col. Width:** 12.4 picas. **Col. Depth:** 14 inches. **Key Personnel:** Joann Kahnt, Editor. **USPS:** 763-570. **Subscription Rates:** $21 individuals; $26 out of area; $27 out of state. **Remarks:** Accepts advertising. **Formerly:** White City Reporter.
Ad Rates: GLR: $.14 **Circ:** Paid 840
BW: $140 Controlled 21
PCI: $2.50

WICHITA†, pop. 279,272.

S KS. Sedgwick Co. 195 mi. SW of Kansas City. Friends University. The Wichita State University. Kansas Newman College. Recreational lakes. Mid-American All Indian Center. Historic Cowtown. Culture Center. Center of rich oil producting and wheat growing region. Manufactures airplanes, airplane supplies, heating and air conditioning units, agricultural and auto equipment, machinery, dairy products, household appliances. Oil refining. Grain storage. Meat packing. Flour milling. Steel fabrication.

12046 Active Aging
631 S. Glenn Phone: (316)264-7353
Wichita, KS 67213 Fax: (316)264-0127

Newspaper serving Wichita metro-area residents over 60. **Founded:** Dec. 1979. **Freq:** Monthly. **Print Method:** Offset. **Trim Size:** 11 1/4 x 17. **Cols./Page:** 4. **Col. Width:** 14 picas. **Col. Depth:** 16 inches. **Key Personnel:** Rebecca A. Funke, Editor; Joe Ludiker, Advertising; Anne Willis, Advertising; Joan Noonan, Office Mgr. **Subscription Rates:** Free persons 55 in Sedgwick, Harvey, Butler counties; $15 elsewhere.
Ad Rates: BW: $1,285.59 **Circ:** Free ‡45,500
4C: $1,735.59
PCI: $27.30

12047 American Bonanza Society—Magazine
American Bonanza Society
PO Box 12888 Phone: (316)945-1700
Wichita Midcontinent Airport Fax: (316)945-1710
Wichita, KS 67277
Publication E-mail: bonanza1@ix.netcom.com

Concerned with the flight and maintenance of Beechcraft Bonanza, Baron, and Travel Air aircraft. Reports on safety, flight regulation, training and travelogues. **Founded:** 1967. **Freq:** Monthly. **Trim Size:** 8 1/2 x 11. **Key Personnel:** Nancy Johnson, Publisher; John Shoemaker, Advertising Mgr., phone (800)773-7798. **ISSN:** 0161-3545. **Subscription Rates:** Included in membership. **Remarks:** Advertising accepted; rates available upon request.
Circ: 10,000

12048 Canfield Family Association
1144 N. Gordon Phone: (316)942-7120
Wichita, KS 67203-6611
Genealogical publication covering information about Canfield, Camfield, and Campfield names. **Founded:** Feb. 1982. **Freq:** Quarterly. **Key Personnel:** Genevieve (Canfield) Martinson, Editor. **ISSN:** 1092-X12X. **Subscription Rates:** $8 individuals; $14 out of country. **Remarks:** Advertising not accepted.
Circ: Paid 130

12049 The Catholic Advance
424 N. Broadway St. Phone: (316)263-8191
Wichita, KS 67202-2310 Fax: (316)269-3936

Catholic. **Founded:** 1901. **Freq:** Weekly (Thurs.). **Print Method:** Offset. **Cols./Page:** 5. **Col. Width:** 11.5 nonpareils. **Col. Depth:** 203 agate lines. **Key Personnel:** Christopher M. Riggs, Editor; Bishop Eugene J. Gerber, Publisher. **Subscription Rates:** $12 individuals. **Remarks:** Accepts advertising.
Ad Rates: GLR: $.30 **Circ:** ‡27,882

12050 El Perico
7804 E. Funston, Ste. 210 Phone: (316)651-0372
Wichita, KS 67207-3107 Fax: (316)651-0436

Community newspaper (Spanish). **Subtitle:** Bilingual Newspaper. **Founded:** 1977. **Freq:** Monthly. **Cols./Page:** 4. **Col. Width:** 3.25 picas. **Col. Depth:** 13.5 picas. **Key Personnel:** Anthony J. Ramirez, Editor. **Subscription Rates:** $15. **Remarks:** Accepts advertising.
Ad Rates: PCI: $6.38 **Circ:** 3,000

12051 International Flying Farmer
International Flying Farmers, Inc.
2120 Airport Rd. Phone: (316)943-4234
PO Box 9124 Fax: (316)943-4235
Wichita, KS 67277
Association magazine covering the activities of people with agricultural and/or aviation interests. **Founded:** 1948. **Freq:** 9/year. **Trim Size:** 8 1/4 x 11. **Cols./Page:** 3. **Col. Width:** 14 picas. **Col. Depth:** 10 inches. **Key Personnel:** Deanne Earwood, Editor; Kathy Marsh, Office Mgr. **ISSN:** 0020-675X. **Subscription Rates:** $25 individuals U.S.; $30 Canada; $35 other countries. **Remarks:** Accepts advertising.
Ad Rates: BW: $350 **Circ:** Controlled ‡1,900
PCI: $30

12052 International Journal of Comparative and Applied Criminal Justice
Wichita State University
Box 95 Phone: (316)978-6517
Wichita, KS 67260-0135 Fax: (316)978-3626

Scholarly journal covering research in criminal justice. **Founded:** 1977. **Freq:** Semiannual. **Trim Size:** 6 x 9. **Key Personnel:** Dr. Dae H. Chang, Editor-in-Chief, dchang@twsuvm.cu.twsu.edu. **ISSN:** 0192-4036. **Remarks:** Advertising not accepted.
Circ: Paid 300

12053 International Women Pilots
The Ninety-Nines, Inc.
807 N. Waco Phone: (316)263-9110
Suite 22 Fax: (316)263-7350
Wichita, KS 67203
Publication E-mail: 102126,135@compuserve.com

Magazine for women pilots. **Founded:** 1933. **Freq:** Bimonthly. **Print Method:** Offset. **Trim Size:** 8 1/2 x 11. **Cols./Page:** 3 and 2. **Col. Width:** 28 and 42 nonpareils. **Col. Depth:** 135 agate lines. **Key Personnel:** Betty Rowley, Editor, phone (316)838-7350; John Shoemaker, Advertising Sales, phone (800)773-7798. **ISSN:** 0273-608X. **Subscription Rates:** $20.00. **Remarks:** Accepts advertising. **Available Online. URL:** http://www.ninety-nines.org. **Formerly:** The 99 News.
Ad Rates: BW: $395 **Circ:** ‡7,000
4C: $800

12054 Kansas Beverage News
2416 E. 37th N Phone: (316)838-6700
Wichita, KS 67219 Fax: (316)838-6795

Liquor trade magazine. **Founded:** 1958. **Freq:** Monthly. **Print Method:** Offset. **Trim Size:** 8 1/2 x 11. **Cols./Page:** 3. **Col. Width:** 24 nonpareils. **Col. Depth:** 126 agate lines. **Key Personnel:** Kathy Decker, Editor and Publisher, kdecker@southwind.net. **USPS:** 875-420. **Subscription Rates:** $12 individuals.
Ad Rates: BW: $525 **Circ:** 2,300
4C: $950

12055 Kansas Economic Report
Center for Economic Development and Business Research
CEDBR
WSU
1845 Fairmount St.
Wichita, KS 67260
Publisher E-mail: cedbr@twsuvm.uc.twsu.edu

Business and economic report. **Founded:** 1971. **Freq:** Quarterly. **Print Method:** Offset. **Cols./Page:** 2. **Col. Width:** 38 nonpareils. **Col. Depth:** 134 agate lines. **Key Personnel:** Carlene Hill, Director; Janet Nickel, Editor/Assoc. Dir. **Subscription Rates:** $50 individuals. **Remarks:** Advertising not accepted. **URL:** http://www.twsu.edu/~cedbrwww. **Formerly:** Business and Economic Report.
Circ: 700

12056 Kansas Hospitality
Kansas Restaurant & Hospitality Association
359 S. Hydraulic St. Phone: (316)267-8383
Wichita, KS 67211-1988 Fax: (316)267-8400

Trade magazine on restaurants and hotels in Kansas. **Subtitle:** Kansas Hospitality. **Founded:** Oct. 1938. **Freq:** Bimonthly. **Print Method:** Offset. **Trim Size:** 8 1/2 x 11. **Cols./Page:** 2. **Col. Width:** 3 1/2 inches. **Col. Depth:** 9 7/8 inches. **Key Personnel:** Dillis Hart II, Editor/Advertising Mgr. **ISSN:** 0022-8753. **Subscription Rates:** included in membership. **Remarks:** Accepts advertising. **Formerly:** The Kansas Restaurant.
Ad Rates: 4C: $800 **Circ:** ‡6,000

12057 Kansas Music Review
Kansas Music Educators Association
Wichita State University Phone: (316)838-3904
School of Music Fax: (316)838-3904
Wichita, KS 67260-0053
Trade magazine covering music. **Founded:** 1936. **Freq:** Quarterly. **Trim Size:** 8 1/2 x 11. **Key Personnel:** J. Hardy, Editor. **Remarks:** Accepts advertising.
Ad Rates: BW: $185 **Circ:** (Not Reported)

Oklahoma Beverage News - See Oklahoma City, Oklahoma

12058 The Sunflower
Wichita State University
1845 N. Fairmount Phone: (316)978-3644
Campus Box 134 Fax: (316)978-3778
Wichita, KS 67208
Publisher E-mail: editor@sunflower.es.twso.edu

Collegiate newspaper. **Founded:** 1896. **Freq:** 3/week. **Print Method:** Offset. **Cols./Page:** 4. **Col. Width:** 29 nonpareils. **Col. Depth:** 210 agate lines. **Key Personnel:** Keena Neal, Editor, phone (316)978-6905; Michael Russio, Advertising Mgr., phone (316)978-6906; David Rollins, Business Mgr., phone (316)978-3640. **USPS:** 053-050. **Subscription Rates:** Free; $43.60 by mail. **Remarks:** Accepts advertising. **URL:** http://artstotle.es.twsu.edu/sunflower.html.
Ad Rates: GLR: $7 **Circ:** Mon. 8,000
BW: $408 Wed. 8,000
4C: $638 Fri. 6,000

12059 Vantage
Kansas Newman College
3100 McCormick St. Phone: (316)942-4291
Wichita, KS 67213-2097 Fax: (316)942-4483
Free: (800)736-7585

Collegiate newspaper. **Founded:** 1961. **Freq:** Weekly (Wed.). **Print Method:** Offset. **Trim Size:** 11 1/2 x 16. **Cols./Page:** 5. **Col. Width:** 11 picas. **Col. Depth:** 82 picas. **Key Personnel:** Del Torkelson, Editor; Blaine Halley, Contact, phone (316)942-4291. **Subscription Rates:** Free; $10 institutions. **Remarks:** Color advertising not accepted.
Ad Rates: BW: $150 **Circ:** Free ‡1,500
PCI: $3 Paid 20

12060 Wichita Business Journal
American City Business Journals
110 S. Main St., Ste. 200 Phone: (316)267-6406
Wichita, KS 67202 Fax: (316)267-8570
Publication E-mail: wichita@amcity.com

Business newspaper. **Founded:** Mar. 17, 1986. **Freq:** Weekly (Fri.). **Print Method:** Offset. **Trim Size:** 11 3/8 x 14. **Cols./Page:** 4. **Col. Width:** 2 3/8 inches. **Col. Depth:** 13 inches. **Key Personnel:** John Ek, Dir. of Advertising/Publisher, phone (316)267-8570, jek@amcity.com; Timothy Hart, Managing Editor, phone (316)267-8570, thart@amcity.com. **Subscription Rates:** $67 individuals /year. **Remarks:** Accepts advertising. **URL:** amcity.com/wichita.
Ad Rates: GLR: $8.50 **Circ:** Paid ★5,172
BW: $2,540
4C: $3,020

12061 Wichita Eagle
Knight-Ridder, Inc.
PO Box 820 Phone: (316)268-6000
Wichita, KS 67201 Fax: (316)268-6627

General newspaper. **Subtitle:** Incorporating the Wichita Beacon. **Founded:** Apr. 12, 1872. **Freq:** Daily and Sunday (morn.). **Print Method:** Letterpress. **Trim Size:** 23 1/2 x 13 1/2. **Cols./Page:** 6. **Col. Width:** 26 nonpareils. **Col. Depth:** 311 agate lines. **Key Personnel:** Rick Thames, Jr., Editor, phone (316)268-6694, fax (316)268-6627, rthames@wichitaeagle.com; Peter Pitz, Publisher, phone (316)268-6503, fax (316)268-6609, ppitz@wichitaeagle.com; Sheri Dill, VP/Marketing, phone (316)268-6633, fax (316)268-6609, sdill@wichitaeagle.com; Ron Davidson, VP/Advertising, phone (316)268-6291, fax (316)268-6658, rdavidson@wichitaeagle.com; Karen Magnuson, Managing Editor, phone (316)268-6405, fax (316)268-6627, kmagnuson@wichitaeagle.com. **ISSN:** 1046-3127. **Subscription Rates:** $191.88 individuals. **Remarks:** Advertising accepted; rates available upon request. **Online:** America Online, Inc.; Dialog (The Dialog Corporation). **URL:** http://www.wichitaeagle.com. **Formerly**: Wichita Eagle-Beacon. **Feature Editors:** Arlice Davenport, *Travel*, phone (316)268-6256, adavenport@wichitaeagle.com; Dion Lefler, *News*, phone (316)268-6527, dlefler@wichitaeagle.com; Lori Linenberger, *Features, Lifestyle*, phone (316)268-6298, llinenberger@wichitaeagle.com; Bo Rader, *Photo*, phone (316)268-6231, brader@wichitaeagle.com; Tom Shine, *News*, phone (316)268-6268, tshine@wichitaeagle.com; Macia Werts, *Education, News*, phone (316)268-6267, mwerts@wichitaeagle.com; Steve Zuckerman, *Financial/Business*, phone (316)268-6312, szuckerman@wichitaeagle.com.
Circ: Mon.-Thurs. ★87,915
Fri. ★104,520
Sat. ★102,539
Sun. ★163,160

12062 Wichita WOMEN
Watson Wordsmiths, Inc.
PO Box 781001
Wichita, KS 67278-1001

Magazine (tabloid) for Wichita women. **Subtitle:** To Ease, Enrich, and Celebrate the Lives of Busy Wichita Women. **Founded:** Oct. 1986. **Freq:** Monthly. **Print Method:** Offset. **Trim Size:** 11 3/8 x 16. **Cols./Page:** 2. **Col. Width:** 4 7/8 inches. **Col. Depth:** 15 inches. **Key Personnel:** Kathleen M. Watson, Editor and Publisher. **Subscription Rates:** $15 individuals. **Remarks:** Accepts advertising.
Ad Rates: BW: $875 **Circ:** Paid ‡38
Non-paid ‡30,000

KAAS-TV - See Salina

12063 KAKE-TV - 10
Box 10 Phone: (316)943-4221
Wichita, KS 67201 Fax: (316)943-5160
E-mail: kaketv@kake.com

Format: Commercial TV. **Networks:** ABC. **Owner:** The Chronicle Publishing Co., 150 Fourth St., Ste.695, San Francisco, CA 94103, (415)777-7057, Fax: (415)777-8893. **Founded:** 1954. **Operating Hours:** Continuous; 55% network, 45% local. **ADI:** Wichita-Hutchinson, KS. **Key Personnel:** Randy Oswald, General Mgr.; Kevin Ragan, News Dir.; Don Golledge, Contact; Mark Chamberlin, Mktg.Dir.; Dale Morrell, Chief Engineer; Joe Miller, Controller; Steve South, Station Mgr.; Kathy Mohn, General Sales Mgr.; Kurt Bartolich, Promotions Dir. **Local Programs:** *Good Day Kansas* 11 a.m. - Noon Monday-Friday. **Ad Rates:** $15-1,000 per unit. **URL:** http://www.kake.com.

12064 KFDI-FM - 101.3
4200 N. Old Lawrence Rd. Phone: (316)838-9141
Wichita, KS 67219 Fax: (316)838-3607

Format: Country. **Networks:** ABC; TNNR (The Nashville Network Radio). **Owner:** F.F. Mike Lynch & Mike Oatman, at above address. **Founded:** 1963. **Operating Hours:** Continuous. **ADI:** Wichita-Hutchinson, KS. **Key Personnel:** F.F. Mike Lynch, President; Mike Oatman, Vice President; Spike Santee, General Sales Mgr. **Wattage:** 100,000 ERP.

12065 KFH-AM - 1330
2120 N. Woodlawn, Ste. 352 Phone: (316)685-2121
Wichita, KS 67208-1847 Fax: (316)685-3314
E-mail: kfh@cis.compuserve.com

Format: Talk. **Networks:** CBS. **Founded:** 1922. **Operating Hours:** Continuous. **ADI:** Wichita-Hutchinson, KS. **Key Personnel:** Jim Worthington, General Mgr.; Tony Duesing, Program Dir.; Rick Parrish, Sales Mgr. **Wattage:** 5000. **Ad Rates:** $30 for 30 seconds; $30 for 60 seconds. **URL:** http://ourworld.compuserve.com/homepages/kfh.

12066 KICT-FM - 95.1
734 N. Maize Rd. Phone: (316)722-5600
Wichita, KS 67212 Fax: (316)722-0722
E-mail: staff@t95.com

Format: Top 40; Alternative/New Music/Progressive. **Networks:** ABC. **Founded:** 1972. **Operating Hours:** Continuous. **ADI:** Wichita-Hutchinson, KS. **Key Personnel:** Barry Gaston, Vice Pres./GM, bgaston@t95.com; Ron Eric Taylor, Program Dir.; Jan Harrison, News Dir., jharrison@t95.com; Sherry McKinnon, Music Dir., smckinnon@t95.com; Kevin Keplar, Promotions Dir., kkeplar@t95.com; Sandy White, Production Dir., swhite@t95.com; Carol Lujano, Office Mgr., clujano@t95.com; Kim Zajkowski, Business Mgr., kzajowski@t95.com; Bill Calvert, General Sales Mgr., bcalvert@t95.com. **Wattage:** 100,000. **URL:** http://www.t95.com.

12067 KMUW-FM - 89.1
3317 E. 17th St. Phone: (316)978-6789
Wichita, KS 67208 Fax: (316)978-3946
E-mail: kmuw@twsu.edu

Format: Classical; Jazz; News. **Networks:** National Public Radio (NPR); Public Radio International (PRI). **Founded:** 1949. **Operating Hours:** Continuous. **ADI:** Wichita-Hutchinson, KS. **Key Personnel:** Ross Pierce, Chief Engineer; Mark McCain, General Mgr.; Lu Stephens, Producer/Director; Joe Vincenza, Program Dir.; Carla Eckels, Announcer/Producer; Frank Dudgeon, Operations Dir.; Sandy Lopez, Accounting Specialist; Pat Hayes, Volunteer & Listener Svcs. Coordinator. **Wattage:** 100,000. **URL:** http://www.kmuw.org.

12068 KNSS-AM - 1240
2402 E. 37th St. N. Phone: (316)832-9600
Wichita, KS 67219 Fax: (316)832-9688

Format: News; Talk. **Networks:** NBC; ABC; CNN Radio. **Owner:** Capstar Broadcasting, Inc., at above address. **Founded:** 1947. **Formerly:** Prism Radio Partners, L.P. **Operating Hours:** Continuous. **ADI:** Wichita-Hutchinson, KS. **Key Personnel:** Tim Link, General Mgr., phone (316)832-9600, fax (316)838-2800; Vernon Riggs, General Sales Mgr., phone (316)832-9600, fax (316)838-2800; Steve McIntosh, Manager, fax (316)838-2800; Mike Kennedy, Sports Dir., phone (316)832-9600, fax (316)832-9688. **Local Programs:** *Morning Newswatch* 6 a.m. - 9 a.m. Monday-Friday, Dave Wilson; *Sports Talk* 6 p.m. - 7 p.m. Monday-Friday, Mike Kennedy. **Wattage:** 1000. **Ad Rates:** $36-85 per unit. Combined advertising rates available with KRZZ-FM. **URL:** http://www.1240knss.com.

12069 KPTS-TV - 8
320 W. 21st St. Phone: (316)838-3090
Wichita, KS 67203 Fax: (316)838-8586
E-mail: tv8@kpts.org

Format: Public TV. **Networks:** Public Broadcasting Service (PBS). **Owner:** Kansas Public Telecommunications Service, Inc., at above address, Fax: (316)838-8586, Free: (800)794-8498. **Founded:** 1970. **Operating Hours:** Continuous. **ADI:** Wichita-Hutchinson, KS. **Key Personnel:** Don Checots, Pres. & G.M.; Dave McClintock, Dir. of Engineering Services; Vera Aikman, Director; Linda Tabakin, Dir. of Learning Services & Outreach; Brenda Keeler, Dir. of Development; Dale Goter, Public Affairs Editor. **Local Programs:** *Kansas Week* 8:30 p.m. Friday; *Kansas Week Focus* 8 p.m. Friday. **Wattage:** 302kw. **Ad Rates:** Noncommercial.

12070 KQAM-AM - 1480
2120 N. Woodlawn, Ste.352 Phone: (316)685-2121
Wichita, KS 67208 Fax: (316)685-3314

Format: Sports. **Networks:** ABC; Mutual Broadcasting System. **Founded:** 1977. **Operating Hours:** Continuous. **ADI:** Wichita-Hutchinson, KS. **Key Personnel:** Rick Parrish, Gen. Sales Mgr.; Tony Duesing, Program Dir.; Jim Worthington, General Mgr.; April McQuilken, Traffic Dir. **Wattage:** 5000 day; 1000 night. **Ad Rates:** $30 per unit.

12071 KRZZ-FM - 96.3
2402 E. 37th St. N. Phone: (316)832-9600
Wichita, KS 67219 Fax: (316)838-2800

Format: Classic Rock; Album-Oriented Rock (AOR). **Founded:** 1985. **Operating Hours:** Continuous. **ADI:** Wichita-Hutchinson, KS. **Key Personnel:** Tim Link, General Mgr.; Jackie Wise, General Sales Mgr.; Greg Bergen, Program Dir.; Lester St. James, Asst. Program Director. **Wattage:** 50,000. **Ad Rates:** $60-80 per unit. Combined advertising rates available with KNSS-AM.

12072 KSAS-TV - 24
316 N. West St. Phone: (316)942-2424
Wichita, KS 67203 Fax: (316)942-8927

Format: Commercial TV. **Networks:** Fox. **Owner:** Clear Channel Broadcasting Inc., P O Box 659512, San Antonio, TX 78265, (210)822-2828, Fax: (210)822-2299. **Founded:** 1985. **Operating Hours:** Continuous; All Fox available/ rest local. **ADI:** Wichita-Hutchinson, KS. **Key Personnel:** Diana Wilkin, General Mgr.; Virginia Edwards, Contact; Michael Hochman, Program Dir.; Ken Whitney, Production Mgr.; Linda Madzey, Public Service; Tom Gateway, Promotions Dir.; Lynn Kingsley, Traffic Mgr. **Wattage:** 3.38 mw. **Ad Rates:** Advertising accepted; rates available upon request. **URL:** http://www.foxkansas.com.

12073 KSGL-AM - 900
3337 W. Central Phone: (316)942-3231
Wichita, KS 67203 Fax: (316)942-9314

Format: Religious. **Networks:** Independent. **Founded:** 1977. **Operating Hours:** Continuous. **ADI:** Wichita-Hutchinson, KS. **Key Personnel:** Terry Atherton, General Mgr. **Wattage:** 250. **Ad Rates:** $6-15 for 30 seconds; $8-18 for 60 seconds. Combined advertising rates available with KMYR-AM.

12074 KSNW-TV - 3
833 N. Main Phone: (316)265-3333
Box 333 Fax: (316)292-1197
Wichita, KS 67201

Format: Commercial TV. **Simulcasts:** KSNK-TV, KSNG-TV, and KSNC-TV. **Networks:** NBC. **Owner:** Lee Enterprises, Inc., 215 N. Main St., Davenport, IA, (319)383-2100, Fax: (319)323-9608. **Founded:** 1955. **Formerly:** KARD-TV. **Operating Hours:** Continuous. **ADI:** Wichita-Hutchinson, KS. **Key Personnel:** Al Buch, General Mgr.; Betty Erickson, Program Dir.

12075 KWCH-TV - 12
2815 E. 37th St. N. Phone: (316)838-1212
Wichita, KS 67219 Fax: (316)838-3524

Format: Commercial TV. **Networks:** CBS. **Owner:** Communications Inc., 250 International Dr., PO Box 1717, Spartanburg, SC 29304. **Founded:** 1953. **Formerly:** KTVH-TV. **Operating Hours:** Continuous Sun.-Thur.; 5 a.m.-2:30 a.m. Fri. and Sat. **ADI:** Wichita-Hutchinson, KS. **Key Personnel:** Sandy DiPasquale, General Mgr.; Randy Pratt, General Sales Mgr.

12076 KZSN-AM - 1480
5610 E. 29th St. N. Phone: (316)683-4566
Wichita, KS 67220 Fax: (316)683-4609

Format: Country; Contemporary Country. **Simulcasts:** KZSN-FM. **Networks:** Independent. **Owner:** Southern Skies Corp., Southern Skies Corporation., PO Box 96, Little Rock, AR 72203, (501)227-9696. **Founded:** 1939. **Formerly:** KLEO-AM (1980). **Operating Hours:** Continuous; 100% local. **ADI:**

Wichita-Hutchinson, KS. **Key Personnel:** Jim Worthington, Contact; Pat Moyer, Program Dir.; Lisa Allan, Sales Mgr. **Wattage:** 5,000 day 1,000 night. **Ad Rates:** Advertising accepted; rates available upon request.

12077 KZSN-FM - 102.1
5610 E. 29th St. N. Phone: (316)683-4566
Wichita, KS 67220 Fax: (316)683-4609

Format: Country; Contemporary Country. **Networks:** Independent. **Owner:** Southern Skies Corp., Box 96, Little Rock, AR 72203, (501)227-9696. **Founded:** 1986. **Formerly:** KSKU-FM. **Operating Hours:** Continuous; 100% local. **ADI:** Wichita-Hutchinson, KS. **Key Personnel:** Pat Moyer, Production Dir.; Jim Worthington, Contact; Lisa Allan, Sales Mgr.; Dan Holiday, Music Dir. **Wattage:** 100,000. **Ad Rates:** $60 for 30 seconds.

12078 KZZD-FM - 90.7
3811 N. Meridian Phone: (316)436-1091
Wichita, KS 67204 Fax: (316)838-0691
E-mail: email@z91.org

Format: Alternative/New Music/Progressive. **Owner:** Word of Life Ministries, Inc., at above address, (316)838-9200. **Formerly:** KGAM-FM. **Operating Hours:** Continuous. **ADI:** Wichita-Hutchinson, KS. **Key Personnel:** Stan Boyd, General Mgr., stan@z91.org; Ken Mann, Station Mgr./Program Dir., ken@z91.org; Dan Wemmer, Chief Station Operator, dan@z91.org. **Wattage:** 25,000. **Ad Rates:** $12 for 30 seconds. **URL:** http://www.z91.org.

12079 Multimedia Cablevision, Inc.
701 E. Douglas Phone: (316)262-4270
Box 3027 Fax: (316)262-2309
Wichita, KS 67201
Free: (800)756-1528

Founded: Dec. 1976. **Formerly:** AirCapital Cablevision (1992). **Key Personnel:** Ron Marnell, Vice President; Lin Harris, Program Dir. **Cities Served:** Wichita, KS: subscribing households 97,758.

WILSON, pop. 978.

C. KS. Ellsworth Co. 55 mi. W. of Salina. Lake. Elevators. Grain, stock, poultry farms. Wheat, maize, cattle.

12080 Wilson World
Elsworth Reporter
PO Box 526 Phone: (913)658-2235
Wilson, KS 67490
Newspaper. **Founded:** 1879. **Freq:** Weekly (Thurs.). **Print Method:** Offset. **Cols./Page:** 6. **Col. Width:** 26 nonpareils. **Col. Depth:** 276 agate lines. **Key Personnel:** Karl K. Gaston, Publisher, phone (785)472-3103, fax (785)472-3268. **Subscription Rates:** $16 individuals.
Ad Rates: GLR: $.20 **Circ:** Paid 926
BW: $355.32

WINFIELD†, pop. 10,736.

SE KS. Cowley Co. 40 mi. SE of Wichita. Southwestern College (Methodist). Manufactures crayons, gas burners, plastic. Aircraft assembly, metal products plants. Oil and gas wells.Diversified farming. Kafir corn, wheat, alfalfa.

12081 International Social Science Review
1001 Millington, Ste. B Phone: (316)221-3128
Winfield, KS 67156 Fax: (316)221-7124
Publisher E-mail: pgm@jinx.sckans.edu

Academic journal covering all social sciences. **Subtitle:** International Social Science Review. **Founded:** 1924. **Freq:** Semiannual. **Print Method:** Offset. **Trim Size:** 6 x 9. **Cols./Page:** 1. **Col. Width:** 60 nonpareils. **Col. Depth:** 115 agate lines. **Key Personnel:** Stephen Simon, Editor, phone (704)262-6018, fax (704)262-4976, simonsj@conrad.appstate.edu. **ISSN:** 0278-2308. **Subscription Rates:** $10 individuals; $18 two years; $5 single issue. **Remarks:** Accepts advertising. **Formerly:** Social Sciences.
Ad Rates: BW: $400 **Circ:** Paid ‡7,000
Non-paid ‡150

12082 Winfield Daily Courier
Winfield Publishing Co.
201 E. 9th Ave. Phone: (316)221-1050
Winfield, KS 67156-2817 Fax: (316)221-1101
Publication E-mail: courier@horizon.hit.net

Newspaper with a Republican orientation. **Founded:** 1872. **Freq:** Mon.-Sat. (eve.). **Print Method:** Offset. **Trim Size:** 13 3/4 x 22 3/4 in. **Cols./Page:** 6. **Col. Width:** 2 1/16 inches. **Col. Depth:** 21 inches. **Key Personnel:** Frederick D. Seaton, Editor and Publisher; Lloyd Craig, Advertising Mgr. **Subscription Rates:** $79.45 individuals. **Remarks:** Accepts advertising. **URL:** http://www.winfieldcourier.
Ad Rates: GLR: $.46 **Circ:** Mon.-Sat. ★5,563
BW: $811.44
4C: $941.44
PCI: $6.44

12083 KSWC-FM - 100.3
Southwestern College Phone: (316)221-8263
Winfield, KS 67156-2499

Format: Urban Contemporary; Classic Rock; Alternative/New Music/Progressive. **Networks:** Independent. **Founded:** 1968. **Operating Hours:** 3 p.m.-midnight; 100% local. **Key Personnel:** Bill DeArmond, General Mgr. **Wattage:** 10. **Ad Rates:** Noncommercial.

12084 Multimedia Cablevision, Inc.
1004 Main Phone: (316)221-6360
Winfield, KS 67156-0725 Fax: (316)221-7789

Owner: Gannett, 1100 Wilson Blvd., Arlington, VA 22234, (703)284-6000. **Founded:** 1972. **Key Personnel:** Allen Goff, General Mgr., phone (316)221-1621; John Ozbun, Technical Operations; Linda Neal, Ad Sales Account Exec.; Linda Nelson, Office Mgr. **Cities Served:** Winfield, KS; Cowley County: 75 channels; 1 community access channel; 168 hours per week community access programming.

YATES CENTER†, pop. 2,124.

SE KS. Woodson Co. 56 mi. N. of Independence. Oil wells. Diversified farming. Corn, wheat, oats, hay.

12085 The Yates Center News
PO Box 285 Phone: (316)625-2181
Yates Center, KS 66783 Fax: (316)625-2081
Publication E-mail: ycn@sekansas.com

Community newspaper. **Founded:** Feb. 1877. **Freq:** Weekly (Thurs.). **Print Method:** Offset. **Cols./Page:** 6. **Col. Width:** 24 nonpareils. **Col. Depth:** 301 agate lines. **Key Personnel:** Randall C. Braden, Editor and Publisher. **Subscription Rates:** $26.50 individuals.
Ad Rates: GLR: $.22 **Circ:** Paid ‡1,998
BW: $464.40 Free ‡100
SAU: $3.60
PCI: $3.60

KENTUCKY

State Capital, FRANKFORT

Kentucky is bounded on the north by Ohio and Indiana, northwest by Illinois, east by West Virginia, south by Tennessee, and west by Missouri. Its greatest breadth from east to west is 409 miles; greatest length, 178 miles; land area, 39,732 square miles. The Appalachian Mountains cross the eastern end of the state and many hills dot the rich and fertile tablelands. Northwest of this section, and in the center of the state, is the famous and productive blue grass region, with a gently undulating upland surface and deep valleys at the rivers. Between the Green and Cumberland Rivers the surface is level and known as the "Barrens" from the scarcity of heavy timber. The western part is generally level, with slight hills. The soil of the whole state is remarkably fertile; that part between Lexington and the Ohio River is known as the "Garden of Kentucky." More than 800 miles of Kentucky soil borders on the Ohio and Mississippi Rivers, and there are other navigable rivers in the state. The Weather Bureau at Louisville gives the temperature (annual average) as 56.1; highest on record, 107; lowest on record, -20. Total annual precipitation is 44.39 inches. Kentucky has long been famed for its horses; its thoroughbreds are unexcelled. It is especially noted, too, for its underground passages and caves. Most celebrated of these is Mammoth Cave, which has about 150 miles of connecting passages. The largest of the state's many institutions of higher education is the University of Kentucky, located in Lexington. The University of Louisville, in Louisville, is the oldest municipal university in the United States.

POPULATION: 3,755,000 (1992). Rank among the states, 24th.

AGRICULTURE: Number of farms: 91,000 (1992). Farm acreage: 14,000,000 (1992). Cash receipts from farm marketings: crops, $1,475,000,000 (1991); livestock and products, $1,704,000,000 (1991).

FORESTS: Total forest land: 2,102,000 acres (1991). Principal woods: oak, beech, yellow poplar, southern yellow pine, maple, hickory, red and sap gum, basswood, hemlock, elm, sycamore, cottonwood, and aspen.

MINERALS: Value of production: $343,000,000 (1991). Principal minerals: stone, lime, cement. Value of petroleum production: $109,000,000 (1991).

MANUFACTURES: Value added by manufacture: $23,714,000,000 (1991). Leading industry groups: food and related products, electrical machinery, chemicals and allied products.

LIST OF COUNTIES

Total number of counties 120

County, Location on Map, and County Seat	Pop.
Adair (SC), Columbia	15,360
Allen (SW), Scottsville	14,628
Anderson (C), Lawrenceburg	14,571
Ballard (SW), Wickliffe	7,902
Barren (SWC), Glasgow	34,001
Bath (NE), Owingsville	9,692
Bell (SE), Pineville	31,506
Boone (N), Burlington	57,589
Bourbon (NEC), Paris	19,236
Boyd (NE), Catlettsburg	51,150
Boyle (C), Danville	25,641
Bracken (NE), Brooksville	7,766
Breathitt (EC), Jackson	15,703
Breckenridge (WC), Hardinsburg	16,312
Bullitt (NWC), Shepherdsville	47,567
Butler (SW), Morgantown	11,245
Caldwell (SW), Princeton	13,232
Calloway (SW), Murray	30,735
Campbell (N), Alexandria	83,866
Carlisle (SW), Bardwell	5,238
Carroll (NW), Carrollton	9,292
Carter (NE), Grayson	25,340
Casey (C), Liberty	14,211
Christian (SW), Hopkinsville	68,941
Clark (NEC), Winchester	29,496
Clay (SE), Manchester	21,746
Clinton (SC), Albany	9,135
Crittenden (SW), Marion	9,196
Cumberland (SC), Burkesville	6,784
Daviess (WC), Owensboro	87,189
Edmonson (SWC), Brownsville	10,357
Elliott (NE), Sandy Hook	6,445
Estill (EC), Irvine	14,615
Fayette (NC), Lexington	225,366
Fleming (NE), Flemingsburg	12,292
Floyd (EC), Prestonburg	43,586
Franklin (NC), Frankfort	43,781
Fulton (SW), Hickman	8,271
Gallatin (N), Warsaw	5,393
Garrard (C), Lancaster	11,579
Grant (N), Williamstown	15,737
Graves (SW), Mayfield	33,500
Grayson (WC), Leitchfield	21,050
Green (SC), Greensburg	10,371
Greenup (NE), Greenup	36,742
Hancock (W)C, Hawesville	7,864
Hardin (WC), Elizabethtown	89,240
Harlan (WC), Harlan	36,574
Harrison (NEC), Cynthiana	16,248
Hart (SWC), Munfordville	14,890
Henderson (WC), Henderson	43,044
Henry (NW), New Castle	12,823
Hickman (SW), Clinton	5,566
Hopkins (SW), Madisonville	46,126
Jackson (EC), McKee	11,995
Jefferson (NW), Louisville	664,937
Jessamine (C), Nicholasville	30,508
Johnson (EC), Paintsville	23,248
Kenton (N), Independence	142,031
Knott (EC), Hindman	17,906
Knox (SE), Barbourville	29,676
Larue (WC), Hodgenville	11,679
Laurel (SEC), London	43,438
Lawrence (NE), Louisa	13,998
Lee (SEC), Beattyville	7,422
Leslie (SE), Hyden	13,642
Letcher (SE), Whitesburg	27,000
Lewis (NE), Vanceburg	13,029
Lincoln (C), Stanford	20,045
Livingston (SW), Smithland	9,062
Logan (SW), Russellville	24,416
Lyon (SW), Eddyville	6,624
Madison (C), Richmond	57,508
Marion (C), Lebanon	16,499
Marshall (SW), Benton	27,205
Martin (EC), Inez	12,526
Mason (NE), Maysville	16,666
McCracken (SW), Paducah	62,879
McCreary (SEC), Whitley City	15,603
McLean (WC), Calhoun	9,628
Meade (WC), Bradenburg	24,170
Menifee (EC), Frenchburg	5,092
Mercer (C), Harrodsburg	19,148
Metcalfe (SC), Edmonton	8,963
Monroe (SC), Tompkinsville	11,401
Montgomery (E), Mount Sterling	19,561
Morgan (SC), West Liberty	11,648
Muhlenberg (SW), Greenville	31,318
Nelson (WC), Bardstown	29,710
Nicholas (NEC), Carlisle	6,725
Ohio (WC), Hartford	21,105
Oldham (NW), La Grange	33,263

Owen (NC), Owenton 9,035
Owsley (SEC), Booneville 5,036
Pendleton (N), Falmouth 12,036
Perry (SE), Hazard 30,283
Pike (E), Pikeville 72,583
Powell (EC), Stanton 11,686
Russell (SC), Jamestown 14,716
Scott (NC), Georgetown 23,867
Shelby (NWC), Shelbyville 24,824
Simpson (SW), Franklin 15,145
Spencer (NWC), Taylorsville 6,801
Taylor (C), Campbellsville 21,146
Todd (SW), Elkton 10,940
Trigg (SW), Cadiz 10,361
Trimble (NW), Bedford 6,090
Union (WC), Morganfield 16,557
Warren (SW), Bowling Green 76,673
Washington (C), Springfield 10,441
Wayne (SC), Monticello 17,468
Webster (WC), Dixon 13,995
Whitley (SE), Williamsburg 33,326
Wolfe (EC), Campton 6,503
Woodford (C), Versailles 19,955

STATISTICS

Newspapers

Period of Issue
Daily 22
Evening Daily 16
Morning Daily 4
Daily with Sunday edition 11
Semiweekly 8
Weekly 113
Biweekly 2
Monthly 2
Bimonthly 1
Quarterly 1
Free or partly free 6
Shopper 7
Total Newspapers 156

Periodicals

Period of Issue
Weekly 6
Biweekly 1
Semimonthly 1
Monthly 47
Bimonthly 14
Quarterly 31
Free or partly free 2
Total Periodicals 117

Total number of publications 273

Radio Stations

AM Stations 97
FM Stations 119
Total Radio Stations 216

TV Stations

Total TV Stations 32

Cable Stations

Total Cable Systems 31

Total number of broadcast listings 279

ALBANY†, pop. 2,083.

Clinton Co. (SC). 100 m SW of Lexington. Oil wells; coal mines; timber. Manufactures flour, feed, cheese, boys' shirts. Truck, poultry, dairy farms. cattle.

12086 Clinton County News
Gibson Printing Co., Inc.
116 Washington St. Phone: (606)387-5144
PO Box 360
Albany, KY 42602
Community newspaper. **Founded:** 1949. **Freq:** Weekly (Thurs.). **Print Method:** Offset. **Cols./Page:** 6. **Col. Width:** 25 nonpareils. **Col. Depth:** 294 agate lines. **Key Personnel:** Alan Gibsen, Editor; Janie Gibson, Advertising Mgr. **ISSN:** 1184-80. **Subscription Rates:** $18 individuals. **Remarks:** Accepts advertising.
Ad Rates: GLR: $.25 **Circ:** ‡3,650
SAU: $3.43

12087 WANY-AM - 1390
PO Box 400 Phone: (606)387-5186
Albany, KY 42602-0400

Format: News; Sports; Country; Religious; Agricultural; Bluegrass. **Networks:** ABC; KyNet. **Owner:** Albany Broadcasting Co., at above address. **Founded:** 1958. **Operating Hours:** 17 hrs daily; 25% network, 75% local. **Key Personnel:** Darrell Speck, Contact; Randy Speck, Contact; Mike Speck, Contact; Robert Huddleston, Chief Engineer; Phyllis Butler, Contact; Patricia Bowlin, Contact. **Wattage:** 1000. **Ad Rates:** Advertising accepted; rates available upon request.

12088 WANY-FM - 106.3
PO Box 400 Phone: (606)387-5186
Albany, KY 42602-0400

Format: News; Sports; Religious; Agricultural; Bluegrass. **Networks:** ABC; KyNet. **Owner:** Albany Broadcasting Co., at above address. **Founded:** 1958. **Operating Hours:** 17 hours Daily; 25% network, 75% local. **Key Personnel:** Sid Scott, Contact; Eddie Coop, News Dir.; Larry Nelson, Chief Engineer; Phyllis Butler, Contact. **Wattage:** 2700. **Ad Rates:** Advertising accepted; rates available upon request.

ASHLAND, pop. 27,064.

Boyd Co. (NE). On Ohio River, 16 m NW of Huntington, W. Va. Manufactures steel, coke, mining equipment, gas, leather, dresses, chemicals. Metal processing. Coal mines. Gas well. Clay pits.

12089 The Daily Independent
Ashland Publishing Co.
22417th St., No. 311 Phone: (606)329-1717
Ashland, KY 41101-7606 Fax: (606)324-8434
Free: (800)955-5860

General newspaper. **Founded:** 1896. **Freq:** Daily and Sunday (eve.). **Print Method:** Offset. **Cols./Page:** 6. **Col. Width:** 24 nonpareils. **Col. Depth:** 294 agate lines. **Key Personnel:** Wickliffe R. Powell, Editor; John W. Del Santo, Publisher. **USPS:** 033-780. **Subscription Rates:** $140.20 individuals. **Remarks:** Accepts advertising.
Ad Rates: BW: $1,669.50 **Circ:** Mon.-Sat. 22,532
4C: $1,899.50 Sun. 25,888
PCI: $13.25

12090 Cox Communications
225 Russell Rd., US 23 N. Phone: (606)329-2990
Box 1357 Fax: (606)329-9579
Ashland, KY 41105

Founded: 1970. **Formerly:** Dimension Cable. **Cities Served:** Ashland and Boyd counties, KY.

12091 WCMI-AM - 1340
PO Box 949 Phone: (606)329-1777
Ashland, KY 41105-0949 Fax: (606)324-3377

Format: Adult Contemporary. **Networks:** ABC. **Founded:** 1935. **Operating Hours:** 5 a.m.-midnight. **Key Personnel:** Dick Martin, Jr., General Mgr.; Bilreka Ferguson, Office Mgr. **Wattage:** 3000.

12092 WKAS-TV - 25
c/o Kentucky Authority for Educational TV Phone: (606)258-7000
Fax: (606)258-7399
600 Cooper Dr.
Lexington, KY 40502

Format: Public TV; Educational. **Networks:** Public Broadcasting Service (PBS); Kentucky Educational Television. **Owner:** Kentucky Authority for Educational TV, at above address, (606)258-7170, Fax: (606)258-7390. **Founded:** 1968. **Operating Hours:** 7 a.m.-midnight. **ADI:** Charleston-Huntington, WV. **Key Personnel:** Craig Cornwell, Contact; L. Hobson, Contact; J. Gorman, Contact; D. Holtzclaw, Business Mgr.; M. Ferguson, Contact; Virginia G. Fox, Contact, gfox@msmail.ket.org; Dick Hoffman, Program Dir.; Donna Moore, Contact; Sally Hamilton, Contact; William Wilson, Contact. **Local Programs:** *At Issue*; *Comment on Kentucky*; *School Reform: Answers for Parents*. **Wattage:** 135. **Ad Rates:** Noncommercial. **URL:** http://www.ket.org.

12093 WTSF-TV - 61
3100 Bath Ave. Phone: (606)329-2700
PO Box 2616 Fax: (606)324-9526
Ashland, KY 41105-2616

Format: Religious. **Networks:** Independent. **Owner:** Tri-State Family Broadcasting, at above address. **Founded:** 1983. **Operating Hours:** Continuous. **ADI:** Charleston-Huntington, WV. **Key Personnel:** E. Maybelle Messinger, President; Gertrude Tackett, Program Dir. **Ad Rates:** $20 for 60 seconds.

BARBOURVILLE†, pop. 3,333.

Knox Co. (SE). On Cumberland River, 30 m NW of Middleboro. Union College (Meth.). Coal mines; hardwood timber. Manufactures corsets, sealants, concrete blocks, electrical fixtures, bricks, door frames. Woodworking plants. Agriculture. Horses, vegetables, strawberries, sorghum.

12094 WYWY-AM - 950
222 Daniel Boone Dr. Phone: (606)546-4128
Barbourville, KY 40906 Fax: (606)546-4138

Format: Country; Gospel. **Networks:** Independent. **Owner:** James Engle, at above address. **Founded:** 1965. **Operating Hours:** Sunrise-sunset. **Key Personnel:** Mildred Engle, Office Mgr.; James Engel, President. **Wattage:** 1000. **Ad Rates:** $2.50-3.30 for 30 seconds; $3.50-5.50 for 60 seconds.

12095 WYWY-FM - 96.1
222 Daniel Boone Dr. Phone: (606)546-4128
Barbourville, KY 40906 Fax: (606)546-4138

Format: Country. **Networks:** Independent. **Founded:** 1974. **Formerly:** WBVL. **Operating Hours:** Continuous. **Key Personnel:** Tad Engle, Office Mgr.; Steve Ferner, Operations Dir.; Randy Brock, Sales Mgr. **Wattage:** 25,000. **Ad Rates:** $4.75-5.30 for 30 seconds; $6-7.50 for 60 seconds. Combined advertising rates available with WYWY-AM.

BARDSTOWN†, pop. 6,155.

Nelson Co. (WC). 39 m SE of Louisville. Manufactures bourbon, paper & plastic cups, plates, women's dresses, plastic building materials, office products. Dairy, beef, Tobacco farming.

12096 Kentucky Standard
Landmark Community Newspapers, Inc.
PO Box 639 Phone: (502)348-9003
Bardstown, KY 40004 Fax: (502)348-1971
Free: (800)928-9003
Publication E-mail: standard@bardstown.com

Newspaper. **Founded:** 1900. **Freq:** 3/week. **Print Method:** Web offset. **Cols./Page:** 6. **Col. Width:** 26 nonpareils. **Col. Depth:** 294 agate lines. **Key Personnel:** Jan Witherspoon, Editor; David Greer, Publisher; Joan Hardin, Advertising Mgr. **Subscription Rates:** $44.52 individuals. **Remarks:** Accepts advertising.
Ad Rates: 4C: $320 **Circ:** 9,500
SAU: $8.79

12097 WBRT-AM - 1320
106 S. 3rd St. Phone: (502)348-3943
Bardstown, KY 40004 Fax: (502)348-4043

Format: Country. **Networks:** ABC; KyNet. **Owner:** Nelson County Broadcasting, at above address. **Founded:** 1954. **Operating Hours:** 6 a.m.-sunset. **ADI:** Louisville, KY. **Key Personnel:** Tom Isaac, Contact; Jeanie Isaac, Sales Mgr.; Rick Howellet, News Dir. **Wattage:** 1000. **Ad Rates:** $4-9.40 for 30 seconds; $5-12 for 60 seconds. $4-$9.40 for 30 seconds; $5-$12 for 60 seconds. Combined advertising rates available with WOKH-FM.

12098 WOKH-FM - 96.7
106 S. 3rd St. Phone: (502)348-3943
Bardstown, KY 40004 Fax: (502)348-4043

Format: Adult Contemporary. **Networks:** ABC. **Owner:** Nelson County Broadcasting Co., Inc., at above address. **Founded:** 1979. **Operating Hours:** 6 a.m.-midnight. **ADI:** Louisville, KY. **Key Personnel:** Tom Isaac, Contact; Jeanie Isaac, Sales Mgr.; Rick Howellet, News Dir. **Wattage:** 3000. **Ad Rates:** $4-9.40 for 30 seconds; $5-12 for 60 seconds. $4-$9.40 for 30 seconds; $5-$12 for 60 seconds. Combined advertising rates available with WBRT-AM.

BEATTYVILLE†.

Lee Co. (EC). 5 m W of St. Helens.

12099 WLJC-TV - 65
PO Box Y Phone: (606)464-3600
Beattyville, KY 41311 Fax: (606)464-5021
E-mail: wljc@tgtel.com

Format: Commercial TV. **Networks:** Independent. **Owner:** Hour of Harvets, Inc., at above address. **Founded:** 1982. **Operating Hours:** Continuous. **ADI:** Lexington, KY. **Key Personnel:** Margaret Drake, President; Jonathan Drake, Vice President; Rachel Drake, Office Mgr. **Local Programs:** *Hour of Harvest* 7:00 pm Tues., Thurs., Fri., and Sat., Margaret Drake, Mailing contact. **Ad Rates:** $75-95 for 30 seconds; $125-145 for 60 seconds.

BEAVER DAM, pop. 3,185.

Ohio Co. (WC). 32 m SE of Owensboro. Coal mining. Furniture, lighting fixtures, plastics manufactured. Agriculture. Grain, tobacco, hay.

12100 Ohio County Messenger
Andy Anderson Corp.
501 N. School St. Phone: (502)274-4949
PO Box 187 Fax: (502)754-9484
Beaver Dam, KY 42320
Newspaper with a Report orientation. **Founded:** 1930. **Freq:** Weekly (Wed.). **Print Method:** Offset. **Cols./Page:** 6. **Col. Width:** 27 nonpareils. **Col. Depth:** 301 agate lines. **Key Personnel:** Mrs. Andy Anderson, Jr., Publisher, phone (502)298-7100, fax (502)298-9572; Mrs. Tressie Brown, Office Mgr. **Subscription Rates:** $8 individuals. **Remarks:** Accepts advertising.
Ad Rates: GLR: $.15 **Circ:** ‡2,100
BW: $252

BEDFORD†, pop. 835.

Trimble Co. (C).

12101 Trimble Banner Democrat
Landmark Community Newspapers, Inc.
PO Box 269 Phone: (502)255-3205
Bedford, KY 40006-0289 Fax: (502)255-7797

County newspaper. **Founded:** 1879. **Freq:** Weekly (Thurs.). **Cols./Page:** 6. **Col. Width:** 2 inches. **Col. Depth:** 12 15/16 inches. **Key Personnel:** Chris Jones, Editor/Advertising Mgr.; Dorothy Abernathy, Publisher; Mabel Richmond, Office Mgr. **Subscription Rates:** $17; $21.50 out of county; $28.50 out of state. **Remarks:** Accepts advertising.
Ad Rates: BW: $379.26 **Circ:** Paid ‡1,800
4C: $679.26
SAU: $3.09

BENTON†, pop. 3,700.

Marshall Co. (SW). 24 m SE of Paducah. Resort Area. Chemicals manufactured. Agriculture.

12102 Leisure Scene
Tribune Courier
308 East 12th St. Phone: (502)527-3162
PO Box 410 Fax: (502)527-4567
Benton, KY 42025
Publisher E-mail: office@tribunecourier.com

Summer tourist magazine. **Founded:** 1970. **Freq:** Weekly. **Print Method:** Offset. **Cols./Page:** 6. **Col. Depth:** 13 inches. **Key Personnel:** Greg Travis, Editor; Terri Dunnigan, Advertising Mgr. **Subscription Rates:** Free. **Remarks:** Accepts advertising.
Ad Rates: BW: $234 **Circ:** Free ‡20,000
4C: $384
PCI: $3

12103 Tribune Courier
308 East 12th St. Phone: (502)527-3162
PO Box 410 Fax: (502)527-4567
Benton, KY 42025
Publication E-mail: tribune@ldd.net
Publisher E-mail: office@tribunecourier.com

Newspaper. **Founded:** 1888. **Freq:** Weekly (Wed.). **Print Method:** Offset. **Trim Size:** 13 x 21. **Cols./Page:** 6. **Col. Width:** 24 nonpareils. **Col. Depth:** 301 agate lines. **Key Personnel:** Tim Hurst, General Mgr.; Greg Travis, Editor; Terri Dunnigan, Advertising Dir. **Subscription Rates:** $24. **Remarks:** Accepts advertising.
Ad Rates: GLR: $.31 **Circ:** Paid 7,400
BW: $466.20 Free 200
4C: $716.20
SAU: $4.85

12104 WCBL-AM - 1290
PO Box 387 Phone: (502)527-3102
Benton, KY 42025 Fax: (502)527-5606

Format: Country. **Networks:** NBC. **Owner:** Purchase Broadcasting Co., at above address. **Founded:** 1954. **Operating Hours:** Sunrise-sunset. **Key Personnel:** Sherry Rickman, Operations Mgr.; Stephanie Waters, News Dir.; Jeff Waters, Sports Dir.; Faye Phillips, Public Service Dir. **Wattage:** 5000.

12105 WCBL-FM - 99.1
PO Box 387 Phone: (502)527-3102
Benton, KY 42025 Fax: (502)527-5606

Format: Oldies. **Networks:** NBC. **Founded:** 1966. **Operating Hours:** Continuous. **ADI:** Paducah,KY-Cape Girardeau,MO-Marion,IL. **Key Personnel:** Jim Freeland, General Mgr.; Sherry Rickman, Operations Mgr. **Wattage:** 3000.

BEREA, pop. 8,226.

Madison Co. (C). 40 m S of Lexington. Berea College. Handcraft industries; rubber rings, pressure gauges, greeting cards, fork lifts, brakes manufactured. Dairy, stock, poultry farms. Corn, tobacco, hay.

12106 Appalachian Heritage
Hutchins Library
Berea College Phone: (606)986-9341
Berea, KY 40404 Fax: (606)986-9494

Literary magazine featuring the southern Appalachian culture. **Founded:** 1973. **Freq:** Quarterly. **Print Method:** Offset. **Trim Size:** 6 x 9. **Cols./Page:** 1. **Col. Width:** 28 1/2 picas. **Col. Depth:** 44 picas. **Key Personnel:** Sidney Saylor Farr, Editor, sidney_ farr@berea.edu. **ISSN:** 0363-2318. **Subscription Rates:** $18. **Remarks:** Accepts advertising. **Alt. Formats:** Microform.
Ad Rates: BW: $250 **Circ:** Paid 700
4C: $350 Non-paid 200

12107 The Berea Alumnus
Berea College
CPO 2302 Phone: (606)986-9341
Berea, KY 40404 Fax: (606)986-4506
Free: (800)457-9846

Magazine for college alumni. **Founded:** 1931. **Freq:** Quarterly. **Print Method:** Offset. **Trim Size:** 8 1/2 x 11. **Cols./Page:** 3. **Col. Width:** 28 nonpareils. **Col. Depth:** 140 agate lines. **Subscription Rates:** $10 individuals. **Remarks:** Advertising not accepted. **URL:** http://www.berea.edu.
Circ: ‡36,000

12108 Berea Citizen
PO Box 207 Phone: (606)986-0959
Berea, KY 40403 Fax: (606)986-0960

Community newspaper. **Founded:** 1899. **Freq:** Weekly (Thurs.). **Print Method:** Offset. **Cols./Page:** 6. **Col. Width:** 26 nonpareils. **Col. Depth:** 301 agate lines. **Key Personnel:** Jack Hall, Editor and Publisher. **Subscription Rates:** $15.95 individuals; $21.95 out of state. **Remarks:** Accepts advertising.
Ad Rates: GLR: $.75 **Circ:** ‡3,600
BW: $459.90
4C: $539.90
PCI: $3.65

12109 Pinnacle
Berea College
CPO 2302 Phone: (606)986-9341
Berea, KY 40404 Fax: (606)986-4506
Free: (800)457-9846

Collegiate newspaper. **Founded:** 1953. **Freq:** Monthly. **Print Method:** Offset. **Trim Size:** 13 x 21. **Cols./Page:** 6. **Col. Width:** 12 3/10 picas. **Col. Depth:** 43 3/10 picas. **Key Personnel:** Heather Mathes, Editor and Publisher; Robert Rudd, Advertising Mgr. **Subscription Rates:** $8 individuals; $11 off campus. **Remarks:** Accepts advertising.
Ad Rates: PCI: $1.90 **Circ:** Paid ‡1,800
Free ‡50

12110 WKXO-FM - 106.7
406 Chestnut St. Phone: (606)986-9321
Box 307 Fax: (606)986-8675
Berea, KY 40403

Format: Country; News. **Networks:** ABC; KyNet. **Founded:** 1990. **Operating Hours:** Continuous; 15% network, 85% local. **Key Personnel:** Bob Spradlin, General Mgr. **Wattage:** 6000. **Ad Rates:** $2.50-4 for 15 seconds; $4-7 for 30 seconds; $6-10 for 60 seconds. $2.50-$4 for 15 seconds; $4-$6 for 30 seconds; $7-$9 for 60 seconds. Combined advertising rates available with WKXO-AM.

BOONEVILLE

12111 Booneville Sentinel
Southfork Publishing Co.
PO Box 129 Phone: (606)593-6627
Booneville, KY 41314 Fax: (606)598-2330

Community newspaper. **Founded:** 1978. **Freq:** Weekly. **Print Method:** Offset. **Cols./Page:** 6. **Col. Width:** 2 inches. **Col. Depth:** 21 inches. **Key Personnel:** Phyllis J. Combs, Editor; James F. Nolan, Jr., Publisher. **USPS:** 352-790. **Subscription Rates:** $15. **Remarks:** Accepts advertising.
Ad Rates: GLR: $.15 **Circ:** ‡2,100
BW: $250
4C: $535
SAU: $3.8

BOWLING GREEN†, pop. 40,450.

Warren Co. (SW). On Barren River, at head of navigation, 65 m NE of Nashville, Tenn. Western Kentucky University. Manufactures electric controls, auto parts, air compressors, space heaters, dry cleaning equipment and chemicals; woodworking and garment industries, flour, and beverage works; meat packing and poultry processing plants. Burley, tobacco market. Tobacco stemmeries.

12112 College Heights Herald
Western Kentucky University
122 Garrett Center Phone: (502)745-2653
Bowling Green, KY 42101 Fax: (502)745-2697

College newspaper. **Founded:** 1925. **Freq:** Semiweekly (Tues. and Thurs.). **Print Method:** Offset. **Cols./Page:** 5. **Col. Width:** 24 nonpareils. **Col. Depth:** 196 agate lines. **Key Personnel:** Bob Adams, Advisor, robert.adams@wku.edu; Jo Ann Thompson, Business Mgr., joann.thompson@wku.edu. **Subscription Rates:** $25 individuals. **Remarks:** Accepts advertising. **URL:** http://www.msc.wku.edu:80/info/pubs/herald/.
Ad Rates: BW: $440 **Circ:** Paid 200
4C: $640 Free 10,800
PCI: $5.50

12113 Country Peddler
PO Box 492 Phone: (502)842-3314
Bowling Green, KY 42102 Fax: (502)842-4220

Shopper (tabloid). **Founded:** Aug. 20, 1971. **Freq:** Weekly (Thurs.). **Print Method:** Offset. **Cols./Page:** 4. **Col. Width:** 2 3/8 inches. **Col. Depth:** 12 3/4 inches. **Key Personnel:** Kyda West, Publisher; Belinda Saltzman, Publisher. **Remarks:** Accepts advertising. **URL:** http://bowlinggreen.ky.net/countrypeddler.
Ad Rates: BW: $482 **Circ:** Free ‡336,000
4C: $812

12114 Daily News
News Publishing Co.
813 College St. Phone: (502)781-1700
PO Box 90012 Fax: (502)781-0726
Bowling Green, KY 42102-9012
Free: (800)599-6397
Publication E-mail: dnews@bgn.mindspring.com

General newspaper. **Founded:** 1854. **Freq:** Daily (eve.), Sunday (morn.). **Print Method:** Offset. **Cols./Page:** 6. **Col. Width:** 2 1/16 inches. **Col. Depth:** 21 inches. **Key Personnel:** Mark Van Patten, General Mgr.; John B. Gaines, President; Mary Gaines, National Advertising Mgr.; Pipes Gaines, Publisher. **Subscription Rates:** $111.10 individuals; $137.80 out of area; $143 out of state. **Remarks:** Accepts advertising. Monday-Saturday: BW: $1,656.90; PCI: $13.15; Sunday: BW: $1,902.12; PCI: $15.12. **URL:** http://bowlinggreen.ky.net/dailynews/.
Circ: Mon.-Fri. 22,013
Sun. 25,945

12115 Daily News Express
Daily News Publishing, Inc.
813 College St. Phone: (502)781-1700
PO Box 90012 Fax: (502)781-0726
Bowling Green, KY 42102
Free: (800)599-6397
Publisher E-mail: dnews@bgn.mindspring.com

Shopper. **Founded:** Apr. 1976. **Freq:** Semiweekly (Wed. and Sun.). **Print Method:** Offset. **Trim Size:** 13 3/4 x 22 1/2. **Cols./Page:** 6. **Col. Width:** 2 1/16 inches. **Col. Depth:** 21 inches. **Key Personnel:** John B. Gaines, President; Roger Jones, Advertising Mgr.; Pipes Gaines, Publisher; Mark Van Patten, General Mgr. **Formerly:** Daily News Shopping Guide.
Ad Rates: BW: $441.00 **Circ:** Wed. 11,500
4C: $384.30 Sun. 20,000
SAU: $3.70
PCI: $3.50

12116 Daily News Shopping Guide
Daily News Publishing, Inc.
813 College St. Phone: (502)781-1700
PO Box 90012 Fax: (502)781-0726
Bowling Green, KY 42102
Free: (800)599-6397
Publisher E-mail: dnews@bgn.mindspring.com

Community newspaper. **Founded:** 1846. **Freq:** Daily. **Print Method:** Offset. **Cols./Page:** 6. **Col. Width:** 2 1/16 inches. **Col. Depth:** 21 inches. **Key Personnel:** Pipes Gaines, Publisher; Mark Van Patten, General Mgr., mvanpatten@mindspring.com. **Subscription Rates:** $111.10 local. **URL:** http://www.this.is/bowlinggreen.
Ad Rates: BW: $1,505.70 **Circ:** Mon.-Sun. 21,000
4C: $1,865.70 Sun. 26,800
SAU: $3.70

12117 International Journal of Organizational Analysis
Center for Advanced Studies in Management
1574 Mallory Ct. Phone: (502)782-2601
Bowling Green, KY 42103-1300 Fax: (502)782-2601
Publication E-mail: mgt2000@aol.com

Scholarly journal covering management. **Founded:** 1993. **Freq:** Monthly. **Key Personnel:** Dr. M. Afzalur Rahim, Editor. **ISSN:** 1055-3185. **Subscription Rates:** $179 institutions; $49 students; $64 Professional. **Remarks:** Accepts advertising.
Ad Rates: BW: $125 **Circ:** Paid 450

12118 Kentucky English Bulletin
Kentucky Council of Teachers of English-Language Arts
Dept. of English Phone: (502)745-5760
Bowling Green, KY 42101 Fax: (502)745-2533
Publication E-mail: Hagamja@wku.edu

Scholarly journal covering English instruction for teachers K-college. **Founded:** 1953. **Freq:** Triennial. **Key Personnel:** John Hagaman, Editor. **ISSN:** 0023-0197. **Subscription Rates:** $15 individuals; $5 single issue. **Remarks:** Advertising not accepted.
Circ: Paid 950

12119 Southern Folklore
University Press of Kentucky
Erika Brady Phone: (502)745-5902
Folklore Program Fax: (502)745-6859
Western Kentucky University
Bowling Green, KY 42101
Academic journal on Southern folklore traditions. **Founded:** 1937. **Freq:** 3/year. **Print Method:** Offset. **Trim Size:** 6 x 9. **Cols./Page:** 1. **Col. Width:** 26 picas. **Col. Depth:** 43 picas. **Key Personnel:** Erika Brady, Editor; Katharine Shaw, Circulation Mgr. **ISSN:** 0899-594X. **Subscription Rates:** $25 individuals; $10 single issue; $28 out of country. **Remarks:** Accepts advertising. **Alt. Formats:** Microfiche. **Formerly:** Southern Folklore Quarterly.
Ad Rates: BW: $75 **Circ:** Paid ‡450
Non-paid ‡20

12120 Intermedia
515 Double Springs Rd. Phone: (502)782-0903
PO Box 659 Fax: (502)782-8355
Bowling Green, KY 42102-0659

Founded: 1981. **Formerly:** Storer Cable Communications of Southern Kentucky (1993); TKR Cable of Southern California (1996). **Key Personnel:** Bill Helmbold, General Mgr.; Rick Williams, Marketing Mgr.; Sheryl Morris, LO/Production Mgr.; Al Partin, OPS Mgr.; Jean Secrest, Advertising Sales Mgr. **Cities Served:** Bowling Green, Oakland, Richpond, Rockfield, Smiths Grove, KY; Bowling Green and Warren counties.: subscribing households 23,000; 78 channels; 5 community access channels.

WAUE-FM - See Brownsville

12121 WBGN-AM - 1340
948 Fairview Ave. Phone: (502)842-1638
Box 900 Fax: (502)782-0767
Bowling Green, KY 42101
E-mail: bggator.com

Format: News; Talk; Sports. **Networks:** USA Radio; EFM. **Owner:** Hilltopper Broadcasting, Inc., at above address. **Founded:** 1959. **Operating Hours:** Continuous. **ADI:** Bowling Green (Campbellsville), KY. **Key Personnel:** Ray Brassfield, News Dir.; Bryan Locke, Operations Mgr.; Barry Williams, General Mgr. **Wattage:** 1000. **Ad Rates:** $7-12 for 30 seconds; $10-14 for 60 seconds.

12122 WBKO-TV - 13
PO Box 13000 Phone: (502)781-1313
Bowling Green, KY 42102-9800 Fax: (502)781-1814
E-mail: wbko@wbko.com

Format: Commercial TV. **Networks:** ABC. **Owner:** Benedek Broadcasting Corp., at above address. **Founded:** 1962.

Formerly: WLTV-TV. **Operating Hours:** 5 a.m.-1 a.m. **ADI:** Bowling Green (Campbellsville), KY. **Key Personnel:** Clyde Payne, Sr. Vice Pres./Gen. Mgr.; Dave Chumley, Chief Engineer; Gene Birk, News Dir.; Barbara Powell, Program Mgr.; Gene Prather, Director of Public Affairs; Chris Allen, Promotions Mgr.; Rick McCue, Sales & Station Mgr. **Local Programs:** *AM Kentucky News Center 13* 6 & 10 p.m. **Wattage:** 316,000. **URL:** http://www.wbko.com.

12123 WBLG-FM - 107.1
948 Fairview Ave. Phone: (502)843-0107
Box 900 Fax: (502)782-0767
Bowling Green, KY 42101
E-mail: bggator.com

Format: Adult Contemporary. **Networks:** NBC. **Owner:** Hilltopper Broadcasting, Inc., at above address. **Founded:** 1986. **Operating Hours:** Continuous. **ADI:** Bowling Green (Campbellsville), KY. **Key Personnel:** Ray Brassfield, News Dir.; Bryan Locke, Operations Mgr.; Barry Williams, General Mgr. **Wattage:** 50,000. **Ad Rates:** $15-20 for 30 seconds; $18-24 for 60 seconds.

12124 WBVR-FM - 96.7
2465 Russellville Rd. Phone: (502)843-3333
Bowling Green, KY 42101 Fax: (502)843-0454
Free: (800)999-WBVR
E-mail: bgsales@mindspring.com

Format: Country. **Simulcasts:** WGBV-FM. **Networks:** ABC. **Owner:** WRUS Inc., PO Box 1740, Russellville, KY 42276, (502)726-3555, Fax: (502)726-3095. **Founded:** June 1994. **Formerly:** WMJM-FM; WBZD-FM. **Operating Hours:** Continuous; 10% network, 90% local. **ADI:** Bowling Green (Campbellsville), KY. **Key Personnel:** Roth Stratton, Contact, phone (502)843-3333, fax (502)843-0454. **Wattage:** 6000. **Ad Rates:** $24 for 30 seconds; $30 for 60 seconds. **URL:** http://www.beaverfm.com.

12125 WCVK-FM - 90.7
PO Box 539 Phone: (502)781-7326
Bowling Green, KY 42102

Format: Religious. **Networks:** USA Radio. **Founded:** 1986. **Operating Hours:** 5 a.m.-midnight. **ADI:** Bowling Green (Campbellsville), KY. **Key Personnel:** Dave Queen, General Mgr. **Wattage:** 14,000.

12126 WDCL-FM - 89.7
Western Kentucky University Phone: (502)745-5489
Bowling Green, KY 42101 Fax: (502)745-2084
Free: (800)599-WKYU
E-mail: wkyufm@wku.edu

Format: Public Radio. **Simulcasts:** WKYU-FM. **Networks:** National Public Radio (NPR); American Public Radio (APR); AP. **Owner:** Western Kentucky University, at above address. **Founded:** 1985. **Operating Hours:** Continuous. **ADI:** Bowling Green (Campbellsville), KY. **Key Personnel:** David Dzikowski, Contact; Dan Modlin, News Dir.; Lee Stott, Music Dir.; D. T. Wilkinson, Dir., Educ. Telecom. **Wattage:** 100,000. **Ad Rates:** Noncommercial.

12127 WDNS-FM - 93.3
804 College Phone: (502)781-2121
PO Box 930 Fax: (502)842-0232
Bowling Green, KY 42102

Format: Country. **Founded:** 1973. **Operating Hours:** Continuous. **ADI:** Bowling Green (Campbellsville), KY. **Key Personnel:** David O. White, V.P. General.; Al Arbogast, News Dir.; Julia Turner, Operations Dir.; David White, Sales Mgr. **Wattage:** 25,000. **Ad Rates:** $13-24 for 30 seconds; $17-31 for 60 seconds. $17-$28 for 30 seconds; $22-$38 for 60 seconds. Combined advertising rates available with WKCT-AM.

12128 WKCT-AM - 930
804 College Phone: (502)781-2121
PO Box 930 Fax: (502)842-0232
Bowling Green, KY 42102

Format: News; Talk; Adult Contemporary; Information. **Networks:** CBS; Mutual Broadcasting System. **Founded:** 1947. **Operating Hours:** Continuous; 70% network, 30% local. **Key Personnel:** David O. White, VP/Gen. Mgr.; Dave White, Sales Mgr.; Al Arborgast, News Dir.; Julia Turner, Operations Dir. **Wattage:** 5000. **Ad Rates:** $11-21 for 30 seconds; $14-27 for 60 seconds. $17-$28 for 30 seconds; $22-$38 for 60 seconds. Combined advertising rates available with WDNS-FM.

12129 WKGB-TV - 53
c/o Kentucky Authority for Educational TV Phone: (606)258-7000
Fax: (606)258-7399
600 Cooper Dr.
Lexington, KY 40502

Format: Public TV. **Networks:** Public Broadcasting Service (PBS); Kentucky Educational Television. **Owner:** Kentucky Authority for Educational TV, at above address, (606)258-7170, Fax: (606)258-7390. **Founded:** 1968. **Operating Hours:** 6:15 a.m.-midnight. **ADI:** Bowling Green (Campbellsville), KY. **Key Personnel:** Craig Cornwell, Contact; L. Hobson, Contact; J. Gorman, Contact; D. Holtzclaw, Business Mgr.; M. Ferguson, Contact; Virginia Gaines Fox, Contact, gfox@msmail.ket.org; Donna Moore, Contact; Sally Hamilton, Contact; William Wilson, Contact; D. Hoffman, Program Mgr.; S. Talbert, Contact; B. Ball, Contact; J. Holbrook, Contact; T. Tucker, Contact. **Local Programs:** *Comment on Kentucky*; *Kentucky Afield*; *Kentucky Life*; *Kentucky Tonight*; *Legislative Weekly*. **Wattage:** 676,000. **Ad Rates:** Noncommercial. **URL:** http://www.ket.org.

12130 WKYU-FM - 88.9
Western Kentucky University Phone: (502)745-5489
Bowling Green, KY 42101 Fax: (502)745-2084
Free: (800)599-WKYU
E-mail: wkyufm@wku.edu

Format: Public Radio. **Simulcasts:** WDCL-FM. **Networks:** National Public Radio (NPR); Public Radio International (PRI); AP. **Owner:** Western Kentucky University, at above address. **Founded:** 1980. **Operating Hours:** Continuous. **ADI:** Bowling Green (Campbellsville), KY. **Key Personnel:** David Dzikowski, Contact; Dan Modlin, News Dir.; Lee Stott, Music Dir.; D. T. Wilkinson, Dir., Educ. Telecom. **Wattage:** 100,000. **Ad Rates:** Noncommercial.

12131 WKYU-TV - 24
Western Kentucky University Phone: (502)745-2400
1 Big Red Way Fax: (502)745-2084
Bowling Green, KY 42101-3576
E-mail: wkyutv@wku.edu

Format: Public TV. **Networks:** Public Broadcasting Service (PBS). **Owner:** Western Kentucky University, at above address. **Founded:** 1989. **Operating Hours:** 14 hrs daily; 14% network, 86% local or other. **ADI:** Bowling Green (Campbellsville), KY. **Key Personnel:** Jerry Barnaby, Station Mgr.; Linda S. Oldham, Program Mgr. **Ad Rates:** Noncommercial. **URL:** http://www.wku.edu/WKYU/24home.htm.

BRANDENBURG†, pop. 1,831.

Meade Co. (WC). On Ohio River, 30 m SW of Louisville. Boat connections. Chemical factory. Oak timber. Diversified farming. Wheat, corn, tobacco.

12132 The Meade County Messenger
235 Main St. Phone: (502)422-2155
PO Box 678 Fax: (502)422-2110
Brandenburg, KY 40108-0612
Publication E-mail: mcmnews@bbtel.com

Newspaper with a Democratic orientation. **Founded:** 1892. **Freq:** Weekly (Wed.). **Print Method:** Offset. **Cols./Page:** 6. **Col. Width:** 26 nonpareils. **Col. Depth:** 301 agate lines. **Key Personnel:** Rena Singleton, Publisher. **Subscription Rates:** $19.90 individuals. **Remarks:** Accepts advertising.
Ad Rates: SAU: $6 **Circ:** 7,000
PCI: $4

12133 WMMG-AM - 1140
1715 By-Pass Rd. Phone: (502)422-3961
Brandenburg, KY 40108-1605 Fax: (502)422-3464

Format: Country. **Simulcasts:** WMMG-FM. **Networks:** ABC; Satellite Music Network; KyNet. **Founded:** 1959. **Operating Hours:** Sunrise-sunset. **Key Personnel:** Gwen Blevins, General Mgr.; Dave Clark, Program/Music Dir.; Gwen Blevins, Sales Mgr.; Bob Horsley, Chief Engineer; Dave Clark, News Dir. **Local Programs:** *Meade County Greenwave Sports*; *Tradio*. **Wattage:** 250. **Ad Rates:** $11 for 30 seconds; $12 for 60 seconds. Combined advertising rates available with WMMG-FM.

12134 WMMG-FM - 93.5
1715 By-Pass Rd. Phone: (502)422-3961
Brandenburg, KY 40108 Fax: (502)422-3464

Format: Country. **Simulcasts:** WMMG-AM. **Networks:** ABC; Satellite Music Network; KyNet; UPI. **Owner:** Meade County Communications Inc., at above address, (502)422-4440. **Founded:** 1972. **Operating Hours:** Continuous. **Key Personnel:** Gwen Blevins, General Mgr.; Dave Clark, Music/News/Traffic Dir.; Gwen Burvins, Sales Mgr.; Bob Horsley, Chief Engineer. **Local Programs:** *Meade County Greenwave Sports*; *Tradio*, Dave Clark. **Wattage:** 3400. **Ad Rates:** $11 for 30 seconds; $12 for 60 seconds.

BROOKSVILLE†, pop. 680.

Bracken Co. (NE). 46 m SE of Newport. Flour mill. Grain, dairy farms. Tobacco, corn, wheat.

12135 Bracken County News
Bay Publishing
Box 68 Phone: (606)735-2198
Brooksville, KY 41004 Fax: (606)735-2199

Community newspaper. **Founded:** 1927. **Freq:** Weekly (Thurs.). **Print Method:** Offset. **Cols./Page:** 6. **Col. Width:** 26 nonpareils. **Col. Depth:** 301 agate lines. **Key Personnel:** Kathy Bay, Publisher; Libby Estill, Editor. **Subscription Rates:** $15; $18 out of area; $21 out of state. **Remarks:** Color advertising not accepted.
Ad Rates: BW: $2.50 **Circ:** ‡2,800
SAU: $3

BROWNSVILLE†, pop. 542.

Edmonson Co. (SWC). On Green River, 21 m N of Bowling Green. Raincoat factory. Feed mill. Stock, dairy, poultry, grain farms. Corn, tobacco, hay.

12136 WAUE-FM - 100.7
1519 Euclid Ave. Phone: (502)781-2067
Bowling Green, KY 42103

Owner: Charles M. Anderson, at above address. **Operating Hours:** Continuous.

BUCKNER

12137 The Dixie Trucker
Fastline
4900 Fox Run Rd. Fax: (502)222-0615
PO Box 248 Free: (800)626-6409
Buckner, KY 40010
Publisher E-mail: fastpub@aol.com

Truck trade magazine covering the southern trucking industry. **Subtitle:** The Florida Edition, The Georgia Edition, The Dixie Edition, The Tenn Edition, The Bluegrass Edition, The Indiana Edition, The Tri State Ed. **Founded:** 1978. **Freq:** Monthly. **Print Method:** Offset. **Trim Size:** 8 3/8 x 10 7/8. **Cols./Page:** 3. **Key Personnel:** William G. Howard, Publisher. **Subscription Rates:** Free to qualified subscribers; $12; $18 two years. **Remarks:** Accepts advertising.
Ad Rates: BW: $495 **Circ:** Non-paid ‡210,000
4C: $690

12138 Fastline–Bluegrass Truck
Fastline
4900 Fox Run Rd. Fax: (502)222-0615
PO Box 248 Free: (800)626-6409
Buckner, KY 40010
Publisher E-mail: fastpub@aol.com

Illustrated buying guide for the trucking industry. **Founded:** 1978. **Freq:** Monthly. **Key Personnel:** William Howard, Publisher/Owner; Amy Brambielt, Advertising Dir.; Chrissy Wyatt, Circulation Mgr. **Subscription Rates:** $8 individuals. **Remarks:** Accepts advertising. **Online:** America Online, Inc.
Ad Rates: BW: $585 **Circ:** 21,000
4C: $810

12139 Fastline–Dakota Farm Edition
Fastline
4900 Fox Run Rd. Fax: (502)222-0615
PO Box 248 Free: (800)626-6409
Buckner, KY 40010
Publisher E-mail: fastpub@aol.com

Trade magazine for the trucking and farming industry in North and South Dakota. **Founded:** June 1978. **Freq:** Monthly. **Print Method:** Offset. **Trim Size:** 7 1/2 x 10 3/4. **Key Personnel:** William Howard, Publisher. **Subscription Rates:** $12 two years. **Remarks:** Accepts advertising.
Ad Rates: BW: $585 **Circ:** Combined ⊕**537,000**
4C: $810

12140 Fastline–Dixie Edition
Fastline
4900 Fox Run Rd. Fax: (502)222-0615
PO Box 248 Free: (800)626-6409
Buckner, KY 40010
Publisher E-mail: fastpub@aol.com

Illustrated buying guide for the trucking industry. **Founded:** 1978. **Freq:** Monthly. **Key Personnel:** William Howard, Publisher/Owner; Amy Brambielt, Advertising Dir.; Chrissy Wyatt, Circulation Mgr. **Subscription Rates:** $8 individuals. **Remarks:** Accepts advertising. **Online:** America Online, Inc.
Ad Rates: BW: $585 **Circ:** 21,000
4C: $810

12141 Fastline–Florida Truck Edition
Fastline
4900 Fox Run Rd. Fax: (502)222-0615
PO Box 248 Free: (800)626-6409
Buckner, KY 40010
Publisher E-mail: fastpub@aol.com

Illustrated buying guide for the trucking industry. **Founded:** 1978. **Freq:** Monthly. **Key Personnel:** William Howard, Publisher/Owner; Chrissy Wyatt, Circulation Mgr. **Subscription Rates:** $8 individuals. **Remarks:** Accepts advertising. **Online:** America Online, Inc.
Ad Rates: BW: $585 **Circ:** 21,000
4C: $810

12142 Fastline–Georgia Truck Edition
Fastline
4900 Fox Run Rd. Fax: (502)222-0615
PO Box 248 Free: (800)626-6409
Buckner, KY 40010
Publisher E-mail: fastpub@aol.com

Illustrated buying guide for the trucking industry. **Founded:** 1978. **Freq:** Monthly. **Key Personnel:** William Howard, Publisher/Owner; Amy Brambielt, Advertising Dir.; Chrissy Wyatt, Circulation Mgr. **Subscription Rates:** $8 individuals. **Remarks:** Accepts advertising. **Online:** America Online, Inc.
Ad Rates: BW: $585 **Circ:** 21,000
4C: $810

12143 Fastline–Illinois Edition
Fastline
4900 Fox Run Rd. Fax: (502)222-0615
PO Box 248 Free: (800)626-6409
Buckner, KY 40010
Publisher E-mail: fastpub@aol.com

Illustrated buying guide for the farming industry. **Founded:** 1978. **Freq:** Monthly. **Key Personnel:** William Howard, Publisher/Owner; Amy Brambielt, Advertising Dir.; Chrissy Wyatt, Circulation Mgr. **Subscription Rates:** $8 individuals. **Remarks:** Accepts advertising. **Online:** America Online, Inc.
Ad Rates: BW: $585 **Circ:** 21,000
4C: $810

12144 Fastline–Indiana Edition
Fastline
4900 Fox Run Rd. Fax: (502)222-0615
PO Box 248 Free: (800)626-6409
Buckner, KY 40010
Publisher E-mail: fastpub@aol.com

Illustrated buying guide for the farming industry. **Founded:** 1978. **Freq:** Monthly. **Key Personnel:** William Howard, Publisher/Owner; Amy Brambielt, Advertising Dir.; Chrissy Wyatt, Circulation Mgr. **Subscription Rates:** $8 individuals. **Remarks:** Accepts advertising. **Online:** America Online, Inc.
Ad Rates: BW: $585 **Circ:** 21,000
4C: $810

12145 Fastline–Iowa Edition
Fastline
4900 Fox Run Rd. Fax: (502)222-0615
PO Box 248 Free: (800)626-6409
Buckner, KY 40010
Publisher E-mail: fastpub@aol.com

Illustrated buying guide for the farming industry. **Founded:** 1978. **Freq:** Monthly. **Key Personnel:** William Howard, Publisher/Owner; Amy Brambielt, Advertising Dir.; Chrissy Wyatt, Circulation Mgr. **Subscription Rates:** $8 individuals. **Remarks:** Accepts advertising. **Online:** America Online, Inc.
Ad Rates: BW: $585 **Circ:** 21,000
4C: $810

12146 Fastline–Kansas Edition
Fastline
4900 Fox Run Rd. Fax: (502)222-0615
PO Box 248 Free: (800)626-6409
Buckner, KY 40010
Publisher E-mail: fastpub@aol.com

Illustrated buying guide for the farming industry. **Founded:** 1978. **Freq:** Monthly. **Key Personnel:** William Howard, Publisher/Owner; Amy Brambielt, Advertising Dir.; Chrissy Wyatt, Circulation Mgr. **Subscription Rates:** $8 individuals. **Remarks:** Accepts advertising. **Online:** America Online, Inc.
Ad Rates: BW: $585 **Circ:** 21,000
4C: $810

12147 Fastline–Kentucky Edition
Fastline
4900 Fox Run Rd. Fax: (502)222-0615
PO Box 248 Free: (800)626-6409
Buckner, KY 40010
Publisher E-mail: fastpub@aol.com

Illustrated buying guide for the farming industry. **Founded:** 1978. **Freq:** Monthly. **Key Personnel:** William Howard, Publisher/Owner; Amy Brambielt, Advertising Dir.; Chrissy Wyatt, Circulation Mgr. **Subscription Rates:** $8 individuals. **Remarks:** Accepts advertising. **Online:** America Online, Inc.
Ad Rates: BW: $585 **Circ:** 21,000
4C: $810

12148 Fastline–MidAtlantic Edition
Fastline
4900 Fox Run Rd. Fax: (502)222-0615
PO Box 248 Free: (800)626-6409
Buckner, KY 40010
Publisher E-mail: fastpub@aol.com

Illustrated buying guide for the farming industry. **Founded:** 1978. **Freq:** Monthly. **Key Personnel:** William Howard, Publisher/Owner; Amy Brambielt, Advertising Dir.; Chrissy Wyatt, Circulation Mgr. **Subscription Rates:** $8 individuals. **Remarks:** Accepts advertising. **Online:** America Online, Inc.
Ad Rates: BW: $585 **Circ:** 21,000
4C: $810

12149 Fastline–MidSouth Edition
Fastline
4900 Fox Run Rd. Fax: (502)222-0615
PO Box 248 Free: (800)626-6409
Buckner, KY 40010
Publisher E-mail: fastpub@aol.com

Illustrated buying guide for the farming industry. **Founded:** 1978. **Freq:** Monthly. **Key Personnel:** William Howard, Publisher/Owner; Amy Brambielt, Advertising Dir.; Chrissy Wyatt, Circulation Mgr. **Subscription Rates:** $8 individuals. **Remarks:** Accepts advertising. **Online:** America Online, Inc.
Ad Rates: BW: $585 **Circ:** 21,000
4C: $810

12150 Fastline–Midwest Edition
Fastline
4900 Fox Run Rd. Fax: (502)222-0615
PO Box 248 Free: (800)626-6409
Buckner, KY 40010
Publisher E-mail: fastpub@aol.com

Illustrated buying guide for the trucking industry. **Founded:** 1978. **Freq:** Monthly. **Key Personnel:** William Howard, Publisher/Owner; Amy Brambielt, Advertising Dir.; Chrissy Wyatt, Circulation Mgr. **Subscription Rates:** $8 individuals. **Remarks:** Accepts advertising. **Online:** America Online, Inc.
Ad Rates: BW: $585 **Circ:** 21,000
4C: $810

12151 Fastline–Minnesota Edition
Fastline
4900 Fox Run Rd. Fax: (502)222-0615
PO Box 248 Free: (800)626-6409
Buckner, KY 40010
Publisher E-mail: fastpub@aol.com

Illustrated buying guide for the farming industry. **Founded:** 1978. **Freq:** Monthly. **Key Personnel:** William Howard, Publisher/Owner; Amy Brambielt, Advertising Dir.; Chrissy Wyatt, Circulation Mgr. **Subscription Rates:** $8 individuals. **Remarks:** Accepts advertising. **Online:** America Online, Inc.
Ad Rates: BW: $585 **Circ:** 21,000
4C: $810

12152 Fastline–Missouri Edition
Fastline
4900 Fox Run Rd. Fax: (502)222-0615
PO Box 248 Free: (800)626-6409
Buckner, KY 40010
Publisher E-mail: fastpub@aol.com

Illustrated buying guide for the farming industry. **Founded:** 1978. **Freq:** Monthly. **Key Personnel:** William Howard, Publisher/Owner; Amy Brambielt, Advertising Dir.; Chrissy Wyatt, Circulation Mgr. **Subscription Rates:** $8 individuals. **Remarks:** Accepts advertising. **Online:** America Online, Inc.
Ad Rates: BW: $585 **Circ:** 21,000
4C: $810

12153 Fastline–Nebraska Edition
Fastline
4900 Fox Run Rd. Fax: (502)222-0615
PO Box 248 Free: (800)626-6409
Buckner, KY 40010
Publisher E-mail: fastpub@aol.com

Illustrated buying guide for the farming industry. **Founded:** 1978. **Freq:** Monthly. **Key Personnel:** William Howard, Publisher/Owner; Amy Brambielt, Advertising Dir.; Chrissy Wyatt, Circulation Mgr. **Subscription Rates:** $8 individuals. **Remarks:** Accepts advertising. **Online:** America Online, Inc.
Ad Rates: BW: $585 **Circ:** 21,000
4C: $810

12154 Fastline–Northeast Edition
Fastline
4900 Fox Run Rd. Fax: (502)222-0615
PO Box 248 Free: (800)626-6409
Buckner, KY 40010
Publisher E-mail: fastpub@aol.com

Illustrated buying guide for the farming industry. **Founded:** 1978. **Freq:** Monthly. **Key Personnel:** William Howard, Publisher/Owner; Amy Brambielt, Advertising Dir.; Chrissy Wyatt, Circulation Mgr. **Subscription Rates:** $8 individuals. **Remarks:** Accepts advertising. **Online:** America Online, Inc.
Ad Rates: BW: $585 **Circ:** 21,000
4C: $810

12155 Fastline–Ohio Edition
Fastline
4900 Fox Run Rd. Fax: (502)222-0615
PO Box 248 Free: (800)626-6409
Buckner, KY 40010
Publisher E-mail: fastpub@aol.com

Illustrated buying guide for the farming industry. **Founded:** 1978. **Freq:** Monthly. **Key Personnel:** William Howard, Publisher/Owner; Amy Brambielt, Advertising Dir.; Chrissy Wyatt, Circulation Mgr. **Subscription Rates:** $8 individuals. **Remarks:** Accepts advertising. **Online:** America Online, Inc.
Ad Rates: BW: $585 **Circ:** 21,000
4C: $810

12156 Fastline–Oklahoma Edition
Fastline
4900 Fox Run Rd. Fax: (502)222-0615
PO Box 248 Free: (800)626-6409
Buckner, KY 40010
Publisher E-mail: fastpub@aol.com

Illustrated buying guide for the farming industry. **Founded:** 1978. **Freq:** Monthly. **Key Personnel:** William Howard, Publisher/Owner; Amy Brambielt, Advertising Dir.; Chrissy Wyatt, Circulation Mgr. **Subscription Rates:** $8 individuals. **Remarks:** Accepts advertising. **Online:** America Online, Inc.
Ad Rates: BW: $585 **Circ:** 21,000
4C: $810

12157 Fastline–Rocky Mountain Edition
Fastline
4900 Fox Run Rd. Fax: (502)222-0615
PO Box 248 Free: (800)626-6409
Buckner, KY 40010
Publisher E-mail: fastpub@aol.com

Illustrated buying guide for the farming industry. **Founded:** 1978. **Freq:** Monthly. **Key Personnel:** William Howard, Publisher/Owner; Amy Brambielt, Advertising Dir.; Chrissy Wyatt, Circulation Mgr. **Subscription Rates:** $8 individuals. **Remarks:** Accepts advertising. **Online:** America Online, Inc.
Ad Rates: BW: $585 **Circ:** 21,000
4C: $810

12158 Fastline–Southeast Edition
Fastline
4900 Fox Run Rd. Fax: (502)222-0615
PO Box 248 Free: (800)626-6409
Buckner, KY 40010
Publisher E-mail: fastpub@aol.com

Illustrated buying guide for the farming industry. **Founded:** 1978. **Freq:** Monthly. **Key Personnel:** William Howard, Publisher/Owner; Amy Brambielt, Advertising Dir.; Chrissy Wyatt, Circulation Mgr. **Subscription Rates:** $8 individuals. **Remarks:** Accepts advertising. **Online:** America Online, Inc.
Ad Rates: BW: $585 **Circ:** 21,000
4C: $810

12159 Fastline–Tennessee Farm Edition
Fastline
4900 Fox Run Rd. Fax: (502)222-0615
PO Box 248 Free: (800)626-6409
Buckner, KY 40010
Publisher E-mail: fastpub@aol.com

Illustrated buying guide for the farming industry. **Founded:** 1978. **Freq:** Monthly. **Key Personnel:** William Howard, Publisher/Owner; Amy Brambielt, Advertising Dir.; Chrissy Wyatt, Circulation Mgr. **Subscription Rates:** $8 individuals. **Remarks:** Accepts advertising. **Online:** America Online, Inc.
Ad Rates: BW: $585 **Circ:** 21,000
4C: $810

12160 Fastline–Tennessee Truck Edition
Fastline
4900 Fox Run Rd. Fax: (502)222-0615
PO Box 248 Free: (800)626-6409
Buckner, KY 40010
Publisher E-mail: fastpub@aol.com

Illustrated buying guide for the trucking industry. **Founded:** 1978. **Freq:** Monthly. **Key Personnel:** William Howard, Pub-

lisher/Owner; Amy Brambielt, Advertising Dir.; Chrissy Wyatt, Circulation Mgr. **Subscription Rates:** $8 individuals. **Remarks:** Accepts advertising. **Online:** America Online, Inc.
Ad Rates: BW: $585 **Circ:** 21,000
4C: $810

12161 Fastline–Texas Edition
Fastline
4900 Fox Run Rd. Fax: (502)222-0615
PO Box 248 Free: (800)626-6409
Buckner, KY 40010
Publisher E-mail: fastpub@aol.com

Illustrated buying guide for the farming industry. **Founded:** 1978. **Freq:** Monthly. **Key Personnel:** William Howard, Publisher/Owner; Amy Brambielt, Advertising Dir.; Chrissy Wyatt, Circulation Mgr. **Subscription Rates:** $8 individuals. **Remarks:** Accepts advertising. **Online:** America Online, Inc.
Ad Rates: BW: $585 **Circ:** 21,000
4C: $810

12162 Fastline–Tri-State Edition
Fastline
4900 Fox Run Rd. Fax: (502)222-0615
PO Box 248 Free: (800)626-6409
Buckner, KY 40010
Publisher E-mail: fastpub@aol.com

Illustrated buying guide for the trucking industry. **Founded:** 1978. **Freq:** Monthly. **Key Personnel:** William Howard, Publisher/Owner; Amy Brambielt, Advertising Dir.; Chrissy Wyatt, Circulation Mgr. **Subscription Rates:** $8 individuals. **Remarks:** Accepts advertising. **Online:** America Online, Inc.
Ad Rates: BW: $585 **Circ:** 21,000
4C: $810

12163 Fastline–Wisconsin Edition
Fastline
4900 Fox Run Rd. Fax: (502)222-0615
PO Box 248 Free: (800)626-6409
Buckner, KY 40010
Publisher E-mail: fastpub@aol.com

Illustrated buying guide for the farming industry. **Founded:** 1978. **Freq:** Monthly. **Key Personnel:** William Howard, Publisher/Owner; Amy Brambielt, Advertising Dlr.; Chrissy Wyatt, Circulation Mgr. **Subscription Rates:** $8 individuals. **Remarks:** Accepts advertising. **Online:** America Online, Inc.
Ad Rates: BW: $585 **Circ:** 21,000
4C: $810

BURKESVILLE†, pop. 1,717.

Cumberland Co. (SC). On Cumberland River, 110 m S of Louisville. Oil wells. Saw mill. Summer resort. Stock, poultry, fruit, grain farms. Corn, hay, tobacco.

12164 Cumberland County News
PO Box 307 Phone: (502)864-3891
Burkesville, KY 42717-0307 Fax: (502)864-3497

Community newspaper. **Founded:** 1919. **Freq:** Weekly (Wed.). **Print Method:** Offset. **Cols./Page:** 6. **Col. Width:** 24 nonpareils. **Col. Depth:** 294 agate lines. **Key Personnel:** Patsy Judd, Publisher; Bruce Henson, Advertising Mgr.; Cyndi Pritchett, Editor. **Subscription Rates:** $14.50 individuals. **Remarks:** Accepts advertising.
Ad Rates: BW: $371.70 **Circ:** 2,900
PCI: $4.00

12165 WKYR-AM - 1570
Box 340 Phone: (502)433-7191
Burkesville, KY 42717 Fax: (502)433-7195

Format: Contemporary Country. **Simulcasts:** WKYR-FM. **Networks:** ABC. **Founded:** 1975. **Operating Hours:** Daytime. **ADI:** Nashville (Cookeville), TN. **Key Personnel:** Ray Mullinix, Contact; Don Johnson, Music Dir.; Louise Curtis, Contact. **Wattage:** 1000. **Ad Rates:** Advertising accepted; rates available upon request.

12166 WKYR-FM - 107.9
Box 340 Phone: (502)433-7191
Burkesville, KY 42717-0340 Fax: (502)433-7195

Format: Contemporary Country. **Networks:** ABC. **Founded:** 1988. **Operating Hours:** Continuous. **ADI:** Nashville (Cookeville), TN. **Key Personnel:** Ray Mullinix, Pres./Gen. Mgr./PD; Don Johnson, Music Dir./Production; Louise Curtis, Sales/Office Mgr.; Larry Nelson, Chief Engineer. **Wattage:** 6000. **Ad Rates:** Advertising accepted; rates available upon request.

CADIZ†, pop. 1,987.

Trigg Co. (SW). 20 m W of Hopkinsville. Manufactures fabricated wire products, hosiery, feed, work clothing. Lumber. Timber. Agriculture. Tobacco, wheat, corn.

12167 The Cadiz Record
A. H. Belo
PO Box 1670 Phone: (502)522-6605
Cadiz, KY 42211 Fax: (502)522-3001
Publication E-mail: cadizrecord@dynasty.net

Local newspaper with a Democratic orientation. **Founded:** Dec. 25, 1880. **Freq:** Weekly (Wed.). **Print Method:** Offset. **Cols./Page:** 6. **Col. Width:** 26 nonpareils. **Col. Depth:** 301 agate lines. **Key Personnel:** Tommy Newton, Editor, phone (502)522-6606, t.newton@dynasty.net; Jan C. Witty, General Mgr., jwitty@dynasty.net. **Subscription Rates:** $24 individuals; $27 out of area; $34 out of state. **Remarks:** Accepts advertising. **Alt. Formats:** CD-ROM.
Ad Rates: SAU: $2.25 **Circ:** ‡4,800
PCI: $2.75

The Cadiz Record - See Cadiz

12168 Herald Ledger
A. H. Belo
PO Box 1670 Phone: (502)522-6605
Cadiz, KY 42211 Fax: (502)522-3001

Community newspaper. **Founded:** 1902. **Freq:** Weekly (Wed.). **Print Method:** Offset. **Cols./Page:** 6. **Col. Width:** 24 nonpareils. **Col. Depth:** 297 agate lines. **Key Personnel:** Cindy Riley, General Mgr. **USPS:** 202-380. **Subscription Rates:** $17.49 individuals; $20.50 out of area. **Remarks:** Accepts advertising.
Ad Rates: GLR: $2.90 **Circ:** ‡3,000
BW: $361.20
4C: $571.20
SAU: $2.80

12169 The Union County Advocate
The Cadiz Record
PO Box 1670 Phone: (502)522-6605
Cadiz, KY 42211 Fax: (502)522-3001
Publication E-mail: ucadvocate@dynasty.net

Local newspaper. **Founded:** 1886. **Freq:** Weekly (Wed.). **Print Method:** Offset. **Cols./Page:** 6. **Col. Width:** 2 1/16 inches. **Col. Depth:** 21 1/2 inches. **Key Personnel:** Tammy Newton, Editor; Jan Witty, General and Ad. Mgr.; Heather Brashears, Circulation and Bookkeeping; Bryan Rogers, Sports. **USPS:** 648-080. **Subscription Rates:** $24 individuals; $27.01 out of area; $34 out of state. **Remarks:** Accepts advertising. **URL:** http://www.ucadvocate.com.
Ad Rates: SAU: $6.50 **Circ:** Paid 5,300
PCI: $5 Free 200

12170 WKDZ-AM - 1110
1487 Will Jackson Rd. Phone: (502)522-3232
Cadiz, KY 42211 Fax: (502)522-1110

Format: Gospel. **Owner:** Ham Broadcasting Co., Inc., at above address. **Founded:** 1966. **Operating Hours:** Sunrise-sunset. **Key Personnel:** D. J. Everett III, President; Beth Mann, General Mgr.; Alan Watts, News Dir. **Wattage:** 1000. **Ad Rates:** $5.50-12 for 30 seconds; $6.50-14 for 60 seconds.

12171 WKDZ-FM - 106.3
PO Box 1900 Phone: (502)522-3232
Cadiz, KY 42211-0316 Fax: (502)522-1110
E-mail: wkdz@commandnet.net

Format: Country. **Networks:** Satellite Music Network; Knowledge Network; ABC. **Founded:** 1972. **Operating Hours:** Continuous. **Key Personnel:** D.J. Everett, President, phone (502)886-1480, fax (502)886-6286; Alan Watts, Operations Mgr.; Beth Mann, General Mgr. **Local Programs:** *Around Town*; *KDZ Country Club High School Sports*. **Wattage:** 3000. **Ad Rates:** $10 per unit. WKDZ-AM.

CAMPBELLSVILLE†, pop. 7,598.

Taylor Co. (C). 70 m S of Louisville. Senior College. Parks. Manufacturer casket, underwear, furniture, interior supply. Cabinet shop. Agriculture. Cattle (dairy & beef), hogs, corn, tobacco.

12172 Central Kentucky Researcher
Taylor County Historical Society
Box 14 Phone: (502)465-7033
Campbellsville, KY 42719
Local historical magazine. **Founded:** 1971. **Freq:** Quarterly. **Trim Size:** 8 1/2 x 11. **Key Personnel:** Aileen McKinley, Editor/Circulation Mgr. **Subscription Rates:** Free to qualified subscribers. **Remarks:** Advertising not accepted.
Circ: Controlled 315

12173 WCKQ-FM - 104.1
PO Box 1053 Phone: (502)789-2401
Campbellsville, KY 42719-1053 Fax: (502)789-1450

Format: Adult Contemporary. **Networks:** CBS. **Owner:** George E. Owen, PO Box 1053, Campbellsville, KY 42719-1053, (502)426-6936. **Founded:** 1963. **Formerly:** WTCO-FM. **Operating Hours:** Continuous; 25% network, 75% local. **ADI:** Louisville, KY. **Key Personnel:** George Owen, General Mgr.; Tom McClendon, Music Dir.; Tom Redmon, News Dir. **Wattage:** 25,000. **Ad Rates:** $4-20 for 30 seconds; $5-25 for 60 seconds. $4-$20 for 30 seconds; $5-$25 for 60 seconds. Combined advertising rates available with WTCO-AM.

12174 WGRB-TV - 34
PO Box 400 Phone: (502)384-4738
Campbellsville, KY 42719-0400 Fax: (502)384-6864

Format: Commercial TV. **Networks:** Warner Brothers Studios. **Owner:** Green River Broadcasting Co., Inc., at above address, (502)349-0738. **Founded:** 1983. **Operating Hours:** Continuous. **ADI:** Bowling Green (Campbellsville), KY. **Key Personnel:** Joey Tucker, Traffic Mgr.; Carol LaFever, General Mgr./Program Dir.; Sue Ann Hall, Public Service Director; Gary Tucker, Station/Production Mgr.; Ramona Pendley. **Local Programs:** *Kentucky Morning* 9 a.m. Friday, Everette Lee; *News Source Kentucky* 6 p.m. **Wattage:** 600,000. **Ad Rates:** $20-220 per unit.

12175 WTCO-AM - 1450
PO Box 1053 Phone: (502)789-1450
Campbellsville, KY 42719 Fax: (502)789-1450

Format: Contemporary Christian; Southern Gospel. **Networks:** CBS. **Owner:** Heartland Communications, Inc., at above address. **Founded:** 1948. **Formerly:** WKXJ-AM. **Operating Hours:** Continuous; 75% network,25% local. **ADI:** Louisville, KY. **Key Personnel:** George Owen, General Mgr.; Tom McClendon, Program Mgr. **Wattage:** 1000. **Ad Rates:** $3-8 for 30 seconds; $3.75-10 for 60 seconds. $3-$8 for 30 seconds; $3.75-$10 for 60 seconds. Combined advertising rates available with WCKQ-FM.

CAMPTON†, pop. 419.

Wolfe Co. (EC). 65 m SE of Lexington. Coal mines. Timber. Agriculture. Tobacco, corn, hay.

12176 Wolfe County News
Courier Publishing
PO Box 129 Phone: (606)662-6145
Campton, KY 41301 Fax: (606)662-4010

Community newspaper. **Founded:** 1938. **Freq:** Weekly (Fri.). **Print Method:** Letterpress and offset. Uses mats. **Cols./Page:** 8. **Col. Width:** 22 nonpareils. **Col. Depth:** 294 agate lines. **Key Personnel:** J.B. Stamper, Editor; Earl Kinner, Jr., Publisher. **Subscription Rates:** $12 individuals; $13 out of area; $14 out of state. **Remarks:** Accepts advertising.
Ad Rates: GLR: $.171 **Circ:** Paid 2,750
BW: $250
4C: $410
SAU: $4.04
PCI: $2.90

CARROLLTON†, pop. 3,884.

Carroll Co. (NW). On Ohio River, 52 m NE of Louisville. General Butler State Resort Park. Recreational and industrial area. Livestock, dairy, poultry, grain farms. Tobacco.

12177 News-Democrat
Landmark Community Newspapers, Inc.
PO Box 60 Phone: (502)732-4261
Carrollton, KY 41008 Fax: (502)633-0453

Community newspaper. **Founded:** 1868. **Freq:** Weekly (Wed.). **Print Method:** Offset. **Cols./Page:** 6. **Col. Width:** 2 inches. **Col. Depth:** 301 agate lines. **Key Personnel:** Lucille Schmucker, Office Mgr. **Subscription Rates:** $21 individuals; $28 out of area; $36.95 out of state. **Remarks:** Accepts advertising.
Ad Rates: GLR: $4.53 **Circ:** 3,615

CATLETTSBURG

12178 WTCR-AM - 1420
1 Radio Park Rd. Phone: (606)739-8427
Catlettsburg, KY 41129 Fax: (606)739-6009
Free: (800)938-1033
E-mail: wtcr@hotmail.com

Format: Contemporary Country. **Networks:** ABC. **Founded:** 1954. **Operating Hours:** Continuous. **Key Personnel:** Judy Jennings-Riffe, General Mgr., phone (304)525-7788, fax (304)525-6281; Colleen Murphy, Marketing Dir., phone (304)525-7788, fax (304)525-6281; Clint McElroy, Program and News Dir.; Karen Johnson, General Sales Mgr., phone (304)525-7788, fax (324)525-6281. **Wattage:** 5000. **Ad Rates:** Advertising accepted; rates available upon request.

12179 WTCR-FM - 103.3
1 Radio Park Rd. Phone: (606)739-8427
Catlettsburg, KY 41129 Fax: (606)739-6009
Free: (800)938-1033
E-mail: wtcr@hotmail.com

Format: Contemporary Country. **Networks:** ABC. **Owner:** Commodore Media, 500 - 5th Ave., Ste. 3000, New York, NY 10110, (212)302-2727, Fax: (212)302-6757. **Founded:** 1966. **Operating Hours:** Continuous. **Key Personnel:** Judy Jennings-Riffe, General Mgr., phone (304)525-7788, fax (304)525-6281; Colleen Murphy, Marketing Dir., phone (304)525-7788, fax (304)525-6281; Chuck Black, Program Dir.; Karen Johnson, General Sales Mgr., phone (304)525-7788, fax (304)525-6281; Clint McElroy, News Dir. **Wattage:** 50,000. **Ad Rates:** Advertising accepted; rates available upon request.

CENTRAL CITY, pop. 5,214.

Muhlenberg Co. (SW). 32 m S of Owensboro. Manufactures wood products, beverages, boxes, explosives. Coal mines. Oil wells. Hardwood timber. Truck, grain farms. Corn, tobacco, hay.

12180 Central City Times-Argus
202 W. Broad st. Phone: (502)754-2331
Central City, KY 42330-1540 Fax: (502)754-1805

Newspaper with a Democratic orientation. **Founded:** 1906. **Freq:** Weekly (Wed.). **Print Method:** Offset. **Cols./Page:** 6. **Col. Width:** 26 nonpareils. **Col. Depth:** 301 agate lines. **Key Personnel:** Mark Stone, Editor and Publisher; Richard L. Deavers, Managing Editor. **USPS:** 630-260. **Subscription Rates:** $13 individuals. **Remarks:** Accepts advertising.
Ad Rates: GLR: $.20 **Circ:** 3,000
BW: $315
4C: $450
SAU: $2.50
PCI: $2.50

12181 WNES-AM - 1050
PO Box 471 Phone: (502)754-3000
Central City, KY 42330-0471 Fax: (502)754-9484

Format: Easy Listening. **Networks:** CBS; KyNet. **Owner:** Muhlenberg Broadcasting Co., Inc., at above address. **Founded:** 1955. **Operating Hours:** 6 a.m.-10 p.m. **Key Personnel:** Stan Barnett, Contact. **Wattage:** 1000. **Ad Rates:** $2.40-4 for 30 seconds; $4.30-6 for 60 seconds.

CLINTON†, pop. 1,720.

Hickman Co. (SW). 45 SW of Paducah. Mississippi River tourist attraction. Manufacturers knitted outerwear. Ham curing. Trucking industry. Ships corn, soybeans, wheat, barley, milo, sorghum, tobacco, fruit, livestock and poultry.

12182 Hickman County Gazette
Lewis Publishing, Inc.
308 S.Washington Phone: (502)653-3381
PO Box 200 Fax: (502)653-3322
Clinton, KY 42031
Newspaper with a Democratic orientation. **Founded:** 1904. **Freq:** Weekly (Thurs.). **Print Method:** Offset. **Cols./Page:** 6. **Col. Width:** 20 nonpareils. **Col. Depth:** 294 agate lines. **Key Personnel:** Larry Lewis, Publisher; Jeane Cromika, Manager. **Subscription Rates:** $17 individuals; $20 out of area. **Remarks:** Accepts advertising.
Ad Rates: GLR: $3 **Circ:** Paid ‡2,150
SAU: $4.25 Free ‡50

COLUMBIA†, pop. 3,710.

Adair Co. (SC). 100 m SE of Louisville. Major sewing industry. Manufactures hydrolic pump, cherry furniture. Lumber mills. Sheet metal works. Agriculture. Tobacco, bell peppers, beef cattle, hogs, horses, fruit, corn, wheat, soybeans.

12183 WAIN-AM - 1270
PO Box 77 Phone: (502)384-2134
Columbia, KY 42728-0077 Fax: (502)384-6722

Format: Country. **Simulcasts:** WAIN-FM. **Networks:** ABC; KyNet. **Owner:** Terry Forcht, Drawer 1450, Corbin, KY 40702, (606)528-9600, Fax: (606)528-8487. **Founded:** 1952. **Operating Hours:** 5 a.m.-midnight. **ADI:** Bowling Green (Campbellsville), KY. **Key Personnel:** Louise Wooten, General Mgr.; Lisa Fisher, News Dir.; Don Salmon, Program Dir. **Local Programs:** *Adair County Spectrum*, Lisa Fisher, (502)380-2134, Fax (502)384-6722; *Farm and Home Extension News*, Lisa Fisher, (502)380-2134, Fax (502)384-6722; *Good Time Friday*, Lisa Fisher, (502)380-2134, Fax (502)384-6722. **Wattage:** 1,000 day; 68 night. **Ad Rates:** $5-7 for 30 seconds; $7-9 for 60 seconds.

12184 WAIN-FM - 93.5
PO Box 69 Phone: (502)384-2134
Columbia, KY 42728 Fax: (502)384-6722

Format: Country. **Simulcasts:** WAIN-AM. **Networks:** ABC; KyNet. **Owner:** Terry Forcht, Drawer 1450, Corbin, KY 40702, (606)528-9600, Fax: (606)528-8487. **Founded:** 1968. **Operating Hours:** 5 a.m.-midnight. **ADI:** Bowling Green (Campbellsville), KY. **Key Personnel:** Louise Wooten, General Mgr.; Lisa Fisher, News Dir.; Don Salmon. **Local Programs:** *Good Time Friday*, Lisa Fisher; *Man About Town*, Ron Cowell; *Spectrum*, Lisa Fisher. **Wattage:** 5200. **Ad Rates:** $5-7 for 30 seconds; $7-9 for 60 seconds.

CORBIN, pop. 8,100.

Whitley Co. (NE). Auto parts, bricks, corn, coal mining.

12185 Times-Tribune
APMS
201 N. Kentucky Ave. Phone: (606)528-2464
PO Box 516 Fax: (606)528-9850
Corbin, KY 40701-1529
Free: (800)739-8878
Publication E-mail: times@kih.net

General newspaper. **Founded:** 1892. **Freq:** Daily (eve.). **Print Method:** Offset. **Cols./Page:** 6. **Col. Width:** 2 1/16 inches. **Col. Depth:** 21 1/2 inches. **Key Personnel:** Rochelle Stidham, Publisher, fax (606)528-4656; John Whitlock, Managing Editor, t@kih.net. **USPS:** 132-480. **Subscription Rates:** $102 individuals. **Remarks:** Accepts advertising. **Formerly:** Corbin Times Tribune.
Ad Rates: GLR: $9.41 **Circ:** 8,500
BW: $1,388.04
4C: $1,626.69
SAU: $10.76
PCI: $6.28

12186 Falcon Cablevision of Corbin Inc.
105 W. 3rd St. Phone: (606)523-3000
Corbin, KY 40701 Fax: (606)528-0671

Formerly: Southern Cablevision of Corbin Inc. **Key Personnel:** Dave Hudson, General Mgr.; Sue Philpot, Contact. **Cities Served:** Boyle County.

12187 WCTT-AM - 680
105 N. Kentucky Ave. Phone: (606)528-4717
Box 372 Fax: (606)528-2068
Corbin, KY 40701
E-mail: t107@zgeton.net

Networks: NBC. **Owner:** Encore Communications, at above address. **Founded:** 1947. **Key Personnel:** Dallas Eubanks, President. **Wattage:** 1000.

12188 WCTT-FM - 107.3
105 N. Kentucky St. Phone: (606)528-4717
PO Box 372 Fax: (606)528-2068
Corbin, KY 40701
E-mail: t107@zgeton.net

Format: Adult Contemporary. **Owner:** Encore Communications, at above address. **Founded:** 1947. **Key Personnel:** Dallas Eubanks, Contact. **Wattage:** 50,000.

12189 WKDP-AM - 1330
400 E. Center St. Phone: (606)528-6617
Corbin, KY 40701 Fax: (606)528-4487
Free: (800)264-6670
E-mail: kdcountry@zgeton.net

Format: Contemporary Christian; Talk. **Networks:** ABC; USA Radio. **Owner:** Dallas Eubanks, PO Box 742, Corbin, KY 40702. **Founded:** 1967. **Formerly:** WYGO-AM (1989). **Operating Hours:** Continuous; 50% network, 50% local. **Key Personnel:** John Holbrook, Operations Mgr.; Kip Jervis, Program Dir.; Lonnie Marcum, Sales Mgr.; Britiney Venable, News Dir.; Derek Eubanks, Chief Engineer. **Wattage:** 5000 day; 22 night. **Ad Rates:** $2-5 for 30 seconds; $3-7 for 60 seconds.

12190 WKDP-FM - 99.5
400 E. Center St. Phone: (606)528-6617
Corbin, KY 40701 Fax: (606)523-0427
Free: (800)264-6670

Format: Country. **Networks:** ABC. **Owner:** Eubanks Broadcasting Inc., PO Box 742, Corbin, KY 40702, (606)528-2818. **Founded:** 1967. **Formerly:** WYGO-FM (1989). **Operating Hours:** Continuous; 5% network, 95% local. **ADI:** Lexington, KY. **Key Personnel:** Lonnie Marcum, Sales Mgr.; Cathy Hall, News Dir.; John Holbrook, Operations Mgr.; Jerry Wilson, Music Dir.; Derek Eubanks, Engineer; Kip Jervis, Program Dir. **Wattage:** 50,000. **Ad Rates:** $9.80-14 for 30 seconds; $12.80-16 for 60 seconds.

COVINGTON†, pop. 49,013.

Kenton Co. (N). On Ohio River, opposite Cincinnati. Six bridges connect with Cincinnati. Manufactures machine tools, prison equipment, paper, petroleum, sheet metal products, medicine cabinets, steel, men's clothing, electric safety switches and motor controls, freight cars, parking meters, furniture, stamping dies, steel doors, candied fruit,

12191 Diarist's Journal
209 E. 38th St. Phone: (606)491-2369
Covington, KY 41015
Journal that publishes excerpts from people's diaries and personal journals. **Founded:** 1988. **Freq:** Quarterly. **Print Method:** Offset. **Cols./Page:** 4. **Col. Width:** 2 1/2 inches. **Col. Depth:** 12 1/2 inches. **Key Personnel:** Joe Peebles, Publisher. **Subscription Rates:** $12 individuals; $17 by mail first class; $20 other countries. **Remarks:** Accepts advertising.
Ad Rates: BW: $50 **Circ:** ‡300
PCI: $5

12192 The Kentucky Post
Scripps Howard, Inc.
421 Madison Ave. Phone: (606)292-2600
PO Box 2678 Fax: (606)291-2525
Covington, KY 41011
Newspaper. **Founded:** 1890. **Freq:** Daily (eve.) and Sat. (morn.). **Print Method:** Offset. **Cols./Page:** 6. **Col. Width:** 25 nonpareils. **Col. Depth:** 300 agate lines. **Key Personnel:** Paul F. Knue, Editor; Sherry Ryle, Sales Mgr. **Subscription Rates:** $107.40 individuals. **Remarks:** Accepts advertising. **Online:** Dialog (The Dialog Corporation); DataTimes Corporation.
Ad Rates: SAU: $29.75 **Circ:** ‡47,742

12193 Online
Database
12 Orphanage Road Phone: (606)331-6345
Covington, KY 41017 Fax: (606)331-7261
Publication E-mail: olmag@onlineinc.com

Professional magazine covering online and CD-ROM databases with practical how-to articles covering the entire online industry. **Subtitle:** The Magazine of Online Information Systems. **Founded:** 1977. **Freq:** Bimonthly. **Trim Size:** 8 1/2 x 11. **Cols./Page:** 2. **Col. Width:** 16 picas. **Col. Depth:** 50 picas. **Key Personnel:** Nancy Garman, Editor, ngarman@iac.net; Jeffery K. Pemberton, Publisher; Jenny C. Pemberton, Exec. V.P.; Andrew Pemberton, Advertising Dir. **ISSN:** 0146-5422. **Subscription Rates:** $55 individuals introductory rate; $110 institutions. **Remarks:** Accepts advertising. **Online:** LEXIS-NEXIS. **URL:** http://www.onlineinc.com/database.
Ad Rates: BW: $1,115 **Circ:** ‡5,500
4C: $1,710

12194 +online user
Online, Inc.
14 Princeton Ave. Phone: (606)331-6345
PO Box 17507
Covington, KY 41017
Publication E-mail: olmag@onlineinc.com
Publisher E-mail: info@onlineinc.com

Magazine covering electronic information sources, such as CD-ROMs, online services, and database producers. **Subtitle:** A Practical Magazine for Knowledge Workers. **Founded:** Oct. 1, 1995. **Freq:** Bimonthly. **Key Personnel:** Jeffery K. Pemberton, Publisher; Nancy Garman, Editor, ngarman@well.com; Paula Hane, Editor. **Subscription Rates:** $24 U.S. and Canada; $46 Mexico and California; $59 other countries. **Available Online.**

12195 The Suspension Press
PO Box 2064
Covington, KY 41012

Black community newspaper. **Founded:** Aug. 21, 1982. **Freq:** Biweekly. **Print Method:** Offset. **Cols./Page:** 5. **Col. Width:** 22 nonpareils. **Col. Depth:** 210 agate lines. **Key Personnel:** Pamela Mullins, Editor; Patricia Humphries Fann, Publisher; Robert Humphries, Advertising Mgr. **Subscription Rates:** $12 individuals. **Remarks:** Advertising not accepted for X-rated material.
Ad Rates: BW: $672 **Circ:** Paid ‡38,000
PCI: $11 Free ‡3,200

12196 Inter Media
717 Madison Ave. Phone: (606)431-7766
Covington, KY 41012 Fax: (606)491-6397

Founded: 1981. **Formerly:** Storer Communications; TKR; TCI. **Key Personnel:** Wes Akers, phone ( )Ext. 289; Dan Pelstring; Don Weber, phone ( )Ext. 296; Trip Topken. **Cities Served:** subscribing households 71,349; 210 channels; 5 community access channels; 84 hours per week community access programming.

12197 WCVN-TV - 54
c/o Kentucky Authority for Educational TV
600 Cooper Dr.
Lexington, KY 40502
Free: (800)926-7765
Phone: (606)258-7000
Fax: (606)258-7399

Format: Public TV. **Networks:** Public Broadcasting Service (PBS); Kentucky Educational Television. **Owner:** Kentucky Authority for Educational TV, at above address, (606)258-7170, Fax: (606)258-7390. **Founded:** 1968. **Operating Hours:** 6:15 a.m.-midnight. **ADI:** Cincinnati, OH. **Key Personnel:** Craig Cornwell, Contact; J. Gorman, Contact; D. Holtzclaw, Contact; M. Ferguson, Contact; S. Talbert, Contact; Virginia Gaines Fox, Contact, gfox@msmail.ket.org; Donna Moore, Contact; Sally Hamilton, Contact; William Wilson, Contact; D. Hoffman, Contact; J. Holbrook, Contact; T. Tucker, Contact; B. Ball, Contact; L. Hudson, Contact. **Local Programs:** *Comment on Kentucky*; *Kentucky Afield*; *Kentucky Life*; *Kentucky Tonight*; *Legislative Weekly*. **Wattage:** 162,000. **URL:** http://www.ket.org.

12198 WTSJ-AM - 1050
641 W. 9th St.
Covington, KY 41011
Phone: (606)491-1050
Fax: (606)491-1069
E-mail: 74513.3446@compuserve.com

Format: Religious; Talk. **Owner:** Salem Communications, PO Box 31440, Cincinnati, OH 45231. **Founded:** 1947. **Formerly:** WZIP-AM; Guardian Communications, Inc. **Operating Hours:** Continuous. **ADI:** Cincinnati, OH. **Key Personnel:** Don Lambert, General Mgr. **Wattage:** 1000 day; 278 night. **Ad Rates:** $8-18 for 30 seconds; $10-20 for 60 seconds.

CROMONA, pop. 700.

Letcher Co. (SE). 10 m NE of Whitesburg. Coal mining. Agriculture. Corn, tobacco, potatoes.

Letcher County Community News-Press - See Jenkins

CUMBERLAND, pop. 3,712.

Harlan Co. (NE). 21 m SSE of Hazard. Mining center.

12199 Tri-City News
PO Box 490
Cumberland, KY 40823-0490
Phone: (606)589-2588
Fax: (606)589-2589

Community newspaper. **Founded:** 1929. **Freq:** Weekly. **Print Method:** Offset. **Trim Size:** 13 x 21 1/2. **Cols./Page:** 6. **Col. Depth:** 21.5 inches. **Key Personnel:** Paul J. Wilder, Editor and Publisher; Lavondia Browning, Advertising Mgr. **USPS:** 638-820. **Subscription Rates:** $15 individuals; $20 out of state. **Remarks:** Accepts advertising.
Ad Rates: BW: $483.75 **Circ:** ‡2,200
4C: $803.75
PCI: $4.50

12200 WCPM-AM - 1280
101 Keller St.
Cumberland, KY 40823
Phone: (606)589-4623

Format: Religious; Country. **Networks:** USA Radio; Jones Satellite. **Founded:** 1951. **Operating Hours:** 6 a.m. sunset; 100% local. **ADI:** Knoxville (Crossville), TN. **Key Personnel:** J. George Bibb, General Mgr.; Laura Hollitt, Contact; Tammy Tuttle, Contact. **Wattage:** 1000. **Ad Rates:** $2.50-3 for 30 seconds; $3-4 for 60 seconds. Combined advertising rates available with WSEH-FM.

12201 WSEH-FM - 102.7
101 Keller St.
Cumberland, KY 40823
Phone: (606)589-4623

Format: Country. **Networks:** Jones Satellite. **Owner:** Cumberland City Broadcasting, Inc., at above address. **Founded:** Dec. 1994. **Operating Hours:** Continuous. **Key Personnel:** Geroge Bibb, Pres./General Mgr.; Laura Hollitt, Traffic. **Wattage:** 6000. **Ad Rates:** $4.50-5.75 for 30 seconds; $5.50-6.75 for 60 seconds. **URL:** http://www.wseh-fm.

CYNTHIANA†, pop. 5,881.

Harrison Co. (NEC). 28 m N of Lexington. Tobacco warehouses and redrying plant; cheese, butter, aluminum fabricating, clothing, fertilizer factories; distillery; screws, planing mill; meat processing plant. Stock, dairy, poultry farms. Tobacco,

12202 WCYN-AM - 1400
PO Box 398
Cynthiana, KY 41031-0398
Free: (800)752-4595
Phone: (606)234-1400
Fax: (606)234-1425

Format: Oldies. **Owner:** Ann Anderson, at above address. **Founded:** 1956. **Operating Hours:** Continuous. **Key Personnel:** Anne Anderson, General Mgr.; Bill Bishop, Asst. Manager/Program Director, billybob@kih.net. **Wattage:** 500 day; 1000 night. **Ad Rates:** $4.90-7.00 for 30 seconds; $6.16-8.80 for 60 seconds. Combined advertising rates available with WCYN-FM.

12203 WCYN-FM - 102.3
P.O. Box 398
Cynthiana, KY 41031-7398
Free: (800)752-4595
Phone: (606)234-1400
Fax: (606)234-1425

Format: Country. **Owner:** Ann Anderson, at above address. **Founded:** 1970. **Operating Hours:** Continuous. **Key Personnel:** Ann Anderson, General Mgr.; Christopher A. Winkle, Asst. Manager/Prog. Director; Bill Bishop, Sports Dir. **Local Programs:** *Coffee Break*, Charlie Garnett; *Spell Bound*, Chris Winkle. **Wattage:** 6,000. **Ad Rates:** $4.90-7 for 30 seconds; $6.16-8.80 for 60 seconds. Combined advertising rates available with WCYN-AM.

DANVILLE†, pop. 12,942.

Boyle Co. (C). 36 m SW of Lexington. Centre College (Presb.). Manufactures farm machinery, gas boilers, conveyors, wire components, trash compactors, auto parts, beverages, automatic ice makers, furniture, glass tubing & incandescent blown bulbs, men's clothing, greeting cards; tobacco warehouse. Stock yards. Agriculture. Tobacco, wheat.

12204 Advocate-Messenger
Advocate-Messenger Co.
330 S. 4th St.
Danville, KY 40422-2033
Free: (800)428-0409
Phone: (606)236-2551
Fax: (606)236-9566
Publication E-mail: advocate@amnews.com

General newspaper. **Founded:** 1865. **Freq:** Daily (eve.). **Print Method:** Offset. **Cols./Page:** 6. **Col. Width:** 25 nonpareils. **Col. Depth:** 301 agate lines. **Key Personnel:** Mary Schurz, Editor and Publisher. **Subscription Rates:** $85 individuals. **Remarks:** Accepts advertising.
Ad Rates: SAU: $8.77 **Circ:** Mon.-Fri. ★**11,038**
Sun. ★**12,718**

12205 Centrepiece
Centre College
600 W. Walnut St.
Danville, KY 40422-1394
Phone: (606)238-5500
Fax: (606)238-5507

College alumni magazine. **Founded:** 1959. **Freq:** Quarterly. **Print Method:** Sheet. **Trim Size:** 8 1/2 11. **Cols./Page:** 4. **Col. Width:** 1 5/8 nonpareils and 3 9/16 inches. **Col. Depth:** 134 agate lines. **Key Personnel:** Diane Johnson, Editor, johnsond@centre.edu. **Subscription Rates:** Free. **Remarks:** Advertising not accepted. **URL:** http://www.centre.edu.
Circ: ‡18,000

12206 WDFB-AM - 1170
3596 Alum Springs Rd.
Danville, KY 40422-9607
Phone: (606)236-9333
Fax: (606)236-3348
E-mail: wdfb@searnet.com

Format: Religious. **Simulcasts:** WDFB-FM. **Networks:** USA Radio; Voice of Christian Youth America. **Owner:** Donald Drake, at above address. **Founded:** 1985. **Operating Hours:** Sunrise-sunset; 5% network, 95% local. **ADI:** Lexington, KY. **Key Personnel:** Donald Drake, President/Mgr., wdfb@scarnet.com; Mildred Drake, V.P./Music Dir./Sec./Tres.; Jim Gaskin, Asst. Mgr./Sales Manager; Cindy Pike, Traffic Mgr. **Local Programs:** *Bible Trivia* 3:00 pm - 5:00 pm Sunday, Mildred Drake, Hostess, (606)236-9332; *Family Altar* 10:30 - 11:30 Monday-Friday; *Trading Post* 4:30 - 4:45 Monday-Friday, Mildred Drake, Hostess, (606)236-9332. **Wattage:** 1000. **Ad Rates:** $4-5.20 for 30 seconds; $5-6.25 for 60 seconds. **URL:** http://www.wdfb.com.

12207 WDFB-FM - 88.1
PO Box 106
Danville, KY 40423
Phone: (606)236-9333
Fax: (606)236-3348
E-mail: wdfb@searnet.com

Format: Religious. **Networks:** USA Radio; Voice of Christian Youth America. **Owner:** Alum Springs Educational Corp., at above address. **Founded:** Nov. 1992. **Operating Hours:** Continuous. **Key Personnel:** Don Drake, President; Mildred Drake, Vice President; Jim Gaskin, Chief Engineer/Salesman; Cindy Pike, Traffic Mgr. **Ad Rates:** Noncommercial. **URL:** http://www.wdfb.com.

12208 WHIR-AM - 1230
2063 Shakertown Rd.
Danville, KY 40422
Phone: (606)236-2711
Fax: (606)236-1461

Format: News; Sports. **Networks:** CBS. **Owner:** Hometown Broadcasting of Danville, Inc., at above address. **Founded:** Oct. 1947. **Operating Hours:** Continuous. **ADI:** Lexington, KY. **Key Personnel:** Robert Wagner, General Mgr., rwagner@kih.net; Jim Parman, News Dir.; Lisa McGrath, Traffic Dir.; Steve Bertram, Sports Dir. **Wattage:** 1000. **Ad Rates:** Advertising accepted; rates available upon request.

DAWSON SPRINGS, pop. 3,275.

Hopkins Co. (SW). 95 m W of Bowling Green. Pennyrile Forest State Resort Park. Coal mines. Manufactures plastics, clothing, wood products. Agriculture. Dairy, fruit, corn, tobacco, hay.

12209 The Dawson Springs Progress
Progress Publishing Co., Inc.
131 S. Main St.
PO Box 460
Dawson Springs, KY 42408
Phone: (502)797-3271
Fax: (502)797-3271

Community newspaper. **Founded:** 1919. **Freq:** Weekly (Thurs.). **Print Method:** Offset. **Cols./Page:** 6. **Col. Width:** 25 nonpareils. **Col. Depth:** 294 agate lines. **Key Personnel:** Jed Dillingham, Editor and Publisher; Niles O. Dillingham, President; Scott N. Dillingham, Publisher. **Subscription Rates:** $10.60 individuals; $20 out of county; $25 out of state. **Remarks:** Accepts advertising.
Ad Rates: SAU: $3.28 **Circ:** 2,600
PCI: $2.60

EDMONTON†, pop. 1,401.

Metcalfe (SC). 50 m W of Bowling Green. Manufactures men's and boy's work clothing, plastics, mulch. Agriculture. Corn, tobacco, dairying.

12210 Herald-News
116 S. Main
PO Box 87
Edmonton, KY 42129
Phone: (502)432-3291
Fax: (502)432-4414

Community newspaper. **Founded:** 1894. **Freq:** Weekly (Tues.). **Print Method:** Offset. **Cols./Page:** 6. **Col. Width:** 24 nonpareils. **Col. Depth:** 294 agate lines. **Key Personnel:** Kandis Harper, Advertising Mgr.; Patsy Judd, Publisher, phone (502)864-5352; Clay Scott, Publisher. **USPS:** 168-300. **Subscription Rates:** $14.50 individuals; $22.50 other. **Remarks:** Accepts advertising.
Ad Rates: GLR: $.28 **Circ:** Paid 3,167
BW: $327.60
SAU: $4.40
PCI: $4.40

12211 WKNK-FM - 99.1
PO Box 457
Glasgow, KY 42142-0457
Phone: (502)432-7600
Fax: (502)432-7601

Format: Country. **Networks:** KyNet. **Owner:** Metcalfe Communications, Inc, at above address. **Founded:** 1990. **Operating Hours:** Continuous. **ADI:** Nashville (Cookeville), TN. **Key Personnel:** Judy Crabtree, President; Judy Crabtree, General Mgr.; Pam Prewitt, Operations Mgr. **Wattage:** 3000. **Ad Rates:** $4-8 for 30 seconds; $5-9 for 60 seconds. $4-$8 for 30 seconds; $5-$9 for 60 seconds. Combined advertising rates available with WHHT-FM.

ELIZABETHTOWN†, pop. 15,380.

Hardin Co. (WC). 48 m S of Louisville. Manufacturers men's slacks, cheese, metal products, ready mix concrete, machinery, package chemicals, fertilizer, fuses, tools, dies, magnets, sealants, adhesives, steel fabrication, sockets, nut runners, telephone cable, beverages, plastics. Limestone quarries. Diversified farming. Corn, wheat, tobacco.

12212 The Virginian Pilot
Landmark Communications, Inc.
408 W. Dixie
Elizabethtown, KY 42701
Phone: (502)769-2312
Fax: (502)865-7318

General newspaper. **Founded:** 1869. **Freq:** Daily and Sunday (morn.). **Print Method:** Offset. **Cols./Page:** 6. **Col. Width:** 20 nonpareils. **Col. Depth:** 301 agate lines. **Key Personnel:** David Greer, Editor; Mike Anders, Publisher; Coleman Love, Advertising Mgr. **USPS:** 172-960. **Subscription Rates:** $76.95 individuals. **Remarks:** Accepts advertising. **Formerly:** News-Enterprise.
Ad Rates: BW: $823.05 **Circ:** Mon.-Fri. ★**197,773**
4C: $1,098.05 Sat. ★**227,016**
SAU: $7.25 Sun. ★**233,391**
PCI: $6.45

12213 Comcast Cable
2919 Ring Rd.
Elizabethtown, KY 42701
Phone: (502)737-4200
Fax: (502)737-3379

Founded: 1965. **Formerly:** TeleScripps Cable Co. **Key Personnel:** Doug McMillan. **Cities Served:** 62 channels; 1 community access channel.

12214 WASE-FM - 103.5
PO Box 2087 Phone: (502)766-1035
Elizabethtown, KY 42702 Fax: (502)769-1052
Free: (888)766-1035
E-mail: wase@kvnet.org

Format: Oldies. **Networks:** Westwood One Radio. **Owner:** J. Michael Badwin/Bill Walters, 519 N. Miles, Etown, Elizabethtown, KY 42701. **Founded:** 1967. **Formerly:** WSAC-FM (1987). **Operating Hours:** Continuous;100% local. **Key Personnel:** Rene Bell, General Mgr., rbell@kvnet.org; Karen Allenn, News Dir.; Bill Walters, President. **Local Programs:** *Comment on the Heartland* 8:00 am Sunday, Karen Allenn, (502)766-1035, Fax (502)769-1052. **Wattage:** 25,000. **Ad Rates:** $21-29.40 for 30 seconds; $21-29.40 for 60 seconds.

12215 WIEL-AM - 1400
406 S. Mulberry
PO Box L
Elizabethtown, KY 42701

Format: Talk; News. **Owner:** Basix Communications, at above address. **Founded:** 1950. **Operating Hours:** Continuous; 75% network, 25% local. **ADI:** Louisville, KY. **Key Personnel:** Ross Becker, President; Barry Black, GM/Program Director. **Wattage:** 1000. **Ad Rates:** $10 for 30 seconds; $11 for 60 seconds. Combined advertising rates available with WRZI, WKMO, WRZI-FM.

12216 WKLE-TV - 46
Kentucky Educational TV Phone: (606)258-7000
600 Cooper Dr. Fax: (606)258-7399
Lexington, KY 40502
Free: (800)258-7399

Format: Public TV. **Networks:** Public Broadcasting Service (PBS); Kentucky Educational Television. **Owner:** Kentucky Authority for Educational TV, at above address. **Founded:** 1968. **Formerly:** WKET-TV (1992); WKIE-TV (1995). **Operating Hours:** 6:15 a.m.-midnight. **ADI:** Louisville, KY. **Key Personnel:** William Wilson, Contact; J. Gorman, Contact; D. Holtzclaw, Contact; M. Ferguson, Contact; S. Talbert, Contact; Virginia Gaines Fox, Contact, gfox@msmail.ket.org; Donna Moore, Contact; Sally Hamilton, Contact; D. Hoffman, Contact; Craig Cornwell, Contact; T. Tucker, Contact; J. Holbrook, Contact; L. Hobson, Contact; B. Ball, Contact. **Local Programs:** *Comment on Kentucky*; *Kentucky Afield*; *Kentucky Life*; *Kentucky Tonight*; *Legislative Weekly*. **Wattage:** 1,260,000. **Ad Rates:** Noncommercial. **URL:** http://www.ket.org.

12217 WKMO-FM - 106.3
406 S. Mulberry Phone: (502)763-0800
PO Box L Fax: (502)769-6349
Elizabethtown, KY 42702
Free: (800)566-1063

Format: Country. **Networks:** CBS; Jones Satellite. **Owner:** Basix Communications, at above address. **Founded:** 1975. **Operating Hours:** Continuous; 100% local. **ADI:** Louisville, KY. **Key Personnel:** Ross Becker, President; Barry A. Black, Operations Dir. **Wattage:** 3000. **Ad Rates:** $17 for 30 seconds; $19-22 for 60 seconds. $8.00-$22.00 for 30 seconds; $11.00-$30.00 for 60 seconds. Combined advertising rates available with WIEL-AM. WRZI-FM. **URL:** http://wwwstarradio.org.

12218 WQXE-FM - 98.3
Box 517 Phone: (502)737-8000
Elizabethtown, KY 42702 Fax: (502)737-7229
Free: (800)905-0983
E-mail: wqxe@skn.net; wqxe983@ne.infi.net

Format: Adult Contemporary. **Networks:** CNN Radio. **Owner:** Hardin Co. Broadcasting, Inc, at above address. **Founded:** 1969. **Operating Hours:** Continuous. **ADI:** Louisville, KY. **Key Personnel:** Cale Tharp, Program Dir.; Bill Evans, Manager; Lee Bramblett, News; Marilyn Evans, Public Relations. **Wattage:** 25,000. **Ad Rates:** $13-20 for 30 seconds; $15-22 for 60 seconds. Combined advertising rates available with WGGC-FM.

ELKTON†, pop. 1,815.

Todd Co. (SW) 20 m E of Hopkinsville. Manufactures men's clothing, die casting, refrigerator doors, concrete products. Meat product plant. Agriculture. Tobacco, grain, fruit. Beef cattle.

12219 Todd County Standard
PO Box 308 Phone: (502)265-2439
Public Sq. Fax: (502)265-2571
Elkton, KY 42220
Community newspaper. **Founded:** 1892. **Freq:** Weekly (Wed.). **Print Method:** Offset. **Cols./Page:** 6. **Col. Width:** 24 nonpareils. **Col. Depth:** 294 agate lines. **Key Personnel:** Mike Finch, Publisher, mfinch@pop3.kih.net. **USPS:** 632-580. **Subscription Rates:** $16 individuals. **Remarks:** Color advertising not accepted.
Ad Rates: GLR: $.27 **Circ:** ‡2,750
BW: $516
4C: $737.00
SAU: $4
PCI: $4.25

12220 WEKT-AM - 1070
Marion St. Phone: (502)265-5636
PO Box 577 Fax: (502)265-5637
Elkton, KY 42220

Format: News; Talk; Southern Gospel; Country. **Networks:** USA Radio. **Founded:** 1989. **Formerly:** WOAM-AM; WSRG-AM. **Operating Hours:** Sunrise-sunset. **Key Personnel:** Marshall E. Sidebottom, Contact. **Wattage:** 500. **Ad Rates:** $3.25-4 for 30 seconds; $5.25-6 for 60 seconds.

FALMOUTH†, pop. 2,482.

Pendleton Co. (N). On Licking River, 34 m S of Newport. Manufactures auto engines, feed. Dairy, poultry, grain farms. Hay, corn, tobacco.

12221 The Falmouth Outlook
Cynthiana Democrat
PO Box 111 Phone: (606)654-3332
Falmouth, KY 41040-0111 Fax: (606)654-4365

Community newspaper. **Founded:** June 1907. **Freq:** Weekly (Tues.). **Print Method:** Offset. **Cols./Page:** 6. **Col. Width:** 2 1/16 inches. **Col. Depth:** 21 1/2 inches. **Key Personnel:** Deborrah Dennie, Editor and Publisher. **ISSN:** 0891-8694. **Subscription Rates:** $22.50 individuals; $31.00 out of county; $40.00 out of state; $.75 single issue. **Remarks:** Accepts advertising. **Alt. Formats:** CD-ROM, MacIntosh; Microform.
Ad Rates: GLR: $6.32 **Circ:** Paid ⊕**4,013**
BW: $700 Free ⊕**8,207**
4C: $1,000
SAU: $6.32

12222 The Shopper's Outlook
Cynthiana Democrat
PO Box 111 Phone: (606)654-3332
Falmouth, KY 41040-0111 Fax: (606)654-4365

Shopper. **Subtitle:** The Shopper's Outlook. **Founded:** Mar. 1986. **Freq:** Weekly (Tues.). **Print Method:** Offset. Uses mats. **Cols./Page:** 6. **Col. Width:** 2 1/16 inches. **Col. Depth:** 21 1/2 inches. **Key Personnel:** Deborrah Dennie, Editor and Publisher, phone (606)654-3332. **Subscription Rates:** Free. **Remarks:** Color advertising accepted; rates available upon request. **Alt. Formats:** CD-ROM, MacIntosh; Microform; Mailing labels.
Ad Rates: GLR: $7.84 **Circ:** Free ‡8,207
BW: $700
4C: $1000
SAU: $7.84

12223 WIOK-FM - 107.5
PO Box 50 Phone: (606)472-6351
Falmouth, KY 41040 Fax: (606)472-2875

Format: Gospel. **Networks:** USA Radio; KyNet. **Owner:** Hammond Broadcasting Corp., at above address. **Founded:** 1981. **Operating Hours:** Continuous. **Key Personnel:** Bruce Edwards, Program Dir.; Jan Hammond, General Mgr.; Benny Bivins, Sales Mgr. **Wattage:** 6,000.

FLEMINGSBURG†, pop. 2,835.

Fleming Co. (NE). 54 m NE of Lexington. Land of covered bridges. Manufactures shoes, kitchen utensils, mobile homes, auto chrome. Agriculture. Cattle, tobacco, corn, chicken hatcheries.

12224 The Fleming Gazette
PO Box 32 Phone: (606)845-9211
Flemingsburg, KY 41041
Community newspaper. **Founded:** 1882. **Freq:** Weekly (Wed.). **Print Method:** Offset. **Cols./Page:** 6. **Col. Width:** 26 nonpareils. **Col. Depth:** 280 agate lines. **Key Personnel:** Lowell O. Denton, Publisher. **Subscription Rates:** $7.50 individuals; $5 students. **Remarks:** Accepts advertising.
Ad Rates: BW: $346.50 **Circ:** 3,600
SAU: $3.50

12225 WFLE-AM - 1060
RR. 3, No.1 Radio Dr. Phone: (606)849-4433
Fleming County Industrial Park Fax: (606)845-9353
Flemingsburg, KY 41041

Format: Country. **Networks:** CNN Radio; KyNet; Motor Sports Racing. **Owner:** Fleming County Broadcasting Co., Inc., at above address. **Founded:** 1985. **Operating Hours:** Sunrise-sunset; 90% network, 10% local. **ADI:** Lexington, KY. **Key Personnel:** Carl Haight, Manager. **Wattage:** 500. **Ad Rates:** $2.50 for 30 seconds; $4.50 for 60 seconds.

WFLE-FM - See Lexington

FLORENCE, pop. 15,586.

Boone Co. (N). 10 m S of Covington. Manufactures switchgears, sheet metal, paper bags. Dairy, poultry farms. Corn, tobacco.

12226 Boone County Recorder
Community Press of N. Kentucky
7736 US 42, Ste. D4 Phone: (606)283-0404
Florence, KY 41042 Fax: (606)283-7285
Free: (800)282-3859
Publication E-mail: rnewspaper@aol.com

Community newspaper. **Founded:** 1875. **Freq:** Weekly (Thurs.). **Print Method:** Offset. **Cols./Page:** 6. **Col. Width:** 12 picas. **Col. Depth:** 301 agate lines. **Key Personnel:** Amy Charley, Editor; Gene Clabes, Publisher. **Subscription Rates:** $18.02 individuals. **Remarks:** Accepts advertising.
Ad Rates: BW: $806.25 **Circ:** 7,800
4C: $1,156.25
SAU: $6.25

12227 Dixie News
Dixie News, Inc.
6603 Dixie Hwy. Phone: (606)371-6177
Florence, KY 41042-2199 Fax: (606)371-6306

Community newspaper. **Founded:** Apr. 1962. **Freq:** Weekly (Thurs.). **Print Method:** Offset. **Cols./Page:** 6. **Col. Width:** 21 nonpareils. **Col. Depth:** 224 agate lines. **Key Personnel:** Lee Thomas, Publisher; Ginny Huffaker, Office Mgr. **Remarks:** Accepts advertising.
Ad Rates: GLR: $0.60 **Circ:** Paid 500
BW: $581.79 Free 22,100
PCI: $9

12228 Kenton County Recorder
Community Press of N. Kentucky
7736 US 42, Ste. D4 Phone: (606)283-0404
Florence, KY 41042 Fax: (606)283-7285
Free: (800)282-3859

Community newspaper. **Founded:** 1977. **Freq:** Weekly (Wed.). **Print Method:** Offset. **Cols./Page:** 6. **Col. Width:** 12 picas. **Col. Depth:** 301 agate lines. **Key Personnel:** Gene Clabes, Publisher; Terry O'Connor, Managing Editor. **Subscription Rates:** $15.50 individuals. **Remarks:** Accepts advertising.
Ad Rates: GLR: $.20 **Circ:** ‡2,500
BW: $460
PCI: $5.75

FORT CAMPBELL

12229 Ft. Campbell Courier
Kentucky New Era
Public Affairs Office Phone: (502)798-6759
2334 19th St. Fax: (502)798-6247
Fort Campbell, KY 42223
Publication E-mail: sandersons@campbell-emh5.army.mil

Newspaper for the personnel of Ft. Campbell 101st Airborne Division (Air Assault) Military Base. **Founded:** 1950. **Freq:** Weekly (Thurs.). **Print Method:** Offset. **Trim Size:** 13 3/4 x 22 3/4. **Cols./Page:** 6. **Col. Width:** 12.2 picas. **Col. Depth:** 301 agate lines. **Key Personnel:** Robert Carter, Publisher; Karen Blick, Advertising Mgr. **Subscription Rates:** $42 individuals. **Remarks:** Accepts advertising. **URL:** http://www.campbell.army.mil/campbell.htm.
Ad Rates: BW: $1,096.50 **Circ:** Free 23,000
4C: $1,271.50
PCI: $8.50

FORT KNOX, pop. 37,700.

Hardin Co. (W) 10 m N. of Radcliff.

12230 Armor
U.S. Army Armor Center
ATZK-TDM Phone: (502)624-2249
Fort Knox, KY 40121-5210 Fax: (502)942-6219
Publication E-mail: armormag@ftknox2-emh3.army.mil

Military news magazine. **Founded:** 1888. **Freq:** Bimonthly. **Print Method:** Letterpress and offset. **Trim Size:** 8 1/4 x 11. **Cols./Page:** 3. **Col. Width:** 41 nonpareils. **Col. Depth:** 133 agate lines. **Key Personnel:** Major David L. Daigle, Editor-in-Chief, phone (502)264-2610, daigled@ftknox4-emh3.army.mit; Jon Clemens, Managing Editor, clemensj@ftknox2.emh3.army.mil. **ISSN:** 0004-2420. **Subscrip-**

tion Rates: $22 individuals; $3.00 single issue; $18 military; $35 other countries. **Remarks:** Advertising not accepted.
Circ: Paid 7,000
Non-paid 7,000

12231 Inside the Turret
News-Enterprise
PO Box 995 Phone: (502)624-1211
Fort Knox, KY 40121-0995 Fax: (502)624-6074

Newspaper for the military and civilian personnel of Ft. Knox. **Founded:** 1948. **Freq:** Weekly (Thurs.). **Print Method:** Offset. **Cols./Page:** 6. **Col. Width:** 2 1/2 inches. **Col. Depth:** 21 1/2 inches. **Key Personnel:** Larry Barnes, Editor; Cindy Smith, Advertising Mgr. **Remarks:** Accepts advertising.
Ad Rates: GLR: $.41 **Circ:** Free ‡20,000
BW: $786.90
4C: $1,026.90
SAU: $7.88
PCI: $6.60

FORT THOMAS, pop. 16,012.

Campbell Co. (E). 5 m NE of Southgate. Residential.

12232 Campbell County Recorder
Stepping Stone Publications
654 Highland Ave.
Fort Thomas, KY 41075

County newspaper. **Founded:** Jan. 12, 1977. **Freq:** Weekly (Wed.). **Print Method:** Offset. **Cols./Page:** 6. **Col. Width:** 2 1/16 inches. **Col. Depth:** 21 inches. **Key Personnel:** Gene Clabes, Publisher; Steve J. Olding, Editor; Sandra Cupps, Advertising Mgr. **Subscription Rates:** $13.78 individuals; $16.80 out of county; $23.10 out of state. **Remarks:** Accepts advertising. **Available Online. Alt. Formats:** CD-ROM.
Ad Rates: GLR: $.27 **Circ:** ‡3,500
SAU: $6

FRANKFORT†, pop. 25,973.

Franklin Co. (NC). The State Capital. On Kentucky River, 26 m W of Lexington. Kentucky State University. Manufactures candy, beef items used in restaurants, whiskey, air brake components, underwear, parts for automotive appliances, bimetallic temperature control devices, thermostats, variety of pumps, valves and transformers, auto parts. Tobacco, dairy, stock farms. Beef, feed.

12233 IAPES News
International Association of Personnel in Employment Security
1801 Louisville Rd. Phone: (502)223-4459
Frankfort, KY 40601 Fax: (502)223-4127

Tabloid on employment security, and association activities. **Founded:** 1941. **Freq:** Bimonthly (Feb., April, May, Aug., Oct., and Dec.). **Print Method:** Offset. **Trim Size:** 10 1/2 x 14. **Cols./Page:** 4. **Col. Width:** 28 nonpareils. **Col. Depth:** 182 agate lines. **Key Personnel:** Michael R. Stone, Editor. **ISSN:** 0020-6008. **Subscription Rates:** $25 individuals. **Remarks:** Accepts advertising. **Available Online. URL:** http://www.psro.com/IAPES.
Ad Rates: BW: $560 **Circ:** ‡22,000
PCI: $10

12234 Journal of Applied Aquaculture
The Haworth Press, Inc.
Kentucky State Univ. Phone: (502)564-9109
Aquaculture Research Ctr. Fax: (502)564-9118
Frankfort, KY 40601
Publisher E-mail: getinfo@haworthpressinc.com

Journal on culture of aquatic animals and plants. **Founded:** 1991. **Freq:** Quarterly. **Trim Size:** 6 x 8 1/2. **Key Personnel:** Carl Daivd Webster, Ph.D, Editor, cwebster@dcr.net; Bill Cohen, Publisher. **ISSN:** 1045-4438. **Subscription Rates:** $40 individuals; $75 institutions; $85 libraries. **Remarks:** Accepts advertising.
Ad Rates: BW: $300 **Circ:** Paid 301

12235 KEA News
Kentucky Education Association
401 Capital Ave. Phone: (502)875-2889
Frankfort, KY 40601 Fax: (502)227-8062

Newspaper (tabloid) for members of the Kentucky Education Association. **Freq:** Monthly (Sept.-June.). **Print Method:** Offset. **Trim Size:** 11 3/8 x 15. **Cols./Page:** 4. **Col. Width:** 2 5/16 inches. **Col. Depth:** 14 inches. **Key Personnel:** Jamie Morton, Editor. **ISSN:** 0165-3959. **Subscription Rates:** Free to qualified subscribers; $7 institutions; $5 libraries. **Remarks:** Accepts advertising.
Ad Rates: BW: $728 **Circ:** Free 39,000
PCI: $26.50

12236 Kentucky Afield
Kentucky Dept. of Fish and Wildlife Resources
Arnold L. Mitchell Bldg. Phone: (502)564-4336
1 Game Farm Rd. Fax: (502)564-6508
Frankfort, KY 40601
Free: (800)858-1549

Magazine focusing on wildlife and natural resources conservation. **Founded:** Dec. 1945. **Freq:** Quarterly plus annual July-June outdoor calendar. **Print Method:** Web offset. **Trim Size:** 8 1/2 x 11. **Cols./Page:** 3 and 2. **Col. Width:** 26 and 40 nonpareils. **Col. Depth:** 154 agate lines. **Key Personnel:** Carolyn Hughes-Lynn, Editor, carolyn.lynn@mail.state.ky.us; Barbara J. Pulliam, Branch Manager. **ISSN:** 1059-9177. **Subscription Rates:** $5 individuals; $9 two years; $2 single issue. **Remarks:** Advertising not accepted. **Alt. Formats:** Audio tape. **Formerly:** Kentucky Afield, The Magazine.
Circ: Paid ‡40,000
Controlled ‡4,000

12237 Kentucky Ancestors
Kentucky Historical Society
100 W. Broadway Phone: (502)564-3016
PO Box 1792 Fax: (502)564-4701
Frankfort, KY 40602-1792
Publication E-mail: tom.stephens@mail.state.ky.us

Journal featuring Kentucky family history. **Founded:** 1965. **Freq:** Quarterly. **Print Method:** Offset. **Trim Size:** 8 x 11 1/2. **Key Personnel:** Thomas E. Stephens, Editor, tom.stephens@mail.state.ky.us. **ISSN:** 0023-0103. **Subscription Rates:** $25 members of Kentucky Historical Society; $30 nonmembers. **Remarks:** Advertising not accepted.
Circ: Paid 4,000

12238 Kentucky Bench & Bar Magazine
Kentucky Bar Association
514 W. Main St. Phone: (502)564-3795
Frankfort, KY 40601-1883 Fax: (502)564-3225

Kentucky law journal. **Freq:** Bimonthly. **Print Method:** Offset. **Trim Size:** 8 1/2 x 11. **Cols./Page:** 3 and 2. **Col. Width:** 13 and 20 picas. **Col. Depth:** 60 picas. **Key Personnel:** Bruce K. Davis, Publisher, bdavis@kybar.org. **ISSN:** 0164-9345. **Subscription Rates:** $15 individuals. **Alt. Formats:** Audio tape; Microform.
Ad Rates: BW: $1,050 **Circ:** ‡12,100

12239 Kentucky Engineer
Kentucky Society of Professional Engineers
160 Democrat Dr. Phone: (502)695-5680
Frankfort, KY 40601 Fax: (502)695-0738
Free: (800)455-5573
Publisher E-mail: kspe@kyengcenter.org

General information for Kentucky engineers. **Subtitle:** The Official Publication of the Kentucky Society of Professional Engineers. **Founded:** 1935. **Freq:** Monthly. **Print Method:** 2 color press. **Trim Size:** 8 1/2 x 11. **Cols./Page:** 3. **Col. Width:** 13.5 picas. **Col. Depth:** 57 picas. **Key Personnel:** George Binder, Editor/Exec. Director, george@kyengcenter.org; Connie Davis, Asst. Editor/Publisher, connie@kyengcenter.org. **ISSN:** 0746-2255. **Subscription Rates:** $3 individuals. **Remarks:** Accepts advertising. **Available Online. URL:** http://www.kyengcenter.org.
Ad Rates: BW: $460 **Circ:** Paid ⊕5,593
4C: $1,010

12240 The Kentucky Journal
Kentucky Center for Public Issues
PO Box 1664 Phone: (502)227-1251
Frankfort, KY 40602-1664 Fax: (502)227-1256
Publication E-mail: kepi@mis.net

Statewide Policy Journal. **Founded:** 1989. **Freq:** Bimonthly. **Trim Size:** 11 1/2 x 15. **Key Personnel:** Diana J. Taylor, Editor, phone (502)226-3245, fax (502)226-2832; Bob Sexton, Publisher; Jennifer L. Bobbitt, Interim Dir. **ISSN:** 1063-9357. **Subscription Rates:** $24. **Remarks:** Accepts advertising.
Ad Rates: BW: $500 **Circ:** Paid 1,450
Non-paid 400

12241 Kentucky Libraries
1501 Twilight Trail Phone: (502)223-5322
Frankfort, KY 40601
Publication E-mail: kylibasn@mis.net

Library journal. **Founded:** 1933. **Freq:** Quarterly. **Print Method:** Offset. **Cols./Page:** 1. **Col. Width:** 54 nonpareils. **Col. Depth:** 98 agate lines. **Key Personnel:** Cecelia Tavanes, Editor. **Subscription Rates:** $18 individuals; $40 other countries.
Ad Rates: BW: $200 **Circ:** 1,800

12242 The Kentucky Pharmacist
Kentucky Pharmacists Association
1228 U.S. 127 S. Phone: (502)227-2303
Frankfort, KY 40601 Fax: (502)227-2258

Magazine on community and institutional pharmacy news. **Founded:** 1907. **Freq:** Monthly. **Print Method:** Offset. **Cols./Page:** 2 and 3. **Col. Width:** 54 and 36 nonpareils. **Col. Depth:** 140 agate lines. **Subscription Rates:** $30 individuals. **Remarks:** Accepts advertising.
Ad Rates: BW: $370 **Circ:** Paid ‡1,800
4C: $700 Non-paid ‡100

12243 Kentucky Prairie Farmer
Farm Progress Companies
10303 Vantage Rd. Phone: (502)266-9556
Jeffersontown, KY 40299 Fax: (502)266-9556

Magazine for commercial row-crop, tobacco, and livestock farmers in Kentucky. **Founded:** July 1989. **Freq:** 15/year. **Print Method:** Offset. **Trim Size:** 8 x 10 3/4. **Cols./Page:** 3. **Col. Width:** 2 1/8 inches. **Col. Depth:** 10 inches. **Key Personnel:** Tim Sickman, Editor, tsickman@chilton.net; Sara Wyant, Vice Pres., Editorial; Allan Johnson, President; Chuck Roth, Advertising Dir.; Paul Queck, Executive Editor; Tom Bechman, Associate Editor. **ISSN:** 0162-7104. **Subscription Rates:** Free to qualified subscribers. **Remarks:** Accepts advertising.
Ad Rates: BW: $1,600 **Circ:** ‡9,535
4C: $2,240
PCI: $17

12244 The Kentucky Press
Kentucky Press Association, Inc.
101 Consumer Ln. Phone: (502)223-8821
Frankfort, KY 40601 Fax: (502)226-3867

Magazine focusing on the newspaper industry. **Founded:** 1929. **Freq:** Monthly. **Print Method:** Offset. **Cols./Page:** 4. **Col. Width:** 14 picas. **Col. Depth:** 182 agate lines. **Key Personnel:** Lisa Carnahan, Editor, lcarnahan@kypress.com. **Subscription Rates:** $8 individuals. **Remarks:** Accepts advertising.
Ad Rates: GLR: $6 **Circ:** ‡750
BW: $300
SAU: $6

12245 Register of Kentucky Historical Society
Kentucky Historical Society
100 W. Broadway Phone: (502)564-3016
PO Box 1792 Fax: (502)564-4701
Frankfort, KY 40602-1792
Historical magazine. **Founded:** 1903. **Freq:** Quarterly. **Print Method:** Offset. **Trim Size:** 6 x 9. **Cols./Page:** 1. **Col. Width:** 30 nonpareils. **Col. Depth:** 102 agate lines. **Key Personnel:** Dr. Thomas H. Appleton, Jr., Editor, tom.appleton@mail.state.ky.us. **ISSN:** 0023-0243. **Subscription Rates:** $25 individuals; $35 institutions. **Remarks:** Advertising not accepted.
Circ: ‡4,400

12246 State Journal
Frankfort Publishing Co.
321 W. Main St. Phone: (502)227-4556
Frankfort, KY 40601-1864 Fax: (502)227-2831

General newspaper. **Founded:** 1912. **Freq:** Daily (eve.), Sunday (morn.). **Print Method:** Offset. **Cols./Page:** 6. **Col. Width:** 25 nonpareils. **Col. Depth:** 301 agate lines. **Key Personnel:** Carl West, Editor; Albert E. Dix, Publisher; C.A. McClain, Advertising Mgr. **Subscription Rates:** $75 individuals. **Remarks:** Accepts advertising.
Ad Rates: SAU: $5.38 **Circ:** Mon.-Fri. 8,829
Sun. 10,600

12247 Workforce Professional
International Association of Personnel in Employment Security
1801 Louisville Rd. Phone: (502)223-4459
Frankfort, KY 40601 Fax: (502)223-4127

Magazine about workforce training issues and employment. **Founded:** Mar. 1998. **Freq:** 8/year. **Print Method:** Offset. **Trim Size:** 11 3/8 x 16. **Cols./Page:** 4. **Col. Width:** 33 picas. **Col. Depth:** 194 picas. **Key Personnel:** Rebecca L. Martin, Editor. **ISSN:** 1063-4363. **Subscription Rates:** $25; $6 single issue. **Remarks:** Accepts advertising. **URL:** http://www.iapes.org. **Formerly:** Workforce; IAPES News; Workforce Journal; Perspective.
Ad Rates: BW: $650 **Circ:** Paid ‡16,000

12248 Frankfort Electric and Water Plant Board
317 W. 2nd Phone: (502)223-3401
Frankfort, KY 40602 Fax: (502)223-3887

Founded: 1952. **Key Personnel:** Warner Caines, General Mgr.; David Sandidge, Business Mgr.; John Higginbotham, Marketing, phone (502)227-4480, fax (502)223-4449, jhigginbotham@fewpb.com. **Cities Served:** Frankfort, Graefenburg,

Millville, Waddy, KY: subscribing households 17,400; 58 channels; 1 community access channel; 60 hours per week community access programming.

12249 WFKY-AM - 1490
1030 Burlington Ln. Phone: (502)223-8281
Frankfort, KY 40602 Fax: (502)223-0723
E-mail: wfky@cbcradio.net

Format: Oldies. **Networks:** CBS. **Owner:** Radio Enterprises, at above address. **Founded:** 1946. **Operating Hours:** 5:30 a.m.-midnight. **Local Programs:** *Focus on Frankfort,* Russ Hatter, Mailing contact; *High School Sports,* Steven King, Mailing contact; *On the Air with Steve King,* Steven King, Mailing contact. **Wattage:** 1000.

12250 WKED-AM - 1130
306 W. Main St., Ste. 509 Phone: (502)875-1130
Frankfort, KY 40601 Fax: (502)875-1225
E-mail: wked@kih.net

Networks: CBS; Westwood One Radio. **Founded:** 1977. **Operating Hours:** Daily. **ADI:** Lexington, KY. **Key Personnel:** Kenneth O. Mitchell, VP/Gen. Mgr.; Ken Mitchell, Sales Mgr.; John Roberts, Operations Manager; Tom Latek, News Dir.; Keith West, Program Dir. **Wattage:** 500. **Ad Rates:** $10-14 for 30 seconds; $12-16 for 60 seconds. Combined advertising rates available with WKED-FM.

12251 WKED-FM - 103.7
306 W. Main St., Ste. 509 Phone: (502)875-1130
Frankfort, KY 40601 Fax: (502)875-1225
E-mail: wked@kih.net

Format: Adult Contemporary. **Networks:** CNN Radio; Westwood One Radio. **Owner:** Commonwealth Broadcasting Corp., at above address. **Founded:** 1991. **Operating Hours:** Continuous. **ADI:** Lexington, KY. **Key Personnel:** Kenneth O. Mitchell, Vice Pres./Gen. Mgr.; Ken Mitchell, Sales Mgr.; John Roberts, Operations Director; Tom Latek, News Dir.; Keith West, Program Dir. **Wattage:** 2500. **Ad Rates:** $10-14 for 30 seconds; $12-16 for 60 seconds. Combined advertising rates available with WKED-AM.

FRANKLIN†, pop. 7,738.

Simpson Co. (SW). 21 m S of Bowling Green. Manufactures catalogs, corrugated boxes, aerosol & plastic containers, automotive parts, lumber, feed, rubber bands, tubing, adhesive tape. Hardwood timber. Agriculture. Tobacco, soybeans, grain, livestock.

12252 WFKN-AM - 1220
103 N. High St. Phone: (502)586-4481
PO Box 309 Fax: (502)586-6031
Franklin, KY 42135-0309

Format: Country. **Networks:** ABC; KyNet. **Owner:** Henderson Gleaner, at above address, (502)827-2000, Fax: (502)827-2765. **Founded:** 1954. **Operating Hours:** Continuous. **Key Personnel:** Henry Stone, General Mgr., phone (502)586-4481, fax (502)586-6031, franklinfavhs@kih.net; Tammie Gary, Contact. **Wattage:** 250. **Ad Rates:** $2.70-5.35 for 15 seconds; $4.10-7.70 for 30 seconds; $5.20-9.35 for 60 seconds.

FULTON, pop. 3,137.

Fulton Co. (SW). 48 m S of Paducah. Manufactures printing forms, car window units, gray iron castings, custiom built trailers, lumber, mechanical contracting, clothing & upholstery steamers, ready mix concrete. Oak timber. Seed packaging. Agricultural. Corn, soybeans, sausage.

12253 The Fulton Leader
Fulton Publishing Co.
Box 1200 Phone: (502)472-1121
Fulton, KY 42041 Fax: (502)472-1129
Publisher E-mail: fultonpub@aol.com

General newspaper. **Founded:** June 6, 1898. **Freq:** Weekly (Thurs.). **Print Method:** Offset. **Trim Size:** 13 1/2 x 22 3/4. **Cols./Page:** 6. **Col. Width:** 12 nonpareils. **Col. Depth:** 301 agate lines. **Key Personnel:** William Mitchell, Editor and Publisher. **Subscription Rates:** $35 individuals. **Remarks:** Accepts advertising.
Ad Rates: GLR: $.25 **Circ:** ‡3,150
BW: $469.56
SAU: $3.64

12254 WKZT-AM - 1270
Middle Rd. Hwy. 166 Phone: (502)472-1270
PO Box 1380 Fax: (502)472-1189
Fulton, KY 42041-0388

Format: Country. **Networks:** Independent. **Founded:** 1951. **Formerly:** WFUL-AM (1988). **Operating Hours:** Continuous. **Key Personnel:** Charles Whitlow, General Mgr.; Scott Bell, Program Dir. **Wattage:** 1000. **Ad Rates:** Advertising accepted; rates available upon request.

GARRISON

12255 WOKE-FM - 98.3
PO Box 889
Blacksburg, VA 24063

Format: Gospel. **Owner:** Big River Radio, Inc., at above address. **Operating Hours:** Continuous. **Key Personnel:** Mike Collins, General Mgr.; Vernon H. Baker, Vice President. **Wattage:** 6,000. **Ad Rates:** Underwriting available.

GEORGETOWN†, pop. 10,972.

Scott Co. (NC). 12 m N of Lexington. Georgetown College (Bapt). Seed cleaning, precision tool, electric wire, auto seat spring factories. Foreign motor industry. Agriculture. Tobacco, corn, wheat, cattle, horses.

12256 The Georgetonian
Georgetown College
400 E. College St. Phone: (502)863-8150
Georgetown, KY 40324-1628 Fax: (502)868-8888

Collegiate newspaper. **Subtitle:** Georgetown College Student Newspaper. **Founded:** 1904. **Freq:** Tuesday. **Print Method:** Offset. **Cols./Page:** 6. **Col. Width:** 18 nonpareils. **Col. Depth:** 224 agate lines. **Key Personnel:** Troy Teegarden, Editor, phone (502)863-8150. **Remarks:** Accepts advertising.
Ad Rates: BW: $150 **Circ:** Free ‡2,000
PCI: $1.75

12257 The Georgetown News Graphic
Georgetown Newspapers, Inc.
1481 Cherry Blossom Way Phone: (502)863-1111
PO Box 490 Fax: (502)863-6296
Georgetown, KY 40324
Publication E-mail: gtwnnews@mis.net

Newspaper. **Founded:** 1950. **Freq:** Sun., Wed., Fri. **Print Method:** Offset. **Cols./Page:** 6. **Col. Width:** 2 1/8 inches. **Col. Depth:** 21 1/2 inches. **Key Personnel:** Curtis M. Scogin, Publisher; Melissa Nipper, Editor. **ISSN:** 0886-5965. **Subscription Rates:** $45 individuals; $60 out of county. **Remarks:** Accepts advertising. **Formerly:** The Georgetown Graphic; The Georgetown News and Times.
Ad Rates: BW: $741.75 **Circ:** 4,500
4C: $916.75
PCI: $6.25

12258 WRVG-FM - 89.9
Georgetown College Phone: (502)863-8109
400 E. College St.
Georgetown, KY 40324
E-mail: mlibs0@gtc.georgeown.ky.us

Format: Eclectic. **Founded:** 1963. **Operating Hours:** Continuous. **Key Personnel:** Troy Teegaren, Contact. **Wattage:** 150.

GLASGOW†, pop. 12,958.

Barren Co. (SWC). 72 m SE of Louisville. Manufactures bearings, truck mirrors, axles, concrete products, capacitor, brush handles, computer cable assemblys, screws, ignition parts, mattresses, ink, overalls, garments. Hardwood timber. Agriculture. Tobacco, corn, poultry & dairy products.

12259 Glasgow Daily Times
Donrey Media Group
100 Commerce Dr. Phone: (502)678-5171
Glasgow, KY 42141 Fax: (502)678-5052

General newspaper. **Founded:** 1865. **Freq:** Daily (eve.), Sunday (morn.). **Print Method:** Letterpress and offset. **Cols./Page:** 6. **Col. Width:** 256 nonpareils. **Col. Depth:** 301 agate lines. **Subscription Rates:** $36 individuals.
Circ: 10,000
Sun. 10,000

12260 Glasgow Republican
Donrey Media Group
100 Commerce Dr. Phone: (502)678-5171
Glasgow, KY 42141-1153 Fax: (502)678-5052

General newspaper. **Freq:** Weekly (Thurs.). **Key Personnel:** Frances Bastien, Editor. **Subscription Rates:** $7 state; $9 out of state.
Circ: 1,500

12261 WGGC-FM - 95.1
510 Happy Valley Rd. Phone: (502)651-2142
Box 2099 Fax: (502)651-2141
Glasgow, KY 42142-0219
Free: (800)275-9442

Format: Country. **Owner:** Billy Evans, at above address. **Founded:** 1961. **Formerly:** WPRX-FM. **Operating Hours:** Continuous. **Key Personnel:** Bill Evans, General Mgr., bill@wggc.com; Darrin Evans, Sales Mgr., darrin@wggc.com; Joey Berry, News Dir., joe@wggc.com; Jim Decesare, Program Dir., jim@wggc.com. **Local Programs:** *U. K. Games & Shows,* Bill Evans, Mailing contact, (502)651-2142, Fax (502)651-2141. **Wattage:** 100,000 ERP. **Ad Rates:** $14-20 for 30 seconds; $17-32 for 60 seconds. Combined advertising rates available with WQXE-FM.

WKNK-FM - See Edmonton

12262 WPTQ-FM - 103.7
PO Box 457 Phone: (502)651-6050
Glasgow, KY 42142-0457 Fax: (502)651-7666

Format: Classic Rock. **Networks:** Unistar; CNN Radio. **Owner:** Newberry Broadcasting, Inc., at above address. **Founded:** 1988. **Formerly:** WHHT-FM. **Operating Hours:** Continuous. **ADI:** Nashville (Cookeville), TN. **Key Personnel:** Steven W. Newberry, President; Derron Steenbergen, General Mgr. **Wattage:** 25,000. **Ad Rates:** $10-12 for 30 seconds; $12-14 for 60 seconds. WOVO-FM, WHHT-FM, WCDS-AM.

GRAYSON†, pop. 3,423.

Carter Co. (NE), 15 m SW of Ashland. Residential.

12263 Grayson Journal-Enquirer
Park Newspapers of Morehead, Inc.
113 S. Hord St. Phone: (606)474-5101
PO Box 578 Fax: (606)474-0013
Grayson, KY 41143
Community newspaper. **Founded:** 1969. **Freq:** Weekly (Wed.). **Print Method:** Offset. **Cols./Page:** 6. **Col. Width:** 12 picas. **Col. Depth:** 21 1/2 inches. **Key Personnel:** Becky Walker, Editor. **Subscription Rates:** $15 individuals. **Remarks:** Accepts advertising.
Ad Rates: SAU: $4.05 **Circ:** Paid ‡3,542
PCI: $3.37

12264 WGOH-AM - 1370
US-60 W. Phone: (606)474-5144
Grayson, KY 41143 Fax: (606)474-7777
E-mail: goradis@kcc.edu

Format: Country. **Networks:** CBS. **Owner:** Carter County Broadcasting, Inc., PO Box 487, Grayson, KY 41143. **Founded:** 1959. **Operating Hours:** 15 hours daily; 90% local. **Key Personnel:** Francis Nash, General Mgr.; Jim Phillips, News Dir.; Jeff Roe, Traffic Mgr. **Wattage:** 5000. **Ad Rates:** $2.20-3 for 15 seconds; $3.20-4 for 30 seconds; $4-5 for 60 seconds.

12265 WKCC-FM - 96.7
617 N. Carol Malone Blvd. Phone: (606)474-3749
Grayson, KY 41143-1123

Format: Religious; Contemporary Christian. **Networks:** USA Radio. **Owner:** Kentucky Christian College, at above address. **Founded:** 1973. **Operating Hours:** 6:30 a.m.-10 a.m. and 2 p.m.-midnight; 80% local. **Key Personnel:** Mic Marshall, General Mgr. **Wattage:** 10. **Ad Rates:** Noncommercial.

12266 WUGO-FM - 102.3
US-60 W. Phone: (606)474-5144
Grayson, KY 41143 Fax: (606)474-7777
E-mail: goradio@koc.edu

Format: Adult Contemporary. **Networks:** CBS. **Owner:** Carter County Broadcasting Co., Inc., PO Box 487, Grayson, KY 41143. **Founded:** 1967. **Operating Hours:** 6 a.m.-midnight. **Key Personnel:** Francis Nash, Manager; Jim Phillips, News Dir.; Jeff Roe, Traffic Dir. **Wattage:** 4800. **Ad Rates:** $2.20-3.50 for 15 seconds; $3.20-4.80 for 30 seconds; $4-6 for 60 seconds.

GREENSBURG†, pop. 2,377.

Green Co. (SC). On Green River, 70 m S of Louisville. Cedar timber; sawmills; wood components, stave, wire and cable, rattan furniture, work clothing, novelties factories; tobacco warehouse; gas chemical stripping plant. Church steeples. Tobacco, grain farms.

12267 Record-Herald
PO Box 130 Phone: (502)932-4381
Greensburg, KY 42743 Fax: (502)932-4441

Newspaper. **Founded:** 1895. **Freq:** Weekly (Thurs.). **Print Method:** Offset. **Cols./Page:** 6. **Col. Width:** 24 nonpareils. **Col. Depth:** 210 agate lines. **Key Personnel:** Walt Gorin,

Publisher. **Subscription Rates:** $10.50 individuals. **Remarks:** Accepts advertising.
Ad Rates: BW: $497.94 **Circ:** 4,587
SAU: $3.86

12268 WAKY-AM - 1550
Box 246 Phone: (502)932-7401
Greensburg, KY 42743 Fax: (502)932-7402

Format: Oldies. **Founded:** 1972. **Formerly:** WGRK-AM. **Operating Hours:** Sunrise-sunset. **Key Personnel:** Michael R. Wilson, Contact; Joy Wilson, Sales Mgr. **Wattage:** 1000.

GREENUP†, pop. 1,386.

Greenup Co. (NE). On Ohio River, 14 m W of Ashland. Steel plant; sawmills. Truck, grain farms.

12269 The Greenup News
Park Newspapers of Morehead, Inc.
PO Box 724 Phone: (606)473-9851
Greenup, KY 41144 Fax: (606)473-7591

Newspaper with a Democratic orientation. **Founded:** 1855. **Freq:** Weekly (Thurs.). **Print Method:** Offset. **Cols./Page:** 6. **Col. Width:** 12 picas. **Col. Depth:** 21.5 inches. **Key Personnel:** Jeffery Fannin, General Mgr. **Subscription Rates:** $12 individuals. **Remarks:** Accepts advertising.
Ad Rates: SAU: $3.66 **Circ:** ‡3,768
PCI: $2.87

12270 WLGC-AM - 1520
PO Box 685 Phone: (606)473-7377
Greenup, KY 41144 Fax: (606)473-5086
Free: (800)551-1057

Format: Sports. **Founded:** 1985. **Formerly:** WTCV-AM (1990). **Operating Hours:** Continuous; 95% network, 5% local. **ADI:** Charleston-Huntington, WV. **Key Personnel:** Robert L. Scheilby, Contact; Kent Robinson, Sports Dir.; Tito LaFrond, News Dir. **Wattage:** 5000. **Ad Rates:** $7-11.20 for 60 seconds.

12271 WLGC-FM - 105.7
Main & Harrison Sts., Ste. A Phone: (606)473-7377
Greenup, KY 41144 Fax: (606)473-5086
Free: (800)551-1057

Format: Country. **Founded:** 1982. **Operating Hours:** Continuous; 100% local. **ADI:** Charleston-Huntington, WV. **Key Personnel:** Robert L. Scheilby, Contact; Mark Justice, Program Dir.; Tito LaFrond, News Dir.; Swifty Salyers, Sports Dir.; Paul Mudrak, General Sales Mgr. **Local Programs:** *The Breakfast Club*, Mark Justice; *Ernie Anderson Show*, Mark Justice; *Ron Meade Show*, Mark Justice. **Wattage:** 25,000. **Ad Rates:** $15 for 60 seconds.

GREENVILLE†.

Muhlenberg Co.

12272 WKYA-FM - 105.5
464 State Rte. 189 S. Phone: (502)338-6655
Greenville, KY 42345 Fax: (502)338-7388

Format: Country. **Operating Hours:** Continuous. **Wattage:** 5000.

HARDINSBURG†, pop. 2,211.

Breckinridge Co. (WC). 50 m SW of Louisville. Residential.

12273 Breckinridge County Herald-News
US 60 E. Phone: (502)756-2109
PO Box 6 Fax: (502)756-1003
Hardinsburg, KY 40143
County newspaper. **Founded:** 1878. **Freq:** Weekly (Wed.). **Print Method:** Offset. **Cols./Page:** 6. **Col. Depth:** 21 inches. **Key Personnel:** Nancy L. Beard, Editor; Brucie Beard, Publisher. **USPS:** 551-040. **Subscription Rates:** $10.60 individuals; $15.90 out of county; $25 out of state. **Remarks:** Accepts advertising.
Ad Rates: GLR: $4.50 **Circ:** Paid ‡5,600
BW: $441
4C: $240
SAU: $3.50

HARLAN†, pop. 3,024.

Harlan Co. (SE). 30 m NE of Middlesboro. Coal mines. Hardwood timber. Manufactures sign and sheet metal fabrication, electrical coils, beverages. Dairy processing plants. Truck farms.

12274 The Harlan Daily Enterprise
American Publishing Co.
1548 S. U.S. Hwy. 421 Phone: (606)573-4510
PO Box E Fax: (606)573-0042
Harlan, KY 40831
General newspaper. **Founded:** 1901. **Freq:** Mon.-Sat. (eve.). **Print Method:** Offset. **Cols./Page:** 6. **Col. Width:** 25 nonpareils. **Col. Depth:** 301 agate lines. **Key Personnel:** Jeff Phillips, Exec. Editor; Joe Ben Oller, Publisher. **ISSN:** 1041-7109. **Subscription Rates:** $75 individuals. **Remarks:** Accepts advertising.
Ad Rates: GLR: $.24 **Circ:** 6,766
BW: $1,180.35
4C: $1,461.15
SAU: $9.15
PCI: $7.85

12275 Harlan Community Television Inc.
1st & Eversole Phone: (606)573-2945
Box 592 Fax: (606)573-6959
Harlan, KY 40831

Key Personnel: Charles Hale, Contact. **Cities Served:** subscribing households 3,250; 32 channels.

12276 WFSR-AM - 970
125 S. Main St. Phone: (606)573-1470
PO Box 818 Fax: (606)573-1473
Harlan, KY 40831

Format: News; Sports; Country; Religious. **Networks:** CNN Radio; Unistar. **Owner:** Mark L. Ford, at above address. **Founded:** 1970. **Operating Hours:** 6 a.m.-midnight. **Key Personnel:** Jeff Capps, General Mgr./Production Dir.; Pat Gross, Public Service Announcement Mgr.; Russ Laferty, Chief Engineer. **Wattage:** 5000. **Ad Rates:** $4.12-5.06 for 15 seconds; $5.50-7.75 for 30 seconds; $6.50-9.75 for 60 seconds. Combined advertising rates available with WTUK-FM. **URL:** http://www.harlanco.com.

12277 WHLN-AM - 1410
PO Box 898 Phone: (606)573-2540
Harlan, KY 40831 Fax: (606)573-7557

Format: Oldies. **Networks:** Jones Satellite. **Owner:** James T. Morgan, at above address. **Founded:** 1941. **Operating Hours:** Sunrise-sunset; 85% network, 15% local. **ADI:** Knoxville (Crossville), TN. **Key Personnel:** James T. Morgan, President; James O. Morgan, Vice President; Dorothy Morgan, Contact. **Wattage:** 5000. **Ad Rates:** Advertising accepted; rates available upon request.

12278 WTUK-FM - 105.1
125 S. Main St. Phone: (606)573-1470
PO Box 818 Fax: (606)573-1473
Harlan, KY 40831

Format: Top 40; Adult Contemporary. **Networks:** Westwood One Radio; CNN Radio. **Owner:** Mark L. Ford, at above address. **Founded:** 1990. **Operating Hours:** Continuous. **Key Personnel:** Jeff Capps, Gen. Mgr./Production Dir.; Pat Gross, Public Service Announcement Mgr.; Russ Laferty, Chief Engineer. **Wattage:** 6000. **Ad Rates:** $4.75-7.75 for 30 seconds; $5.75-9.75 for 60 seconds. Combined advertising rates available with WFSR-AM. **URL:** http://www.harlan.co.com.

HAROLD

Floyd Co.

12279 Inter Mountain Cable Inc.
Box 159 Phone: (606)478-9406
Harold, KY 41635 Fax: (606)478-3650
E-mail: htc@castky.com

Founded: 1965. **Formerly:** Tel Com, Inc. **Key Personnel:** Paul D. Gearhart, Manager. **Cities Served:** Pine Magoffin County, Johnson County, and Floyd County, KY; Mingo County, WV; and Buchanan County, VA.: subscribing households 28,000; 31 channels; 1 community access channel; 18 hours per week community access programming.

HARRODSBURG†, pop. 7,265.

Mercer Co. (C). 30 m SW of Lexington. Manufactures men's coats, cheese, optical glass, bathroomfixtures, air conditioning coils, packaging foam, auto parts, brush and contact manufacture dust arresting equipment. Agriculture. Tobacco, wheat, dairy.

12280 The Harrodsburg Herald
PO Box 68 Phone: (606)734-2726
Harrodsburg, KY 40330-0068 Fax: (606)734-0737
Free: (800)803-1184

Newspaper with a Democratic orientation. **Founded:** 1884. **Freq:** Weekly (Thurs.). **Print Method:** Offset. **Trim Size:** 6 x 21 1/2. **Cols./Page:** 6. **Col. Width:** 26 nonpareils. **Col. Depth:** 297 agate lines. **Key Personnel:** Bill Randolph, Editor. **Subscription Rates:** $28 individuals. **Remarks:** Advertising not accepted for alcoholic beverages.
Ad Rates: GLR: $5.04 **Circ:** Thurs. ★**5,740**
BW: $650.16
PCI: $5.04

12281 TCI North Central Kentucky
Box 218 Phone: (606)734-2305
Harrodsburg, KY 40330 Fax: (606)734-5755
Free: (800)273-8039

Key Personnel: C.B. Roland, Contact; Thomas Johnson, General Mgr. **Cities Served:** subscribing households 15,000; 36 channels; 3 community access channels; 168 hours per week community access programming.

12282 WHBN-AM - 1420
400 Beaumont Ave. Phone: (606)734-4321
PO Box 247 Fax: (606)734-5786
Harrodsburg, KY 40330

Format: Country. **Owner:** Mortenson Broadcasting Company, 3270 Blazer Broadway, Ste. 101, Lexington, KY 40509. **Founded:** 1955. **Formerly:** Fort Harrod Broadcasting Corp. **Operating Hours:** 6 a.m.-midnight. **Key Personnel:** Nadine Cole, General Mgr.; Donna Graham, Station Mgr. **Wattage:** 1000. **Ad Rates:** $3.25-4.90 for 30 seconds; $5.20-7.50 for 60 seconds.

12283 WHBN-FM - 99.3
400 Beaumont Ave. Phone: (606)734-4321
PO Box 247 Fax: (606)734-5786
Harrodsburg, KY 40330

Format: Country. **Owner:** Fort Harrod Broadcasting Corp., at above address. **Founded:** 1969. **Operating Hours:** 6 a.m.-midnight. **Key Personnel:** Robert L. Martin, General Mgr., phone (606)734-4321; Nadine Cole, News Dir., phone (606)734-4321. **Wattage:** 3000 ERP. **Ad Rates:** $3.25-4.900 for 30 seconds; $5.20-7.50 for 60 seconds.

HARTFORD†, pop. 2,512.

Ohio Co. (WC). On Rough River, 25 m E of Owensboro. Oil wells; coal mines; limestone quarries; manufactures gloves, auto parts, chemicals. Agriculture. Corn, tobacco, hay.

12284 Ohio County Times-News
Andy Anderson Inc.
108 Center St. Phone: (502)298-7100
PO Box 226 Fax: (502)298-9572
Hartford, KY 42347
Community newspaper. **Founded:** Oct. 30, 1980. **Freq:** Weekly (Thurs.). **Print Method:** Offset. **Cols./Page:** 6. **Col. Width:** 28 nonpareils. **Col. Depth:** 301 agate lines. **Key Personnel:** Dave McBride, Editor; Mrs. A. Anderson, Publisher. **Subscription Rates:** $8 individuals; $15 institutions. **Remarks:** Accepts advertising.
Ad Rates: GLR: $.26 **Circ:** ‡6,700
BW: $322.50
4C: $200
SAU: $4.02
PCI: $4.02

12285 WSNR-AM - 1600
Box 106 Phone: (502)298-3268
Hartford, KY 42347-0106 Fax: (502)298-9326

Format: News; Sports. **Founded:** 1969. **Formerly:** WLLS-AM. **Operating Hours:** 6 a.m.-sunset. **ADI:** Evansville, IN (Madisonville, KY). **Key Personnel:** Lloyd Spivey, General Mgr. **Wattage:** 1000. **Ad Rates:** $3.30 for 30 seconds; $4.50 for 60 seconds.

HAWESVILLE†, pop. 1,036.

Hancock Co. (WC). On Ohio River, 28 m NE of Owensboro. Aluminum product factories. Paper mill. Coal mines. Oil wells. Agriculture. Tobacco, corn, wheat.

12286 Hancock Clarion
Main St. Phone: (502)927-6945
Hawesville, KY 42348 Fax: (502)927-6947
Free: (800)337-0585

Community newspaper. **Founded:** Mar. 4, 1896. **Freq:** Weekly (Thurs.). **Print Method:** Offset. **Cols./Page:** 6. **Col. Width:** 2.25 picas. **Col. Depth:** 21 inches. **Key Personnel:** Donn K. Wimmer, Editor and Publisher; Cathy Sabelhaus, Advertising Mgr. **Subscription Rates:** $19 individuals. **Remarks:** Accepts advertising.
Ad Rates: BW: $661.50 **Circ:** ‡4,100
4C: $786.50
PCI: $5.25

HAZARD†, pop. 5,429.

Perry Co. (SE). 117 m SE of Lexington. Buckhorn Lake State Resort Park. Coal, oil & natural gas. Hardwood timber. Bottling works. Steel fabrication.

12287 Hazard Herald-Voice
548 Main St. Phone: (606)436-5771
PO Box 869 Fax: (606)436-3140
Hazard, KY 41701
Newspaper. **Founded:** 1911. **Freq:** Weekly (Wed.). **Print Method:** Offset. **Cols./Page:** 6. **Col. Width:** 12 picas. **Col. Depth:** 21.5 inches. **Key Personnel:** Mike Kindahl, Editor and Publisher. **Subscription Rates:** $17 county; $20 county; $23 out of state. **Remarks:** Accepts advertising.
Ad Rates: BW: $838.50 **Circ:** ‡5,126
4C: $1,151.69
SAU: $7.61
PCI: $7.61

12288 Community TV Inc.
364 Riverview Dr. Phone: (606)436-4593
Hazard, KY 41701

12289 WEKH-FM - 90.9
c/o WEKU-FM Phone: (606)622-1655
Eastern Kentucky University Free: (800)621-8890
102 Perkins
Richmond, KY 40475
E-mail: weku@acs.eku.edu

Format: News; Classical; Public Radio. **Networks:** National Public Radio (NPR). **Owner:** Eastern Kentucky University Board of Regents, at above address. **Founded:** 1985. **Operating Hours:** Continuous; 15% network, 85% local. **Key Personnel:** Timothy J. Singleton, Station Mgr., phone (606)622-1655; Marie Mitchell, News Dir.; John Francis, Program Dir. **Wattage:** 33,000. **Ad Rates:** Noncommercial. **URL:** http://www.weku.org/.

12290 WJMD-FM - 104.7
PO Box 7001 Phone: (606)439-3358
Hazard, KY 41702 Fax: (606)436-6118

Format: Religious; Southern Gospel. **Networks:** USA Radio. **Owner:** Hazard Broadcasting Services, Inc., at above address. **Founded:** 1989. **Operating Hours:** Continuous. **ADI:** Lexington, KY. **Key Personnel:** Michael Barnett, General Mgr.; Steve Napier, Operations Mgr.; Lema Barnett, Business Mgr. **Wattage:** 6,000. **Ad Rates:** $5 for 30 seconds; $7 for 60 seconds.

12291 WKHA-TV - 35
c/o Kentucky Educational TV Phone: (606)258-7000
600 Cooper Dr. Fax: (606)258-7399
Lexington, KY 40502
Free: (800)926-7765

Format: Public TV. **Networks:** Public Broadcasting Service (PBS); Kentucky Educational Television. **Owner:** Kentucky Authority for Public TV, at above address, (606)258-7170, Fax: (606)258-7390. **Founded:** 1968. **Operating Hours:** 6:15 a.m.-midnight. **ADI:** Lexington, KY. **Key Personnel:** Craig Cornwell, Contact; J. Gorman, Contact; D. Holtzclaw, Contact; M. Ferguson, Contact; S. Talbert, Contact; Virginia Gaines Fox, Contact, gfox@msmail.ket.org; Donna Moore, Contact; Sally Hamilton, Contact; William Wilson, Contact; D. Hoffman, Contact; B. Ball, Contact; L. Hobson, Contact; J. Holbrook, Contact; T. Tucker, Contact. **Local Programs:** *Comment on Kentucky*; *Kentucky Afield*; *Kentucky Life*; *Kentucky Tonight*; *Legislative Weekly*. **Wattage:** 646,000. **Ad Rates:** Noncommercial. **URL:** http://www.ket.org.

12292 WKIC-AM - 1390
PO Box 7898 Phone: (606)436-2121
Hazard, KY 41702-7898 Fax: (606)436-4172

Format: Contemporary Hit Radio (CHR). **Networks:** ABC; KyNet. **Founded:** 1947. **Operating Hours:** 6 a.m.-sunset. **ADI:** Lexington, KY. **Key Personnel:** Ernest Sparkman, Contact; Faron Sparkman, Music Dir.; Stuart Shane, News Dir.; Paula Campbell, Program Dir.; Julius Lasslo, Sports Dir.; Robert Hale, Chief Engineer; Teresa Grender, Contact. **Wattage:** 5000. **Ad Rates:** $5 for 30 seconds; $7 for 60 seconds.

12293 WQXY-AM - 1560
PO Box 1981 Phone: (606)436-0156
Hazard, KY 41702-1981 Fax: (606)436-0156

Format: Oldies; News. **Networks:** Satellite Music Network. **Owner:** Black Gold Broadcasting, at above address. **Founded:** 1988. **Formerly:** WYZQ-AM. **Operating Hours:** Sunrise-sunset; 70% network, 30% local. **ADI:** Lexington, KY. **Key Personnel:** Carlen E. Dixon, News Dir.; William D. Gorman, Program Dir.; R. Brian Baker, General Mgr.; Loretta Burns, Office Mgr. **Wattage:** 1000. **Ad Rates:** $3.75 for 30 seconds; $5 for 60 seconds.

12294 WSGS-FM - 101.1
PO Box 7898 Phone: (606)436-2121
Hazard, KY 41702

Format: Country. **Networks:** ABC. **Owner:** Mountain Broadcasting Service, Inc., at above address. **Founded:** 1959. **Operating Hours:** Continuous. **ADI:** Lexington, KY. **Key Personnel:** Ernest Sparkman, General Mgr. **Wattage:** 100,000. **Ad Rates:** $8-13 for 30 seconds; $10-17 for 60 seconds. $8-$13 for 30 seconds; $10-$17 for 60 seconds. Combined advertising rates available with WKIC-AM.

12295 WYMT-TV - 57
4 Black Gold Blvd Phone: (606)436-5757
Box 1299
Hazard, KY 41702

Format: Commercial TV. **Networks:** CBS. **Owner:** Gray Communications Systems, 126 N. Washington St., Albany, GA 31701. **Founded:** 1969. **Operating Hours:** 5 a.m.-1 a.m. **ADI:** Lexington, KY. **Key Personnel:** Rita Olinger, Production Mgr.; Ernestine Cornett, General Mgr.; Tony Turner, News Dir.; Sharon Linoon, Programmer; John Lewis, Sports Dir.; Jim Boggs, General Sales Mgr.; Louise Sizemore, Office Mgr.; Doris Craft, Traffic Dir.; Ken Fugate, Production Special Projects; Phil Hayes, Chief Engineer. **Ad Rates:** Advertising accepted; rates available upon request.

HENDERSON†, pop. 24,834.

Henderson Co. (WC). On Ohio River, 7 m S of Evansville, Ind, with bridge connections. Manufactures aluminum, truck axles, tire rims, chemicals plastics, ammonia, furniture, castings, composite cans, wood products, brushes. River terminal for agricultural, petroleum and other products. Agricultural. Soybeans, tobacco, cattle.

12296 The Hill
Henderson Community College
2660 S. Green Phone: (502)827-1867
Henderson, KY 42420-4699 Fax: (502)827-8635
Publication E-mail: thehill@pop.uky.edu

Collegiate tabloid. **Founded:** Sept. 1978. **Freq:** Monthly. **Print Method:** Offset. **Cols./Page:** 5. **Col. Width:** 22 nonpareils. **Col. Depth:** 182 agate lines. **Key Personnel:** Craig Beaven, Editor; Tony Strawn, Publisher; Joe Galloway, Advertising Mgr. **Subscription Rates:** Free. **Available Online. URL:** http://www.hence.uky.edu/thehill.
Ad Rates: BW: $110 **Circ:** Non-paid ‡1,200
PCI: $5

12297 WKDQ-FM - 99.5
Box 435 Phone: (502)827-8995
Henderson, KY 42420-0435 Fax: (502)827-5756

Format: Contemporary Country. **Networks:** ABC. **Owner:** W.L. Nininger, Box 1389, Bristol, VA 24203. **Founded:** 1947. **Operating Hours:** Continuous. **Key Personnel:** Mike Robinson, General Mgr. **Wattage:** 100,000. **Ad Rates:** Advertising accepted; rates available upon request.

12298 WKOH-TV - 31
c/o Kentucky Authority for Educational TV Phone: (606)258-7000
Fax: (606)258-7399
600 Cooper Dr.
Lexington, KY 40502
Free: (800)926-7765

Format: Public TV. **Networks:** Public Broadcasting Service (PBS); Kentucky Educational Television. **Owner:** Kentucky Authority for Educational TV, at above address, (606)258-7170, Fax: (606)258-7390. **Founded:** 1980. **Operating Hours:** 6:15 a.m.-midnight. **ADI:** Evansville, IN (Madisonville, KY). **Key Personnel:** Craig Cornwell, Contact; J. Gorman, Contact; D. Holtzclaw, Contact; M. Ferguson, Contact; S. Talbert, Contact; Virginia Gaines Fox, Contact, gfox@msmail.ket.org; Donna Moore, Contact; Sally Hamilton, Contact; William Wilson, Contact; D. Hoffman, Contact; L. Hobson, Contact; B. Ball, Contact; J. Holbrook, Contact; T. Tucker, Contact. **Local Programs:** *Comment on Kentucky*; *Kentucky Afield*; *Kentucky Life*; *Kentucky Tonight*; *Legislative Weekly*. **Wattage:** 708,000. **Ad Rates:** Noncommercial. **URL:** http:/www.ket.org.

12299 WSON-AM - 860
230 2nd St. Phone: (502)826-3923
PO Box 418 Fax: (502)826-7572
Henderson, KY 42420

Format: News; Sports; Big Band/Nostalgia; Easy Listening; Agricultural; Oldies. **Networks:** Satellite Music Network. **Owner:** Henry G. Lackey, at above address. **Founded:** 1941. **Operating Hours:** Continuous. **Key Personnel:** Henry G. Lackey, Contact; Bill Stephens, Contact; Darlene Daniel, Office Mgr.; Wade Gish, Sales Mgr. **Wattage:** 500. **Ad Rates:** $15-17 for 30 seconds; $18-20 for 60 seconds.

HICKMAN†, pop. 2,894.

Fulton Co. (SW). On Mississippi River, 55 m SW of Paducah. Hunting and fishing area. Graphite products, clothing factories. General cargo loading and unloading facilities. Diversified farming. Soybeans, corn, wheat, hay.

12300 The Hickman Courier
1232 Moscow Ave. Phone: (502)236-2726
Hickman, KY 42050-0070 Fax: (502)236-2726

Community newspaper with a Democratic orientation, includes sections on agriculture. **Founded:** 1859. **Freq:** Weekly (Thurs.). **Print Method:** Offset. **Trim Size:** 7 x 11. **Cols./Page:** 6. **Col. Width:** 12 nonpareils. **Col. Depth:** 294 agate lines. **Key Personnel:** Paul Westpheling, Jr., Publisher; John O. Jones, Editor. **USPS:** 243-200. **Subscription Rates:** $16 individuals; $18 out of area. **Remarks:** Accepts advertising.
Ad Rates: GLR: $.19 **Circ:** ‡2,550
BW: $322.50
4C: $70
SAU: $3.00
PCI: $3.75

HIGHLAND HEIGHTS

12301 WNKU-FM - 89.7
301 Landrum Phone: (606)572-6500
Highland Heights, KY 41076 Fax: (606)572-6604
E-mail: wnku@nku.edu

Format: News; Adult Album Alternative. **Networks:** National Public Radio (NPR); Public Radio International (PRI). **Founded:** 1985. **Operating Hours:** anywhere from 5 a.m.-2 a.m.; 25% network, 75% local. **ADI:** Cincinnati, OH. **Key Personnel:** David Arnold, General Mgr.; Grady Kirkpatrick, Program Dir.; Maryanne Zeleznik, News Dir.; Stacy Owen, Music Dir. **Wattage:** 12,000. **Ad Rates:** Noncommercial. **URL:** http://www.nku.edu/wnku.

HINDMAN†, pop. 876.

Knott Co. (SE). 15 m NE of Hazard. Residential.

12302 Troublesome Creek Times
Knott County Publishing Co., Inc.
PO Box 700 Phone: (606)785-5134
Hindman, KY 41822-0700 Fax: (606)785-0105
Publisher E-mail: possum@tgtel.com

Local newspaper. **Subtitle:** Voice of Knott County. **Founded:** 1980. **Freq:** Weekly (Wed.). **Print Method:** Offset. **Trim Size:** 28. **Cols./Page:** 6. **Col. Width:** 25 nonpareils. **Col. Depth:** 301 agate lines. **Key Personnel:** Ron Daley, Editor and Publisher. **USPS:** 583-210. **Subscription Rates:** $15 individuals. **Remarks:** Accepts advertising.
Ad Rates: GLR: $.21 **Circ:** ‡4,300
BW: $387
4C: $647
SAU: $3.95

12303 TV Service Inc.
Box 698 Phone: (606)785-3450
Hindman, KY 41822 Fax: (606)785-3110

Owner: Robert C. Thacker, at above address. **Founded:** 1966. **Key Personnel:** Archie Everage, Manager. **Cities Served:** Knott, Perry, Floyd, and Letcher Counties: subscribing households 10,300; 31 channels; 2 community access channels; 15 hours per week community access programming.

12304 United Cable Systems Inc.
Box 698 Phone: (606)785-3450
Hindman, KY 41822 Fax: (606)785-3110

Key Personnel: Robert C. Thacker, Contact; Archie Everage, Manager. **Cities Served:** Perry and Letcher Counties: subscribing households 5,153; 35 channels; 1 community access channel; 17 hours per week community access programming.

HODGENVILLE†, pop. 2,459.

Larue Co. (WC). 60 m S of Louisville. Manufactures uniforms, limestone quarries; gas wells. Grist, sawmills; hatchery. Tobacco, corn, stock farms.

12305 LaRue County Herald News
Landmark Community Newspapers, Inc.
40 Shawnee Dr. Phone: (502)358-3118
Hodgenville, KY 42748 Fax: (502)358-4852
Publication E-mail: lcherald@ne.infi.net

Community newspaper. **Founded:** 1885. **Freq:** Weekly (Wed.). **Print Method:** Offset. **Cols./Page:** 6. **Col. Width:** 12 nonpareils. **Col. Depth:** 301 agate lines. **Key Personnel:** Debbie Polly, Editor/Gen. Mgr.; Delphia O'Bryant, Office Mgr.;

Kim Davenport, Sales Rep. **USPS:** 241-220. **Subscription Rates:** $20.14 individuals; $32.50 out of state. **Remarks:** Accepts advertising.
Ad Rates: BW: $568.89 **Circ:** ‡3,975
4C: $793.89
SAU: $5.54
PCI: $4.71

HOPKINSVILLE†, pop. 27,318.

Christian Co. (SW). 50 m W of Bowling Green. University of Kentucky Community College. Manufactures concrete products, automative bumpers, bowling balls, clothing, flour, corn meal, furniture, furniture hardware, precision springs, textiles, magnet wire, industrial fasteners, dairy products, hydraulic pumps, commercial packaging, graphite, agriculture feeds.

12306 Kentucky New Era
1618 E. 9th St. Phone: (502)439-5700
PO Box 1087 Fax: (502)887-3222
Hopkinsville, KY 42240
General newspaper. **Founded:** 1869. **Freq:** Mon.-Sat. (eve.). **Print Method:** Offset. **Trim Size:** 13 3/4 x 22 3/4. **Cols./Page:** 6. **Col. Width:** 25 nonpareils. **Col. Depth:** 301 agate lines. **Key Personnel:** Mike Herndon, Managing Editor; Robert C. Carter, Publisher; Taylor Hayes, Advertising Mgr. **Subscription Rates:** $96 individuals. **Remarks:** Accepts advertising.
Ad Rates: BW: $946.86 **Circ:** Mon.-Sat. ★**12,814**
4C: $1,111.86
PCI: $7.34

12307 WHOP-AM - 1230
PO Box 709 Phone: (502)885-5331
Hopkinsville, KY 42240 Fax: (502)885-2688
E-mail: whopi@hop_ uky.campus.mci.net

Format: Adult Contemporary; News. **Networks:** CBS. **Owner:** Hopkinsville Broadcasting Co., Inc., at above address. **Founded:** 1940. **Operating Hours:** Continuous; 10% network, 90% local. **ADI:** Nashville (Cookeville), TN. **Key Personnel:** Roger E. Jeffers, President; Jim Love, News Dir.; Mike Chadwell, Sports Dir.; Tony Winfield, Program Dir. **Wattage:** 1000. **Ad Rates:** $11-17 for 30 seconds; $14.50-22.50 for 60 seconds. $11-$17 for 30 seconds; $14.50-$22.50 for 60 seconds. Combined advertising rates available with WHOP-FM.

12308 WHOP-FM - 98.7
PO Box 709 Phone: (502)885-5331
Hopkinsville, KY 42240 Fax: (502)885-2688
Free: (800)798-7943
E-mail: whop1@hop_ ukycampus.mci.net

Format: Country. **Networks:** CBS; Knowledge Network. **Owner:** Hopkinsville Broadcasting Co. Inc., at above address, Fax: (502)885-7688. **Founded:** 1948. **Operating Hours:** Continuous. **ADI:** Nashville (Cookeville), TN. **Key Personnel:** Roger Jeffers, President/Gen. Mgr.; Jerry Stegall, Sales Mgr.; Jim Love, News Dir.; Jeff Sisk, Program Dir. **Wattage:** 100,000. **Ad Rates:** $14-30 for 30 seconds; $18-35 for 60 seconds.

12309 WNKJ-FM - 89.3
PO Box 1029 Phone: (502)886-9655
Hopkinsville, KY 42241-1029

Format: Religious. **Networks:** Moody Broadcasting. **Owner:** Pennyrile Christian Community, Inc., at above address. **Founded:** 1981. **Operating Hours:** Continuous; 24% network, 76% local. **Key Personnel:** Jim D. Adams, Jr., General Mgr.; Donald E. Griffey, Chief Engineer; Joseph P. Barner, Music Dir. **Wattage:** 12,000. **Ad Rates:** Noncommercial.

12310 WQKS-AM - 1480
400 Hammond Plz. Phone: (502)886-1480
Hopkinsville, KY 42240-4969 Fax: (502)886-6286
E-mail: oldies@oldies1480.com

Format: Oldies. **Founded:** 1954. **Formerly:** WKOA-AM (1986). **Operating Hours:** Continuous; 90% network, 5% local. **ADI:** Nashville (Cookeville), TN. **Key Personnel:** D.J. Everett, General Mgr., dj@oldies1480.com; Beth Mann, Sales Mgr., bmann@commandnet.net. **Local Programs:** *KISS Wake Up Club* 6 a.m. - 8 a.m. Monday & Friday, Tammy Hancock, Mailing contact; *Local News.* **Wattage:** 1000. **Ad Rates:** $5-9 for 30 seconds; $7-11 for 60 seconds.

HORSE CAVE, pop. 2,045.

Hart Co. (SWC). 81 m S of Louisville. Steel, saw, feed mills; cheese factory; tobacco warehouse. Dairy, stock, poultry, grain farms. Tobacco, corn, wheat.

12311 Hart County News-Herald
570 S Dixie St. Phone: (502)786-1929
PO Box 340 Fax: (502)786-4470
Horse Cave, KY 42749-0340
Publisher E-mail: ccpi@caveland.net

Newspaper reaching all of Hart County. **Founded:** 1878. **Freq:** Weekly (Tues.). **Print Method:** Offset. **Cols./Page:** 8. **Col. Width:** 9 picas. **Col. Depth:** 21.5 picas. **Key Personnel:** Nicole M. Randall, Editor, cubs@c-veland.net; A.C. Wilson, Jr., Editor. **USPS:** 236-180. **Subscription Rates:** $25 out of state; $7.95 individuals. **Remarks:** Advertising not accepted for alcoholic beverages.
Ad Rates: GLR: $.34 **Circ:** Paid ‡8,600
BW: $818.72
SAU: $7.14
PCI: $4.76

12312 The Progress (KY)
Cave County Newspapers
570 S. Dixie Phone: (502)773-3401
PO Box 340 Fax: (502)773-8950
Horse Cave, KY 42749
Community newspaper. **Founded:** 1935. **Freq:** Weekly (Thurs.). **Print Method:** Offset. **Trim Size:** 14 x 22 3/4. **Cols./Page:** 8. **Col. Width:** 9 picas. **Col. Depth:** 301 agate lines. **Key Personnel:** Dorothy D. Wilson, Editor; Aubrey C. Wilson, Publisher; A.C. Wilson, Jr., Advertising Mgr. **ISSN:** 0236-2004. **Subscription Rates:** $6.95 individuals; $16 out of area; $20 out of state. **Remarks:** Advertising not accepted for alcoholic beverages. **Formerly:** Barren County Progress.
Ad Rates: BW: $929.35 **Circ:** Paid ‡5,155
4C: $400 Free ‡3,389
SAU: $7.15

HYDEN†, pop. 488.

Leslie Co. (SE). 15 m NW of Leatherwood.

12313 The Leslie County News
Manchester Enterprises
Box 967 Phone: (606)672-2841
Hyden, KY 41749 Fax: (606)672-7409

Hispanic newspaper. **Founded:** 1963. **Freq:** Weekly (Thurs.). **Print Method:** Offset. **Cols./Page:** 6. **Col. Width:** 21 nonpareils. **Col. Depth:** 287 agate lines. **Key Personnel:** Vernon Baker, Publisher. **Subscription Rates:** $18.55 individuals; $26 out of area. **Remarks:** Accepts advertising.
Ad Rates: GLR: $5.80 **Circ:** 5,600
BW: $5.80
SAU: $8.40
PCI: $5.80

INEZ†, pop. 496.

Martin Co. (EC) 3 m NW of Warfield. Residential.

12314 The Mountain Citizen
New Wave Communications Inc.
Box 1029 Phone: (606)298-7570
Inez, KY 41224 Fax: (606)298-3711
Publication E-mail: mtncit@eastky.net

Local newspaper. **Subtitle:** Martin County's Newspaper. **Founded:** Aug. 8, 1975. **Freq:** Weekly (Wed.). **Print Method:** Offset. **Cols./Page:** 6. **Col. Width:** 27 nonpareils. **Col. Depth:** 297 agate lines. **Key Personnel:** Lisa Stayton, Publisher. **USPS:** 090-430. **Subscription Rates:** $18 individuals; $.50 single issue. **Remarks:** Accepts advertising. **Formerly:** The Martin Countian; The Mercury.
Ad Rates: GLR: $.48 **Circ:** ‡5,800
BW: $503.10
4C: $653.10
SAU: $4.10
PCI: $4.75

IRVINE†, pop. 2,889.

Estill Co. (EC). 50 m W of Salyersville. Residential.

12315 Citizen Voice & Times
Citizen Voice, Inc.
108 Court St. Phone: (606)723-5161
PO Box 660 Fax: (606)723-5509
Irvine, KY 40336
Publisher E-mail: cvt@kih.net

Weekly newspaper. **Founded:** 1890. **Freq:** Weekly (Thurs.). **Print Method:** Offset. **Cols./Page:** 6. **Col. Width:** 12 picas. **Col. Depth:** 21 1/2 inches. **Key Personnel:** Beth Curlin, Editor; Guy Hatfield, Publisher; Teresa Hatfield, Advertising Mgr. **USPS:** 270-120. **Subscription Rates:** $15.95 individuals; $23.95 out of area; $32 out of state. **Remarks:** Accepts advertising.
Ad Rates: GLR: $.34 **Circ:** Paid ‡4,750
BW: $398.61 Free ‡9,700
4C: $652.98
SAU: $4.20

12316 WCYO-FM - 106.1
1030 Winchester Rd. Phone: (606)723-5138
PO Box 281 Fax: (606)723-5180
Irvine, KY 40336
Free: (800)606-1061
E-mail: coyote@kih.net

Format: Contemporary Country. **Networks:** ABC. **Founded:** 1991. **Operating Hours:** Continuous. **ADI:** Lexington, KY. **Key Personnel:** Kelly T. Wallingford, Contact; Vince Richardson, Operations Mgr. **Wattage:** 6000. **Ad Rates:** $7.50-10.50 for 30 seconds; $9.00-12 for 60 seconds. $3-$8.50 for 30 seconds; $4.50-$10 for 60 seconds. Combined advertising rates available with WIRV-AM.

12317 WIRV-AM - 1550
1030 Winchester Rd. Phone: (606)723-5138
PO Box 281 Fax: (606)723-5180
Irvine, KY 40336
Free: (800)606-1061

Format: Oldies. **Networks:** KyNet. **Founded:** 1960. **Operating Hours:** 6 a.m.-6 p.m. **ADI:** Lexington, KY. **Key Personnel:** Kelly T. Wallingford, Contact, fax (606)723-5188. **Wattage:** 1000. **Ad Rates:** $3-3.75 for 30 seconds; $3.50-4.50 for 60 seconds. $3-$3.75 for 30 seconds; $3.50-$4.50 for 60 seconds. Combined advertising rates available with WCYO-FM.

JACKSON

Breathitt Co. (EC). 5 m S of Wolverine.

12318 Beattyville Enterprise
Intermountain Publishing Co.
1001 College Ave. Phone: (606)666-2451
Jackson, KY 41339 Fax: (606)666-5757

Community newspaper. **Founded:** 1883. **Freq:** Weekly (Thurs.). **Print Method:** Offset. **Cols./Page:** 6. **Col. Width:** 12.5 picas. **Col. Depth:** 21 inches. **Key Personnel:** Matt Watterson, Editor and Publisher. **USPS:** 047-080. **Subscription Rates:** $12.60; $23 others. **Remarks:** Accepts advertising.
Ad Rates: GLR: $3.25 **Circ:** 3,000
BW: $409.50

12319 Jackson Times
Intermountain Publishing Co.
1001 College Ave. Phone: (606)666-2451
Jackson, KY 41339 Fax: (606)666-5757

Community newspaper. **Founded:** 1887. **Freq:** Weekly (Thurs.). **Print Method:** Offset. **Cols./Page:** 6. **Col. Width:** 12.5 picas. **Col. Depth:** 21 inches. **Key Personnel:** Glenn Gray, Editor and Publisher. **USPS:** 272-240. **Subscription Rates:** $16; $25 others. **Remarks:** Accepts advertising.
Ad Rates: GLR: $4.88 **Circ:** 6,000
BW: $614.88
SAU: $4.88

12320 WEKG-AM - 810
1024 College Ave. Phone: (606)666-7531
Jackson, KY 41339 Fax: (606)666-4946

Format: Hot Country; Religious; Bluegrass; Oldies. **Networks:** CNN Radio. **Founded:** 1969. **Operating Hours:** Dawn-dusk; 75% network, 25% local. **Key Personnel:** Kevin Davidson, Traffic Mgr.; Johnny C, Promotions Mgr.; Doug Neace, Sales Mgr.; John C. Boggs, Office Mgr.; Kevin Davidson, Traffic Mgr. **Wattage:** 5000. **Ad Rates:** $4-7 for 30 seconds; $5-8 for 60 seconds.

12321 WJSN-FM - 106.5
1024 College Ave. Phone: (606)666-7531
Jackson, KY 41339 Fax: (606)666-4946

Format: Hot Country. **Founded:** 1979. **Operating Hours:** Continuous. **Key Personnel:** James M. Hay, General Mgr.; Johnny C, Promotions Mgr.; Doug Neace, Sales Mgr.; John C. Boggs, Asst. Mgr. **Wattage:** 4,545. **Ad Rates:** $4-7 for 30 seconds; $5-8 for 60 seconds.

JAMESTOWN†, pop. 1,441.

Russell Co. (SC). 95 m S of Lexington. Underwear plant. Diversified farming. Cattle.

12322 WJRS-FM - 104.9
PO Box 800 Phone: (502)343-4444
Jamestown, KY 42629 Fax: (502)866-2060

Format: Country. **Simulcasts:** WJKY-AM. **Networks:** Satellite Music Network. **Founded:** 1966. **Operating Hours:** 5 a.m.-11 p.m. **Key Personnel:** Mae Hoover, General Mgr. **Wattage:** 3000. **Ad Rates:** Combined advertising rates available with WJKY-AM.

JEFFERSONTOWN

Kentucky Prairie Farmer - See Frankfort

JENKINS, pop. 3,200.

Letcher Co. (NE). 22 m SSW of Pikesville. Coal mines.

12323 Letcher County Community News-Press
Superior Printing and Publishing
PO Box 217, Rte. 805 Phone: (606)855-4541
Cromona, KY 41810 Fax: (606)855-9290

Community newspaper. **Founded:** Nov. 1, 1959. **Freq:** Weekly (Wed.). **Print Method:** Offset. **Trim Size:** 14 x 22 1/2. **Cols./Page:** 6. **Col. Width:** 2 inches. **Col. Depth:** 21 inches. **Key Personnel:** Mike Whitaker, Editor/Administration; Charles Whitaker, Publisher. **ISSN:** 0899-1820. **Subscription Rates:** $18 local; $29 out of area. **Remarks:** Advertising not accepted for alcoholic beverages.
Ad Rates: GLR: $.28 **Circ:** ‡2,800
BW: $497.70
PCI: $3.95

KEAVY

12324 WVCT-FM - 91.5
PO Box 381 Phone: (606)528-4671
Rt. 11 Fax: (606)528-4671
Keavy, KY 40737

Format: Religious; Educational. **Owner:** Victory Training School Corp., at above address. **Founded:** 1984. **Operating Hours:** Continuous. **Key Personnel:** Billy R. Hipshen, General Mgr., brhipshen@kih.net. **Wattage:** 3300. **Ad Rates:** $3-6 for 30 seconds. **URL:** http://www.suresite.com/ky/w/wvct.

LA GRANGE†, pop. 2,971.

Oldham Co. (NW). 27 m NE of Louisville. Manufactures copper wire, chemicals, food products, prefabricated pools. Greenhouse. Agriculture. Dairying, tobacco, beef cattle.

12325 The Oldham Era
Landmark Community Newspapers, Inc.
PO Box 5 Phone: (502)222-7183
La Grange, KY 40031-0005
Local newspaper. **Founded:** 1876. **Freq:** Weekly (Thurs.). **Print Method:** Letterpress and offset. **Cols./Page:** 6. **Col. Width:** 12 nonpareils. **Col. Depth:** 301 agate lines. **Key Personnel:** Kit Millay, Editor; Dorothy Abernathy, Publisher; Doris Armstrong, Advertising Mgr. **Subscription Rates:** $20 individuals. **Remarks:** Accepts advertising.
Ad Rates: BW: $592.11 **Circ:** ‡6,900
4C: $817.11
SAU: $4.86

LANCASTER†, pop. 3,365.

Garrard Co. (C). 34 m S of Lexington. Saw, feed mills. Diversified farming. Tobacco, corn, wheat, hay.

12326 Central Record
106 Richmond St. Phone: (606)792-2831
PO Box 492 Fax: (606)792-3448
Lancaster, KY 40444-0492
Newspaper with a Democratic orientation. **Founded:** 1889. **Freq:** Weekly (Thurs.). **Print Method:** Letterpress and offset. **Cols./Page:** 6. **Col. Width:** 24 nonpareils. **Col. Depth:** 294 agate lines. **Key Personnel:** Jim Cox, Editor and Publisher; Marguerite Whittaker, Managing Editor. **Subscription Rates:** $12 individuals. **Remarks:** Accepts advertising. **Alt. Formats:** Microform.
Ad Rates: GLR: $.16 **Circ:** ‡4,700
BW: $378
4C: $578
SAU: $3
PCI: $3

12327 Garrard County News
33 Public Sq. Phone: (606)792-2203
PO Box 650 Fax: (606)792-4839
Lancaster, KY 40444
Community newspaper. **Founded:** Aug. 31, 1972. **Freq:** Weekly. **Cols./Page:** 6. **Col. Width:** 2 inches. **Col. Depth:** 21 inches. **Key Personnel:** Jack Penchoff, Editor and Publisher; Karen Penchoff, General Mgr. **USPS:** 139-400. **Subscription Rates:** $12.50 individuals; $20 out of state. **Remarks:** Accepts advertising.
Ad Rates: GLR: $3.50 **Circ:** Paid ⊕3,960
BW: $375
4C: $425
PCI: $3.50

12328 The Mountain Spirit
Christian Appalachian Project
322 Crab Orchard Rd. Phone: (606)792-3051
Lancaster, KY 40446 Fax: (606)792-6560

Report on mission project activities. **Subtitle:** The Magazine of the Christian Appalachian Project. **Founded:** 1982. **Freq:** Bimonthly. **Print Method:** Web offset. **Trim Size:** 8 1/2 x 11. **Cols./Page:** 2 and 3. **Col. Width:** 13 and 18 picas. **Key Personnel:** Margaret Gabriel, Editor, chrisapp@kih.net; Linda Grider East, Circulation Mgr.; Karen Francis Spivey, Graphic Designer. **Subscription Rates:** $8. **Remarks:** Advertising not accepted.
Circ: Paid 24,000

LATONIA

12329 WCVG-AM - 1320
PO Box 15034 Phone: (606)291-2255
Latonia, KY 41015 Fax: (606)655-4345

Format: Gospel. **Networks:** USA Radio. **Owner:** Richard Plessinger, at above address. **Operating Hours:** Continuous. **Key Personnel:** Tracie Hunter, General Mgr./Program Dir.; Jeff Eldred, Operations Mgr.; Jim Gray, Chief Engineer. **Local Programs:** *Tracie Live* 12:00 pm - 2:00 pm Monday-Friday, Tracie Hunter, (606)291-2255. **Wattage:** 500.

LAWRENCEBURG†, pop. 5,167.

Anderson Co. (E). 12 m S of Frankfort. Distillery, cheese, diversified agriculture.

12330 The Anderson News
Landmark Community Newspapers, Inc.
133 Main St. Phone: (502)839-6906
PO Box 116
Lawrenceburg, KY 40342
Community newspapers. **Freq:** Weekly (Wed.). **Key Personnel:** Don White, Editor. **Subscription Rates:** $13.95 individuals; $12.95 seniors; $17.50 out of area; $22.75 out of state.
Circ: ‡5,755

LEBANON†, pop. 6,590.

Marion Co. (C). 28 m W of Danville. Distillery, meat packing, tobacco.

12331 WLBN-AM - 1590
Box 680 Phone: (502)692-3126
Lebanon, KY 40033 Fax: (502)692-6003

Format: Music of Your Life. **Networks:** Mutual Broadcasting System. **Founded:** 1953. **Operating Hours:** Sunrise-sunset; 10% network, 90% local. **ADI:** Louisville, KY. **Key Personnel:** Tom Rogers, Contact; Bob Ruhill, Contact; Alvin Wren, Contact; Tommy Burress, Program Dir. **Local Programs:** *Back Talk*, Alvin Wren. **Wattage:** 1000. **Ad Rates:** $2.70-4.60 for 30 seconds; $3.75-5.95 for 60 seconds. Combined advertising rates available with WLSK.

12332 WLSK-FM - 100.9
Radio Station Rd., Box 680 Phone: (502)692-3126
Lebanon, KY 40033 Fax: (502)692-6003

Networks: Mutual Broadcasting System. **Owner:** J.T. Whitlock Co., at above address. **Founded:** 1974. **Operating Hours:** Continuous; 10% network, 90% local. **ADI:** Louisville, KY. **Key Personnel:** Tom Roscis, Contact; Bob Rahill, Contact; Alvin Wren, Contact; Tommy Burress, Program Dir. **Wattage:** 15000. **Ad Rates:** $3.30-6 for 30 seconds; $4.30-7.70 for 60 seconds.

LEITCHFIELD†, pop. 4,533.

Grayson Co. (WC). 72 m SW of Louisville. Manufactures electronic components, paper novelties, power tools, concrete products, cheese, lumber. Dairy, poultry, grain farms. Tobacco, corn, hay.

12333 Grayson County News-Gazette
Park Newspapers of Kentucky, Inc.
PO Box 305 Phone: (502)259-9622
Leitchfield, KY 42755-0305 Fax: (502)259-5537

Local newspaper. **Founded:** 1881. **Freq:** Semiweekly (Mon. and Thurs.). **Print Method:** Offset. **Cols./Page:** 6. **Col. Width:** 12 nonpareils. **Col. Depth:** 301 agate lines. **Key Personnel:** Edna Duggins, Editor; Jim Allen, Publisher; Nancy Farmer, Advertising Mgr. **Subscription Rates:** $12 individuals; $20 out of area; $23.50 out of state. **Remarks:** Accepts advertising.
Ad Rates: GLR: $.31 **Circ:** ‡6,220

12334 WMTL-AM - 870
2160 Brandenburg Rd. Phone: (502)259-3165
Leitchfield, KY 42754 Fax: (502)259-5693

Format: Southern Gospel. **Networks:** ABC. **Owner:** Heritage Media of Kentucky, Inc., at above address. **Founded:** 1959. **Operating Hours:** 7 a.m.-7 p.m. **ADI:** Louisville, KY. **Key Personnel:** Mark Buckles, General Mgr.; Dave Thompson, Sports Dir.; Tracie Tomes, Program Dir.; Bo Thorpe, News Dir. **Local Programs:** *Gospel Hour* 7:30-8:30 a.m. Monday-Friday, Dave Thompson; *Tradio* 8:30-9 a.m. Monday-Friday, Dave Thompson. **Wattage:** Night 50. **Ad Rates:** $5-9 for 30 seconds; $8-12 for 60 seconds. Combined advertising rates available with WKHG-FM.

LEXINGTON†, pop. 204,165.

Fayette Co. (NC). 80 m E of Louisville. University of Kentucky; Transylvania University; College of the Bible; Lexington Baptist College. Manufactures tobacco, peanut butter, asphalt paving products, insecticides, crop drying equipment, neon signs, television tuners and boosters, men's suits, women's dresses, medicine, caskets, screens, tools, stoves, electric typewriters and stands, electrical control panels, air conditioning, transistors, airbrake equipment, paper cups, glass, parachutes, livestock feed, motor and machine seals, fork lifts, cranes, furniture. Motor bus shops. Meat packing. Principal outlet for eastern and central Kentucky oil, coal, farm and quarry products. Thoroughbred hoses.

12335 Annals of the Association of American Geographers
University of Kentucky Phone: (606)257-9147
Dept. of Geography Fax: (606)323-1969
Lexington, KY 40506
Publication E-mail: annals@ulccc.uky.edu; gaia@org.com; gaia@aag.org

Geography journal. **Founded:** 1911. **Freq:** Quarterly. **Print Method:** Letterpress. **Trim Size:** 6 7/8 x 10. **Cols./Page:** 2. **Col. Width:** 35 nonpareils. **Col. Depth:** 115 agate lines. **Key Personnel:** John Paul Jones III, Editor, geg172@pop.uky.edu. **ISSN:** 0004-5608. **Subscription Rates:** $95 individuals; $110 other countries. **Remarks:** Accepts advertising. **URL:** http://www.aag.org.
Ad Rates: BW: $525 **Circ:** ‡8,750

12336 ANQ
Heldref Publications
University of Kentucky Phone: (606)257-6975
Dept. of English Fax: (606)323-1072
POT 1215
Lexington, KY 40506-0027
Publication E-mail: anq@heldref.org
Publisher E-mail: revu@heldref.org

Journal covering articles and reviews relating to English-language, literature, and bibliography. **Subtitle:** A Quarterly Journal of Short Articles, Notes, and Reviews. **Founded:** Jan. 1987. **Freq:** Quarterly. **Print Method:** Offset. **Trim Size:** 6 x 9. **Cols./Page:** 1. **Col. Width:** 26 picas. **Col. Depth:** 42 picas. **Key Personnel:** Grant Williams, Production Mgr., advertis@heldref.org; Fred Huber, Circulation Mgr., subs@heldref.org; Jean Kline, Fulfillment Mgr.; Douglas Kirkpatrick, Director. **ISSN:** 0895-769X. **Subscription Rates:** $40 individuals; $74 institutions; other countries add $13 postage. **Remarks:** Accepts advertising. **Online:** EBSCO; Infonautics; UMI. **URL:** http://www.heldref.org. **Alt. Formats:** CD-ROM.
Ad Rates: BW: $155 **Circ:** 496

12337 Around the Town
Box 27 Phone: (606)252-6165
Lexington, KY 40588 Fax: (606)252-5748

Entertainment magazine and restaurant guide. **Founded:** Apr. 1, 1958. **Freq:** Monthly. **Print Method:** Offset. **Trim Size:** 5 x 8. **Cols./Page:** 2. **Col. Width:** 29 nonpareils. **Col. Depth:** 112 agate lines. **Key Personnel:** Wallace C. Jones, Editor and Publisher, fax (606)255-4748; Wallace C. Jones, Jr., Advertising Mgr. **Subscription Rates:** Free. **Remarks:** Accepts advertising.
Ad Rates: BW: $225 **Circ:** Free ‡10,000

12338 Athletics Administration
NALDA
904 N. Broadway Phone: (606)226-4550
Lexington, KY 40505 Fax: (606)226-4575

College athletics magazine. **Founded:** 1966. **Freq:** Bimonthly. **Print Method:** Offset. **Trim Size:** 8 x 10 3/4. **Cols./Page:** 3. **Col. Width:** 13 picas. **Col. Depth:** 60 picas. **Key Personnel:** Laurie Garrison, Editor; Rick Ford, Publisher. **ISSN:** 0044-9873. **Subscription Rates:** $15 individuals; $20 Canada and

Mexico. **Remarks:** Accepts advertising. **Formerly**: Athletic Administration.
Ad Rates: BW: $1,345 **Circ:** ‡5,500
4C: $2,235

12339 The Blood-Horse
The Blood-Horse Publications
1736 Alexandria Dr. Phone: (606)278-2361
Lexington, KY 40504 Fax: (606)276-4450
Publication E-mail: advertise@bloodhorse.com
Publisher E-mail: sbearse@bloodhorse.com

Trade magazine covering thoroughbred racing and breeding. **Founded:** 1916. **Freq:** Weekly. **Trim Size:** 8 1/8 x 10 7/8. **Cols./Page:** 3. **Col. Width:** 2 1/4 inches. **Col. Depth:** 10 inches. **Key Personnel:** Ray Paulick, Editor-in-Chief, phone (606)276-6757, rpaulick@bloodhorse.com; Mr. Stacy V. Bearse, President, phone (606)276-6709, sbearse@bloodhorse.com; Gregory Medley, Advertising Dir., phone (606)276-6744, fax (606)276-6706, gmedley@bloodhorse.com. **ISSN:** 0006-4998. **Subscription Rates:** $125 individuals; $198 Canada; $180.05 other countries; $3.50 single issue. **Remarks:** Accepts advertising. **URL:** http://www.bloodhorse.com.
Ad Rates: BW: $1,521 **Circ:** Paid ★**23,547**
4C: $2,348
PCI: $63

12340 The Chase
1150 Industry Rd. Phone: (606)254-4262
Lexington, KY 40505 Fax: (606)254-3145

Magazine on fox hunting. **Founded:** 1920. **Freq:** Monthly. **Print Method:** Offset. **Trim Size:** 9 x 12. **Cols./Page:** 4. **Col. Width:** 2 inches. **Col. Depth:** 88 inches. **Key Personnel:** Jo Ann Stone, Editor. **ISSN:** 0009-1952. **Subscription Rates:** $20. **Remarks:** Accepts advertising.
Ad Rates: BW: $121 **Circ:** ‡3,300

12341 Cow Country News
Kentucky Cattlemen's Association
176 Pasadena Dr. Phone: (606)278-0899
Lexington, KY 40503 Fax: (606)260-2060
Publisher E-mail: kcatassoc@kia.net

Magazine (tabloid) serving beef cattle industry in Kentucky and surrounding areas. **Subtitle:** Cow Country News. **Founded:** 1978. **Freq:** Monthly. **Print Method:** Web offset. **Trim Size:** 11 3/8 x 15 1/4. **Cols./Page:** 5. **Col. Width:** 2 inches. **Col. Depth:** 14 inches. **Key Personnel:** Doug Eades, Editor, deades@kcattle.org. **Subscription Rates:** Free to qualified subscribers. **Remarks:** Accepts advertising. **URL:** http://www.kycattle.org.
Ad Rates: BW: $575 **Circ:** 27,000
4C: $1025
PCI: $20

12342 The Horse
The Blood-Horse Publications
1736 Alexandria Dr. Phone: (606)278-2361
Lexington, KY 40504 Fax: (606)276-4450
Publisher E-mail: sbearse@bloodhorse.com

Equine magazine dedicated to breeding, raising and training healthy horses of all breeds. **Freq:** Monthly. **Key Personnel:** Stacy V. Bearse, President/Publisher. **Subscription Rates:** $30 individuals.

12343 Horseman and Fair World
Horseman Publishing Co.
PO Box 8480 Phone: (606)276-4026
Lexington, KY 40533 Fax: (606)277-8100
Free: (800)860-8199

Harness racing magazine. **Founded:** 1877. **Freq:** Weekly (Thurs.). **Print Method:** Offset. **Cols./Page:** 3. **Col. Width:** 24 nonpareils. **Col. Depth:** 140 agate lines. **Key Personnel:** Kathy Parker, Editor, kparker@lexton.mindspring.com; Greg Schuler, Advertising Mgr., gschuler@mrs.net. **Subscription Rates:** $80 individuals; $98 other countries; $2.75 single issue. **Remarks:** Accepts advertising.
Ad Rates: BW: $550 **Circ:** ‡7,500
4C: $1,130
PCI: $26

12344 INTERCOM
Kentucky Council of Churches
412 Rose St. Phone: (606)253-3027
Lexington, KY 40508 Fax: (606)231-5028

Religious magazine (tabloid) for church leaders of various denominations in Kentucky, southern Indiana, and southern Ohio. **Founded:** Mar. 1983. **Freq:** 5/year. **Print Method:** Offset. **Cols./Page:** 4. **Col. Width:** 2 1/3 inches. **Col. Depth:** 12 inches. **Key Personnel:** Dr. David Burg, Editor; Rev. Nancy Jo Kemper, Publisher. **USPS:** 134-300. **Subscription Rates:** $3. **Remarks:** Color advertising not accepted. **Formerly**: The Council Courier (Mar. 1983).
Ad Rates: GLR: $1.75 **Circ:** Paid 4,890
BW: $247.50 Non-paid 2,569
PCI: $7

12345 Journal of Caribbean Studies
Association of Caribbean Studies
PO Box 22202 Phone: (606)257-6966
Lexington, KY 40502 Fax: (606)323-1072

Journal on the history, culture, and politics of the Caribbean. **Founded:** 1980. **Freq:** Quarterly. **Print Method:** Offset. **Trim Size:** 5 1/2 x 8 1/2. **Cols./Page:** 1. **Col. Width:** 25 picas. **Col. Depth:** 40 picas. **Key Personnel:** O. R. Dathorne, Editor. **ISSN:** 0190-2008. **Subscription Rates:** $50; $200 institutions. **Remarks:** Accepts advertising.
Circ: 1,000

12346 Kentucky Kernel
Kernel Press, Inc.
University of Kentucky Phone: (606)257-2871
026 Grehan Journalism Bldg. Fax: (606)323-1906
Lexington, KY 40506-0042
Collegiate newspaper. **Founded:** 1894. **Freq:** Daily (during the academic year). **Print Method:** Offset. **Trim Size:** 78.5 pca x 130.5 pca. **Cols./Page:** 6. **Col. Width:** 25 nonpareils. **Col. Depth:** 301 agate lines. **Key Personnel:** Lance Williams, Editor; Kelley Bozeman, Advertising Dir. **Remarks:** Accepts advertising.
Ad Rates: BW: $1,612.50 **Circ:** 17,000
4C: $1,777.50
SAU: $12.50

12347 Kentucky Law Journal
Darby Printing Co.
University of Kentucky College of Law Phone: (606)257-8333
148 Law Bldg. Fax: (606)323-1061
Lexington, KY 40506
Publication E-mail: klj@pop.uky.edu

Journal covering legal issues. **Founded:** 1912. **Freq:** Quarterly. **Print Method:** Offset. **Trim Size:** 6 3/4 x 10. **Cols./Page:** 1. **Col. Width:** 27 picas. **Col. Depth:** 48 picas. **Key Personnel:** Rachel Zahniser, Editor-in-Chief; Sharon Minning, Managing Editor. **ISSN:** 0023-026X. **Subscription Rates:** $28 individuals. **Remarks:** Advertising not accepted. **Available Online.**
Circ: Paid ‡880
Controlled ‡475

12348 Kentucky Review
University of Kentucky Library Associates
Lexington, KY 40506-0039 Phone: (606)257-9421
Fax: (606)257-8379

Scholarly journal covering the humanities. **Founded:** 1979. **Freq:** Semiannual. **Cols./Page:** 1. **Key Personnel:** James E. Burgett, Editor; Gordon Hogg, Editor, gehogg01@ukcc.uky.edu; Mary Vass, Production Mgr.; Joseph Miller, Business Mgr. **ISSN:** 0191-1030. **Subscription Rates:** $10 individuals; $3.50 single issue. **Remarks:** Advertising not accepted.
Circ: (Not Reported)

12349 The Lane Report
Lane Communications Group
269 W. Main St. Phone: (606)244-3522
Lexington, KY 40507 Fax: (606)244-3544
Publication E-mail: lanereport@aol.com

Publication for central Kentucky focusing on business, economics, and politics. **Founded:** 1985. **Freq:** Monthly. **Print Method:** Offset. **Trim Size:** 8 1/2 x 10 7/8. **Cols./Page:** 3. **Col. Width:** 2 5/16 inches. **Col. Depth:** 10 inches. **Key Personnel:** Kevin Depew, Editorial Dir. **Subscription Rates:** $29 individuals; $3.75 single issue. **Remarks:** Accepts advertising.
Ad Rates: BW: $1,295 **Circ:** Paid ★**707**
4C: $1,675 Non-paid ★**6,872**

12350 Leader's Magazine
98 Dennis Dr. Phone: (606)277-6221
Lexington, KY 40503 Fax: (606)277-8059
Free: (800)356-5936

Magazine for the insurance industry. **Subtitle:** The Life Insurance Sales Digest. **Founded:** July 1938. **Freq:** Bimonthly. **Print Method:** Letterpress and offset. **Trim Size:** 5 1/4 x 7. **Cols./Page:** 2. **Col. Width:** 12 picas. **Col. Depth:** 204 agate lines. **Key Personnel:** Fred R. Kissling, Jr., Editor and Publisher; Melissa Lester, Asst. Ed.; Vanessa Bentley, Circulation Mgr. **ISSN:** 0023-9631. **Subscription Rates:** $12.95 individuals U.S.; $20.95 Canada; $40 other countries. **Remarks:** Advertising not accepted.
Circ: ‡9,000

12351 Lexington Herald-Leader
Knight-Ridder, Inc.
100 Midland Ave. Phone: (606)231-3100
Lexington, KY 40508 Fax: (606)254-9738

General newspaper. **Founded:** 1983. **Freq:** Mon.-Sun. (morn.). **Print Method:** Offset. **Trim Size:** 13 x 21 1/2. **Cols./Page:** 6. **Col. Width:** 2 1/16 inches. **Col. Depth:** 21 1/2 inches. **Key Personnel:** Ann Cawlkins, Advertising Dir., phone (606)231-3172, fax (606)231-3454; Tim Kelly, Publisher, phone (606)231-3257, fax (606)231-3454; David Holwerk, Managing Editor, phone (606)231-3224, fax (606)231-3326; Sharon Thompson, phone (606)231-3321; Bettye Lee Mastin, phone (606)231-3250; Todd Van Campen, Religion Reporter, phone (606)231-3252; Beverly Fotune, Gardening Reporter, phone (606)231-3251; Liz Petros, Regional Editor, phone (606)231-3305; Angie Muhs, Frankfort Bureau Chief (Politics), phone (502)227-4390; Mary O'Doherty, City Editor, phone (606)231-3302, fax (606)254-9738; Linda Johnson, Elementary/Secondary Education Reporter, phone (606)221-1317; Holly Stepp, High Education Reporter, phone (606)231-3484; Beverly Fortune, Gardening Reporter, phone (606)231-3251; Andy Mead, Environmental Reporter, phone (606)231-3319; Louise Taylor, Horse Industry Reporter, phone (606)231-3205, fax (062)31-3326; Jamie Butters, Industry Reporter, phone (606)231-3201, fax (606)231-3326; Jim Jordan, Financial Reporter, phone (606)231-3242, fax (606)231-3326; Tom Eblen, Projects Editor, phone (606)231-1415, fax (606)231-3326; Steve Dorsey, Design Editor, phone (606)231-1647; LuAnn Farrar, Librarian, phone (606)231-3335; Charles Bertram, Chief Photographer, phone (606)231-1603. **ISSN:** 0745-4260. **Subscription Rates:** $218.40 individuals; $257.40 out of state mailed in-state; $280.80 out of state. **Remarks:** Accepts advertising. **Online:** Dialog (The Dialog Corporation); America Online, Inc.
Ad Rates: GLR: $8062.50 **Circ:** Mon.-Thurs. ★**113,036**
BW: $8711.50 Fri. ★**137,306**
4C: $7,700.16 Sat. ★**129,324**
SAU: $62.50 Sun. ★**156,427**
PCI: $62.50

12352 Lexington Theological Quarterly
Lexington Theological Seminary
631 S. Limestone St. Phone: (606)252-0361
Lexington, KY 40508 Fax: (606)281-6042

Theological journal. **Founded:** Jan. 1966. **Freq:** Quarterly. **Print Method:** Letterpress and offset. **Trim Size:** 5 1/2 x 8 1/2. **Cols./Page:** 1. **Col. Width:** 48 nonpareils. **Col. Depth:** 98 agate lines. **Key Personnel:** Philip N. Drake, Editor; Jerry Sumney, Book Review Editor, bosworth@ukcc.uky.edu. **Subscription Rates:** Free. **Remarks:** Advertising not accepted. **Alt. Formats:** Microform. **Formerly**: College of the Bible Quarterly.
Circ: Non-paid 2,300

12353 The Phi Gamma Delta
Phi Gamma Delta Fraternity
PO Box 4599 Phone: (606)255-1848
Lexington, KY 40544-4599 Fax: (606)253-0779
Publication E-mail: phigam@mis.net

Fraternity magazine. **Founded:** 1879. **Freq:** Quarterly. **Print Method:** Offset. **Cols./Page:** 3. **Col. Width:** 27 nonpareils. **Col. Depth:** 136 agate lines. **Key Personnel:** William A. Martin III, Editor; Suzanne Cox, Publications Coord. **Remarks:** Advertising not accepted.
Circ: ‡90,000

12354 Spectrum: Journal of State Government
Council of State Governments
2760 Research Park Dr. Phone: (606)244-8000
PO Box 11910 Fax: (606)244-8001
Lexington, KY 40578-1910
Free: (800)800-1910
Publisher E-mail: info@csg.org

State government journal. **Founded:** 1930. **Freq:** Quarterly. **Print Method:** Offset. Uses mats. **Trim Size:** 8 1/2 x 11. **Cols./Page:** 2. **Col. Width:** 39 nonpareils. **Col. Depth:** 121 agate lines. **Key Personnel:** Stephanie Plaisance, phone (616)244-8000, fax (606)244-8001, info@csg.org. **ISSN:** 0039-0097. **Subscription Rates:** $45 individuals. **Remarks:** Accepts advertising. **URL:** http://www.csg.org; http://www.gopher.csg.org.
Ad Rates: BW: $390 **Circ:** 4,000

12355 State Government News
Council of State Governments
2760 Research Park Dr. Phone: (606)244-8000
PO Box 11910 Fax: (606)244-8001
Lexington, KY 40578-1910
Free: (800)800-1910
Publication E-mail: info@csg.org; sgnews@csg.org
Publisher E-mail: info@csg.org

State government magazine. **Founded:** 1958. **Freq:** Monthly. **Print Method:** Web offset. **Trim Size:** 8 1/2 x 10 7/8. **Cols./Page:** 3. **Col. Width:** 24 nonpareils. **Col. Depth:** 138 agate

lines. **Key Personnel:** Phyllis Santos, Advertising, phone (606)244-8111, psantos@csg.org; Elaine Stuart, Managing Editor, phone (606)231-1822, estuart@csg.org. **ISSN:** 0039-0119. **Subscription Rates:** $39 individuals; $6 single issue. **Remarks:** Accepts advertising. **URL:** http://www.csg.org; http://gopher.csg.org. **Alt. Formats:** Mailing labels.
Ad Rates: BW: $1,631 **Circ:** Paid ★669
4C: $3,107 Non-paid ★16,019

12356 Inter Media
2544 Palumbo Dr. Phone: (606)268-1123
Lexington, KY 40509 Fax: (606)269-6990

Founded: 1980. **Formerly:** T.C.I. of Lexington, Inc. **Cities Served:** Fayette County, KY: subscribing households 69,000.

12357 Kentucky Educational TV - 15
600 Cooper Dr. Phone: (502)459-9572
Lexington, KY 40502 Fax: (606)258-7399
E-mail: wkpcvpp@aye.net

Format: Public TV. **Networks:** Public Broadcasting Service (PBS). **Owner:** Fifteen Telecommunications, Inc., at above address. **Founded:** 1958. **Formerly:** WKPC-TV. **Operating Hours:** 6:00 a.m.-midnight; 95% network, 5% local. **ADI:** Louisville, KY. **Key Personnel:** John-Robert Curtin, Contact; Darrell Garrett, Contact. **Wattage:** 589. **URL:** http://www.aye.net/wkpc.

12358 WBBE-AM - 1580
1498 Trade Center Dr.
Lexington, KY 40509-4124

Format: Big Band/Nostalgia. **Founded:** 1958. **Formerly:** WAXU-AM (1982). **Operating Hours:** Sunrise-sunset; 99% network, 1% local. **ADI:** Lexington, KY. **Key Personnel:** Charles Dunn, GM/Sales Manager. **Wattage:** 10,000. **Ad Rates:** $9-15 per unit.

12359 WCGW-AM - 770
3270 Blazer Pkwy., No. 102 Phone: (606)264-9700
Lexington, KY 40509 Fax: (606)264-9705
E-mail: kcn1000@aol.com

Format: Southern Gospel. **Networks:** USA Radio. **Owner:** Mortenson Broadcasting Company, at above address, (606)252-1000. **Founded:** 1986. **Formerly:** WJMM-AM (1987). **Operating Hours:** Sunrise-sunset; 5% network, 95% local. **ADI:** Lexington, KY. **Key Personnel:** Ed Wright, General Mgr.; Greg Laha, Program Dir. **Wattage:** 1000. **Ad Rates:** $10-21 for 30 seconds; $12-24 for 60 seconds. Combined advertising rates available with WJMM-FM, WSTL-FM.

WCVN-TV - See Covington

12360 WFLE-FM - 95.1
RR.3, No. 1 Radio Dr. Phone: (606)849-4433
Fleming County Industrial Park Fax: (606)845-9353
Flemingsburg, KY 41041

Format: Country. **Networks:** CNN Radio; KyNet; Meadows Racing. **Owner:** Fleming County Broadcasting Co., Inc., at above address. **Founded:** 1985. **Operating Hours:** Sunrise-sunset; 90% network, 10% local. **ADI:** Lexington, KY. **Key Personnel:** Carl Haight, Manager. **Wattage:** 6000. **Ad Rates:** $2.50 for 30 seconds; $4.50 for 60 seconds.

12361 WGKS-FM - 96.9
1500 Greendale Rd. Phone: (606)233-1515
Lexington, KY 40511 Fax: (606)233-1517

Format: Adult Contemporary. **Networks:** NBC; ABC; Mutual Broadcasting System. **Founded:** 1968. **Formerly:** WCOZ-FM (1992). **Operating Hours:** Continuous. **ADI:** Lexington, KY. **Key Personnel:** Pam McCarty, Contact; Dave Curtis, General Mgr.; Lynn Martin, President; Michael Cooper, Operations Mgr.; Karen Downey, Traffic Mgr.; Jerry Johnson, Program Dir. **Wattage:** 50,000.

WKAS-TV - See Ashland

WKGB-TV - See Bowling Green

WKHA-TV - See Hazard

WKLE-TV - See Elizabethtown

12362 WKMA-TV - 35
c/o Kentucky Authority for Phone: (606)258-7000
Educational TV Fax: (606)258-7399
600 Cooper Dr.
Lexington, KY 40502
Free: (800)926-7765

Format: Public TV. **Networks:** Public Broadcasting Service (PBS); Kentucky Educational Television. **Owner:** Kentucky Authority for Educational TV, at above address, (606)258-7170, Fax: (606)258-7390. **Founded:** 1968. **Operating Hours:** 6:15 a.m.-midnight. **ADI:** Evansville, IN (Madisonville, KY). **Key Personnel:** Craig Cornwell, Contact; S. Talbert, Contact; J. Gorman, Contact; D. Holtzclaw, Business Mgr.; M. Ferguson, Contact; Virginia Gaines Fox, Contact, gfox@msmail.ket.org; Donna Moore, Contact; Sally Hamilton, Contact; William Wilson, Contact; D. Hoffman, Program Dir.; T. Tucker, Contact; L. Hobson, Contact; B. Ball, Contact; J. Holbrook, Contact. **Local Programs:** *Comment on Kentucky*; *Kentucky Afield*; *Kentucky Life*; *Kentucky Tonight*; *Legislative Weekly*. **Wattage:** 617,000. **Ad Rates:** Noncommercial. **URL:** http:/www.ket.org.

WKMJ-TV - See Louisville

WKMR-TV - See Morehead

WKMU-TV - See Madisonville

WKOH-TV - See Henderson

WKON-TV - See Owenton

12363 WKPD-TV - 29
600 Cooper Dr. Phone: (606)258-7000
Lexington, KY 40502 Fax: (606)258-7399
E-mail: stalbert@ket.org

Format: Public TV. **Networks:** Public Broadcasting Service (PBS); Kentucky Educational Television. **Owner:** Kentucky Authority for Educational TV, at above address, (606)258-7170, Fax: (606)258-7390. **Founded:** 1980. **Operating Hours:** 6 a.m.-midnight. **ADI:** Lexington, KY. **Key Personnel:** Virginia Fox, Contact, gfox@msmail.ket.org; S. Hamilton, Contact; D. Moore, Contact; William Wilson, Contact; C. Cornwell, Contact; L. Hobson, Contact; J. Gorman, Contact; D. Holtzclaw, Contact; M. Ferguson, Contact; D. Hoffman, Contact; S. Talbert, Contact; B. Ball, Contact; J. Holbrook, Contact; T. Tucker, Contact. **Local Programs:** *Kentucky Life*; *Kentucky Tonight*. **Wattage:** 123,000. **URL:** http:/www.ket.org.

WKPI-TV - See Pikeville

12364 WKQQ-FM - 98.1
1498 Trade Center Dr. Phone: (606)252-6694
Lexington, KY 40509-4124 Fax: (606)225-0981

Format: Classic Rock. **Networks:** Independent. **Owner:** Village Companies, PO Box 3300, Chapel Hill, NC 27515. **Founded:** 1969. **Operating Hours:** Continuous. **ADI:** Lexington, KY. **Key Personnel:** Keith Yarber, Contact; Tim Wagner, Contact. **Wattage:** 100,000.

12365 WKSO-TV - 29
c/o Kentucky Authority for Phone: (606)258-7000
Educational Television Fax: (606)258-7399
600 Cooper Dr.
Lexington, KY 40502

Format: Public TV. **Networks:** Public Broadcasting Service (PBS); Kentucky Educational Television. **Owner:** Kentucky Authority for Educational Television, at above address, (606)258-7170, (606)258-7390. **Founded:** 1968. **Operating Hours:** 6:15 a.m.-midnight. **ADI:** Lexington, KY. **Key Personnel:** William Wilson, Contact; J. Gorman, Contact; D. Holtzclaw, Contact; M. Ferguson, Contact; S. Talbert, Contact; Virginia Gaines Fox, Contact, gfox@msmail.ket.org; Craig Cornwell, Contact; Donna Moore, Contact; D. Hoffman, Contact; Sally Hamilton, Contact; L. Hobson, Contact; B. Ball, Contact; J. Holbrook, Contact; T. Tucker, Contact. **Local Programs:** *Comment on Kentucky*; *Kentucky Afield*; *Kentucky Life*; *Kentucky Tonight*; *Legislative Weekly*. **Wattage:** 589,000. **Ad Rates:** Noncommercial. **URL:** http://www.ket.org.

12366 WKYT-TV - 27
2851 Winchester Rd. 40509 Phone: (606)299-0411
PO Box 55037 Fax: (606)299-2494
Lexington, KY 40555
E-mail: wkyt@lex.infi.net

Format: Commercial TV. **Networks:** CBS. **Founded:** 1957. **Operating Hours:** 5:30 a.m.-2:35 a.m. **ADI:** Lexington, KY. **Key Personnel:** Wayne Martin, President, phone (606)299-0411, fax (606)299-5531, martinwlexis-nexis.infi.net; Barbara Carden, Program Dir., fax (606)299-5531; Kathy Plomin, Contact; Wayne Martin, Station Mgr. **Local Programs:** *University of Kentucky Sports*. **Wattage:** 1520. **URL:** http://www.wkyt.com.

12367 WLAP-AM - 630
3549 Russell Cave Rd. Phone: (606)293-0563
Lexington, KY 40511-9506 Fax: (606)299-3898

Format: Sports. **Networks:** ESPN Radio. **Founded:** 1922. **Operating Hours:** Continuous. **ADI:** Lexington, KY. **Key Personnel:** Bob Hogan, General Mgr. **Wattage:** 5000 day; 1000 night. **Ad Rates:** Advertising accepted; rates available upon request.

12368 WLEX-TV - 18
1065 Russell Cave Rd. (40505) Phone: (606)255-4404
PO Box 1457 Fax: (606)255-2418
Lexington, KY 40591

Format: Commercial TV. **Networks:** NBC. **Founded:** 1955. **Operating Hours:** Continuous. **ADI:** Lexington, KY. **Key Personnel:** John A. Duvall, General Mgr.; Marilyn Clark, Contact; Mary Broberg, Contact; Simuel R. Wilson, Contact; Sandy Byron, Contact.

12369 WLRO-FM - 102.5
651 Perimeter Dr., Ste. 102 Phone: (606)269-9540
Lexington, KY 40517-4132 Fax: (606)269-9241

Format: Oldies. **Networks:** ABC. **Founded:** 1988. **Operating Hours:** Continuous. **ADI:** Lexington, KY. **Key Personnel:** Bill Clary, Contact; Cindy Ware, Contact. **Wattage:** 3000. **Ad Rates:** $20-50 per unit.

12370 WLXG-AM - 1300
1300 Greendale Rd. Phone: (606)233-1515
Lexington, KY 40511 Fax: (606)233-1517

Format: News; Talk; Sports. **Networks:** NBC; ABC; Mutual Broadcasting System. **Founded:** 1946. **Operating Hours:** Continuous. **ADI:** Lexington, KY. **Key Personnel:** Scott Pierson, Sports Dir.; Dave Curtis, General Mgr.; Karen Downey, Traffic Mgr.; Lynn Martin, President; Michael Cooper, Operations Mgr.; Bill Kelly, Program Dir. **Wattage:** 1000.

12371 WMXL-FM - 94.5
3549 Russell Cave Rd. Phone: (606)293-0563
Lexington, KY 40511-9506 Fax: (606)299-3898

Format: Adult Contemporary. **Networks:** Independent. **Founded:** 1940. **Formerly:** WLAP-FM (1992). **Operating Hours:** Continuous. **ADI:** Lexington, KY. **Key Personnel:** Doug Hammand, Operations Mgr. **Wattage:** 100,000. **Ad Rates:** Advertising accepted; rates available upon request.

12372 WRFL-FM - 88.1
PO Box 777, University Sta. Phone: (606)257-4636
Lexington, KY 40506-0025 Fax: (606)258-1039

Format: Jazz; News; Eclectic; Country; Bluegrass; Alternative/New Music/Progressive. **Networks:** Independent. **Owner:** University of Kentucky, at above address. **Founded:** 1988. **Operating Hours:** Continuous; 100% local. **ADI:** Lexington, KY. **Key Personnel:** Paul Meyers, Contact; Mark Beaty, Program Dir.; Kakie Urch, Music Dir.; Jack Smith, Production Mgr.; Scott Ward, News Dir.; Paul Miles, Sports Dir.; Rachel Peretz, Operations Dir.; Lisa Cox, Promotions Dir. **Wattage:** 250. **Ad Rates:** Noncommercial; underwriting available.

WSKO-TV - See Somerset

12373 WTKT-FM - 103.3
1498 Trade Center Dr.
Lexington, KY 40509-4124

Format: Oldies. **Networks:** Independent. **Founded:** 1973. **Formerly:** WRMA-FM (1990); WAXU-FM; WMGB-FM. **Operating Hours:** Continuous. **ADI:** Lexington, KY. **Key Personnel:** Gil Dunn, General Mgr.; Stan Isert, Program Dir. **Wattage:** 6000. **Ad Rates:** $34-39 per unit.

12374 WTVQ-TV - 36
6940 Man O War Blvd. Phone: (606)233-3600
PO Box 55590 Fax: (606)293-5002
Lexington, KY 40555

Format: Commercial TV. **Networks:** ABC. **Owner:** Media General Broadcasting, Inc., 100 N. Tampa St., Ste. 3150, Tampa, FL 33602, (813)225-4600, Fax: (813)225-4603, Free: (800)226-0451. **Founded:** 1968. **Formerly:** WBLG-TV. **Operating Hours:** Continuous weekdays; 7 a.m.-2 a.m. Sat.; 7 a.m.-1:30 a.m. Sun. **ADI:** Lexington, KY. **Key Personnel:** D. Christopher Aldridge, Vice Pres./Gen. Mgr.

12375 WUKY-FM - 91.3
University of Kentucky Phone: (606)257-3221
340 McVey Hall Fax: (606)257-6291
Lexington, KY 40506
E-mail: wuky913@ukcc.uky.edu

Format: News; Jazz. **Networks:** National Public Radio (NPR); Public Radio International (PRI). **Founded:** 1941. **Formerly:** WBKY-FM (1941). **Operating Hours:** Continuous; 70% network, 30% local. **ADI:** Lexington, KY. **Key Personnel:** Roger Chesser, General Mgr., phone (606)257-3226, fax (606)257-6291, chesser@pop.uky.edu; Gail Koon-Bennett, Marketing Mgr., phone (606)257-7049, fax (606)257-6291, wukgail@pop.uky.edu; Gordon Brandenburg, phone (606)257-9859, fax (606)257-6291, wukybfw@pop.uky.edu; Brian Wright, News Dir. **Local Programs:** *Weekday*, Curt Mathies. **Wattage:** 95,000. **Ad Rates:** Noncommercial. **URL:** http://wuky.uky.edu.

12376 WVLK-AM - 590
PO Box 1559 Phone: (606)253-5900
Lexington, KY 40507-1621 Fax: (606)253-5903
E-mail: wvlkam.com

Format: Full Service. **Networks:** Westwood One Radio; Mutual Broadcasting System; CBS. **Founded:** 1946. **Operating Hours:** Continuous; 20% network, 80% local. **ADI:** Lexington, KY. **Key Personnel:** Tom Leach, Contact, phone (606)253-5900, fax (606)253-5942; Pam Blackburn, Operations Dir., fax (606)253-5940; Robert Lindsey, Program Dir. **Wattage:** 5000. **Ad Rates:** $24.00-76.00 for 30 seconds. **URL:** http://www.wvlkam.com.

12377 WVLK-FM - 92.9
Broadway & Vine, 3rd Fl. Phone: (606)253-5900
Lexington, KY 40507 Fax: (606)253-5903
E-mail: k93@mis.net

Format: Country. **Owner:** HMH Broadcasting Inc., at above address. **Founded:** 1961. **Operating Hours:** Continuous. **ADI:** Lexington, KY. **Key Personnel:** Ralph E. Hacker, President; Connie Joiner-Sabad, Contact; Matt Austin, Program Dir. **Wattage:** 100,000 ERP.

LIBERTY†, pop. 2,206.

Casey Co. (C).

12378 The Casey County News
Landmark Community Newspapers, Inc.
PO Box 40 Phone: (606)787-7171
Liberty, KY 42539-0040 Fax: (606)787-8306

County newspaper. **Freq:** Weekly (Wed.). **Key Personnel:** Maleena Streeval, Editor. **Subscription Rates:** $13.95 individuals; $17.50 out of area; $23.75 out of state.

12379 WKDO-AM - 1560
Hwy. 1649 Phone: (606)787-7331
Liberty, KY 42539 Fax: (606)787-2166

Format: Country. **Networks:** USA Radio. **Founded:** 1963. **Formerly:** WPHN-AM (1963). **Operating Hours:** 16 hours daily. **Key Personnel:** Carlos Wesley, Manager; Rick Wesley, Music Dir. **Wattage:** 1000. **Ad Rates:** $7 for 60 seconds.

12380 WKDO-FM - 98.7
Hwy. 1649, Box B Phone: (606)787-7331
Liberty, KY 42539 Fax: (606)787-2166

Format: Country; Religious. **Networks:** USA Radio. **Founded:** 1963. **Operating Hours:** 18 hours Daily. **Key Personnel:** Rick Wesley, Program Dir.; Carlos Wesley, General Mgr. **Wattage:** 25,000. **Ad Rates:** $9 for 60 seconds.

LONDON†, pop. 4,002.

Laurel Co. (SEC). 70 m S of Lexington. Manufactures bakery products, fabricated sheet metal, automatic transfer switches, church furniture, non-woven products, business forms, lumber, fertilizer, fluid milk, ice cream. Cattle, pork grain farms.

12381 The Sentinel-Echo
Media General Inc.
PO Box 830 Phone: (606)878-7400
London, KY 40743-0830 Fax: (606)878-7404
Publication E-mail: sentinel@kih.net

Community newspaper. **Subtitle:** Serving Laurel County. **Founded:** 1873. **Freq:** 3/week. **Print Method:** Offset. **Trim Size:** 14 x 22. **Cols./Page:** 6. **Col. Width:** 28 nonpareils. **Col. Depth:** 301 agate lines. **Key Personnel:** Ken Shmitheiser, General Mgr.; Michael Bryant, Advertising Dir. **USPS:** 490-600. **Subscription Rates:** $39 individuals. **Remarks:** Accepts advertising.
Ad Rates: GLR: $.25 **Circ:** ‡7,500
BW: $516
4C: $776
SAU: $5.84
PCI: $4.96

12382 WFTG-AM - 1400
F.T.G. Broadcasting Inc. Phone: (606)864-2148
534 Tobacco Rd. Fax: (606)864-0645
London, KY 40741

Format: Country. **Simulcasts:** WWEL-FM. **Networks:** KyNet. **Owner:** Key Broadcasting, at above address, (606)528-9600. **Founded:** 1955. **Operating Hours:** Continuous. **ADI:** Lexington, KY. **Key Personnel:** Terry Harris, Operations/Production Dir.; Francis Wilholt, General Mgr. **Wattage:** 1000. **Ad Rates:** $3-7 for 15 seconds; $4-8 for 30 seconds; $6-10 for 60 seconds.

12383 WWEL-FM - 103.9
534 Tobacco Rd. Phone: (606)864-2148
London, KY 40741 Fax: (606)864-0645

Format: Country. **Networks:** KyNet. **Owner:** Key Broadcasting, at above address, (606)528-9600. **Founded:** 1970. **Operating Hours:** Continuous. **ADI:** Lexington, KY. **Key Personnel:** Francis Wilholt, General Mgr.; Terry Harris, Operations Dir. **Wattage:** 6,000. **Ad Rates:** Noncommercial. $3-7 for 15 seconds; $4-8 for 30 seconds; $6-10 for 60 seconds. Combined advertising rates available with WFTG-AM.

12384 WWLT-FM - 103.1
100 Thompson Poynter Rd. Phone: (606)878-9958
London, KY 40741-7238 Fax: (606)864-9958

Format: Contemporary Christian. **Owner:** Wilderness Hills Broadcasting Inc., at above address. **Founded:** 1969. **Formerly:** WWXL-FM (1993). **Operating Hours:** Continuous. **Key Personnel:** Brian Douglas, Dir. of Operations. **Local Programs:** *The Friday New Music Hour*, Brian Douglas; *The More Music Morning Show*, Dana Douglas. **Wattage:** 3,000 ERP. **Ad Rates:** $3.25-5 for 30 seconds; $4.50-7.50 for 60 seconds.

12385 WYGE-FM - 92.3
201 E. 2nd St. Phone: (606)877-1326
London, KY 40741 Fax: (606)864-3702
E-mail: gnoutreach@sun-spot.com

Format: Religious. **Owner:** Ethel Huff, at above address. **Founded:** 1994. **Operating Hours:** Continuous. **Key Personnel:** Arlene Zawko, Program Dir.; Leland Worley, News/Weather. **Wattage:** 50,000. **Ad Rates:** $5.20-7.50 per unit.

LOUISA†, pop. 1,832.

Lawrence Co. (NE). On Big Sandy River, 30 m S of Ashland. Manufactures boxes, flour, feed, soft drinks. Oil, gas wells. Coal mines. Fire clay. San pit. Timber. Dairy, stock, poultry farms. Corn, feed, sorghum, tocacco.

12386 The Big Sandy News
PO Box 766 Phone: (606)638-4581
Ricky Skaggs Blvd. Fax: (606)638-9949
Louisa, KY 41230-0766
Community newspaper. **Founded:** 1885. **Freq:** Weekly (Wed.). **Print Method:** Offset. **Cols./Page:** 6 and 8. **Col. Width:** 12 and 9 picas. **Col. Depth:** 21 and 21 inches. **Key Personnel:** Jerry Pennington, Editor; Marjorie Hale, General Mgr. **Subscription Rates:** $20 individuals; $24 out of state. **Alt. Formats:** Microform.
Ad Rates: GLR: $4.75 **Circ:** ‡4,200
BW: $333.90
4C: $400
SAU: $5.00
PCI: $3.00

LOUISVILLE†, pop. 298,451.

Jefferson Co. (NW). On Ohio River, 109 m SW of Cincinnati, Ohio. Boat connections. Five bridges to New Albany, Ind. and Jeffersonville, Ind. University of Louisville, law, medical and dental, theology schools. Kentucky Derby and other race courses. Industrial, financial and educational center. Manufactures electrical appliances, whiskey, cigarettes, bathtubs, plumbing and railway supplies, paint, varnish, barrels, boxes, cabinets, bedding, mattresses, textiles, cement, beer, canned vegetables, biscuits, drying machinery, fire brick, caskets, auto bodies, trailers, steel and wood tanks, shirts, synthetic rubber, aluminum boats, farm machinery, plywood, wood plastics, baseball bats. Meat packing; sugar refining; wood working; creosoting, auto assembly plants; machine shops,oil refineries; phosphate, fluorspar, stone quarries.

12387 All Around Kentucky
Kentucky Farm Bureau Federation
9201 Bunsen Park Way Phone: (502)495-5000
Louisville, KY 40220 Fax: (502)495-5114
Publication E-mail: info@kyfb.win.net

Agriculture magazine reporting farm policy news and information on rural living. **Founded:** 1937. **Freq:** Monthly. **Print Method:** Offset. **Trim Size:** 11 3/8 x 15. **Cols./Page:** 4. **Col. Width:** 14 picas. **Col. Depth:** 14 inches. **Key Personnel:** Gary Huddleston, Editor and Publisher; Judy Crask, Advertising Mgr. **ISSN:** 1082-1570. **Subscription Rates:** $.50 individuals. **Remarks:** Accepts advertising. **Former name:** Kentucky Farm Bureau News.
Ad Rates: BW: $2,690 **Circ:** Paid ‡376,108
4C: $3,290 Controlled ‡1,261
PCI: $38.40

12388 American Conchologist
Conchologists of America
1222 Holsworth Ln. Phone: (502)423-0469
Louisville, KY 40222-6616
Publication E-mail: amconch@ix.netcom.com

Professional journal covering conservation of Molluscan habitats and other topics of interest to shell collectors. **Founded:** 1973. **Freq:** Quarterly. **Trim Size:** 8 x 11. **Cols./Page:** 2. **Col. Width:** 1 3/8 inches. **Col. Depth:** 9 inches. **Key Personnel:** Lynn Scheu, Editor. **ISSN:** 1072-2440. **Remarks:** Accepts advertising Shell related items only. **Former name:** Conchologists of America Bulletin (1987).
Ad Rates: BW: $165 **Circ:** Combined 1,700

12389 American Journal of Italian Studies
The DeSoto Press
4720 S. 2nd St. Phone: (502)366-6305
Louisville, KY 40214 Fax: (502)366-6305

Literary journal. Text in Italian, English, and French. **Founded:** 1977. **Freq:** Semiannual. **Trim Size:** 6 x 9. **Key Personnel:** Stelio Cro, Editor, stelcro@aol.com. **ISSN:** 0705-3002. **Subscription Rates:** $20; $50 institutions. **Remarks:** Accepts advertising. **Former name:** Canadian Journal of Italian Studies.
Ad Rates: BW: $100 **Circ:** 300

12390 The American Voice
332 W. Broadway, Ste. 1215 Phone: (502)562-0045
Louisville, KY 40202
Journal of pan-American literature. **Founded:** 1985. **Freq:** 3/year. **Trim Size:** 6 x 9. **Key Personnel:** Fredrick Smock, Editor; Sallie Bingham, Publisher. **ISSN:** 0884-4356. **Subscription Rates:** $15.
Ad Rates: BW: $100 **Circ:** Non-paid 2,000

12391 Biotechnic & Histochemistry
Lippincott Williams & Wilkins
University of Louisville Phone: (502)852-7550
Dept. of Anatomical Sciences Free: (800)334-8635
and Neurobiology
Health Science Center
Louisville, KY 40292
Journal covering the new materials, apparatus, and methods involved in preparing biological specimens. **Subtitle:** Official Publication of the Biological Stain Commission. **Founded:** 1925. **Freq:** Bimonthly. **Print Method:** Offset. **Trim Size:** 8 1/8 x 10 7/8. **Cols./Page:** 1. **Col. Width:** 58 nonpareils. **Col. Depth:** 110 agate lines. **Key Personnel:** G.S. Nettleton, Ph.D., Editor; David Jones, Representative, phone (410)528-4283, djones@wwilkins.com. **ISSN:** 1052-0295. **Subscription Rates:** $76 individuals; $130 other countries. **Remarks:** Accepts advertising. **Alt. Formats:** Mailing labels.
Ad Rates: BW: $565 **Circ:** Paid ‡1,610
4C: $1,335 Non-paid ‡90

12392 Burroughs Bulletin
Chicago Press Corp.
Burroughs Memorial Collection Phone: (502)852-8729
University of Louisville Library Fax: (502)852-8734
Louisville, KY 40292
Magazine devoted to Edgar Rice Burroughs. Includes feature stories and interviews, bibliography, art, and criticism. **Founded:** July 1947. **Freq:** Quarterly. **Print Method:** Offset. **Trim Size:** 8 1/2 x 11. **Cols./Page:** 1. **Col. Width:** 6 1/2 inches. **Col. Depth:** 9 1/2 inches. **Key Personnel:** George T. McWhorter, Editor/Advertising and Circulation Mgr. **Subscription Rates:** $28 U.S.; $35 elsewhere. **Remarks:** Accepts advertising. **URL:** http://www.virtual.bookshop.com.
Circ: Paid ‡800

12393 Church & Society
National Ministries Division PCUSA
100 Witherspoon St. Phone: (502)569-5810
Louisville, KY 40202-1396 Fax: (502)569-8116

Presbyterian church magazine covering social justice. **Subtitle:** The Journal of Just Thoughts. **Founded:** 1908. **Freq:** Bimonthly. **Print Method:** Offset. **Trim Size:** 6 x 9. **Cols./Page:** 1. **Col. Width:** 49 nonpareils. **Col. Depth:** 96 agate lines. **Key Personnel:** Kathy Lancaster, Editor, kathy_lancaster@pcusa.org. **ISSN:** 0037-7805. **Subscription Rates:** $12; $30 three years. **Remarks:** Advertising not accepted. **Formerly:** Social Progresspre (1970).
Circ: Paid 5,000

12394 The Courier-Journal
Courier-Journal Co.
525 W. Broadway St. Phone: (502)582-4011
Louisville, KY 40202-2137 Fax: (502)582-4075

General newspaper. **Founded:** 1868. **Freq:** Daily and Sunday (morn.). **Print Method:** Letterpress. **Cols./Page:** 6. **Col. Width:** 24 nonpareils. **Col. Depth:** 300 agate lines. **Key Personnel:** David V. Hawpe, Editor; Edward Manassah, Publisher; Stephen Bernard, Advertising Dir. **Subscription Rates:** $132 individuals. **Remarks:** Accepts advertising. **Online:** DataTimes Corporation; LEXIS-NEXIS. **URL:** http://

www.courier-journal.com. **Alt. Formats:** CD-ROM. **Feature Editors:** Ed Bennett, *Travel*, phone (502)582-4615; Harry Bryan, *Sports*, phone (502)582-4060; Al Cross, *Political*, phone (502)875-5136; Tom Dorsey, *Radio, TV*, phone (502)582-4474; Yvonne Eaton, *Garden/Home, Society*, phone (502)582-7068; Judy Egerton, *Farm, Rural Development*, phone (502)582-7088; Roger Fristoe, *Movie*, phone (502)582-4503; Sarah Fritschner, *Food*, phone (502)582-4203; Tom Hardin, *Photo*, phone (502)582-4607; Hunt Helm, *City, Metro, News*, phone (502)582-4691; Pat Howington, *Medical*, phone (502)582-4691; Cindy Inskeep, *Fashion*, phone (502)582-4633; Arlene Jacobson, *Consumer Affairs*, phone (502)582-4651; Michael Jennings, *Education*, phone (502)582-4691; Greg Johnson, *Family, Features, Lifestyle, Living, Saturday, Women's*, phone (502)582-7077; Ric Manning, *Aviation, Science*, phone (502)582-4240; Mark McCormick, *Religion*, phone (502)582-4691; Maureen McNerney, *Drama, Entertainment*, phone (502)582-4684; Andrew Melnykovych, *Environmental*, phone (502)582-4645; William Mootz, *Music*, phone (502)582-7078; Glenn Proctor, *Financial/Business, Real Estate*, phone (502)582-4651; Jeffrey Puckett, *Music*, phone (502)582-4160; Linda Raymond, *Suburban*, phone (502)582-4120; Keith Runyon, *Book, Editorials*, phone (502)582-4594.
Ad Rates: PCI: $120.62 **Circ:** Mon.-Sat. ★**228,144**
Sun. ★**306,096**

12395 The Disability Rag's Ragged Edge Magazine
Advocado Press, Inc.
PO Box 145 Phone: (502)894-9492
Louisville, KY 40201 Fax: (502)899-9562
Publication E-mail: rgarr@iglou.com

Magazine of debate on disability rights issues. **Subtitle:** The Disability Experience in America. **Founded:** 1980. **Freq:** Bimonthly. **Print Method:** Offset. **Trim Size:** 8 x 10 5/8. **Cols./Page:** 3. **Col. Width:** 12 picas. **Col. Depth:** 8 3/4 inches. **Key Personnel:** Mary Johnson, Editor. **ISSN:** 0749-9596. **Subscription Rates:** $17.50 individuals; $3.95 single issue; $42 other countries; $35 institutions. **Remarks:** Accepts advertising. **Available Online. URL:** http://www.iglou.com/why/edge.htm. **Alt. Formats:** Large-print. **Formerly:** The Disability Rag (1993); Disability Rag & Resource.
Ad Rates: BW: $875 **Circ:** 3,500
4C: $1,050

12396 Filson Club History Quarterly
Filson Club
1310 S. 3rd St. Phone: (502)635-5083
Louisville, KY 40208 Fax: (502)635-5086
Publisher E-mail: filson@filson.club.org

Journal covering regional history of Kentucky and adjacent states. **Founded:** 1926. **Freq:** Quarterly. **Print Method:** Photo offset. **Trim Size:** 6 1/8 x 9 1/4. **Cols./Page:** 1. **Col. Width:** 26 picas. **Col. Depth:** 42 picas. **Key Personnel:** Nelson L. Dawson, Ph.D., Editor, dawson@filsonclub.org. **ISSN:** 0015-1874. **Subscription Rates:** $40 individuals. **Remarks:** Accepts advertising.
Ad Rates: BW: $95 **Circ:** Controlled 4,100

12397 Henry James Review
Johns Hopkins University Press
University of Louisville Phone: (502)852-4671
Dept. of English Fax: (502)852-4182
Louisville, KY 40292
Publication E-mail: hjamesr@ulkyvm.louisville.edu
Publisher E-mail: jlinfo@jhupress.jhu.edu

Literary journal. **Founded:** 1979. **Freq:** 3/year. **Print Method:** Offset. **Trim Size:** 7 x 10. **Cols./Page:** 1. **Col. Width:** 26 picas. **Col. Depth:** 7 inches. **Key Personnel:** Susan M. Griffin, Editor. **ISSN:** 0273-0340. **Subscription Rates:** $31.50; $73.50 institutions, industry. **Remarks:** Accepts advertising. **URL:** http://muse.jhu.edu/journals/henry_james_review/index.html.
Ad Rates: BW: $205 **Circ:** ‡970

12398 Horizons
Presbyterian Women in the Presbyterian Church (U.S.A.)
100 Witherspoon St. Phone: (502)569-5379
Louisville, KY 40202-1396 Fax: (502)569-8085
Free: (800)487-4875

Magazine for Presbyterian women and annual Bible study. **Founded:** 1988. **Freq:** Bimonthly. **Trim Size:** 8 x 11. **Key Personnel:** Marie T. Cross, Editor. **ISSN:** 1040-0087. **Subscription Rates:** $14 individuals; $16 other countries. **Remarks:** Advertising not accepted. **Alt. Formats:** Audio tape; Braille; Large-print; Microform. **Formerly:** Concern.
Circ: Paid 28,000
Non-paid 1,000

12399 Journal of the Kentucky Medical Association
Kentucky Medical Association
4965 US Hwy. 42 Phone: (502)426-6200
Louisville, KY 40222-8512 Fax: (502)426-6877

Professional medical journal. **Founded:** 1903. **Freq:** Monthly. **Print Method:** Offset. **Trim Size:** 8 1/4 x 10 7/8. **Cols./Page:** 2. **Col. Width:** 17.5 picas. **Col. Depth:** 49 picas. **Key Personnel:** A. Evan Overstreet, M.D., Editor; Sue Tharp, Managing Editor. **ISSN:** 0023-0294. **Subscription Rates:** $35 individuals; $45 out of country; $4 single issue. **Remarks:** Accepts advertising. **Alt. Formats:** Microfilm.
Ad Rates: BW: $360 **Circ:** Controlled ⊕**6,234**
4C: $1,040

12400 Journal of Musicology
University of California Press/Journals
PO Box 4516
Louisville, KY 40204
Publisher E-mail: journal@ucop.edu

Journal covering the study of music. **Founded:** 1972. **Freq:** Quarterly. **Trim Size:** 6 x 9. **ISSN:** 0277-9269. **Subscription Rates:** $24; $48 institution; $18 student. $6 single issue. **Remarks:** Accepts advertising.
Ad Rates: BW: $225 **Circ:** (Not Reported)

12401 Journal of Urban Affairs
JAI Press, Inc.
Urban Studies Institute Phone: (502)852-6626
University of Louisville Fax: (502)852-7386
426 W. Bloom St.
Louisville, KY 40208
Publication E-mail: 102062-2525@compuserve.com

Subtitle: Official Journal of the Urban Affairs Association. **Founded:** 1979. **Freq:** 4/year. **Print Method:** Offset. **Trim Size:** 6 7/8 x 10. **Cols./Page:** 1. **Key Personnel:** Scott B. Cummings, Editor, phone (502)852-8003, fax (502)852-4558, sbcumm01@ulkyum.louisville.edu. **ISSN:** 0735-2166. **Subscription Rates:** $225 institutions; $245 institutions, other countries; $90 individuals; $110 individuals other countries; $130 individuals other countries, airmail; $60 single issue; $65 single issue other countries; $70 single issue other countries, airmail. **Remarks:** Accepts advertising.
Ad Rates: BW: $300 **Circ:** (Not Reported)

12402 Kentucky Banker
Kentucky Bankers Association
Waterfront Plaza, Ste. 1000 Phone: (502)582-2453
325 W. Main St. Fax: (502)584-6390
Louisville, KY 40202
Publisher E-mail: kba@kybanks.com

Trade magazine for members and advocates of the Kentucky Bankers Association. **Freq:** Monthly. **Key Personnel:** Joe Price, Editor. **Subscription Rates:** $30 individuals. **Remarks:** Accepts advertising.
Circ: Combined 1,600

12403 Kentucky Living
Kentucky Association of Electric Cooperatives
PO Box 32170 Phone: (502)451-2430
Louisville, KY 40232 Fax: (502)459-1611
Free: (800)595-4846

Magazine on people, places, events, and history of Kentucky. **Founded:** Apr. 1948. **Freq:** Monthly. **Print Method:** Offset. **Trim Size:** 8 1/8 x 10 7/8. **Cols./Page:** 3. **Col. Width:** 2 1/4 inches. **Col. Depth:** 10 inches. **Key Personnel:** Paul Wesslund, Editor and Publisher; Stephanie Dumeyer, Advertising Mgr. **ISSN:** 0036-0066. **Subscription Rates:** $15 individuals; $2 single issue. **Remarks:** Advertising not accepted for Alcoholic beverages or tobacco products.
Ad Rates: BW: $4,100 **Circ:** Paid ★**458,028**
4C: $5,125
PCI: $195

12404 Kentucky Plumbing-Heating-Cooling Index
Kentucky Association of Plumbing-Heating-Cooling Contractors
1501 Durrett Ln. Phone: (502)451-5577
Louisville, KY 40213 Fax: (502)451-5551
Free: (800)527-4229

Industry magazine for plumbing, heating, and cooling contractors. **Founded:** 1952. **Freq:** Monthly. **Trim Size:** 11 1/4 x 15. **Cols./Page:** 4. **Col. Width:** 2 3/8 inches. **Col. Depth:** 13 inches. **Key Personnel:** Linda Griffey, Managing Editor. **Remarks:** Accepts advertising.
Ad Rates: BW: $330 **Circ:** ‡2,200

12405 Kentucky Travel Guide
Editorial Services Company
812 South 3rd St. Phone: (502)584-2720
Louisville, KY 40203 Fax: (502)584-2722
Free: (800)888-0695
Publisher E-mail: esc@kytravel.com

Travel publication focusing on attractions, events and facilities for 169 Kentucky cities. **Founded:** 1967. **Freq:** Annual. **Print Method:** Web offset. **Trim Size:** 5 1/2 x 8 1/2. **Cols./Page:** 2. **Col. Width:** 2 1/4 inches. **Key Personnel:** Sara N. Reisz, Editor. **Subscription Rates:** $3 single issue. **Remarks:** Accepts advertising. **URL:** http://www.kytravel.com.
Ad Rates: BW: $5,820 **Circ:** Non-paid 300,000
4C: $6,950

12406 Louisville
Louisville Magazine Inc.
137 W. Muhammad Ali Blvd., Ste. 101 Phone: (502)625-0100
Fax: (502)625-0109
Louisville, KY 40202-1438
Publication E-mail: loumag@loumag.com

Lifestyles magazine about the Louisville, KY area. **Founded:** 1950. **Freq:** Monthly. **Print Method:** Web offset. **Trim Size:** 8 1/8 x 10 7/8. **Cols./Page:** 3. **Col. Width:** 2 15/16 inches. **Col. Depth:** 10 inches. **Key Personnel:** Dan Crutcher, Editor and Publisher, dcrutcher@loumag.com. **ISSN:** 0024-6948. **Subscription Rates:** $15; $2.95 single issue. **Remarks:** Accepts advertising. **Available Online. URL:** http://www.louisville.com.
Ad Rates: BW: $2,220 **Circ:** Paid 18,000
4C: $3,060

12407 Louisville Business First
American City Business Journals
111 W. Washington St., Ste. 400 Phone: (502)583-1731
Fax: (502)587-1703
Louisville, KY 40202
Weekly Business Newspaper. **Subtitle:** The Business Newspaper of Greater Louisville. **Founded:** 1984. **Freq:** Weekly. **Print Method:** Web offset. **Trim Size:** 11 1/4 x 15. **Cols./Page:** 4. **Col. Width:** 2 1/8 inches. **Col. Depth:** 13 1/2 inches. **Key Personnel:** Tom Monahan, Publisher; Carol Timmons, Editor; Lisa Troueblood, Circ. Dir.; Carol Braden, Production Dir.; David Bingham, Dir. of Promotions; Linda Vance, Business Mgr.; Maureen O'Meara, Advertising Dir. **Subscription Rates:** $60 individuals; $1.25 single issue. **Remarks:** Accepts advertising. **URL:** http://www.amcity.com/louisville.
Circ: Paid ★**11,463**

12408 The Louisville Cardinal
University of Louisville
Old Student Center, Ste. 305 Phone: (502)588-6727
Louisville, KY 40292-0001 Fax: (502)588-0700

Collegiate newspaper (tabloid). **Founded:** 1928. **Freq:** Weekly (Thurs.). **Print Method:** Offset. **Trim Size:** 11 x 17. **Cols./Page:** 6. **Col. Width:** 26 nonpareils. **Col. Depth:** 301 agate lines. **Subscription Rates:** Free; $8 by mail. **Remarks:** Accepts advertising.
Ad Rates: BW: $482.50 **Circ:** Free 17,000
PCI: $9.25

12409 Louisville Defender
Consumer Communications Industries
1720 Dixie Hwy. Phone: (502)772-2591
Louisville, KY 40210 Fax: (502)775-8655

Community newspaper. **Founded:** Mar. 1933. **Freq:** Weekly (Thurs.). **Print Method:** Offset. **Trim Size:** 13 x 21 1/2. **Cols./Page:** 6. **Col. Width:** 2 1/16 inches. **Col. Depth:** 21 1/2 inches. **Key Personnel:** Yvonne D. Coleman, Editor; Clarence Leslie, Advertising Mgr. **Subscription Rates:** $16 individuals; $18.20 out of area. **Remarks:** Accepts advertising.
Ad Rates: BW: $1,278.90 **Circ:** Non-paid 134
4C: $2,018.90 Paid 2,211
SAU: $10.15
PCI: $9.10

12410 Monday Morning
General Assembly Council, Presbyterian Church (U.S.A.)
100 Witherspoon St., Rm. 5425-A Phone: (502)569-5755
Fax: (502)569-8073
Louisville, KY 40202-1396
Publication E-mail: monday.morning@pcusa.org; stephen.moulton@pcusa.org

Magazine providing a forum for Presbyterian leaders to debate and discuss issues concerning the Presbyterian church. **Subtitle:** The Magazine for Presbyterian leaders. **Founded:** Jan. 6, 1936. **Freq:** Semimonthly (monthly June, July, and August). **Print Method:** Offset. **Trim Size:** 5 x 7 1/2. **Cols./Page:** 2. **Col. Width:** 1.75 inches. **Col. Depth:** 6 inches. **Key Personnel:** Sue Boardman, Editor, phone (502)569-5502, fax (502)569-8073, sue.boardman@pcusa.org; Judith Steer, Managing Editor, phone (502)569-5770, judy.steer@pcusa.org; Don Cecil, Advertising/Sales Promotion, phone (502)569-5755, don.cecil@pcusa.org. **ISSN:** 0360-6171. **Subscription Rates:** $21 individuals; $15 bulk for 6 or more to same

address. **Remarks:** Accepts advertising. **URL:** http://www.pcusa.org/pcusa/mm/.
Ad Rates: BW: $525 **Circ:** 12,100

12411 National Police Review
National Police Officers Association
7811 Old Tree Run Phone: (502)425-9215
Louisville, KY 40222-4694 Fax: (502)326-3705

Magazine serving as a forum for the Police Officers Association of America. Includes articles on new ideas and procedures in law enforcement, security, crime prevention, reviews of police products and equipment, and association news. **Founded:** July 1991. **Freq:** 4/year. **Print Method:** Offset. **Trim Size:** 8 x 10 3/4. **Cols./Page:** 3. **Key Personnel:** John R. Moore, Editor, divcop@aol.com. **Subscription Rates:** $18 members /year. **Remarks:** Advertising accepted; rates available upon request.
Circ: Paid ‡4,000
Non-paid ‡1,000

12412 Presbyterians Today
Presbyterian Church (U.S.A.)
100 Witherspoon St. Phone: (502)569-5637
Louisville, KY 40202-1396 Fax: (502)569-8632
Publication E-mail: today@pcusa.org

Presbyterian magazine. **Subtitle:** The Magazine for Presbyterians. **Founded:** 1862. **Freq:** 10/year. **Print Method:** Offset. **Trim Size:** 8 1/8 x 10 7/8. **Cols./Page:** 3. **Col. Width:** 28 nonpareils. **Col. Depth:** 140 agate lines. **Key Personnel:** Catherine Cottingham, Managing Editor, phone (502)569-5634; Eva Stimson, Editor, phone (502)569-5635. **ISSN:** 0032-759X. **Subscription Rates:** $12.95 individuals; $9 groups; $6.50 member congregations. **Alt. Formats:** Microform. **Formerly:** Presbyterian Survey.
Ad Rates: GLR: $12 **Circ:** ‡90,000
BW: $2,610
4C: $3,300
PCI: $105

12413 Review and Expositor
Review & Expositor
PO Box 6681 Phone: (502)327-8347
Louisville, KY 40206-0681 Fax: (502)327-8347

Magazine on theology. **Founded:** 1904. **Freq:** Quarterly. **Print Method:** Letterpress. **Trim Size:** 7 x 10. **Cols./Page:** 1. **Col. Width:** 48 nonpareils. **Col. Depth:** 126 agate lines. **Key Personnel:** Dan R. Stiver, Editor; Joel F. Drinkard, Jr., Business Mgr. **ISSN:** 0034-6373. **Subscription Rates:** $24 individuals; $40 institutions; $30 other countries; $9 single issue USA; $10 single issue other countries.
Ad Rates: BW: $120 **Circ:** Paid ‡2,400

12414 Southern Seminary Magazine
Review & Expositor
PO Box 6681 Phone: (502)327-8347
Louisville, KY 40206-0681 Fax: (502)327-8347

News and information about Southern Seminary. **Subtitle:** News About the Southern Baptist Theological Seminary. **Founded:** 1932. **Freq:** Quarterly. **Print Method:** Offset. **Trim Size:** 8 3/8 x 10 7/8. **Cols./Page:** 3. **Col. Width:** 27 nonpareils. **Col. Depth:** 132 agate lines. **Key Personnel:** Dr. Douglas C. Walker, Acting Editor. **ISSN:** 0040-7232. **Subscription Rates:** Free. **Remarks:** Advertising not accepted. **Formerly:** The Tie.
Circ: Controlled 33,000

12415 Tire Retreading/Repair Journal
Tire Industry Publication Service
PO Box 37203 Phone: (502)968-8900
Louisville, KY 40233-7203 Fax: (502)964-7859
Free: (800)426-8835
Publication E-mail: itra@itra.com

Magazine containing technical information on tire retreading and repair. **Founded:** 1956. **Freq:** Monthly. **Print Method:** Offset. **Cols./Page:** 2. **Col. Width:** 24 nonpareils. **Col. Depth:** 94 agate lines. **Key Personnel:** Marvin F. Bozarth, Editor. **ISSN:** 1046-7157. **Subscription Rates:** $50 U.S. and Canada; $60 other countries; $90 two years; multiple subscriptions discounts available. **Remarks:** Accepts advertising. **URL:** http://www.itra.com.
Ad Rates: BW: $550 **Circ:** ‡3,000
4C: $1150

12416 UMI's Banking Information Index
UMI
620 S. 3rd St. Phone: (502)583-4111
Louisville, KY 40205 Fax: (502)589-5572

Index of articles on banking trends, topics, issues, and operations. **Founded:** 1982. **Freq:** Quarterly. **Trim Size:** 8 1/2 x 11. **Cols./Page:** 3. **Key Personnel:** Andy Horvay, Managing Editor; Connee Underwood, Assoc. Editor. **ISSN:** 0736-5659. **Remarks:** Advertising not accepted. **Online:** Proquest Direct. **Formerly:** American Bankers Association Banking Literature Index (1994).
Circ: Paid 410
Non-paid 20

12417 Unique Opportunities The Physician's Resource
UO Inc.
455 S. 4th Ave., No. 1236 Phone: (502)589-8250
Louisville, KY 40202 Fax: (502)587-0848
Publication E-mail: unop@aol.com
Publisher E-mail: UNOP@aol.com

Professional magazine covering career development for physicians. **Subtitle:** The Physician's Resource. **Founded:** Nov. 1991. **Freq:** Bimonthly. **Print Method:** Web offset. **Trim Size:** 8 1/8 x 10 7/8. **Cols./Page:** 3. **Key Personnel:** Mollie Hudson, Editor; Mel Weinberger, Publisher/Advertising; Bett Coffman, Assoc. Ed. **ISSN:** 1059-6100. **Subscription Rates:** $30 individuals; $5 single issue. **Remarks:** Accepts advertising.
Ad Rates: BW: $4,275 **Circ:** Controlled 80,000
4C: $5,125

12418 The Voice-Tribune
Southern Publishing, Inc.
3818 Shelbyville Rd. Phone: (502)897-8900
Louisville, KY 40207-3186 Fax: (502)897-8915

Suburban community newspaper. **Founded:** 1949. **Freq:** Weekly (Wed.). **Print Method:** Offset. **Trim Size:** 13 x 21 1/2. **Cols./Page:** 6. **Col. Width:** 2 1/16 inches. **Col. Depth:** 21 1/2 inches. **Key Personnel:** Steve Rusky, Editor; John H. Harralson, Jr., Publisher; John D. Chalek, Jr., General Mgr. **ISSN:** 0894-8100. **Subscription Rates:** $15.95 individuals. **Remarks:** Accepts advertising. **Formerly:** The New Voice.
Ad Rates: BW: $1,350 **Circ:** Paid ‡11,859
4C: $1,800 Free ‡1,571
SAU: $22.53
PCI: $22.53

12419 Welcome to Greater Louisville
Editorial Services Company
812 South 3rd St. Phone: (502)584-2720
Louisville, KY 40203 Fax: (502)584-2722
Free: (800)888-0695
Publisher E-mail: esc@kytravel.com

Visitor's guide for the greater Louisville area, listing current attractions and shopping and dining establishments. **Founded:** 1951. **Freq:** Biweekly. **Print Method:** Sheetfed offset. **Trim Size:** 5 1/2 x 8 1/2. **Cols./Page:** 2. **Col. Width:** 2 1/4 inches. **Key Personnel:** Sara N. Reisz, Editor. **Subscription Rates:** $30 individuals. **Remarks:** Accepts advertising. **URL:** http://www.kytravel.com.
Ad Rates: BW: $915 **Circ:** Controlled 18,000
4C: $955

Western Recorder - See Middletown

12420 TKR Cable
1536 Story Ave. Phone: (502)584-6111
Louisville, KY 40206 Fax: (502)584-1401

Founded: 1979. **Formerly:** Storer Communications of Jefferson County. **Key Personnel:** Charles King, General Mgr.; Chris Bowling, Contact; Jeffrey Landers, Contact; Doug McKenzie, Business Mgr.; John Pait, Operations Mgr. **Cities Served:** Jefferson County, Oldham County, Anchorage, Audubon Park, Bankcroft, Barboumeade, Beechwood Village, Bellermeade, Bellwood, Briarwood, Broadfields, Broeck Point, Brownsboro Village, Cambridge, Cherrywood Village, Creekside, Crossgate, Devondale, Douglass Hills, Glenview Hills, Glenview Manor, Goose Creek, Graymoor, Green Spring, Hickory Hill, Hills and Dales, Hollow Creek, Hollyvilla, Hurtsbourne Acres, Indian Hills, Jeffersontown, Keeneland, Kingsley, Lincolnshire, Lyndon, Lynnview, Manor Creek, Maryhill Estates, Meadow Vale, Meadowbrook Estates, Middletown, Minor Lane Heights, Mockingbird Valley, Moorland, Norbourne Estates, Northfield, Norwood, Parkway Village, Pewee Valley,.

12421 WAMZ-FM - 97.5
520 W. Chesnut Phone: (502)582-7840
Louisville, KY 40202 Fax: (502)582-7837

Format: Contemporary Country. **Networks:** Independent. **Owner:** Clear Channel Radio, Inc., at above address. **Founded:** 1966. **Operating Hours:** Continuous. **ADI:** Louisville, KY. **Key Personnel:** Robert Scherer, General Mgr. **Wattage:** 100,000.

12422 WAVE-TV - 3
725 S. Floyd St. Phone: (502)585-2201
Louisville, KY 40203 Fax: (502)561-4115

Format: Commercial TV. **Networks:** NBC. **Operating Hours:** 6 a.m.-3 a.m. **ADI:** Louisville, KY. **Key Personnel:** Guy Hempel, General Mgr.

12423 WBNA-TV - 21
3701 Fern Valley Rd. Phone: (502)964-2121
Louisville, KY 40219 Fax: (502)966-9692

Format: Commercial TV. **Networks:** Independent. **Owner:** WORD Broadcasting, Inc., at above address. **Founded:** 1986. **Operating Hours:** Continuous. **ADI:** Louisville, KY. **Key Personnel:** Phil Keith, General Mgr. **Wattage:** 2,200,000.

12424 WDJX-FM - 99.7
612 4th Ave., Ste. 100 Phone: (502)589-4800
Louisville, KY 40202 Fax: (502)587-0212

Format: Contemporary Hit Radio (CHR). **Networks:** Independent. **Owner:** Regent Communications, 50 East River Center Blvd, Covington, KY 41011. **Founded:** 1952. **Operating Hours:** Continuous; 100% local. **ADI:** Louisville, KY. **Key Personnel:** Bill Gentry, General Sales Mgr.; Chris Shebel, Program Dir. **Wattage:** 50,000 ERP. **Ad Rates:** $120-175 for 60 seconds.

12425 WDRB-TV - 41
1 Independence Sq. Phone: (502)584-6441
Louisville, KY 40203 Fax: (502)589-5559

Format: Commercial TV. **Networks:** Fox. **Owner:** Blade Communications, Inc., 541 Superior St., Toledo, OH 43660, (419)245-6000. **Founded:** 1971. **Operating Hours:** Continuous. **ADI:** Louisville, KY. **Key Personnel:** John Dorkin, Pres./General Mgr.; Jack Ratterman, General Sales Mgr./Vice Pres.; Glen Cook, Corp. Eng./Vice Pres.; Hal Stopfel, Vice Pres./News Dir.; Judy McDonald, Program Dir.; Pattie M. Kiray, Treasurer; Kim Grau, National Sales Mgr.; Katrina Very, National Sales Mgr.; David Yearwood, Station Mgr. **Wattage:** 5 meg-ERP. **URL:** http://www.fox41.com.

12426 WFIA-AM - 900
612 4th Ave., No.200 Phone: (502)583-4811
Louisville, KY 40202 Fax: (502)583-4820

Format: Religious. **Networks:** USA Radio. **Owner:** Neon Communications, Inc., at above address. **Founded:** 1947. **Operating Hours:** Continuous; 25% network, 55% national, 20% local. **ADI:** Louisville, KY. **Key Personnel:** Tom Schurr, VP Marketing Mgr.; Bill Gentry, Dir. of Sales; Jim Lawson, Station Mgr. **Wattage:** 1000. **Ad Rates:** $10-14 for 60 seconds.

12427 WFPK-FM - 91.9
301 York St. Phone: (502)574-1640
Louisville, KY 40203-2257 Fax: (502)574-1671
E-mail: wfpk@iglou.com

Format: Adult Album Alternative. **Networks:** National Public Radio (NPR); Public Radio International (PRI). **Founded:** 1954. **Operating Hours:** Continuous; 15% network, 85% local. **ADI:** Louisville, KY. **Key Personnel:** Leslie Stewart, Program Dir.; Gerry Weston, General Mgr. **Wattage:** 100,000. **Ad Rates:** Noncommercial.

12428 WFPL-FM - 89.3
301 York St. Phone: (502)574-1640
Louisville, KY 40203-2205 Fax: (502)574-1671
E-mail: webmaster@wfpl.org

Format: Public Radio; News; Talk. **Networks:** National Public Radio (NPR); Public Radio International (PRI). **Owner:** Public Radio Partnership, at above address. **Founded:** 1950. **Formerly:** Louisville Free Public Library. **Operating Hours:** Continuous; 80% network, 20% local. **ADI:** Louisville, KY. **Key Personnel:** John Gregory, Program Dir.; Gerry Weston, General Mgr., gweston@wfpl.org. **Local Programs:** *It's Your Business*, Scott Dowd, (502)574-1792. **Wattage:** 100,000. **Ad Rates:** Noncommercial.

12429 WHAS-AM - 840
520 W. Chesnut Phone: (502)582-7840
Louisville, KY 40202 Fax: (502)582-7837
E-mail: info@whas.com

Format: News; Talk. **Networks:** ABC. **Owner:** Clear Channel Radio, Inc., at above address. **Founded:** 1922. **Operating Hours:** Continuous. **ADI:** Louisville, KY. **Key Personnel:** Robert Scherer, Vice President. **Local Programs:** *Bob Valvano Show* 6 p.m. - 8 p.m. Sunday, Bob Valvano, (502)582-7842; *Dr. Stan Frager* 9 p.m. - midnight Sunday, Stan Frager, (502)582-7842; *Jane Norris Show* 9 a.m. - 12 noon Monday-Friday, Steve Kirkland, (502)582-7773; *Joe Elliott Show* 9 p.m. - midnight Monday-Friday, Steve Kirkland, (502)582-7842. **Wattage:** 50,000. **Ad Rates:** $20-230 for 30 seconds; $25-265 for 60 seconds.

12430 WHAS-TV - 11
PO Box 1100 Phone: (502)582-7840
Louisville, KY 40201 Fax: (502)582-7279

Format: Commercial TV. **Networks:** ABC. **Owner:** A.H. Belo Corporation, PO Box 655237, Dallas, TX 75265-5237, (214)977-8277. **Founded:** 1950. **Operating Hours:** Continuous Sun.-Thur.; 6 a.m.-3 a.m. Fri. and Sat. **ADI:** Louisville, KY. **Key Personnel:** Ken Middleton, Contact, phone (502)582-7700, fax (502)582-7224, kmiddet@witasll.com; Doug Roberts, General Sales Mgr., phone (502)582-7853, fax (502)582-7861, droberts@witsall.com; Dan Miller, Program Mgr., phone (502)582-7867, fax (502)482-7224, dmiller@whasll.com; Gary Gupton, Sports Dir., phone (502)582-7220, fax (502)589-5592, ggupton@whasll.com; John Blim, Promotions Mgr., phone (502)582-7889, jblim@projo.com; Ann Loofbounow, Controller, phone (502)582-7730, aloofbour@whasll.com; Gil Ludwig, Dir. of Engineering, phone (502)582-7760, gludwig@whasll.com. **URL:** http://www@whas11.com; http://www.whasll.com.

12431 WJIE-FM - 88.5
PO Box 197309 Phone: (502)968-1220
Louisville, KY 40259 Fax: (502)962-3143
Free: (800)433-8958

Format: Contemporary Christian. **Networks:** Sun Radio. **Owner:** Evangel Schools Inc., 5400 Minors Ln., Drawer B, Louisville, KY 40219, (502)964-3304. **Founded:** 1987. **Operating Hours:** Continuous; 20% network, 80% local. **ADI:** Louisville, KY. **Key Personnel:** Gerry Pretorius, General Mgr., gerry@wjie.org; Jim Galipeau, Program Dir., jm@wjie.org; Terry Dismore, Operations Dir. **Wattage:** 25,000. **Ad Rates:** Noncommercial. **URL:** http://www.wjie.org.

12432 WKMJ-TV - 68
c/o Kentucky Authority for Educational TV Phone: (606)258-7000
Fax: (606)258-7399
600 Cooper Dr.
Lexington, KY 40502

Format: Public TV. **Networks:** Public Broadcasting Service (PBS); Kentucky Educational Television. **Owner:** Kentucky Authority for Educational TV, at above address, (606)258-7170, Fax: (608)258-7390. **Founded:** 1968. **Operating Hours:** 6:15 a.m.-midnight. **ADI:** Louisville, KY. **Key Personnel:** Craig Cornwell, Contact; S. Talbert, Contact; J. Gorman, Contact; D. Holtzclaw, Business Mgr.; M. Ferguson, Contact; Victoria Gaines Fox, Contact, gfox@msmail.ket.org; Donna Moore, Contact; Sally Hamilton, Contact; William Wilson, Contact; D. Hoffman, Program Dir.; L. Hobson, Contact; B. Ball, Contact; J. Holbrook, Contact; T. Tucker, Contact. **Local Programs:** *Comment on Kentucky*; *Kentucky Afield*; *Kentucky Life*; *Kentucky Tonight*; *Legislative Weekly*. **Wattage:** 1,170,000. **Ad Rates:** Noncommercial. **URL:** http:/www.ket.org.

12433 WLKY-AM - 970
PO Box 1897 Phone: (502)587-0970
Louisville, KY 40201 Free: (800)848-0318

Format: Top 40. **Networks:** Satellite Music Network; ABC. **Founded:** 1933. **Formerly:** WAVE-AM (1981); WAVG-AM (June 17, 1997). **Operating Hours:** Continuous; 70% network, 30% local. **ADI:** Louisville, KY. **Key Personnel:** Charles Jenkins, Pres./Gen. Mgr.; Ron Chilton, Program Dir.; Claude Wayne, Production Dir.; Bob McIntosh, News Dir. **Local Programs:** *Byline with Bob McIntosh*. **Wattage:** 5000. **Ad Rates:** $44 for 30 seconds; $44 for 60 seconds. Combined advertising rates available with WXVW-AM.

12434 WLKY-TV - 32
1918 Mellwood Ave. Phone: (502)893-3671
PO Box 6205 Fax: (502)897-2384
Louisville, KY 40206
E-mail: wlky@iglou.com

Format: Commercial TV. **Networks:** CBS. **Founded:** 1961. **Operating Hours:** 6 a.m.-2 a.m. **ADI:** Louisville, KY. **Key Personnel:** A. Rabun Matthews, Vice Pres./General Mgr.; Bill Stanley, General Sales Mgr.; Michael Sipes, News Dir.; Bruce Burns, Promotions Dir.; Leisa Korn, Business Mgr.

12435 WLLV-AM - 1240
2001 W. Broadway, No. 13 Phone: (502)581-1240
Louisville, KY 40203-3551 Fax: (502)583-4301

Format: Gospel. **Networks:** Independent. **Founded:** 1940. **Operating Hours:** Continuous. **ADI:** Louisville, KY. **Key Personnel:** Archie Dale, Contact. **Wattage:** 1000.

12436 WNAI-AM - 680
9127 Galene Dr., Ste. 2
Louisville, KY 40223-0106
E-mail: wnairadio@hotmail.com

Format: News; Talk; Sports. **Networks:** CNN Radio. **Owner:** Gore-Overgaard Broadcasting, Inc., at above address. **Founded:** 1993. **Operating Hours:** Continuous. **ADI:** Louisville, KY. **Key Personnel:** Ed Moore, Station Mgr., edwnaimgr@aol.com; Gary Major, Operations Mgr., gmam680@aol.com. **Wattage:** 1000. **Ad Rates:** $25 for 30 seconds; $35 for 60 seconds. **URL:** http://www.wnai.com.

12437 WQMF-FM - 95.7
4010 Dupont Circle Phone: (502)896-4400
Louisville, KY 40207 Fax: (502)896-1496

Format: Classic Rock. **Owner:** Clear Channel Radio, at above address. **Founded:** Feb. 1981. **Operating Hours:** Continuous. **ADI:** Louisville, KY. **Key Personnel:** Doug James, Gen. Mgr.; Michael Lee, Operations Mgr.; Charlie Steele, Program Dir.; Mel Rexroat, Music Dir. **Wattage:** 50,000. **Ad Rates:** $90 per unit. Combined advertising rates available with WIFX-FM.

12438 WRKA-FM - 103.1
10001 Linn Sta. Rd. Phone: (502)423-9752
Louisville, KY 40223 Fax: (502)423-0231

Format: Oldies. **Networks:** CBS. **Founded:** 1964. **Operating Hours:** Continuous. **ADI:** Louisville, KY. **Key Personnel:** Brent E. Millar, General Mgr., phone (502)423-3127, fax (502)423-1113, brentmilla@aol.com; Donna Gamblin, General Sales Mgr., phone (502)423-3122, fax (502)423-3161; Patricia Ferry, Business Mgr., phone (502)423-3124; Theresa Fryer, News Dir., phone (502)423-3128; Gregory Hahn, Chief Engineer, phone (502)423-3147, ghahn89916@aol.com; David B. Smith, Program Dir., phone (502)423-3134; Amy Spaulding, Marketing Dir./Special Events, phone (502)423-3137. **Wattage:** 6000.

12439 WTMT-AM - 620
162 W. Broadway Phone: (502)583-6200
Louisville, KY 40202-2135 Fax: (502)589-2979

Format: Sports. **Networks:** Meadows Racing. **Founded:** 1958. **Operating Hours:** Continuous. **ADI:** Louisville, KY. **Key Personnel:** Lee Stinson, Jr., General Mgr. **Wattage:** 500. **Ad Rates:** $20 for 30 seconds; $25 for 60 seconds.

12440 WUOL-FM - 90.5
Strickler Hall Phone: (502)852-6467
University of Louisville Fax: (502)852-1621
Louisville, KY 40292
E-mail: notes@wuol.org

Format: Classical. **Networks:** Beethoven Satellite; Public Radio International (PRI). **Owner:** University of Louisville, at above address. **Founded:** 1976. **Operating Hours:** Continuous; 35% network, 65% local. **ADI:** Louisville, KY. **Key Personnel:** Bill Underwood, Program Dir.; Vicky Costello, Mktg. Dir.; Phil Bailey, Music Dir.; Rich Miles, Production/Operations Coord. **Local Programs:** *Afternoon Classical*, Bill Underwood, Program Dir., (502)852-1100; *Evening Classical*, Bill Underwood, Program Dir., (502)852-8143; *Morning Classical*, Bill Underwood, Program Dir., (502)852-1100. **Wattage:** 21,000. **Ad Rates:** Noncommercial. **URL:** http://wuol.org.

LOUISVILLLE

12441 Theatre Design & Technology
U.S. Institute for Theatre Technology
3001 Springcrest Dr. Phone: (502)426-1211
Louisvillle, KY 40241 Fax: (502)423-7467
Publisher E-mail: usittno@pppmail.appliedtheory.com

Magazine covering technical advances in theatre, including lighting, sound, scene design, and costuming, as well as health and safety issues. **Founded:** 1965. **Freq:** Quarterly. **Print Method:** Letterpress. **Trim Size:** 8 1/2 x 11. **Cols./Page:** 3. **Key Personnel:** David Roger, Editor. **ISSN:** 1052-6765. **Subscription Rates:** $48 U.S.; $58 other countries. **Remarks:** Accepts advertising. **URL:** http://www.usitt.org. **Formerly:** TD & T.
Ad Rates: BW: $830 **Circ:** Paid ‡4,250
4C: $1,010 Non-paid ‡250

LUDLOW, pop. 4,959.

Kenton Co. (N). 5 m N of Covington. Residential.

12442 Ecumenical Trends
Graymoor Ecumenical Institute
Box 16136
Ludlow, KY 41016

Magazine containing ecumenical and inter-religious commentary and news. **Founded:** Apr. 1972. **Freq:** Monthly. **Print Method:** Offset. **Trim Size:** 8 1/2 x 11. **Cols./Page:** 3. **Key Personnel:** Dr. William D. Carpe, Editor; Rev. Emil Tomaskovic, Publisher. **ISSN:** 0360-9073. **Subscription Rates:** $10; $12 other countries. **Remarks:** Advertising not accepted.
Circ: Paid ‡2,417
Non-paid ‡125

LYNCH

12443 Lynch TV Inc.
PO Box 698 Phone: (606)848-2977
Lynch, KY 40855 Fax: (606)848-7379
E-mail: sirraf@scc-uky.campus.mci.net

Founded: 1950. **Key Personnel:** Linda Goins, Contact; Linda Goins, Sec./Treas. **Cities Served:** Lynch, KY: subscribing households 390; 33 channels.

MADISONVILLE†, pop. 16,979.

Hopkins Co. 45 m S of Evansville. Manufactures mine equipment, heating and air conditioners, jet engine airfoils, commercial laundry equipment, filter paper, explosives, tires, work clothing, beverages, concrete products. Coal mining; oil wells; timber. Dairy, beef cattle, swine & poultry. Corn, tobacco, soybeans.

12444 The Messenger
221 S. Main St. Phone: (502)824-3300
PO Box 529 Fax: (502)821-6855
Madisonville, KY 42431
Free: (800)726-6397

General newspaper. **Founded:** 1917. **Freq:** Tues. - Sun. (morn.). **Print Method:** Offset. **Cols./Page:** 6. **Col. Width:** 12 picas. **Col. Depth:** 21 1/2 inches. **Key Personnel:** Tom Clinton, Editor; Maureen Gliorwell, Advertising Mgr.; Bob Morris, Publisher. **Subscription Rates:** $94.80 individuals. **Remarks:** Advertising accepted; rates available upon request.
Circ: Tues.-Fri. ★9,464
Sat. ★9,464
Sun. ★9,107

12445 Four Rivers Cablecomm
30 Oakdale Ave. Phone: (812)367-1597
Madisonville, KY 42431-3237 Fax: (812)367-2829
Free: (800)852-3450

Owner: TWFANCH ONE-CO, 1873 S. Bellaire St., Ste. 1550, Denver, CO 80222. **Founded:** Sept. 1, 1996. **Formerly:** Tele-Media; Welbac. **Key Personnel:** Nancy Heflin, Office Mgr.; Mark Pickens, Contact. **Cities Served:** subscribing households 7,300.

12446 WFMW-AM - 730
2380 N. Main St. Phone: (502)821-4096
PO Box 338 Fax: (502)821-5954
Madisonville, KY 42431

Format: Country. **Networks:** CNN Radio; Westwood One Radio. **Owner:** Sound Broadcasters, Inc., at above address. **Founded:** 1947. **Operating Hours:** Continuous. **ADI:** Evansville, IN (Madisonville, KY). **Key Personnel:** Bob Kelley, General Mgr.; Dan Koeber, Program Dir. **Local Programs:** *High school football and basketball*; *Western Ky. Live* 7:30 am - 8:30 am Monday. **Wattage:** 500. **Ad Rates:** $6-7 for 10 seconds; $8.75-10.25 for 30 seconds; $11.50-13.50 for 60 seconds. Combined advertising rates available with WKTG.

12447 WHRZ-FM - 97.7
552 E. Center St. Phone: (502)825-1081
PO Box 475 Fax: (502)825-1082
Madisonville, KY 42431

Format: Country. **Networks:** KyNet. **Owner:** Tradwater Broadcasting Co, Inc, at above address. **Founded:** 1976. **Operating Hours:** Continuous. **ADI:** Evansville, IN (Madisonville, KY). **Key Personnel:** Keith Farrell, News Dir.; Ron Walker, Program Dir.; Jai Hughes, Traffic Mgr.; Carolyn S. Hamby, General Mgr. **Wattage:** 6000. **Ad Rates:** $6.12-9.29 for 30 seconds; $9.29-12.35 for 60 seconds.

12448 WKMU-TV - 29
c/o Kentucky Authority for Educational TV Phone: (606)258-7000
Fax: (606)258-7399
600 Cooper Dr.
Lexington, KY 40502
Free: (800)926-7765

Format: Public TV. **Networks:** Public Broadcasting Service (PBS); Kentucky Educational Television. **Owner:** Kentucky Authority for Educational TV, at above address, (606)258-7170, Fax: (606)258-7390. **Founded:** 1968. **Operating Hours:** 6:15 a.m.-midnight. **ADI:** Paducah,KY-Cape Girardeau,MO-Marion,IL. **Key Personnel:** Virginia Gaines Fox, Contact, gfox@msmail.ket.org; J. Gorman, Contact; D. Holtzclaw, Contact; M. Ferguson, Contact; S. Talbert, Contact; Donna Moore, Contact; Sally Hamilton, Contact; William Wilson, Contact; D. Hoffman, Contact; Craig Cornwell, Contact; L. Hobson, Contact; B. Ball, Contact; J. Holbrook, Contact; T. Tucker, Contact. **Local Programs:** *Comment on Kentucky*; *Kentucky Afield*; *Kentucky Life*; *Kentucky Tonight*; *Legislative Weekly*. **Wattage:** 692,000. **Ad Rates:** Noncommercial. **URL:** http://www.ket.org.

12449 WKTG-FM - 93.9
PO Box 338 Phone: (502)821-1156
Madisonville, KY 42431 Fax: (502)821-5954
E-mail: wktgradio@apis.net

Format: Classic Rock. **Networks:** Westwood One Radio. **Owner:** Sound Broadcasters, Inc., at above address. **Founded:** 1950. **Operating Hours:** Continuous. **ADI:** Evansville, IN (Madisonville, KY). **Key Personnel:** Bob Kelley, General Mgr.; Todd Holloman, Program Dir.; Chris Gardner, News Dir. **Wattage:** 50,000. **Ad Rates:** $17 for 60 seconds.

12450 WLCN-TV - 19
27 Grapevine Rd. Phone: (502)821-5433
Madisonville, KY 42431 Fax: (502)821-5343

Format: Commercial TV. **Networks:** Independent. **Owner:** Zoe Broadcasting Corp., Box 1087, Madisonville, KY 42431. **Founded:** 1983. **Operating Hours:** Continuous. **ADI:** Evansville, IN (Madisonville, KY). **Key Personnel:** John Price, General Mgr. **Wattage:** 2,693,000.

12451 WSOF-FM - 89.9
1415 Island Ford Rd. Phone: (502)825-3004
PO Box 1246 Fax: (502)825-3005
Madisonville, KY 42431-9419

Format: Religious. **Networks:** USA Radio. **Founded:** 1977. **Operating Hours:** 18 hours daily; 5% network, 95% local. **ADI:** Chicago (LaSalle), IL. **Key Personnel:** Gary L. Hall, Director; Don Ezell, Jr., Contact. **Wattage:** 15,000 ERP. **Ad Rates:** Noncommercial.

MANCHESTER†, pop. 1,838.

Clay Co. (SE). 75 m S of Lexington. Furniture, tooling factories. Coal mines. Hardwood timber. Lumber mill. Agriculture. Corn, tabacco, hay.

12452 Enterprise
PO Box 449 Phone: (606)598-6174
Manchester, KY 40962 Fax: (606)598-2330

Newspaper. **Founded:** 1890. **Freq:** Weekly (Thurs.). **Print Method:** Letterpress and offset. **Cols./Page:** 6. **Col. Width:** 24 nonpareils. **Col. Depth:** 301 agate lines. **Key Personnel:** James F. Nolan, Publisher; Mrs. J.F. Nolan, Sr., Advertising Mgr. **Subscription Rates:** $8.50 individuals. **Remarks:** Accepts advertising. **Formerly:** Enterprise.
Ad Rates: GLR: $.192 **Circ:** 7,200

12453 WKLB-AM - 1290
106 Richmond Rd. Phone: (606)598-2445
Manchester, KY 40962 Fax: (606)598-2653

Format: Country. **Networks:** ABC. **Owner:** Larry Barker, at above address. **Founded:** 1981. **Operating Hours:** Continuous. **ADI:** Lexington, KY. **Key Personnel:** Larry Barker, Contact. **Local Programs:** *Bob Kingsly Top 40 Countdown* 1:00 pm Saturday, Larry Barker, President; *Bob Page ABC Sports*. **Wattage:** 50,000. **Ad Rates:** $5 for 30 seconds; $10.50 for 60 seconds.

12454 WTBK-FM - 105.7
107 Dickinson St. Phone: (606)598-7559
Manchester, KY 40962 Fax: (606)598-7598

Format: Top 40; Talk; Sports; Classic Rock; Bluegrass. **Networks:** AP. **Owner:** Tim Finley, at above address, (606)598-7588, Fax: (606)598-7548. **Founded:** 1989. **Operating Hours:** Continuous. **Key Personnel:** Tim Finley, President/General Mgr. **Local Programs:** *The Inside Story* 7 p.m. - 10 p.m. Tuesday. **Wattage:** 7500. **Ad Rates:** $5-7 for 30 seconds; $8-9 for 60 seconds.

MARION†, pop. 3,400.

Crittenden Co. (C). 35 m ENE of Paducah. Fluorspar mines.

12455 The Crittenden Press
The Crittenden Press, Inc.
PO Box 191 Phone: (502)965-3191
Marion, KY 42064 Fax: (502)965-2516
Publication E-mail: cpress@kih.net
Publisher E-mail: thepress@apex.net

Community newspaper. **Subtitle:** Shopper The Early Bird. **Founded:** 1876. **Freq:** Weekly. **Print Method:** Offset. **Trim Size:** 7 x 10 1/2. **Cols./Page:** 6. **Col. Width:** 24 nonpareils. **Col. Depth:** 301 agate lines. **Key Personnel:** Chris Evans, General Mgr. **USPS:** 138-260. **Subscription Rates:** $18 individuals; $21 out of area; $23 out of state. **Remarks:** Accepts advertising.
Ad Rates: GLR: $.23 **Circ:** ‡4,250
BW: $451.50
PCI: $3.50

12456 WMJL-AM - 1500
PO Box 68 Phone: (502)965-2271
Marion, KY 42064 Fax: (502)965-2515
E-mail: wmjl.com

Format: Country; News; Sports. **Owner:** Joe Myers Productions, Inc., at above address. **Founded:** 1968. **Operating Hours:** Sunrise-sunset; 100% Local. **Key Personnel:** Joseph W. Myers, Owner. **Wattage:** 250. **Ad Rates:** $6 for 30 seconds; $8 for 60 seconds.

MARTIN

12457 WMDJ-AM - 1440
PO Box 1530 Phone: (606)874-8005
Martin, KY 41649 Fax: (606)874-0057

Format: Country. **Networks:** NBC; Louisiana; Agricultural Broadcasting; Westwood One Radio; CBS. **Owner:** Bob Cupit, at above address. **Founded:** 1984. **Operating Hours:** Sunrise-sunset. **Key Personnel:** Dale McKinney, General Mgr., phone (606)874-8005, fax (606)874-0057; Rick D. Caudill, Station Mgr.; Mona Dingus, Sales Mgr.; Bill Marshall, Program/Music Dir.; Rita Sword, Traffic. **Wattage:** 2500. **Ad Rates:** $7-9 for 30 seconds; $8.50-10.50 for 60 seconds.

MAYFIELD†, pop. 10,705.

Graves Co. (SW). 25 m from each of three rivers, Ohio, Mississippi and Tennessee. Manufactures clothing, tires, lamps, bottles, bricks, furniture, flour, snuff, gasoline, shoes, compressors, Tobacco warehouses. Clay pots. Timber. Diversified farming. Wheat, corn, tobacco, soybeans.

12458 Mayfield Messenger
Messenger Newspapers, Inc.
201 N. 8th St. Phone: (502)247-5223
Box 709 Fax: (502)247-6336
Mayfield, KY 42066-1825
General newspaper. **Founded:** 1901. **Freq:** Mon.-Sat. (eve.). **Print Method:** Offset. **Cols./Page:** 6. **Col. Width:** 25 nonpareils. **Col. Depth:** 301 agate lines. **Key Personnel:** Michael Turley, Editor; Bob T. Shytle, Publisher. **Subscription Rates:** $36 individuals. **Remarks:** Accepts advertising.
Ad Rates: SAU: $10.58 **Circ:** (Not Reported)

12459 WIVR-AM - 1320
PO Box 679 Phone: (502)247-5122
Mayfield, KY 42066 Fax: (502)247-4207

Format: Adult Contemporary. **Simulcasts:** WIVR-FM. **Owner:** West Kentucky Broadcasting Co. Inc., PO Box 679, Mayfield, KY 42066, (606)855-6888, Fax: (606)855-7888. **Founded:** 1947. **Formerly:** WNGO-AM. **Operating Hours:** 6 a.m.-7 p.m. **ADI:** Paducah,KY-Cape Girardeau,MO-Marion,IL. **Key Personnel:** Kim Futrell, News Dir., wivr@wk.net; Jamie Richards, Contact, wvre@wk.net; Randy Gardner, General Mgr., randygardner@wk.nt. **Local Programs:** *Mornings with Knight*, Ms. Bo Knight. **Wattage:** 1000.

12460 WIVR-FM - 94.7
U.S. Hwy. 45 N. Phone: (502)247-5122
Mayfield, KY 42066 Fax: (502)247-4207
Free: (800)455-5122
E-mail: wbln@kih.net

Format: Adult Contemporary. **Networks:** Westwood One Radio. **Owner:** Western Kentucky Radio, L.L.C., PO Box 679, Mayfield, KY 42066, (502)726-2471, Fax: (502)726-3555. **Founded:** 1955. **Formerly:** WXID-FM (1997); WBLN-FM. **Operating Hours:** Continuous; 20% network, 80% local. **ADI:** Paducah,KY-Cape Girardeau,MO-Marion,IL. **Key Personnel:** Kim Furrell, News Dir.; Jamie Richards, Music Dir.; Tammi Mallory, General Mgr. **Wattage:** 50,000. **Ad Rates:** $13 for 30 seconds; $18 for 60 seconds.

12461 WYMC-AM - 1430
197 WYMC Rd. Phone: (502)247-1430
PO Box V Fax: (502)247-1825
Mayfield, KY 42066
E-mail: wymc@apex.net

Format: Middle-of-the-Road (MOR). **Networks:** ABC; NBC; Westwood One Radio; St. Louis Cardinals. **Owner:** JDM Communications, Inc., at above address. **Founded:** 1976. **Operating Hours:** Continuous. **ADI:** Paducah,KY-Cape Girardeau,MO-Marion,IL. **Key Personnel:** Jim Moore, General Mgr.; Joyce Fowler, Traffic Mgr.; Eddie Holmes, Program Dir.; Doc Bennett, News Dir.; Larry McIntosh, Sales. **Wattage:** 1000. **Ad Rates:** $4.50-11 for 30 seconds; $7.50-20 for 60 seconds.

MAYSVILLE†, pop. 7,983.

Mason Co. (NE). On Ohio River, 60 m SE of Cincinnati, Ohio. Tourism. Historic center. Museum. Manufactures condensed milk, gasoline, motor parts, soft drinks, cotton goods, shoes, bricks, pulleys, cigars, bicycles, motorcycles. Tobacco warehouses and curing plant; distilleries; nursery. Agriculture. Livestock, tobacco, wheat, milk.

12462 Advertiser
PO Box 518 Phone: (606)564-9091
Maysville, KY 41056-0518 Fax: (606)564-6893

Shopper. **Founded:** 1969. **Freq:** Weekly (Mon.). **Print Method:** Offset. **Cols./Page:** 6. **Col. Width:** 26 nonpareils. **Col. Depth:** 301 agate lines. **Key Personnel:** Frank Robinson, Editor; Robert Hendrickson, Publisher; Patty Moore, Advertising Mgr. **Remarks:** Accepts advertising.
Ad Rates: GLR: $3.60 **Circ:** Free ‡20,133
BW: $870.75
4C: $1,068.75
SAU: $6.75

12463 The Ledger-Independent
Howard Publications
41-43 W. 2nd Phone: (606)564-9091
PO Box 518 Fax: (606)564-6893
Maysville, KY 41056
Free: (800)264-9091
Publication E-mail: advertising@ntr.net

Newspaper. **Founded:** 1968. **Freq:** Mon.-Sat. (morn.). **Print Method:** Offset. **Cols./Page:** 6. **Col. Width:** 26 nonpareils. **Col. Depth:** 301 agate lines. **Key Personnel:** Robert Hendrickson, Publisher; Matt Stahl, Editor; Patricia Moore, Advertising Mgr. **Subscription Rates:** $69 individuals. **Remarks:** Accepts advertising. **Available Online. URL:** http://www.trib.com/maysville.
Ad Rates: GLR: $2.30 **Circ:** ‡8,200
BW: $774
4C: $998
SAU: $6
PCI: $10

12464 WFTM-AM - 1240
626 Forest Ave. Phone: (606)564-3361
PO Box 100 Fax: (606)564-4291
Maysville, KY 41056
Free: (800)264-3572

Format: News; Sports. **Networks:** CBS; Jones Satellite. **Owner:** Standard Tobacco Co. Inc., at above address. **Founded:** 1948. **Operating Hours:** Continuous; 10% network, 90% local. **ADI:** Cincinnati, OH. **Key Personnel:** Doug McGill, Contact; Danny Weddle, Contact. **Wattage:** 1000. **Ad Rates:** $4.75-7.35 for 30 seconds; $5.30-9.25 for 60 seconds.

12465 WFTM-FM - 95.9
626 Forest Ave. Phone: (606)564-3361
PO Box 100 Fax: (606)564-4291
Maysville, KY 41056

Format: Adult Contemporary. **Networks:** Jones Satellite; CBS. **Owner:** Standard Tobacco Co. Inc., at above address. **Founded:** 1965. **Operating Hours:** Continuous; 10% network, 90% local. **ADI:** Cincinnati, OH. **Key Personnel:** Doug McGill, Contact; Danny Weddle, Contact. **Wattage:** 3000. **Ad Rates:** $4.75-7.35 for 30 seconds; $5.30-9.25 for 60 seconds.

MC KEE

12466 The Jackson County Sun
PO Box 130 Phone: (606)287-7197
Mc Kee, KY 40447 Fax: (606)287-7196

County newspaper. **Founded:** 1926. **Freq:** Weekly (Thurs.). **Print Method:** Web offset. **Trim Size:** 13 x 21 1/2. **Cols./Page:** 6. **Col. Width:** 12 picas. **Col. Depth:** 21 1/2 inches. **Key Personnel:** George Ferrell, Editor; Tammy Spurlock, Office Mgr.; Alice Wilson, Advertising; Marty Roberts, Compositor. **USPS:** 271-940. **Subscription Rates:** $12 individuals; $13.50 out of county; $15 out of state. **Remarks:** Accepts advertising.
Ad Rates: GLR: $.50 **Circ:** Paid 3,650
BW: $258 Free 12
4C: $558
SAU: $3.50
PCI: $3.50

12467 WWAG-FM - 107.9
1680 State Rd. 1071 Phone: (606)287-9924
Tyner, KY 40486

Format: Country. **Networks:** ABC. **Owner:** Dandy Broadcasting, Inc., Star Rt. Box 16, Sandgap, KY 40481. **Founded:** 1990. **Operating Hours:** Continuous. **Key Personnel:** D.C. Clemons, General Mgr.; Sherry Nix, Program Dir. **Wattage:** 3000. **Ad Rates:** $4.40-10 for 60 seconds.

MIDDLESBORO, pop. 12,251.

Bell Co. (SE). 110 m SE of Lexington. National and State parks. Wood products, elastic webbing, shirts, plastic pipe manufactured. Meat packing plant. Tannery, bottling works. Coal mines. Foundry. Machine shop.

12468 Daily News
American Publishing Co.
PO Box 579 Phone: (606)248-1010
Middlesboro, KY 40965 Fax: (606)248-7614

General newspaper. **Founded:** 1911. **Freq:** Daily (eve.) and Sat. (morn.). **Print Method:** Offset. **Cols./Page:** 6. **Col. Width:** 2 1/16 inches. **Col. Depth:** 21 1/2 inches. **Key Personnel:** Wayne Ray, Short, Managing Editor; J.T. Hurst, Publisher; Pat Cheek, Advertising Dir. **Subscription Rates:** $82 individuals; $90.10 KY mail; $85 out of state. **Remarks:** Accepts advertising.
Ad Rates: BW: $1,158.42 **Circ:** Mon.-Fri. 7,200
4C: $1,406.42
SAU: $8.72
PCI: $8.98

12469 WFXY-AM - 1490
2118 Cumberland Ave. Phone: (606)248-1574
PO Box 999 Fax: (606)248-6397
Middlesboro, KY 40965
Free: (800)489-9399
E-mail: wfxy@aol.com

Format: Adult Contemporary; News. **Networks:** ABC; KyNet; Jones Satellite. **Owner:** Countrywide Broadcasters, Inc., at above address, (606)248-6005, Fax: (602)248-0404, Free: (800)280-1561. **Founded:** 1967. **Formerly:** WAFI-AM (1979). **Operating Hours:** Continuous; 75% network, 25% local. **ADI:** Knoxville (Crossville), TN. **Key Personnel:** Jim Gilbert, News Dir.; Kevin Ellis, Program Dir.; Beulah Pursifull, Operations Mgr.; Warren Pursifull, General Mgr.; John Engle, Sports Dir.; Rhonda Rains, Promotions Dir. **Wattage:** 1000. **Ad Rates:** $6 for 30 seconds; $9 for 60 seconds.

12470 WMIK-AM - 560
PO Box 608 Phone: (606)248-5842
Middlesboro, KY 40965 Fax: (606)248-7660

Format: Southern Gospel. **Networks:** USA Radio. **Owner:** Gateway Braodcasting, at above address. **Founded:** 1948. **Operating Hours:** Continuous. **ADI:** Knoxville (Crossville), TN. **Key Personnel:** Michael Jones, Office/Traffic Mgr.; Michael Brooks, President; Richard Siler, Treasurer. **Wattage:** 2500 day; 88 night. **Ad Rates:** $5-6.50 for 60 seconds.

12471 WMIK-FM - 92.7
PO Box 608 Phone: (606)248-5842
Middlesboro, KY 40965 Fax: (606)248-7660

Format: Religious; Contemporary Christian. **Networks:** USA Radio; Moody Broadcasting. **Owner:** Gateway Broadcasting, at above address. **Founded:** 1971. **Operating Hours:** Continuous. **ADI:** Knoxville (Crossville), TN. **Key Personnel:** Michael Jones, Office Mgr.; Michael Brooks, President; Richard Siler, Treasurer. **Local Programs:** *Reaching Out*, William Boyd Bingham, (606)248-5842, Fax (606)248-7660; *Heart & Soul*, Bruce Nettleton, Fax (606)248-7660. **Wattage:** 3000. **Ad Rates:** $3-5.50 for 30 seconds; $4-6.50 for 60 seconds.

MIDDLETOWN, pop. 414.

Jefferson Co. (NW). 14 m E of Louisville. Sawmills. Manufactures ready mixed concrete, lead pencils, crayons, artists materials. Diversfied farming. Tobacco, corn, dairying.

12472 Western Recorder
Western Recorder, Inc.
PO Box 43969 Phone: (502)244-6470
Louisville, KY 40253 Fax: (502)244-6474

Newspaper (tabloid) serving Kentucky Baptist Convention. **Founded:** 1826. **Freq:** Weekly (Tues.). **Print Method:** Offset. **Trim Size:** 11 x 15. **Cols./Page:** 4. **Col. Width:** 12 picas. **Col. Depth:** 140 agate lines. **Key Personnel:** Marv Knox, Editor; Mark Wingfield, News Dir.;-Mauri Smith, Business Mgr. **ISSN:** 0043-4132. **Subscription Rates:** $10.60 individuals. **Remarks:** Accepts advertising.
Ad Rates: 4C: $1,120 **Circ:** Paid 48,500
PCI: $20 Free 1,120

MONTICELLO†, pop. 5,677.

Wayne Co. (SC). 100 m S of Lexington. Coal mines; oil wells; rock quarry; timber. Manufactures staves, flour, wood products, machinery; oil refinery. Agriculture. Corn, tobacco, wheat.

12473 Wayne County Outlook
Wayne County Newspaper Inc.
PO Box 432 Phone: (606)348-3338
Monticello, KY 42633 Fax: (606)348-8848

Community newspaper. **Founded:** 1904. **Freq:** Weekly (Wed.). **Print Method:** Offset. **Cols./Page:** 6. **Col. Width:** 24 nonpareils. **Col. Depth:** 294 agate lines. **Key Personnel:** Melinda Jones, Adv. Mgr./Pub. **Subscription Rates:** $21 individuals; $29 out of area.
Ad Rates: GLR: $.60 **Circ:** 6,000
BW: $561.15
4C: $4.35
PCI: $4.35

12474 Enstar Cable
514 N. Main Phone: (606)348-8416
Monticello, KY 42633 Fax: (606)348-6397
Free: (800)388-8416

Key Personnel: Robert Taylor, General Mgr. **Cities Served:** Cumberland, Greensburg, Jellicle, Russell Springs, Liberty, and Monticello, KY.

12475 WFLW-AM - 1360
Worsham Ln. Phone: (606)348-8427
PO Box 696 Fax: (606)348-3867
Monticello, KY 42633
E-mail: wkym@skn.net

Format: Southern Gospel. **Networks:** KyNet. **Founded:** 1955. **Operating Hours:** 6 a.m.-6 p.m.; 10% network, 90% local. **ADI:** Lexington, KY. **Key Personnel:** Stephen W. Staples, Contact; Debbie Brown, Program Mgr. **Wattage:** 1000. **Ad Rates:** $3-6 for 30 seconds; $4-8 for 60 seconds. Combined advertising rates available with WKYM-FM.

12476 WKYM-FM - 101.7
150 Worsham Ln. Phone: (606)348-7083
PO Box 696 Fax: (606)348-3867
Monticello, KY 42633
E-mail: wkym@skn.net

Format: Oldies; Classic Rock. **Founded:** 1965. **Formerly:** WFLW-FM (1974). **Operating Hours:** Continuous; 100% local. **ADI:** Lexington, KY. **Key Personnel:** Stephen W. Staples, Owner/General Mgr.; Debbie Brown, Promotions Mgr. **Wattage:** 6000. **Ad Rates:** $3-8 for 30 seconds; $4-10 for 60 seconds. $3-$8 for 30 seconds; $4-$10 for 60 seconds. Combined advertising rates available with WFLW-AM.

MOREHEAD†, pop. 7,789.

Rowan Co. (NE). 55 m SW of Ashland. State University. Garment, electric components, concrete products factories. Clay pits. Sawmills. Tobacco warehouse. Diversified farming. Tobacco, cattle.

12477 Menifee County News
772 W. 1st St. Phone: (606)784-4116
Morehead, KY 40351 Fax: (606)484-7337
Publication E-mail: tmnews@kihi.net

County newspaper. **Freq:** Weekly (Wed.). **Cols./Page:** 6. **Col. Width:** 12 picas. **Col. Depth:** 21 1/2 inches. **Key Personnel:** Ronald J. Caudill, Publisher; Stephanie Davis, Editor; Shirley Hood, Advertising Mgr. **Remarks:** Accepts advertising.
Ad Rates: PCI: $3.23 **Circ:** ⊕797

12478 The Morehead News
722 W. 1st St. Phone: (606)784-4116
Morehead, KY 40351 Fax: (606)784-7337
Publication E-mail: crhart@london2skn.net.
Publisher E-mail: tmnews@kih.net

Community newspaper. **Founded:** 1883. **Freq:** Semiweekly (Tues. and Fri.). **Print Method:** Offset. **Cols./Page:** 6. **Col. Width:** 12 picas. **Col. Depth:** 21 agate lines. **Key Personnel:** Stephanie Davis, Editor; Ron Caudill, Publisher; Shirley Hood, Advertising Mgr. **Subscription Rates:** $12.50 individuals. **Remarks:** Accepts advertising.
Ad Rates: SAU: $5.68 **Circ:** Paid ⊕5,629
PCI: $4.98

12479 The Trail Blazer
Morehead State University Board of Student Publications
Dept. of Communication, BR 101 Phone: (606)783-5312
Fax: (606)783-2457
Morehead State University
Morehead, KY 40351
Publisher E-mail: thetrailblazer_ msu@yahoo.com

Collegiate newspaper. **Founded:** 1930. **Freq:** Weekly (Wed.). **Print Method:** Offset. **Cols./Page:** 6. **Col. Width:** 24 1/2 picas. **Col. Depth:** 294 agate lines. **Key Personnel:** Joy Tirey, Editor, jctire01@moorehead-st.edu; Sarah Johnson, Advertising Mgr., phone (606)783-2601, moocow98@hotmail.com. **Subscription Rates:** $10 individuals. **Remarks:** Accepts advertising.
Ad Rates: GLR: $6 **Circ:** Paid 523
BW: $590 Free 7,500
4C: $678
PCI: $6

12480 WKMR-TV - 16
c/o Kentucky Educational TV Phone: (606)258-7000
600 Cooper Dr. Fax: (606)432-0951
Lexington, KY 40502
Free: (800)926-7765

Format: Public TV. **Networks:** Public Broadcasting Service (PBS); Kentucky Educational Television. **Owner:** Kentucky Authority for Educational TV, at above address, (606)258-7230, Fax: (606)258-7390, Free: (800)432-0951. **Founded:** 1968. **Operating Hours:** 6:30 a.m.-midnight. **Key Personnel:** Craig Cornwell, Contact, phone (606)258-7275, ccornwell@ket.org; J. Gorman, Contact, phone (606)258-7150, fax (606)258-7461, jgorman@ket.org; D. Holtzclaw, Contact, phone (606)258-7101, fax (606)258-7390, dholtzclaw@ket.org; M. Ferguson, Contact, phone (606)258-7030, mferguson@ket.org; Virginia Gaines Fox, Contact, phone (606)258-7100, gfox@ket.org; Donna Moore, Contact, phone (606)258-7250, dmoore@ket.org; Sally Hamilton, Contact, phone (606)258-7012, shamilton@ket.org; William Wilson, Contact, phone (606)258-7200, wwilson@ket.org; D. Hoffman, Contact, phone (606)358-7252, fax (606)258-7390, dhoffman@ket.org; L. Hobson, Contact, phone (606)258-7260, fax (606)258-7390, lhobson@ket.org; S. Talbert, Contact, phone (606)258-7172, fax (606)258-7390, stalbert@ket.org; B. Ball, Contact, phone (606)258-7160, bball@ket.org; J. Holbrook, Contact, phone (606)258-7032, jholbrook@ket.org; T. Tucker, Contact, phone (606)258-7120, fax (606)258-7390, ttucker@ket.org; Ed Mastrean, Contact, phone (606)258-7230, emastrean@ket.org. **Local Programs:** *Comment on Kentucky*; *Kentucky Afield*; *Kentucky Life*; *Kentucky Tonight*; *Legislative Weekly*. **Wattage:** 676,000. **Ad Rates:** Noncommercial. **URL:** http://www.ket.org.

12481 WMKY-FM - 90.3
Morehead State University Phone: (606)783-2001
UP0903, 124 Henry Ward Pl. Fax: (606)783-2335
Morehead, KY 40351
E-mail: wmky@morehead-st.edu

Format: News; Classical; Information. **Networks:** National Public Radio (NPR); Public Radio International (PRI); KyNet. **Owner:** Morehead State University, at above address. **Founded:** 1965. **Operating Hours:** 18 hours daily; 58% network, 42% local. **Key Personnel:** Angela Mullins, Development & Promotions Dir., phone (606)783-2394, a.mullins@morehead-st.edu; Chuck Mraz, Asst. Dir. of News Programming, phone (606)783-2395, c.mraz@morehead-st.edu; Paul Hitchcock, Music and Production Dir., phone (606)783-2334, p.hitchc@morehead-st.edu; Janean Freeman, Asst. Music Dir., phone (606)783-2320, j.freema@moerhead-st.edu; David Blankenship, Engineering, phone (606)783-2336, d.blankenship@morehead-st.edu. **Local Programs:** *Afternoon Classics*, Janean Freeman, (606)783-2320, Fax (606)783-2335; *Bluegrass Diversion*, Sandy Knipp, (606)783-2001, Fax (606)783-2335; *Friends & Folk*, Steve Young, (606)783-2001, Fax (606)783-2335. **Wattage:** 37,500. **Ad Rates:** Noncommercial; underwriting available.

12482 WMOR-AM - 1330
113 E. 1st St. Phone: (606)784-4141
PO Box 940
Morehead, KY 40351

Format: Religious. **Networks:** ABC. **Owner:** Deam Enterprises, Inc., at above address. **Founded:** 1955. **Operating Hours:** 6 a.m.-local sunset. **Key Personnel:** Jim Forrest, President; Dreama Forrest, Vice President; Rick Hesterberg, Program Dir. **Wattage:** 1000.

12483 WMOR-FM - 92.1
113 E. 1st St. Phone: (606)784-4141
PO Box 940
Morehead, KY 40351

Format: Adult Contemporary. **Networks:** ABC. **Owner:** Dream Enterprises, Inc., at above address. **Founded:** 1965. **Operating Hours:** Continuous. **Key Personnel:** Jim Forrest, President; Dreama Forrest, Vice President; Merv Lawson, Program Dir. **Wattage:** 3000 ERP.

MORGANFIELD†, pop. 3,781.

Union Co. (WC). 23 m S of Henderson. Manufactures metal partitions, plastic and rubber parts for automobiles, fiber tubes and rolls, rebuilt automobile parts. Coal mines. Seed cleaning plant. Agriculture. Pork, corn, livestock.

12484 Paxton Cable TV
531 US Hwy. 60 E. Fax: (502)389-2459
Morganfield, KY 42437-1275

Founded: 1980. **Formerly:** Union CATV Inc. **Key Personnel:** Alan E. Reed, President. **Cities Served:** subscribing households 2,647; 2 channels; 1 community access channel.

12485 WMSK-AM - 1550
Hwy. 60 S., Box 369 Phone: (502)389-1551
Morganfield, KY 42437 Fax: (502)389-1550

Format: Country; Agricultural. **Networks:** ABC. **Owner:** Union County Broadcasting Co., Inc., at above address. **Founded:** 1960. **Operating Hours:** Sunrise-sunset. **Key Personnel:** J.B. Crawley, President; Elizabeth Crawley, Vice President; Don Sheridan, Contact. **Wattage:** 250. **Ad Rates:** $3.95-4.75 for 30 seconds; $5.25-6.25 for 60 seconds.

12486 WMSK-FM - 95.3
Hwy. 60 S., Box 369 Phone: (502)389-1550
Morganfield, KY 42437 Fax: (502)389-1550

Format: Country; Agricultural. **Networks:** ABC. **Owner:** Union County Broadcasting Co., Inc., at above address. **Founded:** 1966. **Operating Hours:** 5:45 a.m.-10 p.m. **Key Personnel:** J.B. Crawley, President; Elizabeth Crawley, Vice President; John Robinson, Contact. **Wattage:** 3000 ERP. **Ad Rates:** $3.95-5.25 for 30 seconds; $4.75-6.25 for 60 seconds.

MORGANTOWN†, pop. 2,000.

Butler Co. (SW). On Green River, 25 m NE of Bowling Green. Coal mines; oil wells; timber. Lumber, feed mills; men's and boy's clothing, boat machinery factories. Agriculture. Corn, tobacco, soya beans.

12487 The Butler County and Green River Republican Banner
Box 219 Phone: (502)526-4151
Morgantown, KY 42261 Fax: (502)526-3111
Publication E-mail: bcbanner@logantel.com

Community newspaper. **Founded:** 1885. **Freq:** Weekly (Wed.). **Print Method:** Offset. **Cols./Page:** 6. **Col. Width:** 26 nonpareils. **Col. Depth:** 294 agate lines. **Key Personnel:** Deborah T. Givens, Editor. **ISSN:** 0745-7006. **Subscription Rates:** $12 individuals; $16 out of area; $20 out of state. **Remarks:** Accepts advertising.
Ad Rates: BW: $378 **Circ:** ‡5,300
4C: $498
SAU: $3
PCI: $3

MOUNT STERLING†, pop. 5,820.

Montgomery Co. (E). 33 m E of Lexington. Manufactures electric motors & components, dishwashers, underwear and knit goods, tool & die makers, automotive parts, concrete products, men's work clothing; feed mill; poultry and packing plants. Dairy, cattle, poultry, grain farms. Tobacco, corn, bell peppers, wheat.

12488 Mt. Sterling Advocate
40 S. Bank St. Phone: (606)498-2222
PO Box 406 Fax: (606)498-2228
Mount Sterling, KY 40353
Community newspaper. **Founded:** 1890. **Freq:** Weekly (Thurs.). **Print Method:** Offset. **Cols./Page:** 6. **Col. Width:** 25 nonpareils. **Col. Depth:** 301 agate lines. **Key Personnel:** Glen Greene, Publisher; JoAnn Halsey, Advertising Mgr.; Deanna Mascle, Managing Editor. **Subscription Rates:** $19.61 individuals. **Remarks:** Accepts advertising.
Ad Rates: GLR: $.27 **Circ:** 6,350
SAU: $5.50
PCI: $4.68

12489 Mt. Sterling Advocate-Advertiser
Mt. Sterling Advocate
40 S. Bank St. Phone: (606)498-2222
PO Box 406 Fax: (606)498-2228
Mount Sterling, KY 40353
Shopper. **Founded:** 1976. **Freq:** Weekly (Mon.). **Print Method:** Offset. **Cols./Page:** 6. **Col. Width:** 25 nonpareils. **Col. Depth:** 301 agate lines. **Key Personnel:** Glen Greene, Publisher; JoAnn Halsey, Advertising Mgr. **Remarks:** Accepts advertising.
Ad Rates: GLR: $.40 **Circ:** Free 17,400
SAU: $7.92
PCI: $6.74

12490 WMST-AM - 1150
34 Broadway Phone: (606)498-1150
PO Box 381 Fax: (606)498-7930
Mount Sterling, KY 40353

Format: Eclectic. **Networks:** KyNet. **Founded:** 1957. **Operating Hours:** 17 hours Daily. **ADI:** Lexington, KY. **Key Personnel:** Bob Speaks, News Dir.; Linda Denton, News Dir.; Dan Manley, Sports Dir.; Vernice Taylor, General Mgr. **Local Programs:** *Kaleidoscope*, Linda Denton, Mailing contact, (606)498-1150, Fax (606)498-7930. **Wattage:** 500 day; 54 night. **Ad Rates:** $3-5 for 15 seconds; $4-6 for 30 seconds; $5-7 for 60 seconds. $2-$4.50 for 15 seconds; $3-$5.50 for 30 seconds; $4-$6.50 for 60 seconds. Combined advertising rates available with WMST-FM.

12491 WMST-FM - 105.5
34 Broadway Phone: (606)498-1150
Mount Sterling, KY 40353 Fax: (606)498-7930

Format: Eclectic. **Networks:** KyNet. **Founded:** 1968. **Operating Hours:** 6:00 a.m.-11:00 p.m. **ADI:** Lexington, KY. **Key Personnel:** Vernice Taylor, General Mgr.; Bob Speaks, News Dir.; Dan Manley, Sports Dir. **Local Programs:** *Kalidescope* 10 a.m.-11 a.m. Monday-Friday, Linda Denton. **Wattage:** 3,000. **Ad Rates:** $3-5 for 15 seconds; $4-6 for 30 seconds; $5-7 for 60 seconds.

MOUNT VERNON

12492 Mt. Vernon Signal
PO Box 185 Phone: (606)256-2244
Mount Vernon, KY 40456 Fax: (606)256-9526

Community newspaper. **Founded:** 1888. **Freq:** Weekly (Thurs.). **Print Method:** Web offset. **Trim Size:** 13 1/2 x 21 1/2. **Cols./Page:** 6. **Col. Width:** 12 1/5 picas. **Col. Depth:** 21 3/10 inches. **Key Personnel:** Perlina Anderkin, Editor; James Anderkin, Jr., Publisher. **USPS:** 366-000. **Subscription Rates:** $12; $15 out of county; $20 out of state. **Remarks:** Accepts advertising.
Ad Rates: BW: $387 **Circ:** ‡5,400
SAU: $3.50
PCI: $2.80

12493 WRVK-AM - 1460
PO Box 1288 Phone: (606)256-2146
Mount Vernon, KY 40456 Fax: (606)256-9146
Free: (800)895-8441
E-mail: wrvk@sun-spot.com

Format: Country; Talk. **Networks:** UPI; USA Radio. **Owner:** Cumberland Media, Inc., at above address, (606)256-9150, Free: (800)672-0870. **Founded:** 1957. **Operating Hours:** 6 a.m.-8 p.m.; 20% network, 80% local. **Key Personnel:** Larry A. Burdette, Contact; Gail F. Burdette, Contact. **Local Programs:** *Talk-N-Trade Show*, Larry Burdette, (606)256-2146. **Wattage:** 500. **Ad Rates:** $6 for 30 seconds; $8 for 60 seconds.

MUNFORDVILLE†, pop. 1,783.

Hart Co. (SWC). 73 m S of Louisville. Feed, lumber mills. Poultry, dairy, grain farms. Tobacco, corn.

12494 WLOC-AM - 1150
PO Box 307 Phone: (502)524-4111
Munfordville, KY 42765

Format: Eclectic. **Networks:** Unistar; CNN Radio. **Founded:** 1956. **Operating Hours:** 5 a.m.-midnight. **Key Personnel:** Joe Bern, Contact. **Wattage:** 1000. **Ad Rates:** $2-4.50 for 15 seconds; $3-6 for 30 seconds; $5-8 for 60 seconds.

12495 WLOC-FM - 102.3
PO Box 307 Phone: (502)524-4111
Munfordville, KY 42765

Format: Eclectic. **Networks:** Unistar; CNN Radio. **Founded:** 1964. **Operating Hours:** 5 a.m.-midnight. **Key Personnel:** Joe Bern, Contact. **Wattage:** 3000. **Ad Rates:** $2-4.50 for 15 seconds; $3-6 for 30 seconds; $5-8 for 60 seconds.

MURRAY†, pop. 14,248.

Calloway Co. (SW). 42 m SE of Paducah. Murray State University. Manufactures hosiery, lumber, tobacco, dairy products, popcorn processors, chemicals, oil filters, custom springs, asbestos clothing and gloves, toys. Agriculture. Tobacco, popcorn, corn, soybeans, wheat.

12496 Journal of Business and Public Affairs
Murray State University
Murray, KY 42071 Phone: (502)762-6198
Fax: (502)762-3740

Scholarly business journal. **Freq:** Semiannual. **Key Personnel:** Glynn Mangold, Editor. **Formerly:** B & PA.

12497 Murray Ledger and Times
1001 Whitnell Ave. Phone: (502)753-1916
Box 1040 Fax: (502)753-1927
Murray, KY 42071
General newspaper. **Founded:** 1889. **Freq:** Mon.-Sat. (eve.). **Print Method:** Offset. **Cols./Page:** 6. **Col. Width:** 18 nonpareils. **Col. Depth:** 294 agate lines. **Key Personnel:** Amy Wilson, Editor; Walter L. Apperson, Publisher; Jim Green, Advertising Mgr.; Alice Rouse, General Mgr. **Subscription Rates:** $72 individuals. **Remarks:** Accepts advertising.
Ad Rates: 4C: $1,070.75 **Circ:** Paid ‡8,000
PCI: $2.00 Free ‡8,000

12498 The Murray State News
Murray State University
2609 University Sta. Phone: (502)762-2998
Murray, KY 42071 Fax: (502)762-3175
Publication E-mail: thenews@ldd.net

Collegiate newspaper. **Founded:** June 24, 1927. **Freq:** Weekly (Fri.). **Print Method:** Offset. **Trim Size:** 13 1/4 x 22 1/2. **Cols./Page:** 6. **Col. Width:** 12.2 picas. **Col. Depth:** 21 inches. **Key Personnel:** Joe Hedges, Faculty Adviser, jdhedges@msumusik.mursuky.edu; Sara Wight, Editor. **Subscription Rates:** Free; $10 off-campus. **Remarks:** Accepts advertising. **URL:** http://www.thenews.org.
Ad Rates: BW: $378 **Circ:** Paid ‡250
4C: $468 Free ‡7,000
PCI: $4

12499 WFGE-FM - 103.7
1500 Diuquid Phone: (502)753-2400
Murray, KY 42071 Fax: (502)753-9434
Free: (800)455-2400
E-mail: wfge@kih.net

Format: Country. **Networks:** Unistar; CNN Radio; Westwood One Radio. **Founded:** 1967. **Formerly:** WBLN-FM (1967); WAAW-FM. **Operating Hours:** Continuous. **Key Personnel:** Greg Delaney, General Mgr.; Neil Bradley, Sports Dir. **Wattage:** 100,000. **Ad Rates:** $16-34 for 30 seconds; $20-42 for 60 seconds.

12500 WKMS-FM - 91.3
University Sta., Box 2018 Phone: (502)762-4359
Murray, KY 42071 Fax: (502)762-4667
Free: (800)599-4737
E-mail: wkms@ldd.net

Format: Public Radio; Classical; News; Information; Jazz. **Networks:** National Public Radio (NPR). **Owner:** Board of Regents, Murray State University, at above address. **Founded:** 1970. **Operating Hours:** Continuous 32% network, 68% local. **ADI:** Paducah,KY-Cape Girardeau,MO-Marion,IL. **Key Personnel:** Kate Lochte, Manager, phone (502)762-4745, fax (502)762-4667, katae.lochte@murraystate.edu. **Local Programs:** *Morning Classics*, Margaret Hunt, (502)762-4899. **Wattage:** 100,000. **Ad Rates:** Noncommercial; underwriting available. $10 per unit. **URL:** http://www.wkms.org.

12501 WNBS-AM - 1340
1500 Duiguid Dr. Phone: (502)753-2400
Murray, KY 42071 Fax: (502)753-9434
Free: (800)455-2400
E-mail: wfge@kih.net

Format: Oldies. **Owner:** WRUS, Inc., at above address. **Founded:** 1948. **Operating Hours:** Continuous; 95% network, 5% local. **Key Personnel:** Greg Delaney, General Mgr.; Bill Hatchet, Program Dir. **Wattage:** 1000. **Ad Rates:** $8.60-10.60 for 30 seconds; $11.60-13.60 for 60 seconds.

NEW CASTLE†, pop. 832.

Henry Co. (NW). 30 m NW of Frankfort. Grist mill. Agriculture. Corn, hay, tobacco.

12502 Henry County Local
Landmark Community Newspapers, Inc.
PO Box 209 Phone: (502)845-2858
New Castle, KY 40050
Newspaper with a Democratic orientation. **Founded:** 1876. **Freq:** Weekly (Wed.). **Print Method:** Offset. **Cols./Page:** 6. **Col. Width:** 24 nonpareils. **Col. Depth:** 294 agate lines. **Key Personnel:** Dave Eldridge, General Mgr. **USPS:** 240-300. **Subscription Rates:** $16.50 individuals. **Remarks:** Accepts advertising.
Ad Rates: BW: $546.96 **Circ:** ‡4,770
4C: $761.96
PCI: $4.24

12503 Henry County Local & Shopper
Landmark Community Newspapers, Inc.
PO Box 209 Phone: (502)845-2858
New Castle, KY 40050 Fax: (502)845-2921
Publication E-mail: holocal@kih.net

Community newspaper. **Founded:** 1876. **Freq:** Weekly. **Print Method:** Web offset. **Cols./Page:** 6. **Col. Width:** 2 inches. **Col. Depth:** 21 1/2 inches. **Key Personnel:** Jason Hart, General Mgr., jasonhart@usa.ner; Tiffany Clark, Advertising Sales; Matt Tungate, Editor. **Subscription Rates:** $19. **Remarks:** Accepts advertising.
Ad Rates: BW: $580.50 **Circ:** Paid ⊕4,262
4C: $805.50 Controlled ⊕35
SAU: $4.50

NEW HOPE

12504 Fatima Family Messenger
Fatima Family Apostolate
3050 Gap Knob Rd. Phone: (502)325-3829
New Hope, KY 40052 Fax: (502)325-3091

Magazine promoting Catholic family life, and witnessing the truths of Catholic faith to youth. **Founded:** 1987. **Freq:** Quarterly. **Key Personnel:** Rev. Robert J. Fox, Editor. **Formerly:** Messenger of Our Lady (1990).

NICHOLASVILLE†, pop. 10,400.

Jessamine Co. (C). 12 m S of Lexington. Manufactures wire products, paperboard food containers, automotive trim parts, plastic, vehicle mufflers, high security lock systems. Machine works. Dairy, stock, poultry, grain, truck farms. Tobacco, corn, wheat.

12505 French Forum
French Forum Publishers, Inc.
PO Box 130 Phone: (606)885-1446
Nicholasville, KY 40340 Fax: (606)257-3743
Publisher E-mail: rcl@ukcc.uky.edu

Journal covering literary criticism and French literature. **Founded:** 1976. **Freq:** Triennial. **Trim Size:** 5 7/8 x 9. **Cols./Page:** 1. **Key Personnel:** Raymond C. La Charite, rcl@ukcc.uky.edu; Virginia A. La Charite, val@ukcc.uky.edu. **ISSN:** 0098-9355. **Subscription Rates:** $20 individuals. **Remarks:** Accepts advertising.
Ad Rates: BW: $90 **Circ:** Controlled 500

12506 The Jessamine Journal
Republic Newspapers
507 N. Main St. Phone: (606)885-5381
PO Box 8 Fax: (606)887-2966
Nicholasville, KY 40340-0008
Publication E-mail: news@jessaminejournal.com

Newspaper. **Founded:** 1873. **Freq:** Weekly (Thurs.). **Print Method:** Offset. **Cols./Page:** 6. **Col. Width:** 26 nonpareils. **Col. Depth:** 294 agate lines. **Key Personnel:** Dave Eldridge, Publisher; Randy Patrick, Editor. **Subscription Rates:** $20 in-county; $0.50 single issue. **Remarks:** Accepts advertising.
Ad Rates: GLR: $.20 **Circ:** 6,066
BW: $717.24
4C: $912.24
SAU: $5.56
PCI: $5.56

OLIVE HILL, pop. 2,539.

Carter Co. (NE). 22 m N of Lewis. Concrete products, men's and boy's work clothing manufactured. Agriculture. Tobacco, livestock, poultry.

12507 Olive Hill Times
Post Office Bldg. Phone: (606)286-4201
Olive Hill, KY 41164
Community newspaper. **Founded:** 1969. **Freq:** Weekly (Wed.). **Print Method:** Offset. **Cols./Page:** 6. **Col. Width:** 12 picas. **Col. Depth:** 21 1/2 inches. **Key Personnel:** Becky Walker, Editor. **Subscription Rates:** $15 individuals. **Remarks:** Accepts advertising.
Ad Rates: SAU: $4.05 **Circ:** Paid ‡2,905
PCI: $3.37

OWENSBORO†, pop. 54,450.

Daviess Co. (WC). On Ohio River, 38 m SE of Evansville, Ind. Kentucky Wesleyan College; Brescia College. Riverport facilities. Manufactures whiskey, electric lamps, radio tubes, chair, cigars, bricks, iron and steel products, furniture, storm and screen windows, concrete, chemicals, tobacco, flour, oil well supplies, sewer pipes, cheese, canned goods, product bakery, building blocks, stock feeds. Tobacco auction warehouses. Meat and poultry packing plants. Soybean mill. Oil, gas wells. Coal mines. Forgings. Timber. Diversified farming.

12508 Messenger-Inquirer
Owensboro Messenger-Inquirer
1401 Frederica St. Phone: (502)926-0123
PO Box 1480 Fax: (502)685-3446
Owensboro, KY 42301-1480
Free: (800)633-2008
Publisher E-mail: news@messenger-inquirer.com

General newspaper. **Founded:** 1875. **Freq:** Mon.-Sun. (morn.). **Print Method:** Offset. **Cols./Page:** 6. **Col. Width:** 25 nonpareils. **Col. Depth:** 294 agate lines. **Key Personnel:** Robert H. Ashley, Editor, phone (502)691-7292, fax (502)686-7868; T. Edward Riney, Publisher, phone (502)691-7210, fax (502)685-3446; Elaine Morgan, Advertising Dir., phone (502)691-7238, fax (502)691-7244; Linda Hagan, Natl. Advertising Coord., phone (502)691-7234, fax (502)691-7244. **Subscription Rates:** $147.70 individuals. **Remarks:** Accepts advertising. Sunday: BW: $2,898; 4C: $3,358; PCI: $23. **URL:** http://www.messenger-inquirer.com.
Ad Rates: GLR: $2 **Circ:** Mon.-Sat. ★31,767
BW: $2,772 Sun. ★34,991
4C: $3,232
PCI: $22

12509 Century Cable
100 Industrial Dr. Phone: (502)685-2991
Box 21798 Fax: (502)685-0854
Owensboro, KY 42302
Free: (800)248-2434

Formerly: Owensboro On the Air. **Key Personnel:** Jim Voyles, Customer Service Mgr.; Barbara Taylor, Marketing Mgr.; Bud Bristow, Plant Mgr. **Cities Served:** Owensboro, Daviess, Webster, and Henderson counties: subscribing households 24,000; 45 channels.

12510 Century Communications
PO Box 21828 Phone: (502)685-2991
Owensboro, KY 42304-1828 Fax: (502)685-0854
Free: (800)248-2434

Founded: 1967. **Formerly:** Owensboro Cablevision. **Cities Served:** Daviess County, KY.

12511 WKWC-FM - 90.3
3000 Frederica St. Phone: (502)685-5937
Owensboro, KY 42301 Fax: (502)926-3196
E-mail: radio@kwc.edu

Format: Eclectic. **Networks:** Independent. **Owner:** Kentucky Wesleyan College, at above address. **Founded:** 1983. **Operating Hours:** 8 a.m.-midnight weekdays; 9 a.m.-midnight Sat.; 7 a.m.-midnight Sun. **Key Personnel:** Pam Gray, Station Mgr. **Wattage:** 5000. **Ad Rates:** Noncommercial.

12512 WOMI-AM - 1490
3301 Frederica St. Phone: (502)683-1558
Box 1330 Fax: (502)685-2500
Owensboro, KY 42302
Free: (800)666-1031
E-mail: tom@wbkr.com

Format: News; Talk. **Simulcasts:** WVJS. **Networks:** NBC. **Owner:** Brill Media, 420 N.W. 5th St., Evansville, IN 47708, Fax: (812)428-4021. **Founded:** 1938. **Operating Hours:** Continuous. **ADI:** Evansville, IN (Madisonville, KY). **Key Personnel:** Gary Exline, General Mgr.; Jeff Nalley, Contact; Paige Moore, Program Dir. **Local Programs:** *Joe Lowe Morning Show* 6:00 am - 8:00 am Monday-Friday, Joe Lowe, (502)683-1558. **Wattage:** 1000. **Ad Rates:** $3.50-12 for 30 seconds; $5.50-14 for 60 seconds. Combined advertising rates available with WVJS-AM.

12513 WSTO-FM - 96.1
100 Industrial Dr. Phone: (502)685-2991
Box 21828 Fax: (502)685-7098
Owensboro, KY 42301

Format: Contemporary Hit Radio (CHR). **Networks:** ABC. **Owner:** Century Communications, 50 Locust Ave., New Canaan, CT 06840, (203)972-2000. **Founded:** 1948. **Operating Hours:** Continuous. **ADI:** Evansville, IN (Madisonville, KY). **Key Personnel:** Steve Cooke, General Mgr.; Lee Wilson, General Sales Mgr. **Local Programs:** *Alternative Sunday Night*, Tim Michaelson, Mailing contact; *Flashback Cafe*, Cindy Mercer, Mailing contact. **Wattage:** 100,000 ERP. **Ad Rates:** $11-69 for 30 seconds; $15-79 for 60 seconds.

12514 WVJS-AM - 1420
3301 Frederica St. Phone: (502)686-0096
Owensboro, KY 42301-6082 Fax: (502)685-2500
E-mail: paige@wbkr.com

Format: Adult Contemporary. **Networks:** ABC. **Founded:** 1948. **Operating Hours:** Continuous. **Key Personnel:** Paige Moore, Program Dir. **Wattage:** 5000. **Ad Rates:** Combined advertising rates available with WOMI-AM.

OWENTON†, pop. 1,341.

Owen Co. (NC). 30 m N of Frankfort. Agriculture. Tobacco, corn, cattle.

12515 The News-Herald
PO Box 219 Phone: (502)484-3431
Owenton, KY 40359 Fax: (502)484-3221
Publication E-mail: newsheral1@ad.com

Community newspaper. **Founded:** 1868. **Freq:** Weekly (Thurs.). **Print Method:** Offset. **Cols./Page:** 6. **Col. Width:** 24 nonpareils. **Col. Depth:** 294 agate lines. **Key Personnel:** Kelly Menser, Editor. **Subscription Rates:** $16.96 individuals; $20.14 out of area; $22 out of state. **Remarks:** Accepts advertising.
Ad Rates: GLR: $.16 **Circ:** ‡3,300
BW: $315
SAU: $4.28

12516 WKON-TV - 52
c/o Kentucky Authority for Educational TV Phone: (606)258-7000
600 Cooper Dr. Fax: (606)258-7399
Lexington, KY 40502
E-mail: gfox@msmail.ket.org

Format: Public TV. **Networks:** Public Broadcasting Service (PBS); Kentucky Educational Television. **Owner:** Kentucky Authority for Educational TV, at above address, (606)258-7170, Fax: (606)258-7390. **Founded:** 1968. **Operating Hours:** 6:15 a.m.-midnight. **ADI:** Paducah,KY-Cape Girardeau,MO-Marion,IL. **Key Personnel:** Craig Cornwell, Contact; J. Gorman, Contact; D. Holtzclaw, Contact; M. Ferguson, Contact; S. Talbert, Contact; Virginia Gaines Fox, Contact; Donna Moore, Contact; Sally Hamilton, Contact; William Wilson, Contact; D. Hoffman, Contact; B. Ball, Contact; L. Hobson, Contact; J. Holbrook, Contact; T. Tucker, Contact. **Local Programs:** *Comment on Kentucky*; *Kentucky Afield*; *Kentucky Life*; *Kentucky Tonight*; *Legislative Weekly*. **Wattage:** 676,000. **Ad Rates:** Noncommercial. **URL:** http://www.ket.org.

OWINGSVILLE†, pop. 1,419.

Bath Co. (NE). 43 m NE of Lexington. Lumber mill. Agriculture. Tobacco, corn, potatoes.

12517 Bath County News-Outlook
Community News Inc.
Box 577 Phone: (606)674-2181
Owingsville, KY 40360 Fax: (606)674-2181

Community newspaper. **Founded:** 1878. **Freq:** Weekly (Thurs.). **Print Method:** Offset. **Cols./Page:** 6. **Col. Width:** 24 nonpareils. **Col. Depth:** 294 agate lines. **Key Personnel:** Ken E. Mertz, Publisher; Margaret C. Metz, Assoc. Pub./Ad. Mgr. **Subscription Rates:** $14 individuals; $24 out of state; $.50 single issue.
Ad Rates: GLR: $.28 **Circ:** ‡3,400
BW: $567
4C: $360
SAU: $4.50
PCI: $4.50

12518 WKCA-FM - 107.7
PO Box 1010 Phone: (606)674-2266
Owingsville, KY 40360 Fax: (606)674-6700

Format: Contemporary Country. **Networks:** Satellite Music Network; ABC. **Owner:** Gateway Radio Works, Inc., at above address. **Founded:** 1983. **Operating Hours:** Continuous; 80% network, 20% local. **ADI:** Lexington, KY. **Key Personnel:** Hays McMakin, President; Jeff Ray, Station Mgr.; Becky Young, Office Mgr.; Bill Chadwell, News Dir. **Local Programs:** *Bluegrass Fever* 7:00 pm - 9:00 pm Thursday, Eric Highley, Mailing contact. **Wattage:** 6,000. **Ad Rates:** $4-5.50 for 30 seconds; $5-6.50 for 60 seconds.

PADUCAH†, pop. 29,315.

McCracken Co. (SW). On the Ohio River, 80 m SW of Evansville, Ind. Manufactures industrial belting, concrete products, barges, metallurgical coke, automotive radiators, chemicals, textile machinery, radio components, castings, pottery, ladies' wearing apparel, barge & railroad cars covers. Important burley tobacco market. Atomic energy plant. Clay, fluorite, coal mines.

12519 American Quilter
American Quilter's Society
PO Box 3290 Phone: (502)898-7903
Paducah, KY 42002-3290 Fax: (502)898-8890
Free: (800)626-5420
Publisher E-mail: aqsquilt@apex.net

Consumer magazine covering for information for quilters. **Founded:** 1985. **Freq:** Quarterly. **Trim Size:** 8 3/4 x 10 3/4. **Key Personnel:** Victoria Faora, Executive Editor. **ISSN:** 8756-6591. **Subscription Rates:** $18 individuals. **Remarks:** Accepts advertising.
Ad Rates: BW: $1,495 **Circ:** Combined 61,000
4C: $2,150

12520 Carlisle County News
Kentucky Publishing, Inc.
701 Jefferson Phone: (502)442-7389
Paducah, KY 42001 Fax: (502)442-5220

Newspaper with a Democratic orientation. **Subtitle:** Serving as Carlisle County's Newspaper since 1894. **Founded:** 1894. **Freq:** Weekly (Wed.). **Print Method:** Offset. **Cols./Page:** 6.

Col. Width: 24 nonpareils. **Col. Depth:** 294 agate lines. **Key Personnel:** Wendy Bowman, Editor; Chris McGehee, Publisher. **Subscription Rates:** $22 individuals; $25 out of area; $40 out of state. **Remarks:** Accepts advertising.
Ad Rates: PCI: $4.75 **Circ:** ‡3,500

12521 The Paducah Sun
PO Box 2300 Phone: (502)443-1771
Paducah, KY 42002-2300 Fax: (502)442-7859
Free: (800)959-1771

General newspaper. **Founded:** 1871. **Freq:** Daily and Sunday (morn.). **Print Method:** Offset. **Cols./Page:** 6. **Col. Width:** 24 nonpareils. **Col. Depth:** 298 agate lines. **Key Personnel:** James Paxton, Editor; Fred Paxton, Publisher; Jay Frizzo, General Mgr.; Jana Thomasson, Asst. Gen. Mgr. **Subscription Rates:** $195 individuals. **Remarks:** Accepts advertising.
Ad Rates: BW: $2,773.13 **Circ:** Mon.-Sat. ★**28,709**
4C: $3,113.13 Sun. ★**31,716**
PCI: $24

12522 (The Smoke) Signal
Paducah Community College
Alben Barkley Dr. Phone: (502)554-9200
PO Box 7380 Fax: (502)554-6218
Paducah, KY 42002-7380
Collegiate newspaper. **Founded:** 1964. **Freq:** Weekly (Wed.). **Print Method:** Offset. **Trim Size:** 8 x 13. **Cols./Page:** 4. **Col. Width:** 21 nonpareils. **Col. Depth:** 182 agate lines. **Remarks:** Accepts advertising.
Ad Rates: BW: $156 **Circ:** (Not Reported)

12523 Comcast Cablevision of Paducah
800 Broadway Phone: (502)442-6382
Paducah, KY 42001 Fax: (502)442-4071

Founded: 1978. **Cities Served:** Graves, Livingston, Marshall and McCracken counties, KY and Massac County, IL.

12524 WDDJ-FM - 96.9
6000 WKYX WKYQ Rd. Phone: (502)442-8231
Paducah, KY 42003-9213 Fax: (502)442-9723
E-mail: wddj@wkynet.com

Format: Contemporary Hit Radio (CHR); Classic Rock. **Networks:** ABC. **Owner:** Radio Paducah, Inc., at above address. **Founded:** 1946. **Operating Hours:** Continuous. **ADI:** Paducah,KY-Cape Girardeau,MO-Marion,IL. **Key Personnel:** R. Lee Hagan, President; Jamie Richards, Operations Mgr.; Dee Gillihan, Sales Mgr. **Wattage:** 100,000 ERP. **Ad Rates:** $11-22 for 30 seconds; $15-24 for 60 seconds. **URL:** http://www.wkynet.com/paducahnet/wddj/default.html.

12525 WDXR-AM - 1450
No. 1 Executive Blvd. Phone: (502)443-1000
Paducah, KY 42001 Fax: (502)442-1000
Free: (800)942-0943
E-mail: t1669@ldd.net

Format: Sports. **Founded:** 1957. **Operating Hours:** Continuous; 75% network, 25% local. **ADI:** Paducah,KY-Cape Girardeau,MO-Marion,IL. **Key Personnel:** Benda Hawes, General Mgr.; Bob Hopper, News Dir.; Brenda Hawes, Operations Mgr. **Wattage:** 1000. **Ad Rates:** $6-12 for 30 seconds.

12526 WDXR-FM - 94.3
No. 1 Executive Blvd. Phone: (502)443-1000
PO Box 2250 Fax: (502)442-1000
Paducah, KY 42001
Free: (800)942-0943
E-mail: t1669@ldd.net

Format: Oldies. **Simulcasts:** WCBF-FM. **Owner:** Hiltopper Broadcasting Inc., PO Box 2250, Paducah, KY 42002. **Founded:** 1957. **Operating Hours:** 100% local. **ADI:** Paducah,KY-Cape Girardeau,MO-Marion,IL. **Key Personnel:** Brenda Hawes, Operations Mgr.; Brenda Hawes, General Mgr.; Bob Hopper, Sports Dir. **Wattage:** 6000. **Ad Rates:** $11-16 for 30 seconds.

12527 WKYQ-FM - 93.3
6000 WKYQ Rd. Phone: (502)554-0093
Paducah, KY 42003 Fax: (502)554-5468
E-mail: info@wkyq.com

Format: Contemporary Country; Agricultural; News. **Networks:** ABC. **Owner:** Bristol Broadcasting Corp., at above address. **Founded:** 1947. **Operating Hours:** Continuous. **ADI:** Paducah,KY-Cape Girardeau,MO-Marion,IL. **Key Personnel:** Gary Morse, Contact; Bobby Cook, Operations Mgr. **Wattage:** 100,000 ERP. **Ad Rates:** $85-110 per unit.

12528 WKYX-AM - 570
Box 2397 Phone: (502)554-8255
Paducah, KY 42002-2397 Fax: (502)554-5468

Format: Talk; News; Sports; Oldies. **Owner:** Bristol Broadcasting Co., Inc., Box 1389, Bristol, VA 24203, (703)669-8112. **Founded:** 1971. **Operating Hours:** Continuous; 40% network, 60% local. **ADI:** Paducah,KY-Cape Girardeau,MO-Marion,IL. **Key Personnel:** Greg Dunver, Program Dir.; Donna Groves, News Dir.; Gary Morse, General Mgr. **Wattage:** 1000 day; 500 night. **Ad Rates:** $60-120 for 30 seconds; $40-110 for 60 seconds.

12529 WPAD-AM - 1560
PO Box 2397 Phone: (502)442-8231
Paducah, KY 42002-2397 Fax: (502)442-9723
E-mail: wpad@wkynet.com

Format: Adult Album Alternative. **Networks:** Westwood One Radio; Mutual Broadcasting System. **Owner:** Purchase Broadcasting, at above address. **Founded:** 1936. **Operating Hours:** Continuous. 99% network, 1% local. **ADI:** Paducah,KY-Cape Girardeau,MO-Marion,IL. **Key Personnel:** Jamie Richards, Operations Mgr.; R.Lee Hagan, General Mgr.; Dee Gillihan, Sales Mgr. **Wattage:** 10,000. **Ad Rates:** $5-13 for 30 seconds; $8-16 for 60 seconds. **URL:** http://www.wkynet.com/paducahnet/wpad/default.html.

12530 WPSD-TV - 6
PO Box 1197 Phone: (502)415-1900
Paducah, KY 42002-1197 Fax: (502)415-1995
Free: (800)4WPSDTV

Format: Commercial TV. **Networks:** NBC. **Founded:** 1957. **Operating Hours:** Continuous. **ADI:** Paducah,KY-Cape Girardeau,MO-Marion,IL. **Key Personnel:** Bill Evans, News Dir.; Dan Steele, Contact, fax (502)415-2020; Richard Paxton, Station Mgr.; Chuck Voss, Production Mgr.; David Jernigan, General Sales Mgr.

PAINTSVILLE†, pop. 3,815.

Johnson Co. (EC). On Big Sandy River, 50 m S of Ashland. Manufactures plumbing fixtures, tobacco. Coal mines. Oil wells. Bottling works. Poultry stock. Truck, grain farms. Apples.

12531 The Paintsville Herald
PO Box 1547 Phone: (606)789-5315
Paintsville, KY 41240 Fax: (606)789-9717

Newspaper. **Founded:** 1901. **Freq:** Weekly (Wed.). **Print Method:** Offset. **Cols./Page:** 6. **Col. Width:** 12 picas. **Col. Depth:** 21 1/2 inches. **Key Personnel:** Kate B. Dickson, Publisher; Ralph Davis III, Editor. **USPS:** 418-440. **Subscription Rates:** $25 individuals. **Remarks:** Accepts advertising.
Ad Rates: BW: $625.65 **Circ:** ‡6,000
4C: $900.25
PCI: $4.85

12532 Big Sandy TV Cable, Inc.
PO Box 956 Phone: (606)789-3455
Paintsville, KY 41240 Fax: (606)789-5352

Founded: 1960. **Key Personnel:** Paul D. Butcher, President. **Cities Served:** subscribing households 2,750; 36 channels; 1 community access channel.

12533 Tele-Media Cable
Box 547 Phone: (606)789-3236
Paintsville, KY 41240

Owner: Tele-Media Corp., 320 W. College Ave., Pleasant Gap, PA 16823, (814)237-1512. **Key Personnel:** Arthur Reed, General Mgr. **Cities Served:** Paintsville, Staffordsville, Thelma, and Viola, KY.

12534 WSIP-AM - 1490
PO Box 591 Phone: (606)789-5311
Paintsville, KY 41240 Fax: (606)789-7200

Format: Gospel. **Networks:** CNN Radio. **Owner:** Key Broadcasting, PO Box 1450, Corbin, KY 40701. **Founded:** 1949. **Operating Hours:** 5 a.m.-midnight. **Key Personnel:** Mike Fyffe, Operations Mgr.; Marcia Thompson, Sales Mgr.; Jason Bussey, News Dir.; Spike Berkhimer, Sports Dir.; Lewis Berkhimer, Contact; Glenna Adkins, General Mgr. **Local Programs:** *Afternoon Trader*, Marcia Thompson, (606)789-3473; *Marcia Thompson in the Afternoon*; *Spike Berkimer in the Morning*. **Wattage:** 1000. **Ad Rates:** $4.71 for 30 seconds; $9.41 for 60 seconds.

12535 WSIP-FM - 98.9
PO Box 591 Phone: (606)789-5311
Paintsville, KY 41240 Fax: (606)789-7200

Networks: CBS. **Owner:** Key Broadcating Inc., at above address. **Founded:** 1975. **Operating Hours:** Continuous. **ADI:** Lexington, KY. **Key Personnel:** Mike Fyffe, Operations Dir., phone (606)789-3325; Glenna Adkins, General Mgr., phone (606)789-3375; Joanna Keaton, News Dir., phone (606)789-3473; Jason Bussey, PD; Spike Berkhimer, Sports Dir.; Paul Manuel, Music Dir./Engineer. **Local Programs:** *Big Sandy Sportsline*, Spike Berkhimer, (606)789-3473; *Swap Shop*, Ron Smith, (606)789-3473; *Talk of the Town*, Jason Bussey, (606)789-3473. **Wattage:** 100,000. **Ad Rates:** $15 for 30 seconds; $22 for 60 seconds.

PARIS†, pop. 7,935.

Bourbon Co. (NEC). 18 m NE of Lexington. Manufactures clothing, household goods, men's and boy's underwear, barrels, mining and automotive equipment, pumps, concrete products. Fertilizer plant. Ships tobacco, livestock. Stock, dairy, poultry farms. Thoroughbred horses.

12536 Bourbon County Citizen
Advertiser
PO Box 158 Phone: (606)987-1870
Paris, KY 40362-0158 Fax: (606)987-3729

Community newspaper. **Founded:** 1984. **Freq:** Weekly (Wed.). **Print Method:** Offset. **Cols./Page:** 6. **Col. Width:** 24 nonpareils. **Col. Depth:** 294 agate lines. **Key Personnel:** Jimmy Brannon, Editor and Publisher; Bebe Wagoner, Advertising Mgr.; Mrs. Larry Brannon, General Mgr. **Subscription Rates:** $12 individuals. **Remarks:** Accepts advertising.
Ad Rates: GLR: $.36 **Circ:** ‡4,100
BW: $635.04
SAU: $5.04

12537 Citizen-Advertiser
Advertiser
PO Box 158 Phone: (606)987-1870
Paris, KY 40362-0158 Fax: (606)987-3729

Newspaper with a Democratic orientation. **Founded:** 1807. **Freq:** Weekly (Mon.). **Print Method:** Offset. **Cols./Page:** 6. **Col. Width:** 24 nonpareils. **Col. Depth:** 294 agate lines. **Key Personnel:** Mrs. Larry Brannon, General Mgr. **Subscription Rates:** Free. **Remarks:** Accepts advertising.
Ad Rates: GLR: $.36 **Circ:** Free ‡11,400
BW: $635.04
SAU: $5.04

PARK HILLS, pop. 3,500.

Kenton Co. (N). 5 m E of Covington. Residential.

12538 Big Truck Trader
Trader Target Publications, Inc.
1450 Dixie Hwy. Phone: (606)581-5500
Park Hills, KY 41011 Fax: (606)581-6837

Magazine featuring photo ads of trucks and equipment for sale by individuals and dealers. **Founded:** 1977. **Freq:** Weekly (Thurs.). **Print Method:** Offset. Uses mats. **Trim Size:** 8 1/2 x 11. **Cols./Page:** 2. **Col. Width:** 27 nonpareils. **Col. Depth:** 128 agate lines. **Key Personnel:** Bruce Lenhoff, Sales Mgr.; Tom Jaynes, General Mgr. **Subscription Rates:** $3 single issue. **Remarks:** Accepts advertising. **URL:** http://www.traderonline.com.
Ad Rates: BW: $305 **Circ:** Combined ‡45,000
4C: $430

12539 Boat & RV Trader
Trader Target Publications, Inc.
1450 Dixie Hwy. Phone: (606)581-5500
Park Hills, KY 41011 Fax: (606)581-6837

Magazine featuring photo ads of boats, motorcycles, and recreational vehicles for sale. **Founded:** 1985. **Freq:** Weekly (Thurs.). **Print Method:** Offset. **Trim Size:** 8 1/2 x 11. **Cols./Page:** 2. **Col. Width:** 27 nonpareils. **Col. Depth:** 128 agate lines. **Key Personnel:** Tom Jaynes, General Mgr.; Bruce Lenhoff, Sales Mgr. **Subscription Rates:** $3 single issue. **Remarks:** Accepts advertising. **URL:** http://www.traderonline.com.
Ad Rates: BW: $279 **Circ:** ‡25,000
4C: $389

12540 Truck Trader
Trader Target Publications, Inc.
1450 Dixie Hwy. Phone: (606)581-5500
Park Hills, KY 41011 Fax: (606)581-6837

Magazine featuring photo classified ads of automobiles for sale by individuals and dealers. **Founded:** Nov. 21, 1975. **Freq:** Weekly (Thurs.). **Print Method:** Offset. **Trim Size:** 8 1/2 x 11. **Cols./Page:** 2. **Col. Width:** 27 nonpareils. **Col. Depth:** 128 agate lines. **Key Personnel:** Tom Jaynes, General Mgr.; Bruce Lenhoff, Sales Mgr. **Subscription Rates:** $3 single issue. **Remarks:** Accepts advertising.
Ad Rates: BW: $255 **Circ:** ‡25,000
4C: $355

PIKEVILLE†, pop. 4,756.

Pike Co. (E) 5 m. S of Millard. Residential.

12541 Appalachian News Express
Lancaster Management
PO Box 802 Phone: (606)437-4054
Pikeville, KY 41502 Fax: (606)437-4246

Community newspaper. **Founded:** 1914. **Freq:** 3/week. **Print Method:** Offset. **Cols./Page:** 6. **Col. Width:** 2 inches. **Col. Depth:** 294 agate lines. **Key Personnel:** Marty Backus, Pub./Exec. Editor; Paula Whitt, Advertising Mgr.; Larry Martin, Editor. **USPS:** 347-510. **Subscription Rates:** $55 individuals; $90 out of area. **Remarks:** Accepts advertising.
Ad Rates: GLR: $.37 **Circ:** ‡10,800
BW: $780.45
4C: $980.45
SAU: $4.66
PCI: $6.05

12542 Pikeville Review
Pikeville College
Pikeville, KY 41501 Phone: (606)432-9612
Fax: (606)432-9328

Literary magazine covering poetry, fiction, essays, and reviews. **Founded:** 1987. **Freq:** Annual. **Trim Size:** 6 x 8. **Key Personnel:** Elgin M. Ward, Editor, eward@pc.edu. **Subscription Rates:** $4 individuals. **Remarks:** Accepts advertising.
Circ: Paid 500

12543 Mountain Cable TV
1953 State Hwy 194 E. Phone: (606)437-6193
Pikeville, KY 41501 Fax: (606)631-3376

Founded: 1966. **Formerly:** Blackburn Cable TV. **Cities Served:** subscribing households 50; 12 channels.

12544 Tele-Media of KWV
PO Box 3008 Phone: (606)432-0930
Pikeville, KY 41502 Fax: (606)437-6239

Key Personnel: Carol Adkins, General Mgr. **Cities Served:** Small towns in the area of Pikeville, KY.

12545 WDHR-FM - 93.1
1240 Radio Dr. Phone: (606)432-8103
Box 2200 Fax: (606)432-2809
Pikeville, KY 41502
E-mail: wdhr@wdhr.com

Format: Country. **Networks:** ABC; KyNet. **Owner:** East Kentucky Broadcasting Corp., at above address. **Founded:** 1973. **Operating Hours:** Continuous. **ADI:** Charleston-Huntington, WV. **Key Personnel:** Walter E. May, Owner; Cindy May Sargent, General Mgr.; Dave Stanford, Program Dir.; Debbie Lawson, Traffic Dir.; Chrissie Mueller, Continuity; Shannon Deskins, News Dir.; Bryan Crager, Sports Dir.; Walter Dingus, Chief Engineer. **Wattage:** 50,000. **Ad Rates:** $8.50-16.75 for 15 seconds; $11-23.35 for 30 seconds; $13.50-28.75 for 60 seconds. **URL:** http://www.wdhr.com/.

12546 WJSO-FM - 90.1
PO Box 3237 Phone: (606)432-0351
Pikeville, KY 41502

Format: Talk; Religious. **Networks:** Moody Broadcasting. **Founded:** 1989. **Operating Hours:** Continuous; 100% network. **Key Personnel:** Jeff Jacobsen, Manager; Ken Robinson, Chief Engineer. **Wattage:** 3800. **Ad Rates:** Noncommercial. **URL:** http://www.moody.edu.

12547 WKPI-TV - 22
c/o Kentucky Authority for Phone: (606)258-7000
Educational TV Fax: (606)258-7399
600 Cooper Dr.
Lexington, KY 40502
Free: (800)432-0951

Format: Public TV. **Networks:** Public Broadcasting Service (PBS); Kentucky Educational Television. **Owner:** Kentucky Authority for Educational TV, at above address. **Founded:** 1968. **Operating Hours:** 6:30 a.m.-midnight. **ADI:** Charleston-Huntington, WV. **Key Personnel:** Virginia Fox, Executive Dir., gfox@ket.org; Sally Hamilton, Deputy Dir./Administration & Support, shamilton@ket.org; Bill Wilsonlaw, Deputy Dir./Education & Outreach, bwilson@ket.org; Donna Moore, Deputy Dir./Programming & Production, dmoore@ket.org; Doris Holtzclaw, Business Mgr., dholtzclaw@ket.org; Jess Holbrook, Dir. Of Studio Engineering, jholbrook@ket.org; Robert Ball, Dir. of Technical Planning, bball@ket.org; Stu Talbert, Dir. of Transmission Systems, stalbert@ket.org; Liz Hobson, Dir. of Education, lhobson@ket.org; Craig Cornwell, Production Dir., ccornwell@ket.org; Dick Hoffman, Program Dir., dhoffman@ket.org; Mike Clark, Dir. of Programming Operations, mclark@ket.org; Mary Campbell, Dir. of Communications, mcampbell@ket.org. **Local Programs:** *Comment on Kentucky*; *Kentucky Afield*; *Kentucky Life*; *Kentucky Tonight*; *Legislative Weekly*. **Wattage:** 1,320,000. **Ad Rates:** Noncommercial. **URL:** http://www.ket.org.

12548 WLSI-AM - 900
Box 2347 Phone: (606)432-9805
Pikeville, KY 41502 Fax: (606)437-0176

Format: Religious. **Founded:** 1949. **Operating Hours:** Continuous; 100% local. **Key Personnel:** Geraldine Fields, General Mgr. **Wattage:** 5000. **Ad Rates:** $3-3.52 for 15 seconds; $5-5.88 for 30 seconds; $7-8.23 for 60 seconds.

12549 WPKE-AM - 1240
1240 Radio Dr. Phone: (606)437-4051
Box 2200 Fax: (606)432-2809
Pikeville, KY 41502
E-mail: wpke@wpke.com

Format: Contemporary Hit Radio (CHR). **Simulcasts:** WPKE-FM; WBPA-AM. **Networks:** ABC; KyNet. **Owner:** East Kentucky Broadcasting Co., at above address. **Founded:** 1949. **Operating Hours:** Continuous. **Key Personnel:** Walter E. May, President; Cindy May Sargent, General Mgr.; Dave Stanford, Program Dir.; Shannon Deskins, News Dir.; Chrissie Mueller, Continuity; Debbie Lawson, Traffic; Walter Dingus, Chief Engineer. **Wattage:** 1000. **Ad Rates:** $7.00-8.40 for 15 seconds; $8.75-10.50 for 30 seconds; $10.50-12.60 for 60 seconds. **URL:** http://members.aol.com/davehamer/ekb/ekb.htm; http://www.wpke.com.

12550 WPKE-FM - 103.1
1240 Radio Dr. Phone: (606)437-4051
Box 2200 Fax: (606)432-2809
Pikeville, KY 41502
E-mail: wpke@wpke.com

Format: Contemporary Hit Radio (CHR). **Networks:** ABC; KyNet. **Owner:** East Kentucky Broadcasting Co., at above address. **Founded:** 1949. **Operating Hours:** Continuous. **ADI:** Charleston-Huntington, WV. **Key Personnel:** Walter E. May, President; Cindy May Sargent, General Mgr.; Dave Stanford, Program Dir.; Shannon Deskins, News Dir.; Chrissie Mueller, Continuity; Debbie Lawson, Traffic; Walter Dingus, Chief Engineer. **Wattage:** 3000. **Ad Rates:** $7-8.40 for 15 seconds; $8.75-10.50 for 30 seconds; $10.50-12.60 for 60 seconds. **URL:** http://www.wpke.com.

PINEVILLE†, pop. 2,599.

Bell Co. (SE). On Cumberland River, 10 m N of Middlesboro. Summer resort and tourist center. Meat products, furniture factories. Coal mines, Hardwood timber. Limestone quarry. Sawmills.

12551 The Pineville Sun
Associated Publications, Inc.
PO Box 250 Phone: (606)337-2333
Pineville, KY 40977-0250
Community newspaper. **Subtitle:** Bell Co.'s Oldest Established Newspaper. **Founded:** May 1908. **Freq:** Weekly (Thurs.). **Print Method:** Offset. **Trim Size:** 7 x 21 1/2. **Cols./Page:** 8. **Col. Width:** 9 picas. **Col. Depth:** 21 inches. **Key Personnel:** Edd Saylor, Jr., Editor; Glenn Gray, Publisher. **Subscription Rates:** $8.50 individuals; $9.50 out of area; $10.50 out of state. **Remarks:** Accepts advertising. **Formerly:** Cumberland Courier.
Ad Rates: BW: $378 **Circ:** 3,000
4C: $653
SAU: $2.75

12552 Tele-Media Cable
PO Box 1037 Phone: (606)337-3116
Pineville, KY 40977 Fax: (606)337-5569

Key Personnel: Dena Hoskins, General Mgr. **Cities Served:** Clairfield, TN; Surrounding communities of Ingram, Frakes and Chenoa, KY.

PIPPA PASSES

Knott Co.

12553 WWJD-FM - 91.7
100 Purpose Rd. Phone: (606)368-2101
Pippa Passes, KY 41844 Fax: (606)368-2125

Format: Contemporary Christian. **Networks:** Independent. **Founded:** 1985. **Formerly:** WOAL-FM. **Operating Hours:** Continuous. **Key Personnel:** Tom Cody, General Mgr. **Wattage:** 7300.

PRESTONSBURG†, pop. 4,011.

Floyd Co. (EC). 60 m S of Ashland. Coal mines. Diversified farming. Corn and truck crops.

12554 The Floyd County Times
Floyd County Newspapers, Inc.
PO Box 391 Phone: (606)886-8506
Prestonsburg, KY 41653 Fax: (606)886-3603

Community newspaper. **Founded:** 1927. **Freq:** Semiweekly (Wed. and Fri.). **Print Method:** Offset. **Cols./Page:** 6. **Col. Width:** 26 nonpareils. **Col. Depth:** 294 agate lines. **Key Personnel:** Scott Perry, Editor; Janice Shepherd, Managing Editor; Shawn Hamilton, Advertising Mgr. **Subscription Rates:** $28 individuals; $38 out of state.
Ad Rates: BW: $637.50 **Circ:** 11,400
SAU: $5
PCI: $5

12555 Cablevision
2565 S. Lake Dr. Phone: (606)886-2291
PO Box 699 Fax: (606)886-1075
Prestonsburg, KY 41653

Formerly: Rifkin & Assoc. **Key Personnel:** Danny Perry, Contact. **Cities Served:** Surrounding Floyd County communities.: subscribing households 3,100; 31 channels.

12556 WDOC-AM - 1310
Box 309 Phone: (606)886-2338
Prestonsburg, KY 41653 Fax: (606)886-1026

Format: Country; News. **Networks:** USA Radio. **Owner:** WDOC, Inc., at above address. **Founded:** 1957. **Operating Hours:** 6 a.m.-sunset. **Key Personnel:** Gorman Collins, Sr., President; Gorman Collins, Jr., General Mgr.; James Allen, Program Dir. **Wattage:** 5000. **Ad Rates:** $3 for 30 seconds; $5 for 60 seconds.

12557 WQHY-FM - 95.5
Box 309 Phone: (606)886-8409
Prestonsburg, KY 41653 Fax: (606)886-1026

Format: Adult Contemporary; Oldies. **Networks:** ABC. **Owner:** WQHY-FM, at above address. **Founded:** 1962. **Operating Hours:** Continuous. **Key Personnel:** Gorman Collins, Sr., President; Gorman Collins, Jr., General Mgr.; James Allen, Program Dir. **Wattage:** 100,000 ERP. **Ad Rates:** $2.75-12.25 for 30 seconds; $4.58-20.42 for 60 seconds.

PRINCETON†, pop. 7,073.

Caldwell Co. (SW). 60 m S of Owensboro. Fluorspar mines. Manufactures hosiery, shirts, boilers, concrete products, lumber. Diversified farming.

12558 Times Leader
PO Box 439 Phone: (502)365-5588
Princeton, KY 42445 Fax: (502)365-7299
Publication E-mail: times-leader@wrynet.com
Publisher E-mail: timesleader@ziggycom.net

Community newspaper. **Founded:** 1871. **Freq:** Semiweekly (Wed. and Sat.). **Print Method:** Offset. **Cols./Page:** 6. **Col. Width:** 24 nonpareils. **Col. Depth:** 21 1/2 inches. **Key Personnel:** Chip Hutcheson, Publisher. **USPS:** 776-660. **Subscription Rates:** $33 individuals; $39 out of county; $48 out of state. **URL:** http://www.wkynet.com/princetonnet/times-leader/. **Formerly:** Princeton Leader; Caldwell County Times.
Ad Rates: GLR: $442.47 **Circ:** ‡5,700
BW: $442.47
4C: $562.47
SAU: $4.50
PCI: $4.50

12559 WAVJ-FM - 104.9
PO Box 148 Phone: (502)365-2072
Princeton, KY 42445 Fax: (502)365-2073

Format: Hot Country. **Networks:** Independent. **Founded:** 1950. **Operating Hours:** 24 hrs.; 75% local, 25% area. **ADI:** Paducah,KY-Cape Girardeau,MO-Marion,IL. **Key Personnel:** David Glass, Manager. **Wattage:** 250. **Ad Rates:** $6.75-7.50 per unit.

12560 WPKY-AM - 1580
Box 148 Phone: (502)365-2072
Princeton, KY 42445 Fax: (502)365-2073

Format: Country. **Networks:** Independent. **Owner:** Dart Inc., at above address. **Founded:** 1950. **Operating Hours:** 6 a.m.-6 p.m.; 100% local. **ADI:** Paducah,KY-Cape Girardeau,MO-Marion,IL. **Key Personnel:** Casey Kuhn, Program Dir.; Teresa Glass, Sales Mgr. **Wattage:** 250.

PROSPECT, pop. 1,981.

Jefferson Co. (NW). 10 m N of Louisville.

12561 Rainbow-Pcar Reviews On-Line
Falsoft Ink, Inc.
9509 U.S. Hwy. 42 Phone: (502)228-4492
PO Box 385 Fax: (502)228-5121
Prospect, KY 40059-0385
Publication E-mail: editor@rainbowpcur.com
Publisher E-mail: lonnie@rainbowpcur.com

Complete & comprehensive reviews of PC computer hardware & software. **Founded:** July 1983. **Freq:** Monthly. **Key Personnel:** Maggie Bunevitch, Managing Editor; Lawrence C. Falk, Publisher; Graycee Claster, Western Sales Dir.; Kim Lewis, Eastern Sales Dir. **ISSN:** 0747-0460. **Remarks:** Accepts advertising. **Formerly**: PCM.
Ad Rates: BW: $1,420 **Circ:** Paid ‡87,046
4C: $1,970 Controlled ‡351

PROVIDENCE, pop. 4,434.

Webster Co. (WC). 34 m SW of Henderson. Plastic, feed factories; Lumber mills. Coal mines. Oak timber. Agriculture. Tobacco, corn, hay, livestock.

12562 The Journal-Enterprise
PO Box 190 Phone: (502)667-2068
Providence, KY 42450-0190 Fax: (502)667-9160

Community newspaper. **Founded:** 1902. **Freq:** Weekly (Thurs.). **Print Method:** Offset. **Cols./Page:** 6. **Col. Width:** 24 nonpareils. **Col. Depth:** 197 agate lines. **Key Personnel:** Mark Holloway, Editor; Charlie Hust, Managing Editor; William E. Hust, Publisher. **Subscription Rates:** $12 individuals. **Remarks:** Accepts advertising.
Ad Rates: GLR: $.16 **Circ:** ‡4,500
SAU: $2.10

RADCLIFF, pop. 14,519.

Hardin Co. (WC). 35 m S of Louisville. Coating and engraving, concrete block. Agriculture. Tobacco, corn, livestock.

12563 The Sentinel
Royalty Printing Inc.
1558 Hill St. Phone: (502)351-4407
Radcliff, KY 40160 Fax: (502)351-4407

Community newspaper. **Founded:** 1961. **Freq:** Weekly (Thurs.). **Print Method:** Offset. **Cols./Page:** 6. **Col. Width:** 24 nonpareils. **Col. Depth:** 301 agate lines. **Key Personnel:** O.J. Royalty, Editor and Publisher. **USPS:** 490-520. **Subscription Rates:** $7.50 individuals. **Remarks:** Accepts advertising. **Alt. Formats:** Microform.
Ad Rates: GLR: $.221 **Circ:** Paid ⊕3,145
BW: $399.13 Non-paid ⊕**319**
4C: $556.01
PCI: $4.31

12564 TCI Radcliff Inc.
460 W. Lincoln Trail Blvd. Phone: (502)351-4114
Box 459 Fax: (502)351-8907
Radcliff, KY 40160

Founded: 1980. **Formerly**: TeleCable of Radcliffe Inc. **Key Personnel:** Ron Vasquez, Technical Mgr. **Cities Served:** Ft. Knox, Muldraugh, Radcliff, KY: subscribing households 11,600; 50 channels; 1 community access channel; 8 hours per week community access programming.

RICHMOND†, pop. 21,705.

Madison Co. (C). 26 m SE of Lexington. Eastern Kentucky University. White Hall State Shrine and Fort Boonesborough State Park. Electric bulb, ice cream, cement block, electric cubes, tools factories; bottling works; tobacco warehouses. Diversified farming. Tobacco, corn, livestock.

12565 The Eastern Progress
Eastern Kentucky University
117 Donovan Annex Phone: (606)622-1881
Richmond, KY 40475 Fax: (606)622-2354
Publication E-mail: progress@acs.eku.edu

Collegiate newspaper of the Department of Mass Communications. **Founded:** 1922. **Freq:** Weekly (Thurs.). **Print Method:** Offset. Uses mats. **Cols./Page:** 6. **Col. Width:** 25 nonpareils. **Col. Depth:** 301 agate lines. **Key Personnel:** Alyssa Bramlage, Editor, phone (606)622-1572; Lee Potter, Advertising Dir., phone (606)622-1489. **Subscription Rates:** Free; $38 by mail. **Remarks:** Accepts advertising. **URL:** http://www.progress.eku.edu.
Ad Rates: BW: $645 **Circ:** Free ‡10,000
4C: $1,045
PCI: $5

12566 WCBR-AM - 1110
College Park Center Phone: (606)623-1235
PO Box 570 Fax: (606)623-7094
Richmond, KY 40476-0570

Format: Southern Gospel. **Owner:** WCBR Inc., at above address. **Founded:** 1969. **Operating Hours:** Sunrise-sunset; 75% network, 25% local. **Key Personnel:** George Robbins, Contact; David Humes, Vice President. **Wattage:** 250. **Ad Rates:** $5 for 30 seconds; $6.50 for 60 seconds.

WEKH-FM - See Hazard

12567 WEKU-FM - 88.9
Eastern Kentucky University Phone: (606)622-1655
102 Perkins Free: (800)621-8890
Richmond, KY 40475
E-mail: weku@acs.eku.edu

Format: News; Classical; Public Radio. **Networks:** National Public Radio (NPR). **Owner:** Eastern Kentucky University Board of Regents, at above address. **Founded:** 1968. **Operating Hours:** Continuous; 15% network, 85% local. **Key Personnel:** Timothy J. Singleton, Station Mgr., phone (606)622-1655; Marie Mitchell, News Dir.; John Francis, Program Dir. **Wattage:** 50,000. **Ad Rates:** Noncommercial. **URL:** http://www.weku.org/.

12568 WEKY-AM - 1340
128 Big Hill Ave. Phone: (606)623-1340
Richmond, KY 40475 Fax: (606)986-8675

Format: Adult Contemporary; Oldies; Sports; Agricultural. **Networks:** ABC; KyNet. **Founded:** 1953. **Operating Hours:** Continuous; 2% network, 98% local. **Key Personnel:** Bob Sprodlin, General Mgr.; Roger Redmon, Contact; Rich Middleton, Contact; Kyle Sowers, News Dir. **Wattage:** 1000. **Ad Rates:** $3-4 for 15 seconds; $6-10 for 30 seconds; $8-12 for 60 seconds.

RUSSELL SPRINGS, pop. 1,831.

Russell Co. (SC). 5 m N of Jamestown. Residential.

12569 The Times Journal
Russell County Newspapers, Inc.
120 Wilson St. Phone: (502)866-3191
PO Box 190 Fax: (502)866-3198
Russell Springs, KY 42642
Local interest newspaper. **Founded:** 1949. **Freq:** Weekly (Thurs.). **Print Method:** Offset. **Cols./Page:** 6. **Col. Width:** 26 nonpareils. **Col. Depth:** 294 agate lines. **Key Personnel:** Jay Albrecht, Editor and Publisher. **USPS:** 617-680. **Subscription Rates:** $17.57 individuals; $27.11 out of area; $26 out of state; $80 other countries. **Remarks:** Accepts advertising. **Feature Editors:** Connie Mann, *Lifestyle.*
Ad Rates: GLR: $.33 **Circ:** Paid ‡4,015
BW: $535.50 Free ‡235
SAU: $4.60
PCI: $4.60

RUSSELLVILLE†, pop. 7,520.

Logan Co. (SW). 30 m W of Bowling Green. Manufactures aluminum die castings, polyurethane foam, work clothes, motors, metal fasteners, wire, poultry equipment, fertilizer, hosiery. Aluminum can stock, Stone quarries. Timber. Dairy, poultry. stock farms. Tobacco, grain.

12570 Bluegrass Music News
1007 Granville Ln. Phone: (502)726-6427
Russellville, KY 42276 Fax: (502)726-2291

Magazine for school music educators who teach K through university-level. **Founded:** Apr. 1, 1950. **Freq:** Quarterly. **Print Method:** Offset. **Trim Size:** 8 1/2 x 11. **Cols./Page:** 3. **Col. Width:** 28 nonpareils. **Col. Depth:** 140 agate lines. **Key Personnel:** Hazel O. Carver, Editor, hcarver@logantele.com. **ISSN:** 0006-5129. **Subscription Rates:** $15 individuals; $18 Canada; $20 other countries.
Ad Rates: BW: $275 **Circ:** ‡2,000

12571 WVVR-FM - 100.3
PO Box 298 Phone: (502)726-3555
Russellville, KY 42276 Fax: (502)726-3095

Format: Contemporary Country. **Founded:** June 1, 1994. **ADI:** Bowling Green (Campbellsville), KY. **Key Personnel:** Bill McGinnis, Owner; Jeff Boyles, Contact; Myla Thomas, Contact; Alan Austin, Music Dir. **Wattage:** 100,000.

SALYERSVILLE†, pop. 1,352.

Magoffin Co. (C).

12572 Salyersville Independent
7 E. Maple St. Phone: (606)349-2915
PO Box 29 Fax: (606)349-2907
Salyersville, KY 41465-9466
Community newspaper. **Founded:** Nov. 1921. **Freq:** Weekly. **Print Method:** Offset. **Trim Size:** 22 3/4 x 14 1/2. **Cols./Page:** 6. **Col. Width:** 25 1/2 nonpareils. **Col. Depth:** 301 agate lines. **Key Personnel:** Tim C. Bostic, Editor and Publisher, fax (606)349-6256. **Subscription Rates:** $18.02 individuals; $20.14 out of area; $22 out of state. **Remarks:** Accepts advertising.
Ad Rates: GLR: $3.40 **Circ:** ‡4,200
BW: $296.70
PCI: $3

12573 Frank Howard TV Cable
Box 229 Phone: (606)349-3317
Salyersville, KY 41465 Fax: (606)349-6169

Key Personnel: Bella Howard, Office Mgr.; Rick Howard, General Mgr. **Cities Served:** Magoffin County, KY.

12574 WRLV-AM - 1140
PO Box 550 Phone: (606)349-6125
Salyersville, KY 41465-0550 Fax: (606)297-1510

Format: Country. **Networks:** KyNet; ABC. **Owner:** Licking Valley Radio Corp., PO Box 428, Salyersville, KY 41465. **Founded:** 1979. **Operating Hours:** Sunrise-sunset; 10% network, 90% local. **Key Personnel:** C.K. Belhasen, Contact. **Wattage:** 1000. **Ad Rates:** $2.80 for 30 seconds; $4.25 for 60 seconds.

12575 WRLV-FM - 97.3
PO Box 550 Phone: (606)349-6125
Salyersville, KY 41465 Fax: (606)297-1510

Format: Contemporary Country. **Networks:** KyNet; ABC. **Owner:** Licking Valley Radio Corp., PO Box 428, Salyersville, KY 41465. **Operating Hours:** Continuous. **Key Personnel:** Charles Belhasen, Contact. **Wattage:** 6000. **Ad Rates:** $4.45-6.45 for 30 seconds; $6.65-9.45 for 60 seconds.

SCOTTSVILLE†, pop. 4,278.

Allen Co. (SW). 25 m SE of Bowling Green. Overalls, tobacco, drapery, hardware factories. Sawmills. Oil wells. Hardwood timber. Dairy, stock, poultry farms. Tobacco, livestock.

12576 The Citizen-Times
PO Box 310 Phone: (270)237-3441
Scottsville, KY 42164 Fax: (270)237-4943
Free: (888)237-3443

Community newspaper. **Founded:** 1890. **Freq:** Weekly (Thurs.). **Print Method:** Offset. **Trim Size:** 13 x 21 1/2. **Cols./Page:** 6. **Col. Width:** 24 nonpareils. **Col. Depth:** 294 agate lines. **Key Personnel:** Robert B. Pitchford, Editor; Billie P.C. Hatcher, Publisher. **Subscription Rates:** $12 individuals; $15 out of state. **Remarks:** Accepts advertising. **Alt. Formats:** CD-ROM.
Ad Rates: BW: $441 **Circ:** ‡5,900
SAU: $5
PCI: $3.50

12577 WLCK-AM - 1250
104 1/2 Public Sq. Phone: (502)237-3149
PO Box 158 Fax: (502)237-3533
Scottsville, KY 42164
E-mail: wlckwvle@nctc.com

Format: Religious. **Networks:** USA Radio. **Owner:** Sherandan Broadcasting Co., Inc., at above address. **Founded:** 1958. **Operating Hours:** 6 a.m.-9 p.m.; 25% network, 75% local. **ADI:** Nashville (Cookeville), TN. **Key Personnel:** Danny Tabor, Manager; Chris Nelson, News Dir.; Don Meador, Music Dir. **Wattage:** 1000.

12578 WVLE-FM - 99.3
PO Box 158 Phone: (502)237-3148
Scottsville, KY 42164 Fax: (502)237-3533
E-mail: wvlewlck@nctc.com

Format: Country. **Networks:** ABC. **Owner:** Sherandan Broadcasting Co., Inc., at above address. **Founded:** 1967. **Formerly**: WLCK-FM (1981). **Operating Hours:** Continuous. **Key Personnel:** Sherry Tabor, Vice President; Danny Tabor, General Mgr.; Chris Nelson, News Dir. **Wattage:** 6000 ERP. **Ad Rates:** Combined advertising rates available with WLCK-AM.

SEBREE, pop. 1,516.

Webster Co. (WC). 16 m S of Henderson. Aluminum, hybrid seed corn processing plants. Oil, gas wells; timber. Feed mills. Agriculture. Dairying, livestock, soybeans.

12579 The Sebree Banner
Box 36 Phone: (502)835-7521
Sebree, KY 42455 Fax: (502)835-9521

Newspaper with a Democratic orientation. **Founded:** 1892. **Freq:** Weekly (Thurs.). **Print Method:** Offset. **Cols./Page:** 6. **Col. Width:** 24 nonpareils. **Col. Depth:** 294 agate lines. **Key Personnel:** Anthony Lee Catlett, Editor; Betty P. Catlett, Publisher. **Subscription Rates:** $11.66 individuals. **Remarks:** Accepts advertising.
Ad Rates: GLR: $.14 **Circ:** ‡3,800
BW: $346.50
SAU: $3.50
PCI: $2.75

SENECA

12580 Courier Tribune
PO Box 100 Phone: (913)336-2175
Seneca, KY 66538 Fax: (913)336-3475
Publisher E-mail: ctseneca@nvcs.com

Community newspaper. **Founded:** 1862. **Freq:** Weekly (Wed.). **Print Method:** Offset. **Cols./Page:** 6. **Col. Width:** 28 nonpareils. **Col. Depth:** 294 agate lines. **Key Personnel:** Dan Diehl, Editor and Publisher; Janet Diehl, Advertising Mgr. **USPS:** 489-120. **Subscription Rates:** $18.88 individuals; $25 out of area; $.50 single issue. **Remarks:** Accepts advertising.
Ad Rates: BW: $504 **Circ:** ‡3,200
SAU: $4
PCI: $4.25

SHELBYVILLE†, pop. 5,308.

Shelby Co. (NWC). 31 m E of Louisville. Manufactures chemicals, metal fabricating products, food utensils, air filters, men's suits, flour. Oil refinery. Loose leaf tobacco. Agriculture. Tobacco, livestock, corn. Horse farm.

12581 Community Times
Landmark Community Newspapers, Inc.
PO Box 549 Phone: (502)348-9003
Shelbyville, KY 40065 Fax: (502)348-1971

Community newspaper. **Founded:** 1929. **Freq:** Weekly (Wed.). **Print Method:** Letterpress and offset. **Cols./Page:** 6. **Col. Width:** 24 nonpareils. **Col. Depth:** 300 agate lines. **Key Personnel:** Baxter Smith, Editor, phone (410)751-5911; Ron Thomas, Contact. **Subscription Rates:** $23 individuals. **Remarks:** Accepts advertising.
Ad Rates: BW: $1,337.73 **Circ:** Paid 1,294
4C: $1,657.73 Free 9,706
SAU: $10.92

12582 Sentinel-News
Landmark Community Newspapers, Inc.
PO Box 549 Phone: (502)348-9003
Shelbyville, KY 40065 Fax: (502)348-1971
Publication E-mail: sentinelnews@ky1.net

Community newspaper. **Founded:** 1840. **Freq:** Semiweekly. **Print Method:** Offset. **Cols./Page:** 6. **Col. Width:** 21 nonpareils. **Col. Depth:** 301 agate lines. **Key Personnel:** Kelly Menser, Editor; James L. Edelen, Publisher, jedelen@sky1.net. **Subscription Rates:** $36 individuals tri-county. **Remarks:** Accepts advertising.
Ad Rates: BW: $1,079.73 **Circ:** Paid ‡7,853
4C: $1,284.73
SAU: $8.37
PCI: $8.37

12583 WCND-AM - 940
416 Main St. Phone: (502)633-3814
PO Box 248 Fax: (502)633-9923
Shelbyville, KY 40066-0248
E-mail: wthq@wkynet.com

Format: Contemporary Country. **Networks:** Jones Satellite; KyNet. **Owner:** Shelby County Broadcasting, Inc., 122 Hilldale Rd., Paducah, KY 42001, (502)443-8058, Fax: (502)442-1215. **Founded:** 1964. **Operating Hours:** Sunrise-sunset. **ADI:** Louisville, KY. **Key Personnel:** R. Lee Hagan, President; Ron Wainscott, Station Mgr.; Vickie Elliott, Sales Mgr. **Wattage:** 250. **Ad Rates:** $10-16 for 30 seconds; $12-18 for 60 seconds.

12584 WTHQ-FM - 101.7
416 Main St. Phone: (502)633-3814
PO Box 248 Fax: (502)633-9923
Shelbyville, KY 40066-0248
E-mail: wthq@wkynet.com

Format: Country. **Networks:** Jones Satellite; KyNet. **Owner:** Shelby County Broadcasting, Inc., 122 Hilldale Rd., Paducah, KY 42001. **Founded:** 1989. **Formerly:** WCKP-FM (1992). **Operating Hours:** Continuous. **ADI:** Louisville, KY. **Key Personnel:** R. Lee Hagan, President; Ron Wainscott, Station Mgr.; Vickie Elliott, Sales Mgr. **Wattage:** 6000. **Ad Rates:** $10-16 for 30 seconds; $12-18 for 60 seconds.

SHEPHERDSVILLE†, pop. 4,454.

Bullitt Co. (NWC). 20 m S of Louisville. Hardware factory. Sawmills. Distillery. Publishing and printing firm. Diversified farming. Corn, tobacco, dairying.

12585 Pioneer News
Landmark Community Newspapers, Inc.
PO Box 98 Phone: (502)955-9701
Shepherdsville, KY 40165 Fax: (502)955-9704

Community newspaper. **Founded:** 1882. **Freq:** Semiweekly (Mon. and Wed.). **Print Method:** Offset. **Cols./Page:** 6. **Col. Width:** 12 picas. **Col. Depth:** 21 1/2 inches. **Key Personnel:** Thomas Barr, General Mgr.; Pete Mio, General Mgr. **USPS:** 433-740. **Subscription Rates:** $25.95 individuals. **Remarks:** Accepts advertising.
Ad Rates: SAU: $6.01 **Circ:** Paid 6,500
PCI: $7.19 Free 17,000

12586 Pioneer News Extra
Landmark Community Newspapers, Inc.
PO Box 98 Phone: (502)543-2288
Shepherdsville, KY 40165 Fax: (502)955-9704

Community newspaper for Bullitt County. **Founded:** 1882. **Freq:** Semiweekly (Mon. and Wed.). **Print Method:** Web offset. **Cols./Page:** 6. **Col. Width:** 2 1/4 inches. **Col. Depth:** 21 1/2 inches. **Key Personnel:** Tom Barr, Editor. **USPS:** 433-740. **Subscription Rates:** Free shopper; $25.95 individuals. **Remarks:** Accepts advertising.
Ad Rates: GLR: $7.66 **Circ:** Paid ⊕6,324
PCI: $6.41 Controlled ⊕11,132

SMITHLAND†, pop. 512.

Livingston Co. (SW). 13 m NE of Paducah. Manufactures hand and edge tools. Agriculture. Tobacco, corn, strawberries.

12587 The Livingston Ledger
Kentucky Publishing, Inc.
PO Box 129 Phone: (502)928-2182
Smithland, KY 42081 Fax: (502)442-5220

Community newspaper. **Founded:** 1962. **Freq:** Weekly (Thurs.). **Print Method:** Offset. **Cols./Page:** 6. **Col. Width:** 24 nonpareils. **Col. Depth:** 294 agate lines. **Key Personnel:** Terri Stalions, Editor. **Subscription Rates:** $20 individuals. **Remarks:** Accepts advertising.
Ad Rates: GLR: $.17 **Circ:** ‡2,500

SOMERSET†, pop. 10,649.

Pulaski Co. (SC). 79 m S of Lexington. Lake resort area. Manufactures ceramic, glass, charcoal products, fixtures, men's clothing. Flour mills. Hardwood timber. Bottling works. Coal mines. Oil refinery. Creamery. Stock, poultry farms. Corn, tobacco, hay, fruits, vegetables.

12588 Commonwealth-Journal
Park Communications, Inc.
110-112 E. Mount Vernon St. Phone: (606)678-8191
PO Box 859 Fax: (606)679-9225
Somerset, KY 42502
Publication E-mail: kdgreg@som.uky.campus.mci.net

General newspaper. **Founded:** 1895. **Freq:** Daily (eve.), Sunday (morn.). **Print Method:** Offset. **Cols./Page:** 6. **Col. Width:** 25 nonpareils. **Col. Depth:** 301 agate lines. **Key Personnel:** Tim Stratton, General Mgr. **Subscription Rates:** $101 individuals. **Remarks:** Accepts advertising.
Ad Rates: GLR: $6.15 **Circ:** 8,663
BW: $1,039.50 Sun. 8,904
4C: $1,249.50
SAU: $8.95

12589 Lake Cumberland Shopper
Park Communications, Inc.
110-112 E. Mount Vernon St. Phone: (606)678-8191
PO Box 859 Fax: (606)679-9225
Somerset, KY 42502
Publication E-mail: kdgreg@som-uky,campus.mci.net

Shopper. **Founded:** 1976. **Freq:** Weekly (Wed.). **Print Method:** Offset. **Cols./Page:** 6. **Col. Width:** 26 nonpareils. **Col. Depth:** 301 agate lines. **Key Personnel:** Tim Stratton, General Mgr. **Remarks:** Accepts advertising.
Ad Rates: GLR: $4.79 **Circ:** Free 30,000
BW: $1,039.50
PCI: $8.95

12590 The Mirror
Somerset Community College
808 Monticello St. Phone: (606)678-8501
Somerset, KY 42501-2999 Fax: (606)679-5139

Collegiate publication. **Founded:** 1967. **Freq:** Biweekly. **Print Method:** Offset. **Cols./Page:** 5. **Col. Width:** 22 nonpareils. **Col. Depth:** 182 agate lines. **Key Personnel:** Don Orwin, Editor; Alyce Grover, Advisor. **Remarks:** Accepts advertising.
Ad Rates: GLR: $.10 **Circ:** Non-paid ‡1,000
BW: $180
PCI: $3

12591 Somerset Pulaski News Journal
PO Box 1565 Phone: (606)678-0161
Somerset, KY 42502 Fax: (606)678-9032

Community newspaper. **Founded:** 1987. **Freq:** Weekly (Thurs.). **Print Method:** Offset. **Cols./Page:** 6. **Col. Width:** 12 picas. **Col. Depth:** 21 1/2 inches. **Key Personnel:** Stuart Simpson, Publisher, phone (606)679-2624. **Subscription Rates:** $18 in Pulaski County; $28 out of county; $32 out of state. **Remarks:** Accepts advertising. **Formerly:** Pulaski Week (June 5, 1997).
Ad Rates: SAU: $6.50 **Circ:** ‡7,500

12592 WKEQ-AM - 910
PO Box 740 Phone: (606)678-5151
Somerset, KY 42502 Fax: (606)678-2026

Format: Southern Gospel. **Networks:** USA Radio. **Owner:** First Radio, Inc., at above address. **Founded:** 1984. **Operating Hours:** Continuous; 95% network, 5% local. **ADI:** Lexington, KY. **Key Personnel:** Nolan Kenner, President; Mike Tarter, Station Mgr. **Wattage:** 500.

12593 WSCC-FM - 92.1
808 S. Monticello Rd. Phone: (606)679-8501
Somerset, KY 42501

Format: Album-Oriented Rock (AOR). **Founded:** 1967. **Operating Hours:** 8 a.m.-9 p.m. **Key Personnel:** Walt Williams, Contact; Paul Secrest, Station Mgr. **Wattage:** 10. **Ad Rates:** Noncommercial.

12594 WSEK-FM - 97.1
N. Hwy. 1247 Phone: (606)678-5153
Box 740 Fax: (606)678-2026
Somerset, KY 42501

Format: Contemporary Country. **Networks:** Mutual Broadcasting System. **Owner:** First Radio, Inc., at above address. **Founded:** 1964. **Operating Hours:** Continuous. **Key Personnel:** G. Nolan Kenner, Contact; Jim Mercer, Chief Engineer; Nolan Kenner, General Mgr.; Michael Tarter, Station Mgr.; Roger Redmon, News/Sports Dir. **Wattage:** 50,000 ERP.

12595 WSFC-AM - 1240
PO Box 740 Phone: (606)678-5151
Somerset, KY 42502-0740 Fax: (606)678-2026

Format: News; Talk. **Networks:** ABC. **Founded:** 1947. **Operating Hours:** Continuous. **Key Personnel:** Nolan Kenner, General Mgr.; Mike Tarter, Station Mgr.; Roger Redmon, News/Sports Dir.; Jim Mercer, Chief Engineer. **Wattage:** 1000.

12596 WSKO-TV - 29
c/o Kentucky Authority for Phone: (606)258-7000
Educational TV Fax: (606)258-7399
600 Cooper Dr.
Lexington, KY 40502
Free: (800)538-4433
E-mail: gfox@msmail.ket.org

Format: Public TV. **Networks:** Public Broadcasting Service (PBS); Kentucky Educational Television. **Owner:** Kentucky Authority for Educational TV, at above address, (606)258-7170, Fax: (606)258-7390. **Founded:** 1968. **Operating Hours:** 6:15 a.m.-midnight. **ADI:** Paducah,KY-Cape Girardeau,MO-Marion,IL. **Key Personnel:** Virginia Gaines Fox, Contact; Sally Hamilton, Contact; Craig Cornwell, Contact; D. Moore, Contact; William Wilson, Contact; L. Hobson, Contact; D. Holtzclaw, Contact; M. Ferguson, Contact; D. Hoffman, Contact; S. Talbert, Contact; B. Ball, Contact; J. Holbrook, Contact; T. Tucker, Contact. **Local Programs:** *Comment on Kentucky*; *Kentucky Afield*; *Kentucky Life*; *Kentucky Tonight*; *Legislative Weekly*. **Wattage:** 589,000. **Ad Rates:** Noncommercial. **URL:** http://www.ket.org.

12597 WTLO-AM - 1480
290 WTLO Rd. Phone: (606)678-8151
Somerset, KY 42501 Fax: (606)678-8152
E-mail: captain@som-uky.campus.mci.net

Format: Oldies. **Networks:** Satellite Music Network. **Owner:** Cumberland Communications, Inc., PO Drawer 1480, Somerset, KY 42502. **Founded:** 1958. **Operating Hours:** 13 hours daily; 80% network, 20% local. **ADI:** Lexington, KY. **Key**

Personnel: J. Allen Brown, General Mgr.; Brooke Cary, Office Mgr.; Ralph Sherman, Program Dir. **Wattage:** 1000. **Ad Rates:** $12 for 30 seconds; $15 for 60 seconds.

12598 WWOG-FM - 90.9
2034 N. Hwy. 39 Phone: (606)679-6300
Somerset, KY 42501 Fax: (606)679-1342
Free: (800)408-8888

Format: Religious; Educational. **Networks:** USA Radio; Moody Broadcasting. **Owner:** King of Kings Radio Network, 2034 N. Hwy. 39, Somerset, KY 42501. **Founded:** 1994. **Formerly:** WTHL-FM. **Operating Hours:** Continuous. **Key Personnel:** S. David Carr, General Mgr. **Local Programs:** *Songs In The Morning*, David Carr; *Sunday School Hour*, David Carr. **Wattage:** 40,000. **Ad Rates:** Noncommercial.

12599 WWZB-FM - 93.9
PO Box 740 Phone: (606)679-8594
Somerset, KY 42502 Fax: (606)678-2026

Format: Adult Contemporary. **Networks:** CNN Radio. **Owner:** First Radio, Inc., at above address, (606)678-5151, Fax: (606)678-2026. **Founded:** 1984. **Formerly:** WWZB (1998). **Operating Hours:** Continuous; 95% network, 5% local. **ADI:** Lexington, KY. **Key Personnel:** Nolan Kenner, President/General Mgr.; Mike Tarter, Station Mgr. **Wattage:** 50,000.

SPRINGFIELD†, pop. 3,179.

Washington Co. (C). 50 m SE of Louisville. Manufactures plastics, butter, clothing, flour, feed, barrels. Tobacco markets and warehouses. Stock, dairy, poultry, grain farms. Tobacco, corn, wheat.

12600 The Springfield Sun
Landmark Community Newspapers, Inc.
PO Box 31 Phone: (606)336-3716
Springfield, KY 40069 Fax: (606)336-7718

Community newspaper. **Founded:** 1904. **Freq:** Weekly (Wed.). **Print Method:** Offset. **Trim Size:** 13 x 21 1/2. **Cols./Page:** 6. **Col. Width:** 12 picas. **Col. Depth:** 21 1/2 inches. **Key Personnel:** Tim Ballard, Editor; Judy Lassiter, Advertising Mgr. **USPS:** 512-920. **Subscription Rates:** $22 individuals; $29.50 out of area; $40 out of state. **Remarks:** Accepts advertising.
Ad Rates: BW: $438.60 **Circ:** Paid ‡4,500
4C: $738.60 Free ‡50
PCI: $3.53

STANFORD†, pop. 2,764.

Lincoln Co. (C). 40 m SW of Lexington. Walnut timber. Manufactures cheese, butter, wood products, mobile homes. Dairy, stock, grain farms. Tobacco, corn, wheat.

12601 The Interior Journal
PO Box 196 Phone: (606)365-2104
Stanford, KY 40484 Fax: (606)365-2105

Community newspaper. **Founded:** 1860. **Freq:** Weekly (Thurs.). **Print Method:** Offset. **Cols./Page:** 6. **Col. Width:** 24 nonpareils. **Col. Depth:** 294 agate lines. **Key Personnel:** Thomas J. Moore, Publisher; Sharman P. Moore, Advertising Mgr. **USPS:** 929-840. **Subscription Rates:** $15.50 in state; $29.75 out of state. **Remarks:** Accepts advertising.
Ad Rates: BW: $485 **Circ:** 4,314
4C: $785
SAU: $3.85
PCI: $3.85

12602 WRSL-AM - 1520
PO Box 300 Phone: (606)365-2126
Stanford, KY 40484 Fax: (606)365-3247

Format: Southern Gospel. **Networks:** Independent. **Owner:** Jonathan Smith, 102 Bank St., Stanford, KY 40484, (606)365-2668. **Founded:** 1961. **Operating Hours:** Sunrise-sunset. **ADI:** Lexington, KY. **Key Personnel:** Tim Hall, P.D. & Music Director. **Wattage:** 1000. **Ad Rates:** $2-4.50 for 30 seconds; $3.50-6.50 for 60 seconds.

12603 WRSL-FM - 95.9
PO Box 300 Phone: (606)365-2126
Stanford, KY 40484 Fax: (606)365-3247

Format: Country. **Networks:** Independent. **Owner:** Jonathan Smith, 102 Bank St., Stanford, KY 40484, (606)365-2668. **Founded:** 1967. **Operating Hours:** 6 a.m.-10 p.m. **Key Personnel:** Ruth Smith, Contact; Jon Logan, Contact; Joseph Larier, Music Dir. **Wattage:** 3000. **Ad Rates:** $2-4.50 for 30 seconds; $3.50-6.50 for 60 seconds. $2-$4.50 for 30 seconds; $3.50-6.50 for 60 seconds. Combined advertising rates available with WRSL-AM.

STANTON†.

Powell Co. (EC). 5 m S of Clay City.

12604 WSKV-FM - 104.9
PO Box 610 Phone: (606)663-2811
Stanton, KY 40380 Fax: (606)663-2895

Format: Country; Bluegrass. **Networks:** Unistar; KyNet. **Founded:** 1974. **Operating Hours:** Continuous. **Key Personnel:** Walter Parks, Contact. **Local Programs:** *Tradio*, Bud Parks, (606)663-2811, Fax (606)6632895. **Wattage:** 440. **Ad Rates:** $3.65 for 30 seconds; $5.75 for 60 seconds.

STURGIS, pop. 2,293.

Union Co. (WC). 43 m SE of Evansville, Ind. Manufactures clothing, metal, feed. Sawmills. Machine shops. Coal industry. Livestock, grain farms.

12605 News
617 N. Adams St. Phone: (502)333-5545
PO Box 218 Fax: (502)333-9943
Sturgis, KY 42459
Newspaper with a Democratic orientation. **Founded:** 1885. **Freq:** Weekly (Wed.). **Print Method:** Offset. **Cols./Page:** 6. **Col. Width:** 24 nonpareils. **Col. Depth:** 297 agate lines. **Key Personnel:** Paul Monsour, Managing Editor; Betty P. Catlett, Publisher. **Subscription Rates:** $9.54 individuals; $13 out of area; $18 out of state. **Remarks:** Accepts advertising.
Ad Rates: GLR: $.15 **Circ:** 3,200
BW: $378
4C: $543
PCI: $3

TOMPKINSVILLE†, pop. 4,366.

Monroe Co. (SC). 60 m SE of Bowling Green. Timber. Manufactures fertilizer, wire, meat products, work clothes, cheese. Sawmills, pallet mills, beldon wire. Agriculture. Corn, wheat, tobacco, livestock.

12606 Monroe County Citizen
301 N. Main Phone: (502)487-8666
Tompkinsville, KY 42167 Fax: (502)487-8666

Free shopper. **Founded:** 1878. **Freq:** Weekly (Tues.). **Print Method:** Offset. **Trim Size:** 14 x 22 3/4. **Cols./Page:** 8. **Col. Width:** 9 picas. **Col. Depth:** 21 1/2 inches. **Key Personnel:** Gerald Matera, Editor; Aubrey C. Wilson, Sr., Publisher; Barbara R. Logsdon, Advertising Manager. **Subscription Rates:** Free. **Remarks:** Accepts advertising.
Ad Rates: GLR: $34 **Circ:** Non-paid ‡5,169
BW: $818.72
PCI: $476

12607 Tompkinsville News
Monroe County Press, Inc.
105 N. Main St. Phone: (502)487-5576
Tompkinsville, KY 42167-1599 Fax: (502)487-8839

Community newspaper. **Founded:** 1903. **Freq:** Weekly (Thurs.). **Print Method:** Offset. **Cols./Page:** 6. **Col. Width:** 12 picas. **Col. Depth:** 21 inches. **Key Personnel:** Blanche B. Trimble, Managing Editor/Publisher, phone (502)487-8024. **Subscription Rates:** $12 individuals; $16 out of area; $21 out of state. **Remarks:** Accepts advertising. **Feature Editors:** Gina Kinslow, *News*.
Ad Rates: BW: $378 **Circ:** Paid ‡4,513
SAU: $3.75 Free ‡214

TYNER

WWAG-FM - See Mc Kee

VANCEBURG†, pop. 1,939.

Lewis Co. (NE). On Ohio River, 20 m SW of Portsmouth, Ohio. Manufactures shoes, railroad ties, lumber. Dairy, stock, truck farms.

12608 Lewis County Herald
Lewis County Herald Publishing Co.
206 Main St. Phone: (606)796-2331
Vanceburg, KY 41179 Fax: (606)796-3110
Free: (800)572-2685

Community newspaper. **Founded:** 1924. **Freq:** Weekly (Tues.). **Print Method:** Offset. **Cols./Page:** 6. **Col. Width:** 22 nonpareils. **Col. Depth:** 294 agate lines. **Key Personnel:** Dennis K. Brown, Publisher. **Subscription Rates:** $10 individuals; $15 out of county; $20 out of state. **Remarks:** Accepts advertising.
Ad Rates: BW: $308.70 **Circ:** ‡4,500
SAU: $2.45

12609 Century Cable TV
323 Lexington Ave. Phone: (606)796-3490
Vanceburg, KY 41179 Free: (800)451-3116

Owner: Century Communications, 50 Locust Ave., New Canaan, CT 06840, (203)972-2000. **Key Personnel:** Jay Woodard, Plant Manager. **Cities Served:** Blackoak, Green Valley, Vanceburg, KY: subscribing households 1,150; 25 channels.

12610 WKKS-AM - 1570
1106 Fairlane Dr. Phone: (606)796-3031
Vanceburg, KY 41179-1208 Fax: (606)796-6186

Format: Country; Contemporary Country; Bluegrass; Oldies. **Networks:** Satellite Music Network. **Owner:** Brown Communications, Inc., at above address. **Founded:** 1957. **Operating Hours:** 6 a.m.-sunset; 60% network, 40% local. **Key Personnel:** D.K. Brown, General Mgr.; Gary Kidwell, Sports Dir. **Wattage:** 1000. **Ad Rates:** $2.75-3.25 for 30 seconds; $3.75-6 for 60 seconds.

12611 WKKS-FM - 104.9
1106 Fairlane Dr. Phone: (606)796-3031
Vanceburg, KY 41179 Fax: (606)796-6186

Format: Country. **Founded:** 1983. **Key Personnel:** Dennis Brown, Contact. **Wattage:** 3000.

VANCLEVE

Breathitt Co.

12612 WMTC-AM - 730
1003 KY 541 Phone: (606)666-5006
Box 8 Fax: (606)666-7534
Vancleve, KY 41385
E-mail: wmtc@kih.net

Format: Religious; News. **Simulcasts:** WMTC-FM. **Networks:** Independent; USA Radio; Kentucky Agrinet. **Owner:** KMHA, Box 2, Vancleve, KY 41385, (606)666-5008. **Founded:** 1948. **Operating Hours:** 6 a.m.-sunset; 100% local. **Key Personnel:** Seldon Short, General Mgr.; Janet Short, Program Dir.; J. Eldon Neihof, President. **Local Programs:** *Birthday Club*, Sheldon Shout. **Wattage:** 5000. **Ad Rates:** $2.50 for 30 seconds; $5 for 60 seconds.

12613 WMTC-FM - 99.9
1003 KY 541 Phone: (606)666-5006
Box 8 Fax: (606)666-7534
Vancleve, KY 41385
Free: (800)337-5006
E-mail: wmtc@kih.net

Format: Religious; News. **Simulcasts:** WMTC-AM. **Networks:** USA Radio. **Owner:** Kentucky Mountain Holiness Assn., Box 2, Vancleve, KY 41385, (606)666-5008. **Founded:** 1991. **Operating Hours:** 6 a.m.-10 p.m.; 100% local. **Key Personnel:** Seldon Short, General Mgr.; Janet Short, Program Dir.; Paul Merryman, Advertising Dir. **Local Programs:** *Birthday Club*, Seldon Short; *The Manager Speaks*, Seldon Short; *Sunshine Melodies*, Sean Peckinpaugh. **Wattage:** 6000. **Ad Rates:** $3-6 for 60 seconds.

VERSAILLES†, pop. 6,427.

Woodford Co. (C). 12 m W of Lexington. Manufactures work clothing, knit goods, flour, food containers, temperature controls. Dairy, stock, poultry farms. Tobacco, hemp, bluegrass seed.

12614 Woodford Sun
PO Box 29 Phone: (606)873-4131
Versailles, KY 40383-0029 Fax: (606)873-0300

Newspaper. **Founded:** 1869. **Freq:** Weekly (Thurs.). **Print Method:** Offset. **Cols./Page:** 6. **Col. Width:** 27 nonpareils. **Col. Depth:** 294 agate lines. **Key Personnel:** H. Moss Vance, Editor; Albert B. Chandler, Publisher; R. Haywood Alves, Advertising Mgr. **Subscription Rates:** $17 individuals; $21 out of area; $28 out of state. **Remarks:** Accepts advertising.
Ad Rates: BW: $686.70 **Circ:** 5,900
4C: $966.70
SAU: $5.45
PCI: $5.45

12615 WJMM-FM - 106.3
3950 Lexington Rd. Phone: (606)873-8096
Versailles, KY 40383 Fax: (606)873-1318
E-mail: wjmm@aol.com

Format: Religious. **Networks:** USA Radio. **Owner:** Mortenson Broadcasting Co. Of Kentucky, 3270 Blazer Pkwy., Ste. 101, Lexington, KY 40509, (606)264-9700, Fax: (606)264-9705. **Founded:** 1973. **Operating Hours:** Continuous. **ADI:** Lexington, KY. **Key Personnel:** Ed Wright, General Mgr. **Wattage:** 3000.

WARSAW†, pop. 1,328.

Gallatin Co. (N). On Ohio River, 35 m SW of Cincinnati Ohio. Furniture factory, lumber mill. Nurseries. Livestock, corn, tobacco farms.

12616 Gallatin County News
211 3rd St. Phone: (606)567-5051
Box 435 Fax: (606)567-6397
Warsaw, KY 41095
Newspaper. **Founded:** 1880. **Freq:** Weekly (Wed.). **Print Method:** Offset. **Cols./Page:** 6. **Col. Width:** 20 nonpareils. **Col. Depth:** 301 agate lines. **Key Personnel:** Denny K. Warnick, Editor and Publisher. **Subscription Rates:** $18 individuals. **Remarks:** Accepts advertising.
Ad Rates: GLR: $3.25 **Circ:** Paid 2,500
4C: $751
SAU: $3.25
PCI: $3.25

WEST LIBERTY†, pop. 1,381.

Morgan Co. (EC). 78 m E of Lexington. Coal mines. Limestone quarry. Timber. Burley tobacco market. Sawmills. Agriculture. Tobacco, corn, poultry.

12617 The Elliott County News
Courier Publishing Co.
142 Prestonsburg St. Phone: (606)743-3551
PO Box 187 Fax: (606)743-3565
West Liberty, KY 41472
Local newspaper. **Freq:** Weekly. **Print Method:** Offset. **Cols./Page:** 8. **Col. Width:** 1 1/2 inches. **Col. Depth:** 21 inches. **Key Personnel:** Faye Whitley, Editor, phone (606)738-5574; Earl Kinney, Publisher; Sue Kinney, Advertising Mgr. **Subscription Rates:** $8; $9 out of county; $10 out of state. **Remarks:** Accepts advertising.
Ad Rates: GLR: $1.95 **Circ:** ‡1,550
BW: $200
SAU: $3.19

12618 Licking Valley Courier
Courier Publishing Co.
142 Prestonsburg St. Phone: (606)743-3551
PO Box 187 Fax: (606)743-3565
West Liberty, KY 41472
Newspaper. **Founded:** 1910. **Freq:** Weekly (Thurs.). **Print Method:** Offset. **Cols./Page:** 8. **Col. Width:** 22 nonpareils. **Col. Depth:** 294 agate lines. **Key Personnel:** Earl Kinner, Jr., Editor; Delia W. Kinner, Publisher. **Subscription Rates:** $8.50 individuals. **Remarks:** Accepts advertising.
Ad Rates: GLR: $.171 **Circ:** ‡4,000

12619 WLKS-FM - 102.9
129 College St. Phone: (606)743-1029
West Liberty, KY 41472 Fax: (606)743-9557
E-mail: kick1029@aolcom; kick1029@mrtc.com

Format: Hot Country. **Founded:** 1994. **Operating Hours:** Continuous. **Key Personnel:** Barry Michaels, Program Dir., kick1029@mrtc.com; Paul Lyons, Chief Operator, phone (606)743-3145; Gail Benton, Operations Mgr., phone (606)743-3145; Sharon Williams, Sales Mgr., phone (606)743-9640. **Wattage:** 6000. **Ad Rates:** $7 for 30 seconds; $9 for 60 seconds.

WESTPORT

12620 Glass Patterns Quarterly
Glass Patterns Quarterly, Inc.
8300 Hidden Valley Rd. Phone: (502)222-5631
Westport, KY 40077 Fax: (502)222-4527
Publisher E-mail: gpqmag@aol.com

Consumer magazine covering instructional stained glass making for a general and professional audience. **Founded:** 1985. **Freq:** Quarterly. **Print Method:** Web offset. **Trim Size:** 8 1/8 x 10 7/8. **Cols./Page:** 3. **Key Personnel:** Maureen James, Editor; Kathy Gentry, Circulation Mgr. **ISSN:** 1041-6684. **Subscription Rates:** $24 individuals; $43 two years; $61 three yrs. **Remarks:** Accepts advertising. **URL:** http://www.GlassPatterns.com.
Ad Rates: BW: $1,110 **Circ:** Controlled ⊕**45,200**
4C: $1,927

WHITESBURG†, pop. 1,525.

Letcher Co. (E). 30 m SW of Pikeville.

12621 The Mountain Eagle
357B Hazard Rd., Parkway Plaza Phone: (606)633-2252
Fax: (606)633-2843
PO Box 808
Whitesburg, KY 41858-0808
Community newspaper. **Founded:** 1907. **Freq:** Weekly (Wed.). **Print Method:** Offset. **Cols./Page:** 6. **Col. Width:** 12 picas. **Col. Depth:** 21 inches. **Key Personnel:** Tom Gish, Editor and Publisher. **Subscription Rates:** $19.50 individuals; $26.50 out of area.

12622 WEZC-AM - 1480
PO Box 828 Phone: (606)855-7888
Whitesburg, KY 41858 Fax: (606)855-7888
E-mail: jci@kih.com

Format: Contemporary Christian. **Owner:** Jesus Communications, Inc., PO Box 828, Whitesburg, KY 41858, (606)855-4232. **Founded:** 1956. **Operating Hours:** Sunrise-sunset. **Key Personnel:** F.D. Holbrook, Jr, Contact. **Wattage:** 5000. **Ad Rates:** $3.25 for 15 seconds; $2.15-3.60 for 30 seconds; $2.40-4 for 60 seconds.

12623 WIFX-FM - 94.3
PO Box 729 Phone: (606)633-9439
Whitesburg, KY 41858 Fax: (606)633-3314
E-mail: wifx@hotmail.comm

Format: Adult Contemporary; Top 40. **Networks:** ABC. **Owner:** Letcher County Broadcasting, Inc., at above address, (606)633-9430. **Founded:** 1968. **Formerly:** WREM-FM (1981). **Operating Hours:** Continuous; 100% local. **ADI:** Lexington, KY. **Key Personnel:** Garnard Cheldon Kineer, Jr., Manager; Diana Watts, Sales Mgr.; Ted Meadows, Program Dir.; Ernestine Kincer, Contact. **Wattage:** 50,000. **Ad Rates:** $3.50 for 15 seconds; $4.50-6 for 30 seconds; $8.50-10 for 60 seconds.

12624 WMMT-FM - 88.7
306 Madison St. Phone: (606)633-0108
Whitesburg, KY 41858 Fax: (606)633-1009
E-mail: wmmtfm@appalshop.org

Format: Eclectic. **Networks:** Independent. **Founded:** 1985. **Operating Hours:** Continuous; 10% network, 90% local. **Key Personnel:** Tom Hansell, Contact; Jim Webb, Program Dir.; Maxine Kenny, Contact; Rich Kirby, Station Mgr.; Don Mussell, Contact. **Wattage:** 15,000. **Ad Rates:** Noncommercial. **URL:** http://www.appalshop.org.

WHITLEY CITY†, pop. 1,060.

McCreary Co. (SEC). 25 m S of Somerset.

12625 McCreary County Record
Park Newspapers of the Cumberlands
PO Box 9 Phone: (606)376-5356
Whitley City, KY 42653 Fax: (606)376-5357

Community newspaper. **Founded:** 1919. **Freq:** Weekly (Tues.). **Print Method:** Offset. **Cols./Page:** 6. **Col. Width:** 26 nonpareils. **Col. Depth:** 301 agate lines. **Key Personnel:** Ken Smidheiser, Editor. **Subscription Rates:** $14.65 individuals; $30 out of state; $.50 single issue. **Remarks:** Accepts advertising.
Ad Rates: BW: $537.12 **Circ:** ‡4,984
4C: $750
PCI: $4.55

WICKLIFFE†, pop. 1,044.

Ballard Co. (SW). 30 m SW of Paducah. Clay pits; timber; paper mill. Agriculture. Corn, tobacco, dairying.

12626 WBCE-AM - 1200
PO Box 128 Phone: (502)335-5171
Wickliffe, KY 42087-0128

Format: Religious. **Networks:** Independent. **Owner:** Bibletime Ministries, PO Box 128, Wickliffe, KY 42087. **Founded:** 1982. **Operating Hours:** Sunrise-sunset; 100% local. **Key Personnel:** Shelby Baggett, Manager; Jim Baggett, Contact. **Wattage:** 1000. **Ad Rates:** $2.50-4 for 30 seconds; $3-5 for 60 seconds.

12627 WGKY-FM - 95.9
PO Box 500 Phone: (502)335-3696
Wickliffe, KY 42087 Fax: (502)335-3698
Free: (800)493-9696
E-mail: wgky@apex.net

Networks: Jones Satellite. **Owner:** Wickliffer Rental Properties, Inc., at above address. **Founded:** 1986. **Formerly:** WYMC-FM (1991). **Operating Hours:** Continuous; 80% network, 20% local. **ADI:** Paducah,KY-Cape Girardeau,MO-Marion,IL. **Key Personnel:** R. K. Kelley, President; Larry G. Kelley, General Mgr. **Wattage:** 3000. **Ad Rates:** $8-12 for 30 seconds; $12-18 for 60 seconds.

WILLIAMSBURG†, pop. 5,560.

Whitley Co. (SE). On Cumberland River, 30 m NW of Middlesboro. Coal mines; gas wells; hardwood timber. Clothing and outdoor products factories; planing mill; bottling works. Agriculture. Grains, tobacco, livestock.

12628 The Whitley Republican News Journal
Whitley Whiz
PO Box 418 Phone: (606)528-9767
Williamsburg, KY 40769 Fax: (606)528-9779
Publication E-mail: newsjournal@jellocl.com

Newspaper with a Republican orientation. **Founded:** 1908. **Freq:** Weekly (Wed.). **Print Method:** Offset. **Cols./Page:** 6. **Col. Width:** 26 nonpareils. **Col. Depth:** 301 agate lines. **Key Personnel:** Don Estep, Publisher. **Subscription Rates:** $20 individuals. **Remarks:** Color advertising accepted; rates available upon request. **Formerly:** The Whitley Republican.
Ad Rates: GLR: $.46 **Circ:** 8,107
PCI: $6.45

12629 WEKC-AM - 710
Cumberland Regional Mall Phone: (606)549-3000
PO Box 1298 Fax: (606)539-0916
Williamsburg, KY 40769-3298
Free: (888)710-4710
E-mail: wekc@tcnet.net

Format: Gospel. **Networks:** CBS; Meadows Racing. **Owner:** Randy Thompson, PO Box 1298, Williamsburg, KY 40769. **Founded:** 1981. **Operating Hours:** Daytime; 10% network, 90% local. **ADI:** Knoxville (Crossville), TN. **Key Personnel:** Tim Johnson, General Mgr., phone (606)347-0254; Sheila Johnson, Traffic Mgr. **Wattage:** 4200. **Ad Rates:** $4 for 30 seconds; $5.50 for 60 seconds. Combined advertising rates available with WKCB-AM & FM, WQXY-AM. **URL:** http://www.710am.com.

12630 WEZJ-FM - 104.3
522 Main St. Phone: (606)549-2285
Williamsburg, KY 40769 Fax: (606)549-5565
E-mail: david@tcnet.net

Format: Contemporary Country. **Simulcasts:** WEZJ-AM. **Networks:** ABC. **Owner:** Whitley County Broadcasting, Inc., at above address. **Founded:** 1959. **Operating Hours:** 5 a.m.-1 a.m.; 5% network, 95% local. **ADI:** Lexington, KY. **Key Personnel:** Theresa Estes, Contact; David Estes, General Mgr., david@tcnet.net; Paul Estes, President. **Local Programs:** *C.C. Basketball*, David Estes; *Live Wire News*, Theresa Estes; *W.C. Football*, David Estes. **Wattage:** 6000. **Ad Rates:** $8 for 30 seconds; $10.50 for 60 seconds. Combined advertising rates available with WEKX-FM.

WILLIAMSTOWN†, pop. 2,502.

Grant Co. (N). 34 m S of Covington. Ships tobacco, hay, livestock. Dairy, stock, poultry farms.

12631 Grant County News
PO Box 247 Phone: (606)824-3343
Williamstown, KY 41097 Fax: (606)824-5888
Publication E-mail: grantnew@kih.net

Community newspaper. **Founded:** 1906. **Freq:** Weekly (Thurs.). **Print Method:** Offset. **Cols./Page:** 6. **Col. Width:** 26 nonpareils. **Col. Depth:** 301 agate lines. **Key Personnel:** Ken Stone, Publisher; Jamie Baker-Nantz, Editor. **Subscription Rates:** $18.00 individuals. **Remarks:** Accepts advertising.
Ad Rates: BW: $610 **Circ:** Paid ⊕**5,925**
4C: $760 Non-paid ⊕**40**
PCI: $4.89

12632 City of Williamstown Cable
PO Box 147 Phone: (606)824-3633
400 N. Main St. Fax: (606)824-6320
Williamstown, KY 41097-1026
E-mail: wmtwncable@aol.com

Owner: City of Williamstown KY, at above address. **Founded:** 1984. **Key Personnel:** Chuck Hudson, Contact, phone (606)824-3633, fax (606)824-6320. **Cities Served:** Williamstown, KY: subscribing households 990; 40 channels; 1 community access channel; 6 hours per week community access programming.

WILMORE, pop. 3,787.

Jessamine Co. (C). 20 m S of Lexington.

12633 Faith and Philosophy
Society of Christian Philosophers
Department of Philosophy
Asbury College
Wilmore, KY 40390
Publication E-mail: fpjournl@aol.com

Scholarly journal covering the philosophy of religion. **Founded:** 1983. **Freq:** Quarterly. **Trim Size:** 6 x 9. **Subscription Rates:** $30 individuals; $34 Canada; $36 other countries; $45 institutions; $49 institutions Canada; $51 institutions other countries. **URL:** http://www.siu.edu/departments/cola/philos/SCP.

12634 Good News
Forum for Scriptural Christianity, Inc.
308 E. Main St. Phone: (606)858-4661
PO Box 150 Fax: (606)858-4972
Wilmore, KY 40390
Free: (800)487-7784
Publication E-mail: steve@goodnewsmag.org

Religious magazine for evangelical United Methodists. **Subtitle:** The Bi-Monthly Magazine for United Methodists. **Founded:** 1967. **Freq:** Bimonthly. **Print Method:** Offset. **Trim Size:** 8 1/4 x 10 7/8. **Cols./Page:** 3. **Key Personnel:** James V. Heidinger II, Publisher, jim@goodnewsmag.org; Steve Beard, Editor, steve@goodnewsmag.org. **ISSN:** 0436-1563. **Subscription Rates:** $20 individuals. **Remarks:** Accepts advertising. **URL:** http://www.goodnewsmag.org.
Ad Rates: BW: $800 **Circ:** 70,000
4C: $1,050

12635 Missiology
American Society of Missiology
204 N. Lexington Ave. Phone: (606)858-2216
Wilmore, KY 40390-1199 Fax: (606)858-2375

Journal of anthropology, culture, history, theology, and mission studies. **Subtitle:** An International Review. **Founded:** Jan. 1953. **Freq:** Quarterly. **Print Method:** Offset. **Trim Size:** 6 x 9. **Cols./Page:** 2. **Col. Width:** 52 nonpareils. **Col. Depth:** 101 agate lines. **Key Personnel:** Dr. Darrell L. Whiteman, Editor, phone (606)858-2215, fax (630)858-2375, darrell_whiteman@ats.wilmore.ky.us; Kenneth Gill, Publisher, phone (630)752-5533, fax (630)752-5916, kenneth.d.gill@wheaton.edu. **ISSN:** 0091-8296. **Subscription Rates:** $21 individuals; $29 institutions; $17 students; $7 single issue. **Remarks:** Color advertising not accepted. **Formerly:** Practical Anthropology.
Ad Rates: BW: $250 **Circ:** ‡2,000

12636 Snews, The Chimney Sweep News
The Chimney Sweep News
PO Box 98 Phone: (606)986-8001
Wilmore, KY 40390
Trade magazine for North American chimney service technicians. **Founded:** Oct. 1979. **Freq:** 10/year. **Print Method:** Offset. **Key Personnel:** Jay Hensley, Editor; Tim Hensley, Business Mgr. **ISSN:** 0737-2205. **Subscription Rates:** $79 individuals; $89 Canada; $8 single issue. **Remarks:** Accepts advertising.
Ad Rates: BW: $545 **Circ:** Paid 800

WINCHESTER†, pop. 15,216.

Clark Co. (NEC). 18 m E of Lexington. Limestone quarries. Manufactures fertilizer, men's shirts and suits, rubber products, truck axles, bed springs, lumber, seed harvesters, bricks, beverages. Bluegrass seed stripper. Hatcheries. Agriculture. Tobacco, bluegrass seed, livestock.

12637 Weekend Plus
PO Box 4300 Phone: (606)744-3123
Winchester, KY 40391 Fax: (606)745-0638

Community shopper. **Founded:** 1980. **Freq:** Weekly. **Print Method:** Offset. **Trim Size:** 11 x 13. **Cols./Page:** 5. **Col. Width:** 12 1/2 picas. **Col. Depth:** 13 inches. **Key Personnel:** Betty Berryman, Publisher. **Remarks:** Accepts advertising. **Formerly:** Neighbors; Weekend Post.
Ad Rates: BW: $561.60 **Circ:** Non-paid 5,300
4C: $811.60 Paid 7,200
SAU: $8.64

12638 The Winchester Sun
PO Box 4300 Phone: (606)744-3123
Winchester, KY 40392 Fax: (606)745-0638
Publication E-mail: bb@winchestersun.com

Newspaper with a Democratic orientation. **Founded:** Sept. 8, 1878. **Freq:** Daily (eve.). **Print Method:** Offset. **Trim Size:** 14 1/4 x 22 3/4. **Cols./Page:** 6. **Col. Width:** 25 nonpareils. **Col. Depth:** 294 agate lines. **Key Personnel:** William S. Blakeman, Editor; Betty J. Berryman, Publisher, bjberry@aol.com. **Subscription Rates:** $96 individuals; $102 out of area. **Available Online. URL:** http://www.winchestersun.com.
Ad Rates: BW: $1,032 **Circ:** 7,300
4C: $1,282
SAU: $8
PCI: $8

LOUISIANA

State Capital, BATON ROUGE

Louisiana is bounded on the north by Arkansas and Mississippi, east by Mississippi and the Gulf of Mexico, south by the Gulf of Mexico, and west by Texas. Its extreme breadth from east to west is about 300 miles; length, 240 miles; total land area, 43,566 square miles. The surface is generally low and level. There are low hills in the north and northwest, from which the land slopes gradually to the Mississippi and the Gulf. Much of the land along the river is below the water level during the spring freshets and is protected from overflow by levees, which are built on both banks below Baton Rouge and on the west bank throughout the state. Many of the principal rivers and bayous are protected in like manner so that but a small portion of the land is subject to overflow. The soil of the river bottoms is exceedingly fertile and is almost entirely silt brought down by the Mississippi River. It yields large crops of cotton, sugar cane, and rice. The prairies are productive and afford good pasture in places. The hilly section yields good cotton crops, but about half is covered with pine barrens. The climate is semi-tropical, vary warm and moist in summer with little cold weather in winter. The Weather Bureau at New Orleans gives the temperature (annual average) as 68.1; highest on record, 102; lowest on record, 7. Total annual precipitation averages 61.88 inches. New Orleans is the leading city and an important port. This picturesque city is famous as a winter resort and has many historical attractions. Tulane University is located in New Orleans. Louisiana State University, Baton Rouge, is the state's largest institution of higher learning.

POPULATION: 4,287,000 (1992). Rank among the states, 21st.

AGRICULTURE: Number of farms: 30,000 (1992). Farm acreage: 9,000,000 (1992). Cash receipts on farm marketings: crops, $1,172,000,000 (1991); livestock and products, $621,000,000 (1991).

FISHERIES: Total catch: 1,193,000,000 lbs. (1991), $244,000,000 value. Principal fish: shrimp, menhaden, oysters, catfish and bullheads, crabs.

FORESTS: Total forest land: 1,022,000 acres (1991). Principal woods: southern yellow pine, oak, red and sap gum, black and tupelo gum, cottonwood and aspen, cypress, elm, ash, beech, hickory, sycamore, yellow poplar.

MINERALS: Value of production: $352,000,000 (1991). Principal minerals: sulfur, salt, sand and gravel. Value of petroleum production: $2,962,000,000 (1990).

MANUFACTURES: Value added by manufacture: $22,126,000,000 (1991). Leading industry groups: chemical and allied products, food and related products, petroleum and coal products.

LIST OF PARISHES

Total number of parishes 64

Parish, Location on Map, and Parish Seat	Pop.
Acadia (SW), Crowley	55,882
Allen(SW), Oberlin	21,226
Ascension (SE), Donaldsonville	58,214
Assumption (S), Napoleonville	22,753
Avoyelles (E), Marksville	39,159
Beauregard (SW), De Ridder	30,083
Bienville (NW), Arcadia	15,979
Bossier (NW), Benton	86,088
Caddo (NW), Shreveport	248,253
Calcasieu (SW), Lake Charles	168,134
Caldwell (NE), Columbia	9,810
Cameron (SW), Cameron	9,260
Catahoula (EC), Harrisonburg	11,065
Claiborne (N), Homer	17,405
Concordia (EC), Vidalia	20,828
De Soto (W), Mansfield	25,346
East Baton Rouge (SEC), Baton Rouge	380,105
East Carroll (NE), Lake Providence	9,709
East Feliciana (EC), Clinton	19,211
Evangeline (SC), Ville Platte	33 274
Franklin (NE), Winnsboro	22,387
Grant (C), Colfax	17,526
Iberia (S), New Iberia	68,297
Jackson (N), Jonesboro	15,705
Jefferson (SE), Gretna	448,306
Jefferson Davis (SW), Jennings	30,722
Lafayette (SE), Lafayette	164,762
Lafourche (SE), Thibodaux	85,860
LaSalle (C), Jena	13,662
Lincoln (N), Ruston	41,745
Livingston (SE), Livingston	70,526
Madison (NE), Tallulah	12,463
Morehouse (N), Bastrop	31,938
Natchitoches (NW), Natchitoches	36,689
Orleans (SE), New Orleans	496,938
Ouachita (N), Monroe	142,191
Plaquemines (SE), Pointe a la Hache	25,575
Pointe Coupee (SEC), New Roads	22,540
Rapides (C), Alexandria	131,556
Red River (NW), Coushatta	9,387
Richland (NE), Rayville	20,629
Sabine (W), Many	22,646
St. Bernard (SE), Chalmette	66,631
St. Charles (SE), Hahnville	42,437
St. Helena (E), Greensburg	9,876
St. James (SE), Convent	20,879
St. John the Baptist (SE), Edgard	39,996
St. Landry (EC), Opelousas	80,331
St. Martin (S), St. Martinville	43,978
St. Tammany (SE), Covington	144,508
Tangipahoa (SE), Amite	85,709
Tensas (NE), St. Joseph	7,103
Terrebonne (S), Houma	96,982
Union (N), Farmerville	20,690
Vermillion (S), Abbeville	50,055
Vernon (W), Leesville	61,961
Washington (E), Franklinton	43,185
Webster (NW), Minden	41,989
West Baton Rouge (SEC), Port Allen	19,419
West Carroll (NE), Oak Grove	12,093
West Feliciana (EC), St. Francisville	12,915
Winn (NWC), Winnfield	16,269

STATISTICS

Newspapers

Period of Issue	
Daily	20
Evening Daily	13
Morning Daily	9
Daily with Sunday edition	19
Semiweekly	11
Weekly	91
Biweekly	2
Semimonthly	1
Monthly	6
Bimonthly	0
Free or partly free	12
Shopper	5
Total Newspapers	140

Periodicals

Period of Issue	
Weekly	1
Biweekly	1

Monthly	17
Bimonthly	5
Quarterly	30
Free or partly free	1
Total Periodicals	76

Total number of publications	216

Radio Stations

AM Stations	73
FM Stations	107
Total Radio Stations	180

TV Stations

Total TV Stations	32

Cable Stations

Total Cable Systems	26

Total number of broadcast listings	238

ABBEVILLE†, pop. 12,391.

S LA. Vermilion Parish. On Vermilion River, 65 mi. SW of Baton Rouge. Oil and gas wells. Rice mills, sugar and syrup mill. Trapping. Crawfish farming. Agriculture. Livestock, rice, sugar cane.

12639 Abbeville Meridional
318 N. Main St. Phone: (318)893-4223
PO Box 400 Fax: (318)898-9022
Abbeville, LA 70510
General newspaper. **Founded:** 1856. **Freq:** Tues.-Fri. (morn.); Sun. (morn.). **Print Method:** Offset. **Trim Size:** 13 3/4 x 22 7/8. **Cols./Page:** 6. **Col. Width:** 22 nonpareils. **Col. Depth:** 300 agate lines. **Key Personnel:** Gwen Bronssard, Managing Editor; Mike Hebert, General Mgr.; Mike Abbeville, Publisher. **Subscription Rates:** $60 individuals.
Ad Rates: GLR: $.37 **Circ:** Mon.-Fri. 4,802
BW: $819.15 Sun. 5,619
4C: $1,044.15
PCI: $6.35

12640 KROF-AM - 960
Highway 167 N. Phone: (318)893-2531
Box 610 Fax: (318)893-2569
Abbeville, LA 70511-0610

Format: Country; Cajun. **Networks:** Louisiana. **Founded:** 1948. **Operating Hours:** 6am - sunset. **ADI:** Lafayette, LA. **Key Personnel:** Connie Jo Kerr, General Mgr.; Mike Calamari, Program Dir. **Wattage:** 1000. **Ad Rates:** $12-17 for 30 seconds; $15-25 for 60 seconds.

12641 KROF-FM - 105.1
Box 610 Phone: (318)893-2531
Highway 167 N. Fax: (318)893-2569
Abbeville, LA 70511-0610

Format: Oldies. **Networks:** Louisiana. **Founded:** 1974. **Operating Hours:** Continuous. **ADI:** Lafayette, LA. **Key Personnel:** Connie Jo Kerr, General Mgr.; Mike Calamari, Program Dir. **Wattage:** 25,000. **Ad Rates:** $10-17 for 30 seconds; $17-25 for 60 seconds.

ALEXANDRIA†, pop. 51,565.

C LA. Rapides Parish. On Red River, 200 mi. NW of New Orleans. Manufactures valves and instruments, linerboard, lumber, paper products, hardwood flooring, furniture, fertilizer, sashes and doors, chemicals, insecticides, mattresses, pine products, lubricating oil, stoves, gasoline. Foundry, meat packing, cotton ginning, creosoting plants. Forestry. Agriculture. Cotton, corn, sugarcane.

12642 Alexandria Daily Town Talk
Central Newspapers, Inc.
1201 3rd St. Phone: (318)487-6397
P.O. Box 7558 Fax: (318)487-6315
Alexandria, LA 71306
Free: (800)523-8391

General newspaper. **Founded:** Mar. 17, 1883. **Freq:** Mon.-Sun. (morn.). **Print Method:** Offset. **Trim Size:** 13 x 21. **Cols./Page:** 6. **Col. Width:** 25 nonpareils. **Col. Depth:** 294 agate lines. **Key Personnel:** Jim Butler, Editor; John E. Newhouse II, Pres./Publisher; Bill Heirtzler, Advertising Mgr. **Subscription Rates:** $114 individuals; $144 by mail. **Remarks:** Sunday: BW: $2,332.26; 4C: $2,673.26; PCI: $18.51.
Ad Rates: GLR: $2,785.86 **Circ:** Mon.-Sat. 37,631
BW: $2,245.32 Sun. 43,783
4C: $2,586.32
SAU: $22.11
PCI: $22.11

12643 The Alexandria News Weekly
PO Box 608 Phone: (318)443-7664
Alexandria, LA 71309-0608
General newspaper for the black community. **Founded:** 1975. **Freq:** Weekly (Thurs.). **Print Method:** Offset. **Cols./Page:** 6. **Col. Width:** 26 nonpareils. **Col. Depth:** 294 agate lines. **Key Personnel:** Rev. C.J. Bell, Editor; H. Nicholas Stull, Publisher. **Subscription Rates:** $15 individuals. **Remarks:** Color advertising accepted; rates available upon request.
Ad Rates: GLR: $.52 **Circ:** ‡13,750

12644 Forests & People
Louisiana Forestry Association
PO Drawer 5067 Phone: (318)443-2558
Alexandria, LA 71307-5067 Fax: (318)443-1713
Publisher E-mail: laforestry@linknet.net

Magazine for forest products industries, foresters, and forest landowners. **Founded:** 1950. **Freq:** Quarterly. **Print Method:** Offset. **Cols./Page:** 3. **Col. Width:** 27 nonpareils. **Col. Depth:** 129 agate lines. **Key Personnel:** Janet Tompkins, Editor, jtompkins@linknet.net. **USPS:** 456-930. **Subscription Rates:** $11 individuals. **Remarks:** Accepts advertising.
Ad Rates: BW: $429 **Circ:** Combined ‡7,000
4C: $729

12645 Louisiana Baptist Message (LBM)
Louisiana Baptist Convention
PO Box 311 Phone: (318)442-7728
Alexandria, LA 71309 Fax: (318)445-8328
Free: (888)442-7760
Publication E-mail: 70420.21@compuserve.com; baptistmessagel@hotmail.com

Southern Baptist religious newspaper. **Founded:** 1883. **Freq:** Weekly (Thurs.). **Print Method:** Offset. **Trim Size:** 10 1/4 x 13 1/4. **Cols./Page:** 4. **Col. Width:** 14 picas. **Col. Depth:** 13 1/4 inches. **Key Personnel:** Mr. Lynn Clayton, Editor. **Subscription Rates:** $12.75 individuals. **Remarks:** Accepts advertising. **Available Online. URL:** http://www.lacollege.edu/baptist/message/message.html/.
Ad Rates: GLR: $2.50 **Circ:** Paid 45,000
BW: $1,232
PCI: $22

12646 KALB-TV - 5
605-11 Washington St. Phone: (318)445-2456
Alexandria, LA 71301 Fax: (318)442-7427

Format: Commercial TV. **Networks:** NBC. **Owner:** Park Broadcasting of LA, Inc., at above address. **Founded:** 1946. **Operating Hours:** Continuous. **ADI:** Alexandria, LA. **Key Personnel:** Les Golmon, General Mgr.; Jim Reardon, General Sales Mgr.; Charles Neal, Local Sales Mgr.; Jack Frost, News Dir., phone (318)445-6397, fax (318)449-4594; Sharyn Bowen, Program Dir.; John Lindsey, Promotions Dir. **Local Programs:** *News Central 5* 6 p.m and 10 p.m., Jack Frost, Mailing contact, (318)445-2456, Fax (318)442-7427. **Wattage:** Video 100,000; Audio 20,000. **Ad Rates:** $10-750 for 30 seconds; $20-1500 for 60 seconds.

12647 KDBS-AM - 1410
1515 Jackson St. Phone: (318)443-1410
Alexandria, LA 71301 Fax: (318)442-2747
E-mail: krrvl@popalexl.linknet.net

Format: News; Sports; Talk. **Networks:** ABC; Westwood One Radio; ESPN Radio. **Founded:** 1954. **Formerly:** KRRV-AM. **Operating Hours:** Continuous; 98% network, 2% local. **ADI:** Alexandria, LA. **Key Personnel:** Bill Milam, Station Mgr.; Dave Griffiths, Sales Mgr.; Lon Harris, Program Mgr.; Kathy Karson, News Dir. **Wattage:** 1000. **Ad Rates:** Advertising accepted; rates available upon request.

12648 KEZP-FM - 104.3
1847 Sterkx Rd. Phone: (318)449-1999
Alexandria, LA 71301 Fax: (318)487-8173
E-mail: kezp104@iamerica.net

Format: Oldies. **Owner:** Owensville Communications Co., at above address. **Operating Hours:** Continuous. **ADI:** Alexandria, LA. **Key Personnel:** Mark Jones, General Mgr.; Sherry Reynolds, National Sales Mgr.; Randy Reynolds, News Dir.; Clair Glass, Promotions Dir. **Wattage:** 25,000. **Ad Rates:** $30-40 per unit.

12649 KFAD-FM - 93.9
PO Box 5504 Phone: (318)443-9400
Alexandria, LA 71307 Fax: (318)448-3674
E-mail: magic93@centuryinter.net

Format: Oldies; Adult Contemporary. **Owner:** A. E. Fryar, at above address. **Operating Hours:** Continuous. **Key Personnel:** A. E. Fryar, Owner/General Mgr.; Pat Cloud, Operations. **Wattage:** 6000.

12650 KKST-FM - 98.7
1515 Jackson St Phone: (318)443-7454
Alexandria, LA 71301 Fax: (318)442-2747

Format: Adult Contemporary. **Owner:** Capstar Broadcasting Partners Inc., at above address. **Founded:** 1972. **Formerly:** KICR-FM. **Operating Hours:** Continuous. **ADI:** Alexandria, LA. **Key Personnel:** Bill Milam, Station Mgr.; Dave Griffiths, Sales Mgr.; Michael Bailey, Program Mgr.; Kathy Karson, News Dir.; Lon Harris, Operations Mgr. **Local Programs:** *The Wild Wild West*, James West. **Wattage:** 50,000. **Ad Rates:** Advertising accepted; rates available upon request.

12651 KLAX-TV - 31
1811 England Dr. Phone: (318)473-0031
Alexandria, LA 71306 Fax: (318)442-4646
E-mail: 31news@klax-tv.com

Format: Commercial TV. **Networks:** ABC. **Owner:** Pollack/Belz Communications Co., Inc., at above address. **Founded:** 1983. **Operating Hours:** Continuous; 60% network, 40% local. **ADI:** Alexandria, LA. **Key Personnel:** Pat Newberg, General Sales Mgr., fax (318)473-9984; Dan Penny, General Mgr., gn-mgr@klax-tv.com; Bill Bush, Sports Dir., fax (318)445-8855; Bob Madison, News Dir., fax (318)445-8855, 31news@klax-tv.com; Lori K. Davidson, Program Dir., program@klax-tv.com; Peter Petrawski, Promotions, fax (318)442-4646, promos@klax-tv.com. **Local Programs:** *Laqmiappe* 7:25 am & 8:25 am Monday-Friday, Heather Blankenship, Mailing contact; *31 Action News at 6 & 10 p.m.*, Bob Kennon, Mailing contact. **Ad Rates:** $20-6,000 per unit. **URL:** http://www.klax-tv.com.

12652 KLPA-TV - 25
c/o WLPB-TV Phone: (504)767-5660
7733 Perkins Rd. Fax: (504)767-4288
Baton Rouge, LA 70810
Free: (800)272-8161

Format: Public TV. **Simulcasts:** WLPB-TV Baton Rouge, LA. **Networks:** Public Broadcasting Service (PBS); Louisiana Public Broadcasting. **Owner:** Louisiana Public Broadcasting Network, at above address. **Founded:** 1983. **ADI:** Alexandria, LA. **URL:** http://www.lpb.gen.la.us/.

12653 KRRV-FM - 100.3
1515 Jackson St. Phone: (318)443-7454
Alexandria, LA 71301 Fax: (318)442-2747

Format: Country. **Networks:** ABC. **Owner:** Capstar Broadcasting Partners Inc., at above address, Alexandria, LA 71301, (318)442-4462. **Founded:** 1969. **Formerly:** KDBS-FM (1977). **Operating Hours:** Continuous;. **ADI:** Alexandria, LA. **Key Personnel:** Bill Milam, Station Mgr.; Dave Griffiths, Sales Mgr.; Kathy Karson, News Dir.; Lon Harris, Operations Mgr. **Local Programs:** *Live in the Lobby*, Lon Harris; *News Series*, Katrina Tyler. **Wattage:** 100,000. **Ad Rates:** Advertising accepted; rates available upon request.

12654 KSYL-AM - 970
1115 Texas Ave. Phone: (318)445-1234
Alexandria, LA 71301 Fax: (318)445-7321

Format: Adult Contemporary. **Founded:** 1947. **ADI:** Alexandria, LA. **Key Personnel:** Taylor C. Thompson, Contact; Charles J. Soprano, Vice President; Deacon Jones, Music Dir.; Howard Lash, News Dir.; Lenny Dupree, Chief Engineer. **Wattage:** 1000.

12655 KZMZ-FM - 96.9
1515 Jackson St. Phone: (318)443-2543
Alexandria, LA 71301 Fax: (318)443-7306

Format: Classic Rock. **Owner:** LMA with Gulf Star Communications, at above address, (318)443-7454, Fax: (318)442-2747. **Founded:** 1947. **Operating Hours:** Continuous. **ADI:** Alexandria, LA. **Key Personnel:** Bill Milam, General Mgr.; Terry Manning, Program Dir.; Dave Griffiths, General Sales Mgr.; Lan Harris, Operations Mgr. **Wattage:** 100,000. **Ad Rates:** $25-30 for 30 seconds; $28-60 for 60 seconds.

AMITE†, pop. 4,301.

SE LA. Tangipahoa Parish. 45 mi. E. of Baton Rouge. Manufactures prepared feeds, Lumber products, machinery, concrete products. Gravel. Foundry. Ships berries and vegetables. Agriculture. Strawberries, truck crops and dairy farms. Cattle raising.

12656 Amite Tangi-Digest
120 NE Central Phone: (504)748-7156
PO Box 698 Fax: (504)748-7104
Amite, LA 70422
Community newspaper. **Founded:** July 4, 1867. **Freq:** Weekly (Wed.). **Print Method:** Offset. **Cols./Page:** 6. **Col. Depth:** 21 1/2 inches. **Key Personnel:** Trish Adams, Editor; DiAnne Faust, Advertising Mgr.; Carol Brooke, Publisher/Contact; Betty Crowe, Circulation Mgr. **Subscription Rates:** $22.50 individuals; $32.50 individuals out of parish. **Formerly:** News-Digest.
Ad Rates: 4C: $400 **Circ:** ‡2,500
SAU: $4.39
PCI: $4.16

12657 WABL-AM - 1570
Bankston Rd. Phone: (504)748-8385
PO Box 787 Fax: (504)748-3918
Amite, LA 70422
Free: (888)748-8385

Format: Full Service. **Networks:** Louisiana; Mutual Broadcasting System. **Owner:** Amite Broadcasting Co., Inc., at above address. **Founded:** 1956. **Operating Hours:** Sunrise-sunset; 30% network, 70% local. **ADI:** Baton Rouge, LA. **Key Personnel:** Phyliss M. Harrison, General Mgr., pharrison@i_55.com. **Wattage:** 500. **Ad Rates:** $4.50 for 15 seconds; $8 for 30 seconds; $14 for 60 seconds.

ANGOLA

C LA. West Feliciana Parish. 10 mi. SE of Weyanoke.

12658 Angolite
Louisiana State Penitentiary Phone: (504)655-4411
Angola, LA 70712
Prisoner-funded and produced magazine covering prison topics. **Founded:** 1952. **Freq:** Bimonthly. **Print Method:** Offset. **ISSN:** 0402-4249. **Subscription Rates:** $20 individuals; $30 Canada; $40 other countries. **Remarks:** Advertising not accepted.
Circ: (Not Reported)

12659 KLSP-FM - 91.7
Louisiana State Penitentiary Phone: (504)655-4411
Angola, LA 70712 Fax: (504)655-2319

Format: Full Service. **Founded:** 1987. **Operating Hours:** 12 hours daily; 40% network, 60% local. **Key Personnel:** Sheryl Ronatza, Assistant Warden; Cathy Jett, Executive Officer. **Wattage:** 100. **Ad Rates:** Noncommercial.

ARABI, pop. 65,000.

SE LA. Saint Bernard Parish. On Mississippi River, adjoining New Orleans. Oil refineries, aluminum plants. Diversified farming.

12660 Saint Bernard Voice
234 Mehle Ave.
Arabi, LA 70032-1054
Publication E-mail: lastbv@bellsouth.net

Newspaper with a Democratic orientation. **Founded:** 1890. **Freq:** Weekly (Fri.). **Print Method:** Offset. **Trim Size:** 7 x 11. **Cols./Page:** 6. **Col. Width:** 2 1/16 inches. **Col. Depth:** 301 agate lines. **Key Personnel:** Edwin M. Roy, Jr., Editor/Publisher/Contact. **Subscription Rates:** $12 individuals; $14 out of state.
Ad Rates: GLR: $.23 **Circ:** Paid ⊕2,600
BW: $424.41
4C: $400
PCI: $3.29

ARCADIA†, pop. 3,403.

Bienville Parish. 50 mi. E. of Shreveport. Pine timber. Cotton. Salt deposits. Agriculture. Cattle, chickens.

12661 The Arcadia Progress
PO Box 29
Arcadia, LA 71001-0029

Community newspaper. **Founded:** 1985. **Freq:** Weekly (Tues.). **Print Method:** Offset. **Cols./Page:** 6. **Col. Width:** 28 nonpareils. **Col. Depth:** 294 agate lines. **Key Personnel:** Wayne Dring, Publisher; Leslie Harrington, Advertising Mgr. **Subscription Rates:** Free. **Remarks:** Accepts advertising.
Ad Rates: GLR: $4.05 **Circ:** Free ‡4,665
BW: $375.48
4C: $575.48
SAU: $3.44

12662 Bienville Democrat/Ringgold Record
1952 Railroad St. Phone: (318)263-2922
PO Box 29 Fax: (318)263-8897
Arcadia, LA 71001-0029
Community newspaper. **Founded:** 1918. **Freq:** Weekly (Thurs.). **Print Method:** Offset. **Cols./Page:** 6. **Col. Width:** 2 1/16 inches. **Col. Depth:** 21 inches. **Key Personnel:** Wayne Dring, Editor and Publisher; Leslie Harrington, Advertising Mgr. **Subscription Rates:** $25 individuals. **Remarks:** Accepts advertising.
Ad Rates: BW: $375.48 **Circ:** ‡2,700
4C: $575.48
SAU: $4.51
PCI: $3.44

12663 The Ringgold Progress
PO Box 29 Phone: (318)263-2922
Arcadia, LA 71001 Fax: (318)263-8897

Community newspaper. **Founded:** 1982. **Freq:** Weekly (Wed.). **Print Method:** Offset. **Cols./Page:** 6. **Col. Width:** 2 1/16 inches. **Col. Depth:** 21 inches. **Key Personnel:** Waynn E. Dring, Publisher; Leslie Harrington, Advertising Mgr. **Subscription Rates:** Free. **Remarks:** Accepts advertising.
Ad Rates: GLR: $4.05 **Circ:** Free ‡6,630
BW: $510.30
4C: $710.30
SAU: $4.51

BAKER, pop. 12,865.

SEC LA. East Baton Rouge Parish. 10 mi. N. of Baton Rouge. Residential. Chemicals, petro complex, sugarcane, cotton.

12664 Baker Observer
5240 Groom Rd. Phone: (504)775-2315
Baker, LA 70714 Fax: (504)774-9212

Newspaper. **Founded:** 1958. **Freq:** Weekly (Thurs.). **Print Method:** Offset. **Cols./Page:** 6. **Col. Width:** 24 nonpareils. **Col. Depth:** 294 agate lines. **Key Personnel:** Mitchell D. Lynch, Publisher; Mark Smith, Editor; Michelle Gorsch, Circulation Mgr.; Phyllis Wagner, Production Mgr. **Subscription Rates:** $20 individuals.
Ad Rates: BW: $828.18 **Circ:** ‡1,800
PCI: $6.50

12665 TCI of Louisiana
3206 N. Main Phone: (504)774-9400
Baker, LA 70714 Fax: (504)774-4034

Owner: Tele-Communications Inc., 5619 DTC Pkwy., Englewood, CO 80111, (303)267-5500, Fax: (303)779-1228. **Founded:** 1980. **Formerly:** Daniels Cable. **Key Personnel:** Mike Ross, General Mgr.; Kevin Leger, General Mgr. **Cities Served:** Baker, East Baton Rouge Parish (West), Erwinville, Slaughter, Zachary, LA: subscribing households 18,000; 41 channels; 1 community access channel; 158 hours per week community access programming.

12666 WQCK-FM - 92.7
13567 Plank Rd. Phone: (504)774-7780
Baker, LA 70714 Fax: (504)774-7785

Format: Adult Contemporary; Religious. **Networks:** Independent. **Founded:** 1981. **Formerly:** WFEX-FM (1984). **Operating Hours:** Continuous. **ADI:** Baton Rouge, LA. **Key Personnel:** Ronnie Bennett, General Mgr.; Gary Babb, Operations Mgr.; Linda Durham, Office Mgr. **Wattage:** 32,000. **Ad Rates:** $20 for 30 seconds; $25 for 60 seconds.

BALL

12667 KWDF-AM - 840
3735 Rigolette Rd. Phone: (318)640-4373
Pineville, LA 71360 Fax: (318)640-1321

Format: Southern Gospel; Religious. **Networks:** USA Radio. **Founded:** 1986. **Operating Hours:** Sunrise-sunset. **Key Personnel:** Tommy Moore, Contact; Rich Dupree, Contact; Jan Higashi, Contact. **Wattage:** 10,000. **Ad Rates:** $5 for 30 seconds; $6 for 60 seconds.

BASILE, pop. 2,635.

SC LA. Evangeline Parish. 85 mi. W. of Baton Rouge. Residential. Oil. Agriculture.

12668 The Basile Weekly
PO Box 578 Phone: (318)432-6807
Basile, LA 70515 Fax: (318)432-6807

Community newspaper. **Founded:** Sept. 17, 1964. **Freq:** Weekly (Thurs.). **Print Method:** Offset. **Trim Size:** 13 x 22 3/4. **Cols./Page:** 6. **Col. Width:** 2 inches. **Col. Depth:** 21.5 inches. **Key Personnel:** Darrel B. LeJeune, Editor and Publisher. **USPS:** 044-900. **Subscription Rates:** $13 individuals; $17 out of area; $21 out of state. **Remarks:** Accepts advertising.
Ad Rates: BW: $387 **Circ:** Paid ‡1,300
PCI: $3 Free ‡36

BASTROP†, pop. 15,527.

N LA. Morehouse Parish. 29 mi. N. of Monroe. Manufactures paper and paper products, printers ink, varnish, chemicals, farm implements, logging equipment, men's pants. Cotton gins. Diversified farming. Pine, hardwood timber. Gas wells. Cotton, soybeans, rice.

12669 Bastrop Enterprise
Bastrop Newspapers, Inc.
PO Box 311 Phone: (318)281-4421
Bastrop, LA 71221 Fax: (318)283-1699

General newspaper. **Founded:** 1901. **Freq:** Daily (morn.). **Print Method:** Offset. **Cols./Page:** 6. **Col. Width:** 24 nonpareils. **Col. Depth:** 294 agate lines. **Key Personnel:** Cy Wood, Editor and Publisher. **Subscription Rates:** $38.50 individuals. **Remarks:** Accepts advertising.
Ad Rates: PCI: $4.85 **Circ:** (Not Reported)

BATON ROUGE†, pop. 219,486.

SEC LA. East Baton Rouge Parish. 75 mi. NW of New Orleans, on the Mississippi River. The State Capital. Louisiana State University, Southern University A. and M. College. Major port for ocean and river transportation. Manufactures synthetic rubber, aluminum, tetraethyl lead, sulphuric and hydrofluoric acid, alcohol, salt, soda ash, chlorine, chemicals, sashes and doors, steel tanks, concrete pipes, mattresses, soft drinks. Food packing. Oil refining.

12670 The Advocate
Capital City Press
525 Lafayette St. Phone: (504)383-1111
Baton Rouge, LA 70802-5410 Fax: (504)388-0348
Free: (800)960-6397

General newspaper. **Founded:** 1904. **Freq:** Mon.-Sun. (morn.). **Print Method:** Letterpress. **Cols./Page:** 6. **Key Personnel:** Douglas L. Manship, Publisher; David C. Manship, Publisher. **Subscription Rates:** $111.80 Monday-Saturday; $33.80 Sunday. **Remarks:** Accepts advertising. Sunday: BW: $5,272.13; 4C: $6,022.13; PCI: $41.35. **Alt. Formats:** CD-ROM. **Also known as:** Sunday Advocate. **Formerly:** Morning Advocate. **Feature Editors:** Art Adams, *Sunday*, phone (504)383-1111; Bob Anderson, *Environmental*, phone (504)383-1111; Bill Bankston, *Editorials*, phone (504)383-1111; Cynthia Campbell, *Travel*, phone (504)383-1111; Curt Eysink, *Education*, phone (504)383-1111; Kathryn Flournoy, *Financial/Business*, phone (504)383-1111; Dan Hatfield, *Metro, News*, phone (504)383-1111; Mark Keedy, *Photo*, phone (504)383-1111; Karen Martin, *Fashion*, phone (504)383-1111; Butch Muir, *Sports*, phone (504)383-1111; Tommy Simmons, *Food*, phone (504)383-1111; Pat Tessier, *Lifestyle*, phone (504)383-1111; Greg Toney, *Religion*, phone (504)383-1111; John Wirt, *Entertainment, Movie*, phone (504)383-1111; Freda Yarbrough, *Features*, phone (504)383-1111.
Ad Rates: BW: $5,272.13 **Circ:** Mon.-Fri. 96,239
4C: $6,022.13 Sat. 109,897
PCI: $39.08 Sun. 129,706

12671 Baton Rouge Weekly Press
1283 Rosenwald Rd., Ste. 1 Phone: (504)775-2002
Baton Rouge, LA 70807-4173 Fax: (504)775-4216

Minority-based, community newspaper. **Founded:** 1977. **Freq:** Weekly. **Cols./Page:** 6. **Key Personnel:** Ivory J. Payne, Publisher; Walter Dixon, Jr., Editor; Cassie M. Payne, Food Editor; Walter Dixon, Sports & Music Editor. **Subscription Rates:** $26; $14 individuals; $3 single issue. **Remarks:** Accepts advertising. **Alt. Formats:** CD-ROM.
Ad Rates: GLR: $6 **Circ:** Paid 7,500
BW: $10
4C: $400
PCI: $10

12672 The Boardmember
Louisiana School Boards Association
7912 Summa Ave. Phone: (504)769-3191
Baton Rouge, LA 70809 Fax: (504)769-6108
Publication E-mail: isbadb@aol.com

Magazine on education. **Subtitle:** LSBA Official Journal. **Founded:** 1947. **Freq:** Quarterly. **Print Method:** Offset. **Trim Size:** 6 x 9. **Cols./Page:** 1. **Col. Width:** 50 nonpareils. **Col. Depth:** 84 agate lines. **Key Personnel:** W.F. Freddie Whitford, Editor. **Subscription Rates:** $5 individuals. **Remarks:** Advertising not accepted for liquor and tobacco. **Formerly:** The Boardman.
Ad Rates: BW: $90 **Circ:** ‡2,800

12673 The Catholic Commentator
Diocese of Baton Rouge
1800 S. Acadian Thruway Phone: (504)387-0983
PO Box 14746 Fax: (504)336-8789
Baton Rouge, LA 70808-1663
Religious newspaper. **Founded:** 1963. **Freq:** Biweekly. **Print Method:** Offset. **Cols./Page:** 5. **Col. Width:** 21 nonpareils. **Col. Depth:** 196 agate lines. **Key Personnel:** Laura Deavers, Editor; Wanda Koch, Advertising Mgr. **Subscription Rates:** $10 individuals. **Remarks:** Accepts advertising.
Ad Rates: GLR: $.82 **Circ:** ‡50,000
BW: $805
4C: $1,305
PCI: $11.50

12674 The Evangelist
Jimmy Swaggart Ministries
PO Box 262550 Phone: (504)768-8300
Baton Rouge, LA 70826 Fax: (504)769-2244

Religious magazine. **Founded:** 1970. **Freq:** Monthly. **Print Method:** Offset. **Trim Size:** 8 3/8 x 10 7/8. **Cols./Page:** 3. **Col. Width:** 30 nonpareils. **Col. Depth:** 129 agate lines. **Key Personnel:** Donnie Swaggart, Editor, swaggart@jsm.org. **Subscription Rates:** $12. **Remarks:** Advertising not accepted. **URL:** www.jsm.org.
Circ: (Not Reported)

12675 Greater Baton Rouge Business Report
Louisiana Business, Inc.
5757 Corporate Blvd. Phone: (504)928-1700
PO Box 1949 Fax: (504)923-3448
Baton Rouge, LA 70821
Publication E-mail: brbr@businessreport.com

Area business magazine. **Founded:** Sept. 1982. **Freq:** Bi-

weekly. **Print Method:** Offset. **Trim Size:** 11 x 14 3/4. **Cols./Page:** 4. **Col. Width:** 30 nonpareils. **Col. Depth:** 196 agate lines. **Key Personnel:** Paulette Senior, Contact; Rolfe H. McCollister, Jr., Publisher; Julio Melara, President/Assoc Publisher. **ISSN:** 0747-4652. **Subscription Rates:** $46 individuals; $2.00 single issue. **Online:** Premier One Inc. **URL:** http://www.businessreport.com.
Ad Rates: BW: $2,278 **Circ:** Paid ‡3,500
4C: $2,728 Non-paid ‡12,000

12676 International Review of Financial Analysis
Elseiver
College of Business Phone: (504)388-6369
Louisiana State University Fax: (504)388-6366
Baton Rouge, LA 70803
Publication E-mail: 102062.2525@compuserve.com
Publisher E-mail: fcentres@gpu.stv.ualberta.ca

Scholarly journal focusing on global financial issues. **Founded:** 1992. **Freq:** 3/year. **Key Personnel:** George Frankfurter, Editor. **ISSN:** 1057-5219. **Subscription Rates:** $80 individuals; $180 institutions. **Remarks:** Advertising not accepted.
Circ: (Not Reported)

12677 Journal of Macroeconomics
Louisiana State University Press
Louisiana State University Phone: (225)388-6646
College of Business Fax: (225)388-3807
Administration
2113 CEBA Bldg.
Baton Rouge, LA 70803
Publication E-mail: jmacro@unixl.sncc.lsu.edu
Publisher E-mail: uppress@lsuvm.sncc.lsu.edu

Trade journal covering macroeconomics. **Founded:** 1979. **Freq:** Quarterly. **Key Personnel:** David J. Smyth, Funding Editor; W. Douglas McMillin, Editor; Marybeth Theriot, Managing Editor; Margaret Hart, Advertising Mgr.; Becky Brown, Circulation Mgr. **ISSN:** 0164-0704. **Subscription Rates:** $40 individuals; $85 institutions; $85 institutions other countries; add $6 for postage; $22.75 single issue. **Remarks:** Advertising accepted; rates available upon request. **Alt. Formats:** Microfilm.
Circ: Combined ⊕**966**

12678 Journal of Mayan Linguistics
Geoscience Publications
Box 16010 Phone: (504)388-6245
Baton Rouge, LA 70893-6010 Fax: (504)388-4420
Publisher E-mail: gawilc@unix1.sncc.lsu.edu

Scholarly journal covering Mayan linguistics and ethnology. **Founded:** 1978. **Freq:** Irregular. **Print Method:** Offset. **Key Personnel:** Jill Brody, Editor; Esther Shaffer, Managing Editor. **ISSN:** 0195-475X. **Subscription Rates:** $15 individuals. **Remarks:** Advertising not accepted.
Circ: Paid 100

12679 Journal of Winston Churchill
International Churchill Society
1847 Stonewood Dr. Phone: (603)746-4433
Baton Rouge, LA 70816-2861 Fax: (603)746-4260
Publisher E-mail: malakand@aol.com

Journal covering Winston Churchill. **Subtitle:** Finest Hour. **Freq:** Quarterly. **Key Personnel:** Richard Langworth. **Subscription Rates:** $35 individuals. **Remarks:** Accepts advertising.
Circ: (Not Reported)

12680 Knowledge and Policy
Transaction Publishers
Louisana State Universtiy
Sociology Department
Baton Rouge, LA 70803
Publisher E-mail: trans@transactionpub.com

International journal devoted to the development of an interdisciplinary science of knowledge transfer. **Subtitle:** The International Journal of Knowledge Transfer and Utilization. **Founded:** 1988. **Freq:** Quarterly. **Print Method:** Offset. **Trim Size:** 6 3/4 x 10. **Key Personnel:** Esther K. Hicks, Editor-in-Chief. **ISSN:** 0897-1986. **Subscription Rates:** $66 individuals; $132 institutions; $98 individuals other countries; $164 institutions, other countries; $120 two years individuals; $240 two years institutions. **Remarks:** Accepts advertising. **Formerly:** Knowledge in Society.
Ad Rates: BW: $200 **Circ:** Paid 500

12681 LAE News
Louisiana Association of Educators
PO Box 479
Baton Rouge, LA 70821

Educational tabloid. **Founded:** 1977. **Freq:** 4/year. **Print Method:** Offset. **Trim Size:** 11 x 15. **Cols./Page:** 4. **Col. Width:** 30 nonpareils. **Col. Depth:** 214 agate lines. **Key Personnel:** Jeff Simon, Editor, jefflae@aol.com. **Subscription Rates:** $25 individuals. **Remarks:** Accepts advertising.
Ad Rates: BW: $800 **Circ:** ‡21,000

12682 LLA Bulletin
Louisiana Library Association
PO Box 3058 Phone: (504)342-4928
Baton Rouge, LA 70821 Fax: (504)342-3547
Publisher E-mail: lla@pelican.state.lib.la.us

Library science magazine. **Founded:** June 1938. **Freq:** Quarterly. **Print Method:** Offset. **Trim Size:** 6 x 9. **Cols./Page:** 2. **Col. Width:** 42 nonpareils. **Col. Depth:** 112 agate lines. **Key Personnel:** Mary Cosper Le Boeuf, Editor; Carol McMahan, Administrative Officer. **ISSN:** 0024-6867. **Subscription Rates:** $15 individuals; $5 single issue. **Remarks:** Color advertising not accepted.
Ad Rates: BW: $100 **Circ:** Paid ‡1,500
Non-paid ‡50

12683 LOMA Line
Louisiana Oil Marketers Association
PO Box 80357 Phone: (504)926-8300
Baton Rouge, LA 70898 Fax: (504)926-7722

Magazine covering the oil market. **Freq:** Bimonthly. **Print Method:** Offset. Uses mats. **Cols./Page:** 2. **Col. Width:** 42 nonpareils. **Col. Depth:** 133 agate lines.
Circ: Non-paid 600

12684 Louisiana Agriculture Magazine
Louisiana Agricultural Experiment Station
PO Box 25100 Phone: (504)388-2263
Baton Rouge, LA 70894-5100 Fax: (504)388-4524

Agricultural/educational magazine. **Subtitle:** The Magazine of the Louisiana Agricultural Experiment Station. **Founded:** 1958. **Freq:** Quarterly. **Print Method:** Offset. **Trim Size:** 8 7/16 x 11. **Cols./Page:** 3. **Col. Width:** 28 nonpareils. **Col. Depth:** 140 agate lines. **Key Personnel:** Dr. Linda Benedict, Editor, phone (504)388-2937, lbenedict@agctr.lsu.edu. **Subscription Rates:** Free. **Remarks:** Advertising not accepted. **URL:** http://www.agctr.lsu.edu/wwwac.
Circ: Controlled ‡5,900

12685 Louisiana Contractor
McGraw-Hill Companies, Inc./F.W. Dodge Louisiana Contractor
2900 Westfork Dr., Ste. 345 Phone: (225)292-8980
Baton Rouge, LA 70827-0002 Fax: (225)292-5089
Free: (800)786-8980
Publication E-mail: lacsam@aol.com

Trade magazine covering contractors in Louisiana. **Founded:** 1953. **Freq:** Monthly. **Print Method:** Sheetfed offset. **Trim Size:** 8 1/8 x 10 7/8. **Cols./Page:** 3. **Col. Width:** 2 1/8 inches. **Col. Depth:** 10 inches. **Key Personnel:** Sam Barnes, Editor, lacsam@aol.com; M. Kevin Rhodes, Publisher, krhodes@mcgraw-hill.com; Maelane Rhodes, Production Mgr.; Pat Wells, Circulation Mgr. **ISSN:** 0195-7074. **Subscription Rates:** $27 individuals; $5 single issue. **Remarks:** Accepts advertising.
Ad Rates: BW: $920 **Circ:** (Not Reported)
4C: $1,445
PCI: $30

12686 Louisiana Country
Association of Louisiana Electric Cooperatives, Inc.
10725 Airline Hwy. Phone: (504)293-3450
Baton Rouge, LA 70816 Fax: (504)296-0924
Free: (800)355-3450
Publisher E-mail: alec@premier.net

Electric cooperative membership magazine. **Founded:** 1950. **Freq:** Monthly. **Print Method:** Offset. **Trim Size:** 9 3/4 x 13. **Cols./Page:** 4. **Col. Width:** 2.25 inches. **Col. Depth:** 14 inches. **Key Personnel:** Billy Gibson, Dir. of Communications; Randy Pierce, Associate Editor. **USPS:** 473-180. **Subscription Rates:** $5 nonmembers; $2.50 members. **Remarks:** Accepts advertising.
Ad Rates: BW: $1,680 **Circ:** ‡130,000
4C: $800
PCI: $35

12687 Louisiana Engineer & Surveyor Journal
Louisiana Engineering Society
9643 Brookline Ave., Ste. 116 Phone: (225)924-2021
Baton Rouge, LA 70809 Fax: (225)924-2049
Publisher E-mail: les@communique.net

Magazine covering the field of engineering. **Founded:** 1914. **Freq:** Quarterly. **Print Method:** Offset. **Cols./Page:** 3. **Col. Width:** 25 nonpareils. **Col. Depth:** 136 agate lines. **Key Personnel:** Brenda W. Gajan, Editor. **ISSN:** 0024-6794. **Subscription Rates:** $24 individuals. **Remarks:** Accepts advertising. **Formerly:** The Louisiana Engineer.
Ad Rates: BW: $960 **Circ:** Paid 30,000

12688 Louisiana Law Review
Louisiana State University Law Center
Baton Rouge, LA 70803 Phone: (504)388-1685
Fax: (504)388-1683

Scholarly journal covering law. **Founded:** 1940. **Freq:** Quarterly. **Print Method:** Offset. **Trim Size:** 6 3/4 x 10. **Key Personnel:** Todd Leitstein, Editor-in-Chief; Mary Pourciau, Circulation Mgr./Editorial Asst. **ISSN:** 0024-6859. **Subscription Rates:** $42 individuals. **Remarks:** Advertising not accepted. **Online:** LEXIS-NEXIS; Westlaw.
Circ: (Not Reported)

12689 Louisiana Market Bulletin
Louisiana Dept. of Agriculture
Office of Marketing Phone: (504)922-1328
PO Box 3334 Fax: (504)922-1289
Baton Rouge, LA 70821
Trade newspaper featuring agriculture-related articles, advertisements, and recipes. **Founded:** 1908. **Freq:** Semimonthly. **Print Method:** Offset. **Trim Size:** 11 1/2 x 15. **Cols./Page:** 5. **Col. Width:** 10 inches. **Col. Depth:** 13.5 picas. **Key Personnel:** Renee M. Tull, Editor; Rhonda Wyckoff, Advertising Mgr. **Subscription Rates:** $10 two years. **Remarks:** Accepts advertising.
Circ: ‡30,000

12690 Louisiana Municipal Review
Louisiana Municipal Association
700 N. 10th St., Ste. 400
Baton Rouge, LA 70802-4500
Publisher E-mail:
lamunicipalassociation@compuserve.com

Journal covering municipal governments and federal, state and local issues in Louisiana. **Founded:** 1935. **Freq:** Monthly. **Print Method:** Web offset. **Key Personnel:** L. Gordon King, Editor; Tommy Darensbourg, Managing Editor. **ISSN:** 0164-3622. **Subscription Rates:** $12 individuals; $2 single issue. **Remarks:** Accepts advertising. **URL:** http://www.lamunis.org.
Ad Rates: BW: $1,020 **Circ:** (Not Reported)

12691 The Louisiana Pharmacist
Louisiana Pharmacists Association
PO Box 14446
Baton Rouge, LA 70898-4446
Publication E-mail: lpa2000@tlxnet.net
Publisher E-mail: lpa2000@tlxnet.net

Trade journal for registered pharmacists. Official publication of the Louisiana Pharmacists Association. **Subtitle:** The Voice of Pharmacy in Louisiana. **Founded:** Oct. 1943. **Freq:** Bimonthly. **Print Method:** Offset. **Trim Size:** 8 1/2 x 11. **Cols./Page:** 3. **Key Personnel:** Beverly Smiley, Exec. Editor; Adam Thomas, Managing Editor. **USPS:** 588-400. **Subscription Rates:** Included in membership dues; $25 nonmembers. $5 single issue. **Remarks:** Advertising accepted; rates available upon request.
Circ: ‡1,500

12692 Louisiana Rural Economist
Louisiana State University
Dept. of Ag. Economics and Ag. Phone: (504)388-3282
Business Fax: (504)388-2716
Baton Rouge, LA 70803-5604
Magazine covering agricultural economics. **Founded:** 1939. **Freq:** Quarterly. **Print Method:** Offset. **Trim Size:** 6 x 9. **Cols./Page:** 2. **Col. Width:** 27 nonpareils. **Col. Depth:** 112 agate lines. **Key Personnel:** P. Lynn Kennedy, Assoc. Ed., lkennedy@agctr.lsu.edu; Richard Kazmierczok, Editor, rkazmierczok@agctr.lsu.edu. **ISSN:** 8756-6273. **Subscription Rates:** Free. **Remarks:** Advertising not accepted. **URL:** http://rich.agadm.lsu.edu.
Circ: Controlled ‡1,265

12693 LSU Magazine
LSU Alumni Association
3838 W. Lakeshore Dr. Phone: (504)388-1212
Baton Rouge, LA 70808 Fax: (504)388-3816
Publication E-mail: magazine@lsualumni.org

Alumni magazine. **Founded:** 1924. **Freq:** Quarterly. **Print Method:** Sheetfed. **Trim Size:** 8 1/2 x 11. **Cols./Page:** 3. **Col. Width:** 28 nonpareils. **Col. Depth:** 140 agate lines. **Key Personnel:** Andy Crawford, Editor; Kelly Lewis, Account Executive. **Subscription Rates:** Included in membership. **Remarks:** Accepts advertising. **Formerly:** LSU Alumni News.
Ad Rates: BW: $1,205 **Circ:** ‡24,000
4C: $1,565

12694 New Delta Review
Louisiana State University
Baton Rouge, LA 70803-5001 Phone: (504)388-4079

Literary journal covering poetry, fiction, nonfiction and book reviews. **Founded:** 1974. **Freq:** Semiannual. **Print Method:** Offset. **Trim Size:** 6 x 8. **ISSN:** 1050-415X. **Subscription**

Rates: $8.50 individuals; $5 single issue. **Remarks:** Accepts advertising.
Ad Rates: BW: $100 **Circ:** (Not Reported)

12695 The Southern Review
Louisiana State University
43 Allen Hall Phone: (225)388-5108
Baton Rouge, LA 70803-5005 Fax: (225)388-5098

Literature and poetry journal. Publishes fiction, poetry, critical essays, book reviews, and excerpts from novels in progress, with emphasis on contemporary literature in the U.S. and abroad, and with special interest in Southern culture and history. **Founded:** 1965. **Freq:** Quarterly. **Print Method:** Letterpress. **Trim Size:** 6 3/4 x 10. **Cols./Page:** 1. **Col. Width:** 54 nonpareils. **Col. Depth:** 105 agate lines. **Key Personnel:** Dave Smith, Editor; James Olney, Director; Brenda Macon, Business Mgr., bmacon@unix1.sncc.lsu.edu; Michael Griffith, Assoc. Editor. **ISSN:** 0038-4534. **Subscription Rates:** $20 individuals; $40 institutions. **Remarks:** Accepts advertising.
Ad Rates: BW: $250 **Circ:** ‡3,100

12696 Update
Music Educators National Conference
Louisiana State University Phone: (504)388-2593
School of Music
c/o Dr. James L. Byo
Baton Rouge, LA 70803
Publisher E-mail: mbmenc@vais.net

Professional journal covering music for music teachers at all levels. **Subtitle:** Applications of Research in Music Education. **Freq:** Semiannual. **Key Personnel:** Dr. James L. Byo, Contact. **Remarks:** Advertising not accepted.
Circ: (Not Reported)

12697 Urban Education
Corwin Press
Louisiana State Univ. Phone: (504)388-6900
College of Education Fax: (504)388-6918
111 Peabody Hall
Baton Rouge, LA 70803
Publication E-mail: edalomo@lsuvm.sncc.lsu.edu
Publisher E-mail: info@corwinpress.com

Journal covering inner city education. **Founded:** 1966. **Freq:** 5/year. **Print Method:** Offset. **Trim Size:** 5 1/2 x 8 1/2. **Cols./Page:** 1. **Col. Width:** 50 nonpareils. **Col. Depth:** 100 agate lines. **Key Personnel:** Kofi Lomotey, Editor. **ISSN:** 0042-0859. **Subscription Rates:** $70 individuals; $220 institutions; $20 single issue; $50 single issue institutions. **Remarks:** Accepts advertising. **Alt. Formats:** Microform.
Ad Rates: BW: $225 **Circ:** Paid ‡862
Non-paid ‡111

KLPA-TV - See Alexandria

KLPB-TV - See Lafayette

12698 KLSU-FM - 91.1
Louisiana State University Phone: (504)388-6398
39 Hodges Hall Fax: (504)388-1698
Baton Rouge, LA 70803

Format: Alternative/New Music/Progressive. **Networks:** Louisiana; Mutual Broadcasting System. **Owner:** Louisiana State University, Lakeshore Dr., Baton Rouge, LA 70803, (504)388-2160. **Founded:** 1923. **Formerly:** WPLG-FM (1983). **Operating Hours:** Continuous, 5% network, 95% local. **ADI:** Baton Rouge, LA. **Local Programs:** *Nightsounds*, Marc Cohn; *Spontaneous Combustion*, Zia Tamami. **Wattage:** 5000. **Ad Rates:** Noncommercial; underwriting available.

KLTL-TV - See Lake Charles

KLTM-TV - See Monroe

KLTS-TV - See Shreveport

12699 KOOJ-FM - 93.7
8641 United Plaza Blvd., Ste. 208 Phone: (225)922-5045
Fax: (225)922-5046
Baton Rouge, LA 70809
Free: (800)644-0937

Format: Oldies. **Networks:** ABC. **Owner:** Powell Broadcasting Co., 8641 United Plaza Blvd.,, Baton Rouge, LA 70809, Free: (888)922-0937. **Founded:** Jan. 1997. **Formerly:** KDEA-FM; KTBT. **Operating Hours:** Continuous. **ADI:** Lafayette, LA. **Key Personnel:** Todd Sterling, General Mgr., phone (225)922-5109, tlsterl@aol.com; Tricia Cummings, Program Dir.; Lori Hutchinson, Office Mgr., phone (504)922-5128, lorih@eatel.net. **Wattage:** 100,000. **Ad Rates:** $35-45 per unit.

12700 KRVE-FM - 96.1
5555 Hilton Ave., Ste. 500 Phone: (504)231-1860
Baton Rouge, LA 70808 Fax: (504)499-9696
E-mail: river@intersurf.com

Format: Adult Contemporary. **Founded:** 1989. **Formerly:** KIEZ-FM (1989). **Operating Hours:** Continuous. **Key Personnel:** Chris Welmann, General Mgr.; Bob Murphy, Program Dir.; Sam North, Promotions; Jodi Carson, Music Dir. **Wattage:** 50,000. **Ad Rates:** $2.50-60 for 30 seconds; $5-70 for 60 seconds.

12701 TCI
5428 Florida Blvd. Phone: (504)923-0256
Baton Rouge, LA 70896 Fax: (504)925-1668

Founded: 1975. **Formerly:** UAE. **Cities Served:** East Baton Rouge County, Central and East Baton Rouge Parish, LA.

12702 WAFB-TV - 9
844 Government St. Phone: (504)383-9999
Baton Rouge, LA 70802-6090 Fax: (504)379-7891

Format: Commercial TV. **Networks:** CBS. **Founded:** 1953. **Operating Hours:** Continuous. **ADI:** Baton Rouge, LA. **Key Personnel:** Ronald E. Winders, General Mgr.; Ray Sullivan, General Sales Mgr. **Ad Rates:** $10-950 per unit.

12703 WBRH-FM - 90.3
2825 Government St. Phone: (504)383-3243
Baton Rouge, LA 70806 Fax: (504)379-7685

Format: Public Radio; Big Band/Nostalgia. **Networks:** National Public Radio (NPR); Louisiana. **Founded:** 1977. **Operating Hours:** Continuous; 10% network 90% local. **ADI:** Baton Rouge, LA. **Key Personnel:** Danny Dean, General Mgr.; Yvette Hyde, Development Director; Rob Payer, Program/Music Dir. **Wattage:** 7000. **Ad Rates:** Noncommercial. Combined advertising rates available with KBRH-AM.

12704 WBRZ-TV - 2
1650 Highland Rd. (70802) Phone: (504)387-2222
Box 2906 Fax: (504)336-2246
Baton Rouge, LA 70821
E-mail: mis@wbrz.com

Format: Commercial TV. **Networks:** ABC. **Owner:** Richard Manship, at above address. **Founded:** 1955. **Operating Hours:** Continuous. **ADI:** Baton Rouge, LA. **Key Personnel:** Raymond Drago, Production Dir.; Kim Manship, Finance Director; Jamie Politz, Human Resource Director; Clyde Pierce, Engineering Director; Skip Haley, Information Services Director; Richard Manship, President; Pat Cheramie, General Mgr.; Denise Akers, Marketing Director; Jim Daboval, Sales Dir.; Suzanne Marva, Programming Director; John Pastorek, News Dir.; Andrew Shenkan, Sales Mgr. **Wattage:** 100,000.

12705 WDGL-FM - 98.1
PO Box 2231 Phone: (504)388-9898
Baton Rouge, LA 70801-2231 Fax: (504)499-9800

Format: Classic Rock. **Owner:** Guaranty Broadcasting Corp., at above address. **Founded:** 1968. **Formerly:** WAFB-FM (1984); WGGZ-FM. **Operating Hours:** Continuous; 95% local, 5% national. **ADI:** Baton Rouge, LA. **Key Personnel:** Greg Herpin, General Mgr.; Eddie Martiny, Sales Mgr.; Randy Chase, Program Dir.; Johnny A., News Dir.; Matt Patin, Promotions Dir./Administrative Asst. **Local Programs:** *Focal Point*, Kevin Meeks. **Wattage:** 100,000.

12706 WIBR-AM - 1300
9737 N. Winston Ave. Phone: (504)292-9556
Baton Rouge, LA 70809-2531 Fax: (504)291-6420

Format: Sports. **Owner:** Don Nelson, at above address. **Founded:** 1947. **Formerly:** WCLA-AM (1949). **Operating Hours:** Continuous. **ADI:** Baton Rouge, LA. **Key Personnel:** Lew Campbell, Contact; Don Nelson, Contact; Darrell Picou, General Sales Mgr.; Greg Weston, Program Dir. **Wattage:** 5000 day; 1000 night.

12707 WJBO-AM - 1150
5555 Hilton Ave. 5th Fl. Phone: (504)231-1860
Baton Rouge, LA 70806 Fax: (504)231-1869

Format: Talk; News. **Networks:** CBS; EFM; Major Market Radio. **Founded:** 1934. **Operating Hours:** Continuous. **ADI:** Baton Rouge, LA. **Key Personnel:** Manuel R. Broussard, General Mgr.; Jim Thompson, General Sales Mgr. **Local Programs:** *Lawn & Garden Show*, Louis Miller; *Morning News Talk*, Matt Kennedy; *Sports Fan Radio*, Larry Matson. **Wattage:** 5000.

12708 WJFM-FM - 88.5
8919 World Ministry Ave. Phone: (504)768-3867
Baton Rouge, LA 70810 Fax: (504)768-3729

Format: Religious. **Networks:** USA Radio. **Owner:** Jimmy Swaggart Ministries, PO Box 262550, Baton Rouge, LA 70826-2550, (504)768-3202, Fax: (504)768-3729. **Founded:** 1963. **Formerly:** WLUX-AM. **Operating Hours:** Continuous. **ADI:** Baton Rouge, LA. **Key Personnel:** John Santiago, General Mgr., phone (504)768-3202, fax (504)768-3729; John R. Santiago II, Program & Music Director. **Local Programs:** *Jimmy Swaggart Telecast*; *Power House Clubs "Triple Time for Kids"*; *WEF Program*. **Wattage:** 25.5 KW. **Ad Rates:** Advertising accepted; rates available upon request. **URL:** http://www.jsm.org.

12709 WJFM-FM - 88.5
PO Box 262550 Phone: (504)768-3202
Baton Rouge, LA 70826 Fax: (504)768-3729

Format: Gospel. **Owner:** Jimmy Swaggert Ministries, at above address, (504)768-7000. **Operating Hours:** Continuous. **Key Personnel:** John Santiago, Station Mgr./Music Dir.; Harold Steele, Traffic Dir., phone (225)768-3202. **Wattage:** 25,500. **Ad Rates:** Underwriting available. **URL:** http://www.jsm.org.

12710 WKJN-FM - 103.3
9737 N. Winston Ave. Phone: (504)292-9556
Baton Rouge, LA 70804-2531 Fax: (504)291-6420

Format: Contemporary Country. **Networks:** Louisiana. **Owner:** Southern Communications Inc., at above address. **Founded:** 1969. **Formerly:** WTGI-FM (1984). **Operating Hours:** Continuous. **ADI:** Baton Rouge, LA. **Key Personnel:** Gary Hail, Program Dir.; Carla Cowart, Sales Mgr.; Don Nelson, President; Claire Gipson, Business Mgr. **Wattage:** 100,000. **URL:** http://www.challengernet/kajun103.

12711 WLPB-TV - 27
7860 Anselmo Ln. Phone: (225)767-5660
Baton Rouge, LA 70810 Fax: (225)767-4288
Free: (800)272-8161
E-mail: comments@lpb.gen.la.us

Format: Public TV. **Networks:** Public Broadcasting Service (PBS); Louisiana Public Broadcasting. **Owner:** Louisiana Public Broadcasting Network, at above address. **Founded:** 1975. **Operating Hours:** 5:30 a.m.-2 a.m.; 90% network, 10% local. **ADI:** Baton Rouge, LA. **Key Personnel:** Beth Courtney, President, phone (225)767-5660; Jennifer Howze, Program Dir.; Bob Neese, Promotions Dir.; Kent Hatfield, Engineering Dir.; Don Ballard, Operations Mgr.; Homer Dyess, Educational Services Dir.; Ayan Rubin, Educational Services Coord.; Clay Fourrier, Exec. Producer; Cindy Rougeou, CAO. **Local Programs:** *En Francais* 12 noon Sunday, Ken Fowler; *Louisiana: The State We're In* 7 p.m. Friday, Jeff Duhe. **Wattage:** 1,170,000. **URL:** http://www.lpb.gen.la.us/.

12712 WLSS-FM - 102.5
5555 Hilton Ave. 5th Fl. Phone: (504)231-1860
Baton Rouge, LA 70806 Fax: (504)231-1869

Format: Contemporary Hit Radio (CHR). **Networks:** Independent. **Founded:** 1941. **Formerly:** WFMF-FM. **Operating Hours:** Continuous. **ADI:** Baton Rouge, LA. **Key Personnel:** Manuel R. Broussard, General Mgr.; Jim Thompson, General Sales Mgr. **Wattage:** 100,000. **Ad Rates:** Advertising accepted; rates available upon request.

12713 WNDC-AM - 910
3000 Tecumseh St. Phone: (504)357-4571
Baton Rouge, LA 70805 Fax: (504)356-7784

Format: Gospel. **Owner:** New Direction Communications, PO Box 52591, Baton Rouge, LA 70892. **Founded:** 1946. **Operating Hours:** Continuous. **ADI:** Baton Rouge, LA. **Key Personnel:** Dwight Pate, President; Bronwyn Dickson, General Mgr.; Arthur Hoover, Chief Engineer. **Wattage:** 1000. **Ad Rates:** $7-13.50 for 30 seconds; $10-18 for 60 seconds.

12714 WSKR-AM - 1210
5555 Hilton Avenue, Suite 500 Phone: (504)231-1860
Baton Rouge, LA 70808 Fax: (504)231-1869

Format: Sports. **Networks:** CBS; ESPN Radio; Westwood One Radio. **Owner:** Gullstar Communications, at above address. **Founded:** 1960. **Formerly:** WLBI-AM (1984); WBIU-AM (1997). **Operating Hours:** 19 hours daily. **ADI:** Baton Rouge, LA. **Key Personnel:** Jim Thompson, Sales Mgr.; Danny Church, Program Dir.; Terry Easley, News Dir. **Wattage:** 10,000 (day) 1000 (night). **Ad Rates:** $6-8 for 30 seconds; $9-12 for 60 seconds. Combined advertising rates available with KRVE-FM.

12715 WVLA-TV - 33
5220 Essen Ln. Phone: (504)766-3233
P.O. Box 14685 (70898) Fax: (504)768-9191
Baton Rouge, LA 70809

Format: Commercial TV. **Networks:** NBC. **Owner:** Cyril Vetter, at above address. **Founded:** 1971. **Formerly:** WRBT-TV (1987). **Operating Hours:** 6 a.m.-4 a.m. **ADI:** Baton Rouge, LA. **Key Personnel:** Cyril Vetter, Chairman & CEO; Larry Dietz, Vice President; Donnie Picou, Nat'l Sales Mgr.;

Peggy Day, Local Sales Mgr.; Joyce Harvey, Program Dir.; Jason Furrate, Promotions & Marketing Director; Tom Woodside, Chief Engineer. **Ad Rates:** $20-900 per unit.

12716 WXCT-FM - 100.7
929-B Government St. Phone: (504)388-9898
Baton Rouge, LA 70802 Fax: (504)499-9800

Format: Country. **Formerly:** WQXY-FM; WTGE-FM. **Operating Hours:** Continuous. **ADI:** Baton Rouge, LA. **Key Personnel:** Greg Herpin, General Mgr.; Mike Hudson, General Sales Mgr.; Randy Chase, Program Dir.; Bo Hoover, Engineer. **Wattage:** 100,000.

12717 WXOK-AM - 1460
7707 Waco Ave. Phone: (504)926-1106
Baton Rouge, LA 70806 Fax: (504)928-1606

Format: Urban Contemporary. **Networks:** Independent. **Founded:** 1953. **Operating Hours:** Continuous. **ADI:** Baton Rouge, LA. **Key Personnel:** Dennis Lee, General Mgr. **Wattage:** 5000 day; 1000 night.

12718 WYNK-AM - 1380
5555 Hilton Ave., No. 500 Phone: (504)231-1860
Baton Rouge, LA 70808-2597 Fax: (504)231-1869

Owner: Gulfstar Communications Baton Rouge, Inc., at above address, Fax: (504)231-1879. **Operating Hours:** Sunrise-sunset; 9% network, 10% local. **ADI:** Baton Rouge, LA. **Key Personnel:** Chris Wegmann, General Mgr.; Sam North, Promotions Dir.; Danny Church, Program Dir.; Richard Petty, Chief Engineer; Patrick Sorrells, Sales Mgr. **Wattage:** 5000. **Ad Rates:** Combined advertising rates available with WJBO, KRVE, WYNK-FM, WSKR, WLSS.

BELLE CHASSE, pop. 9,000.

SE LA. Plaquemines Parish. 10 mi. S. of New Orleans. Industrial, small business area. Oil and sulpher; commercial fishing. Dairy, fruit - truck farms.

12719 The Plaquemines Gazette
Plaquemines Newspaper Publishing, Inc.
PO Box 700
Belle Chasse, LA 70037

Community newspaper. **Founded:** Jan. 20, 1927. **Freq:** Weekly (Fri.). **Print Method:** Offset. **Trim Size:** 14 3/4 x 21 1/2. **Cols./Page:** 6. **Col. Width:** 14 picas. **Col. Depth:** 21 inches. **Key Personnel:** Dale Benoit, Editor and Publisher; Norris Babin, Publisher. **Subscription Rates:** $20 individuals; $25 out of county; $30 out of state. **Remarks:** Accepts advertising.
Ad Rates: GLR: $.32 **Circ:** ‡3,000
BW: $473.38
SAU: $4.42

12720 The Plaquemines Watchman
Plaquemines Newspaper Publishing, Inc.
7952 HWY 23 Phone: (504)392-1619
Belle Chasse, LA 70037 Fax: (504)393-9327

Local newspaper. **Founded:** May 2, 1981. **Freq:** Weekly (Tues.). **Print Method:** Offset. **Trim Size:** 14 3/4 x 21. **Cols./Page:** 6. **Col. Width:** 14 picas. **Col. Depth:** 301 agate lines. **Key Personnel:** Dale Benoit, Editor and Publisher; Norris Babin, Advertising Mgr. **Subscription Rates:** $20 individuals; $25 out of county; $30 out of state. **Remarks:** Accepts advertising.
Ad Rates: GLR: $.32 **Circ:** ‡3,000
BW: $473.38
SAU: $4.42

12721 KMEZ-FM - 102.9
1450 Poydras St. Phone: (504)593-2171
New Orleans, LA 70112 Fax: (504)593-1865

Format: Urban Contemporary. **Networks:** Satellite Radio. **Founded:** 1990. **Formerly:** KNOK-FM (1991). **Operating Hours:** 9:00 a.m. - 9:30 p.m., school days. **ADI:** New Orleans, LA. **Key Personnel:** Rob Moore, General Mgr.; Nick Ferrera, Program Mgr. **Local Programs:** *Around the Big Eazy*, David Blake; *The Plaquemines Billboard*, Tomeka F. Barrow. **Wattage:** 3000.

BERNICE

12722 Bernice Banner News
Tommy A. Welch
PO Box 568 Phone: (318)285-7424
Bernice, LA 71222 Fax: (318)285-7499

Community newspaper. **Founded:** Sept. 5, 1997. **Freq:** Weekly. **Cols./Page:** 6. **Col. Width:** 12.5 picas. **Key Personnel:** Tina T. Keith, Contact; Violet Lann, Contact. **USPS:** 013-217. **Subscription Rates:** $16 individuals; $20 out of state. **Remarks:** Accepts advertising.
Ad Rates: BW: $504 **Circ:** Paid ⊕598
PCI: $4

BOGALUSA, pop. 16,976.

E LA. Washington Parish. 60 mi. NE of New Orleans. Manufactures lumber, wood and creosoted products, paper, paper boxes and bags, turpentine, tungoil, auto body parts. Yellow pine, hardwood timber. Grain, truck farms. Sugarcane, sweet potatoes, corn, cotton.

12723 The Bogalusa Daily News
Pontchartrain Newspapers
525 Ave. V Phone: (504)732-2565
PO Box 820 Fax: (504)732-4006
Bogalusa, LA 70427-4413
General newspaper. **Founded:** 1931. **Freq:** Daily and Sunday. **Print Method:** Offset. **Cols./Page:** 6. **Col. Width:** 25 nonpareils. **Col. Depth:** 301 agate lines. **Key Personnel:** Lou Major, Publisher. **Subscription Rates:** $99 individuals. **Remarks:** Advertising accepted; rates available upon request.
Circ: ‡7,053

12724 SAC Newsmonthly
PO Box 159 Phone: (504)732-5616
Bogalusa, LA 70429-0159 Fax: (504)732-3744
Free: (800)825-3722

Magazine providing entry information about arts and crafts shows throughout the U.S. **Founded:** 1986. **Freq:** Monthly. **Print Method:** Offset. Uses mats. **Trim Size:** 10 x 13. **Cols./Page:** 4. **Col. Width:** 2 1/2 inches. **Col. Depth:** 13 inches. **Key Personnel:** Wayne Smith, Editor and Publisher. **ISSN:** 0731-2989. **Subscription Rates:** $24 individuals; $3 single issue. **Remarks:** Accepts advertising. **Merged with:** Art & Crafts Catalyst; Southern Arts & Crafts; Craft Show Bulletin; The National Calendar of Open Competitive Exhibitions; Lisa's Report; The National Arts & Crafts Network.
Ad Rates: GLR: $5 **Circ:** Paid ‡2,000
BW: $325 Non-paid ‡30
PCI: $2.5

12725 WIKC-AM - 1490
607 Rio Grande St. Phone: (504)732-4190
Box 638 Fax: (504)732-7594
Bogalusa, LA 70427

Format: Talk; News; Gospel. **Networks:** USA Radio. **Owner:** Gardner S. Adams, Jr., at above address, LA. **Founded:** 1947. **Operating Hours:** Continuous; 50% network, 50% local. **Key Personnel:** G.S. Adams, Jr., Contact. **Wattage:** 1000.

BOSSIER CITY, pop. 49,969.

NW LA. Bossier Parish. 1/2 mi. E. of Shreveport. Manufactures house trailers, air conditioning ducts, electrical parts, boat accessories, mattress, candy, toys. Tie preserving plant. Acid and sulphur. Agriculture. Corn, soybeans, cotton, alfalfa. Cattle, thoroughbred horses.

12726 Bossier Banner-Progress
Bossier Newspapers
PO Box 6267 Phone: (318)747-7900
Bossier City, LA 71171 Fax: (318)747-5298
Publisher E-mail: bpress@ciai.net

Community newspaper. **Founded:** 1859. **Freq:** Weekly (Wed.). **Print Method:** offset. **Cols./Page:** 6. **Col. Width:** 2 inches. **Col. Depth:** 21 inches. **Key Personnel:** Brian Blackley, Editor and Publisher; Pat Culverhouse, Managing Editor; Patrick Morrison, Advertising Dir. **Subscription Rates:** $17.50 in parish; $25 out of parish. **Remarks:** Accepts advertising.
Ad Rates: GLR: $1 **Circ:** ‡500
BW: $1,228.50
4C: $1,478.50
PCI: $6

12727 Bossier Press Tribune
Bossier Newspapers
PO Box 6267 Phone: (318)747-7900
Bossier City, LA 71171 Fax: (318)747-5298
Publisher E-mail: bpress@ciai.net

Community newspaper. **Founded:** 1928. **Freq:** Semiweekly (Mon. and Thurs.). **Print Method:** Offset. **Cols./Page:** 6. **Col. Width:** 12 picas. **Col. Depth:** 21 inches. **Key Personnel:** Brian Blackley, Editor and Publisher; Pat Culverhouse, Managing Editor; Patrick Morrison, Advertising Dir. **Subscription Rates:** $27 in parish; $35 out of parish. **Remarks:** Accepts advertising.
Ad Rates: GLR: $1 **Circ:** Paid 2,000
BW: $1,228.50 Free 300
4C: $1,478.50
PCI: $6.15

12728 UAE
725 Benton Rd. Phone: (318)747-1666
Bossier City, LA 71111 Fax: (318)746-2186

Founded: 1978. **Cities Served:** Bossier County, LA.

12729 United Artists Cable of Bossier City Inc.
Box 5697 Phone: (318)747-1666
Bossier City, LA 71171-5697 Fax: (318)746-2186

Key Personnel: Jim Nisewender, General Mgr.; Lee Anderson, Contact; Diane Bradley, Office Mgr. **Cities Served:** subscribing households 19,000; 1 community access channel.

BOURG

12730 Helicon Cable Communications
PO Box 610 Phone: (504)594-6823
Bourg, LA 70343 Fax: (504)594-7953
Free: (800)504-6823

Owner: 630 Palisade Ave., Englewood Cliffs, NJ 07632, Fax: (201)568-0150, Free: (800)666-2286. **Formerly:** Terrebonne CableVision (1992); Helicon CableVision. **Key Personnel:** Lisa Torbert, phone (504)594-6823, fax (504)594-7953, bourg@iamerica.net. **Cities Served:** subscribing households 11,581; 60 channels; 1 community access channel; 17 hours per week community access programming.

BOUTTE, pop. 500.

SE LA. Saint Charles Parish. 4 mi. NE of Paradis. Residential.

12731 St. Charles Herald-Guide
PO Box 1199 Phone: (504)758-2795
Boutte, LA 70039 Fax: (504)758-7000

Newspaper. **Founded:** 1873. **Freq:** Semiweekly (Wed. and Sat.). **Print Method:** Offset. **Cols./Page:** 6. **Col. Width:** 26 nonpareils. **Col. Depth:** 294 agate lines. **Key Personnel:** Allen J. Lottinger, Publisher; Michael Gorman, Managing Editor; Brent Madere, Advertising Mgr. **USPS:** 475-680. **Subscription Rates:** $10 individuals.
Ad Rates: GLR: $.14 **Circ:** ‡4,550

BOYCE

NC LA. Rapides Parish. 5 mi. S. of Flatwoods.

12732 KBCE-FM - 102.3
Box 69 Phone: (318)793-4003
Boyce, LA 71409 Fax: (318)793-8888

Format: Urban Contemporary. **Networks:** American Urban Radio. **Owner:** Warylene D. Lewis, 604 Windermere Blvd., Alexandria, LA 71303, (318)443-1443. **Founded:** 1982. **Operating Hours:** Continuous. **Key Personnel:** Warylene D. Lewis, President/Gen. Mgr. **Local Programs:** *Issues* 8-9 am. **Wattage:** 21,000. **Ad Rates:** Advertising accepted; rates available upon request.

BURAS

SE LA. Plaquemines Parish. 5 mi. N. of Fort Saint Philip.

12733 KAGY-AM - 1510
Hwy. 23 S. Phone: (504)657-5249
PO Box 1307 Fax: (504)657-5256
Buras, LA 70041
Free: (800)332-5249
E-mail: kagy@cis.compuserve.com

Format: Gospel. **Networks:** Independent. **Owner:** Miracle A/G, PO Box 1307, Buras, LA 70041. **Founded:** 1966. **Operating Hours:** Daytime; 100% local. **Key Personnel:** Max Latham, General Mgr. **Wattage:** 1000. **Ad Rates:** $3-6 for 30 seconds; $8-12 for 60 seconds.

12734 Plaquemines Cablevision
PO Box 7147 Phone: (504)392-4060
Buras, LA 70041-7147 Fax: (504)657-7535

Owner: Cable Management Assoc., PO Box 802068, Dallas, TX 75380, (214)233-9616. **Founded:** 1979. **Key Personnel:** John Helmers, General Mgr. **Cities Served:** subscribing households 5,000; 30 channels; 1 community access channel; 10 hours per week community access programming.

CALHOUN

12735 Journal of Vegetable Crop Production
The Haworth Press, Inc.
PO Box 539 Phone: (318)644-2663
Calhoun, LA 71225 Fax: (318)644-7244
Publisher E-mail: getinfo@haworthpressinc.com

Journal of research about the production of vegetable crops. **Founded:** 1995. **Freq:** Quarterly. **Cols./Page:** 1. **Col. Width:** 4 1/4 inches. **Col. Depth:** 6 1/2 inches. **Key Personnel:** M. LeRon Robbins, Editor, phone (318)644-2662, rrobbins@agctr.lsu.edu; Bill Cohen, Publisher. **ISSN:** 1049-6467. **Subscription Rates:** $24; $32 Industry; $42 libraries. **Remarks:** Accepts advertising.
Ad Rates: BW: $300 **Circ:** (Not Reported)

CHURCH POINT, pop. 4,599.

SW LA. Acadia Parish. 18 mi. NW of Lafayette. Rice mills; cotton gins. Agriculture.

12736 Church Point News
315 N. Main Phone: (318)684-5711
Drawer 319
Church Point, LA 70525
Community newspaper. **Founded:** 1921. **Freq:** Weekly (Wed.). **Print Method:** Offset. **Cols./Page:** 6. **Col. Width:** 26 nonpareils. **Col. Depth:** 301 agate lines. **Key Personnel:** Diane Daigle, Editor; Willie Pitre, Publisher. **Subscription Rates:** $21 individuals; $25 outside parish; $30 out of state. **Remarks:** Accepts advertising.
Ad Rates: GLR: $3.75 **Circ:** 1,600
SAU: $4.31
PCI: $3.75

CLINTON†, pop. 1,919.

C LA. East Feliciana Parish. Cotton gins, dairy farms.

12737 Clinton/East Feliciana Watchman
PO Box 368 Phone: (504)683-5195
Clinton, LA 70722-0368 Fax: (504)683-8982

Regional newspaper. **Founded:** 1878. **Freq:** Weekly. **Print Method:** Offset. **Cols./Page:** 6. **Col. Width:** 2 1/16 inches. **Col. Depth:** 21 1/2 inches. **Key Personnel:** Laura Struck, Editor; Jack Roberts, Publisher; Beverly Stockwell, Advertising Representative. **Subscription Rates:** $19.57 individuals.
Ad Rates: SAU: $3.90 **Circ:** ‡2,250

COLFAX†, pop. 1,680.

C LA. Grant Parish. On Red River, 20 mi. NW of Alexandria. Resort. Fishing, hunting and boating. Pine hardwood timber. Pine bark processing. Stock, truck, grain farms. Soybeans, cotton.

12738 The Chronicle
PO Box 248 Phone: (318)627-3737
Colfax, LA 71417-0248 Fax: (318)627-3019

Community newspaper. **Founded:** July 8, 1876. **Freq:** Weekly (Thurs.). **Print Method:** Offset. **Cols./Page:** 6. **Col. Width:** 26 nonpareils. **Col. Depth:** 294 agate lines. **Key Personnel:** Helen Richards, Editor; W.D. Richards, Jr., Publisher. **USPS:** 121-180. **Subscription Rates:** $11 individuals; $0.35 single issue. **Remarks:** Accepts advertising.
Ad Rates: GLR: $5 **Circ:** ‡3,000
PCI: $5

COLUMBIA†, pop. 687.

N LA. Caldwell Parish. 30 mi. S. of Monroe. Residential.

12739 Caldwell Watchman Progress
PO Box 1269 Phone: (318)649-6411
Columbia, LA 71418 Fax: (318)649-9368

Newspaper with Democratic orientation. **Subtitle:** Legal Journal for Caldwell Parish. **Founded:** 1885. **Freq:** Weekly (Wed.). **Print Method:** Offset. **Trim Size:** 13.75 x 22.0. **Cols./Page:** 6. **Col. Width:** 26 nonpareils. **Col. Depth:** 294 agate lines. **Key Personnel:** Paul Stanton, Mgr./Publisher, phone (318)728-2250; Susan Gartman, Editor, lsncol@aol.com; Amy Daunchl, Ad Rep. **Subscription Rates:** $15 individuals inside Caldwell Parish; $20 elsewhere in Louisiana; $25 out of state. **Remarks:** Accepts advertising.
Ad Rates: BW: $252 **Circ:** Wed. 7,848
4C: $492
SAU: $2
PCI: $3

12740 KCTO-AM - 1540
Box 1319 Phone: (318)649-2756
Columbia, LA 71418

Format: Gospel. **Networks:** Progressive Farmer; Louisiana. **Founded:** 1968. **Operating Hours:** Sunrise-sunset. **Key Personnel:** Tom Gay, Owner/Station Mgr.; Bill Mann, Operations Mgr. **Wattage:** 1000. **Ad Rates:** $2.50 for 30 seconds; $5 for 60 seconds.

COUSHATTA†, pop. 2,084.

NW LA. Red River Parish. On Red River, 45 mi. SE of Shreveport. Appliance and meat pie plants. Oil wells. Timber. Agriculture. Cotton, corn, hay, grain, soybeans. Beef cattle.

12741 The Coushatta Citizen
The Coushatta Citizen Shopper
1703 Ringgold Ave. Phone: (318)932-4201
PO Drawer 1365 Fax: (318)932-4285
Coushatta, LA 71019-2006
Community newspaper. **Founded:** 1871. **Freq:** Weekly (Thurs.). **Print Method:** Offset. **Cols./Page:** 6. **Col. Width:** 28 nonpareils. **Col. Depth:** 294 agate lines. **Key Personnel:** Marsha Loftin, Editor and Publisher. **Subscription Rates:** $18 individuals. **Remarks:** Accepts advertising.
Ad Rates: GLR: $.30 **Circ:** ‡2,900
BW: $635.04
4C: $826.68
SAU: $5.04
PCI: $5.04

12742 The Coushatta Citizen Shopper
1703 Ringgold Ave. Phone: (318)932-4201
PO Drawer 1365 Fax: (318)932-4285
Coushatta, LA 71019-2006
Shopper. **Founded:** 1980. **Freq:** Weekly (Thurs.). **Print Method:** Offset. **Cols./Page:** 6. **Col. Width:** 28 nonpareils. **Col. Depth:** 294 agate lines. **Key Personnel:** Marsha Loftin, Editor and Publisher. **Subscription Rates:** $18; $25 out of state. **Remarks:** Accepts advertising.
Ad Rates: GLR: $1.65 **Circ:** Free ‡3,900
BW: $207.90
4C: $225

12743 KRRP-AM - 950
Rte. 4, Box 197 Phone: (318)932-6704
Coushatta, LA 71019 Fax: (318)932-9700

Format: Classical. **Networks:** CBS. **Owner:** Bethard Broadcasting Corp., at above address. **Founded:** 1981. **Operating Hours:** Continuous. **ADI:** Shreveport, LA-Texarkana, TX. **Key Personnel:** David Graham, Sales Mgr./Production Dir. **Wattage:** 500 days 209 nights. **Ad Rates:** $10-15 for 30 seconds; $12-18 for 60 seconds.

COVINGTON†, pop. 7,892.

SE LA. Saint Tammany Parish. 38 mi. N. of New Orleans. Lumber, concrete products manufactured. Nurseries. Timber. Cattle. Thoroughbred horses.

12744 The News Banner
PO Drawer 90 Phone: (504)892-7980
Covington, LA 70433 Fax: (504)892-8242
Publisher E-mail: banner@neosoft.com

Community newspaper. **Founded:** June 1963. **Freq:** 3/week. **Print Method:** Web offset. **Cols./Page:** 6. **Col. Width:** 13 inches. **Col. Depth:** 21 1/2 inches. **Key Personnel:** Floyd Burckel, Publisher; Don Redman, Managing Editor, dredman@newsbanner.com; Scott Zelden, Business Development Dir., szelden@newsbanner.com. **ISSN:** 1073-9424. **Subscription Rates:** $49 individuals; Free to qualified subscribers. **Remarks:** Accepts advertising. **URL:** tamanet.com.
Ad Rates: GLR: $10.55 **Circ:** Controlled 22,500
BW: $1,360.95
4C: $1,585.95

12745 St. Tammany Farmer
St. Tammany Farmer, Inc.
PO Box 269 Phone: (504)892-2323
321 N. New Hampshire St. Fax: (504)892-2325
Covington, LA 70434
Community newspaper. **Founded:** 1874. **Freq:** Weekly (Wed.). **Print Method:** Offset. **Cols./Page:** 6. **Col. Width:** 25 nonpareils. **Col. Depth:** 294 agate lines. **Key Personnel:** Ellis T. Badon, Editor; Vera Hardman, General Mgr. **USPS:** 477-220. **Subscription Rates:** $15 individuals. **Remarks:** Accepts advertising.
Ad Rates: BW: $661.50 **Circ:** Paid ⊕4,000
4C: $741.50 Free ⊕125
SAU: $5.95
PCI: $5.95

12746 St. Tammany News-Banner
Pontchartrain Newspapers
PO Drawer 90 Phone: (504)892-7980
Covington, LA 70434 Fax: (504)892-8242
Publication E-mail: banner@neosoft.com

Newspaper. **Founded:** 1964. **Freq:** 3/week. **Print Method:** Offset. **Cols./Page:** 6. **Col. Width:** 25 nonpareils. **Col. Depth:** 301 agate lines. **Key Personnel:** Floyd Burckel, Editor and Publisher; Don Readman, Managing Editor; Barbara Eckert, Advertising Mgr.; Scott Zelden, Marketing & Ad Dir. **Subscription Rates:** $49 individuals; $30 six months; $15 three months. **Remarks:** Accepts advertising. **URL:** http://www.tamnet.com.
Ad Rates: GLR: $.25 **Circ:** Paid 5,000
BW: $790.77 Non-paid 17,500
4C: $940.77
SAU: $6.13

CROWLEY†, pop. 16,036.

SW LA. Acadia Parish. 73 mi. SW of Baton Rouge. Manufactures burlap bags, men's slacks, farm machinery, steel - aluminum pipes. Oil, gas wells. Agriculture. Rice, cotton. soybeans. Livestock.

12747 The Crowley Post-Signal
Crowley Post-Signal
602 N. Parkerson Ave. Phone: (318)783-3450
Box 1589 Fax: (318)788-0949
Crowley, LA 70526
Publication E-mail: crowleyps@aol.com

General newspaper. **Founded:** 1898. **Freq:** Tues.-Fri. (eve.); Sun. (morn.). **Print Method:** Letterpress and offset. **Cols./Page:** 6. **Col. Width:** 25 nonpareils. **Col. Depth:** 297 agate lines. **Key Personnel:** Harold Gonzales, Editor; Milo A. Nickel, Publisher. **Subscription Rates:** $84 individuals. **Remarks:** Accepts advertising.
Ad Rates: GLR: $7 **Circ:** 5,878
BW: $903
4C: $1,238.50
SAU: $7

12748 Lake Arthur Sun-Times
Louisiana State Newspapers
602 N. Parkerson Phone: (318)774-2527
Crowley, LA 70526
Community newspaper. **Founded:** 1984. **Freq:** Weekly. **Key Personnel:** Roxi Roy, Manager. **Subscription Rates:** $18.72 local; $80 out of parish; $24 out of state; $18.72 individuals; $.75 single copy. **Remarks:** Accepts advertising.
Ad Rates: GLR: $5 **Circ:** 1,200

12749 Crowley Cable TV
2010 N. Parkerson Ave. Phone: (318)783-5931
Crowley, LA 70526

Key Personnel: Ray Mayo, Manager. **Cities Served:** subscribing households 6,958; 29 channels.

12750 KAJN-FM - 102.9
110 W. 3rd St. Phone: (318)783-1560
Crowley, LA 70526 Fax: (318)783-1674

Format: Religious. **Networks:** USA Radio. **Owner:** Agape Broadcasters, Inc., Box 1469, Crowley, LA 70527. **Founded:** 1977. **Operating Hours:** Continuous; 5% network, 95% local. **ADI:** Lafayette, LA. **Key Personnel:** Barry D. Thompson, Contact; Annette G. Thompson, Vice President; Bryan Riveria, Sales Mgr. **Wattage:** 100,000. **Ad Rates:** $15-22.10 for 30 seconds; $22.20-33.35 for 60 seconds.

12751 KSIG-AM - 1450
320 N. Parkerson Ave. Phone: (318)783-2520
Crowley, LA 70526 Fax: (318)783-5744

Format: Country. **Founded:** 1947. **Key Personnel:** Julius Meax, Contact; Chuck Childress, Program Dir.; Tony Evan, Chief Engineer. **Wattage:** 1000.

DELHI, pop. 3,290.

NE LA. Richland Parish. 30 mi. E. of Monroe. Cotton gins, compresses and warehouses. Manufactures aluminum boats, fiber glass. Oil, gas wells. Hardwood timber. Agriculture. Cotton, oats, corn, soybeans.

12752 The Delhi Dispatch
701 1/2 Broadway Phone: (318)878-2444
PO Box 608 Fax: (318)878-3186
Delhi, LA 71232-0608
Community oriented newspaper. **Founded:** July 11, 1934. **Freq:** Weekly (Thurs.). **Print Method:** Offset. **Trim Size:** 7 x 11. **Cols./Page:** 6. **Col. Width:** 2 1/16 inches. **Col. Depth:** 294 agate lines. **Key Personnel:** Gene Cloninger, Editor. **USPS:** 152-320. **Subscription Rates:** $15 individuals; $26 in state; $25 out of state. **Remarks:** Accepts advertising.
Ad Rates: SAU: $3 **Circ:** ‡1,400

DENHAM SPRINGS, pop. 8,412.

SE LA. Livingston Parish. 16 mi. E. of Baton Rouge. Manufactures wood products, plywood, metal doors, sashes, frames, sewage treatment units. Timber. Poultry, truck farms. Strawberries, sheep, cattle raising.

12753 News
Donham Springs Publishing
688 Hatchell Ln. Phone: (504)665-5176
PO Box 1529 Fax: (504)667-0167
Denham Springs, LA 70727
Newspaper. **Founded:** 1898. **Freq:** Semiweekly (Mon. and Thurs.). **Print Method:** Offset. **Cols./Page:** 6. **Col. Width:** 22 nonpareils. **Col. Depth:** 294 agate lines. **Key Personnel:** James E. Minton, Editor; Jeff M. David, Publisher. **Subscription Rates:** $14 individuals.

DEQUINCY, pop. 3,966.

SW LA. Calcasieu Parish. 25 mi. NW of Lake Charles. Oil, gas wells. Lumber. Rice. Agriculture. Cattle raising.

12754 Cameron Parish Pilot
PO Box 995 Phone: (318)786-8004
DeQuincy, LA 70633 Fax: (318)786-8131
Free: (800)256-7323

Community newspaper. **Founded:** 1956. **Freq:** Weekly (Thurs.). **Print Method:** Offset. **Cols./Page:** 6. **Col. Width:** 24 nonpareils. **Col. Depth:** 295 agate lines. **Key Personnel:** Jerry E. Wise, Editor and Publisher, jwise@mail.ld.centuryinter.net; Jeff Wise, Advertising Mgr. **Subscription Rates:** $15.30 individuals. **Remarks:** Accepts advertising.
Ad Rates: GLR: $.36 **Circ:** ‡2,300
BW: $630.60
SAU: $6.50
PCI: $5

12755 The DeQuincy News
203 E. Harrsion Phone: (318)786-8004
PO Box 995 Fax: (318)786-8131
DeQuincy, LA 70633
Free: (800)256-7323

Community newspaper. **Founded:** 1923. **Freq:** Weekly (Wed.). **Print Method:** Offset. **Trim Size:** 13 x 21. **Cols./Page:** 6. **Col. Width:** 24 nonpareils. **Col. Depth:** 295 agate lines. **Key Personnel:** Jerry E. Wise, Editor and Publisher; Jeffra Wise, Advertising Mgr. **Subscription Rates:** $14.56 individuals; $26 out of state. **Remarks:** Accepts advertising.
Ad Rates: GLR: $.27 **Circ:** ‡3,500
BW: $630
SAU: $6.50

DERIDDER

12756 Beauregard Daily News
News Leader, Inc.
PO Box 698 Phone: (318)462-0616
Deridder, LA 70634-0698 Fax: (318)463-5347

Community newspaper. **Founded:** 1945. **Freq:** 5/week. **Print Method:** Offset. **Cols./Page:** 6. **Col. Width:** 26 nonpareils. **Col. Depth:** 294 agate lines. **Key Personnel:** Bob Houston, Editor; Erbon W. Wise, Publisher; Beaux Victor, Advertising Dir. **Subscription Rates:** $52 individuals. **Remarks:** Accepts advertising.
Ad Rates: GLR: $.69 **Circ:** Paid ‡8,400
BW: $1,234.80 Free ‡5,400
4C: $1,684.80
SAU: $11.05

12757 Guardian
News Leader, Inc.
PO Box 846 Phone: (318)463-6204
Deridder, LA 70634 Fax: (318)463-5347

Military newspaper for Fort Polk and the Joint Readiness Training Center. **Founded:** 1961. **Freq:** Weekly (Fri.) (Tues. and Fri.). **Print Method:** Offset. **Trim Size:** 9 3/4 x 13. **Cols./Page:** 6. **Col. Width:** 9 picas. **Col. Depth:** 13 inches. **Key Personnel:** Linda Thompson, Editor; Al Gensheimer, Publisher; Beavy Victor, Advertising Mgr. **Remarks:** Accepts advertising.
Ad Rates: BW: $900.90 **Circ:** Free ‡15,000
4C: $1,350.90
PCI: $13

12758 KROK-FM - 92.1
PO Box 1180 Phone: (318)463-9292
Deridder, LA 70634 Fax: (318)463-9291
E-mail: krok@krok.com

Format: Adult Album Alternative. **Networks:** Independent. **Owner:** West Central Broadcasting Co., Inc., at above address. **Founded:** 1985. **Operating Hours:** Continuous. **ADI:** Lake Charles, LA. **Key Personnel:** Doug Stannard, General Mgr., doug@krok.com; Sandy Edwards, Music Dir., sandy@krok.com; Doug Stannard, General Sales Mgr., doug@krok.com. **Wattage:** 25,000. **Ad Rates:** $9.41 for 30 seconds; $17.65 for 60 seconds. Combined advertising rates available with KVVP-FM. **URL:** http://www.krok.com.

DODSON

12759 The Piney Woods Journal
Chealaigh Shamrock
PO Box 190
Dodson, LA 71422

Newspaper for the timber, forestry, and forest products industry. **Founded:** June 1997. **Freq:** Monthly. **Print Method:** Offset. **Trim Size:** 11 1/4 x 15. **Cols./Page:** 6. **Col. Width:** 9.6 picas. **Col. Depth:** 14 inches. **Key Personnel:** Troy Thomas Kelly, Editor and Publisher. **Subscription Rates:** $20 individuals. **Remarks:** Accepts advertising.
Ad Rates: PCI: $8.40 **Circ:** Combined 15,000

12760 Quote
Chealaigh Shamrock
PO Box 190
Dodson, LA 71422

Magazine containing humorous, inspirational, and other material for public speakers. **Subtitle:** The Speakers Digest. **Founded:** 1940. **Freq:** Monthly. **Print Method:** Offset. **Trim Size:** 5 1/2 x 8. **Cols./Page:** 2. **Col. Width:** 12 picas. **Col. Depth:** 6.5 inches. **Key Personnel:** T. Thomas Kelly, Editor and Publisher, ttkelly@delphi.com. **ISSN:** 0273-6705. **Subscription Rates:** $37.95 individuals; $45 Canada and Mexico; $55 other countries; $68 two years; $2 single issue. **Remarks:** Accepts advertising.
Ad Rates: BW: $156 **Circ:** ‡5,000
4C: $306
PCI: $15

DONALDSONVILLE†, pop. 7,901.

SE LA. Ascension Parish. On Mississippi River, 63 mi. NW of New Orleans. Syrup mills, foundry, hatchery. Oil and gas refinery. Sugarcane loader, fertilizer, synthetics, tool, aluminum factories. Diversified farming. Sugarcane.

12761 Donaldsonville Chief
402 Railroad Ave. Phone: (225)473-3101
PO Box 309 Fax: (225)473-4060
Donaldsonville, LA 70346
Community newspaper. **Founded:** 1870. **Freq:** Weekly (Thurs.). **Print Method:** Offset. **Cols./Page:** 6. **Col. Width:** 21 nonpareils. **Col. Depth:** 293 agate lines. **Key Personnel:** Ella Metrejean, Publisher; Theresa Cavalier, General Mgr. **Subscription Rates:** $19.50.
Ad Rates: GLR: $4.60 **Circ:** Paid ‡3,000
PCI: $4.60 Non-paid ‡3,000

12762 KKAY-AM - 1590
3365 Hwy. 1 S. Phone: (225)473-6397
Donaldsonville, LA 70346 Fax: (225)474-0073

Format: Gospel. **Networks:** Independent. **Founded:** 1976. **Formerly:** KSMI-AM. **Operating Hours:** Sunrise-sunset. **Key Personnel:** Marcy LeBlanc, General Mgr.; Pat Guillot, Sales Mgr. **Wattage:** 1000. **Ad Rates:** $7-7.50 for 30 seconds; $10.50 for 60 seconds. Combined advertising rates available with KKAY-FM.

12763 KKAY-FM - 104.9
3365 Hwy. 1 S. Phone: (225)473-5764
Donaldsonville, LA 70346-9198 Fax: (225)474-0073

Format: Oldies. **Simulcasts:** KSMI-FM. **Networks:** Independent. **Founded:** 1972. **Formerly:** KSMI-FM. **Operating Hours:** 5:00a.m.-midnight. **Key Personnel:** Twink Alford, Sales Mgr., phone (504)473-6397; Nancy LeBlanc, General Mgr. **Wattage:** 3000. **Ad Rates:** $5-7 for 15 seconds; $8-12 for 30 seconds; $13-16 for 60 seconds. Combined advertising rates available with KKAY-AM.

DRY PRONG

12764 KVDP-FM - 89.1
Box 214 Phone: (318)899-5837
Dry Prong, LA 71423 Fax: (318)899-7624
E-mail: kvdpradio@popalex1.linknet.net

Format: Religious; Educational. **Networks:** Ambassador Inspirational Radio; USA Radio. **Founded:** 1985. **Operating Hours:** Continuous. **Key Personnel:** Coy Edwards, President; Leta Edwards, General Mgr.; Rhonda Edwards, Music Dir.; Lonnie Hutto, Chief Engineer; Rick Hicks, Program Dir. **Wattage:** 4,500.

EUNICE, pop. 12,479.

SC LA. Saint Landry Parish. 45 mi. NW of Lafayette. Sports apparel and furniture manufactured. Processing plants. Oil and gas wells. Rice, cattle, soybeans.

12765 Bayou Bengal
Louisiana State University at Eunice
Box 1129 Phone: (318)550-1211
Eunice, LA 70535 Fax: (318)546-6620

College newspaper. **Founded:** 1967. **Freq:** Monthly. **Print Method:** Web offset. **Trim Size:** 9 3/4 x 13. **Cols./Page:** 5. **Col. Width:** 1 3/4 inches. **Col. Depth:** 13 inches. **Subscription Rates:** Free. **Remarks:** Accepts advertising.
Ad Rates: PCI: $1.75 **Circ:** Non-paid 1,000

12766 The Eunice News
The Moody Co.
251 N. 2nd St. Phone: (318)457-3061
PO Box 989 Fax: (318)457-3122
Eunice, LA 70535-0989
General newspaper. **Founded:** 1904. **Freq:** Tues.-Fri. (eve.); Sun. (morn.). **Print Method:** Offset. **Cols./Page:** 6. **Col. Width:** 25 nonpareils. **Col. Depth:** 301 agate lines. **Key Personnel:** Jerry Hoffpauir, Editor; Gary Miller, Advertising Mgr. **Subscription Rates:** $36 individuals. **Remarks:** Accepts advertising.
Ad Rates: SAU: $4.26 **Circ:** (Not Reported)

12767 KBAZ-FM - 102.1
PO Box 391 Phone: (318)457-3543
Eunice, LA 70535-0391

Format: Country. **Networks:** Satellite Music Network. **Founded:** 1990. **Operating Hours:** Continuous. **Key Personnel:** Robert L. Fontenot, Contact; Jocelyn Bradley, Traffic Mgr.; Missy B. Benoit, Contact; Edna Poullard, Contact. **Wattage:** 25,000. **Ad Rates:** $4.30-5.75 for 30 seconds; $6.45-8.60 for 60 seconds.

12768 KEUN-AM - 105.5
330 W. Waurel Phone: (318)457-3041
PO Box 1049 Fax: (318)457-3081
Eunice, LA 70535

Format: Country; Sports; News; Cajun. **Owner:** Tri Parish Broadcasting, Inc, at above address. **Founded:** 1981. **Operating Hours:** Continuous. **ADI:** Lafayette, LA. **Key Personnel:** Karl Rene de Rouen, Contact; Steve Coppini, Operations Mgr.; Tom Voinche, Sr., Sales Mgr. **Local Programs:** *Coffee Talk* 7:15am -7:50am Monday-Friday, Karl Rene de Rouen. **Wattage:** 1000. **Ad Rates:** $9-12 for 30 seconds; $12-14.25 for 60 seconds. Combined advertising rates available with KJJB-FM.

12769 KJJB-FM - 105.5
PO Box 1049 Phone: (318)457-3041
Eunice, LA 70535 Fax: (318)457-3081

Format: Oldies. **Owner:** Tri-Parish Broadcasting, Inc., at above address. **Founded:** 1980. **Operating Hours:** Continuous. **ADI:** Lafayette, LA. **Key Personnel:** Karl Rene' De Rouen, Pres./General Mgr.; Tom C. Voinche, Compliance Mgr.; Angelle Richard, Traffic Dir.; Steve Coppini, News and Sports Director; Sterling Burleigh, Ethnic Music Dir.; Linda Bellow, Local Sales Mgr. **Local Programs:** *Coffeetalk* 7:15 am - 7:50 am Monday-Friday; *Cajun Music* Sat. - Sun. **Wattage:** 3,000. **Ad Rates:** $11 for 30 seconds; $15 for 60 seconds.

FARMERVILLE

12770 The Gazette
Union Publishing Co.
102 Washington Phone: (318)368-9732
PO Box 722 Fax: (318)368-7331
Farmerville, LA 71241
Community newspaper. **Founded:** 1878. **Freq:** Weekly (Thurs.). **Print Method:** Offset. **Cols./Page:** 6. **Col. Width:** 12.5 picas. **Col. Depth:** 21 inches. **Key Personnel:** Donna Miller, Editor; Carlton White, Publisher. **Subscription Rates:** $20; $25 out of area; $30 out of state. **Remarks:** Accepts advertising. **Formerly:** Farmerville Gazette.
Ad Rates: SAU: $5 **Circ:** ‡4,200

FERRIDAY, pop. 4,472.

NE LA. Concordia Parish. 10 mi. NW of Natchez, MS. Timber, corn.

12771 The Concordia Sentinel
PO Box 312 Phone: (318)757-3646
Ferriday, LA 71334 Fax: (318)757-3001

Community newspaper. **Founded:** 1876. **Freq:** Weekly (Wed.). **Print Method:** offset. **Cols./Page:** 6. **Col. Width:** 2 inches. **Col. Depth:** 21 inches. **Key Personnel:** Sam Hanna, Publisher; Hope Young, Community Editor; Cora Morace, Advertising Mgr. **Subscription Rates:** $20 individuals. **Remarks:** Accepts advertising. **Alt. Formats:** CD-ROM.
Ad Rates: SAU: $4 **Circ:** ‡5,500
PCI: $4.50

12772 KFNV-AM - 1600
PO Box 592 Phone: (318)757-4200
Ferriday, LA 71334 Fax: (318)757-7689
Free: (800)784-1071

Format: Religious. **Networks:** Unistar; Louisiana; Progressive Farmer. **Founded:** 1956. **Operating Hours:** Sunrise-sunset. **Key Personnel:** Hugh Matthews, Manager. **Wattage:** 1000. **Ad Rates:** $5.50 for 30 seconds; $6.50 for 60 seconds.

12773 KFNV-FM - 107.1
PO Box 592 Phone: (318)757-4200
Ferriday, LA 71334 Fax: (318)757-7689
Free: (800)784-1071

Format: Oldies. **Networks:** Louisiana; Westwood One Radio; Mississippi. **Owner:** Desiree' Smith, at above address, (318)649-7959. **Founded:** 1971. **Formerly:** KSTH-FM (1994). **Operating Hours:** Continuous. **Key Personnel:** Desiree Smith, General Mgr.; Jennie Pecanty, Traffic/Program Mgr. **Wattage:** 18,500. **Ad Rates:** $8.50 for 30 seconds; $10 for 60 seconds.

FOLSOM, pop. 319.

E LA. Tammany Parish. 25 mi. SW of Bogalusa. Residential.

12774 Whispering Wind
Written Heritage
PO Box 1390 Phone: (504)796-5433
Folsom, LA 70437-1390 Fax: (504)796-9236
Free: (800)301-8009
Publication E-mail: whiswind@i-55.com
Publisher E-mail: whiswind@i-55.com

Magazine covering historical events, crafts, and material culture of the American Indian. **Subtitle:** American Indian: Past and Present. **Founded:** Oct. 1967. **Freq:** Bimonthly. **Print Method:** Offset. **Trim Size:** 8 1/2 x 11. **Cols./Page:** 2. **Col. Width:** 35 nonpareils. **Col. Depth:** 151 agate lines. **Key Personnel:** Jack B. Heriard, Editor. **ISSN:** 0300-6565. **Subscription Rates:** $20 individuals; $32 other countries; $5 single issue. **Remarks:** Accepts advertising. **Online:** Infonautics Corp. **URL:** whisperingwind.com. **Alt. Formats:** Mailing labels.
Ad Rates: BW: $335 **Circ:** ‡24,000
4C: $835

FRANKLIN†, pop. 9,584.

S LA. Saint Mary Parish. On Bayou Teche. Oil wells, timber. Manufactures lumber, sugar. Agriculture. Sugarcane, rice.

12775 Franklin Banner-Tribune
115 Wilson St. Phone: (318)828-3706
PO Box 566 Fax: (318)828-2874
Franklin, LA 70538-6150
General newspaper. **Founded:** 1885. **Freq:** Daily (eve.). **Print Method:** Offset. **Cols./Page:** 6. **Col. Width:** 24 nonpareils. **Col. Depth:** 294 agate lines. **Key Personnel:** Paul Godfrey, Managing Editor; Allan R. Von Werder, Publisher. **USPS:** 516-320. **Subscription Rates:** $25 individuals. **Remarks:** Accepts advertising.
Ad Rates: BW: $378 **Circ:** Paid 3,280
4C: $678 Non-paid 1,720
PCI: $4.20

FRANKLINTON

12776 Franklinton Era-Leader
The Leader
1137 Main St. Phone: (504)839-9077
PO Drawer F Fax: (504)839-9077
Franklinton, LA 70438
Community newspaper. **Founded:** June 12, 1910. **Freq:** Weekly (Wed.). **Print Method:** Offset. **Cols./Page:** 6. **Col. Width:** 12 1/5 picas. **Col. Depth:** 21 inches. **USPS:** 175-267. **Subscription Rates:** $18. **Remarks:** Accepts advertising.
Ad Rates: PCI: $4.60 **Circ:** 3,485

12777 WFCG-AM - 1110
Box 604 Phone: (504)839-4110
Franklinton, LA 70438 Fax: (504)839-4800

Format: Country. **Simulcasts:** Combined advertising rates available with WFCY-FM. **Networks:** Louisiana. **Owner:** GACO Broadcasting Network, at above address. **Founded:** 1966. **Operating Hours:** Continuous. **Key Personnel:** J.A. Gatewood, Pres./Chief Engineer; Vickie DeCarlo, Sales/Music Dir./News Dir./Mgr.; Vicki DeCarlo, News Dir./Mgr. **Wattage:** 6000. **Ad Rates:** $5 for 30 seconds; $8 for 60 seconds.

GOLDEN MEADOW

12778 Callais Cablevision Inc.
315 Callais Ln. Phone: (504)475-7111
Golden Meadow, LA 70357 Fax: (504)475-6390
Free: (800)256-5665

Key Personnel: Harold Callais, General Mgr. **Cities Served:** Cut Off, Golden Meadow, and Galliano, LA.

GONZALES, pop. 7,287.

SE LA. Ascension Parish. 22 mi. SE of Baton Rouge. Oil wells, timber. Ships vegetables. Truck farms. Sugarcane, strawberries, beans.

12779 Community Mirror
Gonzales Weekly
PO Box 38 Phone: (225)647-4569
Gonzales, LA 70707-0038 Fax: (225)644-8238
Publisher E-mail: gonzwkly@eatel.net

Shopper. **Founded:** 1972. **Freq:** Weekly (Tues.). **Print Method:** Offset. **Cols./Page:** 6. **Col. Width:** 2 inches. **Col. Depth:** 21 1/2 inches. **Key Personnel:** Arlene Bishop, Editor/Mgr.; C.A. Bishop, Publisher. **Subscription Rates:** Free. **Remarks:** Accepts advertising.
Ad Rates: GLR: $.44 **Circ:** Free ‡24,000
BW: $5.82
4C: $143
PCI: $5.82

12780 Gonzales Weekly
PO Box 38 Phone: (225)647-4569
Gonzales, LA 70707-0038 Fax: (225)644-8238
Publisher E-mail: gonzwkly@eatel.net

Newspaper with a Democratic orientation. **Founded:** 1920. **Freq:** Weekly (Fri.). **Print Method:** Offset. **Cols./Page:** 6. **Col. Width:** 2 inches. **Col. Depth:** 21 1/2 inches. **Key Personnel:** C.A. Bishop, Publisher; Arlene Bishop, Editor. **Subscription Rates:** $25 individuals; $30 out of county. **Remarks:** Accepts advertising.
Ad Rates: GLR: $.44 **Circ:** ‡8,000
BW: $5.82
4C: $143
PCI: $5.82

GRAMBLING

12781 KGRM-FM - 91.5
Drawer K Phone: (318)274-6343
Grambling, LA 71245 Fax: (318)274-3245

Format: Urban Contemporary. **Owner:** Grambling State University, at above address. **Founded:** 1974. **Operating Hours:** 6:00 a.m.-midnight. **Key Personnel:** Joyce Evans, Operations/General Mgr., evans;b@vaxo.gram.edu. **Wattage:** 50,000. **Ad Rates:** Noncommercial.

GREENSBURG†, pop. 662.

E LA. Saint Helena Parish. 70 mi. NW of New Orleans. Feed mills. Dairy - truck farms, beef, chicken. Agriculture.

12782 St. Helena Echo
PO Box 190 Phone: (504)222-4541
Greensburg, LA 70441 Fax: (504)708-7104

Community newspaper. **Founded:** 1857. **Freq:** Weekly (Wed.). **Print Method:** Offset. **Cols./Page:** 7. **Col. Width:** 26 nonpareils. **Col. Depth:** 301 agate lines. **Key Personnel:** Carol Brooke, Publisher; Trish Adams, Managing Editor; Fran Snoddy, Customer Service Rep.; Karen McDaniel, Advertising Mgr. **Subscription Rates:** $30 individuals. **Remarks:** Accepts advertising.
Ad Rates: SAU: $4.39 **Circ:** ‡1,900

HAMMOND, pop. 15,043.

SE LA. Tangipahoa Parish. 43 mi. E. of Baton Rouge. Southeastern Louisiana University. Manufactures strawberry crates, mobile homes, plywood, boxes, bricks, foam products, candy, beverages, cabinets, women's wear. Steel mill. Pine, hardwood timber. Truck, dairy, poultry farms. Strawberries.

12783 Hammond Daily Star
Daily Star Publishing Co.
725 S. Morrison Blvd.
Hammond, LA 70404

General newspaper. **Founded:** 1959. **Freq:** Daily (eve.), Sunday (morn.). **Print Method:** Offset. **Trim Size:** 13 3/4 x 22 3/4. **Cols./Page:** 6. **Col. Width:** 2 1/32 inches. **Col. Depth:** 21 1/2 inches. **Key Personnel:** Lil Mirando, Editor; David K. Frazer, Publisher; Liz Black, Advertising Mgr. **Subscription Rates:** $96 individuals; $126.36 by mail. **Remarks:** Accepts advertising.
Ad Rates: BW: $1,149.39 **Circ:** Mon.-Fri. ★12,728
4C: $1,499.39 Sun. ★14,370
SAU: $9.94

12784 Journal of Herpetology
Society for the Study of Amphibians and Reptiles
SE Louisiana University Phone: (504)549-5556
SLU 814 Fax: (504)549-3851
Hammond, LA 70402
Publisher E-mail: ssar@slu.edu

Scientific journal on herpetology of the Society for the Study of Amphibians and Reptiles. **Founded:** 1968. **Freq:** Quarterly. **Key Personnel:** Richard A. Seigel, Editor, rseigel@elu.edu. **ISSN:** 0022-1511. **Subscription Rates:** $40 individuals; $8 single issue plus postage. **Remarks:** Advertising not accepted.
Circ: Combined 2,550

12785 The Lion's Roar
Southeastern Louisiana University
SLU 877 Phone: (504)549-3731
Hammond, LA 70403 Fax: (504)549-3842
Publisher E-mail: mtarver@selw.edu

Collegiate newspaper. **Founded:** 1937. **Freq:** Weekly (Thurs.). **Print Method:** Offset. **Cols./Page:** 6. **Col. Width:** 22 nonpareils. **Col. Depth:** 129 agate lines. **Key Personnel:** Beverly Costanza, Advertising Mgr., bcostanza@selu.edu. **Subscription Rates:** Free; $12 by mail semester.
Ad Rates: PCI: $4 **Circ:** Free ‡5,500

12786 Star Shopping Guide
Daily Star Publishing Co.
PO Box 1149 Phone: (504)345-2333
Hammond, LA 70404-1149 Fax: (504)542-0242
Free: (800)844-2333

Shopper. **Founded:** 1973. **Freq:** Semiweekly (Wed. and Sun.). **Print Method:** Offset. **Cols./Page:** 6. **Col. Width:** 26 nonpareils. **Col. Depth:** 301 agate lines. **Key Personnel:** Lil Mirando, Editor; David K. Frazer, Publisher; Liz Black, Advertising Mgr. **Subscription Rates:** $11.43 individuals; $12.71 institutions. **Remarks:** Accepts advertising. **URL:** http://www.nixonnews.com/star.
Ad Rates: SAU: $5.69 **Circ:** Wed. ‡16,800
Sun. ‡15,900

12787 Charter Communications
PO Box 1478 Phone: (504)542-8969
Hammond, LA 70404 Fax: (504)542-2950
Free: (800)888-2954

Owner: Charter Communications, 12444 Powerscourt Dr., Ste. 100, St. Louis, MO 63131, (314)965-5055. **Founded:** 1994. **Formerly:** Parish Cablevision. **Key Personnel:** Dave Bach, General Mgr. **Cities Served:** Communities in Livingston, Saint Tammany and Tangipahoa Pari shes, LA.: subscribing households 36,000; 56 channels; 1 community access channel.

12788 KSLU-FM - 90.9
Box 783, University Sta. Phone: (504)549-2330
Hammond, LA 70402 Fax: (504)549-3960
E-mail: kslu@i-55.com

Format: Public Radio; Ethnic. **Networks:** Public Radio International (PRI). **Founded:** 1979. **Operating Hours:** Continuous; 35% network, 65% local. **ADI:** Baton Rouge, LA. **Key Personnel:** Ron Nethercutt, General Mgr.; Tim Chauvin, News Dir.; Larry Ward, Chief Engineer; John Pisciotta, Program Dir.; Joyce Savoie, Contact; Shawn Manguno, Music Dir. **Local Programs:** *Morning News*, Shanna Sissom. **Wattage:** 3000 ERP. **Ad Rates:** Noncommercial; underwriting available. **URL:** http://www.i-55.com/kslu.

12789 WFPR-AM - 1400
PO Box 1829 Phone: (504)542-1400
Hammond, LA 70404-1829 Fax: (504)542-9377

Format: Talk; Country. **Owner:** Airweb, Inc., PO Box 1829, Hammond, LA 70404. **Founded:** 1947. **Operating Hours:** Continuous. **Key Personnel:** Steven Chauvin, General Mgr.; Johnny Chaurin, Program Dir.; Nanette Guen, Vice President. **Wattage:** 1000. **Ad Rates:** $15 for 30 seconds; $24 for 60 seconds.

12790 WHMD-FM - 107.1
200 E. Thomas St. Phone: (504)542-1400
Hammond, LA 70403 Fax: (504)542-9377

Format: Country. **Networks:** AP. **Owner:** Airweb, Inc., PO Box 1829, Hammond, LA 70404. **Founded:** 1974. **Operating Hours:** Continuous. **Key Personnel:** Nanette Guerin, Vice President; Steven Chauvin, General Mgr.; Johnny Chaurin, Program Dir. **Wattage:** 3000. **Ad Rates:** $15 for 30 seconds; $24 for 60 seconds.

HARAHAN

12791 Cox Cable Jefferson Parish
338 Edwards Ave. Phone: (504)733-5680
Harahan, LA 70123 Fax: (504)734-0869

Founded: 1979. **Cities Served:** Jefferson and Plaquemines counties, Gretna, Harahan, Jean Lafitte, Kenner Plaquemines Parish, and Westwego, LA.

HAYNESVILLE, pop. 3,454.

N LA. Claiborne Parish. 50 mi. NE of Shreveport. Manufactures work gloves, protective clothing, plywood. Oil, gas wells, timber. Agriculture.

12792 The Haynesville News
PO Box 269
Haynesville, LA 71038

Community and parish newspaper. **Founded:** 1920. **Freq:** Weekly (Thurs.). **Print Method:** Offset. **Trim Size:** 14 x 22 3/4. **Cols./Page:** 6. **Col. Width:** 2 1/16 inches. **Col. Depth:** 21 inches. **Key Personnel:** Paige Reeder, Editor. **USPS:** 238-040. **Subscription Rates:** $14 individuals; $24 out of area; $.35 single issue. **Remarks:** Accepts advertising.
Ad Rates: BW: $403.20 **Circ:** Paid ‡2,754
4C: $578.20 Free ‡35
SAU: $3.5
PCI: $2.24

12793 KWHN-FM - 105.5
714 S. Joliet St.
Joliet, IL 60436-2714

Format: Easy Listening. **Simulcasts:** KLVU-AM. **Founded:** 1984. **Wattage:** 3000.

HOMER†, pop. 4,307.

WC LA. Claiborne Parish. 47 mi. ENE of Shreveport. Trading center of timber section, petroleum deposits.

12794 The Guardian-Journal
PO Box 119 Phone: (318)927-3541
Homer, LA 71040 Fax: (318)927-3542

Community newspaper. **Founded:** 1876. **Freq:** Weekly. **Print Method:** Offset. **Cols./Page:** 6. **Col. Width:** 12 picas. **Key Personnel:** Janice M. Ellis, Editor; Geraldine H. Hightower, Publisher; G. Wesley Spillers, Jr., Advertising Mgr. **Subscription Rates:** $15.60 individuals; $21.84 out of area; $25 out of state. **Remarks:** Accepts advertising.
Ad Rates: BW: $403.20 **Circ:** Paid 2,400
4C: $641.20 Free 1,100
SAU: $3
PCI: $2.20

HOUMA†, pop. 32,602.

S LA. Terrebonne Parish. 53 mi. SW of New Orleans, on the Intracoastal Waterway. Seafood industry; shrimp, oyster, crabs. Commercial fishing. Oil and gas industry. Agriculture. Sugarcane, soybean.

12795 The Bayou Catholic
H.T. Publishing Co.
PO Box 9077 Phone: (504)850-3132
Houma, LA 70361 Fax: (504)850-3215

Official newspaper (tabloid) of the Diocese of Houma-Thibodaux. **Founded:** 1980. **Freq:** Weekly. **Print Method:** Offset. **Trim Size:** Tabloid. **Cols./Page:** 6. **Col. Width:** 9 picas. **Col. Depth:** 13 inches. **Key Personnel:** Louis Aguirre, Editor, phone (504)850-3215, editor@cajun.net; Robert Lindley, Advertising Mgr., phone (504)850-3136, fax (504)850-3215. **ISSN:** 0274-8126. **Subscription Rates:** $13. **Remarks:** Accepts advertising.
Ad Rates: GLR: $.73 **Circ:** Paid ‡22,000
BW: $776.10 Free ‡1,000
4C: $976.10
PCI: $10.15

12796 The Courier
3030 Barrow St. Phone: (504)850-1100
PO Box 2717 Fax: (504)857-2233
Houma, LA 70361
General newspaper. **Founded:** 1878. **Freq:** Daily (eve.), Sunday (morn.). **Print Method:** Offset. **Cols./Page:** 6. **Col. Width:** 2 1/16 inches. **Col. Depth:** 21 inches. **Key Personnel:** Miles Forrest, Publisher, phone (504)857-2231, fax (504)857-2233; Mike Slaughter, Editor, phone (504)857-2202, fax (504)857-2244; Lisa Ferrell, Advertising Dir., phone (504)857-2291, fax (504)857-2229; Mark Gray, Operations Dir., phone (504)857-2236, fax (504)857-2229. **Remarks:** Advertising accepted; rates available upon request. **Formerly:** Houma Daily Courier.
Circ: Mon.-Sat. 19,471
Sun. 21,350

12797 KCIL-FM - 107.5
120 Prevost Phone: (504)851-1020
Houma, LA 70364 Fax: (504)872-4403

Format: Contemporary Country. **Networks:** Unistar; Louisiana. **Owner:** Guaranty Broadcasting, at above address. **Founded:** 1946. **Operating Hours:** Continuous. **ADI:** New Orleans, LA. **Key Personnel:** Michael Stone, General Mgr., mstone@cajun.net; C. J. Kelly, News Dir., cjkelly@cajun.net; Madison Taylor, Promotions Dir., mtaylor@cajun.net; Paul Junior, Production Dir., pauljr@cajun.net. **Wattage:** 100,000. **Ad Rates:** $30-38 for 30 seconds; $34-48 for 60 seconds. Combined advertising rates available with KJIN-AM.

12798 KJIN-AM - 1490
120 Prevost Phone: (504)851-1020
Houma, LA 70364 Fax: (504)872-4403
E-mail: c107@cajun.net

Format: Big Band/Nostalgia. **Founded:** 1946. **Operating Hours:** Continuous. **ADI:** New Orleans, LA. **Key Personnel:** Michael Stone, General Mgr.; Lisa Robinson, Program Dir.; Jan Jackson, Operations Mgr.; Wanda Fos, Sales Mgr. **Wattage:** 1000. **Ad Rates:** $14 for 30 seconds; $18 for 60 seconds. Combined advertising rates available with KCIL.

JEANERETTE, pop. 6,511.

S LA. Iberia Parish. 10 mi. E. of New Iberia. Fresh water fishing, Oil fields. Manufactures machinery and wearing apparel. Sugarcane.

12799 Enterprise
Wicks
PO Box 327 Phone: (318)276-5171
Jeanerette, LA 70544-0327 Fax: (318)369-9640

Newspaper. **Freq:** Weekly (Wed.). **Print Method:** Offset. **Cols./Page:** 6. **Col. Width:** 20 nonpareils. **Col. Depth:** 301 agate lines. **Key Personnel:** Karma Champagne, Editor; Will Chapman, Publisher, phone (318)369-7153. **Subscription Rates:** $30 individuals. **Remarks:** Accepts advertising.
Ad Rates: PCI: $4.56 **Circ:** 4,500

JENA†, pop. 4,332.

C LA. La Salle Parish. 40 mi. NE of Alexandria. Manufactures wire and cable, particle board, cotton. Sawmills. Oil wells. Pine and hardwood timber. Agriculture. Cattle, corn.

12800 KJNA-FM - 99.3
PO Box 1340 Phone: (318)992-4155
Jena, LA 71342

Format: Country. **Networks:** Unistar; Louisiana. **Founded:** 1969. **Operating Hours:** Continuous; 80% network, 20% local. **Key Personnel:** Larry Evans, Station Mgr.; B. Mitchell, Program Dir. **Wattage:** 3000. **Ad Rates:** $10 for 30 seconds; $12 for 60 seconds.

JENNINGS†, pop. 12,401.

SW LA. Jefferson Davis Parish. 30 mi. E. of Lake Charles. Rice mills, water well machinery plants. Oil wells. Oak, gum, pine timber. Agriculture. Rice, cotton, truck crops.

12801 Jennings Daily News
Newspaper Service Co., Inc.
238 Market St. Phone: (318)824-3011
PO Box 910 Fax: (318)824-3019
Jennings, LA 70546
Publication E-mail: jenningsnews@earthlink.net

General newspaper. **Founded:** 1896. **Freq:** Daily (eve.). **Print Method:** Offset. **Cols./Page:** 6. **Col. Width:** 12 1/2 picas. **Col. Depth:** 21 1/2 inches. **Key Personnel:** Dona H. Smith, General Mgr.; Marc Richard, Publisher. **USPS:** 274-300. **Subscription Rates:** $66 individuals. **Remarks:** Accepts advertising.
Ad Rates: BW: $677.25 **Circ:** ‡5,600
4C: $801.45
SAU: $5.05

12802 KJEF-FM - 92.9
PO Box 1008 Phone: (318)824-2934
Jennings, LA 70546 Fax: (318)824-1384

Format: Country; French. **Networks:** NBC. **Owner:** Cajun Country Broadcasting Co., at above address. **Founded:** 1963. **Operating Hours:** Continuous. **ADI:** Lake Charles, LA. **Key Personnel:** Charley Williams, Contact; Bill Bailey, Contact; Sara Commier, Promotions Mgr. **Wattage:** 50,000. **Ad Rates:** $5-12 for 30 seconds; $7-15 for 60 seconds.

JONESBORO†, pop. 5,061.

N LA. Jackson Parish. 40 mi. W. of Monroe. Lumber, pulp, paper mills. Cotton gins. Pine timber. Dairy, poultry, truck farms. Cotton, corn, potatoes.

12803 Jackson Independent
PO Box 520 Phone: (318)259-2551
Jonesboro, LA 71251 Fax: (318)259-8537

Community newspaper. **Founded:** 1892. **Freq:** Weekly (Thurs.). **Print Method:** Offset. **Cols./Page:** 6. **Col. Width:** 25 nonpareils. **Col. Depth:** 294 agate lines. **Key Personnel:** T.L. Colvin Jr., Editor; Kay Colvin, Advertising Mgr. **Subscription Rates:** $28 individuals. **Remarks:** Accepts advertising.
Ad Rates: GLR: $.37 **Circ:** 3,500
BW: $686.70
PCI: $5.45

12804 KTOC-FM - 104.9
Box 690 Phone: (318)259-4600
Jonesboro, LA 71251

Format: Gospel; Country. **Founded:** 1967. **Wattage:** 3000.

12805 TCA Cable TV of Jonesboro
208 Hudson Ave. Phone: (318)259-4447
Jonesboro, LA 71251

Owner: Telecable, Inc., 208 Hudson Ave., Jonesboro, LA. **Founded:** 1971. **Formerly:** Jonesboro Cable Television (1992). **Key Personnel:** W.R. Rogers, General Manager/President. **Cities Served:** East Hodge, Hodge, Jonesboro, North Hodge, Quitman, LA: subscribing households 2,700; 28 channels; 1 community access channel; 2 hours per week community access programming.

JONESVILLE, pop. 2,828.

SC LA. Catahoula Parish. 45 mi. ENE of Alexandria.

12806 Catahoula News-Booster
PO Box 188 Phone: (318)339-7242
Jonesville, LA 71343 Fax: (318)339-7243
Publisher E-mail: catahoulanew@laribay.net

Community news, sports. **Founded:** 1853. **Freq:** Weekly. **Print Method:** Offset. **Cols./Page:** 6. **Col. Width:** 24 nonpareils. **Col. Depth:** 294 agate lines. **Key Personnel:** Bill Clifton, Publisher. **Subscription Rates:** $20 individuals. **Remarks:** Accepts advertising.
Ad Rates: BW: $567 **Circ:** ‡3,600
4C: $807
SAU: $4
PCI: $4.50

KAPLAN, pop. 5,016.

S LA. Vermilion Parish. 25 mi. SW of Lafayette. Gateway to Acadianas' Coastal Wetland. Rice mills, fertilizer factory, garment plant. Agriculture. Sugarcane.

12807 Kaplan Herald
219 N. Cushing Ave. Phone: (318)643-8002
PO Box 236 Fax: (318)643-1382
Kaplan, LA 70548
Community newspaper. **Founded:** Apr. 1, 1965. **Freq:** Weekly (Wed.). **Print Method:** Offset. **Trim Size:** 9 3/4 x 13. **Cols./Page:** 5. **Col. Width:** 1 3/4 inches. **Col. Depth:** 13 inches. **Key Personnel:** Mike Herbert, General Mgr. **USPS:** 291-260. **Subscription Rates:** $10.30 individuals. **Remarks:** Accepts advertising.
Ad Rates: BW: $516 **Circ:** ‡3,500
4C: $796
PCI: $4

KENTWOOD, pop. 2,667.

SE LA. Tangipahoa Parish. 55 mi. NE of Baton Rouge. Bricks manufactured. Lumber mills. Steel mill. Dairy products plants. Cotton gin. Dairy and truck farms.

12808 The Kentwood News-Ledger
Louisiana State Newspapers
202 Ave. F Phone: (504)229-8607
Kentwood, LA 70444 Fax: (504)748-7104

Community newspaper. **Founded:** 1966. **Freq:** Weekly (Thurs.). **Print Method:** Offset. **Cols./Page:** 6. **Col. Depth:** 294 agate lines. **Key Personnel:** Marilyn Crawford, Editor;

Sally Nagle, Advertising Mgr. **Subscription Rates:** $20 individuals; $30 individuals out of parish.
Ad Rates: GLR: $.32 **Circ:** ‡2,300
SAU: $4.39
PCI: $4

12809 Louisiana News
Moody Lafayette Communications
PO Box AD Phone: (504)229-8607
Kentwood, LA 70444 Fax: (504)229-8698

Community newspaper. **Founded:** 1932. **Freq:** Weekly (Thurs.). **Print Method:** Offset. **Cols./Page:** 6. **Col. Width:** 2 1/16 inches. **Col. Depth:** 21 1/2 inches. **Key Personnel:** Charley Vance, Editor/Administration; William K. Irwin, Publisher. **Subscription Rates:** $8.50 individuals. **Remarks:** Accepts advertising. **Formerly:** Kentwood News.
Ad Rates: GLR: $.31 **Circ:** ‡2,100
BW: $546.31
SAU: $4.33

KINDER

12810 Kinder Courier-News
PO Drawer A K Phone: (318)738-5642
Kinder, LA 70648 Fax: (318)738-2118

Community newspaper. **Freq:** Weekly (Thurs.). **Cols./Page:** 6. **Col. Width:** 12 1/5 picas. **Col. Depth:** 21 1/2 inches. **Key Personnel:** Mark Leibson, Managing Editor. **Subscription Rates:** $22 local; $20 senior citizens; $.75 single issue. **Remarks:** Accepts advertising.
Ad Rates: GLR: $.20 **Circ:** 2,700
BW: $545.67
PCI: $4.23

LA PLACE

12811 L'Observateur
L'Observateur
1010 La Place Phone: (504)652-9545
La Place, LA 70069 Fax: (504)652-3885

Newspaper. **Founded:** 1912. **Freq:** Semiweekly (Wed. and Sat.). **Print Method:** Offset. **Cols./Page:** 6. **Col. Width:** 26 nonpareils. **Col. Depth:** 294 agate lines. **Key Personnel:** Sandy Seal, Editor, lobriver@cmq.com; Joy Kennon, Publisher. **Subscription Rates:** $23.40 individuals. **Remarks:** Accepts advertising. **URL:** http://www.lobservateur.com.
Ad Rates: GLR: $.43 **Circ:** Paid 5,000
BW: $8.86 Non-paid 21,580
PCI: $6.56

12812 WADU-AM - 830
1500 E. Airline Hwy. Phone: (504)652-2500
La Place, LA 70068-5238 Fax: (504)652-5004

Format: Easy Listening. **Networks:** USA Radio; Louisiana. **Owner:** River Road Radio, Inc., at above address. **Founded:** 1987. **Operating Hours:** Continuous; 10% network, 90% local. **ADI:** New Orleans, LA. **Key Personnel:** Abele N. du Treil, Contact; Virgie H. du Treil, Contact. **Wattage:** 5000. **Ad Rates:** $2-24 for 30 seconds; $6-28 for 60 seconds.

LAFAYETTE†, pop. 81,961.

S LA. Lafayette Parish. On Vermilion Bayou, 152 mi. W. of New Orleans. University of Southwestern Louisiana. Bricks, oil equipment, cheese, aluminum windows and doors manufactured. Coffee roasters; rice milling; food processing plant; bottling works. Dairy, stock, truck farms. Sugarcane, cotton, corn, rice.

12813 Creole Culture Magazine
Creole Culture Magazine, Inc.
PO Box 92202 Phone: (318)269-1956
Lafayette, LA 70509 Fax: (318)332-4775

Community magazine discussing the cultural heritage, customs, music, cuisine, and language of southwest Louisiana. **Subtitle:** "Serving Southwestern Louisiana and the World". **Founded:** 1990. **Freq:** Monthly. **Trim Size:** 8 1/4 x 10 1/2. **Cols./Page:** 3. **Col. Width:** 3 3/4 inches. **Col. Depth:** 9 1/2 inches. **Key Personnel:** Ruth Foote, Editor and Publisher; Emmette J. Jacob, Jr., Publisher; Dianne Dupas, Advertising Dir. **Subscription Rates:** Free; $15 out of area; $30 other countries; $15 single issue. **Remarks:** Accepts advertising.
Ad Rates: BW: $250 **Circ:** Paid ‡200
PCI: $14 Non-paid ‡9,700

12814 The Daily Advertiser
PO Box 3268 Phone: (318)289-6300
Lafayette, LA 70502 Fax: (318)289-6443
Publication E-mail: acasmg@aol.com

General newspaper. **Founded:** 1865. **Freq:** Daily and Sunday (morn.). **Print Method:** Offset. **Cols./Page:** 6. **Col. Width:** 24 nonpareils. **Col. Depth:** 315 agate lines. **Key Personnel:** John E. Miller, CEO, phone (318)289-6302, fax (318)289-6466, acasmg@aol.com. **Subscription Rates:** $118 individuals. **Remarks:** Accepts advertising.
Ad Rates: 4C: $351 **Circ:** Mon.-Sat. 43,593
SAU: $28.53 Sun. 52,794

12815 Deviant Behavior: An Interdisciplinary Journal
Taylor & Francis
Department of Sociology & Anthropology
University of S.W. Louisiana
Lafayette, LA 70504-0198
Publication E-mail: cep4690@usl.edu
Publisher E-mail: info@taylorandfrancis.com

Journal covering behavioral science and theory in the area of deviant social behavior. **Founded:** 1979. **Freq:** Quarterly. **Print Method:** Offset. **Trim Size:** 6 x 9. **Cols./Page:** 1. **Col. Width:** 52 nonpareils. **Col. Depth:** 99 agate lines. **Key Personnel:** Craig J. Forsyth, Editor. **ISSN:** 0163-9625. **Subscription Rates:** $82 individuals; $165 institutions.
Ad Rates: BW: $425 **Circ:** (Not Reported)
4C: $1,325

12816 Far Gone
PO Box 43745
Lafayette, LA 70504-3745

Poetry magazine. **Founded:** 1995. **Freq:** Annual. **Trim Size:** 8 1/2 x 11. **Key Personnel:** Todd Brendan Fahey, Editor. **Subscription Rates:** $7 individuals.
Circ: Paid 100

12817 Herpetologica
The Herpetologists' League
Dr. Robert Jaeger Phone: (318)482-5235
Dept. of Biology Fax: (318)482-5834
University of Southwestern Louisiana
Lafayette, LA 70504
Publication E-mail: biology@usl.edu

Journal on the study of amphibians and reptiles. **Founded:** 1936. **Freq:** Quarterly. **Print Method:** Offset. **Cols./Page:** 2. **Col. Width:** 31 nonpareils. **Col. Depth:** 93 agate lines. **Key Personnel:** Dr. Robert Jaeger, Editor; Dr. Rebecca Pyles, Treasurer. **ISSN:** 0018-0831. **Subscription Rates:** $95. **Remarks:** Advertising not accepted.
Circ: ‡1,700

12818 In Tune
2851 Johnston St., No. 215 Phone: (318)896-3424
Lafayette, LA 70503 Fax: (318)232-2718

Magazine focusing on music and the arts. **Founded:** Sept. 1993. **Freq:** Monthly. **Print Method:** Web. **Trim Size:** 11 1/2 x 13 1/2. **Cols./Page:** 4. **Col. Width:** 2 1/2 inches. **Col. Depth:** 12 inches. **Key Personnel:** Dominick Cross, Editor/Advertising Director; Dan Willging, Writer. **Subscription Rates:** $12 individuals. **Remarks:** Accepts advertising.
Ad Rates: BW: $300 **Circ:** Paid ‡100
4C: $650 Non-paid ‡20

12819 Louisiana History
Louisiana Historical Association
PO Box 40831 Phone: (318)482-6871
Lafayette, LA 70504-0831 Fax: (318)482-6028
Publication E-mail: rrml554@usl.edu

History magazine. **Founded:** 1960. **Freq:** Quarterly. **Print Method:** Letterpress and offset. **Trim Size:** 6 x 9. **Cols./Page:** 1. **Col. Width:** 51 nonpareils. **Col. Depth:** 98 agate lines. **Key Personnel:** Carl Brasseaux, Managing Editor, phone (318)482-6027, cab944@usl.edu. **ISSN:** 0024-6816. **Subscription Rates:** $25 institutions. **Remarks:** Accepts advertising.
Ad Rates: BW: $100 **Circ:** ‡1,200

12820 Rayne Acadian Tribune
The Daily Advertiser
PO Box 3268 Phone: (318)289-6300
Lafayette, LA 70502 Fax: (318)289-6443

Newspaper with a Democratic orientation. **Founded:** 1894. **Freq:** Semiweekly (Thurs. and Sun.). **Print Method:** Offset. **Cols./Page:** 6. **Col. Width:** 26 nonpareils. **Col. Depth:** 301 agate lines. **Key Personnel:** Steven Bandy, Editor; Myrta Fair Craig, Publisher. **Subscription Rates:** $18 individuals. **Remarks:** Accepts advertising.
Ad Rates: BW: $451.50 **Circ:** 4,512
SAU: $3.50

12821 The Times of Acadiana
Thompson South Louisiana Publishing
PO Box 3528 Phone: (318)237-3560
Lafayette, LA 70502-3528 Fax: (318)261-2630
Publication E-mail: toaletedit@aol.com

Newspaper covering politics, lifestyle, entertainment, and general news. **Founded:** Sept. 18, 1980. **Freq:** Weekly (Wed.). **Print Method:** Offset. **Trim Size:** 10 11/16 x 14 5/8. **Cols./Page:** 4. **Col. Width:** 28 nonpareils. **Col. Depth:** 194 agate lines. **Key Personnel:** Judy Johnson, Editor, judyjay@aol.com; Beth Ardoin, Publisher; Eric Robicheaux, Sales Mgr., ericr@timesofacadiana.com; Judi LaDousa, Program Dir., jladousa@timesofacadiana.com; Odie Terry, Multimedia Div. Dir.; Marti Harrell, Event Marketing Div. Dir., fax (318)233-7484, tslevents@usa.net. **Subscription Rates:** Free; $28.50 by mail. **Remarks:** Accepts advertising.
Ad Rates: BW: $1,358 **Circ:** Non-paid 33,000
4C: $1,738

12822 The Vermilion
University of Southwestern Louisiana
PO Box 4-4813 Phone: (318)482-6960
Lafayette, LA 70504 Fax: (318)482-6959
Publisher E-mail: verm@net-connect.net

Collegiate newspaper. **Founded:** 1904. **Freq:** Weekly (Fri.). **Print Method:** Offset. **Trim Size:** 10 1/2 x 12 1/2. **Cols./Page:** 4. **Col. Width:** 2 5/16 inches. **Col. Depth:** 76 picas. **Key Personnel:** David Paul, Business Mgr. **Subscription Rates:** $6.50 individuals. **Remarks:** Accepts advertising.
Ad Rates: PCI: $4.50 **Circ:** Free ‡12,000

12823 KADN-TV - 15
1500 Eraste Landry Rd. Phone: (318)237-1500
Lafayette, LA 70506 Fax: (318)237-2237

Format: Commercial TV. **Networks:** Fox. **Owner:** Charles Chatelain, at above address. **Founded:** 1980. **Operating Hours:** Continuous. **ADI:** Lafayette, LA. **Key Personnel:** Mike Reed, General Mgr., fax (318)237-2526, miker@kadn.com; Tom Poehler, General Sales Mgr., fax (318)237-2526; Ron High, Program Dir., crew@kadn.com. **Wattage:** 2,300. **Ad Rates:** $15-500 for 30 seconds; $30-1000 for 60 seconds.

12824 KATC-TV - 3
PO Box 63333 Phone: (318)235-3333
Lafayette, LA 70596 Fax: (318)235-9363
E-mail: tvmkte@katc,com

Format: Commercial TV. **Networks:** ABC. **Founded:** Sept. 1962. **Operating Hours:** Continuous Mon. - Thu.; 6 am - 2 am Fri., Sat., Sun. **ADI:** Lafayette, LA. **Key Personnel:** Richard Hardison, General Mgr.

12825 KDYS-AM - 1520
PO Box 3345 Phone: (318)232-2632
Lafayette, LA 70502-3345 Fax: (318)233-3779

Format: Educational. **Owner:** The Powell Group, 8641 United Plaza Blvd., Ste. 300, Baton Rouge, LA 70809, (225)922-4540, Fax: (225)922-4544. **Founded:** 1961. **Formerly:** KXKW-AM (1990); KACY-AM. **Operating Hours:** Continuous. **ADI:** Lafayette, LA. **Key Personnel:** Charles Norman, General Mgr., phone (318)232-1311, fax (318)233-3779; Mary Galyean, Sales Mgr., phone (318)232-1311; Keith LeBlanc, Operations Mgr., phone (318)232-1311; Nina Thibodeaux, Traffic, phone (318)232-1311. **Local Programs:** *Radio Aahs.* **Wattage:** 10,000. **Ad Rates:** Advertising accepted; rates available upon request.

12826 KFXZ-FM - 106.3
3225 Ambassador Caffery Pkwy. Phone: (318)981-0106
Lafayette, LA 70506-7214 Fax: (318)988-0443

Format: Urban Contemporary. **Networks:** ABC. **Owner:** Peter Moncrieff, President, 7707 Waco Dr., Baton Rouge, LA 70802, (504)926-1106, Fax: (504)928-1606. **Founded:** 1985. **Operating Hours:** Continuous; 2% network, 98% local. **ADI:** Lafayette, LA. **Key Personnel:** Keith Moncrieffe, General Mgr.; M. Patton, Chief Engineer; Nedra Jeanlouis, Office Mgr.; Darleen Wesley, News Dir. **Local Programs:** *Guy Broady Morning Show*, Guy Broady. **Wattage:** 6000. **Ad Rates:** $25-56 for 30 seconds; $29-60 for 60 seconds.

12827 KJCB-AM - 770
413 Jefferson St. Phone: (318)233-4262
Lafayette, LA 70501-7057

Format: Jazz; Religious; Urban Contemporary; Oldies. **Networks:** ABC. **Founded:** 1982. **Operating Hours:** Continuous. **ADI:** Lafayette, LA. **Key Personnel:** Joshua Jackson, Sr., President; Horatio Handy, General Mgr. **Wattage:** 1000. **Ad Rates:** $12-26 for 30 seconds.

12828 KLFY-TV - 10
PO Box 90665 Phone: (318)981-4823
Lafayette, LA 70509 Fax: (318)984-8323

Format: Commercial TV. **Networks:** CBS. **Owner:** Young Broadcasting of Louisiana, Inc., 599 Lexington Ave., 47th Fl., 47th Fl., New York, NY 10022, (212)754-7070, Fax: (212)758-1229. **Founded:** 1955. **Operating Hours:** Continuous; 70% network, 30% local. **ADI:** Lafayette, LA. **Key Personnel:** Joseph R. Varholy, Vice President/General Mgr., phone (318)981-4823, fax (318)984-8323; Mike Barras, General Sales Mgr.; Terry Dover, Program Mgr.; Harry Bille, Marketing Dir./Promotions Mgr.; Maria Placer, Vice President-News. **Wattage:** 295,000. **Ad Rates:** $40-750 per unit. **URL:** http://www.klfy.com.

12829 KLPB-TV - 24
c/o WLPB-TV Phone: (504)767-5660
7733 Perkins Rd. Fax: (504)767-4288
Baton Rouge, LA 70810
Free: (800)272-8161

Format: Public TV. **Simulcasts:** WLPB-TV Baton Rouge, LA. **Networks:** Public Broadcasting Service (PBS); Louisiana Public Broadcasting. **Owner:** Louisiana Public Broadcasting Network, at above address. **Founded:** 1981. **Operating Hours:** 6 a.m.-11:30 p.m.; 90% network, 10% local. **ADI:** Lafayette, LA. **Key Personnel:** Beth Courtney, Pres./CEO; Jennifer Howze, Program Dir.; Clay Fourrier, Exec. Producer; Kent Hatfield, Engineering Dir.; Cindy Rougeou, CAO; Homer Dyess, Educational Services Dir.; Ayan Rubin, Educational Services Coord. **URL:** http://www.lpb.gen.la.us/.

12830 KNEK-AM - 1190
3225 Ambassador Caffery Pkwy. Phone: (318)826-3921
Lafayette, LA 70506-7214 Fax: (318)826-3206

Format: Gospel. **Networks:** Louisiana. **Founded:** 1981. **Operating Hours:** 14 hours daily; 5% network, 95% local. **Key Personnel:** Randy Pitre, Program Dir.; Carol Celestri, Office Mgr. **Wattage:** 250. **Ad Rates:** $6.30-9.50 for 30 seconds; $8.60-13.05 for 60 seconds.

12831 KPEL-AM - 1420
1749 Bertrand Dr. Phone: (318)233-7003
Lafayette, LA 70506 Fax: (318)234-7360

Format: Talk. **Networks:** ABC; CBS; NBC. **Owner:** Communications Corp., PO Box 3706, Lafayette, LA 70502, (318)237-1142. **Founded:** 1950. **Operating Hours:** Continuous; 80% network, 20% local. **ADI:** Lafayette, LA. **Key Personnel:** Mike Grimsley, General Mgr.; Ray Suttley, Program Dir.; Jay Walker, Sports Dir.; Terry P. Hebut, General Sales Mgr. **Wattage:** Day 1000; night 750.

12832 KPEL-FM - 105.1
1749 Bertrand Dr. Phone: (318)233-7003
Lafayette, LA 70506 Fax: (318)234-7360
Free: (800)264-5735

Format: News; Talk. **Networks:** CBS; NBC; Mutual Broadcasting System. **Founded:** 1993. **Operating Hours:** Continuous. **ADI:** Lafayette, LA. **Key Personnel:** Mike Grimsley, General Mgr.; Ray Sutley, Program Mgr. **Local Programs:** *KPEL Afternoon Report*, Ray Sutley; *KPEL Morning Request*, Bernadette Lee; *KPEL Primetime*, Bob Hamm. **Wattage:** 25,000.

12833 KSJY-FM - 90.9
PO Box 31086 Phone: (318)837-6225
Lafayette, LA 70593-1086 Fax: (318)837-8860

Format: Adult Contemporary; Gospel. **Founded:** 1988. **Operating Hours:** Continuous; 100% Local. **ADI:** Lafayette, LA. **Key Personnel:** Wendy Christian, General Mgr. **Wattage:** 6,000. **Ad Rates:** Noncommercial.

12834 KSMB-FM - 94.5
PO Box 3345 Phone: (318)232-1311
Lafayette, LA 70502 Fax: (318)233-3779

Format: Top 40. **Networks:** ABC. **Owner:** The Powell Group, 8641 United Plaza Blvd., Ste. 300, Baton Rouge, LA 70809, (225)922-4540, Fax: (225)922-4544. **Founded:** 1964. **Formerly:** KSMB/KDYS Radio Broadcasting Co. **Operating Hours:** Continuous. **ADI:** Lafayette, LA. **Key Personnel:** Charles Norman, General Mgr., phone (318)232-1311, fax (318)233-3779; Mary Galyean, General Sales Mgr.; Bobby Novosad, Program Dir.; Derrick Hayes, Music Dir.; Tony Evans, Chief Engineer; Nina Thibodeaux, Traffic Mgr. **Wattage:** 100,000.

12835 KVOL-AM - 1330
202 Galbert Rd. Phone: (318)233-1330
Lafayette, LA 70506-1806 Fax: (318)237-7733
Free: (800)743-1330
E-mail: planetbuzz@net-connect.net

Format: Sports; Talk. **Simulcasts:** KVOL-FM. **Networks:** ABC. **Owner:** KVOL Radio Broadcasting Co., at above address, (318)232-1311, Fax: (318)233-3779. **Founded:** 1935. **Operating Hours:** Continuous. **ADI:** Lafayette, LA. **Key Personnel:** Charles Norman, General Mgr.; Keith LeBlanc, Operations Mgr.; Jill Johnson, General Sales Mgr., jill1330@hotmail.com; Jill Johnson, Promotions Dir.; Keith LeBlanc, Program Dir.; Nina Thibodeaux, Traffic. **Local Programs:** *Sports Page*, Jimmie Cole, General Sales Mgr. **Wattage:** 5000 day, 1000 night. **Ad Rates:** $25 for 30 seconds; $25 for 60 seconds.

12836 KVOL-FM - 105.9
202 Galbert Rd. Phone: (318)233-1330
Lafayette, LA 70506-1806 Fax: (318)237-7733
Free: (800)743-1330

Format: Talk; Sports. **Simulcasts:** KVOL-AM. **Networks:** Mutual Broadcasting System; NBC. **Owner:** Powell Broadcasting, Inc., at above address. **Founded:** 1989. **Operating Hours:** Continuous. **ADI:** Lafayette, LA. **Key Personnel:** Charles Norman, General Mgr., phone (318)232-1311, fax (318)233-3779; Keith Leblanc, Operations Mgr.; Nina Thibodeaux, Traffic; Jill Johnson, General Sales Mgr.; Keith Leblanc, Program Dir. **Local Programs:** *Afternoon Drive/Zydeco Drive at 5*, Hitman Tommy C.; *The Ofid Day Memory Show*, Carl T. **Wattage:** 6000 ERP. **Ad Rates:** $25 for 30 seconds; $25 for 60 seconds.

LAKE CHARLES†, pop. 75,051.

SW LA. Calcasieu Parish. On Calcasieu River, 62 mi. E. of Beaumont, TX. McNeese State University. Pine hardwood timber. Petroleum refining; plastic basics gasoline, caustic, soda ash, chemicals, anhydrous ammonia, catalyst, chlorine, aluminum, synthetic rubber, lumber, bricks, beverages, concrete products manufactured. Agriculture. Rice, cotton, sugar.

12837 American Mosquito Control Association Journal
American Mosquito Control Association, Inc.
2200 E. Prien Lake Rd. Phone: (318)474-2723
Lake Charles, LA 70601 Fax: (318)478-9434

Professional journal covering mosquitos. **Freq:** Quarterly. **Subscription Rates:** $65 individuals; $17 single issue. **Remarks:** Accepts advertising.
Circ: (Not Reported)

12838 Contraband
McNeese State University
PO Box 91375 Phone: (318)475-5645
Lake Charles, LA 70609-1375 Fax: (318)475-5259

Collegiate newspaper. **Subtitle:** Serving as your Campus Connecton since 1939. **Founded:** Nov. 3, 1939. **Freq:** Weekly (Wed.). **Print Method:** Offset. **Trim Size:** 13 1/8 x 22. **Cols./Page:** 6. **Col. Width:** 12 1/2 picas. **Col. Depth:** 306 agate lines. **Key Personnel:** Todd McCundle, Editor, phone (313)475-5646. **Subscription Rates:** $18 individuals. **Remarks:** Accepts advertising.
Ad Rates: GLR: $4.25 **Circ:** ‡4,500
BW: $378
4C: $600
SAU: $6
PCI: $3

12839 Lake Charles American Press
PO Box 2893 Phone: (318)433-3000
Lake Charles, LA 70602 Fax: (318)494-4008

General newspaper. **Founded:** 1895. **Freq:** Daily and Sunday (morn.). **Print Method:** Offset. **Trim Size:** 13 3/4 x 22 3/4. **Cols./Page:** 6. **Col. Width:** 25 nonpareils. **Col. Depth:** 308 agate lines. **Key Personnel:** James Beam, Editor, phone (318)494-4060, fax (318)494-4070, jbeamamericarican.com; Thomas B. Shearman III, Publisher, phone (318)494-4058, fax (318)494-4050; William Wallace, Advertising Mgr., phone (318)494-4037. **ISSN:** 0739-1196. **Subscription Rates:** $96 individuals. **Remarks:** Accepts advertising. Sunday: GLR: $2.10; SAU: $20.91. **URL:** http://www.americanpress.com.
Ad Rates: GLR: $1.25 **Circ:** Mon.-Sat. ★**36,740**
SAU: $19.50 Sun. ★**41,599**

12840 McNeese Review
McNeese State University
PO Box 91375 Phone: (318)475-5645
Lake Charles, LA 70609-1375 Fax: (318)475-5259

Scholarly journal covering articles and essays in the liberal arts. **Founded:** 1948. **Freq:** Annual. **Print Method:** Offset. **Key Personnel:** Scott Goins, Editor; Carrie Chrisco, Circulation Mgr. **ISSN:** 0885-467X. **Subscription Rates:** $47 individuals. **Remarks:** Advertising not accepted.
Circ: Combined 200

12841 National Forum of Education Administration and Supervision Journal
National Forum Journals
4000 Locke Ln., Tr. 9 Phone: (318)477-0008
Lake Charles, LA 70605-2244 Fax: (318)562-2848

Scholarly journal covering educational management and leadership. **Founded:** 1983. **Freq:** 3/year. **Trim Size:** 6 x 9. **Key Personnel:** William Kritsenis, Ph.D., Editor. **ISSN:** 0888-8132. **Subscription Rates:** $72 institutions and libraries; $36 individuals. **Remarks:** Accepts advertising. **URL:** http://www.nationalforum.com.
Ad Rates: GLR: $25 **Circ:** 7,500
BW: $600

12842 National Forum of Special Education Journal
National Forum Journals
4000 Locke Ln., Tr. 9 Phone: (318)477-0008
Lake Charles, LA 70605-2244 Fax: (318)562-2848

Scholarly electronic journal covering special education. **Subtitle:** Electronic Journal. **Founded:** 1989. **Freq:** Annual. **Trim Size:** 6 x 9. **Key Personnel:** William Kritsenis, Ph.D., Editor. **ISSN:** 1043-2167. **Subscription Rates:** $72 libraries and institutions; $36 individuals. **Remarks:** Accepts advertising.
Ad Rates: GLR: $25 **Circ:** Non-paid 10,000
BW: $600

12843 The Southwest Catholic
Diocese of Lake Charles
PO Box 3223 Phone: (318)439-7430
Lake Charles, LA 70602 Fax: (318)439-7428

Official newspaper of the Diocese of Lake Charles. **Founded:** 1987. **Freq:** Monthly. **Cols./Page:** 5. **Col. Width:** 11.5 picas. **Col. Depth:** 90.6 picas. **Key Personnel:** Most Rev. Jude Speyrer, Publisher, phone (318)439-7400, fax (318)439-7413, jspeyrer@laol.net; Morris LeBleu, Editor, phone (318)439-7434, fax (318)439-7413, mdxdvii@laol.net. **Subscription Rates:** $12. **Remarks:** Advertising not accepted.
Circ: Paid 3,000
Non-paid 1,000

12844 KLCL-AM - 1470
P.O. Box 3067. Phone: (318)433-1641
Lake Charles, LA 70602 Fax: (318)433-2999

Format: Sports. **Owner:** Progressive Communications, Inc., at above address. **Founded:** 1935. **Formerly:** KPLC-AM. **Operating Hours:** Continuous; 80% local. **ADI:** Lake Charles, LA. **Key Personnel:** George Swift, General Mgr.; Don Rivers, Program Dir. **Local Programs:** *In The Zone*, Chad Lemoine; *Probe*, George Swift. **Wattage:** 5000. **Ad Rates:** $14-20 for 30 seconds; $20-28 for 60 seconds.

12845 KLTL-TV - 18
c/o WLPB-TV Phone: (504)767-5660
7860 Anselmo Ln. Fax: (504)767-4288
Baton Rouge, LA 70810
Free: (800)272-8161
E-mail: comments@lpb.gen.la.us

Format: Public TV. **Simulcasts:** WLPB-TV Baton Rouge, LA. **Networks:** Public Broadcasting Service (PBS); Louisiana Public Broadcasting. **Owner:** Louisiana Public Broadcasting Network, at above address. **Founded:** 1981. **ADI:** Lake Charles, LA. **URL:** http://www.lpb.gen.la.us/.

12846 KPLC-TV - 7
320 Division St. Phone: (318)439-9071
PO Box 1488 Fax: (318)437-7600
Lake Charles, LA 70601
E-mail: kplc@aol.com

Format: Commercial TV. **Networks:** NBC. **Founded:** 1954. **Operating Hours:** 6 a.m.-2 a.m.; 75% network, 25% local. **ADI:** Lake Charles, LA. **Key Personnel:** Jim Serra, Contact; James Smith, News Dir.; Robin Dangereau, Program Dir.; Diana Mayo, Operations Mgr.; Roger McGee, Chief Engineer; Tim Bourgeois, Promotions Dir.

12847 KRAW-FM - 107.5
PO Box 3067 Phone: (318)433-1641
Lake Charles, LA 70602 Fax: (318)433-2999

Format: Country. **Owner:** Progressive Communications, at above address. **Operating Hours:** Continuous. **Wattage:** 50,000.

12848 KVHP-TV - 29
129 W. Prien Lake Rd. Phone: (318)474-1316
Lake Charles, LA 70601 Fax: (318)474-9028

Format: Commercial TV. **Networks:** Fox. **Owner:** National Communications, Inc., at above address. **Founded:** 1983. **Operating Hours:** 24hours. **ADI:** Lake Charles, LA. **Key Personnel:** Bruce Hamilton, General Mgr., phone (318)474-1316, fax (318)474-1358, nobadays@aol.com.

12849 KXZZ-AM - 1580
311 Alamo St. Phone: (318)436-7277
Lake Charles, LA 70601 Fax: (318)436-7278

Format: Urban Contemporary. **Networks:** American Urban Radio. **Owner:** Dixie Broadcasters, Inc., at above address. **Founded:** 1947. **Formerly:** KLOU-AM (1985). **Operating Hours:** Continuous; 100% local. **ADI:** Lake Charles, LA. **Key Personnel:** Jerry Goss, VP/Gen. Mgr.; Mike Mitchell, General Sales Mgr.; Brian Robinson, Program Dir. **Wattage:** 1000. **Ad Rates:** $6-17 for 30 seconds; $10-21 for 60 seconds. Combined advertising rates available with KBLU-FM.

12850 KYKZ-FM - 96.1
716 Hodges St. Phone: (318)439-3300
Lake Charles, LA 70601 Fax: (318)433-7701
Free: (800)439-6979

Format: Contemporary Country. **Networks:** ABC. **Owner:** Louisiana Media Interests, Inc., Box 999, Lake Charles, LA 70602. **Founded:** 1976. **Formerly:** KSNS-FM. **Operating Hours:** Continuous. **ADI:** Lake Charles, LA. **Key Personnel:** Eric Cormier, News Dir.; Eric Nielson, Program Dir.; Johnette LaBorde, Sales Mgr.; Dave Chimeno, Chief Engineer. **Wattage:** 100,000.

12851 KZWA-FM - 105.3
PO Box 699 Phone: (318)491-9955
Lake Charles, LA 70602 Fax: (318)433-8097

Format: Urban Contemporary; Adult Contemporary. **Owner:** Faye Brown-Blackwell, at above address. **Founded:** Apr. 1991. **Operating Hours:** Continuous. **Key Personnel:** Faye Brown-Blackwell, General Mgr.; Charles Washson, Sales Mgr.; Anthony Bartie, Traffic Mgr.; Frank Troy, Program Dir.; James Williams, Music Dir. **Wattage:** 50,000. **Ad Rates:** $18-31 for 30 seconds; $20-32 for 60 seconds.

12852 TCI of Louisiana
Box 5365 Phone: (318)477-9674
Lake Charles, LA 70601-8506 Fax: (318)474-3436

Founded: 1967. **Cities Served:** Calcasieu County, LA.

LAKE PROVIDENCE†, pop. 6,361.

NE LA. East Carroll Parish. On Mississippi River, 35 mi. NW of Vicksburg, MS. Cotton gins, warehouse, cooperage, wood products factory. Commercial fisheries. Diversified farming.

12853 Banner-Democrat
313 Lake St. Phone: (318)559-2750
Lake Providence, LA 71254-2688 Fax: (318)559-2750
Newspaper focusing on agricultural interests and community service. **Founded:** 1887. **Freq:** Weekly (Thurs.). **Print Method:** Offset. **Trim Size:** 14 x 22 3/4. **Cols./Page:** 6. **Col. Width:** 26 nonpareils. **Col. Depth:** 294 agate lines. **Key Personnel:** A.C. Carlton, Publisher. **USPS:** 041-380. **Subscription Rates:** $20.60 individuals in county; $25.75 elsewhere in Louisana; $25 out of state. **Remarks:** Accepts advertising.
Ad Rates: GLR: $.25 **Circ:** ‡2,200
BW: $481.32
SAU: $3.82
PCI: $3.82

12854 KLPL-AM - 1050
PO Box 469 Phone: (318)559-2340
Lake Providence, LA 71254-0469 Fax: (318)559-2340

Format: News; Country; Agricultural; Gospel; Classical. **Networks:** Louisiana. **Founded:** 1957. **Operating Hours:** 22 hrs. Daily; 30% network, 70% local. **Key Personnel:** A.L. Thomas, Contact. **Wattage:** 250. **Ad Rates:** $3.50-15 for 30 seconds.

12855 KLPL-FM - 92.7
PO Box 469 Phone: (318)559-2340
Lake Providence, LA 71254-0469 Fax: (318)559-2340

Format: News; Country; Agricultural; Classical; Gospel. **Networks:** Louisiana; Southern States. **Founded:** 1975. **Operating Hours:** 22 hrs. Daily; 30% network, 70% local. **Key Personnel:** A.L. Thomas, Contact. **Wattage:** 3000. **Ad Rates:** $3.50-15 for 30 seconds.

LAROSE, pop. 4,267.

SE LA. Lafourche Parish. 2 mi. N. of Delta.

12856 The Lafourche Gazette
Lafourche Gazette News
PO Box 1450 Phone: (504)693-7229
Larose, LA 70373 Fax: (504)693-8282

Community newspaper. **Founded:** Oct. 27, 1965. **Freq:** Semiweekly (Wed. and Sun.). **Print Method:** Offset. **Trim Size:** 13 x 21. **Cols./Page:** 6. **Col. Width:** 2 inches. **Col. Depth:** 301 agate lines. **Key Personnel:** Earl P. Legendre, Publisher; Vicki M. Chaisson, Advertising Mgr. **Subscription Rates:** $24 non-resident. **Remarks:** Accepts advertising. Sunday: BW: $667.80; 4C: $1,027.80; PCI: $7.27.
Ad Rates: BW: $742.14 **Circ:** Free ‡14,000
4C: $290
PCI: $7.52

12857 KLEB-AM - 1600
11603 Hwy. 308 Fax: (504)798-7793
PO Box 1350
Larose, LA 70373
E-mail: jerryg@cajunnet.com

Founded: 1963. **Operating Hours:** Continuous. **Key Personnel:** Harold Callais, President; Tom Gregory, Program Dir. **Wattage:** 5000 day; 250 night.

LEESVILLE†, pop. 9,054.

W LA. Vernon Parish. 50 mi. SW of Alexandria. Garment factory. Lumber mills. Pine, hardwood timber. Agriculture. Cotton, corn, sweet potatoes.

12858 Leesville Daily Leader
News Leader, Inc.
206 E. Texas Phone: (318)239-3444
PO Box 619 Fax: (318)238-1152
Leesville, LA 71446
Daily newspaper. **Founded:** 1898. **Freq:** Tues.-Fri. (morn.); Sun. (morn.). **Print Method:** Offset. **Cols./Page:** 6. **Col. Width:** 2 1/8 inches. **Col. Depth:** 21 inches. **Key Personnel:** Ben Barkley, Managing Editor; Lewis Cain, Publisher. **Subscription Rates:** $72 individuals; $125 out of area. **Remarks:** Accepts advertising.
Ad Rates: BW: $1,392.30 **Circ:** Paid ‡6,460
4C: $1,842.30 Free ‡9,153
SAU: $11.05

12859 KJAE-FM - 92.7
Box 1323 Phone: (318)238-1956
Leesville, LA 71496-1323 Fax: (318)238-9283
E-mail: kjae@leesville.com

Format: Country. **Networks:** ABC. **Owner:** Penny Scogin, at above address. **Founded:** 1979. **Operating Hours:** Continuous. **Key Personnel:** Steve Elliot, General Mgr.; Cody Keith, Program Dir. **Wattage:** 3000. **Ad Rates:** $6.70-12.65 for 30 seconds; $9.45-14.95 for 60 seconds. **URL:** http://www.leesville.com/kjae.

12860 KLLA-AM - 1570
Box 1323 Phone: (318)238-1956
Leesville, LA 71496-1323 Fax: (318)238-9283
E-mail: klla@leesville.com

Format: Oldies. **Owner:** Penny Scogin Pene Broadcasting Co., Inc., at above address. **Founded:** 1956. **Operating Hours:** 6 a.m.-8 p.m. **Key Personnel:** Penny Scogin, President; Steve Elliot, General Mgr. **Wattage:** 1000. **Ad Rates:** $4.00-6.60 for 30 seconds; $5.15-8.05 for 60 seconds. **URL:** http://www.leesville.com/klla.

12861 KVVP-FM - 105.7
168 KVVP Dr. Phone: (318)537-5887
PO Drawer K Fax: (318)537-4152
Leesville, LA 71446
E-mail: kvvp@kvvp.com

Format: Country. **Networks:** NBC. **Owner:** Stannard Broadcasting Co.,, at above address. **Founded:** 1974. **Operating Hours:** Continuous. **ADI:** Alexandria, LA. **Key Personnel:** Tony McDonald, News Dir./ Promotions Mgr.; Doug Stannard, Station Mgr.; Len Roach, Music Dir.; Paul McCullen, General Sales Mgr. **Wattage:** 25,000. **Ad Rates:** Advertising accepted; rates available upon request. Combined advertising rates available with KROK-FM. **URL:** http://www.kvvp.com.

LOGANSPORT, pop. 1,565.

W LA. De Soto Parish. On Sabine River, 40 mi. SW of Shreveport. Ceramic molds. Sawmill. Gas and oil wells, stock, poultry, truck farms.

12862 KJVC-FM - 92.7
PO Box 700 Phone: (318)697-4000
Logansport, LA 71049 Fax: (318)697-4004

Format: Country. **Owner:** Metropolitan Radio Group, Inc., 1549 Greenbridge, Ozark, MO 65721, (417)581-5595. **Founded:** Sept. 1976. **Operating Hours:** Continuous. **ADI:** Shreveport, LA-Texarkana, TX. **Key Personnel:** Gary L. Acker, President; Gene Fields, General Mgr.; Corey Johnson, Program Dir.; Rick Benson, Chief Engineer. **Wattage:** 3,000.

12863 KORI-FM - 104.7
PO Box 700 Phone: (318)697-4000
Logansport, LA 71049 Fax: (318)697-4004

Format: Country. **Owner:** Metropolitan Radio Group, Inc., 1549 Greenbridge, Ozark, MO 65721, (417)581-5595. **Operating Hours:** Continuous. **ADI:** Shreveport, LA-Texarkana, TX. **Key Personnel:** Gary L. Acker, President; Gene Fields, General Mgr.; Rick Benson, Chief Engineer. **Wattage:** 25,000.

LUTCHER

12864 The Enterprise
Ruhr Publishing, Inc.
PO Drawer 460 Phone: (504)869-5784
Lutcher, LA 70071 Fax: (504)869-4386

Community newspaper. **Founded:** Feb. 1976. **Freq:** Weekly (Wed.). **Cols./Page:** 6. **Col. Width:** 12 1/5 picas. **Col. Depth:** 21 inches. **Key Personnel:** Huey Stein, Editor. **Subscription Rates:** $12.36; $15.45 out of parish; $20 out of state. **Remarks:** Accepts advertising.
Ad Rates: BW: $541.80 **Circ:** 1,900
SAU: $5.18

12865 News Examiner
Ruhr Valley Publishing, Inc.
2290 Texas St. Phone: (504)869-5784
PO Drawer 460 Fax: (504)869-4386
Lutcher, LA 70071
Community newspaper. **Founded:** 1938. **Freq:** Weekly (Thurs.). **Cols./Page:** 6. **Col. Width:** 11 1/2 picas. **Col. Depth:** 21 inches. **Key Personnel:** Huey Stein, Editor; Deborah Reynaud, Publisher; Wilbur Reynaud, Publisher. **Subscription Rates:** $15.45 individuals. **Remarks:** Accepts advertising.
Ad Rates: BW: $652.68 **Circ:** Combined ♦**10,703**
SAU: $5.84
PCI: $4.30

MAMOU, pop. 3,194.

SC LA. Evangeline Parish. 10 mi. N. of Eunice. Manufactures prepared feed, concrete products. Agriculture. Cotton, corn, rice.

12866 Mamou Acadian Press
PO Box 360 Phone: (318)363-2103
Mamou, LA 70554 Fax: (318)363-2841

Newspaper. **Founded:** 1955. **Freq:** Weekly (Thurs.). **Print Method:** Offset. **Cols./Page:** 6. **Col. Width:** 21 1/2 nonpareils. **Col. Depth:** 294 agate lines. **Key Personnel:** Roland Manuel, Editor; Charlene Guillory, Sales Rep. **Subscription Rates:** Free; $16 by mail.
Ad Rates: GLR: $.25 **Circ:** Paid 64
BW: $414.55 Free 2,500
SAU: $3.73

MANSFIELD†, pop. 6,485.

W LA. De Soto Parish. 35 mi. S. of Shreveport. Manufactures lumber, truck trailers, dragline buckets, garments. Pine and hardwood timber. Oil and gas production. Oil refinery. Agriculture. Cotton, soybeans, corn, wheat, dairy and beef cattle.

12867 The Interstate Progress
Natchitoches Times Publications
PO Box 840
Mansfield, LA 71052-0840

Community newspaper. **Subtitle:** Your Hometown Newspaper Since 1889. **Founded:** 1889. **Freq:** Weekly (Thurs.). **Print Method:** Offset. **Cols./Page:** 6. **Col. Width:** 21 nonpareils. **Col. Depth:** 226 agate lines. **Key Personnel:** Sarah Alford, News Editor; Vickie Welborn, Mng. News Editor; Keenan Gingles, Publisher. **Subscription Rates:** $11 individuals; $24 out of area; $36 out of state. **Remarks:** Accepts advertising.
Ad Rates: GLR: $.09 **Circ:** ‡1,800
PCI: $2.37

12868 Mansfield Enterprise-Progress
Keenan Gingles
202 Adams St. Phone: (318)872-4120
PO Box 840 Fax: (318)872-6038
Mansfield, LA 71052
Community newspaper. **Founded:** 1904. **Freq:** Weekly (Thurs.). **Print Method:** Offset. Uses mats. **Cols./Page:** 6. **Col. Width:** 26 nonpareils. **Col. Depth:** 294 agate lines. **Key Personnel:** Keenan C. Gingles, Publisher. **Subscription Rates:** $15 individuals. **Remarks:** Accepts advertising.
Ad Rates: BW: $582.12 **Circ:** ‡4,200
4C: $807.12
SAU: $4.62
PCI: $4.01

MANY†, pop. 3,988.

W LA. Sabine Parish. 68 mi. S. of Shreveport. Tourism. Resort. Recreation. Fishing. Scenic gardens. Museum and park. Lumber mills. Pine, hardwood timber. Oil, gas. Agriculture. Cattle. Dairying. Poultry.

12869 Sabine Index
Box 850 Phone: (318)256-3495
Many, LA 71449 Fax: (318)256-9151

Community newspaper. **Founded:** 1879. **Freq:** Weekly (Wed.). **Print Method:** Offset. **Cols./Page:** 6. **Col. Width:** 22 nonpareils. **Col. Depth:** 290 agate lines. **Key Personnel:** Robert Gentry, Editor and Publisher. **Subscription Rates:** $26 individuals; $39 out of area. **Remarks:** Accepts advertising.
Ad Rates: BW: $880.74 **Circ:** ‡6,200
4C: $1,135.74
PCI: $6.99

12870 Illini Cablevision
595 San Antonio Phone: (318)256-2097
Many, LA 71449 Fax: (318)256-9536

Owner: Ed Baldgridge, at above address. **Founded:** 1963. **Key Personnel:** Ted Dumas, General Mgr. **Cities Served:** Communities in Sabine parish, LA.: 25 channels; 1 community access channel.

12871 KWLA-AM - 1400
605 San Antonio Ave. Phone: (318)256-5177
Many, LA 71449 Fax: (318)256-9536

Format: Oldies. **Networks:** Satellite Music Network; Louisiana. **Founded:** 1962. **Operating Hours:** 5 a.m.-10 p.m. **Key Personnel:** Rhonda Singletary, General Mgr.; Kenny Carter, Chief Engineer. **Wattage:** 1000. **Ad Rates:** $4-8 for 30 seconds; $6-10 for 60 seconds. Combined advertising rates available with KWLU-FM.

12872 KWLV-FM - 107.1
605 San Antonio Ave. Phone: (318)256-5924
Many, LA 71449 Fax: (318)256-9536

Format: Country. **Networks:** Satellite Music Network. **Owner:** WLV-TV, Inc., at above address, Fax: (318)256-0950. **Founded:** 1979. **Operating Hours:** 6 a.m.-10 p.m. **Key Personnel:** Tedd Wayne Dumas, Contact; Rhonda Singletary, General Mgr. **Wattage:** 25,000 ERP. **Ad Rates:** $7-12 for 30 seconds; $9-18 for 60 seconds. Combined advertising rates available with KWLA-A.

MARKSVILLE†, pop. 5,113.

E LA. Avoyelles Parish. 30 mi. SE of Alexandria. Foundry, cotton gin. Hardwood timber. Agriculture. Cotton, corn, sweet potatoes.

12873 Avoyelles Journal
Avoyelles Publishing Co.
100 N. Main St. Phone: (318)253-5413
PO Box 523 Fax: (318)253-7223
Marksville, LA 71351
Community newspaper. **Founded:** 1978. **Freq:** Semiweekly (Wed. and Sun.). **Print Method:** Offset. **Cols./Page:** 6. **Col. Width:** 12 picas. **Key Personnel:** Susan Oecuir, Editor; Kathie Lipe, Advertising Mgr.
Ad Rates: BW: $774 **Circ:** Free 17,600
4C: $1,074
SAU: $6

12874 The Bunkie Record
Avoyelles Publishing Co.
100 N. Main St. Phone: (318)253-5413
PO Box 523 Fax: (318)253-7223
Marksville, LA 71351
Newspaper with a Democratic orientation. **Founded:** 1888. **Freq:** Weekly (Thurs.). **Print Method:** Offset. **Cols./Page:** 6. **Col. Width:** 26 nonpareils. **Col. Depth:** 294 agate lines. **Key Personnel:** Garland Formon, Editor; Kathie Lipe, Advertising Mgr. **Subscription Rates:** $13.50 individuals; $24 out of area; $26 out of state. **Remarks:** Accepts advertising.
Ad Rates: PCI: $4.50 **Circ:** 2,800

12875 Louisiana Roots
Randy DeCur & Assoc.
PO Box 383 Phone: (318)253-5413
Marksville, LA 71351 Fax: (318)253-7223

News magazine for genealogists. **Founded:** 1994. **Freq:** Monthly. **Print Method:** Offset. **Cols./Page:** 5. **Col. Width:** 12 picas. **Col. Depth:** 13 inches. **Key Personnel:** Randy Decuir, Editor and Publisher; Kathie Lipe, Advertising Mgr. **Subscription Rates:** $13.50 by mail. **Formerly:** The Marksville Weekly News.
Ad Rates: BW: $1950 **Circ:** ‡5,000
4C: $295
SAU: $3.50

12876 American Cable Entertainment
403 N. Main St. Phone: (318)253-6504
Marksville, LA 71351 Fax: (318)253-0692

Formerly: Simmons Cablevision. **Key Personnel:** Stanley Poret, General Mgr. **Cities Served:** Marksville, LA.

12877 KAPB-AM - 1370
100 Chester St. Phone: (318)253-5272
PO Box 7
Marksville, LA 71351-0007

Format: Country. **Networks:** Independent. **Owner:** Tom Gay, PO Box 1319, Columbia, LA 71418, (318)649-7959. **Founded:** 1954. **Operating Hours:** 6 a.m.-6 p.m. **ADI:** Cincinnati, OH. **Key Personnel:** Tom Gay, Contact; Johnny Bordelon, Station Mgr.; Pat Tassin, Program Dir. **Local Programs:** *Avoyelles Wildlife Federation Report* 7:45 a.m.-8 a.m. Friday; *Cajun and Zydeco Music* 6 a.m.-9 a.m. Saturday; *Call in Swap Shop* 7:15 a.m.-7:30 a.m.; 12:15 p.m Monday-Friday. **Wattage:** 1000. **Ad Rates:** $7-9.50 for 30 seconds; $10-12.50 for 60 seconds.

12878 KAPB-FM - 97.7
520 Chester Phone: (318)253-9331
Box 7 Fax: (318)253-5262
Marksville, LA 71351

Format: Country. **Networks:** Westwood One Radio; Louisiana. **Owner:** Three Rivers Broadcasting, at above address. **Founded:** 1971. **Operating Hours:** Continuous. **ADI:** Alexandria, LA. **Key Personnel:** DeDe Lemoine, Program/Production Mgr. **Local Programs:** *Avoyelles Wildlife Federation Report* 7:45 a.m.-8 a.m. Friday; *Cajun and Zydeico* 6 a.m.-12 p.m. Saturday; *Call in Swap Shop* 7:15 a.m.-7:30 a.m.; 12:15 p.m Monday-Friday; *Drive Home Show Oldies Country* 4 p.m.-5 p.m. Mon.-Fri. **Wattage:** 6000 ERP. **Ad Rates:** $5-9.50 for 30 seconds; $8-12.50 for 60 seconds.

MARRERO

SE LA. Jefferson Parish. 10 mi. S. of New Orleans.

12879 KGLA-AM - 1540
3521 Industry Phone: (504)347-8491
PO Box 428 Fax: (504)340-4737
Marrero, LA 70072

Format: Hispanic. **Owner:** Ernesto Schweikert, 444 St. Charles Ave., New Orleans, LA 70130. **Founded:** 1969. **Operating Hours:** 6 a.m.-10 p.m. **Key Personnel:** Ernesto Schweikeit, President/Gen. Mgr.; Susan Gray, Sales Mgr. **Wattage:** 1000.

METAIRIE, pop. 135,816.

SE LA. Jefferson Parish. 5 mi. NW of New Orleans. Manufactures fabricated wire, concrete, wood products, automobile parts and accessories, carbon paper, electronic computers, fabricated structural steel. Agriculture. Sugarcane, cotton.

12880 Acres U.S.A.
PO Box 8800 Phone: (504)889-2100
Metairie, LA 70011-8800 Fax: (504)889-2777
Publisher E-mail: info@acresusa.com

Newspaper covering organic/sustainable agriculture, public policy issues, holistic human and veterinary health. **Subtitle:** A Voice for Eco-Agriculture. **Founded:** 1971. **Freq:** Monthly. **Print Method:** Offset. **Trim Size:** 10 3/4 x 15 1/2. **Cols./Page:** 4. **Col. Width:** 2 1/4 inches. **Col. Depth:** 14 inches. **Key Personnel:** Fred C. Walters, Jr., Editor and Publisher, editor@acresusa.com. **ISSN:** 1076-4968. **Subscription Rates:** $24 individuals; $3 single issue. **Remarks:** Accepts advertising.
Ad Rates: BW: $650 **Circ:** 10,000
4C: $850
PCI: $11

12881 Louisiana Life Magazine
111 Veterans Blvd., Ste. 1810 Phone: (504)834-9698
Metairie, LA 70005 Fax: (504)838-7700

Regional magazine. **Founded:** 1981. **Freq:** Quarterly. **Print Method:** Offset. **Trim Size:** 8 1/8 x 10 7/8. **Cols./Page:** 3. **Col. Width:** 31 nonpareils. **Col. Depth:** 133 agate lines. **Key Personnel:** Errol Laborde, Publisher, phone (504)830-7235, elaborde@nopg.com; Cassie Foreman, Publisher, phone (504)830-7233, fax (504)837-2258; Faith Dawson, Assoc. Editor, phone (504)830-7227; Eric Gernhauser, Art Dir., phone (504)830-7269. **ISSN:** 0899-0093. **Subscription Rates:** $15 individuals. **Remarks:** Accepts advertising. **Formerly:** Louisiana Life–Magazine of the Bayou State.
Ad Rates: BW: $3,150 **Circ:** ‡40,001
4C: $3,750

New Orleans Magazine - See New Orleans

12882 Thema
Box 8747 Phone: (504)887-1263
Metairie, LA 70011-8747
Publication E-mail: bothomas@juno.com

Theme-related literary journal. **Founded:** 1988. **Freq:** 3/year. **Print Method:** Offset press. **Trim Size:** 5 1/2 x 8 1/2. **Cols./Page:** 1. **Col. Width:** 3 1/2 inches. **Col. Depth:** 6 inches. **Key Personnel:** Virginia Howard, Editor. **ISSN:** 1041-4851. **Subscription Rates:** $16 individuals; $20 out of country; $8 single issue; $10 out of country. **Remarks:** Advertising not accepted.
Circ: Paid 300
Non-paid 100

12883 WCKW-FM - 92.3
PO Box 5905 Phone: (504)831-8811
Metairie, LA 70009 Fax: (504)831-8885
E-mail: rook923@wckw.com

Format: Album-Oriented Rock (AOR). **Owner:** 222 Corp., 3501 N. Causeway Blvd., Ste. 700, Metairie, LA 70009. **Founded:** 1966. **Operating Hours:** Continuous. **ADI:** New Orleans, LA. **Key Personnel:** Don Pardon, Sales Mgr.; Karol Brandt, Promotions Dir.; Melissa Muzzy, Traffic Dir. **Wattage:** 100,000. **URL:** http://www.wckw.com.

12884 WGSO-AM - 990
3525 N. Causeway Blvd., Ste. 1053 Phone: (504)834-9587
Fax: (504)833-8560
Metairie, LA 70002-3639

Format: News. **Networks:** CNN Radio. **Founded:** 1946. **Formerly:** WYAT-AM. **Operating Hours:** Continuous. **Key Personnel:** Ben Sudduth, News Dir. **Local Programs:** *News Talk - David Tyree Show* 4-6 PM Monday-Friday. **Wattage:** 1000 day; 400 night. **Ad Rates:** $25 per unit.

12885 WLMG-FM - 101.9
3525 N. Causeway Blvd., Ste. 1053 Phone: (504)593-6376
Fax: (504)593-2102
Metairie, LA 70002

Format: Adult Contemporary. **Owner:** Sinclair Radio of New Orleans, 2000 W. 41st St., Baltimore, MD 21211. **Operating Hours:** Continuous. **Key Personnel:** Johnny Andrews, General Mgr. **Wattage:** 100,000.

12886 WLTS-FM - 105.3
3525 N. Causeway Blvd., Ste. 1053 Phone: (504)834-9587
Fax: (504)833-8560
Metairie, LA 70002-7712

Format: Adult Contemporary. **Networks:** Independent. **Founded:** 1970. **Operating Hours:** Continuous. **Key Personnel:** Bob Mitchell, Program Dir. **Wattage:** 100,000.

12887 WMXZ-FM - 95.7
3525 N. Causway Blvd. Ste. 1053 Phone: (504)834-9587
Fax: (504)833-8560
Metairie, LA 70002

Format: Adult Contemporary. **Networks:** Independent. **Founded:** 1957. **Formerly:** WBYU-FM (1988). **Operating Hours:** Continuous; 100% local. **Key Personnel:** Ric Frances, General Mgr.; Ala Strzesniewski, Sales Mgr.; Pamela Sharp-Brown, Contact; Bruce Bond, Program Dir.; Thea Broussard, News Dir. **Wattage:** 100,000. **Ad Rates:** $15-100 for 60 seconds.

12888 WVOG-AM - 600
2730 Loumor Ave. Phone: (504)831-6941
Metairie, LA 70001

Format: Talk; Religious. **Networks:** Independent. **Owner:** F.W. Robbert Broadcasting Co., at above address. **Founded:** 1969. **Formerly:** WWOM-AM (1969). **Operating Hours:** 5:30 a.m.-9:00 p.m.; 100% local. **Key Personnel:** Eric Westenberger, Sales Mgr.; Fred P. Westenberger, Owner; Chris Westenberger, Vice President. **Wattage:** 1000. **Ad Rates:** $8.50 for 30 seconds; $10 for 60 seconds.

MINDEN†, pop. 15,074.

NW LA. Webster Parish. 30 mi. E. of Shreveport. Manufactures processed meat, fishing tackle, portable buildings, rubber roll covers, corrugated containers, air louvers and dampers, electric power, boats, trucks, trailers, generators, logging equipment. Oil wells. Agriculture. Dairying.

12889 Minden Press-Herald
203 Gleason St. Phone: (318)377-1866
PO Box 1339 Fax: (318)377-1895
Minden, LA 71055

Newspaper. **Founded:** 1846. **Freq:** Daily (eve.). **Print Method:** Offset. **Cols./Page:** 6. **Col. Width:** 26 nonpareils. **Col. Depth:** 294 agate lines. **Key Personnel:** Bonnie Koskie, Editor; Pat Culverhouse, General Mgr. **Subscription Rates:** $60 individuals. **Remarks:** Accepts advertising.
Ad Rates: BW: $686.70 **Circ:** Paid 4,844
4C: $896.70 Free 275
SAU: $5.45

12890 KASO-AM - 1240
PO Box 1240 Phone: (318)377-1240
Minden, LA 71058-1240 Fax: (318)377-4619

Format: Music of Your Life. **Simulcasts:** KASO-FM. **Networks:** Mutual Broadcasting System. **Founded:** 1952. **Operating Hours:** Continuous. **Key Personnel:** Mike Cole, Station Mgr.; David Graham, Sales Mgr. **Wattage:** 1000.

12891 KASO-FM - 95.3
412 Lakeshore Dr. Phone: (318)377-1240
Minden, LA 71055 Fax: (318)377-4619

Format: Full Service; Country. **Simulcasts:** KASO-AM. **Networks:** Mutual Broadcasting System. **Founded:** 1978. **Operating Hours:** 5 a.m.-9 p.m. **Key Personnel:** Jesse Lowe, Program Dir.; H.R. Boe Cook, Contact. **Wattage:** 3000.

12892 Minden Cable TV
726 Broadway Phone: (318)377-1978
Box 995 Fax: (318)371-0180
Minden, LA 71055

Key Personnel: Roland Miers, General Mgr. **Cities Served:** Minden, LA: 23 channels. **URL:** http://www.tca-cable.com.

MONROE†, pop. 57,597.

N LA. Ouachita Parish. On Ouachita River, 74 mi. W. of Vicksburg, MS. Northeast Louisiana University. Manufactures auto headlights, slacks, paper products, chemicals, paper, paper containers, store fixtures, furniture, awnings, pumps, bricks, fertilizer, ink, beverages, lumber, foundries. Oil and gas wells. Paper mill and converting equipment.

12893 Journal of Ministry Marketing and Management
The Haworth Press, Inc.
Northeast Louisiana Phone: (318)342-1185
Dept. of Mgt. & Marketing
Monroe, LA 71209
Publisher E-mail: getinfo@haworthpressinc.com

Journal on marketing and management issues in all types of church and ministry settings. **Founded:** 1993. **Freq:** Semiannual. **Trim Size:** 6 x 8 1/2. **Key Personnel:** Robert E. Stevens and David Loudon, PHD, Editor; Bill Cohen, Publisher. **ISSN:** 1057-1523. **Subscription Rates:** $24 individuals; $32 individuals; $48 libraries.
Ad Rates: BW: $300 **Circ:** Paid 119

12894 News-Star
411 N. 4th St., No. 1502 Phone: (318)322-5161
Monroe, LA 71201 Fax: (318)362-0225
Free: (800)259-7788
Publication E-mail: newstar@linknet.net

General newspaper. **Founded:** 1909. **Freq:** Mon.-Sun. (morn.). **Print Method:** Letterpress. **Cols./Page:** 6. **Col. Width:** 24 nonpareils. **Col. Depth:** 301 agate lines. **Key Personnel:** Kathy Spurlock, Exec. ed.; Ed Major, Publisher. **Subscription Rates:** $96 individuals. **Remarks:** Accepts advertising.
Ad Rates: PCI: $28.83 **Circ:** Mon.-Sat. ★**38,092**
Sun. ★**42,968**

12895 The Pow Wow
Northeast Louisiana University
700 University Ave. Phone: (318)342-5450
Monroe, LA 71209 Fax: (318)342-5452
Publication E-mail: powwow@nlu.edu

Collegiate newspaper (broadsheet format). **Founded:** 1931. **Freq:** Weekly (Fri.). **Print Method:** Offset. **Trim Size:** 13 x 21 1/2. **Cols./Page:** 6. **Col. Width:** 14 picas. **Col. Depth:** 196 agate lines. **Key Personnel:** Kristie Keller, Editor, phone (318)342-5457, fax (318)342-5452; Jarrett Reeves, Publications Mgr., phone (318)342-5451; Michael Gray, Advertising Sales Manager, phone (318)342-5454. **USPS:** 440-700. **Subscription Rates:** $10 individuals. **Remarks:** Accepts advertising. **Available Online. Feature Editors:** Shaundricka Tezeno, *Features.*
Ad Rates: 4C: $350 **Circ:** ‡7,000
SAU: $6

12896 KEDM-FM - 90.3
225 Stubbs Hall Phone: (318)342-5556
Monroe, LA 71209-6805 Fax: (318)342-5570
Free: (800)256-4085
E-mail: kedm@alpha.nlu.edu

Format: News; Classical; Jazz; New Age. **Networks:** National Public Radio (NPR); Public Radio International (PRI). **Founded:** 1991. **Operating Hours:** Continuous; 70% network, 30% local. **ADI:** Monroe, LA-El Dorado, AR. **Key Personnel:** Mark Simmons, General Mgr., phone (318)342-5559, fax (318)342-5570, msimmons@spock.nlu.edu; Mark Wilson, Chief Engineer, phone (318)342-5560, mawilson@spock.nlu.edu; Sunny Meriwether, News Dir., phone (318)342-5561, meriweth@spock.nlu.edu; Mark Simmons, Program Dir., phone (318)342-5559; Ray Davidson, Jr, Operations Mgr., phone (318)342-5558, rdavidso@spock.nlu.edu; Susan Allan, Development. Dir, phone (318)342-5557, alllain@spock.nlu.edu. **Local Programs:** *Lagniappe*, Sunny Meriwether, (318)342-5561, Fax (318)342-5570; *Mid Day Classics*, Mark Simmons, (318)342-5559, Fax (318)342-5570; *Straight, No Chaser (Jazz)*, Nick Deriso, (318)342-5556, Fax (318)342-5570. **Wattage:** 87,000. **Ad Rates:** Noncommercial. **URL:** http://www.kedm.nlu.edu.

12897 KJLO-FM - 104.1
PO Box 4808 Phone: (318)388-2323
Monroe, LA 71211-4808 Fax: (318)388-0569
E-mail: kjlo@bayou.com

Format: Country. **Networks:** ABC. **Owner:** New South Communications, PO Box 5797, Meridian, MS 39302, Free: (800)432-1041. **Founded:** 1983. **Formerly:** KWEZ-FM (1986). **Operating Hours:** Continuous. **ADI:** Monroe, LA-El Dorado, AR. **Key Personnel:** Bob Holladay, General Mgr., bobh@bayou.com; Mike Blakeney, Program Dir., mterry@bayou.com; Kerri May, Sales Mgr. **Wattage:** 100,000. **Ad Rates:** $18-33 for 30 seconds; $30-65 for 60 seconds.

12898 KLIC-AM - 1230
1700 Parkview Dr. Phone: (318)387-1230
Monroe, LA 71211

Format: Contemporary Christian; Talk. **Networks:** Moody Broadcasting. **Owner:** Fountain of Love Ministries, at above address. **Operating Hours:** Continuous. **Key Personnel:** Ken Fletcher, President. **Wattage:** 1,000.

12899 KLTM-TV - 13
c/o WLPB-TV Phone: (504)767-5660
7860 Anselmo Ln. Fax: (504)767-4288
Baton Rouge, LA 70810
Free: (800)272-8161
E-mail: comments@lpb.gen.la.us

Format: Public TV. **Simulcasts:** WLPB-TV Baton Rouge, LA. **Networks:** Public Broadcasting Service (PBS); Louisiana Public Broadcasting. **Owner:** Louisiana Public Broadcasting Network, at above address. **Founded:** 1976. **ADI:** Monroe, LA-El Dorado, AR. **URL:** http://www.lpb.gen.la.us/.

12900 KMLB-AM - 1440
Box 4808 Phone: (318)361-0786
Monroe, LA 71211 Fax: (318)388-0569
Free: (800)259-1440
E-mail: kmlb@kmlb.com

Format: News; Talk. **Networks:** ABC; CBS; Mutual Broadcasting System; EFM; ESPN Radio. **Owner:** New South Communications Inc., at above address, (318)388-2323. **Founded:** 1930. **Formerly:** KWEZ-AM (1991). **Operating Hours:** Continuous. **ADI:** Monroe, LA-El Dorado, AR. **Key Personnel:** Ed Holladay, President, phone (601)693-2661, fax (601)483-9826; Bob Holladay, General Mgr., bobh@bayou.com; Mike Downhour, Sales Mgr., miked@bayou.com; Grey Guylas, Program Dir.; Roger Bennet, Chief Engineer, rogerb@bayou.com. **Local Programs:** *Moon Griffon Show*, Greg Guylas, Program Dir., (318)388-2323; *Morning Journal*, Greg Guylas, Program Dir., (318)388-2323; *Soundoff with Lanny James*, Greg Guylas, Program Dir., (318)388-2323. **Wattage:** 5000. **Ad Rates:** $6-13 for 30 seconds; $9-19 for 60 seconds.

12901 KNLU-FM - 91.1
Northeast Louisiana University Phone: (318)342-5659
130 Stubbs Hall
Monroe, LA 71209-8821

Format: Soft Rock. **Founded:** 1973. **Operating Hours:** 18 hrs daily; 100% local. **ADI:** Monroe, LA-El Dorado, AR. **Key Personnel:** Joel Willer, General Mgr.; Mark Wilson, Chief Engineer. **Wattage:** 8500.

12902 KNOE-AM - 540
1400 Oliver Rd. Phone: (318)388-8888
PO Box 4067 Fax: (318)322-8774
Monroe, LA 71201

Format: Adult Contemporary. **Networks:** ABC. **Founded:** 1944. **Operating Hours:** Continuous. **ADI:** Monroe, LA-El Dorado, AR. **Key Personnel:** Randy Minter, General Mgr.; Brian Ringo, Program Dir. **Wattage:** 5000 day, 1000 night. **Ad Rates:** Advertising accepted; rates available upon request.

12903 KNOE-FM - 101.9
1400 Oliver Rd. Phone: (318)388-8888
PO Box 4067 Fax: (318)322-8774
Monroe, LA 71201

Format: Adult Contemporary. **Founded:** 1966. **Operating Hours:** Continuous. **ADI:** Monroe, LA-El Dorado, AR. **Key Personnel:** Randy Minter, General Mgr.; R. Mitchell, Program Dir. **Wattage:** 100,000.

12904 KNOE-TV - 8
1400 Oliver Rd. Phone: (318)388-8888
PO Box 4067 Fax: (318)322-8774
Monroe, LA 71201

Format: Commercial TV. **Networks:** CBS. **Founded:** 1953. **Operating Hours:** Continuous. **ADI:** Monroe, LA-El Dorado, AR. **Key Personnel:** Allen Jones, Station Mgr.; Roy Frostenson, News Dir.; Jerry Harrins, Chief Engineer; Eddie Rayner, Operations Mgr. **Local Programs:** *In Focus* 5-5:30 p.m. Saturday; *Knoe Good Morning Arkansas, Louisiana, Mississippi* 6-8 a.m. Monday-Friday.

12905 KTVE-TV - 10
2909 Kilpatrick Blvd. Phone: (318)323-1300
Monroe, LA 71201 Fax: (318)322-9718
E-mail: regionten@aol.com

Format: Commercial TV. **Networks:** NBC. **Owner:** Gocom Televison, 7621 Little Ave., Ste. 506, Charlotte, NC 28226, (704)341-0944, Fax: (704)341-0945. **Founded:** 1954. **Formerly:** KRBB-TV. **Operating Hours:** Continuous Mon.-Sat.; 5:30 a.m.-2:00 a.m. Sun. **ADI:** Monroe, LA-El Dorado, AR. **Key Personnel:** John Lewis, President, johnnyl@bayou.com. **Wattage:** Full Power VHF.

12906 KYEA-FM - 98.3
1200 N. 18th St., Ste. D Phone: (318)322-1491
Monroe, LA 71201-5449 Fax: (318)325-7203

Format: Urban Contemporary. **Networks:** American Urban Radio; ABC; NBC. **Founded:** 1968. **Operating Hours:** Continuous; 100% local. **ADI:** Monroe, LA-El Dorado, AR. **Key Personnel:** Barbara Dawson-Monk, General Mgr. **Local Programs:** *Old School Sunday*, Rockey Love, Mailing contact, (318)322-1491; *Sunday Evening Blues*, Jay Jaggers, Mailing contact, (318)322-1491. **Wattage:** 50,000. **Ad Rates:** $18-32 for 30 seconds; $28-42 for 60 seconds.

12907 Southwest Cablevision
PO Box 4028 Phone: (318)345-1010
Monroe, LA 71211-4028 Fax: (318)343-5255

Key Personnel: Jack Morgan, Manager. **Cities Served:** North Monroe, South Monroe, Calhoun and Columbia, LA.

MOREAUVILLE

C LA. Avoyelles Parish. 20 mi. NW of Simmesport.

12908 KLIL-FM - 92.1
Hwy I Phone: (318)985-2929
PO Box 365 Fax: (318)985-2995
Moreauville, LA 71355
E-mail: klil@kricket.net

Format: Adult Contemporary; Oldies. **Networks:** Unistar. **Owner:** Cajun Broadcasting, Inc., at above address. **Founded:** 1980. **Operating Hours:** 4 a.m.-10 p.m. Sun.-Thur.; 4 a.m.-midnight Fri.-Sat. **Key Personnel:** Louis B. Coco, Jr., Contact; Ray Kent, Program Dir.; Michael Ricaud, Sales Mgr.; Helen Roy, Traffic Mgr. **Local Programs:** *Farm and Home Show*, Louis Coco; *Greasor Show*, Louis Coco; *Sunrise Seranade*, Louis Coco. **Wattage:** 6000. **Ad Rates:** $3.50-5.25 for 15 seconds; $4.25-6 for 30 seconds; $5.25-7 for 60 seconds. **URL:** http://www.klil.com.

MORGAN CITY, pop. 16,114.

S LA. Saint Mary Parish. On Atchafalaya River, 70 mi. W. of New Orleans. Oyster shell, lumber, fur industries, shipbuilding. Commercial fisheries. Oil and gas wells. Timbers. Truck farms. Sugarcane, asparagus, cabbage.

12909 The Daily Review
1014 Front St. Phone: (504)384-8370
PO Box 948 Fax: (504)384-4255
Morgan City, LA 70381
Publication E-mail: review@petro.net

Community newspaper. **Founded:** 1872. **Freq:** Daily (eve.). **Print Method:** Offset. **Cols./Page:** 6. **Col. Width:** 25 nonpareils. **Col. Depth:** 301 agate lines. **Key Personnel:** Doyle E.

Shirley, Editor and Publisher; Andy Shirley, Advertising Mgr.; Steve Shirley, Publisher. **Subscription Rates:** $52 individuals; $104 by mail. **Remarks:** Accepts advertising.
Ad Rates: GLR: $.45 **Circ:** ‡6,374
BW: $812.70
4C: $1,112.70
PCI: $6.30

12910 St. Mary Journal
1014 Front St. Phone: (504)384-1350
PO Box 31 Fax: (504)384-4255
Morgan City, LA 70381
Publication E-mail: review@iamerica.net
Publisher E-mail: review@iamerica.net

Local newspaper. **Founded:** 1960. **Freq:** Semiweekly (Wed. and Sun.). **Print Method:** Offset. **Cols./Page:** 6. **Col. Width:** 26 nonpareils. **Col. Depth:** 294 agate lines. **Key Personnel:** Doyle E. Shirley, Publisher, phone (504)384-8370; Andy Shirley, Advertising Mgr., phone (504)384-8370. **Subscription Rates:** Free. **Remarks:** Accepts advertising.
Ad Rates: GLR: $.40 **Circ:** Free ‡10,500
BW: $722.40
4C: $1,022.40
SAU: $5.60
PCI: $5.60

12911 Allen's TV Cable Service Inc.
611 Everett Phone: (504)384-8335
PO Box 2643 Fax: (504)384-5243
Morgan City, LA 70381

Founded: 1960. **Key Personnel:** Greg Price, General Mgr. **Cities Served:** Bayou L'Ourse, Belle River, Berwick, Morgan City, Pierre Part, Stephensville, LA: subscribing households 9,000; 45 channels.

12912 KBZE-FM - 105.9
P. O. Drawer N Phone: (504)385-6266
Morgan City, LA 70380 Fax: (504)385-6268

Format: Blues. **Networks:** ABC. **Owner:** Hubcast Broadcasting, Inc., at above address. **Founded:** 1992. **Operating Hours:** Continuous. **Key Personnel:** Howard J. Castay, Jr., Pres./General Mgr.; Darlene L. Castay, Operations Dir.; Lee Condolle, Program Dir. **Wattage:** 6000. **Ad Rates:** Advertising accepted; rates available upon request.

12913 KFXY-FM - 96.7
409 Duke St. Phone: (504)384-1430
Morgan City, LA 70380 Fax: (504)384-2351

Format: Contemporary Hit Radio (CHR). **Founded:** 1967. **Wattage:** 6000.

12914 KMRC-AM - 1430
409 Duke St. Phone: (504)384-1430
Morgan City, LA 70380 Fax: (504)384-2351

Format: Sports. **Owner:** Tiger Island Broadcasting, Inc., at above address. **Founded:** 1954. **Operating Hours:** Continuous. **ADI:** Baton Rouge, LA. **Key Personnel:** Dennis Miller, President/Gen. Manager; Ray Robicheaux, Program and Music Dir., rayr@petronet.net. **Wattage:** 500. **Ad Rates:** $4-12 for 30 seconds; $6-16 for 60 seconds. **URL:** http://www.petronet.net/kfxy.

12915 KQKI-FM - 95.3
128 Pluto St. Phone: (504)395-2853
Morgan City, LA 70380 Fax: (504)395-5094
E-mail: kqki@cajun.net

Format: Country; Ethnic; French. **Networks:** Louisiana. **Owner:** Teche Broadcasting Corp., at above address. **Founded:** 1976. **Operating Hours:** Continuous. **ADI:** Baton Rouge, LA. **Key Personnel:** Paul J. Cook, Contact; Ernest D. Polk, Contact. **Local Programs:** *Saturday Cajun Show*, Bobby Richard; *Trading Post*, Dusty Rhodes. **Wattage:** 25,000. **Ad Rates:** $8.50-15 for 30 seconds; $11.50-18 for 60 seconds. **URL:** http://www.kqki.com.

12916 KWBJ-TV - 39
608 Michigan St. Phone: (504)384-6960
Morgan City, LA 70380 Fax: (504)385-1916

Format: Commercial TV. **Networks:** Warner Brothers Studios. **Owner:** ATVC Inc., at above address. **Founded:** 1986. **Formerly:** K39BJ. **Operating Hours:** Continuous. **ADI:** Baton Rouge, LA. **Key Personnel:** Greg Price, General Mgr., phone (504)384-8335, fax (504)384-5243; Carl Duplantis, Production Mgr.; David Price, Station Mgr.; Leda Booty, Traffic Mgr. **Local Programs:** *South Louisiana Quiz Bowl, NewsDay 39.* **Wattage:** 1000. **Ad Rates:** Advertising accepted; rates available upon request.

NAPOLEONVILLE†, pop. 829.

S LA. Assumption Parish. 55 mi. W. of New Orleans. Sugar factories. Agriculture. Sugarcane, corn, rice, cattle. Soybeans.

12917 The Assumption Pioneer
501 Assumption St. Phone: (504)369-7153
PO Drawer 428 Fax: (504)369-7153
Napoleonville, LA 70390
Community newspaper. **Founded:** 1850. **Freq:** Weekly (Thurs.). **Print Method:** Offset. **Cols./Page:** 6. **Col. Width:** 24 nonpareils. **Col. Depth:** 294 agate lines. **Key Personnel:** Philip Gianelloni, Editor and Publisher, fax (504)369-7157, pgia@aol.com. **USPS:** 034-780. **Subscription Rates:** $7.50 individuals; $0.25 single issue; $10.25 out of state. **Remarks:** Accepts advertising. **Alt. Formats:** Microform; Mailing labels.
Ad Rates: BW: $378.50 **Circ:** ‡2,500
4C: $778.50

NATCHITOCHES†, pop. 16,664.

NW LA. Natchitoches Parish. 68 mi. SE of Shreveport. Northwestern State University of Louisiana. Tourism. Historic landmark district. Manufactures gas, brick, lumber, plywood, paper, mobile homes, cottonseed, oil, cement products, garments, linerboard and laminated wood. Food processing. Fish hatchery, Agriculture.

12918 Current Sauce
Northwestern State University
Box 5306 Phone: (318)357-5213
Natchitoches, LA 71497 Fax: (318)357-6564
Publication E-mail: currentsauce@nsula.edu

Collegiate newspaper. **Founded:** 1914. **Freq:** Weekly (Tues.). **Print Method:** Offset. **Cols./Page:** 6. **Col. Width:** 27 nonpareils. **Col. Depth:** 294 agate lines. **Key Personnel:** Shawn Hornsby, Editor, phone (318)357-5381; John McConnell, Business Mgr.; Tom Whitehead, Advisor. **USPS:** 140-660. **Subscription Rates:** $20 individuals. **Remarks:** Accepts advertising.
Ad Rates: BW: $580.72 **Circ:** ‡3,500
SAU: $4.76

12919 The Natchitoches Times
Natchitoches Times Publications
PO Box 448 Phone: (318)352-3618
Natchitoches, LA 71458 Fax: (318)352-7842
Publication E-mail: andy@nat.1stnet.com

Local newspaper. **Founded:** 1903. **Freq:** Semiweekly (Thurs. and Sun.). **Print Method:** Offset. **Cols./Page:** 6. **Col. Width:** 27 nonpareils. **Col. Depth:** 294 agate lines. **Key Personnel:** Eric P. Jensen, Editor; Lo van B. Thomas, Publisher; Charles R. Norman, Advertising Mgr. **Subscription Rates:** $42 individuals. **Remarks:** Accepts advertising. **URL:** http://www.natchitoches.com.
Ad Rates: BW: $771.12 **Circ:** 8,000
4C: $1,151.12
PCI: $6.12

12920 KDBH-FM - 97.3
505 Royal St., Ste. B Phone: (318)354-4000
Natchitoches, LA 71457 Fax: (318)352-9598

Format: Adult Contemporary. **Networks:** Jones Satellite. **Owner:** Elite Broadcasting Company, at above address. **Founded:** 1965. **Operating Hours:** Continuous. **Key Personnel:** Bill Vance, General Mgr.; John Brewer, National Sales Mgr./Operations Dir.; Rick Beck, Local Sales Mgr. **Wattage:** 25,000. **Ad Rates:** Advertising accepted; rates available upon request. Combined advertising rates available with KNOC-AM. and KSBH-FM.

12921 KNOC-AM - 1450
505 Royal St., Ste. B Phone: (318)354-4000
Natchitoches, LA 71457 Fax: (318)352-9598

Format: Talk; News. **Networks:** ABC; Jones Satellite. **Owner:** Cane River Communications, at above address. **Founded:** 1947. **Operating Hours:** Continuous. **Key Personnel:** Bill Vance, General Mgr.; Rick Beck, Local Sales Mgr.; John Brewer, Ntl. Sales Mgr./Operations Dir. **Wattage:** 1000. **Ad Rates:** Advertising accepted; rates available upon request. Combined advertising rates available with KDBH-FM, KSBH-FM.

12922 KNWD-FM - 91.7
Northwestern State University Phone: (318)357-4180
PO Box 3038 Fax: (318)357-4434
Natchitoches, LA 71497
E-mail: knwd@alpha.nsula.edu

Format: Classic Rock; Alternative/New Music/Progressive; Urban Contemporary. **Networks:** Independent. **Founded:** 1974. **Formerly:** KNSU-FM (1980). **Operating Hours:** Continuous. **Key Personnel:** Casey Shannun, General Mgr.; Paul Ayo, Program Dir.; Mike Mess, Music Dir. **Wattage:** 250.

12923 KSBH-FM - 94.9
505 Royal St., Ste. B Phone: (318)354-4000
Natchitoches, LA 71457 Fax: (318)354-9598

Format: Country. **Owner:** Elite Broadcasting Corp., at above address. **Founded:** 1992. **Operating Hours:** Continuous. **ADI:** Shreveport, LA-Texarkana, TX. **Key Personnel:** Bill Vance, General Mgr.; George Sluppick, News Dir.; Gwen Paige, Traffic Mgr.; Ed Goble, Production Mgr.; John Brewer, National Sales Mgr./Operations Dir.; Rick Beck, Local Sales Mgr. **Wattage:** 25,000. **Ad Rates:** Advertising accepted; rates available upon request.

12924 KZBL-FM - 100.7
1115 Washington St. Phone: (318)352-9696
Natchitoches, LA 71457 Fax: (318)357-9595
E-mail: letters@kzbl.com

Format: Adult Contemporary. **Networks:** CNN Radio. **Founded:** 1985. **Operating Hours:** Continuous. **ADI:** Shreveport, LA-Texarkana, TX. **Key Personnel:** Hal M. Bundrick, Contact; Terry Gilberg, News Dir.; Rod Matthews, Chief Engineer. **Wattage:** 25,000.

NEW IBERIA†, pop. 32,766.

S LA. Iberia Parish. On Bayou Tech., 20 mi. SE of Lafayette. Manufactures oil exploration equipment, carbon black, spices, condiments. Sugar, rice, syrup, steel plants. Sawmills. Bottling works. Canneries. Commercial fisheries. Fur trapping. Salt mines. Oil wells. Timber. Diversified farming.

12925 Daily Iberian
Wick Communications
PO Box 9290 Phone: (318)365-6773
New Iberia, LA 70562-9290 Fax: (318)367-9640
Publication E-mail: dailyiberian@aisp.net

General newspaper. **Founded:** 1893. **Freq:** Daily (eve.), Sat. and Sun. (morn.). **Print Method:** Offset. **Cols./Page:** 6. **Col. Width:** 24 nonpareils. **Col. Depth:** 301 agate lines. **Key Personnel:** Will Chapman, Editor and Publisher. **Subscription Rates:** $102 individuals. **Remarks:** Accepts advertising.
Ad Rates: BW: $1,290 **Circ:** Mon.-Sat. ❑**14,633**
4C: $1,550 Sun. ❑**15,560**
SAU: $10

12926 KANE-AM - 1240
2316 E. Main St. Phone: (318)365-3434
New Iberia, LA 70560 Fax: (318)367-5385

Format: Oldies. **Networks:** ABC; Westwood One Radio. **Owner:** New Iberia Broadcasting Co., Inc., at above address. **Founded:** 1946. **Operating Hours:** Continuous; 11% network, 89% local. **Key Personnel:** Art Suberbielle, President/Gen. Mgr.; Ken Romero, Operations Mgr.; Mitzi Delcambre, Office Mgr. **Local Programs:** *Breakfast Club*, Ken Romero. **Wattage:** 1000. **Ad Rates:** $11-19.50 for 30 seconds; $14.50-26 for 60 seconds.

12927 KNIR-AM - 1360
PO Box 12948 Phone: (318)365-6651
New Iberia, LA 70562-2948 Fax: (318)365-6314

Format: Middle-of-the-Road (MOR). **Networks:** Westwood One Radio. **Owner:** Bonin Broadcasting Corp, at above address. **Founded:** 1969. **Operating Hours:** Continuous. **ADI:** Lafayette, LA. **Key Personnel:** Donald Bonin, President; Eddie Provost, Station Mgr.; Louis Cowen, Sales Mgr.; Dionne Johnson, News Dir. **Wattage:** 1000.

12928 KXKC-FM - 99.1
145 W. Main St. Phone: (318)365-6651
New Iberia, LA 70560 Fax: (318)365-6314
E-mail: kxkc@kxkc.com

Format: Contemporary Country. **Networks:** Independent. **Owner:** Bonin Broadcasting Corp., PO Box 12948, New Iberia, LA 70562. **Founded:** 1969. **Formerly:** KDEA-FM (1969). **Operating Hours:** Continuous. **ADI:** Lafayette, LA. **Key Personnel:** Louis Cowen, Sales Mgr.; Jerry Methvin, Operations Mgr.; Eddie Provost, Station Mgr.; Dionne Johnson, News Dir.; Donald Bonin, President; Patrick Bonin, Marketing & Promotion; Donald M. Bonin, Marketing & Promotion. **Wattage:** 100,000. **URL:** http://www.kxkc.com.

NEW ORLEANS†, pop. 557,482.

SE LA. Orleans Parish. On Lake Pontchartrain and Mississippi River, about 100 mi. above its mouth. Boat connections. Important port, shipping, financial and oil center. Cotton market. Extensive fisheries. Tulane University. Loyola University. Xavier University. University of New Orleans, Dillard Univ. & Southern Univ. at New Orleans. Private schools. Tourist center. Annual Mardi Gras Celebration. Manufactures acoustic materials, adhesives, aluminum, asbestos, cotton, electronics, petroleum refinery products, brick, burlap, cans, chemicals, cigars, coffee, clothing, disinfectants, fish oil and meal, floor tile, furniture, livestock feed, luggage, lumber, oil field supplies, paint, paper boxes, plumbing ware, roofing, sea food, ship building, soap and detergents, steel barrels, sugar, syrup and molasses.

12929 The Black Collegian
Black Collegiate Services, Inc.
140 Carondelet St. Phone: (504)523-0154
New Orleans, LA 70130-2526 Fax: (504)523-0271
Publisher E-mail: leon@black-collegiate.com

Career opportunity magazine featuring job searching, role models, interviews, entertainment, art, and African-American history. **Subtitle:** The Career & Self Development Magazine for African-American Students. **Founded:** 1970. **Freq:** Semi-annual (Oct.- Feb.). **Print Method:** Offset. **Trim Size:** 7 7/8 x 10 3/4. **Cols./Page:** 3. **Col. Width:** 13.5 picas. **Col. Depth:** 9 inches. **Key Personnel:** Preston J. Edwards, Publisher, preston@black-collegiate.com; Melba L. Nevills, Contact. **ISSN:** 0192-3757. **Subscription Rates:** $8 individuals; $4 single issue. **Remarks:** Accepts advertising. **Available Online.** **URL:** http://www.black.collegian.com.
Ad Rates: BW: $6,300 **Circ:** Paid 2,624
4C: $8,400 Non-paid 105,250

12930 Clarion Herald
Clarion Herald Publishing Co., Inc.
1000 Howard Ave. No. 400 Phone: (504)524-1618
New Orleans, LA 70113-1920 Fax: (504)596-3020
Publisher E-mail: clarionherald@clarionherald.org

Catholic newspaper (tabloid). **Founded:** 1963. **Freq:** Biweekly. **Print Method:** Offset. **Trim Size:** 10 3/8 x 14. **Cols./Page:** 4. **Col. Width:** 2 3/8 inches. **Col. Depth:** 14 inches. **Key Personnel:** Peter Finney, Editor; Maureen Austin, Advertising Dir. **Subscription Rates:** $15 individuals; $17 out of state; $23 out of country.
Ad Rates: GLR: $2.04 **Circ:** Paid ‡60,000
BW: $1,260
4C: $1,835
SAU: $31.50
PCI: $28.50

12931 Daily Journal of Commerce
Guide Publishing Co., Inc.
PO Box 52031 Phone: (504)368-8900
New Orleans, LA 70152 Fax: (504)368-8999

Trade newspaper covering construction news in Louisiana and Mississippi. **Founded:** June 1922. **Freq:** 5/week. **Print Method:** Offset. **Trim Size:** 14 1/2 x 23. **Cols./Page:** 6. **Col. Width:** 2 inches. **Col. Depth:** 21 inches. **Key Personnel:** Carlo Ragusa, Editor and Publisher; Paul F. Serpas, Advertising Mgr. **USPS:** 381-800. **Subscription Rates:** $270 individuals. **Remarks:** Color advertising not accepted.
Ad Rates: PCI: $10 **Circ:** (Not Reported)

12932 Dialogue Newsjournal
Box 71221 Phone: (504)581-3336
New Orleans, LA 70172
Journal supporting alternative politics and culture. **Subtitle:** New Orleans' Progressive Community Journal. **Founded:** 1981. **Freq:** Quarterly. **Print Method:** Offset. **Cols./Page:** 3. **Col. Width:** 2 inches. **Col. Depth:** 7 1/2 inches. **Key Personnel:** Brad Ott, Publisher. **Subscription Rates:** Free; $10 out of area. **Remarks:** Advertising accepted; rates available upon request.
Circ: Paid 350
Non-paid 1,650

12933 Fell Swoop
Acre Press
3003 Ponce De Leon St. Phone: (504)943-5198
New Orleans, LA 70119
Literary journal. **Subtitle:** The All Bohemian Review. **Founded:** 1983. **Freq:** 3/year. **Trim Size:** 8 1/2 x 11. **Key Personnel:** X.J. Dailey, Editor. **ISSN:** 1040-5607. **Subscription Rates:** $8. **Remarks:** Advertising not accepted.
Circ: ‡500

12934 Gambit Weekly
Gambit Communications
3923 Bienville St. Phone: (504)486-5900
New Orleans, LA 70119 Fax: (504)483-3156
Publication E-mail: gambitweekly@msn.com

Publication exploring politics, dining, and entertainment in New Orleans. **Founded:** 1980. **Freq:** Weekly. **Cols./Page:** 4. **Col. Width:** 14.5 picas. **Col. Depth:** 77 picas. **Key Personnel:** Margo DuBos, Publisher; Duane Dufrene, Controller; Clancy Dubos, Jr., Executive Editor, fax (504)488-7263; Kathleen Turpel, Advertising Dir., fax (504)483-3159; Eric Coleman, Classified Adv. Mgr., fax (504)483-3153; Mark Karcher, Production Mgr.; Dianne Hubbard, Office Mgr. **ISSN:** 1089-3520. **Subscription Rates:** $52 individuals. **Remarks:** Accepts advertising. **URL:** http://www.bestofneworleans.com. **Formerly:** Gambit.
Ad Rates: BW: $1,539 **Circ:** Free ❑44,714
4C: $1,939 Paid ❑76

12935 Hypertension
Lippincott Williams & Wilkins
Alton Ochsner Medical Foundation Phone: (504)842-4103 Fax: (504)842-4128
1516 Jefferson Highway, BH-514
New Orleans, LA 70121-2484
Publication E-mail: hypertension@comm.net

Journal covering the presentation of scientific investigation in the field of cv regulation as it may affect high blood pressure. **Founded:** 1979. **Freq:** Monthly. **Print Method:** Offset. Uses mats. **Trim Size:** 8 1/8 x 10 7/8. **Cols./Page:** 2. **Col. Width:** 19 picas. **Col. Depth:** 57 picas. **Key Personnel:** Edward Frohlich, MD, Editor; Cara Kaufmann, Publisher, cskaufma@lww.com; Debby K. Smith, Managing Ed. **ISSN:** 0194-911X. **Subscription Rates:** $302 institutions; $213 members; $348 individuals other countries; $281 members other countries; $30 single issue; $40 single issue other countries. **Remarks:** Advertising accepted; rates available upon request. **URL:** http://www.hypertensionaha.org. **Alt. Formats:** CD-ROM; Microfilm.
Circ: ‡4,442

12936 Infant Mental Health Journal
John Wiley and Sons, Inc.
Department of Psychiatry Phone: (504)568-3997
Louisiana State University Fax: (504)568-6246
New Orleans, LA 70112
Publisher E-mail: subinfo@wiley.com

Psychology journal that deals with all aspects of Infancy. **Founded:** 1980. **Freq:** Quarterly. **Print Method:** Offset. **Trim Size:** 6 3/4 x 10. **Cols./Page:** 1. **Col. Width:** 60 nonpareils. **Col. Depth:** 112 agate lines. **Key Personnel:** Joy D. Osofsky, Ph.D., Editor. **ISSN:** 0163-9641. **Subscription Rates:** $64 nonmembers in U.S., Canada, and Mexico; $80 nonmembers in other countries; $136 institutions in U.S.; $148 institutions in other countries. **Remarks:** Accepts advertising.
Ad Rates: BW: $200 **Circ:** Paid ‡1,010
Controlled ‡47

12937 Journal of Couples Therapy
The Haworth Press, Inc.
3500 St. Charles Ave. NW Phone: (504)891-1200
New Orleans, LA 70115
Publisher E-mail: getinfo@haworthpressinc.com

Journal devoted to the study of human bonding and intimacy, for couples, marriage, and family therapists and clinical practitioners. **Founded:** 1989. **Freq:** Quarterly. **Key Personnel:** Barbara Jo Brothers, MSW, Editor; Bill Cohen, Publisher. **Subscription Rates:** $40 U.S.; $52 Canada; $56 other countries; $60 U.S. Institutions; $78 Canada Institutions; $84 other countries Institutions; $125 U.S. Libraries; $162.50 Canada Libraries; $175 other countries Libraries. **Remarks:** Advertising not accepted. **Alt. Formats:** Microfiche.
Circ: 257

12938 The Louisiana Bar Journal
Louisiana State Bar Association
601 St. Charles Ave. Phone: (504)566-1600
New Orleans, LA 70130 Fax: (504)566-0930
Free: (800)421-LSBQ

Professional journal covering law in Louisiana for judges and lawyers. **Freq:** Bimonthly. **Trim Size:** 8 1/2 x 10 7/8. **Key Personnel:** Stephen Lucas, Advertising Sales Rep., phone (504)619-0178; Larry Feldman, Editor, phone (318)226-9100, fax (318)424-5128. **Subscription Rates:** $30 individuals; $6 single issue; $40 other countries. **Remarks:** Accepts advertising. **Online:** West Law, Lexis-Nexis.
Ad Rates: BW: $808 **Circ:** 17,900
4C: $1,333

12939 Louisiana Weekly
PO Box 53008
New Orleans, LA 70113

Black community newspaper. **Founded:** Sept. 25, 1925. **Freq:** Weekly. **Print Method:** Offset. Uses mats. **Cols./Page:** 6. **Col. Width:** 2 1/8 inches. **Col. Depth:** 21 inches. **Key Personnel:** Henry B. Dejoie, Sr. **USPS:** 320-680. **Subscription Rates:** $20 individuals; $.50 single issue. **Remarks:** Accepts advertising.
Ad Rates: GLR: $15 **Circ:** 10,000
BW: $1,890
4C: $2,340
PCI: $17.21

12940 Loyola Law Review
Loyola University School of Law
7214 St. Charles
New Orleans, LA 70118

Professional legal journal. **Freq:** Quarterly. **Key Personnel:** Christie L. Dannewitz, Business Mgr. **ISSN:** 0192-9720. **Subscription Rates:** $20 individuals; $6 single issue; $22 out of country. **Remarks:** Advertising not accepted.
Circ: (Not Reported)

12941 Naval Reservist News
Commander Naval Reserve Force
4400 Dauphine St. Phone: (504)678-6058
New Orleans, LA 70146-5046 Fax: (504)678-5049
Publication E-mail: cnrfpao@cnrf.nola.navy.mil

Tabloid newspaper for members of the Naval Reserve. **Subtitle:** News of the Total Force Navy for the Naval Reserve Community. **Founded:** 1946. **Freq:** Monthly. **Print Method:** Offset(web). **Trim Size:** 11x17. **Col. Width:** 28 nonpareils. **Col. Depth:** 83 agate lines. **Key Personnel:** Patricia S. Antenucci, Editor, phone (504)678-6058, fax (504)678-5049, nrnnews@cnrf.nola.navy.mil; Judy Katzwinkel, Editorial Assistant. **Subscription Rates:** Free to qualified subscribers. **Remarks:** Advertising not accepted. **URL:** http://www.navy.mil/navresfor/.
Circ: Controlled ‡100,000

12942 New Laurel Review
Smoke Bend Publishing
828 Lesseps St. Phone: (504)947-6001
New Orleans, LA 70117
Literary journal covering poetry, fiction, essays, translations, art, and reviews. **Founded:** 1970. **Freq:** Irregular. **Trim Size:** 6 x 9. **Key Personnel:** Lee Meitzen Grue, Editor; Lenny Emanuel, Poetry Editor. **Remarks:** Advertising not accepted.
Circ: (Not Reported)

12943 New Orleans Data News Weekly
Data Enterprises, Inc.
3501 Napolean Ave. Phone: (504)822-4433
New Orleans, LA 70125 Fax: (504)821-0320

Black community newspaper. **Founded:** 1966. **Freq:** Weekly. **Print Method:** Offset. **Cols./Page:** 5. **Col. Width:** 2 inches. **Col. Depth:** 14 inches. **Key Personnel:** Hank Cannon, Editor; Terry Jones, Publisher; Glenn Jones, Circulation Mgr. **ISSN:** 1043-4445. **Subscription Rates:** $21.50. **Remarks:** Accepts advertising. **Formerly:** New Orleans Black Data (1990); Data Newsweekly.
Ad Rates: BW: $1,517.60 **Circ:** Paid ‡380
4C: $600 Free ‡20,000
PCI: $19.71

12944 New Orleans Magazine
New Orleans Publishing Group, Inc.
111 Veterans Blvd., Ste. 1810 Phone: (504)831-3731
Metairie, LA 70005 Fax: (504)838-7700
Publication E-mail: nom@nopg.com

New Orleans lifestyle magazine. **Founded:** Oct. 1, 1966. **Freq:** Monthly. **Print Method:** Offset. **Trim Size:** 8 1/8 x 11. **Cols./Page:** 3. **Col. Width:** 13 picas. **Col. Depth:** 72 picas. **Key Personnel:** Errol Laborde, Publisher, phone (504)830-7235; Faith Dawson, phone (504)830-7227; Eileen Hodgins, Sales Mgr., phone (504)830-7206, fax (504)837-2258; Eric Gernhauser, Art Dir. **ISSN:** 0897-8174. **Subscription Rates:** $19.95 individuals. **Available Online.** **URL:** http://www.neworleans.com/no_ magazine/.
Ad Rates: BW: $3,275 **Circ:** Paid 14,660
4C: $4,300 Non-paid 33,952

12945 New Orleans Menu
New Orleans, Big Bend & Pacific Co., Publishers
PO Box 51831 Phone: (504)524-0348
New Orleans, LA 70151
Publication E-mail: menu@nomenu.com
Publisher E-mail: menu@compuserve.com

Periodical covering food, wine and cooking in New Orleans. **Founded:** Jan. 1977. **Freq:** Quarterly. **Print Method:** Offset. **Trim Size:** 5 1/2 x 8 1/2. **Cols./Page:** 2. **Col. Width:** 2 1/4 inches. **Col. Depth:** 7 inches. **Key Personnel:** Tom Fitzmorris, Publisher. **ISSN:** 8756-498X. **Subscription Rates:** $24 individuals; $10 single issue. **Remarks:** Accepts advertising.
Ad Rates: BW: $250 **Circ:** Combined 3,000

12946 New Orleans Preservation in Print
Preservation Resource Center
604 Julia St. Phone: (504)581-7032
New Orleans, LA 70130 Fax: (504)522-9275
Publisher E-mail: prc@prcno.org

Consumer magazine covering local, historic architecture. **Founded:** 1975. **Freq:** 10/year. **Print Method:** Offset. **Key Personnel:** Patricia H. Gay, Director; Mary Fitzpatrick, Editor; Jackie Derks, Advertising Mgr. **Subscription Rates:** $25 individuals. **Remarks:** Accepts advertising. **Former name:** Preservation Press.
Ad Rates: BW: $920 **Circ:** (Not Reported)
4C: $1,020

12947 New Orleans Review
Loyola University
Box 195 Phone: (504)865-2295
New Orleans, LA 70118 Fax: (504)865-2294
Publication E-mail: noreview@loyno.edu

Literary magazine featuring poetry, fiction, artwork, and literary

and film criticism. **Founded:** Dec. 1968. **Freq:** Quarterly. **Print Method:** Offset. **Trim Size:** 9 x 5 1/2. **Cols./Page:** 1. **Col. Width:** 4 1/2 inches. **Col. Depth:** 7 inches. **Key Personnel:** Ralph Adamo, Editor, adamo@.loyno.edu; Sophia Stone, Associate Editor. **ISSN:** 0028-6400. **Subscription Rates:** $18 individuals; $9 single issue; $21 institutions; $32 out of country. **Remarks:** Advertising accepted; rates available upon request. **Online:** Ingram Periodicals.
Circ: Paid ‡800
Non-paid ‡75

12948 Play Meter Magazine
Skybird Publishing Co., Inc.
PO Box 24170 Phone: (504)488-7003
New Orleans, LA 70184 Fax: (504)488-7083
Publication E-mail: news@playmeter.com

Magazine for the coin-operated entertainment/FEC industry. **Founded:** Dec. 1974. **Freq:** Monthly. **Print Method:** Offset. **Trim Size:** 8 1/2 x 10 7/8. **Cols./Page:** 4. **Col. Width:** 27 nonpareils. **Col. Depth:** 140 agate lines. **Key Personnel:** Valerie Cognevich, Editor; Bonnie T. Theard, Managing Editor; Carol P. Lally, Publisher; Ronald Kogos, Advertising Mgr.; Steven White, Technical Editor. **ISSN:** 1048-8243. **Subscription Rates:** $60 individuals; $5 single issue. **Remarks:** Accepts advertising. **URL:** http://www.playmeter.com.
Ad Rates: BW: $1,195 **Circ:** ‡6,000
4C: $1,745

12949 Preservation in Print
Preservation Resource Center
604 Julia St. Phone: (504)581-7032
New Orleans, LA 70130 Fax: (504)522-9275
Publisher E-mail: prc@prcno.org

Tabloid emphasizing preservation of New Orleans' & Louisiana's historic architecture and neighborhoods. **Founded:** Aug. 1975. **Freq:** Monthly. **Print Method:** Offset. **Trim Size:** 11 x 14. **Cols./Page:** 3. **Col. Width:** 27 nonpareils. **Col. Depth:** 205 agate lines. **Key Personnel:** Mary Fitzpatrick, Editor; Patricia H. Gay, Director. **Subscription Rates:** $15 members. **Remarks:** Accepts advertising. **URL:** http://www.prcno.org.
Ad Rates: BW: $800 **Circ:** Paid ‡9,000
4C: $1,200 Non-paid ‡3,000

12950 The Second Line
New Orleans Jazz Club
828 Royal St., Ste. 265 Phone: (504)455-6847
New Orleans, LA 70116
Traditional jazz magazine. **Founded:** Apr. 1950. **Freq:** Quarterly. **Print Method:** Letterpress and offset. **Trim Size:** 6 x 9. **Cols./Page:** 2. **Col. Width:** 28 nonpareils. **Col. Depth:** 101 agate lines. **Key Personnel:** Don Marquis, Editor. **ISSN:** 0037-0576. **Remarks:** Color advertising not accepted.
Ad Rates: BW: $100 **Circ:** ‡1,000

12951 SENGA
Megasin Publications
7501 Morrison Rd. Phone: (504)242-6022
New Orleans, LA 70126
Journal focusing on issues relating to the assessment and education of black children. **Subtitle:** Sensitive to the Educational Needs of Growing Americans. **Founded:** 1989. **Freq:** Quarterly. **Print Method:** Web offset. **Trim Size:** 8 1/2 x 11. **Cols./Page:** 3. **Col. Width:** 13 1/4 picas. **Col. Depth:** 10 inches. **Key Personnel:** Dorothy J. Aramburo, Editor. **ISSN:** 1044-0275. **Subscription Rates:** $25; $30 other countries. $9 single issue; $11 single issue other countries. **Remarks:** Advertising not accepted.
Circ: (Not Reported)

12952 Sugar Journal
Kriedt Enterprises, Ltd.
129 S. Cortez St. Phone: (504)482-3914
New Orleans, LA 70119 Fax: (504)482-4205
Publication E-mail: sweetpromo@aol.com

Sugar industry magazine. **Founded:** June 1938. **Freq:** Monthly. **Print Method:** Offset. **Trim Size:** 8 1/4 x 11 1/4. **Cols./Page:** 3. **Col. Width:** 13 picas. **Col. Depth:** 10 inches. **Key Personnel:** Romney Kriedt, Publisher. **USPS:** 364-710. **Subscription Rates:** $36 individuals; $71 other countries; $5 single issue. **Remarks:** Accepts advertising.
Ad Rates: BW: $930 **Circ:** Paid ★713
4C: $1,380 Non-paid ★3,459

12953 Surplus Line Reporter & Insurance News
Reporter Publishing Co.
Box 52193 Phone: (504)366-8797
New Orleans, LA 70152-2193 Fax: (504)366-1966
Publisher E-mail: ldleader@worldnetla.net

Tabloid for the insurance trade in Louisiana. **Founded:** Dec. 1982. **Freq:** Monthly. **Print Method:** Offset. **Trim Size:** 11 1/4 x 15 1/2. **Cols./Page:** 4. **Col. Width:** 14 picas. **Col. Depth:** 14 inches. **Key Personnel:** Carol DeGraw, Editor; Charles Hartwell, Publisher. **Subscription Rates:** $18 individuals; $2 single issue. **Remarks:** Accepts advertising.
Ad Rates: BW: $569 **Circ:** Non-paid ‡4,008
4C: $929

12954 Texas Surplus Line Reporter
Reporter Publishing Co.
Box 52193 Phone: (504)366-8797
New Orleans, LA 70152-2193 Fax: (504)366-1966
Publisher E-mail: ldleader@worldnetla.net

Magazine containing general news and photos for the insurance industry in Texas. **Founded:** Mar. 1985. **Freq:** Monthly. **Print Method:** Offset. **Trim Size:** 11 1/4 x 15 1/2. **Cols./Page:** 4. **Col. Width:** 14 picas. **Col. Depth:** 14 inches. **Key Personnel:** Carol DeGraw, Editor; Charles Hartwell, Publisher; Kathy Childress, Advertising Mgr. **Subscription Rates:** $18 individuals. **Remarks:** Accepts advertising.
Ad Rates: BW: $646 **Circ:** Paid ‡835
Non-paid ‡5,110

12955 The Times-Picayune
Times-Picayune Publishing Corp.
3800 Howard Ave. Phone: (504)826-3729
New Orleans, LA 70125-1429 Fax: (504)826-3007
Free: (800)925-0000
Publication E-mail: webmaster@neworleans.net

General newspaper. **Founded:** Jan. 25, 1837. **Freq:** Daily and Sunday (morn.). **Print Method:** Offset. **Cols./Page:** 6. **Col. Width:** 2 1/16 inches. **Col. Depth:** 21 1/4 inches. **Key Personnel:** Jim Amoss, Editor; Ashton Phelps, Jr., Publisher; Robert O'Neill, Advertising Mgr. **Subscription Rates:** $11 daily and Sunday; $7 Sunday; $.50 single issue Daily; $1.50 single issue Sunday. **Online:** Dialog (The Dialog Corporation); DataTimes Corporation; CompuServe Information Service. **URL:** http://www.neworleans.net. **Formerly:** The Times-Picayune/States-Item. **Feature Editors:** Jim Amoss, *News*, phone (504)586-3560; Bettye Anding, *Family*, *Sunday*, phone (504)586-3575; MaryLou Atkinson, *Women's*, phone (504)586-3655; Millie Ball, *Travel*, phone (504)586-3668; Chris Bynum, *Fashion*, phone (504)586-3655; Dale Curry, *Food*, phone (504)586-3575; Valerie Faciane, *Religion*, phone (504)586-3560; Malcolm Forsyth, *Editorials*, phone (504)586-3605; Frank Gagnard, *Music*, phone (504)586-3687; Cindy Hardy, *Features*; Peter Kovacs, *City*, phone (504)586-3560; Mark Lorando, *TV & Radio*, phone (504)586-3665; Bruce Nolan, *Religion*, phone (504)586-3344; Nell Nolan, *Society*, phone (504)586-3655; Dominic Papatola, *Drama*, phone (504)586-3687; Doug Parker, *Photo*, phone (504)586-3686; Renee Peck, *Movie*, phone (504)586-3467; Robert Rhoden, *Aviation*, phone (504)586-3365; Steve Rocca, *Sports*, phone (504)586-3405; Robert Scott, *Financial/Business*, phone (504)586-3418; Greg Thomas, *Real Estate*, phone (504)586-3678.
Circ: Mon.-Sat. ★**259,317**
Sun. ★**296.462**

12956 Tulane Medicine
1430 Tulane Ave., TW 34 Phone: (504)582-7951
New Orleans, LA 70112
Alumni magazine. **Freq:** Semiannual. **Key Personnel:** Stacy Day, Editor, sday@tmcpop.tmc.tulane.edu. **Remarks:** Advertising not accepted.
Circ: (Not Reported)

12957 Tulanian
Tulane Publications
3439 Prytania St., Ste. 400 Phone: (504)865-5714
New Orleans, LA 70115 Fax: (504)865-5621
Publication E-mail: tulanian@mailhost.tcs.tulane.edu

Magazine for college alumni. **Founded:** 1926. **Freq:** Quarterly. **Print Method:** Offset. **Trim Size:** 8 3/8 x 10 7/8. **Cols./Page:** 4. **Col. Width:** 9.5 picas. **Col. Depth:** 120 agate lines. **Key Personnel:** Suzanne Johnson, Editor. **ISSN:** 0041-4026. **Remarks:** Advertising not accepted.
Circ: Controlled 83,000

12958 Xavier Review
Xavier University of Louisiana
Box 110C Phone: (504)483-7481
New Orleans, LA 70125
Literary journal. **Founded:** 1980. **Freq:** Semiannual. **Key Personnel:** Thomas Bonner, Jr., Editor; Robert E. Skinner, Managing Editor, phone (504)483-7303. **ISSN:** 0887-6681. **Subscription Rates:** $10 individuals; $5 single issue. **Remarks:** Advertising not accepted.
Circ: Combined 300

12959 Cox Communications Louisiana
2120 Canal St. Phone: (504)734-7345
New Orleans, LA 70112 Fax: (504)522-0329

Founded: 1982. **Formerly:** Cox Cable of New Orleans. **Cities Served:** Orleans, Jefferson and St. Charles Parishes, LA.: 8 community access channels.

12960 KHOM-FM - 104.1
1001 Howard Ave., Ste. 4200 Phone: (504)524-5158
New Orleans, LA 70113 Fax: (504)522-6544

Format: Contemporary Hit Radio (CHR). **Owner:** Clear Channel Communications, at above address. **Founded:** 1968. **Operating Hours:** Continuous. **ADI:** New Orleans, LA. **Key Personnel:** Bill Thorman, Program Dir.; Kandy Klutch, Asst. Program Dir.; Tom Naylor, Music Dir.; Greg Benefield, Sales Mgr. **Wattage:** 100,000.

12961 KKND-FM - 106.7
929 Howard Ave. Phone: (504)679-7300
New Orleans, LA 70113 Fax: (504)679-7342

Format: Alternative/New Music/Progressive. **Networks:** Westwood One Radio. **Owner:** Clear Channel Radio Inc., 200 Concord Plaza, San Antonio, TX 78216. **Operating Hours:** Continuous. **ADI:** New Orleans, LA. **Key Personnel:** Earnest James, V. P./Marketing Mgr.; Dave Stewart, Operations Mgr. **Wattage:** 100,000. **URL:** http://www.1067theend.com.

KMEZ-FM - See Belle Chasse

12962 KTLN-FM - 90.5
2000 Lakeshore Dr. Phone: (504)280-7000
New Orleans, LA 70148 Fax: (504)280-6061
Free: (800)286-7002

Format: Classical; Public Radio. **Networks:** National Public Radio (NPR). **Owner:** University of New Orleans, at above address. **Founded:** Aug. 1995. **Operating Hours:** Continuous. **Key Personnel:** John S. Batson, General Mgr., jbatson@uno.edu; Ron C. Curtis, Operations Mgr., rcurtis@uno.edu. **Ad Rates:** Noncommercial; underwriting available. **URL:** http://www.wwno.uno.edu.

12963 WBOK-AM - 1230
1639 Gentilly Blvd. Phone: (504)943-4600
New Orleans, LA 70119-2100 Fax: (504)944-4662

Format: Religious. **Networks:** Independent. **Founded:** 1951. **Operating Hours:** Continuous. **ADI:** New Orleans, LA. **Key Personnel:** Annette Pete, General Mgr., phone (504)943-4600, fax (504)944-4662. **Wattage:** 1000.

12964 WBSN-FM - 89.1
3939 Gentilly Blvd. Phone: (504)286-3600
New Orleans, LA 70126

Format: Adult Contemporary; Religious. **Founded:** 1978. **Operating Hours:** Continuous. **ADI:** New Orleans, LA. **Key Personnel:** Rick Funderburk, General Mgr.; Stan Watts, Program Dir.; Brian Sanders, Contact. **Wattage:** 10,000. **Ad Rates:** Noncommercial.

12965 WBYU-AM - 1450
1515 St. Charles Ave. Phone: (504)522-1450
New Orleans, LA 70130-4445 Fax: (504)528-9244

Format: Easy Listening. **Founded:** 1950. **Formerly:** WWIW-AM (1988). **Operating Hours:** Continuous. **ADI:** New Orleans, LA. **Key Personnel:** David Smith, Sales Mgr. **Wattage:** 1000. **Ad Rates:** Advertising accepted; rates available upon request.

12966 WDSU-TV - 6
846 Howard Ave. Phone: (504)679-0600
New Orleans, LA 70113 Fax: (504)679-0733
E-mail: wdsu@com.net

Format: Commercial TV. **Networks:** NBC. **Founded:** 1948. **Operating Hours:** Continuous. **ADI:** New Orleans, LA. **Key Personnel:** Wayne Barnett, General Mgr.; Blaine Mitchell, General Sales Mgr.; Kurt Davis, News Dir.; Carl Bauman, Marketing Mgr.; Brian Norman, Production Mgr.; Fred Steurer, Chief Engineer. **Local Programs:** *Midday* 11:30 a.m., Kurt Davis; *Newscasts* 5 p.m., 6 p.m., 10 p.m., Kurt Davis; *6 News Today* 6 a.m., Kurt Davis. **Wattage:** 100,000. **URL:** http://www.wdsu.com.

12967 WGNO-TV - 26
World Trade Center, Ste. 2800 Phone: (504)581-2600
2 Canal St. Fax: (504)581-2182
New Orleans, LA 70130
E-mail: wgwo-tv@tribune.com

Format: Commercial TV. **Networks:** ABC. **Founded:** 1967. **Formerly:** WWOM-TV. **Operating Hours:** Continuous. **ADI:** New Orleans, LA. **Key Personnel:** William C. Ross, Contact; Micheal LaBonia, General Sales Mgr. **Wattage:** 2.69 mega watts. **Ad Rates:** $50-4,000 per unit.

12968 WLAE-TV - 32
2929 S. Carrollton Ave. Phone: (504)866-7411
New Orleans, LA 70118 Fax: (504)861-5186
Free: (800)725-7411
E-mail: info@wlae.pbs.org

Format: Public TV. **Networks:** Public Broadcasting Service (PBS). **Founded:** 1984. **Operating Hours:** 8:30 a.m.-11 p.m. **ADI:** New Orleans, LA. **Key Personnel:** John Pela, General Mgr.; Shannon Kirkpatrick, Promotions Dir.; Joslyn Yeager, Program Dir.; Mark Coudrain, Operations Mgr. **Wattage:** 2,900,000. **URL:** http://www.pbs.org/wlae.

12969 WNOE-AM - 1060
529 Bienville St. Phone: (504)529-1212
New Orleans, LA 70130-2290 Fax: (504)525-1011

Format: Contemporary Country. **Networks:** Independent. **Founded:** 1925. **Operating Hours:** Continuous. **ADI:** New Orleans, LA. **Key Personnel:** Reggie Bates, Station Mgr. **Wattage:** 50,000 day; 5000 night.

12970 WNOE-FM - 101.1
929 Howard Ave. Phone: (504)679-7300
New Orleans, LA 70113 Fax: (504)679-7345

Format: Contemporary Country. **Networks:** Independent. **Founded:** 1968. **Operating Hours:** Continuous. **ADI:** New Orleans, LA. **Key Personnel:** Richard Turkheimer, General Mgr. **Wattage:** 100,000.

12971 WNOL-TV - 38
1661 Canal St., Ste. 1200 Phone: (504)525-3838
New Orleans, LA 70112-2861 Fax: (504)569-0908
E-mail: wnol@ com.net

Format: Commercial TV. **Networks:** Warner Brothers Studios. **Owner:** Quincy Jones Broadcasting, at above address. **Founded:** 1984. **Operating Hours:** Continuous except Mon. 1 a.m.-6 a.m. **ADI:** New Orleans, LA. **Key Personnel:** Bob Lawrence, Chief Engineer, llawrence@wb38.com; Betty Moore, Business Mgr., fax (504)569-0952, bmoore@wb38.com; Gary Furlow, Production Mgr., fax (504)569-0947, gfurlow@wb38.com.

12972 WODT-AM - 1280
2228 Gravier St. Phone: (504)827-6000
New Orleans, LA 70113

Format: Blues. **Owner:** Clear Channel Radio, at above address. **Operating Hours:** Continuous. **Key Personnel:** Earnest James, VP/Marketing Mgr.; Gerod Stevens, Program Dir.; Connie Macera, Sales Mgr.

12973 WODT-FM - 1280
2228 Gravier Phone: (504)827-6000
New Orleans, LA 70119 Fax: (504)827-6048

Format: Blues. **Networks:** ABC. **Founded:** 1923. **Operating Hours:** Continuous; 100%. **ADI:** New Orleans, LA. **Key Personnel:** Connie Macera, Sales Mgr., cmacera@radioforneworleans.com; Gerod Stevens, Program Dir., fax (504)827-6045; Monica Pierre, News Dir., fax (504)827-6047; Earnest James, Vice Pres./Market Mgr., fax (504)827-6047, eljames@radioforneworleans.com. **Wattage:** 5000.

12974 WQUE-FM - 93.3
2228 Gravier Phone: (504)827-6000
New Orleans, LA 70119 Fax: (504)827-6045

Format: Urban Contemporary. **Networks:** Independent. **Founded:** 1949. **Formerly**: WDSU-FM. **Operating Hours:** Continuous; 100%. **ADI:** New Orleans, LA. **Key Personnel:** Gerod Stevens, Program Dir.; Monica Pierre, News Dir.; Earnest L. James, Vice President/Market Mgr., phone (504)679-7300, eljames@radioforneworleans.com. **Wattage:** 100,000. **Ad Rates:** $95-225 per unit.

12975 WRBH-FM - 88.3
3606 Magazine St. Phone: (504)899-1144
New Orleans, LA 70115-2545 Fax: (504)899-1165

Format: Public Radio. **Networks:** Independent. **Owner:** Radio for the Blind and Print Handicapped, Inc., at above address. **Founded:** 1975. **Operating Hours:** Continuous. **ADI:** New Orleans, LA. **Key Personnel:** Randy A. Savoie, General Mgr.; Katrina Geenen, Office Mgr.; Nora Wall, Development Dir.; Phyllis Jordan, President; Joe Burns, Vice President. **Wattage:** 5300. **Ad Rates:** Underwriting available.

12976 WSHO-AM - 800
1001 Howard Ave., No. 4304 Phone: (504)527-0800
New Orleans, LA 70113-2045 Fax: (504)527-0881
E-mail: wsho@cis.compuserve.com

Format: Talk; Religious; Contemporary Christian. **Networks:** International Broadcasting; Ambassador Inspirational Radio. **Owner:** Shadowlands Communications, L.L.C., at above address. **Founded:** 1926. **Operating Hours:** Continuous; 50% local, 50% network. **ADI:** New Orleans, LA. **Key Personnel:** Jean Epps, Traffic Mgr., phone (504)527-0800, fax (504)527-0881, wsho@cis.compuserve.com; David Gerdes, Program Dir.; William Ainsworth, Station Mgr. **Local Programs:** *Christian Bookshelf* 5:30 pm - 6:00 pm Friday, Jean Epps, Mailing contact. **Wattage:** 1000. **Ad Rates:** $25 for 60 seconds. **URL:** http://www.wsho.com.

12977 WSMB-AM - 1350
1450 Poydras St., Ste. 440 Phone: (504)593-2100
New Orleans, LA 70112 Fax: (504)593-1850

Format: Talk; News. **Networks:** CBS. **Founded:** 1925. **Operating Hours:** Continuous. **ADI:** New Orleans, LA. **Key Personnel:** John Andrews, General Mgr.; Bob Christopher, Operations Dir. **Wattage:** 5000. **Ad Rates:** Advertising accepted; rates available upon request.

12978 WTUL-FM - 91.5
Tulane University Center Phone: (504)865-5887
New Orleans, LA 70118 Fax: (504)862-3072
E-mail: wtul@mailhost.tcs.tulane.edu

Format: Full Service; Public Radio. **Networks:** Independent. **Owner:** Administrators of the Tulane University Educational Fund, at above address. **Founded:** 1961. **Formerly:** WAVE-FM (1961). **Operating Hours:** Continuous; 100% local. **ADI:** New Orleans, LA. **Key Personnel:** Sara Bonisteel, General Mgr.; Igor Siddigui, Program Dir.; Anthony DelRosario, Music Dir.; Chris McStay, Program Dir.; Jake Springfield, Music Dir.; Andy Bizer, Music Dir.; Valeska French, News Dir.; Brandon Cowart, Sponsorship Dir. **Wattage:** 1500. **Ad Rates:** Noncommercial.

12979 WVUE-TV - 8
1025 S. Jefferson Davis Pkwy. Phone: (504)483-1219
New Orleans, LA 70125 Fax: (504)483-1543

Format: Commercial TV. **Networks:** ABC; Fox. **Owner:** Emmis broadcasting Inc., 40 Monument Circle,, Ste.700, Indianapolis, IN 46204, (317)266-0100. **Operating Hours:** Continuous; 25% network, 75% local. **ADI:** New Orleans, LA. **Key Personnel:** Madolyn Bonnot, Vice President, phone (504)486-6161 Ext. 1100, fax (504)483-1107, mbonnot@wvue.emmis.com; Brian Pagragan, VP of Finance, phone (504)486-6161, fax (504)483-1107, bpagragan@wvue.emmis.com; Shela Thompson, General Sales Mgr., sthompson2atswvue.emmis.com; Ann Rogers, Dir. of Marketing/Promotions, arogers@wvue.emmis.com; Dan Wanko, General Sales Mgr. **Local Programs:** *Kidvue*; *News Makers*; *The Players Show*.

12980 WWL-AM - 870
1450 Poydras, Ste. 440 Phone: (504)593-6376
New Orleans, LA 70112-6010 Fax: (504)593-2135

Format: News; Talk; Sports. **Networks:** ABC; CBS. **Founded:** 1922. **Operating Hours:** Continuous. **ADI:** New Orleans, LA. **Key Personnel:** Johnny Andrews, General Mgr. **Wattage:** 50,000.

12981 WWL-TV - 4
1024 N. Rampart St. Phone: (504)529-6204
New Orleans, LA 70116 Fax: (504)529-6471
E-mail: creigert@wwwl-tv.com

Format: Commercial TV. **Networks:** CBS. **Owner:** A.H. Belo Corp., 400 S. Record St., Dallas, TX 75202, (214)977-6606, Fax: (214)977-6603. **Founded:** 1957. **Operating Hours:** Continuous. **ADI:** New Orleans, LA. **Key Personnel:** J. Michael Early, General Mgr., phone (504)529-6200; Jimmie B. Phillips, Station Mgr./General Sales Mgr., phone (504)529-6395. **Local Programs:** *5 PM Eyewitness News*, Jimmie Phillips, (504)529-6395; *6 PM Eyewitness News*, Jimmie Phillips, (504)529-6395; *10 PM Eyewitness News Nightwatch*, Jimmie Phillips, (504)529-6395. **Ad Rates:** Advertising accepted; rates available upon request. **URL:** http://www.wwl-tv.com.

12982 WWNO-FM - 89.9
University of New Orleans Phone: (504)280-7000
New Orleans, LA 70148 Fax: (504)280-6061
Free: (800)286-7002
E-mail: jbatsn@uno.edu

Format: Classical; Jazz; News; Public Radio. **Simulcasts:** KTLN-FM 90.5. **Networks:** National Public Radio (NPR); Public Radio International (PRI). **Founded:** 1972. **Operating Hours:** Continuous; 60% network, 40% local. **ADI:** New Orleans, LA. **Key Personnel:** John S. Batson, General Mgr., phone (504)280-7003, jbatson@uno.edu; Marie-Jeanne Trauth, Development Dir., phone (504)280-7002; Robert Carroll, Chief Engineer, phone (504)280-7000; Ron Curtis, Operations Mgr., phone (504)280-7005, rcurtis@uno.edu; Fred Kasten, Jazz Dir., phone (504)280-7286. **Local Programs:** *Classical New Orleans*, Michael Arnold; *Inside the Arts*, Fred Kasten; *Musica Da Camera*, Michael Arnold. **Wattage:** 50,000. **Ad Rates:** Noncommercial; underwriting available.

12983 WWOZ-FM - 90.7
PO Box 51840 Phone: (504)568-1234
New Orleans, LA 70151-1840 Fax: (504)558-9332
E-mail: mailhost@wwoz.org

Format: Jazz; Blues. **Founded:** 1980. **Operating Hours:** Continuous; 100% local. **ADI:** New Orleans, LA. **Key Personnel:** David Freedman, General Mgr., phone (504)568-1239, david@wwoz.com; Maryse Dejean, Operations Mgr., phone (504)568-1238, fax (504)568-9267; Dwayne Breashears, Program Dir., phone (504)568-1239, fax (504)568-9332. **Wattage:** 4000. **Ad Rates:** Noncommercial; underwriting available. **URL:** http://www.wwoz.org.

12984 WYES-TV - 12
916 Navarre Ave. (70124) Phone: (504)486-5511
PO Box 24026 Fax: (504)483-8408
New Orleans, LA 70184-4026
E-mail: assist@wyes.pbs.org

Format: Public TV. **Networks:** Public Broadcasting Service (PBS). **Founded:** 1957. **Formerly**: WVUE-TV (1970). **Operating Hours:** 7 a.m.-midnight or 1 a.m. **ADI:** New Orleans, LA. **Key Personnel:** Randall Feldman, President; Roy Taglialavore, Dir. of Public Information; Beth Arroyo Utterbeck, Dir. of Broadcasting; Vic Giancola, Dir. of Finance; Judith Holton, Dir. of Development; Randy Davis, Dir. of Engineering. **Wattage:** 316,000 (Visual). **Ad Rates:** Noncommercial. **URL:** http://www.pbs.org/wyes.

12985 WYLD-AM - 940
2228 Gravier St. Phone: (504)827-6000
New Orleans, LA 70119 Fax: (504)827-6048

Format: Religious; Contemporary Christian; Gospel. **Founded:** 1949. **Operating Hours:** Continuous; 100% local. **ADI:** New Orleans, LA. **Key Personnel:** Kris McCoy, Program Dir.; Karen Hence, Promotions Coord.; Earnest James, General Mgr.; Connie Macera, General Sales Mgr. **Wattage:** 10,000. **Ad Rates:** $15-40 for 30 seconds; $50-90 for 60 seconds. Combined advertising rates available with WYLD-FM, WQUE-FM, WODT-AM. **URL:** http://www.am940.com.

12986 WYLD-FM - 98.5
2228 Gravier St. Phone: (504)827-6000
New Orleans, LA 70119 Fax: (504)827-6045

Format: Urban Contemporary. **Networks:** ABC. **Founded:** 1949. **Operating Hours:** Continuous. **ADI:** New Orleans, LA. **Key Personnel:** Earnest James, Vice Pres./Market Mgr.; LeBron Joseph, Program Dir.; Connie Macera, Sales Mgr.; Karen Hence, Promotions Dir.; J.P. Robillard, Chief Engineer. **Wattage:** 10,000 day; 500 night.

NEW ROADS†, pop. 3,924.

SEC LA. Pointe Coupee Parish. 6 mi. from Mississippi River, 22 mi. NW of Baton Rouge. Garment factory. Oil and gas. Commercial fisheries. Diversified farming. Pecans, corn, sugarcane, cotton.

12987 The Pointe Coupee Banner
Pointe Coupee Printing & Publishing Inc.
123 St. Mary St. Phone: (504)638-7155
PO Box 400 Fax: (504)638-8442
New Roads, LA 70760
Community newspaper. **Founded:** 1880. **Freq:** Weekly (Thurs.). **Print Method:** Offset. **Trim Size:** 15 x 22. **Cols./Page:** 6. **Col. Width:** 12 picas. **Col. Depth:** 294 agate lines. **Key Personnel:** Mary Catherine Roy LaCour, Publisher; Brent Roy, Publisher. **ISSN:** 0032-2350. **Subscription Rates:** $20 individuals. **Remarks:** Accepts advertising.
Ad Rates: BW: $535 **Circ:** 5,200
PCI: $4.25

OAK GROVE†, pop. 2,214.

NE LA. West Carroll Parish. 48 mi. NE of Monroe. Cotton. Cannery. Agriculture. Sweet potatoes, tomatoes, soybeans. Cattle.

12988 West Carroll Gazette
North Louisiana Publishing, Inc.
Box 1007 Phone: (318)428-3207
Oak Grove, LA 71263 Fax: (318)428-2747

Community newspaper. **Founded:** 1910. **Freq:** Weekly (Wed.). **Print Method:** Offset. **Cols./Page:** 6. **Col. Width:** 25 nonpareils. **Col. Depth:** 294 agate lines. **Key Personnel:** Johney S. Turner, Editor; Kaye A. Crnkovic, Society Editor; Melba K. West, Office Mgr.; Bill Vaughn, Advertising Mgr.; Paul Stanton, General Mgr.; David Clevenger, Publisher. **Subscription Rates:** $20 individuals; $23 out of area; $29.50 out of state. **Remarks:** Accepts advertising.
Ad Rates: GLR: $.27 **Circ:** ‡2,300
BW: $516
PCI: $4.25

12989 KWCL-FM - 96.7
PO Box 260 Phone: (318)428-9670
Oak Grove, LA 71263 Fax: (318)428-2476

Format: Oldies. **Networks:** Louisiana; ABC; Jones Satellite. **Founded:** 1973. **Operating Hours:** Continuous. **Key Personnel:** Irene Robinson, Contact. **Wattage:** 6900. **Ad Rates:** $4-5 for 30 seconds; $6-8 for 60 seconds.

OAKDALE

12990 Oakdale Journal
PO Box 668 Phone: (318)335-0635
Oakdale, LA 71463-0668 Fax: (318)335-0431

Community newspaper. **Freq:** Weekly (Thurs.). **Cols./Page:** 6. **Col. Width:** 12.5 picas. **Col. Depth:** 21 inches. **Key Personnel:** Barbara Doyle, Editor, barbara@worldnetla.net. **Subscription Rates:** $22; $36. **Remarks:** Accepts advertising.
Ad Rates: SAU: $4.44 **Circ:** 3,000

OPELOUSAS†, pop. 18,903.

SC LA. Saint Landry Parish. 22 mi. N. of Lafayette. Manufactures lumber, brooms, drugs, perfume, salad oil, machinery. Cottonseed oil, meat processing and packing plants. Oil wells. Timber. Diversified farming. Cotton, corn, rice, jams.

12991 Daily World
2781 F49 S. Service Rd. Phone: (318)942-4971
PO Box 1179 Fax: (318)948-6572
Opelousas, LA 70571-1179
Free: (800)256-4522

General newspaper. **Founded:** 1939. **Freq:** Daily (eve.). **Print Method:** Offset. **Cols./Page:** 6. **Col. Width:** 26 nonpareils. **Col. Depth:** 301 agate lines. **Key Personnel:** Harlan Kirgan, Editor; Aaron Parsons, Publisher; Bill Brownlee, Advertising Mgr. **Subscription Rates:** $78 individuals. **Remarks:** Accepts advertising.
Ad Rates: GLR: $.67 **Circ:** Mon.-Fri. 12,558
BW: $1,417.91 Sun. 14,000
4C: $1,807.71
SAU: $10.99

12992 KOGM-FM - 107.1
PO Box 1150 Phone: (318)942-2633
Opelousas, LA 70570 Fax: (318)942-2635
E-mail: kslo@juno.com

Format: Oldies. **Networks:** Jones Satellite. **Founded:** 1965. **Formerly:** KSLO-FM; KOJM-FM. **Operating Hours:** 5 a.m.-11 p.m. **ADI:** Lafayette, LA. **Key Personnel:** Wandell Allegood, Manager; Wally LeBlanc, Chief Engineer; Johnny Wright, Sales Mgr. **Local Programs:** *KOGM's Breakfast Talk* 6am - 8 am Monday-Friday, Johnny Wright. **Wattage:** 3000. **Ad Rates:** $11.95-16.85 for 30 seconds; $14.85-17.90 for 60 seconds. Combined advertising rates available with KSLO.

12993 KSLO-AM - 1230
232 N. Ct. Phone: (318)942-2633
PO Box 1150 Fax: (318)942-2635
Opelousas, LA 70571-1150
E-mail: kslo@juno.com

Format: News; Information; Country; Contemporary Country; Agricultural; French. **Networks:** ABC. **Owner:** KSLO Broadcasting Co., Inc., at above address. **Founded:** 1947. **Operating Hours:** 5 a.m.-11 p.m.; 10% network, 90% local. **ADI:** Lafayette, LA. **Key Personnel:** Wandell Allegood, Manager; Wally LeBlanc, Chief Engineer; Rene Fontenot, Contact; Johnny Wright, Sales Mgr. **Local Programs:** *Church Point Radio Show*, Johnny Wright; *Farm Report*, Steve Benoit; *Ol' Tackle Box*, Johnny Wright. **Wattage:** 1000. **Ad Rates:** $7.80-11.95 for 10 seconds; $11.95-16.85 for 30 seconds; $14.85-17.90 for 60 seconds. Combined advertising rates available with KOGM.

PINEVILLE, pop. 12,034.

C LA. Rapides Parish. Across Red River from Alexandria. Louisiana College. Saw, paper mills. Detergent and chemical plants. Commercial fisheries. Pine, hardwood timber. Diversified farming. Cotton, corn, potatoes.

12994 Wildcat
Louisiana College
1140 College Dr. Phone: (318)487-7212
Pineville, LA 71359 Fax: (318)487-7310
Publication E-mail: wildcat@alex.lacollege.edu
Publisher E-mail: wildcat@alex.lacollege.edu

Collegiate newspaper. **Founded:** 1919. **Freq:** Weekly (during the academic year). **Print Method:** Offset. **Trim Size:** 11 1/2 x 15. **Cols./Page:** 4. **Col. Width:** 14 picas. **Col. Depth:** 196 agate lines. **Key Personnel:** Mike Trice, Adviser, phone (318)487-7220, miketrice@andria.lacollege.edu. **URL:** http://www.lacollege.edu/campus/wildcat/main.html.
Ad Rates: GLR: $4.50 **Circ:** Free 1,000
PCI: $5.85

KWDF-AM - See Ball

PLAQUEMINE†, pop. 7,521.

S LA. Iberville Parish. On Mississippi River, 14 mi. SW of Baton Rouge. Lumber, sugar mills, moss gins, bottling works; foundry, chemical plants. Commercial fisheries. Oil wells; cypress, oak, ash timber. Diversified farming. Rice, sugarcane, corn.

12995 Plaquemine Post-South
Plaquemine Publishing, Inc.
58650 Belleview Dr. Phone: (225)687-3288
PO Box 589 Fax: (225)687-1814
Plaquemine, LA 70764
Publisher E-mail: psnews@ettel.net

Community newspaper. **Founded:** May 9, 1957. **Freq:** Weekly (Thurs.). **Print Method:** Offset. **Trim Size:** 14 x 23. **Cols./Page:** 6. **Col. Width:** 2 1/16 inches. **Col. Depth:** 21 inches. **Key Personnel:** Ellie Hebert, Editor; Joyce S Hebert, Publisher. **USPS:** 576-480. **Subscription Rates:** $20 individuals; $30 out of area. **Remarks:** Accepts advertising.
Ad Rates: GLR: $0.40 **Circ:** Paid 5,872
BW: $705.60 Non-paid 146
4C: $1,105.60
SAU: $5.60
PCI: $5.60

PONCHATOULA, pop. 5,469.

SE LA. Tangipahoa Parish. 40 mi. NW of New Orleans. Lumber, veneer mills, brick, bottling works. Ships, fruit, vegetables. Cypress, hardwood timber. Poultry, truck, fruit farms. Strawberries, beans, peppers.

12996 The Enterprise
PO Box 218 Phone: (504)386-6537
Ponchatoula, LA 70454 Fax: (504)386-6537

Community newspaper. **Founded:** Mar. 11, 1921. **Freq:** Weekly (Wed.). **Print Method:** Offset. **Trim Size:** 7 x 11 1/2. **Cols./Page:** 6. **Col. Width:** 24 nonpareils. **Col. Depth:** 301 agate lines. **Key Personnel:** Don Ellzey, Editor and Publisher; Kate Day, Advertising Mgr. **ISSN:** 0889-0684. **Subscription Rates:** $8 individuals; $12 out of area. **Remarks:** Accepts advertising.
Ad Rates: GLR: $.17 **Circ:** Paid ‡2,100
BW: $290 Free ‡250
4C: $550
SAU: $2.50

12997 The Ponchatoula Times
PO Box 743 Phone: (504)386-2877
Ponchatoula, LA 70454 Fax: (504)386-0458
Publication E-mail: ptimes@ponchatoula.com

Community newspaper. **Subtitle:** The Newspaper of America's Antique City. **Founded:** Oct. 1, 1981. **Freq:** Weekly (Thurs.). **Print Method:** Offset. **Cols./Page:** 6. **Col. Depth:** 21 1/2 inches. **Key Personnel:** Bryan T. McMahon, Editor and Publisher; Terry Ann McMahon, Co-Publisher. **Subscription Rates:** $11; $5.50 students; $5.50 senior citizens. **Remarks:** Accepts advertising. **URL:** http://www.ponchatoula.com/ptimes/.
Ad Rates: BW: $509.55 **Circ:** ‡5,300
4C: $1,009.55
PCI: $3.95

PORT ALLEN†, pop. 6,114.

SEC LA. West Barton Rouge Parish. 1 mi. W. of Baton Rouge. Chemical, iron, steel fabricating plants. Sugar mills. Diversified farming. Sugarcane, rice, corn, cotton.

12998 The Louisiana Cattleman
Louisiana Cattlemen's Association
4921 I-10 Frontage Rd. W. Phone: (504)343-3491
Port Allen, LA 70767 Fax: (504)336-0002

Association magazine. **Founded:** 1967. **Freq:** Monthly. **Print Method:** Sheetfed offset. **Trim Size:** 8 1/2 x 11. **Cols./Page:** 3. **Col. Width:** 13 1/2 picas. **Col. Depth:** 10 inches. **Key Personnel:** Robert H. Felknor, Managing Editor; Sharon Hoffeld, Editor. **USPS:** 588-320. **Subscription Rates:** $25. **Remarks:** Accepts advertising. **Formerly:** The Louisiana Cattleman/The Louisiana Dairyman.
Ad Rates: BW: $515 **Circ:** Paid ‡3,900
4C: $1,010 Non-paid ‡800
PCI: $30

12999 West Side Journal
PO Box 260 Phone: (504)343-2540
Port Allen, LA 70767 Fax: (504)344-0923

Newspaper with a Democratic orientation. **Founded:** 1937. **Freq:** Weekly (Thurs.). **Print Method:** Offset. **Cols./Page:** 6. **Col. Width:** 13 picas. **Col. Depth:** 21 inches. **Key Personnel:** Sherry Romero, General Mgr.; Jeremy Alford, Editor. **Subscription Rates:** $12 individuals in parish; $15 out of parish. **Remarks:** Accepts advertising.
Ad Rates: GLR: $.32 **Circ:** 3,300
BW: $564.48
4C: $789.48
SAU: $4.48

13000 KPAE-FM - 91.5
13028 US Hwy. 190 W. Phone: (504)627-4578
Port Allen, LA 70767 Free: (800)324-1108

Format: Talk; Religious; News; Educational; Middle-of-the-Road (MOR); Gospel; Bluegrass. **Networks:** Moody Broadcasting. **Owner:** Willie F. Kennedy, 13030 U.S. Highway 190 W., Port Allen, LA 70767, (504)627-5801. **Founded:** 1984. **Operating Hours:** Continuous; 60% network, 40% local. **Key Personnel:** Willie F. Kennedy, Pres./Trustee; Arlene Kennedy, Secretary. **Wattage:** 5000. **Ad Rates:** Noncommercial.

RAYNE, pop. 9,066.

SW LA. Acadia Parish. 17 mi. W. of Lafayette. Rice mills, cotton gin. Garment and farm equipment manufactured. Steel fabricating plant. Oil wells. Rice, cotton, sugarcane, frog farms.

13001 The Rayne Independent
The Rayne Independent Newspaper
201 East South 1st St. Phone: (318)334-2128
PO Box 428 Fax: (318)334-2120
Rayne, LA 70578
Community newspaper. **Founded:** Nov. 2, 1967. **Freq:** Weekly (Thurs.). **Print Method:** Offset. **Cols./Page:** 6. **Col. Width:** 26 nonpareils. **Col. Depth:** 298 agate lines. **Key Personnel:** Lillian J. Cart, Editor and Publisher; Walter T. Cart, Advertising Mgr. **Subscription Rates:** $14 individuals; $17 out of area. **Remarks:** Accepts advertising.
Ad Rates: BW: $510 **Circ:** ‡4,160
4C: $660
SAU: $4.00
PCI: $4.00

13002 Tribune Plus
Rayne Acadian Tribune
108 N. Adams Ave. Phone: (318)334-3186
PO Box 260 Fax: (318)334-8474
Rayne, LA 70578
Shopping guide. **Founded:** 1982. **Freq:** Weekly (Wed.). **Print Method:** Offset. **Cols./Page:** 6. **Col. Width:** 2.4 picas. **Col. Depth:** 21 1/2 inches. **Key Personnel:** Frances R. Bihn, Advertising Dir./Contact. **Formerly:** The Tribune Hopper.
Ad Rates: PCI: $4.00 **Circ:** Free 4572

RAYVILLE†, pop. 4,480.

NC LA. Richland Parish. 22 mi. E. of Monroe. Cotton.

13003 Richland Beacon News
PO Box 209 Phone: (318)728-2250
Rayville, LA 71269 Fax: (318)728-5991

Official journal for legal news of the parish. **Freq:** Weekly (Thurs.). **Print Method:** Offset. **Cols./Page:** 6. **Col. Depth:** 21 1/2 inches. **Key Personnel:** Steve Colwell, General Mgr.; Richland Beacon, Publisher. **Subscription Rates:** Free; $11 institutions; $15 out of parish; $20 out of state. **Remarks:** Accepts advertising.
Ad Rates: 4C: $2.50 **Circ:** Paid ‡1,204
PCI: $6 Non-paid ‡1,471

13004 KTJC-FM - 92.3
1207 1/2 Louisa St. Phone: (318)728-5852
Rayville, LA 71269 Fax: (318)728-3571

Format: Religious. **Networks:** USA Radio; Christian Broadcasting (CBN); Louisiana Public Broadcasting. **Founded:** 1984. **Operating Hours:** 6 a.m.-10 p.m. **Wattage:** 26,000.

13005 KXLA-AM - 990
Hwy. 80 Phone: (318)728-6990
Box 990 Fax: (318)728-6990
Rayville, LA 71269

Format: Gospel. **Networks:** American Urban Radio. **Owner:** Red Bear Management, 1990 N. 18th, Suite 330, Monroe, LA 71201, (318)361-0347, Fax: (318)361-9885. **Founded:** 1957. **Formerly:** KRIH-AM. **Operating Hours:** 6 a.m.-12 a.m.; 10% network, 90% local. **Key Personnel:** Derrick Nation, General Mgr. **Wattage:** 1000. **Ad Rates:** $8 for 30 seconds; $12 for 60 seconds.

RUSTON†, pop. 20,585.

N LA. Lincoln Parish. 30 mi. W. of Monroe. Louisiana Tech University, Grambling State University. Manufactures soft drink bottles, chemicals, lumber, bricks, plywood, insulation, mop and broom handles, dairy and petroleum products. Timber, clay pits. Dairy, poultry, fruit, truck farms.

13006 Ruston Daily Leader
212 W. Park Ave., Phone: (318)255-4353
PO Box 520 Fax: (318)255-4006
Ruston, LA 71270-4314
Free: (800)287-4176

General newspaper. **Founded:** 1894. **Freq:** Daily (eve.), Sunday (morn.). **Print Method:** Offset. **Cols./Page:** 6. **Col. Width:** 25 nonpareils. **Col. Depth:** 294 agate lines. **Key Personnel:** Rick Hohlt, Publisher. **Subscription Rates:** $51 individuals. **Remarks:** Accepts advertising.
Ad Rates: SAU: $5.85 **Circ:** Paid ‡6,990
Non-paid ‡7,000

13007 The Tech Talk
Louisiana Tech University
PO Box 10258 Phone: (318)257-4427
Ruston, LA 71272-0045 Fax: (318)257-4558
Publication E-mail: ttalk@latech.edu

Collegiate newspaper. **Founded:** 1925. **Freq:** Weekly (Thurs.). **Print Method:** Offset. **Cols./Page:** 6. **Col. Width:** 26 nonpareils. **Col. Depth:** 298 agate lines. **Key Personnel:** Wiley Hilburn, Adviser. **Subscription Rates:** $25 individuals; Single issue free. **Remarks:** Accepts advertising. **Available Online. URL:** http://eb.journ.latech.edu/techtalk/index.html.
Ad Rates: BW: $765 **Circ:** Paid ‡8,000
PCI: $13.73

13008 KLPI-FM - 89.1
900 Gilman Phone: (318)257-4851
Ruston, LA 71270 Fax: (318)257-5073
E-mail: webmaster@klpi.org

Founded: 1966. **Formerly:** WLPI-FM. **Operating Hours:** 8:00 a.m.-12:00 a.m. **Key Personnel:** Tim Burga, General Mgr., gm@klpi.org; Kevin Berry, Music Dir., phone (318)257-4852, music@klpi.org; Fred McGhee, Program Dir., program@klpi.org. **Wattage:** 4000. **URL:** http://www.klpi.org.

13009 KPCH-FM - 97.7
1319 N. Vienna Phone: (318)251-3697
PO Box 977 Fax: (318)251-0699
Ruston, LA 71273-0977
Free: (800)250-2510

Format: Oldies; Sports. **Networks:** Louisiana. **Owner:** William W. Brown, 2608 N. Trenton, Ruston, LA 71270, (318)251-0699, Free: (800)250-2510. **Founded:** 1984. **Operating Hours:** Continuous. **ADI:** Monroe, LA-El Dorado, AR. **Key Personnel:** William W. Brown, Contact, phone (318)255-7179, fax (318)251-0699; Linda H. Brown, Operations Mgr.; Tommy Moore, Contact, phone (318)424-2769, fax (318)425-3057. **Local Programs:** *Bill Brown Git Down* 8 p.m. - 12 a.m. Saturday, Bill Brown, Mailing contact. **Wattage:** 50,000. **Ad Rates:** $8.82-14.11 for 30 seconds; $14.11-21.76 for 60 seconds.

13010 KRUS-AM - 1490
Box 430 Phone: (318)255-2530
500 N. Monroe St. Fax: (318)225-2100
Ruston, LA 71270

Format: Blues. **Networks:** AP. **Owner:** Ruston Broadcasting Co., Inc., at above address. **Founded:** 1947. **Operating Hours:** 20 hours daily; 1% network, 99% local. **ADI:** Monroe, LA-El Dorado, AR. **Key Personnel:** Dan Hollingsworth, Pres./Gen. Mgr.; James Cooper, Music/Sports Dir. **Wattage:** 1000. **Ad Rates:** $3.54-7.06 for 30 seconds; $7.06-11.77 for 60 seconds.

13011 KXKZ-FM - 107.5
PO Box 430 Phone: (318)255-5000
Ruston, LA 71273 Fax: (318)255-2100
E-mail: kxkz@lamerica.net

Format: Country. **Networks:** AP. **Founded:** 1965. **Formerly:** KRUS-FM (1977). **Operating Hours:** Continuous. **ADI:** Monroe, LA-El Dorado, AR. **Key Personnel:** Dan Hollingsworth, Pres./General Mgr./Chief Engineer; Bob Day, Music Dir.; Karen Jones, News Dir. **Wattage:** 100,000. **Ad Rates:** $26 for 30 seconds; $34 for 60 seconds. $26 for 30 seconds; $32 for 60 seconds.

13012 Ruston Cable TV
Box 737 Phone: (318)255-6594
Ruston, LA 71273 Fax: (318)251-2711

Key Personnel: William R. Rogers, General Mgr. **Cities Served:** Grambling, Simsboro, Vienna, and Ruston, LA.

ST. FRANCISVILLE

13013 St. Francisville Democrat
Louisiana Suburban Press
4749 Johnson St. Phone: (504)635-3366
PO Drawer 1876 Fax: (504)635-3398
St. Francisville, LA 70775-1876
Community newspaper serving West Feliciana Parish. **Founded:** Feb. 3, 1892. **Freq:** Weekly (Thurs.). **Print Method:** Offset. **Cols./Page:** 6. **Col. Width:** 24 nonpareils. **Col. Depth:** 301 agate lines. **Key Personnel:** Susan A. Bush, Editor-in-Chief. **Subscription Rates:** $20 individuals; $25 out of parish; $42 out of state. **Remarks:** Accepts advertising.
Ad Rates: GLR: $5.45 **Circ:** ‡1,900
SAU: $5.45

ST. JOSEPH

13014 The Tensas Gazette
Bastrop Enterprise
PO Box 25 Phone: (318)766-3258
St. Joseph, LA 71366 Fax: (318)766-4273

Newspaper. **Subtitle:** Tensas Gazett. **Founded:** 1852. **Freq:** Weekly. **Print Method:** Offset. **Cols./Page:** 6. **Col. Width:** 12.5 picas. **Col. Depth:** 21 inches. **Key Personnel:** Joseph C. Curtis, Mgr./Editor; Paul Stanton, Publisher, phone (318)728-2250, fax (318)728-5991. **Subscription Rates:** $17 individuals; $22 out of county; $27 out of state. **Available Online.**
Ad Rates: GLR: $3.80 **Circ:** 3,000
BW: $478.80
SAU: $3.80
PCI: $3.80

ST. MARTINVILLE

13015 Teche News
214 N. Main Phone: (318)394-6234
PO Box 69 Fax: (318)394-7511
St. Martinville, LA 70582
Community newspaper. **Founded:** Feb. 27, 1886. **Freq:** Weekly (Wed.). **Print Method:** Offset. **Cols./Page:** 6. **Col. Width:** 12 picas. **Col. Depth:** 21 1/2 inches. **Key Personnel:** Henri C. Bienvenu, Editor and Publisher; Mary Johnson, Advertising Mgr., marykk69@aol.com. **USPS:** 535-600. **Subscription Rates:** $28 individuals; $30 out of state. **Remarks:** Accepts advertising. **Alt. Formats:** Microform.
Ad Rates: BW: $722.40 **Circ:** Paid ⊕6,449
4C: $947.40 Non-paid ⊕53
SAU: $5.60
PCI: $5.60

SHREVEPORT

13016 American Rose
American Rose Society
8877 Jefferson Paige Rd. Phone: (318)938-5402
Shreveport, LA 71119 Fax: (318)938-5405
Publisher E-mail: ars@ars-hq.org

Magazine concerning all aspects of rose growing. **Founded:** 1933. **Freq:** Monthly (Jan.-Dec.). **Print Method:** Offset. **Trim Size:** 8 3/8 x 10 7/8. **Cols./Page:** 3. **Col. Width:** 26 nonpareils. **Col. Depth:** 140 agate lines. **Key Personnel:** Mike Kromer, Editor, mike@ars-hq.org; Beth Smiley, Managing Editor, beth@ars-hq.org; Josephine Carmody, Advertising Dir., josie@ars-hq.org. **ISSN:** 0003-0899. **Subscription Rates:** $32 individuals; $3 single issue. **Remarks:** Accepts advertising. **Former name:** The American Rose Magazine.
Ad Rates: GLR: $.55 **Circ:** Paid ‡22,109
BW: $653 Controlled ‡150
4C: $956
PCI: $50

13017 Loadstar
J & F Publishing, Inc.
Box 30008 Phone: (318)221-8718
Shreveport, LA 71130-0008 Fax: (318)221-8870
Publisher E-mail: judi@loadstar.com

Magazine on diskette for Commodore 64/128 40 column computers. **Founded:** 1984. **Freq:** Monthly. **Key Personnel:** Fender Rucker, Editor. **Subscription Rates:** $69.95 individuals; $7.95 single issue. **Remarks:** Advertising not accepted. **Alt. Formats:** Diskette.
Circ: Paid 1,400

13018 Loadstar Quarterly
J & F Publishing, Inc.
Box 30008 Phone: (318)221-8718
Shreveport, LA 71130-0008 Fax: (318)221-8870
Publisher E-mail: judi@loadstar.com

Magazine on diskette for Commodore 128 80 column computers. **Founded:** 1988. **Freq:** Quarterly. **Key Personnel:** Fender Tucker, Editor. **Subscription Rates:** $24.95 individuals; $7.95 single issue. **Remarks:** Advertising not accepted. **Alt. Formats:** Diskette.
Circ: Combined 600

13019 North Louisiana Historical Association Journal
North Louisiana Historical Association
Box 6701 Phone: (318)797-5355
Shreveport, LA 71136 Fax: (318)797-5122

Journal covering local history. **Founded:** 1952. **Freq:** Triennial. **Key Personnel:** Alan S. Thompson, Editor, athompso@pilot.lsus.edu. **ISSN:** 0739-005X. **Subscription Rates:** $13 individuals; $3 single issue. **Remarks:** Advertising not accepted.
Circ: Paid 500

13020 Poet
PO Box 5646
Shreveport, LA 71135

Publication featuring essays on writing, poetry, and pertinant information on national competitions and awards for poets and writers. **Founded:** 1984. **Freq:** Quarterly. **Trim Size:** 8 1/2 x 11. **Col. Width:** 2 1/4 inches. **Col. Depth:** 10 inches. **Key Personnel:** Peggy Cooper, Managing Editor, phone (440)5949-2020. **ISSN:** 0748-4062. **Subscription Rates:** $24. **Remarks:** Accepts advertising.
Ad Rates: BW: $485 **Circ:** Paid 6,000
PCI: $45

13021 The Shreveport Sun
The Shreveport Sun, Inc.
PO Box 38357 Phone: (318)631-6222
Shreveport, LA 71133-8357
Black community newspaper. **Founded:** 1920. **Freq:** Weekly (Wed.). **Print Method:** Offset. **Cols./Page:** 6. **Col. Width:** 25 nonpareils. **Col. Depth:** 301 agate lines. **Key Personnel:** Sonya Collins Landry, Editor; Ronald Collins, Advertising Mgr. **Subscription Rates:** $15 individuals. **Remarks:** Accepts advertising.
Ad Rates: BW: $959.76 **Circ:** Paid 4,968
SAU: $7.44 Free 102

13022 The Times
222 Lake St. Phone: (318)459-3200
Shreveport, LA 71101 Fax: (318)459-3301
Free: (800)551-8892

General newspaper. **Founded:** 1872. **Freq:** Mon.-Sun. (morn.). **Print Method:** Letterpress. **Cols./Page:** 6. **Col. Width:** 25 nonpareils. **Col. Depth:** 301 agate lines. **Key Personnel:** Mike Whitehead, Editor; Bob Bryan, Managing Editor. **Subscription Rates:** $114 individuals. **Remarks:** Accepts advertising. **Feature Editors:** Sheri Conover, *Travel*, phone (318)459-3200; Bill Cooksey, *TV & Radio*, phone (318)459-3200; Martha Fitzgerald, *Women's*, phone (318)459-3200.
Ad Rates: SAU: $45.38 **Circ:** Mon.-Sat. 77,323
Sun. 95,275

13023 Cablevision of Shreveport
6529 Quilen Rd. Phone: (318)631-3060
Shreveport, LA 71108 Fax: (318)631-1027

Founded: 1976. **Cities Served:** Caddo County, De Soto County, Bethany, and Greenwood, LA; Harrison County and Waskom, TX.

13024 KBCL-AM - 1070
316B Gregg St. Phone: (318)861-1070
Shreveport, LA 71104 Fax: (318)868-0990

Format: Religious; News; Talk. **Networks:** Independent. **Owner:** G. Randy Alewyne, III, at above address. **Founded:** 1957. **Operating Hours:** 6:30a.m.-8 p.m.; 10% network, 90% local. **ADI:** Shreveport, LA-Texarkana, TX. **Key Personnel:** G. Randy Alewyne III, President; J. Scott Carr, Sales Manager/Program Director; Don Hanley, General Mgr.; John Newberry, Public Affairs Coordinator; R.W. Guile, Marketing Director. **Wattage:** 250. **Ad Rates:** $6-15 for 30 seconds; $9-18 for 60 seconds.

13025 KDAQ-FM - 89.9
1 University Pl. Phone: (318)797-5150
Shreveport, LA 71115-2301 Fax: (318)797-5153
Free: (800)552-8502

Format: Public Radio; Jazz; Eclectic; Classical. **Networks:** National Public Radio (NPR). **Owner:** Louisiana State University Board of Supervisors, at above address. **Founded:** 1984. **Operating Hours:** Continuous. **ADI:** Shreveport, LA-Texarkana, TX. **Key Personnel:** Catherine Fraser, Station Mgr. **Wattage:** 100,000.

13026 KEEL-AM - 710
6341 Westport Ave. Phone: (318)688-1130
Shreveport, LA 71129-2498 Fax: (318)687-8574

Format: News; Talk; Big Band/Nostalgia. **Networks:** CNN Radio. **Founded:** 1922. **Operating Hours:** Continuous. **ADI:** Shreveport, LA-Texarkana, TX. **Key Personnel:** Bill Fry, General Mgr. **Local Programs:** *The Larry Ryan Show*, Robin Patterson, (318)425-1490; *Sports with Al LeGrand*, Al LeGrand, (318)687-8574; *Strategies For Living*, Dave McMillian, (318)425-1490. **Wattage:** 50,000. **Ad Rates:** Advertising accepted; rates available upon request.

13027 KFLO-AM - 1300
PO Box 7277 Phone: (318)222-2744
Shreveport, LA 71137-7277 Fax: (318)425-7507

Format: Religious; Sports. **Networks:** Mutual Broadcasting System. **Founded:** 1975. **Operating Hours:** Sunrise-sunset. **ADI:** Shreveport, LA-Texarkana, TX. **Key Personnel:** Tommy Moore, General Mgr. **Wattage:** 5000.

13028 KITT-FM - 93.7
6341 Westport Ave. Phone: (318)688-1130
Shreveport, LA 71129-2498 Fax: (318)687-8574

Format: Hot Country. **Founded:** 1968. **Formerly:** KMBQ-FM. **Operating Hours:** Continuous. **ADI:** Shreveport, LA-Texarkana, TX. **Key Personnel:** Bill Fry, General Mgr. **Wattage:** 100,000. **Ad Rates:** Advertising accepted; rates available upon request.

13029 KLSA-FM - 90.7
1 University Pl. Phone: (318)797-5150
Shreveport, LA 71105 Fax: (318)797-5154
Free: (800)552-8502

Format: Classical; Jazz; News. **Founded:** 1987. **Operating Hours:** Continuous. **ADI:** Shreveport, LA-Texarkana, TX. **Key Personnel:** Catherine Fraser, General Mgr.; Mary Masters, Program Dir.; Greg Carter, News Dir.; Rod Mathews, Chief Engineer. **Wattage:** 100,000.

13030 KLTS-TV - 24
c/o Lousiana Public Broadcasting Network (LPB) Phone: (504)767-5660
Fax: (504)767-4288
7860 Anselmo Ln.
Baton Rouge, LA 70810
Free: (800)272-8161

Format: Public TV. **Simulcasts:** WLPB-TV Baton Rogue, LA. **Networks:** Public Broadcasting Service (PBS); Louisiana Public Broadcasting. **Owner:** LA Educational TV Authority, at above address. **Founded:** 1978. **Operating Hours:** 5 a.m. - 2 a.m. **ADI:** Shreveport, LA-Texarkana, TX. **Key Personnel:** Beth Courtney, President/CEO, phone (504)767-4200, beth_courtney@wlpb.pbs.org; Jennifer Howze, Program Dir., phone (504)767-4211, jennifer_howze@wlpb.pbs.org; Bob Neese, Promotions Dir., phone (504)767-4211, bob_neese@wlpb.pbs.org; Kent Hatfield, Engineering Dir., phone (504)767-4202, fax (504)767-4277, kent_hatfield@wlpb.pbs.org; Don Ballard, Operations Mgr., phone (504)767-4277, fax (504)767-4277, don_ballard@wlpb.pbs.org; Homer Dyess, Educational Services Dir., phone (504)767-4206, fax (504)767-4299, homer_dyess@wlpb.pbs.org; Ayan Rubin, Educational Services Coord., phone (504)767-4207, fax (504)767-4299, ayan_rubin@wlpb.pbs.org; Clay Fourrier, Exec. Producer, phone (504)767-4204, fax (504)767-4277, clay_fourrier@wlpb.pbs.org; Cindy Rougeou, CAO, phone (504)767-4200, cindy_rougeou@wlpb.pbs.org. **URL:** http://www.lpb.org.

13031 KMSS-TV - 33
PO Box 30033 Phone: (318)631-5677
Shreveport, LA 71130 Fax: (318)631-4195

Format: Commercial TV. **Networks:** Fox; Independent. **Owner:** Communications Corp., 3519 Jewella Ave., Shreveport, LA 71130. **Founded:** 1985. **Operating Hours:** Continuous; 26% network, 74% local. **ADI:** Shreveport, LA-Texarkana, TX. **Key Personnel:** Joe Sugg, General Mgr., phone ( )Ext. 113; Doug Ginn, Program Dir., phone ( )Ext. 112; Susan Newman, General Sales Mgr., phone ( )Ext. 117; Margie Bueche, Local Sales Mgr., phone ( )Ext. 129; Dale Beasly, Business Mgr., phone ( )Ext. 114; Eric Peterson, Chief Engineer, phone ( )Ext. 136. **Wattage:** 4,570,000. **Ad Rates:** $5-225 for 10 seconds; $6.50-360 for 15 seconds; $10-550 for 30 seconds; $20-1100 for 60 seconds.

13032 KOKA-AM - 980
PO Box 103 Phone: (318)222-3122
Shreveport, LA 71161 Fax: (318)459-1493

Format: Religious. **Networks:** NBC; American Urban Radio. **Owner:** Cary D. Camp, 949 Poleman Rd., Shreveport, LA 71107. **Formerly:** KLMB-AM (1988). **Operating Hours:** 5 a.m.-midnight. **ADI:** Shreveport, LA-Texarkana, TX. **Key Personnel:** Cary D. Camp, Contact; Diane Camp, General Mgr.; Eddie Giles, Program Dir. **Wattage:** 5000. **Ad Rates:** $18 for 30 seconds; $35 for 60 seconds.

13033 KRMD-AM - 1340
3109 Alexander St. Phone: (318)865-5173
PO Box 41011 Fax: (318)865-3657
Shreveport, LA 71134-1101
E-mail: krmd@prodigy.com

Format: Sports. **Networks:** ABC. **Owner:** Capstar Broadcasting, at above address, (512)340-7850, Fax: (512)340-7895. **Founded:** 1928. **Operating Hours:** Continuous. **ADI:** Shreveport, LA-Texarkana, TX. **Key Personnel:** John A Swan, Operations Mgr.; Jerry Frentress, General Sales Mgr. **Local Programs:** *This Is The ArkLaTex*, Tony King. **Wattage:** 1000. **Ad Rates:** $95 for 30 seconds; $120 for 60 seconds.

13034 KRMD-FM - 101.1
3109 Alexander St. Phone: (318)865-5173
PO Box 41011 Fax: (318)865-3657
Shreveport, LA 71134-1011
E-mail: krmd@prodigy.com

Format: Contemporary Country. **Networks:** ABC. **Owner:** Benchmark Communications, at above address, (410)244-0600, Fax: (410)244-7170. **Founded:** 1948. **Operating Hours:** Continuous. **ADI:** Shreveport, LA-Texarkana, TX. **Key Personnel:** John A. Swan, Contact; Gene Dickerson, Contact; Jerry Frentress, General Sales Mgr.; Rick Stephenson, Music Director. **Local Programs:** *This Is The ArkLaTex*, Tony King. **Wattage:** 100,000. **Ad Rates:** $95 for 30 seconds; $120 for 60 seconds.

13035 KRUF-FM - 94.5
6341 Westport Ave. Phone: (318)688-1130
Shreveport, LA 71129 Fax: (318)687-8574

Format: Contemporary Hit Radio (CHR). **Founded:** 1948. **Formerly:** KWKH-FM (1996); KROK-FM. **Operating Hours:** Continuous. **ADI:** Shreveport, LA-Texarkana, TX. **Key Personnel:** Bill Fry, General Mgr.; Gary Robinson, Operations Mgr.; Cathy McCalister, General Sales Mgr., fax (318)688-9839. **Wattage:** 100,000.

13036 KRVQ-FM - 102.1
208 N. Thomas Dr. Phone: (318)222-0636
Shreveport, LA 71107 Fax: (318)222-2957

Format: Oldies. **Owner:** Ninety-Five Point Seven, Inc., at above address. **Operating Hours:** Continuous. **Key Personnel:** Howard Clark, Program Dir.; Howard Hart, Production Dir.; Hal Bundrick, Operations Mgr.; Cindy Delaney, Sales Mgr. **Wattage:** 25,000. **Ad Rates:** $4-65 per unit. **URL:** http://www.river102.com.

13037 KSCL-FM - 91.3
2911 Centenary Blvd. Phone: (318)869-5296
Shreveport, LA 71104 Fax: (318)869-5294
E-mail: kscl@centenary.edu

Format: Alternative/New Music/Progressive; Jazz; Ethnic; Urban Contemporary. **Networks:** Independent. **Owner:** Centenary College of Louisiana, at above address, LA. **Founded:** 1976. **Operating Hours:** Noon - 12 a.m.; 100% local. **ADI:** Shreveport, LA-Texarkana, TX. **Key Personnel:** Slater McKay, Station Mgr., jmckay@centenary.edu; Johnathan Clay, Music Dir., jclay@centenary.edu; Tommy Welch, Program Dir., twelch@centenary.edu; Jamie Prince, Program Dir., jprince@centenary.edu; Rolin Moe, News Dir., rmoe@centenary.edu; Chris Brown, Music Dir., cebrown@centenary.edu; John Veen, Music Dir.; Nan Matthews, Engineer. **Wattage:** 150. **Ad Rates:** Noncommercial.

13038 KSLA-TV - 12
1812 Fairfield Phone: (318)222-1212
Shreveport, LA 71101 Fax: (318)677-6703

Format: Commercial TV. **Networks:** CBS. **Owner:** Raycom Media, Inc., 201 Monroe St., Ste. 710, Montgomery, AL 36104, (334)206-1400, Fax: (334)206-1555. **Founded:** 1955. **Operating Hours:** 5 a.m.-1:30 or 2 a.m. **ADI:** Shreveport, LA-Texarkana, TX. **Key Personnel:** Ed Bradley, Vice Pres./Gen. Mgr.; Debra Shelton-Little, Local Sales Mgr.; Karl Cole, Operations Mgr.; Cindy Townsend, Business Mgr.; Donna Frank, Program Dir.; James Russel, Chief Engineer. **Ad Rates:** Advertising accepted; rates available upon request.

13039 KSYR-FM - 95.7
208 N. Thomas Phone: (318)222-0636
Shreveport, LA 71107 Fax: (318)222-2957

Format: Adult Contemporary. **Owner:** Ninety-Five Point Seven, Inc., at above address. **Formerly:** KASO-FM. **Operating Hours:** Continuous. **Key Personnel:** Howard Clark, Program Dir.; Howard Hart, Production Dir.; Hal Bundrick, Operations Mgr.; Cindy Delaney, Sales Mgr. **Wattage:** 50,000. **Ad Rates:** $4-65 per unit. **URL:** http://www.star957fm.com.

13040 KTAL-FM - 98.1
3150 N. Market St. Phone: (318)425-2422
Shreveport, LA 71107 Fax: (318)425-2488

Format: Album-Oriented Rock (AOR). **Networks:** ABC. **Founded:** 1945. **Operating Hours:** Continuous. **ADI:** Shreveport, LA-Texarkana, TX. **Key Personnel:** Jim Vidler, General Mgr. **Wattage:** 100,000.

13041 KTAL-TV - 6
PO Box 7428 Phone: (318)425-2422
Shreveport, LA 71137-7428 Fax: (318)425-2488

Format: Commercial TV. **Networks:** NBC. **Founded:** 1953. **ADI:** Shreveport, LA-Texarkana, TX. **Key Personnel:** H. Lee Bryant, President. **Wattage:** 100,000.

13042 KTBS-TV - 3
312 E. Kings Hwy. Phone: (318)861-5800
Box 44227 Fax: (318)862-9434
Shreveport, LA 71134-4227

Format: Commercial TV. **Networks:** ABC. **Owner:** KTBS, Inc., at above address. **Founded:** Sept. 3, 1955. **Operating Hours:** Continuous. **ADI:** Shreveport, LA-Texarkana, TX. **Key Personnel:** Edwin Wray, President/Gen. Manager; Marvin Perry, Program Dir.; Ron Thoma, Production Mgr.; Ken White, News Dir., phone (318)861-5880, fax (318)862-9431; A. Dale Beasley, Controller; George Sirven, General Sales Mgr. & Station Mgr.; David Hendricks, Chief Engineer, phone (318)861-5860, fax (318)862-9435. **Local Programs:** *The Inside Story* 6:30 a.m. Sunday; *KTBS 3 News at 5 Monday - Friday and Sunday*; *KTBS 3 News at 6 and 10 Monday - Sunday*. **Wattage:** 100,000. **URL:** http://www.ktbs.com/ktbs.

13043 KTUX-FM - 98.9
5005 W. Monkhouse Phone: (318)635-9999
Shreveport, LA 71109 Fax: (318)635-6285

Networks: Independent. **Owner:** Ken Stephens, at above address. **Founded:** 1983. **Operating Hours:** Continuous; 100% local. **ADI:** Shreveport, LA-Texarkana, TX. **Key Personnel:** Ken Stephens, General Mgr.; Paul Cannell, Program Dir.; Evan Armstrong, Sales Mgr. **Wattage:** 100,000.

13044 KVKI-FM - 1550
6341 W. Port Ave. Phone: (318)688-1130
Shreveport, LA 71129 Fax: (318)687-8574

Format: Oldies. **Founded:** 1950. **ADI:** Shreveport, LA-Texarkana, TX. **Key Personnel:** David McMillan, General Mgr.; Cindy Delaney, General Sales Mgr. **Wattage:** 500.

13045 KVKI-FM - 96.5
6341 Westport Ave. Phone: (318)688-1130
Shreveport, LA 71130-1130 Fax: (318)687-8574

Format: Adult Contemporary. **Networks:** CBS. **Founded:** 1959. **Operating Hours:** Continuous. **ADI:** Shreveport, LA-Texarkana, TX. **Key Personnel:** William R. Fry, Owner/Mgr. **Wattage:** 100,000.

13046 KWKH-AM - 1130
6341 Westport Ave. Phone: (318)688-1130
Shreveport, LA 71129 Fax: (318)687-8574

Format: News; Country; Agricultural. **Networks:** Mutual Broadcasting System. **Founded:** 1926. **Operating Hours:** Continuous. **ADI:** Shreveport, LA-Texarkana, TX. **Key Personnel:** Bill Fry, General Mgr.; Barney Cannon, Operations Mgr.; Cathy McAllister, General Sales Mgr.; John Lee, News Dir. **Local Programs:** *Cannon's Collectables*, Barny Cannon, (318)688-1130, Fax (318)687-8574; *Country Gold*, Frank Page, (318)688-1130, Fax (318)687-8574; *Gospel Go Round*, Barney Cannon. **Wattage:** 50,000. **URL:** http://www.kwkh1130.com.

SLIDELL

13047 Slidell Sentry-News
Pontchartrain Newspapers
3648 Pontchartrain Dr. Phone: (504)643-4918
PO Box 910 Fax: (504)643-4966
Slidell, LA 70459
Publication E-mail: sentry@neosoft.com

Newspaper. **Freq:** 2/wk (Thursday and Sunday). **Key Personnel:** Terry Madox, Publisher. **Subscription Rates:** $99. **Formerly:** The Daily Sentry-News.
Circ: Sun. 21,252
Thurs. 21,652

13048 Cablevision Industries of Saint Tammany
60097 Hwy 11 Phone: (504)626-1188
Slidell, LA 70458 Fax: (504)649-3250

Founded: 1979. **Cities Served:** Saint Tammany County, Lacombe, Pearl River, and Saint Tammany Parish, LA.

13049 WSLA-AM - 1560
38230 Coast Blvd. Phone: (504)643-1560
PO Box 1175
Slidell, LA 70459

Format: News; Talk; Sports. **Networks:** Mutual Broadcasting System; Louisiana; USA Radio. **Owner:** MAPA Broadcasting, Inc., at above address. **Founded:** 1973. **Formerly:** WSDL-AM (1975). **Operating Hours:** 6 a.m.-7 p.m. **ADI:** New Orleans, LA. **Key Personnel:** Paul Mayoral, President; George Mayoral, General Mgr. **Local Programs:** *High School Football,* Dennis Cousin, (504)643-1560. **Wattage:** 1000. **Ad Rates:** $10 for 30 seconds.

SPRINGHILL

13050 The Advertiser
Springhill Press & News Journal
PO Box 668 Phone: (318)539-3511
Springhill, LA 71075 Fax: (318)539-3512

Community newspaper. **Freq:** Weekly. **Print Method:** Offset. **Cols./Page:** 6. **Col. Width:** 2 1/16 inches. **Col. Depth:** 21 inches. **Key Personnel:** Steve Colwell, Publisher; Kathy Compton, Editor. **Subscription Rates:** Free. **Remarks:** Accepts advertising.
Ad Rates: PCI: $3.44 **Circ:** Free 9,100

13051 Springhill Press & News Journal
PO Box 668 Phone: (318)539-3511
Springhill, LA 71075 Fax: (318)539-3512

Community newspaper. **Freq:** Weekly (Thurs.). **Print Method:** Offset. **Cols./Page:** 6. **Col. Width:** 12.3 picas. **Col. Depth:** 21 inches. **Key Personnel:** Steve Colwell, Publisher. **Subscription Rates:** $21; $31 out of area; $.50 single issue. **Remarks:** Accepts advertising.
Ad Rates: BW: $567 **Circ:** ‡4,000
4C: $690.60
SAU: $4.75
PCI: $4.00

13052 KBSF-AM - 1460
Box 127 Phone: (318)539-4616
Springhill, LA 71075

Format: Oldies. **Networks:** Satellite Music Network; Louisiana. **Owner:** Metropolitan Radio Group, 1549 Greenbridge, Ozark, MO 65721. **Founded:** 1954. **Operating Hours:** 6 a.m.-midnight. **Key Personnel:** Keith Hill, Contact. **Wattage:** 1000. **Ad Rates:** $5.50 for 30 seconds; $6.50 for 60 seconds.

13053 KIOU-AM - 1480
PO Box 127 Phone: (318)222-0272
Springhill, LA 71075-0127 Fax: (318)222-0482

Format: Gospel. **Owner:** Metropolitan Radio Group, 1549 Greenbridge, Ozark, MO 65721. **Formerly:** KJOE-AM (1989); KCIJ-AM. **Operating Hours:** 6 a.m.-6 p.m.; 100% local. **ADI:** Shreveport, LA-Texarkana, TX. **Key Personnel:** Peter Stinson, General Mgr. **Wattage:** 1000 day; 130 night. **Ad Rates:** $6 for 30 seconds; $8 for 60 seconds.

13054 KTKC-FM - 92.7
Box 127 Phone: (318)539-4616
Springhill, LA 71075

Format: Oldies. **Networks:** Louisiana; Satellite Music Network; ABC. **Owner:** Metropolitan Radio Group, 1549 Greenbridge Rd., Ozark, MO 65721, Free: (800)961-5595. **Founded:** 1975. **Operating Hours:** 6 a.m.-midnight. **Key Personnel:** Keith Hill, Contact. **Wattage:** 3000. **Ad Rates:** $5.50 for 30 seconds; $6.50 for 60 seconds.

SULPHUR, pop. 19,709.

SW LA. Calcasieu Parish. 10 mi. W. of Lake Charles. Manufactures concrete and metal products, boats, plastics. Oil refinery. Agriculture. Rice, cattle.

13055 Ft. Polk Guardian
716 E. Napolean Phone: (318)463-6204
PO Box 1999 Fax: (318)463-5347
Sulphur, LA 70664-1999
Newspaper. **Freq:** Weekly. **Print Method:** Offset. **Cols./Page:** 6. **Col. Width:** 1 7/16 inches. **Col. Depth:** 13 inches. **Subscription Rates:** $36. **Remarks:** Accepts advertising.
Ad Rates: GLR: $1.33 **Circ:** Non-paid 15,000
BW: $1,310.40
4C: $1,904.40
SAU: $16.80
PCI: $16.80

13056 The Iowa News
News Leader, Inc.
716 E. Napoleon Phone: (318)527-7075
PO Box 1999 Fax: (318)528-3044
Sulphur, LA 70664-1999
Community newspaper. **Founded:** Nov. 1992. **Freq:** Weekly. **Print Method:** Web offset. **Cols./Page:** 6. **Col. Width:** 2 1/16 inches. **Col. Depth:** 21 inches. **Key Personnel:** Brenda Merchant, Editor; Suzanne Peveto, Advertising Dir. **ISSN:** 1071-5843. **Subscription Rates:** $10.48 individuals. **Remarks:** Accepts advertising.
Ad Rates: SAU: $9.10 **Circ:** Controlled 4,100

13057 Southwest Daily News
News Leader, Inc.
716 E. Napoleon Phone: (318)527-7075
PO Box 1999 Fax: (318)528-3044
Sulphur, LA 70664-1999
Community newspaper. **Founded:** 1939. **Freq:** Mon.-Sun. **Print Method:** Offset. **Trim Size:** 13 5/8 x 21 7/8. **Cols./Page:** 6. **Col. Width:** 26 nonpareils. **Col. Depth:** 273 agate lines. **Key Personnel:** E.W. Wise, Publisher; Ophelia Hayes, V.P. Mktg. **USPS:** 507-520. **Subscription Rates:** $36 individuals. **Remarks:** Accepts advertising.
Ad Rates: GLR: $1.33 **Circ:** Combined ‡16,000
BW: $1,518.30
4C: $2,068.30
SAU: $12.05

The Vinton News - See Vinton

13058 Carlyss Cablevision, Inc.
Box 2447 Phone: (318)583-4973
Sulphur, LA 70664-2447 Fax: (318)583-9854

Founded: 1982. **Key Personnel:** C. J. Lejeune, Manager; Ray Ebersole, Chief Engineer; Meme Reider, Marketing. **Cities Served:** subscribing households 1,333; 30 channels; 1 community access channel.

13059 KEZM-AM - 1310
101 W. Napoleon St. Phone: (318)527-3611
Sulphur, LA 70663-3343 Fax: (318)527-0213

Format: Oldies. **Networks:** Satellite Music Network; ABC. **Owner:** Merchant Broadcasting Inc., at above address, (318)527-9466, Fax: (318)527-0213. **Founded:** 1955. **Operating Hours:** Continuous. **ADI:** Lake Charles, LA. **Key Personnel:** Karen Jackson, Traffic Manager; Kathy Soilew, Sales Mgr.; Bruce Merchant, General Mgr. **Wattage:** 500. **Ad Rates:** $5 for 30 seconds.

13060 KKGB-FM - 101.3
PO Box 2418 Phone: (318)625-7777
Sulphur, LA 70664 Fax: (318)625-7787
E-mail: therock@maas.net

Format: Album-Oriented Rock (AOR); Classic Rock. **Networks:** CNN Radio. **Owner:** 21st Century Communications, at above address. **Founded:** 1990. **Formerly:** KTQQ-FM (1994). **Operating Hours:** Continuous. **ADI:** Lake Charles, LA. **Key Personnel:** Keith Martin, Owner/General Mgr.; Micah Boone, Program Dir.; Dana Puckett, Station/Sales Mgr.; Niki Johns, Music Dir.; Lisa Daniels, Promotions Dir.; Maria Mott, Traffic Mgr. **Local Programs:** *After Dark,* Mark Ruiz. **Wattage:** 25,000. **Ad Rates:** $22-30 for 30 seconds; $28-45 for 60 seconds.

TALLULAH†, pop. 10,392.

NE LA. Madison Parish. 18 mi. NW of Vicksburg, MS. Manufactures uniforms, metal products, chemicals, lumber. Agriculture. Cotton, soybeans, corn milo.

13061 The Madison Journal
300 S. Chestnut St. Phone: (318)574-1405
Tallulah, LA 71282 Fax: (318)574-4219

Community newspaper. **Founded:** 1869. **Freq:** Weekly (Wed.). **Print Method:** Offset. **Cols./Page:** 6. **Col. Width:** 26 nonpareils. **Col. Depth:** 295 agate lines. **Key Personnel:** David Davis, Editor; Bill Sumrall, Reporter. **Subscription Rates:** $20 individuals; $23 out of parish. **Remarks:** Accepts advertising.
Ad Rates: GLR: $.25 **Circ:** ‡3,400
BW: $504
4C: $661
PCI: $4.40

13062 KBYO-FM - 104.9
Hwy. 80 W., Box 1112 Phone: (318)574-1500
Tallulah, LA 71284 Fax: (318)636-7386

Format: Country; Agricultural. **Owner:** Sharing Inc., at above address. **Founded:** 1983. **Operating Hours:** 5 a.m.-midnight. **Key Personnel:** Chris C. Kimbell, Jr., Contact; Hub Turner, Program Dir. **Wattage:** 3000 ERP.

13063 Tallulah Cablevision Corp.
PO Box 1678 Phone: (318)574-0762
Tallulah, LA 71284

Key Personnel: Dale Miller, General Mgr. **Cities Served:** Tallulah and Richmond, LA.

THIBODAUX†, pop. 15,810.

SE LA. Lafourche Parish. On Bayou Lafourche, 45 mi. SW of New Orleans. Nicholls State University. Harvesting equipment factory. Sea food processing plant. Sugar refineries. Foundries. Ships vegetables. Oil, natural gas wells. Truck, dairy farms. Sugarcane, corn, vegetables.

13064 Daily Comet
The Daily Comet
705 W. 5th Ave. Phone: (504)447-4055
PO Box 5238 Fax: (504)448-7606
Thibodaux, LA 70302
Free: (800)256-1305

General newspaper. **Founded:** 1887. **Freq:** Daily (eve.). **Print Method:** Offset. **Cols./Page:** 6. **Col. Width:** 25 nonpareils. **Col. Depth:** 301 agate lines. **Key Personnel:** Jeffrey Zeringue, Managing Editor, phone (504)448-7611; Gary Palmer, Publisher, phone (504)448-7601. **Subscription Rates:** $84 individuals. **Remarks:** Accepts advertising.
Ad Rates: GLR: $1.49 **Circ:** Mon.-Fri. 11,971
BW: $1,442.70
4C: $1,642.70
PCI: $11.45

13065 Louisiana English Journal
Louisiana Council of Teachers of English
Nicholls State University Phone: (504)448-4432
PO Box 2825 Fax: (504)448-4927
Thibodaux, LA 70310
Publisher E-mail: gensomp@nich-nsunet.nich.edu

Scholarly journal covering poetry and fiction from Louisiana. **Founded:** 1992. **Freq:** Semiannual. **Print Method:** Offset. **Trim Size:** 8 1/2 x 11. **Cols./Page:** 2. **Key Personnel:** Olivia M. Pass, Editor. **Subscription Rates:** $20 individuals; $10 single issue. **Remarks:** Accepts advertising.
Circ: (Not Reported)

13066 The Nicholls Worth
Nicholls State University
PO Box 2010 Phone: (504)448-4259
Thibodaux, LA 70310 Fax: (504)448-4267
Publication E-mail: nwads@nich-nsunet.nich.edu; nw@nich-nsunet.nich.edu

Collegiate newspaper. **Founded:** 1955. **Freq:** Weekly (Thurs.). **Print Method:** Offset. **Cols./Page:** 5. **Col. Width:** 2 1/16 inches. **Col. Depth:** 13 13/16 inches. **Key Personnel:** Trish Brunet, Editor, phone (504)448-4258. **Subscription Rates:** $12 individuals.
Ad Rates: SAU: $3 **Circ:** ‡5,500
PCI: $3.25

13067 KNSU-FM - 91.5
Nicholls State University Phone: (504)448-4448
PO Box 2664 Fax: (504)449-7106
Thibodaux, LA 70310
E-mail: knsu@nich-nsunet.nich.edu

Format: Alternative/New Music/Progressive. **Owner:** Nicholls State University, at above address, LA, (504)448-4003. **Founded:** 1972. **Formerly:** KVFG-FM (1985). **Operating Hours:** 7 a.m.-2 a.m. Mon.-Thurs./7a.m.-10 p.m. Fri/10 a.m.-10 p.m. **Key Personnel:** James Ash, Station Mgr.; Corey Clement, Program Dir., phone (504)448-4446; John Price, Music Dir., phone (504)448-4447; James Berreca, News Dir. **Wattage:** 250. **Ad Rates:** Noncommercial.

13068 KTIB-AM - 640
108 Green St. Phone: (504)447-9006
Thibodaux, LA 70301 Fax: (504)446-2338

Format: Oldies; News. **Networks:** NBC. **Owner:** La Terr Broadcasting Corp., at above address. **Founded:** 1953. **Operating Hours:** Continuous; 8% network, 92% local. **ADI:** New Orleans, LA. **Key Personnel:** Raymond Saadi, Vice Pres./Gen. Mgr.; Darin Fontz, Sports & News Dir. **Local Programs:** *Dialogue - Public Affairs* 8:10 a.m. Monday-Friday, Marie Bergeron, (504)447-9006. **Wattage:** 5000. **Ad Rates:** Advertising accepted; rates available upon request.

13069 KXOR-FM - 106.3
106 Ridgefield Rd. Phone: (504)446-5604
Thibodaux, LA 70301 Fax: (504)446-5672

Format: Hot Country. **Networks:** Louisiana Public Broadcasting. **Owner:** Joseph M. Costello III, 4539 I-10 Service Rd., Metairie, LA 70006, (504)889-2424, Fax: (504)889-0602. **Founded:** 1966. **Operating Hours:** Continuous. **Key Person-**

nel: Greg Dumas, General Sales Mgr. **Wattage:** 50,000. **Ad Rates:** $18 for 30 seconds; $25 for 60 seconds.

13070 R Media
1306 Ridgefield Rd. Phone: (504)446-8444
PO Box 5178 Fax: (504)447-9541
Thibodaux, LA 70301

Founded: 1970. **Formerly:** Lafourche Communications; Time Warner. **Key Personnel:** Kip Kraemer, General Mgr. **Cities Served:** Labadieville, Napoleonvile, Paulina, Raceland, Thibodaux, Vacherie, LA: subscribing households 22,467; 62 channels; 1 community access channel; 168 hours per week community access programming.

VIDALIA†.

C LA. Concordia Parish. 2 mi. W. of Natchez.

13071 Aquaculture News
Nelson Publications (Jonesville)
PO Box 610 Phone: (318)336-4660
Vidalia, LA 71373 Fax: (318)336-4644
Publisher E-mail: editor@theaquaculturnews.com

Newspaper. **Founded:** Dec. 1992. **Freq:** Monthly. **Print Method:** Offset. **Key Personnel:** Stanley Nelson, Editor and Publisher; Rebecca Nelson, Office Mgr.; William Atkins, Internet Maintenance. **ISSN:** 1097-2447. **Subscription Rates:** $20 individuals; $35 two years; $50 out of country. **Remarks:** Accepts advertising. **URL:** http://www.theaquaculturenews.com.
Ad Rates: BW: $890 **Circ:** (Not Reported)
4C: $1,190
PCI: $17.50

13072 KVLA-AM - 1400
20 Alabama St. Phone: (318)336-7466
PO Box 1129 Fax: (318)336-7466
Vidalia, LA 71373
E-mail: dcupit@iamerica.net

Format: Country; Talk. **Networks:** CBS. **Owner:** Bob Cupit, at above address. **Founded:** 1984. **Operating Hours:** 5 a.m.-11 p.m. **Key Personnel:** Bob Cupit, General Mgr.; David Cupit, Program Dir., dcupit@iamerica.net; Lou Cupit, Sales Mgr. **Wattage:** 1000. **Ad Rates:** $7-9 for 30 seconds; $8.50-10.50 for 60 seconds.

VILLE PLATTE†, pop. 9,201.

SC LA. Evangeline Parish. 48 mi. S. of Alexandria. Oil field products. Electric generators. Iron works. Agriculture. Cotton, corn, rice, yams.

13073 Ville Platte Gazette
Evanguling Publishing Co.
PO Box 220 Phone: (318)363-3939
Ville Platte, LA 70586 Fax: (318)363-2841

Local newspaper. **Founded:** 1914. **Freq:** Semiweekly. **Print Method:** Offset. **Cols./Page:** 6. **Col. Width:** 2 1/16 inches. **Col. Depth:** 21.5 picas. **Key Personnel:** Carissa Heburt, Editor, vpgaz@asbank.com; Jerry Matt, Advertising Mgr. **Subscription Rates:** $30 individuals; $35 out of area; $40 out of state. **Remarks:** Accepts advertising.
Ad Rates: BW: $890.10 **Circ:** ‡4,000
4C: $990.10
PCI: $6.90

13074 KVPI-AM - 1050
809 W. LaSalle St. Phone: (318)363-2124
PO Drawer J Fax: (318)363-3574
Ville Platte, LA 70586
E-mail: kvpi@centaryinter.net

Format: French. **Networks:** Independent. **Owner:** Ville Platte Broadcasting Co., at above address. **Founded:** 1953. **Operating Hours:** Sunrise-sunset; 100% local. **ADI:** Lafayette, LA. **Key Personnel:** Jim Soileau, General Mgr.; Mark Layne, News Dir.; Scott McDaniel, Sports Dir.; Cheryl DeBaillon, Music Dir.; Chris Lamke, Program Dir. **Wattage:** 250. **Ad Rates:** $5.75-8.60 for 30 seconds; $8.15-11.10 for 60 seconds.

13075 KVPI-FM - 92.5
809 W. LaSalle St. Phone: (318)363-2124
PO Drawer J Fax: (318)363-3574
Ville Platte, LA 70586
E-mail: kvpi@centurymter.net

Format: Oldies. **Networks:** USA Radio. **Owner:** Ville Platte Broadcasting Co., at above address. **Founded:** 1965. **Operating Hours:** 6 a.m.-midnight; 100% local. **ADI:** Lafayette, LA. **Key Personnel:** Jim Soileau, General Mgr.; Martel Ardoin, News Dir.; Scott McDaniel, Sports Dir.; J.L. Sylvester, Chief Engineer; Bonnie Fontenot, Contact; Chris Lamke, Program Dir. **Wattage:** 4800. **Ad Rates:** $5.75-8.60 for 30 seconds; $8.15-11.10 for 60 seconds.

13076 Star Cable TV Co.
1000 W. LaSalle St. Phone: (318)363-5900
Ville Platte, LA 70586 Fax: (318)363-9171
Free: (800)326-8700
E-mail: starlai@centuryinter.net

Owner: Star Cable Associates, 100 Greentree Commons, 318 Mansfield Ave., Pittsburgh, PA 15220, (412)937-0099, Fax: (412)937-0145. **Founded:** 1976. **Key Personnel:** Eulin Guidry, General Mgr., phone (318)363-5900, fax (318)363-9171. **Cities Served:** Iberia, Lydia, Mamou, Parish, Ville Platte, LA; St. Martin and Vermillion parishes: subscribing households 9,304; 46 channels; 1 community access channel; 14 hours per week community access programming.

VINTON, pop. 3,631.

SW LA. Calcasieu Parish. 20 mi. W. of Lake Charles. Agriculture. Cattle, rice, sugarcane.

13077 The Vinton News
News Leader, Inc.
716 E. Napoleon Phone: (318)527-7075
PO Box 1999 Fax: (318)528-3044
Sulphur, LA 70664-1999
Community newspaper. **Founded:** 1961. **Freq:** Weekly (Wed.). **Print Method:** Offset. **Cols./Page:** 6. **Col. Width:** 24 nonpareils. **Col. Depth:** 294 agate lines. **Key Personnel:** Brenda Merchant, Editor; E.W. Wise, Publisher; Ophelia Hayes, V.P. Mktg. **USPS:** 621-540. **Subscription Rates:** $12.48 individuals. **Remarks:** Accepts advertising.
Ad Rates: GLR: $1.33 **Circ:** ‡2,260
BW: $1,045.80
4C: $1,595.80
SAU: $8.30
PCI: $8.30

VIOLET

13078 Cox Communications
7509 St. Bernard Hwy. Phone: (504)682-4690
Violet, LA 70092 Fax: (504)682-4718

Owner: Tele-Communications Inc., 5619 DTC Pkwy., Englewood, CO 80111, (303)267-5500, Fax: (303)779-1228. **Formerly:** TCI of Louisiana. **Key Personnel:** David W. Jones, General Mgr.; Lorrie Blappert, Business Mgr.; Rhonda Mathis, Advertising Mgr.; Frank Franklin, Technical Operations Mgr. **Cities Served:** Arabi, Braitwaithe, Chalmette, Hopedale, Meraux, Shell Beach, St. Bernard, Toca, Violet, LA.

VIVIAN, pop. 4,146.

W LA. Caddo Parish. 32 mi. W. of Crowley. Manufactures mobile homes, garments, boats. Oil and gas refineries. Oil wells. Timber. Agriculture. Cotton, corn.

13079 Caddo Citizen
Box 312 Phone: (318)375-3294
Vivian, LA 71082-0312 Fax: (318)375-4578

Local newspaper. **Founded:** Jan. 1912. **Freq:** Weekly (Thurs.). **Print Method:** Offset. **Cols./Page:** 6. **Col. Width:** 27 nonpareils. **Col. Depth:** 301 agate lines. **Key Personnel:** Coral Titus, Editor; Jill Boswell, Publisher. **Subscription Rates:** $24 individuals; $29 out of parish; $33 out of state.
Ad Rates: BW: $451.50 **Circ:** ‡3,600
4C: $901.50
SAU: $3.50

13080 KNCB-AM - 1320
PO Box 1072 Phone: (318)375-3278
Vivian, LA 71082 Fax: (318)375-3329

Format: Country; Religious. **Networks:** AP; ABC. **Owner:** Ruby S. Collins, at above address. **Founded:** 1966. **Operating Hours:** Pre-sunrise to sunset. **Key Personnel:** Ruby Collins, Contact; Gary Spikes, News Dir.; Carol Martin, Contact; Mike Johnston, Sports Dir.; Cherry McCarty, Music Dir.; Carol Martin, Program Dir. **Local Programs:** *Tell-Talk* 9:00 am - 9:30 am Monday-Friday, Gary Spikes, (318)375-5483. **Wattage:** 5000. **Ad Rates:** $10 for 30 seconds; $14 for 60 seconds. Combined advertising rates available with KNCB-FM.

WASHINGTON

SC LA. Saint Landry Parish. 10 mi. N. of Opelousas.

13081 KNEK-FM - 104.7
PO Box 598 Phone: (318)826-3921
Washington, LA 70589 Fax: (318)826-3206

Format: Urban Contemporary. **Networks:** Louisiana. **Founded:** 1989. **Operating Hours:** Continuous. **Key Personnel:** Tyrone Davis, Program Dir.; Carol Celestine, Office Mgr. **Wattage:** 25,000. **Ad Rates:** $7.30-10.50 for 30 seconds; $9.60-14.05 for 60 seconds.

WELSH, pop. 3,515.

SW LA. Jefferson Davis Parish. 32 mi. W. of Crowley. Manufactures meat products, chemicals. Crude petroleum and natural gas. Agriculture. Cotton, rice, truck crops, soybeans.

13082 Welsh Citizen
Moody Co.
PO Box 796 Phone: (318)734-2891
Welsh, LA 70591 Fax: (318)734-4457

Newspaper. **Founded:** 1951. **Freq:** Weekly (Tues.). **Print Method:** Offset. **Cols./Page:** 8. **Col. Width:** 22 nonpareils. **Col. Depth:** 287 agate lines. **Key Personnel:** Felix Thibodeaux, Editor; Nancy Cormier, Publisher. **Subscription Rates:** $10 individuals. **Remarks:** Accepts advertising.
Ad Rates: SAU: $1.90 **Circ:** (Not Reported)

WEST MONROE, pop. 14,993.

N LA. Ouachita Parish. On the Ouachita River. Manufactures paper bags and boxes, cottonseed oil, veneer, syrup, concrete culverts, lumber. Commercial fisheries. Timber. Gas wells. Dairy, stock, poultry, truck farms. Cotton, corn.

13083 The Ouachita Citizen
PO Box 758 Phone: (318)322-3161
West Monroe, LA 71294 Fax: (318)325-2285
Publication E-mail: ocitizen@idmerce.net

Local newspaper. **Founded:** 1924. **Freq:** Weekly (Thurs.). **Print Method:** Offset. Uses mats. **Cols./Page:** 6. **Col. Width:** 2 1/16 inches. **Col. Depth:** 294 agate lines. **Key Personnel:** Sam Hanna, Sr., Publisher; Sam Hanna, Jr., Publisher/Editor/Advertising. **ISSN:** 0746-7478. **Subscription Rates:** $22 individuals; $31 out of area. **Remarks:** Accepts advertising. **Alt. Formats:** Microform.
Ad Rates: GLR: $6.50 **Circ:** ‡6,000
SAU: $6.50
PCI: $6.30

13084 KARD-TV - 14
102 Thomas Rd., Ste. 400 Phone: (318)323-1972
West Monroe, LA 71291 Fax: (318)322-0926

Format: Commercial TV. **Networks:** Fox. **Founded:** 1984. **Formerly:** KLAA-TV. **Operating Hours:** Continuous. **ADI:** Monroe, LA-El Dorado, AR. **Key Personnel:** Lydia Sandifer, General Mgr.; Mark Hernandez, General Sales Mgr.; J.D. Hammons, Production Mgr.; Gary Miers, Promotions Mgr. **Ad Rates:** Advertising accepted; rates available upon request. **URL:** http://www.kard.com/fox14/; http://www.kard.com.

13085 KMCT-TV - 39
701 Parkwood Phone: (318)322-1399
West Monroe, LA 71291-5435 Fax: (318)323-3783
Free: (800)249-1399

Format: Commercial TV. **Networks:** Independent. **Founded:** 1986. **Operating Hours:** Continuous. **ADI:** Monroe, LA-El Dorado, AR. **Key Personnel:** Charles Reed, General Mgr. **Ad Rates:** Advertising accepted; rates available upon request.

WESTLAKE, pop. 5,246.

SW LA. Calcasieu Parish. 4 mi. W. of Lake Charles. Oil refining, petrochemical, carbon black manufactured. Agriculture. Rice.

13086 Builder News Extra
News Leader, Inc.
PO Box 127 Phone: (318)436-0583
Westlake, LA 70669
Shopper. **Founded:** 1962. **Freq:** Weekly (Wed.). **Print Method:** Offset. **Cols./Page:** 6. **Col. Width:** 26 nonpareils. **Col. Depth:** 294 agate lines. **Key Personnel:** E.W. Wise, Publisher; Ophilia Hayes, V.P. Mktg. **Subscription Rates:** Free. **Formerly:** Westlake/Moss Bluff News Buyer's Guide.
Circ: Free ‡6,909

13087 Westlake/Moss Bluff News
News Leader, Inc.
PO Box 127 Phone: (318)436-0583
Westlake, LA 70669 Fax: (318)436-0584

Community newspaper. **Founded:** 1960. **Freq:** Weekly (Thurs.). **Print Method:** Offset. **Cols./Page:** 6. **Col. Width:** 26 nonpareils. **Col. Depth:** 294 agate lines. **Key Personnel:** Cliff Seiber, Editor, starshadow@csi.com; Lewis Cain, Publisher.

Subscription Rates: $10.48 in parish; $26 out of parish. **Remarks:** Accepts advertising. **Formerly:** The Westlaker.
Ad Rates: GLR: $.34 **Circ:** ‡2,091
BW: $1,209.60
4C: $1,263.90
SAU: $10.25

13088 KHLA-FM - 99.5
Shady Ln. at Guillory St. Phone: (318)433-1641
Westlake, LA 70669 Fax: (318)433-2999

Format: Adult Contemporary. **Owner:** Progressive Communications, at above address. **Founded:** 1965. **Operating Hours:** Continuous. **ADI:** Lake Charles, LA. **Key Personnel:** George Swift, General Mgr.; Don Rivers, Operations Dir. **Wattage:** 100,000 ERP. **Ad Rates:** $25 for 30 seconds; $30 for 60 seconds.

WINNFIELD†, pop. 7,311.

NWC LA. Winn Parish. 45 mi. NW of Alexandria. Lumber, creosote mills. Rock quarry, Oil wells. Truck farms. Corn, cattle.

13089 Winn Parish Enterprise
Pineland Publishing Co.
PO Box 750 Phone: (318)628-2712
Winnfield, LA 71483 Fax: (318)628-6196

Community newspaper. **Founded:** 1925. **Freq:** Weekly (Wed.). **Print Method:** Offset. **Trim Size:** 7 x 11 1/2. **Cols./Page:** 6. **Col. Width:** 12 picas. **Col. Depth:** 294 agate lines. **Key Personnel:** Bob Holeman, Publisher. **Subscription Rates:** $20 individuals. **Remarks:** Accepts advertising.
Ad Rates: BW: $505.26 **Circ:** ‡4200
4C: $745.26
SAU: $4.29

13090 KVCL-AM - 1270
No. 1 KVCL Rd. Phone: (318)628-5822
PO Box 548 Fax: (318)628-7355
Winnfield, LA 71483-0548

Format: Adult Contemporary. **Networks:** Mutual Broadcasting System; Louisiana. **Owner:** Harrison Broadcast Organization Inc., at above address. **Founded:** 1955. **Operating Hours:** Continuous. **Key Personnel:** George B. Harrison, President/Gen. Mgr.; George Feger, General Sales Mgr.; Mike Parker, Program and Music Dir.; Patricia Harrison, V.P./Public Relations; Don Garrett, News Dir.; Meloney Brooks, Traffic Mgr. **Wattage:** 1000.

13091 KVCL-FM - 92.1
No. 1 KVCL Rd. Phone: (318)628-5822
PO Box 548 Fax: (318)628-7355
Winnfield, LA 71483

Format: Country. **Networks:** Mutual Broadcasting System; Louisiana. **Owner:** Harrison Broadcast Organization Inc., at above address. **Founded:** 1955. **Operating Hours:** Continuous. **Key Personnel:** George B. Harrison, President/Gen. Mgr./News Dir.; George Feger, General Sales Mgr.; Mike Parker, Program and Music Dir.; Patricia Harrison, V.P. of Public Relations; Leigh Anne Harrison, Traffic Mgr. **Wattage:** 6000. **Ad Rates:** $6-8 for 30 seconds; $7-9 for 60 seconds.

WINNSBORO†, pop. 5,921.

NE LA. Franklin Parish. 39 mi. SE of Monroe. Fishing. Oil and gas wells. Cotton gins. Compress-warehouse. Sawmill. Timber. Stock, dairy, grain farms. Cotton, yams, beef, cattle.

13092 The Franklin Sun
Hanna Publications
514 Prairie St. Phone: (318)435-4521
PO Box 550 Fax: (318)435-9220
Winnsboro, LA 71295-0550
Publication E-mail: thesun@fsbnet.com

Newspaper. **Founded:** 1856. **Freq:** Weekly (Wed.). **Print Method:** Offset. **Trim Size:** 6 x 21. **Cols./Page:** 6. **Col. Width:** 26 nonpareils. **Col. Depth:** 291 agate lines. **Key Personnel:** Sam Hanna, Publisher, phone (318)757-3647, fax (318)757-3001; Monica Iduff, Advertising Mgr.; Leslie Young, Editor. **Subscription Rates:** $20 individuals; $33.50 out of state; $27.50 elsewhere. **Remarks:** Accepts advertising.
Ad Rates: GLR: $.25 **Circ:** ‡6,200
BW: $500
4C: $550
PCI: $4.50

ZACHARY, pop. 7,297.

SEC LA. East Baton Rouge Parish. 15 mi. N. of Baton Rouge. Residential.

13093 Zachary Plainsman-News
Louisiana Suburban Press
5145 Main St. Phone: (504)654-6841
Suite C Fax: (504)654-8271
Zachary, LA 70791
Local newspaper. **Founded:** 1953. **Freq:** Weekly (Thurs.). **Print Method:** Offset. **Cols./Page:** 6. **Col. Width:** 26 nonpareils. **Col. Depth:** 301 agate lines. **Key Personnel:** Katherine Gilbert, Editor; Mithcell Lynch, General Mgr.; Sherry Romero, Advertising Mgr. **Subscription Rates:** $20 individuals; $25 out of parish. **Remarks:** Accepts advertising.
Ad Rates: GLR: $.21 **Circ:** 2,163
BW: $703.05
4C: $903.05
PCI: $5.45

MAINE

State Capital, AUGUSTA

Maine, largest of the New England states, is bounded on the north by Quebec and New Brunswick, Canada, east by New Brunswick, south by Atlantic Ocean, and west by New Hampshire and Quebec. Its extreme length from north to south is 301 miles; its width varies greatly because of the many shore indentations. The total land area is 30,865 square miles. The northern part is mainly a wilderness of forest land with coniferous trees and mountainous elevation, thinly peopled except in the fertile tracts of Aroostook county. In the northeast, on the St. John River, are several French Canadian settlements. The southern part is varied, the surface seldom much broken. It has tracts of great fertility, and others, especially in the southeast, that are only moderately productive. The climate is cold in winter, mild in summer. The Weather Bureau at Portland gives the temperature (annual average) as 45.4; highest on record, 93; lowest, -23. Total annual precipitation is 44.34 inches. Maine is a fishing, hunting, and summer resort of great popularity. Portland, the chief port, has a large cruiseship tourist traffic in addition to its extensive trade in freight. The state has about 1,300 wooded islands. On one of them, Mt. Desert, are Arcadia National Park and a notable summer colony. Higher education is provided by many colleges, a theological seminary, and a Maritime academy. The University of Maine, the largest, is located at Orono.

POPULATION: 1,235,000 (1992). Rank among the states, 39th.

AGRICULTURE: Number of farms: 7,000 (1992). Farm acreage: 1,000,000 (1992). Cash receipts from farm marketings: crops, $192,000,000 (1991); livestock and products, $252,000,000 (1991).

FISHERIES: Total catch: 192,000,000 lbs. (1991), $155,000,000 value. Principal fish: lobster, ocean perch, herring (sea), clams, scallops.

FORESTS: Total forest land: 93,000 acres (1991). Principal woods: white pine, hemlock, eastern spruce, balsam fir, birch, maple, oak, eastern cedar, beech, ash, basswood, cottonwoods, aspen.

MINERALS: Value of production: $41,000,000 (1991). Principal minerals: sand and gravel, cement, stone.

MANUFACTURES: Value added by manufacture: $5,428,000,000 (1991). Leading industry groups: paper and allied products, leather and leather products, electric and electronic equipment, furniture and fixtures, stone, clay and glass, food and related products.

LIST OF COUNTIES

Total number of counties 16

County, Location on Map, and County Seat	Pop.
Androscoggin (SW), Auburn	105,259
Aroostook (N), Houlton	86,936
Cumberland (SW), Portland	243,135
Franklin (W), Farmington	29,008
Hancock (SE), Ellsworth	46,948
Kennebec (SWC), Augusta	115,904
Knox (S), Rockland	36,310
Lincoln (S), Wiscasset	30,357
Oxford (S), South Paris	53,602
Penobscot (C), Bangor	146,601
Piscataquis (NC), Dover-Foxcroft	18,653
Sagadahoc (S), Bath	33,535
Somerset (NW), Skowhegan	49,767
Waldo (S), Belfast	33,018
Washington (SE), Machias	35,308
York (SW), Alfred	164,587

STATISTICS

Newspapers

Period of Issue	
Daily	7
Evening Daily	2
Morning Daily	5
Daily with Sunday edition	2
Semiweekly	1
Weekly	37
Biweekly...	1
Semimonthly	1
Monthly	3
Bimonthly	1
Quarterly...	1
Free or partly free	7
Shopper	2
Total Newspapers	56

Periodicals

Period of Issue	
Daily	1
Monthly	10
Bimonthly	9
Quarterly	11
Total Periodicals	48

Total number of publications 104

Radio Stations

AM Stations	17
FM Stations	43
Total Radio Stations	60

TV Stations

Total TV Stations 13

Cable Stations

Total Cable Systems 14

Total number of broadcast listings 87

AUBURN†.

Androscoggin Co. (SE). 5 m W of Lewiston.

13094 Cablevision
121 Mill St. Phone: (207)783-2023
Auburn, ME 04210 Fax: (207)786-2563
Free: (800)492-0757

Founded: 1966. **Formerly**: A R Cable Services, Inc. **Cities Served:** Androscoggin County, Oxford County, Auburn, Lisbon, Lisbon Falls, Mechanic Falls, Oxford, and Sabattus, ME.

13095 WLAM-AM - 870
912 Washington St. Phone: (207)784-5401
Auburn, ME 04210 Fax: (207)784-5581
E-mail: themix@megalink.net

Format: Big Band/Nostalgia. **Simulcasts:** WLAM-FM. **Networks:** Westwood One Radio; ABC. **Owner:** The Great Down East Wireless Talking Machine Co., Inc., at above address, (207)786-2496. **Founded:** 1947. **Formerly**: WASY-AM; WJBQ-AM. **Operating Hours:** Continuous; 85% network, 15% local. **ADI:** Portland-Poland Spring, ME. **Key Personnel:** Ron Frizzell, Contact; Chrys Wilson, Sales Mgr.; Mac Dickson, Program Dir.; Eric Marenghi, Station Mgr. **Local Programs:** *Bob Shaw*, Bob Shaw. **Wattage:** 10,000 day; 1,000 night. **Ad Rates:** $20-50 per unit.

13096 WLAM-FM - 106.7
912 Washington St. Phone: (207)784-5401
Auburn, ME 04210 Fax: (207)784-5581
E-mail: themix@megalink.net

Format: Big Band/Nostalgia. **Simulcasts:** WLAM-AM. **Networks:** Westwood One Radio; ABC. **Owner:** The Great Down East Wireless Talking Machine Co., Inc., at above address. **Founded:** 1947. **Formerly**: WVYH-FM. **Operating Hours:** Continuous; 85% network; 15% local. **ADI:** Portland-Poland Spring, ME. **Key Personnel:** Ron Frizzell, Station Mgr.; Mac Dickson, Program Dir.; Eric Marenghi, Station Mgr. **Wattage:** 5000.

13097 WMTW-TV - 8
99 Danville Corner Rd. Phone: (207)782-1800
PO Box 8 Fax: (207)783-7371
Auburn, ME 04210
E-mail: wmtw@wmtw.com

Format: Commercial TV. **Networks:** ABC. **Owner:** Harron Communications Corp., 70 E. Lancaster Ave., Frazer, PA 19355, (215)644-7500. **Founded:** 1954. **Operating Hours:** Continuous. **ADI:** Portland-Poland Spring, ME. **Key Personnel:** David Kaufman, Vice President; David Baer, News Dir.; Jack Conner, Chief Engineer; John Gregory, Production Mgr.; Doug Alpert, National Sales Mgr.; SuzAnne Brown, Business Mgr./Human Resources; Cary O'Neill, Marketing Mgr. **Local Programs:** *Channel 8 News*, Mary Jo Cranmore; *First at Five*, Mary Jo Cranmore.

13098 WMWX-FM - 99.9
912 Washington St. Phone: (207)786-2496
Auburn, ME 04210 Fax: (207)784-5581
Free: (888)333-MIXX
E-mail: themix@wmwx.com

Format: Adult Contemporary. **Networks:** Independent. **Owner:** Ron Frizzell, at above address. **Founded:** 1978. **Formerly**: WWAV-FM (1982); WKZS-FM (1998). **Operating Hours:** Continuous; 100% local. **Key Personnel:** Ron Frizzell, General Mgr.; Chrys Wilson, Sales Mgr., phone (207)797-0780; Mac Dickson, Program Dir.; Eric Marenghi, Station Mgr. **Local Programs:** *Donna and Dickson*, Mac Dickson. **Wattage:** 50,000. **Ad Rates:** $40-60 per unit.

AUGUSTA†, pop. 21,819.

SW ME. Kennebec Co. On Kennebec River, 26 mi. NE of Lewiston. State Capital. Founded 1628 as trading post of Plymouth colony. University of Maine at Augusta. Resort. Manufactures computers, wood and paper products, textiles, shoes; meat processing.

13099 The Christian Civic League Record
Christian Civic League
PO Box 5459 Phone: (207)622-7634
Augusta, ME 04332 Fax: (207)621-0035
Free: (800)769-4132
Publication E-mail: email@cclmaine.org

Magazine on civic action. **Founded:** 1900. **Freq:** Monthly. **Print Method:** Offset. **Cols./Page:** 5. **Col. Width:** 22 nonpareils. **Col. Depth:** 182 agate lines. **Key Personnel:** Cynthia Randall, Editor, cyndee@cclmaine.org. **Subscription Rates:** $10 individuals. **Remarks:** Advertising not accepted.
Circ: Paid ‡3,000
Non-paid ‡300

13100 Fatal Occupational Injuries in Maine
Department of Labor
45 State House Sta. Phone: (207)624-6444
Augusta, ME 04333-0045 Fax: (207)624-6449

Technical publication covering work-related injuries of private and public employees in Maine. **Founded:** 1992. **Freq:** Annual. **Key Personnel:** Robert W. Leighton, Jr., Robert.W.Leighton@state.me.us. **Subscription Rates:** Free. **Remarks:** Advertising not accepted. **Former name**: Report of Fatal Occupational Injuries in Maine.
Circ: Non-paid 1,000

13101 Kennebec Journal
274 Western Ave. Phone: (207)623-3811
PO Box 1052 Fax: (207)623-3811
Augusta, ME 04330-4976
Free: (800)537-5508

General newspaper. **Founded:** 1825. **Freq:** Mon.-Sat. (morn.). **Print Method:** Offset. **Cols./Page:** 6. **Col. Width:** 26 nonpareils. **Col. Depth:** 301 agate lines. **Key Personnel:** Alan Buncher, Exec. Editor; Ronald Uecker, Advertising Dir. **Remarks:** Accepts advertising.
Ad Rates: PCI: $11.06 **Circ:** Mon.-Sat. ★**15,708**
Sun. ★**14,185**

13102 Maine Fish and Wildlife
Maine Dept. of Inland Fisheries and Wildlife
284 State St., No. 41 Phone: (207)287-8000
Augusta, ME 04333 Fax: (207)287-6395

Fish and wildlife conservation periodical. **Founded:** 1959. **Freq:** Quarterly. **Print Method:** Offset. **Trim Size:** 8 1/2 x 11. **Cols./Page:** 3 and 2. **Col. Width:** 27 and 42 nonpareils. **Col. Depth:** 133 agate lines. **Key Personnel:** J. Paul Reynolds, Editor. **ISSN:** 0360-005X. **Subscription Rates:** $9 individuals. **URL:** http://www.state.me.us/ifw.
Circ: Paid 12,500
Non-paid 1,500

13103 Maine Motor Transport News
142 Whitten Rd. Phone: (207)623-4128
PO Box 857 Fax: (207)623-4096
Augusta, ME 04332
Magazine on motor trucks. **Founded:** 1946. **Freq:** 10/year. **Print Method:** Letterpress. **Trim Size:** 8 3/8 x 10 7/8. **Cols./Page:** 3. **Col. Width:** 26 nonpareils. **Col. Depth:** 123 agate lines. **Key Personnel:** Dale E. Hanington, Editor; Gayle P. Baber, Advertising Mgr. **Subscription Rates:** $35 individuals. **Remarks:** Accepts advertising.
Ad Rates: BW: $275 **Circ:** Paid 2,452
4C: $675 Non-paid 1,500

13104 The Maine Sportsman
Box 365 Phone: (207)846-9501
Augusta, ME 04330
Magazine (tabloid) covering Maine hunting and fishing topics. **Founded:** May 1972. **Freq:** Monthly. **Print Method:** Offset. **Trim Size:** 11 x 16. **Cols./Page:** 5. **Col. Width:** 1 7/8 inches. **Col. Depth:** 13 inches. **Key Personnel:** Harry Vanderweide, Editor; Jon Lund, Publisher; George Pulkkenin, Advertising Mgr. **Subscription Rates:** $20 individuals; $2.25 single issue. **Remarks:** Accepts advertising.
Ad Rates: BW: $700 **Circ:** ‡30,000
PCI: $7.50

13105 Maine Trails
Maine Better Transportation Association
146 State St. Phone: (207)622-0526
Augusta, ME 04330 Fax: (207)623-2928

Magazine informing association members and the business community about Maine transportation issues. **Subtitle:** The Magazine of the Maine Better Transportation Assn. **Founded:** 1941. **Freq:** Bimonthly. **Print Method:** Offset. **Trim Size:** 8 1/4 x 10 7/8. **Cols./Page:** 2. **Key Personnel:** Maira R. Fuentes, Editor. **Subscription Rates:** $20. **Remarks:** Accepts advertising. **Formerly**: Transportation Infrastructure Issues with Maine.
Ad Rates: BW: $230 **Circ:** Controlled ‡1,300
4C: $680

13106 State Cable TV Corp.
83 Anthony Ave. Phone: (207)623-5145
Augusta, ME 04330 Fax: (207)623-3407
Free: (800)540-5145
E-mail: info@statecable.com

Owner: Whitcom Investment Company, 1271 Avenue of the Americas, Rm. 4310, New York, NY 10020, (212)582-2300. **Founded:** 1966. **Key Personnel:** Michael Angelakis, President & Chief Executive Officer, phone (207)623-3615; Ken Danielson, V.P. of Finance, phone (207)623-3685; Reggie Clark, Jr, V.P. of Engineering & Tech Operations, phone (207)623-3685; Jennifer Vachon, Marketing Dir., phone (207)623-3685; Kathleen Hounsell, V.P. of Customer Serv./Office Operations, phone (207)623-3695; Roger Gagne, VP/Ad. Sales, phone (207)622-3030, fax (207)622-2386; Ned Lightner, Program Dir., phone (207)622-3030, fax (207)622-7386. **Cities Served:** subscribing households 59,657. **URL:** http://www.statecable.com.

13107 WTVL-AM - 1490
52 Western Ave. Phone: (207)623-4735
Augusta, ME 04330 Fax: (207)626-5948

Format: Adult Contemporary; Soft Rock. **Networks:** ABC. **Owner:** WTVL Corp., at above address. **Founded:** 1946. **Operating Hours:** Continuous; 3% network, 97% local. **Key Personnel:** Douglas D. Warner, Station Mgr.; Jon Paradise, Program Dir.; Eric Leimbach, News Dir. **Wattage:** 1000. **Ad Rates:** $15 for 30 seconds; $25 for 60 seconds.

BANGOR†, pop. 31,643.

C ME. Penobscot Co. On Penobscot River, 60 mi. NE of Augusta. Bangor Theological Seminary. Husson College. University of Maine. Manufactures paper, footwear, wood products, lumber, electronics.

13108 Bangor Daily News
491 Main St. Phone: (207)990-8000
PO Box 1329 Fax: (207)941-0885
Bangor, ME 04402-1329
Free: (800)432-7964
Publication E-mail: Bangornews@aol.com
Publisher E-mail: bdnmail@bangornews.infi.net

General newspaper. **Founded:** 1834. **Freq:** Mon.-Sat. (morn.). **Print Method:** Flexography. **Trim Size:** 13 x 21. **Cols./Page:** 6. **Col. Width:** 25 nonpareils. **Col. Depth:** 301 agate lines. **Key Personnel:** Richard J. Warren, Publisher, phone (207)990-8221, fax (207)941-9476; Robert W. Stairs, VP, Administration, phone (207)990-8223, fax (207)990-8095; A. Mark Woodward, Exec. Ed., phone (207)990-8239, fax (207)941-9476; Wayne A. Lawton, Advertising Dir., phone (207)990-8061; James M. Spox, Circulation Mgr., phone (207)990-8280, fax (207)990-8027; Charles Campo, Librarian, phone (207)990-8160, fax (207)990-8160, bdnlib@bangornews.infi.net. **ISSN:** 0892-8738. **Subscription Rates:** $161.20 individuals. **Remarks:** Accepts advertising. **Online:** Lexis/Nexia,Datatimes. **Alt. Formats:** CD-ROM; Microform. **Feature Editors:** Janine Pineo, *Travel*.
Ad Rates: BW: $5,506.20 **Circ:** Mon.-Fri. ★**69,514**
4C: $6,237.20 Sat. ★**82,870**
PCI: $54.63 Sun. ★**82,870**

13109 Cablevision
149 Target Industrial Circle Phone: (207)942-4661
Box 1405 Fax: (207)942-5426
Bangor, ME 04401
Free: (800)432-1648

Founded: 1971. **Formerly**: A-R Cable Service, Inc. **Key Personnel:** William Fay, General Mgr.; Robert Jones, Contact; Deborah Chapman, Contact; Patti Rollins, Contact. **Cities Served:** subscribing households 24,300; 36 channels; 1 community access channel.

13110 WABI-AM - 910
27 State St. Phone: (207)947-9100
Bangor, ME 04401 Fax: (207)947-2346
E-mail: 971@midmaine.com

Format: Oldies; Middle-of-the-Road (MOR). **Networks:** CNN Radio. **Owner:** Bangor Radio Corp., at above address. **Founded:** 1924. **Operating Hours:** Continuous. **ADI:** Bangor, ME. **Key Personnel:** Tristan G. Richards, General Mgr., trich4524@juno.com; Melissa Pearch, News Dir.; George Hale, Exec./Station Mgr. **Local Programs:** *George Hale Show*, George Hale. **Wattage:** 5000. **Ad Rates:** $10-35 for 30 seconds; $12-40 for 60 seconds. Combined advertising rates available with WWBX-FM.

13111 WABI-TV - 5
35 Hildreth St. Phone: (207)947-8321
Bangor, ME 04401 Fax: (207)941-9378
Free: (800)432-1625

Format: Commercial TV. **Networks:** CBS. **Owner:** Community Broadcasting Services, at above address. **Founded:** 1953. **Operating Hours:** Continuous. **ADI:** Bangor, ME. **Key Personnel:** Michael Young, General Mgr. **URL:** http://www.wabi-tv.com.

13112 WHCF-FM - 88.5
PO Box 5000 Phone: (207)947-2751
Bangor, ME 04401 Fax: (207)947-0010
Free: (800)947-2577
E-mail: fm885@telplus.net

Format: Religious; Talk. **Networks:** Independent; Moody Broadcasting; USA Radio; SkyLight Satellite. **Owner:** Bangor Baptist Church, at above address, (207)947-6576. **Founded:** 1981. **Operating Hours:** Continuous; 20% network, 80% local. **ADI:** Bangor, ME. **Key Personnel:** Thomas Obey,

General Mgr.; Virgil Phinney, News Dir.; Michael Dalton, Program Dir.; Kathy Schroeher, Office Mgr. **Local Programs:** *Maine Agenda*, Steve Strout; *Pastor's Study*, Thomas Obey, General Mgr. **Wattage:** 100,000. **Ad Rates:** Noncommercial. **URL:** http://www.teleplus.net/whcf.

13113 WHSN-FM - 89.3
1 College Circle Phone: (207)947-3987
Bangor, ME 04401 Fax: (207)947-3987

Format: Contemporary Hit Radio (CHR); Alternative/New Music/Progressive. **Networks:** AP. **Owner:** Husson College Trustees, at above address, (207)941-7000. **Founded:** 1974. **Operating Hours:** 6 a.m.-midnight, Sept., May; 10 a.m.-10 p.m.; 100% local. **ADI:** Bangor, ME. **Key Personnel:** Ben Haskell, Gen. Mgr./Faculty Advisor. **Wattage:** 140. **Ad Rates:** Noncommercial; underwriting available.

13114 WJCX-FM - 99.5
2881 Ohio St., Ste 8 Phone: (207)884-6052
Bangor, ME 04401 Free: (800)797-WCJX
E-mail: wjcx@ime.net

Format: Contemporary Christian; Talk. **Owner:** CSN International, at above address. **Operating Hours:** Continuous. **ADI:** Bangor, ME. **Key Personnel:** James R. Lord, Station Mgr.

13115 WLBZ-TV - 2
PO Box 415, Phone: (207)942-4821
329 Mt. Hope Ave Fax: (207)945-6816
Bangor, ME 04402-0415

Format: Commercial TV. **Networks:** NBC. **Founded:** 1954. **Operating Hours:** Continuous. **ADI:** Bangor, ME. **Key Personnel:** Judith Horan, General Mgr.

13116 WMEB-TV - 12
65 Texas Ave. Phone: (207)941-1010
Bangor, ME 04401 Fax: (207)942-2857
E-mail: comments@mpbc.org

Format: Public TV. **Networks:** Public Broadcasting Service (PBS). **Owner:** Maine Public Broadcasting, 1450 Lisbon St., Lewiston, ME 04240, (207)783-9101, Fax: (207)783-5193. **Founded:** 1962. **Operating Hours:** 6 a.m.-midnight. **ADI:** Bangor, ME. **Key Personnel:** Robert H. Gardiner, President, rgardiner@mpbc.org; Chris F. Amann, Dir. of Finance, camann@mpbc.org; Katherine Arno, Dir. of Television Services, karno@mpbc.org; Russell J. Peotter, Dir. of Marketing & Development, rpeotter@mpbc.org; Donald Carrigan, Public Affairs Mgr., dcarrigan@mpbc.org; Charles S. Rose, Advertising & Promotions Mgr., crose@mpbc.org; Melinda Lake, Media Relations Coordinator, mlake@mpbc.org; Alexander G. Maxwell, Dir. of Engineering, amaxwell@mpbc.org; Joyce Moulin, Audience Services. **Ad Rates:** Noncommercial. **URL:** http://www.mpbc.org.

WMEM-TV - See Presque Isle

13117 WPBC-FM - 99.5
727 Hamond St. Phone: (207)947-3600
Bangor, ME 04401 Fax: (207)947-1728

Format: Adult Contemporary. **Networks:** Independent. **Owner:** Penobscot Broadcasting Corp., at above address. **Founded:** 1976. **Operating Hours:** Continuous. **ADI:** Bangor, ME. **Key Personnel:** Alicia Nichols, Sales Mgr.; Jay Lundstrom, Operations Mgr.; James Goff, General Mgr.; Kent Thurston, Program Mgr. **Wattage:** 50,000. **Ad Rates:** $20-45 for 30 seconds.

13118 WVII-TV - 7
371 Target Industrial Circle Phone: (207)945-6457
P.O. Box 1101 Fax: (207)942-0511
Bangor, ME 04401

Format: Commercial TV. **Networks:** ABC. **Founded:** 1965. **Formerly:** WEMT-TV. **Operating Hours:** Continuous. **ADI:** Bangor, ME. **Key Personnel:** Bernard Chase, General Mgr., phone (207)945-6457. **Wattage:** 316,000.

13119 WZON-AM - 620
PO Box 1929 Phone: (207)942-4656
Bangor, ME 04402-1929 Fax: (207)942-4657

Format: Talk; News. **Networks:** CBS; Mutual Broadcasting System; Talknet. **Founded:** 1926. **Formerly:** WLBZ-AM (1977). **Operating Hours:** Continuous. **ADI:** Bangor, ME. **Key Personnel:** Andy Soule, Operations Mgr.; Russ Vanardale, News Dir.; Leo Jonason, Contact. **Wattage:** 5000. **Ad Rates:** $7-20 for 30 seconds; $10-25 for 60 seconds.

BAR HARBOR, pop. 4,124.

SE ME. Hancock Co. On Mount Desert Island, 40 mi. SE of Bangor. Acadia National Park. Resort.

13120 The Bar Harbor Times
Courier Publications
PO Box 68 Phone: (207)288-3311
Bar Harbor, ME 04609-0068 Fax: (207)288-5813
Publication E-mail: bhtimes@downeast.net
Publisher E-mail: cgmail@courierpub.com

Local newspaper. **Founded:** July 11, 1914. **Freq:** Weekly (Thurs.). **Print Method:** Offset. **Trim Size:** 13 x 21. **Cols./Page:** 6 and 4. **Col. Width:** 9 and 14 picas. **Col. Depth:** 15 inches. **Key Personnel:** Earl Brechlin, Editor; David Morse, Publisher; Brian Hewett, Advertising Mgr.; Maureen Baker, Business Mgr. **USPS:** 044-060. **Subscription Rates:** $30 individuals local; $48 out of state. **Remarks:** Accepts advertising.
Ad Rates: SAU: $6.95 **Circ:** Paid ‡8,271
PCI: $10.95 Free ‡500

BATH, pop. 10,246.

S. ME. Sagadahoc Co. On Atlantic Ocean, 22 mi. SE of Lewiston. Marine museum. Shipbuilding. Trade center.

13121 Coastal Journal
PO Box 705 Phone: (207)443-6241
Bath, ME 04530-0705 Fax: (207)443-5605
Free: (800)649-6241
Publication E-mail: coastal@biddeford.com

Community newspaper (tabloid). **Founded:** Oct. 31, 1966. **Freq:** Weekly (Thurs.). **Print Method:** Offset. **Cols./Page:** 5 and 7. **Col. Width:** 2.069 and 1.442 inches. **Col. Depth:** 12 7/8 and 12 7/8 inches. **Key Personnel:** John Brill, General Mgr. **Subscription Rates:** Free; $45 by mail.
Ad Rates: PCI: $10.92 **Circ:** Free 19,000

13122 WJTO-AM - 730
PO Box 308 Phone: (207)443-6671
Bath, ME 04530-0308

Format: Easy Listening. **Networks:** CNN Radio. **Founded:** 1957. **Formerly:** WMMS-AM (1959). **Operating Hours:** Continuous; 99% local. **ADI:** Portland-Poland Spring, ME. **Key Personnel:** Bob Bittner, Oper./Traffic Mgr./Owner/Gen. Mgr.; Tory Gates, News Dir., phone (207)443-6671. **Local Programs:** *Attunements*; *Berean Baptist Church*; *H.S. Sports.* **Wattage:** 1000 day; 29 night. **Ad Rates:** $7.30 per unit.

BELFAST†, pop. 6,243.

S. ME. Waldo Co. A port of entry at head of Penobscot Bay, 40 mi. ENE of Augusta. Resort.

13123 The Republican Journal
Courier Publications
71 High St. Phone: (207)338-3333
PO Box 327 Fax: (207)338-5498
Belfast, ME 04915-0327
Publication E-mail: trjmail@courierpub.com
Publisher E-mail: cgmail@courierpub.com

County newspaper. **Founded:** 1829. **Freq:** Weekly (Thurs.). **Print Method:** Offset. **Cols./Page:** 6. **Col. Width:** 14 picas. **Col. Depth:** 294 agate lines. **Key Personnel:** Lori Groening, Editor; Greg Whitcomb, Advertising Mgr. **Subscription Rates:** $32 out of state; $18 individuals. **Remarks:** Accepts advertising.
Ad Rates: PCI: $7.30 **Circ:** Paid 7,450

BETHEL, pop. 2,340.

W. ME. Oxford Co. On Androscoggin River, 33 mi. NW of Lewiston. Resort.

13124 The Bethel Oxford County Citizen
Lewiston Sun Journal
Box 109 Phone: (207)824-2444
Bethel, ME 04217 Fax: (207)824-2426

Community newspaper. **Founded:** 1895. **Freq:** Weekly (Wed.). **Print Method:** Offset. **Cols./Page:** 6. **Col. Width:** 24 nonpareils. **Col. Depth:** 294 agate lines. **Key Personnel:** Edward Snook, Publisher. **Subscription Rates:** $13 individuals. **Remarks:** Accepts advertising.
Ad Rates: GLR: $.179 **Circ:** 3,100
BW: $285
4C: $600
SAU: $3.50

BIDDEFORD, pop. 19,638.

SE ME. York Co. On Saco River, 14 mi. SSW of Portland. Diversified manufacturing; textiles.

13125 Journal Tribune
Journal Publishing Corp.
PO Box 627 Phone: (207)282-1535
Biddeford, ME 04005 Fax: (207)282-3138
Free: (800)255-7601
Publication E-mail: jtribune@biddeford.com

Independent general newspaper serving York County, ME. **Founded:** 1884. **Freq:** Daily (eve.) and Sat. (morn.). **Print Method:** Offset. **Trim Size:** 13 3/4 x 23 3/4. **Cols./Page:** 6. **Col. Width:** 2 1/16 inches. **Col. Depth:** 21.5 picas. **Key Personnel:** Robert Saunders, Managing Editor; Dennis J. Flaherty, Publisher; Donald Lauzier, Editor; Charles W. Osbon, Circulation Mgr. **ISSN:** 0057-20. **Subscription Rates:** $175 by mail; $130 by carrier. **Remarks:** Accepts advertising. **URL:** http://www.journaltribune.com.
Ad Rates: BW: $1,573.80 **Circ:** Mon.-Fri. ★**10,503**
4C: $475 Sat. ★**12,286**
SAU: $12.20

BLUE HILL, pop. 1,644.

SW ME. Hancock Co. 30 mi. SSE of Bangor. Summer resort.

13126 The Weekly Packet
Penobscot Bay Press, Inc.
PO Box 646 Phone: (207)374-2341
Blue Hill, ME 04614 Fax: (207)374-2343

Community newspaper. **Founded:** 1934. **Freq:** Weekly (Thurs.). **Print Method:** Offset. **Trim Size:** 11 x 17. **Cols./Page:** 4. **Col. Width:** 2 1/2 inches. **Col. Depth:** 15 inches. **Key Personnel:** R. Nathaniel W. Barrows, Editor and Publisher, phone (207)367-2200, fax (207)367-6397; Barbara Audit, News Editor. **USPS:** 624-320. **Subscription Rates:** $24.95 individuals; $33.95 out of state; $.60 single issue. **Remarks:** Accepts advertising.
Ad Rates: BW: $480 **Circ:** Paid 1,984
PCI: $8 Free 53

BOOTHBAY HARBOR, pop. 2,207.

Lincoln Co. (S). 30 m NE of Portland. Summer resort. Shipyards, packing houses. Fisheries.

13127 Boothbay Register
Maine OK Enterprises
PO Box 357
Boothbay Harbor, ME 04538-0357
Publication E-mail: boothbayregister@clinic.net

Community newspaper. **Founded:** Dec. 9, 1876. **Freq:** Weekly (Thurs.). **Print Method:** Offset. **Trim Size:** 15 13/16 x 21. **Cols./Page:** 7. **Col. Width:** 2 1/16 inches. **Col. Depth:** 21 inches. **Key Personnel:** Mary D. Brewer, Managing Editor; Marylouise Cowan, Publisher. **USPS:** 061-120. **Subscription Rates:** $22; $30 out of area. **Available Online. URL:** http://boothbayregister.maine.com.
Ad Rates: BW: $705.60 **Circ:** 5,000
4C: $150
SAU: $6

BREWER, pop. 9,017.

Penobscot Co. (SE). On Penobscot River opposite Bangor. Wood pulp, paper, brick.

13128 WBFB-FM - 104.7
12 Acme Rd., Ste. 207 Phone: (207)989-7364
Brewer, ME 04412-1546 Fax: (207)989-8321

Format: Contemporary Country. **Networks:** Independent. **Founded:** 1986. **Formerly:** WWFX-FM (1997). **Operating Hours:** Continuous; 100% local. **ADI:** Bangor, ME. **Key Personnel:** Mark Osborne, General Mgr.; Jeff Pierce, Music Dir.; Keryn Smith, General Sales Mgr. **Wattage:** 50,000. **Ad Rates:** Advertising accepted; rates available upon request.

13129 WQCB-FM - 106.5
49 Acme Rd. Phone: (207)989-5631
PO Box 100 Fax: (207)989-5685
Brewer, ME 04412
Free: (800)339-1065
E-mail: q1065@telplus.net

Format: Country. **Networks:** AP. **Owner:** Castle Broadcasting, at above address, Free: (800)244-9722. **Founded:** 1985. **Operating Hours:** Continuous; 100% local. **ADI:** Bangor, ME. **Key Personnel:** Bob Duchesne, General Mgr.; Bob Potts, Program Dir.; Cindy Campbell, Music Dir.; Mark Parent, Operations Dir.; Russ VanArsdale, News Dir.; Patsy Pearson, National Sales Manager. **Wattage:** 100,000. **Ad Rates:** $65 for 30 seconds; $70 for 60 seconds. **URL:** http://www.telplus.net/q1065.

BRIDGTON, pop. 3,528.

Cumberland Co. (NW). 39 m NW of Portland. Summer resort. Pine timber. Manufactures synthetic fabric, shoes, wood products. Dairy, poultry, fruit farms.

13130 The Bridgton News
Bridgton News Corp.
42 Main St. Phone: (207)647-2851
PO Box 244
Bridgton, ME 04009
Community newspaper. **Founded:** 1870. **Freq:** Weekly (Thurs.). **Print Method:** Offset. **Cols./Page:** 8. **Col. Width:** 23 nonpareils. **Col. Depth:** 294 agate lines. **Key Personnel:** Michael T. Corrigan, Editor; Henry A. Shorey, Publisher; Gail A. Stretton, Advertising Mgr. **USPS:** 065-020. **Subscription Rates:** $20 individuals; $.50 single issue. **Remarks:** Accepts advertising.
Ad Rates: GLR: $0.30 **Circ:** ⊕**6,783**
BW: $714
PCI: $4.75

BROOKLIN, pop. 619.

Hancock Co. (SE) 20 m S of Ellsworth. Residential

13131 Hope
PO Box 160 Phone: (207)359-4651
Brooklin, ME 04616 Fax: (207)359-8950
Publisher E-mail: info@hopemag.com

Consumer magazine covering social issues. **Subtitle:** People Making a Difference. **Founded:** Mar. 1996. **Freq:** Quarterly. **Print Method:** Web offset. **Trim Size:** 8 1/8 x 10 7/8. **Key Personnel:** Jon Wilson, Pub./Ed.-in-Chief; Kimberly Ridley, Senior Editor. **ISSN:** 1085-228X. **Subscription Rates:** $19.95 individuals; $3.95 single issue. **Remarks:** Accepts advertising.
Ad Rates: BW: $1,125 **Circ:** 18,000
4C: $1,800

13132 Professional BoatBuilder
WoodenBoat Publications, Inc.
Naskeag Rd. Phone: (207)359-4651
PO Box 78 Fax: (207)359-8920
Brooklin, ME 04616
Free: (800)273-SHIP
Publisher E-mail: wbstore@woodenboat.

Magazine for those working in boat design, construction, and repair. **Subtitle:** The Magazine of Boat Production, Construction & Repair. **Founded:** Sept. 1989. **Freq:** Bimonthly. **Print Method:** Web offset. **Trim Size:** 8 1/8 x 10 7/8. **Key Personnel:** Paul Lazarus, Editor; Carl Cramer, Publisher; Paul Lazarus, Editor; Jonathan Wilson, Advertising Mgr.; Barbara Walsh, Managing Editor; Ted Hugger, Director. **ISSN:** 1043-2035. **Subscription Rates:** Free to qualified subscribers. **Remarks:** Accepts advertising. **URL:** http://www.woodenboat.com.
Ad Rates: BW: $3,455 **Circ:** Controlled 23,688
4C: $4,835

13133 WoodenBoat
WoodenBoat Publications, Inc.
Naskeag Rd. Phone: (207)359-4651
PO Box 78 Fax: (207)359-8920
Brooklin, ME 04616
Free: (800)273-SHIP
Publisher E-mail: wbstore@woodenboat.

Magazine covering the design, building, care, preservation, and use of wooden boats, including commercial and pleasure, old and new, sail and power. **Subtitle:** The Magazine for Wooden Boat Owners, Builders, and Designers. **Founded:** Sept. 1, 1974. **Freq:** Bimonthly. **Print Method:** Offset. **Trim Size:** 8 1/8 x 10 7/8. **Cols./Page:** 3. **Col. Width:** 27 nonpareils. **Col. Depth:** 140 agate lines. **Key Personnel:** Matthew Murphy, Editor; Carl Cramer, Publisher. **ISSN:** 0095-0674. **Subscription Rates:** $29 individuals; $5.50 single issue. **Remarks:** Accepts advertising.
Ad Rates: BW: $4,650 **Circ:** Paid ★**109,458**
4C: $6,510

BRUNSWICK, pop. 17,366.

Cumberland Co. (SW). On Androscoggin River, 27 m NE of Portland. Bowdoin College (Co-educational). Summer resort. Naval Air Station. Manufactures paper, art supplies, shoes, children's clothing.

13134 BOWDOIN Magazine
Bowdoin College
4104 College Station Phone: (207)725-3136
Brunswick, ME 04011-8432 Fax: (207)725-3127

Magazine for college alumni. **Founded:** 1927. **Freq:** 3/year. **Print Method:** Offset. **Trim Size:** 8 3/8 x 10 7/8. **Cols./Page:** 3. **Col. Width:** 2 1/4 inches. **Col. Depth:** 9 3/4 inches. **Key Personnel:** Alison M. Bennie, Editor, abennie@bowdoin.edu. **Subscription Rates:** Free. **Remarks:** Accepts advertising.
Ad Rates: BW: $500 **Circ:** Non-paid ‡21,000
4C: $1,100

13135 Brunswick Times Record
Times Record
6 Industry Rd. Phone: (207)729-3311
PO Box 10 Fax: (207)729-5728
Brunswick, ME 04011
Newspaper with a Democratic orientation. **Founded:** Feb. 1, 1967. **Freq:** Daily (eve.). **Print Method:** Offset. **Cols./Page:** 7. **Col. Width:** 24 nonpareils. **Col. Depth:** 301 agate lines. **Key Personnel:** David L. Swearingen, Editor; Campbell B. Niven, Publisher; Marie Almy, Advertising Mgr. **Subscription Rates:** $70.80 individuals. **Remarks:** Accepts advertising.
Ad Rates: PCI: $7.05 **Circ:** Mon.-Thurs. ★**11,633**
Fri. ★**14,301**

13136 Church World
Brunswick Publishing Co.
PO Box 698 Phone: (207)729-3311
Industry Rd. Fax: (207)729-5728
Brunswick, ME 04011
Publication E-mail: churchworld@timesrecord.com

Catholic religious newspaper. **Subtitle:** Maine's Catholic Weekly. **Founded:** 1930. **Freq:** Weekly (Thurs.). **Print Method:** Offset. **Trim Size:** 10 x 15 1/2. **Cols./Page:** 5. **Col. Width:** 2 inches. **Col. Depth:** 15.5 picas. **Key Personnel:** Claire M. Bastien, Editor/Administration, phone (207)729-87532; Thomas J. Kardos, Associate Editor. **ISSN:** 0009-6601. **Subscription Rates:** $25 individuals; $35 other countries. **Remarks:** Accepts advertising.
Ad Rates: GLR: $.48 **Circ:** ‡6,271
BW: $562.50
PCI: $7.50

13137 Casco Cable TV
336 Bath Rd. Free: (800)439-2629
Brunswick, ME 04011-2635

Formerly: American Cable Co. **Key Personnel:** Dan Heydon, General Mgr.; Randy Brown, Chief Engineer; Bonnie Kinney, Office Mgr. **Cities Served:** Alna, Damariscotta, Dresden, Edgecomb, Newcastle, Nobleboro, Waldoboro, West Port Isle, Wiscasset, ME: subscribing households 3,600; 41 channels; 1 community access channel; 12 hours per week community access programming.

13138 WBOR-FM - 91.1
1 College St. Phone: (207)725-3210
Brunswick, ME 04011
E-mail: wbor@polar.bowdoin.edu

Format: Alternative/New Music/Progressive. **Owner:** Bowdoin College, at above address. **Operating Hours:** 7 a.m.-1 a.m. **Key Personnel:** Ben Chiappinelli, Station Mgr., phone (207)728-6839, bchiappi@arctos.bowdoin.edu; Rob Ford, Program Dir., phone (207)373-0356, rford@arctos.bowdoin.edu; Dave Gurney, Music Dir., phone (207)725-5472, dgurney@arctos.bowdoin.edu; Burgie Howard, Advisor, phone (207)725-3536, bhoward@henry.bowdoin.edu. **Wattage:** 300. **URL:** http://www.bowdoin.edu/~wbor/index.html.

CALAIS, pop. 4,262.

Washington Co. (SE). On St. Croix River, 90 m E of Bangor. Summer resort. Bridges to Milltown and St. Stephens, N.B. Manufactures furniture, lumber, pulpwood. Blueberries packed. Truck farms.

13139 The Calais Advertiser
Advertiser Publishing Co.
19 Church St. Phone: (207)454-3561
PO Box 660 Fax: (207)454-3458
Calais, ME 04619-0660
Publication E-mail: calad@nbnet.nb.ca

Community newspaper (tabloid). **Founded:** 1836. **Freq:** Weekly (Thurs.). **Print Method:** Offset. **Trim Size:** 10 x 15. **Cols./Page:** 5. **Col. Width:** 25 nonpareils. **Col. Depth:** 210 agate lines. **Key Personnel:** Ferguson Calder, Editor and Publisher; Maxine Geroux, Advertising Mgr. **Subscription Rates:** $31 out of area; $27 individuals. **Remarks:** Accepts advertising. **Alt. Formats:** CD-ROM.
Ad Rates: BW: $247.50 **Circ:** 4,350
PCI: $3.30

13140 WMED-TV - 13
1450 Lisbon St. Phone: (207)783-9101
Lewiston, ME 04240 Fax: (207)783-5193
Free: (800)884-1717
E-mail: comments@mpbc.org

Format: Public TV. **Simulcasts:** WMEB-TV; WCBB-TV; WMEA-TV. **Networks:** Public Broadcasting Service (PBS). **Founded:** 1963. **Operating Hours:** 6 a.m.-midnight. **Key Personnel:** Robert H. Gardiner, President, rgardiner@mpbc.org; Katherine Arno, Television Services Dir., karno@mpbc.org; Russell J. Peotter, Marketing & Development Dir., rpeotter@mpbc.org; Alexander G. Maxwell, Dir. of Engineering, gmaxwell@mpbc.org; Chris F. Amann, Dir. of Finance, camann@mpbc.org; Donald Carrigan, Public Affairs Mgr., dcarrigan@mpbc.org; Joyce Moulin, Audience Services Coord., jmoulin@mpbc.org. **Local Programs:** *Made in Maine*, Katherine Arno; *MaineWatch*, Bill Maroldo; *True North*, John Greenman. **Ad Rates:** Noncommercial. **URL:** http://www.mpbc.org.

13141 WQDY-FM - 92.7
281 Main St. Phone: (207)454-7545
Calais, ME 04619 Fax: (207)454-3062
E-mail: wqdy@nemaine.com

Format: Full Service; Contemporary Hit Radio (CHR); Contemporary Country. **Simulcasts:** WALZ-FM. **Networks:** ABC. **Owner:** WQDY, Inc., PO Box 403, Calais, ME 04619, Fax: (207)454-3062. **Founded:** 1975. **Operating Hours:** Continuous. **Key Personnel:** Rob Hunter, Public Service Dir.; Michael Goodine, Owner/Pres.; William G. McVicar, Owner/VP; Bill Conley, Program/Music Dir.; June Gillispie, Office Mgr. **Local Programs:** *Open Line*, Bill Conley. **Wattage:** 3000 ERP. **Ad Rates:** $7.50-13.15 for 30 seconds; $9.20-14.95 for 60 seconds.

CAMDEN, pop. 4,584.

Knox Co. (S). On Penobscot Bay, 40 m E of Augusta. Resort. Manufactures felts, electronics, tents, leather and canvas products. Boat building & repairs.

13142 The Camden Herald
Courier Publications
PO Box 248 Phone: (207)236-8511
Camden, ME 04843
Publication E-mail: cherald@courierpub.com
Publisher E-mail: cgmail@courierpub.com

Newspaper. **Founded:** Feb. 6, 1869. **Freq:** Weekly (Thurs.). **Print Method:** Offset. **Cols./Page:** 6. **Col. Width:** 2 1/16 inches. **Col. Depth:** 294 agate lines. **Key Personnel:** Carolyn R. Marsh, Editor, fax (207)236-2816, editor@cherald.acadia.net; David Morse, Publisher, cgmail@courierpub.com; Diane Norton, Advertising Mgr., fax (207)236-2816. **Subscription Rates:** $31; $41.50 out of country. **Remarks:** Accepts advertising. **Formerly:** Coast Papers.
Ad Rates: GLR: $6 **Circ:** 5,000
PCI: $8

13143 Down East Magazine
Down East Enterprise, Inc.
PO Box 679 Phone: (207)594-9544
Camden, ME 04843-0679 Fax: (207)594-7215
Free: (800)766-1670
Publication E-mail: advertising@downeast.com
Publisher E-mail: downeast@midcoast.com

Subtitle: The Magazine of Maine. **Founded:** 1954. **Freq:** Monthly. **Print Method:** Offset. **Trim Size:** 8 1/8 x 10 7/8. **Cols./Page:** 3. **Col. Width:** 27 nonpareils. **Col. Depth:** 140 agate lines. **Key Personnel:** Dale Kuhnert, Editor, dkuhnert@downeast.com; H. Allen Fernald, President, afernald@downeast.com; Kit Parker, Publisher, kparker@downeast.com. **ISSN:** 0012-5776. **Subscription Rates:** $29.90 individuals; $39.90 Canada; $3.50 single issue. **Remarks:** Accepts advertising.
Ad Rates: BW: $2,681 **Circ:** ‡88,000
4C: $3,888

13144 Fly Rod & Reel
Down East Enterprise, Inc.
PO Box 370 Phone: (207)594-9544
Camden, ME 04843 Fax: (207)594-7215
Free: (800)766-1670
Publisher E-mail: downeast@midcoast.com

We focus on all aspects of fly-fishing; travel, equipment, technique. **Subtitle:** Magazine of American Fly-Fishing. **Founded:** 1979. **Freq:** Bimonthly. **Print Method:** Web offset. **Trim Size:** 8 1/8 x 10 7/8. **Cols./Page:** 3. **Col. Width:** 2 1/4 inches. **Col. Depth:** 10 inches. **Key Personnel:** Jim Butler, Editor, jbutler@downeast.com; Kit Parker, Publisher; Bill Anderson, Advertising Mgr. **ISSN:** 1045-0149. **Subscription Rates:** $16.97. **Remarks:** Accepts advertising. **URL:** http://www.flyfishers.com. **Formerly:** Rod & Reel.
Ad Rates: BW: $2,580 **Circ:** Paid 62,514
4C: $3,880

13145 KM World
Knowledge Asset Media, Inc.
18 Bayview St. Phone: (207)236-8524
Camden, ME 04843 Fax: (207)236-6452
Publication E-mail: editor@kmworld.com

Journal focusing on the applications of knowledge management solutions as they apply to business and corporations. **Subtitle:** Creating and Managing the Knowledge-Based Enterprise. **Founded:** Oct. 1997. **Freq:** Monthly. **Print Method:** Web offset. **Trim Size:** 10 1/2 x 13. **Key Personnel:** Andy Moore, Ed. in Chief/Co-Publisher, andy_moore@kmworld.com; Dan Bolita, Executive Ed., dan_bolita@kmworld.com; Jennifer McIntosh, Managing Ed., jennifer_mcintosh@kmworld.com; Bruce Taylor, President/CEO, bruck_taylor@kmworld.com. **ISSN:** 1060-894X. **Subscription Rates:** Free to qualified subscribers U. S., Canada and Mexico only; $60 individuals U. S.; $80 Canada and Mexico; $108 overseas surface mail; $225 U. S. airmail. **URL:** http://www.kmworld.com. **Formerly:** Imaging World.
Ad Rates: BW: $11,000 **Circ:** Non-paid 90,000
4C: $12,200

13146 Maine Boats & Harbors
21 Elm St. Phone: (207)236-8622
Camden, ME 04843 Fax: (207)236-0811
Publisher E-mail: meboats@acadia.net

Consumer magazine covering boating in Maine. **Founded:** Sept. 1984. **Freq:** Bimonthly. **Key Personnel:** John K. Hanson, Jr., Contact. **Subscription Rates:** $17.95 individuals; $37.95 other countries; $27.95 Canada. **Remarks:** Accepts advertising.
Ad Rates: BW: $2,275 **Circ:** Combined 20,000
4C: $3,110

CARIBOU, pop. 9,916.

Aroostook Co. (NE). 13 m N of Presque Isle. Potatoes, sugar beets.

13147 Aroostook Republican & News
Northeast Publishing Co.
PO Box 608 Phone: (207)496-3251
Caribou, ME 04736 Fax: (207)492-4351
Publication E-mail: aroosrep@bangornews.infi.net
Publisher E-mail: printwks@bangornews.infi.net

Local newspaper. **Founded:** 1881. **Freq:** Weekly (Wed.). **Print Method:** Offset. **Trim Size:** 13 x 21 1/2. **Cols./Page:** 6. **Col. Width:** 12 picas. **Col. Depth:** 21 1/2 inches. **Key Personnel:** Paul Gough, Exec. Editor; Pam Lynch, Business Mgr.; Reginald Thompson, Advertising Mgr. **Subscription Rates:** $33.80 individuals; $43 out of area; $45.50 out of state. **Remarks:** Accepts advertising.
Ad Rates: SAU: $7.15 **Circ:** Paid 5,075
PCI: $7.15

13148 WCXU-FM - 97.7
RR 2, Box 2100 Phone: (207)473-7513
E. Green Ridge Rd. Fax: (207)472-3221
Caribou, ME 04736
Free: (800)622-9298

Format: Adult Contemporary. **Networks:** NBC. **Owner:** Canxus Broadcasting, at above address. **Founded:** 1986. **Operating Hours:** Continuous; 20% network, 80% local. **ADI:** Presque Isle, ME. **Key Personnel:** Dennis Curley, General Mgr.; Douglas Christiansen, News Dir.; Mark Stewart, Program Dir.; Richard Chandler, Sports Dir.; Peter Edwards, Promotions Mgr. **Wattage:** 6000. **Ad Rates:** $10-15 for 30 seconds; $12-18 for 60 seconds.

13149 WCXX-FM - 102.3
RR 2, Box 2100 Phone: (207)473-7513
E. Green Ridge Rd. Fax: (207)472-3221
Caribou, ME 04736
Free: (800)660-WCXU

Format: Adult Contemporary. **Networks:** NBC. **Owner:** Canxas Broadcasting Corp., at above address. **Founded:** 1988. **Operating Hours:** Continuous; 15% network, 85% local. **ADI:** Presque Isle, ME. **Key Personnel:** Dennis Curley, General Mgr.; Richard Chandler, Station Mgr.; Peter Doeberer, Sales Mgr.; Douglas Christianson, News Dir.; Mark Stewart, Program Dir. **Wattage:** 3000. **Ad Rates:** $10-15 for 30 seconds; $12-18 for 60 seconds.

CASTINE

13150 Castine Patriot
Penobscot Bay Press
PO Box 205 Phone: (207)326-4383
Castine, ME 04421 Fax: (207)326-4383

Community newspaper. **Founded:** 1980. **Freq:** Weekly (Thurs.). **Print Method:** Offset. **Cols./Page:** 5. **Col. Width:** 15 picas. **Col. Depth:** 15 inches. **Key Personnel:** R. Nathaniel W. Barrows, Publisher, phone (207)367-2200, fax (207)367-6397. **USPS:** 546-410. **Subscription Rates:** $24.95; $33.95 out of state. **Remarks:** Accepts advertising.
Ad Rates: BW: $480 **Circ:** 1,000
PCI: $8

DAMARISCOTTA, pop. 1,493.

Lincoln Co. (S). 45 m NE of Portland. Summer resort. Lumber mills. Dairy, poultry, fruit farms.

13151 Lincoln County News
PO Box 36 Phone: (207)563-3171
Damariscotta, ME 04543 Fax: (207)563-3127
Free: (800)339-5818
Publication E-mail: lcn@lincoln.midcoast.com

Newspaper with a Republican orientation. **Founded:** 1875. **Freq:** Weekly (Thurs.). **Print Method:** Offset. **Trim Size:** 16 1/2 x 22 1/2. **Cols./Page:** 7. **Col. Width:** 12.6 picas. **Col. Depth:** 21 inches. **Key Personnel:** Christopher A. Roberts, Publisher; Judi Finn, Editor. **USPS:** 313-500. **Subscription Rates:** $15 individuals; $18 out of state. **Remarks:** Accepts advertising.
Ad Rates: GLR: $.34 **Circ:** Paid 7,700
SAU: $5 Non-paid 58
PCI: $4.40

DEER ISLE

13152 WomenPolice
RR 1, Box 1 Phone: (207)348-6976
Deer Isle, ME 04627 Fax: (207)348-6171

Trade magazine covering law enforcement. **Founded:** 1958. **Freq:** Quarterly. **ISSN:** 0890-5894. **Subscription Rates:** $25 individuals; $35 out of country. **Remarks:** Accepts advertising. **URL:** http://www.iawp.org.
Circ: Controlled 3,500

DEXTER, pop. 4,286.

Penobscot Co. (C). 30 m NW of Bangor. Summer resort. Manufactures woolen goods, shoes, machinery, Truck, dairy, poultry, fruit farms.

13153 The Eastern Gazette
PO Box 306 Phone: (207)924-7402
Dexter, ME 04930-0306 Fax: (207)924-6215
Free: (800)287-2295
Publication E-mail: gazette@agate.net
Publisher E-mail: gazette@kynd.net

Community newspaper. **Subtitle:** Hometown Advantage. **Founded:** 1853. **Freq:** Weekly (Mon.). **Print Method:** Web. **Cols./Page:** 5. **Col. Width:** 2 1/16 inches. **Col. Depth:** 15 inches. **Key Personnel:** Robert Shank, Editor and Publisher; Janice Shank, Publisher. **USPS:** 165-784. **Subscription Rates:** $35 individuals. **Remarks:** Accepts advertising.
Ad Rates: BW: $660 **Circ:** ‡17,250
4C: $1,200
SAU: $8.80

DOVER FOXCROFT

13154 Maine Magazine
County Wide Communications, Inc.
78 River St. Phone: (207)564-7548
Dover Foxcroft, ME 04426
Consumer magazine featuring information on the people and lifestyles of Maine. **Subtitle:** The Magazine of Maine's Treasures. **Founded:** 1984. **Freq:** Monthly. **Print Method:** Web offset. **Trim Size:** 8 1/2 x 11. **Cols./Page:** 3. **Col. Depth:** 10 inches. **Key Personnel:** Bob Berta, Publisher; Lester Reynolds, Editor. **USPS:** 566-530. **Subscription Rates:** $28 individuals; $3 single issue.
Ad Rates: BW: $450 **Circ:** Paid 16,200
4C: $900

13155 The Piscataquis Observer
Northeast Publishing Co.
PO Box 30 Phone: (207)564-8355
Dover Foxcroft, ME 04426 Fax: (207)564-7056
Publication E-mail: observer@kynd.net

Newspaper. **Founded:** 1838. **Freq:** Weekly (Wed.). **Print Method:** Offset. **Cols./Page:** 6. **Col. Width:** 26 nonpareils. **Col. Depth:** 301 agate lines. **Key Personnel:** Helen Kelly, Reporter, phone (207)564-8458; Hope Witham, Reporter; Martha M. Lostrom, Exec. Editor. **Subscription Rates:** $26.50 individuals; $34 out of area; $36 out of state. **Remarks:** Accepts advertising.
Ad Rates: GLR: $6.90 **Circ:** ‡5,500
SAU: $5.10
PCI: $7.90

13156 WDME-FM - 103.1
118 Union Sq., Ste. D-103 Phone: (207)564-2642
Dover Foxcroft, ME 04426 Fax: (207)564-8905
E-mail: wdme@kynd.net

Format: Adult Contemporary; Sports; News; Information. **Networks:** ABC; AP. **Owner:** Mid-Maine Media, Inc., at above address. **Founded:** 1967. **Operating Hours:** Continuous. **ADI:** Bangor, ME. **Key Personnel:** Richard Thau, General Mgr.; Bob Robinson, Station Mgr.; Mark Young, Operations Mgr.; Steve White, Production; Tinker Richards, Sales Mgr.; Bob Robinson, News; Joyce Wemer, Business Promotions Mgr.; Howard Soule, Engineering. **Local Programs:** *The D-103 Morning Show* 6:00 am - 9:00 am Monday-Friday, Bob Robinson, Mailing contact; *The Drive Home* 4:00 pm - 6:00 pm Monday-Friday, Bob Robinson, Mailing contact. **Wattage:** 6000. **Ad Rates:** $7-10 for 30 seconds; $8-14 for 60 seconds. **URL:** http://www.kynd.com/~wdme/.

EASTPORT, pop. 1,982.

Washington Co. (E). 80 m E of Bangor. Residential.

13157 The Quoddy Tides
123 Water St. Phone: (207)853-4806
PO Box 213 Fax: (207)853-4095
Eastport, ME 04631
Publication E-mail: qtides@nemaine.com

Newspaper reporting community and marine news. **Founded:** Nov. 1968. **Freq:** Biweekly. **Print Method:** Offset. **Cols./Page:** 4. **Col. Width:** 14 picas. **Col. Depth:** 15 inches. **Key Personnel:** Edward French, Editor and Publisher. **USPS:** 453-220. **Subscription Rates:** $22 individuals in Washington County; $25 elsewhere. **Remarks:** Accepts advertising.
Ad Rates: BW: $330 **Circ:** ‡4,866
PCI: $6

ELLSWORTH†, pop. 5,179.

Hancock Co. (SE). On Union River, 25 m S of Bangor. Summer resort. Fishing. Lumber mill. Timber. Truck, fruit, dairy, poultry farms. Blueberries.

13158 The Ellsworth American
30 Water St. Phone: (207)667-2576
PO Box 509 Fax: (207)667-7656
Ellsworth, ME 04605-0509
Publisher E-mail: info@ellsworthamerican.com

Community newspaper. **Founded:** 1851. **Freq:** Weekly (Thurs.). **Print Method:** Offset. **Cols./Page:** 7. **Col. Width:** 26 nonpareils. **Col. Depth:** 298 agate lines. **Key Personnel:** James R. Wiggins, Editor; Terry Young, Advertising Mgr.; Alan L. Baker, Publisher. **USPS:** 173-960. **Subscription Rates:** $27; $33 out of area; $44 out of state. **Remarks:** Accepts advertising. **URL:** http://www.ellsworthamerican.com.
Ad Rates: GLR: $.928 **Circ:** Paid ⊕11,008
BW: $1,400 Free ⊕280
4C: $1,775
PCI: $11.5

13159 WDEA-AM - 1370
68 State St. Phone: (207)667-9555
Box 1129 Fax: (207)667-2436
Ellsworth, ME 04605
Free: (800)439-9965

Format: Big Band/Nostalgia. **Networks:** CBS; Mutual Broadcasting System; ABC. **Founded:** 1958. **Operating Hours:** Continuous. **Key Personnel:** Martha Tod-Dudman, Owner; Amy Rees, Contact; Fred Miller, Contact. **Wattage:** 5000. **Ad Rates:** $5-17 for 30 seconds; $6-22 for 60 seconds.

13160 WKSQ-FM - 94.5
Box 9494 Phone: (207)667-7573
Buttermilk Rd. Fax: (207)667-9494
Ellsworth, ME 04605
E-mail: kiss94@acadia.net

Format: Adult Contemporary. **Founded:** 1982. **Operating Hours:** Continuous. **ADI:** Bangor, ME. **Key Personnel:** Mark Osborne, President; Keryn W. Smith, General Sales Mgr.; Bruce Carpenter, News Dir.; Natalie Knox, Exec. Vice Pres. **Wattage:** 50,000. **Ad Rates:** $25-50 for 30 seconds. Combined advertising rates available with WBFB-FM & WLKE-FM.

13161 WLKE-FM - 99.1
PO Box 9494 Phone: (207)667-7573
Ellsworth, ME 04605 Fax: (207)667-9494
E-mail: lucky99@acadia.net

Format: Country. **Networks:** ABC. **Owner:** Star Broadcasting of Maine, Inc., at above address. **Founded:** 1992. **Operating Hours:** Continuous. **ADI:** Bangor, ME. **Key Personnel:** Natalie Knox, Exec. VP; Keryn Smith, VP/Sales; Chris Powers, Program Dir. **Wattage:** 50,000.

13162 WWMJ-FM - 95.7
68 State St. Phone: (207)667-9555
Box 1129 Fax: (207)667-2436
Ellsworth, ME 04605-1924
Free: (800)439-9965

Format: Oldies. **Networks:** ABC. **Founded:** 1965. **Formerly:** WDEA-FM (1982). **Operating Hours:** Continuous. **Key Personnel:** Martha Tod Dudman, Contact; Amy Rees, Sales VP; Fred Miller, Contact. **Wattage:** 11,500. **Ad Rates:** Advertising accepted; rates available upon request.

FARMINGTON†, pop. 6,730.

Franklin Co. (W). 50 m NE of Lewiston. State Teachers College. Resort. Manufactures ear protectors, skewers, dowels. Dairy, fruit, truck farms. Sweet corn, string beans, apples.

13163 Franklin Journal and Farmington Chronicle
Mt. Blue Publishing Co., Inc.
PO Box 750 Phone: (207)778-2075
Farmington, ME 04938-0750 Fax: (207)778-6970
Free: (888)778-2075
Publisher E-mail: mail@mtbluenewspapers.com

Local newspaper. **Founded:** 1840. **Freq:** Semiweekly (Tues. and Fri.). **Print Method:** Offset. **Cols./Page:** 9. **Col. Width:** 20 nonpareils. **Col. Depth:** 295 agate lines. **Key Personnel:** Greg Davis, Managing Editor; Janet K. Warner, Publisher. **USPS:** 020-838. **Subscription Rates:** $30 individuals; $40 out of state. **Remarks:** Accepts advertising.
Ad Rates: GLR: $4.50 **Circ:** Tues. ⊕**4,590**
BW: $650 Fri. ⊕**5,290**
SAU: $7.50
PCI: $5.00

13164 Maine Genealogist
Maine Genealogical Society
Box 221
Farmington, ME 04938-0221

Trade journal covering history and genealogy in Maine. **Founded:** 1978. **Freq:** Quarterly. **Key Personnel:** Lois W. Thurston, Editor. **Subscription Rates:** $20 members. **Remarks:** Advertising not accepted. **Former name:** The Maine Seine.
Circ: Combined 2,000

13165 Mainestream
University of Maine-Farmington
5 South St. Phone: (207)778-7380
Farmington, ME 04938 Fax: (207)778-7328

Collegiate newspaper. **Founded:** 1929. **Freq:** 3/month. **Print Method:** Letterpress. Uses mats. **Trim Size:** 12 x 15. **Cols./Page:** 4. **Col. Width:** 23 nonpareils. **Col. Depth:** 189 agate lines. **Key Personnel:** Dan Ryder, Editor; Molly Patterson, Asst. Editor; Kerri Bulter, Asst. Editor; Beth Edwards, Advertising Mgr. **Subscription Rates:** Free. **Remarks:** Accepts advertising. **URL:** http://vilet.umfacad.maine.edu/mainstream.
Ad Rates: GLR: $11.25 **Circ:** Free ‡2,000
BW: $270
PCI: $3

13166 WKTJ-FM - 99.3
Voter Hill Rd. Phone: (207)778-3400
PO Box 590 Fax: (207)778-3000
Farmington, ME 04938

Format: Adult Contemporary; Country; Oldies. **Founded:** 1973. **Operating Hours:** 5:30 a.m.-midnight; 100% local. **Key Personnel:** Alfredo Ibarguen, Pres./Engineer; Claire Taylor, General Mgr.; Stephen R. Bull, Sales Mgr.; Mike Pike, Music/News Dir.; Muriel Powers, Station/Traffic Mgr. **Local Programs:** *Grapevine*, Ray Corey, (207)778-4650; *HealthBeat*, Mary Miller. **Wattage:** 1500 ERP. **Ad Rates:** $6-14 for 30 seconds; $8-16 for 60 seconds.

FORT FAIRFIELD, pop. 4,376.

Aroostook Co. (N). On the Aroostook River, 150 m NE of Bangor. Power plant. Agriculture. Potatoes.

13167 Fort Fairfield Review
Eastern Publishing Ltd.
PO Box 411 Phone: (207)472-3111
Fort Fairfield, ME 04742 Fax: (207)473-7977
Publication E-mail: ffreview@ainop.com

Community newspaper. **Founded:** 1892. **Freq:** Weekly (Wed.). **Print Method:** Offset. **Trim Size:** 13 x 21 1/2. **Cols./Page:** 6. **Col. Width:** 12 1/2 picas. **Col. Depth:** 301 agate lines. **Key Personnel:** Marcia M. Reed, Editor; Cathy Bernard, Advertising Mgr. **USPS:** 205-720. **Subscription Rates:** $20.50 individuals; $23 out of county. **Remarks:** Accepts advertising.
Ad Rates: BW: $535.35 **Circ:** Paid 2,103
SAU: $4.30 Free 70
PCI: $4.10

FORT KENT, pop. 4,826.

Aroostook Co. (N). 20 m S of Edmundston, New Brunswick. Residential.

13168 The Bengal Review
University of Maine-Fort Kent
25 Pleasent Phone: (207)834-3162
Fort Kent, ME 04743-1222
Collegiate newspaper. **Founded:** 1983. **Freq:** 7/year. **Print Method:** Offset. **Trim Size:** 11 1/2 x 16. **Cols./Page:** 5. **Col. Width:** 24 nonpareils. **Col. Depth:** 200 agate lines. **Key Personnel:** Julie Bayly, Adviser. **Subscription Rates:** Free. **Remarks:** Accepts advertising.
Ad Rates: PCI: $3 **Circ:** Free ‡1,300

FREEPORT

13169 WMSJ-FM - 89.3
PO Box 432 Phone: (207)865-3448
Freeport, ME 04032 Fax: (207)865-1763
E-mail: wmsj@wmsj.org

Format: Contemporary Christian. **Networks:** USA Radio. **Owner:** Downeast Christian Communications, Inc., at above address. **Operating Hours:** Continuous. **Key Personnel:** John Libby, President; Mark Tordoff, Station Mgr.; Demetrius Webb, Program Dir. **Local Programs:** *Reckless Faith*, Bruce Wilson; *Cleft in the Rock*, Thom Hazel; *Joy Sunday*, Michael Marx. **Wattage:** 5,000. **Ad Rates:** $5 for 30 seconds. **URL:** http://www.wmsj.org.

GARDINER

Kennebee Co. (SW). 15 m S of Augusta.

13170 WABK-FM - 104.3
PO Box 280 Phone: (207)582-3303
Gardiner, ME 04345 Fax: (207)582-8144

Format: Oldies. **Networks:** ABC. **Owner:** Tryon-Seacoast Comm Inc., Northern Ave, PO Box 280, Gardiner, ME 04345. **Founded:** 1974. **Operating Hours:** Continuous; 99% local, 1% other. **Key Personnel:** Richard Walsh, General Mgr.; Steve Smith, Group Program Dir.; Don Bumps, News Dir. **Wattage:** 50,000. **Ad Rates:** $19-39 for 30 seconds; $25-50 for 60 seconds.

13171 WFAU-AM - 1280
PO Box 1280 Phone: (207)582-3303
Gardiner, ME 04345 Fax: (207)582-8144
Free: (800)540-9524

Format: Adult Contemporary; News. **Networks:** Westwood One Radio; CBS. **Founded:** 1946. **Operating Hours:** Continuous. **Key Personnel:** Richard Walsh, Contact; Jim Walker, Operations Mgr.; Steve Smith, Group Prog. Mgr. **Wattage:** 5000. **Ad Rates:** $15.00 for 30 seconds; $12.00 for 60 seconds.

13172 WKCG-FM - 101.3
PO Box 280 Phone: (207)582-3303
Gardiner, ME 04345 Fax: (207)582-8144

Format: Contemporary Country. **Networks:** Jones Satellite. **Owner:** Tryon-Seacoast Comm. Inc, Nothern Ave, PO Box 280, Gardiner, ME 04345. **Founded:** 1968. **Operating Hours:** Continuous; 99% local. **Key Personnel:** Richard Walsh, General Mgr.; Steve Smith, Group Program Dir.; Don Bumpus, News Dir. **Wattage:** 50,000. **Ad Rates:** $25-35 for 30 seconds; $28-50 for 60 seconds.

GREENVILLE

Piscataquis Co. (NC). 5 m N of Shirley Mills.

13173 Moosehead Enterprises
Lakeview St. Phone: (207)695-3337
Box 526
Greenville, ME 04441

Owner: Earl Richardson, at above address. **Founded:** 1964. **Key Personnel:** Earl Richardson, Jr., General Mgr. **Cities Served:** Jackman, Bingham, Greenville, Moscow, Gilford, Rockwood, and Monson, ME.

HALLOWELL, pop. 2,502.

Kennebec (SWC). 6 m S of Augusta. Residential.

13174 Maine Times
PO Box 350 Phone: (207)623-8955
Hallowell, ME 04347 Fax: (207)623-8970
Free: (800)439-8866
Publication E-mail: mainetimes@powerlink.net

Newspaper (tabloid). **Subtitle:** Maine's Weekly Journal of News and Opinion. **Founded:** Oct. 22, 1968. **Freq:** Weekly (Wed.). **Print Method:** Offset. **Trim Size:** 10 1/8 x 12 1/2. **Cols./Page:** 4. **Col. Width:** 19 nonpareils. **Col. Depth:** 210 agate lines. **Key Personnel:** Douglas J. Rooks, Editor and Publisher; Bob Lawson, Business Mgr. **ISSN:** 0025-0783. **Subscription Rates:** $28 individuals; $.95 single issue. **Remarks:** Accepts advertising. **Alt. Formats:** Microform.
Ad Rates: BW: $890 **Circ:** Paid ‡11,000
PCI: $24

HOULTON†, pop. 6,766.

Aroostook Co. (N). Port of entry. 117 m NE of Bangor. Historic area. Manufactures wood products. Dairy. Agriculture. Potatoes, grain.

13175 Houlton Pioneer Times
Northeast Publishing Co.
PO Box 456 Phone: (207)532-2281
Houlton, ME 04730
Publication E-mail: pioneer.timws@houlton.com

Community newspaper. **Founded:** 1857. **Freq:** Weekly (Wed.). **Print Method:** Offset. **Cols./Page:** 6. **Col. Width:** 25 nonpareils. **Col. Depth:** 301 agate lines. **Key Personnel:** Martha M. Lostrom, Exec. Editor, phone (207)764-4471. **Subscription Rates:** $28.50 individuals County; $37 Maine; $39.50 out of ME; $66 other countries. **Remarks:** Accepts advertising.
Ad Rates: SAU: $8.20 **Circ:** ‡5,700

13176 Houlton Cable TV
6 Water St. Phone: (207)532-2579
Box 610 Fax: (207)532-4025
Houlton, ME 04730

Founded: June 1, 1952. **Key Personnel:** Ronald E. Dee, Technician. **Cities Served:** Hodgdon, Houlton, Island Falls, Patten, ME: subscribing households 2,990; 29 channels.

13177 Mattawamkeag Cablevision
PO Box 38 Phone: (207)532-4451
Houlton, ME 04730

Founded: 1988. **Key Personnel:** Don Dee, Operator. **Cities Served:** Mattawamkeg, Winn., ME: subscribing households 340; 26 channels; 1 community access channel.

13178 Sherman Cablevision
54 South St. Phone: (207)532-3320
Box 38
Houlton, ME 04730

Owner: Ronald E. Dee, at above address. **Founded:** Nov. 1986. **Cities Served:** Sherman Mills, Stayville, ME: subscribing households 269; 22 channels.

13179 WHOU-FM - 100.1
PO Box 40 Phone: (207)532-3600
Houlton, ME 04730 Fax: (207)521-0056

Format: Adult Contemporary; Oldies. **Networks:** ABC. **Owner:** County Communications, Inc., at above address. **Founded:** 1976. **Formerly:** WHGS-FM (1994). **Operating Hours:** Continuous; 75% local, 25% network. **Key Personnel:** Dave Moore, President/General Mgr.; Michelle Lord, Operations Mgr.; Sandy Hayner, Chief Engineer; Michael Robinson, Sales Mgr. **Local Programs:** *All Request Party Mix* Saturday; *Elm Tree Diner Birthday Club*, Paul Cleary, (207)532-3600; *Gold Drive at 5*, Shawn Rigby, (207)532-3600, Fax (207)521-0056. **Wattage:** 25,000. **Ad Rates:** $10-15 for 30 seconds; $14-20 for 60 seconds.

KENNEBUNK, pop. 6,621.

York Co. (SW). 25 m SW of Portland. Resort. Fishing community.

13180 York County Coast Star
York County Coast Star, Inc.
PO Box 979 Phone: (207)985-2961
Kennebunk, ME 04043-0979 Fax: (207)985-9050

Newspaper serving Pease Air Force Base, Portsmouth, NH. **Founded:** 1877. **Freq:** Weekly (Fri.). **Print Method:** Offset. **Cols./Page:** 6. **Col. Width:** 18 nonpareils. **Col. Depth:** 221 agate lines. **Key Personnel:** Ed Freakley, Publisher; Marilyn Dempsey, Advertising Mgr. **Subscription Rates:** $15.60 individuals. **Remarks:** Accepts advertising.
Ad Rates: GLR: $.31 **Circ:** Paid ♦**10,557**
Non-paid ♦**109**

13181 Cable TV of the Kennebunks
35 Beach St. Phone: (207)967-5212
Kennebunk, ME 04043 Fax: (207)967-0591
Free: (800)585-3574

Owner: Kenneth R. Thompson, at above address. **Founded:** 1981. **Key Personnel:** Claudia Richards, Operations Mgr. **Cities Served:** Alfred, Arundel, Dayton, Kennebunk, Kennebunkport, Lyman, ME: subscribing households 8,000; 45 channels; 1 community access channel; 20 hours per week community access programming. **URL:** KbunkTV.com.

LAMOINE

13182 The Beloit Poetry Journal
The Beloit Poetry Journal Foundation, Inc.
24 Berry Cove Rd. Phone: (207)667-5598
Lamoine, ME 04605
Magazine presenting new poems without bias as to school, length, form, or subject; including authors such as Albert Goldbarth, Molly Tenenbaum, Sherman Alexie, and Lola Haskins; containing reviews of new books by and about poets. **Founded:** Sept. 30, 1950. **Freq:** Quarterly. **Print Method:** Offset. **Trim Size:** 6 x 9. **Cols./Page:** 1. **Key Personnel:** Marion K. Stocking, Editor. **ISSN:** 0005-8661. **Subscription Rates:** $12 individuals; $18 industry; $4 single issue. **Remarks:** Advertising not accepted.
Circ: Paid ‡655
Non-paid ‡415

LEWISTON, pop. 40,481.

Androscoggin Co. (SW). On Androscoggin River, 36 m N of Portland. Bates College. Lewiston and Auburn adjoin on opposite banks of Androscoggin River, forming practically one city in everything but government. Manufactures cotton, rayon and woolen textiles, woolen blankets, carpeting, shoes, lasts, spools, bobbins, bricks, wood products, machinery, store fixtures, belting and leather products, bleaching chemicals, electrical supplies and equipment, transistors, structural concrete. Brass and iron foundries.

13183 The Bates Student
Bates College Publishing Association
Chase Hall Phone: (207)795-7494
309 Bates College Fax: (207)786-6035
Lewiston, ME 04240
Publication E-mail: gfried@bates.com; thebatesstudent@sales.edu

Student newspaper serving Bates College. Includes news, features, arts, and sports. **Founded:** 1873. **Key Personnel:** Jeremy Breningstall, Editor-in-Chief. **Subscription Rates:** $22. **Remarks:** Accepts advertising. **URL:** http://abacus.bates.edu/˜jvillano/; http://www.sales.edu/people/studpuss/batesstudent.
Circ: (Not Reported)

13184 Lewiston Sun-Journal
104 Park St. Phone: (207)784-5411
Lewiston, ME 04240 Fax: (207)786-3940
Free: (800)482-0753

General newspaper. **Founded:** 1893. **Freq:** Mon.-Sun. (morn.). **Print Method:** Offset. **Cols./Page:** 6. **Col. Width:** 26 nonpareils. **Col. Depth:** 294 agate lines. **Key Personnel:** Stephen M. Costello, Contact. **Subscription Rates:** $179 individuals. **Remarks:** Accepts advertising.
Ad Rates: BW: $3,790.08 **Circ:** Mon.-Sat. ★**38,342**
4C: $6,140.08 Sun. ★**41,462**
SAU: $32.19

13185 WCBB-TV - 10
1450 Lisbon St. Phone: (207)783-9101
Lewiston, ME 04240 Fax: (207)783-5193
Free: (800)884-1717
E-mail: comments@mpbc.org

Format: Public TV. **Networks:** Public Broadcasting Service (PBS). **Owner:** Maine Public Broadcasting Corp., at above address. **Founded:** 1961. **Formerly:** WCDB-TV. **Operating Hours:** 6 a.m.-12 a.m.; 90% network, 10% local. **ADI:** Portland-Poland Spring, ME. **Key Personnel:** Robert H. Gardiner, President, rgardiner@mpbc.org; Chris F. Amann, Dir., Finance, camann@mpbc.org; Donald Carrigan, Public Affairs Dir., dcarrigan@mpbc.org; Russell J. Peotter, Marketing & Development Dir., rpeotter@mpbc.org; Charles S. Rose, Advertising & Promotion Dir., crose@mpbc.org; Katherne Arno, Dir., Television Services, karno@mpbc.org; Melinda Lake, Media Relations Coordinator, mlake@mpbc.org; Alexander G. Maxwell, Dir., Engineering, gmaxwell@mpbc.org. **Local Programs:** *Made in Maine* 8:30 p.m. Thursday, Tami Kennedy; *MaineWatch* 8 o,n, Thursday, William Maroldo. **Ad Rates:** Noncommercial. **URL:** http://www.mpbc.org.

WMED-TV - See Calais

LINCOLN, pop. 5,066.

Penobscot Co. (C). 40 m NE of Bangor. Paper machinery; Manufactures paper; Truck, poultry, dairy farms. Forest products; Recreation.

13186 Lincoln News
PO Box 35 Phone: (207)794-6532
Lincoln, ME 04457 Fax: (207)794-2004
Publisher E-mail: lincnews@midmaine.com

Community newspaper. **Founded:** 1959. **Freq:** Weekly (Thurs.). **Print Method:** Offset. **Trim Size:** 10 x 16. **Cols./Page:** 5. **Col. Width:** 2 inches. **Col. Depth:** 224 agate lines. **Key Personnel:** M. Sheila Tenggren, Editor and Publisher. **USPS:** 313-780. **Subscription Rates:** $26; $29 out of state. **Remarks:** Accepts advertising.
Ad Rates: BW: $400 **Circ:** Paid ‡5,439
PCI: $5 Free ‡20

LINCOLNVILLE

13187 Maine Organic Farmer and Gardener
Maine Organic Farmers and Gardeners Association
RR2, Box 594 Phone: (207)763-3043
Lincolnville, ME 04849
Publication E-mail: mofga@biddeford.com

Newspaper (tabloid) containing environmental and agricultural news and features for farmers, gardeners, and consumers. **Founded:** 1974. **Freq:** Quarterly. **Print Method:** Offset. **Cols./Page:** 6. **Col. Width:** 37 nonpareils. **Col. Depth:** 210 agate lines. **Key Personnel:** Jean English, Editor; Janice Clark, Advertising Mgr. **ISSN:** 0891-9194. **Subscription Rates:** $12 individuals; $18 other countries.
Ad Rates: GLR: $10 **Circ:** Paid ‡5,000
BW: $250 Non-paid ‡100
PCI: $10

13188 Lincolnville Communications
Box 200 Phone: (207)763-9900
Lincolnville, ME 04849 Fax: (207)763-9902
Free: (800)553-4304

Founded: 1989. **Key Personnel:** Shirley Manning, General Mgr.; David Pelletier, Contact; Ruth Laite, Office Mgr. **Cities Served:** subscribing households 800; 36 channels; 1 community access channel.

LIVERMORE FALLS, pop. 3,572.

Androscoggin Co. (SW). On Androscoggin River, 30 m N of Lewiston. Manufactures paper, cotton gloves, foundry and lumber products. Dairy, stock, poultry farms. Corn, beans.

13189 Livermore Falls Advertiser
Mt. Blue Publishing Co., Inc.
PO Box B. Phone: (207)897-4321
Livermore Falls, ME 04254 Fax: (207)897-4322
Publisher E-mail: mail@mtbluenewspapers.com

Community newspaper. **Founded:** 1892. **Freq:** Weekly (Thurs.). **Print Method:** Offset. **Cols./Page:** 9. **Col. Width:** 22 nonpareils. **Col. Depth:** 295 agate lines. **Key Personnel:** Donna Arsenault, Managing Editor; Janet K. Warner, Publisher. **USPS:** 008-020. **Subscription Rates:** $19 in state; $26 out of state. **Remarks:** Accepts advertising.
Ad Rates: GLR: $4.50 **Circ:** Paid ⊕**3,060**
BW: $650 Non-paid ⊕**10**
SAU: $7.50
PCI: $5

MACHIAS†, pop. 2,458.

Washington Co. (SE). On Machias River, 90 m E of Bangor. University of Maine at Machias. Resort. Fishing. Forestry. Blueberries.

13190 County Wide Newspaper
County Wide Communications, Inc.
26 Main St. Phone: (207)564-7548
PO Box 497 Fax: (207)564-7051
Machias, ME 04654
Community newspaper. **Founded:** 1977. **Freq:** Weekly. **Print Method:** Web offset. **Trim Size:** 10 x 15. **Cols./Page:** 5. **Col. Width:** 11 picas. **Col. Depth:** 15 inches. **Key Personnel:** Bob Berta, Publisher; Lerter J. Reynolds, Editor; Joyce Hartford, Advertising Dir. **USPS:** 566-530. **Subscription Rates:** $28 individuals; $34 other countries.
Ad Rates: BW: $325 **Circ:** Paid 4,400
PCI: $4.75 Free 300

13191 Machias Valley News Observer
Machias Valley Publishing Co., Inc.
PO Box 357 Phone: (207)255-6561
Machias, ME 04654-0357 Fax: (207)255-4058
Free: (800)464-6561

Community newspaper. **Founded:** 1853. **Freq:** Weekly (Wed.). **Print Method:** Offset. **Cols./Page:** 5. **Col. Width:** 1 3/4 inches. **Col. Depth:** 14 3/4 inches. **Key Personnel:** Jay B. Hinson, Editor; Nancy N. Hayward, Managing Editor; Joyce Holland, Advertising Mgr. **USPS:** 323-940. **Subscription Rates:** $25; $26 out of country. **Remarks:** Accepts advertising.
Ad Rates: GLR: $.35 **Circ:** Paid 3,221
BW: $285 Non-paid 65
PCI: $4.90

13192 WALZ-FM - 95.3
105 Main St. Phone: (207)255-8321
Machias, ME 04654

Format: Country; Easy Listening. **Networks:** USA Radio. **Owner:** WALZ Radio, at above address. **Founded:** 1978. **Operating Hours:** 5 a.m.-midnight; 100% local. **Key Personnel:** Henry E. Chausse, General Mgr.; Greg A. Maker, Program Dir.; Rosemary A. Chausse, Production Mgr. **Wattage:** 3000. **Ad Rates:** $5.10 for 30 seconds; $6.80 for 60 seconds.

MADAWASKA, pop. 5,282.

Aroostook Co. (N). On St. John River, 2 m S of Edmunston, New Brunswick. Paper mill. Fishing tackle, perfumes, cosmetics manufactured. Dairy, truck farms. Potatoes.

13193 St. John Valley Times
696 W. Main St. Phone: (207)728-3336
PO Box 419 Fax: (207)728-3825
Madawaska, ME 04756
Free: (800)339-9502
Publisher E-mail: sjvt@nci1.net

Community newspaper. **Founded:** Oct. 2, 1957. **Freq:** Weekly (Wed.). **Print Method:** Offset. **Trim Size:** 11 1/2 x 16. **Cols./Page:** 5. **Col. Width:** 2 inches. **Col. Depth:** 15 inches. **Key Personnel:** Don Levesque, Editor and Publisher; Julia Bayly, Managing Editor; Carole Michaud, Advertising Mgr.; Myra A. Bard, Circulation Mgr. **Subscription Rates:** $33 by mail. **Remarks:** Accepts advertising.
Ad Rates: GLR: $.36 **Circ:** Paid 6,500
BW: $288.75 Free 20
4C: $698.75
PCI: $5.05

MILLINOCKET, pop. 7,567.

Penobscot Co. (C) 3 m N of Norcross. Residential.

13194 The Katkahdin Times
Eastern Publishing Ltd.
Penobscot Ave. Phone: (207)723-8118
PO Box 330 Fax: (207)723-4434
Millinocket, ME 04462
Publication E-mail: ktimes@agate.net

Regional newspaper. **Founded:** 1976. **Freq:** Weekly (Tues.). **Print Method:** Offset. **Trim Size:** 13 x 21 1/2. **Cols./Page:** 6. **Col. Width:** 2 1/16 inches. **Col. Depth:** 21 1/2 inches. **Key Personnel:** Barbara Waters, Editor; David S. Henley, Publisher; Diana Daniels, Business Mgr.; Kathy Beaumont, Advertising Mgr. **Subscription Rates:** $24 individuals; $38 out of state; $0.50 single issue. **Remarks:** Accepts advertising.
Ad Rates: GLR: $.30 **Circ:** Paid 4,200
BW: $819.15 Free 160
4C: $1,219.15
SAU: $6.35
PCI: $6.35

NEWPORT

13195 WGUY-FM - 102.1
108 Elm St. Phone: (207)368-1021
Newport, ME 04953 Fax: (207)368-3299

Format: Oldies. **Owner:** Innovative Advertising Consultants, Inc., at above address. **Operating Hours:** Continuous. **ADI:** Bangor, ME. **Key Personnel:** Dan Priestly, General Mgr.; Jeff Hooker, Local Sales Mgr.; Jocelynn Priestly, Station Mgr. **Wattage:** 50,000. **Ad Rates:** $10-12 per unit.

NORWAY, pop. 4,042.

Oxford Co. (W). 48 m NW of Portland. Summer resort. Timber. Manufactures shoes, snowshoes, wooden novelties, electronic parts, dowels, confectionery. Diversified farming. Sweet corn, beans.

13196 Advertiser-Democrat
James Newspaper, Inc.
2 Bridge St. Phone: (207)743-7011
PO Box 269 Fax: (207)743-2256
Norway, ME 04268
Community newspaper. **Founded:** 1826. **Freq:** Weekly (Wed.). **Print Method:** Offset. **Trim Size:** 22 3/4 x 28. **Cols./Page:** 9. **Col. Width:** 16 nonpareils. **Col. Depth:** 297 agate lines. **Key Personnel:** Howard James, Editor and Publisher; Judy James, Sales Mgr.; Susan Arena, Managing Editor. **Subscription Rates:** $15.50 individuals. **Remarks:** Accepts advertising.
Ad Rates: GLR: $.28 **Circ:** ‡7,500
BW: $708.75
SAU: $6.75
PCI: $4.50

13197 WKTQ-AM - 1450
243 Main St. Phone: (207)743-5911
PO Box 72 Fax: (207)743-5913
Norway, ME 04268
Free: (800)386-2132
E-mail: woxo@megalink.net

Format: Talk; Sports. **Simulcasts:** WTME. **Networks:** USA Radio. **Owner:** Gleason Marketing Services, at above address. **Founded:** 1955. **Formerly:** WKTP-AM (1975). **Operating Hours:** Continuous. **Key Personnel:** Richard Gleason, Pres./Gen. Mgr.; Don Mayberry, Station Mgr.; Julie Flowers, Program Mgr. **Wattage:** 1000. **Ad Rates:** $7-13 for 30 seconds; $9-17 for 60 seconds. Combined advertising rates available with WOXO-FM, WTME-AM, WTBM-FM.

13198 WOXO-FM - 92.7
243 Main St. Phone: (207)743-5911
PO Box 72 Fax: (207)743-5913
Norway, ME 04268
Free: (800)386-2132
E-mail: woxo@megalink.net

Format: Contemporary Country. **Simulcasts:** WTBM. **Networks:** Independent. **Owner:** Gleason Marketing Services, Inc., at above address. **Founded:** 1970. **Formerly:** WNWY-FM (1975). **Operating Hours:** Continuous. **Key Personnel:** Don Mayberry, General and Sales Mgr.; Richard Gleason, President; Julie Flowers, Program Dir. **Wattage:** 3000. **Ad Rates:** $9.50-16 for 60 seconds. Combined advertising rates available with WTBM-FM, WKTQ-AM, WTME-AM.

13199 WTME-AM - 1240
243 Main St. Phone: (207)743-5911
PO Box 72 Fax: (207)743-5913
Norway, ME 04268-0072
Free: (800)386-2132
E-mail: woxo@megalink.net

Format: Talk; Sports. **Simulcasts:** WKTQ-AM. **Networks:** USA Radio. **Founded:** 1938. **Formerly:** WXGL-AM (1990). **Operating Hours:** Continuous. **ADI:** Portland-Poland Spring, ME. **Key Personnel:** Richard Gleason, President; Don Mayberry, Manager; Julie Flowers, Program Dir. **Wattage:** 1000. **Ad Rates:** $7-13 for 30 seconds; $9-17 for 60 seconds. Combined advertising rates available with WOXO-FM, WTBM-FM.

OLD TOWN, pop. 8,422.

Penobscot Co. (S). On Penobscot River, 12 m NE of Bangor. Manufactures shoes, paper, lumber, handles, canoes, boats, pulp products. Timber. Agriculture. Potatoes, truck crops.

13200 Penobscot Times, Inc.
400 N. Main St. Phone: (207)827-4451
Old Town, ME 04468 Fax: (207)827-2280
Publication E-mail: penobtimes@aol.com

Newspaper. **Founded:** 1888. **Freq:** Weekly (Wed.). **Print Method:** Offset. **Cols./Page:** 4. **Col. Width:** 29 nonpareils. **Col. Depth:** 210 agate lines. **Key Personnel:** David C. Wollstadt, Editor and Publisher; Beverly King, Advertising Mgr. **Subscription Rates:** $20; $30 out of area. **Remarks:** Accepts advertising. **Formerly:** Old Town Orono Times.
Ad Rates: BW: $198 **Circ:** Paid ‡3,900
PCI: $5 Free ‡200

ORONO, pop. 10,578.

Penobscot Co. (C). On Penobscot River, 8 m NE of Bangor. University of Maine. Textile mill. Manufactures canvas goods, oars, paddles. Aquaculture (live bait). Agriculture. Hay, vegetables.

13201 American Potato Journal
Potato Association of America
Attn: Hugh Murphy Phone: (207)866-4793
241 Main St.
Orono, ME 04473
Publisher E-mail: umpotato@maine.maine.edu

Professional journal for potato research, extension, utilization, and technical workers in all aspects of potato production and utilization throughout the Western Hemisphere (English and Spanish). **Founded:** 1923. **Freq:** Bimonthly. **Print Method:** Offset. **Trim Size:** 6 x 9. **Cols./Page:** 1. **Col. Width:** 54 nonpareils. **Col. Depth:** 98 agate lines. **Key Personnel:** Dr. Hugh J. Murphy, Editor; Ronald Knight, Publisher, phone (207)942-9273; Lorelei Wing, Administrative Assistant. **ISSN:** 0003-0589. **Subscription Rates:** $40 individuals; $65 institutions; $15 graduate students; $300 sustaining members. **Remarks:** Advertising not accepted.
Circ: ‡1,000

13202 Journal of Marriage and the Family
National Council on Family Relations
30 Merrill Hall, University of Maine Phone: (207)581-3103
Fax: (207)581-3120
Orono, ME 04469-5749
Publisher E-mail: ncfr3989@ncfr.com

Publication in the family field featuring original research and theory, research interpretation, and critical discussion related to marriage and the family. **Founded:** 1939. **Freq:** Quarterly. **Print Method:** Offset. **Trim Size:** 6 3/4 x 10. **Cols./Page:** 2. **Col. Width:** 2 inches. **Col. Depth:** 112 agate lines. **Key Personnel:** Robert Milardo, Editor, phone (207)581-3128, fax (207)581-3120, milardo@maine.maine.edu. **ISSN:** 0022-2445. **Subscription Rates:** $50 individuals; $95 institutions; $25 students. **Remarks:** Accepts advertising.
Ad Rates: BW: $715 **Circ:** ‡7,500

13203 The Journal of Mind and Behavior
Institute of Mind and Behavior
University of Maine Phone: (207)581-2057
Dept. of Psychology, Rm. 301
5742 Little Hall
Orono, ME 04469-5742
Journal focusing on psychology and philosophy. **Founded:** Jan. 1980. **Freq:** Quarterly. **Print Method:** Offset. **Trim Size:** 5 1/2 x 8 1/2. **Cols./Page:** 1. **Col. Width:** 52 nonpareils. **Col. Depth:** 104 agate lines. **Key Personnel:** Dr. Raymond C. Russ, Ph.D, Editor; Ingeborg Biller, Advertising Mgr. **ISSN:** 0271-0137. **Subscription Rates:** $46 individuals; $98 institutions; $15 single issue. **Remarks:** Accepts advertising. **URL:** http://www.kramer.ume.maine.edu/~jmb/.
Ad Rates: BW: $250 **Circ:** Paid ‡1,159

13204 Journal of Phycology
Allen Press
University of Maine Phone: (207)581-2895
School of Marine Sciences, Rm. 202 Fax: (207)581-1479
5722 Deering Hall
Orono, ME 04469-5722
Publication E-mail: jphycol@maine.maine.edu

Journal presenting research on algae. **Subtitle:** Bimonthly publication of the Phycological Society of America. **Founded:** 1965. **Freq:** Bimonthly. **Print Method:** Letterpress and offset. **Cols./Page:** 2. **Col. Width:** 39 nonpareils. **Col. Depth:** 133 agate lines. **Key Personnel:** Dr. Susan Brawley, Editor, jphycol@maine.maine.edu; Bill Woodard, Business Mgr., phone (800)627-0326, bwoodard@allenpress.com. **ISSN:** 0022-3646. **Subscription Rates:** $325 libraries; $65 individuals; $35 students. **URL:** http://www.allenpress.com/jphycol.
Circ: 2,100

13205 The Journal of Supercritical Fluids
Elsevier Science Inc.
Dept. of Chemical Engineering Phone: (207)581-2286
University of Maine Fax: (207)581-2323
Orono, ME 04469-5737
Publisher E-mail: usinfo@elsevier.com

Contains articles on theories and fluids. **Founded:** 1988. **Freq:** Bimonthly. **Cols./Page:** 2. **Col. Width:** 19.5 picas. **Col. Depth:** 56 picas. **Key Personnel:** Erdogan Kiran, Editor, kiran@maine.maine.edu. **ISSN:** 0896-8446. **Subscription Rates:** $295; $290 other countries; $68.75 U.S. and Canada; $72.50 elsewhere. **Remarks:** Accepts advertising.
Ad Rates: BW: $200 **Circ:** Paid 229
Controlled 34

13206 Northeast Folklore
Maine Folklife Center
University of Maine Phone: (207)581-1891
5773 S. Stevens Hall Fax: (207)581-1823
Orono, ME 04469-5773
Journal covering folklore in Maine. **Freq:** Annual. **Subscription Rates:** $25 individuals. **Remarks:** Advertising not accepted.
Circ: (Not Reported)

13207 Puckerbrush Review
Puckerbrush Press
76 Main St. Phone: (207)581-3832
Orono, ME 04473
Literary magazine. **Founded:** 1978. **Freq:** Semiannual. **Key Personnel:** Constance Hunting, phone (207)586-3832. **ISSN:** 0890-3433. **Subscription Rates:** $11 individuals; $4 single issue. **Remarks:** Advertising not accepted.
Circ: Paid 300

PORTLAND†, pop. 61,572.

Cumberland Co. (SW). On Casco Bay, 108 m NE of Boston. Important port with extensive foreign and coastwise trade. Manufactures cans, confectionery, crackers and cakes, clay and foundry products, canned goods, fertilizer, potato chips, machinery, screen, elevators, furniture, clothing, paper and wood boxes, stoves, chemicals, hardware, yarn, shoes, sirups, jams, mattresses, paint, burial cases. Cooperage, sardine packing; cold storage plants.

13208 Alaska Fisherman's Journal
Diversified Business Publications
121 Free St. Phone: (207)842-5508
PO Box 7437 Fax: (207)842-5509
Portland, ME 04122
Magazine (tabloid) serving the Alaska commercial fishing industry. **Founded:** 1977. **Freq:** Monthly. **Print Method:** Offset. **Trim Size:** 11 1/2 x 16. **Cols./Page:** 4. **Col. Width:** 28 nonpareils. **Col. Depth:** 210 agate lines. **Key Personnel:** John van Amerongen, Editor, phone (206)283-1150, fax (206)286-8544, jvan@divcom.com; Mike Lodato, Publisher, phone (207)842-5616, mlodato@divcom.com; Robert Barr, Advertising, phone (206)283-1150, fax (206)286-8594, rbarr@divcom.com. **ISSN:** 0164-8330. **Subscription Rates:** $21 individuals; $26 Canada; $70 other countries; $1.95 single issue. **Remarks:** Accepts advertising. **URL:** http://www.afjournal.com.
Ad Rates: BW: $19950 **Circ:** Paid △**1,865**
4C: $2,675 Non-paid △**7,589**
PCI: $51

13209 Audiofile
37 Silver St. Phone: (207)774-7563
Box 109 Fax: (207)775-3744
Portland, ME 04112-0109
Publication E-mail: info@audiofilemagazine.com
Publisher E-mail: info@audiofilemagazine.com

Consumer magazine covering news, reviews and features on audiobooks. **Subtitle:** The Audiobook Review. **Founded:** June 1992. **Freq:** 6/year. **Print Method:** Web offset. **Trim Size:** 8 1/2 x 11. **Key Personnel:** H. Huntington Stehli, Publisher; Robin F. Whitten, Editor; Susan A. Fockler, Advertising Mgr. **ISSN:** 1063-0244. **Subscription Rates:** $24 individuals; $4 single issue. **Remarks:** Accepts advertising.
Ad Rates: BW: $1,175 **Circ:** Combined 10,000
4C: $1,525

13210 The Cafe Review
Yes Books
20 Danforth St. Phone: (207)775-3233
Portland, ME 04101
Journal covering poetry and art. **Founded:** Oct. 1989. **Freq:** Quarterly. **Print Method:** Offset. **Key Personnel:** Steve Luttrell, Editor-in-Chief; W. Atherton, Editor; Alex Fischer, Editor; Chris McKneally, Assoc. Editor. **ISSN:** 1069-7179. **Subscription Rates:** $25 individuals. **Remarks:** Advertising not accepted.
Circ: Controlled 500

13211 Face Magazine
About Face, Inc.
500 Forest Ave., Ste. 2 Phone: (207)774-9703
Portland, ME 04101 Fax: (207)774-3233
Publication E-mail: mail@facemag.com

Newspaper (tabloid) covering entertainment opportunities in central and southern Maine and seacoast New Hampshire. **Founded:** 1988. **Freq:** Semimonthly. **Print Method:** Offset. **Trim Size:** 11 5/8 x 14. **Cols./Page:** 4. **Col. Width:** 2 3/8 inches. **Col. Depth:** 10 1/8 inches. **Key Personnel:** Bennie Green, Editor and Publisher. **Subscription Rates:** $35.
Ad Rates: BW: $665 **Circ:** Free 17,500
4C: $1,050

13212 Maine History
Maine Historical Society
485 Congress St. Phone: (207)774-1822
Portland, ME 04101 Fax: (207)775-4301

Scholarly journal covering local history. **Freq:** Semiannual. **Key Personnel:** Richard Judd, Editor. **ISSN:** 1090-5413. **Subscription Rates:** $20 individuals. **Remarks:** Advertising not accepted. **URL:** http://mainehistory.org.
Circ: (Not Reported)

13213 Maine Sunday Telegram
The Portland Newspapers
390 Congress St. Phone: (207)791-6650
PO Box 1460 Fax: (207)791-6920
Portland, ME 04101-3514
Free: (800)442-6036
Publication E-mail: portlandpaper@server.nlis.net
Publisher E-mail: portlandpaper@scryer.nlis.net

General newspaper. **Founded:** 1887. **Freq:** Weekly (Sun.). **Print Method:** Flexography. **Cols./Page:** 6. **Col. Width:** 25 nonpareils. **Col. Depth:** 301 agate lines. **Key Personnel:** Madeline Corson, Editor; Amanda Schumaker, Publisher; Jodie Krueger, Circulation Mgr.; Bruce Gensmer, President; Steve Coreenlec, feature editor. **Subscription Rates:** $49.95 by mail. **Remarks:** Advertising accepted; rates available upon request. **URL:** http://www.portland.com.
Circ: Paid 145,000

13214 National Fisherman
PO Box 7438 Phone: (207)842-5608
Portland, ME 04112-7438 Fax: (207)842-5609
Publication E-mail: editor@nationalfisherman.com

Magazine covering commercial fishing and boat building. **Founded:** 1903. **Freq:** Monthly. **Print Method:** Offset. **Trim Size:** 11 x 14 1/2. **Cols./Page:** 4. **Col. Width:** 28 nonpareils. **Col. Depth:** 189 agate lines. **Key Personnel:** Ralph Raffio, Editorial Dir.; Scott Allmendinger, Publisher; Clarke Canfield, Executive Editor. **ISSN:** 0027-9250. **Subscription Rates:** $22.95 individuals. **Remarks:** Accepts advertising.
Ad Rates: BW: $3,590 **Circ:** Paid 40,034
4C: $4,855

13215 The Northeast
Episcopal Diocese of Maine
143 State St. Phone: (207)772-1953
Portland, ME 04101 Fax: (207)773-0095
Free: (800)244-6062
Publication E-mail: diomaine@diomaine.org

Tabloid serving as a forum for the exchange of information among members of the Episcopal Diocese of Maine. **Subtitle:** The Oldest Continuous News Journal in the Episcopal Church. **Founded:** 1873. **Freq:** 10/year. **Print Method:** Offset. **Trim Size:** 11 1/2 x 16. **Cols./Page:** 4. **Key Personnel:** Heidi Shott, Editor, hshott@diomaine.org. **Subscription Rates:** Contributions accepted. **Remarks:** Advertising not accepted.
Circ: ‡10,000

13216 Ocean Navigator
Navigator Publishing Corp.
PO Box 569 Phone: (207)772-2466
Portland, ME 04112-0569 Fax: (207)772-2879
Publication E-mail: 76452.3245committeepuserve.com
Publisher E-mail: editors@oceannavigator.com

Magazine on Marine navigation and offshore sailing equipment and techniques. **Subtitle:** The Magazine of Marine Navigation & Ocean Voyaging. **Founded:** 1985. **Freq:** 8/year. **Print Method:** Offset. **Trim Size:** 8 1/4 x 10 7/8. **Cols./Page:** 3. **Col. Width:** 26 nonpareils. **Col. Depth:** 140 agate lines. **Key Personnel:** Tim Queeney, Editor; Alex Agnew, Publisher. **ISSN:** 5669-8721. **Subscription Rates:** $24 individuals. **URL:** http://www.oceannavigator.com.
Ad Rates: BW: $2,697 **Circ:** Paid ‡43,000
4C: $4,034 Non-paid ‡2,000

13217 Portland
578 Congress St.
Portland, ME 04101

Magazine distributed in northern New England and Atlantic Canada featuring lifestyles, business news, real estate updates, performing arts, reviews, and fiction. **Subtitle:** Maine's City Magazine. **Founded:** Mar. 1986. **Freq:** 10/year plus special issues. **Print Method:** Web offset. **Trim Size:** 8 3/8 x 10 7/8. **Cols./Page:** 3. **Col. Width:** 13 1/2 picas. **Key Personnel:** Colin Sargent, Editor and Publisher. **ISSN:** 0887-5340. **Subscription Rates:** $20. $2.95 single issue. **Remarks:** Accepts advertising. **Online:** CompuServe.
Ad Rates: BW: $1,238 **Circ:** Paid ‡10,000
4C: $1,588

13218 Portland Press Herald
The Portland Newspapers
390 Congress St. Phone: (207)791-6650
PO Box 1460 Fax: (207)791-6920
Portland, ME 04101-3514
Free: (800)442-6036
Publication E-mail: herald@portland.com
Publisher E-mail: portlandpaper@scryer.nlis.net

General newspaper. **Founded:** 1862. **Freq:** Mon.-Sat. (morn.). **Print Method:** Letterpress. **Cols./Page:** 6. **Col. Width:** 25 nonpareils. **Col. Depth:** 301 agate lines. **Key Personnel:** Madeline Corson, Publisher; Amanda Schumaker, Advertising Mgr.; Bruce Ceensmer, President; Jodie Krueger, Director. **Subscription Rates:** $129.95 individuals. **Remarks:** Advertising accepted; rates available upon request. **URL:** http://www.portland.com. **Absorbed:** Evening Express.
Circ: Mon.-Sat. ★75,686
Sun. ★124,892

13219 Seafood Business
Journal Publications
PO Box 7438 Phone: (207)842-5600
Portland, ME 04112-7438 Fax: (207)842-5603
Publication E-mail: editor@seafoodbusiness.com

Seafood industry magazine. **Subtitle:** The Magazine for Marketing Success. **Founded:** 1982. **Freq:** Bimonthly. **Print Method:** Web offset. **Trim Size:** 14 7/8 x 11. **Cols./Page:** 3. **Col. Width:** 27 nonpareils. **Col. Depth:** 10 inches. **Key Personnel:** Ralph Raffio, Editorial Dir.; Scott Allmendinger, Publisher; Clarke Canfield, Executive Editor; Deborah Napier, Marketing Dir. **ISSN:** 0889-3217. **Subscription Rates:** $30 U.S. and Canada; $70 other countries; $5 single issue. **Remarks:** Accepts advertising. **Formerly:** Seafood - Capital F.
Ad Rates: BW: $2,390 **Circ:** Paid 960
4C: $3,260 Controlled 15,200

13220 Time Warner Cable
118 Johnson Rd. Phone: (207)775-2381
Box 8180 Fax: (207)775-6422
Portland, ME 04102

Owner: Time Warner Inc., 300 First Stamford Place, Stamford, CT 06902-6732, (203)328-0600, Fax: (203)328-0690. **Founded:** 1973. **Formerly:** Public Cable (1973). **Key Personnel:** Tom Kinney, President, phone (207)775-2381, fax (207)775-6422; Leigh Fisher, Marketing Dir., phone (207)775-2381, fax (207)775-6422. **Cities Served:** Cape Elizabeth, Cumberland, Falmouth, Gorham, New Gloucester, North Yarmouth, Portland, Scarborough, South Portland, Westbrook, Yarmouth, ME: subscribing households 61,000; 80 channels; 3 community access channels.

13221 WBLM-FM - 102.9
1 City Center Phone: (207)774-6364
Portland, ME 04101 Fax: (207)774-8707

Format: Album-Oriented Rock (AOR); Classic Rock. **Networks:** Independent. **Founded:** 1973. **Operating Hours:** Continuous; 100% local. **ADI:** Portland-Poland Spring, ME. **Key Personnel:** Eve Rubins, General Mgr.; Herb Ivy, Operations Mgr.; Mike Sambrook, Station Mgr. **Wattage:** 100,000.

13222 WCSH-TV - 6
1 Congress Sq. Phone: (207)828-6666
Portland, ME 04101 Fax: (207)828-6610

Format: Commercial TV. **Networks:** NBC. **Operating Hours:** 6:30 am-1:30 am weekdays; 6:30 am-3 am Sat.; 6:30 am-midnight Sun. **ADI:** Portland-Poland Spring, ME. **Key Personnel:** Lew Colby, General Mgr.; Carol Scott, Program Dir.

13223 WCYY-FM - 93.9
1 City Center Phone: (207)774-6364
Portland, ME 04101 Fax: (207)774-8707
E-mail: wcyy@wcyy.com

Simulcasts: WCYI-FM. **Networks:** Independent. **Founded:** 1949. **Formerly:** WKFM-FM (1988); WXGL-FM. **Operating Hours:** Continuous; 100% local. **ADI:** Portland-Poland Spring, ME. **Key Personnel:** Micah Malloy, Local Sales Mgr.; Herb Ivy, Operations Mgr.; Mike Sambrook, General Mgr. **Wattage:** 50,000.

13224 WGME-TV - 13
PO Box 1731 Phone: (207)797-9330
Portland, ME 04103 Fax: (207)878-3505
Free: (800)766-9330

Format: Commercial TV. **Networks:** CBS. **Owner:** Guy Gannett Communications, PO Box 1460, Portland, ME 04104, (207)780-9000, Fax: (207)828-8160. **Founded:** 1954. **Formerly:** WGAN-TV (1982). **Operating Hours:** Continuous; 80% network, 20% local. **ADI:** Portland-Poland Spring, ME. **Key Personnel:** Towle Tompkins, Program Dir.; David Rio, Sports Dir.; Towle Tompicins, Promotions Dir.; Craig Clark, Chief Engineer; Gary Lesters, Operations Mgr. **Ad Rates:** $20-2000 per unit.

13225 WJBQ-FM - 97.9
583 Warren Phone: (207)775-6321
Portland, ME 04103 Fax: (207)772-8087

Format: Contemporary Hit Radio (CHR). **Networks:** Independent. **Founded:** 1974. **Formerly:** WJBQ-FM (1986). **Operating Hours:** Continuous; 100% local. **ADI:** Portland-Poland Spring, ME. **Key Personnel:** Robert Caron, General Mgr.; Tim Moore, Operations Mgr., timmoore@wjbq.com; Barbara Cole, Sales Mgr. **Local Programs:** *Jeff Persons*; *Meredith in the Morning*. **Wattage:** 50,000. **Ad Rates:** $40 per unit.

13226 WLOB-AM - 1310
779 Warren Ave. Phone: (207)775-1310
Portland, ME 04103

Format: Religious. **Simulcasts:** WLOB-FM. **Owner:** Carter Broadcasting, 20 Park Plz., Ste. 720, Boston, MA 02116-4303, (617)423-0210, Fax: (617)482-9305. **Founded:** 1956. **Operating Hours:** Continuous. **ADI:** Portland-Poland Spring, ME. **Key Personnel:** Ken Carter, General Mgr., phone (617)423-0210, fax (617)482-9305; Richard Ringenback, Contact, phone (207)775-1310; Steve Callahan, Chief Engineer, phone (617)254-9267. **Wattage:** 5000. **Ad Rates:** $7-13 for 30 seconds; $13-20 for 60 seconds. Combined advertising rates available with WLOB-FM.

13227 WMEA-TV - 26
309 Marginal Way Phone: (207)783-9101
Portland, ME 04101 Fax: (207)783-5193
Free: (800)884-1717
E-mail: comments@mpbc.org

Format: Public TV. **Simulcasts:** WMEB-TV, WCBB-TV. **Networks:** Public Broadcasting Service (PBS). **Owner:** Maine Public Broadcasting, 1450 Lisbon St., Lewiston, ME 04240-3514. **Founded:** Apr. 1974. **Operating Hours:** 6 a.m.-midnight. **ADI:** Portland-Poland Spring, ME. **Key Personnel:** Robert H. Gardiner, President, rgardiner@mpbc.org; Chris F. Amann, Dir. of Finance, camann@mpbc.org; Donald Carrigan, Public Affairs Dir., dcarrigan@mpbc.org; Russell J. Peotter, Dir. of Marketing & Development, rpeotter@mpbc.org; Charles S. Rose, Dir. of Advertising & Promotion, crose@mpbc.org; Katherine Arno, Dir. of Television Services, karno@mpbc.org; Melinda Lake, Media Relations Coordinator, mlake@mpbc.org; Alexander G. Maxwell, Dir. of Engineering, amaxwell@mpbc.org; Joyce Moulin, Audience Services. **Local Programs:** *Made in Maine*, Tami Kennedy; *MaineWatch*, Bill Maroldo; *True North*, John Greenman. **Ad Rates:** Noncommercial. **URL:** http://www.mpbc.org.

13228 WMPG-FM - 90.9
96 Falmouth St. Phone: (207)780-4974
Portland, ME 04103 Fax: (207)780-4590

Format: Eclectic. **Networks:** Pacifica. **Founded:** 1971. **Operating Hours:** Continuous; 5% network; 95% local. **ADI:** Portland-Poland Spring, ME. **Key Personnel:** Jim Rand, Station Mgr. **Wattage:** 1111. **Ad Rates:** $12-15 per unit.

13229 WPOR-AM - 1490
15 Baxter Blvd. Phone: (207)773-8111
Portland, ME 04101-1820 Fax: (207)772-0870
E-mail: wpor@cis.compuserve.com; wpor@aol.com

Format: Country. **Simulcasts:** WPOR-FM. **Networks:** ABC. **Owner:** Saga Communications Inc., at above address. **Founded:** 1947. **Operating Hours:** Continuous; 1% network, 99% local. **ADI:** Portland-Poland Spring, ME. **Key Personnel:** Robert J. Gold, General Mgr.; Bonnie Grant, Dir. of Sales; Jon Shannon, Program Dir.; Amy Rees, Local Sales Mgr. **Wattage:** 1000. **Ad Rates:** $20-105 for 30 seconds; $25-120 for 60 seconds.

13230 WPOR-FM - 101.9
15 Baxter Blvd. Phone: (207)773-8111
Portland, ME 04101-1820 Fax: (207)772-0870
E-mail: wpor@cis.compuserve.com; wpor@aol.com

Format: Country. **Simulcasts:** WPOR-AM. **Networks:** ABC. **Owner:** Saga Communication Inc., at above address. **Founded:** 1967. **Operating Hours:** Continuous; 1% network, 99% local. **ADI:** Portland-Poland Spring, ME. **Key Personnel:** Robert J. Gold, Contact; Amy Rees, Local Sales Mgr.; Jon Shannon, Director; Bonnie Grant, Dir. of Sales. **Wattage:** 50,000. **Ad Rates:** $20-105 for 30 seconds; $25-120 for 60 seconds.

13231 WPXT-TV - 51
2320 Congress St. Phone: (207)774-0051
Portland, ME 04102 Fax: (207)774-6849
E-mail: fox51@wpxt.com

Format: Commercial TV. **Networks:** Fox. **Founded:** 1986. **Operating Hours:** 19 hours daily. **ADI:** Portland-Poland Spring, ME. **Key Personnel:** Doug Finck, General Mgr.; Jennifer VanDerWerf, Program/Promotions Mgr.; Jim Lapiana, General Sales Mgr.; Ann Gagne, Business Mgr.; Roy Ouellette, Chief Engineer; Matt Ledin, News Dir. **Wattage:** 3,300,000. **Ad Rates:** $25-1400 per unit.

13232 WTHT-FM - 107.5
1335 Washington Ave. Phone: (207)797-0780
Portland, ME 04103 Fax: (207)797-0368

Format: Contemporary Hit Radio (CHR). **Networks:** ABC. **Founded:** 1966. **Operating Hours:** Continuous. **ADI:** Portland-Poland Spring, ME. **Key Personnel:** Brian Cliffe, General Mgr. **Wattage:** 50,000.

POWNAL

13233 Fine Tool Journal
Antique and Collectible Tools, Inc.
27 Ficket Rd. Phone: (207)688-4962
Pownal, ME 04069 Fax: (207)688-4152

Trade magazine covering vintage hand tools for users and collectors. **Founded:** 1970. **Freq:** Quarterly. **Trim Size:** 8 1/2 x 11. **Cols./Page:** 2. **Col. Width:** 3 1/4 inches. **Key Personnel:** Clarence Blanchard, Manager/Editor, ftjceb@aol.com. **ISSN:** 0245-6824. **Subscription Rates:** $27 individuals; $7.50 single issue. **Remarks:** Accepts advertising. **URL:** http://www.wowpages.com/ftj.
Ad Rates: BW: $125 **Circ:** Paid 2,000
PCI: $11

PRESQUE ISLE, pop. 11,172.

Aroostook Co. (N). 145 m N of Bangor. University of Maine at Presque Isle. Manufactures fertilizer, starch, barrels. Spruce timber. Agriculture, especially potatoes.

13234 Maine Potato News
Maine Potato Board
PO Box 510 Phone: (207)764-7033
Presque Isle, ME 04769-0510 Fax: (207)764-4499
Free: (800)924-9041
Publisher E-mail: mepotbd@mepotbd.sdi.agate.net

Newspaper reporting agriculture news for the potato industry. **Founded:** 1955. **Freq:** Monthly. **Print Method:** Offset. **Cols./Page:** 5. **Col. Width:** 11.5 picas. **Col. Depth:** 13 inches. **Key Personnel:** Martha Lostrom, Editor. **Subscription Rates:** Free. **Remarks:** Advertising accepted; rates available upon request.
Circ: Free ‡6,250

13235 Star-Herald
Northeast Publishing Co.
40B North St. Phone: (207)768-5431
PO Box 510 Fax: (207)764-7585
Presque Isle, ME 04769
Publication E-mail: starhrld@bangornews.infi.net

Local newspaper. **Founded:** 1889. **Freq:** Weekly (Wed.). **Print Method:** Offset. **Cols./Page:** 6. **Col. Width:** 25 nonpareils. **Col. Depth:** 301 agate lines. **Key Personnel:** Martha M. Lostrom, Exec. Editor; John P. Bishop, Publisher. **USPS:** 519-090. **Subscription Rates:** $28.60 individuals. **Remarks:** Accepts advertising.
Ad Rates: BW: $774 **Circ:** ‡7475
SAU: $7.60
PCI: $7.60

13236 Time Warner Cable of Maine
PO Box 1249 Phone: (207)764-1324
Presque Isle, ME 04769-1249 Fax: (207)764-1299

Owner: 300 First Stanford Pl., Stamford, CT 06902-6732, (203)328-0600. **Founded:** June 1960. **Formerly:** Teleprompter (1983); Group W Cable (1987); Paragon Cable. **Key Personnel:** Barry McCrum, General Mgr. **Cities Served:** Caribou, Caswell, Connor, Fort Fairfield AFB, Limestone, New Sweden, Presque Isle, Westfield, Woodland, ME: subscribing households 9,000; 52 channels; 1 community access channel; 10 hours per week community access programming.

13237 WAGM-TV - 8
201 Parkhust Rd. Phone: (207)764-4461
PO Box 1149 Fax: (207)764-5329
Presque Isle, ME 04769
E-mail: wagmtv@wagm-tv.com

Format: Commercial TV. **Networks:** CBS. **Owner:** Nepsk, at above address. **Founded:** 1956. **Operating Hours:** 5:25 a.m.-2 a.m. **ADI:** Presque Isle, ME. **Key Personnel:** Sue Bernard, News Dir.; Fran Pelletier, Sales Mgr.; Linda Connolly, Traffic Mgr.; Wes Desjardins, Production Mgr.; Catherine Donovan, General Mgr. **Ad Rates:** $90 for 30 seconds.

13238 WBPW-FM - 96.9
PO Box 312 Phone: (207)769-6600
Presque Isle, ME 04769 Fax: (207)764-5274
E-mail: wqhr@agate.net

Format: Hot Country. **Networks:** Westwood One Radio. **Owner:** Pilot Communications, Inc., at above address. **Founded:** 1973. **Operating Hours:** Continuous. **ADI:** Presque Isle, ME. **Key Personnel:** Dave Lyman, General Mgr.; Rick Davis, Program Dir.; Lisa Miles, U.S. Sales Mgr.; Steve Bessant, Canadian Sales Mgr. **Wattage:** 100,000. **Ad Rates:** Advertising accepted; rates available upon request. Combined advertising rates available with WQHR WOZ1.

13239 WMEM-TV - 10
c/o WMEB-TV Phone: (207)941-1010
65 Texas Ave. Fax: (207)942-2857
Bangor, ME 04401
E-mail: comments@mpbc.org

Format: Public TV. **Simulcasts:** WMEB-TV, WCBB-TV. **Networks:** Public Broadcasting Service (PBS). **Owner:** Maine Public Broadcasting, 1450 Lisbon St., Lewiston, ME 04240, (207)783-9101, Fax: (207)783-5193. **Founded:** 1963. **Operating Hours:** 6 a.m.-midnight. **ADI:** Presque Isle, ME. **Key Personnel:** Robert H. Gardiner, President, rgardiner@mpbc.org; Chris F. Amann, Dir. of Finance, camann@mpbc.org; Katherine Arno, Dir. of Television Services, karno@mpbc.org; Russell J. Peotter, Dir. of Marketing & Development, rpeotter@mpbc.com; Donald Carrigan, Public Affairs Mgr., dcarrigan@mpbc.org; Charles S. Rose, Dir. of Advertising & Promotion, crose@mpbc.org; Melinda Lake, Media Relations Coordinator, mlake@mpbc.org; Alexander G. Maxwell, Dir. of Engineering, gmaxwell@mpbc.org. **Ad Rates:** Noncommercial. **URL:** http://www.mpbc.org.

13240 WQHR-FM - 96.1
PO Box 312 Phone: (207)769-6600
Presque Isle, ME 04769 Fax: (207)764-5274
E-mail: wqhr@agate.net

Networks: ABC. **Founded:** 1995. **Operating Hours:** Continuous. **ADI:** Presque Isle, ME. **Key Personnel:** Dave Lyman, General Mgr.; Rick Davis, Program Dir.; Lisa Miles, Sales Mgr.; Steve Bessant, Canadian Sales Mgr. **Wattage:** 100,000. **Ad Rates:** Advertising accepted; rates available upon request. Combined advertising rates available with WBPW WOZ1.

13241 WUPI-FM - 92.1
c/o University of Maine Phone: (207)764-0311
181 Main St.
Presque Isle, ME 04769

Format: Alternative/New Music/Progressive. **Owner:** Board of Trustees of the University of Maine System, 107 Maine Ave., Bangor, ME 04401, (207)947-0336. **Founded:** 1972. **Operating Hours:** Noon-1 a.m. **ADI:** Presque Isle, ME. **Key Personnel:** Brian Massey, Station Mgr.; Scott Gordon, Music Dir. **Wattage:** 10. **Ad Rates:** Noncommercial.

RANGELEY

13242 Orgonomic Functionalism
Wilhelm Reich Infant Trust, Orgonon
PO Box 687
Rangeley, ME 04970
Publication E-mail: wr@rangeley.org

Literary magazine covering the works of Wilhelm Reich. **Founded:** 1990. **Freq:** Annual. **Key Personnel:** Mary Boyd Higgins, Editor. **ISSN:** 1054-075X. **Subscription Rates:** $18.95 single issue.

ROCKLAND†, pop. 7,919.

Knox Co. (S). On Penobscot Bay, 44 m E of Augusta. U.S. Coast Guard Base. Historic area. Museums. Commercial fishing industry.

13243 The Courier-Gazette
Courier-Gazette, Inc.
1 Park Dr. Phone: (207)594-4401
PO Box 249 Fax: (207)596-6981
Rockland, ME 04841
Publication E-mail: cgmail@courierpub.com

Community newspaper. **Founded:** Jan. 22, 1846. **Freq:** 3/week. **Print Method:** Offset. **Trim Size:** 14 x 22 3/4. **Cols./Page:** 6. **Col. Width:** 26 nonpareils. **Col. Depth:** 294 agate lines. **Key Personnel:** David E. Morse, Publisher; Ron Belyea, Advertising Dir.; Michael McGuire, Editor. **Subscription Rates:** $80 individuals; $100 out of state. **Remarks:** Accepts advertising.
Ad Rates: PCI: $9.40 **Circ:** 9,129

13244 Lincoln County Weekly
Courier Publications
PO Box 249 Phone: (207)594-4401
Rockland, ME 04841 Fax: (207)596-6981
Free: (800)559-4401
Publication E-mail: cgmail@courierpub.com
Publisher E-mail: cgmail@courierpub.com

Shopper. **Founded:** Apr. 7, 1987. **Freq:** Weekly (Tues.). **Print Method:** Offset. **Trim Size:** 14 x 22 5/8. **Cols./Page:** 6. **Col. Depth:** 21 inches. **Key Personnel:** Joan Grant, Editor; David Morse, Publisher; David Libby, Advertising Mgr. **Subscription Rates:** $16 individuals; $19 out of state. **Remarks:** Accepts advertising. **Formerly:** The Weekly Courier.
Ad Rates: PCI: $4.75 **Circ:** Free 34,054

13245 FrontierVision
PO Box 1499 Phone: (207)596-6622
Rockland, ME 04841 Fax: (207)596-6365

Founded: 1995. **Formerly:** United Video Cablevision (1995). **Key Personnel:** Brian Gasser, General Mgr.; Valerie Winchenbach, Operations Mgr.; David Winchenbach, Contact. **Cities Served:** Ashland, Belgrade, Blue Hill, Boothbay, Bridgton, Buckfield, Castine, Crocker/Carrabasset, Kenduskeag, Norridgewok, Philips/Avon/Strong, ME; Cornish, Bethel, Calais, Eagle Lake, Easton, Ft. Kent, Freep ort, Green, Hancock, Harpswell, Hermon, Madawaska, Mapleton, Migars, Bristol, Buxton, Hill, Milo, Mt. Desert, N. Anson, Poland, Portage, Rockland, Windham, Sidney, Stockholm, Stockton Springs, Stonington, Van Buren, Vinalhaven, Washburn ME: 1 community access channel; 168 hours per week community access programming.

13246 WMCM-FM - 103.3
415 Main St. Phone: (207)594-1450
Rockland, ME 04841-3305 Fax: (207)594-2234
E-mail: radio@mint.net

Format: Country. **Networks:** ABC; Satellite Music Network. **Owner:** Rockland Radio Corp., at above address. **Founded:** 1968. **Operating Hours:** Continuous; 90% network, 10% local. **Key Personnel:** Peter K. Orne, Sr., President/Gen. Mgr.; Don Shield, News Dir.; Peter Orne, Jr., General Sales Mgr.; David O'Donnell, Program Dir.; Elaine Knowlton, V.P./Business & Traffic Mgr. **Wattage:** 50,000. **Ad Rates:** $23 for 30 seconds; $30 for 60 seconds.

13247 WRKD-AM - 1450
415 Main St. Phone: (207)594-1450
Rockland, ME 04841-3305 Fax: (207)594-2234
E-mail: radio@mint.net

Format: Adult Contemporary. **Networks:** CNN Radio. **Owner:** Rockland Radio Corp., at above address. **Founded:** 1952. **Operating Hours:** Continuous; 90% network, 10% local. **Key Personnel:** Peter K. Orne, Sr., President; Elaine Knowlton, V.P/Admin.; Peter K. Orne, Jr., General Sales Mgr.; Don Shields, News Dir. **Wattage:** 1,000. **Ad Rates:** Advertising accepted; rates available upon request.

ROCKPORT

13248 Fishing Tackle Trade News
Rte. 1 Roxmont Rd. Phone: (207)594-9544
Rockport, ME 04856 Fax: (207)594-5144
Free: (800)766-1670

Magazine for the fishing tackle trade. **Founded:** 1952. **Freq:** Monthly. **Print Method:** Offset. **Trim Size:** 8 1/4 x 10 7/8. **Cols./Page:** 3 and 2. **Col. Width:** 27 and 42 nonpareils. **Col. Depth:** 140 agate lines. **Key Personnel:** Hugh McKellar, Editor; Matthew Mayo, Assoc. Editor. **ISSN:** 0015-3060. **Subscription Rates:** Free to tackle retailers and wholesalers; $45 others. **Remarks:** Accepts advertising.
Ad Rates: BW: $2,820 **Circ:** Non-paid 22,500
4C: $4,360
PCI: $40

RUMFORD

13249 WLLB-AM - 790
100 Congress St. Phone: (207)364-7969
PO Box 40
Rumford, ME 04276

Format: Big Band/Nostalgia. **Networks:** Satellite Music Network. **Owner:** Carter Broadcasting Corp., 20 Park Plaza, Ste. 720, Boston, MA 02116, (617)423-0210. **Founded:** 1953. **Formerly:** WRUM-AM (1997). **Operating Hours:** Continuous; 90% network, 10% local. **Key Personnel:** Michael Breton, Station Mgr. **Wattage:** 1000. **Ad Rates:** $7 for 30 seconds; $12 for 60 seconds.

SACO

13250 WRED-FM - 95.9
110 Main St. Phone: (207)283-1116
Ste 1102 Fax: (207)283-1234
Saco, ME 04072

Format: Contemporary Hit Radio (CHR); News. **Networks:** AP. **Founded:** 1982. **Formerly:** WHYR-FM. **Operating Hours:** Continuous. **Key Personnel:** Harry Bailey, General Mgr.; Astrid Bailey, Contact; Jeff Parsons, Program Dir.; Fred Miller, Sales Mgr. **Wattage:** 6,000. **Ad Rates:** $8-16 for 30 seconds; $9-18 for 60 seconds.

SALSBURY COVE

13251 Mount Desert Island Biological Laboratory
Salsbury Cove, ME 04672

Scientific journal covering biological research. **Freq:** Annual. **Subscription Rates:** $10 individuals. **Former name:** MDIBL Bulletin.

SANFORD

13252 The Sanford News
George J. Foster Co.
PO Box D Phone: (207)324-5986
Sanford, ME 04073 Fax: (207)490-1431

Local newspaper serving Southern Maine. **Founded:** 1980. **Freq:** Weekly. **Print Method:** Offset. **Cols./Page:** 6. **Col. Depth:** 21 1/2 inches. **Key Personnel:** Ellen Todd, Assoc. Editor; Donna Bourque, Advertising Mgr. **Subscription Rates:** $19.99. **Remarks:** Accepts advertising.
Ad Rates: BW: $1,487.37 **Circ:** Paid ‡6,500
SAU: $11.88
CNU: $7.52

13253 WCDQ-FM - 92.1
Box 631 Phone: (207)324-7271
Sanford, ME 04073 Fax: (207)324-2464
E-mail: wcdq@wcdq.com

Format: Classic Rock. **Founded:** 1985. **Formerly:** WEBI-FM. **Operating Hours:** Continuous. **Key Personnel:** Becky Brown, General Mgr.; Russ Dumont, Program Dir.; Jonathan Smith, News Dir.; Becky Brown, Contact. **Wattage:** 3000. **Ad Rates:** $22-40 per unit. Combined advertising rates available with WSME-AM.

13254 WSME-AM - 1220
Box 631 Phone: (207)324-7271
Sanford, ME 04073 Fax: (207)324-2464
E-mail: wcdq@wcdq.com

Format: News; Talk. **Operating Hours:** Continuous. **Key Personnel:** Becky Brown, Sales Mgr.; Russ Dumont, Program Dir. **Wattage:** 1000. **Ad Rates:** $12-30 per unit. Combined advertising rates available with WCDQ-FM.

SCARBOROUGH

Cumberland Co. (SE). 5 m S of Westbrook.

13255 WPKM-FM - 106.3
17 Elmwood Ave. Phone: (207)883-9596
PO Box 610 Fax: (207)883-9530
Scarborough, ME 04070-0610

Format: Classical. **Networks:** Independent. **Founded:** 1988. **Operating Hours:** Continuous; 100% local. **Key Personnel:** Cameron Smith, Program Dir.; Louis Vitali, General Mgr. **Wattage:** 3000. **Ad Rates:** Advertising accepted; rates available upon request. Combined advertising rates available with WBQQ.

SKOWHEGAN†, pop. 8,100.

Somerset Co. (SC). 15 m NNW of Waterville. Shoes, lumber, dairy, truck farms.

13256 WSKW-AM - 1160
Box 159 Phone: (207)474-5171
Middle Rd. Fax: (207)474-3299
Skowhegan, ME 04976-0159

Format: Music of Your Life. **Networks:** Independent. **Founded:** 1956. **Formerly:** WQMR-AM (1988). **Operating Hours:** Continuous. **ADI:** Bangor, ME. **Key Personnel:** Alan W. Anderson, Contact; Mike Estrada, News Dir. **Wattage:** 10,000. **Ad Rates:** $12 per unit.

SOUTH PORTLAND

13257 WGAN-AM - 560
420 Western Ave. Phone: (207)774-4561
South Portland, ME 04106 Fax: (207)774-3788
E-mail: gan56.com

Format: Talk; News. **Networks:** CBS. **Founded:** 1938. **Operating Hours:** Continuous; 60% network, 40% local. **ADI:** Portland-Poland Spring, ME. **Key Personnel:** Dave Winsor, Program Dir.; Cary Pahigan, VP/General Mgr.; Chris Mac, Marketing Dir.; Bill Whitten, Sales Mgr. **Local Programs:** *Kroah and Crocker*, Jesse Quinn. **Wattage:** 5000. **Ad Rates:** Advertising accepted; rates available upon request. Combined advertising rates available with WZAN-AM.

13258 WMGX-FM - 93.1
420 West Ave. Phone: (207)774-4561
South Portland, ME 04106 Fax: (207)774-3788
E-mail: wmgx@aol.com

Format: Adult Contemporary. **Founded:** 1977. **Operating Hours:** Continuous. **Key Personnel:** Cary Panigian, General Mgr.; Randi Kirshbaum, Program Dir.; Ethan Minton, Music Dir.; Chris Mac, Marketing Dir. **Wattage:** 50,000 ERP.

13259 WYNZ-FM - 100.9
420 Western Ave. Phone: (207)774-4561
South Portland, ME 04106-1704 Fax: (207)774-3788

Format: Oldies. **Networks:** CBS. **Owner:** Saga Communications of New England, 73 Kercheval Ave., Grosse Pointe Farms, MI 48236, (313)886-7070, Fax: (313)886-7150. **Founded:** 1977. **Operating Hours:** Continuous. **Key Personnel:** Cary Panigian, General Mgr.; Tina Segerstrom, Sales Mgr.; Ken McGrail, Program Dir. **Wattage:** 25,000.

13260 WZAN-AM - 970
420 Western Ave. Phone: (207)774-4561
South Portland, ME 04106-1704 Fax: (207)774-3788

Format: Talk. **Networks:** CBS. **Owner:** Saga Communications of New England, Inc., 173 Kercheval Ave., Grosse Pointe Farms, MI 48236. **Founded:** 1925. **Formerly:** WCSH-AM (1980); WYNZ-AM (Aug. 1993). **Operating Hours:** Continuous. **ADI:** Portland-Poland Spring, ME. **Key Personnel:** Cary Pahigan, VP/General Mgr.; Dave Winsor, Program Dir.; Bill Whitten, Sales Mgr. **Wattage:** 5000. **Ad Rates:** Advertising accepted; rates available upon request. Combined advertising rates available with WGAN.

SPRINGVALE

13261 New England Cablevision Inc.
72 Pleasant St. Phone: (207)324-3777
Springvale, ME 04083 Fax: (207)490-1697

URL: http://www.necable.com.

STANDISH

13262 WSJB-FM - 91.5
St. Joseph's College Phone: (207)892-6766
278 Whites Bridge Rd. Fax: (207)893-7873
Standish, ME 04084
E-mail: wyates@sjcme.edu

Format: Contemporary Hit Radio (CHR); Eclectic. **Founded:** 1984. **Operating Hours:** 7 a.m.-midnight. **ADI:** Portland-Poland Spring, ME. **Key Personnel:** William Yates, Faculty Adviser, wyates@sjcme.edu. **Wattage:** 365.

STONINGTON, pop. 1,273.

Hancock Co. (SE). On Penobscot Bay, 65 m S of Bangor. Commercial fishing port. Sea food cannery, shipyards.

13263 Commercial Fisheries News
Compass Publications, Inc., Fisheries Division
PO Box 37 Phone: (207)367-2396
Stonington, ME 04681 Fax: (207)367-2490
Free: (800)989-5253
Publication E-mail: comfish@media2.hypernet.com

Magazine for commercial fishermen. **Founded:** 1973. **Freq:** Monthly. **Print Method:** Offset. **Cols./Page:** 4. **Col. Width:** 28 nonpareils. **Col. Depth:** 210 agate lines. **Key Personnel:** Richard W. Martin, Publisher. **ISSN:** 0273-6713. **Subscription Rates:** $21.95 individuals; $2.75 single issue. **Remarks:** Accepts advertising.
Ad Rates: BW: $1,400 **Circ:** 8,500

13264 Fish Farming News
Compass Publications, Inc., Fisheries Division
PO Box 37 Phone: (207)367-2396
Stonington, ME 04681 Fax: (207)367-2490
Free: (800)989-5253
Publication E-mail: comfish@media2.hypernet.com

Business newspaper for North American aquaculturists. **Founded:** 1993. **Freq:** Bimonthly plus annual review and forecast issue. **Print Method:** Offset. **Cols./Page:** 4. **Col. Width:** 28 nonpareils. **Col. Depth:** 210 agate lines. **Key Personnel:** Susan Jones, Editor. **ISSN:** 1047-2525. **Subscription Rates:** $10; $1.95 single issue. **Remarks:** Accepts advertising.
Ad Rates: BW: $1,125 **Circ:** Controlled 8,500
4C: $1,900

13265 Island Ad-Vantages
Penobscot Bay Press, Inc.
PO Box 36 Phone: (207)367-2200
Stonington, ME 04681 Fax: (207)367-6397
Publication E-mail: press@celestat.com

Community newspaper. **Founded:** 1935. **Freq:** Weekly (Thurs.). **Print Method:** Offset. **Trim Size:** 11 x 17. **Cols./Page:** 4. **Col. Width:** 2 1/2 inches. **Col. Depth:** 15 inches. **Key Personnel:** R. Nathaniel W. Barrows, Editor and Publisher. **USPS:** 270-440. **Subscription Rates:** $24.95 individuals; $33.95 out of state. **Remarks:** Accepts advertising.
Ad Rates: BW: $480 **Circ:** 2,491
PCI: $8

13266 Marine Performance and Fisheries Product News
Compass Publications, Inc., Fisheries Division
PO Box 37 Phone: (207)367-2396
Stonington, ME 04681 Fax: (207)367-2490
Free: (800)989-5253
Publication E-mail: comfish@media2.hypernet.com

New product publication for commercial fishermen, seafood processors, and aquaculturists. **Founded:** 1986. **Freq:** Quarterly. **Print Method:** Offset. **Cols./Page:** 4. **Col. Width:** 28 nonpareils. **Col. Depth:** 210 agate lines. **Key Personnel:** Richard W. Martin, Publisher. **ISSN:** 1047-2525. **Remarks:** Accepts advertising. **Formerly:** Product News; Fisheries Product News.
Ad Rates: BW: $1,575 **Circ:** Controlled 14,525
4C: $2,350

THOMASTON

13267 The Northwoods Journal
Northwoods Press
PO Box 298 Phone: (207)354-0998
Thomaston, ME 04861 Fax: (207)354-8953
Publication E-mail: cal@americanletter.org
Publisher E-mail: cal@ime.net

Trade magazine for writers. **Subtitle:** A Magazine for Writers. **Founded:** 1973. **Freq:** Quarterly. **Print Method:** Offset. **Trim Size:** 5 1/2 x 8 1/2. **Key Personnel:** Robert W. Olmsted. **Subscription Rates:** $12.50 individuals; $8.45 single issue. **Remarks:** Accepts advertising. **URL:** http://www.americanbetters.org.
Ad Rates: BW: $70 **Circ:** Paid 350

TOPSHAM, pop. 6,431.

Sagadahoc Co. (S). 28 m NE of Portland. Residential.

13268 WBCI-FM - 105.9
122 Main St. Phone: (207)725-9224
Topsham, ME

Format: Classic Rock. **Owner:** Kaleidoscope, Inc., at above address. **Founded:** Feb. 18, 1991. **Formerly:** WIGY-FM (1989); WKRH-FM. **Operating Hours:** Continuous. **Wattage:** 50,000.

TROY

13269 Potato Eyes
Nightshade Press
Ward Hill Phone: (207)948-3427
PO Box 76 Fax: (207)948-5088
Troy, ME 04987
Publisher E-mail: potatoeyes@uninets.net

Literary arts journal covering rural topics. **Founded:** 1989. **Freq:** Semiannual. **Print Method:** Offset. **Trim Size:** 5 1/4 x 8 1/4. **Key Personnel:** Carolyn Page, Editor. **Subscription Rates:** $12 individuals; $7.95 single issue. **Remarks:** Advertising not accepted.
Circ: Combined 450

WALDOBORO, pop. 3,985.

Lincoln Co. (S) 10 m SE of Jefferson. Residential. Manufactures plastics.

13270 Maine Antique Digest
911 Main St. Phone: (207)832-7534
PO Box 1429 Fax: (207)832-7341
Waldoboro, ME 04572-1429
Publication E-mail: mad@maine.com

Tabloid featuring articles on art, antiques, and Americana. **Founded:** Nov. 1973. **Freq:** Monthly. **Print Method:** Offset. **Cols./Page:** 5. **Col. Width:** 21 nonpareils. **Col. Depth:** 210 agate lines. **Key Personnel:** Samuel C. Pennington, Editor and Publisher; Alice Greene, Advertising Mgr. **USPS:** 019-

630. **Subscription Rates:** $43 individuals; $3.75 single issue. **Remarks:** Accepts advertising.
Ad Rates: BW: $750 PCI: $13.50 **Circ:** Paid ‡33,000 Non-paid ‡1,500

13271 **Maine Water Utilities Association Journal**
Maine Water Utilities Association
PO Box P Phone: (207)832-2263
Waldoboro, ME 04572-0917 Fax: (207)832-2265

Association magazine. **Founded:** 1924. **Freq:** Daily (during the academic year). **Key Personnel:** Jeffrey L. McNelly, Editor. **Remarks:** Advertising accepted; rates available upon request.
Circ: 400

WATERVILLE, pop. 17,779.

Kennebec Co. (SWC). On Kennebec River, 18 m N of Augusta. Colby College. Thomas College. Summer resort. Manufactures pulp, worsted cloth, paper plates, shirts, fibre, meat, foundry products, monuments. Dairy, poultry, truck farms. Potatoes, corn, beans.

13272 **Central Maine Morning Sentinel**
Guy Gannett Publications, Inc.
25 Silver St. Phone: (207)873-3341
Waterville, ME 04901-6648 Fax: (207)873-3341

General newspaper. **Founded:** Mar. 3, 1904. **Freq:** Mon.-Sat. (morn.). **Print Method:** Offset. **Trim Size:** 13 x 21 1/2. **Cols./Page:** 6. **Col. Width:** 24 nonpareils. **Col. Depth:** 301 agate lines. **Key Personnel:** Davis R. Rawson, Editor; Jean Gannett Hawley, Publisher; Ron Uecker, Advertising Mgr. **Subscription Rates:** $109.20 individuals; $132 out of state. **Remarks:** Accepts advertising.
Ad Rates: GLR: $1.39 BW: $2,509.05 4C: $450 SAU: $19.45 PCI: $19.45 **Circ:** Mon.-Sat. 21,243 Sun. 18,645

13273 **Colby**
Colby College
Waterville, ME 04901 Phone: (207)872-3226 Fax: (207)872-3555
Publication E-mail: mag@colby.edu

College alumni magazine. **Founded:** 1911. **Freq:** 4/year. **Print Method:** Sheetfed Offset. **Trim Size:** 8 1/2 x 11. **Cols./Page:** 3. **Col. Width:** 26 nonpareils. **Col. Depth:** 133 agate lines. **Key Personnel:** Stephen B. Collins, Exec. Editor, phone (207)872-3276, sbcollin@colby.edu; Brian D. Speer, Graphic Designer, phone (207)872-3218. **Remarks:** Advertising not accepted. **URL:** http://www.colby.edu:/colby.mag/.
Circ: Non-paid ‡26,000

13274 **Colby Echo**
Colby College
5921 Mayflower Hill Dr. Phone: (207)872-3349
Waterville, ME 04901 Fax: (207)872-3555
Publisher E-mail: echo@colby.edu

Collegiate newspaper. **Founded:** 1877. **Freq:** Weekly (Thurs.). **Print Method:** Offset. **Cols./Page:** 5. **Col. Width:** 23 nonpareils. **Col. Depth:** 220 agate lines. **Subscription Rates:** $40 individuals. **Remarks:** Accepts advertising.
Ad Rates: GLR: $.44 BW: $380 PCI: $6.75 **Circ:** Free 4,000

13275 **WMHB-FM - 90.5**
Colby College Phone: (207)872-3686
Waterville, ME 04901 Fax: (207)872-3785
E-mail: wmhb@colby.edu

Format: Alternative/New Music/Progressive; News. **Networks:** Independent. **Owner:** Mayflower Hill Broadcasting, Inc., at above address. **Founded:** 1958. **Operating Hours:** Continuous; 100% local. **Key Personnel:** Jason M. Tom, General Mgr.; Thomas DiBrita, Asst. Gen. Mgr.; Nyasha Pfukwa, Music Dir.; Mike Baru, Program Dir. **Wattage:** 110. **Ad Rates:** Underwriting available.

WESTBROOK, pop. 14,976.

Cumberland Co. (SW). 6 m W of Portland. Manufactures corrugated paper boxes, coated printing and specialty paper. cotton and silk thread spinning, computers, solid tires, retreaded tires, shoes, dowels, cement blocks. Dairy, truck farms.

13276 **American Journal**
4 Dana St. Phone: (207)854-2577
Westbrook, ME 04092 Fax: (207)854-0018

Community newspaper. **Founded:** Jan. 4, 1950. **Freq:** Weekly (Wed.). **Print Method:** Offset. **Cols./Page:** 5. **Col. Width:** 11 1/2 picas. **Col. Depth:** 15 1/4 inches. **Key Personnel:** Harry T. Foote, Editor and Publisher; Raymond M. Foote, Assistant Publisher. **ISSN:** 0092-119X. **Subscription Rates:** $25 individuals. **Remarks:** Accepts advertising excluding tobacco products.
Ad Rates: GLR: $0.786 BW: $420 4C: $175 PCI: $11 **Circ:** Paid 7,200 Free 122

YARMOUTH, pop. 7,300.

Cumberland Co. (E). On Caseo Bay. 10 m N of Portland. Commercial fisheries.

13277 **Golf Course News**
United Publications, Inc.
106 Lafayette St. Phone: (207)846-0600
Yarmouth, ME 04096 Fax: (207)846-0657
Publication E-mail: golfcoursenews.com

Tabloid covering golf course maintenance. **Subtitle:** The Newspaper for the Golf Course Industry. **Founded:** Feb. 1989. **Freq:** 12/year. **Print Method:** Web offset. **Trim Size:** 10 5/8 x 13 5/8. **Cols./Page:** 4 and 5. **Col. Width:** 2 3/8 and 1 inches. **Col. Depth:** 13 1/2 inches. **Key Personnel:** Hal Phillips, Editor; Mark Leslie, Managing Editor; Charles Von Brecht, Publisher. **ISSN:** 1054-0644. **Subscription Rates:** Free to qualified subscribers.
Ad Rates: BW: $2,735 **Circ:** Controlled ‡22,100

13278 **Gourmet News**
United Publications, Inc.
106 Lafayette St. Phone: (207)846-0600
Yarmouth, ME 04096 Fax: (207)846-0657
Publication E-mail: jfriedrick@gourmetnews.com

Trade newspaper for the gourmet food industry. **Freq:** Monthly. **Key Personnel:** Chris Crocker, Publisher; Joanne Friedrick, Editor; Lori Glickman, Managing Editor; Christina Levere, Asst. Editor. **Subscription Rates:** $65 individuals; Free to qualified subscribers. **Remarks:** Accepts advertising.
Circ: Non-paid 22,000

13279 **HME News**
United Publications, Inc.
106 Lafayette St. Phone: (207)846-0600
Yarmouth, ME 04096 Fax: (207)846-0657

Business newspaper for home medical equipment providers. Editorial coverage focuses on industry news, mergers and acquisitions, governmental and regulatory impact on the HME industry, as well as product reviews and industry trend coverage. **Subtitle:** The Business Newspaper for Home Medical Equipment Providers. **Founded:** May 1995. **Freq:** Monthly. **Key Personnel:** Jim Sullivan, Editor, jsullivan@hmenews.com; Neil Rouda, Publisher, nrouda@hmenews.com. **Remarks:** Accepts advertising.
Ad Rates: BW: $3,485 4C: $4,375 **Circ:** Paid △17,100

13280 **Kitchenware News**
United Publications, Inc.
106 Lafayette St. Phone: (207)846-0600
Yarmouth, ME 04096 Fax: (207)846-0657

Trade magazine covering news of retailers and kitchenware products. **Founded:** Jan. 1994. **Freq:** Monthly. **Print Method:** Web offset. **Trim Size:** 10 5/8 x 13 5/8. **Cols./Page:** 4. **Col. Width:** 2 1/4 inches. **Col. Depth:** 12 5/8 inches. **Key Personnel:** Thyra Porter, Editor; Jim McNeil, Publisher; Brenda Boothby, Circulation Mgr.; Joline Gilman, Production Mgr. **USPS:** 012-625. **Subscription Rates:** $55 individuals; $5.50 single issue. **Remarks:** Accepts advertising. **Alt. Formats:** Microfilm.
Ad Rates: BW: $3,815 4C: $4,740 **Circ:** Combined ‡12,122

13281 **Service News**
United Publications, Inc.
106 Lafayette St. Phone: (207)846-0600
Yarmouth, ME 04096 Fax: (207)846-0657

Tabloid newspaper. **Subtitle:** The Newspaper For Computer Service Support. **Founded:** 1981. **Freq:** Monthly. **Print Method:** Offset. **Trim Size:** 10 5/8 x 14 3/4. **Cols./Page:** 4. **Col. Width:** 13.5 picas. **Col. Depth:** 13 1/4 inches. **Key Personnel:** Brook Taliaferro, President; Joline Gilman, Production Mgr.; Karen Hamilton, Editor; Alison Harris, Publisher. **ISSN:** 1046-1965. **Subscription Rates:** Free to qualified subscribers. **Remarks:** Accepts advertising. **Formerly:** Computer/Electronic Service News.
Ad Rates: BW: $5,160 4C: $6,240 PCI: $65 **Circ:** Controlled ‡45,100

13282 **WCME-FM - 96.7**
PO Box 580 Phone: (207)563-5710
Yarmouth, ME 04096 Fax: (207)865-3299
Free: (800)635-7355

Format: Contemporary Country. **Networks:** Satellite Music Network. **Owner:** Bay Communications, at above address, (207)865-1199. **Founded:** 1984. **Operating Hours:** Continuous; 5% network, 95% local. **Key Personnel:** Marilyn Quinn, General Mgr.; Ken Minot, Program Dir.; Thomas Cole, Chief Engineer. **Local Programs:** *Coastal Country Network*, Matt Fake. **Wattage:** 25,000. **Ad Rates:** $21-24 per unit.

YORK

13283 **The York Weekly**
James Carter Publications, Inc.
17 Woodbridge Rd. Phone: (207)363-4343
PO Box 7 Fax: (207)351-2849
York, ME 03909
Publication E-mail: yorkweekly@cybertowns.com

Community newspaper. **Founded:** Nov. 1890. **Freq:** Weekly (Wed.). **Print Method:** Offset. **Trim Size:** 11 1/2 x 15 1/2. **Cols./Page:** 6. **Col. Width:** 9 1/2 picas. **Col. Depth:** 14 1/2 inches. **Key Personnel:** James E. Carter, Publisher; Deborah McDermott, Editor. **USPS:** 696-220. **Subscription Rates:** $25 individuals. **Remarks:** Accepts advertising. **URL:** http://www.yorkweekly.com.
Ad Rates: PCI: $8.50 **Circ:** Paid ‡4,918 Free ‡175

YORK CENTER

13284 **WXHT-FM - 95.3**
PO Box 150 Phone: (603)430-9500
Portsmouth, NH 03802-0150 Fax: (603)430-9501

Networks: Independent. **Owner:** Atlantic Star Communications, at above address, 7th Fl., Ste. 2. **Founded:** 1987. **Formerly:** WQMI-FM (1989); WCQL-FM (1996). **Operating Hours:** Continuous; 100% local. **ADI:** Boston-Worcester,MA-Derry-Manchester,NH. **Key Personnel:** Kim D. Jones, General Mgr.; Glenn Stewart, Program Dir.; Charles Triest, Sales Mgr.; Kelly Brown, News Dir. **Wattage:** 6000. **Ad Rates:** Advertising accepted; rates available upon request.

MARYLAND

State Capital, ANNAPOLIS

Maryland is bounded on the north by Pennsylvania, east and southeast by Delaware and the Atlantic Ocean, west by West Virginia, and south and southwest by Virginia, West Virginia, and the District of Columbia. The Chesapeake Bay divides the greater portion of it into two unequal parts, known as the Eastern and Western Shores. Its extreme width from east to west on its northern border is 198 miles, and , following the course of the Potomac River, varies from 3 or 4 miles to about 125 miles. Its land area is 9,775 square miles. The surface of the Eastern Shore is mostly level, in parts low and swampy, but towards the north, rocky and broken. The Western Shore, between the Potomac River and Chesapeake Bay, presents the same general features. The northwest is very mountainous, with five or six ridges of the Alleghenies, principally the Blue and Laurel, traversing it. In the extreme west are the beautiful elevated valleys, or glades. The mountainous slopes are thickly wooded. The soil of the Eastern Shore and southern Maryland is alluvial, classed as silt and sandy loam, while the soil of the central and northern parts are made up primarily of loams and silt loams. The Weather Bureau at Baltimore gives the temperature (annual average) as 55.1; highest on record, 105; lowest on record, -7. Total annual precipitation is 40.76 inches. Water and rail transportation are highly developed. Maryland's commerce is confined chiefly to Baltimore, one of the principal ports of the country, and one whose trade is extremely heavy. The Potomac River and Chesapeake Bay are navigable for large vessels, and many smaller rivers and bays are accessible for vessels of light draft. The United States Naval Academy is located at Annapolis; the University of Maryland at College Park. Johns Hopkins University at Baltimore is internationally famous, and its hospital receives patients from all over the world.

POPULATION: 4,908,000 (1992). Rank among the states, 19th.

AGRICULTURE: Number of farms: 16,000 (1992). Farm acreage: 2,000,000 (1992). Cash receipts from farm marketings: crops, $554,000,000 (1991); livestock and products, $779,000,000 (1991).

FISHERIES: Total catch: 81,000,000 lbs. (1991), $47,000,000 value. Principal fish: oysters, clams, striped bass, tuna.

FORESTS: Total forest land: 2,632,000 acres (1987).

MINERALS: Value of production: $348,000,000 (1991). Principal minerals: stone, sand and gravel, cement.

MANUFACTURES: Value added by manufacture: $15,242,000,000 (1991). Leading industry groups: primary metal industries, transportation equipment, food and related products.

LIST OF COUNTIES

Total number of counties 23

County, Location on Map, and County Seat	Pop.
Allegheny (NW), Cumberland	74,946
Anne Arundel (C), Annapolis	427,239
Baltimore (N), Towson, Fullerton	692,134
Calvert (S), Prince Frederick	51,372
Caroline (E), Denton	27,035
Carroll (N), Westminster	123,372
Cecil (NE), Elkton	71,347
Charles (SW), La Plata	101,154
Dorchester (SE), Cambridge	30,236
Frederick (N), Frederick	150,208
Garrett (NW), Oakland	28,138
Harford (NE), Bel Air	182,132
Howard (C), Ellicott City	187,328
Kent (NE), Chestertown	17,842
Montgomery (WC), Rockville	757,027
Prince Georges (SC), Up. Marlboro	729,268
Queen Annes (E), Centerville	33,953
St. Mary's (S), Leonardtown	75,974
Somerset (SE), Princess Anne	23,440
Talbot (E), Easton	30,549
Washington (NW), Hagerstown	121,393
Wicomico (SE), Salisbury	74,339
Worcester (SE), Snow Hill	35,028

STATISTICS

Newspapers

Period of Issue	
Daily	14
Evening Daily	4
Morning Daily	4
Daily with Sunday edition	8
Semiweekly	5
Weekly	61
Biweekly	2
Semimonthly	5
Monthly	8
Bimonthly	3
Quarterly	1
Free or partly free	26
Shopper	2
Total Newspapers	101

Periodicals

Period of Issue	
Weekly	8
Biweekly	1
Triweekly	1
Semimonthly	9
Monthly	115
Bimonthly	69
Quarterly	116
Total Periodicals	381

Total number of publications 482

Radio Stations

AM Stations	44
FM Stations	67
Total Radio Stations	111

TV Stations

Total TV Stations 16

Cable Stations

Total Cable Systems 11

Total number of broadcast listings 138

ABERDEEN

Harford Co. (NE). 2 m S of Havre de Grace.

13285 Harford Business Ledger, Inc.
214 W. Bel Air Ave. Phone: (410)272-4208
Aberdeen, MD 21001-0075 Fax: (410)272-4208
Publication E-mail: hbledger@erols.com

Business newspaper. **Founded:** Oct. 1989. **Freq:** Monthly. **Print Method:** Offset. **Cols./Page:** 4. **Col. Width:** 2 1/4 inches. **Col. Depth:** 13 1/2 inches. **Key Personnel:** Philip Smith, Publisher; Cheryl Mattix, Editor. **USPS:** 013-919. **Subscription Rates:** $20 individuals. **Remarks:** Accepts advertising.
Ad Rates: BW: $1,965 **Circ:** Controlled 5,954
4C: $2,190
PCI: $35

13286 Comcast Cablevision of Harford County
30 N. Parke St. Phone: (410)272-7500
Aberdeen, MD 21001 Fax: (410)272-6203

Owner: Comcast Corp., 1500 Market St., East Tower, Philadelphia, PA 19102, (215)665-1700, Fax: (215)981-7790, Free: (800)477-8383. **Founded:** 1967. **Formerly:** Multiview Cablevision. **Key Personnel:** Mick Jolly, Contact, phone (410)612-0855, fax (410)272-6203; Pat Donovan, Contact, phone (410)612-0702, fax (410)272-6203; Kay Moore, Exec. Sec., phone (410)612-0801, fax (410)272-6203; Jaye Gamble, General Mgr., phone (410)931-4600, fax (410)931-6345. **Cities Served:** Harford County: subscribing households 55,000; 82 channels; 1 community access channel; 168 hours per week community access programming.

13287 WAMD-AM - 970
400 Hiob Ln. Phone: (410)272-4400
PO Box 970
Aberdeen, MD 21001

Format: Talk; Sports; Soft Rock. **Networks:** ABC. **Owner:** Mackk Broadcasting Co., Inc., at above address, (301)272-4400. **Founded:** 1957. **Operating Hours:** 6 a.m.-11 p.m.; 10% network, 90% local. **ADI:** Baltimore, MD. **Key Personnel:** James V. McMahan, Jr., General Mgr.; Jean Brammer, Office Mgr. **Local Programs:** *Auction Block*; *Health Waves*; *Your Money*. **Wattage:** 500. **Ad Rates:** $20 for 30 seconds; $30 for 60 seconds.

ADELPHI

13288 NABJ Journal
National Association of Black Journalists
8701A Adelphi Rd. Phone: (301)445-7100
Adelphi, MD 20783-1716 Fax: (301)445-7101

Professional magazine covering journalism trends and their impact on Afro-American reporters. **Freq:** Quarterly. **Key Personnel:** Yvette Walker, Editor; Debbie R. Chase, Managing Editor, debbie@nabj.org; Gerry Van Treek, Advertising Rep., phone (847)562-8633. **Subscription Rates:** $9 individuals; $1.50 single issue. **Remarks:** Accepts advertising. **URL:** http://www.nabj.org.
Ad Rates: GLR: $6 **Circ:** Paid 3,000
BW: $1,050

ANNAPOLIS†, pop. 31,740.

Anne Arundel Co. (C). The State Capital. On Severn River, 2 m from Chesapeake Bay, 27 m SE of Baltimore. United States Naval Academy; St. John's College. Boat connections. Fish, crab and oyster industries. Boat yards; beverages, controls, concrete products manufactured. Trading center for residents of surrounding summer resorts.

13289 The Capital
Capital Gazette Communications, Inc.
2000 Capital Dr. Phone: (410)268-5000
PO Box 911 Fax: (410)268-4643
Annapolis, MD 21404
Free: (800)327-1583

General newspaper. **Founded:** 1884. **Freq:** Daily (eve.), Sunday (morn.). **Print Method:** Offset. **Trim Size:** 13 5/8 x 22. **Cols./Page:** 6. **Col. Width:** 2 1/16 inches. **Col. Depth:** 21 inches. **Key Personnel:** Edward D. Casey, Editor; Philip Merrill, Publisher; George Cruze, Advertising Mgr. **Subscription Rates:** $91 individuals; $143 out of area. **Remarks:** Accepts advertising. **URL:** http://www.capitalonline.com.
Ad Rates: BW: $1,640.52 **Circ:** Mon.-Sat. ★**46,758**
4C: $2,090.52 Sun. ★**49,466**
PCI: $15.57

13290 Chesapeake Bay Magazine
Chesapeake Bay Communications
1819 Bay Ridge Ave. Phone: (410)263-2662
Annapolis, MD 21403 Fax: (410)267-6924

Boating magazine covering Chesapeake Bay. **Founded:** 1971. **Freq:** Monthly. **Print Method:** Web press. **Trim Size:** 8 1/4 x 10 7/8. **Key Personnel:** Tim Sayles, Editor; Richard Royer, Publisher. **Subscription Rates:** $22.95.
Ad Rates: 4C: $3,950 **Circ:** Paid ★**43,810**

13291 Chesapeake Family
Jefferson Communications
1202 West St., 100 Phone: (410)263-1641
Annapolis, MD 21401 Fax: (410)280-0255
Publication E-mail: chesfam@family.com

Consumer parenting magazine. **Founded:** Sept. 1990. **Freq:** Monthly. **Print Method:** Web. **Trim Size:** 8 1/4 x 10 3/4. **Cols./Page:** 3. **Col. Width:** 2 5/6 inches. **Col. Depth:** 10 inches. **Key Personnel:** Crickett Gibbons, Editor. **Subscription Rates:** $21 individuals. **Remarks:** Accepts advertising. **URL:** http://www.chesapeakefamily.com. **Former name:** Chesapeake Children.
Ad Rates: BW: $1,300 **Circ:** Controlled 40,000
4C: $1,660

13292 Maryland Farmer
Rural Press USA
Rte. 1 Phone: (703)459-3209
POB 432 Fax: (703)459-2401
Maurertown, VA 22644
Agricultural newspaper. **Founded:** 1979. **Freq:** Monthly. **Print Method:** Offset. **Trim Size:** 10 1/2 x 13 1/4. **Cols./Page:** 4. **Col. Width:** 2 1/4 inches. **Col. Depth:** 12 7/8 inches. **Key Personnel:** Julie Gochenour, Editor; Allen Williams, Wittma, Publisher; Don Holland, Advertising Mgr.; Mike Coan, Circulation Mgr.; Kris Wheeler, Managing Editor. **Subscription Rates:** $12 individuals. **Remarks:** Accepts advertising.
Ad Rates: BW: $1,105 **Circ:** ‡14,000
4C: $1,605
PCI: $14

13293 Maryland Register
Division of State Documents
PO Box 2249 Phone: (410)974-2486
Annapolis, MD 21404-2249 Fax: (410)974-2546
Free: (800)633-9657

Magazine on public administration and law. **Founded:** Oct. 17, 1974. **Freq:** Biweekly. **Print Method:** Offset. **Trim Size:** 8 1/2 x 11. **Cols./Page:** 2. **Col. Width:** 40 nonpareils. **Col. Depth:** 126 agate lines. **Key Personnel:** Robert J. Colborn, Editor. **ISSN:** 0360-2834. **Subscription Rates:** $100 individuals 2nd class; $180 1st class; $7 single issue includes Postage. **Remarks:** Advertising not accepted. **Alt. Formats:** Mailing labels.
Circ: Paid ‡1,200
Controlled ‡400

13294 Municipal Maryland
Maryland Municipal League
1212 West St. Phone: (410)268-5514
Annapolis, MD 21401 Fax: (410)268-7004
Publisher E-mail: mml@mdmunicipal.org

Magazine for elected and appointed city and town officials in Maryland. Provides a forum for ideas on municipal affairs. **Founded:** 1972. **Freq:** 10/year. **Print Method:** Offset. **Trim Size:** 8 1/2 x 11. **Cols./Page:** 2 and 3. **Col. Width:** 3.5 and 2 inches. **Col. Depth:** 9 3/8 inches. **Key Personnel:** Karen A. Liskey, Editor. **Subscription Rates:** $21 individuals; $2.50 single issue.
Ad Rates: BW: $345 **Circ:** Paid ‡1,750
Non-paid ‡190

13295 Naval History
U.S. Naval Institute
Preble Hall Phone: (410)268-6110
118 Maryland Ave. Fax: (410)269-7940
Annapolis, MD 21402-5035
Journal devoted to naval history. **Founded:** 1987. **Freq:** Bimonthly. **Print Method:** Web offset. **Trim Size:** 8 1/2 x 11. **Key Personnel:** Fred L. Schultzll, Editor; James A. Barber, Jr., Publisher; James E. Burke, Advertising Mgr. **ISSN:** 1042-1920. **Subscription Rates:** $20; $24 other countries. **Remarks:** Accepts advertising.
Ad Rates: BW: $1,275 **Circ:** 32,000
4C: $1,675

13296 Proceedings
U.S. Naval Institute
Preble Hall Phone: (410)268-6110
118 Maryland Ave. Fax: (410)269-7940
Annapolis, MD 21402-5035
Magazine on naval and maritime news. **Founded:** 1873. **Freq:** Monthly. **Print Method:** Offset. **Trim Size:** 8 1/8 x 10 3/4. **Cols./Page:** 3. **Col. Width:** 12 1/2 picas. **Col. Depth:** 54 picas. **Key Personnel:** Fred H. Rainbow, Editor; James A. Barber, Jr., Publisher; James E. Burke, Advertising Mgr. **ISSN:** 0041-798X. **Subscription Rates:** $30 individuals; $27 U.S.N.I. members; $3 single issue. **Remarks:** Accepts advertising.
Ad Rates: BW: $3,000 **Circ:** ‡125,000
4C: $3,800

13297 The Publick Enterprise
Mainbrace Inc.
PO Box 4520 Phone: (410)268-3527
Annapolis, MD 21403 Fax: (410)268-9867

Community newspaper. **Subtitle:** An Uncommon Newspaper for Uncommon People. **Founded:** Nov. 16, 1978. **Freq:** Semimonthly. **Print Method:** Offset. **Trim Size:** 11 1/2 x 17. **Cols./Page:** 4. **Col. Width:** 14 picas. **Col. Depth:** 15 inches. **Key Personnel:** Nancy Noyes, Managing Editor; Steve Voorhis, Publisher, svoorhis@ix.netcom.com. **Subscription Rates:** Free; $36 by mail. **Remarks:** Advertising not accepted for adoption.
Ad Rates: BW: $681 **Circ:** Paid ‡200
Free ‡11,800

13298 St. John's Reporter
St. John's College, Office of Public Relations
Box 2800
Annapolis, MD 21404

Alumni publication of St. John's College. **Founded:** 1976. **Freq:** Quarterly. **USPS:** 018-750.
Circ: Non-paid 20,000

13299 Shipmate
U.S. Naval Academy Alumni Association
Alumni House Phone: (410)263-4448
247 King George St. Fax: (410)269-0151
Annapolis, MD 21402
Publication E-mail: shipmate@usna.com

Alumni magazine. **Founded:** 1938. **Freq:** 10/year. **Print Method:** Web press. **Trim Size:** 8 1/4 x 10 7/8. **Cols./Page:** 3 and 2. **Col. Width:** 27 and 42 nonpareils. **Col. Depth:** 136 agate lines. **Key Personnel:** Rebekah Chaney, Contact, rg.chaney@usna.com. **ISSN:** 0488-6720. **Subscription Rates:** $30 individuals. **Remarks:** Accepts advertising.
Ad Rates: BW: $770 **Circ:** ‡40,000
4C: $1,220

13300 Business Radio 1190 WBIS - 1190
1081 Bay Ridge Phone: (410)269-0700
Annapolis, MD 21404 Fax: (410)269-0692
E-mail: wbis1190@aol.com

Format: News; Talk. **Networks:** Business Radio. **Owner:** at above address. **Founded:** 1998. **Formerly:** WANN (1998). **Operating Hours:** Sunrise-sunset. **ADI:** Baltimore, MD. **Key Personnel:** M.H. Blum, President; M.W. Pittman, Chief Engineer; Joe Piette, Station Mgr.; Scott Cutty, Operations Mgr. **Wattage:** 10,000. **Ad Rates:** $55-60 for 60 seconds.

13301 WFSI-FM - 107.9
918 Chesapeake Ave. Phone: (410)268-6200
Annapolis, MD 21403

Format: Religious. **Networks:** Family Stations Radio. **Founded:** 1959. **Operating Hours:** Continuous. **Wattage:** 50,000. **Ad Rates:** Noncommercial. **URL:** http://www.wfsiradio.com.

13302 WMPT-TV - 22, 28, 31, 36, 62, 67
c/o Maryland Public Phone: (410)356-5600
Broadcasting Commission Fax: (410)581-4338
11767 Owings Mills Blvd.
Owings Mills, MD 21117

Format: Public TV. **Simulcasts:** WMPB, WCPB, WWPB, WGPT, WFPT. **Networks:** Public Broadcasting Service (PBS); Eastern Educational Television. **Owner:** State of Maryland, at above address. **Founded:** 1969. **Operating Hours:** 3a.m.-1:30a.m. Mon.-Sun. **ADI:** Baltimore, MD. **Key Personnel:** Robert J. Shuman, Pres./CEO; Janice Wilson, Sr. Vice Pres., Marketing & Development; Larry D. Unger, Sr. Vice Pres., Administration & Finance; Gladys M. Kaplan, Vice Pres., Human Resources; Zyl Shoubin, Vice Pres., Programming/Broadcast Serv.; Everett L. Marshburn, Vice Pres., Broadcast Productions; John T. Potthast, Vice Pres., National Productions; Carol Wonsavage, Dir., Regional Communications; Robert J. Sestili, Sr. V.P., COO. **Local Programs:** *MotorWeek*, John Davis, (410)581-4186, Fax (410)581-4113; *Newsnight Maryland* 7:00 pm Monday-Friday, Steve Kremer, (410)581-4054; *Wall Street Week with Louis Rukeyser* Friday, Rich Dubroff, (410)581-4187, Fax (410)581-0980. **Wattage:** 5,000,000. **URL:** http://www.mpt.org.

13303 WNAV-AM - 1430
236 Admiral Dr. Phone: (410)263-1430
Annapolis, MD 21401 Fax: (410)268-5360
E-mail: wnav@toad.net

Format: Full Service; Adult Contemporary. **Networks:** NBC.

Owner: Sajack Broadcasting Corporation, at above address. **Founded:** 1949. **Operating Hours:** 5 a.m.-midnight. **ADI:** Baltimore, MD. **Key Personnel:** Stephen Hopp, General Mgr.; Bill Lusby, Program Dir.; Bryan Nehman, News Dir.; Sheron Slack, Business Mgr. **Local Programs:** *Talk About Kids* 10:00 am - 11:00 am Tuesday, Gloria Goldfaden, Maggie Thomas; *Home Innovations* 11:00 am - 12:00 pm Tuesday, Elaine Mikk; *Mutual Fund Money Talk* 11:00 am Wednesday; *Capital Caucaus* 11:00 am - 11:30 am Wednesday, Joe Miedusiewski; *Talk with the Mayor* 10:00 am - 10:30 am Thursday, Mayor Dean Johnson; *School Talk* 10:30 am - 11:00 am Thursday; *1430 Connection* Fri., 10:00 am - 11:00 am; Sun., 7:00 am - 8:00 am, Bryan Nehman; *Week in Review/Weekend Headliner* 5:00 am - 6:00 am Saturday; *In the Garden* 8:00 am - 10:00 am Saturday, Andre Viette; *America This Week* 6:00 am - 6:30 am Sunday, Jim Bohannon; *Wonderful Words of Life* 6:30 am - 6:45 am Sunday; *Crime Line* 6:45 am - 7:00 am Sunday, Len Stipes; *Family Chat Time* 8:00 am - 8:30 am Sunday, Dr. Samuel Callahan, Maude Callahan; *Jewish Music, News and Views* 9:00 am - 9:30 am Sunday, Larry Goldstein; *Wild About Broadway* 10:00 am - 11:00 am Sunday, Elliott Kanbar; *Salute to Sinatra* 7:00 pm - 9:00 pm Sunday, DJ Pondo; *Big Band Dance Party* 9:00 pm - 12:00 am Sunday, Bo Lewis. **Wattage:** 5000. **URL:** http://www.wnav.com. **Additional Contact Info: Mailing Address:** PO Box 829, Annapolis, MD 21404.

13304 WRNR-FM - 740kc
112 Main St., 3rd Fl. Phone: (410)626-0103
Annapolis, MD 21401

Format: Album-Oriented Rock (AOR). **Networks:** CBS. **Founded:** 1976. **Formerly**: News/Talk/Sports. **Operating Hours:** Continuous. **Key Personnel:** Richard S. Wachtel, General Mgr. **Wattage:** 6000. **Ad Rates:** Advertising accepted; rates available upon request.

13305 WYRE-AM - 810
112 Main St. Phone: (410)626-0103
Annapolis, MD 21401 Fax: (410)267-7634

Format: Country; Oldies. **Networks:** ABC. **Owner:** Maven Broadcasting, 112 Main St., Annapolis, MD 21401. **Founded:** 1946. **Formerly**: WASL-AM; WABW-AM. **Operating Hours:** Sunrise-sunset; 100% local. **ADI:** Baltimore, MD. **Key Personnel:** Jacob Einstein, General Mgr. & Program Dir.; John Rouse, Station Mgr.; Sunny Devese, Sales Mgr.; Jack Edwards, Program Dir. **Local Programs:** *Bring Back the Doo-Wops*, Charlie Coleman; *Live Wire Morning Show*, Bill Lusby; *R 'n B Alley*, Charles Stinchcomb. **Wattage:** 250. **Ad Rates:** $30-40 for 60 seconds. **URL:** http://www.wyreradio.com.

ANNAPOLIS JUNCTION

13306 Cleaning & Restoration
ASCR International
10830 Annapolis Junction Rd., Ste. 312 Phone: (301)604-4411
Fax: (301)604-4713
Annapolis Junction, MD 20701-1120
Free: (800)272-7012
Publisher E-mail: info@ascr.org

Journal covering drapery, rug, upholstery, and carpet cleaning; fire and water damage; and disaster restoration and mechanical systems cleaning and inspection . **Founded:** 1962. **Freq:** Monthly. **Print Method:** Offset. **Trim Size:** 8 1/2 x 11. **Cols./Page:** 3 and 2. **Col. Width:** 24 and 37 agate lines. **Col. Depth:** 122 agate lines. **Key Personnel:** Patricia Harmon, Editor; Kim Howard, Publisher. **ISSN:** 0886-9901. **Subscription Rates:** $27 individuals; $6 single issue. **Remarks:** Accepts advertising. **Formerly**: Voice.
Ad Rates: BW: $450 **Circ:** ‡2,600
4C: $1,200

ARNOLD, pop. 500.

Anne Arundel Co. (C). 5 m N of Annapolis. Residential.

13307 Campus Crier
Anne Arundel Community College
101 College Pkwy. Phone: (410)541-2803
Arnold, MD 21012-1857 Fax: (410)541-2201
Publication E-mail: crier@mail.aacc.cc.md.us

Collegiate newspaper. **Founded:** 1981. **Freq:** Semimonthly. **Print Method:** Offset. **Cols./Page:** 4. **Col. Width:** 30 nonpareils. **Col. Depth:** 182 agate lines. **Key Personnel:** Chris McCreary, Editor-in-Chief; Beki Gambel, Business Mgr. **Subscription Rates:** Free on campus. **Remarks:** Accepts advertising.
Ad Rates: BW: $165 **Circ:** ‡4,000

13308 The German Postal Specialist
German Philatelic Society
Box 779 Phone: (410)757-2344
Arnold, MD 21012 Fax: (410)757-6857
Publisher E-mail: germanyphilatelic@juno.com

Magazine devoted to German philately. **Founded:** 1950. **Freq:** Monthly. **Print Method:** Offset. **Trim Size:** 6 x 9. **Cols./Page:** 2. **Col. Width:** 40 nonpareils. **Col. Depth:** 133 agate lines. **Key Personnel:** Rudolf Anders, Editor. **ISSN:** 0116-8823. **Subscription Rates:** Free to members; $2.50 others. **Remarks:** Accepts advertising.
Ad Rates: BW: $87.50 **Circ:** Paid ‡1,650
Controlled ‡30

BALTIMORE, pop. 786,775.

An independent city not located in a county. On Patapsco River, 12 m from Chesapeake Bay. Important port connection with the sea through Chesapeake Bay and Chesapeake and Delaware Canal. Medical and cultural center, also trading, financial and manufacturing city. Johns Hopkins University and other universities and colleges; many private schools. Manufactures iron, steel, copper products, instruments, fertilizer, chemicals, tin ware, men's clothing, aircraft and parts, spices and flavoring extracts, malt and distilled beverages, soap and soap products, bakery products, electrical and electronic equipment and appliances, wire and cable. Boat and shipyards; dry docks; meat packing; printing and publishing; motor-vehicleassembling; sugar refining; vegetable canning; petroleum refining.

13309 AJNR: American Journal of Neuroradiology
Lippincott Williams & Wilkins
351 W. Camden St. Phone: (410)528-8517
Baltimore, MD 21201-2436 Fax: (410)528-4312
Free: (800)882-0483

Medical journal for neuro-scientists and radiologists. **Founded:** 1980. **Freq:** Bimonthly. **Print Method:** Offset. **Trim Size:** 8 1/8 x 10 7/8. **Cols./Page:** 2. **Col. Width:** 32 nonpareils. **Col. Depth:** 119 agate lines. **Key Personnel:** Michael S. Huckman, M.D., Editor; Sherry Reed, Rep. **ISSN:** 0195-6108. **Subscription Rates:** $133 individuals; $178 foreign. **Remarks:** Accepts advertising.
Ad Rates: BW: $750 **Circ:** Paid ‡5,934
4C: $1,625 Non-paid ‡130

13310 Alternative Press Index
PO Box 33109 Phone: (410)243-2471
Baltimore, MD 21218 Fax: (410)235-5325
Publication E-mail: altpress@igc.apc.org
Publisher E-mail: altpress@igc.apc.org

Index to alternative (progressive) periodicals in humanities, journalism, and social sciences. **Subtitle:** An Index to Alternative and Radical Publications. **Founded:** 1969. **Freq:** Quarterly. **Print Method:** Offset. **Trim Size:** 8 1/2 x 11. **Cols./Page:** 3. **Col. Width:** 27 nonpareils. **Col. Depth:** 130 agate lines. **Key Personnel:** Les Wade, Editor; Charles D'Adamo, Editor, cdadamo@igc.apc.org. **ISSN:** 0002-662X. **Subscription Rates:** $50 reduced personal rate; $250 institutions. **Remarks:** Advertising not accepted. **URL:** http://www.nisc.com. **Alt. Formats:** CD-ROM.
Circ: Paid ‡550
Controlled ‡200

13311 American Journal of Epidemiology
111 Market Place Phone: (410)223-1600
Suite 840 Fax: (410)223-1620
Baltimore, MD 21202-6709
Science research and medicine journal. **Founded:** 1921. **Freq:** Semimonthly 2/mo. **Print Method:** Offset. **Trim Size:** 8 1/8 x 10 7/8. **Cols./Page:** 2. **Col. Width:** 52 nonpareils. **Col. Depth:** 98 agate lines. **Key Personnel:** Moyses Szklo, M.D., Editor-in-Chief. **ISSN:** 0002-9262. **Subscription Rates:** $250 other countries; $258 other countries; $15 single issue. **Remarks:** Accepts advertising. **URL:** http://11phweb.5ph.jhu.edu/pubs/jepi.
Ad Rates: BW: $995 **Circ:** ‡6,100

13312 American Journal of Mathematics
Johns Hopkins University Press
Johns Hopkins University Phone: (410)516-7411
Dept. of Mathematics
Baltimore, MD 21218
Publication E-mail: ajm@chow.mat.jhu.edu
Publisher E-mail: jlinfo@jhupress.jhu.edu

Journal covering applied and pure mathematics. **Founded:** 1878. **Freq:** Bimonthly. **Print Method:** Offset. **Trim Size:** 6 x 9. **Cols./Page:** 1. **Col. Width:** 52 nonpareils. **Col. Depth:** 98 agate lines. **Key Personnel:** Tara Dorai-Berry, Advertising Mgr.; Bernard Shiffman, Editor-in-Chief. **ISSN:** 0002-9327. **Subscription Rates:** $85 individuals; $18 single issue; $250 institutions. **Remarks:** Accepts advertising. **URL:** http://calliope.jhu.edu/journals/american_ journal_ of_ mathema.
Ad Rates: BW: $225 **Circ:** ‡2,100

13313 American Journal of Physical Medicine and Rehabilitation
Lippincott Williams & Wilkins
351 W. Camden St. Phone: (410)528-8517
Baltimore, MD 21201-2436 Fax: (410)528-4312
Free: (800)882-0483

Medical journal. **Subtitle:** Official Journal of the Association of Academic Physiatrists. **Founded:** 1921. **Freq:** Bimonthly. **Print Method:** Offset. **Trim Size:** 8 1/8 x 10 7/8. **Cols./Page:** 2. **Col. Width:** 32 nonpareils. **Col. Depth:** 119 agate lines. **Key Personnel:** Ernest W. Johnson, M.D., Editor; Beth Missett, Rep. **ISSN:** 0894-9115. **Subscription Rates:** $65 individuals; $85 other countries. **Remarks:** Accepts advertising.
Ad Rates: BW: $565 **Circ:** Paid ‡3,854
4C: $1,215 Non-paid ‡157

13314 American Journal of Roentgenology
Lippincott Williams & Wilkins
351 W. Camden St. Phone: (410)528-8517
Baltimore, MD 21201-2436 Fax: (410)528-4312
Free: (800)882-0483

Journal publishing orginal articles on general and diagnostic radiology. **Subtitle:** Official Journal of the American Roentgen Ray Society. **Founded:** 1906. **Freq:** Monthly. **Print Method:** Web offset. **Trim Size:** 8 3/8 x 10 7/8. **Cols./Page:** 2. **Col. Width:** 32 nonpareils. **Col. Depth:** 119 agate lines. **Key Personnel:** Robert N. Berk, M.D., Editor; Sherry Reed, Rep. **ISSN:** 0361-803X. **Subscription Rates:** $125 individuals; $135 other countries. **Remarks:** Accepts advertising.
Ad Rates: BW: $1,340 **Circ:** Paid ‡23,131
4C: $2,540 Non-paid ‡351

13315 Anagram
3505 N. Charles St.
Baltimore, MD 21218
Publication E-mail: anagram@jhunix.hcf-jhu.edu

Literary journal for Asian Americans. **Subtitle:** The Asian American Literary Journal. **Freq:** Annual. **Key Personnel:** Angela Lo, Editor-in-Chief. **Remarks:** Advertising not accepted. **URL:** http://www.jhu.edu/~anagram/index.html. **Formerly**: Asian Voices.
Circ: (Not Reported)

13316 Anesthesia & Analgesia
Lippincott Williams & Wilkins
351 W. Camden St. Phone: (410)528-8517
Baltimore, MD 21201-2436 Fax: (410)528-4312
Free: (800)882-0483

Medical journal. **Subtitle:** Official Journal of the International Anesthesia Research Society. **Founded:** 1921. **Freq:** Monthly. **Print Method:** Offset. **Trim Size:** 8 1/4 x 11. **Cols./Page:** 2. **Col. Width:** 3 1/4 inches. **Col. Depth:** 10 inches. **Key Personnel:** Ronald D. Miller, Editor; David Baker, Advertising Mgr. **ISSN:** 0003-2999. **Subscription Rates:** $157 individuals Domestic; $22 single issue. **Remarks:** Accepts advertising.
Ad Rates: BW: $955 **Circ:** ‡22,084
4C: $2,380

13317 The Annals of Dyslexia
The International Dyslexia Association
8600 LaSalle Rd. Phone: (410)296-0232
Chester Bldg. Fax: (410)321-5069
Suite 382
Baltimore, MD 21286-2044
Free: (800)222-3123

Journal containing scholarly papers presented at the IDA's annual conference. **Founded:** 1950. **Freq:** Annual. **Subscription Rates:** $18 nonmembers. **Remarks:** Advertising not accepted. **Formerly**: Bulletin of the Orton Society.
Circ: 12,000

13318 AUA News
Lippincott Williams & Wilkins
351 W. Camden St. Phone: (410)528-8517
Baltimore, MD 21201-2436 Fax: (410)528-4312
Free: (800)882-0483

Professional journal covering clinical and socio-economic issues regarding urology for urologists. **Founded:** 1996. **Freq:** Bimonthly. **Key Personnel:** Alma Wills, Publisher; Debbie Polly, Editor. **Remarks:** Accepts advertising.
Ad Rates: BW: $2,750 **Circ:** Combined 12,639
4C: $4,465

13319 Avenue News
The Avenue, Inc.
442 Eastern Blvd. Phone: (410)687-7775
Baltimore, MD 21221 Fax: (410)687-7881

Community newspaper (tabloid). **Founded:** 1974. **Freq:** Weekly (Thurs.). **Print Method:** Offset. **Cols./Page:** 6. **Col. Width:** 18 nonpareils. **Col. Depth:** 196 agate lines. **Key**

Personnel: Jay Livingston, Editor; Ken Coldwell, Publisher. **Remarks:** Accepts advertising.
Ad Rates: GLR: $1.11 **Circ:** Free 40,000
PCI: $15.60

13320 Baltimore Afro-American
The Afro-American Co.
2519 N Charles St. Phone: (410)554-8200
Baltimore, MD 21218 Fax: (410)554-8213
Free: (800)AFRO-892

Black community newspaper. **Founded:** 1892. **Freq:** Weekly (Sat.). **Cols./Page:** 6. **Col. Width:** 24 nonpareils. **Col. Depth:** 301 agate lines. **Key Personnel:** John J. Oliver, Publisher. **Subscription Rates:** $26 individuals; $46 two years; $58 three years. **Remarks:** Accepts advertising. **Available Online.**
Ad Rates: BW: $5,646.33 **Circ:** Sat. ★**9,941**
4C: $6,096.33
SAU: $43.77

13321 Baltimore Business Journal
American City Business Journals
111 Market Pl., Ste. 720 Phone: (410)576-1161
Baltimore, MD 21202 Fax: (410)576-3112
Publication E-mail: baltimore@amcity.com

Newspaper reporting Baltimore business news. **Founded:** 1983. **Freq:** Weekly. **Print Method:** Offset. **Trim Size:** 11 1/4 x 15. **Cols./Page:** 4. **Key Personnel:** James Breiner, Publisher, jbreiner@bbjournal.com; Terence O'Hara, Editor, tohara@bbjournal.com; Joanna Sullivan, Managing Editor, jsullivan@bbjournal.com. **Subscription Rates:** $65.71 individuals. **Remarks:** Accepts advertising. **Available Online. URL:** http://www.amcity.com/baltimore.
Ad Rates: GLR: $7.50 **Circ:** Paid ★**9,217**
BW: $3,080
4C: $3,680
PCI: $55

13322 The Baltimore Chronicle
30 W. 25th St. Phone: (410)243-4141
Baltimore, MD 21218
Publication E-mail: baltchron@charm.net

Local newspaper. **Founded:** Apr. 3, 1973. **Freq:** Monthly. **Print Method:** Offset. **Trim Size:** 11 1/2 x 16. **Cols./Page:** 5. **Col. Width:** 24 nonpareils. **Col. Depth:** 194 agate lines. **Key Personnel:** Larry Krause, Editor and Publisher; Alice Cherbonnier, Managing Editor. **Subscription Rates:** $10 by mail. **Remarks:** Accepts advertising. **URL:** http://www.charm.net/~marc/chronicle.
Ad Rates: GLR: $.70 **Circ:** Paid ‡450
BW: $539 Free ‡28,000
PCI: $9.80

13323 Baltimore City Paper
Scranton Times
812 Park Ave. Phone: (410)889-6600
Baltimore, MD 21201-4847 Fax: (410)523-2222

Lifestyle and entertainment newspaper (tabloid). **Founded:** 1978. **Freq:** Weekly (Wed.). **Print Method:** Offset. **Cols./Page:** 5. **Col. Width:** 26 nonpareils. **Col. Depth:** 182 agate lines. **Key Personnel:** Donald Farley, V.P./Gen. Mgr. **Subscription Rates:** Free; $35 by mail. **Remarks:** Accepts advertising.
Ad Rates: BW: $1,975 **Circ:** Non-paid 84,395

13324 Baltimore Gay Paper
Baltimore Gay Paper Inc.
PO Box 22575 Phone: (410)837-7748
Baltimore, MD 21203 Fax: (410)837-8512
Publication E-mail: bgpaper@cris.com

Newspaper publishing news and articles of interest to the Baltimore gay community. **Founded:** Sept. 1979. **Freq:** Semimonthly. **Print Method:** Offset. **Trim Size:** 10 x 14 3/4. **Cols./Page:** 4. **Col. Width:** 14.25 picas. **Col. Depth:** 14 inches. **Key Personnel:** Mike Chase, Editor; Mike Cathy, Assoc. Editor. **Subscription Rates:** Free; $35 by mail. **Remarks:** Color advertising not accepted. **URL:** http://www.cris.com/~bgpaper.
Ad Rates: BW: $495 **Circ:** Paid ‡3,000
PCI: $10.75 Free ‡10,000

13325 The Baltimore Guide
R & B Publishing Co.
526 S. Conkling St. Phone: (410)732-6600
Baltimore, MD 21224 Fax: (410)732-6336
Publication E-mail: ads@ebguide.com

Community newspaper (tabloid). **Founded:** 1927. **Freq:** Weekly (Thurs.). **Print Method:** Offset. **Trim Size:** 10 1/4 x 13 3/4. **Cols./Page:** 5 and 6. **Col. Width:** 22 nonpareils. **Col. Depth:** 195 agate lines. **Key Personnel:** Jacqueline Watts, Editor, phone (410)732-6603, editor@ebguide.com; Richard W. Sandza, Publisher, rbpublisher@ebguide.com. **Subscription Rates:** Free; $15 by mail. **Remarks:** Accepts advertising.
Ad Rates: GLR: $1.15 **Circ:** Paid ♦**202**
BW: $1,120 Non-paid ♦**36,538**
4C: $1,420
PCI: $16.10

13326 Baltimore Magazine
10000 Lancaster St., Ste. 400 Phone: (410)752-4200
Baltimore, MD 21202 Fax: (410)625-0280
Free: (800)935-0838
Publication E-mail: smarge@baltimoremag.com

Magazine on regional news. **Founded:** Oct. 1907. **Freq:** Monthly. **Print Method:** Offset. Uses mats. **Trim Size:** 8 1/8 x 10 7/8. **Cols./Page:** 3. **Col. Width:** 26 nonpareils. **Col. Depth:** 140 agate lines. **Key Personnel:** Dick Basoco, Chief Operating Officer, bdick@baltimoremag.com; Amanda White, Art Director, wamanda@baltimoremag.com; Ken Iglehart, Managing Editor, iken@baltimoremag.com; Georgia Huff, Research Dir., hgeorgia@baltimoremag.com; Margaret Gucoff, Managing Editor, gmeg@baltimoremag.com; Henry Priller, Circulation Mgr., phenry@baltimoremag.com; Jenny Bishop, Advertising Dir., bjenny@baltimoremag.com. **ISSN:** 0005-4453. **Subscription Rates:** $18 individuals; $2.95 single issue. **Remarks:** Accepts advertising. **URL:** http://www.softaid.net/bhtiuore.wag.
Ad Rates: BW: $4,095 **Circ:** Paid ★**60,626**
4C: $6,155
PCI: $95

13327 The Baltimore Sun
501 N. Calvert St. Phone: (410)332-6000
Baltimore, MD 21278-0001 Fax: (410)752-6049
Free: (800)829-8000

General newspaper. **Founded:** 1837. **Freq:** Mon.-Sun. (morn.). **Print Method:** Offset. **Cols./Page:** 6. **Col. Width:** 25 nonpareils. **Col. Depth:** 294 agate lines. **Key Personnel:** Michael Waller, Publisher; John Carroll, Editor, phone (410)332-6496; William Marimow, Managing Editor, phone (410)332-6088; Steve Proctor, Assistant Managing Editor, phone (410)332-6120. **Subscription Rates:** $46.80 morning; $52 Sunday; $52 Sunday. **Remarks:** Accepts advertising. **Online:** DataTimes Corporation; Dialog (The Dialog Corporation); LEXIS-NEXIS; CompuServe Information Service. **Alt. Formats:** CD-ROM. **Feature Editors:** Molly Dunham, *Sports*, phone (410)332-6717; Kim Marcum, *Features*, phone (410)332-6106; John McIntyre, *Columnist*, phone (410)332-6133; Gerald Merrell, *Financial/Business*; Jeff Price, *Travel*, phone (410)332-6748.
Ad Rates: SAU: $140.20 **Circ:** Mon.-Sat. ★**314,033**
Sun. ★**478,516**

13328 Baltimore's Child
11 Dutton Ct. Phone: (410)367-5883
Baltimore, MD 21228 Fax: (410)719-9342
Publication E-mail: baltochild@aol.com

Local parenting magazine. **Founded:** Mar. 1983. **Freq:** Monthly. **Print Method:** Web press. **Cols./Page:** 6. **Col. Width:** 1/9-16 inches. **Col. Depth:** 12 inches. **Key Personnel:** Joanne Giza, Editor, phone (410)367-5883, fax (410)719-9342, plm05026@mindspring.com; Sharon Keech, Publisher. **Subscription Rates:** $15.75 local annual. **Remarks:** Accepts advertising. **Online:** FAMILY COM. **URL:** http://www.baltimoreschild.com.
Ad Rates: BW: $2111 **Circ:** Controlled ‡65,000
4C: $2611
PCI: $30.50

13329 BICYCLE USA
League of American Bicyclists
190 W. Ostend St., No. 120 Phone: (410)539-3399
Baltimore, MD 21230-3755 Fax: (410)539-3496

Magazine including a calendar of cycling events and articles on bicycle touring, legislation, history, riding techniques, and medical and technical topics. **Subtitle:** Membership magazine of the League of American Bicyclists. **Founded:** 1880. **Freq:** 6/year. **Print Method:** Offset. **Trim Size:** 8.25" x 10.75". **Cols./Page:** 4 and 3. **Col. Width:** 20 and 28 nonpareils. **Col. Depth:** 140 agate lines. **Key Personnel:** Donald W. Tighe, Editor. **ISSN:** 0747-0371. **Subscription Rates:** $30 individuals. **Remarks:** Accepts advertising. **Online:** America Online, Inc.
Ad Rates: BW: $875 **Circ:** ‡32,000
4C: $1,325

13330 Bookbird
Morgan State University Phone: (410)319-3958
Dept. Of English and Language Arts Fax: (410)319-3166
Baltimore, MD 21251-4001
Scholarly journal covering topics in children's literature worldwide. **Founded:** 1963. **Freq:** Quarterly. **Print Method:** Offset. **Key Personnel:** Meena Khorana, Editor-in-Chief, meenakh@aol.com; Dennis Butler-Klinghammer, Business Mgr.; Carol Garrett, Circulation Mgr. **ISSN:** 0006-7377. **Subscription Rates:** $40 individuals; $10 single issue. **Remarks:** Accepts advertising.
Ad Rates: BW: $400 **Circ:** Combined 1,650
4C: $750

13331 Braille Monitor
National Federation of the Blind
1800 Johnson St. Phone: (410)659-9314
Baltimore, MD 21230-4898 Fax: (410)685-5653
Publisher E-mail: nfb@iamdigex.net

Magazine covering news, activities, and programs of the National Federation of the Blind. **Freq:** Monthly. **Key Personnel:** Barbara Pierce, Editor. **ISSN:** 0006-8829. **Subscription Rates:** Free to members and visually-impaired individuals. **Remarks:** Advertising not accepted. **URL:** http://www.nfb.org. **Alt. Formats:** Audio tape; Braille.
Circ: Non-paid 40,000

13332 Bulletin of the History of Medicine
Johns Hopkins University Press
Johns Hopkins University Phone: (410)955-3179
316 Welch Medical Library Fax: (410)550-6819
1900 E. Monument St.
Baltimore, MD 21205
Publication E-mail: muse@muse.jhu.edu
Publisher E-mail: jlinfo@jhupress.jhu.edu

Official publication of the American Association for the History of Medicine. Journal covering the Social and Scientific Aspects of the History of Medicine Worldwide. **Founded:** 1933. **Freq:** Quarterly. **Print Method:** Offset. **Trim Size:** 6 x 9. **Cols./Page:** 1. **Col. Width:** 52 nonpareils. **Col. Depth:** 102 agate lines. **Key Personnel:** Gert H. Brieger, Editor; Jerome J. Bylebyl, Editor; Tara Dorai-Berry, Advertising Mgr.; Susan Abrams, Assistant Editor, sab@welchlink.jhu.edu. **ISSN:** 0007-5140. **Subscription Rates:** $32 individuals; $78 single issue; $9.50 institutions. **Remarks:** Accepts advertising. **URL:** http://muse.jhu.edu.
Ad Rates: BW: $285 **Circ:** ‡2,880

13333 The Catholic Review
Cathedral Foundation, Inc.
320 Cathedral St. Phone: (410)547-5380
PO Box 777 Fax: (410)385-0113
Baltimore, MD 21203
Publication E-mail: crletters@aol.com

Newspaper of the Archdiocese of Baltimore. **Founded:** 1913. **Freq:** Weekly (Wed.). **Print Method:** Offset. **Trim Size:** 22 x 27 1/2. **Cols./Page:** 6. **Col. Width:** 2 1/16 inches. **Col. Depth:** 21 inches. **Key Personnel:** Daniel L. Medinger, Editor, dmedinger@aol.com; David Hoeckel, Advertising Mgr. **ISSN:** 0008-8315. **Subscription Rates:** $25 individuals. **Remarks:** Accepts advertising.
Ad Rates: BW: $2,898 **Circ:** ‡68,000
4C: $3,398
PCI: $34

13334 Circulation
Lippincott Williams & Wilkins
351 W. Camden St. Phone: (410)528-8517
Baltimore, MD 21201-2436 Fax: (410)528-4312
Free: (800)882-0483

Journal containing original articles on cardiovascular, clinical, and laboratory investigation. **Founded:** 1950. **Freq:** Weekly. **Print Method:** Offset. **Trim Size:** 8 1/4 x 10 7/8. **Cols./Page:** 2. **Col. Width:** 38 nonpareils. **Col. Depth:** 130 agate lines. **Key Personnel:** James T. Willerson, MD, Editor, phone (713)794-6585, fax (713)794-6810, dstjohn@heart.med.uth.tmc.edu; Cara Kaufman, Publisher, phone (410)528-8514, fax (410)528-4312, cskaufma@lww.com; Joe Jackson, Advertising Mgr., phone (973)403-7677, fax (973)403-7795, bartjack@aol.com. **ISSN:** 0009-7322. **Subscription Rates:** $223; $394 other countries; $20 single issue; $25 single issue other countries. **Remarks:** Accepts advertising. **URL:** http://www.circulationaha.org.
Ad Rates: BW: $2,248 **Circ:** Paid ‡25,000
4C: $1,660

13335 Circulation Research
Lippincott Williams & Wilkins
351 W. Camden St. Phone: (410)528-8517
Baltimore, MD 21201-2436 Fax: (410)528-4312
Free: (800)882-0483

Journal covering basic research on the cardiovascular system. **Founded:** 1953. **Freq:** Semimonthly. **Print Method:** Offset. **Trim Size:** 8 1/8 x 10 7/8. **Cols./Page:** 2. **Col. Width:** 38 nonpareils. **Col. Depth:** 130 agate lines. **Key Personnel:** Stephen Vatner, M.D., Editor, phone (412)359-8088, fax (412)359-8410; Cara Kaufman, Publisher, phone (410)528-8514, fax (410)528-4312, cskaufma@lww.com; Joe Jackson, Advertising Mgr., phone (973)403-7677, fax (973)403-7795, bartjack@aol.com. **ISSN:** 0009-7330. **Subscription Rates:**

$267 U.S. and other countries; $329; $25 single issue; $35 single issue foreign. **URL:** http://www.circresaha.org.
Ad Rates: BW: $756 **Circ:** Paid ‡3,100
4C: $1,380

13336 Critical Care Medicine
Lippincott Williams & Wilkins
351 W. Camden St. Phone: (410)528-8517
Baltimore, MD 21201-2436 Fax: (410)528-4312
Free: (800)882-0483

Interdisciplinary journal for ICU and CCU specialists. **Subtitle:** Official Journal of the Society of Critical Care Medicine. **Founded:** 1973. **Freq:** Monthly. **Print Method:** Offset. **Trim Size:** 8 3/8 x 10 7/8. **Cols./Page:** 2. **Col. Width:** 32 nonpareils. **Col. Depth:** 119 agate lines. **Key Personnel:** Bart Chernow, M.D., Editor; Stacey Fernandez, Rep. **ISSN:** 0090-3493. **Subscription Rates:** $109 individuals; $169 institutions; $64 students; $214 out of country. **Remarks:** Accepts advertising.
Ad Rates: BW: $1,155 **Circ:** Paid 14,089
4C: $2,120 Non-paid ‡351

13337 Current Surgery
Lippincott Williams & Wilkins
351 W. Camden St. Phone: (410)528-8517
Baltimore, MD 21201-2436 Fax: (410)528-4312
Free: (800)882-0483

Professional journal covering continuing education for surgical residents and general surgeons. **Founded:** 1943. **Freq:** 9/year (March/April, July/August, and November/December combined). **Trim Size:** 8 1/8 x 10 7/8. **Key Personnel:** Walter J. Pories, M.D., Editor; Gary Walchli, VP, Advertising Sales; Steve Tauber, Advertising Sales Mgr. **Remarks:** Accepts advertising.
Ad Rates: BW: $800 **Circ:** Combined 1,542
4C: $995

13338 The Daily Record
The Daily Record Co.
11 E. Saratoga St. Phone: (410)752-1717
Baltimore, MD 21202 Fax: (410)332-0698
Free: (800)296-8181
Publication E-mail: adv@mddailyrecord.com

Daily Bussiness Newspaper reporting news and features on business, real estate, technology, healthcare and law. **Subtitle:** Business and Legal News of Maryland. **Founded:** Oct. 2, 1888. **Freq:** Mon.-Sat. **Print Method:** Web offset. **Trim Size:** 11 1/2 x 17 1/2. **Cols./Page:** 4. **Col. Width:** 2 5/16 inches. **Col. Depth:** 15 3/4 inches. **Key Personnel:** Keith I. Girard, Editor, girard@mddailyrecord.com; Christopher Eddings, Publisher, eddings@mddailyrecord.com. **USPS:** 145-120. **Subscription Rates:** $174 individuals. **Remarks:** Accepts advertising. **URL:** http://www.mddailyrecord.com. **Formerly:** Warfield's Business Record.
Ad Rates: BW: $2,600 **Circ:** Paid ‡7,597
PCI: $11.50 Free ‡1,747

13339 Dirty Linen
Box 66600 Phone: (410)583-7973
Baltimore, MD 21239-6600 Fax: (410)337-6735
Publisher E-mail: office@dirtylinen.com

Consumer magazine covering folk and world music. **Founded:** 1983. **Freq:** Bimonthly. **Print Method:** Sheet Fed. **Trim Size:** 8 3/8 x 10 7/8. **Cols./Page:** 3. **Col. Width:** 2 3/8 inches. **Col. Depth:** 9 5/8 inches. **Key Personnel:** Paul Hartman, Editor; Linda Cohn, Advertising Mgr.; Susan Hartman, General Mgr. **ISSN:** 1047-4315. **Subscription Rates:** $22 individuals; $27 Canada; $44 other countries; $5 single issue. **Remarks:** Accepts advertising. **URL:** http://www.dirtylinen.com.
Ad Rates: BW: $1,050 **Circ:** Combined 20,000
4C: $1,475

13340 Disability Notes
Social Security Administration
545 Altmeyer Bldg. Phone: (410)965-9022
Baltimore, MD 21235 Fax: (410)965-6503

Newsletter focusing on disability programs offered by Social Security and other agencies. **Founded:** 1992. **Freq:** Quarterly. **Cols./Page:** 3. **Key Personnel:** Julian A. Maxwell, juliana.maxwell@ssa.gov'. **Subscription Rates:** Free. **Remarks:** Advertising not accepted. **URL:** http://www.ssa.gov. **Alt. Formats:** Braille.
Circ: Non-paid 5,400

13341 English Literary History (ELH)
Johns Hopkins University Press
Department of English Phone: (410)516-8948
Gilman 146
Johns Hopkins University
Baltimore, MD 21218
Publisher E-mail: jlinfo@jhupress.jhu.edu

Journal covering the historical interpretation of major English and American literary works. **Founded:** 1934. **Freq:** Quarterly. **Print Method:** Offset. **Trim Size:** 6 x 9. **Cols./Page:** 1. **Col. Width:** 52 nonpareils. **Col. Depth:** 105 agate lines. **Key Personnel:** Ronald Paulson, Editor; Tara Dorai-Berry, Advertising Mgr. **ISSN:** 0013-8304. **Subscription Rates:** $22 individuals; $7.5 single issue industry; $73 institutions. **Remarks:** Accepts advertising.
Ad Rates: BW: $275 **Circ:** ‡2130

13342 Epidemiology
Lippincott Williams & Wilkins
351 W. Camden St. Phone: (410)528-8517
Baltimore, MD 21201-2436 Fax: (410)528-4312
Free: (800)882-0483

Professional medical journal for epidemiologists and related disciplines. **Founded:** 1990. **Freq:** Bimonthly. **Trim Size:** 8 1/8 x 10 7/8. **Key Personnel:** Kenneth J. Rothman, M.D., Editor; Gary Walchli, VP, Advertising Sales; Steve Tauber, Advertising Sales Mgr.; Carol Brooks, National Sales Mgr., cbrooks@wwilkins.com. **Remarks:** Accepts advertising.
Ad Rates: BW: $495 **Circ:** Combined 1,747
4C: $1,230

13343 Flower of the Forest Black Genealogical Journal
Mullac Publishing
1364 Walker Ave. Phone: (410)323-3883
Baltimore, MD 21239
Journal covering Black genealogical and historical issues. **Founded:** Oct. 1982. **Freq:** Annual. **Subscription Rates:** $7 individuals. **Remarks:** Advertising not accepted.
Circ: (Not Reported)

13344 Foot & Ankle
Lippincott Williams & Wilkins
351 W. Camden St. Phone: (410)528-8517
Baltimore, MD 21201-2436 Fax: (410)528-4312
Free: (800)882-0483

Medical journal. **Subtitle:** Official Journal of the American Orthopaedic Foot and Ankle Society. **Founded:** 1980. **Freq:** Monthly. **Print Method:** Offset. **Trim Size:** 8 1/2 x 11. **Cols./Page:** 2. **Col. Width:** 32 nonpareils. **Col. Depth:** 119 agate lines. **Key Personnel:** Kenneth A. Johnson, M.D., Editor; Stacey Fernandez, Rep. **ISSN:** 1071-1007. **Subscription Rates:** $95 individuals; $12 single issue; $14 single issue Foreign; $110 institutions Domestic; $125 individuals Foreign; $140 institutions, other countries. **Remarks:** Accepts advertising.
Ad Rates: BW: $550 **Circ:** Paid ‡3,941
4C: $1,275 Non-paid ‡48

13345 Future Reflections
National Federation of the Blind
1800 Johnson St. Phone: (410)659-9314
Baltimore, MD 21230-4898 Fax: (410)685-5653
Publisher E-mail: nfb@iamdigex.net

Journal offering practical guidance in the day-to-day aspects of raising blind children of all ages. **Subtitle:** The Natl. Federation of the Blind Magazine for Parents of Blind Children. **Founded:** 1981. **Freq:** Quarterly. **Trim Size:** 8 1/2 x 11. **Cols./Page:** 2. **Col. Width:** 3 1/3 inches. **Col. Depth:** 8 1/2 inches. **Key Personnel:** Barbara Cheadle, Editor and Publisher. **ISSN:** 0883-3419. **Subscription Rates:** $8 individuals; $15 nonmembers. **Remarks:** Advertising not accepted. **URL:** http://www.nfb.org; nfb@iamdigex.net. **Alt. Formats:** Audio tape.
Circ: Combined ‡12,000

13346 The Gazette
Johns Hopkins University
3400 N. Charles St. Phone: (410)516-8514
Baltimore, MD 21218 Fax: (410)516-5251
Publication E-mail: gazette@resource.ca.jhu.edu.

Tabloid containing articles on research and scholarly activities of faculty and information of general interest to faculty, students, and staff of the Johns Hopkins University. **Founded:** Sept. 7, 1971. **Freq:** Weekly (Mon.) (biweekly, June-Aug.). **Print Method:** Offset. **Trim Size:** 11 1/2 x 16. **Cols./Page:** 4. **Col. Width:** 14 picas. **Key Personnel:** Lois Perschetz, Editor, lwp@jhu.edu; Julie Wittlesberger, Advertising Mgr., phone (410)343-3371, fax (410)343-3371, gazellegrp@aol.com. **Subscription Rates:** Free; $26 individuals. **Remarks:** Accepts advertising. **Available Online. URL:** http://www.jhu.edu:80/~gazette/. **Formerly:** Johns Hopkins University Gazette.
Ad Rates: BW: $750 **Circ:** Free ‡16,000

13347 The General
Monarch Avalon, Inc.
4517 Hartford Rd. Phone: (410)254-9200
Baltimore, MD 21214 Fax: (410)254-0991
Publication E-mail: ahgeneral@avalonhill.com
Publisher E-mail: publisher@girlslife.com

Consumer magazine on games and gaming. **Founded:** Apr. 1966. **Freq:** Bimonthly. **Print Method:** Sheetfed lithography. **Trim Size:** 8 1/2 x 11. **Cols./Page:** 3. **Col. Width:** 14.5 picas. **Col. Depth:** 10 inches. **Key Personnel:** Stuart Tucker, Editor; Ed Weiss, Advertising Mgr.; Jack Dott, Circulation Mgr. **ISSN:** 0888-1081. **Subscription Rates:** $18 individuals; $36 Canada and Mexico; $48 other countries; $4.95 single issue. **Remarks:** Accepts advertising.
Ad Rates: 4C: $1,800 **Circ:** Paid 48,500

13348 Girls' Life
Monarch Avalon, Inc.
4517 Hartford Rd. Phone: (410)254-9200
Baltimore, MD 21214 Fax: (410)254-0991
Publication E-mail: editorial@girlslife.com
Publisher E-mail: publisher@girlslife.com

Consumer magazine for girls and Girl Scouts ages 8-14 years. **Founded:** Aug. 1994. **Freq:** Bimonthly. **Print Method:** Web offset. **Trim Size:** 8 1/4 x 10 1/2. **Cols./Page:** 3. **Col. Width:** 2 1/4 inches. **Col. Depth:** 9 1/2 inches. **Key Personnel:** Karen Bokram, Publisher, karen@girlslife.com; Jennifer Brown, Advertising Mgr.; Kelly White, Senior Editor; Edward Weiss, Marketing Dir.; Suzanne Long, Circulation Mgr. **ISSN:** 1078-3326. **Subscription Rates:** $17.85 individuals; $13.45 Girl Scout members; $2.95 single issue. **Remarks:** Accepts advertising.
Ad Rates: BW: $12,375 **Circ:** Combined ‡1,000,000
4C: $13,750

13349 Goucher College Quarterly
Goucher College
1021 Dulaney Valley Rd. Phone: (410)337-6180
Baltimore, MD 21204
College Alumni magazine. **Founded:** 1921. **Freq:** Quarterly. **Print Method:** Letterpress and offset. **Cols./Page:** 3 and 2. **Col. Width:** 27 and 42 nonpareils. **Col. Depth:** 133 agate lines. **Remarks:** Advertising not accepted.
Circ: 15,000

13350 The Greyhound
Loyola College
100 W. Coldspring Ln. T05E Phone: (410)617-2282
Baltimore, MD 21210 Fax: (410)617-2982
Publication E-mail: greyhound@loyola.edu

Collegiate newspaper. **Subtitle:** Celebrating 70 years of Strong Truths Well Lived. **Founded:** 1927. **Freq:** Weekly (Tues.). **Cols./Page:** 5. **Col. Width:** 2 inches. **Col. Depth:** 15 inches. **Key Personnel:** Elizabeth Walker, Editor-in-Chief, phone (410)617-2352, ewalker@loyola.edu; Thomas Panarese, Editor-in-Chief, phone (410)617-2282, tpanarese@loyola.edu. **Subscription Rates:** Free on campus. **Remarks:** Accepts advertising Adoption services.
Ad Rates: BW: $535 **Circ:** Free 3,000
SAU: $8.00

13351 Health Physics
Lippincott Williams & Wilkins
351 W. Camden St. Phone: (410)528-8517
Baltimore, MD 21201-2436 Fax: (410)528-4312
Free: (800)882-0483

Journal presenting information dealing with the protection of man and his environment from unwarranted ionizing and nonionizing radiation exposure. **Subtitle:** Official Journal of the Health Physics Society. **Founded:** 1958. **Freq:** 12/year. **Print Method:** Offset. **Trim Size:** 8 1/4 x 11. **Cols./Page:** 2. **Col. Width:** 35 nonpareils. **Col. Depth:** 123 agate lines. **Key Personnel:** Richard J. Vetter, Editor; Arnold Kranzler, Advertising Mgr. **ISSN:** 0017-9078. **Subscription Rates:** $169 individuals; $633 institutions; $55 single issue. **Remarks:** Accepts advertising.
Ad Rates: BW: $700 **Circ:** 8,860
4C: $1,500

13352 Hispanic Engineer
Career Communications Group, Inc.
729 E. Pratt St., No. 504 Phone: (410)244-7101
Baltimore, MD 21202 Fax: (410)752-1837
Free: (800)932-7101
Publisher E-mail: ccgmag@aol.com

Student/Professional magazine. **Subtitle:** Information Technology. **Founded:** 1984. **Freq:** Quarterly. **Print Method:** Offset. **Trim Size:** 8 1/2 x 11. **Key Personnel:** Carmela Mellado, Editor, phone (213)727-9914, fax (213)727-9384; Tyrone D. Taborn, C.E.O., phone (410)244-7101; Jean Hamilton, Business Mgr. **ISSN:** 7350-9286. **Subscription Rates:** $26. **Remarks:** Accepts advertising. **URL:** http://www.ccg.mag.com. **Alt. Formats:** CD-ROM.
Ad Rates: BW: $3,230 **Circ:** ‡15,000
4C: $4,030

13353 International Chinese Snuff Bottle
International Chinese Snuff Bottle Society
2601 N. Charles St. Phone: (410)467-9400
Baltimore, MD 21218 Fax: (410)243-3451
Publisher E-mail: icsbs@worldnet.att.net

Scholarly publication covering Chinese snuff bottles and

related topics. **Founded:** Dec. 1974. **Freq:** 3/year, May, September, and January. **Trim Size:** 8 1/2 x 11. **Key Personnel:** Berthe Ford, Editor. **ISSN:** 0734-5534. **Subscription Rates:** Included in membership. **Remarks:** Accepts advertising. **URL:** http://www.snuffbottle.org. **Formerly**: Chinese Snuff Bottle Society of America Newsletter (1974).
Circ: (Not Reported)

13354 International Journal of Health Services
Baywood Publishing Co., Inc.
Dr. Vicente Navarro Phone: (410)955-3280
Johns Hopkins University Fax: (410)955-3281
624 N. Broadway, 448 Hampton House
Baltimore, MD 21205-1901
Publisher E-mail: baywood@baywood.com

International health services journal covering social policy, political economy, sociology, history, philosophy, ethics, and law. **Founded:** 1970. **Freq:** Quarterly. **Print Method:** Offset. **Trim Size:** 6 x 9. **Cols./Page:** 1. **Col. Width:** 4 1/2 inches. **Col. Depth:** 7 1/2 inches. **Key Personnel:** Vicente Navarro, Editor; Stuart Cohen, Publisher; Lorna Cohen, Advertising Mgr.; S. Edwards, Circulation Mgr. **ISSN:** 0020-7314. **Subscription Rates:** $40.50 U.S. and Canada; $45.35 other countries; $123.50 Industry; $128.35 Industry, other countries. **Remarks:** Advertising not accepted.
Circ: (Not Reported)

13355 JMPT: Journal of Manipulative and Physiological Therapeutics
Lippincott Williams & Wilkins
351 W. Camden St. Phone: (410)528-8517
Baltimore, MD 21201-2436 Fax: (410)528-4312
Free: (800)882-0483

Medical journal. **Subtitle:** Official Journal of the National College of Chiropractic. **Founded:** 1978. **Freq:** 9/year. **Print Method:** Offset. **Trim Size:** 8 3/8 x 10 7/8. **Cols./Page:** 2. **Col. Width:** 32 nonpareils. **Col. Depth:** 119 agate lines. **Key Personnel:** Dana J. Lawrence, D.C., Editor; Joyce Michael, Rep. **ISSN:** 0161-4754. **Subscription Rates:** $78 individuals; $108 industry. **Remarks:** Accepts advertising.
Ad Rates: BW: $410 **Circ:** Paid ‡3,806
4C: $1,035 Non-paid ‡103

13356 Johns Hopkins Magazine
Johns Hopkins University
3400 N. Charles St. Phone: (410)516-8514
Baltimore, MD 21218 Fax: (410)516-5251

Alumni magazine featuring general interest articles and medical updates. **Founded:** 1950. **Freq:** 5/year. **Print Method:** Offset. **Trim Size:** 8 1/4 x 10 7/8. **Cols./Page:** 3. **Col. Width:** 13 picas. **Col. Depth:** 9 3/8 inches. **Key Personnel:** Sue De Pasquale, Editor. **Subscription Rates:** Free to qualified subscribers; $18 institutions. **Remarks:** Accepts advertising.
Ad Rates: BW: $2,250 **Circ:** Controlled ‡115,000
4C: $3,330

13357 The Johns Hopkins News-Letter
Centaur Press
Shriver Hall 6 Phone: (410)516-6000
3400 N. Charles St. Fax: (410)516-6565
Baltimore, MD 21218
Publication E-mail: news.letter@jhu.edu

College newspaper. **Founded:** 1897. **Freq:** Weekly (Thurs.). **Print Method:** Offset. **Trim Size:** 13 x 21 1/2. **Cols./Page:** 6. **Col. Width:** 2 inches. **Col. Depth:** 21 inches. **Key Personnel:** Gianna Abruzzo, Editor-in-Chief; Doug Steinke, Editor-in-Chief; Andrew Pergam, Business Mgr. **Subscription Rates:** $40 individuals; $25 1/2 year. **Available Online. URL:** http://www.jhu.edu/~newslett.
Ad Rates: BW: $750 **Circ:** Free 7,000
4C: $1,150
SAU: $6.60
PCI: $8

13358 The Josephite Harvest
St. Joseph's Society of the Sacred Heart
1130 N. Calvert St. Phone: (410)727-3386
Baltimore, MD 21202-3802 Fax: (410)752-8571
Publication E-mail: harvestssj@aol.com

Magazine showcasing the work of the Josephite Apostolate. **Founded:** 1888. **Freq:** Quarterly. **Trim Size:** 8 1/2 x 11. **Key Personnel:** Rev. Joseph C. Verrett, S.S.J., Editor. **ISSN:** 0021-7603. **Subscription Rates:** By offering; $5 suggested. **Remarks:** Advertising not accepted.
Circ: Paid 15,000
Free 70,000

13359 Journal of the American Academy of Child and Adolescent Psychiatry
Lippincott Williams & Wilkins
351 W. Camden St. Phone: (410)528-8517
Baltimore, MD 21201-2436 Fax: (410)528-4312
Free: (800)882-0483

Child psychiatry journal. **Founded:** 1962. **Freq:** Bimonthly. **Print Method:** Web offset. **Trim Size:** 8 3/8 x 10 7/8. **Cols./Page:** 2. **Col. Width:** 40 nonpareils. **Col. Depth:** 112 agate lines. **Key Personnel:** John F. McDermott Jr., M.D., Contact; Joyce Michael, Rep. **ISSN:** 0890-8567. **Subscription Rates:** $90 individuals; $115 industry. **Remarks:** Accepts advertising.
Ad Rates: BW: $765 **Circ:** Paid ‡8,045
4C: $1,540 Non-paid ‡116

13360 Journal of the American Geriatrics Society
Lippincott Williams & Wilkins
351 W. Camden St. Phone: (410)528-4000
Baltimore, MD 21201 Fax: (410)528-4312
Free: (800)882-0483

Medical journal reporting developments in the clinical fields of geriatric medicine and gerontology. **Founded:** 1953. **Freq:** Monthly. **Print Method:** Offset. **Trim Size:** 8 1/8 x 10 7/8. **Cols./Page:** 2. **Col. Width:** 3 1/4 inches. **Col. Depth:** 10 inches. **Key Personnel:** William Applegate, Editor, phone (901)448-5903, fax (901)448-7041, wapplegate@utmem1.utmem.edu; Al Lucchesi, Contact, phone (215)238-4403, fax (215)238-4461, alucches@lww.com. **ISSN:** 0002-8614. **Subscription Rates:** $161 individuals; $289 institutions. **Remarks:** Accepts advertising.
Ad Rates: BW: $1,365 **Circ:** ‡9,228
4C: $2,965

13361 The Journal of the Association for Persons with Severe Handicaps
TASH
29 W. Susquehanna Ave., Ste. 210 Phone: (410)828-8274
Baltimore, MD 21204 Fax: (410)828-6706
Free: (800)482-TASH
Publisher E-mail: tash@tash.org

Special education journal presenting articles that report original research, authoritative and comprehensive reviews, and conceptual and practical position papers offering new directions for people with disabilities. **Founded:** Sept. 1975. **Freq:** Quarterly. **Trim Size:** 6 1/4 x 8 3/4. **Key Personnel:** Linda Bambara, Editor, phone (610)758-3271, lmbi@leigh.edu. **ISSN:** 0274-9483. **Subscription Rates:** $88 individuals; $45 parents, self-advocates; $230 schools, libraries, universities, agencies. **Remarks:** Accepts advertising. **Online:** UMI. **Alt. Formats:** Audio tape; Microform. **Formerly**: American Association for the Education of the Severely & Profoundly Handicapped Review (1980).
Ad Rates: BW: $380 **Circ:** Controlled ‡4,000

13362 Journal of Developmental & Behavioral Pediatrics
Lippincott Williams & Wilkins
351 W. Camden St. Phone: (410)528-8517
Baltimore, MD 21201-2436 Fax: (410)528-4312
Free: (800)882-0483

Medical journal covering learning disabilities behavioral reactions of childhood, and family dynamics for pediatricians, child psychiatrists, and special educators. **Subtitle:** Official Journal of the Society of Behavioral Pediatrics. **Founded:** 1980. **Freq:** Bimonthly. **Print Method:** Offset. **Trim Size:** 8 1/2 x 11. **Cols./Page:** 2. **Col. Width:** 39 nonpareils. **Col. Depth:** 130 agate lines. **Key Personnel:** Stanford B. Friedman, M.D., Editor; Jim Burke, Rep. **ISSN:** 0196-206X. **Subscription Rates:** $98 individuals; $118 other countries. **Remarks:** Accepts advertising.
Ad Rates: BW: $365 **Circ:** Paid ‡1,542
4C: $990 Non-paid ‡90

13363 Journal of Endodontics
Lippincott Williams & Wilkins
351 W. Camden St. Phone: (410)528-8517
Baltimore, MD 21201-2436 Fax: (410)528-4312
Free: (800)882-0483

Journal for endodontists and general dentists. **Subtitle:** Official Publication of the American Association of Endodontists. **Founded:** 1975. **Freq:** Monthly. **Print Method:** Offset. **Trim Size:** 8 1/2 x 11. **Cols./Page:** 2. **Col. Width:** 32 nonpareils. **Col. Depth:** 119 agate lines. **Key Personnel:** Henry J. Van Hassel, D.D.S., Editor; Gary Walchli, Advertising Dir.; Stacey Fernandez, Rep. **ISSN:** 0099-2399. **Subscription Rates:** $57 individuals; $82 other countries. **Remarks:** Accepts advertising.
Ad Rates: BW: $840 **Circ:** Paid ‡6,050
4C: $1,565 Non-paid ‡75

13364 Journal of Foot Surgery
Lippincott Williams & Wilkins
351 W. Camden St. Phone: (410)528-8517
Baltimore, MD 21201-2436 Fax: (410)528-4312
Free: (800)882-0483

Medical journal covering clinical advances in foot surgery for podiatrists and orthopaedic foot surgeons. **Subtitle:** Official Publication of the American College of Foot Surgeons. **Founded:** 1961. **Freq:** Bimonthly. **Print Method:** Offset. **Trim Size:** 8 1/2 x 11. **Cols./Page:** 2. **Col. Width:** 32 nonpareils. **Col. Depth:** 119 agate lines. **Key Personnel:** Richard P. Reinharz, D.P.M., Editor; Gary Walchli, Advertising Dir.; Joyce Michael, Rep. **ISSN:** 1067-2516. **Subscription Rates:** $109 individuals; $139 institutions In-training 57. **Remarks:** Accepts advertising.
Ad Rates: BW: $625 **Circ:** Paid ‡6,400
4C: $1,350 Non-paid ‡200

13365 Journal of Health Care Law and Policy
University of Maryland School of Law
500 W. Baltimore St.
Baltimore, MD 21201

Legal journal covering health related issues. **Founded:** May 1, 1998. **Freq:** Semiannual. **Cols./Page:** 1. **Key Personnel:** Carla McGregor, Editor-in-Chief; Eric DeVito, Exec. Editor; Jean-Marie Sylla, Managing Editor. **Remarks:** Accepts advertising. **Online:** LEXIS-NEXIS; Westlaw. **Former name:** Maryland Journal of Contemporary Legal Issues.
Circ: Paid 250

13366 Journal of Human Virology
Lippincott-Raven Publishers
University of Maryland at Baltimore Phone: (410)706-1941
Fax: (410)706-1944
University of Maryland Biotechnology Institute
Institute of Human Virology
Medical Biotechnology Center, 725 W. Lombard St.
Baltimore, MD 21201
Publication E-mail: redfield@umbi.umd.edu

Scholarly medical journal covering human viruses and chronic diseases. **Founded:** Nov. 1997. **Freq:** Bimonthly. **Trim Size:** 8 1/4 x 11. **Cols./Page:** 2. **Col. Width:** 3 3/8 inches. **Col. Depth:** 10 inches. **Key Personnel:** Robert C. Gallo, Consulting Editor; Robert R. Redfield, Editor-in-Chief; William A. Blattner, Editor-in-Chief; Susan Erdson, Ad Sales Mgr. **ISSN:** 1090-9058. **Subscription Rates:** $89 individuals; $129 institutions; $24 single issue. **Remarks:** Accepts advertising.
Ad Rates: BW: $500 **Circ:** (Not Reported)
4C: $890

13367 The Journal of Medical Practice Management
Lippincott Williams & Wilkins
351 W. Camden St. Phone: (410)528-8517
Baltimore, MD 21201-2436 Fax: (410)528-4312
Free: (800)882-0483

Journal covering legislation, litigation, office management and other issues affecting medical practices. **Founded:** 1985. **Freq:** Quarterly. **Print Method:** Offset. **Trim Size:** 8 3/8 x 11. **Cols./Page:** 2. **Col. Width:** 32 nonpareils. **Col. Depth:** 119 agate lines. **Key Personnel:** Richard Cook, Publisher. **ISSN:** 1055-8675. **Subscription Rates:** $59 individuals; $74 other countries; $77 industry; $92 industry, other countries; $19 single issue.
Circ: Paid ‡3,330
Non-paid ‡110

13368 Journal of Nervous and Mental Disease
Lippincott Williams & Wilkins
PO Box 6815 Phone: (410)938-3182
Baltimore, MD 21285 Fax: (410)938-3183
Publication E-mail: journalnmd@hotmail.com

Psychiatry journal publishing studies in related social, behavioral, and neorological sciences. **Founded:** 1874. **Freq:** Monthly. **Print Method:** Offset. **Trim Size:** 8 1/8 x 10 7/8. **Cols./Page:** 2. **Col. Width:** 32 nonpareils. **Col. Depth:** 119 agate lines. **Key Personnel:** Eugene B. Brody, M.D., Editor, phone (410)938-3181, wfmh@erols.com; Gary Walchli, Advertising Dir.; Randy Ezell, Rep.; Kathy McKnight, Managing Editor. **ISSN:** 0022-3018. **Subscription Rates:** $140 individuals; $175 other countries; $230 institutions. **Remarks:** Accepts advertising.
Ad Rates: BW: $425 **Circ:** Paid ‡2,105
4C: $1,100 Non-paid ‡79

13369 The Journal of Neuroscience
Lippincott Williams & Wilkins
351 W. Camden St. Phone: (410)528-8517
Baltimore, MD 21201-2436 Fax: (410)528-4312
Free: (800)882-0483

Medical journal. **Founded:** 1981. **Freq:** Monthly. **Print Meth-**

od: Offset. **Trim Size:** 8 1/2 x 11. **Cols./Page:** 2. **Col. Width:** 32 nonpareils. **Col. Depth:** 119 agate lines. **Key Personnel:** Dale Purves, M.D., Editor; Gary Walchli, Advertising Mgr.; Elizabeth Mosko, Rep. **Subscription Rates:** $710 individuals; $795 other countries. **Remarks:** Accepts advertising.
Ad Rates: BW: $615 **Circ:** Paid ‡3,341
4C: $1,390 Non-paid ‡303

13370 The Journal of Orthopaedic and Sports Physical Therapy (JOSPT)
Lippincott Williams & Wilkins
351 W. Camden St. Phone: (410)528-8517
Baltimore, MD 21201-2436 Fax: (410)528-4312
Free: (800)882-0483

Medical journal. **Founded:** 1979. **Freq:** Monthly. **Print Method:** Web offset. **Trim Size:** 8 3/8 x 10 7/8. **Cols./Page:** 2. **Col. Width:** 32 nonpareils. **Col. Depth:** 119 agate lines. **Key Personnel:** Gary L. Smidt, Ph.D., Contact; Gary Walchli, Advertising Mgr.; Joyce Michael, Rep. **Subscription Rates:** $70 individuals; $100 other countries. **Remarks:** Accepts advertising.
Ad Rates: BW: $800 **Circ:** Paid ‡16,971
4C: $1,625 Non-paid ‡272

13371 Journal of Rehabilitation Research and Development
United States Department of Veterans Affairs
103 S. Gay St. Phone: (410)962-1800
Baltimore, MD 21202-4051 Fax: (410)962-9670
Publication E-mail: puba@balt-rehab.med.va.gov
Publisher E-mail: pubs@vard.org

Journal containing scientific articles and clinical reports on rehabilitation research and development. **Founded:** 1983. **Freq:** Quarterly. **Trim Size:** 8 1/2 x 11. **Cols./Page:** 2. **Col. Width:** 3 1/2 inches. **Key Personnel:** Tamara T. Sowell, Editor, tamara@vard.org; Neil McAleer, Managing Editor, neil@vard.org. **ISSN:** 0007-506X. **Subscription Rates:** Free. **Remarks:** Advertising not accepted. **URL:** http://www.vard.org. **Formerly:** Bulletin of Prosthetics Research.
Circ: Non-paid 25,000

13372 Journal of Trauma
Lippincott Williams & Wilkins
351 W. Camden St. Phone: (410)528-8517
Baltimore, MD 21201-2436 Fax: (410)528-4312
Free: (800)882-0483

Surgery journal. **Founded:** 1961. **Freq:** Monthly. **Print Method:** Offset. **Trim Size:** 8 1/2 x 11. **Cols./Page:** 2. **Col. Width:** 32 nonpareils. **Col. Depth:** 119 agate lines. **Key Personnel:** John H. Davis, M.D., Editor; Gary Walchli, Advertising Dir.; Greg Pessagno, Rep. **Subscription Rates:** $105 individuals; $145 other countries. **Remarks:** Accepts advertising.
Ad Rates: BW: $710 **Circ:** Paid ‡6,436
4C: $1,585 Non-paid ‡278

13373 Journal of Urology
Lippincott Williams & Wilkins
351 W. Camden St. Phone: (410)528-8517
Baltimore, MD 21201-2436 Fax: (410)528-4312
Free: (800)882-0483

Medical journal. **Subtitle:** Official Journal of the American Urological Association, Inc. **Founded:** 1917. **Freq:** Monthly. **Print Method:** Web offset. **Trim Size:** 8 3/8 x 10 7/8. **Cols./Page:** 2. **Col. Width:** 32 nonpareils. **Col. Depth:** 119 agate lines. **Key Personnel:** John T. Grayhack, Editor; Gary Walchli, Advertising Dir.; Steve Tauber, Rep. **ISSN:** 0022-5347. **Subscription Rates:** $229 individuals; $25 single issue; $31 single issue Foreign; $225 institutions Domestic; $330 institutions, other countries; $304 other countries individual. **Remarks:** Accepts advertising.
Ad Rates: BW: $1,835 **Circ:** Paid ‡18,356
4C: $2,030 Non-paid ‡423

13374 Laboratory Investigation
Lippincott Williams & Wilkins
351 W. Camden St. Phone: (410)528-8517
Baltimore, MD 21201-2436 Fax: (410)528-4312
Free: (800)882-0483

Pathology journal. **Founded:** 1952. **Freq:** Monthly. **Print Method:** Web offset. **Trim Size:** 8 3/8 x 10 7/8. **Cols./Page:** 2. **Col. Width:** 32 nonpareils. **Col. Depth:** 119 agate lines. **Key Personnel:** Emanuel Rubin, M.D., Editor; Gary Walchli, Advertising Dir.; Beth Missett, Rep. **ISSN:** 0023-6837. **Subscription Rates:** $147 individuals; $249 institutions In-training 90. **Remarks:** Accepts advertising.
Ad Rates: BW: $725 **Circ:** Paid ‡3,200
4C: $1,500

13375 Lacrosse
US Lacrosse, Inc.
113 W. University Pkwy. Phone: (410)235-6882
Baltimore, MD 21210 Fax: (410)366-6735
Publication E-mail: info@lacrosse.org

Sports magazine. **Founded:** 1978. **Freq:** 8 times/year. **Print Method:** Offset. **Trim Size:** 8 1/8 x 10 7/8. **Cols./Page:** 3 and 2. **Col. Width:** 2.07 and 3.236 inches. **Col. Depth:** 9.342 and 9.342 inches. **Key Personnel:** Marc Bouchard, Editor, mbouchard@lacrosse.org. **ISSN:** 1050-5893. **Subscription Rates:** $35 students; $45 adult; $50 family or international.
Ad Rates: BW: $720 **Circ:** Paid ‡15,000
4C: $1,420 Non-paid ‡1,000

13376 The Lancet (North American Edition)
Lippincott Williams & Wilkins
351 W. Camden St. Phone: (410)528-8517
Baltimore, MD 21201-2436 Fax: (410)528-4312
Free: (800)882-0483

Medical journal. Contents identical to British edition. **Founded:** 1823. **Freq:** Weekly. **Print Method:** Letterpress and offset. **Trim Size:** 8 1/4 x 11. **Key Personnel:** Robin Fox, M.D., Editor; Gary Walchli, Advertising Dir.; Cara Kaufman, Marketing Mgr.; Don Debora, Rep. **Subscription Rates:** $98 individuals.
Ad Rates: BW: $2,080 **Circ:** ‡19,614
4C: $3,070

13377 The Law Forum
University of Baltimore
1420 N. Charles St.
Baltimore, MD 21202

College legal journal covering current law topics. **Freq:** Semiannual. **ISSN:** 0811-5796. **Subscription Rates:** Free to qualified subscribers. **Remarks:** Advertising not accepted.
Circ: Controlled 8,000

13378 Maryland Historical Magazine
Maryland Historical Society
201 W. Monument St. Phone: (410)685-3750
Baltimore, MD 21201 Fax: (410)385-2105

Magazine on Maryland history and culture. **Founded:** 1906. **Freq:** Quarterly. **Print Method:** Offset. **Trim Size:** 6 3/4 x 10. **Cols./Page:** 1. **Col. Width:** 5 inches. **Col. Depth:** 9 1/4 inches. **Key Personnel:** Robert I. Cottom, Jr., Editor, rcottom@mdhs.org; Donna Shear, Managing Editor, dshear@mdhs.org. **ISSN:** 0025-4528. **Subscription Rates:** Free to members; $6 single issue; $30 institutions. **Remarks:** Accepts advertising.
Ad Rates: BW: $425 **Circ:** ‡4,000

13379 Maryland Medical Journal
MedChi
1211 Cathedral St. Phone: (410)539-0872
Baltimore, MD 21201 Fax: (410)547-0915
Publication E-mail: info@mail.medchi.org

Medical journal. **Founded:** 1952. **Freq:** Bimonthly. **Print Method:** Offset. **Trim Size:** 8 1/8 x 10 7/8. **Cols./Page:** 2. **Col. Width:** 42 nonpareils. **Col. Depth:** 132 agate lines. **Key Personnel:** Vivian Smith, Editor; Aliza Rossman, Advertising, alizar@mail.medchi.org. **ISSN:** 0025-4363. **Subscription Rates:** $45 individuals; $57 other countries; $7 single issue. **Remarks:** Accepts advertising. **URL:** http://www.medchi.org.
Ad Rates: BW: $700 **Circ:** ‡7,500
4C: $1,260

13380 Maryland Naturalist
Natural History Society of Maryland
2643 N. Charles St. Phone: (410)235-6116
Baltimore, MD 21218
Scientific journal. **Founded:** 1930. **Freq:** Semiannual. **Print Method:** Offset. **Trim Size:** 8 1/2 x 11. **Key Personnel:** Arnold Norden, Editor; Donell Redman, Editor. **ISSN:** 0096-4158. **Subscription Rates:** $20; $25 other countries. **Remarks:** Advertising not accepted.
Circ: Paid 250
Controlled 40

13381 Maryland Pharmacist
Maryland Pharmacists Association
650 W. Lombard St. Phone: (410)727-0746
Baltimore, MD 21201 Fax: (410)727-2253
Publisher E-mail: mpha@erols.com

Pharmaceutical journal. **Subtitle:** The Official Journal of the Maryland Pharmacists Association. **Founded:** 1925. **Freq:** Quarterly. **Print Method:** Offset. **Trim Size:** 8 1/2 x 11. **Cols./Page:** 2. **Col. Width:** 27 nonpareils. **Col. Depth:** 101 agate lines. **Key Personnel:** Howard Schiff, Program Dir. **ISSN:** 0025-4347. **Subscription Rates:** $15 individuals; $2.50 single issue. **Remarks:** Accepts advertising.
Ad Rates: BW: $350 **Circ:** 1,100

13382 Maryland Poetry Review
Maryland State Poetry and Literary Society
c/o B. Simon Phone: (410)744-0349
99 Smithwood Ave.
Baltimore, MD 21228
Literary arts magazine. **Founded:** 1962. **Freq:** Annual. **Trim Size:** 7 x 11. **Key Personnel:** Rosemary Klein, Editor-in-Chief; B. Simon, Asst. Editor; H. Burgess, Asst. Editor; D. Cuddy, Contributing Editor. **ISSN:** 0892-807X. **Remarks:** Advertising not accepted. **URL:** http://members.aol.com/mdstpoetry. **Alt. Formats:** CD-ROM.
Circ: Paid 500

13383 Maryland Sports, Health and Fitness News
Frontline Communications Group, Inc.
PO Box 32684 Phone: (410)922-1158
Baltimore, MD 21282 Fax: (410)922-8115

Tabloid publication covering sports, health, nutrition, and fitness issues for Maryland residents. **Founded:** 1996. **Freq:** Bimonthly. **Print Method:** Web offset. **Trim Size:** 11 x 15. **Cols./Page:** 4. **Col. Width:** 2 1/4 inches. **Col. Depth:** 14 inches. **Key Personnel:** Dr. Gladson I. Nwanna, Managing Editor; Greg Osita, Advertising Mgr. **ISSN:** 1090-7122. **Subscription Rates:** Free; $15 by mail. **Remarks:** Accepts advertising.
Ad Rates: BW: $1,445 **Circ:** Free 20,000
4C: $2,045

13384 Medicine
Lippincott Williams & Wilkins
The Johns Hopkins Hospital Phone: (410)955-6641
Division of Medical Genetics Fax: (410)955-4999
Blalock 1007
Baltimore, MD 21205
Medical journal. **Founded:** 1922. **Freq:** Bimonthly. **Print Method:** Web offset. **Trim Size:** 8 1/8 x 10 7/8. **Cols./Page:** 2. **Col. Width:** 32 nonpareils. **Col. Depth:** 119 agate lines. **Key Personnel:** Victor A. McKusick, Editor; Gary Walchli, Vice Pres., Advertising Sales; Randy Ezell, Rep., phone (410)361-8004, rezell@wwilkins.com. **Subscription Rates:** $87 individuals; $117 other countries. **Remarks:** Accepts advertising. **Alt. Formats:** Mailing labels.
Ad Rates: BW: $665 **Circ:** Paid ‡3,381
4C: $1,515 Non-paid ‡135

13385 Medicine and Science in Sports and Exercise
Lippincott Williams & Wilkins
351 W. Camden St. Phone: (410)528-8517
Baltimore, MD 21201-2436 Fax: (410)528-4312
Free: (800)882-0483

Medical journal. **Founded:** 1969. **Freq:** Monthly. **Print Method:** Web offset. **Trim Size:** 8 1/8 x 10 7/8. **Cols./Page:** 2. **Col. Width:** 32 nonpareils. **Col. Depth:** 119 agate lines. **Key Personnel:** Peter B. Raven, Ph.D., Editor; Gary Walchli, Vice Pres., Advertising Sales; Sharlene Isaacson, Rep., phone (410)528-8519, sisaacson@wwilkins.com. **Subscription Rates:** $147 individuals; $257 other countries; $23 single issue. **Remarks:** Accepts advertising. **Alt. Formats:** Mailing labels.
Ad Rates: BW: $1,105 **Circ:** Paid ‡16,949
4C: $2,100 Non-paid ‡128

13386 Mid-Atlantic Builder
Home Builders Association of Maryland
1502 Woodlawn Dr. Phone: (410)265-7400
Baltimore, MD 21207-4009 Fax: (410)265-6529

Trade magazine for the building industry in the Mid-Atlantic region. **Founded:** 1984. **Freq:** Bimonthly. **Print Method:** Offset. **Trim Size:** 8 1/2 x 11. **Key Personnel:** Kristin Josephson, Editor; John Kortecamp, Publisher. **Subscription Rates:** $50 individuals. **Remarks:** Accepts advertising.
Ad Rates: BW: $500 **Circ:** ‡3,000
4C: $1,100

13387 The Mission Helper
Mission Helpers of the Sacred Heart
1001 W. Joppa Rd. Phone: (410)823-8585
Baltimore, MD 21204-3787 Fax: (410)825-6355
Publisher E-mail: missionadv@aol.com

Magazine reporting on missionary activities. **Founded:** 1894. **Freq:** Quarterly. **Trim Size:** 8 1/2 x 11. **Cols./Page:** 2 and 3. **Col. Width:** 3 1/2 inches. **Col. Depth:** 9 1/2-10 inches. **Key Personnel:** Mary Ann Krastel, Editor, markrastel@aol.com. **Subscription Rates:** $8 donation. **Remarks:** Advertising not accepted.
Circ: Controlled 7,500

13388 MLN (Modern Language Notes)
Johns Hopkins University Press
Hispanic & Italian Studies Phone: (410)516-7868
John Hopkins Univ. Fax: (410)516-8403
221 Gilman Hall
Baltimore, MD 21218
Publisher E-mail: jlinfo@jhupress.jhu.edu

Journal on the theory, interpretation, and history of modern languages (French, German, Italian, Spanish). **Founded:** 1886. **Freq:** 5/year. **Print Method:** Offset. **Trim Size:** 6 x 9. **Cols./Page:** 1. **Col. Width:** 50 nonpareils. **Col. Depth:** 96 agate lines. **Key Personnel:** Harry Sieber, General editor; Tara Dorai-Berry, Advertising Mgr. **ISSN:** 0026-7910. **Sub-**

scription Rates: $35 individuals; $89 institutions; $9 single issue; $19 single issue institutions. **Remarks:** Accepts advertising. **Available Online. URL:** http://www.press.jhu.edu/journals/mln/.
Ad Rates: BW: $285 **Circ:** ‡1,800

13389 Modernism/Modernity
Johns Hopkins University Press
2715 N. Charles St. Phone: (410)516-6987
Baltimore, MD 21218 Fax: (410)516-3866
Free: (800)548-1784
Publisher E-mail: jlinfo@jhupress.jhu.edu

Scholarly journal covering modernist studies, including art, music, architecture, literary theory, history and related areas. **Founded:** 1995. **Freq:** Triennial. **Trim Size:** 5.5 x 8. **Key Personnel:** Ed. Robert von Hallberg; Lawrence Rainey; Anastasia Scherr, Advertising Mgr., phone (410)516-6988, fax (410)516-3866. **ISSN:** 1071-6068. **Subscription Rates:** $30 individuals; $68 institutions; $11 single issue. **Remarks:** Accepts advertising. **URL:** http://www.press.jhu.edu/press/journals/.
Ad Rates: BW: $185 **Circ:** Combined 740

13390 The Montage
Essex Community College
7201 Rossville Blvd. Phone: (410)780-6576
Baltimore, MD 21237-3898 Fax: (410)686-9503

Collegiate magazine (tabloid). **Founded:** 1978. **Freq:** Tri-weekly (during the academic year). **Print Method:** Offset. **Trim Size:** 11 x 14. **Cols./Page:** 5. **Col. Width:** 2 1/2 inches. **Col. Depth:** 182 agate lines. **Key Personnel:** Gwyneth B. Howard, Editor; Pat Thompson, Advertising Mgr. **Remarks:** Accepts advertising.
Ad Rates: BW: $250 **Circ:** ‡10,500
4C: $570
PCI: $4.69

13391 NAD Case Reports
Council of Better Business Bureaus, Inc.
PO Box 79168 Phone: (301)617-7810
Baltimore, MD 21279-0168 Fax: (301)206-9789

Reports covering advertising case reports containing analysis of challenges against national advertisers by competitors, consumers, local Better Business Bureaus, and the National Advertising Division. **Founded:** 1971. **Freq:** 10/year. **Subscription Rates:** $1,000 individuals; $100 single issue. **URL:** http://www.bbb.org.

13392 Neurosurgery
Lippincott Williams & Wilkins
351 W. Camden St. Phone: (410)528-8517
Baltimore, MD 21201-2436 Fax: (410)528-4312
Free: (800)882-0483

Medical surgery journal. **Founded:** 1977. **Freq:** Monthly. **Print Method:** Web offset. **Trim Size:** 8 3/8 x 10 7/8. **Cols./Page:** 2. **Col. Width:** 32 nonpareils. **Col. Depth:** 119 agate lines. **Key Personnel:** Michael L.J. Apuzzo, M.D., Editor; Gary Walchli, Advertising Dir.; Greg Pessagno, Rep. **Subscription Rates:** $120 individuals; $165 other countries; $17 single issue. **Remarks:** Accepts advertising.
Ad Rates: BW: $915 **Circ:** Paid ‡7,597
4C: $1,765 Non-paid ‡365

13393 Northeast Times Booster
Patuxent Publishing Co.
409 Washington Ave. Phone: (410)337-2400
Towson, MD 21204 Fax: (410)337-2490

Community newspaper. **Founded:** 1947. **Freq:** Weekly (Wed.). **Print Method:** Offset. **Trim Size:** 11 x 15. **Cols./Page:** 5. **Col. Width:** 11 picas. **Col. Depth:** 80.25 picas. **Key Personnel:** Blaise Willig, Editor; S. Zeke Orlinsky, Publisher; David Thomasini, Advertising Dir. **Subscription Rates:** Free; $104 out of area. **Remarks:** Advertising accepted; rates available upon request.
Circ: Paid 21
Non-paid 18,793

13394 Pathology Case Reviews
Lippincott Williams & Wilkins
Dept. of Pathology Phone: (410)328-5072
N2W508 Fax: (410)328-0644
22 S. Greene St.
Baltimore, MD 21201-1595
Publication E-mail: jmerritt@phl.lrpub.com

Each issue examines one theme in the field with peer-reviewed case reports that focus on diagnosis, specimen handling, and reports generation. **Founded:** 1996. **Freq:** Bimonthly. **Print Method:** Sheetfed offset. **Trim Size:** 8 1/2 x 11. **Key Personnel:** Steven G. Silverberg, MD, Editor; Jeffrey A. Kant, M.D., Associate Editor; Jan F. Silverman, M.D., Associate Editor; Kathleen Phelan, Advertising Sales Manager, phone (215)238-4282; Jennifer Bass, National Accounts Manager, phone (215)238-4283; J. Merritt, Contact, jmerritt@phl.lrpub.com. **Subscription Rates:** $99 individuals; $129 institutions; $28 single issue. **Remarks:** Accepts advertising.
Ad Rates: BW: $795 **Circ:** Paid 1,200
4C: $870 Non-paid 1,400

13395 Pediatric Emergency Care
Lippincott Williams & Wilkins
351 W. Camden St. Phone: (410)528-8517
Baltimore, MD 21201-2436 Fax: (410)528-4312
Free: (800)882-0483

Medical journal. **Founded:** 1985. **Freq:** Quarterly. **Print Method:** Offset. **Trim Size:** 8 1/8 x 10 7/8. **Cols./Page:** 2. **Col. Width:** 32 nonpareils. **Col. Depth:** 119 agate lines. **Key Personnel:** Stephen Ludwig, M.D., Editor; Gary Fleischer, M.D., Advertising Mgr.; Donald Pfarr, Advertising Mgr.; Alma Wills, Publisher. **Subscription Rates:** $77 individuals; $97 other countries. **Remarks:** Accepts advertising.
Ad Rates: BW: $425 **Circ:** Paid ‡2,693
4C: $1,100 Non-paid ‡86

13396 Pediatric Infectious Disease
Lippincott Williams & Wilkins
351 W. Camden St. Phone: (410)528-8517
Baltimore, MD 21201-2436 Fax: (410)528-4312
Free: (800)882-0483

Medical journal. **Founded:** 1982. **Freq:** Monthly. **Print Method:** Offset. **Trim Size:** 8 1/8 x 10 7/8. **Cols./Page:** 2. **Col. Width:** 32 nonpareils. **Col. Depth:** 119 agate lines. **Key Personnel:** John D. Nelson, Editor; George H. McCracken, Advertising Mgr.; Greg Pessagno, Rep. **Subscription Rates:** $70 individuals; $105 other countries. **Remarks:** Accepts advertising.
Ad Rates: BW: $975 **Circ:** Paid ‡15,963
4C: $1,850 Non-paid ‡302

13397 Pediatric Research
Lippincott Williams & Wilkins
351 W. Camden St. Phone: (410)528-8517
Baltimore, MD 21201-2436 Fax: (410)528-4312
Free: (800)882-0483

Pediatric research journal. **Founded:** 1967. **Freq:** Monthly. **Print Method:** Offset. **Trim Size:** 8 3/8 x 10 7/8. **Cols./Page:** 2. **Col. Width:** 32 nonpareils. **Col. Depth:** 119 agate lines. **Key Personnel:** Dennis M. Bier, Editor; Gary Walchli, Advertising Mgr.; Alma Wills, Publisher. **Subscription Rates:** $128 individuals; $163 other countries. **Remarks:** Accepts advertising.
Ad Rates: BW: $505 **Circ:** Paid ‡3,593
4C: $1,180 Non-paid ‡23

13398 Philosophy, Psychiatry & Psychology
Johns Hopkins University Press
2715 N. Charles St. Phone: (410)516-6900
Baltimore, MD 21218-4319 Fax: (410)516-3866
Free: (800)548-1784
Publisher E-mail: jlinfo@jhupress.jhu.edu

Scholarly journal covering overlap between philosophy, psychiatry, and psychology. **Freq:** Quarterly. **Key Personnel:** K.W.M. Fulford, Editor; John Z. Sadler, Editor; Anatasia Scherr, Advertising Mgr., phone (410)516-6988. **ISSN:** 1071-6076. **Subscription Rates:** $85 members; $32 students; $22 single issue. **Remarks:** Accepts advertising. **URL:** http://www.press.jhu.edu/press/journals/.
Ad Rates: BW: $200 **Circ:** 570

13399 Physician's Practice Digest
Magazine Works, Inc.
100 S Charles St., 13th Fl. Phone: (410)539-3100
Baltimore, MD 21201 Fax: (410)539-3188
Free: (800)781-2211

Professional magazine covering practice management for physicians. **Founded:** Oct. 1989. **Freq:** Bimonthly. **Print Method:** Web offset. **Trim Size:** 8 1/4 x 10 7/8. **Cols./Page:** 3. **Col. Width:** 2 1/4 inches. **Col. Depth:** 10 inches. **Key Personnel:** Scott Weber, Publisher; Gerry Hartung, Publisher; Cathy Canning, Editor; Abigail Green, Asst. Editor; Jeffrey Furniss, VP, Sales & Mktg.; Karen Lind, Traffic/Production Mgr. **Subscription Rates:** $32 individuals; $60 two years; $8 single issue. **Remarks:** Accepts advertising. **URL:** http://www.ppdnet.com.
Circ: Controlled 100,000

13400 Port of Baltimore
Media Two
1031 Cromwell Bridge Rd. Phone: (410)828-0120
Baltimore, MD 21286 Fax: (410)825-1002

Maritime and shipping magazine. **Founded:** 1928. **Freq:** Monthly. **Print Method:** Web. **Trim Size:** 8 1/8 x 10 7/8. **Cols./Page:** 2 and 3. **Key Personnel:** Merrill Witty, Editor, mcwitty@aol.com; Christine Leo, Advertising Account Exec., media2leo@aol.com. **Subscription Rates:** Free to qualified subscribers. **Remarks:** Accepts advertising.
Ad Rates: BW: $1,295 **Circ:** Controlled ‡11,500
4C: $1,875

13401 Publication of the Astronomical Society of the Pacific
American Institute of Physics (AIP)
Space Telescope Science Institute Phone: (410)516-4273
Fax: (410)516-4191
3700 San Martin Dr.
Baltimore, MD 21218
Publication E-mail: pasp@stsci.edu
Publisher E-mail: subs@aip.org

Journal devoted to astronomical results of a scientific nature and current astronomical research. **Founded:** 1891. **Freq:** Monthly. **Print Method:** Offset. **Trim Size:** 8 1/2 x 11. **Cols./Page:** 2. **Col. Width:** 41 nonpareils. **Col. Depth:** 136 agate lines. **Key Personnel:** Howard E. Bond, Editor. **ISSN:** 0004-6280. **Subscription Rates:** $80 individuals; $190 institutions. **Remarks:** Advertising not accepted.
Circ: ‡2,500

13402 Quicks Professional Journal
The Engineering Society of Baltimore, Inc.
11 W. Mount Vernon Pl. Phone: (410)539-6914
Baltimore, MD 21201 Fax: (410)783-9372

Magazine on engineering, architectural, and construction interests. **Founded:** 1926. **Freq:** Monthly. **Print Method:** Offset. **Trim Size:** 8 1/2 x 11. **Cols./Page:** 3. **Col. Width:** 27 nonpareils. **Col. Depth:** 133 agate lines. **Key Personnel:** Michele D. Bedsaul, Editor. **Subscription Rates:** Free to ESB members; $12 institutions. **Remarks:** Accepts advertising. **Formerly:** Baltimore Engineer.
Ad Rates: BW: $700 **Circ:** Non-paid ‡6,500
4C: $1,300

13403 Radiology
Radiological Society of North America
550 N. Broadway, Ste. 206 Phone: (410)327-0124
Baltimore, MD 21205 Fax: (410)276-0353

Journal focusing on radiology. **Subtitle:** Radiology. **Founded:** 1915. **Freq:** Monthly. **Print Method:** Offset. **Trim Size:** 8 1/4 x 11 1/4. **Cols./Page:** 3. **Col. Width:** 2 1/4 inches. **Col. Depth:** 10 inches. **Key Personnel:** Stanley S. Siegelman, M.D., Editor, phone (410)327-0124; Tom Shimala, Advertising Dir., phone (708)571-7819. **ISSN:** 0033-8419. **Subscription Rates:** $205 individuals; $250 out of country; $25 single issue.
Ad Rates: BW: $2050 **Circ:** ‡36,500
4C: $3475

13404 Red & Black
Catonsville Community College
800 S. Rolling Rd.
Baltimore, MD 21228

Collegiate newspaper. **Subtitle:** The Student Newspaper of Catonsville Community College. **Founded:** 1958. **Freq:** Biweekly. **Print Method:** Offset. **Cols./Page:** 5. **Col. Width:** 22 nonpareils. **Col. Depth:** 197 agate lines. **Key Personnel:** Tammy Coffinberger, Editor, tcoff454@neors.cat.cc.md.us. **Remarks:** Accepts advertising.
Ad Rates: BW: $250 **Circ:** Non-paid ‡4,100
PCI: $4

13405 School Library Media Activities Monthly
LMS Associates
17 E. Henrietta St. Phone: (410)685-8621
Baltimore, MD 21230 Fax: (410)685-0870

School library periodical. **Founded:** Sept. 1984. **Freq:** Monthly. **Key Personnel:** Paula Montgomery, Editor, paulam@clark.net; Debra Goodrich, Production, phone (561)464-2237, dag054@aol.com. **ISSN:** 0889-9371. **Subscription Rates:** $49 individuals; $4.90 single issue. **Remarks:** Accepts advertising.
Circ: Paid 11,500

13406 Serenity
Little Sisters of the Poor
601 Maiden Choice Ln. Phone: (410)744-9367
Baltimore, MD 21228 Fax: (410)788-5614

Magazine making known the apostolate of Little Sisters of the Poor and providing a positive view of the elderly and the respect due them. **Founded:** 1970. **Freq:** Quarterly. **Print Method:** Offset. **Trim Size:** 5 1/2 x 8 1/2. **Key Personnel:** Sr. Constance Veit, Editor. **Subscription Rates:** donations. **Remarks:** Advertising not accepted.
Circ: Free 65,000

13407 Shattered Wig Review
425 E. 31st St. Phone: (410)243-6888
Baltimore, MD 21218-3409
Literary journal covering alternative poetry and nonfiction. **Founded:** Apr. 1988. **Freq:** Semiannual. **Trim Size:** 8 1/2 x 8

1/2. **Key Personnel:** Sonny Bodkin, Editor. **Subscription Rates:** $8 individuals; $5 single issue. **Remarks:** Advertising not accepted. **Former name**: The Gilded Watercress Annual.
Circ: (Not Reported)

13408 Shoe Service
SSIA Service Corp.
5024 R. Campbell Blvd. Phone: (410)931-8100
Baltimore, MD 21236 Fax: (410)931-8111

Magazine for the shoe repair industry. **Subtitle:** The Magazine for the Shoe Service Industry. **Founded:** 1921. **Freq:** Monthly. **Print Method:** Offset. Uses mats. **Trim Size:** 8 1/4 x 11 1/4. **Cols./Page:** 3 and 2. **Col. Width:** 13 and 20 picas. **Col. Depth:** 60 picas. **Key Personnel:** Mitchell Lebovic, Editor, lebovic@aol.com. **ISSN:** 0193-256X. **Subscription Rates:** $18 individuals. **Remarks:** Accepts advertising.
Ad Rates: GLR: $133 **Circ:** ‡17,000
BW: $1,295
4C: $1,795

13409 Social Anarchism
2743 Maryland Ave. Phone: (410)243-6987
Baltimore, MD 21218 Fax: (410)830-2455
Publication E-mail: sociala@nothingness.org

Journal featuring articles and essays focusing on issues such as ecological and feminist anarchy, and anti-authoritarianism. **Subtitle:** A Journal of Practice and Theory. **Founded:** 1983. **Freq:** 2/year. **Trim Size:** 6x9. **ISSN:** 0196-4804. **Subscription Rates:** $14 two years. **URL:** http://www.nothingness.org/sociala/.
Circ: (Not Reported)

13410 Street Voice
101 W Read St., No. 421 Phone: (410)783-5449
Baltimore, MD 21201 Fax: (410)685-9008
Publication E-mail: cansv@igc.apc.org

Tabloid directed toward the homeless, substance users, and low-income people. **Subtitle:** Shop Stewards for the Underclass. **Founded:** 1991. **Freq:** Quarterly. **Print Method:** Offset. **Cols./Page:** 2. **Col. Width:** 5 1/2 inches. **Col. Depth:** 14 1/2 inches. **Key Personnel:** Curtis Price, Contact. **Subscription Rates:** Free. **Remarks:** Accepts advertising.
Circ: Non-paid 4,000

13411 Stroke
Lippincott Williams & Wilkins
351 W. Camden St. Phone: (410)528-8517
Baltimore, MD 21201-2436 Fax: (410)528-4312
Free: (800)882-0483

Journal publishing reports of clinical and basic investigation of any aspect of cerebral circulation and its diseases. **Subtitle:** Journal of the American Stroke Association. **Founded:** 1970. **Freq:** Monthly. **Print Method:** Offset. Uses mats. **Trim Size:** 8 1/8 x 10 7/8. **Cols./Page:** 2. **Col. Width:** 38 nonpareils. **Col. Depth:** 130 agate lines. **Key Personnel:** Mark L. Dyken, M.D., Editor, phone (317)274-0218, fax (317)630-7910, myurk@iupui.edu; Cara Kaufman, Publisher, phone (410)528-8514, fax (410)528-4312, cskaufma@lww.com; Joseph Jackson, Advertising Rep., phone (973)403-7677, fax (973)403-7795, bartjack@aol.com. **ISSN:** 0039-2499. **Subscription Rates:** $213; $289 other countries; $30 single issue; $40 single issue other countries. **Remarks:** Accepts advertising. **URL:** http://www.strokeaha.org. **Alt. Formats:** Microfilm.
Ad Rates: BW: $857 **Circ:** Paid ‡6,500
4C: $1,380

13412 Transplantation
Lippincott Williams & Wilkins
351 W. Camden St. Phone: (410)528-8517
Baltimore, MD 21201-2436 Fax: (410)528-4312
Free: (800)882-0483

Medical research journal. **Subtitle:** Official Journal of the Transplantation Society. **Founded:** 1963. **Freq:** Monthly. **Print Method:** Offset. **Trim Size:** 8 1/2 x 11. **Cols./Page:** 2. **Col. Width:** 32 nonpareils. **Col. Depth:** 119 agate lines. **Key Personnel:** Anthony P. Monaco, M.D., Editor; Gary Walchli, Advertising Dir.; Sherry Reed, Rep. **ISSN:** 0041-1337. **Subscription Rates:** $260 individuals; $21 single issue; $415 institutions Domestic; $330 individuals Foreign; $485 institutions, other countries; $24 single issue Foreign. **Remarks:** Accepts advertising.
Ad Rates: BW: $625 **Circ:** Paid ‡3,877
4C: $1,300 Non-paid ‡132

13413 Truck Sales & Leasing Magazine
Newport Communications East
600 Reisterstown Rd., Suite 404 Phone: (410)486-7430
Baltimore, MD 21208 Fax: (410)486-7478
Publisher E-mail: 7t542@heavytruck.com

Magazine covering truck sales and leasing, including selling techniques, truck technology, sales engineering, vehicle application, vocational and seasonal selling, new products, and industry news. **Founded:** 1983. **Freq:** Bimonthly. **Print Method:** Offset. **Trim Size:** 8 1/8 x 10 7/8. **Cols./Page:** 3. **Key Personnel:** David A. Kolman, Editor and Publisher, phone (410)486-7430. **ISSN:** 0740-3941. **Subscription Rates:** Free to qualified subscribers; $36 Nonqualified. **Formerly**: Heavy Truck Salesman Magazine.
Ad Rates: BW: $5,290 **Circ:** Controlled ‡21,000
4C: $7,650
PCI: $110

13414 U.S. Black Engineer & Information Technology
Career Communications Group, Inc.
729 E. Pratt St., No. 504 Phone: (410)244-7101
Baltimore, MD 21202 Fax: (410)752-1837
Free: (800)932-7101
Publisher E-mail: ccgmag@aol.com

Magazine for black engineers, computer scientists, and professionals involved in the industry. **Founded:** 1980. **Freq:** 4/year. **Print Method:** Offset. **Trim Size:** 8 1/2 x 11. **Key Personnel:** Tyrone D. Taborn, C.E.O./Publisher, tyrone.taborn@ccgmag.com; Marsha Reeves Jews, C.O.O. & Assoc. Publisher, ccgmag@aol.com; Jean Hamilton, CFO/Circulation Mgr.; Garland Thompson, Editorial Director; Guy L. Madison, Dir. of Sales. **ISSN:** 1088-3444. **Subscription Rates:** $26 individuals yearly. **Remarks:** Accepts advertising. **URL:** http://www.ccgmag.com. **Alt. Formats:** CD-ROM. **Formerly**: U.S. Black Engineer.
Ad Rates: BW: $2,755 **Circ:** Non-paid 15,300
4C: $3,555

13415 Vegetarian Journal
The Vegetarian Resource Group
PO Box 1463 Phone: (410)366-8343
Baltimore, MD 21203 Fax: (410)366-8804
Publisher E-mail: vrg@vrg.org

Journal with recipes and news related to vegetarianism. **Founded:** 1982. **Freq:** Bimonthly. **Trim Size:** 8 1/4 x 10 7/8. **Cols./Page:** 2 and 3. **Key Personnel:** Debra Wasserman, Editor. **ISSN:** 0885-7636. **Subscription Rates:** $20 individuals; $30 Canada; $42 other countries; $3.50 single issue. **Remarks:** Advertising not accepted. **URL:** http://www.vrg.org. **Alt. Formats:** Microform.
Circ: 24,000

13416 World Business Review
World Business Research Center
11 E Chase St., No. 6D Phone: (410)332-9970
Baltimore, MD 21202 Fax: (410)332-9972

Consumer magazine covering business, banking, economic issues, and investment worldwide. **Founded:** Feb. 1991. **Freq:** Bimonthly. **Cols./Page:** 3. **Key Personnel:** Dr. Patrick Ngwolo, Editor; Eva Nwulia, Asst. to the Editor. **ISSN:** 1081-3284. **Subscription Rates:** $3.95 single issue; $39.95 two years USA. **Remarks:** Accepts advertising.
Ad Rates: BW: $5,000 **Circ:** Combined 14,000
4C: $8,000

13417 WBAL-AM - 1090
3800 Hooper Ave. Phone: (410)467-3000
Baltimore, MD 21211 Fax: (410)338-6483
Free: (800)467-9225

Format: News; Talk; Sports. **Networks:** ABC; ESPN Radio. **Founded:** 1925. **Operating Hours:** Continuous. **ADI:** Baltimore, MD. **Key Personnel:** Jeff Beauchamp, Contact, phone (410)338-6637, fax (410)366-4166, jbeauchamp@hearst.com; Ed Kiernan, Contact, phone (410)338-6571, ekiernan@hearst.com; Mike Wellbrock, Contact, phone (410)338-6466, fax (410)338-694, mwellbrock@hearst.com. **Local Programs:** *Allen Prell Show* 9:00 pm - 12:00 pm Monday-Friday, Malarie Pinkard, (410)338-6551; *Dave Durian Morning Show* 5:00 am - 9:00 am Monday-Friday, Chris Kendzierski, (410)338-6623; *Ron Smith Show* 3:00 pm - 6:00 pm Monday-Friday, Al Lizmi, (410)338-6653. **Wattage:** 50,000. **URL:** http://www.wbal.com.

13418 WBAL-TV - 11
3800 Hooper Ave. Phone: (410)467-3000
Baltimore, MD 21211 Fax: (410)338-6460

Format: Commercial TV. **Networks:** NBC. **Operating Hours:** Continuous. **ADI:** Baltimore, MD. **Key Personnel:** Kerry Richards, Contact; Hank Volde, Contact; Bru Fiwe, Contact; Bob Feiw, General Sales Mgr.; Emerson Coleman, Contact; Princell Hair, News Dir.

13419 WBFF-TV - 45
2000 W. 41 St. Phone: (410)467-4545
Baltimore, MD 21211 Fax: (410)467-5090
Free: (800)969-8845
E-mail: webmaster@wbff45.com

Format: Commercial TV. **Networks:** Independent; Fox. **Founded:** 1971. **Operating Hours:** Continuous. **ADI:** Baltimore, MD. **Key Personnel:** Darren Shapiro, General Sales Mgr.; Alan Sawyer, Local Sales Mgr.; Joe DeFeo, News Dir., fax (410)467-5093; Steve Marks, Regional Dir., fax (410)662-7964; Robert Epstein, Director of Sales/Mktg; Jeff Rhodes, Promotions Mgr., fax (410)467-4985; Barry Schiffer, Research Mgr. **Wattage:** 400,000. **Ad Rates:** $100-5,000 for 30 seconds; $200-7,500 for 60 seconds. **URL:** http://www.wbff45.com.

13420 WBGR-AM - 860
3000 Druid Park Dr. Phone: (410)367-7773
Baltimore, MD 21215 Fax: (410)367-4702

Format: Gospel. **Networks:** American Urban Radio. **Owner:** Jack Mortenson, Lexington Green, Ste. 6000, 3191 Nicholasville Rd., Lexington, KY 40503, (606)215-1000, Fax: (606)245-1600. **Founded:** 1984. **Formerly**: WAYE-AM. **Operating Hours:** Continuous; 5% network, 95% local. **ADI:** Baltimore, MD. **Key Personnel:** Maurice Hulbert, General Mgr.; Norven Goldsberry, Program Dir.; Su Wood, General Mgr.; Jack Mortenson, President. **Wattage:** 2500.

13421 WBJC-FM - 91.5
2901 Liberty Heights Ave. Phone: (410)462-8444
Baltimore, MD 21215-7893

Format: Classical; Public Radio. **Networks:** Public Radio International (PRI). **Owner:** Baltimore City Community College, at above address. **Founded:** 1951. **Operating Hours:** Continuous; 8% network, 92% local. **ADI:** Baltimore, MD. **Key Personnel:** Cary Smith, General Mgr.; John Kelley, Asst. Manager; Jonathan Palevsky, Program Dir.; Thomas Hill, Operations Dir.; Joe Hutchins, Development Director; Kim Farley, Membership Director; Frank Zeiler, Chief Engineer. **Local Programs:** *Face The Music*, Jonathan Palevsky; *Past Masters*, Jonathan Pavelsky. **Wattage:** 50,000. **Ad Rates:** Noncommercial; underwriting available.

13422 WBMD-AM - 750
305 Washington Ave., 4th Fl. Phone: (410)821-9000
Baltimore, MD 21204-4715 Fax: (410)483-2314

Format: Religious. **Networks:** Independent. **Owner:** American Radio Systems, at above address, Fax: (410)583-2314. **Founded:** 1946. **Operating Hours:** Sunrise-sunset. **ADI:** Baltimore, MD. **Key Personnel:** Clark West, Contact; Mike Magraw, Music Dir. **Wattage:** 1000. **Ad Rates:** Advertising accepted; rates available upon request.

13423 WCAO-AM - 600
1829 Reisterstown Rd., Ste. 420 Phone: (410)653-2200
Baltimore, MD 21208 Fax: (410)486-8057

Format: Gospel. **Networks:** NBC. **Owner:** CBS Radio, 40 W. 57th St., New York, NY 10019, (212)809-2900, Fax: (212)809-4010. **Founded:** 1922. **Operating Hours:** Continuous. **ADI:** Baltimore, MD. **Key Personnel:** Ben Hill, General Mgr.; Steve Goldstein, General Sales Mgr.; Lee Michaels, Program Dir., phone (410)602-9053. **Wattage:** 5000. **Ad Rates:** Advertising accepted; rates available upon request.

13424 WEAA-FM - 88.9
Hillen Rd. & Coldspring Ln. Phone: (443)885-4526
Baltimore, MD 21251 Fax: (410)319-3798

Format: Public Radio; Gospel; Urban Contemporary; Jazz; Talk. **Networks:** National Public Radio (NPR); AP; Corporation for Public Broadcasting. **Owner:** Morgan State University, at above address. **Founded:** Jan. 10, 1977. **Operating Hours:** Continuous; 5% network, 95% local. **ADI:** Baltimore, MD. **Key Personnel:** Maxie C. Jackson, General Mgr., phone (443)885-3807, mjackson@moac.morgan.edu-e-mail; Kyle LaRue, Program Dir., phone (443)885-4528, klarue@moac.morgan.edu-e-mail; Roslyn Nelson, News Dir., rnelson@moac.morgan.edu; Charles Fant, Chief Engineer; Sandi Mallory, Public Affairs Dir., smallory@moac.morgan.edu; Kevin Bradley, Development Dir., kbradley@moac.morgan.edu; Tanya Byrd, Assst. Program Dir./Promotions Dir., tbyrd@moac.morgan.edu. **Local Programs:** *Griot for the Young and Young at Heart*, Lawrence Shorter; *Two Way Talk*, Kevin Fowler. **Wattage:** 12,600. **Ad Rates:** Underwriting available. **URL:** http://www.morgan.edu/weaa.

13425 WERQ-AM - 1010
100 St. Paul St., 4th Fl. Phone: (410)332-8200
Baltimore, MD 21202 Fax: (410)593-4550

Simulcasts: CNN at night and on weekends. **Networks:** CNN Radio. **Owner:** United Broadcasting Co., Inc., 4733 Bethesda Ave., Ste. 808, Bethesda, MD 20814, (301)652-7706. **Founded:** 1981. **Formerly**: WSID-AM (1992); WYST-AM. **Operating Hours:** Continuous. **ADI:** Baltimore, MD. **Key Personnel:** Wendy Corey, News Dir.; Robert Philips, General Sales Mgr.; Hal Martin, Contact; William Hooper, General Mgr.; Mary Speake, Contact. **Wattage:** 1000.

13426 WERQ-FM - 92
100 St. Paul St., 4th Fl. Phone: (410)332-8200
Baltimore, MD 21202 Fax: (410)539-4550

Format: Contemporary Hit Radio (CHR). **Owner:** Radio One, at above address. **Founded:** 1981. **Formerly:** WLPL-FM (1992); WYST-FM. **Operating Hours:** Continuous. **ADI:** Baltimore, MD. **Key Personnel:** Cathy Hughes, CEO, General Manager; Wendy Corey, News Dir.; Tom Calococci, Program Dir.; Malean Alston, Promotions Dir.; Pam Somers, Station Mgr. **Wattage:** 37,000. **Ad Rates:** Advertising accepted; rates available upon request.

13427 WHSW-TV - 24
4820 Seton Dr., Ste. M-N Phone: (410)358-2400
Baltimore, MD 21215 Fax: (410)764-7232

Format: Commercial TV. **Networks:** Home Shopping Network. **Owner:** Silver King Communications, 12425 28th St North No. 300, St. Petersburg, FL 33716, (813)573-0339. **Formerly:** WJKL-TV. **Operating Hours:** Continuous. **ADI:** Baltimore, MD. **Key Personnel:** Kenneth Becker, Vice President/Station Manager; Bonnie McCausey, Program Director. **Ad Rates:** $25-75 for 30 seconds.

13428 WITH-AM - 1230
5 Light St., Ste. 650 Phone: (410)528-1230
Baltimore, MD 21202 Fax: (410)528-1256

Format: Oldies. **Networks:** Mutual Broadcasting System. **Owner:** Guardian Communications, 800 Comptom Rd., No. 33, Cincinnati, OH 45231, (513)931-8080, Fax: (513)931-8108. **Founded:** 1941. **Operating Hours:** Continuous. **ADI:** Baltimore, MD. **Key Personnel:** Gerry Liss, General Mgr.; Bob Mathers, Sales Mgr.; Niles Seaberg, Program/Operations Mgr.; Mark Patey, Promotions Mgr. **Wattage:** 1000. **Ad Rates:** $24-50 for 30 seconds; $30-50 for 60 seconds.

13429 WIYY-FM - 97.9
3800 Hooper Ave. Phone: (410)889-0098
Baltimore, MD 21211-1313 Fax: (410)675-7946
Free: (800)467-9225

Format: Album-Oriented Rock (AOR). **Networks:** ABC. **Founded:** 1958. **Formerly:** WBAL-FM. **Operating Hours:** Continuous. **ADI:** Baltimore, MD. **Key Personnel:** Ed Kiernan, General Mgr., phone (410)467-3000, ekiernan@hearst.com. **Wattage:** 50,000 ERP.

13430 WJCE-AM - 680
2000 W. 41st St. Phone: (901)767-0104
Baltimore, MD 21211 Fax: (901)767-0582

Format: Oldies. **Owner:** Sinclair Radio of Memphis Licensee, at above address. **Operating Hours:** Continuous. **Key Personnel:** Curt Peterson, General Mgr. **Wattage:** 10,000.

13431 WJHU-FM - 88.1
2216 N. Charles St. Phone: (410)516-9548
Baltimore, MD 21218 Fax: (410)516-1976
E-mail: mail@wjhu.org

Format: Talk; Jazz; News. **Networks:** National Public Radio (NPR); Public Radio International (PRI). **Founded:** 1986. **Operating Hours:** 24 hours 80% network; 20% local. **ADI:** Baltimore, MD. **Key Personnel:** Dianne MacLeod, Dir. of Administration; Kevin Donohue, Underwriting Sales Mgr/Development Dir. **Local Programs:** *BSO Casual Concerts*, Judith Schonbach, (410)516-6305; *Marc Steiner Show*, Marc Steiner. **Wattage:** 10,000. **Ad Rates:** Noncommercial; underwriting available. **URL:** www.wjhu.org/.

13432 WJZ-TV - 13
3725 Maldden Ave. Phone: (410)578-7501
TV Hill Fax: (410)578-7502
Baltimore, MD 21211

Format: Commercial TV. **Networks:** CBS. **Operating Hours:** Continuous. **ADI:** Baltimore, MD. **Key Personnel:** Jay Newman, Contact.

13433 WLIF-FM - 101.9
One W. Pennsylvania Ave., Ste. 850 Phone: (410)823-1570
Fax: (410)296-9543
Baltimore, MD 21204

Format: Adult Contemporary. **Founded:** 1970. **Operating Hours:** Continuous; 5% network, 95% local. **ADI:** Baltimore, MD. **Key Personnel:** Ken Stevens, General Mgr.; Mr. Roy Deutschman, General Sales Mgr.; Gary Balaban, Program Dir. **Wattage:** 50,000. **Ad Rates:** Advertising accepted; rates available upon request.

13434 WMAR-TV - 2
6400 York Rd. Phone: (410)377-2222
Baltimore, MD 21212 Fax: (410)377-0493
E-mail: wmartv2@aol.com

Format: Commercial TV. **Networks:** ABC. **Owner:** Scripps Howard Broadcasting Co., 312 Walnut St., 28th Fl., Cincinnati, OH 45201, (513)977-3000, Fax: (513)977-3768, Free: (800)888-3000. **Founded:** 1947. **Operating Hours:** Continuous. **ADI:** Baltimore, MD. **Key Personnel:** Steve Gigliotti, V. Pres./Gen. Mgr., phone (410)372-2300, fax (410)377-3010; Steve Bock, General Sales Mgr., phone (410)372-2370, fax (410)377-0439; Robert Imhoff, Controller, phone (410)372-2409, fax (410)377-0493; Drew Berry, News Dir., phone (410)372-2505; Joseph Bruno, Engineering Dir., phone (410)372-2602; Harry Kakel, Production Mgr., phone (410)372-2602; Lori Grant, Dir. of Public Affairs, phone (41-)372-2656; Dayna Crisco, Dir. of Human Resources, phone (410)372-2305, fax (410)377-3010; Bill Bradley, Dir. of Sales, phone (410)372-2362, fax (410)377-0434. **Local Programs:** *Face to Face* 11 a.m. Saturday, Lori Grant, Public Affairs Dir.; *2 the Point* 7:30 a.m. Sunday, Lori Grant.

13435 WMPB-TV - 67
c/o Maryland Public Broadcasting Commission Phone: (410)356-5600
Fax: (410)581-4338
11767 Owings Mills Blvd.
Owings Mills, MD 21117
Free: (800)223-3678
E-mail: comments@mpt.org

Format: Public TV. **Simulcasts:** WMPT, WCPB, WWPB, WGPT, WFPT. **Networks:** Public Broadcasting Service (PBS); Eastern Educational Television. **Owner:** Maryland Public Broadcasting Commission, at above address. **Founded:** 1969. **Operating Hours:** 3 a.m.-1:30 a.m. **ADI:** Baltimore, MD. **Key Personnel:** Robert J. Shuman, Pres./CEO; Dr. Archie L. Buffkins, Sr. Vice Pres., Broadcasting; Janice Wilson, Sr. Vice Pres., Marketing & Development; Larry D. Unger, Sr. Vice Pres., Administration & Finance; Martin Jacobs, Vice Pres., Finance & Accounting; Gladys M. Kaplan, Vice Pres., Human Resources; Ann Engelman, Vice Pres., Programming/Broadcast Serv.; Everett L. Marshburn, Vice Pres., Broadcast Productions; John T. Potthast, Vice Pres., National Productions; Barry P. Freidly, Vice Pres., Memebership; Hannah Lee Byron, Dir., Corp. Comm. & Gov't Affairs; Carol Wonsavage, Dir., Regional Communications; Sharon Philippart, Dir., National Communications. **Wattage:** 1,000,000. **URL:** http://www.mpt.org.

13436 WNUV-TV - 54
2000 W. 41st St. Phone: (410)467-8854
Baltimore, MD 21211 Fax: (410)235-8450

Format: Commercial TV. **Operating Hours:** Continuous. **ADI:** Baltimore, MD. **Key Personnel:** Robert Gluck, Regional Dir., phone (410)662-1480, fax (410)662-7964; Bill Fanshawe, General Sales Mgr., phone (410)662-1454; Bill Finch, Program Dir.; Barry Schiffer, Research Mgr.; Alan Sawyer, LSM, phone (410)662-1433. **Ad Rates:** $100-2,500 for 30 seconds; $150-4,500 for 60 seconds. **URL:** http://www.wnuv54.com.

13437 WOCT-FM - 104.3
600 Washington Ave., Ste. 201 Phone: (410)825-1043
Baltimore, MD 21204 Fax: (410)583-5557

Format: Classic Rock. **Formerly:** WBSB-FM; WSSF-FM. **Operating Hours:** Continuous. **ADI:** Baltimore, MD. **Key Personnel:** Ardie Gregory, General Mgr.; Jay Supovitz, General Sales Mgr.; Terry Trouyet, Contact. **Wattage:** 50,000. **URL:** http://www.woctfm.com.

13438 WOGY-FM - 94.1
2000 W. 41st St. Phone: (901)767-0104
Baltimore, MD 21211 Fax: (901)767-0582

Format: Country. **Owner:** Sinclair Radio of Memphis Licensee, at above address. **Operating Hours:** Continuous. **Key Personnel:** Curt Peterson, General Mgr. **Wattage:** 50,000.

13439 WPOC-FM - 93.1
711 W. 40th St. Phone: (410)366-3693
Baltimore, MD 21211 Fax: (410)235-3899
E-mail: wpoc93fm@prodigy.com

Format: Country. **Owner:** Nationwide Mutual Insurance Co., 1 Nationwide Plaza, Columbus, OH 43216, (614)249-7676, Fax: (614)249-6995. **Founded:** 1974. **Operating Hours:** Continuous. **ADI:** Baltimore, MD. **Key Personnel:** Shelia Silverstein, Promotions Dir.; Bill Vanko, News Dir.; Jeff Thomas, General Sales Mgr.; Jim Dolan, General Mgr.; Lang Sturgeon, Chief Engineer. **Wattage:** 16,000. **Ad Rates:** Advertising accepted; rates available upon request.

13440 WRBS-FM - 95.1
3600 Georgetown Rd. Phone: (410)247-4100
Baltimore, MD 21227-1698 Fax: (410)247-4533
E-mail: info@wrbs.com

Format: Religious. **Owner:** Peter & John Radio Fellowship, 8713 Liberty Plaza, Randallstown, MD 21133, (410)922-0602. **Founded:** 1964. **Operating Hours:** Continuous; 5% network, 95% local. **ADI:** Baltimore, MD. **Key Personnel:** David Paul, News Dir.; Steve Lawhon, Station Mgr.; Tom Bisset, General Mgr.; Peter Allen, Chief Engineer. **Local Programs:** *Baltimore Speaks Out*, Tom Bisset; *Interviews*, David Paul. **Wattage:** 50,000. **Ad Rates:** $35-75 per unit. **URL:** http://www.wrbs.com.

WSMD-AM - See La Plata

13441 WTMD-FM - 89.7
Towson State University Phone: (410)830-8938
8000 York Rd. Fax: (410)830-2609
Baltimore, MD 21252
E-mail: wtmd@towson.edu

Format: Alternative/New Music/Progressive. **Networks:** Independent. **Founded:** 1976. **Formerly:** WCVT-FM (1992). **Operating Hours:** Continuous. **ADI:** Baltimore, MD. **Key Personnel:** Dr. John R. Turner III, General Mgr., phone (410)830-3604, jturner@towson.edu; Jim Armstrong, Program Dir., phone (410)830-8937, jarmstrong@towson.edu; John Spivey, Music Dir., phone (410)830-8937, jspivey@towson.edu. **Local Programs:** *The Breeze (Format) Music for the 90's.* **Wattage:** 10,000. **Ad Rates:** Noncommercial.

13442 WWIN-AM - 1400
100 St. Paul St. Phone: (410)332-8200
Baltimore, MD 21202 Fax: (410)783-4791

Format: Gospel; Religious. **Networks:** Unistar. **Founded:** 1951. **Operating Hours:** Continuous. **ADI:** Baltimore, MD. **Key Personnel:** Alfred Liggins, General Mgr.; Debbie Edwards, Contact; Karl Goehring, Chief Engineer; Mike Roberts, Program Dir.; Pam Somers, Contact. **Wattage:** 3000.

13443 WWIN-FM - 95.9
100 St. Paul St. Phone: (410)332-8200
Baltimore, MD 21202 Fax: (410)752-2252

Format: Urban Contemporary. **Networks:** Unistar. **Founded:** 1964. **Formerly:** WHTE-FM (1989). **Operating Hours:** Continuous. **ADI:** Baltimore, MD. **Key Personnel:** Alfred Liggins, General Mgr.; Debbie Edwards, Contact; Karl Goehring, Chief Engineer; Terri Avery, Program Dir.; Pam Somers, Contact. **Wattage:** 3000.

13444 WWMX-FM - 106.5
600 Washington Ave., No. 201 Phone: (410)852-1065
Baltimore, MD 21204 Fax: (410)583-1065

Format: Adult Contemporary. **Operating Hours:** Continuous. **ADI:** Baltimore, MD. **Key Personnel:** Robert Lind, General Mgr.; Ardie Gregory, Station Mgr.; Greg Dunkin, Program Dir.; Jay Supovitz, Contact. **Wattage:** 50,000.

13445 WXYV-FM - 102.7
1829 Reistertown Rd. Phone: (410)653-2200
Baltimore, MD 21208 Fax: (410)486-8057

Format: Urban Contemporary. **Networks:** NBC. **Owner:** CBS Radio, 40 W. 47th St., New York, NY 10019, (212)809-2900, Fax: (212)809-4010. **Founded:** 1947. **Operating Hours:** Continuous. **ADI:** Baltimore, MD. **Key Personnel:** Dave Ferguson, Program Dir.; Ben Hill, General Mgr.; Steve Goldstein, General Sales Mgr. **Wattage:** 50,000. **Ad Rates:** Advertising accepted; rates available upon request.

BEL AIR†, pop. 7,814.

Harford Co. 23 m NE of Baltimore. Shoe factory. Horse breeding. Dairy.

13446 Aegis
Homestead Publishing Co., Inc.
10 Hays St. Phone: (410)838-4400
PO Box 189 Fax: (410)638-0357
Bel Air, MD 21014
Free: (888)879-1710

Community newspaper group. **Founded:** 1856. **Freq:** Twice weekly. **Print Method:** Offset. **Cols./Page:** 6. **Col. Width:** 26 nonpareils. **Col. Depth:** 294 agate lines. **Key Personnel:** Ted Hendricks, Exec. Editor; John D. Worthington IV, Publisher; Marianne Pfeffer, Advertising Dir. **Subscription Rates:** $32 local; $40 in state; $45 out of state. **Remarks:** Accepts advertising.
Ad Rates: BW: $1,955.52 **Circ:** Wed. ★**34,390**
4C: $2,280.52 Fri. ★**34,390**
SAU: $15.52
PCI: $15.52

13447 The Weekender
Homestead Publishing Co., Inc.
10 Hays St. Phone: (410)838-4400
PO Box 189 Fax: (410)638-0357
Bel Air, MD 21014
Free: (888)879-1710

Community newspaper. **Founded:** 1986. **Freq:** Weekly. **Print Method:** Web offset. **Trim Size:** 11 1/2 x 14. **Cols./Page:** 5. **Col. Width:** 12 1/2 picas. **Col. Depth:** 13 inches. **Key**

Personnel: Ted Hendricks, Editor; Peter A. Jay, Publisher; Irna M. Jay, Publisher; Philip M. Stoffan, Editor. **Remarks:** Accepts advertising. **Formerly**: The Enterprise (1992); Hartford Democrat.
Ad Rates: BW: $260 **Circ:** ‡10,000
PCI: $4

13448 Clearview Partners
2242 Conwingo Rd. Phone: (410)838-7600
Bel Air, MD 21015 Fax: (410)838-8546

Owner: Clearview Partners, at above address. **Founded:** 1988. **Formerly:** Aireview CATV, Inc. (1995); GS Communications (1996); Clearview CATV, Inc. (1996). **Key Personnel:** William Domurad, President, phone (717)285-3746, fax (717)285-2340; Douglas Nace, General Mgr. **Cities Served:** Harford County, MD; Chanceford Twp., Crossroads Boro, Delta, East Hopewell Twp., Fawn Grove, Fawn Twp., Hopewell Twp., Lower Chanceford Twp., North Hopewell Twp., Peach Bottom Twp., Shrewsbury Twp., Stewartstown, Winterstown Boro, PA; Harford County: subscribing households 10,013; 53 channels; 1 community access channel; 168 hours per week community access programming.

13449 WHFC-FM - 91.1
401 Thomas Run Rd. Phone: (410)836-4305
Bel Air, MD 21015

Format: Classical; Educational; Adult Contemporary. **Founded:** 1972. **Key Personnel:** John Davlin, General Mgr. **Wattage:** 2240.

BELTSVILLE

13450 The Beltsville News
The Beltsville-Vansville District Citizens' Association, Inc.
11328 Montgomery Rd. Phone: (301)937-8962
Beltsville, MD 20705 Fax: (301)937-4509

Community newspaper. **Founded:** 1952. **Freq:** Monthly. **Key Personnel:** Sally A. Ehrle, Managing Editor; Evelyn Adkins, Business Mgr., phone (301)937-7954, fax (301)937-6620; Ted Ladd, Advertising Exec., phone (301)937-6796; Matt Bernota, Advertising Exec., phone (301)937-7259, fax (301)931-8150. **Subscription Rates:** Free; $10 by mail. **Remarks:** Accepts display and classified advertising.
Ad Rates: BW: $437.50 **Circ:** Non-paid ‡14,000
PCI: $6.25

BERLIN

13451 Maryland Coast Dispatch
PO Box 467 Phone: (410)641-4561
Berlin, MD 21811 Fax: (410)641-0488
Publication E-mail: dispatch@dmv.com

Tabloid. **Founded:** 1970. **Freq:** Weekly. **Trim Size:** 10 x 13 1/2. **Cols./Page:** 4. **Col. Width:** 2 3/4 inches. **Col. Depth:** 13 1/2in inches. **Remarks:** Accepts advertising.
Ad Rates: BW: $607.95 **Circ:** Paid ‡25,000
4C: $907.95
SAU: $11

BETHESDA, pop. 78,300.

Montgomery Co. (WC). Adjoins Washington, DC, on the East. Residential. Research and Development, Science and Medical center.

13452 ACSM Bulletin
American Congress on Surveying and Mapping
5410 Grosvenor Ln. Phone: (301)493-0200
Bethesda, MD 20814-2122 Fax: (301)493-8245
Publisher E-mail: barbacsm@mindspring.com

Magazine on new techniques, developments, and projects in surveying, cartography, and geodesy. **Subtitle:** Promoting Advancement in Surveying and Mapping. **Founded:** 1961. **Freq:** Bimonthly. **Print Method:** Web offset. **Trim Size:** 8 1/4 x 10 7/8. **Cols./Page:** 3. **Col. Width:** 28 nonpareils. **Col. Depth:** 140 agate lines. **Key Personnel:** Gail Papa, Editor. **ISSN:** 0747-9417. **Subscription Rates:** $75; $85 other countries. $13 single issue. **Remarks:** Accepts advertising.
Ad Rates: BW: $922 **Circ:** 10,000
4C: $1,622

13453 Advances in Physiology Education
The American Physiological Society
9650 Rockville Pike Phone: (301)530-7070
Bethesda, MD 20814-3991 Fax: (301)571-1814
Publisher E-mail: info@aps.faseb.org

Journal covering physiology education. **Founded:** 1989. **Freq:** 2/year. **Print Method:** Web offset. **Trim Size:** 8 3/8 x 10 7/8. **Cols./Page:** 2. **Col. Width:** 21 picas. **Col. Depth:** 58 picas. **Key Personnel:** P.A. Hansen, Editor. **ISSN:** 1043-4046. **Subscription Rates:** $17; $20 other countries; $25 Industry; $28 Industry, other countries. **Remarks:** Advertising accepted; rates available upon request.
Circ: Paid ‡216
Non-paid ‡40

13454 Agricultural and Environmental Biotechnology Abstracts
Cambridge Scientific Abstracts
7200 Wisconsin Ave., Ste. 601 Phone: (301)961-6700
Bethesda, MD 20814-4823 Fax: (301)961-6720
Free: (800)843-7751
Publication E-mail: market@csa.com
Publisher E-mail: sales@csa.com; journals@csa.com

Scientific journal. **Founded:** 1993. **Freq:** Quarterly plus annual index. **Key Personnel:** Deborah Whitman, Editor, deborah@csa.com; Craig Emerson, Managing Editor; Ted Caris, Publisher. **ISSN:** 1063-1151. **Subscription Rates:** $425 print and electronic; $385 electronic. **Remarks:** Advertising not accepted. **Online:** Dialog (The Dialog Corporation); STN International. **URL:** http://www.csa.com. **Alt. Formats:** CD-ROM. **Formerly**: Biotechnology Research Abstracts.
Circ: (Not Reported)

13455 Algology, Mycology & Protozoology: Microbiology Abstracts, Section C
Cambridge Scientific Abstracts
7200 Wisconsin Ave., Ste. 601 Phone: (877)434-6339
Bethesda, MD 20814 Fax: (301)961-6790
Free: (800)843-7751
Publisher E-mail: market@csa.com

Scientific journal. **Founded:** 1972. **Freq:** Monthly. **Print Method:** Offset. **Trim Size:** 6 1/2 x 9. **Cols./Page:** 2. **Key Personnel:** Roberta Gardner, Editor, roberta@csa.com; Craig Emerson, Managing Editor; Ted Caris, Publisher; Matt Dunie, Vice President of Marketing. **ISSN:** 0301-2328. **Subscription Rates:** $1,115 print and electronic; $950 electronic only. **Remarks:** Advertising not accepted. **Online:** Dialog (The Dialog Corporation); STN International. **URL:** http://www.csa.com. **Alt. Formats:** CD-ROM, SilverPlatter Information Inc.
Circ: (Not Reported)

13456 American Journal of Health-System Pharmacy
American Society of Health-System Pharmacists
7272 Wisconsin Ave. Phone: (301)657-3000
Bethesda, MD 20814 Fax: (301)652-8278
Publication E-mail: ajhp@ashp.org

Journal for pharmacists practicing in health-systems (acute care, ambulatory care, homecare, long term care, HMO's, PPOs, & PBMs). **Founded:** 1943. **Freq:** Bimonthly. **Print Method:** Offset. **Trim Size:** 8 1/8 x 10 7/8. **Cols./Page:** 2. **Col. Width:** 19 picas. **Col. Depth:** 55 picas. **Key Personnel:** C. Richard Talley, Editor, phone (301)657-3000, fax (301)657-1641. **ISSN:** 1079-2082. **Subscription Rates:** $165 individuals; $175 other countries; $195 Canada. **Remarks:** Accepts advertising. **Formerly**: American Journal of Hospital Pharmacy.
Ad Rates: GLR: $3.60 **Circ:** Paid ‡28,765
BW: $3,100 Non-paid ‡10,505
4C: $4,870

13457 The American Journal of Occupational Therapy
American Occupational Therapy Association, Inc. (AOTA)
PO Box 31220 Phone: (301)652-2682
Bethesda, MD 20824-1220 Fax: (301)652-7711
Free: (800)877-1383
Publication E-mail: ajotsis@aota.org

Journal providing a forum for occupational therapy personnel to share research, case studies, and new theory. **Founded:** 1947. **Freq:** Bimonthly. **Print Method:** Offset. **Trim Size:** 8 1/2 x 11. **Cols./Page:** 2 and 3. **Col. Width:** 20 picas. **Col. Depth:** 58 picas. **Key Personnel:** Elaine Viseltear, Editor Emerita; Betty Hasselkus, Editor, phone (301)652-2682; Amy Eutsey, Managing Editor, phone (301)652-2682, amye@aota.org; Stephanie Abrams, Advertising Sales Specialist, sabrams@aota.org. **ISSN:** 0272-9490. **Subscription Rates:** $50 individuals; $120 industry; $130 other countries; $12 single issue. **Remarks:** Accepts advertising. **URL:** http://www.aota.org.
Ad Rates: BW: $1,745 **Circ:** 60,000
4C: $2,445

13458 The American Journal of Pathology
9650 Rockville pike Phone: (301)571-0107
Bethesda, MD 20814 Fax: (301)571-0108
Publication E-mail: ajp@pathol.faseb.org

Journal publishing original experimental and clinical studies in diagnostic and experimental pathology. **Founded:** 1901. **Freq:** Monthly. **Print Method:** Sheetfed offset. **Trim Size:** 8 1/8 x 11. **Cols./Page:** 2. **Col. Width:** 39 nonpareils. **Col. Depth:** 140 agate lines. **ISSN:** 0002-9440. **Subscription Rates:** $165; $90 interns and residents, U.S.; $155 interns and residents, Canada; $230 other countries; $250 Industry; $315 Industry, other countries. $26 single issue. **Remarks:** Accepts advertising. **URL:** http://www.edoc.com/pathology.
Ad Rates: BW: $1,000 **Circ:** ‡5,219
4C: $1,815

13459 American Journal of Physiology: Cell Physiology
The American Physiological Society
9650 Rockville Pike Phone: (301)530-7070
Bethesda, MD 20814 Fax: (301)571-1814
Publisher E-mail: info@aps.faseb.org

Journal promoting contemporary and innovative approaches to the study of cell and general physiology. **Founded:** 1977. **Freq:** Monthly. **Print Method:** Offset. **Trim Size:** 8 3/8 x 10 7/8. **Cols./Page:** 2. **Col. Width:** 21 picas. **Col. Depth:** 56 picas. **Key Personnel:** K.E. Barrett, Editor; Sue Pokray, Advertising Mgr. **ISSN:** 0363-6143. **Subscription Rates:** $248; $288 Canada and Mexico; $328 other countries; $370 industry; $410 Canada and Mexico industry; $450 other countries industry; $124 members. **Remarks:** Accepts advertising.
Ad Rates: BW: $630 **Circ:** Paid 445
4C: $725 Non-paid 93

13460 American Journal of Physiology (Consolidated)
The American Physiological Society
9650 Rockville Pike
Bethesda, MD 20814
Publisher E-mail: info@aps.faseb.org

Physiology journal publishing articles from eight individual journals. **Founded:** 1898. **Freq:** Monthly. **Print Method:** Offset. **Trim Size:** 8 3/8 x 10 7/8. **Cols./Page:** 2. **Col. Width:** 21 picas. **Col. Depth:** 56 picas. **Key Personnel:** Brenda B. Rauner, Exec. Editor. **ISSN:** 0002-9513. **Subscription Rates:** $1,224 individuals; $1,344 Canada and Mexico; $1,524 other countries; $1,835 industry; $1,955 Canada and Mexico industry; $2,135 other countries industry; $612 APS members. **Remarks:** Accepts advertising.
Ad Rates: BW: $350 **Circ:** Paid ‡2336
4C: $955 Non-paid ‡182

13461 American Journal of Physiology: Endocrinology and Metabolism
The American Physiological Society
9650 Rockville Pike Phone: (301)530-7070
Bethesda, MD 20814 Fax: (301)571-1814
Publisher E-mail: info@aps.faseb.org

Journal reporting research on the levels of organization ranging from the molecular, subcellular, and cellular levels to the whole animal, including the human being. **Founded:** 1980. **Freq:** Monthly. **Print Method:** Offset. **Trim Size:** 8 3/8 x 10 7/8. **Cols./Page:** 2. **Col. Width:** 21 picas. **Col. Depth:** 56 picas. **Key Personnel:** J.E. Pessin, Editor; Sue Pokroy, Advertising Mgr. **ISSN:** 0193-1849. **Subscription Rates:** $170; $210 Canada and Mexico; $230 elsewhere; $255 institutions; $295 institutions, Canada and Mexico; $315 institutions, other countries; $85 members APS members. **Remarks:** Accepts advertising. **URL:** http://www.faseb.org/aps.
Ad Rates: BW: $630 **Circ:** Paid 321
4C: $725 Non-paid 88

13462 American Journal of Physiology: Gastrointestinal and Liver Physiology
The American Physiological Society
9650 Rockville Pike
Bethesda, MD 20814-3991
Publisher E-mail: info@aps.faseb.org

Journal publishing original papers dealing with normal or abnormal function of the alimentary canal and its accessory organs. **Founded:** 1980. **Freq:** Monthly. **Print Method:** Offset. **Trim Size:** 8 3/8 x 10 7/8. **Cols./Page:** 2. **Col. Width:** 21 picas. **Col. Depth:** 56 picas. **Key Personnel:** M.F. Kagnoff, Editor; Brenda B. Rauner, Advertising Mgr. **ISSN:** 0193-1857. **Subscription Rates:** $170; $210 Canada and Mexico; $230 other countries; $255 institutions; $295 institutions, Canada and Mexico; $315 institutions, other countries; $85 members. **Remarks:** Accepts advertising.
Ad Rates: BW: $630 **Circ:** Paid 372
4C: $725 Non-paid 88

13463 American Journal of Physiology: Heart and Circulatory Physiology
The American Physiological Society
9650 Rockville Pike Phone: (301)530-7070
Bethesda, MD 20814-3991 Fax: (301)571-1814
Publisher E-mail: info@aps.faseb.org

Journal presenting studies and new descriptions of cardiovascular functions. **Founded:** 1977. **Freq:** Monthly. **Print Method:** Offset. **Trim Size:** 8 3/8 x 10 7/8. **Cols./Page:** 2. **Col. Width:** 21 picas. **Col. Depth:** 56 picas. **Key Personnel:** D.R. Harder, Editor; Sue Pokroy, Advertising Mgr. **ISSN:** 0363-6135. **Subscription Rates:** $334; $167 members; $384 Canada and Mexico; $434 other countries; $500 industry;

$550 Canada and Mexico industry; $600 other countries industry. **Remarks:** Accepts advertising.
Ad Rates: BW: $630 **Circ:** Paid 617
4C: $725 Non-paid 88

13464 American Journal of Physiology: Lung Cellular and Molecular Physiology
The American Physiological Society
9650 Rockville Pike Phone: (301)530-7070
Bethesda, MD 20814 Fax: (301)571-1814
Publisher E-mail: info@aps.faseb.org

Journal publishing original papers on molecular, cellular, and merphological aspects of cells and components of the respiratory system. **Founded:** 1989. **Freq:** Monthly. **Print Method:** Offset. **Trim Size:** 8 3/8 x 10 7/8. **Cols./Page:** 2. **Col. Width:** 21 picas. **Col. Depth:** 56 picas. **Key Personnel:** D.E. Rannels, Editor; Sue Pokroy, Advertising Mgr. **ISSN:** 1040-0605. **Subscription Rates:** $160; $200 Canada and Mexico; $220 other countries; $240 institutions; $280 institutions, Canada and Mexico; $300 institutions, other countries; $80 members. **Remarks:** Accepts advertising.
Ad Rates: BW: $630 **Circ:** Paid 455
4C: $725 Non-paid 69

13465 American Journal of Physiology: Regulatory, Integrative and Comparative Physiology
The American Physiological Society
9650 Rockville Pike Phone: (301)530-7070
Bethesda, MD 20814-3991 Fax: (301)571-1814
Publisher E-mail: info@aps.faseb.org

Journal publishing papers about physiological science. **Founded:** 1977. **Freq:** Monthly. **Print Method:** Offset. **Trim Size:** 8 3/8 x 10 7/8. **Cols./Page:** 2. **Col. Width:** 21 picas. **Col. Depth:** 56 picas. **Key Personnel:** J.E. Hall, Editor; Sue Pokroy, Advertising Mgr. **ISSN:** 0363-6119. **Subscription Rates:** $226; $271 Canada and Mexico; $301 other countries; $340 institutions; $385 institutions, Canada and Mexico; $415 institutions, other countries; $113 members. **Remarks:** Accepts advertising.
Ad Rates: BW: $630 **Circ:** Paid 240
4C: $725 Non-paid 87

13466 American Journal of Physiology: Renal Physiology
The American Physiological Society
9650 Rockville Pike Phone: (301)530-7118
Bethesda, MD 20814 Fax: (301)571-8305
Publisher E-mail: info@aps.faseb.org

Journal covering information on kidney and urinary tract physiology, epithelial cell biology and control of body fluid volume and composition. **Founded:** 1977. **Freq:** Monthly. **Print Method:** Offset. **Trim Size:** 8 3/8 x 10 7/8. **Cols./Page:** 2. **Col. Width:** 21 picas. **Col. Depth:** 56 picas. **Key Personnel:** S.C. Herbert, Editor; Sue Pokroy, Advertising Mgr. **ISSN:** 0363-6127. **Subscription Rates:** $190 U.S.; $225 Canada and Mexico; $247 other countries; $255 institutions; $295 institutions Canada and Mexico; $315 institutions other countries; $95 APS members. **Remarks:** Accepts advertising. **Formerly:** American Journal of Physiology: Renal, Fluid and Electrolyte Physiology.
Ad Rates: BW: $630 **Circ:** Paid 512
4C: $725 Non-paid 89

13467 Animal Behavior Abstracts
Cambridge Scientific Abstracts
7200 Wisconsin Ave., Ste. 601 Phone: (877)434-6339
Bethesda, MD 20814 Fax: (301)961-6790
Free: (800)843-7751
Publication E-mail: sales@csa.com
Publisher E-mail: market@csa.com

Scientific journal covering behavioral and related studies. **Founded:** 1972. **Freq:** Quarterly. **Print Method:** Offset. **Trim Size:** 6 1/2 x 9. **Cols./Page:** 2. **Key Personnel:** Robert Hilton, Editor, robert@csa.com; Craig Emerson, Managing Editor; Ted Caris, Publisher; Matt Dunie, Vice President of Marketing. **ISSN:** 0301-8695. **Subscription Rates:** $740 print and electronic; $630 electronic only. **Remarks:** Advertising not accepted. **Online:** Dialog (The Dialog Corporation); STN International. **URL:** http://www.csa.com. **Alt. Formats:** CD-ROM, SilverPlatter Information Inc.
Circ: (Not Reported)

13468 APMA News
American Podiatric Medical Association
9312 Old Georgetown Rd. Phone: (301)571-9200
Bethesda, MD 20814-1646 Fax: (301)530-2752
Free: (800)ASK-APMA

Non-scientific news for member podiatrists. **Founded:** Nov. 1980. **Freq:** Monthly. **Print Method:** Web heatset. **Trim Size:** 8 1/8 x 10 7/8. **Cols./Page:** 3. **Col. Width:** 2 3/16 inches. **Col. Depth:** 9 inches. **Key Personnel:** David J. Zych, Editor, djzych@apma.org; Jenyfer A. Morris, Advertising Mgr.; Edith A. Caro; Rodney Peele, Contact. **ISSN:** 8750-2585. **Subscription Rates:** $25 individuals; $50 institutions.
Ad Rates: BW: $1,300 **Circ:** Paid ‡12,375
4C: $675 Non-paid ‡125

13469 ASFA 2: Ocean Technology, Policy & Non-Living Resources
Cambridge Scientific Abstracts
7200 Wisconsin Ave., Ste. 601 Phone: (877)434-6339
Bethesda, MD 20814 Fax: (301)961-6790
Free: (800)843-7751
Publication E-mail: sales@csa.com
Publisher E-mail: market@csa.com

Scientific journal covering oceanography, offshore technology and operations. **Subtitle:** Aquatic Sciences and Fisheries Abstracts. **Founded:** 1971. **Freq:** Monthly. **Print Method:** Letterpress and offset. **Trim Size:** 6 1/2 x 9. **Cols./Page:** 2. **Key Personnel:** Craig Emerson, Editor, craig@csa.com; Angela Hitti, VP/Editorial; Ted Caris, Publisher; Matt Dunie, Vice President of Marketing. **ISSN:** 0140-5381. **Subscription Rates:** $995 print and electronic; $845 electronic only. **Remarks:** Advertising not accepted. **Online:** Dialog (The Dialog Corporation); STN International; DIMDI; CAN/OLE; ESA-IRS. **URL:** http://www.csa.com. **Alt. Formats:** CD-ROM, SilverPlatter Information Inc.
Circ: (Not Reported)

13470 ASFA 3: Aquatic Pollution and Environmental Quality
Cambridge Scientific Abstracts
7200 Wisconsin Ave., Ste. 601 Phone: (877)434-6339
Bethesda, MD 20814 Fax: (301)961-6790
Free: (800)843-7751
Publisher E-mail: market@csa.com

Journal containing information on the aquatic environments and marine pollution problems. **Subtitle:** Aquatic Sciences and Fisheries. **Founded:** 1990. **Freq:** Bimonthly. **Print Method:** Letterpress and Offset. **Trim Size:** 6 1/2 x 9. **Key Personnel:** Craig Emerson, Editor, craig@csa.com; Angela Hitti, VP/Editorial; Ted Caris, Publisher. **ISSN:** 1045-6031. **Subscription Rates:** $405 print and electronic; $345 electronic only. **Remarks:** Advertising not accepted. **Online:** Dialog (The Dialog Corporation); ESA-IRS; Dimdi. **URL:** http://www.csa.com. **Alt. Formats:** CD-ROM.
Circ: (Not Reported)

13471 ASFA Aquaculture Abstracts
Cambridge Scientific Abstracts
7200 Wisconsin Ave., Ste. 601 Phone: (877)434-6339
Bethesda, MD 20814 Fax: (301)961-6790
Free: (800)843-7751
Publication E-mail: craig@csa.com; sales@csa.com
Publisher E-mail: market@csa.com

Scientific journal covering aquaculture. **Founded:** 1984. **Freq:** Bimonthly. **Print Method:** Letterset and offset. **Trim Size:** 6 1/2 x 9. **Key Personnel:** Craig Emerson, Editor, craig@csa.com; Angela Hitti, VP/Editorial; Ted Caris, Publisher; Mark Furneaux, Vice President of Marketing. **ISSN:** 0739-814X. **Subscription Rates:** $460 print and electronic; $390 electronic only. **Remarks:** Advertising not accepted. **Online:** Dialog (The Dialog Corporation); STN International; DIMDI; ESA-IRS. **URL:** http://www.csa.com. **Alt. Formats:** CD-ROM, SilverPlatter Information Inc.
Circ: (Not Reported)

13472 ASFA/Aquatic Sciences & Fisheries Abstracts Part 1: Biological Sciences & Living Resources
Cambridge Scientific Abstracts
7200 Wisconsin Ave., Ste. 601 Phone: (877)434-6339
Bethesda, MD 20814 Fax: (301)961-6790
Free: (800)843-7751
Publication E-mail: sales@csa.com
Publisher E-mail: market@csa.com

Scientific journal covering marine, freshwater, and brackish water environments. **Founded:** 1971. **Freq:** Monthly. **Print Method:** Letterpress. **Trim Size:** 6 1/2 x 9. **Cols./Page:** 2. **Key Personnel:** Craig Emerson, Editor, craig@csa.com; Angela Hitti, VP/Editorial; Ted Caris, Publisher. **ISSN:** 0140-5373. **Subscription Rates:** $1,290 print and electronic; $1,095 electronic only. **Remarks:** Advertising not accepted. **Online:** Dialog (The Dialog Corporation); STN International; DIMDI; CAN/OLE; ESA-IRS. **URL:** http://www.csa.com. **Alt. Formats:** CD-ROM, SilverPlatter Information Inc.
Circ: (Not Reported)

13473 ASFA Marine Biotechnology Abstracts
Cambridge Scientific Abstracts
7200 Wisconsin Ave., Ste. 601 Phone: (877)434-6339
Bethesda, MD 20814 Fax: (301)961-6790
Free: (800)843-7751
Publication E-mail: sales@csa.com
Publisher E-mail: market@csa.com

Journal covering the application of molecular biology and molecular genetics to aquatic organisms. **Founded:** 1989. **Freq:** Quarterly. **Key Personnel:** Haleh Samiel, Editor, haleh@csa.com; Angela Hitti, Managing Editor; Ted Caris, Publisher; Mark Furneaux, Vice Pres. of Marketing. **ISSN:** 1043-8971. **Subscription Rates:** $335 U.S. and Canada; $360 other countries. **Remarks:** Advertising not accepted. **Online:** Dialog (The Dialog Corporation); STN International. **URL:** http://www.csa.com. **Alt. Formats:** CD-ROM, SilverPlatter Information Inc.
Circ: (Not Reported)

13474 Association Trends
Martineau Corp.
7910 Woodmont Ave., Ste. 1150 Phone: (301)652-8666
Bethesda, MD 20814-3062 Fax: (301)656-8654
Publication E-mail: assntrends@assntrends.com

Newspaper for staff professionals of volunteer organizations. Covers business, trade associations, and professional societies. **Founded:** 1973. **Freq:** Weekly (Fri.). **Print Method:** Offset. **Trim Size:** 11 x 17. **Cols./Page:** 4. **Col. Width:** 28 nonpareils. **Col. Depth:** 224 agate lines. **Key Personnel:** Jill M. Cornish, Publisher, jill@assntrends.com; Ed Dalere, Managing Editor, edd@assntrends.com. **ISSN:** 0196-1942. **Subscription Rates:** $95 individuals; $165 Canada. **Remarks:** Accepts advertising. **URL:** http://www.assntrends.com.
Ad Rates: BW: $1,810 **Circ:** Paid ‡4,154
4C: $2,895 Free ‡2,997

13475 Bacteriology: Microbiology Abstracts, Section B
Cambridge Scientific Abstracts
7200 Wisconsin Ave., Ste. 601 Phone: (877)434-6339
Bethesda, MD 20814 Fax: (301)961-6790
Free: (800)843-7751
Publisher E-mail: market@csa.com

Scientific journal covering bacterial taxonomy and genetics, microbial ecology, vaccines, and immunology. **Founded:** 1965. **Freq:** Monthly. **Print Method:** Offset. **Trim Size:** 6 1/2 x 9. **Cols./Page:** 2. **Key Personnel:** Roberta Gardner, Editor, roberta@csa.com; Craig Emerson, Managing Editor; Ted Caris, Publisher; Matt Dunie, Vice President of Marketing. **ISSN:** 0300-8398. **Subscription Rates:** $1,205 print and electronic; $1,025 electronic only. **Remarks:** Advertising not accepted. **Online:** Dialog (The Dialog Corporation); STN International. **URL:** http://www.csa.com. **Alt. Formats:** CD-ROM, SilverPlatter Information Inc.
Circ: (Not Reported)

13476 BioEngineering Abstracts
Cambridge Scientific Abstracts
7200 Wisconsin Ave., Ste. 601 Phone: (877)434-6339
Bethesda, MD 20814 Fax: (301)961-6790
Free: (800)843-7751
Publisher E-mail: market@csa.com

Journal containing information on the medical and biological application of engineering knowledge. **Subtitle:** Cambridge Biotechnology Research Series. **Freq:** Bimonthly. **Trim Size:** 8 1/2 x 11. **Key Personnel:** Evelyn Beck, Editor, evelyn@csa.com; Craig Emerson, Managing Editor; Ted Caris, Publisher. **ISSN:** 1068-5693. **Subscription Rates:** $825 print and electronic; $700 electronic only. **Remarks:** Advertising not accepted. **Available Online. URL:** http://www.csa.com. **Alt. Formats:** CD-ROM.
Circ: (Not Reported)

13477 Biophysical Journal
Biophysical Society
9650 Rockville Pike Phone: (301)571-0663
Bethesda, MD 20814
Publication E-mail: bj@biophysics.faseb.org
Publisher E-mail: society@biophysics.faseb.org

Journal focusing on biophysics. **Founded:** 1960. **Freq:** Monthly. **Print Method:** Offset. **Trim Size:** 8 1/2 x 11. **Cols./Page:** 2. **Col. Width:** 39 nonpareils. **Col. Depth:** 124 agate lines. **Key Personnel:** Peter B. Moore, Editor. **ISSN:** 0006-3495. **Subscription Rates:** $770 institutions. **Remarks:** Accepts advertising. **Online:** Highwire Press. **Alt. Formats:** Microform.
Ad Rates: BW: $1,000 **Circ:** ‡6,500
4C: $1,500

13478 Calcium and Calcified Tissue Abstracts
Cambridge Scientific Abstracts
7200 Wisconsin Ave., Ste. 601 Phone: (877)434-6339
Bethesda, MD 20814 Fax: (301)961-6790
Free: (800)843-7751
Publisher E-mail: market@csa.com

Scientific journal covering bone metabolism, tooth development, nerve transmission, and other calcium-related functions. **Founded:** 1969. **Freq:** Quarterly. **Print Method:** Offset. **Trim Size:** 6 1/2 x 9. **Cols./Page:** 2. **Key Personnel:** Janet Padgett, Editor, janet@csa.com; Craig Emerson, Managing Editor; Ted Caris, Publisher; Matt Dunie, Vice President of Marketing. **ISSN:** 1069-5540. **Subscription Rates:** $680 print and electronic; $580 electronic only. **Remarks:** Advertising not

accepted. **Online:** Dialog (The Dialog Corporation); STN International. **URL:** http://www.csa.com. **Alt. Formats:** CD-ROM, SilverPlatter Information Inc. **Formerly:** Calcified Tissue Abstracts (1994).
Circ: (Not Reported)

13479 Cartography and Geographic Information Systems
American Congress on Surveying and Mapping
5410 Grosvenor Ln. Phone: (301)493-0200
Bethesda, MD 20814-2122 Fax: (301)493-8245
Publisher E-mail: barbacsm@mindspring.com

Scholarly journal for cartographers and geographic information systems professionals. **Founded:** 1973. **Freq:** Quarterly. **Print Method:** Offset, sheetfed. **Trim Size:** 8 1/4 x 10 7/8. **Cols./Page:** 2. **Col. Width:** 18.5 picas. **Key Personnel:** Robert C. Cromley, Editor, phone (860)486-3656, fax (860)486-1348, cromley@uconn.edu; Ilse Aupui, Managing Editor, ilseaesm@mindspring.com. **ISSN:** 1050-9844. **Subscription Rates:** $85; $95 other countries. **Remarks:** Accepts advertising. **URL:** http://www.survmap.org. **Formerly:** The American Cartographer (1990).
Ad Rates: BW: $900 **Circ:** 4,000
4C: $1,650

13480 Chemoreception Abstracts
Cambridge Scientific Abstracts
7200 Wisconsin Ave., Ste. 601 Phone: (877)434-6339
Bethesda, MD 20814 Fax: (301)961-6790
Free: (800)843-7751
Publisher E-mail: market@csa.com

Scientific journal covering the neurobiology, chemistry, and physiology of taste, smell, internal chemoreception, and chemotaxis. **Subtitle:** Chemical Senses and Applied Techniques. **Founded:** 1972. **Freq:** Quarterly. **Print Method:** Offset. **Trim Size:** 6 1/2 x 9. **Cols./Page:** 2. **Key Personnel:** Fred Spangler, Editor, fred@csa.com; Craig Emerson, Managing Editor; Ted Caris, Publisher; Matt Dunie, Vice President of Marketing. **ISSN:** 0300-1261. **Subscription Rates:** $555 print and electronic; $470 electronic only. **Remarks:** Advertising not accepted. **Online:** Dialog (The Dialog Corporation); STN International. **URL:** http://www.csa.com. **Alt. Formats:** CD-ROM, SilverPlatter Information Inc.
Circ: (Not Reported)

13481 Chevy Chase Gazette
The Gazette Newspapers
4815 Rugby Ave. Phone: (301)951-4390
Bethesda, MD 20814 Fax: (301)951-4409

Community newspaper. **Freq:** Weekly (Wed.). **Trim Size:** 13 1/2 x 22 3/4. **Cols./Page:** 5. **Col. Width:** 1 5/16 inches. **Col. Depth:** 13 inches. **Key Personnel:** James F. Mannarino, General Mgr.; Miranda Spivack, Deputy Editor. **Subscription Rates:** Free. **Remarks:** Advertising accepted; rates available upon request.
Circ: Combined ❑7,591

13482 Common Boundary Magazine
4905 Del Ray Ave. Ste. 210 Phone: (301)652-9495
Bethesda, MD 20814 Fax: (301)652-0579
Free: (800)548-8737
Publication E-mail: connect@commonboundary.org

Magazine exploring the interface between spirituality, psychotherapy and creativity. **Subtitle:** Exploring Spirituality, Psychotherapy and Creativity. **Founded:** 1980. **Freq:** Bimonthly. **Print Method:** Mini-web. **Trim Size:** 8 1/2 x 11. **Cols./Page:** 3. **Col. Width:** 2 1/8 inches. **Col. Depth:** 9 inches. **Key Personnel:** Anne A. Simpkinson, M.A., Editor; Charles H. Simpkinson, Ph.D., Publisher. **ISSN:** 0885-8500. **Subscription Rates:** $24.95 individuals; $4.95 single issue; $35 out of country surface; $45 two years other countries - airmail. **Remarks:** Accepts advertising. **URL:** http://www.commonboundary.org. **Alt. Formats:** Mailing labels. **Formerly:** Kindred Spirit.
Ad Rates: BW: $1,240 **Circ:** ‡20,000
4C: $1,785

13483 Computer and Information Systems Abstracts Journal
Cambridge Scientific Abstracts
7200 Wisconsin Ave., Ste. 601 Phone: (877)434-6339
Bethesda, MD 20814 Fax: (301)961-6790
Free: (800)843-7751
Publication E-mail: sales@csa.com
Publisher E-mail: market@csa.com

Journal covering computer and information sciences. Jointly published with Engineering Information Inc. **Founded:** 1962. **Freq:** 12/year. **Print Method:** Letterpress and offset. **Trim Size:** 8 1/2 x 11. **Cols./Page:** 2. **Col. Width:** 42 nonpareils. **Col. Depth:** 133 agate lines. **Key Personnel:** Evelyn Beck, Editor, evelyn@csa.com; Craig Emerson, Managing Editor; Ted Caris, Publisher; Bart De Castro, Advertising Mgr.; Matt Dunie, VP, Mktg. **ISSN:** 0191-9776. **Subscription Rates:** $1,275 print and electronic; $1,085 electronic only. **Remarks:** Advertising not accepted. **Online:** STN International. **URL:** http://www.csa.com.
Circ: (Not Reported)

13484 Conference Papers Index
Cambridge Scientific Abstracts
7200 Wisconsin Ave., Ste. 601 Phone: (877)434-6339
Bethesda, MD 20814 Fax: (301)961-6790
Free: (800)843-7751
Publication E-mail: sales@csa.com
Publisher E-mail: market@csa.com

Journal covering worldwide scientific and technical conferences. **Founded:** 1973. **Freq:** Bimonthly. **Print Method:** Letterpress and offset. **Trim Size:** 8 1/2 x 11. **Cols./Page:** 2. **Col. Width:** 43 nonpareils. **Col. Depth:** 126 agate lines. **Key Personnel:** Carla McMillan, Editor, carla@csa.com; Ted Caris, Publisher; Bart De Castro, Advertising Mgr.; Craig Emerson, Managing Editor. **ISSN:** 0162-704X. **Subscription Rates:** $1,170 print and electronic; $995 electronic only. **Remarks:** Advertising not accepted. **Online:** STN International; Dialog. **URL:** http://www.csa.com.
Circ: (Not Reported)

13485 CSA Neurosciences Abstracts
Cambridge Scientific Abstracts
7200 Wisconsin Ave., Ste. 601 Phone: (877)434-6339
Bethesda, MD 20814 Fax: (301)961-6790
Free: (800)843-7751
Publication E-mail: sales@csa.com
Publisher E-mail: market@csa.com

Scientific journal covering all aspects of vertebrate and invertebrate neuroscience, with special emphasis on neural diseases such as Alzheimer's. **Founded:** 1982. **Freq:** Monthly. **Print Method:** Offset. **Trim Size:** 6 1/2 x 9. **Cols./Page:** 2. **Key Personnel:** Fred Spangler, Editor, fred@csa.com; Angela Hitti, Managing Editor; Ted Caris, Publisher; Mark Furneaux, Vice President of Marketing. **ISSN:** 0141-7711. **Subscription Rates:** $800 U.S. and Canada; $895 other countries. **Remarks:** Advertising not accepted. **Online:** Dialog (The Dialog Corporation); STN International. **URL:** http://www.csa.com. **Alt. Formats:** CD-ROM, SilverPlatter Information Inc.
Circ: (Not Reported)

13486 Current Books Magazine
PO Box 34468 Phone: (301)530-8200
Bethesda, MD 20827-0468 Fax: (301)530-8201

Magazine featuring excerpts from the best new fiction and nonfiction books. **Founded:** 1992. **Freq:** Quarterly. **Print Method:** Web. **Trim Size:** 7 1/4 x 10. **Cols./Page:** 2. **Col. Width:** 3 inches. **Col. Depth:** 8 1/2 inches. **Key Personnel:** Edwin S. Grosvenor, Editor and Publisher; Joshua D. Dinman, Marketing Manager; Sara M. Revis, Circulation Mgr. **ISSN:** 1063-9012. **Subscription Rates:** $14.95 individuals; $4.95 single issue. **Remarks:** Accepts advertising.
Ad Rates: BW: $1,600 **Circ:** Paid 8,500
Non-paid 23,100

13487 Ecology Abstracts
Cambridge Scientific Abstracts
7200 Wisconsin Ave., Ste. 601 Phone: (877)434-6339
Bethesda, MD 20814 Fax: (301)961-6790
Free: (800)843-7751
Publisher E-mail: market@csa.com

Scientific journal about ecology. **Founded:** 1974. **Freq:** Monthly. **Print Method:** Offset. **Trim Size:** 6 1/2 x 9. **Cols./Page:** 2. **Key Personnel:** Robert Hilton, Editor, robert@csa.com; Craig Emerson, Managing Editor; Ted Caris, Publisher; Matt Dunie, Vice President of Marketing. **ISSN:** 0143-3296. **Subscription Rates:** $1,165 print and electronic; $990 electronic only. **Remarks:** Advertising not accepted. **Online:** Dialog (The Dialog Corporation); STN International. **URL:** http://www.sca.com. **Alt. Formats:** CD-ROM, SilverPlatter Information Inc.
Circ: (Not Reported)

13488 Education Week
Editorial Projects in Education, Inc.
6935 Arlington Rd., Ste. 100 Phone: (301)280-3100
Bethesda, MD 20814 Fax: (301)280-3250
Publication E-mail: ew@epe.org
Publisher E-mail: ads@epe.org

Professional newspaper for elementary and secondary school educators. **Subtitle:** American Education's Newspaper of Record. **Founded:** 1981. **Freq:** Weekly 43/year. **Print Method:** Offset. **Trim Size:** 11 x 14 5/8. **Cols./Page:** 5. **Key Personnel:** Virginia B. Edwards, Editor and Publisher, fax (301)280-3200; Michael McKenna, Advertising Dir. **ISSN:** 0277-4232. **Subscription Rates:** $69.94 individuals. **URL:** http://www.edweek.org.
Ad Rates: BW: $5,980 **Circ:** Paid ★54,213
4C: $7,910
PCI: $71

13489 EIS: Digests of Environmental Impact Statements
Cambridge Scientific Abstracts
7200 Wisconsin Ave., Ste. 601 Phone: (877)434-6339
Bethesda, MD 20814 Fax: (301)961-6790
Free: (800)843-7751
Publisher E-mail: market@csa.com

Journal abstracting government environmental impact statements. **Founded:** 1970. **Freq:** Bimonthly. **Key Personnel:** Edward Reid, Editor, edfor 30 secondssa.com; Angela Hitti, Managing Editor; Ted Caris, Publisher; Angela Hitti. **ISSN:** 0364-1074. **Subscription Rates:** $625 U.S. and Canada; $695 other countries. **Remarks:** Advertising not accepted. **URL:** http://www.csa.com. **Alt. Formats:** CD-ROM, SilverPlatter Information Inc.
Circ: (Not Reported)

13490 Electrical Contractor
National Electrical Contractors Association
3 Bethesda Metro Center, Ste. 1100 Phone: (301)657-3110
Fax: (301)215-4500
Bethesda, MD 20814-5372
Subtitle: The management magazine for electrical contracting. **Founded:** 1939. **Freq:** Monthly. **Print Method:** Offset. **Trim Size:** 8 1/8 x 10 7/8. **Cols./Page:** 3. **Col. Width:** 14 picas. **Col. Depth:** 57 picas. **Key Personnel:** Joseph Salimando, Publisher; Donna L. Bailey, Business and Promotion; Thomas Naber, Editor. **ISSN:** 0033-5118. **Remarks:** Accepts advertising.
Ad Rates: BW: $4,780 **Circ:** Non-paid ‡71,032
4C: $6,250

13491 Electronics & Communications Abstracts Journal
Cambridge Scientific Abstracts
7200 Wisconsin Ave., Ste. 601 Phone: (877)434-6339
Bethesda, MD 20814 Fax: (301)961-6790
Free: (800)843-7751
Publication E-mail: sales@csa.com
Publisher E-mail: market@csa.com

Journal covering electronics and communications. Jointly published with Engineering Information Inc. **Founded:** 1967. **Freq:** Bimonthly. **Print Method:** Letterpress and offset. **Trim Size:** 8 1/2 x 11. **Cols./Page:** 2. **Col. Width:** 42 nonpareils. **Col. Depth:** 133 agate lines. **Key Personnel:** Evelyn Beck, Editor, evelyn@csa.com; Ted Caris, Publisher; Bart De Castro, Advertising Mgr.; Craig Emerson, Managing Editor; Matt Dunie, V. P. of Mktg. **ISSN:** 0361-3313. **Subscription Rates:** $1,235 print and electronic; $1,050 electronic only. **Remarks:** Advertising not accepted. **Online:** STN International. **URL:** http://www.csa.com.
Circ: (Not Reported)

13492 Entomology Abstracts
Cambridge Scientific Abstracts
7200 Wisconsin Ave., Ste. 601 Phone: (877)434-6339
Bethesda, MD 20814 Fax: (301)961-6790
Free: (800)843-7751
Publication E-mail: robert@csa.com
Publisher E-mail: market@csa.com

Journal containing information on the latest techniques and methodology, anatomy, physiology, etc. of insects and insect-like species. **Founded:** 1969. **Freq:** Monthly. **Print Method:** Offset. **Trim Size:** 6 1/2 x 9. **Key Personnel:** Robert Hilton, Editor; Angela Hitti, Vice President; Ted Caris, Publisher; Craig Emerson, Managing Editor. **ISSN:** 0013-8924. **Subscription Rates:** $1,190 print and electronic rate; $1,010 electronic only. **Remarks:** Advertising not accepted. **URL:** http://www.csa.com. **Alt. Formats:** CD-ROM.
Circ: (Not Reported)

13493 The FASEB Journal
Federation of America Societies for Experimental Biology
Office of Publications Phone: (301)530-7002
9650 Rockville Pike Fax: (301)571-1855
Bethesda, MD 20814-3998
Publication E-mail: faseb.journal@yale.edu
Publisher E-mail: erekas@faseb.org

Journal on multidisciplinary life sciences research. **Subtitle:** A Multidisciplinary Resource for the Life Sciences. **Founded:** July 1987. **Freq:** 15/year. **Print Method:** Offset. **Trim Size:** 8 1/2 x 10 7/8. **Cols./Page:** 2. **Col. Width:** 42 nonpareils. **Col. Depth:** 133 agate lines. **Key Personnel:** Vincent T. Marchesi, M.D., Editor-in-Chief, phone (203)737-2334, fax (203)737-2267, faseb.journal@yale.edu; Edward P. Rekas, Director, phone (301)530-7100, fax (301)571-1855, erekas@faseb.org; Susan Mergenhagen, Advertising Dir., phone (301)530-7103, fax (301)571-0683, adnet@faseb.org. **ISSN:** 0892-6638. **Subscription Rates:** $67 members print only; $132 nonmembers print only; $425 institutions print & online; $445 Mexico and Canada; $32 students; $477 international print & online; $425 international print only. **Remarks:** Accepts advertising. **Formerly:** Federation Proceedings.
Ad Rates: BW: $1,765 **Circ:** 6,000
4C: $2,860

13494 Findex
Cambridge Scientific Abstracts
7200 Wisconsin Ave., Ste. 601 Phone: (877)434-6339
Bethesda, MD 20814 Fax: (301)961-6790
Free: (800)843-7751
Publisher E-mail: market@csa.com

Journal containing information on market and industry studies, surveys and audits, company profiles, consumer studies and multi-client studies in a wide range of subject areas. **Subtitle:** The Worldwide Directory of Market Research Reports, Studies and Surveys. **Founded:** 1978. **Freq:** Annual. **Trim Size:** 8 1/2 x 11. **ISSN:** 0273-4125. **Subscription Rates:** $425 U.S. and Canada. **Remarks:** Advertising not accepted. **Online:** Dialog. **URL:** http://www.findexonline.com. **Alt. Formats:** CD-ROM, Market Research Locator.
Circ: (Not Reported)

13495 Fisheries
American Fisheries Society
5410 Grosvenor Ln,, Ste. 110 Phone: (301)897-8616
Bethesda, MD 20814 Fax: (301)897-8096
Publisher E-mail: main@fisheries.org

Magazine covering fisheries management and aquatic resource issues. **Founded:** Jan. 1976. **Freq:** Monthly. **Print Method:** Offset. Uses mats. **Trim Size:** 8 1/4 x 10 7/8. **Cols./Page:** 2 and 3. **Col. Width:** 40 and 13 picas. **Col. Depth:** 120 agate lines. **Key Personnel:** Kristin Merriman-Clarke, Editor, kclarke@fisheries.org; Amy Fink, Advertising Mgr., afink@fisheries.org; Susan Monseur, Production Editor, smonseur@fisheries.org. **ISSN:** 0363-2415. **Subscription Rates:** $71.50 individuals; $79.50 Canada; $82.50 elsewhere; $35.50 students and retirees; $39.50 Canada students and retirees; $41.50 elsewhere students and retirees. **Remarks:** Accepts advertising.
Ad Rates: BW: $970 **Circ:** ‡9,300

13496 Forest Science
Society of American Foresters
5400 Grosvenor Ln. Phone: (301)897-8720
Bethesda, MD 20814-2198 Fax: (301)897-3690

Magazine publishing research results covering silviculture, soils, biometry, diseases, recreation, photosynthesis, tree physiology, management, harvesting, and policy analysis. **Founded:** Mar. 1955. **Freq:** Quarterly. **Print Method:** Offset. **Trim Size:** 7 x 9. **Cols./Page:** 1. **Col. Width:** 60 nonpareils. **Col. Depth:** 113 agate lines. **Key Personnel:** Cindy Drabick, Advertising Sales Mgr., drabickc@shfnet.org. **ISSN:** 0015-749X. **Subscription Rates:** $50 individuals; $100 institutions. **URL:** http://www.safnet.org.
Ad Rates: BW: $420 **Circ:** 2,000

13497 Futures Research Quarterly
World Future Society
7910 Woodmont Ave., Ste. 450 Phone: (301)656-8274
Bethesda, MD 20814 Fax: (301)951-0394
Free: (800)989-8274
Publication E-mail: schley@tmn.com
Publisher E-mail: wfsinfo@wfs.org; letters@wfs.org

Journal on future studies methodology. **Founded:** 1985. **Freq:** Quarterly. **Print Method:** Offset. **Trim Size:** 6 x 9. **Cols./Page:** 1. **Col. Width:** 50 nonpareils. **Col. Depth:** 94 agate lines. **Key Personnel:** Kenneth J. Hunter, Editor; Timothy Mack, Advertising Mgr.; Audrey Clayton, Editor. **ISSN:** 0049-8092. **Subscription Rates:** $70 individuals; $90 nonmembers libraries; $95 professional members. **Remarks:** Advertising not accepted. **URL:** http://www.wfs.org/wfs.
Circ: ‡1,500

13498 The Futurist
World Future Society
7910 Woodmont Ave., Ste. 450 Phone: (301)656-8274
Bethesda, MD 20814 Fax: (301)951-0394
Free: (800)989-8274
Publisher E-mail: wfsinfo@wfs.org; letters@wfs.org

Magazine exploring social and technological changes. **Subtitle:** A Journal of Forecasts, Trends, and Ideas About the Future. **Founded:** Feb. 1967. **Freq:** Monthly except combined Jun-Jul and Aug-Sept issues. **Print Method:** Offset. **Trim Size:** 8 1/4 x 10 3/4. **Cols./Page:** 3. **Col. Width:** 26 nonpareils. **Col. Depth:** 136 agate lines. **Key Personnel:** Edward S. Cornish, Editor; Jeff Cornish, Advertising Mgr., jcornish@wfs.org. **ISSN:** 0016-3317. **Subscription Rates:** $35 individuals; $4.95 single issue. **Remarks:** Accepts advertising. **Online:** Dialog. **URL:** http://www.wfs.org/wfs. **Alt. Formats:** Microform.
Ad Rates: BW: $1,250 **Circ:** ‡31,000
4C: $1,880

13499 Gastroenterology
W. B. Saunders Co.
AGA National Office Phone: (301)941-9781
7910 Woodmont Ave., 7th Fl. Fax: (301)951-0757
Bethesda, MD 20814
Medical journal examining all aspects of gastroenterology. **Subtitle:** A Journal Devoted to the Clinical and Basic Studies of the Digestive Tract and Liver. **Founded:** 1943. **Freq:** Monthly. **Print Method:** Offset. **Trim Size:** 8 1/4 x 11. **Cols./Page:** 2. **Col. Width:** 20 picas. **Col. Depth:** 56 picas. **Key Personnel:** Daniel K. Podolsky, M.D., Editor; Harry Dean, Publisher; James C. Cunningham, Advertising Mgr. **ISSN:** 0016-5085. **Subscription Rates:** $195 individuals. **Remarks:** Accepts advertising. **Available Online. URL:** http://www.gastro.org.
Ad Rates: GLR: $2.50 **Circ:** 15,851
BW: $1,875
4C: $3,725

13500 Genetics Abstracts
Cambridge Scientific Abstracts
7200 Wisconsin Ave., Ste. 601 Phone: (877)434-6339
Bethesda, MD 20814 Fax: (301)961-6790
Free: (800)843-7751
Publication E-mail: wilma@csa.com
Publisher E-mail: market@csa.com

Scientific journal covering animal and plant genetics. **Founded:** 1968. **Freq:** Monthly. **Print Method:** Offset. **Trim Size:** 6 1/2 x 9. **Key Personnel:** Craig Emerson, Managing Editor, craig@csa.com; Ted Caris, Publisher; Wilma Ek, Editor, wilma@csa.com. **ISSN:** 0016-674X. **Subscription Rates:** $1,220 print and electronic; $1,035 electronic only. **Remarks:** Advertising not accepted. **Online:** Dialog (The Dialog Corporation); STN International. **URL:** http://www.csa.com. **Alt. Formats:** CD-ROM, SilverPlatter Information Inc.
Circ: (Not Reported)

13501 Health Affairs
Project HOPE
7500 Old Georgetown Rd., Suite 600 Phone: (301)656-7401
Fax: (301)654-2845
Bethesda, MD 20814
Publication E-mail: healthaffairs@projhope.org

Journal covering health policy issues. **Subtitle:** The Policy Journal of the Health Sphere. **Founded:** Oct. 1, 1982. **Freq:** Bimonthly. **Print Method:** Offset. **Trim Size:** 6 3/4 x 10. **Cols./Page:** 1. **Col. Width:** 62 nonpareils. **Col. Depth:** 112 agate lines. **Key Personnel:** John K. Iglehart, Editor; Jane Hiebert-White, Exec. Editor. **ISSN:** 0278-2715. **Subscription Rates:** $85 individuals U.S. and Canada; $139 institutions U.S. and Canada; $140 individuals other countries; $175 institutions, other countries; $25 single issue U.S. and Canada; $29 single issue other countries; $160 two years U.S. and Canada; $269 two years institutions in the U.S. and Canada; $239 two years individuals in other countries; $289 two years institutions in other countries. **Remarks:** Advertising not accepted. **Online:** LEXIS-NEXIS.
Circ: Paid ‡8,000
Controlled ‡150

13502 Health and Safety Science Abstracts
Cambridge Scientific Abstracts
7200 Wisconsin Ave., Ste. 601 Phone: (877)434-6339
Bethesda, MD 20814 Fax: (301)961-6790
Free: (800)843-7751
Publication E-mail: sales@csa.com
Publisher E-mail: market@csa.com

Journal covering health and safety research. **Founded:** 1973. **Freq:** Quarterly. **Print Method:** Letterpress and offset. **Trim Size:** 8 1/2 x 11. **Cols./Page:** 2. **Col. Width:** 42 nonpareils. **Col. Depth:** 133 agate lines. **Key Personnel:** Evelyn Beck, Editor, evelyn@csa.com; Craig Emerson, Managing Editor; Ted Caris, Publisher; Mark Furneaux, Vice Pres., Mktg. **ISSN:** 0892-9351. **Subscription Rates:** $925 print and electronic; $785 electronic only. **Remarks:** Advertising not accepted. **Online:** ORBIT-QUESTEL; STN International. **URL:** http://www.csa.com. **Alt. Formats:** CD-ROM, SilverPlatter Information Inc.; CD-ROM, Pol Tox (Silver Platter).
Circ: (Not Reported)

13503 Hearing Loss: The Journal of Self Help for Hard of Hearing People
Self Help for Hard of Hearing People
7910 Woodmont Ave., Ste. 1200 Phone: (301)657-2248
Bethesda, MD 20814 Fax: (301)913-9413
Publication E-mail: national@shhh.org
Publisher E-mail: national@shhh.org

Magazine covering all aspects of hearing loss as well as new technology. **Founded:** 1979. **Freq:** Bimonthly. **Trim Size:** 8 1/2 x 10 7/8. **Cols./Page:** 3. **Col. Width:** 2 1/4 inches. **Col. Depth:** 9 9/16 inches. **Key Personnel:** Barbara Kelley, Editor; Donna L. Sorkin, Executive Dir. **Subscription Rates:** $25 individuals; $35 professionals; $50 libraries and nonprofit organizations; $100 institutions. **URL:** http://www.shhh.org; http://www.shhh.org. **Formerly:** SHHH Journal.
Ad Rates: GLR: $10 **Circ:** Paid 200,000
BW: $2,400
4C: $4,000

13504 Immunology Abstracts
Cambridge Scientific Abstracts
7200 Wisconsin Ave., Ste. 601 Phone: (877)434-6339
Bethesda, MD 20814 Fax: (301)961-6790
Free: (800)843-7751
Publisher E-mail: market@csa.com

Scientific journal covering all aspects of immunology. **Founded:** 1976. **Freq:** Bimonthly. **Print Method:** Offset. **Trim Size:** 6 1/2 x 9. **Cols./Page:** 2. **Key Personnel:** Deborah Whitman, Editor, deborah@csa.com; Craig Emerson, Managing Editor, craig@csa.com; Ted Caris, Publisher; Matt Dunie, Vice President of Marketing. **ISSN:** 0307-112X. **Subscription Rates:** $1,150 print and electronic; $975 electronic only. **Remarks:** Advertising not accepted. **Online:** Dialog (The Dialog Corporation); STN International. **URL:** http://www.csa.com. **Alt. Formats:** CD-ROM, SilverPlatter Information Inc.
Circ: (Not Reported)

13505 Industrial and Applied Microbiology: Microbiology Abstracts, Section A
Cambridge Scientific Abstracts
7200 Wisconsin Ave., Ste. 601 Phone: (877)434-6339
Bethesda, MD 20814 Fax: (301)961-6790
Free: (800)843-7751
Publication E-mail: sales@csa.com
Publisher E-mail: market@csa.com

Scientific journal covering research and applications in agricultural, chemical, pharmaceutical industries. **Founded:** 1965. **Freq:** Monthly. **Print Method:** Offset. **Trim Size:** 6 1/2 x 9. **Cols./Page:** 2. **Key Personnel:** Craig Emerson, Managing Editor; Ted Caris, Publisher; Matt Dunie, Vice Pres., Mktg.; Roberta Cardner, Editor, roberta@csa.com. **ISSN:** 0300-838X. **Subscription Rates:** $1,195 print and electronic; $1,015 electronic only. **Remarks:** Advertising not accepted. **Online:** Dialog (The Dialog Corporation); STN International. **URL:** http://www.csa.com. **Alt. Formats:** CD-ROM, SilverPlatter Information Inc.
Circ: (Not Reported)

13506 International Pharmaceutical Abstracts
American Society of Health-System Pharmacists
7272 Wisconsin Ave. Phone: (301)657-3000
Bethesda, MD 20814 Fax: (301)652-8278

Abstract journal covering approximately 800 worldwide pharmaceutical, medical, and health care publications. Sections range from the clinical, pratical, and theoretical to the economic and scientific aspects of the literature. **Subtitle:** IPA. **Founded:** 1964. **Freq:** Semimonthly. **Print Method:** Offset. **Trim Size:** 8 x 10 1/2. **Cols./Page:** 2. **Col. Width:** 36 nonpareils. **Col. Depth:** 126 agate lines. **Key Personnel:** D.R. Tousignaut, Editor. **ISSN:** 0020-8264. **Subscription Rates:** $425 U.S. and Canada; $450 other countries. **Remarks:** Advertising not accepted. **Online:** Dialog (The Dialog Corporation); OVID; STN; DIMD; DataStar. **Alt. Formats:** CD-ROM; CD-ROM; CD-ROM; CD-ROM; CD-ROM.
Circ: Paid ‡1,300
Non-paid ‡200

13507 Journal of the American Podiatric Medical Association
American Podiatric Medical Association
9312 Old Georgetown Rd. Phone: (301)571-9200
Bethesda, MD 20814-1646 Fax: (301)530-2752
Free: (800)ASK-APMA

Professional journal for podiatrists. **Founded:** 1911. **Freq:** Monthly. **Print Method:** Offset. **Trim Size:** 8 1/8 x 10 7/8. **Cols./Page:** 2. **Col. Width:** 38 nonpareils. **Col. Depth:** 127 agate lines. **Key Personnel:** Annette Theuring, Managing Editor. **ISSN:** 0003-0538. **Subscription Rates:** $100 nonmembers U.S., Canada, Mexico; $120 nonmembers other countries; $10 single issue. **Remarks:** Color advertising accepted; rates available upon request. **Alt. Formats:** CD-ROM.
Ad Rates: BW: $1,300 **Circ:** Paid ‡13,397
4C: $650 Non-paid ‡1,693

13508 Journal of Applied Physiology
The American Physiological Society
9650 Rockville Pike Phone: (301)530-7070
Bethesda, MD 20814-3991 Fax: (301)571-1814
Publisher E-mail: info@aps.faseb.org

Journal covering respiratory, environmental, and exercise physiology. **Founded:** 1948. **Freq:** Monthly. **Print Method:** Offset. **Trim Size:** 8 3/8 x 10 7/8. **Cols./Page:** 2. **Col. Width:** 21 picas. **Col. Depth:** 56 picas. **Key Personnel:** J.E. Remmers, Editor; Brenda B. Rauner, Exec. Editor. **ISSN:** 8750-7587. **Subscription Rates:** $454 individuals; $227 APS members; $494 Canada and Mexico; $680 industry; $544 other countries; $720 Canada and Mexico industry; $770 other countries industry. **Remarks:** Accepts advertising.
Ad Rates: BW: $350 **Circ:** Paid ‡2,750
4C: $955 Non-paid ‡163

13509 Journal of Aquatic Animal Health
American Fisheries Society
5410 Grosvenor Ln., Ste. 110 Phone: (301)897-8616
Bethesda, MD 20814 Fax: (301)897-5080
Publication E-mail: journals@fisheries.org
Publisher E-mail: main@fisheries.org

Journal featuring applied and basic research results relating to the causes, effects, treatments and prevention of disease, particularly of fish and shellfish. **Founded:** 1989. **Freq:** Quarterly. **Print Method:** Offset. **Trim Size:** 7 x 10. **Cols./Page:** 2. **Col. Width:** 16 1/2 picas. **Col. Depth:** 49 picas. **Key Personnel:** Sally Kendall, Journals Mgr., phone (301)897-5080, skendall@fisheries.org. **ISSN:** 0899-7659. **Subscription Rates:** $133 U.S.; $140 elsewhere or; $488 U.S. as part AFS of a 5-journal library package; $523 elsewhere. **Remarks:** Accepts advertising. **URL:** http://www.fisheries.org.
Circ: Paid 1,500

13510 The Journal of Biological Chemistry
American Society for Biochemistry and Molecular Biology, Inc.
9650 Rockville Pike Phone: (301)530-7145
Bethesda, MD 20814 Fax: (301)571-1824
Publisher E-mail: asbmb@asbmb.faseb.org

Biochemistry journal. **Founded:** 1905. **Freq:** Weekly. **Print Method:** Web press. **Trim Size:** 8 3/8 x 10 7/8. **Cols./Page:** 2. **Col. Width:** 32 nonpareils. **Col. Depth:** 119 agate lines. **Key Personnel:** Herbert Tabor, Editor. **ISSN:** 0021-9258. **Subscription Rates:** $400 members; $1,500 institutions; $1,750 other countries. **Remarks:** Accepts advertising. **URL:** http://www.jbc.org.
Ad Rates: GLR: $17 **Circ:** (Not Reported)
BW: $990
4C: $1,945

13511 Journal of Forestry
Society of American Foresters
5400 Grosvenor Ln. Phone: (301)897-8720
Bethesda, MD 20814-2198 Fax: (301)897-3690

Journal covering measurement, protection, management, and use of forests for wildlife, recreation, water, wilderness, and graying, as well as the growing and harvesting for timber and energy. **Founded:** 1902. **Freq:** Monthly. **Print Method:** Offset. **Trim Size:** 8 1/4 x 11 1/4. **Cols./Page:** 3. **Col. Width:** 26 nonpareils. **Col. Depth:** 140 agate lines. **Key Personnel:** Cindy Drabick, Advertising Mgr.; Sally Atwater, Editor, atwaters@safnet.org. **ISSN:** 0022-1201. **Subscription Rates:** $55; $100 institutions. **URL:** http://www.safnet.org.
Ad Rates: BW: $1,820 **Circ:** 20,000
4C: $2,800
PCI: $85

13512 Journal of Neurophysiology
The American Physiological Society
9650 Rockville Pike Phone: (301)530-7118
Bethesda, MD 20814 Fax: (301)571-8305
Publisher E-mail: info@aps.faseb.org

Journal covering the nervous system and its functions. **Founded:** 1938. **Freq:** Monthly. **Print Method:** Offset. **Trim Size:** 8 3/8 x 10 7/8. **Cols./Page:** 2. **Col. Width:** 21 picas. **Col. Depth:** 56 picas. **Key Personnel:** P.L. Strick, Editor; Brenda B. Rauner, Exec. Editor. **ISSN:** 0022-3077. **Subscription Rates:** $434 individuals; $217 APS member; $484 Canada and Mexico; $554 other countries; $650 industry; $700 Canada and Mexico industry; $770 other countries industry. **Remarks:** Accepts advertising.
Ad Rates: BW: $350 **Circ:** Paid ‡1,444
4C: $955 Non-paid ‡137

13513 Journal of Nutrition
Lancaster Publications
9650 Rockville Pike Rd. Phone: (301)530-7050
Bethesda, MD 20814-3990 Fax: (301)571-1892

Journal on nutrition research in the U.S. and abroad. **Founded:** Sept. 1928. **Freq:** Monthly. **Print Method:** Offset. **Trim Size:** 8 1/2 x 11. **Cols./Page:** 2 and 1. **Col. Width:** 42 and 86 nonpareils. **Col. Depth:** 133 agate lines. **Key Personnel:** Willard J. Visek, Editor-in-Chief. **ISSN:** 0022-3166. **Subscription Rates:** $90 nonmembers; $25 students students; $185 institutions; $45 members. **Remarks:** Accepts advertising. **URL:** http://www.nutrition.org.
Ad Rates: BW: $685 **Circ:** Paid ‡4,420
4C: $955 Non-paid ‡204

13514 Lead Detection and Abatement Contractor
IAQ Publications, Inc.
7920 Norfolk Ave., No. 900 Phone: (301)913-0115
Bethesda, MD 20814-2502 Fax: (301)913-0119
Free: (800)394-0115

Trade magazine covering detection and debatement of lead hazards. **Key Personnel:** Susan Valenti, svalenti@iaqpubs.com. **Remarks:** Accepts advertising. **URL:** http://www.iaqpubs.com.
Ad Rates: GLR: $350 **Circ:** Paid 10,000

13515 Linguistics and Language Behavior Abstracts
Cambridge Scientific Abstracts
7200 Wisconsin Ave., Ste. 601 Phone: (877)434-6339
Bethesda, MD 20814 Fax: (301)961-6790
Free: (800)843-7751
Publisher E-mail: market@csa.com

Linguistics publication containing abstracts from over 2,000 serials from 30 languages. **Founded:** 1967. **Freq:** 5/year. **Print Method:** Offset. **Cols./Page:** 2. **Col. Width:** 36 nonpareils. **Col. Depth:** 122 agate lines. **Key Personnel:** Lynette Hunter, Managing Editor. **ISSN:** 0888-8027. **Subscription Rates:** $405. **Remarks:** Advertising not accepted. **Available Online. Alt. Formats:** CD-ROM, SilverPlatter Information, Inc. **Formerly:** Language and Language Behavior Abstracts (1988).
Circ: ‡900

13516 Mechanical Engineering Abstracts
Cambridge Scientific Abstracts
7200 Wisconsin Ave., Ste. 601 Phone: (877)434-6339
Bethesda, MD 20814 Fax: (301)961-6790
Free: (800)843-7751
Publication E-mail: sales@csa.com
Publisher E-mail: market@csa.com

Journal on mechanical engineering. Jointly published with Engineering Information Inc. **Founded:** 1973. **Freq:** Bimonthly. **Print Method:** Letterpress and offset. **Trim Size:** 8 1/2 x 11. **Cols./Page:** 2. **Col. Width:** 42 nonpareils. **Col. Depth:** 133 agate lines. **Key Personnel:** Evelyn Beck, Editor, evelyn@csa.com; Ted Caris, Publisher; Bart De Castro, Advertising Mgr.; Craig Emerson, Managing Editor; Matt Dunie, Vice Pres., Mktg. **ISSN:** 1063-7311. **Subscription Rates:** $1,190 print and electronic; $1,010 electronic only. **Remarks:** Advertising not accepted. **Online:** Dialog (The Dialog Corporation); STN International; ESA-IRS. **URL:** http://www.csa.com. **Alt. Formats:** CD-ROM, SilverPlatter Information Inc. **Formerly:** ISMEC: Mechanical Engineering Abstracts (1993).
Circ: (Not Reported)

13517 Medical and Pharmaceutical Biotechnology Abstracts
Cambridge Scientific Abstracts
7200 Wisconsin Ave., Ste. 601 Phone: (301)961-6700
Bethesda, MD 20814-4823 Fax: (301)961-6720
Free: (800)843-7751
Publication E-mail: market@csa.com
Publisher E-mail: sales@csa.com; journals@csa.com

Scientific journal. **Founded:** 1993. **Freq:** Quarterly plus annual index. **Key Personnel:** Deborah Whitman, Editor, deborah@cas.com; Craig Emerson, Managing Editor; Ted Caris, Publisher. **ISSN:** 1063-1178. **Subscription Rates:** $425 print and electronic; $360 electronic. **Remarks:** Advertising not accepted. **Online:** Dialog (The Dialog Corporation); STN International. **URL:** http://www.csa.com. **Alt. Formats:** CD-ROM. **Formerly:** Biotechnology Research Abstracts (1992).
Circ: (Not Reported)

13518 Military Grocer
Downey Communications, Inc.
4800 Montgomery Ln., Ste. 710 Phone: (301)718-7600
Bethesda, MD 20814-3461 Fax: (301)718-7604
Publication E-mail: grocer@downey-data.com

Trade magazine for Defense Commissary Agency. **Founded:** Oct. 1991. **Freq:** Bimonthly. **Print Method:** Web offset. **Trim Size:** 8 1/8 x 10 7/8. **Cols./Page:** 2 and 3. **Col. Width:** 20 and 13 picas. **Col. Depth:** 56 and 56 picas. **Key Personnel:** Peggy Noonan Reed, Editor; J. Craig Borucki, Art Director. **ISSN:** 1058-8620. **Subscription Rates:** $40. **Alt. Formats:** CD-ROM, Commissary & Exchange Directory.
Ad Rates: BW: $2,950 **Circ:** Controlled 8,000
4C: $3,450

13519 Military Medicine
Association of Military Surgeons of the U.S. (AMSUS)
9320 Old Georgetown Rd. Phone: (301)897-8800
Bethesda, MD 20814 Fax: (301)530-5446
Free: (800)761-9320
Publication E-mail: milmed@amsus.org
Publisher E-mail: alec@premier.net

Journal for professional personnel affiliated with the Federal medical services. **Founded:** 1891. **Freq:** Monthly. **Print Method:** Web press. **Trim Size:** 8 1/8 x 10 7/8. **Cols./Page:** 2 and 1. **Col. Width:** 3 l/2 and 7 inches. **Col. Depth:** 9 2/3 and 4 inches. **Key Personnel:** RADM John C. Duffy, USPHS, Editor; Mark Shute, Editorial Asst., marks@amsus.org; Dr. Frederic Sanford, Publisher, freds@amsus.org; Bill Bride, Advertising Coord. **ISSN:** 0026-4075. **Subscription Rates:** $35 individuals; $40 other countries; $6 single issue. **Remarks:** Accepts advertising. **Alt. Formats:** Microform.
Ad Rates: BW: $1,035 **Circ:** Paid ‡15,783
4C: $2,010 Non-paid ‡947

13520 News in Physiological Sciences (NIPS)
9650 Rockville Pike Phone: (301)530-7070
Bethesda, MD 20814-3991 Fax: (301)571-1814

Professional review journal for physiologists. **Founded:** 1986. **Freq:** Bimonthly. **Print Method:** Offset. **Trim Size:** 8 1/2 x 11. **Cols./Page:** 3. **Col. Width:** 12 picas. **Col. Depth:** 56 picas. **Key Personnel:** S.G. Schultz, Editor; Sue Pokroy, Advertising Mgr., phone (301)530-7015, fax (301)571-8305, spokroy@aps.faseb.org. **Subscription Rates:** $35 IUPS-affiliated societies; $80 nonmembers; $115 institutions. **Remarks:** Accepts advertising.
Ad Rates: BW: $1,050 **Circ:** Paid ‡11,600
4C: $2,145

13521 North American Journal of Fisheries Management
American Fisheries Society
5410 Grosvenor Ln., Ste. 110 Phone: (301)897-8616
Bethesda, MD 20814 Fax: (301)897-5080
Publication E-mail: journals@fisheries.org
Publisher E-mail: main@fisheries.org

Fisheries management journal. **Founded:** 1981. **Freq:** Quarterly. **Print Method:** Offset. **Trim Size:** 7 x 10. **Cols./Page:** 2. **Col. Width:** 32 nonpareils. **Col. Depth:** 114 agate lines. **Key Personnel:** Sally Kendall, Journals Mgr., fax (301)897-5080, skendall@fisheries.org. **ISSN:** 0275-5947. **Subscription Rates:** $488 libraries US; $523 libraries in other countries; as part of 5 journal AFS; library package. **Remarks:** Accepts advertising. **URL:** http://www.fisheries.org. **Alt. Formats:** Mailing labels.
Circ: ‡3,200

13522 Northern Journal of Applied Forestry
Society of American Foresters
5400 Grosvenor Ln. Phone: (301)897-8720
Bethesda, MD 20814-2198 Fax: (301)897-3690
Publication E-mail: staebler@safnet.org

Forestry industry magazine covering an area eastern Kansas and the areas northward and eastward (including all or part of 25 states and 6 provinces of Canada). **Founded:** Mar. 1984. **Freq:** Quarterly. **Print Method:** Offset. **Trim Size:** 8 1/4 x 11 1/4. **Cols./Page:** 3. **Col. Width:** 2 1/8 inches. **Col. Depth:** 10 inches. **Key Personnel:** Kurt Gottschalk, Editor; Cindy Drabick, Advertising Mgr., drabickc@satnet.org. **ISSN:** 0742-6348. **Subscription Rates:** $40 individuals; $85 institutions; $5 single issue. **Remarks:** Accepts advertising. **URL:** http://www.safnet.org.
Ad Rates: BW: $500 **Circ:** 2,000
PCI: $25

13523 Nucleic Acids Abstracts
Cambridge Scientific Abstracts
7200 Wisconsin Ave., Ste. 601 Phone: (877)434-6339
Bethesda, MD 20814 Fax: (301)961-6790
Free: (800)843-7751
Publisher E-mail: market@csa.com

Scientific journal covering molecular biology. **Founded:** 1970. **Freq:** Monthly. **Print Method:** Offset. **Trim Size:** 6 1/2 x 9. **Cols./Page:** 2. **Key Personnel:** Wilma Ek, Editor, wilma@csa.com; Craig Emerson, Managing Editor; Ted Caris, Publisher; Matt Dunie, Vice President of Marketing. **ISSN:** 1070-2466. **Subscription Rates:** $1,065 print and electronic; $905 electronic only. **Remarks:** Advertising not accepted. **Online:** Dialog (The Dialog Corporation); STN International. **URL:** http://www.csa.com. **Alt. Formats:** CD-ROM, SilverPlatter Information Inc. **Formerly:** CSA Biochemistry Abstracts, Part 2: Nucleic Acids (1994).
Circ: (Not Reported)

13524 Oceanic Abstracts
Cambridge Scientific Abstracts
7200 Wisconsin Ave., Ste. 601 Phone: (877)434-6339
Bethesda, MD 20814 Fax: (301)961-6790
Free: (800)843-7751
Publication E-mail: craig@csa.com
Publisher E-mail: market@csa.com

Journal covering oceanography, meteorology, marine biology, offshore engineering, living and non-living resources, law, ship technology, navigation and communications, the shipping industry, geology, geophysics, geochemistry, pollution, and conservation. **Founded:** 1964. **Freq:** Monthly. **Print Method:** Offset. **Trim Size:** 8 1/2 x 11. **Cols./Page:** 2. **Col. Width:** 42 nonpareils. **Col. Depth:** 133 agate lines. **Key Personnel:** Catherine E. Deckard, Editor, kate@csa.com; Ted Caris, Publisher; Bart De Castro, Advertising Mgr.; Craig Emerson, Managing Editor; Matt Dunie, V. P. of Mktg. **ISSN:** 0748-1489. **Subscription Rates:** $1,250 print and electronic; $1,065 electronic only. **Remarks:** Advertising not accepted. **Online:** Dialog (The Dialog Corporation); STN International. **URL:**

http://www.csa.com. **Alt. Formats:** CD-ROM, Marine, Oceanographic & Freshwater Resources (NISC).
Circ: (Not Reported)

13525 Oncogenes & Growth Factors Abstracts
Cambridge Scientific Abstracts
7200 Wisconsin Ave., Ste. 601 Phone: (877)434-6339
Bethesda, MD 20814 Fax: (301)961-6790
Free: (800)843-7751
Publisher E-mail: market@csa.com

Electronic abstracts journal covering the mechanisms that cause cancerous cell growth. Available online only. **Founded:** 1989. **Freq:** Monthly. **Key Personnel:** Deborah Whitman, Editor, deborah@csa.com; Craig Emerson, Managing Editor; Ted Caris, Publisher; Bart DeCastro, Marketing Dir. **ISSN:** 1043-8963. **Subscription Rates:** $215 U.S.; $245 other countries. **Remarks:** Advertising not accepted. **Online:** Dialog (The Dialog Corporation); STN International. **URL:** http://www.csa.com. **Alt. Formats:** CD-ROM.
Circ: (Not Reported)

13526 OT Practice Magazine
American Occupational Therapy Association, Inc. (AOTA)
PO Box 31220 Phone: (301)652-2682
Bethesda, MD 20824-1220 Fax: (301)652-7711
Free: (800)877-1383
Publication E-mail: otpractice@aota.org

Professional magazine covering occupational therapy, health care, and rehabilitation of the American Occupational Therapy Association. **Founded:** Jan. 1996. **Freq:** 10/year. **Print Method:** Web offset. **Trim Size:** 8 1/8 x 10 7/8. **Key Personnel:** Laura Farr Collins, Editor, phone (301)652-2682, laurac@aota.org; Jennifer Irey, Advertising Development Specialist; Stephanie D. Abrams, Advertising Sales Special., sabrams@aota.org; otpracad@aota.org. **ISSN:** 1804-4902. **Subscription Rates:** $50 individuals; $25 students; $85 institutions; $12 single issue. **Remarks:** Accepts advertising. **URL:** http://www.aota.org.
Ad Rates: BW: $2,627 **Circ:** Paid ⊕**44,755**
4C: $3,352 Non-paid ⊕**1,305**

13527 OT Week
AOTA, Inc.
4720 Montgomery Ln. Phone: (301)652-1188
Bethesda, MD 20852-4043 Fax: (301)652-0476

Professional magazine for occupational therapy practitioners. **Founded:** 1987. **Freq:** Weekly. **Key Personnel:** Paula Steib, Editor; David Zuckerman, Managing Editor. **ISSN:** 0893-1712. **Subscription Rates:** $80 individuals. **Remarks:** Accepts advertising.
Circ: (Not Reported)

13528 Parent & Child
7048 Wilson Ln. Phone: (301)652-5383
Bethesda, MD 20817
Parenting newspaper. **Freq:** Bimonthly. **Subscription Rates:** $19.95.
Circ: Free 51,122
Paid 337

13529 PE & RS Photogrammetric Engineering & Remote Sensing
American Society for Photogrammetry and Remote Sensing (ASPRS)
5410 Grosvenor Ln., Ste. 210 Phone: (301)493-0290
Bethesda, MD 20814-2160 Fax: (301)493-0208
Publisher E-mail: asprs@asprs.org

Journal covering photogrammetry, remote sensing, geographic information systems, cartography, and surveying, global positioning systems, digital photogrammetry. **Subtitle:** The Official Journal of the ASPRS!. **Founded:** 1934. **Freq:** Monthly. **Print Method:** Offset. **Trim Size:** 8 3/8 x 10 7/8. **Cols./Page:** 2 and 4. **Col. Width:** 21.5 and 9.6 picas. **Col. Depth:** 56 picas. **Key Personnel:** James B. Case, Technical Editor; Kimberly A. Tilley, Managing Editor; James R. Plasker, Publisher; Stan Morain, Editor. **ISSN:** 0099-1112. **Subscription Rates:** $130. **Remarks:** Accepts advertising.
Ad Rates: BW: $1,318 **Circ:** ‡9,500
4C: $2,618
PCI: $85

13530 Physiological Reviews
The American Physiological Society
9650 Rockville Pike Phone: (301)530-7070
Bethesda, MD 20814-3991 Fax: (301)571-1814
Publisher E-mail: info@aps.faseb.org

Review journal covering physiology, biochemistry, nutrition, biophysics, and neuroscience. **Founded:** 1921. **Freq:** Quarterly. **Print Method:** Offset. **Trim Size:** 8 3/8 x 10 7/8. **Cols./Page:** 2. **Col. Width:** 21 picas. **Col. Depth:** 56 picas. **Key Personnel:** W.F. Boron, Editor; Sue Pokroy, Advertising Mgr. **ISSN:** 0031-9333. **Subscription Rates:** $174 individuals; $209 Canada and Mexico; $260 institutions; $275 institutions, Canada and Mexico; $290 institutions, other countries; $87 members. **Remarks:** Accepts advertising.
Ad Rates: BW: $580 **Circ:** Paid ‡2,684
4C: $775 Non-paid ‡183

13531 Poet Lore
The Writer's Center
4508 Walsh St. Phone: (301)654-8664
Bethesda, MD 20815 Fax: (301)654-8667
Publication E-mail: postmaster@writer.org
Publisher E-mail: postmaster@writer.org

Poetry journal. **Founded:** 1889. **Freq:** Quarterly. **Print Method:** Offset. **Trim Size:** 6 1/4 x 9. **Cols./Page:** 1. **Col. Width:** 60 nonpareils. **Col. Depth:** 100 agate lines. **Key Personnel:** Elizabeth Poliner, Exec. Editor; Jane Fox, Advertising Mgr.; Geraldine Connolly, Exec. Editor. **ISSN:** 0032-1966. **Subscription Rates:** $15 individuals; $24 institutions; $4.50 single issue.
Ad Rates: BW: $100 **Circ:** Paid ‡600
Non-paid ‡10

13532 Pollution Abstracts
Cambridge Scientific Abstracts
7200 Wisconsin Ave., Ste. 601 Phone: (877)434-6339
Bethesda, MD 20814 Fax: (301)961-6790
Free: (800)843-7751
Publication E-mail: evelyn@csa.com; sales@csa.com
Publisher E-mail: market@csa.com

Journal covering environmental pollution. **Founded:** 1970. **Freq:** Monthly. **Print Method:** Letterpress and offset. **Trim Size:** 8 1/2 x 11. **Cols./Page:** 2. **Col. Width:** 42 nonpareils. **Col. Depth:** 133 agate lines. **Key Personnel:** Evelyn Beck, Editor; Craig Emerson, Managing Editor; Ted Caris, Publisher. **ISSN:** 0032-3624. **Subscription Rates:** $1,180 print and electronic; $920 electronic only. **Remarks:** Advertising not accepted. **Online:** Dialog (The Dialog Corporation); STN International; DataStar (Knight-Ridder Information AG); ESA-IRS. **URL:** http://www.csa.com. **Alt. Formats:** CD-ROM, Poltox (Silver Platter); CD-ROM, Pollution (NISC).
Circ: (Not Reported)

13533 The Progressive Fish-Culturist
American Fisheries Society
5410 Grosvenor Ln., Ste. 110 Phone: (301)897-8616
Bethesda, MD 20814 Fax: (301)897-5080
Publication E-mail: journals@fisheries.org
Publisher E-mail: main@fisheries.org

Aquaculture journal. **Founded:** 1932. **Freq:** Quarterly. **Print Method:** Offset. **Trim Size:** 7 x 10. **Cols./Page:** 2. **Col. Width:** 32 nonpareils. **Col. Depth:** 114 agate lines. **Key Personnel:** Sally Kendall, Journals Mgr., skendall@fisheries.org. **ISSN:** 0033-0779. **Subscription Rates:** $133 U.S.; $140 elsewhere; $488 U.S. as part of 5 AFS journal AFS Library package; $523 elsewhere. **Remarks:** Accepts advertising. **URL:** http://www.fisheries.org.
Circ: ‡2,200

13534 Response to the Victimization of Women and Children
4938 Hampden LN No. 255
Bethesda, MD 20814-2962

Journal of research and analysis of data, programs, and legislative responses to child and wife abuse, sexual abuse, pornography, and related topics. **Founded:** 1976. **Freq:** Quarterly. **Print Method:** Offset. **Trim Size:** 8 1/2 x 11. **Cols./Page:** 2. **Col. Width:** 20 picas. **Col. Depth:** 57 picas. **Key Personnel:** Jane Roberts Chapman, Editor and Publisher. **ISSN:** 0894-7597. **Subscription Rates:** $30 individuals; $55 institutions. **Remarks:** Color advertising not accepted.
Ad Rates: BW: $250 **Circ:** 1,600

13535 Risk Abstracts
Cambridge Scientific Abstracts
7200 Wisconsin Ave., Ste. 601 Phone: (877)434-6339
Bethesda, MD 20814 Fax: (301)961-6790
Free: (800)843-7751
Publisher E-mail: market@csa.com

Journal covering the assessment and management of risk. **Founded:** 1984. **Freq:** Quarterly. **Key Personnel:** Jatin Nathwani, Editor; Craig Emerson, Managing Editor; Evelyn Beck, Managing Editor, evelyn@csa.com. **ISSN:** 0824-3336. **Subscription Rates:** $385 print and electronic; $325 electronic only. **Remarks:** Advertising not accepted. **URL:** http://www.csa.com. **Alt. Formats:** CD-ROM.
Circ: (Not Reported)

13536 Sociological Abstracts
Cambridge Scientific Abstracts
7200 Wisconsin Ave., Ste. 601 Phone: (877)434-6339
Bethesda, MD 20814 Fax: (301)961-6790
Free: (800)843-7751
Publisher E-mail: market@csa.com

Publication containing abstracts of sociology publications worldwide. **Founded:** 1953. **Freq:** Bimonthly. **Print Method:** Offset. **Trim Size:** 8 1/2 x 11. **Cols./Page:** 2. **Col. Width:** 49 nonpareils. **Col. Depth:** 135 agate lines. **Key Personnel:** Terry M. Owen, Product Mgr. **ISSN:** 0038-0202. **Subscription Rates:** $635 (including index). **Remarks:** Advertising not accepted. **Online:** Dialog (The Dialog Corporation); DataStar (The Dialog Corporation); DIMDI; OCLC FirstSearch; Ovid Technologies. **URL:** http://www.csa.com. **Alt. Formats:** CD-ROM, SilverPlatter Information, Inc.
Circ: ‡1,900

13537 Solid State and Superconductivity Abstracts
Cambridge Scientific Abstracts
7200 Wisconsin Ave., Ste. 601 Phone: (877)434-6339
Bethesda, MD 20814 Fax: (301)961-6790
Free: (800)843-7751
Publication E-mail: evelyn@csa.com; sales@csa.com
Publisher E-mail: market@csa.com

Journal covering theory, production, and application of solid state materials and devices, including conventional and high-temperature superconductivity. Jointly published with Engineering Information Inc. **Founded:** 1956. **Freq:** Bimonthly. **Print Method:** Letterpress and offset. **Trim Size:** 8 1/2 x 11. **Cols./Page:** 2. **Col. Width:** 42 nonpareils. **Col. Depth:** 133 agate lines. **Key Personnel:** Evelyn Beck, Editor; Ted Caris, Publisher; Bart De Castro, Advertising Mgr.; Craig Emerson, Managing Editor; Matt Dunie, Vice Pres., Mktg. **ISSN:** 0896-5900. **Subscription Rates:** $1,275 print and electronic; $1,085 electronic only. **Remarks:** Advertising not accepted. **Online:** STN International. **URL:** http://www.csa.com.
Circ: (Not Reported)

13538 Southern Journal of Applied Forestry
Society of American Foresters
5400 Grosvenor Ln. Phone: (301)897-8720
Bethesda, MD 20814-2198 Fax: (301)897-3690
Publication E-mail: staebler@afnet.org

Forestry industry magazine covering an area south of Maryland and westward into Texas and Oklahoma and other areas with similar conditions. **Founded:** 1977. **Freq:** Quarterly. **Print Method:** Offset. **Trim Size:** 8 1/4 x 11 1/4. **Cols./Page:** 3. **Col. Width:** 26 nonpareils. **Col. Depth:** 140 agate lines. **Key Personnel:** John Rennie, Editor; Cindy Drabick, Advertising Mgr., drabickc@safnet.org. **ISSN:** 0148-4419. **Subscription Rates:** $40 individuals; $85 institutions. **URL:** http://www.safnet.org.
Ad Rates: BW: $500 **Circ:** 2,000
PCI: $25

13539 Surveying and Land Information Systems
American Congress on Surveying and Mapping
5410 Grosvenor Ln. Phone: (301)493-0200
Bethesda, MD 20814-2122 Fax: (301)493-8245
Publisher E-mail: barbacsm@mindspring.com

Scholarly journal for surveying and land information systems professsionals. **Founded:** 1941. **Freq:** Quarterly. **Print Method:** Offset, sheetfed. **Trim Size:** 8 1/4 x 10 7/8. **Cols./Page:** 2. **Col. Width:** 20 picas. **Key Personnel:** Charles R. Schwarz, Editor. **ISSN:** 0039-6273. **Subscription Rates:** $85; $95 other countries. **Remarks:** Accepts advertising. **Formerly:** Surveying and Mapping (1990).
Ad Rates: BW: $876 **Circ:** Paid 9,000
4C: $1,576

13540 Teacher Magazine
Editorial Projects in Education, Inc.
6935 Arlington Rd., Ste. 100 Phone: (301)280-3100
Bethesda, MD 20814 Fax: (301)280-3250
Publication E-mail: tm@epe.org
Publisher E-mail: ads@epe.org

Professional magazine for elementary and secondary teachers. **Founded:** 1989. **Freq:** 9/year. **Print Method:** Offset. **Trim Size:** 10 3/4 x 14 1/2. **Cols./Page:** 3. **Key Personnel:** Ronald A. Wolk, Editor; Carolyn Kaye, Assoc. Publisher; Michael McKennna, Advertising Dir. **ISSN:** 1046-6193. **Subscription Rates:** $17.94. $3 single issue. **Remarks:** Accepts advertising.
Ad Rates: BW: $4,690 **Circ:** Paid ★**35,353**
4C: $6,265 Non-paid ★**81,569**
PCI: $71

13541 TMA Journal
Treasury Management Association
7315 Wisconsin Ave., Ste. 600 W. Phone: (301)907-2862
Fax: (301)907-2864
Bethesda, MD 20814
Publication E-mail: tma@tma-net.org

Trade magazine on treasury management with emphasis on the corporate point of view. **Subtitle:** Journal for the Treasury Executive. **Founded:** Oct. 1981. **Freq:** Bimonthly. **Print Method:** Offset. **Trim Size:** 8 1/2 x 11. **Cols./Page:** 3. **Key Personnel:** Rebecca Bisgyer, VP of Communications/Mktg.; Ayo I. Mseka, Dir. of Publications/Creative Services. **ISSN:**

0731-1281. **Subscription Rates:** $90 individuals; $100 Canada and Mexico; $120 other countries; $65 libraries. **Remarks:** Accepts advertising. **URL:** http://www.tma-net.org. **Formerly:** Journal of Cash Management (1994).
Ad Rates: BW: $2,500 **Circ:** Paid 12,000
4C: $3,540 Non-paid 200

13542 Toxicology Abstracts
Cambridge Scientific Abstracts
7200 Wisconsin Ave., Ste. 601 Phone: (877)434-6339
Bethesda, MD 20814 Fax: (301)961-6790
Free: (800)843-7751
Publication E-mail: roberta@csa.com; sales@csa.com
Publisher E-mail: market@csa.com

Scientific journal. **Founded:** 1978. **Freq:** Monthly. **Print Method:** Offset. **Trim Size:** 6 1/2 x 9. **Cols./Page:** 2. **Key Personnel:** Roberta Gardner, Editor, roberta@csa.com; Craig Emerson, Managing Editor; Ted Caris, Publisher; Matt Dunie, Vice President of Marketing. **ISSN:** 0140-5365. **Subscription Rates:** $1,070 print and electronic; $910 electronic only. **Remarks:** Advertising not accepted. **Online:** Dialog (The Dialog Corporation); STN International. **URL:** http://www.csa.com. **Alt. Formats:** CD-ROM.
Circ: (Not Reported)

13543 Transactions of the American Fisheries Society
American Fisheries Society
5410 Grosvenor Ln., Ste. 110 Phone: (301)897-8616
Bethesda, MD 20814 Fax: (301)897-5080
Publication E-mail: journals@fisheries.org
Publisher E-mail: main@fisheries.org

Fisheries science journal. **Founded:** 1870. **Freq:** Bimonthly. **Print Method:** Offset. **Trim Size:** 7 x 10. **Cols./Page:** 2. **Col. Width:** 32 nonpareils. **Col. Depth:** 114 agate lines. **Key Personnel:** Sally Kendall, Journals Mgr., fax (301)897-5080, skendall@fisheries.org. **ISSN:** 0002-8487. **Subscription Rates:** $488 libraries US; $523 libraries other countries includes 5 AFS journals. **Remarks:** Accepts advertising. **URL:** http://www.fisheries.org.
Circ: ‡3,700

13544 U.S.A.E.
Custom News, Inc.
4341 Montgomery Ave. Phone: (301)951-1881
Bethesda, MD 20814-4401 Fax: (301)656-2845
Free: (800)627-8723
Publication E-mail: usae@usaenews.com
Publisher E-mail: staff@usaenews.com

Weekly news of associations CVBs and hotels. **Subtitle:** The national independent association newspaper. **Founded:** 1982. **Freq:** Weekly. **Print Method:** Offset. **Trim Size:** 11 x 16. **Cols./Page:** 4. **Col. Width:** 14 picas. **Col. Depth:** 14 inches. **Key Personnel:** Anne Daly Heller, Publisher, anne_ross@usaenews.com. **ISSN:** 0894-8194. **Subscription Rates:** $95 individuals. **Remarks:** Accepts advertising. **URL:** usaenews.com.
Ad Rates: BW: $2,895 **Circ:** 2,000
4C: $3,570

13545 Virology and AIDS Abstracts
Cambridge Scientific Abstracts
7200 Wisconsin Ave., Ste. 601 Phone: (877)434-6339
Bethesda, MD 20814 Fax: (301)961-6790
Free: (800)843-7751
Publication E-mail: roberta@csa.com
Publisher E-mail: market@csa.com

Scientific journal which covers world scientific literature on human, animal, and plant viruses, with emphasis on AIDS. **Founded:** 1967. **Freq:** Monthly. **Print Method:** Offset. **Trim Size:** 6 1/2 x 9. **Cols./Page:** 2. **Key Personnel:** Shawn Lucas, Editor; Angela Hitti, Managing Editor; Ted Caris, Publisher; Mark Furneaux, Vice President of Marketing. **ISSN:** 0896-5919. **Subscription Rates:** $935 U.S. and Canada; $1,015 other countries. **Remarks:** Advertising not accepted. **Online:** Dialog (The Dialog Corporation); STN International. **URL:** http://www.csa.com. **Alt. Formats:** CD-ROM, SilverPlatter Information Inc. **Formerly:** Virology Abstracts (1988).
Circ: (Not Reported)

13546 Western Journal of Applied Forestry
Society of American Foresters
5400 Grosvenor Ln. Phone: (301)897-8720
Bethesda, MD 20814-2198 Fax: (301)897-3690
Publication E-mail: staebler@safnet.org

Journal for forestry professionals and technicians, forest land owners, and others in the industry. Coverage includes Western United States and Canada, east to the western parts of the Dakotas, Kanasas, Nebraska, Texas, and other areas with similar conditions. **Founded:** 1977. **Freq:** Quarterly. **Print Method:** Offset. **Trim Size:** 8 1/4 x 11 1/4. **Cols./Page:** 3. **Col. Width:** 26 nonpareils. **Col. Depth:** 140 agate lines. **Key Personnel:** Cindy Drabick, Advertising Mgr., drabickc@safnet.org. **ISSN:** 0885-6095. **Subscription Rates:** $40; $85 institutions. **URL:** http://www.safnet.org.
Ad Rates: BW: $500 **Circ:** 1,000
PCI: $25

13547 World Calendar
Cambridge Scientific Abstracts
7200 Wisconsin Ave., Ste. 601 Phone: (301)961-6700
Bethesda, MD 20814-4823 Fax: (301)961-6720
Free: (800)843-7751
Publisher E-mail: sales@csa.com; journals@csa.com

International listing of upcoming conferences and exhibitions on metals and engineered materials. **Founded:** 1975. **Freq:** Quarterly. **Print Method:** Offset. **Trim Size:** 8 1/4 x 11 3/4. **Cols./Page:** 2. **Col. Width:** 42 nonpareils. **Col. Depth:** 134 agate lines. **Key Personnel:** Carole Houk, Editor, phone (216)591-9150; Karen Skiba, Editor, kskiba@matinfo.com. **ISSN:** 0263-7987. **Subscription Rates:** $230. **Remarks:** Advertising not accepted.
Circ: (Not Reported)

13548 Writer's Carousel
The Writer's Center
4508 Walsh St. Phone: (301)654-8664
Bethesda, MD 20815 Fax: (301)654-8667
Publisher E-mail: postmaster@writer.org

Tabloid newspaper containing articles about writing and literary activity, and book reviews. **Founded:** Jan. 1977. **Freq:** Bimonthly. **Print Method:** Offset. **Trim Size:** 11 3/8 x 14 1/2. **Cols./Page:** 3. **Key Personnel:** Allan Lefcowitz, Editor, lefty@writer.org; Jean-Marc Favreau, Managing Editor. **Subscription Rates:** $30 individuals; $20 students. **Remarks:** Color advertising not accepted. **URL:** http://www.writer.org. **Former name:** Carousel.
Ad Rates: GLR: $2.50 **Circ:** Paid ‡2,300
BW: $440 Non-paid ‡3,000
PCI: $35

WDCA-TV - See Washington, District of Columbia

BOWIE, pop. 33,695.

Prince George's Co. (SC). 20 m SW of Baltimore. Bowie State College. Site of the Bowie Race Course. Steel mill. Dairy, poultry, truck farms.

13549 Blade-News
Capital Publishing Co.
PO Box 790
Bowie, MD 20718

Newspaper. **Founded:** 1967. **Freq:** Weekly (Thurs.). **Print Method:** Offset. **Cols./Page:** 6. **Col. Width:** 26 nonpareils. **Col. Depth:** 301 agate lines. **Key Personnel:** John L. Rouse, Editor and Publisher, jrouse@dc.infi.net. **Subscription Rates:** $23 individuals. **Remarks:** Accepts advertising. **Available Online. URL:** http://www.capitalonline.com.
Ad Rates: BW: $2,625.25 **Circ:** Thurs. ★13,402
4C: $3,075
PCI: $20.83

13550 The Journal of Histotechnology
Cunningham Associates
4201 Northview Dr., Ste. 502 Phone: (301)262-6221
Bowie, MD 20716-2604 Fax: (301)262-9188
Publication E-mail: histo@nsh.org
Publisher E-mail: fams@holonet.net

Histotechnology and pathology journal. **Subtitle:** Official Journal of the National Society of Histotechnolgy. **Founded:** 1977. **Freq:** Quarterly. **Print Method:** Offset. **Trim Size:** 8 1/4 x 11. **Cols./Page:** 2. **Col. Width:** 39 nonpareils. **Col. Depth:** 133 agate lines. **Key Personnel:** Jules Elias, Editor, phone (503)236-1695, fax (503)236-1750, get9@juno.com. **ISSN:** 0147-8885. **Subscription Rates:** $50. **Remarks:** Accepts advertising.
Ad Rates: BW: $840 **Circ:** Paid ‡4,950
4C: $1,590 Controlled ‡250

13551 The Maryland Gazette
Capital Gazette Printing
6800 Laurel Bowie Rd. Phone: (301)766-3700
Bowie, MD 20715-1709 Fax: (410)768-5189

Community newspaper. **Founded:** 1727. **Freq:** Semiweekly (Wed. and Sat.). **Print Method:** Offset. **Cols./Page:** 6. **Col. Width:** 26 nonpareils. **Col. Depth:** 301 agate lines. **Key Personnel:** Robert L. Goodman, Editor; Eleanor Merrill, Publisher. **Subscription Rates:** $26 individuals. **Remarks:** Accepts advertising.
Ad Rates: SAU: $24.50 **Circ:** 36,573

13552 The Plastic Tower
Box 702
Bowie, MD 20718

Consumer magazine covering poetry. **Founded:** Sept. 1989. **Freq:** Quarterly. **Key Personnel:** Roger Kyle-Keith, Editor; Carol Dyer, Editor. **ISSN:** 1066-6044. **Subscription Rates:** $8 individuals; $2.50 single issue. **Remarks:** Advertising not accepted.
Circ: Combined 250

BRADDOCK HEIGHTS

13553 WJTM-FM - 88.1
PO Box 205 Phone: (301)662-9090
Braddock Heights, MD 21714 Fax: (301)371-8888

Format: Gospel. **Networks:** USA Radio; Moody Broadcasting. **Owner:** Joy Public Broadcasting Corp., at above address. **Founded:** May 1991. **Operating Hours:** Continuous. **ADI:** Baltimore, MD. **Key Personnel:** Michael Graham, Operations Mgr.; James Dove, Engineer; Lowell Bush, Station Mgr., phone (608)723-8888; Wally Vanderswaag, Asst. Manager. **Wattage:** 4000. **Ad Rates:** Noncommercial. **URL:** http://www.wjtm.org.

BRUNSWICK, pop. 4,572.

Frederick Co. (N). 14 m SW of Frederick. Residential.

13554 The Brunswick Citizen
Citizen Communications, Inc.
2 S. Maryland Ave. Phone: (301)834-7722
Brunswick, MD 21716
Local newspaper. **Founded:** 1974. **Freq:** Weekly (Wed.). **Print Method:** Offset. **Cols./Page:** 5. **Col. Width:** 24 nonpareils. **Col. Depth:** 14 agate lines. **Key Personnel:** Julia Maynard, Editor and Publisher. **Subscription Rates:** $12.60 individuals local.
Ad Rates: SAU: $5.85 **Circ:** 3,500

13555 WTRI-AM - 1520
214 13th Ave. Phone: (301)834-6998
Brunswick, MD 21716-0248 Fax: (301)834-7922

Format: Full Service; Eclectic. **Networks:** USA Radio. **Founded:** 1969. **Operating Hours:** Sunrise-sunset; 15% network, 85% local. **Key Personnel:** Liz Roberts, President; Tom Whalen, Contact. **Wattage:** 10,000. **Ad Rates:** $10 for 30 seconds; $15 for 60 seconds.

BRYANTOWN, pop. 300.

Charles Co. (SW). 10 m NE of La Plata. Residential.

13556 TAMS Journal
Token and Medal Society, Inc.
PO Box 366 Phone: (301)274-3441
Bryantown, MD 20617-0366
Magazine on tokens and medals (numismatic items). **Founded:** Apr. 1961. **Freq:** Bimonthly. **Print Method:** Letterpress. **Trim Size:** 8 1/2 x 11. **Cols./Page:** 2. **Col. Width:** 42 nonpareils. **Col. Depth:** 140 agate lines. **Key Personnel:** David E. Schenkman, Editor. **Subscription Rates:** $20 individuals.
Ad Rates: BW: $75 **Circ:** ‡1,600

BURTONSVILLE

Montgomery Co. (WC). 12 m NE of Rockville. Residential.

13557 Sign Language Studies
Linstok Press
4020 Blackburn Ln. Phone: (301)421-0268
Burtonsville, MD 20866-1167 Fax: (301)421-0270
Free: (800)475-4756
Publisher E-mail: signmedia1@aol.com

Magazine concerning the use of primary and alternative sign languages. **Freq:** Quarterly. **Subscription Rates:** $40 individuals; $50 institutions. **Remarks:** Advertising not accepted.
Circ: (Not Reported)

CAMBRIDGE†, pop. 11,703.

Dorchester Co. (SE). On Choptank River, 32 m W of Salisbury. Manufactures lumber, wire cloth, electronics, boats; vegetable, seafood canneries. Commercial fisheries. Oysters and crabs. Frozen fish processing. Metal casting. Printing and publishing. Farming. Tomatoes, wheat, corn, soybeans.

13558 The Daily Banner
Independent Newspapers, Inc.
1000 Goodwill Rd. Phone: (410)228-3133
PO Box 580 Fax: (410)228-6547
Cambridge, MD 21613
General newspaper. **Founded:** 1897. **Freq:** Daily (eve.). **Print Method:** Offset. **Cols./Page:** 6. **Col. Width:** 25 nonpareils. **Col. Depth:** 294 agate lines. **Key Personnel:** Debra Bierbaum, Editor; Tammy Brittingham, Publisher. **Subscription Rates:** $78 individuals.
Ad Rates: BW: $1,120 **Circ:** ‡7,212
4C: $1,320
SAU: $8.10

13559 The Dorchester Star
Chesapeake Publishing Corp.
300 Academy St. Phone: (410)228-0222
Cambridge, MD 21613 Fax: (410)228-0685

Community newspaper. **Freq:** Weekly (Fri.). **Key Personnel:** Richard Weisbach, Circulation Dir. **Subscription Rates:** Free. **Remarks:** Accepts advertising.
Circ: Non-paid 10,487

13560 WCEM-AM - 1240
PO Box 237 Phone: (410)228-4800
Cambridge, MD 21613 Fax: (410)228-0130

Format: Country; News. **Networks:** ABC. **Owner:** Verstandig Broadcasting, Inc., 4850 Connecticut Ave. NW, Washington, DC 20008, (202)244-1422. **Founded:** 1947. **Formerly:** WCMD-AM (1950). **Operating Hours:** Continuous; 45% network, 55% local. **ADI:** Baltimore, MD. **Key Personnel:** Joel Scott, Operations Mgr.; Sharon Palamaras, General Mgr. **Wattage:** 1000. **Ad Rates:** $6.50-20.75 for 30 seconds; $8.50-23.75 for 60 seconds.

CAMP SPRINGS, pop. 2,900.

Prince George's Co. (SC). 5 m E of Washington, DC. Residential.

13561 Seafarers LOG
Seafarers Intl. Union
5201 Auth Way Phone: (301)899-0675
Camp Springs, MD 20746 Fax: (301)899-7355
Publication E-mail: 7112.2615@compuserve.com

Monthly tabloid on maritime labor. **Subtitle:** Official Publication of the Seafarers International Union. **Founded:** 1938. **Freq:** Monthly. **Print Method:** Offset. **Cols./Page:** 4. **Col. Width:** 32 nonpareils. **Col. Depth:** 200 agate lines. **Key Personnel:** Daniel Duncan, Communications Dir. **ISSN:** 0160-2047. **Remarks:** Advertising not accepted.
Circ: Non-paid ‡43,000

CATONSVILLE

13562 Arbutus Times
Patuxent Publishing Co.
757 Frederick Rd., Ste. 103 Phone: (410)788-4500
Catonsville, MD 21228 Fax: (410)788-4103

Suburban community newspaper. **Founded:** 1956. **Freq:** Weekly (Wed.). **Print Method:** Offset. **Cols./Page:** 5. **Col. Width:** 22 nonpareils. **Col. Depth:** 210 agate lines. **Key Personnel:** Jim Joyner, Editor, jjoyner@patuxent.com; John Patinella, President; Beth Ditman, Director. **Subscription Rates:** $12 individuals; $14 out of county; $22 out of state. **Remarks:** Accepts advertising.
Ad Rates: BW: $886 **Circ:** Paid 3,708
4C: $1,486 Non-paid 3,378

13563 Catonsville Times
Patuxent Publishing Co.
757 Frederick Rd., Ste. 103 Phone: (410)788-4500
Catonsville, MD 21228 Fax: (410)788-4103

Suburban community newspaper. **Founded:** 1880. **Freq:** Weekly (Wed.). **Print Method:** Offset. **Trim Size:** 11 x 15. **Cols./Page:** 5. **Col. Width:** 11 picas. **Col. Depth:** 80.25 picas. **Key Personnel:** Jim Joyner, Editor, jjoyner@p0aturent.com; John Patinella, President; Beth Ditman, Advertising Dir. **Subscription Rates:** $18; $22 out of state. **Remarks:** Advertising accepted; rates available upon request.
Circ: Paid 6,794
Non-paid 8,072

13564 WUMD-FM - 560
5401 Willkin Ave. Phone: (301)455-3192
Catonsville, MD 21228

Format: Alternative/New Music/Progressive. **Key Personnel:** Rob Thornton, Music Dir. **Ad Rates:** Noncommercial.

CENTREVILLE†, pop. 2,018.

Queen Anne's Co. (E). 55 m S of Wilmington Del. Industrial trailer factories. Poultry processing plant. Flour and feed mill. Agriculture. Dairy products, wheat, soybeans, corn, tomatoes.

13565 Record Observer
Chesapeake Publishing Corp.
114 Broadway Phone: (410)758-1400
Centreville, MD 21617 Fax: (410)758-1701

Community newspaper. **Freq:** Weekly (Fri.). **Key Personnel:** Richard Weisbach, Circulation Dir. **Remarks:** Accepts advertising.
Circ: Combined 3,317

CHESTERTOWN†, pop. 3,300.

Kent Co. (NE). On Chester River, 45 m S of Wilmington, Del. Washington College. Summer & winter resort. Fertilizer and chemical factories; printing plant. Commercial fisheries. Diversified farming. Dairying. Wheat, corn, tomatoes.

13566 Kent County News
PO Box 30 Phone: (410)778-2011
Chestertown, MD 21620 Fax: (410)778-6522

Community newspaper. **Founded:** Feb. 6, 1946. **Freq:** Weekly (Thurs.). **Print Method:** Offset. **Trim Size:** 13 x 21. **Cols./Page:** 6. **Col. Width:** 12.5 picas. **Col. Depth:** 21 inches. **Key Personnel:** Mary B. Burton, Advertising Mgr.; Patricia McGee, Editor. **USPS:** 292-660. **Subscription Rates:** $23 individuals; $21 senior citizens in county. **Remarks:** Accepts advertising.
Ad Rates: GLR: $.70 **Circ:** Paid 7,468
BW: $1,121.40 Non-paid 103
4C: $1,541.40
SAU: $9.55
PCI: $9

13567 WCTR-AM - 1530
PO Box 700 Phone: (410)778-1530
Chestertown, MD 21620-0700 Fax: (410)778-4800
E-mail: wctr@juno.com

Format: Talk; News; Sports; Adult Contemporary; Agricultural. **Networks:** CNN Radio. **Founded:** 1963. **Operating Hours:** Sunrise-sunset; 40% network, 60% local. **ADI:** Baltimore, MD. **Key Personnel:** Jody Taylor, General Mgr.; John Link, Program Dir.; Ben Caltey, Sports Dir. **Wattage:** 250. **Ad Rates:** $9.10-13.35 for 30 seconds; $10.35-17.65 for 60 seconds.

CHEVY CHASE, pop. 5,307.

Montgomery Co. (WC) on N.W. border of DC. Residential.

13568 Potomac Children
3908 Underwood St. Phone: (301)656-2133
Chevy Chase, MD 20815 Fax: (301)656-7830
Publication E-mail: pchildrn@family.com

Newspaper. **Founded:** Mar. 1984. **Freq:** Monthly. **Cols./Page:** 4. **Col. Width:** 2 3/8 inches. **Subscription Rates:** $17.85. **Remarks:** Accepts advertising.
Ad Rates: BW: $1,150 **Circ:** Free 33,988
4C: $1,625 Paid 72

13569 The Rose Sheet
FDC Reports, Inc.
5550 Friendship Blvd., Ste. 1 Phone: (301)657-9830
Chevy Chase, MD 20815 Fax: (301)664-7259

Trade journal for executives in the toiletries, fragrance, cosmetic, and skin care industries. **Founded:** May 1980. **Freq:** Weekly (Mon.). **Trim Size:** 8 1/2 x 11. **Cols./Page:** 1. **Key Personnel:** Holly Meed, Managing Editor, hmeed@elsevier.com; Tim Harrington, Vice Pres. of Editorial Operations; Rok Nerble, President. **ISSN:** 0279-1110. **Subscription Rates:** $630 individuals. **Remarks:** Advertising not accepted. **Online:** Lexis/Nexis, Data-Star, Dialog, Ovid.
Circ: (Not Reported)

COLLEGE PARK, pop. 23,614.

Prince George's Co. (SC). 8 m N of Washington, DC. University of Maryland. Electronic firms. Sheet metal works. Lumber mill.

13570 American Journalism Review
University of Maryland Phone: (301)405-8803
1117 Journalism Bldg. Fax: (301)405-8323
College Park, MD 20742
Publication E-mail: editor@ajrxumd.edu

Journalism review. **Founded:** 1977. **Freq:** 10/year. **Print Method:** Offset. **Trim Size:** 8 3/8 x 11. **Cols./Page:** 3. **Col. Width:** 14 nonpareils. **Key Personnel:** Rem Rieder, Editor; Ernest Durso, Advertising Mgr.; Chris Harvey, Managing Editor. **ISSN:** 1067-8654. **Subscription Rates:** $24 individuals; $3.95 single issue. **Remarks:** Accepts advertising. **URL:** http://www.ajr.org. **Formerly:** Washington Journalism Review (1993).
Ad Rates: BW: $6,399 **Circ:** Paid 8,447
4C: $7,967 Controlled 18,033

13571 Announcer
American Association of Physics Teachers
One Physics Ellipse Phone: (301)209-3300
College Park, MD 20740-3845 Fax: (301)209-0845
Publication E-mail: aapt-pubs@aapt.org
Publisher E-mail: aapt-pubs@aapt.org

Magazine for physics teachers. **Founded:** 1977. **Freq:** Quarterly. **Print Method:** Web press. **Trim Size:** 8 x 10 3/4. **Cols./Page:** 2. **Col. Width:** 20 picas. **Col. Depth:** 56 picas. **Key Personnel:** Dr. Bernard V. Khoury, Editor, bkhoury@aapt.org; Sina Kniseley, Dir. of Communications, sknisele@aapt.org; Christine Rogers, Contact, crogers@aapt.org. **ISSN:** 1042-0851. **Subscription Rates:** $31 nonmembers; $51 other countries. **Remarks:** Accepts advertising. **Formerly:** Senior Life—Elkhart-Kosciusko Edition.
Ad Rates: BW: $748 **Circ:** Paid ‡11,000
4C: $1573

13572 Applied Physics Letters
American Institute of Physics
1 Physics Ellipse Phone: (301)209-3070
College Park, MD 20740-3843 Fax: (301)209-0843
Publication E-mail: apl@anl.gov
Publisher E-mail: aipinfo@aip.org

Journal focusing on research in applied physics and applications for industry. **Founded:** 1962. **Freq:** Weekly. **Print Method:** Offset. **Trim Size:** 8 1/2 x 11. **Cols./Page:** 2. **Col. Width:** 41 nonpareils. **Col. Depth:** 136 agate lines. **Key Personnel:** Nghi Q. Lam, Editor, phone (630)252-4200, fax (630)252-4973. **ISSN:** 0003-6951. **Subscription Rates:** $820. **Remarks:** Accepts advertising. **Available Online. URL:** http://www.aip.org/ojs/service.html.
Ad Rates: BW: $450 **Circ:** 4,600
4C: $1,000

13573 Current Physics Index
American Institute of Physics (AIP)
One Physics Ellipse Phone: (301)661-9404
College Park, MD 20740-3843 Fax: (301)394-9704
Publisher E-mail: subs@aip.org

Index to AIP and member society journals. **Founded:** 1975. **Freq:** Quarterly. **Print Method:** Offset. **Trim Size:** 8 1/4 x 11. **Cols./Page:** 2. **Col. Width:** 41 nonpareils. **Col. Depth:** 136 agate lines. **Key Personnel:** Debbie McHone, Editorial Supervisor, phone (516)576-2431. **ISSN:** 0098-9819. **Subscription Rates:** $1,305 individuals. **Remarks:** Advertising not accepted.
Circ: ‡279

13574 Diamondback
Maryland Media, Inc./University of Maryland-College Park
3150 S. Campus Dining Hall Phone: (301)314-8200
College Park, MD 20742 Fax: (301)314-8358
Publication E-mail: diamondb@umail.umd.edu

Collegiate newspaper. **Founded:** 1908. **Freq:** Daily (during the academic year). **Print Method:** Offset. **Trim Size:** 13 x 21 1/4. **Cols./Page:** 6 and 6. **Col. Width:** 26 nonpareils and 2 1/16 inches. **Col. Depth:** 298 agate lines and 21 1/4 inches. **Key Personnel:** Elizabeth Cummings, Editor; Polly Manke, Advertising Mgr. **Subscription Rates:** $36 individuals. **Remarks:** Accepts advertising. **URL:** http://www.inform.umd.edu/diamondback.
Ad Rates: BW: $1,657.50 **Circ:** ‡19,000
4C: $1,942.50
SAU: $13
PCI: $13

13575 Feminist Studies
University of Maryland
Women's Studies Program Phone: (301)405-7415
0103 Taliofemo Fax: (301)314-9190
College Park, MD 20742
Publication E-mail: femstud@umail.umd.edu

Scholarly journal discussing women's studies issues. **Founded:** 1972. **Freq:** 3/year. **Key Personnel:** Claire G. Moses, Editor; MJ Povisil, Editorial Asst., mp57@umail.umd.edu. **ISSN:** 0046-3663. **Subscription Rates:** $30; $85 industry; $12 single issue. **Remarks:** Color advertising not accepted.
Ad Rates: BW: $250 **Circ:** 6,000

13576 The Industrial Physicist
American Institute of Physics
1 Physics Ellipse Phone: (301)209-3070
College Park, MD 20740-3843 Fax: (301)209-0843
Publication E-mail: tip@aip.acp.org

Publisher E-mail: aipinfo@aip.org

Trade publication featuring articles of interest to industrial physicists. **Founded:** July 1995. **Freq:** Quarterly. **Print Method:** Web offset. **Trim Size:** 8 1/4 x 10 7/8. **Cols./Page:** 3. **Key Personnel:** Ken McNaughton, Editor; Carol Lucas, Circulation and Fulfillment; Abby Klar, Advertising Mgr. **ISSN:** 1082-1848. **Subscription Rates:** $24 individuals; $48 institutions; $20 single issue. **Remarks:** Accepts advertising.
Ad Rates: BW: $3,750 **Circ:** Controlled 40,000

13577 The Journal of Chemical Physics
American Institute of Physics (AIP)
One Physics Ellipse Phone: (301)661-9404
College Park, MD 20740-3843 Fax: (301)394-9704
Publisher E-mail: subs@aip.org

Journal presenting experimental and theoretical papers. **Founded:** 1931. **Freq:** 48/year. **Print Method:** Offset. **Trim Size:** 8 1/4 x 11. **Cols./Page:** 2. **Col. Width:** 41 nonpareils. **Col. Depth:** 136 agate lines. **Key Personnel:** Don Levy, Editor, phone (312)702-7067, fax (312)702-8314, levy@jcp2.uchicago.edu. **ISSN:** 0021-9606. **Subscription Rates:** $3,480. **Remarks:** Advertising not accepted. **Alt. Formats:** Microfiche.
Circ: ‡3,200

13578 Journal of Counseling Psychology
American Psychological Association
Department of Psychology Phone: (301)405-5917
College Park, MD 20742 Fax: (301)314-9202
Publisher E-mail: webmaster@apa.org

Journal presenting empirical studies about counseling processes and interventions, theoretical articles about counseling, and studies dealing with evaluation of counseling applications and programs. **Founded:** 1954. **Freq:** Quarterly. **Print Method:** Offset. **Trim Size:** 8 1/4 x 11. **Cols./Page:** 2. **Col. Width:** 46 nonpareils. **Col. Depth:** 126 agate lines. **Key Personnel:** Clara E. Hill, Editor; Susan Knapp, Exec. Editor; Jodi Ashcraft, Advertising Mgr.; Juanita Brodie, Circulation Mgr. **ISSN:** 0022-0167. **Subscription Rates:** $31 members; $65 nonmembers; $130 institutions. **Remarks:** Accepts advertising.
Ad Rates: BW: $255 **Circ:** ‡8,500

13579 Lotus Remarque
Lotus Ltd.
Box L Phone: (301)982-4054
College Park, MD 20741
Magazine for Lotus car owners. **Founded:** 1973. **Freq:** Monthly. **Print Method:** Offset. **Trim Size:** 8 1/2 x 11. **Cols./Page:** 2. **Col. Width:** 3 1/2 inches. **Col. Depth:** 10 inches. **Key Personnel:** M.S. Winston, Editor. **Subscription Rates:** $30 new; $20 renewal. **Remarks:** Advertising accepted; rates available upon request.
Circ: Paid ‡1,400
Non-paid ‡45

13580 Physics Today
American Institute of Physics
One Physics Ellipse Phone: (301)209-2440
College Park, MD 20740 Fax: (301)209-0842
Publisher E-mail: aipinfo@aip.org

Journal covering news of physics research and activities that affect physics. **Founded:** 1948. **Freq:** Monthly. **Print Method:** Letterpress. **Trim Size:** 8 1/4 x 10 7/8. **Cols./Page:** 3. **Col. Width:** 2 3/16 inches. **Col. Depth:** 140 agate lines. **Key Personnel:** Stephen G. Benka, Editor; Richard T. Kobel, Advertising Mgr. **ISSN:** 0031-9228. **Subscription Rates:** $2.25 members; $49 members of affiliated societies; $69 nonmembers; $165 institutions; $15 for shipping/handling via surface mail; $30 for international airmail delivery; $20 single issue.
Ad Rates: BW: $5,445 **Circ:** ‡111,205

13581 Prologue
National Archives and Records Administration
8601 Adelphi Rd. Phone: (301)713-7360
College Park, MD 20740-6001 Fax: (301)713-7270
Publisher E-mail: inquire@nara.gov

Periodical covering historical articles based on research in the National Archives and Presidential libraries. **Subtitle:** Quarterly of the National Archives and Records Administration. **Founded:** 1969. **Freq:** Quarterly. **Key Personnel:** Mary Ryan, Managing Editor; Olivia Hylton, Subscriptions. **ISSN:** 0033-1031. **Subscription Rates:** $16 individuals; $4 single issue. **Remarks:** Advertising not accepted. **URL:** http://www.nara.gov/publications/prologue/prologue.html. **Former name:** Prologue: Journal of the National Archives.
Circ: Combined 2,299

13582 Public Relations Review
Elseiver
College of Journalism
University of Maryland
College Park, MD 20742
Publication E-mail: 102062-2525@compuserve.com
Publisher E-mail: fcentres@gpu.stv.ualberta.ca

Communications journal covering public relations education, government, survey research, public policy, history, and bibliographies. **Subtitle:** A Journal of Research and Comment. **Founded:** 1974. **Freq:** 5/year. **Print Method:** Offset. **Trim Size:** 6 7/8 x 10. **Cols./Page:** 1. **Col. Width:** 57 nonpareils. **Col. Depth:** 98 agate lines. **Key Personnel:** Ray E. Hiebert, Editor. **ISSN:** 0363-8111. **Subscription Rates:** $230 institutions; $255 institutions, other countries; $280 institutions, other countries airmail; $100 individuals; $125 other countries; $150 other countries airmail; $50 single issue; $35 single issue other couuntries; $60 single issue other countries airmail. **Remarks:** Accepts advertising.
Ad Rates: BW: $150 **Circ:** Paid ‡1,500
Non-paid ‡55

13583 Science Communication
Sage Publications Inc.
College of Journalism Phone: (301)405-2430
University of Maryland Fax: (301)314-9166
College Park, MD 20742
Publisher E-mail: info@sagepub.com

Social science research journal. **Founded:** 1979. **Freq:** Quarterly. **Print Method:** Offset. **Trim Size:** 5 1/2 x 8 1/2. **Cols./Page:** 1. **Col. Width:** 50 nonpareils. **Col. Depth:** 100 agate lines. **Key Personnel:** Carol L. Rogers, Editor, cr46@umail.umd.edu; Sara Miller McCune, Publisher; Valerie Giràmberk, Circulation Mgr. **ISSN:** 0164-0259. **Subscription Rates:** $55 individuals; $154 institutions; $248 two years institutions; $178 single issue; $34 single issue institutions. **Remarks:** Accepts advertising. **Alt. Formats:** Microform. **Formerly:** Knowledge, Creation, Diffusion, Utilization.
Ad Rates: BW: $195 **Circ:** Paid ‡850
Non-paid ‡82

13584 The Stars and Stripes
The National Tribune Corp.
Box 624 Phone: (301)486-0839
College Park, MD 20740 Fax: (301)486-0817
Publication E-mail: stars@stripes.com

America's oldest national weekly newspaper for veterans. **Subtitle:** The National Tribune. **Founded:** 1877. **Freq:** Bimonthly. **Trim Size:** 13 x 10 3/16. **Cols./Page:** 5. **Col. Width:** 11.5 picas. **Key Personnel:** Margaret Gentry, Contact. **Subscription Rates:** $19. **Remarks:** Accepts advertising. **Online:** Internet.
Ad Rates: BW: $4,650 **Circ:** 10,000
4C: $5,600
PCI: $70

13585 WMUC-FM - 88.1
University of Maryland Phone: (301)314-7865
3130 S. Campus Dining Hall Fax: (301)314-7879
College Park, MD 20742-8431
E-mail: wmuc@wmuc.und.edu

Format: Full Service. **Founded:** 1979. **Operating Hours:** Continuous. **ADI:** Washington, DC. **Key Personnel:** Rachel Weintraub, General Mgr., phone (301)314-7867; Meg Zamula, Program Dir., phone (301)314-7868, mzed@wam.umd.edu; Donny Williams, Promotions Dir., phone (301)314-7865, dgw@wam.umd.edu; Josh Hughes, Sales Mgr., phone (301)314-7865, business@wmuc.und.edu; Kevan Lee, Public Affairs Director, phone (301)3147875, nmkevan@wam.umd.edu. **Wattage:** 10. **Ad Rates:** Advertising accepted; rates available upon request. **URL:** http://www.wmuc.umd.edu.

COLUMBIA, pop. 72,000.

Howard Co. (C). 20 m NE of Rockville. Howard Community College.

13586 Abbey
White Urp Publishing
5360 Fallriver Row Ct. Phone: (410)730-4272
Columbia, MD 21044
Literary journal. **Founded:** 1970. **Freq:** Quarterly. **Print Method:** Photocopier. **Trim Size:** 8 1/2 x 11. **Key Personnel:** David Greisman, Editor, greisman@aol.com; Andre Choutete, Advertising Mgr. **Remarks:** Accepts advertising.
Ad Rates: BW: $20 **Circ:** Controlled 200

13587 American Journal of Dance Therapy
American Dance Therapy Association
2000 Century Plaza, Ste. 108 Phone: (410)997-4040
10632 Little Patuxent Pkwy. Fax: (410)997-4048
Columbia, MD 21044
Publisher E-mail: adta@aol.com

Journal for clinicians, reseachers, and educators in dance therapy. **Freq:** Semiannual.

13588 Baptist Life
Baptist Convention of Maryland/Delaware
10255 Old Columbia Rd. Phone: (410)290-5290
Columbia, MD 21046-1716 Fax: (410)290-6627

Tabloid newspaper for Southern Baptists of Maryland and Delaware. **Founded:** Dec. 9, 1849. **Freq:** Semimonthly. **Print Method:** Offset. **Trim Size:** 11 1/4 x 14 1/2. **Cols./Page:** 5. **Col. Width:** 1.9 inches. **Col. Depth:** 205 agate lines. **Key Personnel:** Ronald K. Chaney, Editor. **ISSN:** 0883-7864. **Subscription Rates:** $7.50 individuals. **Remarks:** Accepts advertising. **Formerly:** Bapist True Union.
Ad Rates: PCI: $15 **Circ:** 10,000

13589 Business Credit
National Association of Credit Management
8815 Centre Park Dr., Ste. 200 Phone: (410)740-5560
Columbia, MD 21045 Fax: (410)740-5574
Free: (800)955-8815
Publication E-mail: bcm@nacm.org
Publisher E-mail: nacm@nacm.org

Magazine covering finance, business credit management, providing information for the extension of credit, maintenance of accounts receivable, and cash asset management. **Subtitle:** The Magazine of Credit and Financial Professionals. **Founded:** 1898. **Freq:** Monthly (July/Aug and Nov/Dec. issues combined). **Print Method:** Web offset. **Trim Size:** 8 1/8 x 10 7/8. **Cols./Page:** 3. **Col. Width:** 13 picas. **Col. Depth:** 67 picas. **Key Personnel:** Katherine Jeschke, VP Communications, katherinej@macm.org. **ISSN:** 0897-0181. **Subscription Rates:** $45 individuals; $41 libraries; $6 single issue. **Remarks:** Accepts advertising. **Alt. Formats:** Microform. **Formerly:** Credit and Financial Management (Dec. 1, 1987).
Ad Rates: BW: $3,215 **Circ:** Paid ‡38,106
4C: $4,165

13590 Columbia Flier
Patuxent Publishing Co.
10750 Little Patuxent Pkwy. Phone: (410)730-3990
Columbia, MD 21044
Suburban community newspaper. **Founded:** 1969. **Freq:** Weekly (Thurs.). **Print Method:** Offset. **Trim Size:** 11 x 15. **Cols./Page:** 5. **Col. Width:** 11 picas. **Col. Depth:** 80.25 picas. **Key Personnel:** Tom Graham, Editor; S. Zeke Orlinsky, Publisher; Don Nunes, Advertising Dir. **Subscription Rates:** Free; $156 out of area.
Ad Rates: BW: $1,412 **Circ:** Paid 187
4C: $1,862 Non-paid 32,382

13591 Columbia Magazine
Patuxent Publishing Co.
10750 Little Patuxent Pkwy. Phone: (410)730-3990
Columbia, MD 21044
Magazine mailed to all local households. **Freq:** Quarterly. **Trim Size:** 8 1/4 x 10 3/4. **Key Personnel:** Susan Connel, Editor; S. Zeke Orlinsky, Publisher. **Subscription Rates:** Free; $8 out of area. $1.50 single issue. **Remarks:** Accepts advertising.
Ad Rates: BW: $2,825 **Circ:** Controlled 33,000
4C: $3,425

13592 Columbia Union Visitor
Columbia Union Conference of Seventh-day Adventists
5427 Twin Knolls Rd. Phone: (301)596-0800
Columbia, MD 21045 Fax: (410)997-7420
Free: (800)438-9600
Publication E-mail: 204315.2145@compuserve.com

Seventh-Day Adventist magazine. **Subtitle:** Official publication of the Seventh-day Adventist church in the Mid- Atlantic States. **Founded:** 1896. **Freq:** Semimonthly. **Print Method:** Offset. **Trim Size:** 8 1/8 x 10 5/8. **Cols./Page:** 3 and 4. **Col. Width:** 26 and 20 nonpareils. **Col. Depth:** 136 agate lines. **Key Personnel:** Richard Duerksen, Editor; Kimberly Luste Maran, Managing Editor. **Subscription Rates:** Free to qualified subscribers; $8.50 institutions. **URL:** http://www.columbiaunion.org.
Ad Rates: BW: $950 **Circ:** Controlled ‡42,000
4C: $1,500
PCI: $35

13593 Food World
Best-Met Publishing Co., Inc.
5537 Twin Knolls Rd., Ste. 438 Phone: (410)730-5013
Columbia, MD 21045 Fax: (410)740-4680
Publisher E-mail: bestmet@crosslink.net

Regional food trade magazine (tabloid). **Founded:** Mar. 1945.

Freq: Monthly. **Print Method:** Offset. **Trim Size:** 10 x 14. **Cols./Page:** 5. **Col. Width:** 24 nonpareils. **Col. Depth:** 196 agate lines. **Key Personnel:** Jeff Metzger, Publisher; Richard J. Bestany, President. **USPS:** 203-920. **Subscription Rates:** $36 individuals. **Remarks:** Accepts advertising.
Ad Rates: BW: $2,846.20 4C: $4,001.20 PCI: $40.66 **Circ:** Non-paid ‡22,000

13594 Howard County Times
Patuxent Publishing Co.
10750 Little Patuxent Pkwy. Phone: (410)730-3990
Columbia, MD 21044
Community newspaper. **Founded:** 1840. **Freq:** Weekly (Thurs.). **Print Method:** Offset. **Trim Size:** 9 13/16 x 12 5/16. **Cols./Page:** 5. **Col. Width:** 11 picas. **Col. Depth:** 74 picas. **Key Personnel:** Tom Graham, Editor; S. Zeke Orlinsky, Publisher; Don Nunes, Advertising Dir. **Subscription Rates:** $16 individuals; $18 out of county; $22 out of state. **Remarks:** Accepts advertising.
Ad Rates: BW: $1,397 4C: $1,747 **Circ:** Paid 12,458 Non-paid 7,304

13595 North County News
Patuxent Publishing Co.
10750 Little Patuxent Pkwy. Phone: (410)730-3990
Columbia, MD 21044
Community newspaper. **Founded:** 1989. **Freq:** Weekly (Thurs.). **Key Personnel:** Patricia Harrington, Circulation Mgr. **Remarks:** Accepts advertising.
Circ: Non-paid 20,055

13596 Northeast Booster
Patuxent Publishing Co.
10750 Little Patuxent Pkwy. Phone: (410)730-3990
Columbia, MD 21044
Community newspaper. **Founded:** 1947. **Freq:** Weekly (Wed.). **Key Personnel:** Patricia Harrington, Circulation Mgr. **Remarks:** Accepts advertising.
Circ: Combined 19,559

13597 Northeast Reporter
Patuxent Publishing Co.
10750 Little Patuxent Pkwy. Phone: (410)730-3990
Columbia, MD 21044
Community newspaper. **Founded:** 1945. **Freq:** Weekly (Wed.). **Key Personnel:** Patricia Harrington, Circulation Mgr. **Remarks:** Accepts advertising.
Circ: Combined 16,395

13598 The Official Guide to Howard County
Patuxent Publishing Co.
10750 Little Patuxent Pkwy. Phone: (410)730-3990
Columbia, MD 21044
Magazine featuring visitor information on Howard County, Maryland. **Freq:** Annual. **Trim Size:** 8 1/4 x 10 3/4. **Key Personnel:** S. Zeke Orlinsky, Publisher; Jean F. Moon, General Mgr.; Susan Connel, Editor. **Subscription Rates:** free. **Remarks:** Accepts advertising.
Ad Rates: BW: $2,942 4C: $3,542 **Circ:** ‡30,000

13599 Uniforum's IT Solutions
UniForum
10440 Shaker Dr., Ste. 203 Phone: (410)715-9500
Columbia, MD 21046 Fax: (301)596-8803
Free: (800)255-5620
Publication E-mail: pubs@uniforum.org
Publisher E-mail: pubs@uniforum.org

Magazine covering the Unix and open systems marketplace. **Subtitle:** UNIX and Open Technologies for the Enterprise. **Founded:** 1981. **Freq:** Monthly. **Print Method:** Web offset. **Trim Size:** 8 1/2 x 11. **Cols./Page:** 3. **Col. Width:** 24 nonpareils. **Col. Depth:** 115 agate lines. **Key Personnel:** Jeff Bartlett, Managing Editor; Richard Shippee, Publisher. **ISSN:** 1069-0417. **Subscription Rates:** Included in membership. **Remarks:** Accepts advertising. **URL:** http://www.uniforum.org. **Formerly:** CommUNIXations (1991); Uniform Monthly.
Ad Rates: BW: $3,095 4C: $4,005 **Circ:** Controlled 30,000

CRISFIELD, pop. 2,924.

Somerset Co. (SE). On Chesapeake Bay, 123 m S of Wilmington, Del. Important sea food shipping center. Manufactures brushes, sea food tools, nets, boxes, barrels, cutlery. Dairy, poultry, stock farms. Strawberries, tomatoes, potatoes.

13600 Crisfield Times
Independent Newspapers, Inc.
914 W. Main St. Phone: (410)968-1188
Crisfield, MD 21817 Fax: (410)968-1197

Local newspaper. **Founded:** 1891. **Freq:** Weekly (Wed.). **Print Method:** Offset. **Trim Size:** 13 x 21 1/2. **Cols./Page:** 6. **Col. Width:** 26 nonpareils. **Col. Depth:** 301 agate lines. **Key Personnel:** Anthony W. Bertino, Jr., Publisher. **Subscription Rates:** $16.80. **Remarks:** Accepts advertising.
Ad Rates: GLR: $2.55 BW: $1,257.75 4C: $1,457.75 PCI: $9.75 **Circ:** 2,102

CUMBERLAND†, pop. 25,933.

Allegany Co. (NW). On Potomac River, at terminal of Chesapeake & Ohio Canal, 130 m W of Baltimore. Alleghany Community College. Manufactures railroad equipment, brick, lumber, drills, plastics, steel shafting, glassware, boxes, macaroni, auto tires. Limestone quarries, coal mines.

13601 Cumberland Times News
McLeansboro Times-Leader
19 Baltimore St. Phone: (301)722-4600
PO Box 1662 Fax: (301)722-4870
Cumberland, MD 21502
Publication E-mail: cth@times-news.com
Publisher E-mail: press@excel.net

General newspaper. **Founded:** 1870. **Freq:** Mon.-Sun. (morn.). **Print Method:** Offset. **Cols./Page:** 6. **Col. Width:** 25 nonpareils. **Col. Depth:** 301 agate lines. **Key Personnel:** Lance White, Managing Editor, phone (302)722-4600; Terry Horne, Publisher, phone (301)722-4600; George Griffin, General Mgr., phone (301)722-4600; Stephen Stouffer, Advertising Mgr. **Subscription Rates:** $51 individuals. **Remarks:** Accepts advertising.
Ad Rates: SAU: $14.80 **Circ:** Mon.-Sat. ★**31,456** Sun. ★**34,040**

13602 WCBC-AM - 1270
35 Baltimore St. Phone: (301)724-5000
Cumberland, MD 21502 Fax: (301)722-8336
E-mail: staff@wcbc1270am.com

Format: Talk; Adult Contemporary; News; Sports; Oldies. **Networks:** ABC. **Owner:** Cumberland Broadcasting Co., at above address. **Founded:** 1976. **Formerly:** WUOK-AM (1976). **Operating Hours:** Continuous; 50% network, 50% local. **ADI:** Hagerstown, MD. **Key Personnel:** David N. Avdelotte, Sr., Contact, dnorman@wcbc1270am.com; James M. Robey, Contact, jrobey@wcbc1270am.com; Mary Clites, Sales Mgr., mclites@wcbc1270am.com. **Wattage:** 5000 day; 1000 night. **Ad Rates:** $4.50-6.90 for 15 seconds; $9.00-13.80 for 30 seconds; $11.70-17.94 for 60 seconds. Combined advertising rates available with WCBC-FM.

WCBC-FM - See Keyser, West Virginia

13603 WKGO-FM - 106.1
350 Byrd Ave. Phone: (301)722-6666
Cumberland, MD 21502 Fax: (301)722-0945

Format: Adult Contemporary. **Networks:** Westwood One Radio. **Owner:** Dix Communications, at above address. **Founded:** 1962. **Operating Hours:** Continuous. **ADI:** Washington, DC. **Key Personnel:** Beda M. Riley, General Mgr.; Tim Martin, Program Dir. **Wattage:** 4000. **Ad Rates:** $15.00 for 30 seconds; $18.00 for 60 seconds.

13604 WNTR-AM - 1230
516 White Ave. Phone: (301)759-3600
Cumberland, MD 21502 Fax: (301)777-5404
E-mail: wrogwntr@miworld.net

Format: News; Sports; Talk; Information. **Networks:** NBC. **Owner:** Tschody Radio, at above address, (301)777-5400, Fax: (301)724-2571. **Founded:** 1948. **Formerly:** WALI-AM. **Operating Hours:** Continuous. **Key Personnel:** Eva Geiger, Office Mgr.; Patrick L. Sullivan, Program Dir.; Rick Williams, Chief Engineer; Kevin Spencer, Asst. Program Dir.; Eva Geiger, General Mgr. **Local Programs:** *Bargain Box*, Kym Kelly. **Wattage:** 1000. **Ad Rates:** $9-14 for 30 seconds; $10-17 for 60 seconds. WROG-FM. **URL:** http://www.wntr.com.

13605 WROG-FM - 102.9
516 White Ave. Phone: (301)777-5400
Cumberland, MD 21502 Fax: (301)777-5404
E-mail: wrogwntr@miworld.net

Format: Country. **Networks:** Jones Satellite; CNN Radio. **Owner:** Tschudy Radio, at above address. **Founded:** 1948. **Formerly:** WJSE-FM. **Operating Hours:** Continuous. **ADI:** Washington, DC. **Key Personnel:** Eva Geiger, General Mgr.; Patrick L. Sullivan, Program Dir.; Eva Geiger, Office Mgr.; Rick Williams, Chief Engineer; Kevin Spencer, Asst. Program Dir. **Local Programs:** *Kevin Spencer Show*, Kevin Spencer; *Little Caesars Drive at Five*, Kevin Spencer; *Pat Sullivan's Morning Program*, Patrick Sullivan. **Wattage:** 50,000. **Ad Rates:** $13-23 for 30 seconds; $17-27 for 60 seconds. $13-$23 for 30 seconds; $17-$27 for 60 seconds. Combined advertising rates available with WALI-AM. **URL:** http://www.wrog.com.

13606 WTBO-AM - 1450
350 Byrd Ave. Phone: (301)722-6666
Cumberland, MD 21502 Fax: (301)722-0945

Format: Big Band/Nostalgia. **Networks:** CNN Radio. **Owner:** Dix Communications, at above address. **Founded:** 1928. **Operating Hours:** Continuous. **ADI:** Washington, DC. **Key Personnel:** Beda M. Riley, General Mgr.; Tim Martin, Program Dir.; Jim Van, News Dir. **Wattage:** 1000. **Ad Rates:** $9-14 for 30 seconds; $11-16 for 60 seconds.

DAMASCUS

– Courier-Gazette – See Gaithersburg.

13607 Damascus Courier-Gazette
The Gazette Newspapers
1200 Quince Orchard Blvd. Phone: (301)253-6161
Gaithersburg, MD 20878 Fax: (301)670-7183

Newspaper. **Founded:** 1977. **Freq:** Weekly (Wed.). **Print Method:** Offset. Uses mats. **Trim Size:** 10 15/16 x 13. **Cols./Page:** 5. **Col. Width:** 26 nonpareils. **Col. Depth:** 182 agate lines. **Key Personnel:** Chuck Lyons, President. **Remarks:** Accepts advertising.
Ad Rates: BW: $507 4C: $777 SAU: $7.80 **Circ:** Combined ❑**7,392**

DENTON†, pop. 1,927.

Caroline Co. (S). On Choptank River (nav.), 48 m NW of Salisbury. Timber. Fruit and vegetable canneries; flour and lumber mills. Diversified farming. Tomatoes, corn, wheat.

13608 WKDI-AM - 840
24580 Station Rd. Phone: (410)479-2288
PO Box 309 Fax: (410)479-2810
Denton, MD 21629
E-mail: wkdibrothersadcast.net

Format: Religious. **Owner:** Bayshore Communications Inc., at above address. **Founded:** 1988. **Operating Hours:** Sunrise-sunset. **Key Personnel:** Michael A. McCoy, General Mgr. **Wattage:** 1000. **Ad Rates:** $6 for 15 seconds; $8 for 30 seconds; $10 for 60 seconds.

DUNDALK, pop. 89,500.

Baltimore Co. (N), 6 m E of Baltimore. Dundalk Community College. Ft. McHenry (historical site). Dundalk Marine Terminal. Auto body factory; steel plant; shipbuilding.

13609 Dundalk Eagle
Kimbel Publication, Inc.
4 N. Center Pl. Phone: (410)288-6060
Dundalk, MD 21222 Fax: (410)288-2712

Community newspaper. **Founded:** May 1969. **Freq:** Weekly (Thurs.). **Print Method:** Offset. **Cols./Page:** 6. **Col. Width:** 20 nonpareils. **Col. Depth:** 210 agate lines. **Key Personnel:** Kimbel E. Oelke, Editor and Publisher. **USPS:** 709-800. **Subscription Rates:** $10 by mail; $20 out of state.
Ad Rates: GLR: $1 BW: $1,594 4C: $1,902 PCI: $15.40 **Circ:** Paid ‡26,000 Free ‡1,200

DUNKIRK

13610 Geocosmic Magazine
National Council for Geocosmic Research, Inc.
PO Box 1220 Phone: (301)812-2583
Dunkirk, MD 20754-1220 Fax: (301)812-2589

Trade magazine on astrology and cosmology. **Founded:** 1972. **Freq:** Semiannual. **Print Method:** Offset. **Trim Size:** 8 1/2 x 11. **Cols./Page:** 2. **Col. Width:** 3 1/4 inches. **Col. Depth:** 9 1/4 inches. **Key Personnel:** Frances McEvoy, Editor, phone (617)484-1882; Arlene Nimark, Advertising Mgr.; Mary Downing, Production Mgr. **ISSN:** 1080-6415. **Subscription Rates:** Included in membership; $10 single issue. **Remarks:** Accepts advertising.
Ad Rates: BW: $350 **Circ:** Paid 3,000

EARLEVILLE

13611 Dress
Costume Society of America
55 Edgewater Dr. Phone: (410)275-1619
PO Box 73 Fax: (410)275-8936
Earleville, MD 21919-0073
Free: (800)CSA-9447
Publication E-mail: 71554.3201@compuserve.com

Magazine containing news and information about the costume

industry and the Costume Society. Includes book reviews. **Founded:** 1975. **Freq:** Annual. **Key Personnel:** Kaye Kittle Boyer, Manager, phone (410)275-1619, fax (410)275-8936. **ISSN:** 0361-2112. **Subscription Rates:** Included in membership. **Remarks:** Advertising not accepted. **URL:** http://www.costumesocietyamerica.com.
Circ: (Not Reported)

EASTON†, pop. 7,536.

Talbot Co. (E). On Tred Avon River, 38 m NW of Salisbury. Nurseries; canned goods, furniture, brick, tile, underwear manufactured. Seafood packing. Diversified farming. Wheat, soybeans, corn, tomatoes.

13612 The Delmarva Farmer
American Farm Publications, Inc.
505 Brookletts Ave. Phone: (410)822-3965
PO Box 2026 Fax: (410)822-5068
Easton, MD 21601
Free: (800)634-5021
Publication E-mail: delfarmer@skipjack.bluecrab.org
Publisher E-mail: farmercirc@skipjack.bluecrab.org

Newspaper (tabloid) featuring news of interest to agricultural concerns in Maryland, Delaware, Virginia, New Jersey, and Pennsylvania. **Subtitle:** The Agribusiness Newspaper of the Mid-Atlantic Region. **Founded:** Mar. 1, 1976. **Freq:** Weekly. **Print Method:** Offset. **Trim Size:** 11 1/4 x 14 1/2. **Cols./Page:** 4. **Col. Width:** 24 nonpareils. **Col. Depth:** 203 agate lines. **Key Personnel:** Mark Powell, Editor; E. Ralph Hostetter, Publisher; Sheila Brittingham, Advertising Mgr.; Marc Van Pelt, VP/Gen. Mgr. **ISSN:** 0194-2964. **Subscription Rates:** $14 individuals; $26 two years. **Remarks:** Accepts advertising.
Ad Rates: BW: $658 **Circ:** Paid ‡6,161
4C: $1,253 Free ‡2,295
PCI: $8.80

13613 The New Jersey Farmer
American Farm Publications, Inc.
505 Brookletts Ave. Phone: (410)822-3965
PO Box 2026 Fax: (410)822-5068
Easton, MD 21601
Free: (800)634-5021
Publication E-mail: njfarmer@skipjack.bluecrab.org
Publisher E-mail: farmercirc@skipjack.bluecrab.org

Tabloid featuring news of interest to agricultural concerns in New Jersey. **Subtitle:** Growing with the Garden State. **Founded:** Apr. 5, 1988. **Freq:** Bimonthly. **Print Method:** Offset. **Trim Size:** 11 1/4 x 14 1/2. **Cols./Page:** 4. **Col. Width:** 24 nonpareils. **Col. Depth:** 203 agate lines. **Key Personnel:** Bruce Hotchkiss, Editor; E. Ralph Hostetter, Publisher; Marc Van Pelt, General Mgr.; Barry Sabo, Circulation Mgr. **ISSN:** 0898-8765. **Subscription Rates:** $13 individuals. **Remarks:** Accepts advertising. **URL:** http://www.american-farm.com.
Ad Rates: BW: $450 **Circ:** Paid ‡1,733
4C: $1,045 Controlled ‡3,143
PCI: $9

13614 WCEI-AM - 1460
306 Port St. Phone: (410)822-3301
Easton, MD 21601-4101 Fax: (410)822-0576
Free: (800)695-2345

Format: Talk; Big Band/Nostalgia; Easy Listening. **Networks:** AP. **Owner:** Clark Broadcasting Company, at above address. **Founded:** 1960. **Formerly:** WEMD-AM (1981). **Operating Hours:** Continuous. **Key Personnel:** James Hammond, General Mgr.; Pam O'Brien, News Dir.; Stephen Hunter, Program Dir.; Julie Reed, Sales Mgr. **Wattage:** 1000. **Ad Rates:** $10.75-23 for 30 seconds; $16.13-34.50 for 60 seconds.

13615 WCEI-FM - 96.7
306 Port St. Phone: (410)822-3301
Easton, MD 21601-4101 Fax: (410)822-0576
Free: (800)695-2345

Format: Adult Contemporary. **Networks:** AP. **Owner:** Clark Broadcasting Co., at above address. **Founded:** 1975. **Formerly:** WEMD-FM (1981). **Operating Hours:** Continuous. **Key Personnel:** James A. Hammond, General Mgr.; Pam O'Brein, News Dir.; Steve Hunter, Program Dir.; Julie Reed, Sales Mgr. **Wattage:** 25,000. **Ad Rates:** $10.75-23 for 30 seconds; $16.13-34.50 for 60 seconds.

ELKTON†, pop. 6,468.

Cecil Co. (NE). 18 m SW of Wilmington, Del. Clay, sand, gravel pits. Manufactures fireworks, explosives, plastics, rubber novelties, chemical compounds, hosiery, paper, dresses, boat building, rocket propellent, automotive parts. Agriculture. Dairy, beef.

13616 Cecil Whig
Chesapeake Publishing Corp.
601 Bridge St. Phone: (410)398-3311
PO Box 429 Fax: (410)398-4044
Elkton, MD 21922-0429
General newspaper. **Founded:** Aug. 7, 1841. **Freq:** Daily. **Print Method:** Web offset. **Trim Size:** 23 x 27. **Cols./Page:** 6. **Col. Width:** 26 nonpareils. **Col. Depth:** 294 agate lines. **Key Personnel:** Terry Peddicord, Editor; Jeffrey Mezzatesta, Publisher. **USPS:** 095-560. **Subscription Rates:** $68 individuals. **Remarks:** Accepts advertising.
Ad Rates: GLR: $.62 **Circ:** Paid ♦12,989
BW: $1,001.70 Non-paid ♦676
4C: $1,251.70
PCI: $8.70

13617 WOEL-FM - 89.9
Box 246 Phone: (410)392-3225
Elkton, MD 21922-0246 Fax: (410)392-3229
Free: (800)226-0869

Format: Religious. **Networks:** USA Radio. **Founded:** 1978. **Operating Hours:** Continuous. **Key Personnel:** Ray Linzy, Operations Mgr. **Wattage:** 3000. **Ad Rates:** Noncommercial.

13618 WSER-AM - 1550
192 Maloney Rd. Phone: (410)398-3883
Elkton, MD 21921 Fax: (410)392-9882

Format: News; Talk. **Networks:** ABC. **Owner:** First Philadelphia Properties, 311 French Rd., Newtown Square, PA 19073, (610)356-3946. **Founded:** 1963. **Operating Hours:** 6 a.m.-6p.m. **ADI:** Baltimore, MD. **Key Personnel:** Mark Crouch, General Mgr.; Gina Dluhos, Traffic Mgr. **Wattage:** 1000. **Ad Rates:** $20-12 for 30 seconds.

ELLICOTT CITY†, pop. 21,800.

Howard Co. (E).

13619 Maryland PHCC News & Views
Maryland Plumbing Heating Cooling Contractors, Inc.
10176 Balto Natl. Pike, No. 205 Phone: (410)461-5977
Ellicott City, MD 21042 Fax: (410)750-2507

Plumbing and heating magazine. **Founded:** 1926. **Freq:** Monthly. **Print Method:** Offset. **Cols./Page:** 2. **Col. Width:** 42 nonpareils. **Col. Depth:** 140 agate lines. **Key Personnel:** Diane P. Kastner, Editor. **Subscription Rates:** Free to qualified subscribers. **Remarks:** Advertising accepted; rates available upon request.
Circ: Non-paid 2,500

13620 Howard Cable TV Assoc. Inc.
3417 Plumtree Dr. Phone: (410)461-1156
Ellicott City, MD 21042 Fax: (410)461-4731

URL: http://www.comcastonline.com.

EMMITSBURG

13621 WMTB-FM - 89.9
Mount St. Mary's College Phone: (301)447-6122
Emmitsburg, MD 21727

Format: Alternative/New Music/Progressive; Rap. **Founded:** 1977. **Formerly:** WMSM-FM (1987). **Operating Hours:** Continuous. **Key Personnel:** Randy Gray, Faculty Advisor. **Wattage:** 10.

FORT MEADE

13622 Soundoff
Patuxent Publishing Co.
Post Public Affairs Office Phone: (301)677-1388
Bldg. 2837, Ernie Pyle St. Fax: (301)799-5911
Fort Meade, MD 20755-5025
Fort Meade military newspaper (tabloid). **Founded:** 1949. **Freq:** Weekly (Thurs.). **Print Method:** Offset. **Trim Size:** 11 x 15. **Cols./Page:** 5. **Col. Width:** 11 inches. **Col. Depth:** 80.25 inches. **Key Personnel:** K.L. Vantran, Editor, vantrank@meade-emhz.army.mil; John Patirella, Publisher; David Tomasini, Advertising Dir. **Subscription Rates:** Free. **Remarks:** Accepts advertising.
Circ: Non-paid 14,070

FREDERICK†, pop. 28,086.

Frederick Co. (N). 45 m N of Baltimore. Frederick Community College. Hood College (Co-Ed). Manufactures glass containers, electronics, aluminum, clothing, foundry, dairy products, lime, fertilizer, lumber, bricks, flour. Agriculture. Dairying.

13623 AOPA Pilot
421 Aviation Way Phone: (301)695-2350
Frederick, MD 21701-4756 Fax: (301)695-2180
Publication E-mail: acpahq@aopa.org

Magazine for general aviation pilots and aircraft owners who are members of the Aircraft Owners and Pilots Assn. Articles are tailored to address the special informational requirements of both recreational and business pilots. **Founded:** Mar. 1958. **Freq:** Monthly. **Print Method:** Offset. **Trim Size:** 8 1/8 x 10 7/8. **Cols./Page:** 3. **Col. Width:** 2 1/4 inches. **Col. Depth:** 10 inches. **Key Personnel:** Thomas B. Haines, Editor and Publisher; Denis C. Beran, Advertising Mgr. **Subscription Rates:** $21 individuals; $5 single issue. **Remarks:** Accepts advertising. **URL:** http://www.aopa.org.
Ad Rates: BW: $10,960 **Circ:** Paid ★329,353
4C: $17,200
PCI: $375

13624 BarleyCorn
George Rivers
PO Box 549 Phone: (301)432-5599
Frederick, MD 21705 Fax: (301)432-5553
Publisher E-mail: grivers668@aol.com

Consumer magazine covering beer brewing. **Subtitle:** Celebrating and Exploring the Brewing Arts. **Founded:** Dec. 1990. **Freq:** 6/year. **Print Method:** Web offset. **Trim Size:** 11 x 15. **Cols./Page:** 4. **Col. Width:** 2 1/4 inches. **Col. Depth:** 12 1/2 inches. **Subscription Rates:** $20 individuals. **Remarks:** Accepts advertising.
Circ: Combined 50,000

13625 Frederick Magazine
Diversions Publications, Inc.
6 East St., No. 301 Phone: (301)662-8171
Frederick, MD 21701-5601 Fax: (301)662-8171
Publication E-mail: frederickmagazine.com

Consumer lifestyle magazine for mid-Maryland. **Founded:** 1985. **Freq:** Monthly. **Print Method:** Web offset. **Trim Size:** 8 1/4 x 10 7/8. **Cols./Page:** 3. **Key Personnel:** Dan Patrell, Managing Editor; Tom Gorsline, Publisher, fax (301)662-8399, tgorslinec@frederickmagazine.com; Amy Lewis, Advertising Dir., alewis@frederickmagazine.com. **USPS:** 006-923. **Subscription Rates:** $19.95 individuals; $2.95 single issue. **Remarks:** Accepts advertising.
Ad Rates: BW: $1,623 **Circ:** Controlled 16,000
4C: $1,973

13626 The Frederick News Post
The Frederick Post
Box 578 Phone: (301)662-1177
Frederick, MD 21701-5666 Fax: (301)662-1615

General newspaper. **Founded:** Dec. 10, 1910. **Freq:** Mon.-Sat. (morn.). **Print Method:** Offset. **Cols./Page:** 6. **Col. Width:** 24 nonpareils. **Col. Depth:** 294 agate lines. **Key Personnel:** Michael Powell, Manager; George B. Delaplaine, Jr., Editor and Publisher; Ed Gaydos, Advertising Mgr.; George E. Randall, Publisher. **Subscription Rates:** $67 individuals. **Formerly:** The Frederick Post.
Circ: Combined ★40,881

13627 Hood Today
Hood College
401 Rosemont Ave. Phone: (301)696-3641
Frederick, MD 21701-8575
Collegiate tabloid. **Founded:** 1986. **Freq:** Monthly. **Print Method:** Offset. **Trim Size:** 11 x 14. **Cols./Page:** 5. **Col. Width:** 11 picas. **Col. Depth:** 70 picas. **Key Personnel:** Kristen Woodruff, Editor; Lora Wilson, Advertising Mgr., fax (301)696-3598. **Subscription Rates:** $6 individuals. **Remarks:** Color advertising not accepted. **Feature Editors:** Kenya Brown, *News*.
Ad Rates: BW: $260 **Circ:** Free ‡1,250
4C: $400
PCI: $4.50

13628 Professional Surveyor
Professional Surveyors Publishing Co., Inc.
1713-J Rosemont Ave. Phone: (301)682-6101
Frederick, MD 21702 Fax: (301)920-6105
Publication E-mail: profsurv@profsurv.com

Magazine for land surveyors, mappers, and civil engineers. **Founded:** Jan. 1981. **Freq:** 10/year. **Print Method:** Web offset. **Trim Size:** 8 3/8 x 10 7/8. **Cols./Page:** 3. **Col. Width:** 28 nonpareils. **Col. Depth:** 112 agate lines. **Key Personnel:** Marc Cheves, Editor, marc@profsurv.com; Johan Boesjes, Publisher, johan.boesjes@gitc.nl; Amy Catherine McEwan, Advertising Dir., ac@profsurv.com; Liz Ingwersen, Promotion Coord., liz@profsurv.com. **ISSN:** 0278-1425. **Subscription Rates:** Free to qualified subscribers. **Remarks:** Accepts advertising. **URL:** http://www.landsurveyor.com/profsurv.
Ad Rates: GLR: $60 **Circ:** Controlled ‡52,000
BW: $3,850
4C: $4,950
PCI: $110

WAFY-FM - See Middletown

13629 WFMD-AM - 930
PO Box 151 Phone: (301)663-4181
Frederick, MD 21705 Fax: (301)663-5494
E-mail: nt930@aol.com

Format: News; Talk. **Networks:** CBS. **Owner:** Jim Gibbons Radio, Inc., at above address. **Founded:** 1936. **Operating Hours:** Continuous. **ADI:** Washington, DC. **Key Personnel:** Frank Mitchell, Program Dir.; Rebecca Matthews, News Dir.; Ron Kitzmiller, Sports Dir.; Terry Gibbons, Gen./Operations Mgr.; Roger Lide, Chief Engineer; Chris King, Production Dir. **Wattage:** 5000 day; 2500 night. **Ad Rates:** Advertising accepted; rates available upon request. Combined advertising rates available with WFRE-FM.

13630 WFPT-TV - 62
c/o Maryland Public Broadcasting Commission Phone: (410)356-5600
Fax: (410)581-4338
11767 Owings Mills Blvd.
Owings Mills, MD 21117
Free: (800)223-3678
E-mail: comments@mpt.org

Format: Public TV. **Simulcasts:** WMPB, WMPT, WCPB, WWPB, WGPT. **Networks:** Public Broadcasting Service (PBS); Eastern Educational Television. **Owner:** Maryland Public Broadcasting Commission, at above address. **Operating Hours:** 3 a.m.-1:30 a.m., Mon.-Sun. **ADI:** Baltimore, MD. **Key Personnel:** Robert J. Shuman, Pres./CEO; Dr. Archie L. Buffkins, Sr. Vice Pres., Broadcasting; Janice Wilson, Sr. Vice Pres., Marketing & Development; Larry D. Unger, Sr. Vice Pres., Administration & Finance; Martin Jacobs, Vice Pres., Finance & Accounting; Gladys M. Kaplan, Vice Pres., Human Resources; Ann Engelman, Vice Pres., Programming/Broadcast Serv.; Everett L. Marshburn, Vice Pres., Broadcast Productions; John T. Potthast, Vice Pres., National Productions; Barry P. Freidly, Vice Pres., Membership; Hannah Lee Byron, Dir., Corp. Comm. & Gov't Affairs; Carol Wonsavage, Dir., Regional Communications; Sharon Philippart, Dir., National Communications. **Wattage:** 3,300,000. **URL:** http://www.mpt.org.

13631 WFRE-FM - 99.9
5966 Grove Hill Rd. Phone: (301)663-4337
Box 151 Fax: (301)663-5494
Frederick, MD 21705-0151

Format: Country. **Owner:** Jim Gibbons Radio, Inc., at above address. **Founded:** 1959. **Operating Hours:** Continuous. **Key Personnel:** Larry Viehmeyer, General Sales Mgr.; Jim Titus, Music Dir. **Local Programs:** *Spectrum*, Rebecca Hicks, News Dir., (301)662-3103. **Wattage:** 9,000.

FROSTBURG

Allegany Co. (NW). 30 m W of Cumberland.

13632 WFRB-AM - 560
242 Finzel Rd. Phone: (301)689-8871
Frostburg, MD 21532 Fax: (301)689-8880
E-mail: wfrb@mail.miworld.net

Format: Country. **Networks:** Mutual Broadcasting System. **Owner:** Dix Communications, at above address. **Founded:** 1958. **Operating Hours:** 6 a.m.-sunset, 2 hours past sunset. **Key Personnel:** Beda M. Riley, General Mgr.; Chris Bagley, Operations Mgr.; Jim Frantz, News Dir.; J.D. Frye, Music Dir. **Wattage:** 5000. **Ad Rates:** $9.55-14.55 for 30 seconds; $12.7-17.9 for 60 seconds.

13633 WFWM-FM - 91.9
Frostburg State University Phone: (301)689-4143
Compton Hall Fax: (301)689-7040
Frostburg, MD 21532
E-mail: wfwm@hotmail.com

Format: Jazz; Classical; Alternative/New Music/Progressive. **Networks:** Independent; National Public Radio (NPR). **Founded:** 1989. **Operating Hours:** Continuous. **Key Personnel:** Rene G. Atkinson, General Mgr. **Wattage:** 1,500. **Ad Rates:** Noncommercial.

13634 WLIC-FM - 97.1
He's Alive Corp. Offices Phone: (301)895-3292
203 Springs Rd. Fax: (301)895-3293
PO Box 540
Grantsville, MD 21536

Format: Southern Gospel; Adult Contemporary. **Networks:** USA Radio. **Owner:** He's Alive Inc., at above address. **Founded:** 1989. **Operating Hours:** 5:30 a.m.-midnight. **Key Personnel:** Dewayne Johnson, President; Wally Weeks, General Mgr.; Scott Reppert, Music Dir. **Wattage:** 145. **Ad Rates:** Noncommercial.

FULTON

13635 Journal of Agricultural and Food Information
The Haworth Press, Inc.
8349 Resevoir Rd. Phone: (301)490-5898
Fulton, MD 20759 Fax: (301)504-6409
Publisher E-mail: getinfo@haworthpressinc.com

Professional journal covering agriculture information technology. **Founded:** 1983. **Freq:** Quarterly. **Trim Size:** 6x8 1/2. **Cols./Page:** 1. **Key Personnel:** Robyn Frank, Editor, phone (503)737-3260, fax (503)737-3453; Bill Cohen, Publisher. **Subscription Rates:** $36 individuals; $50 institutions; $85 libraries. **Remarks:** Accepts advertising. **Alt. Formats:** Microfiche.
Ad Rates: BW: $300 **Circ:** Paid 200

GAITHERSBURG, pop. 26,424.

Montgomery Co. (WC). 20 m NW of Washington, DC. Suburban community. Commercial and financial centers. Forest Oak (a tree known as a historical monument). Agribusiness, research & development.

13636 Advances in Nursing Science
Aspen Publishers, Inc.
200 Orchard Ridge Dr., Ste. 200 Phone: (301)417-7500
Gaithersburg, MD 20878 Fax: (301)417-7550
Publisher E-mail: customer.service@aspenpubl.com

Academic medical journal. **Founded:** 1978. **Freq:** Quarterly. **Trim Size:** 7 x 10. **Cols./Page:** 2. **Col. Width:** 32 nonpareils. **Col. Depth:** 105 agate lines. **Key Personnel:** Peggy Chinn, Editor. **ISSN:** 0161-9268. **Subscription Rates:** $82; $98 out of country; $26 single issue. **Remarks:** Accepts advertising. **URL:** http://www.aspenpub.com.
Ad Rates: BW: $600 **Circ:** 2,343,169
4C: $1,500

13637 Burtonsville Gazette
The Gazette Newspapers
1200 Quince Orchard Blvd. Phone: (301)253-6161
Gaithersburg, MD 20878 Fax: (301)670-7183

Community newspaper. **Freq:** Weekly (Wed.). **Trim Size:** 13 3/4 x 11 1/2. **Cols./Page:** 5. **Col. Width:** 115-116 inches. **Col. Depth:** 13 inches. **Key Personnel:** Judith A. Hruz, Managing Editor. **Subscription Rates:** Free. **Remarks:** Accepts advertising. **Available Online.**
Ad Rates: BW: $811.20 **Circ:** Controlled ❑**17,653**
4C: $1211.20 Paid ❑**6**
PCI: $12.48

13638 Critical Care Nursing Quarterly
Aspen Publishers, Inc.
200 Orchard Ridge Dr., No. 200 Phone: (301)417-7500
Gaithersburg, MD 20878 Fax: (301)417-7650
Free: (800)638-8437
Publisher E-mail: customer.service@aspenpubl.com

Journal providing coverage of advances, procedures, and techniques in the clinical management of the critically ill or injured patient. **Founded:** 1978. **Freq:** Quarterly. **Trim Size:** 7 x 10. **Cols./Page:** 2. **Col. Width:** 16 picas. **Col. Depth:** 45 picas. **Key Personnel:** Janet M. Barber, Editor. **ISSN:** 0887-9303. **Subscription Rates:** $85 individuals; $102 other countries; $27 single issue. **Remarks:** Accepts advertising. **URL:** http://www.aspenpublishers.com. **Alt. Formats:** Microform. **Formerly:** Critical Care Quarterly.
Ad Rates: BW: $600 **Circ:** ‡3,000
4C: $1,500

Damascus Courier-Gazette - See Damascus

13639 EA Journal
National Association of Enrolled Agents
200 Orchard Ridge Dr., No. 302 Phone: (301)212-9608
Gaithersburg, MD 20878-1978 Fax: (301)990-1611
Publisher E-mail: info@naea.org

Magazine containing articles and analyses of technical taxation issues for tax practitioners. Includes articles that help tax practitioners improve their business management and marketing skills. **Founded:** 1983. **Freq:** Bimonthly. **Trim Size:** 8 1/2 x 11. **Key Personnel:** Carol Pettit, Editor, taxlady@aol.com; Cliff Weiss, Managing Editor, cweiss@naea.org. **ISSN:** 8750-7072. **Subscription Rates:** Included in membership; $48 nonmembers. **Remarks:** Accepts advertising. **URL:** http://www.naea.org. **Alt. Formats:** Mailing labels.
Ad Rates: BW: $725 **Circ:** 10,000
4C: $1,400

13640 Equus
Fleet Street Publishing
656 Quince Orchard Rd., Ste. 600 Phone: (301)977-3900
Fax: (301)990-9015
Gaithersburg, MD 20878
Publication E-mail: equuslts@aol.com
Publisher E-mail: dletters@aol.com

Magazine featuring health, care, and understanding of horses. **Founded:** 1977. **Freq:** Monthly. **Print Method:** Offset. **Trim Size:** 8 x 10 3/4. **Cols./Page:** 3. **Col. Width:** 27 nonpareils. **Col. Depth:** 137 agate lines. **Key Personnel:** Ami Shinitzky, Editor and Publisher; Susan Harding, Publisher. **Subscription Rates:** $24 individuals; $3.25 single issue.
Ad Rates: BW: $3,840 **Circ:** Paid ★**145,949**
4C: $6,140

13641 Family & Community Health
Aspen Publishers, Inc.
200 Orchard Ridge Dr., No. 200 Phone: (301)417-7500
Gaithersburg, MD 20878 Fax: (301)417-7650
Free: (800)638-8437
Publisher E-mail: customer.service@aspenpubl.com

Journal on practical and policy matters related to health promotion and maintenance. **Founded:** 1978. **Freq:** Quarterly. **Trim Size:** 7 x 10. **Cols./Page:** 2. **Col. Width:** 16 picas. **Col. Depth:** 45 picas. **Key Personnel:** Jeanette Lancaster, Editor. **ISSN:** 0160-6379. **Subscription Rates:** $121 individuals; $145 out of country; $38 single issue. **Remarks:** Accepts advertising. **URL:** http://www.aspenpublishers.com. **Alt. Formats:** Microform.
Ad Rates: 4C: $1,500 **Circ:** Paid 1,327
Non-paid 106

13642 The Gaithersburg Gazette
The Gazette Newspapers
PO Box Caller No. 6006 Phone: (301)948-3120
Gaithersburg, MD 20884
Newspaper. **Founded:** 1959. **Freq:** Weekly (Wed.). **Print Method:** Offset. Uses mats. **Trim Size:** 10 15/16 x 13. **Cols./Page:** 5. **Col. Width:** 26 nonpareils. **Col. Depth:** 182 agate lines. **Key Personnel:** Charles Lyons, President. **Subscription Rates:** $10 individuals. **Remarks:** Accepts advertising.
Ad Rates: BW: $1,900.60 **Circ:** Combined ❑**31,522**
4C: $2,400.60
SAU: $29.24
PCI: $29.24

The Germantown Gazette - See Germantown

13643 Health Care Management Review
Aspen Publishers, Inc.
200 Orchard Ridge Dr., No. 200 Phone: (301)417-7500
Gaithersburg, MD 20878 Fax: (301)417-7650
Free: (800)638-8437
Publisher E-mail: customer.service@aspenpubl.com

Journal devoted to management issues in health care and administration. **Founded:** 1976. **Freq:** Quarterly. **Trim Size:** 8 1/2 x 11. **Cols./Page:** 2. **Col. Width:** 20 picas. **Col. Depth:** 50 picas. **Key Personnel:** Jane Garwood, Publisher; Sandy Cannon, Acquisition Editor. **ISSN:** 0361-6274. **Subscription Rates:** $140 individuals; $168 out of country; $43 single issue. **Remarks:** Accepts advertising. **Available Online. URL:** http://www.aspenpublishers.com. **Alt. Formats:** Microform.
Ad Rates: BW: $600 **Circ:** Paid ‡4,429
4C: $1,500

13644 The Health Care Supervisor
Aspen Publishers, Inc.
200 Orchard Ridge Dr., No. 200 Phone: (301)417-7500
Gaithersburg, MD 20878 Fax: (301)417-7650
Free: (800)638-8437
Publisher E-mail: customer.service@aspenpubl.com

Journal providing cost-effective solutions and guidance for health care supervisors. **Founded:** 1982. **Freq:** Quarterly. **Trim Size:** 7 x 10. **Cols./Page:** 2. **Col. Width:** 16 picas. **Col. Depth:** 45 picas. **Key Personnel:** Charles R. McConnell, Editor. **ISSN:** 0731-3381. **Subscription Rates:** $125 individuals; $150 out of country; $38 single issue. **Remarks:** Accepts advertising. **URL:** http://www.aspenpublishers.com. **Alt. Formats:** Microform.
Ad Rates: BW: $600 **Circ:** Paid 1,899
4C: $1,500 Free 66

13645 Holistic Nursing Practice
Aspen Publishers, Inc.
200 Orchard Ridge Dr., No. 200 Phone: (301)417-7500
Gaithersburg, MD 20878 Fax: (301)417-7650
Free: (800)638-8437
Publisher E-mail: customer.service@aspenpubl.com

Journal exploring emerging holistic models of clinical practice. **Founded:** 1986. **Freq:** Quarterly. **Trim Size:** 7 x 10. **Cols./Page:** 2. **Col. Width:** 16 picas. **Col. Depth:** 45 picas. **Key Personnel:** Gloria F. Donnelly, Editor. **ISSN:** 0887-9311. **Subscription Rates:** $90 individuals; $108 out of country; $28

single issue. **Remarks:** Accepts advertising. **Available Online. URL:** http://www.aspenpublishers.com. **Alt. Formats:** Microform. **Formerly:** Topics in Clinical Nursing (1988).
Ad Rates: BW: $600 **Circ:** (Not Reported)
4C: $1,500

13646 Home Health Care Management and Practice
Aspen Publishers, Inc.
200 Orchard Ridge Dr., No. 200 Phone: (301)417-7500
Gaithersburg, MD 20878 Fax: (301)417-7650
Free: (800)638-8437
Publisher E-mail: customer.service@aspenpubl.com

Journal covering issues and practical concerns in home health care. **Founded:** 1989. **Freq:** Bimonthly. **Trim Size:** 8 1/2 x 11. **Cols./Page:** 2. **Col. Width:** 16 picas. **Col. Depth:** 45 picas. **Key Personnel:** Barbara Gingerich, RN, Editor; Deborah Ondeck, RN, Editor. **ISSN:** 0893-2190. **Subscription Rates:** $99 individuals; $119 other countries; $31 single issue. **Remarks:** Accepts advertising. **Formerly:** Journal of Home Health Care Practice.
Ad Rates: BW: $600 **Circ:** 1,000
4C: $1,500

13647 Hospital Materiel Management Quarterly
Aspen Publishers, Inc.
200 Orchard Ridge Dr., No. 200 Phone: (301)417-7500
Gaithersburg, MD 20878 Fax: (301)417-7650
Free: (800)638-8437
Publisher E-mail: customer.service@aspenpubl.com

Journal emphasizing the application of practical and cost-effective techniques and procedures to purchasing and materiel management practices. **Founded:** 1979. **Freq:** Quarterly. **Trim Size:** 7 x 10. **Cols./Page:** 2. **Col. Width:** 16 picas. **Col. Depth:** 45 picas. **Key Personnel:** Charles E. Housley, Editor. **ISSN:** 0192-2262. **Subscription Rates:** $130 individuals; $150 other countries; $39 single issue. **Remarks:** Accepts advertising. **Available Online. URL:** http://www.aspenpublishers.com. **Alt. Formats:** Microform.
Ad Rates: BW: $600 **Circ:** Paid 1,571
4C: $1,500 Non-paid 88

13648 Infants and Young Children
Aspen Publishers, Inc.
200 Orchard Ridge Dr. Phone: (301)417-7500
Gaithersburg, MD 20878 Fax: (301)417-7550
Free: (800)638-8437
Publisher E-mail: customer.service@aspenpubl.com

Interdisciplinary publication focusing on young children. **Subtitle:** Interdisciplinary. **Founded:** 1987. **Freq:** Quarterly. **Trim Size:** 7 x 10. **Cols./Page:** 2. **Col. Width:** 16 inches. **Col. Depth:** 45 inches. **Key Personnel:** Michael Brown, Publisher; James A. Blackman, M.D., Editor; Eric Duchinsky, Acquisitions. **ISSN:** 0896-3746. **Subscription Rates:** $82 individuals; $90 out of country; $26 single issue. **URL:** http://www.aspenpublishers.com. **Alt. Formats:** Microform.
Circ: Paid 2,600

13649 Journal of Ambulatory Care Management
Aspen Publishers, Inc.
200 Orchard Ridge Dr., No. 200 Phone: (301)417-7500
Gaithersburg, MD 20878 Fax: (301)417-7650
Free: (800)638-8437
Publisher E-mail: customer.service@aspenpubl.com

Journal devoted to the management information needs of professionals in ambulatory care. **Founded:** 1978. **Freq:** Quarterly. **Trim Size:** 7 x 10. **Cols./Page:** 2. **Col. Width:** 16 picas. **Col. Depth:** 45 picas. **Key Personnel:** Norbert Goldfield, Editor. **ISSN:** 0148-9917. **Subscription Rates:** $135; $162 other countries; $41 single issue. **Remarks:** Accepts advertising. **Available Online. URL:** http://www.aspenpublishers.com. **Alt. Formats:** Microform.
Ad Rates: BW: $600 **Circ:** Paid 2,598
4C: $1,500 Non-paid 123

13650 Journal of Cardiovascular Nursing
Aspen Publishers, Inc.
200 Orchard Ridge Dr., No. 200 Phone: (301)417-7500
Gaithersburg, MD 20878 Fax: (301)417-7650
Free: (800)638-8437
Publisher E-mail: customer.service@aspenpubl.com

Journal dedicated to strengthening the clinical expertise of cardiovascular nurses in every setting: critical care, acute care, ambulatory care, home care, and rehabilitation. **Founded:** 1986. **Freq:** Quarterly. **Trim Size:** 7 x 10. **Cols./Page:** 2. **Col. Width:** 16 inches. **Col. Depth:** 45 inches. **Key Personnel:** Barbara Jean Riegel, Editor; Debra Moser, Editor. **ISSN:** 0889-4655. **Subscription Rates:** $85 individuals; $102 other countries; $27 single issue. **Remarks:** Accepts advertising. **Available Online. URL:** http://www.aspenpublishers.com. **Alt. Formats:** Microform.
Ad Rates: BW: $600 **Circ:** Paid 2,271
4C: $1,500 Non-paid 4

13651 Journal of Head Trauma Rehabilitation
Aspen Publishers, Inc.
200 Orchard Ridge Dr., No. 200 Phone: (301)417-7500
Gaithersburg, MD 20878 Fax: (301)417-7650
Free: (800)638-8437
Publisher E-mail: customer.service@aspenpubl.com

Journal providing an interdisciplinary approach to the clinical management and rehabilitation of persons with head injuries. **Founded:** 1986. **Freq:** Bimonthly. **Trim Size:** 7 x 10. **Cols./Page:** 2. **Col. Width:** 16 picas. **Col. Depth:** 45 picas. **Key Personnel:** Nathaniel Mayer, Editor; Mitchell Rosenthal, Editor; Betsy Sandel, Associate Editor; Bruce Caplan, Associate Editor. **ISSN:** 0885-9701. **Subscription Rates:** $112 individuals; $123 foreign; $23 single issue. **Remarks:** Accepts advertising. **URL:** http://www.aspenpub.com. **Alt. Formats:** Microform. **Formerly:** Head Trauma Rehab.
Ad Rates: BW: $600 **Circ:** Paid 2,500
4C: $1,500 Free 66

13652 Journal of Health Care Finance
Aspen Publishers, Inc.
200 Orchard Ridge Dr., Ste. 200 Phone: (301)417-7500
Gaithersburg, MD 20878 Fax: (301)417-7550
Publisher E-mail: customer.service@aspenpubl.com

Journal offering advice, effective management strategies, and information on new financing alternatives for competing in today's health care financial environment. **Founded:** 1974. **Freq:** Quarterly. **Trim Size:** 7 x 10. **Cols./Page:** 2. **Col. Width:** 16 picas. **Col. Depth:** 45 picas. **Key Personnel:** James Unland, Editor; Judith Baker, Editor. **ISSN:** 0095-3814. **Subscription Rates:** $140; $168 out of country; $42 single issue. **Remarks:** Accepts advertising. **URL:** http://www.aspenpublishers.com. **Alt. Formats:** Microform, UMI. **Formerly:** Topics in Health Care Financing.
Ad Rates: BW: $600 **Circ:** Paid 2,034
4C: $1,500 Non-paid 73

13653 Journal of Nursing Care Quality
Aspen Publishers, Inc.
200 Orchard Ridge Dr., Ste. 200 Phone: (301)417-7500
Gaithersburg, MD 20878 Fax: (301)417-7550
Publisher E-mail: customer.service@aspenpubl.com

Journal providing insight, information, and solutions to major problems and issues faced by nurses in quality assurance. **Founded:** 1986. **Freq:** Quarterly. **Trim Size:** 7 x 10. **Cols./Page:** 2. **Col. Width:** 16 picas. **Col. Depth:** 45 picas. **Key Personnel:** Patricia Schroeder, Editor. **ISSN:** 1057-3631. **Subscription Rates:** $99 individuals; $102 out of country; $34 single issue. **Remarks:** Accepts advertising. **URL:** http://www.aspenpublishers.com. **Alt. Formats:** Microform. **Formerly:** Journal of Nursing Quality Assurance (1991).
Ad Rates: BW: $600 **Circ:** Paid 5,362
4C: $1,500 Non-paid 108

13654 Journal of Perinatal and Neonatal Nursing
Aspen Publishers, Inc.
200 Orchard Ridge Dr., No. 200 Phone: (301)417-7500
Gaithersburg, MD 20878 Fax: (301)417-7650
Free: (800)638-8437
Publisher E-mail: customer.service@aspenpubl.com

Journal on issues and practical concerns in perinatal and neonatal clinical practice. **Founded:** 1987. **Freq:** Quarterly. **Trim Size:** 7 x 10. **Cols./Page:** 2. **Col. Width:** 16 picas. **Col. Depth:** 45 picas. **Key Personnel:** Diane J. Angelini, Editor; Susan Blackburn, Editor. **ISSN:** 0893-2190. **Subscription Rates:** $85 individuals; $102 other countries; $27 single issue. **Available Online. URL:** http://www.aspenpublishers.com. **Alt. Formats:** Microform, UMI.
Ad Rates: BW: $600 **Circ:** Paid 2,501
4C: $1,500 Non-paid 92

13655 Journal of Therapeutic Horticulture
American Horticultural Therapy Association
362A Christopher Ave. Phone: (301)948-3010
Gaithersburg, MD 20879-1280 Fax: (301)869-2397

Journal containing articles on the therapeutic aspects of gardening and agriculture for persons with disabilities. **Founded:** 1986. **Freq:** Annual. **Key Personnel:** Steven H. Davis, Staff Editor. **ISSN:** 1088-3487. **Subscription Rates:** $15 nonmembers. **Remarks:** Advertising not accepted.
Circ: Paid 900

13656 Managed Care Quarterly
Aspen Publishers, Inc.
200 Orchard Ridge Dr. Phone: (301)417-7500
Gaithersburg, MD 20878 Fax: (301)417-7550
Free: (800)638-8437
Publisher E-mail: customer.service@aspenpubl.com

Journal providing current information to health care executives who require in-depth material on specific managed care issues. **Founded:** 1991. **Freq:** Quarterly. **Trim Size:** 8 1/2 x 11. **Cols./Page:** 2. **Col. Width:** 20 inches. **Col. Depth:** 54 inches. **Key Personnel:** Allan Fine, Editor. **ISSN:** 1064-5454. **Subscription Rates:** $120 individuals; $36 single issue; $144 out of country. **Remarks:** Advertising accepted; rates available upon request. **Available Online. URL:** http://www.aspenpubrishers.com. **Alt. Formats:** Microform.
Circ: 2200

13657 Nursing Administration Quarterly
Aspen Publishers, Inc.
200 Orchard Ridge Dr., No. 200 Phone: (301)417-7500
Gaithersburg, MD 20878 Fax: (301)417-7650
Free: (800)638-8437
Publisher E-mail: customer.service@aspenpubl.com

Journal presenting information on the management of nursing services. **Founded:** 1976. **Freq:** Quarterly. **Print Method:** Offset. **Trim Size:** 7 x 10. **Cols./Page:** 2. **Col. Width:** 16 picas. **Col. Depth:** 45 picas. **Key Personnel:** Barbara Brown, Editor. **ISSN:** 0363-9568. **Subscription Rates:** $119 individuals; $143 other countries; $37 single issue. **Remarks:** Accepts advertising. **URL:** http://www.aspenpublishers.com. **Alt. Formats:** Microform.
Ad Rates: BW: $600 **Circ:** Paid 4,239
4C: $1,500 Non-paid 47

13658 Outdoor America
Izaak Walton League of America
707 Conservation Ln. Phone: (301)548-0150
Gaithersburg, MD 20878-2983 Fax: (301)548-0146
Publisher E-mail: general@iwla.com

Association magazine on outdoor recreation and the conservation of America's natural resources. **Founded:** 1922. **Freq:** Quarterly. **Print Method:** Offset. **Trim Size:** 8 1/4 x 10 7/8. **Cols./Page:** 3. **Col. Width:** 27 nonpareils. **Col. Depth:** 135 agate lines. **Key Personnel:** Zachary Hoskins, Editor, zachh@iwla.org. **ISSN:** 0021-3314. **Subscription Rates:** $25 individuals. **Remarks:** Accepts classified advertising.
Ad Rates: GLR: $.75 **Circ:** 45,000
BW: $1,150
4C: $1,600

13659 Pharmacy Practice Management Quarterly
Aspen Publishers, Inc.
200 Orchard Ridge Dr., No. 200 Phone: (301)417-7500
Gaithersburg, MD 20878 Fax: (301)417-7650
Free: (800)638-8437
Publisher E-mail: customer.service@aspenpubl.com

Journal devoted to the management of hospital pharmacy services. **Founded:** 1981. **Freq:** Quarterly. **Trim Size:** 7 x 10. **Cols./Page:** 2. **Col. Width:** 16 picas. **Col. Depth:** 45 picas. **Key Personnel:** Andrew L. Wilson, Editor. **ISSN:** 0271-1206. **Subscription Rates:** $130; $150 out of country; $39 single issue. **Remarks:** Accepts advertising. **URL:** http://www.aspenpublishers.com. **Formerly:** Topics in Hospital Pharmacy Management.
Ad Rates: BW: $600 **Circ:** Paid 1,213
4C: $1,500 Non-paid 78

13660 Poolesville Gazette
The Gazette Newspapers
1200 Quince Orchard Blvd. Phone: (301)253-6161
Gaithersburg, MD 20878 Fax: (301)670-7183

Community newspaper. **Freq:** Weekly (Wed.). **Trim Size:** 10 3/4w x 13 3/4d. **Cols./Page:** 5. **Col. Width:** 2 1/16 inches. **Col. Depth:** 13 inches. **Key Personnel:** William Schlossenberg, Publisher. **Subscription Rates:** Free. **Remarks:** Accepts advertising.
Ad Rates: BW: $501.80 **Circ:** Combined ❑**4,144**
4C: $801.80
PCI: $7.77

13661 Quality Management in Health Care
Aspen Publishers, Inc.
200 Orchard Ridge Dr. Phone: (301)417-7500
Gaithersburg, MD 20878 Fax: (301)417-7550
Free: (800)638-8437
Publisher E-mail: customer.service@aspenpubl.com

Journal providing a forum to explore and assist in the theoretical, technical, and strategic elements of quality management in health care. **Founded:** 1991. **Freq:** Quarterly. **Trim Size:** 8 1/2 x 11. **Cols./Page:** 2. **Col. Width:** 20 picas. **Col. Depth:** 54 picas. **Key Personnel:** Jean Carroll, Editor. **ISSN:** 1063-8628. **Subscription Rates:** $142 individuals; $170 out of country; $44 single issue. **Remarks:** Advertising not accepted. **URL:** http://www.aspenpub.ellishers.com. **Alt. Formats:** Microform.
Circ: Paid 1,400

13662 Silver Spring Gazette
The Gazette Newspapers
1200 Quince Orchard Blvd. Phone: (301)253-6161
Gaithersburg, MD 20878 Fax: (301)670-7183

Community newspaper. **Freq:** Weekly (Wed.). **Key Person-**

nel: Gary T. Socha, Publisher; Judith A. Hruz, Managing Editor. **Subscription Rates:** Free.
Circ: Combined ❑**24,558**

13663 Sweeping
National Chimney Sweep Guild
16021 Industrial Dr., Ste. 8 Phone: (301)963-5600
Gaithersburg, MD 20877 Fax: (301)963-0838
Free: (800)536-0118

Trade magazine covering technical information for chimney sweeps and venting technologists. **Founded:** 1977. **Freq:** Monthly. **Print Method:** Sheetfed offset. **Key Personnel:** Calli Schmidt, Editor; Dolores Ridout, Advertising Mgr. **ISSN:** 1041-6692. **Subscription Rates:** $42 individuals. **Remarks:** Accepts advertising. **URL:** http://www.ncsg.org.
Ad Rates: BW: $540 **Circ:** Paid ⊕**1,200**
4C: $700

13664 Topics in Clinical Chiropractic
Aspen Publishers, Inc.
200 Orchard Ridge Dr., No. 200 Phone: (301)417-7500
Gaithersburg, MD 20878 Fax: (301)417-7650
Free: (800)638-8437
Publisher E-mail: customer.service@aspenpubl.com

Professional medical journal covering rehabilitation. **Founded:** 1994. **Freq:** Quarterly. **Trim Size:** 8 x 11. **Cols./Page:** 2. **Col. Width:** 41.5 picas. **Col. Depth:** 58 picas. **Key Personnel:** Robert Mootz, Editor. **ISSN:** 1073-2837. **Subscription Rates:** $79 individuals; $25 single issue. **Remarks:** Accepts advertising. **URL:** http://www.aspenpub.com. **Alt. Formats:** Microform.
Ad Rates: BW: $600 **Circ:** 1,037

13665 Topics in Clinical Nutrition
Aspen Publishers, Inc.
200 Orchard Ridge Dr., Ste. 200 Phone: (301)417-7500
Gaithersburg, MD 20878 Fax: (301)417-7550
Publisher E-mail: customer.service@aspenpubl.com

Journal addressing the challenges and problems of dietitians and others involved in dietary care in a health care setting. **Founded:** 1986. **Freq:** Quarterly. **Trim Size:** 7 x 10. **Cols./Page:** 2. **Col. Width:** 16 picas. **Col. Depth:** 45 picas. **Key Personnel:** Margaret Simko, Editor; Judith Gilbride, Editor. **ISSN:** 0883-5691. **Subscription Rates:** $82; $36 students; $90 other countries; $26 single issue. **Remarks:** Accepts advertising. **URL:** http://www.aspenpub.com. **Alt. Formats:** Microform.
Ad Rates: BW: $600 **Circ:** Paid 1,400
4C: $1,500 Non-paid 86

13666 Topics in Emergency Medicine
Aspen Publishers, Inc.
200 Orchard Ridge Dr. Phone: (301)417-7500
Gaithersburg, MD 20878 Fax: (301)417-7550
Free: (800)638-8437
Publisher E-mail: customer.service@aspenpubl.com

Journal serving as an interdisciplinary guide to the latest developments in clinical emergency care. **Founded:** 1979. **Freq:** Quarterly. **Trim Size:** 7 x 10. **Cols./Page:** 2. **Col. Width:** 16 picas. **Col. Depth:** 45 picas. **Key Personnel:** Carmen Germaine Warner, Editor; Anthony Albano, Editor. **ISSN:** 0164-2340. **Subscription Rates:** $105 individuals; $126 other countries; $33 single issue. **Remarks:** Accepts advertising. **Available Online. URL:** http://www.aspenpub.com. **Alt. Formats:** Microform.
Ad Rates: BW: $600 **Circ:** Paid 2,000
4C: $1,500

13667 Topics in Geriatric Rehabilitation
Aspen Publishers, Inc.
200 Orchard Ridge Dr. Phone: (301)417-7500
Gaithersburg, MD 20878 Fax: (301)417-7550
Free: (800)638-8437
Publisher E-mail: customer.service@aspenpubl.com

Journal presenting clinical, basic, and applied research, as well as theoretical information, for the health care professional practicing in the area of geriatric rehabilitation. **Founded:** 1985. **Freq:** Quarterly. **Trim Size:** 7 x 10. **Cols./Page:** 2. **Col. Width:** 16 picas. **Col. Depth:** 45 picas. **Key Personnel:** Carole Bernstein Lewis, Editor. **ISSN:** 0882-7524. **Subscription Rates:** $82; $90 out of country; $26 single issue. **Remarks:** Accepts advertising. **URL:** http://www.aspenpublishers.com. **Alt. Formats:** Microform.
Ad Rates: BW: $600 **Circ:** Paid 1,768
4C: $1,500 Non-paid 70

13668 Topics in Health Information Management
Aspen Publishers, Inc.
200 Orchard Ridge Dr., No. 200 Phone: (301)417-7500
Gaithersburg, MD 20878 Fax: (301)417-7650
Free: (800)638-8437
Publisher E-mail: customer.service@aspenpubl.com

Journal focusing on the information needs of the medical record practitioner. **Founded:** 1985. **Freq:** Quarterly. **Trim Size:** 7 x 10. **Cols./Page:** 2. **Col. Width:** 16 picas. **Col. Depth:** 45 picas. **Key Personnel:** Melanie S. Brodnik, Editor. **ISSN:** 1065-0989. **Subscription Rates:** $115 individuals; $138 out of country; $34 single issue. **Available Online. URL:** http://www.aspenpublishers.com. **Alt. Formats:** Microform, UMI. **Formerly:** Topics in Health Record Management.
Ad Rates: BW: $600 **Circ:** 1,500
4C: $1,500

13669 Topics in Language Disorders
Aspen Publishers, Inc.
200 Orchard Ridge Dr., No. 200 Phone: (301)417-7500
Gaithersburg, MD 20878 Fax: (301)417-7650
Free: (800)638-8437
Publisher E-mail: customer.service@aspenpubl.com

Journal intending to clarify the application of theory to practice in the treatment, rehabilitation, and education of individuals with language disorders. **Founded:** 1980. **Freq:** Quarterly. **Trim Size:** 7 x 10. **Cols./Page:** 2. **Col. Width:** 16 picas. **Col. Depth:** 45 picas. **Key Personnel:** Katharine G. Butler, Editor. **ISSN:** 0271-8294. **Subscription Rates:** $76 individuals; $84 other countries; $24 single issue. **Remarks:** Accepts advertising. **Online:** UMI. **URL:** http://www.aspenpublishers.com. **Alt. Formats:** Microform.
Ad Rates: BW: $600 **Circ:** Paid 3,278
4C: $1,500 Non-paid 78

13670 Topics in Stroke Rehabilitation
Aspen Publishers, Inc.
200 Orchard Ridge Dr., No. 200 Phone: (301)417-7500
Gaithersburg, MD 20878 Fax: (301)417-7650
Free: (800)638-8437
Publisher E-mail: customer.service@aspenpubl.com

Professional medical journal covering stroke rehabilitation. **Founded:** 1994. **Freq:** Quarterly. **Trim Size:** 7 x 10. **Cols./Page:** 2. **Col. Width:** 16 picas. **Col. Depth:** 44 picas. **Key Personnel:** Eliot J. Roth, Editor; Don A. Olson, Editor. **ISSN:** 1074-9357. **Subscription Rates:** $82 individuals; $26 single issue; $990 U.S. and other countries. **Remarks:** Accepts advertising. **URL:** http://www.aspenpub.com; http://www.aspenpublishers.com.
Ad Rates: BW: $500 **Circ:** Paid 1,000

13671 Western Maryland Genealogy
GenLaw Resources
PO Box 9187 Phone: (301)947-5572
Gaithersburg, MD 20898-9187 Fax: (301)977-8062
Publisher E-mail: genlaw@mindspring.com

Trade journal covering local genealogy. **Founded:** Jan. 1985. **Freq:** Quarterly. **Print Method:** Offset. **Key Personnel:** Donna Valley Russell, Contributing Editor; Patricia Abelard Andersen, Editor and Publisher. **ISSN:** 0747-7805. **Subscription Rates:** $20 individuals; $30 Canada. **Remarks:** Advertising not accepted.
Circ: Controlled 704

13672 WMET-AM - 1150
8945 N. Westland Dr. Phone: (301)921-0093
Gaithersburg, MD 20877

Format: News. **Simulcasts:** media general cable 28 audio. **Networks:** Business Radio. **Owner:** Sondra Linden, at above address, MD. **Founded:** 1983. **Formerly:** WJOK-AM; WMTG-AM. **Operating Hours:** Continuous. **Key Personnel:** Sondra Linden, Owner/Pres., phone (301)9210093. **Wattage:** 1000 day; 500 night. **Ad Rates:** $40-60 for 30 seconds; $15 for 4 seconds; $50-60 for 60 seconds. www.audionet.

GAMBRILLS

13673 Jones Communications
815 Rte. 3 Phone: (410)987-3900
Box 267 Fax: (410)923-3568
Gambrills, MD 21054

Founded: 1983. **Formerly:** Jones Intercable, Inc. **Key Personnel:** Darren Fox, Production Mgr. **Cities Served:** Anne Arundel County, MD: subscribing households 51,500; 62 channels; 1 community access channel; 168 hours per week community access programming.

GERMANTOWN

13674 The Germantown Gazette
The Gazette Newspapers
1200 Quince Orchard Blvd. Phone: (301)253-6161
Gaithersburg, MD 20878 Fax: (301)670-7183

Newspaper. **Founded:** 1959. **Freq:** Weekly (Wed.). **Print Method:** Offset. Uses mats. **Trim Size:** 10 15/16 x 13. **Cols./Page:** 5. **Col. Width:** 26 nonpareils. **Col. Depth:** 182 agate lines. **Key Personnel:** Chuck Lyons, President. **Subscription Rates:** $10 individuals. **Formerly:** Gazette (1992).
Ad Rates: BW: $1,710.80 **Circ:** Combined ❑**20,099**
4C: $2,210.80
SAU: $26.32
PCI: $26.32

GLEN BURNIE, pop. 38,608.

Anne Arundel Co. (C). 10 m S of Baltimore. Fort Meade. Furniture, toy, concrete block factories; sheet metal works; machinery, boat building; electronics. Diversified farming.

13675 WJRO-AM - 1590
PO Box 159 Phone: (410)761-1590
Glen Burnie, MD 21060-0159

Format: Religious; Ethnic; Polka. **Networks:** Independent. **Founded:** 1963. **Operating Hours:** Continuous. **Key Personnel:** Larnell Philips, General Mgr. **Wattage:** 1000.

GRANTSVILLE

13676 WAIJ-FM - 90.3
203 Springs Rd. Phone: (301)895-3292
PO Box 540 Fax: (301)895-3293
Grantsville, MD 21536

Format: Southern Gospel; Contemporary Christian. **Networks:** USA Radio. **Owner:** He's Alive, Inc., at above address. **Founded:** 1984. **Operating Hours:** 5:30 a.m.-midnight. **Key Personnel:** Dewayne Johnson, President; Wally Weeks, General Mgr.; Claire Saulpaw, Contact; Scott Reppert, Music Dir. **Wattage:** 10,000. **Ad Rates:** Noncommercial.

WLIC-FM - See Frostburg

WRIJ-FM - See Masontown, Pennsylvania

GREENBELT, pop. 17,332.

Prince Georges Co. (SC). 9 m NE of Washington, D. C. Residential.

13677 Greenbelt News Review
Greenbelt Cooperative Publishing Association, Inc.
15 Crescent Rd., Ste. 100 Phone: (301)474-4131
Greenbelt, MD 20770-1887 Fax: (301)474-5880

Community newspaper. **Founded:** Nov. 24, 1937. **Freq:** Weekly (Thurs.). **Print Method:** Letterpress and offset. **Trim Size:** 11 x 17. **Cols./Page:** 5. **Col. Width:** 24 nonpareils. **Col. Depth:** 196 agate lines. **Key Personnel:** Mary Lou Williamson, Editor; James Giese, Publisher, phone (301)441-2662. **Subscription Rates:** $32 individuals. **Remarks:** Accepts advertising.
Ad Rates: GLR: $.54 **Circ:** Paid ‡100
BW: $600 Free ‡10,900
4C: $30
PCI: $7.50

13678 Spectrum (Greenbelt)
National Association of Black Accountants, Inc.
7249-A Hanover Pkwy. Phone: (301)474-6222
Greenbelt, MD 20770-3653 Fax: (301)474-3114

Professional magazine of the National Association of Black Accountants, Inc. **Founded:** June 1970. **Freq:** Annual. **Trim Size:** 8 1/2 x 11. **Cols./Page:** 2. **Col. Width:** 3 1/4 inches. **Col. Depth:** 9 inches. **Key Personnel:** Thomas Hampton, Editor. **Subscription Rates:** $20 individuals. **Remarks:** Accepts advertising.
Ad Rates: BW: $1,000 **Circ:** Controlled 2,750

WPGC-AM - See Washington, District of Columbia

WPGC-FM - See Washington, District of Columbia

HAGERSTOWN†, pop. 34,132.

Washington Co. (NW). 72 m NW of Baltimore. Hagerstown Junior College. Manufactures aircraft parts, truck engines, shoes, women's and children's dresses, sand blast and dust collecting equipment, furniture, ribbon, hosiery, underwear, leather goods, rubber heels and soles, cold storage doors, pipe organs and supplies, paper boxes, plastic pipes, paint, seashore erosion forms, creamery, mayonnaise products. Slate quarries.

13679 Ambulatory Medicine Letter
J.B. Lippincott Co.
PO Box 1590 Phone: (800)777-2295
Hagerstown, MD 21741 Fax: (301)824-7390
Publication E-mail: lrorders@phl.lrpub.com

Journal focusing on ambulatory medicine. **Freq:** Semimonthly. **ISSN:** 0897-554X. **Subscription Rates:** $84; $105 other countries. $6 single issue. **URL:** http://www.lrpub.com. **Alt. Formats:** CD-ROM.

13680 American Jails
American Jail Association
2053 Day Rd., Ste. 100 Phone: (301)790-3930
Hagerstown, MD 21740-9795 Fax: (301)790-2941
Publisher E-mail: jails@worldnet.att.net

Criminal justice magazine. **Founded:** 1987. **Freq:** Bimonthly. **Trim Size:** 8 1/4 x 11. **Cols./Page:** 3. **Key Personnel:** Ken Kerle, Managing Editor. **ISSN:** 1056-0319. **Subscription Rates:** $30 members. **Remarks:** Accepts advertising.
Ad Rates: BW: $1,095 **Circ:** Paid 4,800
4C: $1,995 Non-paid 2,500

13681 The Daily-Mail
The Herald-Mail Co.
PO Box 439 Phone: (301)733-5131
Hagerstown, MD 21741 Fax: (301)733-7264
Free: (800)626-6397
Publication E-mail: news@herald-mail.com

General newspaper. **Founded:** 1828. **Freq:** Daily (eve.). **Print Method:** Offset. **Cols./Page:** 6. **Col. Width:** 26 nonpareils. **Col. Depth:** 301 agate lines. **Key Personnel:** John W. League, Editor and Publisher, jleague@herald-mail.com; Dave Elliott, Personnel Dir., phone (301)791-7496, fax (301)739-7518, davee@herald-mail.com; Gloria George, Exec. Editor, gloriag@herald-mail.com; Marlene Russell, Asst. to the Publisher, marlener@herald-mail.com; Stuart Trueax, Controller; Celeste Snavely, Circulation Dir., celestes@herald-mail.com; Terry McDaniel, Advertising Dir., terrym@herald-mail.com. **Subscription Rates:** $134 individuals. **Remarks:** Accepts advertising. **URL:** http://www.herald-mail.com.
Ad Rates: GLR: $2.45 **Circ:** Mon.-Fri. 15,601
BW: $3,247.83 Sat. 35,725
SAU: $25.18 Sun. 39,849

13682 Lippincott's Reviews: Radiology
J.B. Lippincott Co.
PO Box 1590 Phone: (800)777-2295
Hagerstown, MD 21741 Fax: (301)824-7390
Publication E-mail: lrorders@phl.lrpub.com

Journal focusing on radiology. **Freq:** Quarterly. **ISSN:** 1059-2156. **Subscription Rates:** $45; $95 individual; $105 Industry; $125 individual other countries; $135 Industry other countries. $34 single issue. **URL:** http://www.lrpub.com.

13683 Listen
55 West Oak Ridge Dr. Phone: (301)791-7000
Hagerstown, MD 21740 Fax: (301)791-9734
Free: (800)548-8700

Magazine promoting drug awareness and other teen issues. **Subtitle:** Celebrating Positive Choices. **Founded:** 1947. **Freq:** Monthly. **Print Method:** Offset. **Trim Size:** 8 x 10 5/8. **Cols./Page:** 2. **Col. Width:** 47 nonpareils. **Col. Depth:** 127 agate lines. **Key Personnel:** Lincoln Steed, Editor, lsteed@rhpa.org. **ISSN:** 0024-435X. **Subscription Rates:** $24.97 individuals; $2.50 single issue. **Remarks:** Accepts advertising.
Ad Rates: 4C: $1,200 **Circ:** ‡35,000

13684 Message
Review and Herald Publishing Association
55 W. Oak Ridge Dr. Phone: (301)393-3000
Hagerstown, MD 21740 Fax: (301)393-3292
Free: (800)765-6955
Publisher E-mail: message@rhpa.org

Religious magazine for African-Americans. **Subtitle:** A Christian Magazine of Contemporary Issues. **Founded:** 1898. **Freq:** Bimonthly. **Print Method:** Offset. **Trim Size:** 8 1/8 x 10 5/8. **Cols./Page:** 3. **Col. Width:** 2 1/8 inches. **Col. Depth:** 9 1/4 inches. **Key Personnel:** Rhoda K. Johnson, Editorial Secretary; Dr. Ron Smith, Editor. **ISSN:** 0026-0231. **Subscription Rates:** $12.97 individuals. **Remarks:** Accepts advertising. **Formerly:** Message Magazine.
Ad Rates: BW: $1,107 **Circ:** Paid ‡78,273
4C: $1,382 Non-paid ‡56

13685 The Morning Herald
The Herald-Mail Co.
PO Box 439 Phone: (301)733-5131
Hagerstown, MD 21741 Fax: (301)733-7264
Free: (800)626-6397
Publication E-mail: news@herald-mail.com

General newspaper. **Founded:** 1873. **Freq:** Mon.-Sun. (morn.). **Print Method:** Offset. **Cols./Page:** 6. **Col. Width:** 26 nonpareils. **Col. Depth:** 301 agate lines. **Key Personnel:** John W. League, Editor and Publisher; Gloria George, Executive Editor; Terry McDaniel, Advertising Dir.; Celeste Snavely, Circulation Dir.; Dave Elliott, Personnel Dir.; Stuart Trueax, Comptroller. **Subscription Rates:** $120. **Remarks:** Accepts advertising. **URL:** http://www.herold-mail.com.
Ad Rates: GLR: $1.71 **Circ:** Mon.-Fri. 21,348
BW: $3,098.55 Sat. 35,725
SAU: $23.95 Sun. 39,849

13686 Nurse Educator
J.B. Lippincott Co.
PO Box 1590 Phone: (800)777-2295
Hagerstown, MD 21741 Fax: (301)824-7390
Publication E-mail: lrorders@phl.lrpub.com

Journal containing information on both the practical and the theoretical aspects of nursing education. **Freq:** Bimonthly. **Key Personnel:** Suzanne Smith Blancett, Editor-in-Chief. **ISSN:** 0363-3624. **Subscription Rates:** $45 individuals; $85 institutions; $18 single issue. **URL:** http://www.lrpub.com.

13687 Vibrant Life
Review and Herald Publishing Association
55 W. Oak Ridge Dr. Phone: (301)393-3000
Hagerstown, MD 21740 Fax: (301)393-3292
Free: (800)765-6955
Publication E-mail: vleditor@rhpa.org
Publisher E-mail: message@rhpa.org

Christian magazine for 25- to 45-year olds. Emphasizes preventative medicine and covers physical, mental, and spiritual health topics. **Subtitle:** A magazine for healthful living. **Founded:** 1885. **Freq:** Bimonthly. **Print Method:** Offset. **Trim Size:** 10 3/4 x 8 1/4. **Cols./Page:** 3. **Col. Width:** 26 nonpareils. **Col. Depth:** 129 agate lines. **Key Personnel:** Larry Becker, Editor. **ISSN:** 0749-3509. **Subscription Rates:** $15.97 individuals; $3.25 single issue. **Remarks:** Accepts advertising. **URL:** http://www.rhpa.org.
Ad Rates: BW: $1,050 **Circ:** ‡50,000
4C: $1,450

13688 The Winner
The Health Connection
55 W. Oak Ridge Dr. Phone: (301)790-9735
Hagerstown, MD 21740 Free: (800)548-8700

Magazine for K-6th graders that focuses on health issues, including substance abuse. **Founded:** 1956. **Freq:** Monthly (Sept-May). **Print Method:** Offset. **Trim Size:** 8 x 10 5/8. **Key Personnel:** Lincoln Steed, Editor, lsteed@rhpa.org. **ISSN:** 0043-5937. **Subscription Rates:** $9.97. **Remarks:** Advertising not accepted.
Circ: Paid 15,000

13689 Antietam Cable TV
1000 Willow Circle Phone: (301)797-5000
Hagerstown, MD 21740 Fax: (301)797-4829

Key Personnel: Gene Hager, General Mgr.; Mary Michaels, Office Mgr.; Steven Tritle, Sales Mgr. **Cities Served:** subscribing households 28,000; 50 channels; 1 community access channel.

13690 WARK-AM - 1490
880 Commonwealth Ave. Phone: (301)733-4500
Hagerstown, MD 21740-6881 Fax: (301)733-0040
Free: (800)222-9279

Format: Talk; Oldies. **Networks:** Westwood One Radio. **Owner:** Manning Broadcasting Inc., at above address. **Founded:** 1947. **Operating Hours:** Continuous; 90% network, 10% local. **ADI:** Hagerstown, MD. **Key Personnel:** Eugene J. Manning, Contact, gmanning@warx.com; Fred Manning, Vice President; Stacy Drake, Program Dir. **Wattage:** 1000. **Ad Rates:** $5-8 for 30 seconds; $7-10 for 60 seconds. **URL:** http://www.warx.com.

13691 WARX-FM - 106.9
880 Commonwealth Ave. Phone: (301)733-4500
Hagerstown, MD 21740 Fax: (301)733-0040
Free: (800)222-9279

Format: Oldies. **Networks:** Mutual Broadcasting System; Westwood One Radio. **Owner:** Manning Broadcasting Inc., at above address. **Founded:** 1957. **Formerly:** WARK-FM (1975). **Operating Hours:** Continuous; 10% Network, 90% Local. **ADI:** Hagerstown, MD. **Key Personnel:** Eugene J. Manning, Contact, gmanning@warx.com. **Wattage:** 50,000. **Ad Rates:** $18-35 for 30 seconds; $25-45 for 60 seconds. **URL:** http://www.warx.com.

13692 WHAG-AM - 1410
1250 Maryland Ave. Phone: (301)797-7300
Hagerstown, MD 21740-7244 Fax: (301)797-2659

Format: Talk; Sports; News. **Networks:** ABC; ESPN Radio. **Owner:** Gemini Broadcast Group, at above address. **Founded:** 1962. **Operating Hours:** 6 a.m.-12 midnight; 90% network, 10% local. **ADI:** Washington, DC. **Key Personnel:** Kibby Albright, General Mgr.; Will Kauffman, News Dir. **Wattage:** 1000. **Ad Rates:** $16.00-40.00 for 30 seconds. Combined advertising rates available with WQCM-FM.

13693 WHAG-TV - 25
13 E. Washington St. Phone: (937)797-4400
Hagerstown, MD 21740 Fax: (937)733-1735
E-mail: wcsfoto@kis.hoe.net

Format: Commercial TV. **Networks:** NBC. **Owner:** Quorum Broadcasting Inc., 18 Newberg St., Boston, MA 02115. **Founded:** 1970. **Operating Hours:** Continuous; 50% network, 50% local. **ADI:** Hagerstown, MD. **Key Personnel:** Chuck Noland, Program/Operations Dir., cnoland@nbc25.com; Glen Fortinberry, News Dir., fax (301)745-4093; Marcus Anderson, Chief Engineer; Hugh Breslin, Vice Pres./Gen. Mgr., hbreslin@nbc25.com; Michelle Mong, Accounting Mgr.; Nancy Vanhouten, Office Mgr., nvan@nbc25.com. **Ad Rates:** $5-4000 per unit. **URL:** www.nbc25.com.

13694 WJEJ-AM - 1240
1135 Haven Rd. Phone: (301)739-2323
Hagerstown, MD 21742 Fax: (301)797-7408
Free: (800)265-0057

Format: Full Service; Talk; Adult Contemporary; Oldies. **Networks:** CBS. **Owner:** Hagerstown Broadcasting Co., Inc., at above address. **Founded:** 1932. **Operating Hours:** 5 a.m.-2 a.m.; 10% network, 90% local. **ADI:** Hagerstown, MD. **Key Personnel:** John T. Staub, Pres./Gen. Mgr.; Louis J. Scally, Chief Engineer; Tom Bradley, News Dir.; Kenneth Forsythe, Promotions Mgr.; Jackie Hall, Traffic Mgr.; Bob Tantillo, Sales Mgr. **Wattage:** 1000. **Ad Rates:** $10-15 for 30 seconds; $12-20 for 60 seconds. Combined advertising rates available with WWMD-FM.

WQCM-FM - See Halfway

13695 WWMD-FM - 104.7
1135 Haven Rd. Phone: (301)739-2323
Hagerstown, MD 21742 Fax: (301)797-7408
Free: (800)265-0057

Format: Easy Listening. **Owner:** Hagerstown Broadcasting Co., Inc., at above address. **Founded:** 1946. **Formerly:** WJEJ-FM (1977). **Operating Hours:** 5 a.m.-2 a.m.; 1% network, 99% local. **ADI:** Hagerstown, MD. **Key Personnel:** John T. Staub, Pres./Gen. Mgr.; Dan Wilson, Sales Mgr.; Louis J. Scally, Chief Engineer; Tom Bradley, News Dir.; Kenneth Forsythe, Promotions Mgr.; Jackie Hall, Traffic Mgr. **Wattage:** 75,000. **Ad Rates:** $13-18 for 30 seconds; $16-25 for 60 seconds. Combined advertising rates available with WJEJ-AM.

13696 WWPB-TV - 31
c/o Maryland Public Television Phone: (410)356-5600
11767 Owings Mills Blvd. Fax: (410)581-4338
Owings Mills, MD 21117-1499
Free: (800)223-3678
E-mail: comments@mpt.org

Format: Public TV. **Simulcasts:** WMPB, WMPT, WCPB, WGPT, WFPT. **Networks:** Public Broadcasting Service (PBS); Eastern Educational Television. **Owner:** Maryland Public Broadcasting Commission, at above address. **Operating Hours:** 3 a.m.-1:30 a.m., Mon.-Sun. **ADI:** Hagerstown, MD. **Key Personnel:** Robert J. Shuman, Pres./CEO; Dr. Archie L. Buffkins, Sr. Vice Pres., Broadcasting; Janice Wilson, Sr. Vice Pres., Marketing & Development; Larry D. Unger, Sr. Vice Pres., Administration & Finance; Martin Jacobs, Vice Pres., Finance & Accounting; Gladys M. Kaplan, Vice Pres., Human Resources; Ann Engelman, Vice Pres., Programming/Broadcast Serv.; Everett L. Marshburn, Vice Pres., Broadcast Production; John T. Potthast, Vice Pres., National Productions; Barry P. Freidly, Vice Pres., Membership; Hannah Lee Byron, Dir., Corp. Comm. & Gov't Affairs; Carol Wonsavage, Dir., Regional Communications; Sharon Philippart, Dir., National Communications. **Wattage:** 4,070,000. **URL:** http://www.mpt.org.

HALFWAY

13697 WQCM-FM - 96.7
1250 Maryland Ave. Phone: (301)797-7300
Hagerstown, MD 21740 Fax: (301)797-2659

Format: Classic Rock. **Networks:** ABC. **Owner:** Gemini Broadcast Group, at above address. **Founded:** 1968. **Operating Hours:** Continuous. **ADI:** Washington, DC. **Key Personnel:** Kibby Albright, General Mgr.; David Miller, Program Dir. **Wattage:** 4800. **Ad Rates:** $19-40 for 30 seconds. Combined advertising rates available with WHAG-AM.

HANCOCK, pop. 1,887.

Washington Co. (NW). On Potomac River, 27 m W of Hagerstown. Sand quarries; timber. Garment and trailer factories. Poultry, fruit, grain farms. Apples, peaches, corn, wheat.

13698 The Hancock News
263 Pennsylvania Ave. Phone: (301)678-6255
Hancock, MD 21750 Fax: (301)678-5520

Community newspaper. **Founded:** 1914. **Freq:** Weekly (Wed.). **Print Method:** Letterpress. **Cols./Page:** 6. **Col. Width:** 24 nonpareils. **Col. Depth:** 294 agate lines. **Key Personnel:** J. Warren Buzzerd, Editor, phone (304)258-1800, fax (304)258-8441; James S. Buzzerd, Publisher. **Subscription Rates:** $16.80 individuals. **Remarks:** Accepts advertising.
Ad Rates: GLR: $.50 **Circ:** ‡2,600
BW: $327.60
PCI: $3

13699 Satire
PO Box 340 Phone: (301)678-6999
Hancock, MD 21750-0340
Publication E-mail: satire@intrepid.net

Magazine devoted to satire, (short stories, essays, articles, poetry, cartoons). **Subtitle:** The Quarterly Journal of Contemporary Satire. **Founded:** 1994. **Freq:** 4/year. **Trim Size:** 8 1/2 x 11. **Key Personnel:** Larry Logan, Editor. **ISSN:** 1073-6522. **Subscription Rates:** $16 individuals; $5 single issue. **Remarks:** Advertising accepted; rates available upon request. **URL:** http://www.intrepid.net/satire.
Circ: 400

HANOVER

13700 Maryland Pennysaver
1342 Charwood Rd Phone: (410)684-2700
Hanover, MD 21076 Fax: (410)684-2065
Free: (800)736-6972

Shopper. **Founded:** Aug. 22, 1979. **Freq:** Weekly. **Print Method:** Offset. **Trim Size:** 7 1/2 x 10 1/2. **Cols./Page:** 3. **Col. Width:** 27 nonpareils. **Col. Depth:** 142 agate lines. **Key Personnel:** Denny Guastaferro, Pub./Chief Operating Officer, phone (410)684-2600, fax (410)865-4545. **Subscription Rates:** Free. **Remarks:** Accepts advertising. **URL:** http://www.mdpennysaver.com. **Alt. Formats:** Mailing labels.
Circ: Free ‡926,000

HAVRE DE GRACE

13701 WXCY-FM - 103.7
707 Revolution St. Phone: (410)939-1100
PO Box 269 Fax: (410)939-1104
Havre de Grace, MD 21078
Free: (800)788WXCY

Format: Contemporary Country. **Networks:** Unistar. **Founded:** 1960. **Operating Hours:** Continuous. **Key Personnel:** Bob Bloom, General Mgr.; Rico Richards, Promotions Dir.; Jane Belmeir, News Dir.; Dave Hovel, Program Dir. **Wattage:** 50,000. **Ad Rates:** $36-40 for 30 seconds; $45-50 for 60 seconds.

HOLLYWOOD

13702 American Cable T.V. of St. Mary's Co.
10 Airport View Dr. Phone: (301)373-3201
PO Box 159 Fax: (301)373-3757
Hollywood, MD 20636
Free: (800)427-0705

Owner: American Cable T.V. Investors Ltd., 5619 DTC Pkwy., Englewood, CO 80111. **Founded:** 1968. **Formerly:** Cable TV of Leonardtown; United Cable TV of Lexington; Simmons Communications, Inc. **Key Personnel:** Phil Spindt, General Mgr.; Jerry Orris, Contact; Mike Laigle, Contact. **Cities Served:** subscribing households 16,000; 40 channels.

HUNT VALLEY

13703 WGRX-FM - 100.7
11350 Mccormick Rd., Ste EPIII701 Phone: (410)771-8484
Fax: (410)771-1616
Hunt Valley, MD 21031-1002

Format: Country. **Networks:** ABC. **Owner:** Shamrock Communications, 149 Penn Ave., Scranton, PA 18503, (717)348-9100. **Formerly:** WTIR-FM. **Operating Hours:** Continuous. **ADI:** Baltimore, MD. **Key Personnel:** Roy Deutschman, General Mgr.; Dave Anthony, Program Dir.; Dave Stenner, Promotions Dir.; Ray Ciafardini, General Sales Mgr. **Local Programs:** *Ann Phibian; David Hopperfield/Splash Gordon; Hopalong Cassidy.* **Wattage:** 16,000 ERP.

HURLOCK

13704 WAAI-FM - 100.9
6301 Meadow Dr. Phone: (410)754-3032
PO Box 1300 Fax: (410)754-3032
Hurlock, MD 21643

Format: Country. **Networks:** USA Radio. **Owner:** Apex Associates Inc., at above address. **Founded:** 1989. **Operating Hours:** Continuous. **Key Personnel:** Keith Mayo, President, kmayo@dmv.com; Troy D. Hill, Station Mgr. **Wattage:** 1300. **Ad Rates:** Advertising accepted; rates available upon request. **URL:** http://www.waai-duck.com.

HYATTSVILLE, pop. 12,709.

Prince George's Co. (SC). 7 m NE of Washington, DC. Manufactures cinder blocks, auto bodies, plastics, motor vehicles, aircraft parts, bricks. Residential. Truck, dairy, poultry, fruit farms.

13705 Advance Data
U.S. Department of Health and Human Services
National Center for Health Statistics
6525 Belcrest Rd., Rm. 1064
Hyattsville, MD 20782
Publisher E-mail: nchsquery@cdc.gov

Serial containing statistical data on health. **Freq:** Irregular. **Subscription Rates:** Free. **Remarks:** Advertising not accepted. **URL:** http://www.cdc.gov/nchshome.htm.
Circ: Non-paid 15,000

13706 Catholic Standard
Carroll Publishing Co.
5001 Eastern Ave. Phone: (301)853-4599
Hyattsville, MD 20782 Fax: (301)853-4599
Publisher E-mail: custsvc@carrollpub.com

Religious newspaper. **Subtitle:** Weekly Newspaper for the Archdiocese of Washington. **Founded:** Nov. 1951. **Freq:** Weekly (Thurs.). **Print Method:** Offset. **Trim Size:** 11 3/8 x 14 1/2. **Cols./Page:** 5. **Col. Width:** 11 picas. **Col. Depth:** 13 1/2 inches. **Key Personnel:** Thomas Schmidt, General Mgr.; Marty Valentine, Advertising Dir.; Mark Zimmermann, Editor; Linda Milo, Circulation Mgr. **ISSN:** 0411-2741. **Subscription Rates:** $31 individuals. **Remarks:** Advertising not accepted for political advertisements.
Ad Rates: BW: $1,958 **Circ:** ‡51,000
4C: $2,456
PCI: $29

13707 National Vital Statistics Report
National Center for Health Statistics
6525 Belcrest Rd., No. 1064 Phone: (301)436-8500
Hyattsville, MD 20782-2003
Magazine covering population studies; includes vital statistics on mortality, natality, marriage, and divorce. **Founded:** 1950. **Freq:** Irregular. **Print Method:** Offset. **Cols./Page:** 2. **Col. Width:** 42 nonpareils. **Col. Depth:** 123 agate lines. **Remarks:** Advertising not accepted. **URL:** http://www.cdc.gov/nchswww/. **Formerly:** Monthly Vital Statistics Report.
Circ: Non-paid ‡9,000

13708 WHFS-FM - 99.1
8201 Corporate Dr., Ste. 550 Phone: (301)306-0991
Hyattsville, MD 20785 Fax: (301)731-0431
Free: (800)321-WHFS

Format: Alternative/New Music/Progressive. **Founded:** 1968. **Operating Hours:** Continuous. **ADI:** Washington, DC. **Key Personnel:** Phil Zachary, V.P./General Mgr.; Bill Parshall, General Sales Mgr.; Robert Benjamin, Program Dir.; Mary Kay Lemay, Promotions Dir.; Bob Waugh, Music Dir. **Local Programs:** *Now Hear This*, Dave Marsh, Production Mgr.; *Sunday Papers*, Rob Timm, News Dir. **Wattage:** 50,000. **URL:** http://www.whfs.com.

IJAMSVILLE

13709 The Word Among Us
The Word Among Us Press
9639 Dr. Perry Rd., No. 126 Phone: (301)831-1262
Ijamsville, MD 21754 Fax: (301)831-1188
Free: (800)775-WORD

Magazine containing articles to help Catholics read, understand, and act on the teachings of scripture and live the Christian life. **Founded:** 1981. **Freq:** 11/year. **Print Method:** Web. **Trim Size:** 5 3/8 x 8 3/8. **Cols./Page:** 2. **Col. Width:** 2 1/4 inches. **Col. Depth:** 7 inches. **Key Personnel:** Jeff Smith, Publisher; Leo Zanchettin, Editor. **ISSN:** 0742-4639. **Subscription Rates:** $18 individuals; $2.50 single issue. **Remarks:** Advertising not accepted.
Circ: Paid 200,000

JOPPA

13710 National Association of Document Examiners Journal
National Association of Document Examiners, Inc.
Box 324 Phone: (410)679-8257
Joppa, MD 21085 Fax: (410)538-8548
Publisher E-mail: fordocexam@aol.com

Association journal. **Freq:** Semiannual. **Key Personnel:** Katherine Koppenhauer, Editor. **Subscription Rates:** $15 individuals; $18 out of country. **Remarks:** Accepts advertising. **Also known as:** NADE Journal.
Circ: Paid 135

KENSINGTON, pop. 1,822.

Montgomery Co. (WC). 10 m N of Bethesda.

13711 BC&T News
Bakery, Confectionery, and Tobacco Workers International Union
10401 Connecticut Ave. Phone: (301)933-8600
Kensington, MD 20895-3961 Fax: (301)946-8452

Subtitle: Publication of the Bakery Confectionery, and Tobacco Workers International Union. **Founded:** 1978. **Freq:** 9/year. **Print Method:** Offset. **Cols./Page:** 5. **Col. Width:** 23 nonpareils. **Col. Depth:** 217 agate lines. **Subscription Rates:** Free to qualified subscribers.
Circ: Controlled 135,000

13712 The Journal of Afro-Latin American Studies and Literatures
Department of Language and Modern Literature
5313 Flanders Ave. Phone: (301)946-9503
Kensington, MD 20895-1140
Publication that examines the contributions of African decendants to the development of the U.S. **Freq:** 2/year. **Key Personnel:** Rosangela Maria Vieira, Editor; Kathleen Palombo King, Editor.

13713 Taxi and Livery Management
International Taxicab and Livery Association
3849 Farragut Ave. Phone: (301)946-5701
Kensington, MD 20895 Fax: (301)946-4641
Publication E-mail: itla1997@aol.com
Publisher E-mail: itla@itla-info.org

Magazine for owners and operators of taxicab, limousine, livery, van, and minibus fleets. Includes information on vehicles, marketing, public relations, legal issues, industry meetings and conventions, industry products and more. **Freq:** Quarterly. **Print Method:** Sheetfed offset. **Trim Size:** 8 1/2 x 11. **Cols./Page:** 3. **Col. Width:** 13 1/2 picas. **Key Personnel:** Nancy Murphy, Editor/Contact; Alfred LaGasse, Publisher. **ISSN:** 0040-0426. **Subscription Rates:** $16 individuals; $4 single issue. **Formerly:** Taxicab Management.
Ad Rates: BW: $995 **Circ:** ‡5,500
4C: $1,595

13714 Undersea & Hyperbaric Medicine
Undersea and Hyperbaric Medical Society
10531 Metropolitan Ave. Phone: (301)942-2980
Kensington, MD 20895 Fax: (301)942-7804
Publisher E-mail: uhms@uhms.org

Scientific journal covering diving physiology and clinical hyperbaric medicine. **Founded:** 1974. **Freq:** Quarterly. **Trim Size:** 8 1/2 x 11. **Cols./Page:** 2. **Key Personnel:** Tom S. Neuman, Editor. **ISSN:** 1066-2936. **Subscription Rates:** $85 individuals; $20 single issue. **Remarks:** Advertising not accepted. **Formerly:** Undersea Biomedical Research.
Circ: Controlled 2,200

LA PLATA†, pop. 2,484.

Charles Co. (SW). 25 m S of Washington, DC. Charles County Community College. Bottling works. Timber. Tobacco. Metal works. Diversified farming.

13715 WKIK-FM - 102.9
PO Box 2470 Phone: (301)870-5550
La Plata, MD 20646 Fax: (301)884-0280

Format: Country. **Networks:** ABC. **Owner:** Somar Communications, Inc., at above address. **Founded:** Nov. 1, 1994. **Formerly:** WRFK-FM (Dec. 31, 1996). **Operating Hours:** Continuous.

13716 WSMD-AM - 1560
c/o S. Fruin and J. Schaller
7 St. Paul St., Ste. 1400
Baltimore, MD 21202

Format: Adult Contemporary. **Founded:** 1965. **ADI:** Baltimore, MD. **Key Personnel:** Nancy Sinclair, General Mgr.; Bob Cannon, Program Dir. **Wattage:** 1000.

LANDOVER HILLS

13717 Vision
National Catholic Office for the Deaf
7202 Buchanan St. Phone: (301)577-1684
Landover Hills, MD 20784-2236 Fax: (301)577-1690
Publisher E-mail: ncod@erols.com

Journal for persons involved in ministry to deaf people. **Founded:** 1977. **Freq:** 4/year. **Trim Size:** 7 1/2 x 10. **Key Personnel:** Arvilla Rank, Editor. **Subscription Rates:** $15 individuals; $25 two years; $17 other countries; $27 two years other countries. **Formerly:** Listening (1992).
Ad Rates: BW: $250 **Circ:** 1,000

LANHAM, pop. 9,400.

Prince George's Co. (SC) 4 m S College Park. Residential.

13718 American Entomologist
Entomological Society of America
9301 Annapolis Rd. Phone: (301)731-4535
Lanham, MD 20706 Fax: (301)731-4538
Publication E-mail: pubs@entsoc.org
Publisher E-mail: sales@entsoc.org

A quarterly magazine of general interest to entomologists. **Founded:** 1954. **Freq:** Quarterly. **Print Method:** Offset. **Trim Size:** 8 1/2 x 11. **Cols./Page:** 3. **Col. Width:** 14 picas. **Col. Depth:** 59 picas. **Key Personnel:** J.E. McPherson, Jr., Editor; Raymond L. Everngam, JR., Managing Editor; David DeCouto, Advertising Mgr. **ISSN:** 0013-8754. **Subscription Rates:** $15 individuals; $30 nonmembers; $55 institutions. **Remarks:** Accepts advertising. **Formerly**: Bulletin of the Entomological Society of America.
Ad Rates: BW: $735 **Circ:** Paid 8300
4C: $1535

13719 Annals of the Entomological Society of America
Entomological Society of America
9301 Annapolis Rd. Phone: (301)731-4535
Lanham, MD 20706 Fax: (301)731-4538
Publication E-mail: pubs@entsoc.org
Publisher E-mail: sales@entsoc.org

Entomology journal. **Founded:** 1908. **Freq:** Bimonthly. **Print Method:** Offset. **Trim Size:** 6 7/8 x 10. **Cols./Page:** 2. **Col. Width:** 17 picas. **Col. Depth:** 52 picas. **Key Personnel:** Leo Lachance, Editor; C.W. Schaefer, Editor; Raymond L. Everngam, Jr., Managing Editor; David DeCouto, Advertising Mgr. **ISSN:** 0013-8746. **Subscription Rates:** $25 individuals; $65 nonmembers; $110 institutions.
Circ: 2,100

13720 CORRECTIONS TODAY
American Correctional Association
4380 Forbes Blvd. Phone: (301)918-1800
Lanham, MD 20706-4322 Fax: (301)918-1900
Free: (800)222-5646
Publisher E-mail: admin@aca.org

Magazine covering corrections, law enforcement, and rehabilitation. **Founded:** 1938. **Freq:** 7/year. **Print Method:** Offset. **Trim Size:** 8 1/2 x 11. **Cols./Page:** 3 and 2. **Col. Width:** 27 and 40 nonpareils. **Col. Depth:** 140 agate lines. **Key Personnel:** Gabriella M. Daley, Publisher, fax (301)918-1886, gdaley@aca.org. **ISSN:** 0190-2563. **Subscription Rates:** $25 individuals. **Remarks:** Accepts advertising. **Alt. Formats:** Microfiche.
Ad Rates: BW: $885 **Circ:** ‡25,000
4C: $1,810

13721 Environmental Entomology
Entomological Society of America
9301 Annapolis Rd. Phone: (301)731-4535
Lanham, MD 20706 Fax: (301)731-4538
Publication E-mail: pubs@entsoc.org; esa@entsoc.org
Publisher E-mail: sales@entsoc.org

Entomology journal focusing on enviornmental issues. **Founded:** 1972. **Freq:** Bimonthly. **Print Method:** Offset. **Trim Size:** 6 7/8 x 10. **Cols./Page:** 2. **Col. Width:** 17 picas. **Col. Depth:** 52 picas. **Key Personnel:** Dr. Karen M. Clancy, Editor, phone (520)556-2105, fax (520)556-2130, kmc@alpine.for.nau.edu; Dr. Timothy J. Lysyk, Editor, phone (403)327-4561, fax (403)382-3156, lysyk@abrsle.agr.ca; Dr. Jesse A. Logan, Editor, phone (801)755-3573, fax (801)755-3563, jlogan@cc.usu.edu; Dr. Frank J. Messina, Editor, phone (801)797-2528. **ISSN:** 0046-225X. **Subscription Rates:** $30 individuals; $84 nonmembers; $162 institutions. **Remarks:** Accepts advertising. **URL:** http://esa.edoc.com.
Ad Rates: BW: $410 **Circ:** 2,739

13722 Journal of Economic Entomology
Entomological Society of America
9301 Annapolis Rd. Phone: (301)731-4535
Lanham, MD 20706 Fax: (301)731-4538
Publication E-mail: pubs@entsoc.org
Publisher E-mail: sales@entsoc.org

Entomology journal focusing on economic issues. **Founded:** 1908. **Freq:** Bimonthly. **Print Method:** Offset. **Trim Size:** 6 7/8 x 10. **Cols./Page:** 2. **Col. Width:** 17 picas. **Col. Depth:** 52 picas. **Key Personnel:** Dr. Richard A. Butts, Editor, phone (403)327-4561, fax (403)382-3156, butts@em.agr.ca; Dr. John D. Stark, Editor, phone (253)445-4519, fax (253)445-4669, starkj@wsu.edu; Dr. James E. Throne, Editor, phone (785)776-2796, fax (785)776-2792, throne@usgrmrl.ksu.edu; Dr. Julie L. Todd, Editor, phone (515)294-2405, fax (515)294-5957, jtodd@iastate.edu; Dr. Sandra A. Allan, Editor, phone (352)392-4700, fax (352)392-9704, allans@mail.vetmed.ufl.edu; Dr. Matthew H. Greenstone, Editor, phone (405)478-8638, pardosa@ibm.net. **ISSN:** 0022-0493. **Subscription Rates:** $30 individuals; $95 nonmembers; $194 institutions. **URL:** http://esa.edoc.com.
Circ: 3,388

13723 Journal of Medical Entomology
Entomological Society of America
9301 Annapolis Rd. Phone: (301)731-4535
Lanham, MD 20706 Fax: (301)731-4538
Publication E-mail: pubs@entsoc.org
Publisher E-mail: sales@entsoc.org

Journal on systematics and biology of insects, acarines, and other arthropods of public health and veterinary significance. **Founded:** 1964. **Freq:** Bimonthly. **Print Method:** Offset. **Trim Size:** 6 7/8 x 10. **Cols./Page:** 2. **Col. Width:** 17 picas. **Col. Depth:** 52 picas. **Key Personnel:** Dr. William K. Reisen, Editor, phone (805)589-0891, fax (805)589-4913, arbo@lightspeed.net; Dr. C. Dayton Steelman, Editor, phone (501)575-2510, dsteelman@comp.uark.edu. **ISSN:** 0022-2585. **Subscription Rates:** $30 individuals; $81 nonmembers; $156 institutions. **URL:** http://esa.edoc.com.
Circ: 1,412

13724 The National AMVET
AMVETS
4647 Forbes Blvd. Phone: (301)459-9600
Lanham, MD 20706 Fax: (301)459-7924
Publication E-mail: amvets@amvets.org

Magazine containing service-related infromation and data for veterans. **Founded:** 1946. **Freq:** Quarterly. **Print Method:** Offset. **Trim Size:** 8 1/8 x 10 7/8. **Cols./Page:** 3. **Col. Width:** 13 picas. **Col. Depth:** 55 1/2 picas. **Key Personnel:** Richard W. Flanagan, Editor, dflanagan@amvets.org. **ISSN:** 0027-853X. **Subscription Rates:** $10 nonmembers. **Remarks:** Accepts advertising.
Ad Rates: BW: $1,953 **Circ:** Paid ‡175,000
4C: $3,161 Controlled ‡4,000
PCI: $150

13725 The North American Deer Farmer
North American Deer Farmer
9301 Anapolis Rd., No. 206 Phone: (301)459-7708
Lanham, MD 20706 Fax: (301)459-7864
Publisher E-mail: info@nadefa.org

Trade journal covering deer farming and ranching. **Subtitle:** The Official Journal of the North American Deer farmers Association. **Founded:** 1992. **Freq:** Quarterly. **Trim Size:** 8 x 11. **Key Personnel:** Barbara Fox, Editor. **ISSN:** 1084-0583. **Subscription Rates:** $195 individuals. **Remarks:** Accepts advertising.
Ad Rates: BW: $350 **Circ:** Combined 1,200
4C: $525

13726 Nozzle & Wrench
WMDA Service Station & Auto Repair Association
9420 Annapolis Rd., Ste. 307 Phone: (301)577-2875
Lanham, MD 20706-3021 Fax: (301)306-0523
Free: (800)492-0329

Automotive repair magazine representing the independent automotive aftermarket of Maryland, Delaware, and the District of Columbia. **Freq:** Monthly. **Print Method:** Offset. **Trim Size:** 8 1/2 x 11. **Cols./Page:** 2. **Key Personnel:** Roy Littlefield, Editor; Joie Kohl-Collier, Assoc. Ed. **Remarks:** Accepts advertising. **Formerly**: The Nozzle.
Ad Rates: BW: $375 **Circ:** Controlled ‡3,000

13727 Prospects
UNESCO
4611-F Assembly Dr. Phone: (301)459-2255
Lanham, MD 20706-4391 Fax: (301)459-0056
Free: (800)865-3450
Publication E-mail: order@bernan.com

Journal serving as a review of education around the world. **Subtitle:** Quarterly Review of Education. **Freq:** Quarterly. **Print Method:** Offset. **Key Personnel:** Z. Morsy, Editor. **ISSN:** 0033-1538. **Subscription Rates:** $40 individuals. **Remarks:** Advertising not accepted.
Circ: (Not Reported)

13728 The UNESCO Courier
UNESCO
4611-F Assembly Dr. Phone: (301)459-2255
Lanham, MD 20706-4391 Fax: (301)459-0056
Free: (800)865-3450
Publication E-mail: info@bernan.com

General interest magazine. Prints editions in English, French, Spanish, Russian, German, Italian, Arabic, Hindi, Tamil, Persian, Turkish, Japanese, Portuguese, Dutch, Urdu, Catalan, Malay, Korean, and Swahili. **Founded:** 1948. **Freq:** Monthly. **Print Method:** Offset. **Cols./Page:** 2. **Col. Width:** 40 nonpareils. **Col. Depth:** 147 agate lines. **Subscription Rates:** $59 individuals. **Remarks:** Advertising not accepted.
Circ: (Not Reported)

13729 Voice of Youth Advocates
Scarecrow Press, Inc.
4720 Boston Way, Ste. A Phone: (301)459-3366
Lanham, MD 20706 Fax: (301)459-2118
Free: (800)462-6420
Publisher E-mail: orders@scarecrowpress.com

Journal for professionals covering books for young adults. **Founded:** Apr. 1978. **Freq:** Bimonthly. **Print Method:** Web. **Trim Size:** 8 3/8 x 10 7/8. **Cols./Page:** 2. **Key Personnel:** Cathi Dunn MacRae, Editor, cmacrae@scarecrowpress.com; Shirley Lambert, Publisher, slambert@scarecrowpress.com; Dawn Stotzfus, Book Review Editor, dstotzfus@scarecrowpress.com; Linda Benson, Circulation Mgr., lbenson@scarecrowpress.com. **ISSN:** 0160-4201. **Subscription Rates:** $38.50 individuals. **Remarks:** Accepts advertising.
Circ: Combined 4,669

13730 Maryland Cable
9609 Anapolis Rd. Phone: (301)306-5700
Lanham, MD 20706 Fax: (301)731-7822

Owner: Jones Communications, 9315 Largo Dr. W., Upper Marlboro, MD 20774, (301)306-5810. **Founded:** 1980. **Formerly**: Storer Cable (1983); Prime Cable (1987); MultiVision Cable TV (1993). **Key Personnel:** Jeffrey Patrick, Production Mgr. **Cities Served:** subscribing households 81,000; 88 channels; 9 community access channels.

13731 WOL-AM - 1450
5900 Pricess Garden Pkwy., Ste. 800 Phone: (301)306-1111
Lanham, MD 20706 Fax: (301)306-1149

Format: News; Talk. **Simulcasts:** WOLB-AM. **Networks:** ABC; Shadow Traffic. **Owner:** Radio One, Inc., at above address. **Founded:** 1924. **Operating Hours:** Continuous. **Key Personnel:** Alfred Liggins, President; Joe Madison, Program Dir., phone (301)429-2631; Anthony Washington, General Mgr.; Shellie Bowers, Jr., Dir. of Board Operations; Cathy Hughes, Owner. **Wattage:** 1000. **Ad Rates:** Combined advertising rates available with WMMJ-FM.

LAUREL, pop. 12,103.

Prince George's Co. (SC). 16 m NE of Washington, DC. Manufactures paints, electric housewares, fans. Diversified farming. Dairy products.

13732 Johns Hopkins APL Technical Digest
Johns Hopkins University Applied Physics Laboratory
11100 Johns Hopkins Rd. Phone: (240)228-5625
Laurel, MD 20723-6099
Publisher E-mail: laura.tye@jhuapl.edu

Technical journal covering research and programs at Johns Hopkins University Applied Physics Laboratory. **Founded:** Jan. 1980. **Freq:** Quarterly. **Print Method:** Sheetfed offset. **Key Personnel:** Kishin Moorjani, Editor-in-Chief; Karen M. Belton, Managing Editor; Jack W. Mothershead, Art Dir. **ISSN:** 0270-5214. **Subscription Rates:** Free to qualified subscribers. **Remarks:** Advertising not accepted. **URL:** http://www.jhuapl.edu/digest/.
Circ: Controlled ⊕4,330

13733 Laurel Leader
Patuxent Publishing Co.
615 Main St. Phone: (301)725-2000
Laurel, MD 20707 Fax: (301)725-7344

Suburban community newspaper. **Founded:** Sept. 17, 1897. **Freq:** Weekly (Thurs.). **Print Method:** Offset. **Cols./Page:** 5. **Col. Width:** 12.5 nonpareils. **Key Personnel:** Joe Murchison, Editor; S. Zeke Orlinsky, Publisher; Jodi McMannis, Advertising Dir. **ISSN:** 0748-528X. **Subscription Rates:** Free; $16

institutions; $18 out of county; $22 out of state. **Remarks:** Accepts advertising.
Ad Rates: BW: $1,608 4C: $2,058 **Circ:** Paid 419 Non-paid 27,622

13734 NAfIM Journal
National Apostolate for Inclusion Ministry
PO Box 3070 Phone: (301)776-9900
Laurel, MD 20709 Fax: (301)776-7800
Publisher E-mail: naim-usa@erols.com

Journal covering the advocation of inclusion of persons with mental retardation in the Catholic Church. **Founded:** 1967. **Freq:** Quarterly. **Key Personnel:** Cheryl Hall, Executive Dir.; Jill Johnson, Editor. **Subscription Rates:** $35 individuals. **Remarks:** Accepts advertising. **Former name:** NAPMR Quarterly.
Ad Rates: BW: $750 **Circ:** (Not Reported)

13735 WILC-AM - 900
Rte. 197 & Briarwood Rd. Phone: (301)419-2122
PO Box 42 Fax: (301)419-2409
Laurel, MD 20725

Format: Hispanic. **Networks:** Independent. **Founded:** 1985. **Formerly:** WLMD-AM (1965). **Operating Hours:** 6 a.m.-10 p.m. **Key Personnel:** Alejandro Carrasco, General Mgr. **Wattage:** 1900. **Ad Rates:** $15-30 for 15 seconds; $25-48 for 30 seconds; $30-60 for 60 seconds.

LEXINGTON PARK, pop. 9,136.

St. Mary's Co. 55 m SE of Washington, DC. On Patuxent River. Diversified farming.

13736 St. Mary's Enterprise
Chesapeake Publishing Corp.
PO Box 700 Phone: (301)862-2111
Lexington Park, MD 20653 Fax: (301)737-2896

Local newspaper. **Founded:** 1883. **Freq:** Semiweekly (Wed. and Fri.). **Trim Size:** 13 x 21. **Cols./Page:** 6. **Col. Width:** 12 picas. **Col. Depth:** 21 inches. **Key Personnel:** Richard H. Boyd, Editor; Ralph Martin, Publisher; Mickey Carlock, Advertising Mgr. **Subscription Rates:** $30.
Ad Rates: PCI: $7.70 **Circ:** ‡15,000

13737 WMDM-AM - 1690
PO Box 600 Phone: (301)475-8383
Lexington Park, MD 20653 Fax: (301)475-7832

Format: News; Talk. **Networks:** ABC; Westwood One Radio; Talknet. **Founded:** 1953. **Formerly:** WPTX-AM (1998). **Operating Hours:** Continuous. **Key Personnel:** Alisa Riley, General Mgr., alisa_riley@hotmail.com; Tomas Cuellar, Operations Mgr., tc@olg.com; Stacy Reynolds, Program Dir., stacy@olg.com. **Wattage:** 5000 day; 1000 night. **URL:** http://www.thebaynet.com.

13738 WMDM-FM - 97.7
PO Box 600 Phone: (301)475-8383
Lexington Park, MD 20653 Fax: (301)475-7832

Format: Country. **Networks:** ABC; Westwood One Radio. **Owner:** Patuxent Radio Partners Ltd., at above address. **Founded:** 1976. **Operating Hours:** Continuous. **Key Personnel:** Stacy Reynolds, Program Dir., stacy@olg.com; Tomas Cuellar, Operations Mgr., tc@olg.com. **Wattage:** 3000. **URL:** http://www.977thebay.com.

LINTHICUM

13739 Emergency Medicine
Cadmus Journal Services
Airport Sq. No. & Fax: (410)691-6203
940 Elkedgelanding Free: (800)257-5529
Linthicum, MD 21090-2908
Trade magazine on the business of generating, transmitting and distributing electric power. **Subtitle:** Acute Medicine for the Primary Care Physician. **Founded:** 1969. **Freq:** Monthly (2/mo. in Feb., Apr., June, and Sept.). **Print Method:** Web offset. **Trim Size:** 7 7/8 x 10 3/4. **Cols./Page:** 3 and 2. **Col. Width:** 2 1/8 and 4 inches. **Col. Depth:** 10 inches. **Key Personnel:** Robert Schwieger, Editor-in-Chief; John Slater, Publisher; Joanne Sohn, Promotions Mgr. **ISSN:** 0013-6654. **Subscription Rates:** $60; $80 Canada and Mexico; $100 other countries; $50 physicians; $37 students. $6 single issue. **Remarks:** Accepts advertising.
Ad Rates: BW: $4,765 4C: $6,390 **Circ:** Paid 3,110 Non-paid 48,258

LINTHICUM HEIGHTS

13740 Management Science
The Institute for Operations Research and the Management Sciences
901 Elkridge Landing Rd., Ste. 400 Phone: (410)850-0300 Fax: (410)684-2963
Linthicum Heights, MD 21090
Free: (800)446-3676
Publication E-mail: publications@informs.org
Publisher E-mail: informs@jhuvms.hcf.jhu.edu

Professional journal covering business and management. **Founded:** 1954. **Freq:** Monthly. **Print Method:** Offset. **Key Personnel:** Hau Lee, Ph.D., Editor-in-Chief. **ISSN:** 0025-1909. **Subscription Rates:** Included in membership. **Remarks:** Accepts advertising.
Circ: (Not Reported)

13741 Operations Research
The Institute for Operations Research and the Management Sciences
901 Elkridge Landing Rd., Ste. 400 Phone: (410)850-0300 Fax: (410)684-2963
Linthicum Heights, MD 21090
Free: (800)446-3676
Publisher E-mail: informs@jhuvms.hcf.jhu.edu

Journal publishing new operations research for practitioners and Operations Research Society of America members. **Founded:** 1952. **Freq:** Bimonthly. **Print Method:** Offset. **Trim Size:** 8 x 10 13/16. **Cols./Page:** 2. **Col. Width:** 37 nonpareils. **Col. Depth:** 123 agate lines. **Key Personnel:** Donald Ratliff, Editor. **ISSN:** 0030-364X. **Subscription Rates:** $109 individuals; $122 out of country; $172 institutions; $185 institutions out of country. **URL:** http://www.informs.org.
Ad Rates: BW: $550 **Circ:** Paid ‡10,789

LUTHERVILLE

13742 Music Monthly
Maryland Musician Publications
1144 York Rd. Phone: (410)494-0566
Lutherville, MD 21093-6201 Fax: (410)494-0565
Publication E-mail: musmonthly@aol.com

Consumer magazine covering music, regionally and nationally. **Founded:** Sept. 1984. **Freq:** Monthly. **Print Method:** Web offset. **Trim Size:** 11 x 17. **Cols./Page:** 4. **Col. Width:** 2 1/4 inches. **Col. Depth:** 12 1/2 inches. **Key Personnel:** Susan Mudd, Publisher; M. Kelly Connelly, Editor; Mark Bounds, Senior Editor. **Subscription Rates:** $25 individuals. **Remarks:** Accepts advertising.
Ad Rates: BW: $695 4C: $2,500 **Circ:** Controlled 35,000

13743 Times-Herald
1205 York Rd., Ste. 10A Phone: (410)296-4895
Lutherville, MD 21093 Fax: (410)296-4898
Publication E-mail: thpaper@erols.com

Community newspaper. **Founded:** 1962. **Freq:** Biweekly. **Print Method:** Offset. **Trim Size:** 13 3/4 x 22 3/4. **Cols./Page:** 6. **Col. Width:** 2 inches. **Col. Depth:** 21 inches. **Key Personnel:** Marina Brockmann, Publisher. **Subscription Rates:** Free; $50 by mail. **Remarks:** Accepts advertising. **Formerly:** Essex Times.
Ad Rates: BW: $1,149 4C: $1,524 SAU: $11.75 **Circ:** 32,000

MECHANICSVILLE

13744 WSMD-FM - 98.3
28095 Three Notch Rd., Ste. 2-B Phone: (301)870-5550 Fax: (301)884-0280
Mechanicsville, MD 20659

Format: Classic Rock; News; Sports. **Networks:** ABC. **Founded:** 1988. **Formerly:** WQMR-FM (1991). **Operating Hours:** Continuous. **Key Personnel:** Patrick Wood, News Dir., phone (301)870-5550; Roy Robertson, Program Dir. **Wattage:** 3000 ERP.

MIDDLETOWN, pop. 1,748.

Frederick Co. (N). 8 m W of Frederick. Diversified farming. Dairy products, wheat, corn.

13745 The Middletown Valley Citizen
Citizen Communications, Inc.
1220 Marker Rd. Phone: (301)371-9399
Middletown, MD 21769
Community newspaper. **Founded:** 1990. **Freq:** Weekly. **Print Method:** Offset. **Cols./Page:** 5. **Col. Width:** 2 inches. **Col. Depth:** 14 inches. **Key Personnel:** Julie Maynard, Editor; Comfort Grandi, Assoc. Ed. **ISSN:** 1056-7674. **Subscription Rates:** $12; $17 out of area. **Remarks:** Accepts advertising.
Ad Rates: PCI: $5.50 **Circ:** Paid ‡1,600 Non-paid ‡35

13746 WAFY-FM - 103.1
5742 Industry Ln. Phone: (301)620-7700
Frederick, MD 21704 Fax: (301)696-0509
Free: (301)620-1031

Format: Adult Contemporary. **Founded:** 1990. **Operating Hours:** Continuous. **Key Personnel:** Barbara Marmet, General Mgr.; Rob Marmet, Sales Mgr. **Wattage:** 3000.

MILLERSVILLE, pop. 500.

Anne Arundel Co. (C). 5 m N of Annapolis. Residential.

13747 Intermedia
406 Headquarters Dr., Ste. 201 Phone: (410)987-8400
Millersville, MD 21108 Fax: (410)987-4890

Owner: Intermedia Partners, 235 Montgomery St., No. 4, San Francisco, CA 94104. **Founded:** 1979. **Formerly:** Acton Corp. North Arundel CATV. **Key Personnel:** Paul Janson, General Mgr.; Craig Malang, Contact; Patricia Archibald, Office Mgr. **Cities Served:** North Anne Arundel County: subscribing households 50,000; 80 channels; 2 community access channels; 168 hours per week community access programming.

MONTGOMERY

13748 Cable TV of Montgomery
20 W. Gude Dr. Phone: (301)294-7600
Rockville, MD 20850-1151 Fax: (301)294-7697

Founded: 1984. **Cities Served:** Montgomery County, Prince Georges County, Barnesville, Battery Park, Bethesda, Boyds, Brookville, Burtonsville, Chevy Chase, Damascus, Derwood, Friendship Heights, Gaithersburg, Garrett Park, Germantown, Glen Echo, Kensington, North White Oak, Oakmont, Olney, Poolesville, Potomac, Rockville, Silver Spring, Somerset, South White Oak, Tacoma Park, Washington Grove, and West Bethesda, MD.

MOUNTAIN LAKE PARK, pop. 1,597.

Garrett Co. (NW). 3 m S of Oakland. Residential.

13749 WKHJ-FM - 98.9
PO Box 2337 Phone: (301)334-4272
Mountain Lake Park, MD 21550 Fax: (301)334-2152

Format: Adult Contemporary. **Networks:** CNN Radio. **Founded:** 1990. **Operating Hours:** Continuous. **ADI:** Pittsburgh, PA. **Key Personnel:** Terry King, General Mgr.; Cathy L. Clocker, Sales Mgr. **Wattage:** 3000 ERP. **Ad Rates:** $5.20-6.25 for 15 seconds; $8.60-10.35 for 30 seconds; $11.70-14.50 for 60 seconds.

NORTH EAST

13750 The Mariner
Chesapeake Publishing Corp.
500 S. Main St. Phone: (410)287-9430
North East, MD 21901 Fax: (410)287-9442
Publication E-mail: Themariner@dpnet.net

Consumer magazine covering boating and leisure. **Founded:** 1980. **Freq:** Semimonthly. **Print Method:** Web offset. **Trim Size:** 10 x 13. **Cols./Page:** 5. **Col. Width:** 1 7/8 inches. **Col. Depth:** 11 1/2 inches. **Key Personnel:** Ira Black, Editor. **Subscription Rates:** $25 individuals; Free single copy.
Ad Rates: BW: $540 4C: $765 **Circ:** Combined 33,000

OAKLAND†, pop. 1,994.

Garrett Co. (NW). 50 m SW of Cumberland. Summer & winter resorts. Maple sugar and syrup, wood products, lens manufactured. Feed, lumber, flour mills. Dairy, truck, grain farms. Potatoes, buckwheat, corn & green beans.

13751 The Republican
Sincell Publishing Co., Inc.
PO Box 326 Phone: (301)334-3963
Oakland, MD 21550 Fax: (301)334-5904
Publication E-mail: republican@gcnet.net

Community newspaper. **Founded:** Mar. 4, 1877. **Freq:** Weekly (Thurs.). **Print Method:** Offset. **Cols./Page:** 8. **Col. Width:** 22 nonpareils. **Col. Depth:** 294 agate lines. **Key Personnel:** Donald W. Sincell, Editor; Lisa Rook, Advertising Mgr.; Robert

B. Sincell, Manager. **Subscription Rates:** $16.28 individuals. **Remarks:** Accepts advertising.
Ad Rates: BW: $453.60 **Circ:** Thurs. 11,102
4C: $775.25
PCI: $3.95

13752 WGPT-TV - 36
c/o Maryland Public Broadcasting Commission
11767 Owings Mills Blvd.
Owings Mills, MD 21117
Phone: (410)356-5600
Fax: (410)581-4338
Free: (800)233-3678

Format: Public TV; Eclectic. **Simulcasts:** WMPB, WMPT, WCPB, WWPB, WFPT. **Networks:** Public Broadcasting Service (PBS); Eastern Educational Television. **Owner:** Maryland Public Broadcasting Commission, at above address. **Operating Hours:** 3a.m.-1:30a.m. Mon.-Sun. **ADI:** Baltimore, MD. **Key Personnel:** Robert J. Shuman, Pres./CEO; Dr. Archie L. Buffkins, Sr. Vice Pres., Broadcasting; Janice Wilson, Sr. Vice Pres., Marketing & Development; Larry D. Unger, Sr. Vice Pres., Administration & Finance; Martin Jacobs, Vice Pres., Finance & Accounting; Gladys M. Kaplan, Vice Pres., Human Resources; Ann Engelman, Vice Pres., Programming/Broadcast Ser.; Everett L. Marshburn, Vice Pres., Broadcast Production; John T. Potthast, Vice Pres., National Productions; Barry P. Freidly, Vice Pres., Membership; Hannah Lee Byron, Dir., Corp. Comm. & Gov't. Affairs; Carol Wonsavage, Dir., Regional Communications; Sharon Philippart, Dir., National Communications. **Wattage:** 250,000. **URL:** http://www.mpt.org.

13753 WMSG-AM - 1050
PO Box 271
Oakland, MD 21550
Phone: (301)334-3800
Fax: (301)334-5800

Format: Country; Gospel. **Networks:** CBS. **Owner:** Oakland Media Group, PO Box 449, Oakland, MD 21550. **Founded:** 1963. **Operating Hours:** 6 a.m.-11 p.m. **Key Personnel:** James Butscher, Contact. **Wattage:** 1000 day; 75 night. **Ad Rates:** $2.75-5.70 for 10 seconds; $4.05-8.15 for 30 seconds; $5.50-11.35 for 60 seconds. $2.75-$5.70 Tennessee; $4.05-$8.15 for 30 seconds; $5.50-$11.35 for 60 seconds. Combined advertising rates available with.

13754 WXIE-FM - 92.3
PO Box 271
Oakland, MD 21550
Phone: (301)334-1100
Fax: (301)334-5800

Format: Classic Rock. **Networks:** ABC. **Owner:** Oakland Media Group, PO Box 449, Oakland, MD 21550. **Founded:** 1966. **Operating Hours:** Continuous. **Key Personnel:** James Butscher, Contact. **Wattage:** 990. **Ad Rates:** $2.75-5.70 for 10 seconds; $4.05-8.15 for 30 seconds; $5.50-11.35 for 60 seconds. $2.75-$5.70 Tennessee; $4.05-$8.15 for 30 seconds; $5.50-$11.35 for 60 seconds. Combined advertising rates available with.

OCEAN CITY, pop. 4,946.

Worchester Co. (SE). on Atlantic Ocean, 23 m E of Salisbury. Summer beach resort. Light industries. Commercial and sport fishing.

13755 Maryland Times-Press
Thomson-Chesapeake Publications
214 16th St.
PO Box 479
Ocean City, MD 21842
Phone: (410)289-6834
Fax: (410)289-6838
Publication E-mail: atlantic@shore.intercom.net

Community newspaper. **Founded:** 1923. **Freq:** Weekly (Wed.). **Print Method:** Offset. **Cols./Page:** 6. **Col. Width:** 2 1/16 inches. **Col. Depth:** 21 1/2 inches. **Key Personnel:** Joseph Harris, Editor; Chris Eddings, Publisher. **USPS:** 166-160. **Subscription Rates:** $9.95 individuals; $18 other countries. **Formerly:** Ocean City Times (Oct. 1986); Maryland Coast Press.
Ad Rates: BW: $1,212.16 **Circ:** Paid 5,500
4C: $1,472.60
PCI: $9.40

13756 Oceana Magazine
PO Box 2070
Ocean City, MD 21843-2070
Phone: (302)539-6313
Fax: (302)539-6815
Publication E-mail: oceana@beachin.net

Magazine. **Founded:** 1978. **Freq:** Weekly. **Print Method:** Web offset. **Trim Size:** 10 x 15. **Cols./Page:** 4. **Col. Width:** 14 picas. **Col. Depth:** 84 picas. **Key Personnel:** Elizabeth Brownell, Editor. **Subscription Rates:** $55. **Remarks:** Accepts advertising. **URL:** http://www.oceanamagazine.com.
Ad Rates: GLR: $10 **Circ:** Non-paid ‡27,000
BW: $395
4C: $470
PCI: $12

13757 TCI Cablevision of Eastern Shore
8301 Coastal Hwy.
Ocean City, MD 21842
Phone: (410)524-3401
Fax: (410)524-2335

Owner: Tele-Communications Inc., Terrace Tower II, 5619 DTO Pkwy., Englewood, CO 80111, (303)267-5500, Fax: (303)779-1228. **Formerly:** United Cable; United Artists. **Key Personnel:** David Kane, General Mgr. **Cities Served:** Berlin, Fenwick Island, Ocean City, West Ocean City, MD.

OLNEY, pop. 4600.

Montgomery Co. (WC). 10 m N of Bethesda. Residential

13758 Deleading
Weil Communications and Marketing, Inc.
PO Box 535
Olney, MD 20830
Phone: (301)924-5490
Fax: (301)924-0265
Publication E-mail: weilcm@erols.com
Publisher E-mail: weilcm@erols.com

Trade magazine covering testing, abatement, and worker safety concerns in lead base paint activities in multi-unit housing and institutional facilities. **Freq:** Monthly. **Print Method:** Offset. **Trim Size:** 11 1/4 x 14 3/4. **Cols./Page:** 4. **Col. Width:** 14 picas. **Col. Depth:** 13 1/2 inches. **Key Personnel:** Stephen Weil, Publisher, weilcki@erols.com; Shannon Thomas Kennedy, Editor, stk350@aol.com. **Subscription Rates:** $35 individuals. **Alt. Formats:** Mailing labels.
Ad Rates: BW: $1,500 **Circ:** Paid ‡1,600
4C: $1,950 Non-paid 9,000

13759 Housing Operations Manager
Weil Communications and Marketing, Inc.
PO Box 535
Olney, MD 20830
Phone: (301)924-5490
Fax: (301)924-0265
Publisher E-mail: weilcm@erols.com

Trade magazine covering issues of public housing authority management and facility maintenance, energy conservation, and other facility management issues intended for multi-unit housing and institutional administrators. **Founded:** Sept. 1981. **Freq:** Monthly. **Print Method:** Offset. **Trim Size:** 11 1/4 x 14 3/4. **Cols./Page:** 4. **Col. Width:** 28 nonpareils. **Col. Depth:** 189 agate lines. **Key Personnel:** Shannon Thomas Kennedy, Editor, stk350@aol.com; Stephen Weil, Publisher, weilcis@erols.com. **Subscription Rates:** $50 individuals. **Remarks:** Accepts advertising. **Alt. Formats:** Mailing labels. **Formerly:** Maintenance and Modernization Supervisor; Facility Nehs.
Ad Rates: BW: $1,500 **Circ:** Paid ‡1,600
4C: $1,950 Non-paid ‡7,400

13760 Petroleum Marketer
GCI Publishing Co., Inc.
PO Box 1110
Olney, MD 20830-1110

Magazine for oil marketing equipment and merchandising industry. **Subtitle:** The Equipment Book. **Founded:** 1933. **Freq:** Bimonthly. **Print Method:** Web offset. **Trim Size:** 8 1/8 x 10 7/8. **Cols./Page:** 2 and 3. **Col. Width:** 40 and 26 nonpareils. **Col. Depth:** 140 agate lines. **Key Personnel:** Louise Classon, Editor; Paula Jacobs, Advertising Mgr. **ISSN:** 0362-7799. **Subscription Rates:** $24 individuals; $30 two years. **Remarks:** Accepts advertising. **URL:** http://www.gcipub.com.
Ad Rates: BW: $2,495 **Circ:** ‡15,000
4C: $3,995
PCI: $2.25

13761 World Coffee & Tea
GCI Publishing Co., Inc.
PO Box 1110
Olney, MD 20830-1110

Trade magazine covering the speciality coffee and gourmet tea market and related products/services. **Founded:** 1960. **Freq:** Monthly. **Print Method:** Web offset. **Trim Size:** 8 1/4 x 11. **Cols./Page:** 3. **Col. Width:** 26 nonpareils. **Col. Depth:** 140 agate lines. **Key Personnel:** Ken Silverstein, Publisher; Colin Campbell, Editor; Cathy John, Advertising Mgr.; Susie Parker, Advertising Mgr. **ISSN:** 0043-8340. **Subscription Rates:** $24 individuals; $40 two years; $5 single issue. **Remarks:** Accepts advertising. **URL:** http://www.gcipub.com.
Ad Rates: BW: $1,350 **Circ:** Non-paid ‡9,500
4C: $2,100

OWINGS MILLS, pop. 7,500.

Baltimore Co. (N). 3m N of Pikesville. Light industrial.

13762 Amazon Times
PO Box 135
Owings Mills, MD 21117

Publication featuring dialogue on all topics of interest to lesbians. **Founded:** 1990. **Freq:** Quarterly. **Key Personnel:** Charlotte Zinser, Editor. **Subscription Rates:** $20; $25 Industry. **Remarks:** Advertising not accepted.
Circ: (Not Reported)

13763 WCBM-AM - 680
11 Music Fair Rd.
Owings Mills, MD 21117
Phone: (410)356-3003
Fax: (410)581-0150
E-mail: hottalk@wcbm.com

Format: Talk. **Networks:** ABC. **Operating Hours:** Continuous. **Key Personnel:** Nick Mangione, Jr., General Mgr.; Bob Pettit, General Sales Mgr.; Sean Casey, Program Dir.; Berlin Smart, Business Mgr.; Ken Maylath, News Dir. **Local Programs:** *Les Kinsolving*, Gary St. Ours, Mailing contact; *The Morning Show*, Sean Casey, Mailing contact; *The 20th Show*, Gary St. Ours, Mailing contact. **Wattage:** 10,000 day; 5000 night. **Ad Rates:** $20-120 per unit.

WCPB-TV - See Salisbury

WFPT-TV - See Frederick

WGPT-TV - See Oakland

WMPB-TV - See Baltimore

WMPT-TV - See Annapolis

WWPB-TV - See Hagerstown

PASADENA

13764 Minerva
The Minerva Center
20 Granada Rd.
Pasadena, MD 21122-2708
Phone: (410)437-5379
Fax: (914)693-2834
Publisher E-mail: minervacen@aol.com

Journal featuring articles, reviews, fiction, and poetry. **Subtitle:** Quarterly Report on Women in the Military. **Founded:** Mar. 1983. **Freq:** Quarterly. **Print Method:** Offset. **Trim Size:** 5 1/2 x 8 1/2. **Cols./Page:** 1. **Col. Width:** 42 nonpareils. **Col. Depth:** 98 agate lines. **Key Personnel:** Linda Grant DePauw, Editor and Publisher. **ISSN:** 0736-718X. **Subscription Rates:** $50 individuals; $75 institutions. **Remarks:** Advertising accepted; rates available upon request.
Circ: Paid ‡500
Non-paid ‡20

13765 Minerva's Bulletin Board
The Minerva Center
20 Granada Rd.
Pasadena, MD 21122-2708
Phone: (410)437-5379
Fax: (914)693-2834
Publisher E-mail: minervacen@aol.com

News magazine for military women and female veterans. **Founded:** 1988. **Freq:** Quarterly. **Print Method:** Offset. **Trim Size:** 8 1/2 x 11. **Cols./Page:** 2. **Col. Width:** 3 inches. **Col. Depth:** 8 inches. **Key Personnel:** Linda Grant De Pauw, Editor and Publisher. **ISSN:** 0897-6104. **Subscription Rates:** $25 individuals; $50 institutions. **Remarks:** Accepts advertising.
Ad Rates: BW: $500 **Circ:** 400

POCOMOKE CITY, pop. 3,558.

Worcester Co. (SE). On Pocomoke River, 21 m S of Salisbury. Tourism, Shopping and docking areas. Manufactures flour, feed, canned goods, crates, baskets, fertilizer, foundry products, lumber. Pine and oak timber. Diversified farming. Poultry, potatoes, corn, beans, tomatoes.

13766 Worcester County Messenger
Chesapeake Publishing Corp.
PO Box 388
Pocomoke City, MD 21851
Phone: (410)957-1700
Fax: (410)957-4314

Newspaper. **Founded:** 1869. **Freq:** Weekly (Wed.). **Print Method:** Offset. **Cols./Page:** 6. **Col. Width:** 28 nonpareils. **Col. Depth:** 301 agate lines. **Key Personnel:** William H. Kerbin, Editor; Donna Bloxom, Advertising Mgr. **Subscription Rates:** $18 individuals; $30 other countries plus sales tax.
Ad Rates: BW: $1,103 **Circ:** Paid 3,200
4C: $1,500
SAU: $8.80
PCI: $8.80

POTOMAC, pop. 2,000.

Montgomery Co. (WC). 5 m S. of Rockville. Residential.

13767 Aviation Maintenance
Phillips Business Information, Inc.
1201 Seven Locks Rd., Ste. 300
Potomac, MD 20854
Phone: (301)340-7788
Fax: (301)340-3847
Free: (800)777-5006
Publication E-mail: am@phillips.com

Publisher E-mail: clientservices.pbi@phillips.com

Magazine covering aviation maintenance. **Founded:** 1982. **Freq:** Monthly. **Print Method:** Offset. **Trim Size:** 8 x 10 3/4. **Cols./Page:** 3 and 2. **Col. Width:** 26 and 40 nonpareils. **Col. Depth:** 126 agate lines. **Key Personnel:** Clifton C. Stroud II, Editor. **Subscription Rates:** Free to qualified subscribers. **Remarks:** Accepts advertising. **Formerly**: Aviation Equipment Maintenance.
Ad Rates: BW: $5,545 **Circ:** Controlled ‡40,000
4C: $6,720

13768 Avionics Magazine
Phillips Business Information, Inc.
1201 Seven Locks Rd., Ste. 300 Phone: (301)340-7788
Potomac, MD 20854 Fax: (301)340-3847
Free: (800)777-5006
Publication E-mail: avionics@phillips.com
Publisher E-mail: clientservices.pbi@phillips.com

Magazine about aviation electronics for commercial and military aircraft. **Founded:** Jan. 1976. **Freq:** Monthly. **Print Method:** Offset. **Trim Size:** 8 1/8 x 10 7/8. **Cols./Page:** 3. **Col. Width:** 26 nonpareils. **Col. Depth:** 126 agate lines. **Key Personnel:** Scott Chase, Publisher; David W. Robb, Editor/Assoc. Publisher. **ISSN:** 0273-7639. **Subscription Rates:** Free to qualified subscribers. **Remarks:** Accepts advertising.
Ad Rates: BW: $5,625 **Circ:** Controlled 23,000
4C: $6,825
PCI: $185

13769 Communications
Phillips Business Information, Inc.
1201 Seven Locks Rd., Ste. 300 Phone: (301)340-7788
Potomac, MD 20854 Fax: (301)340-3847
Free: (800)777-5006
Publication E-mail: ctmagazine@aol.com
Publisher E-mail: clientservices.pbi@phillips.com

Magazine catering to cable TV industry's technical community; written by industry engineers, technicians, managers, and professionals. **Subtitle:** Official Trade Journal of the Society of Cable Television Engineers. **Founded:** Mar. 1984. **Freq:** Monthly. **Print Method:** Offset. **Trim Size:** 8 3/8 x 10 7/8. **Cols./Page:** 2 and 3. **Col. Width:** 21.5 and 14 picas. **Col. Depth:** 9 3/4 inches. **Key Personnel:** Alex Zavistovich, Contact; Toni I. Barnett, Contact; Charles Castellani, Contact. **ISSN:** 0884-2272. **Subscription Rates:** Free to qualified subscribers. **Remarks:** Accepts advertising.
Ad Rates: BW: $3,955 **Circ:** Controlled ‡25,000
4C: $4,955
PCI: $1.60

13770 In-Motion
Phillips Business Information, Inc.
1201 Seven Locks Rd., Ste. 300 Phone: (301)340-7788
Potomac, MD 20854 Fax: (301)340-3847
Free: (800)777-5006
Publisher E-mail: clientservices.pbi@phillips.com

Magazine covering information on talent, technology, and services of film and video production. **Founded:** Jan. 1, 1981. **Freq:** Monthly.

13771 Mobile Products Europe
Phillips Business Information, Inc.
1201 Seven Locks Rd., Ste. 300 Phone: (301)340-7788
Potomac, MD 20854 Fax: (301)340-3847
Free: (800)777-5006
Publisher E-mail: clientservices.pbi@phillips.com

Product tabloid describing cellular paging products. **Founded:** Mar. 1, 1991. **Freq:** 8/year. **Trim Size:** 10 7/8 x 15 3/4. **Key Personnel:** Lisa Porther Fasold, Editor. **ISSN:** 1065-9188. **Subscription Rates:** Free to qualified subscribers. **Formerly**: Mobile Products International.

13772 Potomac Gazette
The Gazette Newspapers
10220 River Rd., No. 111 Phone: (301)299-2570
Potomac, MD 20854 Fax: (301)299-8542

Community newspaper. **Freq:** Weekly (Wed.). **Trim Size:** 13 1/2 x 22 3/4. **Cols./Page:** 5. **Col. Width:** 1 5/16 inches. **Col. Depth:** 13 inches. **Key Personnel:** James F. Mannarino, General Mgr.; Miranda Spivack, Deputy Editor. **Subscription Rates:** Free. **Remarks:** Advertising accepted; rates available upon request.
Circ: Combined ❑16,189

13773 The Public Manager
The Bureaucrat, Inc.
12007 Titian Way Phone: (301)279-9445
Potomac, MD 20854 Fax: (301)251-5872

Subtitle: The New Bureaucrat. **Founded:** 1972. **Freq:** Quarterly. **Print Method:** Offset. **Trim Size:** 8 3/8 x 11. **Cols./Page:** 2. **Col. Width:** 40 nonpareils. **Col. Depth:** 136 agate lines. **Key Personnel:** Thomas W. Novotny, Editor. **ISSN:** 1061-7639. **Subscription Rates:** $28; $50 institutions. **Formerly**: The Bureaucrat (1992).
Ad Rates: BW: $500 **Circ:** ‡5,000

13774 Rotor & Wing
Phillips Business Information, Inc.
1201 Seven Locks Rd., Ste. 300 Phone: (301)340-1520
Potomac, MD 20854 Fax: (301)340-0542
Publisher E-mail: clientservices.pbi@phillips.com

Magazine covering helicopters. **Founded:** 1967. **Freq:** Monthly. **Print Method:** Offset. **Trim Size:** 8 x 10 3/4. **Cols./Page:** 3. **Col. Width:** 27 nonpareils. **Col. Depth:** 140 agate lines. **Key Personnel:** Scott Chase, Publisher; Kathy Kocks, Editor. **ISSN:** 0191-6408. **Subscription Rates:** $49 individuals; $80 other countries; $6.95 single issue. **Remarks:** Accepts advertising.
Ad Rates: BW: $6,470 **Circ:** Paid 7,738
4C: $8,695 Non-paid 31,786
PCI: $160

13775 Telecommunications Regulatory Monitor
Phillips Business Information, Inc.
1201 Seven Locks Rd., Ste. 300 Phone: (301)340-7788
Potomac, MD 20854 Fax: (301)340-3847
Free: (800)777-5006
Publisher E-mail: clientservices.pbi@phillips.com

Looseleaf service for telecommunication industry regulation. **Founded:** 1984. **Freq:** Quarterly. **Print Method:** Offset. **Cols./Page:** 1. **Col. Width:** 54 nonpareils. **Col. Depth:** 133 agate lines. **Key Personnel:** David A. Irwin, Editor; Thomas Phillips, Publisher. **Subscription Rates:** $450 individuals.

13776 Via Satellite
Phillips Business Information, Inc.
1201 Seven Locks Rd., Ste. 300 Phone: (301)340-7788
Potomac, MD 20854 Fax: (301)340-3847
Free: (800)777-5006
Publisher E-mail: clientservices.pbi@phillips.com

Communication satellite industry magazine. **Founded:** 1986. **Freq:** Monthly. **Print Method:** Web. **Trim Size:** 8 3/8 x 10 7/8. **Cols./Page:** 3. **Col. Width:** 2 1/4 inches. **Col. Depth:** 9 3/4 inches. **Key Personnel:** Joe Rosone, Advertising Contact, jrosone@phillips.com. **ISSN:** 1041-0643. **Subscription Rates:** $49 United States and Canada; $69 other countries. **Remarks:** Accepts advertising.
Ad Rates: BW: $3,445 **Circ:** 24,000
4C: $3,870
PCI: $60

13777 Wireless Product News
Phillips Business Information, Inc.
1201 Seven Locks Rd., Ste. 300 Phone: (301)340-7788
Potomac, MD 20854 Fax: (301)340-3847
Free: (800)777-5006
Publication E-mail: ddeker@phillips.com
Publisher E-mail: clientservices.pbi@phillips.com

Trade magazine covering the wireless communications products industry. **Subtitle:** Incorporating Mobile Product News. **Founded:** 1985. **Freq:** Monthly. **Print Method:** Offset. **Trim Size:** 10 7/8 x 15 3/4. **Cols./Page:** 4. **Col. Width:** 27 nonpareils. **Col. Depth:** 125 agate lines. **Key Personnel:** Tom Phillips, President. **ISSN:** 1044-1190. **Subscription Rates:** Free to qualified subscribers. **Remarks:** Accepts advertising. **Formerly**: Mobile Communications Business; Mobile Product News.
Ad Rates: BW: $5,180 **Circ:** Controlled ‡28,000
4C: $6,080

13778 WCTN-AM - 950
7825 Tuckerman Ln., No. 211 Phone: (301)299-7026
Potomac, MD 20854 Fax: (301)299-5301
E-mail: wctn@wctn.net

Format: Religious; Contemporary Christian. **Networks:** USA Radio; Moody Broadcasting; Ambassador Inspirational Radio. **Owner:** Seven Locks Broadcasting Co., at above address. **Founded:** 1973. **Operating Hours:** Continuous. **Key Personnel:** Rebecca Wong, Operations and Traffic Mgr., rebecca@wctn.net; John Vogt, General Mgr., johnvogt@wctn.net; Bob Allen, Chief Engineer. **Local Programs:** *Community Focus*, Tanya Brown, (301)299-7026, Fax (301)299-5301; *Wake-Up Call*, Joan Veon, (301)924-2056. **Wattage:** 2500. **Ad Rates:** $20-35 for 30 seconds; $25-40 for 60 seconds. **URL:** http://www.wctn.net.

PRINCE FREDERICK†, pop. 400.

Calvert Co. (S). On Patuxent River, 41 m SE of Washington, DC. Tourism. Fish, crab industries. Agriculture. Tobacco, corn.

13779 The Calvert
The Washington Times Co.
PO Box 910 Phone: (410)535-1575
Prince Frederick, MD 20678 Fax: (301)855-9071

Newspaper with a independent orientation. **Founded:** 1940. **Freq:** Weekly (Wed.). **Print Method:** offset. **Cols./Page:** 6. **Col. Width:** 25 nonpareils. **Col. Depth:** 294 agate lines. **Key Personnel:** Sandra Worsham, Advertising Mgr.; Chales L. Mister, Advertising Mgr.; Richard McIntire, Editor. **USPS:** 086-620. **Subscription Rates:** $15.75 individuals Calvert county only; $18.75 out of county. **Remarks:** Accepts advertising.
Ad Rates: GLR: $.29 **Circ:** Paid ‡8710
BW: $818 Non-paid ‡120
4C: $1168
PCI: $6.49

13780 The Calvert Independent
The Washington Times Co.
PO Box 910 Phone: (301)855-1000
Prince Frederick, MD 20678 Fax: (301)855-9070

Community newspaper. **Founded:** 1940. **Freq:** Weekly. **Cols./Page:** 6. **Col. Width:** 2 1/16 inches. **Col. Depth:** 21 inches. **Key Personnel:** Charles L. Mister, General Mgr.; Joe Norris, Editor, phone (410)535-1575, fax (410)535-2436. **Subscription Rates:** $15.75. **Remarks:** Accepts advertising.
Ad Rates: BW: $818 **Circ:** Paid 9,308
4C: $1,168
SAU: $18.40

13781 The Recorder
Chesapeake Publishing Corp.
440 Main St. Phone: (410)535-1234
PO Box 485 Fax: (410)535-5883
Prince Frederick, MD 20678
Community newspaper. **Founded:** Apr. 15, 1971. **Freq:** Semiweekly (Wed. and Fri.). **Print Method:** Offset. **Trim Size:** 13 x 21. **Cols./Page:** 6. **Col. Width:** 28 nonpareils. **Col. Depth:** 294 agate lines. **Key Personnel:** Kevin Conron, Editor; Ralph Martin, Publisher; Jeannie Green, Advertising Mgr. **Subscription Rates:** $23.10 in county. **Remarks:** Accepts advertising.
Ad Rates: GLR: $6.22 **Circ:** 8,625
BW: $783.12
4C: $1,283.12
PCI: $6.22

13782 Star-Democrat & Sunday Star
Chesapeake Publishing Corp.
440 Main St. Phone: (410)535-1234
PO Box 485 Fax: (410)535-5883
Prince Frederick, MD 20678
Publication E-mail: mail@stardem.com

General newspaper. **Founded:** 1799. **Freq:** Daily and Sunday. **Print Method:** Offset. **Cols./Page:** 6. **Col. Width:** 2 1/16 inches. **Col. Depth:** 21 inches. **Key Personnel:** Denise Riley, Editor; Larry E. Effingham, Publisher; David Fike, Advertising Dir.; Leon Rebuck, Circulation Mgr.; Diane Ferguson, Classified Mgr.; Kent Smith, Editor. **ISSN:** 1065-2345. **Subscription Rates:** $84 individuals; $126 out of area. **Remarks:** Accepts advertising. **URL:** http://www.stardem.com.
Ad Rates: PCI: $16.20 **Circ:** Mon.-Fri. 17,021
Sun. 16,995

13783 WMJS-FM - 92.7
3950 Hallowing Point Phone: (410)535-2201
Box 547
Prince Frederick, MD 20678

Format: Soft Rock. **Networks:** Independent. **Founded:** 1971. **Operating Hours:** 5 a.m.-midnight. **Key Personnel:** Ada Gollub, Sales Mgr.; Melvin Gollub, General Mgr. **Wattage:** 6000. **Ad Rates:** $10-13 for 30 seconds; $17.80-32 for 60 seconds.

PRINCESS ANNE†, pop. 1,499.

Somerset Co. (SE). On Manokin River, 12 m S of Salisbury. University of Maryland-Eastern Shore. Fruit and vegetable canneries. Manufactures needles, shirts, lumber, modular homes, flour, feed. Nurseries. Agriculture. Poultry. Potatoes, strawberries, tomatoes, beans.

13784 Maryland Music Educator
Maryland Music Educators Association
c/o Ray H. Zeigler Phone: (410)651-9359
1021 Old Princess Anne Rd. Fax: (410)651-9359
Princess Anne, MD 21853
Publication E-mail: raybach@aol.com

Professional journal covering music education for the Maryland Music Educator's Association. **Founded:** 1954. **Freq:** Quarterly. **Trim Size:** 8 1/2 x 11. **Cols./Page:** 3. **Col. Width:** 13 picas. **Key Personnel:** Dr. Ray H. Zeigler, Jr., Editor/

Advertising Mgr., RayBach@aol.com. **Subscription Rates:** $10 individuals. **Remarks:** Accepts advertising.
Ad Rates: BW: $160 **Circ:** Combined 1,400
PCI: $20

13785 Somerset/Crisfield Express
Chesapeake Publishing Corp.
PO Box 310 Phone: (410)289-6834
Princess Anne, MD 21853 Fax: (410)289-6838

Shopping guide. **Founded:** Oct. 1986. **Freq:** Weekly. **Print Method:** Offset. **Cols./Page:** 5. **Col. Width:** 12 picas. **Col. Depth:** 13 inches. **Key Personnel:** R. Crumbacker, Editor; Darel LaPrade, Publisher; Tom Sexton, Advertising Mgr. **Remarks:** Accepts advertising.
Ad Rates: PCI: $7.40 **Circ:** Free ‡1,700

13786 Somerset Herald
Thomson-Chesapeake Publications
PO Box 310 Phone: (410)651-1600
Princess Anne, MD 21853 Fax: (410)651-3785
Publication E-mail: herald@shore-source.com

Community newspaper. **Founded:** 1826. **Freq:** Weekly (Wed.). **Print Method:** Offset. **Cols./Page:** 6. **Col. Width:** 12 picas. **Col. Depth:** 21 1/2 inches. **Key Personnel:** Liz Holland, Editor; Gary Grossman, Publisher; Jodie Racine, Advertising Mgr. **ISSN:** 8756-6397. **Subscription Rates:** $18.90 individuals; $30 out of area. **Remarks:** Accepts advertising. **Formerly**: Marylander & Herald (1984).
Ad Rates: GLR: $7.28 **Circ:** Paid 3,000
BW: $729 Free 3,000
4C: $1,135
PCI: $6.60

13787 WESM-FM - 91.3
University of Maryland, Eastern Shore
Backbone Rd.
Princess Anne, MD 21853
E-mail: wesm@umes3.umd.edu

Format: Jazz; Blues; Gospel; Big Band/Nostalgia; News. **Networks:** Public Radio International (PRI); National Public Radio (NPR). **Owner:** University of Maryland, Eastern Shore, at above address, (301)651-2200. **Founded:** 1987. **Key Personnel:** Anthony J. Hunt, General Mgr., phone (410)651-7092, ajhunt@mail.umes.edu; Yancy L. Carrigan, Music Dir., phone (410)652-7924, ylcarrigan@mail.umes.edu; Mark Bohnett, Engineer, phone (410)543-9652; Marva Lovett, Program Dir., phone (410)651-7944, mrlovett@mail.umes.edu; Greg L. Handy, Operations Dir., phone (410)651-7903, glhandy@mail.umes.edu; Bruce D. Copeland, Production Dir., phone (410)651-7904, bdcopeland@mail.umes.edu. **Wattage:** 50,000. **Ad Rates:** Noncommercial; underwriting available. **URL:** http://www.wesm.umes.edu.

13788 WOLC-FM - 102.5
Crisfield Ln. Phone: (410)543-9652
PO Box 130 Fax: (410)651-9652
Princess Anne, MD 21853-0130
E-mail: wolc@wolc.org

Format: Religious. **Networks:** Ambassador Inspirational Radio; SkyLight Satellite; Sun Radio. **Owner:** Maranatha, Inc., at above address. **Founded:** 1976. **Operating Hours:** Continuous; 40% network, 60% local. **ADI:** Salisbury, MD. **Key Personnel:** James G. East, General Mgr., jeast@wolc.org; Greg Fentress, Program Dir., gfentres@wolc.org; Mark Bohnett, Chief Engineer, mbohnett@wolc.org; Joe Lachuiti, Sales/Development Mgr. **Local Programs:** *Contact Delmarva*, Jim East; *Joy in the Morning*, Greg Fentress; *Joy Ride*, Bill White. **Wattage:** 50,000. **Ad Rates:** $12-15 for 30 seconds; $17-20 for 60 seconds. **URL:** http://www.wolc.org.

RANDALLSTOWN

13789 Kite Lines
Aeolus Press, Inc.
PO Box 466 Phone: (410)922-1212
Randallstown, MD 21133-0466 Fax: (410)922-4262
Publication E-mail: Kitelines@compuserve.com
Publisher E-mail: kitelines@compuserve.com

Publication containing news and reviews, plans, techniques, profiles, and articles for adult kite enthusiasts. **Subtitle:** The International Kite Journal. **Founded:** 1977. **Freq:** Quarterly. **Print Method:** Web. **Trim Size:** 8 3/8 x 10 7/ 8. **Cols./Page:** 3. **Col. Width:** 14 picas. **Col. Depth:** 60 picas. **Key Personnel:** Valerie Govig, Editor and Publisher; Steve McKerrow, Asst. Ed.; Leonard M. Conover, Assoc. Editor. **ISSN:** 0192-3439. **Subscription Rates:** $16 individuals; $22 other countries; $4.50 single issue. **Remarks:** Accepts advertising. **Alt. Formats:** Microform.
Ad Rates: BW: $914 **Circ:** ‡13,000
4C: $1,775

ROCKVILLE†, pop. 43,811.

Montgomery Co. (WC). 17 m N of Washington, D.C. Residential & commercial. Research and development center.

13790 Asha
American Speech-Language-Hearing Association
10801 Rockville Pike Phone: (301)897-5700
Rockville, MD 20852 Fax: (301)571-0457

Magazine on hearing, language, and speech. **Founded:** Sept. 1959. **Freq:** Quarterly (June/July combined). **Print Method:** Offset. **Trim Size:** 8 1/8 x 10 7/8. **Cols./Page:** 3 and 4. **Col. Width:** 13 1/2 inches and 10 picas. **Col. Depth:** 57 1/2 and 57 1/2 picas. **Key Personnel:** Joanne Jessen, Ph.D., Managing Editor; Pamela J. Leppin, Advertising Mgr. **ISSN:** 0001-2475. **Subscription Rates:** $60 individuals; $90 other countries; $90 institutions; $110 institutions, other countries; $9 single issue. **Remarks:** Accepts advertising. **URL:** http://www.asha.org/asha/.
Ad Rates: BW: $1,705 **Circ:** ‡94,000
4C: $3,250

13791 Automotive Services Retailer
Graphics Concepts
1801 Rockville Pike, Ste. 330 Phone: (301)984-4000
Rockville, MD 20852 Fax: (301)984-7340

Trade magazine for professionals in the quick lube industry. **Founded:** Jan. 1987. **Freq:** Bimonthly. **Print Method:** Web offset. **Trim Size:** 8 1/4 x 10 7/8. **Cols./Page:** 3 and 2. **Col. Width:** 13 and 20 picas. **Col. Depth:** 54 3/5 picas. **Key Personnel:** Louise Classon, Editor; David Gerchen, Advertising Mgr. **Remarks:** Accepts advertising. **Formerly**: Convenient Automotive Services Retailer.
Ad Rates: BW: $2,100 **Circ:** Non-paid 16,900
4C: $3,300

13792 BNAC Communicator
BNA Communications, Inc.
9493 Key West Ave. Phone: (301)948-0540
Rockville, MD 20850 Fax: (301)948-2085
Free: (800)233-6067

Tabloid providing news and information to human resource professionals, safety, environment, and EEO compliance officers. **Subtitle:** Topics and Resources for Training. **Founded:** 1980. **Freq:** Quarterly. **Print Method:** Offset. **Trim Size:** 11 1/2 x 15. **Cols./Page:** 4. **Col. Width:** 14 picas. **Col. Depth:** 13 13/16 inches. **Key Personnel:** Tony Cornish, Editor; Theresa McGrail, Circulation Mgr. **ISSN:** 1051-208X. **Subscription Rates:** Controlled. **Remarks:** Advertising not accepted. **Available Online**. **URL:** http://www.bna.com/bnac.
Circ: Controlled ‡150,000

13793 Challenge Magazine
Disabled Sports, USA
451 Hungerford Dr., Ste. 100 Phone: (301)217-0960
Rockville, MD 20850 Fax: (301)217-0968
Publisher E-mail: dsusa@dsusa.org

Magazine providing information on sports for people with physical disabilities. **Freq:** Quarterly. **Key Personnel:** Karen Rountree, Contact. **Subscription Rates:** Included in membership. **Remarks:** Accepts advertising. **Formed by the merger of**: Handicapped Sport Report.
Circ: Paid 30,000

13794 Clinical Psychiatry News
International Medical News Group
12230 Wilkins Ave. Phone: (301)816-8700
Rockville, MD 20852 Fax: (301)816-8738
Publication E-mail: cpnews@imng.com

Medical and psychiatry tabloid. **Founded:** 1973. **Freq:** Monthly. **Print Method:** Offset. **Trim Size:** 11 1/4 x 14 3/8. **Cols./Page:** 4. **Col. Width:** 14 picas. **Col. Depth:** 13 1/4 inches. **Key Personnel:** Johanna H. Weekley, Editor-in-Chief; Gary Gyss, Publisher. **ISSN:** 0270-6644. **Subscription Rates:** $60. **Remarks:** Accepts advertising.
Ad Rates: BW: $4065 **Circ:** Controlled 32,946
4C: $5475

13795 Family Practice News
International Medical News Group
12230 Wilkins Ave. Phone: (301)816-8700
Rockville, MD 20852 Fax: (301)816-8738
Publication E-mail: fpnews@imng.com

Family physician medical tabloid. **Founded:** 1971. **Freq:** 2/mo. **Print Method:** Offset. **Trim Size:** 11 1/4 x 14 3/8. **Cols./Page:** 4. **Col. Width:** 14 picas. **Col. Depth:** 13 1/4 inches. **Key Personnel:** Johanna H. Weekley, Editor-in-Chief; George J. Lister, Publisher. **ISSN:** 0300-7073. **Subscription Rates:** $96. **Remarks:** Accepts advertising.
Ad Rates: BW: $7735 **Circ:** Controlled 72,625
4C: $9565

13796 411
United Communications Group
11300 Rockville Pike, Ste. 1100 Phone: (301)287-2700
Rockville, MD 20852-3030 Fax: (301)287-2049
Free: (800)929-4824
Publication E-mail: mccormick@ucg.com
Publisher E-mail: customer@ucg.com

Publication offering strategies for improving telecommunications systems efficiency. **Subtitle:** The Telecom Manager's Money-Saving Guide to Services, Technologies and Equipment. **Founded:** 1979. **Freq:** Semimonthly. **Trim Size:** 8 1/2 x 11. **Key Personnel:** Betty Lehnus, Editor. **Subscription Rates:** $339. **Remarks:** Advertising not accepted. **Formerly**: Telephone Angles.
Circ: (Not Reported)

13797 German Life
Zeitgeist Publishing, Inc.
226 North Adams St. Phone: (301)294-9081
Rockville, MD 20850 Fax: (301)294-7821
Free: (800)875-2997
Publication E-mail: info@germanlife.com

Magazine on German-speaking culture, past and present, and on German-American topics. **Founded:** July 1994. **Freq:** Bimonthly. **Trim Size:** 8 1/8 x 10 7/8. **Cols./Page:** 3. **Col. Width:** 2 1/8 inches. **Col. Depth:** 9 3/4 inches. **Key Personnel:** Lisa A. Fitzpatrick, Publisher, lfitzpatrick@germanlife.com; Heidi L. Whitesell, Editor, hwhitesell@germanlife.com; Karen F. Brewer, Advertising Mgr., phone (301)746-6246, fax (301)746-6469, kbrewer@germanlife.com. **ISSN:** 1075-2382. **Subscription Rates:** $19.95 individuals; $24.65 out of country; $15.95 students; $4.95 single issue. **Remarks:** Accepts advertising. **URL:** http://www.germanlife.com.
Ad Rates: BW: $2,940 **Circ:** Paid 25,000
4C: $3,675 Controlled 20,000

13798 Hazard Technology
EIS International
1401 Rockville Pike, Ste. 500 Phone: (301)738-6900
Rockville, MD 20852 Fax: (301)738-1026
Free: (800)999-5009
Publisher E-mail: inof@eisint.com

Tabloid environmental and emergency management. **Founded:** 1980. **Freq:** 2/year. **Print Method:** Offset. Uses mats. **Trim Size:** 11 x 15. **Cols./Page:** 4. **Col. Width:** 36 nonpareils. **Col. Depth:** 96 agate lines. **Key Personnel:** Leslie Atkin, Editor. **ISSN:** 0742-6410. **Subscription Rates:** Free. **Remarks:** Accepts advertising. **URL:** http://www.eisintl.com. **Formerly**: Hazard Monthly.
Ad Rates: BW: $500 **Circ:** ‡55,000

13799 IEEE Circuits and Devices
The Institute of Electrical & Electronics Engineers, Inc.
FDA/CDRH, HFZ-134 Phone: (301)827-4688
12725 Twinbrook Pkwy. Fax: (301)827-4677
Rockville, MD 20857
Publisher E-mail: customer.service@ieee.org

Publication featuring information on electro-optics, PC components and programs for engineers, and application oriented articles. **Founded:** 1985. **Freq:** Bimonthly. **Key Personnel:** Ronald Waynant, Editor, r.waynant@ieee.org; John Lowell, Editor, j.lowell@ieee.org; Brian Benbrook, Managing Editor, b.benbrook@ieee.org. **ISSN:** 8755-3996. **Subscription Rates:** $21; $14 students single issue; $10 IEEE Student-Market; $120 nonmembers. **Remarks:** Advertising accepted; rates available upon request. **URL:** http://www.erols.com/circuits.
Circ: Paid 7,500

13800 Interchange (Rockville)
Transportation Communications International Union
3 Research Pl. Phone: (301)948-4910
Rockville, MD 20850 Fax: (301)330-7661

Trade magazine for transportation union members. **Founded:** 1899. **Freq:** Bimonthly. **Print Method:** Offset. **Key Personnel:** R. A. Scardelletti, Editor; L.E. Bosher, Managing Editor; D. S. Curry, Executive Dir. **ISSN:** 0885-5889. **Subscription Rates:** $10 individuals. **Remarks:** Advertising not accepted. **Former name:** Railway Clerk/Interchange.
Circ: Controlled 95,000

13801 Internal Medicine News
International Medical News Group
12230 Wilkins Ave. Phone: (301)816-8700
Rockville, MD 20852
Publication covering clinical developments for practicing internists. **Freq:** Semimonthly. **Key Personnel:** Mary Jo Dales, Editor. **Subscription Rates:** $96 individuals; $6 single issue. **Remarks:** Accepts advertising.
Ad Rates: BW: $5,805 **Circ:** Paid 101,608
4C: $7,565

13802 Language, Speech, and Hearing Services in Schools
American Speech-Language-Hearing Association
10801 Rockville Pike Phone: (301)897-5700
Rockville, MD 20852 Fax: (301)571-0457

Journal pertaining to speech, hearing, and language services for children, particularly in schools. **Founded:** Jan. 1970. **Freq:** Quarterly. **Print Method:** Offset. **Trim Size:** 8 1/8 x 10 7/8. **Cols./Page:** 2. **Col. Width:** 20 picas. **Col. Depth:** 55 picas. **Key Personnel:** Elaine Silliman, Ph.D., Editor, phone (813)974-9812, fax (813)974-8421, silliman@luna.cas.usf.edu; Pam Leppin, Advertising Mgr., phone (301)897-0121, fax (301)897-7348, pleppin@asha.org. **ISSN:** 0161-1461. **Subscription Rates:** $35 individuals; $45 individuals other countries; $85 institutions; $95 institutions, other countries other countries. **Remarks:** Accepts advertising. **URL:** http://www.asha.org/asha/.
Ad Rates: BW: $1,475 **Circ:** ‡55,000
4C: $3,000

13803 Montgomery County Sentinel
Montgomery County Sentinel Newspapers
PO Box 1272 Phone: (301)948-4630
Rockville, MD 20849-1272 Fax: (301)417-1210

Community tabloid newspaper. **Founded:** 1855. **Freq:** Weekly (Thurs.). **Print Method:** Offset. **Trim Size:** 14 1/2 x 10 1/2. **Cols./Page:** 4. **Col. Width:** 14.3 picas. **Col. Depth:** 14 inches. **Key Personnel:** Kenneth McIntyre, Editor; Bernard Kapiloff, Publisher; Rick Levine, Advertising Mgr. **Subscription Rates:** Free; $15 by mail; $29 out of state. **Remarks:** Accepts advertising.
Ad Rates: GLR: $.83 **Circ:** Paid 8,076
BW: $684 Free 1,245
4C: $1,284
SAU: $12

13804 The Montgomery Journal
The Montgomery Journal Newspaper
1 Research Ct. Phone: (301)670-1400
Rockville, MD 20850-3285 Fax: (301)670-1421

General newspaper. **Founded:** 1973. **Freq:** Daily (morn.). **Print Method:** Offset. **Cols./Page:** 6. **Col. Width:** 26 nonpareils. **Col. Depth:** 301 agate lines. **Key Personnel:** Mark Tapscott, Editor; Karl Spain, Publisher; Diane Macioce, Assoc. Publisher; Joe Gatto, Advertising Mgr., phone (301)670-1490, fax (301)670-7971. **Subscription Rates:** $65 individuals. **Remarks:** Accepts advertising. **URL:** http://www.jrnl.com.
Ad Rates: GLR: $2.36 **Circ:** Mon.-Fri. ★**30,659**
BW: $3,741
4C: $4,316
PCI: $29

13805 Mutual Funds Update
Wiesenberger
1455 Research Blvd. Phone: (301)545-4000
Rockville, MD 20851 Fax: (301)545-6400
Free: (800)232-2285
Publisher E-mail: wies@cda.com

Professional journal covering mutual funds financial information. **Founded:** 1990. **Freq:** Monthly. **Trim Size:** 8 1/2 x 11. **Key Personnel:** Daniel L. Phelps, Editor; Dawn Kahler, Managing Editor, phone (301)545-4415, dawn.kahler@cda.com. **Subscription Rates:** $295 individuals. **Remarks:** Advertising not accepted.
Circ: Combined 2,500

13806 New Homes Register
Bartow Communications
12156 Parklawn Dr. Phone: (301)468-7001
Rockville, MD 20852 Fax: (301)468-7005

Publication containing new home real estate information. **Founded:** Mar. 1993. **Freq:** 23/year. **Print Method:** Offset. **Trim Size:** 8 x 10 3/4. **Cols./Page:** 1. **Col. Width:** 7 inches. **Key Personnel:** Randy Bartow, Editor. **Subscription Rates:** $25 individuals. **Remarks:** Accepts advertising.
Ad Rates: BW: $425 **Circ:** Non-paid 17,000
4C: $475

13807 Ob Gyn News
International Medical News Group
12230 Wilkins Ave. Phone: (301)816-8700
Rockville, MD 20852
Publication E-mail: obnews@imng.com

Obstetrics and gynecology tabloid distributed to obstetricians a nd gynecologists. **Subtitle:** Tabloid covering obstetrics and gynecology distributed to ob/gyns. **Founded:** 1966. **Freq:** Semimonthly. **Print Method:** Offset. **Trim Size:** 11 1/4 x 14 3/8. **Cols./Page:** 4. **Col. Width:** 14 picas. **Col. Depth:** 13 1/4 inches. **Key Personnel:** Johanna H. Weekley, Editor; Gary Gyss, Publisher.
Ad Rates: BW: $4,185 **Circ:** Controlled 32,131
4C: $6,020

13808 Optometric Education
Association of Schools & Colleges of Optometry
6110 Exec. Blvd., No. 510 Phone: (301)231-5944
Rockville, MD 20852 Fax: (301)770-1828

Optometric journal. **Founded:** 1975. **Freq:** Quarterly. **Print Method:** Offset. **Trim Size:** 8 1/2 x 11. **Cols./Page:** 3. **Col. Width:** 29 nonpareils. **Col. Depth:** 136 agate lines. **Key Personnel:** Felix M. Barker O.D., M.S.; Patricia C. O'Rourke, Advertising Mgr. **ISSN:** 0098-6917. **Subscription Rates:** $20 individuals; $30 other countries. **Formerly**: Journal of Optometric Education.
Ad Rates: BW: $570 **Circ:** ‡2,800
4C: $1,170

13809 Pediatric News
International Medical News Group
12230 Wilkins Ave. Phone: (301)816-8700
Rockville, MD 20852-1834 Fax: (301)816-8738
Publication E-mail: pdnews@imng.com

Tabloid covering pediatric medicine and distributed to pediatricians. **Founded:** 1967. **Freq:** Monthly. **Print Method:** Offset. **Trim Size:** 11 1/4 x 14 3/8. **Cols./Page:** 4. **Col. Width:** 14 picas. **Col. Depth:** 13 1/4 inches. **Key Personnel:** Johanna H. Weekley, Editor; Gary Gyss, Publisher. **Subscription Rates:** $60. **Remarks:** Accepts advertising.
Ad Rates: BW: $3190 **Circ:** Controlled 37,058
4C: $4730

13810 Pharmacopeial Forum
U.S. Pharmacopeial Convention Inc.
12601 Twinbrook Pkwy. Phone: (301)881-0666
Rockville, MD 20852 Fax: (301)816-8236
Free: (800)822-8772

Journal on drug standards. **Founded:** 1975. **Freq:** Bimonthly. **Print Method:** Offset. **Trim Size:** 8 1/2 x 11. **Cols./Page:** 2 and 1. **Col. Width:** 38 and 76 nonpareils. **Col. Depth:** 136 agate lines. **Key Personnel:** Keith A. Seabaugh, Editor, phone (301)998-6820, fax (301)816-8373, kas@usp.org. **ISSN:** 0363-4655. **Subscription Rates:** $340 individuals. **Remarks:** Advertising not accepted.
Circ: Paid ‡2,000
Non-paid ‡200

13811 The Plant Cell
American Society of Plant Physiologists
15501 Monona Dr. Phone: (301)251-0560
Rockville, MD 20855-2768 Fax: (301)279-2996
Publisher E-mail: aspp@aspp.org

Academic research journal reporting major advances in plant cellular and molecular biology. **Founded:** 1989. **Freq:** Monthly. **Print Method:** Sheet-fed, letterpress. **Trim Size:** 10 1/2 x 8 1/2. **Cols./Page:** 2. **Col. Width:** 19 picas. **Col. Depth:** 51 picas. **Key Personnel:** Judith E. Grollman, Managing Editor, phone (301)251-0560, fax (301)279-2996, grollman@aspp.org; Brian A. Larkins, Editor, phone (602)621-9958, fax (602)621-3692. **ISSN:** 1040-4651. **Subscription Rates:** $1,225 institutions; $75 single issue; $110 members; $80 students. **Remarks:** Advertising accepted; rates available upon request. **Available Online. URL:** http://www.aspp.org.
Circ: ‡5,000

13812 Plant Physiology
American Society of Plant Physiologists
15501 Monona Dr. Phone: (301)251-0560
Rockville, MD 20855-2768 Fax: (301)279-2996
Publisher E-mail: aspp@aspp.org

Journal on botanical sciences. **Founded:** 1924. **Freq:** Monthly. **Print Method:** Offset. **Trim Size:** 8 1/8 x 10 7/8. **Cols./Page:** 2. **Col. Width:** 3 5/16 inches. **Col. Depth:** 9 inches. **Key Personnel:** Maarten Chrispeels, Editor-in-Chief, phone (619)534-2571, fax (619)534-4052, mchrispeels@ucsd.edu; Deborah Weiner, Managing Editor, fax (301)309-9196, dweiner@aspp.org. **ISSN:** 0032-0889. **Subscription Rates:** $1300 institutions bundled with The Plant Cell. **Remarks:** Color advertising accepted; rates available upon request. **URL:** http://www.plantphysiol.org/.
Ad Rates: BW: $600 **Circ:** ‡5,000

13813 Prevention Pipeline
National Clearinghouse for Alcohol and Drug Information
PO Box 2345 Phone: (301)294-3319
Rockville, MD 20847-2345 Fax: (301)468-6433

Trade magazine covering alcohol and drug abuse prevention information. **Freq:** Bimonthly. **Key Personnel:** Barbara Ryan, Editor; Craig Steinburg, Managing Editor, phone (301)468-2600, csteinburg@health.org; Juanita Hardy, Circulation Mgr. **Subscription Rates:** $28 individuals; $32 out of country. **Remarks:** Advertising not accepted. **URL:** httpl://www.health.org.
Circ: (Not Reported)

13814 Schizophrenia Bulletin
U.S. Government Printing Office
Room 17C-20 Phone: (301)443-9772
Public Health Services Fax: (301)443-6000
Dept. of Health and Human Services
National Insitute of Health
Rockville, MD 20857
Report providing information and abstracts of recent literature on schizophrenia. **Founded:** 1969. **Freq:** Quarterly. **Print Method:** Letterpress. **Cols./Page:** 2. **Col. Width:** 26 1/2 nonpareils. **Col. Depth:** 105 agate lines. **Key Personnel:** David Shore, Managing Editor, phone (301)443-3683. **ISSN:** 0586-7614. **Subscription Rates:** $20 U.S.; $25 other countries. **Remarks:** Advertising not accepted. **Alt. Formats:** Microform.
Circ: ‡4,800

13815 Skin & Allergy News
International Medical News Group
12230 Wilkins Ave. Phone: (301)816-8700
Rockville, MD 20852 Fax: (301)816-8738
Publication E-mail: sknews@imng.com

Dermatology/allergy tabloid. **Founded:** 1970. **Freq:** Monthly. **Print Method:** Offset. **Trim Size:** 11 1/4 x 14 3/8. **Cols./Page:** 4. **Col. Width:** 14 picas. **Col. Depth:** 13 1/4 inches. **Key Personnel:** Johanna H. Weekley, Editor-in-Chief; Gary Gyss, Publisher. **Subscription Rates:** $70. **Remarks:** Accepts advertising.
Ad Rates: BW: $1705 **Circ:** Controlled 18,782
4C: $2875

13816 Strange Magazine
Box 2246 Phone: (301)460-4789
Rockville, MD 20847 Fax: (301)460-1959
Publisher E-mail: strange1@strangemag.com

Consumer magazine covering strange phenomena. **Founded:** Oct. 1987. **Freq:** Semiannual. **Print Method:** Web offset. **Trim Size:** 8 3/16 x 10 11/16. **Key Personnel:** Mark Chorvinsky, Editor. **ISSN:** 0894-8968. **Subscription Rates:** $21.95 individuals; $7.95 single issue. **Remarks:** Accepts advertising. **URL:** http://www.strangemag.com.
Circ: Combined 15,500

13817 Telling It Like It Is
Transportation Communications International Union
3 Research Pl. Phone: (301)948-4910
Rockville, MD 20850 Fax: (301)330-7661

Trade magazine for transportation union members. **Founded:** 1991. **Freq:** Bimonthly. **Print Method:** Offset. **Key Personnel:** R. A. Scardelletti, Editor; D. S. Curry, Exec. Dir., Publications. **Remarks:** Advertising not accepted. **Former name**: Leadership Action Lines.
Circ: (Not Reported)

13818 Washington Jewish Week
12300 Twinbrook Pkwy., Ste. 250 Phone: (301)230-2222
Fax: (301)881-6362
Rockville, MD 20852
Publication E-mail: 7138201@mcimail.com

Jewish interests Newspaper. **Founded:** 1930. **Freq:** Weekly (Thurs.). **Print Method:** Offset. **Cols./Page:** 5. **Col. Width:** 27 nonpareils. **Col. Depth:** 200 agate lines. **Key Personnel:** Jonathan Kapiloff, Publisher; Dr. Diana Davis, General Mgr.; Eric Rozenman, Managing Editor. **Subscription Rates:** $26 local; $28 out of state. **Remarks:** Accepts advertising.
Ad Rates: BW: $1,250 **Circ:** ‡20,000
4C: $1,750
PCI: $19.50

13819 The Winning Edge
Transportation Communications International Union
3 Research Pl. Phone: (301)948-4910
Rockville, MD 20850 Fax: (301)330-7661

Trade magazine covering the transportation industry for union members. **Founded:** 1992. **Freq:** Quarterly. **Key Personnel:** R. A. Scardelletti, Editor; D. S. Curry, Exec. Dir. of Publications. **ISSN:** 1070-2415. **Subscription Rates:** Free to qualified subscribers. **Remarks:** Advertising not accepted.
Circ: (Not Reported)

Cable TV of Montgomery - See Montgomery

13820 WARW-FM - 94.7
5912 Hubbard Dr. Phone: (301)984-6000
Rockville, MD 20852 Fax: (301)468-2490

Format: Adult Contemporary. **Networks:** CBS. **Founded:** 1946. **Formerly**: WJMD-FM (1983); WLTT-FM (1994). **Operating Hours:** Continuous. **Key Personnel:** Sarah W. Taylor, General Mgr.; Craig Astwood, Program Dir.; Joanne Tombrakos, General Sales Mgr. **Wattage:** 50,000 ERP.

13821 WBIG-FM - 100.3
11300 Rockville Pike, Ste. 905 Phone: (301)468-1800
Rockville, MD 20852 Fax: (301)770-0236
Free: (800)493-0236
E-mail: oldie@mindspring.com

Format: Oldies. **Owner:** Chancellor Media Licensee Co., at above address. **Founded:** 1993. **Operating Hours:** Continuous. **ADI:** Washington, DC. **Key Personnel:** Catherine Melay, General Mgr./VP, cmelay@oldies100.com; Lesley Bowers, General Sales Mgr.; Steve Allan, Program Dir., sallan1@juno.com; Brandan Hurly, Marketing. **Wattage:** 36,000. **URL:** http://www.oldies100.com.

13822 WGAY-FM - 99.5
1801 Rockville Pike, 6th Fl. Phone: (301)468-9429
Rockville, MD 20852

Founded: 1960. **Operating Hours:** Continuous. **Key Personnel:** Darren Davis, Program Dir., phone (301)255-4302, fax (301)255-4332, softrocker@aol.com. **Wattage:** 21,000. **Ad Rates:** Advertising accepted; rates available upon request.

13823 WTEM-AM - 980
11300 Rockville Pike, Ste. 707 Phone: (301)231-7798
Rockville, MD 20852-3089 Fax: (301)881-8030
E-mail: phohmann@aerols.com

Format: Sports; Talk. **Founded:** 1946. **Formerly:** WGMS-AM (1992). **Operating Hours:** Continuous. **Key Personnel:** Bennett Zier, VP/Gen.Mgr., phone (301)230-3548, fax (301)770-6036, bluezebra@aol.com; Jim Weiskopf, General Sales Mgr., phone (301)230-3535, fax (301)770-1570, weistop@aol.com; Tod Castleberry, Operations Mgr., phone (301)230-3537, fax (301)881-8030, tcastle@erols.com; David Talley, Dir. of Finance, phone (301)225-4364, fax (301)468-3509; Ben Milton, Chief Engineer, phone (301)468-3509, fax (301)881-0830. **Wattage:** 50,000 day; 5,000 night.

13824 WTOP-FM - 94.3
Radio Center Phone: (301)424-9292
12216 Parklawn Dr., Ste. 203 Fax: (301)424-8266
Rockville, MD 20852

Format: Oldies. **Owner:** Radio Broadcast Communications, Inc., at above address. **Founded:** 1947. **Operating Hours:** Continuous. **Key Personnel:** Bill Parris, General Mgr. **Wattage:** 3000. **Ad Rates:** Advertising accepted; rates available upon request.

SALISBURY

13825 The Daily Times
115 E. Carroll St. Phone: (410)749-7171
Salisbury, MD 21802 Fax: (410)543-8736
Publication E-mail: newsroom@shore.intercom.net
Publisher E-mail: times@shore-source.com

General newspaper. **Founded:** 1923. **Freq:** Mon.-Sun. (morn.). **Print Method:** Offset. **Cols./Page:** 6. **Col. Width:** 24 nonpareils. **Col. Depth:** 301 agate lines. **Key Personnel:** Gary Grossman, Publisher, phone (410)341-6537; Peter Lynch, Advertising Mgr., phone (410)341-6532; Peter Mio, Advertising Dir., phone (410)341-6539; Cly de Pinson, Advertising Dir. **Subscription Rates:** $34.13 individuals; $44.36 by mail. **Remarks:** Accepts advertising. **URL:** http://www.shore-source.com. **Formerly:** The Daily News.
Ad Rates: BW: $2,189.13 **Circ:** Mon.-Sat. 27,263
4C: $2,738.13 Sun. 30,894
SAU: $14.23
PCI: $16.97

13826 The Flyer
Salisbury State University
Box 3183 Phone: (410)543-6191
Salisbury, MD 21801-6860 Fax: (410)548-2800
Publication E-mail: flyer@ssu.edu

Collegiate newspaper. **Founded:** 1949. **Freq:** Weekly. **Print Method:** Offset. **Cols./Page:** 4. **Col. Depth:** 13 inches. **Key Personnel:** Jen Abbatiello, Editor, jxa9882@students.ssu.edu. **Subscription Rates:** $10 semester. **Remarks:** Accepts advertising.
Ad Rates: BW: $200 **Circ:** Free ‡2,500

13827 Literature Film Quarterly
Salisbury State University
Salisbury, MD 21801 Phone: (410)543-6446
Fax: (410)543-6068
Publication E-mail: litfilmquart@ssu.edu

Magazine covering film adaptations of literature. **Founded:** 1973. **Freq:** Quarterly. **Print Method:** Offset. **Trim Size:** 6 x 9. **Cols./Page:** 1. **Col. Width:** 52 nonpareils. **Col. Depth:** 105 agate lines. **Key Personnel:** James M. Welsh, Editor, jxwelsh@ssu.edu; Anne R. Welsh, Business Mgr., phone (410)334-3495, arwelsh@ssu.edu; Thomas L. Erskine, Associate Editor, phone (410)543-6371, tlerskine@ssu.edu. **ISSN:** 0090-4260. **Subscription Rates:** $20 individuals; $40 institutions; $42 out of country; $48 by mail airmail overseas. **URL:** http://www.ssu.edu. **Alt. Formats:** Microform.
Ad Rates: GLR: $125 **Circ:** ‡800
BW: $90
4C: $50

13828 Salisbury News & Advertiser
Independent Newspapers, Inc.
307 E. Market St. Phone: (410)749-0272
Salisbury, MD 21801 Fax: (410)749-5073
Publication E-mail: snapaper@aol.com

Local newspaper. **Founded:** 1867. **Freq:** Weekly (Wed.). **Print Method:** Offset. **Trim Size:** 13.5 x 22.8. **Cols./Page:** 6. **Col. Width:** 12 picas. **Col. Depth:** 21.5 inches. **Key Personnel:** Anthony W. Bertino, Jr., Publisher, awbjr@aol.com. **Subscription Rates:** $15 individuals; Free.
Ad Rates: GLR: $4.50 **Circ:** Free 13,660
BW: $1,973.70
4C: $2,173.70
PCI: $15.30

13829 WBOC-TV - 16
WBOC Box 2057 Phone: (410)749-1111
Salisbury, MD 21802 Fax: (410)749-2361

Format: Commercial TV. **Networks:** CBS. **Owner:** Thomas Draper, at above address. **Operating Hours:** 6 a.m.-2 a.m. **ADI:** Salisbury, MD. **Key Personnel:** Bill Kenton, General Mgr.; Charlie Timmons, Sales Mgr.; Marilyn Buerkle, News Dir. **Ad Rates:** $35-575 per unit.

13830 WCPB-TV - 28
c/o Maryland Public Phone: (410)356-5600
Broadcasting Commission Fax: (410)581-4338
11767 Owings Mills Blvd.
Owings Mills, MD 21117
Free: (800)223-3678
E-mail: comments@mpt.org

Format: Public TV. **Simulcasts:** WMPB, WMPT, WWPB, WGPT, WFPT. **Networks:** Public Broadcasting Service (PBS); Eastern Educational Television. **Owner:** Maryland Public Broadcasting Commission, at above address. **Operating Hours:** 3 a.m.-1:30 a.m., Mon.-Sun. **ADI:** Salisbury, MD. **Key Personnel:** Robert J. Shuman, Pres./CEO; Dr. Archie L. Buffkins, Sr. Vice Pres., Broadcasting; Janice Wilson, Sr. Vice Pres., Marketing & Development; Larry D. Unger, Sr. Vice Pres., Administration & Finance; Martin Jacobs, Vice Pres., Finance & Accounting; Gladys M. Kaplan, Vice Pres., Human Resources; Ann Engelman, Vice Pres., Programming/Broadcast Serv.; Everett L. Marshburn, Vice Pres., Broadcast Production; John T. Potthast, Vice Pres., National Productions; Barry P. Freidly, Vice Pres., Membership; Hannah Lee Byron, Dir., Corp. Comm. & Gov't Affairs; Carol Wonsavage, Dir., Regional Communications; Sharon Philippart, Dir., National Communications. **Wattage:** 2,300,000. **URL:** http://www.mpt.org.

13831 WDIH-FM - 90.3
PO Box 186 Phone: (410)546-7772
Salisbury, MD 21801

Format: Adult Contemporary. **Founded:** 1990. **ADI:** Hagerstown, MD. **Key Personnel:** George Copeland, General Mgr. **Wattage:** 378.

13832 WICO-AM - 1320
Box 909 Phone: (410)742-3212
Salisbury, MD 21803 Fax: (410)548-1543
E-mail: wico@radiocenter.com

Format: Talk; News; Sports. **Networks:** EFM; Daynet; ABC; CNN Radio. **Founded:** 1957. **Operating Hours:** Continuous. **ADI:** Salisbury, MD. **Key Personnel:** Michael Reath, General Mgr., dbcone@dmv.com. **Wattage:** 1000. **Ad Rates:** Combined advertising rates available with WICO-FM.

13833 WICO-FM - 94.3
Box 909 Phone: (410)742-3212
Salisbury, MD 21803 Fax: (410)548-1543
E-mail: catcountry@radiocenter.com

Format: Contemporary Country. **Simulcasts:** WXJN-FM. **Networks:** Independent. **Founded:** 1969. **Operating Hours:** Continuous. **Key Personnel:** Michael Reath, General Mgr., miker@radiocenter.com. **Wattage:** 3000. **Ad Rates:** Combined advertising rates available with WICO-AM, WQJA-FM.

13834 WJDY-AM - 1470
1633 N. Division St. Phone: (410)742-5191
Salisbury, MD 21801-3805 Fax: (410)749-9079

Format: Urban Contemporary. **Networks:** CBS. **Founded:** 1958. **Operating Hours:** Sunrise-sunset. **ADI:** Hagerstown, MD. **Key Personnel:** J.P. Connor, Jr., General Mgr.; Brad Connor, Sales Mgr. **Wattage:** 5000.

13835 WMDT-TV - 47
202 Downtown Plaza Phone: (410)742-4747
Salisbury, MD 21801 Fax: (410)742-5767
E-mail: wmdt@wmdt.com

Format: Commercial TV. **Networks:** NBC; CNN Radio. **Founded:** 1980. **Operating Hours:** Continuous. **ADI:** Salisbury, MD. **Key Personnel:** Kathleen McLain, General Mgr., kathleen_mclain@wmdt.com; Teri Monahan, General Sales Mgr., teri_monahan@wmdt.com. **Local Programs:** *Dimension 47*; *Showcase of Homes*. **Ad Rates:** Advertising accepted; rates available upon request.

13836 WQHQ-FM - 104.7
Box U Phone: (410)742-1923
Salisbury, MD 21802-1197 Fax: (410)742-2329
Free: (800)762-0105

Format: Adult Contemporary. **Networks:** Independent. **Owner:** H.V.S. Partners of Salisbury, at above address. **Founded:** 1965. **Operating Hours:** Continuous. **ADI:** Hagerstown, MD. **Key Personnel:** Ron J. Gillenardo, General Mgr.; Sandi Alexander, Operations Mgr. **Wattage:** 50,000. **Ad Rates:** Advertising accepted; rates available upon request.

13837 WSBY-FM - 98.9
1633 N. Division St. Phone: (410)742-5191
Salisbury, MD 21801

Format: Oldies. **Founded:** 1958. **ADI:** Hagerstown, MD. **Key Personnel:** Rick Kimball, Program Dir. **Wattage:** 6000.

13838 WSCL-FM - 89.5
Box 2596 Phone: (410)543-6895
Salisbury, MD 21802-2596 Fax: (410)548-3000
E-mail: wscl@ssu.edu

Format: Classical; News. **Networks:** National Public Radio (NPR); AP; Public Radio International (PRI). **Owner:** Salisbury State University Foundation, Inc., at above address. **Founded:** 1987. **Operating Hours:** Continuous; 50% network, 50% local. **ADI:** Salisbury, MD. **Key Personnel:** Fred Marino, General Mgr.; Pam Andrews, Program Dir.; Bruce Blanchard, Chief Engineer; Kevin Meerschaert, News Dir. **Wattage:** 33,000. **Ad Rates:** Noncommercial; underwriting available.

13839 WSDL-FM - 90.7
PO Box 2596 Phone: (410)543-6895
Salisbury, MD 21802

Format: Classical; News. **Networks:** National Public Radio (NPR). **Owner:** Salisbury State University Foundation, Inc., at above address. **Founded:** Feb. 14, 1998. **Operating Hours:** Continuous. **Key Personnel:** Fred Marino, General Mgr., ffmarino@ssu.edu; Pam Andrews, Program Dir., psandrews@ssu.edu; Bruce Blanchard, Chief Engineer, wmbukowski@ssu.edu; M. E. Vest, Program Asst., mevest@ssu.edu. **Ad Rates:** Noncommercial.

13840 WTGM-AM - 960
213-219 W. Main St. Phone: (410)742-1923
Salisbury, MD 21801 Fax: (410)742-2329
Free: (800)242-9589
E-mail: wave@shore.intercom.net

Format: Sports. **Networks:** Westwood One Radio; ESPN Radio. **Owner:** H.V.S. Partners of Salisbury, at above address. **Founded:** 1930. **Formerly:** WBOC-AM (1982); WLVW-AM (1994). **Operating Hours:** Continuous; 20% local, 80% network. **ADI:** Salisbury, MD. **Key Personnel:** Ron J. Gillenardo, General Mgr.; Jim Whittemore, Program Dir.; Don Bailey, General Sales Mgr. **Local Programs:** *High School Football & Basketball Play by Play*, Jim Whittemore, Mailing contact, (410)742-1923, Fax (410)742-2329; *Salisbury State Football & Basketball Play by Play*, Jim Whittemore, Mailing contact, (410)742-1923, Fax (410)742-2329. **Wattage:** 5,000.

13841 WWFG-FM - 99.9
2326 Goddard Pkwy Phone: (410)860-2200
Salisbury, MD 21801 Fax: (410)860-0599

Format: Country. **Networks:** Independent. **Owner:** Benchmark Communications, at above address. **Founded:** 1978. **Formerly:** WKHI-FM. **Operating Hours:** Continuous; 100% local. **ADI:** Hagerstown, MD. **Key Personnel:** Joyce Marshall, General Mgr.; Bill Hoder, General Sales Mgr.; Tracy Townsend, Office Mgr. **Wattage:** 50,000.

SILVER SPRING

13842 Adventist Review
General Conference of Seventh-Day Adventists
12501 Old Columbia Pike Phone: (301)680-6510
Silver Spring, MD 20904 Fax: (301)680-6502

Seventh Day Adventist magazine. **Founded:** 1850. **Freq:** Weekly (Thurs.). **Print Method:** Offset. **Trim Size:** 8 1/8 x 10 3/8. **Cols./Page:** 4. **Col. Width:** 21 nonpareils. **Col. Depth:**

135 agate lines. **Key Personnel:** William Johnsson, Editor; Mark B. Thomas, Advertising Mgr. **ISSN:** 0161-1119. **Subscription Rates:** $38.20 individuals; $.95 single issue. **Remarks:** Accepts advertising.
Ad Rates: BW: $1,032 **Circ:** ‡47,000
4C: $1,432

13843 Chinese American Forum
Chinese American Forum, Inc.
606 Brantford Ave. Phone: (301)622-3053
Silver Spring, MD 20904 Fax: (301)622-3053

Non-profit magazine promoting cultural exchange and open communication for the purpose of education. **Founded:** May 1984. **Freq:** Quarterly. **Trim Size:** 8 1/2 x 11. **Cols./Page:** 2. **Col. Width:** 3 1/2 inches. **Col. Depth:** 9 1/2 inches. **Key Personnel:** S. Yen Lee, Ph.D., Editor and Publisher; T. C. Peng, Ph.D., Vice President. **ISSN:** 0895-4690. **Subscription Rates:** $14 individuals; $20 institutions; $3.50 single issue. **Remarks:** Color advertising not accepted.
Ad Rates: BW: $160 **Circ:** Paid ‡500
Non-paid ‡50

13844 Excalibur
Montgomery College
Takoma Park Campus Phone: (301)650-1490
7600 Takoma Ave. Fax: (301)650-1550
Takoma Park, MD 20912
Collegiate newspaper (tabloid). **Founded:** Sept. 14, 1946. **Freq:** 10/year (during the academic year). **Cols./Page:** 4. **Col. Width:** 28 nonpareils. **Col. Depth:** 196 agate lines.
Ad Rates: BW: $300 **Circ:** Free ‡2,000
PCI: $5 Free 500

13845 Fabricare
International Fabricare Institute
12251 Tech Rd. Phone: (301)622-1900
Silver Spring, MD 20904 Fax: (301)236-9320
Free: (800)638-2627
Publisher E-mail: communications@ifi.org

Trade magazine for the drycleaning industry. **Founded:** 1971. **Freq:** Monthly. **Print Method:** Sheetfed offset. **Trim Size:** 8 x 11. **Cols./Page:** 3. **Col. Width:** 14 picas. **Col. Depth:** 58 picas. **Key Personnel:** David J. Uchic, VP, Communications. **Subscription Rates:** $25 individuals. **Remarks:** Accepts advertising. **Alt. Formats:** CD-ROM.
Ad Rates: BW: $1,725 **Circ:** Paid 8,800
4C: $2,625

13846 Fabricare—International Fabricare Institute
International Fabricare Institute
12251 Tech Rd. Phone: (301)622-1900
Silver Spring, MD 20904 Fax: (301)236-9320
Free: (800)638-2627
Publisher E-mail: communications@ifi.org

Trade magazine for dry cleaners, launderers, and other groups in the industry worldwide. **Freq:** Monthly. **Trim Size:** 8 1/2 x 11. **Cols./Page:** 3. **Key Personnel:** David J. Uchic, Communications VP; Ruby Burns, Editorial Asst. **ISSN:** 0184-6778. **Subscription Rates:** $65 members. **Remarks:** Accepts advertising. **URL:** http://www.ifi.org-or-Communications@ifi.org. **Former name:** Fabricare News.
Circ: (Not Reported)

13847 Government Computer News
Cahners Publishing Company
8601 Georgia Ave., Ste. 300 Phone: (301)650-2000
Silver Spring, MD 20910 Fax: (301)650-2111

Magazine for government technical and management executives responsible for managing and buying information technology products and services. Covers computer/communications news, trends, applications, and products impacting government operations. **Subtitle:** The National Newspaper of Government Computing. **Founded:** 1982. **Freq:** 30/year. **Print Method:** Offset. **Trim Size:** 13 1/2 x 10 3/4. **Cols./Page:** 4. **Col. Width:** 28 nonpareils. **Col. Depth:** 189 agate lines. **Key Personnel:** Thomas R. Temin, Editor; Gary R. Squires, Publisher; Franke Pass, Jr., Production Dir.; Elaine Ross, Business Mgr.; Linda Carpenter, Editorial Asst. **ISSN:** 0738-4300. **Subscription Rates:** $99.90 individuals; $10 single issue. **Remarks:** Accepts advertising. **Online:** Lexus-Nexus. **URL:** http://www.gcn.com. **Alt. Formats:** CD-ROM.
Ad Rates: BW: $8,700 **Circ:** Free 81,289
4C: $10,170

13848 Guild Reporter
The Newspaper Guild, AFL-CIO, CLC
8611 2nd Ave. Phone: (301)585-2990
Silver Spring, MD 20910 Fax: (301)585-0668

Union journal on news industry economics and labor relations. **Founded:** 1933. **Freq:** Monthly. **Print Method:** Offset. **Cols./Page:** 5. **Col. Width:** 23 nonpareils. **Col. Depth:** 210 agate lines. **Key Personnel:** Liz McConnell, Editor. **ISSN:** 0017-5404. **Subscription Rates:** $20 individuals. **Remarks:** Advertising not accepted. **URL:** http://www.newsguild.org; http://www.mvpc.com.
Circ: Paid ‡850
Controlled ‡32,500

13849 Homily Service
Liturgical Conference
8750 Georgia Ave. Phone: (301)495-0885
Ste. 123 Fax: (301)495-5945
Silver Spring, MD 20910-3621
Free: (800)394-0885
Publisher E-mail: litconf@aol.com

Ecumenical religious magazine providing exegetical analysis, psychological insights, and theological reflections on the Sunday lectionary. **Subtitle:** An Ecumenical Resource for Sharing the Word. **Founded:** 1968. **Freq:** Monthly. **Print Method:** Offset. **Trim Size:** 6 x 9. **Cols./Page:** 1. **Col. Width:** 52 nonpareils. **Col. Depth:** 103 agate lines. **Key Personnel:** Virginia Sloyan, Editor. **Subscription Rates:** $60 individuals; $5.50 single issue.
Ad Rates: BW: $400 **Circ:** ‡4,200

13850 INFORM
Association for Information and Image Management
1100 Wayne Ave., Ste. 1100 Phone: (301)587-8202
Silver Spring, MD 20910 Fax: (301)587-2711
Free: (800)477-2246

Magazine for the information management professional, covering applications of micrographic, optical, and computer technology and systems. **Founded:** Jan. 10, 1987. **Freq:** 10/year. **Print Method:** Letterpress. **Trim Size:** 8 3/8 x 10 7/8. **Cols./Page:** 3. **Col. Width:** 30 nonpareils. **Col. Depth:** 131 agate lines. **Key Personnel:** R.V. Head, Editor. **ISSN:** 0892-3876. **Subscription Rates:** $85 individuals. **Remarks:** Accepts advertising. **URL:** http://www.aiim.org.
Ad Rates: BW: $2,340 **Circ:** Non-paid ‡40,000
4C: $3,340

13851 JazzTimes
Jazz Times
8737 Colesville Rd., 5th Fl. Phone: (301)588-4114
Silver Spring, MD 20910-3921 Fax: (301)588-5531
Free: (800)866-7664
Publication E-mail: jtimes@aol.com

Magazine incorporating all genres of jazz music for professionals and fans. **Subtitle:** America's Jazz Magazine. **Founded:** Nov. 9, 1970. **Freq:** 10/year. **Print Method:** Web offset. **Trim Size:** 8 1/2 x 10 3/4. **Cols./Page:** 3. **Col. Width:** 2 1/4 inches. **Col. Depth:** 10 inches. **Key Personnel:** Mike Joyce, Editor; Glenn Sabin, Publisher; Lee Mergner, Assoc. Publisher. **ISSN:** 0272-572X. **Subscription Rates:** $21.95 individuals; $3.95 single issue. **Available Online.** **URL:** http://www.jazzcentralstation.com. **Alt. Formats:** Microform.
Ad Rates: BW: $2,515 **Circ:** Paid ‡80,898
4C: $3,220 Non-paid ‡9,000
PCI: $60

13852 The Journal of Adventist Education
Department of Education, General Conference of Seventh-Day Adventists
12501 Old Columbia Pike Phone: (301)680-5075
Silver Spring, MD 20904-6600 Fax: (301)622-9627

Professional journal for teachers and educational administrators in the Seventh-day Adventist Church. **Founded:** 1939. **Freq:** 5/year (combined June/Sept. issue). **Print Method:** Offset. **Trim Size:** 8 1/8 x 10 3/4. **Cols./Page:** 2 and 3. **Col. Width:** 26 and 36 nonpareils. **Col. Depth:** 128 agate lines. **Key Personnel:** Beverly J. Rumble, Editor; Beverly J. Rumble. **ISSN:** 0021-8480. **Subscription Rates:** $17.25 individuals; $3.50 single issue. **Remarks:** Accepts advertising.
Ad Rates: BW: $795 **Circ:** Paid ‡7,500
4C: $1,500 Non-paid ‡250

13853 Journal of Practical Nursing
National Association for Practical Nurse Education & Service
1400 Spring St., No. 330 Phone: (301)588-2491
Silver Spring, MD 20910-2735 Fax: (301)588-3667
Publisher E-mail: napnes@bellatlantic.net

Journal providing information on licensed practical nursing for LPNs, PN educators, and students. **Subtitle:** The Voice of Practical/Vocational Nursing. **Founded:** 1951. **Freq:** Quarterly. **Print Method:** Offset. **Trim Size:** 8 3/8 x 11. **Cols./Page:** 2 and 3. **Col. Width:** 19 and 13 picas. **Col. Depth:** 59.5 picas. **Key Personnel:** Helen Larsen, Editor, fax (301)588-2839. **ISSN:** 0022-3867. **Subscription Rates:** $20. **Remarks:** Accepts advertising.
Ad Rates: BW: $695 **Circ:** Paid ‡8,000
4C: $1,345

13854 JPEN: Journal of Parenteral and Enteral Nutrition
American Society for Parenteral and Enteral Nutrition
8630 Fenton St., Ste. 412 Phone: (301)587-6315
Silver Spring, MD 20910-3805 Fax: (301)587-3323
Publisher E-mail: aspen@nutr.org

Scientific peer review journal. **Founded:** 1976. **Freq:** Bimonthly. **Print Method:** Web press. **Trim Size:** 8 3/8 x 10 7/8. **Cols./Page:** 2. **Col. Width:** 32 nonpareils. **Col. Depth:** 119 agate lines. **Key Personnel:** John L. Rombeau, Editor; Keith Dillon, Mktg. Director, keithd@aspen.nutr.org. **ISSN:** 0148-6071. **Subscription Rates:** $90 individuals; $145 institutions. **Remarks:** Accepts advertising. **URL:** http://www.clinnutr.org.
Ad Rates: BW: $1,400 **Circ:** Paid ‡9,129
4C: $2,300 Non-paid ‡620

13855 Labor's Heritage
The George Meany Memorial Archives
10000 New Hampshire Ave. Phone: (301)431-5457
Silver Spring, MD 20903 Fax: (301)431-0385

Magazine featuring historical articles and photographs for laypersons. **Founded:** Jan. 1989. **Freq:** Quarterly. **Print Method:** Offset. **Trim Size:** 8 1/2 x 11. **Cols./Page:** 2. **Col. Width:** 3 3/8 inches. **Col. Depth:** 7 3/8 inches. **Key Personnel:** Robert Reynolds, Managing Editor, rreynold@capcon.net; Pat Costello, Customer Service. **ISSN:** 1041-5904. **Subscription Rates:** $19.95. **Remarks:** Advertising not accepted.
Circ: 9,000

13856 Liberty
Review and Herald Publishing Association
12501 Old Columbia Pike Phone: (301)680-6448
Silver Spring, MD 20904-6600
Publisher E-mail: message@rhpa.org

Magazine concerning religious freedom. **Founded:** 1888. **Freq:** Bimonthly. **Print Method:** Offset. **Trim Size:** 8 1/8 x 10 5/8. **Cols./Page:** 3. **Col. Width:** 40 nonpareils. **Col. Depth:** 131 agate lines. **Key Personnel:** Roland R. Hegstad, Editor; Ted N. C. Wilson, Jr., Publisher. **ISSN:** 0024-2055. **Subscription Rates:** $6.25 individuals. **Remarks:** Advertising not accepted.
Circ: (Not Reported)

13857 Liturgy
Liturgical Conference
8750 Georgia Ave., Ste. 123 Phone: (301)495-0885
Silver Spring, MD 20910-3621 Fax: (301)495-5945
Free: (800)394-0885
Publisher E-mail: litconf@aol.com

Journal with religious and ecumenical themes. **Founded:** 1956. **Freq:** Quarterly. **Print Method:** Offset. Uses mats. **Trim Size:** 7 x 10. **Cols./Page:** 1. **Col. Width:** 5 inches. **Col. Depth:** 8 inches. **Key Personnel:** David Philippart, Editor, phone (773)486-8970, dphilipp@ltp.org. **ISSN:** 0458-063X. **Subscription Rates:** $45.00 individuals; $10.95 single issue. **Remarks:** Advertising not accepted.
Circ: 2,300

13858 Manager's Source Guide
The Adler Group, Inc.
8601 Georgia Ave., 7th Fl. Phone: (301)588-0681
Silver Spring, MD 20910 Fax: (301)588-0924
Publication E-mail: adlerinfo@prodigy.net

Magazine for managers and property owners of offices, apartments, and retail and industrial parks. **Subtitle:** Serving the Decision Makers of Income Producing Properties. **Founded:** 1984. **Freq:** Annual. **Trim Size:** 11 x 15. **Cols./Page:** 5. **Col. Width:** 2 inches. **Col. Depth:** 13 inches. **Key Personnel:** Bridget Russell, Publisher, bridgetagi@aol.com; Karen Kemble, Adv. Coord., klkemble@aol.com. **Subscription Rates:** $109. **Remarks:** Accepts advertising. **Formerly:** Property Management Monthly.
Ad Rates: BW: $1,650 **Circ:** 10,000
4C: $2,290

13859 Mental Health Report
Business Publishers, Inc.
8737 Colesville Rd., Ste. 1100 Phone: (301)589-5103
Silver Spring, MD 20910 Fax: (301)587-4530
Free: (800)274-6737
Publisher E-mail: bpinews@bpinews.com

Magazine reporting on legislation affecting the mentally ill and their families. **Freq:** 26/year. **Subscription Rates:** $325 individuals. **Remarks:** Advertising not accepted.
Circ: (Not Reported)

13860 Ministry
General Conference of Seventh-Day Adventists
12501 Old Columbia Pike Phone: (301)680-6510
Silver Spring, MD 20904 Fax: (301)680-6502
Publication E-mail: 74532.2425@compuserve.com

International journal for clergy. **Subtitle:** International Journal for Clergy. **Founded:** 1928. **Freq:** Monthly. **Print Method:** Offset. **Trim Size:** 8 x 11. **Cols./Page:** 3. **Col. Width:** 27 nonpareils. **Col. Depth:** 138 agate lines. **Key Personnel:** Willmore D. Eva, Editor, phone (301)680-6506; Jeannette Calbi, Subscription & Circultation, phone (301)680-6503; Julia Norcott, Asst. Editor. **ISSN:** 0026-5314. **Subscription Rates:** $29.95 individuals. **Remarks:** Advertising accepted; rates available upon request.
Circ: Paid ‡20,000
Controlled ‡50,000

13861 The NAD Broadcaster
National Association of the Deaf
814 Thayer Ave. Phone: (301)587-1788
Silver Spring, MD 20910-4500 Fax: (301)587-1791

Newspaper for deaf and hard of hearing people, and their parents and educators. **Founded:** 1978. **Freq:** Monthly. **Print Method:** Web. **Trim Size:** 11 x 17. **Cols./Page:** 3. **Col. Width:** 28 nonpareils. **Col. Depth:** 140 agate lines. **Subscription Rates:** Free to members; $20 nonmembers. **Remarks:** Accepts advertising.
Circ: ‡22,000

13862 The Nautilus
Bailey-Matthews Shell Museum
PO Box 7279 Phone: (202)786-2073
Silver Spring, MD 20907-7279 Fax: (202)357-2343

Zoological (mollusks) magazine. **Founded:** July 1886. **Freq:** Quarterly. **Trim Size:** 8 1/2 x 11. **Cols./Page:** 2. **Col. Width:** 36 nonpareils. **Col. Depth:** 96 agate lines. **Key Personnel:** M.G. Harasewych, Editor, phone (202)786-2073, fax (202)357-2343, harasewych@nmnh.si.edi; J.H. Leal, Managing Editor, phone (941)395-2233, fax (941)395-6706, leal@water.net. **ISSN:** 0028-1344. **Subscription Rates:** $40 individuals. **Remarks:** Advertising not accepted.
Circ: ‡700

13863 NCP: Nutrition in Clinical Practice
American Society for Parenteral and Enteral Nutrition
8630 Fenton St., Ste. 412 Phone: (301)587-6315
Silver Spring, MD 20910-3805 Fax: (301)587-3323
Publisher E-mail: aspen@nutr.org

Clinical nutrition journal. **Founded:** 1985. **Freq:** Bimonthly. **Print Method:** Sheet fed. **Trim Size:** 8 3/8 x 10 7/8. **Cols./Page:** 2. **Col. Width:** 32 nonpareils. **Col. Depth:** 119 agate lines. **Key Personnel:** Peggi Guenter, Ph.D., RN, CNSN, Editor; Keith Dillon, Sales and Marketing Dir., keithd@aspen.nutr.org. **ISSN:** 0884-5336. **Subscription Rates:** $42 individuals; $88 institutions. **Remarks:** Accepts advertising. **URL:** http://www.clinnutr.org.
Ad Rates: BW: $1,135 **Circ:** Paid ‡7,609
4C: $2,035 Non-paid ‡520

13864 Prensa Hispana
The Spanish Speaking Community of Maryland, Inc.
8519 Piney Branch Rd. Phone: (301)587-7217
Silver Spring, MD 20901 Fax: (301)589-1397

Community newspaper (Spanish). **Freq:** Monthly. **Key Personnel:** Emilio Perche Rivas, Editor.

13865 Uno Mas Magazine
Jim Saah
Box 1832 Fax: (301)770-3250
Silver Spring, MD 20915
Popular culture magazine featuring literature, art, photography, and music. **Founded:** Oct. 1990. **Freq:** Quarterly. **Print Method:** Offset. **Trim Size:** 8-1/2 x 11. **Cols./Page:** 3. **Col. Width:** 2 1/5 inches. **Col. Depth:** 10 inches. **Key Personnel:** Jim Saah, Editor. **Subscription Rates:** $11 individuals; $3 single issue. **Remarks:** Accepts advertising. **URL:** http://www.unomas.com.
Ad Rates: BW: $200 **Circ:** Paid 4,500
4C: $300

13866 WMDO-AM - 1540
962 Wayne Ave., 9th Fl. Phone: (301)589-4800
Silver Spring, MD 20910 Fax: (301)495-9556

Format: Hispanic. **Networks:** Cadena Radio Centro (CRC). **Owner:** Los Cerezos Broadcasting Company, at above address. **Founded:** 1981. **Operating Hours:** Sunrise-sunset. **ADI:** Washington, DC. **Key Personnel:** Rudy Guernica, General Mgr.; Oscar Burgos, Sports Dir.; Mini Capers, Business Mgr.; Eu Allegria, Contact; Elio Aguilar, Sales Mgr.; Antonio Aguilar, Program Dir.; Violeta Munoz, Traffic Mgr. **Wattage:** 5000. **Ad Rates:** $30 for 30 seconds; $70 for 60 seconds.

13867 WWDC-AM - 1260
8750 Brookville Rd. Phone: (301)587-7100
Silver Spring, MD 20910-1822 Fax: (301)587-5267

Format: Music of Your Life. **Networks:** Independent. **Founded:** 1941. **Operating Hours:** Continuous. **Key Personnel:** Richard Mack, General Mgr.; Bob Duckman, Program Dir.; Shryl Whigham, Promotions Dir.; Melissa Kelly, General Sales Mgr. **Wattage:** 5000.

13868 WWDC-FM - 101.1
8750 Brookville Rd. Phone: (301)587-7100
Silver Spring, MD 20910 Fax: (301)587-0225

Format: Album-Oriented Rock (AOR). **Networks:** Independent. **Founded:** 1947. **Operating Hours:** Continuous. **Key Personnel:** Richard Mack, General Mgr.; Bob Neumann, Program Dir.; Shryl Whigham, Promotions Dir.; Melissa Kelly, General Sales Mgr. **Wattage:** 22,500.

13869 WWRC-AM - 980
8121 Georgia Ave. Phone: (301)587-4900
Silver Spring, MD 20910-4933 Fax: (301)587-5759

Format: Talk. **Networks:** CNN Radio. **Founded:** 1923. **Operating Hours:** Continuous. **ADI:** Washington, DC. **Key Personnel:** Dianne Robinson, Contact; Shandelle Barton, Promotions Dir.; Dennis Reese, Sales Mgr.; Eric Jennings, Business Mgr.; Diana Silman, Program Dir.; David Howard, General Sales Mgr.; Melissa Kelly, Local Sales Mgr.; Bob Deutsch, Promotions Mgr.; Leslie Brown, Business Mgr. **Local Programs:** *Joe Madison Show*, Ann Sawyer. **Wattage:** 50,000 daytime/5000 night. **Ad Rates:** Advertising accepted; rates available upon request.

TAKOMA PARK

13870 Employment in the Mainstream
Mainstream, Inc.
6930 Carroll Ave., Ste. 240 Phone: (301)891-8777
Takoma Park, MD 20912 Fax: (301)891-8778
Publisher E-mail: info@mainstreaminc.org

Magazine providing information on various employment issues that affect people with disabilities. **Founded:** 1975. **Freq:** 4/year. **Trim Size:** 8 1/2 x 11. **Cols./Page:** 3. **Col. Width:** 2 1/4 inches. **Col. Depth:** 9 3/4 inches. **Key Personnel:** Fritz Rumpel, Contact. **ISSN:** 0888-9724. **Subscription Rates:** $25 individuals. **Remarks:** Accepts advertising. **Alt. Formats:** Audio tape. **Formerly:** In the Mainstream.
Ad Rates: BW: $550 **Circ:** Paid 1,400

13871 Environmental Action Magazine
Environmental Action Foundation
6930 Carroll Ave., Ste. 600
Takoma Park, MD 20912

Magazine. **Founded:** 1970. **Freq:** Quarterly. **Print Method:** Offset. **Trim Size:** 8 1/2 x 11. **Key Personnel:** Barbara Ruben, Editor; David Lapp, Advertising Mgr. **ISSN:** 0013-922X. **Subscription Rates:** $25; $30 for-profit institutions. **Remarks:** Accepts advertising. **Online:** Dialog (The Dialog Corporation); LEXIS-NEXIS.
Ad Rates: BW: $600 **Circ:** Paid 12,000
Non-paid 2,000

Excalibur - See Silver Spring

13872 WGTS-FM - 91.9
7600 Flower Ave. Phone: (301)891-4200
Takoma Park, MD 20912-7796 Fax: (301)270-9191
E-mail: wgts@cuc.edu

Owner: Columbia Union College Broadcasting Inc., at above address. **Founded:** 1956. **Operating Hours:** Continuous. **ADI:** Washington, DC. **Key Personnel:** John E. Konrad, General Mgr.; Ben Milton, Operations Dir.; Sharon Kay Kendall, Music Dir. **Local Programs:** *Music for Awhile*, Richard Carter; *Plant Talk*, Terry Pogue; *Saturday Seminar*, Gerry Fuller. **Wattage:** 29,500. **Ad Rates:** Noncommercial; underwriting available. **URL:** http://www.wsts.org.

TEMPLE HILLS, pop. 3,300.

Prince George's Co. (SC) 5 m SE of D.C. Residential.

13873 Sergeants
Air Force Sergeants Association
PO Box 50 Phone: (301)899-3500
Temple Hills, MD 20757-0050 Fax: (301)899-8136
Free: (800)638-0594
Publisher E-mail: afsahq@internetmci.com

Military magazine. **Founded:** 1966. **Freq:** Monthly. **Print Method:** Offset. **Trim Size:** 8 1/8 x 10 3/4. **Cols./Page:** 3. **Col. Width:** 28 nonpareils. **Col. Depth:** 129 agate lines. **Key Personnel:** David L. Barrette, Exec. Editor; James Staton, Publisher. **ISSN:** 0360-7364. **Subscription Rates:** $24 individuals; $2 single issue. **Remarks:** Advertising accepted; rates available upon request.
Circ: Non-paid ‡131,000

THURMONT, pop. 2,934.

Frederick Co. (N). 17 m N of Frederick. Catoctin Mountain National Park. Manufactures shoes, clothing, salesbooks. Graineries. Dairy and poultry farms. Wheat, truck crops, peaches, apples.

13874 WTHU-AM - 1450
10 Radio Ln. Phone: (301)271-2188
Thurmont, MD 21788-1645

Format: News; Talk. **Networks:** Unistar; CNN Radio; Agrinet Farm Radio. **Owner:** Chuck Walmer, at above address. **Founded:** 1968. **Formerly:** WFCO-AM (1987). **Operating Hours:** Continuous. **Key Personnel:** Chuck Walmer, Contact. **Wattage:** 500. **Ad Rates:** $8-14 for 30 seconds.

TIMONIUM

13875 Food Production Management
CTI Publications, Inc.
2 Oakway Rd. Phone: (410)308-2080
Timonium, MD 21093-4247 Fax: (410)308-2079
Publisher E-mail: sales@ctipubs.com

Magazine on food processing and individual packing news for management, sales, and production personnel in the canning, glass packing, aseptic, and frozen food industries. **Founded:** 1878. **Freq:** Monthly. **Print Method:** Sheetfed offset. **Trim Size:** 8 3/8 x 10 7/8. **Cols./Page:** 2 and 3. **Col. Width:** 41 and 26 nonpareils. **Col. Depth:** 137 agate lines. **Key Personnel:** Arthur I. Judge II, Editor; W. Randall Gerstmyer, Publisher. **ISSN:** 0191-6181. **Subscription Rates:** $35 individuals; $15 single issue. **Remarks:** Accepts advertising. **Alt. Formats:** Mailing labels.
Ad Rates: BW: $1,575 **Circ:** Paid ★253
4C: $2,425 Non-paid ★3,881

13876 The Maryland Horse
Maryland Horse Breeders Association
30 East Padonia Rd. Phone: (410)252-2100
Timonium, MD 21093 Fax: (410)560-0503
Publication E-mail: mdhorse@access.digex.com
Publisher E-mail: mdhobr@erols.com

Magazine on the entire spectrum of Maryland's diverse horse industry. **Founded:** July 1936. **Freq:** Monthly. **Print Method:** Offset. **Trim Size:** 8 3/8 x 10 7/8. **Cols./Page:** 2 and 3. **Col. Width:** 13 and 20 picas. **Col. Depth:** 54.5 picas. **Key Personnel:** Timothy T. Capps, Editor and Publisher; Barrie Reightler, Directory of Publications; Anne Warner, Circulation Mgr. **ISSN:** 0025-4274. **Remarks:** Advertising not accepted.
Circ: Paid ‡695
Non-paid ‡240

13877 Mid-Atlantic Thoroughbred
Maryland Horse Breeders Association
30 E. Padonia Rd.
Timonium, MD 21093
Publication E-mail: mdhorse@access.digex,com
Publisher E-mail: mdhobr@erols.com

Magazine for people in the thoroughbred industry. **Founded:** 1991. **Freq:** Monthly. **Print Method:** Offset sheetfed. **Trim Size:** 8 3/8 x 10 7/8. **Cols./Page:** 3. **Col. Width:** 13 picas. **Col. Depth:** 56 picas. **Key Personnel:** Timothy T. Capps, Editor; Barrie Reightler, Director; Anne Warner, Circulation. **ISSN:** 1056-3245. **Subscription Rates:** $30; $42 other countries; $3.50 single issue. **Remarks:** Accepts advertising.
Ad Rates: GLR: $6 **Circ:** Paid ‡10,200
BW: $600
4C: $1,200
PCI: $55

TOWSON, pop. 73,053.

Baltimore Co. (NC) 5 m North of Baltimore. Goucher College; Towson State University.

13878 The Baltimore Messenger
Patuxent Publishing Co.
409 Washington Ave. Phone: (410)337-2400
Towson, MD 21204 Fax: (410)337-2490

Community newspaper. **Founded:** 1976. **Freq:** Weekly (Wed.). **Print Method:** Offset. **Cols./Page:** 5 and 7. **Col. Width:** 11 picas. **Col. Depth:** 182 agate lines. **Key Personnel:** Elizabeth Eck, Editor. **Subscription Rates:** Free. **Remarks:** Advertising accepted; rates available upon request.
Circ: Non-paid 13,204
Paid 58

13879 Jeffersonian
Patuxent Publishing Co.
409 Washington Ave. Phone: (410)337-2425
Towson, MD 21204 Fax: (410)337-2490

Community newspaper. **Founded:** 1858. **Freq:** Weekly

(Thurs.). **Print Method:** Offset. **Trim Size:** 15 x 23. **Cols./Page:** 6. **Col. Width:** 26 nonpareils. **Col. Depth:** 294 agate lines. **Key Personnel:** Cynthia Prairie, Editor, phone (410)337-2425, cprairie@patuxent.com; John Patinella, Publisher; Beth Ditman, Advertising Mgr. **Subscription Rates:** $15.75 /year; $25 out of state /year. **URL:** http://lifegoeson.com.
Ad Rates: BW: $2,246 **Circ:** Paid 3,700
4C: $2,596 Non-paid 878

13880 JNMS: Journal of the Neuromusculoskeletal System
Data Trace Publishing Co.
110 West Rd., Ste. 227 Phone: (410)494-4994
Towson, MD 21204 Fax: (410)494-0515
Free: (800)342-0454
Publisher E-mail: info@datatrace.com

Professional journal covering neuromusculoskeletal function and dysfunction for chiropractors and related medical practitioners. **Founded:** 1993. **Freq:** Quarterly. **Print Method:** Web offset. **Trim Size:** 8 3/8 x 10 7/8. **Cols./Page:** 2. **Key Personnel:** Cindy Lee Floyd, Production Mgr. **ISSN:** 1067-8239. **Subscription Rates:** $58 individuals; $118 institutions; $35 resident; $15 single issue. **Remarks:** Accepts advertising.
Ad Rates: BW: $1,180 **Circ:** Paid 10,000
4C: $1,875

Northeast Times Booster - See Baltimore

13881 Owings Mills Times
Patuxent Publishing Co.
409 Washington Ave. Phone: (410)337-2400
Towson, MD 21204 Fax: (410)337-2490

Suburban community newspaper. **Founded:** 1976. **Freq:** Weekly (Thurs.). **Print Method:** Offset. **Trim Size:** 11 x 15. **Cols./Page:** 5. **Col. Width:** 11 picas. **Col. Depth:** 74 picas. **Key Personnel:** Elizabeth Eck, Editor; John Patinella, Times Mirror Publisher, phone (410)730-3620. **Subscription Rates:** Free. **Remarks:** Advertising accepted; rates available upon request. **Formerly:** Owings Mills Flier (1989).
Circ: Paid 173
Non-paid 32,210

13882 The Towerlight
Towson University
University Union, Rm. 313 Phone: (410)830-2288
Towson, MD 21286 Fax: (410)830-3862
Publication E-mail: towerlight@towson.edu

Community newspaper. **Founded:** Sept. 14, 1947. **Freq:** Semiweekly (Mon. and Thurs.). **Print Method:** Offset. **Cols./Page:** 5. **Key Personnel:** Mike Raymond, Advertising Dir. **Remarks:** Accepts advertising. **URL:** http://www.towson.edu/towerlight/.
Ad Rates: PCI: $7.40 **Circ:** ‡10,000

13883 Towson Times
Patuxent Publishing Co.
409 Washington Ave. Phone: (410)337-2400
Towson, MD 21204 Fax: (410)337-2490

Suburban community newspaper. **Founded:** 1948. **Freq:** Weekly (Wed.). **Print Method:** Offset. **Trim Size:** 11 x 15. **Cols./Page:** 5. **Col. Width:** 11 picas. **Col. Depth:** 74 picas. **Key Personnel:** Paul Milton, Editor; S. Zeke Orlinsky, Publisher; Don Nunes, Advertising Dir. **Subscription Rates:** Free; $104 by mail.
Ad Rates: BW: $2,324 **Circ:** Paid 318
4C: $2,674 Non-paid 35,379

13884 WQSR-FM - 105.7
305 Washington Ave., 4th Fl. Phone: (410)825-1000
Towson, MD 21204-4715 Fax: (410)825-3800

Format: Oldies. **Networks:** Independent. **Founded:** 1963. **Operating Hours:** Continuous. **ADI:** Baltimore, MD. **Key Personnel:** Alan Hay, V Pres./Gen. Mgr. **Wattage:** 50,000.

UPPER FAIRMOUNT

13885 Art Calendar
PO Box 199 Phone: (410)651-9150
Upper Fairmount, MD 21867 Fax: (410)651-5313
Free: (800)597-5988
Publisher E-mail: barbdoug@dmv.com

Marketing journal for visual artists. **Subtitle:** The Business Magazine for Visual Artists. **Founded:** 1986. **Freq:** Monthly. **Print Method:** Offset. **Trim Size:** 8 1/2 x 11. **Cols./Page:** 3. **Col. Width:** 2.25 inches. **Col. Depth:** 9.8 inches. **Key Personnel:** Barbara Dougherty, Publisher, phone (410)651-9151, barb@artcalendar.com; Drew Sreis, Editor, phone (410)651-9151, drew@artcalendar.com. **ISSN:** 0893-3901. **Subscription Rates:** $32. $5 single issue. **Available Online. URL:** http://www.artcalendar.com. **Alt. Formats:** Mailing lists.
Ad Rates: BW: $1,800 **Circ:** Paid ‡22,000

UPPER MARLBORO†, pop. 828.

Prince George's Co. (SC). 18 m E of Washington, DC. Packing plants. Agriculture. Tobacco, corn, feed, wheat.

13886 Enquirer Gazette
Chesapeake Publishing Corp.
PO Box 30 Phone: (301)627-2833
Upper Marlboro, MD 20773 Fax: (301)627-2835
Publication E-mail: gazette3@erols.com

Community newspaper. **Founded:** 1851. **Freq:** Weekly (Thurs.). **Print Method:** Offset. **Cols./Page:** 6. **Col. Width:** 30 nonpareils. **Col. Depth:** 294 agate lines. **Key Personnel:** John Driscoll, Editor; Ralph Martin, Publisher. **Subscription Rates:** $6 individuals. **Remarks:** Accepts advertising.
Ad Rates: GLR: $.31 **Circ:** Paid 3,866
Non-paid 1,002

13887 InVitro Cellular & Developmental Biology - PLANT
Society for In Vitro Biology
9315 Largo Dr. W., Ste. 255 Phone: (301)324-5054
Upper Marlboro, MD 20774 Fax: (301)324-5057
Free: (800)741-7476
Publisher E-mail: sivb@sivb.org

Journal devoted solely to plant manuscripts with emphasis on developmental, molecular and cellular biology of cells, tissues, and organs. **Founded:** 1991. **Freq:** Quarterly. **Print Method:** Offset. **Trim Size:** 8 1/4 x 11. **Cols./Page:** 2. **Col. Width:** 40 nonpareils. **Col. Depth:** 121 agate lines. **Key Personnel:** T. Thorpe, Editor, phone (403)289-9311, fax (403)289-9311, tthorpe@acs.ucalgary.ca; Denise McCall, Publications Mgr., phone (301)324-5054, sivb@sivb.org. **ISSN:** 1054-5476. **Subscription Rates:** $115 individuals. **Remarks:** Accepts advertising. **Alt. Formats:** Mailing labels.
Ad Rates: BW: $400 **Circ:** ‡900
4C: $900

WALDORF, pop. 6,500.

Charles Co. (S) 20 m S.E. of Washington, DC.

13888 Cochran's Corner
1003 Tyler Ct. Phone: (301)870-1664
Waldorf, MD 20602
Literary journal covering fiction and poetry. **Founded:** July 1982. **Freq:** Monthly. **Trim Size:** 8 x 11. **Cols./Page:** 3. **Key Personnel:** Jeanie Saunders, Exec. Editor, phone (724)733-0664. **Subscription Rates:** $30 individuals; $5 single issue. **Remarks:** Accepts advertising.
Ad Rates: BW: $65 **Circ:** Combined 7,000

13889 Maryland Independent
Chesapeake Publishing Corp.
7 Industrial Park Phone: (301)645-9480
Waldorf, MD 20602 Fax: (301)884-9403
Free: (800)843-3357

County newspaper. **Founded:** 1872. **Freq:** Semiweekly (Wed. and Fri.). **Print Method:** Offset. **Cols./Page:** 6. **Col. Width:** 12 picas. **Col. Depth:** 21 1/2 inches. **Key Personnel:** John Driscoll, Editor; Ralph Martin, Publisher; Greg Runyan, Advertising Mgr. **Subscription Rates:** $25 individuals; $35 out of state.
Ad Rates: GLR: $12.82 **Circ:** Paid 22,714
4C: $1,837.66 Non-paid 353
PCI: $11.41

13890 Jones Intercable, Inc. of Charles County
336 Post Office Rd. Phone: (301)843-9759
Waldorf, MD 20602 Fax: (301)843-7212

Owner: Jones Intercable, Inc., 9697 E. Mineral Ave., Englewood, CO 80112, (303)792-3111. **Founded:** 1964. **Key Personnel:** Nina Kern, General Mgr.; Robert Walker, Chief Engineer; J. Ben Painter, Contact; Audrey Damon, Office Mgr. **Cities Served:** subscribing households 19,600; 35 channels.

WALKERSVILLE

13891 Bible and Spade
Associates for Biblical Research
31 E Frederick St., Ste. 468 Phone: (301)898-9358
Walkersville, MD 21793-8234 Fax: (301)898-9358
Publisher E-mail: abrocf@msn.com

Consumer magazine covering archaeology and biblical research. **Founded:** 1972. **Freq:** Quarterly. **Print Method:** Offset. **Trim Size:** 5 5/16 x 8 7/16. **Cols./Page:** 2. **Col. Width:** 2 1/8 inches. **Col. Depth:** 7 inches. **Key Personnel:** Bryant G. Wood, Editor. **ISSN:** 1079-6959. **Subscription Rates:** $35 individuals. **Remarks:** Advertising not accepted.
Circ: Paid 800

WESTMINSTER†, pop. 8,808.

Carroll Co. (N). 28 m NW of Baltimore. Western Maryland College; Carroll County Farm Museum. Manufactures car assembly parts, clothing, fertilizer, soft drinks. Crafts distribution. Meat packing. Agriculture. Dairy products, peaches, apples.

13892 Carroll County Times
Landmark Community Newspapers, Inc.
201 Railroad Ave. Phone: (410)848-4400
PO Box 346 Fax: (410)857-8749
Westminster, MD 21157-4823
General newspaper. **Founded:** Oct. 2, 1911. **Freq:** Mon.-Sun. (morn.). **Print Method:** Offset. **Trim Size:** 13 3/4 x 22 3/4. **Cols./Page:** 6. **Col. Width:** 24 nonpareils. **Col. Depth:** 301 agate lines. **Key Personnel:** Jim Lee, Editor, phone (410)857-7878, fax (410)857-8749, ccfeatr@cot.infl.net; Robin Saul, Publisher, phone (410)857-7870, fax (410)857-1176; Charles Baker, Advertising Mgr. **Subscription Rates:** $105 individuals. **Remarks:** Accepts advertising. **Online:** Carroll County Online. **URL:** http://www.carrollcounty.com.
Ad Rates: GLR: $15.43 **Circ:** Mon.-Sat. 22,554
BW: $1,990.47 Sun. 23,909
4C: $1,699.44
SAU: $11.24

13893 Miniature Donkey Talk
Pheasant Meadow Farm
1338 Hughes Shop Rd. Phone: (410)875-0118
Westminster, MD 21158 Fax: (410)857-9145
Publication E-mail: minidonk@qis.net

Trade magazine covering animal health care, management, and training. **Founded:** Oct. 1987. **Freq:** Bimonthly. **Print Method:** Web offset. **Trim Size:** 7 3/4 x 10 3/4. **Cols./Page:** 2. **Col. Width:** 3 1/4 inches. **Col. Depth:** 9 1/4 inches. **Key Personnel:** Bonnie Gross, Editor; Mike Gross, Advertising/Circulation Mgr. **ISSN:** 1058-7063. **Subscription Rates:** $25 individuals; $5 single issue. **Remarks:** Accepts advertising. **URL:** http://www.qis.net/~minidonk/donktext.htm.
Ad Rates: BW: $220 **Circ:** Combined 7,300
4C: $375

13894 The Phoenix
The Phoenix, WMC
2 College Hill Phone: (410)751-8600
Westminster, MD 21157 Fax: (410)857-2729
Publisher E-mail: phoenix@ns1.wmdc.edu

Collegiate newspaper. **Founded:** 1922. **Freq:** Semimonthly. **Print Method:** Letterpress and offset. **Trim Size:** 10 1/4 x 15. **Cols./Page:** 5. **Col. Width:** 24 nonpareils. **Col. Depth:** 196 agate lines. **Key Personnel:** Kate Hampson, Editor, phone (410)751-8294, kch002@wmdc.edu. **Subscription Rates:** $15 individuals. **Remarks:** Accepts advertising. **Formerly:** The Gold Bug; The Scrimshaw.
Ad Rates: GLR: $.15 **Circ:** ‡1,500
BW: $472.50
PCI: $6.30

13895 WTTR-AM - 1470
101 WTTR Ln. Phone: (410)848-5511
Westminster, MD 21158 Fax: (410)876-5907
E-mail: wttr@qis.net; wttr@juno.com

Format: Full Service; Sports; Agricultural; Oldies. **Networks:** ABC. **Owner:** Shamrock Communications, 149 Penn Ave., Scranton, PA 18503, (717)348-9103. **Founded:** 1953. **Operating Hours:** 24hrs 60% network, 40% local. **ADI:** Baltimore, MD. **Key Personnel:** Dwight Dingle, Station Mgr., phone (410)848-5511, fax (410)876-5095, wttr@juno.com; Mark Woodworth, News Dir.; Fred Klimes, Chief Engineer; Jeff Laird, General Mgr. **Local Programs:** *Carroll Community Forum*, Mark Woodworth, (410)876-1515. **Wattage:** 1000. **Ad Rates:** $10-30 for 30 seconds; $12-37 for 60 seconds. Combined advertising rates available with WGRX-FM.

WHALEYSVILLE

13896 WOCQ-FM - 103.9
11210 Bell Rd. Phone: (410)641-0001
Whaleysville, MD 21872-2005 Fax: (410)641-0930
E-mail: oc104@ce.net

Format: Contemporary Hit Radio (CHR). **Networks:** ABC. **Founded:** 1981. **Operating Hours:** Continuous; 95% local. **ADI:** Salisbury, MD. **Key Personnel:** Darryl Nixon, President; Ed Fennessy, Sales Mgr.; George Kreiner, Program Dir.; Skip McClosky, News Dir. **Wattage:** 3000. **Ad Rates:** $5-40 for 30 seconds; $7-50 for 60 seconds.

WHEATON, pop. 73,800.

Montgomery Co. (WC). 5 m N of Washington, DC. Residential

13897 The Washington Diplomat
The Washington Diplomat, Inc.
PO Box 1345 Phone: (301)933-3552
Wheaton, MD 20915-1345 Fax: (301)949-0065
Publication E-mail: news@washdiplomat.com
Publisher E-mail: eflash@crosslink.net

Newspaper for the international and diplomatic community in Washington, D.C. **Founded:** Nov. 1994. **Freq:** Monthly. **Print Method:** Web Offset. **Trim Size:** 2 x 9. **Key Personnel:** Victor Shiblie, Editor-in-Chief. **Subscription Rates:** $25 individuals; $45 two years. **Remarks:** Accepts advertising.
Ad Rates: BW: $1,200 **Circ:** Combined 25,000
4C: $1,700

WILLIAMSPORT

Washington Co. (NW). 5 m S of Hagerstown.

13898 WCRH-FM - 90.5
PO Box 439 Phone: (301)582-0285
Williamsport, MD 21795 Fax: (301)582-2707
E-mail: wcrh@crosslink.net

Format: Religious. **Networks:** Moody Broadcasting; Ambassador Inspirational Radio. **Owner:** Cedar Ridge Ministries, at above address. **Founded:** 1976. **Operating Hours:** Continuous; 50% network, 50% local. **ADI:** Hagerstown, MD. **Key Personnel:** Ward Childerston, General Mgr.; Robert Dunkle, News Dir.; Susanna Scott, Music Dir. **Wattage:** 10,000. **Ad Rates:** Noncommercial.

WYII-FM - See Martinsburg, West Virginia

WORTON

13899 WKHS-FM - 90.5
Box 905 Phone: (410)778-4249
Worton, MD 21678 Fax: (410)778-3802

Format: Adult Contemporary. **Networks:** Independent. **Owner:** Kent County Board of Education, 215 Washington Ave., Chestertown, MD 21620, (410)778-1595. **Founded:** 1973. **Operating Hours:** Continuous. **Key Personnel:** Steve Kramarck, Station Mgr. **Wattage:** 17,500. **Ad Rates:** Noncommercial.

MASSACHUSETTS

State Capital, BOSTON

Massachusetts is bounded on the north by Vermont and New Hampshire, east by the Atlantic Ocean, south by the Atlantic Ocean and by Rhode Island and Connecticut, and west by New York. Its extreme breadth is 160 miles, its length from 47 to 90 miles; land area, 7,838 square miles. The surface is greatly diversified: mountainous in the extreme west, hilly and broken in the east and northeast, and in the southeast mainly low and sandy. Toward the west is the fertile valley of the Connecticut River. The mountains are the Taconic and the Hoosac (continuations of the Green Mountain ranges of Vermont) with detached members of the White Mountains. The Weather Bureau at Boston gives the temperature (annual average) as 51.3; highest on record, 104; lowest on record, -18. Total annual precipitation is 41.51 inches. The state has abundant rail and coastside shipping facilities. The Cape Cod Canal, an eight-mile cut between Buzzards Bay and Sandwich, enables coasting vessels to avoid the long trip around the Cape Cod peninsula, shortening the distance between Boston and New York by 70 miles. The North Shore above Boston, Cape Cod, the hill towns west of the Connecticut River, and the valley of the Housatonic, in Berkshire county, are popular summer resorts. Boston is one of the greatest fishing ports in the country. There are a great many colleges in the state, including some of the country's most famous. Harvard University, the oldest in the country, is located at Cambridge, as is the Massachusetts Institute of Technology. Nearly all of Massachusetts is rich in historical interest. At Provincetown, in 1620, the Mayflower made its first landing, going from there to Plymouth.

POPULATION: 5,998,000 (1992): Rank among the states, 13th.

AGRICULTURE: Number of farms: 7,000 (1992). Farm acreage: 1,000,000 (1992). Cash receipts from farm marketings: crops, $355,000,000 (1991); livestock and products, $121,000,000 (1991).

FISHERIES: Total catch: 289,000,000 lbs. (1991), $296,000,000 value. Principal fish: haddock, scallops, flounder, cod, lobster, ocean perch, clams, whiting.

FORESTS: Total forest land: 3,097,000 acres (1987). Principal woods: white pine, hemlock, oak, maple, eastern spruce, beech, birch, ash, balsam, fir, cherry, southern yellow pine, eastern cedar.

MINERALS: Value of production: $112,000,000 (1991). Principal minerals: stone, sand and gravel, lime.

MANUFACTURES: Value added by manufacture: $34,472,000,000 (1991). Leading industry groups: electrical machinery, machinery (except electrical), food and related products, fabricated metal products.

LIST OF COUNTIES

Total number of counties 14

County, Location on Map, and County Seat	Pop.
Barnstable (E), Barnstable	186,605
Berkshire (W), Pittsfield	139,352
Bristol (SE), Taunton	506,325
Dukes (SE), Edgartown	11,639
Essex (NE), Salem	670,080
Franklin (NW), Greenfield	70,092
Hampden (SW), Springfield	456,310
Hampshire (WC), Northampton	146,568
Middlesex (NE), Cambridge	1,398,468
Nantucket (SE), Nantucket	6,012
Norfolk (E), Dedham	616,087
Plymouth (SE), Plymouth	435,276
Suffolk (E), Boston	663,906
Worcester (C), Worcester	709,705

STATISTICS

Newspapers

Period of Issue	
Daily	40
Evening Daily	30
Morning Daily	5
Daily with Sunday edition	14
Semiweekly	4
Weekly	215
Biweekly	8
Semimonthly	6
Monthly	8
Bimonthly	3
Quarterly	4
Free or partly free	54
Shopper	7
Total Newspapers	291

Periodicals

Period of Issue	
Weekly	16
Biweekly	6
Semimonthly	7
Monthly	81
Bimonthly	63
Quarterly	134
Free or partly free	1
Total Periodicals	401

Total number of publications 692

Radio Stations

AM Stations	56
FM Stations	99
Total Radio Stations	155

TV Stations

Total TV Stations 18

Cable Stations

Total Cable Systems 29

Total number of broadcast listings 202

ABINGTON, pop. 13,517.

SE MA. Plymouth Co. 5 mi. SE of Brockton. Residential.

13900 Abington/Rockland Mariner
Mariner Newspapers
165 Enterprise Dr. Phone: (617)837-3500
Marshfield, MA 02050-2132 Fax: (617)837-4540
Free: (800)649-6661
Publisher E-mail: cmathis@cnc.com

Community newspaper. **Founded:** 1876. **Freq:** Weekly (Thurs.). **Print Method:** Offset. **Trim Size:** 11 3/8 x 17. **Cols./Page:** 5. **Col. Width:** 15 1/2 inches. **Col. Depth:** 2 1/8 inches. **Key Personnel:** Bob Flavell, Editor; Jack Powers, Advertising Mgr.; Margaret Smorgiewicz, Publisher; Judy McCaffrey Perry, Advertising Dir.; Maria Tedme, Circulation Mgr. **USPS:** 088-760. **Subscription Rates:** $18. **Remarks:** Combined advertising rates available with other Mariner Newspapers.
Ad Rates: BW: $942.40 **Circ:** Paid 2,461
4C: $1,300 Non-paid 86
PCI: $8.25

ACTON, pop. 17,544.

NE MA. Middlesex Co. 18 mi. NW of Cambridge. Manufactures concrete, chemical products, motors, generators, mechanical measuring and controlling instruments, calculators, textiles. Truck, poultry, fruit, dairy farms.

13901 Robb Report
1 Acton Pl. Phone: (978)263-7749
Acton, MA 01720 Fax: (978)263-0722
Free: (800)229-7622
Publication E-mail: robb@robbreport.com

Lifestyle magazine focusing on vintage and exotic automobiles, lifestyle and interiors, upscale travel, boating, investment opportunities, technology, profiles, and recreation. **Subtitle:** For the Luxury Lifestyle. **Founded:** 1976. **Freq:** Monthly. **Print Method:** Offset. **Trim Size:** 8 1/8 x 10 7/8. **Cols./Page:** 3. **Col. Width:** 2 1/4 inches. **Col. Depth:** 9 3/4 inches. **Key Personnel:** Steven Caste, Editor; Dan Phillips, Publisher, fax (978)263-3812; Rick Sedler, Advertising Dir., fax (978)263-3812. **ISSN:** 0279-1447. **Subscription Rates:** $65 individuals. **Remarks:** Advertising accepted; rates available upon request. **Available Online. URL:** http://www.robbreport.com.
Circ: Paid ★105,526

13902 WHAB-FM - 89.1
96 Hayward Rd. Phone: (508)264-4700
Acton, MA 01720 Fax: (508)263-8409

Format: Eclectic. **Founded:** 1979. **Key Personnel:** Donald R. Gilberti, General Mgr.; Patrick Mullaney, Program Dir. **Wattage:** 9.1.

ADAMS

13903 WCDC-TV - 19
c/o WTEN-TV Phone: (518)436-4822
341 Northern Blvd. Fax: (518)462-6065
Albany, NY 12204

Format: Commercial TV. **Simulcasts:** WTEN-TV Albany, NY. **Networks:** ABC. **Owner:** Young Broadcasting of Albany, Inc., 599 Lexington Ave., 47th Fl., New York, NY 10022, (212)754-7070, Fax: (212)758-1229. **ADI:** Albany-Schenectady-Troy, NY. **Key Personnel:** Robert M. Peterson, Contact; Rob Puglisi, News Dir.; Dan Murphy, Sports Dir.; Vera Hope, General Sales Mgr.

ALLSTON

13904 Cablevision of Boston
28 Travis St. Phone: (617)787-6600
Allston, MA 02134 Fax: (617)787-6606

Founded: 1982. **Cities Served:** Suffolk County, Allston, Black Bay, Beacon Hill, Brighton, Charlestown, Chinatown, Dorchester, East Boston, Fenway, Hyde Park, Jamaica Plain, Mattapan, North End, Roslindale, Roxbury, South Boston, South End, and West Roxbury, MA.

AMESBURY

13905 Amesbury News
Community Newspaper Company
16 Millyard Phone: (508)834-3150
Amesbury, MA 01913 Fax: (508)834-3151
Publication E-mail: amesburynews@cnc.com

Community newspaper (tabloid). **Founded:** 1888. **Freq:** Weekly (Fri.). **Print Method:** Offset. **Trim Size:** 11 3/8 x 17. **Cols./Page:** 5. **Col. Width:** 2 1/16 inches. **Col. Depth:** 16 inches. **Key Personnel:** Chuck Goodrich, Exec. Publisher, phone (508)739-1301; Michael Moses, Advertising Mgr., phone (508)739-1350; Donna M. Greene, Editor, phone (508)834-3145; Jim Malone, Editor-in-Chief, phone (508)412-1560. **ISSN:** 0192-8910. **Subscription Rates:** $21 individuals; $27 two years; $17 students (9 months). **Remarks:** Accepts advertising.
Ad Rates: GLR: $3.75 **Circ:** Combined 3,299
BW: $644
PCI: $8

13906 Merrimack Valley Sunday
Community Newspaper Company
16 Millard Phone: (508)834-3150
Amesbury, MA 01913 Fax: (508)834-3151
Free: (800)880-1812
Publication E-mail: musunday@cnc.com

Community newspaper (tabloid). **Founded:** 1986. **Freq:** Weekly (Sun.). **Print Method:** Offset. **Trim Size:** 11 3/8 x 17. **Cols./Page:** 5. **Col. Width:** 2 1/16 inches. **Col. Depth:** 16 inches. **Key Personnel:** Donna Greene, Editor, phone (508)834-3145; Chuck Goodrich, Exec. Publisher, phone (508)739-1301; Michael Moses, Advertising Mgr., phone (508)739-1350; Jim Malone, Editor-in-Chief, phone (508)412-1560. **USPS:** 003-076. **Subscription Rates:** $35; $24 6 months; $17 students. **Remarks:** Accepts advertising.
Ad Rates: GLR: $3.75 **Circ:** Sun. 5,951
BW: $908
4C: $1,251
PCI: $10

AMHERST, pop. 33,229.

WC MA. Hampshire Co. 4 mi. E. of Connecticut River, 14 mi. N. of Holyoke. Amherst College (coed); Hampshire College (co-ed). University of Massachusetts. Publishing industry. Dairy and poultry farms. Tobacco, onions, apples.

13907 American Journal of Physics
American Association of Physics Teachers
Merrill Science Bldg.
Amherst College
Amherst, MA 01002
Publisher E-mail: aapt-pubs@aapt.org

Journal devoted to the instructional and cultural aspects of physics. **Founded:** 1933. **Freq:** Monthly. **Print Method:** Offset. **Trim Size:** 8 1/2 x 11. **Cols./Page:** 2. **Col. Width:** 41 nonpareils. **Col. Depth:** 136 agate lines. **Key Personnel:** Dr. Robert H. Romer, Editor. **ISSN:** 0002-9505. **Subscription Rates:** $205; $225 other countries. **Remarks:** Accepts advertising. **Formerly**: The American Physics Teacher (1940).
Ad Rates: BW: $726 **Circ:** 8,100
4C: $1,526

13908 Amherst
Amherst College
Amherst, MA 01002 Phone: (413)542-2335
Fax: (413)542-2117

College alumni publication. **Founded:** 1949. **Freq:** Quarterly. **Print Method:** Offset. **Cols./Page:** 3. **Col. Width:** 26 nonpareils. **Col. Depth:** 130 agate lines. **Key Personnel:** Douglas Wilson, Editor.

13909 Amherst Bulletin
H.S. Gere & Sons, Inc.
55 University Dr. Phone: (413)549-2000
Amherst, MA 01002 Fax: (413)549-8181

General newspaper. **Freq:** Weekly. **Print Method:** Offset. **Trim Size:** 13 3/4 x 22 3/4. **Cols./Page:** 6. **Col. Width:** 24 agate lines. **Col. Depth:** 301 nonpareils. **Key Personnel:** Nick Grabbe, Editor, phone (413)549-2000, fax (413)549-8181, amherst@gazettenet.com; John Ebbets, Advertising Dir., phone (413)584-5000, fax (413)585-5293; Bonnie Wells, Arts Editor, phone (415)549-2000, fax (413)549-8181, amherst@gazettenet.com. **ISSN:** 0192-8449. **Subscription Rates:** Free; $36 by mail. **Remarks:** Accepts advertising.
Ad Rates: BW: $1,104.24 **Circ:** Controlled 13,000
4C: $1,554.24
PCI: $11.05

13910 Amherst Student
Amherst College
Box 1816 Phone: (413)542-2304
Amherst, MA 01002-5000 Fax: (413)542-2305
Publication E-mail: student@amherst.edu

College newspaper. **Founded:** 1868. **Freq:** Weekly. **Print Method:** Web. **Cols./Page:** 5. **Subscription Rates:** $30 individuals; $80 two years. **Remarks:** Accepts advertising.
Ad Rates: BW: $320 **Circ:** Controlled 2,500
PCI: $5

13911 Contemporary Sociology
University of Arizona
University of Massachusetts Phone: (413)545-5974
W-34 Machmer Hall Fax: (413)545-1994
Amherst, MA 01003
Publication E-mail: consoc@sadri.umass.edu
Publisher E-mail: edwards@asanet.org

Journal containing reviews of scholarly essays on sociology and related topics. **Founded:** Jan. 1972. **Freq:** Bimonthly. **Print Method:** Offset. **Trim Size:** 6 3/4 x 9 7/8. **Cols./Page:** 2. **Col. Width:** 2 5/8 inches. **Col. Depth:** 8 1/2 inches. **Key Personnel:** Dan Clawson, Editor; Nancy Sylvester, Advertising Mgr. **ISSN:** 0094-3061. **Subscription Rates:** $25 members; $50 nonmembers; $105 institutions. **Remarks:** Accepts advertising.
Ad Rates: BW: $400 **Circ:** ‡7,200

13912 Dickens Quarterly
University of Massachusetts
Dept. of English Phone: (413)545-1914
Amherst, MA 01003 Fax: (413)545-3880
Publication E-mail: cgtp@atuvm.atu.edu
Publisher E-mail: paroissien@english.umass.edu

Scholarly journal covering the life and works of Charles Dickens. **Subtitle:** Life, Times and Works of Charles Dickens. **Founded:** 1970. **Freq:** 4x/yr. **Trim Size:** 7 x 9. **Cols./Page:** 1. **Col. Width:** 4 1/4 inches. **Col. Depth:** 7 inches. **Key Personnel:** Troy Philpotts, phone (501)968-0809. **ISSN:** 0742-5473. **Subscription Rates:** $20 individuals; $25 out of country; $5 single issue. **Remarks:** Accepts advertising. **Former name**: Dickens Studies Newsletter.
Ad Rates: GLR: $75 **Circ:** Paid 560
BW: $75

13913 English Literary Renaissance
PO Box 2300 Phone: (413)577-3603
Amherst, MA 01004 Fax: (413)577-3605

Scholarly journal covering literature in England from 1485-1666. **Founded:** 1971. **Freq:** Triennial. **Print Method:** Photo offset. **Trim Size:** 6 1/2 x 9. **Cols./Page:** 1. **Key Personnel:** Arthur F. Kinney, Editor; Kirby Farrell, Editor; Lynne Boden, Editorial Asst. **ISSN:** 0013-8312. **Subscription Rates:** $35 institutions; $20 individuals; $16 students; $12 single issue. **Remarks:** Accepts advertising.
Ad Rates: BW: $100 **Circ:** Combined 1,450

13914 The Herb, Spice, and Medicinal Plant Digest
The Haworth Press, Inc.
Dept. of Plant and Soil Sciences Phone: (413)545-2347
12 A Stockbridge Hall Fax: (413)545-3958
University of Massachusetts
Amherst, MA 01003
Publisher E-mail: getinfo@haworthpressinc.com

Professional journal with referred papers. **Founded:** 1982. **Freq:** Semiannual. **Trim Size:** 8 1/2 x 11. **Key Personnel:** Lyle Craker, Ph.D., Editor, craker@pssci.umass.edu. **ISSN:** 1048-3160. **Subscription Rates:** $10 U.S.; $17 other countries. **Remarks:** Advertising not accepted. **URL:** http://www.unix.oit.umass.edu/~herbdig. **Formerly**: Journal of Herbs, Spices, and Medicinal Plants.
Circ: 1,000

13915 International Quarterly of Community Health Education
Baywood Publishing Co., Inc.
Dr. George Cernada Phone: (413)545-1314
University of Massachusetts
School of Public Health
Amherst, MA 01003
Publisher E-mail: baywood@baywood.com

Publication on the relationship between community health education and social change. **Subtitle:** A Journal of Policy and Applied Research. **Founded:** 1981. **Freq:** Quarterly. **Print Method:** Offset. **Trim Size:** 6 x 9. **Cols./Page:** 1. **Col. Width:** 4 1/2 inches. **Col. Depth:** 7 1/2 inches. **Key Personnel:** George P. Cernada, Editor; Stuart Cohen, Publisher; Michelle Satchell, Advertising Mgr.; S. Edwards, Circulation Mgr. **ISSN:** 0272-684X. **Subscription Rates:** $48.50 U.S. and Canada; $53.75 other countries; $152.50 institutions; $157.75 other countries institutions. **Remarks:** Advertising not accepted.
Circ: (Not Reported)

13916 Journal of Computing in Higher Education
Norris Publishers
PO Box 34640 Phone: (413)545-4232
Amherst, MA 01003-4640 Fax: (413)545-3203

Contains information on technologies that improve the teaching and learning process. Includes scholarly essays, reviews, reports, and research articles. **Founded:** 1989. **Freq:** Semiannual. **Trim Size:** 9 x 6. **Key Personnel:** Carol MacKnight, Editor, cmacknight@oit.umass.edu. **ISSN:** 1042-1726. **Subscription Rates:** $35 individuals; $60 institutions; $80 foreign;

$35 students. **Remarks:** Accepts advertising. **URL:** http://www-unix.oit.umass.edu/~carolm/jche/.
Ad Rates: BW: $50 **Circ:** Paid 200
Non-paid 200

13917 Journal of Tree Fruit Production
The Haworth Press, Inc.
University of Massachusetts Phone: (413)545-2963
Dept. of Plant and Soil Sciences Fax: (413)545-0260
Bowditch Hall
Amherst, MA 01003
Publisher E-mail: getinfo@haworthpressinc.com

Journal on tree fruit production. **Founded:** 1994. **Freq:** Biennial. **Trim Size:** 6x8 1/2. **Key Personnel:** Wesley R. Autio, PHD, Editor; Bill Cohen, Publisher. **ISSN:** 1055-1387. **Subscription Rates:** $36 individuals 30% more for Canada; 40% more for other countries; $60 institutions 30% more for Canada; 40% more for other countries; $95 libraries 30% more for Canada; 40% more for other countries. **Remarks:** Accepts advertising.
Ad Rates: BW: $300 **Circ:** Paid 96

13918 Journal of Turf Grass Management
The Haworth Press, Inc.
University of Massachusetts Phone: (413)545-2860
Dept. of Plant and Soil Science
Stockbridge Hall
Amherst, MA 01003
Publisher E-mail: getinfo@haworthpressinc.com

Journal on turfgrass management. **Founded:** 1993. **Freq:** Quarterly. **Trim Size:** 6 x 8 1/2. **Key Personnel:** William A. Torello, Editor; Bill Cohen, Publisher. **ISSN:** 1070-437X. **Subscription Rates:** $90 libraries; $36 individuals; $48 industry. **Remarks:** Accepts advertising.
Ad Rates: BW: $300 **Circ:** Paid 127

13919 Law & Society Review
Law and Society Association
Hampshire House Phone: (413)545-4617
University of Massachusetts Fax: (413)545-1640
PO Box 33615
Amherst, MA 01003-3615
Publisher E-mail: lsa@legal.umass.edu

Journal on law and society. **Founded:** 1966. **Freq:** Quarterly. **Print Method:** Offset. **Trim Size:** 6 1/2 x 9 3/4. **Cols./Page:** 1. **Col. Width:** 52 nonpareils. **Col. Depth:** 115 agate lines. **Key Personnel:** Susan S. Silbey, Editor. **ISSN:** 0023-9216. **Subscription Rates:** $124 U.S.; $139 other countries. **Remarks:** Accepts advertising. **Alt. Formats:** Microform.
Ad Rates: BW: $250 **Circ:** ‡2,400

13920 Main Group Chemistry News
University of Massachusetts
Amherst, MA 01003 Phone: (413)545-2422
Fax: (413)545-4490
Publication E-mail: lan.mellanby@gbriap.com

Scholarly journal covering science. **Founded:** 1993. **Freq:** Quarterly. **Trim Size:** 166 x 242 mm. **Cols./Page:** 2. **Key Personnel:** Prof. Robert Holmes, Contact. **ISSN:** 1068-3119. **Subscription Rates:** $48 individuals. **Remarks:** Accepts advertising.
Ad Rates: BW: $1,480 **Circ:** (Not Reported)
4C: $2,880

13921 Massachusetts Daily Collegian
University of Massachusetts
113 Campus Center Phone: (413)545-3500
Amherst, MA 01003 Fax: (413)545-1592

Collegiate newpaper in New England. **Founded:** 1879. **Freq:** Daily. **Print Method:** Offset. **Cols./Page:** 6. **Col. Width:** 12.5 picas. **Col. Depth:** 21 inches. **Key Personnel:** Jacob W. Michaels, Editor-in-Chief. **Subscription Rates:** $50.
Ad Rates: BW: $2,394 **Circ:** Free ‡17,000
4C: $500
PCI: $19

13922 The Massachusetts Review
University of Massachusetts
South College Phone: (413)545-2689
Amherst, MA 01003 Fax: (413)577-0740

Magazine of literature, arts, and current affairs. **Founded:** 1959. **Freq:** Quarterly. **Print Method:** Offset. **Trim Size:** 6 x 9. **Cols./Page:** 1. **Col. Width:** 6 inches. **Key Personnel:** Mary Heath, Editor; Jules Chametzky, Editor; Paul Jenkins, Editor; Ellen Watson, Managing Editor, ewatson@external.umass.edu. **ISSN:** 0025-4878. **Subscription Rates:** $18 individuals. **Remarks:** Accepts advertising. **URL:** massrev@external.umass.edu.
Ad Rates: BW: $125 **Circ:** Paid ‡1,400
Non-paid ‡300

13923 Peregrine
Amherst Writers & Artists Press, Inc.
PO Box 1076 Phone: (413)253-7764
Amherst, MA 01004 Fax: (413)253-7764
Publisher E-mail: awapress@javanet.com

Literary journal covering poetry, fiction, translations, essays and reviews. **Founded:** 1984. **Freq:** Annual. **Trim Size:** 6 x 9. **Key Personnel:** Nancy Rose, Managing Editor. **ISSN:** 0890-622X. **Subscription Rates:** $7 single issue. **Remarks:** Advertising not accepted.
Circ: (Not Reported)

13924 POLITY
Polity Publications, Inc.
University of Massachusetts Phone: (413)545-1354
426 Thompson Hall Fax: (413)545-4902
Amherst, MA 01003-7520
Publication E-mail: polity@polsci.umass.edu

Journal of political science. **Subtitle:** The Journal of the Northeastern Political Science Association. **Founded:** Sept. 1968. **Freq:** Quarterly. **Print Method:** Offset. **Trim Size:** 6 x 9. **Cols./Page:** 3. **Col. Width:** 27 nonpareils. **Col. Depth:** 140 agate lines. **Key Personnel:** M.J. Peterson, Editor, phone (413)545-6193, mjp@polsci.umass.edu; Patricia Bachand, Bus. Mgr./CON, p.bachand@umass.edu. **ISSN:** 0032-3497. **Subscription Rates:** $25 individuals; $45 institutions. **Remarks:** Color advertising not accepted. **Alt. Formats:** Microfilm.
Ad Rates: BW: $100 **Circ:** Paid ‡1,000
Non-paid ‡100

13925 Theatre Topics
University of Massachusetts
Dept. of English Phone: (413)545-1914
Amherst, MA 01003 Fax: (413)545-3880
Publisher E-mail: paroissien@english.umass.edu

Journal covering all aspects of the theater. Published in cooperation with the Association for Theatre in Higher Education. **Founded:** 1991. **Freq:** Semiannual. **Key Personnel:** Harley Erdman, Editor; Jeffrey Eric Jenkins, Advertising Mgr. **ISSN:** 1054-8378. **Subscription Rates:** $18; $29 institutions. **Remarks:** Accepts advertising.
Ad Rates: BW: $215 **Circ:** 2,300

13926 Transitions Abroad
PO Box 1300 Phone: (413)256-3414
Amherst, MA 01004-1300 Fax: (413)256-0373
Free: (800)293-0373
Publication E-mail: info@transitionsabroad.com
Publisher E-mail: info@transitionsabroad.com

Magazine providing current and detailed practical information for the independent, international traveler on employment, study, special interest travel, and living overseas. Each issue focuses on one country or region. Annual directory, published separately in January (19.95). **Subtitle:** The Guide to Learning, Living, and Working Overseas. **Founded:** May 15, 1977. **Freq:** Bimonthly. **Print Method:** Offset. **Trim Size:** 8 1/2 x 11. **Cols./Page:** 3. **Col. Width:** 27 nonpareils. **Col. Depth:** 140 agate lines. **Key Personnel:** Clayton A. Hubbs, Editor and Publisher, editor@transitionsabroad.com; Michael Slaff, Advertising Mgr., phone (413)247-3300, fax (413)247-5758, mslaff@javanet.com; David Cline, Managing Editor. **ISSN:** 0276-4717. **Subscription Rates:** $24.95 individuals; $6.25 single issue. **URL:** http://www.transabroad.com.
Ad Rates: BW: $1,025 **Circ:** Paid ‡18,000

13927 UMASS Magazine
University of Massachusetts
Munson Hall Phone: (413)545-2991
Amherst, MA 01003 Fax: (413)545-3824
Publisher E-mail: umassmag@umassp.edu

Magazine containing collegiate and alumni news. **Subtitle:** The Magazine for Alumni & Friends of the University. **Founded:** 1920. **Freq:** Quarterly. **Print Method:** Offset. **Trim Size:** 8 1/2 x 11. **Cols./Page:** 3. **Col. Width:** 28 nonpareils. **Col. Depth:** 210 agate lines. **Key Personnel:** Patricia Wright, Editor, pwright@urd.umass.edu. **Remarks:** Advertising not accepted. **URL:** http://www.umass.edu/umassmag/. **Formerly:** Contact, Massachusetts Magazine.
Circ: Free ‡140,000

13928 WAMH-FM - 89.3
Amherst College Phone: (413)542-2224
Box 2171 Fax: (413)542-8250
Amherst, MA 01002-5000
E-mail: wamh@amherst.edu

Format: Full Service. **Networks:** Independent. **Owner:** Trustees of Amherst College, at above address, (413)542-2352. **Founded:** 1948. **Formerly:** WAMF-FM (1971). **Operating Hours:** Continuous; 100% local. **Key Personnel:** Jason Eugene Heindl, General Mgr.; Becky Siegel, Program Dir.; Matt Fagin, Music Dir. **Wattage:** 150.

13929 WFCR-FM - 88.5
Hampshire House Phone: (413)545-0100
University of Massachusetts Fax: (413)545-2546
Amherst, MA 01003-3630
Free: (800)639-8850
E-mail: wfcr@external.umass.edu

Format: Classical; Jazz; News; Folk; Public Radio. **Simulcasts:** WTTT-AM. **Networks:** National Public Radio (NPR); Public Radio International (PRI). **Owner:** University of Massachusetts, at above address. **Founded:** 1961. **Operating Hours:** Continuous. **ADI:** Springfield, MA. **Key Personnel:** Martin Miller, General Mgr. **Wattage:** 13,000. **Ad Rates:** Noncommercial.

13930 WMUA-FM - 91.1
University of Massachusetts Phone: (413)545-2876
105 Campus Center Fax: (413)545-0682
Amherst, MA 01003
E-mail: wmua@stuaf.umas.edu

Format: Eclectic. **Networks:** AP. **Founded:** 1949. **Operating Hours:** Continuous. **Key Personnel:** Brad Davidson, General Mgr.; Dave duCille, Programmer; Glenn Siegel, Advisor. **Local Programs:** *Jazz, Not Jazz*, Roger Fega, (413)545-2876, Fax (413)545-0682; *Jazz in Silhouette*, Glen Siegel, (413)545-2876, Fax (413)545-0682; *Polka Bandstand*, Billy Belina, Mailing contact, (413)545-2876, Fax (413)545-0682. **Wattage:** 1000. **Ad Rates:** Underwriting available.

ANDOVER, pop. 26,370.

NE MA. Essex Co. 3 mi. S. of Lawrence. Manufactures electronics, card cloth, dyestuffs and chemicals.

13931 The Andover Townsman
33 Chestnut St. Phone: (508)475-1943
Andover, MA 01810 Fax: (508)475-5731
Publication E-mail: townsman@aol.com

Newspaper with a Republican orientation. **Founded:** Oct. 14, 1887. **Freq:** Weekly (Thurs.). **Print Method:** Offset. **Trim Size:** 10 3/8 x 12 3/4. **Cols./Page:** 7. **Col. Width:** 1 3/8 inches. **Col. Depth:** 12 3/4 inches. **Key Personnel:** Taylor Armerding, Editor, tarmerding@andovertownsman.com; Irving E. Rogers III, Publisher; Michael A. Masessa, Jr., Business Mgr. **USPS:** 025-440. **Subscription Rates:** $40.
Ad Rates: GLR: $11.50 **Circ:** ⊕8,401
BW: $1,026.38
4C: $1,426.38
PCI: $11.50

13932 The Long Term View
Massachusetts School of Law
Woodland Park Phone: (978)681-0800
500 Federal St. Fax: (978)681-6330
Andover, MA 01810
Publication E-mail: ltv@msl.edu
Publisher E-mail: neb@mslaw.edu

Journal of public policy. **Subtitle:** A Journal of Informed Opinion. **Founded:** 1992. **Freq:** Quarterly. **Key Personnel:** Lawrence R. Velvel, Editor; Nancy Bernhard, Editor, neb@mslaw.edu. **ISSN:** 1066-1182. **Subscription Rates:** $10; $3.95 single issue. **Remarks:** Advertising not accepted. **URL:** http://www.longterm.mslaw.edu.
Circ: Non-paid 5,000

13933 Work
Gold
5 Possem Hollow Rd.
Andover, MA 01810-2445

Journal covering current work practices. **Subtitle:** A Journal of Prevention, Assessment, & Rehabilitation. **Freq:** Quarterly. **Subscription Rates:** $60 individuals; $95 institutions. **Remarks:** Advertising accepted; rates available upon request.
Circ: (Not Reported)

13934 WPAA-FM - 91.7
Phillips Academy Phone: (508)749-4384
Andover, MA 01810 Fax: (508)749-4123

Format: Eclectic. **Owner:** Phillips Academy, at above address. **Founded:** 1965. **Operating Hours:** Weekdays: 6:30-8 a.m, 5 p.m.-midnight Weekends 8:00 a.m.-midnight. **Key Personnel:** Kelly Trainor, General Mgr. **Wattage:** 10,000.

ARLINGTON, pop. 48,219.

NE MA. Middlesex Co. 7 mi. NW of Boston. Residential. Small business.

13935 American Shoemaking
Shoe Trades Publishing Co.
61 Massachusetts Ave. Phone: (781)648-8160
Arlington, MA 02474 Fax: (781)646-9832
Publisher E-mail: info@shoetrades.com

Magazine reporting on shoe manufacturing. **Founded:** 1896. **Freq:** Monthly. **Print Method:** Offset. **Trim Size:** 8 1/8 x 11 1/4. **Cols./Page:** 3. **Col. Width:** 30 nonpareils. **Col. Depth:** 136 agate lines. **Key Personnel:** James D. Sutton, Editor; John J. Moynihan, Publisher. **Subscription Rates:** $55 individuals annual; $10 single issue. **Remarks:** Accepts advertising.
Ad Rates: BW: $2,370 **Circ:** Paid 1,836
4C: $3,270 Non-paid 719
PCI: $55

13936 Arlington Advocate
Community Newspaper Company
254 Second Ave Phone: (781)433-7800
Needham, MA 02192 Fax: (781)433-8202
Publisher E-mail: townonline.com

Local newspaper. **Founded:** Dec. 16, 1871. **Freq:** Weekly (Thurs.). **Print Method:** Offset. **Trim Size:** 13 3/4 x 22 1/2. **Cols./Page:** 6. **Col. Width:** 12 nonpareils. **Col. Depth:** 21 inches. **Key Personnel:** Carol Beggy, Editor; Asa Cole, Publisher; Fred Splaine, Advertising Mgr. **Subscription Rates:** Free; $20 by mail; $15 students; $34 out of county.
Ad Rates: BW: $1,418.76 **Circ:** Paid 9,711
4C: $1,718.76 Free 433
SAU: $12.44

13937 Exponent II
Exponent II, Inc.
Box 128 Phone: (617)862-1928
Arlington, MA 02174 Fax: (617)868-3464

Newspaper for Mormon women. **Founded:** 1974. **Freq:** Quarterly. **Print Method:** Web offset. **Trim Size:** 11 1/4 x 17. **Cols./Page:** 3 and 4. **Key Personnel:** Jennifer Atkinson, Editor. **Subscription Rates:** $10. **Remarks:** Advertising not accepted.
Circ: 4,000

13938 Galilean Electrodynamics
141 Rhinecliff St. Phone: (781)643-3155
Arlington, MA 02476-7331 Fax: (781)646-8114
Publisher E-mail: dwhitney@mit.edu

Professional journal covering physics. **Founded:** Jan. 1990. **Freq:** Bimonthly and two special issues in 1999. **Trim Size:** 8 x 11. **Cols./Page:** 2. **Col. Width:** 3.63 inches. **Col. Depth:** 9.7 inches. **Key Personnel:** Cynthia K. Whitney, Editor, dwhitney@mit.edu; Howard C. Hayden, Assoc. Editor. **ISSN:** 1047-4811. **Subscription Rates:** $40 individuals; $54 for 6 regular & 2 special issues in 1999. **Remarks:** Advertising not accepted.
Circ: Combined ‡320

13939 The Leather Manufacturer
Shoe Trades Publishing Co.
61 Massachusetts Ave. Phone: (781)648-8160
Arlington, MA 02474 Fax: (781)646-9832
Publisher E-mail: info@shoetrades.com

Magazine on tanning and finishing leather. **Founded:** 1883. **Freq:** Monthly. **Print Method:** Offset. **Trim Size:** 8 1/2 x 11 1/2. **Cols./Page:** 3. **Col. Width:** 26 nonpareils. **Col. Depth:** 136 agate lines. **Key Personnel:** James Sutton, Editor; John J. Moynihan, Publisher. **Subscription Rates:** $52 individuals. **Remarks:** Accepts advertising. **URL:** http://www.shoetrades.com.
Ad Rates: BW: $1,545 **Circ:** ‡2,000
4C: $2,345
PCI: $60

13940 the new renaissance
Friends of the New Renaissance, Inc.
26 Heath Rd., No. 11
Arlington, MA 02474-3645

Literary magazine covering poetry, fiction, art, lead articles, reviews, and essays worldwide. **Subtitle:** An International Magazine of Ideas & Opinions, Emphasizing Literature and the Arts. **Founded:** Oct. 1968. **Freq:** Semiannual. **Print Method:** Offset. **Trim Size:** 6 x 9. **Key Personnel:** Louise T. Reynolds, Editor-in-Chief; David Hamasher, Circulation Mgr.; Patricia Michaud, Assoc. Editor, wmichaud@givi.net; Michal Ann Kuchouski, Assoc. Editor. **ISSN:** 0028-6575. **Subscription Rates:** $24 individuals USA; $10 individuals single issue. **Remarks:** Advertising not accepted.
Circ: Combined 710

ASHLAND, pop. 9,165.

NE MA. Middlesex Co. 10 mi. SW of Wellesley. Residential.

13941 The Ashland Tab
Community Newspaper Company
254 2nd Ave. Phone: (781)433-7828
Needham, MA 02192-9114 Fax: (781)433-7835

Community newspaper (tabloid). **Founded:** Oct. 1988. **Freq:** Weekly (Tues.). **Print Method:** Offset. **Trim Size:** 10 x 16. **Cols./Page:** 7. **Col. Width:** 8 picas. **Key Personnel:** John Wilpers, Editor; Russel Pergament, Advertising Mgr.; Stephen Cummings, Publisher; Lisa Flicop, Editor; Kirk A. Davis, Publisher, phone (617)433-8262, fax (617)969-3302. **URL:** http://townonline.com. **Formerly**: The Ashland/Holliston Gazette.
Circ: Non-paid 3,494

ATHOL, pop. 10,634.

C. MA. Worcester Co. 29 mi. W. of Fitchburg. Manufactures mechanical tools, drills, cutters, shoes, artificial leather, leather findings, celluloid goods, wooden toys, textile machinery, window blinds, furniture, metal and wooden novelties, plastic extrusions, paper boxes.

13942 Athol Daily News
Athol Press
PO Box 1000 Phone: (508)249-3535
Athol, MA 01331 Fax: (508)249-9630
Publication E-mail: adn@tiac.net

General newspaper. **Founded:** Nov. 1, 1934. **Freq:** Mon.-Sat. (eve.). **Print Method:** Offset. **Cols./Page:** 6. **Col. Width:** 25 nonpareils. **Col. Depth:** 294 agate lines. **Key Personnel:** B.B. Cummings, Editor; Richard J. Chase, Publisher; Dan Mahoney, Advertising Mgr. **Subscription Rates:** $96 individuals. **Remarks:** Accepts advertising. **Alt. Formats:** Microform.
Ad Rates: BW: $756 **Circ:** ‡5,684
SAU: $6
PCI: $6

ATTLEBORO, pop. 34,196.

SE MA. Bristol Co. 8 mi. N. of Pawtucket, RI. Manufactures jewelry and jewelry findings, bleach, dyes, reinforced paper, gold and silver plate, tools, nuclear fuel, electronic components, optical goods, paper boxes, rubber stamps, metal specialties, labels and seals, badges.

13943 The Sun Chronicle
34 S. Main St. Phone: (508)222-7000
Box 600 Fax: (508)226-5851
Attleboro, MA 02703
General newspaper. **Founded:** 1889. **Freq:** Daily (eve.), Sat. and Sun. (morn.). **Print Method:** Offset. **Cols./Page:** 6. **Col. Width:** 2 1/6 inches. **Col. Depth:** 21 1/4 inches. **Key Personnel:** Ned Bristol, Editor; Paul Rixon, Publisher; Oreste D'Arconte, General Mgr. **Subscription Rates:** $157 individuals. **Remarks:** Accepts advertising.
Ad Rates: BW: $1,295 **Circ:** Mon.-Sat. 22,638
4C: $1,630 Sun. 23,566
SAU: $10.15

13944 Inland Cable Communications
8 N. Main St. Phone: (508)761-9239
Attleboro, MA 02703 Fax: (508)223-4616

Owner: Continental Cablevision, at above address. **Founded:** 1981. **Key Personnel:** Stephen Cronin, General Mgr.; Chris Miller, Advertising Sales; Don Charlebois, Pay-per-view Coord.; Mark Godin, Chief Technician; Chris Miller, Program Dir. **Cities Served:** Attleboro, Rehoboth, MA: subscribing households 15,000; 75 channels; 4 community access channels; 20 hours per week community access programming.

13945 WARA-AM - 1320
45 West St. Phone: (508)222-9272
Attleboro, MA 02703 Fax: (508)222-8284
E-mail: talk@am1320wara.com

Format: Talk; News; Sports. **Networks:** AP; CNN Radio. **Founded:** 1950. **Operating Hours:** Continuous. **Key Personnel:** Joe Mangiacotti, VP/General Manager; Steve Winslow, Operations; Richard Lunt, News Dir. **Wattage:** 5000. **Ad Rates:** Advertising accepted; rates available upon request.

AUBURN, pop. 14,845.

C. MA. Worcester Co. 5 mi. S. of Worcester. Manufactures lumber, building materials, tools, steel, industrial equipment, and wool.

13946 Auburn News
Stonebridge Press, Inc.
1 St. Mark St. Phone: (508)832-2222
Auburn, MA 01501 Fax: (508)832-2431

Newspaper. **Founded:** 1949. **Freq:** Weekly (Wed.). **Print Method:** Offset. Uses mats. **Cols./Page:** 6. **Col. Width:** 19 nonpareils. **Col. Depth:** 224 agate lines. **Key Personnel:** Fran Boutilier, Contact; Ron MacGilvray, Contact. **Subscription Rates:** $10.50 individuals. **Remarks:** Accepts advertising. **Formerly**: Worester County Newspapers.
Ad Rates: SAU: $7.06 **Circ:** ‡2,728

AVON, pop. 5,026.

E. MA. Norfolk Co. 20 mi. S. of Boston. Manufactures shoe soles, heels and shanks, moccasin cutting dies and machinery, recapped tires. Agriculture.

13947 Avon Messenger
Associated Newspapers
7 Cabot Pl. Phone: (781)878-1111
PO Box 441 Fax: (781)878-3333
Stoughton, MA 02072
Publisher E-mail: aweeklies@aol.com

Community newspaper. **Founded:** 1929. **Freq:** Weekly (Wed.). **Print Method:** Offset. **Cols./Page:** 6. **Col. Width:** 9.5 picas. **Col. Depth:** 16 inches. **Key Personnel:** Richard R. Dailey, Publisher. **Subscription Rates:** $17.50 individuals. **Remarks:** Accepts advertising.
Ad Rates: BW: $10.53 **Circ:** ‡1,140
4C: $10.77
PCI: $10.53

AYER, pop. 6,993.

NE MA. Middlesex Co. 13 mi. E. of Fitchburg. Manufactures garment machinery, cutlery, paper products, furniture, electronics. Apple packing; cannery. Timber. Diversified farming. Apples, truck crops.

13948 Fort Devens Dispatch
Nashoba Publications, Inc.
69 Fitchburg Rd. Phone: (978)772-0777
Ayer, MA 01432-0362 Fax: (978)772-4012
Free: (800)445-5635
Publisher E-mail: editor@nashobapub.com

Newspaper for military personnel of Ft. Devens. **Founded:** 1965. **Freq:** Weekly (Wed.). **Print Method:** Web offset. **Cols./Page:** 8. **Col. Width:** 24 nonpareils. **Col. Depth:** 294 agate lines. **Key Personnel:** Frank Hartnett, Sr., Publisher. **Remarks:** Accepts advertising.
Ad Rates: GLR: $.178 **Circ:** Free 5,200

13949 The Public Spirit
Nashoba Publications, Inc.
69 Fitchburg Rd. Phone: (978)772-0777
Ayer, MA 01432-0362 Fax: (978)772-4012
Free: (800)445-5635
Publisher E-mail: editor@nashobapub.com

Community newspaper. **Founded:** 1869. **Freq:** Weekly (Wed.). **Print Method:** Offset. **Cols./Page:** 8. **Col. Width:** 24 nonpareils. **Col. Depth:** 294 agate lines. **Key Personnel:** Frank Hartnett, Jr., Editor; Frank Hartnett, Sr., Publisher. **Subscription Rates:** $25 individuals. **Remarks:** Accepts advertising.
Ad Rates: GLR: $.267 **Circ:** 12,000

Times-Free Press - See Pepperell

BABSON PARK

13950 Babson Bulletin
Babson College
Millea Hall Phone: (781)239-5256
Babson Park, MA 02457 Fax: (781)239-5989
Publisher E-mail: alumnews@babson.edu

Magazine for college alumni. **Founded:** 1932. **Freq:** Quarterly. **Print Method:** Offset. **Trim Size:** 8 3/4 x 11. **Cols./Page:** 2 and 4. **Col. Width:** 26 nonpareils. **Col. Depth:** 135 agate lines. **Key Personnel:** Melinda Lamb Theodore, Editor, theodore@babson.edu. **USPS:** 898-140. **Remarks:** Advertising not accepted.
Circ: Controlled 32,000

BARRE, pop. 4,102.

C. MA. Worcester Co. 22 mi. NW of Worcester. Machine shop and foundry. Dairy farms.

13951 Barre Gazette
5 Exchange St. Phone: (508)355-4000
Barre, MA 01005 Fax: (508)355-6274

Community newspaper. **Founded:** May 1834. **Freq:** Weekly (Thurs.). **Print Method:** Offset. **Trim Size:** 13 x 21. **Cols./Page:** 8. **Col. Width:** 1 1/2 inches. **Col. Depth:** 294 agate lines. **Key Personnel:** Marilyn A. Haynes, Editor-in-Chief; Patrick H. Turley, Publisher, phone (413)283-8393; Tim Mara,

Advertising Mgr. **USPS:** 044-560. **Subscription Rates:** $21 individuals; $34 two years. **Remarks:** Accepts advertising.
Ad Rates: GLR: $.334 **Circ:** ‡2,500
BW: $1,008
4C: $1,308
PCI: $6.00

BECKET

13952 Anais
Anais Nin Foundation
PO Box 276
Becket, MA 01223

Scholarly journal covering the works of Anais Nin and related writers. **Subtitle:** An International Journal. **Founded:** 1983. **Freq:** Annual. **Print Method:** Offset. **Trim Size:** 6 x 9. **Cols./Page:** 1. **Key Personnel:** Gunther Stuhlmann, Editor. **ISSN:** 8755-3910. **Subscription Rates:** $8 individuals; $9 out of country; $12.50 institutions; $14 institutions out of country. **Remarks:** Advertising not accepted.
Circ: Paid 1,000

BEDFORD

13953 Bedford Minute Man
Community Newspaper Company/Northwest
150 Baker Ave., Ste. 305 Phone: (978)371-5754
PO Box 9191 Fax: (978)371-9058
Concord, MA 01742-9191
Community newspaper. **Founded:** 1959. **Freq:** Weekly (Thurs.). **Print Method:** Offset. **Cols./Page:** 6. **Col. Width:** 21 nonpareils. **Col. Depth:** 294 agate lines. **Key Personnel:** Jon Towne, Managing Editor; Steve Dines, President; Lisa Comins, Advertising Mgr. **USPS:** 047-740. **Subscription Rates:** $24 individuals; $36 out of county. **Remarks:** Accepts advertising.
Ad Rates: PCI: $8.80 **Circ:** Paid 3,254
Non-paid 19

13954 Hobby Greenhouse
Hobby Greenhouse Association
8 Glen Terr. Phone: (781)275-0377
Bedford, MA 01730-2048
Publisher E-mail: jhale@world.std.com

Trade magazine covering greenhouse construction and greenhouse growing for members. **Founded:** 1976. **Freq:** Quarterly. **Trim Size:** 8 x 11. **Cols./Page:** 3. **Col. Width:** 2 1/4 inches. **Key Personnel:** Janice L. Hale, Editor, jhale@world.std.com; Linda Vanaria, Advertising Mgr. **ISSN:** 1040-6212. **Subscription Rates:** $19 individuals; $3.50 single issue. **Remarks:** Accepts advertising. **Former name:** The Planter (1985).
Ad Rates: BW: $125 **Circ:** Combined 2,000

BELCHERTOWN

NW MA. Hampshire Co. 10 mi. SE of Amherst.

13955 Amrac Clearview
40 Daniel Shays Hwy. Phone: (413)323-9203
Belchertown, MA 01007 Fax: (413)323-7466

Owner: Amrac Telecommunications, 470 Totten Pond Rd., Waltham, MA 02154, (617)890-9191, Fax: (617)890-6239, Free: (800)585-0039. **Founded:** 1985. **Key Personnel:** Sid Whiting, Contact; Karl Whiting, Operations Mgr.; David Slivka, Contact; David Whiting, Tech Mgr.; Gail Valentine, Office Mgr. **Cities Served:** Belchertown, Hadley, MA: subscribing households 4,827; 41 channels; 1 community access channel; 6 hours per week community access programming.

BELMONT, pop. 26,100.

NE MA. Middlesex Co. 6 mi. NW of Boston. (Branch of Boston P.O.) Residential.

13956 Phenomenological Inquiry
World Phenomenology Intitute
348 Payson Rd. Phone: (617)295-3487
Belmont, MA 02478 Fax: (617)295-5963

Journal containing scholarly articles relating to phenomenology. **Founded:** 1976. **Freq:** Annual. **Key Personnel:** Anna-Teresa Tymieniecka, Ph.D, Editor. **ISSN:** 8885-3886. **Subscription Rates:** $40 individuals. **Remarks:** Accepts advertising. **Formerly:** Phenomenology Information Bulletin.
Circ: Paid 400
Non-paid 200

BEVERLY, pop. 37,655.

NE MA. Essex Co. On an inlet of the Atlantic Ocean, 20 mi. NE of Boston. Summer resort. Manufactures shoe machinery and findings, wood and metal products, textiles, sails, electronic tubes.

13957 Oil and Energy
New England Fuel Institute
PO Box 37 Phone: (978)927-1541
Beverly, MA 01915 Fax: (978)927-8862
Publisher E-mail: grey@shore.net

Magazine for the independent fuel and heating contractor. **Subtitle:** Serving the Independent Fuel and Heating Contractor. **Founded:** June 1, 1957. **Freq:** Monthly. **Print Method:** Offset. Uses mats. **Trim Size:** 8 1/4 x 11. **Cols./Page:** 3. **Col. Width:** 13 picas. **Col. Depth:** 10 inches. **Key Personnel:** Keith Lewis, Managing Editor. **ISSN:** 0044-0205. **Subscription Rates:** $15 Free to qualified subscribers; $15 institutions. **Formerly:** Yankee Oilman Magazine.
Ad Rates: GLR: $9 **Circ:** Controlled ‡6,583
BW: $1,230 Paid ‡2,038
4C: $2,015

13958 Salem Evening News
32 Dunham Rd. Phone: (978)922-1234
Beverly, MA 01915 Fax: (978)922-4330
Publisher E-mail: sen@ecnnews.com

Newspaper. **Founded:** 1893. **Freq:** Mon.-Sat. (eve.). **Print Method:** Offset. **Cols./Page:** 6. **Col. Width:** 25 nonpareils. **Col. Depth:** 294 agate lines. **Key Personnel:** David Marcus, Editor, dmarcus@ecnnews.com; John Kinney, Publisher, fax (978)927-7596, jkinney@ecnnews.com. **Subscription Rates:** $165 by mail. **Remarks:** Accepts advertising. **Formerly:** Beverly Times; Salem News.
Ad Rates: SAU: $32.50 **Circ:** Mon.-Sat. 36,446

13959 WBOQ-FM - 104.9
8 Enon St. Phone: (508)927-1049
Beverly, MA 01915 Fax: (508)921-2635
Free: (800)370-1049
E-mail: webmaster@wbach.com

Format: Classical. **Networks:** Concert Music Network (CMN). **Founded:** 1964. **Formerly:** WVCA-FM (1988). **Operating Hours:** Continuous. **ADI:** Boston-Worcester,MA-Derry-Manchester,NH. **Key Personnel:** Alan Tolz, General Mgr.; Steve Murphy, Operations Mgr.; Karl Alan, Music Dir. **Local Programs:** *Best of Boston*, Karl Alan, Music Dir.; *Broadway Classics*, Karl Alan, Music Dir.; *North Shore Issues*, Bob Miot, Mailing contact. **Wattage:** 3000. **Ad Rates:** $35-65 for 60 seconds. **URL:** http://www.wbach.com.

13960 WNSH-AM - 1570
376 Hale St. Phone: (508)927-9674
Beverly, MA 01915-2096

Format: Full Service; Ethnic; Adult Contemporary; Top 40; Oldies; Middle-of-the-Road (MOR). **Networks:** Independent. **Owner:** FSAM Corp., at above address. **Founded:** 1967. **Formerly:** WMLO-AM. **Wattage:** 500. **Ad Rates:** Advertising accepted; rates available upon request.

BILLERICA, pop. 36,727.

NC MA. Middlesex Co. 6 mi. S. of Lowell.

13961 The Billerica News
Community Newspapers Inc.
360 Summer St. Fax: (508)670-5299
Somerville, MA 02144
Community newspaper. **Founded:** 1928. **Freq:** Weekly (Thurs.). **Print Method:** Offset. **Cols./Page:** 5. **Col. Width:** 22 nonpareils. **Col. Depth:** 224 agate lines. **Subscription Rates:** $15. **Remarks:** Accepts advertising.
Ad Rates: GLR: $.21 **Circ:** Non-paid 4,129
BW: $320
PCI: $5

13962 Boundary Elements Communications
Computational Mechanics Inc.
25 Bridge St. Phone: (978)667-5841
Billerica, MA 01821 Fax: (978)667-7582
Publication E-mail: cmina@ix.netcom.com; cmp@cmp.co.uk
Publisher E-mail: cmina@ix.netcom.com

Engineering journal. **Founded:** 1989. **Freq:** Bimonthly. **Print Method:** Offset. **Trim Size:** 8 1/4 x 11 21/32. **Cols./Page:** 2. **Col. Width:** 3 3/8 inches. **Col. Depth:** 9 1/2 inches. **Key Personnel:** M.H. Aliabadi, Editor; C.A. Brebbia, Editor; J. Mackerle, Editor. **ISSN:** 1353-825X. **Subscription Rates:** $296 Included in membership. **Remarks:** Accepts advertising. **Formerly:** Boundry Element Abstracts and Newsletter; Boundary Elements Communications; International Journal of Boundary Elements Communications.
Circ: (Not Reported)

13963 Metronome Magazine
PO Box 921 Phone: (978)957-0925
Billerica, MA 01821
Consumer magazine covering music of all types. **Founded:** Jan. 1, 1986. **Freq:** Monthly. **Print Method:** Web offset. **Trim Size:** 10 x 13. **Cols./Page:** 4. **Col. Width:** 2 1/2 inches. **Key Personnel:** Brian Michael Owens, Contact. **Subscription Rates:** $20 individuals. **Remarks:** Accepts advertising.
Ad Rates: GLR: $15 **Circ:** Controlled 30,000
BW: $500
PCI: $15

BOSTON†, pop. 562,994.

E. MA. Suffolk Co. On Massachusetts Bay. The State Capital. Noted educational center with more than 200 private schools and colleges in Boston and immediate vicinity. Many historical features. Important seaport. Foremost fishing port and wool market. The industrial center of New England and center of one of the largest suburban areas in the United States. More than 200,000,000 pounds of fish are landed annually. Extensive fish freezing and cold storage plants. Important industries; printing and publishing, ship building, sugar refining, manufacture of boots and shoes; electrical machinery, textiles, bakery products, confectionery, cutlery, leather, plastics, chemicals, furniture, wooden and paper boxes, foundry and machine shop products, woolens, worsteds, meat packing.

13964 Adweek/New England
Adweek LP
100 Boylston St., Ste. 210 Phone: (617)482-0876
Boston, MA 02116 Fax: (617)482-2921

News magazine serving the advertising, marketing, and media industries in New England. **Founded:** 1965. **Freq:** Weekly. **Print Method:** Offset. **Trim Size:** 8 3/8 x 10 7/8. **Cols./Page:** 3. **Key Personnel:** Judy Warner, Editor; Ronald Kolgraf, Publisher. **ISSN:** 0888-0840. **Subscription Rates:** $125 individuals; $62.50 members. **Remarks:** Accepts advertising.
Ad Rates: BW: $2,507.50 **Circ:** Paid ‡7,538
4C: $4,309.50
PCI: $90

13965 AGNI
Boston University Phone: (617)353-7135
236 Bay State Rd. Fax: (617)353-7136
Boston, MA 02215-1403
Publication E-mail: agni@bu.edu

Journal of literature and ideas. **Founded:** 1972. **Freq:** Semiannual. **Trim Size:** 4 3/4 x 7 7/8. **Key Personnel:** Askold Melnyczuk, Editor; Valerie Duff, Managing Editor, phone (617)353-7135, fax (617)353-7136. **ISSN:** 0191-3352. **Subscription Rates:** $18 individuals; $38 institutions; $40 2 yrs. **Remarks:** Accepts advertising. **URL:** http://www.webdelsol.com/agni/. **Formerly:** AGNI Review.
Ad Rates: 4C: $330 **Circ:** Paid 2,000
Non-paid 500

13966 AMC Outdoors
Appalachian Mountain Club
5 Joy St. Phone: (617)523-0636
Boston, MA 02108 Fax: (617)523-0722
Publication E-mail: amcoutdoors@amcinfo.org

Outdoor recreation and conservation magazine. **Subtitle:** The Magazine of the Appalachian Mountain Club. **Founded:** 1910. **Freq:** 10/year. **Print Method:** Web. **Trim Size:** 8 x 10 3/4. **Cols./Page:** 3 and 4. **Col. Width:** 40 and 20 nonpareils. **Col. Depth:** 126 agate lines. **Key Personnel:** Jane Roy Brown, jroybrown@amcinfo.org wow; Madeline Eno, Publisher, meno@amcinfo.org. **ISSN:** 0003-6587. **Subscription Rates:** $40 members. **Remarks:** Accepts advertising. **Formerly:** Appalachian Bulletin.
Ad Rates: GLR: $1.95 **Circ:** Paid ‡78,000
BW: $2,090 Non-paid ‡1,000
4C: $2,950
PCI: $45

13967 American Journal of Law & Medicine
American Society of Law, Medicine & Ethics, Inc.
765 Commonwealth Ave., Ste. 1672
Boston, MA 02215
Publisher E-mail: aslme@bu.edu

Law review publishing scholarly and professional articles, student cases and notes, and annotations of recent health-care-related court decisions. **Founded:** 1975. **Freq:** Quarterly. **Print Method:** Web/Perfect bound. **Trim Size:** 6 3/4 x 10. **Cols./Page:** 1. **Col. Width:** 29 1/2 picas. **Col. Depth:** 49 picas. **Key Personnel:** Jeremy Johnson, Editor-in-Chief; Michael Vasko, Dir. of Publications, phone (617)262-4990, mvasko@alsme.org. **ISSN:** 0098-8588. **Subscription Rates:** $90 individuals; $170 institutions; other countries add $30 for postage. **Online:** Lexis; Westlaw; Ebsco; Index Medious; Embase: Excespta Medica. **URL:** http://www.alsme.org. **Alt. Formats:** Microform; Mailing labels.
Ad Rates: BW: $600 **Circ:** 3,700

13968 Animals Magazine
Massachusetts Society for the Prevention of Cruelty to Animals and the American Human Education Society
350 S. Huntington Ave. Phone: (617)541-5065
Boston, MA 02130 Fax: (617)522-4885
Free: (800)998-0797
Publication E-mail: animals@americast.com

Magazine on wildlife, pets, animal welfare, and environmental issues. **Founded:** 1868. **Freq:** Bimonthly. **Print Method:** Web offset. **Trim Size:** 8 1/4 x 10 7/8. **Cols./Page:** 3. **Col. Width:** 2 3/16 inches. **Col. Depth:** 10 inches. **Key Personnel:** Joni Praded, Directory/Editor, phone (617)541-5067, jpraded@mspca.org; Joseph E. Kaknes, Advertising Mgr., phone (617)541-5090, jkaknes@mspca.org. **ISSN:** 0030-6835. **Subscription Rates:** $19.94 individuals; $24.94 other countries; $2.95 single issue. **Remarks:** Accepts advertising. **Online:** American Cybercasting Corporation. **Alt. Formats:** Microform.
Ad Rates: BW: $3,050 **Circ:** Paid 100,000
4C: $4,500

13969 The Atlantic Monthly
The Atlantic Monthly Co.
77 N. Washington St. Phone: (617)854-7700
Boston, MA 02114 Fax: (617)854-7876

General interest magazine. **Founded:** 1857. **Freq:** Monthly. **Print Method:** Offset. **Trim Size:** 8 1/16 x 10 7/8 in. **Cols./Page:** 3 and 2. **Col. Width:** 27 and 40 nonpareils. **Col. Depth:** 138 agate lines. **Key Personnel:** William Whitworth, Editor-in-Chief. **ISSN:** 0276-9077. **Subscription Rates:** $17.94 individuals. **Online:** LEXIS-NEXIS. **URL:** http://www.theatlantic.com. **Formerly:** The Atlantic.
Ad Rates: BW: $20,640 **Circ:** Paid 454,278
4C: $30,980

13970 Bay Windows
631 Tremont St. Phone: (617)266-6670
Boston, MA 02118-1201 Fax: (617)266-5973

Magazine covering gay male and lesbian news and literature. **Founded:** 1983. **Freq:** Weekly. **Print Method:** Wel offset. **Trim Size:** 10 1/8 x 15 1/2. **Cols./Page:** 6. **Key Personnel:** Jeff Epperly, Editor; Serge Gojkovich, Display Advertising; James G. Hoover, Publisher. **Subscription Rates:** $110 by mail first class; $50 by mail third class.
Circ: Non-paid 24,500

13971 The Beacon Hill Times
83 Phillips St. Phone: (617)523-9490
Boston, MA 02114 Fax: (617)523-8668

Newspaper covering two neighborhoods, Beacon Hill and Charles River Park, in the Boston, MA, area. **Founded:** Sept. 1, 1995. **Freq:** Biweekly. **Key Personnel:** Karen Cord, Editor and Publisher, editor@beaconhilltimes.com; Elizabeth Thomson, Assoc. Editor/Publisher, editor@beaconhilltimes.com. **Subscription Rates:** Free to qualified subscribers; $40 out of area. **Remarks:** Accepts advertising. **URL:** http://www.beaconhilltimes.com.
Ad Rates: BW: $704 **Circ:** Paid 100
PCI: $11 Non-paid 12,500

13972 Berklee Today
Berklee Press Publications
1140 Boylston St. Phone: (617)747-2325
Boston, MA 02215 Fax: (617)247-8788
Publisher E-mail: msmall@berklee.edu

College alumni magazine covering music and other issues. **Founded:** June 1989. **Freq:** 3/year. **Print Method:** Web offset. **Trim Size:** 8 1/8 x 10 7/8. **Cols./Page:** 3. **Col. Width:** 2 1/4 inches. **Col. Depth:** 9 1/2 inches. **Key Personnel:** Mark Small, Editor. **ISSN:** 1052-3839. **Subscription Rates:** $25 individuals; Free to qualified subscribers. **Remarks:** Accepts advertising.
Ad Rates: BW: $1,100 **Circ:** Non-paid ‡32,500
4C: $1,400

13973 Boston Business Journal
MCP, Inc.
200 High St. Phone: (617)330-1000
Boston, MA 02110 Fax: (617)330-1016

Business newspaper specializing in local and regional business for upper management and CEO's of large and mid-sized businesses. **Founded:** May 1980. **Freq:** Weekly. **Print Method:** Offset. **Trim Size:** 10 1/8 x 13 1/2. **Cols./Page:** 4. **Col. Width:** 14.3 picas. **Key Personnel:** Chuck Heschmeyer, Editor; James Menneto, Publisher; Mike Olivier, Advertising Mgr.; Sean Ryan, Circulation Mgr. **ISSN:** 0746-4975. **Subscription Rates:** $64 individuals.
Ad Rates: BW: $3,975 **Circ:** Paid ★17,202
4C: $4,575

13974 The Boston Globe
New York Times Co./Globe Newspaper Co.
135 Morrissey Blvd. Phone: (617)929-2935
PO Box 2378 Fax: (617)929-3192
Boston, MA 02107-3310
General newspaper. **Founded:** 1872. **Freq:** Mon.-Sun. (morn.). **Print Method:** Offset. Uses mats. **Cols./Page:** 6. **Col. Width:** 24 nonpareils. **Col. Depth:** 294 agate lines. **Key Personnel:** Matthew V. Storen, Editor; William O. Taylor, Publisher; Benjamin B. Taylor, President; Mary Jane Patrone, Vice Pres. of Marketing. **Remarks:** Accepts advertising. **Online:** Dialog (The Dialog Corporation); DataTimes Corporation; CompuServe Information Service; LEXIS-NEXIS; America Online, Inc. **Alt. Formats:** CD-ROM. **Feature Editors:** Jerry Ackerman, *Environmental*, phone (617)929-3157; Vin Alabiso, *Photo*, phone (617)929-3173; Alison Arnett, *Sunday*, phone (617)929-2948; Steve Bailey, *Financial/Business*, phone (617)929-2924; John Burke, *Metro*, phone (617)929-3138; Jay Carr, *Movie*, phone (617)929-2811; Muriel Cohen, *Education*, phone (617)929-3067; William Davis, *Travel*, phone (617)929-2944; Vince Doria, *Sports*, phone (617)929-2840; Richard Dyer, *Music*, phone (617)929-2782; James Franklin, *Religion*, phone (617)929-3075; Julie Hatfield, *Fashion*, phone (617)929-2803; Peter Hotton, *Garden/Home*, phone (617)929-2946; Mary Jane Wilkinson, *Living*, phone (617)929-2913; John King, *Real Estate*, phone (617)929-2907; Richard Knox, *Medical*, phone (617)929-3078; Lincoln Millstein, *Features*, phone (617)929-2800; Tom Mulvoy, *News*, phone (617)929-3216; Gail Perrin, *Food*, phone (617)929-2802; Ed Siegel, *TV & Radio*, phone (617)929-2832.
Ad Rates: SAU: $184.25 **Circ:** Mon.-Fri. ★**470,825**
Sat. ★**457,442**
Sun. ★**751,021**

13975 Boston Herald
PO Box 2096 Phone: (617)426-3000
Boston, MA 02106-2096 Fax: (617)542-1315
Free: (800)225-2040

General newspaper. **Founded:** 1982. **Freq:** Mon.-Sun. (morn.). **Print Method:** Letterpress. Uses mats. **Cols./Page:** 5. **Col. Width:** 17 nonpareils. **Col. Depth:** 200 agate lines. **Key Personnel:** Ken Chandler, Editor, phone (617)542-1315; Patrick Purcell, Publisher; Shaun Butler, Advertising Vice Pres.; Bill Weber, Asst. Managing Editor; Andrew F. Costello, Jr., Executive Editor; Kevin Convey, Managing Editor; Andrew Gully, Managing Editor; Sonia Turek, Deputy Managing Editor; Andy Tomolonis, Deputy Managing Editor; Ted Bunker, Asst. Managing Editor; Gwen Gage, Vice Pres., Promotions; Randy Hano, National Sales Mgr.; Bob Sheehan, Retail Advertising Mgr.; Tom Libby, Dir., Information Technology; John Hoarty, Vice Pres., Circulation; Amanda Anderson, Marketing Mgr., Circulation; Gerry Sher, Mgr., Home Delivery. **Remarks:** Accepts advertising. **Online:** DataTimes Corporation. **URL:** http://www.bostonherald.com. **Feature Editors:** Dana Bisbee, *Society*; Howie Carr, *News*; Mark Chapman, *Book, Travel*; Rachelle Cohen, *Editorials*; Kevin Cole, *Photo*; Monica Collins, *TV*; Jane Dornbusch, *Food*; Margery Eagan, *News*; Joe Fitzgerald, *News*; Peter Gelzinis, *News*; Leonard Greene, *News*; Larry Katz, *Music*; Eric Norment, *Sunday*; Walter Roche, *Political*; Dan Rosenfeld, *City*; James Verniere, *Movie*; Janet Walsh, *City*; Bill Weber, *Entertainment*.
Ad Rates: PCI: $174.50 **Circ:** Mon.-Fri. ★**271,425**
Sat. ★**218,975**
Sun. ★**177,139**

13976 The Boston Jewish Times
15 School St. Phone: (617)442-9680
Boston, MA 02108-4307 Fax: (617)367-9310

Jewish-oriented newspaper (tabloid). **Founded:** Sept. 1945. **Freq:** Semimonthly. **Print Method:** Offset. Uses mats. **Cols./Page:** 5. **Col. Width:** 24 nonpareils. **Col. Depth:** 224 agate lines. **Key Personnel:** Sten B. Lukin, Editor and Publisher; Sarabeth Lukin, Advertising Mgr. **ISSN:** 8750-1961. **Subscription Rates:** $12 individuals. **Remarks:** Accepts advertising.
Ad Rates: GLR: $.43 **Circ:** ‡11,000
BW: $432
SAU: $6

13977 Boston Magazine
300 Massachusetts Ave. Phone: (617)262-9700
Boston, MA 02115 Fax: (617)262-4925
Publication E-mail: artj@bostonmagazine.com

Magazine covering business, politics, and lifestyle in the Boston metropolitan area. **Founded:** Sept. 1962. **Freq:** Monthly. **Print Method:** Offset. **Trim Size:** 8 x 10 7/8. **Cols./Page:** 3. **Col. Width:** 27 nonpareils. **Col. Depth:** 140 agate lines. **Key Personnel:** Craig Vnger, Editor; Alan J. Klein, Publisher; Susan Watson, Marketing Director; Mary Kaye Chryssicas, Advertising Dir. **Subscription Rates:** $15 individuals; $3.50 single issue. **Remarks:** Accepts advertising. **URL:** http://www.bostonmagazine.com.
Ad Rates: BW: $7,242 **Circ:** Paid ★127,339
4C: $10,353

13978 The Boston Parent's Paper
The Parents' Plus, Inc.
PO Box 1777
Boston, MA 02130
Publication E-mail: tbpp@parentsplus.com

Magazine. **Founded:** July 1984. **Freq:** Monthly. **Trim Size:** 10 x 12 3/8. **Key Personnel:** Betsy Weaver, President; William Lindsay, Editor-in-Chief; Deirde Wilson, Managing Editor; Barbara Smith Decker, Sr. Editor, Depts.; Kaleel Sakakeeny, Travel Editor. **Subscription Rates:** $15. **Remarks:** Accepts advertising.
Ad Rates: BW: $2,940 **Circ:** Free 65,417
4C: $3,540 Paid 771

13979 The Boston Phoenix
Phoenix Media Group
126 Brookline Ave. Phone: (617)536-5390
Boston, MA 02215 Fax: (617)536-1463

Metropolitan newspaper. **Founded:** 1966. **Freq:** Weekly (Thurs.). **Print Method:** Offset. **Trim Size:** 11 x 17. **Cols./Page:** 6. **Col. Width:** 11 picas. **Col. Depth:** 16 inches. **Key Personnel:** Peter Kadzis, Editor; Stephen Mindich, Publisher; William Risteen, Advertising Dir. **Subscription Rates:** $41.50 individuals.
Ad Rates: GLR: $6.43 **Circ:** Paid 68,000
BW: $8,385 Free 50,000
4C: $9,635
PCI: $87.35

13980 Boston Seniority
Mayor's Commission on Affairs of the Elderly
One City Hall Pl., Rm. 271 Phone: (617)635-2712
Boston, MA 02201 Fax: (617)635-3213

Newspaper for senior Bostonians. **Founded:** 1977. **Freq:** Monthly. **Trim Size:** 8 1/2 x 11. **Cols./Page:** 3. **Col. Width:** 2 5/16 inches. **Col. Depth:** 9 3/4 inches. **Key Personnel:** Carrie Dawe, Editor, carrie.dawe@ci.boston.ma.us. **Subscription Rates:** Free. **Remarks:** Advertising not accepted.
Circ: Free ‡20

13981 Boston University Today
Boston University
236 Bay State Rd. Phone: (617)353-2505
Boston, MA 02215
Collegiate newspaper (tabloid). **Subtitle:** A Weekly Newspaper for The Boston University Community. **Freq:** Weekly. **Print Method:** Offset. Uses mats. **Trim Size:** 11 5/16 x 17 1/16. **Cols./Page:** 4. **Col. Width:** 14 1/2 picas. **Col. Depth:** 92 picas. **Key Personnel:** Michael Shavelson, Editorial, phone (617)353-5791; Marissa Mediate, Advertising, phone (617)353-5390; Joan Frank, Subscriptions, phone (617)353-2055. **Subscription Rates:** $25 individuals. **Remarks:** Accepts advertising.
Ad Rates: BW: $492 **Circ:** Paid ‡500
SAU: $8 Free ‡16,000

13982 Bulletin of the AMS
American Meteorological Society
45 Beacon St. Phone: (617)227-2425
Boston, MA 02108 Fax: (617)742-8718
Publisher E-mail: amspubs@ametsoc.org

Magazine containing official American Meteorological Society professional articles, membership news, and book reviews. **Founded:** 1920. **Freq:** Monthly. **Print Method:** Offset. **Trim Size:** 7 3/4 x 10 1/2. **Cols./Page:** 2. **Col. Width:** 39 nonpareils. **Col. Depth:** 126 agate lines. **Key Personnel:** Ronald McPherson, Editor and Publisher. **ISSN:** 0003-0007. **Subscription Rates:** $30 individuals; $80 nonmembers; $15 single issue. **Remarks:** Accepts advertising. **URL:** http://www.ams.allenpress.com. **Alt. Formats:** CD-ROM, The AMS Journal; Bulletin Archive.
Ad Rates: BW: $845 **Circ:** ‡12,585
4C: $2,625

13983 Business History Review
60 Harvard Way Phone: (617)495-6154
Boston, MA 02163 Fax: (617)496-5985
Publication E-mail: bhr@hbs.edu

Journal covering business and economic history. **Founded:** 1926. **Freq:** Quarterly. **Print Method:** Letterpress and offset. Uses mats. **Trim Size:** 6 x 9. **Cols./Page:** 1. **Col. Width:** 50 nonpareils. **Col. Depth:** 98 agate lines. **Key Personnel:** Thomas K. McCraw, Editor; Kelcey Wilson, Production Mgr., kwilson@hbs.edu; Walter A. Friedman, Assoc. Editor, phone (617)495-6954. **ISSN:** 0007-6805. **Subscription Rates:** $50 individuals; $15 single issue; $100 institutions, other countries; $115 other countries. **Remarks:** Accepts advertising.
Ad Rates: BW: $200 **Circ:** Paid 2,000
Non-paid 300

13984 CFO
CFO Publishing
253 Summer St. Phone: (617)345-9700
Boston, MA 02210 Fax: (617)951-9306

Chief Financial Officer. Business magazine for small to mid-sized companies. **Subtitle:** Magazine for Senior Financial Executives. **Founded:** Feb. 1985. **Freq:** Monthly. **Print Method:** Web offset. **Trim Size:** 8 1/8 x 10 3/4. **Cols./Page:** 3. **Col. Depth:** 2 1/4 inches. **Key Personnel:** Julia Homer, Editor; David Laird, Publisher; Laurie Finnie, Advertising Mgr. **Subscription Rates:** $19; $5 single issue. **Remarks:** Accepts advertising.
Ad Rates: BW: $22,670 **Circ:** Controlled ‡350,000
4C: $32,080

13985 The Christian Science Journal
The Christian Science Publishing Society
1 Norway St. Phone: (617)450-2000
Boston, MA 02115
Publication E-mail: journal@csps.com

An ongoing record of Christian Science healing includes Worldwide directory of churches and Christian Science practitioners. **Subtitle:** Official Publication of The First Church of Christ, Scientist. **Founded:** Apr. 1883. **Freq:** Monthly. **Print Method:** Offset. **Trim Size:** 8 1/8 x 10 3/4. **Cols./Page:** 1 and 3. **Col. Width:** 28.75 and 12.3 picas. **Col. Depth:** 58.3 picas. **Key Personnel:** William E. Moody, Editor. **ISSN:** 0009-5613. **Subscription Rates:** $43 individuals; $4 single issue. **Remarks:** Advertising not accepted.
Circ: (Not Reported)

13986 The Christian Science Monitor
The Christian Science Publishing Society
1 Norway St. Phone: (617)450-2000
Boston, MA 02115
National daily newspaper. **Founded:** 1908. **Freq:** Daily (morn.). **Print Method:** Offset. **Trim Size:** 11 x 14. **Cols./Page:** 6. **Col. Width:** 20 nonpareils. **Col. Depth:** 192 agate lines. **Key Personnel:** David Cook, Editor. **Subscription Rates:** $144 individuals. **Remarks:** Accepts advertising. **Online:** DataTimes Corporation; Dialog (The Dialog Corporation); LEXIS-NEXIS; Compuserve Information Service. **URL:** http://www.csmonitor.com. **Alt. Formats:** CD-ROM. **Feature Editors:** April Austin, *Entertainment, Movie*, phone (617)450-2452; Alan Bunce, *TV & Radio*, phone (617)450-2463; David Francis, *Financial/Business*, phone (617)450-2380; Marilyn Gardner, *Women's*, phone (617)450-2468; Lawrence Goodrich, *Features*, phone (617)450-2437; Jane Lampmann, *News*, phone (617)450-2410; Peter Spotts, *Editorials*, phone (617)450-2370; Ruth Wales, *Religion*, phone (617)450-2440.
Ad Rates: BW: $3,600 **Circ:** Mon.-Fri. ★**71,924**
4C: $4,000

13987 Christian Science Quarterly-Bible Lessons
The Christian Science Publishing Society
1 Norway St. Phone: (617)450-2000
Boston, MA 02115
Publication E-mail: journal@rsps.com

Religious magazine for daily study of the Bible. Editions printed in Danish, Dutch, English, French, Greek, German, Indonesian, Italian, Japanese, Norwegian, Polish, Portuguese, Spanish, and Swedish; also a monthly English Braille edition. **Subtitle:** For Daily Study of the Bible. **Founded:** 1898. **Freq:** Quarterly. **Print Method:** Offset. **Trim Size:** 4.75 x 7. **Cols./Page:** 1. **Key Personnel:** Noel Fischer, Mng. Pub., phone (800)288-7095, fischerm@csps.com. **ISSN:** 0145-7365. **Subscription Rates:** $23.50 individuals; $33 study edition; $2.50 Braille edition. **Remarks:** Advertising not accepted. **Alt. Formats:** Audio tape; Braille; Large-print.
Circ: (Not Reported)

13988 Christian Science Sentinel
The Christian Science Publishing Society
The Christian Science Publishing Society Phone: (617)450-2700
Fax: (617)450-2707
One Norway St.
P-602
Boston, MA 02115-3122
Free: (800)288-7090

Christian Science magazine. Inspiring non-fiction and testimonies of Christian healing. **Founded:** 1898. **Freq:** Weekly (Mon.). **Print Method:** Offset. **Trim Size:** 5 3/8 x 7 5/8. **Cols./Page:** 1. **Col. Width:** 25 picas. **Col. Depth:** 36 picas. **Key Personnel:** William E. Moody, Editor. **ISSN:** 0009-563X. **Subscription Rates:** $54 individuals; $2 single issue; $64 other countries. **Remarks:** Advertising not accepted. **Alt. Formats:** Audio tape.
Circ: (Not Reported)

13989 Civil Engineering Practice
Boston Society of Civil Engineers Section
Engineering Center Phone: (617)227-5551
1 Walnut St. Fax: (617)227-6783
Boston, MA 02108
Professional magazine covering civil engineering. **Subtitle:** Journal of the Boston Society of Civil Engineers. **Founded:** 1986. **Freq:** Semiannual. **Print Method:** Sheetfed offset. **Trim Size:** 7 1/4 x 10. **Cols./Page:** 2. **Col. Width:** 17 picas. **Col. Depth:** 61 picas. **Key Personnel:** Gian Lombardo, Editor. **ISSN:** 0886-9685. **Subscription Rates:** $28 individuals; $15 single issue. **Remarks:** Accepts advertising. **Former name:** Journal of the Boston Society of Civil Engineers.
Circ: Paid 3,000

13990 Community Support Network News
Center for Psychiatric Rehabilitation
930 Commonwealth Ave., 2nd Fl. Phone: (617)353-3549
Fax: (617)353-7700
Boston, MA 02215
Magazine promoting the exchange of information on services for adults with long-term mental illness. **Founded:** 1983. **Freq:** Quarterly. **Subscription Rates:** $20 individuals. **Remarks:** Advertising not accepted.
Circ: (Not Reported)

13991 Congregational Library Bulletin
Congregational Library
14 Beacon St. Phone: (617)523-0470
Boston, MA 02108 Fax: (617)523-0491
Publisher E-mail: blwhfw@aol.com

Journal covering religious works of the library. **Founded:** 1949. **Freq:** Triennial. **Print Method:** Offset. **Key Personnel:** Harold F. Worthley, Editor. **ISSN:** 0010-5821. **Subscription Rates:** $10 individuals. **Remarks:** Advertising not accepted.
Circ: Paid 925

13992 Connection: New England's Journal of Higher Education & Economic Development
The New England Board of Higher Education
45 Temple Place Phone: (617)357-9620
Boston, MA 02111 Fax: (617)338-1577
Publication E-mail: pubinfo@nebhe.org

Journal of higher education and economic development. **Founded:** 1986. **Freq:** Quarterly. **Trim Size:** 8 1/2 x 11 1/2. **Key Personnel:** John O. Harney, Editor, jharney@nebhe.org; John C. Hoy, Publisher, jch@nebhe.org; Charlotte Stratton, Manager, cstratton@nebhe.org; Susan Martin, Asst. Editor, smartin@nebhe.org; Christine Quinlan, Adv. Dir. and Marketing, cquinlan@nebhe.org. **ISSN:** 0895-6405. **Subscription Rates:** $20; $3.95 single issue. **Remarks:** Accepts advertising. **URL:** http://www.nebhe.org. **Alt. Formats:** CD-ROM; Microform.
Ad Rates: GLR: $150 **Circ:** Controlled 13,500
BW: $1,320
4C: $1,925

13993 Consolidated Returns Tax Reports
R.I.A. Group
31 St. James Ave. Phone: (617)423-2020
Boston, MA 02116-4101 Fax: (617)574-9445
Free: (800)950-1205

Business journal. **Founded:** 1990. **Freq:** Monthly. **Cols./Page:** 2. **Key Personnel:** Lawrence M. Axelrod, Editor. **ISSN:** 1047-8949. **Subscription Rates:** $345.

13994 Corporate Controller
R.I.A. Group
31 St. James Ave. Phone: (617)423-2020
Boston, MA 02116-4101 Fax: (617)574-9445
Free: (800)950-1205

Journal on corporate accounting including auditing, operations, technology, controls, and management. **Founded:** 1988. **Freq:** Bimonthly. **Key Personnel:** Joan Reinbott, Editor; Marie Gallagher, Advertising Mgr. **ISSN:** 0899-0174. **Subscription Rates:** $115. **Remarks:** Accepts advertising.
Ad Rates: BW: $875 **Circ:** 4,000
4C: $1,675

13995 DVS Guide
Descriptive Video Service
WGBH Phone: (617)492-2777
125 Western Ave. Fax: (617)783-8668
Boston, MA 02134
Free: (800)333-1203
Publication E-mail: dvs@wgbh.org

Magazine listing updates and programs available from the Descriptive Video Service, a free national service that makes television programs, cable programming and movies accessible to blind or visually impaired individuals. **Freq:** Quarterly. **Subscription Rates:** Free. **Remarks:** Advertising not accepted. **URL:** http://www.wgbh.org/dvs. **Alt. Formats:** Braille; Large-print.
Circ: Combined 24,688

13996 EIDOS
PO Box 96 Phone: (617)262-0096
Boston, MA 02137-0096 Fax: (617)364-0096
Publisher E-mail: eidos@eidos.org
"Pansexual rights-oriented periodical for free thinking consenting adults who value liberty and privacy.". **Subtitle:** Sexual Freedom and Erotic Entertainment for Consenting Adults. **Founded:** Jan. 1984. **Freq:** Quarterly. **Print Method:** Web. **Trim Size:** 8 1/2 x 11. **Key Personnel:** Brenda Loew, Publisher. **ISSN:** 0740-8307. **Subscription Rates:** $25 U.S., Canada, and Mexico; $31 Europe; $33 other countries; $7 single issue; $125 lifetime. **Remarks:** Accepts advertising. **URL:** http://www.eidos.org.
Ad Rates: BW: $125 **Circ:** 12,000

13997 El Mundo
408 S. Huntington Ave. Phone: (617)522-5060
Boston, MA 02130-4814 Fax: (617)524-5886

Community newspaper (Spanish). **Founded:** 1972. **Freq:** Weekly. **Print Method:** Offset. **Cols./Page:** 5. **Col. Width:** 11 picas. **Col. Depth:** 16 inches. **Key Personnel:** Alberto Vasallo, Jr., Editor and Publisher; Maria R. Vasallo, Management Supervisor, mvasallo@prodigy.net; Alberto Vasallo III, Advertising Mgr. **Subscription Rates:** $60. **Remarks:** Accepts advertising.
Ad Rates: GLR: $1.21 **Circ:** 27,000
BW: $560
4C: $1,560
PCI: $9

13998 The Episcopal Times
Episcopal Diocese of Massachusetts
138 Tremont St. Phone: (617)482-5800
Boston, MA 02111-1319 Fax: (617)482-8431

Religious newspaper. **Founded:** Sept. 1, 1976. **Freq:** 8/year. **Print Method:** Offset. **Trim Size:** 11 x 12. **Cols./Page:** 4. **Col. Width:** 28 nonpareils. **Col. Depth:** 196 agate lines. **Key Personnel:** Jay Cormier, Editor. **Subscription Rates:** Free; $10 (outside of diocese). **Remarks:** Accepts advertising.
Ad Rates: BW: $1,000 **Circ:** Free ‡40,000

13999 Fag Rag
Fag Rag Books
PO Box 15331, Kenmore Sta. Phone: (617)661-7534
Boston, MA 02215
Consumer magazine covering poetry, fiction and essays for a gay audience. **Founded:** 1971. **Print Method:** Web offset. **Subscription Rates:** $10 single issue. **Remarks:** Accepts advertising.
Circ: Non-paid 5,000

14000 Fast Company
77 N Washington St. Phone: (617)973-0300
Boston, MA 02114 Fax: (617)973-0373
Publication E-mail: loop@fastcompany.com
Publisher E-mail: advertising@fastcompany.com

Business magazine covering the changes underway in how business competes, and the practices that shape how work gets done. Also profiles the people, teams, products, and ideas that define the emerging world of business. **Founded:** Nov. 1995. **Print Method:** Offset. **Trim Size:** 8 3/4 x 10 7/8. **Key Personnel:** Thomas R. Evans, President; Alan M. Webber, Editor; William C. Taylor, Editor. **Subscription Rates:** $14.95 individuals. **Remarks:** Accepts advertising. **URL:** http://www.fastcompany.com.
Ad Rates: BW: $7,838 **Circ:** Paid ★**256,348**
4C: $11,700

14001 Federal Reserve Bank of Boston Regional Review
Federal Reserve Bank of Boston
PO Box 2076 Phone: (617)973-3397
Boston, MA 02106-2076 Fax: (617)973-4292

Magazine covering economic and business issues. **Founded:** 1990. **Freq:** Quarterly. **Trim Size:** 12 1/4 x 8 1/8. **Cols./Page:** 3. **Key Personnel:** John Campbell, Editor-in-Chief; Jane Katz, Editor; Miriam Wasserman, Assoc. Editor. **ISSN:** 1062-1865. **Subscription Rates:** Free. **Remarks:** Advertising not accepted. **URL:** http://www.bos.frb.org.
Circ: Controlled 20,000

14002 Foodservice East
The Newbury Street Group, Inc.
294 Washington St., No. 1032 Phone: (617)695-9080
Boston, MA 02108-4608 Fax: (617)695-9080
Free: (800)852-5212

Tabloid covering trends and analysis of the foodservice industry in the Northeast. **Founded:** Apr. 1926. **Freq:** 6/year. **Print Method:** Offset. **Trim Size:** 10 7/8 x 14 1/2. **Cols./Page:** 5. **Col. Width:** 11 1/2 picas. **Col. Depth:** 190 agate lines. **Key Personnel:** Susan Holaday, Editor; Richard E. Dolby, Publisher. **ISSN:** 0885-6877. **Subscription Rates:** $20 individuals. **Remarks:** Accepts advertising.
Ad Rates: GLR: $3.58 **Circ:** ‡22,000
BW: $2,891
4C: $3,716

14003 Game Pro
IDG
One Exeter Plaza, 15th Fl. Phone: (617)534-1200
Boston, MA 02116-2851 Fax: (617)262-2300

Magazine for S.W.A.T. Pro users. **Freq:** Bimonthly. **Trim Size:** 8 1/4 x 14. **Remarks:** Accepts advertising. **Formerly:** S.W.A.T. Pro.
Ad Rates: 4C: $3,000 **Circ:** Paid 55,000

14004 Gayme
P.O. Box 15645 Phone: (617)695-8015
Kenmore Sta.
Boston, MA 02215
Magazine concerning gay lifestyle and culture. **Founded:** 1993. **Freq:** Annual. **Print Method:** Offset. **Trim Size:** 8 x 11. **Cols./Page:** 2. **Col. Width:** 3 inches. **Col. Depth:** 10 inches. **Key Personnel:** Bill Andriette, Contact, bill@bronze.lcs.mit.edu. **ISSN:** 1071-8427. **Subscription Rates:** $14 individuals; $9.95 single issue. **Remarks:** Advertising not accepted.
Circ: Paid 600
Non-paid 6,400

14005 Government Information Quarterly
Elseiver
Graduate School of Library & Information Science Phone: (617)521-2798
Fax: (617)521-3192
Simmons College
Boston, MA 02118
Publication E-mail: 102062-2525@compuserve.com
Publisher E-mail: fcentres@gpu.stv.ualberta.ca

Refereed scholarly journal. **Subtitle:** An International Journal of Policies, Resources Services, and Practices. **Founded:** 1984. **Freq:** Quarterly. **Print Method:** Offset. **Trim Size:** 6 7/8 x 10. **Cols./Page:** 1. **Key Personnel:** Peter Hernon, Editor, phone (617)521-2794, pheronevm@simmons.edu. **ISSN:** 0740-624X. **Subscription Rates:** $180 institutions; $200 institutions, other countries; $220 institutions, other countries airmail; $80 individuals; $100 other countries; $120 other countries airmail; $47.50 single issue; $52.50 single issue other couuntries; $57.50 single issue other countries airmail. **Remarks:** Accepts advertising.
Ad Rates: BW: $300 **Circ:** (Not Reported)

14006 The Guide
Fidelity Publishing
Box 990593
Boston, MA 02199
Publisher E-mail: theguide@guidemag.com

Consumer magazine covering travel, entertainment, politics and sex for gay men. **Subtitle:** Gay Travel, Entertainment, Politics and Sex. **Founded:** 1981. **Freq:** Monthly. **Print Method:** Web offset. **Trim Size:** 7 3/4 x 10 3/4. **Key Personnel:** French Wall, Editor, french@guidemag.com. **ISSN:** 1047-8906. **Subscription Rates:** $30 individuals; $5 single issue. **Remarks:** Accepts advertising. **URL:** http://www.guidemag.com.
Ad Rates: BW: $795 **Circ:** Combined 30,000
4C: $1,650

14007 Harvard Business Review
Harvard Business School Publishing Corp.
60 Harvard Way Phone: (617)495-6800
Boston, MA 02163 Fax: (617)495-9933
Publication E-mail: hbr_ editorial@hbsp.harvard.edu

Magazine for business executives. **Founded:** 1922. **Freq:** Bimonthly. **Print Method:** Offset. **Trim Size:** 8 3/16 x 10 3/4. **Cols./Page:** 3 and 2. **Col. Width:** 27 and 41 nonpareils. **Col. Depth:** 140 agate lines. **Key Personnel:** Stephen Sykes, Assoc. Publisher, phone (617)496-8166; Peter Van Leight, Advertising Dir., phone (212)872-9280, fax (212)838-6535. **ISSN:** 0017-8012. **Subscription Rates:** $85 individuals; $145 other countries; $13.50 single issue; $95 Canada and Mexico. **Remarks:** Accepts advertising. **Online:** Dailog; Lexis, Nexis. **URL:** http://www.hosp.harvard.edu.
Ad Rates: BW: $13,500 **Circ:** Paid ★**235,652**
4C: $16,500

14008 Health and Human Rights
Harvard School for Public Health
651 Huntington Ave., 7th Fl. Phone: (617)432-4311
Boston, MA 02115 Fax: (617)432-4310
Publisher E-mail: fxbcenter@igc.apc.org

Journal covering the relationship between human rights and health worldwide. **Subtitle:** An International Journal. **Founded:** 1994. **Freq:** Semiannual. **Trim Size:** 6 x 9. **ISSN:** 1079-0969. **Subscription Rates:** $36 individuals; $12 single issue. **Remarks:** Advertising not accepted.
Circ: (Not Reported)

14009 The Herald of Christian Science
The Christian Science Publishing Society
1 Norway St. Phone: (617)450-2000
Boston, MA 02115
Christian Science magazine with articles and testimonies of Christian healing (German, French, Spanish, Portuguese, Norwegian, Swedish, Danish, Dutch, Italian, Indonesian, Japanese, and Greek; and braille). **Founded:** 1903. **Freq:** Monthly and Quarterly, depending on language. **Print Method:** Offset. **Trim Size:** 5 3/8 x 7 1/2. **Cols./Page:** 1. **Col. Width:** 50 nonpareils. **Col. Depth:** 91 agate lines. **Key Personnel:** William E. Moody, Editor; Mary Trammel, Assoc. Editor. **ISSN:** 0145-7578. **Subscription Rates:** $23 individuals. **Remarks:** Advertising not accepted. **Alt. Formats:** Audio tape; Braille.
Circ: (Not Reported)

14010 The Horn Book Guide to Children's and Young Adult Books
The Horn Book, Inc.
56 Roland St., Ste. 200 Phone: (617)628-0225
Boston, MA 02129 Fax: (617)628-0882
Free: (800)325-1170
Publisher E-mail: info@hbook.com

Journal that offers critical reviews of approximately 4,000 children's and young adult books per year. **Subtitle:** to Children's and Young Adult Books. **Founded:** Feb. 1990. **Freq:** 2/year. **Trim Size:** 8 1/2 x 11. **Key Personnel:** Jennifer Brabander, Executive Editor, jbrabander@hbook.com; Karen Walsh, Advertising Mgr., kwalsh@hbook.com. **ISSN:** 1044-405X. **Subscription Rates:** $42; $25 single issue. **Remarks:** Accepts advertising. **Available Online. Alt. Formats:** CD-ROM; Microform.
Ad Rates: BW: $1,320 **Circ:** Paid 4,500
Non-paid 500

14011 The Horn Book Magazine
The Horn Book, Inc.
56 Roland St., Ste. 200 Phone: (617)628-0225
Boston, MA 02129 Fax: (617)628-0882
Free: (800)325-1170
Publisher E-mail: info@hbook.com

Magazine covering children's literature. **Founded:** 1924. **Freq:** Bimonthly. **Print Method:** Offset. **Trim Size:** 6 x 9. **Cols./Page:** 1. **Col. Width:** 48 nonpareils. **Col. Depth:** 98 agate lines. **Key Personnel:** Roger Sutton, Editor, rsutton@hbook.com; Karen Walsh, Marketing Manager, phone (617)227-4709, kwalsh@hbook.com. **ISSN:** 0018-5078. **Subscription Rates:** $40 individuals; $50 institutions $24.95 new subscription; $8.50 single issue. **Remarks:** Accepts advertising.
Ad Rates: BW: $1,320 **Circ:** Combined 22,500

14012 Horticulture
Primedia Special Interest Publication
98 N. Washington St. Phone: (617)742-5600
Boston, MA 02114 Fax: (617)367-6364
Publication E-mail: feedback@hortmag.com

Magazine for the amateur gardener. **Subtitle:** American Gardening at Its Best. **Founded:** 1904. **Freq:** 8/year. **Print Method:** Offset. **Trim Size:** 8 x 10 1/2. **Cols./Page:** 3. **Col. Width:** 2.25 nonpareils. **Col. Depth:** 9.576 agate lines. **Key Personnel:** Thomas C. Cooper, Editor; Joel P. Toner, Publisher; Dena Heisner, Production Mgr.; Pam Conrad, Art Dir. **ISSN:** 0018-5329. **Subscription Rates:** $28 individuals; $4.95 single issue. **Remarks:** Accepts advertising. **URL:** http:/ /www.hortmag.com.
Ad Rates: BW: $11,570 **Circ:** Paid 275
4C: $15,250

14013 The Improper Bostonian
Improper Publications, Inc.
45 Newbury St., Ste. 509 Phone: (617)859-1446
Boston, MA 02116 Fax: (617)859-1446
Publication E-mail: improperb@aol.com

Newspaper. **Founded:** Aug. 1991. **Freq:** Biweekly. **Trim Size:** 10 x 17 3/4. **Cols./Page:** 4. **Col. Width:** 2 5/16 inches. **Col. Depth:** 12 3/4 inches. **Key Personnel:** Mark Semonian, Publisher; Nancy Gaines, Editor; Jim Pite, VP Sales/Marketing. **Subscription Rates:** $40 individuals via first-class mail.
Ad Rates: BW: $3,517 **Circ:** 80,000
4C: $4,398

14014 Inc. Magazine
The Goldhirsh Group
38 Commercial Wharf Phone: (617)248-8000
Boston, MA 02110 Fax: (617)248-8090
Free: (800)842-1343
Publication E-mail: editors@inc.com

Business and finance magazine for business owners and managers. **Subtitle:** The Magazine for Growing Companies. **Founded:** 1979. **Freq:** Monthly. **Print Method:** Offset. **Trim Size:** 8 1/8 x 10 3/4. **Cols./Page:** 3. **Col. Width:** 27 nonpareils. **Col. Depth:** 140 agate lines. **Key Personnel:** George Gendron, Editor; Riley McDonaugh, Publisher; Gary Mirkin, Advertising Dir. **ISSN:** 0162-8968. **Subscription Rates:** $25 individuals; $3 single issue. **Remarks:** Accepts advertising. **URL:** http://www.inc.com.
Ad Rates: GLR: $12.95 **Circ:** Paid ★**662,381**
BW: $38,690
4C: $59,195
PCI: $900

14015 Inc. Technology
The Goldhirsh Group
38 Commercial Wharf Phone: (617)248-8000
Boston, MA 02110 Fax: (617)248-8090
Free: (800)842-1343
Publication E-mail: tech@inc.com

Magazine covering technological issues for small to mid-size companies. **Founded:** Nov. 15, 1994. **Freq:** Quarterly. **Key Personnel:** Emily Esterson, Assoc. Ed.; Thea Singer, Articles Editor. **Subscription Rates:** $19 individuals; $4 single issue. **Remarks:** Advertising accepted; rates available upon request. **URL:** http://www.inc.com; http://www.inc.com.
Circ: Paid 640,000

14016 Internal Auditing
Warren, Gorham & Lamont R.I.A. Group
31 St. James Ave. Fax: (617)423-1914
Boston, MA 02116
Publisher E-mail: rgallagher@riag.com

Journal for the professional internal auditor. Covers operations, financial, and EDP auditing, department administration, and relationships with external auditors, management, and the board. **Founded:** 1986. **Freq:** Quarterly. **Print Method:** Offset. **Trim Size:** 7 1/2 x 10. **Cols./Page:** 2. **Col. Width:** 2 5/8 inches. **Col. Depth:** 9 inches. **Key Personnel:** Stephen H. Collins, Editor, phone (212)367-6398, fax (212)367-6718; Meg Chomicz, Advertising Mgr. **ISSN:** 0897-0378. **Subscription Rates:** $92 individuals. **Remarks:** Accepts advertising. **URL:** http://www.riag.com; http://www.riagax.com.
Ad Rates: BW: $500 **Circ:** Paid ‡4,380
4C: $1,130 Non-paid ‡630

14017 International Ophthalmology Clinics
Little, Brown, and Co., Inc.
34 Beacon St. Phone: (617)859-5607
Boston, MA 02108 Fax: (617)859-0629
Free: (800)628-4221

Clinical review articles for ophthalmologists. **Founded:** 1961. **Freq:** Quarterly. **Print Method:** Offset. **Trim Size:** 8 1/8 x 10 7/8. **Cols./Page:** 1. **Col. Width:** 80 nonpareils. **Col. Depth:** 140 agate lines. **Key Personnel:** Gil Smolin, M.D., Editor; Mitchell Friedlaender, M.D., Contact. **ISSN:** 0020-8167. **Subscription Rates:** $150 individuals. **Remarks:** Advertising not accepted.
Circ: ‡2,677

14018 Inventors' Digest
JMH Publishing Co.
310 Franklin St., No. 24 Phone: (617)367-4540
Boston, MA 02110 Fax: (617)723-6988
Free: (800)838-8808
Publication E-mail: inventorsd@aol.com

Magazine covering the invention process including development and marketing. **Subtitle:** America's Leading Inventors Magazine. **Founded:** 1985. **Freq:** Bimonthly. **Print Method:** Offset. **Trim Size:** 8 1/2 x 10 7/8. **Cols./Page:** 3. **Key Personnel:** Joanne M. Hayes-Rines, Editor and Publisher. **ISSN:** 0883-9859. **Subscription Rates:** $27; $32 Canada; $45 overseas. **Remarks:** Accepts advertising. **URL:** http://www.inventorsdigest.com.
Ad Rates: BW: $1,166 **Circ:** ‡20,000
4C: $1,566

14019 The Journal of Academic Librarianship
Elseiver
Graduate School of Library and Information Science Phone: (617)521-2800
Fax: (617)521-3192
Simmons College
Boston, MA 02118
Publication E-mail: 102062.2525@compuserve.com; phernonevmsvax.summons.edu
Publisher E-mail: fcentres@gpu.stv.ualberta.ca

Professional library journal. **Founded:** 1974. **Freq:** Bimonthly. **Print Method:** Offset. **Trim Size:** 8 12 x 11. **Cols./Page:** 3. **Col. Width:** 14 inches. **Col. Depth:** 57 inches. **Key Personnel:** Peter Hernon, Editor-in-Chief, phone (617)521-2794, pheronevm@simmons.edu. **ISSN:** 0099-1333. **Subscription Rates:** $75; $195 institutions. **Remarks:** Accepts advertising. **Online:** Ebsco; UMI.
Circ: (Not Reported)

14020 Journal of Aging and Social Policy
The Haworth Press, Inc.
University of Massachusetts-Boston Phone: (617)287-7300
Gerontology Institute Fax: (617)287-7080
100 Morrissey Blvd.
Boston, MA 02125-3393
Publication E-mail: norton@umbsky.cc.umb.edu
Publisher E-mail: getinfo@haworthpressinc.com

Forum for analysis, argument, research, and advocacy of social policy as it affects the aging population. **Subtitle:** A Journal Devoted to Aging and Social Policy. **Founded:** 1989. **Freq:** Quarterly. **Trim Size:** 6x8 1/2. **Key Personnel:** Francis G. Caro, Ph.D., Editor, frank.caro@umb.edu; Robert Morris, DSW, Editor; Bill Cohen, Publisher; Jill R. Norton, Managing Editor, jill.norton@umb.edu. **ISSN:** 0895-9420. **Subscription Rates:** $40 individuals; $80 institutions; $175 libraries. **Remarks:** Accepts advertising. **Alt. Formats:** Microfiche.
Ad Rates: BW: $300 **Circ:** 448

14021 Journal of Applied Meteorology
American Meteorological Society
45 Beacon St. Phone: (617)227-2425
Boston, MA 02108 Fax: (617)742-8718
Publication E-mail: amspubs@ametsoc.org
Publisher E-mail: amspubs@ametsoc.org

Journal exploring the applications of the atmospheric sciences to operational and practical goals. **Founded:** Mar. 1962. **Freq:** Monthly. **Print Method:** Offset. **Trim Size:** 7 3/4 x 10 1/2. **Cols./Page:** 2. **Col. Width:** 39 nonpareils. **Col. Depth:** 126 agate lines. **Key Personnel:** Ronald McPherson, Publisher. **ISSN:** 0894-8763. **Subscription Rates:** $335 individuals. **Remarks:** Advertising not accepted. **URL:** http://www.ams.allenpress.com.
Circ: ‡2,721

14022 Journal of Atmospheric and Oceanic Technology
American Meteorological Society
45 Beacon St. Phone: (617)227-2425
Boston, MA 02108 Fax: (617)742-8718
Publication E-mail: amspubs@ametsoc.org
Publisher E-mail: amspubs@ametsoc.org

Journal describing the instrumentation and methodology used in atmospheric and oceanic research. **Founded:** Mar. 1984. **Freq:** Monthly. **Print Method:** Offset. **Trim Size:** 7 3/4 x 10 1/2. **Cols./Page:** 2. **Col. Width:** 39 nonpareils. **Col. Depth:** 126 agate lines. **Key Personnel:** Ronald McPherson, Publisher. **ISSN:** 0739-0572. **Subscription Rates:** $240 individuals. **Remarks:** Advertising not accepted. **URL:** http://www.ams.allenpress.com. **Alt. Formats:** CD-ROM, The AMS Bulletin; Bulletin Archive.
Circ: ‡1,588

14023 Journal of Climate
American Meteorological Society
45 Beacon St. Phone: (617)227-2425
Boston, MA 02108 Fax: (617)742-8718
Publisher E-mail: amspubs@ametsoc.org

Journal presenting articles on climate, atmospheric variability, and the impact of climate change on society. **Founded:** 1988. **Freq:** Monthly. **Print Method:** Offset. **Trim Size:** 7 3/4 x 10 1/2. **Cols./Page:** 2. **Col. Width:** 39 nonpareils. **Col. Depth:** 126 agate lines. **Key Personnel:** Ronald McPherson, Exec. Dir. **ISSN:** 0894-8755. **Subscription Rates:** $395 individuals. **Remarks:** Advertising not accepted. **URL:** http://www.ams.allenpress.com. **Alt. Formats:** CD-ROM, The AMS Journal; Bulletin Archive. **Formerly:** Journal of Climate and Applied Meteorology (1988).
Circ: ‡2,481

14024 Journal of Clinical Psychopharmacology
Lippincott Williams & Wilkins
Tufts University Phone: (617)636-6897
School of Medicine
Dept. of Pharmacology
136 Harrison Ave.
Boston, MA 02111
Medical journal. **Founded:** 1981. **Freq:** Bimonthly. **Print Method:** Offset. **Trim Size:** 8 1/2 x 11. **Cols./Page:** 2. **Col. Width:** 32 nonpareils. **Col. Depth:** 119 agate lines. **Key Personnel:** Richard I. Shader, M.D., Editor-in-Chief; Kathleen Malamphy, National Sales Manager, phone (410)528-4424, kmalamphy@wwilkins.com; Lynn Gibson, Production Manager, phone (410)528-4281. **ISSN:** 0271-0749. **Subscription Rates:** $114 individuals; $149 other countries; $174 industry; $209 industry, other countries; $24 single issue. **Remarks:** Accepts advertising. **Alt. Formats:** Microform; Mailing labels.
Ad Rates: BW: $725 **Circ:** Paid ‡8,614
4C: $1,500 Non-paid ‡163

14025 Journal of Health Communication
Taylor & Francis
Emerson-Tufts Program in Health Communication Phone: (617)824-7831
Emerson College Fax: (617)824-8912
100 Beacon St.
Boston, MA 02116
Publication E-mail: jhc@emerson.edu
Publisher E-mail: info@taylorandfrancis.com

Peer-reviewed journal publishing qualitative and quantitative studies, ethical essays, case studies, and book reviews that present developments in health communications. **Subtitle:** International Perspectives. **Founded:** 1996. **Freq:** Quarterly. **Print Method:** Offset. **Key Personnel:** Scott Ratzan, MD, Editor-in-Chief, phone (617)824-8745. **ISSN:** 1081-0730. **Remarks:** Accepts advertising. **URL:** www.emerson.edu/jhealth-com/.
Ad Rates: BW: $650 **Circ:** (Not Reported)
4C: $1,550

14026 The Journal of Law, Medicine & Ethics
American Society of Law, Medicine & Ethics, Inc.
765 Commonwealth Ave., Ste. 1634 Phone: (617)262-4990
Boston, MA 02215 Fax: (617)437-7596
Publisher E-mail: aslme@bu.edu

Journal for lawyers, doctors and other health care professionals. Articles cover such medicolegal issues as access to health care, health care reform, managed care, advance directives, genetics, informed consent, managed care, pain management, futility, AIDS, abortion, reproductive and children's health, and assisted suicide. Includes book reviews, cases and policy decisions. **Founded:** 1973. **Freq:** Quarterly. **Print Method:** Offset. **Trim Size:** 8 1/2 x 11. **Cols./Page:** 2 and 3. **Col. Width:** 20 and 13 picas. **Col. Depth:** 54 picas. **Key Personnel:** Ellen Wright Clayton, Editor; Bernard Lo, Editor; Michael Vasko, Managing Editor, mvasko@alsme.org. **ISSN:** 0277-8459. **Subscription Rates:** $90 individuals; $170 institutions; $25 single issue; $30 single issue Outside the USA. **Remarks:** Color advertising not accepted. **Online:** Westlaw; Lexis-Nexis; Medlind; Ebsco; Information Access. **URL:** http://www.alsme.org. **Alt. Formats:** Microform; Mailing labels. **Formerly:** Law, Medicine & Health Care.
Ad Rates: BW: $600 **Circ:** ‡5,000

14027 Journal of Physical Oceanography
American Meteorological Society
45 Beacon St. Phone: (617)227-2425
Boston, MA 02108 Fax: (617)742-8718
Publication E-mail: amspubs@ametsoc.org
Publisher E-mail: amspubs@ametsoc.org

Journal presenting original research and survey papers devoted to the communication of knowledge concerning the physics and chemistry of the oceans and of the processes coupling the sea to the atmosphere. **Founded:** Jan. 1971. **Freq:** Monthly. **Print Method:** Offset. **Trim Size:** 7 3/4 x 10 1/2. **Cols./Page:** 2. **Col. Width:** 39 nonpareils. **Col. Depth:** 126 agate lines. **Key Personnel:** Ronald McPherson, Publisher. **ISSN:** 0022-3670. **Subscription Rates:** $405 individuals. **Remarks:** Advertising not accepted. **URL:** http://www.ams.allenpress.com. **Alt. Formats:** CD-ROM.
Circ: ‡2,067

14028 Journal of Progressive Human Services
The Haworth Press, Inc.
School of Social Work Phone: (617)353-3752
264 Bay State Rd. Fax: (617)353-5612
Boston, MA 02215
Publisher E-mail: getinfo@haworthpressinc.com

Journal on social problems and human services from the progressive perspective. **Founded:** 1990. **Freq:** Biannual. **Trim Size:** 6x81/2. **Key Personnel:** Cheryl Hyde, Ph.D, Editor; Bill Cohen, Publisher. **ISSN:** 0890-7064. **Subscription Rates:** $36 individuals 30% more for Canada; 40% more for other countries; $48 institutions 30% more for Canada; 40% more for other countries; $95 libraries 30% more for Canada; 40% more for other countries. **Remarks:** Accepts advertising.
Ad Rates: BW: $300 **Circ:** Controlled ‡1,099

14029 Journal of Transnational Management Development
The Haworth Press, Inc.
Dept. of Administrative Sciences Phone: (617)353-3016
Boston University Fax: (617)353-6840
808 Commonwealth Ave.
Boston, MA 02215
Publication E-mail: kgecker@bu.edu
Publisher E-mail: getinfo@haworthpressinc.com

Journal on transnational management development issues. **Founded:** 1994. **Freq:** Quarterly. **Trim Size:** 6x8 1/2. **Key Personnel:** Kip Becker, Ph.D, Editor, kbecker@bu.edu; Bill Cohen, Publisher. **ISSN:** 1068-6061. **Subscription Rates:** $45 individuals; $80 institutions; $175 libraries. **Remarks:** Accepts advertising.
Ad Rates: BW: $300 **Circ:** Paid 107

14030 Lawyer's Journal
Massachusetts Bar Association
20 West St. Phone: (617)338-0516
Boston, MA 02111-1218 Fax: (617)338-0650

Professional journal covering legal issues. **Subtitle:** Massachusetts Bar Association. **Founded:** 1980. **Freq:** Monthly. **Key Personnel:** Robert C. Pedzewick, Sales Mgr., pedzewick@massbpe.org. **Subscription Rates:** Included in membership. **Remarks:** Accepts advertising. **Online:** LEXIS-NEXIS.
Circ: Controlled 19,000

14031 Massachusetts Bar Association Lawyers Journal
Massachusetts Bar Association
20 West St. Phone: (617)338-0516
Boston, MA 02111-1218 Fax: (617)338-0650
Publication E-mail: communications@massbar.org

Professional newspaper covering law. **Founded:** Oct. 1993. **Freq:** Monthly.
Circ: Controlled 18,000

14032 Massachusetts Beverage Business
New Beverage Publications, Inc.
55 Clarendon St. Phone: (617)482-2531
Boston, MA 02116-4067 Fax: (617)482-2531

Publication for the retail beverages industry. **Subtitle:** Massachusetts Beverage Business. **Founded:** 1944. **Freq:** Monthly. **Print Method:** Offset. **Trim Size:** 8 1/2 x 11. **Cols./Page:** 3. **Col. Width:** 27 nonpareils. **Col. Depth:** 140 agate lines. **Key Personnel:** S.I. Stone, Publisher, phone (617)423-2531, fax (617)482-7163, sistone@beveragebusiness; P.I. Stone, Executive Editor, fax (617)482-2531, pistone@beveragebusiness. **ISSN:** 1084-1113. **Subscription Rates:** $52 individuals. **Remarks:** Accepts advertising. **URL:** http://www.beveragebusiness.com; http://beveragebusiness.com. **Formerly:** Massachusetts Beverage Journal.
Ad Rates: BW: $1,515 **Circ:** Paid ‡7,248
4C: $3,030 Non-paid ‡605
PCI: $95

14033 Massachusetts CPA Review Online
Massachusetts Society of Certified Public Accountants, Inc.
105 Chauncey St., 10th Fl. Phone: (617)556-4000
Boston, MA 02111-1742 Fax: (617)556-4126
Free: (800)392-6145
Publication E-mail: mscpa@mscpaonline.org

Newsletter covering business, tax issues, and technology. **Subtitle:** The Newsletter of the Massachusetts Society of Certified Public Accountants, Inc. **Founded:** Nov. 1990. **Freq:** Bimonthly. **Trim Size:** 8.5 x 11. **Key Personnel:** Cheryl McCloud, Editor-in-Chief, cmcloud@mscpaonline.org; Amy Kaiser, Editor/Adversting Mgr., akaiser@mscpaonline.org; Erin Danehy, Editorial Assistant, edanehy@mscpaonline. **Remarks:** Accepts advertising. **URL:** http://www.MSCPAonline.org.
Circ: (Not Reported)

14034 Massachusetts Lawyers Weekly
Lawyers Weekly Publications
41 West St. Phone: (617)451-7300
Boston, MA 02111 Fax: (617)451-7324
Free: (800)444-5297
Publication E-mail: natsales@lweekly.com

Newspaper (tabloid) reporting Massachusetts legal news. **Founded:** 1972. **Freq:** Weekly. **Trim Size:** 11 1/2 x 17. **Cols./Page:** 4. **Key Personnel:** Paul J. Martinek, Editor. **ISSN:** 0196-7509. **Subscription Rates:** $259 individuals. **Remarks:** Advertising accepted; rates available upon request. **Available Online. URL:** http://www.masslaw.com.
Circ: ‡16,000

14035 Monthly Weather Review
American Meteorological Society
45 Beacon St. Phone: (617)227-2425
Boston, MA 02108 Fax: (617)742-8718
Publication E-mail: amspubs@ametsoc.org
Publisher E-mail: amspubs@ametsoc.org

Journal presenting original research and survey papers concerned with weather analysis and forecasting. **Founded:** 1873. **Freq:** Monthly. **Print Method:** Offset. **Trim Size:** 7 3/4 x 10 1/2. **Cols./Page:** 2. **Col. Width:** 39 nonpareils. **Col. Depth:** 126 agate lines. **Key Personnel:** Ronald McPherson, Publisher. **ISSN:** 0027-0644. **Subscription Rates:** $445 individuals. **Remarks:** Advertising not accepted. **URL:** http://www.ams.allenpress.com. **Alt. Formats:** CD-ROM, The AMS Journal; Bulletin Archive.
Circ: ‡2,972

14036 The Municipal Advocate
Massachusetts Municipal Association
60 Temple Pl. Phone: (617)426-7272
Boston, MA 02111 Fax: (617)695-1314
Free: (800)882-1498

Magazine covering municipal issues such as law, insurance, finance, public safety, public works, and land use. **Founded:** 1980. **Freq:** Quarterly. **Print Method:** Offset, sheetfed. **Trim Size:** 8 1/2 x 11. **Cols./Page:** 3. **Col. Width:** 2 1/4 inches. **Col. Depth:** 9 3/4 inches. **Key Personnel:** Geoffrey Beckwith, Publisher; John Ouellette, Editor, advocate_editor@mma.org. **ISSN:** 1046-2422. **Subscription Rates:** $25 members; $49 nonmembers. **Remarks:** Accepts advertising. **Formerly:** Municipal Forum.
Ad Rates: BW: $730 **Circ:** Combined 5,884
4C: $1,030

14037 Mutual Fund Market News
600 Atlantic Ave. Phone: (617)723-6400
Boston, MA 02210 Fax: (617)624-7200
Publication E-mail: mfmn@dalbar.com

Magazine featuring news and information about the mutual fund industry. **Freq:** Weekly. **Key Personnel:** Susan Weiner, Editor; Olivia Grant, Circulation Mgr.; Thomas Cunningham, Advertising Contact; Kelly Doherty, Advertising Contact; John Harrington, Advertising Contact. **Subscription Rates:** $1,250 individuals. **Remarks:** Accepts advertising. **Formerly:** FACS of the Week.
Circ: (Not Reported)

14038 My Friend
Pauline Books & Media
50 St. Paul's Ave. Phone: (617)522-8911
Jamaica Plain Fax: (617)541-9805
Boston, MA 02130
Publication E-mail: myfriend@pauline.org
Publisher E-mail: editorial@pauline.org

Magazine teaching Christian values and basic Catholic doctrine to children ages 7-12. **Subtitle:** The Catholic Magazine for Kids. **Founded:** Jan. 1979. **Freq:** 10/year. **Print Method:** Offset. **Trim Size:** 8 1/8 x 10 7/8. **Cols./Page:** 3. **Col. Width:** 13 picas. **Col. Depth:** 58 1/2 picas. **Key Personnel:** Sr. Kathryn James Hermes, FSP, Editor/Contact, phone (617)522-8911, fax (617)541-9805. **ISSN:** 0164-3568. **Subscription Rates:** $18 individuals; $2 single issue. **Remarks:** Advertising not accepted. **URL:** htpp://www.pauline.org.
Circ: ‡11,500

14039 New England Economic Indicators
Federal Reserve Bank of Boston
PO Box 2076 Phone: (617)973-3397
Boston, MA 02106-2076 Fax: (617)973-4292
Publication E-mail: boston.library@bos.frborg

Statistical publication. **Freq:** Monthly. **Trim Size:** 8 1/2 x 11. **Key Personnel:** Nanette Furg, Editor, nannette.y.fung@bos.frb.org. **ISSN:** 0458-4448. **Subscription Rates:** Free. **Remarks:** Advertising not accepted. **URL:** http://www.bos.frb.org/economic/rcei/reei.htm.
Circ: (Not Reported)

14040 New England Economic Review
Federal Reserve Bank of Boston
PO Box 2076 Phone: (617)973-3397
Boston, MA 02106-2076 Fax: (617)973-4292

Economics and business journal. **Founded:** 1919. **Freq:** Bimonthly. **Print Method:** Offset. **Cols./Page:** 2. **Col. Width:** 39 nonpareils. **Col. Depth:** 119 agate lines. **Key Personnel:** Joan T. Poskanzer, Editor. **Subscription Rates:** Free. **Remarks:** Advertising not accepted.
Circ: Non-paid ‡15,000

14041 New England Historical and Genealogical Register
New England Historic Genealogical Society
101 Newbury St. Phone: (617)536-5740
Boston, MA 02116-3007 Fax: (617)536-7307
Publisher E-mail: anovick@nehgs.org

Scholarly Journal focusing on genealogy and history. **Founded:** Jan. 1847. **Freq:** Quarterly. **Print Method:** Offset. **Trim Size:** 6 x 9. **Cols./Page:** 1. **Col. Width:** 48 nonpareils. **Col. Depth:** 98 agate lines. **Key Personnel:** Jane F. Fiske, Editor, jfiske@nehgs.org; Aileen Novick, Assistant, anovick@nehgs.org. **ISSN:** 0028-4785. **Subscription Rates:** Free to qualified subscribers; $40 institutions. **Remarks:** Accepts advertising. **Alt. Formats:** CD-ROM.
Ad Rates: BW: $425 **Circ:** ‡18,500

14042 The New England Journal of Medicine
10 Shattuck St. Phone: (617)893-3000
Boston, MA 02115-6094 Fax: (617)893-0413
Free: (800)843-6356
Publication E-mail: nejmcust@mms.org

Journal for the medical profession. **Founded:** Jan. 1812. **Freq:** Weekly (Thurs.). **Print Method:** Offset. **Trim Size:** 8 x 10 7/8. **Cols./Page:** 2. **Col. Width:** 39 nonpareils. **Col. Depth:** 140 agate lines. **Key Personnel:** Jerome P. Kassirer, M.D., Editor-in-Chief; Robert D. Boverschulte, VP Publishing. **ISSN:** 0028-4795. **Subscription Rates:** $119 individuals; $182 other countries. **Remarks:** Accepts advertising. **URL:** http://www.nejm.org. **Alt. Formats:** CD-ROM.
Ad Rates: BW: $4,750 **Circ:** Paid ‡230,000
4C: $6,450 Non-paid ‡10,132
PCI: $310

14043 New England Law Review
New England School of Law
154 Stuart St. Phone: (404)344-2665
Boston, MA 02116 Fax: (404)346-3332

Professional journal covering law. **Freq:** Quarterly. **Key Personnel:** Erin Coffman, Business Managing Editor. **ISSN:** 0028-4823. **Subscription Rates:** $20 individuals. **Remarks:** Advertising not accepted.
Circ: (Not Reported)

14044 The New England Quarterly: A Historical Review of New England Life and Letters
Northeastern University
Meserve Hall, No. 239 Phone: (617)373-2734
360 Huntington Ave. Fax: (617)373-2661
Boston, MA 02115
Publication E-mail: neq@lynx.neu.edu

Journal carrying articles in the fields of literature, history, and culture relating to New England. **Subtitle:** A Historical Review of New England Life and Letters. **Founded:** 1928. **Freq:** Quarterly. **Print Method:** Offset. **Trim Size:** 6 x 9. **Cols./Page:** 1. **Col. Width:** 4 inches. **Col. Depth:** 7 inches. **Key Personnel:** William M. Fowler, Jr., Editor, phone (617)536-1608, fax (617)859-0074, wfowler@masshist.org; Linda Smith Rhoads, Editor. **ISSN:** 0028-4866. **Subscription Rates:** $20 individuals; $25 institutions; $7 single issue. **Remarks:** Color advertising not accepted.
Ad Rates: BW: $150 **Circ:** Paid ‡2,000
Non-paid ‡400

14045 The Noise
74 Jamaica St. Phone: (617)524-4735
Boston, MA 02130
Publisher E-mail: tmaxnoise@aol.com

Fanzine covering Boston area rock music. **Subtitle:** Rock Around Boston. **Founded:** 1981. **Freq:** Monthly (except August & January). **Print Method:** Web offset. **Trim Size:** 8 3/8 x 10 3/4. **Cols./Page:** 2. **Col. Width:** 3 5/8 inches. **Col. Depth:** 10 inches. **Key Personnel:** T. Max, Editor and Publisher, tmaxnoise@aol.com; Francis DiMenno, Editor, fdimenno@providence.edu; Mikey Dee, Editor, mickey@planetarygroup.com; H. Einstein, Editor, heinstein@aol.com; Lianna Ness, Editor, lness@aims.turningpoint.com. **Subscription Rates:** $16 by mail; $2 single issue. **Remarks:** Accepts advertising. **URL:** http://www.rockopera.com/thenoise.html.
Ad Rates: BW: $227 **Circ:** Paid ‡5000

14046 The Northeastern News
Northeastern University
434 Curry Student Center Phone: (617)373-4343
360 Huntington Ave. Fax: (617)373-2649
Boston, MA 02115
Publication E-mail: nunews@nu-news.com

Collegiate newspaper (tabloid). **Founded:** 1921. **Freq:** Weekly (Wed.). **Print Method:** Offset. **Trim Size:** 10 x 16. **Cols./Page:** 5. **Col. Width:** 2 inches. **Col. Depth:** 16 inches. **Key Personnel:** Christine Walsh, Editor-in-Chief, phone (617)373-4789, editor@nu-news.com; Kate Arsenault, Advertising Mgr., phone (617)373-4343, advertising@nu-news.com; Jeremy Walters, Business Mgr., phone (617)373-4343, business@nu-news.com; Sarah Johnson, Managing Editor, phone (617)373-2648, news@nu-new.com. **Subscription Rates:** $25 individuals. **Remarks:** Accepts advertising. **URL:** http://www.nu-news.com.
Ad Rates: BW: $660 **Circ:** Free ‡10,000
4C: $985
PCI: $8.25

14047 Nutrition Reviews
International Life Sciences Institute-Nutrition Foundation
USDA Human Nutrition Phone: (617)556-3202
Research Center on Aging Fax: (617)556-3005
Tufts University
711 Washington St.
Boston, MA 02111
Journal on nutrition research and policy issues. **Founded:** 1942. **Freq:** Monthly. **Print Method:** Offset. **Trim Size:** 8 1/6 x 11. **Cols./Page:** 2. **Col. Width:** 32 nonpareils. **Col. Depth:** 112 agate lines. **Key Personnel:** Dr. Irwin H. Rosenberg, Editor; Dr. Robert Russell, Assoc. Editor; Dr. Richard Wood, Assoc. Editor; Jennifer Hellwig, M.S., Senior Staff Editor, hellwig_nr@email.hnrc.tufts.edu. **ISSN:** 0029-6643. **Subscription Rates:** $75 individuals; $125 institutions; $105 other countries. **Remarks:** Advertising not accepted.
Circ: ‡6,500

14048 The Older American
Massachusetts Association of Older Americans
110 Arlington St. Phone: (617)426-0804
Boston, MA 02116 Fax: (617)426-0070

Newspaper (tabloid) containing information on issues of concern to the elderly. **Founded:** Feb. 1975. **Freq:** Quarterly. **Print Method:** Offset. **Trim Size:** 10 x 16. **Cols./Page:** 4. **Col. Width:** 27 nonpareils. **Col. Depth:** 224 agate lines. **Key Personnel:** Phyllis Galante, Editor. **ISSN:** 0738-9639. **Subscription Rates:** free w/membership; $15 individuals membership; $50 for organizations. **Remarks:** Color advertising not accepted.
Ad Rates: GLR: $8 **Circ:** Paid ‡9,000
BW: $515 Controlled ‡3,000

14049 Organic Preparations and Procedures International
Organic Preparations and Procedures, Inc.
University of Massachusetts
Boston
Dept. of Chemistry
Boston, MA 02125-3393

Scholarly journal covering organic synthesis. **Subtitle:** The New Journal for Organic Synthesis. **Founded:** Feb. 1972. **Freq:** Bimonthly. **Print Method:** Photo offset. **Trim Size:** 7 x 10 1/4. **Key Personnel:** Prof. J. P. Anselme, Editor; M. C. Anselme, Circulation Mgr.; F. Madsen, Advertising Mgr. **ISSN:** 0030-4948. **Subscription Rates:** $235 institutions postage; $120 individuals postage. **Remarks:** Advertising accepted; rates available upon request.
Circ: (Not Reported)

14050 Our Special
National Braille Press, Inc.
88 St. Stephen St. Phone: (617)266-6160
Boston, MA 02115 Fax: (617)437-0456
Free: (800)548-7323
Publisher E-mail: orders@nbp.org

General interest Braille magazine for blind women. **Founded:** 1930. **Freq:** 6/year. **Print Method:** Braille. **Key Personnel:** Jeanne Neale, Editor; Diane Croft, Marketing Mgr., dcroft@nbp.org. **Subscription Rates:** $15. **Remarks:** Advertising not accepted.
Circ: ‡2,000

14051 Panorama
Jerome Press Publications, Inc.
332 Congress St. Phone: (617)423-3400
Boston, MA 02210 Fax: (617)423-7108

Visitor's guide distributed for guests at 63 hotels in the Boston area. **Subtitle:** Boston's Offical Bi-Weekly Guide. **Founded:** 1951. **Freq:** Biweekly. **Print Method:** Offset. **Trim Size:** 5 5/8 x 8 3/8. **Cols./Page:** 2. **Col. Width:** 2 5/16 inches. **Col. Depth:** 7 3/4 inches. **Key Personnel:** Joyce B. Sirota, Editor/Advertising Mgr.; Rita K. Fucillo, Publisher. **ISSN:** 0048-282X. **Remarks:** Accepts advertising.
Ad Rates: BW: $490 **Circ:** Non-paid ‡28,745
4C: $640

14052 Partisan Review
236 Bay State Rd. Phone: (617)353-4260
Boston, MA 02215 Fax: (617)353-7444
Publisher E-mail: partisan@bu.edu

Magazine featuring literary, cultural, and political articles, reviews, fiction, and poetry. **Founded:** 1934. **Freq:** Quarterly. **Print Method:** Offset. **Trim Size:** 6 x 9. **Cols./Page:** 1. **Col. Width:** 51 nonpareils. **Col. Depth:** 96 agate lines. **Key Personnel:** William Phillips, Editor and Publisher. **ISSN:** 0031-2525.
Ad Rates: BW: $200 **Circ:** ‡8,200

14053 Pharmacotherapy
Pharmacotherapy Publications, Inc.
750 Washington Ave. Phone: (617)636-5390
NEMC Box 806 Fax: (617)636-5318
Boston, MA 02111
Publication E-mail: ppijournal@aol.com

Magazine presenting original research articles on all aspects of human pharmacology and reviews of articles on druge and drug therapy. **Subtitle:** The Journal of Human Pharmacology and Drug Therapy. **Founded:** July 1981. **Freq:** Monthly. **Print Method:** Offset. **Trim Size:** 8 1/8 x 10 7/8. **Cols./Page:** 2. **Col. Width:** 37 nonpareils. **Col. Depth:** 135 agate lines. **Key Personnel:** Richard T. Scheife, Editor and Publisher; Ann E. Chella-Nigh, Business Mgr., phone (617)636-5390, fax (617)636-5318; Wendy R. Cramer, Assoc. Ed.; Minhoai Lam, Production Mgr. **ISSN:** 0277-0008. **Subscription Rates:** $65 individuals; $95 institutions; $45 students; $80 other countries; $110 institutions, other countries; $60 students, other coun-

tries. **Remarks:** Accepts advertising. **URL:** http://www.healthgate.com. **Alt. Formats:** Microform.
Ad Rates: BW: $1,200 **Circ:** ‡6,600
4C: $2,550

14054 The Pilot
Catholic Diocese of Boston
49 Franklin St. Phone: (617)482-4316
Boston, MA 02110-1304 Fax: (617)482-5647

Official Roman Catholic Archdiocesan newspaper of Boston. **Founded:** 1829. **Freq:** Weekly (Fri.). **Print Method:** Offset. **Cols./Page:** 5. **Col. Width:** 9 7/8 inches. **Col. Depth:** 13 inches. **Key Personnel:** Cardinal Bernard Law, Publisher; Rev. Peter V. Conley, Editor; Joan T. Allister. **Subscription Rates:** $20. **Remarks:** Accepts advertising.
Ad Rates: GLR: $1.60 **Circ:** 31,000
BW: $1,500
PCI: $22.40

14055 PLAYS
Plays, Inc.
120 Boylston St. Phone: (617)423-3157
Boston, MA 02116 Fax: (617)423-2168
Publisher E-mail: plays@user1.channel1.com

Magazine for schools, libraries or drama groups containing one-act plays for holiday celebrations and special patriotic occasions, plays with modern settings and modern situations. Features comedies, dramas, skits, puppet plays, and dramatized classics. **Subtitle:** The Drama Magazine for Young People. **Founded:** Sept. 1941. **Freq:** 7/year (Jan /Feb. issues combined). **Print Method:** Offset. **Trim Size:** 5 1/2 x 8 3/8. **Cols./Page:** 2. **Col. Width:** 28 nonpareils. **Col. Depth:** 101 agate lines. **Key Personnel:** Sylvia K. Burack, Editor; Elizabeth Preston, Managing Editor. **USPS:** 473-810. **Subscription Rates:** $29 individuals; $3.50 single issue. **Remarks:** Accepts advertising. **Online:** UMI; Information Access. **Alt. Formats:** Audio tape; Large-print; Microform.
Ad Rates: BW: $1,000 **Circ:** ‡13,000
PCI: $80

14056 Post-Gazette
5 Prince St. Phone: (617)227-8929
Box 135
Boston, MA 02113
Newspaper. **Founded:** July 1896. **Freq:** Weekly (Fri.). **Print Method:** Offset. **Cols./Page:** 5. **Col. Width:** 23 nonpareils. **Col. Depth:** 223 agate lines. **Key Personnel:** Pamela Donnaruma, Publisher. **Subscription Rates:** $20 individuals. **Remarks:** Accepts advertising.
Ad Rates: PCI: $20 **Circ:** Paid 15,900

14057 Psychiatric Rehabilitation Journal
930 Commonwealth Ave. Phone: (617)353-3549
Boston, MA 02215 Fax: (617)353-9209

Journal discussing issues, programs, and research on psychiatric rehabilitation. **Founded:** 1979. **Freq:** Quarterly. **Trim Size:** 8 1/2 x 11. **Key Personnel:** LeRoy Spaniol, Ph.D., Executive Publisher. **ISSN:** 1095-158X. **Subscription Rates:** $50 individuals; $93 institutions; $60 Canada; $70 other countries; $26 members. **Alt. Formats:** Braille; Mailing labels. **Formerly:** Psychosocial Rehabilitation Journal/Innovations & Research.
Ad Rates: BW: $1,000 **Circ:** Paid 4,000

14058 Public Health Reports
U.S. Government Printing Office
Rm. 1855, JFK Federal Bldg. Phone: (617)565-1440
Boston, MA 02203 Fax: (617)565-4260
Publication E-mail: phr@nlm.nih.gov

Publication reporting on policies, research, and services in public health. **Founded:** 1878. **Freq:** Bimonthly. **Print Method:** Letterpress. **Trim Size:** 8 1/2 x 11. **Cols./Page:** 2. **Col. Width:** 39 nonpareils. **Col. Depth:** 126 agate lines. **Key Personnel:** Dr. Anthony Robbins, Editor, phone (617)5651440, fax (565)4260, robbins@nlm.nih.gov. **ISSN:** 0033-3549. **Subscription Rates:** $15. **Remarks:** Advertising not accepted.
Circ: 7,500

14059 Sampan
Asian-American Civic Association
105 Chauncy St., Lower Level Phone: (617)426-9492
Boston, MA 02111 Fax: (617)482-2316

Newspaper serving the Asian American community. **Founded:** Oct. 1972. **Freq:** Semimonthly. **Cols./Page:** 6. **Col. Width:** 1 3/4 inches. **Col. Depth:** 15 inches. **Key Personnel:** Evelyn Tang, Manager, tten@hotmail.com; Chau-ming Lee, Executive Dir. **Subscription Rates:** $30; $60 by first class mail; single issue free. **Remarks:** Accepts advertising.
Ad Rates: BW: $520 **Circ:** Controlled 16,000
4C: $1,020
PCI: $10

14060 Simmons Review
Simmons College
300 The Fenway Phone: (617)521-2363
Boston, MA 02115 Fax: (617)521-3193
Free: (800)246-0573
Publisher E-mail: millikan@simmons.edu

Collegiate magazine. **Founded:** 1947. **Freq:** 3/year. **Print Method:** Offset. **Trim Size:** 8 1/2 x 11. **Cols./Page:** 2. **Col. Width:** 39 nonpareils. **Col. Depth:** 128 agate lines. **Key Personnel:** Harriet Petrocelli, Editor, phone (617)521-2369, hpetrocelli@simmons.edu. **ISSN:** 0049-0512. **Remarks:** Advertising not accepted. **URL:** http://www.simmons.edu.
Circ: Non-paid 35,000

14061 Slat Water Sportsman
Times Mirror Magazines, Inc.
77 Franklin St., 10th Fl. Phone: (617)338-2300
Boston, MA 02110 Fax: (617)338-2309
Publication E-mail: swsfish@ultranet.com

Magazine on salt water fishing and boating. **Subtitle:** The Fishing Authority. **Founded:** 1939. **Freq:** Monthly. **Print Method:** Offset. **Trim Size:** 7 7/8 x 10 3/4. **Cols./Page:** 3. **Col. Width:** 27 nonpareils. **Col. Depth:** 143 agate lines. **Key Personnel:** Colin M. Cunningham, Jr., Editor-in-Chief/Publisher; Barry Gibson, Editor; Jaye McAuliffe, Assoc. Pub. **ISSN:** 0036-3618. **Subscription Rates:** $3.50 single issue. **Remarks:** Accepts advertising. **Available Online. URL:** http://www.saltwatersportsman.com.
Ad Rates: BW: $8,160 **Circ:** Paid 146,213
4C: $12,170

14062 The South End News
631 Tremont St. Phone: (617)266-6670
Boston, MA 02118-1201 Fax: (617)266-5973

Local newspaper. **Founded:** Feb. 10, 1980. **Freq:** Weekly (Thurs.). **Print Method:** Offset. **Trim Size:** 10 1/8 x 15 1/2. **Key Personnel:** Peter Steele, Editor; James G. Hoover, Publisher. **ISSN:** 0738-9108. **Subscription Rates:** Free; $25 by mail. **Remarks:** Accepts advertising.
Ad Rates: PCI: $11.18 **Circ:** Paid 300
Free 18,500

14063 South Shore News
Franklin Publishing Co., Inc.
99 High St. Phone: (781)878-3333
Boston, MA 02110-2320
Newspaper. **Founded:** 1859. **Freq:** Weekly (Mon.). **Print Method:** Offset. **Trim Size:** 10 1/4 x 16. **Cols./Page:** 6. **Col. Width:** 21 nonpareils. **Col. Depth:** 224 agate lines. **Key Personnel:** John Anderson, Advertising Mgr.; Barbara Marcott, Office Mgr. **Subscription Rates:** $35 individuals. **Remarks:** Accepts advertising.
Ad Rates: GLR: $.86 **Circ:** 73,003
PCI: $19.50

14064 The Standard
Standard Publishing Corp.
155 Federal St., 13th Fl. Phone: (617)457-0600
Boston, MA 02110 Fax: (617)482-7820
Free: (800)682-5759
Publication E-mail: stnd@earthlink.net

Trade newspaper covering insurance events, legislation, regulatory hearings, and court sessions for independent insurance agents in New England. **Subtitle:** New England's Insurance Weekly. **Founded:** 1865. **Freq:** Weekly (Fri.). **Print Method:** Offset. **Trim Size:** 8 1/2 x 11. **Cols./Page:** 3. **Col. Width:** 2.25 picas. **Col. Depth:** 140 agate lines. **Key Personnel:** Paul T. Tetrault, Jr., Editor; John C. Cross, Publisher; Barbara Crockett, Advertising Mgr. **ISSN:** 0038-9390. **Subscription Rates:** $55 individuals. **Remarks:** Accepts advertising.
Ad Rates: BW: $1,122 **Circ:** 5,123
4C: $1,755
PCI: $47

14065 Strategic Review
U.S. Strategic Institute
PO Box 15618, Kenmore Sta. Phone: (617)353-8700
Boston, MA 02215-0011 Fax: (617)353-7330
Publication E-mail: stratrev@bu.edu
Publisher E-mail: stratrev@bu.edu

Military and political magazine. **Founded:** 1973. **Freq:** Quarterly. **Print Method:** Offset. **Trim Size:** 8 1/4 x 11. **Cols./Page:** 2. **Col. Width:** 19 picas. **Col. Depth:** 54 picas. **Key Personnel:** Benjamin F. Schemmer, Editor-in-Chief, phone (941)649-1445, fax (941)649-0960, zoorfu@aol.com; Abigail DuBois, Managing Editor, gdubois@bu.edu. **ISSN:** 0091-6846. **Subscription Rates:** $35 individuals; $25 individuals govt. and libraries; $7.50 single issue. **Remarks:** Advertising not accepted.
Circ: Paid ‡3,000
Non-paid ‡500

14066 Studies in Romanticism
Boston University
236 Bay State Rd. Phone: (617)353-2505
Boston, MA 02215
Literary journal. **Founded:** 1961. **Freq:** Quarterly. **Print Method:** Offset. **Trim Size:** 6 x 9 1/8. **Cols./Page:** 1. **Col. Width:** 53 nonpareils. **Col. Depth:** 96 agate lines. **Key Personnel:** David Wagenknecht, Editor; Deborah Swedberg, Managing Editor. **ISSN:** 0039-3762. **Subscription Rates:** $23 individuals; $60 institutions; $6 single issue. **Remarks:** Accepts advertising. **Online:** UMI. **Alt. Formats:** Microform.
Ad Rates: BW: $200 **Circ:** ‡1,800

14067 Syndicated Columnists Weekly
National Braille Press, Inc.
88 St. Stephen St. Phone: (617)266-6160
Boston, MA 02115 Fax: (617)437-0456
Free: (800)548-7323
Publisher E-mail: orders@nbp.org

Newspaper covering syndicated columnists from major U.S. papers in Braille. **Founded:** Aug. 1984. **Freq:** Weekly. **Key Personnel:** Diane Croft. **Subscription Rates:** $20.80. **Remarks:** Advertising not accepted. **Alt. Formats:** Braille.
Circ: Combined 1,500

14068 Teen Voices Magazine
Women Express, Inc.
316 Huntington Ave. Phone: (617)262-2434
Boston, MA 02115 Fax: (617)262-8937
Publisher E-mail: womenexp@teenvoices.com

Magazine featuring educational articles for teenage girls and young adult women. **Subtitle:** Because You're More than Just a Pretty Face. **Founded:** 1990. **Freq:** Quarterly. **Trim Size:** 8 1/4 x 10 3/4. **Cols./Page:** 2. **Col. Width:** 3.75 inches. **Col. Depth:** 8.75 inches. **Key Personnel:** Alison Amoroso, Director; Shannon Benging, Managing Editor. **ISSN:** 1074-7494. **Subscription Rates:** $20. **Remarks:** Accepts advertising. **URL:** http://www.teenvoices.com.
Ad Rates: BW: $400 **Circ:** Paid 3,000
Non-paid 7,000

14069 Walking
Reader's Digest Publications
9-11 Horcourt Street Phone: (617)266-3322
Boston, MA 02116
Publication E-mail: walkingmag@aol.comp

Magazine for recreational and fitness walkers; includes articles on health, fitness, nutrition, travel, gear and equipment, and events. **Founded:** May 27, 1986. **Freq:** Bimonthly. **Print Method:** Offset. **Trim Size:** 7.87 x 10.5. **Cols./Page:** 3. **Col. Width:** 27 nonpareils. **Col. Depth:** 140 agate lines. **Key Personnel:** Seth Bauer, Editor. **ISSN:** 1042-2102. **Subscription Rates:** $14.95 individuals; $2.99 single issue; foreign, $20.95.
Ad Rates: BW: $22,580 **Circ:** Paid ★**658,034**
4C: $28,190
PCI: $540

14070 Weather and Forecasting
American Meteorological Society
45 Beacon St. Phone: (617)227-2425
Boston, MA 02108 Fax: (617)742-8718
Publisher E-mail: amspubs@ametsoc.org

Original research and survey papers related to operational forecasting. **Founded:** Sept. 1985. **Freq:** Bimonthly. **Print Method:** Offset. **Trim Size:** 7 3/4 x 10 1/2. **Cols./Page:** 2. **Col. Width:** 39 nonpareils. **Col. Depth:** 126 agate lines. **Key Personnel:** Ronald McPherson, Publisher. **ISSN:** 0022-4928. **Subscription Rates:** $140 individuals. **Remarks:** Advertising not accepted. **URL:** http://www.ams.allenpress.com. **Alt. Formats:** CD-ROM, The AMS Journal; Bulletin Archive.
Circ: ‡2,985

14071 The Woman Rebel
PO Box 2474 Phone: (617)623-4141
Boston, MA 02208
Magazine for women with a slant on activism. **Subtitle:** The Magazine for the Female Iconoclast. **Founded:** 1995. **Freq:** Bi-annual. **Trim Size:** 8 1/2 x 11. **Key Personnel:** Diane Glass, Editor, dmglass@aol.com; Rachael Burger, Editor, rlburger@aol.com. **Subscription Rates:** $10 individuals; $3 single issue. **URL:** http://www.mindspring.com/˜wrebel.
Ad Rates: BW: $300 **Circ:** Paid 2000

14072 The World
Unitarian Universalist Association
25 Beacon St. Phone: (617)742-2100
Boston, MA 02108 Fax: (617)367-3237
Publication E-mail: worldmag@uua.org

Religious news magazine. **Subtitle:** Journal of the Unitarian Universalist Association. **Founded:** 1987. **Freq:** Bimonthly. **Print Method:** Offset. **Trim Size:** 8 1/8 x 10 1/2. **Cols./Page:** 3. **Col. Width:** 2 3/16 inches. **Col. Depth:** 9 3/8 inches. **Key Personnel:** Amy Hoffman, Editor, ahoffman@uua.org; Myha

Nguyen, Advertising Mgr., fax (617)742-7025, bfrasier@uua.org; Irene Greene, Circulation Mgr., igreene@vva.org. **ISSN:** 0892-2462. **Subscription Rates:** Free to qualified subscribers; $21 individuals; $4.50 single issue. **Remarks:** Accepts advertising.
Ad Rates: BW: $3,100 **Circ:** Controlled ‡117,000
PCI: $120 Paid ‡1,000

14073 The WorldPaper
World Times, Inc.
210 World Trade Center Phone: (617)439-5400
Boston, MA 02210 Fax: (617)439-5415
Publication E-mail: editorial@worldtimes.com

An international editorial supplement to newspapers and magazines featuring writers who write about their native countries (English, Spanish, Russian, Chinese, Japenese). **Subtitle:** Global Themes from Regional Perspectives. **Founded:** Apr. 1978. **Freq:** Monthly. **Print Method:** Letterpress and offset. **Trim Size:** 15 x 22 3/4. **Cols./Page:** 6 and 3. **Col. Width:** 2 1/2 and 2 inches. **Col. Depth:** 22 3/4 inches. **Key Personnel:** Crocker Snow, Jr., Pres./Editor-in-Chief, phone (617)439-5410, csnow@worldtimes.com; Cameron Brandt, Editor, phone (617)439-5442, cbrandt@worldtimes.com; Lena Granberg, Publisher, phone (617)439-5413, lgranberg@worldtimes.com. **Subscription Rates:** $24. **Remarks:** Accepts advertising. **URL:** http://www.worldpaper.com.
Ad Rates: BW: $39,000 **Circ:** Paid 1,800,000
SAU: $40
PCI: $245

14074 The Writer Magazine
The Writer, Inc.
120 Boylston St. Phone: (617)423-3157
Boston, MA 02116 Fax: (617)423-2168
Publication E-mail: writer@user1.channel1.com
Publisher E-mail: writer@user1.channel1.com

Magazine for free-lance writers. Publishing practical information and advice on how to write publishable material and where to sell it. **Subtitle:** The Pioneer (Oldest) Magazine for Writers. **Founded:** Apr. 1887. **Freq:** Monthly. **Print Method:** Offset. **Trim Size:** 7 1/2 x 10 1/2. **Cols./Page:** 2. **Col. Width:** 34 nonpareils. **Col. Depth:** 119 agate lines. **Key Personnel:** Sylvia K. Burack, Editor; Elizabeth Preston, Managing Editor. **ISSN:** 0043-9517. **Subscription Rates:** $28 individuals; $3.50 single issue. **Remarks:** Accepts advertising. **Alt. Formats:** Audio tape; CD-ROM; Large-print; Microform.
Ad Rates: BW: $1,600 **Circ:** ‡53,000
PCI: $125

14075 Zion's Herald
Boston Wesleyan Association
The United Methodist Center Phone: (617)266-3900
566 Commonwealth Fax: (617)266-4619
Boston, MA 02215-2520
Magazine featuring United Methodist Church news. **Founded:** Jan. 9, 1823. **Freq:** Semimonthly. **Print Method:** Offset. **Cols./Page:** 4. **Col. Width:** 14.5 picas. **Col. Depth:** 207 agate lines. **Key Personnel:** Ann Greene Whiting, Editor. **Subscription Rates:** $15 individuals.
Ad Rates: PCI: $7 **Circ:** ‡6,000
7,200

14076 Continental Cablevision, Inc.
Pilot House, Lewis Wharf Phone: (617)742-9500
Boston, MA 02110 Fax: (617)742-0530

Founded: 1963. **Key Personnel:** Amos B. Hostetter, Jr., Chairman/CEO; Timothy P. Neher, Vice Chairman; Michel J. Ritter, Pres. and COO; Henry R. James, Dir. of Corporate Communications. **Cities Served:** Various communities in Maine, New Hampshire, Massachusetts, Connecticut, Michigan, Iowa, New York, Virginia, Florida, Ohio, Illinois.: subscribing households 3,000,000; 54 channels.

14077 WABU-TV - 68
1660 Soldiers Field Rd. Phone: (617)787-6868
Boston, MA 02135 Fax: (617)562-4280

Format: Commercial TV. **Networks:** Independent. **Owner:** Boston University, at above address. **Founded:** July 1993. **Formerly:** WQTV-TV. **Operating Hours:** Continuous. **ADI:** Boston-Worcester,MA-Derry-Manchester,NH. **Key Personnel:** Robert D. Gordon, Pres./Gen. Mgr.; Will Meyl, Vice Pres./Sales Mgr.; Bill Spitzer, Vice President; Anne Lootens, Program Mgr.; Paul Wilson, Local Sales Mgr.; Peter Fiedler, Operations Mgr.; Joan Sheridan, Business Mgr.; Joe Sweeney, Engineering Dir.; Glenn Koch, Production Mgr.

14078 WBCN-FM - 104.1
1265 Boylston St. Phone: (617)266-1111
Boston, MA 02215-3480 Fax: (617)247-2266

Format: Album-Oriented Rock (AOR). **Networks:** Independent. **Founded:** 1968. **Operating Hours:** Continuous. **ADI:** Boston-Worcester,MA-Derry-Manchester,NH. **Key Personnel:** Tony Berardini, General Mgr. **Wattage:** 24,500.

14079 WBCS-FM - 96.9
330 Stuart St. Phone: (617)542-0241
Boston, MA 02116 Fax: (617)542-5809

Format: Adult Contemporary. **Networks:** Independent. **Founded:** 1945. **Formerly:** WJIB-FM (1992). **Operating Hours:** Continuous. **ADI:** Boston-Worcester,MA-Derry-Manchester,NH. **Key Personnel:** David Lebow, General Mgr. **Wattage:** 50,000.

14080 WBMX-FM - 98.5
116 Huntington Ave., 10th Fl. Phone: (617)236-6898
Boston, MA 02116 Fax: (617)236-6832

Format: Adult Contemporary. **Owner:** American Radio Systems Inc., 116 Huntington Ave., 11th Fl., Boston, MA 02116, (617)375-7500, Fax: (617)375-7575. **Founded:** 1948. **Formerly:** WROR-FM. **Operating Hours:** Continuous. **ADI:** Boston-Worcester,MA-Derry-Manchester,NH. **Key Personnel:** Greg Strassel, Program Dir., phone (617)236-6888, fax (617)236-6864; Jenny McCann, Contact, phone (617)236-6831, fax (617)236-6864; Amy Doyle, Music Dir., phone (617)236-6860. **Wattage:** 50,000.

14081 WBOS-FM - 92.9
1200 Soldiers Field Rd. Phone: (617)254-9267
Boston, MA 02134-1004 Fax: (617)782-8757
E-mail: wbosonline@aol.comm

Format: Album-Oriented Rock (AOR). **Networks:** Independent. **Owner:** Greater Media, Inc., 2 Kennedhy Blvd., East Brunswick, NJ 08816, (732)247-6161, Fax: (732)247-0215. **Founded:** 1954. **Operating Hours:** Continuous. **ADI:** Boston-Worcester,MA-Derry-Manchester,NH. **Key Personnel:** John R. Laton, Station Mgr.; James T. Herron, Program Dir.; Patrica L. Baker, General Sales Mgr.; Steven J. Callahan, Chief Engineer; Louise A. Sullivan, Business Mgr.; Peter H. Smyth, V.P./GM, phone (617)542-0241; Adam R. Klein, Promotions Dir.; Marcie Mills, phone (617)542-0241. **Local Programs:** *Brookline Today*, Sue Cope. **Wattage:** 50,000. **Ad Rates:** $200-350 per unit.

14082 WBUR-FM - 90.9
890 Commonwealth Ave. Phone: (617)353-0909
Boston, MA 02215 Fax: (617)353-4747

Format: News; Information; Eclectic. **Networks:** National Public Radio (NPR); Public Radio International (PRI). **Founded:** 1950. **Operating Hours:** Continuous. **ADI:** Boston-Worcester,MA-Derry-Manchester,NH. **Key Personnel:** Jane Christo, General Mgr.; George Boosey, Program Mgr.; Mary Fronk, Underwriting Sales Mgr.; Sam Fleming, News Dir.; Jay Clayton, Marketing Mgr.; Steve Elman, Assistant Gen. Mgr. **Local Programs:** *The Connection*, Mary McGrath; *Morning Edition*, Tim Allik. **Wattage:** 7200. **Ad Rates:** Noncommercial.

14083 WBZ-AM - 1030
1170 Soldiers Field Rd. Phone: (617)787-7000
Boston, MA 02134-1092 Fax: (617)787-7060

Format: News; Talk. **Networks:** ABC; AP. **Founded:** 1921. **Operating Hours:** Continuous. **ADI:** Boston-Worcester,MA-Derry-Manchester,NH. **Key Personnel:** John Spinola, General Mgr.; Brian Whittemore, News Dir. **Wattage:** 50,000.

14084 WBZ-TV - 4
1170 Soldiers Field Rd. Phone: (617)787-7000
Boston, MA 02134 Fax: (617)787-5969

Format: Commercial TV. **Networks:** NBC. **Founded:** 1948. **Operating Hours:** Continuous. **ADI:** Boston-Worcester,MA-Derry-Manchester,NH. **Key Personnel:** Debra Zeyen, Contact; Kim Harbin, Contact.

14085 WEEI-AM - 850
116 Huntington Ave. Phone: (617)375-8000
Boston, MA 02116-5749 Fax: (617)375-8019

Format: Sports. **Networks:** CBS. **Founded:** 1924. **Operating Hours:** Continuous. **ADI:** Boston-Worcester,MA-Derry-Manchester,NH. **Key Personnel:** John Maguire, Station Mgr.; Glenn Ordway, Program Dir.; Bill Ebben, General Sales Mgr. **Local Programs:** *Big Show*, Jason Wolpe; *A Team*, Paul Serino; *Ted Nation*, Rene Marchando. **Wattage:** 50,000.

14086 WERS-FM - 88.9
126 Beacon St. Phone: (617)824-8892
Boston, MA 02116 Fax: (617)824-8804

Format: Eclectic. **Networks:** Independent. **Owner:** Emerson College, at above address, (617)578-8891. **Founded:** 1949. **Operating Hours:** 6 a.m.- 2 a.m.; 100% local. **ADI:** Boston-Worcester,MA-Derry-Manchester,NH. **Key Personnel:** Art Singer, General Mgr., fax (617)824-8856, asinger@emerson.edu; Richard Levy, Chief Engineer; Mark Walsh, Program Dir., phone (617)824-8891, fax (617)824-8804. **Wattage:** 4000. **Ad Rates:** Noncommercial.

14087 WEZE-AM - 1260
PO Box 9121 Phone: (617)328-0880
North Quincy, MA 02171 Fax: (617)328-0375
Free: (800)243-1260

Format: Religious; Talk. **Networks:** Independent. **Founded:** 1922. **Operating Hours:** Continuous. **Key Personnel:** Alex Canavan, General Mgr.; Mark Carey, Program Dir. **Wattage:** 5000.

14088 WGBH-FM - 89.7
125 Western Ave. Phone: (617)492-2777
Boston, MA 02134 Fax: (617)864-7927

Format: Classical; Jazz; Folk; News; Public Radio. **Networks:** National Public Radio (NPR); Public Radio International (PRI). **Owner:** WGBH Educational Foundation, at above address. **Founded:** 1951. **Operating Hours:** Continuous. **ADI:** Boston-Worcester,MA-Derry-Manchester,NH. **Key Personnel:** Marita Rivero, General Mgr.; Ron Jones, Program Dir., ron_jones@wgbh.org; John Voci, Operations Dir.; Jon Solins, Music Projects Dir.; Carl Watanabe, Program Mgr. **Local Programs:** *Classical Performances*, Richard Knisely; *Classics in the Morning*, Ron Della Chiesa; *Jazz with Eric in the Evenings*, Eric Jackson. **Wattage:** 100,000. **Ad Rates:** Noncommercial. **URL:** http://www.wgbh.org.

14089 WGBH-TV - 2
125 Western Ave. Phone: (617)492-2777
Boston, MA 02134 Fax: (617)787-0714

Format: Public TV. **Networks:** Public Broadcasting Service (PBS). **Owner:** WGBH Educational Foundation, at above address. **Founded:** 1955. **Operating Hours:** 6 a.m. to 1 a.m. **ADI:** Boston-Worcester,MA-Derry-Manchester,NH. **Key Personnel:** David Liroff, Station Mgr.; Henry Becton, Contact; Dan Everett, Contact; Jeanne Hopkins, Contact. **Ad Rates:** Noncommercial.

14090 WGBX-TV - 44
125 Western Ave. Phone: (617)492-2777
Boston, MA 02134 Fax: (617)787-0714

Format: Public TV. **Networks:** Public Broadcasting Service (PBS). **Owner:** WGBH Educational Foundation, at above address. **Founded:** 1967. **Operating Hours:** 7 a.m.-1 a.m. **ADI:** Boston-Worcester,MA-Derry-Manchester,NH. **Key Personnel:** Henry Becton, Contact; David B. Liroff, Contact; Jeanne Hopkins, Contact; Dan Everett, Contact; Steve Bass, Station Mgr. **Ad Rates:** Noncommercial. **URL:** www.wgbh.org.

14091 WHDH-TV - 7
7 Bulfinch Pl. Phone: (617)725-0777
Boston, MA 02114 Fax: (617)227-4782

Format: Commercial TV. **Networks:** NBC. **Formerly:** WNEV-TV. **Operating Hours:** Continuous. **ADI:** Boston-Worcester,MA-Derry-Manchester,NH. **Key Personnel:** Michael Carson, VP/General Manager; Peter Hennessey, General Sales Mgr.; Patricia Barraza.vos, Dir. of P.R./Communications; Joan McCready, Program Services Director; Laura Hale, VP/Programming & Creative Services Dir.; Bill Pohovey, News Dir.; John Bell, Managing Editor; Jim Shultis, Chief Engineer; Cheryl Garthwait, Research Director. **Local Programs:** *Boston Common*; *Urban Update*. **URL:** http://www.whdh.com.

14092 WILD-AM - 1090
90 Warren St. Phone: (617)427-2222
Boston, MA 02119 Fax: (617)427-2677

Format: Urban Contemporary; Adult Contemporary. **Networks:** American Urban Radio; ABC. **Owner:** Nash Communications Corp., at above address. **Founded:** 1946. **Operating Hours:** Sunrise-sunset. **ADI:** Boston-Worcester,MA-Derry-Manchester,NH. **Key Personnel:** Bernadine Foster Nash, Pres./CEO; Michael McDernott, General Mgr.; Eugenia Nicholas, General Sales Mgr.; Ken Johnson, Program Dir.; Steve Gousby, Music Coor. **Local Programs:** *In Unison*, Nina Arimah; *Time Tunnel*, Ken Johnson. **Wattage:** 5000. **Ad Rates:** $72 for 30 seconds; $90 for 60 seconds. **URL:** http://www.wildam1090.com.

14093 WLVI-TV - 56
75 Morrissey Blvd. Phone: (617)265-5656
Boston, MA 02125 Fax: (617)265-2538

Format: Commercial TV. **Networks:** Warner Brothers Studios. **Founded:** Dec. 1966. **Operating Hours:** Continuous. **ADI:** Boston-Worcester,MA-Derry-Manchester,NH. **Key Personnel:** John J. Vitanovec, V.P. and Gen. Mgr.; Fran Perdisatt, General Sales Mgr.; Graceyn Brown, Program Dir.; Greg Caputo, News Dir. **Local Programs:** *Boston's Big Screen*; *Star Trek*; *10 O'Clock News*. **Wattage:** 120 kw.

14094 WMEX-AM - 1150
330 Stuart St. Phone: (617)542-0241
Boston, MA 02116 Fax: (617)542-5809

Format: Adult Contemporary. **Simulcasts:** WMJX-FM. **Net-**

works: ABC. **Founded:** 1979. **Operating Hours:** Continuous. **ADI:** Boston-Worcester,MA-Derry-Manchester,NH. **Key Personnel:** Candy Oteri, Contact; Molly O'Brien, Contact; Nancy Quill, Music Dir.; Sue Oberg, Traffic Dir.; Tim Stansky, Contact; Peter Smyth, General Mgr.; Don Kelley, Operations Mgr.; Frank Kelley, General Sales Mgr.; Alex Klemmer, Contact; Jaime Weiser, Promotions Dir. **Wattage:** 5000.

14095 WMFP-TV - 62
One Beacon St. 35th Fl. Phone: (617)720-1062
Boston, MA 02108

Format: Public TV. **Networks:** Independent. **Owner:** Shop At Home Inc., at above address, (423)688-0300, Fax: (423)689-5067. **Founded:** 1987. **Operating Hours:** Continuous. **ADI:** Boston-Worcester,MA-Derry-Manchester,NH. **Key Personnel:** Bill Desmond, Chief Engineer; Lou James, General Mgr. **Wattage:** 5000. **Ad Rates:** Advertising accepted; rates available upon request.

14096 WMJX-FM - 106.7
330 Stuart St. Phone: (617)542-0241
Boston, MA 02117 Fax: (617)542-0620

Format: Adult Contemporary. **Simulcasts:** WMEX-AM. **Owner:** Greater Media Inc., at above address. **Founded:** 1981. **Operating Hours:** Continuous. **ADI:** Boston-Worcester,MA-Derry-Manchester,NH. **Key Personnel:** Peter Smyth, General Mgr.; Jim Berry, Promotions Dir.; Frank Kelley, General Sales Mgr.; Don Kelley, Operations Mgr.; Candy O'Terry, Program Coordinator. **Local Programs:** *Bay State Forum*, Gay Vernon; *Boston Life*, Gay Vernon; *Exceptional Women*, Gay Vernon. **Wattage:** 50,000.

14097 WNBU-TV -
1660 Soldiers Field Rd.
Boston, MA 02135

Owner: Boston University Communications, Inc., at above address.

14098 WODS-FM - 103.3
1170 Soldiers Field Rd. Phone: (617)787-7522
Boston, MA 02134 Fax: (617)787-7523

Format: Oldies. **Networks:** CBS. **Owner:** CBS Inc., 51 W. 52nd St., New York, NY 10019, (212)975-4321. **Founded:** 1948. **Formerly**: WEEI-FM (1984); WHTT-FM (1986); WMRQ-FM (1987). **Operating Hours:** Continuous. **ADI:** Boston-Worcester,MA-Derry-Manchester,NH. **Key Personnel:** Ted Jordan, General Mgr., phone (617)787-7570; Debra Harris O'Hearn, General Sales Mgr., phone (617)787-7575; Rick Shockley, Program Dir., phone (617)787-7572; Karen Reddington, Promotions Dir., phone (617)787-7537; Dave Faneuf, News, phone (617)787-7529; Joanne Adduci, National Sales Mgr. **Wattage:** 50,000.

14099 WQLL-FM - 96.5
73 Kercheval Ave.
Grosse Pointe Farms, MI 48236

Format: Oldies; Full Service. **Owner:** Saga Communications Inc., at above address. **Former name**: WOXF-FM. **Operating Hours:** Continuous. **ADI:** Boston-Worcester,MA-Derry-Manchester,NH. **Key Personnel:** Ray Garon, VP/General Mgr.; Tom Kallechey, Programs and Operations Dir.; J. C. Haze, Program Dir.; Katie Ojanen, Local Sales Mgr. **Wattage:** 6000. **Ad Rates:** Advertising accepted; rates available upon request.

14100 WRBB-FM - 104.9
360 Huntington Ave. Phone: (617)373-4338
Boston, MA 02115-5096 Fax: (617)373-5095

Format: Eclectic. **Founded:** 1971. **Operating Hours:** Continuous. **ADI:** Boston-Worcester,MA-Derry-Manchester,NH. **Key Personnel:** Christian Del Prete, Program Dir.; Greg Pretranzio, Sports Dir.; Lou Conrad, Contact; Chris Adams, Contact; Matt White, Music Dir.; Scott Souza, News Dir. **Wattage:** 10. **Ad Rates:** Underwriting available.

14101 WRKO-AM - 680
116 Huntington Ave., 10th Fl. Phone: (617)236-6800
Boston, MA 02116 Fax: (617)236-6889

Format: Talk. **Networks:** ABC. **Owner:** American Radio Systems Inc., at above address, (617)375-7500, Fax: (617)375-7575. **Founded:** 1922. **Operating Hours:** Continuous. **ADI:** Boston-Worcester,MA-Derry-Manchester,NH. **Key Personnel:** Brad Murray, General Mgr.; Kevin Straley, Program Dir. **Local Programs:** *Clapprood and Whitley*, Peter Skrupka, (617)375-8098, Fax (617)236-6889; *Howie Carr*, Doug Goudie, (617)375-8098, Fax (617)236-6889; *Two Chicks Dishing*, Paul Brennan, (617)236-6818, Fax (617)236-6889. **Wattage:** 50,000. **Ad Rates:** Advertising accepted; rates available upon request.

14102 WSBK-TV - 38
83 Leo Birmingham Pkwy. Phone: (617)783-3838
Boston, MA 02135 Fax: (617)783-1875

Format: Commercial TV. **Networks:** United Paramount Network; Independent. **Owner:** Paramount Stations Group, 5555 Melrose Ave, Los Angeles, CA 90038. **Founded:** 1964. **Operating Hours:** Continuous; 100% local. **ADI:** Boston-Worcester,MA-Derry-Manchester,NH. **Key Personnel:** Scott McGavick, Contact; Stuart P. Tauber, VP/General Mgr.; John Viall, Operations Mgr.; Meg LaVigne, Program Mgr.; Mark Lund, General Sales Mgr.; Julie Bruno; Jeff Reed, Sales Mgr.; Douglas Wheeler, Contact; Jim McCarthy, Chief Engineer; Virgnia Jones, Contact; Scott McGavick, Sales Mgr.; Julie Bruno, Sales Mgr.; Jeff Reed, Sales Mgr. **Local Programs:** *Boston Bruins*, Doug Wheeler; *Boston Celtics*; *UPN 38 Prime News*, Meg LaVigne.

14103 WSJZ-FM - 96.9
1200 Soldiers Field Rd. Phone: (617)254-9267
Boston, MA 02134-1004 Fax: (617)782-8757
E-mail: oasis99.5@aol.comm

Format: Jazz. **Networks:** Westwood One Radio. **Owner:** Greater Media, Inc., 2 Kennedy Blvd., East Brunswick, NJ 08816, (732)247-6161, Fax: (732)247-0215. **Founded:** 1947. **Absorbed**: WKLB-FM (Aug. 23, 1997). **Formerly**: WOAZ-FM (Aug. 23, 1997); WSSH-FM. **Operating Hours:** Continuous. **ADI:** Boston-Worcester,MA-Derry-Manchester,NH. **Key Personnel:** John R. Laton, Station Mgr.; Karen Gagne Ball, General Sales Mgr.; Steven J. Callahan, Chief Engineer; Shirley Maldonado, Program Dir.; Adam R. Klein, Promotions Dir.; Louise A. Sullivan, Business Mgr.; Marcie Mills, National Sales Mgr., phone (617)542-0241; Peter H. Smyth, VP/GM, phone (617)542-0241. **Local Programs:** *Lowell Journal*, Sue Cope. **Wattage:** 50,000. **Ad Rates:** $175-350 per unit.

14104 WSSS-FM - 104.7
116 Huntington Ave.
Boston, MA 02116

Format: Oldies; Contemporary Hit Radio (CHR). **Owner:** EZ Charlotte, Inc., at above address. **Founded:** 1969. **Former name**: WMXC (1994). **Operating Hours:** Continuous. **Key Personnel:** Gary Brobst, VP/General Mgr., phone (704)561-4850; Craig Mundy, General Sales Mgr., phone (704)561-4892; Don Schaeffer, Program Dir., phone (704)561-4846. **Wattage:** 100,000. **URL:** http://www.wsss.com.

14105 WUMB-FM - 91.9
University of Massachusetts at Boston Phone: (617)287-6900
Boston, MA 02125-3393 Fax: (617)287-6916
Free: (800)573-2100
E-mail: wumb@umbsky.cc.umb.edu

Format: Folk; Jazz. **Founded:** 1982. **Operating Hours:** 5 a.m.-1 a.m.; 100% local. **ADI:** Boston-Worcester,MA-Derry-Manchester,NH. **Key Personnel:** Patricia A. Monteith, General Mgr.; Noel Johnson, Promotions Dir.; Brian Quinn, Program Dir.; Grady Moates, Chief Engineer. **Wattage:** 1000. **Ad Rates:** Noncommercial.

14106 WUNR-AM - 1600
160 N. Washington St. Phone: (617)367-9003
Boston, MA 02114-2142 Fax: (617)367-2265

Format: Ethnic. **Networks:** Independent. **Owner:** Herbert S. Hoffman, at above address. **Founded:** 1948. **Operating Hours:** Continuous; 100% local. **ADI:** Boston-Worcester,MA-Derry-Manchester,NH. **Key Personnel:** Jane A. Clarke, Contact; Stephen C. Lalli, Contact; Suzanne Pellegrini, Contact; Norman Ruby, Operations Mgr. **Wattage:** 5000. **Ad Rates:** $15-26 for 30 seconds; $19-32 for 60 seconds.

14107 WZBU-TV -
1660 Soldiers Field Rd.
Boston, MA 02135

Owner: Boston University Communications Inc., at above address.

14108 WZLX-FM - 100.7
The Prudential Tower Phone: (617)267-0123
Suite 2450 Fax: (617)421-9305
Boston, MA 02199

Format: Classic Rock. **Founded:** 1979. **Operating Hours:** Continuous. **ADI:** Boston-Worcester,MA-Derry-Manchester,NH. **Key Personnel:** Jerry Cham, General Mgr.; Buzz Knight, Program Dir.; Chris Paquin, Sales Mgr.; Amy Hull, Business Mgr. **Local Programs:** *Common Ground*, Debbie Enblom, News Dir. **Wattage:** 20,000.

BOURNE, pop. 15,730.

NW MA. Barnstable Co. On Cape Cod Canal, 14 mi. W. of Barnstable. Summer resort.

14109 Bourne Courier
Community Newspaper
5 Namskaket Rd. Phone: (508)398-0123
PO Box 2776 Fax: (508)760-3387
Orleans, MA 02653-6776
Free: (800)660-8999

Community newspaper. **Founded:** 1894. **Freq:** Weekly (Wed.). **Print Method:** Offset. **Trim Size:** 16 1/2 x 11. **Cols./Page:** 5. **Col. Width:** 21 nonpareils. **Col. Depth:** 224 agate lines. **Key Personnel:** Eric Hartell, Editor; Jeanne Moore-Yount, Advertising Mgr. **Subscription Rates:** $13 individuals; $21 out of county. **Remarks:** Accepts advertising.
Ad Rates: GLR: $.38 **Circ:** Paid 2,114
BW: $424 Free 482
4C: $1,024
PCI: $5.30

14110 The Bourne Enterprise
Falmouth Publishing Co.
50 Depot Ave. Phone: (508)548-4700
Falmouth, MA 02540 Fax: (508)540-8407
Free: (800)286-7744

Local newspaper. **Founded:** 1985. **Freq:** Weekly. **Print Method:** Offset. **Trim Size:** 14 x 23. **Cols./Page:** 6. **Col. Width:** 21 nonpareils. **Col. Depth:** 294 agate lines. **Key Personnel:** William H. Hough, Exec. Editor; Margaret Hough Russell, Publisher; Janice Walford, Managing Editor; Christopher Megan, Sales Dir. **Subscription Rates:** $41.60 individuals; $.40 single issue. **Remarks:** Accepts advertising.
Ad Rates: BW: $1,168.65 **Circ:** Paid 10,087
SAU: $7.25
PCI: $7.25

BRADFORD

14111 The Alliance Newspaper
PO Box 5164 Phone: (508)373-3291
Bradford, MA 01835 Fax: (508)373-3291

Focusing on health and human services for health care and human service professionals, their clients, and the general public. **Founded:** Jan. 1994. **Freq:** Bimonthly. **Key Personnel:** Mark W. McKellar, Marketing Manager. **Remarks:** Advertising accepted; rates available upon request.
Circ: Free 14,000
Paid 1,000

BRAINTREE, pop. 36,337.

E. MA. Norfolk Co. 10 mi. S. of Boston. Historical area. Manufactures leather goods, pipes, valves, linoleum, rubber tile, petroleum products, beverages, potato chips. Shipbuilding.

14112 Braintree Forum
Mariner Newspapers
PO Box K Phone: (617)843-2937
Braintree, MA 02184 Fax: (617)849-3319
Publisher E-mail: cmathis@cnc.com

Community newspaper. **Founded:** 1878. **Freq:** Weekly (Wed.). **Print Method:** Offset. **Cols./Page:** 6. **Col. Width:** 18 nonpareils. **Col. Depth:** 224 agate lines. **Subscription Rates:** $20 individuals.
Ad Rates: BW: $767.25 **Circ:** Paid 4,508
4C: $1,167.25 Non-paid 189
PCI: $8.25

14113 Braintree Gazette
Associated Newspapers
7 Cabot Pl. Phone: (781)878-1111
PO Box 441 Fax: (781)878-3333
Stoughton, MA 02072
Publisher E-mail: aweeklies@aol.com

Community newspaper. **Founded:** 1984. **Freq:** Weekly (Wed.). **Print Method:** Offset. **Cols./Page:** 6. **Col. Width:** 9.5 picas. **Col. Depth:** 16 inches. **Key Personnel:** Richard R. Dailey, Publisher. **Subscription Rates:** $10 individuals. **Remarks:** Accepts advertising.
Ad Rates: BW: $10.53 **Circ:** ‡1,605
4C: $10.77
PCI: $10.53

14114 DEC Magazine
Duane Publishing Co.
PO Box 850769 Phone: (617)848-6150
Braintree, MA 02185 Fax: (617)848-6160
Publication E-mail: info@decmagazine.com

Magazine on demolition and environmental remediation. **Subtitle:** Demolition & Environmental Contractors. **Founded:** 1967. **Freq:** Monthly. **Print Method:** Offset. **Trim Size:** 8 1/8 x 10 7/8. **Cols./Page:** 3. **Col. Width:** 2 1/4 inches. **Col. Depth:** 10 inches. **Key Personnel:** Herbert T. Duane III, Editor-in-Chief; Susan Cellucci, Jr., Managing Editor and Advertising;

Robin Hammond, News and Circulation; Katherine Duane, President; Herbert T. Duane, Jr., Publisher. **Subscription Rates:** $72 other countries; $35 individuals. **Remarks:** Accepts advertising. **Formerly:** Wrecking & Salvage Journal.
Ad Rates: BW: $650 **Circ:** Controlled ‡16,292
4C: $1,200
PCI: $35

14115 Cablevision
197 Quincy Ave. Phone: (781)848-2350
Braintree, MA 02184 Fax: (781)848-9719

Founded: 1984. **Key Personnel:** John Havenstein, Dir. of Sales/Marketing, phone (617)787-6600, fax (617)787-6066, jhaven@cablevision.com; Kathleen Mayo, General Mgr., phone (617)787-6600, fax (617)787-6606, kmayo@cablevision.com; Cathy Brisson, Marketing Mgr., cbrisson@cablevision.com; Earnestine Daley, Marketing Supervisor, edaley@cablevision.com. **Cities Served:** subscribing households 10,448; 80 channels; 5 community access channels. **URL:** http://www.cablevision.com; http://www.ma.cablevision.com.

BREWSTER

14116 Brewster Oracle
Community Newspaper
5 Namskaket Rd. Phone: (508)398-0123
PO Box 2776 Fax: (508)760-3387
Orleans, MA 02653-6776
Free: (800)660-8999

Community newspaper. **Founded:** 1987. **Freq:** Weekly (Wed.). **Print Method:** Offset. **Trim Size:** 11 x 16 1/2. **Cols./Page:** 5. **Col. Width:** 21 inches. **Col. Depth:** 224 agate lines. **Key Personnel:** Eric Hartell, Editor; Jeanne Moore-Yount, Advertising Mgr. **Subscription Rates:** Free; $25 (mail). **Remarks:** Accepts advertising.
Ad Rates: GLR: $.39 **Circ:** Non-paid 1,666
BW: $436
4C: $1,036
PCI: $5.45

14117 WFCC-FM - 107.5
One Villages Dr. Phone: (508)896-9322
Brewster, MA 02631 Fax: (508)896-8380

Format: Classical. **Networks:** Concert Music Network (CMN). **Owner:** Allan Stanley, at above address. **Founded:** 1987. **Operating Hours:** 6 a.m.-midnight. **Key Personnel:** Allan Stanley, General Mgr.; Ed Cochran, Sales Mgr.; Janice Gray, Program Dir.; Tina Gorgone, Traffic Mgr. **Wattage:** 50,000. **Ad Rates:** Advertising accepted; rates available upon request.

BRIDGEWATER, pop. 17,202.

SE MA. Plymouth Co. 7 mi. S. of Brockton. State College. Shoe, leatherboard and nail factories; foundry; brickyard; machine shops. Truck, poultry, dairy farms. Potatoes, corn, tomatoes.

14118 Bridgewater Independent
Associated Newspapers
PO Box 156 Phone: (508)697-2881
Bridgewater, MA 02324 Fax: (508)947-1763
Publisher E-mail: aweeklies@aol.com

Community newspaper. **Founded:** 1812. **Freq:** Weekly (Thurs.). **Print Method:** Offset. **Cols./Page:** 6. **Col. Width:** 1 9/16 inches. **Col. Depth:** 16 inches. **Key Personnel:** Terry Egan, Managing Editor; Rhonda Connesso, Office Mgr.; John Anderson, Advertising Mgr. **USPS:** 064-980. **Subscription Rates:** $17.50. **Remarks:** Accepts advertising. **Formerly:** Bridgewater Townsman.
Ad Rates: PCI: $5.65 **Circ:** ‡3,481

14119 Bridgewater Townsman
Mariner Newspapers
165 Enterprise Dr. Phone: (617)837-3500
Marshfield, MA 02050-2132 Fax: (617)837-4540
Free: (800)649-6661
Publisher E-mail: cmathis@cnc.com

Community newspaper. **Freq:** Weekly (Thurs.). **Print Method:** Offset. **Trim Size:** 11 3/8 x 17. **Cols./Page:** 3. **Col. Depth:** 15 1/2 inches. **Key Personnel:** Bob Flavell, Editor; Jack Powers, General Mgr. **Subscription Rates:** $9. **Remarks:** Combined advertising rates available with other Mariner Newspapers.
Ad Rates: BW: $767.25 **Circ:** Paid 1,566
4C: $1,167.25 Non-paid 125
PCI: $8.25

14120 East Bridgewater Citizen
Associated Newspapers
7 Cabot Pl.
PO Box 156
Bridgewater, MA 02324
Publisher E-mail: aweeklies@aol.com

Community newspaper. **Founded:** 1883. **Freq:** Weekly (Wed.). **Print Method:** Offset. **Cols./Page:** 6. **Col. Width:** 9.5 picas. **Col. Depth:** 16 inches. **Key Personnel:** Richard R. Dailey, Publisher. **Subscription Rates:** $17.50. **Remarks:** Accepts advertising.
Ad Rates: BW: $10.53 **Circ:** ‡1,811
4C: $10.77
PCI: $1,053

14121 East Bridgewater Star
Associated Newspapers
PO Box 156 Phone: (781)585-5981
Bridgewater, MA 02324
Publisher E-mail: aweeklies@aol.com

Community newspaper. **Founded:** 1812. **Freq:** Weekly (Thurs.). **Print Method:** Offset. **Cols./Page:** 6. **Col. Width:** 1 9/16 inches. **Col. Depth:** 16 inches. **Key Personnel:** Terry Egan, Managing Editor. **USPS:** 104-360. **Subscription Rates:** $17.50 in county. **Remarks:** Accepts advertising.
Ad Rates: PCI: $5.65 **Circ:** Paid ‡2,185

14122 Lincoln Herald
Lincoln Memorial University Press
Bridgewater State College Phone: (508)697-1388
Bridgewater, MA 02324 Fax: (508)279-6167
Publication E-mail: tturner@bridgew.edu; lmuseum@centryinter.net

Journal covering research in Lincolniana and the Civil War and promoting Abraham Lincoln's ideals in American education. **Founded:** 1938. **Freq:** Quarterly. **Print Method:** Letterpress and offset. **Trim Size:** 7 1/4 x 10 1/4. **Cols./Page:** 2. **Col. Width:** 30 nonpareils. **Col. Depth:** 112 agate lines. **Key Personnel:** Frank Coburn, Managing Editor, phone (615)869-6384; Steven K. Rogstad, Review Editor, 414681-4973. **ISSN:** 0024-3671. **Subscription Rates:** $20; $5 single issue; $35 International. **Remarks:** Accepts advertising.
Ad Rates: BW: $270 **Circ:** ‡780

14123 WBIM-FM - 91.5
Bridgewater State College Phone: (508)697-1366
Rondileau Campus Center Fax: (508)697-1705
Bridgewater, MA 02325

Format: Alternative/New Music/Progressive. **Founded:** 1971. **Operating Hours:** 8 a.m.-midnight. **Key Personnel:** David Boutchie, Station Mgr.; Russ Benoit, Program Dir.; Mikel Strom, Music Dir.; Meghan Blake, Promotions Dir.; Amy Hall, News Dir.; Nicole D'Andrea, Public Service Dir.; Tim Higgins, Production Dir.; Rafael Avellan, Underwriting Dir. **Local Programs:** *The Basement*, Tim Higgins; *Kansas City*; *The Local Show*, Russ Benoit. **Wattage:** 180. **Ad Rates:** Noncommercial.

BROCKTON, pop. 95,172.

SE MA. Plymouth Co. 20 mi. S. of Boston. Manufactures shoe findings and tools, textiles, boxes, metal products, plastics, electronics, machine tools.

14124 Brockton News Tribune
Associated Newspapers
7 Cabot Pl. Phone: (781)878-1111
PO Box 441 Fax: (781)878-3333
Stoughton, MA 02072
Publisher E-mail: aweeklies@aol.com

Community newspaper. **Founded:** 1985. **Freq:** Weekly (Wed.). **Print Method:** Offset. **Cols./Page:** 6. **Col. Width:** 9.5 picas. **Col. Depth:** 16 inches. **Key Personnel:** Richard R. Dailey, Publisher. **Subscription Rates:** $10 individuals. **Remarks:** Accepts advertising.
Ad Rates: BW: $10.53 **Circ:** ‡3,500
4C: $10.77
PCI: $10.53

14125 The Enterprise
Enterprise
60 Main St. Phone: (508)586-6200
PO Box 1450 Fax: (508)427-4949
Brockton, MA 02303
Free: (800)462-5569
Publication E-mail: enternews@aol.com; entnews@aol.com
Publisher E-mail: entad@aol.com

General newspaper. **Founded:** 1880. **Freq:** Daily (eve.), Sat. and Sun. (morn.). **Print Method:** Letterpress and flexography. **Cols./Page:** 6. **Col. Width:** 2 1/16 inches. **Col. Depth:** 21 inches. **Key Personnel:** Ray Lacaillade, Advertising Dir., phone (508)427-4008, fax (508)427-4949, entad-dept@aol.com; James F. Plugh, Publisher, phone (508)427-4004, fax (508)427-4005; Paul A. Labreche, General Mgr., phone (508)427-4040, fax (508)427-4005. **ISSN:** 0744-2114. **Subscription Rates:** $124.80 Sunday only; $335.40 7-day. **Remarks:** Accepts advertising. **URL:** southofboston.com. **Feature Editors:** John Murphy, *City*, phone (508)427-4045, fax (508)586-6506, enternews@aol.com.
Ad Rates: GLR: $2.61 **Circ:** Mon.-Fri. 46,804
BW: $3,908.52 Sat. 46,430
4C: $4,368.52 Sun. 57,982
PCI: $31.02

14126 Continental Cablevision
4 Main St. Phone: (508)588-2434
Brockton, MA 02401 Fax: (508)588-5168

Founded: 1983. **Key Personnel:** Richard Donaghue, General Mgr.; Lou Russo, Contact; T.J. Lacey, Contact; Jack Orpen, Contact; Renea Jeffers, Contact. **Cities Served:** subscribing households 34,500; 70 channels; 3 community access channels.

14127 WBET-AM - 1460
60 Main St. Phone: (508)587-2400
PO Box 787 Fax: (508)587-4786
Brockton, MA 02403

Format: News; Talk. **Networks:** CNN Radio. **Founded:** 1946. **Operating Hours:** Continuous; 5% network, 95% local. **ADI:** Boston-Worcester,MA-Derry-Manchester,NH. **Key Personnel:** Charles K. Bergeron, Station Mgr.; Peter Rivora, Program Dir. **Wattage:** 5000 day; 1000 night. **Ad Rates:** $14-20 for 30 seconds; $18-24 for 60 seconds.

14128 WCAV-FM - 97.7
60 Main St. Phone: (508)587-2400
Brockton, MA 02403 Fax: (508)587-4786
E-mail: wcav@juno.com

Format: Country. **Networks:** Westwood One Radio. **Owner:** KJI Broadcasting, at above address. **Founded:** 1948. **Formerly:** WBET-FM (1975). **Operating Hours:** Continuous. **ADI:** Providence, RI-New Bedford, MA. **Key Personnel:** Charles K. Bergeron, Station Mgr.; Frank Fitz, Program Dir. **Local Programs:** *Homegrown Tomatoes* 2:00 pm - 3:00 pm Sunday, Rod Morrison, Producer/Host. **Wattage:** 3000. **Ad Rates:** $30 for 60 seconds. Combined advertising rates available with WBET-AM. **URL:** http://www.wcavfm.com.

14129 WMSX-AM - 1410
288 Linwood St. Phone: (508)587-1410
Brockton, MA 02401 Fax: (508)587-1903

Format: Talk. **Networks:** USA Radio. **Founded:** 1961. **Operating Hours:** 6 a.m.-11 p.m. **Key Personnel:** Mike Mand, Operations; Dan Collier, Station Mgr. **Local Programs:** *Good Afternoon with Mark Santos*, Mark Santos, Mailing contact; *Morning Show with Ron Peterson*, Ron N. Peterson, Mailing contact; *Pat Barnes Show*, Mike Mann, Mailing contact. **Wattage:** 1000. **Ad Rates:** $10-15 for 30 seconds.

BROOKLINE, pop. 55,062.

E. MA. Norfolk Co. 3 mi. SW of Boston. (Branch of Boston P.O.) Residential. Manufactures greeting cards, shades and curtains.

14130 Arion
Boston University
10 Lenox St. Phone: (617)353-6480
Brookline, MA 02446 Fax: (617)353-5905
Publication E-mail: arion@acs.bu.edu

Literary journal covering poetry, translations, and reviews. **Subtitle:** A Journal of Humanities and the Classics. **Founded:** 1962. **Freq:** 3/year. **Key Personnel:** Herbert Golder, Editor; Nicholas Poburko, Managing Editor; Jennifer Vilaga, Senior Production Asst. **ISSN:** 0095-5909. **Subscription Rates:** $19 individuals; $10.50 single issue; $12 students; $35 institutions. **Remarks:** Accepts advertising. **URL:** http://www.bu.edu/arion.
Circ: Paid 425

14131 BOSTONIA
Boston University
10 Lenox St.
Brookline, MA 02146

Boston University alumni magazine. **Founded:** 1900. **Freq:** Quarterly. **Print Method:** Web offset. **Trim Size:** 8 1/8 x 10 7/8. **Cols./Page:** 3. **Col. Width:** 27 nonpareils. **Col. Depth:** 129 1/2 agate lines. **Key Personnel:** Jerrold Hickey, Editor. **ISSN:** 0264-1441. **Remarks:** Advertising not accepted.
Circ: Paid 2,000
Non-paid 200,000

14132 The Brookline Tab
Community Newspaper Company
254 2nd Ave. Phone: (781)433-7828
Needham, MA 02192-9114 Fax: (781)433-7835

Community newspaper (tabloid). **Founded:** 1979. **Freq:** Weekly (Tues.). **Print Method:** Offset. **Trim Size:** 10 x 16. **Cols./Page:** 7. **Col. Width:** 8 picas. **Key Personnel:** John Wilpers, Editor; Russel Pergament, Publisher; Stephen Cummings, Publisher; Lisa Flicop, Advertising Mgr.
Circ: Non-paid 15,156

14133 Greek Orthodox Theological Review
Holy Cross Orthodox Press
50 Goddard Ave. Phone: (617)731-3500
Brookline, MA 02146 Fax: (617)850-1460

Academic journal for the Orthodox Christian community and theologians. **Founded:** 1954. **Freq:** Quarterly. **Print Method:** Offset. **Trim Size:** 6 x 9. **Cols./Page:** 1. **Col. Width:** 55 nonpareils. **Col. Depth:** 81 agate lines. **Key Personnel:** Anton Vrame, Business Mgr.; George D. Dragas, Editor, fax (617)232-7819. **ISSN:** 0017-3894. **Subscription Rates:** $25 individuals; $27 other countries; $30 foreign. **Remarks:** Advertising not accepted.
Circ: ‡800

14134 Handcraft Illustrated
17 Station St. Phone: (617)232-1000
Brookline, MA 02146 Fax: (617)232-1572
Publication E-mail: handcraftillustrated@bcpress.com

Magazine covering step-by-step, do-it-yourself craft projects. **Founded:** 1994. **Freq:** Quarterly. **Key Personnel:** Carol Sterbenz, Editor. **Subscription Rates:** $19.95 individuals; $4 single issue. **Remarks:** Advertising not accepted.
Circ: 150,000

14135 Journal of Modern Hellenism
Hellenic College Press
50 Goddard Ave. Phone: (617)731-3500
Brookline, MA 02146 Fax: (617)566-9075

Scholarly journal covering Greek studies. **Founded:** 1985. **Freq:** Annual. **Trim Size:** 6 x 9. **Cols./Page:** 7. **Col. Width:** 4 inches. **Col. Depth:** 7 inches. **Key Personnel:** Anton C. Vrame, Manager; Harry Psomiades, Editor. **ISSN:** 0743-7749. **Subscription Rates:** $15 individuals. **Remarks:** Advertising not accepted.
Circ: Combined 650

14136 Massachusetts Civil Service Reporter
Landlaw Specialty Publishers
374 Boylston St. Phone: (617)277-4455
Brookline, MA 02146 Fax: (617)277-7375
Free: (800)637-6330

Professional magazine covering civil service and law. **Freq:** Triennial. **Subscription Rates:** $210 individuals.

14137 Massachusetts Discrimination Law Reporter
Landlaw Specialty Publishers
374 Boylston St. Phone: (617)277-4455
Brookline, MA 02146 Fax: (617)277-7375
Free: (800)637-6330

Professional magazine covering discrimination law. **Freq:** Monthly. **Subscription Rates:** $330 individuals.

14138 Medicine & Global Survival
M & G S
10 Brookline Place West
Brookline, MA 02146

Journal examining issues such as war, civil conflict, disaster, the environment, public health and development and human rights. **Founded:** Mar. 1994. **Freq:** Quarterly. **Trim Size:** 8 x 10 7/8. **Key Personnel:** Jennifer Leaning, M.D., Editor-in-Chief. **ISSN:** 1051-2438. **Subscription Rates:** $38 individuals; $120 other. **Remarks:** Advertising not accepted. **Formerly:** The PSR Quarterly.
Circ: (Not Reported)

14139 Plastic and Reconstructive Surgery
Lippincott Williams & Wilkins
1101 Beacon St. Phone: (617)232-7523
Brookline, MA 02146 Fax: (617)730-5525

Medical journal. **Founded:** 1946. **Freq:** 14/year. **Print Method:** Web offset. **Trim Size:** 8 1/8 x 10 7/8. **Cols./Page:** 2. **Col. Width:** 32 nonpareils. **Col. Depth:** 119 agate lines. **Key Personnel:** Robert Goldwyn, M.D., Editor; Gary Walchli, Vice Pres., Advertising Sales; Joyce Michaelan, Rep., phone (410)528-4294, jmichael@wwilkins.com. **Subscription Rates:** $159 individuals; $214 other countries. **Remarks:** Accepts advertising. **Alt. Formats:** Mailing labels.
Ad Rates: BW: $1,325 **Circ:** Paid ‡13,240
4C: $2,625 Non-paid ‡315

BROOKLINE VILLAGE

14140 Natural Health
Natural Health Books
PO Box 1200 Phone: (617)232-1000
Brookline Village, MA 02147 Fax: (617)232-1572

Magazine of alternative medicine, natural foods and products, and self-care. **Subtitle:** The Guide to Well-Being. **Founded:** 1971. **Freq:** Bimonthly. **Print Method:** Offset. **Trim Size:** 8 1/4 x 10 7/8. **Cols./Page:** 3. **Col. Width:** 2 1/4 inches. **Col. Depth:** 9 3/4 inches. **Key Personnel:** Ann D'Alesandro, Advertising Dir.; Chris Kimball, Publisher; Anne Alexander, Editor. **ISSN:** 0888-1375. **Subscription Rates:** $24 individuals; $4 single issue. **Remarks:** Accepts advertising. **Formerly:** East West Journal.
Ad Rates: BW: $7,9000 **Circ:** ‡320,000
4C: $9,500

CAMBRIDGE†, pop. 95,322.

NE MA. Middlesex Co. On Charles River, 3 mi. W. of Boston. (Branch of Boston P.O.) Harvard University; Massachusetts Institute of Technology; Radcliffe College. Manufactures rubber goods, electrical machinery, foundry products, furniture. Printing, publishing and electronic research industries.

14141 Advances in Theoretical and Mathematics Physics
International Press of Boston Inc.
PO Box 38-2872 Phone: (617)491-6560
Cambridge, MA 02238-2872 Fax: (617)491-6779
Publication E-mail: costas@math.harvard.edu
Publisher E-mail: hugh@descartes.intlpress.com

Academic journal covering mathematics and physics. **Founded:** 1997. **Freq:** Quarterly. **Key Personnel:** Abhay Ashtekar, Editor-in-Chief; Shing-Tung Yau, Editor-in-Chief. **ISSN:** 1095-0761. **Subscription Rates:** $80 single issue; $300 institutions; $40 single issue. **Remarks:** Accepts advertising. **Available Online. URL:** http://www.intlpress.com.
Ad Rates: GLR: $50 **Circ:** (Not Reported)
BW: $250
4C: $500

14142 American Journal of Ancient History
Harvard University
Robinson Hall Phone: (617)496-5881
Cambridge, MA 02138 Fax: (617)496-3425

Scholarly journal covering Greek and Roman history. **Founded:** 1976. **Freq:** Semiannual. **Print Method:** Offset. **Trim Size:** 8 1/2 x 5 1/2. **Key Personnel:** E. Badian, Editor; W. Lurie, Asst. **ISSN:** 0362-8914. **Subscription Rates:** $24 U.S. and Canada; $28 other countries. **Remarks:** Accepts advertising.
Ad Rates: BW: $125 **Circ:** Paid 600

14143 The American Prospect
New Prospect, Inc.
PO Box 383080
Cambridge, MA 02238-3080

Political journal covering public policy. **Subtitle:** Journal for the Liberal Imagination. **Founded:** 1990. **Freq:** Semimonthly. **Print Method:** Web offset. **Key Personnel:** Robert Kuttner, Editor; Scott Stossel, Exec. Editor; Kelley Cronin, Business Mgr.; Devin McCloskey, Circulation Dir. **ISSN:** 1049-7285. **Subscription Rates:** $25 individuals; $60 institutions; $4.95 single issue. **Remarks:** Accepts advertising. **Online:** LEXIS-NEXIS. **URL:** http://epn.org/prospect.html.
Ad Rates: BW: $740 **Circ:** (Not Reported)

14144 Appendx
PO Box 382806 Phone: (617)495-4247
Cambridge, MA 02238 Fax: (617)495-8916
Publisher E-mail: appendx@gsd.harvard.edu

Professional journal covering architecture criticism. **Founded:** May 1996. **Freq:** Annual. **Trim Size:** 8 x 10. **Key Personnel:** Darell Fields, Contact; Milton Curry, Contact; Kevin Fuller, Contact. **Remarks:** Accepts advertising. **URL:** http://www.appendx.org.
Ad Rates: BW: $250 **Circ:** (Not Reported)
4C: $400

14145 Asian American Policy Review
Harvard University
79 John F. Kennedy St., T269
Cambridge, MA 02138
Publication E-mail: aapr@harvard.edu

Journal covering Asian Pacific American public policy. **Founded:** 1989. **Freq:** Annual. **ISSN:** 1062-1830. **Subscription Rates:** $15 individuals; $35 institutions. **Remarks:** Accepts advertising.
Ad Rates: BW: $200 **Circ:** Combined 700

14146 Asian Journal of Mathematics
International Press of Boston Inc.
PO Box 38-2872 Phone: (617)491-6560
Cambridge, MA 02238-2872 Fax: (617)491-6779
Publication E-mail: ajm@math.cuhk.edu.hk
Publisher E-mail: hugh@descartes.intlpress.com

Academic journal for mathematicians. **Founded:** 1997. **Freq:** Quarterly. **Print Method:** Offset. **Trim Size:** 7 x 9. **Key Personnel:** Shing-Tung Yau, Editor-in-Chief; Raymond H. Chan, Editor-in-Chief. **ISSN:** 1093-6106. **Subscription Rates:** $60 individuals; $180 institutions; $30 single issue. **Remarks:** Accepts advertising.
Ad Rates: GLR: $50 **Circ:** Combined 1,100
BW: $250
4C: $500

14147 Astrophysical Journal
University of Chicago Press
Harvard-Smithsonian Center for Astrophysics Phone: (617)495-4479
60 Garden St.
Cambridge, MA 02138
Scientific journal covering the field of astronomy and astronomical physics. **Founded:** 1895. **Freq:** 3/month. **Print Method:** Offset. Accepts mats. **Trim Size:** 8 1/2 x 11 1/2. **Cols./Page:** 1 and 2. **Col. Width:** 7 1/2 and 3 1/2 inches. **Col. Depth:** 9 inches. **Key Personnel:** Dr. A. Dalgarno, Editor; Dr. E.H. Avrett, Deputy Editor. **Subscription Rates:** $695 individuals; $155 members. **Remarks:** Advertising not accepted.
Circ: Paid ‡2,800
Non-paid ‡60

14148 Bad Attitude
PO Box 390110
Cambridge, MA 02139

Journal for women who are interested in lesbian lifestyles. Features erotic fiction. **Founded:** 1984. **Freq:** Quarterly. **Key Personnel:** Jasmine Sterling, Editor. **Subscription Rates:** $35 individuals six issues; $60 other countries overseas; $7 single issue. **Remarks:** Advertising accepted; rates available upon request.
Circ: Paid ‡5,000

14149 The Boston Book Review
The Boston Book Review LTD
30 Brattle St., 4th Fl. Phone: (617)497-0344
Cambridge, MA 02138 Fax: (617)497-0394
Publisher E-mail: bbr-info@bostonbookreview.org

Literary arts magazine featuring book reviews, interviews and essays, poetry and fiction. **Founded:** Nov. 1993. **Freq:** 10/year. **Print Method:** Offset. **Trim Size:** 11 x 14. **Cols./Page:** 4. **Col. Width:** 2 1/2 inches. **Col. Depth:** 13 inches. **Key Personnel:** Kiril Alexandrov, President; Theo C. Theoharis, Editor. **ISSN:** 1072-8317. **Subscription Rates:** $24 individuals; $50 out of country; $3.25 single issue. **Remarks:** Accepts advertising. **URL:** http://www.bostonbookreview.org.
Ad Rates: GLR: $4.97 **Circ:** Combined ‡10,000
BW: $590
4C: $840
PCI: $12.61

14150 Boston Review
30 Wadsworth Ave., No. E53-407 Phone: (617)253-3642
Fax: (617)252-1549
MIT
Cambridge, MA 02139-4307
Publication E-mail: bostenreview@mit.edu

Magazine focusing on culture and politics. **Subtitle:** A political and literary forum. **Founded:** 1975. **Freq:** Bimonthly. **Print Method:** Offset. **Trim Size:** 11 3/8 x 14 1/2. **Cols./Page:** 4. **Key Personnel:** Joshua Cohen, Editor, cohen@mit.edu; Matthew Howard, Managing Editor, howard@mit.edu. **Subscription Rates:** $15; $18 institutions. $5 single issue. **Remarks:** Accepts advertising. **URL:** http://www-polisci.mit.edu/bostonreview; http://www.polisci.mit.edu/bostonreview.
Ad Rates: GLR: $25 **Circ:** Paid ‡10,000
BW: $800 Non-paid ‡25,000

14151 Cable in the Classroom
CCI/Crosby Publishing
141 Portland St., Ste. 7100 Phone: (617)494-4997
Cambridge, MA 02139 Fax: (617)494-4898

Magazine directing teachers to quality educational television programs. **Founded:** 1991. **Freq:** Monthly. **Trim Size:** 8 x 10 3/4. **Key Personnel:** Stephen P. Crosby, Publisher; Al Race, Editor; Nina Bohn, Sales Dir.; Bill Whalen, Project Mgr. **ISSN:** 1054-5409. **Subscription Rates:** $20 individuals; $3 single issue. **Remarks:** Accepts advertising.
Ad Rates: BW: $5,590 **Circ:** Paid 112,600
4C: $6,995

14152 Cambridge Chronicle
Community Newspaper Company
360-366 Summer St. Phone: (617)868-7400
Somerville, MA 02144-3132 Fax: (617)629-3381

Community newspaper. **Founded:** 1846. **Freq:** Weekly (Thurs.). **Print Method:** Offset. **Cols./Page:** 6. **Col. Width:** 26 nonpareils. **Col. Depth:** 294 agate lines. **Key Personnel:** John Breneman, Editor; Steve Levinsky, Publisher; Chris Warren, Advertising Dir. **Subscription Rates:** $21 by mail. **Remarks:** Accepts advertising.
Ad Rates: GLR: $3.75 **Circ:** Paid 8,106
BW: $2,431.80 Non-paid 1,589
SAU: $19.30
PCI: $19.30

14153 Careers and the College Grad
Crimson & Brown Associates
201 Broadway Phone: (617)577-7790
Cambridge, MA 02139 Fax: (617)577-7799
Free: (800)CBA-FORU
Publisher E-mail: careers_magazines@cba.kaplan.com

Recruitment magazine covering career advice and company profiles. **Founded:** 1987. **Print Method:** Web offset. **Trim Size:** 8 1/8 x 10 7/8. **Key Personnel:** Liz Matson, Editor; Ellen Conte, Advertising Mgr. **Subscription Rates:** $17.45 individuals. **Remarks:** Accepts advertising. **URL:** http://www.cbacareers.com.
Ad Rates: BW: $5,100 **Circ:** Controlled 24,000
4C: $6,400

14154 Careers and the Engineer
Crimson & Brown Associates
201 Broadway Phone: (617)577-7790
Cambridge, MA 02139 Fax: (617)577-7799
Free: (800)CBA-FORU
Publisher E-mail: careers_magazines@cba.kaplan.com

National recruitment magazine aimed at top engineering, computing and information-system undergraduates. **Founded:** 1989. **Freq:** Semiannual. **Print Method:** Web offset. **Trim Size:** 8 1/8 x 10 7/8. **Key Personnel:** Kathleen Grimes, Publisher, kathleen_grimes@kaplan.com; Maureen Coler, Editor, maureen_coler@kaplan.com; Jeff Wallace, Advertising Rep., jeff_wallace@kaplan.com; Ellen Conte, Advertising Mgr., ellen_conte@cba.kaplan.com. **Subscription Rates:** $17.45 single issue. **Remarks:** Accepts advertising.
Ad Rates: BW: $5,500 **Circ:** Non-paid 30,000
4C: $6,700

14155 Careers and the MBA
Crimson & Brown Associates
201 Broadway Phone: (617)577-7790
Cambridge, MA 02139 Fax: (617)577-7799
Free: (800)CBA-FORU
Publisher E-mail: careers_magazines@cba.kaplan.com

Career resource magazine for MBA students featuring company profiles, feature articles, and career bios. **Founded:** 1968. **Freq:** Semiannual. **Trim Size:** 8 1/2 x 10 7/8. **Key Personnel:** Kathleen Grimes, Dir. of Publishing; Liz Matson, Asst. Editor. **Subscription Rates:** $12.95 single issue plus 4.50 s/h. **Remarks:** Accepts advertising.
Ad Rates: BW: $4,750 **Circ:** Paid 4,000
4C: $6,000 Non-paid 18,500

14156 Cell
Cell Press
1050 Massachusetts Ave. Phone: (617)661-7057
Cambridge, MA 02138 Fax: (617)661-7061
Publication E-mail: advertisingcell@cell.com
Publisher E-mail: blewin@cell.com

Journal on molecular and cell biology. **Founded:** 1974. **Freq:** Biweekly. **Print Method:** Sheetfed. **Trim Size:** 8 1/2 x 11. **Cols./Page:** 2. **Col. Width:** 40 nonpareils. **Col. Depth:** 120 agate lines. **Key Personnel:** Benjamin Lewin, Editor; Elizabeth Wardell, Advertising Mgr., ewardell@cell.com. **ISSN:** 0092-8674. **Subscription Rates:** $115 individuals U.S.; $230 other countries; $200 Canada; $595 institutions; $720 institutions, other countries; $680 institutions, Canada. **Remarks:** Accepts advertising. **Available Online. URL:** http://www.cell.com.
Ad Rates: BW: $2,200 **Circ:** Combined ‡17,181
4C: $3,300

14157 Computer Music Journal
The MIT Press
5 Cambridge Center Phone: (617)253-5646
Cambridge, MA 02142 Fax: (617)258-6779
Free: (800)356-0343
Publisher E-mail: webmistress@mitpress.mit.edu

Journal for musicians, composers, scientists, engineers, and computer enthusiasts interested in contemporary and electronic music and computer generated sound. **Founded:** 1976. **Freq:** Quarterly. **Print Method:** Offset. **Trim Size:** 8 1/2 x 11. **Cols./Page:** 2. **Col. Width:** 36 nonpareils. **Col. Depth:** 126 agate lines. **Key Personnel:** Stephen Pope, Editor; Rebecca McLeod, Advertising Mgr.; Curtis Roads, Assoc. Editor. **ISSN:** 0148-9267. **Remarks:** Accepts advertising.
Ad Rates: GLR: $1.33 **Circ:** ‡3,700
BW: $425
4C: $1,000

14158 Crank!
Broken Mirrors Press
Box 473
Cambridge, MA 02238

Magazine covering science fiction and fantasy literature. **Key Personnel:** Bryan Cholfin, Editor. **Subscription Rates:** $3.50 individuals.

14159 Critical Review
Critical Review Foundation, Inc.
PO Box 380015
Cambridge, MA 02238
Publication E-mail: info@criticalreview.com

Uses political science, history, psychology, sociology, economics, and anthropology to explore the effects of different social systems on human well-being. **Subtitle:** An Interdisciplinary Journal of Politics and Society. **Founded:** 1987. **Freq:** Quarterly. **Print Method:** Offset. **Trim Size:** 5 1/2 x 8 1/2. **Cols./Page:** 1. **Key Personnel:** Dawn Herron, Business Mgr. **ISSN:** 0891-3811. **Subscription Rates:** $29; $59 libraries; $10 single issue; $15 students.
Ad Rates: BW: $75 **Circ:** Paid ‡1,500
Non-paid ‡500

14160 Cultural Survival Quarterly
Cultural Survival, Inc.
96 Mt. Auburn St. Phone: (617)441-4500
Cambridge, MA 02138 Fax: (617)441-5417
Publisher E-mail: csinc@cs.org

Magazine for general public and policy makers intended to stimulate action for ethnic minorities and indigenous peoples. **Subtitle:** World Report on The Rights of Indigenous People and Ethnic Minorities. **Founded:** 1982. **Freq:** Quarterly. **Print Method:** Web. **Trim Size:** 8 3/8 x 10 7/8. **Cols./Page:** 3. **Col. Width:** 13 1/2 picas. **Key Personnel:** Amy Stoll, Managing Editor, phone (617)441-5413. **ISSN:** 0740-3291. **Subscription Rates:** $45; $5 single issue; $25 students and seniors.
Ad Rates: BW: $600 **Circ:** Paid 10,000
4C: $800

14161 DAEDALUS
American Academy of Arts & Sciences
136 Irving St. Phone: (617)491-2600
Cambridge, MA 02138 Fax: (617)576-5088
Publication E-mail: daedalus@amacad.org

Interdisciplinary journal. **Subtitle:** Journal of the American Academy of Arts and Sciences. **Founded:** 1958. **Freq:** Quarterly. **Print Method:** Offset. **Trim Size:** 6 x 9. **Cols./Page:** 1. **Col. Width:** 52 nonpareils. **Col. Depth:** 103 agate lines. **Key Personnel:** Stephen R. Graubard, Editor; Phyllis S. Bendell, Managing Editor. **ISSN:** 0011-5266. **Subscription Rates:** $33 individuals; $10.95 single issue; $49.50 institutions. **Remarks:** Advertising not accepted.
Circ: ‡20,000

14162 Design Quarterly
The MIT Press
5 Cambridge Center Phone: (617)253-5646
Cambridge, MA 02142 Fax: (617)258-6779
Free: (800)356-0343
Publisher E-mail: webmistress@mitpress.mit.edu

Journal covering architecture, design, and contemporary graphics. **Founded:** 1946. **Freq:** Quarterly. **Print Method:** Offset. **Trim Size:** 8 1/2 x 11. **Cols./Page:** 1. **Col. Width:** 35 1/2 picas. **Col. Depth:** 49 picas. **Key Personnel:** Martin Filler, Editor; Susan Packard, Asst. Editor. **ISSN:** 0011-9415. **Subscription Rates:** $28 individuals; $60 Institutions. **Remarks:** Advertising not accepted.
Circ: Paid ‡3,400
Non-paid ‡20

14163 The Drama Review
The MIT Press
5 Cambridge Center Phone: (617)253-5646
Cambridge, MA 02142 Fax: (617)258-6779
Free: (800)356-0343
Publisher E-mail: webmistress@mitpress.mit.edu

Journal on the performing arts covering the social, economic, and political contexts of performances with an emphasis on the experimental, the avant-garde, the intercultural, and the interdisciplinary. **Founded:** 1955. **Freq:** Quarterly. **Print Method:** Offset. **Trim Size:** 7 x 10. **Cols./Page:** 1. **Col. Width:** 60 nonpareils. **Col. Depth:** 112 agate lines. **Key Personnel:** Richard Schechner, Editor; Laura Ayr, Advertising Mgr. **ISSN:** 0012-5962.
Circ: 4,800

14164 Econometrica
The Econometric Society
Department of Economics Phone: (617)496-5895
Harvard University
Cambridge, MA 02138
Journal concerning economic theory in relation to statistics and mathematics. **Founded:** 1933. **Freq:** Bimonthly. **Key Personnel:** Drew Fudenberg, Editor; Dorothy Hodges, Managing Editor; Julie Gordon, Executive Dir. **Subscription Rates:** $68 members including subscriptions; $20 students; $169 institutions.
Ad Rates: BW: $350 **Circ:** ‡7,000

14165 15 Minutes
Harvard Crimson, Inc.
14 Plympton St. Phone: (617)576-6565
Cambridge, MA 02138 Fax: (617)576-6363
Free: (888)CRI-MSON
Publisher E-mail: crimson@thecrimson.com

Arts and entertainment tabloid. **Founded:** 1979. **Freq:** Weekly (Thurs.). **Print Method:** Offset. **Cols./Page:** 4. **Col. Width:** 27 nonpareils. **Col. Depth:** 168 agate lines. **Key Personnel:** Sameer Chishin, Business Mgr. **Remarks:** Accepts advertising.
Ad Rates: PCI: $7 **Circ:** Non-paid ‡10,000

14166 Growing Without Schooling
Holt Associates, Inc.
2380 Massachusetts Ave., Ste. 104 Phone: (617)864-3100
Cambridge, MA 02140 Fax: (617)864-9235
Publisher E-mail: holtgws@aol.com

Magazine about teaching and learning outside of school. **Founded:** Aug. 1977. **Freq:** Bimonthly. **Print Method:** Laser printing, offset final print. **Trim Size:** 8 1/2 x 11. **Cols./Page:** 3. **Col. Width:** 2.5 inches. **Col. Depth:** 10 inches. **Key Personnel:** Susannah Sheffer, Editor; Patrick Farenga, Publisher. **ISSN:** 0745-5305. **Subscription Rates:** $25 individuals; $6 single issue. **Remarks:** Accepts advertising. **URL:** http://www.holtgws.com. **Alt. Formats:** Microfiche.
Ad Rates: BW: $700 **Circ:** Paid 5,500
PCI: $45 15,000

14167 Harvard Advocate
21 South St. Phone: (617)495-0737
Cambridge, MA 02138
Publication E-mail: advocate@hcs.harvard.edu

Literary journal. **Founded:** 1866. **Freq:** Quarterly (during the academic year). **Print Method:** Letterpress and offset. **Cols./Page:** 2 and 3. **Col. Width:** 26 and 41 nonpareils. **Col. Depth:** 133 agate lines. **Key Personnel:** Etienne Benson, President, ebenson@fas.harvard.edu; Franklin Leonard, Publisher, leonard@fas.harvard.edu; Saadi Soudavar, President, soudavar@fas.harvard.edu. **ISSN:** 0017-8004. **Subscription Rates:** $25 individuals; $5 single issue unmailed; $30 institutions; $35 other countries. **Remarks:** Accepts advertising. **Available Online. URL:** http://www.hcs.harvard.edu/~advocate. **Alt. Formats:** Microform.
Ad Rates: BW: $250 **Circ:** Paid ‡300
Non-paid ‡3,000

14168 Harvard Crimson
Harvard Crimson, Inc.
14 Plympton St. Phone: (617)576-6565
Cambridge, MA 02138 Fax: (617)576-6363
Free: (888)CRI-MSON
Publication E-mail: news@thecrimson.com
Publisher E-mail: crimson@thecrimson.com

Collegiate newspaper. **Founded:** 1873. **Freq:** Daily (morn.). **Print Method:** Letterpress and offset. **Cols./Page:** 6. **Col. Width:** 27 nonpareils. **Col. Depth:** 294 agate lines. **Key Personnel:** Matthew Granade, President, granade@thecrimson.com. **Subscription Rates:** $69 individuals. **Remarks:** Accepts advertising. **URL:** http://www.thecrimson.com.
Ad Rates: SAU: $11 **Circ:** ‡10,000
PCI: $12

14169 Harvard Design Magazine
Graduate School of Design (GSD)
48 Quincy St. Phone: (617)495-7814
Cambridge, MA 02138 Fax: (617)496-3391
Publication E-mail: hdm@gsd.harvard.edu

Magazine covering school events and news related to the teaching and study of architecture, landscape architecture, and urban planning and design. Features articles on the work of students, faculty, and alumni, and announces results of design competitions, awards and programs. **Founded:** 1971. **Freq:** 3x/year. **Trim Size:** 10 1/2 x 13 1/2. **Key Personnel:** William Saunders, Editor; Nancy Levinson, Editor; Jeffrey Gonyeau, Business and Circulation Coord. **ISSN:** 1093-4421. **Subscription Rates:** Free to students and alumni; $25 others; $35 other countries. **Formerly:** GSD News.
Ad Rates: BW: $3,000 **Circ:** 15,000

14170 Harvard Educational Review
Harvard University
6 Appian Way Phone: (617)495-3432
Gutman Library, Ste. 349 Fax: (617)496-3584
Cambridge, MA 02138
Free: (800)513-0763
Publication E-mail: hepg@hugse1.harvard.edu

Scholarly journal in education; publishes articles and book reviews. **Founded:** Feb. 1931. **Freq:** Quarterly. **Print Method:** Offset. **Trim Size:** 6 3/4 x 10. **Cols./Page:** 1. **Col. Width:** 5 inches. **Col. Depth:** 7 1/2 inches. **Key Personnel:** Karen E. Maloney, General Mgr.; Joan Gorman, Advertising Mgr. **ISSN:** 0017-8055. **Subscription Rates:** $39 individuals; $58 2 years individual; $79 institutions; $118 two years 2 years institutional. **Remarks:** Accepts advertising.
Ad Rates: BW: $475 **Circ:** ‡10,000

14171 The Harvard Independent
Harvard University
79 John F. Kennedy Phone: (617)495-3682
Cambridge, MA 02138-5808 Fax: (617)496-3692

Collegiate newspaper. **Founded:** 1969. **Freq:** Weekly (Thurs.). **Print Method:** Offset. **Cols./Page:** 4. **Col. Width:** 25 nonpareils. **Col. Depth:** 196 agate lines. **Key Personnel:** Ellie Grossman, President; Jason Petruis, Editor-in-Chief. **Subscription Rates:** Free; $15 individuals. **Remarks:** Accepts advertising.
Ad Rates: BW: $544 **Circ:** Paid ‡300
PCI: $10 Free ‡6,000

14172 Harvard International Review
PO Box 401 Phone: (617)495-9607
Cambridge, MA 02238-0401 Fax: (617)496-4472

Publication focusing on current international events. **Founded:** 1979. **Freq:** Quarterly. **Key Personnel:** Geordie Dukas, Editor-in-Chief, dukas@fas.harvard.edu. **ISSN:** 0739-1854. **Subscription Rates:** $16; $26 other countries; $26 Industry; $30 two years. $4.95 single issue. **Remarks:** Accepts advertising. **Alt. Formats:** CD-ROM.
Circ: (Not Reported)

14173 Harvard Journal of Asiatic Studies
Harvard-Yenching Institute
2 Divinity Ave. Phone: (617)495-2758
Cambridge, MA 02138 Fax: (617)495-7798

Scholarly journal covering languages, literature, cultures, and the history of Eastern and Central Asia. **Founded:** 1936. **Freq:** Semiannual. **Print Method:** Photo offset. **Trim Size:** 9 1/8 x 6 1/8. **Key Personnel:** Howard S. Hibbett, Editor; Joanna Handlin Smith, Exec. Editor. **ISSN:** 0073-0548. **Subscription Rates:** $30 individuals; $45 institutions prepaid; $15 single issue. **Remarks:** Advertising not accepted.
Circ: Paid 1,100

14174 Harvard Journal of Legislation
William S. Hein & Co., Inc.
Harvard University Phone: (617)495-4400
Harvard University Law School Fax: (617)496-2148
Publications Center
Hastings Hall
Cambridge, MA 02138
Publication E-mail: hlsjol@law.harvard.edu
Publisher E-mail: wsheinco@class.org

Scholarly journal covering legislation. **Founded:** 1964. **Freq:** Semiannual. **ISSN:** 0017-808X. **Subscription Rates:** $28 individuals; $34 out of country; $14 single issue; $17 single issue out of country. **Remarks:** Advertising not accepted.
Circ: 800

14175 Harvard Law Review
1511 Massachusetts Ave. Phone: (617)495-4650
Cambridge, MA 02138 Fax: (617)495-2748

Journal publishing legal scholarship. **Founded:** 1887. **Freq:** 8/year (monthly, Nov.-June). **Print Method:** Offset. **Cols./Page:** 1. **Col. Width:** 78 nonpareils. **Col. Depth:** 136 agate lines. **Key Personnel:** Susan Walker, Business Mgr.; Collen Verner, Circulation Mgr. **ISSN:** 0017-811X. **Subscription Rates:** $45 individuals annual; $10 single issue; $51 other countries; $115 Air mail. **Remarks:** Accepts advertising. **Online:** LEXIS-NEXIS; WESTLAW.
Ad Rates: BW: $350 **Circ:** ‡5,275

14176 Harvard Magazine
7 Ware St. Phone: (617)495-5746
Cambridge, MA 02138 Fax: (617)495-0324
Free: (800)648-4499

Alumni magazine. **Founded:** 1898. **Freq:** Bimonthly. **Print Method:** Offset. **Trim Size:** 8 3/8 x 10 7/8. **Cols./Page:** 3. **Col. Width:** 26 nonpareils. **Col. Depth:** 135 agate lines. **Key Personnel:** John S. Rosenberg, Editor, phone (617)496-6707, john_ rosenberg@harvard.edu; Ed Antos, Advertising Dir., phone (617)496-6658, ed_ antos@harvard.edu; Bob Fitta, Advertising Account Mgr., phone (617)496-6631, bob_ fitta@harvard.edu; Eriko Ogawa, Dir. of Marketing, phone (617)496-6687, eriko_ ogawa@harvard.edu; Karline Kosdrosky, NE Regional Advertising Mgr., phone (617)496-4032, karline_ kosdrosky@harvard.edu; Felecia Carter, Dir. of Circulation, phone (617)496-6694, felecia_ carter@harvard.edu. **ISSN:** 0095-2427. **Subscription Rates:** $30 individuals; $4.95 single issue. **Remarks:** Accepts advertising. **URL:** www.harvard_ magazine.com.
Ad Rates: BW: $9,130 **Circ:** Paid ‡23,906
4C: $13,335 Non-paid ‡188,027
PCI: $300

14177 Harvard Review
Harvard College Library
Poetry Room
Cambridge, MA 02138

Literary journal covering fiction, nonfiction, book reviews, and poetry. **Founded:** May 1992. **Freq:** Semiannual. **Print Method:** Offset. **Trim Size:** 6 x 9. **Cols./Page:** 1. **Col. Width:** 5 inches. **Col. Depth:** 7 inches. **Key Personnel:** Stratis Haviaras, Editor. **ISSN:** 1077-2901. **Subscription Rates:** $16 individuals; $24 out of country; $10 single issue. **Remarks:** Accepts advertising.
Ad Rates: BW: $330 **Circ:** Controlled 2,300

14178 Harvard Theological Review
Harvard Divinity School
45 Francis Ave. Phone: (617)495-5786
Cambridge, MA 02138-1994 Fax: (617)495-9489

Scholarly magazine covering theology, ethics, and history. **Founded:** 1908. **Freq:** Quarterly. **Trim Size:** 6 x 9. **Cols./Page:** 1. **Key Personnel:** Helmut Koester, Editor; Marianne Bonz, Managing Editor, mbonz@div.harvard.edu. **ISSN:** 0017-8160. **Subscription Rates:** $30 individuals; $50 institutions. **Remarks:** Accepts advertising. **Alt. Formats:** Microform; Mailing labels.
Ad Rates: BW: $200 **Circ:** 6,000

14179 Harvard University Gazette
Harvard University
Holyoke Center 1060 Phone: (617)495-1585
1350 Massachusetts Ave. Fax: (617)495-0754
Cambridge, MA 02138
Community newspaper. **Freq:** Weekly. **Key Personnel:** John Lenger, Editor. **Subscription Rates:** $25 individuals; $32 out of country. **Remarks:** Advertising not accepted. **URL:** http://www.news-harvard.edu.
Circ: (Not Reported)

14180 Immunity
Cell Press
1050 Massachusetts Ave. Phone: (617)661-7057
Cambridge, MA 02138 Fax: (617)661-7061
Publication E-mail: blewin@cell.com; immunity@cell.com
Publisher E-mail: blewin@cell.com

Journal that encompasses all systems that contribute to, or interact with, the immune response of the organism. **Founded:** 1994. **Freq:** Monthly. **Print Method:** Sheetfed. **Trim Size:** 8 1/2 x 11. **Subscription Rates:** $105 individuals; $155 individuals out of country; $495 institutions; $550 institutions out of country. **Remarks:** Accepts advertising. **URL:** http://www.immunity.com.
Ad Rates: BW: $400 **Circ:** 3,000
4C: $1,300

14181 Immunodeficiency Reviews
Harwood Academic Publishers GmbH
F. S. Rosen
Harvard Medical School
Dept. of Pediatrics
Children's Hospital
Cambridge, MA 02138

Medical journal. **Freq:** Quarterly. **Key Personnel:** Fred S. Rosen, Editor; Maxime Seligmann, Advertising Mgr. **ISSN:** 0893-5300.

14182 The International Journal of Robotics Research
The MIT Press
5 Cambridge Center Phone: (617)253-5646
Cambridge, MA 02142 Fax: (617)258-6779
Free: (800)356-0343
Publisher E-mail: webmistress@mitpress.mit.edu

Journal for researchers, scientists, and students in robotics, artificial intelligence, applied mathematics, computer science, electrical engineering, and related fields. **Founded:** 1982. **Freq:** Bimonthly. **Print Method:** Offset. **Trim Size:** 8 1/2 x 11. **Cols./Page:** 2. **Col. Width:** 36 nonpareils. **Col. Depth:** 126 agate lines. **Key Personnel:** M. Brady, Editor; Rebecca McLeod, Advertising Mgr. **ISSN:** 0278-3649. **Subscription Rates:** $65 individuals; $135 institutions; $50 students and retired; persons; $58 other countries; $15 single issue. **Remarks:** Accepts advertising.
Ad Rates: GLR: $1.33 **Circ:** (Not Reported)
BW: $400

14183 International Organization
The MIT Press
5 Cambridge Center Phone: (617)253-5646
Cambridge, MA 02142 Fax: (617)258-6779
Free: (800)356-0343
Publisher E-mail: webmistress@mitpress.mit.edu

Journal on international politics and economics including political economy, foreign policy, history, and comparative politics. **Founded:** 1947. **Freq:** Quarterly. **Print Method:** Offset. **Trim Size:** 6 x 9 1/2. **Cols./Page:** 1. **Col. Width:** 54 nonpareils. **Col. Depth:** 105 agate lines. **Key Personnel:** Steven D. Krasner, Editor; Cathy Maretz, Advertising Mgr. **ISSN:** 0020-8183. **Subscription Rates:** $22.50 individuals; $47 institutions; $13 single issue. **Remarks:** Accepts advertising.
Ad Rates: BW: $220 **Circ:** ‡2,800

14184 International Security
The MIT Press
BCSIA (Belfer Center for Phone: (617)495-1914
Science & International Affairs) Fax: (617)496-4403
79 JFK St.
Cambridge, MA 02138
Publication E-mail: is@harvard.edu
Publisher E-mail: webmistress@mitpress.mit.edu

Scholarly journal of essays on international affairs and isssues of defense, security, arms control, and use of force, from all political viewpoints. **Founded:** 1976. **Freq:** Quarterly. **Trim Size:** 6 3/4 x 10. **Cols./Page:** 1. **Col. Width:** 74 nonpareils. **Col. Depth:** 133 agate lines. **Key Personnel:** Steven E. Miller, Editor-in-Chief, phone (617)495-1411, steven_ miller@harvard.edu; Owen Cote, Editor, phone (617)258-7428, fax (617)258-5028, owencote@mit.edu; Rebecca McLeod, Advertising Mgr., phone (617)253-2866, fax (617)258-5028, mcleod@mit.edu; Meara Keegan Zaheer, Editorial Assist., phone (617)495-1914, meara_ zaheer@harvard.edu; Michael E. Brown, Editor, phone (202)687-5727, fax (202)687-5175, michael_ brown@harvard.edu; Sean M. Lynn-Jones, Editor, phone (617)495-1463, sean_ lynn-jones@harvard.edu; Diane McCree, Deputy Editor, phone (617)495-1403, diane_ mccree@havard.edu. **ISSN:** 0162-2889. **Subscription Rates:** $30 U.S. and Canada; $20 students and retirees; $44 other countries; $75 institutions Institutions; $10 single issue; $20 back issues. **Remarks:** Accepts advertising.
Ad Rates: BW: $400 **Circ:** ‡4,600

14185 Journal of the American Association of Variable Star Observers
American Association of Variable Star Observers
25 Birch St. Phone: (617)354-0484
Cambridge, MA 02138 Fax: (617)354-0665
Publication E-mail: journal@aavso.org
Publisher E-mail: aavso@aavso.org

Scientific journal covering variable star astronomy and related topics and association news. **Founded:** 1962. **Freq:** Semiannual. **Print Method:** Web offset. **Trim Size:** 5 x 8. **ISSN:** 0271-9053. **Subscription Rates:** $25 individuals; $40 institutions; $10 single issue. **Remarks:** Advertising not accepted.
Circ: (Not Reported)

14186 Journal of Differential Geometry
International Press of Boston Inc.
PO Box 38-2872 Phone: (617)491-6560
Cambridge, MA 02238-2872 Fax: (617)491-6779
Publication E-mail: hugh@intlpress.com
Publisher E-mail: hugh@descartes.intlpress.com

Academic journal devoted to research in differential geometry and related subjects. **Founded:** 1995. **Freq:** 9/year. **Key Personnel:** C.C. Hsiung, Editor-in-Chief; S.T. Yau, Editor-in-Chief. **ISSN:** 0022-040X. **Subscription Rates:** $100 individuals; $409 institutions; $11 single issue individuals; $45 single issue institutions. **Remarks:** Accepts advertising. **URL:** http://www.intlpress.com.
Ad Rates: GLR: $50 **Circ:** Combined 1,250
BW: $250
4C: $500

14187 Journal of Functional and Logic Programming
The MIT Press
5 Cambridge Center Phone: (617)253-5646
Cambridge, MA 02142 Fax: (617)258-6779
Free: (800)356-0343
Publisher E-mail: webmistress@mitpress.mit.edu

Scholarly journal covering functional and logic programming. **ISSN:** 1080-5230. **Subscription Rates:** $30 individuals; $125 institutions. **URL:** http://www.cs.tu-berlin.de/journal/jflp.

14188 The Journal of Interdisciplinary History
The MIT Press
5 Cambridge Center Phone: (617)253-5646
Cambridge, MA 02142 Fax: (617)258-6779
Free: (800)356-0343
Publisher E-mail: webmistress@mitpress.mit.edu

Journal includes substantive articles, research notes, review essays, and book reviews relating historical research and work in economics and demographics. **Founded:** 1969. **Freq:** Quarterly. **Print Method:** Offset. **Trim Size:** 5 7/8 x 9. **Cols./Page:** 1. **Col. Width:** 54 nonpareils. **Col. Depth:** 105 agate lines. **Key Personnel:** R. Rotberg, Editor; T. Rabb, Advertising Mgr.; Laura Ayr, Advertising Mgr. **Subscription Rates:** $28 individuals; $65 institutions; $24 students and senior; citizens.; $15 single issue. **Remarks:** Accepts advertising.
Ad Rates: BW: $165 **Circ:** (Not Reported)

14189 Journal of Sedimentary Research
Rutgers University
MIT Phone: (918)493-3361
Deapt. of Earth, Planetary & Atmospheric Sciences
77 Massachusetts Ave.
Cambridge, MA 02139
Scientific journal of sedimentary geology. **Founded:** 1931. **Freq:** Bimonthly. **Print Method:** Offset. **Trim Size:** 8 1/2 x 11. **Cols./Page:** 2. **Col. Width:** 3 1/2 inches. **Col. Depth:** 9 inches. **Key Personnel:** Gail M. Ashley, Editor, phone (617)253-3397, fax (617)253-6208; Christine V. Alfano, Editorial Assistant. **ISSN:** 0022-4472. **Subscription Rates:** $70 individuals. **Remarks:** Accepts advertising. **Formerly:** Journal of Sedimentary Petrology.
Ad Rates: BW: $500 **Circ:** 6,000
4C: $1,700

14190 Linguistic Inquiry
The MIT Press
5 Cambridge Center Phone: (617)253-5646
Cambridge, MA 02142 Fax: (617)258-6779
Free: (800)356-0343
Publisher E-mail: webmistress@mitpress.mit.edu

Journal on advanced linguistics research and theory, including phonology, syntax, semantics, and morphology. **Founded:** 1970. **Freq:** Quarterly. **Print Method:** Offset. **Trim Size:** 7 x 9. **Cols./Page:** 1. **Col. Width:** 60 nonpareils. **Col. Depth:** 98 agate lines. **Key Personnel:** S. Jay Keyser, Editor; Laura Ayr, Advertising Mgr. **ISSN:** 0024-3892. **Subscription Rates:** $37 U.S. and Canada; $75 institutions; $25 students and retired; persons; $43 other countries; $15 single issue. **Remarks:** Accepts advertising.
Ad Rates: BW: $250 **Circ:** (Not Reported)

14191 Methods and Applications of Analysis
International Press of Boston Inc.
PO Box 38-2872 Phone: (617)491-6560
Cambridge, MA 02238-2872 Fax: (617)491-6779
Publisher E-mail: hugh@descartes.intlpress.com

Academic journal covering research in applied mathematics with applications to the sciences. **Founded:** 1992. **Freq:** Quarterly. **Key Personnel:** Robert M. Miura, Editor-in-Chief; Roderick Wong, Editor-in-Chief. **ISSN:** 1073-2772. **Subscription Rates:** $100 individuals; $200 institutions; $75 single issue. **Remarks:** Accepts advertising.
Ad Rates: GLR: $50 **Circ:** Combined 100
BW: $250
4C: $500

14192 Neural Computation
The MIT Press
5 Cambridge Center Phone: (617)253-5646
Cambridge, MA 02142 Fax: (617)258-6779
Free: (800)356-0343
Publisher E-mail: webmistress@mitpress.mit.edu

Disseminating research results in the neural computation field. **Founded:** 1989. **Freq:** Bimonthly. **Print Method:** Offset. **Trim Size:** 6 x 9. **Cols./Page:** 1. **Col. Width:** 26 picas. **Col. Depth:** 43 picas. **Key Personnel:** Terrence J. Sejnowski, Editor; Rosemary Miller, Managing Editor. **ISSN:** 0899-7667. **Subscription Rates:** $65; $150 Industry; $40 students and senior citizens; $28 single issue. **Remarks:** Accepts advertising.
Ad Rates: GLR: $.33 **Circ:** Paid ‡1,309
BW: $450 Non-paid ‡102

14193 Neuron
Cell Press
1050 Massachusetts Ave. Phone: (617)661-7057
Cambridge, MA 02138 Fax: (617)661-7061
Publication E-mail: neuron@cell.com
Publisher E-mail: blewin@cell.com

Journal encompassing all areas of experimental neuroscience. **Founded:** 1988. **Freq:** Monthly. **Print Method:** Web Press. **Trim Size:** 8 1/2 x 11. **Key Personnel:** Dr. Gregory Gasic, Editor, fax (617)661-7061, ggasic@cell.com. **Subscription Rates:** $110 individuals U.S.; $170 out of country; $475 institutions; $535 institutions, other countries. **URL:** http://www.neuron.org.
Ad Rates: BW: $600 **Circ:** Combined ‡4,146
4C: $1,500

14194 New England Folk Almanac
Folk Arts Network, Inc.
Box 380867 Phone: (617)522-7522
Cambridge, MA 02238-0867
Publication E-mail: nefolk@aol.com
Publisher E-mail: fan@world.std.com

Newspaper featuring folk arts topics, CD reviews and a comprehensive calendar for the New England area. **Freq:** Bimonthly. **Print Method:** Web press. **Cols./Page:** 4. **Col. Width:** 2 3/8 inches. **Key Personnel:** Marcia Young Palmater, Editor; Kathleen Frey, Graphic Arts Designer. **Subscription Rates:** $18 individuals; $25 Canada and Mexico; $35 elsewhere. **Remarks:** Advertising accepted; rates available upon request.
Circ: (Not Reported)

14195 Nieman Reports
Nieman Foundation
1 Francis Ave. Phone: (617)495-2237
Cambridge, MA 02138 Fax: (617)495-8976
Publication E-mail: nreditor@harvard.edu

Trade magazine covering journalism. **Founded:** 1947. **Freq:** Quarterly. **Key Personnel:** Robert H. Phelps, Editor. **Subscription Rates:** $20 individuals; $30 out of country; $5 single issue. **Remarks:** Advertising not accepted. **URL:** http://www.nieman.harvard.edu/nieman.html.
Circ: Combined 5,664

14196 Nucleus
Union of Concerned Scientists
2 Brattle Sq. Phone: (617)547-5552
PO Box 9105 Fax: (617)864-9405
Cambridge, MA 02238-9105
Publisher E-mail: ucs@ucsusa.org

Magazine covering UCS issues (energy policy, global resources, arms control, nuclear power safety, transportation policy, and sustainable agriculture). **Subtitle:** The Quarterly Magazine of the Union of Concerned Scientists. **Founded:** 1976. **Freq:** Quarterly. **Trim Size:** 8 1/2 x 11. **Key Personnel:** Stuart Kiang, Editor. **ISSN:** 0888-5729. **Subscription Rates:** $20 individuals. **Remarks:** Advertising not accepted.
Circ: (Not Reported)

14197 October
The MIT Press
5 Cambridge Center Phone: (617)253-5646
Cambridge, MA 02142 Fax: (617)258-6779
Free: (800)356-0343
Publisher E-mail: webmistress@mitpress.mit.edu

Journal on contemporary art. **Founded:** 1976. **Freq:** Quarterly. **Print Method:** Offset. **Trim Size:** 7 x 9. **Cols./Page:** 1. **Col. Width:** 72 nonpareils. **Col. Depth:** 98 agate lines. **Key Personnel:** Douglas Crimp, Editor; R. Krauss, Advertising Mgr.; A. Michelson, Editor; Laura Ayr, Advertising Mgr. **ISSN:** 0162-2870. **Remarks:** Color advertising not accepted.
Ad Rates: BW: $220 **Circ:** ‡3,300

14198 Perspective
PO Box 2439 Phone: (617)495-4290
Cambridge, MA 02238 Fax: (617)495-4688
Publisher E-mail: perspy@hcs.harvard.edu

Political magazine written and published by students. **Subtitle:** Harvard-Radcliffe's Liberal Monthly. **Founded:** 1985. **Freq:** Monthly. **Trim Size:** 10 x 16. **Cols./Page:** 4. **Col. Width:** 2 1/4 inches. **Col. Depth:** 16 inches. **Key Personnel:** Rita Lin, President; Dan Hopkins, Managing Editor; Ethan Ard, Managing Editor. **Subscription Rates:** $10; $15 institutions; $25 other countries; $1 single issue. **Remarks:** Accepts advertising.
Ad Rates: BW: $352 **Circ:** Controlled 10,000
4C: $300
PCI: $5.50

14199 Presence
The MIT Press
5 Cambridge Center Phone: (617)253-5646
Cambridge, MA 02142 Fax: (617)258-6779
Free: (800)356-0343
Publisher E-mail: webmistress@mitpress.mit.edu

Scholarly journal on teleopertors and virtual environments. **Subtitle:** Teleoperators and Virtual Environments. **Founded:** 1992. **Freq:** Quarterly. **Trim Size:** 8 1/2 x 11. **Key Personnel:** Thomas B. Sheridan, Editor; Thomas A. Furness III, Editor; Nathaniel I. Durlach, Managing Editor; Doug Allen, Managing Editor. **ISSN:** 1054-7460. **Subscription Rates:** $50; $40 students and seniors; $125 Industry.

14200 Pressed Streets
7 Speridakis Terrace Phone: (617)497-7724
Cambridge, MA 02139
Street/homeless journal focusing on the arts. **Founded:** Nov. 1995. **Freq:** Monthly. **Print Method:** Web offset. **Trim Size:** 8 1/2 x 11. **Cols./Page:** 2. **Col. Width:** 3 1/2 inches. **Col. Depth:** 10 3/4 inches. **Key Personnel:** Marc D. Goldfinger, Editor; Leland James, Layout; Deb Byrne, Ad Designer. **Subscription Rates:** $40 individuals; $4 single issue, Canada by mail; $3 single issue, Canada at news-stands. **Remarks:** Advertising accepted; rates available upon request.
Circ: Paid 2,000

14201 Psyche
Cambridge Entomological Club
26 Oxford St. Phone: (617)496-1034
Cambridge, MA 02138-2902 Fax: (617)495-1224
Publication E-mail: psyche@oeb.harvard.edu

Entomology academic journal. **Subtitle:** Journal of Entomology. **Founded:** 1874. **Freq:** Quarterly. **Print Method:** Offset. **Trim Size:** 6 x 9. **Cols./Page:** 1. **Col. Width:** 48 nonpareils. **Col. Depth:** 84 agate lines. **Key Personnel:** Kathleen Horton, Managing Editor. **ISSN:** 0033-2615. **Subscription Rates:** $35 individuals; $45 institutions. **Remarks:** Advertising not accepted.
Circ: 700

14202 The Quarterly Journal of Economics
The MIT Press
Littauer Center 227 Phone: (617)495-2142
Cambridge, MA 02138 Fax: (617)495-7730
Publisher E-mail: webmistress@mitpress.mit.edu

Journal of analytical articles in economic theory. **Founded:** 1886. **Freq:** Quarterly. **Print Method:** Offset. **Trim Size:** 6 x 9. **Cols./Page:** 1. **Key Personnel:** Olivier Blanchard, Editor; Lawrence F. Katz, Editor; Andrei Shleifer, Editor; Rebecca McLeod, Advertising Mgr., phone (617)253-2866. **ISSN:** 0033-5533. **Subscription Rates:** $40 individuals; $130 institutions; $24 student/retired. **Remarks:** Color advertising not accepted.
Ad Rates: BW: $400 **Circ:** ‡4,900

14203 Radcliffe Quarterly
Radcliffe College Office of Communications
10 Garden St. Phone: (617)495-8608
Cambridge, MA 02138 Fax: (617)495-8422

Alumni magazine. **Founded:** 1916. **Freq:** Quarterly. **Print Method:** Offset. **Trim Size:** 8 1/2 x 10 7/8. **Cols./Page:** 4. **Col. Width:** 34 nonpareils. **Col. Depth:** 140 agate lines. **Key Personnel:** Diane Sherlock, Editor; Pat Harrison, Associate Editor; Ruth Prince, Production Editor. **ISSN:** 0033-7528. **Remarks:** Accepts advertising.
Circ: Free ‡33,500

14204 Radical Teacher
PO Box 383316 Phone: (617)492-3468
Cambridge, MA 02238-3316
Periodical containing articles, photos, interviews, and book reviews on radical feminist theory and practice in education. **Founded:** 1975. **Freq:** 3/year. **Key Personnel:** Susan O'Malley, Editor; Louis Kampf, Circulation Mgr. **ISSN:** 0191-4847. **Subscription Rates:** $10.
Circ: 3,000

14205 Review of Economics and Statistics
The MIT Press
Harvard University Phone: (617)495-2111
111 Littauer Ctr. Fax: (617)495-7730
Economics Dept.
Cambridge, MA 02138
Publication E-mail: restate@arrow.fas.harvard.edu; restat@arrow.fas.harvard.edu
Publisher E-mail: webmistress@mitpress.mit.edu

Economics journal. **Founded:** 1918. **Freq:** Quarterly. **Print Method:** Offset. **Trim Size:** 8 1/4 x 10 3/4. **Cols./Page:** 2. **Col. Width:** 36 nonpareils. **Col. Depth:** 119 agate lines. **Key Personnel:** James H. Stock, Editor; Robert Pindyck, Editor; George J. Borjas, Editor; John Y. Campbell, Editor. **ISSN:** 0034-6535. **Subscription Rates:** $45 individuals; $25 students. **Remarks:** Accepts advertising.
Ad Rates: BW: $310 **Circ:** 4,000

14206 Roundel Magazine
BMW Car Club of America, Inc.
2130 Massachusetts Ave. Phone: (617)492-2500
Cambridge, MA 02140 Fax: (617)876-3424
Free: (800)878-9292
Publisher E-mail: BMWCclub@aol.com

Magazine for BMW enthusiasts. **Founded:** 1969. **Freq:** Monthly. **Print Method:** Web offset. **Trim Size:** 8 1/8 x 10 7/8. **Cols./Page:** 3. **Col. Width:** 2 1/16 inches. **Col. Depth:** 10 inches. **Key Personnel:** Satch Carlson, Editor, phone (907)345-1195, satch@alaska.net; Mark Luckman, Publisher, mluckman@aol.com; Michael Slaff, Advertising Mgr., phone (413)247-3300, fax (413)247-5758, mslaff@javanet.com.

ISSN: 0889-3225. **Subscription Rates:** $35. **Remarks:** Accepts classified advertising. **Available Online.**
Ad Rates: BW: $1341 **Circ:** Paid 48,000
4C: $1848

14207 Sky & Telescope
Sky Publishing Corp.
49 Bay State Rd. Phone: (617)864-7360
Cambridge, MA 02138 Fax: (617)864-6117
Free: (800)253-0245
Publication E-mail: skytel@skypub.com

Magazine on astronomy and space science. **Subtitle:** The Essential Magazine of Astronomy. **Founded:** Nov. 1941. **Freq:** Monthly. **Print Method:** Offset. **Trim Size:** 8 3/16 x 10 7/8. **Cols./Page:** 3. **Col. Width:** 2 5/16 inches. **Col. Depth:** 9 7/8 inches. **Key Personnel:** Leif J. Robinson, Editor, lrobinson@skypub.com; Kimberly Bennett, Advertising Sales Dir, kbennett@skypub.com; Susan Lit, Assoc. Pub, sblit@skypub.com. **ISSN:** 0037-6604. **Subscription Rates:** $39.95 individuals; $29.95 students; $4.50 single issue. **Remarks:** Accepts advertising. **URL:** http://www.skypub.com. **Alt. Formats:** Microfilm; Microform.
Ad Rates: BW: $3,390 **Circ:** Paid ★125,706
4C: $5,085

14208 Sloan Management Review
Massachusetts Institute of Technology
77 Massachusetts Ave E60-100 Phone: (617)253-7170
Cambridge, MA 02139 Fax: (617)258-9739
Publication E-mail: smr@mit.edu

Business journal highlighting trends and practical techniques for managers. **Founded:** Apr. 1960. **Freq:** Quarterly. **Print Method:** Offset. **Trim Size:** 8 3/8 x 10 7/8. **Cols./Page:** 2. **Col. Width:** 19.5 picas. **Col. Depth:** 125 agate lines. **Key Personnel:** Jane Gebhart, Editor. **ISSN:** 0019-848X. **Subscription Rates:** $79 individuals; $99 Canada and Mexico; $125 Other countries. **Remarks:** Accepts advertising. **URL:** http://web.mit.edu/smr-online.
Ad Rates: BW: $3,195 **Circ:** ‡25,000
4C: $3,545

14209 Sonus
24 Avon Hill Phone: (617)868-0215
Cambridge, MA 02140 Fax: (617)868-0215

Trade journal covering music worldwide. **Subtitle:** Journal of Global Musical Possibilities. **Founded:** 1980. **Freq:** Semiannual. **Trim Size:** 5 1/2 x 8 1/2. **Key Personnel:** Pozzi Escot, Contact. **ISSN:** 0739-229X. **Subscription Rates:** $25 individuals; $30 libraries; $15 single issue. **Remarks:** Advertising not accepted.
Circ: Paid 500

14210 Spare Change
Homeless Empowerment Project, Inc.
1151 Massachusetts Ave. Phone: (617)497-1595
Cambridge, MA 02138
New England periodical for the homeless. **Founded:** 1992. **Freq:** Biweekly. **Cols./Page:** 4. **Col. Width:** 2 inches. **Key Personnel:** Linda Larson, Editor; Fred Ellis, Advertising/Circulation. **Subscription Rates:** $40. **Remarks:** Accepts advertising.
Circ: Paid 25,000

14211 Speculum, A Journal of Medieval Studies
Medieval Academy of America
1430 Massachusetts Ave. Phone: (617)491-1622
Cambridge, MA 02138 Fax: (617)492-3303
Publisher E-mail: maa@fas.harvard.edu

Scholarly journal containing reviews and articles pertaining to all disciplines of medieval studies. **Founded:** 1926. **Freq:** Quarterly. **Print Method:** Offset. **Trim Size:** 6 3/4 x 10. **Cols./Page:** 1. **Col. Width:** 58 nonpareils. **Col. Depth:** 115 agate lines. **Key Personnel:** Luke Wenger, Editor. **ISSN:** 0038-7134. **Subscription Rates:** $55 individuals; $80 institutions, libraries; $20 single issue. **Remarks:** Color advertising not accepted.
Ad Rates: BW: $400 **Circ:** ‡5,500

14212 The Tech
PO Box 397029 Phone: (617)253-1541
Cambridge, MA 02139 Fax: (617)258-8226
Publication E-mail: general@the-tech.mit.edu

Collegiate newspaper (tabloid). **Subtitle:** The Newspaper of the Students of the Massachusetts Institute of Technology. **Founded:** Nov. 17, 1881. **Freq:** Semiweekly (Tues. and Fri.; during the academic year). **Print Method:** Offset. **Trim Size:** 17 x 22. **Cols./Page:** 5. **Col. Width:** 24 nonpareils. **Col. Depth:** 224 agate lines. **Key Personnel:** Josh Bittrer, Chairman; Dan McGuire, Editor-in-Chief; Joey Dieckhans, Business Mgr., phone (617)258-8324; Daniel C. Stevenson, Chairman; Erica Pfister, Managing Editor; Jennifer Lane, Executive Ed.; Joel Rosenberg, Arts Editor. **ISSN:** 0148-9607. **Subscription Rates:** $45 by mail third class; $105 by mail first class. **Remarks:** Accepts advertising tobacco. **Available Online.** **URL:** http://www.the-tech.mit.edu.
Ad Rates: BW: $1,600 **Circ:** Paid ‡500
4C: $1,100 Free ‡8,500
PCI: $11

14213 Technology Review
201 Vassar St. Phone: (617)253-8250
Cambridge, MA 02139 Fax: (617)258-5850
Publication E-mail: trcomments@mit.edu

Magazine reviewing new developments in technology with an emphasis on economic, political, and social implications. Not a new product publication. **Founded:** Jan. 1899. **Freq:** 6/year. **Print Method:** Offset. **Trim Size:** 8 x 10 3/4. **Cols./Page:** 2 and 3. **Col. Width:** 3.25 and 2.5 picas. **Col. Depth:** 9.5 picas. **Key Personnel:** John Benditt, Editor, phone (617)258-7888, fax (617)258-8778; R. Bruce Journey, Publisher/CEO, phone (617)253-2708. **Subscription Rates:** $30 individuals; $3.75 single issue; $42 other countries; $3.75 single issue.
Ad Rates: BW: $5,040 **Circ:** ‡93,000
4C: $7,200
PCI: $35

14214 Transition
Duke University Press
1430 N. Massachusetts Ave., 4th Fl. Phone: (617)496-2847
Fax: (617)496-2871
Cambridge, MA 02138
Publication E-mail: amylee@acpub.duke.edu
Publisher E-mail: dukepress@duke.edu

Magazine on African and African-American issues. **Subtitle:** An International Review. **Founded:** 1961. **Freq:** Quarterly. **Trim Size:** 6 7/8 x 9 3/4. **Cols./Page:** 2. **Col. Width:** 2 1/2 inches. **Col. Depth:** 7 13/16 inches. **Key Personnel:** Henry Louis Gates, Jr., Editor; Kwame Anthony Appiah, Editor; Wole Soyinka, Chair of Edit. Bd. **Subscription Rates:** $24 individuals; $60 institutions; $10 single issue. **Remarks:** Accepts advertising.
Ad Rates: BW: $300 **Circ:** Paid 1,500
Non-paid 1,000

14215 VooDoo Magazine
MIT Phone: (617)293-4575
77 Massachusetts Ave., Rm. 50-309
Cambridge, MA 02139
Publication E-mail: voodoo@mit.edu

Collegiate humor magazine containing articles and comics. **Subtitle:** The M.I.T. Journal of Humour. **Founded:** 1921. **Freq:** Quarterly. **Trim Size:** 8 x 10 3/4. **Cols./Page:** 2. **Key Personnel:** James Tanabe, Editor; Lex Nemzer, Contact. **ISSN:** 1066-2499. **Subscription Rates:** $10; $3 single issue. **Remarks:** Accepts advertising. **URL:** http://web.mit.edu/voodoo/www.
Ad Rates: BW: $500 **Circ:** Non-paid 8,000
4C: $3,000
PCI: $10

14216 WCRI Research Briefs
Workers Compensation Research Institute
101 Main St. Phone: (617)494-1240
Cambridge, MA 02142 Fax: (617)494-5240

Magazine concerning original research on workers' compensation. **Freq:** Monthly. **Subscription Rates:** $195 individuals. **Remarks:** Advertising not accepted.
Circ: (Not Reported)

14217 Worldprofit Online Magazine
Worldprofit, Inc.
PO Box 38-2767 Phone: (617)547-6372
Cambridge, MA 02238 Fax: (617)547-0061

Business development magazine of particular interest to small businesses. Available online only. **Founded:** 1995. **Freq:** Monthly. **Key Personnel:** Dr. Jeffrey Lant, Contact, drjlant@worldprofit.com. **Subscription Rates:** Free. **Remarks:** Advertising not accepted. **URL:** http://www.worldprofit.com.
Circ: Non-paid 600,000

14218 Continental Cablevision
88 Sherman St. Phone: (617)876-5005
Cambridge, MA 02140 Fax: (617)876-8613

Founded: 1985. **Cities Served:** Middlesex County, and Arlington, MA.

14219 WHRB-FM - 95.3
389 Harvard St. Phone: (617)495-4818
Cambridge, MA 02138 Fax: (617)496-3990
E-mail: whrb@hcs.harvard.edu

Format: Full Service. **Owner:** Harvard Radio Broadcasting Inc., at above address. **Founded:** 1940. **Operating Hours:** Continuous. **Key Personnel:** Matthew Price, General Mgr.; Nailah Robinson, News Dir.; Matthew Weissman, Publicity Dir.; David Elma, Program Dir.; Mary Sadanaga, Sports Dir.; Peter Rojas, Music Dir. **Wattage:** 3000. **Ad Rates:** $12-30 for 30 seconds; $30-40 for 60 seconds. **URL:** http://hcs.harvard.edu/nuhrb.

14220 WJIB-AM - 740
443 Concord Ave. Phone: (617)868-7400
Cambridge, MA 02138

Format: Easy Listening. **Owner:** Bob Bittner Broadcasting, Inc., at above address. **Founded:** 1991. **Former name:** WCAS-AM (1987); WLVG-AM (1991). **Operating Hours:** Continuous. **ADI:** Boston-Worcester,MA-Derry-Manchester,NH. **Key Personnel:** Bob Bittner, General Mgr. **Wattage:** 1000. **Ad Rates:** $20 for 30 seconds; $30 for 60 seconds.

14221 WMBR-FM - 88.1
3 Ames St. Phone: (617)253-4000
Cambridge, MA 02142-1305
E-mail: info@wmbr.mit.edu

Format: Full Service. **Networks:** Independent. **Owner:** Technology Broadcasting Corp., at above address. **Founded:** 1961. **Formerly:** WTBS-FM. **Operating Hours:** 6 a.m.-2:30 a.m.; 95% local. **Key Personnel:** Adam Weintraub, General Mgr.; Ted Young, Chief Engineer; Shawn Mamros, Controller; Andrew Sparks, Station Mgr.; Russ Newman, Program Dir. **Local Programs:** *Breakfast of Champions*, Jon Bernhardt; *Late Risers' Club*, Joanie Lindstrom; *Pipeline*, Bob DuBrow. **Wattage:** 720. **Ad Rates:** Noncommercial. **URL:** http://wmbr.mit.edu/.

14222 WRCA-AM - 1330
552 Mass Ave., Ste. 201 Phone: (617)492-3300
Cambridge, MA 02139-1562 Fax: (617)492-2800

Format: Ethnic; Hispanic. **Networks:** Independent. **Founded:** 1948. **Formerly:** WDLW-AM (1992). **Operating Hours:** Continuous. **Key Personnel:** Peter Arpin, General Mgr.; Stu Fink, Station & Operations Mgr. **Local Programs:** *Carribean Connection*, David Martin, (617)492-3300; *Radiolandia*, Alberto Vasallo III, (617)876-4293. **Wattage:** 5000. **Ad Rates:** $35 for 60 seconds.

CANTON, pop. 18,182.

E. MA. Norfolk Co. 15 mi. SW of Boston. Residential.

14223 Canton Journal
Mariner Newspapers
12 Revere St. Phone: (617)828-0006
PO Box 254 Fax: (617)828-3340
Canton, MA 02021-0254
Publication E-mail: cmathis@cnc.com
Publisher E-mail: cmathis@cnc.com

Community newspaper. **Founded:** 1876. **Freq:** Weekly (Thurs.). **Print Method:** Offset. **Trim Size:** 11 3/8 x 17. **Cols./Page:** 3. **Col. Depth:** 15 1/2 inches. **Key Personnel:** Mike Berger, Editor; David Cutler, President. **USPS:** 088-760. **Subscription Rates:** $18 individuals.
Ad Rates: BW: $651 **Circ:** Paid 2,786
4C: $1,051 Non-paid 156
SAU: $7

14224 Canton Register
Associated Newspapers
7 Cabot Pl. Phone: (781)878-1111
PO Box 441 Fax: (781)878-3333
Stoughton, MA 02072
Publisher E-mail: aweeklies@aol.com

Community newspaper. **Founded:** 1982. **Freq:** Weekly (Wed.). **Print Method:** Offset. **Cols./Page:** 6. **Col. Width:** 9.5 picas. **Col. Depth:** 16 inches. **Key Personnel:** Richard R. Dailey, Publisher. **Subscription Rates:** $17.50 individuals. **Remarks:** Accepts advertising.
Ad Rates: BW: $10.53 **Circ:** ‡1,102
4C: $10.77
PCI: $10.53

CAPE COD

14225 Cape Cod News
Community Newspaper
5 Namskaket Rd. Phone: (508)398-0123
PO Box 2776 Fax: (508)760-3387
Orleans, MA 02653-6776
Free: (800)660-8999

Community newspaper. **Founded:** 1964. **Freq:** Weekly (Wed.). **Print Method:** Offset. **Trim Size:** 16 1/2 x 11. **Cols./Page:** 5. **Col. Width:** 21 nonpareils. **Col. Depth:** 224 agate lines. **Key Personnel:** Eric Hartell, Exec. Editor; Jeanne

Moore-Yount, Vice Pres. Marketing/Sales. **Subscription Rates:** Free; $25 by mail. **Remarks:** Accepts advertising.
Ad Rates: GLR: $.80 **Circ:** (Not Reported)
BW: $896
4C: $1,296
PCI: $11.20

CARLISLE, pop. 3,306.

NE MA. Middlesex Co. 6 mi. NW of Concord. Residential.

14226 Carlisle Mosquito
Carlisle Communications, Inc.
PO Box 616 Phone: (508)369-8313
Carlisle, MA 01741 Fax: (508)369-3569

Local newspaper. **Founded:** July 1983. **Freq:** Weekly. **Print Method:** Offset. **Trim Size:** 10 x 15 1/2. **Cols./Page:** 5. **Col. Width:** 2 nonpareils. **Col. Depth:** 238 agate lines. **Key Personnel:** Sylvia Williard, Advertising Mgr.; Jackie Frey, Advertising Mgr. **Subscription Rates:** $15 local; $10 students.
Ad Rates: GLR: $6 **Circ:** Free ‡1,850
BW: $418.40
SAU: $6
PCI: $6.75

CARVER

14227 Carver Reporter
MPG Newspapers
9 Long Pond Rd. Phone: (508)746-5555
PO Box 959 Fax: (508)747-2148
Plymouth, MA 02362-0959
Free: (800)242-0264
Publisher E-mail: newsroom@mpgnews.com

Community newspaper. **Founded:** 1988. **Freq:** Weekly (Thurs.). **Print Method:** Offset. **Trim Size:** 16 1/2 x 11. **Cols./Page:** 5. **Col. Width:** 21 nonpareils. **Col. Depth:** 224 agate lines. **Key Personnel:** Phyllis Hughes, Publisher, fax (508)747-6616, phughes@mpgnews.com. **Subscription Rates:** $18 in county; $32 out of country. **Remarks:** Accepts advertising. **URL:** http://www.mpgnews.com.
Ad Rates: GLR: $.52 **Circ:** Combined ♦**2,606**
BW: $608
4C: $1008
PCI: $7.60

CHARLESTOWN

SE MA. Middlesex Co. On Boston Harbor.

14228 Charlestown Patriot & Somerville Chronicle
Charlestown Patriot Publications Inc.
1 Thompson Sq. Phone: (617)241-9511
Charlestown, MA 02129
Community newspaper. **Founded:** Sept. 1958. **Freq:** Weekly. **Print Method:** Offset. **Trim Size:** 8 1/2 x 11. **Cols./Page:** 6. **Col. Width:** 18 nonpareils. **Col. Depth:** 224 agate lines. **Key Personnel:** Gloria S. Conway, Contact; Sioux Gerow, Advertising Mgr. **Subscription Rates:** $50. **Remarks:** Color advertising not accepted.
Ad Rates: GLR: $.37 **Circ:** ‡4,500
BW: $499.20
PCI: $5.20

14229 WBPS-AM - 890
197 8th St., Ste.500 Phone: (617)242-1800
Charlestown, MA 02129 Fax: (617)241-9044

Format: Ethnic; Sports. **Owner:** Douglas Broadcasting, Inc., 499 Hamilton Ave. Ste 140, Palo Alto, CA 94301, (415)324-5888, Fax: (415)688-1166. **Founded:** Mar. 1995. **Formerly:** WBIV-AM. **Operating Hours:** Continuous. **Key Personnel:** Patrice Donley, General Mgr.; Marc Gardner, Business Mgr. **Wattage:** 25,000.

CHATHAM, pop. 6,430.

SE MA. Barnstable Co. On Atlantic Ocean, 18 mi. E. of Barnstable. Resort town.

14230 Chatham Current
Community Newspaper
5 Namskaket Rd. Phone: (508)398-0123
PO Box 2776 Fax: (508)760-3387
Orleans, MA 02653-6776
Free: (800)660-8999

Community newspaper. **Founded:** 1987. **Freq:** Weekly (Wed.). **Print Method:** Offset. **Trim Size:** 11 x 16 1/2. **Cols./Page:** 5. **Col. Width:** 21 inches. **Col. Depth:** 224 agate lines. **Key Personnel:** Eric Hartell, Editor; Jeanne Moore-Yount, Advertising Mgr. **Subscription Rates:** Free; $25 (mail). **Remarks:** Accepts advertising.
Ad Rates: GLR: $.46 **Circ:** Non-paid 1,677
BW: $520
4C: $1,120
PCI: $6.50

CHESTNUT HILL

NE MA. Middlesex Co. 6 mi. SW of Boston. (Branch of Boston P.O.) Residential.

14231 Educational Policy
Corwin Press
Boston College Phone: (617)552-4236
Campion Hall Fax: (617)552-8422
Chestnut Hill, MA 02167
Publisher E-mail: info@corwinpress.com

Journal providing research on educational policy and practice at the local, national and international level. **Founded:** 1985. **Freq:** Bimonthly. **Trim Size:** 5 1/4 x 8 1/2. **Key Personnel:** Philip G. Altbach, Editor, altbach@bc.edu. **ISSN:** 0895-9048. **Subscription Rates:** $75 individuals; $225 institutions; $20 single issue individuals; $50 single issue institutions. **Remarks:** Accepts advertising.
Ad Rates: BW: $225 **Circ:** Paid 700
Non-paid 30

14232 The Heights
Boston College
McElroy Commons, No. 113 Phone: (617)552-2220
Chestnut Hill, MA 02167 Fax: (617)552-4823

Collegiate newspaper. **Subtitle:** The Independent Student Weekly of Boston College. **Founded:** 1919. **Freq:** Weekly (Mon.). **Print Method:** Offset. **Cols./Page:** 5. **Col. Width:** 24 nonpareils. **Col. Depth:** 196 agate lines. **Key Personnel:** Lori Lefarre, Editor, phone (617)552-2223; Stephen Barwikowski, Managing Editor. **Subscription Rates:** Free; $50 by mail. **Remarks:** Accepts advertising. **Available Online. URL:** http://www.bcheights.com.
Ad Rates: PCI: $8.50 **Circ:** Free 10,000

14233 Method
Lonergan Institute at Boston College
Bapst Library Phone: (617)552-8095
Boston College Fax: (617)552-0510
Chestnut Hill, MA 02167-3806
Scholarly journal covering the writings of Bernard Lonergan. **Subtitle:** Journal of Lonergan Studies. **Founded:** 1983. **Freq:** Semiannual. **Trim Size:** 6 x 9. **Key Personnel:** Patrick Byrne, Editor; Charles Hefling, Editor; Mark Morelli, Editor. **Subscription Rates:** $16 individuals; $28 libraries and institutions; $8 single issue. **Remarks:** Advertising not accepted.
Circ: Combined 500

14234 Philosophy & Social Criticism
Boston College
McElroy Commons, No. 113 Phone: (617)552-2220
Chestnut Hill, MA 02167 Fax: (617)552-4823

International journal focusing on continental thought, American philosophy, ethics, law, hermeneutics, literary theory, cultural critique, politics, modernity and postmodernity. **Subtitle:** An International, Inter-disciplinary Quarterly Journal. **Freq:** Quarterly. **Key Personnel:** David M. Rasmussen, Editor. **Subscription Rates:** $80 libraries; $30 individuals; $25 students.

14235 WZBC-FM - 90.3
Boston College Phone: (617)552-3511
McElroy 107 Fax: (617)552-2158
Chestnut Hill, MA 02167
E-mail: wzbc@wzbc.org

Format: Alternative/New Music/Progressive. **Networks:** Independent. **Founded:** 1973. **Formerly:** WVBC-FM (1978). **Operating Hours:** 6 a.m.-2 a.m.; 100% local. **Key Personnel:** Dan Figenshu, General Mgr., fax (617)552-1738; Sandra Barrett, Music Dir., phone (617)552-4685; Meg Croke, Promotions Dir., phone (617)552-4684; Tyler Walsh, Sports Dir.; Caroline Paray, News Dir. **Wattage:** 1000. **Ad Rates:** Noncommercial. **URL:** http://www.wzbc.org.

CHICOPEE, pop. 55,112.

SW MA. Hampden Co. 4 mi. S. of Holyoke. Residential.

14236 National Engineer
National Association of Power Engineers
One Springfield St. Phone: (413)592-6273
Chicopee, MA 01013-2624 Fax: (413)592-1998

Subtitle: Magazine of the National Association of Power Engineers. **Founded:** 1897. **Freq:** Monthly. **Print Method:** Offset. **Trim Size:** 8 1/2 x 11. **Cols./Page:** 3. **Col. Width:** 26 nonpareils. **Col. Depth:** 140 agate lines. **Key Personnel:** William F. Judd, Editor. **ISSN:** 0027-9218. **Subscription Rates:** $25 individuals; $3 single issue. **Remarks:** Accepts advertising.
Ad Rates: BW: $787 **Circ:** Paid ‡5,422
4C: $1,312 Controlled ‡56
PCI: $50

14237 WACE-AM - 730
326 Chicopee St. Phone: (413)594-6654
Chicopee, MA 01013

Format: Religious; Talk. **Networks:** Independent. **Owner:** Carter Broadcasting Corp., 20 Park Plaza, Ste. 720, Boston, MA 02116, (617)423-0210. **Founded:** 1946. **Operating Hours:** Continuous. **Key Personnel:** Cal McLain, Program/News/Music; Michael D., Office Mgr.; Ken Carter, Pres./Gen. Mgr.; Ken Carter, Pres./Gen. Mgr. **Local Programs:** *In the Public Interest* Saturday, Cal McLain, Mailing contact. **Wattage:** 5000.

CLINTON, pop. 12,771.

C. MA. Worcester Co. On Nashua River, 12 mi. N. of Worchester. Manufactures flashlights, metal, concrete and wire goods, dyestuffs, chemicals, plastics, cereals, books, carpets, looms, furniture, radiators, luminous signs. Fruit, dairy, poultry farms. Apples, peaches.

14238 The Item
The Coulter Press
156 Church St. Phone: (508)368-0176
Clinton, MA 01510 Fax: (508)368-1151

General newspaper. **Founded:** 1893. **Freq:** Weekly. **Print Method:** Offset. **Trim Size:** 13 3/4 x 21 1/2. **Cols./Page:** 6. **Col. Width:** 25 nonpareils. **Col. Depth:** 300 agate lines. **Key Personnel:** Frank Hewitt, Publisher; Ron Chapdelaine, Advertising Mgr. **USPS:** 118-580. **Subscription Rates:** $52 individuals. **Remarks:** Accepts advertising.
Ad Rates: BW: $1,046 **Circ:** ‡6,100
PCI: $9.40

14239 Item Extra
The Coulter Press
156 Church St. Phone: (508)368-0176
Clinton, MA 01510 Fax: (508)368-1151

Shopper. **Founded:** 1931. **Freq:** Weekly. **Print Method:** Offset. **Trim Size:** 13 3/4 x 21 1/2. **Cols./Page:** 6. **Col. Width:** 25 nonpareils. **Col. Depth:** 300 agate lines. **Key Personnel:** Frank Hewitt, Publisher; Ron Chapdelaine, Advertising Mgr. **Remarks:** Accepts advertising.
Circ: Free ‡7,000

CONCORD, pop. 16,293.

NE MA. Middlesex Co. On Concord River, 20 mi. NW of Boston. Rich in historical and literary interest. Dairy, poultry, truck and fruit farms.

14240 The Beacon
Community Newspaper Company/Northwest
150 Baker Ave., Ste. 305 Phone: (978)371-5754
PO Box 9191 Fax: (978)371-9058
Concord, MA 01742-9191
Community newspaper. **Founded:** 1945. **Freq:** Weekly (Thurs.). **Print Method:** Offset. **Cols./Page:** 6. **Col. Depth:** 21 inches. **Key Personnel:** Dorris Hilberg, Editor; Mark O'Neil, Publisher; Jack Simko, Advertising Dir. **USPS:** 034-380. **Subscription Rates:** $29 individuals; $45 out of country. **Remarks:** Accepts advertising.
Ad Rates: GLR: $4.50 **Circ:** Paid 5,669
BW: $2000 Non-paid 44
4C: $2400
SAU: $16.70
PCI: $16.70

Bedford Minute Man - See Bedford

14241 Chelmsford Independent
Community Newspaper Company
PO Box 9191 Phone: (508)256-7196
Concord, MA 01742-9191 Fax: (508)256-6111

Community newspaper. **Founded:** 1980. **Freq:** Weekly (Thurs.). **Print Method:** Offset. **Cols./Page:** 7. **Col. Width:** 28 nonpareils. **Col. Depth:** 196 agate lines. **Key Personnel:** Marlene Switzer, Managing Editor; Richard Lombardi, Editor; Christopher Eddings, Publisher; Mark O'Neil, Advertising Mgr. **USPS:** 677-030. **Subscription Rates:** $22 individuals; $30 out of country. **Remarks:** Accepts advertising. **URL:** http://townonline.com.
Ad Rates: PCI: $7.80 **Circ:** Paid 5,219
Non-paid 35

14242 Lexington Minuteman
Community Newspaper Company/Northwest
PO Box 9191 Phone: (617)861-9110
Concord, MA 01742-9191 Fax: (617)863-8662

Community newspaper. **Founded:** 1965. **Freq:** Weekly (Thurs.). **Print Method:** Offset. **Cols./Page:** 6. **Col. Width:** 20 nonpareils. **Col. Depth:** 294 agate lines. **Key Personnel:** Jon Towne, Managing Editor; Steve Dines, President; Lisa Comins, Advertising Mgr. **USPS:** 331-340. **Subscription Rates:** $24 individuals; $36 out of county. **Remarks:** Accepts advertising.
Ad Rates: PCI: $12.50 **Circ:** Paid 8,292
Non-paid 36

Littleton Independent - See Littleton

The Maynard Beacon - See Maynard

14243 Perspective
Association of Professional Directors of YMCAs in the U.S.
Kendall & Co. Phone: (978)369-6393
4A Damonmill Sq. Fax: (978)371-7117
Concord, MA 01742
Magazine containing administrative, managerial, fund-raising, program, and philosophical material for YMCA professionals. **Founded:** 1975. **Freq:** 8/year. **Print Method:** Offset. Uses mats. **Trim Size:** 8 1/2 x 11. **Cols./Page:** 3. **Key Personnel:** Steven A. Kendall, Editor, kendallnco@aol.com; Paul C. Carr, Advertising Mgr. **ISSN:** 0745-3027. **Remarks:** Accepts advertising.
Ad Rates: BW: $963 **Circ:** ‡5,000
4C: $1,713

Tewksbury Advertiser - See Tewksbury

The Westford Eagle - See Westford

14244 WIQH-FM - 88.3
500 Walden St. Phone: (508)369-2440
Concord, MA 01742

Format: Album-Oriented Rock (AOR); Alternative/New Music/Progressive. **Founded:** 1971. **Key Personnel:** Gillian R. Holcomb, General Mgr. **Wattage:** 10.

CUMMAQUID

14245 TIE (The International Educator)
The International Educator's Institute
PO Box 513 Phone: (508)362-1414
Cummaquid, MA 02637 Fax: (508)362-1411
Publication E-mail: tie@capecod.net

Magazine (tabloid) reporting job listings from schools around the world. Includes information on salary, benefits, terms and conditions of employment, and application instructions also news on global education and general education information. **Subtitle:** Official Publication of the International Educator's Institute. **Founded:** 1986. **Freq:** 5/year. **Print Method:** Offset. **Trim Size:** 10 1/4 x 16. **Cols./Page:** 5. **Col. Width:** 2 inches. **Col. Depth:** 16 inches. **Key Personnel:** Sherry Calef, Editor, phone (617)662-3411, fax (781)662-2629, tiedit@aol.com. **ISSN:** 1044-3509. **Subscription Rates:** $30. **Remarks:** Accepts advertising.
Ad Rates: BW: $1,950 **Circ:** 14,000
PCI: $50

DANVERS, pop. 24,100.

NE MA. Essex Co. 3 mi. N. of Peabody. Residential.

Hamilton-Wenham Chronicle - See Hamilton

14246 North Shore Sunday
Community Newspaper Company
152 Sylvan St. Phone: (508)774-0505
Danvers, MA 01923 Fax: (508)762-0450

Community newspaper (tabloid). **Founded:** 1977. **Freq:** Weekly (Sun.). **Print Method:** Offset. **Trim Size:** 11 3/8 x 17. **Cols./Page:** 5. **Col. Width:** 2 1/16 inches. **Col. Depth:** 16 inches. **Key Personnel:** Taylor Armerding, Editor; Chuck Goodrich, Publisher; Robert Tisi, Ad. Mgr. **Subscription Rates:** $36 individuals; Free single copy. **Remarks:** Accepts advertising.
Ad Rates: GLR: $1.59 **Circ:** Paid 50
BW: $2,232 Free 90,000
SAU: $27.90

DEDHAM†, pop. 25,298.

E. MA. Norfolk Co. On Charles River, 9 mi. SW of Boston. Residential. Manufactures control mechanisms, greeting cards, corrugated boxes.

14247 Daily Transcript
Community Newspaper Company
254 Second Ave Phone: (781)433-7800
Needham, MA 02192 Fax: (781)433-8202
Publisher E-mail: townonline.com

General newspaper. **Founded:** 1973. **Freq:** Daily (eve.). **Print Method:** Offset. **Cols./Page:** 6. **Col. Width:** 25 nonpareils. **Col. Depth:** 300 agate lines. **Key Personnel:** James Harder, Editor; Kirk Davis, Publisher. **Subscription Rates:** $91 individuals; $110 out of area. **Remarks:** Accepts advertising. **Formerly:** Dedham Transcript (1989).
Ad Rates: GLR: $1.42 **Circ:** Mon.-Fri. 7,805
BW: $1,134
4C: $1,434
SAU: $9

14248 The Dedham Times
395 Washington St. Phone: (781)329-5553
Dedham, MA 02026 Fax: (781)329-8291

Community newspaper. **Founded:** Aug. 16, 1993. **Freq:** Weekly (Fri.). **Trim Size:** 11 1/4 x 17. **Cols./Page:** 5. **Col. Width:** 1 7/8 inches. **Key Personnel:** Hana Janjigian Heald, Editor-in-Chief; Elizabeth F. Martin, Business Mgr.; James E. Heald, Publisher. **Subscription Rates:** Free to qualified subscribers; $24 individuals; $30 out of area.
Ad Rates: BW: $375 **Circ:** Paid ⊕2,400
4C: $485
PCI: $5

14249 WFXT-TV - 25
25 Fox Dr. Phone: (617)467-2525
PO Box 9125 Fax: (617)467-7210
Dedham, MA 02027-9125

Format: Commercial TV. **Networks:** Fox. **Founded:** Oct. 10, 1977. **Formerly:** WXNE-TV (1986). **Operating Hours:** Continuous; 21% network, 79% local. **ADI:** Boston-Worcester,MA-Derry-Manchester,NH. **Key Personnel:** Jim Byrne, Dir. Programming and Promotion, phone (617)467-1470, fax (617)467-7206; Rich Golden, VP/General Sales Mgr., phone (617)467-1430, fax (617)467-7201; Coleen Marren, VP/General Mgr., phone (617)467-1310, fax (617)467-7209; Deborah Picardi, Public Affairs Director, phone (617)467-1475, fax (617)467-7206. **Local Programs:** *Fox News Boston* 10 p.m.

DEERFIELD

NW MA. Franklin Co. 4 mi. S. of Greenfield.

14250 WGAJ-FM - 91.7
PO Box 248 Phone: (413)774-1850
Deerfield, MA 01342-0248 Fax: (413)772-1100

Format: Alternative/New Music/Progressive; Urban Contemporary; Jazz; Album-Oriented Rock (AOR); Classic Rock. **Networks:** Independent. **Founded:** 1981. **Operating Hours:** 7 a.m.-8 a.m.,3 p.m.-midnight weekdays; 7 a.m.-midnight Saturday and Sunday; 100% local. **Key Personnel:** Bibby Howell, General Mgr.; Ame Igharo, Station Mgr.; Tucker McCormick, Studio Mgr.; Matt Ouderkirk, Network Mgr.; Leigh Merrigan, Business Mgr.; Chad Walker, Asst. General Mgr.; Kate O'Rourke, Sales Dir.; Kareem Rabie, Music Dir.; Todd Yates, Music Dir.; Mike Brown, Sports Dir.; Quincy Perkins, Sports Dir. **Wattage:** 100. **Ad Rates:** Noncommercial.

DORCHESTER

SE MA. Suffolk Co. Ward of city of Boston.

14251 Dorchester Argus-Citizen
South Boston Tribune
PO Box 6 Phone: (617)268-3440
South Boston, MA 02127 Fax: (617)268-6420

Local newspaper. **Founded:** 1927. **Freq:** Weekly (Thurs.). **Print Method:** Offset. **Cols./Page:** 9. **Col. Width:** 9 1/2 picas. **Col. Depth:** 308 agate lines. **Key Personnel:** Daniel J. Horgan, Publisher. **Subscription Rates:** $14 individuals; $17 out of area. **Remarks:** Accepts advertising.
Ad Rates: GLR: $.52 **Circ:** ‡7,350
SAU: $6.90

DOVER

14252 The Dover Tab
Community Newspaper Company
254 2nd Ave. Phone: (781)433-7828
Needham, MA 02192-9114 Fax: (781)433-7835

Community newspaper (tabloid). **Founded:** Oct. 1985. **Freq:** Weekly (Tues.). **Print Method:** Offset. **Trim Size:** 10 x 16. **Cols./Page:** 7. **Col. Width:** 8 picas. **Key Personnel:** John Wilpers, Editor; Russel Pergament, Advertising Mgr.; Stephen Cummings, Publisher; Lisa Flicop, Editor. **URL:** http://townonline.com. **Formerly:** The Dover/Sherborn Gazette.
Circ: Non-paid 2,255

DOVER-SHERBORN

14253 Dover-Sherborn Suburban Press
Suburban World, Inc.
992 Great Plain Ave. Phone: (508)653-4460
PO Box 358 Fax: (781)444-1795
Needham, MA 02192
Free: (800)847-NEWS
Publication E-mail: dover@suburbanworld.com; sherborn@suburbanworld.com

Newspaper. **Founded:** 1968. **Freq:** Weekly (Thurs.). **Print Method:** Offset. **Trim Size:** 11 x 17. **Cols./Page:** 5. **Col. Width:** 10 1/4 picas. **Col. Depth:** 16 inches. **Key Personnel:** Christine Leonard, Editor; William Barrett, Publisher; Dave Petruska, Advertising Mgr. **Subscription Rates:** $22 individuals; $27 out of area; $18 students. **Remarks:** Accepts advertising.
Ad Rates: GLR: $.58 **Circ:** Combined 2,077

DRACUT, pop. 24,040.

NC MA. Middlesex Co. 2 mi. N. of Lowell.

14254 The Dracut Dispatch
The Dispatch Publishing Co., Inc.
434 Textile Ave. Phone: (508)957-0007
PO Box 1 Fax: (508)957-1051
Dracut, MA 01826
Local newspaper. **Founded:** 1973. **Freq:** Weekly (Thurs.). **Print Method:** Offset. **Trim Size:** 10 x 16. **Cols./Page:** 7. **Col. Width:** 1 5/16 inches. **Col. Depth:** 224 agate lines. **Key Personnel:** Geraldine Katin, Editor; William J. Themelis, Publisher. **ISSN:** 8750-1341. **Subscription Rates:** Free; $14 by mail.
Ad Rates: PCI: $7.00 **Circ:** Paid ‡3,600
Free ‡3,000

DUDLEY

14255 The Times
West County Newspapers
Rte. 12
Schofield Ave.
Dudley, MA 01571

Community newspaper. **Founded:** Mar. 17, 1859. **Freq:** Weekly (Wed.). **Print Method:** Offset. Uses mats. **Cols./Page:** 6. **Col. Width:** 16 nonpareils. **Key Personnel:** Martin Fry, Editor; Ernest Mayotte, Publisher. **USPS:** 617-200. **Subscription Rates:** $18 individuals; $21.50 other. **Remarks:** Accepts advertising.
Ad Rates: BW: $859 **Circ:** ‡8,164
SAU: $6.42
PCI: $8.95

DUXBURY, pop. 11,807.

SE MA. Plymouth Co. On Duxbury Bay, 30 mi. SE of Boston. Residential.

14256 Duxbury Clipper
The Mariner
PO Box 1656 Phone: (617)934-2811
Duxbury, MA 02331 Fax: (617)934-5917

Community newspaper (tabloid). **Founded:** May 11, 1950. **Freq:** Weekly (Wed.). **Print Method:** Offset. **Trim Size:** 11 1/2 x 17. **Cols./Page:** 6. **Col. Width:** 1 1/2 inches. **Col. Depth:** 15 1/2 inches. **Key Personnel:** John Henry Cutler, Publisher; Priscilla Sangster, Advertising Mgr. **USPS:** 163-260. **Subscription Rates:** $15 individuals; $25 out of area. **Remarks:** Accepts advertising.
Ad Rates: GLR: $.43 **Circ:** Paid ‡4,500
BW: $380 Free ‡150
4C: $780
PCI: $4.65

14257 Duxbury Reporter
MPG Newspapers
9 Long Pond Rd. Phone: (508)746-5555
PO Box 959 Fax: (508)747-2148
Plymouth, MA 02362-0959
Free: (800)242-0264
Publisher E-mail: newsroom@mpgnews.com

Community newspaper. **Founded:** 1987. **Freq:** Weekly (Wed.). **Print Method:** Offset. **Trim Size:** 16 1/2 x 11. **Cols./Page:** 5. **Col. Width:** 21 nonpareils. **Col. Depth:** 224 agate lines. **Key Personnel:** Phyllis Hughes, Publisher, phughes@mpgnews.com. **Subscription Rates:** Free; $32

(out of county). **Remarks:** Accepts advertising. **URL:** http://www.mpgnews.com.
Ad Rates: GLR: $.53 **Circ:** Combined ♦2,929
BW: $596
4C: $996
PCI: $7.45

14258 Journal of Turkish Studies/Turkluk Bilgisi Arastirmalari
Harvard University
Box 1447 Phone: (781)585-8796
Duxbury, MA 02331 Fax: (781)585-8796

Scholarly journal covering history, literature, and language of the Turkic peoples of the Middle East and Central Asia. **Founded:** 1977. **Freq:** Annual. **Trim Size:** 8 1/2 x 11. **Cols./Page:** 1. **Key Personnel:** Prof. Sinasi Tekin; Prof. Gdnul Tekin. **Subscription Rates:** $200 individuals. **Remarks:** Accepts advertising.
Ad Rates: BW: $1,000 **Circ:** (Not Reported)

EAST BOSTON, pop. 30,000.

E. MA. Suffolk Co. Section of Boston on E. side of Charles River estuary.

14259 Air Travel Journal
256 Marginal St. Phone: (617)561-4000
East Boston, MA 02128-2823 Fax: (617)561-2821

Business traveler newspaper of Logan Airport, Boston, MA. **Founded:** Nov. 1972. **Freq:** Semimonthly. **Print Method:** Offset. **Trim Size:** 10 x 16. **Cols./Page:** 6. **Col. Width:** 1 9/16 inches. **Col. Depth:** 16 inches. **Key Personnel:** Robert H. Weiss, Editor and Publisher. **Subscription Rates:** $30 individuals. **Remarks:** Accepts advertising.
Ad Rates: GLR: $.70 **Circ:** Non-paid 18,000
BW: $936
PCI: $9.75

14260 East Boston Times
Wakefield Item Co.
40 William Kennedy Sq. Phone: (617)567-9600
East Boston, MA 02128
Publication E-mail: dailyitem@aol.com

Newspaper. **Founded:** 1886. **Freq:** Weekly (Wed.). **Print Method:** Offset. **Cols./Page:** 8. **Col. Width:** 22 nonpareils. **Col. Depth:** 294 agate lines. **Key Personnel:** Louis D. Torrone, Editor; John Torrone, Publisher. **Remarks:** Accepts advertising.
Ad Rates: GLR: $.40 **Circ:** Free ‡15,500

EAST LONGMEADOW, pop. 12,905.

SW MA. Hampden Co. 12 mi. S. of Westfield. Residential.

14261 Childsplay
Reminder Publications
280 N. Main St. Phone: (413)525-6661
East Longmeadow, MA 01028 Fax: (413)525-5882
Publication E-mail: chldplay@famil.com

Magazine on parenting. **Subtitle:** The Parenting Magazine of Western Massachusetts. **Founded:** 1984. **Freq:** Bimonthly. **Print Method:** offset. **Trim Size:** 8 1/2 x 11. **Cols./Page:** 3. **Col. Width:** 2 1/4 inches. **Col. Depth:** 9 7/8 inches. **Key Personnel:** Christopher Buendo, Publisher, cbuendo@thereminder.com. **Subscription Rates:** $15. **Remarks:** Accepts advertising. **URL:** http://www.family.com.
Ad Rates: BW: $1,000 **Circ:** Paid 552
4C: $1,500 Free 9,448

14262 The Reminder
Reminder Publications, Inc.
280 N. Main St. Phone: (413)525-6661
East Longmeadow, MA 01028-1865 Fax: (413)525-5882
Community newspaper for the East Longmeadow, Longmeadow, Hampden, Wilbraham, and Sixteen Acres and Forest Park sections of Springfield, MA. **Founded:** Nov. 2, 1962. **Freq:** Weekly (Mon.). **Print Method:** Offset. **Trim Size:** 11 1/2 x 14. **Cols./Page:** 5. **Col. Width:** 2 inches. **Col. Depth:** 182 agate lines. **Key Personnel:** Ann Carver, Editor; Daniel Buendo, Sales Mgr.; Christopher Buendo, General Mgr., cbuendo@thereminder.com. **Subscription Rates:** Free; $15 by mail. **Remarks:** Accepts advertising. **Available Online. URL:** http://www.thereminder.com.
Ad Rates: GLR: $1.05 **Circ:** Free ‡30,000
BW: $825
4C: $1,125
SAU: $14
PCI: $14

14263 WAQY-AM - 1600
45 Fisher Ave. Phone: (413)525-4141
East Longmeadow, MA 01028 Fax: (413)525-4334

Format: Classic Rock. **Simulcasts:** WAQY-FM. **Founded:** 1947. **Formerly:** WIXY-AM. **Operating Hours:** Daytime Only. **Key Personnel:** Glenn Stewart, Program Dir.; Larry Goldberg, General Mgr. **Wattage:** 2500. **Ad Rates:** Advertising accepted; rates available upon request.

14264 WAQY-FM - 102.1
45 Fisher Ave. Phone: (413)525-4141
East Longmeadow, MA 01028 Fax: (413)525-4334
E-mail: rock102.com

Format: Classic Rock. **Networks:** Independent. **Founded:** 1966. **Operating Hours:** Continuous. **Key Personnel:** Lawrence Goldberg, General Mgr., lgoldberg@rock102.com; Glenn Stewart, Program Dir.; Judith Anderson, General Sales Mgr., janderson@rock102.com. **Wattage:** 50,000. **Ad Rates:** Advertising accepted; rates available upon request.

EAST SANDWICH

14265 WSDH-FM - 91.5
Sandwich High School Phone: (508)888-0420
365 Quaker Meetinghouse Rd. Fax: (508)833-8392
East Sandwich, MA 02537
E-mail: wsdh@sandwich.k12.ma.us

Format: Contemporary Hit Radio (CHR). **Networks:** Independent. **Owner:** Sandwich Public Schools, 16 Dewey Ave., Sandwich, MA 02563, (508)888-1054. **Founded:** 1977. **Operating Hours:** 10 a.m.-4 p.m.; 100% local. **Key Personnel:** Richard Rose, General Mgr.; Kassia Waskiewicz, Station Mgr., nsyncccc@aol.com. **Wattage:** 310. **Ad Rates:** Noncommercial.

EASTHAM

14266 Eastham-Wellfleet Oracle
Community Newspaper
5 Namskaket Rd. Phone: (508)398-0123
PO Box 2776 Fax: (508)760-3387
Orleans, MA 02653-6776
Free: (800)660-8999

Community newspaper. **Founded:** 1987. **Freq:** Weekly. **Print Method:** Offset. **Trim Size:** 11 x 16 1/2. **Cols./Page:** 5. **Col. Width:** 21 inches. **Col. Depth:** 224 agate lines. **Key Personnel:** Eric Hartell, Editor; Jeanne Moore-Yount, Advertising Mgr. **Subscription Rates:** Free; $25 (mail). **Remarks:** Accepts advertising.
Ad Rates: GLR: $39 **Circ:** Non-paid 1,659
BW: $440
4C: $1,040
PCI: $5.50

EASTON

14267 Easton Bulletin
Associated Newspapers
7 Cabot Pl. Phone: (781)878-1111
PO Box 441 Fax: (781)878-3333
Stoughton, MA 02072
Publisher E-mail: aweeklies@aol.com

Community newspaper. **Founded:** 1929. **Freq:** Weekly (Thurs.). **Print Method:** Offset. **Cols./Page:** 6. **Col. Width:** 9.5 picas. **Col. Depth:** 16 inches. **Key Personnel:** Richard R. Dailey, Publisher. **Subscription Rates:** $17.50. **Remarks:** Accepts advertising.
Ad Rates: BW: $10.53 **Circ:** ‡1,916
4C: $10.77
PCI: $10.53

EDGARTOWN†, pop. 2,204.

SE MA. Dukes Co. On E. shore of Martha's Vineyard Island. Ferry connections with Woods Hole via Vineyard Haven. Summer resort. Shell fisheries, deep water fishing industry.

14268 Martha's Vineyard Magazine
34 S. Summer St. Phone: (508)627-4311
PO Box 66 Fax: (508)627-7444
Edgartown, MA 02539
Publication E-mail: news@mvgazette.com

Magazine covering the history, art, poetry, lifestyles, and culture of Martha's Vineyard. **Founded:** 1985. **Freq:** Quarterly. **Print Method:** Web offset. **Trim Size:** 8 1/8 x 10 7/8. **Cols./Page:** 3. **Col. Width:** 2 1/4 inches. **Col. Depth:** 9 5/16 inches. **Key Personnel:** Richard Reston, Publisher; Mary Jo Reston, Publisher; Laurence Michie, Editor. **ISSN:** 1052-5785. **Subscription Rates:** $15 individuals; $3.95 single issue. **Remarks:** Accepts advertising.
Ad Rates: BW: $1,370 **Circ:** Paid ‡7,600
4C: $1,770 Non-paid ‡4,400

14269 Vineyard Gazette
Vineyard Gazette, Inc.
34 S. Summer St. Phone: (508)627-4311
PO Box 66 Fax: (508)627-7444
Edgartown, MA 02539
Publication E-mail: news@mvgazette.con

Resort and local newspaper. **Founded:** May 1846. **Freq:** Weekly Tues. & Fri. (summers only), plus Friday year-round. **Print Method:** Offset. **Cols./Page:** 7. **Col. Width:** 26 nonpareils. **Col. Depth:** 294 agate lines. **Key Personnel:** Richard F. Reston, Editor and Publisher; Mary Jo Reston, Publisher; Eileen Holley, Advertising Mgr. **USPS:** 659-940. **Subscription Rates:** $41 individuals; $53 Off the island. **Remarks:** Accepts advertising. **URL:** http://www.mvgazette.com.
Ad Rates: PCI: $18.75 **Circ:** 13,478

EVERETT, pop. 37,195.

NE MA. Middlesex Co. 3 mi. N. of Boston. (Branch of Boston P.O.) Manufactures paint and varnish, chemicals, refined oil products, cans, tanks, truck bodies, steel racks, shoes, foundry and coal tar products, candy.

14270 Leader-Herald and News Gazette
Leader Publishing Co., Inc.
28 Church St. Phone: (617)387-4570
Everett, MA 02149 Fax: (617)387-0409

Community newspaper. **Founded:** 1885. **Freq:** Weekly (Thurs.). **Print Method:** Offset. **Cols./Page:** 8. **Col. Width:** 21 nonpareils. **Col. Depth:** 301 agate lines. **Key Personnel:** Joseph Curnane, Jr., Editor. **Subscription Rates:** Free; $40 by mail. **Remarks:** Accepts advertising.
Ad Rates: GLR: $.34 **Circ:** Free ‡15,000
BW: $840
PCI: $5

FAIRHAVEN

14271 The Advocate
Hathaway Publishing
130 Main St. Phone: (508)961-2243
Fairhaven, MA 02719 Fax: (508)961-2245

Community newspaper. **Founded:** 1978. **Freq:** Weekly (Thurs.). **Print Method:** Offset. **Trim Size:** 13 x 21 1/2. **Cols./Page:** 6. **Col. Width:** 2 inches. **Col. Depth:** 224 agate lines. **Key Personnel:** Ray Hopkins, General Mgr.; Lori Rebello, Editor. **Subscription Rates:** $21 individuals; $40 out of country. **Remarks:** Advertising accepted; rates available upon request.
Circ: Paid ‡2,900

14272 WBSM-AM - 1420
22 Sconticut Neck Rd. Phone: (508)993-1767
Fairhaven, MA 02719 Fax: (508)999-1420

Format: Talk; News. **Networks:** CBS; AP. **Owner:** H and D Entertainment Inc., 2 Stanford Dr., Farmington, CT 06032, (203)357-1464. **Founded:** 1949. **Operating Hours:** Continuous; 20% network, 80% local. **Key Personnel:** Steven Bogue, General Mgr.; Cathy Correll, Sales Mgr.; James Marshall, Program Dir. **Local Programs:** *Pat DesMaris* 3p.m.-7p.m., Pat DesMaris; *Pete Braley & Co.* 6a.m.-9a.m., Pete Borley; *Stan Lipp* 9a.m.-Noon, Stan Lipp. **Wattage:** 5000 day; 1000 night. **Ad Rates:** $24-30 for 30 seconds; $24-45 for 60 seconds.

14273 WFHN-FM - 107.1
22 Sconticut Neck Rd. Phone: (508)999-6690
Fairhaven, MA 02719 Fax: (508)999-1420

Format: Contemporary Hit Radio (CHR). **Networks:** Independent. **Founded:** 1989. **Operating Hours:** Continuous; 100% local. **Key Personnel:** Steven Bogue, General Mgr.; J.R. Reitz, Program Mgr.; Jeanmarie Manning, Sales Mgr. **Wattage:** 3000. **Ad Rates:** $26-43 for 30 seconds; $32-48 for 60 seconds.

FALL RIVER, pop. 92,574.

SE MA. Bristol Co. On Tauton River, at mouth of Mount Hope Bay, 18 mi. SE of Providence, RI. Foreign and domestic trade. Manufactures cotton goods, thread and yarns, rayon and silk products, textiles, lighting fixtures curtains, rubber and latex products, paper boxes, plastics, textile machinery, luggage, rope and cord, leather belting, fiberglass boats. Cotton, cloth bleaching plants.

14274 The Anchor
887 Highland Ave. Phone: (508)675-7151
PO Box 7 Fax: (508)675-7048
Fall River, MA 02722
Publisher E-mail: anchorpress@sneplanet.com

Catholic newspaper (tabloid). **Founded:** Apr. 11, 1957. **Freq:** Weekly (Fri.). **Print Method:** Offset. **Cols./Page:** 5. **Col. Width:** 22 nonpareils. **Col. Depth:** 204 agate lines. **Key Personnel:** Ref. John F. Moore, Editor; Most Rev. Sean P. O'Malley, OFM, Publisher; Rosemary Dussault, General Mgr. **USPS:** 545-020. **Subscription Rates:** $14 individuals. **Remarks:** Accepts advertising. **Alt. Formats:** Microform.
Ad Rates: GLR: $.85 **Circ:** ‡30,011
BW: $500
PCI: $11.75

14275 Herald News
Northeast Publishing, Inc.
207 Pocasset St. Phone: (508)676-8211
Box 2410 Fax: (508)676-2566
Fall River, MA 02722
General newspaper. **Founded:** 1872. **Freq:** Daily (eve.), Sat. and Sun. (morn.). **Print Method:** Letterpress. Uses mats. **Cols./Page:** 8. **Col. Width:** 26 nonpareils. **Col. Depth:** 301 agate lines. **Key Personnel:** Bernard F. Sulivan, Editor; Edward F. St. John, Publisher; Paul D. Gelinas, Advertising Mgr. **Remarks:** Accepts advertising.
Ad Rates: PCI: $15.30 **Circ:** Mon.-Sat. ★**27,168**
Sun. ★**29,148**

FALMOUTH, pop. 23,640.

E. MA. Barnstable Co. On sea coast, 39 mi. SE of New Bedford. Resort. Marine Biological Laboratory and Oceanographic Institution. Commercial fisheries. Agriculture. Strawberries, cranberries.

14276 Arts and Entertainment Tourist Guide
Falmouth Publishing Co.
50 Depot Ave. Phone: (508)548-4700
Falmouth, MA 02540 Fax: (508)540-8407
Free: (800)286-7744

Tabloid features guide to Cape Cod and local news of interest to the tourist. **Founded:** 1985. **Freq:** Weekly (Fri.). **Print Method:** Offset. **Trim Size:** 11 1/2 x 16. **Cols./Page:** 5. **Col. Width:** 15 nonpareils. **Col. Depth:** 210 agate lines. **Key Personnel:** William H. Hough, Exec. Editor; Margaret Hough Russell, Editor; John T. Hough, Publisher; Danielle Guay, Advertising Mgr. **ISSN:** 0747-0142. **Subscription Rates:** $31.20 individuals. **Remarks:** Accepts advertising. **Formerly:** At Your Leisure Tourist Guide (1992).
Ad Rates: BW: $576 **Circ:** Paid 10,000
4C: $856 Non-paid 13,241
SAU: $13.50
PCI: $10.59

The Bourne Enterprise - See Bourne

FITCHBURG†, pop. 39,580.

C. MA. Worcester Co. On Nashua River, 46 mi. NW of Boston. Fitchburg State College. Manufactures electrical equipment, paper, shoes, cotton and woolen goods, saws, machine knives, plastic goods, screen plates, curtains, air conditioning equipment, boxes, luggage, textiles, brass and iron castings, furniture, hardware.

14277 Pioneer
Raivaaja Publishing Co.
147 Elm St.
Fitchburg, MA 01420
Publisher E-mail: raivaaja@netplus.com

Newspaper serving the Finnish-American community (Finnish and English). **Founded:** 1905. **Freq:** Weekly (Wed.). **Print Method:** Offset. **Cols./Page:** 5. **Col. Width:** 11 picas. **Col. Depth:** 88 picas. **Key Personnel:** Marita Cauthen, Editor; Jonathan Ratila, Business Mgr. **ISSN:** 1059-4779. **Subscription Rates:** $28 individuals. **Remarks:** Accepts advertising. **Foreign language name:** Raivaaja.
Ad Rates: GLR: $.70 **Circ:** ‡2,000
BW: $500
PCI: $4.50

14278 Sentinel & Enterprise
808 Main St. Phone: (508)343-6911
Fitchburg, MA 01420 Fax: (508)342-1158

General newspaper. **Founded:** 1838. **Freq:** Daily (eve.). **Print Method:** Offset. **Cols./Page:** 6. **Col. Width:** 24 nonpareils. **Col. Depth:** 301 agate lines. **Key Personnel:** Ann Connery Frantz, Editor; William A. White, Publisher; Janet Banville, Advertising Dir. **Subscription Rates:** $143 individuals. **Remarks:** Accepts advertising.
Ad Rates: GLR: $1.30 **Circ:** Mon.-Sat. ★**19,723**
BW: $2101.41 Sun. ★**20,146**
4C: $2411.41
SAU: $16.29
PCI: $15.66

14279 WEIM-AM - 1280
762 Water St. Phone: (978)343-3766
PO Box 727 Fax: (978)345-6397
Fitchburg, MA 01420
E-mail: news@weim.com

Format: Sports; Adult Contemporary; News; Talk. **Networks:** ABC. **Owner:** WEIM Corp., at above address, MA. **Founded:** 1941. **Operating Hours:** 19 hrs. Daily; 15% network, 85% local. **ADI:** Boston-Worcester,MA-Derry-Manchester,NH. **Key Personnel:** Frank Filippone, Contact; Jack Raymond, Program Dir. **Wattage:** 5000. **Ad Rates:** $20-25 for 30 seconds; $30-35 for 60 seconds. **URL:** http://www.weim.com.

14280 WXPL-FM - 91.3
160 Pearl St. Phone: (978)665-3692
Fitchburg, MA 01420 Fax: (978)665-3693
E-mail: wxpl@fsc.edu

Format: Alternative/New Music/Progressive. **Owner:** Fitchburg State College, at above address, (978)345-2151. **Founded:** 1985. **Formerly:** WFRC-FM. **Operating Hours:** 8:30 a.m.- 2 a.m. **Key Personnel:** Sheri Emerson, Station Mgr.; Jason St. Amand, Asst. Station Mgr.; Rick Melo, Program Dir.; Jeff Firnhaber, Music Dir.; Christina Giadone, Public Relations Director. **Wattage:** 110. **Ad Rates:** Noncommercial.

FLORENCE

14281 Perspectiva
Educational News Service
PO Box 60478 Phone: (413)586-4490
Florence, MA 01062-0478 Fax: (413)586-3448
Free: (800)600-4494
Publisher E-mail: info@ednews.com

Educational magazine for those learning Spanish. **Subtitle:** World News in Intermediate Spanish for Language Learning. **Founded:** May 1990. **Freq:** Monthly. **Trim Size:** 8 x 10 3/8. **Cols./Page:** 3. **Col. Width:** 2.25 inches. **Col. Depth:** 9 inches. **Key Personnel:** Sarah Clay, Publisher; Bonifacio Contreras, Publisher. **ISSN:** 1059-0536. **Subscription Rates:** $25; $35 Canada; $50 other countries; group discounts available. **Remarks:** Accepts advertising.
Ad Rates: BW: $900 **Circ:** 15,000
PCI: $55

FOXBORO, pop. 14,148.

E. MA. Norfolk Co. 22 mi. SW of Boston. Manufactures indicating and recording instruments.

14282 The Foxboro Reporter
The Sun Chronicle
36 Mechanic St.
PO Box 289
Foxboro, MA 02035

Community newspaper. **Founded:** 1884. **Freq:** Weekly (Thurs.). **Print Method:** Offset. **Trim Size:** 13 x 21 1/2. **Cols./Page:** 6. **Col. Width:** 2 1/16 inches. **Col. Depth:** 21 inches. **Key Personnel:** Jeffrey Peterson, Editor; Paul Rixon, Publisher; Edward J. Wilson, Advertising Mgr. **Subscription Rates:** $17 individuals. **Remarks:** Accepts advertising.
Ad Rates: GLR: $.335 **Circ:** ‡5,200
BW: $606.30
4C: $976.30
SAU: $4.70

14283 Time Warner Cable
85 E. Belcher Rd. Phone: (508)543-8650
Foxboro, MA 02035 Fax: (508)698-0601
Free: (800)452-8488

Founded: 1983. **Formerly:** CVI-Cablevision Industries. **Key Personnel:** Steve Grossman, General Mgr.; Mary Anderson, Sales and Marketing Mgr.; Brian Joyce, Chief Technician; Betty Maloney, Operations and Customer Service Mgr.; Wes Rea, Programming Mgr.; Laura Cornell, Office Mgr. **Cities Served:** Bristol, Middlesex, Norfolk, Plymouth, and Worcester countie s, MA.: subscribing households 72,600; 66 channels; 3 community access channels; 25 hours per week community access programming.

FRAMINGHAM, pop. 65,113.

NE MA. Middlesex Co. 21 mi. SW of Boston. State College. Residential. Retailing center.

14284 CIO Magazine
International Data Group
492 Old Connecticut Path Phone: (508)872-0080
PO Box 9208 Fax: (508)879-7784
Framingham, MA 01701-9208
Free: (800)942-4672

Publication for Chief Information Officers (CIOs) and other senior executives. **Subtitle:** The Magazine For Information Executives. **Founded:** 1987. **Freq:** 21/year. **Print Method:** Web offset. **Trim Size:** 8 1/8 x 10 3/4. **Cols./Page:** 3. **Key Personnel:** Lew McCreary, Editorial Director, phone (508)935-4618, mccreary@cio.com; Joe Levy, Publisher, phone (508)935-4274, fax (508)872-3759, jlevy@cio.com; Cathy O'Leary Hayes, Mktg. Vice Pres., phone (508)935-4521, fax (508)877-0618, chayes@cio.com; Abbie Lundberg, Editor, phone (508)935-4731, lundberg@cid.com. **ISSN:** 0894-9301. **Subscription Rates:** $75 individuals; $8 single issue. **URL:** http://www.cio.com.
Ad Rates: BW: $13,450 **Circ:** Paid ‡6,982
4C: $18,950 Controlled ‡90,000

14285 Computerworld
International Data Group
500 Old Connecticut Path Phone: (508)879-0700
Framingham, MA 01701 Fax: (508)875-8931

Newspaper for information systems executives. **Founded:** 1967. **Freq:** Weekly. **Print Method:** Offset. Uses mats. **Trim Size:** 10 3/8 x 13. **Key Personnel:** Paul Gillin, Editor; Mike Rogers, Publisher. **ISSN:** 0010-4841. **Subscription Rates:** $48 individuals. **Remarks:** Accepts advertising. **Available Online. URL:** http://www.computerworld.com.
Ad Rates: BW: $26,000 **Circ:** Paid ★**170,031**
4C: $30,775

14286 ComputerWorld Campus Edition
ComputerWorld Inc.
500 Old Connecticut Path Phone: (508)879-0700
Framingham, MA 01701-4649 Fax: (508)875-3202
Free: (800)343-6474

Magazine containing computer career information for graduating college and university students. **Founded:** 1988. **Freq:** 2/year. **Key Personnel:** Paul Gillin, Editor-in-Chief; John Corrigan, Vice President; Derek Hulitzky, derek_hulitzky@cw.com. **Subscription Rates:** Free to students. **Remarks:** Accepts advertising. **URL:** http://careers.computerworld.com.
Ad Rates: BW: $9,800 **Circ:** Non-paid **100,000**
4C: $12,400

14287 EOS/ESD Technology
The Brinton Group Inc.
49 Eaton Rd., Ste. 100
Framingham, MA 01701-2727

Publication covering electrostatic discharge products and services. **Subtitle:** The Magazine for ESD-Control Professionals in the Electronics Industry. **Founded:** 1987. **Freq:** Bimonthly. **Print Method:** Web offset. **Trim Size:** 8 1/2 x 11. **Cols./Page:** 3. **Col. Width:** 2 1/8 inches. **Col. Depth:** 10 inches. **Key Personnel:** James B. Brinton, Publisher; Lisa Gillette, Editor; Michael Newton, Circulation Mgr. **Subscription Rates:** $65. **Remarks:** Accepts advertising.
Ad Rates: BW: $4,373 **Circ:** Non-paid ‡31,000
4C: $5,265

14288 The Framingham Tab
Community Newspaper Company
254 2nd Ave. Phone: (781)433-7828
Needham, MA 02192-9114 Fax: (781)433-7835

Community newspaper (tabloid). **Founded:** Oct. 1986. **Freq:** Weekly (Tues.). **Print Method:** Offset. **Trim Size:** 10 x 16. **Cols./Page:** 7. **Col. Width:** 8 picas. **Key Personnel:** John Wilpers, Editor; Russel Pergament, Advertising Mgr.; Stephen Cummings, Publisher; Lisa Flicop, Editor. **URL:** http://townonline.com.
Circ: Non-paid 15,778

14289 The Gatepost
Framingham State College
100 State St. Phone: (508)626-4605
Framingham, MA 01701 Fax: (508)626-4939
Publication E-mail: pniessen@fsc.mass.edu

Collegiate newspaper. **Subtitle:** Independent Student Newspaper of Framingham State College. **Founded:** Mar. 1932. **Freq:** Weekly. **Trim Size:** 11 1/2 x 17. **Cols./Page:** 5. **Col. Width:** 1 15/16 inches. **Key Personnel:** Kerri Hosmer, Editor-in-Chief. **Available Online.**
Ad Rates: BW: $470 **Circ:** Free ‡2,500
PCI: $7

14290 Hellenic Chronicle
Hellenic Publishing
5-6 Franklin Commons Phone: (508)820-9700
Framingham, MA 01701-6637 Fax: (508)820-0952

Newspaper for the Greek-American community. **Founded:** 1950. **Freq:** Weekly (Thurs.). **Print Method:** Offset. **Cols./Page:** 6. **Col. Width:** 21 nonpareils. **Col. Depth:** 294 agate lines. **Key Personnel:** George Anagnostos, Managing Editor; Nancy Agris Savage, News/Foreign Editor; A.A. Agris, Publisher; Peter James Agris, Advertising Mgr. **Subscription Rates:** $25 individuals. **Remarks:** Accepts advertising.
Ad Rates: BW: $1,827 **Circ:** 21,252
4C: $2,167
SAU: $14.50

14291 InfoWorld Direct
International Data Group
5 Speen St. Phone: (508)879-0700
PO Box 9171 Fax: (508)875-8931
Framingham, MA 01701
Free: (800)343-4935

Magazine focusing on purchasing software and hardware products. **Freq:** Monthly. **Trim Size:** 10 x 13. **Remarks:** Accepts advertising.
Ad Rates: BW: $6,930 **Circ:** Paid 100,000

14292 Metrowest
Middlesex News Publishing Co.
33 New York Ave. Phone: (508)626-3800
Framingham, MA 01701 Fax: (508)626-4400

Community newspaper. **Freq:** Weekly (Fri.).
Circ: Non-paid ‡73,928

14293 The Middlesex News
Community Newspaper Company
33 York Ave. Phone: (508)626-3800
Framingham, MA 01701 Fax: (508)626-4400
Publisher E-mail: townonline.com

General newspaper. **Founded:** 1897. **Freq:** Daily (eve.). **Print Method:** Offset. **Cols./Page:** 6. **Col. Width:** 25 nonpareils. **Col. Depth:** 300 agate lines. **Key Personnel:** Richard A. Holmes, Editor; Bill Gulledge, Publisher; Mark O'Neil, Advertising Mgr. **Subscription Rates:** $156 individuals. **Remarks:** Accepts advertising. **Feature Editors:** Adam Gaffin, *Environmental, Medical, Science*, phone (508)626-3968; Jan Gardener, *City*, phone (508)626-3858; Jan Gardner, *Metro*, phone (508)626-3858; Tim Greene, *Political*, phone (508)626-3988; Rick Holmes, *News*, phone (508)626-3932; Art Illman, *Photo*, phone (508)626-3608; Lisa LaBlanca, *Education*, phone (508)626-3930; Rus Lodi, *Sports*, phone (508)626-3872; Paul McNamara, *Editorials*, phone (508)626-3932; Cate Prato, *Drama, Entertainment, Fashion, Features, Food, Garden/Home, Lifestyle, Movie, Music, Society, TV & Radio, Travel*, phone (508)626-3969; Rick Saia, *Saturday*, phone (508)626-3930; Maureen Sullivan, *Religion*, phone (508)626-4406; Neal Weinberg, *Financial/Business, Real Estate*, phone (508)626-3876.
Ad Rates: BW: $2677.5 **Circ:** Mon.-Fri. 47,974
4C: $3077.5 Sat. 33,316
SAU: $25 Sun. 41,220
PCI: $21.25

14294 Network World
International Data Group
161 Worcester Rd. Phone: (508)875-6400
PO Box 9172 Fax: (508)820-3467
Framingham, MA 01701-9172
Free: (800)622-1108

The newsweekly of enterprise network computing. **Subtitle:** The Newsweekly of Enterprise Network Computing. **Founded:** Mar. 24, 1986. **Freq:** Weekly (Mon.). **Print Method:** Offset. **Trim Size:** 10 9/16 x 13 1/4. **Cols./Page:** 5. **Col. Width:** 1 13/16 inches. **Col. Depth:** 14 inches. **Key Personnel:** John Gallant, Editor; Colin Ungaro, CEO; Ann Finn, Production Mgr.; Evilec Thibeault, Publisher. **ISSN:** 0887-7661. **Subscription Rates:** $95 individuals. **Remarks:** Accepts advertising. **Available Online. URL:** http://www.nwtusion.com. **Formerly:** Computer World on Communications; On Communications.
Ad Rates: BW: $21,950 **Circ:** ‡150,208
4C: $26,050

Southborough Villager - See Southborough

14295 Cablevision of Framingham
1253 Worcester Rd. Phone: (508)872-6300
Framingham, MA 01701 Fax: (508)875-1846

Formerly: Framingham Cable TV; Framingham Cablevision Associates. **Key Personnel:** Mike Klein, Program Dir., phone (508)875-5434. **Cities Served:** subscribing households 16,000; 80 channels; 2 community access channels.

14296 WDJM-FM - 91.3
Framingham State Coll. Phone: (508)626-4623
100 State St. Fax: (508)626-4939
Framingham, MA 01701-2460

Format: Alternative/New Music/Progressive. **Networks:** Independent. **Founded:** 1972. **Formerly:** WFSB-FM. **Operating Hours:** 9 a.m.-2 a.m.; 100% local. **Key Personnel:** Cris Chiaravallot, General Mgr.; Kerry Schmidt, Program Dir.; Melissa Burt, Asst. Program Dir.; L Lawrence Goldstein, Public Service Dir.; Jason Heasley, Music Dir.; Eileen Cronin, Public Relations. **Wattage:** 100.

14297 WKOX-AM - 1200
100 Mt. Wayte Ave. Phone: (508)820-2400
Framingham, MA 01702-5705 Fax: (508)820-2458

Format: News; Talk; Ethnic. **Networks:** ABC. **Founded:** 1947. **Operating Hours:** Continuous. **ADI:** Boston-Worcester,MA-Derry-Manchester,NH. **Key Personnel:** Scott Gibbons, Station Mgr. **Wattage:** 10,000. **Ad Rates:** $25-75 for 60 seconds.

FRANKLIN, pop. 18,217.

NE MA. Norfolk Co. 8 mi. E. of Milford. Residential.

14298 Collision Magazine
Jason Krusa
PO Box M Phone: (508)528-6211
Franklin, MA 02038-0822 Fax: (508)541-8600

Magazine discussing auto body shops, dealers, and insurance claims settling practices. **Founded:** 1960. **Freq:** 6/year. **Print Method:** Sheetfed offset. **Trim Size:** 8 1/8 x 10 7/8. **Cols./Page:** 3 and 4. **Col. Width:** 13 and 9 picas. **Col. Depth:** 10 inches. **ISSN:** 0739-7437. **Subscription Rates:** $18 overseas add $30 postage. **Remarks:** Accepts advertising. **Absorbed:** Tow Age Magazine.
Ad Rates: BW: $1,600 **Circ:** Paid ‡7,900
4C: $2,600 Controlled ‡3,000

14299 Glass Scene
Massachusetts Glass Dealers Association
PO Box 389 Phone: (508)541-8600
Franklin, MA 02038-0389 Fax: (508)541-8600

Trade publication covering news for glass installers who sell and repair architectural and auto glass. **Founded:** 1978. **Freq:** Quarterly. **Print Method:** Offset. **Trim Size:** 8 x 11. **Key Personnel:** Jay Kruza, Editor. **Subscription Rates:** $15. **Remarks:** Accepts advertising.
Ad Rates: BW: $650 **Circ:** Paid 1,200

14300 The Sharon Advocate
Norfolk Community Newspapers Inc.
1000 Franklin Village Dr. Phone: (508)528-2600
PO Box 612 Fax: (508)528-2676
Franklin, MA 02038
Community newspaper. **Founded:** 1873. **Freq:** Weekly (Thurs.). **Print Method:** Offset. **Trim Size:** 14 3/16 x 21 5/16. **Cols./Page:** 6. **Col. Width:** 2 1/16 inches. **Col. Depth:** 21 1/2 inches. **Key Personnel:** Melody Howard, Editor; Stuart Green, Managing Editor; Jack Shea, Publisher. **USPS:** 491-900. **Subscription Rates:** $17.50; $14 senior citizens; $21 out of area; $24 out of state. **Remarks:** Accepts advertising.
Ad Rates: GLR: $7.75 **Circ:** Paid 4,085
BW: $892.50 Non-paid 159
PCI: $6.50

14301 Wheelings -New England Mechanic
Jason Krusa
PO Box M Phone: (508)528-6211
Franklin, MA 02038-0822 Fax: (508)541-8600

Tabloid serving manufacturers, jobbers, auto dealers, and automotive repair technicians. **Founded:** Jan. 1972. **Freq:** 4/year. **Print Method:** Offset. **Trim Size:** 11 x 17. **Cols./Page:** 4. **Col. Width:** 27 nonpareils. **Col. Depth:** 224 agate lines. **Key Personnel:** J. A. Kruza, Editor; Mike Zingraff, Managing Editor. **Subscription Rates:** $22 in USA. **Remarks:** Accepts advertising.
Ad Rates: BW: $900 **Circ:** Paid ‡8,000
Controlled ‡1,000

14302 WGAO-FM - 88.3
99 Main St. Phone: (508)528-4210
Franklin, MA 02038 Fax: (508)541-1922

Format: Contemporary Christian; Eclectic; Album-Oriented Rock (AOR); Classic Rock; Alternative/New Music/Progressive. **Networks:** AP. **Owner:** Dean College, at above address. **Founded:** 1975. **Operating Hours:** 8 a.m.- 12 a.m. 10% network, 90% local. **Key Personnel:** Vic Michaels, General Mgr., phone (508)541-1623; Richard Pezzuolo, Contact, phone (508)541-1621. **Local Programs:** *Let's Talk*, Stefan Cline, (508)528-4210; *Sports Overtime*, Nakia Keizer, (508)528-4210. **Wattage:** 175. **Ad Rates:** Noncommercial.

GARDNER, pop. 17,900.

C. MA. Worcester Co. 58 mi. W. of Boston. Environmental control systems, molded plastics, foundry and machine shop products, steel and metal tubing, yarn. Dairy farms.

14303 WGAW-AM - 1340
PO Box 87 Phone: (508)632-1340
Gardner, MA 01440-0087

Format: Adult Contemporary. **Networks:** AP. **Founded:** 1946. **Key Personnel:** Don Wilson, General Mgr.; Mark Rossi, Contact. **Wattage:** 1000.

GLOUCESTER, pop. 27,768.

NE MA. Essex Co. On S. side of Cape Ann Peninsula, 28 mi. NE of Boston. Summer resort. Catching, canning, freezing and shipping of fish, especially cod, haddock, halibut, mackerel and ocean perch. Manufactures glue, nets and seines, ink, isinglass, cod liver oil, oiled clothing, paint, wooden boxes, textiles.

14304 Old-House Interiors
Gloucester Publishers
2 Main St. Phone: (978)283-3200
Gloucester, MA 01930-5726 Fax: (978)283-4629

Consumer magazine covering interior design. **Founded:** 1996. **Freq:** Quarterly. **Print Method:** Offset. **Trim Size:** 8 3/16 x 10 7/8. **Cols./Page:** 3. **Col. Width:** 42 nonpareils. **Key Personnel:** Patricia Poore, Editor; William O'Donnell, Publisher; Becky Bernie, National Sales Mgr. **ISSN:** 1079-3941. **Subscription Rates:** $18 individuals; $4.95 single issue. **Remarks:** Accepts advertising. **URL:** http://www.oldhouseinteriors.com.
Ad Rates: BW: $5,465 **Circ:** Paid 120,000
4C: $7,285

14305 Old-House Journal
DoveTale Publishers
2 Main St. Phone: (508)283-3200
Gloucester, MA 01930 Fax: (508)283-4629

Magazine containing practical articles about the restoration, decoration, and maintenance of houses built before 1940. **Founded:** Oct. 1973. **Freq:** Bimonthly. **Print Method:** Offset. **Trim Size:** 8 3/16 x 10 7/8. **Cols./Page:** and 3. **Key Personnel:** Patricia Poore, Editor; Bill O'Donnell, Publisher. **ISSN:** 0094-0178. **Subscription Rates:** $27 individuals; $4 single issue. **Remarks:** Accepts advertising.
Ad Rates: BW: $3,995 **Circ:** Paid 143,343
4C: $5,595

14306 Times
The Ottaway Newspapers
Whittemore St. Phone: (508)283-7000
Gloucester, MA 01930 Fax: (508)281-5748

General newspaper. **Founded:** 1857. **Freq:** Mon.-Sat. (eve.). **Print Method:** Offset. **Cols./Page:** 8. **Col. Width:** 22 nonpareils. **Col. Depth:** 294 agate lines. **Key Personnel:** William McCulloch, Editor; Frank O. King, Publisher. **Subscription Rates:** $45 individuals. **Remarks:** Accepts advertising.
Ad Rates: PCI: $10.08 **Circ:** Mon.-Sat. 11,646

14307 New England Cablevision Inc.
38 Blackburn Center Phone: (508)281-0811
Gloucester, MA 01930 Fax: (508)281-8679

Founded: 1982. **Key Personnel:** Henry Zacchini, General Mgr. **Cities Served:** subscribing households 12,500; 52 channels; 2 community access channels; 30 hours per week community access programming.

GRAFTON

14308 Spirit of Change Magazine
PO Box 410 Phone: (508)839-2228
Grafton, MA 01519 Fax: (508)839-1173

Consumer magazine covering holistic health and New Age issues. **Founded:** Oct. 1987. **Freq:** Bimonthly. **Print Method:** Web. **Trim Size:** 10 7/8 x 13 5/8. **Cols./Page:** 4. **Col. Width:** 2 1/4 inches. **Col. Depth:** 12 1/4 inches. **Key Personnel:** Carol Bedrosian, Editor and Publisher; Sosie Sagherian, Advertising Dir.; Linda Smolenski, General Mgr. **Subscription Rates:** $25 individuals; $5 single issue. **Remarks:** Accepts advertising.
Ad Rates: BW: $1,135 **Circ:** Combined 70,000
4C: $1,585

GREAT BARRINGTON, pop. 7,405.

W. MA. Berkshire Co. On Housatonic River, 20 mi. SW of Pittsfield. Summer resort. Paper mills; log homes. Manufactures nuclear components. Dairy, poultry farms.

14309 Berkshire Record
21 Elm St. Phone: (413)528-5380
Great Barrington, MA 01230 Fax: (413)528-9449
Publication E-mail: berkrec@bcn.net

Community newspaper. **Founded:** 1989. **Freq:** Weekly (Fri.). **Print Method:** Web offset. **Trim Size:** 14 x 23. **Cols./Page:** 6. **Col. Width:** 6 inches. **Col. Depth:** 21 1/2 inches. **Key Personnel:** Anthony Prisendorf, Publisher; Donna Jones, Editor; Jim Hurley, Advertising Mgr. **USPS:** 004-483. **Subscription Rates:** $22; $24 out of area. **Remarks:** Accepts advertising.
Ad Rates: BW: $1,100 **Circ:** ‡4,500
4C: $1,500
SAU: $9.10
CNU: $9.10
PCI: $7.90

14310 Hikane: The Capable Woman
PO Box 841
Great Barrington, MA 01230-0841

Magazine serving as a networking/grassroots tool for disabled lesbians and their "wimmin" allies. Available in print, cassette, and braille. **Founded:** 1989. **Freq:** Quarterly. **Print Method:** Offset. **Trim Size:** 8 1/2 x 11. **Subscription Rates:** $14; $24 institution.

14311 Orion
195 Main St. Phone: (413)528-4422
Great Barrington, MA 01230 Fax: (413)528-0676
Publication E-mail: orion@orionsociety.org
Publisher E-mail: orion@orionsociety.org

Magazine centering on issues related to nature. **Subtitle:** People and Nature. **Founded:** 1982. **Freq:** Quarterly. **Print Method:** Offset. **Trim Size:** 8 1/2 x 11. **Key Personnel:** George K. Russell, Editor; H. Emerson Blake, Managing Editor. **ISSN:** 1058-3130. **Subscription Rates:** $30 individuals; $30 institutions; $50 two years; $70 three years. **Remarks:** Advertising not accepted. **URL:** http://www.orionsociety.org. **Formerly:** Orion Nature Quarterly.
Circ: Paid ‡15,000
Controlled ‡200

14312 Southern Berkshire Shopper's Guide
35 Bridge St. Phone: (413)528-0095
PO Box 89 Fax: (413)528-4805
Great Barrington, MA 01230
Shopper. **Founded:** Apr. 15, 1968. **Freq:** Weekly (Wed.). **Print Method:** Offset. **Cols./Page:** 6. **Col. Width:** 20 nonpareils. **Col. Depth:** 224 agate lines. **Key Personnel:** John T. Raifstanger, Publisher; Jean Raifstanger, Advertising Mgr. **Remarks:** Accepts advertising.
Ad Rates: BW: $480 **Circ:** Controlled ‡19,500
PCI: $5 Free ‡5,500

14313 WSBS-AM - 860
Box 297 Phone: (413)528-0860
Great Barrington, MA 01230 Fax: (413)528-2162

Format: Adult Contemporary; Full Service. **Networks:** CNN Radio. **Owner:** Berkshire Broadcasting Co., Inc., at above address. **Founded:** 1956. **Operating Hours:** 5:30 a.m.-7 p.m.; 10% network, 90% local. **Key Personnel:** Donald A. Thurston, President; Richard Lindsay, News Dir.; Gerard Reardon, Program Dir. **Wattage:** 2700. **Ad Rates:** $11-20 for 30 seconds; $14-25 for 60 seconds. WNAW-AM, WMNB-FM, and WBBS-FM.

GREENFIELD†, pop. 18,436.

NW MA. Franklin Co. On Connecticut River, 20 mi. N. of Northampton. Franklin Co. (NW). On Connecticut River, 20 m N of Northampton. Manufactures dies, machine tools, grinding and finishing machinery, sterling silver tableware, shovels, rakes, paper boxes. Agriculture. Corn, cucumbers, squash, cabbage, apples, potatoes.

14314 The Athol/Orange Town Crier
The Town Crier Community Newspapers
PO Box 1435 Phone: (413)774-7226
Greenfield, MA 01302 Fax: (413)774-6809
Free: (800)448-9595
Publication E-mail: gtcrier@crocker.com
Publisher E-mail: printinc@vermontel.com

Community newspaper. **Founded:** 1987. **Freq:** Weekly (Fri.). **Print Method:** Offset. **Trim Size:** 11 5/16 x 15. **Cols./Page:** 8. **Col. Width:** 1 3/16 inches. **Col. Depth:** 13 3/4 inches. **Key Personnel:** Pat Finnell, Advertising Mgr., phone (802)257-7771, fax (802)257-2211. **Subscription Rates:** Free; $26 by mail. **Online:** ADONE. **URL:** http://www.adone.com/tcrier/.
Ad Rates: BW: $550 **Circ:** Free ♦12,268
PCI: $6.40

14315 The Greenfield Town Crier
The Town Crier Community Newspapers
PO Box 1435 Phone: (413)774-7226
Greenfield, MA 01302 Fax: (413)774-6809
Free: (800)448-9595
Publication E-mail: gtcrier@crocker.com
Publisher E-mail: printinc@vermontel.com

Community newspaper. **Founded:** 1967. **Freq:** Weekly (Fri.). **Print Method:** Offset. **Trim Size:** 11 5/16 x 15. **Cols./Page:** 8. **Col. Width:** 1 3/16 inches. **Col. Depth:** 13 3/4 inches. **Key Personnel:** Jim Gildea, Editor; Roger Miller, Publisher, phone (802)257-7777. **Subscription Rates:** Free; $26 by mail. **Online:** ADONE. **URL:** http://www.adone.com/tcrier/.
Ad Rates: BW: $700 **Circ:** Free ♦19,869
PCI: $7.40

14316 Markers
Association for Gravestone Studies
278 Main St., Ste. 207 Phone: (413)772-0836
Greenfield, MA 01301-3230
Publisher E-mail: ags@javanet.com

Scholarly journal covering gravestone history, art and folklore. **Founded:** 1979. **Freq:** Annual. **Key Personnel:** Richard E. Meyer, meyerr@wou.edu. **ISSN:** 0277-8726. **Subscription Rates:** $37 single issue. **Remarks:** Advertising not accepted.
Circ: Paid 200

14317 The Recorder
14 Hope St. Phone: (413)772-0261
PO Box 1367 Fax: (413)774-5511
Greenfield, MA 01302-1367
General newspaper. **Founded:** Feb. 1, 1792. **Freq:** Mon.-Sat. (morn.). **Print Method:** Offset. **Trim Size:** 13 3/4 x 22 3/4. **Cols./Page:** 6. **Col. Width:** 25 nonpareils. **Col. Depth:** 298 agate lines. **Key Personnel:** Tim Blagg, Editor; Kay Berenson, Publisher; Rich Fahey, Advertising Dir. **Subscription Rates:** $140.40 individuals. **Remarks:** Accepts advertising.
Ad Rates: SAU: $8.65 **Circ:** Mon.-Sat. 14,849

14318 WGAM-AM - 1520
267 Main St. Phone: (413)772-2522
PO Box 520 Fax: (413)772-2322
Greenfield, MA 01301

Format: Easy Listening. **Owner:** Radio Akutnik Inc., at above address. **Founded:** 1980. **Formerly:** WPOE-AM (1986); Howard Communication Co. **Operating Hours:** Sunrise-sunset; 80% network, 40% local. **Key Personnel:** Ed Skutnik, Station Mgr.; Ed Skutnik, General Sales Mgr.; Ed Skutnik, Contact; Ed Skutnik, News Dir. **Wattage:** 10,000. **Ad Rates:** $15-20 for 30 seconds; $20-40 for 60 seconds.

14319 WHAI-AM - 1240
PO Box 32 Phone: (413)774-4301
Greenfield, MA 01302 Fax: (413)773-5637

Format: Adult Contemporary. **Simulcasts:** WHAI-FM. **Networks:** CBS. **Founded:** 1938. **Operating Hours:** Continuous; 8% network, 92% local. **ADI:** Springfield, MA. **Key Personnel:** Ann Banash, General Mgr.; Jay Deane, Program Dir.; Chris Collins, News Dir.; Jeff Tirrell, Sports Dir.; Bob Diamond, Sales Mgr.; Jay Deane, Music Dir.; Amy Valinski, Contact. **Wattage:** 1000. **Ad Rates:** $7.50-21.65 for 15 seconds; $10.70-30.90 for 30 seconds; $14-38.60 for 60 seconds.

14320 WHAI-FM - 98.3
PO Box 32 Phone: (413)774-4301
Greenfield, MA 01302 Fax: (413)773-5637
E-mail: whai@celinet.com

Format: Adult Contemporary. **Simulcasts:** WHAI-AM. **Networks:** CBS. **Founded:** 1948. **Operating Hours:** Continuous; 8% network, 92% local. **ADI:** Springfield, MA. **Key Personnel:** Ann Banash, General Mgr.; Jay Fidanza, Program Dir.; Chris Collins, News Dir.; Jeff Tirrell, Sports Dir.; Bob Diamond, Sales Mgr.; Jay Deane, Music Dir.; Carrie Giard, Contact. **Wattage:** 3000. **Ad Rates:** $7.50-21.65 for 15 seconds; $10.70-30.90 for 30 seconds; $14-38.60 for 60 seconds.

14321 WRSI-FM - 95.3
158 Main St. Phone: (413)774-2321
PO Box 910 Fax: (413)772-6400
Greenfield, MA 01302

Format: Eclectic. **Simulcasts:** WMTT Wilmington, VT. **Founded:** 1981. **Operating Hours:** 24 hrs. **Key Personnel:** Jean O'Mealy, Contact. **Local Programs:** *Women of Note* 8:00 am - 11:00 am Saturday, Will Stanley. **Wattage:** 320. **Ad Rates:** $20-29 for 60 seconds. Combined advertising rates available with WSSH, WHDQ,WKXE, WNHV, WTSV. **URL:** http://www.wrsi.com.

HALIFAX

14322 Halifax/Plympton Reporter
MPG Newspapers
9 Long Pond Rd. Phone: (508)746-5555
PO Box 959 Fax: (508)747-2148
Plymouth, MA 02362-0959
Free: (800)242-0264
Publisher E-mail: newsroom@mpgnews.com

Community newspaper. **Founded:** 1984. **Freq:** Weekly (Thurs.). **Print Method:** Offset. **Trim Size:** 16 1/2 x 11. **Cols./Page:** 5. **Col. Width:** 21 nonpareils. **Col. Depth:** 224 agate lines. **Key Personnel:** Phyllis Hughes, Publisher, phughes@mpgnews.com. **Subscription Rates:** $20 in county; $32 out of area. **Remarks:** Accepts advertising. **URL:** http://www.mpgnews.com.
Ad Rates: GLR: $.49 **Circ:** Combined ♦1,734
BW: $576
4C: $976
PCI: $7.45

HAMILTON, pop. 6,960.

NE MA. Essex Co. 3 mi. NE of Wenham. Residential.

14323 Hamilton-Wenham Chronicle
Community Newspaper Company
152 Sylvan St. Phone: (978)739-8513
Danvers, MA 01923 Fax: (978)739-8501
Publication E-mail: hwchronicle@cnc.com

Community newspaper (tabloid). **Founded:** 1949. **Freq:** Weekly (Wed.). **Print Method:** Offset. **Trim Size:** 11 3/8 x 17. **Cols./Page:** 5. **Col. Width:** 2 1/16 inches. **Col. Depth:** 16 inches. **Key Personnel:** T.R. Wadsworth, Editor; Chuck Goodrich, Publisher; Jim Nolan, Advertising Dir. **USPS:** 068-550. **Subscription Rates:** $23 individuals; $33 out of area. **Remarks:** Accepts advertising.
Ad Rates: BW: $980 **Circ:** Paid 2,831
4C: $1,480 Free 163
SAU: $12.25
PCI: $12.25

HANOVER, pop. 11,358.

SE MA. Plymouth Co. 30 mi. S. of Boston. Residential.

14324 Hanover Branch
Associated Newspapers
7 Cabot Pl. Phone: (781)878-1111
PO Box 441 Fax: (781)878-3333
Stoughton, MA 02072
Publisher E-mail: aweeklies@aol.com

Community newspaper. **Founded:** 1908. **Freq:** Weekly (Thurs.). **Print Method:** Offset. **Cols./Page:** 6. **Col. Width:** 9.5 picas. **Col. Depth:** 16 inches. **Key Personnel:** Richard R. Dailey, Publisher. **Subscription Rates:** $10 individuals. **Remarks:** Accepts advertising.
Ad Rates: BW: $10.53 **Circ:** ‡1,750
4C: $10.77
PCI: $10.53

14325 Hanover Mariner
Mariner Newspapers
165 Enterprise Dr. Phone: (617)837-3500
Marshfield, MA 02050-2132 Fax: (617)837-4540
Free: (800)649-6661
Publisher E-mail: cmathis@cnc.com

Community newspaper. **Freq:** Weekly (Wed.). **Print Method:** Offset. **Trim Size:** 11 3/8 x 17. **Cols./Page:** 5. **Col. Width:** 2 1/8 inches. **Col. Depth:** 15 1/2 inches. **Key Personnel:** Margaret Smoragiewicz, Publisher; Judy McCaffrey Perry, Advertising Dir. **Subscription Rates:** $22. **Remarks:** Combined advertising rates available with other Mariner Newspapers.
Ad Rates: BW: $942.40 **Circ:** Paid 2,381
4C: $1,300.00 Non-paid 124
PCI: $8.25

HANSON

14326 Hanson Town Crier
Associated Newspapers
7 Cabot Pl. Phone: (781)878-1111
PO Box 441 Fax: (781)878-3333
Stoughton, MA 02072
Publisher E-mail: aweeklies@aol.com

Community newspaper. **Founded:** 1983. **Freq:** Weekly (Thurs.). **Print Method:** Offset. **Cols./Page:** 6. **Col. Width:** 9.5 picas. **Col. Depth:** 16 inches. **Key Personnel:** Richard R. Dailey, Publisher. **Subscription Rates:** $17.50. **Remarks:** Accepts advertising.
Ad Rates: PCI: $10.53 **Circ:** ‡1,388

HARWICH

14327 Harwich Oracle
Community Newspaper
5 Namskaket Rd. Phone: (508)398-0123
PO Box 2776 Fax: (508)760-3387
Orleans, MA 02653-6776
Free: (800)660-8999

Community newspaper. **Founded:** 1986. **Freq:** Weekly (Wed.). **Print Method:** Offset. **Trim Size:** 11 x 16 1/2. **Cols./Page:** 5. **Col. Width:** 21 inches. **Col. Depth:** 224 agate lines. **Key Personnel:** Eric Hartell, Editor; Jeanne Moore-Yount, Advertising Mgr. **Subscription Rates:** Free; $25 (mail). **Remarks:** Accepts advertising.
Ad Rates: GLR: $.50 **Circ:** Non-paid 3,425
BW: $564
4C: $1,164
PCI: $7.05

14328 WCCT-FM - 90.3
Pleasant Lake Ave. Phone: (508)432-4500
Harwich, MA 02645 Fax: (508)432-7916

Format: News; Eclectic. **Simulcasts:** Rebroadcasts WBUR-FM. **Networks:** National Public Radio (NPR). **Owner:** Cape Cod Regional Technical High School, at above address. **Founded:** 1989. **Operating Hours:** Continuous. **Key Personnel:** Burt Fisher, Manager, fischer@meol.mass.edu. **Wattage:** 800.

HATFIELD, pop. 3,045.

WC MA. Hampshire Co. 9 mi. E. of Williamsburg. Residential.

14329 Valley Advocate
87 School St. Phone: (413)247-9301
Hatfield, MA 01038-9732 Fax: (413)247-5439

Community newspaper. Prints editions for Greenfield, Northhampton, and Greater Springfield. **Founded:** 1973. **Freq:** Weekly (Wed.). **Print Method:** Offset. **Cols./Page:** 5. **Col. Width:** 11 picas. **Col. Depth:** 177 agate lines. **Key Personnel:** Christine Austin, Editor and Publisher, CAustin@newmassmedia.com; Geoffrey A. Robinson, Publisher, GRobinson@newmassmedia.com; DoHan Allen, Advertising Mgr., DAllen@newmassmedia.com. **Subscription Rates:** $30 individuals. **Remarks:** Accepts advertising. **URL:** http://www.valleyadvocate.com; http://www.newmassmedia.com.
Ad Rates: GLR: $1.71 **Circ:** Free 26,558

HAVERHILL, pop. 46,865.

NE MA. Essex Co. On Merrimack River, 33 mi. N. of Boston. Manufactures shoes, heels, soles, counters, plastics, chemicals leather goods, coin operated machines, paper boxboard, electric coils, machinery.

14330 The Haverhill Gazette
Havenhill Gazette
447 W. Lowell Ave. Phone: (508)374-0321
PO Box 991 Fax: (508)521-6970
Haverhill, MA 01831
Publication E-mail: hgazette@tiac.com

Community newspaper. **Founded:** 1821. **Freq:** Weekly (Thurs.). **Print Method:** Offset. **Cols./Page:** 5. **Col. Width:** 1 15/16 inches. **Col. Depth:** 12 3/4 inches. **Key Personnel:** Ellen Wolslegel, General Mgr. **Subscription Rates:** $20. **URL:** http://www.hgazette.com.
Ad Rates: SAU: $7.15 **Circ:** 8,000

14331 WXRV-FM - 92.5
30 How St. Phone: (508)374-4733
PO Box 1490 Fax: (508)373-8023
Haverhill, MA 01831

Format: Alternative/New Music/Progressive. **Networks:** Westwood One Radio. **Owner:** Northeast Broadcasting Co., at above address. **Founded:** 1959. **Formerly:** WLYT-FM (1996). **Operating Hours:** Continuous. **Key Personnel:** Joe Faletra, Operations Mgr.; Joanne Doody, Program Dir.; Mike Mullaney, Music Dir. **Wattage:** 25,000. **Ad Rates:** $65 for 60 seconds.

HINGHAM

14332 Hingham Journal
The Hingham
73 South St. Phone: (617)749-0031
Hingham, MA 02043 Fax: (617)740-8955

Community newspaper. **Freq:** Weekly. **Key Personnel:** Henry W. Bosworth, Jr., Editor and Publisher.

14333 Hingham Mariner
Mariner Newspapers
165 Enterprise Dr. Phone: (617)837-3500
Marshfield, MA 02050-2132 Fax: (617)837-4540
Free: (800)649-6661
Publisher E-mail: cmathis@cnc.com

Community newspaper. **Freq:** Weekly (Thurs.). **Print Method:** Offset. **Cols./Page:** 6. **Col. Width:** 2 1/8 inches. **Col. Depth:** 20.5 inches. **Key Personnel:** Margaret Smoragiewicz, Publisher; Judy McCaffrey Perry, Advertising Dir. **Subscription Rates:** $22. **Remarks:** Combined advertising rates available with other Mariner Newspapers.
Ad Rates: GLR: $11.78 **Circ:** Paid 4,038
BW: $1,448.94 Non-paid 166
4C: $1,800.00
PCI: $8.25

HOLBROOK

14334 The Holbrook Sun
Mariner Newspapers
PO Box 355 Phone: (617)767-4000
Holbrook, MA 02343 Fax: (617)849-3319
Publisher E-mail: cmathis@cnc.com

Community newspaper. **Founded:** Apr. 1958. **Freq:** Weekly (Wed.). **Print Method:** Offset. **Trim Size:** 8 1/2 x 11. **Cols./Page:** 4 and 6. **Col. Width:** 14.5 and 9 picas. **Col. Depth:** 15 1/2 inches. **USPS:** 247-120. **Subscription Rates:** $20. **Remarks:** Accepts advertising.
Ad Rates: BW: $767.25 **Circ:** Paid 1,871
4C: $1,167.25 Non-paid 173
PCI: $8.25

14335 Holbrook Times
Associated Newspapers
7 Cabot Pl. Phone: (781)878-1111
PO Box 441 Fax: (781)878-3333
Stoughton, MA 02072
Publisher E-mail: aweeklies@aol.com

Community newspaper. **Founded:** 1929. **Freq:** Weekly (Wed.). **Print Method:** Offset. **Cols./Page:** 6. **Col. Width:** 9.5 picas. **Col. Depth:** 16 inches. **Key Personnel:** Richard R. Dailey, Publisher. **Subscription Rates:** $17.50. **Remarks:** Accepts advertising.
Ad Rates: BW: $10.53 **Circ:** Paid ‡1,446
4C: $10.77
PCI: $10.53

HOLDEN, pop. 13,750.

C. MA. Worcester Co. 8 mi. NNW of Worcester.

14336 The Landmark
The Holden Landmark Corp.
1650 Main St. Phone: (508)829-5981
PO Box 546 Fax: (508)829-5984
Holden, MA 01520
Publisher E-mail: editor@thelandmark.com

Community newspaper serving a five town region. **Founded:** Jan. 1976. **Freq:** Weekly. **Print Method:** Offset. **Trim Size:** 11 x 16. **Cols./Page:** 6. **Col. Width:** 1 9/16 inches. **Col. Depth:** 15 1/2 inches. **Key Personnel:** Joanne G. Root, Editor and Publisher, editor@thelandmark.com; Sharon Morgan, Contact; Elaine Real, Contact. **ISSN:** 3039-3000. **Subscription Rates:** $23 individuals; $27 out of state; $14 students; $25 out of state senior citizens; $15 students. **Remarks:** Accepts advertising. **Available Online.** **URL:** http://www.thelandmark.com. **Alt. Formats:** Microform. **Formerly:** The Holden Landmark.
Ad Rates: BW: $805.44 **Circ:** ‡8,905
4C: $1,197.39
SAU: $11.76
PCI: $8.39

HOLLISTON, pop. 12,622.

NE MA. Middlesex Co. 12 mi. W. of Quincy. Residential.

14337 The Holliston Tab
Community Newspaper Company
254 2nd Ave. Phone: (781)433-7828
Needham, MA 02192-9114 Fax: (781)433-7835

Community newspaper (tabloid). **Founded:** 1988. **Freq:** Weekly (Tues.). **Print Method:** Offset. **Trim Size:** 10 x 16. **Cols./Page:** 7. **Col. Width:** 8 picas. **Key Personnel:** John Wilpers, Editor; Russel Pergament, Advertising Mgr.; Stephen Cummings, Publisher; Lisa Flicop, Editor. **URL:** http://townonline.com. **Formerly:** The Ashland Holliston Gazette.
Circ: Non-paid 3,447

14338 WHHB-FM - 91.5
Holliston High School
Holliston, MA 01746
E-mail: whhb@vsq.net

Format: Eclectic. **Founded:** 1979. **Operating Hours:** Daily, 6:00 am - 7:30 am, 2:00 pm - 10:00 pm. **Key Personnel:** William Curboy, General Mgr. **Wattage:** 10. **Ad Rates:** Noncommercial. **URL:** http://www. listen.to/whhb.

HOLYOKE, pop. 44,678.

SW MA. Hampden Co. On Connecticut River, 10 mi. N. of Springfield. Prominent in the manufacturing of fine writing papers and paper converting. Manufactures air compressors, air conditioners, electronics, cotton, silk, rayon, synthetic fabrics, fabricated steel products, leather belting, detergent, optical and paper mill equipment, roller chains, rubber products, sporting goods.

14339 Tracings
Sisters of Providence
Gamelin St. Phone: (413)536-7511
Holyoke, MA 01040-4083 Fax: (413)536-7917

Tabloid spreading mission awareness and reporting on the activities of the Sisters of Providence. **Founded:** 1980. **Freq:** Quarterly. **Key Personnel:** Patricia St. Amand, Editor. **Subscription Rates:** Free. **Remarks:** Advertising not accepted.
Circ: Free ‡3,250

14340 WCCH-FM - 103.5
303 Homestead Ave. Phone: (413)552-2488
Holyoke, MA 01040 Fax: (413)534-8975

Owner: Holyoke Community College, at above address, (413)552-2600. **Operating Hours:** 6 a.m.-11 p.m. **Key Personnel:** Steven J. Knachel, General Mgr. **Wattage:** 10. **Ad Rates:** Noncommercial.

14341 WRNX-FM - 100.9 FM
98 Lower Westfield Rd., 3rd Fl. Phone: (413)536-1105
Holyoke, MA 01040-2712 Fax: (413)536-1153
Free: (800)977-1009
E-mail: wrnx@javanet.com

Format: Adult Album Alternative. **Networks:** AP. **Founded:** 1963. **Formerly:** WTTT-AM; Hampshire County Broadcasting, Inc. **Operating Hours:** 8:30a.m.-5:00p.m. **Key Personnel:** Tom Davis, Manager; Dave Withaus, Program Dir.; Bruce Stebbins, Operations Mgr.; Lesa Poplawski, Traffic Mgr. **Local Programs:** *Good Sports*, Rob Burke; *Swaps*, Brian McCullough; *Your Money Matters*, Rob Burke. **Wattage:** 5000.

HUBBARDSTON

14342 New England Golf
New England Golfer Magazine, Inc.
148 Old Westminster Rd. Phone: (978)928-5300
Hubbardston, MA 01452 Fax: (508)840-3209

Regional golf magazine covering six New England states. **Founded:** Aug. 1990. **Freq:** Monthly. **Print Method:** Web offset. **Trim Size:** 11 x 14 1/2. **Key Personnel:** Marx Mitchell, Publisher; Tom Davis, Editor. **Subscription Rates:** $12. $1.75 single issue. **Remarks:** Accepts advertising.
Ad Rates: BW: $1,500 **Circ:** Paid 38,000
4C: $2,000 Controlled 15,000

HUDSON, pop. 16,408.

NE MA. Middlesex Co. 5 mi. NW of Malboro. Manufactures footwear, aircraft parts and auxiliary equipment, woolens, rubber products, hand and edge tools, electronic equipment, lumber, nonferous castings, machine parts. Truck, poultry, fruit, dairy farms.

14343 A-R Cable Investments, Inc.
577 Main St. Phone: (508)562-3885
Hudson, MA 01749 Fax: (508)562-7591

Owner: Cablevision Systems Corp., 1 Media Crossways, Woodbury, NY 11797, (516)364-8450, Fax: (516)496-1780. **Formerly:** A-R Cable Services Inc. **Key Personnel:** Audrey M. Hall, General Mgr., phone (978)562-1675, ahall@cablevision.com; David Green, Dir., Govt. Relations, dgreen@cablevision.com; Carl Andersen, Dir. of Sales/Marketing, canders1@cablevision.com; Tom Garcia, Dir. of Engineering, phone (978)562-1675, tgarcia@cablevision.com. **Cities Served:** Acton, Hudson, Maynard, Stow, Sudbury, MA: subscribing households 18,708; 69 channels; 2 community access channels.

14344 Cablevision of Suburban Massachusetts
577 Main St. Phone: (508)562-1675
Hudson, MA 01749 Fax: (508)562-7591

Owner: Cablevision Systems Corp., 1 Media Crossways, Woodbury, NY 11797, (516)364-8450, Fax: (516)496-1780. **Formerly:** Adams-Russell Cablevision. **Key Personnel:** Audrey M. Hall, General Mgr.; David Green, Asst. Gen. Mgr.; Bob Lindenfelzer, Dir. of Sales 1 Mkt.; Tom Garcia, Dir. of Engineering; Rob Travers, Dir. of Programming. **Cities Served:** Acton, Ashburnham, Ashby, Ayer, Bedford, Belmont, Boxborough, Braintree, Carlisle, Concord, Danvers, Fitchburg, Framingham, Gardner, Georgetown, Groveland, Haverhill, Hudson, Leominster, Lexington, Lincoln, Littleton, Lunenberg, Lynnfield, Maynard, Norwood, Peabody, Shirley, Stow, Sudbury, Templeton, Townsend, Tyngsborough, Westminster, Westwood, MA: subscribing households 185,000; 65 channels; 17 community access channels.

14345 WHSH-TV - 66
71 Parmenter Rd. Phone: (508)562-0660
Hudson, MA 01749 Fax: (508)562-1166

Format: Commercial TV. **Networks:** Home Shopping Network. **Owner:** USA Broadcasting, Inc., 1 HSN Dr., Saint Petersburg, FL 33729, (813)572-8585, Fax: (813)572-1488. **Founded:** Feb. 12, 1985. **Formerly:** WVJV-TV. **Operating Hours:** Continuous; 92% network, 8% local. **ADI:** Boston-Worcester,MA-Derry-Manchester,NH. **Key Personnel:** Francesca Bryden, Operations Mgr.; Mark Arpino, Chief Engineer.

HYANNIS, pop. 6,847.

E. MA. Barnstable Co. 45 mi. SE of Boston. Manufactures lumber, packaging machinery, bayberry candles. Fisheries. Summer resort. Agriculture. Cranberries.

14346 The Barnstable Patriot
The Barnstable Patriot Newspaper, Inc.
4 Barnstable Rd. Phone: (508)771-1427
PO Box 1208 Fax: (508)790-3997
Hyannis, MA 02601
Publication E-mail: barnpat@cape.com

Community newspaper. **Founded:** June 26, 1830. **Freq:** Weekly (Thurs.). **Print Method:** Offset. **Cols./Page:** 6. **Col. Width:** 21 nonpareils. **Col. Depth:** 126 agate lines. **Key Personnel:** David Still II, Editor; Robert F. Sennott, Jr., Co-Publisher; Anne Gile Sennott, Co-Publisher; Lucinda S. Harrison, Advertising Dept. **Subscription Rates:** $25. **Remarks:** Accepts advertising. **URL:** http://www.barnstablepatriot.com.
Ad Rates: BW: $1,212.75 **Circ:** ‡3,200
PCI: $9.90

14347 Cape Cod Times
319 Main St. Phone: (508)775-1200
Hyannis, MA 02601 Fax: (508)775-7337

General newspaper. **Founded:** 1936. **Freq:** Mon.-Sun. (morn.). **Print Method:** Offset. **Trim Size:** 13 x 21 1/4. **Cols./Page:** 6. **Col. Width:** 12 1/2 picas. **Col. Depth:** 21 1/4 inches. **Key Personnel:** William J. Breisky, Editor; Timothy O. White, Managing Editor; Scott Himstead, Publisher; Peter Meyer, General Mgr.; Gloria Bowman, Advertising Dir.; Donald Waterman, Circulation Dir. **USPS:** 089-120. **Subscription Rates:** $130; $78 Sunday only. **Remarks:** Accepts advertising. Monday-Saturday: GLR: $2.57; BW: $3,474.38; 4C: $3,764.38; PCI: $27.25; SAU: $27.25; Sunday: SAU: $31.88; PCI: $31.88. **Feature Editors:** Alicia Blaisdell-Bannon, *Lifestyle*; William Higgins, *Sports*; Tim Miller, *Entertainment*; William Smith, *Editorials*, phone (508)775-1200; Mark Sullivan, *News*.
Circ: Mon.-Sat. ★53,098
Sun. ★64,636

14348 WCIB-FM - 101.9
154 Barnstable Rd. Phone: (508)778-2888
Hyannis, MA 02601 Fax: (508)778-9651
Free: (877)COOL102
E-mail: cool@capecod.net

Format: Classic Rock. **Owner:** Radio Falmouth, Inc., at above address. **Founded:** 1971. **Operating Hours:** Continuous. **ADI:** Boston-Worcester,MA-Derry-Manchester,NH. **Key Personnel:** Albert Makkay, President; Dana Panepinto, Station Mgr.; Mark Schmit, Sales Mgr.; Albert J. Makkay, General Mgr.; Steve Soloman, Operations Mgr. **Wattage:** 50,000. **Ad Rates:** Advertising accepted; rates available upon request.

14349 WOCN-FM - 103.9
760 Main St. Phone: (508)771-1224
Hyannis, MA 02601 Fax: (508)775-2605
E-mail: wocn@hotmail.com

Format: Adult Contemporary. **Networks:** CBS. **Owner:** Cape Cod Broadcasting Corp., at above address. **Founded:** 1994. **Former name:** WATB-FM (1994). **Operating Hours:** Continuous. **Key Personnel:** Gregory D. Bone, Owner/General Mgr.; William H. Densberger, Marketing Dir.; Steven Colella, Sales Mgr.; Wayne White, Operations Mgr. **Wattage:** 3000. **Ad Rates:** $45 per unit. **URL:** http://www.ocean104.com.

14350 WPXC-FM - 102.9
154 Barnstable Rd. Phone: (508)778-2888
Hyannis, MA 02601-2930 Fax: (508)778-9651

Format: Album-Oriented Rock (AOR); Classic Rock. **Networks:** Independent. **Owner:** Albert Makkay, at above address. **Founded:** 1987. **Operating Hours:** Continuous. **ADI:** Boston-Worcester,MA-Derry-Manchester,NH. **Key Personnel:** Albert Makkay, General Mgr.; Bill Lowell, News Dir.; Peter Winfield, Station Mgr.; Brad Goodwin, General Sales Mgr.; Suzanne Tonnaire, Program Dir. **Local Programs:** *Home Grown*, Suzanne Tonnaire, (508)778-2888. **Wattage:** 50,000.

14351 WQRC-FM - 99.9
737 W. Main St. Phone: (508)771-1224
Hyannis, MA 02601-3499 Fax: (508)775-2605

Format: Full Service; Adult Contemporary. **Networks:** AP. **Founded:** 1970. **Operating Hours:** Continuous; 2% network, 98% local. **ADI:** Boston-Worcester,MA-Derry-Manchester,NH. **Key Personnel:** Gregory D. Bone, General Mgr.; Janet Birchfeld, Production Dir.; Matt Pitta, News Dir.; William H. Denuberger, Contact; Stephen M. Colella, Sales Mgr.; Wayne W. White, Program Dir. **Wattage:** 50,000. **Ad Rates:** $60-100 per unit.

14352 WYST-FM - 93.5
745 W. Main St. Phone: (508)760-5252
Hyannis, MA 02601 Fax: (508)760-5353

Format: Contemporary Hit Radio (CHR). **Networks:** Westwood One Radio. **Owner:** Boch Broadcasting, at above address. **Founded:** 1989. **Formerly:** WFXR-FM (1996); WJCO-FM (1998). **Operating Hours:** Continuous. **Key Personnel:** Randy Bush, General Mgr.; Diane Rundle, Sales Mgr.; Chris Boles, Program Mgr., phone (508)775-5678, fax (508)775-3420. **Wattage:** 3000 ERP.

HYDE PARK

14353 Hyde Park Mattapan Tribune
Tribune Publishing Co.
1261 Hyde Park Ave. Phone: (617)361-6500
Hyde Park, MA 02136 Fax: (617)361-8909

Newspaper. **Founded:** 1935. **Freq:** Weekly (Thurs.). **Print Method:** Offset. Uses mats. **Cols./Page:** 9. **Col. Width:** 9 1/2 picas. **Col. Depth:** 308 agate lines. **Key Personnel:** Daniel J. Horgan, Publisher; Alice O'Leary, Editor. **Subscription Rates:** $15 individuals. **Remarks:** Accepts advertising.
Ad Rates: GLR: $.52 **Circ:** Paid ‡5,330
PCI: $7 Free ‡539

Jamaica Plain/Roxbury Citizen - See Jamaica Plain

Milton Record Transcript - See Milton

INDIAN ORCHARD

14354 Titanic Commutator
Titanic Historical Society, Inc.
PO Box 51053 Phone: (413)543-4770
Indian Orchard, MA 01151-0053
Publication E-mail: titanicinfo@mail.titanic1.org

Journal spotlighting historical ocean liners, including White Star Line Titanic. **Founded:** Sept. 1963. **Freq:** Quarterly. **Print Method:** Offset. **Trim Size:** 8-1/2 x 11. **Col. Width:** 3 1/2 inches. **Col. Depth:** 10 inches. **Key Personnel:** Karen Kamuda; Ed Kamuda. **ISSN:** 0040-8182. **Subscription Rates:** $40 individuals. **Remarks:** Accepts advertising.
Circ: (Not Reported)

IPSWICH, pop. 11,158.

NE MA. Essex Co. 25 mi. N. of Boston. Summer resort. Manufactures electronic and electrical products, leather. Shellfish industries.

14355 Georgetown Record
Community Newspaper Company
2 Washington St. Phone: (508)356-5141
Ipswich, MA 01938 Fax: (508)356-9188
Free: (800)924-5141

Community newspaper (tabloid). **Founded:** 1983. **Freq:** Weekly (Wed.). **Print Method:** Offset. **Trim Size:** 11 3/8 x 17. **Cols./Page:** 5. **Col. Width:** 2 1/16 inches. **Col. Depth:** 16 inches. **Key Personnel:** Ted Wadsworth, Editor; Chuck Goodrich, Publisher; John Vistorino, Advertising Dir. **USPS:** 746-610. **Subscription Rates:** $20; $15 students; $33 out of area.
Circ: Paid 1,646
Free 151

14356 Ipswich Chronicle
55 Market St. Phone: (978)412-1800
Ipswich, MA 01938 Fax: (978)412-1801
Publisher E-mail: ipschronicle@chc.com

Community newspaper (tabloid). **Founded:** 1872. **Freq:** Weekly (Thurs.). **Print Method:** Offset. **Trim Size:** 11 3/8 x 17. **Cols./Page:** 5. **Col. Width:** 2 1/16 inches. **Col. Depth:** 16 inches. **Key Personnel:** Susan Hershey, Editor; Chuck Goodrich, Publisher; Jim Nolan, Advertising Dir. **USPS:** 269-640. **Subscription Rates:** $19 individuals; $14 students; $31 out of area. **Remarks:** Accepts advertising.
Ad Rates: BW: $980 **Circ:** Paid 4,615
4C: $1,480 Free 351
PCI: $12.25

14357 Perspectives on Science and Christian Faith
American Scientific Affiliation
PO Box 668 Phone: (978)356-5656
Ipswich, MA 01938 Fax: (978)356-4375
Publisher E-mail: asa@newl.com

Academic science and Christian theology journal. **Subtitle:** Journal of the ASA. **Founded:** 1949. **Freq:** Quarterly. **Print Method:** Offset. **Trim Size:** 8 1/2 x 11. **Cols./Page:** 2. **Col. Width:** 19 picas. **Col. Depth:** 22 picas. **Key Personnel:** Dr. John W. Haas, Jr., Editor; Lyn Berg, Managing Editor. **ISSN:** 0892-2675. **Subscription Rates:** $30 individuals; $45 institutions; $8 single issue. **Formerly**: Journal of the American Scientific Affiliation (1987).
Ad Rates: BW: $410 **Circ:** ‡2,800
PCI: $35

JAMAICA PLAIN

14358 Arnoldia
Harvard University
125 Arbor Way Phone: (617)524-1718
Jamaica Plain, MA 02130-2795 Fax: (617)524-1418
Publication E-mail: arnoldia@arnarb.harvard.edu
Publisher E-mail: arnarb@harvard.edu

Trade magazine of the Arnold Arboretum covering horticulture, botany, and the history of landscape design. **Subtitle:** Magazine of the Arnold Arboretum. **Founded:** 1911. **Freq:** Quarterly. **Print Method:** Offset. **Key Personnel:** Karen Madsen, Editor, khmadsen@arnarb.harvard.edu. **ISSN:** 0042-633. **Subscription Rates:** $20 individuals; $25 out of country; $5 single issue. **Remarks:** Advertising not accepted. **Formerly**: Bulletin of Public Information.
Circ: 4,450

14359 Jamaica Plain/Roxbury Citizen
Tribune Publishing Co.
1261 Hyde Park Ave. Phone: (617)361-6500
Hyde Park, MA 02136 Fax: (617)361-8909

Newspaper. **Founded:** 1935. **Freq:** Weekly (Thurs.). **Print Method:** Offset. Uses mats. **Cols./Page:** 9. **Col. Width:** 9 1/2 picas. **Col. Depth:** 308 agate lines. **Key Personnel:** Daniel J. Horgan, Jr, Publisher; Alice O'Leary, Editor. **Subscription Rates:** $15 individuals. **Remarks:** Accepts advertising.
Ad Rates: GLR: $.52 **Circ:** ‡3,700
SAU: $7

14360 The Rhode Island Parents' Paper
The Parents' Plus, Inc.
670 Centre St., Ste. 9, 3rd Fl. Phone: (617)522-1515
Jamaica Plain, MA 02130 Fax: (617)522-1694
Free: (800)733-3771
Publication E-mail: ripp@parentsplus.com

Newsmagazine for parents of young children. **Founded:** Aug. 1989. **Freq:** Monthly. **Print Method:** Web offset. **Trim Size:** 10 x 12 3/8. **Cols./Page:** 4. **Col. Width:** 2 3/8 inches. **Col. Depth:** 12 3/8 inches. **Key Personnel:** Jodi Leavy, Reg. Sales Dir., leavy@parentsplus.com. **Subscription Rates:** $16. **Remarks:** Accepts advertising. **URL:** http://www.parenting-qa.com; http://www.parentsplus.com.
Ad Rates: GLR: $15 **Circ:** Paid 71
BW: $1,465 Free 35,000
4C: $1,965
PCI: $41.50

14361 Sojourner
Sojourner Feminist Institute, Inc.
42 Seaverns Ave. Phone: (617)524-0415
Jamaica Plain, MA 02130-2865
Publication E-mail: info@sojourner.org; sojourn@tiac.net

Magazine covering political, cultural, and social issues from a wide range of feminist perspectives. **Subtitle:** The Women's

Forum. **Founded:** Sept. 1975. **Freq:** Monthly. **Print Method:** Offset. **Trim Size:** 11 x 16. **Cols./Page:** 5. **Col. Width:** 1 7/8 inches. **Col. Depth:** 15 inches. **Key Personnel:** Stephanie Poggi, Editor, spoggi@sojourner.org; Christa Lyoni, Adver., advertising@sojourner.org; Kate Hogan, Exec. Dir., kate@sojourner.org. **ISSN:** 0191-8699. **Subscription Rates:** $21 individuals; $31 institutions. **Remarks:** Color advertising not accepted. **Alt. Formats:** Audio tape; CD-ROM, Softline Information.
Ad Rates: GLR: $24 **Circ:** 40,000
PCI: $22

KINGSTON

14362 Kingston Independent Voice
Mariner Newspapers
165 Enterprise Dr. Phone: (617)837-3500
Marshfield, MA 02050-2132 Fax: (617)837-4540
Free: (800)649-6661
Publisher E-mail: cmathis@onc.com

Community newspaper. **Freq:** Weekly (Wed.). **Print Method:** Offset. **Trim Size:** 11 3/8 x 17. **Cols./Page:** 5. **Col. Width:** 2 1/8 inches. **Col. Depth:** 16 inches. **Key Personnel:** Margaret Smoragiewicz, Publisher; Judy McCaffrey Perry, Advertising Dir. **Subscription Rates:** Free. **Remarks:** Combined advertising rates available with other Mariner Newspapers.
Ad Rates: GLR: $11.78 **Circ:** ‡3,000
BW: $942.40
4C: $1,300.00
PCI: $8.25

14363 Kingston Reporter
MPG Newspapers
9 Long Pond Rd. Phone: (508)746-5555
PO Box 959 Fax: (508)747-2148
Plymouth, MA 02362-0959
Free: (800)242-0264
Publisher E-mail: newsroom@mpgnews.com

Community newspaper. **Founded:** 1984. **Freq:** Weekly (Thurs.). **Print Method:** Offset. **Cols./Page:** 5. **Col. Width:** 2 inches. **Key Personnel:** Phyllis Hughes, Publisher, phughes@mpgnews.com. **Subscription Rates:** Free; $32 by mail. **Remarks:** Accepts advertising. **URL:** http://www.mpgnews.com.
Ad Rates: GLR: $.53 **Circ:** Combined ♦**4,047**
BW: $624
4C: $1,024
PCI: $7.60

14364 South Shore Baby Journal
Riverside Publishing
2 Riverside Dr. Phone: (781)585-7472
Kingston, MA 02364
Consumer magazine covering parenting, children, and family life. **Founded:** Sept. 1991. **Freq:** Monthly. **Trim Size:** 10 x 16. **Cols./Page:** 5. **Col. Width:** 2 inches. **Col. Depth:** 16 inches. **Key Personnel:** Barbara Chandler, Editor and Publisher. **Subscription Rates:** $9 individuals. **Remarks:** Accepts advertising.
Ad Rates: BW: $995 **Circ:** Combined 16,000

LAWRENCE, pop. 63,175.

NE MA. Essex Co. On Merrimack River, 27 mi. NW of Boston. Manufactures electronics, paper products, rubber products, leather goods, textiles, rugs, shoes, soap, chemicals, mattresses, plastics, machinery, boxes, boats, furniture, cosmetics.

14365 The Eagle-Tribune
Eagle-Tribune
PO Box 100 Phone: (508)685-1000
Lawrence, MA 01842 Fax: (508)685-1588
Publication E-mail: news@eagletribune.com

General newspaper. **Founded:** 1868. **Freq:** Daily (eve.), Sat. and Sun. (morn.). **Print Method:** Offset. **Trim Size:** 13 x 21 1/2. **Cols./Page:** 6. **Col. Width:** 2 1/16 inches. **Col. Depth:** 21 1/2 inches. **Key Personnel:** Daniel Warner, Editor, phone (978)685-1000, fax (978)687-6045, dwarner@eagletribune.com; Irving E. Rogers III, Publisher; Vincent P. Cottone, Advertising Dir.; Andrew Eick, Circulation Mgr. **Subscription Rates:** $182; $250 by mail. **URL:** http://www.eagletribune.com. **Formerly:** Lawrence Eagle-Tribune (1991). **Feature Editors:** Russ Conway, *Sports*, nonway@eagletribune.com; Ken Johnson, *Editorials*, kjohnson@eagletribune.com; John Macone, *State*, jmacone@eagletribune.com; Susan Scully, *Art, Features*, sscully@eagletribune.com; Marjory Sherman, *Medical*, msherman@; Alan White, *City*, awhite@eagletribune.com.
Ad Rates: GLR: $1.90 **Circ:** Mon.-Sat. ★**55,491**
BW: $3,857 Sun. ★**60.603**
4C: $4,386
SAU: $28.46
PCI: $29.90

14366 The Long Story
18 Eaton St. Phone: (978)686-7638
Lawrence, MA 01843-1110
Literary magazine covering fiction and poetry. **Founded:** Apr. 1983. **Freq:** Annual. **Print Method:** Offset. **Trim Size:** 5 1/2 x 8 1/2. **Cols./Page:** 1. **Key Personnel:** R. P. Burham, Editor, rpbtls@aol.com. **ISSN:** 0741-4242. **Subscription Rates:** $6 individuals; $11 two years. **Remarks:** Advertising not accepted.
Circ: Combined 1,100

14367 Continental Cablevision
92 Glenn St. Phone: (508)687-2288
Lawrence, MA 01843 Fax: (508)687-7932
E-mail: ccnctv3@aol.com

Owner: Continental Cablevision Inc., The Pilot House, Lewis Wharf, Boston, MA 02110. **Founded:** 1973. **Key Personnel:** Brian Lambert, General Mgr.; Brian Bane, Technioal Operations Mgr.; Cathy Maloney, Community Relations; Barrett Lester, Programming Mgr. **Cities Served:** Lawrence, Methvew, North Andover, MA: subscribing households 34,000; 64 channels; 1 community access channel; 10 hours per week community access programming.

LEE, pop. 6,247.

W. MA. Berkshire Co. 3 mi. E. of Intelaken. Residential. Industrial.

14368 The Berkshire Penny Saver
J.W. McWhirk Publishers, Inc.
14 Park Pl. Phone: (413)243-2341
PO Box 300 Fax: (413)243-4662
Lee, MA 01238-0300
Shopper. **Founded:** June 21, 1963. **Freq:** Weekly (Tues.). **Print Method:** Offset. **Trim Size:** 10 1/4 x 12 1/2. **Cols./Page:** 6. **Col. Width:** 21 nonpareils. **Col. Depth:** 12 inches. **Key Personnel:** Dani J. Holmes, Publisher; Peter E. Czaja, Jr., Advertising Mgr. **Subscription Rates:** Free. **Remarks:** Accepts advertising.
Ad Rates: GLR: $.15 **Circ:** Free ‡16,000
BW: $435
PCI: $6.04

14369 Residential Treatment for Children and Youth
The Haworth Press, Inc.
RR 1, Box 561 Phone: (413)298-3194
Lee, MA 01238-9602
Publisher E-mail: getinfo@haworthpressinc.com

Journal covering the theory and practice of residential treatment. **Subtitle:** A Journal of Professional Practice. **Founded:** 1986. **Freq:** Quarterly. **Trim Size:** 6x8 1/2. **Key Personnel:** Gordon Northrup, M.D., Editor, phone (413)298-3194, northrup@berkshire.net; Bill Cohen, Publisher. **ISSN:** 0886-571X. **Subscription Rates:** $45 individuals; $120 institutions; $200 libraries. **Remarks:** Accepts advertising. **Alt. Formats:** Microfiche.
Ad Rates: BW: $300 **Circ:** Paid 799

LENOX, pop. 6,550.

WC MA. Bershire Co. 7 mi. S. of Pittsville. Summer resort.

14370 Ski America
PO Box 737 Phone: (413)637-9810
Lenox, MA 01240 Fax: (413)637-9873

Magazine on skiing. **Founded:** Oct. 1972. **Freq:** Quarterly. **Print Method:** Web offset. **Trim Size:** 8 1/8 x 10 3/4. **Cols./Page:** 3. **Col. Width:** 2 3/8 inches. **Col. Depth:** 10 inches. **Key Personnel:** Barry Hollister, Editor and Publisher; B. Robert Wadsworth, Senior Vice Pres. Advertising. **Subscription Rates:** $5 individuals. **Remarks:** Accepts advertising.
Ad Rates: GLR: $2.75 **Circ:** ‡250,000
BW: $11,000
4C: $11,440
PCI: $350

14371 What Is Enlightenment?
Moksha Press
Attn: Marketing Phone: (413)637-6000
PO Box 2360 Fax: (413)637-6015
Lenox, MA 01240
Free: (800)376-3210
Publication E-mail: wie@moksha.org; wie@wie.org
Publisher E-mail: wie@mokshapress.org

Explores questions facing contemporary spiritual seekers. **Subtitle:** An inquiry into the most important spiritual questions of our time. **Founded:** 1991. **Freq:** Semiannual. **Print Method:** Web press. **Trim Size:** 8 1/2 x 11. **Key Personnel:** Michelle Hemingway, CEO; Kathy Bayer, Editor; Susan Brandle, Editor. **ISSN:** 1080-3432. **Subscription Rates:** $12 individuals; $6.95 single issue. **URL:** http://www.moksha.org./wie.
Ad Rates: BW: $590 **Circ:** Paid 30,000
4C: $1,675

LEXINGTON, pop. 29,479.

NE MA. Middlesex Co. 11 mi. NW of Boston. (Branch of Boston P.O.) Residential town of historical interest. Research, light industry. Nurseries.

14372 BYTE
The McGraw-Hill Companies, Inc.
29 Hartwell Ave. Phone: (617)860-6336
Lexington, MA 02173-3154 Fax: (617)860-6179

BYTE gives computer professionals the crucial information needed to satisfy their companies present, and future technology objectives. BYTE tracks and analyzes emerging technologies and products for multi-platform environments with editorial focus on building networked applications, Internet/Intranet/Extranet strategies, managing data, and network integration. BYTE's worldwide, paid circulation totals nearly 1.5 million. **Founded:** 1975. **Freq:** Monthly. **Print Method:** Web offset. **Trim Size:** 7 3/4 x 10 1/2. **Cols./Page:** 2 and 3. **Key Personnel:** Kevin McPherson, Publisher, phone (781)860-6020, fax (781)860-6179, kmcphers@mcgraw-hill.com; Mark Schlack, Editor-in-Chief, phone (781)860-6827, fax (781)860-6572, mschlack@mcgraw-hill.com. **ISSN:** 0360-5280. **Subscription Rates:** $24.95; $3.95 single issue. **Remarks:** Accepts advertising. **Online:** Dow Jones News-Retrieval. **URL:** http://www.byte.com. **Alt. Formats:** CD-ROM.
Ad Rates: BW: $25,410 **Circ:** Paid 442,553
4C: $3,875

14373 CryoGas International
J.R. Campbell & Associates, Inc.
5 Militia Dr. Phone: (781)862-0624
Lexington, MA 02173 Fax: (781)863-9411
Publication E-mail: cryogas@tiac.net

Professional magazine focusing on the business of industrial gases. **Subtitle:** Over 35 Years of Reporting on Cryogenics, Industrial Gases, and Related Systems. **Founded:** 1962. **Freq:** 11/year (Aug. and Sept. issues combined). **Print Method:** Offset. **Trim Size:** 8 1/2 x 11. **Cols./Page:** 2. **Col. Width:** 3 2/5 inches. **Col. Depth:** 9 inches. **Key Personnel:** Bob Keeley, Editor/Assoc. Publisher; Lori Campbell-Frieling, Advertising Mgr.; Toby Marshall, Senior Editor. **ISSN:** 1052-0139. **Subscription Rates:** $150 individuals; $200 out of country; $25 single issue. **Remarks:** Accepts advertising. **URL:** http://www.cryogas.oom. **Formerly:** Cryogenic Information Report (Sept. 1989).
Ad Rates: BW: $902 **Circ:** Non-paid 36
4C: $1,752

14374 The Northern Light
Supreme Council, Scottish Rite, NMJ, USA
PO Box 519 Phone: (781)862-4410
Lexington, MA 02420 Fax: (781)863-1833

Magazine containing articles of interest to Masons and their families. **Subtitle:** A Window for Freemasonry. **Founded:** Jan. 1970. **Freq:** Quarterly. **Print Method:** Offset. **Trim Size:** 8 1/8 x 10 7/8. **Cols./Page:** 3. **Col. Width:** 27 nonpareils. **Col. Depth:** 136 agate lines. **Key Personnel:** Richard H. Curtis, Editor, dcurtis@supremecouncil.org. **ISSN:** 1088-4416. **Subscription Rates:** $10 Included in membership. **Remarks:** Advertising not accepted.
Circ: Paid ‡645
Non-paid ‡320,000

14375 WIN News
Women's International Network
187 Grand St. Phone: (781)862-9431
Lexington, MA 02173 Fax: (781)862-1734
Publication E-mail: winnews@igc.org

Journal by, for, and about women, reporting on the status of women and women's rights around the globe. **Subtitle:** Women's International Network News. **Founded:** 1975. **Freq:** Quarterly. **Print Method:** Letterpress and offset. **Trim Size:** 7 x 11. **Cols./Page:** 2. **Col. Width:** 36 nonpareils. **Col. Depth:** 140 agate lines. **Key Personnel:** Fran P. Hosken, Editor. **ISSN:** 0145-7985. **Subscription Rates:** $35 individuals; $48 institutions; $5 single issue. **Remarks:** Accepts advertising. **Alt. Formats:** CD-ROM.
Ad Rates: BW: $300 **Circ:** ‡1,100

LEXINGTON PARK

14376 The Enterprise
Chesapeake Publishing Corp.
22652 3 Notch Rd.
Lexington Park, MA 20653

Community newspaper. **Founded:** 1884. **Freq:** Semiweekly (Wed. and Fri.). **Print Method:** Offset. **Cols./Page:** 6. **Col.**

Width: 12 picas. **Col. Depth:** 21 inches. **Key Personnel:** Dave Palmer, General Mgr.; Ralph Martin, Publisher. **Subscription Rates:** $36.
Ad Rates: GLR: $1.48 **Circ:** Paid 14,230
BW: $1493.90 Free 18
4C: $1778.90
PCI: $12.65

LINCOLN CENTER

14377 Home Automation
Seaside Education Associates, Inc.
Home Tech Project Free: (800)899-3804
PO Box 6341
Lincoln Center, MA 01773
Magazine focusing on home control technology for people with disabilities. **Subtitle:** Home Controls for All Abilities. **Freq:** Monthly. **Key Personnel:** Boots Garrett, Editor; James McCormack, Executive Director. **Subscription Rates:** Free. **Remarks:** Advertising not accepted. **URL:** http://www.seaside.org/.
Circ: Non-paid 4,200

LITTLETON, pop. 6,970.

NE MA. Middlesex Co. 4 mi. N. of Harvard. Residential.

14378 Littleton Independent
Community Newspaper Company/Northwest
150 Baker Ave., Ste. 305 Phone: (978)371-5754
PO Box 9191 Fax: (978)371-9058
Concord, MA 01742-9191
Community newspaper. **Founded:** 1960. **Freq:** Weekly (Thurs.). **Print Method:** Offset. **Cols./Page:** 6. **Col. Width:** 20 nonpareils. **Col. Depth:** 294 agate lines. **Key Personnel:** Dorris Hilberg, Managing Editor; Darrow Tully, Publisher; Bob Shomphe, Advertising Mgr. **USPS:** 315-800. **Subscription Rates:** $24; $36 out of county.
Ad Rates: BW: $786 **Circ:** Paid 2,009
4C: $1,186 Non-paid 13
SAU: $7.80
PCI: $7

14379 Meteorological & Geoastrophysical Abstracts
Inforonics
25 Porter Rd. Phone: (978)698-7358
Littleton, MA 01460 Fax: (978)698-7500
Publication E-mail: mga@inforonics.com

Journal presenting abstrcts of current world literature in meteorology, climatology, aeronomy, planetary atmospheres, solar-terrestrial relations, hydrology, oceanography, glaciology. **Founded:** Jan. 1950. **Freq:** Monthly. **Print Method:** Offset. **Trim Size:** 8 1/2 x 11. **Cols./Page:** 2. **Key Personnel:** Richard E. Hallgren, Publisher; Lawrence F. Buckland, Editorial Mgr., lfb@inforonics.com. **ISSN:** 0026-1130. **Subscription Rates:** $1275 print; $1650 CD-ROM; $3000 Web. **Remarks:** Advertising not accepted. **URL:** http://www.mganet.org. **Alt. Formats:** CD-ROM, MGA.
Circ: ‡350

LOWELL†, pop. 92,418.

NE MA. Middlesex Co. On Merrimack River, at mouth of Concord River, 25 mi. NW of Boston. University of Lowell. Urban National Cultural Park. Manufactures textile machines, knit products, plastics, textiles. Electronic printing and publishing industries.

14380 New Solutions
Baywood Publishing Co., Inc.
c/o Mary Lee Dunn/Charles Levenstein, Editors Phone: (508)934-3268
Fax: (508)452-5711
University of Massachusetts Lowell
Work Environment Program
Lowell, MA 01854
Publisher E-mail: baywood@baywood.com

Professional journal covering health, work, and the environment. **Subtitle:** A Journal of Environmental and Occupational Health Policy. **Freq:** Quarterly. **Trim Size:** 6 x 9. **Cols./Page:** 1. **Col. Width:** 4 inches. **Col. Depth:** 7 inches. **Key Personnel:** Dr. Charles Levenstein, Editor; Mary Lee Dunn, Asst. Editor. **ISSN:** 1048-2911. **Subscription Rates:** $40 individuals; $75 institutions. **Remarks:** Advertising not accepted.
Circ: (Not Reported)

14381 Sun
Lowell Sun Publishing Co.
15 Kearney Sq. Phone: (508)458-7100
Lowell, MA 01853 Fax: (508)970-4800
Free: (800)694-7100

General newspaper. **Founded:** 1878. **Freq:** Daily (eve.), Sat. and Sun. (morn.). **Print Method:** Letterpress. **Cols./Page:** 6. **Col. Width:** 25 nonpareils. **Col. Depth:** 301 agate lines. **Key Personnel:** John H. Costello, Jr., Editor and Publisher, phone (508)970-4621; Jonathan F. Kellogg, Sr., Exec. Editor, phone (508)970-4622; Kendall Wallace, General Mgr., phone (508)970-4627; James Campanini, Exec. News Editor, phone (508)970-4652; David McArdle, National News Editor, phone (508)970-4638; Paul A. Schwabe, Advertising Mgr., phone (508)970-4663; Frank Standley, Natl. Advertising MG. **USPS:** 321-180. **Subscription Rates:** $.35 institutions, Canada daily, single copy; $1.40 Sunday, single copy. **Remarks:** Accepts advertising. **Feature Editors:** John Greenwald, *Sunday*, phone (508)970-4637; David Gregory, *Photo*, phone (508)970-4663; Carol McQuaid, *Lifestyle, Women's*, phone (508)970-4631; Gail Ross, *Financial/Business*, phone (508)970-4660; Charles St. Armand, *City*, phone (508)970-4645; Dennis Whitton, *Sports*, phone (508)970-4628; Thomas Zuppa, *Suburban*, phone (508)970-4644.
Ad Rates: BW: $3,960.30 **Circ:** Mon.-Fri. 52,508
4C: $4610.30 Sat. 51,915
SAU: $30.70 Sun. 55,806
PCI: $30.70

14382 UMASS Lowell Connector
University of Massachusetts at Lowell
100 Pawtucket St. Phone: (978)934-5009
Lowell, MA 01854 Fax: (978)934-3031
Publisher E-mail: connector@uml.edu

Collegiate newspaper. **Founded:** 1950. **Freq:** Weekly. **Print Method:** Offset. **Cols./Page:** 5. **Col. Width:** 22 nonpareils. **Col. Depth:** 215 agate lines. **Key Personnel:** Mary Ann Karabatsos, Office Mgr.; Brad Duquette, Editor-in-Chief; Jennifer Ross, Managing Editor; Katie Hennessey, A & E Editor; Patrick Buckley, Advertising Editor; Susan Bolduc, Office Asst. **Subscription Rates:** $0 Free; $0 Free. **Remarks:** Accepts advertising. **Formerly:** The Text.
Ad Rates: PCI: $5 **Circ:** Free ‡4,000

14383 Lowell Cable TV Co., Inc.
12 Washer St. Phone: (508)459-3313
Lowell, MA 01852-5355 Fax: (508)454-6910

Founded: 1979. **Cities Served:** subscribing households 47,000.

14384 WCAP-AM - 980
243 Central St. Phone: (508)454-0404
Lowell, MA 01852 Fax: (508)458-9124

Format: News; Talk. **Networks:** ABC. **Founded:** 1951. **Operating Hours:** Continuous. **Key Personnel:** Maurice Cohen, General Mgr.; Kevin Dunn, Operations Mgr. **Local Programs:** *Saturday Morning Live* 6:00 am - 10:00 am Saturday, Warren Shaw; *At Dawn With Dunn* 6:00 am - 9:00 am Monday-Friday, Kevin Dunn; *The Computer Report* 7:00 am - 8:30 am Sunday, Dave Scuito. **Wattage:** 5000.

14385 WJUL-FM - 91.5
1 University Ave. Phone: (508)452-9073
Lowell, MA 01854 Fax: (508)934-3031
E-mail: jrodden@cs.uml.edu

Format: Alternative/New Music/Progressive. **Owner:** University of Massachusetts at Lowell, at above address. **Founded:** 1952. **Formerly:** WLTI-FM. **Operating Hours:** 6 a.m.-2 a.m. **Key Personnel:** Jessica Rodden, General Mgr.; Paul Vaughan, Music Dir.; Erik Scott, Promotions Mgr.; Dan Taylor, Program Dir.; Glen Anderson, Chief Engineer. **Wattage:** 1400. **Ad Rates:** Noncommercial.

14386 WLLH-AM - 1400
40-44 Church St. Phone: (508)458-8486
PO Box 1818 Fax: (508)452-0980
Lowell, MA 01853

Format: Adult Contemporary. **Networks:** ABC. **Founded:** 1934. **Operating Hours:** 5 a.m.-2 a.m.; 100% local. **Key Personnel:** Perry Kapiloff, General Mgr.; Mark Sawyer, Program Dir.; Bob Ellis, Operations Mgr.; Paul Brennan, Music Dir.; Frank Messina, General Sales Mgr. **Wattage:** 2000.

LUNENBURG

14387 Button
Thimble Press
Box 26
Lunenburg, MA 01462
Publication E-mail: buttonx26@aol.com

Consumer magazine covering poetry, fiction, and literature. **Founded:** June 1993. **Freq:** Semiannual. **Print Method:** Offset. **Trim Size:** 4 x 5. **Cols./Page:** 1. **Col. Width:** 18 picas. **Col. Depth:** 23 picas. **Key Personnel:** S. Cragin, Publisher; D. E. Bell, Poetry Editor; A. Dawes, Fiction Editor. **Subscription Rates:** $5 two years; $2 single issue. **Remarks:** Accepts advertising.
Ad Rates: BW: $100 **Circ:** Combined 1,200

LYNN, pop. 78,471.

NE MA. Essex Co. On Massachusetts Bay, 10 mi. NE of Boston. Large trade center. Manufactures electrical and electronic equipment, aircraft jet engines, steam turbines and gears, shoes and allied products, shoe welding, folding, and taping machinery, incandescent lamps, leather goods and dressing, plastics, rubber goods moulds, wire and foundry products, upholstery springs. Lobster fisheries.

14388 Daily Evening Item
Hastings & Sons
38 Exchange St. Phone: (617)593-7700
PO Box 951 Fax: (617)581-3178
Lynn, MA 01903
Publication E-mail: lynnitem@shore.nte

General newspaper. **Founded:** 1877. **Freq:** Daily (eve.) and Sat. (morn.). **Print Method:** Letterpress. **Cols./Page:** 6. **Col. Width:** 25 nonpareils. **Col. Depth:** 298 agate lines. **Key Personnel:** Allan T. Kort, Managing Editor; Bryan C. Thayer, Publisher; Kevin Kelly, Advertising Mgr.; Molly Evans, Mkg. Dir.; Brian P. Lacy, Circulation Dir.; Peter L. Chipman, Operations Dir.; Arthur C. Carr, Controller. **USPS:** 142-820. **Subscription Rates:** $120 individuals; $165 by mail. **Remarks:** Accepts advertising.
Ad Rates: BW: $3,181.13 **Circ:** Mon.-Fri. 21,055
4C: $3,481.13 Sat. 18,715
SAU: $244.95

14389 Sunday Post
Lynn Sunday Post
619 Chestnut St. Phone: (617)592-4600
Lynn, MA 01904 Fax: (617)592-1811

Newspaper. **Founded:** 1960. **Freq:** Weekly (Sun.). **Print Method:** Offset. Uses mats. **Cols./Page:** 7. **Col. Width:** 24 nonpareils. **Col. Depth:** 301 agate lines. **Key Personnel:** Arthur Belleville, Editor; Bernard A. McGovern, Publisher. **Remarks:** Accepts advertising.
Ad Rates: SAU: $.70 **Circ:** (Not Reported)

14390 Warner Cable Communications, Inc.
26 Tremont St. Phone: (617)397-8400
Lynn, MA 01902 Fax: (617)599-4309

Founded: 1980. **Cities Served:** Essex County, MA.

14391 WFNX-FM - 101.7
25 Exchange St. Phone: (617)595-6200
Lynn, MA 01901 Fax: (617)595-3810
E-mail: wfnx@wfnx.com

Format: Alternative/New Music/Progressive. **Founded:** 1983. **Operating Hours:** Continuous. **ADI:** Boston-Worcester,MA-Derry-Manchester,NH. **Key Personnel:** Stephen Mindich, Owner; Andrew Kingston, General Manager; Mame Glasheen, National Sales Mgr.; David Coppola, Operations Dir.; Kelly Graml, Marketing Manager; Laurie Gail, Music Dir. **Wattage:** 3000. **URL:** http://www.wfnx.com.

LYNNFIELD, pop. 11,267.

N. MA. Essex Co. 12 mi. NE of Boston. Residential.

14392 Essex Genealogist
Essex Society of Genealogists
Box 313 Phone: (978)664-9279
Lynnfield, MA 01940-0313
Publisher E-mail: essexsoc@aol.com

Genealogical magazine covering Essex County, Massachusetts. **Founded:** Feb. 1981. **Freq:** Quarterly. **Key Personnel:** Marcia Lindberg, Editor; Nancy Hayward, Managing Editor. **ISSN:** 0279-067X. **Subscription Rates:** $18 individuals; $5 single issue. **Remarks:** Advertising not accepted.
Circ: Paid 800

14393 The Lynnfield Villager
Great Oak Publications, Inc.
55 Salem St. Phone: (781)334-6319
Lynnfield, MA 01940 Fax: (978)664-4761

Community newspaper. **Founded:** 1973. **Freq:** Weekly (Wed.). **Print Method:** Offset. **Cols./Page:** 5. **Col. Width:** 22 nonpareils. **Col. Depth:** 224 agate lines. **Key Personnel:** Albert E. Sylvia, Jr., Editor and Publisher, phone (617)334-6319. **ISSN:** 1077-2308. **Subscription Rates:** $17 individuals; $20 out of area. **Remarks:** Accepts advertising.
Ad Rates: GLR: $.42 **Circ:** Paid 1,840
BW: $400 Non-paid 184
SAU: $5.90
PCI: $5.90

14394 Women's Circle
House of White Birches
PO Box 299
Lynnfield, MA 01940-0299

Magazine containing stories on home-based female entrepreneurs, readers' letters, craft and needlework, designs, and other features. **Founded:** 1957. **Freq:** Bimonthly. **Print Method:** Offset. **Trim Size:** 8 x 10 3/4. **Cols./Page:** 3. **Col. Width:** 13 1/2 picas. **Col. Depth:** 58 picas. **Key Personnel:** Marjorie Pearl, Editor; Sharly Berry, Advertising Mgr. **ISSN:** 0509-089X. **Subscription Rates:** $12.97 individuals; $1.95 single issue. **Remarks:** Advertising accepted; rates available upon request.
Circ: ‡49,749

MALDEN, pop. 53,386.

NE MA. Middlesex Co. On Malden River, 5 mi. N. of Boston. (Branch of Boston P.O.) Manufactures rubber boots, fire hoses, paints, varnishes, drugs, radio and electronic parts, shoes, spices, sheet steel, aluminum products, auto bodies, seat covers, draperies, furniture.

14395 Malden Evening News
Eastern Middlesex Press Publications, Inc.
277 Commercial St. Phone: (617)321-8000
Malden, MA 02148 Fax: (617)321-8008
Publication E-mail: newsmerc@user1.channel1.com

General newspaper. 5 days Mon thru Fri. **Founded:** 1892. **Freq:** Daily (eve.). **Print Method:** Offset. **Cols./Page:** 6. **Col. Width:** 25 nonpareils. **Col. Depth:** 294 agate lines. **Key Personnel:** Tom Daly, General Mgr. **Subscription Rates:** $118 individuals. **Remarks:** Accepts advertising. **Absorbed:** Maiden Evening News (1989); Melrose Evening News (1989); Medford Daily (1989); Medford Mercury (1989). **Formerly:** Daily News Mercury.
Ad Rates: BW: $1,512 **Circ:** ‡15,000
4C: $2,312
SAU: $12

MANCHESTER, pop. 5,424.

NE MA. Essex Co. On Atlantic Ocean, 23 mi. NE of Boston. Residential. Boat yards.

14396 The Manchester Cricket
Cricket Press, Inc.
PO Box 357 Phone: (978)526-7131
Manchester, MA 01944-0357 Fax: (978)526-8193
Publisher E-mail: cricket@cricketpress.com

Community newspaper. **Founded:** May 19, 1888. **Freq:** Weekly (Fri.). **Print Method:** Offset. **Trim Size:** 13 3/4 x 23. **Cols./Page:** 6. **Col. Width:** 12 picas. **Col. Depth:** 21 inches. **Key Personnel:** Daniel B. Slade, Editor; Harry E. Slade, Jr., Publisher. **USPS:** 327-420. **Subscription Rates:** $20 individuals; $10 students. **Remarks:** Accepts advertising. **Alt. Formats:** Mailing labels.
Ad Rates: SAU: $9 **Circ:** ‡2,515
PCI: $7

MANSFIELD, pop. 13,453.

SE MA. Bristol Co. 24 mi. SW of Boston. Residential. Chemicals, truck farms.

14397 The Mansfield News
Norfolk Community Newspapers Inc.
154 Copeland Dr. Phone: (508)339-8977
Mansfield, MA 02048
Community newspaper. **Founded:** 1873. **Freq:** Weekly. **Print Method:** Offset. **Trim Size:** 13 x 16. **Cols./Page:** 5. **Col. Width:** 2 1/16 inches. **Col. Depth:** 16 inches. **Key Personnel:** Asa Cole, Publisher; Donna Whitehead, Managing Editor, phone (508)339-8977; Sean Burke, Advertising Dir., phone (508)528-2600, fax (508)528-2676. **USPS:** 328-280. **Subscription Rates:** $21; $27 out of area. **Remarks:** Accepts advertising.
Ad Rates: BW: $460 **Circ:** Paid 3,611
SAU: $5.75 Non-paid 215

14398 Mansfield Reporter
Associated Newspapers
7 Cabot Pl. Phone: (781)878-1111
PO Box 441 Fax: (781)878-3333
Stoughton, MA 02072
Publication E-mail: aweeklies@aol.com
Publisher E-mail: aweeklies@aol.com

Community newspaper. **Founded:** 1989. **Freq:** Weekly (Thurs.). **Print Method:** Offset. **Cols./Page:** 6. **Col. Width:** 9.5 picas. **Col. Depth:** 16 inches. **Key Personnel:** Richard R. Dailey, Publisher. **Subscription Rates:** $10 individuals; $35 out of state. **Remarks:** Accepts advertising.
Ad Rates: BW: $10.53 **Circ:** Paid ‡1,425
4C: $10.77
PCI: $10.53

14399 The Norton Mirror
Norfolk Community Newspapers Inc.
154 Copeland Dr. Phone: (508)339-8977
Mansfield, MA 02048
Community newspaper. **Founded:** 1987. **Freq:** Weekly. **Print Method:** Offset. **Trim Size:** 11 x 17. **Cols./Page:** 5. **Col. Width:** 2 1/6 inches. **Col. Depth:** 16 inches. **Key Personnel:** Asa Cole, Publisher; Sean Burke, Advertising Dir.; Donna Whithead, Managing Editor, phone (508)339-8977, fax (508)528-2676; Chris Warren, Advertising Dir. **Subscription Rates:** $17 individuals; $23 out of area. **Remarks:** Accepts advertising.
Ad Rates: BW: $361.60 **Circ:** Paid 1,616
PCI: $5.65 Non-paid 82

MARBLEHEAD

14400 Marblehead Reporter
Community Newspaper Company
PO Box 468 Phone: (617)631-7700
Marblehead, MA 01945 Fax: (617)639-2830
Publication E-mail: sweditor@shore.net

Community newspaper (tabloid). **Founded:** 1964. **Freq:** Weekly (Thurs.). **Print Method:** Offset. **Trim Size:** 11 3/8 x 17. **Cols./Page:** 5. **Col. Width:** 2 1/16 inches. **Col. Depth:** 16 inches. **Key Personnel:** Diana Montgomery, Editor; Chuck Goodrich, Publisher; John Vistorino, Advertising Mgr.; Robert Tuttle, Contact. **Subscription Rates:** Free in county; $31 out of county. **Remarks:** Accepts advertising.
Ad Rates: GLR: $3.20 **Circ:** Paid 740
BW: $800 Free 10,086
4C: $1,250
SAU: $12.45

Swampscott Reporter - See Swampscott

14401 WLYN-AM - 101.7
8 Bartlett St. Phone: (617)595-6200
Marblehead, MA 01945-2720 Fax: (617)595-3810

Format: Ethnic. **Networks:** Independent. **Founded:** 1947. **Operating Hours:** Sunrise-sunset. **Key Personnel:** Paul Allen, General Mgr.; Ed White, News Dir. **Wattage:** 1000.

MARLBOROUGH, pop. 30,617.

NE MA. Middlesex Co. 27 mi. W. of Boston. Manufactures shoes and slippers, miners lamps, paper, wire and foundry products, electronic equipment, feed. Metal stampings. Dairy and fruit farms.

14402 Hudson Daily Sun
Marlboro Enterprise
230 Maple St. Phone: (508)490-7450
Marlborough, MA 01752 Fax: (508)490-7471

Community newspaper. **Freq:** Mon.-Sat. (morn.). **Print Method:** Offset. **Key Personnel:** Rick Lombardi, Editor; Steve Dines, Publisher; Bob Shompe, Advertising Mgr. **Remarks:** Accepts advertising.
Ad Rates: PCI: $8.30 **Circ:** Combined 6,227

14403 Marlboro Enterprise
230 Maple St. Phone: (508)490-7450
Marlborough, MA 01752 Fax: (508)490-7471

Local newspaper. **Founded:** 1889. **Freq:** Weekly (Thurs.). **Print Method:** Offset. **Cols./Page:** 5. **Col. Width:** 12 picas. **Col. Depth:** 13 inches. **Key Personnel:** Marilyn Spencer, Editor, phone (508)490-7455, mspencer@cnc.com; Charles Goodrich, Publisher; Robert Shompe, Advertising Mgr. **USPS:** 330-360. **Subscription Rates:** $96; $132 out of area. **Remarks:** Accepts advertising.
Ad Rates: PCI: $8.30 **Circ:** Combined 6,227

14404 WSRO-AM - 1470
48 Fitchburg St. Phone: (508)485-9291
Marlborough, MA 01752-1262 Fax: (508)624-6496
E-mail: wsro@wsro.com

Format: Full Service. **Networks:** USA Radio. **Founded:** 1958. **Operating Hours:** Continuous. **ADI:** Boston-Worcester,MA-Derry-Manchester,NH. **Key Personnel:** Dave O'Gara, General Mgr. **Wattage:** 5000. **URL:** http://www.wsro.com/.

MARSHFIELD, pop. 20,916.

SE MA. Plymouth Co. 30 mi. SE of Boston. Residential.

Abington/Rockland Mariner - See Abington

Bridgewater Townsman - See Bridgewater

Hanover Mariner - See Hanover

Hingham Mariner - See Hingham

Kingston Independent Voice - See Kingston

14405 Marshfield Mariner
Mariner Newspapers
165 Enterprise Dr. Phone: (617)837-3500
Marshfield, MA 02050-2132 Fax: (617)837-4540
Free: (800)649-6661
Publisher E-mail: cmathis@cnc.com

Community newspaper. **Freq:** Weekly (Wed.). **Print Method:** Offset. **Trim Size:** 11 3/8 x 17. **Cols./Page:** 5. **Col. Width:** 2 1/8 inches. **Col. Depth:** 15 1/2 inches. **Key Personnel:** Margaret Smorgiewicz, Publisher; Judy McCaffrey Perry, Advertising Dir. **Subscription Rates:** $22. **Remarks:** Combined advertising rates available with other Mariner Newspapers.
Ad Rates: BW: $942.40 **Circ:** Paid 4,399
4C: $1,300.00 Non-paid 175
PCI: $8.25

14406 Marshfield Reporter
MPG Newspapers
9 Long Pond Rd. Phone: (508)746-5555
PO Box 959 Fax: (508)747-2148
Plymouth, MA 02362-0959
Free: (800)242-0264
Publisher E-mail: newsroom@mpgnews.com

Community newspaper. **Founded:** 1987. **Freq:** Weekly (Thurs.). **Print Method:** Offset. **Trim Size:** 16 1/2 x 11. **Cols./Page:** 5. **Col. Width:** 21 nonpareils. **Col. Depth:** 224 agate lines. **Key Personnel:** Phyllis Hughes, Publisher, phughes@mpgnews.com. **Subscription Rates:** Free; $32 out of county. **Remarks:** Accepts advertising. **URL:** http://www.mgpnews.com.
Ad Rates: GLR: $.53 **Circ:** Combined ♦**4,334**
BW: $596
4C: $996
PCI: $7.45

Norwell Mariner - See Norwell

Pembroke Mariner - See Pembroke

Randolph Mariner - See Randolph

Scituate Mariner - See Scituate

14407 South Look
Mariner Newspapers
165 Enterprise Dr. Phone: (617)837-3500
Marshfield, MA 02050-2132 Fax: (617)837-4540
Free: (800)649-6661
Publisher E-mail: cmathis@cnc.com

Community newspaper. **Founded:** 1876. **Freq:** Weekly. **Print Method:** Offset. **Trim Size:** 11 3/8 x 17. **Cols./Page:** 3. **Col. Width:** 15 1/2 inches. **Key Personnel:** Bob Flavell, Editor; Jack Powers, General Mgr. **USPS:** 088-760. **Subscription Rates:** $18. **Remarks:** Combined advertising rates available with other Mariner Newspapers.
Ad Rates: BW: $767.25 **Circ:** Paid 54,000
4C: $1,167.25 Free 2,500
PCI: $8.25

14408 Stoughton Journal
Mariner Newspapers
165 Enterprise Dr. Phone: (617)837-3500
Marshfield, MA 02050-2132 Fax: (617)837-4540
Free: (800)649-6661
Publisher E-mail: cmathis@cnc.com

Community newspaper. **Founded:** 1987. **Freq:** Weekly (Thurs.). **Print Method:** Offset. **Trim Size:** 11 3/8 x 17. **Cols./Page:** 5. **Col. Width:** 1 7/8 inches. **Col. Depth:** 16 inches. **Key Personnel:** Asa Cole, Publisher; Amy Dwyer, Advertising Dir. **Subscription Rates:** $24 individuals. **Remarks:** Combined advertising rates available with other Mariner Newspapers. **URL:** http://www.airmax.net/perspective. **Feature Editors:** Marilyn Jackson, *Financial/Business*, phone (617)828-0006, fax (617)828-9039, marilyn.jackson@cnc.com.
Ad Rates: BW: $942.40 **Circ:** Paid 2,037
4C: $1,300 Non-paid 39
PCI: $8.25

Whitman/Hanson Mariner - See Whitman

14409 WATD-FM - 95.9
130 Enterprise Dr. Phone: (617)837-1166
Marshfield, MA 02050 Fax: (617)837-1978

Format: Adult Contemporary. **Networks:** Independent. **Owner:** Ed Perry, at above address. **Founded:** 1977. **Operating**

Hours: Continuous. **Key Personnel:** Bob Stone, News Dir.; Carol Perry, Promotions Dir. **Local Programs:** *A Feast of Irish Music*, S. Mulligan; *The World of Blues*, Peter Black. **Wattage:** 3000. **Ad Rates:** $18-28 for 30 seconds; $22-32 for 60 seconds.

MASHPEE, pop. 5,940.

SW MA. Barnstable Co. On Cape Cod.

14410 Mashpee Messenger
Community Newspaper
5 Namskaket Rd. Phone: (508)398-0123
PO Box 2776 Fax: (508)760-3387
Orleans, MA 02653-6776
Free: (800)660-8999

Community newspaper. **Founded:** 1985. **Freq:** Weekly (Wed.). **Print Method:** Offset. **Trim Size:** 11 x 16 1/2. **Cols./Page:** 5. **Col. Width:** 21 inches. **Col. Depth:** 224 agate lines. **Key Personnel:** Eric Hartwell, Editor; Jeanne Moore-Yount, Advertising Mgr. **Subscription Rates:** Free; $25 (mail). **Remarks:** Accepts advertising.
Ad Rates: GLR: $.38 **Circ:** Non-paid 2,290
BW: $424
4C: $1,024
PCI: $5.30

MATTAPAN

14411 Survival News
95 Standard St. Phone: (617)327-4219
Mattapan, MA 02126 Fax: (617)327-4219
Publisher E-mail: masswelf@aol.com

Founded: 1987. **Freq:** Semiannual. **Print Method:** Web offset. **Cols./Page:** 2. **Col. Width:** 5 inches. **Col. Depth:** 15 1/2 inches. **Subscription Rates:** Free; $10 by mail; $25 institutions. **Remarks:** Advertising accepted; rates available upon request.
Circ: Paid 750
Free ⊕9,000

MAYNARD, pop. 9,590.

NE MA. Middlesex Co. 18 mi. NW of Cambridge. Residential.

14412 Association Meetings
Adams Business Media
60 Main St. Phone: (978)897-5552
Maynard, MA 01754-2011 Fax: (978)897-6824

Magazine for association meeting planners. **Subtitle:** The Independent Voice of the Association Industry. **Founded:** 1989. **Freq:** Bimonthly. **Print Method:** Offset. Uses mats. **Trim Size:** 8 1/8 x 11. **Cols./Page:** 3. **Col. Width:** 27 nonpareils. **Col. Depth:** 140 agate lines. **Key Personnel:** Regina McGee, Editor; J. Peter Huestis, Sr. Vice Pres./Group Publisher; Chari A. O'Rourke, Circulation Mgr.; Mark Adams, President; Virginia Lofft, Vice Pres./Publishing Dir.; Melissa Fromento, Advertising Sales Dir.; Betsy Bair, Editorial Dir.; Georgi Mueller, Sales & Marketing Operations Mgr.; Sue Noble, Production Mgr.; Karen Kranak Waxman, Traffic Mgr. **ISSN:** 8750-1686. **Subscription Rates:** $56 individuals. **Remarks:** Accepts advertising.
Ad Rates: BW: $4,570 **Circ:** Controlled ‡22,000
4C: $6,090

14413 Corporate Meetings & Incentives
Adams Business Media
60 Main St. Phone: (978)897-5552
Maynard, MA 01754-2011 Fax: (978)897-6824

Magazine for executives and travel professionals responsible for choosing sites and destinations for meeting and incentive travel programs. **Subtitle:** The Senior Executives Guide to Decision Making. **Founded:** 1980. **Freq:** Monthly. **Print Method:** Web offset. **Trim Size:** 8 1/8 x 10 7/8. **Cols./Page:** and 3. **Key Personnel:** Barbara Scofidio, Editor, phone (978)448-8211, fax (978)448-8212, bscofidio@mail.aip.com; Betsy Bair, Editorial Dir., phone (978)448-0582, fax (978)448-2646, bbair@mail.aip.com; Melissa Fromento, Advertising Sales Dir., phone (212)827-4733, fax (212)827-4730, mfromento@mail.aip.com; Georgi Mueller, Sales & Marketing Operatinos Mgr., phone (978)897-5552, fax (978)897-6824, gmueller@mail.aip.com. **ISSN:** 0745-1636. **Subscription Rates:** $65 per year; $9.50 single issue; $121 out of country. **Remarks:** Accepts advertising. **Online:** AOL. **URL:** http://www.acp.com.
Ad Rates: BW: $5,505 **Circ:** Controlled ‡36,776
4C: $7,405

14414 Insurance Conference Planner
Adams Business Media
60 Main St. Phone: (978)897-5552
Maynard, MA 01754-2011 Fax: (978)897-6824

Magazine on insurance meeting and conference planning. **Subtitle:** The Executive's Guide to Incentive Travel and Meetings. **Founded:** 1965. **Freq:** Bimonthly. **Print Method:** Offset. **Trim Size:** 8 1/8 x 11. **Cols./Page:** 3. **Col. Width:** 27 nonpareils. **Col. Depth:** 140 agate lines. **Key Personnel:** Susan Hatch, Editor, sghatch@aol.com; J. Peter Huestis, Publisher; Chari A. O'Rourke, Circulation Mgr. **ISSN:** 0193-0516. **Subscription Rates:** $56 individuals. **Remarks:** Accepts advertising. **URL:** http://www.meetingsnet.com.
Ad Rates: BW: $2,600 **Circ:** Controlled ‡8,500
4C: $1,340

14415 The Maynard Beacon
Community Newspaper Company/Northwest
150 Baker Ave., Ste. 305 Phone: (978)371-5754
PO Box 9191 Fax: (978)371-9058
Concord, MA 01742-9191
Publication E-mail: maynard@cmc.com

Community newspaper. **Founded:** 1965. **Freq:** Weekly (Thurs.). **Print Method:** Offset. **Cols./Page:** 6. **Col. Width:** 20 nonpareils. **Col. Depth:** 294 agate lines. **Key Personnel:** Lucille Daniel, Managing Editor, phone (508)371-5738; Thomas Marquis, Publisher, phone (508)371-5757, fax (508)371-5215; Jom Towme. **USPS:** 006-152. **Subscription Rates:** $29 individuals; $40 out of country. **Remarks:** Accepts advertising.
Ad Rates: BW: $2,000 **Circ:** Paid 3,700
4C: $2,400 Non-paid 14
SAU: $16.70
PCI: $16.70

14416 Medical Meetings
Adams Business Media
60 Main St. Phone: (978)897-5552
Maynard, MA 01754-2011 Fax: (978)897-6824

Magazine covering medical meetings and conference planning. **Subtitle:** The International Guide for Healthcare Meeting Planners. **Founded:** 1973. **Freq:** 8/year. **Print Method:** Offset. **Trim Size:** 8 1/8 x 10 7/8. **Cols./Page:** 3. **Col. Width:** 27 nonpareils. **Col. Depth:** 140 agate lines. **Key Personnel:** David Erickson, Editor; Virgina M. Lofft, Vice Pres./Publishing Dir.; Betsy Bair, Editorial Dir.; Mark Adams, President; J. Peter Huestis, Sr. Vice President/Publishing Dir.; Melissa Fromento, Advertising Sales Dir.; Georgi Mueller, Sales & Marketing Operations Mgr.; Sue Noble, Production Mgr.; Karen Kranak Waxman, Traffic Mgr.; Chari A. O'Rourke, Circulation Mgr. **ISSN:** 0093-1314. **Subscription Rates:** $56 individuals; $8 single issue; $105 other countries. **Remarks:** Accepts advertising. **Online:** AOL. **URL:** http://www.meetingsnet.com.
Ad Rates: BW: $3,710 **Circ:** Controlled ‡12,500
4C: $5,205

MEDFIELD

14417 Jazz Player
Dorn Publications, Inc.
93 West St.
Medfield, MA 02052

Trade magazine for jazz musicians. **Freq:** Bimonthly. **Subscription Rates:** $45 individuals; $60 out of country; $85 two years; $110 two years out of country.

14418 Medfield Suburban Press
Suburban World, Inc.
992 Great Plain Ave. Phone: (508)653-4460
PO Box 358 Fax: (781)444-1795
Needham, MA 02192
Free: (800)847-NEWS

Community newspaper (tabloid). **Founded:** 1929. **Freq:** Weekly (Thurs.). **Print Method:** Offset. **Trim Size:** 11x 17. **Cols./Page:** 6. **Col. Width:** 10.25 picas. **Col. Depth:** 16 inches. **Key Personnel:** Gareth Charter, Exec. Editor; William Barrett, Publisher; Susan Robinson, Advertising Mgr. **Subscription Rates:** $22 individuals; $27 out of area; $18 students. **Remarks:** Accepts advertising.
Ad Rates: GLR: $.58 **Circ:** Combined 3,091

14419 Saxophone Journal
Dorn Publications, Inc.
93 West St.
Medfield, MA 02052

Trade magazine for professional saxophone players. **Freq:** Bimonthly. **Subscription Rates:** $45 individuals; $60 out of country; $85 two years; $110 two years out of country; $5 single issue.

MEDFORD, pop. 58,076.

NE MA. Middlesex Co. On Mystic River, 5 mi. NW of Boston. (Branch of Boston P.O.); Tufts University. Manufactures paper boxes, leather, textile oil and soap, wire and iron products, jointing compounds, wax and polish, valves, waterproof sheeting, mattresses, commercial pumps, containers, concrete blocks, dental materials, fruit syrup, truck and trailer bodies.

14420 Applied Biochemistry and Biotechnology
Humana Press, Inc.
c/o David R. Walt, Exec. Editor Phone: (617)627-3470
Tufts University Fax: (617)627-3443
Dept. of Chemistry
Medford, MA 02155
Publication E-mail: dwalt@emerald.tufts.edu
Publisher E-mail: humana@humanapr.com

Scientific journal covering biochemistry and biotechnology. **Subtitle:** Enzyme Engineering & Biotechnology. **Freq:** 21/year. **Trim Size:** 7 x 10. **Key Personnel:** David R. Walt, Exec. Editor. **ISSN:** 0273-2289. **Subscription Rates:** $885 individuals; $40 single issue. **Remarks:** Accepts advertising.
Circ: (Not Reported)

14421 Daily Mercury
Associated Newspapers
7 Cabot Pl. Phone: (781)878-1111
PO Box 441 Fax: (781)878-3333
Stoughton, MA 02072
Publisher E-mail: aweeklies@aol.com

General newspaper. **Founded:** 1880. **Freq:** Daily (eve.). **Print Method:** Offset. **Cols./Page:** 6. **Col. Width:** 256 nonpareils. **Col. Depth:** 294 agate lines. **Key Personnel:** David Brickman, Editor and Publisher; Jim Mitchell, Advertising Mgr. **Subscription Rates:** $118 individuals.
Circ: ‡4,995

14422 The Fletcher Forum of World Affairs
Fletcher School of Law & Diplomacy
160 Packard Ave. Phone: (617)623-3610
Medford, MA 02155 Fax: (617)623-3979

Journal of contemporary, legal, political, economic, and diplomatic aspects of international affairs. **Founded:** 1976. **Freq:** Semiannual. **Trim Size:** 6 1/2 x 9 1/2. **Key Personnel:** Carlisle Levine, Editor-in-Chief; Chris Williams, Managing Editor; Meg Donovan, Circulation Mgr.; Kate Houghton, Production Mgr. **ISSN:** 1046-1868. **Subscription Rates:** $8 single issue magazine rates; $16 individuals; $25 institutions. **URL:** forum@emerald.tufts.edu.
Ad Rates: BW: $200 **Circ:** Paid 2,000

14423 PC Week
Ziff-Davis Publishing Co.
10 Presidents Landing Phone: (617)393-3700
Medford, MA 02155-5146 Free: (800)451-1032

Tabloid featuring microcomputer products and developments. **Subtitle:** The National Newspaper of Corporate Microcomputing. **Founded:** 1983. **Freq:** Weekly. **Print Method:** Web offset. **Trim Size:** 10 3/4 x 14. **Cols./Page:** 4. **Key Personnel:** Eric Lindquist, Editor, elindquist@pcweek.ziff.com; Donald J. Byrnes, Publisher. **Subscription Rates:** Free to qualified subscribers; $195 individuals; $250 Canada and Mexico; $395 other countries; $6 single issue. **Remarks:** Accepts advertising. **Online:** CompuServe Information Service; LEXIS-NEXIS; ZiffNet Information Service. **URL:** http://www.pcweek.com. **Alt. Formats:** CD-ROM; Microform.
Ad Rates: BW: $14,790 **Circ:** Controlled 128,277

14424 WMFO-FM - 91.5
Cutris Hall Phone: (617)625-0800
Tufts College Fax: (617)625-6072
Medford, MA 02155

Format: Full Service. **Owner:** Tufts College, 490 Boston Ave., Medford, MA 02155. **Founded:** 1960. **Formerly:** WTUR-AM (1971). **Operating Hours:** Continuous; 100% local. **Key Personnel:** Mikey Dee, Contact; Akira Kamiya, News Dir.; Steve Clay, Sports Dir.; Sean Murphy, Contact; John Grebe, Operations Dir.; Derek Smith, Music Dir.; Kurt Maitland, General Mgr.; Ashley Seratta, Program Dir.; Steve Cantor, Contact; Holly Harris, Contact; Shawn Patrick, Contact. **Wattage:** 125.

14425 WXKS-AM - 1430
99 Revere Beach Pkwy. Phone: (617)396-1430
PO Box 128 Fax: (617)391-3064
Medford, MA 02155

Format: Big Band/Nostalgia. **Networks:** Independent. **Founded:** 1952. **Operating Hours:** Continuous. **Key Personnel:** Matt Mills, General Mgr. **Wattage:** 5000 day; 1000 night.

🎙 **14426 WXKS-FM - 107.9**
Box 128 Phone: (617)396-1430
Medford, MA 02155 Fax: (617)391-3064
E-mail: bevois@aol

Format: Contemporary Hit Radio (CHR). **Networks:** Independent. **Owner:** Evergreen Media, 99 Revere Beach Parkway, Medford, MA 02155, (617)393-7715, Fax: (617)393-7897. **Founded:** 1979. **Operating Hours:** Continuous. **ADI:** Boston-Worcester,MA-Derry-Manchester,NH. **Key Personnel:** Janet Karger, General Mgr.; John Ivey, Program Dir.; Lisa Fell, General Sales Mgr.; Jim de Casro, President; Beverly Tilden, Marketing Director. **Wattage:** 50,000.

MELROSE, pop. 30,055.

NE MA. Middlesex Co. 8 mi. N. of Boston. Manufactures chemicals, radios, electronics, lighting.

📖 **14427 Advertiser**
Community Newspaper
40 W. Foster St. Phone: (617)233-2040
Melrose, MA 02176-3811 Fax: (617)231-8064

Newspaper. **Founded:** 1888. **Freq:** Weekly (Thurs.). **Print Method:** Letterpress and offset. **Cols./Page:** 6. **Col. Width:** 23 nonpareils. **Col. Depth:** 294 agate lines. **Key Personnel:** David Weldon, Editor; Frank Yetter, Publications Dir. **Subscription Rates:** $15. **Remarks:** Accepts advertising.
Ad Rates: GLR: $.27 **Circ:** 5,800
BW: $26.10
SAU: $8.90
PCI: $8.90

📖 **14428 Malden Observer**
Community Newspaper Company
40 West Foster St. Phone: (617)655-4001
Melrose, MA 02176 Fax: (617)655-2195

Community newspaper (tabloid). **Founded:** 1988. **Freq:** Weekly. **Print Method:** Offset. **Trim Size:** 11 3/8 x 17. **Cols./Page:** 5. **Col. Width:** 2 1/16 inches. **Col. Depth:** 16 inches. **Key Personnel:** Pete Chianco, Editor; Jim Nolan, Advertising Dir.; Chuck Goodrich, Publisher. **USPS:** 001-093. **Subscription Rates:** Free. **Remarks:** Accepts advertising. **Formerly:** Prime Times.
Ad Rates: BW: $1,352 **Circ:** Non-paid 12,433
4C: $1,852
SAU: $16.90
PCI: $16.90

📖 **14429 Melrose Free Press**
Community Newspaper Company
40 W. Foster St. Phone: (617)665-4001
Melrose, MA 02176 Fax: (617)665-2195

Community newspaper (tabloid). **Founded:** 1901. **Freq:** Weekly. **Print Method:** Offset. **Trim Size:** 14 x 22 3/4. **Cols./Page:** 6. **Col. Width:** 2 inches. **Col. Depth:** 21 inches. **Key Personnel:** Dan Ryan, Editor; Frank Yetter, Advertising Mgr.; Chuck Goodrich, Publisher. **USPS:** 338-340. **Subscription Rates:** $19; $30 out of area. **Remarks:** Accepts advertising. **Formerly:** Melrose Observer (1992); Prime Times.
Ad Rates: BW: $644 **Circ:** Paid 5,667
PCI: $8.05 Free 642

📖 **14430 Saugus Advertiser**
Community Newspaper Company
40 West Foster St. Phone: (617)665-4001
Melrose, MA 02176 Fax: (617)665-2195

Community newspaper. **Founded:** 1879. **Freq:** Weekly. **Print Method:** Offset. **Trim Size:** 14 x 22 3/4. **Cols./Page:** 6. **Col. Width:** 2 inches. **Col. Depth:** 21 inches. **Key Personnel:** Dawn Souza, Editor; Chuck Goodrich, Publisher; Jim Nolan, Advertising Dir. **USPS:** 609-400. **Subscription Rates:** $15; $14 students; $31 out of area. **Remarks:** Accepts advertising.
Ad Rates: BW: $1,543.50 **Circ:** Paid 4,524
4C: $2,043.50 Free 260
SAU: $12.25
PCI: $12.25

METHUEN, pop. 36,700.

W. MA. Essex Co. 9 mi. NE of Lowell. Industrial.

📖 **14431 Journal of Innovative Management**
GOAL/QPC
13 Branch St. Phone: (508)685-3900
Methuen, MA 01844 Fax: (508)685-6151

Journal focusing on news and information on quality management, systems thinking, and creativity and innovation. **Founded:** 1995. **Freq:** Quarterly. **Print Method:** Offset. **Trim Size:** 8 x 11. **Cols./Page:** 2. **Key Personnel:** Laurence R. Smith, Editor, lsmith@shore.net. **ISSN:** 1081-0714. **Subscription Rates:** $139 individuals; $149 Canada; $159 other countries; $39 single issue. **Remarks:** Advertising not accepted.
Circ: Paid 2,500
Non-paid 1,000

🎙 **14432 WCCM-AM - 800**
462 Merriman St. Phone: (978)683-7171
Methuen, MA 01844 Fax: (978)687-1180

Format: News; Talk. **Networks:** CNN Radio. **Owner:** Costa-Eagle Radio, at above address. **Founded:** 1947. **Formerly:** Curt Gowdy Broadcasting. **Operating Hours:** 24 hrs. **ADI:** Boston-Worcester,MA-Derry-Manchester,NH. **Key Personnel:** John Bassett, General Mgr.; Bruce Arnold, Program Dir. **Local Programs:** *Bruce Arnold Program*, Bruce Arnold; *Hotline*, Craig Roberts; *Let's Talk Sports*, Frank Benjamin. **Wattage:** 1000. **Ad Rates:** $17-30 for 30 seconds; $20-45 for 60 seconds.

🎙 **14433 WHAV-AM - 1490**
462 Merrimack St. Phone: (508)689-2900
Methuen, MA 01844 Fax: (508)373-8023

Format: Hispanic; News; Talk. **Networks:** Home Shopping Network. **Owner:** Costa Eagle Radio, at above address. **Founded:** 1947. **Operating Hours:** Continuous. **Key Personnel:** Frankie Foxx, Music Dir.; Brian Webster, Program Dir.; Tricia Taskey, News Dir. **Wattage:** 1000.

MIDDLEBORO, pop. 16,404.

SE MA. Plymouth Co. 10 mi. E. of Tauton. Manufactures shoes, varnish, fire fighting equipment, heating pads, calendars, photo finishing, bricks. Cranberry canning. Dairy farms.

📖 **14434 Middleboro Gazette**
Hathaway Publishing
148 W. Grove St. Phone: (617)947-1760
PO Box 551 Fax: (617)942-9426
Middleboro, MA 02346
Newspaper. **Founded:** 1852. **Freq:** Weekly (Wed.). **Print Method:** Offset. **Cols./Page:** 6. **Col. Width:** 24 nonpareils. **Col. Depth:** 301 agate lines. **Key Personnel:** Jane Lopes, Editor; Warren G. Hathaway, Publisher. **Subscription Rates:** $13 individuals. **Remarks:** Accepts advertising.
Ad Rates: GLR: $.46 **Circ:** 5,860

MILFORD, pop. 23,390.

C. MA. Worcester Co. 12 mi. SW of Framington. Manufactures computers, rubber goods, elastic webbing, ceramic tile, glass, tools, concrete, dies, metal stampings, construction materials, paints. Dairy, truck farms.

📖 **14435 Journal of the New England Water Works Association**
New England Water Works Association
64 Dilla St. Phone: (508)478-6996
Milford, MA 01757-1104 Fax: (508)634-8643

Technical journal reporting on association events as well as meetings and information of interest to the waterworks industry. **Founded:** 1886. **Freq:** Quarterly. **Print Method:** Offset. **Trim Size:** 7 1/4 x 10. **Cols./Page:** 2. **Col. Width:** 3 inches. **Col. Depth:** 8 inches. **Key Personnel:** Peter C. Karalekas, Jr., Editor; Melissa Fortin, Adver. & Circulation Mgr. **ISSN:** 0028-1939. **Subscription Rates:** $20 Free to qualified subscribers; $32 other countries; $28 other countries.
Ad Rates: BW: $330 **Circ:** Paid ‡2,800
4C: $850 Non-paid ‡243

📖 **14436 Milford Daily News**
Alta Group
159 S. Main St. Phone: (508)473-1111
PO Box 160 Fax: (508)634-7512
Milford, MA 01757
General newspaper. **Founded:** Sept. 1, 1887. **Freq:** Mon.-Sat. (eve.). **Print Method:** Offset. Uses mats. **Trim Size:** 13 x 21 1/2. **Cols./Page:** 6. **Col. Width:** 2 1/16 inches. **Col. Depth:** 301 agate lines. **Key Personnel:** Andrea Haynes, Editor, phone (508)634-7567, fax (508)634-7514; Dennis Fitzgerald, Advertising Mgr., phone (508)634-7503, fax (508)634-7511. **USPS:** 144-320. **Subscription Rates:** $104 individuals. **Remarks:** Accepts advertising.
Ad Rates: GLR: $1.32 **Circ:** Mon.-Sat. 12,679
SAU: $12.35

📖 **14437 Neighbors**
159 S. Main St. Phone: (508)473-1111
Milford, MA 01757 Fax: (508)478-8769

Local newspaper (tabloid). **Founded:** Feb. 1986. **Freq:** Weekly (Tues.). **Print Method:** Offset. **Cols./Page:** 5. **Col. Width:** 24 nonpareils. **Col. Depth:** 224 agate lines. **Key Personnel:** John T. Hourihan, Editor; Thomas C. Sawyer, Publisher; Richard Rae, Advertising Mgr. **Remarks:** Accepts advertising. **Formerly:** News Plus (1992).
Ad Rates: BW: $573.75 **Circ:** Free ‡25,581
PCI: $8.50

📖 **14438 Sticks & Mallets**
DORN Publications
PO Box 716 Fax: (508)359-7988
Milford, MA 01757 Free: (800)527-6647

Music magazine for percussionists. **Subtitle:** The Magazine for all Percussionists. **Freq:** Bimonthly. **Subscription Rates:** $45 individuals; $85 two years; $60 out of country individuals; $110 two years out-of-country; $8 single issue. **Former name:** Drummer.

🎙 **14439 WMRC-AM - 1490**
258 Main St. Phone: (508)473-1490
PO Box 421 Fax: (508)478-2200
Milford, MA 01757

Format: Full Service; Adult Contemporary. **Networks:** ABC. **Owner:** Thomas M. McAuliffe, at above address. **Founded:** 1956. **Operating Hours:** full time; 20% local, 80% network/satellite. **Key Personnel:** Ed Thompson, News Dir.; Tom McAuliffe II, General Mgr.; Rick Michaels, Program Dir.; Suzanne McAuliffe, Office Mgr. **Local Programs:** *Conversations*; *Sports Talk Live*; *Spotlight on Law & Business*; *Talking Health*. **Wattage:** 1000. **Ad Rates:** $14-20 for 30 seconds; $17-24 for 60 seconds. **URL:** http://www.uwmrc.com; http://www.wmrc@dfront.com.

MILLBURY, pop. 11,808.

C. MA. Worcester Co. 6 mi. SE of Worcester. Manufactures woolens, wire, felt, shoe thread, textile supplies, machinery, edged tools, shuttles, heddles and frames. Fish hatcheries. Dairy, poultry, truck, fruit farms.

📖 **14440 Dairy World**
IBA, Inc.
19 River St. Phone: (508)865-2507
Millbury, MA 01527 Fax: (508)865-5891

Dairy farming magazine. **Subtitle:** A Magazine Especially for the Dairy Farmer. **Founded:** 1967. **Freq:** Bimonthly. **Print Method:** Offset. **Trim Size:** 8 1/2 x 11. **Cols./Page:** 3. **Col. Width:** 26 nonpareils. **Col. Depth:** 138 agate lines. **Key Personnel:** Joseph Scolaro, Editor; Patricia Forkell, Asst. Editor. **Subscription Rates:** $12 individuals. **Remarks:** Accepts advertising.
Ad Rates: BW: $1,000 **Circ:** Non-paid ‡40,999
4C: $1,800

📖 **14441 Sheltie Pacesetter**
117 Park Hill Ave. Phone: (508)753-8500
Millbury, MA 01527
Trade magazine covering Shetland Sheepdogs (Shelties). **Founded:** 1977. **Freq:** Bimonthly. **Print Method:** Sheetfed offset. **Trim Size:** 8 1/2 x 11. **Key Personnel:** Nancy Lee Cathcart, Editor; Nancy Pratt, Editor, npratt@ma.ultramet.com. **ISSN:** 0774-6608. **Subscription Rates:** $44 individuals; $10 single issue. **Remarks:** Accepts advertising. **URL:** http://www.sheltie.com.
Ad Rates: BW: $165 **Circ:** Combined ⊕**2,810**
4C: $945

MILLERS FALLS, pop. 1,200.

W. MA. Franklin Co. 3 mi. N. of Erving. Residential.

📖 **14442 The Renovator's Supply**
Renovator's Old Mill Phone: (413)659-3773
Millers Falls, MA 01349 Fax: (413)659-3796

Home service magazine. **Founded:** 1978. **Freq:** Bimonthly. **Print Method:** Offset. **Trim Size:** 6 x 10 7/8. **Cols./Page:** 2. **Col. Depth:** 140 agate lines. **Key Personnel:** Clau de Jeanloz, Editor and Publisher. **Subscription Rates:** $5 individuals; $2 single issue. **Remarks:** Accepts advertising.
Ad Rates: BW: $22,350 **Circ:** ‡8,000,000

MILLVILLE

📖 **14443 Je Me Souviens**
American-French Genealogical Society
PO Box 171 Phone: (508)885-4316
Millville, MA 01529
Publisher E-mail: afgs@ids.net

Genealogical journal. **Founded:** 1978. **Freq:** Semiannual. **Print Method:** Offset. **Trim Size:** 5 x 8. **Cols./Page:** 2. **Col. Width:** 2 inches. **Key Personnel:** Paul P. Delisle, Editor, delislep@juno.com. **ISSN:** 0195-7384. **Subscription Rates:** $30 individuals. **Remarks:** Accepts advertising.
Ad Rates: BW: $50 **Circ:** Combined 1,700

MILTON, pop. 25,860.

E. MA. Norfolk Co. 6 mi. S. of Boston. (Branch of Boston P.O.) Residential. Manufactures crackers, cocoa, chocolate, ice cream.

14444 Milton Record Transcript
Tribune Publishing Co.
1261 Hyde Park Ave. Phone: (617)361-6500
Hyde Park, MA 02136 Fax: (617)361-8909

Community newspaper. **Founded:** 1900. **Freq:** Weekly (Fri.). **Print Method:** Offset. **Cols./Page:** 9. **Col. Width:** 9 1/2 picas. **Col. Depth:** 308 agate lines. **Key Personnel:** Daniel J. Horgan, Jr., Publisher. **Subscription Rates:** $20 individuals. **Remarks:** Accepts advertising.
Ad Rates: GLR: $.52 **Circ:** ‡5,900
PCI: $7

14445 Milton Townsman
Associated Newspapers
7 Cabot Pl. Phone: (781)878-1111
PO Box 441 Fax: (781)878-3333
Stoughton, MA 02072
Publisher E-mail: aweeklies@aol.com

Community newspaper. **Founded:** 1985. **Freq:** Weekly (Thurs.). **Print Method:** Offset. **Cols./Page:** 6. **Col. Width:** 9.5 picas. **Col. Depth:** 16 inches. **Key Personnel:** Richard R. Dailey, Publisher. **Subscription Rates:** $10. **Remarks:** Accepts advertising.
Ad Rates: PCI: $10.53 **Circ:** 1,640

14446 WMLN-FM - 91.5
1071 Blue Hill Ave. Phone: (617)333-0311
Milton, MA 02186 Fax: (617)333-2792

Format: Alternative/New Music/Progressive; News; Sports. **Networks:** NBC. **Founded:** 1975. **Operating Hours:** Continuous; 5% network, 95% local. **Key Personnel:** Alan Frank, Contact, phone (617)333-2139, fax (617)333-2386, afrank@curry.edu; Josh Easler, Station Mgr., phone (617)333-2386. **Local Programs:** *Local Focus*, Josh Easler. **Wattage:** 170. **Ad Rates:** Noncommercial.

NANTUCKET†, pop. 5,087.

SE MA. Nantucket Co. On N. shore of Nantucket Island, 25 mi. SE of Hyannis. Boat connections. Resort.

14447 The Hemingway Review
University of Idaho Press
c/o Susan F. Beegel Phone: (508)325-7157
180 Polpis Rd. Fax: (508)325-7157
Nantucket, MA 02554
Academic journal covering the work and life of Ernest Hemingway. **Founded:** 1971. **Freq:** Semiannual. **Print Method:** Photo offset. **Trim Size:** 6 x 9. **Key Personnel:** Susan F. Beegel, Editor, sbeegel@aol.com. **ISSN:** 0276-3362. **Subscription Rates:** $20 individuals; $10 single issue. **Remarks:** Advertising not accepted. **Former name:** Hemingway Notes.
Circ: Combined 1,200

14448 The Inquirer and Mirror
Ottaway Publishing Co.
Milestone Rd. Phone: (508)228-0001
Box 1198 Fax: (508)325-5089
Nantucket, MA 02554
Publication E-mail: inkynews@aol.com

Community newspaper. **Founded:** June 23, 1821. **Freq:** Weekly (Thurs.). **Print Method:** Offset. **Cols./Page:** 8. **Col. Width:** 22 nonpareils. **Col. Depth:** 287 agate lines. **Key Personnel:** Marianne Giffin Stanton, Editor/Co-Mgr.; Gael Polchinski, Co-Mgr.; Carla K. Powers, Advertising Mgr.; Amy Bowman, Circulation Mgr. **ISSN:** 0891-8686. **Subscription Rates:** $30 individuals; $36 out of area; $131 other countries. **Remarks:** Accepts advertising. **URL:** http://www.nantucket.net/inkym/.
Ad Rates: GLR: $.49 **Circ:** Paid ♦**9,336**
BW: $1,131.60 Non-paid ♦**36**
PCI: $8

14449 Nantucket Magazine
Nantucket Journal, Inc.
2 Greglen Ave., Ste. 408 Phone: (508)228-8700
Nantucket, MA 02554 Fax: (508)228-9063

Consumer magazine covering Nantucket Island. **Founded:** 1989. **Freq:** Quarterly. **Print Method:** Web offset. **Trim Size:** 8 1/8 x 10 7/8. **Cols./Page:** 3. **Col. Width:** 2 1/8 inches. **Col. Depth:** 9 3/16 inches. **Key Personnel:** Stephen Sheppard, Editor; Michele Lindstedt, Advertising Mgr.; C. S. Lovelace, Circulation Mgr. **ISSN:** 1074-1763. **Subscription Rates:** $15.95 individuals; $3.95 single issue. **Remarks:** Accepts advertising. **Former name:** Nantucket Journal.
Ad Rates: BW: $990 **Circ:** Combined 6,393
4C: $1,555

14450 Renaissance Magazine
Phantom Press Publications
13 Appleton Rd. Phone: (508)325-0411
Nantucket, MA 02554 Fax: (508)325-5992
Publisher E-mail: renzine@aol.com

Magazine about the world of Renaissance fairs, roleplaying, and re-enactment. Includes articles on culinary and herbal arts, history, costuming, and castles. **Founded:** Jan. 1, 1996. **Freq:** Quarterly. **Print Method:** Web. **Trim Size:** 8.5 x 11. **Cols./Page:** 6. **Key Personnel:** Kim Guarnaccia, Editor and Publisher. **Subscription Rates:** $17 individuals; $6 single issue; $32 two years. **Remarks:** Accepts advertising.
Ad Rates: BW: $950 **Circ:** Paid ‡20,000
4C: $1,250 Non-paid ‡2,000

14451 Yesterday's Island
Yesterday's Island, Inc.
PO Box 626 Phone: (508)228-9165
Nantucket, MA 02554 Fax: (508)228-1348

Tourist guide. **Founded:** 1971. **Freq:** Weekly. **Print Method:** Offset. Cols 5. **Col. Width:** 24 nonpareils. **Col. Depth:** 224 agate lines. **Key Personnel:** Suzanne M. Daub, Editor; Jerry T. Daub, Publisher. **Subscription Rates:** $25 individuals; $30 outside continental U.S. **Remarks:** Accepts advertising.
Ad Rates: GLR: $1 **Circ:** Non-paid 350,000

14452 TCI of Nantucket
1 Monomoy Rd. Phone: (508)228-2008
Nantucket, MA 02554 Fax: (508)228-9004

Owner: TCI, 4643 S. Ulster St., Ste. 400, Denver, CO 80237. **Founded:** 1973. **Formerly:** Nantucket Cablevision (1992). **Key Personnel:** Ronald E. Russell, Contact. **Cities Served:** subscribing households 4,300; 32 channels; 1 community access channel.

NATICK, pop. 29,461.

NE MA. Middlesex Co. 18 mi. W. of Boston. Manufactures electronic equipment, boxes and boxboard, baseballs, softballs, band saws, machine parts, electric clocks. Foundry.

14453 BioTechniques
Eaton Publishing
154 E. Central St. Phone: (508)655-8282
Natick, MA 01760 Fax: (508)655-9910

Research journal. **Subtitle:** The Journal of Laboratory Technology for Bioresearch. **Founded:** 1983. **Freq:** Monthly. **Print Method:** Web offset. **Trim Size:** 8 1/4 x 10 7/8. **Cols./Page:** 3. **Col. Width:** 2 3/16 inches. **Col. Depth:** 10 inches. **Key Personnel:** James Ellingboe, Editor; Francis Eaton, Publisher; Susan Starratt, Advertising Mgr.; Karen Shulman, Editor. **Subscription Rates:** $95; $125 other countries. $13 single issue. **Available Online. URL:** bitechniques.com; http://www.biotechniques.com.
Ad Rates: BW: $4,620 **Circ:** 60,000
4C: $5,820

14454 Experimental Mathematics
A K Peters, Ltd.
63 South Ave. Phone: (508)655-9933
Natick, MA 01760 Fax: (508)655-5847
Publication E-mail: editorial@expmath.org
Publisher E-mail: service@akpeters.com

Journal devoted to developing mathematical theory and insight. **Founded:** 1992. **Freq:** Quarterly. **Trim Size:** 8 1/2 x 11. **Cols./Page:** 2. **Col. Width:** 3 5/16 inches. **Col. Depth:** 8 1/8 inches. **Key Personnel:** David B.A. Epstein, Editor-in-Chief, dbae@maths.warwick.ac.uk; Silvio Levy, Editor, levy@math.berkeley.edu; Carolyn Artin, Editor, editorial@akpeters.com; Carolyn Astin, Editor. **ISSN:** 1058-6458. **Subscription Rates:** $225 institutions; $60 single issue; $95 individuals; $65 members of American Mathematical Society. **Remarks:** Advertising not accepted. **URL:** http://www.akpeters.com; http://www.expmath.com.
Circ: Paid 500

14455 Journal of Graphics Tools
A K Peters, Ltd.
63 South Ave. Phone: (508)655-9933
Natick, MA 01760 Fax: (508)655-5847
Publication E-mail: editorial@akpeters.com
Publisher E-mail: service@akpeters.com

Journal containing research ideas for computer graphics professionals. **Founded:** 1996. **Freq:** Quarterly. **Trim Size:** 7 x 10. **Cols./Page:** 1. **Key Personnel:** Ronen Barzel, Editor-in-Chief, ronen@pixar.com; Andrew Glassner, Founding Editor, glassner@microsoft.com; David Salesin, Consulting Editor, salesin@cs.washington.edu; Jenny Rogers, Asst. Editor. **ISSN:** 1086-7651. **Subscription Rates:** $40 individuals; $35 members of ACM; $98 institutions in U.S. and Canada; $30 single issue; $60 other countries; $118 institutions, other countries. **Remarks:** Advertising not accepted. **URL:** http://www.acm.org/jgt.
Circ: (Not Reported)

14456 Natick Bulletin
Suburban World, Inc.
992 Great Plain Ave. Phone: (508)653-4460
PO Box 358 Fax: (781)444-1795
Needham, MA 02192
Free: (800)847-NEWS

Newspaper. **Founded:** 1865. **Freq:** Weekly (Thurs.). **Print Method:** Offset. **Cols./Page:** 6. **Col. Width:** 20 nonpareils. **Col. Depth:** 224 agate lines. **Key Personnel:** Ellen Prihodko, Editor; William Barrett, Publisher; Robert M. Shomphe, Jr., Advertising Mgr. **Subscription Rates:** $18 individuals. **Remarks:** Accepts advertising. **URL:** http://www.suburbanworld.
Ad Rates: GLR: $.62 **Circ:** Combined 2,556

14457 The Natick Tab
Community Newspaper Company
254 2nd Ave. Phone: (781)433-7828
Needham, MA 02192-9114 Fax: (781)433-7835

Community newspaper. **Founded:** Oct. 1985. **Freq:** Weekly. **Print Method:** Offset. **Trim Size:** 10 x 16. **Cols./Page:** 8. **Col. Width:** 8 picas. **Col. Depth:** 16 inches. **Key Personnel:** John Wilpers, Editor; Russel Pergament, Publisher; Stephen Cummings, Publisher; Lisa Flicop, Editor. **URL:** http://townonline.com.
Circ: Non-paid 8,325

14458 Peptide Research
Eaton Publishing
154 E. Central St. Phone: (508)655-8282
Natick, MA 01760 Fax: (508)655-9910

Interdisciplinary journal for the rapid publication of articles describing original research on peptides. **Subtitle:** The Journal of Peptide Application, Synthesis and Analysis. **Founded:** 1988. **Freq:** Bimonthly. **Print Method:** Web offset. **Trim Size:** 8 3/4 x 10 7/8. **Cols./Page:** 3. **Col. Width:** 2 3/16 inches. **Col. Depth:** 10 inches. **Key Personnel:** James Ellingboe, Editor; Francis Eaton, Publisher; Christine McAndrews, Advertising Mgr.; Karen Shulman, Circulation Mgr. **ISSN:** 1040-5704. **Subscription Rates:** $75 individuals; $95 Canada; $110 other countries; $15 single issue. **Remarks:** Accepts advertising. **Online:** Biotechnet. **URL:** http://www.biotechniques.com.
Ad Rates: BW: $1,380 **Circ:** 3,000
4C: $1,880

NEEDHAM, pop. 27,901.

E. MA. Norfolk Co. 12 mi. SW of Boston. (Branch of Boston P.O.) Manufactures knit goods, dental and surgical instruments, textiles, electronic products.

Arlington Advocate - See Arlington

The Ashland Tab - See Ashland

The Brookline Tab - See Brookline

Daily Transcript - See Dedham

Dover-Sherborn Suburban Press - See Dover-Sherborn

The Dover Tab - See Dover

The Framingham Tab - See Framingham

The Holliston Tab - See Holliston

14459 The Journal of Bone and Joint Surgery
20 Pickering St. Phone: (781)449-9780
Needham, MA 02192 Fax: (781)449-9787
Publication E-mail: edit@jbss.org

Magazine covering orthopaedic surgical techniques. **Founded:** 1903. **Freq:** Monthly. **Print Method:** Offset. **Trim Size:** 8 5/16 x 10 7/8. **Cols./Page:** 2. **Col. Width:** 40 nonpareils. **Col. Depth:** 140 agate lines. **Key Personnel:** Amber Howard, Advertising Mgr., phone (781)449-9745, fax (781)449-9742, howarda@jbjs.org. **ISSN:** 0021-9355. **Subscription Rates:** $96 individuals. **Remarks:** Accepts advertising. **URL:** http://www.jbjs.org. **Alt. Formats:** CD-ROM.
Ad Rates: BW: $1,680 **Circ:** Paid ‡37,396
4C: $2,880 Non-paid 429

Medfield Suburban Press - See Medfield

Natick Bulletin - See Natick

The Natick Tab - See Natick

14460 NCGR Journal
National Council for Geocosmic Research, Inc.
c/o Lorraine Welsh Phone: (617)444-4428
42 Garland Rd.
Needham, MA 02192
Technical journal covering cosmology and astrology. **Founded:** 1972. **Freq:** Semiannual. **Print Method:** Offset. **Trim Size:** 8 1/2 x 11. **Cols./Page:** 2. **Col. Width:** 3 1/4 inches. **Col. Depth:** 9 1/4 inches. **Key Personnel:** Lorraine Welsh, Editor; Arlene Nimark, Advertising Mgr.; Mark Downing, Production Editor. **ISSN:** 1080-6423. **Subscription Rates:** Included in membership; $10 single issue. **Remarks:** Accepts advertising.
Ad Rates: BW: $350 **Circ:** Paid 3,100

14461 Needham TAB
Community Newspaper Company
254 Second Ave Phone: (781)433-7800
Needham, MA 02192 Fax: (781)433-8202
Publisher E-mail: townonline.com

Local newspaper. **Founded:** 1874. **Freq:** Weekly (Wed.). **Print Method:** Offset. **Cols./Page:** 6. **Col. Width:** 25 nonpareils. **Col. Depth:** 300 agate lines. **Key Personnel:** Maria Buckley, Editor, mbuckley@cnc.com; Kirk Davis, Publisher. **Subscription Rates:** Free. **Remarks:** Accepts advertising.
Ad Rates: BW: $2,142 **Circ:** Free 10,316
4C: $2,802

14462 Needham Times
Suburban World, Inc.
992 Great Plain Ave. Phone: (508)653-4460
PO Box 358 Fax: (781)444-1795
Needham, MA 02192
Free: (800)847-NEWS
Publication E-mail: needham@suburbanworld.com

Local newspaper. **Founded:** 1932. **Freq:** Weekly (Thurs.). **Print Method:** Offset. **Trim Size:** 11 x 17. **Cols./Page:** 6. **Col. Width:** 10 1/4 picas. **Col. Depth:** 16 inches. **Key Personnel:** William Barrett, Publisher, phone (781)444-1706; David Petruska, Circulation Mgr., phone (781)444-1706; Elizabeth Banks, Exec. Editor, phone (781)444-1706, editor@suburbanworld.com. **Subscription Rates:** $30 out of area; $22 students.
Ad Rates: PCI: $10.98 **Circ:** Free 11,700

News Tribune - See Waltham

Newton Graphic - See Newton

14463 The Newton Tab
Community Newspaper Company
254 2nd Ave. Phone: (781)433-7828
Needham, MA 02192-9114 Fax: (781)433-7835

Community newspaper (tabloid). **Founded:** 1979. **Freq:** Weekly (Tues.). **Print Method:** Offset. **Trim Size:** 10 x 16. **Cols./Page:** 7. **Col. Width:** 8 picas. **Key Personnel:** John Wilpers, Editor; Russel Pergament, Publisher; Stephen Cummings, Publisher; Lisa Flicop, Advertising Mgr.
Circ: Non-paid 20,945

14464 Offshore Magazine
Offshore Communications, Inc.
220-9 Reservoir St. Phone: (781)449-6204
PO Box 817 Fax: (781)449-9702
Needham, MA 02194-0979
Publication E-mail: oshore@aol.com

Boating magazine. **Subtitle:** Northeast Boating At Its Best. **Founded:** 1976. **Freq:** Monthly. **Print Method:** Offset. Uses mats. **Trim Size:** 8 1/8 x 10 7/8. **Cols./Page:** 3. **Col. Width:** 30 nonpareils. **Col. Depth:** 161 agate lines. **Key Personnel:** Richard Royer, Publisher; Betsy Frawley Haggerty, Editor; Al Black, Advertising Dir. **ISSN:** 0274-9394. **Subscription Rates:** $19.95 individuals. **Remarks:** Accepts advertising.
Ad Rates: 4C: $2,762.50 **Circ:** ‡32,000

14465 Parkway Transcript
Community Newspaper Company
254 Second Ave Phone: (781)433-7800
Needham, MA 02192 Fax: (781)433-8202
Publisher E-mail: townonline.com

Community newspaper. **Founded:** 1930. **Freq:** Weekly (Wed.). **Print Method:** Offset. **Cols./Page:** 6. **Col. Width:** 25 nonpareils. **Col. Depth:** 300 agate lines. **Key Personnel:** Kirk Davis, Publisher. **Subscription Rates:** $20 individuals; $12.50 students; $25 out of county. **Remarks:** Accepts advertising.
Ad Rates: BW: $2,142 **Circ:** Paid 2,540
4C: $2,802 Free 97

The Sherborn Tab - See Sherborn

The Sudbury Town Crier & TAB - See Sudbury

The Wayland Tab - See Wayland

The Wellesley Tab - See Wellesley

14466 The Wellesley Townsman
Community Newspaper Company
254 Second Ave Phone: (781)433-7800
Needham, MA 02192 Fax: (781)433-8202
Publisher E-mail: townonline.com

Community newspaper. **Founded:** 1906. **Freq:** Weekly (Thurs.). **Print Method:** Offset. **Cols./Page:** 6. **Col. Width:** 18 nonpareils. **Col. Depth:** 294 agate lines. **Key Personnel:** Kirk Davis, Editor; Cathy Brauner, Publisher. **Subscription Rates:** $20; $16 senior citizens and students; $27 out of area. **Remarks:** Advertising not accepted for tobacco products.
Ad Rates: PCI: $9 **Circ:** Paid 6,671
Non-paid 492

14467 West Roxbury Transcript
Community Newspaper Company
254 Second Ave Phone: (781)433-7800
Needham, MA 02192 Fax: (781)433-8202
Publisher E-mail: townonline.com

Community newspaper. **Founded:** 1944. **Freq:** Weekly (Wed.). **Print Method:** Offset. **Cols./Page:** 6. **Col. Width:** 25 nonpareils. **Col. Depth:** 300 agate lines. **Key Personnel:** James Harder, Editor; Kirk Davis, Publisher. **Subscription Rates:** $20 individuals; $12.50 students; $25 out of county. **Remarks:** Accepts advertising.
Ad Rates: BW: $2,142 **Circ:** Paid 4,032
4C: $2,802 Free 190

The Weston Tab - See Weston

14468 Continental Cablevision of Massachusetts, Inc.
95 Wexford St. Phone: (617)449-6960
Needham, MA 02194 Fax: (617)455-8693

Founded: 1981. **Cities Served:** Middlesex and Norfolk counties, MA.

14469 WCVB-TV - 5
5 TV Pl. Phone: (781)449-0400
Needham, MA 02194 Fax: (781)449-0260

Format: Commercial TV. **Networks:** ABC. **Owner:** Hearst-Argyle Television, Inc., 888 7th Ave., New York, NY 10106. **Founded:** 1972. **Operating Hours:** Continuous. **ADI:** Boston-Worcester,MA-Derry-Manchester,NH. **Key Personnel:** Paul LaCamera, President/General Mgr., phone (781)433-4000; A. Hoffman, VP/General Sales Mgr., phone (781)433-4165; J. Wertlieb, Local Sales Mgr., phone (781)433-4155; Lisa Goyette, National Sales Mgr., phone (781)433-4150; Marc J. Mekler, Commercial Operations Mgr., phone (781)433-4108; Adrienne Lotoski, Research Dir., phone (781)433-4181; Rena Salzman, Sales Marketing Dir., phone (781)433-4157; Amy Goode, Sales Promotion Mgr., phone (781)433-4177; Tom Bringola, VP/Business Mgr., phone (781)433-4014; Liz Cheng, Dir., Programming and Public Relations, phone (781)433-4008; Patrick Baldwin, Creative Services Dir., phone (781)433-4226; Caroline Waddel, Public Relations Mgr., phone (781)433-4771; Karen Holmes Ward, Executive Producer/Public Affairs; Mike Keller, VP of Engineering, phone (781)433-4774. **Wattage:** 100,000. **URL:** http://www.wcvb.com.

NEEDHAM HEIGHTS

NE MA. Norfolk Co. 10 mi. E. of Wellesley.

14470 Contractors Equipment Guide
50 Central Ave. Phone: (781)449-1250
PO Box 324 Fax: (781)449-7768
Needham Heights, MA 02494
Free: (800)225-8448
Publisher E-mail: cegsells@worldnet.att.net

Trade magazine on new and used construction equipment. **Founded:** July 1960. **Freq:** Biweekly. **Print Method:** Web offset. **Trim Size:** 10 1/8 x 16. **Cols./Page:** 5. **Col. Width:** 1 7/8 inches. **Col. Depth:** 225 agate lines. **Key Personnel:** J. LaCamera, Editor. **ISSN:** 0300-6514. **Subscription Rates:** $70 individuals; $130 two years first class; $3 single issue. **Remarks:** Accepts advertising.
Ad Rates: BW: $955 **Circ:** ‡26,262
PCI: $33

NEW BEDFORD, pop. 98,478.

SE MA. Bristol Co. On Buzzards Bay at mouth of Acushnet River, 56 mi. S. of Boston. Bridge to Fairhaven. Port of entry, with good harbor. Resort. Shopping center for Cape Cod, Martha's Vineyard and Nantucket. One of the largest fishing ports on the Atlantic coast. Freezing plants. Manufactures fine cotton and silk goods, tire fabrics, drills, screws, copper, eyelets and tacks, capacitors, rubber goods, paper products, rope, twine, lubricating oil, paint, electrical goods, golf balls, textile-mill supplies and machinery, cable, wire, camera film.

14471 The Standard-Times
Standard-Times Publishing Co.
25 Elm St. Phone: (508)997-7411
New Bedford, MA 02740-6235 Fax: (508)997-7852
Free: (800)288-4896

General newspaper. **Founded:** 1850. **Freq:** Daily (eve.), Sat. and Sun. (morn.). **Print Method:** Offset. **Trim Size:** 14 x 22 3/4. **Cols./Page:** 6. **Col. Width:** 13 1/8 inches. **Col. Depth:** 21 1/2 inches. **Key Personnel:** James M. Ragsdale, Editor; Orren B. Robbins, Publisher; Rita Thieme, Advertising Mgr. **USPS:** 518-380. **Subscription Rates:** $130 individuals. **Remarks:** Accepts advertising. **URL:** http://www.s-t.com. **Feature Editors:** Michael Bailey, *Rural Development, Saturday, Suburban*, phone (508)997-7411; Robert Barcellos, *Religion*, phone (508)997-7411; Mike Conery, *News, Political*, phone (508)997-7411; Steve DeCosta, *Financial/Business*, phone (508)997-7411; Anne Eisenmenger, *Travel*, phone (508)997-7411; Brad Hathaway, *Drama, Entertainment, Fashion, Features, Food, Lifestyle, Living, Medical, Movie, Music, Science, Society*, phone (508)997-7411; Richard Lodge, *City, Metro*, phone (508)997-7411; George Patisteas, *Photo*, phone (508)997-7411; Susan Pawlack-Seaman, *Education*, phone (508)997-7411; Bob Stern, *Sports*, phone (508)997-7411; Rachel Thomas, *Consumer Affairs*, phone (508)997-7411; Steve Urbon, *Editorials*, phone (508)997-7411; Steve Varnum, *TV*, phone (508)997-7411; Natalie White, *Environmental*, phone (508)997-7411.
Ad Rates: GLR: $1.23 **Circ:** Mon.-Sat. ★**39,190**
BW: $2,212.35 Sun. ★**44,043**
4C: $2,462.35
SAU: $17.15
PCI: $17.15

14472 Colony Cablevision
630 Mt. Pleasant St. Phone: (508)998-9000
New Bedford, MA 02740 Fax: (508)998-3329

Founded: 1975. **Formerly:** Whaling City Cable TV. **Cities Served:** Bristol County and Dartmouth, MA.

14473 WJFD-FM - 97.3
270 Union St. Phone: (508)997-2929
New Bedford, MA 02740 Fax: (508)990-3893

Format: Ethnic. **Networks:** Independent. **Founded:** 1949. **Operating Hours:** Continuous. **Key Personnel:** Edmund Dinis, General Mgr. **Wattage:** 50,000. **Ad Rates:** $5-9 for 10 seconds; $7-13.50 for 30 seconds; $9-16 for 60 seconds.

NEWBURYPORT, pop. 15,900.

NE MA. Essex Co. On Merrimac River, 3 mi. from ocean, 35 mi. NE of Boston. Major historic sights. Manufactures electronics, semi-conductors, silverware, machine shop products. Fisheries. Truck farms.

14474 Nautical Research Journal
Nautical Research Guild, Inc.
62 Marlboro St. Phone: (978)462-6970
Newburyport, MA 01950-3134
Magazine for ship modelers covering historical maritime data. **Founded:** 1948. **Freq:** Quarterly. **Print Method:** Offset. **Trim Size:** 8 1/2 x 11. **Cols./Page:** 2. **Col. Width:** 20 nonpareils. **Col. Depth:** 132 agate lines. **Key Personnel:** Rob Napier, Editor. **ISSN:** 0738-7245. **Subscription Rates:** $30 individuals; $7.50 single issue. **Remarks:** Accepts advertising. **Alt. Formats:** Microform.
Ad Rates: BW: $150 **Circ:** ‡1,700

14475 Newburyport Daily News
Essex County Newspaper
23 Liberty St. Phone: (508)462-6666
Newburyport, MA 01950 Fax: (508)465-8505

General newspaper. **Founded:** 1888. **Freq:** Mon.-Sat. (eve.). **Cols./Page:** 6. **Col. Width:** 25 nonpareils. **Col. Depth:** 294 agate lines. **Key Personnel:** Calhoun J. Killeen, Jr., Editor; Frank O. King, Publisher. **Subscription Rates:** $30 individuals. **Remarks:** Accepts advertising. **URL:** http://www.newburyportnews.com.
Ad Rates: SAU: $10.08 **Circ:** Mon.-Sat. ★**13,758**

14476 Open Wheel Magazine
65 Parker St., Ste. 2 Phone: (978)463-3787
Newburyport, MA 01950 Fax: (978)463-3250

Open Wheel Racing Magazine. **Founded:** 1981. **Freq:** Monthly. **Print Method:** Offset. **Trim Size:** 8 1/8 x 10 3/4. **Cols./Page:** 3. **Col. Width:** 27 nonpareils. **Col. Depth:** 140 agate lines. **Key Personnel:** Dick Berggen, Exec. Editor; Doug Gore, Technical Editor; Ros Sneddon, Editor. **Subscription**

Rates: $18.95 individuals; $27.95 Canada; $30.95 out of country; $3.99 single issue.
Ad Rates: BW: $2,625 **Circ:** Paid ★71,703
4C: $4,230

14477 Stock Car Racing
General Media
65 Parker St., Ste. 2 Phone: (978)463-3787
Newburyport, MA 01950 Fax: (978)463-3250

Magazine covering stock car racing. **Founded:** 1966. **Freq:** Monthly. **Print Method:** Offset. **Trim Size:** 8 1/8 x 10 3/4. **Cols./Page:** 3. **Col. Width:** 27 nonpareils. **Col. Depth:** 140 agate lines. **Key Personnel:** Dick Berggren, Editor; Doug Gore, Technical Editor. **ISSN:** 0734-7340. **Subscription Rates:** $18.95 individuals; $3.99 single issue.
Ad Rates: BW: $6,305 **Circ:** Paid ★229,305
4C: $10,230

14478 WNBP-AM - 1450
6 Federal St. Phone: (508)462-1450
Newburyport, MA 01950-2804 Fax: (508)462-0333

Format: Adult Contemporary. **Networks:** USA Radio. **Owner:** Damon Radio, Inc., at above address. **Founded:** 1957. **Operating Hours:** 5 a.m.-11 p.m. **Key Personnel:** Win Damon, General Mgr.; Matt Stevens, Program Dir.; John Evans, News Dir. **Wattage:** 1000.

NEWTON, pop. 83,622.

NE MA. Middlesex Co. 7 mi. SW of Boston. (Branch of Boston P.O.) Andover Newton Theological School; Boston College; Mt. Ida Jr. College; Aquinas Jr. College; LaSell Jr. College. Residential. Manufactures radio tubes, railway signals, yarn, knit goods, electronics, fans, plastics.

14479 Alledger
Boston College School of Law
885 Centre St. Phone: (617)552-4339
Newton, MA 02159 Fax: (617)552-2615
Publication E-mail: bcalledger@aol.com

Newspaper circulated to law students. **Founded:** 1981. **Freq:** Semimonthly. **Print Method:** Offset. **Trim Size:** 10 x 16. **Cols./Page:** 4. **Col. Width:** 27 nonpareils. **Col. Depth:** 224 agate lines. **Key Personnel:** Jason Bassett, Editor-in-Chief; Ann Snyder, Managing Editor. **Remarks:** Accepts advertising.
Ad Rates: BW: $390 **Circ:** Non-paid 2,000
PCI: $6.50

14480 Boston College Environmental Affairs Law Review
Boston College School of Law
885 Centre St. Phone: (617)552-4339
Newton, MA 02159 Fax: (617)552-2615

Academic journal covering environmental law. **Founded:** 1973. **Freq:** Quarterly. **Trim Size:** 6 x 9. **ISSN:** 0190-7034. **Subscription Rates:** $23 individuals; $6 single issue. **Remarks:** Advertising not accepted.
Circ: Paid 800

14481 CPI Purchasing
Cahners Publishing Company
275 Washington St. Phone: (617)558-2119
Newton, MA 02458 Fax: (617)558-4700

Magazine serves qualified buyers in the chemical/process industries. **Founded:** 1984. **Freq:** Monthly. **Print Method:** Offset. **Cols./Page:** 3. **Col. Width:** 30 nonpareils. **Col. Depth:** 140 agate lines. **Key Personnel:** David Erickson, Editor; Gary R. Squires, Publisher. **Remarks:** Accepts advertising.
Ad Rates: BW: $3,160 **Circ:** Non-paid ‡40,007
4C: $4,650

14482 Datamation
Cahners Publishing Company
275 Washington St. Phone: (617)558-2119
Newton, MA 02458 Fax: (617)558-4700
Publication E-mail: bsemich@cahners.com

Magazine on computers and information processing. **Subtitle:** The Emerging Technologies Magazine for Today's IS. **Founded:** 1957. **Freq:** Semimonthly. **Print Method:** Offset. **Trim Size:** 7 7/8 x 10 1/2. **Cols./Page:** 3. **Col. Width:** 27 nonpareils. **Col. Depth:** 140 agate lines. **Key Personnel:** Carole Sacino, Publisher; Regina Twiss, Marketing Manager; J. William Semich, Editor-in-Chief; Ellen Romanow, Editor. **ISSN:** 0011-6963. **Subscription Rates:** $69. $10 single issue. **Remarks:** Accepts advertising. **Online:** CompuServe Information Service; "Plug In" Datamation. **URL:** http://www.datamation.com.
Ad Rates: BW: $14,845 **Circ:** Paid 2,168
4C: $17,845 Non-paid 160,052

14483 Design News
Cahners Publishing Company
275 Washington St. Phone: (617)558-2119
Newton, MA 02458 Fax: (617)558-4700
Publication E-mail: dn@chners.com

Magazine covering design engineering. **Founded:** 1946. **Freq:** Semimonthly. **Print Method:** Offset. **Trim Size:** 8 x 10 3/4. **Cols./Page:** 3. **Col. Width:** 26 nonpareils. **Col. Depth:** 135 agate lines. **Key Personnel:** Larry Maloney, Publisher. **Subscription Rates:** $55 individuals. **Remarks:** Accepts advertising.
Ad Rates: BW: $6,375 **Circ:** Non-paid ‡182,000
4C: $8,120

14484 Digital News & Review
Cahners Publishing Company
275 Washington St. Phone: (617)558-2119
Newton, MA 02458 Fax: (617)558-4700

Subtitle: The Independent Newspaper and Test Lab of Open Computing for DEC Sites. **Founded:** Oct. 1983. **Freq:** Semimonthly. **Print Method:** Offset. **Trim Size:** 10 3/4 x 13 1/2. **Cols./Page:** 4. **Col. Width:** 2 1/4 inches. **Col. Depth:** 13 inches. **Key Personnel:** Paul Nesdore, Editor; Steve Twombly, Publisher; Wayne Howe, Advertising Dir.; Gwen Brady, Contact; Jennifer London, Sales Coord. **ISSN:** 0734-4314. **Subscription Rates:** Free to qualified subscribers. **Remarks:** Accepts advertising. **Alt. Formats:** CD-ROM. **Formerly:** Digital Review.
Ad Rates: BW: $7,580 **Circ:** Controlled ‡90,000
4C: $1,814
PCI: $475

14485 E D N China
Cahners Publishing Company (Newton)
275 Washington St. Phone: (852)965-1553
Newton, MA 02158-1630 Fax: (852)976-0706

Trade magazine covering design-oriented electronics. **Founded:** Sept. 1994. **Freq:** Monthly. **Key Personnel:** William Zhang, wmzhang@public.bta.net.com; Adonis Mak. **Remarks:** Accepts advertising. **Former name:** EDN China.
Circ: Controlled 20,400

14486 EDN Magazine Edition
Cahners Publishing Co.
275 Washington St. Phone: (617)964-3030
Newton, MA 02158 Fax: (617)558-4700

Magazine for electronic design engineers and engineering managers. **Founded:** 1956. **Freq:** Biweekly. **Print Method:** Offset. **Trim Size:** 7 7/8 x 10 1/2. **Cols./Page:** 3 and 2. **Col. Width:** 14 and 20.5 picas. **Col. Depth:** 60 picas. **Key Personnel:** Michael Markowitz, Editor, phone (617)558-4214, fax (617)558-4470, m.markowitz@cahners.com; Tom Tobeck, Publisher, phone (617)558-4454, fax (617)558-4470, ttobek@edn.cahners.com; Lauren Elsaesser, Promotion Coordinator. **Subscription Rates:** $140 individuals; $20 single issue; $209 Canada. **Remarks:** Accepts advertising. **URL:** http://www.ednmag.com.
Ad Rates: BW: $9,930 **Circ:** Non-paid 161,523
4C: $12,330 Paid 3,131

14487 EDN Products and Careers
Cahners Publishing Company
275 Washington St. Phone: (617)558-2119
Newton, MA 02458 Fax: (617)558-4700

Newspaper (tabloid) of technology, products, and careers for engineers and engineering managers. **Founded:** 1986. **Freq:** Biweekly. **Print Method:** Web offset. **Trim Size:** 10 3/4 x 14 1/2. **Cols./Page:** 5 and 6. **Col. Width:** 11 and 9 picas. **Col. Depth:** 86 picas. **Key Personnel:** Jon Titus, Editorial Dir.; Roy Forsberg, Publisher; Jeffrey Patterson, Sales Mgr. **ISSN:** 0012-7515. **Subscription Rates:** Free to qualified subscribers. **Remarks:** Accepts advertising. **Formerly:** EDN News Edition.
Ad Rates: BW: $7,695 **Circ:** Controlled ‡131,000
4C: $9,240

14488 Electronic Business Today
Cahners Publishing Company
275 Washington St. Phone: (617)558-2119
Newton, MA 02458 Fax: (617)558-4700

Magazine for purchasing managers and buyers of electronic components and materials used in end product manufacture. **Subtitle:** The Magazine for High Technology Buying. **Founded:** Sept. 1986. **Freq:** Monthly. **Print Method:** Offset. **Trim Size:** 8 1/2 x 11. **Cols./Page:** 3. **Col. Width:** 13 picas. **Col. Depth:** 63 picas. **Key Personnel:** John Kerr, Editor; Jack O'Connor, Publisher. **ISSN:** 0889-0196. **Subscription Rates:** Free to qualified readers; $40 nonqualified; $50 Canada and Mexico. **Remarks:** Accepts advertising. **Formerly:** Electronic Purchasing; Electronic Business Buyer.
Ad Rates: BW: $4,755 **Circ:** Non-paid ‡56,023
4C: $5,850
PCI: $112

14489 Industrial Distribution
Cahners Business Information
275 Washington St. Phone: (617)964-3030
Newton, MA 02458 Fax: (617)558-4700

Magazine covering industrial supplies marketing, management, sales, telecommunications, computers, inventory, and warehouse management. **Subtitle:** The Business Magazine for Industrial Distributors. **Founded:** Jan. 1911. **Freq:** Monthly. **Print Method:** Offset. **Trim Size:** 7 7/8 X 10 1/2. **Cols./Page:** 3. **Col. Width:** 26 nonpareils. **Col. Depth:** 133 agate lines. **Key Personnel:** Jack Keough, Assoc. Publisher/Editor, phone (617)558-4432, fax (617)630-3922, jkeough@cahners.com; Rusty Piersons, Group Publisher, phone (617)558-4564, fax (617)630-3922, rpiersons@cahners.com. **Remarks:** Accepts advertising. **URL:** http://www.inddist.com.
Ad Rates: BW: $7,400 **Circ:** Non-paid ‡41,500
4C: $9,250

14490 Interior Design
Cahners Publishing Company
275 Washington St. Phone: (617)558-2119
Newton, MA 02458 Fax: (617)558-4700

Interior designing and furnishings magazine. **Founded:** 1932. **Freq:** Monthly. **Print Method:** Offset. **Trim Size:** 8 3/8 x 10 7/8. **Cols./Page:** 2. **Col. Width:** 42 nonpareils. **Col. Depth:** 140 agate lines. **Key Personnel:** Stan Abercrombie, Chief Editor; Lester Dundes, V.P./Publishing Director; Cara David, Advertising Mgr.; Bill Ash, Publisher. **ISSN:** 0020-5508. **Subscription Rates:** $47.95.
Circ: Paid ★55,361

14491 Logistics Management and Distribution Report
Logistics Management & Distribution Report
275 Washington St. Phone: (617)558-4473
Newton, MA 02458 Fax: (617)558-4327
Publication E-mail: lm@cahners.com

Publication covering the areas of logistics, transportation, and supply-chain management. **Founded:** 1962. **Freq:** Monthly. **Print Method:** Offset. **Trim Size:** 7 7/5 x 10 1/2. **Cols./Page:** 3. **Col. Width:** 27 nonpareils. **Col. Depth:** 130 agate lines. **Key Personnel:** Peter Bradley, Editor and Publisher. **ISSN:** 1098-7355. **Subscription Rates:** $83.90. **Remarks:** Accepts advertising. **URL:** http://www.logisticsmgmt.com. **Former name:** Logistics Management (Jan. 1, 1998); Traffic Management.
Ad Rates: BW: $8,820 **Circ:** Non-paid ‡83,243
4C: $9,545

14492 Modern Materials Handling
Cahners Publishing Company
275 Washington St. Phone: (617)558-2119
Newton, MA 02458 Fax: (617)558-4700

Publication featuring materials handling. **Founded:** 1946. **Freq:** 14/year. **Print Method:** Offset. Uses mats. **Cols./Page:** 3 and 2. **Col. Width:** 27 and 40 nonpareils. **Col. Depth:** 140 agate lines. **Key Personnel:** Ray Kulwiec, Editor; William G. Sbordon, Publisher. **Remarks:** Accepts advertising.
Ad Rates: BW: $4,940 **Circ:** Non-paid ‡105,841
4C: $6,095

14493 Musical Merchandise Review
The Larkin Group
100 Wells Ave. Phone: (617)964-5100
Newton, MA 02159-9103 Fax: (617)964-2752
Free: (800)869-7469

Magazine on musical instruments and accessories. **Founded:** 1879. **Freq:** Monthly. **Print Method:** Offset. **Trim Size:** 8 1/2 x 11. **Cols./Page:** 3. **Col. Width:** 28 nonpareils. **Col. Depth:** 140 agate lines. **Key Personnel:** Don Johnson, Editor; Sid Davis, Publisher. **Subscription Rates:** Free to qualified subscribers; $24 individuals. **Remarks:** Accepts advertising. **Formerly:** EDT; Accent.
Ad Rates: GLR: $1,690 **Circ:** Paid 1,803
BW: $1,535 Non-paid 9,035
4C: $2,135
PCI: $1,190

14494 NARPPS Journal and News
National Association of Rehabilitation Professionals in the Private Sector (NARPPS)
313 Washington St., No. 302
Newton, MA 02158

Journal concerning rehabilitation. **Freq:** 4/year. **Subscription Rates:** $59 individuals.

14495 Newton Graphic
Community Newspaper Company
254 Second Ave Phone: (781)433-7800
Needham, MA 02192 Fax: (781)433-8202
Publisher E-mail: townonline.com

Community newspaper. **Founded:** 1872. **Freq:** Weekly (Wed.). **Print Method:** Offset. **Cols./Page:** 6. **Col. Width:** 25 nonpareils. **Col. Depth:** 300 agate lines. **Key Personnel:** Ellen Ushkanian, Editor; Kirk Davis, Publisher. **Subscription Rates:** $20 individuals; $12.50 students; $25 out of county. **Remarks:** Accepts advertising.
Ad Rates: BW: $1,276.38 4C: $2,802 SAU: $10.10 PCI: $11.25
Circ: Paid 323 Free 28,018

14496 Nostoc Magazine
Arts End Books
PO Box 162 Phone: (508)885-9904
Newton, MA 02468
Publisher E-mail: artsend@ma.ultranet.com

Literary arts magazine. **Founded:** 1972. **Freq:** Irregular. **Print Method:** Offset. **Key Personnel:** Marshall Brooks, Editor. **Subscription Rates:** $20 individuals; $4 single issue. **Remarks:** Accepts advertising.
Circ: Non-paid 500

14497 Purchasing Magazine
Cahners Business Information
275 Washington St. Phone: (617)964-3030
Newton, MA 02458 Fax: (617)558-4700

Magazine for buying professionals. **Subtitle:** The Magazine of Total Supply Chain Management. **Founded:** 1915. **Freq:** Semimonthly (monthly Jan., Aug., July and Dec.). **Print Method:** Offset. **Trim Size:** 8 x 10 3/4. **Cols./Page:** 3. **Col. Width:** 27 nonpareils. **Col. Depth:** 140 agate lines. **Key Personnel:** Kevin Fitzgerald, Editor, phone (617)558-4224, fax (617)558-4327, kevinf@cahners.com; John F. O'Connor, Publisher, jo'connor@cahners.com. **ISSN:** 0033-4448. **Subscription Rates:** $65. **Remarks:** Accepts advertising. **URL:** http://www.purchasing.com.
Ad Rates: BW: $6,850 4C: $8,475
Circ: Non-paid ‡100,203

14498 R & D Magazine
Cahners Publishing Company
275 Washington St. Phone: (617)558-2119
Newton, MA 02458 Fax: (617)558-4700

Magazine covering the field of applied research and development. **Founded:** 1959. **Freq:** Monthly. **Print Method:** Web offset. **Trim Size:** 8 x 10 3/4. **Cols./Page:** 3. **Col. Width:** 2 1/8 inches. **Col. Depth:** 10 inches. **Key Personnel:** Rob Cassidy, Editor. **ISSN:** 0746-9179. **Subscription Rates:** $69.95. $20 single issue. **Remarks:** Accepts advertising. **Formerly:** Industrial Research and Development.
Ad Rates: BW: $7,750 4C: $9,535
Circ: Paid 1,703 Non-paid 108,500

14499 Test & Measurement Europe
Cahners Business Information
275 Washington St. Phone: (617)964-3030
Newton, MA 02458 Fax: (617)558-4700
Publication E-mail: ednkerridge@mcimail.com

Professional magazine for electronics engineers responsible for test, measurement, inspection, and quality control in Europe. **Founded:** 1993. **Freq:** Bimonthly. **Print Method:** Web offset. **Key Personnel:** Roy Forsberg, Publisher; Brian Kerridge, Editor; Peter Micheli, Marketing Dir. **Subscription Rates:** Free to qualified subscribers. **Remarks:** Accepts advertising. **URL:** http://www.tmworld.com.
Ad Rates: BW: $4,565 4C: $5,540 PCI: $205
Circ: Controlled ‡25,000

14500 Test & Measurement World
Cahners Business Information
275 Washington St. Phone: (617)964-3030
Newton, MA 02458 Fax: (617)558-4700
Publication E-mail: tmw@cahners.com

Electronic engineering magazine specializing in test, measurement, and inspection of electronic products. **Subtitle:** The Magazine for Quality in Electronics. **Founded:** 1981. **Freq:** Monthly. **Print Method:** Web offset. **Trim Size:** 7 7/8 x 10 1/2. **Cols./Page:** 3. **Col. Width:** 13 2/5 picas. **Col. Depth:** 60 picas. **Key Personnel:** Jonathan Titus, Editor, phone (617)558-4573, fax (617)558-4470, jontitus@cahners.com; Roy Forsberg, Publisher, phone (617)558-4367, roy.forsberg@tmw.cahners.com; Peter Micheli, Mktg. Dir., phone (617)558-4813, fax (617)558-4470, pmicheli@ttmw.cahners.com; A. Darlene Fisher, Publisher's Asst., phone (617)558-4363, dfisher@tmw.cahners.com. **ISSN:** 0744-1657. **Subscription Rates:** $77.90 nonmembers. **Remarks:** Accepts advertising. **URL:** http://www.tmworld.com.
Ad Rates: BW: $6,475 4C: $7,870 PCI: $230
Circ: Controlled ‡74,300

14501 WNTN-AM - 1550
143 Rumford Ave. Phone: (617)969-1550
Newton, MA 02166

Format: Talk; Ethnic. **Networks:** Independent. **Owner:** Colt Communications, LLC, at above address. **Founded:** 1968. **Operating Hours:** Sunrise-sunset; 100% local. **Key Personnel:** Robert Rudnick, Station Mgr.; John Frassica, News Dir.; Sybil Tonkonogy, Public Affairs Director. **Local Programs:** *1550 Magazine* 11:00 am - 12:00 noon Monday-Friday. **Wattage:** 10,000. **URL:** http://www.wtcbfm.com.

NEWTON CENTER, pop. 83,622.

SE MA. Middlesex Co. 7 mi. W. of Boston. Mt. Ida Junior College.

14502 Show Reporter
335 Boylston St.
Newton Center, MA 02159-2843

Footwear and related industries publication. **Founded:** Aug. 1968. **Freq:** 3/year. **Print Method:** Offset. **Trim Size:** 11 x 16. **Cols./Page:** 5. **Col. Width:** 1 7/8 inches. **Col. Depth:** 14 inches. **Key Personnel:** Irving B. Roberts, Editor and Publisher; H.W. Davenport, Advertising Mgr. **Subscription Rates:** Free. **Remarks:** Accepts advertising.
Ad Rates: BW: $1,450 4C: $2,325
Circ: Free ‡10,000

NORTH ADAMS, pop. 18,063.

W. MA. Berkshire Co. Near W. end of Hoosac tunnel, 18 mi. NE of Pittsfield. State College; Williams College. Limestone quarries. Manufactures electronics components, wire, machinery, textiles, shoes, papers, chemical products.

14503 The Advocate
Berkshire Advocate, Inc.
87 Marshall St. Phone: (413)664-6900
PO Box 95 Fax: (413)664-7900
North Adams, MA 01247
Regional newspaper (tabloid). **Subtitle:** Newsweekly for the Berkshires and Southwestern Vermont. **Founded:** 1981. **Freq:** Weekly. **Print Method:** Offset. **Trim Size:** 11 1/2 x 17. **Cols./Page:** 6. **Col. Width:** 1 1/2 inches. **Col. Depth:** 16 inches. **Key Personnel:** Mark Rondeau, Editor; Ellen J. Bernstein, Publisher; Carol Allan, Advertising Dir. **Subscription Rates:** $100 individuals.
Ad Rates: BW: $955 4C: $1,300 PCI: $9.95
Circ: Paid ‡97 Free ‡21,000

14504 Transcript
North Adams Publishing Co.
Box 473 Phone: (413)663-3741
North Adams, MA 01247 Fax: (413)662-2792

General newspaper. **Founded:** 1843. **Freq:** Daily (eve.) and Sat. (morn.). **Print Method:** Offset. Uses mats. **Trim Size:** 14 x 22. **Cols./Page:** 6. **Key Personnel:** David E. Nahan, Editor and Publisher. **Subscription Rates:** $102.
Ad Rates: PCI: $9.71
Circ: Mon.-Fri. ★**8,157** Sat. ★**9,014**

14505 WJJW-FM - 91.1
Massachusetts College of Liberal Arts Phone: (413)662-5405 Fax: (413)662-5010
Merdock Hall
North Adams, MA 01247

Format: Jazz; Ethnic; Religious; Urban Contemporary; Oldies; Alternative/New Music/Progressive. **Networks:** Independent. **Founded:** 1974. **Formerly:** N. Adams State College. **Operating Hours:** 7 a.m.-3 a.m. **Key Personnel:** Alisha Cropper, General Mgr.; Scott Fleishman; Liz Frederick, Pop, Rock Alternative Music; Joe Yerdon, Music Dir.; Al Wiggins, Music Dir.; Chris Cattel, Music Dir.; Ramon Gonzalez, Music Dir. **Wattage:** 423. **Ad Rates:** Noncommercial.

14506 WMNB-FM - 100.1
Box 707 Phone: (413)663-6567
North Adams, MA 01247 Fax: (413)662-2143
E-mail: wnaw@bcn.net

Format: Easy Listening. **Networks:** CNN Radio; AP. **Owner:** Berkshire Broadcasting Co., Inc., at above address. **Founded:** 1964. **Operating Hours:** 5:30 a.m.-midnight. **Key Personnel:** Dave Fierro, Program Mgr.; Corydon L. Thurston, Contact; Paula Markland, PSA Director; Ron Plock, News Dir. **Local Programs:** *Opinion* 8:30 a.m.-9 a.m. Monday-Friday, Ron Plock. **Wattage:** 3000. **Ad Rates:** $11-20 for 30 seconds; $14-25 for 60 seconds. WNAW-AM, WSBS-AM, and WBBS-FM. **URL:** http://www.wmnbfm.com.

14507 WNAW-AM - 1230
Box 707 Phone: (413)663-6567
North Adams, MA 01247 Fax: (413)662-2143
E-mail: wnaw@bcn.net

Format: Adult Contemporary; News; Top 40; Oldies. **Networks:** AP. **Owner:** Berkshire Broadcasting Co., Inc., at above address. **Founded:** 1947. **Formerly:** WMNB-AM (1987). **Operating Hours:** 5:30 a.m.-midnight Mon.-Sat.; 7 a.m.-midnight Sun. **Key Personnel:** Ron Plock, News Dir.; Dave Fierro, Program Dir.; Paula Markland, PSA Director; Corydon L. Thurston, Contact. **Local Programs:** *Opinion* 8:30 a.m.-9 a.m. Monday-Friday, Ronald Plock, News Dir. **Wattage:** 1000. **Ad Rates:** $16-20 for 30 seconds; $20-25 for 60 seconds. WMNB-FM, WSBS-AM. **URL:** http://www.bcn.net/wnaw_ radio.

NORTH EASTON, pop. 6,100.

E. MA. Bristol Co. 5 mi. S. of Stoughton. Stonehill College. Residential.

14508 Speedway Scene
Hockomock Publishing
50 Washington St. Phone: (508)238-7016
PO Box 300 Fax: (508)230-2381
North Easton, MA 02356
Tabloid covering circle track racing from Winston Cup to local events. **Subtitle:** Winston Cup Beat. **Founded:** June 1971. **Freq:** Weekly. **Print Method:** Offset. **Trim Size:** 11 x 14. **Cols./Page:** 6. **Col. Width:** 1 5/8 inches. **Col. Depth:** 13 inches. **Key Personnel:** Val LeSieur, Editor and Publisher, vales@aol.com; Tim Christopher, Advertising Mgr. **USPS:** 920-360. **Subscription Rates:** $35; $52 Canada.
Ad Rates: BW: $1,008 4C: $1,483 PCI: $12
Circ: ‡52,500

14509 The Summit
Stonehill College
320 Washington St. No. 1974 Phone: (508)230-7830
North Easton, MA 02357 Fax: (508)230-8268

Collegiate newspaper. **Founded:** 1948. **Freq:** Weekly (during the academic year). **Print Method:** Offset. **Cols./Page:** 5. **Col. Width:** 24 nonpareils. **Col. Depth:** 224 agate lines. **Key Personnel:** Francis Diaz, Editor-in-Chief, fdiaz@student.stonehill.edu. **USPS:** 010-795. **Subscription Rates:** $10 non-students.
Ad Rates: BW: $320
Circ: Free 2,350

14510 WSHL-FM - 91.3
Stonehill College Phone: (508)238-2612
North Easton, MA 02357 Fax: (508)238-5722

Format: Alternative/New Music/Progressive. **Owner:** Stonehill College, at above address. **Founded:** 1973. **Formerly:** WSTO-FM. **Operating Hours:** Continuous. **Key Personnel:** Daniel R. Gerow, General Mgr.; Christopher Chapman, Music Dir.; Patricia Bauer, Program Dir.; Stephanie Shea, Underwriting Dir.; Matt Buchanan, Promotions; Ted Sharkey, Promotions; Brendon Snyder, Production Dir.; Josh Harlow, News Dir.; Marc MacGuillivray, Rap/Urban; Jason Nusbaum, RPM Dir.; Jon Newton, Metal Dir.; Ryan Asselta, Sports Dir.; Peter Q. George, Chief Engineer. **Wattage:** 100. **Ad Rates:** Noncommercial; underwriting available.

NORTH QUINCY

WEZE-AM - See Boston

NORTH READING, pop. 11,455.

NE MA. Middlesex Co. 18 mi. NW of Boston. Residential. Poultry farms.

14511 North Reading Transcript
Great Oak Publications, Inc.
7 Bow St. Phone: (978)664-4761
North Reading, MA 01864 Fax: (978)664-4954

Community newspaper. **Founded:** 1956. **Freq:** Weekly (Thurs.). **Print Method:** Offset. **Cols./Page:** 5. **Col. Width:** 26 nonpareils. **Col. Depth:** 224 agate lines. **Key Personnel:** Albert E. Sylvia, Publisher; Robert Turosz, Editor; Albert E. Sylvia, Jr., Managing Editor. **USPS:** 394-700. **Subscription Rates:** $22 annually locally; $25 out of area annually.
Ad Rates: GLR: $.45 BW: $508 4C: $440 SAU: $6.35 PCI: $6.35
Circ: Paid 4,052 Non-paid 226

14512 Stoneham Independent
Great Oak Publications, Inc.
7 Bow St. Phone: (978)664-4761
North Reading, MA 01864 Fax: (978)664-4954

Community newspaper. **Founded:** 1870. **Freq:** Weekly (Wed.). **Print Method:** Offset. **Trim Size:** 13 x 21. **Cols./Page:** 6. **Col. Width:** 13 picas. **Col. Depth:** 21 inches. **Key Personnel:** Jeff Gutridge, Editor; Mark J. Haggerty, Publisher. **USPS:** 522-400. **Subscription Rates:** $20; $22 out of area; $24 out of state. **Remarks:** Accepts advertising.
Ad Rates: GLR: $0.48 **Circ:** Paid 4,322
BW: $850.50 Non-paid 31
PCI: $6.75

NORTHAMPTON†, pop. 29,286.

WC MA. Hampshire Co. 17 mi. NW of Springfield. Smith College (women). Manufactures cutlery, wire cable, toothbrushes, caskets, optical merchandise, indelible ink, tracer paper. Agriculture. Tobacco, onions, potatoes.

14513 Daily Hampshire Gazette
H.S. Gere & Sons, Inc.
PO Box 299
Northampton, MA 01061

General newspaper. **Founded:** 1786. **Freq:** Daily (eve.) and Sat. (morn.). **Print Method:** Offset. **Trim Size:** 13 3/4 x 22 3/4. **Cols./Page:** 6. **Col. Width:** 24 agate lines. **Col. Depth:** 301 nonpareils. **Key Personnel:** James Foudy, Editor; John Ebbets, Advertising Dir. **ISSN:** 0739-3506. **Subscription Rates:** $180 individuals. **Remarks:** Accepts advertising. **URL:** http://www.gazettenet.com.
Ad Rates: GLR: $.70 **Circ:** Mon.-Sat. 20,502
BW: $1,754.40
4C: $2,204.40
PCI: $13.60

14514 Smith Alumnae Quarterly
Alumnae Association of Smith College
Smith College Phone: (413)585-2020
Alumnae House Fax: (413)585-2073
Northampton, MA 01063-0001
Free: (800)526-2023
Publication E-mail: alumnae@ais.smith.edu

College alumnae magazine. **Founded:** 1909. **Freq:** Quarterly. **Print Method:** Offset. **Trim Size:** 8 1/2 x 11. **Cols./Page:** 3. **Col. Width:** 28 nonpareils. **Col. Depth:** 133 agate lines. **Key Personnel:** Sarah Barrett, Co-Editor; John MacMillan, Co-Editor; Karin Fischer, Asst. Editor/Contact. **USPS:** 499-000. **Subscription Rates:** Free. **Remarks:** Advertising not accepted.
Circ: ‡40,000

14515 The Sophian
Smith College
Capen Annex Phone: (413)585-4972
Northampton, MA 01060 Fax: (413)585-2075

Collegiate newspaper. **Founded:** 1952. **Freq:** Weekly. **Trim Size:** 11 x 17. **Cols./Page:** 5. **Col. Width:** 2 inches. **Col. Depth:** 16 inches. **Subscription Rates:** $35; $55 (mail). **Remarks:** Accepts advertising.
Ad Rates: BW: $360 **Circ:** ‡4,500
SAU: $7.78
PCI: $5.50

14516 WHMP-AM - 1400
15 Hampton Ave. Phone: (413)586-7400
PO Box 268 Fax: (413)585-0927
Northampton, MA 01060

Format: News; Talk; Information; Sports. **Networks:** NBC. **Owner:** Multi-Market Radio of Northamptom, Inc., at above address. **Founded:** 1950. **Operating Hours:** Continuous; 10% network, 90% local. **ADI:** Springfield, MA. **Key Personnel:** Rick Heideman, General Mgr.; Mike Dion, Operations Mgr.; Rick Heideman, Sales Mgr.; Ted Baker, Program Dir. **Wattage:** 1000. **Ad Rates:** $7-26 per unit.

14517 WHMP-FM - 99.3
15 Hampton Ave. Phone: (413)586-7400
PO Box 268 Fax: (413)585-0927
Northampton, MA 01060

Format: Contemporary Hit Radio (CHR). **Owner:** Multi-Market Radio of Northampton, Inc., at above address. **Founded:** 1956. **Key Personnel:** Rick Heideman, General Mgr. **Wattage:** 3000.

14518 WOZQ-FM - 91.9
Smith College Phone: (413)585-4956
Northampton, MA 01063-0100 Fax: (413)585-2075
E-mail: wozq@sophia.smith.edu

Format: Alternative/New Music/Progressive; Eclectic. **Owner:** Smith College, at above address, (413)584-2700. **Founded:** 1983. **Formerly:** WRSC-FM. **Operating Hours:** Continuous; 100% local. **Key Personnel:** Sara Shaw, Contact; Terri Rosenblatt, Music Dir.; Sara Shaw, Station Mgr.; Alyssa Chadburn, Program Dir.; Tamar Brown, Contact; Alyssa Anderson, Contact; Alyssa Gerber, Contact; Malicé Grant, Contact. **Wattage:** 400. **URL:** http://www.smith.edu/wozq.

NORTHFIELD

NC MA. Franklin Co. 5 mi. N. of Warwick.

14519 WNMH-FM - 91.5
206 Main St. Phone: (413)498-3603
Northfield, MA 01360 Fax: (413)498-3664

Format: News; Contemporary Hit Radio (CHR); Alternative/New Music/Progressive. **Networks:** ABC. **Owner:** Trustee of Northfield Mount Hermon School, at above address. **Founded:** 1984. **Formerly:** WMHS-FM (1984). **Operating Hours:** Continuous. **Key Personnel:** Nathaniel Webb, Station Dir.; Bill Hattendorf, Advisor/GM, phone (413)498-5470; Preston Lau, Operations Dir.; Aaron Lanou, Promotions Dir.; Brian Pressman, Music Dir.; Jamila Marie Patten, News Dir.; Kevin Barrett, Sports Dir.; Thomas Olajos, Technical Dir. **Wattage:** 235. **Ad Rates:** Noncommercial; underwriting available.

NORTON, pop. 12,690.

SE MA. Bristol Co. 8 mi. NW of Taunton. Wheaton College (women). Pine, oak timber. Manufactures paper and wooden boxes, box boards. Agriculture. Turkeys.

14520 Feminist Teacher
Ablex Publishing Corp.
Wheaton College Phone: (508)286-3732
Norton, MA 02766 Fax: (508)285-8270
Publication E-mail: feminist_ teacher@wheatonma.edu; coheegai@esumail.emporia.edu

Magazine containing articles, news, and resources for feminist educators. **Founded:** 1984. **Freq:** 2/year. **Trim Size:** 8 1/2 x 11. **Cols./Page:** 2. **Col. Width:** 42 picas. **Key Personnel:** Paula Krebs, phone (508)286-3652, fax (508)285-8270; Gail Cohee, phone (316)341-5542, coheegai@esumail.emporia.edu. **ISSN:** 0882-4843. **Subscription Rates:** $18 individuals; $33 out of country; $37.50 institutions; $47.50 institutions, other countries; $6 single issue. **Remarks:** Accepts advertising.
Circ: Paid 900

14521 Norton Courier
Associated Newspapers
7 Cabot Pl. Phone: (781)878-1111
PO Box 441 Fax: (781)878-3333
Stoughton, MA 02072
Publisher E-mail: aweeklies@aol.com

Community newspaper. **Founded:** 1991. **Freq:** Weekly (Thurs.). **Print Method:** Offset. **Cols./Page:** 6. **Col. Width:** 9.5 picas. **Col. Depth:** 16 inches. **Key Personnel:** Richard R. Dailey, Publisher. **Subscription Rates:** $17.50. **Remarks:** Accepts advertising.
Ad Rates: PCI: $10.53 **Circ:** 1,500

14522 Wheaton Wire
Wheaton College
Norton, MA 02766 Phone: (508)285-7722
Fax: (508)285-2908

Collegiate newspaper (tabloid). **Founded:** Oct. 8, 1987. **Freq:** Daily (during the academic year). **Print Method:** Offset. **Trim Size:** 9 1/2 x 14. **Cols./Page:** 5. **Key Personnel:** Nicole Hebert, Publisher. **Subscription Rates:** $20 off campus. **Remarks:** Accepts advertising.
Ad Rates: BW: $200 **Circ:** (Not Reported)
PCI: $5

NORWELL, pop. 9,240.

NE MA. Plymouth Co. 12 mi. ENE of Brockton. Agriculture.

14523 Aquaculture International
Chapman & Hall Inc.
101 Philip Dr. Free: (800)842-3636
Norwell, MA 02061-1615
Publisher E-mail: order@chaphall.com

Journal concerning the quality of aqua products, such as cultured fish, crustaceans, mollusks, and plants. **Freq:** Quarterly. **ISSN:** 0967-6120. **Subscription Rates:** $210 annual.

14524 DDIN International
Larson Associates
95 Mt. Blue St. Phone: (781)659-2115
Norwell, MA 02061 Fax: (781)659-2411
Free: (800)229-3346
Publisher E-mail: larson@dieco.com

Trade magazine covering diecutting process. **Founded:** Sept. 1986. **Freq:** Quarterly. **Print Method:** Web offset. **Trim Size:** 8 1/2 x 11. **Cols./Page:** 3. **Key Personnel:** Robert Larson, Contact, larson@dicco.com. **ISSN:** 1078-6902. **Subscription Rates:** $48 individuals U.S. and Mexico; $86 two years U.S. and Mexico; $65 other countries; $120 two years other countries. **Remarks:** Accepts advertising. **URL:** http://www.dieco.com. **Former name:** DDIN North America.
Ad Rates: BW: $1275 **Circ:** Combined 6,000
PCI: $1925

14525 Ecotoxicology
Chapman & Hall Inc.
101 Philip Dr. Free: (800)842-3636
Norwell, MA 02061-1615
Publisher E-mail: order@chaphall.com

Journal covering the effects of toxic chemicals on population, communities and ecosystems. **Freq:** Quarterly. **ISSN:** 0963-9292. **Subscription Rates:** $190 annual.

14526 The EDI Law Review
Kluwer Law International
101 Philip Dr. Phone: (617)354-0140
Norwell, MA 02061 Fax: (617)354-8595

Journal on theoretical biology. **Freq:** Quarterly. **Key Personnel:** P. Dullemeijer, Editor; D. Ludwig, Editor. **Subscription Rates:** $221.

14527 International Play Journal
Chapman & Hall Inc.
101 Philip Dr. Free: (800)842-3636
Norwell, MA 02061-1615
Publisher E-mail: order@chaphall.com

Journal geared towards those who work to serve children and children's play. **Freq:** Triannual. **ISSN:** 0965-2531. **Subscription Rates:** $195 annual.

14528 Journal of Programming Languages
Chapman & Hall Inc.
101 Philip Dr. Free: (800)842-3636
Norwell, MA 02061-1615
Publisher E-mail: order@chaphall.com

Journal providing research in high level language design and implementation. **Freq:** Quarterly. **ISSN:** 0963-9306. **Subscription Rates:** $210 annual.

14529 Journal of Strategic Marketing
Chapman & Hall Inc.
101 Philip Dr. Free: (800)842-3636
Norwell, MA 02061-1615
Publisher E-mail: order@chaphall.com

Journal containing articles on the relationship between marketing and management. **Freq:** Quarterly. **ISSN:** 0965-254X. **Subscription Rates:** $194 annual.

14530 MAGMA
Chapman & Hall Inc.
101 Philip Dr. Free: (800)842-3636
Norwell, MA 02061-1615
Publisher E-mail: order@chaphall.com

Journal on magnetic resonance techniques and applications to physics, medicine and biology. **Founded:** 1993. **Freq:** Quarterly. **Key Personnel:** Dean Smith, Publisher; Nancy Fogarty, Advertising Dir. **ISSN:** 0968-5243. **Subscription Rates:** $195 annual. **Remarks:** Advertising accepted; rates available upon request.
Circ: (Not Reported)

14531 New England Real Estate Journal
East Coast Publications
57 Washington St.
Norwell, MA 02061
Publication E-mail: nerej@ix.net.com

Newspaper publishing commercial, industrial, and investment real estate news. **Founded:** Jan. 17, 1963. **Freq:** Weekly (Fri.). **Print Method:** Offset. **Trim Size:** 10 1/4 x 16. **Cols./Page:** 5. **Col. Width:** 2 inches. **Col. Depth:** 16 inches. **Key Personnel:** Benjamin Summers, Managing Editor; Roland Hopkins, Sr., Publisher; Linda Christman, Assistant to Publisher; Brian Heneghan, Sales Mgr. **ISSN:** 0028-4890. **Subscription Rates:** $139 individuals per year. **Remarks:** Accepts advertising. **Online:** Netcom-Centernet.
Ad Rates: BW: $1,171 **Circ:** Paid ‡8,000
4C: $1,621 Free ‡1,200

14532 New York R.E. Journal
East Coast Publications
57 Washington St. Phone: (617)878-4540
Norwell, MA 02061-1715 Fax: (617)871-1853
Free: (800)654-4993
Publication E-mail: nere,@ix.netcom.com

Commercial real estate journal. **Founded:** June 1989. **Freq:** Bimonthly. **Print Method:** Web offset. **Trim Size:** 10 1/4 x 13 1/4. **Cols./Page:** 5. **Col. Width:** 2 inches. **Col. Depth:** 13 inches. **Key Personnel:** Brian Heneghan, Editor; Linda Christman, Advertising Mgr.; Sue Bailey, Circulation Director. **ISSN:** 1057-2104. **Subscription Rates:** $60 individuals per year; $3 single issue. **URL:** http://www.centerent.com//rejouranl.htm.
Ad Rates: BW: $995 **Circ:** Paid 3,700
4C: $1,445

14533 Norwell Mariner
Mariner Newspapers
165 Enterprise Dr. Phone: (617)837-3500
Marshfield, MA 02050-2132 Fax: (617)837-4540
Free: (800)649-6661
Publisher E-mail: cmathis@cnc.com

Community newspaper. **Freq:** Weekly (Wed.). **Print Method:** Offset. **Trim Size:** 11 3/8 x 17. **Cols./Page:** 5. **Col. Width:** 2 1/8 inches. **Col. Depth:** 15 1/2 inches. **Key Personnel:** Margaret Smoragiewicz, Publisher; Judy McCaffrey Perry, Advertising Dir. **Subscription Rates:** $22. **Remarks:** Combined advertising rates available with other Mariner Newspapers.
Ad Rates: GLR: $11.78 **Circ:** Paid 2,188
BW: $942.40 Non-paid 104
4C: $1,300.00
PCI: $8.25

NORWOOD, pop. 29,711.

E. MA. Norfolk Co. 3 mi. S. of Dedham. Residential.

14534 CIM Construction Journal
Construction Industries of Massachusetts
1500 Providence Hwy. Phone: (617)551-0182
PO Box 667 Fax: (617)551-0916
Norwood, MA 02062
Publication E-mail: cim@ix.netcomp.comp

Magazine on heavy and highway construction. **Founded:** 1921. **Freq:** Weekly (Sat.). **Print Method:** Offset. **Trim Size:** 8 1/2 x 11. **Cols./Page:** 2. **Col. Width:** 42 nonpareils. **Col. Depth:** 139 agate lines. **Key Personnel:** John M. Pourbaix, Editor and Publisher; Elizabeth Duhig, Advertising Mgr.; Mark J. Drummey, Advertising Mgr.; Mark J. Drummey, Advertising Mgr. **Remarks:** Accepts advertising.
Ad Rates: BW: $300 **Circ:** ‡3,200
4C: $825

14535 Clinical Laboratory MarketPlace
Market Place Publications
89 Access Rd. Phone: (617)762-6600
Norwood, MA 02062 Fax: (617)762-1300

Direct response service for clinical supervisory personnel. **Founded:** 1968. **Freq:** Bimonthly. **Print Method:** Offset. **Trim Size:** 6 x 10 13/16. **Key Personnel:** Kevin M. Curran, Editor. **Subscription Rates:** $50. **Remarks:** Accepts advertising.
Ad Rates: BW: $2,765 **Circ:** 61,555
4C: $3,615

14536 Journal of Electronic Defense
Horizon House Publications, Inc.
685 Canton St. Phone: (781)769-9750
Norwood, MA 02062 Fax: (781)769-9884
Publication E-mail: jed@jedonline.com

Defense electronics magazine. **Subtitle:** Official Publication of the Association of Old Crows. **Founded:** July 1978. **Freq:** Monthly. **Print Method:** Offset. **Trim Size:** 7 13/16 x 10 3/4. **Cols./Page:** 3. **Col. Width:** 26 nonpareils. **Col. Depth:** 140 agate lines. **Key Personnel:** H. Gershanoff, Editor and Publisher, hgershanoff@jedonline.com; Peter Slingluff, Sales Dir., pslingluff@jedonline.com. **Subscription Rates:** $125 individuals; $200. **Remarks:** Accepts advertising. **URL:** http://www.jedonline.com.
Ad Rates: BW: $6,518 **Circ:** Paid ‡16,894
4C: $7,893

14537 Meeting Planners MarketPlace
Market Place Publications
89 Access Rd. Phone: (617)762-6600
Norwood, MA 02062 Fax: (617)762-1300

Direct response service for meeting planners. **Founded:** 1970. **Freq:** Bimonthly. **Print Method:** Offset. **Trim Size:** 6 x 10 13/16. **Key Personnel:** Kevin M. Curran, Editor. **Remarks:** Accepts advertising.
Ad Rates: BW: $3,975 **Circ:** 78,817
4C: $3,975

14538 Microwave Journal
Horizon House Publications, Inc.
685 Canton St. Phone: (781)769-9750
Norwood, MA 02062 Fax: (781)769-9884

Electronic engineering magazine. **Subtitle:** Microwave - RF & Lightwave Technology. **Founded:** 1958. **Freq:** Monthly. **Print Method:** Offset. **Trim Size:** 7 13/16 x 10 3/4. **Cols./Page:** 3 and 2. **Col. Width:** 26 and 40 nonpareils. **Col. Depth:** 140 agate lines. **Key Personnel:** Harlan Howe, Editor and Publisher. **ISSN:** 0192-6225. **Subscription Rates:** Free to qualified subscribers; $75. **Remarks:** Accepts advertising. **Available Online. URL:** http://www.mwjournal.com/mwj/html.
Ad Rates: BW: $5,360 **Circ:** Paid 1,241
4C: $6,225 Controlled 54,050

14539 The New Advocate
Christopher-Gordon Publishers Inc.
1502 Providence Highway, Ste. 12 Phone: (781)762-5577
Fax: (781)762-2110
Norwood, MA 02062
Free: (800)934-8322

Professional journal covering children's literature in education for teachers. **Founded:** 1989. **Freq:** Quarterly. **Print Method:** Offset. **Trim Size:** 6 3/4 X 10. **Key Personnel:** Kathy Short, Editor, phone (520)621-1311, fax (520)621-1853; Dana Fox, Editor. **ISSN:** 0895-1381. **Subscription Rates:** $30 individuals prepaid; $45 individuals purchase order; $40 Canada. **Remarks:** Accepts advertising.
Circ: 3,500

14540 Telecommunications Magazine
Horizon House Publications, Inc.
685 Canton St. Phone: (781)769-9750
Norwood, MA 02062 Fax: (781)769-9884
Publication E-mail: tcs@telecoms.mag.com

Magazine on international voice, data, and image networks communications. **Subtitle:** The Technology and Business Monthly for Communications Professionals. **Founded:** 1967. **Freq:** Monthly. **Print Method:** Offset. **Trim Size:** 8 3/16 x 10 7/8. **Cols./Page:** 3. **Col. Width:** 2 1/8 inches. **Col. Depth:** 10 inches. **Key Personnel:** Jack Pazzanese, Assoc. Pub.; Tom Valovic, Editor-in-Chief; William Bazzy, President. **ISSN:** 0278-4831. **Subscription Rates:** Free to qualified subscribers; $95 individuals. **Remarks:** Accepts advertising. **URL:** http://www.telecoms-mag.com. **Alt. Formats:** Microform.
Ad Rates: BW: $11,830 **Circ:** Paid 1,735
4C: $14,070 Controlled 80,000

ORANGE

NC MA. Franklin Co. 5 mi. N. of Wendell Depot.

14541 WCAT-AM - 700
660 E. Main St. Phone: (508)544-2321
PO Box 90
Orange, MA 01364

Format: Talk; News. **Owner:** PS Broadcasting, Inc., at above address. **Founded:** 1956. **Formerly:** WPNS-AM (1987). **Operating Hours:** Sunrise-sunset; 75% network, 25% local. **Key Personnel:** Jean Partridge, Pres./Gen.Mgr. **Local Programs:** *North Quabbin Business Journal*, Tom Kussey. **Wattage:** 2500. **Ad Rates:** $6-9 for 30 seconds; $7-12 for 60 seconds.

14542 WCAT-FM - 99.9
660 E. Main St. Phone: (978)544-2321
PO Box 90
Orange, MA 01364

Format: Adult Contemporary. **Networks:** ABC; Satellite Music Network. **Owner:** P & S Broadcasting, Inc., at above address. **Founded:** 1989. **Operating Hours:** Continuous. **ADI:** Boston-Worcester,MA-Derry-Manchester,NH. **Key Personnel:** Jean S. Partridge, Pres./Gen. Mgr. **Wattage:** 3000. **Ad Rates:** $8-14 for 30 seconds; $9-20 for 60 seconds. WCAT-AM.

ORLEANS, pop. 5,306.

E. MA. Barnstable Co. 40 mi. SE of Plymouth. Fishing.

14543 Best Read Guide
PO Box 1958 Phone: (508)240-1212
Orleans, MA 02653 Fax: (508)240-2912
Publication E-mail: bestread@capecod.com

Magazine aiding vacationing families in Cape Cod, **Founded:** 1988. **Freq:** Monthly. **Print Method:** Web offset. **Trim Size:** 5 1/4 x 7 1/2. **Cols./Page:** 2. **Col. Width:** 2 1/4 inches. **Col. Depth:** 7 inches. **Key Personnel:** Walter Brooks, Publisher; Julie Brooks, Managing Editor. **Subscription Rates:** $18 individuals; $3 single issue. **Remarks:** Accepts advertising. **URL:** http://www.capecod.com. **Formerly:** Best Read Guide–Cape Cod (1992).
Ad Rates: BW: $2,000 **Circ:** Controlled ‡1.3 million annually
4C: $2,800

Bourne Courier - See Bourne

Brewster Oracle - See Brewster

Cape Cod News - See Cape Cod

14544 The Cape Codder
Community Newspaper
5 Namskaket Rd. Phone: (508)398-0123
PO Box 2776 Fax: (508)760-3387
Orleans, MA 02653-6776
Free: (800)660-8999

Local newspaper. **Founded:** 1946. **Freq:** Semiweekly (TUE and Fri.). **Print Method:** Offset. **Cols./Page:** 5. **Col. Width:** 20 nonpareils. **Col. Depth:** 224 agate lines. **Key Personnel:** Greg O'Brien, Editor; Jack Powers, Gen. Mgr. Adv. **Subscription Rates:** $.75. **Remarks:** Accepts advertising.
Ad Rates: SAU: $15.55 **Circ:** Paid 14,988

Chatham Current - See Chatham

Eastham-Wellfleet Oracle - See Eastham

Harwich Oracle - See Harwich

Mashpee Messenger - See Mashpee

14545 Orleans Oracle
Community Newspaper
5 Namskaket Rd. Phone: (508)398-0123
PO Box 2776 Fax: (508)760-3387
Orleans, MA 02653-6776
Free: (800)660-8999

Community newspaper. **Founded:** 1987. **Freq:** Weekly (Thurs.). **Print Method:** Offset. **Trim Size:** 11 x 16 1/2. **Cols./Page:** 5. **Col. Width:** 21 inches. **Col. Depth:** 224 agate lines. **Key Personnel:** Eric Hartell, Editor; Jeanne Moore-Yount, Advertising Mgr. **Subscription Rates:** Free; $25 (mail). **Remarks:** Accepts advertising. **Formerly:** Cape Cod Oracle.
Ad Rates: GLR: $.45 **Circ:** Free 1,094
BW: $500
4C: $1,100
PCI: $6.25

14546 The Register
Community Newspaper
5 Namskaket Rd. Phone: (508)398-0123
PO Box 2776 Fax: (508)760-3387
Orleans, MA 02653-6776
Free: (800)660-8999

Newspaper. **Founded:** 1836. **Freq:** Weekly (Thurs.). **Print Method:** Offset. **Cols./Page:** 5. **Col. Width:** 21 nonpareils. **Col. Depth:** 224 agate lines. **Key Personnel:** Doug Bergen, Editor; Greg O'Biren, Publisher. **Subscription Rates:** $18.50. **Remarks:** Accepts advertising.
Ad Rates: GLR: $1.05 **Circ:** ‡9,274
BW: $1,152
4C: $1,552
PCI: $14.40

Wellfleet Oracle - See Wellfleet

14547 WKPE-AM - 1170
Radio Center Phone: (508)255-3220
Orleans, MA 02653 Fax: (508)255-9787
E-mail: rock1047@rock1047.com

Format: Album-Oriented Rock (AOR). **Founded:** 1970. **Operating Hours:** Sunrise-sunset, **ADI:** Boston-Worcester,MA-Derry-Manchester,NH. **Key Personnel:** Susan Pickering, General Mgr.; Michelle Dodd, Station Mgr.; Dan Towers; Wendy Hartman. **Wattage:** 1,000. **Ad Rates:** $50-120 for 30 seconds; $50-125 for 60 seconds. **URL:** http://www.rock1047.com.

14548 WKPE-FM - 104.7
Radio Center Phone: (508)255-3220
Orleans, MA 02653 Fax: (508)255-9787
Free: (800)497-1047
E-mail: wkpefm@ix.netcom.com

Format: Album-Oriented Rock (AOR). **Simulcasts:** WKPE-AM. **Owner:** GranCam Communications, 25 Bog Hollow Rd., Orleans, MA 02653. **Founded:** 1970. **Former name:** CAPE 104. **Operating Hours:** Continuous. **ADI:** Boston-Worcester,MA-Derry-Manchester,NH. **Key Personnel:** Susan Pickering, General Mgr.; Michelle Dodd, Sales Mgr.; Dan Towers, Program Dir.; Wendy Hartman, Promotions Dir. **Wattage:** 50,000. **Ad Rates:** $50-120 for 30 seconds; $50-125 for 60 seconds. **URL:** http://www.rock1047.com.

PALMER, pop. 11,389.

SW MA. Hampden Co. 15 mi. E. of Springfield. Manufactures

plastic products, wire goods, metal culverts, ladders, cosmetics, fire trucks, brushes. Dairy, poultry, fruit farms. Apples.

14549 The Harvard Salient
Turley Publications
24 Water St. Phone: (413)283-8393
Palmer, MA 01069-1840 Fax: (413)289-1977
Free: (800)824-6648

Voice of conservation at America's premier university. **Founded:** 1981. **Freq:** Semimonthly. **Print Method:** Offset. **Cols./Page:** 4. **Col. Width:** 2 1/4 inches. **Col. Depth:** 15 inches. **Key Personnel:** Corwyn Hopke, President, phone (617)493-3276; Matt Bruce, Jr., Editor, phone (617)493-2411; Colin Kennedy, Business Mgr., phone (617)493-2550. **Subscription Rates:** $20; $30 other countries. **Remarks:** Accepts advertising. **Online:** Internet.
Ad Rates: BW: $200 **Circ:** 4,500
4C: $500
PCI: $5

14550 Journal Register
Turley Publications
24 Water St. Phone: (413)283-8393
Palmer, MA 01069-1840 Fax: (413)289-1977
Free: (800)824-6648

Newspaper. **Founded:** 1850. **Freq:** Weekly (Thurs.). **Print Method:** Letterpress and offset. **Cols./Page:** 8. **Col. Width:** 20 nonpareils. **Col. Depth:** 294 agate lines. **Key Personnel:** Thomas Turley, Editor; Patrick Turley, Publisher. **Subscription Rates:** $23. **Remarks:** Accepts advertising.
Ad Rates: GLR: $.183 **Circ:** 4,700

PEABODY, pop. 45,976.

NE MA. Essex Co. 15 mi. NE of Boston. Tanning, finishing of leather and sheepskin. Manufactures gelatin, corrugated boxes, nails, shoe machinery, fibre and leather innersoles, resinous chemicals, plastics.

14551 New England Bride
New England Bride Inc.
215 Newbury St., Ste. 207 Phone: (508)535-4186
Peabody, MA 01960 Fax: (508)535-3090
Publication E-mail: neb@wedex.com; tom@wedex.com

Magazine for brides-to-be in six New England states. **Subtitle:** America's Only Monthly Bridal Magazine. **Founded:** Sept. 1972. **Freq:** Monthly. **Print Method:** Offset. **Trim Size:** 8 1/8 x 10 7/8. **Cols./Page:** 3. **Col. Width:** 27 nonpareils. **Col. Depth:** 140 agate lines. **Key Personnel:** Thomas J. Parello, Publisher; J. Gail Parello, Publisher; Christine Hennigan, Art Director; Matthew J. Demeis, Asst. Editor. **ISSN:** 0744-6861. **Subscription Rates:** Free to qualified subscribers brides-to-be 18 mon. before; their weddings; $36 individuals. **URL:** http://www.wedex.com; http://www.wed.com.
Ad Rates: BW: $2,495 **Circ:** Non-paid ‡15,075

PEMBROKE, pop. 13,487.

SE MA. Plymouth Co. 12 mi. E. of Brocton. Residential.

14552 Pembroke Mariner
Mariner Newspapers
165 Enterprise Dr. Phone: (617)837-3500
Marshfield, MA 02050-2132 Fax: (617)837-4540
Free: (800)649-6661
Publisher E-mail: cmathis@cnc.com

Community newspaper. **Freq:** Weekly (Wed.). **Print Method:** Offset. **Trim Size:** 11 3/8 x 17. **Cols./Page:** 5. **Col. Width:** 2 1/8 inches. **Col. Depth:** 15 1/2 inches. **Key Personnel:** Paul Woodhull, Editor; Margaret Smorgiewicz, Publisher; Judy McCaffrey Perry, Advertising Dir. **Subscription Rates:** $16. **Remarks:** Combined advertising rates available with other Mariner Newspapers.
Ad Rates: BW: $942.40 **Circ:** Paid 1,531
4C: $1,300.00 Non-paid 178
PCI: $8.25

14553 Pembroke Reporter
MPG Newspapers
9 Long Pond Rd. Phone: (508)746-5555
PO Box 959 Fax: (508)747-2148
Plymouth, MA 02362-0959
Free: (800)242-0264
Publisher E-mail: newsroom@mpgnews.com

Community newspaper. **Founded:** 1983. **Freq:** Weekly (Thurs.). **Print Method:** Offset. **Trim Size:** 16 1/2 x 11. **Cols./Page:** 5. **Col. Width:** 21 nonpareils. **Col. Depth:** 224 agate lines. **Key Personnel:** Phyllis Hughes, Publisher, phughes@mpgnews.com. **Subscription Rates:** $20 in county; $32 out of area. **Remarks:** Accepts advertising. **URL:** http://www.mpgnews.com.
Ad Rates: GLR: $.49 **Circ:** Combined ♦1,813
BW: $560
4C: $960
PCI: $7.45

14554 Plymouth County Business Review
Plymouth County Development Council
PO Box 1620 Phone: (781)826-3136
Pembroke, MA 02359 Fax: (781)826-0444
Publication E-mail: info@plymouth-1620.com

Trade business review covering regional business trends and stories. **Founded:** 1982. **Freq:** Semiannual. **Subscription Rates:** Free to qualified subscribers; $2 single issue. **Remarks:** Accepts advertising.
Circ: Non-paid 5,000

PEPPERELL, pop. 8,061.

NE MA. Middlesex Co. 18 mi. W. of Lowell.

14555 Times-Free Press
Nashoba Publications, Inc.
69 Fitchburg Rd. Phone: (978)772-0777
Ayer, MA 01432-0362 Fax: (978)772-4012
Free: (800)445-5635
Publisher E-mail: editor@nashobapub.com

Newspaper with a Democratic orientation. **Founded:** 1920. **Freq:** Weekly (Wed.). **Print Method:** Offset. **Cols./Page:** 9. **Col. Width:** 14 nonpareils. **Col. Depth:** 294 agate lines. **Key Personnel:** Frank Hartnett, Editor and Publisher. **Subscription Rates:** $15. **Remarks:** Accepts advertising.
Ad Rates: GLR: $.35 **Circ:** 9,700

14556 What's the Point?
PO Box 1575
Pepperell, MA 01463

Arts and entertainment magazine for people in their 20s. **Founded:** Aug. 1996. **Freq:** Bimonthly. **Print Method:** Web offset. **Trim Size:** 11 x 14. **Cols./Page:** 5. **Col. Width:** 2 inches. **Col. Depth:** 14 inches. **Key Personnel:** J.M. Hirsch, Editor-in-Chief. **ISSN:** 1089-702X. **Subscription Rates:** Free; $12 by mail. **Remarks:** Accepts advertising.
Ad Rates: BW: $260 **Circ:** Non-paid 5,000
4C: $460
PCI: $4

PITTSFIELD†, pop. 51,974.

W. MA. Berkshire Co. 58 mi. NW of Springfield. Publishing center. Summer and winter resorts. Manufactures electrical equipment, wooden pallets and skids, textiles, machinery, cement blocks, steel fabric, tools and dies, paper, control systems, plastics, missiles.

14557 The Berkshire Courier
Berkshire Courier Inc.
74 North St., No. 612
Pittsfield, MA 01201-5116

Community newspaper. **Founded:** 1834. **Freq:** Weekly (Thurs.). **Print Method:** Offset. **Cols./Page:** 6. **Col. Width:** 2 1/16 inches. **Col. Depth:** 21 1/4 inches. **Key Personnel:** Eileen W. Mooney, Editor; John W.P. Mooney, Publisher. **USPS:** 051-380. **Subscription Rates:** $24 individuals; $45 two years. **Remarks:** Accepts advertising.
Ad Rates: BW: $750 **Circ:** ‡3,200
4C: $975
SAU: $7

14558 The Berkshire Eagle
Pittsfield Publications, Inc.
PO Box 1171 Phone: (413)447-7311
Pittsfield, MA 01201 Fax: (413)499-3419
Publication E-mail: eagle@berkshirenet.com

General newspaper. **Founded:** 1789. **Freq:** Mon.-Sun. (morn.). **Print Method:** Offset. **Trim Size:** 12 1/2 x 22 1/2. **Cols./Page:** 6. **Col. Width:** 12.3 picas. **Col. Depth:** 21 1/4 inches. **Key Personnel:** Martin Langfield, Publisher; David Scribner, Editor. **ISSN:** 0895-8193. **Subscription Rates:** $134.20. **Remarks:** Accepts advertising. **URL:** http://www.berkshieeagle.com.
Ad Rates: GLR: $1.56 **Circ:** Mon.-Sat. 30,340
BW: $2,537.25 Sun. 34,771
4C: $2,887.25
SAU: $19.90

14559 Berkshire Summer
The Pittsfield Gazette, Inc.
PO Box 2236 Phone: (413)443-2010
Pittsfield, MA 01202 Fax: (413)443-2445

Weekly summer newspaper included as a pullout section of The Pittsfield Gazette and distributed independently in nearby communities. **Freq:** Weekly summer months only. **Trim Size:** 11 1/2 x 17. **Cols./Page:** 5. **Col. Width:** 1 11/12 inches. **Col. Depth:** 16 inches. **Key Personnel:** Jonathan Levine, Editor and Publisher; Anthony Fyden, Asst. Editor; Richard Houdek, Spec.Corr.; Carol Perkins, Spec.Corr.
Ad Rates: BW: $500 **Circ:** (Not Reported)
SAU: $7.00

14560 Catholic Library World
Catholic Library Association
100 N St., Ste. 224 Phone: (413)443-2252
Pittsfield, MA 01201-5109 Fax: (413)443-2252

Professional, referreed journal covering libraries. **Subtitle:** Official Journal of the Catholic Library Association. **Founded:** 1921. **Freq:** Quarterly. **Print Method:** Offset. **Trim Size:** 8 1/2 x 11. **Cols./Page:** 3. **Col. Width:** 26 nonpareils. **Col. Depth:** 140 agate lines. **Key Personnel:** Allen Gruenke, Editor, phone (313)388-7429, allencd@flash.net. **ISSN:** 0008-820X. **Subscription Rates:** $60. **Remarks:** Accepts advertising. **Alt. Formats:** Microform.
Ad Rates: BW: $300 **Circ:** ‡1,200
4C: $660

14561 Photonics Spectra
Laurin Publishing Co. Inc.
Berkshire Common Phone: (413)499-0514
PO Box 4949 Fax: (413)442-3180
Pittsfield, MA 01202-4949
Free: (800)553-0051
Publication E-mail: photonics@laurin.com; photonics@mci.mail.com
Publisher E-mail: photonics@laurin.com

Magazine covering optics, fiber, electro-optics, lasers, imaging and optical computing. **Founded:** 1967. **Freq:** Monthly. **Print Method:** Offset. **Trim Size:** 8 1/4 x 10 7/8. **Cols./Page:** 3 and 2. **Col. Width:** 26 and 40 nonpareils. **Col. Depth:** 140 agate lines. **Key Personnel:** Stephanie Weiss, Senior Editor; T.C. Laurin, Exec. Publisher; Wendy Laurin, Vice Pres. Mktg. **ISSN:** 0731-1230. **Subscription Rates:** $103 individuals; $11 single issue. **Remarks:** Accepts advertising. **Alt. Formats:** CD-ROM.
Ad Rates: BW: $6,420 **Circ:** Controlled ‡86,500
4C: $7,990

14562 WBEC-AM - 1420
PO Box 958 Phone: (413)499-3333
Pittsfield, MA 01202 Fax: (413)442-1590
E-mail: cj@am1420wbec.com

Format: Full Service; News; Talk. **Networks:** ABC. **Owner:** Aritaur Communications, Inc., at above address. **Founded:** 1947. **Operating Hours:** Continuous. **ADI:** Albany-Schenectady-Troy, NY. **Key Personnel:** Howard Frost, Engineer; Laura Freed, Sales Mgr.; Curt Preisser, News Dir.; Sandra Greenspan, Controller. **Wattage:** 1000. **Ad Rates:** Advertising accepted; rates available upon request. **URL:** am1420wbec.com.

14563 WBEC-FM - 105.5
PO Box 958 Phone: (413)499-3333
Pittsfield, MA 01202 Fax: (413)442-1590
Free: (800)221-9232
E-mail: cj@live105wbec.com

Format: Contemporary Hit Radio (CHR). **Owner:** Aritaur Communications, Inc., at above address. **Founded:** 1963. **Operating Hours:** Continuous. **ADI:** Albany-Schenectady-Troy, NY. **Key Personnel:** Carl Blake, Program Dir.; Laura Freed, Station Mgr.; Curt Preisser, News Dir.; Howard Frost, Engineer; Sandra Greenspan, Controller. **Wattage:** 3000. **Ad Rates:** Advertising accepted; rates available upon request. **URL:** live105wbec.com.

14564 WBRK-AM - 1340
100 North St. Phone: (413)442-1553
Pittsfield, MA 01201 Fax: (413)445-5294

Format: Adult Contemporary. **Networks:** CBS; Mutual Broadcasting System. **Owner:** WBRK, Inc., at above address. **Operating Hours:** Continuous. **Key Personnel:** William Graulty, News Dir.; Michael J. Bunn, Contact; Robert W. Shade, Contact; Richard Weinberg, Contact. **Wattage:** 1000. **Ad Rates:** $9.75 for 30 seconds; $30.50 for 60 seconds.

14565 WRCZ-FM - 101.7
100 North St. Phone: (413)442-1553
Pittsfield, MA 01201 Fax: (413)445-5294

Format: Contemporary Hit Radio (CHR). **Founded:** 1970. **Key Personnel:** Richard Weinberg, Contact. **Wattage:** 3000.

14566 WUHN-AM - 1110
501 East St. Phone: (413)499-1100
PO Box 1265 Fax: (413)499-1800
Pittsfield, MA 01201

Format: Country. **Owner:** Weiner Broadcasting, Inc., at above address. **Founded:** 1971. **Operating Hours:** Sunrise-sunset. **Key Personnel:** Philip Weiner, General Mgr. **Wattage:** 5000.

14567 WUPE-FM - 95.9
501 East St. Phone: (413)499-1100
Pittsfield, MA 01201 Fax: (413)499-1800

Format: Adult Contemporary. **Networks:** Westwood One Radio. **Owner:** Weiner Broadcasting, Inc., at above address. **Founded:** 1975. **Operating Hours:** Continuous. **Key Personnel:** Philip Weiner, General Mgr. **Wattage:** 1000.

PLYMOUTH†, pop. 35,913.

SE MA. Plymouth Co. On Plymouth Bay, 37 mi. SE of Boston. Rich in historical interest, oldest town in New England. Landing place of the Pilgrims in 1620. Museums, whale watches, fishing boats.

Carver Reporter - See Carver

Duxbury Reporter - See Duxbury

Halifax/Plympton Reporter - See Halifax

Kingston Reporter - See Kingston

Marshfield Reporter - See Marshfield

14568 Old Colony Memorial
MPG Newspapers
9 Long Pond Rd. Phone: (508)746-5555
PO Box 959 Fax: (508)747-2148
Plymouth, MA 02362-0959
Free: (800)242-0264
Publisher E-mail: newsroom@mpgnews.com

Community newspaper. **Founded:** 1822. **Freq:** Weekly (Thurs.). **Print Method:** Offset. **Trim Size:** 14 x 22 3/4. **Cols./Page:** 6. **Col. Width:** 26 nonpareils. **Col. Depth:** 301 agate lines. **Key Personnel:** Phyllis Hughes, Publisher, phughes@mpgnews.com. **Subscription Rates:** $29 in county; $42 out of area. **Remarks:** Accepts advertising. **URL:** http://www.mpgnews.com.
Ad Rates: GLR: $1.28 **Circ:** Combined ♦**12,388**
BW: $2,299.50
4C: $2,699.50
PCI: $18.25

Pembroke Reporter - See Pembroke

14569 WPLM-AM - 1390
PO Box 1390 Phone: (508)746-1390
Plymouth, MA 02362 Fax: (508)830-1128

Simulcasts: WPLM-FM. **Networks:** Westwood One Radio. **Owner:** Plymouth Rock Broadcast, at above address. **Founded:** 1955. **Operating Hours:** Continuous. **ADI:** Boston-Worcester,MA-Derry-Manchester,NH. **Key Personnel:** Steve Williams, Program Dir.; Alan W. Anderson, General Mgr. **Wattage:** 5000.

14570 WPLM-FM - 99.1
PO Box 1390 Phone: (508)746-1390
Plymouth, MA 02362 Fax: (508)830-1128
Free: (977)327-9991
E-mail: staff@wplm.com

Format: Easy Listening. **Simulcasts:** WPLM-AM. **Networks:** Westwood One Radio. **Owner:** Plymouth Rock Broadcast, at above address. **Founded:** 1961. **Operating Hours:** Continuous. **ADI:** Boston-Worcester,MA-Derry-Manchester,NH. **Key Personnel:** Alan W. Anderson, General Mgr.; Jack Brady, Program Dir. **Wattage:** 50,000.

PROVINCETOWN, pop. 3,536.

E. MA. Barnstable Co. At tip of Cape Cod, 55 mi. by water SE of Boston. Historic spot where the Mayflower first landed. Summer theatre and resort. Boat building. Artist colony.

14571 Outlander
Omdega Press
PO Box 1546
Provincetown, MA 02657

Magazines containing articles, fiction, non-fiction, and letters. **Founded:** 1994. **Freq:** Irregular. **Trim Size:** 8-1/2 x 11. **Key Personnel:** Robert Seaver Gebelein, Contact. **Subscription Rates:** $10; $1 single issue. **Remarks:** Advertising not accepted.
Circ: Paid 10
Non-paid 50

14572 The Provincetown Advocate
100 Bradford St. Phone: (617)487-1170
Box 93 Fax: (508)487-3878
Provincetown, MA 02657-0093
Local newspaper. **Founded:** 1869. **Freq:** Weekly (Thurs.). **Print Method:** Offset. **Cols./Page:** 6. **Col. Width:** 18 nonpareils. **Col. Depth:** 224 agate lines. **Key Personnel:** Duane Steele, Editor and Publisher; Rose M. Steele, Advertising Mgr. **Subscription Rates:** $18.25.
Circ: 8,398

14573 Provincetown Arts
Provincetown Arts, Inc.
650 Commercial St. Phone: (508)487-3167
Provincetown, MA 02657 Fax: (508)487-8634

Journal covering the arts and literature. **Founded:** 1985. **Freq:** Annual. **Print Method:** Web offset. **Trim Size:** 9 x 12. **Cols./Page:** 3. **Key Personnel:** Christopher Busa, Editorial Dir. **ISSN:** 1053-5012. **Subscription Rates:** $10 individuals; $20 two years; Free to qualified subscribers; $6.5 single issue; $100 lifetime subscription. **Remarks:** Accepts advertising.
Ad Rates: BW: $990 **Circ:** Combined 10,000

14574 WOMR-FM - 92.1
14 Center St. Phone: (508)487-2106
PO Box 975 Fax: (508)487-5524
Provincetown, MA 02657
Free: (800)921-9667
E-mail: jbwomr921@capecod.net

Format: Eclectic; Blues; Jazz; Folk; Classical; Bluegrass. **Founded:** 1982. **Operating Hours:** Continuous. **Key Personnel:** Bob Seay, Exec. Dir.; Jeanne Brossart, Production Mgr. **Local Programs:** *The Irene Rabinowitz Show*, Irene Rabinowitz, Mailing contact; *The Joe Poire Show*, Joe Poire, Mailing contact; *Talking Together*, Robert Levy, Mailing contact. **Wattage:** 6,000. **Ad Rates:** Noncommercial; underwriting available. **URL:** http://www.capecodaccess.com/womr/; http://www.capecod.net/~jbrossar/.

QUINCY, pop. 84,743.

E. MA. Norfolk Co. On the sea coast, 8 mi. S. of Boston. Eastern Nazarene College. Ship building yards. Manufactures weighing, packaging, mattress and surfacing machinery, plastics, paper, rubber products, iron products, electron tubes, crystal diodes, chemicals, paint, gears, telephones, builders' supplies. Foundry.

14575 Fire Technology
National Fire Protection Association (NFPA)
1 Batterymarch Park Phone: (617)770-3000
Quincy, MA 02269-9101 Fax: (617)770-0700
Free: (800)344-3555
Publication E-mail: firetech@nfpa.org

Scientific journal covering fire protection research and applications. **Founded:** Feb. 1965. **Freq:** Quarterly. **Print Method:** Offset. **Trim Size:** 6 x 9. **Cols./Page:** 1. **Col. Width:** 27 picas. **Col. Depth:** 45 picas. **Key Personnel:** John M. Watts, Jr., Editor; Kathie Robinson, Editorial Dir.; Sheryl Doyle, Circulation. **ISSN:** 0015-2684. **Subscription Rates:** $44.50; $50.50 Canada; $54.50 other countries. **Remarks:** Advertising not accepted.
Circ: ‡4,000

14576 Nature Photographer
PO Box 2019 Phone: (617)847-0095
Quincy, MA 02269 Fax: (617)847-0952
Publication E-mail: mjsquincy@pipeline.com

Consumer magazine covering nature photography. **Founded:** 1990. **Freq:** Bimonthly. **Print Method:** Web offset. **Trim Size:** 8 3/8 x 10 7/8. **Cols./Page:** 3. **Col. Width:** 2 1/4 inches. **Col. Depth:** 10 inches. **Key Personnel:** EvaMarie Mathaey, Editor, evamarie.flinet.com; Helen Longest-Slaughter, Photo Editor. **Subscription Rates:** $16.45 individuals; $3.50 single issue. **Remarks:** Accepts advertising.
Circ: Combined ‡15,020

14577 NFPA Journal
National Fire Protection Association (NFPA)
1 Batterymarch Park Phone: (617)770-3000
Quincy, MA 02269-9101 Fax: (617)770-0700
Free: (800)344-3555

Magazine concerning fire protection, prevention. **Subtitle:** The Official Magazine of the National Fire Protection Association. **Founded:** Jan. 1907. **Freq:** Bimonthly. **Print Method:** Offset. **Trim Size:** 8 1/8 x 10 7/8. **Cols./Page:** 3. **Col. Width:** 13.6 picas. **Col. Depth:** 57.5 picas. **Key Personnel:** Kathleen Robinson, Editorial Dir., phone (617)984-7565, krobinson@nfpa.org; Marilyn Freel, Advertising Mgr., phone (617)984-7517, mfreel@nfpa.org. **ISSN:** 1054-8793. **Subscription Rates:** $95 individuals. **Remarks:** Accepts advertising. **Formerly:** Fire Journal; Fire Command.
Ad Rates: BW: $5,300 **Circ:** ‡66,000
4C: $6,790
PCI: $230

14578 The Patriot Ledger
PO Box 9159 Phone: (617)786-7000
Quincy, MA 02269-9159 Fax: (617)786-7298
Free: (800)972-5070
Publication E-mail: newsroom@ledger.com

General newspaper. **Founded:** Jan. 7, 1837. **Freq:** Daily (eve.). **Print Method:** Letterpress. **Trim Size:** 13 x 22. **Cols./Page:** 6. **Col. Width:** 2 1/16 inches. **Col. Depth:** 22 inches. **Key Personnel:** William Ketter, Editor; K. Prescott Low, Publisher. **Subscription Rates:** $.75 single issue M-F; $1 single issue Sat. **Remarks:** Accepts advertising. **Online:** DataTimes Corporation; America Online; Nexis; Dow Jones. **Feature Editors:** Vicki Fitzgerald, *Food*, phone (617)786-7083; Jon Lehman, *Entertainment*, phone (617)786-7066; Vera Vida, *Fashion*, phone (617)786-7080.
Ad Rates: GLR: $3.38 **Circ:** Mon.-Fri. ★**74,031**
BW: $6,255.48 Sat. ★**90,353**
SAU: $47.39

14579 Sun
The Quincy Sun Publishing Co., Inc.
1372 Hancock St. Phone: (617)471-3100
Quincy, MA 02169 Fax: (617)472-3963

Newspaper. **Founded:** 1968. **Freq:** Weekly (Thurs.). **Print Method:** Offset. **Cols./Page:** 6. **Col. Width:** 18 nonpareils. **Col. Depth:** 224 agate lines. **Key Personnel:** Robert H. Bosworth, Editor; Henry W. Bosworth, Jr., Publisher. **USPS:** 453-060. **Subscription Rates:** $13 individuals. **Remarks:** Accepts advertising.
Ad Rates: GLR: $.59 **Circ:** Paid ‡6,150
BW: $792 Free ‡440
4C: $1,192
SAU: $9
PCI: $8.25

14580 Continental Cablevision
81 School St. Phone: (617)471-3200
Quincy, MA 02169 Fax: (617)472-7350

Founded: 1982. **Cities Served:** Norfolk County, MA.

14581 WJDA-AM - 1300
PO Box 690626 Phone: (617)479-1300
Quincy, MA 02269-0626 Fax: (617)479-0622

Format: News; Sports. **Networks:** Independent. **Owner:** South Shore Broadcasting Co., at above address. **Founded:** 1947. **Operating Hours:** 6 a.m.-9 p.m. Mon.-Sat.; 6 a.m.-6 p.m. Sun. **Key Personnel:** James Asher, President, jdasher@aol.com; John Nicolson, Contact; Roy Lind, Program Dir.; Michael Benjamin, Sales Mgr. **Wattage:** 1000. **Ad Rates:** $16-24 for 30 seconds; $20-30 for 60 seconds.

RANDOLPH, pop. 28,218.

E. MA. Norfolk Co. 14 mi. S. of Boston. Residential. Manufactures paper boxes, business machines.

14582 Moneysaver
355 Union St. Phone: (617)963-8267
PO Box 1
Randolph, MA 02368-0001
Shopper. **Founded:** 1952. **Freq:** Weekly (Wed.). **Print Method:** Offset. **Cols./Page:** 4. **Col. Width:** 22 nonpareils. **Col. Depth:** 140 agate lines. **Key Personnel:** B. Paul March, Editor and Publisher. **Subscription Rates:** Free; $46 out of area. **Remarks:** Accepts advertising.
Ad Rates: PCI: $10.88 **Circ:** Free ‡18,500

14583 Randolph Herald
Associated Newspapers
7 Cabot Pl. Phone: (781)878-1111
PO Box 441 Fax: (781)878-3333
Stoughton, MA 02072
Publisher E-mail: aweeklies@aol.com

Community newspaper. **Founded:** 1929. **Freq:** Weekly (Wed.). **Print Method:** Offset. **Cols./Page:** 6. **Col. Width:** 9.5 picas. **Col. Depth:** 16 inches. **Key Personnel:** Richard R. Dailey, Publisher. **Subscription Rates:** $10 individuals. **Remarks:** Accepts advertising.
Ad Rates: BW: $10.53 **Circ:** Paid ‡1,421
4C: $10.77
PCI: $10.53

14584 Randolph Mariner
Mariner Newspapers
165 Enterprise Dr. Phone: (617)837-3500
Marshfield, MA 02050-2132 Fax: (617)837-4540
Free: (800)649-6661
Publisher E-mail: cmathis@cnc.com

Community newspaper. **Freq:** Weekly (Wed.). **Print Method:** Offset. **Trim Size:** 11 3/8 x 17. **Cols./Page:** 5. **Col. Width:** 2 1/8 inches. **Col. Depth:** 16 inches. **Key Personnel:** Margaret Smoragiewicz, Publisher; Judy McCaffrey Perry, Advertising Dir. **Subscription Rates:** $22. **Remarks:** Combined advertising rates available with other Mariner Newspapers.
Ad Rates: GLR: $11.78 **Circ:** Paid 1,565
BW: $942.40 Non-paid 88
4C: $1,300.00
PCI: $8.25

RAYNHAM

14585 Raynham Journal
Associated Newspapers
7 Cabot Pl. Phone: (781)878-1111
PO Box 441 Fax: (781)878-3333
Stoughton, MA 02072
Publisher E-mail: aweeklies@aol.com

Community newspaper. **Founded:** 1976. **Freq:** Weekly (Thurs.). **Print Method:** Offset. **Cols./Page:** 6. **Col. Width:** 9.5 picas. **Col. Depth:** 16 inches. **Key Personnel:** Richard R. Dailey, Publisher. **Subscription Rates:** $17.50 in county. **Remarks:** Accepts advertising.
Ad Rates: BW: $10.53 **Circ:** Paid 1,774
4C: $10.77
PCI: $10.53

READING, pop. 22,678.

NE MA. Middlesex Co. 12 mi. NW of Boston. Manufactures stoves, plastic fabrics, neckwear, text books. Poultry, fruit, truck farms.

14586 Daily Chronicle
PO Box 240 Phone: (617)944-2200
Reading, MA 01867 Fax: (617)942-0884

General newspaper. **Founded:** 1870. **Freq:** Daily (eve.). **Print Method:** Offset. **Cols./Page:** 6. **Col. Width:** 21 nonpareils. **Col. Depth:** 294 agate lines. **Key Personnel:** Richard P. Haggerty, General Mgr. **Subscription Rates:** $191.75. **Remarks:** Accepts advertising.
Ad Rates: SAU: $8.25 **Circ:** Paid ‡14,215
Controlled 2,092

REHOBOTH

Bristol Co.

14587 WNAC-TV - 64
33 Pine St. Phone: (508)252-9711
Rehoboth, MA 02769 Fax: (508)252-6210
Free: (800)548-0064

Format: Commercial TV. **Networks:** Fox; Independent. **Owner:** Argyle TV Holdings, Inc, 9220 Sunset Blvd., Los Angeles, CA 90069, (310)271-9700. **Founded:** 1984. **Formerly:** WSTG-TV (1986). **Operating Hours:** 6am-2am weekdays; 6am-2am Sat.; 6 am-12:30 am Sun. **ADI:** Providence, RI-New Bedford, MA. **Key Personnel:** Jonathan Barcelo, National Sales Mgr.; Thomas Viall, Production Mgr.; Deborah Koller, Promotions Mgr.; Jeff Rosser, V.Pres./Gen. Mgr.; Keith Folz, Station Mgr.; Shawn O'Rourke, General Sales Mgr.; Rich Sweitzer, Chief Engineer.

REVERE, pop. 42,423.

E. MA. Suffolk Co. On Massachusetts Bay, 6 mi. NE of Boston. (Branch of Boston P.O.) Summer resort. Residential. Manufactures air conditioning, electrical controls, heating equipment, paint, furniture, textiles, wood heels, electric pumps, hotel, restaurant, kitchen, and farm equipment, machine parts, chemicals, spices, beverages, brass.

14588 Revere Journal
Journal Transcript Newspapers
327 Broadway Phone: (617)284-2400
Revere, MA 02151 Fax: (617)289-5352

Community newspaper. **Founded:** 1881. **Freq:** Weekly (Wed.). **Print Method:** Offset. **Trim Size:** 14 x 22 3/4. **Cols./Page:** 6. **Col. Width:** 12.5 picas. **Col. Depth:** 294 agate lines. **Key Personnel:** Richard Powers, Editor; Neil P. Collins, Publisher; Lou McGrew, Publisher. **Subscription Rates:** $13; $20 out of area. **Remarks:** Accepts advertising.
Ad Rates: SAU: $6.65 **Circ:** Paid 6,974
Non-paid 397

14589 Continental Cablevision
41 Marble St. Fax: (617)286-1542
Revere, MA 02151 Free: (800)876-6988

Key Personnel: Dave Dane, General Mgr.; Russ Hanagan, Program Dir.; Tami Benedick, Contact. **Cities Served:** subscribing households 57; 2 channels; 2 community access channels.

ROCHESTER

14590 Cranberries
PO Box 190 Phone: (508)763-8080
Rochester, MA 02770-0190 Fax: (508)763-4141
Publisher E-mail: cranberries@mediaone.net

Magazine covering growing, processing, and marketing of cranberries. **Subtitle:** The National Cranberry Magazine. **Founded:** 1936. **Freq:** 11/year. **Print Method:** Offset. **Trim Size:** 8 1/2 x 11. **Cols./Page:** 3. **Col. Width:** 24 nonpareils. **Col. Depth:** 126 agate lines. **Key Personnel:** Carolyn Gilmore, Editor and Publisher. **ISSN:** 0011-0787. **Subscription Rates:** $25 individuals USA; $3 single issue.
Ad Rates: BW: $185 **Circ:** ‡1,375
4C: $250
PCI: $22

ROCKLAND

14591 Abington Standard
Associated Newspapers
800 Hingham St.
PO Box 309
Rockland, MA 02370
Publisher E-mail: aweeklies@aol.com

Community newspaper. **Founded:** 1981. **Freq:** Weekly (Wed.). **Print Method:** Offset. **Cols./Page:** 6. **Col. Width:** 9.5 picas. **Col. Depth:** 16 inches. **Key Personnel:** Richard R. Dailey, Publisher. **Subscription Rates:** $17.50 individuals. **Remarks:** Accepts advertising.
Ad Rates: BW: $10.53 **Circ:** ‡1,694
4C: $10.77
PCI: $10.53

14592 The Griffin Report of Food Marketing
Griffin Publishing Co., Inc.
1099 Hingham St. Phone: (617)878-5300
Rockland, MA 02370 Fax: (617)871-4721
Publisher E-mail: griffinpub@aol.com

Trade newspaper (tabloid) covering the retail supermarket and convenience store industry in the six state New England and upstate New York markets. **Founded:** 1966. **Freq:** Monthly. **Print Method:** Offset. **Trim Size:** 11 x 17. **Cols./Page:** 5. **Col. Width:** 24 nonpareils. **Col. Depth:** 224 agate lines. **Key Personnel:** Stephen M. Griffin, Publisher/Pres.; Ed Gunderson, VP, Sales/Mktg.; Craig Faucher, Editor; Rachel Wolff, Production Mgr. **ISSN:** 0192-4400. **Subscription Rates:** Free to qualified subscribers; $42 individuals. **Remarks:** Accepts advertising.
Ad Rates: BW: $2,217.60 **Circ:** Paid 3,500
4C: $3,267.60 Free 9,000
PCI: $29.96

14593 Modern Food Service
Griffin Publishing Co., Inc.
1099 Hingham St. Phone: (617)878-5300
Rockland, MA 02370 Fax: (617)871-4721
Publisher E-mail: griffinpub@aol.com

Magazine for restaurateurs, chefs, caterers, and purchasing agents in the food service industry. **Founded:** 1977. **Freq:** Monthly. **Print Method:** Web offset. **Trim Size:** 11 x 15. **Cols./Page:** 5. **Col. Width:** 2 inches. **Col. Depth:** 14 inches. **Key Personnel:** Stephen M. Griffin, Publisher/Pres.; Bob Vosburgh, Editor; Kevin Gallagher, Vice President; Rachel Wolff, Production Mgr. **ISSN:** 0888-7829. **Remarks:** Accepts advertising. **Formerly:** Modern Food Service News; Restaurant Exchange News.
Ad Rates: BW: $1,950 **Circ:** ‡20,615
4C: $2,950
PCI: $30

14594 Rockland Standard
Associated Newspapers
800 Hingham St. Phone: (781)878-1111
Rockland, MA 02370 Fax: (781)878-3333
Publisher E-mail: aweeklies@aol.com

Community newspaper. **Founded:** 1853. **Freq:** Weekly (Wed.). **Print Method:** Offset. **Cols./Page:** 6. **Col. Width:** 9.5 picas. **Col. Depth:** 16 inches. **Key Personnel:** Richard R. Dailey, Publisher. **Subscription Rates:** $10 individuals. **Remarks:** Accepts advertising.
Ad Rates: BW: $10.53 **Circ:** Paid 1,405
4C: $10.77
PCI: $10.53

14595 Yankee Food Service
Griffin Publishing Co., Inc.
1099 Hingham St. Phone: (617)878-5300
Rockland, MA 02370 Fax: (617)871-4721
Publisher E-mail: griffinpub@aol.com

Newspaper (tabloid) covering business news, personnel changes, food trends, and trade events of the New England food service industry. **Founded:** 1979. **Freq:** Monthly. **Print Method:** Offset. **Trim Size:** 11 x 17. **Cols./Page:** 5. **Col. Width:** 24 nonpareils. **Col. Depth:** 224 agate lines. **Key Personnel:** Stephen Griffin, Publisher/Pres.; Ed Gunderson, Dir. of Sales; Kirsten Whitten, Editor; Julie Irvine, VP/General Mgr.; Rachel Wolff, Production Mgr. **ISSN:** 0195-2552. **Subscription Rates:** Free to qualified subscribers To qualified subscribers; $40 individuals. **Remarks:** Accepts advertising.
Ad Rates: BW: $2,160 **Circ:** Paid ‡3,000
4C: $3,210 Non-paid ‡20,000
PCI: $27.50

14596 WRPS-FM - 88.3
34 MacKinley Way Phone: (617)871-0724
Rockland, MA 02370
E-mail: wrps@rockland.mec.edu

Format: Public Radio. **Founded:** 1974. **Key Personnel:** Stephen J. Budkiewicz, General Mgr. **Wattage:** 100. **Ad Rates:** Noncommercial.

RUSSELL

14597 Russell Municipal Cable TV
Town Hall, 65 Main St. Phone: (413)862-4707
Box 408 Fax: (413)862-3103
Russell, MA 01071
E-mail: russell3@exit.com

Owner: Town of Russell, Massachusetts, at above address. **Founded:** 1987. **Key Personnel:** Susan B. Maxwell, Manager; Louis E. Garlo, Commissioner; William Herman, Commissioner. **Cities Served:** Russell, MA: subscribing households 460; 36 channels; 1 community access channel.

SALEM†, pop. 38,220.

Essex Co. On the Atlantic Ocean, 16 mi. NE of Boston. State College. One of the oldest cities in the state. Manufactures incandescent bulbs, fluorescent tubes and fixtures, games, confectionery, leather shoes, steam valves, chemicals, leather novelties, mattresses. Lobster fisheries.

14598 The American Neptune
Peabody Essex Museum
East India Sq. Phone: (508)745-1876
Salem, MA 01970 Fax: (508)774-6776
Publication E-mail: dori_ phillips@pem.org

Magazine covering maritime history and arts. **Subtitle:** A Quarterly Journal of Maritime History and Arts. **Founded:** Jan. 1941. **Freq:** Quarterly. **Trim Size:** 8 1/2 x 11. **Cols./Page:** 2. **Col. Width:** 60 nonpareils. **Col. Depth:** 102 agate lines. **Key Personnel:** Donald S. Marshall, Publisher; Geraldine M. Ayers. **ISSN:** 0003-0155. **Subscription Rates:** $39 individuals; $45 institutions; $42 other countries; $48 institutions, other countries. **Remarks:** Advertising accepted; rates available upon request. **Available Online.**
Circ: ‡1,300

14599 Essex County Newspapers
Salem News Publishing Co.
155 Washington St. Phone: (508)744-0600
Salem, MA 01970 Fax: (508)744-1010

General newspaper. **Founded:** 1880. **Freq:** Mon.-Sat. (eve.). **Print Method:** Offset. **Trim Size:** 13 13/16 x 22 1/2. **Cols./Page:** 6. **Col. Width:** 2 1/32 inches. **Col. Depth:** 21 inches. **Key Personnel:** John P. Kinney, President and Publisher; Peter Watson, General Mgr.; David Marcus, Editor; Paul Briand, Asst. to the Publisher; Brent Connolly, Dir. of Sales and Marketing; Robert Babcock, Ad. Mgr.; Margo Wagner, Classified Dir.; David Lodge, Retail Ad. Mgr.; Rino Vitolo, Circulation Mgr. **Subscription Rates:** $16.50. **Remarks:** Accepts advertising. **Formerly:** Salem Evening News; Beverly Times; Peabody Times.
Ad Rates: BW: $205 **Circ:** Mon.-Sat. 37,924
SAU: $26.56
PCI: $23.25

14600 Gulf of Maine Times
PO Box 4524 Phone: (978)740-2998
Salem, MA 01970 Fax: (978)740-3180

Newspaper covering environmental, economic, and social issues in the Gulf of Maine watershed. **Subtitle:** Promoting Cooperation to maintain and Enhance Environmental Quality in the Gulf of Maine. **Founded:** Mar. 1997. **Freq:** Quarterly. **Print Method:** Web. **Trim Size:** 17 x 23. **Cols./Page:** 4. **Col. Width:** 2 1/4 inches. **Col. Depth:** 14 inches. **Key Personnel:**

Anne Donovan, Editor-in-Chief, phone (617)727-9530, fax (617)723-5408, anne.donovan@state.ma.us; Suzy Fried, Editor, sfried@world.std.com. **Subscription Rates:** Free. **Remarks:** Advertising not accepted Call editor for info. **Available Online. URL:** http://www.gulfofmaine.org/times.
Circ: Controlled 13,000

14601 The Jewish Journal/North of Boston
North Shore Jewish Press
201 Washington St. Phone: (508)745-4111
PO Box 555 Fax: (508)745-5333
Salem, MA 01970
Publication E-mail: salemjrnal@aol.com

Jewish newspaper. **Subtitle:** Serving the Communities North of Boston. **Founded:** 1977. **Freq:** Biweekly. **Print Method:** Offset. **Trim Size:** 11 x 17. **Cols./Page:** 5. **Col. Width:** 1 3/4 inches. **Col. Depth:** 16 inches. **Key Personnel:** Bette Keva, Editor; Gerald Posner, Publisher. **ISSN:** 1040-0095. **Subscription Rates:** $12 individuals; $20 out of area. **Remarks:** Accepts advertising.
Ad Rates: BW: $1160 **Circ:** 13500
PCI: $14.50

14602 Journal of Business and Economic Studies
Salem State College
352 Lafayette St. Phone: (978)542-9316
Salem, MA 01970
Professional journal covering all aspects of business. **Freq:** Semiannual. **Key Personnel:** David M. Jacobson, Editor; Kathy Dow, Asst. Editor; Kim Underhill. **ISSN:** 3185-214. **Subscription Rates:** $25 individuals. **Remarks:** Advertising not accepted.
Circ: Paid 1,700

14603 The Salem State Log
Salem College
352 Lafayette Phone: (508)741-6448
Salem, MA 01970
Collegiate newspaper. **Subtitle:** The Log. **Founded:** 1927. **Freq:** Semimonthly. **Print Method:** Offset. **Cols./Page:** 5. **Col. Width:** 22 nonpareils. **Col. Depth:** 224 agate lines. **Remarks:** Accepts advertising.
Ad Rates: GLR: $.36 **Circ:** Free ‡4,000
BW: $360
PCI: $7

14604 WESX-AM - 1230
PO Box 710 Phone: (508)744-1230
Salem, MA 01970 Fax: (508)744-1853

Format: Big Band/Nostalgia; Oldies; Adult Contemporary; Talk; News; Sports. **Networks:** AP. **Owner:** North Shore Broadcasting Corp., at above address. **Founded:** 1939. **Operating Hours:** Continuous; 5%network, 95% local. **Key Personnel:** Allen Needham, Jr., News Dir.; Betty C. Stavis, Jr., Traffic Mgr./Public Affairs Dir.; James D. Asher, President; Stuart Egenberg, Sales Mgr.; Larry Burnham, Program Dir. **Local Programs:** *Party-Line*, Al Needham. **Wattage:** 1000. **Ad Rates:** $17-24 for 30 seconds; $35-30 for 60 seconds.

14605 WMWM-FM - 91.7
352 Lafayette St. Phone: (978)745-9401
Salem, MA 01970 Fax: (978)741-9433
E-mail: wmwm@star.net

Format: Alternative/New Music/Progressive. **Networks:** Independent. **Owner:** Salem State College Board of Trustees, at above address, (508)741-6000, Fax: (978)741-6000. **Founded:** 1979. **Operating Hours:** 7 a.m.-12 a.m. **Key Personnel:** Shilo MacDonald, General Mgr.; Ben Woart, Program Dir.; Gretchen Shae, Music Dir.; Bob Nelson, Contact. **Local Programs:** *Commin' Atcha*, Joe Kelley. **Wattage:** 130. **Ad Rates:** Noncommercial. **URL:** http://www.star.net; http://wmwm.star.net.

SCITUATE, pop. 17,317.

SE MA. Plymouth Co. On Massachusetts Bay, 3 mi. E. of Norwell. Residential.

14606 Scituate Mariner
Mariner Newspapers
165 Enterprise Dr. Phone: (617)837-3500
Marshfield, MA 02050-2132 Fax: (617)837-4540
Free: (800)649-6661
Publisher E-mail: cmathis@cnc.com

Community newspaper. **Freq:** Weekly (Wed.). **Print Method:** Offset. **Trim Size:** 11 3/8 x 17. **Cols./Page:** 5. **Col. Width:** 2 1/8 inches. **Col. Depth:** 15 1/2 inches. **Key Personnel:** Margaret Smoragiewicz, Publisher; Judy McCaffrey Perry, Advertising Dir. **Subscription Rates:** $22. **Remarks:** Combined advertising rates available with other Mariner Newspapers.
Ad Rates: BW: $942.40 **Circ:** Paid 3,777
4C: $1,300.00 Non-paid 130
PCI: $8.25

SHARON, pop. 13,601.

E. MA. Norfolk Co. 17 mi. SW of Boston. Residential. Manufactures electronics, steel dies. Stamping mills. Resort.

14607 Sharon Sentinel
Associated Newspapers
7 Cabot Pl. Phone: (781)878-1111
PO Box 441 Fax: (781)878-3333
Stoughton, MA 02072
Publisher E-mail: aweeklies@aol.com

Community newspaper. **Founded:** 1972. **Freq:** Weekly (Thurs.). **Print Method:** Offset. **Cols./Page:** 6. **Col. Width:** 9.5 picas. **Col. Depth:** 16 inches. **Key Personnel:** Richard R. Dailey, Publisher. **Subscription Rates:** $17.50. **Remarks:** Accepts advertising.
Ad Rates: PCI: $10.53 **Circ:** 3,172

SHEFFIELD, pop. 2,660.

SW MA. Berkshire Co. 24 mi. S. of Pittsfield. Resort.

14608 WBSL-FM - 91.7
245 Undermountian Rd. Phone: (413)229-6683
Sheffield, MA 01257 Fax: (413)229-3178

Format: Full Service; Public Radio; Jazz; Classic Rock; Oldies; Folk; Alternative/New Music/Progressive. **Owner:** Berkshire Schools, Inc., at above address, (413)229-8511. **Founded:** 1972. **Operating Hours:** 2:30 p.m.-1 a.m.; 100% local. **Key Personnel:** Tom Jaworski, Contact; Tom Jay, Contact. **Wattage:** 250. **Ad Rates:** Noncommercial.

SHELBURNE FALLS, pop. 2,002.

NW MA. Franklin Co. 8 mi. NW of Greenfield. Residential. Agriculture.

14609 Shelburne Falls and West County News
West County News
73 Bridge St. Phone: (413)625-9417
PO Box 218 Fax: (413)625-2158
Shelburne Falls, MA 01370
Community newspaper (tabloid). **Founded:** 1979. **Freq:** Weekly (Fri.). **Print Method:** Offset. **Trim Size:** 11 1/2 x 16. **Cols./Page:** 5. **Col. Width:** 1 7/8 inches. **Col. Depth:** 16 inches. **Key Personnel:** Richard Matthews, Editor and Publisher; Marjorie Matthews, Publisher/General Mgr.; Fred Bourassa, Advertising Mgr.; Jeremy Rogers, Managing Editor. **USPS:** 520-290. **Subscription Rates:** $32.50 individuals; $35 out of state.
Ad Rates: BW: $472 **Circ:** ‡2,800
PCI: $5.90

14610 Charlemont TV
56 Bridge St. Phone: (413)339-6685
Shelburne Falls, MA 01370 Fax: (413)625-6017

Key Personnel: Earl Crowningshield, General Mgr. **Cities Served:** Readsboro, VT.

SHERBORN, pop. 4,260.

SW MA. Middlesex Co. 16 mi. SW of Boston. Manufactures shoes.

14611 The Sherborn Tab
Community Newspaper Company
254 2nd Ave. Phone: (781)433-7828
Needham, MA 02192-9114 Fax: (781)433-7835

Community newspaper. **Founded:** Oct. 1985. **Freq:** Weekly (Tues.). **Print Method:** Offset. **Trim Size:** 10 x 16. **Cols./Page:** 8. **Col. Width:** 8 picas. **Key Personnel:** John Wilpers, Editor; Russell Pergament, Publisher; Stephen Cummings, Publisher; Lisa Flicop, Advertising Mgr. **Formerly:** The Dover/Sherborn Gazette.
Circ: Non-paid 1,799

SHREWSBURY

NC MA. Worcester Co. 10 mi. S. of Boylston.

14612 Journal of Intensive Care Medicine
Blackwell Science, Inc.
21 N. Quinsiganmond Ave. Phone: (508)756-1306
Shrewsbury, MA 01545
Publisher E-mail: http://www.blackwell-science.com/usa

Medical journal for specialists working in intensive care units. **Founded:** Jan. 1986. **Freq:** Bimonthly. **Print Method:** Offset. **Trim Size:** 8 1/8 x 10 7/8. **Cols./Page:** 2. **Col. Width:** 3 3/8 inches. **Col. Depth:** 10 inches. **Key Personnel:** James Rippe, M.D., Editor; James Krosschell, Publisher, phone (617)876-7500, fax (617)876-7022. **ISSN:** 0885-0666. **Subscription Rates:** $85 individuals. **Remarks:** Advertising accepted; rates available upon request.
Circ: ‡2,200

14613 Shrewsbury's Community Cablevision
100 Maple Ave. Phone: (508)845-4881
Shrewsbury, MA 01545 Fax: (508)842-9419
E-mail: cmurray@ci.shrewsbury.ma.us

Founded: 1983. **Formerly:** Shrewsbury Electric Light Plant (1992). **Key Personnel:** Thomas R. Josie, General Mgr. **Cities Served:** Shrewsbury, MA: subscribing households 10,139; 69 channels; 2 community access channels; 35 hours per week community access programming. **URL:** http://www.co.shrewsbury.ma.us.

SOMERSET, pop. 18,813.

SE MA. Bristol Co. On Taunton River, 6 mi. N. of Fall River. (Branch of Fall River P.O.) Residential.

14614 The Spectator
Hathaway Publishing
780 County St. Phone: (508)674-4656
Somerset, MA 02726 Fax: (508)677-1210

Community newspaper. **Founded:** 1932. **Freq:** Weekly (Wed.). **Print Method:** Letterpress and offset. **Cols./Page:** 6. **Col. Depth:** 21 1/2 inches. **Key Personnel:** Sheila Weinberg, Editor; W.G. Hathaway, Publisher; R.P. Hopkins, Advertising Mgr.; Warren G. Hathaway, Publisher; Warren G. Hathaway, Publisher. **Subscription Rates:** $20. **Remarks:** Accepts advertising.
Ad Rates: SAU: $8.25 **Circ:** Paid 7,247
PCI: $8.25 Non-paid 325

14615 WHTB-AM - 1400
1 Home St. Phone: (508)678-9727
Somerset, MA 02725 Fax: (508)673-0310

Format: Ethnic; Talk. **Owner:** SNE Broadcasting Ltd., PO Box 927, Fall River, MA 02722. **Founded:** 1948. **Formerly:** WALE-AM. **Operating Hours:** 5:15 a.m.-11:30 p.m. **ADI:** Providence, RI-New Bedford, MA. **Key Personnel:** Carole W. Fiola, VP/Gen. Mgr.; Paul W. Gelzinis, Sales Mgr.; Rick Edwards, Program Dir.; Rene R. Charest, Producer; Hector A. Gauthier, Jr., Chief Engineer; Anne-Marie Massicotte, Financial and Job Compliance Mgr.; Robert A. Silvia, Sales and Marketing Coord.; Paul W. Gelzinis, Sales Mgr.; Hector A. Gauthier, Jr., Chief Engineer. **Local Programs:** *Amizade Sonora* 4:00 pm - 6:30 pm; *The Lou Perreira Show* 6:30 pm - 9:00 pm; *Voz do Emigrante* 10:00 am - 4:00 pm; *The Rosary* 11:30 pm - 11:50 pm. **Wattage:** 1,000. **Ad Rates:** $12-24 for 60 seconds. Combined advertising rates available with WSAR-AM.

14616 WSAR-AM - 1480
1 Home St. Phone: (508)678-9727
Somerset, MA 02725 Fax: (508)673-0310
E-mail: wsar1480@aol.com

Format: News; Talk; Sports. **Networks:** ABC. **Owner:** Bristol County Broadcasting Inc., PO Box 927, Fall River, MA 02722. **Founded:** 1921. **Operating Hours:** Continuous; 25% network, 75% local. **Key Personnel:** Carol W. Fiola, VP/Gen. Mgr.; Paul W. Gelzinis, Sales Mgr.; Rick Edwards, Program Dir.; Rene Charest, Producer; Peter Legace, News Dir.; Hector A. Gauthier, Jr., VP of Operations; Mary Murphy, Jr., Traffic Manager; Robert A. Silvia, Sales & Marketing Coordinator; Anne-Marie Massicotte, Financial and Job Compliance Mgr.; Robert Silvia, Sales and Marketing Coord. **Wattage:** 5000. **Ad Rates:** $20-40 for 60 seconds. Combined advertising rates available with WHTB-AM. **URL:** http://www.wsar.com.

SOMERVILLE, pop. 77,372.

NE MA. Middlesex Co. Suburb of Boston on the Mystic River. (Branch of Boston P.O.) Manufactures paper products, caskets, industrial oil and tanning materials, vinegar, ladders and woodenware, spraying equipment, furniture, metal stamps, tools and dies, novelties, ornamental iron, suitcases and bags, wagon and truck bodies, piano tuners' supplies, textiles, brooms, food processing and packaging.

14617 B&M Bulletin
Boston & Maine Railroad Historical Society Inc.
32 Tower St.
Somerville, MA 02143-1427

Magazine containing articles, data, and photos describing the history of the Boston & Maine Railroad and its predecessor

lines, equipment, and people. **Founded:** Sept. 1971. **Freq:** Quarterly. **Print Method:** Offset. **Trim Size:** 8 1/2 x 11. **Cols./Page:** 2. **Col. Width:** 21 picas. **Col. Depth:** 140 agate lines. **Key Personnel:** John Alan Roderick, Editor. **ISSN:** 0362-2711. **Subscription Rates:** $25 included in annual membership. $5.95 single issue. **Remarks:** Advertising not accepted.
Circ: ‡2,200

The Billerica News - See Billerica

Cambridge Chronicle - See Cambridge

14618 Danvers Herald
Community Newspaper Company
240A Elm St Phone: (617)733-8200
Somerville, MA 02144 Fax: (617)433-8285
Free: (800)880-1812
Publication E-mail: sweditor@shore.net

Community newspaper (tabloid). **Founded:** 1870. **Freq:** Weekly (Thurs.). **Print Method:** Offset. **Trim Size:** 11 3/8 x 17. **Cols./Page:** 5. **Col. Width:** 2 1/16 inches. **Col. Depth:** 16 inches. **Key Personnel:** Howard Iverson, Editor; Chuck Goodrich, Publisher; John Vistorino, Advertising Mgr. **Subscription Rates:** $18 individuals; $14 students; $31 out of area. **Remarks:** Accepts advertising. **URL:** http://www.townonline.com.
Ad Rates: BW: $644 **Circ:** Paid 4,604
SAU: $8.05 Free 750

14619 Dollar Saver
Community Newspapers Inc.
240 Elm St., Ste. 22 Phone: (617)628-3380
Somerville, MA 02144 Fax: (617)629-3381

Shopper. **Print Method:** Offset. **Cols./Page:** 6. **Col. Width:** 26 nonpareils. **Col. Depth:** 294 agate lines. **Key Personnel:** William P. Dole, Publisher; Don Morse, Editor.

14620 Dollars & Sense
Economic Affairs Bureau
1 Summer St. Phone: (617)628-8411
Somerville, MA 02143 Fax: (617)628-2025
Free: (888)736-7377
Publication E-mail: dollars@igc.org

Magazine providing left-wing perspectives on current economic affairs. **Subtitle:** What's Left in Economics. **Founded:** Oct. 1974. **Freq:** 6/year. **Print Method:** Offset. **Trim Size:** 8 1/2 x 11. **Cols./Page:** 2. **Col. Width:** 20 picas. **Col. Depth:** 8 3/4 inches. **Key Personnel:** Marc Breslow, Editor; Abby Scher, Editor; Jeremy Smith, Advertising; Randal Divinski, Circulation Mgr. **ISSN:** 0012-5245. **Subscription Rates:** $22.95; $39 two years; $42 institutions; $3.95 single issue; $35.95 other countries surface mail; $48.95 other countries air mail. **Remarks:** Accepts advertising. **Online:** SIRS, Inc.; LEXIS-NEXIS. **URL:** http://www.igc.apc.org/dollars/. **Alt. Formats:** CD-ROM, PAIS Select.
Ad Rates: BW: $550 **Circ:** ‡8,400
4C: $1,150
PCI: $30

14621 Mass Bay Antiques
Community Newspaper Company
240A Elm St Phone: (617)733-8200
Somerville, MA 02144 Fax: (617)433-8285
Free: (800)880-1812

Magazine for antique dealers and collectors. **Founded:** Apr. 1, 1980. **Freq:** Monthly. **Print Method:** Offset. **Cols./Page:** 5. **Col. Width:** 12 nonpareils. **Col. Depth:** 224 agate lines. **Key Personnel:** Betti Babine, Publisher; Ann Whittier, Editor. **Subscription Rates:** $15 individuals. **Remarks:** Advertising accepted; rates available upon request.
Circ: ‡22,000

14622 Newsweekly
Community Newspapers Inc.
240 Elm St., Ste. 22 Phone: (617)628-3380
Somerville, MA 02144 Fax: (617)629-3381

Shopper. **Founded:** 1956. **Freq:** Weekly (Wed.). **Remarks:** Accepts advertising. **Formerly:** Merrimack Valley Advertiser (Chelmsford Edition).
Ad Rates: BW: $588 **Circ:** Free ‡12,435
PCI: $7.35

14623 North Andover Citizen
Community Newspaper Company
240A Elm St Phone: (617)733-8200
Somerville, MA 02144 Fax: (617)433-8285
Free: (800)880-1812
Publication E-mail: nsnews@shore.net

Community newspaper (tabloid). **Founded:** 1965. **Freq:** Weekly (Thurs.). **Print Method:** Offset. **Trim Size:** 11 3/8 x 17. **Cols./Page:** 4. **Col. Width:** 30 nonpareils. **Col. Depth:** 182 agate lines. **Key Personnel:** John Macone, Editor; Chuck Goodrich, Publisher; John Vistorino, Advertising Mgr. **USPS:** 450-630. **Subscription Rates:** $19; $14 students; $31 out of area. **Remarks:** Accepts advertising.
Ad Rates: BW: $644 **Circ:** Paid 2,818
SAU: $8.05 Free 1,013

14624 Radical America
Alternative Education Project
237 A Holland Phone: (617)628-6585
Somerville, MA 02143 Fax: (617)628-6585

Socialist-feminist journal of politics and culture specializing in radical, labor, and women's history and theory, grassroots and community organizing, peace and disarmament issues, and African-American, Third World, and gay and lesbian issues. **Founded:** May 1967. **Freq:** Quarterly. **Print Method:** Offset. **Trim Size:** 7 x 10. **Cols./Page:** 2. **Col. Width:** 3 inches. **Col. Depth:** 8 1/4 inches. **Key Personnel:** Marla Erlien, Staff. **ISSN:** 0033-7617. **Subscription Rates:** $22; $28 other countries. **Remarks:** Color advertising not accepted.
Ad Rates: BW: $225 **Circ:** Controlled 5,000
Non-paid 1,000

14625 Somerville Journal
Community Newspapers Inc.
360-366 Summer St.
Somerville, MA 02144

Community newspaper. **Founded:** 1870. **Freq:** Weekly (Thurs.). **Print Method:** Offset. **Cols./Page:** 6. **Col. Width:** 26 nonpareils. **Col. Depth:** 294 agate lines. **Key Personnel:** Timothy Lundergan, Editor; Frank Yetter, Publisher; Ed Vargas, Advertising Dir. **Subscription Rates:** $21 individuals Local. **Remarks:** Accepts advertising.
Ad Rates: GLR: $3.75 **Circ:** Paid 8,206
BW: $2,431.80 Non-paid 2,003
SAU: $19.30
PCI: $19.30

14626 The Somerville News
7 Davis Sq. Phone: (617)666-4010
Somerville, MA 02144-2917 Fax: (617)666-2974

Community newspaper. **Founded:** 1969. **Freq:** Monthly. **Print Method:** Letterpress. **Trim Size:** 10 x 16. **Cols./Page:** 5. **Col. Width:** 22 nonpareils. **Col. Depth:** 220 agate lines. **Key Personnel:** Robert J. L. Publicover, Publisher. **Subscription Rates:** $20. **Remarks:** Accepts advertising.
Ad Rates: BW: $1,320 **Circ:** Combined ‡14,000
SAU: $10.95
PCI: $15.07

14627 Technology & Conservation of Art, Architecture & Antiquities
The Technology Organization, Inc.
76 Highland Ave. Phone: (617)623-4488
Somerville, MA 02143
Magazine on art, architecture, and archeology. **Founded:** 1976. **Freq:** Quarterly. **Print Method:** Offset. **Trim Size:** 8 1/2 x 11. **Cols./Page:** 3. **Col. Width:** 25 nonpareils. **Col. Depth:** 140 agate lines. **Key Personnel:** S.E. Schur, Editor and Publisher. **ISSN:** 0146-1214. **Remarks:** Accepts advertising.
Ad Rates: BW: $1,600 **Circ:** Non-paid ‡15,000
4C: $2,250

Watertown Press - See Watertown

SOUTH BOSTON

Dorchester Argus-Citizen - See Dorchester

14628 South Boston Tribune
PO Box 6 Phone: (617)268-3440
South Boston, MA 02127 Fax: (617)268-6420

Community newspaper. **Founded:** 1938. **Freq:** Weekly (Thurs.). **Print Method:** Offset. **Cols./Page:** 8. **Col. Width:** 24 nonpareils. **Col. Depth:** 294 agate lines. **Key Personnel:** Daniel J. Horgan, Jr., Publisher. **Subscription Rates:** $13 individuals. **Remarks:** Accepts advertising.
Ad Rates: GLR: $.26 **Circ:** ‡8,000
4C: $1,000
SAU: $5.40

SOUTH DARTMOUTH

SE MA. Bristol Co. 5 mi. S. of New Bedford. Residential.

14629 The Chronicle
Hathaway Publishing
45 Slocum Rd. Phone: (508)992-1522
PO Box 80268 Fax: (508)992-1689
South Dartmouth, MA 02748-0268
Newspaper. **Founded:** 1966. **Freq:** Weekly. **Print Method:** Offset. **Cols./Page:** 6. **Col. Width:** 24 nonpareils. **Col. Depth:** 301 agate lines. **Key Personnel:** Susan Gonsalves, Editor; R.P. Hopkins, General Mgr. **Subscription Rates:** $21. **Remarks:** Accepts advertising.
Ad Rates: BW: $1,322.25 **Circ:** 6,000
4C: $1,722.25
SAU: $11.55
PCI: $11.25

14630 Hair to Stay
Winter Publishing Inc.
PO Box 80667 Phone: (508)999-0078
South Dartmouth, MA 02748 Fax: (508)984-4040
Publication E-mail: squirrel@hairtostay.com

Magazine for people who love and appreciate female body hair. **Founded:** 1994. **Freq:** Quarterly. **Trim Size:** 8 1/2 x 11. **Key Personnel:** Pam Winter, Editor, pam@hairtostay.com. **Subscription Rates:** $50 individuals; $12 single issue plus $3 postage; $50 Canada; $70 other countries. **Remarks:** Accepts advertising.
Circ: Paid 10,000

SOUTH HADLEY, pop. 16,399.

WC MA. Hampshire Co. 4 mi. N. of Holyoke. Mount Holyoke College (women). Residential.

14631 WMHC-FM - 91.5
Mount Holyoke College Phone: (413)538-2019
Blanchard Center Fax: (413)538-2431
South Hadley, MA 01075

Format: Eclectic. **Networks:** Independent. **Owner:** Mount Holyoke College Trustees, at above address. **Founded:** 1940. **Operating Hours:** 6 a.m.-4 a.m. **Key Personnel:** Sarah Lachane, General Mgr., sclachan@mtholyoke.edu; Angelly Shadani, Assistant General Manager, anshahan@mtholyoke.edu; Abbey Clymer, Business, ahchymer@mtholyoke.edu; Erica Brown, Program Dir., ejbrown@mtholyoke.edu; Gillian Beck, Underwriter, ggbeck@mtholyoke.edu; Jessica Macie, Promotions, jlmacie@mtholyoke.edu; Cassandra White, Engineer, cewhite@mtholyoke.edu; Claire Micklin, Traffic, cemickli@mtholyoke.edu; Katherine Sullivan, Music Dir., klsulliv@mtholyoke.edu; Nadya Ruschak, Music Dir., nbruscha@mtholyoke.edu; Noe Carmichael, Music Dir., ncarmich@mtholyoke.edu; Laura Draper, Music Dir., lbdraper@mtholyoke.edu; Tina Driscoll, Music Dir., tmdrisco@mtholyoke.edu. **Wattage:** 100. **Ad Rates:** Noncommercial. **URL:** http://www.mtholyoke.edu.

SOUTH YARMOUTH

14632 WCOD-FM - 106.1
851 Main St., Ste. 1 Phone: (508)760-5252
South Yarmouth, MA 02664-5275 Fax: (508)760-5353

Format: Adult Contemporary. **Owner:** Boch Broadcasting, 278 South Sea Ave., West Yarmouth, MA 02673, (508)775-5678, Fax: (508)771-3420. **Founded:** 1967. **Operating Hours:** Continuous; 100% local. **ADI:** Boston-Worcester,MA-Derry-Manchester,NH. **Key Personnel:** Chris Boles, Program Dir., phone (508)775-5678, fax (508)771-3420; Randy Bush, General Mgr.; Dave Gellar, Dir. of Sales; Chris Barnes, News Dir., phone (508)862-6397, fax (508)862-6297. **Wattage:** 50,000. **Ad Rates:** $30-70 per unit.

14633 WWKJ-FM - 101.1
851 Main St., Ste. 1 Phone: (508)760-5252
South Yarmouth, MA 02664-5275 Fax: (508)760-5353

Format: Classic Rock. **Networks:** Westwood One Radio. **Founded:** 1987. **Formerly:** WFAL-FM. **Operating Hours:** Continuous; 100% local. **Key Personnel:** Randy Bush, General Mgr.; Gavin Spittle, Program Dir., phone (508)775-5678, fax (508)771-3420; Steve Dines, Publisher; Diane Rice Rindle, General Sales Mgr. **Local Programs:** *Cape Politics.* **Wattage:** 6000. **Ad Rates:** $14-18 for 30 seconds; $20-24 for 60 seconds.

SOUTHBOROUGH, pop. 6,193.

S. MA. Worcester Co. 4 mi. SE of Marlborough. Residential.

14634 Southborough Villager
33 New York Ave. Phone: (508)485-5200
Framingham, MA 01701-8880 Fax: (508)485-2133
Free: (800)982-4023

Community newspaper. **Founded:** Nov. 30, 1979. **Freq:** Weekly. **Print Method:** Offset. **Cols./Page:** 6. **Col. Width:** 12 picas. **Col. Depth:** 21 inches. **Key Personnel:** Glenda A. Hazard, Editor; Steve Dines, Publisher; Bob Shompe, Advertising Mgr. **USPS:** 528-250. **Subscription Rates:** $24; $36 out of county. **Remarks:** Accepts advertising.
Ad Rates: PCI: $5 **Circ:** Paid 1,299
Non-paid 29

SOUTHBRIDGE, pop. 16,665.

C. MA. Worcester Co. 21 mi. S. of Worcester. Manufactures optical goods, cutlery, worsteds. Dairy farms.

14635 The Southbridge Evening News
Stonebridge Press Inc.
25 Elm St. Phone: (508)764-4325
Southbridge, MA 01550 Fax: (508)764-8015
Free: (800)367-9898
Publication E-mail: sbnews@mega.net
Publisher E-mail: sbnews@hey.net

General newspaper. **Founded:** 1923. **Freq:** Daily. **Print Method:** Offset. **Cols./Page:** 6. **Col. Width:** 1 1/2 inches. **Col. Depth:** 16 inches. **Key Personnel:** David Cutler, Editor. **USPS:** 504-380. **Subscription Rates:** $80.60. **Remarks:** Accepts advertising. **Formerly**: The News.
Ad Rates: GLR: $10 **Circ:** Paid ‡5,400
BW: $1,099
PCI: $9

14636 WQVR-FM - 100.1
100 Foster St. Phone: (508)765-0100
Southbridge, MA 01550-2537 Fax: (508)764-2682

Format: Country. **Networks:** NBC. **Owner:** Eastern Media, at above address. **Founded:** 1968. **Operating Hours:** Continuous. **Key Personnel:** Don Fitzgibbons, General Mgr.; Joe Grivalski, Operations Mgr. **Wattage:** 3000. **Ad Rates:** $40 for 60 seconds.

SPENCER, pop. 10,774.

S. MA. Worcester Co. 10 mi. W. of Worcester. Manufactures chemicals, plastics, wire products, lumber, paper board boxes. Dairying. Poultry farms.

14637 The New Leader
Stonebridge Press Inc.
369 Main St. Phone: (508)885-9402
PO Box 911 Fax: (508)885-4213
Spencer, MA 01562
Publisher E-mail: sbnews@hey.net

Community newspaper (tabloid). **Founded:** 1977. **Freq:** Weekly (Thurs.). **Print Method:** Offset. **Cols./Page:** 6. **Col. Width:** 21 nonpareils. **Col. Depth:** 189 agate lines. **Key Personnel:** Robert Scarbeau, Editor; Michele Ferro, Publisher. **Subscription Rates:** $18. **Remarks:** Accepts advertising.
Ad Rates: PCI: $6.25 **Circ:** 4,000

SPRINGFIELD†, pop. 152,319.

SW MA. Hampden Co. On Connecticut River, 98 mi. SW of Boston. American International College; Springfield College; Western New England College; Springfield Technical Community College. Manufactures electrical machinery and equipment, computer components, games toys, school supplies, fibre products, matches, drop forgings, proprietary medicine, machine tools, firearms, packaging machinery, stationery, chains, textiles, saws, plastics, chemicals and allied products, leather goods, wire, castings and patterns, brass and brass goods, tools.

14638 The Catholic Observer
Catholic Observer, Inc.
65 Elliot St. Phone: (413)732-3175
PO Box 1570 Fax: (413)747-0273
Springfield, MA 01101-1570
Catholic newspaper (tabloid). **Founded:** 1954. **Freq:** Biweekly. **Print Method:** Offset. **Cols./Page:** 5. **Col. Width:** 1 13/16 inches. **Col. Depth:** 165 agate lines. **Key Personnel:** Sharon Roulier, Executive Editor; Anita Tucker, Business Mgr.; Ray Burke, Advertising Mgr. **Subscription Rates:** $12. **Remarks:** Advertising not accepted for alcohol, cigarettes, or political causes.
Ad Rates: GLR: $.91 **Circ:** 14,456
BW: $828.75
4C: $1,078.75
PCI: $12.75

14639 Union-News & Sunday Republican
1860 Main St. Phone: (413)788-1000
Springfield, MA 01101 Fax: (413)788-1301

General newspaper. **Founded:** 1824. **Freq:** Mon.-Sat. (morn.). **Print Method:** Letterpress. **Cols./Page:** 6. **Col. Width:** 26 nonpareils. **Col. Depth:** 301 agate lines. **Key Personnel:** Arnold Friedman, Editor; David Starr, Publisher; Dwight Brouillard, Advertising Dir. **Subscription Rates:** $100 daily; $65 Sunday. **Remarks:** Accepts advertising. **URL:** http://www.masslive.com. **Feature Editors:** Phyllis Andreoni, *Education*, phone (413)788-1269; John Appleton, *Political*, phone (413)788-1288; Laurie Bobskill, *Medical*, phone (413)788-1338; Robert Chipkin, *State*, phone (413)788-1201; William Freebairn, *Education*, phone (413)788-1269; Stan Freeman, *Environmental, Science*, phone (413)788-1264; Arnold Friedman, *Book*, phone (413)788-1212; Jame Gillen, *Metro*, phone (413)788-1303; James Gillen, *Suburban*, phone (413)788-1303; Joseph Hopkins, *Editorials*, phone (413)788-1255; Kevin McGurk, *Consumer Affairs*, phone (413)788-1335; Ruth O'Brien, *TV*, phone (413)788-1293; Jean O'Connell, *Fashion, Food*, phone (413)788-1298; Richard Osgood, *Sports*, phone (413)788-1210; Mimi Rigali, *Family, Features, Garden/Home, Lifestyle, Real Estate, Society, Travel, Women's*, phone (413)788-1291; Larry Rivais, *City, Rural Development*, phone (413)788-1304; Carolyn Robbins, *Financial/Business*, phone (413)788-1298; Norman Roy, *Photo*, phone (413)788-1045; Doris Schmidt, *Entertainment, Movie, Music*, phone (413)788-1331; Dorris Schmidt, *Drama*, phone (413)788-1279; Lawrence Sullivan, *News*, phone (413)788-1342.
Ad Rates: 4C: $1,063 **Circ:** Mon.-Sat. ★**94,572**
SAU: $43.05 Sun. ★**141,253**

14640 Yellow Jacket
American International College
1000 State St. Phone: (413)737-5331
Springfield, MA 01109-3189
Collegiate newspaper. **Founded:** 1934. **Freq:** Semimonthly (during the academic year). **Print Method:** Offset. **Trim Size:** 11 x 14. **Cols./Page:** 4. **Col. Width:** 24 nonpareils. **Col. Depth:** 185 agate lines. **Key Personnel:** Nicole Phillips, Editor. **Remarks:** Accepts advertising.
Ad Rates: BW: $200 **Circ:** 800
PCI: $20

14641 Continental Cablevision, Inc. of Springfield
3303 Main St. Phone: (413)730-4500
Springfield, MA 01107 Fax: (413)734-9243
Free: (800)952-2253

Founded: 1982. **Cities Served:** Hampden County, MA.

14642 WAIC-FM - 91.9
1000 State St. Phone: (413)736-7662
Springfield, MA 01109 Fax: (413)737-2803

Format: Adult Contemporary; Jazz; Religious; Urban Contemporary. **Networks:** Independent. **Owner:** American International College, at above address, (413)737-7000. **Founded:** 1964. **Operating Hours:** 6 a.m.-midnight; 100% local. **ADI:** Springfield, MA. **Key Personnel:** Gilen A. Forbes, Program Dir.; Robert Brownlee, Music Dir.; Kim Fowlkes, General Mgr. **Wattage:** 440.

14643 WDMR-TV - 65
974 Main St. Phone: (413)746-6565
Springfield, MA 01105 Fax: (413)956-6834

Networks: Telemundo. **Owner:** Channel 13 Televisions, Inc., 886 Maple Ave., Hartford, CT 06114, (860)956-1303. **Founded:** June 13, 1990. **Formerly**: WBX-TV. **Operating Hours:** Continuous. **ADI:** Springfield, MA. **Key Personnel:** Lucio C. Ruzzier, President; Sal Minniti, Chief Engineer; Gaetano Leone, General Mgr.; William Newton, Vice Pres., Sales. **Local Programs:** *Adelante*, William Newton, (860)956-1303, Fax (860)956-6834; *L'Italia D'America*, Lucio C. Ruzzier, (860)956-1303, Fax (860)956-6834; *Specials*, William Newton, (860)956-1303, Fax (860)956-6834. **Wattage:** 1000 - Radiating 33,000. **Ad Rates:** Advertising accepted; rates available upon request.

14644 WGBY-TV - 57
44 Hampden St. Phone: (413)781-2801
Springfield, MA 01103 Fax: (413)731-5093

Format: Public TV. **Networks:** Public Broadcasting Service (PBS). **Founded:** 1971. **Operating Hours:** 7:30 a.m.-midnight. **ADI:** Springfield, MA. **Key Personnel:** Ray Miller, Chief Engineer, rmiller@wgby.org; Deborah Onslow, General Mgr., donslow@wgby.org; Kevin Crane, Program Mgr., kcrane@wgby.org; William Rhodes, Production Mgr., brhodes@wgby.org; William Gonyea, Mgr. of Business Affairs, bgonyea@wgby.org. **Ad Rates:** Noncommercial.

14645 WGGB-TV - 40
1300 Liberty St. Phone: (413)733-4040
Box 40 Fax: (413)781-1363
Springfield, MA 01102-0040

Format: Commercial TV. **Networks:** ABC. **Founded:** 1953. **Formerly**: WHYN-TV (1976). **Operating Hours:** Continuous. **ADI:** Springfield, MA. **Key Personnel:** Kevin LeRoux, Contact; Mike Moran, Station Mgr.; Dan Salamone, News Dir. **Ad Rates:** $50-1500 per unit.

14646 WMAS-AM - 1450
PO Box 9500 Phone: (413)737-1414
Springfield, MA 01102 Fax: (413)737-1488
Free: (800)YES-WMAS

Format: Music of Your Life; Middle-of-the-Road (MOR). **Networks:** Mutual Broadcasting System; ABC. **Owner:** Lappin Communications, Inc., PO Box 9500, Springfield, MA 01102. **Founded:** 1932. **Operating Hours:** Continuous; 5% network, 95% local. **ADI:** Springfield, MA. **Key Personnel:** Bruce Peckover, Contact; Chris Carr, Program Dir.; Jonathan Evans, News Dir.; Chuck Herlihy, Chief Engineer. **Wattage:** 1000.

14647 WMAS-FM - 94.7
PO Box 9500 Phone: (413)737-1414
Springfield, MA 01102 Fax: (413)737-1488

Format: Adult Contemporary. **Networks:** Independent. **Owner:** Lappin Communications, Inc., PO Box 1139, Springfield, MA 01101. **Founded:** 1947. **Operating Hours:** Continuous; 5% network, 95% local. **ADI:** Springfield, MA. **Key Personnel:** Joseph Rizza, Contact; Tom Holt, Program Dir.; Chuck Herlihy, Chief Engineer. **Wattage:** 50,000.

14648 WNEK-FM - 105.1
Western New England College Phone: (413)782-1582
1215 Wibraham Rd. Fax: (413)796-2111
Springfield, MA 01119

Format: Full Service; Educational. **Networks:** ABC; AP. **Owner:** Western New England College, at above address. **Founded:** 1970. **Formerly**: WTRZ-FM (1977). **Operating Hours:** 8 a.m.-midnight. **ADI:** Springfield, MA. **Key Personnel:** Dan Bruno, Operations Dir.; Rob Jacque, Metal Coordinator; Heather McFarland, Alternate Coordinator; Ed Stankovich, R&B Coordinator; Becky Lauber, Traffic Dir.; Brian Noel, Public Service Coordinator; Michelle Smith, Financial Dir.; Charles Clerke, Underwriting Coordinator; Nick Wolkowicz, Public Relations Coordinator. **Wattage:** 13.

14649 WNNZ-AM - 640
PO Box 15640 Phone: (413)736-6400
Springfield, MA 01115 Fax: (413)858-1958
Free: (800)736-4640

Format: Talk. **Networks:** Unistar; CBS; ABC. **Owner:** Celia Communications, Inc., at above address. **Founded:** 1987. **Operating Hours:** Continuous; 100% local. **ADI:** Springfield, MA. **Key Personnel:** Curtis H. Hahn, President; Celia F. Hahn, Contact; John Baibak, News Dir.; Kevin Casey, Program Dir. **Local Programs:** *Curt Hahn Show*, Curt Hahn; *Michael Harrison Show*, Michael Harrison. **Wattage:** 50,000. **Ad Rates:** $35-60 for 30 seconds; $35-60 for 60 seconds.

14650 WSCB-FM - 89.9
263 Alden St. Phone: (413)748-3131
Springfield, MA 01109 Fax: (413)748-3473

Format: Eclectic. **Founded:** 1958. **Operating Hours:** Continuous. **ADI:** Springfield, MA. **Key Personnel:** Richard Levy, General Mgr. **Wattage:** 100. **Ad Rates:** Noncommercial.

14651 WTCC-FM - 90.7
1 Armory Sq. Phone: (413)781-6628
Springfield, MA 01105 Fax: (413)781-3747
E-mail: sepia45@aol.com

Format: Ethnic; Eclectic; Religious; Oldies. **Networks:** Independent. **Founded:** 1972. **Operating Hours:** Continuous; 100% local. **ADI:** Springfield, MA. **Key Personnel:** Ernest Johnson, General Mgr.; Denise Gore, Contact; Fred Krampits, Chief Engineer; Evelyn Tumulac, News Dir., phone (413)785-1629. **Wattage:** 4000. **Ad Rates:** $10 for 30 seconds.

14652 WVNE-AM - 760
70 James St., Ste. 201 Phone: (508)831-9863
Worcester, MA 01603-1000 Fax: (508)831-7964
E-mail: wvne@aol.com

Format: Religious; Talk. **Networks:** USA Radio; Sun Radio; Ambassador Inspirational Radio. **Owner:** Blount Masscom, Inc., at above address. **Founded:** 1990. **Operating Hours:** Sunrise-sunset. **ADI:** Boston-Worcester,MA-Derry-Manchester,NH. **Key Personnel:** Steve Tuzeneu, Operations Mgr.; Dave Young, Vice Pres./Gen. Mgr.; Bill Blount, President. **Wattage:** 25,000. **Ad Rates:** $10-14 for 30 seconds; $18-21 for 60 seconds. **URL:** http://www.lifechangingradio.com.

14653 WWLP-TV - 22
PO Box 2210 Phone: (413)786-2200
Springfield, MA 01102 Fax: (413)786-7144

Format: Commercial TV. **Networks:** NBC. **Owner:** Adams Communication Corp., PO Box 2617, Clearwater, FL 34615, (813)449-1500. **Operating Hours:** 6 a.m.-1:30 a.m. **ADI:** Springfield, MA. **Key Personnel:** William M. Pepin, General Mgr.

STOCKBRIDGE, pop. 2,328.

W. MA. Berkshire Co. 10 mi. S. of Pittsfield. Residential.

14654 The Association of Marian Helpers Bulletin
Marian Helpers Center
Eden Hill Phone: (413)298-3691
Stockbridge, MA 01263 Fax: (413)298-3583
Free: (800)462-7426
Publication E-mail: dmintl@aol.com

Official magazine of the Association of Marian Helpers. **Founded:** 1947. **Freq:** Quarterly. **Key Personnel:** Fr. Joseph Joseph, M.I.C., Director and Publisher; Vinny Flinn, Exec. Editor. **Subscription Rates:** Free to qualified subscribers. **Remarks:** Advertising not accepted. **URL:** http://www.marian.org; http://www.carian.org.
Circ: Controlled 600,000

14655 Roze Maryi
Congregation of Marians
Eden Hill Phone: (413)298-3691
Stockbridge, MA 01263 Fax: (413)298-3583
Free: (800)462-7426
Publisher E-mail: mhc@marian.org

Magazine of the Assn. of Marian Helpers, a spiritual benefit society of the Congregations of Marians. (Polish). **Founded:** 1944. **Freq:** Quarterly. **Print Method:** Offset. **Trim Size:** 8 1/4 x 10 3/4. **Cols./Page:** 2. **Col. Width:** 27 nonpareils. **Col. Depth:** 105 agate lines. **Key Personnel:** Bro. Andrew Maczynski, M.I.C., Editor, fr.joseph@marian.org; Maciej P. Talar. **ISSN:** 0745-3299. **Subscription Rates:** $10; $15 Europe; $20 other continents. **Remarks:** Advertising not accepted. **URL:** http://www.marian.org.
Circ: Paid ‡6,000
Controlled ‡1,500

STOUGHTON, pop. 26,710.

E. MA. Norfolk Co. 19 mi. S. of Boston. Manufactures woolen knit goods, elastic webbing, shoes, rubber specialties, plastics, machine tools, raincoats.

Avon Messenger - See Avon

Braintree Gazette - See Braintree

Brockton News Tribune - See Brockton

Canton Register - See Canton

Daily Mercury - See Medford

Easton Bulletin - See Easton

Hanover Branch - See Hanover

Hanson Town Crier - See Hanson

Holbrook Times - See Holbrook

Mansfield Reporter - See Mansfield

Milton Townsman - See Milton

Norton Courier - See Norton

Randolph Herald - See Randolph

Raynham Journal - See Raynham

Sharon Sentinel - See Sharon

14656 Stoughton Chronicle
Associated Newspapers
7 Cabot Pl. Phone: (781)878-1111
PO Box 441 Fax: (781)878-3333
Stoughton, MA 02072
Publication E-mail: aweeklies@aol.com
Publisher E-mail: aweeklies@aol.com

Community newspaper. **Founded:** 1861. **Freq:** Weekly (Wed.). **Print Method:** Offset. **Cols./Page:** 6. **Col. Width:** 9.5 picas. **Col. Depth:** 16 inches. **Key Personnel:** Richard R. Dailey, Publisher. **Subscription Rates:** $17.50. **Remarks:** Accepts advertising.
Ad Rates: BW: $10.53 **Circ:** Paid 2,450
4C: $10.77
PCI: $10.53

14657 Suburban News
Franklin Publishing Co., Inc.
PO Box 441
Stoughton, MA 02072-0441

Newspaper. **Founded:** 1974. **Freq:** Weekly. **Print Method:** Offset. **Cols./Page:** 6. **Col. Width:** 1 9/16 inches. **Col. Depth:** 16 inches. **Key Personnel:** Rose Thompson, Editor; Paul Mack, Publisher. **Subscription Rates:** $17.50. **Remarks:** Color advertising accepted; rates available upon request.
Ad Rates: GLR: $1.45 **Circ:** Free 30,000
BW: $1,200
SAU: $23.50
PCI: $19.95

West Bridgewater Times - See West Bridgewater

Weymouth Dispatch - See Weymouth

Whitman Times - See Whitman

STURBRIDGE, pop. 5,976.

SW MA. Worcester Co. 18 mi. SW of Worcester. Industrial.

14658 Old Sturbridge Visitor
Old Sturbridge, Inc.
1 Old Sturbridge Village Rd. Phone: (508)347-3362
Sturbridge, MA 01566-1198 Fax: (508)347-0377
Publisher E-mail: langdon@osv.org

Magazine covering museum research, collecting and programs for museum members. **Freq:** Quarterly. **Key Personnel:** Alberta Sebolt George, President; Jack Larkin, Senior Editor. **ISSN:** 0485-6724. **Subscription Rates:** Free to qualified subscribers; $25 nonmembers. **Remarks:** Advertising not accepted. **Former name:** Rural Visitor (1982).
Circ: Combined 10,000

SUDBURY, pop. 14,027.

NE MA. Middlesex Co. 16 mi. W. of Cambridge. Residential. Manufactures machinery equipment. Nurseries.

14659 Bonsai Today
Stone Lantern Publishing Co.
PO Box 816 Phone: (978)443-7110
Sudbury, MA 01776 Fax: (978)443-9115
Publication E-mail: order@stonelantern.com

Magazine on bonsai. **Founded:** 1989. **Freq:** Bimonthly. **Trim Size:** 8 1/4 x 11 3/8. **Cols./Page:** 3. **Col. Width:** 2 3/8 inches. **Col. Depth:** 7 3/8 inches. **Key Personnel:** W. John Palmer, Publisher, jpalmer@stonelantern.com. **ISSN:** 1044-2529. **Subscription Rates:** $42; $48 Canada; $52.50 other countries. $7.95 single issue. **Remarks:** Advertising accepted; rates available upon request.
Circ: ‡8,012

14660 Radiology Management
Cryan Associates
c/o Theresa V. Cryan Phone: (508)443-6911
PO Box 910 Fax: (508)443-0197
Sudbury, MA 01776
Publication E-mail: cryanassoc@fiam.net
Publisher E-mail: ahraonline.org

Magazine covering non-medical radiology operations. **Founded:** 1979. **Freq:** Quarterly 6/year. **Print Method:** Offset. Uses mats. **Trim Size:** 8 1/2 x 11. **Cols./Page:** 2. **Col. Width:** 42 nonpareils. **Col. Depth:** 126 agate lines. **Key Personnel:** David Woodford, Editor. **ISSN:** 0198-7097. **Subscription Rates:** $54 individuals.
Ad Rates: 4C: $2,754 **Circ:** 4,445

14661 The Sudbury Town Crier & TAB
Community Newspaper Company
254 2nd Ave. Phone: (781)433-7828
Needham, MA 02192-9114 Fax: (781)433-7835

Community newspaper. **Founded:** 1997. **Freq:** Weekly (Thurs.). **Print Method:** Offset. **Trim Size:** 10 x 16. **Cols./Page:** 5. **Col. Width:** 12 picas. **Key Personnel:** Darienne Hosley, Editor, darienne.hosley@cnc.com. **Remarks:** Accepts advertising. **URL:** http://www.townonline.com. **Formerly:** The Wayland/Sudbury Gazette; The Sudbury Tab; The Sudbury Town Crier.
Circ: Paid 3,761

14662 The WANT ADvertiser
WANT AD Publications, Inc.
128 Boston Post Rd. Phone: (978)443-7007
Sudbury, MA 01776-3330 Fax: (978)443-3340
Free: (800)242-9433
Publisher E-mail: thewantad@aol.com

Classified ad magazine. **Founded:** 1957. **Freq:** Weekly (Tues.). **Print Method:** Offset. **Trim Size:** 8 x 10 3/4. **Cols./Page:** 4. **Col. Width:** 18 nonpareils. **Col. Depth:** 120 agate lines. **Key Personnel:** Kimberly Grellier, Editor, phone (978)443-4778, fax (978)443-5033. **Subscription Rates:** $195 individuals; $1.75 single issue. **Remarks:** Accepts advertising. **URL:** http://www.wantadvertiser.com.
Ad Rates: GLR: $10 **Circ:** 65,000
BW: $425
PCI: $60

14663 Wheels, Etc.
WANT AD Publications, Inc.
128 Boston Post Rd. Phone: (978)443-7007
Sudbury, MA 01776-3330 Fax: (978)443-3340
Free: (800)242-9433
Publisher E-mail: thewantad@aol.com

Automobile classified ad magazine containing photos. **Founded:** 1984. **Freq:** Weekly (Tues.). **Print Method:** Offset. **Trim Size:** 8 1/4 x 11. **Cols./Page:** 2. **Col. Width:** 3 1/2 inches. **Col. Depth:** 10 inches. **Key Personnel:** Patricia Halter, Editor; Kimberly Grellier, Circulation Mgr. **Subscription Rates:** $120; $1.50 single issue. **Remarks:** Accepts advertising. **Formerly:** Wheels and Keels.
Ad Rates: BW: $300 **Circ:** ‡17,000

14664 WYAJ-FM - 97.7
Lincoln Sundbury Regional High School Phone: (998)443-3531
Fax: (978)443-8824
390 Lincoln Rd.
Sudbury, MA 01776

Format: Full Service; Alternative/New Music/Progressive. **Networks:** Independent. **Owner:** Sudbury Valley Broadcasting Foundation, at above address. **Founded:** 1979. **Operating Hours:** 3 p.m.-11 p.m. weekdays, 6:30 a.m.-7:55 am weekdays; 100% local. **Key Personnel:** Carl Rutman, General Mgr., carl_ Rutman@isrhs.net. **Wattage:** 10.

SWAMPSCOTT, pop. 13,837.

NE MA. Essex Co. 11 mi. NE of Boston. (Branch of Lynn P.O.) Residential.

14665 Swampscott Reporter
Community Newspaper Company
40 South St. Phone: (617)631-7700
Marblehead, MA 01945 Fax: (617)639-2830
Publication E-mail: sweditor@shore.net

Community newspaper (tabloid). **Founded:** 1965. **Freq:** Weekly (Thurs.). **Print Method:** Offset. Uses mats. **Trim Size:** 11 3/8 x 17. **Cols./Page:** 5. **Col. Width:** 2 inches. **Col. Depth:** 16 inches. **Key Personnel:** John Ouellette, Editor; Chuck Goodrich, Publisher; John Vistorino, Advertising Mgr. **ISSN:** 0893-3634. **Subscription Rates:** $18 individuals; $15 students; $31 out of area. **Remarks:** Accepts advertising.
Ad Rates: BW: $740 **Circ:** Paid 3,495
SAU: $11.50 Non-paid 490

TAUNTON†, pop. 45,001.

SE MA. Bristol Co. On Tauton River, 32 mi. S. of Boston. Diversified industry. Manufactures sailboats, plastics, curtains, wire, felt, yarn, metal buildings.

14666 Taunton Daily Gazette
5 Cohannet St. Phone: (508)880-9000
Taunton, MA 02780-3903 Fax: (508)824-3487
Publication E-mail: tdg@ini.net

General newspaper. **Founded:** 1848. **Freq:** Daily and Sat. (morn.). **Print Method:** Offset. **Trim Size:** 12 x 21 1/2. **Cols./Page:** 6. **Col. Width:** 1 7/8 inches. **Col. Depth:** 301 agate lines. **Key Personnel:** Terrence Mercer, Editor; John Lamp, Advertising Mgr.; Tim Hogan, Publisher; J. William Dean, Circulation Dir. **Subscription Rates:** $132.60 individuals. **Remarks:** Accepts advertising.
Ad Rates: BW: $1,284.84 **Circ:** Mon.-Sat. ★**14,536**
4C: $240 Sun. ★**13,703**
PCI: $14.55

14667 WPEP-AM - 1570
41 Taunton Green Phone: (508)822-1570
Taunton, MA 02780-3233

Format: News; Talk. **Networks:** UPI. **Founded:** 1949. **Operating Hours:** Continuous. **ADI:** Providence, RI-New Bedford, MA. **Key Personnel:** George Colajezzi, Vice President/General Manager; Mike Logan, News Dir.; Donna Colajezzi, Contact; Irene C. Peacock, Sales Mgr. **Local Programs:** *Donna Colajezzi Show*; *Bob Jacobs Show*; *Robert Parent Show*. **Wattage:** 1000. **Ad Rates:** $14-22 for 30 seconds; $16-30 for 60 seconds.

TEWKSBURY, pop. 24,635.

NE MA. Middlesex Co. 5 mi. SE of Lowell. Manufactures printing inks, wood products. Nurseries.

14668 The Oblate World and Voice of Hope
Missionary Oblates of Mary Immaculate
486 Chandler St. Phone: (978)858-0434
PO Box 680 Fax: (978)858-3661
Tewksbury, MA 01876
Newspaper covering the Eastern, Western, and Northern

provinces. **Founded:** 1939. **Freq:** Bimonthly. **Key Personnel:** Rev. Wm. O'Donnell, O.M.I., Editor.

14669 Tewksbury Advertiser
Community Newspapers Inc.
Box 9191 Phone: (508)667-2156
Concord, MA 01742-9191 Fax: (508)262-9947

Community newspaper. **Founded:** 1957. **Freq:** Weekly (Wed.). **Print Method:** Offset. **Cols./Page:** 6. **Col. Width:** 21 nonpareils. **Col. Depth:** 294 agate lines. **Key Personnel:** Laurie Glasheen, Editor; William P. Dole, Publisher; Beth A. Lancaster, Advertising Mgr. **Subscription Rates:** Free; $15 (mail). **Remarks:** Accepts advertising. **Formerly:** Merrimack Valley Advertiser (Tewksbury Edition) (1992).
Ad Rates: BW: $2,412.90 **Circ:** Free 5,060
PCI: $19.15

14670 Wilmington-Tewksbury Town Crier
Daily Times
104 Lowell Street
Wilmington, MA 01887
Publication E-mail: towncrier1@aol.com

Community newspaper. **Founded:** 1955. **Freq:** Weekly. **Print Method:** Offset. **Cols./Page:** 6. **Col. Width:** 12 picas. **Col. Depth:** 21 inches. **Key Personnel:** C. Stuart Neilson, General Mgr.; Frank Amato, Editor. **USPS:** 635-340. **Subscription Rates:** $20; $24 out of area; $5 single issue. **Remarks:** Accepts advertising.
Ad Rates: GLR: $.65 **Circ:** Paid ♦**5,868**
BW: $819 Non-paid ♦**544**
4C: $1200
SAU: $9
PCI: $9

TISBURY

SE MA. Dukes Co. On Martha's Vineyard.

14671 WMVY-FM - 92.7
Box 1148 Phone: (508)693-5000
Tisbury, MA 02568 Fax: (508)693-8211
Free: (800)477-WMVY

Format: Album-Oriented Rock (AOR); Album-Oriented Rock (AOR); Classical; Jazz. **Networks:** AP. **Owner:** Broadcast Properties, Inc., Box 1148, Vineyard Haven, MA 02568. **Founded:** 1981. **Operating Hours:** 5:30 a.m.-2 a.m.; 5% network, 95% local. **Key Personnel:** Andy Brunk, General Mgr.; Barbara Dacey, Program & Music Director/ Station Mgr.; Joe Pulman, News Dir. **Wattage:** 3000. **Ad Rates:** $20-45 for 30 seconds.

TOPSFIELD

14672 Tri-Town Transcript
Community Newspaper Company
58 Main St. Phone: (508)887-2727
Topsfield, MA 01983 Fax: (508)887-0791

Community newspaper (tabloid). **Founded:** 1960. **Freq:** Weekly (Thurs.). **Print Method:** Offset. Uses mats. **Trim Size:** 11 3/8 x 17. **Cols./Page:** 5. **Col. Width:** 2 1/16 inches. **Col. Depth:** 16 inches. **Key Personnel:** Faye Raynard, Editor; Chuck Goodrich, Publisher; John Vistorino, Advertising Dir. **USPS:** 311-430. **Subscription Rates:** $19; $14 students; $31 out of area. **Remarks:** Accepts advertising.
Ad Rates: BW: $644 **Circ:** Paid 4,244
SAU: $8.05 Free 637
PCI: $8.05

14673 WBMT-FM - 88.3
20 Endicott Rd. Phone: (508)887-8830
Topsfield, MA 01983-2013

Format: Album-Oriented Rock (AOR); Classic Rock. **Owner:** Masconomet Regional High School, at above address, (508)887-2323. **Founded:** 1978. **Operating Hours:** 9 a.m.-9 p.m. weekdays; noon-8 p.m. Saturday and Sunday; 100% local. **Key Personnel:** Glenn Walker, General Mgr.; Aimee Jefferson, Station Mgr.; Mike Sanger, Contact; Rebecca Schricker, Contact; Betsy Hopkins, Music Dir.; Melissa Maxfield, Production Dir.; Chris Meniates, Program Dir.; Tim Jalbert, Chief Engineer. **Wattage:** 825. **Ad Rates:** Noncommercial.

VINEYARD HAVEN

14674 Adelphia Cable of MV
Box 2109 Phone: (508)693-6644
Vineyard Haven, MA 02568 Fax: (508)693-3669

Owner: Tele-Media Corp., 251 E. College Ave., Box 90, State College, PA 16801, (814)238-8314. **Founded:** 1995. **Formerly:** Tele-media Co. of MV (1984). **Key Personnel:** Ken Goldberg, Contact/Sales Manager; Michael McLaughin, Studio Mgr. **Cities Served:** Vineyard Haven, MA: subscribing households 4,800; 56 channels; 1 community access channel; 2 hours per week community access programming.

WABAN

14675 Parents' Choice
Parents' Choice Foundation
1935 Beacon St. Phone: (617)965-5913
Waban, MA 02168-1461 Fax: (617)965-4516

Subtitle: Since 1978, The Only Nonprofit Consumer Guide to Children's Home Video, Books, Toys, Computer Software, Audio, TV, and Movies. **Founded:** 1978. **Freq:** Quarterly. **Print Method:** Web offset. **Trim Size:** 11 1/2 x 17 1/8. **Cols./Page:** 4. **Col. Width:** 2 3/8 inches. **Col. Depth:** 15 inches. **Key Personnel:** Diana Huss Green, Editor. **ISSN:** 0161-8146. **Subscription Rates:** $18. **Remarks:** Accepts advertising. **Online:** starwave.
Ad Rates: BW: $1,335 **Circ:** 300,000

WAKEFIELD, pop. 24,895.

NE MA. Middlesex Co. 10 mi. N. of Boston. Manufactures shoes, textiles, lead, iron pipe. Residential.

14676 Item
Wakefield Item Co.
26 Albion St. Phone: (781)245-0080
Wakefield, MA 01880 Fax: (781)246-0061

General newspaper. **Founded:** 1894. **Freq:** Daily (eve.). **Key Personnel:** Peter Rossi, Editor; Robert P. Dolbeare, Publisher. **Subscription Rates:** $72. **Remarks:** Accepts advertising.
Ad Rates: PCI: $8.20 **Circ:** (Not Reported)

14677 128 News
Rieder Communications
382 Lowell St., Ste. 203
Wakefield, MA 01880

Business newspaper for Massachusetts high tech and business communities. **Founded:** 1985. **Freq:** Monthly. **Print Method:** Web press. **Cols./Page:** 4. **Col. Width:** 2 3/8 inches. **Col. Depth:** 15 1/2 inches. **Key Personnel:** Martin Rieder, Editor, phone (978)525-3081; Jude McKinnon, Editor, Columns, phone (978)525-3081; Ed Rader, Tech. Dir. **Subscription Rates:** $18 individuals. **Remarks:** Accepts advertising.
Ad Rates: BW: $1,050 **Circ:** Controlled 25,000

WALPOLE, pop. 18,859.

E. MA. Norfolk Co. 12 mi. SW of Braintree. Residential.

14678 The Walpole Times
Mariner
962 Main St. Phone: (617)668-0243
PO Box 388 Fax: (508)668-5174
Walpole, MA 02081-0388
Community newspaper. **Founded:** 1915. **Freq:** Weekly (Thurs.). **Print Method:** Offset. **Cols./Page:** 6. **Col. Width:** 26 nonpareils. **Col. Depth:** 294 agate lines. **Key Personnel:** Paul Clerici, Editor; Albie Nudel, Advertising Mgr. **Subscription Rates:** $22. **Remarks:** Accepts advertising.
Ad Rates: GLR: $.41 **Circ:** Paid 5,700
BW: $787.50 Free 121
PCI: $5.75

14679 WSRB-FM - 91.5
275 Common St.
Walpole, MA 02081

Format: Top 40; Album-Oriented Rock (AOR); Classic Rock; Alternative/New Music/Progressive. **Networks:** Independent. **Owner:** Town of Walpole, at above address. **Founded:** 1974. **Formerly:** WWWA-FM. **Operating Hours:** 2:00-5:00 p.m. **Wattage:** 10.

WALTHAM, pop. 58,200.

NE MA. Middlesex Co. 10 mi. W. of Boston. Brandeis University; Bentley College. Manufactures radio and TV transmitting apparatus, x-ray, electronic components, photographic equipment, computing equipment, soft drinks, machinery.

14680 American Jewish History
American Jewish Historical Society
2 Thornton Rd. Phone: (617)891-8110
Waltham, MA 02154 Fax: (617)899-9208
Publisher E-mail: ajhs@ajhs.org

Journal on American Jewish history. **Founded:** Dec. 1892. **Freq:** Quarterly. **Print Method:** Uses mats. Letterpress and offset. **Trim Size:** 6 x 9. **Cols./Page:** 1. **Col. Width:** 52 nonpareils. **Col. Depth:** 100 agate lines. **Key Personnel:** Marc Lee Raphael, Editor; Michael Feldberg, Exec. Dir. **ISSN:** 0164-0178. **Subscription Rates:** $50 individuals; $69 libraries; $15 single issue. **Remarks:** Accepts advertising. **Alt. Formats:** Microfilm; Microform.
Ad Rates: BW: $200 **Circ:** ‡3,550

14681 The American Journal of Sports Medicine
230 Calvary St. Phone: (781)736-0707
Waltham, MA 02453 Fax: (781)736-0607

Medical journal. **Founded:** 1972. **Freq:** Bimonthly. **Print Method:** Web press. **Trim Size:** 8 3/8 x 10 7/8. **Cols./Page:** 2. **Col. Width:** 32 nonpareils. **Col. Depth:** 119 agate lines. **Key Personnel:** Robert E. Leach, M.D., Editor; E. Ann Donaldson, Managing Editor. **ISSN:** 0363-5465. **Subscription Rates:** $85 individuals; $100 out of country Industry; $100 institutions; $16 single issue industry. **Remarks:** Accepts advertising. **Alt. Formats:** CD-ROM; Microform.
Ad Rates: BW: $970 **Circ:** Paid ‡12,717
4C: $1,090 Non-paid ‡125

14682 Bentley Observer
Bentley College
175 Forest St. Phone: (781)891-2241
Waltham, MA 02154-4705 Fax: (781)891-3165

College alumni magazine. **Freq:** Quarterly. **Print Method:** Sheetfed offset. **Key Personnel:** Susan Simpson, Editor. **Remarks:** Advertising not accepted.
Circ: Controlled 38,000

14683 Forced Exposure
PO Box 9102 Phone: (617)562-0507
Waltham, MA 02254-9102 Fax: (617)562-0533

Magazine covering music, science fiction, and fiction. **Founded:** 1982. **Freq:** Quarterly. **Print Method:** Offset. **Trim Size:** 8 1/2 x 11. **Key Personnel:** Jimmy Johnson, Editor. **Subscription Rates:** $13. $3.95 single issue.

14684 Journal of Neurogenetics
Harwood Academic Publishers GmbH
Dept. of Biology
Brandeis University
Waltham, MA 02154

Science journal. **Freq:** Quarterly. **Key Personnel:** Jeffrey C. Hall, Editor-in-Chief. **ISSN:** 0167-7063.

14685 the Justice
Brandeis University
Usdan Student Center 7
Waltham, MA 02254-9110
Publication E-mail: justice@pip.cc.brandeis.edu

Collegiate newspaper. **Founded:** 1949. **Freq:** Weekly (Tues.). **Print Method:** Offset. **Cols./Page:** 5. **Col. Width:** 22 nonpareils. **Col. Depth:** 224 agate lines. **Key Personnel:** Dani Benel, Editor-in-Chief, phone (781)736-3751; Adam Lieb, Managing Editor, phone (781)736-3751; Arye Elfenbein, News Editor, phone (781)376-3752; Susanna Chilnick, Photography Editor, phone (781)736-3751; Jodi Eichler, Features Editor, phone (781)736-3754; Jesse Friedman, Advertising Editor, phone (781)736-3755; Allan Burstyn, Forum Editor, phone (781)736-3754; Brian Lowe, Sports Editor, phone (781)736-3753; Corinna Lesser, Arts Editor, phone (781)736-3753; Brian Irwin, Subscriptions Mgr., phone (781)736-3751. **Subscription Rates:** $25 per year; $15 per semester. **Remarks:** Accepts advertising.
Ad Rates: BW: $6.50 **Circ:** Paid 300
PCI: $6.50 Free 4,200

14686 News Tribune
Community Newspaper Company
254 Second Ave Phone: (781)433-7800
Needham, MA 02192 Fax: (781)433-8202
Publisher E-mail: townonline.com

General newspaper. **Founded:** 1863. **Freq:** Daily (eve.). **Print Method:** Offset. **Cols./Page:** 6. **Col. Width:** 25 nonpareils. **Col. Depth:** 300 agate lines. **Key Personnel:** Ellen Ishkanian, Editor; Kirk Davis, Publisher. **Subscription Rates:** $91; $110 out of area. **Remarks:** Accepts advertising. **Feature Editors:** Jeanne Washington, *Financial/Business, Food, Regional.*
Ad Rates: GLR: $1.42 **Circ:** Mon.-Fri. 8,581
BW: $1,134
4C: $1,434
SAU: $9

14687 Proof Texts
Johns Hopkins University Press
NEJS Department Phone: (617)736-2960
Brandeis University Fax: (617)736-2070
Waltham, MA 02254
Publisher E-mail: jlinfo@jhupress.jhu.edu

Journal. **Subtitle:** A Journal of Jewish Literary History. **Founded:** 1981. **Freq:** 3/year. **Print Method:** Offset. **Trim Size:** 6 x 9. **Cols./Page:** 1. **Col. Width:** 26 picas. **Col. Depth:** 7 inches. **Key Personnel:** Tara Dorai-Berry, Advertising Mgr.;

Alan Mintz, Editor; David G. Roskies, Editor. **ISSN:** 0272-9601. **Subscription Rates:** $25; $57.5 institutions. **Remarks:** Accepts advertising.
Ad Rates: BW: $200 **Circ:** ‡960

14688 Reseller Management
Post-Newsweek Business Information
800 South St., Ste. 305 Phone: (781)692-1055
Waltham, MA 02154 Fax: (781)692-1077

Computer trade magazine for computer dealers and value added resellers, emphasizing reseller management issues. **Subtitle:** Selling Technology and Services for Profit. **Founded:** 1978. **Freq:** Monthly. **Print Method:** Web offset. **Trim Size:** 8 1/4 x 10 7/8. **Cols./Page:** 2 and 3. **Key Personnel:** G. Hale, Editor-in-Chief, ghale@resellermgmt.com; S. Biolous, Associate Publisher, sbiolous@ix.netcom.com; W. Bryan Wadworth, Executive Editor, bwadworth@resellermgmt.com; Kate Zwald, Managing Editor, kzwald@resellermgmt.com. **ISSN:** 1042-7325. **Subscription Rates:** Free to qualified resellers. **Remarks:** Accepts advertising. **Available Online. URL:** http://www.resellermgmt.com.
Ad Rates: BW: $10,740 **Circ:** Non-paid ‡85,060

14689 Transgender Tapestry
International Foundation for Gender Education
PO Box 229 Phone: (781)899-2212
Waltham, MA 02254-0229 Fax: (781)899-5703
Publication E-mail: tgmag@ifge.org
Publisher E-mail: info@ifge.org

Consumer magazine covering gender expressions and identity, including crossdressing and transsexualism. **Founded:** 1987. **Freq:** Quarterly. **Key Personnel:** Nancy Nangeroni, Editor; Mykaez Hawley, Editor. **Subscription Rates:** $40 individuals; $55 out of country; $12 single issue. **Remarks:** Accepts advertising. **URL:** http://www.ifge.org.
Ad Rates: BW: $1,000 **Circ:** Combined 8,000
4C: $1,700

14690 The Vanguard
Bentley College
LaCava Campus Center, Rm. 169 B Phone: (781)891-2912
Waltham, MA 02452 Fax: (781)891-2574
Publication E-mail: vanguard@bentley.edu

College newspaper (tabloid). **Founded:** 1975. **Freq:** Weekly (Thurs.). **Print Method:** Offset. **Trim Size:** 11 x 17. **Cols./Page:** 5. **Col. Width:** 11 picas. **Col. Depth:** 16 inches. **Key Personnel:** Stacey Hart, Editor-in-Chief, phone (781)891-2912, fax (781)891-2754, hart_stac@bentley.edu. **Subscription Rates:** $12.50 per semester. **Remarks:** Accepts advertising. **URL:** http://www.bnet.bentley.edu/vanguard. **Formerly:** The Inferno (Mar. 1985).
Ad Rates: BW: $280 **Circ:** Free ‡5,000
SAU: $6
PCI: $8.70

14691 WBRS-FM - 100.1
415 South St. Phone: (617)736-5277
Waltham, MA 02254-9110 Fax: (617)736-4787
E-mail: wbrs@binah.cc.brandeis.edu

Format: Eclectic. **Owner:** Trustees of Brandeis University, at above address. **Founded:** 1968. **Operating Hours:** Continuous. **Key Personnel:** Adam Guttell, General Mgr.; Jeremy Sholvitz, Program Dir. **Wattage:** 25. **Ad Rates:** Noncommercial. **URL:** http://www.wbrs.org.

14692 WCRB-FM - 102.5
750 South St. Phone: (781)893-7080
Waltham, MA 02154 Fax: (781)893-0038
E-mail: wcrb@wcrb.com

Format: Classical. **Networks:** Independent. **Owner:** Charles River Broadcasting Company, at above address. **Founded:** 1948. **Operating Hours:** Continuous. **ADI:** Boston-Worcester,MA-Derry-Manchester,NH. **Key Personnel:** Christopher Jones, President, jones@wcrb.com; Terri Gamble, General Sales Mgr., fax (781)899-1676, gamble@wcrb.com; Mario Mazza, Program Dir., mazza@wcrb.com. **Wattage:** 50,000.

14693 WJMN-FM - 94.5
235 Bear Hill Rd. Phone: (617)290-0009
Waltham, MA 02154-1014 Fax: (617)290-0722
E-mail: jamn.com

Format: Urban Contemporary. **Networks:** Independent. **Owner:** Chancellor Media, 433 E. Las Colinas, No. 1130, Irving, TX 75039. **Founded:** 1948. **Formerly:** WZOU-FM (May 1993). **Operating Hours:** Continuous. **Key Personnel:** Alan Chartrand, General Sales Mgr., phone (781)663-2500, fax (781)290-0721, alan945@aol.com; Matt Mills, General Mgr., phone (617)663-2500, fax (781)290-0722, mattm945@aol.com; "Cadillac Jack" McCartney, Program Dir., phone (781)663-2500, fax (781)290-0722; Tom Pappas, Business Mgr., phone (617)663-2500, fax (781)290-0722; Bob Wotiz, Chief Engineer, phone (617)396-1430, fax (781)391-3064. **Wattage:** 11,500. **Ad Rates:** Advertising accepted; rates available upon request. **URL:** http://www.jamn.com.

WARE, pop. 8,953.

WC MA. Hampshire Co. 27 mi. NE of Springfield. Manufactures cotton goods, woolens, gummed paper, iron castings, hydraulic equipment, ice skates, athletic shoes.

14694 New England Antiques Journal
Turley Publications
4 Church St. Phone: (413)967-3505
PO Box 120 Fax: (413)967-6009
Ware, MA 01082
Free: (800)432-3505

Magazine covering antiques. **Founded:** 1982. **Freq:** Monthly. **Print Method:** Production method desktop. **Trim Size:** 11 x 16. **Cols./Page:** 6. **Col. Width:** 1 1/2 inches. **Col. Depth:** 15 3/4 inches. **Key Personnel:** Jody Young, General Mgr.; Julie Murkette, Managing Editor. **ISSN:** 0897-5795. **Subscription Rates:** Free to qualified subscribers; $19.95. $1.50 single issue. **Remarks:** Accepts advertising.
Ad Rates: BW: $550 **Circ:** Paid 6,000
PCI: $8 Controlled 11,000

14695 Ware River News
Turley Publications
4 Church St. Phone: (413)967-3505
PO Box 120 Fax: (413)967-6009
Ware, MA 01082
Free: (800)432-3505

Community newspaper. **Founded:** 1887. **Freq:** Weekly (Thurs.). **Print Method:** Offset. **Cols./Page:** 8. **Col. Width:** 18 nonpareils. **Col. Depth:** 294 agate lines. **Key Personnel:** Glenn H. Ickler, Editor; Patrick H. Turley, Publisher, phone (413)283-8393; Peg Stacy, Advertising Mgr. **USPS:** 666-100. **Subscription Rates:** $21 individuals. **Remarks:** Accepts advertising.
Ad Rates: GLR: $.33 **Circ:** ‡4,600
BW: $1,058.40
PCI: $6.30

14696 WARE-AM - 1250
90 South St. Phone: (413)967-6231
PO Box 210 Fax: (413)967-4456
Ware, MA 01082

Format: Country. **Networks:** ABC. **Founded:** 1946. **Operating Hours:** Continuous; 5% network; 95% local. **Key Personnel:** Robert C. Costello, General Mgr.; Butch Day, Program Dir.; Jean Fairbanks, News Dir. **Wattage:** 5000. **Ad Rates:** $13-18 for 30 seconds; $20-35 for 60 seconds.

WATERTOWN, pop. 34,384.

NE MA. Middlesex Co. 8 mi. W. of Boston. (Branch of Boston P.O.) Fisher Jr. College; Perkins School for the Blind. Residential. Manufactures fabricated metal products, electrical and other machinery, medical instruments, rubber products, electronic equipment, chemical products.

14697 The Armenian Mirror-Spectator
Baikar Association, Inc.
755 Mt. Auburn St. Phone: (617)924-4420
Watertown, MA 02172 Fax: (617)924-3860
Publication E-mail: armmirror@aol.com

Community newspaper (Armenian and English). **Founded:** 1932. **Freq:** Weekly. **Print Method:** Offset. **Cols./Page:** 4. **Col. Width:** 22 nonpareils. **Col. Depth:** 224 agate lines. **Key Personnel:** Barbara Merguerian, Editor. **ISSN:** 0004-234X. **Subscription Rates:** $60.
Ad Rates: GLR: $3 **Circ:** 2,800
BW: $325
PCI: $6

14698 The Armenian Weekly
Hairenik Association, Inc.
80 Bigelow Ave. Phone: (617)926-3974
Watertown, MA 02172-2012 Fax: (617)926-1750

Tabloid on Armenian interests. **Founded:** 1934. **Freq:** Weekly (Sat.). **Print Method:** Offset. **Trim Size:** 10 x 16. **Cols./Page:** 5. **Key Personnel:** Vahe Habeshian, Editor; Shakeh Baghdassarian, Advertising Mgr. **ISSN:** 0148-2971. **Subscription Rates:** $60 individuals. **Remarks:** Color advertising not accepted.
Ad Rates: BW: $400 **Circ:** Paid ‡2,200
PCI: $10 Free ‡300

14699 Business Consumer Guide
Beacon Research Group, Inc.
125 Walnut St. Phone: (617)924-0044
Watertown, MA 02172 Fax: (617)924-0055

National publication featuring evaluations of office products and services aimed at the business community. **Founded:** Nov. 1992. **Freq:** Monthly. **Key Personnel:** Mie-Yun Lee, Editor, mylee@buyerszone.com; Gregg Kavet, Publisher. **ISSN:** 1078-2400. **Subscription Rates:** $159 individuals; $25 single issue. **Remarks:** Advertising not accepted. **Available Online. URL:** http://www.buyerszone.com.
Circ: (Not Reported)

14700 New Age
New Age Publishing
42 Pleasant St. Phone: (617)926-0200
Watertown, MA 02172 Fax: (617)926-5021
Publication E-mail: editor@newage.com

New Age Journal reports on leading-edge ideas in the areas of health, natural living, self-improvement, psychology, publishing and music. It is written for readers who are not limited by conventional thinking and are seeking to improve their lives and society. **Subtitle:** The Journal for Holistic Living. **Founded:** Nov. 1974. **Freq:** 6/year. **Print Method:** Offset. **Trim Size:** 7 7/8 x 10 1/2. **Cols./Page:** 3. **Col. Width:** 2 1/8 inches. **Col. Depth:** 9 1/4 inches. **Key Personnel:** Joan Duncan Oliver, Editor; David H. Thorne, Publisher. **ISSN:** 0746-3618. **Subscription Rates:** $24 individuals; $4.95 single issue. **URL:** http://www.newage.com/home/newage/. **Formerly:** Health, Environment, Fitness, Spirituality Nutrition, Alternative Medicine.
Ad Rates: BW: $5,325 **Circ:** Paid 261,000
4C: $6,750 Non-paid 14,000

14701 Watertown Press
Community Newspapers Inc.
360-366 Summer St. Phone: (617)629-3387
Somerville, MA 02144-3132 Fax: (617)629-3381

Community newspaper. **Founded:** 1955. **Freq:** Weekly (Thurs.). **Print Method:** Offset. **Cols./Page:** 6. **Col. Width:** 26 nonpareils. **Col. Depth:** 294 agate lines. **Key Personnel:** Ms. Tommy Peterson, Editor, fax (617)628-6624; Frank Yetter, Publisher, fax (617)628-6624; Catherine Nelson, Advertising Dir., fax (617)628-6624. **Subscription Rates:** $21 by mail Local. **Remarks:** Accepts advertising.
Ad Rates: GLR: $3.75 **Circ:** Paid 2,653
BW: $1,688.40 Non-paid 1,545
SAU: $13.40
PCI: $13.40

WAYLAND, pop. 12,170.

NE MA. Middlesex Co. 12 mi. W. of Cambridge. Residential. Chemical and electronic research. Electrical instruments, electronics manufactured. Nurseries.

14702 Electronic House
EH Publishing, Inc.
PO Box 340 Phone: (508)358-3400
Wayland, MA 01778 Fax: (508)358-5195
Publication E-mail: kmoyes@ehpub.com

Magazine for high-tech homeowners. **Subtitle:** Advanced Housing and Home Automation. **Founded:** 1986. **Freq:** Bimonthly. **Print Method:** Offset. **Trim Size:** 8 1/4 x 10 1/2. **Cols./Page:** 3. **Col. Width:** 28 nonpareils. **Col. Depth:** 147 agate lines. **Key Personnel:** Julie Jacobson, Managing Editor, jacobson@ehpub.com. **ISSN:** 0886-6643. **Subscription Rates:** $23.95 individuals; $39.95 two years. **Remarks:** Accepts advertising. **URL:** www.electronichouse.com.
Ad Rates: GLR: $99 **Circ:** ‡25,000
BW: $5,400
4C: $6,500

14703 Medievalia Et Humanistica
Medieval and Renaissance Society
PO Box 5074 Phone: (781)899-3194
Wayland, MA 01778 Fax: (781)899-5500
Free: (800)462-6420

Scholarly journal covering Medieval and Renaissance studies. **Subtitle:** Studies in Medieval and Renaissance Culture. **Founded:** 1946. **Freq:** Annual. **Print Method:** Hard Bound. **Key Personnel:** Paul Clogan, Editor, clogan@unt.edu. **ISSN:** 0076-6127. **Subscription Rates:** $56 single issue. **Remarks:** Advertising not accepted.
Circ: Paid 2,000

14704 Popular Home Automation
EH Publishing, Inc.
PO Box 340 Phone: (508)358-3400
Wayland, MA 01778 Fax: (508)358-5195

Magazine providing home improvement projects and product information on computers, home automation software, whole-house wiring, home theaters, music systems, security systems, and residential telecommunications. **Subtitle:** The How-to Guide to Home Technology. **Founded:** Aug. 1, 1996. **Freq:** Bimonthly. **Print Method:** Web/Offset. **Trim Size:** 8 x 10 7/8. **Key Personnel:** Leo Soderman, soderman@ehpub.com. **ISSN:** 1089-7925. **Subscription Rates:** $29.95 individuals.

Remarks: Accepts advertising. **URL:** http://www.pophome.com.
Ad Rates: BW: $3,600 **Circ:** Paid ‡19,889
4C: $4,700

14705 The Wayland Tab
Community Newspaper Company
254 2nd Ave. Phone: (781)433-7828
Needham, MA 02192-9114 Fax: (781)433-7835

Community newspaper (tabloid). **Founded:** Oct. 1985. **Freq:** Weekly (Tues.). **Print Method:** Offset. **Trim Size:** 10 x 16. **Cols./Page:** 7. **Col. Width:** 8 picas. **Key Personnel:** John Wilpers, Editor; Russel Pergament, Advertising Mgr.; Stephen Cummings, Publisher; Lisa Flicop, Editor. **URL:** http://townonline.com. **Formerly:** The Wayland/Sudbury Gazette.
Circ: Non-paid 3,184

WEBSTER, pop. 14,480.

C. MA. Worcester Co. On French River, 18 mi. S. of Worcester. Lake resort. Manufactures textiles, shoes. Dairy, fruit farms.

14706 WGFP-AM - 940
27 Douglas Rd. Phone: (508)943-9400
Webster, MA 01570 Fax: (508)943-0405

Format: News; Talk. **Networks:** ABC. **Owner:** Chowder Broadcast Group LLC, at above address. **Founded:** 1980. **Operating Hours:** 6 a.m.-6 p.m.; 70% network, 30% local. **ADI:** Boston-Worcester,MA-Derry-Manchester,NH. **Key Personnel:** Doc Siddell, Operations Mgr.; Nancy Reyburn, Office Mgr. **Local Programs:** *Public Forum*, Kevin Casey, Operations Mgr. **Wattage:** 1000. **Ad Rates:** Advertising accepted; rates available upon request.

WELLESLEY, pop. 27,209.

E. MA. Norfolk Co. 15 mi. SW of Boston. Wellesley College (women); Babson College (men); Mass. Bay Community College.

14707 Wellesley Magazine
Wellesley College
106 Central St. Phone: (617)283-2331
Wellesley, MA 02181-8201 Fax: (617)283-3638

Magazine for college alumnae. **Founded:** 1916. **Freq:** Quarterly (during the academic year). **Print Method:** Offset. **Cols./Page:** 3. **Col. Width:** 30 nonpareils. **Col. Depth:** 133 agate lines. **Key Personnel:** Laura Katz, Acting Editor, lkatz@wellesley.edu. **Remarks:** Advertising not accepted. **Formerly:** Alumnae Magazine (1992).
Circ: ‡32,000

14708 The Wellesley Tab
Community Newspaper Company
254 2nd Ave. Phone: (781)433-7828
Needham, MA 02192-9114 Fax: (781)433-7835

Community newspaper (tabloid). **Founded:** Oct. 1985. **Freq:** Weekly (Tues.). **Print Method:** Offset. **Trim Size:** 10 x 16. **Cols./Page:** 7. **Col. Width:** 8 picas. **Key Personnel:** John Wilpers, Editor; Russel Pergament, Advertising Mgr.; Stephen Cummings, Publisher; Lisa Flicop, Editor. **URL:** http://townonline.com.
Circ: Non-paid 5,622

14709 The Women's Review of Books
Wellesley College
Center for Research on Women
Wellesley College
Wellesley, MA 02481
Publication E-mail: iganiner@wellesleu/edi

Magazine on feminist thinking and writing. **Subtitle:** Book Review. **Founded:** 1983. **Freq:** Monthly (except August). **Print Method:** Offset. **Trim Size:** 10 x 15. **Cols./Page:** 4. **Col. Width:** 28 nonpareils. **Col. Depth:** 210 agate lines. **Key Personnel:** Linda Gardiner, Editor and Publisher, phone (781)283-2535, lgardiner@wellesley.edu; Anita D. McClellan, Advertising Mgr., phone (781)283-2560, amcclellan@wellesley.edu; Nancy Wechsler, Customer Service, phone (781)283-2087, nwechsler@wellesley.edu. **ISSN:** 0738-1433. **Subscription Rates:** $25; $45 two years. **Remarks:** Color advertising not accepted. **URL:** http://www.wellesley.edu/WCW/CRW/WROB/welcome.html. **Alt. Formats:** CD-ROM; Microform.
Ad Rates: BW: $1,995 **Circ:** Paid ‡12,000
PCI: $47 Non-paid ‡600

14710 WZLY-FM - 91.5
Wellesley College Phone: (617)283-2690
Wellesley, MA 02181 Fax: (617)283-2678

Format: Eclectic. **Networks:** AP. **Founded:** 1976. **Operating Hours:** 9 a.m.-3 a.m. **Key Personnel:** Lauren McDade, General Mgr.; Jennifer Spillane, Program Dir. **Wattage:** 10. **Ad Rates:** Noncommercial.

WELLESLEY HILLS

14711 City Trees
Society of Municipal Arborists
PO Box 364 Fax: (978)535-3899
Wellesley Hills, MA 02481
Trade magazine covering urban forestry. **Founded:** 1964. **Freq:** Bimonthly. **Print Method:** Offset. **Trim Size:** 8 1/2 x 11. **Key Personnel:** Leonard Phillips, Editor. **Subscription Rates:** $20 individuals. **Remarks:** Accepts advertising.
Ad Rates: BW: $110 **Circ:** Controlled 2,500
4C: $550

14712 Contingency Planning and Recovery Journal (CPR-J)
Management Advisory Publications
PO Box 81151 Phone: (781)235-2895
Wellesley Hills, MA 02181 Fax: (781)235-5757

Business magazine for managers, disaster recovery planners, auditors, security officers and contingency planning coordinators, users dependent on computers, LAN Administrators, and year 2000 project managers. **Founded:** 1987. **Freq:** Quarterly. **Print Method:** Offset. **Trim Size:** 8 1/2 x 11. **Cols./Page:** 2. **Col. Width:** 3.4 inches. **Col. Depth:** 9 inches. **Key Personnel:** Javier F. Kuong, Editor; C.M. Winters, Advertising Mgr.; N. Lagos, Editor; A. Llana, Contact. **ISSN:** 0899-4595. **Subscription Rates:** $65 nonmembers US and Canada; $83 other countries. **Remarks:** Accepts advertising.
Ad Rates: GLR: $5 **Circ:** (Not Reported)
BW: $700

WELLFLEET

14713 Wellfleet Oracle
Community Newspaper
5 Namskaket Rd. Phone: (508)398-0123
PO Box 2776 Fax: (508)760-3387
Orleans, MA 02653-6776
Free: (800)660-8999

Community newspaper. **Founded:** 1987. **Freq:** Weekly (Thurs.). **Print Method:** Offset. **Trim Size:** 11 x 16 1/2. **Cols./Page:** 5. **Col. Width:** 21 inches. **Col. Depth:** 224 agate lines. **Key Personnel:** Eric Hartell, Editor; Jeanne Moore-Yount, Advertising Mgr. **Subscription Rates:** Free; $25 (mail). **Remarks:** Accepts advertising.
Ad Rates: GLR: $.39 **Circ:** Paid 97
BW: $440 Free 1,417
4C: $1,040
PCI: $5.50

WEST BARNSTABLE

SE MA. Barnstable Co. 10 mi. SE of Hyannis.

14714 WKKL-FM - 90.7
Cape Cod Community College Phone: (508)375-4030
Rte. 132 Fax: (508)375-4020
West Barnstable, MA 02668
E-mail: wkkl@capecod.net

Format: Adult Contemporary; Jazz; News; Talk; World Beat; Heavy Metal; Blues. **Networks:** Independent. **Owner:** Cape Cod Community College, at above address, (617)362-2131. **Founded:** 1977. **Operating Hours:** 10 a.m.-4 p.m. Mon.-Fri.;10 a.m.-1 p.m. Sat.-Sun.; NPR 1 a.m. **Key Personnel:** Lisa Anne Zinsius, General Mgr. **Local Programs:** *Local Music Show*, Michael Tinker; *Tinkers Blues Revue*, Michael Tinker; *Voice of Liberty*, Kendra Mahoney. **Wattage:** 305.

WEST BRIDGEWATER

14715 West Bridgewater Times
Associated Newspapers
7 Cabot Pl. Phone: (781)878-1111
PO Box 441 Fax: (781)878-3333
Stoughton, MA 02072
Publisher E-mail: aweeklies@aol.com

Community newspaper. **Founded:** 1976. **Freq:** Weekly (Wed.). **Print Method:** Offset. **Cols./Page:** 6. **Col. Width:** 9.5 picas. **Col. Depth:** 16 inches. **Key Personnel:** Richard R. Dailey, Publisher. **Subscription Rates:** $17.50. **Remarks:** Accepts advertising.
Ad Rates: BW: $10.53 **Circ:** 494
4C: $10.77
PCI: $10.53

WEST QUINCY

14716 Bay State Nurse News
KLM Communications, Inc.
45 Willard St. Phone: (617)984-2631
West Quincy, MA 02169 Fax: (617)328-7571
Publisher E-mail: klmcomm@aol.com

Professional publication covering nursing in Massachusetts, New Hampshire and Vermont. **Founded:** Apr. 1992. **Freq:** Monthly. **Print Method:** Web offset. **Key Personnel:** Michael R. McCaffrey, Publisher. **ISSN:** 1083-8090. **Subscription Rates:** $20 individuals; $2.50 single issue. **Remarks:** Accepts advertising. **Former name:** Boston Nurse News.
Ad Rates: GLR: $5 **Circ:** Combined 17,000
BW: $3,600
PCI: $60

WEST SPRINGFIELD, pop. 27,042.

WC MA. Hampden Co. Across Connecticut River from Springfield. Manufactures paper, boxes, plastic products, wire, electronic equipment, fabricated metal products. Smelting and machine works, bindery. Agriculture.

14717 West Springfield Record
West Springfield Record, Inc.
516 Main St. Phone: (413)736-1587
PO Box 357 Fax: (413)739-2477
West Springfield, MA 01090
Community newspaper (tabloid). **Founded:** 1953. **Freq:** Weekly (Thurs.). **Print Method:** Offset. **Cols./Page:** 6. **Col. Width:** 20 nonpareils. **Col. Depth:** 224 agate lines. **Key Personnel:** Thomas M. Coburn, Editor and Publisher. **Subscription Rates:** $13; $26 out of country. **Remarks:** Accepts advertising.
Ad Rates: GLR: $.20 **Circ:** 5,600
SAU: $3.47

14718 WACM-AM - 1490
34 Sylvan St. Phone: (413)781-5200
West Springfield, MA 01089 Fax: (413)734-2240

Format: Hispanic. **Networks:** Spanish Broadcasting System. **Founded:** 1949. **Operating Hours:** Continuous. **Key Personnel:** Tony Gois, General Mgr.; Helena Gois, Office Mgr. **Local Programs:** *Nuestra Comunidad Talk Show*, Tony Gois; *Nuestra Escuela Talk Show*, Tony Gois; *Personalidades Talk Show*, Tony Gois. **Wattage:** 1000. **Ad Rates:** $12.50-22.50 for 30 seconds; $15-25 for 60 seconds.

WEST STOCKBRIDGE

14719 Lingo Magazine
Hard Press, Inc.
PO Box 184 Phone: (413)232-4690
West Stockbridge, MA 01266-0184 Fax: (413)232-4675
Publication E-mail: editors@hardpress.com

Magazine including poetry, art, photographs, music, and fiction. **Subtitle:** A Journal of the Arts. **Founded:** Sept. 1993. **Freq:** Biennial. **Trim Size:** 8 1/2 x 11. **Key Personnel:** Jon Gams, Editor, jongams@handpress.com; Chad Odefey, Asst. Editor; Ned Depew, Mktg. **ISSN:** 1081-1419. **Subscription Rates:** $20; $12.50 single issue. **URL:** http://www.handpress.com.
Ad Rates: BW: $800 **Circ:** 3,500,000
4C: $1,200

WEST YARMOUTH

14720 WUOK-AM - 1240
278 S. Sea Ave. Phone: (508)775-7400
West Yarmouth, MA 02673 Fax: (508)771-3420
E-mail: wxtk@capecod.net

Format: Sports. **Founded:** 1940. **Formerly:** WOCB-AM (1992). **Operating Hours:** Continuous. **Key Personnel:** Ernie Boch, President; Kurt Sanborn, Operations Mgr.; Cary L. Pahigian, VP/General Mgr.; Pam Perrault, Business Mgr. **Wattage:** 1000. **Ad Rates:** $25 for 30 seconds; $30 for 60 seconds.

WESTBOROUGH, pop. 13,619.

C. MA. Worcester Co. 3 mi. SE of Woodville. Residential.

14721 Client/Server Computing
Sentry Technology Group
One Research Dr. Phone: (508)366-2031
Suite 400-B Fax: (508)836-4732
Westborough, MA 01581-3907
Free: (800)225-9218
Publication E-mail: clientserver@mcimail.com

Magazine providing information to client/server decision mak-

ers in large organizations. **Founded:** Sept. 1991. **Freq:** Monthly. **Print Method:** Web offset. **Trim Size:** 8 x 10 3/4. **Key Personnel:** John Kerr, Editor-in-Chief; Bill Orth, National Sales Manager; Mary-Ann Gajewski, Production Mgr.; Kathleen Kenny, Circulation Mgr. **ISSN:** 1059-3470. **Subscription Rates:** $75 Individuals; $85 Canada; $135 other countries. **Remarks:** Accepts advertising. **Online:** EBSCO & Information Access. **URL:** http://www.sentrytech.com.
Ad Rates: BW: $10,700 **Circ:** Controlled 95,000
4C: $12,900

14722 Software Magazine
Sentry Technology Group
One Research Dr., Ste. 400B Phone: (508)366-2031
Westborough, MA 01581 Fax: (508)366-8104
Publication E-mail: softwaremagazine@mcimail.com

Computer magazine. **Subtitle:** For Managers of Corporate Software. **Founded:** May 1, 1981. **Freq:** Monthly. **Print Method:** Web offset. **Trim Size:** 8 x 10 3/4. **Cols./Page:** 3. **Col. Width:** 22 nonpareils. **Col. Depth:** 189 agate lines. **Key Personnel:** Don Fagan, Publisher; Patrick Porter, Editor; Kym Gilhooly, Managing Editor; Deborah Radcliff, West Coast Editor; Dave Brousell, Editorial Dir.; Daniela Cimino, Assoc. Editor; Susan Mael, New Products Editor; Kathleen Kenny, Circulation Mgr.; Julekha Dash, Staff Writer; Julie D'Errico, Design Asst.; Mary-Ann Gajewski, Production Mgr.; Dave Swanson, Design Director. **ISSN:** 0897-8085. **Subscription Rates:** $75 individuals; $85 Canada; $135 other countries. **Remarks:** Accepts advertising. **URL:** http://www.sentrytech.com. **Formerly**: Software News.
Ad Rates: BW: $11,180 **Circ:** Controlled 105,000
4C: $13,440

14723 The Westborough News
10 E. Main St. Phone: (508)366-1511
Westborough, MA 01581 Fax: (508)366-5265

Community newspaper. **Founded:** 1974. **Freq:** Weekly. **Print Method:** Offset. **Cols./Page:** 6. **Col. Width:** 9 1/2 picas. **Col. Depth:** 16 inches. **Key Personnel:** Phyllis T. Jones, Editor and Publisher. **ISSN:** 0893-3782. **Subscription Rates:** $12 individuals; $22 out of area. **Remarks:** Accepts advertising.
Ad Rates: PCI: $7.50 **Circ:** Paid 4,300

14724 WAAF-AM - 1440
2 Westborough Business Park, Ste. 4000 Phone: (508)836-9223
Westborough, MA 01581 Fax: (508)366-0745

Format: Adult Contemporary. **Networks:** ABC; Univision. **Founded:** 1926. **Operating Hours:** Continuous. **Key Personnel:** John Sutherland, General Mgr. **Wattage:** 5000.

14725 WAAF-FM - 107.3
2 Westbourough Business Park, Ste. 4000 Phone: (508)836-9223
Westborough, MA 01581 Fax: (508)366-0745

Format: Album-Oriented Rock (AOR). **Networks:** Unistar. **Founded:** 1961. **Operating Hours:** Continuous. **Key Personnel:** Bruce Mittman, Contact. **Wattage:** 50,000.

WESTFIELD, pop. 36,465.

SW MA. Hampden Co. 10 mi. W. of Springfield. State College. Manufactures bicycles, boilers, plastic molds, rifles, sports arms, machinery, fish line, abrasives, paper, foundry products, whips, whip lashes, brass valves, brushes and polishes, metal nuts, cigars, digital computers. Agriculture. Tobacco.

14726 The Longmeadow News
Westfield News Advertiser, Inc.
62 School St., No. 64 Phone: (413)562-4181
Westfield, MA 01085-2835 Fax: (413)562-4185

Community newspaper. **Founded:** July 1990. **Freq:** Weekly (Thurs.). **Print Method:** Offset. Uses mats. **Cols./Page:** 4. **Col. Width:** 16 nonpareils. **Col. Depth:** 224 agate lines. **Key Personnel:** Yvonne Prestwich, Editor; Christopher Larsen, Publisher. **USPS:** 746-869. **Subscription Rates:** $14 individuals. **Remarks:** Accepts advertising.
Ad Rates: PCI: $5.50 **Circ:** ‡1,930

14727 The Wallace Pennysaver
Westfield News Advertiser, Inc.
62 School St., No. 64 Phone: (413)562-4181
Westfield, MA 01085-2835 Fax: (413)562-4185

Shopper. **Founded:** 1969. **Freq:** Weekly (Sun.).
Circ: Free ‡26,837

14728 The Westfield Evening News
Westfield News Advertiser, Inc.
62 School St., No. 64 Phone: (413)562-4181
Westfield, MA 01085-2835 Fax: (413)562-4185

General newspaper. **Founded:** 1932. **Freq:** Daily (eve.) and Sat. (morn.). **Print Method:** Offset. **Cols./Page:** 6. **Col. Width:** 24 nonpareils. **Col. Depth:** 297 agate lines. **Key Personnel:** George O'Brien, Managing Editor; E. Carol Mazza, Publisher. **Subscription Rates:** $48. **Remarks:** Accepts advertising. **Formerly**: The News.
Ad Rates: SAU: $7.10 **Circ:** (Not Reported)

14729 Continental Cablevision
1110 E. Mountain Rd. Phone: (413)562-9923
Westfield, MA 01085 Fax: (413)568-6625

Founded: 1970. **Cities Served:** Hampden and Hampshire counties, MA.

14730 WSKB-FM - 89.5
Western Ave. Phone: (413)572-5427
Westfield, MA 01085 Fax: (413)562-3613

Format: Alternative/New Music/Progressive. **Owner:** University of Massachusetts, at above address, (413)568-3311. **Founded:** 1968. **Formerly**: WWED-AM (1979). **Operating Hours:** 9 a.m.-1 a.m.; 100% local. **Key Personnel:** Rob Stone, Music Dir.; Mike Swgen, Music Dir.; Mike Cortiz, Asst. Music Director; Daryl Durken, Production Dir. **Wattage:** 100.
Ad Rates: Noncommercial.

WESTFORD

14731 The Westford Eagle
Community Newspaper Company/Northwest
PO Box 9191 Phone: (508)256-7196
Concord, MA 01742-9191 Fax: (508)256-6111

Community newspaper. **Founded:** 1970. **Freq:** Weekly (Thurs.). **Print Method:** Offset. **Cols./Page:** 9. **Col. Width:** 20 nonpareils. **Col. Depth:** 294 agate lines. **Key Personnel:** Marlene Switzer, Managing Editor; Gail Ferney, Editor; Christopher Edding, Publisher; Mark O'Neil, Advertising Mgr. **USPS:** 787-740. **Remarks:** Accepts advertising.
Ad Rates: PCI: $9 **Circ:** Paid 4,536
Non-paid 18

14732 Nashoba Cable
4 Liberty Way Phone: (508)692-1906
Westford, MA 01886 Fax: (508)692-9491

Founded: 1984. **Key Personnel:** Bill Schuler, Contact; Alan Davis, Contact. **Cities Served:** subscribing households 35,000; 59 channels.

WESTON, pop. 11,169.

NE MA. Middlesex Co. 12 mi. W. of Boston. Regis College (women). Residential.

14733 American Journal of Alzheimers Disease
Prime National Publishing Corp.
470 Boston Post Rd. Phone: (781)899-2702
Weston, MA 02493 Fax: (781)899-4900

Professional medical journal covering Alzheimers Disease. **Founded:** 1985. **Freq:** Bimonthly. **Print Method:** Offset. **Trim Size:** 8 7/8 x 10 3/8. **Key Personnel:** Richard A. DeVito, Sr., PUB; Eileen DeVito, President; Nancy Stone, Managing Editor; Dr. Daniel A. Pollen, Editor-in-Chief; Carol Zeigler, Production Mgr.; Jack Stolz, Circulation Mgr. **ISSN:** 1082-5207. **Subscription Rates:** $106 individuals; $148 institutions; $30 single issue. **Remarks:** Accepts advertising. **Former name:** American Journal of Alzheimer's Care and Related Disorders and Research.
Ad Rates: BW: $2,035 **Circ:** Paid ‡2,200
4C: $3,525

14734 American Journal of Hospice and Palliative Care
Prime National Publishing Corp.
470 Boston Post Rd. Phone: (781)899-2702
Weston, MA 02493 Fax: (781)899-4900

Professional journal of hospice practitioners. Provides information to physicians, nurses, clergy, social workers, and volunteers providing care to the terminally ill. **Founded:** Nov. 1984. **Freq:** Bimonthly. **Print Method:** Offset. **Trim Size:** 10 7/8 x 8 3/8. **Cols./Page:** 3. **Col. Width:** 26 nonpareils. **Col. Depth:** 122 agate lines. **Key Personnel:** Dennis Ricci, Editor; Richard A. DeVito, Publisher. **ISSN:** 1049-9091. **Subscription Rates:** $106 individuals; $148 institutions and Library. **Remarks:** Accepts advertising. **Formerly**: The American Journal of Hospice Care.
Ad Rates: BW: $2,380 **Circ:** Paid ‡2,152
4C: $3,875 Non-paid ‡827

14735 Healing Ministry
Prime National Publishing Corp.
470 Boston Post Rd. Phone: (781)899-2702
Weston, MA 02493 Fax: (781)899-4900

Professional medical journal covering care for the physically and psychologically ill and dying. **Founded:** 1994. **Freq:** Bimonthly. **Key Personnel:** Richard A. DeVito, Sr., PUB; Eileen DeVito, President; Scott A. Aubrey, Managing Editor; Michele Spilberg, Staff Editor; Carol Zeigler, Production Mgr.; Jack Stolz, Circulation Mgr. **ISSN:** 0895-5336. **Subscription Rates:** $52 individuals; $82 institutions; $25 single issue. **Remarks:** Accepts advertising.
Ad Rates: BW: $2,030 **Circ:** 1,100
4C: $3,525

14736 Journal of Healthcare Safety, Compliance & Infection Control
Prime National Publishing Corp.
470 Boston Post Rd. Phone: (781)899-2702
Weston, MA 02493 Fax: (781)899-4900

Professional journal covering healthcare safety and compliance under federal regulatory agencies. **Founded:** 1997. **Freq:** 10/year. **Print Method:** Offset. **Trim Size:** 10 7/8 x 8 3/8. **Key Personnel:** Richard A. DeVito, Sr., PUB; Eileen DeVito, President; Earl J. Forman, Managing Editor; Michele Spilberg, Staff Editor; Dennis Ricci, Staff Editor; Carol Zeigler, Production Mgr.; Jack Stolz, Circulation Mgr. **ISSN:** 1096-3707. **Subscription Rates:** $148 individuals; $25 single issue. **Remarks:** Accepts advertising. **URL:** http://www.pnpco.com.
Ad Rates: BW: $7,030 **Circ:** (Not Reported)
4C: $3,875

14737 Journal of Neurovascular Disease
Prime National Publishing Corp.
470 Boston Post Rd. Phone: (781)899-2702
Weston, MA 02493 Fax: (781)899-4900

Professional medical journal covering neurosurgery, neurology, neuroradiology, and rehabilitation. **Founded:** 1996. **Freq:** Bimonthly. **Key Personnel:** Richard A. DeVito, Sr., PUB; Eileen DeVito, President; Scott A. Aubrey, Managing Editor; Michele Spilberg, Staff Editor; Carol Zeigler, Production Mgr.; Jack Stolz, Circulation Mgr. **ISSN:** 1087-5670. **Subscription Rates:** $120 individuals; $195 institutions; $25 single issue. **Remarks:** Accepts advertising.
Circ: (Not Reported)

14738 Nursingworld Journal
Prime National Publishing Corp.
470 Boston Post Rd. Phone: (781)899-2702
Weston, MA 02493 Fax: (781)899-4900

Magazine for the nursing profession. **Founded:** 1975. **Freq:** Monthly. **Print Method:** Offset. **Cols./Page:** 5. **Col. Width:** 22 nonpareils. **Col. Depth:** 224 agate lines. **Key Personnel:** Ira Alterman, Editor; Richard A. De Vito, Publisher; Jim O'Hara, Advertising Mgr. **Subscription Rates:** $22.
Circ: Paid ‡5,600
Non-paid ‡35,000

14739 Running Wild
494 North Ave. Phone: (617)899-9896
Weston, MA 02193-1806
Outdoor magazine for runners. **Subtitle:** the trailrunners magazine. **Freq:** Bimonthly. **Key Personnel:** Peter W. Severance, Publisher. **ISSN:** 1067-5094. **Subscription Rates:** $18.

14740 Seismological Research Letters
Seismological Society of America
Boston College Phone: (617)552-8300
Weston Observatory Fax: (617)522-8388
381 Concord Rd.
Weston, MA 02193
Publisher E-mail: publications@seismosoc.org

Scholarly journal covering seismology and earthquake engineering. **Founded:** 1930. **Freq:** Bimonthly. **Print Method:** Offset. **Trim Size:** 8 1/2 x 11. **Cols./Page:** 2. **Col. Width:** 3 2/5 inches. **Col. Depth:** 9 3/10 inches. **Key Personnel:** John E. Ebel, Editor-in-Chief, ebel@bcvms.bc.edu; Christine A. Powell, Eastern Section Editor; Janice Sellers, Administration/Circulation. **ISSN:** 0012-8287. **Subscription Rates:** $85 individuals. **Remarks:** Advertising not accepted. **Former name**: Earthquake Notes.
Circ: (Not Reported)

14741 The Weston Tab
Community Newspaper Company
254 2nd Ave. Phone: (781)433-7828
Needham, MA 02192-9114 Fax: (781)433-7835

Community newspaper (tabloid). **Founded:** Oct. 1986. **Freq:** Weekly (Tues.). **Print Method:** Offset. **Trim Size:** 10 x 16. **Cols./Page:** 7. **Col. Width:** 8 picas. **Key Personnel:** John Wilpers, Editor; Russel Pergament, Advertising Mgr.; Stephen Cummings, Publisher; Lisa Flicop, Editor. **Remarks:** Accepts advertising. **URL:** http://townonline.com.
Ad Rates: GLR: $.55 **Circ:** Non-paid 2,424
BW: $659

WEYMOUTH, pop. 55,601.

E. MA. Norfolk Co. 15 mi. SE of Boston. (Branch of Boston P.O.) Manufactures shoes, shoe counters, belting, electronics components, paper boxes, industrial resins and chemicals.

14742 Weymouth Dispatch
Associated Newspapers
7 Cabot Pl. Phone: (781)878-1111
PO Box 441 Fax: (781)878-3333
Stoughton, MA 02072
Publisher E-mail: aweeklies@aol.com

Community newspaper. **Founded:** 1986. **Freq:** Weekly (Wed.). **Print Method:** Offset. **Cols./Page:** 6. **Col. Width:** 9.5 picas. **Col. Depth:** 16 inches. **Key Personnel:** Richard R. Dailey, Publisher. **Subscription Rates:** $17.50. **Remarks:** Accepts advertising.
Ad Rates: BW: $10.53 **Circ:** 1,288
4C: $10.77
PCI: $10.53

14743 Weymouth News
Mariner Newspapers
PO Box 330 Phone: (617)337-1944
Weymouth, MA 02188-0330 Fax: (617)849-3319
Publisher E-mail: cmathis@cnc.com

Community newspaper. **Founded:** 1867. **Freq:** Weekly (Wed.). **Print Method:** Offset. **Cols./Page:** 6. **Col. Width:** 18 nonpareils. **Col. Depth:** 224 agate lines. **Key Personnel:** Patricia Murray, Editor; David S. Cutler, Publisher. **Subscription Rates:** $18. **Remarks:** Accepts advertising.
Ad Rates: GLR: $.59 **Circ:** Paid 4,692
BW: $767.25 Non-paid 208
4C: $1,216.32
PCI: $8.25

14744 Media One
83 Moore Rd.
Weymouth, MA 02189

Founded: 1981. **Formerly**: Dimension Cable Services; Cox Communications. **Key Personnel:** Marianne Healy, Customer Services Supervisor. **Cities Served:** Weymouth, MA: subscribing households 18,000; 93 channels; 3 community access channels; 12 hours per week community access programming.

WHITINSVILLE, pop. 4,210.

C. MA. Worcester Co. 16 mi. SE of Worcester. Manufactures textile machinery, ring spinners. Dairy farms.

14745 Blackstone Valley Tribune
Stonebridge Press
PO Box 210
Whitinsville, MA 01588

Community newspaper. **Founded:** 1950. **Freq:** Semiweekly (Wed. and Fri.) (WED and Fri.). **Print Method:** Offset. **Cols./Page:** 6. **Col. Width:** 19 nonpareils. **Col. Depth:** 189 agate lines. **Key Personnel:** David Cutler, Publisher; Michael Macinnis, Sales/Adv. Coord. **Subscription Rates:** $24. **Remarks:** Advertising not accepted for tobacco products.
Ad Rates: GLR: $8 **Circ:** Wed. ‡5,300
BW: $1,175 Fri. ‡12,996
4C: $1,975
PCI: $10.50

WHITMAN

14746 Whitman/Hanson Mariner
Mariner Newspapers
165 Enterprise Dr. Phone: (617)837-3500
Marshfield, MA 02050-2132 Fax: (617)837-4540
Free: (800)649-6661
Publisher E-mail: cmathis@cnc.com

Community newspaper. **Founded:** 1876. **Freq:** Weekly (Wed.). **Print Method:** Offset. **Trim Size:** 11 3/8 x 17. **Cols./Page:** 3. **Col. Width:** 15 1/2 inches. **Key Personnel:** Bob Flavell, Editor; Jack Powers, Advertising Mgr. **Subscription Rates:** $20; $18 senior citizens and students; $25 out of area. **Remarks:** Combined advertising rates available with other Mariner Newspapers.
Ad Rates: BW: $767.25 **Circ:** Paid 1,730
4C: $1,167.25 Non-paid 39
PCI: $8.25

14747 Whitman Times
Associated Newspapers
7 Cabot Pl. Phone: (781)878-1111
PO Box 441 Fax: (781)878-3333
Stoughton, MA 02072
Publisher E-mail: aweeklies@aol.com

Community newspaper. **Founded:** 1883. **Freq:** Weekly (Thurs.). **Print Method:** Offset. **Cols./Page:** 6. **Col. Width:** 9.5 picas. **Col. Depth:** 16 inches. **Key Personnel:** Richard R. Dailey, Publisher. **Subscription Rates:** $17.50 in county. **Remarks:** Accepts advertising.
Ad Rates: BW: $10.53 **Circ:** 1,251
4C: $10.77
PCI: $10.53

WILBRAHAM

14748 Showcase Real Estate Magazine
PO Box 846 Phone: (413)596-9550
Wilbraham, MA 01095 Fax: (413)596-9807

Magazine for home buyers. **Founded:** 1983. **Freq:** Monthly. **Print Method:** Offset. **Trim Size:** 8 1/2 x 11. **Cols./Page:** 2. **Col. Width:** 42 nonpareils. **Col. Depth:** 140 agate lines. **Key Personnel:** Jim DeForest, Owner; Sharron DeForest, Owner. **Remarks:** Accepts advertising. **Formerly**: Showcase of Homes.
Ad Rates: BW: $195 **Circ:** Non-paid ‡40,000
4C: $500

WILLIAMSTOWN, pop. 8,741.

W. MA. Berkshire Co. On Hoosac River, 18 mi. N. of Pittsfield. Williams College. Manufactures wire.

14749 Williams Alumni Review
Alumni Society of Williams College
880 Main St. Phone: (413)597-4278
PO Box 676 Fax: (413)597-4158
Hopkins Hall
Williamstown, MA 01267-0676
Publication E-mail: alumni.review@williams.edu

Magazine for collegiate alumni, parents, and friends. **Founded:** 1909. **Freq:** Quarterly (during the academic year). **Print Method:** Web. **Trim Size:** 8 1/2 x 11. **Cols./Page:** 2 and 3. **Col. Width:** 40 and 26 nonpareils. **Col. Depth:** 138 agate lines. **Key Personnel:** Thomas W. Bleezarde, Editor/Contact, thomas.w.bleezarde@williams.edu. **USPS:** 684-580. **Subscription Rates:** Free. **Remarks:** Advertising not accepted. **URL:** http://www.williams.edu:803/alumrel/review.html.
Circ: Free ‡28,744

14750 The Williams Record
Williams College
SU Box 1018 Phone: (413)597-2289
Williamstown, MA 01267 Fax: (413)597-2450
Publication E-mail: record@record.williams.edu

Collegiate newspaper. **Founded:** 1904. **Freq:** Weekly (Tues.) (during the academic year). **Print Method:** Offset. **Cols./Page:** 6. **Col. Width:** 2 1/8 inches. **Col. Depth:** 21 1/4 inches. **Key Personnel:** Reed Wiedower, Editor-in-Chief, phone (413)547-2400; John Wiedower, Business Mgr. **USPS:** 684-680. **Subscription Rates:** $45 by mail. **Remarks:** Color advertising not accepted. **URL:** http://record.williams.edu.
Ad Rates: GLR: $.40 **Circ:** Paid ‡1,500
BW: $680 Free ‡2,500
PCI: $5.75

14751 WCFM-FM - 91.9
Williams College
Williamstown, MA 01267 Phone: (413)597-3265 Fax: (413)597-2259
E-mail: wcfmbd@wso.williams.edu

Format: Alternative/New Music/Progressive. **Networks:** Independent. **Founded:** 1940. **Operating Hours:** Continuous 95% local. **Key Personnel:** Audrey Watkins, General Mgr.; John Putnam, News/Community Affairs Dir.; Kara Roggenkamp, Program Dir.; Ross Hammond, Technical Dir.; Erik Klemetti, Music Dir. **Wattage:** 1110. **Ad Rates:** Noncommercial. **URL:** http://wso.williams.edu/orgs/wcfm/index.html.

WILMINGTON, pop. 17,471.

NE MA. Middlesex Co. 15 mi. NW of Boston. Manufactures paper, plastic products, lacquer, and machinery. Research and development; warehousing distribution centers.

14752 Property Digest and Economic Development Magazine
Barry, Inc.
PO Box 551 Phone: (978)658-0441
Wilmington, MA 01887-0551 Fax: (978)657-8691
Publication E-mail: propdig@barryinc.com
Publisher E-mail: usrer@barryinc.com

Magazine listing availability of properties nationwide. **Founded:** 1991. **Freq:** Semiannual. **Print Method:** Offset. **Trim Size:** 8 x 11. **Cols./Page:** 3. **Col. Width:** 2 1/4 inches. **Col. Depth:** 10 inches. **Key Personnel:** Joan Carrns, Editor; Therese DiBlasi, Advertising Mgr.; Elizabeth Cannon, Circulation Mgr. **ISSN:** 1088-5811. **Subscription Rates:** $20 SNG. **Remarks:** Accepts advertising. **URL:** http://www.barryinc.com. **Formerly**: Property Digest; Literature Review.
Ad Rates: GLR: $50 **Circ:** Controlled ‡6,000
BW: $2,200
4C: $4,200

Wilmington-Tewksbury Town Crier - See Tewksbury

WINCHENDON, pop. 7,019.

C. MA. Worcester Co. 18 mi. NW of Fitchburg. Recreation State Park. Timber. Manufactures furniture, plastics, toys, tools, novelties, woodenware, bobbins and spools, tubs and pails. Poultry, dairy farms. Camping sites.

14753 The Winchendon Courier
Stonebridge Press Inc.
110 Front St. Phone: (508)297-0050
Winchendon, MA 01475-1749 Fax: (508)297-2177
Publisher E-mail: sbnews@hey.net

Newspaper. **Founded:** 1878. **Freq:** Weekly (Wed.). **Print Method:** Offset. **Cols./Page:** 6. **Col. Depth:** 301 agate lines. **Key Personnel:** David Cutter, Publisher. **Subscription Rates:** $24 individuals. **Remarks:** Accepts advertising. **Formerly**: Jaffrey-Ridge Chronicles.
Ad Rates: PCI: $5.50 **Circ:** 2,000

14754 WINQ-FM - 97.7
3 Central St. Phone: (508)297-3698
Winchendon, MA 01475 Fax: (508)297-9970

Format: Alternative/New Music/Progressive; Contemporary Hit Radio (CHR). **Networks:** AP. **Owner:** Central Broadcasting Corp., at above address. **Founded:** 1983. **Operating Hours:** Continuous. **ADI:** Boston-Worcester,MA-Derry-Manchester,NH. **Key Personnel:** Bill Maxwell, General Mgr.; Greg Vine, News and Director of Operations; Bob Walker, Music Dir.; Scott Bingham, General Sales Mgr. **Local Programs:** *First 5 at 5*, Bill Maxwell, General Mgr. **Wattage:** 3000 ERP. **Ad Rates:** $20-30 per unit. **URL:** http://www.winqfm.com.

WINCHESTER, pop. 20,701.

NE MA. Middlesex Co. 8 mi. NW of Boston. Residential. Manufactures pointers for automotive instrument panels.

14755 The Quarterly Review of Wines
QRW Publishing
24 Garfield Ave. Phone: (781)729-7132
Winchester, MA 01890 Fax: (781)721-0572
Publication E-mail: qrwinc@tiac.net

Consumer magazine on fine wines and selected spirits. **Founded:** Sept. 1, 1977. **Freq:** Quarterly. **Print Method:** Web offset. **Trim Size:** 8 1/2x10 7/8. **Cols./Page:** 3. **Col. Width:** 2.25 picas. **Col. Depth:** 9 3/4 inches. **Key Personnel:** Richard L. Elia, Editor and Publisher; Beth Hamilton, Sales/Circulation; Jack Lynch, Advertising Mgr. **ISSN:** 0740-1248. **Subscription Rates:** $14.95; $3.95 single issue. **Remarks:** Accepts advertising. **Online:** TIAC. **URL:** http://www.qrw.com.
Ad Rates: GLR: $133 **Circ:** Paid ‡78,725
BW: $5,000 Non-paid ‡51,400
4C: $7,250

14756 WHSR-FM - 91.9
80 Skillings Rd. Phone: (617)721-7004
Winchester, MA 01890

Format: Alternative/New Music/Progressive; Educational; Top 40. **Founded:** 1956. **Key Personnel:** Arnold Goldstein, General Mgr.; Debbie Williams, Program Dir. **Wattage:** 10.

WOBURN, pop. 36,626.

NE MA. Middlesex Co. 10 mi. NW of Boston. Manufactures mattresses, plastics, chemical and aluminum products, leather, leatherworking machinery, gears, tools, electronics, automotive parts, rubber rolls, belt knives and band saws. Floriculture.

14757 Aboriginal Science Fiction
Second Renaissance Foundation Inc.
PO Box 2449 Phone: (617)935-7326
Woburn, MA 01888-0849
Science fiction literary magazine. **Subtitle:** Tales of the Human Kind. **Founded:** 1986. **Freq:** Quarterly. **Print Method:** Web offset. **Trim Size:** 8 3/8 x 10 7/8. **Cols./Page:** 2 and 3. **Col. Width:** 3 1/4 and 2 inches. **Col. Depth:** 10 inches. **Key Personnel:** Charles C. Ryan, Editor. **ISSN:** 0895-3198. **Subscription Rates:** $18. $3.95 single issue. **Remarks:** Accepts advertising.
Ad Rates: BW: $750 **Circ:** Paid 23,121
4C: $1,200 Non-paid 197
PCI: $30

14758 Daily Times Chronicle
Woburn Daily Times, Inc.
1 Arrow Dr. Phone: (781)933-3700
Woburn, MA 01801-2090
Publisher E-mail: news@woburnonline.com

Suburban community newspaper. **Founded:** 1901. **Freq:** Daily (eve.). **Print Method:** Offset. **Cols./Page:** 6. **Col. Width:** 2 1/16 inches. **Col. Depth:** 294 agate lines. **Key Personnel:** James D. Haggerty III, Editor; Peter M. Haggerty, Publisher; Thomas Kirk, Advertising Mgr. **USPS:** 689-360. **Subscription Rates:** $165.75 individuals; $191.75 out of area. **Remarks:** Accepts advertising.
Ad Rates: GLR: $1.07 **Circ:** Paid 11,570
BW: $1,890 Non-paid 85
4C: $450
SAU: $15
PCI: $15

14759 European Journal of Purchasing and Supply Management
Butterworth-Heinemann
225 Wildwood Ave. Phone: (617)928-2500
Woburn, MA 01801-2025 Fax: (617)933-6333
Free: (800)366-2665

Journal encouraging the development of conceptual thinking and practical approaches within the field of purchasing and supply management. **Freq:** Quarterly. **Key Personnel:** Prof. Richard Lamming, Editor. **ISSN:** 0969-7012. **Subscription Rates:** $120 individuals annual British pounds; $110 other countries British pounds.

14760 Journal of Air Transport Management
Butterworth-Heinemann
225 Wildwood Ave. Phone: (617)928-2500
Woburn, MA 01801-2025 Fax: (617)933-6333
Free: (800)366-2665

Journal offering an international forum for the discussion and analysis of key issues relating to air transport. **Freq:** Quarterly. **Key Personnel:** Prof. Rigas Doganis, Editor. **ISSN:** 0969-6997. **Subscription Rates:** $125 individuals annual British pounds; $115 other countries British pounds.

14761 Journal of Retailing and Consumer Services
Butterworth-Heinemann
225 Wildwood Ave. Phone: (617)928-2500
Woburn, MA 01801-2025 Fax: (617)933-6333
Free: (800)366-2665

Journal focusing on consumer behavior and decision making by managers and policy makers. **ISSN:** 0969-6989. **Subscription Rates:** $170 individuals annual British pounds; $160 other countries British pounds.

14762 Journal of Vocational Rehabilitation
Butterworth-Heinemann
225 Wildwood Ave. Phone: (617)928-2500
Woburn, MA 01801-2025 Fax: (617)933-6333
Free: (800)366-2665

Peer-review journal spotlighting current research issues in the field of vocational rehabilitation. **Freq:** Quarterly. **Key Personnel:** Paul Wehman, Editor. **Subscription Rates:** $60 individuals; $95 institutions. **Remarks:** Advertising accepted; rates available upon request.
Circ: (Not Reported)

14763 The Knee
Butterworth-Heinemann
225 Wildwood Ave. Phone: (617)928-2500
Woburn, MA 01801-2025 Fax: (617)933-6333
Free: (800)366-2665

Journal centering on anatomy, biochemistry of bone and soft tissues, surgery and rehabilitation. **Freq:** Quarterly. **Print Method:** Sheetfed offset. **Trim Size:** 210 x 297 mm. **Key Personnel:** Malcolm M.S. Glasgow, Editor; Richard S. Laskin, Editor. **ISSN:** 0968-0160. **Subscription Rates:** $110 annual British pounds; $105 other countries annual British pounds.
Circ: ‡2,250

14764 Supramolecular Science
Butterworth-Heinemann
225 Wildwood Ave. Phone: (617)928-2500
Woburn, MA 01801-2025 Fax: (617)933-6333
Free: (800)366-2665

Journal providing a forum uniting supramolecular research from a wide range of disciplines, including materials science chemistry, physics, and polymer science. **Freq:** Quarterly. **Key Personnel:** Wolfgang Knoll, Editor-in-Chief. **ISSN:** 0968-5677. **Subscription Rates:** $170 annual British pounds; $160 other countries British pounds.

14765 Transport Policy
Butterworth-Heinemann
225 Wildwood Ave. Phone: (617)928-2500
Woburn, MA 01801-2025 Fax: (617)933-6333
Free: (800)366-2665

Journal providing a bridge between theory and practice in transport policy development and implementation. **Key Personnel:** Dr. Phil Goodwin, Editor. **ISSN:** 0967-070X. **Subscription Rates:** $115 individuals annual British pounds; $110 other countries British pounds.

14766 Ultrasonics Sonochemistry
Butterworth-Heinemann
225 Wildwood Ave. Phone: (617)928-2500
Woburn, MA 01801-2025 Fax: (617)933-6333
Free: (800)366-2665

Journal centering on ultrasonics sonochemistry. **Key Personnel:** T. Ando, Editor; T. Mason, Editor; K. Suslick, Editor. **ISSN:** 1350-4177. **Subscription Rates:** $75 individuals annual British pounds; $65 other countries British pounds.

14767 Winchester Star
Community Newspaper Company
186 Cambridge Rd.
Woburn, MA 01801-4793
Publisher E-mail: townonline.com

Local newspaper. **Founded:** 1880. **Freq:** Weekly (Thurs.). **Print Method:** Offset. **Trim Size:** 13 3/4 x 22 1/2. **Cols./Page:** 6. **Col. Width:** 2 1/16 inches. **Col. Depth:** 21 inches. **Key Personnel:** Ellen Fanning, Editor; Asa Cole, Publisher; Fred Splaine, Advertising Dir. **Subscription Rates:** $20; $15 students; $34 out of area. **Remarks:** Accepts advertising.
Ad Rates: BW: $1,369.62 **Circ:** Paid 4,626
SAU: $10.87 Free 385

WOLLASTON

14768 Campus Camera
Eastern Nazarene College
25 E. Elm St.
Wollaston, MA 02170

Campus newspaper. **Founded:** Sept. 12, 1997. **Freq:** Biweekly. **Key Personnel:** Joyce Sampson, Editor; Meradee Jarvis, Advertising Mgr. **Subscription Rates:** $20 individuals. **Remarks:** Accepts advertising.
Ad Rates: BW: $260 **Circ:** (Not Reported)
PCI: $9

WOODS HOLE

SW MA. Barnstable Co. 16 mi. ESE of New Bedford. Whaling, goat guilding. Residential.

14769 The Biological Bulletin
Marine Biological Laboratory
Woods Hole, MA 02543 Phone: (508)289-7149
Fax: (508)457-1924
Publisher E-mail: subscriptions@mbl.edu

Professional journal covering original research in neurobiology and behavior, cell biology, development and reproduction, physiology, and ecology and evolution. **Founded:** 1897. **Freq:** Bimonthly. **Print Method:** Web offset. **Trim Size:** 8 1/4 x 11. **Cols./Page:** 2. **Col. Width:** 3 1/4 inches. **Col. Depth:** 8 1/2 inches. **Key Personnel:** Pamela Clapp, Editor, pclapp@mbl.edu; Charles Lynch, Advertising Mgr., phone (781)848-9396; Patty Burns, Circulation Mgr., fax (508)457-1924, pburns@mbl.edu. **ISSN:** 0006-3185. **Subscription Rates:** $95 individuals; $205 institutions; $40 single issue. **Remarks:** Accepts advertising. **URL:** http://www.mbl.edu/BIOLOGICALBULLETIN.
Ad Rates: BW: $1,100 **Circ:** Controlled 1,690
4C: $2,300

14770 Oceanus Magazine
Woods Hole Oceanographic Institution
MS No. 5 Phone: (508)289-3516
Woods Hole, MA 02543 Fax: (508)457-2156
Publication E-mail: oceanusmag@whoi.edu

Subtitle: Reports on Research at the Woods Hole Oceanographic Institution. **Founded:** 1952. **Freq:** Semiannual. **Print Method:** Sheetfed. **Trim Size:** 8 1/2 x 11. **Cols./Page:** 2. **Col. Width:** 17 picas. **Col. Depth:** 59 picas. **Key Personnel:** Jane A. Hopewood, Contact; Vicky Cullen, Editor, phone (508)289-2719. **ISSN:** 0029-8182. **Subscription Rates:** $15. **Remarks:** Advertising not accepted. **Alt. Formats:** Microform.
Circ: Controlled 5,000

14771 WCAI-FM - 90.1
PO Box 82 Phone: (508)548-9600
Woods Hole, MA 02543

Format: Public Radio. **Networks:** National Public Radio (NPR). **Owner:** WGBH Educational Foundation, at above address. **Operating Hours:** Continuous. **Key Personnel:** John Voci, Contact, john_ voci@wgbh.org. **Wattage:** 6,500.

WORCESTER†, pop. 161,799.

C. MA. Worcester Co. 40 mi. W. of Boston. College of the Holy Cross (Catholic); Clark University; Worcester Polytechnic Institute; Assumption College; State College; other schools. Manufacturing.

14772 The Catholic Free Press
The Roman Catholic Diocese of Worcester
51 Elm St. Phone: (508)757-6387
Worcester, MA 01609 Fax: (508)756-8315

Religious newspaper. **Founded:** May 4, 1951. **Freq:** Weekly (Fri.). **Print Method:** Offset. **Cols./Page:** 6. **Col. Width:** 26 nonpareils. **Col. Depth:** 294 agate lines. **Key Personnel:** Gerard E. Goggins, Exec. Editor; Rev. T.J. Harrington, Publisher. **ISSN:** 0008-8056. **Subscription Rates:** $19. **Remarks:** Accepts advertising.
Ad Rates: GLR: $.89 **Circ:** ‡24,500
BW: $149.52
SAU: $15.85

14773 The Crusader
College of the Holy Cross
PO Box 32-A Phone: (508)793-2668
Worcester, MA 01610 Fax: (508)793-3020
Publication E-mail: crusader@holycross.edu

Collegiate newspaper. **Founded:** 1925. **Freq:** Weekly (Fri.) (during the academic year). **Print Method:** Offset. **Trim Size:** 10 x 16. **Cols./Page:** 4. **Col. Width:** 28 nonpareils. **Col. Depth:** 224 agate lines. **Key Personnel:** Michael E. Neagle, Editor-in-Chief. **Subscription Rates:** $20 individuals.
Ad Rates: BW: $439.04 **Circ:** ‡4,000
PCI: $5.50

14774 Economic Geography
Clark University
950 Main St. Phone: (508)793-7311
Worcester, MA 01610 Fax: (508)793-8881
Publication E-mail: econman@clarku.edu

Geographic journal. **Founded:** Mar. 1925. **Freq:** Quarterly. **Print Method:** Letterpress. **Cols./Page:** 2. **Col. Width:** 30 nonpareils. **Col. Depth:** 112 agate lines. **Key Personnel:** Susan Hanson, Editor; David Angel, Editor. **ISSN:** 0013-0095. **Subscription Rates:** $40 individuals; $15 single issue; $52 Domestic; $55 other countries; $22 students Domestic; $43 individuals Foreign; individuals. **Remarks:** Advertising not accepted.
Circ: ‡2,500

14775 Hanover News
440 Lincoln St.
Worcester, MA 01653-0002

Community newspaper. **Founded:** Oct. 1877. **Freq:** Weekly (Wed.). **Cols./Page:** 6. **Col. Width:** 12 picas. **Col. Depth:** 21 inches. **Key Personnel:** R.L. Sand and Dora Sand, Publisher. **Subscription Rates:** $13.50 individuals; $14.50 in state; $15.50 out of state. **Remarks:** Accepts advertising.
Ad Rates: BW: $252 **Circ:** 1,000
PCI: $2.10

14776 International Figure Skating
44 Front St., no. 280 Phone: (508)756-2595
Worcester, MA 01608 Fax: (508)792-5981
Publication E-mail: ifsmag@aol.com

News magazine for figure skating. **Founded:** Oct. 1993. **Freq:** 6/year. **Print Method:** WEB. **Trim Size:** 8 1/2 x 11. **Key Personnel:** Lois Elfman, Editor-in-Chief, phone (212)799-3517, fax (212)712-9814, elfmaned1@aol.com; Mark Lund, Publisher. **ISSN:** 1070-9568. **Subscription Rates:** $22.95 U.S.; $28 Canada; $39 other countries; $3.95 single issue. **Remarks:** Accepts advertising.
Ad Rates: BW: $1,500 **Circ:** Paid 52,000
4C: $2,500

14777 Jewish Chronicle
Mar-Len Publications
131 Lincoln St. Phone: (508)752-2512
Worcester, MA 01605 Fax: (508)752-9057

Local Ethnic paper. **Founded:** 1926. **Freq:** Biweekly. **Print Method:** Offset. **Cols./Page:** 6. **Col. Width:** 22 nonpareils. **Col. Depth:** 224 agate lines. **Key Personnel:** Sondra Shapiro, Exec. Editor; Philip Davis, Publisher. **Subscription Rates:** $15. **Remarks:** Accepts advertising.
Ad Rates: GLR: $.37 **Circ:** ‡4000
BW: $1,056
4C: $2,400
PCI: $11

14778 The Scarlet
Clark University
950 Main St. Phone: (508)793-7311
Worcester, MA 01610-1477 Fax: (508)793-8881
Publication E-mail: scarlet@vax.clarku.edu
Publisher E-mail: econman@clarku.edu

Collegiate newspaper. **Subtitle:** The Student Newspaper of Clark University. **Founded:** 1945. **Freq:** Weekly (during the academic year). **Print Method:** Offset. **Cols./Page:** 5. **Col. Width:** 1 3/4 inches. **Col. Depth:** 30 nonpareils. **Key Personnel:** Rebecca Kirszner, Editor; Ciji Jones, Business Mgr. **Subscription Rates:** $24. **Remarks:** Accepts advertising. **URL:** http://scarlet.clark.edu/~scarlet/scarlethome.htm. **Alt. Formats:** Mailing labels.
Ad Rates: BW: $320 **Circ:** Free 2,000
PCI: $6.60

14779 The Senior Advocate
Mar-Len Publications
131 Lincoln St. Phone: (508)752-2512
Worcester, MA 01605 Fax: (508)752-9057

Newspaper for senior citizens. **Founded:** 1975. **Freq:** Biweekly. **Print Method:** Offset. **Cols./Page:** 6. **Col. Width:** 22 nonpareils. **Col. Depth:** 224 agate lines. **Key Personnel:** Sondra Shapiro, Editor; Philip Davis, Publisher; Philip Davis, Publisher. **Subscription Rates:** $14 individuals. **Remarks:** Accepts advertising.
Ad Rates: BW: $6,048 **Circ:** Free 87,630
4C: $7,848 Paid 1,303
PCI: $63

14780 The Senior Times
Senior Times Inc.
1102 Pleasant St., Ste. 814 Phone: (508)798-2706
Worcester, MA 01602 Fax: (508)798-2706

Community newspaper. **Founded:** 1977. **Freq:** Monthly. **Print Method:** Photo offset. **Key Personnel:** Edwin Gledhill, Publisher.
Circ: Combined 3,349

14781 Telegram & Gazette
20 Franklin St. Phone: (508)793-9100
PO Box 15012 Fax: (508)793-9281
Worcester, MA 01615-0012
Publisher E-mail: info@telegram.com

General newspaper. **Founded:** 1866. **Freq:** Mon.-Sun. **Print Method:** Flex. **Trim Size:** 13 3/4 x 22 3/4. **Cols./Page:** 6. **Col. Width:** 2 1/16 inches. **Col. Depth:** 21 1/2 inches. **Key Personnel:** Bruce S. Bennett, President and Publisher; Robert Z. Nemeth, Editorial Page Editor; Harry T. Whitin, Editor; Thomas F.X. Cole, Marketing Services Director; Robert N. Recore, Advertising Dir.; Nancy Cahalen-Bayley, Asst. Advertising Sales Dir.; Anthony J. Simollardes, Advertising Operations Mgr.; Maurice J. Guarini, National Advertising Mgr.; Edward J. Bauer, Classified Display Mgr.; Ron Wolfram, Zone Sales Division Mgr.; Barry R. LaRoche, Circulation Mgr.; Peter H. Horstmann, Director of Human Resources; Sheila M. Battles, Personnel Mgr.; Robert R. Beatty, Director Finance/MIS; Joseph E. Sgro, Controller; Leah M. Lamson, Managing Editor; Lee J. Merkel, News Editor; Kathleen Pierce, Special Sections Editor; Averil Capers, Research Editor; Sheila Croteau, Education Mgr.; Thomas Hunt, Graphic Design Mgr.; Cheryl Haskins, Audiotex Mgr.; Kurt Parent, Plant Mgr.; Ronald Corriveau, Production Superintendent; Wayne P. Shepard, Mailroom Mgr.; Steven Erikson, Transportation Mgr.; James Denman, Facilities Mgr. **USPS:** 005-046. **Subscription Rates:** $96.20; $65 Sunday. **Remarks:** Accepts advertising. **Online:** DataTimes Corporation. **URL:** http://www.telegram.com. **Formed by the merger of:** Worcester Telegram (1989); The Evening Gazette (1989); The Saturday Paper (1989); The Sunday Telegram (1989). **Feature Editors:** Barbara Houle, *Food*; Leonard J. Lazure, *Photo*; Frank Magiera, *Art*; David Mawson, *Features, Music*; John J. Monahan, *Environmental*; David Natham, *Sports*; Diana Scott, *Travel*; Kathleen Shaw, *Religion*.
Ad Rates: BW: $9,840.60 **Circ:** Mon.-Sat. ★**105,896**
4C: $1,0525.60 Sun. ★**132,992**
SAU: $75.25
PCI: $78.10

14782 Worcester Business Journal
172 Shrewsbury St. Phone: (508)755-8004
Worcester, MA 01604-4636 Fax: (508)755-4734
Free: (800)925-8004

Regional magazine covering business in central Massachusetts. **Subtitle:** The Business Paper of Central Massachusetts. **Founded:** Mar. 1990. **Freq:** Biweekly. **Print Method:** Web offset. **Trim Size:** 11 x 14. **Cols./Page:** 4. **Col. Width:** 2 3/8 inches. **Key Personnel:** Steven Jones-D'Agostino, Editor, sjd@wbjournal.com. **ISSN:** 1063-6595. **Subscription Rates:** $39.95 individuals; $1.25 single issue. **Remarks:** Accepts advertising. **URL:** http://www.wbjournal.com. **Formerly:** Business Worcester.
Ad Rates: BW: $2,680 **Circ:** Combined 11,000

14783 Worcester Magazine
Worcester Business Journal
172 Shrewsbury St. Phone: (508)755-8004
Worcester, MA 01604-4636 Fax: (508)755-4734
Free: (800)925-8004

Regional tabloid. **Subtitle:** Worcester's Alternative Newsweekly. **Founded:** 1976. **Freq:** Weekly (Wed.). **Print Method:** Offset. **Trim Size:** 11 x 15. **Cols./Page:** 4. **Col. Width:** 28 nonpareils. **Col. Depth:** 238 agate lines. **Key Personnel:** Walter Crockett, Editor; Peter Stanton, Publisher. **ISSN:** 0191-4960. **Subscription Rates:** Free to qualified subscribers; $26 by 3rd class mail; $65 by 1st class mail. **Remarks:** Accepts advertising.
Ad Rates: BW: $1,695 **Circ:** Paid 42
4C: $2,220 Non-paid 38,182

14784 WPI Journal
Worcester Polytechnic Institute
100 Institute Rd. Phone: (508)831-5609
Worcester, MA 01609-2280 Fax: (508)831-5820
Publication E-mail: wpi-journal@wpi.edu

College alumni magazine. **Founded:** 1897. **Freq:** Quarterly. **Print Method:** Offset. **Trim Size:** 8 1/2 x 11. **Cols./Page:** 3. **Col. Width:** 27 nonpareils. **Col. Depth:** 133 agate lines. **Key Personnel:** Michael W. Dorsey, Editor, mwdorsey@wpi.edu; Bonnie Gelbwasser, Managing Editor, phone (508)831-5706, fax (508)831-5820, big@wpi.edu. **ISSN:** 0148-6128. **Remarks:** Advertising not accepted. **URL:** http://www.wpi.edu/journal.
Circ: Non-paid ‡25,000

14785 WPI Newspeak
Worcester Polytechnic Institute
100 Institute Rd. Phone: (508)831-5609
Worcester, MA 01609-2280 Fax: (508)831-5820
Publication E-mail: newspeak@wpi.edu

Collegiate newspaper. **Subtitle:** The Student Newspaper of Worcester Polytechnic Institute. **Founded:** 1909. **Freq:** Weekly (Tues.). **Print Method:** Letterpress. **Trim Size:** 8 1/2 x 11. **Cols./Page:** 4. **Col. Width:** 2 3/8 inches. **Col. Depth:** 16 inches. **Key Personnel:** Justin D. Greenough, Editor-in-Chief; Jared Auclair, Circulation Mgr.; Brandon Ngo, Advertising Mgr. **ISSN:** 1093-0081. **Subscription Rates:** $20. **Remarks:** Accepts advertising. **URL:** http://www.wpi.edu/~newspeak. **Alt. Formats:** Microform. **Formerly:** Newspeak.
Ad Rates: GLR: $.50 **Circ:** Paid ‡100
BW: $276 Free ‡2,650
PCI: $5.75

14786 Greater Media Cable
95 Higgins St. Phone: (508)853-1515
Worcester, MA 01606-1913 Fax: (508)854-5042

Founded: 1969. **Formerly:** Greater Worcester Cablevision. **Key Personnel:** Richard Tuthill, Contact; Art Goody, Contact; Allan Eisenberg, Contact. **Cities Served:** subscribing households 110,000; 58 channels; 3 community access channels.

14787 WCHC-FM - 88.1
Holy Cross College Phone: (508)793-2475
Box G Fax: (508)783-2471
Worcester, MA 01610
E-mail: wchc@holycross.edu

Format: Alternative/New Music/Progressive; Urban Contemporary. **Operating Hours:** 7 a.m.-2 a.m. **ADI:** Boston-Worcester,MA-Derry-Manchester,NH. **Key Personnel:** Damien Berthiaume, Station Mgr.; Trevor Atwell Mark O'Connell, Music Dir.; Brian Foclera, Program Dir.; Jessica Lagios, News Dir.; Amanda Condon, Announcing Dir; Mike Foley, Public Service Announcment Dir; Marc Anastasia, Promotions Dir. **Wattage:** 100.

14788 WCUW-FM - 91.3
910 Main St. Phone: (508)753-1012
Worcester, MA 01610

Format: Ethnic; News; Eclectic. **Networks:** Independent. **Owner:** WCUW, Inc., at above address. **Founded:** 1973. **Operating Hours:** Continuous; 100% local. **ADI:** Boston-Worcester,MA-Derry-Manchester,NH. **Key Personnel:** Joe Cutroni, Station Mgr. **Wattage:** 630. **Ad Rates:** Underwriting available.

14789 WICN-FM - 90.5
6 Chatham St. Phone: (508)752-0700
Worcester, MA 01609 Fax: (508)752-7518

Format: Public Radio; Jazz; News; Classical. **Networks:** National Public Radio (NPR); Public Radio International (PRI). **Owner:** WICN Public Radio, Inc., at above address. **Founded:** 1969. **Operating Hours:** Continuous; 40% network, 60% local. **ADI:** Boston-Worcester,MA-Derry-Manchester,NH. **Key Personnel:** Eugene R. Petit, Program Dir.; Steve Charbonneau, Jazz Dir.; Catherine Fuller, Classical Music Dir.; Drew Watson, Operations Mgr. **Local Programs:** *Jazz Matinee Jazz* 12 p.m.-4 p.m., Gene Petit, Program Dir., (508)752-0700, Fax (508)752-7518; *Serenade - Classical Music* 8 p.m.-midnight, Gene Petit, Program Dir., (508)752-0700, Fax (508)752-7518; *A Tasteful Blend Jazz* 6 a.m.-10 a.m., Steve Charbonneau, (508)752-0700, Fax (508)752-7518. **Wattage:** 8100. **Ad Rates:** Noncommercial; underwriting available.

14790 WORC-AM - 1310
108 Grove St., No. 17A Phone: (508)799-0581
Worcester, MA 01605-2629 Fax: (508)756-4851

Format: Talk. **Networks:** USA Radio. **Owner:** Davis Radio Corp., at above address. **Founded:** 1925. **Operating Hours:** Continuous; 85% network, 15% local. **ADI:** Boston-Worcester,MA-Derry-Manchester,NH. **Key Personnel:** Rich Green, Program Dir.; Alan Berman, General Sales Mgr. **Local Programs:** *Financial Hour*, Mike McDonald, Mailing contact; *Gun Owners Action League*, Mike Yuscino, Mailing contact; *Nick Manzello Sports Page*, Nick Manzello, Mailing contact. **Wattage:** 5000 day; 1000 night. **Ad Rates:** $17-50 per unit.

14791 WSRS-FM - 96.1
Box 961, West Side Sta. Phone: (508)757-9696
Worcester, MA 01602 Fax: (508)757-1779
E-mail: wsrsfm@aol.com

Format: Adult Contemporary. **Networks:** Independent. **Founded:** 1940. **Operating Hours:** Continuous. **ADI:** Boston-Worcester,MA-Derry-Manchester,NH. **Key Personnel:** Bud Paras, V.P./General Mgr.; Jennifer Antaya, General Sales Mgr.; Steve Peck, P.D. **Wattage:** 25,000.

14792 WTAG-AM - 580
PO Box 58, West Side Sta. Phone: (508)795-0580
Worcester, MA 01602 Fax: (508)757-1779

Format: Talk; Sports. **Networks:** CBS. **Founded:** 1924. **Operating Hours:** Continuous. **ADI:** Boston-Worcester,MA-Derry-Manchester,NH. **Wattage:** 5000.

WVNE-AM - See Springfield

14793 WXLO-FM - 104.5
250 Commercial St. Phone: (508)752-1045
Worcester, MA 01608 Fax: (508)793-0824
E-mail: wxlo@wxlo.com

Format: Adult Contemporary. **Networks:** AP. **Owner:** Montachusett Broadcasting, Inc., at above address. **Founded:** 1979. **Formerly:** WFMP-FM (1982). **Operating Hours:** Continuous; 10% network, 90% local. **ADI:** Boston-Worcester,MA-Derry-Manchester,NH. **Key Personnel:** Jim Cande, Sales Mgr.; Steve Gallagher, General Mgr.; Robyn Pallis, Group Controller; Sid Schweiger, Chief Engineer; Matt Blake, Operations Mgr.; Frank Foley, News Dir. **Wattage:** 50,000. **Ad Rates:** $75-150 per unit. **URL:** http://www.wxlo.com.

YARMOUTH PORT

14794 The Register
Community Newspaper Company
923G Rte. 6A Phone: (508)375-4990
Box 400 Fax: (508)375-4901
Yarmouth Port, MA 02675
Community newspaper. **Founded:** 1896. **Freq:** Weekly. **Print Method:** Offset. **Trim Size:** 10 3/8 x 15 5/16. **Cols./Page:** 3. **Col. Width:** 3 1/4 inches. **Col. Depth:** 15 inches. **Key Personnel:** Ben Gagnon, Managing Editor, phone (508)375-4943. **Subscription Rates:** $20.95; $26.95 out of area. **Remarks:** Accepts advertising. **URL:** http://www.townonline.com.
Ad Rates: GLR: $.75 **Circ:** ‡8,900
BW: $865.92
4C: $1,365.92
PCI: $6.69

MICHIGAN

State Capital, LANSING

Michigan is bounded on the north by Lake Superior, east by Lakes Huron, St. Clair, and Erie and their connecting Rivers, south by Ohio and Indiana, and west by Wisconsin and Lake Michigan. Its land area is 56,809 square miles. The state consists of two peninsulas, of which the southern is, north to south, about 300 miles; width about 200. Here manufacturing has grown to chief importance. This part of the state is level to undulating, abounding in lakes and streams, with extensive forest of pine and other timber in the north, mixed hardwoods in the south, and fruit-growing in the southwest. There are over 11,000 lakes, large and small, which are popular resorts of anglers and summer visitors. The northern peninsula is more rugged in surface and its chief industries are tourism, copper and iron mining, and timber operations. The Weather Bureau at Detroit gives the temperature (annual average) as 48.6; highest on record, 105; lowest on record, -24. Total annual precipitation is 32.62 inches. The great extent of its water boundary line, about 3,100 miles, gives Michigan a commanding position in lake commerce. The ship canal between Lake Huron and Lake Superior at Sault Ste. Marie handles more tonnage than the Panama Canal or any other canal in the United States and Canada. Detroit, noted throughout the world as a major center of automobile manufacture, is also a great commercial center. A very large tonnage of freight traffic passes through the Detroit River. There are many institutions of higher education in the state, among them being the Michigan State University, East Lansing; and the University of Michigan, Ann Arbor.

POPULATION: 9,437,000 (1992). Rank among the states, 8th.

AGRICULTURE: Number of farms: 54,000 (1992). Farm acreage: 11,000,000 (1992). Cash receipts from farm marketings: crops, $1,793,000,000 (1991); livestock and products, $1,288,000,000 (1991).

FORESTS: Total forest land: 4,855,000 acres (1991). Principal woods: maple, hemlock, birch, white pine, cottonwood and aspen, oak, elm, beech, basswood, ash, eastern cedar.

MINERALS: Value of production: $1,503,000,000 (1991). Principal minerals: iron ore, cement, sand and gravel. Value of petroleum production: $348,000,000 (1991).

MANUFACTURES: Value added by manufacture: $63,351,000,000 (1991). Leading industry groups: transportation equipment, machinery (except electrical), primary metal industries, fabricated metal products.

LIST OF COUNTIES

Total number of counties 83

County, Location on Map, and County Seat	Pop.
Alcona (NE), Harrisville	10,145
Alger (NC Up. Penin.), Munising	8,972
Allegan (NE), Allegan	90,509
Alpena (NE), Alpena	30,605
Antrim (NW), Bellaire	18,185
Arenac (E), Standish	14,931
Baraga (N Up. Penin.), L'Anse	7,954
Barry (SW), Hastings	50,057
Bay (EC), Bay City	11,723
Benzie (NW), Beulah	12,200
Berrien (SW), St. Joseph	161,378
Branch (S), Coldwater	41,502
Calhoun (S), Marshall	135,982
Cass (SW), Cassopolis	49,477
Charlevoix (N), Charlevoix	21,468
Cheboygan (N), Cheboygan	21,398
Chippewa (NE Up. Penin.), Sault Ste. Marie	34,604
Clare (N), Harrison	24,952
Clinton (SC), St. Johns	57,883
Crawford (N), Grayling	12,260
Delta (S Up. Penin.), Escanaba	37,780
Dickinson (SW Up. Penin.), Iron Mountain	26,831
Eaton (S), Charlotte	92,879
Emmet (N), Petoskey	25,040
Genesee (SEC), Flint	430,459
Gladwin (NEC), Gladwin	21,896
Gogebic (NW Up. Penin.), Bessemer	18,052
Grand Traverse (NW), Traverse City	64,273
Gratiot (C), Ithaca	38,982
Hillsdale (S), Hillsdale	43,431
Houghton (NW Up. Penin.), Houghton	35,446
Huron (E), Bad Axe	34,951
Ingham (S), Mason	281,912
Ionia (SWC), Ionia	57,024
Iosco (NE), Tawas City	30,209
Iron (W Up. Penin.), Crystal Falls	13,175
Isabella (C), Mount Pleasant	54,624
Jackson (S), Jackson	149,756
Kalamazoo (SW), Kalamazoo	223,411
Kalkaska (NW), Kalkaska	13,497
Kent (W), Grand Rapids	500,631
Keweenaw (N Up. Penin.), Eagle River	1,701
Lake (W), Baldwin	8,583
Lapeer (S), Lapeer	74,768
Leelanau (NW), Leland	16,527
Lenawee (S), Adrian	91,476
Livingston (SE), Howell	115,645
Luce (N Up. Penin.), Newberry	5,763
Mackinac (E Up. Penin.) St. Ignace	10,674
Macomb (SE), Mount Clemens	717,400
Manistee (NW), Manistee	21,265
Marquette (NWC Up. Penin.), Marquette	70,887
Mason (W), Ludington	25,537
Mecosta (WC), Big Rapids	37,308
Menominee (SW Up. Penin.), Menominee	24,920
Midland (EC), Midland	75,651
Missaukee (NC), Lake City	12,147
Monroe (SE), Monroe	133,600
Montcalm (SC), Stanton	53,059
Montmorency (NE), Atlanta	8,936
Muskegon (W), Muskegon	158,983
Newaygo (W), White Cloud	38,202
Oakland (SE), Pontiac	1,083,592
Oceana (W), Hart	22,454
Ogemaw (NE), West Branch	18,681
Ontonagon (NW Up. Penin.), Ontonagon	8,854
Osceola (NWC), Reed City	20,146
Oscoda (NE), Mio	7,842
Otsego (N), Gaylord	17,957
Ottawa (W), Grand Haven	187,768
Presque Isle (NE), Rogers City	13,743
Roscommon (NC), Roscommon	19,776
Saginaw (EC), Saginaw	211,946
St. Clair (E), Port Huron	145,607
St. Joseph (S), Centerville	58,913
Sanilac (E), Sandusky	39,928
Schoolcraft (EC Up. Penin.), Manistique	8,302
Shiawassee (SEC), Corunna	69,770
Tuscola (E), Caro	55,498
Van Buren (SW), Paw Paw	70,060
Washtenaw (SE), Ann Arbor	282,937
Wayne (SE), Detroit	2,111,687
Wexford (NW), Cadillac	26,360

STATISTICS

Newspapers

Period of Issue	
Daily	50
Evening Daily	36

Morning Daily	12
Daily with Sunday edition	23
Semiweekly	18
Weekly	267
Biweekly	9
Semimonthly	1
Monthly	12
Free or partly free	62
Shopper	63
Total Newspapers	370

Periodicals

Period of Issue

Weekly	13
Biweekly	5
Semimonthly	2
Monthly	55
Bimonthly	34
Quarterly	66
Total Periodicals	236

Total number of publications 606

Radio Stations

AM Stations	124
FM Stations	176
Total Radio Stations	300

TV Stations

Total TV Stations 43

Cable Stations

Total Cable Systems 36

Total number of broadcast listings 379

ADA

14795 Ada/Forest Hills Advance
Advance Newspapers
2141 Port Sheldon Rd. Phone: (616)669-2700
PO Box 9 Fax: (616)669-1162
Jenison, MI 49428-9301
Free: (800)439-0960

Community newspaper. **Founded:** 1966. **Freq:** Weekly (Wed.). **Print Method:** Offset. **Cols./Page:** 6. **Col. Width:** 9 1/2 picas. **Key Personnel:** Joel Holland, Publisher, fax (616)669-3930. **Subscription Rates:** $25. **Remarks:** Combined advertising rates available with other Advance Newspapers. **Formerly:** East Grand Rapids Advance.
Ad Rates: BW: $643.20 **Circ:** Combined 12,662
4C: $943.20
SAU: $8.04
PCI: $6.70

ADRIAN

14796 Access
Access Communications, Inc.
155 N. Winter Phone: (517)263-0800
Adrian, MI 49221 Fax: (517)263-8809

Shopper covering Lenawee County. **Founded:** July 1977. **Freq:** Weekly (Mon.). **Print Method:** Offset. **Trim Size:** 13 3/4 x 11 1/4. **Cols./Page:** 8. **Col. Width:** 7 1/4 picas. **Col. Depth:** 177 agate lines. **Key Personnel:** Bruce Gotts, Publisher/Owner. **Subscription Rates:** $50 individuals.
Ad Rates: GLR: $.71 **Circ:** Free 35,372
BW: $650
4C: $975.00
PCI: $10.00

14797 The Daily Telegram
133 N. Winter St. Phone: (517)265-5111
PO Box 647 Fax: (517)263-4152
Adrian, MI 49221
Free: (800)968-5111

General newspaper. **Founded:** 1892. **Freq:** Daily (eve.). **Print Method:** Offset. **Cols./Page:** 6. **Col. Width:** 2 inches. **Col. Depth:** 21 1/2 inches. **Key Personnel:** Stephen Staloch, Publisher; Michelle Micklewright, Editor. **Subscription Rates:** $156. **Formerly:** Adrian Daily Telegram.
Ad Rates: BW: $168 **Circ:** Mon.-Sat. 17,263
4C: $304 Sun. 16,874
SAU: $13.22

14798 Michigan Christian Advocate
316 Springbrook Ave. Phone: (517)265-2075
Adrian, MI 49221-2099 Fax: (517)263-7422
Publisher E-mail: Michigan_Christian_Advocate@ecunet.org

United Methodist tabloid. **Founded:** Nov. 1873. **Freq:** 26/year. **Print Method:** Offset. **Key Personnel:** Ann Whiting, Editor, Michigan.Christian.Advocate@ecunct.org. **Subscription Rates:** $9. **Remarks:** Accepts advertising.
Ad Rates: GLR: $2.50 **Circ:** ‡11,000
BW: $550
PCI: $18

14799 The National Gleaner Forum
Gleaner Life Insurance Society
PO Box 1894
Adrian, MI 49221-7894

Fraternal insurance magazine. **Founded:** 1894. **Freq:** Quarterly. **Print Method:** Offset. **Trim Size:** 5 3/8 x 8. **Cols./Page:** 2. **Col. Width:** 26 nonpareils. **Col. Depth:** 95 agate lines. **Key Personnel:** Jennifer Allman, Coordinator of Communications, gleaner@gleanerlife.com. **USPS:** 373-200. **Subscription Rates:** Free to qualified subscribers. **Remarks:** Advertising not accepted.
Circ: ⊕**31,000**

14800 WABJ-AM - 1490
121 W. Maumee St. Phone: (517)265-1500
Adrian, MI 49221 Fax: (517)263-4525
E-mail: wabj@dmci.net

Format: News; Talk. **Networks:** ABC; Michigan Farm Radio; Talknet. **Owner:** Friends Communications of Michigan, Inc., at above address. **Founded:** 1947. **Operating Hours:** Continuous; 10% network, 90% local. **ADI:** Toledo, OH. **Key Personnel:** Steve Porter, Contact; Scott Shigley, Contact; John Sebastian, Program/News/Sports Dir. **Local Programs:** *Lenaweee Insider*, Jonas Myers, (517)265-1500, Fax (517)263-4525. **Wattage:** 1000. **Ad Rates:** Advertising accepted; rates available upon request. **URL:** http://www.radiofriends.com.

14801 WLEN-FM - 103.9
242 W. Maumee St. Phone: (517)263-1039
Adrian, MI 49221 Fax: (517)265-5362

Format: Adult Contemporary. **Networks:** Mutual Broadcasting System. **Owner:** Lenawee Broadcasting Co., at above address. **Founded:** 1965. **Operating Hours:** Continuous; 10% network, 90% local. **ADI:** Detroit, MI. **Key Personnel:** Julie Koehn, General Mgr.; Dale Gaertner, Program Dir.; Patt Hayes, Sales Mgr. **Wattage:** 3000.

14802 WQTE-FM - 95.3
121 W. Maumee St. Phone: (517)265-9500
Adrian, MI 49221 Fax: (517)263-4525
E-mail: q95@dmci.net

Format: Contemporary Country. **Networks:** ABC. **Owner:** Friends Communications of Michigan, Inc., at above address. **Founded:** 1976. **Operating Hours:** Continuous; 10% network, 90% local. **ADI:** Toledo, OH. **Key Personnel:** Steve Porter, Contact; Scott Shigley, Contact; Ryan Horn, News Dir.; Greg Green, P.D. **Local Programs:** *Q-95 weekend*, Greg Green, (517)265-9500, Fax (517)263-4525. **Wattage:** 3000. **Ad Rates:** Advertising accepted; rates available upon request. **URL:** http://www.radiofriends.com.

14803 WVAC-FM - 107.9
Adrian College Phone: (517)265-5161
110 S. Madison St. Fax: (517)264-3331
Adrian, MI 49221

Format: Full Service. **Networks:** Independent. **Founded:** 1983. **Operating Hours:** Continuous; 100% local. **Key Personnel:** Steve Shehan, General Mgr.; Bill Kressback, Chief Engineer. **Wattage:** 10.

ALBION

14804 Albion Recorder
111 W. Center St. Phone: (517)629-3984
Albion, MI 49224-1755 Fax: (517)629-5790

Local newspaper. **Founded:** 1904. **Freq:** Mon.-Sat. (morn.). **Print Method:** Offset. **Cols./Page:** 6. **Col. Width:** 25 nonpareils. **Col. Depth:** 301 agate lines. **Key Personnel:** Terry Fitzwater, Editor and Publisher. **Subscription Rates:** $86. **Remarks:** Accepts advertising.
Ad Rates: GLR: $1.50 **Circ:** Paid 3,100
BW: $1,354 Non-paid 10,000
4C: $350
SAU: $11.49

14805 Morning Star: The Shopping Guide
Salesmen Publications
125 E. Cass St. Phone: (517)629-2127
PO Box 5 Fax: (517)629-8831
Albion, MI 49224
Free: (800)589-2127

Shopper. **Founded:** 1925. **Freq:** Weekly (Wed.). **Print Method:** Offset. **Trim Size:** 11 3/8 x 16 3/4. **Cols./Page:** 6. **Col. Width:** 19 nonpareils. **Col. Depth:** 224 agate lines. **Key Personnel:** George R. Raymond, Editor. **Remarks:** Color advertising accepted; rates available upon request.
Ad Rates: BW: $345 **Circ:** Free 9,366
PCI: $4

14806 WUFN-FM - 96.7
13799 Donovan Rd. Phone: (517)531-4478
Albion, MI 49224 Fax: (517)531-5009
Free: (800)776-1020
E-mail: wufn@flc.org

Format: Religious. **Networks:** Ambassador Inspirational Radio. **Owner:** Family Life Communications, Inc., PO Box 35300, Tucson, AZ 85740, (520)742-6976, Fax: (520)742-6979, Free: (800)776-1070. **Founded:** 1971. **Operating Hours:** Continuous. **Key Personnel:** Randy Carlson, President; David Jones, Operations Mgr.; Dave Kersey, Vice President of Broadcasting; Rod Robison, Vice President of Development; Dave Shough, Controller; Ken Peel, Music Dir.; Dave Phelps, General Mgr. **Local Programs:** *Sunrise Sounds* 6:00 am - 9:00 am Weekdays, Dave Dawson, Mailing contact; *Midday Cafe* 12:00 noon Weekdays, David Jones, Mailing contact; *In The Pastors Study* 7:30 am & pm Weekdays, Dave Phelps. **Wattage:** 3000 ERP. **Ad Rates:** Noncommercial. **URL:** http://www.flc.org/wufn.

ALLEGAN

14807 The Allegan County News
Kaechele Publications, Inc.
231 Trowbridge Phone: (616)673-5534
PO Box 189 Fax: (616)673-5535
Allegan, MI 49010
Publication E-mail: email@allegannews.com
Publisher E-mail: allnews@accn.org

Regional newspaper. **Founded:** 1887. **Freq:** Weekly (Thurs.). **Print Method:** Offset. **Cols./Page:** 6. **Col. Width:** 26 nonpareils. **Col. Depth:** 21 1/2 inches. **Key Personnel:** Cheryl Kaechele, Publisher; Dave Trinka, Editor, editor@allegannews.com. **USPS:** 013-700. **Subscription Rates:** $18 individuals; $23 out of area; $27 out of state; $13.50 students. **Remarks:** Accepts advertising. **Formerly:** Allegan County News & Gazette.
Ad Rates: SAU: $7.76 **Circ:** 5,500

14808 Allegan Flashes
Stauffer Communications, Inc.
595 Jenner Dr. Phone: (616)673-2141
Allegan, MI 49010-1567 Fax: (616)673-4761
Free: (800)968-4415
Publisher E-mail: fpi595@aol.com

Shopper. **Founded:** 1935. **Freq:** Weekly (Mon.). **Print Method:** Offset. **Trim Size:** 11 3/8 x 13 3/4. **Cols./Page:** 4. **Col. Width:** 2 7/16 inches. **Col. Depth:** 12 1/2 inches. **Key Personnel:** David H. Moored, General Mgr.; Allen Louks, Sales Mgr. **Subscription Rates:** Free; $14 by mail.
Ad Rates: GLR: $6 **Circ:** Free ❑**16,340**
BW: $551.04 Paid ❑**7**
4C: $250 space
PCI: $8.61 unit

14809 Lakeshore Flashes Shopping Guide
Stauffer Communications, Inc.
595 Jenner Dr. Phone: (616)673-2141
Allegan, MI 49010-1567 Fax: (616)673-4761
Free: (800)968-4415
Publisher E-mail: fpi595@aol.com

Shopper/weekly newspaper. **Subtitle:** Lakeshore Flashes. **Founded:** 1950. **Freq:** Weekly (Mon.). **Print Method:** Offset. **Trim Size:** 11 3/8 x 13 3/4. **Cols./Page:** 4. **Col. Width:** 2 7/16 inches. **Col. Depth:** 12 inches. **Key Personnel:** David H. Moored, General Mgr.; Allen Louks, Sales Mgr. **Subscription Rates:** $14 individuals; Free.
Ad Rates: GLR: $6 **Circ:** Controlled ❑**9,329**
BW: $469.12 Paid ❑**2**
4C: $250 space
PCI: $7.33 unit

14810 Senior Times (Kalamazoo)
Stauffer Communications, Inc.
595 Jenner Dr. Phone: (616)673-2141
Allegan, MI 49010-1567 Fax: (616)673-4761
Free: (800)968-4415
Publisher E-mail: fpi595@aol.com

Newspaper for senior citizens in Kalamazoo, MI. **Founded:** 1989. **Freq:** Monthly. **Print Method:** Offset. **Trim Size:** 10 3/8 x 16. **Cols./Page:** 6. **Col. Width:** 1 5/8 inches. **Col. Depth:** 16 inches. **Key Personnel:** Jack Hendericks, Publisher; Allen Decent, Editor. **Subscription Rates:** Free; $6 (mail). **Remarks:** Accepts advertising.
Ad Rates: BW: $720 **Circ:** Free 21,856

14811 West Michigan Senior Times
595 Jenner Dr. Phone: (616)673-2141
Allegan, MI 49010 Fax: (616)673-4761
Free: (800)968-4415
Publisher E-mail: tpisgs@aol.com

Newspaper for senior citizens. **Subtitle:** A Newspaper For and About Area Senior Adults. **Founded:** 1989. **Freq:** Monthly 12/year. **Print Method:** Offset. **Trim Size:** 11 3/8 x 17. **Cols./Page:** 6. **Col. Width:** 1 5/8 inches. **Col. Depth:** 16 inches. **Key Personnel:** Rebecca Roe, Editor; David H. Moored, General Mgr.; Tina Loomis, Marketing Coordinator; Allen Louks, Sales Mgr. **Subscription Rates:** $14 individuals. **URL:** http://www.wowcom.net. **Formerly:** Senior Times.
Ad Rates: GLR: $6 **Circ:** Free 25,000
BW: $794
4C: $969

14812 Zeeland Flashes Shopping Guide
Stauffer Communications, Inc.
595 Jenner Dr. Phone: (616)673-2141
Allegan, MI 49010-1567 Fax: (616)673-4761
Free: (800)968-4415
Publisher E-mail: fpi595@aol.com

Shopper/weekly newspaper. **Founded:** 1958. **Freq:** Weekly (Mon.). **Print Method:** Offset. **Trim Size:** 11 3/8 x 13 3/4. **Cols./Page:** 4. **Col. Width:** 2 7/16 inches. **Col. Depth:** 12 1/2 inches. **Key Personnel:** David H. Moored, General Mgr.; Allen Louks, Sales Mgr. **Subscription Rates:** Free; $14 (mail).
Ad Rates: GLR: $6 **Circ:** Controlled ❑**9,853**
BW: $481.92 Paid ❑**2**
4C: $250 space
PCI: $7.53 unit

14813 Allegan County Cablevision Inc.
1169 26th St. Phone: (616)673-3812
Allegan, MI 49010-9064 Fax: (616)673-3578

Key Personnel: Mark Scott, General Mgr. **Cities Served:** Allegan, Plainwell, Otsego, Gobels, Martin, Hamilton, and Hopkins, MI.

ALLENDALE

14814 WTLJ-TV - 54
10290 48th Ave. Phone: (616)895-4154
Allendale, MI 49401

Format: Religious. **Founded:** 1986. **Operating Hours:** Continuous. **ADI:** Grand Rapids-Kalamazoo-Battle Creek, MI. **Key Personnel:** Vic VanDeventer, General Mgr.; Frank Ayre, Chief Engineer; Ronda Price, Production Mgr. **Wattage:** 4,400,000.

ALMA

14815 WFYC-AM - 1280
PO Box 669 Phone: (517)463-3175
Alma, MI 48801-0669 Fax: (517)463-6674
Free: (800)995-9111
E-mail: jacom@nethawk.com

Format: Sports. **Networks:** USA Radio. **Owner:** Jacom, Inc., at above address. **Founded:** 1948. **Operating Hours:** 6 a.m.-11 p.m.; 75% network, 25% local. **ADI:** Flint-Saginaw-Bay City, MI. **Key Personnel:** James P. Sommerville, Contact. **Wattage:** 1000. **Ad Rates:** $10.00 for 30 seconds; $13.00 for 60 seconds.

14816 WMLM-AM - 1520 AM
4170 N. State Rd. Phone: (517)463-4013
Alma, MI 48801
E-mail: wmlm@nethawk.com

Format: Country. **Networks:** ABC. **Owner:** Siefker Broadcasting Corp., at above address. **Founded:** 1977. **Operating Hours:** 6 am - 11 pm; 5% network, 95% local. **ADI:** Flint-Saginaw-Bay City, MI. **Key Personnel:** Gregory W. Siefker, Pres./Gen. Mgr. **Wattage:** 1000. **Ad Rates:** $5.75-9 for 30 seconds; $6.75-10.25 for 60 seconds.

14817 WQBX-FM - 104.9
PO Box 669 Phone: (517)463-3175
Alma, MI 48801-0669 Fax: (517)463-6674

Format: Oldies. **Networks:** ABC; Unistar; ABC. **Founded:** 1948. **Formerly:** WFYC-FM. **Operating Hours:** 6 a.m.-11 p.m.; 95% network, 5% local. **Key Personnel:** David W. Sommerville, General Mgr.; James P. Sommerville, Contact. **Wattage:** 3000.

ALPENA

14818 Alpena News
Alpena News Publishing Co.
130 Park Pl. Phone: (517)354-3111
PO Box 367 Fax: (517)354-2096
Alpena, MI 49707
Free: (800)448-0254
Publication E-mail: alpenanews@oweb.com

General newspaper. **Founded:** 1899. **Freq:** Mon.-Sat. (morn.). **Print Method:** Offset. **Trim Size:** 6 x 21 1/2. **Cols./Page:** 6. **Col. Width:** 25 nonpareils. **Col. Depth:** 301 agate lines. **Key Personnel:** Bill Speer, Editor and Publisher. **Subscription Rates:** $148. **Remarks:** Accepts advertising. **URL:** http://www.oweb.com/upnorth.
Ad Rates: BW: $1,220.94168.74 **Circ:** Mon.-Sat. ★**11,588**
4C: $200
SAU: $15.22
PCI: $9.69

14819 Alpena Star
Star Publications
PO Box 620 Phone: (517)732-5125
Gaylord, MI 49734 Fax: (517)732-9323
Free: (800)782-7237
Publisher E-mail: starads@northland.lib.mi.us

Shopper (tabloid). **Founded:** 1972. **Freq:** Weekly (Sun.). **Print Method:** Offset. Uses mats. **Trim Size:** 11 1/8 x 17 1/2. **Cols./Page:** 6. **Col. Width:** 21 nonpareils. **Col. Depth:** 224 agate lines. **Key Personnel:** Dave Baragrey, Publisher; Mike Adams, Sales Mgr. **Subscription Rates:** Free; $10 (mail). **Remarks:** Accepts advertising. **Formerly:** Alpena Star Advertiser.
Ad Rates: GLR: $.32 **Circ:** Combined 18,921
BW: $430.08
4C: $610.08
PCI: $6.23

14820 WATZ-AM - 1450
123 Prentiss St. Phone: (517)354-8400
PO Box 536 Fax: (517)354-3436
Alpena, MI 49707

Format: News; Talk; Sports. **Networks:** ABC. **Owner:** Watz Radio, Inc, at above address. **Founded:** 1946. **Operating Hours:** 5:30 a.m.-1 a.m. **ADI:** Alpena, MI. **Key Personnel:** Mike Centala, Contact, mcentala@freeway.net; Steve Wright, Program Dir., watz@watz.com; Bruce Johnson, News Dir., phone (572)356-0355; Don Parteka, Contact. **Wattage:** 1000. **Ad Rates:** $6 for 30 seconds; $9 for 60 seconds. Combined advertising rates available with WATZ-FM.

14821 WATZ-FM - 99.3
123 Prentiss St. Phone: (517)354-8400
PO Box 536 Fax: (517)354-3436
Alpena, MI 49707
E-mail: watznews@watz.com

Format: Contemporary Country. **Networks:** ABC. **Owner:** WATZ Radio, Inc., at above address. **Founded:** 1967. **Formerly:** WATZ-FM. **Operating Hours:** 5:30 a.m.-1 a.m. **ADI:** Alpena, MI. **Key Personnel:** Mike Centala, Contact, phone (517)354-8400, fax (517)354-3436, mcentala@freeway.net; Steve Wright, Program Dir., watz@watz.com; Bruce Johnson, News Dir., phone (517)356-0365. **Wattage:** 50,000 ERP. **Ad Rates:** $7-11.50 for 10 seconds; $13-17 for 30 seconds; $17-23 for 60 seconds. Combined advertising rates available with WATZ-AM.

14822 WBKB-TV - 11
1390 Bagley St. Phone: (517)356-3434
Alpena, MI 49707

Format: Commercial TV. **Networks:** CBS. **Founded:** 1975. **Operating Hours:** 6:30-1:00 a.m. **ADI:** Alpena, MI. **Key Personnel:** Curtis W. Smith, Contact.

14823 WCML-FM - 91.7
Central Michigan University Phone: (517)774-3105
Public Broadcasting Center Fax: (517)774-4427
3965 E. Broomfield Rd.
Mount Pleasant, MI 48859
Free: (800)999-5656
E-mail: pubcast@cmich.edu

Format: Jazz; News; Classical. **Founded:** 1978. **ADI:** Alpena, MI. **Key Personnel:** Thomas Hunt, General Mgr.; Ray Ford, Program Dir.; Art Curtis, Underwriting. **Wattage:** 100,000.

14824 WCML-TV - 6
c/o WCMU-TV Phone: (517)774-3105
Central Michigan University Fax: (517)774-4427
3965 E. Broomfield
Mount Pleasant, MI 48859

Format: Public TV. **Networks:** Public Broadcasting Service (PBS). **Owner:** Central Michigan University, at above address. **Founded:** 1975. **Operating Hours:** 6 a.m.-midnight. **ADI:** Alpena, MI. **Key Personnel:** Monte Higgins, Station Mgr.; Rick Schudiske, Program Dir. **Ad Rates:** Noncommercial.

14825 WHSB-FM - 107.7
1491 M-32 W. Phone: (517)354-4611
Alpena, MI 49707 Fax: (517)354-4014

Format: Adult Contemporary. **Networks:** ABC. **Owner:** Daraka Broadcasting Inc., at above address. **Founded:** 1964. **Operating Hours:** Continuous. **ADI:** Alpena, MI. **Key Personnel:** Mark Thomas, General Mgr.; Donna Waltz-Jaskolski, National Sales Manager; Darrell Kelly, Contact. **Wattage:** 100,000. **Ad Rates:** $13-18 for 30 seconds; $18-25 for 60 seconds. Combined advertising rates available with WBMI-FM; WHAK-AM; WHAK-FM; WHST-FM.

ANN ARBOR

14826 AI EDAM
Cambridge University Press
The University of Michigan Phone: (313)936-1590
Ann Arbor, MI 48109-2110 Fax: (313)763-1260
Publication E-mail: clive-dym@hmc.edu; journals_marketing@cup.org; wpb@eecsu.mich.edu

Journal focusing on artificial intelligence technologies. **Subtitle:** Artificial Intelligence for Engineering Design, Analysis, and Manufacturing. **Founded:** Jan. 1995. **Freq:** 5/year. **Trim Size:** 8 1/4 x 11. **Key Personnel:** William P. Birmingham, Editor. **ISSN:** 0890-0604. **Subscription Rates:** $224 institutions; $98 individuals; $49 single issue. **Remarks:** Accepts advertising.
Ad Rates: BW: $400 **Circ:** Paid ‡237
Non-paid ‡67

14827 The Ann Arbor News
340 E. Huron St. Phone: (313)994-6989
Ann Arbor, MI 48104 Fax: (313)994-6879

General newspaper. **Founded:** 1835. **Freq:** Daily (eve.), Sat. and Sun. (morn.). **Print Method:** Letterpress. **Cols./Page:** 6. **Col. Width:** 26 nonpareils. **Col. Depth:** 308 agate lines. **Key Personnel:** Ed Petykiewicz, Editor; David D. Wierman, Publisher; Joe Grech, Advertising Dir.; David Bishop, Assoc. Editor and Ombudsman, phone (313)994-6825; Al Bliss, Graphics Editor and Art Dir., phone (313)994-6820; Grace Purvas, Librarian, phone (313)994-6852. **Subscription Rates:** $132. **Remarks:** Accepts advertising. **URL:** http://www.mlive.com. **Feature Editors:** Karl Bates, *Environmental*, phone (313)994-6825; Jud Branam, *Education*; Steve Cagle, *Fashion, Food, Travel*, phone (313)994-6701; Steve Cain, *Education*, phone (313)994-6820; Andy Chapelle, *News, Political*, phone (313)994-6858; Don Faber, *Religion*, phone (313)994-6873; Rick Fitzgerald, *Metro*, phone (313)994-6862; Mike Kersmarki, *Automotive, Financial/Business, Real Estate*, phone (313)994-6872; Geoff Larcom, *Sports*; Bruce Martin, *Entertainment, Movie*, phone (313)994-6838; Judy Nies Tell, *Photo*, phone (313)994-6823; Kay Semion, *Editorials*, phone (313)994-6863; Julie Wiernik, *Lifestyle, Living, Medical, Science, Women's*, phone (313)994-6872.
Ad Rates: PCI: $23.84 **Circ:** Mon.-Sat. ★**57,694**
Sun. ★**74,526**

14828 Ann Arbor Observer
Ann Arbor Observer Co.
201 Catherine St. Phone: (313)769-3175
Ann Arbor, MI 48104 Fax: (313)769-3375

City magazine offering in-depth features, profiles, historical articles, items on new business, restaurant reviews, and a listing of events and exhibits. **Founded:** July 1976. **Freq:** Monthly. **Print Method:** Offset. Uses mats. **Trim Size:** 10 1/2 x 13 1/2. **Cols./Page:** 4. **Col. Width:** 27 nonpareils. **Col. Depth:** 182 agate lines. **Key Personnel:** John Hilton, Editor, hilton@observer.com; Patricia Garcia, Publisher, pg@observer.com; Vikki J. Enos, Advertising Mgr. **Subscription Rates:** $16. **URL:** http://www.arborweb.com.
Ad Rates: BW: $1,761 **Circ:** Paid 4,852
4C: $2,161 Non-paid 53,963

14829 Automobile Magazine
Primedia Publishing
120 E. Liberty St. Phone: (734)994-3500
Ann Arbor, MI 48104-4193 Fax: (734)994-1153
Publication E-mail: autoletters@primediamags.com

Automotive magazine. **Founded:** Apr. 1986. **Freq:** Monthly. **Print Method:** Offset. **Trim Size:** 8 x 10 13/18. **Cols./Page:** 3. **Col. Width:** 24 nonpareils. **Col. Depth:** 138 agate lines. **Key Personnel:** David E. Davis, Jr., Editor/Publication Dir. **Subscription Rates:** $20 individuals. **Remarks:** Accepts advertising. **URL:** http://www.automobilemag.com. **Additional Contact Info: Advertising:** 575 Lexington Ave., 24th Fl., New York, NY 10022.
Ad Rates: BW: $39,110 **Circ:** Paid ★**618,996**
4C: $55,870

14830 Bulletin of the American Society of Papyrologists
Scholars Press
434 S. State St.
Ann Arbor, MI 48109
Publisher E-mail: scholars@emory.edu

Official journal of the American Society of Papyrologists; including texts, literature, and articles on inscriptions and subjects in Greek, Roman, and Egyptian history. **Founded:** 1963. **Freq:** Quarterly. **Print Method:** Offset. **Trim Size:** 6 x 9. **Cols./Page:** 1. **Col. Width:** 54 nonpareils. **Col. Depth:** 96 agate lines. **Key Personnel:** Terry G. Wilfong, Editor; Timothy Renner, Editorial Board; John Whitehorne, Editorial Board. **ISSN:** 0003-1186. **Subscription Rates:** $40. **Remarks:** Advertising not accepted.
Circ: 500

14831 The Collectors Club Philatelist
Collectors Club, Inc.
PO Box 3501 Phone: (734)665-7166
Ann Arbor, MI 48106-3501 Fax: (734)665-5816
Publisher E-mail: collectorsclub@nac.net

Magazine devoted to philatelic study and research. **Founded:** Jan. 1923. **Freq:** Bimonthly. **Print Method:** Offset. **Trim Size:** 6 x 9. **Cols./Page:** 1. **Col. Width:** 52 nonpareils. **Col. Depth:** 118 agate lines. **Key Personnel:** P.A.S. Smith, Editor, phone (734)665-7166, passmith@umich.edu; Richard Pounder, Advertising Mgr. **ISSN:** 0010-0838. **Subscription Rates:** $42. $7 single issue. **Remarks:** Accepts advertising.
Ad Rates: BW: $300 **Circ:** ‡1,300

14832 Comparative Studies in Society & History
Cambridge University Press
102 Rackham Bldg. Phone: (734)764-6362
Univ. of Mich. Fax: (734)647-2105
Ann Arbor, MI 48109-1070
Publication E-mail: cssh@umich.edu

Journal focusing on anthropology, sociology, history, political science. **Founded:** 1959. **Freq:** Quarterly. **Print Method:** Offset. **Cols./Page:** 1. **Col. Width:** 52 nonpareils. **Col. Depth:** 104 agate lines. **Key Personnel:** Thomas Trautmann, Editor; James Schaefer, Senior Editor. **ISSN:** 0010-4175. **Subscription Rates:** $93 institutions; $37 individuals; $23 single issue U.S., Canada, Mexico. **Remarks:** Accepts advertising. **URL:** http://www.umich.edu/~cssh.
Ad Rates: BW: $500 **Circ:** Paid ‡2028

14833 The Education Digest
Prakken Publications, Inc.
3970 Varsity Dr. Phone: (734)975-2800
PO Box 8623 Fax: (734)975-2787
Ann Arbor, MI 48107-8623
Free: (800)530-WORD
Publication E-mail: ededit@cyberzone-inc.com
Publisher E-mail: publisher@cybezone-inc.com

Journal containing condensed articles from educational publications focusing on key issues, policies, practices, and research, with regular monthly columns and features aimed primarily at professional educators. **Subtitle:** Outstanding Articles Condensed for Quick Review. **Founded:** Nov. 1935. **Freq:** 9/year (Sept.-May). **Print Method:** Web Offset. **Trim Size:** 5 1/2 x 8. **Cols./Page:** 2. **Col. Width:** 24 nonpareils. **Col. Depth:** 92 agate lines. **Key Personnel:** George F. Kennedy, Publisher; Alice B. Klock, Advertising Mgr., tdedv@teddirections.com; Kenneth Schroeder, Managing Editor. **ISSN:** 0013-127X. **Subscription Rates:** $48 individuals. **Remarks:** Accepts advertising. **Alt. Formats:** CD-ROM, University Microfilms; EBSCO Publishing; Microform; Mailing labels.
Ad Rates: BW: $666 **Circ:** ‡22,000
PCI: $50

14834 Endangered Species Update
University of Michigan
430 E. University, Dana Bldg. Phone: (734)763-3243
Ann Arbor, MI 48109-1115 Fax: (734)936-2195
Publication E-mail: esupdate@umich.edu

Technical environmental journal. **Founded:** Dec. 1983. **Freq:** Bimonthly. **Trim Size:** 8 x 11. **Cols./Page:** 3. **Col. Width:** 5.5 centimeters. **Col. Depth:** 24 centimeters. **Key Personnel:** Misty McPhee, Editor, phone (734)936-2195, mmcphee@umich.edu; Andrew Hayes, Editorial Asst. **ISSN:** 1081-3705. **Remarks:** Advertising not accepted. **URL:** http://www.umich.edu/~esupdate.
Circ: Controlled 1,450

14835 Great Lake Entomologist
Michigan Entomological Society
c/o Mark F. O'Brien
University of Michigan
Museum of Zoology, Insect Div.
Ann Arbor, MI 48109-1079

Scientific journal covering entomology. **Founded:** 1966. **Freq:** Quarterly. **Key Personnel:** Mark F. O'Brien, Editor; M. C. Nielsen, Treas. **ISSN:** 0090-0222. **Subscription Rates:** $30 individuals; $6 single issue. **Former name:** The Michigan Entomologist.
Circ: Combined 715

14836 Great Lakes Pilot News
Don Kleinschmidt
1219 Van Dusen Phone: (734)439-8847
Ann Arbor, MI 48103 Fax: (734)769-6471

Trade journal covering aviation. **Founded:** 1990. **Freq:** Bimonthly. **Print Method:** Web offset. **ISSN:** 1081-406X. **Subscription Rates:** $12; Free to qualified subscribers. **Remarks:** Accepts advertising. **URL:** http://www.pilotnews.com.
Ad Rates: BW: $550 **Circ:** Non-paid 14,000

14837 HUES
New Moon Publishing
PO Box 7778 Phone: (313)971-0023
Ann Arbor, MI 48107 Fax: (313)971-0450
Publisher E-mail: newmoon@newmoon.org

Consumer magazine covering identity issues for women. **Freq:** Quarterly. **Print Method:** Sheetfed offset. **Trim Size:** 8 x 11. **Key Personnel:** Nancy Gruver, Publisher; Joe Kelly, Publisher; Ophira Edut, Editor-in-Chief; Tali Edut, Editor-in-Chief; Dyann Logwood, Editor-in-Chief. **ISSN:** 1081-8219. **Subscription Rates:** $19.99 individuals; $3.95 single issue. **Remarks:** Accepts advertising.
Ad Rates: BW: $1,200 **Circ:** Paid 1,400
4C: $1,750

14838 Japanophile
Japanophile Press
PO Box 7977 Phone: (734)930-1553
Ann Arbor, MI 48107 Fax: (734)930-9968
Publisher E-mail: jpnhand@japanophile.com

Literary journal covering Japanese culture with a western perspective. **Founded:** Jan. 1977. **Freq:** Quarterly. **Trim Size:** 5 1/2 x 8 1/2. **Cols./Page:** 1. **Col. Width:** 4 1/4 inches. **Col. Depth:** 6 1/2 inches. **Key Personnel:** Susan Lapp, Editor and Publisher; Sayoko Smith, Circulation Mgr. **ISSN:** 1071-4227. **Subscription Rates:** $14 individuals; $20 out of country; $4 single issue. **Remarks:** Accepts advertising.
Ad Rates: BW: $100 **Circ:** Controlled 450

14839 Journal of Anthroposophical Medicine
Physicians Association for Anthroposophical Medicine
1923 Geddes Ave. Phone: (734)930-9462
Ann Arbor, MI 48104 Fax: (734)662-1727

Professional medical journal covering anthroposophically-extended medicine. **Freq:** Quarterly. **Print Method:** Offset. **Trim Size:** 6 1/4 x 9 1/2. **Key Personnel:** Candace Escalada, Circulation Mgr.; Edwin Funk, MD, Managing Editor; Christa Van Tellingen, MD, Editor. **ISSN:** 1067-4640. **Subscription Rates:** $50 individuals; $60 out of country. **Remarks:** Accepts advertising.
Circ: Controlled 400

14840 Journal of Cuneiform Studies
Scholars Press
University of Michigan Phone: (313)936-2679
Dept. of Near Eastern Studies
c/o Piotr Michalowski
3074 Frieze Bldg.
Ann Arbor, MI 48109
Publisher E-mail: scholars@emory.edu

Scholarly journal covering technical and general information on the history of languages of ancient literate cultures. **Founded:** 1947. **Freq:** Annual. **Print Method:** Offset. **Trim Size:** 8 1/2 x 11. **Cols./Page:** 2. **Col. Width:** 3 inches. **Col. Depth:** 8 3/8 inches. **Key Personnel:** Piotr Michalowski, Editor, piotrm@umich.edu; Pat Johnston, Circulation Mgr. **ISSN:** 0022-0256. **Subscription Rates:** $45 individuals; $55 institutions; $60 out of country. **Remarks:** Advertising not accepted.
Circ: Paid 500

14841 Journal of Great Lakes Research
International Association for Great Lakes Research
c/o R. Stephen Schneider, Phone: (734)763-1520
Managing Editor Fax: (734)647-2748
University of Michigan
745 Dennison Bldg.
502 E. University
Ann Arbor, MI 48109-1090
Publication E-mail: rssch@umich.edu

Interdisciplinary, technical journal covering large lakes worldwide. **Founded:** 1975. **Freq:** Quarterly. **Print Method:** Offset. **Trim Size:** 8 1/2 x 11. **Cols./Page:** 2. **Col. Width:** 20 picas. **Col. Depth:** 53 picas. **Key Personnel:** Gerald Matisoff, Editor, gxm4@po.cwru.edu; Stephen Schneider, Managing Editor, rssch@umich.edu; Wendy Foster, Business Office. **ISSN:** 0380-1330. **Subscription Rates:** $50 individuals; $100 libraries. **Remarks:** Advertising not accepted. **URL:** http://www.geog.buffalo.edu/iaglr.
Circ: (Not Reported)

14842 Journal of Housing for the Elderly
The Haworth Press, Inc.
2226 Art & Architecture Bldg., Phone: (313)763-9560
The Univ of Michigan Fax: (313)763-2322
Ann Arbor, MI 48109-2069
Publisher E-mail: getinfo@haworthpressinc.com

Magazine dealing with issues on housing for the elderly. **Founded:** 1983. **Freq:** Biennial. **Trim Size:** 6x8 1/2. **Key Personnel:** Leon A. Pastalan, Editor. **ISSN:** 0276-3893. **Subscription Rates:** $48 individuals; $120 institutions; $200 libraries. **Remarks:** Accepts advertising. **Alt. Formats:** Microfiche.
Ad Rates: BW: $300 **Circ:** 1,250

14843 Mathematical Reviews
American Mathematical Society
416 4th St. Phone: (313)996-5250
PO Box 8604 Fax: (313)996-2916
Ann Arbor, MI 48107-8604
Publication E-mail: mathrev@math.ams.org
Publisher E-mail: pub@ams.org

Journal containing reviews and abstracts of current mathematical literature. **Founded:** 1940. **Freq:** Monthly. **Print Method:** Offset. **Trim Size:** 9 x 12. **Cols./Page:** 2. **Col. Width:** 3 5/8 inches. **Col. Depth:** 10 3/4 inches. **Key Personnel:** R. Keith Dennis, Executive Editor. **ISSN:** 0025-5629. **Subscription Rates:** $389 plus $5460 data access fee; $4368 institutional members. **Remarks:** Advertising not accepted. **Online:** Dialog (The Dialog Corporation); NACSIS. **URL:** http://www.ams.org/mathscinet/. **Alt. Formats:** CD-ROM, MathSciDisk; Magnetic tape; Microform.
Circ: Paid ‡1,500

14844 Michigan Alumnus
University of Michigan
200 Fletcher St. Phone: (734)764-0384
Ann Arbor, MI 48109-1007 Fax: (734)764-4506
Free: (800)847-4764

Collegiate magazine. **Founded:** 1894. **Freq:** Quarterly. **Print Method:** Letterpress and offset. **Trim Size:** 8 1/2 x 11. **Cols./Page:** 3. **Col. Width:** 40 nonpareils. **Col. Depth:** 134 agate lines. **Key Personnel:** Noreen Ferris Wolcott, Editor; Marie L. Frost, Advertising Coord., phone (734)763-9706, frostm@umich.edu. **Subscription Rates:** $40. **Remarks:** Accepts advertising.
Ad Rates: BW: $1,400 **Circ:** 100,000
4C: $2,500

14845 Michigan Botanist
Michigan Botanical Club, Inc.
University of Michigan Herbarium
North University Bldg.
Ann Arbor, MI 48109-1057

Journal covering botany in the Great Lakes region. **Freq:** Quarterly. **Key Personnel:** Barbara J. Madsen, Editor; Thomas Clough, Business and Circulation Mgr. **ISSN:** 0026-203X. **Subscription Rates:** $16 individuals; $4 single issue.
Circ: Combined ⊕**800**

14846 The Michigan Daily
University of Michigan
420 Maynard St. Phone: (313)764-0552
Ann Arbor, MI 48109 Fax: (313)764-4275
Publication E-mail: daily@umich.edu

Collegiate newspaper. **Founded:** 1890. **Freq:** Daily (morn.) (during the academic year). **Print Method:** Letter press. **Cols./Page:** 6. **Col. Width:** 26 nonpareils. **Col. Depth:** 301 agate lines. **Key Personnel:** Heather Kamins, Editor-in-Chief. **Subscription Rates:** $180 individuals; $100 Fall only; $105 Winter only. **Remarks:** Accepts advertising. **Available Online. URL:** http://www.pub.umich.edu/daily/.
Ad Rates: GLR: $2.75 **Circ:** Free ‡18,000
PCI: $11.50

14847 Michigan Feminist Studies
University of Michigan
234 West Hall Phone: (734)763-9791
Ann Arbor, MI 48109-1092 Fax: (734)647-4943
Publication E-mail: mfseditors@umich.edu

Interdisciplinary, feminist journal produced and edited by graduate students at the University of Michigan. **Founded:** 1978. **Freq:** Annual. **Key Personnel:** Cari Carpenter, Editor; Karen Miller, Editor. **Subscription Rates:** $5 individuals; $12 institutions. **Remarks:** Accepts advertising. **Former name:** Occasional Papers in Women's Studies.
Ad Rates: BW: $50 **Circ:** Controlled 250

14848 Michigan Law Review
Michigan Law Review Association
Hutchins Hall Phone: (734)763-5870
625 S. State St. Fax: (734)647-5817
Ann Arbor, MI 48109-1215
Publisher E-mail: dkz@umich.edu

Legal journal. **Founded:** 1902. **Freq:** 8/year. **Print Method:** Offset. **Trim Size:** 6 3/4 x 10. **Cols./Page:** 1. **Col. Width:** 56 nonpareils. **Col. Depth:** 106 agate lines. **Key Personnel:** Dorothy A. Kelly, Business Mgr., dkz@umich.edu. **ISSN:** 0026-2234. **Subscription Rates:** $50 individuals; $60 out of country with $1 per subscription agency discount. **Remarks:** Advertising not accepted. **Online:** Westlaw; LEXIS-NEXIS. **URL:** http://www.law.umich.edu/pubs/journals/mlr. **Alt. Formats:** Microform.
Circ: ‡2,138

14849 Michigan Mathematical Journal
University of Michigan
525 E. University Phone: (248)647-4462
Ann Arbor, MI 48109-1109 Fax: (248)763-0938
Publisher E-mail: michigan.math.j@umich.edu

Scholarly journal covering research in mathematics. **Founded:** 1952. **Freq:** Triennial. **Trim Size:** 6 x 9. **Cols./Page:** 1. **Col. Width:** 4 1/2 inches. **Col. Depth:** 7 1/2 inches. **Key Personnel:** Gopal Prasad, Managing Editor; Suzanne Jackson, Editorial Asst. **ISSN:** 0026-2285. **Subscription Rates:** $100 individuals. **Remarks:** Advertising not accepted.
Circ: Paid 900

14850 Michigan Municipal Review
Michigan Municipal League
PO Box 1487 Phone: (734)662-3246
Ann Arbor, MI 48106-1487 Fax: (734)662-8083
Free: (800)653-2483
Publisher E-mail: league@mml.org

Magazine for the exchange of ideas and information between officials of Michigan's cities and villages. **Subtitle:** The Offical Magazine of the Michigan Municipal League. **Founded:** 1928. **Freq:** 10/year. **Print Method:** Offset. **Trim Size:** 8 1/2 x 11. **Cols./Page:** 3. **Col. Width:** 13 picas. **Col. Depth:** 57 picas. **Key Personnel:** Judi Lintott, Editor, jlintott@mnol.org; George D. Goodman, Publisher; Colleen Layton, Managing Editor; Jeanette Westhead, Graphic Designer; Carmen Tippett, New Subscriptions. **ISSN:** 0026-2331. **Subscription Rates:** $24; $3 single issue. **Remarks:** Accepts advertising.
Ad Rates: BW: $600 **Circ:** ‡11,300
4C: $2,350

14851 Michigan Quarterly Review
University of Michigan
3032 Rackham Bldg. Phone: (734)764-9265
Ann Arbor, MI 48109-1070
Publication E-mail: dorisk@umich.edu; michigan.quarterly.review@umich.edu

Journal publishing cultural and literary commentary and reviews, essays, memoirs, fiction, and poetry. **Founded:** 1962. **Freq:** Quarterly. **Print Method:** Offset. **Trim Size:** 6 x 9. **Cols./Page:** 1. **Col. Width:** 52 nonpareils. **Col. Depth:** 103 agate lines. **Key Personnel:** Laurence Goldstein, Editor. **ISSN:** 0026-2420. **Subscription Rates:** $18. **Remarks:** Accepts advertising.
Ad Rates: BW: $100 **Circ:** ‡1,400

14852 Planning for Higher Education
Society for College and Planning (SCUP)
4251 Plymouth Rd. Phone: (734)998-7832
Ann Arbor, MI 48105-2785 Fax: (734)998-6532

Magazine on higher education. **Freq:** Quarterly September, December, March, and June. **ISSN:** 0736-0983. **Subscription Rates:** $50 individuals; $62 Canada and Mexico; $68 elsewhere. **URL:** http://www.scup.org.

14853 Research News
University of Michigan
Division of Research Phone: (313)763-5587
Development & Administration Fax: (313)763-4053
3003 S State St.
Ann Arbor, MI 48109-1274
Publication E-mail: researchnews@umich.edu

Magazine about research developments in science, engineering, medicine, the arts, social sciences, and the humanities written for the non-specialist. **Founded:** 1948. **Freq:** 4/year. **Print Method:** Offset. **Trim Size:** 8 1/2 x 11. **Cols./Page:** 3. **Col. Width:** 14 1/2 picas. **Col. Depth:** 9 inches. **Key Personnel:** Suzanne Tainter, Editor. **ISSN:** 0041-9842. **Subscription Rates:** Free; $6 Canada & Mexico; $15 other countries. **Remarks:** Advertising not accepted. **URL:** http://www.drda.umich.edu/ovpr/researchnews/rn.html.
Circ: Controlled ‡8,000

14854 Tech Directions
Prakken Publications, Inc.
3970 Varsity Dr. Phone: (734)975-2800
PO Box 8623 Fax: (734)975-2787
Ann Arbor, MI 48107-8623
Free: (800)530-WORD
Publication E-mail: tdedit@techdirections.com
Publisher E-mail: publisher@cybezone-inc.com

Magazine covering industrial education, technology education, trade and industry, and vocational-technical education. Articles are geared for teacher and administrator use and reference from elementary school through postsecondary levels. **Subtitle:** Linking Education to Careers. **Founded:** 1941. **Freq:** 10/year. **Print Method:** Web offset. **Trim Size:** 8 x 10 7/8. **Cols./Page:** 3 and 2. **Col. Width:** 27 and 41 nonpareils. **Col. Depth:** 140 agate lines. **Key Personnel:** Tony Bowden, Managing Editor; George F. Kennedy, Publisher; Alice B. Klock, Advertising Mgr., tdadv@techdirections.com. **ISSN:** 1062-9351. **Subscription Rates:** Free to qualified subscribers; $30 individuals (U.S.). **Remarks:** Accepts advertising. **URL:** http://www.techdirections.com/. **Alt. Formats:** CD-ROM, University Microfilms, EBSCO Publishing; Microform; Mailing labels. **Formerly:** School Shop (1989); School Shop/Tech Directions (1992).
Ad Rates: BW: $4,185 **Circ:** Paid 279
4C: $5,490 Controlled 44,301
PCI: $215

14855 University of Michigan Museums of Art and Archaeology Bulletin
University of Michigan Museum of Art
434 S. State St. Phone: (734)647-3307
Ann Arbor, MI 48109-1390 Fax: (734)763-8976

Scholarly journal covering the collections of the University of Michigan museums of art and archaeology. **Founded:** 1978. **Freq:** Semiannual. **Print Method:** Offset. **Trim Size:** 7 1/2 x 10. **Key Personnel:** Margaret A. Lourie, Managing Editor. **ISSN:** 0076-8391. **Remarks:** Advertising not accepted.
Circ: (Not Reported)

14856 Media One
2505 S. Industrial Phone: (313)973-2266
PO Box 998 Fax: (313)973-0078
Ann Arbor, MI 48104

Owner: Columbia Cable of Michigan, at above address. **Founded:** 1972. **Key Personnel:** Ronald Harmon, Contact; Wayne Gambin, Operations Mgr.; Richard Allen, Contact; Laura Rodgers, Contact; Jim Bowen, Contact. **Cities Served:** subscribing households 64,600; 65 channels.

14857 WAAM-AM - 1600
4230 Packard Rd. Phone: (734)971-1600
Ann Arbor, MI 48108 Fax: (734)973-2916

Format: Talk; News; Middle-of-the-Road (MOR). **Networks:** NBC; Mutual Broadcasting System. **Owner:** Whitehall Broadcasting, at above address. **Founded:** 1947. **Formerly:** WHRV-AM (1961). **Operating Hours:** Continuous; 42% network, 58% local. **Key Personnel:** Catherine A. Kalman, General Mgr.; Chris Caris, News Dir.; Ken Kelly, Program Dir.; Phil Keren, Contact. **Local Programs:** *Ken Kelly Show* 4:00 pm - 6:00 pm Monday-Friday, Eric Brown; *Ted Heusel Show* 9:00 am - 12:00 noon Monday-Friday, Phil Keren; *Morning Show* 7:00 am - 9:00 am Monday-Friday, Phil Keren, Mailing contact. **Wattage:** 5000. **Ad Rates:** $14-33 for 30 seconds; $16-38 for 60 seconds.

14858 WBSX-TV - 31
3975 Varsity Dr. Phone: (313)973-7900
Ann Arbor, MI 48108 Fax: (313)973-7906

Format: Commercial TV. **Owner:** Blackstar Communications of Michigan, Inc., PO Box 2267, Ann Arbor, MI 48106. **Founded:** 1981. **Formerly:** WIHT-TV. **Operating Hours:** Continuous; 85% network, 15% local. **ADI:** Detroit, MI. **Key Personnel:** Christopher Webb, VP/Gen. Mgr.; Robert Thompson, Chief Engineer; Jerry Samons, Production Mgr. **Local Programs:** *Black Perspective* 7 a.m., Tyrone Bynum; *Spot Light* 8 a.m. Sunday, Chris Webb. **Wattage:** 1,222. **Ad Rates:** $25-150 for 30 seconds.

14859 WIQB-FM - 102.9
PO Box 300 Phone: (313)930-0103
Ann Arbor, MI 48106 Fax: (313)930-9500
Free: (800)762-5103
E-mail: wiqb@branch.com

Format: Album-Oriented Rock (AOR). **Networks:** Westwood One Radio. **Founded:** 1962. **Operating Hours:** Continuous; 100% local. **ADI:** Detroit, MI. **Key Personnel:** John Vance, Operations Dir.; Jennifer Sabo, News/Promotions Dir.; Dave Paulus, General Mgr.; Janet Jablonski, General Sales Mgr. **Wattage:** 50,000. **Ad Rates:** $50-85 per unit. **URL:** http://wiqb.branch.com.

14860 WQKL-FM - 107.1
24 Frank Lloyd Wright Phone: (313)930-0107
Box 300 Fax: (313)741-1071
Ann Arbor, MI 48106
E-mail: wiqb@branch.com

Format: Oldies. **Owner:** Arbor Radio LP, at above address. **Founded:** 1988. **Formerly:** WAMX-FM. **Operating Hours:** Continuous; 5% network, 95% local. **ADI:** Lansing (Ann Arbor), MI. **Key Personnel:** Dave Paulus, General Mgr.; John Vance, Program Dir.; Sheila Croce, Business Mgr.; Tom Peterson, Chief Engineer; Janet Jablonski, Sales Mgr.; Bob Kolan, Sales Mgr. **Wattage:** 3000. **Ad Rates:** $60 for 30 seconds; $75 for 60 seconds. **URL:** http://wiqb.branch.com.

14861 WTKA-AM - 1050
24 Frank Lloyd Wright Dr. Phone: (313)930-0107
PO Box 300 Fax: (313)741-1071
Ann Arbor, MI 48106
E-mail: wiqb@branch.com

Format: Talk; News; Sports. **Networks:** ABC. **Founded:** 1947. **Formerly:** WPAG-AM (1983); WPZA-AM. **Operating Hours:** Continuous; 20% network, 80% local. **ADI:** Lansing (Ann Arbor), MI. **Key Personnel:** Dave Paulus, General Mgr.; John Vance, Program Dir.; Ellen Mohan, News Dir.; Doug Karsch, Sports Dir.; Janet Jablonski, Sales Mgr. **Local Programs:** *Michigan Farm Radio Network*, Bob Driscoll, (313)439-7749. **Wattage:** 10,000. **Ad Rates:** $25-30 for 30 seconds; $35-40 for 60 seconds. **URL:** http://wiqb.branch.com.

14862 WUOM-FM - 91.7
5000 LSA Bldg. Phone: (313)764-9210
Ann Arbor, MI 48109
E-mail: annat@umich.edu

Format: Public Radio; Classical; News; Jazz; Information. **Networks:** National Public Radio (NPR); AP; American Public Radio (APR). **Founded:** 1948. **Operating Hours:** Continuous. **ADI:** Lansing (Ann Arbor), MI. **Key Personnel:** Donovan Reynolds, Station Mgr.; Joan Siefert Rose, Program Dir.; Shelley MacMillan, Development/Mktg. Director; Steve Graham, Chief Engineer; Joan Siefert Rose, News Dir.; Harriet Teller, Promotions Dir. **Local Programs:** *Desert Island Discs*, Joel Seguine; *4:30 Report*, Bob Whitman; *Today's World*, Bob Whitman. **Wattage:** 93,000. **Ad Rates:** Noncommercial. **URL:** http://www.umich.edu/wuom.

WVGR-FM - See Grand Rapids

ARMADA

14863 Armada Times
PO Box 915 Phone: (313)784-5551
Armada, MI 48005-0915 Fax: (313)784-8710

Community newpaper. **Founded:** 1886. **Freq:** Weekly (Wed.). **Print Method:** Letterpress and offset. **Cols./Page:** 5. **Col. Width:** 11 picas. **Col. Depth:** 14 inches. **Key Personnel:** James Mitchell, Editor. **USPS:** 032-200. **Subscription Rates:** $15 individuals. **Remarks:** Accepts advertising.
Ad Rates: BW: $250 **Circ:** 2,400
4C: $585
PCI: $4

ATLANTA

14864 Montmorency County Tribune
PO Box 186 Phone: (517)785-4214
Atlanta, MI 49709 Fax: (517)785-3118

Community newspaper. **Founded:** 1886. **Freq:** Weekly (Wed.). **Print Method:** Offset. **Trim Size:** 11 1/2 x 17. **Cols./Page:** 6. **Col. Width:** 19 nonpareils. **Col. Depth:** 224 agate lines. **Key Personnel:** Thomas C. Young, Editor and Publisher. **Subscription Rates:** $19. **Remarks:** Accepts advertising.
Ad Rates: GLR: $0.40 **Circ:** ‡5,350
BW: $475.20
SAU: $6.86
PCI: $5.86

AUBURN HILLS

14865 WAHS-FM - 89.5
2800 Waukegan Phone: (248)852-4278
Auburn Hills, MI 48326 Fax: (248)852-0595

Format: Educational. **Owner:** Avondale School District, at above address. **Founded:** 1976. **Operating Hours:** 6:30 a.m.-9:30 p.m. **ADI:** Detroit, MI. **Key Personnel:** Toni Shoemaker, Faculty Advisor, msshoe@aol.com. **Wattage:** 100. **Ad Rates:** Noncommercial.

BAD AXE

14866 Huron Daily Tribune
211 N. Heisterman St. Phone: (517)269-6461
Bad Axe, MI 48413 Fax: (517)269-9893
Free: (800)322-1184

General newspaper. **Founded:** 1875. **Freq:** Daily (eve.). **Print Method:** Offset. **Cols./Page:** 6. **Col. Width:** 22 nonpareils. **Col. Depth:** 301 agate lines. **Key Personnel:** Sandra J. Sutton, Editor; Allen Wamsley, Publisher. **Subscription Rates:** $102 per year. **Remarks:** Accepts advertising. **URL:** http://www.info.com.
Ad Rates: BW: $844.95 **Circ:** Mon.-Fri. ★**7,691**
4C: $1,069.95 Sun. ★**8,079**
PCI: $6.55

14867 WLEW-AM - 1340
935 S. Van Dyke Rd. Phone: (517)269-9931
Bad Axe, MI 48413 Fax: (517)269-7702

Format: Contemporary Country. **Networks:** CNN Radio. **Owner:** Thumb Broadcasting, Inc., at above address. **Founded:** 1950. **Operating Hours:** Continuous; 100% local. **ADI:** Flint-Saginaw-Bay City, MI. **Key Personnel:** Richard Aymen, President/Gen. Mgr.; Tom Meyer, Station Mgr.; Matt Aymen, Sales Mgr./V.P.; Jack Thomas, Music Dir.; Craig Routzhn, News Dir.; Max Koch, Continuity Dir. **Local Programs:** *Ladies Line*, Matt Aymen; *Polka Connection*, Matt Aymen; *What Do You Think?*, Matt Aymen. **Wattage:** 1000. **Ad Rates:** $14.80-14 for 30 seconds; $18.50 for 60 seconds. Combined advertising rates available with WLEW-FM.

14868 WLEW-FM - 102.1
935 S. Van Dyke Rd. Phone: (517)269-9931
Bad Axe, MI 48413 Fax: (517)269-7702

Format: Adult Contemporary; Classic Rock. **Networks:** CNN Radio. **Owner:** Thumb Broadcasting, Inc., at above address. **Founded:** 1950. **Operating Hours:** Continuous; 100% local. **ADI:** Flint-Saginaw-Bay City, MI. **Key Personnel:** Richard A. Aymen, President/Gen. Mgr.; Tom Meyer, Station Mgr.; Matt Aymen, VP/Sales Mgr.; Jack Thomas, Music Dir.; Craig Routhzhn, News Dir.; Max Koch, Operations Mgr. **Local Programs:** *Jack Thomas - J.T. in the Mid-Morning*, Matt Aymen, Mailing contact; *Max Koch - Drive Morning*, Matt Aymen, Mailing contact; *Max in the Morning*, Matt Aymen, Mailing contact. **Wattage:** 50,000. **Ad Rates:** $17 for 30 seconds; $21.20 for 60 seconds.

BALDWIN

14869 Lake County Star
The Pioneer Group
851 Michigan Phone: (616)745-4635
PO Box 399 Fax: (616)745-7733
Baldwin, MI 49304
Shopping guide. **Freq:** Weekly (Thurs.). **Print Method:** Offset. **Cols./Page:** 7. **Col. Width:** 1 3/8 inches. **Col. Depth:** 16 inches. **Key Personnel:** John A. Batdorff, Publisher. **Remarks:** Combined advertising rates available with other Pioneer Group newspapers.
Ad Rates: SAU: $7.75 **Circ:** Free ‡4,154

BATTLE CREEK

14870 Battle Creek Enquirer
Gannett Co., Inc.
155 W. Van Buren St. Phone: (616)964-0299
Battle Creek, MI 49017-3093 Fax: (616)964-8242

General newspaper. **Founded:** 1900. **Freq:** Daily (eve.), Sat. and Sun. (morn.). **Print Method:** Urbanite offset press. **Trim Size:** 13 x 21 1/4. **Cols./Page:** 6. **Col. Width:** 25 nonpareils. **Col. Depth:** 308 agate lines. **Key Personnel:** Ellen Leifeld, Exec. Editor; R.B. Miller, Jr., Contact; Jim Barnes, Publisher. **Subscription Rates:** $143 (carrier); $156 (motor carrier); $146 out of state; $1.75 single issue daily; $2.50 single issue Sun. **Remarks:** Accepts advertising.
Ad Rates: GLR: $20.35 **Circ:** Mon.-Sat. ★**26,367**
BW: $252 Sun. ★**35,579**
4C: $545
SAU: $27

14871 Battle Creek Shopper News
J-Ad Corp.
1361 E. Columbia Ave. Phone: (616)965-3955
Battle Creek, MI 49014 Fax: (616)968-8586
Publisher E-mail: j-ad@voyager.com

Community newspaper (tabloid). **Founded:** Oct. 16, 1967. **Freq:** Weekly (Thurs.). **Print Method:** Offset. **Trim Size:** 11 3/8 x 18. **Cols./Page:** 6. **Col. Width:** 10 picas. **Col. Depth:** 16 inches. **Key Personnel:** Joyce Ryan, Editor; Fred Jacobs, Publisher. **Subscription Rates:** Free; $21 by mail. **Remarks:** Accepts advertising. **Formerly:** Beacon Preview.
Ad Rates: GLR: $.43 **Circ:** Free 50,855
BW: $590.40
4C: $7.40
PCI: $7.40

14872 Children's Literature Association Quarterly
Children's Literature Association
PO Box 138 Phone: (616)965-8180
Battle Creek, MI 49016 Fax: (616)965-3568
Publisher E-mail: chla@mlc.lib.mi.us

Children's literature scholarly journal. **Founded:** 1982. **Freq:** Quarterly. **Print Method:** Offset. **Cols./Page:** 2. **Col. Width:** 42 nonpareils. **Col. Depth:** 135 agate lines. **Key Personnel:** Marilynn Olson, Editor, mo03@swt.edu. **ISSN:** 0885-0429. **Subscription Rates:** $70 individuals; $110 institutions.
Ad Rates: BW: $250 **Circ:** ‡750

14873 WBCK-AM - 930
390 Golden Ave. Phone: (616)963-5555
Battle Creek, MI 49015 Fax: (616)963-5185

Format: News; Talk; Information. **Networks:** ABC. **Owner:** Central Star Broadcasting, 425 2nd St. SE., Ste. 450, Cedar Rapids, IA 52401. **Founded:** 1948. **Operating Hours:** Continuous. **ADI:** Grand Rapids-Kalamazoo-Battle Creek, MI. **Key Personnel:** Tom McHale, News Dir.; Bill Gray, Sports Dir.; Jack McDevitt, General Mgr.; Kathy Wagman, General Sales Mgr.; Tim Collins, Operations Mgr., tcollins@battlecreekradio.com. **Local Programs:** *Dave Eddy Morning Show*, Dave Eddy, (616)963-5555, Fax (616)963-5185; *Morning News*, Tom McHale, (616)963-6397, Fax (616)963-5185; *Saturday Morning Show*, Chris Simmons, (616)963-5555, Fax (616)963-5185. **Wattage:** 5000/1000. **Ad Rates:** $8-34 for 30 seconds; $6-40 for 60 seconds. **URL:** http://www.battlecreekradio.com.

14874 WBXX-FM - 95.3
390 Golden Ave. Phone: (616)963-5555
Battle Creek, MI 49015 Fax: (616)963-5185

Format: Adult Contemporary. **Owner:** Central Star Broadcasting, 425 2nd St. SE, Ste. 450, Cedar Rapids, IA 52401. **Founded:** 1976. **Formerly:** WMJC-FM. **Operating Hours:** Continuous. **ADI:** Grand Rapids-Kalamazoo-Battle Creek, MI. **Key Personnel:** Tim Collins, Operations Mgr., tcollins@battlecreekradio.com; Kathy Wagaman, Sales Mgr.; Jack McDevitt, General Mgr.; John Patrick, Program Dir. **Wattage:** 3000.

14875 WNWN-FM - 98.5
25 W. Michigan Ave., 4th Fl. Phone: (616)968-1991
Battle Creek, MI 49017 Fax: (616)968-1881
E-mail: wnwn@net-link.net

Format: Contemporary Country. **Networks:** ABC. **Owner:** Midwest Radio Group, at above address. **Founded:** 1949. **Operating Hours:** Continuous. **ADI:** Grand Rapids-Kalamazoo-Battle Creek, MI. **Key Personnel:** Peter Tanz, General Mgr.; P.J. Lacey, Program Dir.; Jim Whelan, News Dir.; Cindy Ireland, Sales Mgr. **Wattage:** 50,000. **Ad Rates:** $45-80 for 60 seconds. Combined advertising rates available with WFAT-FM.

14876 WOLY-AM - 1500
15074 6 1/2 Mile Rd. Phone: (616)965-1515
Battle Creek, MI 49017 Fax: (616)965-1315

Format: Religious. **Networks:** USA Radio. **Founded:** 1963. **Formerly:** WVOC-AM (1982). **Operating Hours:** Sunrise-sunset. **ADI:** Grand Rapids-Kalamazoo-Battle Creek, MI. **Key Personnel:** Larry Langman, General Mgr.; Jim Elsman, President/Owner. **Wattage:** 1000. **Ad Rates:** $8 for 30 seconds; $12 for 60 seconds.

14877 WOTV-TV - 41
5200 W. Dickman Rd., Box 1616 Phone: (616)968-9341
Battle Creek, MI 49016 Fax: (616)966-6837
E-mail: wotv@wotv.com

Format: Commercial TV. **Networks:** ABC. **Owner:** Channel 41, Inc., at above address. **Founded:** 1971. **Formerly:** WUHQ-TV. **Operating Hours:** 5 a.m.-2 a.m. **ADI:** Grand Rapids-Kalamazoo-Battle Creek, MI. **Key Personnel:** Jerry P. Colvin, Contact, phone (616)966-6804, fax (616)966-6819. **Wattage:** 5,000,000. **Ad Rates:** Advertising accepted; rates available upon request.

14878 WRCC-AM - 1400
390 Golden Ave. Phone: (616)963-5555
Battle Creek, MI 49015 Fax: (616)963-5185

Networks: ABC. **Owner:** Central Star Broadcasting, 425 2nd St. SE, Ste. 450, Cedar Rapids, IA 52401. **Founded:** 1926. **Formerly:** WELL-AM (1996); WWKN-AM. **Operating Hours:** Continuous. **ADI:** Grand Rapids-Kalamazoo-Battle Creek, MI. **Key Personnel:** Tim Collins, Operations Mgr., tcollins@battlecreekradio.com; Jack McDevitt, General Mgr.; Kathy Wagaman, General Sales Mgr. **Wattage:** 1000.

14879 WWKN-FM - 104.9
390 Golden Ave. Phone: (616)963-5555
Battle Creek, MI 49015 Fax: (616)963-5185

Format: Oldies. **Networks:** ABC. **Owner:** Central Star Broadcasting, 425 2nd St. SE. Ste. 450, Cedar Rapids, IA 52401. **Founded:** 1969. **Formerly:** WELL-FM (1996); WRCC-FM. **Operating Hours:** Continuous. **ADI:** Grand Rapids-Kalamazoo-Battle Creek, MI. **Key Personnel:** Jack McDevitt, General Mgr.; Dan McClintock, Program Dir.; Kathy Wagaman, General Sales Mgr.; Tim Collins, Operations Dir., tcollins@battlecreekradio.com. **Wattage:** 6000.

BAY CITY

14880 The Bay City Times
311 5th St. Phone: (517)894-9630
Bay City, MI 48708 Fax: (517)893-0649

General newspaper. **Founded:** 1873. **Freq:** Daily (eve.), Sat. and Sun. (morn.). **Print Method:** Letterpress. **Cols./Page:** 6. **Col. Width:** 24 nonpareils. **Col. Depth:** 298 agate lines. **Key Personnel:** Paul M. Keep, Editor, keepp@bc-times.com; C. Kevin Dykema, Publisher; Archie Duncan, Advertising Mgr. **Subscription Rates:** $137 mail; $135 motor route. **Remarks:** Accepts advertising.
Ad Rates: GLR: $236 **Circ:** Mon.-Sat. ★**37,225**
BW: $3,487.13 Sun. ★**48,662**
4C: $4,145.97
PCI: $24.82

14881 Valley Farmer
905 S. Henry Phone: (517)893-6507
Bay City, MI 48706
Agricultural newspaper with classified and auction listings. **Founded:** 1929. **Freq:** Weekly (Thurs.). **Print Method:** Offset. **Trim Size:** 11 1/2 x 16 in. **Cols./Page:** 6. **Col. Width:** 18 nonpareils. **Col. Depth:** 210 agate lines. **Key Personnel:** Mark Schanhals, Editor; David B. Hebert, Publisher. **Subscription Rates:** $18 individuals. **Remarks:** Accepts advertising. **Feature Editors:** Jeff Hebert, *Sports*.
Ad Rates: GLR: $.50 **Circ:** ‡1,900
BW: $275
SAU: $6.10
PCI: $4.65

14882 WCHW-FM - 91.3
1624 Columbus Ave. Phone: (517)892-1741
Bay City, MI 48706 Fax: (517)892-7946
E-mail: wchw@mailexcite.com

Format: Album-Oriented Rock (AOR). **Founded:** 1973. **Operating Hours:** 8:00 am - 5:00 pm; Mon. - Fri. **ADI:** Flint-Saginaw-Bay City, MI. **Key Personnel:** Bryan Bishop, Program Dir./Station Mgr., bucksweep@hotmail.com. **Wattage:** 100. **Ad Rates:** Noncommercial.

BEAR LAKE

14883 WZTU-FM - 100.1
12013 West St.
Bear Lake, MI 49614
E-mail: wztu@hotmail.com

Format: Alternative/New Music/Progressive. **Networks:** Westwood One Radio. **Owner:** Roger L. Hoppe II, at above address. **Founded:** 1987. **Formerly:** WRQT-FM (1991). **Operating Hours:** Continuous. **ADI:** Traverse City-Cadillac, MI. **Key Personnel:** Jayna R. Childs, Operations Mgr.; Marie Osborn, Production Dir. **Wattage:** 3000. **Ad Rates:** $7-7.50 for 30 seconds; $9-11 for 60 seconds.

BELLAIRE

14884 Antrim County News
Up North Publications, Inc.
PO Box 337 Phone: (616)533-8523
Bellaire, MI 49615
Community newspaper. **Founded:** 1946. **Freq:** Weekly (Wed.). **Print Method:** Offset. **Trim Size:** 13 1/4 x 21. **Cols./Page:** 6. **Col. Width:** 2 1/16 inches. **Col. Depth:** 21 inches. **Key Personnel:** Jeffrey Hallburg, Publisher. **Subscription Rates:** $22; $25 out of area. **Remarks:** Accepts advertising.
Ad Rates: GLR: $0.45 **Circ:** ‡5,600
BW: $793.80
4C: $953.80
SAU: $6.30
PCI: $6.30

BELLEVILLE

14885 The Belleville Enterprise
Michigan Community Newspapers
35540 Michigan Ave. Phone: (313)729-4000
PO Box 578 Fax: (313)729-6880
Wayne, MI 48184
Community newspaper. **Founded:** 1886. **Freq:** Weekly (Thurs.). **Print Method:** Offset. **Cols./Page:** 6. **Col. Width:** 12 picas. **Col. Depth:** 21 1/2 inches. **Key Personnel:** Mike Wilcox, Publisher; Kathy Wilcox, Owner; Joan Dyer-Zinner, General Mgr.; Rita Bedell, Classified Manager; Ron Spielman, Advertising Mgr.; Justin Wilcox, Circulation Mgr. **Subscription Rates:** $48. **Remarks:** Accepts advertising.
Ad Rates: SAU: $4.68 **Circ:** Paid 1,110
Non-paid 2,683

BENTON HARBOR

14886 Lake Michigan Journal
Lake Michigan College
2755 E. Napier Ave. Phone: (616)927-3571
Benton Harbor, MI 49022-1899 Fax: (616)927-4491

Collegiate newspaper. **Founded:** 1950. **Freq:** Weekly. **Print Method:** Offset. **Cols./Page:** 6. **Col. Width:** 18 nonpareils. **Col. Depth:** 206 agate lines. **Subscription Rates:** $6.50. **Remarks:** Accepts advertising.
Ad Rates: BW: $378 **Circ:** (Not Reported)

14887 Twin City Trade Lines Shopper's Guide
Dickson Media, Inc.
115 Main St. Phone: (616)461-6941
Eau Claire, MI 49111 Fax: (616)461-6816

Shopper. **Founded:** 1969. **Freq:** Weekly (Mon.). **Print Method:** Offset. **Trim Size:** 11 x 17. **Cols./Page:** 6. **Col. Width:** 20

nonpareils. **Col. Depth:** 225 agate lines. **Key Personnel:** Lee Borkowski, Publisher. **Remarks:** Accepts advertising.
Ad Rates: GLR: $.35 **Circ:** Free 32,386
BW: $60
PCI: $4.90

14888 Consolidated Cablevision
206 W. Main St. Phone: (616)926-1197
Benton Harbor, MI 49022 Fax: (616)926-2582

Owner: Joppa Assoc; LP, 288 Clayton St. No. 302, Denver, CO 80206, (303)355-4300. **Key Personnel:** Steve Williams, General Mgr. **Cities Served:** subscribing households 8,700; 42 channels; 1 community access channel.

14889 WHFB-AM - 1060
2100 Fairplain Ave. Phone: (616)925-9300
PO Box 608 Fax: (616)925-0065
Benton Harbor, MI 49022

Format: Classic Rock. **Networks:** CNN Radio. **Founded:** 1947. **Operating Hours:** Continuous. **ADI:** South Bend-Elkhart, IN. **Key Personnel:** Tom Weidle, General Mgr.; Bill Stanley, Operations Dir.; Lindy Bartholmey, Sales Mgr. **Local Programs:** *Academic Challenge*; *Coaches Corner*, *For the Record*. **Wattage:** 5000. **Ad Rates:** $15-25 for 30 seconds; $15-25 for 60 seconds. Combined advertising rates available with WHFB-FM.

14890 WHFB-FM - 99.9
2100 Fairplane Ave. Phone: (616)925-9300
Benton Harbor, MI 49022 Fax: (616)925-0065

Format: Adult Contemporary. **Networks:** CNN Radio. **Founded:** 1947. **Operating Hours:** Continuous. **Key Personnel:** Tom Weidle, President/Gen. Mgr.; Dan Mason, Program Dir.; Lindy Bartholmey, Local Sales Mgr.; Ed Skonie, News Dir.; Michele Stone, Promotions Dir. **Wattage:** 50,000. **Ad Rates:** $27-41 per unit.

BERRIEN SPRINGS

14891 The Journal Era
Perry Publications
PO Box 98 Phone: (616)473-5421
Berrien Springs, MI 49103-0098 Fax: (616)471-1362

Community newspaper. **Founded:** 1874. **Freq:** Weekly (Wed.). **Print Method:** Offset. **Cols./Page:** 5. **Col. Width:** 23 nonpareils. **Col. Depth:** 224 agate lines. **Key Personnel:** D. Michael Perry, Publisher. **Subscription Rates:** $15; $18 out of county; $75 other countries. **Remarks:** Accepts advertising.
Ad Rates: BW: $260 **Circ:** ‡3,800
SAU: $3.64
PCI: $3.25

14892 Lake Union Herald
Lake Union Conference of Seventh-Day Adventists
PO Box C Phone: (616)473-8242
Berrien Springs, MI 49103 Fax: (616)473-8209

Religious magazine containing news for members of Seventh-Day Adventist Church in the Great Lakes area. **Founded:** 1908. **Freq:** Monthly. **Print Method:** Offset. **Trim Size:** 8 x 10 5/8. **Cols./Page:** 3. **Col. Width:** 2 1/4 inches. **Col. Depth:** 9 5/8 inches. **Key Personnel:** Richard Dower, Editor; Nadine Dower, Managing Editor. **ISSN:** 0194-908X. **Subscription Rates:** $50 single issue; $7.50 individuals. **Remarks:** Accepts advertising members only.
Ad Rates: BW: $633 **Circ:** Paid 28,500
4C: $1,570 Non-paid 949
PCI: $30

14893 Student Movement
Andrews University Press
213 Info Services Bldg. Phone: (616)471-6915
Berrien Springs, MI 49104-1700 Fax: (616)471-6224
Publication E-mail: smeditor@andrews.edu
Publisher E-mail: aupress@andrews.edu

Collegiate newspaper. **Founded:** 1915. **Freq:** Weekly (Wed.). **Print Method:** Offset. **Trim Size:** 11 x 17. **Cols./Page:** 5. **Col. Depth:** 210 agate lines. **Key Personnel:** Marshal Horman, Advertising Mgr.; Shereen Devadas, Editor. **Subscription Rates:** Free. **Remarks:** Accepts advertising.
Ad Rates: BW: $225 **Circ:** Free 2,500

BEULAH

14894 Ad-Visor
PO Box 797 Phone: (616)882-9613
Beulah, MI 49617 Fax: (616)882-9615

Community newspaper (tabloid). **Founded:** 1967. **Freq:** Weekly (Mon.). **Print Method:** Offset. **Cols./Page:** 6. **Col. Width:** 20 nonpareils. **Col. Depth:** 224 agate lines. **Key Personnel:** Deb Hawkins, Editor; Frank Noverr, Publisher. **Subscription Rates:** $20. **Remarks:** Accepts advertising.
Ad Rates: PCI: $4.78 **Circ:** 8,500

BIG RAPIDS

14895 Ferris State Torch
Ferris State University
ASC 3080 Phone: (616)592-5946
820 Campus Dr.
Big Rapids, MI 49307
Collegiate newspaper. **Founded:** 1931. **Freq:** Weekly. **Print Method:** Offset. **Cols./Page:** 5. **Col. Width:** 23 nonpareils. **Col. Depth:** 196 agate lines. **Key Personnel:** Julia Quillan, Advertising Mgr., j-a-quillan@ferris.edu. **Subscription Rates:** Free; $45 (mail). **Remarks:** Accepts advertising.
Ad Rates: PCI: $5 0 **Circ:** Free ‡6,000

14896 Manistee County Pioneer Press
The Pioneer Group
502 N. State St. Phone: (616)796-4831
Big Rapids, MI 49307-1469 Fax: (616)796-1152
Free: (800)968-1114

Community newspaper. **Founded:** 1888. **Freq:** Weekly (Wed.). **Print Method:** Offset. **Cols./Page:** 5. **Col. Width:** 12.5 picas. **Col. Depth:** 21 inches. **Key Personnel:** Pauline J. Jaquish, Editor; John A. Batdorff, Publisher. **USPS:** 327-900. **Subscription Rates:** $20 individuals; $26 out of area; $36 out of state. **Remarks:** Color advertising accepted; rates available upon request.
Ad Rates: BW: $360 **Circ:** ‡1,500
4C: $510
SAU: $4.50

14897 Nova Review
Nova Media Inc.
1724 N. State St. Phone: (616)796-4637
Big Rapids, MI 49307-9073
Publication E-mail: trund@nov.com
Publisher E-mail: trund@nov.com

Journal publishing literary works and criticism, art and health issues especially regarding drug culture plus rehabilitation techniques. **Founded:** Jan. 1995. **Freq:** Quarterly. **Print Method:** Offset and web. **Cols./Page:** 5. **Col. Width:** 1 7/8 inches. **Col. Depth:** 11 inches. **Key Personnel:** Thomas J. Rundquist, Editor, trund@nov.com; Karen Wilson, Editor. **ISSN:** 1079-8374. **Subscription Rates:** $20 individuals; $5 single issue. **Remarks:** Accepts advertising. **URL:** http://www.nov.com.
Ad Rates: BW: $100 **Circ:** Paid 100
4C: $400 Non-paid 12,000
PCI: $8.35

14898 The Pioneer
The Pioneer Group
502 N. State St. Phone: (616)796-4831
Big Rapids, MI 49307-1469 Fax: (616)796-1152
Free: (800)968-1114

General newspaper. **Founded:** Apr. 17, 1862. **Freq:** Mon.-Sat. (morn.). **Print Method:** Offset. **Trim Size:** 14 x 22 3/4. **Cols./Page:** 9. **Col. Width:** 21 nonpareils. **Col. Depth:** 399 agate lines. **Key Personnel:** Judy Hale, Editor; John A. Batdorff, Publisher; John A. Batdorff II, C.O.O.; Denise Classen, Advertising Mgr. **ISSN:** 8750-5533. **Subscription Rates:** $80 individuals. **Remarks:** Accepts advertising.
Ad Rates: SAU: $9.35 **Circ:** Paid 5,859
PCI: $5.35 Free 24

14899 Tri-County Shoppers Guide
The Pioneer Group
502 N. State St. Phone: (616)796-4831
Big Rapids, MI 49307-1469 Fax: (616)796-1152
Free: (800)968-1114

Shopper. **Founded:** 1955. **Freq:** Weekly (Mon.). **Print Method:** Offset. **Trim Size:** 10 1/16 x 16. **Cols./Page:** 7. **Col. Width:** 16 nonpareils. **Col. Depth:** 224 agate lines. **Key Personnel:** John A. Batdorff, Publisher; John A. Batdorff II, C.O.O.; Denise Clasen, Advertising Mgr. **Remarks:** Accepts advertising.
Ad Rates: GLR: $9.90 **Circ:** Free ‡16,658
BW: $95
PCI: $5.55

14900 WBRN-AM - 1460
13574 Northland Dr. Phone: (616)796-7684
PO Box 1158
Big Rapids, MI 49307
E-mail: wbrn@wbrn.com

Format: Adult Contemporary; Oldies; Classic Rock. **Simulcasts:** WBRN-FM. **Networks:** UPI. **Owner:** RH Communications, Inc., at above address. **Founded:** 1953. **Operating Hours:** Continuous. **Key Personnel:** Robert J. Hampson, Jr., President; Monte D. Johnson, Operations Mgr.; William Beckwith, Program Dir.; Robert Willson, Chief Engineer. **Wattage:** 5000. **Ad Rates:** $13.60 for 30 seconds; $17 for 60 seconds.

14901 WBRN-FM - 100.9
13574 Northland Dr. Phone: (616)796-7684
PO Box 1158 Fax: (616)796-6227
Big Rapids, MI 49307
E-mail: wbrn@wbrn.com

Format: Adult Contemporary; Oldies; Classic Rock. **Simulcasts:** WBRN-AM. **Networks:** UPI. **Owner:** RH Communications, Inc., at above address. **Founded:** 1964. **Operating Hours:** Continuous; 100% local. **Key Personnel:** Robert J. Hampson, Jr., President; Monte D. Johnson, Operations Mgr.; William Beckwith, Program Dir.; Robert Willison, Chief Engineer. **Local Programs:** *News and Focus*, John Smith, News Dir. **Wattage:** 6000. **Ad Rates:** $13.60 for 30 seconds; $17 for 60 seconds.

BINGHAM FARMS

14902 Michigan Natural Resources Magazine
Kolka and Robb
30600 Telegraph Rd., Ste 1255 Phone: (810)642-9580
Bingham Farms, MI 48025-4531 Fax: (810)642-5290

Publication focusing on environmental education, wildlife, and outdoor recreation. **Founded:** 1931. **Freq:** Bimonthly. **Print Method:** Web Offset. **Trim Size:** 8 3/8 x 10 7/8. **Cols./Page:** 2. **Col. Width:** 27 nonpareils. **Col. Depth:** 140 agate lines. **Key Personnel:** Richard Morscheck, Editor; Vicki Robb, Publisher. **ISSN:** 0275-8180. **Subscription Rates:** $12 individuals. **URL:** http//www.dnr.state.mi.us.
Ad Rates: BW: $2,800 **Circ:** Paid 67,459
4C: $4,000

BIRMINGHAM

14903 Balance
Balance Publishing, Inc.
200 Elm St., Ste. 200 Phone: (810)645-9207
Birmingham, MI 48009 Fax: (810)642-7849
Free: (800)287-8888
Publication E-mail: balancemag@aol.com

Magazine focusing on fitness for men and women. **Subtitle:** A Lifetime of Fitness for Men & Women. **Founded:** Aug. 1996. **Print Method:** Web offset. **Trim Size:** 8 1/8 x 10 7/8. **Cols./Page:** 3. **Col. Width:** 2 1/4 inches. **Col. Depth:** 10 1/8 inches. **Key Personnel:** Kim Oberlin, Editor; Julie Becker, Assistant Editor/Circulation Mgr. **Subscription Rates:** $12.90 individuals; $23.40 two years; $2.95 single issue; $17.70 one year. **Remarks:** Accepts advertising.
Ad Rates: BW: $1,952 **Circ:** (Not Reported)
4C: $2,733

14904 Lightworks
Lightworks Magazine, Inc.
Box 1202 Phone: (248)626-8026
Birmingham, MI 48012-1202 Fax: (248)737-0046

Magazine covering new and experimental arts forms. **Subtitle:** Illuminating New and Experimental Art. **Founded:** 1975. **Freq:** Irregular. **Print Method:** Sheetfed offset. **Trim Size:** 8 1/2 x 11. **Key Personnel:** Charlton Burch, Editor & Designer; Andrea D. Martin, Business Mgr. **ISSN:** 0161-4223. **Remarks:** Advertising not accepted.
Circ: Combined 2,000

14905 Northeast Detroiter Harper Woods Herald
2648 Dorchester Phone: (248)649-0749
Birmingham, MI 48009
Community newspaper. **Founded:** May 1946. **Freq:** Weekly (Thurs.). **Print Method:** Offset. **Trim Size:** 14 1/2 x 22 1/2. **Cols./Page:** 8. **Col. Width:** 19 nonpareils. **Col. Depth:** 301 agate lines. **Key Personnel:** Lloyd Saulter, Editor and Publisher; Kevin Saulter, Advertising Mgr. **Subscription Rates:** $6; $8 out of state. **Remarks:** Accepts advertising.
Ad Rates: PCI: $6 **Circ:** ‡12,604

BLISSFIELD

14906 The Advana
River Raisin Publications, Inc.
121 Newspaper St. Phone: (517)486-4290
Blissfield, MI 49228 Fax: (517)486-2400

Community newspaper. **Founded:** Mar. 1874. **Freq:** Weekly (Wed.). **Print Method:** Offset. **Trim Size:** 11 x 17. **Cols./Page:** 6 and 8. **Col. Width:** 1 5/8 inches. **Col. Depth:** 16 inches. **Key Personnel:** Marcia Loader, Owner/Publisher, phone (517)486-2400, fax (517)486-4675; Doug Goodnough, Editor, phone (517)486-2400, fax (517)486-4675. **Subscrip-**

tion Rates: $20 individuals; $30 out of area. **Remarks:** Accepts advertising. **Formerly:** Blissfield Advance.
Ad Rates: BW: $350.80 **Circ:** Paid 2,197
SAU: $5.80 Free 134
PCI: $6.46

BLOOMFIELD

14907 CAM Magazine
Construction Association of Michigan
1625 S. Woodward Phone: (248)972-1000
PO Box 3204 Fax: (248)972-1001
Bloomfield, MI 48302-3204
Publisher E-mail: marketing@cam-online.com

Magazine featuring construction industry trends and information. **Subtitle:** The Voice of the Construction Industry. **Founded:** 1980. **Freq:** Monthly. **Print Method:** Sheetfed offset. **Trim Size:** 8 1/2 x 11. **Cols./Page:** 3. **Col. Width:** 14 picas. **Col. Depth:** 9 1/2 inches. **Key Personnel:** Phyllis Brooks, Editor; Mary Kremposky, Assoc. Editor; Amanda Tackett, Adv. Senior Account Exec./Contact; Michael Lawson, Assoc. Editor; Bob Harley, Acct. Exec. **ISSN:** 0883-7880. **Subscription Rates:** $36; $20 members; $3 single issue.
Ad Rates: BW: $990 **Circ:** Paid 4,125
4C: $1,650 Non-paid 350

BLOOMFIELD HILLS

14908 Roeper Review
Roeper School
PO Box 329 Phone: (248)203-7321
Bloomfield Hills, MI 48303 Fax: (248)203-7350

Journal focussing on issues relating to the education of gifted and talented children. Articles are written by teachers, scholars and students. **Subtitle:** A Journal on Gifted Child Education. **Founded:** Aug. 1977. **Freq:** Quarterly. **Trim Size:** 8 1/2 x 11. **Key Personnel:** Ruthan Brodsky, Editor, ruthan@aol.com. **ISSN:** 0278-3193. **Subscription Rates:** $46.75 individuals; $70 institutions. **Remarks:** Accepts advertising. **Online:** ERIC. **URL:** http://www.roeper.org. **Alt. Formats:** Microform; Microform.
Ad Rates: BW: $350 **Circ:** Paid 2,200
Non-paid 200

14909 James Communications, Inc.
710 N. Woodward Phone: (810)647-1080
Ste. 180 Fax: (810)647-1321
Bloomfield Hills, MI 48304

Key Personnel: William R. James, General Mgr. **Cities Served:** West Lake, LA; High Springs, FL; Hawkinsville and Eatonton, GA; Wartburg, TN; Grayson, KY; Guin and Roanoke, AL; Jacksboro, TX; Durant, OK; and Platte River, CO.

14910 WBFH-FM - 88.1
4200 Andover Rd. Phone: (248)645-4740
Bloomfield Hills, MI 48302 Fax: (248)645-4744

Format: Alternative/New Music/Progressive; Classic Rock; Educational. **Founded:** Oct. 1, 1976. **Operating Hours:** Continuous. **Key Personnel:** Pete Bowers, General Mgr., phone (248)645-4742, pbowers@mail.bloomfield.org; Paul L. Gaba, Asst. Mgr., phone (248)645-4743, pgaba@mail.bloomfield.org. **Local Programs:** *Somewhere in Time*; *Sportscan*; *Voices of Bloomfield*. **Wattage:** 360. **Ad Rates:** Noncommercial. **URL:** http://www.bloomfield.k12mi.us/wbfb/wbfh.html.

14911 WPON-AM - 1460
2222 Franklin Rd. Phone: (810)332-8883
Bloomfield Hills, MI 48302 Fax: (810)332-5470
E-mail: wpon@wpon.com

Format: Talk. **Networks:** Independent. **Founded:** 1940. **Operating Hours:** 18 hours Daily; 100% local. **Key Personnel:** Maria Fotion, General Mgr. **Wattage:** 1000. **Ad Rates:** $15 for 10 seconds; $25 for 30 seconds; $40 for 60 seconds.

BOYNE CITY

14912 The Citizen
112 S. Park St. Phone: (616)582-6761
PO Box A Fax: (616)582-6762
Boyne City, MI 49712
Community newspaper. **Founded:** Mar. 3, 1879. **Freq:** Weekly (Wed.). **Print Method:** Offset. **Trim Size:** 13 x 21. **Cols./Page:** 6. **Col. Width:** 12 picas. **Col. Depth:** 21 inches. **Key Personnel:** Hugh Conklin, Publisher. **Subscription Rates:** $22 (mail); $32 out of area. **Remarks:** Accepts advertising. **Formerly:** Charlevoix County Press.
Ad Rates: BW: $776.16 **Circ:** Paid ‡2,700
4C: $1,008.52
SAU: $6.16
PCI: $5.85

14913 Outstate Business
Harbor House Publishers, Inc.
221 Water St. Phone: (616)582-2814
Boyne City, MI 49712 Fax: (616)582-3392
Free: (800)491-1760
Publisher E-mail: harbor@harborhouse.com

Articles pertain to business in Michigan outside of the Metropolitan Detroit area. **Subtitle:** The Magazine of Michigan Business and Industry. **Founded:** 1987. **Freq:** Quarterly. **Print Method:** Offset. **Trim Size:** 8 1/2 x 11. **Cols./Page:** 2 and 3. **Col. Width:** 19 and 13 picas. **Col. Depth:** 7 inches. **Key Personnel:** David L. Knight, Editor; Michelle Cortright, Publisher; Ray Peurasaari, Advertising Mgr. **ISSN:** 1064-3621. **Subscription Rates:** $10. **Remarks:** Accepts advertising. **Alt. Formats:** Microfilm. **Formerly:** North Force Magazine.
Ad Rates: BW: $1,980 **Circ:** Non-paid ‡10,000
4C: $2,555

14914 Seaway Review
Harbor House Publishers, Inc.
221 Water St. Phone: (616)582-2814
Boyne City, MI 49712-1244 Fax: (616)582-3392
Free: (800)491-1760
Publisher E-mail: harbor@harborhouse.com

Magazine on maritime transportation, business, and international and economic news and analyses. **Subtitle:** The International Business Transportation Magazine of the Great Lakes/St. Lawrence System. **Founded:** 1970. **Freq:** Quarterly. **Print Method:** Offset. **Trim Size:** 8 3/8 x 10 7/8. **Cols./Page:** 3 and 2. **Col. Width:** 20 and 28 nonpareils. **Col. Depth:** 140 agate lines. **Key Personnel:** Michelle Cortright, Managing Editor; Jacques Les Strang, Publisher. **ISSN:** 0037-0487. **Subscription Rates:** $20. **Remarks:** Accepts advertising. **Available Online. Alt. Formats:** CD-ROM, UMI.
Ad Rates: BW: $1,745 **Circ:** Paid ‡10,200
4C: $2,355 Non-paid ‡400

14915 Snowscope
112 S. Park St. Phone: (616)582-6761
PO Box A
Boyne City, MI 49712
Winter tourist publication for skiers, snowmobilers, etc. **Founded:** 1981. **Freq:** Monthly (December-March). **Print Method:** Offset. **Cols./Page:** 5. **Col. Width:** 2 1/4 inches. **Col. Depth:** 13 inches. **Subscription Rates:** $18. **Remarks:** Accepts advertising.
Ad Rates: GLR: $.56 **Circ:** Paid ‡3,354
BW: $493.92 Non-paid ‡13,646
4C: $743.92
SAU: $7.84
PCI: $7.84

BRIGHTON

14916 The Engravers Journal
PO Box 318 Phone: (810)229-5725
26 Summit St. Fax: (810)229-8320
Brighton, MI 48116
Publication E-mail: info@engraversjournal.com

Magazine covering awards, trophies, and advertising specialties, published for the advancement of the recognition and identification industry. **Founded:** 1975. **Freq:** 12/year. **Print Method:** Offset. Uses mats. **Trim Size:** 8 1/2 x 11. **Cols./Page:** 2 and 3. **Col. Width:** 2 1/8 and 43 nonpareils. **Col. Depth:** 114 agate lines. **Key Personnel:** Michael J. Davis, Publisher. **Subscription Rates:** $49. **Remarks:** Accepts advertising.
Ad Rates: BW: $1,380 **Circ:** (Not Reported)
4C: $1,905

BRONSON

14917 The Bronson Journal
PO Box 38 Phone: (517)369-5085
Bronson, MI 49028
Community newspaper. **Founded:** 1881. **Freq:** Weekly (Thurs.). **Print Method:** Offset. **Cols./Page:** 6. **Col. Width:** 12.5 picas. **Col. Depth:** 21 1/2 inches. **Key Personnel:** Scott D. McGraw, Editor and Publisher. **Subscription Rates:** $20 individuals; $26 out of country. **Remarks:** Accepts advertising.
Ad Rates: BW: $516 **Circ:** ‡2,250
4C: $716
SAU: $4

BROOKLYN

14918 The Exponent
Exponent
160 S. Main Phone: (517)592-2122
Brooklyn, MI 49230 Fax: (517)592-3241
Publisher E-mail: exponews@frontiernet.net

Local newspaper. **Founded:** Sept. 1, 1881. **Freq:** Weekly (Tues.). **Print Method:** Web. **Cols./Page:** 5. **Col. Width:** 23 nonpareils. **Col. Depth:** 224 agate lines. **Key Personnel:** Patty Meyers-Wilkens, Editor; Matthew Schepeler, Publisher. **Subscription Rates:** $25. **Remarks:** Accepts advertising.
Ad Rates: 4C: $800 **Circ:** Paid ‡6,000
PCI: $5.75

14919 Irish Hills Cablevision LP
113 Lane St.
PO Box 633
Brooklyn, MI 49230

Owner: N-Com Holding Corp., 11401 Joseph Campau, Hamtramck, MI 48212, (313)365-0760, Fax: (313)365-2170. **Founded:** 1983. **Formerly:** Columbia Cable. **Key Personnel:** Robert Robinson, Systems Tech.; Pamela J. Rider, Systems Mgr.; Pam Lowry, Office Mgr. **Cities Served:** Brooklyn, Cambridge Township, Cement City, Columbia Township, Franklin Township, Norvell, Onsted, Somerset Township, MI: subscribing households 3860; 45 channels; 1 community access channel; 20 hours per week community access programming.

BROWN CITY

14920 The Brown City Banner
4241 Main St. Phone: (810)346-2753
Box 250 Fax: (810)346-2579
Brown City, MI 48416-9701
Community newspaper. **Founded:** 1891. **Freq:** Weekly (Mon.). **Cols./Page:** 5. **Col. Width:** 1 3/4 inches. **Key Personnel:** Bernice Hilman, Editor; Louise Gilman, Office Mgr.; Janet Balyo, Advertising Mgr. **Subscription Rates:** $15.50 individuals. **Remarks:** Accepts advertising.
Circ: (Not Reported)

BUCHANAN

14921 Berrien County Record
109 Days Ave. Phone: (616)695-3878
PO Box 191 Fax: (616)695-3880
Buchanan, MI 49107
Community newspaper. **Founded:** 1867. **Freq:** Weekly (Wed.). **Print Method:** Offset. **Cols./Page:** 6. **Col. Width:** 12.25 picas. **Col. Depth:** 21 1/2 inches. **Key Personnel:** David W. Holmes, Publisher; R. Cloud, Assoc. Editor; Mark Anderson, Managing Editor. **USPS:** 051-600. **Subscription Rates:** $25; $32 other. **Absorbed:** Lake County Chronicle (May 1, 1990).
Ad Rates: BW: $600 **Circ:** Paid 2,600
4C: $90.00 Free 350
SAU: $6.00
PCI: $4.80

BURTON

14922 WWBN-FM - 101.7
G 3338 E.Bristol Rd. Phone: (810)742-1470
PO Box 1470 Fax: (810)742-5170
Burton, MI 48529
E-mail: wwbn@aol.com

Format: Album-Oriented Rock (AOR). **Networks:** Independent. **Owner:** Faircom Flint, Inc., at above address. **Founded:** 1953. **Formerly:** WKMF-AM. **Operating Hours:** Continuous. **Key Personnel:** John Risher, Contact; J. Patrick, Program Dir. **Wattage:** 5000 day; 1000 night. **URL:** http://www.wwbn.com.

CADILLAC

14923 Buyers Guide
Central Michigan Newspapers, Inc.
112-A Beech St. Phone: (616)775-3361
Cadillac, MI 49601 Fax: (616)775-3382
Publisher E-mail: cmn@cmnnet.com

Shopper. **Founded:** 1976. **Freq:** Weekly (Mon.). **Print Method:** Offset. **Cols./Page:** 6. **Col. Width:** 9 picas. **Col. Depth:** 96 picas. **Key Personnel:** Paige P. O'Neal, General Mgr. **Subscription Rates:** Free. **Remarks:** Accepts advertising.
Ad Rates: GLR: $0.54 **Circ:** Free ‡21,500
BW: $774
4C: $891
PCI: $7.55

14924 Cadillac News
130 N. Mitchell St. Phone: (616)775-6565
Cadillac, MI 49601-1865 Fax: (616)775-8790

General newspaper. **Founded:** 1872. **Freq:** Mon.-Sat. (morn.). **Print Method:** Offset. **Trim Size:** 14 x 22 3/4. **Cols./Page:** 6. **Col. Width:** 2 1/16 inches. **Col. Depth:** 22 inches. **Key Personnel:** Thomas C. Huckle, Editor and Publisher; James Stevenson, Marketing Mgr.; Mark W. Lagerwey, Managing Editor; Chris Huckle, Marketing Mgr., phone (616)779-5200, huckle@cadillacnews.com; Matt Seward, Contact.

USPS: 082-500. **Subscription Rates:** $112.47. **Remarks:** Advertising not accepted for alcoholic beverages. **URL:** http://www.cadillacnews.com.
Ad Rates: PCI: $17.32 **Circ:** Mon.-Fri. ‡9,792
Sat. ‡10,956
Free ‡16,638

14925 Northern Michigan News
130 N. Mitchell St. Phone: (616)775-6565
PO Box 640 Fax: (616)775-8790
Cadillac, MI 49601-1856
Community newspaper. **Founded:** 1972. **Freq:** Weekly (Mon.). **Print Method:** Offset. **Trim Size:** 14 x 22 3/4. **Cols./Page:** 6. **Col. Width:** 26 nonpareils. **Col. Depth:** 308 agate lines. **Key Personnel:** Thomas C. Huckle, Editor and Publisher; Chris Huckle, Marketing Mgr. **Subscription Rates:** $12. **Remarks:** Accepts advertising.
Ad Rates: BW: $1,848 **Circ:** Paid ‡9,747
4C: $2,265 Free ‡16,638
PCI: $17.32

14926 WATT-AM - 1240
PO Box 520 Phone: (616)775-1263
Cadillac, MI 49601 Fax: (616)779-2844

Format: Talk; News. **Networks:** Westwood One Radio; EFM. **Owner:** MacDonald Broadcasting Co., 7825 S. Mackinaw Trail, Cadillac, MI 49601. **Founded:** 1945. **Operating Hours:** Continuous. **ADI:** Traverse City-Cadillac, MI. **Key Personnel:** Trish Garber, General Mgr., phone (616)347-8713, fax (616)347-9920; Shane Mcintosh, News Dir., phone (616)775-1263, fax (616)779-2844. **Wattage:** 1000. **Ad Rates:** $5 for 30 seconds. Combined advertising rates available with WLXV.

14927 WCMV-TV - 27
c/o WCMU-TV Phone: (517)774-3105
Central Michigan University Fax: (517)774-4427
3965 E. Broomfield
Mount Pleasant, MI 48859

Format: Public TV. **Networks:** Public Broadcasting Service (PBS). **Owner:** Central Michigan University, at above address. **Founded:** 1984. **Operating Hours:** 6 a.m.-midnight; 90% network, 10% local. **ADI:** Traverse City-Cadillac, MI. **Key Personnel:** Monte Higgins, Station Mgr.; Rick Schudiske, Program Dir.; Linda Hyde, Contact. **Ad Rates:** Noncommercial.

14928 WGKI-TV - 33/45
7669 S. 45th Rd. Phone: (616)775-9813
Cadillac, MI 49601 Fax: (616)775-1898
E-mail: info@fox33.net

Format: Commercial TV. **Networks:** Fox; United Paramount Network. **Owner:** GRK Productions Joint Venture, at above address. **Founded:** 1983. **Operating Hours:** Continuous; 25% network, 75% local. **ADI:** Traverse City-Cadillac, MI. **Key Personnel:** Charlie McCain, Sales Mgr.; Gary Knapp, Pres./General Mgr.; Ron Roth, Production Mgr.; Amy Nimeth, Traffic Mgr.; Dan Somes, Operations Mgr.; Julie Brines, Program Dir.; Shane Mcintosh, Promotions Mgr. **Wattage:** 776,000.

14929 WGKU-TV - 33/45
7669 S. 45 Rd. Phone: (616)775-9813
Cadillac, MI 49601 Fax: (616)775-1898
E-mail: info@fox33.net

Format: News; Sports. **Simulcasts:** WGKI. **Networks:** Fox; United Paramount Network. **Owner:** GRK Productions Joint Venture, at above address. **Founded:** 1989. **Operating Hours:** Continuous. **ADI:** Traverse City-Cadillac, MI. **Key Personnel:** Charlie McCain, Sales Mgr.; Gary Knapp, Pres./General Mgr.; Ron Roth, Production Mgr.; Amy Nimeth, Traffic Mgr.; Dan Somes, Operations Mgr.; Julie Brines, Program Dir.; Shane McIntosh, Promotions Mgr. **Wattage:** 851,000.

14930 WKJF-AM - 1370
1111 S. Mitchell Phone: (616)775-0143
Cadillac, MI 49601 Fax: (616)775-5217

Format: Talk. **Networks:** ABC. **Founded:** 1968. **Formerly:** WWAM-AM (1979). **Operating Hours:** 5:30 a.m.-1 a.m.; 5% network, 95% local. **ADI:** Traverse City-Cadillac, MI. **Key Personnel:** Ross Biederman, President. **Local Programs:** *On Line with Ron Jolly*, Ron Jolly, (616)947-7675, Fax (616)929-3988. **Wattage:** 5000 day; 1000 night.

14931 WWTV-TV - 9 & 10
PO Box 627 Phone: (616)775-3478
22320 130th Ave. Fax: (616)775-3671
Cadillac, MI 49601
Free: (800)782-7910
E-mail: info@9and10news.com

Format: Commercial TV. **Networks:** CBS. **Owner:** Heritage Broadcasting Co. of Michigan, at above address. **Founded:** 1954. **Operating Hours:** 24 hrs. **ADI:** Traverse City-Cadillac, MI. **Key Personnel:** Mario Iacobelli, President, mario@9and10news.com; William Kring, Station Mgr., kringer@9and10news.com; Sherri McKinley, Program Dir., sherrimckinley@9and10news.com; Jennifer Sutterfield, Creative Services Dir.; Jon-Michial Carter, News Dir., newsdirector@9and10news.com. **Local Programs:** *Michigan This Morning*, Curt Sutterfield, (616)775-3478; *Nightside*, Bob Walters, (616)775-3478. **Wattage:** 316,000 visual; 31,600 aural. **Ad Rates:** Oombined advertising rates available with WWUP-TV. **URL:** http://www.9and10news.com.

CALEDONIA

14932 Caledonia/Gaines Township Advance
Advance Newspapers
2141 Port Sheldon Rd. Phone: (616)669-2700
PO Box 9 Fax: (616)669-1162
Jenison, MI 49428-9301
Free: (800)439-0960

Suburban community newspaper (tabloid). **Founded:** 1966. **Freq:** Weekly (Tues.). **Print Method:** Offset. **Cols./Page:** 6. **Col. Width:** 16 nonpareils. **Col. Depth:** 224 agate lines. **Key Personnel:** Joel Holland, Publisher. **Subscription Rates:** $25. **Remarks:** Accepts advertising.
Ad Rates: BW: $336 **Circ:** Controlled 6,811
4C: $497.60 Paid 11
PCI: $3.50

CAMDEN

14933 The Farmers' Advance
Camden Publications, Inc.
130 S. Main St. Phone: (517)368-5201
PO Box 8 Fax: (517)368-5131
Camden, MI 49232
Free: (800)222-6336

Agricultural newspaper. **Subtitle:** Your Farm and Auction Weekly. **Founded:** Nov. 1898. **Freq:** Weekly (Wed.). **Print Method:** Offset. **Trim Size:** 10 9/16 x 16. **Cols./Page:** 8. **Col. Width:** 14 nonpareils. **Col. Depth:** 224 agate lines. **Key Personnel:** Kurt Greenhoe, Publisher. **Subscription Rates:** $27. **Remarks:** Accepts advertising.
Ad Rates: BW: $1,459.20 **Circ:** Paid ‡19,315
4C: $1,859.20 Free ‡2,512
PCI: $11.40

CANTON

14934 Canton Eagle
Michigan Community Newspapers
35540 Michigan Ave. Phone: (313)729-4000
PO Box 578 Fax: (313)729-6880
Wayne, MI 48184
Community newspaper. **Founded:** 1945. **Freq:** Weekly (Thurs.). **Print Method:** Offset. **Cols./Page:** 6. **Col. Width:** 12 picas. **Col. Depth:** 21 1/2 inches. **Key Personnel:** Mike Wilcox, Publisher; Kathy Wilcox, Owner; Joan Dyer-Zinner, Managing Editor; Rita Bedell, Classified Manager; Ron Spielman, Advertising Mgr.; Justin Wilcox, Circulation Mgr. **Subscription Rates:** $48. **Remarks:** Accepts advertising.
Ad Rates: SAU: $5.85 **Circ:** Paid 145
Non-paid 4,022

14935 Canton Observer
Observer & Eccentric Newspapers
36251 Schoolcraft Rd. Phone: (313)591-2300
Livonia, MI 48150-1216 Fax: (313)953-2232

Community newspaper. **Founded:** 1976. **Freq:** Semiweekly (Mon. and Thurs.). **Print Method:** Offset. **Cols./Page:** 9. **Col. Width:** 17 nonpareils. **Col. Depth:** 301 agate lines. **Key Personnel:** Richard Aginian, Publisher. **Subscription Rates:** $23. **Remarks:** Accepts advertising.
Ad Rates: GLR: $2.62 **Circ:** Paid 8,299
Non-paid 1,347

14936 WSDP-FM - 88.1
46181 Joy Rd. Phone: (313)416-7732
Canton, MI 48187

Format: Album-Oriented Rock (AOR); Alternative/New Music/Progressive. **Founded:** 1972. **Operating Hours:** 16 hours daily; 100% local. **Key Personnel:** Bill Keith, Station Mgr., bkeith@edcen.ehhs.cmich.edu. **Local Programs:** *The Sanctuary*, Jessica Rasmussen, (313)416-7732. **Wattage:** 200. **Ad Rates:** Noncommercial.

CARO

14937 Shopper's Guide
Caro Publishing
344 N. State Phone: (517)673-3181
Box 106 Fax: (517)673-5662
Caro, MI 48723
Free: (800)221-SOLD
Publication E-mail: tca@century.net

Combined Community Newspaper and Shopper. **Founded:** 1870. **Freq:** Published Mon., Wed., and Sat. **Print Method:** Offset. **Trim Size:** 10 x 16. **Cols./Page:** 7. **Col. Width:** 24 nonpareils. **Col. Depth:** 210 agate lines. **Key Personnel:** Britt McLaughlin, Publisher. **Subscription Rates:** Free. **Remarks:** Accepts advertising.
Ad Rates: GLR: $.32 **Circ:** Combined 42,600
BW: $5
4C: $175
PCI: $5

14938 Tuscola County Advertiser
A Division of Caro Publishing
PO Box 106 Phone: (517)673-3181
Caro, MI 48723 Fax: (517)673-5662
Free: (800)821-7653
Publication E-mail: tca@centuryinter.net

Local newspaper. **Founded:** Aug. 21, 1868. **Freq:** Semiweekly (Wed. and Sat.). **Print Method:** Offset. **Cols./Page:** 8. **Col. Width:** 18 nonpareils. **Col. Depth:** 294 agate lines. **Key Personnel:** Brett M. McLaughlin, Publisher; Jamie McCoy, Advertising Mgr.; Nancy Barringer, News Editor. **Subscription Rates:** $32. **Remarks:** Accepts advertising.
Ad Rates: GLR: $.28 **Circ:** ⊕10,000
BW: $848.40
4C: $1,088.40
SAU: $5.87
PCI: $5.05

14939 WIDL-FM - 92.1
1184 Cleaver Rd. Phone: (517)673-9435
PO Box 151
Caro, MI 48723

Format: Classic Rock. **Networks:** ABC. **Founded:** 1974. **Operating Hours:** Continuous; 90% network, 10% local. **Key Personnel:** Bill Jackson, General Mgr. **Wattage:** 6000. **Ad Rates:** $9-15 for 30 seconds; $12-17 for 60 seconds. Combined advertising rates available with WKYO-AM.

14940 WKYO-AM - 1360
1184 Cleaver Rd. Phone: (517)673-2136
PO Box 151
Caro, MI 48723

Format: Full Service; Country; Agricultural. **Networks:** ABC. **Founded:** 1962. **Operating Hours:** Continuous; 75% network, 25% local. **Key Personnel:** Bill Jackson, General Mgr. **Wattage:** 1000. **Ad Rates:** $9-13 for 30 seconds; $12-16 for 60 seconds.

CARSON CITY

14941 Carson City Gazette
Greenville News Inc.
211 W. Main
Carson City, MI 48811-9728

Community newspaper. **Founded:** Mar. 1881. **Freq:** Weekly (Mon.). **Print Method:** Offset. Uses mats. **Cols./Page:** 6. **Col. Width:** 18 nonpareils. **Col. Depth:** 192 agate lines. **Key Personnel:** John Stafford, Publisher; Barbara Sutherland, Editor; John Norton, General Mgr. **Remarks:** Accepts advertising.
Ad Rates: BW: $422.40 **Circ:** Paid ‡273
4C: $721.32 Free ‡9,730
SAU: $6.95
PCI: $4.40

CASEVILLE

14942 Harron Cable TV
6912 Main St. Phone: (517)856-2231
PO Box 1287 Fax: (517)856-3985
Caseville, MI 48725
Free: (800)772-7548

Owner: Paul Harron, 70 E. Lancaster, Frazer, PA 19355, (610)993-1000. **Founded:** 1988. **Key Personnel:** Donald V. Pascarella, General Mgr. **Cities Served:** Worth Township, Hume Township, Caseville Township.: subscribing households 12,000; 35 channels; 1 community access channel.

CASS CITY

14943 Cass City Chronicle
6550 Main St. Phone: (517)872-2010
Cass City, MI 48726 Fax: (517)872-3810

Community newspaper. **Founded:** 1881. **Freq:** Weekly (Tues.). **Print Method:** Offset. **Cols./Page:** 8. **Col. Width:** 19 nonpareils. **Col. Depth:** 294 agate lines. **Key Personnel:** Clarke Haire, Editor and Publisher. **Subscription Rates:** $15. **Remarks:** Accepts advertising.
Ad Rates: SAU: $5.32 **Circ:** ‡3,454

CENTRAL LAKE

14944 The Torch
PO Box 575 Phone: (616)544-2345
Central Lake, MI 49622
Local newspaper. **Founded:** 1892. **Freq:** Weekly (Thurs.). **Print Method:** Offset. **Cols./Page:** 5. **Col. Width:** 19 nonpareils. **Col. Depth:** 231 agate lines. **Key Personnel:** Jeff Hallberg, Editor and Publisher. **USPS:** 097-660. **Subscription Rates:** $22 individuals; $25 out of area. **Remarks:** Accepts advertising.
Ad Rates: BW: $260 **Circ:** 2,050
PCI: $3.25

CHARLEVOIX

14945 Charlevoix Courier
112 Mason St. Phone: (616)547-6558
PO Box 117 Fax: (616)547-4992
Charlevoix, MI 49720-0117
Community newspaper. **Founded:** 1883. **Freq:** Weekly (Wed.). **Print Method:** Offset. **Trim Size:** 13 1/2 x 22 1/2. **Cols./Page:** 5. **Col. Width:** 12 picas. **Col. Depth:** 13 inches. **Key Personnel:** Laurie Lounsbury, Editor; Kim Taylor, Advertising Mgr.; Ken Winter, General Mgr. **USPS:** 135-220. **Subscription Rates:** $39.00 individuals; $50.80 out of area; $33.20 senior citizens and servicemen.
Ad Rates: BW: $2522.52 **Circ:** 2305
4C: $3056.52
PCI: $21.65
PCI: $8.60

14946 The North Woods Call
Rte. 1, 00509 Turkey Run Rd. Phone: (616)547-9797
Charlevoix, MI 49720 Fax: (616)547-0367

Tabloid on natural resources, nature, and the outdoors. **Founded:** Oct. 1953. **Freq:** Semimonthly. **Print Method:** Offset. **Trim Size:** 11 1/2 x 16. **Cols./Page:** 5. **Col. Width:** 1 7/8 inches. **Col. Depth:** 15 inches. **Key Personnel:** Glen L. Sheppard, Editor and Publisher, shep@freeway.net. **Subscription Rates:** $25; $44 two years.
Ad Rates: PCI: $7.06 **Circ:** ‡12,000

14947 Star Advertiser
Star Publications
PO Box 620 Phone: (517)732-5125
Gaylord, MI 49734 Fax: (517)732-9323
Free: (800)782-7237
Publisher E-mail: starads@northland.lib.mi.us

Shopper (tabloid). **Founded:** 1970. **Freq:** Weekly (Sun.). **Print Method:** Offset. **Trim Size:** 11 1/8 x 17 1/2. **Cols./Page:** 6. **Col. Width:** 21 nonpareils. **Col. Depth:** 224 agate lines. **Key Personnel:** David Baragrey, Publisher. **Remarks:** Accepts advertising. **Available Online.**
Ad Rates: GLR: $4 **Circ:** Free 12,844
BW: $542.40
4C: $738.40
PCI: $5.65

CHARLOTTE

14948 WLCM-AM - 1390
PO Box 338 Phone: (517)543-8200
Charlotte, MI 48813 Fax: (517)543-7779

Format: Religious. **Networks:** Interstate Radio. **Owner:** Midwest Broadcasting Inc, at above address. **Founded:** 1956. **Formerly:** WCER-AM; WGWY-AM; WNLF-AM; WNNY-AM. **Operating Hours:** 6am-sunset. **ADI:** Lansing (Ann Arbor), MI. **Key Personnel:** David Huva, Station Mgr. **Wattage:** 5000. **Ad Rates:** $6-6 for 15 seconds; $10-10 for 30 seconds; $12-12 for 60 seconds. Combined advertising rates available with WLQV, WSNL, WLYV.

CHEBOYGAN

14949 Daily Tribune
Cheboygan Daily Tribune, Inc.
308 N. Main Phone: (616)627-7144
PO Box 290 Fax: (616)627-5331
Cheboygan, MI 49721
Local newspaper. **Founded:** 1875. **Freq:** Daily (morn.). **Print Method:** Offset. **Cols./Page:** 6. **Col. Width:** 25 nonpareils. **Col. Depth:** 294 agate lines. **Key Personnel:** Rip Woodin, Publisher; Roy Trahan, General Mgr. **Subscription Rates:** $78. **Remarks:** Accepts advertising.
Ad Rates: PCI: $5.50 **Circ:** Paid 4,550
Non-paid 450

14950 Shoppers Fair
Cheboygan Daily Tribune, Inc.
308 N. Main Phone: (616)627-7144
PO Box 290 Fax: (616)627-5331
Cheboygan, MI 49721
Shopper. **Founded:** 1964. **Freq:** Weekly (Sun.). **Print Method:** Offset. **Cols./Page:** 5. **Col. Width:** 21 nonpareils. **Col. Depth:** 224 agate lines. **Key Personnel:** Rip Woodin, Publisher; Roy Trahan, General Mgr. **Subscription Rates:** $5.25. **Remarks:** Accepts advertising.
Ad Rates: GLR: $.39 **Circ:** Free ‡24,000
BW: $470.40
SAU: $5.88
PCI: $5.60

14951 WCBY-AM - 1240
1356 Mackinaw Ave. Phone: (616)627-2341
Cheboygan, MI 49721 Fax: (616)627-7000
Free: (800)348-1051

Format: Middle-of-the-Road (MOR). **Networks:** ABC. **Owner:** Northern Star Broadcasting, at above address. **Founded:** 1954. **Operating Hours:** 6:00 a.m-midnight. **ADI:** Lansing (Ann Arbor), MI. **Key Personnel:** Mike Grisdale, Program Dir.; Chris Monk, VP/Gen.Mgr. **Wattage:** 1000. **Ad Rates:** $10-15 for 30 seconds.

14952 WIDG-AM - 940
1356 Mackinaw Ave. Phone: (906)643-9494
Cheboygan, MI 49721-1003 Fax: (616)627-7000

Format: Oldies. **Networks:** NBC; Jones Satellite. **Founded:** 1966. **Formerly:** WLVM-AM (1984). **Operating Hours:** Sunrise-sunset; 10% network, 90% local. **ADI:** Traverse City-Cadillac, MI. **Key Personnel:** Del Reynolds, Contact, reynolds@freway.com; Mary Reynolds, Contact. **Wattage:** 5000. **Ad Rates:** $6-16 per unit.

CHELSEA

14953 Personnel Management Abstracts
704 Island Lake Rd. Phone: (313)475-1979
Chelsea, MI 48118
Publication E-mail: personnel_ mgt_ abstracts@msn.com

Index to articles from academic and trade journals dealing with the management of people and organizational behavior. Arranged by subject and author. **Founded:** 1955. **Freq:** Quarterly (annual supplement). **Print Method:** Offset. **Trim Size:** 8 1/2 x 11. **Cols./Page:** 3. **Col. Width:** 2 1/4 inches. **Col. Depth:** 8 inches. **Key Personnel:** Gloria J. Reo, Editor. **ISSN:** 0031-577X. **Subscription Rates:** $180 individuals; $186 other countries; $340 two years; $352 two years other countries. **Remarks:** Advertising not accepted.
Circ: ‡645

CLARE

14954 The Clare Sentinel
112 W. 4th St. Phone: (517)386-9937
Clare, MI 48617 Fax: (517)386-9938

Community newspaper. **Founded:** 1878. **Freq:** Weekly (Wed.). **Print Method:** Offset. **Cols./Page:** 6. **Col. Width:** 2 inches. **Col. Depth:** 21 inches. **Key Personnel:** Alfred R. Bransdorfer, Editor and Publisher. **Subscription Rates:** $19.50. **Remarks:** Accepts advertising.
Ad Rates: GLR: $.24 **Circ:** ‡3,200
SAU: $5.86

CLARKSTON

14955 The Clarkston News
Sherman Publications, Inc.
5 S. Main Phone: (248)625-3370
Clarkston, MI 48346 Fax: (248)625-0706

Local newspaper. **Founded:** 1929. **Freq:** Weekly (Wed.). **Print Method:** Offset. **Cols./Page:** 6. **Col. Width:** 18 nonpareils. **Col. Depth:** 210 agate lines. **Key Personnel:** Annette Kingsbury, Editor; Eric Lewis, Advertising Dir.; Jim Sherman, Jr., Publisher. **Subscription Rates:** $16 individuals. **Remarks:** Accepts advertising. **Alt. Formats:** Microform.
Ad Rates: GLR: $.62 **Circ:** Paid 4,000
BW: $823.50
SAU: $8.19
PCI: $9.15

CLIMAX

14956 Crescent
150 Main St. Phone: (616)746-4331
Olimax, MI 49034
Community newspaper. **Founded:** 1912. **Freq:** Weekly (Fri.). **Print Method:** Offset. **Cols./Page:** 4. **Col. Width:** 24 nonpareils. **Col. Depth:** 175 agate lines. **Key Personnel:** Bruce Rolfe, Editor and Publisher., Editor and Publisher. **USPS:** 118-120. **Subscription Rates:** $10. **Remarks:** Accepts advertising.
Ad Rates: GLR: $.12 **Circ:** ‡850
PCI: $2.25

CLINTON

14957 The Clinton Local
108 Tecumseh St. Phone: (517)456-4100
PO Box B Fax: (517)456-6372
Clinton, MI 49236
General newspaper. **Founded:** 1884. **Freq:** Weekly (Thurs.). **Print Method:** Offset. **Cols./Page:** 6. **Col. Width:** 1 3/4 inches. **Col. Depth:** 203 agate lines. **Key Personnel:** Maryann Habrick, Editor and Publisher. **Subscription Rates:** $15; $17 out of area.
Ad Rates: 4C: $90 **Circ:** ‡1,700
SAU: $3.50

CLINTON TOWNSHIP

14958 WADL-TV - 38
22590 15 Mile Rd. Phone: (810)790-3838
Clinton Township, MI 48035 Fax: (810)790-3841

Format: Commercial TV. **Simulcasts:** WJBK-TV. **Networks:** Independent. **Owner:** Adell Broadcasting Corp., at above address. **Founded:** 1989. **ADI:** Detroit, MI. **Key Personnel:** Frank Adell, Contact.

WUFL-AM - See Sterling Heights

CLIO

14959 WEYI-TV - 25
2225 W. Willard Rd., Box 250 Phone: (810)687-1000
Clio, MI 48420 Fax: (810)687-4925

Format: Commercial TV. **Networks:** CBS. **Founded:** 1953. **Formerly:** WKNX-TV (1971). **Operating Hours:** Continuous; 95% network, 5% local. **ADI:** Flint-Saginaw-Bay City, MI. **Key Personnel:** Beverly Knickerbocker, Production Mgr.; Eric S. Land, Contact; Jon L. Bengtson, Program Dir.; Dave Barber, Contact; James Barnes, Contact; Don Weatherup, Promotions Mgr. **Ad Rates:** Advertising accepted; rates available upon request.

COLDWATER

14960 The Daily Reporter
15 W. Pearl St. Phone: (517)278-2318
Coldwater, MI 49036-1912 Fax: (517)278-6041
Publisher E-mail: publisher@thedailyreporter.com

Local newspaper. **Founded:** Feb. 10, 1896. **Freq:** M-F (evening); Saturday (morning). **Print Method:** Offset. **Cols./Page:** 6. **Col. Width:** 1.76 inches. **Col. Depth:** 21 1/4 inches. **Key Personnel:** Robert A. Jodon, Publisher, rwjodon@thedaileyreporter.com; Chris Balusik, Managing Editor. **ISSN:** 0745-6794. **Subscription Rates:** $104. **Remarks:** Accepts advertising. **Formerly:** Coldwater Daily Reporter (June 1988).
Ad Rates: BW: $1,190.07 **Circ:** ‡6,000
4C: $1,340.67
PCI: $9.23

14961 WTVB-AM - 1590
PO Box 1600 Phone: (517)279-9767
Coldwater, MI 49036 Fax: (517)279-4695

Format: Adult Contemporary. **Networks:** ABC; Satellite Music Network. **Owner:** MWC, Inc., at above address. **Founded:** 1947. **Operating Hours:** Continuous; 60% network, 40% local. **Key Personnel:** Peter Tanz, General Mgr.; Jim Whelan, News Dir.; Ken Delaney, Program Dir. **Wattage:** 5000. **Ad Rates:** $10-20.50 for 30 seconds; $14-24 for 60 seconds.

COLEMAN

14962 WPRJ-FM - 101.7
227 Jackson Rd. Phone: (517)465-9775
PO Box 236 Fax: (517)465-1060
Coleman, MI 48618
E-mail: wprj@junu.com

Format: Religious; Contemporary Christian. **Owner:** Come Together Ministries, Inc., at above address. **Founded:** 1992. **Operating Hours:** Continuous. **ADI:** Flint-Saginaw-Bay City, MI. **Key Personnel:** Gary H. Bugh, Pres./Gen. Mgr.; Brian "Doc" Erwin, Music Dir.; Lisa Huss, Office Pro.; Connie Wieber, Operations Mgr.; Jeff Schultz, Underwriter. **Local Programs:** *Cheff Jeff* 8 a.m. Friday, Jeff Schultz; *Daybreak* 6 a.m.-9 a.m. Monday-Friday, Jeff Schultz. **Wattage:** 6,000. **Ad Rates:** Noncommercial.

COLON

14963 The Express
216 E. State St. Phone: (616)432-3488
PO Box 816
Colon, MI 49040-0816
Community newspaper. **Founded:** Oct. 1, 1886. **Freq:** Weekly (Wed.). **Print Method:** Offset. **Cols./Page:** 6. **Col. Width:** 12 picas. **Col. Depth:** 21 inches. **Key Personnel:** Skip Plath, Editor and Publisher. **Subscription Rates:** $15; $17.50 out of area; $20 out of state. **Remarks:** Accepts advertising.
Ad Rates: SAU: $11.90 **Circ:** ‡1,136
PCI: $1.82

COMMERCE

14964 Commerce Spinal Column Newsweekly
Spinal Column Publications
7196 Cooley Lake Rd. Phone: (248)360-6397
PO Box 14 Fax: (248)360-4711
Union Lake, MI 48387-0014
Local newspaper. **Founded:** 1960. **Freq:** Weekly. **Print Method:** Offset. **Trim Size:** 10 1/2 x 15. **Cols./Page:** 8. **Col. Width:** 7 picas. **Col. Depth:** 14 inches. **Key Personnel:** David D. Hohendorf, Publisher; James W. Fancy, Publisher; Laurie Wallace, Advertising Mgr. **Remarks:** Accepts advertising.
Ad Rates: GLR: $6.88 **Circ:** Free ‡9,800
BW: $770.56
PCI: $13.76

CROSWELL

14965 Jeffersonian
14 Wells St. Phone: (810)679-4500
Croswell, MI 48422 Fax: (810)679-4504

Local newspaper. **Founded:** 1858. **Freq:** Weekly (Mon.). **Print Method:** Offset. **Cols./Page:** 6. **Col. Width:** 21 nonpareils. **Col. Depth:** 210 agate lines. **Key Personnel:** John D. Johnson, Editor and Publisher. **Subscription Rates:** $22.95. **Remarks:** Accepts advertising.
Ad Rates: GLR: $.32 **Circ:** Combined ‡20,700

CRYSTAL

14966 Crystal Cable TV
122 Lake St. Phone: (517)235-6100
Box 365 Fax: (517)235-6247
Crystal, MI 48818
E-mail: cctv@glccmi.com

Owner: Rex Skea, 1033 Senator Rd., Crystal, MI 48818, (517)235-6695, Fax: (517)235-6247. **Founded:** 1988. **Key Personnel:** Rex Skea, President, phone (517)235-6100, fax (517)235-6247, rskea@glccmi.com; Allen Horak, Vice President, ahorak@glccmi.com; Kim Marks, Sec./Treas., kmark@glccmi.com; Mark Winslow, General Mgr., markw@glccmi.com. **Cities Served:** Crystal, MI: subscribing households 600; 38 channels; 1 community access channel; 168 hours per week community access programming. **URL:** http://www.cctv/glccmi.com.

CRYSTAL FALLS

14967 Indiana Law Reporter
Law Reporter Co.
209 Michigan Ave. Phone: (906)875-6970
PO Box 270
Crystal Falls, MI 49920
Professional journal covering legal issues in Indiana. **Founded:** 1978. **Freq:** Semiannual. **Key Personnel:** John A. Sundquist, Editor. **ISSN:** 0279-5558. **Subscription Rates:** $225 individuals. **Remarks:** Advertising not accepted.
Circ: Combined 222

14968 Crystal Falls CATV
401 Superior Ave. Phone: (906)875-6650
Crystal Falls, MI 49920 Fax: (906)875-3767

Key Personnel: Walter Hagglund, General Mgr.; Angelo Diqui, Contact. **Cities Served:** 20 channels.

DAVISON

14969 The Davison Index
220 N. Main St. Phone: (810)653-3511
PO Box 100
Davison, MI 48423-0100
Newspaper. **Founded:** 1889. **Freq:** Weekly (Wed.). **Print Method:** Offset. **Trim Size:** 11 3/8 x 16 1/4. **Cols./Page:** 6. **Col. Width:** 20 nonpareils. **Col. Depth:** 210 agate lines. **Key Personnel:** Don Schelske, Editor; James A. Sherman, Jr., Publisher. **Subscription Rates:** $15 individuals.
Ad Rates: GLR: $.37 **Circ:** 11,000
BW: $540
PCI: $6

14970 Davison Cablevision Ltd.
217 Shopper's Alley Phone: (810)653-0966
Davison, MI 48423 Fax: (810)653-8287
Free: (800)783-4578

Owner: D.F. Deleware, Ltd. Partnership, 1876 S. Bellaires, Ste. 1550, Denver, CO 80222, (303)756-5600. **Founded:** 1979. **Key Personnel:** Tom Haner, General Mgr.; Tracy Jensen, Chief Engineer. **Cities Served:** Almont, Atlas, Davison, Dryden, Goodrich, Grand Blanc, Imlay City, Mount Morris, North Branch, Otisville, Richfield, MI: subscribing households 7,215; 38 channels; 1 community access channel.

DE WITT

14971 WQHH-FM - 96.5
101 Northcrest Rd., Ste. 4 Phone: (517)484-9600
Lansing, MI 48906-1262 Fax: (517)484-9699

Format: Urban Contemporary. **Founded:** 1988. **Operating Hours:** Continuous. **ADI:** Lansing (Ann Arbor), MI. **Key Personnel:** Helena Dubose, Contact. **Wattage:** 3000. **Ad Rates:** $30-50 per unit. Combined advertising rates available with WXLA-AM.

DEARBORN

14972 Dearborn Press & Guide
Heritage Newspapers
15340 Michigan Ave. Phone: (313)943-4250
Dearborn, MI 48126-2917 Fax: (313)846-5531

Community newspaper. **Founded:** June 14, 1918. **Freq:** Weekly (Tues.). **Print Method:** Offset. **Trim Size:** 13 3/4 x 22 1/2. **Cols./Page:** 6. **Col. Width:** 2 1/16 inches. **Col. Depth:** 21 inches. **Key Personnel:** Gary Woronchak, Editor; Robert Riddell, Publisher; Judy Rogers, Advertising Dir. **Subscription Rates:** $26; $36 out of area. **Remarks:** Accepts advertising.
Ad Rates: GLR: $2.14 **Circ:** Paid 5,328
BW: $3,867.42 Non-paid 19,824
SAU: $33.25
PCI: $29.98

14973 Forming & Fabricating
Society of Manufacturing Engineers
1 SME Dr. Phone: (313)271-1500
PO Box 930 Fax: (313)271-2861
Dearborn, MI 48121-0930
Free: (800)733-4SME
Publication E-mail: Kleiart@sme.org

Trade magazine for manufacturing companies that form and fabricate sheet metal, plate, tube, and pipe in producing products. **Founded:** Jan. 1994. **Freq:** Monthly. **Print Method:** Web offset. **Key Personnel:** Art Klein, Editor; John Coleman, Publisher; John Poswalk, Circulation Mgr. **ISSN:** 1075-3699. **Subscription Rates:** $100 individuals. **Remarks:** Accepts advertising.
Ad Rates: BW: $4,260 **Circ:** Controlled 65,496
4C: $5,310

14974 Journal of Manufacturing Systems
Society of Manufacturing Engineers
1 SME Dr. Phone: (313)271-1500
PO Box 930 Fax: (313)271-2861
Dearborn, MI 48121-0930
Free: (800)733-4SME
Publication E-mail: journals@sme.org

Journal publishing refereed research papers with the aim of intergrating established and developed manufacturing processes, equipment, and software. **Founded:** 1982. **Freq:** Bimonthly. **Print Method:** Offset. **Trim Size:** 8 1/2 x 11. **Cols./Page:** 2. **Col. Width:** 20 picas. **Col. Depth:** 8 3/4 inches. **Key Personnel:** Ellen Kehoe, Sr. Editor, kehoell@sme.org. **ISSN:** 0278-6125. **Subscription Rates:** $240 individuals; $210 members; $40 single issue. **Remarks:** Accepts advertising.
Ad Rates: PCI: $85 **Circ:** Paid 1,500

14975 Leaves
Mariannhill Mission Society
PO Box 87 Phone: (313)561-2330
Dearborn, MI 48121-0087
Magazine providing religious and spiritual encouragement for families. **Founded:** 1938. **Freq:** Bimonthly. **Print Method:** Offset. **Key Personnel:** Rev. Thomas Heier, C.M.M., Editor-in-Chief. **ISSN:** 0714-4113. **Subscription Rates:** Free. **Remarks:** Advertising not accepted.
Circ: Free 120,000

14976 Michigan Living
AAA Automobile Club of Michigan
1 Auto Club Dr. Phone: (313)336-1506
Dearborn, MI 48126 Fax: (313)336-1344
Publication E-mail: michliving@aol.com

Magazine covering travel, recreation and lifestyle activities in Michigan, the U.S., and around the world. Also reports on highway and home safety. **Founded:** July 1918. **Freq:** 10/year. **Print Method:** Offset. **Trim Size:** 7 7/8 x 10 7/8. **Cols./Page:** 3. **Col. Width:** 28 nonpareils. **Col. Depth:** 138 agate lines. **Key Personnel:** Ronald E. Garbinski, Editor, phone (248)816-9265, fax (248)816-2251, regarbo@aol.com; Khristi Zimmeth, Sr. Editor. **ISSN:** 0745-1798. **Subscription Rates:** $9; $1 single issue. **Remarks:** Accepts advertising. **Available Online. URL:** http://www.aaamich.com.
Ad Rates: BW: $17,850 **Circ:** Paid ★1,015,754
4C: $20,420
PCI: $745

Times-Herald - See Dearborn Heights

14977 WDOZ-AM - 1310
PO Box 1310 Phone: (313)846-8500
15001 Michigan Ave. Fax: (313)846-1068
Dearborn, MI 48121

Format: Blues. **Networks:** Independent. **Founded:** 1946. **Formerly:** WKNH-AM. **Operating Hours:** 6 a.m.-midnight. **ADI:** Detroit, MI. **Key Personnel:** Gary Fischer, Contact. **Wattage:** 5000.

14978 WHFR-FM - 89.3
Henry Ford Community College Phone: (313)845-9676
5101 Evergreen Fax: (313)845-6321
Dearborn, MI 48128

Format: Alternative/New Music/Progressive; Eclectic; Jazz. **Networks:** Independent. **Owner:** Henry Ford Community College, at above address, (313)845-9600. **Founded:** 1985. **Operating Hours:** Continuous. **ADI:** Detroit, MI. **Key Personnel:** Jay B. Korinek, Station Advis., phone (313)845-6477; Susan McGraw, Asst. General Mgr., phone (313)845-9842. **Local Programs:** *Highway 61* 3:00 pm - 7:00 pm Friday, Joanna Korczynska, (313)845-9676. **Wattage:** 270. **Ad Rates:** Noncommercial; underwriting available. **URL:** http://www.henryford.cc.mi.us/events/whfr/index.html.

14979 WNIC-FM - 100.3
PO Box 1310 Phone: (313)846-8500
Dearborn, MI 48121 Fax: (313)846-3722

Format: Adult Contemporary. **Networks:** Independent. **Owner:** Evergreen Media Corp., 433 E. Las Colinas Blvd., Suite 1130, Irving, TX 75039. **Founded:** 1946. **Operating Hours:** Continuous. **Key Personnel:** Gary Fischer, Contact; John Long, Contact; Robert Schutt, General Sales Mgr.; Jim Harper, Program Dir.; Dave Lockhart, News Dir. **Wattage:** 50,000.

DEARBORN HEIGHTS

14980 Hockey Weekly
25042 W. Warren Rd. Phone: (313)563-9130
Dearborn Heights, MI 48127 Fax: (313)563-9538
Publication E-mail: puck@amateurhockey.com

Amateur hockey tabloid. **Founded:** 1974. **Freq:** 30/year. **Print Method:** Offset. **Trim Size:** 11 x 14 1/2. **Cols./Page:** 4. **Col. Width:** 23 nonpareils. **Col. Depth:** 192 agate lines. **Key Personnel:** Padraic Mullin, Editor; Johanna Mullin, Publisher; Laurie Rowed, Managing Editor. **Subscription Rates:** $32 individuals. **Remarks:** Accepts advertising. **URL:** http://www.amateurhockey.com. **Alt. Formats:** Mailing labels.
Ad Rates: BW: $500 **Circ:** Combined ‡10,000
4C: $850

14981 The New Age Patriot
New Age Patriot
PO Box 419 Phone: (313)563-3192
Dearborn Heights, MI 48127 Fax: (313)563-3192
Publisher E-mail: nap@mail.wwnet.com

Magazine concerning marijuana legalization advocacy. **Founded:** Jan. 1980. **Freq:** Quarterly. **Trim Size:** 8 1/2 x 11. **Cols./Page:** 3. **Col. Width:** 3 inches. **Subscription Rates:** $12 individuals. **Remarks:** Accepts advertising.
Circ: Paid 300
Non-paid 4,000

14982 Times-Herald
13730 Michigan Ave. Phone: (313)584-4000
Dearborn, MI 48126 Fax: (313)584-1357
Publisher E-mail: dbntherald@aol.com

Community newspaper. **Founded:** 1963. **Freq:** Semiweekly (Wed. and Sun.). **Print Method:** Offset. **Cols./Page:** 6. **Col. Width:** 12 1/2 picas. **Col. Depth:** 21 inches. **Key Personnel:** Scott Bewick, Editor; Michael Bewick, Publisher; Louise Parker, Advertising Mgr.; Tom J. Edwards, Editor. **USPS:** 193-230. **Subscription Rates:** $24.95 individuals; $39 out of area.

Remarks: Accepts advertising. **Formerly**: Heights Independent (1991).
Ad Rates: BW: $3,031.50 **Circ:** ‡27,000
4C: $3,481.50
SAU: $23.50

DECATUR

14983 Decatur Republican
Box 36 Phone: (616)423-2411
Decatur, MI 49045
Community newspaper. **Freq:** Weekly (Thurs.). **Key Personnel:** David D. Moorman, Editor.
Circ: 1,600

DECKERVILLE

14984 The Deckerville Recorder
Regentin Publishing
3520 Main Phone: (810)376-3805
PO Box 519 Fax: (810)376-4058
Deckerville, MI 48427
Community newspaper. **Founded:** Oct. 1892. **Freq:** Weekly (Wed.) 1XT (Tues.). **Print Method:** Offset. **Cols./Page:** 6. **Col. Width:** 9 1/2 picas. **Col. Depth:** 15 inches. **Key Personnel:** Douglas Regentin, Editor. **USPS:** 457-960. **Subscription Rates:** $13.50 out of state. **Remarks:** Accepts advertising. **Absorbed**: Carsonville-Port Sanilac Journal (1989).
Ad Rates: GLR: $.11 **Circ:** ‡2,189
BW: $336
SAU: $5
PCI: $4

DETROIT

14985 The Adcrafter
Adcraft Club of Detroit
1249 Washington Blvd., Ste. 2630 Phone: (313)962-7225
Fax: (313)962-3599
Detroit, MI 48226-1852
Publication E-mail: adcraft@adcraft.com
Publisher E-mail: adcraft@adcraft.org

Magazine for the advertising industry. **Subtitle:** The Voice of Advertising in Detroit. **Founded:** 1907. **Freq:** Weekly (Fri.). **Print Method:** Offset. **Trim Size:** 8 1/2 x 11. **Cols./Page:** 3. **Col. Width:** 14 picas. **Col. Depth:** 140 agate lines. **Key Personnel:** Robert Guerrini, Editor. **ISSN:** 0001-8066. **Subscription Rates:** $30. **Remarks:** Accepts advertising.
Ad Rates: BW: $700 **Circ:** ‡4,800
4C: $1,600
PCI: $21

14986 Against the Current
Center for Changes
7012 Michigan Ave. Phone: (313)841-0161
Detroit, MI 48210 Fax: (313)841-8884
Publication E-mail: cfc@igc.apc.org

Magazine oriented toward movements for social and political change. Emphasizes labor, national minorities, feminist issues, and international solidarity. Supports socialist democracy and workers' control, worldwide. **Founded:** 1979. **Freq:** Bimonthly. **Print Method:** Offset. **Trim Size:** 8 1/2 x 11. **Cols./Page:** 3. **Col. Width:** 27 nonpareils. **Col. Depth:** 133 agate lines. **Key Personnel:** David Finkel, Editor. **ISSN:** 0739-4853. **Subscription Rates:** $25 individuals; $25 institutions; $40 two years individual; $50 institutions. **Remarks:** Accepts advertising. **Formerly**: Changes Socialist Monthly (1985).
Circ: Paid ‡1,600

14987 American-Arab Message
17514 Woodward Ave. Phone: (313)868-2266
Detroit, MI 48203 Fax: (313)868-2267

Religious and political magazine printed in Arabic and English. **Founded:** May 1937. **Freq:** Weekly (Fri.). **Print Method:** Letterpress and offset. **Cols./Page:** 5. **Col. Width:** 24 nonpareils. **Col. Depth:** 301 agate lines. **Key Personnel:** Rev. (Imam) M.A. Hussein, Publisher, imam4@juno.com. **Subscription Rates:** $25. **Remarks:** Accepts advertising.
Ad Rates: GLR: $17.75 **Circ:** ‡8,750
BW: $700

14988 Annals of Scholarship
Wayne State University Press
Leonard N. Simons Bldg. Phone: (313)577-6120
4809 Woodward Ave. Fax: (313)577-6131
Detroit, MI 48201-1309
Free: (800)978-7323

Scholarly journal of the humanities and social sciences. **Founded:** 1980. **Freq:** Quarterly. **Trim Size:** 6 x 9. **Key Personnel:** Marie-Rose Logan, General Editor. **Remarks:** Advertising accepted; rates available upon request.
Circ: Paid 150

14989 Automotive Industries
Cahners Business Information
2600 Fisher Bldg. Phone: (313)875-2090
Detroit, MI 48202 Fax: (313)875-8148
Publisher E-mail: marketaccess@cahners.com

Magazine serving original equipment manufacturers in the automotive industry. **Founded:** 1895. **Freq:** Monthly. **Print Method:** Offset. **Trim Size:** 8 x 10 3/4. **Cols./Page:** 3. **Col. Width:** 25 nonpareils. **Col. Depth:** 140 agate lines. **Key Personnel:** John McElroy, Editor, jmcelroy@chilton.net; James E. Henne, Publisher. **ISSN:** 0273-656X. **Subscription Rates:** Free to qualified subscribers; $55; $110 other countries. **Remarks:** Accepts advertising.
Ad Rates: BW: $7,200 **Circ:** Non-paid ‡105,000
4C: $9,195
PCI: $150

14990 Automotive News
Crain Communications, Inc.
1400 Woodbridge Ave. Phone: (313)446-6000
Detroit, MI 48207-3187 Fax: (313)446-0347
Free: (800)678-9595
Publication E-mail: autonews@crain.com

Tabloid reporting on all facets of the automotive and truck industry, as well as related businesses. **Founded:** 1925. **Freq:** Weekly. **Print Method:** Offset. **Trim Size:** 11 x 14 1/2. **Cols./Page:** 5. **Col. Width:** 2 inches. **Col. Depth:** 196 agate lines. **Key Personnel:** Peter Brown, Editor, phone (313)446-1600, pbrown@crain.com; Keith E. Crain, Publisher; Tony Merpi, Advertising Dir., phone (313)446-6030, fax (313)446-8030, tmerpi@crain.com. **Subscription Rates:** $109 individuals; $3 single issue; $169 Canada; $288 other countries. **Remarks:** Accepts advertising.
Ad Rates: BW: $10,775 **Circ:** Paid ★**81,376**
4C: $13,845
PCI: $176

14991 AutoWeek
Crain Communications, Inc.
1400 Woodbridge Ave. Phone: (313)446-6000
Detroit, MI 48207-3187 Fax: (313)446-0347
Free: (800)678-9595
Publication E-mail: letters@autoweek.com; adsales@autoweek.com

Magazine for car enthusiasts includes news coverage and features on vehicles, personalities, and events. Provides coverage of Formula One, CART, NASCAR, and IMSA races. **Founded:** 1957. **Freq:** Weekly. **Print Method:** Letterpress and offset. **Trim Size:** 8 1/4 x 10 3/4. **Cols./Page:** 3. **Col. Width:** 2 1/4 inches. **Col. Depth:** 140 agate lines. **Key Personnel:** Dutch Mandel, Editor, phone (313)446-0318, fax (313)446-1027, dmandel@crain.com; Leon Mandel, Publisher, phone (313)446-6040, lmandel@crain.com; Jeff Nellett, Advertising Dir., phone (313)446-0355, jnellett@crain.com. **ISSN:** 0192-9674. **Subscription Rates:** $32 individuals; $2.50 single issue. **Remarks:** Accepts advertising. **Online:** LEXIS-NEXIS. **URL:** htttp://www.autoweek.com.
Ad Rates: BW: $17,405 **Circ:** Paid ★**294,214**
4C: $27,110
PCI: $6

14992 Babyfish...Lost Its Momma
PO Box 11589
Detroit, MI 48211
Publication E-mail: babyfish@umich.edu

A current events magazine containing poetry, articles, book and music reviews, recipes, and fiction. **Key Personnel:** Craig Sunfrog, Editor. **URL:** http://www-personal.umich.edu/~babyfish/fishnet_toc.html.

14993 Bulletin of the Detroit Institute of Arts
Detroit Institute of Arts
5200 Woodward Ave. Phone: (313)833-7900
Detroit, MI 48202 Fax: (313)833-3926
Publication E-mail: web@dia.org

Scholarly journal covering the collection of the Detroit Institute of Arts. **Founded:** 1919. **Freq:** Semiannual. **Print Method:** Sheetfed offset. **Trim Size:** 9 1/2 x 10. **Cols./Page:** 3. **Col. Width:** 2 1/2 inches. **Col. Depth:** 7 inches. **Key Personnel:** Maya Hoptman, Editor, phone (313)833-1368, fax (313)833-9169. **ISSN:** 0011-9636. **Subscription Rates:** $16 individuals; $10 members; $8 single issue; Free to qualified subscribers. **Remarks:** Advertising not accepted.
Circ: Combined 5,000

14994 The Citizen
11901 Joseph Campau Ave. Phone: (313)365-9500
Hamtramck, MI 48212
Local newspaper. **Founded:** Sept. 1934. **Freq:** Weekly (Thurs.). **Print Method:** Offset. **Trim Size:** 13 x 21 1/2. **Cols./Page:** 6. **Col. Width:** 12 picas. **Col. Depth:** 298 agate lines. **Key Personnel:** Karen Spang, Editor and Publisher. **ISSN:** 1042-6906. **Subscription Rates:** $18; $21 out of county. **Remarks:** Accepts advertising.
Ad Rates: GLR: $.45 **Circ:** ‡10,242
BW: $1,324.80
4C: $1,950
SAU: $17

14995 Co-Ette Magazine
Co-Ette Club Inc.
2020 W. Chicago Blvd. Phone: (313)867-0880
Detroit, MI 48206
Consumer club magazine covering local activities, culture, and philanthropy. **Founded:** 1959. **Freq:** Annual. **Key Personnel:** Mary-Agnes Miller Davis, Editor/Coordinator. **Remarks:** Accepts advertising.
Ad Rates: GLR: $200 **Circ:** (Not Reported)

14996 Crain's Detroit Business
Crain Communications, Inc.
1400 Woodbridge Ave. Phone: (313)446-6000
Detroit, MI 48207-3187 Fax: (313)446-0347
Free: (800)678-9595

Local business tabloid covering Wayne, Macomb, Oakland, Livingston, and Washtenaw counties. **Founded:** Feb. 4, 1985. **Freq:** Weekly (Mon.). **Print Method:** Offset. **Trim Size:** 11 x 14 3/4. **Cols./Page:** 5. **Col. Width:** 2 inches. **Col. Depth:** 14 inches. **Key Personnel:** Mary Kramer, Assoc. Publisher, phone (313)446-0399, fax (313)446-1687, mkramer@crain.com; Keith Crain, Publisher; Susan Cascade, Advertising Dir., phone (313)446-6032, fax (313)393-0997, scascade@crain.com. **ISSN:** 0882-1992. **Subscription Rates:** $49 /year. **Remarks:** Accepts advertising. **Online:** LEXIS-NEXIS. **URL:** http://www.crainsdetroit.com.
Ad Rates: BW: $8,260 **Circ:** Paid ★**36,167**
4C: $9,785

14997 Criticism
Wayne State University Press
Dept. of English Phone: (313)577-2450
Wayne State University Fax: (313)577-8618
Detroit, MI 48202
Journal on literature and the arts. **Subtitle:** A Quarterly for Literature and the Arts. **Founded:** 1959. **Freq:** Quarterly. **Print Method:** Offset. **Trim Size:** 6 x 9. **Cols./Page:** 1. **Col. Width:** 4 1/4 inches. **Col. Depth:** 6 5/8 inches. **Key Personnel:** Renata R. M. Wasserman, Editor, phone (313)577-3409, rwasser@cms.cc.wayne.edu; Arthur Evans, Publisher; Ann Schwartz, Contact. **ISSN:** 0011-1589. **Subscription Rates:** $28 individuals; $50 institutions; $15 single issue. **Remarks:** Accepts advertising.
Ad Rates: BW: $200 **Circ:** ‡1,200

14998 D.A.C. News
Detroit Athletic Club
241 Madison Ave. Phone: (313)963-5993
Detroit, MI 48226 Fax: (313)963-8891

Magazine reporting on club activities and including articles about sports, finance, travel, and personalities. **Subtitle:** Offical Magazine of Detroit Athletic Club. **Founded:** 1916. **Freq:** 9/year. **Print Method:** Offset. **Trim Size:** 8 1/2 x 11. **Cols./Page:** 3 and 2. **Col. Width:** 28 and 42 nonpareils. **Col. Depth:** 140 agate lines. **Key Personnel:** Albert C. Cochrane, Advertising Mgr.; John A. Bluth, Editor and Publisher. **ISSN:** 0011-4707. **Subscription Rates:** $36 individuals. **Remarks:** Accepts advertising.
Ad Rates: BW: $715 **Circ:** ‡4,114
4C: $1,410

14999 Detroit Free Press
Knight-Ridder, Inc.
321 W. Lafayette Blvd. Phone: (313)222-6400
Detroit, MI 48226 Fax: (313)222-5981
Free: (800)678-6400

General newspaper. Publishes combined weekend and holiday editions with the Detroit News under 1989 Joint Operating Agreement. **Founded:** May 1, 1831. **Freq:** Mon.-Sun. (morn.). **Print Method:** Offset. **Cols./Page:** 6. **Col. Width:** 13 picas. **Col. Depth:** 21 3/4 inches. **Key Personnel:** Joe Stroud, Editor, phone (313)222-6583, fax (313)222-6774; Heath J. Meriwether, Publisher, phone (313)222-5794, fax (313)222-8874; Robert G. McGruder, Exec. Editor, phone (313)222-6821, fax (313)222-5981; Chip Visci, Managing Editor, phone (313)222-8850, fax (313)222-5981; Jerry Teagan, Vice President and Business Mgr., phone (313)222-6595, fax (313)222-8874; Laura Varon Brown, Graphics Dir., phone (313)222-5002, fax (313)222-5981; Ron Dzwonkowski, Projects Editor, phone (313)222-6635, fax (313)222-5981; Carole Leigh Hutton, Deputy Managing Editor/News, phone (313)222-6606, fax (313)222-5981; Lawrence DeVine, Theater Critic, phone (313)222-6517, fax (313)223-4726; Mike Davis, Design Dir., phone (313)222-6792, fax (313)222-5981; Nancy Laughlin, National/World Desk Editor, phone (313)223-4743, fax (313)223-5981; Mike Smith, Photography Dir., phone (313)222-8893, fax (313)222-5981; Julie Topping, Universal Desk Chief, phone (313)223-4473, fax (313)223-5985; David Kushma, Assoc. Editor, phone (313)222-6583, fax (313)222-

6774. **Subscription Rates:** $343.20; $371.80 out of state; $150.80 Sunday edition only; $158.60 out of state Sunday edition only. **Remarks:** Accepts advertising. **Online:** Dialog (The Dialog Corporation); CompuServe Information Service. **URL:** http://www.freep.com. **Alt. Formats:** CD-ROM, Dialog (The Dialog Corporation). **Feature Editors:** Pat Anstett, *Medical*, phone (313)222-5021, fax (313)222-5397; Leesa Bainbridge, *City*, phone (313)222-6582, fax (313)222-5981; Alex Cruden, *News*, phone (313)222-6465, fax (313)222-5981; David Crumm, *Religion*, phone (313)223-4626, fax (313)223-5981; Mike Duffy, *TV*, phone (313)222-6520, fax (313)222-4726; Thom Fladung, *Lifestyle*, phone (313)223-4272, fax (313)223-5397; Marty Hair, *Garden/Home*, phone (313)222-6610, fax (313)223-4726; Patty LaNouns Stearns, *Food*, phone (313)222-5026, fax (313)223-4726; Linnea Lannon, *Book*, phone (313)222-6620, fax (313)223-4726; Chris Ledbetter, *Entertainment*, phone (313)222-6619, fax (313)223-4726; Mike Lupo, *City*, phone (313)222-6806, fax (313)222-5981; Hugh McDiarmid, *Political*, phone (313)223-4470, fax (313)223-5981; Gene Myers, *Sports*, phone (313)222-6736, fax (313)222-5983; Kathy O'Gorman, *Education*, phone (313)222-6651, fax (313)222-5981; Dale Parry, *Features*, phone (313)222-6549, fax (313)223-4726; Gerry Volgenau, *Travel*, phone (313)222-6521, fax (313)223-4726; Tom Walsh, *Financial/Business*, phone (313)222-8767, fax (313)222-5992.
Ad Rates: GLR: $19.86; BW: $53,113.50; 4C: $61,973.50; PCI: $407
Circ: Mon.-Fri. ★**378,256**; Sat. ★**600,786**; Sun. ★**805,405**

15000 The Detroit Jewish News
27676 Franklin Rd. Phone: (248)354-6060
Southfield, MI 48034-8203 Fax: (248)354-6069
Publication E-mail: thedjn@aol.com

Jewish interest newspaper. **Founded:** 1942. **Freq:** Weekly (Fri.). **Print Method:** Offset. **Trim Size:** 11 x 14. **Cols./Page:** 5. **Col. Depth:** 13 inches. **Key Personnel:** Gary Rosenblatt, Editor; Charles Buerger, Publisher; Arthur Horwitz, Advertising Mgr. **USPS:** 275-520. **Subscription Rates:** $34; $45 out of area. **Remarks:** Accepts advertising. **URL:** http://www.detroitjewishnews.com.
Ad Rates: PCI: $21.25
Circ: Paid 20,555; Free 300

15001 The Detroit Journal
B & Y Publications
11000 W. McNichols, Ste. 210 Phone: (313)342-1717
Detroit, MI 48221 Fax: (313)312-9078

Black community newspaper (tabloid). **Founded:** 1992. **Freq:** Monthly. **Print Method:** Offset. **Key Personnel:** Walter Johnson, Editor and Publisher. **Subscription Rates:** Free. **Formerly:** The Detroit Times.
Circ: Free 20,000

15002 Detroit Labor News
Metropolitan Detroit AFL-CIO
2550 W. Grand Blvd. Phone: (313)896-2600
Detroit, MI 48208 Fax: (313)896-1078

Labor tabloid. **Founded:** Apr. 3, 1914. **Freq:** Biweekly. **Print Method:** Offset. **Trim Size:** 10 x 13. **Cols./Page:** 4. **Col. Width:** 14 1/2 picas. **Col. Depth:** 182 picas. **Key Personnel:** Aldo Vagnozzi, Editor. **USPS:** 462-990. **Subscription Rates:** $11. **Remarks:** Advertising not accepted for anti-union companies. **Alt. Formats:** Microform.
Ad Rates: GLR: $.72; BW: $500; 4C: $600; PCI: $10
Circ: Paid ⊕**4,770**; Non-paid ⊕**100**

15003 Detroit Legal News
Detroit Legal News Co.
2001 W. Lafayette Phone: (313)961-3949
Detroit, MI 48216 Fax: (313)961-7817
Free: (800)875-5275

Legal and financial newspaper. **Founded:** 1895. **Freq:** Daily (morn.) M-F. **Print Method:** Offset. **Trim Size:** 15 1/2 x 22. **Cols./Page:** 7. **Col. Width:** 1 7/8 inches. **Col. Depth:** 21 inches. **Key Personnel:** Eric Pope, Editor, editor@legalnews.com. **USPS:** 155-580. **Subscription Rates:** $140 annually. **Remarks:** Accepts advertising. **Available Online. URL:** http://www.legalnews.com.
Ad Rates: BW: $970; 4C: $1,690; PCI: $18
Circ: ⊕**1,850**

15004 Detroit Medical News
Wayne County Medical Society
1010 Antietam Phone: (313)567-1640
Detroit, MI 48207-2899 Fax: (313)567-2065

Magazine for the medical profession. **Founded:** 1902. **Freq:** Weekly. **Print Method:** Offset. Uses mats. **Trim Size:** 8 1/2 x 11. **Cols./Page:** 3. **Col. Width:** 27 nonpareils. **Col. Depth:** 112 agate lines. **Key Personnel:** Susan H. Adelman, M.D., Editor; Marlise A. Michael, Managing Editor. **Subscription Rates:** $40. **Remarks:** Accepts advertising.
Ad Rates: BW: $254; PCI: $34
Circ: ‡4,500

15005 Detroit Metropolitan Woman
Metropolitan Woman Inc.
North Park Plaza Phone: (248)443-6500
17117 W. 9 Mile Rd., Ste. 1115 Fax: (248)443-6501
Southfield, MI 48075-4517
Magazine containing news, features, and information for women in the metropolitan Detroit area. **Founded:** 1991. **Freq:** Monthly. **Print Method:** Web press. **Trim Size:** 8 x 10 3/4. **Cols./Page:** 3. **Key Personnel:** Alice F. Sieloff, Publisher. **Subscription Rates:** $18; $2 single issue. **Remarks:** Accepts advertising.
Ad Rates: BW: $2,375; 4C: $2,520
Circ: Paid ‡10,000; Non-paid ‡20,000

15006 The Detroit News
Gannett Co., Inc.
615 W. Lafayette Blvd. Phone: (313)222-2300
Detroit, MI 48226-3197 Fax: (313)222-2335
Free: (800)678-4115

General newspaper. Publishes combined weekend and holiday editions with the Detroit Free Press under 1989 Joint Operating Agreement. **Founded:** 1873. **Freq:** Mon.-Sun. (morn.). **Print Method:** Offset. **Cols./Page:** 6. **Col. Width:** 2 1/16 inches. **Col. Depth:** 22 1/4 inches. **Key Personnel:** Mark Silverman, Editor and Publisher; Robert Giles, Editor; Christina Bradford, Managing Editor. **Remarks:** Accepts advertising. **Online:** DataTimes Corporation. **Alt. Formats:** CD-ROM, NewsBank, Inc. **Feature Editors:** Tom Bray, *Editorials*; Marge Colburn, *Garden/Home*; Phil Laciura, *Sports*; Rhonda Rudd, *Art*, *Religion*; Susan Stark, *Movie*.
Ad Rates: SAU: $281.07
Circ: Mon.-Fri. ★**245,351**; Sat. ★**600,786**; Sun. ★**805,405**

15007 Detroit Society for Genealogical Research Magazine
Detroit Society for Genealogical Research, Inc.
The Burton Historical Collection Phone: (313)833-1480
Detroit Public Library
5201 Woodward Ave. & Kirby
Detroit, MI 48202-4093
Genealogy magazine. **Founded:** 1936. **Freq:** Quarterly. **Print Method:** Letterpress and offset. **Trim Size:** 8 1/2 x 11. **Cols./Page:** 1. **Key Personnel:** Patricia Ibbotson, Editor, pibbotso@aol.com. **ISSN:** 0011-9687. **Subscription Rates:** $20 individuals. **Remarks:** Advertising not accepted. **URL:** http://dsgr.org.
Circ: ‡900

15008 Detroiter
Detroit Regional Chamber
1 Woodward Ave., Ste. 1700 Phone: (313)964-4000
PO Box 33840 Fax: (313)964-0531
Detroit, MI 48232-0840
Publisher E-mail: research@detroitchamber.com

Magazine focusing on Metro Detroit business news. **Subtitle:** For Business in Regional Detroit. **Founded:** 1910. **Freq:** Monthly. **Print Method:** Offset. **Trim Size:** 7 3/8 x 9 7/8. **Cols./Page:** 3. **Col. Width:** 28 nonpareils. **Col. Depth:** 139 agate lines. **Key Personnel:** Chris W. Mead, Editor, phone (313)596-0373, cmead@detroitchamber.com; Valerie Bollin, Sr. Dir. of Advertising, vbollin@detroitchamber.com. **ISSN:** 0011-9709. **Subscription Rates:** $18 individuals. **Remarks:** Accepts advertising. **URL:** http://www.detroitchamber.com.
Ad Rates: BW: $1,495; 4C: $2,349
Circ: Paid 18,535; Controlled 2,000

15009 Drug Metabolism and Disposition
Lippincott Williams & Wilkins
The Institute of Chemical Toxicology Phone: (313)577-4068
Wayne State University Fax: (313)577-0082
2727 2nd Ave., Rm. 4000
Detroit, MI 48201-2564
Medical journal. **Subtitle:** The Biological Fate of Chemicals. **Founded:** 1973. **Freq:** Monthly. **Print Method:** Offset. **Trim Size:** 8 3/8 x 10 7/8. **Cols./Page:** 2. **Col. Width:** 32 nonpareils. **Col. Depth:** 119 agate lines. **Key Personnel:** Raymond F. Novak, Ph.D., Editor; C. Valton, Rep., cvalton@wwilkins.com. **ISSN:** 0090-9556. **Subscription Rates:** $85 individuals; $105 other countries. **Remarks:** Accepts advertising. **Alt. Formats:** Mailing labels; Mailing labels.
Ad Rates: BW: $345; 4C: $1,085
Circ: Paid ‡1,016; Non-paid ‡93

15010 Family Relations
National Council on Family Relations
Wayne State University Phone: (313)873-5032
87 E. Ferry St. Fax: (313)871-9383
Detroit, MI 48202
Free: (888)781-9331
Publication E-mail: fr@iog.wayne.edu
Publisher E-mail: ncfr3989@ncfr.com

Publication for family practitioners and academics on relationships across the life cycle with implications for intervention, education and public policy. **Subtitle:** Interdisciplinary Journal of Applied Family Studies. **Founded:** 1968. **Freq:** Quarterly. **Print Method:** Offset. **Trim Size:** 8 1/2 x 11. **Cols./Page:** 2. **Key Personnel:** Jeffrey Dwyer, Editor, dwyer@iog.wayne.edu. **ISSN:** 0197-6664. **Subscription Rates:** $45 individuals; $85 institutions; $20 students Non-US add $12. **Remarks:** Accepts advertising. **URL:** http://www.iog.wayne.edu/fr. **Formerly:** Family Relations: Journal of Applied Family of Child Studies.
Ad Rates: BW: $600
Circ: ‡5,000

15011 Fifth Estate
4632 2nd Ave. Phone: (313)831-6800
Detroit, MI 48201
Magazine covering anarchism and radical environmentalism. **Founded:** 1965. **Freq:** Quarterly. **Print Method:** Web offset. **Cols./Page:** 4. **ISSN:** 0015-0800. **Subscription Rates:** $8 U.S.; $10 other countries; Free to prisoners; $12 libraries; $50 corporations, government agencies. **Remarks:** Advertising not accepted.
Circ: Paid 5,000

15012 Human Biology
Wayne State University Press
The Leonard N. Simons Bldg. Phone: (313)577-6120
4809 Woodward Ave. Fax: (313)577-6131
Detroit, MI 48201-1309
Free: (800)978-7323

Journal on population genetics, evolutionary and genetic demography, and behavioral genetics. **Subtitle:** The International Journal of Population Biology and Genetics. **Founded:** 1929. **Freq:** Bimonthly. **Print Method:** Offset. **Trim Size:** 6 x 9. **Cols./Page:** 1. **Col. Width:** 4 1/2 inches. **Col. Depth:** 7 inches. **Key Personnel:** Michael H. Crawford, Editor. **ISSN:** 0018-7143. **Subscription Rates:** $75 individuals; $140 institutions. **Remarks:** Advertising not accepted.
Circ: 1,800

15013 Journal of Aging and Ethnicity
Springer Publishing Co.
c/o Donald E. Gelfand, Ph. D., Editor Phone: (313)577-0774
Department of Sociology Fax: (313)577-2735
2228 F/AB Wayne State University
Detroit, MI 48202
Publisher E-mail: springer@springerpub.com

Scholarly journal for researchers and professionals in gerontology and geriatrics, emphasizing the ethnic population of North America. **Founded:** 1996. **Trim Size:** 7 x 10. **Cols./Page:** 1. **Col. Width:** 5 inches. **Col. Depth:** 8 inches. **Key Personnel:** Donald E. Gelfand, Ph.D., Editor; Rafael Ortiz, Advertising Mgr.; Cory Sklaire, Circulation Mgr.; Matt Fenton, Production Mgr. **ISSN:** 1076-1624. **Subscription Rates:** $26 individuals; $62 two years; $49 individuals out of country; $74 two years out of country; $70 institutions; $105 institutions two years; $79 institutions out of country; $119 institutions two years out of country; $15 single issue. **Remarks:** Accepts advertising.
Ad Rates: BW: $300
Circ: Combined 150

15014 Journal of Analytic Social Work
The Haworth Press, Inc.
Wayne State Univ. Phone: (313)577-4447
School of Social Work Fax: (313)577-8770
Detroit, MI 48202
Publisher E-mail: getinfo@haworthpressinc.com

Journal on social work. **Founded:** 1993. **Freq:** Quarterly. **Trim Size:** 6x8 1/2. **Key Personnel:** Jerrold R. Brandell, Ph.D., Editor; Bill Cohen, Publisher. **ISSN:** 1052-9950. **Subscription Rates:** $36 individuals; $48 institutions; $95 libraries. **Remarks:** Accepts advertising.
Ad Rates: BW: $300
Circ: Paid 569

15015 Journal of Organizational Behavior-Management
The Haworth Press, Inc.
Univ. of Detroit Mercy Phone: (313)993-1000
College of Business & Adminstration Fax: (313)271-4910
4001 W. McNichols
Detroit, MI 48221-9987
Publisher E-mail: getinfo@haworthpressinc.com

Journal on behavior management in organizations. **Founded:** 1977. **Freq:** Biannual. **Trim Size:** 6x8 1/2. **Key Personnel:** Thomas Mawhinney, Ph.D., Editor; Bill Cohen, Publisher. **ISSN:** 0160-8061. **Subscription Rates:** $32 individuals; $140 institutions; $250 libraries. **Remarks:** Accepts advertising.
Ad Rates: BW: $300
Circ: Controlled ‡583

15016 Journal of Stroke and Cerebrovascular Diseases
National Stroke Association (NSA)
Henry Ford Hospital Phone: (313)876-2665
Dept. Of Neurology Fax: (313)876-1466
2799 W. Grand Blvd.
Detroit, MI 48202
Publisher E-mail: info@stroke.org

Professional journal covering information related to stroke and cerebrovascular disease for the medical community. **Freq:** Bimonthly. **Cols./Page:** 2. **Key Personnel:** Dr. K.M.A. Welch, M.D., Editor-in-Chief; Susan E. MacPhee, Managing Editor. **ISSN:** 1052-3057. **Subscription Rates:** $99 individuals; $44 single issue. **Remarks:** Accepts advertising.
Circ: (Not Reported)

15017 Merrill-Palmer Quarterly
Wayne State University Press
The Leonard N. Simons Bldg. Phone: (313)577-6120
4809 Woodward Ave. Fax: (313)577-6131
Detroit, MI 48201-1309
Free: (800)978-7323

Journal presenting original experimental, theoretical, and review papers on issues of human development. **Subtitle:** Journal of Developmental Psychology. **Founded:** 1954. **Freq:** Quarterly. **Print Method:** Offset. **Trim Size:** 6 x 9. **Cols./Page:** 1. **Col. Width:** 26. picas. **Col. Depth:** 42 picas. **Key Personnel:** Keith Stanovich, Assoc. Editor, phone (416)961-8758; Nicki Crick, Assoc. Editor, phone (612)625-8879; Charlotte Patteron, Assoc. Editor, phone (804)924-0665; Carolyn U. Shantz, Editor, phone (313)577-0653, fax (313)577-7636, cshantzsunday.science.wayne.edu; Ann Schwartz, Advertising Mgr. **ISSN:** 0272-930X. **Subscription Rates:** $45; $86 institutions; single issue. **Remarks:** Accepts advertising.
Ad Rates: BW: $225 **Circ:** Paid ‡1,200
Non-paid ‡100

15018 Metro Times
Metro Times, Inc.
733 Saint Antoine St. Phone: (313)961-4060
Detroit, MI 48226-2936 Fax: (313)961-6598
Publication E-mail: metrotimes@aminc.com
Publisher E-mail: metrotimes@metrotimes.com

Newspaper. **Subtitle:** News, Arts, and Entertainment in Metro Detroit. **Founded:** 1980. **Freq:** Weekly (Wed.). **Print Method:** Offset. **Trim Size:** 10 3/8 x 13. **Cols./Page:** 6. **Col. Width:** 20 nonpareils. **Col. Depth:** 182 agate lines. **Key Personnel:** Jim McCarter, Publisher, jmccarter@aminc.com; Larry Gabriel, Editor, lgabriel@aminc.com. **Subscription Rates:** Free; $50; $80 (mail). **Remarks:** Accepts advertising. **Available Online. URL:** http://www.metrotimes.com. **Feature Editors:** Alisa Gordaneer, *Environmental, Food, Travel*, agordaneer@metrotimes.com.
Ad Rates: GLR: $4.72 **Circ:** Non-paid 106,805
BW: $1,795
4C: $2,395
SAU: $33
CNU: $34.20

15019 The Michigan Catholic
305 Michigan Ave. Phone: (313)224-8000
Detroit, MI 48226 Fax: (313)224-8009

Religious newspaper (tabloid). **Founded:** 1873. **Freq:** Weekly (Fri.). **Print Method:** Offset. **Trim Size:** 11 1/4 x 14 1/2. **Cols./Page:** 5. **Col. Width:** 2 inches. **Col. Depth:** 12 3/4 inches. **Key Personnel:** Msgr. F Gerald Martin, Associate Publisher; Ken Shoemaker, Director of Marketing; Kristine L. Persinger, Managing Editor. **USPS:** 344-740. **Subscription Rates:** $20. **Remarks:** Accepts advertising.
Ad Rates: GLR: $.90 **Circ:** ‡35,000
BW: $939.12
4C: $1,339.12

15020 Michigan Chronicle
Sengestacke Newspaper Corp.
479 Ledyard St. Phone: (313)963-5522
Detroit, MI 48201 Fax: (313)963-8788
Free: (800)203-2229
Publication E-mail: chronicle4@aol

Black community newspaper. **Subtitle:** Michigan Chronicle. **Founded:** 1936. **Freq:** Weekly (Wed.). **Print Method:** Offset. **Cols./Page:** 6. **Col. Width:** 21 nonpareils. **Col. Depth:** 126 inches. **Key Personnel:** Samuel Logan, Publisher; John H. Sengstacke, Chmn. of the Board; Alisa M. Giddens, Business Mgr. **Subscription Rates:** $25 individuals newspaper rates; $14 6 months; $46 two years; $.50 single issue magazine rates. **Alt. Formats:** CD-ROM, Softline; CD-ROM, Ethnic News Watch; Microform.
Ad Rates: GLR: $37.75 **Circ:** ‡47,428
BW: $4,756.50
4C: $1,147.90

15021 Michigan Contractor and Builder
Contractor Publishing Co.
1629 W. Lafayette Phone: (313)962-3337
Detroit, MI 48216 Fax: (313)962-4560

Magazine providing information on highway, airport, bridge, sewer, water-works, and heavy public and private building construction. **Founded:** 1907. **Freq:** Weekly (Sat.). **Print Method:** Offset. **Trim Size:** 8 1/8 x 10 7/8. **Cols./Page:** 3 and 2. **Col. Width:** 26 and 42 nonpareils. **Col. Depth:** 140 agate lines. **Key Personnel:** Guy Snyder, Editor, guysny@aol.com; J.D. Mertz, Publisher; Roy Jones, Advertising Mgr. **USPS:** 997-740. **Subscription Rates:** $115 individuals. **Remarks:** Accepts advertising.
Ad Rates: BW: $584 **Circ:** Paid 2,708
4C: $909 Non-paid 298

15022 Michigan Industry
Contractor Publishing Co.
1629 W. Lafayette Phone: (313)962-3337
Detroit, MI 48216 Fax: (313)962-4560

Magazine serving readers in the Michigan industrial sector–metalworking, manufacturing, plastics, woodworking, material handling, and specialized equipment fields. **Founded:** Apr. 1968. **Freq:** Bimonthly. **Print Method:** Offset. **Trim Size:** 8 1/4 x 11. **Cols./Page:** 3. **Col. Width:** 13 picas. **Col. Depth:** 60 picas. **Key Personnel:** Guy Snyder, Editor, guysny@aol.com; John D. Mertz, Publisher; Roy Jones, Advertising Mgr. **ISSN:** 0746-911X. **Remarks:** Accepts advertising. **Formerly:** Michigan Plant and Equipment.
Ad Rates: BW: $758 **Circ:** Non-paid ‡16,000
4C: $1,258
PCI: $43

15023 The Monitor
Downtown Detroit Monitor, Inc.
33490 Groesbeck Phone: (810)296-6007
Fraser, MI 48026 Fax: (810)296-6072

City-wide newspaper (tabloid) emphasizing downtown Detroit; covers entertainment, music, sports, and educational opportunities. **Founded:** Dec. 1963. **Freq:** Weekly (Thurs.). **Print Method:** Offset. **Trim Size:** 11 1/2 x 14. **Cols./Page:** 5. **Col. Width:** 11.5 picas. **Col. Depth:** 12 3/4 inches. **Key Personnel:** Horst Mann, Editor; Joseph R. Zerilli, Publisher. **Subscription Rates:** Free; $40 by mail. **Remarks:** Color advertising accepted; rates available upon request. **Formerly:** Detroit Monitor (1990).
Ad Rates: GLR: $1 **Circ:** Free ‡47,000
BW: $750
PCI: $14

15024 Motorbooty
Clownskull Graphics
Box 02007 Phone: (313)871-8419
Detroit, MI 48202 Fax: (313)871-4840
Publication E-mail: motorb@motorbooty.com

Consumer magazine covering underground culture and satire. **Subtitle:** The Better Magazine. **Founded:** Sept. 1987. **Freq:** Irregular. **Print Method:** Offset. **Key Personnel:** Mark Dancey, Editor and Publisher; David Merline, Managing Editor; Mike Rubin, Senior Editor. **Subscription Rates:** $16 individuals; $7 single issue. **Remarks:** Accepts advertising. **URL:** http://www.motorbooty.com.
Ad Rates: BW: $1,500 **Circ:** Paid 25,000
4C: $2,500

15025 Neurological Research
Forefront Publishing
Wayne State University Phone: (313)745-4661
University Health Center, 6E Fax: (313)745-4099
Department of Neurosurgery
4201 St. Antoine
Detroit, MI 48201
Publisher E-mail: zapdoib@prodigy.com

Professional medical journal covering research and reviews on neurosurgery, neurology, and neurosciences. **Founded:** 1979. **Freq:** 8/year. **Print Method:** Sheetfed offset. **Trim Size:** 8 1/2 x 11. **Cols./Page:** 2. **Col. Width:** 20 picas. **Col. Depth:** 60 picas. **Key Personnel:** George M. Austin, MD, Editor; Manuel Dujovny, MD, Editor, dujovny@neurosurg.wayne.edu. **ISSN:** 0161-6412. **Subscription Rates:** $125 individuals; $675 institutions; $98 students. **Remarks:** Accepts advertising.
Ad Rates: BW: $565 **Circ:** (Not Reported)
4C: $1,265

15026 PIME World
PIME Missionaries
17330 Quincy St. Phone: (313)342-4066
Detroit, MI 48221-2765 Fax: (313)342-6816

Magazine reporting on missionary activities. **Founded:** 1954. **Freq:** Monthly (except July-August). **Trim Size:** 8 1/8 x 10 3/4. **Cols./Page:** 3. **Col. Width:** 13 1/2 picas. **Col. Depth:** 9 1/4 inches. **Key Personnel:** Paul W. Witte, Managing Editor, pimemiss@flash.net; Bruno Piccolo, Publisher. **ISSN:** 0008-8218. **Subscription Rates:** $5. **Remarks:** Advertising not accepted. **Alt. Formats:** Microfilm. **Formerly:** Catholic Life.
Circ: 26,000

15027 Place
Dawson Publications, Inc.
American Institute of Architects Phone: (313)965-4100
Michigan Chapter Fax: (313)965-1501
553 E. Jefferson St.
Detroit, MI 48226
Professional magazine covering architecture by local architects. **Freq:** Quarterly. **Key Personnel:** Tim Casai; Cathy Mosley, Circulation Mgr. **Subscription Rates:** $2.50 single issue. **Remarks:** Accepts advertising.
Ad Rates: BW: $1,200 **Circ:** Controlled 3,500

15028 The Pyramid
2211 Cass Ave. Phone: (313)961-9148
Detroit, MI 48201 Fax: (313)961-9052

Magazine containing temple information for members of the Shriner organization. **Founded:** 1893. **Freq:** Quarterly. **Print Method:** Letterpress and offset. **Key Personnel:** Ivory M. Buck, Jr., Editor; Fred Williams, Advertising Mgr. **Remarks:** Advertising not accepted.
Circ: Paid 28,000
Non-paid 25

15029 Resource Sharing & Information Networks
The Haworth Press, Inc.
3100 Adamany Library Phone: (313)577-4021
Wayne State Univ. Fax: (313)577-7563
Detroit, MI 48202
Publication E-mail: aa3805@wayne.edu
Publisher E-mail: getinfo@haworthpressinc.com

Journal on recent developments in the area of interlibrary cooperation in all types of libraries. **Freq:** 2/year. **Trim Size:** 6x8 1/2. **Key Personnel:** Robert P. Holley, PhD, Editor, fax (313)577-5725, aa3805@wayne.edu. **ISSN:** 0737-7797. **Subscription Rates:** $42 individuals; $125 institutions; $150 libraries.
Ad Rates: BW: $300 **Circ:** Paid 424

15030 Signal
Detroit Educational Television Foundation
7441 2nd Blvd. Phone: (313)873-7200
Detroit, MI 48202 Fax: (313)876-8118
Publication E-mail: viewer_ services@wtvs.org

Detroit public television program guide. **Freq:** Monthly. **Trim Size:** 8 1/2 x 11. **Key Personnel:** Sandy Jaszczak, Editor, phone (313)876-8161, sandy_ jaszczak@wtvs.org. **USPS:** 000-183. **Subscription Rates:** $40. **Remarks:** Color advertising accepted; rates available upon request. **URL:** http://www.wtvs.org. **Formerly:** Signal 56.
Ad Rates: BW: $1,930 **Circ:** ‡70,000
4C: $2,530

15031 Solidarity
International Union, U.A.W.
8000 E. Jefferson Ave. Phone: (313)926-5291
Detroit, MI 48214 Fax: (313)331-1520
Publisher E-mail: uaw@uaw.org

Labor magazine. **Founded:** 1954. **Freq:** 10/year. **Print Method:** Rotogravure. **Trim Size:** 9 3/8 x 11 1/2. **Cols./Page:** 3. **Col. Width:** 17 picas. **Col. Depth:** 68 picas. **Key Personnel:** David Elsila, Editor. **ISSN:** 0164-856X. **Subscription Rates:** $5. **Remarks:** Advertising not accepted. **URL:** http://www.uaw.org.
Circ: Non-paid ‡1,315,000

15032 The South End
Wayne State University Student Newspapers Publishing Board
6001 Cass Ave. Phone: (313)577-3494
Detroit, MI 48202 Fax: (313)577-6546
Publication E-mail: jennifer@southend.wayne.edu

Collegiate newspaper. **Founded:** 1918. **Freq:** Daily (during the academic year); 2/week (May-Aug.). **Print Method:** Offset. **Cols./Page:** 5. **Col. Width:** 20 nonpareils. **Col. Depth:** 189 agate lines. **Key Personnel:** Terri Nichols, Editor-in-Chief, terri@southend.wayne.edu; Robert Sharp, Advertising Mgr. **Subscription Rates:** Free; $70 by mail. **Available Online. URL:** http://www.southend.wayne.edu. **Formerly:** The Daily Collegian.
Ad Rates: BW: $388 **Circ:** Free ‡10,000
4C: $868
SAU: $7.50
PCI: $8

15033 Struggle
Tim Hall
Box 13261 Phone: (313)273-9039
Detroit, MI 48213-0261
Literary magazine covering poetry, fiction, essays, and related

literature. **Subtitle:** A Magazine of Proletarian Revolutionary Literature. **Founded:** 1985. **Freq:** Quarterly. **Print Method:** 8 1/2 x 5 3/4. **Key Personnel:** Tim Hall, Editor. **ISSN:** 1094-9399. **Subscription Rates:** $10 individuals; $12 institutions; $15 institutions out of country; $2.50 single issue. **Remarks:** Advertising not accepted.

Circ: Combined 450

15034 Varsity News
University of Detroit-Mercy
3800 Puritan Phone: (313)993-3300
Detroit, MI 48238 Fax: (313)993-1120

College newspaper. **Founded:** 1918. **Freq:** Weekly. **Print Method:** Offset. **Cols./Page:** 6. **Col. Width:** 12.5 picas. **Col. Depth:** 20.5 inches. **Key Personnel:** Matthew Mio, Editor, miomj@ujmercy.edu; Bret Mantyk, Advertising Mgr. **Subscription Rates:** Free.
Ad Rates: BW: $386 **Circ:** Free ‡5,000
4C: $780
PCI: $9

15035 Wayne State Magazine
Wayne State University
441 Ferry Mall Phone: (313)577-6044
Detroit, MI 48202-3619 Fax: (313)577-6044

Student interest magazine. **Founded:** 1934. **Freq:** Quarterly. **Print Method:** Laserprinter. **Trim Size:** 8 1/2 x 11. **Cols./Page:** 3. **Col. Width:** 2.5 picas. **Col. Depth:** 7 inches. **Key Personnel:** Deborah D. Suitt, Editor. **Subscription Rates:** Free to qualified subscribers; $12. **Remarks:** Accepts advertising.
Ad Rates: BW: $350 **Circ:** Non-paid 2,000
4C: $800

15036 The Witness
The Episcopal Church Publishing Co.
7000 Michigan Ave. Phone: (313)841-1967
Detroit, MI 48210-2872 Fax: (313)841-1956

Ecumenical journal addressing issues of faith and social justice through art, poetry, book reviews, profiles and essays. **Founded:** 1917. **Freq:** 10/year. **Print Method:** Offset. **Trim Size:** 9 x 10. **Cols./Page:** 3. **Col. Width:** 28 nonpareils. **Col. Depth:** 115 agate lines. **Key Personnel:** Jeanie Wylie-Kellermann, Co-Editor; Julie Wortman, Co-Editor. **ISSN:** 0197-8896. **Subscription Rates:** $25 individuals; $15 limited income; $30 other countries; $3 single issue. **Remarks:** Advertising not accepted. **Alt. Formats:** Microform.

Circ: Paid ‡4,500
Non-paid ‡500

15037 Booth American Co.
333 W. Fort St., Ste. 1230 Phone: (313)965-3360
Detroit, MI 48226 Fax: (313)965-1160

Founded: 1939. **Key Personnel:** Richard Lesley, Contact. **Cities Served:** Kernville, CA; Madeira, FL; Bingham Farms, Birmingham, Bloomfield Hill, Jackson, MI; Boone, NC; Andersonville, SC; Watertown, SD; Blacksburg, Salem, VA: subscribing households 141,761.

15038 Comcast Cablevision
12775 Lyndon Ave. Phone: (313)934-2600
Detroit, MI 48227 Fax: (313)934-9490

Founded: 1982. **Formerly:** Barden Cablevision. **Key Personnel:** Don H. Barden, President; Yvonne Murray, General Mgr.; John Barden, Contact; Robert Hood, Operations Mgr. **Cities Served:** subscribing households 4,100; 38 channels; 1 community access channel.

15039 WCSX-FM - 94.7
1 Radio Plaza Phone: (248)398-7600
Detroit, MI 48220 Fax: (248)542-8800

Format: Classic Rock. **Owner:** Greater Media, Inc., 2 Kennedy Blvd., East Brunswick, NJ 08816. **Founded:** 1967. **Formerly:** WMJC-FM. **Operating Hours:** Continuous. **ADI:** Detroit, MI. **Key Personnel:** Tom Bender, Sr. Vice Pres./Regional General Mgr.; Mike Chires, Dir. of Sales; Allen Gantman, General Sales Mgr.; Michael T. Mayer, National Sales Mgr. **Local Programs:** *The Peter Werbe Show*, Peter Werbe; *Radio Microscope*, Lisa Dillon. **Wattage:** 50,000. **Ad Rates:** Advertising accepted; rates available upon request. **URL:** http://www.wcsx.com.

15040 WDET-FM - 101.9
4600 Cass Phone: (313)577-4146
Detroit, MI 48201 Fax: (313)577-1300
E-mail: wdetfm@wdet.wayne.edu

Format: Eclectic; Jazz; News; Folk; Blues. **Networks:** National Public Radio (NPR); Michigan Public Radio. **Owner:** Wayne State University, 4249 Faculty Administation Bldg., Detroit, MI 48202, (313)577-2268. **Founded:** 1952. **Operating Hours:** Continuous; 25% network, 75% local. **ADI:** Detroit, MI. **Key Personnel:** Caryn G. Mathes, General Mgr.; Judy Adams, Program Dir.; Jeri Griffin-Buboltz, Business Mgr.; Debra Clayton, Public Relations & Promotions Dir.; Roger Adams, News Dir.; Renee Bulanda, Membership Dir; Lynn Fauth, Development & Mktg. Dir.; Martin Bandyke, Music Dir. **Wattage:** 48,000. **Ad Rates:** Noncommercial; underwriting available. **URL:** http://www.wdet.org.

15041 WDFN-AM - 1130
2930 E. Jefferson Phone: (313)259-5440
Detroit, MI 48207 Fax: (313)259-1885
E-mail: wuggiefan@aol.com

Format: Sports. **Networks:** Westwood One Radio; ABC. **Founded:** 1939. **Formerly:** WCXI-AM (1992); WWWW-AM (July 5, 1994). **Operating Hours:** Continuous. **ADI:** Detroit, MI. **Key Personnel:** Phil Lamka, General Mgr.; Mark Wuggazer, Program Dir.; Gregg Henson, Exec. Producer. **Wattage:** 50,000. **URL:** http://www.wdfn.com.

15042 WDIV-TV - 4
550 W. Lafayette Blvd. Phone: (313)222-0444
Detroit, MI 48231 Fax: (313)222-0471

Format: Commercial TV. **Networks:** NBC. **Formerly:** WWJ-TV. **Operating Hours:** Continuous. **ADI:** Detroit, MI. **Key Personnel:** Alan Frank, VP/General Manager. **URL:** http://www.wdiv.com.

15043 WDTR-FM - 90.9
9345 Lawton Ave. Phone: (313)596-3507
Detroit, MI 48206 Fax: (313)596-3517

Format: Information; Educational. **Owner:** Detroit Public Schools, 5057 Woodward, Detroit, MI 48202, (313)494-1000. **Founded:** 1948. **Operating Hours:** 6:30 a.m.-8:30 p.m.; 95% local. 8:30 to 8:30pm (sat,sun). **ADI:** Detroit, MI. **Key Personnel:** Cliff Russell, General Mgr. **Wattage:** 47,000.

15044 WDWB-TV - 20
27777 Franklin Rd., Ste. 1220 Phone: (248)355-2020
Southfield, MI 48034 Fax: (248)355-0368

Format: Commercial TV. **Networks:** Warner Brothers Studios. **Owner:** Granite Broadcasting Corp., 767 3rd Ave,34M Fl, New York, NY 10017, (212)826-2530, Fax: (212)826-2858. **Founded:** 1968. **Formerly:** WXON-TV (Oct. 1997). **Operating Hours:** Continuous; 100% local. **ADI:** Detroit, MI. **Key Personnel:** Sarah Norat-Phillips, President/General Mgr.; Jeffrey Guilbert, Station Mgr./VP of Sales. **Wattage:** 1.2 Million. **URL:** http://www.wb20detroit.com.

15045 WGPR-FM - 107.5
3146 E. Jefferson Ave. Phone: (313)259-8862
Detroit, MI 48207 Fax: (313)259-6662

Format: Urban Contemporary. **Networks:** CBS. **Owner:** International Free and Accepted Modern Masons & O.E.S., 2101 Gratiot Ave, Detroit, MI, (313)259-5817. **Founded:** 1961. **Operating Hours:** Continuous. **ADI:** Detroit, MI. **Key Personnel:** George Mathews, President. **Wattage:** 50,000. **Ad Rates:** $39-88 for 30 seconds; $44-110 for 60 seconds.

15046 WGPR-TV - 62
3140-3146 E. Jefferson Ave. Phone: (313)259-8862
Detroit, MI 48207 Fax: (313)259-6662

Format: Commercial TV. **Networks:** CBS. **Founded:** 1975. **Operating Hours:** Continuous. **ADI:** Detroit, MI. **Key Personnel:** George Mathews, Pres./Gen. Mgr.; D. Roger Williams, Admin. Asst.; Michelle DeSouza, Admin. Asst.; Joseph Spencer, Program Dir.; Patricia Watson, Sales Mgr.; Lucia Marvin, News Dir.; James O. Dogan, Station Mgr. **Ad Rates:** $35-150 per unit.

15047 WJBK-TV - 2
16550 W. 9 Mile Phone: (248)557-2000
Southfield, MI 48037-4705 Fax: (248)552-0280
E-mail: fox2detroit@ameritech.net

Format: Commercial TV. **Networks:** Fox. **Owner:** Fox Television Stations, Inc., 1999 S. Bundy Dr., Los Angeles, CA 90025-5235. **Founded:** Oct. 24, 1948. **Operating Hours:** Continuous. **ADI:** Detroit, MI. **Key Personnel:** James A. Clayton, Vice Pres./General Mgr.; Bernadette A. Prudente, Vice Pres. of Finance; Jeff Murri, Vice Pres. of Sales; Sheila Bruce, Local Sales Mgr.; Kelly Collins, Research Dir.; Michael Caver, Traffic/Continuity Dir.; Terry D'Esposito, Dir. of Marketing; Neil Goldstein, Vice Pres. of News; Dana McDaniel, Asst. News Dir.; Robin Tracey, Production Mgr.; Audrey Fish, Vice Pres. of Creative Services; Katy Baetz Matthews, Community Service Dir.; Debra Lawson, Public Relations Dir. **URL:** http://www.fox2detroit.com. **Additional Contact Info: Mailing Address:** Box 2000, Southfield, MI 48037-2000.

15048 WJLB-FM - 97.9
645 Griswold St., Suite 633 Phone: (313)965-2000
Detroit, MI 48226-4177 Fax: (313)965-9970

Format: Urban Contemporary. **Owner:** Chancellor Media Corporation, 433 E. Las Colinas Blvd., Ste. 1130, Irving, TX 75039, (214)869-9020, Fax: (214)869-3671. **Founded:** 1939. **Operating Hours:** Continuous; 100% local. **ADI:** Detroit, MI. **Key Personnel:** Verna S. Green, Sr. VP/General Mgr., fax (313)965-9970; Shel Leshner, General Sales Mgr., fax (313)965-8721; Michael Saunders, Program Dir., fax (313)965-3965; Tory Innis-Jackson, News Dir. **Local Programs:** *Talk Back*, Mildred Gassis, Fax (313)965-3965. **Wattage:** 50,000. **Ad Rates:** $45-585 for 30 seconds; $50-650 for 60 seconds.

15049 WJR-AM - 760
2100 Fisher Bldg. Phone: (313)875-4440
Detroit, MI 48202 Fax: (313)875-9022
Free: (800)859-0957

Format: News; Talk. **Networks:** ABC. **Founded:** 1922. **Operating Hours:** Continuous. **ADI:** Detroit, MI. **Key Personnel:** Mike Fezzey, Pres./General Mgr., fax (313)875-3519; Bob Schick, Local Sales Mgr., fax (313)875-8760; Dick Haefner, News Dir.; Al Mayers, Operations Mgr., fax (313)875-1988; John Gallagher, General Sales Mgr., phone (313)875-4440, fax (313)875-8760; Doug Johnston, National Sales Mgr., fax (313)875-8760; Cindy Cooper, Programming Asst., fax (313)875-1988; Kassie Kretzschmar, Dir. of Marketing & Promotion, fax (313)875-1988; Steve Stewart, Regional Sales Mgr. **Local Programs:** *Albom in the Afternoon* 4-6 p.m., Joan Isabella; *Ken Calvert Show* 10 a.m.-noon, Mike Skiels; *Paul W. Smith* 6 a.m.-10 a.m., Mike Shields. **Wattage:** 50,000. **Ad Rates:** Advertising accepted; rates available upon request. **URL:** http://www.wjr.net.

15050 WJZZ-FM - 105.9
2994 E. Grand Blvd. Phone: (313)871-0590
Detroit, MI 48202 Fax: (313)871-8770

Format: Jazz. **Networks:** Independent. **Owner:** Bell Broadcasting Co., at above address. **Founded:** 1963. **Formerly:** WCHD-FM (1974). **Operating Hours:** Continuous; 100% local. **ADI:** Detroit, MI. **Key Personnel:** Mary Bell, President; Wendell Cox, Vice President; Eric B. Bass, General Sales Mgr.; Robert Bass, Contact; Terry Arnold, Program Dir.; Treva Bass, Chief Engineer; Deborah F. Copeland, Contact. **Wattage:** 20,000. **Ad Rates:** $50-270 for 30 seconds; $50-300 for 60 seconds.

15051 WMKM-AM - 1440
1514 E. Jefferson Phone: (313)393-1044
Detroit, MI 48207 Fax: (313)393-1878

Format: Gospel. **Owner:** Michael J. Gallagher, at above address. **Founded:** 1990. **Formerly:** WCHB-AM (1989). **Operating Hours:** Continuous; 100% local. **ADI:** Detroit, MI. **Key Personnel:** Michael Gallagher, President; Crystal Sampson, General Mgr. **Wattage:** 1000. **Ad Rates:** $35-45 per unit.

15052 WMUZ-FM - 103.5
12300 Radio Pl. Phone: (313)272-3434
Detroit, MI 48228

Format: Religious; Contemporary Christian; Talk. **Networks:** Independent. **Founded:** 1958. **Operating Hours:** Continuous. **ADI:** Detroit, MI. **Key Personnel:** Frank Franciosi, General Mgr. **Wattage:** 50,000.

15053 WMXD-FM - 92.3
645 Griswold Phone: (313)965-2000
Detroit, MI 48226 Fax: (313)965-9970

Format: Adult Contemporary; Urban Contemporary. **Networks:** Independent. **Founded:** 1964. **Formerly:** WVAE-FM. **Operating Hours:** Continuous. **ADI:** Detroit, MI. **Key Personnel:** Verna Green, General Mgr./Sr. VP. **Wattage:** 50,000.

15054 WOMC-FM - 104.3
2201 Woodward Heights Blvd. Phone: (248)546-9600
Detroit, MI 48220 Fax: (248)546-5446

Format: Oldies. **Networks:** Westwood One Radio. **Founded:** 1948. **Operating Hours:** Continuous. **ADI:** Detroit, MI. **Key Personnel:** Elaine Baker, General Mgr.; Jean Harding, Promotions Dir.; Jack Johnson, General Sales Mgr.; Carolyn Zorwick, Contact; Bill Stedman, Program Dir. **Wattage:** 190,000. **Ad Rates:** Advertising accepted; rates available upon request.

15055 WPLT-FM - 96.3
2100 Fisher Bldg. Phone: (313)871-3030
Detroit, MI 48202 Fax: (313)875-9636
E-mail: planet963@planet963.com

Networks: ABC. **Founded:** 1948. **Formerly:** WHYT-FM (1982). **Operating Hours:** Continuous. **ADI:** Detroit, MI. **Key Personnel:** Mike Fezzey, General Mgr.; Garett Michaels, Program Dir.; Mark Wuggazer, Mktg. Dir.; Alex Tear, Music Dir. **Local Programs:** *Johnny In The Morning*, Chris Zito, (313)873-9863. **Wattage:** 20,000. **URL:** http://www.963theplanet.com.

15056 WQBH-AM - 1400
Penobscot Bldg. Phone: (313)965-4500
Detroit, MI 48226 Fax: (313)965-4608

Format: Urban Contemporary; Blues; Jazz. **Founded:** 1941. **Operating Hours:** Continuous. **ADI:** Detroit, MI. **Wattage:** 1000.

15057 WTVS-TV - 56
7441 2nd Blvd. Phone: (313)873-7200
Detroit, MI 48202 Fax: (313)876-8118

Format: Public TV. **Networks:** Public Broadcasting Service (PBS). **Founded:** 1953. **Operating Hours:** Continuous; 60% network, 5% local, 35% other. **ADI:** Detroit, MI. **Key Personnel:** Steven Antoniotti, Pres./Gen. Mgr.; Dan Krichbaum, Vice President; Dan Alpert, Station Mgr.; David Devereaux, Vice President; Bob Scott, Vice President; Jay Nelson, Production Dir.; Bob Rossbach, director education & outreach; Nancy Ewing, Vice President; Catherine Anderson, Vice President; Diane Bliss, Vice President. **Local Programs:** *Back to Back* 5 p.m. Wednesday, Jennifer Corney; *Black Journal* 7:30 p.m. Wednesday, Tony Mottley; *City for Youth*. **Wattage:** 1,550,000. **Ad Rates:** Noncommercial; underwriting available. **URL:** www.wtvs.org.

15058 WWWW-FM - 106.7
2930 E. Jefferson Phone: (313)259-4323
Detroit, MI 48207

Format: Country. **Networks:** Unistar. **Owner:** Shamrock Broadcasting, 4444 Lakeside Dr., Burbank, CA 91505-4017, (818)845-4444. **Founded:** 1981. **Operating Hours:** Continuous. **ADI:** Detroit, MI. **Key Personnel:** Phil Lamka, General Mgr. **Wattage:** 61,000.

DOWAGIAC

15059 Dowagiac Daily News
Dowagiac Daily News Inc.
205 Spaulding St. Phone: (616)782-2101
Box 30 Fax: (616)782-5290
Dowagiac, MI 49047-1474
Community newspaper. **Founded:** 1897. **Freq:** Daily (eve.). **Print Method:** Offset. **Cols./Page:** 8. **Col. Width:** 22 nonpareils. **Col. Depth:** 294 agate lines. **Key Personnel:** John Eby, Editor; Danny Dean, Publisher. **Subscription Rates:** $42. **Remarks:** Accepts advertising.
Ad Rates: PCI: $3.93 **Circ:** (Not Reported)

15060 WDOW-AM - 1440
Marcellus Hwy. Phone: (616)782-5106
PO Box 150 Fax: (616)782-5107
Dowagiac, MI 49047
E-mail: hawk@wvhq.com

Format: Country. **Networks:** Michigan Farm Radio; Michigan; ABC. **Founded:** 1960. **Operating Hours:** Continuous. **ADI:** South Bend-Elkhart, IN. **Key Personnel:** Doug Hawkes, General Mgr.; Micki Johnson, General Sales Mgr., micki@wvhq.com. **Wattage:** 1000. **Ad Rates:** $7.50-10 for 30 seconds; $10.50-12 for 60 seconds. Combined advertising rates available with WVHQ-FM.

15061 WVHQ-FM - 92.1
PO Box 150 Phone: (616)782-5106
Dowagiac, MI 49047 Fax: (616)782-5107

Format: Adult Contemporary; Oldies. **Networks:** ABC. **Founded:** 1960. **Formerly:** WDOW-FM. **Operating Hours:** Continuous. **ADI:** South Bend-Elkhart, IN. **Key Personnel:** Doug Hawkes, General Mgr., hawk@wvhq.com; Micki Johnson, General Sales Mgr., micki@wvhq.com. **Local Programs:** *Hawkes & Company*, Doug Hawkes. **Wattage:** 3000. **Ad Rates:** $15 per unit. Combined advertising rates available with WDOW-AM. **URL:** http://www.wvhq.com.

EAST GRAND RAPIDS

15062 On the Town
On the Town Publications
705 Bagley SE, Ste. 102 Phone: (616)451-0361
East Grand Rapids, MI 49506 Fax: (616)454-4666
Publication E-mail: townmag@aol.com

Arts and entertainment magzine for West Michigan. **Subtitle:** West Michigan's Only Arts & Entertainment Magazine. **Founded:** Sept. 1982. **Freq:** Monthly. **Print Method:** Web offset. **Trim Size:** 10 3/4 x 14. **Cols./Page:** 4. **Col. Width:** 2 1/4 inches. **Col. Depth:** 12 3/4 inches. **Key Personnel:** Joanne Bailey, Editor; Michelle Jake, Assoc. Ed.; Joel Holland, Publisher. **Subscription Rates:** $13 individuals.
Ad Rates: BW: $1,337 **Circ:** Controlled 35,000
4C: $1,562

EAST JORDAN

15063 Michigan Snowmobiler
01615 Advance-East Jordan Rd. Phone: (616)536-2371
PO Box 417 Fax: (616)536-7691
East Jordan, MI 49727
Publication E-mail: michsnow@freeway.com

Magazine on snowmobiling. **Founded:** 1967. **Freq:** 6/year (monthly, Sept.-Feb.). **Print Method:** Web offset. **Trim Size:** 9 13/16 x 12 1/2. **Cols./Page:** 5. **Col. Width:** 1 13/16 inches. **Col. Depth:** 12 1/2 inches. **Key Personnel:** Lyle Shipe, Editor and Publisher. **ISSN:** 0746-2298. **Subscription Rates:** $12; $20 two years. **Remarks:** Accepts advertising.
Ad Rates: GLR: $21 **Circ:** ‡26,000
BW: $1,100
4C: $1,475
PCI: $21

EAST LANSING

15064 Agricultural Economics Report
Michigan State University
Reference Rm. Phone: (517)355-6650
East Lansing, MI 48824-1039 Fax: (517)432-1800
Publisher E-mail: AGECON@mainlib3.lib.msu.edu

Publication covering farm management and agricultural economics for researchers. **Founded:** 1965. **Freq:** Irregular. **Trim Size:** 8 1/2 x 11. **ISSN:** 0065-4442. **Remarks:** Advertising not accepted.
Circ: Non-paid 70

15065 Behavioral Research in Accounting
American Accounting Association
Broad College of Business
Dept. of Accounting
N270 N. Business
East Lansing, MI 48824
Publisher E-mail: aaahq@packnet.net

Academic journal covering research in accounting. **Founded:** 1988. **Freq:** Annual. **Trim Size:** 5 7/8 x 9. **Cols./Page:** 1. **Key Personnel:** Susan F. Haka, Editor, phone (517)432-2920, fax (517)423-1101; James DeLa, AAA Publications Coord. **ISSN:** 1050-4753. **Subscription Rates:** $20 individuals. **Remarks:** Advertising not accepted.
Circ: Paid 1,800

15066 Celestinesca
Michigan State University
East Lansing, MI 48824-1112 Phone: (517)355-8350
Fax: (517)432-3844

Scholarly journal covering Spanish literature. **Founded:** 1977. **Freq:** Semiannual. **Print Method:** Web offset. **Trim Size:** 6 x 9. **Cols./Page:** 1. **Key Personnel:** Joseph T. Snow, Editor, snow@pilot.msu.edu. **Subscription Rates:** $4 single issue. **Remarks:** Advertising not accepted.
Circ: Controlled 412

15067 Communication Outlook
Artificial Language Laboratory
405 Computer Center Phone: (517)353-0870
East Lansing, MI 48824-1042 Fax: (517)353-4766
Publisher E-mail: artlang@pilot.msu.edu

Magazine reporting on the newest developments in the application of technology for neurologically impaired persons. **Founded:** 1978. **Freq:** Quarterly. **Subscription Rates:** $18 individuals. **Remarks:** Advertising accepted; rates available upon request.
Circ: Paid 1,500

15068 The Historian
Michigan State University Press
c/o History Dept. Phone: (517)432-5040
Michigan State University Fax: (517)432-3629
301 Morrill Hall
East Lansing, MI 48824
Publication E-mail: historia@pilot.msu.edu

Journal of the Phi Alpha Theta National Honor Society in History. **Founded:** 1937. **Freq:** Quarterly. **Trim Size:** 6 x 9. **Cols./Page:** 1. **Key Personnel:** Linda Cooke Johnson, Editor, historic@pilot.msu.edu; Carol Cole, Copy Editor; Richard Spall, Book Review Editor, phone (740)368-3642, fax (740)368-3643, brhistor@cc.owu.edu; Laura Luptowski, Managing Editor. **ISSN:** 0018-2370. **Subscription Rates:** $30 individuals; $25 members. **Remarks:** Accepts advertising.
Ad Rates: BW: $500 **Circ:** Combined 16,000

15069 Ingham County News
Ingham Newspaper Co.
210 Abbott St., Ste. 28 Phone: (517)333-7272
PO Box 1568 Fax: (517)333-7275
East Lansing, MI 48826
Community newspaper. **Founded:** 1859. **Freq:** Weekly (Wed.). **Print Method:** Offset. **Cols./Page:** 5. **Key Personnel:** Teresa Fitzwater, Editor and Publisher. **Subscription Rates:** $17.50.
Circ: ‡2,702

15070 Journal for Farming Systems Research-Extension (AFSRE)
Michigan State University
313 Natural Resource Bldg. Phone: (517)353-8994
East Lansing, MI 48824-1222 Fax: (517)353-8994

Contains information for farming system researchers and extensionists. **Founded:** 1991. **Freq:** Semiannual. **Trim Size:** 6 x 9. **Cols./Page:** 1. **Col. Width:** 4.5 inches. **Col. Depth:** 7.25 inches. **Key Personnel:** George Axinn, Editor, axinn@pilot.msu.edu. **ISSN:** 1051-6786. **Subscription Rates:** $20 students and developing countries; $65 developed countries; $125 institutions. **Remarks:** Accepts advertising.
Ad Rates: BW: $60 **Circ:** 500

15071 Journal of Hospitality and Leisure Marketing
Springer-Verlag New York, Inc.
The School of Hospitality Business Phone: (517)353-9211
Fax: (517)484-1170
The Eli Broad College of Business/Management
Michigan State Univ.
235 Eppley Ctr.
East Lansing, MI 48824-1121
Publisher E-mail: journals@springer-ny.com

Academic and industry journal dealing with marketing issues in the hospitality and leisure industries. **Founded:** 1992. **Freq:** Quarterly. **Trim Size:** 6x8 1/2. **Key Personnel:** Bonnie Knutson, Editor, drbonnie@pilot.msu.edu. **ISSN:** 1050-7051. **Subscription Rates:** $38 individuals; $45 institutions; $125 libraries. **Alt. Formats:** Microfiche.
Ad Rates: BW: $300 **Circ:** 396

15072 Journal of South Asian Literature
Michigan State University
201 Morrill Hall Phone: (517)355-9571
East Lansing, MI 48824 Fax: (517)353-3755

Scholarly journal covering South Asian literature. **Founded:** 1968. **Freq:** Semiannual. **Key Personnel:** Surjit Dulai, Editor/Manager. **ISSN:** 0091-5637. **Subscription Rates:** $22 individuals; $27 institutions; $11 single issue. **Remarks:** Accepts advertising.
Circ: Paid 400

15073 MEA Voice
Michigan Education Association
1216 Kendale Blvd. Phone: (517)332-6551
Box 2573 Fax: (517)337-5414
East Lansing, MI 48826-2573
Free: (800)292-1934
Publication E-mail: drk@mea.org

Educational tabloid for teachers union. **Founded:** Sept. 1, 1969. **Freq:** Monthly. **Print Method:** Web press. **Trim Size:** 11 x 13 1/2. **Cols./Page:** 4 and 4. **Col. Width:** 14 picas. **Col. Depth:** 12.5 inches. **Key Personnel:** Dennis Keenon, Editor, dkeenan1@aol.com. **ISSN:** 0883-573X. **Subscription Rates:** $15. **URL:** http://www.mea.org. **Formerly:** Teacher's Voice; Voice.
Ad Rates: BW: $2,780 **Circ:** ‡143,000
4C: $2,780
PCI: $82

15074 Michigan Medicine
Michigan State Medical Society
PO Box 950 Phone: (517)337-1351
East Lansing, MI 48826-0950 Fax: (517)337-2490
Publisher E-mail: msms@msms.org

Medical magazine. **Subtitle:** The Journal of the Michigan State Medical Society. **Founded:** 1902. **Freq:** Monthly. **Print Method:** Web offset. **Trim Size:** 8 1/4 x 10 7/8. **Cols./Page:** 3. **Col. Width:** 26 nonpareils. **Col. Depth:** 136 agate lines. **Key Personnel:** Kristen Lare, Managing Editor, phone (517)337-1351, fax (517)336-5797, klare@msms.org. **ISSN:** 0026-2293. **Subscription Rates:** $100.
Ad Rates: BW: $639 **Circ:** ‡14,000
4C: $1,689
PCI: $62

15075 MSU Alumni Magazine
Michigan State University Alumni Association
MSU Union Phone: (517)355-8314
East Lansing, MI 48824-1029 Fax: (517)355-5265
Publication E-mail: ala12@msu.edu

Alumni association magazine. **Founded:** 1955. **Freq:** Quarterly (during the academic year). **Print Method:** Offset. **Cols./Page:** 3 and 2. **Col. Width:** 28 and 40 nonpareils. **Col. Depth:** 133 agate lines. **Key Personnel:** Robert Bao, Editor, phone

(517)432-1889, baor@pilot.msu.edu. **Subscription Rates:** Included in membership.
Ad Rates: BW: $1,000 **Circ:** 37,000

15076 Northeast African Studies
Michigan State University Press
Michigan State University
319 Morrill Hall
East Lansing, MI 48824-1036
Publication E-mail: ethiopia@hs7.hst.msu.edu

Scholarly journal covering Northeast African studies. **Founded:** 1994. **Freq:** Triennial. **Cols./Page:** 1. **Key Personnel:** Harold G. Marcus, Editor. **ISSN:** 0740-9133. **Subscription Rates:** $30 individuals; $48 out of country. **Remarks:** Advertising not accepted.
Circ: (Not Reported)

15077 Red Cedar Review
Red Cedar Press
17C Morrill Hall Phone: (517)355-9656
Dept. of English
East Lansing, MI 48824
Publication E-mail: rcreview@pilot.msu.edu
Publisher E-mail: rcreview@pilot.msu.edu

Literary magazine covering fiction and poetry. **Founded:** 1963. **Freq:** Biennial. **Key Personnel:** Carrie Preston, Poetry Editor, presto21@pilot.msu.edu; David Sheridan, Fiction Editor. **Subscription Rates:** $10 individuals; $5 single issue. **Remarks:** Accepts advertising.
Ad Rates: BW: $100 **Circ:** (Not Reported)

15078 The State News
State News, Inc.
343 Student Service Bldg. Phone: (517)355-8252
East Lansing, MI 48824-1113 Fax: (517)353-2599

Collegiate newspaper. **Founded:** 1906. **Freq:** Daily (morn.). **Print Method:** Offset. **Trim Size:** 14 x 22 7/8. **Cols./Page:** 6. **Col. Width:** 25 nonpareils. **Col. Depth:** 294 agate lines. **Key Personnel:** Robert Bullard, Advertising Mgr. **USPS:** 520-260. **Subscription Rates:** $55. **Remarks:** Accepts advertising. **URL:** http://www.statenews.com.
Ad Rates: GLR: $.95 **Circ:** ‡33,000
BW: $1,682
4C: $2,132
PCI: $13.35

15079 The Towne Courier
Ingham Newspaper Co.
210 Abbott St., Ste. 28 Phone: (517)333-7272
PO Box 1568 Fax: (517)333-7275
East Lansing, MI 48826
Community newspaper. **Founded:** 1962. **Freq:** Weekly (Wed.). **Print Method:** Offset. **Trim Size:** 11 x 17. **Cols./Page:** 5. **Key Personnel:** Teresa Fitzwater, Editor and Publisher. **Subscription Rates:** $17.50.
Circ: ‡4,982

15080 Williamston Enterprise
Ingham Newspaper Co.
210 Abbott St., Ste. 28 Phone: (517)333-7272
PO Box 1568 Fax: (517)333-7275
East Lansing, MI 48826
Community newspaper. **Founded:** 1872. **Freq:** Weekly (Wed.). **Print Method:** Offset. Uses mats. **Trim Size:** 11 x 17. **Cols./Page:** 5. **Col. Width:** 19 nonpareils. **Col. Depth:** 189 agate lines. **Key Personnel:** Teresa Fitzwater, Editor and Publisher. **Subscription Rates:** $17.50.
Circ: ‡2,400

15081 WDBM-FM - 88.9
Michigan State University Phone: (517)353-4414
G-4 Holden Hall Fax: (517)355-6552
East Lansing, MI 48824

Format: Eclectic. **Founded:** 1988. **Operating Hours:** Continuous; 100% local. **Key Personnel:** Gary Reid, Contact; Sean Hanley, Station Mgr.; Lindsay Peters, Program Dir.; Chris Santiago, Music Dir.; Mike Vitale, Sports Dir.; Joel Chaiken, News Dir. **Wattage:** 2000. **Ad Rates:** Noncommercial. **URL:** http://www.www.wdbm.msu.edu.

15082 WKAR-AM - 870
Michigan State University Phone: (517)355-6540
283 Communications Arts Bldg. Fax: (517)353-7124
East Lansing, MI 48824

Format: Talk; News; Information. **Networks:** National Public Radio (NPR). **Owner:** Michigan State University Board of Trustees, at above address. **Founded:** 1922. **Operating Hours:** Daytime; 50% network, 50% local. **ADI:** Lansing (Ann Arbor), MI. **Key Personnel:** Steve Meuche, General Mgr.; Gary Blievernicht, Chief Engineer; Diane Hutchens, Promotions Dir.; Curt Gilleo, Contact; Jayne Marsh, Contact; Hal Prentice, Music Dir. **Wattage:** 10,000. **Ad Rates:** Noncommercial.

15083 WKAR-TV - 23
212 Communication Arts Bldg. Phone: (517)432-9527
East Lansing, MI 48824-1212 Fax: (517)353-7124
E-mail: mail@wkar.msu.edu

Format: Public TV. **Networks:** Public Broadcasting Service (PBS). **Founded:** 1954. **Operating Hours:** 6:45 a.m.-12:30 a.m.; 95% network, 5% local. **ADI:** Lansing (Ann Arbor), MI. **Key Personnel:** Steve Meuche, General Mgr.; Jayne Marsh, Sales Mgr.; Doug Schrems, Production Mgr.; Mary Jane Wilson, Program Mgr.; Tim Zeko, Exec. Producer; Nancy Gilleo, Business Mgr.; Jeanie Croope, Promotions Mgr.; Gary Blievernicht, Chief Engineer. **URL:** http://www.wkar.msu.edu.

15084 WWDX-FM - 92.1
220 Mac Ave., Ste. 101 Phone: (517)332-8700
East Lansing, MI 48823-4392 Fax: (517)332-6418

Format: Album-Oriented Rock (AOR). **Networks:** Independent. **Founded:** 1972. **Formerly:** WLNZ-FM (1991); WGOR-FM (1991); WXMX-FM (1994). **Operating Hours:** Continuous; 100% local. **Key Personnel:** Mike Thomas, General Mgr.; Chris Brunt, Program Dir.; Melissa Ayzy, Sales Mgr.; Janna Walsch, News and Public Service Dir. **Wattage:** 6000. **Ad Rates:** $25 for 60 seconds.

EAST TAWAS

15085 Iosco County News Herald
News-Press Publishing Co., Inc.
110 W. State St. Phone: (517)362-3456
Box 72 Fax: (517)362-6601
East Tawas, MI 48730-0072
Community newspaper. **Founded:** 1940. **Freq:** Weekly (Wed.). **Print Method:** Offset. **Trim Size:** 11 x 17 1/2. **Cols./Page:** 5. **Col. Width:** 24 nonpareils. **Col. Depth:** 231 agate lines. **Key Personnel:** Neal R. Miller, Editor, nmiller@voyager.net. **USPS:** 268-520. **Subscription Rates:** $25; $30; $35 out of state. **Remarks:** Accepts advertising.
Ad Rates: GLR: $5.22 **Circ:** ‡7,790
SAU: $5.22

15086 WHST-FM - 107.3
130 Newman St., Ste. B Phone: (517)362-6149
East Tawas, MI 48730-1210 Fax: (517)362-6351
Free: (800)743-6424

Format: Adult Contemporary. **Networks:** CBS. **Owner:** Tawas City Broadcasting Co., at above address. **Founded:** 1973. **Formerly:** WDBI-FM. **Operating Hours:** Continuous; 5% network, 95% local. **Key Personnel:** Don Backus, President. **Wattage:** 3000. **Ad Rates:** Advertising accepted; rates available upon request.

EASTPOINTE

15087 The Advisor
21st Century Newspapers, Inc.
100 Macomb Daily Dr.
Mount Clemens, MI 48046

Community newspaper serving Eastpointe, Roseville, and St. Clair Shores, MI. **Freq:** Weekly (Sun.). **Print Method:** Offset. **Cols./Page:** 6. **Col. Width:** 2 1/16 inches. **Col. Depth:** 21 1/2 inches. **Key Personnel:** Frank Sheperd, President/CEO, phone (810)469-4510, fax (810)469-4512; Wayne Oehmke, Publisher, fax (810)731-2522; Phillip Marien, General Mgr.; Joseph Warner, Editor; Chris Troszak, Advertising Mgr. **Subscription Rates:** Free; $80 out of area. **Remarks:** Accepts advertising. **Former name:** Macomb-North Clinton Advisor.
Ad Rates: BW: $1,999.50 **Circ:** Free ‡42,803
SAU: $15.50

15088 Propeller Magazine
American Power Boat Association
17640 E. 9 Mile Rd. Phone: (810)773-9700
Eastpointe, MI 48021-0377 Fax: (810)773-6490
Publisher E-mail: apbahq@aol.com

Power boating magazine. **Founded:** 1915. **Freq:** Monthly. **Print Method:** Offset. **Trim Size:** 8 1/2 x 11. **Cols./Page:** 3. **Col. Width:** 30 nonpareils. **Col. Depth:** 170 agate lines. **Key Personnel:** Michele Weston Rowe, Exec. Editor. **ISSN:** 0194-6218. **Subscription Rates:** $25; $50 other countries. **Remarks:** Accepts advertising. **Available Online. URL:** http://www.goracing.com/apba/.
Ad Rates: BW: $598 **Circ:** ‡7,000
4C: $1,000

EATON RAPIDS

15089 Flashes Shoppers Guide & News
115 Grand St. Phone: (517)663-2361
PO Box 156 Fax: (517)663-2381
Eaton Rapids, MI 48827
Free: (877)212-4615

Shopper (tabloid). **Founded:** Nov. 1945. **Freq:** Weekly (Tues.). **Print Method:** Offset. **Trim Size:** 11 x 17. **Cols./Page:** 6. **Col. Width:** 1 5/8 inches. **Col. Depth:** 16 inches. **Key Personnel:** Rod McLaughlin, Owner. **Subscription Rates:** $20. **Remarks:** Accepts advertising. **Formerly:** Flashes Shoppers Guide.
Ad Rates: GLR: $0.40 **Circ:** Free ‡12,500
BW: $365.76
4C: $665.76
PCI: $5.45

EAU CLAIRE

15090 Central County Trade Lines Shopper's Guide
Michiana Publications, Inc.
115 Main St. Phone: (616)461-4411
Eau Claire, MI 49111 Fax: (616)461-6816

Shopper. **Founded:** 1949. **Freq:** Weekly (Mon.). **Print Method:** Offset. **Cols./Page:** 6. **Col. Width:** 20 nonpareils. **Col. Depth:** 225 agate lines. **Key Personnel:** Reva E. Murphy, Publisher. **Remarks:** Accepts advertising.
Ad Rates: GLR: $.25 **Circ:** Free 14,149
BW: $50
PCI: $3.60

Twin City Trade Lines Shopper's Guide - See Benton Harbor

EDWARDSBURG

15091 Argus
217 N. 4th St.
Niles, MI 49120-2301

Newspaper. **Founded:** 1875. **Freq:** Weekly (Thurs.). **Print Method:** Offset. **Cols./Page:** 8. **Col. Width:** 15 nonpareils. **Col. Depth:** 294 agate lines. **Key Personnel:** Teresa Youngdale, Editor; Danny Dean, Publisher; Sandy Garver, Advertising Mgr. **Subscription Rates:** $12.
Circ: 1,800

ELK RAPIDS

15092 The Town Meeting
Up North Publications, Inc.
PO Box 335 Phone: (616)264-9711
Elk Rapids, MI 49629
Community newspaper. **Founded:** 1974. **Freq:** Weekly. **Print Method:** Offset. **Key Personnel:** Amy Whitaker, Editor. **Subscription Rates:** $22; $25 out of area. **Remarks:** Accepts advertising.
Ad Rates: GLR: $.23 **Circ:** Paid 2,000
BW: $260.00
4C: $360.00
SAU: $3.25

ELSIE

15093 WOES-FM - 91.3
8989 Colony Rd. Phone: (517)862-4237
Elsie, MI 48831 Fax: (517)862-4463

Format: Polka. **Founded:** 1978. **Operating Hours:** Continuous. **Key Personnel:** George Bishop, General Mgr.; Kevin Somers, Operations Mgr. **Wattage:** 535.

ESCANABA

15094 The Daily Press
600 Ludington St., No. 2 Phone: (906)786-2021
Escanaba, MI 49829-3830 Fax: (906)786-3752

General newspaper. **Founded:** 1909. **Freq:** Daily (eve.) and Sat. (morn.). **Print Method:** Offset. **Key Personnel:** Peggy Bryson, Editor; Robert B. Gregg, Publisher; Thomas Dufour, Advertising Mgr. **Remarks:** Accepts advertising.
Ad Rates: PCI: $10.03 **Circ:** 11,842

15095 The Delta Reporter
600 Ludington St., No. 2 Phone: (906)789-9122
Escanaba, MI 49829-3830 Fax: (906)789-9006

Community newspaper. **Founded:** Apr. 1887. **Freq:** Weekly (Wed.). **Print Method:** Offset. **Cols./Page:** 5. **Col. Width:** 23 nonpareils. **Col. Depth:** 182 agate lines. **Key Personnel:**

Christine Pepin, Editor; Bob Gregg, Publisher. **Subscription Rates:** $20. **Remarks:** Accepts advertising.
Ad Rates: PCI: $9.69 **Circ:** 3,420

15096 KYKX-FM - 104.7
604 Ludington St. Phone: (906)786-3800
Escanaba, MI 49829 Fax: (906)789-9959

Format: Country. **Networks:** Satellite Music Network. **Owner:** KMB Broadcasting, at above address. **Founded:** 1978. **Operating Hours:** Continuous. **Key Personnel:** Alice Sabuco, General Mgr.; Kim Rabitoy, Sales Mgr.; Polly Flinders, News Dir.; Ken Curtis, Program Dir. **Wattage:** 100,000. **Ad Rates:** Advertising accepted; rates available upon request.

15097 WCHT-AM - 600
524 Ludington St., Ste. 300 Phone: (906)789-0600
Escanaba, MI 49829 Free: (800)866-0097

Format: Talk. **Networks:** ABC; ESPN Radio. **Owner:** Lakes Radio, Inc., at above address. **Founded:** 1958. **Formerly:** WLST-AM (1985); WBDN-AM. **Operating Hours:** Continuous; 70% network, 30% local. **Key Personnel:** Richard A. Duerson, VP/General Mgr.; Nick Sawyer, Sales Mgr.; Jeff Gerber, Station Mgr. **Wattage:** 570 day; 134 night. **Ad Rates:** $6.50-9 for 15 seconds; $7.50-10 for 30 seconds; $8.50-15 for 60 seconds.

15098 WDBC-AM - 680
604 Ludington St. Phone: (906)786-6144
Escanaba, MI 49829 Fax: (906)789-9959

Format: Adult Contemporary. **Networks:** CBS; Mutual Broadcasting System. **Owner:** KMB Broadcasting, at above address. **Founded:** 1941. **Operating Hours:** 5 a.m.-1 a.m.; 10% network, 90% local. **Key Personnel:** Alice Sabuco, General Mgr.; Polly Finders, News Dir.; Kevin Scannell, Music/Program Dir.; Kim Rabitoy, Sales Mgr. **Wattage:** 10,000. **Ad Rates:** $6.50-9.50 for 15 seconds; $9.50-15.50 for 30 seconds; $10.50-19.50 for 60 seconds. Combined advertising rates available with WDBC-AM.

15099 WJMN-TV - 3
c/o CBS, Inc. Phone: (414)437-5411
PO Box 19055 Fax: (414)437-4576
Green Bay, WI 54307-9055
E-mail: wfrv@dct.com

Format: Commercial TV. **Simulcasts:** WFRV-TV Green Bay, WI. **Networks:** CBS. **Owner:** CBS, Inc., at above address. **Founded:** 1969. **Operating Hours:** Continuous. **ADI:** Marquette, MI. **Key Personnel:** R. Perry Kidder, VP/General Mgr.; Jackie Stewart, General Sales Mgr.; Lee Hitter, News Dir. **Ad Rates:** Advertising accepted; rates available upon request.

EVART

15100 Evart Review
The Pioneer Group
101 W. Slosson Phone: (616)832-5566
Reed City, MI 49677 Fax: (616)832-5558

Community newspaper. **Founded:** Oct. 1872. **Freq:** Weekly. **Print Method:** Offset. **Trim Size:** 13 x 21 1/2. **Cols./Page:** 9. **Col. Width:** 1 3/8 inches. **Col. Depth:** 21 1/2 inches. **Key Personnel:** Jim Bruskotter, Editor; John A. Batdorff, Publisher. **Remarks:** Accepts advertising.
Ad Rates: SAU: $6.50 **Circ:** ‡2,183
PCI: $3.35

FARMINGTON

15101 Farmington Observer & Eccentric
Observer & Eccentric Newspapers
36251 Schoolcraft Rd. Phone: (313)591-2300
Livonia, MI 48150-1216 Fax: (313)953-2232

Community newspaper. **Founded:** 1886. **Freq:** Semiweekly (Mon. and Thurs.). **Print Method:** Offset. **Cols./Page:** 9. **Col. Width:** 17 nonpareils. **Col. Depth:** 301 agate lines. **Key Personnel:** Richard Aginian, Publisher. **Subscription Rates:** $21. **Remarks:** Accepts advertising.
Ad Rates: GLR: $2.62 **Circ:** Paid 5,688
Non-paid 6,524

FARMINGTON HILLS

15102 ACI Structural Journal
American Concrete Institute
PO Box 9094 Phone: (248)848-3700
Farmington Hills, MI 48333 Fax: (248)848-3701

Journal containing information on structural design and analysis of concrete elements and structures; includes design and analysis theory, and related ACI standards and committee reports. **Subtitle:** Journal of the American Concrete Institute. **Founded:** Jan. 1987. **Freq:** Bimonthly. **Print Method:** Offset. **Trim Size:** 8 1/8 x 10 7/8. **Cols./Page:** 2. **Col. Width:** 40 nonpareils. **Col. Depth:** 140 agate lines. **Key Personnel:** Rebecca A. Hartford, Managing Editor. **ISSN:** 0889-3241. **Subscription Rates:** $118 individuals U.S. & possessions; $126 out of country; $8.75 members; $21.50 nonmembers. **Remarks:** Advertising not accepted. **URL:** http://www.aci-int.org.
Circ: ‡16,400

15103 Building Business & Apartment Management
Building Industry Association of Southeastern Michigan
30375 Northwestern Hwy., Ste. 100 Phone: (248)737-4477
Fax: (248)737-5741
Farmington Hills, MI 48334
Construction and apartment industry magazine. **Founded:** 1937. **Freq:** Monthly. **Print Method:** Offset. **Trim Size:** 8 1/2 x 11. **Cols./Page:** 3. **Col. Width:** 21 inches. **Col. Depth:** 140 inches. **Key Personnel:** Susan Adler, Editor, susanadler@compuserve.com; Irvin H. Yackness, Executive Editor. **Remarks:** Accepts advertising. **Formerly:** Bildor.
Ad Rates: BW: $1,375 **Circ:** Paid ‡11,000
4C: $1,575 Controlled ‡100

15104 Concrete Abstracts
American Concrete Institute
PO Box 9094 Phone: (248)848-3700
Farmington Hills, MI 48333 Fax: (248)848-3701

Magazine summarizing and indexing U.S. and international publications that report developments in concrete and concrete technology. **Founded:** July 1971. **Freq:** Bimonthly. **Print Method:** Offset. **Trim Size:** 8 1/2 x 11. **Cols./Page:** 2. **Col. Width:** 21 picas. **Col. Depth:** 60 picas. **Key Personnel:** Helayne H. Beavers, Editor. **ISSN:** 0045-8007. **Subscription Rates:** $153 members; $180 nonmembers. **Remarks:** Advertising not accepted. **Alt. Formats:** CD-ROM.
Circ: ‡676

15105 Concrete International
American Concrete Institute
38800 Country Club Dr. Phone: (248)848-3737
Farmington Hills, MI 48331 Fax: (248)848-3701

Trade magazine covering engineering, construction, structural design, and the technology of concrete. **Founded:** Jan. 1979. **Freq:** Monthly. **Print Method:** Offset. **Trim Size:** 8 1/8 x 10 7/8. **Cols./Page:** 3. **Col. Width:** 26 nonpareils. **Col. Depth:** 140 agate lines. **Key Personnel:** Roger Wood, Sr. Editor, phone (248)848-3738, rwood@aci-int.org; William J. Semioli, Editor-in-Chief, bsemioli@aci-int.org; Diane Pociask, Publishing Asst., phone (248)848-3736, dpociask@aci-int.org; Paula G. Schmalzriedt, Production Editor, phone (248)848-3734, pschmalz@aci-int.org; Susan C. McCraven, Engineering Editor, phone (248)848-3742, smccarven@aci-int.org; Keith A. Tosolt, Sr. Assoc. Editor, phone (248)848-3735, ktosolt@aci-int.org; Nicholas Moretti, Assoc. Editor, phone (248)848-3761, nmoretti@aci-int.org. **ISSN:** 0162-4075. **Subscription Rates:** $112. **Remarks:** Accepts advertising. **URL:** http://www.aci-int.inter.net. **Alt. Formats:** Mailing labels. **Formerly:** Concrete International: Design & Construction.
Ad Rates: GLR: $95 **Circ:** Paid 104
BW: $2,470 Controlled 17,268
4C: $3,420
PCI: $95

15106 NTEA Technical Report
National Truck Equipment Association
37400 Hills Tech Dr. Phone: (248)489-7090
Farmington Hills, MI 48331-3414 Fax: (248)489-8590
Free: (800)441-6832
Publisher E-mail: info@ntea.com

Technical periodical covering the truck and transport equipment industry. **Freq:** Monthly (as needed). **Print Method:** Offset. **Subscription Rates:** $24 members; $48 nonmembers; $2 single issue members; $4 single issue non-members. **Remarks:** Advertising not accepted.
Circ: Paid 1,600

15107 Witness
Oakland Community College
27055 Orchard Lake Rd. Phone: (248)471-7740
Farmington Hills, MI 48334
Magazine blending the features of a literary and issue-oriented publication. **Founded:** 1987. **Freq:** Semiannual. **Print Method:** Offset. **Trim Size:** 6 x 9. **Cols./Page:** 1. **Col. Width:** 6 inches. **Col. Depth:** 9 inches. **Key Personnel:** Peter Stine, Editor, phone (734)996-5732. **ISSN:** 0891-1371. **Subscription Rates:** $15 individuals one year; $22 institutions one year. **Remarks:** Accepts advertising.
Ad Rates: BW: $100 **Circ:** Paid ‡1,500
Controlled ‡1,500

15108 Time Warner Cable
37635 Enterprise Ct. Phone: (810)553-7300
Farmington Hills, MI 48331 Fax: (810)553-4829

Founded: 1983. **Cities Served:** Oakland County, MI.

15109 WLLZ-FM - 98.7
31555 14 Mile Rd., Ste. 102 Phone: (810)855-5100
Farmington Hills, MI 48334 Fax: (810)855-1302

Format: Album-Oriented Rock (AOR). **Founded:** 1961. **Operating Hours:** Continuous. **Key Personnel:** Jay Clark, Program Dir.; Leslie Quinn, News Dir.; Kevin T. Smith, Contact; Russell Van Houten, Station Mgr.; George Kenyon, Contact; Gary Palmer, Music Dir.; Mike Isabella, Contact. **Wattage:** 50,000.

15110 WORB-FM - 90.3
27055 Orchard Lake Rd. Phone: (810)471-7718
Farmington Hills, MI 48334

Format: Alternative/New Music/Progressive; Eclectic. **Founded:** 1975. **Operating Hours:** 8 a.m.-10 p.m. weekdays; 8 a.m.-5:30 p.m. Saturday and Sunday. **Key Personnel:** Ronald Burda, Contact; Jonathan Moshier, Station Mgr.; Alex Stoherine, Program Dir.; Rich Stringfellow, Music Dir. **Wattage:** 10. **Ad Rates:** Noncommercial.

FERNDALE

15111 Jam Rag
Jam Rag Press
Box 20076 Phone: (248)542-8090
Ferndale, MI 48220
Publication E-mail: rdlnews@ruston_ leader.com
Publisher E-mail: jamrag@usamail.com

Community newspaper covering rock music in the Detroit area. **Founded:** 1985. **Freq:** Monthly 4 special editions. **Print Method:** Web offset. **Trim Size:** 7 1/2 x 10 1/2. **Cols./Page:** 4. **Col. Width:** 1 1/2 inches. **Key Personnel:** Tom Ness, Publisher; Sue Ness, Publisher. **ISSN:** 1094-9488. **Subscription Rates:** Free to qualified subscribers; $23 individuals. **Remarks:** Accepts advertising.
Ad Rates: BW: $339 **Circ:** Non-paid 15,000
4C: $529
PCI: $14

FLINT

15112 The Catholic Times
GLS Diocesan Reports
1045 Darling St. Phone: (810)767-6525
Flint, MI 48532 Fax: (810)767-6567
Publication E-mail: ctedition@aol.com

Religious newspaper covering the local, national, and international church. **Subtitle:** Official Publication of the Diocese of Lansing. **Founded:** Nov. 22, 1991. **Freq:** Weekly (Fri.). **Print Method:** Offset. **Trim Size:** 13 3/8 x 22 3/4. **Cols./Page:** 8. **Col. Width:** 9 picas. **Col. Depth:** 294 agate lines. **Key Personnel:** Mark A. Myczkowiak, General Mgr.; Evelyn Barella, Editor. **USPS:** 007-686. **Subscription Rates:** $23.95 individuals. **Formerly:** The Catholic Weekly (1991).
Ad Rates: GLR: $.52 **Circ:** Paid 7,967
BW: $1,176 Non-paid 101
4C: $1,576
PCI: $6.76

15113 The Flint Journal
200 E. 1st St. Phone: (313)766-6100
Flint, MI 48502 Fax: (313)767-7518

General newspaper. **Founded:** 1876. **Freq:** Daily (eve.), Sat. and Sun. (morn.). **Print Method:** Letterpress. **Cols./Page:** 6. **Col. Width:** 25 nonpareils. **Col. Depth:** 308 agate lines. **Key Personnel:** Carlton Winfrey, Opinion Page Editor; Dave Poniers, Sports Editor; John Dickson, Photo Director; Marcia Mattson, Health Writer, phone (313)766-6326; Ron Krueger, Food Writer, phone (313)766-6241; Tom Lindley, Editor, phone (313)766-6189; Danny R. Gaydou, Publisher, phone (313)766-6324; Roger Samuel, Advertising Dir., phone (313)766-6330; Roger Van Noord, Managing Editor, phone (313)766-6241; Michael Riha, Metro Editor, phone (313)766-6374; Rhonda Sanders, Features Editor, phone (313)766-6241; Brooke Rausch, Assoc. Editor. **Subscription Rates:** $110. **Remarks:** Accepts advertising. **Feature Editors:** Elizabeth Brenner, *Medical*, phone (313)766-6330; John Dickson, *Lifestyle*, phone (313)766-6241; Jennifer Kildee, *Food*, phone (313)766-6117; David Poniers, *Sports*, phone (313)766-6186; Michael Riha, *Women's*, phone (313)766-6241.
Ad Rates: BW: $4,055.04 **Circ:** Mon.-Sat. ★**93,603**
4C: $4,842.12 Sun. ★**112,091**
PCI: $30.72

The Flushing Observer - See Flushing

15114 The FORUM Magazine
Mico Graphics & Advertising, Inc.
1739 N. Saginaw, Ste. A Phone: (810)767-7769
Flint, MI 48505 Fax: (810)767-1364

Magazine focusing on issues in the Flint, Michigan, area. Issues of interest throughout Michigan and U.S. **Founded:**

1989. **Freq:** Monthly. **Print Method:** Sheet fed. **Trim Size:** 8-1/2 x 11. **Cols./Page:** 3. **Col. Width:** 2 1/4 inches. **Col. Depth:** 10 inches. **Key Personnel:** Loretta Wofford-Milow, Editor; Fred Milow, Advertising Mgr., phone (810)767-6578. **Subscription Rates:** $14.95 individuals; $3 single issue. **Remarks:** Accepts advertising.
Ad Rates: BW: $1,335 **Circ:** Paid ‡2,000
4C: $2,280 Non-paid ‡8,000

15115 Journal of Leadership Studies
Baker College
1050 W. Bristol Rd. Phone: (810)766-4390
Flint, MI 48507 Fax: (810)766-4399
Free: (800)469-3165
Publisher E-mail: journal@baker.edu

Scholarly journal covering leadership studies. **Founded:** 1993. **Freq:** Quarterly. **Key Personnel:** Richard Hodgetts, Editor. **ISSN:** 1071-7919. **Subscription Rates:** $65 individuals; $20 single issue. **Remarks:** Accepts advertising.
Ad Rates: BW: $500 **Circ:** (Not Reported)

15116 MCC Post
Mott Community College
1401 E. Court St. Phone: (313)239-8224
Flint, MI 48503-2089 Fax: (313)762-0257

Collegiate magazine. **Subtitle:** Mott Community College Post. **Founded:** 1929. **Freq:** Biweekly. **Print Method:** Offset. **Cols./Page:** 5. **Col. Width:** 23 nonpareils. **Col. Depth:** 196 agate lines. **Key Personnel:** Jim Crawford, Editor; Paul Rozycki, Advisor. **Remarks:** Accepts advertising.
Ad Rates: GLR: $.30 **Circ:** Non-paid ‡4,200
BW: $125
PCI: $4

15117 The Suburban News
Advance Newspapers
5085 Miller Rd.
Flint, MI 48507-1071

Suburban newspaper. **Founded:** Feb. 7, 1973. **Freq:** Semiweekly (Sun. and Thurs.). **Print Method:** Offset. **Cols./Page:** 6. **Col. Width:** 2 1/8 inches. **Col. Depth:** 21 inches. **Key Personnel:** Robert Bement, Editor; Henry Hogan, Publisher; Robert Natzel, Advertising Dir. **Subscription Rates:** $34.95. **Remarks:** Accepts advertising.
Ad Rates: BW: $1,076.04 **Circ:** ‡15,200
4C: $1,526.04
PCI: $8.54

15118 Comcast Cablevision of Flint
3008 Airpark Dr. S. Phone: (810)235-9200
Flint, MI 48507 Fax: (810)235-9205

Founded: 1966. **Cities Served:** Genesee County, Oakland County, Burton, Clio, Flint Twp., Flushing, Grand Blanc, Holly Village, Mount Morris, Swartz Creek, and Vienna Twp., MI.

15119 WCRZ-FM - 107.9
3338 E. Bristol Rd. Phone: (810)743-1080
Flint, MI 48501 Fax: (810)742-5170

Format: Adult Contemporary. **Networks:** CBS. **Founded:** 1961. **Operating Hours:** Continuous. **ADI:** Flint-Saginaw-Bay City, MI. **Key Personnel:** Jay Patrick, Operations Mgr. **Wattage:** 50,000. **URL:** http://www.wcrz.com; http://www.wcrz@aol.com.

15120 WDZZ-FM - 92.7
120 E. 1st. St., Ste.1830 Phone: (810)767-7300
Flint, MI 48502 Fax: (810)238-7310

Format: Urban Contemporary. **Networks:** CBS. **Founded:** 1979. **Operating Hours:** Continuous. **ADI:** Flint-Saginaw-Bay City, MI. **Key Personnel:** Roger Moorman, General Mgr.; Ross Holland, Program Dir.; Mark Hiller, Sales Mgr. **Wattage:** 3000. **Ad Rates:** $70-82 per unit. Combined advertising rates available with WFDF-AM.

15121 WFBE-FM - 95.1
923 E. Kearsley St. Phone: (810)760-1148
Flint, MI 48503-1974 Fax: (810)760-6790

Format: Public Radio; Full Service; Eclectic. **Networks:** American Public Radio (APR). **Owner:** Flint Board of Education, 923 Kearsley St., Flint, MI 48503, (810)762-1000. **Founded:** 1953. **Operating Hours:** 5 a.m.-1 a.m.; 45% network, 55% local. **ADI:** Flint-Saginaw-Bay City, MI. **Key Personnel:** Tom Butts, Station Mgr./Program Dir.; Pam Bakken, Contact. **Wattage:** 50,000.

15122 WFDF-AM - 910
120 E. 1st. St. Phone: (810)238-7300
Genesee Towers, Ste. 1830 Fax: (810)238-7310
Flint, MI 48502

Format: Talk; News; Sports. **Networks:** CBS; Satellite Music Network. **Owner:** Connoisseur Communications of Flint,, at above address. **Founded:** 1922. **Formerly:** WFCF-AM (1989). **Operating Hours:** Continuous. **ADI:** Flint-Saginaw-Bay City, MI. **Key Personnel:** Roger Moosman, General Mgr.; Les Root, News Dir.; Mark Hilles, Sales Mgr. **Local Programs:** *Dave Barber Show, Lehto's Law.* **Wattage:** 5000. **Ad Rates:** $70-82 per unit.

15123 WFLT-AM - 1420
317 S. Averill Phone: (810)239-5733
Flint, MI 48506 Fax: (810)239-7134

Format: Religious; Gospel. **Networks:** Independent. **Founded:** 1955. **Operating Hours:** Continuous. **ADI:** Flint-Saginaw-Bay City, MI. **Key Personnel:** A.J. Pointer, President; J.C. Curry, Vice President; Suette Brown, Traffic Dir.; Rory Cavette, Operations Mgr. **Wattage:** 500. **Ad Rates:** $12.50-20 for 30 seconds; $15-25 for 60 seconds.

15124 WFUM-FM - 91.1
303 E. Kearsley St. Phone: (810)762-3028
1001 Mott Memorial Bldg. Fax: (810)233-6017
Flint, MI 48502-2186
Free: (800)728-WFUM

Format: Public Radio; Jazz; Classical. **Simulcasts:** WUOM-FM. **Networks:** National Public Radio (NPR). **Founded:** 1985. **Operating Hours:** 5:30 am-1 am weekdays, 6:30 am-1 am Saturday and Sunday; 30% network, 70% local. **ADI:** Flint-Saginaw-Bay City, MI. **Key Personnel:** Gordon Lawrence, Station Mgr. **Wattage:** 15,000. **Ad Rates:** Advertising accepted; rates available upon request. Combined advertising rates available with WCRZ-FM.

15125 WFUM-TV - 28
The University of Michigan-Flint Phone: (810)762-3028
1321 E. Court St. Fax: (810)233-6017
Flint, MI 48502-2186

Format: Public TV. **Networks:** Public Broadcasting Service (PBS). **Founded:** 1980. **Operating Hours:** 7 a.m.-1 a.m.; 70% network, 30% local. **ADI:** Flint-Saginaw-Bay City, MI. **Key Personnel:** Diane Parker, Contact; Jim Gaver, Program Mgr.; Gordon Lawrence, Station Mgr.; Ray Miller, Operations Mgr.; Wayne Henderson, Chief Engineer; Carolyn Meldrum, Contact.

15126 WJRT-TV - 12
2302 Lapeer Rd. Phone: (810)233-3130
Flint, MI 48503 Fax: (810)257-2834
E-mail: wjrt@cris.com

Format: Commercial TV. **Networks:** ABC. **Owner:** ABC, Inc., 77 W. 66th St., New York, NY 10036, (212)456-7777. **Founded:** 1958. **Operating Hours:** Continuous, weekdays, 6 a.m.-2:30 a.m., Saturday and Sunday; 50% network, 50% local. **ADI:** Flint-Saginaw-Bay City, MI. **Key Personnel:** Tom Bryson, President; Jim Bleicher, News Dir.; Sara Jo Gallock, Program Dir.; Dan Aube, General Sales Mgr.; Ed Phelps, Sports Dir.; Diane Parker, Business Mgr. **Wattage:** 316kw.

15127 WSMH-TV - 66
G 3463 W. Pierson Rd. Phone: (810)785-8866
Flint, MI 48504 Fax: (810)785-8963

Format: Commercial TV. **Networks:** Fox. **Owner:** Sinclair Broadcasting, Inc., 2000 W. 43rd St., Baltimore, MD 21211, (410)467-4545. **Founded:** 1984. **Operating Hours:** Continuous. **ADI:** Flint-Saginaw-Bay City, MI. **Key Personnel:** Aaron Olander, General Mgr.; Denise Poosch, Nat'l Sales Mgr.; John Grover, Chief Engineer; Sharon Croner, Promotions Mgr.; Jeanette Reynolds, Traffic Mgr. **Wattage:** 1170.

15128 WWCK-AM - 105.5
3217 Lapeer Rd. Phone: (810)744-1570
Flint, MI 48503 Fax: (810)743-2500

Format: Contemporary Hit Radio (CHR). **Networks:** Independent. **Owner:** Marc Steenbarger, at above address. **Founded:** 1946. **Operating Hours:** Continuous. **ADI:** Flint-Saginaw-Bay City, MI. **Key Personnel:** Marc Steenbarger, Contact; Scott Seipel, Program Dir.; Jack Steenbarger, Contact. **Wattage:** 3000.

FLUSHING

15129 The Flushing Observer
Advance Newspapers
5085 Miller Rd.
Flint, MI 48507-1071

Suburban newspaper. **Founded:** 1882. **Freq:** Semiweekly (Thurs. and Sun.). **Print Method:** Offset. **Cols./Page:** 6. **Col. Depth:** 294 agate lines. **Key Personnel:** William Vanaman, Editor; Henry Hogan, Publisher; Robert Natzel, Advertising Dir. **Subscription Rates:** $34.95. **Remarks:** Accepts advertising.
Ad Rates: BW: $834.12 **Circ:** ‡7,500
4C: $1,284.12
PCI: $6.62

FOWLERVILLE

15130 Fowlerville Shopper
Hometown Newspapers
323 E. Grand River Phone: (517)548-2000
PO Box 230 Fax: (517)548-3005
Howell, MI 48843
Shopper (tabloid). **Founded:** 1874. **Freq:** Weekly (Wed.). **Print Method:** Offset. **Trim Size:** 11 1/2 x 17. **Cols./Page:** 5. **Col. Width:** 2 1/16 inches. **Col. Depth:** 16 inches. **Key Personnel:** Roland Peterson, Publisher; Mike Preville, Advertising Mgr. **Remarks:** Accepts advertising.
Ad Rates: BW: $395.20 **Circ:** Combined ♦**9,457**
4C: $595.20
SAU: $4.94

FRANKENMUTH

15131 Frankenmuth News
231 Hubinger Phone: (517)652-3246
PO Box 252 Fax: (517)652-3247
Frankenmuth, MI 48734-1703
Local newspaper. **Founded:** 1906. **Freq:** Weekly (Wed.). **Print Method:** Offset. **Cols./Page:** 8. **Col. Width:** 19 nonpareils. **Col. Depth:** 301 agate lines. **Key Personnel:** Scott Wenzel, Editor; Steven Grainger, Publisher; John Ozerites, Advertising Mgr. **USPS:** 207-960. **Subscription Rates:** $22.50. **Remarks:** Accepts advertising.
Ad Rates: GLR: $.45 **Circ:** ‡4,950
BW: $601.80
4C: $1,101.80
SAU: $4.20
PCI: $3.54

15132 WKNX-AM - 1250
306 W. Genesee St. Phone: (517)652-4500
Frankenmuth, MI 48734 Fax: (517)652-4600

Format: Middle-of-the-Road (MOR). **Networks:** USA Radio. **Founded:** 1947. **Operating Hours:** Continuous. **Key Personnel:** John W. Blehm, Pres./Gen. Mgr./Program Dir.; Bob Fiedle, Chief Engineer; Dana Macvay, Sales Mgr.; Bob Dyer, Promotions Dir.; Bob Samuel, News Dir.; Kathy Blehm, Station Manager. **Wattage:** 1000-Day, 50-Night. **Ad Rates:** $10-12 for 30 seconds; $12-15 for 60 seconds.

FRANKFORT

15133 Benzie County Record-Patriot
The Pioneer Group
417 Main St. Phone: (616)352-9659
PO Box 673 Fax: (616)352-7874
Frankfort, MI 49635
Community newspaper. **Subtitle:** Benzie Co. Record Patroit. **Founded:** 1888. **Freq:** Weekly (Wed.). **Print Method:** Offset. **Cols./Page:** 5. **Col. Width:** 21 nonpareils. **Col. Depth:** 182 agate lines. **Key Personnel:** Roland Halliday, Editor; Jack Batdorff, CEO; Dick Bowman, Advertising Mgr.; Terry J. Fitzwater, Publisher. **Subscription Rates:** $20 individuals a year; $28 out of country; $38 out of state.
Ad Rates: SAU: $6.50 **Circ:** ‡4,427

15134 WBNZ-FM - 99.3
1532 Forrester Rd. Phone: (616)352-9603
Frankfort, MI 49635 Fax: (616)352-7877
Free: (800)974-9269

Format: Adult Contemporary; News; Sports. **Owner:** Crystal Clear Communications, Inc., at above address. **Founded:** 1978. **Operating Hours:** Continuous. **ADI:** Traverse City-Cadillac, MI. **Key Personnel:** Marc McGuire, Gen./Sales Mgr.; John Rutherford, P.D.; Chuck Randal, News/Sports Dir. **Wattage:** 50,000. **Ad Rates:** $7-12 for 30 seconds; $9-14 for 60 seconds.

FRASER

The Monitor - See Detroit

FREEPORT

15135 Freeport News
129 Division St. Phone: (616)765-8511
Freeport, MI 49325
Community newspaper. **Founded:** 1926. **Freq:** Weekly (Thurs.). **Print Method:** Letterpress. **Cols./Page:** 5. **Col. Width:** 24 nonpareils. **Col. Depth:** 224 agate lines. **Key Personnel:** Charles H. Geiger, Editor and Publisher. **Subscription Rates:** $6.

15136 Record
Freeport News
129 Division St. Phone: (616)765-8511
Freeport, MI 49325
Newspaper with a Republican orientation. **Founded:** 1893. **Freq:** Weekly (Thurs.). **Print Method:** Letterpress. Uses mats. **Cols./Page:** 5. **Col. Width:** 24 nonpareils. **Col. Depth:** 210 agate lines. **Key Personnel:** Charles H. Geiger, Editor and Publisher. **Subscription Rates:** $6.
Circ: 600

FREMONT

15137 Hi-Lites Shoppers Guide
Hi-Lites Graphics, Inc.
1212 Locust Phone: (616)924-0630
Fremont, MI 49412 Fax: (616)924-5580
Free: (800)482-5262

Shopper (tabloid). **Founded:** 1948. **Freq:** Weekly (Mon.). **Print Method:** Offset. **Trim Size:** 11 x 17. **Cols./Page:** 6. **Col. Width:** 20 nonpareils. **Col. Depth:** 244 agate lines. **Key Personnel:** B. Jon Sovinski, Publisher; Karen Baird, Advertising Mgr.; Tom Kowalski, Circulation Mgr. **Subscription Rates:** Free; $20 by mail.
Ad Rates: BW: $360 **Circ:** Free 20,000
4C: $570
PCI: $4.65

15138 Times-Indicator
T.I. Publications
44 W. Main Phone: (616)924-4400
PO Box 7 Fax: (616)924-4066
Fremont, MI 49412-0007
Local newspaper covering Newaygo County and adjacent areas. **Founded:** 1878. **Freq:** Weekly (Wed.). **Print Method:** Offset. **Cols./Page:** 8. **Col. Width:** 18 nonpareils. **Col. Depth:** 301 agate lines. **Key Personnel:** Richard C. Wheater, Sr., Editor; Debby Reinhold, Advertising Mgr. **Subscription Rates:** $22 individuals.
Ad Rates: BW: $590 **Circ:** 7,500
4C: $800
SAU: $7.25

15139 WSHN-AM - 1550
PO Box 190 Phone: (616)924-4700
Fremont, MI 49412 Fax: (616)924-9746
Free: (877)924-4700
E-mail: wshn@riverview.net

Format: Talk; News; Sports. **Networks:** CNN Radio. **Owner:** WSHN Inc., at above address. **Founded:** 1960. **Formerly:** WMIV-AM. **Operating Hours:** Sunrise-sunset; 95% network, 5% local. **ADI:** Grand Rapids-Kalamazoo-Battle Creek, MI. **Key Personnel:** Christine Zimmer, Office/Traffic Mgr.; Don Noordyk, Sales Mgr.; Christine Zimmer, Production; Jon Russell, News Dir.; Don Noordyk, Pres./Gen. Mgr. **Wattage:** 5000. **Ad Rates:** $2-10 for 30 seconds; $4-12 for 60 seconds.

15140 WSHN-FM - 100.1
PO Box 190 Phone: (616)924-4700
Fremont, MI 49412 Fax: (616)924-9746
Free: (877)924-4700
E-mail: wshn@riverview.net

Format: Country. **Networks:** Westwood One Radio. **Owner:** WSHN Inc., at above address. **Founded:** 1960. **Operating Hours:** Continuous. **ADI:** Grand Rapids-Kalamazoo-Battle Creek, MI. **Key Personnel:** Christine Zimmer, Office/Traffic Manager; Christine Zimmer, Production; James Richard, Sales Mgr.; Jon Russell, News Dir.; Don Noordyk, Pres./General Mgr. **Wattage:** 5000. **Ad Rates:** $12-15 for 30 seconds; $18-28 for 60 seconds.

FULTON

15141 Artery
Artery Publishing Co.
13998 W Ave. E. Phone: (616)496-8308
Fulton, MI 49052-0165
Journal covering biomedical research in heart disease. **Founded:** 1974. **Freq:** Bimonthly. **Print Method:** Letterpress and offset. Uses mats. **Trim Size:** 6 x 9. **Cols./Page:** 1. **Col. Width:** 51 nonpareils. **Col. Depth:** 98 agate lines. **Key Personnel:** Charles E. Day, Editor; Claudia Sandrella, Publisher. **ISSN:** 0098-6127. **Subscription Rates:** $18 single issue; $85 individuals per volume; $95 out of country per volume. **Remarks:** Advertising not accepted.
Circ: (Not Reported)

GARDEN CITY

15142 Garden City Observer
Observer & Eccentric Newspapers
36251 Schoolcraft Rd. Phone: (313)591-2300
Livonia, MI 48150-1216 Fax: (313)953-2232

Community newspaper. **Founded:** 1962. **Freq:** Semiweekly (Mon. and Thurs.). **Print Method:** Offset. **Cols./Page:** 9. **Col. Width:** 17 nonpareils. **Col. Depth:** 301 agate lines. **Key Personnel:** Richard Aginian, Publisher. **Subscription Rates:** $23. **Remarks:** Accepts advertising.
Ad Rates: GLR: $2.62 **Circ:** Paid 2,603
Free 3,235

15143 WCAR-AM - 1090
32500 Park Ln. Phone: (313)525-1111
Garden City, MI 48135 Fax: (313)525-3608

Format: Eclectic. **Founded:** 1963. **Formerly:** WIID-AM (1979). **Operating Hours:** Continuous. **ADI:** Detroit, MI. **Key Personnel:** Susan McGraw, General Mgr.; Susan Papera, Operations Mgr. **Wattage:** 500. **Ad Rates:** $28 for 30 seconds; $54 for 60 seconds.

GAYLORD

Alpena Star - See Alpena

15144 Charlevoix Co. Star
Star Publications
PO Box 620 Phone: (517)732-5125
Gaylord, MI 49734 Fax: (517)732-9323
Free: (800)782-7237
Publisher E-mail: starads@northland.lib.mi.us

Shopper. **Freq:** Weekly (Sun.). **Print Method:** Offset. Uses mats. **Trim Size:** 11 1/8 x 17 1/2. **Cols./Page:** 6. **Col. Width:** 21 nonpareils. **Col. Depth:** 224 agate lines. **Key Personnel:** David Baragrey, Publisher, phone (616)347-8186, fax (616)347-5744; Dan McDonald, Advertising Mgr. **Subscription Rates:** Free. **Remarks:** Accepts advertising.
Ad Rates: GLR: $4 **Circ:** Non-paid 10,794
BW: $577.92
4C: $773.92
PCI: $6.02

15145 Gaylord Herald Times
Otsego County Herald Times, Inc.
PO Box 598 Phone: (517)732-1111
Gaylord, MI 49734 Fax: (517)732-3490
Publisher E-mail: pub@gaylordheraldtimes.com

Community newspaper. **Founded:** 1875. **Freq:** Weekly (Thurs.). **Print Method:** Offset. **Cols./Page:** 6. **Col. Width:** 24 nonpareils. **Col. Depth:** 301 agate lines. **Key Personnel:** Jeff Hogan, News Editor; James L. Grisso, Publisher; Chris Jenkins, Editor; James Cook, Sports Editor; Marilyn Kaczanowski, Assistant to the Publisher; Colette Hogan, Production Mgr.; J.A. Thompson, Circulation Mgr. **Subscription Rates:** $35.00 individuals; $47.50 out of area. **Remarks:** Accepts advertising.
Ad Rates: SAU: $10.22 **Circ:** Paid ‡7,010
Free ‡140

15146 Market Place Up North
Otsego County Herald Times, Inc.
PO Box 598 Phone: (517)732-1111
Gaylord, MI 49734 Fax: (517)732-3490
Publication E-mail: ht@fr
Publisher E-mail: pub@gaylordheraldtimes.com

Shopper (tabloid) also covering local news. **Founded:** 1976. **Freq:** Weekly (Sat.). **Print Method:** Offset. **Trim Size:** 10 x 16. **Cols./Page:** 5. **Col. Width:** 12 1/2 picas. **Col. Depth:** 16 1/2 inches. **Key Personnel:** Colette Hogan, Production Dir.; James L. Grisso, Publisher; Beth Norton, Advertising Mgr.; Marilyn Kaczanowski, Asst. to the Publisher; J.A. Thompson, Circulation Mgr. **Subscription Rates:** Free. **Remarks:** Accepts advertising. **Formerly:** ADZ.
Ad Rates: SAU: $10.22 **Circ:** Free ‡20,000

15147 Northern Lights
Otsego County Herald Times, Inc.
PO Box 598 Phone: (517)732-1111
Gaylord, MI 49734 Fax: (517)732-3490
Publisher E-mail: pub@gaylordheraldtimes.com

Magazine promoting tourism in Michigan's northern lower peninsula. **Founded:** 1990. **Freq:** Monthly. **Print Method:** Offset. **Trim Size:** 11 x 10 1/4. **Cols./Page:** 5. **Col. Width:** 12.5 picas. **Key Personnel:** James L. Grisso, Publisher; Chris Jenkins, Editor, chris@gaylordheraldtimes.com; Marilyn Kachznowski, Asst. to the Publisher, marilyn@gaylordheraldtimes.com; Jeff Hogan, News Editor. **Remarks:** Accepts advertising. **Formerly:** Gaylord Magazine; North Country Magazine.
Ad Rates: PCI: $10.91 **Circ:** Non-paid 15,000

15148 Northern Star
Star Publications
PO Box 620 Phone: (517)732-5125
Gaylord, MI 49734 Fax: (517)732-9323
Free: (800)782-7237
Publisher E-mail: starads@northland.lib.mi.us

Shopper (tabloid). **Founded:** 1960. **Freq:** Weekly (Sun.). **Print Method:** Offset. Uses mats. **Trim Size:** 11 1/8 x 17 1/2. **Cols./Page:** 6. **Col. Width:** 21 nonpareils. **Col. Depth:** 224 agate lines. **Key Personnel:** David Baragrey, Publisher; Angela Love, Advertising Mgr. **Remarks:** Accepts advertising. **URL:** http://www.star-ads.com.
Ad Rates: BW: $618.24 **Circ:** Non-paid 17,944
4C: $817.24
PCI: $6.44

15149 Petoskey Star Advertiser
Star Publications
PO Box 620 Phone: (517)732-5125
Gaylord, MI 49734 Fax: (517)732-9323
Free: (800)782-7237
Publication E-mail: starads@northland.lib.mi.us
Publisher E-mail: starads@northland.lib.mi.us

Shopper. **Freq:** Weekly (Sun.). **Print Method:** Offset. Uses mats. **Trim Size:** 11 1/8 x 17 1/2. **Cols./Page:** 6. **Col. Width:** 21 nonpareils. **Col. Depth:** 224 agate lines. **Key Personnel:** David Baragrey, Publisher, phone (616)347-8186, fax (616)347-5744; Dan McDonald, Advertising Mgr. **Subscription Rates:** Free. **Remarks:** Accepts advertising. **Former name:** Emmet Advertiser.
Ad Rates: GLR: $4 **Circ:** Non-paid 12,807
BW: $618.24
4C: $814.24
PCI: $6.44

Presque Isle Star - See Rogers City

Star Advertiser - See Charlevoix

Star Buyer's Guide - See West Branch

Straits Area Star - See St. Ignace

15150 WKPK-FM - 106.7
PO Box 190 Phone: (616)516-4485
Gaylord, MI 49735 Fax: (616)546-4490
E-mail: peak1067@gt11.com

Format: Top 40. **Networks:** Westwood One Radio. **Owner:** Northern Radio of Gaylord, at above address. **Founded:** 1972. **Formerly:** WWRM-FM (1984). **Operating Hours:** Continuous. **ADI:** Traverse City-Cadillac, MI. **Key Personnel:** John Dew, General Mgr.; Bob Scott, Regional Sales Manager; Rob Weaver, Program Dir.; Brent Carey, News/Music Director; Scott McDonald, Promotions Dir.; Bob Sheen, Business Mgr. **Wattage:** 100,000. **Ad Rates:** $15-22 per unit. **URL:** http://www.wkpk.com.

15151 WOLW-FM - 91.1
Box 695 Phone: (517)732-6274
Gaylord, MI 49734-0695 Fax: (517)732-8171
Free: (800)545-8857
E-mail: ncr@ncradio.org

Format: Religious. **Simulcasts:** WPHN-FM. **Networks:** Moody Broadcasting. **Owner:** Northern Christian Radio, Inc., at above address. **Founded:** 1988. **Operating Hours:** Continuous; 60% local, 40% network. **ADI:** Traverse City-Cadillac, MI. **Key Personnel:** David A. Malin, General Mgr., dmanlin@ncradio.org; George A. Lake, Jr., Chief Engineer, glake@ncradio.org; Doug Smith, Program Dir., dougs@ncradio.org. **Wattage:** 50,000. **Ad Rates:** Noncommercial.

15152 WPHN-FM - 90.5
1511 M-32 E. Phone: (517)732-6274
Box 695 Fax: (517)732-8171
Gaylord, MI 49734-0695
Free: (800)545-8857
E-mail: ncr@ncradio.org

Format: Religious. **Networks:** Moody Broadcasting. **Owner:** Northern Christian Radio, Inc., at above address. **Founded:** 1985. **Operating Hours:** Continuous; 40% network, 60% local. **ADI:** Alpena, MI. **Key Personnel:** David A. Malin, General Mgr., dmalin@ncradio.org; George A. Lake, Jr., Chief Engineer, glake@ncradio.org; Doug Smith, Program Dir., doug@ncradio.org. **Wattage:** 100,000. **Ad Rates:** Noncommercial.

15153 WSNQ-AM - 900
650 E. Main Phone: (517)732-2341
PO Box 1766 Fax: (517)732-6202
Gaylord, MI 49735

Format: Oldies. **Founded:** 1950. **Formerly:** WATC-AM; WMJZ-AM. **Operating Hours:** Continuous. **Key Personnel:**

Kent Smith, President; Mike Reling, Program Dir.; Chris Hebel, General Mgr.; Kay Burson, Traffic/Production Dir.; Maria Smith, Operations Mgr. **Wattage:** 1000. **Ad Rates:** $7 for 30 seconds; $9 for 60 seconds. Combined advertising rates available with WMJZ-FM.

GLADWIN

15154 Gladwin Buyers Guide
Central Michigan Newspapers, Inc.
215 N. Main St. Phone: (517)426-9351
PO Box 447 Fax: (517)426-0551
Mount Pleasant, MI 48804-0447
Free: (800)616-6397
Publisher E-mail: cmn@cmnnet.com

Shopper. **Freq:** Weekly. **Print Method:** Offset. Uses mats. **Cols./Page:** 6. **Col. Width:** 20 nonpareils. **Col. Depth:** 224 agate lines. **Key Personnel:** Paige O'Neal, General Mgr. **Remarks:** Accepts advertising. **Online:** AO SEND.
Ad Rates: GLR: $6.90 **Circ:** Free ❑17,200
BW: $580.80
4C: $655
PCI: $6.90

15155 Gladwin County Record and Beaverton Clarion
700 E. Cedar Ave. Phone: (517)426-9411
PO Box 425 Fax: (517)426-2023
Gladwin, MI 48624
Publication E-mail: edit@gladcorec.com

Community newspaper. **Founded:** 1877. **Freq:** Weekly (Wed.). **Print Method:** Offset. **Trim Size:** 13 x 21 1/2. **Cols./Page:** 6. **Col. Width:** 2 inches. **Col. Depth:** 21 1/2 inches. **Key Personnel:** Michael Drey, Publisher. **USPS:** 219-100. **Subscription Rates:** $24.95 by mail. **Remarks:** Accepts advertising. **URL:** http://www.gladcorec.com.
Ad Rates: GLR: $7.75 **Circ:** Paid ‡8,200
SAU: $7.75 Free ‡60

15156 WGDN-AM - 1350
3601 W. Woods Rd. Phone: (517)426-1350
Gladwin, MI 48624 Fax: (517)426-9436

Format: Easy Listening; Adult Contemporary. **Simulcasts:** WGDN-FM. **Networks:** USA Radio. **Owner:** Apple Broadcasting Co., at above address. **Founded:** 1974. **Formerly:** WJEB-AM (1986). **Operating Hours:** 5 a.m.-midnight. **Key Personnel:** Steve Coston, General Mgr. **Wattage:** 1000. **Ad Rates:** $6 for 30 seconds; $7 for 60 seconds.

15157 WGDN-FM - 103.1
3601 W. Woods Rd. Phone: (517)426-1031
Gladwin, MI 48624

Format: Country. **Networks:** USA Radio. **Founded:** 1987. **Formerly:** WGMM-FM. **Operating Hours:** Continuous. **ADI:** Flint-Saginaw-Bay City, MI. **Key Personnel:** Steve Coston, General Mgr. **Wattage:** 25,000. **Ad Rates:** $10 for 30 seconds; $12 for 60 seconds.

GRAND BLANC

15158 WSNL-AM - 600
6171 S. Center Rd. Phone: (810)694-4146
Grand Blanc, MI 48439 Fax: (810)694-0661
Free: (800)600-4146
E-mail: wsnl600@mailcity.com

Format: Religious; Adult Contemporary. **Networks:** Independent; USA Radio. **Owner:** Midwest Broadcasting Corp., at above address. **Founded:** 1946. **Formerly:** WTAC-AM (Mar. 1997). **Operating Hours:** Continuous. **Key Personnel:** Jon Yinger, General Mgr.; Jenifer Carll, Program Dir.; Sally Freel, Office Mgr.; Jim Grondin, Sales Mgr. **Wattage:** 1000. **Ad Rates:** $12-15 for 30 seconds; $14-18 for 60 seconds.

GRAND HAVEN

15159 Tribune
Grand Haven Publishing Corp.
301 N. 3rd St. Phone: (616)842-6400
Grand Haven, MI 49417 Fax: (616)842-9584
Publication E-mail: ghnews@novagate.com

General newspaper. **Founded:** 1885. **Freq:** Daily (eve.) and Sat. (morn.). **Print Method:** Offset. **Trim Size:** 13 x 21. **Cols./Page:** 6. **Col. Width:** 12.3 picas. **Col. Depth:** 21 inches. **Key Personnel:** Fred Van den Brand, Editor; Paul Bedient, Advertising Mgr. **Subscription Rates:** $65; $86 out of area. **Remarks:** Accepts advertising.
Ad Rates: BW: $9.65 **Circ:** Mon.-Sat. 10,135
SAU: $11.35

15160 WGHN-AM - 1370
1 S. Harbor Phone: (616)842-8110
Grand Haven, MI 49417 Fax: (616)842-4350

Format: Adult Contemporary. **Networks:** CBS. **Owner:** WGHN, Inc., at above address. **Founded:** 1956. **Operating Hours:** Continuous; 5% network, 95% local. **ADI:** Grand Rapids-Kalamazoo-Battle Creek, MI. **Key Personnel:** William J. Struyk, Contact; Ron Stevens, News Dir. **Wattage:** 500. **Ad Rates:** $13-21 per unit.

15161 WGHN-FM - 92.1
1 South Harbor Phone: (616)842-8110
Grand Haven, MI 49417

Format: Adult Contemporary. **Networks:** CBS. **Owner:** WGHN, Inc., at above address. **Founded:** 1969. **Operating Hours:** Continuous; 5% network, 95% local. **ADI:** Grand Rapids-Kalamazoo-Battle Creek, MI. **Key Personnel:** William J. Struyk, Contact; Ron Stevens, News Dir. **Wattage:** 3000. **Ad Rates:** $13-21 per unit.

GRAND LEDGE

15162 Charlotte Shopping Guide
Community Newspapers
219 S. Bridge Phone: (517)627-6085
Grand Ledge, MI 48837 Fax: (517)627-3497
Free: (800)646-6397

Community newspaper (tabloid). **Founded:** 1947. **Freq:** Weekly (Tues.). **Print Method:** Offset. **Trim Size:** 11 1/2 x 17 1/2. **Cols./Page:** 6. **Col. Width:** 9.5 picas. **Col. Depth:** 16 inches. **Key Personnel:** Joe Warner, Editor; Tricia Johnson, Publisher. **Subscription Rates:** $104 individuals. **Remarks:** Accepts advertising. **Formed by the merger of:** Eaton County Newschronicle (1989); The Shopper's Guide (1989). **Formerly:** Charlotte Shopping Guide and Eaton County News.
Ad Rates: GLR: $2.58 **Circ:** Combined 13,748
BW: $629.76
4C: $909.76
SAU: $8.53
PCI: $6.56

15163 Delta Waverly Community News
Community Newspapers
219 S. Bridge Phone: (517)627-6085
Grand Ledge, MI 48837 Fax: (517)627-3497
Free: (800)646-6397

Community newspaper. **Founded:** 1984. **Freq:** Weekly (Sun.). **Print Method:** Offset. **Trim Size:** 10 1/4 x 16. **Cols./Page:** 6. **Col. Width:** 9.5 picas. **Col. Depth:** 16 inches. **Key Personnel:** Nancy Zeimen, Editor; Terence J. Fitzwater, Publisher. **Subscription Rates:** $104 by mail. **Remarks:** Accepts advertising. **Formerly:** Delta Waverly News Herald.
Ad Rates: GLR: $2.58 **Circ:** Paid 86
BW: $625.92 Non-paid 8,881
4C: $775.92
SAU: $8.47
PCI: $6.52

15164 DeWitt Bath Review
Community Newspapers
219 S. Bridge Phone: (517)627-6085
Grand Ledge, MI 48837 Fax: (517)627-3497
Free: (800)646-6397

Community newspaper. **Founded:** 1978. **Freq:** Weekly (Sun.). **Print Method:** Offset. **Cols./Page:** 6. **Col. Width:** 9.5 picas. **Col. Depth:** 224 agate lines. **Key Personnel:** Preston E. Odette, Publisher; Lynn Sutfin, Editor; Peter Cantine, VP & GM. **Subscription Rates:** $17.50; $14.50 senior citizens; $27.50 out of state. **Remarks:** Accepts advertising.
Ad Rates: GLR: $.66 **Circ:** Combined 7,348
BW: $744
4C: $999
SAU: $9.30
PCI: $10.40

15165 Eaton Rapids Community News
Community Newspapers
219 S. Bridge Phone: (517)627-6085
Grand Ledge, MI 48837 Fax: (517)627-3497
Free: (800)646-6397

Shopping guide. **Founded:** Feb. 1993. **Freq:** Weekly (Sat.). **Print Method:** Offset. **Trim Size:** 11 1/4 x 17. **Cols./Page:** 6. **Col. Width:** 9.5 picas. **Col. Depth:** 16 inches. **Key Personnel:** Tricia Johnson, Publisher; Joe Warner, Editor. **Subscription Rates:** $104 individuals. **Remarks:** Combined advertising rates available with other Community Newspapers. **Formerly:** The Advantage; Eaton County News.
Ad Rates: GLR: $2.58 **Circ:** Combined 17,477
BW: $629.76 Free 16,567
4C: $909.76
SAU: $8.53
PCI: $6.56

15166 The Grand Ledge Independent
Community Newspapers
219 S. Bridge Phone: (517)627-6085
Grand Ledge, MI 48837 Fax: (517)627-3497
Free: (800)646-6397

Community newspaper. **Subtitle:** Grand Ledge Independent. **Founded:** 1869. **Freq:** Weekly (Tues.). **Print Method:** Offset. **Cols./Page:** 6. **Col. Width:** 9.5 picas. **Col. Depth:** 16 inches. **Key Personnel:** Nancy Zeimen, Editor; Terry Fitzwater, Publisher. **Subscription Rates:** $104. **Remarks:** Accepts advertising.
Ad Rates: GLR: $2.58 **Circ:** Combined 12,509
BW: $615
4C: $775.92
SAU: $10
PCI: $6.25

Portland Review & Observer - See Portland

GRAND RAPIDS

15167 Aquinas Times
Aquinas College Publications Board
1607 Robinson Rd. SE Phone: (616)459-8281
Grand Rapids, MI 49506-1799 Fax: (616)732-4487
Publication E-mail: aqtimes_ editor@aquinas.edu

Collegiate newspaper. **Subtitle:** Aquinas College Student Press. **Founded:** 1970. **Freq:** Biweekly. **Print Method:** Offset. **Trim Size:** 11 1/4 x 14 1/2. **Cols./Page:** 5. **Col. Width:** 1 3/4 inches. **Col. Depth:** 13 inches. **Key Personnel:** Heather M. Karal, Editor, karalhea@aquinas.edu; Heather Young, Asst. Editor, younghea@aquinas.edu; Karen Smith, Business Mgr., aqtimes_ advertising@aquinas.edu. **Subscription Rates:** Free; $5 (mail). **Remarks:** Accepts advertising. **Formerly:** Aquinas Sunrise. **Feature Editors:** Joshua Cochran, *News*; Elizabeth Dudek, *Entertainment*; Chris Manning, *Features*; Nate Thomas, *Sports*.
Ad Rates: GLR: $10 **Circ:** Non-paid ‡1,500
BW: $140

15168 The Banner
CRC Publications
2850 Kalamazoo Ave. SE Phone: (616)224-0831
Grand Rapids, MI 49560 Fax: (616)224-0834
Free: (800)333-8300
Publication E-mail: banner@crcaol.com; banner@crcna.org
Publisher E-mail: crcpublications.org

Magazine of the Christan Reformed Church in America. **Founded:** 1866. **Freq:** Biweekly. **Print Method:** Offset. **Trim Size:** 8 1/2 x 11. **Cols./Page:** 3 and 4. **Col. Depth:** 10 inches. **Key Personnel:** Rev. John Suk, Editor. **ISSN:** 0005-5557. **Subscription Rates:** $34.95 individuals; $57.73 Canada. **Remarks:** Accepts advertising. **URL:** http://thebanner.org.
Ad Rates: GLR: $7.25 **Circ:** Paid ‡30,000
BW: $1,350 Controlled ‡255
4C: $1,650
PCI: $60

15169 Cadence
Valley Media, Inc.
705 Bagley SE Phone: (616)454-9456
Grand Rapids, MI 49506 Fax: (616)454-4666

Community newspaper. **Founded:** 1975. **Freq:** Weekly (Wed.). **Print Method:** Letterpress and offset. **Cols./Page:** 6. **Col. Width:** 18 nonpareils. **Col. Depth:** 217 agate lines. **Key Personnel:** Mike Wyngarden, Editor, phone (616)669-2700, fax (616)669-4848; Joel Holland, Publisher. **Subscription Rates:** $20 individuals; $30 out of area. **Remarks:** Accepts advertising.
Ad Rates: BW: $418.50 **Circ:** ‡5,400
4C: $493.50
PCI: $7.65

15170 Chimes
Calvin College
3201 Burton SE Phone: (616)957-7031
Grand Rapids, MI 49546-4388 Fax: (616)957-8551
Publication E-mail: chimes@calvin.edu

Collegiate newspaper. **Founded:** 1906. **Freq:** Weekly (Fri.). **Print Method:** Offset. **Cols./Page:** 5. **Col. Width:** 24 nonpareils. **Col. Depth:** 210 agate lines. **Key Personnel:** Sarah Potter, General Mgr. **Subscription Rates:** $15. **Remarks:** Accepts advertising. **URL:** http://www.calvin.edu.
Ad Rates: GLR: $13 **Circ:** Paid ‡90
BW: $500 Free ‡3,500
SAU: $7
PCI: $14

15171 Christian Home & School
Christian Schools International
3350 E. Paris Ave., SE Phone: (616)957-1070
Grand Rapids, MI 49512-3054 Fax: (616)957-5022
Free: (800)635-8288
Publisher E-mail: chrschint@aol.com

Magazine addressing issues of concern to contemporary Christian families; particularly aimed at parents who support Christian education. **Founded:** 1922. **Freq:** Bimonthly. **Trim Size:** 8 1/2 x 11. **Cols./Page:** 3. **Col. Width:** 13 1/2 picas. **Col. Depth:** 55 picas. **Key Personnel:** Gordon L. Bordewyk, Exec. Editor, gbordewyk@aol.com; Roger Schmurr, Sr. Editor, rogers@csionline.org; Lori Feenstra, Advertising Mgr. **ISSN:** 0095-5389. **Subscription Rates:** $11.95 individuals; $14.95 Canada. **URL:** http://www.christianschoolsint.com.
Ad Rates: BW: $1,818 **Circ:** Paid ‡1,000
4C: $2,339 Controlled ‡63,000

15172 The Collegiate
Grand Rapids Community College
143 Bostwick NE Phone: (616)771-4000
Grand Rapids, MI 49503 Fax: (616)771-4005

Collegiate tabloid. **Founded:** 1940. **Freq:** 13/year (during the academic year). **Print Method:** Offset. **Trim Size:** 10 x 15. **Cols./Page:** 5. **Col. Width:** 24 nonpareils. **Col. Depth:** 213 agate lines. **Remarks:** Accepts advertising.
Ad Rates: BW: $250 **Circ:** Free ‡3,500
SAU: $3.50
PCI: $6

15173 East Grand Rapids Cadence
Advance Newspapers
2141 Port Sheldon Rd. Phone: (616)669-2700
PO Box 9 Fax: (616)669-1162
Jenison, MI 49428-9301
Free: (800)439-0960

Community newspaper. **Founded:** 1966. **Freq:** Weekly (Wed.). **Print Method:** Offset. **Cols./Page:** 6. **Col. Width:** 9 1/2 picas. **Key Personnel:** Joel Holland, Publisher, fax (616)669-3930. **Subscription Rates:** $25. **Remarks:** Accepts advertising. **Formerly:** East Grand Rapids Advance.
Ad Rates: BW: $734.40 **Circ:** Free 3,715
4C: $1,034.40 Paid 858
SAU: $9.18
PCI: $7.65

15174 Grand Rapids Advance
Advance Newspapers
2141 Port Sheldon Rd. Phone: (616)669-2700
PO Box 9 Fax: (616)669-1162
Jenison, MI 49428-9301
Free: (800)439-0960

Community newspaper. **Founded:** 1985. **Freq:** Weekly (Tues.). **Print Method:** Offset. **Trim Size:** 10 3/8 x 15 7/8. **Cols./Page:** 6. **Col. Width:** 1 5/8 inches. **Key Personnel:** Joel Holland, Publisher, fax (616)669-3930. **Subscription Rates:** $25. **Remarks:** Accepts advertising.
Ad Rates: BW: $758.40 **Circ:** Free 12,047
4C: $1,058.40 Paid 32
SAU: $9.48
PCI: $7.90

15175 Grand Rapids Magazine
Gemini Publications
549 Ottawa Ave. NW, Ste. 201 Phone: (616)459-4545
Grand Rapids, MI 49503-1444 Fax: (616)459-4800
Publication E-mail: info@geminipub.com
Publisher E-mail: info@geminipub.com

Regional general interest magazine. **Founded:** Apr. 1964. **Freq:** Monthly. **Print Method:** Offset. **Trim Size:** 8 3/8 x 10 7/8. **Cols./Page:** 3. **Col. Width:** 28 nonpareils. **Col. Depth:** 140 agate lines. **Key Personnel:** Carole Valade Copenhauer, Editor; John H. Zwarensteyn, Publisher; Randy Prichard, Sales Mgr.; Amy Staskey, Circulation Mgr.; Dottie Rhodes, Production Mgr. **ISSN:** 1055-5145. **Subscription Rates:** $19. **Remarks:** Advertising not accepted for pornography.
Ad Rates: BW: $1,990 **Circ:** Paid 12,400
4C: $2,320 Non-paid 3,600

15176 The Grand Rapids Press
Booth Newspapers, Inc.
155 Michigan St. NW Phone: (616)459-1400
Grand Rapids, MI 49503-2302 Fax: (616)459-1502

General newspaper. **Founded:** 1890. **Freq:** Daily (eve.). **Print Method:** Letterpress. **Cols./Page:** 6. **Col. Width:** 24 nonpareils. **Col. Depth:** 308 agate lines. **Key Personnel:** Michael Lloyd, Editor. **Subscription Rates:** $116. **Remarks:** Accepts advertising. **Online:** DataTimes Corporation. **Feature Editors:** Andy Angelo, *City, News*, phone (616)459-1456; Bob Becker, *Sports*, phone (616)459-1674; Cathy Bissell, *Fashion*, phone (616)459-1501; Hank Bornheimer, *Travel*, phone (616)459-1490; Ruth Butler, *TV & Radio*, phone (616)459-1586; Ann Byle, *Book*, phone (616)459-1612; Joe Crawford, *Editorials*, phone (616)459-1483; John Douglas, *Movie*, phone (616)459-1631; Ed Golder, *Religion*, phone (616)459-1613; Jim Harger, *Financial/Business, Real Estate*, phone (616)459-1592; Bob Keveney, *Sunday*, phone (616)459-1489; Chris Meehan, *Medical*, phone (616)459-1461; David Nicolette, *Drama*, phone (616)459-1594; Ted Roelofs, *Political*, phone (616)459-1497; Sue Schroder, *Family, Garden/Home*, phone (616)459-1627; Susan Schroder, *Features, Lifestyle, Society, Women's*, phone (616)459-1627; John Sinkevics, *Environmental*, phone (616)459-1471; Jim Starkey, *Photo*, phone (616)459-1619; Tracy Supert, *Education*, phone (616)459-1492; Sue Wallace, *Entertainment, Music*, phone (616)459-1604; Ann Wells, *Food*, phone (616)459-1503.
Ad Rates: SAU: $34.83 **Circ:** Mon.-Sat. ★**139,703**
Sun. ★**190,219**

15177 The Grand Rapids Times
PO Box 7258 Phone: (616)245-8737
Grand Rapids, MI 49510-7258 Fax: (616)245-1026

Newspaper targeted for black population in Grand Rapids, Muskegon, Battle Creek and Kalamazoo, Michigan. **Founded:** 1959. **Freq:** Weekly. **Print Method:** Web offset. **Trim Size:** 9 5/16 x 15. **Cols./Page:** 5. **Col. Width:** 2 inches. **Col. Depth:** 15 inches. **Key Personnel:** Patricia Pulliam, Editor and Publisher; Yergan Pulliam, Publisher. **Subscription Rates:** $12. **Remarks:** Accepts advertising.
Ad Rates: BW: $450 **Circ:** (Not Reported)
4C: $750
SAU: $5.99

15178 Missionary Monthly
Missionary Monthly, Inc.
c/o I.D.E.A. Ministries Phone: (616)698-8393
4595 Broadmoor Ave. SE, No. 237 Fax: (616)698-3080
Grand Rapids, MI 49512
Publisher E-mail: ideamin@ideaministries.org

Magazine on evangelical Christian churches and missions worldwide. **Founded:** 1896. **Freq:** 9/year. **Print Method:** Offset. **Trim Size:** 7 x 10. **Cols./Page:** 2. **Col. Width:** 32 nonpareils. **Col. Depth:** 120 agate lines. **Key Personnel:** Dr. Dick L. Van Halsema, Editor and Publisher. **ISSN:** 0161-7133. **Subscription Rates:** $15 individuals; $1.75 single issue.
Ad Rates: BW: $325 **Circ:** Paid ‡3,000
Non-paid ‡1,000

15179 Our Daily Bread
RBC Ministries
3000 Kraft Ave., SE Phone: (616)942-6770
Grand Rapids, MI 49555 Fax: (616)957-5741

Religious magazine. **Founded:** Apr. 1956. **Freq:** Quarterly. **Trim Size:** 4 x 6. **Cols./Page:** 1. **Key Personnel:** Kurt DeHaan, Managing Editor. **Subscription Rates:** Free. **Remarks:** Advertising not accepted. **URL:** http://www.odb.org. **Alt. Formats:** Large-print.
Circ: (Not Reported)

15180 TCI
PO Box 128901
Grand Rapids, MI 49512-8901

Founded: 1976. **Formerly:** UAE. **Cities Served:** Allegan County, Kent County, Ottowa County, Ada, Cascade, East Grand Rapids, Grandville, Kentwood, and Wyoming, MI.

15181 WBBL-AM - 1340
60 Monroe Center Phone: (616)456-5461
Grand Rapids, MI 49503 Fax: (616)451-3299

Format: Sports. **Founded:** 1940. **Formerly:** WLAV-AM (May 1, 1994). **Operating Hours:** Continuous. **ADI:** Grand Rapids-Kalamazoo-Battle Creek, MI. **Key Personnel:** Bart Brandmiller, General Mgr.; Tom Marshall, Contact. **Wattage:** 1000. **Ad Rates:** $3-40 per unit.

15182 WBMX-AM - 640
1345 Thomas St. SE
Grand Rapids, MI 49506-2651

Format: Adult Contemporary; Middle-of-the-Road (MOR); News. **ADI:** Grand Rapids-Kalamazoo-Battle Creek, MI. **Key Personnel:** Robert S. Van Prooyen, Contact; David Bradley, Contact. **Wattage:** 1000 day; 250 night.

15183 WBYW-FM - 89.9
PO Box 2892 Phone: (616)453-3711
Grand Rapids, MI 49501-2892

Format: Big Band/Nostalgia; Country; Alternative/New Music/Progressive. **Networks:** Independent. **Founded:** 1978. **Formerly:** WEHB-FM. **Operating Hours:** Continuous; 100% local. **ADI:** Grand Rapids-Kalamazoo-Battle Creek, MI. **Key Personnel:** Al Lane, Contact; John A. Lubinskas, Station Mgr. **Wattage:** 4000.

15184 WCSG-FM - 91.3
1159 E. Beltline Ave. NE Phone: (616)942-1500
Grand Rapids, MI 49505 Fax: (616)942-7078
Free: (800)968-4543
E-mail: wcsg@cornerstone.edu

Format: Religious. **Networks:** USA Radio. **Owner:** Cornerstone Baptist Educational Ministries, 1001 E. Beltline Ave. NE, Grand Rapids, MI 49505. **Founded:** 1973. **Operating Hours:** Continuous. **ADI:** Grand Rapids-Kalamazoo-Battle Creek, MI. **Key Personnel:** Lee Geysbeek, General Mgr.; Jack Haveman, Contact; Becky Carlson, News Dir.; Chris Lenke, Operations Mgr. **Wattage:** 37,000. **Ad Rates:** Noncommercial.

15185 WCUZ-FM - 101.3
77 Monroe Center, Ste. 1000 Phone: (616)459-1919
Grand Rapids, MI 49503 Fax: (616)242-9373

Format: Country. **Networks:** ABC. **Founded:** 1973. **Formerly:** WFFX-FM. **Operating Hours:** Continuous; 100% local. **ADI:** Grand Rapids-Kalamazoo-Battle Creek, MI. **Key Personnel:** Skip Essick, V.P./General Mgr.; Doug Montgomery, Operations Mgr./Program Dir.; Rob Sanford, News Dir.; Rich Berry, Sales Mgr.; Tim Hygh, National Sales Mgr.; Don Missad, Chief Engineer. **Wattage:** 50,000.

15186 WFUR-AM - 1570
PO Box 1808 Phone: (616)451-9387
Grand Rapids, MI 49501 Fax: (616)451-8460

Format: Religious. **Simulcasts:** WFUR FM/ 1200a - 600am M - S. **Networks:** USA Radio. **Owner:** William E. Kuiper, Sr., at above address. **Founded:** 1948. **Operating Hours:** Continuous; 8% network, 92% local. **ADI:** Grand Rapids-Kalamazoo-Battle Creek, MI. **Key Personnel:** Roger Peuler, Sales Mgr.; William E. Kuiper, Sr., Owner; Dave Kuiper, News Dir.; Steve Kuiper, Program Dir.; Doug Wentworth, Sports Dir.; William Kuiper, Jr., Contact. **Wattage:** 1000 day; 300 night. **Ad Rates:** $6-10 for 30 seconds; $7.50-12 for 60 seconds. WFUR-FM $18.00 to $30.00.

15187 WGRD-FM - 97.9
38 W. Fulton, Ste. 200 Phone: (616)459-4111
Grand Rapids, MI 49503 Fax: (616)454-5530

Format: Adult Album Alternative. **Founded:** 1962. **Operating Hours:** Continuous. **ADI:** Grand Rapids-Kalamazoo-Battle Creek, MI. **Key Personnel:** Joel Schaaf, General Mgr.; Margaret Smith, Program Dir.; Darla Jaye, News Dir.; Pamela Kyle, Business Mgr.; Jeff Morton, Sales Mgr. **Wattage:** 13,000. **Ad Rates:** $10-200 per unit. **URL:** http://www.wgrd.com.

15188 WGVK-TV - 52
301 W. Fulton Phone: (616)771-6666
Grand Rapids, MI 49504-6492 Fax: (616)771-6625
Free: (800)442-2771
E-mail: wgvu@gvsu.edu

Format: Public TV. **Networks:** Public Broadcasting Service (PBS). **Founded:** 1972. **Operating Hours:** 6:30 a.m.-1 a.m.; 90% network, 10% local. **ADI:** Grand Rapids-Kalamazoo-Battle Creek, MI. **Key Personnel:** Carrie Corbin, Program Mgr.; Gary Kesler, Promotions Mgr.; Michael T. Walenta, General Mgr.; Chuck Furman, Contact; Bob Lumbert, Dir. of Engineering; Peg Van Nevel, Development Mgr.; Steve Chrypinski, Underwriting Mgr. **Local Programs:** *Ethics in View*, Tim Scarpino. **Ad Rates:** Noncommercial; underwriting available.

15189 WGVU-AM - 1480
301 W. Fulton Phone: (616)771-6666
Grand Rapids, MI 49504-6492 Fax: (616)336-7204
E-mail: wgvu@gvsu.edu

Format: News; Information. **Networks:** AP; American Public Radio (APR); National Public Radio (NPR). **Founded:** 1954. **Formerly:** WMAX-AM. **Operating Hours:** Continuous. **ADI:** Grand Rapids-Kalamazoo-Battle Creek, MI. **Key Personnel:** Michael T. Walenta, General Mgr.; Gary Kesler, Promotions Mgr.; Robert Lumbert, Chief Engineer. **Wattage:** 1000 day; 5000 night. **Ad Rates:** Noncommercial; underwriting available.

15190 WGVU-FM - 88.5
301 W. Fulton Phone: (616)771-6666
Grand Rapids, MI 49504-6492 Fax: (616)336-7204
Free: (800)442-2771
E-mail: wgvu@gvsu.edu

Format: Public Radio; Jazz; News; Information. **Networks:** National Public Radio (NPR); AP. **Founded:** 1983. **Formerly:** WGVC-FM (1987). **Operating Hours:** Continuous; 25% network, 75% local. **ADI:** Grand Rapids-Kalamazoo-Battle Creek, MI. **Key Personnel:** Michael T. Walenta, General Mgr.; Ken Kolbe, News Dir.; David Moore, Contact. **Wattage:** 3000. **Ad Rates:** Noncommercial; underwriting available. $8-16 per unit.

15191 WGVU-TV - 35
301 W. Fulton Phone: (616)771-6666
Grand Rapids, MI 49504-6492 Fax: (616)771-6625
Free: (800)442-2771
E-mail: wgvu@gvsu.edu

Format: Public TV. **Networks:** Public Broadcasting Service (PBS). **Founded:** 1972. **Operating Hours:** 6:30 a.m.-1:00 a.m.; 90% network, 10% local. **ADI:** Grand Rapids-Kalamazoo-Battle Creek, MI. **Key Personnel:** Michael T. Walenta, General Mgr.; Chuck Furman, Contact; Gary Kesler, Promotions Mgr.; Carrie Corbin, Program Mgr.; Phil Lane, Production Supervisor; Bob Lumbert, Dir. of Engineering; Steve Chrypinski, Underwriting Mgr. **Local Programs:** *Ask The . .*, Phil Lane, Mailing contact; *Good Thyme Cooking*, Phil Lane, Mailing contact; *West Michigan Week*, Phil Lane, Mailing contact. **Ad Rates:** Noncommercial; underwriting available.

15192 WKLQ-FM - 94.5
60 Monroe Center NW, Ste. 1000 Phone: (616)774-8461
Fax: (616)774-0351
Grand Rapids, MI 49503

Format: Classic Rock. **Networks:** ABC. **Owner:** Michigan Media, Inc., at above address. **Founded:** 1921. **Operating Hours:** Continuous. **ADI:** Grand Rapids-Kalamazoo-Battle Creek, MI. **Key Personnel:** Bart Brandmiller, General Mgr., bab945@iserv.net; Rob Kozel, General Sales Mgr., rkozel@iserv.net; Tony Gates, Program Dir., gates@wlav.com; Ron Steenwyk, Technical Mgr., mmiron@iserv.net. **Wattage:** 50,000. **Ad Rates:** $40-130 per unit. Combined advertising rates available with WLAV-FM, WBBL-AM. **URL:** http://www.wklq.com.

15193 WKWM-AM - 1140
2610 Horizon SE, Ste., F Phone: (616)956-3323
Grand Rapids, MI 49546 Fax: (616)956-9321

Format: Urban Contemporary. **Networks:** American Urban Radio. **Owner:** Goodrich Radio Marketing, Inc., at above address, (616)698-7733. **Founded:** 1978. **Operating Hours:** Sunrise-sunset; 100% local. **ADI:** Grand Rapids-Kalamazoo-Battle Creek, MI. **Key Personnel:** Robert Goodrich, General Mgr. **Wattage:** 5000. **Ad Rates:** $15-40 for 60 seconds.

15194 WLAV-FM - 96.9
60 Monroe Center Phone: (616)456-5461
Grand Rapids, MI 49503 Fax: (616)451-3299

Format: Classic Rock. **Founded:** 1947. **Operating Hours:** Continuous. **ADI:** Grand Rapids-Kalamazoo-Battle Creek, MI. **Key Personnel:** Bart Brandmiller, President; Kelly Norton, General Sales Mgr.; Tony Gates, Program Dir. **Wattage:** 50,000. **Ad Rates:** Combined advertising rates available with WKLQ-FM, WBBL-AM. **URL:** http://www.wlav.com.

15195 WLHT-FM - 95.7
PO Box 96 Phone: (616)451-4800
Grand Rapids, MI 49501 Fax: (616)451-0113
E-mail: wlht.com@i-serv

Format: Adult Contemporary. **Networks:** ABC. **Founded:** 1962. **Operating Hours:** Continuous. **ADI:** Grand Rapids-Kalamazoo-Battle Creek, MI. **Key Personnel:** Phil Catlett, General Mgr.; Bill Bailey, Program Dir.; Bruce Parrott, Marketing Dir. **Wattage:** 41,000. **Ad Rates:** Combined advertising rates available with WRCV-AM. **URL:** http://www.wlht.com.

15196 WMFN-AM - 640
2422 Burton St. S.E. Phone: (616)949-8585
Grand Rapids, MI 49546-4806 Fax: (616)949-9262

Format: Sports. **Networks:** CBS. **Owner:** Cook Media II, at above address. **Founded:** 1995. **Formerly**: WBYY-AM (1991). **Operating Hours:** 24HRS. **ADI:** Grand Rapids-Kalamazoo-Battle Creek, MI. **Key Personnel:** Ken Jacoby, Program Mgr.; Roger Munyon, News/Public Affairs Director; Mike Marshall, General Mgr. **Wattage:** 1250. **Ad Rates:** $20 for 30 seconds; $25 for 60 seconds.

15197 WNWZ-AM - 1410
PO Box 96 Phone: (616)451-4800
Grand Rapids, MI 49501 Fax: (616)451-4807

Format: News. **Networks:** CNN Radio. **Owner:** Capstar Broadcast Partners, 600 Congress Ave., Ste. 1400, Austin, TX 78701. **Founded:** 1962. **Former name:** WRCV-AM (1998). **Operating Hours:** Continuous. **Key Personnel:** Phil Catlett, General Mgr., catlettp@iserv.net; Bruce Parrott, Program Dir., parrottb@iserv.net; Glenn Eckelkamp, Sales Mgr., eckelkampg@aserv.net. **Wattage:** 1000. **Ad Rates:** $25 per unit.

15198 WODJ-FM - 107.3
2610 Horizon Dr., Ste. F Phone: (616)956-3323
Grand Rapids, MI 49546 Fax: (616)956-3424
E-mail: wodj@wodj.com

Format: Oldies. **Networks:** Westwood One Radio. **Founded:** 1989. **Operating Hours:** Continuous. **ADI:** Grand Rapids-Kalamazoo-Battle Creek, MI. **Key Personnel:** Len O'Kelly, Program Dir.; Tom Wilson, Prod. Dir.; Nancy Faasse, Bus. Mgr./Nat. Sales Mgr., Reg. Sales, nfaasse@wodj.com; Tom Wilson, Production Dir.; Scott Fredericks, Promotions Dir. **Wattage:** 50,000. **Ad Rates:** $55-90 for 60 seconds. Combined advertising rates available with WSNX, WKWM, WSHZ, WMHG, WMRR.

15199 WOOD-AM - 1300
77 Monroe Center St. N.W., No. 1000 Phone: (616)459-1919
Fax: (616)242-6599
Grand Rapids, MI 49503-2903
E-mail: info@woodradio.com

Format: Full Service; Talk. **Networks:** Independent. **Founded:** 1924. **Formerly**: WEBK-AM (1924). **Operating Hours:** Continuous; 50% network, 50% local. **ADI:** Grand Rapids-Kalamazoo-Battle Creek, MI. **Key Personnel:** Skip Essick, V.P./General Mgr.; Phil Tower, Operations Mgr./Program Dir.; Rob Sanford, News Dir.; Henry Capogna, Sales Mgr.; Tim Hygh, National Sales Mgr.; Kate Folkertsma, Business Manager; Don Missad, Chief Engineer; Kay Jaarsma, Traffic Mgr. **Local Programs:** *Afternoon Journal*, Rob Sanford; *WOOD Good Morning Show*, Gary Allen. **Wattage:** 5,000. **Ad Rates:** Advertising accepted; rates available upon request.

15200 WOOD-FM - 105.7
77 Monroe Center, Ste. 1000 Phone: (616)459-1919
Grand Rapids, MI 49503 Fax: (616)242-6599
E-mail: info@woodradio.com

Format: Adult Contemporary. **Networks:** Independent. **Owner:** Clear Channel Radio, Inc., at above address, San Antonio, TX. **Founded:** 1962. **Operating Hours:** Continuous; 100% local. **ADI:** Grand Rapids-Kalamazoo-Battle Creek, MI. **Key Personnel:** Juli Agacinski, Promotions Mgr.; Stan Atkinson, Operations Mgr.; Paul Boscarino, Sales Mgr.; Dick Stoimenoff, Natl. Sales Manager; Kate Folkertsma, Business Mgr.; Don Missad, Chief Engineer; Skip Essick, Vice Pres./General Mgr.; Chris Moubray, Traffic Mgr. **Wattage:** 265,000. **Ad Rates:** Advertising accepted; rates available upon request.

15201 WOOD-TV - 8
120 College Ave., SE Phone: (616)456-8888
Grand Rapids, MI 49501 Fax: (616)456-9169

Format: Commercial TV. **Networks:** NBC. **Owner:** LCH Communications, 120 College SE, Grand Rapids, MI 49501. **Founded:** 1949. **Formerly**: WOTV-TV. **Operating Hours:** Continuous; 44% network, 56% local. **ADI:** Grand Rapids-Kalamazoo-Battle Creek, MI. **Key Personnel:** Scott Blumenthal, Contact; Jerry Colvin, Contact; Craig Cole, Program Dir.; Molly Kelley, Promotions Dir.; Michael Laemers, Chief Engineer; Daniel Caldwell, Business Mgr.

15202 WSNX-FM - 104.5
2610 Horizon SE, Ste. F Phone: (616)956-6696
Grand Rapids, MI 49546 Fax: (616)956-9321

Format: Contemporary Hit Radio (CHR). **Networks:** Unistar. **Owner:** Goodrich Radio Marketing, 4417 Broadmoor, Kentwood, MI 49512, (616)698-7733. **Founded:** 1971. **Formerly**: WTRU-FM. **Operating Hours:** Continuous. **ADI:** Grand Rapids-Kalamazoo-Battle Creek, MI. **Key Personnel:** Mike St. Cyr, Operations Mgr.; Mark McClure, General Sales Mgr. **Wattage:** 50,000. **Ad Rates:** Advertising accepted; rates available upon request. **URL:** http://www.snx.com.

15203 WTKG-AM - 1230
77 Monroe Center, Ste. 1000 Phone: (616)459-1919
Grand Rapids, MI 49503 Fax: (616)242-6599
E-mail: wcuz@wcuz.com

Format: Talk. **Networks:** ABC; Westwood One Radio; People's Network; USA Radio. **Founded:** 1945. **Formerly**: WJEF-AM; WCUZ-AM. **Operating Hours:** Continuous. **ADI:** Grand Rapids-Kalamazoo-Battle Creek, MI. **Key Personnel:** Skip Essick, V.P./General Mgr.; Phil Tower, Operations Mgr./Program Dir.; Rob Sanford, News Dir.; Henry Capogna, Sales Mgr.; Tim Hygh, National Sales Mgr.; Don Missad, Chief Engineer; Gail Walters, Traffic Mgr. **Local Programs:** *High School Sports*, Rick Berkey, (616)451-2551, Fax (616)451-0931; *Midday Show*, Dennis Sutton, (616)451-2551, Fax (616)451-0931. **Wattage:** 1000. **Ad Rates:** Advertising accepted; rates available upon request. **URL:** http://www.wcuz.com.

15204 WTRV-FM - 100.5
PO Box 96 Phone: (616)451-4800
Grand Rapids, MI 49501 Fax: (616)451-4807

Format: Easy Listening. **Owner:** Capstar Broadcast Partners, 600 Congress Ave., Ste. 1400, Austin, TX 78701. **Founded:** 1994. **Former name:** WQPN-FM (1998). **Operating Hours:** Continuous. **Key Personnel:** Phil Catlett, General Mgr., catlettp@iserv.net; Mike Benson, Program Dir., mbenson@capstarbroadcast.com; Margaret Lathuis, General Sales Mgr., matthuis@capstarbroadcast.com. **Wattage:** 3000. **Ad Rates:** $50-75 per unit.

15205 WVGR-FM - 104.1
c/o WUOM-FM Phone: (313)764-9210
5000 LSA Bldg. Fax: (313)747-3488
Ann Arbor, MI 48109-1352

Format: Public Radio; News; Classical; Jazz. **Networks:** National Public Radio (NPR); American Public Radio (APR). **Founded:** 1961. **Operating Hours:** Continuous. **ADI:** Lansing (Ann Arbor), MI. **Key Personnel:** Donovan Reynolds, Station Mgr.; Joan Siefert Rose, Program/News Dir.; Steve Graham, Chief Engineer; Itarriet Teller, Promotions Dir.; Shelly MacMillan, Development/Marketing Dir.; Bob Whitham, News Dir. **Local Programs:** *Desert Island Discs*, Joel Seguine; *4:30 Report*, Bob Whitman; *Today's World*, Bob Whitman. **Wattage:** 108,000. **Ad Rates:** Noncommercial.

15206 WXMI-TV - 17
3117 Plaza Dr. NE Phone: (616)364-8722
Grand Rapids, MI 49525 Fax: (616)364-8506

Format: Commercial TV. **Networks:** Fox; Independent. **Owner:** Dudley Communications Corporation, 500 3rd St., Ste. 17, Wausau, WI 54401. **Founded:** 1982. **Operating Hours:** 6 a.m.-2 a.m.; 99% network and syndicated, 1% local. **ADI:** Grand Rapids-Kalamazoo-Battle Creek, MI. **Key Personnel:** Mark Krause, Program Mgr.; Pat Mullen, General Mgr.; Bonnie Hunter, Director of Admin. Operations; Ed Fernandez, Director of Sales; Pennie Westers, Director of Creative Services; Dale Scholten, Director of Engineering. **Ad Rates:** $40-2,500 per unit.

15207 WZZM-TV - 13
Box Z Phone: (616)785-1313
Grand Rapids, MI 49501 Fax: (616)785-1301

Format: Commercial TV. **Networks:** ABC. **Operating Hours:** 6 a.m.-12:30 a.m. or sign off. **ADI:** Grand Rapids-Kalamazoo-Battle Creek, MI. **Key Personnel:** Richard F. Appleton, Contact; Buss Kunst, General Sales Mgr.; Al Forist, Contact; Ken Kolbe, News Dir.; Roberta Tepper, Contact; Karen Horstmanshof, Contact; Chuck Mikowski, Chief Engineer.

GRANDVILLE

15208 The Something Better News
Something Better Publications, Inc.
3300 28th St. SW Phone: (616)530-3957
Grandville, MI 49418 Fax: (616)530-0728

Christian community newspaper. **Subtitle:** Christian Community News. **Founded:** Aug. 1991. **Freq:** Monthly. **Key Personnel:** Jerry Fennell, President and Editor. **Subscription Rates:** Free; $20 by mail. **URL:** http://www.somebetnews.com.
Ad Rates: GLR: $10.57 **Circ:** Combined 75,000
BW: $10.57
4C: $12.57
PCI: $10.57

15209 Voice
IFCA International
3520 Fairlanes Phone: (616)531-1840
Box 810 Fax: (616)531-1814
Grandville, MI 49418-1536
Free: (800)347-1840
Publication E-mail: margieifca@aol.com

Religious magazine. **Subtitle:** The IFCA - Serving Independent Churches. **Founded:** 1930. **Freq:** Bimonthly. **Print Method:** Offset. **Trim Size:** 8 3/8 x 10 3/4. **Cols./Page:** 3. **Col. Width:** 13 picas. **Col. Depth:** 10 inches. **Key Personnel:** Dr. Richard I. Gregory, Editor. **USPS:** 662-140. **Subscription Rates:** $7.50 individuals. **URL:** www.ifca.org.
Ad Rates: BW: $195 **Circ:** Paid ‡7,000
4C: $850 Non-paid ‡3,000
PCI: $8.25

GRAYLING

15210 Crawford County Avalanche
102 Michigan Ave. Phone: (517)348-6811
PO Box 490 Fax: (517)348-6806
Grayling, MI 49738
Community newspaper. **Founded:** 1878. **Freq:** Weekly (Thurs.). **Print Method:** Offset. **Cols./Page:** 6. **Col. Width:** 21 nonpareils. **Col. Depth:** 294 agate lines. **Key Personnel:** Linda Golnick, General Mgr.; Howard Madsen, Associate Publisher. **Subscription Rates:** $16 individuals; $24 out of area. **Remarks:** Accepts advertising.
Ad Rates: BW: $554.40 **Circ:** ‡5,000
4C: $814.40
SAU: $4.40
PCI: $4.40

15211 WGRY-AM - 1230
6514 Old Lake Rd. Phone: (517)348-6171
Grayling, MI 49738 Fax: (517)348-6181

Format: Adult Contemporary. **Simulcasts:** WQON-FM. **Net-**

works: Mutual Broadcasting System. **Founded:** 1970. **Operating Hours:** Continuous; 3.7% network, 96.3% local. **ADI:** Traverse City-Cadillac, MI. **Key Personnel:** William Gannon, General Mgr.; Pete Michaels, Operations Mgr.; Angela Lorenc, Sales Mgr. **Local Programs:** *Daves Coffee Club*, Dave Sherbert; *Trading Post*. **Wattage:** 1000. **Ad Rates:** $13-16.50 for 30 seconds; $16-20.50 for 60 seconds. Combined advertising rates available with WGRY-FM: $4-$11.25 for 30 seconds; $5-$14 for 60 seconds.

15212 WGRY-FM - 100.3
6514 Old Lake Rd. Phone: (517)348-6171
Grayling, MI 49738 Fax: (517)348-6181

Format: Country. **Networks:** Mutual Broadcasting System. **Owner:** Gannon Broadcasting, 6514 Old Lake Rd, Grayling, MI 49738. **Founded:** 1989. **Operating Hours:** Continuous; 3.7% network, 96.3% local. **ADI:** Traverse City-Cadillac, MI. **Key Personnel:** William Gannon, General Mgr.; Pete Michaels, Operations Mgr.; Angela Lorenc, Sales Mgr. **Wattage:** 60,000. **Ad Rates:** $13-16.50 for 30 seconds; $16-20.50 for 60 seconds. Combined advertising rates available with WGRY-AM: $4-$11.25 for 30 seconds; $5-$14 for 60 seconds.

GREENVILLE

15213 The Buy Line
109 N. Lafayette St. Phone: (616)754-9301
PO Box 340 Fax: (616)754-8559
Greenville, MI 48838
Free: (800)968-9301

Shopper. **Founded:** 1982. **Freq:** Weekly (Mon.). **Print Method:** Offset. **Cols./Page:** 6. **Col. Width:** 18 nonpareils. **Col. Depth:** 224 agate lines. **Key Personnel:** Brenda Johnson, Advertising Mgr.; Robert Stafford, General Mgr.; John Stafford, Publisher; Larry Carbonell, President; Doug McAvoy, Circulation Mgr.; Kelly Campbell, Marketing Mgr. **Remarks:** Accepts advertising. **URL:** http://staffordgroup.com.
Ad Rates: BW: $1,577.25 **Circ:** Free ‡37,605
4C: $2,252.28
SAU: $25.55
PCI: $16.43

15214 The Daily News
109 N. Lafayette St. Phone: (616)754-9301
PO Box 340 Fax: (616)754-8559
Greenville, MI 48838-9998
Free: (800)968-9301

General newspaper. **Founded:** 1854. **Freq:** Mon.-Sat. (eve.). **Print Method:** Offset. **Trim Size:** 14 x 22 3/4. **Cols./Page:** 8. **Col. Width:** 9 picas. **Col. Depth:** 21 inches. **Key Personnel:** Larry Carbonell, President; Rob Stafford, General Mgr.; Alan Blanchard, Editor; John Stafford, Publisher; Brenda Johnson, Advertising Mgr.; Kelly Campbell, Marketing Mgr.; Doug McAvoy, Circulation Mgr.; David Pelts, Editor. **USPS:** 144-220. **Subscription Rates:** $115.20 individuals; $127.20 out of area. **Remarks:** Accepts advertising. **URL:** http://staffordgroup.com.
Ad Rates: BW: $1,201.20 **Circ:** Paid 9,050
4C: $1,426.20
SAU: $11.20
PCI: $7.15

15215 Cable Michigan
1202 W. Benton Fax: (616)754-5344
Greenville, MI 48838-0187 Free: (800)545-0994

Founded: 1976. **Key Personnel:** David M. Young, Contact. **Cities Served:** subscribing households 20,000; 45 channels; 3 community access channels; 504 hours per week community access programming. **URL:** http://www.cablemichigan.com.

15216 WPLB-AM - 1380
9181 S. Greenville Phone: (616)754-3656
Greenville, MI 48838 Fax: (616)754-2390

Format: Country; Sports. **Networks:** Great Lakes; Michigan Farm Radio. **Founded:** 1960. **Operating Hours:** Continuous. **Key Personnel:** Jeff Kortes, General Mgr.; Jim St. Clair, Program Dir. **Wattage:** 1000. **Ad Rates:** $10-19 for 30 seconds; $11-19 for 60 seconds.

GROSSE ILE

15217 The Ile Camera
Heritage Newspapers
8801 Maoomb Phone: (313)676-0515
PO Box 233 Fax: (313)676-0638
Grosse Ile, MI 48138
Local newspaper. **Founded:** 1945. **Freq:** Weekly. **Print Method:** Offset. Uses mats. **Cols./Page:** 5. **Col. Width:** 11 1/2 picas. **Col. Depth:** 13 inches. **Key Personnel:** Sheila R. McAfee, Editor; Fred Manuel, Publisher; Carlee Atkinson, Advertising Mgr., phone (313)246-0887, fax (313)246-2727. **Subscription Rates:** $24 individuals. **Remarks:** Accepts advertising.
Ad Rates: GLR: $.39 **Circ:** ‡3,700
BW: $409.50
4C: $929.00
SAU: $6.30

GROSSE POINTE FARMS

15218 The Connection
Anteebo Publishers
96 Kercheval Ave. Phone: (313)882-0294
Grosse Pointe Farms, MI 48236 Fax: (313)882-1585
Publisher E-mail: jminnis@grossepointenews.com

Community newspaper. **Founded:** 1992. **Freq:** Weekly (Thurs.). **Print Method:** Photo offset. **Key Personnel:** Robert G. Edgar, Publisher.
Circ: Combined ♦**34,880**

15219 Grosse Pointe News
Anteebo Publishers
96 Kercheval Ave. Phone: (313)882-0294
Grosse Pointe Farms, MI 48236 Fax: (313)882-1585
Publisher E-mail: jminnis@grossepointenews.com

Community newspaper. **Founded:** Nov. 1940. **Freq:** Weekly (Thurs.). **Print Method:** Offset. **Trim Size:** 12 5/8 x 21 1/2. **Cols./Page:** 6. **Col. Width:** 26 nonpareils. **Col. Depth:** 294 agate lines. **Key Personnel:** John Minnis, Editor, phone (313)343-5590, jminnis@grossepointenews.com; Robert G. Edgar, Publisher, phone (313)343-5588; Roger Hages, Advertising Mgr., phone (313)343-5580, rhages@grosspointenews.com; Margie Smith, Editor, phone (313)343-5594, msmith@grossepointenews.com. **USPS:** 230-400. **Subscription Rates:** $31 individuals; $38 out of state. **Remarks:** Accepts advertising. **URL:** http://grossepointenews.com.
Ad Rates: GLR: $17.64 **Circ:** Thurs. ♦**15,629**
BW: $2,222.64
4C: $2,622.64
SAU: $16
PCI: $16

WQLL-FM - See Boston, Massachusetts

HAMTRAMCK

The Oitizen - See Detroit

15220 The Polish World
Polish Daily News, Inc.
11903 Joseph Campau St. Phone: (313)365-1990
Hamtramck, MI 48212 Fax: (313)365-0850
Publisher E-mail: sszcze4594@aol.com

Community newspaper (Polish & English). **Founded:** Mar. 1, 1904. **Freq:** Weekly. **Print Method:** Web. **Trim Size:** 11 x 17. **Cols./Page:** 6. **Col. Width:** 1 1/2 inches. **Key Personnel:** Bruno Nowicki, President. **Subscription Rates:** $1 single issue; $35. **Remarks:** Accepts advertising. **Foreign language name:** Swiat Polski.
Ad Rates: GLR: $3 **Circ:** ‡4,000
BW: $800
SAU: $17.25
CNU: $21
PCI: $12.75

HANCOCK

15221 WMPL-AM - 920
PO Box 547 Phone: (906)482-3700
Hancock, MI 49930 Fax: (906)482-1540

Format: Talk; News. **Networks:** USA Radio. **Founded:** 1957. **Operating Hours:** 6 a.m.-midnight. **Key Personnel:** W.G. Blake, President. **Wattage:** 1000. **Ad Rates:** $3.20-4 for 15 seconds; $4.50-6.25 for 30 seconds; $8-10 for 60 seconds.

HARBOR BEACH

15222 Times
123 N. 1st St. Phone: (517)479-3605
Harbor Beach, MI 48441-1102
Newspaper. **Founded:** 1882. **Freq:** Weekly (Thurs.). **Print Method:** Letterpress and offset. **Cols./Page:** 6. **Col. Width:** 20 nonpareils. **Col. Depth:** 196 agate lines. **Key Personnel:** David Busch, Editor and Publisher. **Subscription Rates:** $11. **Remarks:** Accepts advertising.
Ad Rates: GLR: $.14 **Circ:** (Not Reported)

HARBOR SPRINGS

15223 Harbor Springs Harbor Light
North Country Publishing Corp.
211 E. 3rd St. Phone: (616)526-2191
Harbor Springs, MI 49740 Fax: (616)526-7634
Publication E-mail: news@ncpublish.com

Community newspaper. **Subtitle:** The Newspaper of Harbor Springs. **Freq:** Weekly (Wed.). **Print Method:** Offset. **Cols./Page:** 6. **Col. Width:** 2 1/16 inches. **Col. Depth:** 21 inches. **Key Personnel:** Charles O'Neill, General Mgr.; Kevin O'Neill, Publisher. **USPS:** 938-000. **Subscription Rates:** $31; $52 out of county. **Remarks:** Accepts advertising.
Ad Rates: SAU: $8.90 **Circ:** ‡2,000

HARRISON

15224 WKKM-FM - 92.1
209 E. Spruce St. Phone: (517)539-7105
PO Box 549
Harrison, MI 48625-0549

Format: Country. **Networks:** ABC. **Owner:** David A. Carmine, at above address. **Founded:** 1975. **Operating Hours:** Continuous; 5% network, 95% local. **ADI:** Flint-Saginaw-Bay City, MI. **Key Personnel:** David A. Carmine, General Mgr. **Wattage:** 6000. **Ad Rates:** $4.75 for 60 seconds.

HARRISVILLE

15225 Alcona County Review
111 Lake St. Phone: (517)724-6384
PO Box 548 Fax: (517)724-6655
Harrisville, MI 48740
Free: (877)873-8439
Publication E-mail: acr@northland.lib.mi.us

Community newspaper. **Founded:** 1877. **Freq:** Weekly (Wed.). **Print Method:** Offset. **Trim Size:** 11 1/2. **Cols./Page:** 5. **Col. Width:** 2 inches. **Col. Depth:** 16 inches. **Key Personnel:** Cheryl Peterson, Publisher. **USPS:** 012-90. **Subscription Rates:** $15 individuals; $18 out of country. **Remarks:** Accepts advertising. **Alt. Formats:** Mailing labels.
Ad Rates: BW: $520 **Circ:** ‡3,400
PCI: $6.50

HART

15226 Oceana's Herald-Journal
Oceana's Herald
123 State St. Phone: (616)873-5602
Hart, MI 49420-0190 Fax: (616)873-4775

Community newspaper. **Founded:** 1869. **Freq:** Weekly (Thurs.). **Print Method:** Offset. **Trim Size:** 15 x 22. **Cols./Page:** 6. **Col. Width:** 13 picas. **Col. Depth:** 21 inches. **Key Personnel:** Mary Sanford, Editor; James O. Young, Advertising Mgr. **Subscription Rates:** $18; $21 out of area; $26 out of state. **Remarks:** Accepts advertising.
Ad Rates: BW: $768.60 **Circ:** ‡7,560
4C: $976.80
PCI: $6.10

15227 WCXT-FM - 105.3
220 Polk Phone: (616)873-7129
Hart, MI 49420 Fax: (616)873-7120

Format: Adult Contemporary. **Founded:** 1983. **Operating Hours:** Continuous. **Key Personnel:** Yvette Jernudd, Office Mgr.; Mark Waters, Program Dir. **Wattage:** 100,000 ERP.

HARTFORD

15228 Shoppers Guide
515 E. Main Phone: (616)621-4415
PO Box 265
Hartford, MI 49057-0265
Shopper. **Founded:** 1958. **Freq:** Weekly (Tues.). **Print Method:** Offset. **Cols./Page:** 6. **Col. Width:** 22 nonpareils. **Col. Depth:** 224 agate lines. **Key Personnel:** William McLaughlin, Editor and Publisher.
Circ: Free ‡11,000

HARTLAND

15229 Hartland Shopper
Hometown Newspapers
323 E. Grand River Phone: (517)548-2000
PO Box 230 Fax: (517)548-3005
Howell, MI 48843
Shopping guide. **Freq:** Weekly (Wed.). **Key Personnel:** Rich Perlberg, General Mgr.; John A. Kaake, Editor.
Circ: Non-paid 7,520

HASLETT

15230 Michigan News
Michigan State Grange
1730 Chamberlain Phone: (517)339-2171
Haslett, MI 48840 Fax: (517)339-3636
Free: (800)337-1502
Publication E-mail: msgrange@voyager.net

Agricultural magazine. **Founded:** 1917. **Freq:** 10/year. **Print Method:** Offset. **Trim Size:** 8 1/2 x 11. **Cols./Page:** 3. **Col. Width:** 42 nonpareils. **Col. Depth:** 140 agate lines. **Key Personnel:** Robert E. Brown, Editor; Peggy L. Johnston. **USPS:** 345-580. **Subscription Rates:** Free to qualified subscribers. **Remarks:** Accepts advertising. **Formerly:** Michigan Patron.
Ad Rates: BW: $140 **Circ:** ‡1,500

HASTINGS

15231 The Hastings Banner
J-Ad Corp.
PO Box B
Hastings, MI 49058
Publisher E-mail: j-ad@voyager.com

Community newspaper. **Founded:** 1856. **Freq:** Weekly (Thurs.). **Print Method:** Offset. **Trim Size:** 14 1/4 x 22 1/2. **Cols./Page:** 5. **Col. Width:** 13 1/2 picas. **Col. Depth:** 21 inches. **Key Personnel:** David Young, Editor; John P. Jacobs, Publisher; Scott Ommen, Advertising Mgr. **Subscription Rates:** $25 in county; $29 out of county.
Ad Rates: BW: $345.45 **Circ:** ‡7,000
4C: $495.45
SAU: $4.50
PCI: $3.10

15232 Hastings Reminder
J-Ad Corp.
1952 N. Broadway Phone: (616)945-9554
PO Box B Fax: (616)945-5192
Hastings, MI 49058
Free: (800)870-7085
Publisher E-mail: j-ad@voyager.com

Community newspaper. **Founded:** 1945. **Freq:** Weekly (Tues.). **Print Method:** Offset. **Cols./Page:** 6. **Col. Width:** 20 nonpareils. **Col. Depth:** 224 agate lines. **Key Personnel:** Frederic J. Jacobs; Scott Ommen, Advertising Mgr. **Subscription Rates:** Free. **Remarks:** Accepts advertising.
Ad Rates: BW: $572 **Circ:** Free 28,450
4C: $828
SAU: $8.11
PCI: $5.45

Lakewood News - See Lake Odessa

15233 Maple Valley News
J-Ad Corp.
1952 N. Broadway Phone: (616)945-9554
PO Box B Fax: (616)945-5192
Hastings, MI 49058
Free: (800)870-7085
Publisher E-mail: j-ad@voyager.com

Community newspaper. **Founded:** 1873. **Freq:** Weekly (Tues.). **Print Method:** Offset. **Trim Size:** 11 x 17. **Cols./Page:** 6. **Col. Width:** 10 picas. **Col. Depth:** 16 inches. **Key Personnel:** Frederick Jacobs, Publisher; David Young, Editor; Scott Ommen, Advertising Mgr. **Subscription Rates:** $20. **Remarks:** Accepts advertising.
Ad Rates: BW: $216 **Circ:** Free ‡3,200
4C: $416
SAU: $4.70
PCI: $2.75

15234 The Sun & News
J-Ad Corp.
1952 N. Broadway Phone: (616)945-9554
PO Box B Fax: (616)945-5192
Hastings, MI 49058
Free: (800)870-7085
Publisher E-mail: j-ad@voyager.com

Local newspaper. **Founded:** 1870. **Freq:** Weekly (Tues.). **Print Method:** Offset. **Trim Size:** 11 x 17. **Cols./Page:** 6. **Col. Width:** 10 picas. **Col. Depth:** 16 inches. **Key Personnel:** David Young, Editor; Frederick Jacobs, Publisher; Scott Ommen, Advertising Mgr. **Subscription Rates:** $20. **Remarks:** Accepts advertising.
Ad Rates: BW: $307.50 **Circ:** ‡8,000
4C: $507.20
SAU: $5.28
PCI: $4.25

15235 WBCH-AM - 1220
119 W. State St. Phone: (616)945-3414
PO Box 88 Fax: (616)945-3470
Hastings, MI 49058

Format: Hot Country. **Networks:** ABC; Westwood One Radio. **Owner:** Kenneth Radant, at above address. **Founded:** 1958. **Operating Hours:** Continuous. **ADI:** Grand Rapids-Kalamazoo-Battle Creek, MI. **Key Personnel:** Ken Radant, Contact; Steve Radant, Music Dir.; George Youngs, News Dir. **Wattage:** 250. **Ad Rates:** Advertising accepted; rates available upon request.

15236 WBCH-FM - 100.1
PO Box 88 Phone: (616)945-3414
Hastings, MI 49058 Fax: (616)945-3470
E-mail: wbch@wbch.com

Format: Country. **Networks:** ABC. **Owner:** Kenneth Radant, at above address. **Founded:** 1958. **Operating Hours:** Continuous. **ADI:** Grand Rapids-Kalamazoo-Battle Creek, MI. **Key Personnel:** Ken Radant, Contact; Steve Radant, Music Dir.; Dave McIntye, News Dir. **Wattage:** 3000. **Ad Rates:** Advertising accepted; rates available upon request.

HIGHLAND

15237 Highland Shopping Guide
Sliger/Livingston Publications, Inc.
323 E. Grand River Phone: (517)548-2000
Howell, MI 48843 Fax: (517)548-3005
Publisher E-mail: m.sturt@htonline.com

Shopping guide. **Freq:** Weekly (Mon.). **Key Personnel:** Rich Perlberg, General Mgr.; John A. Kaake, Editor. **URL:** http://www.htonline.com.
Circ: Free ‡14,121

15238 Highland Spinal Column Newsweekly
Spinal Column Publications
7196 Cooley Lake Rd. Phone: (248)360-6397
PO Box 14 Fax: (248)360-4711
Union Lake, MI 48387-0014
Local newspaper. **Founded:** 1960. **Freq:** Weekly. **Print Method:** Offset. **Trim Size:** 10 1/2 x 15. **Cols./Page:** 8. **Col. Width:** 7 picas. **Col. Depth:** 14 inches. **Key Personnel:** David D. Hohendorf, Publisher; James W. Fancy, Publisher; Laurie Wallace, Advertising Mgr. **Remarks:** Accepts advertising.
Ad Rates: GLR: $4.75 **Circ:** Free ‡3,950
BW: $532
PCI: $9.50

HIGHLAND PARK

15239 Michigan Citizen
New Day Publishing Enterprises
211 Glendale, Ste. 216 Phone: (313)869-0033
Highland Park, MI 48203 Fax: (313)869-0430
Publication E-mail: micitizen@aol.com

Newspaper serving African-American communities in Michigan. **Subtitle:** America's Most Progressive Newspaper. **Founded:** Nov. 25, 1978. **Freq:** Weekly. **Print Method:** Offset. **Cols./Page:** 6. **Col. Width:** 12 picas. **Col. Depth:** 21 inches. **Key Personnel:** Teresa Maxwell-Kelly, Editor; Charles D. Kelly, Publisher. **ISSN:** 1072-2041. **Subscription Rates:** $21 individuals; $36 two years. **Remarks:** Accepts advertising. **Formerly:** The Citizen (Mar. 1986).
Ad Rates: 4C: $3,739.00 **Circ:** Paid 51,442
PCI: $26.50 Free 918

15240 WHPR-FM - 88.1
15851 Woodward Ave. Phone: (313)868-8812
Highland Park, MI 48203 Fax: (313)868-8725

Format: Jazz; Urban Contemporary. **Owner:** R.J.'s Late Night Entertainment Corp., at above address. **Founded:** 1954. **Key Personnel:** R.J. Watkins, Contact; Geo. Hutcherson, Contact; Henry Tyler, Contact. **Wattage:** 10.

HILLSDALE

15241 Hillsdale Daily News
Division of Stauffer Communications
33 McCollum St. Phone: (517)437-7351
PO Box 287 Fax: (517)437-3963
Hillsdale, MI 49242-0287
Publication E-mail: hillsdnews@dmci.net

General newspaper. **Founded:** 1909. **Freq:** Daily (eve.) and Sat. (morn.). **Print Method:** Offset. **Trim Size:** 13 3/4 x 22 3/4. **Cols./Page:** 6. **Col. Width:** 2 1/16 inches. **Col. Depth:** 21 1/2 inches. **Key Personnel:** William K. Turner, Publisher; Judy Gabriele, Advertising Mgr.; Jeff West, Operations Coordinator; David Holcomb, Business Mgr.; Kelly Compton, Circulation Coord.; Marlanea Stemen, Advertising Coord. **USPS:** 245-700. **Subscription Rates:** $83.70; $144 out of area. **Remarks:** Accepts advertising. **URL:** http://www.hillsdale.net.
Ad Rates: BW: $780 **Circ:** Paid ⊕7679
4C: $1,005 Free ⊕5
SAU: $8.28
PCI: $7.20

15242 Comcast Cablevision of Hillsdale
4 S. Howell St. Phone: (517)437-2656
PO Box 223 Fax: (517)437-2767
Hillsdale, MI 49242-0223

Owner: Comcast Corp., 1500 Market St., East Tower, Philadelphia, PA 19102-2148, (215)665-7000, Fax: (215)981-7790. **Founded:** Jan. 1, 1966. **Formerly:** Twin Valley CATV. **Key Personnel:** Roger L. Nevins, Operations Mgr. **Cities Served:** Hillsdale, Jonesville Village, Mosherville, North Adams, Osseo, Pittsford, Waldron, MI: 40 channels; 1 community access channel. **URL:** http://www.comcast.com.

15243 WCSR-AM - 1340
170 N. West St. Phone: (517)437-4444
PO Box 273 Fax: (517)437-7461
Hillsdale, MI 49242
E-mail: wcsr@dmic.net

Format: Adult Contemporary. **Owner:** WCSR Inc., at above address. **Founded:** 1955. **Operating Hours:** 6 a.m.-midnight; 99% local, 1% network. **ADI:** Lansing (Ann Arbor), MI. **Key Personnel:** Tony Flynn, Contact; Parke Hayes, News Dir.; Mike Flynn, Assistant Mgr.; Gary Floyd, Sales Mgr. **Wattage:** 500 day; 250 night. **Ad Rates:** $11-18.25 for 30 seconds; $13.75-22.50 for 60 seconds.

15244 WCSR-FM - 92.1
170 N. West St. Phone: (517)437-4444
PO Box 273 Fax: (517)437-7461
Hillsdale, MI 49242
E-mail: wcsr@dmci.net

Format: Adult Contemporary. **Owner:** WCSR, Inc., at above address. **Founded:** 1955. **Operating Hours:** 6 a.m.-midnight; 99% local, 1% network. **ADI:** Lansing (Ann Arbor), MI. **Key Personnel:** Tony Flynn, Contact; Parke Hayes, News Dir.; Mike Flynn, Assistant Mgr.; Gary Floyd, Sales Mgr. **Wattage:** 6000. **Ad Rates:** $11-18.25 for 30 seconds; $13.75-22.50 for 60 seconds.

HOLLAND

15245 Holland Flashes Shopping Guide
Stauffer Communications, Inc.
437 136th Ave. Phone: (616)396-2394
Holland, MI 49424 Fax: (616)396-4710
Free: (800)968-2525
Publication E-mail: fpisgs@aol.com
Publisher E-mail: fpi595@aol.com

Shopper/weekly newspaper. **Subtitle:** Flashes (Holland). **Founded:** 1966. **Freq:** Weekly (Mon.). **Print Method:** Offset. **Trim Size:** 10 3/8 x 12 1/2. **Cols./Page:** 4. **Col. Width:** 2 7/16 inches. **Col. Depth:** 12 1/2 inches. **Key Personnel:** Mark Dalman, Manager, mdalman@flashespublishers.com. **Subscription Rates:** Free; $14 (mail). **Remarks:** Accepts advertising.
Ad Rates: BW: $700.80 **Circ:** Free □30,142
4C: $280
PCI: $10.95

15246 The Holland Sentinel
54 W. 8th St. Phone: (616)392-2311
Holland, MI 49423 Fax: (616)392-3526
Free: (800)968-3497

General newspaper. **Founded:** 1896. **Freq:** Daily (morn.). **Print Method:** Offset. Uses mats. **Cols./Page:** 6. **Col. Width:** 24 nonpareils. **Col. Depth:** 301 agate lines. **Key Personnel:** Jim Timmermann, Managing Editor, jtimmerman@sentinelnet.com; Ron Wallace, Publisher, rwallace@sentinelnet.com; Michael Assink, Advertising Mgr., massink@sentinel.net.com; Steve Kimono, Circulation Mgr., skimono@sentelnet.com. **Subscription Rates:** $120 individuals. **Remarks:** Accepts advertising. **Alt. Formats:** CD-ROM.
Ad Rates: GLR: $.74 **Circ:** Mon.-Sat. 19,760
BW: $1773 Sun. 19,084
4C: $2044
SAU: $129
PCI: $14.60

15247 WEVS-FM - 92.7
476 N. 120th Phone: (616)396-0977
Holland, MI 49424 Fax: (616)396-9907

Format: Adult Contemporary; Oldies; Classic Rock. **Networks:** Westwood One Radio; ABC. **Owner:** Conrad Communications Corp., at above address. **Founded:** 1987. **Operating Hours:** Continuous. **ADI:** Grand Rapids-Kalamazoo-Battle Creek, MI. **Key Personnel:** Dale Ray, Program Dir.; Shannon

Lowe, News Dir. **Wattage:** 3000. **Ad Rates:** $9-16 for 30 seconds.

15248 WHTC-AM - 1450
PO Box 1467 Phone: (616)392-3121
Holland, MI 49422 Fax: (616)392-8066
E-mail: whtc@whtc.com

Format: Full Service. **Networks:** CBS. **Owner:** Holland Communications, Inc., 87 Central Ave., Holland, MI 49423. **Founded:** 1948. **Operating Hours:** 19 hours daily; 5% network, 95% local. **ADI:** Grand Rapids-Kalamazoo-Battle Creek, MI. **Key Personnel:** Mike Walton, President; Kevin J. Oswald, General Sales Mgr., oswald@whtc.com; Ken Evans, Operations Dir., evans@whtc.com; Zane Hunt, News Dir., news@whtc.com. **Local Programs:** *Ken Evans Show* 5:00 am - 9:30 am Monday-Friday, Ken Evans; *Talk of the Town* 9:30 am - 11:30 am Monday-Friday, Juke Vanoss. **Wattage:** 1000. **Ad Rates:** $25 for 30 seconds; $29 for 60 seconds. **URL:** http://www.whtc.com.

15249 WJQK-FM - 99.3
5658 143rd Ave. Phone: (616)394-1260
Holland, MI 49423 Fax: (616)394-9008
Free: (800)567-8993

Format: Religious; Contemporary Christian. **Networks:** ABC. **Owner:** Leslie J. Lanser, at above address. **Founded:** 1987. **Formerly:** WZND-FM (1986). **Operating Hours:** Continuous. **ADI:** Grand Rapids-Kalamazoo-Battle Creek, MI. **Key Personnel:** Leslie J. Lanser, President/Sales Manager; Troy West, Program Dir.; Jack Moelker, News Dir.; Roger Allen, Sports Dir.; Brad Lanser, Vice President. **Wattage:** 5100. **Ad Rates:** $12-20 for 15 seconds; $15-26 for 30 seconds; $20-36 for 60 seconds. $12-$20 for 15 seconds; $15-$26 for 30 seconds; $20-$36 for 60 seconds. Combined advertising rates available with WWJQ-AM. **URL:** http://www.wjq.com.

15250 WTHS-FM - 89.9
DeWitt Centre Phone: (616)395-7878
141 E. 12th St. Fax: (616)305-7922
PO Box 9000
Holland, MI 49422-9000
E-mail: wthsmd@hope.edu

Format: Public Radio; Alternative/New Music/Progressive. **Networks:** Mutual Broadcasting System. **Owner:** Trustees of Hope College, at above address, Fax: (616)395-7958. **Founded:** 1985. **Operating Hours:** 6 a.m.-2 a.m.; 100% local. **Key Personnel:** Eric Hultgren, General Mgr.; Lorraine Gardner, Programming; Amy Hall, Personnel Dir., phone (616)395-6545; Joe Kolk, Production; Katy Balcer, Music Dir., phone (616)395-4830; Brent VanderKolk, Underwriting Dir., phone (616)355-6276; Jenn Dorn, Program Dir., phone (616)395-4830; Jeff Bates, Business Dir., phone (616)355-0435; Jon Pott, Production Dir., phone (616)395-4875; Michael McCune, Traffic Dir., phone (616)395-6413; Nathan Oostendorp, Admin. Asst., phone (616)395-6884. **Local Programs:** *Friday Night Jams*, Michael McCune, (616)395-6413; *New Music Show*, Katy Balcer, (616)395-4830; *The Upper Room*, Amy Hall, (616)395-6545. **Wattage:** 1000. **Ad Rates:** Noncommercial. **URL:** http://www.hope.edu/~beckman/wths/.

15251 WWJQ-AM - 1260
5658 143rd Ave. Phone: (616)394-1260
Holland, MI 49423 Fax: (616)394-9008
Free: (800)567-8993

Format: Religious. **Networks:** ABC. **Owner:** Lanser Broadcasting Corp., at above address, Free: (888)993-1260. **Founded:** 1956. **Formerly:** WJBL-AM (1983). **Operating Hours:** Continuous. **ADI:** Grand Rapids-Kalamazoo-Battle Creek, MI. **Key Personnel:** Leslie J. Lanser, President & Sales Mgr.; Jack Moelker, News Dir.; Troy West, Program Dir.; Brad Lanser, Vice President; Roger Allen, Sports Dir. **Wattage:** 5000 day; 1000 night. **Ad Rates:** $12-20 for 15 seconds; $15-26 for 30 seconds; $20-36 for 60 seconds. $12-$20 for 15 seconds; $15-$26 for 30 seconds; $20-$36 for 60 seconds. Combined advertising rates available with WJQK-FM. **URL:** http://www.wjq.com.

HOLLY

15252 The Herald Advertiser
4048 Grange Hall Rd. Phone: (248)634-8219
Holly, MI 48442
Community newspaper. **Founded:** 1877. **Freq:** Weekly (Thurs.). **Print Method:** Offset. **Trim Size:** 12 1/2 x 21. **Cols./Page:** 7. **Col. Width:** 1 3/4 inches. **Col. Depth:** 21 inches. **Key Personnel:** Alan C. Campbell, Editor and Publisher; Donald J. Campbell, Advertising Mgr. **Subscription Rates:** $15 individuals; $21 out of area; $24 out of state. **Remarks:** Accepts advertising.
Ad Rates: PCI: $4.10 **Circ:** Paid 1,455
Non-paid 848

HOLT

15253 WXIK-FM - 94.1
2495 N. Cedar Phone: (517)699-0994
Holt, MI 48842 Fax: (517)699-0794
Free: (800)786-7106

Format: Country. **Networks:** ABC. **Founded:** Dec. 1993. **Formerly:** WIBM-FM; WBHR-FM. **Operating Hours:** Continuous. **ADI:** Lansing (Ann Arbor), MI. **Key Personnel:** Mike Thomas, General Mgr., phone (517)699-0111, fax (517)699-1880; Jay J. McCrae, Program Dir., phone (517)699-0111, fax (517)699-1880; John Sterling, General Sales Mgr., phone (517)699-0111, fax (517)699-1880. **Wattage:** 50,000. **Ad Rates:** Advertising accepted; rates available upon request.

HOMER

15254 The Homer Index
Index Media, Inc.
122 E. Main St. Phone: (517)568-4646
Box 236 Fax: (517)568-4346
Homer, MI 49245
Community newspaper. **Subtitle:** Serving the Homer and Litchfield Areas. **Founded:** Dec. 1871. **Freq:** Weekly (Wed.). **Print Method:** Offset. **Trim Size:** 13 x 21 1/2. **Cols./Page:** 6. **Col. Width:** 26 nonpareils. **Col. Depth:** 308 agate lines. **Key Personnel:** Susan Cook, Editor; Cynthia Kirkbride, Advertising Mgr. **ISSN:** 0891-1398. **Subscription Rates:** $15. **Remarks:** Accepts advertising.
Ad Rates: GLR: $.14 **Circ:** 1,900
BW: $327.60
SAU: $3.06
PCI: $2.60

HOUGHTON

15255 The Daily Mining Gazette
206 Shelden Ave. Phone: (906)482-1500
Houghton, MI 49931 Fax: (906)482-2726
Free: (800)682-7607

General newspaper. **Founded:** 1858. **Freq:** Daily (eve.). **Print Method:** Offset. **Trim Size:** 13 x 21 1/2. **Cols./Page:** 6. **Col. Width:** 27 nonpareils. **Col. Depth:** 301 agate lines. **Key Personnel:** Cyndi Perkins, Editor; Karen Callaway, Advertising Mgr. **Subscription Rates:** $120 individuals. **Remarks:** Accepts advertising. **Available Online. URL:** http://www.gazedt@up.net.
Ad Rates: GLR: $.83 **Circ:** Mon.-Sat. ★**11,018**
BW: $1,558.32
4C: $1,963.32
SAU: $12.08

15256 Michigan Tech Lode
Michigan Technological University
Memorial Union Bldg., Rm. 106 Phone: (906)487-2404
Houghton, MI 49931 Fax: (906)487-3125
Publication E-mail: lode@mtu.edu

Collegiate newspaper. **Subtitle:** Michigan Tech Lode. **Founded:** 1921. **Freq:** Weekly (Fri.). **Print Method:** Offset. **Trim Size:** 2 x 21. **Cols./Page:** 6. **Col. Width:** 2 inches. **Col. Depth:** 21 1/2 inches. **Key Personnel:** Shawn Martin, Business Mgr. **Subscription Rates:** $10 individuals; $8 by mail. **URL:** http://www.grp.mtu.edu/lode/.
Ad Rates: 4C: $300 **Circ:** Free 6,000
PCI: $6.50

15257 WCCY-AM - 1400
313 Montezuma Ave. Phone: (906)482-7700
Houghton, MI 49931 Fax: (906)482-7751
E-mail: wolf@op.net

Format: Contemporary Country. **Networks:** ABC. **Owner:** Justin Marzke, 142 Woodland, Laurium, MI 49913, (906)337-3481. **Founded:** 1929. **Formerly:** WHDF-AM. **Operating Hours:** Continuous; 20% network, 80% local. **ADI:** Marquette, MI. **Key Personnel:** Kevin Ericson, Program Dir.; Dick Strom, News Dir.; Norm Koski, Sports Dir.; Justin M. Marzke, General Mgr. **Wattage:** 1000. **Ad Rates:** $7.50-11.90 for 60 seconds.

15258 WGGL-FM - 91.1
Academic Offices Bldg. Phone: (906)482-8912
Michigan Technological University Fax: (906)482-1207
Houghton, MI 49931

Format: Public Radio; News; Classical. **Networks:** American Public Radio (APR); National Public Radio (NPR); Minnesota Public Radio. **Owner:** Minnesota Public Radio, 45 E. 7th St., St. Paul, MN 55101, (612)290-1500. **Founded:** 1968. **Operating Hours:** Continuous. **Key Personnel:** Jill Burkland, Station Mgr. **Wattage:** 100,000. **Ad Rates:** Noncommercial.

15259 WOLV-FM - 97.7
313 E. Montezuma Ave. Phone: (906)482-7700
Houghton, MI 49931 Fax: (906)486-7751
E-mail: wolf@up.net

Format: Adult Contemporary. **Owner:** To-Mar Broadcasting, 142 Woodland, Laurium, MI 49913, (906)337-3481. **Founded:** 1981. **Formerly:** WHUH-FM (1989); WOLF-FM (Apr. 1994). **Operating Hours:** Continuous. **ADI:** Marquette, MI. **Key Personnel:** Dick Storm, News Dir.; Kevin Ericson, Program Dir.; Norm Koski, Sports Dir.; Ed Janisse, Promotions Dir. **Local Programs:** *Copper Country Today*, Dick Storm. **Wattage:** 3500. **Ad Rates:** $10-16.50 for 60 seconds.

HOUGHTON LAKE

15260 The Houghton Lake Resorter
4049 W. Houghton Lake Dr. Phone: (517)366-5341
PO Box 248 Fax: (517)366-4472
Houghton Lake, MI 48629
Local newspaper. **Founded:** 1939. **Freq:** Weekly (Thurs.). **Print Method:** Offset. **Trim Size:** 14 1/2 x 22 3/4. **Cols./Page:** 6. **Col. Width:** 24 nonpareils. **Col. Depth:** 301 agate lines. **Key Personnel:** Thomas W. Hamp, Editor and Publisher. **Subscription Rates:** $18 individuals; $22 out of area. **Remarks:** Accepts advertising.
Ad Rates: GLR: $.34 **Circ:** Paid ⊕**7,751**
BW: $774 Non-paid ⊕**58**
4C: $1,074
SAU: $6.00

HOWARD CITY

15261 River Valley News Shopper
The Pioneer Group
491 Shaw St. Phone: (616)937-4740
PO Box 407 Fax: (616)937-4048
Howard City, MI 49329
Shopping guide with local news and features. **Founded:** 1865. **Freq:** Weekly (Mon.). **Print Method:** Offset. **Cols./Page:** 7. **Col. Width:** 1 3/8 inches. **Col. Depth:** 16 inches. **Key Personnel:** John A. Batdorff, Publisher. **Remarks:** Accepts advertising. **Formerly:** The Record (1990).
Ad Rates: BW: $504 **Circ:** Free ‡15,975
SAU: $6.50
PCI: $4.50

HOWELL

15262 Brighton Argus
Hometown Newspapers
323 E. Grand River Phone: (517)548-2000
PO Box 230 Fax: (517)548-3005
Howell, MI 48843
Community newspaper. **Founded:** 1880. **Freq:** Weekly (Wed.). **Print Method:** Offset. **Trim Size:** 13 3/4 x 22 1/2. **Cols./Page:** 6. **Col. Width:** 2 1/16 inches. **Col. Depth:** 21 1/2 inches. **Key Personnel:** Dennis Keenon, Editor; Rolly Peterson, Publisher; Mike Preville, Advertising Mgr. **Subscription Rates:** $18 local; $22 in state; $25 out of state. **Remarks:** Accepts advertising.
Ad Rates: BW: $1,044.90 **Circ:** Combined ♦**13,116**
4C: $1,244.90
SAU: $8.10

Fowlerville Shopper - See Fowlerville

Hartland Shopper - See Hartland

Highland Shopping Guide - See Highland

15263 Home Town News
Hometown Newspapers
323 E. Grand River Phone: (517)548-2000
PO Box 230 Fax: (517)548-3005
Howell, MI 48843
Community newspaper. **Freq:** Weekly.
Circ: Paid 10,503
Free 11,321

15264 The Lakes Area Shopping Guide
Hometown Newspapers
323 E. Grand River Phone: (517)548-2000
PO Box 230 Fax: (517)548-3005
Howell, MI 48843
Shopper. **Freq:** Weekly.
Circ: Free ‡38,000

15265 Livingston County Press
Hometown Newspapers
PO Box 230
Howell, MI 48844

Community newspaper. **Founded:** 1843. **Freq:** Weekly (Wed.). **Print Method:** Offset. **Trim Size:** 13 3/4 x 22 1/2. **Cols./Page:** 6. **Col. Width:** 2 1/16 inches. **Col. Depth:** 21 1/2 inches. **Key Personnel:** Dennis Keenon, Editor; Roland

Peterson, Publisher; Mike Preville, Advertising Mgr. **Subscription Rates:** $18; $22 in state; $25 out of state. **Remarks:** Accepts advertising.
Ad Rates: BW: $1,199.70 **Circ:** Combined ♦**14,720**
4C: $1,399.70
SAU: $9.30
PCI: $9.30

15266 Monday Green Sheet
Hometown Newspapers
323 E. Grand River Phone: (517)548-2000
PO Box 230 Fax: (517)548-3005
Howell, MI 48843
Shopper. **Founded:** 1982. **Freq:** Weekly (Mon.). **Print Method:** Offset. **Trim Size:** 13 3/4 x 22 1/2. **Cols./Page:** 6. **Col. Width:** 2 1/16 inches. **Col. Depth:** 21 1/2 inches. **Key Personnel:** Roland Peterson, Publisher; Mike Preville, Advertising Mgr. **Remarks:** Accepts advertising.
Ad Rates: BW: $2,060.13 **Circ:** Non-paid ♦**55,098**
4C: $2,460.13
SAU: $15.97
PCI: $15.97

The Pinckney Shopper - See Pinckney

15267 WHMI-FM - 93.5
1372 W. Grand River Phone: (517)546-0860
PO Box 935 Fax: (517)546-1758
Howell, MI 48844
Free: (800)WHMI-935
E-mail: whmi935@ismi.net

Format: Adult Contemporary. **Networks:** ABC. **Owner:** The Livingston Radio Co., Inc., at above address, Free: (888)WHMI935. **Founded:** 1977. **Operating Hours:** 24hrs. **ADI:** Detroit, MI. **Key Personnel:** Marcia Jablonski, General Mgr.; Greg Jablonski, President; Reed Kittredge, Operations Mgr.; Todd Kulman, News Dir.; Doug Manaker, Sports Dir.; Rob Otto, Music Dir.; Debbie Whitaker-Platt, Sales Mgr. **Wattage:** 5200. **Ad Rates:** Advertising accepted; rates available upon request. **URL:** http://www.whmi.com.

HUDSON

15268 Bi-County Herald
115 S. Church St. Phone: (517)448-2201
PO Box 87 Fax: (517)448-2201
Hudson, MI 49247
Shopper. **Founded:** 1934. **Freq:** Weekly (Tues.). **Print Method:** Offset. **Cols./Page:** 8. **Col. Width:** 20 nonpareils. **Col. Depth:** 301 agate lines. **Key Personnel:** John W. Monahan, Editor and Publisher. **Subscription Rates:** Free; $25 (mail). **Remarks:** Accepts advertising. **Alt. Formats:** CD-ROM, MacIntosh-Pagemaker.
Ad Rates: GLR: $3.75 **Circ:** Free ‡11,500
BW: $4.60
SAU: $3

15269 Hudson Post Gazette
113 S. Market St. Phone: (517)448-2611
PO Box 70
Hudson, MI 49247
Community newspaper. **Founded:** 1858. **Freq:** Weekly (Thurs.). **Cols./Page:** 6. **Col. Width:** 2 inches. **Col. Depth:** 21 inches. **Key Personnel:** Edward Potter, Editor and Publisher. **USPS:** 253-600. **Subscription Rates:** $20; $23 out of area. **Remarks:** Accepts advertising.
Ad Rates: SAU: $4.50 **Circ:** 2,000

IMLAY CITY

15270 Tri-City Times
Page One Corp.
PO Box 278 Phone: (810)724-2615
Imlay City, MI 48444 Fax: (810)724-8552

Community newspaper serving Imlay City, Almont, Capac, Dryden, and surrounding townships in Lapeer and St. Clair counties, Michigan. **Founded:** 1980. **Freq:** Weekly (Wed.). **Print Method:** Offset. **Cols./Page:** 9. **Col. Width:** 18 nonpareils. **Col. Depth:** 301 agate lines. **Key Personnel:** John C. Ashe, Editor; Randy Jorgensen, General Mgr.; Delores Heim, Publisher. **Subscription Rates:** $10 single issue.
Circ: 6,200

INDIAN RIVER

15271 Straitsland Resorter
3691 Club Rd. Phone: (616)238-7362
PO Box 579 Fax: (616)238-1290
Indian River, MI 49749
Publication E-mail: editor@resorter.com

Community newspaper. **Founded:** 1958. **Freq:** Weekly (Thurs.). **Print Method:** Offset. **Cols./Page:** 6. **Col. Width:** 1.5 inches. **Col. Depth:** 16 inches. **Key Personnel:** Kathy Swanson, Publisher. **USPS:** 523-040. **Subscription Rates:** $18 individuals; $22 out of area; $27 out of state.
Ad Rates: BW: $460 **Circ:** ‡3,200
SAU: $4.60
PCI: $2.80

INKSTER

15272 Inkster Ledger Star
Michigan Community Newspapers
35540 Michigan Ave. Phone: (313)729-4000
PO Box 578 Fax: (313)729-6880
Wayne, MI 48184
Community newspaper. **Founded:** 1945. **Freq:** Weekly (Thurs.). **Print Method:** Offset. **Cols./Page:** 6. **Col. Width:** 12 picas. **Col. Depth:** 21 1/2 inches. **Key Personnel:** Mike Wilcox, Publisher; Kathy Wilcox, Owner; Joan Dyer-Zinner, Managing Editor; Rita Bedell, Classified Manager; Ron Spielman, Advertising Mgr.; Justin Wilcox, Circulation Mgr. **Subscription Rates:** $48. **Remarks:** Accepts advertising.
Ad Rates: SAU: $4.68 **Circ:** Paid 1,695
Non-paid 889

INTERLOCHEN

15273 WIAA-FM - 88.7
Interlochen Center For The Arts Phone: (616)276-4400
Interlochen, MI 49643 Fax: (616)276-4417
Free: (800)441-9422
E-mail: ipr@interlochen.k12.mi.us

Format: Classical. **Simulcasts:** WIZY-FM. **Networks:** Michigan Public Radio; Public Radio International (PRI); National Public Radio (NPR). **Owner:** Interlochen Center For The Arts, at above address. **Founded:** 1963. **Operating Hours:** Continuous. **Key Personnel:** Thom Paulson, General Mgr.; David Srebnik, Program Dir. **Local Programs:** *IPR Report*, Bob Allen; *Saturday Morning Radio*, Edward Catton. **Wattage:** 100,000. **Ad Rates:** Noncommercial. **URL:** http://www.interlochen.k12.mi.us/ipr/.

IONIA

15274 WION-AM - 1430
Box 143 Phone: (616)527-4400
Ionia, MI 48846 Fax: (616)527-4402

Format: News; Middle-of-the-Road (MOR). **Networks:** ABC. **Owner:** MacPherson Broadcasting, at above address. **Founded:** 1953. **Operating Hours:** Continuous; 60% network, 40% local. **Key Personnel:** Robert Driscoll, Sales & General Manager, phone (616)427-4400, fax (616)527-4402. **Wattage:** 5000. **Ad Rates:** $6.60-10.50 for 30 seconds; $7-12.50 for 60 seconds.

IRON MOUNTAIN

15275 The Daily News
215 E. Ludington St. Phone: (906)774-2772
PO Box 460 Fax: (906)774-1285
Iron Mountain, MI 49801-2917
Free: (800)743-2088
Publication E-mail: dnews@up.lib.mi.us

General newspaper. **Founded:** Apr. 11, 1921. **Freq:** Daily (eve.) and Sat. (morn.). **Print Method:** Offset. **Trim Size:** 13 x 21 1/2. **Cols./Page:** 6. **Col. Width:** 2 inches. **Col. Depth:** 301 agate lines. **Key Personnel:** Blaine Hyska, Editor; Robert J. Johnson, Publisher, phone (906)774-7660; Jon Cantrell, Advertising Dir., phone (906)774-9545; Jerry Newhouse, Circulation Dir. **Subscription Rates:** $137 individuals; $147 by mail. **Remarks:** Accepts advertising.
Ad Rates: BW: $2,034.33 **Circ:** Mon.-Sat. 10,019
4C: $2,404.33
SAU: $15.77

15276 WJNR-FM - 101.5
212 W. J Street Phone: (906)774-5731
Iron Mountain, MI 49801 Fax: (906)774-4542

Format: Hot Country. **Networks:** ABC. **Owner:** Results Broadcasting of Michigan, Inc., at above address, (906)774-4542. **Founded:** 1972. **Operating Hours:** Continuous; 40% network, 60% local. **ADI:** Green Bay-Appleton (Suring), WI. **Key Personnel:** Rick Sawer, Program Dir.; John Koehler, Sports Dir.; Aaron Harper, News Dir.; Carrie Toretta, Sales Mgr. **Wattage:** 100,000. **Ad Rates:** $5.00-7.00 for 15 seconds; $6-20 for 30 seconds; $10-30 for 60 seconds.

15277 WMIQ-AM - 1450
101 E. Kent St. Phone: (906)774-4321
PO Box 10 Fax: (906)774-7799
Iron Mountain, MI 49801
E-mail: krockin@up.lib.mi.us; krock@uplogon.com

Format: Full Service; News; Talk. **Networks:** Canadian Broadcasting Corporation (CBC)/Societe Radio-Canada (SRC); CNN Radio. **Owner:** Iron Zepher Broadcasting Co., at above address. **Founded:** 1947. **Operating Hours:** Continuous; 80% network, 20% local. **Key Personnel:** Pete Frecchio, Operations Mgr.; Veronica Roberts, General Mgr. **Local Programs:** *My Show*, Pete Frecchio, (906)774-4321. **Wattage:** 1000. **Ad Rates:** $2-8 for 15 seconds; $3-10 for 30 seconds; $4.50-13 for 60 seconds.

IRON RIVER

15278 Iron River Reporter
Northland Publishers, Inc.
801 W. Adams Phone: (906)265-9927
PO Box 311 Fax: (906)265-5755
Iron River, MI 49935
Publication E-mail: reporter@up.net

Community newspaper. **Founded:** 1885. **Freq:** Weekly (Wed.). **Print Method:** Offset. **Cols./Page:** 6. **Col. Width:** 12 picas. **Col. Depth:** 21 1/2 inches. **Key Personnel:** Marion Nelson III, Managing Editor, mvolek@up.net. **Subscription Rates:** $30 individuals; $39 out of area. **Remarks:** Accepts advertising.
Ad Rates: BW: $500 **Circ:** ‡7,200
4C: $600
SAU: $4.45

15279 WIKB-AM - 1230
328 W. Genesee St. Phone: (906)265-5104
Iron River, MI 49935

Format: Oldies. **Networks:** NBC. **Founded:** 1949. **Operating Hours:** 5 a.m.-11 p.m. Mon.-Sat., 7 a.m.-10 p.m. Sun.; 3% network. **Key Personnel:** Jay Barry, Contact; Bill Leonoff, Operations Mgr.; Bill Leonoff, News Dir. **Wattage:** 1000. **Ad Rates:** $26 for 60 seconds.

IRONWOOD

15280 Ironwood Daily Globe
Globe Publishing Co.
118 E. McLeod Ave. Phone: (906)932-2211
Ironwood, MI 49938-2120 Fax: (906)932-5358
Free: (800)236-2887

General newspaper. **Founded:** 1919. **Freq:** Mon.-Sat. (eve.). **Print Method:** Offset. **Cols./Page:** 6. **Col. Width:** 2 inches. **Col. Depth:** 301 agate lines. **Key Personnel:** Gary A. Lamberg, Editor. **Subscription Rates:** $98 individuals.
Ad Rates: SAU: $8.22 **Circ:** ‡8,585

15281 North Country Sun
North Country Sun, Inc.
PO Box 425 Phone: (906)932-3530
Ironwood, MI 49938 Fax: (906)932-3074
Publication E-mail: evergreen@win.bright.net

Shopper. **Subtitle:** Shopping News for the U.P. & N. Wisconsin. **Founded:** 1978. **Freq:** Weekly (Mon.). **Print Method:** Offset. **Trim Size:** 11 1/2 x 17 1/2. **Cols./Page:** 6. **Col. Width:** 19 nonpareils. **Col. Depth:** 231 agate lines. **Key Personnel:** Gary LaPean, Publisher, phone (715)682-8131, fax (715)-682-6400; Richard Barringer, General Mgr. **Subscription Rates:** $25 individuals. **Remarks:** Accepts advertising.
Ad Rates: BW: $653.40 **Circ:** Non-paid ♦**17,208**
4C: $803.40
PCI: $6.60

15282 WIMI-FM - 99.7
PO Box 250 Phone: (906)932-2411
Ironwood, MI 49938 Fax: (906)932-2485

Format: Adult Contemporary. **Networks:** CBS. **Owner:** Roberts Broadcasting, Inc., at above address. **Founded:** 1974. **Operating Hours:** Continuous. **Key Personnel:** Gary Aho, Sports Dir.; Scott Jaeger, General Sales Mgr.; Kelly Klein, News Dir.; Steve Reznick, Contact; Edward Rickard, General Mgr. **Wattage:** 100,000. **Ad Rates:** $3.38-5.25 for 15 seconds; $4.50-7 for 30 seconds; $6.30-9.80 for 60 seconds.

15283 WJMS-AM - 590
PO Box 250 Phone: (906)932-2411
Ironwood, MI 49938 Fax: (906)932-2485
Free: (800)352-3541

Format: Talk; Country; Contemporary Country. **Networks:** CBS. **Owner:** Roberts Broadcasting, Inc., at above address. **Founded:** 1931. **Operating Hours:** Continuous. **Key Personnel:** Gary Aho, Sports Dir.; Scott Jaeger, General Sales Mgr.; Kelly Klein, News Dir.; Steve Reznick, Contact; Edward Rickard, General Mgr. **Wattage:** 5000 day; 1000 night. **Ad Rates:** $3.38-5.25 for 15 seconds; $4.50-7 for 30 seconds; $6.30-9.80 for 60 seconds.

ISHPEMING

15284 WIAN-AM - 1240
PO Box 700 Phone: (906)225-1313
845 W. Washington St. Fax: (906)225-1324
Marquette, MI 49855

Format: News; Talk; Sports. **Simulcasts:** WDMJ-AM. **Networks:** ABC. **Founded:** 1947. **Formerly:** WJPD-AM (1992). **ADI:** Marquette, MI. **Key Personnel:** Steven Handrich, General Mgr. **Wattage:** 1000. **Ad Rates:** $15-20 for 60 seconds.

15285 WMQT-FM - 107.7
1710 Ash St. Phone: (906)485-5523
PO Box 467 Fax: (906)485-4585
Ishpeming, MI 49849
E-mail: q107wmqt@aol.com

Format: Adult Contemporary. **Networks:** NBC. **Founded:** 1974. **Operating Hours:** Continuous. **ADI:** Marquette, MI. **Key Personnel:** William J. Blake, Contact; Tom Mogush, General Mgr. **Wattage:** 100,000. **Ad Rates:** $20-26 for 30 seconds; $24-30 for 60 seconds. Combined advertising rates available with WZAM.

15286 WZAM-AM - 970
1710 Ash St. Phone: (906)485-5523
Ishpeming, MI 49849 Fax: (906)485-4585

Format: News. **Founded:** 1959. **Formerly:** WMVN-AM. **Operating Hours:** 6 a.m.-7 p.m. **Key Personnel:** Tom Mogush, General Mgr. **Wattage:** 5000.

ITHACA

15287 Gratiot County Herald
MacDonald Publications
123 N. Main St. Phone: (517)875-4151
PO Box 10 Fax: (517)875-3159
Ithaca, MI 48847
Free: (800)519-6418

Local newspaper. **Founded:** 1869. **Freq:** Weekly (Thurs.). **Print Method:** Offset. **Cols./Page:** 5. **Col. Width:** 18 nonpareils. **Col. Depth:** 301 agate lines. **Key Personnel:** Tom MacDonald, Publisher. **Subscription Rates:** $23 individuals. **Remarks:** Accepts advertising.
Ad Rates: GLR: $0.60 **Circ:** ‡7,100
BW: $532
4C: $932
SAU: $6.65

JACKSON

15288 Blazer News
The Blazer News
PO Box 806 Phone: (517)788-4600
Jackson, MI 49204 Fax: (517)788-5300

Black community newspaper. **Founded:** 1963. **Freq:** Weekly (Wed.). **Print Method:** Offset. **Cols./Page:** 5. **Col. Width:** 23 nonpareils. **Col. Depth:** 224 agate lines. **Key Personnel:** Ron Davis, Editor. **Subscription Rates:** $50 individuals; $75 business. **Remarks:** Accepts advertising. **Alt. Formats:** Mailing labels. **Formerly:** Jackson Blazer.
Ad Rates: GLR: $.50 **Circ:** ‡2,000
BW: $960
4C: $1,200
SAU: $12.50
PCI: $14

15289 The Jackson Citizen Patriot
Booth Newspapers
214 S. Jackson St. Phone: (517)781-2300
Jackson, MI 49201-2282 Fax: (517)787-9711
Free: (800)878-6397

General newspaper. **Founded:** 1837. **Freq:** Daily (eve.). **Print Method:** Offset. **Cols./Page:** 6. **Col. Width:** 25 nonpareils. **Col. Depth:** 304 agate lines. **Key Personnel:** Sandy Petykiewicz, Editor; F.T. Weaver, Publisher. **Subscription Rates:** $160.
Ad Rates: SAU: $21.22 **Circ:** Mon.-Sat. 36,118
Sun. 41,428

15290 Jackson County Legal News
Remvue
304 Francis Phone: (517)782-0825
Box 1090 Fax: (517)782-4996
Jackson, MI 49204
Publication E-mail: legalnews@jacksonmi.com

Legal newspaper. **Founded:** 1965. **Freq:** Weekly (Mon.). **Print Method:** Offset. **Cols./Page:** 5. **Col. Width:** 22 nonpareils. **Col. Depth:** 224 agate lines. **Key Personnel:** Ronald C. Kohls, Editor and Publisher. **USPS:** 271-860. **Subscription Rates:** $31 individuals. **Remarks:** Accepts advertising.
Ad Rates: PCI: $3 **Circ:** 1,900

15291 Legacies in Time
Proving Grounds International, Inc.
PO Box 1074
Jackson, MI 49204

Magazine covering history, current African affairs, African history, and philosophy. **Founded:** 1990. **Freq:** Quarterly. **Trim Size:** 8 1/2 x 11. **Cols./Page:** 3. **Col. Width:** 2.1 inches. **Col. Depth:** 10 inches. **Key Personnel:** Carolyn Okerchiri, Editor. **ISSN:** 1049-1864. **Subscription Rates:** $18. $5 single issue. **Remarks:** Accepts advertising.
Ad Rates: GLR: $4 **Circ:** Paid ‡400
BW: $110 Non-paid ‡250
4C: $240
PCI: $19.95

15292 Photo Marketing
Photo Marketing Association International
3000 Picture Pl. Phone: (517)788-8100
Jackson, MI 49201 Fax: (517)788-8371
Publisher E-mail: pma-publications@amai.org

Trade magazine for photo/video dealers and photo finishers. **Founded:** June 1924. **Freq:** Monthly. **Print Method:** Offset. **Trim Size:** 8 1/8 x 10 3/4. **Cols./Page:** 3. **Col. Width:** 27 nonpareils. **Col. Depth:** 140 agate lines. **Key Personnel:** Gary Pageau, Executive Editor, gpageau@pmai.org; Roy S. Pung, Publisher; Bruce H. Aldrich, Publisher. **ISSN:** 0031-8531. **Subscription Rates:** $30 individuals; $35 Canada; $50 international. **URL:** http://www.pmai.org.
Ad Rates: BW: $3,555 **Circ:** Controlled 17,021
4C: $4,455
PCI: $63

15293 The Spectator
State Prison of Southern Michigan
4000 Cooper St. Phone: (517)780-6000
Jackson, MI 49201-7519 Fax: (517)780-6021

Prison newspaper. **Founded:** 1930. **Freq:** Weekly (Fri.). **Print Method:** Letterpress and offset. **Cols./Page:** 5. **Col. Width:** 22 nonpareils. **Col. Depth:** 190 agate lines. **Key Personnel:** John D. Ketzner, Editor. **Subscription Rates:** $10. **Remarks:** Accepts advertising.
Ad Rates: GLR: $.107 **Circ:** (Not Reported)

15294 WIBM-AM - 1450
1700 Glenshire Dr. Phone: (517)787-9546
Jackson, MI 49201 Fax: (517)787-7517
E-mail: wkhm@wkhm.com

Format: Easy Listening. **Owner:** Jackson Radio Works, Inc., at above address. **Founded:** 1925. **Formerly:** WXCI-AM (1996). **Operating Hours:** Continuous. **Key Personnel:** Bruce Goldsen, General Mgr.; Sue Goldsen, General Sales Mgr.; Kathy Beauchamp, Traffic; Tom Patrick, News Dir. **Wattage:** 750. **Ad Rates:** Advertising accepted; rates available upon request. Combined advertising rates available with WKHM-AM, WKHM-FM.

15295 WKHM-AM - 970
1700 Glenshire Dr. Phone: (517)787-9546
Jackson, MI 49201 Fax: (517)787-7517
E-mail: wkhm@wkhm.com

Format: News; Talk; Sports. **Networks:** ABC. **Owner:** Jackson Radio Works, Inc., at above address. **Founded:** 1952. **Operating Hours:** Continuous. **ADI:** Lansing (Ann Arbor), MI. **Key Personnel:** Bruce Goldsen, President; Bruce Goldsen, General Mgr.; Dave Weatherwax, Program Dir., phone (517)787-3397, dwax@dmci.net; Jennifer Guy, News Dir., phone (517)787-2346, news@wkhm.com. **Local Programs:** *AM Jackson* 6:00 am - 9:00 am Monday-Friday, Dave Weatherwax, Mailing contact. **Wattage:** 1000. **Ad Rates:** Combined advertising rates available with WKHM-FM, WIBM-AM. **URL:** http://www.wkhm.com.

JENISON

Ada/Forest Hills Advance - See Ada

Caledonia/Gaines Township Advance - See Caledonia

East Grand Rapids Cadence - See Grand Rapids

Grand Rapids Advance - See Grand Rapids

15296 Grand Valley Advance
Advance Newspapers
2141 Port Sheldon Rd. Phone: (616)669-2700
PO Box 9 Fax: (616)669-1162
Jenison, MI 49428-9301
Free: (800)439-0960

Suburban community newspaper (tabloid). **Founded:** 1966. **Freq:** Weekly (Tues.). **Print Method:** Offset. **Trim Size:** 10 3/8 x 15 7/8. **Cols./Page:** 6. **Col. Width:** 16 nonpareils. **Col. Depth:** 224 agate lines. **Key Personnel:** Joel Holland, Publisher, fax (616)669-3930. **Subscription Rates:** $25. **Remarks:** Accepts advertising.
Ad Rates: BW: $921.60 **Circ:** Free 18,219
4C: $1,261.60 Paid 6,028
SAU: $11.52
PCI: $9.60

Kentwood Advance - See Kentwood

15297 Northfield Advance
Advance Newspapers
2141 Port Sheldon Rd. Phone: (616)669-2700
PO Box 9 Fax: (616)669-1162
Jenison, MI 49428-9301
Free: (800)439-0960

Community newspaper. **Founded:** 1966. **Freq:** Weekly (Wed.). **Print Method:** Offset. **Trim Size:** 10 3/8 x 15 7/8. **Cols./Page:** 6. **Col. Width:** 9 1/2 picas. **Key Personnel:** Joel Holland, Publisher. **Subscription Rates:** $25. **Remarks:** Accepts advertising.
Ad Rates: BW: $686.40 **Circ:** Free 19,933
4C: $804.80 Paid 87
SAU: $8.12
PCI: $7.15

15298 Ottawa Advance
Advance Newspapers
2141 Port Sheldon Rd. Phone: (616)669-2700
PO Box 9 Fax: (616)669-1162
Jenison, MI 49428-9301
Free: (800)439-0960

Suburban tabloid newspaper. **Founded:** 1966. **Freq:** Weekly (Tues.). **Print Method:** Offset. **Trim Size:** 10 3/8 x 15 7/8. **Cols./Page:** 6. **Col. Width:** 16 nonpareils. **Col. Depth:** 224 agate lines. **Key Personnel:** Joel Holland, Publisher, fax (616)669-3930. **Subscription Rates:** $25 individuals. **Remarks:** Accepts advertising.
Ad Rates: BW: $705.60 **Circ:** Free 8,820
4C: $1,005.60 Paid 60
SAU: $8.82
PCI: $7.35

Rockford/Cedar Springs Advance - See Rockford

15299 South Advance
Advance Newspapers
2141 Port Sheldon Rd. Phone: (616)669-2700
PO Box 9 Fax: (616)669-1162
Jenison, MI 49428-9301
Free: (800)439-0960

Suburban community newspaper (tabloid). **Founded:** 1966. **Freq:** Weekly (Tues.). **Print Method:** Offset. **Trim Size:** 10 3/8 x 15 7/8. **Cols./Page:** 6. **Col. Width:** 16 nonpareils. **Col. Depth:** 224 agate lines. **Key Personnel:** Joel Holland, Publisher. **Subscription Rates:** $25. **Remarks:** Accepts advertising. **Formerly:** Byron Center/Dorr Advance.
Ad Rates: BW: $384 **Circ:** Controlled 7,958
4C: $564.80 Paid 22
PCI: $4.35

Sparta/Kent City Advance - See Sparta

Walker/Westside Advance - See Walker

Wyoming Advance - See Wyoming

JONESVILLE

15300 Jonesville Independent
Independent Newspapers
253 E. Chicago St., Ste. A Phone: (517)849-9880
PO Box 96 Fax: (517)849-7401
Jonesville, MI 49250
Community newspaper. **Founded:** 1835. **Freq:** Weekly (Fri.). **Print Method:** Offset. **Trim Size:** 13 1/4 x 21 1/2. **Cols./Page:** 6. **Col. Width:** 2 inches. **Col. Depth:** 21 inches. **Key Personnel:** Scott McGraw, Contact. **Subscription Rates:** $12. **Remarks:** Accepts advertising.
Ad Rates: BW: $341.85 **Circ:** 1,200
4C: $541.85
SAU: $2.65
PCI: $2.50

KALAMAZOO

15301 ADVANCES
Fetzer Institute
9292 W. KL Ave. Phone: (616)375-2000
Kalamazoo, MI 49009-9398 Fax: (616)372-2163
Publication E-mail: advances@fetzer.org

Journal focusing on the understanding of mind-body health. **Subtitle:** The Journal of Mind-Body Health. **Founded:** 1983. **Freq:** Quarterly. **Trim Size:** 7 x 10. **Cols./Page:** 2. **Col. Width:** 2 7/8 inches. **Col. Depth:** 8 7/8 inches. **Key Person-**

nel: Harris Dienstfrey, Editor; Linda Bell Grdina, Managing Editor. **ISSN:** 0741-9783. **Subscription Rates:** $50 individuals; $80 institutions student; $25 students; $68 Canada; $75 other countries. **Remarks:** Advertising not accepted. **Online:** EBSCO PUBLISHING-HOMEWORK HELPER. **Alt. Formats:** CD-ROM.

Circ: Paid ‡4,971
Non-paid ‡929

15302 Bloodlines
United Kennel Club, Inc.
100 E. Kilgore Rd. Phone: (616)343-9020
Kalamazoo, MI 49002-5584 Fax: (616)343-7037
Publisher E-mail: ukclub@net.link.net

Magazine devoted to working, showing, and training breeds of dogs. **Subtitle:** An International Journal Devoted to Pure Bred Dogs. **Founded:** 1905. **Freq:** 6/year. **Print Method:** Offset. **Trim Size:** 8 1/8 x 10 7/8. **Cols./Page:** 3. **Col. Width:** 27 nonpareils. **Col. Depth:** 136 1/2 agate lines. **Key Personnel:** Vicki Rand, Managing Editor; Fred Miller, Publisher; Rosalie Reeves, Advertising Mgr. **USPS:** 058-220. **Subscription Rates:** $24 individuals; $34 other countries; $6 single issue. **Remarks:** Accepts advertising.
Ad Rates: GLR: $13 **Circ:** Paid ‡5,200
BW: $162 Non-paid ‡190
4C: $350
PCI: $8

15303 Business Outlook for West Michigan
W.E. Upjohn Institute for Employment Research
300 S. Westnedge Ave. Phone: (616)343-5541
Kalamazoo, MI 49007-4686 Fax: (616)343-7310
Publisher E-mail: publications@we.upjohninst.org

Business magazine containing economic analyses, statistics, and forecasts for western Michigan. **Founded:** 1984. **Freq:** Quarterly. **Print Method:** Offset. **Trim Size:** 8 1/2 x 11. **Cols./Page:** 2. **Col. Width:** 40 nonpareils. **Col. Depth:** 127 agate lines. **Key Personnel:** George Erickcek, Editor. **ISSN:** 0748-4216. **Subscription Rates:** $25; $40 two years. **Remarks:** Advertising not accepted. **URL:** http://www.upjohninst.org.
Circ: Paid ‡300
Controlled ‡300

15304 Chinese Language Teachers Association Journal
Chinese Language Teachers Association
Kalamazoo College Phone: (616)337-7001
1200 Academy St. Fax: (616)337-7251
Kalamazoo, MI 49006
Publisher E-mail: clta@kzoo.edu

Scholarly journal covering the teaching and learning of Chinese language and literature. **Founded:** 1966. **Freq:** Triennial. **Key Personnel:** Madeline Chu, Executive Dir., phone (616)337-7325, chu@kzoo.edu; Shou-hsin Teng, Editor, steng@ccntnu.edu.tw. **Subscription Rates:** $80 individuals; $80 institutions; $85 Canada; $100 other countries.
Circ: 650

15305 Comparative Drama
Medieval Institute
Western Michigan University Phone: (616)387-8832
1201 Oliver St. Fax: (616)387-8750
Kalamazoo, MI 49008-3801
Journal for comparative and interdisciplinary study of drama. **Founded:** Mar. 1967. **Freq:** Quarterly. **Print Method:** Offset. **Trim Size:** 6 x 9. **Cols./Page:** 1. **Col. Width:** 4 1/8 inches. **Col. Depth:** 7 inches. **Key Personnel:** Luis Gamez, Editor-in-Chief, phone (616)387-2601, fax (616)387-2562, gamez@wmich.edu; Luis Gamez, phone (616)387-2601. **ISSN:** 0010-4078. **Subscription Rates:** $18 individuals; $32 institutions; $35 other countries. **Remarks:** Advertising not accepted.
Circ: Paid ‡850
Controlled ‡50

15306 Coonhound Bloodlines
United Kennel Club, Inc.
100 E. Kilgore Rd. Phone: (616)343-9020
Kalamazoo, MI 49002-5584 Fax: (616)343-7037
Publisher E-mail: ukclub@net.link.net

Magazine about coonhound field trials and hunting; including information about training, veterinary care, upcoming events, stories, event results and rules. **Subtitle:** The Complete Magazine for the Houndsman. **Founded:** Jan. 1973. **Freq:** Monthly. **Print Method:** Offset. **Trim Size:** 8 1/8 x 10 7/8. **Cols./Page:** 2 and 3. **Col. Width:** 43 and 28 nonpareils. **Col. Depth:** 136 1/2 agate lines. **Key Personnel:** Fred T. Miller, Publisher; Vicki Rand, Managing Editor; Rosalie Reeves, Advertising Mgr. **USPS:** 017-690. **Subscription Rates:** $20 individuals; $3 single issue; $1.50 S/H. **Remarks:** Accepts advertising.
Ad Rates: GLR: $18 **Circ:** Paid 20,700
BW: $260
4C: $400
PCI: $18

15307 Early Drama, Art, and Music Review
Medieval Institute Publications
Kalamazoo, MI 49008-3851 Phone: (616)387-8755
Fax: (616)387-8750

Scholarly journal covering studies in early drama and relation to other arts. **Founded:** 1978. **Freq:** Semiannual. **Print Method:** Offset. **Key Personnel:** Clifford Davidson, Editor, davidson@wmich.edu. **ISSN:** 0148-9401. **Subscription Rates:** $8 individuals. **Remarks:** Advertising not accepted. **Former name:** EDAM Newsletter.
Circ: Combined 150

15308 Flashes Kalamazoo Shopper
Stauffer Communications, Inc.
7837 Sprinkle Rd. Phone: (616)324-1000
Kalamazoo, MI 49002 Fax: (616)324-1005
Free: (800)968-2527
Publisher E-mail: fpi595@aol.com

Shopper/weekly newspaper. **Subtitle:** Kalamazoo, Village Area, Postage, and Westside Flashes. **Founded:** 1975. **Freq:** Weekly (Mon.). **Print Method:** Offset. **Trim Size:** 10 3/8 x 12 1/2. **Cols./Page:** 4. **Col. Width:** 2 7/16 inches. **Col. Depth:** 12 1/2 inches. **Key Personnel:** Dave Moored, General Mgr., dmoored@flashespublishers.com; Allen Louks, Sales Mgr., acmnlouks@aol.com; Tony Fales, Team Leader, fax (616)262-9288. **Subscription Rates:** Free; $18 by mail. **Remarks:** Accepts advertising.
Ad Rates: BW: $1,785.60 **Circ:** Free 84,950
4C: $330
PCI: $27.90

15309 Hunting Retriever
United Kennel Club, Inc.
100 E. Kilgore Rd. Phone: (616)343-9020
Kalamazoo, MI 49002-5584 Fax: (616)343-7037
Publisher E-mail: ukclub@net.link.net

Magazine featuring hunting retrievers. **Founded:** 1984. **Freq:** Bimonthly. **Print Method:** Offset. **Trim Size:** 8 1/2 x 11. **Cols./Page:** 3. **Col. Width:** 2 3/8 inches. **Col. Depth:** 9 3/4 inches. **Key Personnel:** Vicki Rand, Managing Editor; Rosalie Reeves, Assistant Sales Mgr. **ISSN:** 8750-6629. **Subscription Rates:** $25 U.S.; $30 other countries. **Remarks:** Accepts advertising.
Ad Rates: BW: $200 **Circ:** Paid 3,500
4C: $485 Non-paid 50
PCI: $15

15310 Journal of Asia-Pacific Business
The Haworth Press, Inc.
Dept. of Marketing
Haworth College of Business
Western Michigan University
Kalamazoo, MI 49008
Publisher E-mail: getinfo@haworthpressinc.com

Journal featuring managerially oriented as well as academic articles centered on the Asia-Pacific region. **Founded:** 1993. **Freq:** Quarterly. **Key Personnel:** Zahir A. Quraeshi, Editor; Bill Cohen, Publisher. **ISSN:** 1059-9231. **Subscription Rates:** $24; $48 Industry; $75 libraries. **Remarks:** Accepts advertising.
Ad Rates: BW: $300 **Circ:** (Not Reported)

15311 Journal of International Accounting, Auditing and Taxation
Elseiver
Haworth College of Business Phone: (616)387-5259
Western Michigan University Fax: (616)387-5710
Kalamazoo, MI 49008
Publication E-mail: 102062.2525@compuserve.com
Publisher E-mail: fcentres@gpu.stv.ualberta.ca

Focuses on global issues in accounting. **Founded:** 1992. **Freq:** Semiannual. **Key Personnel:** Kathleen Sinning, Editor, kathleen.sinning@wmich.edu; Hans Dykxhoorn, Editor, hansdykxdhoorn@wmich.edu. **ISSN:** 1061-9518. **Subscription Rates:** $75 individuals; $180 institutions. **Remarks:** Advertising not accepted.
Circ: (Not Reported)

15312 Journal of Sociology and Social Welfare
Western Michigan University Phone: (616)387-3205
School of Social Work Fax: (616)387-3217
Kalamazoo, MI 49008-5034
Journal presenting a broad range of articles which analyze social welfare institutions, policies, or problems from a social scientific perspective. **Founded:** 1973. **Freq:** Quarterly. **Print Method:** Offset. **Trim Size:** 6 x 9. **Cols./Page:** 1. **Col. Width:** 4.25 inches. **Col. Depth:** 7 inches. **Key Personnel:** Robert D. Leighninger, Jr., Editor, phone (504)388-5887, leighnin@erols.com; Frederick MacDonald, Ph.D., Managing Editor, phone (616)387-3191, frederick.macdonald@wmich.edu. **ISSN:** 0191-5096. **Subscription Rates:** $35; $40 out of area Industry; $75 institutions; $85 institutions outside U.S. **Remarks:** Advertising not accepted.
Circ: ‡650

15313 Kalamazoo Gazette
Booth Newspapers
401 S. Burdick St. Phone: (616)345-3511
Kalamazoo, MI 49007-5279 Fax: (616)345-0583

General newspaper. **Founded:** 1837. **Freq:** Mon.-Sat. (eve.). **Print Method:** Letterpress. **Cols./Page:** 6. **Col. Width:** 24 nonpareils. **Col. Depth:** 308 agate lines. **Key Personnel:** James R. Mosby, Jr., Editor; James Pulliam, Advertising Mgr. **Subscription Rates:** $87. **Remarks:** Accepts advertising. **URL:** http://www.mlive.com. **Feature Editors:** Jeff Alexander, *Environmental*; Kathy Doud, *Book, Drama, Music*; Peggy Guthaus, *Fashion, Food*; Tom Haroldson, *TV & Radio*; Paul Keep, *Financial/Business, Real Estate*; Mary Kramer, *Metro*; Bill Krasean, *Medical*; Robert Maxwell, *Photo*; Jack Moss, *Sports*; Becky Payne, *Education*; Larry Pratt, *Travel*; Doug Pullen, *Movie*; Harold Smith, *Sunday*; Norman Sparks, *Garden/Home*; Tom Thinnes, *Editorials*; Craig Thomas, *Religion*; Mary Wade, *Entertainment, Family, Features, Lifestyle*.
Ad Rates: SAU: $22.08 **Circ:** Mon.-Fri. **★59,477**
Sat. **★68,156**
Sun. **★75,210**

15314 Medieval Prosopography
Medieval Institute
Western Michigan University Phone: (616)387-8832
1201 Oliver St. Fax: (616)387-8750
Kalamazoo, MI 49008-3801
Scholarly journal covering biography and family history in the medieval period. **Subtitle:** History and Collective Biography. **Founded:** 1980. **Freq:** Annual. **Trim Size:** 7 x 10. **Cols./Page:** 1. **Key Personnel:** Candace Porath, Senior Editor, candace.porath@wmich.edu. **ISSN:** 0198-9405. **Subscription Rates:** $30 individuals; $37.50 libraries and institutions. **Remarks:** Advertising not accepted.
Circ: (Not Reported)

15315 Reading Horizons
Western Michigan University
Kalamazoo, MI 49008 Phone: (616)387-3470
Fax: (616)387-2882

Academic publication covering education. **Founded:** 1960. **Freq:** Quarterly. **Key Personnel:** Karen Thomas, Editor; Paul Wilson, Editor. **ISSN:** 0034-0502. **Subscription Rates:** $20 individuals; $5 single issue. **Remarks:** Advertising not accepted.
Circ: (Not Reported)

15316 Third Coast
Western Michigan Univ. Phone: (616)387-2675
Dept. of English Fax: (616)387-2562
Kalamazoo, MI 49008-5092
Magazine containing poetry, nonfiction, and parts of novels. **Founded:** 1995. **Freq:** Semiannual. **Trim Size:** 6 x 9. **Key Personnel:** Kathleen McGookey, Managing Editor, phone (616)387-2616, 96mcgookey@wmich.edu; Tony Spicer, Poetry Editor; Scott Bade, Poetry Editor; Janice Robertson, Fiction Editor; Pedro Ponce, Fiction Editor. **Subscription Rates:** $11 /year; $6 single issue; $5 back issue. **Remarks:** Accepts advertising. **URL:** http://www.wmich.edu/thirdcoast.
Circ: Paid 100

15317 Western Herald
Western Michigan University
1523 Fanuce Student Service Bldg. Phone: (616)383-1600
Fax: (616)387-2267
Kalamazoo, MI 49008
Collegiate newspaper. **Founded:** 1916. **Freq:** 4/wk (Mon.-Thurs. during the academic year). **Print Method:** Offset. **Cols./Page:** 6. **Col. Width:** 26 nonpareils. **Col. Depth:** 294 agate lines. **Key Personnel:** O'Ryan Rickard, Contact, phone (616)387-2110, oryan.rickard@umich.edu. **Subscription Rates:** $29 individuals; $31 out of state. **Remarks:** Accepts advertising. **Available Online. URL:** http://www.wmich.edu/herald.
Ad Rates: 4C: $1,351.70 **Circ:** Combined 12,500
PCI: $7.95

15318 WMU, The Magazine
Western Michigan University
1201 Oliver St. Phone: (616)387-8400
Kalamazoo, MI 49008-3899 Fax: (616)387-8422

Alumni magazine. **Founded:** 1930. **Freq:** Quarterly. **Print Method:** Offset. **Trim Size:** 8 1/4 x 10 3/4. **Cols./Page:** 3. **Col. Width:** 40 nonpareils. **Col. Depth:** 224 agate lines. **Key Personnel:** David H. Smith, Contact, phone (616)387-8431, david.h.smith@wmich.edu; Jeanne Baron, Contact, phone (616)387-8433, jeanne.baron@wmich.edu. **ISSN:** 0279-3628. **Subscription Rates:** Free to alumni association members and friends of WMU. **Remarks:** Advertising not accepted. **URL:** http://www.wmich.edu. **Formerly:** The Westerner.
Circ: Free 75,000

15319 SBM Communications
750 E. Vine St. Phone: (616)345-0109
Kalamazoo, MI 49007-1874 Fax: (616)345-0100

Founded: 1981. **Formerly:** Cable TV of Kalamazoo. **Key Personnel:** Earl Drake, General Mgr.; Lori A. Lamb, Vice President. **Cities Served:** Kalamazoo, MI: subscribing households 50; 26 channels; 6 community access channels.

15320 WFAT-FM - 96.5
6021 S. Westnedge Ave. Phone: (616)327-7600
Kalamazoo, MI 49002-2811 Fax: (616)327-0726
E-mail: wfat@netlink.net

Format: Adult Contemporary. **Networks:** Unistar. **Owner:** Midwest Radio Group, at above address. **Founded:** 1986. **Formerly:** WHEZ-AM (1990). **Operating Hours:** Continuous. **ADI:** Grand Rapids-Kalamazoo-Battle Creek, MI. **Key Personnel:** Peter Tanz, General Mgr.; Dan Mason, Program Dir.; Greg Barton, Sales Mgr. **Wattage:** 3,400. **Ad Rates:** $30-80 for 60 seconds. Combined advertising rates available with WNWN-FM.

15321 WIDR-FM - 89.1
Western Michigan University Phone: (616)387-6301
1511 Faunce Fax: (616)387-0958
Kalamazoo, MI 49008-5070

Format: Alternative/New Music/Progressive. **Networks:** Independent. **Founded:** 1952. **Operating Hours:** Continuous; 100% local. **ADI:** Grand Rapids-Kalamazoo-Battle Creek, MI. **Key Personnel:** Stan Fracker, General Mgr.; Amy Lane, Business Mgr.; Chad Zupke, Program Dir.; Kelly Argyle, Music Dir.; Derek Ricca, News Dir. **Wattage:** 100. **Ad Rates:** Noncommercial.

15322 WKDS-FM - 89.9
606 E. Kilgore Phone: (616)337-0899
Kalamazoo, MI 49001 Fax: (616)337-0251
E-mail: wicds@remclz.klz.mi.us

Format: Full Service. **Networks:** Independent. **Founded:** 1983. **Operating Hours:** 8 a.m.-9 p.m.; 100% local. **Key Personnel:** Robert Kucera, General Mgr.; Kris Kirkpatrick, Program Dir., phone (610)337-0220, fax (616)337-0251, wkds@remc12.k12.mi.us. **Wattage:** 100. **Ad Rates:** Noncommercial.

15323 WKFR-FM - 103.3
4154 Jennings Dr. Phone: (616)344-0111
PO Box 50911 Fax: (616)344-4223
Kalamazoo, MI 49005

Format: Top 40. **Networks:** Westwood One Radio. **Owner:** Cumulus Broadcasting, at above address. **Operating Hours:** Continuous. **ADI:** Grand Rapids-Kalamazoo-Battle Creek, MI. **Key Personnel:** Ed Sackley, Market Mgr., ed.sackley@cumulusb.com; Dave Michaels, Program Dir., drdave@wkfr.com; Mark Anderson, Asst. Program Dir., mark@wkfr.co,; Dave Benson, Promotions Dir., benson@wkfr.com; Craig Russell, Music Dir., craig@wkfr.com. **Local Programs:** *On the Verge*, Jeff Green; *Hometown Countdown*, Dave Benson; *Retro Lunch*, Mark Anderson. **Wattage:** 50,000. **URL:** http://www.wkfr.com.

15324 WKMI-AM - 1360
4154 Jennings Dr. Phone: (616)344-0111
PO Box 50911 Fax: (616)344-4223
Kalamazoo, MI 49005-0911
E-mail: radio@wkmi.com; news@wkmi.com

Format: Talk; News. **Networks:** ABC. **Owner:** Cumulus Broadcasting Inc., at above address. **Founded:** 1946. **Formerly:** Crystal Radio Group, Inc. **Operating Hours:** Continuous. **ADI:** Grand Rapids-Kalamazoo-Battle Creek, MI. **Key Personnel:** Ed Sackley, Pres./GM, ed.sackley@cumulusb.com; Joe Daugherty, Operations Mgr., joed@wkmi.com; Steve Stoimenoff, General Sales Mgr., steve.stoimenoff@cumulusb.com; Jodi Victor, News Dir., news@wkmi.com. **Wattage:** 5000. **Ad Rates:** Combined advertising rates available with WRKR-FM, WKFR-FM. **URL:** http://www.wkmi.com.

15325 WKPR-AM - 1420
2244 Ravine Rd. Phone: (616)381-1420
PO Box 50867
Kalamazoo, MI 49004

Format: Middle-of-the-Road (MOR); Religious. **Networks:** USA Radio. **Owner:** Kalamazoo Broadcasting Co., Inc., WFUR Radio, 399 Garfield Ave. SW, Grand Rapids, MI 49501, (616)451-9387. **Founded:** 1960. **Operating Hours:** 6 a.m.-sunset, winter; 6 a.m.-7 p.m., summer. **ADI:** Grand Rapids-Kalamazoo-Battle Creek, MI. **Key Personnel:** William E. Kuiper, Sr., President; Kip Odell, Contact; Kip Odell, Office Mgr. **Local Programs:** *Update*, Rick Fortaine. **Wattage:** 1000. **Ad Rates:** $6-7 for 30 seconds; $7-8 for 60 seconds.

15326 WKZO-AM - 590
4200 W. Main,St. Phone: (616)345-7121
Kalamazoo, MI 49006 Fax: (616)345-1436
Free: (800)873-1074
E-mail: am590@cis.compuserve.com

Format: News; Talk. **Networks:** CBS; ESPN Radio. **Founded:** 1931. **Operating Hours:** Continuous. **ADI:** Grand Rapids-Kalamazoo-Battle Creek, MI. **Key Personnel:** Stephen Trivers, General Mgr.; Ken Lanphear, Operations Mgr.; Dennis Martin, Sales Mgr.; Richard Piet, Program/News Director. **Wattage:** 5000. **Ad Rates:** Combined advertising rates available with WQLR-FM & WQSN-AM, WKLZ-AM. **URL:** http://www.wkzo.com.

15327 WLLA-TV - 64
7048 E. Kilgore Phone: (616)345-6421
PO Box 3157 Fax: (616)345-5665
Kalamazoo, MI 49003

Format: Commercial TV. **Networks:** Independent; Warner Brothers Studios. **Founded:** 1987. **Operating Hours:** Continuous. **ADI:** Grand Rapids-Kalamazoo-Battle Creek, MI. **Key Personnel:** Richard Hawkins, General Mgr. **Wattage:** 2,500,000. **Ad Rates:** $12-75 for 30 seconds.

15328 WMUK-FM - 102.1
Western Michigan University Phone: (616)387-5715
Kalamazoo, MI 49008 Fax: (616)387-4630

Format: Classical; News; Jazz; Public Radio; Bluegrass. **Networks:** National Public Radio (NPR); Michigan Public Radio. **Owner:** Western Michigan University, at above address. **Founded:** 1951. **Formerly:** WMCR-FM. **Operating Hours:** 5:30 a.m.-2 a.m. Sun.-Sat. **ADI:** Grand Rapids-Kalamazoo-Battle Creek, MI. **Key Personnel:** Garrard Macleod, General Mgr., phone (616)387-5719, macleod@wmich.edu; Klay Woodworth, Operations Dir., phone (616)387-5725; Floyd Pientka, Program Dir., phone (616)387-5724; Tony Griffin, News Dir., phone (616)387-5717; Mark Tomlonson, Chief Engineer, phone (616)387-5738. **Local Programs:** *Afternoon Edition*, Lorraine Goodrich. **Wattage:** 50,000. **Ad Rates:** Noncommercial.

15329 WQLR-FM - 106.5
4200 W. Main St. Phone: (616)345-7121
Kalamazoo, MI 49006 Fax: (616)345-1436
Free: (800)873-1074
E-mail: qlite@cis.compuserve.com

Format: Adult Contemporary. **Owner:** Fairfield Broadcasting Co., at above address. **Founded:** 1972. **Operating Hours:** Continuous. **ADI:** Grand Rapids-Kalamazoo-Battle Creek, MI. **Key Personnel:** Stephen Trivers, Contact; William Wertz, Contact; Dennis Martin, Sales Mgr.; Kenneth Lanphear, Contact; Richard Piet, News Dir. **Wattage:** 33,000. **Ad Rates:** Combined advertising rates available with WKZO-AM, WQSN-AM, WKLZ-AM. **URL:** http://www.qlite.com.

15330 WQSN-AM - 1660
4200 W. Main St. Phone: (616)345-7121
Kalamazoo, MI 49007-2729 Fax: (616)345-1436
Free: (800)873-1074
E-mail: wqsn@compuserve.com

Format: Sports. **Owner:** Fairfield Broadcasting Co., at above address. **Founded:** 1985. **Operating Hours:** Continuous. **ADI:** Grand Rapids-Kalamazoo-Battle Creek, MI. **Key Personnel:** Stephen C. Trivers, Pres./Gen. Mgr.; William J. Wertz, Exec. VP; Ken Lanphear, Operations Dir.; Richard Piet, News Dir.; Tim Abramowski, PSA Dir.; Gary Lange, Sports Dir. **Wattage:** 10,000 a day; 1,.000 night. **Ad Rates:** Advertising accepted; rates available upon request. Combined advertising rates available with WQLR-FM, WKZO-AM,WKLZ-AM.

15331 WRKR-FM - 107.7
4154 Jennings Dr. Phone: (616)344-0111
P.O. Box 50911 Fax: (616)344-4800
Kalamazoo, MI 49005-0911
E-mail: radio@wrkr.com

Format: Classic Rock; Album-Oriented Rock (AOR). **Networks:** ABC. **Owner:** Cumulus Broadcasting, Inc., at above address. **Founded:** 1988. **Formerly:** Crystal Radio Group Inc. **Operating Hours:** Continuous. **ADI:** Grand Rapids-Kalamazoo-Battle Creek, MI. **Key Personnel:** Ed Sackley, Pres./Gen. Mgr., ed.sackley@cumulusb.com; Steve Stoimenoff, General Sales Mgr., steve.stoiimenoff@cumulusb.com; Mike Ferris, Program Dir., ferris@wrkr.com; Dave Doran, Asst. Program Dir., doran@wrkr.com; Jodi Victor, News Dir., news@wrkr.com. **Wattage:** 50,000. **Ad Rates:** Combined advertising rates available with WKMI-AM, WKFR-FM. **URL:** http://www.wrkr.com.

15332 WWMT-TV - 3
590 W. Maple St. Phone: (616)388-3333
Kalamazoo, MI 49008 Fax: (616)388-8228

Format: Commercial TV. **Networks:** CBS. **Owner:** Granite Broadcasting Corp., 767 3rd Ave., 34th Fl., New York, NY 10017, (212)826-2530, Fax: (212)826-2858. **Founded:** 1950. **Formerly:** WKZO-TV. **Operating Hours:** Continuous. **ADI:** Grand Rapids-Kalamazoo-Battle Creek, MI. **Key Personnel:** Richard F. Appleton, President/General Mgr.; Nancy Kern, Programming; Mike King, General Sales Mgr. **Ad Rates:** Advertising accepted; rates available upon request. **URL:** http://www.wwmt.com/.

KALKASKA

15333 The Leader and the Kalkaskian
318 N. Cedar St. Phone: (616)258-4600
Kalkaska, MI 49646
County newspaper. **Subtitle:** 1869. **Freq:** Weekly. **Print Method:** Offset. **Trim Size:** 13 1/4 x 21. **Cols./Page:** 6. **Col. Width:** 2 1/16 inches. **Col. Depth:** 21 inches. **Key Personnel:** Jeff Hallberg, Publisher, phone (616)533-8523, fax (616)533-6803; Jim Bumpus, Editor; Janet Sieting, Advertising Mgr. **ISSN:** 5454-2000. **Subscription Rates:** $22; $25 out of area; $16 armed forces. **Remarks:** Accepts advertising. **URL:** http://www.upnorthpub.com.
Ad Rates: GLR: $.42 **Circ:** 3,900
BW: $737.10
4C: $897.10
SAU: $5.85

15334 WKAL-FM - 1420
PO Box 580
Kalkaska, MI 49646
E-mail: rowellroost@torchlake.com

Format: Alternative/New Music/Progressive; Album-Oriented Rock (AOR). **Owner:** Kalkaska Area Educational Foundation, Inc., at above address. **Operating Hours:** Sunrise-sunset. **Key Personnel:** G. M. Kurygier, Station Mgr.; Jeff Rowell, Program Dir. **Wattage:** 500.

KENTWOOD

15335 Kentwood Advance
Advance Newspapers
2141 Port Sheldon Rd. Phone: (616)669-2700
PO Box 9 Fax: (616)669-1162
Jenison, MI 49428-9301
Free: (800)439-0960

Suburban newspaper (tabloid). **Founded:** 1966. **Freq:** Weekly (Tues.). **Print Method:** Offset. **Trim Size:** 10 5/8 x 15 7/8. **Cols./Page:** 6. **Col. Width:** 16 nonpareils. **Col. Depth:** 224 agate lines. **Key Personnel:** Joel Holland, Publisher, fax (616)669-3930. **Subscription Rates:** $25. **Remarks:** Accepts advertising.
Ad Rates: BW: $830.40 **Circ:** Free 15,058
4C: $1,130.40 Paid 258
SAU: $10.38
PCI: $8.65

15336 Old Mill News
670 - 56th St. SE, No. 5 Phone: (616)455-0609
Kentwood, MI 49548-5814
Publisher E-mail: wdenton@qtm.net

Journal of the Society for the Preservation of Old Mills. **Founded:** Oct. 1972. **Freq:** Quarterly. **Print Method:** Computer. **Trim Size:** 8 1/2 x 11. **Cols./Page:** 2. **Col. Width:** 42 nonpareils. **Col. Depth:** 136 agate lines. **Key Personnel:** Esther A. Middlewood, Editor and Publisher, eamedit@aol.com; Frank Woods, Advertising Mgr., phone (401)884-8476. **ISSN:** 0276-3338. **Subscription Rates:** $21 U.S.; $20 out of country. **Remarks:** Accepts advertising.
Circ: ‡2,300

KINGSFORD

15337 WEUL-FM - 98.1
130 Carmen Dr. Phone: (906)249-1423
Marquette, MI 49855

Format: Religious. **Founded:** 1990. **ADI:** Marquette, MI. **Key Personnel:** W. Curtis Marker, Contact. **Wattage:** 240.

LAKE CITY

15338 Waterfront
101 N. Main St. Phone: (616)839-4315
PO Box L Fax: (616)839-4994
Lake City, MI 49651-0912
Local newspaper. **Founded:** 1968. **Freq:** Weekly (Tues.). **Print Method:** Offset. **Cols./Page:** 5. **Col. Width:** 22 nonpareils. **Col. Depth:** 182 agate lines. **Key Personnel:** Robert Redman, Publisher. **USPS:** 623-720. **Subscription Rates:** $16 individuals.
Ad Rates: SAU: $3.10 **Circ:** ‡4,500

LAKE ODESSA

15339 Lakewood News
J-Ad Corp.
1952 N. Broadway Phone: (616)945-9554
PO Box B Fax: (616)945-5192
Hastings, MI 49058
Free: (800)870-7085
Publisher E-mail: j-ad@voyager.com

Local paper of Lake Odessa, Woodland, Sunfield, Mulliken, and Clarksville Freeport. **Founded:** 1988. **Freq:** Weekly. **Print Method:** Web offset. **Cols./Page:** 6. **Col. Width:** 1 5/8 inches. **Col. Depth:** 16 inches. **Key Personnel:** Frederick Jacobs, Publisher; David Young, Editor; Scott Ammen, Advertising Mgr. **Subscription Rates:** Free; $20 (mail). **Remarks:** Accepts advertising.
Ad Rates: BW: $307.20 **Circ:** Paid 70
4C: $507.20 Free 6,000
SAU: $5.28
PCI: $4.25

LAKE ORION

15340 AFAS Quarterly
Bort Productions
PO Box 325 Phone: (810)814-0627
Lake Orion, MI 48361-0325 Fax: (810)814-0627

Automotive Fine Arts Society magazine dedicated to educating the public about the aesthetic value of automotive fine art and to keeping collectors informed of field trends. **Subtitle:** A Journal by the Automotive Fine Arts Society. **Founded:** Jan. 1989. **Freq:** Annual. **Print Method:** Sheetfed offset. **Trim Size:** 8 1/2 x 11. **Cols./Page:** 3. **Col. Width:** 2 3/8 inches. **Col. Depth:** 9 7/8 inches. **Key Personnel:** Jack Juratovic, Publisher; Jan Taylor, Editor. **ISSN:** 0899-9171. **Subscription Rates:** $24 2/yr.; $12 single issue; $32 Canada; $40 rest of the world. **Remarks:** Accepts advertising. **Formerly:** Automotive Fine Arts Society.
Ad Rates: BW: $565 **Circ:** 5,000
4C: $1,325

15341 Lake Orion Review
30 N. Broadway Phone: (248)693-8331
Lake Orion, MI 48362 Fax: (248)628-9750

Newspaper. **Founded:** 1881. **Freq:** Weekly (Wed.). **Print Method:** Offset. **Cols./Page:** 6. **Col. Width:** 18 nonpareils. **Col. Depth:** 210 agate lines. **Key Personnel:** Elaine Steib, Editor; James A. Sherman, Publisher; Eric Lewis, Advertising Mgr.; Don Rush, General Mgr. **Subscription Rates:** $21 individuals. **Alt. Formats:** Microform.
Ad Rates: BW: $396 **Circ:** 3,400
PCI: $4.40

LAKEVIEW

15342 Lakeview Enterprise
The Pioneer Group
327 Lincoln Ave. Phone: (517)352-6026
PO Box 500 Fax: (517)352-8210
Lakeview, MI 48850
Publication E-mail: enterprise@pioneergroup.net

Community newspaper. **Founded:** 1879. **Freq:** Weekly (Wed.). **Print Method:** Offset. **Cols./Page:** 9. **Col. Width:** 1 3/8 inches. **Col. Depth:** 21 inches. **Key Personnel:** John A. Batdorff, Publisher; Mike Taylor, Editor. **Subscription Rates:** $19.95 individuals; $31.95 out of area; $42.95 out of state. **Remarks:** Combined advertising rates available with other Pioneer Group newspapers. **URL:** http://www.pioneergroup.net.
Ad Rates: SAU: $6.50 **Circ:** ‡1,685
PCI: $3.75

LANSE

15343 L'Anse Sentinel
L'Anse Sentinel Inc.
202 N. Main Phone: (906)524-6194
PO Box 7 Fax: (906)524-6197
Lanse, MI 49946
Local newspaper. **Founded:** 1880. **Freq:** Weekly (Wed.). **Print Method:** Offset. **Cols./Page:** 6. **Col. Width:** 30 nonpareils. **Col. Depth:** 301 agate lines. **Key Personnel:** Barry Drue, Editor; Ed Danner, Publisher; Polly Kahkonen, Advertising Mgr. **Subscription Rates:** $34. **Remarks:** Accepts advertising.
Ad Rates: GLR: $.36 **Circ:** ‡4,241
SAU: $5.96

LANSING

15344 The Bottom Line
Alcohol Research Information Service
1106 E. Oakland Ave. Phone: (517)485-9900
Lansing, MI 48906 Fax: (517)485-1928

Journal on substance abuse problems and alcohol-related issues. **Subtitle:** on Alcohol in Society. **Founded:** 1977. **Freq:** Quarterly. **Print Method:** Offset. **Trim Size:** 5 1/2 x 8 1/2. **Cols./Page:** 1. **Col. Width:** 27 picas. **Col. Depth:** 44 picas. **Key Personnel:** Robert Hammond, Editor. **Subscription Rates:** $20; $30 other countries. **Remarks:** Advertising not accepted.
Circ: Paid ‡2,000
Non-paid ‡500

15345 The Conservative News
919.5 W. Washtenaw St. Phone: (517)887-8775
PO Box 11099
Lansing, MI 48901
General interest newspaper which includes local and national news and coverage of art and sports. **Freq:** Monthly. **Print Method:** Letterpress. **Cols./Page:** 7. **Key Personnel:** Vera Watts, Editor; Linus Watts, Editor; Marsha Ann Morrow, Editor; Melvin C. Morrow II, Editor-in-Chief.
Circ: 13,000

15346 Journal of the Michigan Dental Association
Michigan Dental Association
230 N. Washington Ave., Ste. 208 Phone: (517)372-9070
Fax: (517)372-0008
Lansing, MI 48933
Free: (800)589-2632
Publisher E-mail: mda@michigandental.org

Journal of The Michigan Dental Association. **Founded:** 1919. **Freq:** 9/year. **Print Method:** Offset. **Trim Size:** 8 1/2 x 11. **Cols./Page:** 3. **Col. Width:** 13 picas. **Col. Depth:** 62 picas. **Key Personnel:** William Chase, DDS, Editor; David Foe, Managing Editor, dfoe@michigandental.org. **Subscription Rates:** $70.
Ad Rates: BW: $445 **Circ:** Paid 5,969
4C: $1,145 Non-paid 348

15347 Journal of Small Business
Small Business Association of Michigan
222 N. Washington Sq., Ste. 310 Phone: (517)482-8788
Fax: (517)482-4205
PO Box 16158
Lansing, MI 48901-6158
Free: (800)362-5461

Publication (tabloid) covering general small business news of the state and region including legislative issues. **Founded:** 1995. **Freq:** Bimonthly. **Print Method:** Sheetfed offset. **Trim Size:** 8.5 x 11. **Cols./Page:** 3 and 4. **Col. Depth:** 10 inches. **Key Personnel:** Dennis L. Larson, Director of Communications & Editor, dllarson@aol.com. **ISSN:** 1084-3639. **Available Online. URL:** sbam.org.
Ad Rates: BW: $935 **Circ:** Non-paid 9,000

15348 Lansing State Journal
120 E. Lenawee Phone: (517)377-1000
Lansing, MI 48919-0001 Fax: (517)377-1298

General newspaper. **Founded:** 1855. **Freq:** Mon.-Sun. (morn.). **Print Method:** Letterpress. **Cols./Page:** 6. **Col. Width:** 26 nonpareils. **Col. Depth:** 308 agate lines. **Key Personnel:** Zack Binkley, Editor; W. Curtis Riddle, Publisher; Ron Carpretia, Advertising Mgr. **Subscription Rates:** $175. R $175. **Remarks:** Accepts advertising. **URL:** http://www.lansinglife.com. **Feature Editors:** Jean Aikin, *Photo*, phone (517)377-1072; Chris Andrews, *Political*, phone (517)377-1054; Karen Douglas, *Fashion*, phone (517)377-1063; Janet Geissler, *Food*, phone (517)377-1065; Mike Hughes, *Drama, Entertainment, Movie, Music, Radio*, phone (517)377-1156; Norris Ingells, *Aviation, Travel*, phone (517)377-1155; Steve Klein, *Sports*, phone (517)377-1071; Elaine Kulhanek, *Metro*, phone (517)377-1053; Kathy Lavey, *Book, Family, Garden/Home, Lifestyle, Society, Women's*, phone (517)377-1249; Mark Nixon, *Editorials*, phone (517)377-1038; Chaz Osburn, *News*, phone (517)377-1017; Dennis Raymo, *TV*, phone (517)377-1073; Sheila Schimpf, *Religion*, phone (517)377-1050; Les Smith, *Financial/Business, Real Estate*, phone (517)377-1056.
Ad Rates: GLR: $2.99 **Circ:** Mon.-Sat. ★**69,951**
BW: $5,518.92 Sun. ★**91,388**
4C: $6,315.92
SAU: $41.81

15349 Media Spectrum
Michigan Association for Media in Education
6810 S. Cedar, Ste. 8 Phone: (517)699-1717
Lansing, MI 48911 Fax: (517)694-9303
Publication E-mail: bhbrooks@aol.com

Professional magazine for library media specialists in Michigan schools. **Founded:** 1974. **Freq:** 3/year. **Print Method:** Letterpress and offset. **Trim Size:** 8 1/2 x 11. **Cols./Page:** 3. **Col. Width:** 28 nonpareils. **Col. Depth:** 130 agate lines. **Key Personnel:** Peter Butts, Editor, phone (616)393-7530; Mary James, Editor, phone (616)261-6534, fax (616)261-6462; Ginger Sisson, phone (616)261-6450, fax (616)261-6501. **ISSN:** 0731-3675. **Subscription Rates:** $25; $30 other countries. **Remarks:** Accepts advertising. **URL:** http://www.mame.gen.mi.us.
Ad Rates: BW: $155 **Circ:** ‡1,500

15350 Michigan AFL-CIO News
Michigan State AFL-CIO
419 Washington Sq. S., Ste. 200 Phone: (517)487-5966
Fax: (517)487-5213
Lansing, MI 48933-2138
Tabloid reporting political and legislative news concerning Michigan labor leaders. **Founded:** Sept. 4, 1939. **Freq:** Monthly. **Print Method:** Offset. **Trim Size:** 11 1/2 x 15. **Cols./Page:** 4. **Col. Width:** 14 picas. **Col. Depth:** 84 picas. **Key Personnel:** Jon B. Ogar, Editor, jogar@voyager.net. **ISSN:** 0026-1998. **Subscription Rates:** $2.50. **Remarks:** Accepts advertising. **URL:** http://www.miaflcio.org. **Alt. Formats:** Microfilm; Microform.
Ad Rates: BW: $2,500 **Circ:** ‡30,000

15351 Michigan Banker Magazine
PO Box 12236 Phone: (517)332-7800
Lansing, MI 48901-2236 Fax: (517)332-7806

Magazine reporting banking news. Aimed exclusively at Michigan's commercial banking industry. **Subtitle:** Edited for Commercial Banks in Michigan. **Founded:** 1989. **Freq:** Monthly. **Print Method:** Sheet-fed offset. **Trim Size:** 8 1/2 x 11. **Cols./Page:** 3. **Col. Width:** 14 picas. **Col. Depth:** 10 inches. **Key Personnel:** Jerome H. O'Neil, Editor and Publisher, phone (517)382-7800; Mrs. Loy Gee, Sales Director; Pat Loesel, Production Mgr. **ISSN:** 0193-0257. **Subscription Rates:** $92.50. **Remarks:** Accepts advertising. **Formerly:** Michigan Banking and Business News (1989).
Ad Rates: BW: $595 **Circ:** Paid ‡650
4C: $1,095
PCI: $25

15352 Michigan Bar Journal
State Bar of Michigan
306 Townsend St. Phone: (517)372-9030
Lansing, MI 48933
Publisher E-mail: webmeister@michbar.org

Legal magazine. **Founded:** 1921. **Freq:** Monthly. **Print Method:** Web offset. **Trim Size:** 8 1/2 x 11. **Cols./Page:** 3. **Col. Width:** 28 nonpareils. **Col. Depth:** 136 agate lines. **Key Personnel:** Nancy F. Brown, Editor; Nichole Kelley, Editorial Assistant, nkelley@michbar.org. **ISSN:** 0164-3576. **Subscription Rates:** $45 individuals; $55 other countries. **Remarks:** Accepts advertising.
Ad Rates: BW: $790 **Circ:** ‡31,600
4C: $1,370

15353 Michigan Farm News
Michigan Farm Bureau
7373 W. Saginaw Hwy. Phone: (517)323-7000
PO Box 30960 Fax: (517)323-6541
Lansing, MI 48909-8460
Free: (800)292-2680
Publisher E-mail: mfbinfo@aol.com

Agribusiness publication for Michigan farmers. **Founded:** 1928. **Freq:** Semimonthly. **Print Method:** Web offset. **Trim Size:** 11 x 17. **Cols./Page:** 4. **Col. Width:** 2 3/8 inches. **Col. Depth:** 10 inches. **Key Personnel:** Sue Stuever Battel, Editor.
Ad Rates: BW: $1,900 **Circ:** Paid 44,565
4C: $2,300

15354 Michigan Florist
Michigan Floral Association
5815 Executive Dr., Ste B Phone: (517)394-2900
Lansing, MI 48911 Fax: (517)394-3011
Publication E-mail: rcrittenden@voyager.net

Magazine for retail florists, wholesalers and growers; covering products, industry services, floral arrangements, floral business, and related concerns. **Subtitle:** A publication of the Michigan Floral Association. **Founded:** July 1948. **Freq:** Bimonthly. **Print Method:** Offset. **Trim Size:** 8 1/2 x 11. **Cols./Page:** 3. **Col. Width:** 2 1/4 inches. **Col. Depth:** 10 inches. **Key Personnel:** Tracy Michael, Editor. **ISSN:** 0026-217X. **Subscription Rates:** $50 associate members. $5 single issue.
Ad Rates: BW: $470 **Circ:** Controlled ‡10,000
4C: $970

15355 Michigan Food News
Michigan Grocers Association
221 N. Walnut Phone: (517)372-6800
Lansing, MI 48933 Fax: (517)372-3002
Free: (800)947-6237

Magazine focusing on retail and wholesale grocery food industry. **Subtitle:** Michigan Food News. **Founded:** 1946. **Freq:** Monthly. **Print Method:** Sheet fed. **Trim Size:** 10 x 14. **Cols./Page:** 5. **Col. Width:** 17 nonpareils. **Col. Depth:** 224 agate lines. **Key Personnel:** Linda M. Gobler, Publisher; Kevin Gray, Editor; Cherie Smith, Advertising Mgr. **Subscription Rates:** $25 individuals; $4 single issue. **Remarks:** Accepts advertising.
Ad Rates: BW: $850 **Circ:** Controlled 9,000
4C: $1,500
PCI: $25

15356 Michigan History Magazine
Michigan Department of State
717 W. Allegan St. Phone: (517)373-3703
Lansing, MI 48918-1805 Fax: (517)373-0851
Free: (800)366-3703

Magazine on Michigan history. Includes special articles and regular features on all facets of Michigan's past. **Founded:** 1917. **Freq:** Bimonthly. **Print Method:** Web press. **Trim Size:** 8 1/2 x 11. **Key Personnel:** Roger L. Rosentreter, Editor, phone (517)373-3704; Diana Paiz Engle, Advertising Mgr., phone (517)335-2716; Joni Russell, Circ. Clerk. **ISSN:** 0026-2196. **Subscription Rates:** $12.95; $23.95 two years. **Remarks:** Advertising not accepted. **URL:** http://www.sos.state.mi-us/history/mag/mag.html.
Circ: 32,000

15357 Michigan Hospitals
Michigan Hospital Association
6215 W. St. Joseph Hwy. Phone: (517)323-3443
Lansing, MI 48917-4846 Fax: (517)323-0913

Trade magazine for Michigan hospital leaders and healthcare policy makers. **Founded:** 1965. **Freq:** Bimonthly. **Print Method:** Offset. **Trim Size:** 8 1/2 x 11. **Cols./Page:** 2 and 3. **Col. Width:** 4 7/8 and 3 inches. **Key Personnel:** Karel Juhl, Editor; Pat Horan, Advertising Mgr. **ISSN:** 0026-220X. **Subscription Rates:** $18; $65 other countries. **Remarks:** Accepts advertising.
Ad Rates: GLR: $.45 **Circ:** ‡1,750
BW: $400
4C: $1,300

15358 Michigan Lawyers Weekly
333 S. Washington St., Ste. 300 Phone: (517)374-6200
Lansing, MI 48933 Fax: (517)374-6222
Free: (800)678-5297
Publication E-mail: michlwkly@aol.com

Case summaries for the legal profession; includes all Michigan courts. **Founded:** 1986. **Freq:** Weekly. **Trim Size:** 10 x 15 3/4. **Cols./Page:** 4. **Col. Width:** 2 1/2 inches. **Col. Depth:** 16 inches. **Key Personnel:** Diane Smith, Publisher/Editor-in-Chief; Ed Wesoloski, Executive Opinion Editor; Lisa Archambeau, Circulation Mgr. **ISSN:** 0897-618X. **Subscription Rates:** $269 individuals. **Remarks:** Accepts advertising. **Online:** America Online, Inc. **Alt. Formats:** Diskette.
Ad Rates: BW: $1,420 **Circ:** Paid ‡4,700
4C: $1,990 Controlled ‡17,000

15359 Michigan Master Plumber and Mechanical Contractor
Michigan Plumbing and Mechanical Contractors Association (MPMCA)
400 N. Walnut St. Phone: (517)484-5500
Lansing, MI 48933 Fax: (517)484-5225
Free: (800)292-1044

Magazine for plumbing contractors and mechanical contractors. **Founded:** Feb. 1953. **Freq:** Monthly. **Print Method:** Offset. Uses mats. **Trim Size:** 8 1/2 x 11. **Cols./Page:** 3. **Col. Width:** 42 nonpareils. **Col. Depth:** 140 agate lines. **Key Personnel:** Cindy Hall-Maher, Editor and Publisher. **Remarks:** Accepts advertising.
Ad Rates: BW: $425 **Circ:** Controlled ‡3,100
4C: $990

15360 The Michigan Optometrist
Michigan Optometric Association
530 W. Ionia St., Ste. A Phone: (517)482-0616
Lansing, MI 48933-1062 Fax: (517)482-1611
Publisher E-mail: mioptoassn@aol.com

Professional magazine. **Founded:** Jan. 1, 1921. **Freq:** Monthly. **Print Method:** Offset. **Trim Size:** 8 1/2 x 11. **Cols./Page:** 2. **Col. Width:** 39 nonpareils. **Col. Depth:** 126 agate lines. **Key Personnel:** William D. Dansby, C.A.E., Editor; Linda A. Derose, Advertising Mgr. **ISSN:** 1071-1627. **Subscription Rates:** $15. **Remarks:** Accepts advertising.
Ad Rates: BW: $271 **Circ:** Paid ‡796
PCI: $16 Controlled ‡99

15361 Michigan Out-of-Doors
Michigan United Conservation Clubs
Box 30235 Phone: (517)371-1041
Lansing, MI 48909 Fax: (517)371-1505
Publisher E-mail: mucc@mucc.org

Magazine focusing on conservation, hunting, and fishing. **Founded:** Jan. 1947. **Freq:** Monthly. **Print Method:** Offset. **Trim Size:** 8 1/8 x 10 3/4. **Cols./Page:** 3. **Col. Width:** 27 nonpareils. **Col. Depth:** 196 agate lines. **Key Personnel:** Dennis Knickerbocker, Editor; Richard L. Jameson, Publisher; William Donahue, Advertising Mgr. **ISSN:** 0026-2382. **Subscription Rates:** $25; $2.50 single issue. **Remarks:** Advertising not accepted for partisan politics.
Ad Rates: GLR: $5.36 **Circ:** Paid 98,182
BW: $1,935 Non-paid 6,501
4C: $2,585
PCI: $75

15362 Michigan Overseas Veteran
Department of Michigan Veterans of Foreign Wars
Box 20036
Lansing, MI 48901
Publication E-mail: barry@mivfw.org
Publisher E-mail: webmaster@mivfw.org

Publication reporting on legislation and programs for veterans. **Subtitle:** MOV. **Founded:** Nov. 1923. **Freq:** 8/year. **Print Method:** Offset. **Trim Size:** 14 x 22 3/4. **Cols./Page:** 5. **Col. Width:** 20 nonpareils. **Col. Depth:** 294 agate lines. **Key Personnel:** Val Cemonceli, Contact. **ISSN:** 1067-0661. **Subscription Rates:** $4. **Remarks:** Advertising not accepted.
Circ: Paid ‡89,000
Controlled ‡250

15363 Michigan Pharmacist
Michigan Pharmacists Association
815 N. Washington Ave. Phone: (517)484-1466
Lansing, MI 48906 Fax: (517)484-4893
Publication E-mail: mpa1@worldnet.att.net

Regional professional magazine for hospital, independent, community and consultant pharmacists, pharmacy students and technicians, and pharmaceutical representatives, wholesalers and companies. **Founded:** 1963. **Freq:** Monthly. **Print Method:** Offset. **Trim Size:** 8 1/2 x 11. **Cols./Page:** 3 and 2. **Col. Width:** 28 and 42 nonpareils. **Col. Depth:** 140 agate lines. **Key Personnel:** Jennifer Pakkala, Managing Editor. **ISSN:** 1045-6481. **Subscription Rates:** $40. **Remarks:** Accepts advertising. **Formerly:** Journal Michigan Pharmacist.
Ad Rates: BW: $630 **Circ:** ‡3,900
4C: $600
PCI: $30

15364 Michigan Roads and Construction
535 N. Clippert, Ste. B Phone: (517)332-7600
PO Box 25007 Fax: (517)332-7336
Lansing, MI 48909-5007
Highways and public works magazine. **Founded:** 1905. **Freq:** Weekly (Thurs.). **Print Method:** Offset. **Trim Size:** 8 1/4 x 11 1/4. **Cols./Page:** 3 and 2. **Col. Depth:** 120 agate lines. **Key Personnel:** Bud Baker, Editor; John Lux, Editor. **Subscription Rates:** $35. **Remarks:** Accepts advertising.
Ad Rates: BW: $140 **Circ:** Paid ★1,043
Non-paid ★436

15365 Michigan Sportsman
Game & Fish Publications, Inc.
2250 Newmarket Pkwy., Ste. 110 Phone: (770)953-9222
PO Box 721 Fax: (770)933-9510
Marietta, GA 30061-0741
State-specific/regional sports magazine with an emphasis on hunting and fishing. **Freq:** Monthly. **Print Method:** Offset. **Trim Size:** 8 1/2 x 11. **Key Personnel:** Dennis Schmidt, Editor; Steven W. Vaughn, Publisher. **ISSN:** 0539-8908. **Subscription Rates:** $11.95; $18.95 two years; $27.95 three years.

15366 Service Quarterly
Service Station Dealers Association of Michigan, Inc.
200 N. Capitol, Ste. 420, L-30 Phone: (517)484-4096
Lansing, MI 48933-1314 Fax: (517)484-5705
Publisher E-mail: ssdami@sojourn.com

Magazine for service station dealers in Michigan. **Founded:** Jan. 1929. **Freq:** Quarterly. **Print Method:** Offset. **Trim Size:** 9 1/4 x 14. **Cols./Page:** 4. **Col. Width:** 2 1/8 inches. **Col. Depth:** 14 inches. **Key Personnel:** Terry Burns, Publisher. **ISSN:** 1043-7053. **Subscription Rates:** Free to qualified subscribers; $110. $10 single issue. **Remarks:** Accepts advertising. **Formerly:** Retail Gasoline Dealers News; SSDA-MI News.
Ad Rates: BW: $595 **Circ:** Non-paid 6,500
SAU: $145

15367 Shaw Annual
Pennsylvania State University Press
1034 Hickory St. Phone: (517)487-2087
Lansing, MI 48912-1711
Publisher E-mail: sgt3@psu.edu

Scholarly journal covering Shaw and Shaviana. **Freq:** Annual. **Key Personnel:** Fred Crawford, Editor. **ISSN:** 0741-5842. **Subscription Rates:** $35 individuals; $41 out of country. **Remarks:** Advertising not accepted.
Circ: (Not Reported)

15368 TRACKS MAGAZINE
Michigan United Conservation Clubs
2101 Wood St. Phone: (517)346-6493
PO Box 30235 Fax: (517)371-1505
Lansing, MI 48909
Free: (800)777-6720
Publisher E-mail: mucc@mucc.org

Wildlife magazine which discusses conservation issues (targeted at young audience). **Founded:** 1978. **Freq:** Monthly (Sept.-May). **Print Method:** Web offset. **Trim Size:** 9 x 11 1/2. **Key Personnel:** Christie Bleck, Editor. **ISSN:** 0238-8810. **Subscription Rates:** $2 (rates for 10 or more per address); $5 individuals; $1.50 half-year (rates for 10 or more per address). **Remarks:** Advertising not accepted.
Circ: 63,000

15369 way station magazine
1319 S. Logan St. Phone: (517)374-7735
Lansing, MI 48910
Publication E-mail: waystationmag@juno.com

Literary journal covering poetry, fiction and art. **Founded:** 1989. **Freq:** Quarterly. **Print Method:** Offset. **Trim Size:** 8 1/2 x 11. **Cols./Page:** 4. **Key Personnel:** Randy Glumm, Editor and Publisher. **Subscription Rates:** $18 individuals; $6 single issue. **Remarks:** Accepts advertising.
Ad Rates: BW: $275 **Circ:** Combined 1,040

15370 YES Quarterly
Young Entomologists' Society, Inc.
Minibeast Zooseum & Educational Ctr. Phone: (517)886-0630
6907 W. Grand River Ave. Fax: (517)886-0630
Lansing, MI 48906-9131
Publisher E-mail: yesbugs@aol.com

Professional journal covering insects, spiders, and other invertebrates. **Freq:** Quarterly. **Trim Size:** 5 1/2 x 8 1/2. **Cols./Page:** 1. **Key Personnel:** Gary A. Dunn, Education Dir.; Deborah Thirkhill, Editor. **ISSN:** 0884-6677. **Subscription Rates:** $45 individuals; $2 single issue. **Remarks:** Accepts advertising.
Ad Rates: BW: $50 **Circ:** Paid 700

15371 WHZZ-FM - 101.7
PO Box 25008 Phone: (517)393-1320
Lansing, MI 48909-5008 Fax: (517)393-0882

Format: Contemporary Hit Radio (CHR). **Owner:** MacDonald Broadcasting Co., at above address. **Founded:** 1947. **Formerly:** WLYY-FM (1991); WILS-FM. **Operating Hours:** Continuous. **ADI:** Lansing (Ann Arbor), MI. **Key Personnel:** Ken MacDonald, General Mgr. **Wattage:** 3000.

15372 WILS-AM - 1320
PO Box 25008 Phone: (517)393-1320
Lansing, MI 48909-5008 Fax: (517)393-0882

Format: Adult Contemporary. **Networks:** Satellite Music Network. **Owner:** MacDonald Broadcasting, at above address. **Founded:** 1947. **Operating Hours:** Continuous. **ADI:** Lansing (Ann Arbor), MI. **Key Personnel:** Ken MacDonald, General Mgr. **Wattage:** 5000.

15373 WILX-TV - 10
P.O. Box 30380 Phone: (517)393-0110
Lansing, MI 48909 Fax: (517)393-8555

Format: Commercial TV. **Networks:** NBC. **Owner:** Brissett TV of Lansing, Inc., at above address. **Founded:** 1959. **Operating Hours:** Continuous. **Key Personnel:** Chris Cornelius, President/Gen. Manager.

15374 WJIM-AM - 1240
3420 Pine Tree Rd. Phone: (517)394-7272
Lansing, MI 48911 Fax: (517)394-3391

Format: News; Talk. **Simulcasts:** WFMK-FM, WITL-FM. **Networks:** NBC. **Founded:** 1934. **Operating Hours:** Continuous. **Key Personnel:** Rod Krol, VP/General Mgr.; Jack Robbins, Program Dir.; Mike Gordon, Dir. of Sales. **Local Programs:** *Chris Holman Morning Show* 6:00 am - 9:00 am Monday-Friday, Scott Moore, Producer; *Phil Arthur Hultz* 5:00 pm - 9:00 pm Monday-Friday, Phil Arthurhultz, Host. **Wattage:** 1000. **Ad Rates:** $25-50 for 60 seconds. Combined advertising rates available with WJIM-FM, WMMQ-FM, WVFN-AM. **URL:** http://www.wjim.com.

15375 WJIM-FM - 97.5
3420 Pine Tree Rd. Phone: (517)394-7272
Lansing, MI 48911 Fax: (517)394-3391

Format: Oldies. **Simulcasts:** WVFN-AM. **Networks:** ABC. **Founded:** 1960. **Operating Hours:** Continuous. **Key Personnel:** Mike Gordon, Dir. of Sales; Tim Kiesling, Program Dir. **Wattage:** 45,000. **Ad Rates:** $75-100 for 60 seconds. Combined advertising rates available with WJIM-AM, WITL-FM, WMMQ-FM.

15376 WLNS-TV - 6
2820 E. Saginaw Phone: (517)372-8282
Lansing, MI 48912 Fax: (517)374-7610

Format: Commercial TV. **Networks:** CBS. **Owner:** Young Broadcasting Inc., 3 E. 54th St., New York, NY 10022. **Founded:** 1950. **ADI:** Lansing (Ann Arbor), MI. **Key Personnel:** Grant A. Santimore, General Mgr.

15377 WLNZ-FM - 89.7
PO Box 40010 Phone: (517)483-1710
Lansing, MI 48901-7210 Fax: (517)483-9781
E-mail: wlnz@alpha.lansing.cc.mi.us

Format: Jazz; Blues. **Owner:** Lansing Community College, at above address. **Former name:** WLCC-FM (1994). **Operating Hours:** 6 a.m.-2 a.m. **ADI:** Lansing (Ann Arbor), MI. **Key Personnel:** Dave Downing, Station Mgr.; Lyn Peraino, Program Dir.; Dennis Edwards, Music Dir. **Wattage:** 200. **Ad Rates:** Noncommercial.

15378 WMMQ-FM - 94.9
3420 Pine Tree Phone: (517)393-1010
Lansing, MI 48911 Fax: (517)394-3391
E-mail: wmmq.com

Format: Classic Rock. **Owner:** Liggett Broadcast, Inc., at above address. **Founded:** 1963. **Formerly:** WVIC-FM. **Operating Hours:** Continuous. **Key Personnel:** Rod Krol, General Mgr., phone (517)394-7272; Mark Stevens, Program Dir.; Mike Gordon, Dir. of Sales. **Wattage:** 50,000. **Ad Rates:** $75-125 for 30 seconds. Combined advertising rates available with WJIM-AM/FM, WVFN-AM, WITL-FM, WFMK-FM.

WQHH-FM - See De Witt

15379 WSYM-TV - 47
600 W. St. Joseph St., Ste. 47 Phone: (517)484-7747
Lansing, MI 48933 Fax: (517)484-3144
E-mail: kenney@journalbroadcastgrove.com

Format: Commercial TV. **Networks:** Fox. **Owner:** Journal Broadcast Group, Inc., 720 E. Capitol Dr., Milwaukee, WI, (414)967-9611. **Founded:** 1982. **Formerly:** WFSL-TV (1986). **Operating Hours:** 8 a.m.-5 p.m. **ADI:** Lansing (Ann Arbor), MI. **Key Personnel:** Judy Kenney, Contact, kenney@journalbroadcastgroup.com; Bill Shipley, Operations Mgr., shipley@journalbroadcastgroup.com; Kip Bohne, Marketing Mgr., bohne@journalbroadcastgroup.com; Gary Baxter, General Sales Mgr., fax (517)484-9750, baxter@journalbroadcastgroup.com; Bill Tessman, Chief Engineer, tessman@journalbroadcastgroup.com; Jami Anderson, Contact, anderson@journalbroadcastgroup.com. **Local Programs:** *Fox 47 News at 10* 10:00 pm Mon.-Sun.

15380 WVFN-AM - 730
3420 Pine Tree Phone: (517)394-7272
Lansing, MI 48911 Fax: (517)394-3391

Format: Sports; Talk. **Owner:** Liggett Broadcast, Inc., at above address. **Founded:** 1964. **Formerly:** WVIC-AM. **Operating Hours:** Continuous. **Key Personnel:** Rod Krol, VP/General Mgr., phone (517)394-7272, fax (517)394-3391; Mike Gordon, Dir. of Sales; Jack Robbins, Program Dir. **Local Programs:** *Staudt on Sports* 12:00 - 1:00 pm Monday-Friday, Tim Staudt, Host; *Sports Guys* 5:00 pm - 6:00 pm Monday-Friday. **Wattage:** 500 day; 50 night. **Ad Rates:** $10-25 for 60 seconds. Combined advertising rates available with WMMQ-FM, WFMK-FM, WJIM-AM, WJIM-FM, WITL-FM.

15381 WXLA-AM - 1180
101 Northcrest Rd., Ste. 4 Phone: (517)484-9600
Lansing, MI 48906-1262 Fax: (517)484-9699

Format: Oldies; Urban Contemporary. **Networks:** Independent. **Owner:** Mid Michigan Diamond Broadcasters, at above address. **Founded:** 1977. **Operating Hours:** Sunrise-sunset. **ADI:** Lansing (Ann Arbor), MI. **Key Personnel:** Helena Dubose, General Mgr. **Wattage:** 1000. **Ad Rates:** $21-26 per unit.

LAPEER

15382 Lapeer County Buyer's Guide
415 Nepessing Phone: (810)664-1877
Lapeer, MI 48446 Fax: (810)664-4320
Free: (800)462-9966
Publication E-mail: boothpub@greatlakes.net

Shopping guide. **Subtitle:** Lapeer Buyer's Guide. **Founded:** 1975. **Freq:** Weekly (Mon.). **Print Method:** Offset. **Trim Size:** 16 x 22 1/2. **Cols./Page:** 6. **Col. Width:** 19 nonpareils. **Col. Depth:** 210 agate lines. **Key Personnel:** Doug Finkbeiner, Publisher; Rick Henry, Pres./Gen. Mgr.; Teressa Robbins, Sales Mgr. **Subscription Rates:** Free; $22 (mail). **Remarks:** Accepts advertising.
Ad Rates: BW: $630 **Circ:** Free 30,165
4C: $567
PCI: $6.50

15383 Lapeer County Press
1521 Imlay City Rd. Phone: (810)664-0811
Lapeer, MI 48446 Fax: (810)664-5852
Publication E-mail: co-press@tir.com

County newspaper. **Founded:** 1839. **Freq:** Semiweekly (Wed. and Sun.). **Print Method:** Offset. **Cols./Page:** 6. **Col. Width:** 25 nonpareils. **Col. Depth:** 300 agate lines. **Key Personnel:** Mark Haney, Editor; Ernest Slade, Publisher; Nancy Ransom, Advertising Mgr. **Subscription Rates:** $34.50 individuals. **Remarks:** Accepts advertising.
Ad Rates: GLR: $.85 **Circ:** Wed. 15,542
BW: $2,087.22 Sun. 16,169
4C: $2,587.22
SAU: $16.18

15384 The Thumb Blanket
1521 Imlay City Rd. Phone: (810)664-0811
Lapeer, MI 48446 Fax: (810)664-5852
Free: (800)269-9918
Publisher E-mail: tblanket@auci.net

Shopper. **Founded:** Jan. 15, 1980. **Freq:** Weekly (Sun.) Sun. **Print Method:** Offset. **Trim Size:** 11 1/4 x 16. **Cols./Page:** 6. **Col. Width:** 21 nonpareils. **Col. Depth:** 210 agate lines. **Key Personnel:** Barbara Buchholz, Office Mgr.; John Guza, General Mgr. **Subscription Rates:** $25 by mail. **Remarks:** Accepts advertising.
Ad Rates: BW: $540 **Circ:** Non-paid 18,650
4C: $725
PCI: $6.20

15385 WLSP-AM - 1530
286 W. Nepessing St. Phone: (810)664-8555
Lapeer, MI 48446 Fax: (810)664-8990

Format: Sports; Talk. **Networks:** ESPN Radio; Westwood One Radio. **Founded:** 1962. **Formerly:** WDEY-AM (1990); WWGZ-AM (1994). **Operating Hours:** Sunrise-sunset. **ADI:** Detroit, MI. **Key Personnel:** Don Weber, General Mgr.; Jay Alexander, Program Dir. **Local Programs:** *High School Football Game of the Week*, Jay Alexander, Mailing contact; *Morning Sports Page Show*, Karl Lawson, Mailing contact. **Wattage:** 5000. **Ad Rates:** $12 for 30 seconds; $15 for 60 seconds.

15386 WMPC-AM - 1230
1800 N. Lapeer Rd. Phone: (810)664-6211
Lapeer, MI 48446 Fax: (810)664-5361
E-mail: wmpc@tir.com

Format: Religious. **Networks:** SkyLight Satellite; AP. **Owner:** Calvary Bible Church, 923 S. Main, Lapeer, MI 48446, (810)664-2838. **Founded:** 1926. **Operating Hours:** Continuous; 55% network, 45% local. **Key Personnel:** Arnold L. Bracy, General Mgr., phone (810)664-2838, fax (810)664-5361; Judy McDonald, Office Mgr., phone (810)664-6211, fax (810)664-5361; Bill Hetchler, Chief Operator, phone (810)664-6211, fax (810)664-5261, hetchler@tir.com. **Local Programs:** *Off The Bookshelf* 10:05 am Monday-Friday, Bill Hetchler, Chief Oper. **Wattage:** 1000. **Ad Rates:** Noncommercial. **URL:** http://www.wmpc.org.

15387 WRXF-FM - 103.1
286 W. Nepessing St. Phone: (810)664-8555
Lapeer, MI 48446 Fax: (810)664-8990

Format: Classic Rock. **Simulcasts:** WLSP. **Networks:** Independent; Westwood One Radio. **Founded:** 1968. **Formerly:** WDEY-FM (1990); WWGZ-FM (1998). **Operating Hours:** Continuous. **ADI:** Detroit, MI. **Key Personnel:** Don Weber, General Mgr.; Jay Alexander, Operations Mgr.; Tony LaBrie, Program Dir., info@wings103.com. **Local Programs:** *Attitude Adjustment*, Tony Labrie, Mailing contact; *Request Heaven*, Zach Powers, Mailing contact; *Sunday Night Session*, Tony Labrie, Mailing contact. **Wattage:** 3000. **Ad Rates:** $20 for 30 seconds; $26 for 60 seconds.

LELAND

15388 Leelanau Enterprise & Tribune
Leelanau Publishing Co., Inc.
112 Chandler St. Phone: (616)256-9827
Leland, MI 49654
Local newspaper. **Founded:** Oct. 1877. **Freq:** Weekly (Thurs.). **Print Method:** Offset. **Cols./Page:** 5. **Col. Width:** 11.6 picas. **Col. Depth:** 16 inches. **Key Personnel:** R.C. Kerr, Editor and Publisher; Kath Bierer, Display Advt.; Bill O'Brien, News Editor; Dick Kerr, Editor; W. J. O'Brien, Managing Editor. **USPS:** 309-000. **Subscription Rates:** $17 individuals; $33 out of county. **Remarks:** Accepts advertising.
Ad Rates: BW: $500 **Circ: 8,005**
PCI: $6.75

LESLIE

15389 Leslie Local Independent
S. & G. Publications
109 Carney Phone: (517)589-8228
Box 617 Fax: (517)589-8526
Leslie, MI 49251-0617
Community newspaper. **Founded:** 1869. **Freq:** Weekly (Thurs.). **Print Method:** Offset. **Cols./Page:** 6. **Col. Width:** 16 nonpareils. **Col. Depth:** 238 agate lines. **Key Personnel:** Larry Hook, Jr., Editor; Joan Hill, General Mgr. **Subscription Rates:** $12; $14 out of state.
Ad Rates: BW: $283.50 **Circ:** Paid ‡1,600
SAU: $6.48 Free ‡7,000
PCI: $5.24

LINDEN

15390 Michigan ComputerUser Magazine
Prime Time Press
500 Hickory Phone: (810)735-9720
PO Box 597 Fax: (810)735-9720
Linden, MI 48451
News for business computer users in Michigan. **Subtitle:** Metro Detroit's Computer-Related Buying Resource. **Founded:** Mar. 1992. **Freq:** Monthly. **Print Method:** Newsprint web. **Trim Size:** 10 x 14 max image. **Cols./Page:** 4. **Col. Width:** 2 1/4 inches. **Col. Depth:** 14 inches. **Key Personnel:** Robert Gramer, Editor and Publisher. **ISSN:** 1087-481X. **Subscription Rates:** $12 third class; Free to qualified subscribers. **Remarks:** Accepts advertising. **URL:** http://www.michcu.com.
Ad Rates: BW: $1,406 **Circ:** Controlled ‡65,000
4C: $1,856

LIVONIA

15391 Audecibel
International Hearing Society
16880 Middlebelt Rd., Ste. 4 Phone: (734)522-7200
Livonia, MI 48154 Fax: (734)522-0200

Magazine publishing technical articles and product announcements on hearing aids and hearing. **Subtitle:** Official Journal of the International Hearing Society. **Founded:** Oct. 1952. **Freq:** Quarterly. **Print Method:** Offset. **Trim Size:** 8 1/4 x 11. **Cols./Page:** 3. **Col. Width:** 28 nonpareils. **Col. Depth:** 133 agate lines. **Key Personnel:** Cindy J. Helms, Editor. **ISSN:** 0004-7473. **Subscription Rates:** $35 U.S.; $45 elsewhere. **Alt. Formats:** Microform.
Ad Rates: BW: $1,050 **Circ:** Controlled ‡3,025
4C: $1,640
PCI: $80

Canton Observer - See Canton

15392 Ceramic Arts & Crafts
Scott Publications
30595 Eight Mile Rd. Phone: (810)477-6650
Livonia, MI 48152-1798 Fax: (810)447-6795
Free: (800)458-8237
Publisher E-mail: 104137.1254@compuserve.com

Magazine for the hobby ceramic industry; includes color photos and step-by-step instructions to complete projects. **Subtitle:** The Bible of the Ceramic Hobbyists Since 1955. **Founded:** 1955. **Freq:** Monthly. **Print Method:** Offset. **Trim Size:** 5 1/2 x 8 1/2. **Cols./Page:** 2. **Col. Width:** 13.5 picas. **Col. Depth:** 8 3/4 inches. **Key Personnel:** Bill Thompson, Editor; Robert H. Keessen, Publisher; Shannon Colby, Advertising Mgr.; Jeanette Foxe, Distribution Mgr. **ISSN:** 0009-0190. **Subscription Rates:** $23.50 individuals; $30.90 out of country. **Remarks:** Accepts advertising.
Ad Rates: BW: $675 **Circ:** (Not Reported)
4C: $1,330

15393 Contemporary Doll Collector (Magazine)
Scott Publications
30595 8 Mile Rd. Phone: (248)477-6650
Livonia, MI 48152-1798 Fax: (248)477-6795
Free: (800)458-8237
Publisher E-mail: 104137.1254@compuserve.com

Magazine featuring contemporary doll art. **Subtitle:** The Only Magazine Devoted to Contemporary Doll Art. **Founded:** 1990. **Freq:** Bimonthly. **Print Method:** Offset. **Trim Size:** 8 1/2 x 11. **Cols./Page:** 3. **Col. Width:** 2 1/4 inches. **Col. Depth:** 9 3/4 inches. **Key Personnel:** Robert Keessen, Publisher. **ISSN:** 1052-486X. **Subscription Rates:** $19.90; $4.95 single issue. **Remarks:** Accepts advertising. **Formerly:** Contemporary Doll Magazine.
Ad Rates: BW: $1,040 **Circ:** ‡49,000
4C: $1,845

15394 Doll Crafter
Scott Publications
30595 8 Mile Rd. Phone: (248)477-6650
Livonia, MI 48152-1798 Fax: (248)477-6795
Free: (800)458-8237
Publisher E-mail: 104137.1254@compuserve.com

Dollcrafting magazine focusing on porcelain dollmaking with emphasis on reproductions. **Founded:** 1983. **Freq:** 12/year. **Print Method:** Offset. **Trim Size:** 8 1/2 x 11. **Cols./Page:** 3. **Col. Width:** 13.5 picas. **Col. Depth:** 9 3/4 inches. **Key Personnel:** Barbara Campbell, Editor; Robert H. Keessen, Publisher; Shannon Colby, Advertising Mgr.; Jeanette Foxe, Distributor Mgr. **ISSN:** 0746-9624. **Subscription Rates:** $38.80 individuals. **Remarks:** Accepts advertising.
Ad Rates: BW: $1,510 **Circ:** ‡94,000
4C: $2,680

15395 Dollar Saver
33523 8 Mile Rd., No. C Phone: (810)477-8981
Livonia, MI 48152-4104 Fax: (313)476-2793

Shopper. **Subtitle:** Your Weekly Want Ad Newspaper.

Farmington Observer & Eccentric - See Farmington

Garden City Observer - See Garden City

15396 Livonia Observer
Observer & Eccentric Newspapers
36251 Schoolcraft Rd. Phone: (313)591-2300
Livonia, MI 48150-1216 Fax: (313)953-2232

Community newspaper. **Founded:** 1942. **Freq:** Semiweekly (Mon. and Thurs.). **Print Method:** Offset. **Cols./Page:** 9. **Col. Width:** 17 nonpareils. **Col. Depth:** 301 agate lines. **Key Personnel:** Richard Aginian, Publisher. **Subscription Rates:** $23. **Remarks:** Accepts advertising.
Ad Rates: GLR: $2.62 **Circ:** Paid 19,554
Non-paid 2,722

Plymouth Observer - See Plymouth

Redford Observer - See Redford

Rochester Observer - See Rochester

Southfield Eccentric - See Southfield

Troy Observer - See Troy

West Bloomfield Eccentric - See West Bloomfield

Westland Observer - See Westland

15397 MetroVision of Livonia, Inc.
Box CN3305 Phone: (313)422-2810
Livonia, MI 48151 Fax: (313)422-2239

Founded: 1984. **Cities Served:** Wayne County, MI.

15398 WLQV-AM - 1500
29200 Vassar Dr., Ste. 650 Phone: (810)477-4600
Livonia, MI 48152 Fax: (810)477-6911

Format: Religious. **Networks:** International Broadcasting; USA Radio; Talknet. **Founded:** 1925. **Operating Hours:** Continuous. **ADI:** Detroit, MI. **Key Personnel:** Jon Yinger, CEO/Gen. Mgr.; Mark Ennis, Operations Mgr. **Wattage:** 50,000 day; 5000 night.

LOWELL

15399 Buyers' Guide
Buyer's Guide
202 W. Main St., No. 247 Phone: (616)897-9555
Lowell, MI 49331-1608 Fax: (616)728-7192

Shopper. **Founded:** 1972. **Freq:** Weekly (Thurs.). **Print Method:** Offset. **Cols./Page:** 6. **Col. Width:** 20 nonpareils. **Col. Depth:** 224 agate lines. **Key Personnel:** Dale A. Bush, Publisher. **Remarks:** Accepts advertising.
Ad Rates: GLR: $5.55 **Circ:** Free ‡20,000
BW: $459.35
PCI: $5.55

15400 Lowell Ledger
PO Box 128 Phone: (616)897-9261
Lowell, MI 49331 Fax: (616)897-4809

Community newspaper. **Freq:** Weekly (Wed.). **Cols./Page:** 6. **Col. Width:** 9 1/2 picas. **Col. Depth:** 16 inches. **Key Personnel:** Roger K. Brown, Editor and Publisher.
Circ: 2,200

15401 Lowell Cable TV
127 N. Broadway Phone: (616)897-8405
PO Box 229 Fax: (616)897-4082
Lowell, MI 49331-0229
E-mail: lowcable@gateway.net

Owner: Lowell Light and Power Co., at above address. **Founded:** 1982. **Key Personnel:** Ron Holcomb, General Mgr.; Chris Simmons, Customer Rep.; Tom Richards, Dir. Cable Services, phone (616)897-8477, fax (616)897-8449. **Cities Served:** Lowell, MI: subscribing households 2,290; 49 channels; 1 community access channel; 168 hours per week community access programming.

LUDINGTON

15402 Ludington Daily News
202 N. Rath St. Phone: (616)845-5181
PO Box 340 Fax: (616)843-4011
Ludington, MI 49431-1663
Free: (800)748-0407

General newspaper. **Founded:** 1869. **Freq:** Daily (eve.) and Sat. (morn.). **Print Method:** Offset. **Cols./Page:** 6. **Col. Width:** 24 nonpareils. **Col. Depth:** 301 agate lines. **Key Personnel:** Steve Beqnoche, Editor; David R. Jackson, Publisher; James Frost, Advertising Mgr. **Subscription Rates:** $.50.
Ad Rates: BW: $2,913.12 **Circ:** Mon.-Sat. ★**8,638**
4C: $3,555.12
SAU: $23.12

15403 WKLA-AM - 1450
5941 W. U.S. 10 Phone: (616)843-3438
Ludington, MI 49431-2447 Fax: (616)843-1886

Format: Middle-of-the-Road (MOR). **Networks:** ABC. **Owner:** Roger K. Baerwolf, at above address. **Founded:** 1944. **Operating Hours:** Continuous. **Key Personnel:** Lynn Baerwolf, Business Mgr.; Ray Cummins, News Dir.; Mike Baerwolf, Chief Engineer. **Wattage:** 1000. **Ad Rates:** $8-17 for 30 seconds; $10-22 for 60 seconds.

15404 WKLA-FM - 106.3
5941 W. U.S. 10 Phone: (616)843-3438
Ludington, MI 49431-2447 Fax: (616)843-1886

Format: Adult Contemporary. **Networks:** ABC. **Owner:** Roger K. Baerwolf, at above address. **Founded:** 1971. **Operating Hours:** Continuous. **ADI:** Traverse City-Cadillac, MI. **Key Personnel:** Lynn Baerwolf, Business Mgr.; Mike Baerwolf, Chief Engineer; Jason Wilder, Production Mgr.; Ray Cummins, News Dir. **Local Programs:** *Birthday Book*; *Oldies Brunch.* **Wattage:** 6000. **Ad Rates:** $11-25 for 30 seconds; $14-32 for 60 seconds. Combined advertising rates available with WKLA-AM: $6.60-$12 for 30 seconds, $8.25-$15 for 60 seconds.

MACKINAC ISLAND

15405 The Mackinac Island Town Crier
Maurer Publishing Co.
359 Reagon St. Phone: (906)643-9150
PO Box 277 Fax: (906)643-9122
St. Ignace, MI 49781
Community newspaper. **Subtitle:** A Weekly Newspaper Serving the Makinac Island Community. **Founded:** 1953. **Freq:** Weekly (Sat.). **Print Method:** Offset. **Trim Size:** 11 1/2 x 17. **Cols./Page:** 5. **Col. Width:** 12 picas. **Col. Depth:** 16 inches. **Key Personnel:** Wesley H. Maurer, Jr., Editor and Publisher. **Subscription Rates:** $16.50 individuals.
Ad Rates: GLR: $.40 **Circ:** ‡3,600
BW: $440
PCI: $5.50

MADISON HEIGHTS

15406 Better Investing
National Association of Investors Corp.
711 West Thirteen Mile Rd. Phone: (810)583-6242
Madison Heights, MI 48071 Fax: (810)583-4880

Magazine focusing on investing in long-term common stock. **Founded:** 1951. **Freq:** Monthly. **Print Method:** Web offset. **Trim Size:** 8 1/4 x 10 7/8. **Cols./Page:** 3. **Col. Width:** 27 nonpareils. **Col. Depth:** 138 agate lines. **Key Personnel:** Donald E. Danko, Editor; Martha F. Stephens, Advertising Mgr. **Subscription Rates:** $24 individuals. **Remarks:** Accepts advertising. **URL:** http://www.better-investing.org.
Ad Rates: GLR: $18 **Circ:** Paid 450,000
BW: $6,645 Non-paid ‡10,000
4C: $13,350
PCI: $252

15407 The County Line
Italian Tribune
1415 12 Mile Rd. Phone: (810)541-6744
Madison Heights, MI 48071 Fax: (810)541-6890

Newspaper serving Oakland and Macomb counties, Michigan. **Founded:** 1988. **Freq:** Biweekly. **Print Method:** Offset. **Trim Size:** 10 x 13 1/4. **Cols./Page:** 6. **Col. Width:** 1.5 picas. **Col. Depth:** 13 inches. **Key Personnel:** Edward M. Baker, Publisher; Dr. Richard E. Klein, Publisher; Marlene Baker, Managing Editor.
Ad Rates: GLR: $9 **Circ:** Free 10,000
BW: $729

MANCHESTER

15408 Manchester Enterprise
109 E. Main Phone: (313)428-8173
PO Box 37
Manchester, MI 48158
Community newspaper. **Founded:** 1867. **Freq:** Weekly (Thurs.). **Print Method:** Offset. **Cols./Page:** 5. **Col. Width:** 23 nonpareils. **Col. Depth:** 224 agate lines. **Key Personnel:** Teresa Benedict, Editor. **USPS:** 327-460. **Subscription Rates:** $20 individuals; $25 out of area. **Remarks:** Accepts advertising.
Ad Rates: GLR: $.50 **Circ:** ‡1,800
BW: $275
4C: $475
SAU: $6.25
PCI: $3.50

MANISTEE

15409 Manistee News Advocate
The Pioneer Group
75 Maple St. Phone: (616)723-3592
PO Box 317 Fax: (616)723-4733
Manistee, MI 49660
Local newspaper. **Founded:** 1883. **Freq:** Mon.-Sat. **Print Method:** Web offset. **Trim Size:** 6 x 21 1/2. **Cols./Page:** 8. **Col. Width:** 25 nonpareils. **Col. Depth:** 294 agate lines. **Key Personnel:** Ken Grabowski, Managing Editor; Terry Fitzwater, Publisher; Marilyn Barker, Advertising Mgr. **Subscription Rates:** $84 individuals; $0.50 single issue. **Remarks:** Accepts advertising.
Ad Rates: BW: $838.50 **Circ:** ‡5,898
4C: $1,238.50
SAU: $8.50

15410 West Shore Shoppers Guide
The Pioneer Group
75 Maple St. Phone: (616)723-3592
PO Box 317 Fax: (616)723-4733
Manistee, MI 49660
Shopper. **Founded:** 1972. **Freq:** Weekly (Mon.). **Print Method:** Offset. **Trim Size:** 12 x 13. **Cols./Page:** 6. **Col. Width:** 13 nonpareils. **Col. Depth:** 78 agate lines. **Remarks:** Accepts advertising.
Ad Rates: SAU: $8.50 **Circ:** Free 17,700

15411 WCMW-TV - 21
c/o WCMU-TV Phone: (517)774-3105
Central Michigan University Fax: (517)774-4427
3965 E. Broomfield
Mount Pleasant, MI 48859

Format: Public TV. **Networks:** Public Broadcasting Service (PBS). **Owner:** Central Michigan University, at above address. **Founded:** 1984. **Operating Hours:** 6 a.m.-midnight; 90% network, 10% local. **ADI:** Traverse City-Cadillac, MI. **Key Personnel:** Monte Higgins, Station Mgr.; Rick Schudiske, Program Mgr.; Linda Hyde, Contact. **Ad Rates:** Noncommercial.

15412 WMTE-FM - 97.7
350 River St. Phone: (616)723-9906
Manistee, MI 49660-0190 Fax: (616)723-9908

Format: Album-Oriented Rock (AOR); Classic Rock. **Networks:** NBC; Mutual Broadcasting System; Westwood One Radio. **Formerly:** WRRK-FM. **Operating Hours:** 5 a.m.-1 a.m. **Key Personnel:** Laurie Foster, General Mgr.; Suzanne Stevens, Sales Mgr.; Bernie Schroeder, News Dir. **Wattage:** 3000. **Ad Rates:** $4-8 for 30 seconds; $5-9 for 60 seconds.

MANISTIQUE

15413 Pioneer-Tribune
212 Walnut St. Phone: (906)341-5200
Manistique, MI 49854
Publication E-mail: pioneer@up.net

Community newspaper. **Founded:** 1880. **Freq:** Weekly (Thurs.). **Print Method:** Offset. **Cols./Page:** 8. **Col. Depth:** 300 agate lines. **Key Personnel:** Lisa A. Demers, Publisher. **Subscription Rates:** $20 individuals; $25 out of area. **Remarks:** Accepts advertising.
Ad Rates: GLR: $3.50 **Circ:** 4,000
BW: $350

15414 WTIQ-AM - 1490
1501 Deer St. Phone: (906)341-8444
PO Box 220 Fax: (906)341-6222
Manistique, MI 49854
Free: (800)947-9266
E-mail: wtiq@upmail.com

Format: Oldies. **Networks:** ABC. **Owner:** Great Lakes Radio, Inc., 101 Huron Court, Negaunee, MI 49866, (906)228-9700, Fax: (906)228-9717. **Founded:** 1964. **Operating Hours:** Continuous. **Key Personnel:** Dick Ketcik, Sports Dir.; Annette Cox, Traffic/Billing Mgr., hamster@iceware.com; Todd Noordyk, Pres./General Mgr., tnoordyk@iceware.com; Paul Olson, News Dir. **Local Programs:** *Community Focus* 12:30 p.m. Tues. and Thurs. **Wattage:** 1000. **Ad Rates:** $4-7.50 for 30 seconds; $5-9 for 60 seconds. Combined advertising rates available with WCMM-FM, WGLC-FM, WCHT-AM.

MARCELLUS

15415 Marcellus News
PO Box 277 Phone: (616)646-2101
Marcellus, MI 49067
Community newspaper. **Freq:** Weekly (Thurs.). **Cols./Page:** 8. **Col. Width:** 9.5 picas. **Col. Depth:** 21 inches. **Key Personnel:** Donald D. Moormann, Editor and Publisher.
Circ: 1,400

MARLETTE

15416 Leader
Box 338 Phone: (517)635-2435
Marlette, MI 48453 Fax: (517)635-3769

Local newspaper. **Founded:** 1877. **Freq:** Weekly (Wed.). **Print Method:** Offset. **Cols./Page:** 6. **Col. Width:** 24 nonpareils. **Col. Depth:** 301 agate lines. **Key Personnel:** John Frazier, Editor; H. Allan Wamsley, Publisher. **Subscription Rates:** $10 individuals. **Remarks:** Accepts advertising.
Ad Rates: SAU: $6.50 **Circ:** ‡2,000

MARQUETTE

15417 Action Shopper
1010 W. Washington Phone: (906)228-8920
Marquette, MI 49855 Fax: (906)228-5777

Community newspaper. **Founded:** May 16, 1972. **Freq:** Weekly (Wed.). **Print Method:** Offset. **Trim Size:** 11 1/4 x 17. **Cols./Page:** 7. **Col. Width:** 8 picas. **Col. Depth:** 223 agate lines. **Key Personnel:** Richard Havican, General Mgr. **Subscription Rates:** Free.
Ad Rates: GLR: $9.35 **Circ:** Free ‡30,000
BW: $812.25
4C: $1,037.25
PCI: $9.26

15418 Single Shot Rifle Journal
American Single Shot Rifle Association
625 Pine St. Phone: (906)225-1828
Marquette, MI 49855 Fax: (906)227-1819

Magazine on single-shot rifles. **Founded:** 1948. **Freq:** Bimonthly. **Print Method:** Offset. **Trim Size:** 8 1/2 x 11. **Cols./Page:** 3. **Col. Width:** 28 nonpareils. **Col. Depth:** 140 agate lines. **Key Personnel:** Rudi Prusok, Editor, rprusok@nmu.edu. **ISSN:** 0734-5801. **Subscription Rates:** $25 / year. **Remarks:** Accepts advertising. **URL:** http://www.shooters.com. **Formerly**: American Single Shot Rifle News.
Ad Rates: GLR: $1 **Circ:** Paid ‡2,500
BW: $150 Controlled ‡100
PCI: $5

15419 The U.P. Catholic
The UP Catholic
347 Rock St. Phone: (906)226-8821
PO Box 548 Fax: (906)226-6941
Marquette, MI 49855
Free: (800)675-1335

Catholic newspaper. **Subtitle:** The Newspaper of the Diocese of Marquette. **Founded:** 1946. **Freq:** Semimonthly. **Print Method:** Offset. **Cols./Page:** 4. **Col. Width:** 2 3/8 inches. **Col. Depth:** 16 inches. **Key Personnel:** Joseph K. Zyble, Editor; Most Rev. James H. Garland, Publisher; Sandra L. Paull-Numikoski, Business Mgr.; Dan Sullivan, Editorial Assistant. **ISSN:** 1063-4525. **Subscription Rates:** $20 /year; $1.50 single issue.
Ad Rates: BW: $432 **Circ:** Paid 5,200
PCI: $6.75

15420 WCMM-FM - 94.7
2025 US 41 West Phone: (906)288-9702
Marquette, MI 49855 Fax: (906)228-9717
Free: (800)947-9266
E-mail: wcmm@upmail.com

Format: Country. **Networks:** ABC. **Owner:** Great Lakes Radio, Inc., 101 Huron Ct., Negaunee, MI 49866, (906)228-9700, Fax: (906)228-9717. **Founded:** 1991. **Formerly:** WTIQ-FM (1992). **Operating Hours:** Continuous. **ADI:** Marquette, MI. **Key Personnel:** Annette Cox, Traffic Mgr., annette@wkqs.com; Todd Noordyk, Pres./Corporate Mgr., tnoordyk@superior.iceware.com; David Vaughan, Station Mgr.; Annette Cox, Office Mgr.; Jay Scott, Music Dir.; Nick Sawyer, Sales Mgr., nick@wkqs.com. **Wattage:** 100,000. **Ad Rates:** $10-12 for 30 seconds; $14-16 for 60 seconds. Combined advertising rates available with WGLQ-FM, WTIQ-AM, WKQS-FM, WCHT-AM. **URL:** http://www.wcmm.com.

15421 WDMJ-AM - 1320
PO Box 700 Phone: (906)225-1313
845 W. Washington St. Fax: (906)225-1324
Marquette, MI 49855

Format: News; Talk; Sports. **Simulcasts:** WIAN-AM. **Networks:** ABC. **Owner:** Goetz Broadcasting, Eaton Ave., PO Box 94, Fort Atkinson, WI 53538. **Founded:** 1931. **Operating Hours:** Continuous.2% network, 98% local. **ADI:** Marquette, MI. **Key Personnel:** Steven W. Handrich, General Mgr. **Wattage:** 5000 day; 1000 night. **Ad Rates:** $15-20 for 60 seconds.

WEUL-FM - See Kingsford

15422 WFXD-FM - 103.3
832 W. Washington St. Phone: (906)228-6800
Marquette, MI 49855 Fax: (906)228-5766
E-mail: fox@superior.iceware.com

Format: Oldies. **Networks:** Mutual Broadcasting System; Satellite Music Network. **Founded:** 1974. **Formerly:** WUUN-FM (1986); WRUP-FM. **Operating Hours:** Continuous; 80% network, 20% local. **ADI:** Marquette, MI. **Key Personnel:** David Peterson, General Mgr. **Wattage:** 100,000. **Ad Rates:** Advertising accepted; rates available upon request.

15423 WHWL-FM - 95.7
130 Carmen Dr. Phone: (906)249-1423
Marquette, MI 49855

Format: Religious. **Owner:** Gospel Opportunities Inc., at above address. **Founded:** 1975. **Operating Hours:** 5:50 a.m.-midnight. **ADI:** Marquette, MI. **Key Personnel:** Curt Marker, General Mgr. **Wattage:** 100,000. **Ad Rates:** Noncommercial.

WIAN-AM - See Ishpeming

15424 WNMU-FM - 90.1
Northern Michigan Univeristy Phone: (906)227-2600
Marquette, MI 49855 Fax: (906)227-2905
Free: (800)227-9668
E-mail: pr90@nmu.edu

Format: Full Service; Classical; News; Jazz. **Simulcasts:** WNMU-TV. **Networks:** National Public Radio (NPR); Public Radio International (PRI); AP. **Owner:** Northern Michigan University, at above address. **Founded:** 1963. **Formerly:** WNMR-FM (1975). **Operating Hours:** Continuous. **ADI:** Marquette, MI. **Key Personnel:** Gregg Beukema, Promotions Dir., phone (906)227-2642, gbeukema@nmu.edu; Susan Sherman, Station Mgr., phone (906)227-2633, ssherman@nmu.edu; Hans Ahlstrom, Music Producer, hahlstrom@nmu.edu; Bill Hart, Operations Mgr., wehart@nmu.edu; Stan Wright, Producer, swright@nmu.edu; Scott K. Seaman, General Mgr., sseaman@nmu.edu. **Local Programs:** *Humeresque*, Stan Wright; *Night Studio Jazz*, Hans Ahlstrom; *Weekday*, Bill Hart. **Wattage:** 100,000. **Ad Rates:** Noncommercial.

15425 WNMU-TV - 13
Northern Michigan University Phone: (906)277-1300
Marquette, MI 49855 Fax: (906)227-2905
Free: (800)227-WNMU
E-mail: wnmu@nmu.edu; tv13@nmu.edu

Format: Public TV. **Simulcasts:** WNMU-FM. **Networks:** Public Broadcasting Service (PBS). **Owner:** Board of Control of Northern Michigan University, at above address. **Founded:** 1972. **Formerly**: WNPB-TV (1974). **Operating Hours:** 7:15 a.m.-12:30 a.m.; 90% network, 10% local. **ADI:** Marquette, MI. **Key Personnel:** Scott K. Seaman, General Mgr.; Bruce S. Turner, Station Mgr. **Local Programs:** *Ask The . (Doctors, Dentists, Lawyers)* 8 p.m Thursday, Bob Thomson, Mailing contact; *High School Bowl* 8 p.m Saturday, Bob Thomson, Mailing contact; *Media Meet* 9:30 p.m. Friday, Sonya Chrisman, Mailing contact. **Wattage:** 316 visual; 63.1 aural. **Ad Rates:** Noncommercial.

15426 WUPX-FM - 91.5
Northern Michigan University Phone: (906)227-1844
Marquette, MI 49855-5301 Fax: (906)227-2344
E-mail: wupx@nmu.edu

Format: Alternative/New Music/Progressive. **Owner:** Northern Michigan University Board of Control, 606 Cohodas Administrative Center, NMU, Marquette, MI 49855. **Founded:** 1971. **Formerly**: WBKX-FM (1992). **Operating Hours:** Continuous. **ADI:** Marquette, MI. **Key Personnel:** Bridgette Jaakola, General Mgr.; James Moran, Station Mgr.; Charles Ganzert, Faculty Advisor; Paul White, Administrative Advisor. **Local Programs:** *Music Mailbox*, Mike Porter, Mailing contact; *New Age Cafe*, Sandra Peake, Mailing contact; *Room 104*, E. Dean. **Wattage:** 200. **Ad Rates:** Noncommercial.

MARSHALL

15427 Marshall Community Advisor
J-Ad Corp.
215 W. Michigan Phone: (616)781-5444
Marshall, MI 49068-0111 Fax: (616)781-7766
Publisher E-mail: j-ad@voyager.com

Community newspaper (tabloid). **Founded:** 1966. **Freq:** Weekly (Wed.). **Print Method:** Offset. **Cols./Page:** 6. **Col. Width:** 20 nonpareils. **Col. Depth:** 224 agate lines. **Key Personnel:** John Jacobs, Editor and Publisher. **Subscription Rates:** Free.
Ad Rates: BW: $302.40 **Circ:** Free 18,791
4C: $502.40
SAU: $5.26
PCI: $3.40

MASON

15428 WUNN-AM - 1110
1571 Tonlinson Rd. Phone: (517)676-2488
PO Box 288 Fax: (517)676-3705
Mason, MI 48854
Free: (800)776-1020

Format: Religious. **Owner:** Family Life Broadcasting, PO Box 35300, Tucson, AZ 85740, (520)742-6976, Fax: (520)742-6979. **Founded:** 1967. **Operating Hours:** Sunrise-sunset; 49% network, 51% local. **Key Personnel:** Dave Phelps, General Mgr. **Local Programs:** *FLR Open Forum*, Dave Phelps. **Wattage:** 1000. **Ad Rates:** Noncommercial.

MAYVILLE

15429 Mayville Monitor
PO Box 299 Phone: (517)843-6441
Mayville, MI 48744-0299 Fax: (517)843-0054
Free: (800)330-6441

Community newspaper. **Founded:** Mar. 26, 1884. **Freq:** Weekly (Thurs.). **Print Method:** Offset. **Trim Size:** 11 1/2 x 16. **Cols./Page:** 6. **Col. Width:** 9 1/2 picas. **Col. Depth:** 15 inches. **Key Personnel:** Gale Langford, Editor and Publisher; Debra Langford, Publisher. **USPS:** 334-680. **Subscription Rates:** $13 individuals in county; $15 out of area; $18 out of state. **Remarks:** Accepts advertising.
Ad Rates: BW: $260 **Circ:** Paid 1,200
4C: $496
SAU: $4
PCI: $3

MENOMINEE

15430 WAGN-AM - 1340
413 10th Ave. Phone: (906)863-5551
PO Box 365 Fax: (906)863-5679
Menominee, MI 49858
Free: (800)633-5815

Format: Middle-of-the-Road (MOR); Oldies. **Networks:** ABC; Mutual Broadcasting System; CBS. **Founded:** 1953. **Operating Hours:** Continuous. **ADI:** Green Bay-Appleton (Suring), WI. **Key Personnel:** William Sauve, Owner/Sales; James Callow, News Dir.; Chuck Patrick, Operations Mgr. **Wattage:** 1000. **Ad Rates:** $4.75-8 for 30 seconds; $6.75-10 for 60 seconds.

15431 WHYB-FM - 103.9
413 10th Ave. Phone: (906)863-5551
PO Box 365 Fax: (906)863-5679
Menominee, MI 49858
Free: (800)633-5815

Format: Country. **Networks:** Satellite Music Network; AP. **Owner:** Good Neighbor Broadcasting, Inc, at above address. **Founded:** 1984. **Formerly:** WCJL-FM (1992). **Operating Hours:** Continuous. **ADI:** Green Bay-Appleton (Suring), WI. **Key Personnel:** Chuck Patrick, General Mgr.; Jim Callow, Operations Mgr. **Wattage:** 3000. **Ad Rates:** $7-14 for 30 seconds; $9-16 for 60 seconds. $7-$14 for 30 seconds; $9-$16 for 60 seconds. Combined advertising rates available with WAGN-AM: $6-$11 for 30 seconds; $8-$13.

MIDLAND

15432 Midland Daily News
PO Box 432 Phone: (517)835-7171
Midland, MI 48640-5161 Fax: (517)835-6991

General newspaper. **Founded:** 1857. **Freq:** Daily (eve.). **Print Method:** Offset. **Cols./Page:** 6. **Col. Width:** 25 nonpareils. **Col. Depth:** 301 agate lines. **Key Personnel:** John H. Telfer II, Editor; Gordon Hall, Publisher; Jenny L. Anderson, General Mgr. **USPS:** 347-700. **Subscription Rates:** $117 individuals.
Ad Rates: GLR: $1.75 **Circ:** Mon.-Sat. ★**16,412**
BW: $2,276.85 Sun. ★**18,086**
4C: $2,751.85
PCI: $17.65

15433 Phi Rho Sigma Journal
Phi Rho Sigma Medical Society
c/o James L. Jackson, MD, FACS
4011 orchard Dr., Ste. 2020
Midland, MI 48640
Publication E-mail: hrodenbe@wpc.iupui.edu

Membership journal. **Freq:** Quarterly. **Key Personnel:** James L. Jackson, M.D., Editor, jjack@cris.com. **Subscription Rates:** Included in membership. **Remarks:** Advertising not accepted.
Circ: Non-paid 12,500

15434 WMPX-AM - 1490
1510 Bayliss St. Phone: (517)631-1490
PO Box 1513 Fax: (517)631-6357
Midland, MI 48641-1513

Format: Big Band/Nostalgia. **Networks:** ABC. **Owner:** Steel Broadcasting, Inc., at above address. **Founded:** 1948. **Operating Hours:** Continuous Mon.-Sat.; 5 a.m.-midnight Sun. **Key Personnel:** Thomas J. Steel, Contact; Tom Schelich, Sales Mgr.; Katherine Morse, PSA Dir. **Wattage:** 1000.

15435 WMRX-FM - 97.7
1510 Bayliss St. Phone: (517)435-4844
PO Box 1513 Fax: (517)631-6357
Midland, MI 48640-1513

Format: Big Band/Nostalgia; Adult Contemporary. **Networks:** Satellite Music Network. **Owner:** Steel Broadcasting, Inc., at above address. **Founded:** 1984. **Operating Hours:** Continuous (Mon.-Sat.); 5 a.m.-midnight Sun. **Key Personnel:** Tom Steel, Contact. **Wattage:** 6000.

MILFORD

15436 Milford Spinal Column Newsweekly
Spinal Column Publications
7196 Cooley Lake Rd. Phone: (248)360-6397
PO Box 14 Fax: (248)360-4711
Union Lake, MI 48387-0014
Local newspaper. **Founded:** 1960. **Freq:** Weekly. **Print Method:** Offset. **Trim Size:** 10 1/2 x 15. **Cols./Page:** 8. **Col. Width:** 7 picas. **Col. Depth:** 14 inches. **Key Personnel:** David D. Hohendorf, Publisher; James W. Fancy, Publisher; Laurie Wallace, Advertising Mgr. **Remarks:** Accepts advertising.
Ad Rates: GLR: $4.59 **Circ:** Free ‡2,500
BW: $514.08
PCI: $9.18

15437 Milford Times
Hometown Newspapers
405 N. Main St. Phone: (810)685-1507
Milford, MI 48381
Community newspaper. **Founded:** 1971. **Freq:** Weekly (Thurs.). **Print Method:** Offset. **Trim Size:** 14 x 22 1/2. **Cols./Page:** 6. **Col. Width:** 1 3/8 inches. **Col. Depth:** 21 inches. **Key Personnel:** Chris Carroll, Editor; Ben Gumm, Publisher; Salley McLaren, Advertising Mgr. **Remarks:** Accepts advertising.
Ad Rates: GLR: $.80 **Circ:** Combined ♦**5,436**
BW: $1,263
4C: $1,863
SAU: $11.23

15438 WEXL-AM - 1340
3351 Roanoke Dr. Phone: (810)544-2200
Milford, MI 48381-3377

Format: Religious. **Networks:** Independent. **Founded:** 1923. **Operating Hours:** 5:30 a.m.-2 a.m. **Key Personnel:** G.B. Sparks, General Mgr. **Wattage:** 1000. **Ad Rates:** $17-23 for 30 seconds; $23-29 for 60 seconds.

MINDEN CITY

15439 Minden City Herald
1524 Main St. Phone: (517)864-3630
Minden City, MI 48456 Fax: (517)864-5363

Community newspaper. **Founded:** 1888. **Freq:** Weekly (Thurs.). **Print Method:** Offset. **Trim Size:** 11 1/2 x 15. **Cols./Page:** 5. **Col. Width:** 2 inches. **Col. Depth:** 15 inches. **Key Personnel:** Paul A. Engel, Editor and Publisher. **USPS:** 350-620. **Subscription Rates:** $13.50 individuals. **Remarks:** Accepts advertising.
Ad Rates: BW: $225 **Circ:** Paid 1450
SAU: $4.50 Free 100

MONROE

15440 The Monroe Evening News/The Monroe Sunday News
Monroe Publishing Co.
20 W. 1st Phone: (734)242-1100
PO Box 1176 Fax: (734)242-3175
Monroe, MI 48161
General newspaper. **Founded:** 1825. **Freq:** Daily (eve.), Sat. and Sun. (morn.). **Print Method:** Web atlas offset press. **Trim Size:** 13 3/4 x 23 3/4. **Cols./Page:** 6. **Col. Width:** 26 nonpareils. **Col. Depth:** 21 inches. **Key Personnel:** Grattan Gray, Chairman of the Board; Steve Gray, President; Lonnie Peppler, VP/Publisher, lonnie@monroenews.com; Deborah Saul, Editor, saul@monroenews.com; Shirley Hyden, Business Mgr.; Tom Pottorff, Circulation Mgr.; Bob Spoons, Retail Advertising Mgr.; Beth Salow, Classified Advertising Mgr. **USPS:** 359-400. **Subscription Rates:** $148.20 individuals. **Remarks:** Accepts advertising. Monday-Saturday: PCI: $13.05; Sunday: PCI: $13.47. **URL:** http://www.monroenews.com.
Circ: Mon.-Sat. ‡23,621
Sun. ‡25,085

15441 The Monroe Guardian
Heritage Newspapers
23 W. 1st St. Phone: (313)243-2100
PO Box 1426 Fax: (313)243-5196
Monroe, MI 48161
Newspaper. **Founded:** 1878. **Freq:** Sunday. **Print Method:** Offset. **Trim Size:** 11 x 21 1/2. **Cols./Page:** 6. **Col. Width:** 16 nonpareils. **Col. Depth:** 301 agate lines. **Key Personnel:** Daniel Rowe, Editor & Gen. Mgr.; Fred Manuel, Publisher. **Remarks:** Accepts advertising.
Ad Rates: GLR: $.74 **Circ:** Combined 9,484
BW: $1,167.45
4C: $1,602.45
SAU: $9.05

15442 Spinnaker
IHM Sisters
610 W. Elm St. Phone: (313)241-3660
Monroe, MI 48161 Fax: (313)457-1890

Newspaper covering activities of the IHM Sisters and their associates in ministry. **Founded:** 1984. **Freq:** 5/year. **Print Method:** Offset. **Cols./Page:** 4. **Key Personnel:** Ann Oestreich, S.S.J., Editor. **Subscription Rates:** $4. **Remarks:** Advertising not accepted.
Circ: Paid 1,250

15443 River Raisin Cable
1145 S. Telegraph Rd. Phone: (734)243-9350
Monroe, MI 48161 Fax: (734)243-2366
Free: (800)875-9350

Key Personnel: Mark Dineen, Vice-Pres. Michigan Operations, phone (616)846-4822, fax (616)846-0797; Cliff Cleland, Regional System Mgr., phone (734)243-9462, fax (734)243-2366; Pat Kirby, Office Mgr. **Cities Served:** subscribing households 16,451; 60 channels; 1 community access channel.

15444 WEJY-FM - 97.5
1275 N. Macomb St. Phone: (313)241-1491
Monroe, MI 48161 Fax: (313)457-3990

Format: Eclectic. **Owner:** Monroe Public Schools, at above address, (734)241-0330. **Founded:** 1978. **Operating Hours:** 6:30 a.m.-8 p.m. Mon.-Fri. **Key Personnel:** Eric Diroff, Chief Engineer, phone (734)241-1663, fax (734)457-0990; Eric Diroff, Contact. **Wattage:** 10.

15445 WTWR-FM - 98.3
7 S. Monroe St. Phone: (313)242-6600
Monroe, MI 48161 Fax: (313)242-6599

Format: Contemporary Hit Radio (CHR); Adult Contemporary; News; Eclectic. **Networks:** Independent. **Founded:** 1982. **Operating Hours:** Continuous; 100% local. **ADI:** Toledo, OH. **Key Personnel:** Tom Treece, Contact; Terri McCormick, Contact; Lisa Way, News Dir.; Sandy Avery, Office Mgr. **Local Programs:** *All Request Lunch Hour*, Terry McCormick; *The Fringe*, Lisa Way, (313)242-6397; *Quiet Storm*, Steve Marshall. **Wattage:** 3000. **Ad Rates:** $25 for 30 seconds; $30 for 60 seconds. **URL:** http://www.tower98.com.

MORENCI

15446 The Morenci Observer
120 North St. Phone: (517)458-6811
Morenci, MI 49256 Fax: (517)458-6811

Community newspaper. **Founded:** 1872. **Freq:** Weekly (Wed.). **Print Method:** Offset. **Cols./Page:** 6. **Col. Width:** 26 nonpareils. **Col. Depth:** 294 agate lines. **Key Personnel:** Jeffrey Johnston, Editor; David G. Green, Publisher. **Subscription Rates:** $14. **Remarks:** Accepts advertising.
Ad Rates: BW: $312 **Circ:** Paid ‡2,500
SAU: $2.85

MOUNT CLEMENS

15447 The Advisor
21st Century Newspapers, Inc.
100 Macomb Daily Dr.
Mount Clemens, MI 48046

Community newspaper serving Mt. Clemens, Macomb, Clinton Township, Harrison Township, and Fraser, MI. **Freq:** Weekly (Sun.). **Print Method:** Offset. **Cols./Page:** 6. **Col. Width:** 2 1/16 inches. **Col. Depth:** 21 1/2 inches. **Key Personnel:** Frank Shepherd, President/CEO, phone (810)469-4510, fax (810)469-4512; Wayne Oehmke, Publisher, fax (810)731-2522; Phillip Marien, General Mgr.; Josesph Warner, Editor; Chris Troszak, Advertising Mgr. **Subscription Rates:** Free; $80 out of area. **Remarks:** Accepts advertising. **Formerly:** Mount Clemens-South Clinton Advisor (1990); Mt. Clemens, South Clinton, Harrison Advisor.
Ad Rates: BW: $2,580 **Circ:** Non-paid ‡34,199
4C: $3,705
SAU: $20

The Advisor - See Eastpointe

The Advisor - See Mount Clemens

15448 Macomb County Legal News
21st Century Newspapers, Inc.
100 Macomb Daily Dr.
Mount Clemens, MI 48046

Legal newspaper. **Founded:** 1956. **Freq:** Weekly (Fri.). **Print Method:** Offset. **Cols./Page:** 6. **Col. Width:** 25 nonpareils. **Col. Depth:** 301 agate lines. **Key Personnel:** Diane Kish, Editor; Bill Thomas, Publisher. **ISSN:** 0024-9289. **Subscription Rates:** $25. **Remarks:** Accepts advertising.
Ad Rates: BW: $1,244.85 **Circ:** 950
SAU: $9.65

15449 The Macomb Daily
100 Macomb Daily Dr. Phone: (810)469-4510
PO Box 707 Fax: (810)469-2892
Mount Clemens, MI 48046
Publisher E-mail: edit@macombdaily.com

General newspaper. **Founded:** 1840. **Freq:** Daily and Sunday (morn.). **Print Method:** Offset. **Cols./Page:** 6. **Col. Width:** 12.6 picas. **Col. Depth:** 21 1/2 inches. **Key Personnel:** Phil Van Hulle, Editor, phone (810)783-0226; Ken Kish, Managing Editor, News, phone (810)783-0228; Niky Hachigian, Lifestyles Editor, phone (810)783-0323. **Subscription Rates:** $135.20 (home delivery). **Remarks:** Advertising not accepted for X-rated films. Monday-Saturday: BW: $5,031; 4C: $5,636; SAU: $39; Sunday: BW: $5,721.15; 4C: $6,326.15; SAU: $44.35. **Feature Editors:** Frank DeFrank, *Education*, phone (810)783-0309; Bill Fleming, *Financial/Business*, phone (810)783-0253; Niky Hachigian, *Real Estate*, phone (810)783-0323; Mitch Kehetian, *Editorials*, phone (810)783-0327; Debbie Komar, *Entertainment, Food, Medical*, phone (810)783-0251; George Pohly, *Sports*, phone (810)783-0270; Bob Selna, *Religion*, phone (810)783-0229; Chad Selweski, *Political*, phone (810)783-0218.
Circ: Mon.-Fri. 58,944
Sat. 56,236
Sun. 84,193

Sterling Heights Source - See Sterling Heights

Warren Advisor - See Warren

MOUNT MORRIS

15450 Genesee County Herald
PO Box 127 Phone: (810)686-3842
Mount Morris, MI 48458 Fax: (810)686-9181

Community newspaper. **Freq:** Weekly (Wed.). **Cols./Page:** 6. **Col. Width:** 9 1/2 picas. **Col. Depth:** 16 inches. **Key Personnel:** Jeff Harrington, Editor and Publisher.
Circ: 2,000

MOUNT PLEASANT

15451 Alma Reminder
Central Michigan Newspapers, Inc.
215 N. Main St. Phone: (517)426-9351
PO Box 447 Fax: (517)426-0551
Mount Pleasant, MI 48804-0447
Free: (800)616-6397
Publisher E-mail: cmn@cmnnet.com

Shopper. **Founded:** 1938. **Freq:** Weekly (Mon.). **Print Method:** Offset. Uses mats. **Cols./Page:** 6. **Col. Width:** 20 nonpareils. **Col. Depth:** 224 agate lines. **Key Personnel:** Tammy Fisher, General Mgr. **Subscription Rates:** Free. **Remarks:** Accepts advertising. **Online:** AO SEND.
Ad Rates: GLR: $6.85 **Circ:** Free ❑**20,447**
BW: $600
4C: $765
PCI: $6.85

15452 Buyers Guide
Mt. Pleasant Buyers Guide
215 N. Main Phone: (517)772-2971
PO Box 447 Fax: (517)773-0382
Mount Pleasant, MI 48804-0447
Free: (800)616-6397
Publication E-mail: cmn@cmnet.com

Shopping guide. **Founded:** 1946. **Freq:** Weekly (Mon.). **Print Method:** Offset. Uses mats. **Cols./Page:** 6. **Col. Width:** 20 nonpareils. **Col. Depth:** 224 agate lines. **Key Personnel:** Ray Pike, Publisher, fax (517)773-2762, rpike@cmnet.com; Kathy Simon, Advertising Mgr., fax (517)772-2971, glove@cmnet.com. **Subscription Rates:** Free. **Remarks:** Accepts advertising.
Ad Rates: GLR: $2.95 **Circ:** Free ‡28,660
BW: $859.20
4C: $1,039.20
SAU: $6.02

15453 Carson City Reminder
Central Michigan Newspapers, Inc.
215 N. Main St. Phone: (517)426-9351
PO Box 447 Fax: (517)426-0551
Mount Pleasant, MI 48804-0447
Free: (800)616-6397
Publisher E-mail: cmn@cmnnet.com

Shopper. **Founded:** 1968. **Freq:** Weekly (Mon.). **Print Method:** Offset. Uses mats. **Cols./Page:** 6. **Col. Width:** 20 nonpareils. **Col. Depth:** 224 agate lines. **Key Personnel:** Robert Natzel, General Mgr. **Remarks:** Accepts advertising. **Online:** AO SEND.
Ad Rates: BW: $316.80 **Circ:** Free ❑**10,680**
4C: $424.80
PCI: $4

15454 Central Michigan Life
Central Michigan University
8 Anspach Hall Phone: (517)774-3493
Mount Pleasant, MI 48859 Fax: (517)774-7805
Publication E-mail: cmlife@cmuvm.csv.cmich.edu

Collegiate newspaper. **Founded:** 1919. **Freq:** 3/week. **Print Method:** Offset. **Cols./Page:** 6 and 6. **Col. Width:** 28 nonpareils and 2 1/8 inches. **Col. Depth:** 294 agate lines and 21 inches. **Key Personnel:** Liz Whishaw, Editor; Cynthia Sedlak, Advertising Dir., cynthia.a.sedlak@cmich.edu. **Subscription Rates:** $65 individuals. **Remarks:** Accepts advertising. **URL:** http://141.209.72.12.
Ad Rates: GLR: $11.25 **Circ:** Paid ‡700
BW: $1,417.50 Free ‡14,900
4C: $1,657.50
SAU: $11.25

15455 Clare County Buyers Guide
Central Michigan Newspapers, Inc.
215 N. Main St. Phone: (517)426-9351
PO Box 447 Fax: (517)426-0551
Mount Pleasant, MI 48804-0447
Free: (800)616-6397
Publisher E-mail: cmn@cmnnet.com

Shopper. **Freq:** Weekly (Mon.). **Print Method:** Offset. Uses mats. **Cols./Page:** 6. **Col. Width:** 20 nonpareils. **Col. Depth:** 224 agate lines. **Key Personnel:** Kathy Simon, General Mgr., fax (517)773-2762, alove@cmnnet.com; Ray Pike, Publisher, rpike@cmnnet.com. **Subscription Rates:** Free. **Online:** ADSEND.
Ad Rates: GLR: $4.95 **Circ:** Free ‡16,100
BW: $432
4C: $612
PCI: $4.95

15456 The Edmore Advertiser
Central Michigan Newspapers, Inc.
215 N. Main St. Phone: (517)426-9351
PO Box 447 Fax: (517)426-0551
Mount Pleasant, MI 48804-0447
Free: (800)616-6397
Publisher E-mail: cmn@cmnnet.com

Shopper. **Founded:** 1951. **Freq:** Weekly (Mon.). **Print Method:** Offset. Uses mats. **Cols./Page:** 6. **Col. Width:** 20 nonpareils. **Col. Depth:** 224 agate lines. **Key Personnel:** Tammy Fisher, General Mgr. **Subscription Rates:** Free. **Remarks:** Accepts advertising. **Online:** ADSEND.
Ad Rates: GLR: $4.65 **Circ:** Free ❑**15,897**
BW: $360
4C: $468
PCI: $4.65

Gladwin Buyers Guide - See Gladwin

15457 Hemlock Shoppers Guide
Central Michigan Newspapers, Inc.
215 N. Main St. Phone: (517)426-9351
PO Box 447 Fax: (517)426-0551
Mount Pleasant, MI 48804-0447
Free: (800)616-6397
Publisher E-mail: cmn@cmnnet.com

Shopper. **Founded:** 1976. **Freq:** Weekly (Mon.). **Print Method:** Offset. **Cols./Page:** 6. **Col. Width:** 1 1/2 inches. **Col. Depth:** 16 inches. **Key Personnel:** Tammy Fisher, General Mgr. **Remarks:** Accepts advertising.
Ad Rates: BW: $346.56 **Circ:** Free ❑**12,316**
4C: $586.56
PCI: $4.22

15458 Michigan Oil and Gas News
206 W. Michigan, Ste. 200 Phone: (517)772-5181
PO Box 250 Fax: (517)773-2970
Mount Pleasant, MI 48804-0250
Publisher E-mail: mogn@sensible-net.com

Magazine reporting drilling activities in Michigan; includes permit information. **Founded:** 1932. **Freq:** Weekly (Fri.). **Print Method:** Offset. **Trim Size:** 8 1/2 x 11. **Cols./Page:** 3. **Col. Width:** 27 nonpareils. **Col. Depth:** 140 agate lines. **Key Personnel:** Jack Westbrook, Editor and Publisher. **USPS:** 405-780. **Subscription Rates:** $100 individuals.
Ad Rates: BW: $425 **Circ:** ‡2,050
4C: $950 Non-paid ‡85

15459 Midland Buyer's Guide
Central Michigan Newspapers, Inc.
PO Box 464 Free: (800)616-6397
215 N. Main St.
Mount Pleasant, MI 48804-0464
Publisher E-mail: cmn@cmnnet.com

Shopper. **Freq:** Weekly (Mon.). **Print Method:** Offset. Uses mats. **Trim Size:** 16.75 x 11. **Cols./Page:** 6. **Col. Width:** 20 nonpareils. **Col. Depth:** 224 agate lines. **Key Personnel:** Ray Pike, Publisher, rpike@cmnnet.com; Kathy Simon, Dir. of Sales & Marketing, ksimon@cmnnet.com; Sue Bonstelle, General Mgr., sbonstelle@cmnnet.com. **Subscription Rates:** Free.
Ad Rates: BW: $8.55 **Circ:** Free ❑**27,901**
PCI: $10.30

15460 The Morning Sun
Central Michigan Newspapers, Inc.
PO Box 447 Phone: (517)772-2971
Mount Pleasant, MI 48804-0447 Fax: (517)773-0382
Publisher E-mail: cmn@cmnnet.com

General newspaper. **Founded:** 1864. **Freq:** Daily (morn.) Sun.-Fri. **Print Method:** Offset. **Cols./Page:** 8. **Col. Width:** 1 1/2 inches. **Col. Depth:** 301 agate lines. **Key Personnel:** B. Ray Pike, Publisher, fax (517)773-2762, rpike@cmnnet.com; Rick Mills, Editor, rmills@cmnnet.com; Kathy Simon, Director, ksimon@cmnnet.com. **Subscription Rates:** $145.08 by mail per year. **Remarks:** Accepts advertising. **Online:** AOSEND.
Ad Rates: GLR: $9.80 **Circ:** Mon.-Fri. 11,327
BW: $1,251.60 Sun. 12,814
4C: $1,451.60
SAU: $11.89

15461 WCEN-AM - 1150
Box 407, Isabella Rd. Phone: (517)773-5961
Mount Pleasant, MI 48804-0407 Fax: (517)772-9420

Format: Big Band/Nostalgia; Talk; News. **Networks:** Mutual Broadcasting System. **Owner:** Richard Sommerville, at above address. **Founded:** 1949. **Operating Hours:** 6 a.m. - 6 p.m. **ADI:** Flint-Saginaw-Bay City, MI. **Key Personnel:** Richard Sommerville, General Mgr.; Jim Sommerville, Contact; Tina Sawyer, News Dir. **Wattage:** 1000. **Ad Rates:** $26-36 for 60 seconds. $20-$30 per unit. Combined advertising rates available with WCEN-FM.

15462 WCEN-FM - 94.5
Box 407, Bluegrass Rd. Phone: (517)773-5961
Mount Pleasant, MI 48804-0407 Fax: (517)772-9420

Format: Country. **Networks:** Mutual Broadcasting System. **Owner:** Richard Sommerville, at above address. **Founded:** 1963. **Operating Hours:** Continuous. **ADI:** Flint-Saginaw-Bay City, MI. **Key Personnel:** Richard Sommerville, Contact; Jim Sommerville, Contact; Tina Sawyer, News Dir. **Wattage:** 100,000. **Ad Rates:** $26-36 for 60 seconds. $20-$30 per unit. Combined advertising rates available with WCEN-AM.

WCML-FM - See Alpena

WCML-TV - See Alpena

15463 WCMU-FM - 89.5
Public Broadcasting Center Phone: (517)774-3105
Central Michigan University Fax: (517)774-4427
3965 E. Broomfield Rd.
Mount Pleasant, MI 48859
Free: (800)999-5656
E-mail: pubscast@cmich.edu

Format: Jazz; Blues; News; Classical; Public Radio. **Networks:** National Public Radio (NPR). **Founded:** 1964. **Operating Hours:** Continuous; 25% network, 75% local. **ADI:** Flint-Saginaw-Bay City, MI. **Key Personnel:** Thomas Hunt, Station Mgr.; Raymond Ford, Program Dir.; Art Curtis, Underwriting. **Wattage:** 100,000. **Ad Rates:** Noncommercial. $9-13 per unit.

15464 WCMU-TV - 14
Central Michigan University Phone: (517)774-3105
3965 E. Broomfield Fax: (517)774-4427
Mount Pleasant, MI 48859

Format: Public TV. **Networks:** Public Broadcasting Service (PBS). **Owner:** Central Michigan University, at above address. **Founded:** 1967. **Operating Hours:** 6 a.m.-midnight; 90% network, 10% local. **ADI:** Flint-Saginaw-Bay City, MI. **Key Personnel:** Monte Higgins, Station Mgr., phone (517)774-3105, fax (517)774-4427, monte.higgins@cmich.edu; Rick Schudiske, Program Mgr.; Linda Hyde, Contact. **Ad Rates:** Noncommercial.

WCMV-TV - See Cadillac

WCMW-TV - See Manistee

15465 WCZY-FM - 104.3
4065 E. Wing Rd. Phone: (517)772-9664
Mount Pleasant, MI 48858 Fax: (517)773-5000
E-mail: wczy@sensible-net.com

Format: Soft Rock. **Networks:** Jones Satellite. **Owner:** Central Michigan Communications, Inc., at above address. **Founded:** 1991. **Operating Hours:** Continuous; 90% network, 10% local. **Key Personnel:** Mike Carey, General Mgr./Owner; Dan Bragg, Program Dir.; Lisa Johnson, Office Mgr.; Kim Chiodo, News Dir. **Wattage:** 2600. **Ad Rates:** $6-7.75 for 15 seconds; $7.75-9.50 for 30 seconds; $9.25-11 for 60 seconds. Combined advertising rates available with WMMI-AM.

15466 WMHW-FM - 91.5
Central Michigan University Phone: (517)774-7287
180 Moore Hall Fax: (517)774-2426
Mount Pleasant, MI 48859
E-mail: wmhw@cmich.edu

Format: Alternative/New Music/Progressive. **Owner:** Central Michigan University Board of Trustees, at above address, (517)774-3851. **Founded:** 1963. **Operating Hours:** Continuous; 100% local. **Key Personnel:** Dr. Jerry Henderson, Radio Operations Manager, phone (517)774-7284, hende1jd@mail.cmich.edu. **Wattage:** 300. **Ad Rates:** Noncommercial. **URL:** http://www.bca.cmich.edu/modern_rock_91.htm.

15467 WMMI-AM - 830
4065 E. Wing Rd. Phone: (517)772-9664
Mount Pleasant, MI 48858 Fax: (517)773-5000
E-mail: wczy@sensible-net.com

Format: Oldies. **Networks:** Jones Satellite. **Owner:** Central Michigan Communications, Inc., at above address. **Founded:** 1987. **Operating Hours:** Sunrise-sunset; 90% network, 10% local. **Key Personnel:** Mike Carey, Owner; Dan Bragg, Program Dir.; Lisa Johnson, Office Mgr.; Kim Chiodo, News Dir. **Local Programs:** *Tiger Baseball*, Mike Carcy; *MSU Football*, Mike Carcy. **Wattage:** 1000. **Ad Rates:** $7-7.75 for 15 seconds; $8.75-9.50 for 30 seconds; $10.25-11 for 60 seconds. Combined advertising rates available with WCZY-FM: 15 $10-$10.75; 30 $11.75-$12.50 60 $13.25-$14.

MUNISING

15468 The Alger County Shopper
113 W. Superior Phone: (906)387-3282
PO Box 38
Munising, MI 49862
Shopper (tabloid). **Founded:** 1989. **Freq:** Weekly (Mon.). **Trim Size:** 10 1/4 x 15. **Cols./Page:** 6. **Col. Width:** 1 1/2 inches. **Col. Depth:** 15 inches. **Key Personnel:** Willie J. Peterson, Publisher. **Subscription Rates:** $25 out of area. **Remarks:** Accepts advertising.
Ad Rates: SAU: $6 **Circ:** ‡5,000
PCI: $3

15469 The Munising News
The Munising News Pub. Co., Inc.
PO Box 38 Phone: (906)387-3282
Munising, MI 49862
Community newspaper. **Founded:** 1896. **Freq:** Weekly (Wed.). **Print Method:** Offset. **Trim Size:** 15 1/4 x 21 1/2. **Cols./Page:** 9. **Col. Width:** 21 nonpareils. **Col. Depth:** 301 agate lines. **Key Personnel:** Willie J. Peterson, Publisher. **Subscription Rates:** $25; $30 out of country. **Remarks:** Accepts advertising.
Ad Rates: SAU: $6 **Circ:** Paid ‡3,075
PCI: $350 Free ‡65

15470 WHCH-FM - 98.3
110 W. Onota St. Phone: (906)387-4000
Munising, MI 49862 Fax: (906)387-5161
Free: (800)236-4007

Format: Contemporary Country. **Networks:** Westwood One Radio. **Owner:** Mid Pen Broadcasting, Inc., 307 S. Front St., Marquette, MI 49855. **Founded:** 1974. **Formerly:** WQXO-FM (1992). **Operating Hours:** Continuous. **ADI:** Marquette, MI. **Key Personnel:** Brian Steinhoff, General Mgr. **Wattage:** 50,000. **Ad Rates:** $7.00-11.00 for 30 seconds; $11.00-15.00 for 60 seconds.

15471 WQXO-AM - 1400
110 W. Onota St. Phone: (906)387-4000
PO Box 100 Fax: (906)387-5161
Munising, MI 49862
Free: (800)236-4007

Format: Adult Contemporary. **Networks:** Westwood One Radio. **Founded:** 1955. **Operating Hours:** Continuous. **Key Personnel:** Brian Steinhoff, General Mgr. **Wattage:** 1000. **Ad Rates:** $3-4 for 30 seconds; $5.50-6.50 for 60 seconds. Combined advertising rates available with WHCH-FM.

MUSKEGON

15472 Miniature Collector
Scott Publications
1060 W. Norton Phone: (616)780-3302
Muskegon, MI 49441 Fax: (616)780-3561
Publisher E-mail: 104137.1254@compuserve.com

Magazine for collectors and makers of dollhouses, dollhouse furnishings, and other miniatures. Articles include profiles of top artists, visits to private and public collections, and how-to projects. **Founded:** Apr. 1977. **Freq:** 8/year. **Print Method:** Offset. **Trim Size:** 8 1/2 x 11. **Cols./Page:** 3. **Col. Width:** 26 nonpareils. **Col. Depth:** 140 agate lines. **Key Personnel:** Ruth Keessen, Publisher; Barbara J. Aardema, Editor. **ISSN:** 0199-9184. **Subscription Rates:** $25.95; $33.95 other countries. **Remarks:** Accepts advertising.
Ad Rates: BW: $895 **Circ:** 40,000
4C: $1,360

15473 The Muskegon Chronicle & The Sunday Chronicle
981 3rd St. Phone: (616)722-3161
PO Box 59 Fax: (616)728-3330
Muskegon, MI 49443
Free: (800)783-3161

General newspaper. **Founded:** 1857. **Freq:** Daily (eve.), Sat. and Sun. (morn.). **Print Method:** Letterpress. **Trim Size:** 13 1/2 x 22 3/4. **Cols./Page:** 6. **Col. Width:** 25 nonpareils. **Col. Depth:** 308 agate lines. **Key Personnel:** D. Gunnar Carlson, Editor, phone (616)725-6355, fax (616)722-2552; Gary Ostrom, Publisher, phone (616)725-6350, fax (616)722-2552; Kevin Newton, Advertising Dir., phone (616)725-6311, fax (616)726-3434; Kimberly Ahrens, Controller, phone (616)725-6300; J.D. Wallace, Cir. Director, phone (616)725-6336, fax (616)722-3323; Dale Swartz, Pre-Press Mgr., phone (616)725-6330; Martha L. Mattson, NIE/Promotion Coord., phone (616)725-6390; Tom Schaub, Promotion/Marketing Mgr.; Linda Odette, phone (616)725-6367. **Subscription Rates:** $11 individuals; $11.50 out of area. **Remarks:** Accepts advertising. Sunday: GLR: $33.66; BW: $4,443.12; 4C: $5,123.12.
Ad Rates: GLR: $29.95 **Circ:** Mon.-Sat. ★**48,029**
BW: $3,953.40 Sun. ★**52,342**
4C: $4,633.40

15474 TCI Cable Vision
Box 978 Phone: (616)733-0818
Muskegon, MI 49443 Fax: (616)733-0426

Founded: 1966. **Formerly:** WestMarc Cable. **Cities Served:** Muskegon, Newaygo, and Ottawa counties, MI.

15475 WKBZ-AM - 850
592 W. Pontaluna Rd. Phone: (616)798-2141
Muskegon, MI 49444 Fax: (616)798-3677

Format: News; Talk. **Networks:** CBS; Mutual Broadcasting System. **Founded:** 1926. **Operating Hours:** Continuous. **Key Personnel:** Frank Landingham, General Mgr.; Doug Cirner, Operations Mgr.; Lucy Nalley, Sales Mgr.; John Hughs, News Dir. **Local Programs:** *The Talk of the Town.* **Wattage:** 1,000. **Ad Rates:** Advertising accepted; rates available upon request.

15476 WKBZ-FM - 95.3
592 W. Pontaluna Rd. Phone: (616)798-2141
Muskegon, MI 49444 Fax: (616)798-3677

Format: Urban Contemporary; Full Service. **Founded:** 1975. **Formerly:** WRNF-FM; WCNF-FM. **Operating Hours:** Continuous. **Key Personnel:** Frank Landingham, General Mgr.; Frank Landingham, Station Mgr.; Doug Cirner, Operations Mgr.; Lucy Nalley, Sales Mgr.; John Hughs, News Dir. **Wattage:** 3,000. **Ad Rates:** Advertising accepted; rates available upon request.

15477 WLCS-FM - 98.3
851 W. Laketon Ave. Phone: (616)759-0544
Muskegon, MI 49441-2964 Fax: (616)759-3410

Format: Oldies. **Networks:** ABC. **Founded:** 1983. **Formerly:** WIMM-FM (1986). **Operating Hours:** Continuous. **ADI:** Grand Rapids-Kalamazoo-Battle Creek, MI. **Key Personnel:** Bob Bolton, Vice Pres./General Mgr. **Wattage:** 3000. **Ad Rates:** $9 for 15 seconds; $18 for 30 seconds; $22 for 60 seconds. Combined advertising rates available with WEFG-FM & WVBR-AM.

15478 WMHG-AM - 1600
875 E. Summit Ave. Phone: (616)733-1616
Muskegon, MI 49444 Fax: (616)739-9037

Format: Middle-of-the-Road (MOR). **Networks:** ABC. **Owner:** Goodrich Radio Marketing, 4417 Broadmoor, Kentwood, MI 49512, (616)698-7733, Fax: (616)698-7220. **Founded:** 1949. **Formerly:** WTRU-AM; WSNX-AM; WSFN-AM. **Operating Hours:** Continuous. **ADI:** Grand Rapids-Kalamazoo-Battle Creek, MI. **Key Personnel:** Mike St.Cyr, General Mgr.; Caroljean Scheidt, Sales Mgr. **Wattage:** 5000. **Ad Rates:** Advertising accepted; rates available upon request. Combined advertising rates available with WMRR-FM, WSHZ-FM.

15479 WMUS-AM - 1090
Lakeview Center Phone: (616)722-2091
3565 Green St. Fax: (616)733-1107
Muskegon, MI 49442
Free: (800)304-3528
E-mail: 107mus@novagate.com

Format: Contemporary Country. **Networks:** ABC. **Owner:** Radio One, at above address. **Founded:** 1947. **Operating Hours:** Continuous; 1% network, 99% local. **ADI:** Grand Rapids-Kalamazoo-Battle Creek, MI. **Key Personnel:** Harvey Nedeau, Pres. & Chairman of the Board; Bob Kozel, Sales Mgr.; Mark Dixon, Operations Mgr.; Pam Roberts, Asst. Program Dir. & Promotions Dir.; Scott Stick, Asst. Program Dir. & Music Dir.; Gene Gregory, News & Creative Services. **Wattage:** 1000. **Ad Rates:** Combined advertising rates available with WMUS-FM.

15480 WMUS-FM - 106.9
3565 Green St. Phone: (616)744-1671
Muskegon, MI 49442 Fax: (616)733-1107
Free: (800)304-3528
E-mail: 107mus@novagate.com

Format: Contemporary Country. **Networks:** ABC. **Founded:** 1947. **Operating Hours:** Continuous; 1% network, 99% local. **ADI:** Grand Rapids-Kalamazoo-Battle Creek, MI. **Key Personnel:** Harvey Nedeau, Pres. & Chairman of the Board; Bob Kozel, Sales Mgr.; Mark Dixon, Operations Mgr.; Pam Roberts, Asst. Program Dir. & Promotions Dir.; Scott Stick, Asst. Program Dir. & Music Dir.; Gene Gregory, News & Creative Services. **Wattage:** 50,000. **Ad Rates:** Combined advertising rates available with WMUS-AM.

15481 WQWQ-AM - 1520
592 W. Pontaluna Rd. Phone: (616)798-2141
Muskegon, MI 49444 Fax: (616)798-3677
Free: (800)652-1520

Format: Contemporary Christian. **Networks:** Satellite Music Network. **Owner:** WLC Broadcasting Inc., at above address. **Founded:** 1963. **Formerly:** WKJR-AM. **Operating Hours:** Continuous. **ADI:** Marquette, MI. **Key Personnel:** Frank Landingham, VP/Gen. Mgr.; Doug Cirner, VP, Operations; Lucy Nalley, General Sales Mgr.; John Hughs, News Dir. **Local Programs:** *Artist of the Week*, Al Flogg, (616)798-2245, Fax (616)798-3819. **Wattage:** 10,000 day; 1000 night. **Ad Rates:** Advertising accepted; rates available upon request.

15482 WUBR-AM - 1490
851 Laketon Ave. Phone: (616)759-0544
Muskegon, MI 49441 Fax: (616)759-3410
Free: (800)968-7529

Format: Music of Your Life. **Networks:** Jones Satellite; Unistar. **Founded:** 1981. **Formerly:** WPBK-AM (1992); WEFG-AM. **Operating Hours:** Continuous; 100% network. **Key Personnel:** Bob Bolton, General Mgr.; Jim Schlichting, Sales Mgr.; Oscar Osbo, Program Dir. **Wattage:** 1000. **Ad Rates:** Combined advertising rates available with WEFG-FM, WLCS-FM. **URL:** http://www.virst.com.

NEGAUNEE

15483 WKQS-FM - 101.9
101 Huron Ct. Phone: (906)227-7777
Negaunee, MI 49866 Fax: (906)228-9717
E-mail: todd@wkqs.com

Format: Adult Contemporary. **Networks:** ABC. **Owner:** Great Lakes Radio, Inc., at above address. **Founded:** Jan. 4, 1997. **Operating Hours:** Continuous. **ADI:** Marquette, MI. **Key Personnel:** Mark Evans, Station Mgr., mark@wkqs.com; Jennifer Richards, Program and Music Dir.; Walt Lindala, News Dir., news@wkqs.com. **Wattage:** 50,000. **Ad Rates:** $10 for 30 seconds; $14 for 60 seconds. **URL:** http://www.wkqs.com.

15484 WLUC-TV - 6
177 U.S. Hwy. 41 East Phone: (906)475-4161
Negaunee, MI 49866 Fax: (906)475-4824
Free: (800)562-9776
E-mail: tv6sales@wluctv6.com

Format: Commercial TV. **Networks:** NBC. **Owner:** Raycom Media, RSA Tower, 201 Monroe St., Ste. 710, Montgomery, AL 36104, (334)206-1400, Fax: (334)206-1555. **Founded:** 1956. **Operating Hours:** 5:30 a.m.-2 a.m. **ADI:** Marquette, MI. **Key Personnel:** Brad Van Sluyters, Vice President/GM, bvansluyters@raycommedia.com. **Wattage:** 100,000. **Ad Rates:** Advertising accepted; rates available upon request. **URL:** http://wluctv6.com.

NEW BALTIMORE

15485 The Voice
Voice Communications Corp.
PO Box 760 Phone: (810)987-6464
New Baltimore, MI 48047 Fax: (810)949-2217

Community newspaper. **Founded:** Apr. 1983. **Freq:** Weekly. **Print Method:** Web. **Cols./Page:** 5. **Col. Width:** 2 inches. **Col. Depth:** 15 inches. **Key Personnel:** Donna Reamer, Editor; Debbie Loggins, Advertising Mgr. **Subscription Rates:** $24 individuals. **Remarks:** Accepts advertising.
Ad Rates: PCI: $42 **Circ:** Free 62,024

NEW BUFFALO

15486 New Buffalo Times
P.O. Box 369 Phone: (616)469-1100
102 S. Whittaker Fax: (616)469-6397
New Buffalo, MI 49117
Community newspaper. **Founded:** 1942. **Freq:** Weekly (Wed.). **Print Method:** Offset. **Trim Size:** 12 x 14 1/2. **Cols./Page:** 4. **Col. Width:** 14 1/2 picas. **Col. Depth:** 13 inches. **Key Personnel:** M.B. Moriarty, Editor and Publisher. **USPS:** 377-960. **Subscription Rates:** $26; $39 out of area. **Remarks:** Accepts advertising. **Formerly:** New Buffalo Times & Bridgeman Times (1990).
Ad Rates: GLR: $10 **Circ:** ‡5,000
PCI: $10

NEWBERRY

15487 Newberry News
Newberry News Inc.
PO Box 46 Phone: (906)293-8401
Newberry, MI 49868 Fax: (906)293-8815

Community newspaper. **Founded:** 1886. **Freq:** Weekly

(Wed.). **Cols./Page:** 6. **Col. Width:** 2 inches. **Col. Depth:** 21 inches. **Key Personnel:** Nancy Diem, Editor and Publisher, updiems@aol.com. **USPS:** 383-980. **Subscription Rates:** $22 local; $29 outside of Luce County. **Remarks:** Accepts advertising.
Ad Rates: SAU: $3 **Circ:** 3,600
PCI: $3.30

15488 WNBY-AM - 1450
Hwy. M-123 S. Phone: (906)293-3221
PO Box 501 Fax: (906)293-8275
Newberry, MI 49868

Format: Easy Listening. **Networks:** ABC; Jones Satellite. **Owner:** Gerald Feutz, at above address. **Founded:** 1966. **Operating Hours:** Continuous; 80% network, 20% local. **Key Personnel:** Gerald Feutz, Contact; Sandy Feutz, Contact; Vickie Holcomb, Contact. **Wattage:** 1000. **Ad Rates:** $7 for 30 seconds; $9 for 60 seconds.

15489 WNBY-FM - 93.7
Hwy. M-123 S. Phone: (906)293-3221
PO Box 501 Fax: (906)293-8275
Newberry, MI 49868

Format: Oldies. **Networks:** ABC; Satellite Music Network; Jones Satellite. **Owner:** Gerald Feutz, at above address. **Founded:** 1966. **Operating Hours:** Continuous. **Key Personnel:** Gerald Feutz, Contact; Saundra Feutz, Contact; Vickie Holcomb, Contact. **Wattage:** 6000. **Ad Rates:** $9.50 for 30 seconds; $12 for 60 seconds.

NILES

Argus - See Edwardsburg

15490 Hometown News
Hometown
314 E. Main St. Phone: (616)684-8844
PO Box 549 Fax: (616)684-6115
Niles, MI 49120
Community newspaper. **Founded:** 1988. **Freq:** Weekly. **Print Method:** Offset. **Trim Size:** 13 3/4 x 23 1/4. **Col. Width:** 2 inches. **Col. Depth:** 22 inches. **Key Personnel:** Lyle Sumerix, Editor. **Subscription Rates:** Free. **Remarks:** Advertising not accepted.
Circ: Free ‡27,000

15491 Niles Daily Star
Argus
217 N. 4th St.
Niles, MI 49120-2301

General newspaper. **Founded:** 1886. **Freq:** Mon.-Sat. (morn.). **Print Method:** Offset. **Cols./Page:** 8. **Col. Width:** 21 nonpareils. **Col. Depth:** 294 agate lines. **Key Personnel:** Danny Dean, Editor and Publisher; Polli M. Smith-Ryder, Advertising Mgr. **Subscription Rates:** $48. **Remarks:** Accepts advertising.
Ad Rates: PCI: $4.80 **Circ:** (Not Reported)

15492 WAOR-FM - 95.3
210 S. Philip Rd. Phone: (616)683-6123
PO Box 370 Fax: (616)683-2758
Niles, MI 49120
E-mail: waor@waor.com

Format: Classic Rock. **Founded:** 1957. **Operating Hours:** Continuous. **ADI:** South Bend-Elkhart, IN. **Key Personnel:** Patricia Redd, General Mgr.; Pam Reed, Sales Mgr.; Shelley Morgan, Program Dir. **Local Programs:** *Michiana Today* 7:30-8:00 a.m. Sunday. **Wattage:** 3300. **Ad Rates:** $45-70 per unit. Combined advertising rates available with WNIL-AM. **URL:** http://www.waor.com.

15493 WNIL-AM - 1290
210 S. Phillip Rd. Phone: (616)683-6123
PO Box 370 Fax: (616)683-2758
Niles, MI 49120

Format: Oldies. **Networks:** Mutual Broadcasting System; Jones Satellite. **Owner:** Niles Broadcasting Co, at above address. **Founded:** 1956. **Operating Hours:** 6 a.m.-6 p.m., winter; Sunrise-sunset, summer; 80% network, 20% local. **ADI:** South Bend-Elkhart, IN. **Key Personnel:** Patrick Redd, General Mgr.; Pam Reed, Sales Mgr.; Sara Charisse, News Dir.; Ric Clingman, Program Dir. **Local Programs:** *Fabulous Sports Babe* 10 a.m. - 2 p.m. Monday-Friday; *Michiana Today* 9:30 a.m. - 10 a.m. Monday-Friday; *One on One Sports* 2 p.m. - 8 p.m. Monday-Friday. **Wattage:** 500. **Ad Rates:** $10-20 for 60 seconds. WAOR-FM.

NORTH BRANCH

15494 Cable Properties Inc.
PO Box 386 Phone: (810)688-3059
North Branch, MI 48461 Fax: (810)793-4669
Free: (800)950-3059

Founded: Jan. 1988. **Key Personnel:** J. David Giesy, President; Carol M. Davis, Vice President. **Cities Served:** Applegate, Attica, Clifford, Deckeville, Deford, Forester, Forestville, Kingston, Lum, Munger, Silverwood, MI; Rives Junction, Minden City, Ruth, Berville, Otterlake, Mayv ille, Fostoria, Goodells: subscribing households 2,279; 42 channels; 2 community access channels; 2 hours per week community access programming.

NORTHVILLE

15495 The Northville Record
Hometown Newspapers
104 W. Main Phone: (313)369-1700
Northville, MI 48167-1521 Fax: (810)349-1050

Community newspaper. **Founded:** 1869. **Freq:** Semiweekly (Mon. and Thurs.). **Print Method:** Offset. **Trim Size:** 13 3/4 x 22 1/2. **Cols./Page:** 6. **Col. Width:** 2 1/16 inches. **Col. Depth:** 21 1/2 inches. **Key Personnel:** Lee Snider, Editor; Rich Perlberg, Publisher; Gary Kelber, Advertising Mgr. **Subscription Rates:** $18; $22 in state; $25 out of state. **Remarks:** Accepts advertising.
Ad Rates: GLR: $13.17 **Circ:** Combined ♦5,886
BW: $1,698.93
4C: $1,898.93
SAU: $13.17
PCI: $13.17

Novi News - See Novi

NORWAY

15496 City of Norway CATV
915 Brown St. Phone: (906)563-9641
Box 99 Fax: (906)563-7502
Norway, MI 49870

Owner: City of Norway, 915 Main St., PO Box 99, Norway, MI 49870, (906)563-8015, Fax: (906)563-7502. **Founded:** 1954. **Key Personnel:** Tom Pearman, Chief Technician, phone (906)563-9961, fax (906)563-7502. **Cities Served:** Norway, MI; Norway Township, MI: subscribing households 1,633; 37 channels; 1 community access channel; 168 hours per week community access programming.

NOVI

15497 American Tool, Die & Stamping News
Eagle Publications, Inc.
42400 Grand River, Ste. 103 Phone: (248)347-3486
Novi, MI 48375-2572 Fax: (248)347-3492
Free: (800)783-3491
Publication E-mail: amertdsn@ismi.net

Magazine focusing on tool, die, stamping, and EDMing. **Founded:** 1973. **Freq:** Bimonthly. **Print Method:** Web offset. **Trim Size:** 8 1/2 x 11. **Cols./Page:** 2 and 3. **Col. Width:** 28 and 42 nonpareils. **Col. Depth:** 98 agate lines. **Key Personnel:** Gail Dawson, Advertising, amertdsn@ismi.net; Arthur E. Brown, Editor; Joan Oakley, Circulation. **ISSN:** 0192-5709. **Subscription Rates:** $80 other countries. **Remarks:** Accepts advertising. **URL:** http://www.ismi.net/tool-die. **Formerly:** Die-making, Stamping and EDMing; EDM Digest.
Ad Rates: BW: $2,275 **Circ:** Controlled 37,000
4C: $3,075

15498 Filtration News
Eagle Publications, Inc.
42400 Grand River, Ste. 103 Phone: (248)347-3486
Novi, MI 48375-2572 Fax: (248)347-3492
Free: (800)783-3491
Publication E-mail: filtnews@ismi.net

Magazine focusing on industrial particulate removal. **Founded:** 1982. **Freq:** Bimonthly. **Print Method:** Web offset. **Trim Size:** 8 1/2 x 11. **Cols./Page:** 2 and 3. **Col. Width:** 38 and 25 nonpareils. **Col. Depth:** 98 agate lines. **Key Personnel:** Carol Brown, Editor; Arthur Brown, Publisher; Joseph Driscoll, Advertising Mgr. **Remarks:** Accepts advertising.
Ad Rates: BW: $2,275 **Circ:** Controlled ‡29,000
4C: $2,775
PCI: $75

15499 Novi News
Hometown Newspapers
104 W. Main Phone: (810)349-1700
Northville, MI 48167 Fax: (810)349-1050

Community newspaper. **Founded:** 1955. **Freq:** Weekly (Thurs.) Thursday only. **Print Method:** Offset. **Trim Size:** 13 3/4 x 22 1/2. **Cols./Page:** 6. **Col. Width:** 2 1/16 inches. **Col. Depth:** 21 1/2 inches. **Key Personnel:** Rich Perlberg, Publisher; Mike Malott, Managing Editor, mikem@aeonline.com; Gary Kelber, Advertising Mgr. **Subscription Rates:** $22 local; $27 in state; $30 out of state. **Remarks:** Accepts advertising.
Ad Rates: GLR: $12.98 **Circ:** Combined ♦5,541
BW: $1,674.42
4C: $1,874.42
SAU: $12.98

15500 Novi Spinal Column Newsweekly
Spinal Column Publications
7196 Cooley Lake Rd. Phone: (248)360-6397
PO Box 14 Fax: (248)360-4711
Union Lake, MI 48387-0014
Local newspaper. **Founded:** 1960. **Freq:** Weekly. **Print Method:** Offset. **Trim Size:** 10 1/2 x 15. **Cols./Page:** 8. **Col. Width:** 7 picas. **Col. Depth:** 14 inches. **Key Personnel:** David D. Hohendorf, Publisher; James W. Fancy, Publisher; Laurie Wallace, Advertising Mgr. **Remarks:** Accepts advertising.
Ad Rates: GLR: $5.82 **Circ:** Free ‡4,150
BW: $651.84
PCI: $11.64

15501 Royal Oak Courier
Anne C. Rose
31210 Portside Dr., No. 3201
Novi, MI 48377

Weekly community newspaper. **Founded:** 1996. **Freq:** Weekly. **Print Method:** Web offset. **Trim Size:** 11 x 17. **Cols./Page:** 3. **Key Personnel:** Anne C. Rose, Publisher. **Subscription Rates:** $25.

15502 WCAF-AM - 1530
31210 Portside Dr., No. 3201
Novi, MI 48377

Format: Classical. **Founded:** 1996. **Operating Hours:** Continuous. **Key Personnel:** Anne C. Rose, General Mgr. **Wattage:** 1000. **Ad Rates:** $12-25 for 30 seconds.

15503 WOVI-FM - 89.5
24062 Taft Rd. Phone: (810)449-1526
Novi, MI 48375 Fax: (810)449-1519
E-mail: wovi@hs.novi.k12.mi.us

Format: Adult Album Alternative. **Networks:** Independent. **Founded:** 1978. **Operating Hours:** 7 a.m.-3 p.m.; 100% local. **Key Personnel:** David A. Legg, Station Mgr. **Wattage:** 100 ERP. **Ad Rates:** Noncommercial. **URL:** http://hs.novi.k12.mi.us/wovi/.

OAK PARK

15504 Bridge
The Bridge
14050 Vernon St.
Oak Park, MI 48237

Literary magazine containing fiction, poetry, and reviews. **Subtitle:** A Journal of Fiction & Poetry. **Founded:** Dec. 1990. **Freq:** Semiannual. **Print Method:** Letterpress. **Trim Size:** 5 1/2 x 8 1/2. **Cols./Page:** 1. **Key Personnel:** Jack Zucker, Contact; Helen Zucker, Contact, hzucker@oakland.edu; Mitzi Alvin, Contact. **Subscription Rates:** $13 individuals; $7 single issue.
Circ: Paid 600
Non-paid 100

15505 WHND-AM - 560
22150 Greenfield Rd. No. 200 Phone: (810)968-4100
Oak Park, MI 48237 Fax: (810)968-4103

Format: Oldies. **Networks:** Unistar. **Owner:** Radio Group, Inc., 640 Fifth Ave., New York, NY 10019. **Founded:** 1956. **Formerly:** WQTE-AM. **Operating Hours:** Sunrise-sunset. **Key Personnel:** Dino Valle, General Sales Mgr. **Wattage:** 500. **Ad Rates:** Advertising accepted; rates available upon request.

15506 WKQI-FM - 95.5
15401 W. 10 Mile Rd. Phone: (248)967-3750
Oak Park, MI 48237 Fax: (248)967-0840

Format: Contemporary Hit Radio (CHR); Adult Contemporary. **Owner:** Chancellor Media Corp., 300 Crescent Ct., Ste. 600, Dallas, TX 75201. **Founded:** 1949. **Formerly:** WCZY-FM (1989). **Operating Hours:** Continuous. **ADI:** Detroit, MI. **Key Personnel:** Dave Kerr, Vice Pres./General Mgr., phone (214)922-8700; Charlie Fritz, General Sales Mgr.; Tom O'Brien, Program Dir.; Teresa Tomeo, Contact. **Wattage:** 100,000.

OKEMOS

15507 The Corporate Board
Vanguard Publications, Inc.
4440 S. Hagadorn Rd. Phone: (517)336-1700
Okemos, MI 48864 Fax: (517)336-1705
Publication E-mail: info@corporateboard.com

Journal covering corporate directorship issues. **Subtitle:** Journal of Corporate Governance. **Founded:** 1980. **Freq:** Bimonthly. **Print Method:** Offset. **Trim Size:** 8 1/2 x 11. **Cols./Page:** 2. **Col. Width:** 39 nonpareils. **Col. Depth:** 122 agate lines. **Key Personnel:** Ralph Ward, Editor, phone (517)833-7615, fax (517)833-7615, editor@corporateboard.com. **ISSN:** 0746-8652. **Subscription Rates:** $450 individuals; $2,695 corporate. **Remarks:** Advertising not accepted. **Formerly:** The Corporate Director (1983).
Circ: ‡3,300

15508 Michigan Christmas Tree Journal
Michigan Christmas Tree Association
PO Box 1215 Phone: (517)332-5511
Okemos, MI 48805-1215 Fax: (517)332-4848
Free: (800)589-TREE

Magazine of the Michigan Christmas Tree Assn. **Founded:** 1958. **Freq:** Quarterly. **Cols./Page:** 3. **Col. Width:** 2 1/4 inches. **Col. Depth:** 10 inches. **Key Personnel:** Laurie Koelling, Editor. **Subscription Rates:** Included in association membership.
Ad Rates: BW: $275 **Circ:** 1,200
4C: $750
PCI: $25

15509 Michigan Country Lines
Michigan Electric Cooperative Association
2859 W. Jolly Rd. Phone: (517)351-6322
Okemos, MI 48864 Fax: (517)351-6396

Magazine on rural lifestyles and home energy use. **Founded:** 1980. **Freq:** Bimonthly. **Print Method:** Web offset. **Trim Size:** 8 x 10 1/2. **Cols./Page:** 3. **Col. Width:** 2 5/16 inches. **Col. Depth:** 10 inches. **Key Personnel:** Michael F. Buda, Executive Editor, mbuda@countrylines.com; Gail Knudtson, Editor; Deena Carlson, Editorial Asst.; Alison Lahti, Advertising Asst. **USPS:** 591-710. **Subscription Rates:** $4. **Remarks:** Accepts advertising. **URL:** http://www.countrylines.com.
Ad Rates: BW: $3,450 **Circ:** 216,000
4C: $3,850
PCI: $180

15510 Triad
Michigan Osteopathic Association
2445 Woodlake Circle Phone: (517)347-1555
Okemos, MI 48864-5941 Fax: (517)347-1566
Free: (800)657-1556
Publisher E-mail: moa@com.msu.edu

Professional journal of the Michigan Osteopathic Association. **Founded:** 1988. **Freq:** Quarterly. **Trim Size:** 8 1/2 x 11. **Key Personnel:** John Everett, D.O., Editor; Heather E. Puskala, Managing Editor; Cheri Rugh, Advertising Exec. **ISSN:** 1046-4948. **Subscription Rates:** $50 individuals. **Remarks:** Accepts advertising.
Ad Rates: BW: $475 **Circ:** Paid ⊕**3,500**
4C: $1,300

OLIVET

15511 Shipherd's Record
Olivet College
Olivet, MI 49076 Phone: (616)749-7630
Fax: (616)749-6629

College alumni magazine. **Founded:** 1980. **Freq:** Quarterly. **Print Method:** Offset. **Trim Size:** 16 1/4 x 11 1/4. **Cols./Page:** 3. **Col. Width:** 28 nonpareils. **Col. Depth:** 134 agate lines. **Key Personnel:** Charles W. Sheaffer, Editor, csheaffer@olivetnet.edu. **USPS:** 407-860.
Circ: Non-paid 10,000

15512 WOCR-FM - 89.7
105A Mott Center Phone: (616)749-7398
Olivet College Fax: (616)749-7121
Olivet, MI 49076

Format: Contemporary Hit Radio (CHR). **Networks:** Independent. **Founded:** 1975. **Operating Hours:** 7 a.m.-2 a.m. 100% local. **Key Personnel:** Stuart Blacklaw, Contact; Carlos Sims, General Mgr.; Richard Craig, Station Mgr.; Mike Adams, Station Mgr. **Local Programs:** *AM Mayem*, Alex Demott; *Lunch Box Jam*, Sam Quintella; *Softnotes*, Brian Ward. **Wattage:** 125. **Ad Rates:** Noncommercial.

ONAWAY

15513 The Onaway Outlook
Presque Newspaper
PO Box 176 Phone: (517)734-2105
Onaway, MI 49765-0176
Community newspaper. **Founded:** 1974. **Freq:** Weekly (Wed.). **Print Method:** Offset. **Cols./Page:** 6. **Col. Width:** 19 nonpareils. **Col. Depth:** 224 agate lines. **Key Personnel:** Richard W. Lamb, General Mgr. **Subscription Rates:** $22 individuals. **Remarks:** Accepts advertising.
Ad Rates: GLR: $220.80 **Circ:** ‡2,400
PCI: $3

15514 Presque Isle County Advance
Presque Newspaper
PO Box 176 Phone: (517)734-2105
Onaway, MI 49765-0176
Community newspaper. **Founded:** 1879. **Freq:** Weekly (Thurs.). **Print Method:** Offset. **Cols./Page:** 8. **Col. Width:** 20 nonpareils. **Col. Depth:** 294 agate lines. **Key Personnel:** Richard Lamb, Editor/Gen. Mgr.; Dick Higgs, Managing Editor. **Subscription Rates:** $23 individuals. **Remarks:** Accepts advertising.
Ad Rates: GLR: $500 **Circ:** 4,400
BW: $1,144
4C: $1,750
SAU: $5
PCI: $3.50

ONTONAGON

15515 The Ontonagon Herald
326 River St. Phone: (906)884-2826
Ontonagon, MI 49953 Fax: (906)884-2939

Community newspaper. **Founded:** 1881. **Freq:** Weekly (Wed.). **Print Method:** Web offset. **Trim Size:** 14 x 22. **Cols./Page:** 6. **Col. Width:** 2 1/16 inches. **Col. Depth:** 21 inches. **Key Personnel:** Maureen Guzek, Editor and Publisher. **Subscription Rates:** $33 individuals.
Ad Rates: BW: $693 **Circ:** 3,750
PCI: $5.50

15516 WOAS-FM - 88.5
701 Parker Phone: (906)884-4422
Ontonagon, MI 49953 Fax: (906)884-2742
E-mail: kraisane@goisd.k12.mi.us

Format: Full Service. **Networks:** Independent. **Owner:** Ontonagon Area Schools, at above address. **Founded:** 1979. **Operating Hours:** 10 a.m.-3:30 p.m. **Key Personnel:** K. Raisanen, Acting Mgr.; C. Zielinski, Acting Mgr. **Wattage:** 10. **Ad Rates:** Advertising accepted; rates available upon request.

15517 WUPY-FM - 101.1
610 Greenland Rd. Phone: (906)884-9668
Ontonagon, MI 49953-1422 Fax: (906)884-4985
E-mail: wupy@up.net

Format: Oldies; News; Sports; Religious. **Networks:** Michigan; CBS; ABC. **Owner:** S & S Broadcasting, at above address. **Founded:** 1986. **Formerly:** WONT-FM. **Operating Hours:** Continuous. **Key Personnel:** Skip Schulz, General Sales Mgr., sshultz@up.net; Jackie Dobbins, Program Dir., jdobbins@up.net; Heather Store, News Dir., hstore@up.net; Sandy Schulz, General Sales Manager, sshulz@up.net; Bob Peltola, Sports Dir., wupy@up.net. **Wattage:** 30,000. **Ad Rates:** $5-8 for 30 seconds; $7-10 for 60 seconds.

ORTONVILLE

15518 The County Line Reminder
Lapeer County Press
48 South St., Ste. 101 Phone: (248)627-2843
Ortonville, MI 48462 Fax: (248)627-3473

Local newspaper. **Founded:** 1952. **Freq:** Weekly (Sun.). **Print Method:** Offset. **Cols./Page:** 6. **Col. Width:** 2 1/16 inches. **Col. Depth:** 21 inches. **Key Personnel:** Ernest Slade, Publisher. **Subscription Rates:** $79 out of area. **Remarks:** Accepts advertising.
Ad Rates: GLR: $9.10 **Circ:** Paid ‡200
BW: $535 Free ‡10,000
4C: $1,080
SAU: $8.12

OSCODA

15519 Oscoda Press
News Press Publishing Co.
311 S. State St. Phone: (517)739-2055
PO Box 663 Fax: (517)739-3201
Oscoda, MI 48750
Local newspaper. **Freq:** Weekly (Wed.). **Cols./Page:** 5. **Col. Width:** 2 1/4 inches. **Col. Depth:** 16 1/2 inches. **Key Personnel:** J. Berkeley Smith, Editor and Publisher. **USPS:** 412-840. **Subscription Rates:** $25 individuals; $30 out of area; $35 out of state. **Remarks:** Accepts advertising.
Ad Rates: SAU: $4.20 **Circ:** 5,900

OTISVILLE

15520 The Daze
Daze Inc.
10271 S. State Rd. Phone: (313)631-4593
Otisville, MI 48463 Fax: (313)631-4567
Free: (800)336-9927

Magazine (tabloid) on antique and collectible glass and china pottery pieces made in America between 1920 and 1950. **Founded:** Mar. 1971. **Freq:** Monthly. **Print Method:** Offset. **Cols./Page:** 7. **Col. Width:** 17 nonpareils. **Col. Depth:** 180 agate lines. **Key Personnel:** Teri Steele, Editor and Publisher; Jill Farnsworth, Managing Editor. **ISSN:** 0895-3961. **Subscription Rates:** $21. $2 single issue. **Remarks:** Accepts advertising. **Online:** DG Daze. **Formerly:** Depression Glass Daze, Inc.
Ad Rates: BW: $614 **Circ:** ‡18,000
PCI: $9.50

OTSEGO

15521 Shoppers Guide
Community Shoppers Guide Inc.
117 N. Farmer St. Phone: (616)694-9431
PO Box 168 Fax: (616)694-9145
Otsego, MI 49078-0168
Shopper. **Founded:** 1940. **Freq:** Weekly (Sat.). **Print Method:** Offset. **Trim Size:** 10 1/2 x 12 1/2. **Cols./Page:** 4. **Col. Width:** 2.47 inches. **Col. Depth:** .68 inches. **Key Personnel:** Ron Bennett, Editor and Publisher. **Remarks:** Accepts advertising. **Alt. Formats:** CD-ROM.
Ad Rates: BW: $608 **Circ:** Free ‡12,500
4C: $400
PCI: $9.50

15522 WQXC-AM - 980
Box 980 Fax: (616)692-6861
Otsego, MI 49078

Format: Adult Contemporary. **Simulcasts:** WQXC-FM. **Networks:** AP. **Founded:** 1958. **Operating Hours:** Continuous. **ADI:** Grand Rapids-Kalamazoo-Battle Creek, MI. **Key Personnel:** Robert P. Brink, Contact. **Wattage:** 1000 day; 100 night. **Ad Rates:** Advertising accepted; rates available upon request.

15523 WQXC-FM - 100.9
PO Box 80 Phone: (616)692-6851
Otsego, MI 49078-0080 Fax: (616)692-6861

Format: Oldies. **Networks:** AP. **Founded:** 1981. **Operating Hours:** Continuous. **ADI:** Grand Rapids-Kalamazoo-Battle Creek, MI. **Key Personnel:** Robert P. Brink, Contact. **Wattage:** 3000. **Ad Rates:** Advertising accepted; rates available upon request.

OWOSSO

15524 The Argus-Press
The Argus-Press Co.
201 E. Exchange St.
PO Box 399
Owosso, MI 48867

General newspaper. **Founded:** 1854. **Freq:** Daily (eve.), Sat. and Sun. (morn.). **Print Method:** Offset. **Trim Size:** 13 3/4 x 22 3/4. **Cols./Page:** 6. **Col. Width:** 12 picas. **Col. Depth:** 301 agate lines. **Key Personnel:** Richard E. Campbell, Editor; Thomas E. Campbell, Publisher; G. Mark Cudington, Advertising Dir. **USPS:** 416-280. **Subscription Rates:** $.50; $.75.
Ad Rates: GLR: $.75 **Circ:** Paid ‡12,000
BW: $1,341.60
4C: $1,626.60
SAU: $10.40

15525 The Durand Express
The Argus-Press Co.
201 E. Exchange St.
PO Box 399
Owosso, MI 48867

Community newspaper. **Founded:** July 12, 1888. **Freq:** Weekly (Thurs.). **Print Method:** Offset. **Cols./Page:** 6. **Col. Width:** 12 picas. **Col. Depth:** 21 1/2 inches. **Key Personnel:** Helen Granger, Editor; Thomas Campbell, Publisher. **USPS:** 162-920. **Subscription Rates:** $18; $30 out of state. **Remarks:** Accepts advertising.
Ad Rates: GLR: $.44 **Circ:** Paid 2,133
BW: $793.35 Non-paid 65
4C: $1,078.35
SAU: $6.15

15526 WOAP-AM - 1080
2301 N. Shiawassee St. Phone: (517)725-8196
PO Box 128 Fax: (517)725-6626
Owosso, MI 48867

Format: Country. **Networks:** Satellite Music Network; ABC. **Owner:** Michigan Radio Group, Inc., at above address, (810)744-1570, Fax: (810)743-2500. **Founded:** 1948. **Operating Hours:** Sunrise-sunset; 90% network, 10% local. **ADI:** Flint-Saginaw-Bay City, MI. **Key Personnel:** Art Kinsey, General Mgr. **Wattage:** 1000. **Ad Rates:** $7.10-14.20 for 30 seconds; $8.30-16.50 for 60 seconds.

OXFORD

15527 The Oxford Leader
Sherman Publications, Inc.
PO Box 108 Phone: (248)628-4801
Oxford, MI 48371 Fax: (248)628-9750

Community newspaper. **Founded:** 1898. **Freq:** Weekly (Wed.). **Print Method:** Offset. **Trim Size:** 11 x 16. **Cols./Page:** 6. **Col. Width:** 9 1/2 picas. **Col. Depth:** 15 inches. **Key Personnel:** James A. Sherman, Publisher; Eric Lewis, Advertising Mgr. **Subscription Rates:** $18 individuals; $20 out of area; $30 out of state. **Remarks:** Accepts advertising.
Ad Rates: GLR: $.27 **Circ:** Paid ‡3,297
BW: $396 Free ‡36
PCI: $4.40

PAW PAW

15528 The Courier-Leader
PO Box 129 Phone: (616)657-3072
Paw Paw, MI 49079-0129 Fax: (616)657-5723

Newspaper covering local agriculture and industry. **Founded:** 1843. **Freq:** Weekly (Fri.). **Print Method:** Offset. **Cols./Page:** 6. **Col. Width:** 12 1/2 nonpareils. **Col. Depth:** 290 agate lines. **Key Personnel:** Felix A. Racette, Editor and Publisher. **USPS:** 564-620. **Subscription Rates:** $14 individuals. **Remarks:** Accepts advertising.
Ad Rates: BW: $567 **Circ:** Paid ⊕**4,069**
4C: $300 Free 45
SAU: $4.84
PCI: $3

PETOSKEY

15529 The AD-vertiser
The AD-vertiser, Inc.
600 Charlevoix Ave. Phone: (616)347-8186
PO Box 826 Fax: (616)347-5744
Petoskey, MI 49770
Free: (800)735-5729

Regional shopper (tabloid) for Emmet County, western tip of northern Lower Michigan. **Founded:** 1956. **Freq:** Weekly (Sun.). **Print Method:** Offset. **Cols./Page:** 6. **Col. Width:** 1 5/8 inches. **Col. Depth:** 16 inches. **Key Personnel:** James Glasser, Publisher. **Remarks:** Accepts advertising. **Alt. Formats:** CD-ROM. **Formerly:** Emmet County AD-Vertiser (Jan. 1, 1987).
Ad Rates: GLR: $0.51 **Circ:** Free ‡13,382
BW: $690.24
4C: $915.24
PCI: $7.19

15530 The Graphic
Petoskey News-Review, Super Shopper, and Graphic
319 State St. Phone: (616)347-2544
PO Box 528 Fax: (616)347-6833
Petoskey, MI 49770-0528
Publisher E-mail: petoskeynews@petoskeynews.com

Entertainment resort newspaper. **Founded:** 1960. **Freq:** Weekly. **Print Method:** Offset. **Trim Size:** 11 3/8 x 14. **Cols./Page:** 5. **Col. Width:** 5 inches. **Col. Depth:** 13 inches. **Key Personnel:** Ken Winter, Editor; Kirk Schaller, Publisher; Dena Sydow, Advertising Mgr. **Subscription Rates:** Free. **Remarks:** Advertising accepted; rates available upon request.
Circ: Free 17,000

15531 Petoskey News-Review
Petoskey News-Review, Super Shopper, and Graphic
319 State St. Phone: (616)347-2544
PO Box 528 Fax: (616)347-6833
Petoskey, MI 49770-0528
Publisher E-mail: petoskeynews@petoskeynews.com

Local newspaper. **Founded:** 1875. **Freq:** Daily (eve.). **Print Method:** Offset. **Trim Size:** 14 x 22 3/4. **Cols./Page:** 6. **Col. Width:** 12 picas. **Col. Depth:** 21 inches. **Key Personnel:** Ken Winter, Editor/Gen. Mgr.; Kirk Schaller, Publisher; Dena Sydow, Advertising Mgr. **USPS:** 387-660. **Subscription Rates:** $121.70 individuals; $180.20 out of area.
Ad Rates: BW: $3,240.72 **Circ:** Mon.-Fri. ★**11,735**
4C: $3,882
SAU: $25.72

15532 Super Shopper
Petoskey News-Review, Super Shopper, and Graphic
319 State St. Phone: (616)347-2544
PO Box 528 Fax: (616)347-6833
Petoskey, MI 49770-0528
Publisher E-mail: petoskeynews@petoskeynews.com

Shopper. **Founded:** 1972. **Freq:** Weekly (Sun.). **Print Method:** Offset. **Trim Size:** 11 1/2 x 17. **Cols./Page:** 5. **Col. Width:** 24 nonpareils. **Col. Depth:** 224 agate lines. **Key Personnel:** Kirk Schaller, Publisher; Dena Sydow, Advertising Mgr.; Ken Winter, Ed./Gen.Mgr. **Subscription Rates:** Free.
Ad Rates: BW: $3,240.72 **Circ:** ‡30,000
4C: $3,882
SAU: $25.72

15533 WAIR-FM - 92.5
322 Bay St. Phone: (616)348-2000
Petoskey, MI 49770 Fax: (616)348-2092
Free: (800)297-9247
E-mail: wair@wair.com

Format: Oldies. **Networks:** ABC. **Owner:** Northern Bottling Co., at above address. **Founded:** 1988. **Operating Hours:** Continuous; 3% network, 97% local. **ADI:** Traverse City-Cadillac, MI. **Key Personnel:** Stan Campbell, Station Mgr., scamp@wair.com; Tom Pluister, Operations Mgr. **Wattage:** 100,000. **Ad Rates:** $12-26 for 30 seconds; $19-33 for 60 seconds.

15534 WJML-AM - 1110
2175 Click Rd. Phone: (616)348-5000
Petoskey, MI 49770
E-mail: talk@wjml.com

Format: News; Talk; Oldies. **Networks:** CBS; People's Network; Mutual Broadcasting System; Westwood One Radio. **Owner:** Stone Communications, Inc., at above address. **Founded:** 1966. **Operating Hours:** Continuous. **ADI:** Traverse City-Cadillac, MI. **Key Personnel:** Richard D. Stone, President. **Local Programs:** *Bits of Life*, B. J. Mogg. **Wattage:** 10,000. **URL:** http://www.wjml.com.

15535 WJNL-AM - 1110
2175 Click Rd. Phone: (616)348-5000
Petoskey, MI 49770
E-mail: talk@wjml.com

Format: News; Talk. **Networks:** CBS. **Owner:** Stone Communications, Inc., at above address. **Founded:** 1966. **Operating Hours:** Continuous. **Key Personnel:** Richard D. Stone, Pres./General Mgr., rick@wjml.com. **Wattage:** 10,000. **URL:** http://www.wjml.com.

15536 WKLZ-FM - 98.9
322 Bay St. Phone: (616)348-2000
Petoskey, MI 49770-2407 Fax: (616)348-7002

Format: Adult Contemporary; Soft Rock. **Simulcasts:** WKLT-FM. **Networks:** AP; ABC. **Owner:** Petoskey Broadcasting, at above address. **Founded:** 1965. **Formerly:** WJML-FM (1991). **Operating Hours:** Continuous. **ADI:** Traverse City-Cadillac, MI. **Key Personnel:** Marion Kalbfleisch, Station Mgr. **Wattage:** 52,000.

15537 WMBN-AM - 1340
PO Box 286 Phone: (616)347-8713
Petoskey, MI 49770 Fax: (616)347-9920

Format: Oldies. **Networks:** ABC. **Owner:** MacDonald Garber Broadcasting Inc., at above address. **Founded:** 1947. **Operating Hours:** Continuous. **ADI:** Traverse City-Cadillac, MI. **Key Personnel:** Trish Garber, General Mgr.; Tom Clemens, Sales Mgr. **Wattage:** 1000.

PIGEON

15538 The Newsweekly
Great Lakes Media, Inc.
7232 E. Michigan Ave. Phone: (517)453-3100
Pigeon, MI 48755 Fax: (517)453-3877
Free: (800)733-4780

Newspaper. **Founded:** 1890. **Freq:** Weekly (Tues.). **Print Method:** Letterpress and offset. **Trim Size:** 10 1/4 x 15. **Cols./Page:** 6. **Col. Width:** 9 picas. **Col. Depth:** 15 inches. **Key Personnel:** Tony Fisher, Editor. **ISSN:** 4878-6000. **Subscription Rates:** $21; $31 out of state. **Remarks:** Accepts advertising. **Formerly:** News Weekly.
Ad Rates: GLR: $.30 **Circ:** Paid 5,900
PCI: $5.10

PINCKNEY

15539 The Pinckney Shopper
Hometown Newspapers
323 E. Grand River Phone: (517)548-2000
PO Box 230 Fax: (517)548-3005
Howell, MI 48843
Shopper (tabloid). **Founded:** 1977. **Freq:** Weekly (Wed.). **Print Method:** Offset. **Trim Size:** 11 1/2 x 17. **Cols./Page:** 5. **Col. Width:** 2 1/16 inches. **Col. Depth:** 16 inches. **Key Personnel:** Roland Peterson, Publisher; Mike Preville, Advertising Mgr. **Remarks:** Accepts advertising. **Formed by the merger of:** Pickney Shopping Guide; Pickney Express. **Formerly:** The Shopper Express and Pinckney Post.
Ad Rates: BW: $395.20 **Circ:** Non-paid ♦**13,176**
4C: $595.20
SAU: $4.94
PCI: $4.94

PINCONNING

15540 Pinconning Journal
110 3rd St. Phone: (517)879-3811
PO Box 626 Fax: (517)879-5529
Pinconning, MI 48650
Community newspaper. **Founded:** 1892. **Freq:** Weekly (Wed.). **Print Method:** Offset. **Cols./Page:** 6. **Col. Width:** 12 1/2 picas. **Col. Depth:** 21 1/2 inches. **Key Personnel:** Thomas Johnson, Editor and Publisher. **Subscription Rates:** $15; $17 out of county in MI; $20 out of state. **Remarks:** Accepts advertising.
Ad Rates: BW: $380.55 **Circ:** 1,950
PCI: $2.95

PITTSFORD

15541 WPCJ-FM - 91.1
9400 Beecher Rd. Phone: (517)523-3427
Pittsford, MI 49271 Fax: (517)523-3427
E-mail: freedomfarm@dmci.net

Format: News; Religious; Information. **Networks:** Moody Broadcasting. **Owner:** Pittsford Educational Broadcasting Foundation, at above address. **Founded:** 1985. **Operating Hours:** 15.5 hours Daily; 25% network, 75% local. **Key Personnel:** Richard Krage, Station Mgr.; Ed Trombley, Chief Engineer; Tim Neinas, Asst. Mgr. **Wattage:** 280.

PLAINWELL

15542 The Union Enterprise
Kaechele Publications, Inc.
PO Box 417 Phone: (616)685-9571
Plainwell, MI 49080 Fax: (616)685-2686
Publisher E-mail: allnews@accn.org

Community newspaper (tabloid). **Freq:** Weekly (Thurs.). **Print Method:** Offset. **Cols./Page:** 5. **Col. Width:** 2 1/8 inches. **Col. Depth:** 16 inches. **Key Personnel:** Cheryl Kaechele, Publisher. **USPS:** 413-600. **Subscription Rates:** $15; $18 out of county; $22 out of state. **Remarks:** Accepts advertising.
Ad Rates: SAU: $6.06 **Circ:** Paid 755

PLYMOUTH

15543 The Community Crier
821 Penniman Ave. Phone: (313)453-6900
Plymouth, MI 48170
Local newspaper. **Founded:** Feb. 5, 1974. **Freq:** Weekly (Wed.). **Print Method:** Offset. **Cols./Page:** 4. **Col. Width:** 28 nonpareils. **Col. Depth:** 193 agate lines. **Key Personnel:** W. Edward Wendover, Publisher; Bryon Martin, Editor. **USPS:** 304-150. **Subscription Rates:** $40 individuals. **Remarks:** Accepts advertising.
Ad Rates: BW: $1,439 **Circ:** Paid ‡5,687
4C: $1,864 Free ‡14,128

15544 Plymouth Observer
Observer & Eccentric Newspapers
36251 Schoolcraft Rd. Phone: (313)591-2300
Livonia, MI 48150-1216 Fax: (313)953-2232

Community newspaper. **Founded:** 1888. **Freq:** Semiweekly (Mon. and Thurs.). **Print Method:** Offset. **Cols./Page:** 9. **Col. Width:** 17 nonpareils. **Col. Depth:** 301 agate lines. **Key Personnel:** Richard Aginian, Publisher. **Subscription Rates:** $23. **Remarks:** Accepts advertising.
Ad Rates: GLR: $2.62 **Circ:** Paid 1,060
Non-paid 3,153

15545 MediaOne
14909 Beck Rd. Phone: (734)254-1500
PO Box 8009C Fax: (734)254-1780
Plymouth, MI 48170

Founded: 1978. **Formerly:** Continental Cablevision (May 1997). **Key Personnel:** Bill Black, fax (734)254-1869, bblack@mediaone.com. **Cities Served:** Cleveland, Dayton, OH: subscribing households 354,000; 80 channels. **URL:** http://www.mediaone.com.

PONTIAC

15546 The Oakland County Legal News
The Oakland County Legal News Publishing Co., Inc.
500 W. Huron, Ste. 102 Phone: (810)338-4567
PO Box 430238 Fax: (810)338-4240
Pontiac, MI 48343-0238
Free: (800)310-4800

Magazine containing legal, business, and financial news. **Founded:** 1927. **Freq:** Weekly (Fri.). **Print Method:** Offset. **Trim Size:** 15 1/2 x 23. **Cols./Page:** 6. **Col. Width:** 1 3/4 inches. **Col. Depth:** 21 inches. **Key Personnel:** Melanie Brown, Managing Editor. **ISSN:** 0739-0203. **Subscription Rates:** $45 local; $52 in state; $60 out of state. **Remarks:** Accepts advertising. **Formerly:** The Pontiac-Oakland County Legal News.
Ad Rates: BW: $1,344 **Circ:** Paid ‡1,412
CNU: $8.91 Non-paid ‡35
PCI: $8

15547 Oakland Press
Oakland Press Co.
48 W. Huron St., No. 436009 Phone: (313)332-8181
PO Box 9 Fax: (313)332-8284
Pontiac, MI 48342-2101
General newspaper. **Founded:** 1843. **Freq:** Mon.-Sun. (morn.). **Print Method:** Letterpress. **Cols./Page:** 6. **Col. Width:** 2 1/16 inches. **Col. Depth:** 21 1/2 inches. **Key Personnel:** William Thomas, Editor; Bruce H. McIntyre, Publisher. **Subscription Rates:** $85.80. **Remarks:** Accepts advertising. **Feature Editors:** Susan Belniak, *City*; Sandra Birdiett, *Religion*; Daniel Grantham, *Financial/Business*; Jody Headlee, *Garden/Home*; Susan Hood, *News*; Kenn Jones, *Drama, Entertainment, Movie, Music*; Keith Langlois, *Sports*; Sybil Little, *Fashion, Food, Society*; Neil Munro, *Editorials*; Ed Noble, *Photo*; Holly Shreve, *Features*; Steve Spalding, *Political*.
Ad Rates: SAU: $31.50 **Circ:** Mon.-Sat. ★**80,645**
Sun. ★**97,657**

PORT HURON

15548 Times Herald
The Times Herald Co.
911 Military St. Phone: (810)985-7171
Port Huron, MI 48060 Fax: (810)989-6294
Free: (800)462-4057
Publication E-mail: tmshrld@ic.net

General newspaper. **Founded:** 1869. **Freq:** Daily (eve.). **Print Method:** Offset. **Cols./Page:** 6. **Col. Width:** 25 nonpareils. **Col. Depth:** 301 agate lines. **Key Personnel:** Patrick Rice, Editor, phone (810)989-6256, fax (810)989-6294; Mike Scobey, Publisher, phone (810)989-6236; Cindy George, Advertising Dir., phone (810)989-6267, fax (810)989-6294. **Subscription Rates:** $154. **Remarks:** Accepts advertising. **Alt. Formats:** Microform.
Ad Rates: BW: $2,702.87 **Circ:** Mon.-Sat. 30,999
4C: $3,097.87 Sun. 42,448
SAU: $24.65

15549 Woman's Life
Woman's Life Insurance Society
1338 Military St. Phone: (810)985-5191
PO Box 5020 Fax: (810)985-6970
Port Huron, MI 48061-5020
Free: (800)521-9292

Magazine for members of Woman's Life Insurance Society, a fraternal benefit society. **Subtitle:** Key Information Vital to Every Woman's Fiscal and Physical Health. **Founded:** 1892. **Freq:** Quarterly. **Print Method:** Offset. **Trim Size:** 8 3/8 x 10 7/8. **Cols./Page:** 3. **Col. Width:** 13 picas. **Col. Depth:** 53 picas. **Key Personnel:** Janice U. Whipple, Editor and Publisher; Wendy L. Krabach, Dir. of Communications/Fraternal Svcs. **ISSN:** 0027-5689. **Subscription Rates:** Free to members. **Remarks:** Advertising not accepted. **Formerly:** Review.
Circ: Non-paid 34,000

15550 WBTI-FM - 96.9
2379 Military St. Phone: (810)987-4100
Port Huron, MI 48060

Format: Adult Contemporary. **Networks:** Independent. **Owner:** Hanson Communications, Inc., at above address. **Founded:** 1991. **Operating Hours:** Continuous. **Wattage:** 5000. **Ad Rates:** Advertising accepted; rates available upon request.

15551 WHLS-AM - 1450
808 Huron Ave. Phone: (810)987-1450
PO Box 807 Fax: (810)987-9380
Port Huron, MI 48061-0807

Format: Oldies. **Networks:** AP; Jones Satellite. **Owner:** Wismer Broadcasting, Inc., at above address. **Founded:** 1938. **Operating Hours:** Continuous. **ADI:** Detroit, MI. **Key Personnel:** John F. Wismer, Owner/Pres.; Matt Brown, Operations Mgr.; Lawrence Smith, Sales Mgr.; Gary Girard, News Dir. **Local Programs:** *Let's Talk About It*, K.C. Norman, Mailing contact; *Let's Talk Sports*, Dennis Stockey, Mailing contact; *Special Edition*, K.C. Norman, Mailing contact. **Wattage:** 1000. **Ad Rates:** $6-24.50 for 30 seconds; $7-27.50 for 60 seconds.

15552 WHYT-AM - 1590
2379 Military St. Phone: (810)987-4100
Port Huron, MI 48060

Format: Country. **Networks:** ABC. **Owner:** Hancom LLC, at above address. **Founded:** 1952. **Formerly:** WDOG; WSMD; Hanson Communications, Inc.; WISN. **Operating Hours:** Continuous. **Key Personnel:** Lee C. Hanson, Contact. **Local Programs:** *The Good Morning Show*, Dene Tyrrell. **Wattage:** 1000. **Ad Rates:** Advertising accepted; rates available upon request. Combined advertising rates available with WBTI-FM, WPHM-AM.

15553 WNFA-FM - 88.3
2865 Maywood Dr. Phone: (810)985-3260
Port Huron, MI 48060 Fax: (810)985-7712
Free: (800)989-9637
E-mail: wnradio@aol.com

Format: Religious. **Networks:** Moody Broadcasting; SkyLight Satellite; USA Radio. **Founded:** 1986. **Operating Hours:** Continuous; 50% network, 50% local. **Key Personnel:** Tom Winn, Station Mgr.; Ellyn Davey, Contact; Lori McNaughton, Operations Mgr. **Wattage:** 1300. **Ad Rates:** Noncommercial.

15554 WSAQ-FM - 107.1
808 Huron Ave. Phone: (810)987-1450
Port Huron, MI 48061-0807 Fax: (810)987-9380
E-mail: wsaq@mail.rc.net

Format: Contemporary Country. **Networks:** Westwood One Radio. **Owner:** Wismer Broadcasting, Inc., at above address. **Founded:** 1964. **Operating Hours:** Continuous. **Key Personnel:** John F. Wismer, Owner/Pres.; Brian Harper, Program Dir.; Lawrence Smith, Sales Mgr. **Local Programs:** *Morning Show*, Brian Harper, Mailing contact; *Saturday Night House Party*, Leslie James, Mailing contact; *Sunday Morning Classics*, Brian Harper, Mailing contact. **Wattage:** 6,000 ERP.

15555 WSGR-FM - 91.3
323 Erie St. Phone: (810)984-5064
Port Huron, MI 48061-5015

Format: Eclectic. **Founded:** 1971. **Operating Hours:** 8 a.m.-2 a.m. Daily. **Key Personnel:** John Hill, General Mgr.; Lance Billow, Program Dir. **Wattage:** 100.

PORTAGE

15556 Cablevision Michigan, Inc.
4176 Commercial Ave. Phone: (616)323-2236
Portage, MI 49002 Fax: (616)323-0580

Owner: Cablevision Systems Corp., One Media Crossways, Woodbury, NY 11797, (516)364-8450. **Founded:** 1966. **Key Personnel:** Gary Kaser, Branch Systems Manager. **Cities Served:** Kalamazoo County: subscribing households 52,000; 44 channels; 4 community access channels; 674 hours per week community access programming.

PORTLAND

15557 Portland Review & Observer
Community Newspapers
219 S. Bridge Phone: (517)627-6085
Grand Ledge, MI 48837 Fax: (517)627-3497
Free: (800)646-6397

Community newspaper. **Founded:** 1854. **Freq:** Weekly (Mon.). **Print Method:** Offset. **Cols./Page:** 6. **Col. Width:** 9 1/2 picas. **Col. Depth:** 224 agate lines. **Key Personnel:** Nan Simons, Editor; Nancy Zeimen, Publisher.
Ad Rates: GLR: $.36 **Circ:** Combined 5,703
BW: $342.72
4C: $657.72
SAU: $6.55
PCI: $5.04

PRUDENVILLE

15558 WUPS-FM - 98.5
PO Box 468 Phone: (517)366-5364
Prudenville, MI 48651-0468 Fax: (517)366-6200
Free: (800)365-4487

Format: Adult Contemporary. **Networks:** ABC. **Owner:** Northlands Communications, Inc., at above address. **Founded:** 1953. **Formerly:** WJGS-FM (1988). **Operating Hours:** Continuous; 2% network, 98% local. **Key Personnel:** John M. Salov, Contact; Barbra Rigling, Contact. **Wattage:** 100,000. **Ad Rates:** $12-18 for 30 seconds; $15-20 for 60 seconds.

REDFORD

15559 Redford Observer
Observer & Eccentric Newspapers
36251 Schoolcraft Rd. Phone: (313)591-2300
Livonia, MI 48150-1216 Fax: (313)953-2232

Community newspaper. **Founded:** 1958. **Freq:** Semiweekly (Mon. and Thurs.). **Print Method:** Offset. **Cols./Page:** 9. **Col. Width:** 17 nonpareils. **Col. Depth:** 301 agate lines. **Key Personnel:** Dick Isham, Publisher. **Subscription Rates:** $23. **Remarks:** Accepts advertising.
Ad Rates: BW: $2.62 **Circ:** Paid 1,094
Non-paid 3,607

15560 Time Warner Cable
25000 Capital Phone: (313)538-1313
Box 39178 Fax: (313)538-1237
Redford, MI 48239
E-mail: bxjw62b@prodigy.com

Founded: Jan. 1, 1980. **Formerly:** MetroVision of Redford, Inc. **Key Personnel:** Kirk D. Smith, General Mgr.; Russ Priebe, Chief Engineer; Paul Secwald, Service Mgr.; Chuck Barker, Program Dir. **Cities Served:** Redford Township, MI: subscribing households 14,000; 76 channels; 4 community access channels; 15 hours per week community access programming.

REED CITY

Evart Review - See Evart

15561 Freeway Shoppers Guide
The Pioneer Group
101 W. Slosson Phone: (616)832-5566
PO Box 117 Fax: (616)832-5558
Reed City, MI 49677
Shopping guide. **Freq:** Weekly (Mon.). **Print Method:** Offset. **Cols./Page:** 7. **Col. Width:** 1 3/8 inches. **Col. Depth:** 16 inches. **Key Personnel:** John A. Batdorff, Publisher. **Subscription Rates:** Free. **Remarks:** Combined advertising rates available with other Pioneer Group newspapers. **Online:** Adsend.
Ad Rates: SAU: $7.60 **Circ:** Free ‡10,425

15562 The Herald-News
The Pioneer Group
101 W. Slosson Phone: (616)832-5566
PO Box 117 Fax: (616)832-5558
Reed City, MI 49677
Community newspaper. **Founded:** 1872. **Freq:** Weekly (Thurs.). **Print Method:** 13 x 22. Offset. **Cols./Page:** 9. **Col. Width:** 1 3/8 inches. **Col. Depth:** 294 agate lines. **Subscription Rates:** $16 individuals. **Remarks:** Accepts advertising.
Ad Rates: SAU: $3.65 **Circ:** (Not Reported)
PCI: $7.15

15563 WDEE-AM - 1500
101 S Higbee St. Phone: (616)832-1600
Reed City, MI 49677-1103

Format: Country. **Founded:** 1981. **Operating Hours:** Sunrise-sunset. **Key Personnel:** Steven V. Beilfuss, Contact. **Wattage:** 250. **Ad Rates:** Advertising accepted; rates available upon request.

RICHMOND

15564 Review
Richmond Newspaper Group
68834 S. Main St. Phone: (810)727-3745
Richmond, MI 48062 Fax: (810)727-3929
Free: (800)686-7388

Newspaper. **Subtitle:** Chesterfield Review, Richmond Review, Independent Press. **Founded:** 1876. **Freq:** Weekly (Mon.). **Print Method:** Offset. **Cols./Page:** 6. **Col. Width:** 62 picas. **Col. Depth:** 183 agate lines. **Key Personnel:** Phil Allmen, Editor; John D. Johnson, Publisher. **Subscription Rates:** $16.
Ad Rates: PCI: $12.60 **Circ:** 43,628

ROCHESTER

15565 Clarion
429 Walnut St Phone: (810)651-9021
Rochester, MI 48307 Fax: (810)651-8243

Newspaper. **Subtitle:** Rochester Clarion, Inc. **Founded:** 1898. **Freq:** Weekly (Thurs.). **Print Method:** Offset. **Trim Size:** 2 1/16 x 21. **Cols./Page:** 6. **Col. Width:** 2 inches. **Col. Depth:** 21 inches. **Key Personnel:** Justin Wilcox, Publisher. **Subscription Rates:** $19.
Ad Rates: BW: $1,820.70 4C: $1,970.70 SAU: $14.45 PCI: $14.45 **Circ:** Paid 10,500

15566 Eastern Basketball Magazine
PO Box 370. Phone: (313)879-1676
Rochester, MI 48308-0370 Fax: (313)879-1977

College basketball and high school recruiting newspaper. **Founded:** 1976. **Freq:** 11/year. **Print Method:** Offset. **Cols./Page:** 4. **Col. Width:** 27 nonpareils. **Col. Depth:** 140 agate lines. **Key Personnel:** Larry Donald, Publisher; Mike Sheridan, Managing Editor. **Subscription Rates:** $35. **Remarks:** Accepts advertising.
Ad Rates: BW: $1,100 4C: $1,540 **Circ:** Paid ‡10,000 Free ‡1,250

15567 Rochester Observer
Observer & Eccentric Newspapers
36251 Schoolcraft Rd. Phone: (313)591-2300
Livonia, MI 48150-1216 Fax: (313)953-2232

Community newspaper. **Founded:** 1972. **Freq:** Semiweekly (Mon. and Thurs.). **Print Method:** Offset. **Cols./Page:** 9. **Col. Width:** 17 nonpareils. **Col. Depth:** 301 agate lines. **Key Personnel:** Richard Aginian, Publisher. **Subscription Rates:** $21. **Remarks:** Accepts advertising.
Ad Rates: GLR: $2.62 **Circ:** Paid 1,041 Non-paid 8,813

15568 WXOU-FM - 88.3
Oakland University Phone: (248)370-4273
65 Oakland Center Fax: (248)370-4272
Rochester, MI 48309
E-mail: wxou@oakland.edu

Format: Eclectic. **Founded:** 1972. **Formerly:** WOUX-FM (1994). **Operating Hours:** Continuous. **Key Personnel:** Allison K. Spicer, General Mgr., akspicer@oakland.edu; Matthew McLean, Program Dir., mdmclean@oakland.edu; Stephen Cramer, Public Affairs Dir., secramer@oakland.edu; Chris McCullen, Music Dir.; Clay Flaim, Sports Dir.; Mario Suau, Chief Announcer, mrsuan@oakland.edu; Mario Suau, Promotions Dir., mrsuau@oakland.edu; Erin Brown, Public Service Dir., eebrown@oakland.edu; Tom Dicenna, Faculty Advisor; Jim Miller, Contact, uonomake@oakland.edu. **Local Programs:** *Breaking the Glass*; *Out of Bounds Sports Shows*, Jason Lee, (248)370-4273; *Picacco for the Ears*, Lisa Belanger, (248)370-4273. **Wattage:** 110. **Ad Rates:** Noncommercial.

ROCKFORD

15569 Rockford/Cedar Springs Advance
Advance Newspapers
2141 Port Sheldon Rd. Phone: (616)669-2700
PO Box 9 Fax: (616)669-1162
Jenison, MI 49428-9301
Free: (800)439-0960

Community newspaper (tabloid). **Freq:** Weekly (Tues.). **Print Method:** Offset. **Cols./Page:** 6. **Col. Width:** 16 nonpareils. **Col. Depth:** 224 agate lines. **Key Personnel:** Joel Holland, Publisher. **Remarks:** Combined advertising rates available with other Advance Newspapers. **Formerly:** East Grand Rapids Advance.
Ad Rates: BW: $480 PCI: $5.30 **Circ:** Free 14,495 Paid 97

ROGERS CITY

15570 Presque Isle Star
Star Publications
PO Box 620 Phone: (517)732-5125
Gaylord, MI 49734 Fax: (517)732-9323
Free: (800)782-7237
Publisher E-mail: starads@northland.lib.mi.us

Shopper (tabloid). **Founded:** 1988. **Freq:** Weekly (Sun.). **Print Method:** Offset. Uses mats. **Trim Size:** 11 1/8 x 17 1/2. **Cols./Page:** 6. **Col. Width:** 21 nonpareils. **Col. Depth:** 224 agate lines. **Key Personnel:** David Baragrey, Publisher, phone (517)356-2121, fax (517)354-8275; Mike Adams, Sales Mgr. **Subscription Rates:** Free. **Remarks:** Accepts advertising. **Available Online**. **Formerly:** The Northern Advertiser (1989).
Ad Rates: GLR: $4 BW: $450.24 4C: $646.24 PCI: $4.55 **Circ:** Free 7,353

15571 WHAK-AM - 960
5667 M-68 Hwy. Phone: (517)734-9960
Rogers City, MI 49779 Fax: (517)734-2603

Format: Contemporary Country. **Networks:** ABC; AP. **Owner:** Dr. Robert Currier, 1491 M-32 West, Alpena, MI 49707, (517)354-4611, Fax: (517)734-2603. **Founded:** 1949. **Operating Hours:** Sunrise-sunset; 10% network, 90% local. **ADI:** Traverse City-Cadillac, MI. **Key Personnel:** Dr. Robert Currier, Owner; Peter JaKey, Contact; Donna Smith, Contact; Bob Edwards, Program Dir./Music Dir.; Amy Grohowski, Sales. **Wattage:** 5000. **Ad Rates:** $4.70-6.50 for 15 seconds; $7.05-8.85 for 30 seconds; $8.85-10.60 for 60 seconds.

15572 WMLQ-FM - 96.7
4814 County Rd. 441 Phone: (517)734-4797
PO Box 297 Fax: (517)734-7804
Rogers City, MI 49779

Format: Big Band/Nostalgia. **Networks:** Satellite Music Network. **Owner:** President - John D. Degroat, at above address. **Founded:** 1984. **Operating Hours:** 18 hours daily. **Key Personnel:** Ken Smolinski, Station Mgr. **Wattage:** 26,000. **Ad Rates:** $6-11 for 30 seconds; $8-13 for 60 seconds.

ROMEO

15573 The Countryman
The Romeo Observer
124 W. St. Clair Phone: (810)752-3524
Box 96
Romeo, MI 48065-0096
Community newspaper. **Founded:** 1969. **Freq:** Weekly. **Print Method:** Offset. **Trim Size:** 2 1/16. **Cols./Page:** 6. **Col. Depth:** 21 1/2 inches. **Subscription Rates:** Free. **Remarks:** Accepts advertising.
Ad Rates: BW: $1,120.30 4C: $1,372.30 SAU: $8.70 **Circ:** Non-paid ‡7,130

15574 The Romeo Observer
124 W. St. Clair Phone: (810)752-3524
Box 96
Romeo, MI 48065-0096
Community newspaper. **Founded:** May 3, 1866. **Freq:** Weekly (Wed.). **Print Method:** Offset. **Cols./Page:** 6. **Col. Width:** 2 1/16 inches. **Col. Depth:** 301 agate lines. **Key Personnel:** Melvin E. Bleich, Editor and Publisher. **USPS:** 470-340. **Subscription Rates:** $10. **Remarks:** Accepts advertising.
Ad Rates: GLR: $8.95 BW: $1,154.55 4C: $1,404.55 **Circ:** Paid 6,918 Free 7,130

ROMULUS

15575 Romulus Roman
Michigan Community Newspapers
35540 Michigan Ave. Phone: (313)729-4000
PO Box 578 Fax: (313)729-6880
Wayne, MI 48184
Community newspaper. **Founded:** 1892. **Freq:** Weekly (Thurs.). **Print Method:** Offset. **Cols./Page:** 6. **Col. Width:** 12 picas. **Col. Depth:** 21 1/2 inches. **Key Personnel:** Mike Wilcox, Publisher; Kathy Wilcox, Owner; Joan Dyer-Zinner, Managing Editor; Rita Bedell, Classified Manager; Ron Spielman, Advertising Mgr.; Justin Wilcox, Circulation Mgr. **Subscription Rates:** $48. **Remarks:** Accepts advertising.
Ad Rates: SAU: $4.68 **Circ:** Paid 1,084 Non-paid 2,758

15576 WCHB-AM - 1200
32790 Henry Ruff Rd. Phone: (313)278-1440
Romulus, MI 48174 Fax: (313)722-8495

Format: Religious; Blues. **Networks:** Independent. **Owner:** Bell Broadcasting Co., 2994 E. Grand Blvd., Detroit, MI 48202, (313)871-0590. **Founded:** 1956. **Operating Hours:** Continuous; 2% network, 98% local. **Key Personnel:** Mary Bell, President; Wendell Cox, Contact; Eric Bass, General Sales Mgr.; Terry Arnold, Program Dir.; Treva Bass, Chief Engineer. **Wattage:** 1000.

ROSCOMMON

15577 Roscommon County Herald-News
905 Lake Ave. Phone: (517)275-5100
Box 8
Roscommon, MI 48653-0905
Newspaper with a community orientation. **Founded:** 1885. **Freq:** Weekly (Sun.). **Print Method:** Offset. **Cols./Page:** 5. **Col. Width:** 12.5 picas. **Col. Depth:** 210 agate lines. **Key Personnel:** Amy Goodrich, Editor; Robert Perlberg, Publisher; Jan Anderson, Advertising Mgr. **Subscription Rates:** $25. **Remarks:** Accepts advertising.
Ad Rates: GLR: $.17 BW: $420.00 4C: $645.00 SAU: $7.00 PCI: $7.00 **Circ:** Non-paid ‡14,500

ROSEVILLE

15578 Movie Collector's World
Arena Publishing Co.
17230 13 Mile Rd. Phone: (810)774-4311
Roseville, MI 48066 Fax: (810)774-5450
Free: (800)273-6883
Publisher E-mail: arenapub@ic.net

Magazine for movie poster and memorabilia collectors. **Founded:** 1976. **Freq:** Biweekly. **Print Method:** Web offset. **Trim Size:** 11 x 14. **Cols./Page:** 4. **Col. Width:** 2 1/8 inches. **Col. Depth:** 13 inches. **Key Personnel:** Brian A. Bukantis, Publisher. **ISSN:** 8750-5401. **Subscription Rates:** $45 individuals; $5 single issue.
Ad Rates: BW: $175 4C: $450 **Circ:** Paid ‡4,800 Controlled ‡200

ROYAL OAK

15579 Alarm Clock
PO Box 1551 Phone: (313)593-9677
Royal Oak, MI 48068 Fax: (313)593-9306

Magazine focusing primarily on women in music. **Subtitle:** Featuring Women in Music. **Founded:** 1991. **Freq:** Quarterly. **Trim Size:** 5 1/2 x 8 1/2. **Key Personnel:** Allan Salyer, Contact, asalyer@uta.com. **Subscription Rates:** $6 three issues. **Remarks:** Advertising not accepted.
Circ: Non-paid 200

15580 Cruise Entertainment Magazine
Tony Rome Enterprises, Inc.
PO Box 398 Phone: (248)545-9040
Royal Oak, MI 48068-0398 Fax: (248)545-1073

Consumer magazine covering news and entertainment for a local gay and lesbian community. **Founded:** Mar. 1979. **Freq:** Weekly. **Print Method:** Sheetfed offset. **Trim Size:** 5 1/2 x 8 1/2. **Cols./Page:** 2. **Col. Width:** 2 1/8 inches. **Col. Depth:** 4 1/2 inches. **Key Personnel:** Tony Rome, Publisher; Phillip O'Jibway, Editor. **ISSN:** 1086-2986. **Remarks:** Accepts advertising.
Ad Rates: BW: $235 **Circ:** Non-paid 5,000

15581 The Daily Tribune
Independent Newspapers Inc.
210 E. 3rd St. Phone: (313)541-3000
Royal Oak, MI 48067-2603 Fax: (313)541-7041

General newspaper. **Founded:** 1902. **Freq:** Daily (eve.), Sunday (morn.). **Print Method:** Offset. **Cols./Page:** 6. **Col. Width:** 25 nonpareils. **Col. Depth:** 301 agate lines. **Key Personnel:** Keith Strand, Publisher; Michael A. Beeson, Editor; Steve Finlay, City Editor. **Subscription Rates:** $72.80; $105 in state; $114.40 out of state. **Remarks:** Accepts advertising.
Ad Rates: GLR: $28.82 BW: $3,160.50 4C: $3,855.50 SAU: $24.50 **Circ:** Mon.-Fri. 19,462 Sun. 21,650

15582 Orbit Magazine
Popular Amusement, Inc.
919 S. Main St., Ste. 2001 Phone: (248)541-3900
Royal Oak, MI 48067
Publication E-mail: orbit@mich.com

Newsprint magazine covering entertainment in metropolitan Detroit. **Subtitle:** The Magazine Dedicated to the Art of Having Fun. **Founded:** Aug. 1990. **Freq:** Monthly. **Trim Size:** 11 1/2 x 13 1/2. **Cols./Page:** 6. **Col. Width:** 1 5/8 inches. **Col. Depth:** 13 inches. **Key Personnel:** Jerry Peterson, Editor and Publisher; Katy McNerney, Managing Editor. **Subscription Rates:** $17.95. **Remarks:** Accepts advertising. **URL:** http://www.orby.com/orbit.
Ad Rates: BW: $1,665 4C: $2,015 PCI: $25 **Circ:** Controlled ‡50,000

15583 TCI Cablevision
4500 Delemere Blvd. Phone: (810)549-2100
Royal Oak, MI 48073 Fax: (810)549-6289

Founded: 1983. **Formerly:** UAE. **Cities Served:** Oakland County, MI.

SAGINAW

15584 The Catholic Weekly
GLS Diocesan Reports
1520 Court St. Phone: (517)793-7661
PO Box 1405 Fax: (517)793-7663
Saginaw, MI 48605-1405
Publication E-mail: cwedit1@aol.com; glsdiorepo@aol.com

Religious newspaper covering the local, national, and international church. **Subtitle:** Official Publication of the Dioceses of Saginaw and Gaylord. **Founded:** May 5, 1940. **Freq:** Weekly (Fri.). **Print Method:** Offset. **Trim Size:** 13 3/8 x 22 3/4. **Cols./Page:** 8. **Col. Width:** 9 picas. **Col. Depth:** 294 agate lines. **Key Personnel:** Kathleen A. Socha, Gaylord Editor; Mark A. Myczkowiak, General Mgr.; Dan Digmann, Saginaw Editor. **USPS:** 376-750. **Subscription Rates:** $23.95 individuals. **Remarks:** Accepts advertising.
Ad Rates: GLR: $.52 **Circ:** Paid ⊕**11,464**
BW: $1,176 Free 583
4C: $1,576
PCI: $6.76

15585 Michigan Dry Bean Digest
Michigan Bean Shippers Association
2435 Midland Rd. Phone: (517)790-3010
PO Box 6008 Fax: (517)790-3747
Saginaw, MI 48608
Publisher E-mail: mbsa@concentric.net

Magazine containing information for and about people engaged in the production, processing, canning, packaging, and marketing of Michigan grown dry bean products. **Subtitle:** Dry Bean Digest. **Founded:** 1976. **Freq:** Quarterly. **Print Method:** Offset. **Trim Size:** 8 1/2 x 11. **Cols./Page:** 2 and 3. **Col. Width:** 22 and 14 picas. **Key Personnel:** John A. McGill, Jr., Editor and Publisher; Ann M. Watters, Advertising Mgr. **ISSN:** 0885-6060. **Subscription Rates:** $25; $35 other countries overseas; $7.50 single issue. **Remarks:** Accepts advertising. **URL:** http://www.concentric.net/~mbsa.
Ad Rates: BW: $1,250 **Circ:** Paid ‡547
4C: $1,500 Non-paid ‡4,779

15586 Review Magazine
318 S. Hamilton Phone: (517)799-6078
Saginaw, MI 48602 Fax: (517)799-6162
Publication E-mail: ackdpen@cns.com

News and entertainment magazine. **Founded:** 1979. **Freq:** Biweekly. **Print Method:** Offset. **Cols./Page:** 6. **Col. Width:** 19 nonpareils. **Col. Depth:** 210 agate lines. **Key Personnel:** Robert E. Martin, Editor and Publisher. **Subscription Rates:** Free; $15. **Remarks:** Accepts advertising. **Available Online. URL:** http://www.cris.com/~acidpen. **Formerly**: Bay Area Review.
Ad Rates: GLR: $1 **Circ:** Paid 200
BW: $375 Non-paid 25,000
4C: $575
PCI: $8.50

15587 The Saginaw News
203 S. Washington Ave. Phone: (517)752-7171
Saginaw, MI 48607 Fax: (517)752-3115
Free: (800)875-6397

General newspaper. **Founded:** 1859. **Freq:** Daily (eve.). **Print Method:** Letterpress. **Cols./Page:** 6. **Col. Width:** 24 nonpareils. **Col. Depth:** 308 agate lines. **Key Personnel:** Paul Chaffee, Editor; Ray Thatcher, Publisher; Gene Bobic, Advertising Mgr. **USPS:** 475-440. **Subscription Rates:** $10; $11.25 (mail); $11.75 out of state. **Remarks:** Accepts advertising. **URL:** http://www.sa.mlive.com. **Feature Editors:** Jim Buckley, *Sports*, phone (517)776-9770; Zada Cambridge, *Religion*, phone (517)776-9668; Paul Chaffee, *Saturday, Sunday*, phone (517)776-9764; Mary Foreman, *Food*, phone (517)776-9676; Fred Garrett, *Rural Development*, phone (517)776-9711; Rob Handeyside, *Metro*, phone (517)776-9678; Brian Hlavaty, *News*, phone (517)776-9700; Mary Jean Babic, *Political*, phone (517)776-9685; Steve Jessmore, *Photo*, phone (517)776-9773; Jeri Kornegay, *Environmental, Saturday, Sunday*, phone (517)776-9695; Curt Leece, *Photo*, phone (517)776-9689; Janet Martineau, *Book, Drama, Entertainment, Movie, Music*, phone (517)776-9707; John Puravs, *Editorials*, phone (517)776-9684; Tara Ransom, *Financial/Business, Real Estate*, phone (517)776-9674; Paul Rau, *Education*, phone (517)776-9695; Ken Tabacsko, *Family, Fashion, Features, Garden/Home, Lifestyle, Society, TV & Radio, Travel, Women's*, phone (517)776-9705; Mike Thompson, *Political*, phone (517)776-9725.
Ad Rates: BW: $3,517.80 **Circ:** Mon.-Sat. ★**50,541**
4C: $4,142.80 Sun. ★**60,635**
PCI: $26.65

15588 The Saginaw Press
410 Hancock St. Phone: (517)793-8070
PO Box 1836 Fax: (517)793-7225
Saginaw, MI 48605-1836
Community newspaper. **Founded:** 1912. **Freq:** Weekly (Fri.). **Print Method:** Use line/halftone engraving for photos. Letterpress. **Cols./Page:** 6. **Col. Width:** 28 nonpareils. **Col. Depth:** 273 agate lines. **Key Personnel:** G.W. Baxter III, Editor and Publisher; G.W. Baxter IV, Advertising Mgr. **USPS:** 047-546. **Subscription Rates:** $12; $17.50 out of area; $25 out of state. **Remarks:** Accepts advertising.
Ad Rates: GLR: $5.04 **Circ:** Paid ⊕**522**
BW: $589.68 Free ⊕**6**
SAU: $5.04

15589 Cox Cable Saginaw
720 N. Bates St. Phone: (517)799-8030
Saginaw, MI 48602 Fax: (517)799-7829

Founded: 1973. **Cities Served:** Saginaw County, Buena Vista Township, Carrollton Township, Saginaw Township, Spaulding Township, and Zilwaukee, MI.

15590 WAQP-TV - 49
2865 Trautner Dr. Phone: (517)249-5969
Saginaw, MI 48604
E-mail: tct@tct-net.org

Format: Commercial TV; Religious. **Networks:** Independent. **Owner:** Tri-State Christian TV, PO Box 1010, Marion, IL 62959, (618)997-9333. **Founded:** 1985. **Operating Hours:** Continuous; 60% network, 40% local. **ADI:** Flint-Saginaw-Bay City, MI. **Key Personnel:** Mike Socier, Contact; Ronald Booth, Chief Engineer; Albert E. Baldwin, Jr., Public Affairs. **Local Programs:** *Ask the Pastor* 11:30 a.m. Tues and Thurs., Annette Carnes, Mailing contact; *Michigan Alive* 11:30 a.m. - 12:30 p.m. Friday; *Public Report* Mondays 10 a.m., Wednesday 2 p.m., Charisse Piwowarski, Mailing contact. **Wattage:** 1,000,000. **URL:** http://www.waqp@tct-net.org.

15591 WGER-FM - 106.3
6165 Bay Rd. Phone: (517)792-1063
Saginaw, MI 48604 Fax: (517)792-1977

Format: Adult Contemporary; Soft Rock. **Founded:** 1964. **Operating Hours:** Continuous; 100% local. **ADI:** Flint-Saginaw-Bay City, MI. **Key Personnel:** Jerry O'Donnell, Program Dir.; Ray Nelson, General Sales Mgr.; Nancy Dymond, Vice President. **Wattage:** 3000. **Ad Rates:** $25-55 for 30 seconds.

15592 WHNN-FM - 96.1
5196 State St. Phone: (517)799-1000
Saginaw, MI 48603 Fax: (517)790-1942
E-mail: oldies96whnn@compuserve.com

Format: Oldies. **Networks:** Westwood One Radio. **Owner:** Liggett Broadcast, 3420 Pine Tree Rd., Lansing, MI 48911, (517)394-4404. **Founded:** 1947. **Formerly**: WBCM-FM (1983). **Operating Hours:** Continuous; 5% network, 95% local. **ADI:** Flint-Saginaw-Bay City, MI. **Key Personnel:** Jim Spangenberg, General Sales Mgr.; Scott Stine, Program Dir.; Jennifer Gough, Office Mgr.; Dan Martin, News Dir. **Wattage:** 100,000. **Ad Rates:** $40-100 per unit.

15593 WIOG-FM - 102.5
1795 Tittabawassee Phone: (517)752-3456
Saginaw, MI 48605 Fax: (517)754-5046
E-mail: wiog@cris.com

Format: Adult Contemporary. **Networks:** ABC. **Founded:** 1969. **Operating Hours:** Continuous. **ADI:** Flint-Saginaw-Bay City, MI. **Key Personnel:** Nancy Dymond, General Mgr.; Mike Macdonald, Program Dir.; Keith Kelly, Music Dir. **Wattage:** 86,000.

15594 WKCQ-FM - 98.1
Box 1776 Phone: (517)752-8161
Saginaw, MI 48605 Fax: (517)752-8102
Free: (800)262-0098
E-mail: wkcq@cris.com

Format: Country. **Networks:** ABC. **Operating Hours:** Continuous. **ADI:** Flint-Saginaw-Bay City, MI. **Key Personnel:** Kenneth H. MacDonald, Jr., General Mgr.; Duane Alverson, Sales Mgr.; Rick Walker, Operations Mgr. **Wattage:** 50,000.

15595 WKQZ-FM - 93.3
3190 Christy Way Phone: (517)695-5115
Suite No. 5 Fax: (517)695-5376
Saginaw, MI 48603

Format: Album-Oriented Rock (AOR); Classic Rock. **Networks:** ABC. **Owner:** WKQZ L.L.C., at above address, (517)337-2877, Fax: (517)337-0883. **Formerly**: WRCI-FM (1986). **Operating Hours:** Continuous; 100% local. **ADI:** Flint-Saginaw-Bay City, MI. **Key Personnel:** Annette Stensrud, General Sales Mgr.; Rick Church, Program Dir.; Mike Thomas, General Mgr. **Wattage:** 39,000. **Ad Rates:** Advertising accepted; rates available upon request.

15596 WNEM-TV - 5
PO Box 531, 107 N. Franklin St. Phone: (517)755-8191
Fax: (517)758-2110
Saginaw, MI 48606

Format: Commercial TV. **Networks:** CBS. **Founded:** 1954. **Operating Hours:** Continuous. **ADI:** Flint-Saginaw-Bay City, MI. **Key Personnel:** Paul Virciglio, Vice Pres./Gen. Mgr.; Peggy Madigan, Ad. Contact.

15597 WSAM-AM - 1400
Box 1776 Phone: (517)752-8161
Saginaw, MI 48605 Fax: (517)752-8102
E-mail: wkcq@cris.com

Format: Middle-of-the-Road (MOR). **Networks:** ABC; CNN Radio; Westwood One Radio. **Founded:** 1940. **Operating Hours:** Continuous. **ADI:** Flint-Saginaw-Bay City, MI. **Key Personnel:** Kenneth H. MacDonald, Jr., General Mgr.; Duane Alverson, Sales Mgr.; Rick Walker, Operations Mgr./Program Dir. **Local Programs:** *Sam Morning Edition*, Ted Maddox. **Wattage:** 1000.

15598 WSGW-AM - 790
1795 Tittabawassee Phone: (517)752-3456
Saginaw, MI 48605 Fax: (517)754-5046
E-mail: wsgw@concentric.net

Format: News; Talk. **Networks:** CBS; NBC. **Founded:** 1950. **Operating Hours:** Continuous; 25% network, 75% local. **ADI:** Flint-Saginaw-Bay City, MI. **Key Personnel:** Dave Maurer, Program Dir.; Terry Lenz, Sports Dir.; Nancy Dymond. **Wattage:** 5000.

15599 WTLZ-FM - 107.1
126 N. Franklin St., Ste. 514 Phone: (517)754-1071
Saginaw, MI 48607 Fax: (517)754-4292

Format: Jazz; Ethnic; Religious; Urban Contemporary. **Networks:** ABC; Satellite Radio. **Owner:** WTL, Inc., at above address. **Founded:** 1988. **Formerly**: WWWS-FM (1988). **Operating Hours:** Continuous; 10% network, 90% local. **ADI:** Flint-Saginaw-Bay City, MI. **Key Personnel:** Jack Lich, Contact; Kermit Crockett, Program Dir.; D'Ante Toussaint, Contact; Rosa Chaffer, Contact; Chris Banks, Contact. **Wattage:** 6000. **Ad Rates:** $16-26 for 60 seconds.

ST. IGNACE

The Mackinac Island Town Crier - See Mackinac Island

15600 The St. Ignace News
Maurer Publishing Co.
359 Reagon St. Phone: (906)643-9150
PO Box 277 Fax: (906)643-9122
St. Ignace, MI 49781
Community newspaper. **Founded:** 1878. **Freq:** Weekly (Wed.). **Print Method:** Offset. **Cols./Page:** 6. **Col. Width:** 12 1/2 picas. **Col. Depth:** 294 agate lines. **Key Personnel:** Wesley H. Maurer, Jr., Editor and Publisher. **USPS:** 462-380. **Subscription Rates:** $34. **Remarks:** Accepts advertising.
Ad Rates: GLR: $.49 **Circ:** 7,000
BW: $864.36
SAU: $6.86

15601 Straits Area Star
Star Publications
PO Box 620 Phone: (517)732-5125
Gaylord, MI 49734 Fax: (517)732-9323
Free: (800)782-7237
Publisher E-mail: starads@northland.lib.mi.us

Shopper (tabloid). **Founded:** 1987. **Freq:** Weekly (Sun.). **Print Method:** Offset. Uses mats. **Trim Size:** 11 1/8 x 17 3/4. **Cols./Page:** 6. **Col. Width:** 21 nonpareils. **Col. Depth:** 224 agate lines. **Key Personnel:** David Baragrey, Publisher; Sue Duffiney, Editor, phone (616)627-3151, fax (616)627-6244. **Subscription Rates:** Free. **Remarks:** Accepts advertising. **Available Online. Formerly**: Community Shopper.
Ad Rates: GLR: $4 **Circ:** Free 15,369
BW: $604.80
4C: $653.80
PCI: $6.30

ST. JOHNS

15602 The Clinton County News
Community Newspapers
320 N. Clinton Phone: (517)224-2361
St. Johns, MI 48879 Fax: (517)224-4452

Community newspaper. **Founded:** 1856. **Freq:** Weekly (Sun.). **Print Method:** Offset. **Cols./Page:** 6. **Col. Width:** 9.5 picas. **Col. Depth:** 224 agate lines. **Key Personnel:** Lynn

Suffin, Editor; Pres Odette, Publisher. **Subscription Rates:** Free; $17.50 out of area. **Remarks:** Accepts advertising.
Ad Rates: GLR: $.69 **Circ:** Combined 12,319
BW: $936
4C: $1,101
SAU: $9.75
PCI: $12.40

15603 St. Johns Reminder
109 W. Higham St. Phone: (517)224-8356
PO Box 473 Fax: (517)224-9458
St. Johns, MI 48879-0473
Shopper/Community News. **Founded:** 1949. **Freq:** Weekly (Sat.). **Print Method:** Offset. **Cols./Page:** 6. **Col. Width:** 20 nonpareils. **Col. Depth:** 294 agate lines. **Key Personnel:** Rebecca M. Wood, Publisher; Sue Knickerbocker, Editor; Joseph J. Humenik, Advertising Mgr. **Subscription Rates:** $32 individuals. **Remarks:** Accepts advertising.
Ad Rates: GLR: $.33 **Circ:** Free ❑**16,200**
BW: $355.20
4C: $606.40
PCI: $3.70

15604 WWSJ-AM - 1580
PO Box 276 Phone: (517)224-9592
St. Johns, MI 48879 Fax: (517)224-9592

Format: Talk. **Networks:** Michigan Farm Radio; USA Radio. **Founded:** 1959. **Formerly:** WRBJ-AM. **Operating Hours:** 6 a.m.-10 p.m. **ADI:** Lansing (Ann Arbor), MI. **Key Personnel:** R. Ditmer, Contact. **Local Programs:** *1580 Farm Talk.* **Wattage:** 1000 night, 3 day. **Ad Rates:** $5 for 30 seconds; $8.85 for 60 seconds.

ST. JOSEPH

15605 Agricultural Engineering
American Society of Agricultural Engineers
2950 Niles Rd. Phone: (616)429-0300
St. Joseph, MI 49085 Fax: (616)429-3852
Free: (800)371-2723
Publisher E-mail: hq@asae.org

Magazine covering technology for food and agriculture. **Subtitle:** Engineering and Technology for a Sustainable World. **Founded:** 1994. **Freq:** Monthly. **Print Method:** Offset. **Trim Size:** 8 1/4 x 10 7/8. **Cols./Page:** 3. **Col. Width:** 13 1/2 nonpareils. **Col. Depth:** 131 agate lines. **Key Personnel:** Lorraine Hanover, Editor, phone (616)428-6325, hanover@asae.org; Donna Hull, Publisher, phone (616)428-6326, hull@asae.org; Pam Bakken, Advertising Mgr., phone (616)428-6337, bakken@asae.org. **ISSN:** 1076-3333. **Subscription Rates:** $56.00. **Remarks:** Accepts advertising. **URL:** http://www.asae.org. **Formerly:** Magazine Covering.
Ad Rates: BW: $995 **Circ:** ‡9,000
4C: $1,295

15606 Applied Engineering in Agriculture
American Society of Agricultural Engineers
2950 Niles Rd. Phone: (616)429-0300
St. Joseph, MI 49085 Fax: (616)429-3852
Free: (800)371-2723
Publisher E-mail: hq@asae.org

Peer-reviewed journal focused on practical applications of current research related to engineering for agricultural, food and biological systems. **Founded:** 1985. **Freq:** Bimonthly. **Trim Size:** 8 1/2 x 11. **Key Personnel:** Pam Devore-Hansen, Editor, phone (517)833-5045, p.hansen@nethawk.com; Donna M. Hull, Publisher, phone (616)428-6326, hull@asae.org. **ISSN:** 0883-8542. **Subscription Rates:** $84.00 individuals; $44.50 members. **Remarks:** Advertising not accepted.
Circ: Paid ‡700

15607 The Herald-Palladium
3450 Hollywood Rd. Phone: (616)429-2400
St. Joseph, MI 49085 Fax: (616)429-7661
Free: (800)356-4262

General newspaper. **Founded:** 1858. **Freq:** Daily (eve.), Sat. and Sun. (morn.). **Print Method:** Offset. **Trim Size:** 13 3/4 x 22 3/4. **Cols./Page:** 6. **Col. Width:** 26 nonpareils. **Col. Depth:** 301 agate lines. **Key Personnel:** David Harrison, Publisher; R. D. Farrell, Advertising Dir. **USPS:** 387-440. **Subscription Rates:** $135.20.
Ad Rates: BW: $2,920.56 **Circ:** Mon.-Sat. ★**30,202**
4C: $3,396.56 Sun. ★**31,783**
SAU: $22.64
PCI: $22.64

15608 Transactions of the ASAE
American Society of Agricultural Engineers
2950 Niles Rd. Phone: (616)429-0300
St. Joseph, MI 49085 Fax: (616)429-3852
Free: (800)371-2723
Publisher E-mail: hq@asae.org

Agricultural engineering peer-reviewed research journal. **Founded:** 1958. **Freq:** Bimonthly. **Print Method:** Offset. **Trim Size:** 8 1/2 x 11. **Cols./Page:** 2. **Col. Width:** 40 nonpareils. **Col. Depth:** 140 agate lines. **Key Personnel:** Pam DeVore Hansen, Editor, p.hansen@nethawk.com; Donna M. Hull, phone (616)428-6326, hull@asae.org. **ISSN:** 0001-2351. **Subscription Rates:** $81.00 members; $238 nonmembers. **Remarks:** Advertising not accepted. **URL:** http://www.asae.org.
Circ: ‡1,200

15609 WIRX-FM - 107.1
PO Box 107 Phone: (616)925-1111
St. Joseph, MI 49085 Fax: (616)925-1011
E-mail: wirx@wirx.com

Format: Album-Oriented Rock (AOR). **Founded:** 1966. **Operating Hours:** Continuous. **ADI:** South Bend-Elkhart, IN. **Key Personnel:** Gayle Olson, General Mgr.; John Vances, Program Dir.; Bob Bolak, Dir. of Sales. **Wattage:** 3000 ERP. **URL:** http://www.wirx.com.

15610 WSJM-AM - 1400
PO Box 107 Phone: (616)925-1111
St. Joseph, MI 49085 Fax: (616)925-1011
E-mail: wsjm@wssm.com

Format: News; Talk. **Networks:** ABC; Talknet; CNN Radio. **Founded:** 1956. **Operating Hours:** Continuous. **Key Personnel:** Gayle Olson, General Mgr.; Phil McDonald, Contact; Bob Bolak, Dir. of Sales. **Wattage:** 1000.

SALINE

15611 Milan News
The Reporter Papers
106 W. Michigan Ave. Fax: (313)429-3621
Saline, MI 48176
Community newspaper. **Founded:** 1985. **Freq:** Weekly (Wed.). **Print Method:** Offset. **Trim Size:** 11 1/4 x 15. **Cols./Page:** 6. **Col. Width:** 1 5/8 inches. **Col. Depth:** 14 inches. **Key Personnel:** Laura Crossey, Editor; Paul L. Tull, Publisher. **Subscription Rates:** $8 local; $10 out of area. $2 discount service personnel and senior citizens. **Remarks:** Accepts advertising.
Ad Rates: BW: $273 **Circ:** ‡2,200
PCI: $3.40

15612 Mr. Mazoo
The Reporter Papers
106 W. Michigan Ave. Fax: (313)429-3621
Saline, MI 48176
Shopper news. **Founded:** 1978. **Freq:** Weekly (Mon.). **Print Method:** Offset. **Trim Size:** 11 3/8 x 15. **Cols./Page:** 6. **Col. Width:** 1 5/8 inches. **Col. Depth:** 14 inches. **Key Personnel:** Tom Kirvan, Editor; Paul Tull, Publisher. **Remarks:** Accepts advertising.
Ad Rates: BW: $504 **Circ:** Free ‡15,065
PCI: $6

15613 The Saline Reporter, Inc.
The Reporter Papers
106 W. Michigan Ave. Fax: (313)429-3621
Saline, MI 48176
Community newspaper. **Founded:** 1948. **Freq:** Weekly (Wed.). **Print Method:** Offset. **Cols./Page:** 8. **Col. Width:** 20 nonpareils. **Col. Depth:** 294 agate lines. **Key Personnel:** Tom Kirvan, Editor; Paul L. Tull, Publisher. **Subscription Rates:** $14, $17 out of area. **Remarks:** Accepts advertising.
Ad Rates: PCI: $5.65 **Circ:** 4,800

SANDUSKY

15614 Official Michigan
Official Michigan, Inc.
432 S. Sandusky Phone: (517)635-3000
Sandusky, MI 48471 Fax: (517)635-3000

Political newspaper for legislators, lawyers, and judges and interested individuals. **Founded:** 1954. **Freq:** Weekly (Mon.). **Print Method:** Letterpress and offset. **Trim Size:** 10 x 15. **Cols./Page:** 6. **Col. Width:** 1 1/2 inches. **Col. Depth:** 210 agate lines. **Key Personnel:** Don Kilts, Editor; John Johnson, Publisher; Ken O'Dell, Advertising Mgr.; Jane Vanderpel, Office Mgr. **Subscription Rates:** $32.50; $39.00 out of state. **Remarks:** Accepts advertising.
Ad Rates: PCI: $7 **Circ:** Paid 800
Free 100

15615 Sanilac County Buyer's Guide
30 E. Sanilac Ave. Phone: (810)648-9900
PO Box 72 Fax: (810)664-7572
Sandusky, MI 48471
Free: (800)462-9966

Shopper. **Subtitle:** Sanilac Buyer's Guide. **Founded:** 1969. **Freq:** Weekly (Sun.). **Print Method:** Offset. **Trim Size:** 16 x 22 1/2. **Cols./Page:** 6. **Col. Width:** 19 nonpareils. **Col. Depth:** 210 agate lines. **Key Personnel:** Doug Finkbeiner, Publisher; Rick Henry, General Mgr., rhenry@greatlakes.net; Teressa Robbins, Sales Mgr., trobbins@greatlakes.net. **Subscription Rates:** Free; $22 (mail). **Remarks:** Accepts advertising.
Ad Rates: BW: $477 **Circ:** Free 19,086
PCI: $6.00

15616 Sanilac County News
432 S. Sandusky Rd. Phone: (313)648-4000
Sandusky, MI 48471 Fax: (313)648-4002

Community newspaper. **Founded:** 1971. **Freq:** Weekly (Wed.). **Print Method:** Offset. **Cols./Page:** 6. **Col. Width:** 20 nonpareils. **Col. Depth:** 201 agate lines. **Key Personnel:** John D. Johnson, Publisher. **Subscription Rates:** Free; $18.95 in country, $39.95 in Michigan, $49.95 outside Michigan. **Remarks:** Accepts advertising.
Ad Rates: GLR: $.32 **Circ:** Paid ‡9,400
Free ‡16,900

15617 WMIC-AM - 660
19 S. Elk Phone: (810)648-2700
Sandusky, MI 48471 Fax: (810)648-3242

Format: Full Service. **Networks:** ABC. **Owner:** Sanilac Broadcasting Co., at above address. **Founded:** 1968. **Operating Hours:** 6 a.m.-sunset. **ADI:** Flint-Saginaw-Bay City, MI. **Key Personnel:** Bob Armstrong, General Mgr. **Wattage:** 1000. **Ad Rates:** $8-12 for 30 seconds; $10-14 for 60 seconds.

15618 WTGV-FM - 97.7
19 S. Elk Phone: (810)648-2700
Sandusky, MI 48471 Fax: (810)648-3242

Format: Middle-of-the-Road (MOR). **Networks:** ABC. **Founded:** 1971. **Operating Hours:** Continuous. **ADI:** Flint-Saginaw-Bay City, MI. **Key Personnel:** Bob Armstrong, General Mgr. **Wattage:** 3000. **Ad Rates:** $8-12 for 30 seconds; $10-14 for 60 seconds.

SAUGATUCK

15619 The Commercial Record
Kaechele Publications, Inc.
790 Lake St. Phone: (616)857-2570
PO Box 246 Fax: (616)857-4637
Saugatuck, MI 49453
Publisher E-mail: allnews@accn.org

Community newspaper. **Founded:** 1868. **Freq:** Weekly (Thurs.). **Print Method:** Offset. **Cols./Page:** 5. **Col. Width:** 2 1/8 inches. **Col. Depth:** 16 inches. **Key Personnel:** Cheryl Kaechele, Publisher; Daniel Osborn, Editor. **USPS:** 125-700. **Subscription Rates:** $15; $18 out of county; $21 out of state. **Remarks:** Accepts advertising.
Ad Rates: SAU: $6.24 **Circ:** Paid 2,000
Free 100

SAULT SAINTE MARIE

15620 Evening News
American Publishing of Michigan
109 Arlington St. Phone: (906)632-2235
Sault Sainte Marie, MI 49783-1901 Fax: (906)632-1222
General newspaper. **Founded:** 1879. **Freq:** Daily (eve.), Sunday (morn.). **Print Method:** Offset. **Trim Size:** 13 3/4 x 22 1/2. **Cols./Page:** 6. **Col. Width:** 25 nonpareils. **Col. Depth:** 21 inches. **Key Personnel:** Ken Fazzari, Editor; Richard Beadle, Advertising Mgr. **Subscription Rates:** $95. **Remarks:** Accepts advertising.
Ad Rates: GLR: $.60 **Circ:** 9,213
BW: $1,073.28
4C: $275
SAU: $8.32

15621 Tri-County Buyers' Guide
American Publishing of Michigan
109 Arlington St. Phone: (906)632-2235
Sault Sainte Marie, MI 49783-1901 Fax: (906)632-1222
Shopper. **Founded:** 1966. **Freq:** Weekly (Sun.). **Print Method:** Offset. **Cols./Page:** 5. **Col. Width:** 25 nonpareils. **Col. Depth:** 224 agate lines. **Key Personnel:** Patrick Egan, Publisher; Jack Mitchell, Advertising Mgr. **Remarks:** Accepts advertising.
Ad Rates: GLR: $518.96 **Circ:** Free ‡19,770

15622 WKNW-AM - 1400
1402 Ashmun St. Phone: (906)635-0995
Sault Sainte Marie, MI 49783 Fax: (906)635-1216

Format: Oldies; Talk; News; Sports. **Networks:** Mutual Broadcasting System; NBC; CBS; EFM. **Owner:** Algoma Broadcasting Co., at above address. **Founded:** 1990. **Operating Hours:** Continuous. **ADI:** Traverse City-Cadillac, MI. **Key Personnel:** John Bell, Program Dir.; Jeffery Delvany, General Mgr.; Brian Davies, News Dir. **Local Programs:** *Open Line*

12:35 pm Monday-Friday, A.J. Cummings. **Wattage:** 250. **Ad Rates:** Combined advertising rates available with WYSS-FM.

15623 WSOO-AM - 1230
PO Box 1230 Phone: (906)632-2231
Sault Sainte Marie, MI 49783

Format: Adult Contemporary. **Networks:** ABC; Michigan. **Founded:** 1940. **Operating Hours:** Continuous. **Key Personnel:** Tom Ewing, General Mgr.; Paul Stabile, Program Dir.; Larry McNeal, News Dir. **Wattage:** 1000.

15624 WSUE-FM - 101.3
PO Box 1230 Phone: (906)632-2231
Sault Sainte Marie, MI 49783

Format: Classic Rock. **Founded:** 1940. **Operating Hours:** Continuous. **Key Personnel:** Tom Ewing, General Mgr.; Paul Stabile, Program Dir.; Larry McNeal, News Dir. **Wattage:** 90,000. **Ad Rates:** $7-7.25 for 30 seconds; $9.75-10.75 for 60 seconds.

15625 WYSS-FM - 99.5
1402 Ashmun Phone: (906)635-0995
Sault Sainte Marie, MI 49783 Fax: (906)635-1216

Format: Contemporary Hit Radio (CHR). **Networks:** Westwood One Radio. **Owner:** Algoma Broadcasting, at above address. **Founded:** 1972. **Formerly:** WSMM-FM (1977). **Operating Hours:** Continuous. **ADI:** Traverse City-Cadillac, MI. **Key Personnel:** Michael T. Boldt, General Mgr.; Terry Carr, Program Dir.; Ron Dewey, News Dir. **Wattage:** 26,500.

SEBEWAING

15626 The Michigan Lutheran
Lutheran Church, Missouri Synod, Michigan District
PO Box 683 Phone: (517)883-3100
Sebewaing, MI 48759 Fax: (517)883-9211

Lutheran church publication presenting the work of the Mich. Dist. **Founded:** 1922. **Freq:** Monthly. **Print Method:** Letterpress and offset. **Trim Size:** 14 1/2 x 23. **Cols./Page:** 6. **Col. Width:** 22 nonpareils. **Col. Depth:** 210 agate lines. **Key Personnel:** Walt Rummel, Editor; Alice Pearson, Advertising Mgr., phone (810)651-1129; Betty Guenther, Asst. Editor, phone (517)883-2753. **Subscription Rates:** $6. **Remarks:** Accepts advertising.
Ad Rates: BW: $936 **Circ:** ‡60,000
PCI: $12

15627 Underground Zine Scene
316 E. Main St. Phone: (517)883-9383
Sebewaing, MI 48759
Publication E-mail: zscewe@juno.com

Consumer magazine covering music. **Founded:** June 1995. **Freq:** Semiannual. **Print Method:** Xerox. **Trim Size:** 8 1/2 x 11. **Subscription Rates:** $2 single issue. **Remarks:** Accepts advertising. **Former name:** Independent Underground.
Circ: Controlled 225

SENEY

15628 Grand Marais Pilot & Pictured Rocks Review
PO Box 123 Phone: (906)499-3318
Seney, MI 49883 Fax: (906)499-3321

Local newspaper (tabloid). **Subtitle:** Folklore, Fables & Features of the Upper Peninsula and Other Famous Places. **Founded:** 1971. **Freq:** Monthly. **Print Method:** Offset. **Trim Size:** 11 x 13 1/2. **Cols./Page:** 5. **Col. Width:** 2 inches. **Col. Depth:** 12 inches. **Key Personnel:** Enrico Capogrossa, Editor and Publisher. **Subscription Rates:** $20 individuals. **Remarks:** Accepts advertising.
Ad Rates: GLR: $.089 **Circ:** ‡35,000
BW: $445
PCI: $8.50

SHEPHERD

15629 Shepherd Argus
PO Box 459 Phone: (517)828-6360
Shepherd, MI 48883 Fax: (517)828-5361

Community newspaper. **Freq:** Weekly (Wed.). **Cols./Page:** 6. **Col. Width:** 10 picas. **Col. Depth:** 16 inches. **Key Personnel:** Geraldine Grim, Editor; George Grim, Publisher.
Circ: 2,000

SOUTH HAVEN

15630 South Haven Daily Tribune
American Publishing Co.
950 Bailey Ave., No. 4 Phone: (616)637-1104
South Haven, MI 49090 Fax: (616)637-8415
Publication E-mail: shaven@accn.org

Local newspaper. **Founded:** May 8, 1899. **Freq:** Daily (morn.) Ecept Sat.,& Sun. **Print Method:** Offset. Uses mats. **Trim Size:** 14 x 23. **Cols./Page:** 6. **Col. Width:** 27 nonpareils. **Col. Depth:** 308 agate lines. **Key Personnel:** Cathy Sisson, Editor; Mary Deemer, General Mgr. **USPS:** 146-700. **Subscription Rates:** $82.80 individuals.
Ad Rates: GLR: $.42 **Circ:** Paid ‡2,125
BW: $1,009.80 Mon. ‡14,300
4C: $1,244.80 Paid ‡2,100
SAU: $8 Mon. 13,600

15631 WCSY-FM - 98.3
510 Williams St. Phone: (616)637-6397
South Haven, MI 49090 Fax: (616)637-2675
E-mail: cosy@cybersol.com

Format: Adult Contemporary. **Networks:** ABC. **Owner:** WSJM Inc., at above address. **Founded:** 1961. **Formerly:** WJOR-FM (1980). **Operating Hours:** Continuous. **Key Personnel:** Paul Layendecker, Station Mgr.; Dick Shier, News Dir.; Denise Guerero, Asst. P.D. **Local Programs:** *The Breakfast Club*, Dick Shier. **Wattage:** 3000.

SOUTH LYON

15632 The South Lyon Herald
Hometown Newspapers
101 N. Lafayette Phone: (248)437-2011
South Lyon, MI 48178 Fax: (248)437-3386

Community newspaper. **Founded:** 1879. **Freq:** Weekly (Thurs.). **Print Method:** Offset. **Trim Size:** 13 3/4 x 22 1/2. **Cols./Page:** 6. **Col. Width:** 2 1/16 inches. **Col. Depth:** 21 1/2 inches. **Key Personnel:** Rick Byrne, Editor; Richard Perlberg, Publisher; Bob Peri, Advertising Mgr. **USPS:** 503-600. **Subscription Rates:** $22; $27 out of area; $30 out of state. **Remarks:** Accepts advertising.
Ad Rates: BW: $819.15 **Circ:** Combined ♦**6,523**
4C: $1,019.15
SAU: $6.35

SOUTHFIELD

15633 BMWE Journal
Brotherhood of Maintenance of Way Employees
26555 Evergreen Rd., Ste. 200 Phone: (248)948-1010
Southfield, MI 48076-4225 Fax: (248)948-7150

Railroad labor tabloid. **Founded:** 1891. **Freq:** Monthly. **Print Method:** Offset. **Key Personnel:** Mac A. Fleming, Editor; Susan L. Creswell, sue@bmwe. **ISSN:** 1049-3921. **Subscription Rates:** $20. **Remarks:** Advertising not accepted.
Circ: ‡60,000

The Detroit Jewish News - See Detroit

Detroit Metropolitan Woman - See Detroit

15634 Employee Assistance Quarterly
The Haworth Press, Inc.
24725 W. 12 Mile Rd., Ste. 310
Southfield, MI 48034
Publisher E-mail: getinfo@haworthpressinc.com

Deals with psychological aspects of management including handling alcoholism issues in the workplace. **Founded:** 1971. **Freq:** Quarterly. **Key Personnel:** Keith McClellan, Editor; Marjorie J. Middle, Advertising Mgr. **Subscription Rates:** $38; $90 Industry. $125 libraries and subscription agencies. **Formerly:** Labor-Management Alcoholism Journal (1983).

15635 Lawrence Technological University Magazine
Lawrence Technological University
21000 W. 10 Mile Rd. Phone: (248)204-4000
Southfield, MI 48075-1058 Fax: (248)204-3727
Publication E-mail: alumni@ltu.edu

Magazine for alumni and friends of Lawrence Technological University covering higher education. **Founded:** 1977. **Freq:** Semiannual. **Print Method:** Web offset. **Trim Size:** 8 1/2 x 11. **Cols./Page:** 4. **Col. Width:** 10.5 picas. **Col. Depth:** 9 inches. **Key Personnel:** Bruce Annett, Editor. **Subscription Rates:** Free to qualified subscribers. **Remarks:** Advertising not accepted. **Former name:** Lawrence Institute of Technology Magazine.
Circ: Non-paid 27,000

15636 Metro Parent Magazine
All Kids Considered Ltd.
24567 Northwestern Hwy., No. 150 Phone: (248)352-0990
Fax: (248)352-5066
Southfield, MI 48075
Publication E-mail: metropar@family.com

Consumer magazine covering parenting in Southeast Michigan. **Founded:** Sept. 1986. **Freq:** Monthly. **Print Method:** Web offset. **Trim Size:** 10 1/2 x 12 1/2. **Cols./Page:** 4. **Col. Width:** 2 1/4 inches. **Col. Depth:** 11 1/4 inches. **Subscription Rates:** $25 individuals. **Remarks:** Accepts advertising. **URL:** http://www.metroparent.com.
Ad Rates: BW: $2,515 **Circ:** Controlled 66,000
4C: $2,865

15637 phenomeNEWS
18444 W. 10 Mile, Ste. 105 Phone: (248)569-3888
Southfield, MI 48075 Fax: (248)569-4512

Inspirational, motivational, holistic health, metaphysics. **Subtitle:** Michigan's Body, Mind, Spirit Connection. **Founded:** June 1978. **Freq:** Monthly. **Cols./Page:** 4. **Col. Width:** 14 picas. **Key Personnel:** Gerri Magee, Advertising/Public Relations Dir.; Cindy Saul, Editor and Publisher. **Subscription Rates:** Free; $14 subscription.
Ad Rates: BW: $555 **Circ:** Free 50,000

15638 Southfield Eccentric
Observer & Eccentric Newspapers
36251 Schoolcraft Rd. Phone: (313)591-2300
Livonia, MI 48150-1216 Fax: (313)953-2232

Community newspaper. **Founded:** 1939. **Freq:** Semiweekly (Mon. and Thurs.). **Print Method:** Offset. **Cols./Page:** 9. **Col. Width:** 17 nonpareils. **Col. Depth:** 301 agate lines. **Key Personnel:** Dick Isham, Publisher. **Subscription Rates:** $21. **Remarks:** Accepts advertising.
Ad Rates: GLR: $2.62 **Circ:** Paid 3,490
Non-paid 5,780

15639 Supercharger
Society of Automotive Engineers - Detroit Section
21000 W. Ten Mile Rd. Phone: (248)357-3340
Southfield, MI 48075 Fax: (248)357-1824

Magazine containing subjects of current interest for members of the Society of Automotive Engineers. **Founded:** 1927. **Freq:** 8/year (1/month Oct.-May). **Print Method:** Offset. **Trim Size:** 5 1/2 x 8 1/2. **Cols./Page:** 2. **Col. Width:** 2 inches. **Col. Depth:** 7 inches. **Key Personnel:** Dan Markey, Editor; Michele Tinson, Circulation Mgr. **Remarks:** Accepts advertising.
Ad Rates: BW: $1,290 **Circ:** Paid 16,687
4C: $2,610

15640 Tech News
Lawrence Technological University
21000 W. 10 Mile Rd. Phone: (248)204-4000
Southfield, MI 48075-1058 Fax: (248)204-3727

Collegiate publication. **Founded:** 1932. **Freq:** Monthly. **Print Method:** Web. **Trim Size:** 11 3/8 x 14 3/8. **Cols./Page:** 5. **Col. Width:** 27 nonpareils. **Col. Depth:** 189 agate lines. **Key Personnel:** Bill King, Staff Advisor, bking@ltu.edu.
Ad Rates: GLR: $.04 **Circ:** Non-paid ‡3,000
BW: $216
PCI: $4

15641 Ward's Auto World
Ward's Communications
3000 Town Center, Ste. 2750 Phone: (248)357-0800
Southfield, MI 48075-1212 Fax: (248)357-0810
Publication E-mail: wards@wardsauto.com

Business magazine containing news and analysis for middle and upper management within all disciplines of the automotive OEM. **Founded:** 1965. **Freq:** Monthly. **Print Method:** Web offset. **Trim Size:** 8 x 10 3/4. **Cols./Page:** 2 and 3. **Col. Width:** 40 and 26 nonpareils. **Col. Depth:** 130 agate lines. **Key Personnel:** David C. Smith, Editor-in-Chief; Roger K. Powers, Publisher; Michael A. Arnholt, Managing Editor. **ISSN:** 0043-0315. **Subscription Rates:** $10 single issue; $55 individuals. **Remarks:** Accepts advertising. **URL:** http://www.wardsauto.com. **Alt. Formats:** Microfilm.
Ad Rates: BW: $8,400 **Circ:** Controlled 100,520
4C: $10,660

15642 Ward's Automotive Yearbook
Ward's Communications
3000 Town Center, Ste. 2750 Phone: (248)357-0800
Southfield, MI 48075-1212 Fax: (248)357-0810

Trade journal featuring articles and statistics on the automotive industry including sales, production, and development. **Founded:** 1938. **Freq:** 1/year. **Trim Size:** 8 1/4 x 11. **Key Personnel:** Deebe Farris, Editor; Roger K. Powers, Publisher.

Subscription Rates: $385 single issue. **Remarks:** Accepts advertising. **URL:** http://www.wardsauto.com.
Ad Rates: GLR: $33 **Circ:** Paid 5,000
BW: $2,800
4C: $3,650

15643 Continental Cablevision
27800 Franklin Rd. Phone: (810)353-3905
Southfield, MI 48034 Fax: (810)353-0141

Founded: 1982. **Cities Served:** Oakland County, Keego Harbor, Lathrup Village, Oak Park, Orchard Lake, Royal Oak Township, Sylvan Lake, and West Bloomfield Township, MI.

15644 WDRQ-FM - 93.1
28411 Northwestern Hwy., Ste. 1000 Phone: (810)354-9300
Southfield, MI 48034 Fax: (810)354-1474

Format: Adult Contemporary. **Networks:** Independent. **Owner:** Viacom International, Inc., 1515 Broadway, New York, NY 10036, (212)258-6000. **Founded:** 1947. **Formerly**: WLTI-FM. **Operating Hours:** Continuous; 100% local. **Key Personnel:** George Kenyon, Vice Pres./Gen. Mgr.; Marcy Cyburt, General Sales Mgr.; Dan Zako, Sales Mgr.; Nikki Van Doran, Marketing Director; Mark Phelps, Chief Engineer. **Wattage:** 26,500. **Ad Rates:** $65-350 per unit.

WDWB-TV - See Detroit

WJBK-TV - See Detroit

15645 WKBD-TV - 50
26905 W. 11 Mile Rd., Box 50 Phone: (810)350-5050
Southfield, MI 48037-0050 Fax: (810)355-2692

Format: Commercial TV. **Networks:** United Paramount Network. **Owner:** Paramount Stations Group, Inc., 5555 Melrose Ave., Hollywood, CA 90038-3197, (213)956-8100. **Founded:** 1965. **Operating Hours:** Continuous; 5% network, 95% local. **ADI:** Detroit, MI. **Key Personnel:** Mike Dunlop, General Mgr.; Roland Trombley, Sales Mgr.; Tom Bell, News Dir.; Paul Prange, Program Mgr.; Tim Swore, Sports Dir.; Toby Cunningham, Contact. **Ad Rates:** $25-10,000 for 30 seconds.

15646 WKRK-FM - 97.1
16550 W. 9 Mile Rd. Phone: (248)395-9797
PO Box 5005 Fax: (248)423-7725
Southfield, MI 48086-5005
E-mail: extremeradio.com

Networks: CBS. **Founded:** 1941. **Formerly**: WJOI-FM (Sept. 2, 1994); WYST-FM (1997). **Operating Hours:** Continuous; 100% local. **ADI:** Detroit, MI. **Key Personnel:** Mike Stern, Program Dir., phone (248)423-3389, mstern@971.cbs.com. **Wattage:** 15,000.

15647 WSHJ-FM - 88.3
24675 Lahser Rd. Phone: (810)746-8630
Southfield, MI 48034

Format: Full Service. **Networks:** ABC. **Owner:** Southfield Public Schools, at above address, (810)746-8600. **Founded:** 1967. **Operating Hours:** 8 a.m.-10 p.m. weekdays; 10% network, 90% local. **Key Personnel:** Jon Fruytier, General Mgr.; Max Peelman, Program Dir.; Jon Jackson, Operations Dir. **Wattage:** 125.

15648 WWJ-AM - 950
16550 W. 9 Mile Rd. Phone: (248)423-3300
Southfield, MI 48086 Fax: (248)423-3326
E-mail: wwjnews.950@cbs.com

Format: News; Sports. **Networks:** CBS; AP. **Founded:** 1920. **Operating Hours:** Continuous; 10% network, 90% local. **ADI:** Detroit, MI. **Key Personnel:** Rich Homberg, VP/Gen. Mrg., phone (248)423-3322, fax (248)423-3303; Tom O'Brien, Station Mgr., phone (248)423-3330, fax (248)423-3438; Stephen Kay, News & Programming, phone (248)423-3331; Rick Burkhardt, General Sales Mgr., phone (810)423-3330. **Wattage:** 5000. **URL:** wwj.com.

15649 WXDG-FM - 105.1
28588 Northwestern Hwy., Ste. 200 Phone: (248)355-1051
Southfield, MI 48034 Fax: (248)355-3485
E-mail: studio@radioedge.com

Owner: Greater Michigan Radio, at above address. **Founded:** 1960. **Formerly**: WQRS-FM. **Operating Hours:** Continuous. **Key Personnel:** Bruce J. Stoller, Contact. **Wattage:** 50,000.

15650 WXYT-AM - 1270
15600 W. 12 Mile Rd. Phone: (248)569-8000
Southfield, MI 48076 Fax: (248)569-4514
E-mail: wxyt.com

Format: Talk. **Networks:** CNN Radio. **Owner:** Infinity Broadcasting, at above address. **Founded:** 1925. **Formerly**: WXYZ-AM (1985). **Operating Hours:** Continuous. **ADI:** Detroit, MI. **Key Personnel:** Rich Homberg, General Mgr., fax (248)569-4514; Doug Gondek, Program Dir./Operations Mgr., gondex@wxyt.com; Mark Nicholson, General Sales Mgr. **Wattage:** 5000. **Ad Rates:** $150-2,000 for 60 seconds. **URL:** http://www.wxyt.com.

15651 WXYZ-TV - 7
20777 W. 10 Mile Rd., Box 789 Phone: (810)827-7777
Southfield, MI 48037-0789 Fax: (810)827-4454

Format: Commercial TV. **Networks:** ABC. **Owner:** Scripps-Howard Broadcasting Inc., 1100 Central Trust Tower, Cincinnati, OH 45202, (513)977-3000, Fax: (513)977-3966. **Founded:** 1948. **Operating Hours:** Continuous; 45% network, 55% local. **ADI:** Detroit, MI. **Key Personnel:** Tom Griesdorn, Contact; Marla Drutz, Program Acquisition and Mktg. Dir.; Walter Kraft, News Dir.; Grace Gilchrist, Station Mgr.; Mimmi Mathis, Program Development and Ad Dir.; Mike Doback, Engineering Mgr.; Bob Sliva, General Sales Mgr.; Joe Trondle, Local Sales Mgr.; Al Upchurch, Assistant News Dir.; Bob Giles, Dir. of News Operations; Gary Schlaff, Research Dir. **Ad Rates:** Advertising accepted; rates available upon request.

SOUTHGATE

15652 News Herald
Heritage Newspapers, Inc.
1 Heritage Pl., Ste. 100 Phone: (313)246-0800
Southgate, MI 48195 Fax: (313)284-2028

Community newspaper. **Founded:** 1879. **Freq:** Semiweekly (Wed. and Sun.). **Print Method:** Offset. **Cols./Page:** 6. **Col. Width:** 12.5 picas. **Col. Depth:** 21 1/2 inches. **Key Personnel:** Karl Ziomek, Editor; Donald W. Thurlow, Publisher; Bill Dillingham, Advertising Mgr.; Lynn Hemphill, Editor; Sue Nations, Circulation Mgr.; Bonnie Klimowicz, Circulation Mgr. **Subscription Rates:** $39. **Remarks:** Accepts advertising. **URL:** http://www.heritage.com.
Ad Rates: GLR: $3.70 **Circ:** Wed. 84,143
BW: $6,682.20
4C: $7,832.20
PCI: $51.80

SPARTA

15653 Great Lakes Fruit Growers News
Great American Publishing Co.
343 S. Union Phone: (616)887-9008
PO Box 128 Fax: (616)887-2666
Sparta, MI 49345
Publisher E-mail: glp@iserv.net

Agricultural tabloid. **Founded:** 1961. **Freq:** Monthly. **Print Method:** Offset. **Trim Size:** 11 1/2 x 17. **Cols./Page:** 5. **Key Personnel:** Matt McCallum, Publisher; Dee Rau, Advertising Mgr.; Lee Dean, Managing Editor. **Subscription Rates:** $9.50. **Remarks:** Accepts advertising.
Ad Rates: BW: $900 **Circ:** Paid ‡12,345
4C: $1,890
PCI: $11.25

15654 Great Lakes Vegetable Growers News
Great American Publishing Co.
343 S. Union Phone: (616)887-9008
PO Box 128 Fax: (616)887-2666
Sparta, MI 49345
Publisher E-mail: glp@iserv.net

Agricultural tabloid. **Founded:** 1966. **Freq:** Monthly. **Print Method:** Offset. **Trim Size:** 11 1/2 x 17. **Cols./Page:** 5. **Col. Width:** 22 nonpareils. **Col. Depth:** 224 agate lines. **Key Personnel:** Matt McCallum, Publisher; Dee Rau, Advertising Mgr.; Lee Dean, Managing Editor. **Subscription Rates:** $9.50 individuals. **Remarks:** Accepts advertising.
Ad Rates: BW: $900 **Circ:** Combined ‡14,415
4C: $1,890
PCI: $11.25

15655 Sparta/Kent City Advance
Advance Newspapers
2141 Port Sheldon Rd. Phone: (616)669-2700
PO Box 9 Fax: (616)669-1162
Jenison, MI 49428-9301
Free: (800)439-0960

Community newspaper (tabloid). **Founded:** 1966. **Freq:** Weekly (Tues.). **Print Method:** Offset. **Cols./Page:** 6. **Col. Width:** 16 nonpareils. **Col. Depth:** 224 agate lines. **Key Personnel:** Joel Holland, Publisher, fax (616)669-3930. **Subscription Rates:** $25 individuals. **Remarks:** Combined advertising rates available with other Advance Newspapers. **Formerly**: Ada/Cascade/Forest Hills Advance.
Ad Rates: BW: $494.40 **Circ:** Controlled 12,225
4C: $794.40 Paid 243
SAU: $6.18
PCI: $5.15

SPRING ARBOR

15656 Spring Arbor College Journal
Spring Arbor College
106 E. Main St. Phone: (517)750-1200
Spring Arbor, MI 49283-9799 Fax: (517)750-3837

College alumni magazine. **Founded:** 1976. **Freq:** Quarterly. **Print Method:** Offset. **Trim Size:** 8 1/2 x 11. **Cols./Page:** 3. **Col. Width:** 20 nonpareils. **Col. Depth:** 125 agate lines. **Key Personnel:** Shannon L. Scholten, Editor. **Subscription Rates:** Free. **Remarks:** Advertising not accepted.
Circ: Controlled 11,000

15657 KTGG-AM - 1540
Spring Arbor College Phone: (517)750-6540
Spring Arbor, MI 49283 Fax: (517)750-6619
Free: (800)750-9723
E-mail: wsae@admin.arbor.edu

Format: Religious. **Networks:** SkyLight Satellite. **Owner:** Spring Arbor College Communications, Inc., at above address. **Founded:** 1985. **Operating Hours:** Sunrise-sunset; 100% local. **Key Personnel:** Michelle Dawson, General & Program Mgr., phone (517)750-6543. **Local Programs:** *Sundy Sounds* 10:00 am - 10:30 am Sunday, Michelle Dawson, Mailing contact; *Sunday Sacred Classics* 8:30 - 9:30 am Sunday. **Wattage:** 500. **Ad Rates:** Noncommercial. **URL:** http://www.arbor.edu/wsae.

15658 WSAE-FM - 106.9
Spring Arbor College Phone: (517)750-6540
106 Main St. Fax: (517)750-6619
Sayre Hall
Spring Arbor, MI 49283
Free: (800)750-9723
E-mail: wsae@admin.arbor.edu

Format: Contemporary Christian. **Networks:** SkyLight Satellite. **Owner:** Spring Arbor College Communications, at above address, Fax: (517)750-6619. **Founded:** 1963. **Operating Hours:** Continuous. **Key Personnel:** Michelle Dawson, General Mgr., phone (517)750-6543. **Local Programs:** *Sunday Sounds* 10:00 am - 10:30 am Sunday, Michelle Dawson, General Mgr.; *Sunday Sacred Classics* 8:30 am 9:30 am Sunday. **Wattage:** 3900. **Ad Rates:** Noncommercial. **URL:** http://www.arbor.edu/wsae.

SPRINGPORT

15659 Signal
104 Maple St. Phone: (517)857-2500
Box 157
Springport, MI 49284
Newspaper. **Founded:** 1876. **Freq:** Weekly (Thurs.). **Print Method:** Letterpress and offset. **Cols./Page:** 5. **Col. Width:** 24 nonpareils. **Col. Depth:** 203 agate lines. **Key Personnel:** Helen F. Prine, Editor and Publisher. **Subscription Rates:** $8. **Remarks:** Accepts advertising.
Ad Rates: GLR: $.17 **Circ:** (Not Reported)

STANDISH

15660 Arenac County Independent
203 E. Cedar Phone: (517)846-4531
PO Box 699 Fax: (517)846-9868
Standish, MI 48658
Free: (800)831-7669

Community newspaper. **Founded:** 1883. **Freq:** Weekly (Wed.). **Print Method:** Offset. **Cols./Page:** 6. **Col. Width:** 25 nonpareils. **Col. Depth:** 301 agate lines. **Key Personnel:** E.J. Perlberg and Robert Perlberg, Publisher. **Subscription Rates:** $10.
Ad Rates: GLR: $.27 **Circ:** ‡6,156
BW: $709.50
SAU: $5.50

15661 WSTD-FM - 96.9
1670 Able Rd. Phone: (517)654-2400
PO Box 969 Fax: (517)654-2440
Sterling, MI 48659-0969
Free: (800)422-9690

Format: Full Service; Adult Contemporary. **Networks:** Unistar; Mutual Broadcasting System. **Founded:** 1989. **Operating Hours:** Continuous. **Key Personnel:** Edwin H. Eichler, General Mgr.; Pam Cousineau, Assistant General Mgr. **Wattage:** 3000. **Ad Rates:** $8-13 for 30 seconds; $10.50-15 for 60 seconds.

STERLING

WSTD-FM - See Standish

STERLING HEIGHTS

15662 Sterling Heights Source
21st Century Newspapers, Inc.
100 Macomb Daily Dr.
Mount Clemens, MI 48046

Community newspaper. **Founded:** 1972. **Freq:** Weekly (Sun.). **Print Method:** Offset. **Cols./Page:** 6. **Col. Width:** 2 1/16 inches. **Col. Depth:** 21 1/2 inches. **Key Personnel:** Frank Sheperd, President/CEO, phone (810)469-4510; Wayne Oehmke, Publisher; Chris Troszak, Retail Advertising Mgr.; Joe Warner, Managing Editor. **Subscription Rates:** $80. **Remarks:** Accepts advertising. **Formerly**: Sterling/Utica/Shelby Advisor (1989).
Ad Rates: PCI: $35 **Circ:** (Not Reported)

15663 Comcast Cablevision of Southeast Michigan
6095 Wall St. Phone: (810)978-8780
Sterling Heights, MI 48312 Fax: (810)978-1511
Free: (800)660-8780

Owner: Comcast Cable Communications Inc., 1234 Market St., Philadelphia, PA 19107-2480, (215)665-1700. **Key Personnel:** Dave Wells, General Mgr. **Cities Served:** All of Macomb County except the city of Roseville.

15664 WUFL-AM - 1030
42669 Garfield Rd., Ste. 328 Phone: (810)263-1030
Clinton Township, MI 48038 Fax: (810)228-1030
Free: (800)733-1030

Format: Religious. **Networks:** USA Radio. **Owner:** Family Life Broadcasting System, PO Box 35300, Tucson, AZ 85740, (602)742-6976. **Founded:** 1988. **Operating Hours:** Sunrise-sunset. **Key Personnel:** Steven K. Wright, General Mgr.; Gary Lundy, News/Public Affairs Editor; Greg Kinzy, Asst. Mgr.; Cornelius Henderson, Community Relations Dir. **Wattage:** 5000. **Ad Rates:** Noncommercial.

STURGIS

15665 Sturgis Journal
Hometown Communications, Inc.
209 John St. Phone: (616)651-5407
Box 660 Fax: (616)651-2296
Sturgis, MI 49091-1459
Free: (800)686-5653

General newspaper. **Founded:** 1859. **Freq:** Daily (eve.) and Sat. (morn.). **Print Method:** Offset. **Cols./Page:** 6. **Col. Width:** 24 nonpareils. **Col. Depth:** 301 agate lines. **Key Personnel:** Richard A. Piatt, Editor and Publisher. **Subscription Rates:** $78. **Remarks:** Accepts advertising.
Ad Rates: PCI: $9.67 **Circ:** ‡7,687

15666 WMSH-AM - 1230
70808 S. Nottawa Phone: (616)651-2383
P.O. Box 7080 Fax: (616)659-1111
Sturgis, MI 49091
E-mail: wmsh@voyager.net

Format: Oldies. **Simulcasts:** WMSH-FM. **Networks:** ABC. **Owner:** Lake Cities Broadcasting Corp., PO Box 9990, Angola, IN 46703, (219)692-6851, Fax: (219)692-6861. **Founded:** 1951. **Formerly**: WSTR-AM (1989). **Operating Hours:** Continuous. **ADI:** Grand Rapids-Kalamazoo-Battle Creek, MI. **Key Personnel:** Tom Flynn, General Mgr., tflynn@voyager.net. **Wattage:** 1000. **Ad Rates:** $6-12 for 30 seconds; $7-15 for 60 seconds. Combined advertising rates available with WTHD-FM, WLKI-FM.

15667 WMSH-FM - 99.3
70808 S. Nottawa Phone: (616)651-2383
P.O. Box 7080 Fax: (616)659-1111
Sturgis, MI 49091
E-mail: wmsh@voyager.net

Format: Oldies. **Simulcasts:** WMSH-AM. **Networks:** ABC. **Owner:** Lake Cities Broadcasting Corp., PO Box 999, Angola, IN 46703, (219)692-6851, Fax: (219)692-6861. **Founded:** 1951. **Formerly**: WSTR-FM (1991). **Operating Hours:** Continuous. **Key Personnel:** Tom Flynn, General Mgr., phone (616)651-2383, fax (616)659-1111, tflynn@voyager.net. **Wattage:** 3000. **Ad Rates:** $6-12 for 30 seconds; $7-15 for 60 seconds. Combined advertising rates available with WTHD-FM, WLKI-FM.

SUNFIELD

15668 The Sunfield Sentinel
Sunfield Sentinel Publishing
PO Box 8 Phone: (517)566-8500
Sunfield, MI 48890 Fax: (517)566-8873

Farming community newspaper. **Founded:** 1888. **Freq:** Weekly. **Print Method:** Offset. **Cols./Page:** 6. **Col. Width:** 12 picas. **Col. Depth:** 280 agate lines. **Key Personnel:** Connie Speaks, Editor; Art Kimball, Publisher. **Subscription Rates:** $9 individuals; $10 out of state. **Remarks:** Color advertising not accepted.
Ad Rates: BW: $240 **Circ:** ‡900

SWARTZ CREEK

15669 Fireplug
Michigan State Fireman's Association
9001 Miller Rd., Ste. 10 Phone: (517)322-2424
Swartz Creek, MI 48473-0405 Fax: (517)322-2235
Publication E-mail: MSFAssoc@AOL.com
Publisher E-mail: msfassoc@aol.com

Trade magazine for firemen. **Freq:** Quarterly. **Key Personnel:** Joseph J. Edgerton. **ISSN:** 0273-6101. **Subscription Rates:** $20 individuals; $75 fire departments. **Remarks:** Accepts advertising.
Ad Rates: BW: $300 **Circ:** (Not Reported)

TAWAS CITY

15670 The Northeastern Shopper
129 E. North St. Phone: (517)362-6111
Box 447 Fax: (517)362-7080
Tawas City, MI 48764-0447
Shopper. **Founded:** Apr. 14, 1954. **Freq:** Sunday. **Print Method:** Offset. **Trim Size:** 11 x 17. **Cols./Page:** 6. **Col. Width:** 21 nonpareils. **Col. Depth:** 224 agate lines. **Key Personnel:** William L. Ezo, Publisher. **Remarks:** Accepts advertising.
Ad Rates: BW: $1237.44 **Circ:** Free ‡40,252
PCI: $12.89

15671 WIOS-AM - 1480
PO Box 549 Phone: (517)362-3417
Tawas City, MI 48764-0549 Fax: (517)362-4544

Format: Easy Listening; Talk; Sports. **Networks:** ABC. **Owner:** Carroll Broadcasting, Inc., at above address, (517)362-3627. **Founded:** 1958. **Operating Hours:** Sunrise-sunset. **ADI:** Flint-Saginaw-Bay City, MI. **Key Personnel:** John Carroll, General Mgr.; Tim Carroll, Sales Mgr.; Mike Mitchell, News Dir.; Kevin Allen, Program Dir.; Karen Costle, Contact. **Wattage:** 1000. **Ad Rates:** Advertising accepted; rates available upon request. Combined advertising rates available with WKJC-FM.

15672 WKJC-FM - 104.7
PO Box 549 Phone: (517)362-3417
Tawas City, MI 48764-0549 Fax: (517)362-4544

Format: Country; Sports. **Networks:** ABC. **Owner:** Carroll Broadcasting, at above address, (517)362-3627. **Founded:** 1958. **Operating Hours:** Continuous. **ADI:** Flint-Saginaw-Bay City, MI. **Key Personnel:** John Carroll, General Mgr.; Tim Carroll, Sales Mgr.; Mike Mitchell, News Dir.; Kevin Allen, Program Dir.; Karen Castle, Contact. **Wattage:** 50,000. **Ad Rates:** Advertising accepted; rates available upon request.

TAYLOR

15673 Comcast Cable TV
24744 Eureka Rd. Phone: (734)946-6010
Taylor, MI 48180 Fax: (734)946-1924

Founded: 1980. **Formerly**: Maclean Hunter Cable TV (1995). **Key Personnel:** Kathleen Ebli, General Mgr.; Joe Bellance, Sales Mgr. **Cities Served:** Allen Park, Berlin, Brownstown, Ecorse, Flat Rock, Garden City, Grosse Ile, Inkster, Melvindale, River Rouge, Rockwood, South Rockwood, Southgate, Taylor, MI; Downriver in Wayne County: subscribing households 70,000; 80 channels; 3 community access channels; 36 hours per week community access programming.

TECUMSEH

15674 The Tecumseh Herald
PO Box 218 Phone: (517)423-2174
110 E. Logan Fax: (517)423-6258
Tecumseh, MI 49286
Free: (800)832-6443

Community newspaper. **Founded:** 1850. **Freq:** Weekly (Thurs.). **Print Method:** Offset. **Cols./Page:** 8. **Col. Width:** 18 nonpareils. **Col. Depth:** 294 agate lines. **Key Personnel:** James L. Lincoln, Editor; James C. Lincoln, Publisher. **Subscription Rates:** $22 individuals. **Remarks:** Accepts advertising.
Ad Rates: GLR: $.23 **Circ:** ‡5,500
SAU: $6.80

TEMPERANCE

15675 Bedford Cablevision Ltd.
8212 Lewis Ave. Phone: (313)847-0546
Box 340 Fax: (313)847-4112
Temperance, MI 48182

Owner: Phoenix Cable Inc., 10 S. Franklin Turnpike, Ramsey, NJ 07446. **Founded:** Apr. 15, 1982. **Key Personnel:** Jim Feeney, Exec. Vice Pres.; Charles Himelrich, Asst. Vice Pres.; John Finley, Dir. of Marketing. **Cities Served:** Bedford, Ida, Temperance, Whiteford, MI: subscribing households 6,950; 47 channels; 1 community access channel; 168 hours per week community access programming.

THREE OAKS

The Other Side of the Lake - See Chicago, Illinois

15676 South County Gazette and Shopper
Artistic Energy Group, Inc.
505 W. Locust St. Phone: (616)756-2421
PO Box 303 Fax: (616)756-7220
Three Oaks, MI 49128
Free community newspaper. **Subtitle:** Michigan's Best Weekly 1991. **Founded:** 1929. **Freq:** Weekly (Mon.). **Print Method:** Offset. **Trim Size:** 11 3/8 x 13 3/4. **Cols./Page:** 4. **Col. Width:** 2 1/4 inches. **Col. Depth:** 12 1/2 inches. **Key Personnel:** Marlsue Hojnacki, Editor; Michael Hojnacki, Editor and Publisher; Marlene Reid, Advertising Mgr. **Subscription Rates:** $15 individuals; $25 out of area. **Remarks:** Accepts advertising. **Formerly**: The Gazette; Galien River Gazette. **Merged with:** Shore & Country Shopper (1996).
Ad Rates: BW: $450 **Circ:** Combined ‡11,002
4C: $600
SAU: $10

THREE RIVERS

15677 The Shoppers Guide of Three Rivers
130 W. Michigan Ave. Phone: (616)279-7448
Three Rivers, MI 49093 Fax: (616)279-7440

Shoppers Guide. **Subtitle:** Midweek Shopper. **Founded:** 1958. **Freq:** Weekly (Wed.). **Print Method:** Offset. **Trim Size:** 10 3/4 x 16. **Cols./Page:** 6. **Col. Width:** 20 nonpareils. **Col. Depth:** 224 agate lines. **Key Personnel:** Jerry J. Wright, Publisher; E.R. DeWitt, Advertising Mgr.; Jane Harmon, General Mgr. **Subscription Rates:** Free. **Remarks:** Accepts advertising.
Ad Rates: GLR: $0.30 **Circ:** Free ‡19,000
BW: $532.80
4C: $832.80
PCI: $5.55

15678 Three Rivers Commercial-News
Three Rivers Commerical News
124 N. Main St. Phone: (616)279-7488
Three Rivers, MI 49093 Fax: (616)279-6007

Local newspaper. **Founded:** 1895. **Freq:** Daily (eve.) and Sat. (morn.). **Print Method:** Offset. **Cols./Page:** 8. **Col. Width:** 18 nonpareils. **Col. Depth:** 301 agate lines. **Key Personnel:** Dick Milliman II, Editor and Publisher; Joe Albertson, General Mgr. **Subscription Rates:** $65. **Remarks:** Accepts advertising.
Ad Rates: GLR: $6.35 **Circ:** Paid 4,503
BW: $860 Free ‡17,100
4C: $1,080
SAU: $7.10
PCI: $5.30

15679 Jones Intercable
414 W. Hoffman Phone: (616)273-8408
Box 128 Fax: (616)279-5254
Three Rivers, MI 49093

Owner: Jones Intercable Inc., 9697 E. Mineral Ave., Englewood, CO 80112, (303)792-3111. **Formerly**: Omega Cable (1974). **Key Personnel:** Sharon Bachinski, General Mgr.; Marla Hurse, Marketing Mgr. **Cities Served:** Centreville, Coloma, Constantine, Dowagiac, Schoolcraft, Three Rivers, Vicksburg, Watervliet, White Pigeon, MI: subscribing households 15,800; 49 channels.

15680 WLKM-AM - 1510
59750 Constantine Rd. Phone: (616)278-1815
Three Rivers, MI 49093

Format: Talk; News; Agricultural. **Networks:** Michigan Farm Radio; UPI; Westwood One Radio. **Owner:** Voice of Three Rivers, Inc., at above address. **Founded:** 1962. **Operating Hours:** Sunrise-sunset. **ADI:** Grand Rapids-Kalamazoo-Battle Creek, MI. **Key Personnel:** Dennis Rumsey, General Mgr. **Wattage:** 500. **Ad Rates:** $3.00 for 30 seconds; $4.50 for 60 seconds.

15681 WLKM-FM - 95.9
59750 Constantine Rd. Phone: (616)278-1815
Three Rivers, MI 49093 Fax: (616)273-7975

Format: Soft Rock; News; Agricultural. **Networks:** Michigan Farm Radio; Mutual Broadcasting System. **Owner:** Voice of Three Rivers, Inc., at above address. **Founded:** 1975. **Operating Hours:** Continuous. **ADI:** Grand Rapids-Kalamazoo-Battle Creek, MI. **Key Personnel:** Dennis Rumsey, General Mgr.; Jack Baker, News Dir.; Kathy Loker, Sales Mgr. **Wattage:** 3000. **Ad Rates:** $8.30-13.80 for 30 seconds; $9.70-16.15 for 60 seconds.

TRAVERSE CITY

15682 The Home Shop Machinist
2779 Aero Park Dr. Phone: (616)946-3712
Traverse City, MI 49684 Fax: (616)946-3289
Free: (800)447-7367
Publication E-mail: vpshop@aol.com
Publisher E-mail: villagepre@aol.com

Magazine for the amateur small shop machinist. **Founded:** 1982. **Freq:** Bimonthly. **Print Method:** Offset. **Trim Size:** 8 1/2 x 11. **Key Personnel:** Joe D. Rice, Editor; Robert L. Goff, Publisher; Lori Gardyko, Advertising Mgr., fax (616)946-9588. **ISSN:** 0744-6640. **Subscription Rates:** $26.50 individuals. **URL:** http://members.aol.com/vpshop/hsm.htm.
Ad Rates: BW: $1,021 **Circ:** Paid ‡33,400
Non-paid ‡82

15683 Independent Publisher
Jenkins Group, Inc.
121 E. Front St., 4th Fl. Phone: (616)933-0445
Traverse City, MI 49684 Fax: (616)933-0448

Magazine containing book reviews and articles about independent publishing. **Subtitle:** The Magazine of Independent Publishing. **Founded:** 1983. **Freq:** Bimonthly. **Print Method:** Offset. Uses mats. **Trim Size:** 8 1/2 x 11. **Cols./Page:** 4. **Col. Width:** 22 nonpareils. **Col. Depth:** 224 agate lines. **Key Personnel:** Jerrold R. Jenkins, Publisher; Victoria Sutherland, Advertising Dir.; Mardi Link, Exec. Editor; Barb Pittman, Art Dir.; Tim Watson, Circulation Mgr. **ISSN:** 0000-0485. **Subscription Rates:** $34 individuals; $5.95 single issue. **Remarks:** Accepts advertising. **Formerly:** Small Press.
Ad Rates: GLR: $19.50 **Circ:** Paid 10,000
BW: $1,075 Non-paid 3,000
4C: $2,020
PCI: $59

15684 Live Steam
Village Press Publications
PO Box 629
Traverse City, MI 49685
Publication E-mail: steambook@aol.com

Magazine covering steam powered engines for hobbyists. **Founded:** 1966. **Freq:** Bimonthly. **Print Method:** Offset. **Trim Size:** 8 1/2 x 11. **Cols./Page:** 3. **Col. Width:** 14 picas. **Col. Depth:** 60 picas. **Key Personnel:** Joe D. Rice, Editor; Robert L. Goff, Publisher; Kathy Booth, Advertising Mgr. **ISSN:** 0364-5177. **Subscription Rates:** $37 individuals. **Available Online. URL:** http://www.villagepress.com.
Ad Rates: BW: $635 **Circ:** Paid ‡11,221
4C: $1135 Non-paid ‡382

15685 Machinist's Workshop
Village Press Publications
2779 Aero Park Dr.
Traverse City, MI 49684

Magazine describing metal working techniques and projects for hobby machinists. **Founded:** 1988. **Freq:** Bimonthly. **Print Method:** Offset. **Trim Size:** 8 1/2 x 11. **Cols./Page:** 3. **Col. Width:** 2 1/2 inches. **Col. Depth:** 10 inches. **Key Personnel:** Joe Rice, Editor, phone (800)327-7377, jrice@villagepress.com; Clover McKinley, Asst. Editor, phone (800)327-7377; Lori Gardyko, Advertising Mgr., phone (800)327-7377. **ISSN:** 0897-070X. **Subscription Rates:** $23; $4.50 single issue. **Remarks:** Accepts advertising. **URL:** http://www.villagepress.com. **Alt. Formats:** Microfiche. **Formerly:** Projects in Metal.
Ad Rates: BW: $704 **Circ:** Paid ‡18,696
Non-paid ‡73

15686 Psychology in the Schools
Clinical Psychology Publishing Co., Inc.
PO Box 4150 Phone: (616)946-3606
Traverse City, MI 49685 Fax: (616)946-4916

Journal focusing on the use of psychology in schools. **Founded:** Jan. 1964. **Freq:** Quarterly. **Print Method:** Offset. **Trim Size:** 6 3/4 x 10. **Cols./Page:** 1. **Col. Width:** 61 nonpareils. **Col. Depth:** 111 agate lines. **Key Personnel:** G.B. Fuller, Editor. **ISSN:** 0033-3085. **Subscription Rates:** $35; $100 institutions; $111 other countries. **Remarks:** Accepts advertising.
Ad Rates: BW: $200 **Circ:** Paid ‡1,684
Non-paid ‡78

15687 Publishing Entrepreneur
Jenkins Group, Inc.
121 E. Front St., 4th Fl. Phone: (616)933-0445
Traverse City, MI 49684 Fax: (616)933-0448
Publication E-mail: jenkins.group@smallpress.com

Magazine featuring articles on information and publishing technology. **Subtitle:** Profit Strategies for the Information & Publishing Industry. **Founded:** 1994. **Freq:** Bimonthly. **Trim Size:** 8 1/4 x 10 7/8. **Key Personnel:** Mardi Link, Editor; Victoria Sutherland, Advertising Dir.; Barb Pittman, Art Dir.; Tim Watson, Circulation Mgr. **ISSN:** 1092-7270. **Subscription Rates:** $28 individuals; $3.50 single issue. **Remarks:** Advertising accepted; rates available upon request. **Formerly:** Information Entrepreneur.
Circ: (Not Reported)

15688 Traverse City Record-Eagle
Herald & Record Co.
120 W. Front St. Phone: (616)946-2000
PO Box 632 Fax: (616)946-8273
Traverse City, MI 49685-4968
General newspaper. **Founded:** 1858. **Freq:** Daily (morn.). **Print Method:** Offset. **Trim Size:** 14 x 21. **Cols./Page:** 6. **Col. Width:** 24 nonpareils. **Col. Depth:** 300 agate lines. **Key Personnel:** Zeke Fleet, General Mgr.; Frank B. Senger, Publisher; Ken Hall, Executive Editor; Michael Nau, Controller; Steve Knape, Circulation Mgr.; Thomas Bunch, Circulation Mgr. **Subscription Rates:** $189.85 by mail /annual. **URL:** http://www.record-eagle.com.
Ad Rates: GLR: $2.15 **Circ:** Mon.-Sat. ★**28,726**
BW: $2,480.67 Sun. ★**40,142**
4C: $2,925.67
SAU: $21
PCI: $19.30

15689 Traverse, Northern Michigan's Magazine
Prism Publications, Inc.
148 E. Front St. Phone: (616)941-8174
Traverse City, MI 49684 Fax: (616)941-8391
Free: (800)678-3416
Publication E-mail: traverse@freshwater.com

Regional lifestyle features magazine. **Subtitle:** Northern Michigan's Magazine. **Founded:** June 1981. **Freq:** Monthly. **Print Method:** Offset. **Trim Size:** 8 3/8 x 10 7/8. **Cols./Page:** 3. **Key Personnel:** Deborah W. Fellows, Founder; Jodi Simpson, Director of Circulation & Marketing; Nile Young, Jr., Dir of art. **ISSN:** 1071-3719. **Subscription Rates:** $28 individuals; $3.50 single issue; $38 Foreign. **Remarks:** Accepts advertising. **URL:** http://freshwater.com/traverse. **Formerly:** TRAVERSE the Magazine.
Ad Rates: BW: $2,115 **Circ:** ‡22,000
4C: $2,530

15690 Higgins Lake Cable TV
PO Box 1029 Phone: (517)821-5567
Traverse City, MI 49685-1029

Founded: 1987. **Cities Served:** Beaver Creek Township, Gerrish Township, Lake Township, Lyon Township, Markey Township, Roscommon Township, MI: subscribing households 3,500; 36 channels.

15691 WBCM-FM - 93.5
314 E. Front St. Phone: (616)947-7675
Traverse City, MI 49684 Fax: (616)929-3988
E-mail: wtcm@wtcmradio.com

Format: Country. **Networks:** ABC. **Owner:** WBCM Radio, Inc., at above address. **Founded:** 1978. **Formerly:** WCLX-FM (1992); WTCM-FM. **Operating Hours:** Continuous. **ADI:** Traverse City-Cadillac, MI. **Key Personnel:** Ross Biederman, General Mgr. **Wattage:** 50,000. **Ad Rates:** $8 for 30 seconds; $10 for 60 seconds.

15692 WBYB-FM - 94.3
745 S. Garfield Ave. Phone: (616)947-0003
Traverse City, MI 49685 Fax: (616)947-4290
Free: (888)442-8943

Format: Country. **Owner:** Northern Michigan Radio, Inc., at above address. **Founded:** Nov. 25, 1997. **Former name:** WIAR-FM. **Operating Hours:** Continuous. **Key Personnel:** D. C. Cavender, Program Dir., phone (616)947-5383, dccav@hotmail.com; Susan Melton, Promotions Dir., phone (616)947-9085, susancole@yahoo.com; A. J. Allan, PSA Dir. **Wattage:** 15,000. **URL:** http://www.10943.com.

15693 WCCW-FM - 107.5
308 E. Front Phone: (616)946-6211
Traverse City, MI 49684 Fax: (616)946-1914
Free: (800)833-1075

Format: Oldies. **Networks:** Satellite Music Network. **Founded:** 1960. **Operating Hours:** Continuous. **ADI:** Traverse City-Cadillac, MI. **Key Personnel:** Hal Payne, General Mgr. **Wattage:** 50,000. **Ad Rates:** $15-25 for 30 seconds; $18-28 for 60 seconds. Combined advertising rates available with WCCW-AM, WKJF-AM.

15694 WGTU-TV - 29
201 E. Front St. Phone: (616)946-2900
Traverse City, MI 49684 Fax: (616)946-1600
E-mail: wgtuwgtq@aol.com

Format: Commercial TV. **Networks:** ABC. **Owner:** Scanlan Communications, at above address. **Founded:** 1971. **Operating Hours:** 24 hrs. **ADI:** Traverse City-Cadillac, MI. **Key Personnel:** Todd Runovavaara, Contact; Thomas Scanlan, Contact; James Domagalski, Program Dir. **Local Programs:** *Rita Melotti-Live* 6:30 a.m. - 7 a.m. Monday-Friday, Rita Melotti, Mailing contact. **Ad Rates:** $30-800 per unit. **URL:** http://www.wgtu.com.

15695 WIFN-AM - 1590
517 1/2 S. Union St. Phone: (810)765-8893
Traverse City, MI 49684-3246 Fax: (810)765-8894
E-mail: wifn@aol.com

Format: News; Talk. **Networks:** Mutual Broadcasting System; ABC. **Owner:** Barr/Schremp Communications, at above address. **Founded:** 1951. **Formerly:** WDOG-AM (1965); WSMA-AM. **Operating Hours:** Continuous. **ADI:** Detroit, MI. **Key Personnel:** David Barr, Operations Mgr./Sales Dir./Gen. Mgr. **Wattage:** 1000. **Ad Rates:** $9-13 for 10 seconds; $11-15 for 30 seconds; $13-17 for 60 seconds.

15696 WKLT-FM - 97.5
745 S. Garfield Phone: (616)947-0003
Traverse City, MI 49684 Fax: (616)947-7002
E-mail: wklt.com

Format: Album-Oriented Rock (AOR); Classic Rock. **Simulcasts:** WKLZ-FM (98.9). **Networks:** ABC. **Owner:** Northern Broadcasting Inc, at above address. **Founded:** 1979. **Operating Hours:** Continuous; 5% network, 95% local. **ADI:** Traverse City-Cadillac, MI. **Key Personnel:** DeeAnn Davis, National Sales Mgr., ddavis928@aol.com; John Dew, General Mgr., dewline1@wklt.com; Terri Ray, Program Dir., tray@wklt.com; Ben Ludka, Promotions Dir., luds@wklt.com. **Local Programs:** *Ellis & Company*, Pete Misiak; *Lunch at Leetsville*, Terri Ray; *The Renegade*, Dave Clapper. **Wattage:** 32,000. **Ad Rates:** Advertising accepted; rates available upon request. Combined advertising rates available with WKPK-FM, WBYB-FM, WAIR-FM. **URL:** http://www.wklt.com.

15697 WLDR-FM - 101.9
118 S. Union St. Phone: (616)947-3220
Traverse City, MI 49684 Fax: (616)947-7201
E-mail: wldr@traverse.com

Format: Adult Contemporary. **Networks:** Westwood One Radio; CNN Radio. **Owner:** Donald J. Wiitala, 6300 Singletree Ln., Williamsburg, MI 49690. **Founded:** 1966. **Operating Hours:** Continuous. **ADI:** Traverse City-Cadillac, MI. **Key Personnel:** Dave Maxson, News Dir.; Vic Browning, Music Dir.; Jon Forton, Sales Mgr.; Donald J. Wiitala, Owner; Tina Martin, Office Mgr.; Tina Martin, Office Mgr.; Vic Browning, Program Dir. **Wattage:** 100,000. **Ad Rates:** $16-23 for 30 seconds; $20-27 for 60 seconds.

15698 WLJN-AM - 1400
Box 1400 Phone: (616)946-1400
Traverse City, MI 49685 Fax: (616)946-3959
Free: (800)968-1400
E-mail: wljn@juno.com

Format: Religious. **Networks:** Moody Broadcasting; USA Radio; Ambassador Inspirational Radio; Voice of Christian Youth America; SkyLight Satellite. **Owner:** Good News Media, Inc., at above address. **Founded:** 1982. **Operating Hours:** Continuous; 85% network, 15% local. **ADI:** Traverse City-Cadillac, MI. **Key Personnel:** Brian S. Harcey, Manager; Don Parker, Chief Engineer; Pete Lathrop, Program Dir.; Evelyn Purdy, Music Dir. **Wattage:** 640.

15699 WLJN-FM - 89.9
Box 1400 Phone: (616)946-1400
Traverse City, MI 49685 Fax: (616)946-3959
Free: (800)968-1400
E-mail: wljn@juno.com

Format: Religious. **Networks:** Moody Broadcasting; Ambassador Inspirational Radio; USA Radio; Voice of Christian Youth America. **Owner:** Good News Media, Inc., at above address. **Founded:** 1988. **Operating Hours:** Continuous; 55% network, 45% local. **ADI:** Traverse City-Cadillac, MI. **Key**

Personnel: Brian S . Harcey, Manager; Don Parker, Chief Engineer; Pete Lathrop, Program Dir.; Evelyn Purdy, Music Dir. **Wattage:** 12,500.

15700 WNMC-FM - 90.7
1701 E. Front St. Phone: (616)922-1091
Traverse City, MI 49686 Fax: (616)922-8963

Format: Jazz; Blues; Ethnic; Urban Contemporary; Alternative/New Music/Progressive; Talk; Folk. **Networks:** IBS. **Owner:** Northwestern Michigan College, at above address, (616)922-1000. **Founded:** 1967. **Operating Hours:** 20 hours Daily; 100% local. **ADI:** Traverse City-Cadillac, MI. **Key Personnel:** Teresa O'Hara, General Mgr.; Sammy Stamper, Business Director; Keith Schwartz, Program Dir. **Local Programs:** *Folks Like Us*, Mike Sullivan, (616)922-1090; *Pow Wow Highway*, Teresa O'Hara; *Tertulia*, Keith Schwartz, (616)922-1182. **Wattage:** 600. **Ad Rates:** $5 per unit.

15701 WPBN-TV - 7
8581 M-72 W. Phone: (616)947-7770
P.O. Box 546 Fax: (616)947-0354
Traverse City, MI 49685

Format: Commercial TV. **Networks:** NBC. **Owner:** Federal Broadcasting Company., 1533 N. Woodward, Ste. 240, Bloomfield Hills, MI 48304, (810)645-8930. **Founded:** 1954. **Operating Hours:** Continuous; 70% network, 30% local. **ADI:** Traverse City-Cadillac, MI. **Key Personnel:** Greg Wittland, General Mgr.; Linda Kimbel, General Sales Mgr.; Mike Conway, News Dir.; Wendy Kuemin, Business Mgr.

15702 WTCM-AM - 580
314 E. Front St. Phone: (616)947-7675
Traverse City, MI 49684 Fax: (616)929-3988
E-mail: wtcm@wtcmradio.com

Format: Talk; News. **Networks:** ABC. **Owner:** Midwestern Broadcasting, at above address. **Founded:** 1941. **Operating Hours:** Continuous. **ADI:** Traverse City-Cadillac, MI. **Key Personnel:** Ross Biederman, Contact. **Local Programs:** *On Line with Ron Jolly*, Ron Jolly, Mailing contact, (616)947-7675, Fax (616)929-3988. **Wattage:** 15,000 day; 500 night. **Ad Rates:** $19-36 for 30 seconds; $23-44 for 60 seconds.

15703 WTOM-TV - 4
8518 M-72 W. Phone: (616)947-7770
PO Box 546 Fax: (616)947-0354
Traverse City, MI 49684

Format: Commercial TV. **Networks:** NBC. **Founded:** 1954. **Operating Hours:** Continuous. **ADI:** Traverse City-Cadillac, MI. **Key Personnel:** Gregory A. Wittland, Contact; Linda Kimbel, General Sales Mgr.; Mike Conway, News Dir.; Wendy Kuemin, Business Mgr.

TROY

15704 Air Conditioning, Heating and Refrigeration News
Business News Publishing Co.
755 W. Big Beaver Rd., Ste. 1000 Phone: (248)362-3700
Troy, MI 48084 Fax: (248)244-6439
Publisher E-mail: beardenk@bnp.com

Tabloid for HVAC and commercial refrigeration contractors, wholesalers, manufacturers, engineers, and owners/managers. **Founded:** 1926. **Freq:** Weekly. **Print Method:** Offset. **Trim Size:** 11 x 15 3/8. **Cols./Page:** 5. **Col. Width:** 23 nonpareils. **Col. Depth:** 197 agate lines. **Key Personnel:** Wayne Johnson, Editor; M.A. Miller, Publisher; Laurie Tomczak, Advertising Mgr. **ISSN:** 0002-2276. **Subscription Rates:** $82 individuals. **URL:** http://www.bnp.com.
Ad Rates: BW: $8,539 **Circ:** Paid ★**24,166**
4C: $1,580 Non-paid ★**8,952**
PCI: $156

15705 Detroit Lutheran
Lutheran Center Association
6336 Donaldson Dr. Phone: (810)879-7610
Troy, MI 48098-1532 Fax: (810)879-7610

Lutheran newspaper containing church and Lutheran high school news and events in the southeast Michigan area and national syndical news and state district news. **Subtitle:** Lutheran High School Assn. "News and Views". **Founded:** 1941. **Freq:** Monthly. **Print Method:** Offset. **Cols./Page:** 5. **Col. Width:** 23 nonpareils. **Col. Depth:** 186 agate lines. **Key Personnel:** Betty J. Mueller, Editor/Advertising Mgr. **ISSN:** 1521-1444. **Subscription Rates:** $8. **Formerly:** Tri-County Lutheran; TLC Lutheran News.
Ad Rates: BW: $350 **Circ:** Paid ‡8,500
PCI: $6.75 Free ‡46

15706 EAP Digest
Performance Resource Press, Inc.
1270 Rankin Dr., Ste. F Phone: (248)588-7733
Troy, MI 48083 Fax: (248)588-6633
Free: (800)453-7733
Publisher E-mail: sapeap@ix.netcom.com

Magazine covering planning, development, and administration of employee assistance programs. **Subtitle:** The Voice of Employee Assistance Programs. **Founded:** Nov. 1980. **Freq:** Bimonthly. **Print Method:** Offset. **Trim Size:** 8 5/8 x 10 7/8. **Cols./Page:** 3. **Col. Width:** 13 picas. **Col. Depth:** 9 1/4 inches. **Key Personnel:** Brent Chartier, Managing Editor; George T. Watkins, Publisher; Janet Miloian, Advertising Mgr. **ISSN:** 0273-8910. **Subscription Rates:** $8 single issue; $36 U.S.; $45 Canada, Hawaii, and Alaska; $55 other countries; $65 air mail, other countries. **Remarks:** Accepts advertising.
Ad Rates: BW: $1,200 **Circ:** Paid ‡3,700
4C: $1,600 Controlled ‡6,000
PCI: $70

15707 Electronic Products
Hearst Business Media Corp./IMN Division
5700 Crooks Rd. Phone: (313)828-7000
PO Box 7032 Fax: (313)828-7008
Troy, MI 48007-7032
Free: (800)544-0929
Publication E-mail: rpell@hearstelectelectroweb.com

Magazine for electronic design engineers and management. **Founded:** July 1957. **Freq:** 12/year. **Print Method:** Offset. **Trim Size:** 8 x 10 3/4. **Cols./Page:** 3 and 2. **Col. Width:** 24 and 40 nonpareils. **Col. Depth:** 140 agate lines. **Key Personnel:** Frank Egan, Editor and Publisher. **Subscription Rates:** Free to qualified subscribers. **Remarks:** Accepts advertising. **URL:** http://electronicproducts.com.
Ad Rates: BW: $8,135 **Circ:** Controlled ‡123,788
4C: $9,605

15708 Engineered Systems
Business News Publishing Co.
755 W. Big Beaver Rd., Ste. 1000 Phone: (248)362-3700
Troy, MI 48084 Fax: (248)244-6439
Publisher E-mail: beardenk@bnp.com

Publication focusing on heating and cooling systems design, operations, and maintenance for commercial, industrial, and institutional applications. **Subtitle:** Practical Applications for Innovative HVAC System Engineers. **Founded:** 1984. **Freq:** Monthly. **Trim Size:** 8 x 10 3/4. **Cols./Page:** 3. **Col. Width:** 2 1/4 inches. **Col. Depth:** 10 inches. **Key Personnel:** Mark P. Skaer, Editor, phone (248)244-6446, skaermebnp.com; Kathy Janes, Advertising Mgr., phone (248)244-6457, janeskebnp.com; Peter Moran, Publisher, phone (914)776-9241, fax (914)776-5217, pemlengsys@aol.com. **ISSN:** 0891-9976. **Subscription Rates:** $45. **Remarks:** Accepts advertising. **URL:** http://www.bnp.com.
Ad Rates: GLR: $93 **Circ:** Paid 93
BW: $5,178 Controlled 57,521
4C: $6,478
PCI: $120

15709 The Fear Finder
Halloween Events, Inc.
36393 Dequindre Phone: (248)524-9782
Troy, MI 48083 Fax: (248)524-1320

Newspaper covering local Halloween events and news. **Founded:** 1993. **Freq:** Annual. **Print Method:** Photo offset. **Trim Size:** 11 x 13 5/8. **Key Personnel:** Edward Terebus, Owner. **Subscription Rates:** Free.
Circ: Combined 500,000

15710 Modern Woodworking
Business News Publishing Co.
755 W. Big Beaver Rd., Ste. 1000 Phone: (248)362-3700
Troy, MI 48084 Fax: (248)244-6439
Publisher E-mail: beardenk@bnp.com

Magazine for management in the primary and secondary wood products industry. **Founded:** 1989. **Freq:** Monthly. **Print Method:** Web offset. **Trim Size:** 10 7/8 x 14 1/2. **Key Personnel:** David Welch, Editor, phone (901)818-0608, fax (901)818-0703, dlwelchmw@aol.com; Dave Lurie, Group Publisher, phone (248)244-2461, fax (248)244-6439, luried@bnp.com. **Subscription Rates:** $24. $5 single issue. **Remarks:** Accepts advertising. **URL:** http://www.modernwoodworking.com. **Formerly:** Furniture and Cabinet Manufacturing.
Ad Rates: BW: $2,450 **Circ:** 57,000
4C: $3,650
PCI: $50

15711 Motor Magazine
Hearst Business Media Corp./IMN Division
5700 Crooks Rd. Phone: (313)828-7000
PO Box 7032 Fax: (313)828-7008
Troy, MI 48007-7032
Free: (800)544-0929

Magazine for the automotive aftermarket trade, professional mechanics and shop owners. **Subtitle:** The Magazine for the Responsible Automotie Technician. **Founded:** 1903. **Freq:** Monthly. **Print Method:** Offset. **Trim Size:** 7 7/8 x 10 5/8. **Cols./Page:** 3 and 2. **Col. Width:** 27 and 42 nonpareils. **Col. Depth:** 140 agate lines. **Key Personnel:** John Lyden, Editor, jlyden@motor.com; Richard Laimbeer, Publisher. **ISSN:** 0027-1748. **Subscription Rates:** $48 individuals.
Ad Rates: BW: $9,525 **Circ:** ‡140,000
4C: $13,065

15712 Paint & Coatings Industry
755 W. Big Beaver Rd., Ste. 1000 Phone: (248)244-6461
Troy, MI 48084 Fax: (248)244-6439
Trade journal. **Founded:** 1985. **Freq:** 12/year. **Print Method:** Offset. **Trim Size:** 8 1/8 x 10 3/4. **Cols./Page:** 3. **Col. Width:** 2 1/8 inches. **Key Personnel:** Harper Henderson, Publisher, phone (248)244-6478, hendersonh@bnp.com; Donna Campbell, Sales Mgr., phone (610)650-4050, fax (610)650-4051, donnabnp@aol.com; Darlene Brezinski, Editor, phone (906)779-9498, darpaint@aol.com; Evelyn Allen, Production Mgr., phone (248)244-6434, fax (248)244-6439, allene@bnp.com; David Lurie, Group Publisher, luried@bnp.com. **ISSN:** 0884-3848. **Remarks:** Advertising accepted; rates available upon request. **Available Online. URL:** http://www.bnp.com/pci. **Alt. Formats:** Microform.
Circ: Non-paid ‡20,000

15713 P.O.B. (Point of Beginning)
Business News Publishing Co.
755 W. Big Beaver Rd. Phone: (248)244-6419
Ste. 1000 Fax: (248)362-5103
Troy, MI 48084
Free: (800)565-0707
Publisher E-mail: beardenk@bnp.com

Magazine printing technical, business, trade, and general interest news for mapping and surveying professionals and technicians. **Founded:** Oct. 1975. **Freq:** Monthly. **Print Method:** Offset. **Trim Size:** 8 1/4 x 10 3/4. **Cols./Page:** 3 and 2. **Col. Width:** 26 and 40 nonpareils. **Col. Depth:** 10 inches. **Key Personnel:** Taggart E. Henderson, Group Publisher; Walt Walkowski, Publisher; Beth Wierzbinski, Editor; Dean Dimitrieski, Advertising Mgr., phone (248)244-1277; James Carswell, Production Mgr. **ISSN:** 0739-3865. **Subscription Rates:** Free to qualified subscribers; $5 single issue.
Ad Rates: GLR: $18 **Circ:** Controlled ‡40,030
BW: $4,160
4C: $5,310
PCI: $117

15714 Snips Magazine
755 W. Big Beaver Rd., 10th Fl. Phone: (248)362-3700
Troy, MI 48084-4903 Fax: (248)362-0317
Publication E-mail: base@bnp.com

Magazine for the sheet metal, warm-air heating, ventilating, and air conditioning industry. **Founded:** Mar. 1932. **Freq:** Monthly. **Print Method:** Offset. **Trim Size:** 8 1/4 x 11 1/4. **Cols./Page:** 3 and 2. **Col. Width:** 27 and 41 nonpareils. **Col. Depth:** 140 agate lines. **Key Personnel:** Ed Bas, Editor and Publisher, phone (248)244-6467. **ISSN:** 0037-7457. **Subscription Rates:** $18 individuals; $2 single issue.
Ad Rates: BW: $2,440 **Circ:** Paid 1,151
4C: $3,407 Controlled 27,312
PCI: $78

15715 Student Assistance Journal
Performance Resource Press, Inc.
1270 Rankin Dr., Ste. F Phone: (248)588-7733
Troy, MI 48083 Fax: (248)588-6633
Free: (800)453-7733
Publisher E-mail: sapeap@ix.netcom.com

Magazine carrying information on student assistance programs, including substance abuse, for school administrators, counselors, educators, treatment professionals, and others who work with youths. Covers planning, development, administration, and evaluation. **Subtitle:** The Voice of Student Assistance Programs. **Founded:** 1988. **Freq:** 5/year. **Print Method:** Offset. **Trim Size:** 8 5/8 x 10 7/8. **Cols./Page:** 3. **Col. Width:** 13 picas. **Col. Depth:** 9.25 picas. **Key Personnel:** Susan Hipsley, Editor; George T. Watkins, Publisher; Kim Peake, Advertising Mgr. **Subscription Rates:** $34 U.S.; $43 Canada, Hawaii, and Alaska; $52 other countries; $62 air mail, other countries. **Remarks:** Accepts advertising.
Ad Rates: BW: $1,190 **Circ:** Paid ‡8,000
4C: $1,590 Controlled ‡7,000
PCI: $50

15716 Troy Observer
Observer & Eccentric Newspapers
36251 Schoolcraft Rd. Phone: (313)591-2300
Livonia, MI 48150-1216 Fax: (313)953-2232

Community newspaper. **Founded:** 1970. **Freq:** Semiweekly (Mon. and Thurs.). **Print Method:** Offset. **Cols./Page:** 6. **Col. Width:** 12.5 picas. **Col. Depth:** 21 inches. **Key Personnel:** Tom Baer, Editor; Monica Dicola, Advertising Mgr. **Subscription Rates:** $24.20; $18 senior citizens. **Remarks:** Accepts advertising.
Ad Rates: BW: $1,562.19 **Circ:** Paid 1,254
4C: $2,262.19 Non-paid 6,885
SAU: $12.11

15717 Troy-Somerset Gazette
Gazette Newspapers, Inc.
1903 E. Wattles Phone: (810)524-4868
Troy, MI 48098 Fax: (810)524-9140

Community newspaper (tabloid). **Founded:** Sept. 1980. **Freq:** Weekly. **Print Method:** Offset. **Trim Size:** 11 1/2 x 30. **Cols./Page:** 5. **Col. Width:** 11.06 picas. **Col. Depth:** 13 1/2 inches. **Key Personnel:** Cynthia Kmett, Editor; Claire Weber, Publisher. **Subscription Rates:** Free; $26 (mail). **Alt. Formats:** Microform.
Ad Rates: BW: $857 **Circ:** Free ‡24,500
4C: $957
SAU: $12.95
PCI: $12.95

15718 Walls & Ceilings
Business News Publishing Co.
755 W. Big Beaver Rd., Ste. 1000 Phone: (248)362-3700
Troy, MI 48084 Fax: (248)244-6439
Publisher E-mail: beardenk@bnp.com

Trade magazine for contractors, suppliers, and distributors of drywall, plaster, stucco, EIFS, acoustics, metal framing, and ceilings. **Subtitle:** Voice of the Industry since 1938. **Founded:** Feb. 1938. **Freq:** Monthly. **Print Method:** Offset. **Trim Size:** 8 3/8 x 10 7/8. **Cols./Page:** 3. **Col. Width:** 2 1/6 inches. **Col. Depth:** 10 inches. **ISSN:** 0043-0161. **Subscription Rates:** Free to qualified subscribers. **Remarks:** Advertising accepted; rates available upon request. **URL:** http://www.wconline.com.
Circ: Controlled ‡25,030
Paid ‡243

Wayland-Weston Town Crier - See Wayland

15719 WDZR-FM - 102.7
850 Stephenson Hwy., No. 405 Phone: (248)589-7900
Troy, MI 48083 Fax: (248)589-8295

Format: Album-Oriented Rock (AOR). **Networks:** ABC. **Owner:** Syndicated Communications, 8401 Colesville 300, Silver Spring, MD 20910, (301)608-3203, Fax: (301)608-3302. **Founded:** 1978. **Formerly:** WKSG-FM (1984). **Operating Hours:** Continuous. **ADI:** Detroit, MI. **Key Personnel:** Bruce Hogan, Business Mgr., mhogan2671@aol.com; Joe Bevilacqua, Program Dir.; Bill Mullen, Chief Engineer; Robert Striker, General Mgr. **Wattage:** 50,000.

TWIN LAKE

15720 WBLV-FM - 90.3
Blue Lake Fine Arts Camp Phone: (616)894-2616
Rt. 2
Twin Lake, MI 49457
E-mail: radio@bluelake.org

Format: Public Radio; Classical; Jazz; News. **Networks:** National Public Radio (NPR); American Public Radio (APR); Michigan Public Radio. **Owner:** Blue Lake Fine Arts Camp, 300 E. Crystal Lake Rd., Twin Lake, MI 49457, (616)894-1966. **Founded:** 1982. **Operating Hours:** Continuous; 21% network, 79% local. **ADI:** Grand Rapids-Kalamazoo-Battle Creek, MI. **Key Personnel:** Dave Myers, General Mgr.; Sandy Krupp, Office Mgr.; Steve Albert, Program Dir. **Wattage:** 100,000. **Ad Rates:** Noncommercial; underwriting available. $8-20 per unit. $12-25 per unit. **URL:** http://www.bluelake.org.

UNION CITY

15721 Register-Tribune
314 N. Broadway Phone: (517)741-8451
Box 8 Fax: (517)369-2225
Union City, MI 49094
Community newspaper. **Founded:** Feb. 1869. **Freq:** Weekly (Thurs.). **Print Method:** Offset. **Cols./Page:** 6. **Col. Width:** 26 nonpareils. **Col. Depth:** 301 agate lines. **Key Personnel:** Raymond W. Smith, Editor and Publisher. **Subscription Rates:** $9; $11 out of area. **Remarks:** Accepts advertising.
Ad Rates: SAU: $2.90 **Circ:** Paid ‡1,256
PCI: $2.90 Free ‡20

15722 Tribune
314 N. Broadway Phone: (517)741-8451
PO Box F Fax: (517)369-2225
Union City, MI 49094
Newspaper. **Founded:** 1888. **Freq:** Weekly (Wed.). **Print Method:** Offset. **Cols./Page:** 6. **Col. Width:** 21 nonpareils. **Col. Depth:** 224 agate lines. **Key Personnel:** Larry A. Key, Editor; Dorothy M. Key, Publisher. **Remarks:** Accepts advertising.
Ad Rates: BW: $316.80 **Circ:** Free 2,456
SAU: $3.64

UNION LAKE

Commerce Spinal Column Newsweekly - See Commerce

Highland Spinal Column Newsweekly - See Highland

Milford Spinal Column Newsweekly - See Milford

Novi Spinal Column Newsweekly - See Novi

Waterford Spinal Column Newsweekly - See Waterford

West Bloomfield Spinal Column Newsweekly - See West Bloomfield

White Lake Spinal Column Newsweekly - See White Lake

UNIVERSITY CENTER

15723 WDCP-TV - 35
Delta College Phone: (517)686-9350
University Center, MI 48710 Fax: (517)686-0155
Free: (800)388-1935
E-mail: wdcq@alpha.delta.edu

Format: Public TV. **Networks:** Independent. **Founded:** 1986. **Formerly:** WUCX-TV. **Operating Hours:** 6:30 a.m.-12:30 a.m. **ADI:** Flint-Saginaw-Bay City, MI. **Key Personnel:** Barry G. Baker, GM/Dir. of Broadcasting, phone (517)686-9346, fax (517)686-0155, bgbaker@alpha.delta.edu. **Local Programs:** *The Professionals* 8:00 pm Wednesday. **URL:** http:/www.delta.edu/˜tldtvradio.

15724 WDCQ-TV - 19
Delta Rd. Phone: (517)686-9350
University Center Fax: (517)686-0155
University Center, MI 48710
Free: (800)388-1935
E-mail: wdcq@alpha.delta.edu

Format: Public TV. **Networks:** Independent. **Founded:** 1962. **Formerly:** WUCM-TV. **Operating Hours:** 6:30 a.m.-12:30 a.m. **ADI:** Flint-Saginaw-Bay City, MI. **Key Personnel:** Barry G. Baker, GM/Dir. of Broadcasting, phone (517)686-9346, fax (517)686-0155, bgbaker@alpha.delta.edu. **Local Programs:** *The Professional* 8:00 pm Wednesday. **URL:** http://www.delta.edu/tv˜tvradio.

UTICA

15725 Romeo-Washington Source
21st Century Newspapers, Inc.
48075 Van Dyke Phone: (810)731-1000
PO Box 168
Utica, MI 48317
Community newspaper. **Founded:** 1972. **Freq:** Weekly (Sun.). **Print Method:** Offset. **Cols./Page:** 6. **Col. Width:** 2 1/16 inches. **Col. Depth:** 21 1/2 inches. **Key Personnel:** Frank Shepherd, President/CEO, phone (810)469-4510, fax (810)469-4512; Wayne Oehmke, Publisher, fax (810)731-2522; Phillip Marien, General Mgr.; Joseph Warner, Editor; Chris Troszak, Advertising Mgr. **Subscription Rates:** $80 (mail). **Remarks:** Accepts advertising. **Formerly:** Romeo-Washington Advisor.
Ad Rates: BW: $1,360.95 **Circ:** Non-paid 6,976
4C: $1,645.95
SAU: $10.55

VANDERBILT

15726 Our Home Town
540 E. Main St. Phone: (517)732-7167
PO Box 101 Fax: (517)732-7167
Vanderbilt, MI 49795
Publication E-mail: ourhometown@hotmail.com

Community newspaper. **Founded:** June 1956. **Freq:** Weekly. **Print Method:** Offset. **Trim Size:** 11 x 16. **Cols./Page:** 3. **Col. Width:** 3 inches. **Col. Depth:** 16 inches. **Key Personnel:** Tom Serino, Editor and Publisher, edmrlca@hotmail.com. **Subscription Rates:** $14; $17 out of state. **Remarks:** Accepts advertising.
Ad Rates: BW: $160 **Circ:** Paid ‡1,200
4C: $600 Free ‡100
SAU: $5
PCI: $8.20

VASSAR

15727 Cass River Trader
PO Box 1653 Phone: (517)823-8651
Vassar, MI 48768 Fax: (517)823-2531

Shopper. **Founded:** 1967. **Freq:** Weekly (Mon.). **Print Method:** Offset. **Trim Size:** 11 1/2 x 16. **Cols./Page:** 6. **Col. Width:** 20 nonpareils. **Col. Depth:** 210 agate lines. **Key Personnel:** Daniel L. Bilbey, Publisher; Deana Jacoby, Manager.
Ad Rates: BW: $414 **Circ:** Free 18,000
PCI: $4.95

15728 Vassar Pioneer Times
Hearst Corp.
113 S. Main Phone: (517)823-8579
Box 69 Fax: (517)823-8778
Vassar, MI 48768
Local newspaper. **Founded:** 1857. **Freq:** Weekly. **Trim Size:** 11 1/2 x 13 3/4. **Cols./Page:** 5. **Col. Width:** 2 1/16 inches. **Col. Depth:** 13 inches. **Key Personnel:** Sandy Walker, Managing Editor; Al Wamsley, Publisher. **Subscription Rates:** $12 Tuscola, Saginaw and Bay counties; $14 out of area; $16 out of state. **Remarks:** Color advertising accepted; rates available upon request.
Ad Rates: GLR: $4.71 **Circ:** 2,000
PCI: $3.85

VICKSBURG

15729 The Broadcast
Vicksburg Publications, Inc.
109 S. Main Phone: (616)649-2333
Box 154 Fax: (616)649-2335
Vicksburg, MI 49097
Shopping guide. **Founded:** 1936. **Freq:** Weekly. **Print Method:** Web offset. **Trim Size:** 10 1/2 x 15 1/2. **Cols./Page:** 6. **Col. Width:** 1 3/8 inches. **Col. Depth:** 217 agate lines. **Key Personnel:** Jackie Lawrence, Publisher; Betsy Myers, Sales Mgr. **Subscription Rates:** Free. **Remarks:** Accepts advertising.
Ad Rates: BW: $449.30 **Circ:** Free ‡10,500
4C: $400
PCI: $4.45

15730 Commercial-Express
South County Communications
109 S Main, Box 154 Phone: (616)649-2333
Vicksburg, MI 49097 Fax: (616)649-2335

Community newspaper. **Founded:** Jan. 20, 1879. **Freq:** Weekly (Wed.). **Print Method:** Offset. Uses mats. **Trim Size:** 10 1/2 x 15 1/2. **Cols./Page:** 6. **Col. Width:** 1 3/8 inches. **Col. Depth:** 217 agate lines. **Key Personnel:** Scott McGraw, Editor and Publisher. **Subscription Rates:** $18 individuals; $22 out of area. **Remarks:** Accepts advertising.
Ad Rates: BW: $296 **Circ:** 2,350
SAU: $4.11

WALKER

15731 Walker/Westside Advance
Advance Newspapers
2141 Port Sheldon Rd. Phone: (616)669-2700
PO Box 9 Fax: (616)669-1162
Jenison, MI 49428-9301
Free: (800)439-0960

Suburban community newspaper (tabloid). **Founded:** 1966. **Freq:** Weekly (Tues.). **Print Method:** Offset. **Trim Size:** 10 5/8 x 15 7/8. **Cols./Page:** 6. **Col. Width:** 16 nonpareils. **Col. Depth:** 224 agate lines. **Key Personnel:** Joel Holland, Publisher, fax (616)669-3930. **Subscription Rates:** $25. **Remarks:** Accepts advertising.
Ad Rates: BW: $998.40 **Circ:** Free 22,111
4C: $1,298.40 Paid 669
SAU: $12.48
PCI: $10.40

WALLED LAKE

15732 TCI Cablevision of West Oakland County
3166 Martin Rd. Phone: (248)669-3900
Walled Lake, MI 48390 Fax: (248)669-8260

Owner: Tele-Communication Inc., 5619 DTC Pkwy., Englewood, CO 80111, (303)267-5500. **Key Personnel:** Deborah Messerknecht, General Mgr.; Deana Mondock, Office Mgr. **Cities Served:** Commerce Township, Highland Township, Lyon Township, Milford, New Hudson, Northville, Walled Lake,

White Lake, Wixom, MI: subscribing households 22,000; 64 channels; 3 community access channels; 52 hours per week community access programming.

WARREN

15733 Chevy Outdoors
C. E. Publishing
30400 Van Dyke Phone: (810)574-9100
Warren, MI 48093-2368 Fax: (810)575-9328

Motorist magazine. **Subtitle:** A Celebration of American Recreation and Leisure. **Founded:** Apr. 1986. **Freq:** Quarterly. **Print Method:** Web offset. **Trim Size:** 8 x 10 3/4. **Cols./Page:** 3. **Col. Width:** 2 1/4 inches. **Col. Depth:** 140 agate lines. **Key Personnel:** Steve Wilke, Editor. **ISSN:** 0893-2778. **Subscription Rates:** $8. **Remarks:** Accepts advertising. **Formerly:** Chevy Camper (1986).
Ad Rates: BW: $15,960 **Circ:** Paid 80
4C: $20,200 Non-paid 999,950

15734 Corvette Quarterly
C. E. Publishing
30400 Van Dyke Phone: (810)574-9100
Warren, MI 48093-2368 Fax: (810)575-9328

Magazine for Corvette enthusiasts. **Subtitle:** The Official Journal of America's World-Class Sports Car. **Founded:** 1988. **Freq:** Quarterly. **Print Method:** Web offset. **Trim Size:** 8 x 10 1/2. **Cols./Page:** 3. **Col. Width:** 2 1/4 inches. **Col. Depth:** 140 agate lines. **Key Personnel:** Marla Burdock, Editor, phone (810)558-7276, fax (810)558-5897, mburdock@cecom.com; Rick Lafave, Publisher, phone (810)558-4164, rlafave@cecom.com. **ISSN:** 0891-4179. **Subscription Rates:** $29.95 for 12 issues; $21.95 for 8 issues; $11.95 for 4 issues; $4 single issue. **Remarks:** Accepts advertising. **Formerly:** Corvette News (1990).
Ad Rates: BW: $9,750 **Circ:** Non-paid ‡230,000
4C: $13,900

15735 Eastside Advertister Times
C&G Publishing
8204 E. Nine Mile Phone: (313)756-8800
Warren, MI 48089 Fax: (313)756-2783

Community newspaper. **Freq:** Biweekly. **Cols./Page:** 4. **Col. Width:** 10 5/16 inches. **Col. Depth:** 13 1/2 inches. **Key Personnel:** Michael Raveane, Managing Editor; Charlotte and Gilbert Demers, Publisher. **Remarks:** Accepts advertising. **URL:** http://www.totheworld.com.
Ad Rates: BW: $1,061 **Circ:** Controlled ‡31,428

15736 Eastsider
C&G Publishing
8204 E. Nine Mile Phone: (313)756-8800
Warren, MI 48089 Fax: (313)756-2783

Community newspaper. **Freq:** Biweekly. **Cols./Page:** 4. **Col. Width:** 10 5/16 inches. **Col. Depth:** 13 1/2 inches. **Key Personnel:** Michael Raveane, Managing Editor; Charlotte and Gilbert Demers, Publisher. **Remarks:** Accepts advertising. **URL:** http://www.totheworld.com.
Ad Rates: BW: $999 **Circ:** Controlled **♦34,312**

15737 Fraser-Clinton-Macomb Chronicle
C&G Publishing
8204 E. Nine Mile Phone: (313)756-8800
Warren, MI 48089 Fax: (313)756-2783

Community newspaper. **Freq:** Biweekly. **Cols./Page:** 4. **Col. Width:** 10 5/16 inches. **Col. Depth:** 13 1/2 inches. **Key Personnel:** Michael Raveane, Managing Editor; Charlotte and Gilbert Demers, Publisher. **Remarks:** Accepts advertising. **URL:** http://www.totheworld.com.
Ad Rates: BW: $953 **Circ:** Controlled ‡35,613

15738 Friendly Exchange
Farmers Insurance Group of Companies
30400 Van Dyke
Warren, MI 48093-2316

General interest lifestyle magazine. **Subtitle:** The Magazine of the Farmers Insurance Group of Companies. **Founded:** Feb. 1981. **Freq:** Quarterly. **Print Method:** Roto and offset. **Trim Size:** 8 x 10 1/2. **Cols./Page:** 3. **Col. Width:** 2 1/4 inches. **Col. Depth:** 10 inches. **Key Personnel:** Dan Grantham, Editor, phone (810)558-7225, dgrantha@cecom.com; Tom Krempel, Advertising Mgr., phone (810)558-7148; Deanne Olive, Managing Editor, phone (810)558-7272; Rebecca Yops, Art Dir., phone (810)558-7254. **Subscription Rates:** Free to qualified subscribers; $5 individuals; $20 nonmembers. **Remarks:** Advertising not accepted for tobacco products and alcoholic beverages. **Available Online. URL:** http://www.friendlyexchange.com.
Ad Rates: BW: $74,350 **Circ:** Controlled ‡5,700,000
4C: $82,590
PCI: $2,360

15739 Grosse Pointe Times
C&G Publishing
8204 E. Nine Mile Phone: (313)756-8800
Warren, MI 48089 Fax: (313)756-2783

Community newspaper. **Freq:** Biweekly. **Cols./Page:** 4. **Col. Width:** 10 5/16 inches. **Col. Depth:** 13 1/2 inches. **Key Personnel:** Michael Raveane, Managing Editor; Charlotte and Gilbert Demers, Publisher. **Remarks:** Accepts advertising. **URL:** http;//www.totheworld.com.
Ad Rates: BW: $829 **Circ:** Controlled **♦21,355**

15740 The Journal
C&G Publishing
8204 E. Nine Mile Phone: (313)756-8800
Warren, MI 48089 Fax: (313)756-2783

Community newspaper. **Freq:** Weekly. **Cols./Page:** 4. **Col. Width:** 10 5/16 inches. **Col. Depth:** 13 1/2 inches. **Key Personnel:** Michael Raveane, Managing Editor; Charlotte and Gilbert Demers, Publisher. **Remarks:** Advertising accepted; rates available upon request. **URL:** http://www.totheworld.com.
Circ: Controlled ‡30,970

15741 Madison-Park News
C&G Publishing
8204 E. Nine Mile Phone: (313)756-8800
Warren, MI 48089 Fax: (313)756-2783

Community newspaper. **Freq:** Biweekly. **Cols./Page:** 4. **Col. Width:** 10 5/16 inches. **Col. Depth:** 13 1/2 inches. **Key Personnel:** Michael Raveane, Managing Editor; Charlotte and Gilbert Demers, Publisher. **Remarks:** Accepts advertising.
Ad Rates: BW: $706 **Circ:** Controlled **♦21,200**

15742 The Megarian
The Mega Society
4177 Garrick Ave.
Warren, MI 48091

Publication for individuals with exceptionally high IQs. The Journal of the Mega Society. **Freq:** Monthly. **Print Method:** Offset. **Trim Size:** 5 1/2 x 8 1/2. **Cols./Page:** 2. **Key Personnel:** Dr. Romero Anton XIV Montalban-Anderssen, Editor; Marilyn Mach vos Savant, Publisher. **Subscription Rates:** $20. **Remarks:** Advertising not accepted.
Circ: Paid 52

15743 The Music Index
Harmonie Park Press
23630 Pinewood Phone: (810)755-3080
Warren, MI 48091 Fax: (810)755-4213
Free: (800)886-3080
Publisher E-mail: hpp@wwnet.com

Music bibliography magazine. **Subtitle:** A Subject-Author Guide to Music Periodical Literature. **Founded:** 1949. **Freq:** Quarterly. **Print Method:** Offset. **Trim Size:** 8 1/2 x 11. **Cols./Page:** 3. **Col. Width:** 31 nonpareils. **Col. Depth:** 117 agate lines. **Key Personnel:** Sonja Hempseed, Editor, hpp2@wwnet.com. **ISSN:** 0027-4348. **Remarks:** Advertising not accepted. **Alt. Formats:** CD-ROM.
Circ: ‡750

15744 New Center News
31201 Chicago Rd. S. Phone: (810)939-6800
Ste. B-300 Fax: (810)939-5850
Warren, MI 48093
Local newspaper. **Founded:** 1933. **Freq:** Weekly (Mon.). **Print Method:** Offset. **Trim Size:** 13 x 26. **Cols./Page:** 6. **Col. Width:** 2.5 inches. **Col. Depth:** 300 agate lines. **Key Personnel:** Bill Springer, Publisher. **Remarks:** Accepts advertising.
Ad Rates: SAU: $6.50 **Circ:** Free 7000
PCI: $6.50

15745 St. Clair Shores Sentinel
C&G Publishing
8204 E. Nine Mile Phone: (313)756-8800
Warren, MI 48089 Fax: (313)756-2783

Community newspaper. **Freq:** Weekly. **Cols./Page:** 4. **Col. Width:** 10 5/16 inches. **Col. Depth:** 13 1/2 inches. **Key Personnel:** Michael Raveane, Managing Editor; Charlotte and Gilbert Demers, Publisher. **URL:** http://www.totheworld.com.
Ad Rates: BW: $999 **Circ:** Controlled **♦28,089**

15746 Shelby Utica News
C&G Publishing
8204 E. Nine Mile Phone: (313)756-8800
Warren, MI 48089 Fax: (313)756-2783

Community newspaper. **Freq:** Biweekly. **Cols./Page:** 4. **Col. Width:** 10 5/16 inches. **Col. Depth:** 13 1/2 inches. **Key Personnel:** Michael Raveane, Managing Editor; Charlotte and Gilbert Demers, Publisher. **Remarks:** Accepts advertising. **URL:** http://www.totheworld.com.
Ad Rates: BW: $774 **Circ:** Controlled **♦25,775**

15747 Tech Center News
Monday Morning Newspapers, Inc.
31201 Chicago Rd., Ste. B-300 Phone: (810)939-6800
Warren, MI 48093 Fax: (810)939-5850

Newspaper containing automotive and business news for the business community, including General Motors Technical Center, Warren, Michigan. **Founded:** Sept. 1976. **Freq:** Weekly. **Print Method:** Offset. **Trim Size:** 13 x 126. **Cols./Page:** 6. **Col. Width:** 2.5 inches. **Col. Depth:** 300 agate lines. **Key Personnel:** Peter Salinas, Editor; Bill Springer, Publisher. **Subscription Rates:** Free.
Ad Rates: SAU: $12.75 **Circ:** Controlled ‡16,000
PCI: $12.75

15748 Troy Times
C&G Publishing
8204 E. Nine Mile Phone: (313)756-8800
Warren, MI 48089 Fax: (313)756-2783

Community newspaper. **Freq:** Biweekly. **Cols./Page:** 4. **Col. Width:** 10 5/16 inches. **Col. Depth:** 13 1/2 inches. **Key Personnel:** Michael Raveane, Managing Editor; Charlotte and Gilbert Demers, Publisher. **Remarks:** Accepts advertising. **URL:** http://www.totheworld.com.
Ad Rates: BW: $890 **Circ:** Controlled **♦30,748**

15749 Vista USA
C. E. Publishing
30400 Van Dyke Phone: (810)574-9100
Warren, MI 48093-2368 Fax: (810)575-9328

Magazine of the Exxon Travel Club. **Founded:** 1965. **Freq:** Quarterly. **Print Method:** Offset. **Trim Size:** 8 1/2 x 10 7/8. **Cols./Page:** 2 and 3. **Col. Width:** 27 and 42 nonpareils. **Col. Depth:** 130 agate lines. **Key Personnel:** Martha J. Mendez, Editor. **ISSN:** 0507-1577. **Subscription Rates:** $3. $.75 single issue. **Remarks:** Accepts advertising.
Ad Rates: BW: $13,320 **Circ:** 572,102
4C: $16,650

15750 Warren Advisor
21st Century Newspapers, Inc.
100 Macomb Daily Dr.
Mount Clemens, MI 48046

Community newspaper. **Freq:** Weekly (Sun.). **Print Method:** Offset. **Cols./Page:** 6. **Col. Width:** 2 1/16 inches. **Col. Depth:** 21 1/2 inches. **Key Personnel:** Frank Sheperd, President/CEO, phone (810)469-4510, fax (810)469-4512; Wayne Oehmke, Publisher, fax (810)731-2522; Phillip Marien, General Mgr.; Joseph Warner, Editor; Chris Troszak, Advertising Mgr. **Subscription Rates:** Free; $80 out of area. **Remarks:** Accepts advertising.
Ad Rates: BW: $1,999.50 **Circ:** Non-paid ‡29,819
4C: $3,124.50
SAU: $15.50

15751 WPHS-FM - 89.1
30333 Hoover Rd. Phone: (810)751-FM89
Warren, MI 48093 Fax: (810)751-3755
E-mail: wphs@wphs.com

Format: Alternative/New Music/Progressive. **Owner:** Warren Consolidated Schools, 31300 Anita, Warren, MI 48093, (810)825-2400, Fax: (810)825-2059. **Founded:** 1964. **Operating Hours:** 7:00 a.m. - 9 p.m. **ADI:** Detroit, MI. **Key Personnel:** Jennifer Stanczyk, Contact, phone (810)574-3137, indigoes@hotmail.com; Jeremy Olstyn, Contact, indigoes@hotmail.com. **Wattage:** 100. **Ad Rates:** Noncommercial; underwriting available. **URL:** http://www.wphs.com.

WATERFORD

15752 Waterford Spinal Column Newsweekly
Spinal Column Publications
7196 Cooley Lake Rd. Phone: (248)360-6397
PO Box 14 Fax: (248)360-4711
Union Lake, MI 48387-0014
Local newspaper. **Founded:** 1960. **Print Method:** Weekly (Wed.). **Trim Size:** 10 1/2 x 15. **Cols./Page:** 8. **Col. Width:** 7 picas. **Col. Depth:** 14 inches. **Key Personnel:** David D. Hohendorf, Publisher; James W. Fancy, Publisher; Laurie Wallace, Advertising Mgr. **Remarks:** Accepts advertising.
Ad Rates: GLR: $7.75 **Circ:** Free ‡13,600
BW: $868.88
PCI: $15.50

WATERVLIET

15753 Tri-City Record
Box 7 Phone: (616)463-6397
Watervliet, MI 49098 Fax: (616)463-8329

Local newspaper. **Founded:** 1882. **Freq:** Weekly (Wed.). **Print Method:** Offset. **Cols./Page:** 6. **Col. Width:** 12.3 picas. **Col. Depth:** 21.5 inches. **Key Personnel:** Karl B. Bayer,

Editor and Publisher. **USPS:** 869-340. **Subscription Rates:** $18; $21 out of area; $23 out of state.
Ad Rates: BW: $903 **Circ:** ‡2,637
4C: $65
SAU: $7

WAYLAND

15754 Penasee Globe
Wayland Printing, Inc.
133 E. Superior St. Phone: (616)792-2271
Wayland, MI 49348 Fax: (616)792-2030
Free: (800)554-8800

Community newspaper. **Founded:** Sept. 19, 1884. **Freq:** Weekly. **Print Method:** Offset. **Trim Size:** 11 1/2 x 17. **Cols./Page:** 6. **Col. Width:** 20 nonpareils. **Col. Depth:** 224 agate lines. **Key Personnel:** Nila Aamoth, Editor, phone (616)792-0735, naamoth@penasee.com; Nila Aamoth Carlson, Publisher, phone (616)992-0765, ncarlson@penasee.com; Ron Carlson, Publisher, phone (616)792-8141, rcarlson@penasee.com; Mandy Sikkema, Advertising Mgr., msikkema@penasee.com. **ISSN:** 0895-8580. **Subscription Rates:** $16 individuals; $20 out of state. **Remarks:** Accepts advertising. **Formerly:** The Wayland Globe/Penasee Press (Sept. 1987).
Ad Rates: BW: $696 **Circ:** ‡18,500
4C: $946
SAU: $8.70
SAU: $11
PCI: $7.25

15755 Wayland-Weston Town Crier
Cummins Publishing Co., Inc.
6557 Forest Park Dr., No. 135 Phone: (810)932-2966
Troy, MI 48098-1954 Fax: (313)358-3965
Free: (800)552-5110

Community newspaper (tabloid). **Founded:** 1951. **Freq:** Weekly (Thurs.). **Print Method:** Offset. **Cols./Page:** 5. **Col. Width:** 2 1/16 inches. **Col. Depth:** 15 1/2 inches. **Key Personnel:** Marilyn Spencer, Editor; Kirk Davis, Publisher. **Subscription Rates:** $25; $21 senior citizens and students; $27 out of area; $30 out of state. **Remarks:** Advertising not accepted for tobacco products. **Formerly:** Wayland and Weston Town Crier.
Ad Rates: SAU: $9.83 **Circ:** Paid 4,951
Non-paid 169

WAYNE

The Belleville Enterprise - See Belleville

Canton Eagle - See Canton

Inkster Ledger Star - See Inkster

Romulus Roman - See Romulus

15756 Wayne Eagle
Michigan Community Newspapers
35540 Michigan Ave. Phone: (313)729-4000
PO Box 578 Fax: (313)729-6880
Wayne, MI 48184
Community newspaper. **Founded:** 1945. **Freq:** Weekly (Thurs.). **Print Method:** Offset. **Cols./Page:** 6. **Col. Width:** 12 picas. **Col. Depth:** 21 1/2 inches. **Key Personnel:** Mike Wilcox, Owner; Kathy Wilcox, Owner; Joan Dyer-Zinner, Managing Editor; Ron Spielman, Advertising Manager; Rita Bedell, Classified Manager; Justin Wilcox, Circulation Mgr. **Subscription Rates:** $24. **Remarks:** Accepts advertising.
Ad Rates: SAU: $12.24 **Circ:** Paid 1,347
Non-paid 2,257

15757 Westland Eagle
Michigan Community Newspapers
35540 Michigan Ave. Phone: (313)729-4000
PO Box 578 Fax: (313)729-6880
Wayne, MI 48184
Community newspaper. **Founded:** 1945. **Freq:** Weekly (Thurs.). **Print Method:** Offset. **Cols./Page:** 6. **Col. Width:** 12 picas. **Col. Depth:** 21 1/2 inches. **Key Personnel:** Mike Wilcox, Owner; Kathy Wilcox, Owner; Joan Dyer-Zinner, Managing Editor; Ron Spielman, Advertising Manager; Rita Bedell, Classified Manager; Justin Wilcox, Circulation Mgr. **Subscription Rates:** $48. **Remarks:** Accepts advertising.
Ad Rates: SAU: $5.85 **Circ:** Paid 850
Non-paid 10,397

WEST BLOOMFIELD

15758 West Bloomfield Eccentric
Observer & Eccentric Newspapers
36251 Schoolcraft Rd. Phone: (313)591-2300
Livonia, MI 48150-1216 Fax: (313)953-2232

Community newspaper. **Freq:** Semiweekly (Mon. and Thurs.). **Print Method:** Offset. **Cols./Page:** 9. **Col. Width:** 17 nonpareils. **Col. Depth:** 301 agate lines. **Key Personnel:** Dick Isham, Publisher. **Subscription Rates:** $21. **Remarks:** Accepts advertising. **Formerly:** West Bloomfield Observer & Eccentric.
Ad Rates: GLR: $2.62 **Circ:** Paid 3,502
Non-paid 9,195

15759 West Bloomfield Spinal Column Newsweekly
Spinal Column Publications
7196 Cooley Lake Rd. Phone: (248)360-6397
PO Box 14 Fax: (248)360-4711
Union Lake, MI 48387-0014
Local newspaper. **Founded:** 1960. **Freq:** Weekly. **Print Method:** Offset. **Trim Size:** 10 1/2 x 15. **Cols./Page:** 8. **Col. Width:** 7 picas. **Col. Depth:** 14 inches. **Key Personnel:** David D. Hohendorf, Publisher; James W. Fancy, Publisher; Laurie Wallace, Advertising Mgr. **Remarks:** Accepts advertising.
Ad Rates: GLR: $8.11 **Circ:** Free ‡9,900
BW: $908.32
PCI: $16.22

15760 WBLD-FM - 89.3
4925 Orchard Lake Rd. Phone: (810)851-8930
West Bloomfield, MI 48323

Format: Eclectic. **Owner:** West Bloomfield Board of Education, 2930 Commerce Rd., West Bloomfield, MI 48324, (810)682-3555. **Founded:** 1974. **Operating Hours:** 11 a.m.-7 p.m. Mon.-Fri., 100% local. **Key Personnel:** Paul S. Townley, Station Mgr.; Randy G. Long, Chief Engineer. **Wattage:** 10. **Ad Rates:** Noncommercial.

WEST BRANCH

15761 Ogemaw County Herald
Ogeman County Herald
215 W. Houghton Ave. Phone: (517)345-0044
PO Box 247 Fax: (517)345-0342
West Branch, MI 48661-1219
Newspaper. **Founded:** 1879. **Freq:** Weekly (Thurs.). **Print Method:** Offset. **Cols./Page:** 6. **Col. Width:** 21 1/2 nonpareils. **Col. Depth:** 301 agate lines. **Key Personnel:** Robert E. Perlberg, Publisher. **Subscription Rates:** $25. **Remarks:** Accepts advertising.
Ad Rates: GLR: $.39 **Circ:** (Not Reported)
BW: $709.50
SAU: $5.50

15762 Star Buyer's Guide
Star Publications
PO Box 620 Phone: (517)732-5125
Gaylord, MI 49734 Fax: (517)732-9323
Free: (800)782-7237
Publisher E-mail: starads@northland.lib.mi.us

Shopper (tabloid). **Founded:** 1972. **Freq:** Weekly (Sun.). **Print Method:** Offset. Uses mats. **Trim Size:** 11 1/8 x 17 1/2. **Cols./Page:** 6. **Col. Width:** 21 nonpareils. **Col. Depth:** 224 agate lines. **Key Personnel:** David Baragrey, Publisher. **Subscription Rates:** Free. **Remarks:** Accepts advertising.
Ad Rates: GLR: $.44 **Circ:** Free 29,301
BW: $900
4C: $1,216
SAU: $4
PCI: $9.38

WESTLAND

15763 Westland Observer
Observer & Eccentric Newspapers
36251 Schoolcraft Rd. Phone: (313)591-2300
Livonia, MI 48150-1216 Fax: (313)953-2232

Community newspaper. **Founded:** 1962. **Freq:** Semiweekly (Mon. and Thurs.). **Print Method:** Offset. **Cols./Page:** 9. **Col. Width:** 17 nonpareils. **Col. Depth:** 301 agate lines. **Key Personnel:** Dick Isham, Publisher. **Subscription Rates:** $23. **Remarks:** Accepts advertising.
Ad Rates: GLR: $2.62 **Circ:** Paid 1,783
Non-paid 4,667

WHITE LAKE

15764 White Lake Spinal Column Newsweekly
Spinal Column Publications
7196 Cooley Lake Rd. Phone: (248)360-6397
PO Box 14 Fax: (248)360-4711
Union Lake, MI 48387-0014
Local newspaper. **Founded:** 1960. **Freq:** Weekly. **Print Method:** Offset. **Trim Size:** 10 1/2 x 15. **Cols./Page:** 8. **Col. Width:** 7 picas. **Col. Depth:** 14 inches. **Key Personnel:** David D. Hohendorf, Publisher; James W. Fancy, Publisher; Laurie Wallace, Advertising Mgr. **Remarks:** Accepts advertising.
Ad Rates: GLR: $5.47 **Circ:** Free ‡5,900
BW: $612.64
PCI: $10.94

WHITEHALL

15765 White Lake Beacon
PO Box 98 Phone: (616)894-5356
Whitehall, MI 49461 Fax: (616)894-2174

Community newspaper. **Founded:** Apr. 1983. **Freq:** Weekly (Mon.). **Print Method:** Offset. **Trim Size:** 15 x 21. **Cols./Page:** 6. **Col. Width:** 28 nonpareils. **Col. Depth:** 199 agate lines. **Key Personnel:** Greg Means, Editor; Richard Lound, Publisher; James O. Young, Advertising Mgr.; Karen Henderson, Editor. **Subscription Rates:** Free; $26 by mail. **Remarks:** Accepts advertising.
Ad Rates: GLR: $.40 **Circ:** Paid ‡815
BW: $774.90 Free ‡9,885
4C: $1,029.90
SAU: $6.15

WILLIAMSTON

15766 Out Your Backdoor
4686 Meridian Rd. Phone: (517)347-1689
Williamston, MI 48895 Fax: (517)349-5912
Publication E-mail: jp@glpbooks.com

Magazine focusing on bicycling, adventure, culture, the outdoors, hobbies, and sports. **Subtitle:** For the Avante Garde in Affordable Adventure and Informal Culture. **Founded:** 1991. **Freq:** Semiannual. **Print Method:** Web offset. **Trim Size:** 8 x 10. **Cols./Page:** 2. **Col. Width:** 3 inches. **Col. Depth:** 7 1/2 inches. **Key Personnel:** Jeff Potter, Editor and Publisher. **Subscription Rates:** $8 individuals; $3 single issue. **Remarks:** Accepts advertising. **URL:** http://www.glpbooks.com/oyb.
Ad Rates: BW: $100 **Circ:** Paid 1,000
Non-paid 4,000

WYANDOTTE

15767 Wyandotte Municipal Services
3005 Biddle Ave. Phone: (313)282-7100
Wyandotte, MI 48192 Fax: (313)282-7100

Key Personnel: Thomas M. Daly, General Mgr. **Cities Served:** Wyandotte, MI: subscribing households 9,942; 56 channels; 4 community access channels.

WYOMING

15768 Wyoming Advance
Advance Newspapers
2141 Port Sheldon Rd. Phone: (616)669-2700
PO Box 9 Fax: (616)669-1162
Jenison, MI 49428-9301
Free: (800)439-0960

Suburban tabloid newspaper. **Founded:** 1966. **Freq:** Weekly (Tues.). **Print Method:** Offset. **Trim Size:** 10 3/8 x 15 7/8. **Cols./Page:** 6. **Col. Width:** 16 nonpareils. **Col. Depth:** 224 agate lines. **Key Personnel:** Joel Holland, Publisher. **Subscription Rates:** $25. **Remarks:** Accepts advertising.
Ad Rates: BW: $796.80 **Circ:** Free 20,009
4C: $900.80 Paid 2,540
SAU: $9.41
PCI: $8.30

15769 WYCE-FM - 88.1
2820 Clyde Park Ave. SW Phone: (616)261-4315
Wyoming, MI 49509-2995 Fax: (616)534-8944

Format: Full Service; Hispanic; Ethnic. **Owner:** Grand Rapids Cable Access, Inc., 50 Library Plaza NE, Grand Rapids, MI 49503, (616)459-GRTV, Fax: (616)457-4788. **Founded:** 1984. **Operating Hours:** Continuous; 100% local. **ADI:** Grand Rapids-Kalamazoo-Battle Creek, MI. **Key Personnel:** Phil Tower, Station Mgr.; Thom Bland, Program Dir.; Julie Swanson, Development Dir. **Wattage:** 1000. **Ad Rates:** Underwriting available. **URL:** http://www.grcmc.org.

15770 WYGR-AM - 1530
PO Box 9591 Phone: (616)475-9947
Wyoming, MI 49509 Fax: (616)248-0176

Format: Hispanic. **Owner:** WYGR Broadcasting, at above address. **Founded:** 1964. **Formerly:** WTKG-AM (1986). **Operating Hours:** Sunrise-sunset. **ADI:** Grand Rapids-Kalamazoo-Battle Creek, MI. **Key Personnel:** Roland Rusticus, General and General Sales Mgr. **Local Programs:** *Radio Exitos - AM Drive* 7:00 am - 11:00 am Monday-Friday, R. Rustians, (616)248-9947; *Radio Exitos - Afternoons* 2:00 pm -

4:00 pm Monday-Friday, R. Rusticus. **Wattage:** 500. **Ad Rates:** $7-30 for 30 seconds; $12-40 for 60 seconds.

YALE

15771 Yale Expositor
21 S. Main St. Phone: (313)387-2300
PO Box 158 Fax: (810)387-2300
Yale, MI 48097
Community newspaper. **Subtitle:** JOB PRINTING. **Founded:** May 1882. **Freq:** Weekly (Wed.). **Cols./Page:** 5. **Col. Width:** 11 picas. **Col. Depth:** 15 inches. **Key Personnel:** Bonnie Brown, Editor; Arthur Brown, Publisher. **Subscription Rates:** $15 individuals. **Remarks:** Accepts advertising.
Ad Rates: BW: $375 **Circ:** 2,760

YPSILANTI, pop. 24,031.

Washtenaw Co. (SE). On Huron River, 8 m E of Ann Arbor. Eastern Michigan University, Cleary College. Manufactures auto parts, automobiles, paper, plastics, ladders, sheet metal machinery. Diversified farming. Corn, oats, wheat.

15772 Eastern Echo
Eastern Michigan University
18-B Goddard Phone: (313)487-1010
Ypsilanti, MI 48197 Fax: (313)487-1241
Publication E-mail: eastern.echo@emich.edu

Collegiate newspaper. **Founded:** 1901. **Freq:** 3/week. **Print Method:** Offset. **Cols./Page:** 6. **Col. Width:** 12 picas. **Col. Depth:** 294 agate lines. **Key Personnel:** Cathy Jentoft, Director, fax (734)487-1241, cathyjentoft@emich.edu. **Subscription Rates:** $65 individuals. **Remarks:** Accepts advertising. **URL:** http://www.eastern-echo.emich.edu.
Ad Rates: BW: $1,008 **Circ:** Free ‡10,000
4C: $400
SAU: $8
PCI: $8

15773 Industrial Worker
Industrial Workers of the World (IWW)
103 W. Michigan Ave. Phone: (734)483-3548
Ypsilanti, MI 48197-5438
Publisher E-mail: iww@igc.apc.org

World labor news paper. **Founded:** 1909. **Freq:** Monthly. **Print Method:** Offset. **Cols./Page:** 4. **Col. Width:** 14.5 picas. **Col. Depth:** 217 agate lines. **Key Personnel:** Jon Bekken, jbekken@parsons.iww.org. **ISSN:** 0019-8870. **Subscription Rates:** $15 individuals. **Remarks:** Accepts advertising. **Available Online. URL:** http://www.parsons.iww.org/~iw/. **Alt. Formats:** Microform.
Ad Rates: PCI: $10 **Circ:** Paid ‡5,000
Non-paid ‡80

15774 WEMU-FM - 89.1
PO Box 350 Phone: (313)487-2229
Ypsilanti, MI 48197 Fax: (313)487-1015
E-mail: wemu@emich.edu

Format: Public Radio; Jazz; News; Eclectic. **Networks:** National Public Radio (NPR). **Owner:** Eastern Michigan University, at above address. **Founded:** 1965. **Operating Hours:** Continuous; 27% network, 73% local. **ADI:** Detroit, MI. **Key Personnel:** Linda Yohn, Music Dir.; Clark Smith, News Dir.; Mary Motherwell, Contact; Arthur J. Timko, Station Mgr., arthur.timk.@emich.edu. **Wattage:** 16,000. **Ad Rates:** Noncommercial. **URL:** http://www.emich.edu/public/wemu.

15775 WSDS-AM - 1480
580 W. Clark Rd. Phone: (734)484-1480
Ypsilanti, MI 48198 Fax: (734)484-5313
E-mail: wsds@wsds1480.com

Format: Country. **Simulcasts:** Jones Radio Network. **Networks:** Mutual Broadcasting System. **Founded:** 1962. **Formerly:** WYSI-AM (1968). **Operating Hours:** 5:30 a.m.-midnight weekdays; 7 a.m.-midnight Sun.; 6 a.m.-midnight, Sat. **ADI:** Detroit, MI. **Key Personnel:** George Koch, Contact, gkoch@wsos1480.com; Anorea Nash, Manager, anash@wsds1480.com; Michael Callanan, mcallanan@wsos1480.com. **Wattage:** 1000 day; 5000 night. **Ad Rates:** $5-11 for 10 seconds; $12-21 for 30 seconds; $14-25 for 60 seconds. **URL:** http://www.wsds.1480.com.

15776 WWCM-AM - 990
17 N. Huron Phone: (313)482-4000
Ypsilanti, MI 48197 Fax: (313)482-4995
E-mail: ahqe50c@prodigy.com

Format: Religious; Contemporary Christian. **Founded:** 1962. **Formerly:** WYNZ-AM (1974). **Operating Hours:** Continuous. **Key Personnel:** Lou Velker, General Mgr.; Hugh Duncan, Contact; Daniel Poole, President; Chris Yates, General Sales Mgr.; Janet Raeburn, Office Mgr. **Wattage:** 9,200 day; 250 night. **Ad Rates:** $14 for 30 seconds; $28 for 60 seconds. **URL:** http://www.wwcm.com.

ZEELAND

15777 Zeeland Record
The Zeeland Record Co.
16-22 S. Elm St. Phone: (616)772-2131
Zeeland, MI 49464
Local newspaper. **Founded:** 1893. **Freq:** Weekly (Thurs.). **Print Method:** Web offset. **Cols./Page:** 8. **Col. Width:** 11.5 picas. **Col. Depth:** 15 inches. **Key Personnel:** Kurtis Van Koevering, Editor; Paul Van Koevering, Publisher. **Subscription Rates:** $15 individuals; $16 out of area; $17 out of state.
Ad Rates: GLR: $.50 **Circ:** ‡2,200
PCI: $5

15778 WGNB-FM - 89.3
3764 84th Ave. Phone: (616)772-7300
PO Box 40 Fax: (616)772-9663
Zeeland, MI 49464
Free: (800)968-8930
E-mail: wgnb@moody.edu

Format: Religious. **Networks:** Moody Broadcasting; Sun Radio. **Owner:** Moody Bible Institute of Chicago, at above address, (312)329-2041, Fax: (312)329-8980. **Founded:** 1989. **Formerly:** WXYB-FM. **Operating Hours:** Continuous; 40% network, 60% local. **ADI:** Grand Rapids-Kalamazoo-Battle Creek, MI. **Key Personnel:** Scott Keegan, Contact. **Local Programs:** *The Clockwatcher*, Scott Curtis; *Prime Time West Michigan*; *Your City & Mine.* **Wattage:** 30,000. **Ad Rates:** Noncommercial.

MINNESOTA

State Capital, ST. PAUL

Minnesota is bounded on the north by Ontario and Manitoba, Canada, east by Wisconsin and Lake Superior, south by Iowa, and west by North and South Dakota. Its extreme length from north to south is 406.4 miles; its breadth varies from 183 miles, in the center, to 262 in the south and 330 on the north borders. Its land area is 79,617 square miles. It is a state of wide natural resources and rapidly developing wealth. The surface is generally undulating and diversified with plains, timber belts, and extensive prairies dotted with lakes and groves. The northeast is generally hilly, has great deposits of iron ore, and was formerly entirely covered with immense forests. This region also contains innumerable lakes, abounding in fish and affording popular summer resorts. In the southeast there is a beautiful rolling region, heavily wooded, and from it the surface rises gradually to the Hauteur de Terres or Heights of Land in the northwest. The climate is particularly healthful, and extremely favorable to the growth of vegetation, especially grain crops. The Weather Bureau of Minneapolis gives the temperature (annual average) as 44.9; highest on record, 108; lowest on record, -34. Total annual precipitation is 28.32 inches. The state's shipping, both by water and rail, is immense. The Great Lakes, with Duluth as an advantageously located port, provide an excellent waterway to the Atlantic, and railroads branch in every direction. Minneapolis is the largest cash grain market in the world and second only to Chicago as a grain future market. The University of Minnesota, at Minneapolis, is one of the great universities of the country.

POPULATION: 4,480,000 (1992). Rank among the states, 20th.

AGRICULTURE: Number of farms: 88,000 (1992). Farm acreage: 30,000,000 (1992). Cash receipts from farm marketings: crops, $3,359,000,000 (1991); livestock and products, $3,577,000,000 (1991).

FORESTS: Total forest land: 5,467,000 acres (1991).

MINERALS: Value of production: $1,019,000,000 (1991). Principal minerals: iron ore, sand and gravel, stone.

MANUFACTURES: Value added by manufacture: $25,042,000 (1991). Leading industry groups: food and related products, machinery (except electrical), electrical machinery.

LIST OF COUNTIES

Total number of counties 87

County, Location on Map, and County Seat	Pop.
Aitkin (NEC), Aitkin	12,425
Anoka (SEC), Anoka	243,641
Becker (WC), Detroit Lakes	27,881
Beltrami (NW), Bemidji	34,384
Benton (SC), Foley	30,185
Big Stone (WC), Ortonville	6,285
Blue Earth (SC), Mankato	54,044
Brown (SC), New Ulm	26,984
Carlton (EC), Carlton	29,259
Carver (SC), Chaska	47,915
Cass (NC), Walker	21,791
Chippewa (SW), Montevideo	13,228
Chisago (EC), Center City	30,521
Clay (WC), Moorhead	50,422
Clearwater (NW), Bagley	8,309
Cook (NE), Grand Marais	3,868
Cottonwood (SW), Windom	12,694
Crow Wing (C), Brainerd	44,249
Dakota (SE), Hastings	275,227
Dodge (SE), Mantorville	15,731
Douglas (WC), Alexandria	28,674
Faribault (SC), Blue Earth	16,937
Fillmore (SE), Preston	20,777
Freeborn (SC), Abert Lea	33,060
Goodhue (SE), Red Wing	40,690
Grant (WC), Elbow Lake	6,246
Hennepin (SE), Minneapolis	1,032,431
Houston (SE), Caledonia	18,497
Hubbard (NC), Park Rapids	14,939
Isanti (EC), Cambridge	25,921
Itasca (NC), Grand Rapids	40,863
Jackson (SW), Jackson	11,677
Kanabec (EC), Mora	12,802
Kandiyohi (SWC), Willmar	38,761
Kittson (NW), Hallock	5,767
Koochiching (NC), International Falls	16,299
Lac qui Parle (SW), Madison	8,924
Lake (NE), Two Harbors	10,415
Lake of the Woods (NW), Baudette	4,076
Le Sueur (SC), Le Center	23,239
Lincoln (SW), Ivanhoe	6,890
Lyon (SW), Marshall	24,789
Mahnomen (NW), Mahnomen	5,044
Marshall (NW), Warren	10,993
Martin (SC), Fairmont	22,194
McLeod (SC), Glencoe	32,030
Meeker (SC), Litchfield	20, 846
Mille Lacs (EC), Milaca	18,670
Morrison (C), Little Falls	29,604
Mower (SE),Austin	37,385
Murray (SW), Slayton	9,660
Nicollet (SC), St. Peter	28,076
Nobles (SW), Worthington	20,098
Norman (NW), Ada	7,975
Olmsted (SE), Rochester	106,470
Otter Tail (WC), Fergus Falls	50,714
Pennington (NW), Thief River Falls	13,306
Pine (EC), Pine City	21,269
Pipestone (SW), Pipestone	10,491
Polk (NW), Crookston	32,498
Pope (NW), Glenwood	10,745
Ramsay (SE), St. Paul	485,765
Red Lake (NW), Red Lake Falls	4,525
Redwood (SW), Redwood Falls	17,254
Renville (SW), Olivia	17,673
Rice (SE), Faribault	49,183
Rock (SW), Luverne	9,806
Roseau (NW), Roseau	15,026
St. Louis (NE), Duluth and Hibbing	198,213
Scott (SE), Shakopee	57,846
Sherburne (SEC), Elk River	41,945
Sibley (SC), Gaylord	14,366
Stearns (C), Saint Cloud	118,791
Steele (SE), Owatonna	30,729
Stevens (WC), Morris	10,634
Swift (SW), Benson	10,724
Todd (C), Long Prairie	23,363
Traverse (WC), Wheaton	4,463
Wabasha (SE), Wabasha	19,744
Wadena (WC), Wadena	13,154
Waseca (SC), Waseca	18,079
Washington (SE), Stillwater	145,896
Watonwan (SC), St. James	11,682
Wilkin (WC), Breckenridge	7,516
Winoma (SE), Winoma	47,828
Wright (SEC), Buffalo	68,710
Yellow Medicine (SW), Granite Falls	11,684

STATISTICS

Newspapers

Period of Issue	
Daily	22
Evening Daily	13
Morning Daily	11
Daily with Sunday edition	13
Semiweekly	10
Weekly	305

Biweekly 4
Semimonthly 4
Monthly 9
Free or partly free 56
Shopper 38
Total Newspapers 365

Periodicals

Period of Issue
Weekly 12
Biweekly 0
Semimonthly 2
Monthly 63
Bimonthly 32
Quarterly 31
Total Periodicals 205

Total number of publications 570

Radio Stations

AM Stations 83
FM Stations 122
Total Radio Stations 205

TV Stations

Total TV Stations 23

Cable Stations

Total Cable Systems 43

Total number of broadcast listings 271

ADA†, pop. 1,971.

NW MN. Norman Co. 45 mi. NE of Fargo, ND. Feed manufacturer. Elevators. Agriculture. Grain, potatoes, sugar beets, sunflowers, soybeans. Dairy products.

15779 Norman County Index
307 W. Main St. Phone: (218)784-2541
PO Box 148 Fax: (218)784-2551
Ada, MN 56510-0148
Publication E-mail: nci@means.net
Publisher E-mail: nci@x.means.net

Community newspaper. **Founded:** 1880. **Freq:** Weekly. **Print Method:** Offset. **Cols./Page:** 6. **Col. Width:** 24 nonpareils. **Col. Depth:** 301 agate lines. **Key Personnel:** Ross D. Pfund, Publisher; Tim Halle, Editor. **ISSN:** 391 -780. **Subscription Rates:** $24 individuals; $28 out of area; $34 out of state.
Ad Rates: BW: $511.56 **Circ:** ‡2,350
PCI: $4.06

15780 KRJB-FM - 106.3
312 W. Main St. Phone: (218)784-2844
Ada, MN 56510 Fax: (218)784-3749

Format: Full Service. **Networks:** CNN Radio. **Owner:** R & J Broadcasting, at above address. **Founded:** 1985. **Formerly:** KMCA-FM (1987). **Operating Hours:** Continuous; 15% network, 85% local. **ADI:** Fargo, ND. **Key Personnel:** Jim Birkemeyer, Owner/Gen. Mgr./Sports Dir.; Jarred Scadden, News Dir.; Keyla Hegreberg, Music Dir.; Woody Rolly, Program Dir. **Local Programs:** *Kalidescope*, Woody Roux. **Wattage:** 3000. **Ad Rates:** $9 for 30 seconds; $18 for 60 seconds.

15781 Loretel Cablevision
13 E. 4th Ave. Phone: (218)784-7171
PO Box 72 Fax: (218)784-2706
Ada, MN 56510-0072
Free: (800)642-1306
E-mail: loretel@means.net

Founded: Mar. 1991. **Formerly:** Ada Cable Assn.; Hastad Cable. **Key Personnel:** Steven W. Katka, General Mgr., skat@means.net; Wayne Sourdif, CATV Supervisor, phone (218)784-5158; Mark Potucek, Marketing Manager. **Cities Served:** Ada, Borup, Climax, Felton, Fertile, Fisher, Gary, Halstad, Hendrum, Hitterdal, Shelly, Ulen, MN: subscribing households 1,930; 36 channels; 1 community access channel; 168 hours per week community access programming.

ADRIAN, pop. 1,336.

SW MN. Notles Co. 40 mi. E. of Sioux Fall, SD. Nobles Co. Creamery. Plastics, cement block factory; elevator. Grain, stock, dairy, poultry farms.

15782 Nobles County Review
PO Box 160 Phone: (507)483-2213
Adrian, MN 56110 Fax: (507)483-2219
Publisher E-mail: ncreview@prairie.lakes.com

Community newspaper. **Founded:** 1890. **Freq:** Weekly (Wed.). **Print Method:** Offset. **Trim Size:** 15 x 21. **Cols./Page:** 8. **Col. Width:** 21 nonpareils. **Col. Depth:** 21 inches. **Key Personnel:** Kathy Burzlaff, Editor; Jerry Johnson, Publisher. **Subscription Rates:** $25 individuals; $31 out of state. **Remarks:** Color advertising accepted; rates available upon request. **Formerly:** Ellsworth Voice.
Ad Rates: GLR: $3.50 **Circ:** ‡1,400
BW: $450
PCI: $3.25

AITKIN†, pop. 1,770.

NEC MN. Aitkin Co. On Mississippi River, 88 mi. SW of Duluth. Aitkin Co. Summer & winter resort. Manufactures pallets, wooden boxes, crates. Timber. Truck, turkey, grain, wild rice, dairy farms.

15783 Aitkin Independent Age
Independent Age Newspapers, Inc.
213 Minnesota Ave. N. Phone: (218)927-3761
PO Box 259 Fax: (218)927-3763
Aitkin, MN 56431-0259
Publication E-mail: age@emily.net

County newspaper. **Founded:** 1883. **Freq:** Weekly Offset. **Cols./Page:** 6. **Col. Width:** 2 inches. **Col. Depth:** 21 1/2 inches. **Key Personnel:** Ann Schwartz, Editor; Dick Norlander, Publisher, dick@emily.net; Jeff Tidholm, Advertising Mgr.; Sharon Dotzler, Circulation Mgr. **Subscription Rates:** $27 individuals; $32 out of area; $37 out of state. **Remarks:** Combined advertising rates available with Bargain Hunter.
Ad Rates: GLR: $6.75 **Circ:** ‡6,105
BW: $585
4C: $765
SAU: $3.90
PCI: $6.75

15784 Bargain Hunter
Independent Age Newspapers, Inc.
213 Minnesota Ave. N. Phone: (218)927-3761
PO Box 259 Fax: (218)927-3763
Aitkin, MN 56431-0259
Publication E-mail: age@emily.net

Shopper. **Freq:** Weekly. **Print Method:** Offset. **Trim Size:** 10 1/2 x 15. **Cols./Page:** 5. **Col. Width:** 24 nonpareils. **Col. Depth:** 210 agate lines. **Key Personnel:** Ann Schwartz, Editor; Dick Norlander, Publisher; Jeff Tidholm, Advertising Mgr.; Sharon Dotzler, Circulation Mgr. **Subscription Rates:** Free. **Remarks:** Accepts advertising.
Ad Rates: BW: $585 **Circ:** Free ‡21,000
4C: $785
SAU: $9.25

15785 KKIM-FM - 94.3
PO Box 140 Phone: (218)927-2344
Aitkin, MN 56431 Fax: (218)927-2100
Free: (800)450-5546

Format: Country. **Networks:** Westwood One Radio. **Owner:** Elite Broadcasting Corp., at above address, (888)404-9555, Fax: (218)927-4090. **Founded:** 1972. **Formerly:** KEZZ-FM. **Operating Hours:** Continuous. **ADI:** Duluth, MN-Superior, WI. **Key Personnel:** Terry Dee, General Mgr.; Al Qubynstrom, President; John Tholen, News Dir.; Jan Hall, Operations Mgr. **Wattage:** 25,000. **Ad Rates:** $7-9 for 30 seconds; $8-10 for 60 seconds.

15786 KKIN-AM - 930
PO Box 140 Phone: (218)927-2344
Aitkin, MN 56431 Fax: (218)927-4090
Free: (800)450-5546

Format: Middle-of-the-Road (MOR). **Networks:** USA Radio; Westwood One Radio; Minnesota News. **Owner:** Elite Broadcasting Corp., at above address, Free: (888)404-9555. **Founded:** 1961. **Operating Hours:** Continuous; 80% network, 20% local. **ADI:** Duluth, MN-Superior, WI. **Key Personnel:** Terry Dee, General Mgr.; Al Quarnstrom, President; John Tholen, News Dir.; Jan Hall, Operations Mgr. **Wattage:** 2500. **Ad Rates:** $7-9 for 30 seconds; $8-11 for 60 seconds.

ALBANY, pop. 1,569.

C MN. Stearns Co. 20 mi. NW of Saint Cloud. Residential.

15787 Stearns-Morrison Enterprise
Stearn-Morrison
Box 310 Phone: (320)845-2700
Albany, MN 56307
Newspaper. **Founded:** 1914. **Freq:** Weekly (Tues.). **Print Method:** Offset. **Cols./Page:** 7. **Col. Width:** 24 nonpareils. **Col. Depth:** 294 agate lines. **Key Personnel:** Michael J. Kosik, Editor; Don R. Larson, Publisher; John Olson, Advertising Mgr. **Subscription Rates:** $11. **Remarks:** Accepts advertising.
Ad Rates: GLR: $.28 **Circ:** 4,500

15788 KASM-AM - 1150
Box 390 Phone: (612)845-2184
Albany, MN 56307 Fax: (612)845-2187

Format: Talk; Ethnic; Country; Polka; Agricultural; Big Band/Nostalgia. **Networks:** Independent. **Owner:** KASM of Minnesota, Inc., at above address. **Founded:** 1950. **Operating Hours:** Daytime; 100% local. **ADI:** Minneapolis-St. Paul, MN. **Key Personnel:** Barbara Gretsch, General Mgr.; Terry Hamil, Sports Dir.; Cliff Mitchell, Contact. **Wattage:** 2500. **Ad Rates:** Advertising accepted; rates available upon request.

ALBERT LEA†, pop. 19,190.

SC MN. Freeborn Co. 100 mi. S. of Minneapolis. Freeborn Co. Manufactures stoves, lamps, meat, dairy products, road machinery, beverages, hay tools, poultry equipment, iron shears, store fixtures. Diversified farming.

15789 Tribune
Albert Lea Publishing Co.
808 W. Front St., No. 60 Phone: (507)373-1411
Albert Lea, MN 56007 Fax: (507)373-0333
Free: (800)657-4996

General newspaper. **Founded:** 1897. **Freq:** Daily (eve.), Sunday (morn.). **Print Method:** Offset. **Cols./Page:** 6. **Col. Width:** 25 nonpareils. **Col. Depth:** 301 agate lines. **Key Personnel:** Geri McShane, Editor; Kathy Tighe, Advertising Mgr. **Subscription Rates:** $97.75. **Remarks:** Accepts advertising.
Ad Rates: SAU: $9.55 **Circ:** Mon.-Fri. 7,708
Sun. 7,940

15790 KATE-AM - 1450
305 S. 1st Ave. Phone: (507)373-2338
Albert Lea, MN 56007 Fax: (507)373-4736
E-mail: sales@kate1450.com

Format: News; Talk; Information; Middle-of-the-Road (MOR). **Networks:** ABC; Minnesota News. **Founded:** 1937. **Operating Hours:** Continuous. **ADI:** Rochester, MN-Mason City, IA-Austin, MN. **Key Personnel:** Dave Nolander, General Mgr.; Vern Rassmusen, Sales Mgr.; Al Carstens, Farm Director; Mike Woitas, Operations/News Dir.; Irene Nelson, Public Service Director; Mike Sullivan, Sports Dir. **Wattage:** 1000. **Ad Rates:** $15-70 per unit. Combined advertising rates available with KCPI-FM, KYTC-FM.

15791 KCPI-FM - 94.9
305 S. 1st Ave. Phone: (507)373-2338
Albert Lea, MN 56007 Fax: (507)373-4736
E-mail: sales@kate1450.com

Format: Adult Contemporary. **Networks:** ABC. **Founded:** 1974. **Formerly:** KCPI-FM. **Operating Hours:** Continuous. **ADI:** Rochester, MN-Mason City, IA-Austin, MN. **Key Personnel:** Dave Nolander, General Mgr.; Al Carstens, Farm Director; Mike Sullivan, Sports Dir.; Mike Woitas, Operations/News Dir.; Irene Nelson, Public Service Director. **Wattage:** 3500. **Ad Rates:** $17-29 per unit. Combined advertising rates available with KATE-AM, KYTC-FM.

15792 KYTC-FM - 102.7
305 S. 1st Ave. Phone: (507)373-2338
Albert Lea, MN 56007 Fax: (507)373-4736

Format: Oldies. **Owner:** Nolander Broadcasting Inc., at above address. **Operating Hours:** Continuous. **Key Personnel:** Dave Nolander, Pres./General Mgr.; Vern Rasmussen, General Sales Mgr.; Mike Woitas, Operations/Production Dir.; June Goodnature, Controller. **Wattage:** 25,000. **Ad Rates:** Advertising accepted; rates available upon request.

ALDEN, pop. 687.

SC MN. Freeborn Co. 25 mi. W. of Austin. Residential.

15793 The Alden Advance
150 E. Main Phone: (507)874-3440
Box 485 Fax: (507)874-3440
Alden, MN 56009
Publication E-mail: aldenadv.@clear.lakes.com

Community newspaper. **Founded:** 1891. **Freq:** Weekly (Thurs.). **Print Method:** Offset. **Cols./Page:** 6. **Col. Width:** 2 1/8 inches. **Col. Depth:** 21 1/2 inches. **Key Personnel:** Dave Gehake, Publisher. **ISSN:** 0898-526X. **Subscription Rates:** $18.50 individuals; $20 out of area; $23 out of state. **Remarks:** Accepts advertising.
Ad Rates: BW: $283.80 **Circ:** ‡1,080
PCI: $3.30

ALEXANDRIA†, pop. 7,608.

WC MN. Douglas Co. 65 mi. NW of Saint Cloud. Resort. Manufactures aircraft & parts, abrasives, plastics and concrete products. Diversified farming. Dairying, soybeans, beef cattle, hogs, corn.

15794 The Echo/Press
Alexandria Printing Co.
225 7th Ave. E. Phone: (320)763-3133
PO Box 549 Fax: (320)763-3258
Alexandria, MN 56308
Publication E-mail: echo@rea-alp.com

Community newspaper. **Founded:** 1946. **Freq:** Semiweekly (Wed. and Fri.). **Print Method:** Offset. **Trim Size:** 13 x 21 1/2. **Cols./Page:** 6. **Col. Width:** 29 nonpareils. **Col. Depth:** 301 agate lines. **Key Personnel:** Al Edenloff, Editor; Jon Haaven, Publisher; Judy Hanson, Advertising Mgr. **Subscription Rates:** $41 individuals. **Remarks:** Accepts advertising. **Available Online. URL:** http://www.echopress.com. **Formerly:** Lake Region Echo/Press.
Ad Rates: GLR: $8 **Circ:** Fri. ❑**10,167**
BW: $1,032 Wed. ❑**9,388**
4C: $1,287

15795 Lakeland Shopping Guide
Alexandria Printing Co.
225 7th Ave. E. Phone: (320)763-3133
PO Box 549 Fax: (320)763-3258
Alexandria, MN 56308
Publication E-mail: echo@rea-alp.com

Shopper. **Founded:** 1967. **Freq:** Weekly (Sun.). **Print Meth-**

od: Offset. **Trim Size:** 10 1/4 x 15. **Cols./Page:** 6. **Col. Width:** 20 nonpareils. **Col. Depth:** 210 agate lines. **Key Personnel:** Jon Haaven, Publisher; Jody Hanson, Advertising Mgr. **Subscription Rates:** $41 individuals. **Remarks:** Accepts advertising.
Ad Rates: BW: $675 **Circ:** Free 31,000
4C: $930
SAU: $8
PCI: $8

15796 KCCO-TV - 7
720 Hawthorne St. Phone: (612)763-5166
Alexandria, MN 56308 Fax: (612)763-4991
Free: (800)934-5221

Format: Commercial TV. **Networks:** CBS. **Founded:** 1958. **Formerly**: KCMT-TV (1987). **Operating Hours:** Continuous. **ADI:** Minneapolis-St. Paul, MN. **Key Personnel:** Jan McDaniel, General Mgr.; Mari Leuthner, Stn. Admin.; Wayne Quernemoen, Dir. Tech. Oper.; Greg Keck, Contact. **Wattage:** 316,000.

15797 KIKV-FM - 100.7
604 3rd Ave. W. Phone: (320)762-2154
Box 1024 Fax: (320)762-2156
Alexandria, MN 56308

Format: Country; Agricultural. **Networks:** ABC; Linder Farm. **Founded:** 1970. **Formerly**: KCMT-FM. **Operating Hours:** Continuous. **Key Personnel:** Lou Buron, President; Dave Vagle, General Mgr.; Trudy Blanshan, General Sales Mgr.; Rick Blanshan, Program Dir.; Wendel Sowers, Chief Engineer. **Wattage:** 100,000.

15798 KSAX-TV - 42
415 Filmore Ave. Phone: (320)763-5729
Box 189 Fax: (320)763-4627
Alexandria, MN 56308
Free: (800)584-9803
E-mail: ksax.com

Format: Commercial TV. **Networks:** ABC. **Owner:** Hubbard Broadcasting, 3415 University Ave., St. Paul, MN 55114, (612)646-5535, Fax: (651)642-4170. **Founded:** 1987. **Operating Hours:** Continuous; 50% network, 50% local. **ADI:** Minneapolis-St. Paul, MN. **Key Personnel:** Susan Anderson, Station Mgr.; Jason Hirsch, Operations Mgr., jhirsch@ks.com; Mark Vanderwerf, News Dir., mvanderwerf@ksax.com; Corliss Stark, Contact, cslark@hbi.com. **Wattage:** 2,700,000. **Ad Rates:** $30-600 for 30 seconds.

15799 KSTQ-FM - 99.3
Kenwood Plaza, Ste. 105 Phone: (612)763-6515
418 3rd Ave., E Fax: (612)763-6516
PO Box 1114
Alexandria, MN 56308

Format: Adult Contemporary; Soft Rock. **Networks:** Jones Satellite. **Owner:** Branstock Communications, BOX 241, 105 NE 2nd Av. Suite 200, Glenwood, MN 56334, (612)634-5358, Fax: (612)763-5999. **Founded:** 1984. **Operating Hours:** Continuous. **Key Personnel:** Steve Nestor, President; John Messenger, Program Dir.; Dave McClurg, Sports Dir. **Wattage:** 6000. **Ad Rates:** $5.50-12.50 for 30 seconds; $9.50-16.50 for 60 seconds.

ANNANDALE

15800 Annandale Advocate
73 Oak Ave. Phone: (320)274-3052
PO Box D Fax: (320)274-2301
Annandale, MN 55302
Publication E-mail: annadvoc.@lkdllink.net

Community newspaper. **Freq:** Weekly (Wed.). **Cols./Page:** 6. **Col. Width:** 12.2 picas. **Col. Depth:** 21 1/2 inches. **Key Personnel:** John Fisher, Editor; Steve Prinsen, Publisher.

APPLE VALLEY

15801 Apple Valley/Rosemount/Lakeville Sun Current
Sun Newspapers
10917 Valley View Rd. Phone: (612)829-0797
Eden Prairie, MN 55344 Fax: (612)392-6802
Publication E-mail: applevalleysuncurrent@mnsunpub.com
Publisher E-mail: suncurrentsouth@mnsunpub.com

Community newspaper (tabloid). **Freq:** Weekly (Wed.). **Print Method:** Offset. **Cols./Page:** 4. **Col. Width:** 2 1/2 inches. **Col. Depth:** 15 inches. **Key Personnel:** Frank Chilinski, Publisher, phone (612)392-6851. **URL:** http://www.mnsun.com.
Circ: Free 15,168

APPLETON, pop. 1,842.

SW MN. Swift Co. On Pomme de Terre River, 150 mi. W. of Minneapolis. Electronic plant. Elevator. Grain, dairy, stock, poultry farms. Wheat, oats, corn, beans, soybeans.

15802 Appleton Press
241 W. Snelling
Appleton, MN 56208

Newspaper with a Democratic orientation. **Founded:** 1880. **Freq:** Weekly (Wed.). **Print Method:** Offset. **Cols./Page:** 6. **Col. Width:** 26 nonpareils. **Col. Depth:** 301 agate lines. **Key Personnel:** Loren G. Johnson, Editor; Curtis B. Johnson, Publisher. **Subscription Rates:** $22. **Remarks:** Accepts advertising.
Ad Rates: BW: $509.60 **Circ:** 2,950
SAU: $2.40

15803 KWCM-TV - 10
120 W. Schlieman Phone: (612)289-2622
Appleton, MN 56208 Fax: (612)289-2634
Free: (800)726-3178
E-mail: yourtv@pioneer.org

Format: Public TV. **Networks:** Public Broadcasting Service (PBS). **Founded:** 1966. **Operating Hours:** Continuous. **ADI:** Minneapolis-St. Paul, MN. **Key Personnel:** Suzanne Christopher, Finance Dir.; Dean Orton, Development Dir.; Ansel Doll, General Mgr.; Jon Hegland, Production Dir.; Ronae O'Connor, Membership; Linda Nelson, Programming.

ARLINGTON, pop. 1,779.

SC MN. Sibley Co. 40 mi. N. of Mankato. Manufactures canned vegetables, cement blocks and silos. Heating equipment. Electric transformer rebuilding.

15804 Arlington Enterprise
402 W. Alden St. Phone: (507)964-5547
Arlington, MN 55307 Fax: (507)964-5547

Community newspaper. **Founded:** 1884. **Freq:** Weekly (Thurs.). **Print Method:** Offset. **Trim Size:** 8 x 11 1/2. **Cols./Page:** 7. **Col. Width:** 28 nonpareils. **Col. Depth:** 301 agate lines. **Key Personnel:** Kurt Menk, Editor; Gail Kill, Publisher. **USPS:** 031-980. **Subscription Rates:** $22; $30 out of state. **Remarks:** Color advertising accepted; rates available upon request.
Ad Rates: BW: $325 **Circ:** 1,550
SAU: $2.75
PCI: $4.70

ASKOV, pop. 350.

EC MN. Pine Co. 47 mi. SW of Duluth. Nursery. Agriculture. Dairy products, eggs.

15805 Askov American
PO Box 275 Phone: (612)838-3151
Askov, MN 55704 Fax: (612)838-3152
Publisher E-mail: askovam@wans.net

Community newspaper. **Founded:** 1914. **Freq:** Weekly (Thurs.). **Print Method:** Offset. **Cols./Page:** 7. **Col. Width:** 12 picas. **Col. Depth:** 21.5 picas. **Key Personnel:** David Heiller, Editor and Publisher. **USPS:** 034-140. **Subscription Rates:** $20; $24 out of area. **Remarks:** Accepts advertising.
Ad Rates: GLR: $.20 **Circ:** ‡2,000
PCI: $3.16

ATWATER

15806 Atwater Herald
116 3rd St. Phone: (320)974-8817
PO Box 756
Atwater, MN 56209
Community newspaper. **Freq:** Weekly (Wed.). **Cols./Page:** 6. **Col. Width:** 14 picas. **Col. Depth:** 21 1/2 inches. **Key Personnel:** Dennis Baker, Editor and Publisher.
Circ: 1,200

AUSTIN†, pop. 23,020.

SE MN. Mower co. 100 mi. S. of Minneapolis. Meat packing and canned foods. Manufactures paper boxes, concrete products, business forms, water pollution control equipment, burial vaults, folding cartons, plastic pipes, animal feed, fertilizers. Dairy, stock, truck, poultry farms.

15807 Austin Daily Herald
1310 2nd St. NE Phone: (507)433-8851
PO Box 578 Fax: (507)437-8644
Austin, MN 55912-3436
General newspaper. **Founded:** 1891. **Freq:** Daily (eve.), Sunday (morn.). **Print Method:** Offset. **Cols./Page:** 6. **Col. Width:** 25 nonpareils. **Col. Depth:** 295 agate lines. **Key Personnel:** Mike Mahoney, Editor; Jim Negen, Publisher. **Subscription Rates:** $70.20. **Remarks:** Accepts advertising.
Ad Rates: SAU: $7.62 **Circ:** Mon.-Fri. 8,500
Sun. 8,440

15808 KAAL-TV - 6
1701 10th Pl. NE, Box 577 Phone: (507)437-6666
Austin, MN 55912 Fax: (507)433-9560
E-mail: mail@kaal-tv.co.net; news@kaal-tv.co.net

Format: Commercial TV. **Networks:** ABC. **Owner:** Eastern Broadcasting Corp., at above address, Austin, MN 55912. **Founded:** July 27, 1953. **Formerly**: KAUS-TV (1975). **Operating Hours:** Continuous. **ADI:** Rochester, MN-Mason City, IA-Austin, MN. **Key Personnel:** Dave Tillery, General Mgr.; Pat St. George, General Sales Mgr.; Dean Adams, News Dir.; Patti Schlichter, Program Coordinator. **Wattage:** 100,000. **URL:** http://kaal-tv.co.net.kaal.

15809 KSMQ-TV - 15
2000 8th Ave. NW Phone: (507)433-0678
Austin, MN 55912 Fax: (507)433-0670
Free: (800)658-2539

Format: Public TV. **Networks:** Public Broadcasting Service (PBS). **Owner:** Independent School District No. 492, 202 4th Ave. NE, Austin, MN 55912. **Founded:** 1972. **Formerly**: KATV-TV. **Operating Hours:** 6.00 a.m.-11:00 p.m.; 7:00 a.m. - 12:00 Sat. & Sun. **ADI:** Rochester, MN-Mason City, IA-Austin, MN. **Key Personnel:** Richard Sailors, General Manager. **Ad Rates:** Underwriting available. **URL:** http://www.ksmq.org.

BABBITT

15810 Babbitt Weekly News
PO Box 267 Phone: (218)827-2363
Babbitt, MN 55706 Fax: (218)827-2363

Community newspaper. **Freq:** Weekly (Sat.). **Cols./Page:** 5. **Col. Width:** 2 inches. **Col. Depth:** 14 inches. **Key Personnel:** William E. Proznik, Jr., Publisher. **Subscription Rates:** $18 local annual; $.50 single issue. **Remarks:** Accepts advertising.
Ad Rates: SAU: $5 **Circ:** 1,600
PCI: $4

BAGLEY†, pop. 1,321.

NW MN. Clearwater Co. 170 mi. W. of Duluth. Hunting, fishing & camping. Lumber mills. Timber. Agriculture. Potatoes, wild rice, alfalfa seed, sunflower. Lake resort.

15811 Farmers Independent
PO Box 130 Phone: (218)694-6265
Bagley, MN 56621 Fax: (218)694-6015

Community newspaper. **Founded:** 1918. **Freq:** Weekly (Wed.). **Print Method:** Offset. **Trim Size:** 15 x 22 1/2. **Cols./Page:** 6. **Col. Width:** 2 1/4 inches. **Col. Depth:** 21 1/2 inches. **Key Personnel:** Tom Burford, Manager. **USPS:** 187-720. **Subscription Rates:** $17.50 individuals; $21.50 out of county; $22.50 out of state. **Remarks:** Accepts advertising.
Ad Rates: GLR: $.175 **Circ:** ‡2,600
BW: $450
4C: $320
SAU: $4
PCI: $4

15812 Bagley Public Utilities
18 Main Ave. S. Phone: (218)694-2300
PO Box M Fax: (218)694-6632
Bagley, MN 56621

Owner: Bagley Public Utilities, at above address. **Founded:** 1976. **Key Personnel:** Michael Monsrud, Contact. **Cities Served:** subscribing households 536; 20 channels.

BALATON, pop. 752.

SW MN. Lyon Co. 70 mi. NE of Sioux Falls, SD. Creamery; elevators. Dairy, poultry, grain, beef raising farms.

15813 Balaton-Press-Tribune
Balaton Publishing
PO Box 310 Phone: (507)734-5421
Balaton, MN 56115-0310 Fax: (507)734-2316
Publisher E-mail: balapub@rconnect.com

Community newspaper. **Founded:** 1902. **Freq:** Weekly (Thurs.). **Print Method:** Offset. **Cols./Page:** 6. **Col. Width:** 14 picas. **Col. Depth:** 21 1/2 inches. **Key Personnel:** Jennifer Ringkob, Editor; Seth Schmidt, Publisher. **Subscription Rates:** $22 individuals; $28 out of area. **Remarks:** Accepts

advertising. **Formerly**: Balaton-Russell-Press-Tribune-Record.
Ad Rates: BW: $367.65 **Circ:** ‡1,000
SAU: $2.52
PCI: $2.85

BATTLE LAKE, pop. 708.

WC MN. Otter Trail Co. On a lake of the same name, 17 mi E. of Fergus Falls. Resort. Elevators. Grain, dairy, poultry farms.

15814 Battle Lake Review
Review Enterprises, Inc.
114 Lake Ave. Phone: (218)864-5952
PO Box 98 Fax: (218)864-5212
Battle Lake, MN 56515
Free: (800)340-0426

Community newspaper. **Founded:** May 29, 1884. **Freq:** Weekly (Wed.). **Print Method:** Offset. **Cols./Page:** 7. **Col. Width:** 28 nonpareils. **Col. Depth:** 301 agate lines. **Key Personnel:** Jon A. Tamke, Editor. **Subscription Rates:** $20 individuals; $24 out of area; $28 out of state. **Remarks:** Accepts advertising.
Ad Rates: GLR: $.25 **Circ:** Paid ‡2,215
SAU: $4.53 Free ‡70
PCI: $4.20

BAUDETTE†, pop. 1,170.

NW MN. Lake of the Woods Co. On Rainy River, 180 mi NW of Duluth. Pharmaceutical laboratory. Summer resort. Timber. Dairy, grain farms. Grass seed, seed potatoes.

15815 The Baudette Region
Drawer C Phone: (218)634-1722
Baudette, MN 56623 Fax: (218)634-1224

Community newspaper. **Founded:** 1902. **Freq:** Weekly (Wed.). **Print Method:** Offset. **Trim Size:** 13 x 21 1/2. **Cols./Page:** 6. **Col. Width:** 12 picas. **Key Personnel:** John C. Oren, Editor/Publisher/Contact. **USPS:** 045-500. **Subscription Rates:** $21.50 individuals; $27.50 out of area.
Ad Rates: GLR: $4.50 **Circ:** Paid ‡2,195
BW: $430 Free ‡5
SAU: $4.50

BELGRADE

15816 Belgrade Observer
PO Box 279 Phone: (320)254-8250
Belgrade, MN 56312 Fax: (320)254-3215

Community newspaper. **Freq:** Weekly (Wed.). **Cols./Page:** 5. **Col. Width:** 11 1/2 picas. **Col. Depth:** 15 inches. **Key Personnel:** James R. Lemmer, Publisher.
Circ: 1,200

BELLE PLAINE

15817 Belle Plaine Herald
108 S. Meridian Phone: (612)873-2261
PO Box 7
Belle Plaine, MN 56011
Community newspaper. **Freq:** Weekly (Wed.). **Cols./Page:** 6. **Col. Width:** 14 picas. **Col. Depth:** 21 inches. **Key Personnel:** Edward Townsend, Publisher.
Circ: 3,500

BEMIDJI†, pop. 10,949.

NW MN. Beltrami co. On Lake Bemidji, 140 mi. NE of Fargo, ND. Bemidji State University. Summer resort, in center of The Thousand Lakes region. Computer industry. Woolen mills. Forestry & timber products. Lumber, cement, bricks, woolen goods.

15818 Germanic Notes and Reviews
Bemidji State University
Bemidji, MN 56601 Phone: (218)751-6265
Fax: (218)751-2958
Publication E-mail: gnreve@paulrunyan.net

Scholarly Germanic journal. **Founded:** 1968. **Freq:** Semiannual. **Key Personnel:** R. F. Krummel, Editor. **ISSN:** 0016-8882. **Subscription Rates:** $14 individuals; $18 institutions; $16 out of country; $20 institutions out of country. **Remarks:** Accepts advertising.
Circ: (Not Reported)

15819 Oshkaabewis Native Journal
American Indian Studies Center
Sanford Hall
Bemidji State University
1500 Birchmont Dr., NE, No. 19
Bemidji, MN 56601-2699

Academic journal covering Ojibwe language and linguistics. **Founded:** 1990. **Freq:** Semiannual. **Trim Size:** 6 x 9. **Cols./Page:** 2. **Key Personnel:** Dr. Anton Trener, Editor. **Subscription Rates:** $36 individuals; $.50 single issue. **Remarks:** Accepts advertising. **URL:** http://www.glrain.net/glrain/onj.htm. **Alt. Formats:** Audio tape.
Ad Rates: BW: $250 **Circ:** (Not Reported)

15820 The Pioneer
Forum Communications Co.
Box 455 Phone: (218)751-3740
Bemidji, MN 56619 Fax: (218)751-6914

General newspaper. **Founded:** 1896. **Freq:** Daily and Sunday (morn.). **Print Method:** Offset. **Trim Size:** 13 1/2 x 22 3/4. **Cols./Page:** 6. **Col. Width:** 27 nonpareils. **Col. Depth:** 294 agate lines. **Key Personnel:** Omar Forberg, Contact; Brad Swenson, Managing Editor; Jeff Halverson, Contact. **ISSN:** 0899-1812. **Subscription Rates:** $96 individuals.
Ad Rates: BW: $1,070.70 **Circ:** Mon.-Fri. 8,406
4C: $1,285.70 Sun. 9,153
SAU: $8.85
PCI: $8.30

15821 Poetic Space
Bemidji State University
Bemidji, MN 56601 Phone: (218)751-6265
Fax: (218)751-2958

Literary magazine covering poetry and fiction. **Subtitle:** A Magazine of Poetry and Fiction. **Founded:** 1983. **Freq:** Semiannual. **Print Method:** Offset. **Key Personnel:** Don Hildenbrand, Editor; Thomas Strand, Fiction Editor. **ISSN:** 1067-3733. **Subscription Rates:** $7 individuals; $13 two years; $4 single issue. **Remarks:** Accepts advertising.
Circ: Paid 200

15822 KAWE-TV - 9
1500 Birchmont Dr. NE Phone: (218)751-3407
BSU, Box 9 Fax: (218)751-3142
Bemidji, MN 56601-2699

Format: Commercial TV. **Networks:** Public Broadcasting Service (PBS). **Owner:** Northern Minnesota Public Television, Inc., at above address. **Founded:** June 1980. **Operating Hours:** Continuous. **Key Personnel:** Emily K. Lahti, General Mgr., elahti@nmptv.org; Bill Sanford, Chief Engineer, bsanford@nmptv.org; Deb McGregor-Pfleger, Development Mgr., dpfleger@nmptv.org; Mark Brewer, Program and Product Mgr., mbrewer@nmptv.org; Dennis Weimann, News Dir., dweimann@nmptv.org. **Ad Rates:** Noncommercial. **URL:** http://www.nmptv.org.

15823 KBHP-FM - 101.1
502 Beltrami Ave., NW Phone: (218)751-4120
Bemidji, MN 56601 Fax: (218)751-8091
E-mail: kbhpkbun@kbhpkbun.com

Format: Country; Contemporary Country. **Networks:** ABC; Minnesota News. **Owner:** Paul Bunyan Broadcasting Co., PO Box 1656, Bemidji, MN 56619-1656. **Founded:** 1972. **Operating Hours:** Continuous. **ADI:** Minneapolis-St. Paul, MN. **Key Personnel:** Lou Buron, Owner/President/GM; Peggy Hanson, Sales Mgr.; Todd Haugen, Program Dir.; Mary Campbell, Owner/V.P.; Mardy Karger, News Dir.; Kevin Jackson, Sports Dir. **Local Programs:** *Chat About*, Mardy Karger. **Wattage:** 100,000. **Ad Rates:** Advertising accepted; rates available upon request. Combined advertising rates available with KBUN-AM.

15824 KBSB-FM - 89.7
1500 Birchmont Dr. NE Phone: (218)755-2059
Box D-2E Fax: (218)755-4119
Bemidji, MN 56601
E-mail: fm90@vax1.bemidji.msus.edu

Format: Contemporary Hit Radio (CHR); Album-Oriented Rock (AOR); Bluegrass; Alternative/New Music/Progressive. **Founded:** 1968. **Operating Hours:** Continuous. **Key Personnel:** Adam Kendall, Sales Dir.; Carrie Lewis, Music Dir.; Kevin Van Dyck, News Dir.; Jen Wright, Station Mgr.; Andy Hill, Program Dir. **Wattage:** 115. **Ad Rates:** $3 for 30 seconds; $5 for 60 seconds. Combined advertising rates available with KDRG-FM; KBSU-TV. **URL:** http://vaxl.bemidji.msus.edu/~fm90/fm90.html.

15825 KBUN-AM - 1450
502 Beltrami Ave., NW Phone: (218)751-4120
PO Box 1656 Fax: (218)751-8091
Bemidji, MN 56619-1656
E-mail: kbhpkbun@kbhpkbun.com

Format: Sports; Talk. **Networks:** Mutual Broadcasting System; ESPN Radio; Minnesota News. **Owner:** Paul Bunyan Broadcasting Co., at above address. **Founded:** 1946. **Operating Hours:** Continuous. **ADI:** Minneapolis-St. Paul, MN. **Key Personnel:** Lou Buron, President/GM; Peggy Hanson, Sales Mgr.; Mary Campbell, Owner/V.P.; Mardy Karger, News Dir.; Kevin Jackson, Sports and Program Dir. **Local Programs:** *Chat About*, Mardy Karger; *Fishing Paul Bunyan Country*, Kevin Jackson. **Wattage:** 1000. **Ad Rates:** Advertising accepted; rates available upon request. Combined advertising rates available with KBHP-FM.

15826 KCRB-FM - 88.5
PO Box 578 Phone: (218)751-8864
Bemidji, MN 56601-0578 Fax: (218)751-8640
E-mail: kcrb@mpr.org

Format: Public Radio; Classical; News; Jazz. **Networks:** Minnesota Public Radio; National Public Radio (NPR); American Public Radio (APR). **Owner:** Minnesota Public Radio, 45 E. 7th St., St. Paul, MN 55101, (612)290-1500. **Founded:** 1982. **Operating Hours:** Continuous; 97% network, 3% local. **Key Personnel:** Kristi Booth, Station Mgr.; Ellen Barr, Marketing & Development Assistant, ebarr@mpr.org; Tom Robertson, News Dir. **Wattage:** 95,000. **Ad Rates:** Noncommercial; underwriting available.

15827 KKBJ-AM - 1360
2115 Washington Ave. S. Phone: (218)751-7777
Bemidji, MN 56601 Fax: (218)759-0658
E-mail: kkbjwbji@northernnet.com

Format: Talk. **Networks:** ABC. **Founded:** 1977. **Operating Hours:** 5 a.m. - 12 p.m. **Key Personnel:** Curt Peterson, Program Mgr.; Dan Voss, Sales Mgr.; Marla Sanford, Office Mgr. **Wattage:** 5000. **Ad Rates:** $4-10 for 30 seconds; $6-15 for 60 seconds. $4-$10 for 30 seconds; $6-$15 for 60 seconds. Combined advertising rates available with KKBJ-FM. **URL:** http://www.mnradio.com.

15828 Midwest Cable Communications Inc.
Box 337 Phone: (218)751-5507
Bemidji, MN 56601 Fax: (218)751-8455

Owner: John Langhout, at above address. **Key Personnel:** John Langhout, Contact. **Cities Served:** Bemidji and Cass Lake, MN.

BENSON†, pop. 3,656.

WC MN. Swift Co. 10 mi. N. of De Graff. Dairy.

15829 Swift County Monitor-News
101 12th St. S. Phone: (320)843-4111
PO Box 227 Fax: (320)843-3246
Benson, MN 56215
Community newspaper. **Freq:** Weekly (Wed.). **Cols./Page:** 6. **Col. Width:** 14 picas. **Col. Depth:** 21 1/2 inches. **Key Personnel:** Reed Anfinson, Publisher; Ronald Anfinson, Publisher.
Circ: 3,200

15830 KSCR-AM - 1290
105 13th St. N. Phone: (320)843-3290
Benson, MN 56215 Fax: (320)843-3955
Free: (800)870-7066

Format: Adult Contemporary; Middle-of-the-Road (MOR). **Networks:** Minnesota News; Satellite Music Network. **Founded:** 1958. **Formerly:** KBMO-AM. **Operating Hours:** 6 a.m. - sunset. **Key Personnel:** Jason Brandt, Program Dir.; Amy Jobgen, Traffic Control; Paul Estenson, Pres./Owner. **Local Programs:** *This Morning on KSCR*, Jason Brandt. **Wattage:** 500. **Ad Rates:** $11-13 for 30 seconds; $17-19.50 for 60 seconds. Combined advertising rates available with KSCR-FM.

15831 KSCR-FM - 93.5
105 13th St. N. Phone: (320)843-3290
Benson, MN 56215 Fax: (320)843-3955
Free: (800)870-7066

Format: Middle-of-the-Road (MOR); Adult Contemporary. **Networks:** Minnesota News; Satellite Music Network. **Founded:** 1968. **Operating Hours:** Continuous;. **Key Personnel:** Jason Brandt, Program Dir.; Amy Jobgen, Traffic Control; Paul Estenson, Contact. **Local Programs:** *This Morning on KSCR*, Jason Brandt. **Wattage:** 6000. **Ad Rates:** $11-13 for 30 seconds; $17-19.50 for 60 seconds. Combined advertising rates available with KSCR-AM.

BIG LAKE, pop. 2,210.

SEC MN. Sherbourne Co. 7 mi W. of Elk River. Residential.

15832 West Sherburne Tribune
29 S. Lake St. Phone: (612)263-3602
PO Box 276 Fax: (612)263-8458
Big Lake, MN 55309
Community interest newspaper. **Founded:** 1979. **Freq:** Weekly (Sat.). **Print Method:** Offset. **Cols./Page:** 6. **Col. Width:** 13 1/2 picas. **Col. Depth:** 224 agate lines. **Key Personnel:** Gary Meyer, Publisher. **Subscription Rates:** $5.20. **Remarks:** Accepts advertising.
Ad Rates: GLR: $5.20 **Circ:** Paid ♦137
SAU: $6.20 Non-paid ♦12,456
PCI: $5.20

BIWABIK, pop. 1,428.

NE MN. St. Louis Co. 64 mi. N. of Duluth. Iron mines.

15833 Biwabik Times
PO Box 169 Phone: (218)865-6265
Biwabik, MN 55708 Fax: (218)865-6265

Community newspaper. **Founded:** 1907. **Freq:** Weekly (Thurs.). **Print Method:** Letterpress. Uses mats. **Cols./Page:** 4. **Col. Width:** 28 nonpareils. **Col. Depth:** 210 agate lines. **Key Personnel:** Kitty Anderson, Editor and Publisher. **Subscription Rates:** $14; $16 out of area. **Remarks:** Accepts advertising.
Ad Rates: GLR: $.18 **Circ:** 1,200
BW: $180
PCI: $3

BLACKDUCK, pop. 653.

NW MN. Beltrami Co. 25 mi. N. of Bemidji. Summer & winter resorts. Pulpwood & lumber products. Dairy & beef cattle.

15834 The American
209 Main St. Phone: (218)835-4211
Blackduck, MN 56630 Fax: (218)835-4211

Community newspaper. **Founded:** 1901. **Freq:** Weekly (Sun.). **Print Method:** Offset. **Cols./Page:** 6. **Col. Width:** 2 inches. **Col. Depth:** 21 1/2 inches. **Key Personnel:** Paula Bauman, Editor and Publisher. **Subscription Rates:** $24; $26 out of state. **Remarks:** Accepts advertising. **Formerly:** Blackduck American / Blackduck Publ. Co.
Ad Rates: GLR: $3.50 **Circ:** 1,327
BW: $574.05
4C: $714.05
SAU: $5.50
PCI: $5.50

15835 The Black Duck American
Forum Communications Co.
Drawer M Phone: (218)835-4211
Blackduck, MN 56630
Newspaper. **Freq:** Weekly. **Cols./Page:** 6. **Col. Width:** 2 1/16 inches. **Col. Depth:** 21 1/2 inches. **Key Personnel:** Paula Bauman, Contact; Karin Parker, Contact. **Subscription Rates:** $24.
Circ: Paid 1,369

15836 Blackduck Cablevision Inc.
50 Margaret Ave. E. Phone: (218)835-7890
Box 325 Fax: (218)835-3299
Blackduck, MN 56630-0325
E-mail: bdtele@blackduck.net

Owner: Blackduck Telephone Co., at above address. **Founded:** 1983. **Key Personnel:** Herb Lien, Manager. **Cities Served:** Blackduck, MN: subscribing households 400; 23 channels; 1 community access channel; 168 hours per week community access programming.

BLAINE, pop. 28,558.

SEC MN. Anoka Co. 25 mi. N. of Minneapolis. Residential.

15837 Blaine Spring Lake Park Life
Anoka County Shopper
4101 Coon Rapids Blvd. Phone: (612)421-4444
Coon Rapids, MN 55433-2585 Fax: (612)421-4315

Local newspaper. **Founded:** 1963. **Freq:** Weekly (Fri.). **Print Method:** Offset. **Cols./Page:** 6. **Col. Width:** 26 nonpareils. **Col. Depth:** 308 agate lines. **Key Personnel:** Arch G. Pease, Publisher; Hugh Campbell, Advertising Mgr. **Subscription Rates:** $10. **URL:** http://www.ecm-inc.com.
Circ: ‡2,251

BLOOMING PRAIRIE, pop. 1,969.

SE MN. Steele Co. 20 mi. SE of Owatonna.

15838 Blooming Prairie Times
411 E. Main St. Phone: (507)583-4431
PO Box 247 Fax: (507)583-4445
Blooming Prairie, MN 55917
Local newspaper. **Founded:** 1893. **Freq:** Weekly (Tues.). **Print Method:** Web offset. **Cols./Page:** 6. **Col. Width:** 2 1/16 inches. **Col. Depth:** 21 inches. **Key Personnel:** Elsie Slinger, Publisher. **Subscription Rates:** $24; $28 out of state. **Remarks:** Accepts advertising. **Formerly:** Blooming Prairie News.
Ad Rates: BW: $475 **Circ:** ‡1,600
SAU: $3.77

BLOOMINGTON, pop. 81,831.

SE MN. Hennepin Co. 25 mi. SW of Saint Paul. Residential.

15839 Bloomington Sun Current
Minnesota Sun Publications
7831 E. Bush Lake Rd. Phone: (612)896-4700
Bloomington, MN 55439 Fax: (612)896-4728

Community newspaper (tabloid). **Founded:** 1984. **Freq:** Weekly (Wed.). **Print Method:** Offset. **Cols./Page:** 4. **Col. Width:** 2 1/2 inches. **Col. Depth:** 15 inches. **Key Personnel:** John Gannet Hawley, Publisher; Robert Stjern, Advertising Mgr.
Circ: Non-paid 19,744
Paid 4,255

Brooklyn Center Sun-Post - See Brooklyn Center

15840 Brooklyn Park Sun-Post
Minnesota Sun Publications
7831 E. Bush Lake Rd. Phone: (612)896-4700
Bloomington, MN 55439 Fax: (612)896-4728

Community newspaper (tabloid). **Founded:** 1962. **Freq:** Weekly (Wed.). **Print Method:** Offset. **Cols./Page:** 4. **Col. Width:** 2.5 inches. **Col. Depth:** 15 inches. **Remarks:** Accepts advertising.
Circ: Free 17,171

Burnsville/Savage Sun Current - See Burnsville

Chanhassen Excelsior - See Chanhassen

Eagan Sun Current - See Eagan

15841 East Bloomington Sun Current
Minnesota Sun Publications
7831 E. Bush Lake Rd. Phone: (612)896-4700
Bloomington, MN 55439 Fax: (612)896-4728

Community newspaper (tabloid). **Freq:** Weekly (Wed.). **Print Method:** Offset. **Cols./Page:** 5. **Col. Width:** 1 15/16 inches. **Col. Depth:** 16 inches. **Key Personnel:** John Gannet Hawley, Publisher; Robert Stjern, Advertising Mgr. **Remarks:** Accepts advertising.
Ad Rates: BW: $816 **Circ:** Non-paid 9,455
4C: $1,291 Paid 1,043
PCI: $10.20

Eden Prairie Sun Current - See Eden Prairie

Edina Sun Current - See Edina

Excelsior/Shorewood Sun-Sailor - See Excelsior

15842 Hardware Trade
Hardware Trade, Inc.
10617 France Ave. S, No. 225 Phone: (612)944-3172
Bloomington, MN 55431-3538 Fax: (612)941-3543
Publication E-mail: hrdwrtrade@aol.com

Magazine covering hardware, housewares, lumber, auto, and building materials. **Founded:** 1891. **Freq:** Bimonthly. **Print Method:** Offset. Uses mats. **Trim Size:** 8 1/8 x 11. **Cols./Page:** 3. **Col. Width:** 13 picas. **Col. Depth:** 60 picas. **Key Personnel:** Sue Connelly, Publisher; Pat Peterson, Editor; Kevin Connelly, Advertising Mgr. **Subscription Rates:** $24 individuals; $4 single issue. **Remarks:** Accepts advertising. **Formerly:** Nothern Hardware Trade.
Ad Rates: BW: $2,500 **Circ:** Non-paid 19,294

Hopkins Minnetonka Sailor-Sun - See Hopkins

15843 The Hymn
The Hymn Society in the U.S. & Canada
c/o Carol A. Pemberton, Editor Phone: (612)832-6571
Normandale Community College
9700 France Ave. S.
Bloomington, MN 55431
Publication E-mail: hymneditor@worldnet.att.net
Publisher E-mail: hymnsoc@bu.edu

Trade journal covering hymnological research and congregational song. **Subtitle:** A Journal of Congregational Song. **Founded:** Oct. 1949. **Freq:** Quarterly. **Print Method:** Web offset. **Trim Size:** 8 x 11. **Cols./Page:** 2. **Col. Depth:** 70 picas. **Key Personnel:** Carol A. Pemberton, Editor; David P. Schaap, Advertising, phone (914)338-2816. **ISSN:** 0018-8271. **Subscription Rates:** $45 individuals. **Remarks:** Accepts advertising. **Former name:** Hymn Society of America.
Ad Rates: BW: $500 **Circ:** Paid ⊕2,847
4C: $750

15844 The InterStudy Competitive Edge
InterStudy
2001 Killebrew Dr., No. 122 Phone: (612)474-1176
Bloomington, MN 55425-1884 Fax: (612)474-1613
Publication E-mail: isypubs@ix.netcom.com

National HMO census, reporting growth, enrollment, and other managed care trends. **Subtitle:** Biannual Report of the Managed Health Care Industry. **Founded:** 1980. **Freq:** Semiannual. **Key Personnel:** Richard Hamer, Director; Shawn D. Schwartz, Asst.Dir. **ISSN:** 1058-1294. **Subscription Rates:** $700 for year; $350 per edition-prepaid price. **Remarks:** Advertising not accepted. **Online:** as part of database DIALOG; Dialog (The Dialog Corporation). **Alt. Formats:** CD-ROM; Database.
Circ: Paid 2000
Non-paid 1,000

15845 Midwest Retailer
8528 Columbus Ave. S. Phone: (612)854-7610
Bloomington, MN 55420-2460 Fax: (612)854-6460

Tabloid containing news for retail dealers of floor coverings. **Founded:** 1971. **Freq:** Monthly. **Print Method:** Offset. **Trim Size:** 9 1/2 x 14 1/2. **Cols./Page:** 6. **Col. Width:** 1 1/2 inches. **Col. Depth:** 14 1/2 inches. **Key Personnel:** John A. Thomasberg, Publisher. **Subscription Rates:** Free. **Remarks:** Accepts advertising.
Ad Rates: BW: $1,456 **Circ:** Non-paid ‡6,500

Minnetonka Sun-Sailor - See Minnetonka

New Hope/Golden Valley Sun-Post - See New Hope

15846 North Minneapolis Sun-Post
Minnesota Sun Publications
7831 E. Bush Lake Rd. Phone: (612)896-4700
Bloomington, MN 55439 Fax: (612)896-4728

Community newspaper (tabloid). **Founded:** 1962. **Freq:** Weekly (Wed.). **Print Method:** Offset. **Cols./Page:** 4. **Col. Width:** 2.5 inches. **Col. Depth:** 15 inches. **Subscription Rates:** Free; $60 out of area. **Remarks:** Accepts advertising.
Circ: Free 9,195

Plymouth Wayzata, Orono, Long Lake Sun-Sailor - See Plymouth

Richfield Sun Current - See Richfield

St. Louis Park Sun-Sailor - See St. Louis Park

South St. Paul/Inver Grove Heights Sun Current - See South St. Paul

Sun-Sailor - See Westonka

15847 West Bloomington Sun-Current
Minnesota Sun Publications
7831 E. Bush Lake Rd. Phone: (612)896-4700
Bloomington, MN 55439 Fax: (612)896-4728

Community newspaper (tabloid). **Freq:** Weekly (Wed.). **Print Method:** Offset. **Col. Width:** 1 15/15 inches. **Col. Depth:** 16 inches. **Key Personnel:** John Gannet Hawley, Publisher; Robert Stjern, Advertising Mgr. **Remarks:** Accepts advertising.
Ad Rates: BW: $1,184 **Circ:** Free 16,790
4C: $1,729 Paid 2,439
PCI: $14.80

BLUE EARTH†, pop. 4,132.

SC MN. Faribault Co. 40 mi. S. of Mankato. Manufactures monuments, electronics parts, running boards, truck boxes. Cannery. Grain, stock, poultry, dairy farms. Corn, oats, barley, soybeans.

15848 KBEW-AM - 1560
PO Box 278 Phone: (507)526-2181
Blue Earth, MN 56013 Fax: (507)526-7468

Format: Oldies; Information. **Networks:** ABC. **Founded:** 1963. **Operating Hours:** Sunrise-sunset; 5% network, 95% local. **Key Personnel:** Kevin Benson, Manager. **Wattage:** 1000. **Ad Rates:** $6.45-9.65 for 30 seconds.

15849 KJLY-FM - 104.5
PO Box 72 Phone: (507)526-3233
Blue Earth, MN 56013 Fax: (507)526-3235
E-mail: kjly@kjly.com

Format: Religious. **Networks:** Moody Broadcasting; USA Radio. **Owner:** Minn.-Iowa Christian Broadcasting, Inc., at above address. **Founded:** 1983. **Operating Hours:** Continuous; 40% network, 60% local. **Key Personnel:** Rick Boyd, Program Dir.; Matthew Dorfner, Exec. Director. **Local Programs:** *Wings of Worship* 9:00 pm Monday-Friday, Gina Frandle. **Wattage:** 50,000. **Ad Rates:** Noncommercial. **URL:** http://www.kjly.com.

BRAINERD†, pop. 11,489.

C MN. Crow Wing Co. On Mississippi River, 53 mi. N. of Saint Cloud. Lake resort region. Pulp, paper, lumber mills. Dairy, poultry, grain farms.

15850 Dispatch
Brainerd Dispatch Newspaper Co.
PO Box D Phone: (218)829-4705
Brainerd, MN 56401 Fax: (218)829-7735

General newspaper. **Founded:** 1881. **Freq:** Daily (eve.), Sunday (morn.). **Print Method:** Offset. **Cols./Page:** 6. **Col. Width:** 24 nonpareils. **Col. Depth:** 301 agate lines. **Key Personnel:** Roy Miller, Editor; T.J. McCollough, Publisher. **Subscription Rates:** $68. **Remarks:** Accepts advertising. **URL:** http://www.brainerddispatch.com.
Ad Rates: PCI: $8 **Circ:** Mon.-Fri. 12,866
Sun. 16,807

15851 The In-Fisherman
In-Fisherman
Two In-Fisherman Dr. Phone: (218)829-1648
Brainerd, MN 56425 Fax: (218)829-3091
Publication E-mail: scottl@in-fisherman.com

For Freshwater Anglers; from beginners to professionals. **Subtitle:** The Journal of Freshwater Fishing. **Founded:** 1975. **Freq:** 7/year. **Print Method:** Offset. **Trim Size:** 7 x 9 7/16. **Cols./Page:** 3. **Col. Width:** 2 1/8 inches. **Col. Depth:** 9 7/16 inches. **Key Personnel:** Stu Legaard, Publisher, phone (218)825-2548, stul@in-fisherman.com. **ISSN:** 0276-9905. **Subscription Rates:** $16 individuals; $3.99 single issue. **Remarks:** Accepts advertising. **Available Online. URL:** http://www.in-fisherman.com.
Ad Rates: BW: $10,290 **Circ:** Paid ★**324,206**
4C: $13,890

15852 Walleye In-Sider
In-Fisherman
Two In-Fisherman Dr. Phone: (218)829-1648
Brainerd, MN 56425-8098 Fax: (218)829-2371

Consumer magazine focusing on Walleye fishing techniques and equipment. **Subtitle:** The First & Last Word In Walleye Fishing. **Founded:** 1989. **Freq:** Bimonthly. **Print Method:** Offset. **Trim Size:** 7 x 10. **Cols./Page:** 3. **Col. Width:** 2 1/4 inches. **Col. Depth:** 10 inches. **Key Personnel:** Stu Legaard, Publisher. **ISSN:** 1068-2112. **Subscription Rates:** $9.97; $3.50 single issue; $17 Canada. **Remarks:** Accepts advertising. **URL:** http://www.in-fisherman.com.
Ad Rates: BW: $2,900 **Circ:** Paid ★**74,659**
4C: $3,920
PCI: $110

15853 KBPR-FM - 90.7
501 W. College Dr., Ste. 402 Phone: (218)829-1072
Brainerd, MN 56401 Fax: (612)363-4948

Format: Public Radio; Eclectic; Classical; News; Information. **Networks:** National Public Radio (NPR); American Public Radio (APR); Minnesota Public Radio. **Owner:** Minnesota Public Radio, 45 E. 7th St., St. Paul, MN 55101, (612)290-1500. **Founded:** 1988. **Operating Hours:** Continuous. **Key Personnel:** Robb Daly, Chief Engineer; Tim Walstrom, General Mgr.; Amy Walstrom, Contact; Tim Kelly, News Dir. **Wattage:** 34,000. **Ad Rates:** Noncommercial.

15854 KLIZ-AM - 1380
602 Laurel St. Phone: (218)829-2853
Box 980 Fax: (218)829-6983
Brainerd, MN 56401
Free: (800)922-5666

Format: Adult Contemporary. **Networks:** CNN Radio. **Founded:** 1945. **Operating Hours:** Continuous; 16% network, 84% local. **ADI:** Minneapolis-St. Paul, MN. **Key Personnel:** Mike Overton, Vice President; Jeff Hilborn, Sales Mgr.; Dave Torkelson, Operations Mgr. **Wattage:** 5000. **Ad Rates:** $6-8.50 for 30 seconds; $8-11.50 for 60 seconds.

15855 WJJY-FM - 106.7
410 Front St. Phone: (218)828-1244
Brainerd, MN 56401 Fax: (218)828-3421

Format: Adult Contemporary. **Networks:** Mutual Broadcasting System. **Owner:** James R. Pryor, at above address. **Founded:** 1978. **Operating Hours:** Continuous; 15% network, 85% local. **Key Personnel:** James R. Pryor, Sales Mgr.; Tom Lucas, Program Dir.; Hugh Phillips, News Dir. **Wattage:** 100,000. **Ad Rates:** $7.50-11.50 for 30 seconds; $11-15.50 for 60 seconds.

15856 WWWI-AM - 1270
305 W. Washington St. Phone: (218)828-9994
Brainerd, MN 56401 Fax: (218)828-8327

Format: News; Talk; Sports. **Networks:** CBS. **Owner:** Tower Broadcasting Corp., at above address. **Founded:** 1987. **Formerly:** WJJY-AM (1994). **Operating Hours:** Continuous 25: local, 7% network. **Key Personnel:** James R. Pryor, President & General Sales Mgr.; Mary P. Pryor, VP & Traffic Director. **Local Programs:** *Brainerd Lakes Today*, Dave Johnson. **Wattage:** 5000. **Ad Rates:** $4-6.50 for 30 seconds; $6.40-10.40 for 60 seconds.

BREEZY POINT, pop. 384.

C MN. Crow Wing Co. 5 mi. S. of Crosslake.

15857 KLKS-FM - 104.3
PO Box 300 Phone: (218)562-4884
Breezy Point, MN 56472 Fax: (218)562-4058
E-mail: klks@uslink.net

Format: Middle-of-the-Road (MOR). **Networks:** CNN Radio. **Owner:** Allen Gray, at above address. **Founded:** 1984. **Operating Hours:** 5 a.m.-1 a.m.; 10%network, 90% local. **Key Personnel:** Bob Bundgaard, General Mgr.; Tom Kenow, General Sales Mgr. **Wattage:** 50,000. **Ad Rates:** $9.75-18 for 30 seconds; $12.75-24 for 60 seconds.

BRICELYN, pop. 487.

SC MN. Faribault Co. 30 mi. SE of Blue Earth.

15858 Cannon Valley Cablevision
250 1st St. Phone: (507)653-4444
Box 337 Fax: (507)653-4449
Bricelyn, MN 56014

Owner: Cannon Valley Communications, at above address. **Key Personnel:** Scott W. Johnson, General Mgr. **Cities Served:** Frost, Bricelyn, Kiester, Morristown, and Warsaw, MN.

BROOKLYN CENTER

15859 Brooklyn Center Sun-Post
Minnesota Sun Publications
7831 E. Bush Lake Rd. Phone: (612)896-4700
Bloomington, MN 55439 Fax: (612)896-4728
Publication E-mail:
brooklyncentersunpost@mnsunpub.com

Community newspaper. **Founded:** 1955. **Freq:** Weekly (Wed.). **Print Method:** Offset. **Cols./Page:** 4. **Col. Width:** 2 1/2 inches. **Col. Depth:** 15 inches. **Key Personnel:** Doug Dance, Publisher, phone (612)896-4787, ddane@mnsunpub.com; Pamela Austin, Editor, phone (612)897-5486; Tom Losey, Marketing Dir. **Subscription Rates:** $15. **URL:** http://www.mnsunpub.com.
Circ: Non-paid 6,689
Paid 1,041

BROOKLYN PARK, pop. 43,332.

SE MN. Hernepin Co. 10 mi. N. of Minneapolis. Residential.

15860 King Videocable Co.
6901 Winnetka Ave. N. Phone: (612)533-8347
Brooklyn Park, MN 55428 Fax: (612)531-4445

Founded: 1982. **Key Personnel:** Jim Commers, General Mgr.; Lori James, Advertising Sales Mgr. **Cities Served:** Hennepin County, MN: subscribing households 92,000; 62 channels; 9 community access channels.

BROWNS VALLEY, pop. 906.

SW MN. Traverse Co. 22 mi. SW of Wheaton.

15861 Valley News
PO Box 339 Phone: (320)695-2570
Browns Valley, MN 56219
Local newspaper. **Freq:** Weekly. **Trim Size:** 16 x 22 1/2. **Cols./Page:** 7. **Col. Width:** 12.5 picas. **Col. Depth:** 21 1/2 inches. **Key Personnel:** Jean Labs, Publisher. **Subscription Rates:** $10; $12 out of area. **Remarks:** Accepts advertising.
Ad Rates: SAU: $2.25 **Circ:** Paid 1,375
Free 30

BROWNTON, pop. 688.

SW MN. McLeod Co. 20 mi. WSW of Glencoe.

15862 The Bulletin
McLeod Publishing, Inc.
134 4th Ave. N. Phone: (612)328-4444
Brownton, MN 55312
Community newspaper. **Founded:** Sept. 8, 1892. **Freq:** Weekly. **Print Method:** Offset. **Trim Size:** 21 1/2 x 32. **Cols./Page:** 7. **Col. Width:** 12 picas. **Col. Depth:** 21.5 inches. **Key Personnel:** Lori A. Copler, Managing Editor; Tom Hauer, Advertising Mgr., tomh@glencoenews.com. **USPS:** 068-020. **Subscription Rates:** $22 individuals; $24 out of area; $32 out of state. **Remarks:** Accepts advertising. **Formerly:** Brownton Bulletin.
Ad Rates: BW: $376.25 **Circ:** ‡1,086
SAU: $3.35

BUFFALO†, pop. 4,560.

SEC MN. Wright Co. On Buffalo Lake, 38 mi. NW of Minneapolis. Grain, livestock. Resort. Poultry, stock, dairy, grain farms.

15863 The Drummer
Wright County Journal Press
108 Central Ave. Phone: (612)682-1221
PO Box 159 Fax: (612)682-5458
Buffalo, MN 55313
Shopper. **Founded:** 1971. **Freq:** Weekly (Sun.). **Print Method:** Offset. **Cols./Page:** 8. **Col. Width:** 21 nonpareils. **Col. Depth:** 301 agate lines. **Key Personnel:** James P. McDonnell, Jr., Editor.
Circ: Non-paid 40,100

15864 KRWC-AM - 1360
Box 267 Phone: (612)682-4444
Buffalo, MN 55313 Fax: (612)682-3542
Free: (800)380-1360
E-mail: 1360krwc@uslink.net

Format: Full Service. **Networks:** NBC; Minnesota News. **Founded:** 1971. **Operating Hours:** 6 a.m.-6:30 p.m. **Key Personnel:** Joe Carlson, Pres./Gen. Mgr.; Tim Matthews, Program Dir.; Gary Lee, News Dir./Outdoors Editor. **Local Programs:** *Spotlight*, Tim Matthews. **Wattage:** 500. **Ad Rates:** $7.75-9.75 for 30 seconds; $9.75-11.75 for 60 seconds.

BUFFALO LAKE, pop. 782.

SW MN. Renville Co. 20 mi E. of Olivia. Residential.

15865 News Mirror
100 Main N. Phone: (612)833-2001
Box 1280 Fax: (320)833-2077
Buffalo Lake, MN 55314-0128
Publication E-mail: newsmirror@aol.com

Community newspaper. **Founded:** 1892. **Freq:** Weekly (Wed.). **Print Method:** Offset. **Cols./Page:** 6. **Col. Width:** 28 nonpareils. **Col. Depth:** 301 agate lines. **Key Personnel:** Ken Hubin, Editor and Publisher, kennews@aol.com; John Hubin, Publisher. **USPS:** 069-520. **Subscription Rates:** $24 individuals; $27 out of area; $32 out of state. **Remarks:** Accepts advertising.
Ad Rates: GLR: $.26 **Circ:** ‡2,800
BW: $483
4C: $825

BURNSVILLE, pop. 35,674.

SE MN. Dakota Co. 12 mi. S. of Saint Paul. Residential.

15866 Burnsville/Savage Sun Current
Minnesota Sun Publications
7831 E. Bush Lake Rd. Phone: (612)896-4700
Bloomington, MN 55439 Fax: (612)896-4728
Publication E-mail: burnsvillesuncurrent@mnsunpub.com

Community newspaper (tabloid). **Founded:** 1984. **Freq:** Weekly (Wed.). **Print Method:** Offset. **Cols./Page:** 4. **Col. Width:** 2 1/2 inches. **Col. Depth:** 15 inches. **Key Personnel:** Doug Dane, Publisher, phone (612)896-4787; Pamela Austib, Advertising Dir., phone (612)897-5486. **URL:** http://www.mnsun.com.
Circ: Free 29,698

15867 Dakota County Tribune
Dakota County Tribune, Inc.
1525 E. Hwy. 13 Phone: (612)894-1111
Burnsville, MN 55337 Fax: (612)894-1859
Publisher E-mail: btemple@summittpoint.com

Community newspaper. **Founded:** 1884. **Freq:** Weekly (Thurs.). **Print Method:** Offset. **Cols./Page:** 5. **Col. Width:** 15.25 nonpareils. **Col. Depth:** 218 agate lines. **Key Personnel:** Joseph R. Clay, Publisher; Daniel H. Clay, Publisher. **Subscription Rates:** $24. **Remarks:** Accepts advertising.
Ad Rates: GLR: $.72 **Circ:** ‡1,084
BW: $674.05
PCI: $8.84

CALEDONIA†, pop. 2,691.

SW MN. Houston Co. 23 mi. SW of LaCrosse, WI. Butter factory; lumber, grist mills; iron works. Hatcheries. Hardwood timber. Stock, dairy, poultry farms. Agricultural trade center.

15868 Argus
Caledonia Publishing Co., Inc.
121 W. Main St. Phone: (507)724-3475
Box 227
Caledonia, MN 55921
Community newspaper. **Founded:** 1862. **Freq:** Weekly (Tues.). **Print Method:** Offset. **Cols./Page:** 7. **Col. Width:** 12 picas. **Col. Depth:** 301 agate lines. **Key Personnel:** Thomas Murphy, Editor. **ISSN:** 2350-2600. **Subscription Rates:** $23.50; $26 out of state. **Remarks:** Accepts advertising.
Ad Rates: GLR: $.32 **Circ:** 3,295
BW: $674.24
4C: $854.58
PCI: $4.48

CAMBRIDGE†, pop. 3,170.

EC MN. Isanti Co. 40 mi. N. of Minneapolis. Creamery; woolen mill. Agriculture. Potatoes, oats, corn, soybeans.

15869 Cambridge Star
North Star Media
PO Box 512 Phone: (612)689-1181
Cambridge, MN 55008 Fax: (612)689-1185

Community newspaper. **Founded:** 1905. **Freq:** Weekly (Wed.). **Print Method:** Offset. **Cols./Page:** 6. **Col. Width:** 26 nonpareils. **Col. Depth:** 301 agate lines. **Key Personnel:** Linda Craig, Editor; Bob Swantek, Publisher. **Subscription Rates:** $18. **Remarks:** Accepts advertising.
Ad Rates: GLR: $.75 **Circ:** Free 9,545
4C: $865 Paid 603
PCI: $7.25

15870 County News
ECM Group
234 S. Main St. Phone: (612)689-1981
PO Box 352 Fax: (612)689-4372
Cambridge, MN 55008-0352
Free: (800)473-1981

Community newspaper. **Founded:** 1900. **Freq:** Weekly. **Print Method:** Offset. **Cols./Page:** 6. **Col. Depth:** 21 inches. **Key Personnel:** Evelyn M. Puffer, Editor; Elmer L. Andersen, Publisher; Marcy Overby, Advertising Rep. **ISSN:** 8750-2267. **Subscription Rates:** $29; $25 senior citizens; $36 out of state. **Remarks:** Accepts advertising. **Formerly**: Isanti County News.
Ad Rates: BW: $450 **Circ:** 10,600
PCI: $6.00

15871 Scotsman
ECM Group
234 S. Main St. Phone: (612)689-1981
PO Box 352 Fax: (612)689-4372
Cambridge, MN 55008-0352
Free: (800)473-1981
Publication E-mail: print.cambridge@ecm.inc.com

Shopper. **Founded:** 1963. **Freq:** Weekly (Sun.). **Print Method:** Offset. **Trim Size:** 11 1/2 x 16. **Cols./Page:** 6. **Col. Width:** 24 nonpareils. **Col. Depth:** 224 agate lines. **Key Personnel:** Marge Winkelman, Editor; Julian L. Andersen, Publisher. **Subscription Rates:** Free; $37 by mail. **Remarks:** Accepts advertising. **URL:** http://www.ecm-inc.com.
Ad Rates: GLR: $.83 **Circ:** Paid ‡508
BW: $1,719 Free ‡60,000
4C: $2,019
PCI: $19.10

15872 WREV-FM - 105.3
540 N. Emerson Ave. Phone: (612)689-1055
Cambridge, MN 55008 Fax: (612)339-3163

Format: Full Service; Middle-of-the-Road (MOR). **Founded:** 1973. **Formerly**: KABG-FM (1991); KXLV-FM. **Operating Hours:** Continuous. **Key Personnel:** Todd J. Garamella, Contact. **Wattage:** 25,000. **Ad Rates:** $7-12 for 15 seconds; $10-15 for 30 seconds; $12-18 for 60 seconds.

CANNON FALLS, pop. 2,653.

SE MN. Goodhue Co. Goodhue Co. (SE). 22 m W of Red Wing. Manufactures stock feed, malt & barley products, farm products. Stock, dairy, poultry, grain farms.

15873 Beacon
120 S. 4th St. Phone: (507)263-3991
Cannon Falls, MN 55009
Newspaper with Report orientation. **Founded:** Aug. 4, 1876. **Freq:** Weekly (Thurs.). **Print Method:** Offset. **Cols./Page:** 6. **Col. Width:** 2 inches. **Col. Depth:** 21.5 picas. **Key Personnel:** Richard Dalton, Editor. **Subscription Rates:** $21 individuals; $24 out of area. **Remarks:** Accepts advertising.
Ad Rates: GLR: $.20 **Circ:** ‡4,200
PCI: $4.95

15874 Cannon Shopper
Beacon
120 S. 4th St. Phone: (507)263-3991
Cannon Falls, MN 55009
Shopper. **Founded:** 1976. **Freq:** Weekly (Mon.). **Print Method:** Offset. **Cols./Page:** 6. **Col. Width:** 27 nonpareils. **Col. Depth:** 294 agate lines. **Key Personnel:** G. Richard Dalton, Editor; Dave Templin, Advertising Mgr. **Subscription Rates:** Free. **Remarks:** Accepts advertising.
Ad Rates: GLR: $.24 **Circ:** Free ‡8,800
PCI: $6.40

CASS LAKE

15875 Cass Lake Times
Olson Communications, Inc.
PO Box 398 Phone: (218)335-2290
Cass Lake, MN 56633
Community newspaper. **Founded:** Apr. 26, 1899. **Freq:** Weekly (Thurs.). **Print Method:** Offset. **Cols./Page:** 6. **Col. Width:** 1 5/8 inches. **Col. Depth:** 16 inches. **Key Personnel:** Victor W. Olson, Editor and Publisher, phone (218)652-3475. **USPS:** 092-800. **Subscription Rates:** $22; $26 out of area. **Remarks:** Accepts advertising.
Ad Rates: BW: $355.20 **Circ:** 1,450
4C: $595.20
PCI: $3.70

CHAMPLIN

15876 Champlin Dayton Press
Larson Publications, Inc.
33 2nd St. NE Phone: (612)425-3323
Box 280 Fax: (612)425-1360
Osseo, MN 55369
Publication E-mail: pressnews@mr.net

Community newspaper. **Founded:** 1974. **Freq:** Weekly (Tues.). **Print Method:** Offset. **Cols./Page:** 7. **Col. Width:** 24 nonpareils. **Col. Depth:** 294 agate lines. **Key Personnel:** Don R. Larson, Publisher. **Remarks:** Accepts advertising.
Ad Rates: PCI: $14 **Circ:** Paid 2,220
Free 5,338

15877 Sidewalks
PO Box 321 Phone: (612)824-6734
Champlin, MN 55316-0321
Literary magazine containing poetry, short prose, and art. **Founded:** 1991. **Freq:** Semiannual. **Trim Size:** 5 1/2 x 8 1/2. **Key Personnel:** Tom Heie, Editor. **ISSN:** 1059-2210. **Subscription Rates:** $9 individuals; $6 single issue; $12 institutions. **Remarks:** Advertising not accepted.
Circ: Paid 250
Non-paid 50

CHANHASSEN

15878 Chanhassen Excelsior
Minnesota Sun Publications
7831 E. Bush Lake Rd. Phone: (612)896-4700
Bloomington, MN 55439 Fax: (612)896-4728

Community newspaper (tabloid). **Founded:** 1988. **Freq:** Weekly (Wed.). **Print Method:** Offset. **Cols./Page:** 4. **Col. Width:** 2 1/2 inches. **Col. Depth:** 15 inches. **Key Personnel:** Don Thurlow, Publisher; Paul Johnson, Editor.
Circ: Free 5,485

15879 The Chanhassen Villager
Southwest Suburban Publishing
80 W. 78th St. Phone: (612)934-5045
PO Box 99 Fax: (612)934-7690
Chanhassen, MN 55317
Community newspaper. **Founded:** 1987. **Freq:** Weekly (Thurs.). **Print Method:** Offset. **Trim Size:** 13 x 21 1/2. **Cols./Page:** 6. **Col. Width:** 2 1/8 inches. **Key Personnel:** Dean Trippler, Editor; Mark Weber, Publisher; Gary Klatt, Advertising Mgr.; Peter Holzer, Editor. **Subscription Rates:** Free; $20 (mail); $33 out of area. **Remarks:** Accepts advertising. **Formerly**: Villager (1991).
Ad Rates: BW: $967.50 **Circ:** Paid ‡85
4C: $1,467.50 Free ‡4,290
PCI: $7.50

CHASKA†, pop. 8,346.

SC MN. Carver Co. On Minnesota River, 20 mi. SW of Minneapolis. Manufactures beet sugar, sauerkraut, pickles, butter. Truck, dairy farms.

15880 Chaska Herald
Southwest Suburban Publishing
123 W. 2nd St. Phone: (612)448-2650
PO Box 113 Fax: (612)448-3146
Chaska, MN 55318
Publication E-mail: editor@chaskaherald.com

Community newspaper. **Founded:** 1862. **Freq:** Weekly (Thurs.). **Print Method:** Offset. **Trim Size:** 13 x 21. **Cols./Page:** 6. **Col. Width:** 28 nonpareils. **Col. Depth:** 301 agate lines. **Key Personnel:** Robert Siegel, Editor; Stan Rolfsrud, Publisher; Gary Klatt, Advertising Dir.; Ruby Mohlin, Circulation Mgr. **Subscription Rates:** $26 individuals; $38 out of area. **Remarks:** Accepts advertising. **Formerly**: Carver County Herald (1990).
Ad Rates: BW: $851.40 **Circ:** Free 400
4C: $1,141.40 Paid 4,200
PCI: $6.60

Engineering Contacts - See Minneapolis

15881 Minnesota Insurance
Meusey Communications
1107 Hazeltine Blvd., Ste. 539 Phone: (612)448-8816
Chaska, MN 55318-1008
Insurance magazine. **Founded:** Dec. 1982. **Freq:** Monthly. **Print Method:** Offset. **Trim Size:** 8 1/2 x 11. **Cols./Page:** 3. **Col. Width:** 26 nonpareils. **Col. Depth:** 140 agate lines. **Key Personnel:** Jack Meusey, Editor and Publisher. **Subscription Rates:** $17.
Ad Rates: BW: $598 **Circ:** Non-paid ‡3,987
4C: $898

15882 KSMM-AM - 1530
1107 Hazeltine Blvd., Ste.520 Phone: (612)361-5526
Chaska, MN 55318 Fax: (612)361-5529
E-mail: kkcman@internetmci.com

Format: Jazz. **Networks:** Mutual Broadcasting System. **Owner:** NorthStar Broadcasting, 1209 Pacific Ave., Benson, MN 56215, (320)843-4344. **Founded:** 1963. **Formerly**: KSMM-AM (1986); KKCM-AM. **Operating Hours:** Continuous. **ADI:** Minneapolis-St. Paul, MN. **Key Personnel:** John R. Hull, General Mgr., ksmmradio@excite.com; Louise Krohn, Office Mgr. **Wattage:** 8600. **Ad Rates:** $6 for 15 seconds; $12-15 for 30 seconds; $15-18 for 60 seconds. **URL:** http://www.kwmm.com.

CHISHOLM, pop. 5,930.

NE MN. St. Louis Co. 8 mi. NW of Hibblings. Tourism. Manufactures outerware, tools, specialty meat products, noodles, spaghetti sauces. Iron mines; timber; trucks. Dairy farms. Agriculture. Potatoes, vegetables, hay.

15883 The Chisholm Tribune-Press
216 W. Lake St. Phone: (218)254-4432
Chisholm, MN 55719-1138 Fax: (218)254-7141

Community newspaper. **Founded:** 1901. **Freq:** Weekly (Wed.). **Print Method:** Letterpress and offset. **Cols./Page:** 6. **Col. Width:** 2 inches. **Col. Depth:** 21 inches. **Key Personnel:** Brian K. Anderson, Editor. **Subscription Rates:** $22 individuals; $26 out of area. **Remarks:** Accepts advertising. **Formed by the merger of**: Tribune-Press; Free Press.
Ad Rates: GLR: $.40 **Circ:** ‡2,700
BW: $415.30
4C: $515.80
SAU: $3.92
PCI: $3.30

CHOKIO, pop. 559.

WC MN. Stevens Co. 10o mi. W. of Saint Cloud. Grain farms.

15884 Chokio Review
PO Box 96 Phone: (320)324-2405
Chokio, MN 56221 Fax: (320)324-2449
Publication E-mail: hcreview@runestone.net

Community newspaper. **Subtitle:** The Chokio Review. **Founded:** 1897. **Freq:** Weekly (Thurs.). **Print Method:** Offset. **Trim Size:** 8 x 11. **Cols./Page:** 5. **Col. Width:** 23 nonpareils. **Col. Depth:** 210 agate lines. **Key Personnel:** Ronda Asmus,

Editor; Nick Ripperger, Publisher, ripnican@infolink.morris.mn.us; Anne Ripperger, Publisher, ripnican@atsinfolink.morris.mn.us. **USPS:** 106-300. **Subscription Rates:** $16 individuals; $21 out of area. **Remarks:** Accepts advertising.
Ad Rates: BW: $200 **Circ:** ‡1,000
4C: $320
SAU: $3.04
PCI: $2.85

CLARA CITY, pop. 1,574.

SW MN. Chippewa Co. 100 mi. W. of Minneapolis. Grain, stock, poultry farms. Corn, sugar beets, barley, oats.

15885 Clara City Herald
Box 458 Phone: (612)847-3130
Clara City, MN 56222 Fax: (320)847-2630

General newspaper. **Founded:** 1895. **Freq:** Weekly (Wed.). **Print Method:** Offset. **Cols./Page:** 6. **Col. Width:** 26 nonpareils. **Col. Depth:** 301 agate lines. **Key Personnel:** T.J. Almen, Publisher. **USPS:** 115-080. **Subscription Rates:** $17. **Remarks:** Accepts advertising.
Ad Rates: SAU: $3.00 **Circ:** ‡1,490
PCI: $3

CLARISSA

15886 Independent News Herald
310 Main St. Phone: (218)756-2131
Clarissa, MN 56440 Fax: (218)756-2126
Publisher E-mail: inhnews@means.net

Newspaper. **Founded:** 1891. **Freq:** Weekly (Wed.). **Print Method:** Offset. **Cols./Page:** 6. **Col. Width:** 2 inches. **Col. Depth:** 301 agate lines. **Key Personnel:** Ernest Silbernagel, Publisher; Diane Silbernagel, Publisher. **USPS:** 163-640. **Subscription Rates:** $20 individuals; $36 out of state. **URL:** http://www.inhnews.com. **Absorbed**: Clarissa Independent (1993).
Ad Rates: BW: $265 **Circ:** 2,700
SAU: $4.45

CLINTON, pop. 622.

WC MN. Big Stone Co. 10 mi. N. of Ortonville. Farming community.

15887 Northern Star
Box 368 Phone: (320)325-5152
Clinton, MN 56225 Fax: (612)839-3761

Local newspaper serving the communities of Clinton, Graceville, and Beardsley, MN. **Founded:** May 1, 1965. **Freq:** Weekly (Thurs.). **Print Method:** Offset. **Cols./Page:** 6. **Col. Width:** 26 nonpareils. **Col. Depth:** 301 agate lines. **Key Personnel:** Lois Torgerson, Editor; J.D. Kaercher, Publisher, phone (320)839-6163; Denese Gustafson, Advertising Mgr. **Subscription Rates:** $20 individuals; $26 out of area. **Remarks:** Accepts advertising. **Formerly**: Graceville Enterprise, Clinton Advocate.
Ad Rates: PCI: $4.50 **Circ:** Paid 1,990
Non-paid 20

CLOQUET, pop. 11,142.

EC MN. Carlton Co. 18 mi. W. of Duluth. Manufactures paper, knitted garments, matches, insulation materials, building board, chemicals. Dairy, poultry farms.

15888 The Cloquet Billboard
Cloquet Newspapers
1418 Hwy. 33 S. Phone: (218)879-6761
PO Box 236 Fax: (218)879-6696
Cloquet, MN 55720
Newspaper-Twice weekly, Time Shopper-Saturday. **Founded:** 1884. **Freq:** twice weekly, Wed. & Sat. **Print Method:** Offset. **Cols./Page:** 6. **Col. Width:** 12.3 picas. **Col. Depth:** 21 1/2 inches. **Key Personnel:** Scott Elwood, Publisher. **ISSN:** 0890-5703. **Subscription Rates:** $.50 single issue; $30 In county; $40 out of area. **Remarks:** Accepts advertising.
Ad Rates: GLR: $8 **Circ:** Free ‡3,500
BW: $8 Sat. ‡16,000
4C: $1,000
SAU: $8

15889 The Pine Knot
Cloquet Newspapers
1418 Hwy. 33 S. Phone: (218)879-6761
PO Box 236 Fax: (218)879-6696
Cloquet, MN 55720
Community newspaper. **Founded:** 1884. **Freq:** Semiweekly (Wed. and Sat.). **Print Method:** Web offset. **Cols./Page:** 6. **Col. Width:** 12.3 picas. **Col. Depth:** 21 1/2 inches. **Key Personnel:** Pat Faherty, Editor; Scott Elwood, Publisher. **Subscription Rates:** $30 individuals; $40 out of country. **Remarks:** Accepts advertising.
Ad Rates: PCI: $9.50 **Circ:** Combined ⊕**20,000**

15890 KMFG-FM - 102.9
1104 Cloquet Ave. Phone: (218)263-7531
Cloquet, MN 55720

Format: Classic Rock. **Networks:** Satellite Music Network. **Owner:** Q. V. II, Inc., 702 Poplar Ave., Cloquet, MN 55720. **Operating Hours:** Continuous. **Key Personnel:** Dennis Martin, General Mgr. **Wattage:** 25,000.

COLD SPRING, pop. 2,336.

SE MN. Stearns Co. 15 mi. SW of Saint Cloud.

15891 Cold Spring Record
Cold Spring Record Inc.
PO Box 456 Phone: (612)685-8621
Cold Spring, MN 56320 Fax: (612)685-8885
Publisher E-mail: csrecord@means.net

Local newspaper. **Founded:** 1899. **Freq:** Weekly. **Print Method:** Offset. **Trim Size:** 16 x 23. **Cols./Page:** 6. **Col. Width:** 28 nonpareils. **Col. Depth:** 301 agate lines. **Key Personnel:** Michael E. Austreng, Editor and Publisher. **USPS:** 121-020. **Subscription Rates:** $15. **Remarks:** Accepts advertising.
Ad Rates: SAU: $4.60 **Circ:** Paid ‡3,600
PCI: $4.05 Free ‡25

COLERAINE

15892 Coleraine Cable Communications System
302 Roosevelt Ave. Phone: (218)245-2112
PO Box 670 Fax: (218)245-2123
Coleraine, MN 55722

Owner: City of Coleraine, at above address. **Founded:** Jan. 1, 1992. **Key Personnel:** Temper Payne, Technician. **Cities Served:** Coleraine, MN: subscribing households 374; 41 channels; 2 community access channels; 168 hours per week community access programming.

COLLEGEVILLE, pop. 3,075.

C MN. Stearns Co. 12 mi. NW of Saint Cloud. St. John's University. Dairy farms.

15893 Sisters Today
The Liturgical Press
Attn: Jean Zenzen Phone: (612)363-2718
PO Box 7500 Fax: (612)363-3278
Collegeville, MN 56321-7500
Free: (800)858-5450
Publication E-mail: sales@litpress.org
Publisher E-mail: sales@litpress.org

Journal presenting reflections on theology and various aspects of spirituality, social justice, growth in the Church, and personal development. **Subtitle:** Exploring the vision of women and the Church in our time. **Founded:** Sept. 1929. **Freq:** Bimonthly. **Print Method:** Offset. **Trim Size:** 6 x 9. **Cols./Page:** 1 and 2. **Col. Width:** 4 5/8 inches. **Col. Depth:** 7 1/2 inches. **Key Personnel:** S. Mary Anthony Wagner, O.S.B., Editor, swagner@csbsju.edu; Jean Zenzen, Advertising Mgr., phone (320)363-2718, fax (320)363-3278, sales@litpress.org. **ISSN:** 0037-590X. **Subscription Rates:** $22 individuals; $40 two years; $24 out of country; $4.50 single issue. **Remarks:** Accepts advertising. **Formerly**: Sponsa Regis.
Ad Rates: BW: $330 **Circ:** Paid 3,500

15894 Worship
The Liturgical Press
St. John's Abbey Phone: (612)363-2213
Pox 7500 Fax: (800)445-5899
Collegeville, MN 56321
Free: (800)858-5450
Publication E-mail: litpress@osb.org
Publisher E-mail: sales@litpress.org

Liturgical studies magazine. **Founded:** Nov. 1926. **Freq:** Bimonthly. **Print Method:** Offset. **Trim Size:** 6 x 9 1/4. **Cols./Page:** 1. **Col. Width:** 52 nonpareils. **Col. Depth:** 98 agate lines. **Key Personnel:** R. Kevin Seasoltz, Editor; Michelle Verkuilen, Advertising Mgr. **ISSN:** 0043-941X. **Subscription Rates:** $26 individuals; $51; $28 other countries; $36 institutions; $4.50 single copy. **Remarks:** Accepts advertising. **URL:** http://www.osborg/litpress.
Ad Rates: BW: $345 **Circ:** 5,000

15895 KJNB-FM - 99.9
St. Johns University Phone: (612)363-3380
Box 1255 Fax: (612)363-3492
Collegeville, MN 56321
E-mail: kjnb@csbsju.edu

Format: News; Alternative/New Music/Progressive; Sports. **Founded:** 1977. **Formerly**: KSJU-FM (1977). **Operating Hours:** 9 a.m.-1 a.m., Sept.-May. **Key Personnel:** Joe Cragg, Gen. Mgr./Programming Dir.; Keri Phillips, Assoc. Program Dir.; Chris Polikowsky, Assoc. Program Dir.; Mike Sersch, Assoc. Program Dir.; Andrew Ayers, Gen. Mgr./Music Dir.; Tom Loftus, Assoc. Music Dir.; Sean Peterson, Assoc. Music Dir.; Heath Pochucha, Assoc. Music Dir.; Josh Raub, Assoc. Music Dir.; Amy Hoelmer, Accountant; John Murphy, Marketing Dir.; Joe Reilly, Marketing Dir.; Katie Cerney, Fundraising Dir.; Matt Blaisdell, News Dir.; Craig Maki, Sports Dir.; Tony Baumert, General Staff Rep.; Matt Michels, Engineer. **URL:** http://www.users.cbsju.edu/~kjnb.

15896 KNSR-FM - 88.9
PO Box 7011 Phone: (320)363-7702
St. John's University Fax: (320)363-4948
Collegeville, MN 56321

Format: Public Radio; News; Information. **Networks:** National Public Radio (NPR); American Public Radio (APR); Minnesota Public Radio. **Founded:** 1988. **Operating Hours:** Continuous. **Key Personnel:** Mike Olson, General Mgr.; Laura McCallum, News Dir. **Wattage:** 100,000. **Ad Rates:** Noncommercial.

15897 KSJR-FM - 90.1
St. John's University Phone: (612)363-7702
PO Box 7011 Fax: (612)363-4948
Collegeville, MN 56321

Format: Public Radio; Classical. **Networks:** Minnesota Public Radio; American Public Radio (APR). **Owner:** Minnesota Public Radio, 45 E. 7th St., St. Paul, MN 55101, (612)290-1500. **Founded:** 1967. **Operating Hours:** Continuous. **Key Personnel:** Laura McCallum, News Dir.; Michael Olson, General Mgr., molson@mpr.org. **Wattage:** 100,000. **Ad Rates:** Noncommercial.

COOK, pop. 687.

NC MN. Saint Louis Co. 25 mi. NNW of Virginia.

15898 Cook News-Herald
Cook News
PO Box 1179 Phone: (218)666-5944
Cook, MN 55723 Fax: (218)666-5609
Publication E-mail: cnh@vermilionnet.com

Community newspaper. **Founded:** 1903. **Freq:** Weekly. **Print Method:** Offset. **Trim Size:** 11 x 15. **Cols./Page:** 4. **Col. Width:** 14 picas. **Key Personnel:** Gary D. Albertson, Editor and Publisher. **Subscription Rates:** $22 local. **Remarks:** Accepts advertising.
Ad Rates: PCI: $4.68 **Circ:** 3,652

COON RAPIDS, pop. 35,826.

SEC MN. Anoka Co. 11 mi. N of Minneapolis. Residential.

15899 Anoka County Shopper
4101 Coon Rapids Blvd. Phone: (612)421-4444
Coon Rapids, MN 55433-2585 Fax: (612)421-4315

Shopper. **Founded:** 1934. **Freq:** Weekly (Wed.). **Print Method:** Offset. **Cols./Page:** 6. **Col. Width:** 26 nonpareils. **Col. Depth:** 308 agate lines. **Key Personnel:** Arch G. Pease, Publisher; Hugh Campbell, Advertising Mgr. **Subscription Rates:** $10.
Circ: Free 62,553

15900 Anoka County Union
Anoka County Shopper
4101 Coon Rapids Blvd. Phone: (612)421-4444
Coon Rapids, MN 55433-2585 Fax: (612)421-4315

Local newspaper. **Founded:** 1865. **Freq:** Weekly (Fri.). **Print Method:** Offset. **Cols./Page:** 6. **Col. Width:** 26 nonpareils. **Col. Depth:** 308 agate lines. **Key Personnel:** Kathryn Cassidy, Editor; Arch G. Pease, Publisher; Hugh Campbell, Advertising Mgr. **Subscription Rates:** $10.
Circ: ‡5,329

Blaine Spring Lake Park Life - See Blaine

15901 Coon Rapids Herald
Anoka County Shopper
4101 Coon Rapids Blvd. Phone: (612)421-4444
Coon Rapids, MN 55433-2585 Fax: (612)421-4315

Local newspaper. **Founded:** 1866. **Freq:** Weekly (Fri.). **Print Method:** Offset. **Cols./Page:** 6. **Col. Width:** 26 nonpareils. **Col. Depth:** 308 agate lines. **Key Personnel:** Peter Bodley,

Editor; Arch G. Pease, Publisher; Hugh Campbell, Advertising Mgr. **Subscription Rates:** $10.
Circ: ‡3,430

COTTAGE GROVE, pop. 18,994.

SE MN. Washington Co. 10 mi. SE of Saint Paul, on the Mississippi River. Residential. Manufactures chemicals, reflective & printing products. Dairy, poultry, truck farms.

15902 South Washington County Bulletin
7584 80th St., S Phone: (651)459-3434
Cottage Grove, MN 55016 Fax: (651)459-9491
Publication E-mail:
sowashingtoncountybulletin@fishnet.com

Newspaper. **Founded:** 1958. **Freq:** Weekly (Wed.). **Print Method:** Offset. **Cols./Page:** 6. **Col. Width:** 24 nonpareils. **Col. Depth:** 294 agate lines. **Key Personnel:** Steve Messick, Publisher; Jeff Patterson, General Mgr.; Keith Neis, Editor. **Subscription Rates:** $28. **Remarks:** Accepts advertising. **Formerly**: Washington County Bulletin.
Ad Rates: BW: $1,064.25 **Circ:** ⊕10,462
4C: $1,364.25
PCI: $8.25

COTTONWOOD, pop. 794.

NE MN. Lyon Co. 13 mi. NNE of Marshall.

15903 Tri-County News
74 W. Main Phone: (507)423-6239
PO Box 76 Fax: (507)423-6230
Cottonwood, MN 56229
Local newspaper. **Subtitle:** Tri-County News. **Founded:** 1892. **Freq:** Weekly. **Print Method:** Offset. **Trim Size:** 14 x 21. **Cols./Page:** 6. **Col. Width:** 2 1/8 inches. **Col. Depth:** 21 inches. **Key Personnel:** Jeff Meyer, Publisher; Rae Yost, Editor. **Subscription Rates:** $20 individuals; $22 out of area; $25 out of state. **Remarks:** Accepts advertising. **Formerly:** Independent/Current/Enterprise News (1989); Tri-County Advocate (1990).
Ad Rates: BW: $387 **Circ:** 2,200
4C: $587
PCI: $3.35

CROOKSTON†, pop. 8,628.

NW MN. Polk Co. 25 mi. SE of Grand Forks, ND. Manufactures wind energy components, aluminum castings, custom drapes and quilts, agricultural fertilizers and chemicals, agricultural equipment, precast concrete items. Agriculture. Grain, sugar beets, sunflowers, potatoes, livestock, wheat.

15904 Crookston Daily Times
Crookston Times Printing Co.
124 S. Broadway Phone: (218)281-2730
PO Box 615 Fax: (218)281-7234
Crookston, MN 56716-1955
General newspaper. **Founded:** 1885. **Freq:** Daily (eve.). **Print Method:** Offset. **Cols./Page:** 6. **Col. Width:** 2 1/16 inches. **Col. Depth:** 21 1/2 inches. **Key Personnel:** Twylla Altepeter, Editor; Randy Hultgren, Publisher. **Subscription Rates:** $94. **Remarks:** Accepts advertising.
Ad Rates: GLR: $1.08 **Circ:** Paid 4,195
BW: $899.13 Free 250
4C: $190
SAU: $6.42

15905 Our Northland Diocese
1200 Memorial Dr. Fax: (218)281-3328
PO Box 610
Crookston, MN 56716
Catholic tabloid. **Founded:** Oct. 1946. **Freq:** Semimonthly. **Print Method:** Offset. **Cols./Page:** 5. **Col. Width:** 1 3/4 inches. **Col. Depth:** 13 inches. **Key Personnel:** Carol Evenson, Editor; Diocese of Crookston, Publisher. **Subscription Rates:** $11 individuals. **Remarks:** Accepts advertising.
Ad Rates: BW: $335 **Circ:** ‡14,200
PCI: $6.25

15906 KROX-AM - 1260
208 S. Main Phone: (218)281-1140
PO Box 620 Fax: (218)281-5036
Crookston, MN 56716

Format: News; Talk. **Networks:** NBC; Minnesota News. **Owner:** Gopher Communications Co., at above address. **Founded:** 1948. **Operating Hours:** 5:30 a.m.-midnight; 10% network, 90% local. **Key Personnel:** Frank Fee, Contact; Mary Ann Simmons, News Dir.; Raymond Lee, Program Dir.; Chris Melbye, Music Dir. **Local Programs:** *Coaches Corner, Focus on Education*, MaryAnn Simmons, (218)281-1140; *Steve & Ray Show*, Steve Krueger, (218)281-1140. **Wattage:** 1000. **Ad Rates:** $5.60-10 for 30 seconds; $7.30-12.45 for 60 seconds.

CROSBY, pop. 2,218.

C MN. Crow Wing Co. 15 mi. NW of Brainerd. Lake resort. Timber. Manufacturing.

15907 Crosby-Ironton Courier
Crosby-Ironton Courier, Inc.
12 E. Main St. Phone: (218)546-5029
Box 67 Fax: (218)546-8352
Crosby, MN 56441
Community newspaper. **Founded:** 1911. **Freq:** Weekly (Wed.). **Print Method:** Offset. **Cols./Page:** 6. **Col. Width:** 12 picas. **Col. Depth:** 21 1/2 inches. **Key Personnel:** Amy Sharpe, Managing Editor; Dina McDonough, News Editor; Thomas M. Swensen, Publisher. **USPS:** 138-480. **Subscription Rates:** $20; $25 out of state. **Remarks:** Accepts advertising.
Ad Rates: SAU: $7 **Circ:** Paid 4,282
PCI: $7 Free 51

DASSEL, pop. 1,066.

SC MN. Meeker Co. 54 mi. W. of Minneapolis. Lake resort. Hospital signal systems, portable lake docks & crop drier factories. Hatcheries. Seed corn. Grain, dairy, poultry farms.

15908 Enterprise Dispatch
Cardan, Inc.
261 Atlantic Ave. Phone: (320)275-2192
PO Box 340 Fax: (320)275-2193
Dassel, MN 55325
Publication E-mail: danholje@cmgate.com
Publisher E-mail: dednews@cmgate.com

Community newspaper. **Founded:** 1918. **Freq:** Weekly (Wed.). **Print Method:** Offset. **Cols./Page:** 6. **Col. Width:** 28 nonpareils. **Col. Depth:** 301 agate lines. **Key Personnel:** Carolyn H. Holje, Editor. **USPS:** 120-800. **Subscription Rates:** $22; $26 out of area; $30 out of state. **Remarks:** Advertising not accepted for alcoholic beverages. **Formerly**: Cokato Enterprise; Dassel Dispatch.
Ad Rates: GLR: $.06 **Circ:** 3,500
BW: $593.40
4C: $788.25
SAU: $4.25
PCI: $4.60

DAWSON, pop. 1,901.

SW MN. Lac qui Parle Co. On Lac qui Parle River, 150 mi. W. of Minneapolis. Trucking. elevators; soybean-processing, feed plants. Milk and cheese processing. Ships livestock and grain. Stock, grain, poultry and dairy farms.

15909 Sentinel
PO Box 1015
Dawson, MN 56232

Newspaper with a Republican orientation. **Founded:** 1884. **Freq:** Weekly (Wed.). **Print Method:** Offset. **Cols./Page:** 6. **Col. Width:** 26 nonpareils. **Col. Depth:** 301 agate lines. **Key Personnel:** Steve J. Holland, Editor and Publisher. **Subscription Rates:** $19. **Remarks:** Accepts advertising.
Ad Rates: BW: $325 **Circ:** Paid ‡2,150
PCI: $4 Free ‡15

DEER RIVER, pop. 815.

SC MN. Itasca Co. 14 mi. WNW of Grand Rapids.

15910 Western Itasca Review
Deer River Publishing
PO Box 427 Phone: (218)246-8533
Deer River, MN 56636 Fax: (218)246-8540
Publisher E-mail: drpublsh@paulbunyan.net

Local newspaper. **Founded:** Apr. 1898. **Freq:** Weekly. **Print Method:** Tab. **Trim Size:** 11 1/4 x 15. **Cols./Page:** 6. **Col. Width:** 1 5/8 inches. **Col. Depth:** 14 inches. **Key Personnel:** Bob Barnacle, Editor and Publisher. **Subscription Rates:** $22; $29 out of area; $31 out of state. **Remarks:** Accepts advertising. **Formed by the merger of**: Deer River News; Itasca Progressive.
Ad Rates: BW: $277.20 **Circ:** Paid 1,622
PCI: $2.85 Free 23

DETROIT LAKES†, pop. 7,106.

WC MN. Becker Co. 50 mi. E. of Fargo, ND. Manufactures furnace fittings, silos, boats, sausage. Resort. Mink ranching; hatchery. Stock, dairy, truck, poultry farms. Potatoes.

15911 Becker County Record
Forum Communications Co.
PO Box 826 Phone: (218)847-3151
Detroit Lakes, MN 56502 Fax: (218)847-9409
Free: (800)422-1409
Publisher E-mail: digitali@dlprinting.com

Local newspaper. **Founded:** 1871. **Freq:** Weekly (Wed.). **Print Method:** Offset. Uses mats. **Cols./Page:** 6. **Col. Width:** 25 nonpareils. **Col. Depth:** 301 agate lines. **Key Personnel:** Jamie Marks, Editor, jamiem@dlprinting.com; Dennis Winskowski, Publisher, dennisw@dlprinting.com; David Aune, Advertising Mgr. **Subscription Rates:** Free. **Remarks:** Accepts advertising.
Ad Rates: BW: $1,354.50 **Circ:** Free ❑12,092
4C: $1,679.50 Paid ❑471
SAU: $10.50
PCI: $10.50

15912 Detroit Lakes Tribune
Forum Communications Co.
511 Washington Phone: (218)847-3151
Detroit Lakes, MN 56502 Fax: (218)847-9409
Publisher E-mail: digitali@dlprinting.com

Local newspaper. **Founded:** 1907. **Freq:** Weekly (Sun.). **Print Method:** Offset. Uses mats. **Cols./Page:** 6. **Col. Width:** 25 nonpareils. **Col. Depth:** 301 agate lines. **Key Personnel:** Jamie Marks, Editor, jamiem@dlprinting.com; Dennis Winskowski, Publisher, dennisw@dlprinting.com; David Aune, Advertising Mgr. **Subscription Rates:** $22 local; $24 in state; $41 out of state. **Remarks:** Accepts advertising.
Ad Rates: BW: $1,354.50 **Circ:** Combined ❑5,855
4C: $1,679.50
SAU: $10.50
PCI: $10.50

15913 KBOT-FM - 104.1
PO Box 746 Phone: (218)847-5624
Detroit Lakes, MN 56501 Fax: (218)847-7657
Free: (800)545-1041

Format: Hot Country. **Networks:** Westwood One Radio. **Owner:** Leighton Enterprises, at above address. **Founded:** 1994. **Operating Hours:** Continuous; 100% local. **ADI:** Fargo, ND. **Key Personnel:** Joel Swanson, General Mgr., jswansonkdlm@yahoo.com; Dick Beardsley, Program Dir.; Jeff Leighton, Sales Mgr., kbot1041@yahoo.com. **Wattage:** 50,000. **Ad Rates:** $16.50 for 60 seconds. Combined advertising rates available with KDLM-AM.

15914 KDLM-AM - 1340
PO Box 746 Phone: (218)847-5624
Detroit Lakes, MN 56501 Fax: (218)847-7657

Format: Adult Contemporary; News; Information; Sports. **Networks:** CBS. **Owner:** Leighton Enterprises, at above address. **Founded:** 1951. **Operating Hours:** Continuous; 5% network, 95% local. **ADI:** Fargo, ND. **Key Personnel:** Joel Swanson, General Mgr., jswansonkdlm@yahoo.com; Jeff Leighton, Sales Mgr.; Andy Lia, Operations Mgr. **Local Programs:** *Hodge Podge* 8:35 am Monday-Friday, Dan Ochsner, News Dir. **Wattage:** 1000. **Ad Rates:** $11 for 30 seconds; $16.50 for 60 seconds. Combined advertising rates available with KBOT-FM.

DODGE CENTER, pop. 1,816.

SE MN. Dodge Co. 20 mi. W. of Rochester. Manufactures cement trucks. Fishing tackle, corn, pea canning factories. Grain, dairy, truck farms.

15915 Dodge Center Star-Record
40 W. Main St. Phone: (507)374-6531
Box 279 Fax: (507)374-9327
Dodge Center, MN 55927
Newspaper with Report orientation. **Founded:** 1870. **Freq:** Weekly (Tues.). **Print Method:** Offset. **Trim Size:** 8 x ll. **Cols./Page:** 6. **Col. Width:** 2 inches. **Col. Depth:** 21 1/2 inches. **Key Personnel:** Tony Pierfkalla, Publisher; Rosemary Miller, Advertising Mgr. **Subscription Rates:** $13. **Remarks:** Accepts advertising.
Ad Rates: BW: $341.85 **Circ:** Paid 1,450
4C: $80 Free 50
SAU: $4.85
PCI: $2.85

DULUTH†, pop. 92,811.

NE MN. St. Louis Co. On N. end of Lake Superior, 5 mi. N. of Superior WI. University of Minnesota (at Duluth). College of Saint Scholastica. Manufacturing. Paper mill. Trade in iron ore, taconite, grain, and dairy products. Grain elevators, coal, stone, cement, and ore docks. Commercial and industrial center.

15916 The Catholic Outlook
c/o Carlson and Kirwan Phone: (218)722-7220
118 E Superior St. Fax: (218)722-3358
Duluth, MN 55802
Publication E-mail: rsvpck@cp.duluth.mn.us

Official magazine of the Diocese of Duluth. **Founded:** 1970. **Freq:** Monthly. **Print Method:** Photo offset litho. **Key Personnel:** Julie Zenner, Associate Editor, phone (218)722-7220, fax (218)722-3358; Most Rev. Roger Schwietz, Publisher. **Subscription Rates:** $7. **Remarks:** Advertising not accepted.
Circ: 31,484

15917 CSS Cable
College of St. Scholastica
1200 Kenwood Phone: (218)723-6187
Duluth, MN 55811 Fax: (218)723-6290
Publication E-mail: cable1@css.edu

Collegiate magazine. **Freq:** Weekly (Fri.). **Print Method:** Offset. **Cols./Page:** 4. **Col. Width:** 24 nonpareils. **Col. Depth:** 182 agate lines. **Key Personnel:** Nicole Miller, Editor-in-Chief; Keegan Chaput, News Dir.; Erik Johnson, Advertising Mgr. **Subscription Rates:** $9. **Remarks:** Accepts advertising.
Ad Rates: BW: $260 **Circ:** Controlled ‡1,000
PCI: $7.50

15918 Duluth Budgeteer News
5807 Grand Ave. Phone: (218)624-3665
Duluth, MN 55807 Fax: (218)624-7927
Publication E-mail: budgeteer@mx3.com

Local newspaper. **Subtitle:** Duluth's Newspaper. **Founded:** 1931. **Freq:** 2x/week Sun./Wed. **Print Method:** Offset. **Cols./Page:** 6. **Col. Width:** 26 nonpareils. **Col. Depth:** 301 agate lines. **Key Personnel:** Jeff Swor, General Mgr. **Subscription Rates:** $35 individuals.
Ad Rates: BW: $1,399.65 **Circ:** Paid 1,318
4C: $1,675.25 Free 47,551
SAU: $15.95

15919 Duluth News-Tribune
Knight-Ridder, Inc.
424 W. 1st St. Phone: (218)723-5313
Duluth, MN 55802-1516 Fax: (218)720-4120
Free: (800)456-8282
Publication E-mail: newstrib@duluth.infi.net

General newspaper. **Founded:** 1892. **Freq:** Mon.-Sun. (morn.). **Print Method:** Flexo. **Trim Size:** 13 3/4 x 22 3/4. **Cols./Page:** 6. **Col. Width:** 12 2/5 picas. **Col. Depth:** 21 inches. **Key Personnel:** Craig Gemoules, Managing Editor, phone (218)720-4167; Mary Jacobus, Pres./Publisher, phone (218)723-5420, fax (218)723-5339; Curt Peterson, Circulation Dir., phone (218)723-5252, fax (218)720-4150; Bill Albrecht, Advertising Dir., phone (800)456-7979, fax (218)723-5295; Andrea Novel, Exec. City Editor, phone (218)723-4120; Connie Wirta, City Editor, phone (218)723-5341; Diana Faherty, City Editor, phone (218)723-5310; Chris Miller, Sports Editor, phone (218)723-5312; Bob King, Chief Photographer, phone (218)723-5363; Virgil Swing, Editorial Page Editor, phone (218)723-5301; David Holwerk, Exec. Editor, phone (218)723-5239. **USPS:** 162-180. **Subscription Rates:** $125.84 city; $128.44 motor route; $146.12 mail. **Remarks:** Accepts advertising. **URL:** http://www.duluthnews.com. **Alt. Formats:** Microform. **Formerly:** News-Tribune and Herald (1986).
Ad Rates: BW: $3,645.18 **Circ:** Mon.-Sat. ★**51,223**
4C: $4,555.18 Sun. ★**79,231**
PCI: $28.93

15920 The Duluthian
Duluth Chamber of Commerce
118 E. Superior St. Phone: (218)722-5501
Duluth, MN 55802 Fax: (218)722-3223
Publisher E-mail: chamber@commerce.duluth.mn.us

Chamber of Commerce magazine with business and community orientation. **Founded:** 1965. **Freq:** Bimonthly. **Print Method:** Letterpress and offset. **Trim Size:** 8 1/4 x 11. **Cols./Page:** 3. **Col. Width:** 26 nonpareils. **Col. Depth:** 140 agate lines. **Key Personnel:** Marc Mansfield, Publisher; Gina Chiodi Greene, Editor. **ISSN:** 0012-7116. **Subscription Rates:** $12 members; $3 single issue. **Remarks:** Accepts advertising from members only. **Alt. Formats:** Mailing labels.
Ad Rates: BW: $455 **Circ:** ‡1,800
4C: $755

15921 Labor World
Duluth AFL-CIO Central Labor Body
2002 London Rd., No. 110 Phone: (218)728-4469
Duluth, MN 55812 Fax: (218)724-1413
Publication E-mail: labrwrld@cpinternet.com

Labor newspaper. **Founded:** 1896. **Freq:** Biweekly. **Print Method:** Offset. **Trim Size:** 11 1/2 x 13 3/4. **Cols./Page:** 5. **Col. Depth:** 12 3/4 inches. **Key Personnel:** Larry Sillanpa, Editor. **ISSN:** 0023-6667. **Subscription Rates:** $15. **Remarks:** Accepts advertising.
Ad Rates: BW: $511 **Circ:** Paid ‡13,900
PCI: $8.05

15922 Lake Superior Magazine
Lake Superior Port Cities Inc.
325 Lake Ave. S, 600 Phone: (218)722-5002
Duluth, MN 55802-2323 Fax: (218)722-4096
Free: (888)244-5253
Publication E-mail: edit@lakesuperior.com
Publisher E-mail: reader@lakesuperior.com

Consumer magazine featuring articles and photography about the Lake Superior region. **Founded:** 1979. **Freq:** 7/year. **Print Method:** Offset. **Trim Size:** 8 1/8 x 11. **Cols./Page:** 3. **Col. Width:** 13 picas. **Col. Depth:** 59 picas. **Key Personnel:** Paul Hayden, Editor, plh@lakesuperior.com; James R. Marshall, Publisher, jr@lakesuperior.com; Hugh Bishop, Managing Editor, hb@lakesuperior.com. **ISSN:** 0890-3050. **Subscription Rates:** $21.95; $3.95 single issue. **URL:** http://www.lakesuperior.com.
Ad Rates: BW: $1,435 **Circ:** Paid ‡20,000
4C: $1,735

15923 LP-Gas
Advanstar Communications
131 W. First St. Free: (800)346-0085
Duluth, MN 55802
Publisher E-mail: fulfill@superfil.com

Magazine serving the licensed petroleum gas industry. **Founded:** 1940. **Freq:** Monthly. **Print Method:** Letterpress and offset. **Trim Size:** 8 x 10 3/4. **Cols./Page:** 3. **Col. Width:** 26 nonpareils. **Col. Depth:** 140 agate lines. **Key Personnel:** Zane Chastain, Editor and Publisher. **ISSN:** 0024-7103. **Subscription Rates:** $15. **Remarks:** Advertising accepted; rates available upon request.
Circ: Paid ★**4,606**
Non-paid ★**10,352**

15924 New Moon
New Moon Publishing
PO Box 3620 Phone: (218)728-5507
Duluth, MN 55803-3620 Fax: (218)728-0314
Publication E-mail: newmoon@computerpro.com
Publisher E-mail: newmoon@newmoon.org

Magazine edited by and directed toward girls aged 8-14. **Subtitle:** The Magazine for Girls and Their Dreams. **Founded:** Sept. 1993. **Freq:** Bimonthly. **Print Method:** Sheetfed. **Trim Size:** 7 x 9. **Key Personnel:** Nancy Gouver, Publisher; Joe Kelly, Publisher; Barbara Stretchberry, Managing Editor; Bridget Grosser, Asst. Managing Editor. **ISSN:** 1069-238X. **Subscription Rates:** $29 individuals; $34 Canada; $41 other countries; $6.50 single issue. **Remarks:** Advertising not accepted.
Circ: Paid 22,500

15925 North Coast Review
Poetry Harbor
PO Box 103 Phone: (218)733-1294
Duluth, MN 55801
Regional poetry magazine. **Founded:** 1992. **Freq:** Semiannual. **Print Method:** Offset. **Key Personnel:** Patrick McKinnon, Editor-in-Chief. **ISSN:** 1073-7553. **Subscription Rates:** $4.95 single issue. **Remarks:** Accepts advertising. **URL:** http://www.poharb@toofarnorth.com.
Ad Rates: BW: $90 **Circ:** Controlled 1,000

15926 Skillings' Mining Review
1st Bank Place, Ste. 728 Phone: (218)722-2310
130 W. Superior St. Fax: (218)722-0134
Duluth, MN 55802-2083
Trade magazine for mining business technology, mineral processing, and related fields. **Founded:** June 1, 1912. **Freq:** Weekly. **Print Method:** Offset. **Trim Size:** 8 1/4 x 11 1/4. **Cols./Page:** 3. **Col. Width:** 2 1/16 inches. **Col. Depth:** 10 inches. **Key Personnel:** David N. Skillings, Jr., Editor and Publisher. **USPS:** 376-329. **Subscription Rates:** $30 individuals. **Remarks:** Accepts advertising.
Ad Rates: BW: $920 **Circ:** Paid 2,370
4C: $1,964 Controlled 60
PCI: $44

15927 UMD Statesman
University of Minnesota
118 Kirby Student Center Phone: (218)726-8154
Duluth, MN 55812 Fax: (218)726-8246
Publication E-mail: statesman@d.umn.edu

Collegiate newspaper. **Founded:** 1947. **Freq:** Weekly (Thurs.). **Print Method:** Offset. **Cols./Page:** 5. **Col. Width:** 24 nonpareils. **Col. Depth:** 210 agate lines. **Key Personnel:** Stephanie Engelberth, Editor, phone (218)726-7113; Andrew Galarneault, Advertising Mgr.; Dan Knutson, Business Mgr. **USPS:** 647-340. **Subscription Rates:** $12 individuals /qtr. **Remarks:** Accepts advertising.
Ad Rates: BW: $367.50 **Circ:** 6,000
PCI: $5

15928 Bresnan Communications Co.
302 E. Superior St. Phone: (218)722-2288
Duluth, MN 55802 Fax: (218)726-1008

Owner: Bresnan Communications Co., at above address. **Founded:** 1973. **Key Personnel:** Kevin Lloyd, General Mgr.; Alan Seifert, Plant Manager; Dorothy Kray, Office Mgr.; Steven Netzel, Marketing Manager; Ken Schley, Advertising Mgr. **Cities Served:** Duluth, MN; Lake Nebagamon, Superior, WI: subscribing households 27,200; 116 channels; 4 community access channels.

15929 KBJR-TV - 6
230 E. Superior St. Phone: (218)727-8484
Duluth, MN 55802 Fax: (218)727-9699
E-mail: channel6@kbjr.com

Format: Commercial TV. **Networks:** NBC. **Owner:** Granite Broadcasting Corp., 767 3rd Ave. 34th Fl., New York, NY 10017, (212)826-2530, Fax: (212)826-2858. **Founded:** 1954. **Formerly:** WDSM-TV (1974). **Operating Hours:** Continuous. **ADI:** Duluth, MN-Superior, WI. **Key Personnel:** Robert J. Wilmers, Jr., Gen. Mgr./Pres., rwilmers@kbjr.com; Carl Keller, General Sales Mgr., ckeller@kbjr.com. **Wattage:** 100 KW ERP. **Ad Rates:** $25-1,500 for 30 seconds. **URL:** http://www.kbjr.com.

15930 KDAL-AM - 610
715 E. Central Entrance Phone: (218)722-4321
Duluth, MN 55811 Fax: (218)722-5423

Format: Adult Contemporary; News; Information. **Networks:** CBS. **Founded:** 1936. **Operating Hours:** Continuous. **ADI:** Duluth, MN-Superior, WI. **Key Personnel:** Deb Messer, General Mgr. **Wattage:** 5000.

15931 KDAL-FM - 95.7
715 E. Central Entrance Phone: (218)722-4321
Duluth, MN 55811 Fax: (218)772-5423

Format: Soft Rock; Adult Contemporary. **Networks:** Independent. **Founded:** 1989. **Operating Hours:** Continuous. **ADI:** Duluth, MN-Superior, WI. **Key Personnel:** Deb Messer, General Mgr. **Wattage:** 100,000.

15932 KDDS-AM - 1490
2001 London Rd. Phone: (218)728-6421
Duluth, MN 55812 Fax: (218)728-5809

Format: Classic Rock. **Simulcasts:** KQDS-FM. **Founded:** 1963. **Formerly:** KQDS-AM. **Operating Hours:** Continuous. **ADI:** Duluth, MN-Superior, WI. **Key Personnel:** Ivan Hohnstadt, General Mgr. **Wattage:** 1000.

15933 KDLH-TV - 3
425 Superior St. W. Phone: (218)733-0303
Duluth, MN 55802 Fax: (218)727-7515
E-mail: news@kdlh.com

Format: Commercial TV. **Networks:** CBS. **Owner:** Benedek Broadcasting, 100 Park Ave., Rockford, IL 61101. **Founded:** 1954. **Formerly:** KDAL-TV (1977). **Operating Hours:** 18.5 hours Daily; 70% network, 30% local. **ADI:** Duluth, MN-Superior, WI. **Key Personnel:** Gil Buether, General Mgr./Program Dir.; John Schuldt, News Dir.; Terry VanDell, Chief Engineer; Dan Stein, Program Dir.; Marty Weintraub, Creative Services Mgr.; Dana Dallum, Business Mgr.; Bobbi Lund, Collections Mgr.; Mark Hotchkiss, General Sales Mgr. **Ad Rates:** $10-1000 per unit.

15934 KDNW-FM - 97.3
1101 E. Central Entrance Phone: (218)722-6700
Duluth, MN 55811 Fax: (218)722-1092

Format: Religious. **Networks:** SkyLight Satellite; AP. **Owner:** Northwestern College, 3003 Snelling Ave. N., St. Paul, MN 55113, (612)631-5100. **Founded:** 1983. **Operating Hours:** Continuous; 60% network, 25% local, 15% syndicated. **ADI:** Duluth, MN-Superior, WI. **Key Personnel:** Paul Harkness, Station Mgr.; Gordon Mesedahl, News Dir. **Local Programs:** *Day Brightener*, Paul Harkness; *Our Bits & Pieces*, Edna Blake. **Wattage:** 40,000 ERP. **Ad Rates:** Noncommercial.

15935 KQDS-FM - 94.9
2001 London Rd. Phone: (218)728-6421
Duluth, MN 55812 Fax: (218)728-5809

Format: Classic Rock. **Simulcasts:** KDDS-AM. **Founded:** 1976. **Operating Hours:** Continuous. **ADI:** Duluth, MN-Superior, WI. **Key Personnel:** Ivan Hohnstadt, General Mgr. **Wattage:** 100,000.

15936 KRBR-FM - 102.5
715 E. Central Entrance Phone: (218)722-4321
Duluth, MN 55811 Fax: (218)722-5423

Owner: WDSM, at above address. **Founded:** 1979. **Formerly:** KZIO. **Operating Hours:** Continuous. **ADI:** Duluth, MN-Superior, WI. **Key Personnel:** Deb Messer, General Mgr. **Wattage:** 100,000. **Ad Rates:** $11-21 for 30 seconds; $17-26 for 60 seconds. Combined advertising rates available with KDAL-AM/FM. **URL:** http://www.krbr.com.

15937 KUMD-FM - 103.3
130 Humanities Bldg. Phone: (218)726-7181
Duluth, MN 55812 Fax: (218)726-6571
E-mail: kumd@d.umn.edu

Format: Public Radio; Alternative/New Music/Progressive; News; Information. **Networks:** Public Radio International (PRI). **Owner:** Regents of the University of Minnesota, at above address. **Founded:** 1956. **Operating Hours:** 5 am-3 am weekdays; 6 am-3 am Saturday and Sunday; 20% network, 80% local. **ADI:** Duluth, MN-Superior, WI. **Key Personnel:** Paul Schmitz, Station Mgr.; John Ziegler, Program Dir.; Stephanie Hemphill, Contact. **Wattage:** 95,000. **Ad Rates:** Noncommercial.

15938 WDIO-TV - 10
10 Observation Rd. Phone: (218)727-6864
PO Box 16897 Fax: (218)727-4415
Duluth, MN 55811-0897
E-mail: wdio@aol.com

Format: Commercial TV. **Networks:** ABC. **Owner:** WDIO-TV LLC, 3415 University Ave., St. Paul, MN 55114. **Founded:** 1966. **Operating Hours:** 5 a.m.-1 a.m.; 80% network, 20% local. **ADI:** Duluth, MN-Superior, WI. **Key Personnel:** James (Joe) Golden, General Sales Mgr.; Diane Sargent, Traffic Mgr.; George Couture, General Mgr.; Steve Bolf, Local Sales Mgr.; Steve Goodspeed, News Dir.; Dave Poirier, Program Dir.; Mike Hatlestad, Chief Engineer. **Wattage:** 316,000. **Ad Rates:** $7-12 per unit.

15939 WDSE-TV - 8
1202 E. University Circle Phone: (218)724-8567
Duluth, MN 55811-2420 Fax: (218)724-4269
E-mail: email@wdse.org

Format: Public TV. **Networks:** Public Broadcasting Service (PBS). **Owner:** Duluth-Superior Educational Television Corp., at above address. **Founded:** 1964. **Operating Hours:** 6 a.m.-2:00 a.m. **ADI:** Duluth, MN-Superior, WI. **Key Personnel:** Allen D. Harmon, General Mgr.; Ronald F. Anderson, Program Dir. **Wattage:** 316,000. **Ad Rates:** Underwriting available. **URL:** http://www.wdse.org.

15940 WDSM-AM - 710
715 E. Central Entrance Phone: (218)722-4321
Duluth, MN 55811 Fax: (218)722-5423
E-mail: sports@discover-net.net

Format: Country; Contemporary Country; News; Sports. **Networks:** CNN Radio. **Owner:** Shockley Communications, at above address. **Founded:** 1939. **Operating Hours:** Continuous; 80% network, 20% local. **ADI:** Duluth, MN-Superior, WI. **Key Personnel:** Mark Fleischer, Program Dir.; Deb Messer, General Mgr.; Kristi Guerink, News Dir. **Local Programs:** *Googs & Fleisher*, Chris Mehring, (218)728-6406, Fax (218)728-4317. **Wattage:** 10,000. **Ad Rates:** $10-21 for 30 seconds; $16.50-25 for 60 seconds. **URL:** http://www.duluthradio.com.

15941 WEBC-AM - 560
1001 E. 9th St. Phone: (218)728-4484
Duluth, MN 55805 Fax: (218)728-1779
E-mail: talk@56webc.com

Format: Talk; News. **Networks:** ABC; NBC; Talknet. **Owner:** Brill Media, at above address, (812)423-6200, Fax: (812)428-4021. **Founded:** 1924. **Operating Hours:** Continuous; 75% network, 25% local. **ADI:** Duluth, MN-Superior, WI. **Key Personnel:** Charles Norman, General Mgr.; Dave Walter, Program Dir. **Wattage:** 5000. **URL:** http://www.56webc.com.

15942 WIRR-FM - 90.9
224 Holiday Center Phone: (218)722-9411
Duluth, MN 55802 Fax: (218)720-4900
E-mail: mail@mpr.org

Format: Public Radio; Classical. **Networks:** Minnesota Public Radio. **Owner:** Minnesota Public Radio, 45 E. 7th St., St. Paul, MN 55101, (612)290-1500. **Founded:** 1984. **Operating Hours:** Continuous. **ADI:** Duluth, MN-Superior, WI. **Key Personnel:** John R. Snee, General Mgr.; Bob Kelleher, News Dir.; Carol Howe, Development Dir. **Wattage:** 22,000. **Ad Rates:** Noncommercial; underwriting available. **URL:** http://www.mpr.org.

WIRT-TV - See Hibbing

15943 WNCB-FM - 89.3
425 West Superior St., Ste. 300 Phone: (218)722-3017
Duluth, MN 55802 Fax: (218)722-1650
E-mail: staff@wncb.com

Format: Contemporary Christian. **Owner:** North-Central Christian Broadcasting, at above address. **Founded:** 1971. **Operating Hours:** Continuous; 100% local. **ADI:** Duluth, MN-Superior, WI. **Key Personnel:** Brett M. Gibson, General Mgr., gibber@wncb.com; Paul A. Hitchcock, President; Dave St. John, Program Dir., dave@wncb.com. **Wattage:** 2400. **Ad Rates:** Noncommercial.

15944 WSCD-FM - 92.9
224 Holiday Center Phone: (218)722-9411
Duluth, MN 55802 Fax: (218)720-4900
E-mail: mail@mpr.org

Format: Public Radio; Classical. **Networks:** Minnesota Public Radio. **Owner:** Minnesota Public Radio, 45 E. 7th St., St. Paul, MN 55101, (612)290-1500. **Founded:** 1975. **Operating Hours:** Continuous. **ADI:** Duluth, MN-Superior, WI. **Key Personnel:** John R. Snee, General Mgr.; Carol Howe, Development Dir.; Bob Kelleher, News Dir. **Wattage:** 70,000. **Ad Rates:** Noncommercial. **URL:** http://www.mpr.org.

15945 WWJC-AM - 850
PO Box 2199 Phone: (218)626-2738
Duluth, MN 55808-2199

Format: Religious. **Networks:** USA Radio; International Broadcasting. **Founded:** 1963. **Operating Hours:** Sunrise-sunset. **ADI:** Duluth, MN-Superior, WI. **Key Personnel:** Ted Elm, General Mgr. **Wattage:** 10,000. **Ad Rates:** $3.25-6 for 30 seconds; $4.50-7.50 for 60 seconds.

DUNDAS

15946 Dime Novel Roundup
PO Box 226 Phone: (507)645-5711
Dundas, MN 55019-0226 Fax: (507)646-3734

Magazine devoted to the collecting, preservation and study of old-time dime and nickel novels, popular story papers, series books, and pulp magazines. **Founded:** Jan. 1931. **Freq:** Bimonthly. **Print Method:** Offset. **Trim Size:** 5 1/2 x 8 1/2. **Cols./Page:** 1. **Col. Width:** 54 nonpareils. **Col. Depth:** 105 nonpareils. **Key Personnel:** J. Randolph Cox, Editor and Publisher, cox@stolaf.edu. **ISSN:** 0012-2874. **Subscription Rates:** $15 individuals; $3 single issue. **Remarks:** Color advertising not accepted.
Ad Rates: BW: $25 **Circ:** ‡250
PCI: $4

EAGAN

15947 Eagan Sun Current
Minnesota Sun Publications
7831 E. Bush Lake Rd. Phone: (612)896-4700
Bloomington, MN 55439 Fax: (612)896-4728
Publication E-mail: eagansuncurrent@mnsunpub.com

Community newspaper (tabloid). **Freq:** Weekly (Wed.). **Print Method:** Offset. **Cols./Page:** 4. **Col. Width:** 2 1/2 inches. **Col. Depth:** 15 inches. **Key Personnel:** Doug Dane, Publisher, phone (612)896-4787; Pamela Austin, Advertising Dir., phone (612)897-5486. **URL:** http://www.mnsun.
Circ: Free 270

EAST GRAND FORKS, pop. 8,537.

NW MN. Polk Co. 80 mi. directly N. of Fargo, ND. Beet sugar refinery. Manufactures sugar, potato chips. Agriculture. Wheat, potatoes, barley.

15948 Exponent
PO Box 285 Phone: (218)773-2808
East Grand Forks, MN 56721-0285 Fax: (218)773-9212
Publication E-mail: exponent@grandforks.polaristel.net

Community newspaper. **Founded:** July 11, 1979. **Freq:** Weekly (Wed.). **Print Method:** Offset. **Cols./Page:** 6. **Col. Width:** 12 picas. **Col. Depth:** 21.5 inches. **Key Personnel:** Rollin Bergman, Publisher; Julie Gillie, Publisher; Pete Myszkowski, Editor. **USPS:** 490-890. **Subscription Rates:** $19 individuals; $25 out of area. **Remarks:** Accepts advertising.
Ad Rates: BW: $378 **Circ:** ‡2,300
SAU: $3.25
PCI: $3.25

EDEN PRAIRIE, pop. 16,263.

ST MN. Hennepin Co. 15 mi. SW of Minneapolis. Residential.

Apple Valley/Rosemount/Lakeville Sun Current - See Apple Valley

15949 Eden Prairie News
Southwest Suburban Publishing
PO Box 44220 Phone: (612)934-5045
Eden Prairie, MN 55344 Fax: (612)949-3960

Community newspaper. **Founded:** Aug. 5, 1974. **Freq:** Weekly. **Print Method:** Offset. **Cols./Page:** 6. **Col. Width:** 2 inches. **Col. Depth:** 21 inches. **Key Personnel:** Mark Weber, Publisher, phone (612)829-0265; Gary Klatt, Advertising Dir., phone (612)934-5045; Ruby Mohlin, Circulation Mgr., phone (612)445-3333. **Subscription Rates:** $20 individuals; $30 out of area. **Remarks:** Accepts advertising.
Ad Rates: BW: $1,315.00 **Circ:** Free 11,000
4C: $1,605
PCI: $11.40

15950 Eden Prairie Sun Current
Minnesota Sun Publications
7831 E. Bush Lake Rd. Phone: (612)896-4700
Bloomington, MN 55439 Fax: (612)896-4728

Community newspaper (tabloid). **Founded:** 1984. **Freq:** Weekly (Wed.). **Print Method:** Offset. **Cols./Page:** 5. **Col. Width:** 1 15/16 inches. **Col. Depth:** 16 inches. **Key Personnel:** Don Thurlow, Publisher; Ed Shur, Editor; Paul Johnson, Advertising Dir.; Bonnie Laux, Sales Mgr. **Subscription Rates:** $20 Biannual voluntary subscription. **Remarks:** Accepts advertising. **Formerly:** Sun Prarie Sailor.
Ad Rates: GLR: $14 **Circ:** Free 13,289
BW: $1,120 Paid 77
PCI: $11.90

15951 Game Informer Magazine
Sunrise Publications, Inc.
10120 W. 76th St. Phone: (612)946-7256
Eden Prairie, MN 55344-3744 Fax: (612)946-8155
Publisher E-mail: gamers@winternet.com

Consumer magazine covering video and computer game information and reviews. **Founded:** 1991. **Freq:** Monthly. **Print Method:** Web offset. **Trim Size:** 8 x 10 3/4. **Key Personnel:** Andy McNamara, Editor; Kim Benike, Advertising Sales; Terrie Maley, Circulation and Marketing Mgr.; Rich Cihak, Publisher. **ISSN:** 1067-6392. **Subscription Rates:** $19.98 individuals; $3.95 single issue. **Remarks:** Accepts advertising. **URL:** http://www.gameinformer.com.
Ad Rates: BW: $4,954 **Circ:** Paid 143,782
4C: $6,140

Wayzata Sun-Sailor - See Wayzata

West Saint Paul/Mendota Heights Sun Current - See West Saint Paul

15952 KMSP-TV - 9
11358 Viking Dr. Phone: (612)944-9999
Eden Prairie, MN 55344-7258 Fax: (612)942-0286
E-mail: upn@kmspq.com

Format: Commercial TV. **Networks:** United Paramount Network. **Owner:** United Television, 5801 Wilshire Blvd., No. 340, Beverly Hills, CA 90211, (310)854-0426, Fax: (310)659-8121. **Founded:** 1955. **Operating Hours:** Continuous. **ADI:** Minneapolis-St. Paul, MN. **Key Personnel:** Stuart Swartz, General Mgr., phone (612)946-5601.

EDEN VALLEY, pop. 763.

SC MN. Meeker Co. 35 mi. SW of Saint Cloud. Lake resort. Dairy, poultry farms. Tobacco, small grains, corn, mink ranching.

15953 Journal
PO Box 347 Phone: (612)453-2460
Eden Valley, MN 55329
Community newspaper. **Founded:** July 1890. **Freq:** Weekly (Wed.). **Print Method:** Offset. **Cols./Page:** 7. **Col. Width:** 12 picas. **Col. Depth:** 21 1/2 inches. **Key Personnel:** Steven J. Swenson, Editor and Publisher. **USPS:** 167-600. **Subscription Rates:** $9 local; $10 in state; $13 out of state. **Remarks:** Accepts advertising.
Ad Rates: GLR: $.105 **Circ:** ‡1,375
BW: $263.38
4C: $475
PCI: $1.75

EDGERTON, pop. 1,123.

SW MN. Pipestone Co. 50 mi NE of Sioux Falls, SD. Manufactures vehicle stabilizers, gold mining equipment, plastic products. Stock, grain farms. Corn, soybeans, oats, flax, tobacco.

15954 The Edgerton Enterprise
Edgerton Enterprise
831 Main St. Phone: (507)442-6161
PO Box 397 Fax: (507)442-6161
Edgerton, MN 56128
Publication E-mail: edgent@front.ernet.net

Community newspaper. **Founded:** 1883. **Freq:** Weekly (Wed.). **Print Method:** Offset. **Trim Size:** 16 x 22 3/4. **Cols./Page:** 7. **Col. Width:** 2 1/16 inches. **Col. Depth:** 21 1/2 inches. **Key Personnel:** Melvin DeBoer, Editor and Publisher. **USPS:** 167-880. **Subscription Rates:** $22; $28 out of area. **Remarks:** Advertising not accepted for alcoholic beverages.
Ad Rates: BW: $510 **Circ:** Paid 1,950
4C: $600 Free 13
SAU: $3.70
PCI: $3.70

EDINA, pop. 46,073.

W MN. Hennepin Co. Adjoins Minneapolis on SW. Residential.

15955 Edina Sun Current
Minnesota Sun Publications
7831 E. Bush Lake Rd. Phone: (612)896-4700
Bloomington, MN 55439 Fax: (612)896-4728

Community newspaper (tabloid). **Founded:** 1984. **Freq:** Weekly (Wed.). **Print Method:** Offset. **Cols./Page:** 4. **Col. Width:** 2 1/2 inches. **Col. Depth:** 15 inches. **Key Personnel:** John Gannet Hawley, Publisher; Robert Stjern, Advertising Mgr.
Circ: Paid 2,463
Non-paid 10,839

15956 Minnesota Golfer
The Publishing Group, Inc.
6550 York Ave., Ste.211 Phone: (612)927-4643
Edina, MN 55435
Consumer magazine covering golf and golf related events throughout Minnesota. **Subtitle:** Official publication of the Minnesota Golf Association. **Freq:** Bimonthly. **Print Method:** Heat offset. **Trim Size:** 8 1/4 x 10 7/8. **Cols./Page:** 3. **Col. Width:** 2 1/4 inches. **Col. Depth:** 9 1/2 inches. **Key Personnel:** Chris Geer, Editor. **ISSN:** 1062-1105. **Subscription Rates:** $11.80. **Remarks:** Accepts advertising.
Ad Rates: BW: $3,095 **Circ:** Paid ⊕**60,000**
4C: $3,500
PCI: $87.89

15957 Specialty Law Digest: Health Care
Specialty Digest Publications, Inc.
PO Box 24439 Phone: (612)780-3157
Edina, MN 55424-0439
Medical and health care law journal. **Founded:** 1979. **Freq:** Monthly. **Print Method:** Offset. **Trim Size:** 6 x 9. **Cols./Page:** 2. **Col. Width:** 32 nonpareils. **Col. Depth:** 126 agate lines. **Key Personnel:** Clayton R. Smalley, Editor. **Subscription Rates:** $370.

15958 Swedish American Genealogist
Swenson Swedish Immigration Research Center
c/o Dr. James E. Erickson Phone: (612)925-1008
7008 Bristol Blvd.
Edina, MN 55435-4108
Publisher E-mail: sag@augustana.edu

Professional journal covering Swedish American genealogy, biography, and personal history. **Founded:** Mar. 1981. **Freq:** Quarterly. **Trim Size:** 6 x 9. **Cols./Page:** 1. **Key Personnel:** Dr. James E. Erickson, Editor, j.erickson@nr.cc.mn.us; Jill Seaholm, Circulation Mgr., swseaholm@augustana.edu. **ISSN:** 0275-9314. **Subscription Rates:** $25 individuals. **Remarks:** Accepts advertising.
Circ: Controlled 900

15959 Wildlife Art
Pothole Publications, Inc.
PO Box 390026 Phone: (612)835-5353
Edina, MN 55439 Fax: (612)835-5554
Free: (800)221-6547

Magazine for wildlife art collectors. **Subtitle:** The Art Journal of the Natural World. **Founded:** 1982. **Freq:** 6/year. **Print Method:** Web offset. **Trim Size:** 8 1/4 x 10 13/16. **Cols./Page:** 3. **Key Personnel:** Robert J. Koenke, Publisher; Emily Proskin, Circulation Mgr. **ISSN:** 0746-9640. **Subscription Rates:** $28.95; $6.95 single issue. **Remarks:** Accepts advertising. **URL:** http://www.wildlifeartmag.com. **Formerly:** Wildlife Art News.
Ad Rates: BW: $1,795 **Circ:** ‡65,000
4C: $2,435

ELK RIVER†, pop. 6,785.

SEC MN. Sherburne Co. On Mississippi River, at mouth of Elk River, 30 mi. NW of Saint Paul. Concrete products, berry crates manufactured. Dairy farms.

15960 Elk River Star News
Princeton Publishing
649 Main St. Phone: (612)441-3500
PO Box 330 Fax: (612)441-6401
Elk River, MN 55330
Community newspaper. **Founded:** 1875. **Freq:** Weekly (Wed.). **Print Method:** Offset. **Cols./Page:** 6. **Col. Width:** 30 nonpareils. **Col. Depth:** 274 agate lines. **Key Personnel:** Elmer L. Andersen, Publisher; Dan Herpman, Advertising Mgr. **Subscription Rates:** $18 out of area. **Remarks:** Accepts advertising.
Ad Rates: BW: $711.90 **Circ:** Paid ‡15,055
SAU: $5.69 Free ‡11,935
PCI: $5.65

15961 Elk River Star Shopper
Princeton Publishing
649 Main St. Phone: (612)441-3500
PO Box 330 Fax: (612)441-6401
Elk River, MN 55330
Shopper. **Founded:** 1987. **Freq:** Weekly (Sun.). **Print Method:** Offset. **Key Personnel:** Elmer L. Andersen, Publisher; Dan Herpman, Editor. **Remarks:** Accepts advertising.
Ad Rates: BW: $311.25 **Circ:** (Not Reported)
PCI: $4.15

ELY, pop. 4,820.

NE MN. St. Louis Co. 48 mi. NE of Virginia. Lake resort. Fishing and canoe areas. Wood products.

15962 Ely Echo
Milestones, Inc.
2 E. Sheridan Phone: (218)365-3141
Ely, MN 55731 Fax: (218)365-3142
Free: (800)492-3555
Publication E-mail: elyecho@aol.com
Publisher E-mail: elyecho@aol.com

Community newspaper. **Founded:** Oct. 25, 1972. **Freq:** Weekly (Mon.). **Print Method:** Offset. **Trim Size:** 13 x 21 1/2. **Cols./Page:** 6. **Col. Width:** 25 nonpareils. **Col. Depth:** 298 agate lines. **Key Personnel:** Tom Coombe, Editor; Anne Swenson, Publisher; Nick Wognum, General Mgr. **ISSN:** 0746-7087. **Subscription Rates:** $20 individuals; $30 out of area; $40 out of state. **Remarks:** Accepts advertising.
Ad Rates: BW: $578.60 **Circ:** 4,726
SAU: $6.65
PCI: $5.35

15963 North Country Angler
Milestones, Inc.
2 E. Sheridan Phone: (218)365-3141
Ely, MN 55731 Fax: (218)365-3142
Free: (800)492-3555
Publication E-mail: elyecho@aol.com
Publisher E-mail: elyecho@aol.com

Summer fishing newspaper. **Founded:** 1975. **Freq:** Weekly. **Print Method:** Web offset. **Trim Size:** Tabloid. **Cols./Page:** 4. **Col. Width:** 2 1/4 inches. **Col. Depth:** 13 inches. **Key Personnel:** Bob Cary, Editor; Anne Swenson, Publisher. **Subscription Rates:** $15 individuals. **Remarks:** Accepts advertising.
Ad Rates: BW: $520 **Circ:** Free ‡8,000
SAU: $10
PCI: $10

15964 North Country Saver
Milestones, Inc.
2 E. Sheridan Phone: (218)365-3141
Ely, MN 55731 Fax: (218)365-3142
Free: (800)492-3555
Publication E-mail: elyecho@aol.com
Publisher E-mail: elyecho@aol.com

Shopper. **Founded:** 1980. **Freq:** Weekly (Mon.). **Print Method:** Offset. Uses mats. **Cols./Page:** 4. **Col. Width:** 27 nonpareils. **Col. Depth:** 203 agate lines. **Key Personnel:** Anne Swenson, Editor and Publisher; Tom Coombe, Editor; Nick Wognum, General Mgr.; Anne Swenson, Publisher. **Subscription Rates:** Free. **Remarks:** Accepts advertising.
Ad Rates: BW: $280.88 **Circ:** Free 9,000
SAU: $7.85
PCI: $7.25

ELYSIAN, pop. 454.

SC MN. Le Sueur Co. 21 mi. E. of Mankato. Lake resort. Dairy, poultry, grain, stock farms.

15965 The Elysian Enterprise
PO Box 119 Phone: (507)267-4323
Elysian, MN 56028-0028 Fax: (507)362-4458

Community newspaper. **Founded:** 1893. **Freq:** Weekly (Thurs.). **Print Method:** Offset. **Cols./Page:** 6. **Col. Width:** 30 nonpareils. **Col. Depth:** 301 agate lines. **Key Personnel:** Jay Schneider, Managing Editor; Chuck Wann, Owner-Publisher. **Subscription Rates:** $20 individuals. **Remarks:** Accepts advertising.
Ad Rates: GLR: $.14 **Circ:** Paid ‡480
SAU: $3.50 Free ‡27

EMILY

15966 Emily Cooperative Telephone Co. CATV Div.
PO Box 100 Phone: (218)763-3000
Emily, MN 56447 Fax: (218)763-2042
Free: (800)450-1036

Founded: Oct. 1983. **Key Personnel:** Tim Hills, General Mgr., thills@emily.net; Don Anderson, Cable Supervisor; Jane Hann, Business Mgr. **Cities Served:** Emily, Fifty Lakes, Outing, MN: subscribing households 850; 23 channels; 2 community access channels.

ERSKINE, pop. 585.

NW MN. Polk Co. 58 mi. E. of Grand Forks, ND. Manufactures hay bale loaders and conveyors, snow plows, dairy products. Agriculture. Wheat, potatoes.

15967 Erskine Echo
309 1st St. Phone: (218)687-3775
Box A Fax: (218)687-3744
Erskine, MN 56535
Community newspaper. **Founded:** 1899. **Freq:** Weekly (Wed.). **Print Method:** Offset. **Cols./Page:** 6. **Col. Width:** 24 nonpareils. **Col. Depth:** 301 agate lines. **Key Personnel:** Robert Hole, Editor and Publisher. **USPS:** 178-580. **Subscription Rates:** $18 individuals; $20 out of state. **Remarks:** Accepts advertising.
Ad Rates: SAU: $3.75 **Circ:** ‡1,030

EVELETH, pop. 5,042.

NE MN. Saint Louis Co. 5 mi SW of Gilbert.

15968 WEVE-AM - 1340
Box 650 Phone: (218)741-5922
Eveleth, MN 55734 Fax: (218)741-7302
Free: (800)247-0089

Format: Adult Contemporary. **Networks:** ABC. **Owner:** Lewis Latto, 5732 Eagle View Dr., Duluth, MN 55803, (218)729-9888. **Founded:** 1947. **Operating Hours:** Continuous. **ADI:** Duluth, MN-Superior, WI. **Key Personnel:** Jerry Sylvester, General Mgr.; Steve Carlson, News Dir.; Dennis Jerrold, Program Dir.; Julie Rappucci, Operations Mgr. **Wattage:** 1000. **Ad Rates:** Advertising accepted; rates available upon request.

15969 WEVE-FM - 97.9
Box 650 Phone: (218)741-5922
Eveleth, MN 55734 Fax: (218)741-7302
Free: (800)247-0089

Format: Adult Contemporary. **Simulcasts:** WEVE-AM. **Networks:** ABC. **Owner:** Lew Latto Group, 419 W. Michigan St., Duluth, MN 55802, (218)727-7271. **Founded:** 1978. **Operating Hours:** Continuous. **ADI:** Duluth, MN-Superior, WI. **Key Personnel:** Jerry Sylvester, General Mgr.; Dennis Yourczek, Program Dir. **Wattage:** 71,000. **Ad Rates:** Advertising accepted; rates available upon request.

EXCELSIOR, pop. 2,523.

SE MN. Hennepin Co. 25 mi. W. of Saint Paul. Residential.

15970 Excelsior/Shorewood Sun-Sailor
Minnesota Sun Publications
7831 E. Bush Lake Rd. Phone: (612)896-4700
Bloomington, MN 55439 Fax: (612)896-4728

Community newspaper (tabloid). **Freq:** Weekly (Wed.). **Print Method:** Offset. **Cols./Page:** 4. **Col. Width:** 2 1/2 inches. **Col. Depth:** 15 inches. **Key Personnel:** Don Thurlow, Publisher; Paul Johnson, Advertising Mgr.
Circ: Combined 5,485

FAIRFAX, pop. 1,405.

SW MN. Renville Co. 55 mi. NW of Mankato. Manufactures audio, electronic components, tool and die parts. Dairy, stock, grain farms.

15971 Fairfax Standard
102 SE 1st Phone: (507)426-7235
Box 589 Fax: (507)426-7264
Fairfax, MN 55332
NRO. **Founded:** 1897. **Freq:** Weekly (Wed.). **Print Method:** Offset. **Cols./Page:** 7. **Col. Width:** 28 nonpareils. **Col. Depth:**

301 agate lines. **Key Personnel:** Steven J. Palmer, Editor; Charles H. Warner, Publisher. **USPS:** 184-140. **Subscription Rates:** $18. **Remarks:** Accepts advertising.
Ad Rates: GLR: $.20 **Circ:** ‡1,382
BW: $541.80
PCI: $3.60

FAIRMONT†, pop. 11,506.

SC MN. Martin Co. 50 mi. SW of Mankato. Manfactures railway maintenance equipment, frozen and canned foods, ribbon, plastics, frozen gourmet foods, electronics, cement blocks, feed. Grain, dairy, poultry, stock farms. Lake resort.

15972 Fairmont Photo Press
112 E. 1st St. Phone: (507)238-9456
PO Box 973 Fax: (507)238-9457
Fairmont, MN 56031-0973
Local shopper/newspaper. **Founded:** May 16, 1963. **Freq:** Weekly (Wed.). **Print Method:** Offset. **Trim Size:** 11 3/8 x 16. **Cols./Page:** 6. **Col. Width:** 20 nonpareils. **Col. Depth:** 213 agate lines. **Key Personnel:** Sherman L. Kumba, Editor; Wayne L. Schroeder, Publisher; Randy Chirpich, Advertising Mgr. **Subscription Rates:** Free; $22.50 (mail). **Remarks:** Accepts advertising.
Ad Rates: BW: $388.88 **Circ:** Free 11,800
PCI: $4.25

15973 Sentinel
64 Downtown Plaza Phone: (507)235-3303
PO Box 681 Fax: (507)235-3718
Fairmont, MN 56031
Publication E-mail: sentnews@rconnect.com

General newspaper. **Founded:** 1874. **Freq:** Mon.-Sat. (morn.). **Print Method:** Offset. **Cols./Page:** 6. **Col. Width:** 24 nonpareils. **Col. Depth:** 301 agate lines. **Key Personnel:** Russ Roberts, Editor; Gary Andersen, Publisher. **Subscription Rates:** $90 individuals. **Remarks:** Accepts advertising.
Ad Rates: GLR: $.72 **Circ:** Mon.-Sat. 8,923
4C: $200
SAU: $1,549.29
PCI: $12.01

15974 KFMC-FM - 106.5
1371 W. Lair Rd. Phone: (507)235-5595
PO Box 491 Fax: (507)235-3299
Fairmont, MN 56031
E-mail: kfmc@beucomm.net

Format: Adult Contemporary; Contemporary Hit Radio (CHR). **Owner:** Woodward Broadcasting Inc., at above address. **Founded:** 1979. **Operating Hours:** Continuous; 2% network, 98% local. **ADI:** Minneapolis-St. Paul, MN. **Key Personnel:** Charles V. Woodward III, President, woody@beucomm.net; Don Kliewer, Contact, doni@bcucomm.net; Mike Murphy, Contact; Jill Morris, Operations Mgr.; Rod Halverson, News Dir. **Wattage:** 100,000. **Ad Rates:** $16-30 for 30 seconds; $20-35 for 60 seconds. Combined advertising rates available with KSUM-AM. **URL:** http://www.kfmc.com.

15975 KSUM-AM - 1370
1371 W. Lair Rd. Phone: (507)235-5595
PO Box 491 Fax: (507)235-3299
Fairmont, MN 56031
E-mail: ksum@beucomm.net

Format: Agricultural; News; Sports; Contemporary Country. **Networks:** CNN Radio. **Owner:** Woodward Broadcasting Inc., at above address. **Founded:** 1949. **Operating Hours:** Continuous; 10% network, 90% local. **ADI:** Minneapolis-St. Paul, MN. **Key Personnel:** Charles V. Woodward III, President, woody@beucomm.net; Don Kliewer, Contact, doni@beucomm.net; Mike Murphy, Contact; Patrick Murphy, Operations Mgr.; Rod Halverson, News Dir. **Wattage:** 1000. **Ad Rates:** $16-60 for 30 seconds; $20-70 for 60 seconds. Combined advertising rates available with KFMC-FM.

FALCON HEIGHTS

15976 Minnesota Horticulturist
Minnesota State Horticultural Society
1755 Prior Ave. N. Phone: (651)643-3601
Falcon Heights, MN 55113 Fax: (651)643-3638
Free: (800)676-6747
Publication E-mail: info@gardenmn.org

Gardening information magazine. **Subtitle:** The Magazine of Northern Gardening. **Founded:** 1866. **Freq:** 9/year. **Print Method:** Sheet fed. **Trim Size:** 8 3/8 x 10 7/8. **Cols./Page:** 3. **Col. Width:** 26 nonpareils. **Col. Depth:** 129 agate lines. **Key Personnel:** Lynn M. Steiner, Editor; Terry Goodfellow-Heyer, Director. **ISSN:** 0026-5500. **Subscription Rates:** $25. $3.50 single issue. **Remarks:** Accepts advertising.
Ad Rates: BW: $750 **Circ:** ‡60,000
4C: $990
PCI: $.50

FARIBAULT†, pop. 16,241.

SE MN. Rice Co. 53 mi. S. of Saint Paul. Resort area. Lakes. Manufactures floor trucks, ice cube making machines, air conditioners, concrete products, woolens, amusement park equipment, fabricated casings for computing machines, hoes, silos, lumber, plastic plumbing fixtures, tile, butter, blue cheese. Turkey processing and cannery plants. Foundry. Nurseries; hatchery. Stock, dairy, poultry farms.

15977 News
PO Box 249 Phone: (507)334-1853
Faribault, MN 55021 Fax: (507)334-8569

General newspaper. **Founded:** 1914. **Freq:** Daily (eve.). **Print Method:** Offset. **Cols./Page:** 6. **Col. Width:** 24 nonpareils. **Col. Depth:** 301 agate lines. **Key Personnel:** Michael Cooper, Managing Editor; Dave Balcom, Publisher; Dale Hellickson, Advertising Mgr. **Subscription Rates:** $81. **Remarks:** Accepts advertising.
Ad Rates: SAU: $6.70 **Circ:** ‡7,772

15978 Rice County Shopper
514 Central Ave. Phone: (507)334-9321
PO Box 249 Fax: (507)334-8569
Faribault, MN 55021
Community shopper. **Founded:** 1977. **Freq:** Weekly (Sun.). **Print Method:** Offset. **Trim Size:** 10 1/4 x 13. **Cols./Page:** 4. **Col. Width:** 14 picas. **Col. Depth:** 8.5 picas. **Key Personnel:** Jim Huckle, Editor and Publisher; Dale Hellickson, Advertising Mgr. **Subscription Rates:** Free.
Ad Rates: BW: $741 **Circ:** Free 18,821
4C: $941

15979 KDHL-AM - 920
601 Central Ave. Phone: (507)334-0061
Box 30 Fax: (507)334-7057
Faribault, MN 55021-0030
Free: (800)369-5345
E-mail: kdhl@radiominnesota.com

Format: Oldies; Country; News; Information. **Networks:** ABC; Minnesota News. **Owner:** Radio Ingstad Minn Inc., at above address. **Founded:** 1948. **Operating Hours:** Continuous. **Key Personnel:** John Taylor, Program Dir.; Jeff Kurtz, General Mgr.; Kymn Anderson, Sales Mgr.; Robert Buck, Music Dir.; Gordy Kosfeld, News Dir.; Mike Morrissey, Sports Dir.; Paul Benzick, Traffic Mgr.; Robert Ingstad, Owner. **Local Programs:** *A.M. Minnesota* 9:30-10:00 a.m. Monday-Friday, Gordy Kosfeld. **Wattage:** 5000. **Ad Rates:** Advertising accepted; rates available upon request. **URL:** http://www.radiominnesota.com.

FERGUS FALLS†, pop. 12,519.

WC MN. Otter Trail Co. On Red River, 200 mi. E. of Duluth. Manufactures cabinets, dairy, bakery products, flour, farm machinery, fertilizer, protein meal. Summer resort. Dairy, livestock, grain farms.

15980 Faith and Fellowship
Faith & Fellowship Press
704 W. Vernon Ave. Phone: (218)736-7357
Fergus Falls, MN 56537-2633 Fax: (218)736-2200

Lutheran magazine. **Founded:** 1933. **Freq:** 12/year. **Print Method:** Offset. **Trim Size:** 8 x 10 1/2. **Cols./Page:** 2. **Col. Width:** 40 nonpareils. **Col. Depth:** 125 agate lines. **Key Personnel:** Rev. David Rinden, Editor. **USPS:** 184-600. **Subscription Rates:** $15. **Remarks:** Advertising not accepted.
Circ: Paid ‡7,600
Controlled ‡100

15981 Journal
Fergus Journal Co.
914 E. Channing Ave. Phone: (218)736-7511
PO Box 506 Fax: (218)736-5919
Fergus Falls, MN 56537
Free: (800)726-1781

General newspaper. **Founded:** 1883. **Freq:** Mon-Fri. (eve.) & Sat. (morn.). **Print Method:** Offset. **Cols./Page:** 6. **Col. Width:** 24 nonpareils. **Col. Depth:** 301 agate lines. **Key Personnel:** Jim Morgan, Publisher; Richard Hensley, Editor. **Subscription Rates:** $120 yearly (.75 stand price). **Remarks:** Accepts advertising.
Ad Rates: PCI: $7.93 **Circ:** Mon.-Sat. 9,409

15982 KBRF-AM - 1250
728 Western Ave. N. Phone: (218)736-7596
Fergus Falls, MN 56537 Fax: (218)736-2836
Free: (800)931-9103
E-mail: kbrfkzcr@prtel.com

Format: Contemporary Country; Talk; Agricultural; News; Information. **Networks:** Mutual Broadcasting System; Minnesota News. **Founded:** 1926. **Formerly:** KOTE-AM; KGDE-AM. **Operating Hours:** Continuous; 12% network, 88% local. **ADI:** Fargo, ND. **Key Personnel:** Sue Tate, Acting General Mgr.; Charlie Kampa, Program Dir.; Jim Sturgeon, News Dir.; Jeff Swedberg, Sports Dir.; Charlie Kampa, Farm Dir. **Local Programs:** *In Your Interest* 9:35 a.m. Monday-Friday, Mary Dolan. **Wattage:** 5000. **Ad Rates:** $4-7.70 for 15 seconds; $6-11.80 for 30 seconds; $9.50-17.65 for 60 seconds. Combined advertising rates available with KZCR-FM, KJJK-AM & FM, KPRW-FM.

15983 KJJK-AM - 1020
PO Box 495 Phone: (218)736-5408
Fergus Falls, MN 56538 Fax: (218)736-5400
Free: (888)303-5596
E-mail: kbrfkzcr@prtel.com

Format: Oldies. **Networks:** ABC. **Founded:** 1986. **Operating Hours:** Continuous. **ADI:** Fargo, ND. **Key Personnel:** Sue Tate, Acting General Mgr. **Local Programs:** *In Focus*, Mark Johnson; *Talkin' Sports*, Craig Olson. **Wattage:** 2000. **Ad Rates:** $8-12 for 30 seconds; $12-18 for 60 seconds. Combined advertising rates available with KJJK-FM, KBRF-AM, KZCR-FM, KPRW-FM.

15984 KJJK-FM - 96.5
PO Box 495 Phone: (218)736-5408
Fergus Falls, MN 56538-0495 Fax: (218)736-2836
Free: (888)303-5596
E-mail: kbrfkzcr@prtel.com

Format: Hot Country. **Networks:** ABC. **Owner:** Result Radio, at above address. **Founded:** 1981. **Operating Hours:** Continuous. **ADI:** Fargo, ND. **Key Personnel:** Sue Tate, Acting General Mgr. **Local Programs:** *Talkin' Sports*, Craig Olson. **Wattage:** 100,000. **Ad Rates:** $8-12 for 30 seconds; $12-18 for 60 seconds. Combined advertising rates available with KJJD-AM, KBRF-AM, KZCR-FM, KPRW-FM.

15985 KZCR-FM - 103.3
728 Western Ave. N. Phone: (218)736-5553
Fergus Falls, MN 56537 Fax: (218)736-2836
Free: (800)931-9103
E-mail: kbrfkzcr@prtel.com

Format: Classic Rock. **Owner:** Result Radio Group, Box 767, Winona, MN 55987, (507)452-4000, Fax: (507)452-9494. **Founded:** 1968. **Formerly:** KBRF-FM (1993). **Operating Hours:** Continuous; 100% local. **ADI:** Fargo, ND. **Key Personnel:** Sue Tate, Acting General Mgr.; Stan Comeau, Operations Mgr.; Jim Sturgeon, News Dir.; Jeff Swedberg, Sports Dir. **Local Programs:** *Bumper to Bumper Classic Jam*, Barbara Vangrud. **Wattage:** 100,000. **Ad Rates:** $6-11.80 for 30 seconds; $9.15-17.65 for 60 seconds. Combined advertising rates available with KBRF-AM, KJJK-AM & FM, KPRW-FM.

FLOODWOOD, pop. 650.

SW MN. Saint Louis Co. 40 mi. WNW of Duluth.

15986 The Forum
Floodwood Printing
PO Box 286 Phone: (218)476-2232
112 W. 7th Ave. Fax: (218)476-2232
Floodwood, MN 55736
Publication E-mail: the_ forum@juno.com

Community newspaper (tabloid). **Subtitle:** Only Official Newspaper published in South St. Louis County. **Founded:** 1936. **Freq:** Weekly (Fri.). **Print Method:** Offset. **Cols./Page:** 5. **Col. Width:** 11 picas. **Col. Depth:** 15 inches. **Key Personnel:** Nancy Raihala, Editor and Publisher. **USPS:** 573-580. **Subscription Rates:** $17 individuals; $19 out of state. **Remarks:** Accepts advertising. **Formerly:** Floodwood Forum.
Ad Rates: BW: $273.75 **Circ:** Paid ‡1,335
SAU: $3.65 Free ‡60
PCI: $3.15

FOLEY†, pop. 1,606.

C MN. Berton Co. 14 mi. E. of Saint Cloud. Dairy, stock, poultry, truck farms. Potatoes, corn, beans.

15987 Benton County News
220 Broadway Phone: (320)968-7220
Foley, MN 56329 Fax: (320)968-7220

Community newspaper. **Founded:** 1932. **Freq:** Weekly (Tues.). **Print Method:** Offset. **Cols./Page:** 7. **Col. Width:** 24 nonpareils. **Col. Depth:** 280 agate lines. **Key Personnel:** Ronald F. Youso, Editor and Publisher. **Remarks:** Accepts advertising.
Ad Rates: GLR: $.18 **Circ:** (Not Reported)

FOREST LAKE, pop. 4,596.

SE MN. Washington Co. 25 mi. N. of Saint Paul. Summer

resort. Manufactures tools, snow and lawn fences, protective helmets & gear, wood products, component electronic parts; feed, hammer mills. Creamery. Dairy, poultry, truck farms. Aluminum utensils, fixtures.

15988 St. Croix Valley Peach
ECM Publishers, Inc. - Forest Lake
880 SW 15th St. Phone: (612)464-4601
Forest Lake, MN 55025 Fax: (612)464-4605
Publication E-mail: peach.fl@ecm-inc.com
Publisher E-mail: editor.forestlaketimes@ecm-inc.com

Shopping guide. **Founded:** 1953. **Freq:** Weekly (Sun.). **Print Method:** Offset. **Cols./Page:** 6. **Col. Width:** 20 nonpareils. **Col. Depth:** 15 inches. **Key Personnel:** Howard Lestrud, General Mgr.; Roxie Muehlberg, Ad. Sales Mgr. **Subscription Rates:** Free; $86 individuals per year. **Remarks:** Accepts advertising.
Ad Rates: GLR: $11.95 **Circ:** Free ‡32,000
SAU: $13.28
PCI: $9.80

15989 The Times
ECM Publishers, Inc. - Forest Lake
880 SW 15th St. Phone: (612)464-4601
Forest Lake, MN 55025 Fax: (612)464-4605
Publication E-mail: editor.fl@ecm-inc.com
Publisher E-mail: editor.forestlaketimes@ecm-inc.com

Community newspaper. **Founded:** 1903. **Freq:** Weekly (Thurs.). **Print Method:** Offset. **Cols./Page:** 6. **Col. Width:** 77 picas. **Col. Depth:** 21 inches. **Key Personnel:** Howard Lestrud, General Mgr.; Carol Deitner, Advertising Mgr. **USPS:** 205-080. **Subscription Rates:** Free; $31 out of area; $36 out of state; $29 in area. **Remarks:** Accepts advertising. **Available Online**.
Ad Rates: GLR: $6.25 **Circ:** Paid 798
SAU: $9.95 Free 11,402
PCI: $9.95

15990 WLKX-FM - 95.9
15226 W. Freeway Dr. Phone: (612)464-6796
Forest Lake, MN 55025

Format: Talk; News; Sports; Country; Contemporary Christian. **Networks:** USA Radio. **Owner:** Joanne Rusch-Cary, at above address. **Founded:** 1978. **Operating Hours:** Continuous; 33% network, 67% local. **ADI:** Minneapolis-St. Paul, MN. **Key Personnel:** Doug Hammer, Sales Mgr.; Cathleen Cary, General Mgr. **Local Programs:** *Auction Show.* **Wattage:** 3000. **Ad Rates:** $7-16 for 30 seconds; $11.50-26.50 for 60 seconds.

FOSSTON, pop. 1,599.

NW MN. Polk Co. 68 mi. E of Grand Forks, ND. Creamery. Dairy, stock, grain farms.

15991 Thirteen Towns
C & K Publishing, Inc.
116 W. 2nd St. Phone: (218)435-1313
Fosston, MN 56542 Fax: (218)435-1309

Community newspaper. **Founded:** 1884. **Freq:** Weekly (Mon.). **Print Method:** Offset. **Cols./Page:** 6. **Col. Width:** 12 picas. **Col. Depth:** 21 1/2 inches. **Key Personnel:** David S. Carr, Editor. **Subscription Rates:** $16; $20 out of area. **Remarks:** Accepts advertising.
Ad Rates: SAU: $5 **Circ:** Paid ‡3,100

15992 City of Fosston Cable TV
220 E. 1st St. Phone: (218)435-1737
Fosston, MN 56542 Fax: (218)435-1961
E-mail: fosston@fosston.polaristel.net

Owner: City of Fosston Cable TV, at above address. **Founded:** 1977. **Key Personnel:** Russell W. Earls, Contact; Charles Lucken, Contact. **Cities Served:** subscribing households 605; 1 channel.

15993 KKCQ-AM - 1480
Hwy. 2 E. Phone: (218)435-1919
PO Box 606 Fax: (218)435-1480
Fosston, MN 56542-0606

Format: Country. **Simulcasts:** KKCQ-FM. **Networks:** AP; ABC. **Founded:** 1966. **Formerly:** KEHG-AM. **Operating Hours:** Continuous. **Key Personnel:** Larry E. Roed, Gen. Mgr./Pres.; Phil Ehlke, General Sales Mgr.; Tom Lano, Program Dir.; Phyllis Sjulson, Traffic Dir.; Dan Kendall, News Dir. **Local Programs:** *Food for Thought,* David Seudin. **Wattage:** 5000 day; 2500 night. **Ad Rates:** $5-6.50 for 30 seconds; $7.15-9.30 for 60 seconds.

15994 KKEQ-FM - 107.1
Hwy. 2 E. Phone: (218)435-1919
PO Box 606 Fax: (218)435-1480
Fosston, MN 56542-0606
Free: (800)435-1071
E-mail: q107@means.net

Format: Adult Contemporary; Religious. **Networks:** ABC. **Founded:** 1969. **Formerly:** KKCQ-FM. **Operating Hours:** Continuous. **ADI:** Minneapolis-St. Paul, MN. **Key Personnel:** Larry E. Roed, Pres./Gen. Mgr.; Phil Ehlke, General Sales Mgr.; Phyllis Sjulson, Traffic Dir.; Kevin Arvidson, Program Dir. **Local Programs:** *Ministry in Action* 9:45 am Monday-Friday, Kevin Arvidson, Program Dir. **Wattage:** 50,000. **Ad Rates:** $7.50 for 30 seconds. Combined advertising rates available with KKCQ-FM; KKCQ-AM. **URL:** http://www.christianradio.com/q107.

FULDA

15995 Fulda Free Press
PO Box 439 Phone: (507)425-2303
Fulda, MN 56131 Fax: (507)425-2501

Community newspaper. **Founded:** 1881. **Freq:** Weekly (Wed.). **Print Method:** Offset. **Cols./Page:** 8. **Col. Width:** 10.5 picas. **Col. Depth:** 21 1/2 inches. **Key Personnel:** Gerald Johnson, Publisher. **USPS:** 211-500. **Subscription Rates:** $22; $30 out of area. **Remarks:** Accepts advertising.
Ad Rates: BW: $602 **Circ:** ‡1,400
SAU: $3.75
PCI: $3.25

GAYLORD†, pop. 1,933.

SC MN. Sibley Co. 30 mi. N. Mankato. Manufactures coats, jackets, doors, fresh & frozen egg products. Grain farms. Dairy, corn, soybeans.

15996 Hub
PO Box 208 Phone: (507)237-2476
Gaylord, MN 55334
Community newspaper. **Founded:** 1886. **Freq:** Weekly (Thurs.). **Print Method:** Offset. **Cols./Page:** 7. **Col. Width:** 21 nonpareils. **Col. Depth:** 301 agate lines. **Key Personnel:** James E. Deis, Editor and Publisher. **Subscription Rates:** $22; $25 out of area; $32 out of state. **Remarks:** Accepts advertising.
Ad Rates: BW: $381.87 **Circ:** ‡2,260
4C: $581.87
PCI: $3

GIBBON, pop. 877.

SW MN. Sibley Co. 15 mi. W. of Gaylord.

15997 The Gibbon Gazette
Gibbon Gazette
PO Box 456 Gibbone Phone: (507)834-6966
Gibbon, MN 55335-0456 Fax: (507)834-6966

Community newspaper. **Founded:** 1894. **Freq:** Weekly (Thurs.). **Print Method:** Broadsheet. Offset. **Cols./Page:** 7. **Col. Width:** 11 1/2 picas. **Col. Depth:** 301 agate lines. **Key Personnel:** Charles Warner, Publisher. **Subscription Rates:** $18 individuals; $20 out of area; $24 out of state. **Remarks:** Accepts advertising. **Alt. Formats:** Audio tape.
Ad Rates: BW: $300 **Circ:** Paid 950
PCI: $3 Free 20

GLENCOE†, pop. 4,396.

SC MN. McLeod Co. 45 mi. NW of Mankato. Creamery; cheese factory; corn and pea cannery. Dairy, cattle, poultry, grain farms. Sugar beets, peas, corn. Ships.

15998 The Glencoe Enterprise
831 11th St. Phone: (320)864-4715
PO Box 97 Fax: (320)864-4715
Glencoe, MN 55336
Community newspaper. **Founded:** 1873. **Freq:** Weekly (Thurs.). **Print Method:** Offset. **Cols./Page:** 6. **Col. Width:** 28 nonpareils. **Col. Depth:** 294 agate lines. **Key Personnel:** Annamarie Tudhope, Editor and Publisher. **Subscription Rates:** $22 individuals; $25 out of state. **Remarks:** Accepts advertising.
Ad Rates: GLR: $.412 **Circ:** ‡3,200
BW: $46.10
PCI: $4.25

15999 McLeod County Chronicle
McLeod Publishing, Inc.
PO Box 188 Phone: (320)864-5518
Glencoe, MN 55336 Fax: (612)864-5510

Community newspaper. **Founded:** 1980. **Freq:** Weekly. **Print Method:** 15 x 21 1/2. Offset. **Cols./Page:** 7. **Col. Width:** 2 inches. **Col. Depth:** 21.5 inches. **Key Personnel:** Rich Glennie, Editor, rich@glencoenews.com; William C. Ramige, Publisher, billr@glencoenews.com; Tom Hauer, Advertising Mgr., tomh@glencoenews.com. **Subscription Rates:** $40 individuals. **Remarks:** Accepts advertising.
Ad Rates: BW: $586.95 **Circ:** Paid ‡3,181
SAU: $4.90 Free 56

16000 Jones Intercable
2104 E. 10th St. Phone: (612)864-5612
Box 7 Fax: (612)864-5612
Glencoe, MN 55336

Owner: Jones Intercable Inc., 9697 E. Mineral Ave., Englewood, CO 80112, (303)792-3111. **Key Personnel:** Connie Ruth, Regional Mgr.; Tim Erickson, Chief Engineer; Don Czeck, Chief Technician. **Cities Served:** Glencoe, MN: subscribing households 1,100; 38 channels; 1 community access channel; 158 hours per week community access programming.

GLENWOOD†, pop. 2,523.

WC MN. Pope Co. On Lake Minnewaska, 69 mi. NW of Saint Cloud. Summer resort. Museum (Indian artifacts). Fabricating and machine parts factories. Fish Hatchery. Dairy, stock, grain farms.

16001 Pope County Tribune
108 S. Franklin Phone: (320)634-4571
Glenwood, MN 56334 Fax: (320)634-5522

Local newspaper. **Founded:** Sept. 1, 1920. **Freq:** Weekly (Mon.). **Print Method:** Offset. **Cols./Page:** 6. **Col. Width:** 28 nonpareils. **Col. Depth:** 301 agate lines. **Key Personnel:** John R. Stone, Publisher. **Subscription Rates:** $28 individuals. **Remarks:** Accepts advertising.
Ad Rates: GLR: $.25 **Circ:** Paid ‡4,100
SAU: $4.25 Free ‡100
PCI: $5.36

GOLDEN VALLEY, pop. 22,775.

SE MN. Hennepin Co. 28 mi. NW of Bemidji. Residential.

16002 KXXR-FM - 93.7
917 N. Lilac Phone: (612)545-5601
Golden Valley, MN 55422 Fax: (612)595-4940

Networks: ABC. **Founded:** 1949. **Formerly:** KRXX-AM (1994); KEGE-FM (Nov. 1997). **Operating Hours:** Continuous. **Key Personnel:** Mark Steinmetz, Contact; Amy Waggoner, Contact; Lori Moen, Contact; Wendy Ellis, Contact; Mary L. Koecher, Contact; Wade Linder, Contact. **Local Programs:** *Morning Show,* Mike Dousette. **Wattage:** 100,000.

GONVICK, pop. 362.

NW MN. Clearwater Co. 45 mi NW of Bemidji. Dairy, stock, grain farms.

16003 Leader-Record
Richards Publishing Co., Inc.
PO Box 159 Phone: (218)487-5225
Gonvick, MN 56644 Fax: (218)487-5251
Free: (800)835-8496
Publisher E-mail: richards@gonvick.polaristel.net

Community newspaper. **Founded:** 1901. **Freq:** Weekly (Wed.). **Print Method:** Offset. **Cols./Page:** 6. **Col. Width:** 10 picas. **Col. Depth:** 224 agate lines. **Key Personnel:** Richard D. Richards, Publisher; Corrine J. Richards, Editor. **Subscription Rates:** $18 individuals; $23 out of country. **Remarks:** Accepts advertising.
Ad Rates: SAU: $2.97 **Circ:** Paid 2,000
PCI: $2.25

GOODHUE

16004 The Country Shopper
Grimsrud Publishing, Inc.
225 Main St. Phone: (507)732-7617
PO Box 97 Fax: (507)732-7619
Zumbrota, MN 55992
Free: (800)772-5384

Community newspaper. **Freq:** Weekly (Wed.). **Print Method:** Offset. **Key Personnel:** David Grimsrud, Publisher; Peter Grimsrud, Editor. **Remarks:** Accepts advertising.
Ad Rates: BW: $258 **Circ:** (Not Reported)
PCI: $3.25

16005 Rag Mag
Black Hat Press
508 Second Ave., Box 12 Phone: (651)923-4590
Goodhue, MN 55027
Scholarly magazine covering poetry, prose, and art. **Founded:**

1982. **Freq:** Semiannual. **Trim Size:** 6 x 9. **Key Personnel:** Beverly Voldseth. **ISSN:** 0742-2768. **Subscription Rates:** $10 individuals; $6 single issue.
Circ: Combined 300

GRAND MARAIS, pop. 1,289.

NE MN. Cook Co. 112 mi. NE of Duluth. Summer & winter sports resort. Logging. Timber.

16006 WTIP-FM - 90.7
PO Box 1005 Phone: (218)387-1070
Grand Marais, MN 55604 Fax: (218)387-1120
E-mail: cccomradio@aol.com

Format: Adult Contemporary. **Owner:** Cook County Community Radio Corp, at above address. **Operating Hours:** 5:00 a.m.-2:00 p.m. **Key Personnel:** Mike Raymond, President, phone (218)387-9599; Sue Maijala, Program Dir. **Wattage:** 25,000.

GRAND RAPIDS†, pop. 7,934.

NC MN. Itasca Co. On Mississippi River, 36 mi. SW of Hibbing. Resort. Industrial park. Light manufacturing. Manufactures paper and wood products. Iron Ore mining. Dairy, potato and beef cattle farming.

16007 Herald-Review
301 1st Ave. NW Phone: (218)326-6623
PO Box 220 Fax: (218)326-6627
Grand Rapids, MN 55744
Free: (888)515-6623
Publisher E-mail: herald@grandrapids.mn.com

Newspaper. **Founded:** 1894. **Freq:** Semiweekly (Wed. and Sun.). **Print Method:** Offset. **Trim Size:** Tabloid. **Cols./Page:** 5. **Col. Width:** 11.5 picas. **Col. Depth:** 16 1/2 inches. **Key Personnel:** Wanda Moeller, Editor; Charles Johnson, Publisher; Steve Lynch, Advertising Mgr.; Ron Oleheiser, General Mgr. **Subscription Rates:** $40 individuals per year; $0.75 single issue. **Remarks:** Accepts advertising.
Ad Rates: GLR: $2 **Circ:** 8,700
BW: $780
4C: $1,100
SAU: $9.75

16008 KAXE-FM - 91.7
1841 E. Hwy. 169 Phone: (218)326-1234
Grand Rapids, MN 55744 Fax: (218)326-1235
E-mail: kaxe@kaxe.org

Format: Public Radio; Eclectic. **Networks:** National Public Radio (NPR); Public Radio International (PRI). **Owner:** Northern Community Radio, Inc., at above address. **Founded:** 1976. **Operating Hours:** 5 a.m.-1 a.m.; 45% network, 55% local. **Key Personnel:** Maggie Montgomery, Station Mgr., mmontgom@kaxe.org; Mark Tarner, Dir. of BRG, markt@kaxe.org; Scott Hall, News Dir., shall@kaxe.org; Sharon McKeever, Business Mgr., smckeeve@kaxe.org; John Bauer, Developement Dir., jbauer@kaxe.org. **Wattage:** 100,000. **Ad Rates:** Noncommercial.

16009 KMFY-FM - 96.9
507 SE 11th St. Phone: (218)326-0307
Box 597 Fax: (218)326-3448
Grand Rapids, MN 55744

Format: Adult Contemporary. **Networks:** ABC; Minnesota News; Satellite Music Network. **Owner:** Kirwin Broadcasting, Inc., at above address. **Founded:** 1975. **Formerly:** KNNS-FM (1989). **Operating Hours:** Continuous. **Key Personnel:** Dale Randalls, Contact; Bill Kirwin, Contact; Mike Zimmerli, Program Dir. **Wattage:** 100,000. **Ad Rates:** $5.75-9 for 30 seconds; $7.75-11 for 60 seconds. Combined advertising rates available with KOZY-AM.

16010 KOZY-AM - 1320
Box 597 Phone: (218)326-3446
Grand Rapids, MN 55744 Fax: (218)326-3448

Format: Oldies; News. **Networks:** ABC. **Owner:** Kirwin Broadcasting Inc., at above address. **Founded:** 1948. **Formerly:** KBZY-AM (1952). **Operating Hours:** Continuous. **Key Personnel:** Bill Kirwin, Contact; Dale Randall, Operations Mgr. **Local Programs:** *Kozy Scene*, Dale Randall, (218)3763446, Fax (218)3763448. **Wattage:** 5000. **Ad Rates:** $5.75-9 for 30 seconds; $7.75-11 for 60 seconds. Combined advertising rates available with KMFY-FM.

16011 Triax Cablevision
1105 N.W. 4th St. Phone: (218)326-0900
Grand Rapids, MN 55744 Fax: (218)326-6705

Owner: Intermedia Media Partners, 235 Montgomery, Ste. 420, San Francisco, CA 94104, (415)397-4121, Fax: (415)397-4706. **Formerly:** Northland Cablevision. **Key Personnel:** Scott Walters, Regional Mgr.; Bob Muhich, Area Mgr.; Lee Frahm, Plant Mgr. **Cities Served:** Grand Rapids, Keewatin, Nashwauk, MN; Harris Township, Grand Rapids Township: subscribing households 5,300; 37 channels; 4 community access channels; 54 hours per week community access programming.

GRANITE FALLS†, pop. 3,451.

SW MN. Yellow Medicine Co. On Minnesota River, 123 mi. W. of Minneapolis. Manufactures oilers, hydraulic equipment; rock crushing plants. Dairy, stock, mink, grain farms. Corn, wheat, hogs.

16012 The Advocate-Tribune
PO Box 99 Phone: (612)669-7449
Granite Falls, MN 56241-0099 Fax: (612)564-4293

Community newspaper. **Founded:** 1902. **Freq:** Weekly (Thurs.). **Print Method:** Offset. **Cols./Page:** 6. **Col. Width:** 21 nonpareils. **Col. Depth:** 226 agate lines. **Key Personnel:** Byron Higgin, Editor and Publisher; Tom Cherney, News Editor; Anita Schuler, Advertising. **Subscription Rates:** $22.50; $28 out of state. **Remarks:** Accepts advertising. **Formerly:** Advocate; Tri-County Advocate; The Clarkfield Advocate; Granite Falls Tribune.
Ad Rates: GLR: $5.45 **Circ:** Paid ‡3,700
BW: $450 Free ‡100
4C: $500
PCI: $4.25

GREENBUSH

16013 New River Record
PO Box F Phone: (218)782-2275
Greenbush, MN 56726 Fax: (218)782-2277
Publication E-mail: tribune@means.net

Community newspaper. **Founded:** Jan. 1904. **Freq:** Weekly (Wed.). **Print Method:** Offset. **Cols./Page:** 6. **Col. Depth:** 20 3/4 inches. **Key Personnel:** Terry Lorenson, General Mgr.; Rollin Bergman, Publisher. **ISSN:** 0747-4407. **Subscription Rates:** $19 individuals; $25 out of area. **Remarks:** Accepts advertising. **Alt. Formats:** CD-ROM, Metro.
Ad Rates: BW: $451 **Circ:** Paid ‡540
PCI: $3.50 Free ‡25

GRYGLA, pop. 216.

NW MN. Marshall Co. 40 mi. NE of Thief River Falls. Hunters paradise. Center of Agricultural services.

16014 The Grygla Eagle
Richards Publishing Co., Inc.
PO Box 17 Phone: (218)294-6220
Grygla, MN 56727
Publisher E-mail: richards@gonvick.polaristel.net

Community newspaper. **Founded:** Aug. 1973. **Freq:** Weekly (Thurs.). **Print Method:** Letterpress and offset. **Cols./Page:** 6. **Col. Width:** 20 nonpareils. **Col. Depth:** 224 agate lines. **Key Personnel:** Joy Nordby, Editor; Richard Richards, Publisher. **Subscription Rates:** $18 individuals. **Remarks:** Accepts advertising.
Ad Rates: GLR: $.33 **Circ:** ‡750
BW: $216
SAU: $3.25
PCI: $2.25

HALLOCK†, pop. 1,405.

NW MN. Kittson Co. 60 mi. N. of Grand Forks, ND. Stock, dairy, poultry, grain farms. Wheat, sugar beets.

16015 Kittson County Enterprise
Kittson County Enterprise Co.
109 S. 3rd St. Fax: (218)843-2312
Hallock, MN 56728
Community newspaper. **Founded:** 1884. **Freq:** Weekly. **Print Method:** Offset. **Cols./Page:** 6. **Col. Width:** 12 picas. **Col. Depth:** 21 1/4 inches. **Key Personnel:** Gail Norland, Publisher. **Subscription Rates:** $22 individuals. **Remarks:** Accepts advertising. **Formerly:** Northern Media.
Ad Rates: GLR: $4.20 **Circ:** Paid ‡1,885
BW: $541.80
4C: $621.80
SAU: $5.00
PCI: $4.20

HALSTAD, pop. 690.

NW MN. Norman Co. 38 mi. N. of Fargo, ND. Grain farm. Wheat, potatoes, soybeans.

16016 The Shopper
Shopper Diversified
Box 267 Phone: (218)456-2133
Halstad, MN 56548 Fax: (218)456-2567

Shopper. **Founded:** 1975. **Freq:** Weekly (Mon.). **Print Method:** Offset. **Cols./Page:** 6. **Col. Width:** 19 nonpareils. **Col. Depth:** 217 agate lines. **Key Personnel:** Harold V. Nelson, Editor and Publisher. **Subscription Rates:** Free. **Remarks:** Accepts advertising.
Ad Rates: GLR: $1.08 **Circ:** Free ‡40,220

HANSKA, pop. 429.

SC MN. Brown Co. 100 mi. SW of Minneapolis. Stock, dairy, poultry farms. Hogs, soybeans, corn.

16017 The Hanska Herald
PO Box 45 Phone: (507)439-6214
Hanska, MN 56041-0045
Community newspaper. **Founded:** 1901. **Freq:** Weekly (Thurs.). **Print Method:** Offset. **Trim Size:** 16 x 22 1/2. **Cols./Page:** 7. **Col. Width:** 2 1/16 inches. **Col. Depth:** 21 inches. **Key Personnel:** Bernice E. Becken, Editor; Ross Becken, Publisher. **USPS:** 234-680. **Subscription Rates:** $18 individuals. **Remarks:** Accepts advertising.
Ad Rates: BW: $382.20 **Circ:** Paid ⊕772
SAU: $2.60 Free ⊕28

HARMONY, pop. 1,133.

SE MN. Fillmore Co. 15 mi. S. of Preston.

16018 Harmony Cable Inc.
35 1st Ave. NE Phone: (507)886-2525
PO Box 308 Fax: (507)886-2500
Harmony, MN 55939

Founded: 1984. **Key Personnel:** Kenneth Halverson, Contact. **Cities Served:** subscribing households 385; 36 channels; 1 community access channel.

HASTINGS†, pop. 12,827.

SE MN. Dakota Co. On Mississippi River, 20 mi SE of Saint Paul. Manufactures flour, sprayers, dusters, filing equipment, wire specialties, scotch tape, reflective sheeting, petroleum products, ammonia, ready-to-mix concrete. Dairy, poultry, grain farms. Corn, wheat, rye. Paper, clay products.

16019 Hastings Star Gazette
Trade Winds
PO Box 277 Phone: (612)437-6153
Hastings, MN 55033 Fax: (612)437-5911

Community newspaper. **Founded:** 1969. **Freq:** Weekly (Thurs.). **Print Method:** Offset. **Cols./Page:** 6. **Col. Width:** 30 nonpareils. **Col. Depth:** 294 agate lines. **Key Personnel:** Michael J. O'Connor, Editor. **Subscription Rates:** $16. **Remarks:** Accepts advertising.
Ad Rates: GLR: $.20 **Circ:** ‡5,600

16020 KDWA-AM - 1460
PO Box 215 Phone: (612)437-1460
514 Vermillion St. Fax: (612)438-3042
Hastings, MN 55033

Format: Oldies; News; Sports; Talk. **Networks:** Minnesota News. **Owner:** K & M Broadcasting of Minnesota, at above address. **Founded:** 1963. **Operating Hours:** Continuous; 15% network, 85% local. **ADI:** Minneapolis-St. Paul, MN. **Key Personnel:** Roy K. Kline, Jr., Contact; Dan Massman, Contact; Jim Gallup, News Dir. **Local Programs:** *Local Sports*; *Teen Time*. **Wattage:** 1000. **Ad Rates:** $10 for 30 seconds; $15 for 60 seconds.

HAWLEY, pop. 1,634.

WC MN. Clay Co. 23 mi. E. of Fargo, ND. Agriculture equipment manufactured. Grain and dairy products.

16021 Hawley Herald
608 Main St. Phone: (218)483-3306
PO Box 709 Fax: (218)483-4457
Hawley, MN 56549
Newspaper. **Founded:** 1890. **Freq:** Weekly (Mon.). **Print Method:** Offset. **Cols./Page:** 6. **Col. Width:** 21 nonpareils. **Col. Depth:** 301 agate lines. **Key Personnel:** James Martodam, Editor; Gene Prim, Publisher. **Subscription Rates:** $18. **Remarks:** Accepts advertising.
Ad Rates: SAU: $4.75 **Circ:** Paid ‡2,400
Free ‡50

HAYFIELD

16022 Hayfield Herald
108 E. Main Phone: (507)477-2232
PO Box 85 Fax: (507)374-9327
Hayfield, MN 55940
Community newspaper. **Freq:** Weekly (Tues.). **Cols./Page:** 6. **Col. Width:** 10 1/2 picas. **Col. Depth:** 21 1/2 inches. **Key Personnel:** Brad Friswold, Editor. **Subscription Rates:** $16 individuals; $18 out of area; $20 out of state. **Remarks:** Accepts advertising.
Ad Rates: BW: $341.85 **Circ:** ‡1,750
4C: $416.85
SAU: $5.65
PCI: $2.65

HECTOR

16023 Bird Island Union
Hubin Publishing Co., Inc.
Box 278 Phone: (320)365-3266
Hector, MN 55342 Fax: (320)365-4506
Free: (888)325-0196

Community newspaper. **Founded:** Aug. 22, 1879. **Freq:** Weekly (Wed.). **Cols./Page:** 6. **Col. Width:** 26 nonpareils. **Col. Depth:** 301 agate lines. **Key Personnel:** Bren McDowell, Managing Editor; John Hubin, Publisher, phone (320)848-2248, fax (320)848-2249, jnhubin@means.net. **Subscription Rates:** $24 U.S.; $27 out of country; $32 out of state. **Remarks:** Accepts advertising.
Ad Rates: BW: $300 **Circ:** ‡1,100
PCI: $3.25

16024 News Mirror
PO Box 278 Phone: (320)848-2248
Hector, MN 55342 Fax: (320)848-2249
Free: (888)325-0196

Community newspaper. **Founded:** 1891. **Freq:** Weekly. **Print Method:** Offset. **Cols./Page:** 6. **Col. Width:** 14 picas. **Col. Depth:** 21 1/2 inches. **Key Personnel:** Ken Hubin, Editor, phone (320)833-2001, fax (320)833-2077; John Hubin, Publisher, jnh@means.net. **Subscription Rates:** $24 individuals; $27 out of area; $32 out of state. **Remarks:** Accepts advertising.
Ad Rates: BW: $483.75 **Circ:** Paid 2,500
PCI: $3.90 Free 200

HENDERSON

16025 Closing the Gap
Box 68 Phone: (507)248-3294
Henderson, MN 56044 Fax: (507)248-3810
Publication E-mail: info@closingthegap.com
Publisher E-mail: info@closingthegap.com

Magazine exploring the use of computers for people with disabilities. **Founded:** 1982. **Freq:** 6/year. **Trim Size:** 12x 16. **Key Personnel:** Megan Turek, mturek@closingthegap.com. **ISSN:** 0886-1935. **Subscription Rates:** $31 individuals. **Remarks:** Advertising accepted; rates available upon request. **Alt. Formats:** Diskette, ASCII text.
Circ: Paid 10,000

HENNING, pop. 832.

WC MN. Otter Trail Co. 34 mi. E. of Fergus Falls. Lake resort. Wood products industry. Hatchery. Dairy, poultry, grain farms.

16026 The Henning Advocate
400 Douglas Ave. Phone: (218)583-2935
PO Box 35 Fax: (218)583-2909
Henning, MN 56551-0035
Community newspaper. **Founded:** Mar. 12, 1891. **Freq:** Weekly (Wed.). **Print Method:** Offset. **Cols./Page:** 6. **Col. Width:** 27 nonpareils. **Col. Depth:** 301 agate lines. **Key Personnel:** Andrew Barr, Publisher. **USPS:** 240-180. **Subscription Rates:** $22.50. **Remarks:** Accepts advertising.
Ad Rates: BW: $619 **Circ:** ‡1,511
SAU: $4.03

HERMAN, pop. 600.

WC MN. Grant Co. 40 mi. S. of Fergus Falls. Stock, dairy, grain farms. Soybeans, corn, barley, sugarbeets.

16027 Herman Review
Box E Phone: (320)677-2229
Herman, MN 56248 Fax: (320)677-2229
Publisher E-mail: ripnican@infolink.morris.mn.us

Community newspaper. **Founded:** 1900. **Freq:** Weekly (Thurs.). **Print Method:** Offset. **Trim Size:** 8 x 11. **Cols./Page:** 5. **Col. Width:** 23 nonpareils. **Col. Depth:** 210 agate lines. **Key Personnel:** Nick Ripperger, Publisher; Anne Ripperger, Advertising. **USPS:** 242-180. **Subscription Rates:** $16; $21 out of area. **Remarks:** Accepts advertising.
Ad Rates: GLR: $.178 **Circ:** ‡1,275
BW: $200
4C: $340
SAU: $2.98
CNU: $3.51
PCI: $2.77

HERMANTOWN

16028 Hermantown Star
4850 Miller Trunk, Ste. 4B Phone: (218)727-0419
Hermantown, MN 55811 Fax: (218)722-5821

Local newspaper. **Founded:** Sept. 1977. **Freq:** Weekly (Fri.). **Print Method:** Offset. **Cols./Page:** 6. **Col. Width:** 12 picas. **Col. Depth:** 21 1/2 inches. **Key Personnel:** Keith Hansen, Editor and Publisher, hansen@cpinternet.com. **USPS:** 408-310. **Subscription Rates:** $24.00 individuals. **Remarks:** Accepts advertising.
Ad Rates: BW: $300 **Circ:** Paid 1,313
SAU: $7.50 Free 97
PCI: $7.50

HERON LAKE, pop. 777.

NW MN. Jackson Co. 21 mi. NW of Jackson.

16029 Tri-County News
Tri County News Phone: (507)793-2327
PO Box 227 Fax: (507)793-2327
Heron Lake, MN 56137
Community newspaper. **Founded:** 1886. **Freq:** Weekly. **Print Method:** Offset. **Cols./Page:** 8. **Col. Width:** 1 3/4 inches. **Col. Depth:** 23 inches. **Key Personnel:** Carol Schreiber, Editor; Gerald Johnson, Publisher. **ISSN:** 0273-5482. **Subscription Rates:** $22.00 local; $28 out of area & state. **Remarks:** Accepts advertising.
Ad Rates: GLR: $.24 **Circ:** Paid ‡1,000
SAU: $4.42 Free ‡25
PCI: $3.50

HIBBING†, pop. 21,193.

NE MN. St. Louis Co. 78 mi. NW of Duluth. Hibbing Community College. National historic site. Taconite mining. Foundry, iron ore deposits.

16030 Hibbing Daily Tribune
HTC, Inc.
2142 1st Ave. Phone: (218)262-1011
PO Box 38 Fax: (218)262-4318
Hibbing, MN 55746-1805
Free: (800)477-7093

General newspaper. **Founded:** 1899. **Freq:** Daily (eve.), Sunday (morn.). **Print Method:** Offset. **Cols./Page:** 6. **Col. Width:** 24 nonpareils. **Col. Depth:** 301 agate lines. **Key Personnel:** Alan Zdon, Editor; John Murphy, Publisher. **Subscription Rates:** $70.20. **Remarks:** Accepts advertising.
Ad Rates: SAU: $7.35 **Circ:** (Not Reported)

16031 WIRT-TV - 10
c/o WDIO-TV Phone: (218)727-6864
10 Observation Rd. Fax: (218)727-4415
Duluth, MN 55811
E-mail: wdio@aol.com

Format: Commercial TV. **Simulcasts:** WDIO-TV Duluth, MN. **Networks:** ABC. **Owner:** WDIO-TV LLC, 3415 University Ave., St. Paul, MN 55114. **ADI:** Duluth, MN-Superior, WI. **Key Personnel:** James (Joe) Golden, General Sales Mgr.; Diane Sargent, Traffic Mgr.; George Couture, General Mgr.; Steve Bolf, Local Sales Mgr.; Steve Goodspeed, News Dir.; Dave Poirier, Program Dir.; Mike Hatlestad, Chief Engineer.

16032 WMFG-AM - 1240
807 W. 37th St. Phone: (218)263-7531
Hibbing, MN 55746 Fax: (218)263-6112

Format: Sports. **Owner:** Sounds Unlimited Inc., at above address. **Founded:** 1935. **Operating Hours:** Continuous. **ADI:** Duluth, MN-Superior, WI. **Key Personnel:** Dennis Martin, General Mgr.; Janice Rooney, Office Mgr.; Connie Theising, Office Mgr.; Joe Lancello, News/Sports. **Local Programs:** *Let's Talk About It*, Joe Luncello; *One-on-One Sports*, Joe Lancello, Mailing contact; *Polka Party*, Joe Cuek, Mailing contact. **Wattage:** 1000. **Ad Rates:** $8-12 for 30 seconds; $10-16 for 60 seconds. Combined advertising rates available with WMFG-FM & KMFG-FM.

16033 WMFG-FM - 106.3
807 W. 37th St. Phone: (218)863-7531
Hibbing, MN 55746

Format: Oldies. **Networks:** Satellite Music Network. **Owner:** Sounds Unlimited, Inc., 702 Poplar Ave., Cloquet, MN 55720. **Founded:** 1923. **Operating Hours:** Continuous. **Key Personnel:** Dennis Martin, General Mgr.; Craig Coombs, Sales Mgr.

16034 WNMT-AM - 650
PO Box 1060 Phone: (218)262-4545
Hibbing, MN 55746 Fax: (218)262-2407

Format: News; Talk; Sports. **Networks:** ABC. **Owner:** Midwest Radio Network, at above address. **Founded:** 1975. **Formerly:** WKKQ-AM (1998). **Operating Hours:** Continuous; 95% network, 5% local. **Key Personnel:** Craig Holgate, News Dir.; Melisa Rolfe, Business Mgr. **Wattage:** 10,000. **Ad Rates:** $12-22 for 30 seconds; $13-27 for 60 seconds. Combined advertising rates available with WKKQ.

HILLS

16035 The Hills Crescent
Crescent Publishing
PO Box 457 Phone: (507)962-3230
Hills, MN 56138 Fax: (507)962-3211

Rural community newspaper (tabloid). **Founded:** 1893. **Freq:** Weekly. **Print Method:** Offset. **Cols./Page:** 5. **Col. Width:** 1 7/8 inches. **Col. Depth:** 16 inches. **Key Personnel:** Chad Mickelson, Editor; Preston VerMeer, Publisher. **ISSN:** 8750-0787. **Subscription Rates:** $25 individuals; $27.50 out of area. **Remarks:** Accepts advertising.
Ad Rates: BW: $225 **Circ:** ‡800
SAU: $2.75
PCI: $2.95

HINCKLEY, pop. 963.

EC MN. Pire Co. 80 mi. SW of Duluth. Wood pallet & photo engineering plants. Dairy,

16036 The Hinckley News
The Hinckley News, Inc.
115 Main St. Phone: (320)384-6188
PO Box 310 Fax: (320)384-6188
Hinckley, MN 55037
Publication E-mail: timb@pinenet.com
Publisher E-mail: hinckley.news@pinenet.com

Community newspaper. **Founded:** 1890. **Freq:** Weekly (Thurs.). **Print Method:** Offset. **Cols./Page:** 7. **Col. Width:** 2 inches. **Col. Depth:** 20 inches. **Key Personnel:** Tim Burkhardt, Editor. **USPS:** 245-940. **Subscription Rates:** $16. **Remarks:** Accepts advertising.
Ad Rates: SAU: $4.50 **Circ:** ‡2,000

HOPKINS, pop. 15,336.

SE MN. Hennepin Co. 6 mi. SW of Minneapolis. Manufactures farm machinery; berry crates. Greenhouses. Fruit truck farms. Raspberries, celery, vegetables.

16037 Hopkins Minnetonka Sailor-Sun
Minnesota Sun Publications
7831 E. Bush Lake Rd. Phone: (612)896-4700
Bloomington, MN 55439 Fax: (612)896-4728

Community newspaper (tabloid). **Freq:** Weekly (Wed.). **Print Method:** Offset. **Cols./Page:** 5. **Col. Width:** 1 15/16 inches. **Col. Depth:** 16 inches. **Key Personnel:** Don Thurlow, Publisher; Paul Johnson, Advertising Dir. **Remarks:** Accepts advertising.
Ad Rates: GLR: $24.94 **Circ:** Free 5,337
BW: $696
4C: $1,473
PCI: $21

16038 Mirror News Magazine
Market Power, Inc.
103 2nd St. N.
Hopkins, MN 55343

Journal focusing on manufacturing, merchandising, designing techniques, and procedures of the mirror industry including measuring, fabrication, installation, tools, and machinery. **Founded:** 1960. **Freq:** Quarterly. **Print Method:** Offset. **Trim Size:** 8 1/4 x 10 7/8. **Cols./Page:** 3. **Col. Width:** 28 nonpareils. **Col. Depth:** 143 agate lines. **Key Personnel:** W.L. Tiller, Editor and Publisher. **Subscription Rates:** $16. **Remarks:** Accepts advertising.
Ad Rates: BW: $877 **Circ:** Paid ‡42,230
4C: $1,420 Non-paid ‡5,660

HOWARD LAKE, pop. 1,240.

SEC MN. Wright Co. 43 mi. W. of Minneapolis. Resort. Diversified farming.

16039 Howard Lake Herald
PO Box 190 Phone: (320)543-2131
Howard Lake, MN 55349 Fax: (320)543-2135
Publication E-mail: herald@herald-journal.com

Community newspaper. **Founded:** 1878. **Freq:** Weekly (Mon.). **Print Method:** Offset. **Cols./Page:** 7. **Col. Width:** 2 inches. **Col. Depth:** 21 1/2 inches. **Key Personnel:** Andrea Vargo, Editor; Dale Kovar, General Mgr.; Chris Schultz, Advertising Mgr. **Subscription Rates:** $22 individuals; $26 institutions; $31 out of state. **Remarks:** Accepts advertising.
Ad Rates: BW: $617.05 **Circ:** ‡1,300
SAU: $4.50

16040 Laker Shopper
Howard Lake Herald
PO Box 190 Phone: (320)543-2131
Howard Lake, MN 55349 Fax: (320)543-2135
Publication E-mail: herald@herald-journal.com

Shopper. **Founded:** 1984. **Freq:** Weekly. **Print Method:** Offset. **Cols./Page:** 7. **Col. Width:** 2 inches. **Col. Depth:** 21 1/2 inches. **Key Personnel:** Chris Schultz, Advertising Mgr. **Subscription Rates:** Free. **Formerly:** Howard Laker.
Ad Rates: BW: $865.38 **Circ:** Free ‡6,000
SAU: $8

HUTCHINSON, pop. 9,244.

SC MN. McLeod Co. 58 mi. W. of Minneapolis. Manufactures counters, fixtures, farm machinery, wood, concrete products, beverages, cellophane, electronic components, audio and video magnetic tape. Cold storage plant. Dairy, grain, stock, truck farms.

16041 Hutchinson Leader
Hutchinson Leader, Inc.
36 Washington Ave. W. Phone: (320)587-5000
Hutchinson, MN 55350 Fax: (320)587-6104
Free: (888)326-2476
Publication E-mail: hulead@hutchtel.net
Publisher E-mail: leader@hutchtel.net

Community newspaper. **Founded:** 1880. **Freq:** 2/week. **Print Method:** Offset. **Cols./Page:** 6 and 6. **Col. Width:** 24 nonpareils and 13 inches. **Col. Depth:** 301 agate lines and 21 1/2 inches. **Key Personnel:** Matt McMillan, Publisher; Richard Crawford, Editor; Tina Berglund, Advertising Dir. **USPS:** 254-800. **Subscription Rates:** $45.50 individuals.
Ad Rates: GLR: $6.61 **Circ:** Paid ‡5,500
BW: $852.69
4C: $1,012.69
SAU: $6.61
PCI: $6.61

INTERNATIONAL FALLS†, pop. 5,611.

NC MN. Koochiching Co. On Rainy River, 165 mi. NW of Duluth. Manufactures paper, lumber. Summer resort. Pine, spruce timber. Dairy, truck farms. Clover, alfalfa seed, potatoes, vegetables.

16042 The Daily Journal
North Star Publishing Co.
500 3rd St. Phone: (218)285-7411
PO Box 951 Fax: (218)285-7206
International Falls, MN 56649
Community newspaper. **Founded:** 1911. **Freq:** Daily (eve.). **Print Method:** Offset. **Trim Size:** 14 x 23. **Cols./Page:** 6. **Col. Width:** 26 nonpareils. **Col. Depth:** 294 agate lines. **Key Personnel:** Tom Klein, Editor; Dave Ramnes, General Mgr.; Harry Swenson, Advertising Dir. **Subscription Rates:** $87.60 individuals. **Remarks:** Accepts advertising.
Ad Rates: GLR: $0.40 **Circ:** 4,456
BW: $722.40
4C: $922.40
PCI: $5.60

16043 CFOB-AM - 640
Box 1250 Phone: (218)283-4420
International Falls, MN 56649

Format: Adult Contemporary. **Owner:** Fawcett Broadcasting Ltd, at above address. **Founded:** 1944. **Operating Hours:** Continuous. **Key Personnel:** Hugh Syrja, Manager. **Wattage:** 1000. **Ad Rates:** $13.65-19.20 for 30 seconds.

16044 KGHS-AM - 1230
201 3rd St. Phone: (218)283-3481
Box 591 Fax: (218)283-3087
International Falls, MN 56649

Format: Classic Rock; News. **Networks:** Minnesota News; ABC. **Owner:** Communications International Associates, Inc., at above address. **Founded:** 1959. **Operating Hours:** Continuous; 20% network, 80% local. **ADI:** Duluth, MN-Superior, WI. **Key Personnel:** LuVerne Walter, Station/Sales Mgr.; Roger Johnson, News Dir.; Roger Jerome, Sports Dir. **Local Programs:** *Radio-Active-Morning Talk*, Jerry Franzen, Mailing contact. **Wattage:** 500 day; 250 night. **Ad Rates:** $8-12 for 30 seconds; $12-18 for 60 seconds. $8.50-$12.50 for 60 seconds. Combined advertising rates available with KSDM-FM.

16045 KSDM-FM - 104.1
201 3rd St. Phone: (218)283-2622
Box 591 Fax: (218)283-3087
International Falls, MN 56649

Format: Country. **Networks:** Minnesota News; ABC. **Owner:** Communications International Associates, Inc., at above address, (218)283-3481. **Founded:** 1979. **Operating Hours:** Continuous; 15% network, 85% local. **ADI:** Duluth, MN-Superior, WI. **Key Personnel:** Garrett Bishop, Program Dir.; LuVerne Walter, Station Mgr.; Roger Johnson, News Dir.; LuVerne Walter, Sales Mgr.; Roger Jerome, Sports Dir. **Wattage:** 8500. **Ad Rates:** $8-12 for 30 seconds; $12-18 for 60 seconds. $7.50-$10.50 for 30 seconds; $8.50-$12.50 for 60 seconds. Combined advertising rates available with KGHS-AM.

INVER GROVE HEIGHTS

16046 The Clergy Journal
6160 Carmen Ave. E. Phone: (612)451-9945
Inver Grove Heights, MN 55076 Fax: (612)457-4617

Homiletic and church management journal. **Subtitle:** Your Practical Guide to Church Leadership and Personal Growth. **Founded:** 1924. **Freq:** 10/year. **Print Method:** Letterpress and offset. **Cols./Page:** 3. **Col. Width:** 32 nonpareils. **Col. Depth:** 140 agate lines. **Key Personnel:** Clyde J. Steckel, Jr., Editor; Sarilyn Figueroa, Managing Editor; J. May, Marketing/Media, phone (847)823-4545. **ISSN:** 0009-6431. **Subscription Rates:** $29.95 individuals. **Remarks:** Accepts advertising. **Formerly:** Church Management: The Clergy Journal.
Ad Rates: BW: $600 **Circ:** Paid ‡10,000
4C: $1,650

ISLE, pop. 573.

EC MN. Mille Lacs Co. 38 mi. E. of Brainerd. Manufactures wood products, fishing tackle, boats, metal plating. Resort. Granite quarries; timber. Dairy, stock, poultry farms.

16047 Mille Lacs Messenger
Box 26 Phone: (320)676-3123
Isle, MN 56342 Fax: (320)676-8450
Publication E-mail: mlmess@upstel.net

Community newspaper. **Founded:** 1913. **Freq:** Weekly (Wed.). **Print Method:** Offset. **Trim Size:** 9 3/4 x 15. **Cols./Page:** 5. **Col. Width:** 11 picas. **Col. Depth:** 15 inches. **Key Personnel:** Jim Baden, Editor, jamesbad@upstel.net; Richard W. Norlander, Publisher, phone (218)927-3761, fax (218)927-3763, age@emily.net; Kevin Anderson, General Mgr. **Subscription Rates:** $27 individuals; $32 out of area; $38 out of state.
Ad Rates: GLR: $.257 **Circ:** 5,600
BW: $450
4C: $600
SAU: $8
PCI: $6.75

IVANHOE†, pop. 761.

SW MN. Lincoln Co. 90 mi. NE of Sioux Falls, SD. Dairy, stock, poultry, grain farms. Corn, barley, oats, soybeans.

16048 Ivanhoe Times
PO Box 100 Phone: (507)694-1246
Ivanhoe, MN 56142 Fax: (507)694-1246

Newspaper with a Democratic orientation. **Founded:** 1900. **Freq:** Weekly (Thurs.). **Print Method:** Offset. **Cols./Page:** 6. **Col. Width:** 26 nonpareils. **Col. Depth:** 287 agate lines. **Key Personnel:** Brent Beck, Publisher; Ellen Beck, Publisher. **Subscription Rates:** $25 individuals. **Remarks:** Accepts advertising.
Ad Rates: GLR: $.145 **Circ:** Paid 1,100
BW: $200 Non-paid 55
SAU: $3
PCI: $3.50

JACKSON†, pop. 3,797.

SW MN. Jackson Co. On Des Moines River, 62 mi. SW of Mankato. Manufactures spraying equipment, electronic components. Agriculture. Hog, beef, dairy products, poultry. Grain. Corn, soybeans.

16049 Jackson County Livewire
Livewire Printing Co.
310 2nd St. Phone: (507)847-3771
PO Box 208 Fax: (507)847-5822
Jackson, MN 56143-1640
Free: (800)658-2393
Publisher E-mail: info@livewireprinting.com

Shopper. **Founded:** 1936. **Freq:** Weekly (Mon.). **Print Method:** Offset. **Trim Size:** 11 3/8 x 16. **Cols./Page:** 5. **Col. Width:** 1 7/8 inches. **Col. Depth:** 15 inches. **Key Personnel:** Tim Gallagher, Editor, fax (507)847-5892, timg@livewireprinting.com; Dallas Luhmann, Advertising Mgr., dallasl@livewireprinting.com. **Subscription Rates:** Free; $14 by mail. **Remarks:** Accepts advertising. **URL:** http://www.livewireprinting.com.
Ad Rates: BW: $498.75 **Circ:** Paid ‡321
4C: $698.75 Free ‡9,570
SAU: $6.45
PCI: $6.45

16050 Jackson County Pilot
Jackson County Publishers, Inc.
310 2nd St. Phone: (507)847-3771
PO Box 208 Fax: (507)847-5822
Jackson, MN 56143-1640
Free: (800)658-2393
Publisher E-mail: info@livewireprinting.com

Community newspaper. **Founded:** 1889. **Freq:** Weekly (Thurs.). **Print Method:** Offset. **Trim Size:** 16 x 22 8/10. **Cols./Page:** 7. **Col. Width:** 21 nonpareils. **Col. Depth:** 301 agate lines. **Key Personnel:** Tim Gallagher, Editor, timg@livewireprinting.com; James Keul, Publisher, jimk@livewireprinting.com. **USPS:** 271-880. **Subscription Rates:** $25.50 individuals; $33.95 out of area. **Remarks:** Accepts advertising. **URL:** http://www.livewire-pilot.com/pilot.
Ad Rates: GLR: $.38 **Circ:** Paid ‡2,426
BW: $782.60 Free ‡100
4C: $200
SAU: $6.45
PCI: $5.20

16051 Jackson Municipal TV System
80 W. Ashley Phone: (507)847-3225
Jackson, MN 56143 Fax: (507)847-5586

Founded: 1957. **Key Personnel:** Curtis G. Egeland, Operations Mgr.; Steve Jenson, Technician. **Cities Served:** Jackson, MN: subscribing households 1,538; 34 channels; 1 community access channel; 6 hours per week community access programming.

16052 KKOJ-AM - 1190
Box 29 Phone: (507)847-5400
Jackson, MN 56143 Fax: (507)847-5745

Format: Contemporary Country. **Networks:** USA Radio. **Founded:** 1980. **Operating Hours:** Sunrise-sunset; 25% network, 75% local. **Key Personnel:** Doug Johnson, General Mgr.; Terry Wheeler, Music Dir.; Steve Schwaller, News Dir. **Wattage:** 5000. **Ad Rates:** $6-18 for 30 seconds; $9-27 for 60 seconds.

JANESVILLE, pop. 1,897.

SE MN. Waseca Co. 18 mi. E. of Mankato. Manufactures feed. Dairy, hog, grain farms. Corn, soybeans.

16053 Janesville Argus
Box 220 Phone: (507)234-6651
Janesville, MN 56048 Fax: (507)234-6390

Community newspaper. **Founded:** 1873. **Freq:** Weekly (Wed.). **Print Method:** Uses mats. Offset. **Cols./Page:** 6. **Col. Width:** 27 nonpareils. **Col. Depth:** 301 agate lines. **Key Personnel:** Judy A. Winter, Publisher. **Subscription Rates:** $26; $35 out of state.
Ad Rates: SAU: $4.15 **Circ:** 1,400
CNU: $50
PCI: $3.50

JASPER, pop. 731.

SW MN. Pipestone Co. 27 mi. NE of Sioux Falls, SD. Manufactures stone products. Silica quarries. Stock, grain farms. Corn.

16054 Jasper Journal
PO Box 188 Phone: (507)348-4176
Jasper, MN 56144-0188 Fax: (507)825-2168

Community newspaper. **Founded:** July 1888. **Freq:** Weekly (Mon.). **Print Method:** Offset. **Trim Size:** 10 3/4 x 15. **Cols./Page:** 5. **Col. Width:** 12 picas. **Col. Depth:** 15 inches. **Key Personnel:** Elaine Sestak, Editor; Charles Draper, Publisher; Deloris Quissell, Advertising Mgr. **ISSN:** 0744-3110. **Sub-**

scription Rates: $18 individuals; $22.50 out of area. **Formerly**: Journal (1991).
Ad Rates: PCI: $3.25 **Circ:** ‡1,010

JORDAN, pop. 2,663.

SE MN. Scott Co. 29 mi. Sw of Minneapolis. Manufactures wheelchairs. Sand and gravel pits. Dairy, stock, poultry, grain farms.

16055 Jordan Independent
Southwest Suburban Publishing
109 Rice St. S. Phone: (612)492-2224
Jordan, MN 55352
Community newspaper. **Founded:** 1884. **Freq:** Weekly (Thurs.). **Print Method:** Offset. **Cols./Page:** 6. **Col. Width:** 2 1/8 inches. **Col. Depth:** 21 1/2 inches. **Key Personnel:** Charlene J. Koepp, Editor; Craig Theis, Advertising Mgr.; Gary Klatt, Advertising Dir.; Ruby Mohlin, Circulation Mgr. **Subscription Rates:** $20; $33 out of area. **Remarks:** Accepts advertising.
Ad Rates: BW: $528.90 **Circ:** Paid ⊕**1,500**
4C: $903.90 Free 67
PCI: $4.50

KARLSTAD, pop. 934.

NW MN. Kiltson Co. 40 mi. SW of Roseau.

16056 North Star News
Box 158 Phone: (218)436-2157
Karlstad, MN 56732 Fax: (218)436-3271
Free: (800)874-5386
Publication E-mail: northstar@grandforks.polaristel.net

Community newspaper. **Founded:** 1900. **Freq:** Weekly (Thurs.). **Print Method:** Offset. **Cols./Page:** 6. **Col. Width:** 25 nonpareils. **Col. Depth:** 301 agate lines. **Key Personnel:** Daniel L. Nordine, Editor and Publisher. **USPS:** 598-500. **Subscription Rates:** $17.50. **Remarks:** Accepts advertising. **URL:** http://www.rrv.net/page1pub.
Ad Rates: SAU: $3.85 **Circ:** Paid ‡2,487
Free ‡75

KASSON, pop. 2,827.

SE MN. Dodge Co. 15 mi. W. of Rochester. Medical Branch of the Mayo Clinic. Dairy, grain, stock farms. Corn, oats, soybeans.

16057 Dodge County Independent
PO Box 367 Phone: (507)634-2661
105 1st Ave. NW Fax: (507)634-4446
Kasson, MN 55944
Community newspaper. **Subtitle:** Plus Weekly Shopper. **Founded:** 1867. **Freq:** Weekly (Wed.). **Print Method:** Offset. **Cols./Page:** 6. **Col. Width:** 28 nonpareils. **Col. Depth:** 301 agate lines. **Key Personnel:** Randy Carlsen, Publisher; Folmer Carlsen, Publisher. **USPS:** 159-340. **Subscription Rates:** $18. **Remarks:** Accepts advertising.
Ad Rates: BW: $250 **Circ:** ‡2,300
SAU: $3.75

KENYON, pop. 1,529.

SE MN. Goodhue Co. 14 mi. E. of Faribault. Mattresses and wood products manufactured; canned corn. Grain, dairy, stock, poultry farms. Corn, wheat, barley, soybeans.

16058 The Kenyon Leader
638 2nd St. Phone: (507)789-6161
Kenyon, MN 55946 Fax: (507)789-5040
Publication E-mail: kleader@clear.lakes.com

Community newspaper. **Founded:** June 15, 1885. **Freq:** Weekly (Wed.). **Print Method:** Offset. **Cols./Page:** 6. **Col. Width:** 24 nonpareils. **Col. Depth:** 301 agate lines. **Key Personnel:** Robert D. Noah, Publisher; Douglas A. Noah, Editor. **USPS:** 293-580. **Subscription Rates:** $20 individuals; $22 out of area; $26 out of state. **Remarks:** Accepts advertising.
Ad Rates: GLR: $.285 **Circ:** Paid 1,968
BW: $451.50 Free 46
SAU: $3.30

KERKHOVEN, pop. 761.

SW MN. Swift Co. 16 mi. SE of Benson.

16059 The Kerkhoven Banner
1003 Atlantic Ave. Phone: (320)264-3071
PO Box 148 Fax: (320)264-3070
Kerkhoven, MN 56252
Local newspaper. **Founded:** July 1896. **Freq:** Weekly (Thurs.). **Print Method:** Offset. **Cols./Page:** 6. **Col. Width:** 2 1/8 nonpareils. **Col. Depth:** 301 agate lines. **Key Personnel:** Theodore J. Almen, Editor and Publisher. **USPS:** 293-700. **Subscription Rates:** $16 individuals.
Ad Rates: GLR: $.15 **Circ:** 1,500
BW: $270.90
SAU: $3
PCI: $3

KIESTER, pop. 670.

SC MN. Faribault Co. 25 mi SW of Albert Lea. Feed mill. Stock, dairy, poultry, grain farms. Corn, oats, barley, soybeans.

16060 The Courier-Sentinel
405 W. Center St. Phone: (507)294-3400
Kiester, MN 56051
Community newspaper. **Founded:** 1981. **Freq:** Weekly (Thurs.). **Print Method:** Offset. **Trim Size:** 16 x 23. **Cols./Page:** 7. **Col. Width:** 21 nonpareils. **Col. Depth:** 294 agate lines. **Key Personnel:** Cynthia A. Matson, Editor and Publisher. **Subscription Rates:** $16; $18. **Remarks:** Accepts advertising.
Ad Rates: GLR: $.15 **Circ:** 1,778
SAU: $2.92

KIMBALL, pop. 651.

C MN. Stearns Co. 18 mi. SW of Saint Cloud. Lakes. Ski recreation area. Resort. Manufactures concrete products, truck and trailer equipment. Dairy, poultry farms.

16061 Tri-County News
Box 220 Phone: (320)398-5000
Kimball, MN 55353
Community newspaper. **Founded:** 1948. **Freq:** Weekly (Thurs.). **Print Method:** Offset. **Cols./Page:** 5. **Col. Width:** 22 nonpareils. **Col. Depth:** 210 agate lines. **Key Personnel:** Steve Prinsen, Publisher; Janet Robinson, Editor. **Subscription Rates:** $10; $11 out of state. **Remarks:** Accepts advertising.
Ad Rates: SAU: $2.30 **Circ:** Paid 1,375
Free 25

LA CRESCENT, pop. 3,674.

SE MN. Houston Co. 3 mi. W. of La Crosse, WI, on Mississippi River. Recreation, sports area. Manufactures concrete. Apple orchards. Dairy farms.

16062 Houston County News
104 S. Walnut, Ste. 2 Phone: (507)895-2940
PO Box 205 Fax: (507)895-2942
La Crescent, MN 55947
Community newspaper (tabloid). **Founded:** 1882. **Freq:** Weekly (Thurs.). **Print Method:** Offset. Uses mats. **Trim Size:** 8 1/2 x 11. **Cols./Page:** 6. **Col. Width:** 9 1/2 picas. **Col. Depth:** 155 agate lines. **Key Personnel:** Thomas J. Van der Linden, Publisher, tom@lacrescent.com; Jean Silberman, Publisher, jean@lacrescent.com. **USPS:** 252-700. **Subscription Rates:** $25.50 individuals; $32.50 out of state. **Remarks:** Accepts advertising.
Ad Rates: GLR: $6.60 **Circ:** 2,025
BW: $409.20
4C: $550
SAU: $6.60
PCI: $4.75

16063 WXOW-TV - 19
3705 Hwy. 25 Phone: (507)895-9969
La Crescent, MN 55947 Fax: (507)895-8124
E-mail: wxow@wxow.com

Format: Commercial TV. **Networks:** ABC. **Owner:** Shockley Communications Corporation, 5727 Tokay Blvd., Madison, WI 53719, (608)288-3040. **Founded:** 1970. **Operating Hours:** 6 a.m.-1 a.m.; 60% network, 40% local. **ADI:** La Crosse-Eau Claire, WI. **Key Personnel:** Deb Simonis, Program Dir.; Sean Dwyer, News Dir., phone (507)895-1919, fax (507)895-6196; Chuck Roth, General Mgr. **Wattage:** 630,000 visual, 63,000. **Ad Rates:** Advertising accepted; rates available upon request.

LAFAYETTE, pop. 507.

SC MN. Nicollet Co. 36 mi. NW of Mankato. Manufactures cement blocks, tiles. Agriculture. Corn, oats, barley, wheat, soybeans.

16064 Lafayette-Nicollet Ledger
Ledger Publishing Co.
631 Main Ave. Phone: (507)228-8985
Lafayette, MN 56054 Fax: (507)228-8779

Community newspaper. **Founded:** 1904. **Freq:** Weekly (Thurs.). **Print Method:** Offset. **Cols./Page:** 7. **Col. Width:** 24 nonpareils. **Col. Depth:** 301 agate lines. **Key Personnel:** Ruth Klossner, Editor; Doug Hanson, Publisher. **USPS:** 301-420. **Subscription Rates:** $25; $30 out of state. **Remarks:** Accepts advertising.
Ad Rates: GLR: $.50 **Circ:** 1,240
SAU: $4

16065 South Central Living
Ledger Publishing Co.
631 Main Ave. Phone: (507)228-8985
Lafayette, MN 56054 Fax: (507)228-8779

Shopper. **Founded:** 1988. **Freq:** Monthly. **Trim Size:** Broad sheet. **Cols./Page:** 7. **Col. Width:** 2 inches. **Col. Depth:** 21 1/2 inches. **Key Personnel:** Doug Hanson, Publisher. **USPS:** 301-420. **Subscription Rates:** Free. **Remarks:** Accepts advertising.
Ad Rates: BW: $512 **Circ:** Free ‡9,143
SAU: $4

LAKE BENTON, pop. 869.

SW MN. Lincoln Co. 25 mi. N. of Pipestone. Residential.

16066 Lincoln County Valley Journal
Valley Journal
115 S. Center Phone: (507)368-4275
Lake Benton, MN 56149
Local newspaper. **Freq:** Weekly (Wed.). **Print Method:** Uses mats. Offset. **Cols./Page:** 6. **Col. Width:** 21 nonpareils. **Col. Depth:** 238 agate lines. **Key Personnel:** Marlin D. Thompson, Editor and Publisher. **Subscription Rates:** $12.
Circ: 960

LAKE CITY, pop. 4,505.

SE MN. Wabasha Co. On Lake Pepin, 58 mi. SE of Saint Paul. Manufactures iron and aluminum pistons, flour, precision tools. Nurseries. Resort. Grain, dairy, stock, poultry farms.

16067 Lake City Graphic
107 S. Lakeshore Dr. Phone: (651)345-3316
PO Box 469 Fax: (651)345-4200
Lake City, MN 55041
Community newspaper. **Founded:** 1861. **Freq:** Weekly (Thurs.). **Print Method:** Offset. **Trim Size:** 14 1/2 x 22 3/4. **Cols./Page:** 6. **Col. Width:** 12.5 picas. **Col. Depth:** 21 1/2 inches. **Key Personnel:** Rich Ousky, Editor; Dennis Schumacher, Publisher; Dean Schumacher, Advertising Mgr. **Subscription Rates:** $22 individuals; $27 out of area.
Ad Rates: GLR: $.48 **Circ:** ‡3,200
BW: $870.75
SAU: $6.75
PCI: $6.75

16068 Lake City Shopper
107 S. Lakeshore Dr. Phone: (651)345-3316
PO Box 469 Fax: (651)345-4200
Lake City, MN 55041
Free shopper. **Founded:** 1967. **Freq:** Weekly (Tues.). **Print Method:** Offset. **Trim Size:** 14 1/2 x 22 3/4. **Cols./Page:** 6. **Col. Width:** 12.5 picas. **Col. Depth:** 21 1/2 inches. **Key Personnel:** Rich Ousky, Editor; Dennis Schumacher, Publisher; Dean Schumacher, Advertising Mgr. **Remarks:** Accepts advertising.
Ad Rates: GLR: $.48 **Circ:** Free ‡7,200
BW: $870.75
SAU: $6.75
PCI: $6.75

LAKEFIELD, pop. 1,845.

SW MN. Jackson Co. 80 mi. SW of Mankato. Heat woodburning furnace production. Egg-packing plant. Dairy, stock, poultry, grain farms.

16069 Lakefield Standard
403 Main Phone: (507)662-5555
Box 249 Fax: (507)662-6770
Lakefield, MN 56150
Publication E-mail: lakepub@rconnect.,com

General newspaper. **Founded:** 1884. **Freq:** Weekly (Thurs.). **Print Method:** Offset. **Cols./Page:** 7. **Col. Width:** 1 7/8 inches. **Col. Depth:** 21 1/2 inches. **Key Personnel:** Mark Ericson, Publisher. **USPS:** 302-980. **Subscription Rates:** $18; $21.50 out of area. **Remarks:** Accepts advertising.
Ad Rates: GLR: $.185 **Circ:** Paid ‡1,950
BW: $406 Free ‡12
4C: $600
SAU: $3.90
PCI: $3.15

LAKEVILLE, pop. 14,790.

SE MN. Dakota Co. 22 mi S. of Saint Paul. Industrial area.

16070 Farm Show
Farm Show Publishing, Inc.
20088 Kenwood Trail Phone: (612)469-5572
Box 1029
Lakeville, MN 55044
Magazine reporting on new products and product evaluations. **Founded:** Jan. 1977. **Freq:** Bimonthly. **Print Method:** Offset. **Cols./Page:** 4. **Col. Width:** 27 nonpareils. **Col. Depth:** 192 agate lines. **Key Personnel:** Mark Newhall, Editor and Publisher. **Subscription Rates:** $15.95. **Remarks:** Advertising not accepted.
Circ: ‡150,000

16071 Lakeville Life & Times
Lakeville Publishing, Inc.
20777 Holyoke Ave. W. Phone: (612)469-2181
PO Box 549 Fax: (612)469-2184
Lakeville, MN 55044
Publisher E-mail: lkvlpub@aol.com

Community newspaper. **Founded:** Feb. 1979. **Freq:** Weekly (Sat.). **Print Method:** Offset. **Trim Size:** 11 1/2 x 16. **Cols./Page:** 4. **Col. Width:** 14.5 picas. **Col. Depth:** 15 inches. **Key Personnel:** Richard M. Sherman, Editor and Publisher; Jonette Hubred, Managing Editor; Ginny Lee, Sales Mgr. **Subscription Rates:** $1.50 per week. **Remarks:** Accepts advertising.
Ad Rates: GLR: $.961 **Circ:** Free ‡19,961
BW: $802
4C: $1,052
SAU: $12.64
PCI: $13.37

LAMBERTON, pop. 1,032.

SW MN. Redwood Co. 75 mi. W. of Mankato. Grain, stock, dairy farms. Corn, soybeans.

16072 Lamberton News
218 E. Main St. Phone: (507)752-7181
PO Box 308 Fax: (507)752-7181
Lamberton, MN 56152
Community newspaper. **Founded:** Nov. 14, 1929. **Freq:** Weekly (Wed.). **Print Method:** Offset. **Cols./Page:** 6. **Col. Width:** 24 nonpareils. **Col. Depth:** 301 agate lines. **Key Personnel:** Joseph G. Dietl, Editor and Publisher. **USPS:** 303-640. **Subscription Rates:** $17.50 individuals; $20 out of area; $22.50 out of state.
Ad Rates: GLR: $.15 **Circ:** Paid 1,703
BW: $387 Free 50
SAU: $3
PCI: $3

LE CENTER†, pop. 1,967.

SC MN. Le Sueur Co. 26 mi. NE of Mankato. Manufactures formica counter tops, polyethelene liquid containers, electrical generators, dehydrated alfalfa products. Diversified farming. Dairying, corn, livestock, soybeans, wheat.

16073 Le Center Leader
Minnesota Valley News Publishing, LLC
PO Box 68 Phone: (320)357-2233
Le Center, MN 56057-1502 Fax: (320)357-6656
Publication E-mail: lcleader@prarie.lakes.com

Community newspaper. **Founded:** 1896. **Freq:** Weekly (Wed.). **Print Method:** Offset. **Cols./Page:** 6. **Col. Width:** 13 picas. **Col. Depth:** 301 agate lines. **Key Personnel:** Teresa Emmers-McMillen, Editor and Publisher. **Subscription Rates:** $30 individuals; $42 out of state. **Remarks:** Accepts advertising.
Ad Rates: BW: $774 **Circ:** Paid 2,000
SAU: $6 Free 20
PCI: $6

LE ROY, pop. 937.

SE MN. Mower Co. 23 mi. SE of Austin. State Park. Manufactures plastic & nylon coating of metals, electrical assemblies, plaques. Creamery. Lumber. Dairy, beef, hog, grain farms. Soybeans, oats, corn.

16074 Le Roy Independent
Evans Printing & Publishing
PO Box 89 Phone: (507)324-5325
Le Roy, MN 55951 Fax: (507)324-5267

Community newspaper. **Founded:** 1875. **Freq:** Weekly (Thurs.). **Print Method:** Offset. **Cols./Page:** 6. **Col. Width:** 2.16 inches. **Col. Depth:** 21 inches. **Key Personnel:** Daniel Evans, Publisher. **USPS:** 310-330. **Subscription Rates:** $25.00; $27.00 other. **Remarks:** Accepts advertising.
Ad Rates: BW: $200 **Circ:** ‡1,300
4C: $350
SAU: $3.00
PCI: $3.00

LE SUEUR, pop. 3,763.

SC MN. Le Sueur Co. On Minnesota River, 50 mi. S. of Minneapolis. Cheese factory. Aluminum foundry. Food packing and canning.

16075 Le Sueur News-Herald
Le Sueur Publishing
101 Bridge St.
Le Sueur, MN 56058

Local newspaper. **Founded:** 1880. **Freq:** Weekly (Tues.). **Print Method:** Offset. **Cols./Page:** 6. **Col. Width:** 28 nonpareils. **Col. Depth:** 301 agate lines. **Key Personnel:** Sarah Johnson Malchow, Editor; William Clark, Publisher; Kevin Lindquist, Advertising Mgr. **Subscription Rates:** $16. **Remarks:** Accepts advertising.
Ad Rates: GLR: $.61 **Circ:** ‡2,600

16076 Valley
Le Sueur Publishing
101 Bridge St.
Le Sueur, MN 56058

Local newspaper. **Founded:** 1976. **Freq:** Weekly (Mon.). **Print Method:** Offset. **Cols./Page:** 6. **Col. Width:** 28 nonpareils. **Col. Depth:** 301 agate lines. **Key Personnel:** Sarah Johnson Malchow, Editor; William Clark, Publisher; Kevin Lindquist, Advertising Mgr. **Remarks:** Accepts advertising.
Ad Rates: GLR: $.61 **Circ:** Free ‡7,500

LINDSTROM, pop. 1,260.

EC MN. Chisago Co. 38 mi. NE of Saint Paul. Lake Resort. Plastic products. Fishing. Dairy, grain farms. Potatoes.

16077 Chicago County Press
Box 748 Phone: (651)257-5115
Lindstrom, MN 55045-0748 Fax: (651)257-5500

Community newspaper. **Founded:** June 1898. **Freq:** Weekly (Thurs.). **Print Method:** Offset. **Cols./Page:** 6. **Col. Width:** 28 nonpareils. **Col. Depth:** 294 agate lines. **Key Personnel:** John A. Silver, Editor and Publisher. **USPS:** 106-140. **Subscription Rates:** $38 individuals; $40.50 out of country. **Remarks:** Accepts advertising. **Alt. Formats:** Microform.
Ad Rates: GLR: $.45 **Circ:** Paid ‡3,839
BW: $679.14 Free ‡36
SAU: $6.35
PCI: $6.35

16078 Search Shopper
PO Box 748 Phone: (651)257-5115
Lindstrom, MN 55045-0748 Fax: (651)257-5500

Shopping guide. **Founded:** 1972. **Freq:** Weekly. **Print Method:** Offset. **Cols./Page:** 6. **Col. Width:** 28 nonpareils. **Col. Depth:** 294 agate lines. **Key Personnel:** John A. Silver, Publisher. **Subscription Rates:** Free.
Ad Rates: GLR: $.66 **Circ:** Free ‡16,565
BW: $989.10
SAU: $9.35
PCI: $9.35

LITCHFIELD

16079 Litchfield Independent-Review
PO Box 921 Phone: (320)693-3266
Litchfield, MN 55355 Fax: (320)693-9177

Community newspaper. **Founded:** 1876. **Freq:** Weekly (Thurs.). **Print Method:** Web offset. **Cols./Page:** 8. **Col. Width:** 10 picas. **Col. Depth:** 21 1/2 inches. **Key Personnel:** Vernon Madson, Co-publisher; Stan Roeser, Co-publisher. **Subscription Rates:** $21 within county and adjoining counties. **Remarks:** Accepts advertising.
Ad Rates: SAU: $6.40 **Circ:** 3,800
PCI: $5.17

16080 KLFD-AM - 1410
234 N. Sibley Ave. Phone: (320)693-3281
Litchfield, MN 55355

Format: Full Service. **Owner:** Mid Minnesota Broadcasting, at above address. **Founded:** 1959. **Operating Hours:** Continuous. **Key Personnel:** Bob Greenhow, President; Steve Neighbors, Vice President; Tim Bergstrom, News Dir.; Brad Anderson, Sports Dir. **Wattage:** 500.

LITTLE FALLS†, pop. 7,250.

C MN. Morrison Co. On Mississippi River, 33 mi. NW of Saint Cloud. Resort. Manufactures plastic planting pots, pulp and newsprint, boats, snowplows, conveyors, food ingredients, monuments, furniture, bricks, cement blocks, Hatcheries. Dairy, stock, poultry, truck farms.

16081 Morrison County Record
216 SE 1st St. Phone: (320)632-2345
Little Falls, MN 56345 Fax: (320)632-2348
Free: (888)637-2345
Publication E-mail: mcrecord@littlefall.net

County newspaper (tabloid). **Founded:** 1969. **Freq:** Weekly (Sun.). **Print Method:** Offset. **Trim Size:** 10 x 15. **Cols./Page:** 5. **Col. Width:** 20 nonpareils. **Col. Depth:** 210 agate lines. **Key Personnel:** Carolyn Hoheisel, Publisher, carolh@littlefalls.net; Larry Ehoff, Editor. **Subscription Rates:** $52. **Remarks:** Accepts advertising. **URL:** http://www.mcrecord.com.
Ad Rates: BW: $401.25 **Circ:** Free 16,500
4C: $300 Paid 543
SAU: $6.69
PCI: $6.49

16082 KFML-FM - 94.1
70 N. E. First Ave. Phone: (320)632-2992
Little Falls, MN 56345 Fax: (320)632-2571
E-mail: fallsradio@fallsnet.com

Format: Adult Contemporary; Oldies. **Owner:** KLTF/KFML, Inc., at above address. **Founded:** 1988. **Operating Hours:** Continuous. **Key Personnel:** Jack Hansen, President; Alan Arquette, Program Dir.; Jane Meyer, News Dir. **Wattage:** 3,000. **Ad Rates:** $9 for 30 seconds; $13.50 for 60 seconds. **URL:** http://www.fallsradio.com.

16083 KLTF-AM - 960
70 NE 1st Ave. Phone: (320)632-5414
Little Falls, MN 56345 Fax: (320)632-2571

Format: Adult Contemporary; Country; Talk. **Networks:** CNN Radio. **Owner:** KLTF/KFML Inc., at above address, (320)632-2992. **Founded:** 1950. **Operating Hours:** Continuous. **ADI:** Minneapolis-St. Paul, MN. **Key Personnel:** Jack Hansen, Owner/Gen. Mgr.; Janee Meyer, News Dir.; Gary Block, Contact; Harriet Turner, Contact. **Local Programs:** *Party Line*, Gary Block. **Wattage:** 5000. **Ad Rates:** $10.70 for 30 seconds; $16 for 60 seconds.

LONG PRAIRIE†, pop. 2,859.

SC MN. Todd Co. 23 mi. ENE of Alexandria.

16084 Long Prairie Leader
PO Box 479 Phone: (320)732-2151
Long Prairie, MN 56347 Fax: (320)732-2152

County newspaper. **Founded:** 1882. **Freq:** Weekly. **Print Method:** 14 3/4 x 21. Offset. **Cols./Page:** 6. **Col. Width:** 32 nonpareils. **Col. Depth:** 294 agate lines. **Key Personnel:** Susan Farmer, Editor; Gary R. Brown, Publisher. **Subscription Rates:** $39; $4.50; $49; $30. **Remarks:** Color advertising accepted; rates available upon request.
Ad Rates: BW: $436.50 **Circ:** 3,500
SAU: $4.50

16085 KEYL-AM - 1400
PO Box 187 Phone: (612)732-2164
221 Central Ave. Fax: (612)732-2284
Long Prairie, MN 56347

Format: Country; Full Service. **Networks:** ABC; Satellite Music Network; Minnesota News. **Founded:** 1959. **Operating Hours:** Continuous; 45% local, 55% network. **ADI:** Minneapolis-St. Paul, MN. **Key Personnel:** Gene Sullivan, General Mgr.; Mary Stencel, Contact; Clif Cline, Contact. **Wattage:** 1000. **Ad Rates:** $3.50 for 15 seconds; $5.00-9.00 for 30 seconds; $8.50-12 for 60 seconds. Combined advertising rates available with KXOL-FM.

16086 KXDL-FM - 99.7
PO Box 187 Phone: (612)732-2164
221 Central Ave. Fax: (612)732-2284
Long Prairie, MN 56347

Format: Oldies. **Networks:** Satellite Music Network; ABC. **Founded:** 1992. **Operating Hours:** Continuous. **ADI:** Minneapolis-St. Paul, MN. **Key Personnel:** Gene Sullivan, P/GM; Mary Stencel, Secretary; Cliff Cline, V.P/Operations Mgr. **Wattage:** 6000. **Ad Rates:** $3.50 for 15 seconds; $5-9 for 30 seconds; $8.50-12 for 60 seconds. Combined advertising rates available with KEYL-AM.

LUVERNE†, pop. 4,568.

SW MN. Rock Co. 30 mi. E. of Sioux Falls, SD. Manufactures fire apparatus, butter, silos, automatic feeders, water softeners, ventilating equipment. Dairy, stock, poultry, grain farms, livestock.

16087 Luverne Announcer
Announcer-Star Herald
117 W. Main Phone: (507)283-2333
Box 327 Fax: (507)283-2335
Luverne, MN 56156-1843
Shopper. **Founded:** Jan. 1931. **Freq:** Weekly (Mon.). **Print Method:** Offset. **Cols./Page:** 6. **Col. Width:** 24 nonpareils. **Col. Depth:** 294 agate lines. **Key Personnel:** Christopher Kuffel, Editor; Roger Tollefson, Publisher. **Remarks:** Accepts advertising.
Ad Rates: GLR: $.23 **Circ:** Free 10,122

16088 Rock County Star Herald
Announcer-Star Herald
117 W. Main Phone: (507)283-2333
Box 327 Fax: (507)283-2335
Luverne, MN 56156-1843
Community newspaper. **Founded:** May 23, 1873. **Freq:** Weekly (Thurs.). **Print Method:** Offset. **Cols./Page:** 6. **Col. Width:** 24 nonpareils. **Col. Depth:** 294 agate lines. **Key Personnel:** Lynn Taylor, Editor; Roger S. Tollefson, Publisher. **Subscription Rates:** $20; $25 out of area. **Remarks:** Accepts advertising.
Ad Rates: GLR: $.23 **Circ:** 3,000

16089 KLQL-FM - 101.1
PO Box 599 Phone: (507)283-4444
Hwy. 16 E Fax: (507)283-4445
Luverne, MN 56156

Format: Country; Agricultural. **Networks:** ABC. **Founded:** 1983. **Operating Hours:** Continuous. **ADI:** Sioux Falls-Mitchell, SD. **Key Personnel:** Steve Graphenteen, General Mgr.; Bruce Thalhuber, Operations Mgr. **Wattage:** 100,000 ERP. **Ad Rates:** $8-15 for 30 seconds; $10-17 for 60 seconds. **URL:** http://www.k101.net.

16090 KQAD-AM - 800
Cty. Rd. 4 East Phone: (507)283-4444
PO 599 Fax: (507)283-4445
Luverne, MN 56156

Format: Middle-of-the-Road (MOR); News; Big Band/Nostalgia; Sports; Agricultural. **Networks:** ABC; Westwood One Radio. **Founded:** 1971. **Operating Hours:** Continuous; 20% local, 80% network. **ADI:** Sioux Falls-Mitchell, SD. **Key Personnel:** Steve Graphenteen, General Mgr.; Keith Maine, Program; Scott Van Aartsen, News Dir. **Wattage:** 500. **Ad Rates:** $4-7 for 15 seconds; $6-9 for 30 seconds; $8-11 for 60 seconds.

MABEL

16091 News-Record
Phillips Publishing, Inc.
102 Fillmore Phone: (507)493-5204
PO Box 307 Fax: (507)495-5204
Mabel, MN 55954
Community newspaper. **Freq:** Weekly (Thurs.). **Print Method:** Offset. **Trim Size:** 14 1/2 x 23. **Cols./Page:** 6. **Col. Width:** 12.5 picas. **Col. Depth:** 21 1/2 inches. **Key Personnel:** David Phillips, Publisher; Melissa Vander Plas, Editor. **USPS:** 323-800. **Subscription Rates:** $18; $22 out of area. **Remarks:** Accepts advertising. **Formerly:** Harmony News; Mabel Record.
Ad Rates: BW: $374.10 **Circ:** ‡1,900
SAU: $3.50
PCI: $3.50

MADELIA, pop. 2,130.

SC MN. Watonwan Co. 24 mi. SW of Mankato. Cement tile, frozen foods, feed mills. Grain, stock, poultry, truck farms.

16092 Southern Minnesota Peach
Madelia Media, Inc.
Box 159 Phone: (507)642-3636
Madelia, MN 56062 Fax: (507)642-3535

Shopper. **Founded:** 1952. **Freq:** Weekly. **Print Method:** Offset. **Cols./Page:** 6. **Col. Width:** 10 inches. **Col. Depth:** 15 inches. **Key Personnel:** Mike Whalen, Editor. **Remarks:** Accepts advertising.
Ad Rates: BW: $436 **Circ:** Non-paid ‡15,500
4C: $575
PCI: $4.25

16093 Times-Messenger
Madelia Media, Inc.
Box 159 Phone: (507)642-3636
Madelia, MN 56062 Fax: (507)642-3535

Community newspaper. **Founded:** 1870. **Freq:** Weekly (Tues.). **Print Method:** Offset. **Cols./Page:** 6. **Col. Width:** 24 nonpareils. **Col. Depth:** 21 1/2 inches. **Key Personnel:** Mike Whalen, Publisher. **Subscription Rates:** $22 individuals. **Remarks:** Accepts advertising.
Ad Rates: GLR: $3.50 **Circ:** Paid ‡2,100
BW: $416
4C: $615
SAU: $2.60
CNU: $4.75
PCI: $3.50

MADISON†, pop. 2,212.

SW MN. Lac qui Parle Co. 90 mi. S. of Fergus Falls. Manufactures flour, fertilizer. Grain, dairy, poultry, stock farms. Corn, rye, wheat, oats, barley, soybeans.

16094 Western Guard
PO Box 183 Phone: (612)598-7521
Madison, MN 56256-0183
Community newspaper. **Founded:** 1890. **Freq:** Weekly (Wed.). **Print Method:** Offset. **Cols./Page:** 6. **Col. Width:** 26 nonpareils. **Col. Depth:** 301 agate lines. **Key Personnel:** Richard Gail, Editor and Publisher. **Subscription Rates:** $17; $20 out of state. **Remarks:** Accepts advertising.
Ad Rates: GLR: $.22 **Circ:** ‡3,500
SAU: $2.90

16095 KLQP-FM - 92.1
PO Box 70 Phone: (320)598-7301
Madison, MN 56256 Fax: (320)598-7955
E-mail: klqpfm@frontiernet.net

Format: Country. **Networks:** CNN Radio. **Owner:** Lac qui Parle Broadcasting Co., Inc., at above address. **Founded:** 1983. **Operating Hours:** Continuous; 100% local. **Key Personnel:** Maynard R. Meyer, General Mgr., mmeyer@frontiernet.net; Kristi Kuechenmeister, Assistant Manager; Terry Overlander, Sales Mgr. **Wattage:** 25,000. **Ad Rates:** $4 for 30 seconds; $7.25 for 60 seconds.

MADISON LAKE, pop. 592.

SC MN. Blue Earth Co. 12 mi. E. of Mankato. Summer resort. Dairy, grain, stock farms.

16096 Lake Region Times
509 Main Phone: (507)243-3031
PO Box 128 Fax: (507)243-3122
Madison Lake, MN 56063-0128
Community newspaper. **Founded:** 1915. **Freq:** Weekly (Wed.). **Print Method:** Letterpress and offset. **Cols./Page:** 6. **Col. Width:** 22 nonpareils. **Col. Depth:** 210 agate lines. **Key Personnel:** Marie Groebner, Editor and Publisher. **USPS:** 001-940. **Subscription Rates:** $10 individuals. **Remarks:** Accepts advertising.
Ad Rates: BW: $245.70 **Circ:** Paid 870
SAU: $2.25 Free 31
PCI: $1.95

MAHNOMEN†, pop. 1,283.

NW MN. Mahnomen Co. 58 mi. NE of Fargo. Manufactures butter, lumber. Timber. Dairy, grain farms.

16097 Pioneer
Box 219 Phone: (218)935-5296
Mahnomen, MN 56557
Community newspaper. **Founded:** 1905. **Freq:** Weekly (Thurs.). **Print Method:** Letterpress and offset. **Cols./Page:** 6. **Col. Width:** 25 nonpareils. **Col. Depth:** 301 agate lines. **Key Personnel:** Barb Nelson Agnew, Editor; Patrick D. Kelly, Publisher; Brian Kelly, Manager. **Subscription Rates:** $17 individuals.
Ad Rates: BW: $451.50 **Circ:** ‡2,800
4C: $85
SAU: $4.50

MANKATO†, pop. 28,651.

SC MN. Blue Earth Co. On Minnesota and Blue Earth Rivers, 80 mi. SW of Minneapolis. Mankato State University, Bethany Lutheran College. Manufactures flour, cement, stone products, electronic components, tools, hydraulic equipment, soft drinks, paper boxes, power hammers, farm machinery, sashes, doors, incubators. Stone quarries. Agriculture. Livestock, dairy products, corn, barley. Building materials, oil refinery, breweries.

16098 Favorite Westerns & Serial World
Westerns and Serials Fan Club
527 S. Front St. Phone: (507)549-3677
Mankato, MN 56001-3718 Fax: (507)549-3788
Publisher E-mail: kietzer@mctcnet.net

Magazine for fans of old westerns and serial movies. **Founded:** 1974. **Freq:** Semiannual. **Print Method:** Web offset. **Trim Size:** 8 1/2 x 11. **Cols./Page:** 3. **Col. Width:** 12 picas. **Col. Depth:** 10 inches. **Key Personnel:** Norman Kietzer, Editor. **USPS:** 324-390. **Subscription Rates:** $12; $16 other countries; $8 single issue. **Remarks:** Accepts advertising. **Formerly:** Serial World; Favorite Westerns.
Ad Rates: BW: $75 **Circ:** 2,000

16099 Free Press
Ottaway Newspapers
PO Box 3287 Phone: (507)625-4451
Mankato, MN 56002-3287 Fax: (507)388-4355
Free: (800)657-4662
Publication E-mail: freepress@k.mankato.mn.us

General newspaper. **Founded:** 1887. **Freq:** Mon.-Sat. (morn.). **Print Method:** Offset. **Cols./Page:** 6. **Col. Width:** 26 nonpareils. **Col. Depth:** 301 agate lines. **Key Personnel:** Debra J. Flemming, Editor; E. Joe Vanderhoof, Publisher; Jay Thompson, Marketing Director. **Subscription Rates:** $114.40 individuals carrier delivery.
Ad Rates: BW: $1,806 **Circ:** Mon.-Sat. 25,585
4C: $1,991
SAU: $14

16100 Home Magazine
215 Maxfield Phone: (507)387-7953
PO Box 2 Fax: (507)387-4775
Mankato, MN 56001
Shopper. **Founded:** 1971. **Freq:** Weekly. **Print Method:** Offset. **Trim Size:** 11 x 16. **Cols./Page:** 6. **Col. Width:** 21 nonpareils. **Col. Depth:** 210 agate lines. **Key Personnel:** Quinn McDonald, Publisher; Tom Murray, Advertising Mgr. **Subscription Rates:** Free. **Remarks:** Accepts advertising.
Ad Rates: BW: $957 **Circ:** Combined 39,925
4C: $1,287
PCI: $10.63

16101 The Land
Free Press Co., Inc.
PO Box 3169 Phone: (507)345-4523
Mankato, MN 56001
Farm magazine. **Founded:** 1976. **Freq:** Weekly. **Print Method:** Offset. **Cols./Page:** 6. **Col. Width:** 10 picas. **Col. Depth:** 13 inches. **Key Personnel:** Kevin Schulz, Editor, phone (507)344-6342; Randy Frahm, General Mgr. **Subscription Rates:** Free to qualified subscribers Free to farmers in circ. $17 otherwise.
Ad Rates: BW: $1,265 **Circ:** Non-paid ‡41,500
4C: $1,632.50
PCI: $16.50

16102 The Lion and the Unicorn
Johns Hopkins University Press
Mankato State University Phone: (507)389-2117
English Dept. Fax: (507)389-5887
Box 53
Mankato, MN 56002-8400
Free: (800)548-1784
Publisher E-mail: jlinfo@jhupress.jhu.edu

Literary studies journal. **Subtitle:** A Critical Journal of Children's Literature. **Founded:** 1982. **Freq:** 3/year. **Print Method:** Offset. **Trim Size:** 6 x 9. **Cols./Page:** 1. **Col. Width:** 26 picas. **Col. Depth:** 7 inches. **Key Personnel:** Jack Zipes, Editor; Louisa Smith, Editor; Tara Dorai-Berry, Advertising Mgr. **ISSN:** 0147-2593. **Subscription Rates:** $21 individuals; $41 institutions. **Remarks:** Accepts advertising. **Online:** MUSE through Johns Hopkins.
Ad Rates: GLR: $210 **Circ:** ‡1,290
BW: $200

16103 Reporter
Mankato State University
Mankato State University Phone: (507)389-1776
MSU Box 38 Fax: (507)389-5812
Mankato, MN 56002
Collegiate newspaper. **Founded:** Mar. 26, 1926. **Freq:** Semiweekly (Tues. and Thurs. during the academic year). **Print Method:** Letterpress and offset. **Cols./Page:** 5. **Col. Width:** 1 3/4 inches. **Key Personnel:** Richard Price, Editor, phone (507)389-5454; Ken Steverner, Advertising Mgr., phone (507)389-5451. **Subscription Rates:** $25.
Ad Rates: BW: $273.75 **Circ:** Free 7,500
4C: $536.25
PCI: $3.95

16104 Cable Network, Inc.
PO Box 3248 Phone: (507)387-1151
Mankato, MN 56002 Fax: (507)387-6776

Owner: Mankato Citizens Telephone Co., at above address. **Founded:** 1984. **Formerly:** Mid-Communications Cablevision Inc. **Key Personnel:** Tom Borchert, General Mgr.; Tom Riley, V.P./Sales & Mktg. **Cities Served:** subscribing households 288; 36 channels; 2 community access channels.

16105 KDOG-FM - 96.7
Hwy. 14 E. Phone: (507)345-4537
Box 1420 Fax: (507)345-5364
Mankato, MN 56001

Format: Contemporary Hit Radio (CHR). **Networks:** ABC. **Owner:** Minnesota Valley Broadcasting, at above address, (507)625-9197. **Founded:** 1985. **Operating Hours:** Continuous; 5% network, 95% local. **ADI:** Mankato, MN. **Key Personnel:** Dan Hatter, Operations Mgr.; Mark Ring, General Mgr., kitamark@prairie.labes.com. **Wattage:** 25 kw. **Ad Rates:** $10-14.50 for 30 seconds; $12-18 for 60 seconds.

16106 KEEZ-FM - 99.1
102 Capital Rd. Phone: (507)345-4646
PO Box 3345 Fax: (507)345-3299
Mankato, MN 56002
E-mail: keez@keez.com

Format: Adult Contemporary; Sports; News. **Networks:** Mutual Broadcasting System. **Owner:** Mike Nolan, at above address. **Founded:** 1977. **Formerly:** KEYC-FM (1977). **Operating Hours:** Continuous; 10% network, 90% local. **ADI:** Mankato, MN. **Key Personnel:** Mike Nolan, General Mgr.; Jim Gullickson, General Sales Mgr.; Mark Spangler, News Dir.; Jeff Nixx, Music Dir.; JoEllen Bakos, Traffic Mgr. **Wattage:** 100,000. **Ad Rates:** $18-36 for 30 seconds; $21-42 for 60 seconds.

16107 KEYC-TV - 12
1570 Lookout Dr. Phone: (507)625-7905
PO Box 128 Fax: (507)625-5745
Mankato, MN 56001
E-mail: cbs@keyc.com

Format: Commercial TV. **Networks:** CBS. **Founded:** 1960. **Operating Hours:** 6.00 a.m.-1 a.m. **ADI:** Mankato, MN. **Key Personnel:** Tom Schultz, News Dir., tvtom@keyc.com; Sharon Freitag, Business Mgr., tvsharon@kayc.com; Dennis Wahlstrom, General Mgr., tvdenny@keyc.com; Elaine Peterson, Operations Dir.; Dave Hooge, Chief Engineer; John Ginther, Sales Mgr.; Jeff Poole, Production Mgr. **Local Programs:** *Bandwagon News 12*. **Wattage:** 316,000 visual; 100,000 aural. **Ad Rates:** $25-700 per unit. **URL:** http://www.keyc.com.

16108 KMSU-FM - 89.7
Box 153 Phone: (507)389-5678
Mankato, MN 56001 Fax: (507)389-1705

Format: Public Radio; Eclectic. **Networks:** National Public Radio (NPR). **Owner:** Mankato State University, Box 8400, Mankato, MN 56001. **Founded:** 1963. **Operating Hours:** 20 hrs. Daily; 70% network, 30% local. **ADI:** Mankato, MN. **Key Personnel:** William McGinley, General Mgr.; Marilee Richard, News Dir.; Ron Dick, Chief Engineer; Fred Vette, Operations Dir.; Henry Busse, Contact. **Wattage:** 20,000. **Ad Rates:** Noncommercial.

16109 KTOE-AM - 1420
Box 1420 Phone: (507)345-4537
Mankato, MN 56001 Fax: (507)345-5363

Format: Adult Contemporary; News; Talk. **Networks:** Talknet. **Founded:** 1950. **Operating Hours:** Continuous; 30% network; 70% local. **ADI:** Mankato, MN. **Key Personnel:** Mark Ring, General Mgr., kitnmark@prairie.lakes.com; Mark Ring, General Sales Mgr.; Pete Steiner, Program Dir. **Wattage:** 5000. **Ad Rates:** $23 for 30 seconds; $34 for 60 seconds.

MAPLE GROVE

16110 Archery Business
Ehlert Publishing Group, Inc.
6420 Sycamore Ln. Phone: (612)476-2200
Maple Grove, MN 55369 Fax: (612)476-8065
Free: (800)848-6247

Trade magazine covering the business side of archery and bowhunting. **Subtitle:** The Voice of the Archery Industry. **Founded:** 1976. **Freq:** Bimonthly. **Print Method:** Offset. Uses mats. **Trim Size:** 8 x 10 3/4. **Cols./Page:** 3. **Col. Width:** 27 nonpareils. **Col. Depth:** 140 agate lines. **Key Personnel:** Mike Strandlund, Editor, mike-s@mail.epginc.com; Steve Hedlund, Publisher; Dave Clayton, Sales Mgr., dave-c@mail.epginc.com; Patty Brady, Sales Mgr., patty@mail.epginc.com. **Subscription Rates:** $24.95 individuals. **Remarks:** Accepts advertising.
Ad Rates: BW: $2,470 **Circ:** Controlled 11,000
4C: $3,770

16111 Bowhunting World
Ehlert Publishing Group, Inc.
6420 Sycamore Ln. Phone: (612)476-2200
Maple Grove, MN 55369 Fax: (612)476-8065
Free: (800)848-6247

Magazine for all-season bowhunters and competitive archers. **Subtitle:** The Archer Equipment Authority. **Founded:** 1952. **Freq:** Monthly 9/year. **Print Method:** Offset. **Trim Size:** 8 x 10 1/2. **Cols./Page:** 3. **Col. Width:** 27 nonpareils. **Col. Depth:** 140 agate lines. **Key Personnel:** Mike Strandlund, Editor; Dave Clayton, Sr. Sales Representative; Patty Brady, Sr. Sales Rep. **ISSN:** 1043-5492. **Subscription Rates:** $20 individuals. **Remarks:** Accepts advertising. **Formerly:** Archery World.
Ad Rates: BW: $3,380 **Circ:** ‡125,000
4C: $4,950

16112 Powersports Business
Ehlert Publishing Group, Inc.
6420 Sycamore Ln. Phone: (612)476-2200
Maple Grove, MN 55369 Fax: (612)476-8065
Free: (800)848-6247

Powersports trade magazine. **Founded:** 1967. **Freq:** 18/year. **Print Method:** Web Offset. **Trim Size:** 10 7/8 x 15. **Cols./Page:** 4. **Col. Width:** 2 3/8 inches. **Col. Depth:** 13 7/8 inches. **Key Personnel:** Joe Dehmont, Editor; Stephen M. Hedlund, President; Brian Searles, Associate Publisher; David Voll, Sales Mgr. **ISSN:** 0883-8259. **Subscription Rates:** Free to qualified subscribers. **Remarks:** Accepts advertising. **Formerly:** Snow Goer Trade; Snowmobile Business; Watercraft Business.
Ad Rates: BW: $3,350 **Circ:** Controlled ‡16,000
4C: $4,275

16113 Snow Week
Ehlert Publishing Group, Inc.
6420 Sycamore Ln. Phone: (612)476-2200
Maple Grove, MN 55369 Fax: (612)476-8065
Free: (800)848-6247

Magazine for experienced snowmobile enthusiasts; featuring news, events, competition coverage, and technical/mechanical aspects of the sport. **Founded:** 1973. **Freq:** 18/year. **Trim Size:** 11 3/8 x 15. **Cols./Page:** 4. **Col. Width:** 14 picas. **Col. Depth:** 78 picas. **Key Personnel:** John Prusak, Editor; Stephen M. Hedlund, President; Dick Hendricks, Sr. Vice Pres./Group Publisher; David Bortner, Publisher; Dave Bortner, President. **ISSN:** 0164-7342. **Subscription Rates:** $22 individuals; $2.25 single issue.
Ad Rates: BW: $4,010 **Circ:** 24,160
4C: $5,670

MAPLE LAKE, pop. 1,240.

SEC MN. Wright Co. 45 mi. W. of Minneapolis. Lake resort. Stock, dairy farms.

16114 Messenger
Box 817 Phone: (612)963-3813
Maple Lake, MN 55358 Fax: (612)963-6114

Newspaper with a Republican orientation. **Founded:** 1895. **Freq:** Weekly (Wed.). **Print Method:** Offset. **Cols./Page:** 6. **Col. Width:** 28 nonpareils. **Col. Depth:** 301 agate lines. **Key Personnel:** Harold Brutlag, Editor and Publisher. **ISSN:** 3285-6000. **Subscription Rates:** $15; $17 out of county. **Remarks:** Accepts advertising.
Ad Rates: GLR: $2.97 **Circ:** ‡1,750
BW: $339.20
4C: $579.29
SAU: $2.65
PCI: $3.25

MARSHALL†, pop. 11,161.

SW MN. Lyons Co. 30 mi. NW of Springfield. Southwest State University. Dairy products, diversified agriculture.

16115 Independent
Marshall Independent Corp.
508 W. Main Phone: (507)537-1551
PO Box 411 Fax: (507)537-1557
Marshall, MN 56258
General newspaper. **Founded:** 1874. **Freq:** Mon.-Sat. (morn.). **Print Method:** Offset. **Cols./Page:** 6. **Col. Width:** 24 nonpareils. **Col. Depth:** 301 agate lines. **Key Personnel:** Sherrie Wilson, Editor; Connie Nuese, Advertising Mgr. **Subscription Rates:** $55.20. **Remarks:** Accepts advertising.
Ad Rates: PCI: $8.82 **Circ:** Mon.-Sat. 8,151

16116 Independent Regional Shopper
Marshall Independent Corp.
508 W. Main Phone: (507)537-1551
PO Box 411 Fax: (507)537-1557
Marshall, MN 56258
Shopper. **Founded:** 1965. **Freq:** Weekly (Thurs.). **Print Method:** Offset. **Cols./Page:** 6. **Col. Width:** 23 nonpareils. **Col. Depth:** 210 agate lines. **Key Personnel:** Sherrie Wilson, Editor; Roger Smed, Publisher; Connie Nuese, Advertising Mgr. **Remarks:** Accepts advertising.
Ad Rates: BW: $848.82 **Circ:** Free ‡15,279
4C: $992.82

16117 Bresnan Communications
1104 E. College Dr. Phone: (507)532-5747
Marshall, MN 56258 Fax: (507)537-1572

Owner: Bresnan Communication, 709 Westchester Ave., White Plains, NY 10604, (914)993-6600, Fax: (914)993-6601. **Founded:** Apr. 1965. **Formerly:** Marshall Cable (1986); American Cablevision. **Key Personnel:** Mary Larson, General Mgr.; Dick Letcher, Chief Technician; Sue Olson, Office Mgr. **Cities Served:** Marshall, MN: subscribing households 5,200; 54 channels; 2 community access channels; 120 hours per week community access programming.

16118 KARZ-FM - 107.5
1414 E. College Dr. Phone: (507)532-2282
PO Box 61 Fax: (507)532-3739
Marshall, MN 56258

Simulcasts: KBJJ-FM. **Owner:** Paradis Broadcasting of Marshall, Inc., PO Box 520, Marshall, MN 56258. **Founded:** 1986. **Formerly:** KBJJ-FM. **Operating Hours:** Continuous, 100% local. **ADI:** Sioux Falls-Mitchell, SD. **Key Personnel:** Brad Strootman, Station Mgr.; Scott O'Brien, Program Dir., scottie@kmhl.com. **Wattage:** 9900. **Ad Rates:** $4-6.25 for 15 seconds; $6-9.40 for 30 seconds; $8-12.50 for 60 seconds. Combined advertising rates available with KMHL-AM, KKCK-FM.

16119 KKCK-FM - 99.7
1414 E. College Dr. Phone: (507)532-2282
Marshall, MN 56258 Fax: (507)532-3739

Format: Top 40. **Networks:** ABC. **Owner:** KMHL Broadcasting Co., at above address. **Founded:** 1967. **Operating Hours:** Continuous. **Key Personnel:** Brad Strootman, General Mgr.; Jerry Marquardt, Sports Dir.; Nick Barlow, News Dir.; Tom Hager, Program Mgr. **Wattage:** 100,000. **Ad Rates:** $7.75-9.25 for 15 seconds; $9.75-13.50 for 30 seconds; $11.25-17.25 for 60 seconds.

16120 KMHL-AM - 1400
1414 E. College Dr. Phone: (507)532-2282
PO Box 61 Fax: (507)532-3739
Marshall, MN 56258

Format: News; Sports; Agricultural; Information; Country. **Simulcasts:** KARL-FM. **Networks:** ABC; Linder Farm. **Owner:** KMHL Broadcasting Co., at above address. **Founded:** 1946. **Operating Hours:** Continuous; 18% network, 82% local. **Key Personnel:** Brad Strootman, General Mgr.; Jerry Marquardt, Sports Dir.; Greg Schultz, News Dir.; Val Braun, Business Mgr.; Greg Schultz, Informational Programming. **Local Programs:** *Joyce & Jerry Show* 7 a.m.- 9 a.m., Jerry Marquardt, Mailing contact; *PM Focus*, Greg Schultz, Mailing contact. **Wattage:** 1000. **Ad Rates:** $7.50 for 15 seconds; $9.50-18.50 for 30 seconds; $10.50-24 for 60 seconds. Combined advertising rates available with KKCK-FM, KARL-FM, KARZ-FM.

MAYER

16121 Annals of Balloon History and Museology
15155 County Rd. 32
Mayer, MN 55360

Trade journal covering history of balloons and ballooning. **Founded:** 1991. **Freq:** Irregular. **Print Method:** Letterpress. **Key Personnel:** Paul Maravelas, Editor and Publisher, phone (612)657-2237. **Remarks:** Advertising not accepted.
Circ: (Not Reported)

MEDINA

16122 Woodworker's Journal
Rockler Press
4365 Willow Dr. Phone: (612)478-8232
Medina, MN 55340 Fax: (612)478-8396

Magazine featuring projects, tips and techniques for novice and experienced woodworking hobbyists. **Founded:** 1978. **Freq:** Bimonthly. **Print Method:** Web offset. **Trim Size:** 7 7/8 x 10 1/2. **Cols./Page:** 3. **Col. Width:** 2 1/8 inches. **Key Personnel:** Rob Johnston, Assoc. Editor, phone (612)478-8255, editor@woodworkersjournal.com; Nancy Ammend, Managing Editor; Michelle Scribner, Circulation Coordinator, phone (612)478-8276; J.F. Van Gilder, Co. Publisher's Rep., jimvg@flash.net. **ISSN:** 1041-8113. **Subscription Rates:** $19.95 individuals; $4.95 single issue. **Remarks:** Accepts advertising. **URL:** http://todayswoodworker.com. **Formerly:** Today's Woodworker.
Ad Rates: BW: $5,090 **Circ:** Paid ‡200,795
4C: $5,850 Non-paid ‡812
PCI: $125

MELROSE, pop. 2,409.

C MN. Stearns Co. 30 mi. NW of Saint Cloud. Manufactures

dairy products, monuments. Turkey processing plant. Lake resorts. Dairy, poultry, stock farms.

16123 Bargain Searchlight
Melrose Beacon
PO Box 186 Phone: (612)256-3240
Melrose, MN 56352-0186 Fax: (612)256-3363

Shopper. **Founded:** 1984. **Freq:** Weekly (Wed.). **Print Method:** Offset. **Cols./Page:** 7. **Col. Width:** 24 nonpareils. **Col. Depth:** 301 agate lines. **Key Personnel:** Don Larson, Publisher; Carole Larson, Publisher; Larry Notman, Advertising Mgr.
Circ: Free 1,600

16124 Beacon
Melrose Beacon
PO Box 186 Phone: (612)256-3240
Melrose, MN 56352-0186 Fax: (612)256-3363

Newspaper. **Founded:** 1890. **Freq:** Weekly (Wed.). **Print Method:** Offset. **Cols./Page:** 7. **Col. Width:** 24 nonpareils. **Col. Depth:** 301 agate lines. **Key Personnel:** Don Larson, Publisher; Carole Larson, Publisher. **Subscription Rates:** $20. **Remarks:** Accepts advertising.
Ad Rates: BW: $465.05 **Circ:** 3,000
4C: $765.05

MILACA†, pop. 2,104.

EC MN. Mille Lacs Co. 30 mi. NE of Saint Cloud. Manufactures butter, powdered milk, garments, plastic products. Dairy, poultry farms. Potatoes, oats.

16125 Mille Lacs County Times
Mille Lacs County Time
225 SW 2nd St. Phone: (320)983-6111
PO Box 9 Fax: (320)983-6112
Milaca, MN 56353
Newspaper. **Founded:** 1892. **Freq:** Weekly (Wed.). **Print Method:** Offset. **Cols./Page:** 6. **Col. Width:** 35 nonpareils. **Col. Depth:** 294 agate lines. **Key Personnel:** Gary Larson, Editor; Elmer L. Andersen, Publisher. **Subscription Rates:** $10. **Remarks:** Accepts advertising.
Ad Rates: GLR: $.17 **Circ:** (Not Reported)

MILAN, pop. 417.

SW MN. Chippewa Co. 135 mi. W. of Minneapolis. Stock, dairy, poultry, grain farms. Wheat, corn, barley.

16126 Milan Standard-Watson Journal
Box 190 Phone: (320)734-4458
Milan, MN 56262 Fax: (320)289-2702

Community newspaper. **Founded:** 1896. **Freq:** Weekly (Wed.). **Print Method:** Offset. **Cols./Page:** 5. **Col. Width:** 25 nonpareils. **Col. Depth:** 210 agate lines. **Key Personnel:** Loren Johnson, Publisher. **Subscription Rates:** $14; $15 out of area; $16 out of state. **Remarks:** Accepts advertising.
Ad Rates: GLR: $.10 **Circ:** ‡950
BW: $129
PCI: $1.50

MINNEAPOLIS†, pop. 370,951.

SE MN. Hennepin Co. On Mississippi River, adjacent to Saint Paul. Important grain and milling center. University of MinnesotaAugsburg College, Minneapolis College of Art and Design, North Central Bible College, Saint Mary's Junior College, Minneapolis Communit College. Financial Center. Medical Center. Manufactures food, dairy products, electronic computers, structural steel, thermostatic controls, conveyor equipment, medical electronics equipment, farm machinery, ball bearings, gears, electric portable tools, construction machinery, boilers, tanks, burglar alarm systems, bases and concentrates, textiles, packaging, garden tools, power lawn mowers, sprinklers.

16127 Akademiska Dzive/Academic Life
1 Vincent Ave. S Phone: (612)374-3009
Minneapolis, MN 55405-1953
Scholarly, scientific journal covering Latvian culture. **Founded:** 1958. **Freq:** Annual. **Trim Size:** 7 x 10. **Key Personnel:** Dr. Aina G. Dravnieks, Editor. **ISSN:** 0516-3145. **Subscription Rates:** $10 individuals. **Remarks:** Advertising not accepted.
Circ: Controlled 800

16128 Appellate Courts Edition
Dolan Media Co.
333 S. 7th St., Ste. 2180 Phone: (612)333-4244
Minneapolis, MN 55402-2432
Legal publication serving Minnesota. **Freq:** Weekly. **Key Personnel:** James Dolan, President.

16129 Architecture Minnesota
275 Market St., Ste. 54 Phone: (612)338-6763
Minneapolis, MN 55405-1621 Fax: (612)338-7981
Publication E-mail: aiamnoff@aol.com

Regional design arts magazine. **Founded:** 1954. **Freq:** Bimonthly. **Print Method:** Webb. **Trim Size:** 8 1/4 x 11. **Cols./Page:** 3. **Col. Width:** 27 nonpareils. **Col. Depth:** 138 agate lines. **Key Personnel:** Eric Kudalis, Editor; Peter Rand, Publisher; Judith Van Dyne, Advertising Mgr. **ISSN:** 0149-9106. **Subscription Rates:** $18 individuals; $3.50 single issue. **Remarks:** Accepts advertising.
Ad Rates: BW: $1,185 **Circ:** Paid ‡3,000
4C: $1,635 Controlled ‡4,000

16130 BEEF
Webb Division, Intertec Publishing Corp.
7900 International Dr., 3rd Fl. Phone: (612)851-9329
Minneapolis, MN 55425-1510 Fax: (612)851-4601
Free: (800)722-5334
Publication E-mail: beef@intertec.com

Subtitle: The Business Publication of the Cattle Industry. **Founded:** Sept. 1964. **Freq:** Monthly. **Print Method:** Offset. **Trim Size:** 8 x 10 3/4. **Cols./Page:** 3. **Col. Width:** 26 nonpareils. **Col. Depth:** 140 agate lines. **Key Personnel:** Joe Roybal, Editor; Wayne Bollum, Publisher. **ISSN:** 0005-7738. **Subscription Rates:** Free to qualified subscribers; $30; $40 other countries. **Remarks:** Accepts advertising. **URL:** http://www.homefarm.com.
Ad Rates: BW: $7,990 **Circ:** Controlled ‡100,119
4C: $9,895

16131 Bench & Bar of Minnesota
Minnesota State Bar Association
514 Nicollet Mall, Ste. 300 Phone: (612)333-1183
Minneapolis, MN 55402-1021 Fax: (612)333-4927
Free: (800)882-6722
Publication E-mail: jhaver@statebar.gen.mn.us

Official magazine of Minnesota State Bar Association. Includes editorial on issues of law and law practice, and human interest material of interest to Minnesota lawyers. **Founded:** Dec. 1943. **Freq:** 11/year. **Print Method:** Web Offset. **Trim Size:** 8 3/8 x 10 7/8. **Cols./Page:** 3. **Col. Width:** 2 5/16 inches. **Col. Depth:** 10 inches. **Key Personnel:** Judson P. Haverkamp, Editor, phone (612)673-6333, fax (612)3335194, jhaver@statebar.gen.mn.us; Julie Schaefer, Advertising Sales Rep., phone (612)473-9677, jschaefer8@compuserve.com. **ISSN:** 0276-1505. **Subscription Rates:** $25 individuals. **Remarks:** Accepts advertising. **URL:** http://www.mbar.org. **Alt. Formats:** Mailing labels.
Ad Rates: BW: $953 **Circ:** Paid ‡14,460
4C: $1,403 Non-paid ‡1,385

16132 The Bible Friend
Osterhus Publishing House, Inc.
4500 W. Broadway Phone: (612)537-8335
Minneapolis, MN 55422 Fax: (612)537-9585

Religious magazine. **Founded:** 1903. **Freq:** 10/year. **Print Method:** Offset. **Trim Size:** 9 1/2 x 12. **Cols./Page:** 3. **Col. Width:** 32 nonpareils. **Col. Depth:** 154 agate lines. **Key Personnel:** Mr. Daniel Osterhus, Editor. **Subscription Rates:** $4. **Remarks:** Advertising not accepted.
Circ: Paid 8,000
Non-paid 3,000

16133 Building Material Retailer
National Lumbermens Publishing Corp.
1405 Lilac Dr. N, No. 131 Phone: (612)544-1597
Minneapolis, MN 55422 Fax: (612)544-0820
Free: (800)328-9125
Publication E-mail: bmr@bmrmag.com

Official magazine of National Lumber & Building Material Dealers Association, issued in five regional editions. Includes articles on management, marketing, and merchandising strategies for profitable yard and store operation. **Founded:** July 1984. **Freq:** Monthly. **Print Method:** Offset. **Trim Size:** 8 1/4 x 10 7/8. **Cols./Page:** 3. **Col. Width:** 27 nonpareils. **Col. Depth:** 140 agate lines. **Key Personnel:** Ray Lorenz, Executive editor; Gary Donnelly, Publisher; Chuck Mowrey, Sales Mgr. **USPS:** 997-960. **Subscription Rates:** $24 U.S. and Canada; $60 other countries; $2 single issue. **Remarks:** Accepts advertising.
Ad Rates: BW: $3,300 **Circ:** Controlled ‡29,242
4C: $4,500

16134 Business Ethics
2845 Harriet Ave., Ste. 207 Phone: (612)879-0695
PO Box 8439 Fax: (612)879-0699
Minneapolis, MN 55408
Publication E-mail: bizethics@aol.com

Business newsletter. **Subtitle:** The Insider's Report on Corporate Responsibility. **Founded:** 1987. **Freq:** Bimonthly. **Print Method:** 1/2 web saddle stitched. **Trim Size:** 8 1/2 x 10 3/4. **Cols./Page:** 3. **Key Personnel:** Marjorie Kelly, Editor and Publisher. **ISSN:** 0894-6582. **Subscription Rates:** $49; $9.95 single issue. **Remarks:** Accepts advertising. **Formerly:** Business Ethics: The Magazine of Socially Responsible Business.
Ad Rates: BW: $2,095 **Circ:** Paid 6,000
4C: $2,395 Non-paid 6,000
PCI: $250

16135 Cake
2401 University Ave. NE. Phone: (612)781-9141
Minneapolis, MN 55418 Fax: (612)781-9181

Music and pop culture magazine serving the Minneapolis, MN, area. **Subtitle:** Non-music Music Zine. **Founded:** 1990. **Freq:** Bimonthly. **Trim Size:** 10 x 12. **Key Personnel:** Todd Bennington, Editor; Liz Klaens, Advertising Mgr. **Subscription Rates:** Free to qualified subscribers; $3 single issue. **Remarks:** Accepts advertising.
Ad Rates: BW: $120 **Circ:** Paid 2,000
4C: $1,800 Non-paid 18,000
PCI: $25

16136 Casual Living
Bolger Publications, Inc.
3301 Como Ave. SE Phone: (612)645-6311
Minneapolis, MN 55414 Fax: (612)642-2900
Free: (800)999-6311

Trade magazine for the casual furnishings industry. **Founded:** 1960. **Freq:** 11/year. **Print Method:** Offset. **Trim Size:** 8 1/8 x 10 7/8. **Cols./Page:** 2 and 3. **Col. Width:** 40 and 27 nonpareils. **Col. Depth:** 140 agate lines. **Key Personnel:** Tammy Galvin, Editor, tgalvin@casualliving.com; Judy Rudrud, Publisher, jrudrud@casualliving.com; Gina Wilharber, Publication Asst. **Subscription Rates:** $20. $4 single issue. **Remarks:** Accepts advertising.
Ad Rates: BW: $2,505 **Circ:** 13,000
4C: $3,720

16137 The Circle
1530 E. Franklin Ave. Phone: (612)871-4749
Minneapolis, MN 55404-2136 Fax: (612)871-6878

Newspaper serving Minneapolis-St.Paul area. **Subtitle:** News from a Native American Perspective. **Founded:** Mar. 1, 1980. **Freq:** Monthly. **Print Method:** Web press. **Trim Size:** 11 1/2 x 13 1/2. **Cols./Page:** 6. **Col. Width:** 1 9/16 inches. **Col. Depth:** 12 1/2 inches. **Key Personnel:** Joe Allen, Editor, phone (612)879-1760; Tod LeGarde, Business Manager, phone (612)879-1757; Barbara Nelson, Advertising Sales, phone (612)879-1758. **Subscription Rates:** $18 individuals; $30 two years. **Remarks:** Accepts advertising. **Online:** LEXIS-NEXIS. **Alt. Formats:** CD-ROM.
Ad Rates: GLR: $3 **Circ:** Paid 1,000
BW: $750 Non-paid 24,000
4C: $950

16138 City Pages
City Pages, Inc.
PO Box 59183 Phone: (612)375-1015
Minneapolis, MN 55459-0183 Fax: (612)372-3737
Publication E-mail: adinfo@citypages.com

News and arts Weekly. **Subtitle:** The Alternative News and Arts Weekly of the Twin Cities. **Founded:** Aug. 1, 1979. **Freq:** Weekly (Wed.). **Print Method:** Offset. **Trim Size:** 11 1/2 x 13 1/2. **Cols./Page:** 6. **Col. Width:** 21 nonpareils. **Col. Depth:** 175 agate lines. **Key Personnel:** Tom Finkel, Editor, tfinkel@citypages.com; Mark Bartel, Publisher, mbartel@citypages.com; Jerry Gloe, Advertising Dir., phone (612)372-3743, fax (612)372-3737, jgloe@citypages.com. **ISSN:** 0744-0456. **Subscription Rates:** Free; $52 /year. **Available Online. URL:** http://www.citypages.com.
Ad Rates: BW: $3,495 **Circ:** Free 100,710
4C: $4,645
SAU: $62.84
PCI: $48.23

16139 Classic Cookbooks
Pillsbury Co.
200 6th St., M.S. 28M7 Phone: (612)330-4475
Minneapolis, MN 55402 Fax: (612)330-4875

Magazine containing new recipes. **Founded:** 1979. **Freq:** Monthly. **Print Method:** Web. **Trim Size:** 5 11/16 x 9. **Cols./Page:** 2. **Key Personnel:** Sally Peters, Publisher; William Monn, Manager. **ISSN:** 1089-0432. **Subscription Rates:** $24.95; $2.99 single issue. **Remarks:** Accepts advertising.
Ad Rates: 4C: $10,000 **Circ:** Paid 450,000

16140 Collector
American Collectors Association, Inc.
4040 W. 70th St. Phone: (612)926-6547
Minneapolis, MN 55435
Publisher E-mail: aca@collector.com

Magazine on consumer debt collection services. **Subtitle:** The Official Publication of the American Collectors Association. **Founded:** 1939. **Freq:** Monthly. **Print Method:** Offset. **Trim Size:** 8 1/2 x 11. **Cols./Page:** 3 and 2. **Col. Width:** 26 and 41

nonpareils. **Col. Depth:** 140 agate lines. **Key Personnel:** Tim Dressen, Editor, dressen@collector.com. **Subscription Rates:** $60 individuals.
Ad Rates: BW: $1,400 **Circ:** ‡5,500
4C: $2,150
PCI: $1,000

16141 Computer User
MSP Communications
220 S. 6th St., Ste. 500 Phone: (612)339-7571
Minneapolis, MN 55402-4507 Fax: (612)339-5806
Free: (800)788-0204

Tabloid sized news magazine covering computers in business and office automation. **Subtitle:** Business Technology, Professional Development, the Internet. **Founded:** 1981. **Freq:** Monthly. **Print Method:** Offset. **Cols./Page:** 4. **Key Personnel:** James Matherson, Editor, weditor@usinternet.com; Frank Sisser, Publisher; Michele Wachter, Advertising Mgr. **ISSN:** 0742-5902. **Subscription Rates:** $24.95. **Remarks:** Advertising accepted; rates available upon request.
Circ: Non-paid ‡50,000

16142 Corporate Report Minnesota
105 S. 5th St., Ste. 100 Phone: (612)338-4288
Minneapolis, MN 55402 Fax: (612)373-0195
Publication E-mail: editorial@corpreport.com

Business magazine. **Subtitle:** The Magazine of Minnesota Business. **Founded:** 1969. **Freq:** Monthly. **Print Method:** Offset. **Trim Size:** 8.125 x 10.875. **Cols./Page:** 3. **Col. Width:** 26 nonpareils. **Col. Depth:** 147 agate lines. **Key Personnel:** Beth Ewen, Editor, bethe@corpreport.com; Lisa Bormaster, Publisher, lbormaster@corpreport.com. **ISSN:** 0279-5299. **Subscription Rates:** $34 individuals; $2.95 single issue. **Remarks:** Accepts advertising. **URL:** http://citymedia.com/crm/.
Ad Rates: BW: $4,150 **Circ:** Paid ★7,814
4C: $4,550

16143 Cross Country Skier
Collins Chase Publications
PO Box 50120 Phone: (612)377-0312
Minneapolis, MN 55405 Fax: (612)381-9182
Free: (800)827-0607

Magazine emphasizing touring, destinations, and technique in cross-country skiing. **Founded:** 1976. **Freq:** Monthly. **Print Method:** Web offset. **Trim Size:** 8 x 10 3/4. **Cols./Page:** 3. **Col. Width:** 13 picas. **Col. Depth:** 56 picas. **ISSN:** 0278-9213. **Subscription Rates:** $14.97. **Remarks:** Accepts advertising. **Available Online. URL:** http://www.crosscountryskier.com/.
Ad Rates: BW: $4,040 **Circ:** ‡75,000
4C: $6,060

16144 Dancing USA
DOT Publications, Inc.
10600 University Ave. NW Phone: (612)757-4414
Minneapolis, MN 55448-6166 Fax: (612)757-6605
Free: (800)290-1307
Publication E-mail: ballroom@dancingusa.com

Magazine devoted to music and ballroom dancing for the social dancer, including Latin and Swing. Dance step technique, history and ballrooms/big bands of today and yesterday. Where to go dancing. **Subtitle:** Dancing USA for the Romance of ballroom, Latin, swing and tango dancing. **Founded:** 1982. **Freq:** Bimonthly. **Print Method:** Offset. **Trim Size:** 10 1/2 x 8 3/8. **Cols./Page:** 3. **Col. Width:** 2 1/4 inches. **Col. Depth:** 8 inches. **Key Personnel:** LeAnn Bamford, Publisher, phone (612)767-8768, fax (612)767-8092; Patti Johnson, Editor. **ISSN:** 1053-5454. **Subscription Rates:** $24.97 individuals; $4.50 single issue U.S.; $42.97 two years. **Alt. Formats:** Mailing labels. **Formerly:** Ballroom Dancing Across the USA.
Ad Rates: BW: $1,360 **Circ:** Paid ‡7,000
4C: $1,789 Non-paid ‡13,000
Combined ‡20,000

16145 Decision
The Billy Graham Evangelistic Association
PO Box 779 Phone: (612)338-0500
Minneapolis, MN 55440 Fax: (612)335-1299

Religious magazine. (Also available in a braille edition.). **Founded:** Nov. 1960. **Freq:** Monthly (July/Aug. combined issue). **Print Method:** Offset. **Trim Size:** 8 3/8 x 10 3/4. **Cols./Page:** 3 and 2. **Col. Width:** 27 and 42 nonpareils. **Col. Depth:** 140 agate lines. **Key Personnel:** Roger Palms, Editor. **ISSN:** 0011-7307. **Subscription Rates:** Free to qualified subscribers; $7. **Remarks:** Advertising not accepted.
Circ: Paid 350,000
Non-paid 1,300,000

16146 EI Digest
Environmental Information Ltd.
4801 W. 81st St., No. 119 Phone: (612)831-2473
Minneapolis, MN 55437-1111 Fax: (612)831-6550
Publication E-mail: ei@mr.net
Publisher E-mail: ei@mr.net

Journal covering issues on industrial and hazardous waste management. **Subtitle:** Hazardous Waste Market Place. **Founded:** Jan. 1989. **Freq:** Monthly. **Key Personnel:** Mr. Cary L. Perket, President. **Subscription Rates:** $895 individuals annual. **Remarks:** Advertising not accepted. **URL:** http://www.envirobiz.com.
Circ: (Not Reported)

16147 Engineering Contacts
Meusey Communications
1107 Hazeltine Blvd., Ste. 539 Phone: (612)448-8816
Chaska, MN 55318-1008
Magazine for Minnesota engineers. **Founded:** 1975. **Freq:** Monthly. **Print Method:** Offset. **Trim Size:** 8 1/2 x 11. **Cols./Page:** 3. **Key Personnel:** Jim Meusey, Publisher. **Remarks:** Accepts advertising.
Ad Rates: BW: $467 **Circ:** Non-paid ‡4,000

16148 The Evangelical Beacon
The Evangelical Free Church of America
901 E. 78th St. Phone: (612)854-1300
Minneapolis, MN 55420-1334
Evangelical Christian magazine. **Founded:** 1931. **Freq:** Monthly. **Print Method:** Offset. **Trim Size:** 8 1/2 x 11. **Cols./Page:** 3. **Col. Width:** 30 nonpareils. **Col. Depth:** 140 agate lines. **Key Personnel:** Carol Madison, Editor. **ISSN:** 0014-3332. **Subscription Rates:** $12. **Remarks:** Accepts advertising.
Ad Rates: BW: $1,200 **Circ:** 37,500
4C: $1,650
PCI: $75

16149 The Family Handyman
Home Service Publications, Inc.
7900 International Dr., Ste. 950 Phone: (612)854-3000
Minneapolis, MN 55425 Fax: (612)854-8009

Do-it-yourself home improvement magazine. **Founded:** 1951. **Freq:** 10/year. **Print Method:** Offset. **Trim Size:** 8 x 10 3/4. **Cols./Page:** 3. **Col. Width:** 27 nonpareils. **Col. Depth:** 140 agate lines. **Key Personnel:** Gary Havens, Editor; Thomas Ph. Witschi, Publisher. **ISSN:** 0014-7230. **Subscription Rates:** $19.97 individuals. **Remarks:** Advertising not accepted for tobacco products.
Ad Rates: BW: $29,440 **Circ:** Paid ★1,108,882
4C: $42,695

16150 Farm Industry News
Webb Division, Intertec Publishing Corp.
7900 International Dr., 3rd Fl. Phone: (612)851-9329
Minneapolis, MN 55425-1510 Fax: (612)851-4601
Free: (800)722-5334
Publication E-mail: fin@intertec.com

Agriculture trade magazine covering new products and technology. **Founded:** 1967. **Freq:** 12/year. **Print Method:** Offset. **Trim Size:** 8 1/2 x 11. **Cols./Page:** 3. **Key Personnel:** Kurt Lawton, Editor, kurt_lawton@intertec.com; Ron Sorensen, Publisher, ron_sorensen@intertec.com; Bob Moraczewski, Vice President, bob_moraczewski@intertec.com. **Subscription Rates:** $28.
Ad Rates: BW: $15,410 **Circ:** Non-paid ‡255,000
4C: $19,320
PCI: $501

16151 Farm Supply Retailing
Quirk Enterprises, Inc.
PO Box 23536 Phone: (612)854-5101
Minneapolis, MN 55423-0536 Fax: (612)854-8191
Publisher E-mail: quirk19@mail.idt.net

Magazine including information on sales strategies, ways to improve profits, marketing techniques, and product data for farm supply retailers. **Founded:** Apr. 1, 1993. **Freq:** 10/year. **Trim Size:** 8 x 10 7/8. **Cols./Page:** 3. **Col. Width:** 2 9/16 inches. **Col. Depth:** 10 inches. **Key Personnel:** Joseph Rydholm, Editor; Tom Quirk, Publisher. **ISSN:** 1072-903. **Remarks:** Accepts advertising.
Ad Rates: BW: $2,400 **Circ:** Controlled 20,000
4C: $3,325

16152 Finance and Commerce
Finance & Commerce, Inc.
730 2nd Ave., No. 100 Phone: (612)333-4244
Minneapolis, MN 55402-3400 Fax: (612)333-3243
Free: (800)397-4348

Business newspaper. **Founded:** 1887. **Freq:** Tues.-Sat. **Print Method:** Offset. **Trim Size:** 16 1/2 x 22 3/4. **Cols./Page:** 6. **Col. Width:** 2 3/16 inches. **Col. Depth:** 21 3/16 inches. **Key Personnel:** Debra J. Quaal, Publisher. **USPS:** 190-580. **Subscription Rates:** $145 individuals. **Remarks:** Accepts advertising. **Absorbed:** Register-Mirror (Apr. 11, 1988).
Ad Rates: GLR: $2.15 **Circ:** ‡1,500
BW: $738
PCI: $15

16153 The Five Owls
Five Owls
2004 Sheridan Ave. S Phone: (612)377-2004
Minneapolis, MN 55405 Fax: (612)377-4816

Professional magazine covering children's books for teachers and others. **Founded:** Sept. 1986. **Freq:** 5/year. **Print Method:** Offset. **Trim Size:** 8 1/2 x 11. **Cols./Page:** 2. **Col. Width:** 3 1/4 inches. **Col. Depth:** 9 3/4 inches. **Key Personnel:** Dan Dailey, Publisher; Cheri Moon, Managing Editor. **ISSN:** 0892-6735. **Subscription Rates:** $35 individuals; $8 single issue. **Remarks:** Accepts advertising.
Ad Rates: BW: $1,150 **Circ:** Combined 3,500

16154 Format Magazine
Decker Publications, Inc.
PO Box 29488
Minneapolis, MN 55429
Publication E-mail: format2@aol.com

Magazine for advertising and media professionals in Minnesota. **Subtitle:** For Media, Advertising & Technologies. **Founded:** 1954. **Freq:** Monthly. **Trim Size:** 8 1/4 x 10 7/8. **Cols./Page:** 4. **Col. Width:** 1 5/8 inches. **Col. Depth:** 10 inches. **Key Personnel:** Sheri O'Meara, Editor; Dale Decker, Publisher; Deb Gustafson, Publisher. **ISSN:** 0279-6058. **Subscription Rates:** $18.95 individuals; $1.95 single issue.
Ad Rates: BW: $1,375 **Circ:** Non-paid 3,000
4C: $1,825

16155 Hay & Forage Grower
Webb Division, Intertec Publishing Corp.
7900 International Dr., 3rd Fl. Phone: (612)851-9329
Minneapolis, MN 55425-1510 Fax: (612)851-4601
Free: (800)722-5334

Trade magazine for large-acreage producers of forage crops. **Founded:** 1986. **Freq:** Quarterly. **Print Method:** Offset. **Key Personnel:** Neil Tietz, Editor; Ron Sorensen, Publisher. **Subscription Rates:** $9.95 individuals annual. **Remarks:** Accepts advertising. **URL:** http://www.homefarm.com/.
Ad Rates: BW: $6,400 **Circ:** Non-paid ‡90,000
4C: $7,960

16156 Hospital Practice
McGraw-Hill Healthcare Information Group
4530 W. 77th St. Phone: (612)835-3222
Minneapolis, MN 55435 Fax: (612)835-3460

Magazine providing information on developments and problem areas in medicine and clinical research. Emphasizes application of medical knowledge to the direct care of patients. **Founded:** Oct. 1966. **Freq:** Monthly. **Print Method:** Offset. **Trim Size:** 7 7/8 x 10 3/4. **Cols./Page:** 3. **Col. Width:** 25 nonpareils. **Col. Depth:** 128 agate lines. **Key Personnel:** Janis Cohen, VP/Publisher, phone (212)512-2125; Gretchen Drasner, Senior Mktg. Mgr., phone (612)832-7877; M. James Dougherty, Group Vice President, phone (612)832-7876; Lee Powers, Exec. Editor, phone (612)832-7839; Nancy Souza, Director of Sales, phone (212)512-3492; Rita Beale, Vice President of Sales, phone (212)512-3634; Monica Brent, Acct. Mgr., phone (312)616-3308; Brett Talbott, Mktg. Assoc., btalbott@mcgraw-hill.com. **ISSN:** 8750-2836. **Subscription Rates:** Free to qualified subscribers; $54 other countries; $6 single issue. **Remarks:** Accepts advertising. **Online:** National Library of Medicine. **URL:** http://www.hosppract.com.
Ad Rates: BW: $5,021 **Circ:** Controlled ‡136,183
4C: $6,689

16157 Illustrator
Art Instruction Schools
3309 Broadway NE Phone: (612)362-5121
Minneapolis, MN 55413 Fax: (612)362-5260

Trade magazine covering artwork and past graduates of art instruction schools. **Founded:** 1914. **Freq:** Annual. **Print Method:** Litho. **Trim Size:** 8 1/4 x 10 7/8. **Key Personnel:** Steve Unverzagt, Editor, steveu@visi.com. **ISSN:** 0019-2465. **Subscription Rates:** $2.50 individuals. **Remarks:** Advertising not accepted.
Circ: (Not Reported)

16158 The James White Review
PO Box 3356, Butler Qtr. Sta. Phone: (612)339-8317
Minneapolis, MN 55403
Publication E-mail: jwrmail@aol.com

Gay men's literary journal containing poetry, short stories, book reviews, and art. **Subtitle:** A Gay Men's Literary Quarterly. **Founded:** Oct. 10, 1983. **Freq:** Quarterly. **Print Method:** Offset. **Trim Size:** 11 x 17. **Key Personnel:** Philip Willkie, Publisher; Clif Mayhood, Poetry Editor. **ISSN:** 0891-5393. **Subscription Rates:** $14 individuals; $24 two years; $16 Canada; $20 other countries. **Remarks:** Color advertising not accepted.
Ad Rates: BW: $400 **Circ:** ‡4,500

16159 Journal of Andrology
American Society of Andrology
4-144 Jackson Hall Phone: (612)625-1488
321 Church St., SE Fax: (612)625-1163
Minneapolis, MN 55455
Publication E-mail: andrology@med.umn.edu

Journal covering clinical and laboratory research in the structure and function of the male reproductive system and male gametes. **Founded:** 1980. **Freq:** Bimonthly. **Print Method:** Sheetfed offset. **Trim Size:** 8 1/2 x 11. **Cols./Page:** 2. **Col. Width:** 39 nonpareils. **Col. Depth:** 140 agate lines. **Key Personnel:** Dr. David W. Hamilton, Editor-in-Chief; Dr. Jon L. Pryor, Editor-in-Chief; Lauren Fox, Editoral Assistant; Carol Parlette, ASA Exec. Dir., phone (415)764-4823, fax (415)764-4915, 105037.1120@compuserve.com; Marissa Barlow, Managing Editor, mbarlow@allenpress.com; Onkar Sandal, Marketing, osandal@allenpress.com. **ISSN:** 0196-3635. **Subscription Rates:** $205 individuals; $264 Industry; $287 other countries Industry; $40 single issue; $222 other countries. **Remarks:** Accepts advertising. **URL:** http://www.allenpress.com.
Ad Rates: BW: $475 **Circ:** ‡1,200
4C: $755

16160 Journal of Economic Perspectives
American Economic Association
Humphrey Institute of Public Affairs Phone: (612)626-7695
Fax: (612)625-3513
301 19th Ave. S
Minneapolis, MN 55455
Publication E-mail: jep@hhh.umn.edu
Publisher E-mail: aeainfo@ctrvax.vanderbilt.edu

Economics and finance journal. **Founded:** 1987. **Freq:** Quarterly. **Trim Size:** 7 x 10. **Key Personnel:** Alan B. Krueger, Editor. **ISSN:** 0895-3309. **Subscription Rates:** $130 (joint subscription with Journal). **Remarks:** Accepts advertising.
Ad Rates: BW: $875 **Circ:** Paid 27,000

16161 Journal of Psychology and Human Sexuality
The Haworth Press, Inc.
1300 S. 2nd St. Phone: (612)625-1500
Minneapolis, MN 55414-1092 Fax: (612)626-8311
Free: (800)342-9678
Publisher E-mail: getinfo@haworthpressinc.com

Founded: 1988. **Freq:** Quarterly. **Key Personnel:** Eli Coleman, Ph.D., Editor, coleman001@macoon.tc.umn.edu; Bill Cohen, Publisher. **ISSN:** 0890-7064. **Subscription Rates:** $40 individuals; $120 Industry; $150 libraries. **Remarks:** Accepts advertising.
Ad Rates: BW: $300 **Circ:** 226

16162 Labor Studies Journal
Transaction Publishers
Labor Education Service Phone: (612)624-6343
321-19th Ave. S., 3-300 Fax: (612)624-1585
Minneapolis, MN 55455
Publication E-mail: lsjournal@csom.umn.edu
Publisher E-mail: trans@transactionpub.com

Journal exploring the role of the trade union movement in forging American economic and social policy. **Founded:** 1976. **Freq:** Quarterly. **Print Method:** Offset. **Trim Size:** 5 x 9. **Key Personnel:** Joyce Hegstrom, Editorial Ass., phone (612)624-5020, jhegstrom@csom.umn.edu; John Remington, Editor, phone (612)624-7863, jremington@csom.umn.edu. **ISSN:** 0160-449X. **Subscription Rates:** $36 individuals; $80 institutions; $98 individuals other countries; $112 institutions, other countries; $64 two years individuals; $144 two years institutions. **Remarks:** Accepts advertising.
Ad Rates: BW: $200 **Circ:** ‡800

16163 Latina
PO Box 581546 Phone: (612)623-4305
Minneapolis, MN 55458-1546 Fax: (612)623-4305

Bilingual magazine on the economy, people, entertainment, and the arts. **Subtitle:** Minnesota's Hispanic Bilingual Publication. **Founded:** Sept. 1990. **Freq:** Monthly. **Trim Size:** 8 x 10. **Cols./Page:** 3. **Key Personnel:** Randy Melcher, Editor. **Subscription Rates:** $20. **Remarks:** Accepts advertising.
Ad Rates: BW: $800 **Circ:** Paid ★135,915
4C: $1,275

16164 Let's Play Hockey
Let's Play, Inc.
2721 E. 42nd St. Phone: (612)729-0023
Minneapolis, MN 55406 Fax: (612)729-0259
Publication E-mail: letsplay@letsplayhockey.com

Consumer publication covering all levels of hockey in the U.S. **Founded:** Dec. 1972. **Freq:** Weekly. **Print Method:** Cold web offset. **Trim Size:** 10 7/8 x 16 1/2. **Cols./Page:** 4. **Col. Width:** 2 3/8 inches. **Col. Depth:** 16 inches. **Key Personnel:** Shane Frederick, Editor; Doug Johnson, Publisher; Mike Thill, Photo Editor. **ISSN:** 0889-4795. **Subscription Rates:** $40 individuals. **Remarks:** Accepts advertising.
Ad Rates: BW: $950.40 **Circ:** Paid 11,867
4C: $1,330.40
PCI: $14.85

16165 Let's Play Softball
Let's Play, Inc.
2721 E. 42nd St. Phone: (612)729-0023
Minneapolis, MN 55406 Fax: (612)729-0259

Magazine about softball. **Founded:** Feb. 1987. **Freq:** Monthly. **Print Method:** Cold Web offset. **Trim Size:** 10 7/8 x 16 1/2. **Cols./Page:** 4. **Col. Width:** 2 3/8 inches. **Col. Depth:** 16 inches. **Key Personnel:** Shane Frederick, Editor; Doug Johnson, Publisher; Mike Thill, Photo Editor. **ISSN:** 0892-9440. **Subscription Rates:** $12.
Ad Rates: BW: $832 **Circ:** Controlled 6,533
4C: $1,212
PCI: $13.00

16166 The Loon
Minnesota Ornithologists' Union
James Ford Bell Museum of Natural History
University of Minnesota
10 Church St. SE
Minneapolis, MN 55455-0104
Publication E-mail: mou@biosci.cbs.umn.edu
Publisher E-mail: moumembers@aol.com

Scientific journal covering ornithology and natural history. **Founded:** 1929. **Freq:** Quarterly. **Print Method:** Offset. **Trim Size:** 6 x 9. **Cols./Page:** 2. **Col. Width:** 15 picas. **Col. Depth:** 45 picas. **Key Personnel:** Elizabeth Bell, Membership Secretary, phone (651)459-4150, fax (651)459-6621; Anthony Hertzel, Editor. **Subscription Rates:** $20 individuals; $30 family; $50 supporting; $15 youth through age 17; $25 Canada and foreign, U.S. funds. **Remarks:** Advertising not accepted. **URL:** http://biosci.cbs.umn.edu/mou/.
Circ: Combined 1,400

16167 Lutheran Journal
Macalester Park Publishing Company
7317 Cahill Rd., Ste. 201 Phone: (612)561-1234
Minneapolis, MN 55439 Fax: (612)941-3010
Free: (800)407-9078

Religious magazine. **Founded:** 1936. **Freq:** Quarterly. **Print Method:** Offset. **Trim Size:** 8 1/2 x 11. **Cols./Page:** 2. **Col. Width:** 42 nonpareils. **Col. Depth:** 131 agate lines. **Key Personnel:** Rev. Armin U. Deye, Editor; Michael L. Beard, Publisher. **Subscription Rates:** $6 individuals. **Remarks:** Accepts advertising.
Ad Rates: BW: $1,100 **Circ:** Paid ‡550
4C: $1,500 Non-paid ‡120,000

16168 Lutheran Woman Today
Augsburg Fortress, Publishers
100 S. Fifth St., Ste. 700 Phone: (612)330-3300
PO Box 1209 Fax: (612)330-3455
Minneapolis, MN 55440-1209
Free: (800)426-0115
Publisher E-mail: afp_ bookstore.topic@ecunet.org

Women of the Evangelical Lutheran Church bible study magazine. **Founded:** 1908. **Freq:** 11/year. **Print Method:** Offset. **Trim Size:** 5 3/8 x 8 3/8. **Cols./Page:** 2. **Col. Width:** 30 nonpareils. **Col. Depth:** 122 agate lines. **Key Personnel:** Nancy Stelling, Editor. **ISSN:** 0896-209X. **Subscription Rates:** $10 individuals. **Remarks:** Advertising not accepted. **Alt. Formats:** Audio tape; Braille; Large-print. **Formerly:** Scope (1961); Lutheran Women (1987).
Circ: Paid 232,901

16169 Maize, A Lesbian Country Magazine
Word Weavers
PO Box 8742
Minneapolis, MN 55408-0742

Magazine focusing on the rural lesbian experience and strategies for economic survival and community building. Topics include food, shelter, agriculture, environmental issues, and healing arts. Contains essays, news, book reviews, interviews, and how-to articles. **Freq:** Quarterly. **Subscription Rates:** $10.

16170 Maryland Construction
Dolan Media Co.
333 S. 7th St., Ste. 2180 Phone: (612)333-4244
Minneapolis, MN 55402-2432
Magazine serving the building and contracting industries. **Freq:** Weekly. **Key Personnel:** James Dolan, President.

16171 Maryland Lawyer
Dolan Media Co.
333 S. 7th St., Ste. 2180 Phone: (612)333-4244
Minneapolis, MN 55402-2432
Magazine serving the legal community. **Freq:** Weekly. **Key Personnel:** James Dolan, President.

16172 Midwest Home & Garden
Minnesota Monthly Publications, Inc.
10 S. 5th St., Ste. 1000 Phone: (612)371-5800
Minneapolis, MN 55402-1012 Fax: (612)371-5801

Supplement to Minnesota Monthly. **Subtitle:** A Supplement Magazine to Minnesota Monthly Magazine. **Founded:** 1991. **Freq:** Bimonthly. **Print Method:** Offset. **Trim Size:** 8 3/8 x 11. **Cols./Page:** 3. **Col. Width:** 2 1/4 inches. **Col. Depth:** 10 inches. **Key Personnel:** Jan Senn, Editor, phone (612)371-5833, jsenn@mnmo.com; Steve Fox, Publisher. **Subscription Rates:** $15. $2.50 single issue. **Remarks:** Accepts advertising.
Ad Rates: BW: $3,395 **Circ:** Paid 82,898
4C: $4,375

16173 Minneapolis Labor Review
MPLS Central Labor Union Council
312 Central Ave., Ste. 526 Phone: (612)379-4725
Minneapolis, MN 55414-1077 Fax: (612)379-1307

Labor newspaper. **Founded:** 1907. **Freq:** Semimonthly. **Print Method:** Offset. **Cols./Page:** 6. **Col. Width:** 19 nonpareils. **Col. Depth:** 205 agate lines. **Key Personnel:** Wallace Nelson, Editor. **ISSN:** 0274-9017. **Subscription Rates:** $10. **Remarks:** Accepts advertising.
Ad Rates: BW: $1,200 **Circ:** ‡56,000

16174 Minneapolis St. Paul
MSP Communications
220 S. 6th St., Ste. 500 Phone: (612)339-7571
Minneapolis, MN 55402-4507 Fax: (612)339-5806
Free: (800)788-0204

Metropolitan lifestyle magazine. **Subtitle:** The Magazine of the Twin Cities. **Founded:** 1972. **Freq:** Monthly. **Print Method:** Offset-Web. **Trim Size:** 8 x 10 7/8. **Cols./Page:** 3. **Col. Width:** 26 nonpareils. **Col. Depth:** 140 agate lines. **Key Personnel:** Brian Anderson, Editor; Burton Cohen, Publisher; Pat Mathews, Publisher; Gary Johnson, Publisher. **ISSN:** 0162-6655. **Subscription Rates:** $18. $2.50 single issue. **Remarks:** Accepts advertising.
Ad Rates: BW: $4,270 **Circ:** Paid ★**64,259**
4C: $5,750
PCI: $135

16175 Minneapolis/St. Paul City Business
City Business Twin Cities, Inc.
527 Marquette Ave. S., Ste. 300 Phone: (612)288-2100
Minneapolis, MN 55402 Fax: (612)288-2121

Regional business journal. **Subtitle:** The Business Journal. **Founded:** 1983. **Freq:** Weekly. **Print Method:** Web Offset. **Trim Size:** 10 1/3 x 13 1/4. **Cols./Page:** 4. **Col. Width:** 14.5 picas. **Col. Depth:** 78 picas. **Key Personnel:** Stuart A. Chamblin III, Publisher, phone (612)591-2661; Kevin Maler, Editor, phone (612)591-2644; Leonard Fischer, Art Production Director, phone (612)591-2542. **Subscription Rates:** $64 individuals. **Remarks:** Accepts advertising. **Available Online.**
Ad Rates: BW: $3,471 **Circ:** Paid ★**10,718**
4C: $3,921

16176 Minneapolis Spokesman
3744 4th Ave. S. Phone: (612)827-4021
Minneapolis, MN 55409 Fax: (612)827-0577
Publication E-mail: srclass1@aol.com
Publisher E-mail: srpub2@aol.com

Black community newspaper. **Founded:** 1934. **Freq:** Weekly (Thurs.). **Print Method:** Offset. **Cols./Page:** 6. **Col. Width:** 21 nonpareils. **Col. Depth:** 218 agate lines. **Key Personnel:** Launa Newman, Editor and Publisher, phone (612)827-4921; Tracey Williams, Advertising Mgr., phone (612)824-4452; Gayle Anderson, Editor. **Subscription Rates:** $20 out of state; $25. **Remarks:** Accepts advertising.
Ad Rates: GLR: $19.82 **Circ:** Paid ‡3,790
BW: $2,637.18 Free ‡517
SAU: $17.59
PCI: $10.22

16177 Minnesota
University of Minnesota Alumni Association
501 Coffman Memorial Union Phone: (612)624-2323
300 Washington Ave. SE Fax: (612)626-8167
Minneapolis, MN 55455-0396
Free: (800)UM-ALUMS

University alumni magazine. **Founded:** 1901. **Freq:** Bimonthly. **Print Method:** Web offset. **Trim Size:** 8 1/4 x 10 13/16. **Cols./Page:** 3. **Col. Width:** 28 nonpareils. **Col. Depth:** 124 agate lines. **Key Personnel:** Tom Garrison, Executive Ed., phone (612)626-4854, garri009@tc.umn.edu; Shelly Fling,

Editor, phone (612)626-4864, fling003@tc.umn.edu; Chris Coughlin-Smith, Associate Ed., phone (612)625-0474, cough003@tc.umn.edu; Mike Lee, Graphic Designer, phone (612)625-7125, leexx253@tc.umn.edu; Shelly Horstman, Ad Production Coord., phone (612)626-4856, horst005@tc.umn.edu; Michael Armel, Advertising Sales Rep., phone (612)337-9898, fax (612)337-0004. **ISSN:** 0164-9450. **Subscription Rates:** $40 individuals. **Remarks:** Accepts advertising. **URL:** http://www.umaa.umn.edu.
Ad Rates: BW: $2,980 **Circ:** 40,000
4C: $3,955

16178 The Minnesota Daily
University of Minnesota
10 Murphy Hall Phone: (612)627-4080
206 Church St. SE Fax: (612)627-4159
Minneapolis, MN 55414-3070
Collegiate newspaper (tabloid). **Founded:** May 1, 1900. **Freq:** MXF (morn.). **Print Method:** Offset. **Cols./Page:** 5. **Col. Width:** 1 7/8 inches. **Col. Depth:** 16 inches. **Key Personnel:** Blake Morrison, Editor; Mark Strong, Business Mgr. **USPS:** 351-480. **Subscription Rates:** $45. **Remarks:** Accepts advertising.
Ad Rates: BW: $799.20 **Circ:** Free ‡27,000
4C: $1,249.20
PCI: $9.99

16179 Minnesota Law & Politics
Law & Politics Media, Inc.
220 S. 6th St., Ste. 500 Phone: (612)335-8808
Minneapolis, MN 55402-4507 Fax: (612)335-8809
Publisher E-mail: letters@lawandpolitics.com

Professional magazine covering law and politics in Minnesota. **Founded:** Apr. 1990. **Freq:** Monthly. **Print Method:** Web offset. **Trim Size:** 10 x 12. **Key Personnel:** William C. White, Publisher, phone (612)313-1761; Steven Kaplan, Editor-in-Chief, phone (612)313-1762; Adam Wahlberg, Editor, phone (612)313-1760. **Subscription Rates:** $29 individuals; $2.95 single issue. **Remarks:** Accepts advertising. **URL:** http://www.lawandpolitics.com. **Former name**: Minnesota's Journal of Law & Politics.
Ad Rates: BW: $2,582 **Circ:** Controlled 22,000
4C: $3,132 Paid 2,000

16180 Minnesota Law Review
University of Minnesota Phone: (612)625-9330
229 19th Ave. S. Fax: (612)625-3478
Minneapolis, MN 55455-0444
Publication E-mail: mnlawrev@maroon.tc.umn.edu

Legal journal. **Founded:** 1917. **Freq:** Bimonthly. **Print Method:** Letterpress. **Cols./Page:** 1. **Col. Width:** 54 nonpareils. **Col. Depth:** 112 agate lines. **Key Personnel:** James Poradek, Editor; Nancy King, Administrator. **ISSN:** 0026-5535. **Subscription Rates:** $30. **Remarks:** Accepts advertising.
Circ: 1,345

16181 Minnesota Medicine
Minnesota Medical Association
3433 Broadway St., NE, Ste. 300 Phone: (612)378-1875
Fax: (612)378-3875
Minneapolis, MN 55413-1761
Free: (800)DIAL-MMA
Publication E-mail: mm@mnmed.org
Publisher E-mail: mma@mnmed.org

Magazine on medical, socioeconomic, public health, medical-legal, and biomedical ethics issues of interest to physicians. **Subtitle:** A Journal of Clinical and Health Affairs. **Founded:** Jan. 1918. **Freq:** Monthly. **Print Method:** Web. **Trim Size:** 8 1/8 x 10 7/8. **Cols./Page:** 2 and 3. **Col. Width:** 19 1/2 and 13 picas. **Col. Depth:** 140 agate lines. **Key Personnel:** Charles R. Meyer, M.D., Editor-in-Chief; Meredith McNab, Managing Editor. **ISSN:** 0026-556X. **Subscription Rates:** $40 individuals; $3.50 single issue; $70 out of country. **Remarks:** Accepts advertising. **Online:** MMA. **URL:** http://www.mma@mnmed.org.
Ad Rates: BW: $830 **Circ:** ‡9,500
4C: $1,315

16182 Minnesota Monthly
Minnesota Monthly Publications, Inc.
10 S. 5th St., Ste. 1000 Phone: (612)371-5800
Minneapolis, MN 55402-1012 Fax: (612)371-5801

Regional magazine. **Founded:** 1968. **Freq:** Monthly. **Print Method:** Offset. **Trim Size:** 8 x 10 7/8. **Cols./Page:** 3. **Col. Width:** 13 1/2 picas. **Col. Depth:** 60 picas. **Key Personnel:** David Mahoney, Editor; Steve Fox, Publisher; Tom Whelan, Assoc. Publisher/Advertising Dir. **ISSN:** 0739-8700. **Subscription Rates:** $17.95 individuals; $2.50 single issue. **URL:** http://www.mnmo.com.
Ad Rates: BW: $3,950 **Circ:** Paid ★68,800
4C: $5,100

16183 Minnesota Parent
Stern Publishing
401 N. 3rd St. Ste. 550 Phone: (612)375-1203
Minneapolis, MN 55401 Fax: (612)372-3782
Publication E-mail: adinfo@mnparent.com

Newspaper. **Subtitle:** The Complete Monthly Resource for Families. **Founded:** Feb. 1986. **Freq:** Monthly. **Trim Size:** 11 x 13 1/2. **Cols./Page:** 6. **Key Personnel:** Tom Imbertson, Circulation Mgr., phone (612)372-3713, timbertson@mnparent.com; Mark Bartel, Publisher, phone (612)372-3729, fax (612)372-3737, mbartel@mnparent.com; Jeannine Ouellette Howitz, Editor, phone (612)372-3752, jhowitz@mnparent.com; Carrie Kirkpatrick, Sales Mgr./Associate Publisher, phone (612)372-3748: **ISSN:** 1075-8305. **Subscription Rates:** $25. **Remarks:** Accepts advertising. **URL:** http://www.mparent.com.
Ad Rates: GLR: $7.95 **Circ:** Free 66,900
BW: $2,620
4C: $3,670
SAU: $63.83

16184 Minnesota Sports
Skyway Publications, Inc.
15 S. 5th St., No. 800 Phone: (612)375-9222
Minneapolis, MN 55402 Fax: (612)375-9208

Magazine about sports in Minnesota. **Freq:** 11/year. **Key Personnel:** Glenn R. Hansen, Editor; Shelly Fling, Managing Editor; Ann Bjorlin, Editor. **Subscription Rates:** $15. **Remarks:** Advertising accepted; rates available upon request.
Circ: (Not Reported)

16185 Minnesota Technolog
IT Board of Publications
5 Lind Hall Phone: (612)624-9816
207 Church St. SE Fax: (612)626-0261
Minneapolis, MN 55455
Publication E-mail: itbop@gold.tc.umn.edu
Publisher E-mail: itbop@tc.umn.edu

Official undergraduate magazine of the University of Minnesota's Institute of Technology. **Founded:** Nov. 1920. **Freq:** 5/year. **Print Method:** Offset. **Trim Size:** 8 1/2 x 11. **Cols./Page:** 3. **Key Personnel:** Jacqueline Couillard, Editor/Advertising Mgr., coui0004@maroon.tc.umn.edu; Fred Beecher, beec0018@tc.umn.edu; Dorothea Czernik, President. **ISSN:** 0026-5691. **Subscription Rates:** $12. **Remarks:** Accepts advertising. **URL:** http://www.umn.edu/nlhome/itbop/technology. **Alt. Formats:** Mailing labels.
Ad Rates: GLR: $1.75 **Circ:** Non-paid ‡3,000
BW: $250
4C: $1,000
PCI: $13

16186 MIS Quarterly
MIS Research Center
University of Minnesota Phone: (612)624-7803
Carlson School of Management Fax: (612)624-2056
321 19th Ave. S.
Minneapolis, MN 55455
Publication E-mail: misq@csom.umn.edu

Refereed research journal for academics and practitioners in the management information systems field. **Founded:** Mar. 1977. **Freq:** Quarterly. **Print Method:** Offset. **Trim Size:** 7 x 10. **Cols./Page:** 2. **Col. Width:** 16 picas. **Col. Depth:** 48 picas. **Key Personnel:** Allen Lee, Contact; Susan Scanlan, Managing Editor and Administration, sscanlan@csom.umn.edu; Dr. Gordon B. Davis, Executive Editor. **ISSN:** 0276-7783. **Subscription Rates:** $60 individuals; $50 students; $80 institutions. **Remarks:** Accepts advertising.
Ad Rates: BW: $275 **Circ:** Paid 4,500
Non-paid 100

16187 The Mississippi Rag
The Mississippi Rag, Inc.
1401 W. 76th St., No. 250 Phone: (612)861-2446
Minneapolis, MN 55423 Fax: (612)861-4621
Publication E-mail: editor@mississippirag.com

Magazine containing historical features, stories on current traditional jazz and ragtime events and performances, book and record reviews, photo features on festivals, and club and jazz ragtime listings. **Subtitle:** The Voice of Traditional Jazz and Ragtime. **Founded:** Nov. 1973. **Freq:** Monthly. **Print Method:** Offset. **Trim Size:** 11 3/8 x 16 1/4. **Cols./Page:** 4 and 3. **Col. Width:** 14 and 19 picas. **Col. Depth:** 87 picas. **Key Personnel:** Leslie Johnson, Editor and Publisher, lesliemrag@aol.com. **ISSN:** 0742-4612. **Subscription Rates:** $22 individuals USA; $28 out of country. **Remarks:** Accepts advertising. **URL:** http://www.mississippirag.com.
Ad Rates: BW: $300 **Circ:** Paid ‡4,300

16188 Mythos Journal
Mythos Institute
4509 Drew Ave. S Phone: (612)345-5488
Minneapolis, MN 55410 Fax: (612)922-0546

Interdisciplinary journal of mythology, folklore, and dreamwork. **Founded:** 1993. **Freq:** Semiannual. **Trim Size:** 8 1/2 x 11. **Cols./Page:** 2. **Key Personnel:** Ted Tollefson, Editor; Dr. James W. Maertens, Assoc. Editor, phone (612)924-9266, maert003@maroon.tc.umn.edu. **Subscription Rates:** $30 individuals; $50 other countries; $50 institutions; $6 single issue. **Remarks:** Accepts advertising.
Ad Rates: BW: $100 **Circ:** Paid 500

16189 National Hog Farmer
Webb Division, Intertec Publishing Corp.
7900 International Dr., 3rd Fl. Phone: (612)851-9329
Minneapolis, MN 55425-1510 Fax: (612)851-4601
Free: (800)722-5334
Publication E-mail: nhf@intertec.com

Trade magazine for pork producers. **Founded:** 1956. **Freq:** Monthly. **Print Method:** Offset. **Trim Size:** 8 x 10 3/4. **Cols./Page:** 3. **Col. Width:** 2 1/8 inches. **Col. Depth:** 140 agate lines. **Key Personnel:** Dale Miller, Editor; Wayne Bollum, Publisher. **ISSN:** 0027-9447. **Subscription Rates:** Free to qualified subscribers; $30; $40 other countries. **Remarks:** Accepts advertising. **URL:** http://www.homefarm.com.
Ad Rates: BW: $7,240 **Circ:** Controlled ‡87,154
4C: $9,055
PCI: $290

16190 Northeaster & Northnews
Northeaster
2304 Central Ave., NE Phone: (612)788-9003
Minneapolis, MN 55418 Fax: (612)788-3299

Community newspaper. **Founded:** 1978. **Freq:** Semimonthly. **Print Method:** Web offset. **Cols./Page:** 5. **Col. Width:** 5 picas. **Col. Depth:** 15 inches. **Key Personnel:** Kerry Ashmore, Publisher. **Subscription Rates:** $10. **Remarks:** Accepts advertising. **Formerly**: Northeaster.
Ad Rates: GLR: $4 **Circ:** Non-paid ‡33,000
SAU: $21
PCI: $18.75

16191 Northern Breezes Sailing Magazine
Northern Breezes, Inc.
245 Brunswick Ave. S Phone: (612)542-9707
Minneapolis, MN 55416 Fax: (612)542-8998
Publisher E-mail: thomnbreeze@aol.com

Consumer magazine covering sailing in the Upper Midwest U.S. **Founded:** 1989. **Freq:** Monthly. **Print Method:** Web offset. **Trim Size:** 8 1/4 x 10 1/4. **Cols./Page:** 3. **Col. Width:** 2 1/4 inches. **Key Personnel:** Thom Burns, Contact, thomnbreez@aol.com. **Subscription Rates:** $15 individuals; $2 single issue. **Remarks:** Accepts advertising. **URL:** http://www.sailingbreezes.com.
Ad Rates: BW: $586 **Circ:** Paid ‡2,500
4C: $765 Non-paid ‡17,800
PCI: $23

16192 Northwestern Financial Review
NFR Communications, Inc.
3407 W 44th St. Phone: (612)929-8110
Minneapolis, MN 55410 Fax: (612)929-8146
Publisher E-mail: nfrcomm@means.net

Trade publication covering commercial banking. **Founded:** 1894. **Freq:** Weekly. **Print Method:** Offset. **Trim Size:** 8 1/4 x 11. **Cols./Page:** 3. **Col. Width:** 12 picas. **Col. Depth:** 58 picas. **Key Personnel:** Tom Bengtson, Editor and Publisher; Robert Cronin, Sales Mgr.; Brenda Van Dyck, Managing Editor; Jacqueline Hilgert, Production and Ad Mgr. **ISSN:** 1042-1254. **Subscription Rates:** $75 individuals; $135 two years; $4 single issue. **Remarks:** Accepts advertising. **URL:** http://www.nfrcom.com. **Formerly**: Northwestern Banker; Commercial West.
Ad Rates: BW: $1,125 **Circ:** Paid 2,000
4C: $2,100

16193 NST: Nature, Society and Thought
MEP Publications
University of Minnesota Phone: (612)922-7993
Physics Bldg. Fax: (612)922-0858
116 Church St. SE
Minneapolis, MN 55455-0112
Publisher E-mail: marqu002@tc.umn.edu

Journal dealing interdisciplinary Marxist theory and practice. **Subtitle:** A Journal of Dialectical and Historical Materialism. **Founded:** 1987. **Freq:** Quarterly. **Print Method:** Photo offset. **Trim Size:** 5 1/2 x 8 1/2. **Cols./Page:** 1. **Col. Width:** 4 inches. **Col. Depth:** 7 inches. **Key Personnel:** Erwin Marquit, Editor, marqu002@tc.umm.edu. **ISSN:** 0890-6130. **Subscription Rates:** $15; $28 Industry. $5 single issue; $10 single issue for Industry. **Remarks:** Accepts advertising.
Ad Rates: BW: $100 **Circ:** 500

16194 The Physician and Sportsmedicine
McGraw-Hill Healthcare Information Group
4530 W. 77th St. Phone: (612)835-3222
Minneapolis, MN 55435 Fax: (612)835-3460

A peer-reviewed journal on the medical aspects of sports, exercise, and fitness. **Founded:** 1973. **Freq:** Monthly. **Print Method:** Web offset. **Trim Size:** 7 3/4 x 10 3/4. **Cols./Page:** 3 and 2. **Col. Width:** 16 and 12 picas. **Col. Depth:** 140 agate lines. **Key Personnel:** Gretchen Drasner, Senior Marketing Mgr.; Janis Cohen, Assoc. Group Publisher; M. James Dougherty, Group VP; Susan Hawthorne, Executive Editor, susan_hawthor@mcgraw-hill.com. **ISSN:** 0091-3847. **Subscription Rates:** $46. **Remarks:** Accepts advertising. **Online:** Dialog; Dow Jones Interactive; Lexis-Nexis. **URL:** http://www.physsportsmed.com.
Ad Rates: BW: $5,374 **Circ:** Controlled ‡97,000
4C: $7,184 Paid 15,000

16195 Pillsbury Fast & Healthy Magazine
Pillsbury Co.
200 6th St., M.S. 28M7 Phone: (612)330-4475
Minneapolis, MN 55402 Fax: (612)330-4875

Food magazine featuring healthy 30-minute recipes for active people. **Subtitle:** The Magazine for Fast, Low-Fat Cooking. **Founded:** 1992. **Freq:** Bimonthly. **Print Method:** Offset. **Trim Size:** 5 5/16 x 8 1/2. **Cols./Page:** 2. **Key Personnel:** Betsy Wray, Editor; Sally Peters, Publisher; Diane B. Anderson, Manager; Karen Goodsell, Circulation Mgr. **ISSN:** 1059-8073. **Subscription Rates:** $16.95; $2.99 single issue. **Remarks:** Accepts advertising.
Ad Rates: BW: $3,710 **Circ:** Paid 152,514
4C: $4,950

16196 Postgraduate Medicine
McGraw-Hill Healthcare Information Group
4530 W. 77th St. Phone: (612)835-3222
Minneapolis, MN 55435 Fax: (612)835-3460

Magazine for primary care physicians; presents original clinical articles stressing diagnosis and treatment of practical problems encountered in general medical practice. **Founded:** 1947. **Freq:** 12/year. **Print Method:** Offset. **Trim Size:** 7 3/4 x 10 3/4. **Cols./Page:** 3. **Col. Width:** 30 nonpareils. **Col. Depth:** 136 agate lines. **Key Personnel:** M. James Dougherty, Group Vice President, jdougher@mcgraw-hill.com; Peter A. Setness, MD, Editor-in-Chief, psetness@mcgraw-hill.com; Patricia Flynn, Executive Editor, flynn@mcgraw-hill.com. **ISSN:** 0032-5481. **Subscription Rates:** $54 individuals Free to qualified subscribers. **Remarks:** Accepts advertising. **Online:** Dialog (The Dialog Corporation); Dow Jones News-Retrieval; McGraw-Hill Publications Online. **URL:** http://www.postgradmed.com.
Ad Rates: BW: $5,889 **Circ:** Controlled 140,579
4C: $7,557

16197 Powder and Bulk Engineering
CSC Publishing, Inc.
1300 E. 66th St. Phone: (612)866-2242
Minneapolis, MN 55423-2642 Fax: (612)866-1939

Journal serving chemical, food, plastics, pulp and paper, and electronic industries. **Founded:** 1987. **Freq:** Monthly. **ISSN:** 0897-6627. **Remarks:** Accepts advertising.
Ad Rates: BW: $3,695 **Circ:** Free ‡35,669
4C: $4,995

16198 Presentations Magazine
Lakewood Publications, Inc.
50 S. 9th St. Phone: (612)333-0471
Minneapolis, MN 55402 Fax: (612)333-6521
Free: (800)328-4329
Publication E-mail: presmag@aol.com
Publisher E-mail: justask@lakewoodpub.com

Magazine for presentation managers. **Subtitle:** Technology & Techniques For Effective Communications. **Founded:** Sept. 1988. **Freq:** Monthly. **Print Method:** Web offset. **Trim Size:** 8 x 10 7/8. **Key Personnel:** Larry Tuck, Editor. **ISSN:** 1041-9780. **Subscription Rates:** $24.95 individuals; $5 single issue. **Remarks:** Accepts advertising. **URL:** http://www.lakewoodpub.com.
Ad Rates: BW: $5,955 **Circ:** Controlled ‡70,000
4C: $7,230

16199 Profane Existence
Box 8722 Phone: (612)813-1216
Minneapolis, MN 55408 Fax: (612)813-1219

Consumer magazine covering punk music, radical politics, and alternative issues. **Subtitle:** Making Punk a Threat Again. **Founded:** Nov. 30, 1989. **Freq:** Quarterly. **Print Method:** Spiral web offset. **Trim Size:** 8 1/4 x 10 3/4. **Cols./Page:** 3. **Col. Width:** 2.5 inches. **Col. Depth:** 7.5 inches. **Subscription Rates:** $18 individuals; $3 single issue. **Remarks:** Accepts advertising.
Ad Rates: BW: $60 **Circ:** Combined 9,500

16200 Quirk's Marketing Research Review
Quirk Enterprises, Inc.
PO Box 23536 Phone: (612)854-5101
Minneapolis, MN 55423-0536 Fax: (612)854-8191
Publisher E-mail: quirk19@mail.idt.net

Trade publication for the marketing research industry. **Subtitle:** Practical Applications in Marketing Research. **Founded:** Oct. 1, 1986. **Freq:** 11/year (Aug./Sept.). **Print Method:** Web. **Trim Size:** 8 x 10 7/8. **Cols./Page:** 2 and 3. **Col. Width:** 3 1/2 and 2 9/16 inches. **Col. Depth:** 10 inches. **Key Personnel:** Joseph Rydholm, Editor; Tom Quirk, Publisher; Evan Tweed, Marketing Dir. **ISSN:** 0893-7451. **Subscription Rates:** $70. **Remarks:** Accepts advertising. **Available Online. URL:** http://www.quirks.com.
Ad Rates: BW: $1,820 **Circ:** Non-paid 15,500
4C: $2,480
PCI: $100

16201 Shots
PO Box 390429
Minneapolis, MN 55439
Publication E-mail: shots1234@aol.com.

Informal photography magazine. **Subtitle:** a journal about the art of fine photography. **Founded:** 1986. **Freq:** 4/year. **Print Method:** Web offset. **Trim Size:** 8-11. **Key Personnel:** Robert Owen, Contact. **ISSN:** 1048-793x. **Subscription Rates:** $20 annual; $35 two years.
Circ: Paid 900
Non-paid 900

16202 Skyway News
Skyway Publications, Inc.
15 S. Fifth St., Ste. 800 Phone: (612)375-9222
Minneapolis, MN 55402 Fax: (612)375-9208

Local newspaper serving St. Paul and Minneapolis and south, west and southwest suburbs. **Founded:** 1970. **Freq:** Weekly (Thurs.). **Print Method:** Offset. **Trim Size:** 11 x 13 1/2. **Cols./Page:** 6. **Col. Width:** 1 1/2 inches. **Col. Depth:** 196 agate lines. **Key Personnel:** Karen Baker, Editor; Mari Adamson-Bray, Publisher; Jodie Ahern, Managing Editor; Mary Jo Davis, Advertising Mgr. **ISSN:** 1078-131. **Subscription Rates:** $40. **Formerly:** Skyway News (Minneapolis Edition).
Ad Rates: GLR: $4.40 **Circ:** Free 44,546
BW: $3,132
4C: $575
PCI: $41.76

16203 The Sons of Norway Viking
Sons of Norway
1455 W. Lake St. Phone: (612)827-3611
Minneapolis, MN 55408 Fax: (612)827-0658

Official Sons of Norway magazine reporting on fraternal society's programs and activities. It also features Norwegian and Norwegian-American history and culture. **Founded:** 1904. **Freq:** Monthly. **Print Method:** Web offset. **Trim Size:** 7 1/4 x 9 3/4. **Cols./Page:** 3. **Col. Width:** 2 1/4 inches. **Key Personnel:** Martha Parsons, Editor, phone (612)339-7571, fax (612)339-5806; Kathy Rumpza, Advertising Contact; Terri Purcell, Art Dir.; Suzy Vescio, Production Mgr. **ISSN:** 0038-1462. **Subscription Rates:** $20. **Remarks:** Accepts advertising. **URL:** http://www.sofn.com.
Ad Rates: BW: $1,630 **Circ:** Combined ‡56,000
4C: $2,015

16204 Soviet Biographical Service
J. L. Scherer
4900 18th Ave. S. Phone: (612)722-2947
Minneapolis, MN 55417
Scholarly journal covering the former Soviet Republics. **Founded:** 1985. **Freq:** Quarterly. **Subscription Rates:** $100 U.S.; $110 other countries. **Remarks:** Advertising not accepted.
Circ: (Not Reported)

16205 Soybean Digest
7900 International Dr., 3rd Fl. Phone: (612)851-9329
Minneapolis, MN 55425 Fax: (612)851-4601
Free: (800)722-5334
Publication E-mail: sbd@intertec.com

Magazine offering production, marketing, and management information for farmers who grow soybeans in rotation with other crops. **Founded:** Nov. 1940. **Freq:** Monthly. **Print Method:** Offset. **Trim Size:** 8 x 10 3/4. **Cols./Page:** 3. **Col. Width:** 26 nonpareils. **Col. Depth:** 140 agate lines. **Key Personnel:** Ron Sorensen, Publisher, phone (612)851-4690, ron_sorensen@intertec.com; Syl Marking, Editor, phone (612)851-4640, syl_marking@intertec.com; Neil Tietz, Managing Editor, phone (612)851-4677, neil_tietz@intertec.com; Lynn Chadek, Production Coord., phone (612)851-4622, lynn_chadek@intertec.com. **ISSN:** 0038-6014. **Subscription Rates:** $25; $40 foreign, including Canada. **Remarks:** Accepts advertising. **Alt. Formats:** CD-ROM; Microform.
Ad Rates: BW: $11,770 **Circ:** Controlled ‡218,000
4C: $15,010
PCI: $305

16206 Star Tribune
425 Portland Ave. S. Phone: (612)673-4000
Minneapolis, MN 55488 Fax: (612)673-7138

General newspaper. **Subtitle:** Newspaper of the Twin Cities. **Founded:** 1920. **Freq:** Mon.-Sun. (morn.). **Print Method:** Letterpress. **Cols./Page:** 6. **Col. Width:** 25 nonpareils. **Col. Depth:** 301 agate lines. **Key Personnel:** Tim J. McGuire, Exec. Editor; Joel Kramer, Publisher. **ISSN:** 0895-2825. **Subscription Rates:** $137.80. **Remarks:** Accepts advertising. **Online:** DataTimes Corporation; LEXIS-NEXIS; Dialog (The Dialog Corporation). **URL:** http://www.startribune.com. **Alt. Formats:** CD-ROM, NewsBank, Inc. **Formerly:** Minneapolis Star and Tribune. **Feature Editors:** Michael Anthony, *Music*, phone (612)673-4445; Rosalind Bentley, *Women's*, phone (612)673-7844; Jon Bream, *Music*, phone (612)673-1719; Roger Buoen, *News*, phone (612)673-1729; Ann Burckhardt, *Food*, phone (612)673-1726; Lew Cope, *Science*, phone (612)673-4426; Julie Engebrecht, *Sports*, phone (612)673-4283; Kent Gardner, *Metro*, phone (612)673-4414; John Habich, *Features, Sunday*, phone (612)673-1736; Noel Holston, *TV & Radio*, phone (612)673-4866; Mary Jane Smetanka, *Education*, phone (612)673-7380; Jim Kelly, *Political*, phone (612)673-4397; Liz McConnell, *Garden/Home*, phone (612)673-7208; Darlene Pfister, *Photo*, phone (612)673-4280; Dean Rebuffoni, *Environmental*, phone (612)673-7388; Martha Sawyer Allen, *Religion*, phone (612)673-4139; Sharon Schmickle, *Rural Development*, phone (612)673-4361; Gordy Slovut, *Medical*, phone (612)673-4128; Michael Steele, *Drama*, phone (612)673-7389; Jeff Strickler, *Movie*, phone (612)673-7392; Ingrid Sundstrom, *Real Estate*, phone (612)673-7242; Kristin Tillotson, *Fashion*, phone (612)673-7844; Catherine Watson, *Travel*, phone (612)673-4282; Larry Werner, *Financial/Business*, phone (612)673-4468; Robert White, *Editorials*, phone (612)372-4477; Dave Wood, *Book*, phone (612)673-4430.
Ad Rates: BW: $21,717 **Circ:** Mon.-Sat. ★**735,113**
4C: $23,597 Sun. ★**670,890**
PCI: $172.39

16207 Surprises
The Publishing Group, Inc.
1200 N. 7th St. Phone: (612)881-3183
Minneapolis, MN 55411-4400 Fax: (612)881-2172

Interactive magazine for children ages 5-12 years. **Founded:** 1984. **Freq:** Bimonthly. **Trim Size:** 8 x 11. **Key Personnel:** Tim Drake, Editor. **ISSN:** 0890-3573. **Subscription Rates:** $15.95 individuals; $3.95 single issue. **Remarks:** Accepts advertising. **URL:** http://www.surprises.com. **Former name:** Children's Surprises.
Ad Rates: BW: $1,900 **Circ:** Paid 112,321
4C: $2,500

16208 Sweden & America
Swedish Council of America
2600 Park Ave. Phone: (612)871-0593
Minneapolis, MN 55407 Fax: (612)871-8682
Publisher E-mail: swedcoun@swedishcouncil.org

Consumer magazine covering Swedish culture and Swedish Americans. **Founded:** Jan. 1987. **Freq:** Quarterly. **Key Personnel:** Teresa Scalzo, Editor; Jan Wiggs, Advertising Mgr. **ISSN:** 1042-1777. **Subscription Rates:** $12 individuals; $3.95 single issue. **Remarks:** Accepts advertising.
Ad Rates: BW: $700 **Circ:** Paid 16,000
4C: $1,100

16209 Terrorism (Minneapolis)
4900 18th Ave. S.
Minneapolis, MN 55417

Magazine covering statistics and other information on terrorism, crime, and political violence. **Founded:** 1986. **Freq:** Quarterly. **Subscription Rates:** $45 U.S.; $50 out of country. **Remarks:** Advertising not accepted.
Circ: (Not Reported)

16210 Transfusion
American Association of Blood Banks
University of Minnesota/ Phone: (612)626-3313
Transfusion Fax: (612)624-5411
Box 198
Rm. D211 MAYO
Minneapolis, MN 55455
Publication E-mail: publications@aabb.org

Journal containing original manuscripts and preliminary reports in all fields relating to clinical transfusion, blood groups, immunology, genetics, anthropology and marrow and stem cell transplantation. **Subtitle:** Official Publication of The American Association of Blood Banks. **Founded:** 1961. **Freq:** 11/year. **Print Method:** Sheetfed offset. **Trim Size:** 8 5/8 x 11

1/8. **Cols./Page:** 2. **Col. Width:** 39 nonpareils. **Col. Depth:** 140 agate lines. **Key Personnel:** Jeffery McCullough, M.D., Editor. **ISSN:** 0041-1132. **Subscription Rates:** $150 individuals; $224 institutions; $195 other countries; $385 institutions, other countries; $29 single issue. **Remarks:** Accepts advertising.
Ad Rates: GLR: $12 BW: $1,635 4C: $2,835 **Circ:** Paid ‡13,790 Non-paid ‡158

16211 TRENDS in College Media
National Scholastic Press Association
University of Minnesota Phone: (612)625-8335
Rarig Center Fax: (612)626-0720
330 21st Ave. S.
Minneapolis, MN 55455
Publication E-mail: info@studentpress.journ.umn.edu

Journalism education newspaper. **Founded:** 1921. **Freq:** 4/year (Oct., Dec. March, May). **Print Method:** Offset. **Trim Size:** 8 3/4 x 11 3/8. **Cols./Page:** 5. **Col. Width:** 22 nonpareils. **Col. Depth:** 129 agate lines. **Key Personnel:** Tom E. Rolnicki, Editor; Tom Keekley, Managing Editor; Ross Namaste, Managing Editor. **ISSN:** 1046-2163. **Subscription Rates:** $10; $18 two years. **Remarks:** Accepts advertising. **Available Online. URL:** http://www.studentpress.journ.umn.edu. **Formerly**: Scholastic Editor's Trends in Publications (1990).
Ad Rates: BW: $360 **Circ:** ‡2,500

16212 TRENDS in High School Media
National Scholastic Press Association
620 Rarig Center Phone: (612)625-8335
330 21st Ave. S. Fax: (612)626-0720
Minneapolis, MN 55455
Publication E-mail: info@studentpress.journ.umn.edu

Journalism education newspaper. **Founded:** 1921. **Freq:** 4/year (Oct., Dec., March, May). **Print Method:** Offset. **Trim Size:** 8 3/4 x 11 3/8. **Cols./Page:** 5. **Col. Width:** 22 nonpareils. **Col. Depth:** 129 agate lines. **Key Personnel:** Tom E. Rolnicki, Editor; Tom Keekley, Managing Editor; Ross Namaste, Managing Editor. **ISSN:** 1046-2155. **Subscription Rates:** $10; $18 two years. $2.50 single issue. **Remarks:** Accepts advertising. **Available Online. URL:** http://www.studentpress.journ.umn.edu. **Formerly**: Scholastic Editor's Trends in Publications (1990).
Ad Rates: BW: $360 **Circ:** Paid ‡2,500 Non-paid ‡100

16213 U.S. ART
MSP Communications
220 S. 6th St., Ste. 500 Phone: (612)339-7571
Minneapolis, MN 55402-4507 Fax: (612)339-5806
Free: (800)788-0204

Magazine for collectors of limited-edition prints. For professional and general audiences. **Subtitle:** All The News That Fits Print. **Founded:** 1982. **Freq:** Monthly. **Print Method:** Offset. **Trim Size:** 10 x 12. **Cols./Page:** 4. **Col. Width:** 2 inches. **Col. Depth:** 10 1/2 inches. **Key Personnel:** Frank J. Sisser, Publisher, fsisser@mspcommunications.com; Sara Gilbert, Editor, sgilbert@mspcommunications.com; Laurie Scheel, Advertising Dir.; Betsy Yarosh, Advertising Dir. **ISSN:** 0744-6217. **Subscription Rates:** $32.25; $42.25 other countries. **Remarks:** Accepts advertising. **Formerly**: Midwest Art (1988); U.S. Art, The Magazine of Realism in America.
Ad Rates: 4C: $2,230 **Circ:** Controlled 55,000

16214 Utne Reader
Lens Publishing Co., Inc.
1624 Harmon Pl., Ste. 330 Phone: (612)338-5040
Minneapolis, MN 55403
Publication E-mail: info@utne.com

Digest of original articles and material reprinted from alternative and independent media. Keeps readers abreast of new ideas and emerging issues. **Subtitle:** The Best of the Alternative Media. **Founded:** 1984. **Freq:** Bimonthly. **Print Method:** Offset. **Trim Size:** 7 5/8 x 10. **Cols./Page:** 3. **Col. Width:** 2 1/8 inches. **Col. Depth:** 9 inches. **Key Personnel:** Cathy Madison, Editor, editor@utne.com; Eric Utne, Chm., utne@utne.com; Jeanne Gallaher, Circulation Dir., gallaher@utne.com; Tom McKusick, Advertising Dir., mctom@utne.com; Robert Welsch, President. **ISSN:** 8750-0256. **Subscription Rates:** $19.97 individuals; $4.99 single issue. **Remarks:** Accepts advertising. **Alt. Formats:** Microform.
Ad Rates: BW: $10,060 4C: $14,585 **Circ:** Paid ★**261,055**

16215 Where Twin Cities
Minnesota Monthly Publications, Inc.
10 S. 5th St., Ste. 1000 Phone: (612)371-5800
Minneapolis, MN 55402-1012 Fax: (612)371-5801

Consumer visitor guide for Minnesota. **Founded:** 1967. **Freq:** Monthly. **Key Personnel:** Michelle Baltus, Editor; Steve Fox, Publisher. **Subscription Rates:** $48 individuals; $4 single issue. **Remarks:** Accepts advertising.
Circ: (Not Reported)

16216 Wicazo Sa Review/Red Pencil Review
Wicazo Sa Review
University of Minnesota Press Phone: (612)627-1970
Mill Place, Ste. 290 Fax: (612)627-1980
111 Third Ave. S.
Minneapolis, MN 55401-2520
Scholarly journal covering Native American studies. **Founded:** 1984. **Freq:** Semiannual. **Key Personnel:** Todd Orjala, Acquisitions Ed.; Elizabeth Cook-Lynn, Managing Editor. **Subscription Rates:** $20 individuals; $10 single issue. **Remarks:** Advertising accepted; rates available upon request.
Circ: (Not Reported)

16217 Xcp: Cross Cultural Poetics
Xcp: Cross Cultural Poetics Press
College of St. Catherine-Minneapolis Phone: (612)690-7747
Fax: (612)690-7849
601 25th Ave. S
Minneapolis, MN 55454
Scholarly journal covering poetry, ethnography and cultural and ethnic studies. **Founded:** 1997. **Freq:** Semiannual. **Print Method:** Offset. **Trim Size:** 6 x 9. **Cols./Page:** 1. **Key Personnel:** Mark Nowak, Editor, manowak@stkate.edu. **ISSN:** 1086-9611. **Subscription Rates:** $25 individuals; $40 institutions; $9 single issue. **Remarks:** Accepts advertising. **URL:** http://www.state.edu/xcp/.
Ad Rates: BW: $125 **Circ:** Combined 700

16218 KARE-TV - 11
8811 Olson Memorial Hwy. Phone: (612)546-1111
Minneapolis, MN 55427 Fax: (612)546-8590
E-mail: kare11@kare11.com

Format: Commercial TV. **Networks:** NBC. **Founded:** 1954. **Formerly**: WUSA-TV. **Operating Hours:** Continuous. **ADI:** Minneapolis-St. Paul, MN. **Key Personnel:** John Remes, General Mgr.; Tim Stanko, Mgr. of Mktg. & Promotion, fax (612)546-8606; Tom Lindner, News Dir.; Kiki Rosatti, Community Affairs Dir.; Paula Sergot, Programming/Research; Jill Altmeyer, Business Mgr., fax (612)546-0338; Jerry Ness, General Sales Mgr., fax (612)542-9752; Mike Tamme, Dir. of Engineering. **Local Programs:** *Whatever* 10:00 am.

16219 KBEM-FM - 88.5
1555 James Ave.
Minneapolis, MN 55411
E-mail: kbem@mpls.k12.mn.us

Format: Information; Jazz. **Networks:** Public Radio International (PRI); AP. **Owner:** Minneapolis Public Schools, 807 NE Broadway, Minneapolis, MN 55413, (612)668-1735, Fax: (612)668-1766. **Founded:** 1972. **Operating Hours:** Continuous; 5% network, 95% local. **ADI:** Minneapolis-St. Paul, MN. **Key Personnel:** J.D. Ball, Station Mgr., phone (612)668-1745, fax (612)668-1766; Terry Walker, Program Dir., phone (612)668-1743; Ted Allison, Development Dir., phone (612)668-1748. **Wattage:** 2180. **Ad Rates:** Noncommercial. **URL:** http://www.mpls.k12.mn.us/kbem/index.html.

16220 KDIZ-AM - 1440
917 N. Lilac Dr. Phone: (612)595-4998
Minneapolis, MN 55422 Fax: (612)595-4940

Format: Educational. **Networks:** ABC. **Owner:** Capital Cities/ABC, Inc. A Division of the Walt Disney Companies., at above address. **Founded:** 1948. **Formerly**: KQRS-AM. **Operating Hours:** Continuous. **ADI:** Minneapolis-St. Paul, MN. **Key Personnel:** Brian Acker, Station Mgr., phone (612)886-3277, fax (612)886-0434. **Wattage:** 5000 day; 500 night. **Ad Rates:** $30-50 per unit.

16221 KDWB-FM - 101.3
100 N. 64th St., Ste. 306C Phone: (612)340-9000
Minneapolis, MN 55403 Fax: (612)330-9377

Format: Contemporary Hit Radio (CHR). **Owner:** Chancellor Broadcasting Company, 12655 N. Central Expressway, Ste. 405, Dallas, TX 75243, (214)239-6220. **Founded:** 1959. **Formerly**: WYOO-FM (1976). **Operating Hours:** Continuous; 100% local. **ADI:** Minneapolis-St. Paul, MN. **Key Personnel:** Lee Valsvik, News Dir.; Dan Kieley, Program Dir.; John O'Connell, Promotions Dir.; Rob Morris, Music Dir.; Marc Kalman, Pres./General Mgr.; Thomas Garry, Director of Sales; Mickey Moore, Local Sales Mgr.; Scott Fransen, General Sales Mgr. **Wattage:** 100,000. **Ad Rates:** Advertising accepted; rates available upon request.

16222 KEEY-FM - 102.1
7900 Xerxes Ave. S., No. 102 Phone: (612)820-4200
Minneapolis, MN 55431 Fax: (612)820-4241
E-mail: k102@k102.com

Format: Country. **Owner:** Chancellor Media, 300 Crescent Ct., Ste. 600, Dallas, TX 75201, (214)922-8700. **Founded:** 1983. **Operating Hours:** Continuous. **Key Personnel:** Mick Anselmo, V. P./General Mgr., phone (612)820-4218, manselmo@k102.com; Gregg Swedoerg, Program Dir., phone (612)820-4247, gsk102@k102.com. **Wattage:** 100,000. **URL:** http://www.k102.com.

16223 KFAI-FM - 90.3
1808 Riverside Ave. Phone: (612)341-3144
Minneapolis, MN 55407

Format: Full Service; Eclectic; Ethnic. **Networks:** Pacifica. **Owner:** Fresh Air Inc., at above address. **Founded:** 1978. **Operating Hours:** Continuous; 2% network, 98% local. **ADI:** Minneapolis-St. Paul, MN. **Key Personnel:** Denise Mayotte, General Mgr., phone (612)341-3144; Mike Wassenaar, Program Dir.; Colin Turner, Fundraising Director; Eric Bailey, Volunteer Coordinator; Maris Strautmanis, News Director; Rebecca Swim, Music Dir. **Wattage:** 125 (translator 175). **Ad Rates:** Noncommercial.

16224 KFAN-AM - 1130
PO Box 20731
Minneapolis, MN 55420-0731

Format: Sports. **Networks:** Mutual Broadcasting System. **Founded:** 1923. **Formerly**: WDGY-AM. **Operating Hours:** Continuous; 30% network, 70% local. **ADI:** Minneapolis-St. Paul, MN. **Key Personnel:** David Haeg, General Sales Mgr.; Linda Gorman, Contact; Mark Gunther, Exec. Producer; John Thomas, Station Mgr.; Dan Seeman, Contact; Chad Hartman, Sports Dir.; Judy Dibble, Promotions Dir. **Wattage:** 50,000.

16225 KMOJ-FM - 89.9
501 Bryant Ave. N. Phone: (612)377-0594
Minneapolis, MN 55405 Fax: (612)377-6919

Format: Urban Contemporary. **Founded:** 1973. **Operating Hours:** Continuous. **ADI:** Minneapolis-St. Paul, MN. **Key Personnel:** Vusumuzi Zulu, Station Mgr., vzulu@msn.com; Walter Banks Jr., Program Dir.; J R Maddox, Music Dir.; Vanessa Morris, Contact; Connie Jameson, Traffic & Continuity. **Wattage:** 1000. **Ad Rates:** Noncommercial; underwriting available.

16226 KQQL-FM - 107.9
60 S 6th St., Ste. 930 Phone: (612)333-8118
Minneapolis, MN 55402-4409 Fax: (612)333-1616

Format: Oldies. **Owner:** Chancellor Broadcasting Co., 60 S. 6th St. Ste. 920, Minneapolis, MN 55402, (612)373-0110, Fax: (612)338-8356. **Founded:** 1988. **Operating Hours:** Continuous. **ADI:** Minneapolis-St. Paul, MN. **Key Personnel:** Tom Garry, General Mgr.; Bob Wod, Program Mgr.; Mary O'Neill, Promotions Mgr.; Ben Johnston, Chief Engineer; Thomas Mooney, Controller. **Local Programs:** *Anoka Now*, Mark O'Connell; *Twin Cities Viewpoint*. **Wattage:** 100,000.

16227 KQRS-FM - 92.5
917 N. Lilac Dr. Phone: (612)545-5601
Minneapolis, MN 55422 Fax: (612)595-4940

Format: Album-Oriented Rock (AOR). **Networks:** ABC. **Founded:** 1948. **Operating Hours:** Continuous. **ADI:** Minneapolis-St. Paul, MN. **Key Personnel:** Mark Steinmetz, Contact; Amy Waggoner, Contact; Lori Moen, Contact; Kim Perry, Contact; Sophie Woodle, Promotions Dir.; Mary Lou Koecher, Contact; Dave Hamilton, Program Dir.; Reed Endersbe, Music Dir. **Local Programs:** *Morning Show*, Terri Traen; *On Point*, Kim Perry. **Wattage:** 100,000. **URL:** http://www.92kqrs.com.

16228 KSGS-AM - 950
7001 France Ave. S., No. 200 Phone: (612)836-1041
Minneapolis, MN 55435-4202 Fax: (612)915-9781

Format: Urban Contemporary. **Networks:** Independent. **Formerly**: KJJO-AM (1989). **Operating Hours:** Continuous. **Key Personnel:** Rolf Pepple, General Mgr.; Freddie Bell, Operations Mgr., bellf@ksgs.cbs.com. **Wattage:** 1000.

16229 KSTP-FM - 94.5
3415 University Ave. Phone: (612)642-4141
Minneapolis, MN 55414 Fax: (612)642-4142

Format: Adult Contemporary. **Owner:** Hubbard Broadcasting, at above address. **Founded:** 1965. **Operating Hours:** Continuous. **ADI:** Minneapolis-St. Paul, MN. **Key Personnel:** Virginia Morris, President. **Wattage:** 100,000. **Ad Rates:** Advertising accepted; rates available upon request.

16230 KTCZ-FM - 97.1
Butler Sq., Ste. 306C Phone: (612)339-0000
100 N. 6th St. Fax: (612)349-6230
Minneapolis, MN 55403

Format: Album-Oriented Rock (AOR). **Networks:** Independent. **Operating Hours:** Continuous. **ADI:** Minneapolis-St. Paul, MN. **Key Personnel:** Marc Kalman, General Mgr.; Thomas Garry, Director of Sales; Jeff Barin, Sales Mgr.; Jeff Framke, National Sales Manager; Lauren Marleash, Program Dir.; Scott Fransen, General Sales Mgr. **Wattage:** 100,000.

16231 KUOM-AM - 770
University of Minnesota Phone: (612)625-3500
550 Rarig Center Fax: (612)625-2112
330 21st Ave. S.
Minneapolis, MN 55455-0415
E-mail: amarlow@mail.cee.umn.edu

Format: Alternative/New Music/Progressive. **Networks:** AP. **Owner:** University of Minnesota, Morrill Hall, Minneapolis, MN 55455. **Founded:** 1922. **Absorbed:** WMMR-FM (1946). **Operating Hours:** Sunrise-sunset. 100% local. **ADI:** Minneapolis-St. Paul, MN. **Key Personnel:** Andrew J. Marlow, Station Mgr., amarlow@mail.cee.umn.edu; Larry Oberg, Chief Engineer, loberg@mail.cee.umn.edu; David Lee Olson, News Dir., dolson@mail.cee.umn.edu; Stuart C. Sanders, Development Dir., ssanders@mail.cee.umn.edu; Mark Wheat, Program Dir., mwheat@mail.cee.umn.edu. **Wattage:** 5000. **Ad Rates:** Noncommercial. **URL:** http://www.radiok.org.

16232 KYCR-AM - 1570
5501 Excelsior Blvd. Phone: (612)925-4363
Minneapolis, MN 55401 Fax: (612)926-9479
E-mail: kycr@myhometown.net

Format: Religious; Contemporary Christian. **Networks:** USA Radio; Sun Radio. **Owner:** Childrens Broadcasting Corp., 724 1st St. N., 4th Fl., Minneapolis, MN 55401, (612)338-3300, Fax: (612)338-4318. **Founded:** 1963. **Formerly:** KUXL-AM. **Operating Hours:** Continuous. **ADI:** Minneapolis-St. Paul, MN. **Key Personnel:** Christopher T. Dahl, President; Brian Fisher, Program/Music Director; Sylvia Harder, Public Affairs Dirertor; Scott Allen, Office Mgr.; David Ernewein, Chief Engineer. **Wattage:** 3800 day, 236 night. **Ad Rates:** $13-29 for 30 seconds; $15-33 for 60 seconds.

16233 Paragon Cable
801 Plymouth Ave. North Phone: (612)522-5200
Minneapolis, MN 55411 Fax: (612)521-7626

Founded: 1983. **Cities Served:** Hennepin County, Eden Prairie, Edina, Hopkins, Minnetonka, and Richfield, MN.

16234 WCCO-AM - 830
625 2nd Ave. S. Phone: (612)370-0611
Minneapolis, MN 55402 Fax: (612)370-0683

Format: Full Service. **Networks:** CBS; AP. **Founded:** 1924. **Operating Hours:** Continuous. **ADI:** Minneapolis-St. Paul, MN. **Key Personnel:** Brian Whittemore, VP/Gen. Mgr., phone (612)370-0610, whittemb@wccoradio.cbs.com; Chuck Dickemann, Operations Mgr., phone (612)370-0620, fax (612)370-0159, chuckd@minn.cbs.wec.com; Allen Eitzel, General Sales Mgr., phone (612)370-0611, fax (612)370-0666. **Wattage:** 50,000. **URL:** http://www.wcco.com; http://www.wcco.com.

16235 WCCO-TV - 4
90 S. 11th St. Phone: (612)339-4444
Minneapolis, MN 55403 Fax: (612)330-2603

Format: Commercial TV. **Networks:** CBS. **Operating Hours:** Continuous. **ADI:** Minneapolis-St. Paul, MN. **Key Personnel:** Jim Rupp, Contact.

16236 WFTC-TV - 29
1701 Broadway St. NE Phone: (612)379-2929
Minneapolis, MN 55413 Fax: (612)379-2900
E-mail: feedback@fox29.com

Format: Commercial TV. **Networks:** Fox. **Founded:** 1982. **Formerly:** KITN-TV. **Operating Hours:** Continuous. **ADI:** Minneapolis-St. Paul, MN. **Key Personnel:** Steve Spendlove, General Mgr.; Julie O'Neil, Program Mgr.; Randa Minkarah, General Sales Mgr. **URL:** http://www.fox29.com.

16237 WLTE-FM - 102.9
625 2nd Ave. S., Ste. 550 Phone: (612)339-1029
Minneapolis, MN 55402-1912 Fax: (612)339-5653

Format: Adult Contemporary. **Owner:** CBS, Inc., 51 West 52nd St., New York, NY 10019, (212)975-4321. **Operating Hours:** Continuous. **ADI:** Minneapolis-St. Paul, MN. **Key Personnel:** Rolf Pepple, Contact, fax (612)339-1181; Gary Nolan, Program Dir.; Joe McCormack, Contact; Dave Munson, General Sales Mgr.; Dave Bestler, Contact, phone (612)673-1130, fax (612)339-1181; Steve Brown, Chief Engineer; Kristine Volkman, Business Mgr. **Local Programs:** *Sunday Special*, Robin Anderson. **Wattage:** 100.

16238 WRQC-FM - 100.3
60 S. 6th St., Ste. 930 Phone: (612)330-0100
Minneapolis, MN 55402-4409 Fax: (612)330-0897
E-mail: wrqc@aol.com

Format: Album-Oriented Rock (AOR). **Founded:** 1965. **Formerly:** WCTS-FM (1992); WBOB-FM. **Operating Hours:** Continuous. **ADI:** Minneapolis-St. Paul, MN. **Key Personnel:** Marc Kalman, General Mgr., phone (612)330-9319, fax (612)330-9377; Shelly Malecha-Wilkes, General Sales Mgr.; Lauren MacLeash, Program Mgr.; Thomas Mooney, Controller, fax (612)338-8356. **Wattage:** 100,000. **Ad Rates:** Advertising accepted; rates available upon request.

16239 WXPT-FM - 104.1
7001 France Ave. S., No. 200 Phone: (612)836-1041
Minneapolis, MN 55435-4202 Fax: (612)915-6781
E-mail: kmjz@usinternet.com

Format: Adult Contemporary. **Networks:** ABC. **Founded:** 1962. **Formerly:** KJJO-FM; WXPT-FM; KJJO. **Operating Hours:** Continuous. **Key Personnel:** John Gehron, Vice President; Rolf Pepple, General Mgr.; Dusty Hayes, Program Dir.; Dusty Hayes, Local Sales Mgr.; Dave Bestler, General Sales Mgr. **Wattage:** 100,000. **Ad Rates:** Combined advertising rates available with KSGS-AM. **URL:** http://www.kmjz.com.

MINNEOTA, pop. 1,470.

SW MN. Lyon Co. 15 mi NW of Marshall.

16240 Minneota Mascot
201 N. Jefferson Phone: (507)872-6492
PO Box 8 Fax: (507)872-6492
Minneota, MN 56264
Community newspaper. **Freq:** Weekly (Wed.). **Cols./Page:** 6. **Col. Width:** 2 inches. **Col. Depth:** 21 inches. **Key Personnel:** Jon Guttorm, Publisher.
Circ: 1,400

MINNESOTA LAKE, pop. 744.

SC MN. Faribault Co. 28 mi. SE of Mankato. Stock, poultry, grain farms. Corn, oats, soybeans.

16241 Tribune
Box 308 Phone: (507)462-3575
Minnesota Lake, MN 56068
Community newspaper. **Founded:** June 1, 1894. **Freq:** Weekly (Thurs.). **Print Method:** Offset. **Trim Size:** 11 1/2 x 16. **Cols./Page:** 5. **Col. Width:** 11 picas. **Col. Depth:** 15 inches. **Key Personnel:** Kenneth A. Hiscock, Editor and Publisher. **Subscription Rates:** $10. **Remarks:** Accepts advertising.
Ad Rates: GLR: $.10 **Circ:** ‡900

MINNETONKA, pop. 38,683.

SE MN. Hennepin Co. 5 mi. W. of Minneapolis. Residential.

16242 American How-To
North American Outdoor Group, Inc.
12301 Whitewater Dr., Ste. 260 Phone: (612)988-7117
Minnetonka, MN 55343 Fax: (612)936-9169
Free: (800)688-7611
Publication E-mail: handymanclub@pclink.com
Publisher E-mail: addept@naoginc.com

Do-it-yourself home improvement magazine. **Subtitle:** Official Publication of the Handyman Club of America. **Founded:** Dec. 1993. **Freq:** Bimonthly. **Print Method:** Offset. **Trim Size:** 7 3/4 x 10 1/2. **Cols./Page:** 3. **Col. Width:** 2 1/4 inches. **Col. Depth:** 10 inches. **Key Personnel:** Tom Sweeney, Editor, phone (612)988-7290; Sheila Riley Becker, Publisher, phone (612)988-7114; Russell M. Nolan, Group Publisher. **ISSN:** 1071-3980. **Subscription Rates:** $18 U.S.; $24 Canada. **Remarks:** Accepts advertising. **URL:** http://www.handymanclub.com.
Ad Rates: BW: $21,130 **Circ:** Paid ★**813,296**
4C: $30,850
PCI: $1,200

16243 Art of the West
Duerr and Tierney Ltd.
15612 Hwy. 7, Ste. 235 Phone: (612)935-5850
Minnetonka, MN 55345 Fax: (612)935-6546
Free: (800)937-9194
Publication E-mail: aotw@.aotw.com

Magazine featuring art of the West, including cowboys, landscapes, and western wildlife. **Founded:** Nov. 1987. **Freq:** Bimonthly. **Print Method:** Web. **Trim Size:** 8 1/4 x 10 7/8. **Cols./Page:** 3. **Col. Width:** 13 picas. **Col. Depth:** 58 picas. **Key Personnel:** Vicki Stavig, Editor; Allan J. Duerr, Publisher; Tom F. Tierney, Publisher. **ISSN:** 1047-4994. **Subscription Rates:** $24; $43 two years. **Remarks:** Accepts advertising. **URL:** http://www.aotw.com.
Ad Rates: BW: $2,110 **Circ:** Paid ‡25,000
4C: $2,320 Non-paid ‡5,000

16244 Feedstuffs
Miller Publishing Co.
12400 Whitewater Dr., Ste. 160 Phone: (612)930-4391
Minnetonka, MN 55343 Fax: (612)938-1832

Magazine serving the grain and feed industries and animal agriculture. **Founded:** 1929. **Freq:** Weekly. **Print Method:** Uses mats. Offset. **Trim Size:** 10 x 14. **Cols./Page:** 4. **Col. Width:** 26 nonpareils. **Col. Depth:** 193 agate lines. **Key Personnel:** Sarah Muirhead, Editor, phone (612)930-4346, smuirhead@chilton.net; Gary Ashbacher, Advertising Mgr., phone (612)930-4349, gashbacher@chilton.net. **Subscription Rates:** $109. **Remarks:** Accepts advertising. **URL:** http://www.feedstuffs.com.
Ad Rates: BW: $4,665 **Circ:** Paid ★**13,437**
4C: $6,140 Non-paid ★**2,834**
PCI: $150

16245 Minnetonka Sun-Sailor
Minnesota Sun Publications
7831 E. Bush Lake Rd. Phone: (612)896-4700
Bloomington, MN 55439 Fax: (612)896-4728

Community newspaper (tabloid). **Freq:** Weekly (Wed.). **Print Method:** Offset. **Cols./Page:** 5. **Col. Width:** 1 15/16 inches. **Col. Depth:** 16 inches. **Key Personnel:** Don Thurlow, Publisher; Paul Johnson, Advertising Mgr. **Remarks:** Accepts advertising.
Ad Rates: GLR: $19.88 **Circ:** Free 16,683
BW: $1,352 Paid 1,511
4C: $1,473
PCI: $16.90

16246 North American Fisherman
North American Outdoor Group, Inc.
12301 Whitewater Dr., Ste. 260 Phone: (612)988-7117
Minnetonka, MN 55343 Fax: (612)936-9169
Free: (800)688-7611
Publication E-mail: fishingclub@pclink.com
Publisher E-mail: addept@naoginc.com

Fishing magazine. **Subtitle:** Official Publication of the North American Fishing Club. **Founded:** 1988. **Freq:** 7/year. **Print Method:** Offset. **Trim Size:** 7 3/4 x 10 1/2. **Cols./Page:** 3. **Col. Width:** 2 1/4 inches. **Col. Depth:** 10 inches. **Key Personnel:** Steve Pennaz, Editor, phone (612)988-7228; Rich Sundberg, Publisher; Russell Nolan, Group Publisher. **ISSN:** 1043-2450. **Subscription Rates:** $18. **Remarks:** Accepts advertising. **URL:** http://www.fishingclub.com.
Ad Rates: BW: $14,110 **Circ:** Paid ‡500,000
4C: $18,345

16247 North American Hunter
North American Outdoor Group, Inc.
12301 Whitewater Dr., Ste. 260 Phone: (612)988-7117
Minnetonka, MN 55343 Fax: (612)936-9169
Free: (800)688-7611
Publisher E-mail: addept@naoginc.com

Hunting magazine. **Founded:** Sept. 1978. **Freq:** 8/year. **Print Method:** Offset. **Trim Size:** 7 3/4 x 10 1/2. **Cols./Page:** 3. **Col. Width:** 2 1/4 inches. **Col. Depth:** 10 inches. **Key Personnel:** Gregg Gutschow, Editor, phone (612)988-7225; Tom Perrier, Publisher; Russell M. Nolan, Group Publisher. **USPS:** 462-130. **Subscription Rates:** $18. **Remarks:** Accepts advertising. **URL:** http://www.huntingclub.com.
Ad Rates: BW: $15,525 **Circ:** Paid ★**150,362**
4C: $22,715
PCI: $75

16248 REQUEST
Request Media Inc.
10400 Yellow Circle Dr. Phone: (612)931-8740
Minnetonka, MN 55343 Fax: (612)931-8490
Free: (800)325-0075
Publication E-mail: staff@requestline.com

Music magazine distributed at record stores. **Subtitle:** The Best New Music Magazine. **Founded:** 1989. **Freq:** Monthly. **Print Method:** Offset. **Trim Size:** 10 x 11 5/8. **Cols./Page:** 4. **Col. Width:** 2 inches. **Col. Depth:** 10 5/8 inches. **Key Personnel:** Susan Hamre, Editor. **ISSN:** 1045-0084. **Subscription Rates:** $12.95 by mail; $2.95 single issue. **Remarks:** Accepts advertising. **URL:** http://www.requestline.com.
Ad Rates: BW: $12,750 **Circ:** Paid 1,880
4C: $15,000 Non-paid 503,767

16249 Supertrax International Magazine
Supertrax Publishing LLC
3432 Hwy. 101 Phone: (612)473-7870
Minnetonka, MN 55345 Fax: (612)473-7805
Free: (800)905-8729
Publication E-mail: supertrax@aol.com
Publisher E-mail: trax@ican.net

Magazine for snowmobilers. **Subtitle:** Pulse of Snowmobiling. **Founded:** 1991. **Freq:** 4/year. **Print Method:** Web offset. **Trim Size:** 8 1/8 x 10 7/8. **Cols./Page:** 3. **Col. Width:** 13 picas. **Col. Depth:** 60 picas. **Key Personnel:** C.J. Ramstad, Publisher. **Subscription Rates:** $10 for four issues; $2.95 single issue. **Remarks:** Accepts advertising.
Ad Rates: BW: $14,945 **Circ:** Paid 10,500
4C: $20,160 Non-paid 269,500

16250 Tack'n Togs Merchandising
Miller Publishing Co.
12400 Whitewater Dr., Ste. 160 Phone: (612)930-4391
Minnetonka, MN 55343 Fax: (612)938-1832

International trade magazine for marketers of products for horse and rider. **Founded:** 1970. **Freq:** Monthly. **Print Method:** Web offset. Uses mats. **Trim Size:** 8 x 10 3/4. **Cols./Page:** 3. **Col. Width:** 40 nonpareils. **Col. Depth:** 140 agate lines. **Key Personnel:** Dan DeWeese, Editor; Robert M. Clarity, Publisher; William Poehler, Managing Editor; Steve Joss, Circulation Mgr. **Subscription Rates:** Free to qualified subscribers; $18. **Remarks:** Accepts advertising.
Ad Rates: BW: $2,684 **Circ:** Controlled ‡22,170
4C: $3,584
PCI: $177

MONTEVIDEO†, pop. 5,845.

SW MN. Chippewa Co. On Minnesota River, 133 mi. W. of Minneapolis. Manufactures electronic components, mobile homes, stock feed. Creameries. Stock, dairy, poultry, grain, hog & cattle farms.

16251 American News
Montevideo Publishing Co.
Box 736 Phone: (612)269-2156
223 1st St. Fax: (612)269-2159
Montevideo, MN 56265
Community newspaper. **Subtitle:** Montevideo American News. **Freq:** Weekly (Thurs.). **Print Method:** Web. **Cols./Page:** 6. **Col. Width:** 26 nonpareils. **Col. Depth:** 301 agate lines. **Key Personnel:** Pat Schmidt, Editor; Louie Seese, President. **USPS:** 360-880. **Subscription Rates:** $28.50 individuals; $33.50 out of area; $39.50 out of state. **Remarks:** Accepts advertising.
Ad Rates: GLR: $0.44 **Circ:** Paid 4,566
BW: $806.25 Free 30
4C: $981.25
SAU: $6.25
PCI: $6.25

16252 KDMA-AM - 1460
PO Box 738 Phone: (612)269-8815
Montevideo, MN 56265 Fax: (612)269-8449
E-mail: kdma@lakes.com

Format: Adult Contemporary; Information; News; Sports. **Networks:** ABC. **Owner:** David Ramage, at above address. **Founded:** 1951. **Operating Hours:** 24 hrs. **Key Personnel:** Deanne Hodge, General Mgr.; D. Hodge, News; Dwight Mulder, Program Dir.; Randy Clausen, Sports Dir.; Roger Hill, Sales Mgr. **Wattage:** 1000. **Ad Rates:** $8-9.45 for 30 seconds; $11.95-14.20 for 60 seconds. Combined advertising rates available with KMGM, KKRC.

16253 KMGM-FM - 105.5
PO Box 738 Phone: (612)269-8815
Montevideo, MN 56265 Fax: (612)269-8449
E-mail: kdma@lakes.com

Format: Oldies. **Networks:** ABC. **Owner:** David Ramage, at above address. **Founded:** 1982. **Operating Hours:** Continuous. **Key Personnel:** Deanna Hodge, General Mgr.; D. Hodge, News Dir.; Dwight Mulder, Program Dir.; Rondy Clausen, Sports Dir.; Roger Hill, Sales Mgr. **Wattage:** 3000. **Ad Rates:** $8-9.45 for 30 seconds; $11.95-14.20 for 60 seconds.

MONTGOMERY, pop. 2,349.

SC MN. Le Sueur Co. 22 mi. W. of Faribault. Corn and peas canneries. Steel products and farm equipment manufactured. Dairy, poultry, stock, grain farms.

16254 Montgomery Messenger
Suel Printing Co., Inc.
310 1st St. S. Phone: (612)758-4435
PO Box 49 Fax: (507)364-8602
Montgomery, MN 56069
Community newspaper. **Founded:** 1888. **Freq:** Weekly (Wed.). **Print Method:** Offset. **Cols./Page:** 6. **Col. Width:** 26 nonpareils. **Col. Depth:** 301 agate lines. **Key Personnel:** John J. Keohen, Editor; E. Charles Wann, Publisher; Jerry F. Keohen, Publisher. **USPS:** 361-200. **Subscription Rates:** $14.50 in state; $20 out of state; $26 out of country. **Remarks:** Accepts advertising.
Ad Rates: GLR: $.16 **Circ:** ‡2,500
PCI: $3.15

MONTICELLO, pop. 3,111.

SEC MN. Wright Co. On Mississippi River, 35 mi. NW of Minneapolis. Manufactures heaters, ballpoints, screwdrivers. Egg producing plant. Dairy, beef, grain & potato farms.

16255 Dairy Today
Farm Journal, Inc.
PO Box 1167 Phone: (612)271-3363
261 East Broadway Fax: (612)271-3360
Monticello, MN 55362
Publication E-mail: dairytoday@aol.com

Agricultural magazine for dairy managers and producers. **Subtitle:** The Magazine of American Dairy Producers. **Founded:** 1985. **Freq:** 10/year. **Print Method:** Offset. **Trim Size:** 8 x 10 1/2. **Cols./Page:** 3. **Col. Width:** 2 1/4 inches. **Col. Depth:** 140 agate lines. **Key Personnel:** Jim Dickrell, Editor; Roger D. Randall, President, phone (215)557-8932, rrandall@farmjournal.com; Jerry Gunderson, Publisher, phone (215)557-5769, jgunderson@farmjournal.com. **ISSN:** 1056-1382. **Subscription Rates:** Free to qualified subscribers. **Remarks:** Accepts advertising. **URL:** http://www.dairytoday.com. **Alt. Formats:** Mailing labels. **Formerly:** Dairy Extra (1987).
Ad Rates: BW: $6,570 **Circ:** Non-paid 92,000
4C: $7,750

16256 Monticello Shopper
Monticello Times and Shopper
Box 548 Phone: (612)295-3131
Monticello, MN 55362 Fax: (612)295-3080
Publication E-mail: montimes@biglake.polaristel.net

Shopper. **Founded:** 1958. **Freq:** Weekly (Sun.). **Print Method:** Offset. **Cols./Page:** 6. **Col. Width:** 12.6 picas. **Col. Depth:** 301 nonpareils. **Key Personnel:** Donald Q. Smith, Editor and Publisher; Sherrie T. White, Advertising Mgr. **Subscription Rates:** $32. **Remarks:** Accepts advertising. **URL:** http://www.montitimes.comm. **Formerly:** Monticello Big Lake Shopper (1992).
Ad Rates: 4C: $280 **Circ:** Paid ‡50
PCI: $7.50 Free ‡18,450

16257 Times
Monticello Times and Shopper
Box 548 Phone: (612)295-3131
Monticello, MN 55362 Fax: (612)295-3080
Publication E-mail: montimes@biglake.polaristel.net

Community newspaper. **Founded:** May 1857. **Freq:** Weekly (Thurs.). **Print Method:** Offset. **Cols./Page:** 6. **Col. Width:** 12.6 picas. **Col. Depth:** 21 1/2 inches. **Key Personnel:** Donald Q. Smith, Publisher; Sherrie J. White, Advertising Mgr. **USPS:** 361-660. **Subscription Rates:** $28; $32.50 out of area; $35 out of state. **Remarks:** Accepts advertising. **URL:** http://www.montitimes.comm.
Ad Rates: PCI: $6.20 **Circ:** ‡3,050

MOORHEAD†, pop. 29,998.

WC MN. Clay Co. On REd River, adjacent to Fargo, ND. Concordia College; Moorhead State University. Trade center. Butter, sugar,cheese, boat factories; bottling, sheet metal works; elevator. Ships potatoes, grain. Agriculture. Grain, potatoes, sugar beets.

16258 Alumnews
Moorhead State University
Box 306 Phone: (218)236-2551
Moorhead, MN 56563-0001 Fax: (218)236-4662

College alumni magazine. **Freq:** three times/year. **Print Method:** Offset. **Cols./Page:** 5. **Col. Width:** 22 nonpareils. **Col. Depth:** 210 agate lines. **Key Personnel:** Glenn Tornell, Editor; Ron Matthies, Publisher. **Remarks:** Advertising not accepted.
Circ: Non-paid ‡30,000

16259 The Concordian
Concordia College
PO Box 104 Phone: (218)299-3826
Moorhead, MN 56562 Fax: (218)299-4196
Publication E-mail: concordian@gloria.cord.edu

Collegiate newspaper (tabloid). **Founded:** 1908. **Freq:** Weekly (Fri.). **Print Method:** Offset. **Trim Size:** 11 x 17. **Cols./Page:** 5. **Col. Width:** 1 7/8 inches. **Col. Depth:** 16 inches. **Key Personnel:** Darrell E. Ehrlick, Jr., Editor; Allison Bangs, Business Mgr.; Matthew Peterson, Advertising Manager. **Subscription Rates:** $10. **Remarks:** Accepts advertising. **Available Online. URL:** http://www.cord.edu/dept/concord.
Ad Rates: PCI: $4.50 **Circ:** ‡4000

16260 Moorhead State University Advocate
Moorhead State University
1104 7th Ave. S. Fax: (218)236-4662
Box 306
Moorhead, MN 56563
Publication E-mail: advocate@mhd1.moorhead.msus.edu

Collegiate newspaper (tabloid). **Founded:** 1971. **Freq:** Weekly (Thurs.). **Print Method:** Offset. **Cols./Page:** 5. **Col. Width:** 24 nonpareils. **Col. Depth:** 196 agate lines. **Key Personnel:** Glenn Tornell, Publisher, phone (218)236-2204; Sarah Henning, Editor. **Subscription Rates:** $16. **Remarks:** Accepts advertising. **URL:** http://www.moorhead.msus.edu/~advocate/.
Ad Rates: BW: $3.55 **Circ:** Free ‡5,500
PCI: $4.75

16261 KCCD-FM - 90.3
Concordia College Phone: (218)299-3666
901 S. 8th St. Fax: (218)299-3418
Moorhead, MN 56562

Format: News; Information. **Owner:** Minnesota Public Radio, 45 E. 7th St., St. Paul, MN 55101, (612)290-1500. **Founded:** 1992. **Operating Hours:** Continuous. **Key Personnel:** Vern Goodin, General Mgr.; Dan Gunderson, News Dir. **Wattage:** 100,000. **Ad Rates:** Noncommercial. **URL:** http://www.mpr.org.

16262 KCCM-FM - 91.1
Concordia College Phone: (218)299-3666
901 S. 8th St. Fax: (218)299-3418
Moorhead, MN 56562

Format: Classical; Public Radio. **Networks:** Minnesota Public Radio; National Public Radio (NPR); American Public Radio (APR). **Owner:** Minnesota Public Radio, 45 E. 7th St., St. Paul, MN 55101, (612)290-1500, Free: (800)228-7123. **Founded:** 1971. **Operating Hours:** Continuous; 95% network, 5% local. **Key Personnel:** Vern Goodin, General Mgr., ygoodin@mpr.org; Dan Gunderson, News Dir., dgunderson@mpr.org; Brian Graftaas, Contact, bgraftaas@mpr.org; Deborah Davy, Administrative Assistant. **Wattage:** 67,000. **Ad Rates:** Noncommercial. **URL:** http://www.mpr.org.

16263 KNTN-FM - 102.7
Concordia College Phone: (218)299-3666
901 S. 8th St. Fax: (218)299-3418
Moorhead, MN 56562

Format: News; Information. **Owner:** Minnesota Public Radio, 45 E. 7th St., St. Paul, MN 55101, (612)290-1500. **Founded:** 1991. **Operating Hours:** Continuous. **Key Personnel:** Vern Goodin, General Mgr., vgoodin@mpr.org; Dan Gunderson, News Dir., dgunderson@mpr.org; Brian Graftaas, Development Dir., bgraftaas@mpr.org; Karen Nitzkorski, Promotions Dir. **Wattage:** 100,000. **Ad Rates:** Noncommercial. **URL:** http://www.mpr.org.

16264 KQMN-FM - 91.1
Concordia College Phone: (218)299-3666
901 S. 8th St. Fax: (218)299-3418
Moorhead, MN 56562

Format: Classical. **Owner:** Minnesota Public Radio, 45 E. 7th St., St. Paul, MN 55101, (612)290-1500. **Founded:** 1990. **Operating Hours:** Continuous. **Key Personnel:** Vern Goodin, General Mgr., vgoodin@mpr.org; Dan Gunderson, News Dir., dgunderson@mpr.org; Brian Graftaas, Development Dir., bgraftaas@mpr.org; Deborah Davy, Administrative Assistant, ddavy@mpr.org. **Wattage:** 84,000. **Ad Rates:** Noncommercial. **URL:** http://www.mpr.org; http://www.mpr.org.

MOOSE LAKE, pop. 1,408.

EC MN. Carlton Co. 43 mi. SW of Duluth. Resort. Butter, tile, fishing tackle, pottery, timber products manufactured. Dairy, poultry farms.

16265 Star-Gazette
308 Elm St. Phone: (218)485-4406
Box 449 Fax: (218)485-0237
Moose Lake, MN 55767
Free: (800)247-0882

Community newspaper. **Founded:** 1895. **Freq:** Weekly (Thurs.). **Print Method:** Offset. **Cols./Page:** 7. **Col. Width:** 28 nonpareils. **Col. Depth:** 301 agate lines. **Key Personnel:** Jerry DeRungs, Editor and Publisher. **ISSN:** 0746-2980. **Subscription Rates:** $24 individuals. **Remarks:** Accepts advertising.
Ad Rates: BW: $285 **Circ:** Paid 2,850
SAU: $4.00

MORA†, pop. 2,890.

EC MN. Karabec Co. 60 mi. N. of Minneapolis. Manufactures plastic products, precious metals fabrication, fiberglass pleasure cruisers, steel fabricating, poultry feeds, milk drying equipment. Stock, dairy, poultry farms. Small grains.

16266 Kanabec County Times
107 Park St. S. Phone: (320)679-2661
Mora, MN 55051-1459 Fax: (320)679-2663

Community newspaper. **Founded:** 1884. **Freq:** Weekly (Thurs.). **Print Method:** Offset. **Cols./Page:** 5. **Col. Width:** 23 nonpareils. **Col. Depth:** 210 agate lines. **Key Personnel:**

Wade Weber, Editor and Publisher. **Subscription Rates:** $18. **Remarks:** Accepts advertising.
Ad Rates: GLR: $.246 **Circ:** Paid ‡3,000
Free ‡11,000

📖 **16267 Mora Advertisers**
Karabee Publications
107 Park St. S. Phone: (320)679-2661
Mora, MN 55051-1459 Fax: (320)679-2663

Shopper (tabloid). **Founded:** Feb. 20, 1949. **Freq:** Weekly (Mon.). **Print Method:** Offset. **Trim Size:** 11 1/2 x 16 1/2. **Cols./Page:** 6. **Col. Width:** 21 nonpareils. **Col. Depth:** 217 agate lines. **Key Personnel:** Robert H. Beck, Editor and Publisher. **Subscription Rates:** $25 (out of area). **Remarks:** Accepts advertising. **Formerly**: Mora Advertiser.
Ad Rates: GLR: $.16 **Circ:** Paid ‡192
BW: $225 Free ‡10,554
PCI: $2.95

MORRIS†, pop. 5,367.

WC MN. Stevens Co. 80 mi. directly W. of Saint Cloud. University of Minnesota USDA Agricultural Research Regional Center. Manufactures butter, ice-cream. Agriculture. Livestock, corn, soybeans, small grains.

📖 **16268 Conradiana**
Texas Tech University Press
c/o Dwight Purdy, Editor Phone: (320)589-6265
Department of Humanities
University of Minnesota-Morris
Morris, MN 56267
Publisher E-mail: ttup@ttu.edu

Scholarly journal covering the life and works of British writer Joseph Conrad. **Founded:** 1968. **Freq:** Triennial. **Trim Size:** 6 x 9. **Key Personnel:** Dwight Purdy, Editor, purdydh@caa.mrs.umn.edu. **ISSN:** 0010-6356. **Subscription Rates:** $21 individuals; $35 institutions; $28 out of country individual; $44 out of country institutions. **Remarks:** Accepts advertising.
Circ: (Not Reported)

📖 **16269 Tribune**
108 E. 6th St. Phone: (612)589-2525
PO Box 470 Free: (888)589-2525
Morris, MN 56267
Publisher E-mail: general@aocs.org

Community newspaper. **Founded:** 1877. **Freq:** Weekly (Thurs.). **Print Method:** Offset. **Cols./Page:** 6. **Col. Width:** 14 ems. **Col. Depth:** 21.5 inches. **Key Personnel:** James S. Morrison, Publisher; Terry Manney, Advertising Mgr. **Subscription Rates:** $29 individuals; $36 out of area. **Remarks:** Accepts advertising.
Ad Rates: BW: $567.60 **Circ:** Paid ‡3,523
4C: $807.60 Free ‡58
SAU: $4.70
PCI: $4.70

🎙 **16270 KMRS-AM - 1230**
Box 570 Phone: (320)589-3131
Morris, MN 56267 Fax: (320)589-2715
E-mail: kmrskkok@info-link.net

Format: Middle-of-the-Road (MOR); Agricultural. **Networks:** ABC; Minnesota News. **Founded:** 1956. **Operating Hours:** 5;30 a.m.- 12 a.m. M-Sa, 6 a.m. - 12 a.m. Sun. **Key Personnel:** Bruce Thom, President; Deborah Mattheis, General Mgr.; Bill Eckersen, Program Dir.; Sue Deiter, News Dir.; Marty Berlinger, Chief Engineer. **Wattage:** 1000.

🎙 **16271 KUMM-FM - 89.7**
University of Minnesota-Morris Phone: (320)589-6076
Morris, MN 56267 Fax: (320)589-6075
E-mail: kumm@cda.mrs.umn.edu

Format: Alternative/New Music/Progressive. **Owner:** University of Minnesota-Morris, at above address. **Founded:** 1972. **Operating Hours:** Continuous. **Key Personnel:** Michael Hener, Station Mgr.; Christy Stalker, Program Dir.; Alex Barrett, News Dir.; Josh Kovach, Music Dir.; Josh Majisturski, Publicity Director; Robert Fitzgerald, Production Mgr.; Abe Welle, Secretary. **Wattage:** 225.

MOUND

📖 **16272 The Laker**
J.D. Barreth Pub.
2365 Commerce Blvd. Phone: (612)472-1140
PO Box 82 Fax: (612)472-0516
Mound, MN 55364
Community newspaper. **Founded:** 1972. **Freq:** Weekly (Mon.). **Print Method:** Offset. **Cols./Page:** 6. **Col. Width:** 12 picas. **Col. Depth:** 21 1/2 inches. **Key Personnel:** Bill Holm, Editor; James Berreth, Publisher. **Subscription Rates:** $20. **Remarks:** Accepts advertising.
Ad Rates: BW: $565.55 **Circ:** ‡9,200
PCI: $5.48

MOUNTAIN LAKE, pop. 2,277.

WC MN. Cottonwood Co. 50 mi. W. of Mankato. Farm & stock feeding equipment, hydraulic cylinders & pumps, dairy products manufactured. Stock, grain, poultry farms. Corn, oats, soybeans, flax.

📖 **16273 Mountain Lake/Butterfield Observer/ Advocate**
Central Publications
237 11th St. N. Phone: (507)427-2725
Mountain Lake, MN 56159 Fax: (507)427-2724
Publication E-mail: obsad@rconnect.com

Community newspaper. **Founded:** 1893. **Freq:** Weekly (Wed.). **Print Method:** Offset. **Cols./Page:** 6. **Col. Width:** 28 nonpareils. **Col. Depth:** 301 agate lines. **Key Personnel:** Susan Meissner, Editor. **Subscription Rates:** $28.95 individuals; $36.95 out of area.
Ad Rates: BW: $4.40 **Circ:** ‡2,200

NASHWAUK, pop. 1,419.

NC MN. Itasca Co. 75 mi. NW of Duluth. Residential.

📖 **16274 Eastern Itascan**
310 Central Ave. Phone: (218)885-2100
Nashwauk, MN 55769-1132 Fax: (218)885-1222

Community newspaper. **Subtitle:** Your Newspaper. **Founded:** 1909. **Freq:** Weekly (Thurs.). **Print Method:** Offset. Uses mats. **Trim Size:** 11 1/2 x 18. **Cols./Page:** 6. **Col. Width:** 21 nonpareils. **Col. Depth:** 196 agate lines. **Key Personnel:** Dan Brim, Owner; Karen Brim, Owner. **USPS:** 165-880. **Subscription Rates:** $18; $25 out of area; $29 out of state; $30 other countries. **Remarks:** Accepts advertising.
Ad Rates: BW: $184.80 **Circ:** Paid 1,757
4C: $359.80
SAU: $4.21
PCI: $3.40

NEVIS, pop. 332.

NO MN. Hubbard Co. 13 mi. NE of Park Rapids.

📖 **16275 Northwoods Press**
PO Box 28 Phone: (218)652-3475
Nevis, MN 56467 Fax: (218)652-3475

Community newspaper. **Founded:** 1962. **Freq:** Weekly (Thurs.). **Print Method:** Offset. **Cols./Page:** 6. **Col. Width:** 1 5/8 inches. **Col. Depth:** 16 inches. **Key Personnel:** Victor W. Olson, Editor and Publisher. **USPS:** 580-180. **Subscription Rates:** $23 individuals; $27 out of area. **Remarks:** Accepts advertising. **Formerly**: Hubbard County Independent.
Ad Rates: BW: $299.25 **Circ:** Paid 1462
4C: $479.25 Free 44
PCI: $3.60

NEW BRIGHTON, pop. 23,269.

SE MN. Ramsey Co. 9 mi. NW of Saint Paul. International school. Seminary. Manufactures computers, heart pacemakers.

📖 **16276 New Brighton-Mounds View Bulletin**
Lillie Suburban Newspapers
PO Box 120608 Phone: (612)633-2777
New Brighton, MN 55112 Fax: (612)633-3846

Local newspaper. **Founded:** 1956. **Freq:** Weekly (Wed.). **Print Method:** Letterpress and offset. Uses mats. **Trim Size:** Broadsheet. **Cols./Page:** 6. **Col. Width:** 21 nonpareils. **Col. Depth:** 294 agate lines. **Key Personnel:** Mary Lee Hagert, Managing Editor; N. T. Lillie, Publisher; Jeffery Enright, Publisher; Mark Beckstrom, Advertising Mgr.; Pat Colburn, Circulation Mgr.; James Schwartz, Editor. **Subscription Rates:** $25.95 elsewhere. **Remarks:** Accepts advertising. **Formerly**: New Brighton Bulletin.
Ad Rates: SAU: $22.70 **Circ:** Paid 129
Free 10,077

St. Anthony Bulletin - See St. Anthony

Shoreview-Arden Hills Bulletin - See Shoreview

NEW HOPE

📖 **16277 Construction Bulletin Magazine**
Chapin Publishing Co.
9443 Science Center Dr. Phone: (612)537-7730
New Hope, MN 55428-3636 Fax: (612)537-1363
Free: (800)328-4827

Magazine covering Minnesota, North Dakota, and South Dakota construction activities. **Subtitle:** The Weekly Jobs Book. **Founded:** 1893. **Freq:** Weekly. **Print Method:** Film. **Trim Size:** 8 1/2 x 11. **Cols./Page:** 3. **Col. Width:** 13 picas. **Col. Depth:** 60 picas. **Key Personnel:** George R. Rekela, Editor; Chris Casey, Publisher; Ray Turner, Sales; John Saunders, Sales; Jane Sanem, Circulation Mgr. **USPS:** 130-060. **Subscription Rates:** $160; $3.75 single issue. **Remarks:** Accepts advertising.
Ad Rates: BW: $985 **Circ:** Paid 2,854
4C: $1,435 Non-paid 362
PCI: $45

📖 **16278 New Hope/Golden Valley Sun-Post**
Minnesota Sun Publications
7831 E. Bush Lake Rd. Phone: (612)896-4700
Bloomington, MN 55439 Fax: (612)896-4728
Publication E-mail: goldenvalleysunpost@mnsunpub.com

Community newspaper (tabloid). **Founded:** 1963. **Freq:** Weekly (Wed.). **Print Method:** Offset. **Key Personnel:** Doug Dane, Publisher, phone (612)896-4787; Pamela Austin, Advertising Mgr., phone (612)897-5486.
Circ: Paid 10,775

NEW PRAGUE, pop. 2,952.

SC MN. Le Sueur Co. 40 mi. SW of Minneapolis. Medical Center. Manufactures flour, butter, space and cryogenic equipment, printed paper products. Diversified farming. Dairy products, livestock, grain.

📖 **16279 AG Retailer Magazine**
AG Retailer
120 W. Main St., Ste. 200 Phone: (612)758-5812
New Prague, MN 56071 Fax: (612)758-5813
Publication E-mail: agretail@aol.com

Magazine for crop protection/plant nutrient professionals. **Subtitle:** For Crop Input Professional. **Founded:** 1959. **Freq:** 10/year. **Print Method:** Web offset. **Trim Size:** 8 1/8 x 10 7/8. **Cols./Page:** 3 and 2. **Col. Width:** 26 and 40 nonpareils. **Col. Depth:** 134 agate lines. **Key Personnel:** John Appleton, Publisher, phone (336)545-0281, fax (336)282-9991; Den Gardner, Editor, gard2@aol.com. **ISSN:** 1072-9267. **Subscription Rates:** $40 individuals; $7 single issue. **Remarks:** Accepts advertising. **Formerly**: Solutions.
Ad Rates: BW: $2,600 **Circ:** Non-paid 21,598
4C: $3,500

📖 **16280 New Prague Times**
200 E. Main St. Phone: (612)758-4435
PO Box 25 Fax: (612)758-4135
New Prague, MN 56071
Community newspaper. **Founded:** 1889. **Freq:** Weekly (Thurs.). **Cols./Page:** 6. **Col. Width:** 13 picas. **Col. Depth:** 21.5 picas. **Key Personnel:** Lois Wann, Editor; Chuck Wann, Publisher.
Circ: 4,300

🎙 **16281 KCHK-AM - 1350**
PO Box 251 Phone: (612)758-2571
New Prague, MN 56071 Fax: (612)758-3170
Free: (888)758-2575

Format: Oldies. **Networks:** ABC. **Founded:** 1969. **Formerly**: KTMF-AM. **Operating Hours:** Continuous; 90% network, 10% local. **Key Personnel:** Jack B. Ludescher, General Mgr.; Dave Ernewein, Program Dir.; Andy Regensheid, Sports Dir. **Wattage:** 500. **Ad Rates:** $14 for 30 seconds; $15 for 60 seconds.

🎙 **16282 KCHK-FM - 95.5**
25821 Langford Ave. Phone: (612)758-2571
PO Box 251 Fax: (612)758-3170
New Prague, MN 56071
Free: (888)758-2575

Format: Oldies. **Networks:** ABC. **Founded:** 1989. **Operating Hours:** Continuous; 90% network, 10% local. **Key Personnel:** Jack B. Ludescher, General Mgr.; Dave Ernewein, Program Dir. **Wattage:** 3000. **Ad Rates:** $14 for 30 seconds; $15 for 60 seconds.

NEW ULM†, pop. 13,755.

SC MN. Brown Co. 75 mi. S. of Minneapolis. Dr. Martin Luther College. Manufactures cheese, dairy products, beer,- asbestos, plastic, micro film. Greenhouses. Diversified farming. Wheat, corn, barley, soybeans.

16283 Journal
303 N. Minnesota St. Phone: (507)359-2911
Box 487 Fax: (507)359-7362
New Ulm, MN 56073
Free: (800)967-1760
Publication E-mail: journal@ic.newulm.mn.us

General newspaper. **Founded:** 1937. **Freq:** Mon.-Sun. (morn.). **Print Method:** Offset. **Cols./Page:** 6. **Col. Width:** 24 nonpareils. **Col. Depth:** 301 agate lines. **Key Personnel:** Kevin Sweeney, Editor; Bruce Fenske, Publisher; Marian Peterson, Advertising Dir.; Steve Grosam, Circulation Mgr. **Subscription Rates:** $89. **Remarks:** Accepts advertising.
Ad Rates: SAU: $9.66 **Circ:** Mon.-Sat. ★**9,627**
PCI: $13.21 Sun. ★**10,087**

16284 Prairie Catholic
1400 6th St. N. Phone: (507)359-2966
New Ulm, MN 56073-2099 Fax: (507)354-3667

Official newspaper of the Diocese of New Ulm. **Founded:** 1971. **Freq:** Monthly. **Key Personnel:** Paula Marti, Editor, dnucomm@ic.new-ulm.mn.us. **Remarks:** Advertising not accepted.
Circ: Combined ⊕**26,500**

16285 Amzak Cable
200 N. Minnesota St. Phone: (507)354-4191
New Ulm, MN 56073 Fax: (507)354-4192

Key Personnel: Mike Kazma, General Mgr. **Cities Served:** New Ulm, Madelia, New Prague, and Jordan, MN.

16286 KNSG-FM - 94.7
210 N. Minnesota Phone: (507)723-5000
New Ulm, MN 56073 Fax: (507)723-5604
Free: (800)444-5685
E-mail: radioone@ic.new-ulm.mn.us

Format: Country. **Owner:** Cumulus Broadcasting, at above address. **Founded:** July 1995. **Operating Hours:** Continuous. **Key Personnel:** James Bartels, General Mgr., phone (507)359-2921, jimbartels@cumulusb.com; Marj Frederickson, Sales Mgr., phone (507)359-2921, radioone@ic.new-ulm.mn.us; Brian Filzer, Program Dir., phone (507)359-2921. **Wattage:** 50,000. **URL:** http://www.radiooneminnesota.com.

16287 KNUJ-AM - 860
Grand Hotel Phone: (507)359-2921
210 N. Minnesota Fax: (507)359-4520
PO Box 368
New Ulm, MN 56073
E-mail: radioone@ic.new-ulm.mn.us

Format: Talk; Big Band/Nostalgia; News; Sports; Agricultural; Country. **Networks:** NBC; Minnesota News. **Owner:** James Ingstad Broadcasting, at above address. **Founded:** 1949. **Operating Hours:** Continuous; 30% network, 70% local. **Key Personnel:** Jim Bartels, General Mgr.; Brian Filzen, Program Dir.; Darrel Wilson, News Dir.; Tom Wheeler, Sports Dir.; Lynn Rubie, Farm director; Marj Frederickson, Sales Mgr. **Wattage:** 1000. **Ad Rates:** $19-65 for 30 seconds; $24-75 for 60 seconds.

NEW YORK MILLS, pop. 972.

WC MN. Otter Tail Co. 40 mi. NW of Fergus Falls. Lake resort. Boat factory; lumber mill. Timber. Grain, dairy, poultry farms. Potatoes.

16288 Herald
PO Box 158 Phone: (218)385-2275
New York Mills, MN 56567 Fax: (218)385-3626

Community newspaper. **Founded:** 1915. **Freq:** Weekly (Thurs.). **Print Method:** Offset. **Cols./Page:** 6. **Col. Width:** 28 nonpareils. **Col. Depth:** 301 agate lines. **Key Personnel:** Michael A. Parta, Publisher. **USPS:** 383-100. **Subscription Rates:** $22; $24 out of area; $26 out of state. **Remarks:** Accepts advertising.
Ad Rates: SAU: $5.10 **Circ:** ‡2,000

NORTH BRANCH, pop. 1,597.

EC MN. Chisago Co. 45 mi. N. of Saint Paul.

16289 ECM Post-Review
ECM Publishers, Inc. - North Branch
612 Main St. Phone: (612)464-4601
North Branch, MN 55056 Fax: (612)464-4605

Community newspaper. **Founded:** 1875. **Freq:** Weekly (Wed.). **Print Method:** Offset. **Trim Size:** 11 3/8 x 16. **Cols./Page:** 6. **Col. Width:** 20 nonpareils. **Col. Depth:** 210 agate lines. **Key Personnel:** Twyla Ring, Editor, editor.fl@ecm-inc.com; Elmer Andersen, Publisher; Mary Eslinger, Advertising Mgr. **Subscription Rates:** $24; $27 out of area. **Remarks:** Accepts advertising.
Ad Rates: BW: $495 **Circ:** Paid ‡2,495
SAU: $7.80
PCI: $5.50

NORTH MANKATO, pop. 9,145.

SC MN. Nicollet Co. 5 mi. N. of Skyline.

16290 KXLP-FM - 93.1
1807 Lee Blvd. Phone: (507)388-2900
North Mankato, MN 56003 Fax: (507)345-4675

Format: Classic Rock. **Owner:** Pro Radio Group, at above address. **Founded:** 1986. **Operating Hours:** Continuous. **Key Personnel:** Jo Guck Bailey, General Mgr.; Chris Painter, Station Mgr.; Mary Kay Degrood, Sales Mgr.; Jim Winston, News Dir.; Terry Cooley, Program Dir.; Mike Kalinowski, Promotions. **Wattage:** 100,000. **Ad Rates:** $30 for 30 seconds; $45 for 60 seconds.

16291 KYSM-AM - 1230
1807 Lee Blvd. Phone: (507)388-2900
North Mankato, MN 56003 Fax: (507)345-4675

Format: Classic Rock; Music of Your Life. **Networks:** Minnesota News; Satellite Music Network. **Owner:** Ingstad Mankato Inc., at above address. **Founded:** 1948. **Operating Hours:** Continuous. **ADI:** Mankato, MN. **Key Personnel:** Jo Guck Bailey, General Mgr.; Mary Kay Degrood, Sales Mgr.; Jim Winston, News Dir.; Terry Cooley, Program Dir.; Joel Koetke, Promotions/Asst. Prog. Dir. **Wattage:** 1000. **Ad Rates:** $18 for 30 seconds; $25 for 60 seconds.

16292 KYSM-FM - 103.5
1807 Lee Blvd. Phone: (507)388-2900
North Mankato, MN 56003 Fax: (507)345-4675

Format: Hot Country. **Networks:** Westwood One Radio. **Owner:** Ingstad Mankato Inc., at above address. **Founded:** 1948. **Operating Hours:** Continuous. **ADI:** Mankato, MN. **Key Personnel:** Jo Guck Bailey, General Mgr., jgbmedia@i.c.mankato.mnusa; Mary Kay Degrood, Sales Mgr.; Jim Winston, News Dir.; Terry Cooley, Program Dir. **Wattage:** 100,000. **Ad Rates:** $35 for 30 seconds; $50 for 60 seconds. Combined advertising rates available with KXLP-FM & KYSM-AM.

NORTH ST. PAUL

16293 East Side Review
Lillie Suburban Newspapers
2515 7th Ave. East Phone: (612)777-8800
North St. Paul, MN 55109 Fax: (612)777-8288

Community newspaper. **Founded:** 1984. **Freq:** Weekly (Mon.). **Print Method:** Offset. **Cols./Page:** 6. **Col. Width:** 21 nonpareils. **Col. Depth:** 294 agate lines. **Key Personnel:** Mary Lee Hagert, Managing Editor; N. T. Lillie, Publisher; Jeffery Enright, Publisher; Mark Beckstrom, Advertising Mgr.; Pat Colburn, Circulation Mgr.; Amy Sherman, Editor. **Subscription Rates:** Free. **Remarks:** Accepts advertising.
Ad Rates: BW: $1,134 **Circ:** Free 20,128
SAU: $13.70
PCI: $12.45

16294 Lillie Suburban Shopping Review
Lillie Suburban Newspapers
2515 E. 7th Ave. Phone: (612)777-8800
North St. Paul, MN 55109 Fax: (612)777-8288

Area shopper. **Freq:** Weekly (Mon.). **Print Method:** Offset. **Trim Size:** Broadsheet. **Cols./Page:** 6. **Col. Width:** 21 nonpareils. **Col. Depth:** 294 agate lines. **Key Personnel:** Mary Lee Hagert, Managing Editor; N.T. Lillie, Publisher; Jeffery R. Enright, Publisher; Mark Beckstrom, Advertising Mgr.; Pat Colburn, Circulation Mgr. **Subscription Rates:** Free. **Remarks:** Accepts advertising.
Ad Rates: SAU: $22.70 **Circ:** Mon. 23,353

16295 Maplewood Review
Lillie Suburban Newspapers
2515 E. 7th Ave. Phone: (612)777-8800
North St. Paul, MN 55109 Fax: (612)777-8288

Local newspaper. **Founded:** 1920. **Freq:** Weekly (Wed.). **Print Method:** Offset. Uses mats. **Trim Size:** Broadsheet. **Cols./Page:** 6. **Col. Width:** 21 nonpareils. **Col. Depth:** 294 agate lines. **Key Personnel:** Mary Lee Hagert, Managing Editor; N. T. Lillie, Publisher; Jeffery Enright, Publisher; Mark Beckstrom, Advertising Mgr.; Pat Colburn, Circulation Mgr.; Holly Wenzel, Editor. **Subscription Rates:** $19.95. **Remarks:** Accepts advertising.
Ad Rates: SAU: $22.70 **Circ:** Paid 1,077
Free 192

16296 Oakdale-Lake Elmo Review
Lillie Suburban Newspapers
2515 E. 7th Ave. Phone: (612)777-8800
North St. Paul, MN 55109 Fax: (612)777-8288

Local newspaper. **Founded:** 1920. **Freq:** Weekly (Wed.). **Print Method:** Offset. Uses mats. **Trim Size:** Broadsheet. **Cols./Page:** 6. **Col. Width:** 21 nonpareils. **Col. Depth:** 294 agate lines. **Key Personnel:** Mary Lee Hagert, Managing Editor; N. T. Lillie, Publisher; Jeffery Enright, Publisher; Mark Beckstrom, Advertising Mgr.; Pat Colburn, Circulation Mgr.; Holly Wenzel, Editor. **Subscription Rates:** $19.95. **Remarks:** Accepts advertising. **Formerly:** Washington County Review.
Ad Rates: SAU: $22.70 **Circ:** Paid 910
Free 128

16297 Ramsey County Review
Lillie Suburban Newspapers
2515 E. 7th Ave. Phone: (612)777-8800
North St. Paul, MN 55109 Fax: (612)777-8288

Local newspaper. **Founded:** 1920. **Freq:** Weekly (Wed.). **Print Method:** Offset. **Trim Size:** Broadsheet. **Cols./Page:** 6. **Col. Width:** 21 nonpareils. **Col. Depth:** 294 agate lines. **Key Personnel:** Jeffery Enright, Publisher; N.T. Lillie, Publisher; Mary Lee Hagert, Managing Editor; Mark Beckstrom, Advertising Mgr.; Pat Colburn, Circulation Mgr.; Holly Wenzel, Editor. **Subscription Rates:** $19.95. **Remarks:** Accepts advertising.
Ad Rates: SAU: $22.70 **Circ:** Wed. 1,335

16298 Roseville Review
Lillie Suburban Newspapers
2515 E. 7th Ave. Phone: (612)777-8800
North St. Paul, MN 55109 Fax: (612)777-8288

Local newspaper. **Founded:** 1973. **Freq:** Weekly (Tues.). **Print Method:** Offset. Uses mats. **Trim Size:** Broadsheet. **Cols./Page:** 6. **Col. Width:** 21 nonpareils. **Col. Depth:** 294 agate lines. **Key Personnel:** Mary Lee Hagert, Managing Editor; N. T. Lillie, Publisher; Jeffery Enright, Publisher; Mark Beckstrom, Advertising Mgr.; Pat Colburn, Circulation Mgr.; Amelia Swisher, Editor. **Remarks:** Accepts advertising.
Ad Rates: SAU: $14 **Circ:** Free 15,866

16299 South-West Review
Lillie Suburban Newspapers
2515 E. 7th Ave. Phone: (612)777-8800
North St. Paul, MN 55109 Fax: (612)777-8288

Community newspaper. **Founded:** 1977. **Freq:** Weekly (Sun.). **Print Method:** Offset. **Trim Size:** Broadsheet. **Cols./Page:** 6. **Col. Width:** 21 nonpareils. **Col. Depth:** 294 agate lines. **Key Personnel:** Mary Lee Hagert, Managing Editor; N. T. Lillie, Publisher; Jeffery Enright, Publisher; Mark Beckstrom, Advertising Mgr.; Pat Colburn, Circulation Mgr.; Brian Darsow, Editor. **Subscription Rates:** Free. **Remarks:** Accepts advertising.
Ad Rates: SAU: $18 **Circ:** Free 23,389

16300 Woodbury-South Maplewood Review
Lillie Suburban Newspapers
2515 E. 7th Ave. Phone: (612)777-8800
North St. Paul, MN 55109 Fax: (612)777-8288

Community newspaper. **Founded:** 1980. **Freq:** Weekly (Mon.). **Print Method:** Offset. **Trim Size:** Broadsheet. **Cols./Page:** 6. **Col. Width:** 21 nonpareils. **Col. Depth:** 294 agate lines. **Key Personnel:** Mary Lee Hagert, Managing Editor; N. T. Lillie, Publisher; Jeffery Enright, Publisher; Mark Beckstrom, Adv. Editor & Adv. Mgr.; Pat Colburn, Circulation Mgr.; Brad Bromley, Editor. **Subscription Rates:** Free. **Remarks:** Accepts advertising.
Ad Rates: SAU: $8.80 **Circ:** Free 12,674

NORTHFIELD, pop. 12,562.

SE MN. Rice Co. 30 mi. S. of Minneapolis. Carleton College; St. Olaf College. Manufactures woodworking machinery, cereal, snack foods, spiral freezing, building products, plastic fabrication of industrial laminates & flexible circuitry, conveyor systems. Agricultural crop research. Dairy, stock, poultry, grain farms.

16301 The Carletonian
Carleton College
300 N. College St. Phone: (507)646-4158
Northfield, MN 55057 Fax: (507)646-4146
Publication E-mail: carletonian@carleton.edu

Student newspaper. **Founded:** 1877. **Freq:** Weekly. **Cols./Page:** 6. **Col. Width:** 2 1/8 inches. **Col. Depth:** 21 inches. **Key Personnel:** Kate Gratiot, Contact. **Subscription Rates:** $38. **Remarks:** Accepts advertising. **Available Online. URL:** http://www.carletonian.carleton.edu.
Ad Rates: BW: $300 **Circ:** Paid 500
PCI: $5 Non-paid 2,500

16302 Manitou Messenger
St. Olaf College
1520 St. Olaf Ave. Phone: (507)646-3275
Northfield, MN 55057-1098 Fax: (507)663-3549

Collegiate newspaper. **Founded:** 1887. **Freq:** Weekly (Fri.). **Print Method:** Offset. Broadsheet. **Cols./Page:** 6. **Col. Depth:** 21 inches. **Key Personnel:** Jean Edhlund, Editor, edhlund@stolaf.edu; Melanie Margolis, Editor; Sara Nymo, Business Mgr.; Adrianne Morse, Ad Sales. **Subscription Rates:** $20. **Remarks:** Accepts advertising.
Ad Rates: BW: $200 **Circ:** Free ‡3,800

16303 Northfield News
115 W. 5th St. Phone: (507)645-5615
PO Box 58 Fax: (507)645-6005
Northfield, MN 55057
Publication E-mail: webmaster@northfield.org

Community newspaper. **Founded:** 1876. **Freq:** Semiweekly. **Print Method:** Offset. **Trim Size:** 21 1/2 x 13. **Cols./Page:** 6. **Col. Width:** 28 nonpareils. **Col. Depth:** 300 agate lines. **Key Personnel:** Evelyn Hoover, Editor, editor@northfield.org; Rich Kleber, Publisher, kleber@northfield.org. **Subscription Rates:** $42. **URL:** http://www.northfield.org. **Alt. Formats:** CD-ROM.
Ad Rates: BW: $964.28 **Circ:** Paid 5,790
4C: $1,264.28 Free 375
SAU: $7.48

16304 Northfield Shopper
Northfield News
115 W. 5th St. Phone: (507)645-5615
PO Box 58 Fax: (507)645-6005
Northfield, MN 55057
Publication E-mail: kleber@northfield.org

Shopper. **Founded:** 1938. **Freq:** Weekly (Sun.). **Print Method:** Offset. **Trim Size:** 21 1/2 x 13. **Cols./Page:** 6. **Col. Width:** 26 nonpareils. **Col. Depth:** 294 agate lines. **Key Personnel:** Evelyn Hoover, Managing Editor, editor@northfield.org; Susan Stewart, Advertising Mgr., advertising@northfield.org; Rich Kleber, Publisher, kleber@northfield.org. **Subscription Rates:** Free. **Remarks:** Accepts advertising. **Alt. Formats:** CD-ROM.
Ad Rates: GLR: $.29 **Circ:** Free 12,000
BW: $999.75
4C: $1,249.95
SAU: $7.75

16305 Norwegian-American Studies
Norwegian-American Historical Association (NAHA)
St. Olaf College Library Phone: (507)646-3221
1510 St. Olaf Ave. Fax: (507)646-3734
Northfield, MN 55057
Publisher E-mail: naha@stolaf.edu

Journal covering Norwegian-American life. **Founded:** 1926. **Freq:** Irregular. **Remarks:** Advertising not accepted.
Circ: (Not Reported)

16306 KYMN-AM - 1080
1985 320th St. W. Phone: (507)645-5695
Northfield, MN 55057 Fax: (507)645-9768
E-mail: kymnradio@aol.com

Format: Adult Contemporary; News; Sports. **Networks:** NBC; Mutual Broadcasting System; Motor Racing. **Owner:** KYMN, Inc., at above address. **Founded:** 1968. **Operating Hours:** Sunrise-sunset. **Key Personnel:** Wayne T. Eddy, President/Gen. Mgr.; Roger O'Day, News Dir.; Bob Matheson, Sales Mgr.; Rich Harris, Program Dir.; Jeff Johnson, Sports Dir.; Christian Dady, Music Dir. **Local Programs:** *Community Rpt.*, Roger O'Day; *Tuesday Talk*, Rich Harris, Producer; *Wayne Eddy Affair*. **Wattage:** 1000. **Ad Rates:** $8-18 for 30 seconds; $11.50-22.00 for 60 seconds. **URL:** http://www.kymn.com.

16307 WCAL-FM - 89.3
1520 St. Olaf Ave. Phone: (612)798-9225
Northfield, MN 55057 Fax: (612)798-8614
Free: (888)798-9225
E-mail: wcal@stolaf.edu

Format: Public Radio; Classical. **Networks:** National Public Radio (NPR). **Owner:** St. Olaf College, at above address. **Founded:** 1918. **Operating Hours:** Continuous; 67% network, 33% local. **Key Personnel:** Tom Nelson, Chief Engineer; Stephen Davis, Announcer/Producer; Melissa Ousley, Announcer/Producer; Steve Staruch, Announcer/Producer; Heather Ferguson, Operations Mgr.; Paul Peterson, Manager; Paul Krause, Business Mgr.; Marty Pelikan, Program Dir.; Sarah Entenmann, Promotions Dir.; Deborah Ward, Membership Dir. **Local Programs:** *Sing of Joy*, Paul Krause, Mailing contact, (612)798-8603; *Top of the Day*, Marty Pelikan, Mailing contact, (612)798-8608; *Weekend Notes*, Stephen Davis, Mailing contact, (612)798-8613. **Wattage:** 100,000. **Ad Rates:** Noncommercial.

NORWOOD, pop. 1,219.

SC MN. Carver Co. 40 mi. SW of Minneapolis. Manufactures dairy products, cheese. Grain, dairy, stock, poultry farms. Corn, oats, hay. soybeans.

16308 Norwood-Young America Times
Berreth Publications
Box 67 Phone: (612)467-2271
Norwood, MN 55368 Fax: (612)467-2294

Local newspaper. **Founded:** 1890. **Freq:** Weekly. **Cols./Page:** 12. **Col. Width:** 12 picas. **Col. Depth:** 21 inches. **Key Personnel:** Tim Larson, Editor; James Berreth, Publisher. **Subscription Rates:** $16. **Remarks:** Accepts advertising.
Ad Rates: PCI: $2.82 **Circ:** Paid ‡2,272
Free ‡138

OKLEE, pop. 536.

NW MN. Red Lake Co. 80 mi. NE of Fargo, ND. Creamery; Elevators. Agriculture. Sweet clover seed, flax, oats.

16309 The Oklee Herald
PO Box 9 Phone: (218)796-5181
Oklee, MN 56742 Fax: (218)487-5252

Community newspaper. **Founded:** 1914. **Freq:** Weekly (Wed.). **Print Method:** Offset. **Trim Size:** 11 x 17. **Cols./Page:** 6. **Col. Width:** 20 nonpareils. **Col. Depth:** 224 agate lines. **Key Personnel:** Marilyn Whyte, Editor; Dick Richards, Publisher. **Subscription Rates:** $15; $20 out of county. **Remarks:** Accepts advertising. **Available Online.**
Ad Rates: SAU: $2.90 **Circ:** (Not Reported)
PCI: $2

OLIVIA†, pop. 2,802.

SW MN. Renville Co. 100 mi. W. of Minneapolis. Manufactures plastic binders, concrete products, sunflower seeds, fiberglass shower stalls, custom welding products. Hatcheries. Dairy, stock, poultry, grain farms. Corn, beets, flax, oats, soybeans.

16310 Olivia Times-Journal
Renco Publishing, Inc.
816 E. Lincoln Phone: (320)523-2032
Olivia, MN 56277 Fax: (320)523-2033

Newspaper. **Founded:** 1872. **Freq:** Weekly (Mon.). **Print Method:** Offset. **Cols./Page:** 7. **Col. Width:** 28 nonpareils. **Col. Depth:** 301 agate lines. **Key Personnel:** Heather Thompson, Editor, otj@re.rencopub.com; Rose Hettig, Publisher. **Subscription Rates:** $28 individuals. **Alt. Formats:** CD-ROM, Claris; CD-ROM, Quark Express Documents.
Ad Rates: GLR: $5.29 **Circ:** Paid ‡1,300
BW: $796.15 Non-paid ‡445

ORTONVILLE†, pop. 2,550.

WC MN. Big Stone Co. On Big Stone Lake, 124 mi. S. of Fargo, ND. Manufactures monuments, cheese, butter; canned corn. Summer resort. Granite quarries. Dairy, grain, stock farms.

16311 The Ortonville Independent
Kaercher Publications
Box 336 Phone: (320)839-6163
Ortonville, MN 56278 Fax: (320)839-3761

Community newspaper. **Subtitle:** Ortonville Independent. **Founded:** 1920. **Freq:** Weekly (Tues.). **Print Method:** Letterpress and offset. **Trim Size:** 13 3/4 x 21 1/2. **Cols./Page:** 6. **Col. Width:** 26 nonpareils. **Col. Depth:** 301 agate lines. **Key Personnel:** James D. Kaercher, Editor and Publisher; Suzette Kaercher, Editor. **ISSN:** 4108-3226. **Subscription Rates:** $25; $33 other. **Remarks:** Accepts advertising.
Ad Rates: BW: $400 **Circ:** ‡3,650
4C: $800
SAU: $5
PCI: $5.50

16312 KDIO-AM - 1350
264 Rte. One Phone: (612)839-2581
Ortonville, MN 56278

Format: Talk; News; Sports; Agricultural. **Networks:** CBS; Linder Farm. **Owner:** Donald P. Egert, at above address. **Founded:** 1956. **Operating Hours:** 6 a.m.-8 p.m.; 10% network, 90% local. **ADI:** Minneapolis-St. Paul, MN. **Key Personnel:** Donald P. Egert, President; James R. Egert, General Mgr. **Wattage:** 1000. **Ad Rates:** $4.25-6.25 for 30 seconds; $6.35-8.90 for 60 seconds.

OSAKIS, pop. 1,267.

WC MN. Douglas and Todd Co's. 10 mi. SE of Alexandria.

16313 KBHL-FM - 103.9
PO Box 247 Phone: (612)859-3000
Osakis, MN 56360 Fax: (612)859-3010

Format: Religious. **Networks:** Moody Broadcasting; SkyLight Satellite. **Founded:** 1985. **Operating Hours:** Continuous; 40% network, 60% local. **Key Personnel:** David McIver, Program Dir.; Ivan Tesch, Operations Dir.; Todd Atwater, News Dir.; Pat Brueske, Music Dir. **Wattage:** 6,000. **Ad Rates:** Noncommercial.

OSSEO, pop. 2,974.

SE MN. Hennepin Co. 25 mi. N. of Minnetonka. Agriculture, feed mill.

Champlin Dayton Press - See Champlin

16314 Delano Eagle
Larson Publications, Inc.
33 2nd St. NE Phone: (612)425-3323
Box 280 Fax: (612)425-1360
Osseo, MN 55369
Community newspaper. **Freq:** Weekly. **Print Method:** Offset. **Cols./Page:** 7. **Col. Width:** 2 inches. **Col. Depth:** 294 agate lines. **Key Personnel:** Carole J. Larson, Editor; Don R. Larson, Publisher; Bruce Treichler, Advertising Mgr. **Subscription Rates:** Free; $20. **Remarks:** Accepts advertising. **URL:** pressnews@mr.net.
Circ: Paid 1,300
Free 1,051

16315 North Crow River News
Larson Publications, Inc.
33 2nd St. NE Phone: (612)425-3323
Box 280 Fax: (612)425-1360
Osseo, MN 55369
Publication E-mail: pressnews@mr.net

Community newspaper. **Founded:** 1962. **Freq:** Weekly (Mon.). **Print Method:** Offset. **Cols./Page:** 7. **Col. Width:** 2 inches. **Col. Depth:** 294 agate lines. **Key Personnel:** Carole J. Larson, Editor; Don R. Larson, Publisher; Bruce Treichler, Advertising Mgr. **Subscription Rates:** $24. **Remarks:** Accepts advertising.
Ad Rates: PCI: $14 **Circ:** Paid 2,500
Free 4,645

16316 Osseo-Maple Grove Press
Larson Publications, Inc.
33 2nd St. NE Phone: (612)425-3323
Box 280 Fax: (612)425-1360
Osseo, MN 55369
Community newspaper. **Founded:** 1922. **Freq:** Weekly (Wed.). **Print Method:** Offset. **Cols./Page:** 7. **Col. Width:** 2 inches. **Col. Depth:** 301 agate lines. **Key Personnel:** Carole Larson, Editor; Don R. Larson, Publisher; Bruce Treichler, Advertising Mgr. **Subscription Rates:** $26. **Remarks:** Accepts advertising. **URL:** pressnews@mr.net.
Ad Rates: PCI: $14 **Circ:** Paid 5,500
Free 11,285

16317 Rockford Area News Leader
Larson Publications, Inc.
33 2nd St. NE Phone: (612)425-3323
Box 280 Fax: (612)425-1360
Osseo, MN 55369
Community newspaper. **Founded:** 1982. **Freq:** Weekly (Mon.). **Print Method:** Offset. **Cols./Page:** 7. **Col. Width:** 2 1/16 inches. **Col. Depth:** 21 inches. **Key Personnel:** Bruce Treichler, Editor. **Subscription Rates:** $20. **Remarks:** Accepts advertising other Larson newspapers.
Circ: Paid ♦**501**

16318 South Crow River News
Larson Publications, Inc.
33 2nd St. NE Phone: (612)425-3323
Box 280 Fax: (612)425-1360
Osseo, MN 55369
Publication E-mail: pressnews@mr.net

Community newspaper. **Founded:** 1963. **Freq:** Weekly (Mon.). **Cols./Page:** 7. **Col. Width:** 2 inches. **Col. Depth:** 21 inches. **Key Personnel:** Carole Larson, Editor. **Subscription Rates:** $19. **Remarks:** Combined advertising rates available with other Larson newspapers.
Circ: Paid 1,200
Free 4,048

OWATONNA†, pop. 18,632.

SE MN. Steele Co. 15 mi. S. of Faribault. Pillsbury College. Manufactures jewelry, tools farm machinery, ventilating, testing forms, exerise equipment, butter, cement, tile, leather gloves, dried milk products, service tools for auto industry, beverages, band accessories, canned goods, tannery, glass lamination and tempering. Nurseries. Dairy. Agriculture, machinery, truck farms.

16319 North American Lily Society Quarterly
North American Lily Society, Inc.
PO Box 272 Phone: (507)451-2170
Owatonna, MN 55060 Fax: (507)455-0087
Publisher E-mail: gilman@ll.net

Publication covering horticultural issues on lilies for members. **Freq:** Quarterly. **Print Method:** Offset. **Subscription Rates:** Free to qualified subscribers; $20 /year; $55 /3 year. **Remarks:** Accepts advertising.
Ad Rates: BW: $100 **Circ:** Paid 1,500

16320 Owatonna Area Shopper
Huckle Publishing, Inc.
135 West Pearl Phone: (507)451-2840
Owatonna, MN 55060
Shopper. **Freq:** Weekly. **Cols./Page:** 4. **Col. Width:** 10 1/2 inches. **Col. Depth:** 12 1/2 inches. **Key Personnel:** Ron Ensley, Publisher, phone (507)451-2840. **Remarks:** Accepts advertising. **Formerly:** Owatonna Weekly Shopper.
Ad Rates: BW: $778 **Circ:** Free 14,500
4C: $978
PCI: $47

16321 Owatonna People's Press
Box 346 Phone: (507)451-2840
Owatonna, MN 55060-0346 Fax: (507)451-3282

General newspaper. **Founded:** 1874. **Freq:** Tues.-Sun. (morn.). **Print Method:** Offset. **Cols./Page:** 6. **Col. Width:** 2 1/16 inches. **Col. Depth:** 21 1/2 inches. **Key Personnel:** Ron Ensley, Publisher, phone (507)444-2367, rensley@owatonna.com; Grant Gross, Managing Editor, phone (507)444-2371; Holly Sobrack, Advertising Mgr., phone (507)444-2386. **ISSN:** 0890-2860. **Subscription Rates:** $110.
Ad Rates: BW: $1,451.25 **Circ:** Tues. 7,533
4C: $1,706.25 Sat. 7,533
SAU: $11.25 Sun. 7,730

PARK RAPIDS†, pop. 3,000.

SW MN. Hubbard Co. 40 mi. S. of Bemidji. Dairy farms.

16322 Park Rapids Enterprise
PO Box 111 Phone: (218)732-3364
Park Rapids, MN 56470 Fax: (218)732-8757

Community newspaper for Hubbard County. **Founded:** July 25, 1882. **Freq:** Semiweekly. **Print Method:** Offset. **Cols./Page:** 6. **Col. Width:** 13 3/4 inches. **Col. Depth:** 21 3/4 inches. **Key Personnel:** LuAnn Hurd-Lof, Editor; Dennis Winskowski, Publisher; Candy Parks, Advertising Mgr. **Subscription Rates:** $32 individuals; $47 out of area.
Ad Rates: BW: $928.80 **Circ:** Combined 5,767
4C: $1,198.80
PCI: $7.20

16323 KDKK-FM - 97.5
Box 49 Phone: (218)732-3306
Park Rapids, MN 56470 Fax: (218)732-3307
E-mail: kprmkdkk@unitelc.com

Format: News; Religious; Oldies; Easy Listening. **Simulcasts:** KPRM-AM. **Networks:** Jones Satellite; NBC; Music of Your Life/Fairwest. **Owner:** Ed De La Hunt, Jr., at above address, (218)732-4948. **Founded:** 1967. **Formerly:** KPRM-FM (1990). **Operating Hours:** 18.25 hours Daily; 80% network, 20% local. **Key Personnel:** Ed De La Hunt, Jr., Contact, phone (218)732-3306, fax (218)732-3307; Bernadine Schumacher, Station Mgr.; Dave De La Hunt, Sports Dir. **Local Programs:** *Coffeetime* 9:30 am - 10:00 am Mon. - Sat., Ed DelaHunt, Owner. **Wattage:** 100,000. **Ad Rates:** $6-8.25 for 15 seconds; $8-11 for 30 seconds; $10-13 for 60 seconds. Combined advertising rates available with KPRM-AM.

16324 KPRM-AM - 870
Box 49 Phone: (218)732-3306
Park Rapids, MN 56470 Fax: (218)732-3307

Format: Talk; News; Country; Contemporary Country; Religious; Agricultural. **Networks:** NBC; Mutual Broadcasting System. **Owner:** Ed De La Hunt, Jr., at above address. **Founded:** 1962. **Operating Hours:** 18.25 hours daily; 32% network, 68% local. **Key Personnel:** Ed De La Hunt, Jr., Contact; Bernadine Schumacher, Station Mgr.; David Delahunt, Chief Engineer; Carol Delahunt, Accounts Payable; Karen Lepenski, Traffic Mgr.; Dave Roberts, Air/News. **Local Programs:** *Coffeetime*, Ed De La Hunt; *Curiosity Time*, Bernie Schumacher. **Wattage:** 25,000. **Ad Rates:** $5-7 for 15 seconds; $8-20 for 30 seconds; $9-20 for 60 seconds.

PARKERS PRAIRIE

16325 Parkers Prairie Independent
117 N. Otter Ave. Phone: (218)338-2741
Parkers Prairie, MN 56361 Fax: (218)338-2741

Community newspaper. **Subtitle:** The Independent. **Founded:** 1902. **Freq:** Weekly (Wed.). **Print Method:** Offset. **Trim Size:** 22 3/4 x 16. **Cols./Page:** 6. **Col. Width:** 2 1/16 inches. **Col. Depth:** 21 1/2 inches. **Key Personnel:** Thomas Myers, Editor and Publisher; Shryl Kimners, Publisher. **USPS:** 260-760. **Subscription Rates:** $15, $17, $19 out of country. **Remarks:** Accepts advertising.
Ad Rates: BW: $376.25 **Circ:** 1,800
SAU: $2.50
PCI: $2.50

16326 Data Video Systems Inc.
222 Clayborn Ave. S Phone: (218)338-4000
PO Box 45 Fax: (218)338-3297
Parkers Prairie, MN 56361
E-mail: allmis@parkersprairie.polaristel.net

Founded: 1983. **Key Personnel:** Geo M. Revering, Manager; Rodney Scheel, CEO; David Lehrke, Vice President; Mark Roach, Controller. **Cities Served:** Eagle Bend, Miltona, Parkers Prairie, Urbank, MN: subscribing households 606; 27 channels; 2 community access channels; 10 hours per week community access programming.

PELICAN RAPIDS, pop. 1,867.

WC MN. Otter Tail Co. On Pelican River, 40 mi. SE of Fargo, ND. Resort. Modular homes manufactured; turkey processing plants. Dairy, poultry, stock, grain farms.

16327 Pelican Rapids Press
29 W. Mill Phone: (218)863-1421
Box L Fax: (218)863-1423
Pelican Rapids, MN 56572-0632
Local newspaper. **Founded:** 1897. **Freq:** Weekly (Wed.). **Print Method:** Offset. **Cols./Page:** 6. **Col. Width:** 27 nonpareils. **Col. Depth:** 301 agate lines. **Key Personnel:** Gary E. Peterson, Editor and Publisher; Richard E. Peterson, Publisher. **USPS:** 424-960. **Subscription Rates:** $17 individuals; $22 out of area. **Remarks:** Accepts advertising.
Ad Rates: SAU: $5.25 **Circ:** Paid 3,369
PCI: $5.25 Free 26

PEQUOT LAKES, pop. 681.

C MN. Crow Wing Co. 40 mi. NE of Wadena.

16328 Echoland Shopper
Echo Publishing & Printing, Inc.
PO Box 240 Phone: (218)568-8521
Pequot Lakes, MN 56472 Fax: (218)568-5407
Free: (800)450-8521
Publisher E-mail: echonews@uslink.net

Shopper. **Founded:** 1975. **Freq:** Weekly. **Print Method:** Offset. **Trim Size:** 11 1/2 x 16. **Cols./Page:** 6. **Col. Width:** 21 nonpareils. **Col. Depth:** 210 agate lines. **Key Personnel:** Peter Anderson, Editor. **Remarks:** Accepts advertising. **Feature Editors:** Betty Ryan, *Travel*, phone (218)568-7317.
Ad Rates: GLR: $4.50 **Circ:** Free ‡22,373
BW: $544.50
4C: $644.50
SAU: $7.88
PCI: $7.88

16329 KTIG-FM - 102.7
Box 409 Phone: (218)568-4422
Pequot Lakes, MN 56472 Fax: (218)568-5950
E-mail: radio@ktig.org

Format: Religious. **Networks:** Moody Broadcasting; Ambassador Inspirational Radio; Sun Radio. **Owner:** Minnesota Christian Broadcasters, Inc., at above address. **Founded:** 1978. **Operating Hours:** Continuous; 33.5% network, 66.5% local. **Key Personnel:** Mike Heuberger, General Mgr., mike@ktig.org; Chuck Heaberger, Program Dir., chuck@ktig.org. **Local Programs:** *Heartland*, Tom Bonar, (218)568-4422, Fax (218)568-5950; *Rise and Shine*, Mike Heuberger; *Touch of Tradition*, Marietta Heuberger. **Wattage:** 50,000. **Ad Rates:** Noncommercial.

PERHAM, pop. 2,086.

WC MN. Otter Tail Co. 22 mi. NW of Wadena. Feed mills. Manufactures dog food, dried milk; poultry products processing plants. Creamery. Greenhouse. Resort. Stock, dairy, poultry farms. Potatoes, corn, small grains.

16330 Contact
PO Box 288 Phone: (218)346-5900
Perham, MN 56573 Fax: (218)346-5901
Publication E-mail: perhameb@eot.com

Shopper. **Freq:** Weekly (Sun.). **Print Method:** Offset. **Trim Size:** 15 1/4 x 21 1/2. **Cols./Page:** 7. **Col. Width:** 26 nonpareils. **Col. Depth:** 294 agate lines. **Key Personnel:** Jim Arno, General Mgr., jimarno@cot.com; Michael Parta, Publisher. **Subscription Rates:** $22; $24 out of area; $26 out of state. **Remarks:** Color advertising accepted; rates available upon request.
Ad Rates: GLR: $.41 **Circ:** Free 10,000
4C: $70
PCI: $6.65

16331 Perham Enterprise Bulletin
Box 288 Phone: (218)346-5900
Perham, MN 56573 Fax: (218)346-5901
Publication E-mail: perhameb@eot.com

Community newspaper. **Founded:** 1882. **Freq:** Weekly (Thurs.). **Print Method:** Offset. **Cols./Page:** 7. **Col. Width:** 26 nonpareils. **Col. Depth:** 294 agate lines. **Key Personnel:** Charles Johnson, Editor; Michael Parta, Publisher; James Arno, Manager, jimarno@eot.com. **Subscription Rates:** $22; $24 out of area; $26 out of state. **Remarks:** Accepts advertising.
Ad Rates: SAU: $5.65 **Circ:** 3450

16332 Tekstar Cablevision Inc.
150 2nd Ave. SW Phone: (218)346-2288
Perham, MN 56573 Fax: (218)346-5544
Free: (800)262-0414

Owner: Arvig Enterprises, Inc., at above address, (248)346-5500. **Founded:** 1986. **Formerly:** Lakeland Cablevision (1986); Town & Country Video. **Key Personnel:** David Pratt, General Mgr., dpratt@arvig.com; James Walter, Chief Technician, jwalter@arvig.com. **Cities Served:** subscribing households 16,100; 36 channels; 1 community access channel.

PINE CITY†, pop. 2,489.

EC MN. Pine Co. 65 mi. N. of Saint Paul. Manufactures computer components, wood stoves, soft drinks, recreational vehicles. Dairy, poultry, grain farms. Corn, hay, oats.

16333 Pine City Pioneer
405 E. 2nd Ave Phone: (320)629-6771
Pine City, MN 55063 Fax: (320)629-6772
Publication E-mail: pioneer@pinenet.com
Publisher E-mail: pioneer@pinecitymn.com

Community newspaper. **Founded:** 1885. **Freq:** Weekly (Thurs.). **Print Method:** Offset. **Cols./Page:** 6. **Col. Width:** 26 nonpareils. **Col. Depth:** 294 agate lines. **Key Personnel:** Cindy Rolain, Editor. **Subscription Rates:** $24. **Remarks:** Accepts advertising. **Formerly:** Pioneer (1990).
Ad Rates: BW: $395 **Circ:** ‡3,532
SAU: $5.45
PCI: $5.50

16334 WCMP-AM - 1350
RR 2 Phone: (320)629-7575
Pine City, MN 55063 Fax: (320)629-3933

Format: Full Service; Middle-of-the-Road (MOR). **Networks:** ABC. **Owner:** Patty McNulty, at above address. **Founded:** 1957. **Operating Hours:** 6 a.m.-midnight; 10% network, 90% local. **Key Personnel:** Sam Countoy, News Dir.; Mike Hughes, Operations Mgr.; Jim Erickson, Sports Dir.; Dave Chmiel, General Sales Mgr. **Wattage:** 1000. **Ad Rates:** $9.96-12.83 for 30 seconds; $13-18.59 for 60 seconds.

16335 WCMP-FM - 100.9
RR 2 Phone: (320)629-7575
Pine City, MN 55063 Fax: (320)629-3933

Format: Contemporary Country. **Networks:** ABC. **Owner:** Patty McNulty, at above address. **Founded:** 1978. **Operating Hours:** Continuous; 5% network, 95% local. **Key Personnel:** Dave Chmiel, General Sales Mgr.; Mike Hughes, Operations Mgr.; Jim Erickson, Sports Dir.; Sam Country, News Dir. **Wattage:** 25,000. **Ad Rates:** $10-13 for 30 seconds; $13-19 for 60 seconds.

PINE ISLAND, pop. 1,986.

SE MN. Goodhue Co. 15 mi. NW of Rochester.

16336 Kumquat Meringue
Penumbra Press
PO Box 736 Phone: (507)367-4430
Pine Island, MN 55963
Publisher E-mail: moodyriver@aol.com

Literary magazine featuring poetry. **Subtitle:** Dedicated to the Memory of Richard Brautigan. **Founded:** Apr. 1991. **Freq:** Irregular. **Print Method:** Litho. **Key Personnel:** Christian Nelson, Editor and Publisher. **Subscription Rates:** $5 single issue. **Remarks:** Advertising not accepted. **URL:** http://www.geostar.com/kumquatcastle.
Circ: Paid 600

16337 Pine Island Telephone Co.
Box 588 Phone: (507)356-8302
Pine Island, MN 55963 Fax: (507)356-4001

Founded: 1982. **Key Personnel:** Richard Keane, Manager. **Cities Served:** subscribing households 944; 25 channels; 1 community access channel.

PINE RIVER, pop. 881.

NC MN. Cass Co. 30 mi. N. of Brainerd. Lake Resort. Manufactures reels, wood products, timber. Sawmill. Dairy.

16338 Pine River Journal
215 Norway Ave. Phone: (218)587-2360
Box 370 Fax: (218)587-2331
Pine River, MN 56474
Publication E-mail: echonews@uslink.net

Community newspaper. **Founded:** 1935. **Freq:** Weekly (Thurs.). **Print Method:** Offset. **Cols./Page:** 6. **Col. Width:** 9 1/2 picas. **Col. Depth:** 210 agate lines. **Key Personnel:** Louis Hoglund, Editor, phone (218)568-8521, fax (218)568-5407; Peter Anderson, Publisher. **Subscription Rates:** $24. **Remarks:** Accepts advertising. **Available Online. URL:** http://www.uslink.net~echonews.
Ad Rates: GLR: $2 **Circ:** ‡2,410
BW: $436.50
4C: $706.50
SAU: $6.32
PCI: $4.85

PIPESTONE†, pop. 4,887.

SW MN. Pipestone Co. 42 mi. NE of Sioux Falls SD. Light manufacturing. Stock, dairy, poultry, grain farms.

16339 The Civil War Lady
622 Third Ave., SW
Pipestone, MN 56164

Journal covering Victorian era history, clothing, and social history. **Founded:** 1994. **Freq:** Quarterly. **Print Method:** Offset. **Key Personnel:** Joy Melcher, Editor-in-Chief. **Subscription Rates:** $21 individuals; $4 single issue. **Remarks:** Accepts advertising.
Circ: (Not Reported)

16340 Pipestone County Star
Pipestone Publishing Co.
101 2nd St. NE Phone: (507)825-3333
Box 277 Fax: (507)825-2168
Pipestone, MN 56164-0277
Publisher E-mail: pipepub@pipestonestar.com

Community newspaper. **Founded:** 1879. **Freq:** Weekly (Thurs.). **Print Method:** Offset. **Trim Size:** 16 x 22 3/4. **Cols./Page:** 7. **Col. Width:** 2 1/16 inches. **Col. Depth:** 301 agate lines. **Key Personnel:** Charles Draper, Editor and Publisher, cdvaper@pipestonestar.com; Ray Fuder, Advertising Mgr. **USPS:** 433-940. **Subscription Rates:** $28. **Remarks:** Accepts advertising.
Ad Rates: BW: $820.23 **Circ:** Paid 3,714
4C: $1,060.55 Non-paid 99
SAU: $5.10

16341 KISD-FM - 98.7
Box 456 Phone: (507)825-4282
Pipestone, MN 56164 Fax: (507)825-3364

Format: Oldies. **Networks:** Satellite Music Network. **Owner:** Wallace Christensen Broadcasting, at above address. **Founded:** 1968. **Operating Hours:** Continuous. **Key Personnel:** Bernie Wieme, Music Dir. **Wattage:** 100,000. **Ad Rates:** $5-10 for 30 seconds; $8-18 for 60 seconds.

16342 KLOH-AM - 1050
W. Hwy. 30 Phone: (507)825-4282
PO Box 456 Fax: (507)825-3364
Pipestone, MN 56164

Format: Full Service; Country; Agricultural; Information. **Networks:** ABC; Satellite Music Network. **Owner:** Wallace Christensen Broadcasting, at above address. **Founded:** 1955. **Operating Hours:** Continuous. **Key Personnel:** Diane Carlson, News Dir.; Steve Collins, Sports Dir.; Mylan Ray, Music Dir. **Wattage:** 9000. **Ad Rates:** $5-10 for 30 seconds; $8-18 for 60 seconds.

PLAINVIEW, pop. 2,416.

SE MN. Watasha Co. 10 mi. NE of Rochester. Creamery; cannery. Grain, dairy, poultry, beef cattle farms.

16343 Plainview News
Mack Publishing Co.
409 W. Broadway, No. 457 Phone: (507)534-3121
Plainview, MN 55964-0457 Fax: (507)534-3920

Community newspaper. **Founded:** 1874. **Freq:** Weekly (Tues.). **Print Method:** Offset. **Cols./Page:** 6. **Col. Width:** 28 nonpareils. **Col. Depth:** 301 agate lines. **Key Personnel:** Timothy Mack, Publisher; Janet M. Mack, Editor and Administration. **Subscription Rates:** $12.50. **Remarks:** Accepts advertising.
Ad Rates: GLR: $.23 **Circ:** 3,380

PLYMOUTH, pop. 31,615.

SE MN. Hennepin Co. NW of Minneapolis.

16344 The Inside Line
ARK Media
3030 Harbor Ln. N., No. 131 Phone: (612)551-1915
Plymouth, MN 55447 Fax: (612)551-0449
Publication E-mail: asitze@insideline.com

Trade magazine for buyers, engineers, and managers in the electronics industry. **Founded:** Jan. 1988. **Freq:** 10/year. **Print Method:** Web offset. **Trim Size:** 10 x 13. **Cols./Page:** 4. **Key Personnel:** Amy Sitze, Editor; Alice Tanghe, Publisher. **Subscription Rates:** Free to qualified subscribers. **Remarks:** Accepts advertising. **URL:** http://www.insideline.com.
Circ: Non-paid 42,000

16345 Plymouth Wayzata, Orono, Long Lake Sun-Sailor
Minnesota Sun Publications
7831 E. Bush Lake Rd. Phone: (612)896-4700
Bloomington, MN 55439 Fax: (612)896-4728

Community newspaper (tabloid). **Founded:** 1974. **Freq:** Weekly (Wed.). **Print Method:** Offset. **Cols./Page:** 4. **Col. Width:** 2 1/2 inches. **Col. Depth:** 15 inches. **Key Personnel:** Don Thurlow, Publisher; Paul Johnson, Advertising Director. **Formerly:** Plymouth Post.
Circ: Paid 17,965
Non-paid 14,204

16346 WCTS-AM - 1030
900 Forestview Ln. N. Phone: (612)529-1003
Plymouth, MN 55441-5934 Fax: (612)522-9663

Format: Religious. **Networks:** AP. **Owner:** Central Baptist Theological Seminary of Minneapolis, at above address. **Founded:** 1965. **Formerly:** WMIN-AM. **Operating Hours:** 5:30 a.m.-midnight. **ADI:** Minneapolis-St. Paul, MN. **Key Personnel:** Dr. Douglas R. McLachlan, President; Dennis Whithead, General Mgr., dwhitehead@wavefront.com; Jeff Werth, Announcer; Peter Silseth, News Dir.; John Goetz, Announcer. **Local Programs:** *Christianity in a Changing Culture*, Peter Silseth, Mailing contact. **Wattage:** 50,000. **Ad Rates:** Noncommercial.

PRESTON†, pop. 1,478.

SE MN. Fillmore Co. 37 mi. SE of Rochester. Manufactures butter, flour. Poultry dressing plant. Ships livestock. Hardwood timber. Diversified farming. Hogs, cattle, corn. Dairy farms.

16347 KFIL-AM - 1060
PO Box 370 Phone: (507)765-3856
Preston, MN 55965 Fax: (507)765-2738

Format: Contemporary Country. **Networks:** Mutual Broadcasting System. **Founded:** 1966. **Operating Hours:** 6 a.m.-sunset; 10% network, 90% local. **Key Personnel:** Michael Borgen, General Mgr.; Jeff Borgen, Sales Mgr.; Bruce Fishlaugher, Station Mgr.; Mike Sveen, Music Dir. **Wattage:** 1000. **Ad Rates:** $6.50-8 for 30 seconds; $8.35-10.50 for 60 seconds.

16348 KFIL-FM - 103.1
Box 370 Phone: (507)765-3856
Preston, MN 55965 Fax: (507)765-2738

Format: Country. **Networks:** Mutual Broadcasting System; Linder Farm. **Founded:** 1970. **Operating Hours:** Continuous. **Key Personnel:** Michael Borgen, General Mgr.; Jeff Borgen, Sales Mgr.; Bruce Fishaougher, Station Mgr. **Ad Rates:** $6.50-8.50 for 30 seconds; $8.35-10.50 for 60 seconds.

PRINCETON, pop. 3,146.

EC MN. Mille Lacs Co. 50 mi. NW of Minneapolis. Manufactures school furniture, custom cabinets. Auto parts rebuilding. Dairy, poultry farms. Potatoes, corn, rye.

16349 Princeton Union-Eagle
E.C.M. Publishers, Inc.
208 N. La Grande Ave. Phone: (612)389-1222
Princeton, MN 55371-0278 Fax: (612)389-1728
Free: (800)631-1222
Publication E-mail: editor.unioneagle@eem-inc.com

Community newspaper. **Founded:** 1876. **Freq:** Weekly (Thurs.). **Print Method:** Offset. **Cols./Page:** 6. **Col. Width:** 28 nonpareils. **Col. Depth:** 294 agate lines. **Key Personnel:** Luther Dorr, Editor; Julian L. Andersen, Publisher; Timothy J. Enger, Advertising Mgr., tim.enger@ecm-inc.com. **USPS:** 445-060. **Subscription Rates:** $30 individuals. **Remarks:** Accepts advertising.
Ad Rates: BW: $661.50 **Circ:** Paid 3,666
4C: $775 Free 70
SAU: $4
PCI: $5.25

16350 Town and Country Shopper
E.C.M. Publishers, Inc.
208 N. La Grande Ave. Phone: (612)389-1222
Princeton, MN 55371-0278 Fax: (612)389-1728
Free: (800)631-1222

Shopper. **Founded:** 1974. **Freq:** Weekly (Mon.). **Print Method:** Offset. **Trim Size:** 11 1/2 x 16. **Cols./Page:** 5. **Col. Width:** 61 picas. **Col. Depth:** 180 agate lines. **Key Personnel:** Timothy J. Enger, Editor/Administration; Julian L. Andersen, Publisher. **Subscription Rates:** Free. **Remarks:** Accepts advertising.
Ad Rates: GLR: $.53 **Circ:** Free ‡13,420
BW: $488 Free 12,098
4C: $650
SAU: $6
PCI: $6.50

16351 WQPM-AM - 1300
PO Box 106 Phone: (612)389-1300
Princeton, MN 55371 Fax: (612)389-1359
Free: (800)850-1061

Format: Contemporary Country. **Networks:** ABC. **Founded:** 1967. **Formerly:** WKPM-AM (1978). **Operating Hours:** Continuous.; 2% network, 98% local. **Key Personnel:** Paul Stagg, General Mgr.; Neil Freeman, Program Dir.; Susan Schmidgall, Sales Mgr.; Steve Koranda, Operations Mgr. **Wattage:** 1000. **Ad Rates:** Advertising accepted; rates available upon request.

16352 WQPM-FM - 106.1
PO Box 106 Phone: (612)389-1300
Princeton, MN 55371 Fax: (612)389-1359
Free: (800)850-1061

Format: Contemporary Country. **Networks:** ABC. **Founded:** 1992. **Operating Hours:** Continuous.; 2% network, 98% local. **ADI:** Minneapolis-St. Paul, MN. **Key Personnel:** Paul Stagg, Owner; Neil Freeman, Program Dir.; Susan Schmidgall, Owner/Manager; Steve Koranda, Operations Dir. **Wattage:** 50,000. **Ad Rates:** Advertising accepted; rates available upon request.

PRIOR LAKE, pop. 7,284.

SE MN. Scott Co. 7 mi. SE of Shakopee. Residential. Manufactures cabinets, machine parts, signs.

16353 Prior Lake American
Southwest Suburban Publishing
PO Box 538 Phone: (612)447-6669
Prior Lake, MN 55372 Fax: (612)447-6671

Local newspaper. **Founded:** 1960. **Freq:** Weekly (Sat.). **Print Method:** Offset. **Trim Size:** 13 x 21 1/2. **Cols./Page:** 6. **Col. Width:** 2 inches. **Col. Depth:** 21 1/2 inches. **Key Personnel:** Jim Riccioli, Editor; Laurie Hartmann, Publisher; Gary Klatt, Advertising Dir. **Subscription Rates:** $25 out of area; $20 individuals. **Remarks:** Accepts advertising.
Ad Rates: BW: $1,070.70 **Circ:** ⊕**7,300**
4C: $1,445.70
SAU: $7.92
PCI: $9.20

PROCTOR, pop. 3,500.

NE MN. St. Louis Co. 10 mi. W. of Duluth. Tourist attractions. Iron ore sorting yard. Dairy, truck farms.

16354 Proctor Journal
215 5th St. Phone: (218)624-3344
Proctor, MN 55810 Fax: (218)624-7037
Publication E-mail: pjournal@cp.duluth.mn.us

Newspaper. **Founded:** 1906. **Freq:** Weekly (Thurs.). **Print Method:** Web offset. **Cols./Page:** 5. **Col. Width:** 22 nonpareils. **Col. Depth:** 210 agate lines. **Key Personnel:** Jake P.

Benson, Editor and Publisher. **USPS:** 445-800. **Subscription Rates:** $25 individuals. **Remarks:** Accepts advertising.
Ad Rates: SAU: $4 **Circ:** Paid 1,950
PCI: $5.10 Free 50

RAYMOND, pop. 723.

SW MN. Kardiyohi Co. 85 mi. NW of Minneapolis. Residential.

16355 The Raymond-Prinsburg News
204 Spicer Ave. Phone: (320)967-4244
PO Box 157 Fax: (320)967-4244
Raymond, MN 56282
Community newspaper. **Founded:** 1900. **Freq:** Weekly (Wed.). **Print Method:** Offset. **Trim Size:** 13 1/2 x 21 1/2. **Cols./Page:** 6. **Col. Width:** 2 1/8 inches. **Col. Depth:** 301 agate lines. **Key Personnel:** Ted Almen, Publisher. **USPS:** 456-000. **Subscription Rates:** $18; $22 out of area; $24 out of state. **Remarks:** Advertising accepted; rates available upon request. **Formerly:** Raymond News.
Circ: ‡943

RED LAKE FALLS†, pop. 1,732.

NW MN. Red Lake Co. 48 mi. E. pf Grand Forks, ND. Mobile homes manufactured. Diversified farming. Wheat, livestock.

16356 Gazette
PO Box 370 Phone: (218)253-2594
Red Lake Falls, MN 56750 Fax: (218)253-4114

Community newspaper. **Founded:** 1883. **Freq:** Weekly (Wed.). **Print Method:** Offset. **Cols./Page:** 6. **Col. Width:** 26 nonpareils. **Col. Depth:** 297 agate lines. **Key Personnel:** Keith O. Axvig, Editor and Publisher. **USPS:** 458-320. **Subscription Rates:** $25 individuals. **Remarks:** Accepts advertising.
Ad Rates: BW: $722.40 **Circ:** ‡1,599
4C: $50
SAU: $5.60
PCI: $4.20

RED WING†, pop. 13,736.

SE MN. Goodhue Co. On Mississippi River, 35 mi. SE of Saint Paul. Manufactures leather, rubber goods, footwear,marine engines, pottery, kitchen cabinets, nuclear power, shoes, malt, flour, soybean, linseed oil, trophies, ice & roller skates, rubber goods, insulation, concrete blocks, utility light poles, farm feed. Dairy, stock, grain farms.

16357 Republican-Eagle
2760 No. Service Dr. Phone: (612)388-8235
Box 82 Fax: (612)388-8912
Red Wing, MN 55066
Free: (800)535-1660
Publication E-mail: reedit@win.bright.net

Community newspaper. **Founded:** 1857. **Freq:** Daily (eve.) and Sat. (morn.). **Print Method:** Offset. **Trim Size:** 14 x 22 3/4. **Cols./Page:** 6. **Col. Width:** 2 inches. **Col. Depth:** 21 1/2 inches. **Key Personnel:** Jim Pumarlo, Editor; Arlin Albecht, Publisher; Vickie Winge, Advertising Mgr.; Mark Poss, General Mgr. **USPS:** 145-760. **Subscription Rates:** $94. **Remarks:** Accepts advertising.
Ad Rates: GLR: $0.82 **Circ:** Mon.-Sat. ★7,732
BW: $1,470.42
4C: $1,794.42
PCI: $11.67

16358 KCUE-AM - 1250
474 Guernsey Ln. Phone: (612)388-7151
Red Wing, MN 55066 Fax: (612)388-7153

Format: News; Talk; Country. **Networks:** ABC; Mutual Broadcasting System; Minnesota News; NBC; Business Radio. **Owner:** Sorenson Broadcasting, 604 N. Kiwanis, Sioux Falls, SD 57104, (605)334-1117, Fax: (605)338-0326. **Founded:** 1949. **Formerly:** KAAA-AM (1956). **Operating Hours:** Continuous; 50% network, 50% local. **Key Personnel:** Frank Hanford, General Mgr.; Paul Reding, Sales Mgr.; Trent Allens, Program Dir. **Wattage:** 1000. **Ad Rates:** $6.75-11.30 for 30 seconds; $10.15-16.95 for 60 seconds.

REDWOOD FALLS†, pop. 5,210.

SW MN. Redwood Co. On Redwood River, 115 mi. SW of Minneapolis. Manufactures computer components, metal fabricating, mobile homes, rehabilitation equipment, concrete products. Stock, dairy, poultry, grain farms. Corn, soybeans. Diversified agriculture.

16359 Redwood Gazette
Redwood Gazette, Inc.
140 E. 2nd St. Phone: (507)637-2929
PO Box 299 Fax: (507)637-3175
Redwood Falls, MN 56283
Community newspaper. **Founded:** 1869. **Freq:** Semiweekly (Tues. and Thurs.). **Print Method:** Offset. **Cols./Page:** 6. **Col. Width:** 28 nonpareils. **Col. Depth:** 301 agate lines. **Key Personnel:** Rick Petersen, Editor and Publisher; Peggy Dalland, Advertising Mgr. **Subscription Rates:** $26.50; $35.50 out of area. **Remarks:** Accepts advertising.
Ad Rates: GLR: $.29 **Circ:** ‡5,100
PCI: $4.50

16360 Comfrey Cable TV
PO Box 109 Phone: (507)637-8351
Redwood Falls, MN 56283 Fax: (507)637-8351

Owner: M-Tek Systems, at above address. **Founded:** 1972. **Formerly:** Sleepy Eye CATV. **Key Personnel:** Magdalen Maserek, Manager. **Cities Served:** Belview, Clements, Comfrey, Courtland, Echo, Hanska, Nicollet, Wood Lake, MN: subscribing households 65; 24 channels.

16361 Courtland Cable TV
PO Box 129 Phone: (507)637-8351
Redwood Falls, MN 56283 Fax: (507)637-8351

Owner: M-Tek Systems, at above address. **Founded:** 1972. **Formerly:** Sleepy Eye CATV. **Key Personnel:** Magdalen Maserek, Manager. **Cities Served:** Belview, Clements, Comfrey, Courtland, Echo, Hanska, Nicollet, Wood Lake, MN: subscribing households 130; 24 channels.

16362 Echo Cable TV
PO Box 109 Phone: (507)637-8351
Redwood Falls, MN 56283 Fax: (507)637-8351

Founded: 1972. **Formerly:** Sleepy Eye CATV. **Cities Served:** Echo: subscribing households 94; 25 channels.

16363 Hanska Cable TV
PO Box 109 Phone: (507)637-8351
Redwood Falls, MN 56283

Owner: M-Tek Systems, at above address. **Founded:** 1972. **Key Personnel:** Magdalen Maserek, Manager. **Cities Served:** Comfrey, Courtland, Echo, Hanska, Nicollet, Wood Lake, MN: subscribing households 118; 27 channels.

16364 KLGR-AM - 1490
Hwy. 19 W., Box 65 Phone: (507)637-2989
Redwood Falls, MN 56283 Fax: (507)637-5347
E-mail: klgr@means.net

Format: News; Sports; Agricultural; Country. **Networks:** ABC. **Founded:** 1954. **Operating Hours:** 5:30 a.m.-1:00 a.m.; 16% network, 83% local. **Key Personnel:** Mike Neudecker, General Mgr.; Jim Maurice, Program Dir.; Bruce Tolzmann, News Dir.; Brian Langeland, Farm Director. **Wattage:** 1000. **Ad Rates:** Advertising accepted; rates available upon request.

16365 KLGR-FM - 97.7
Hwy. 19 W., Box 65 Phone: (507)637-2989
Redwood Falls, MN 56283 Fax: (507)637-5347
E-mail: klgr@rconnect.com

Format: Adult Contemporary; News; Sports; Agricultural. **Networks:** Independent. **Founded:** 1974. **Operating Hours:** 5:30 a.m.-1 a.m.; 100% local. **Key Personnel:** Mike Neudecker, General Mgr.; Bruce Tolzmann, News Dir.; Brian Langeland, Farm Director. **Wattage:** 3000.

16366 M-Tek Systems Inc.
PO Box 109 Phone: (507)637-8351
Redwood Falls, MN 56283 Fax: (507)637-8351

Owner: LaVerne Maserek, at above address. **Founded:** 1972. **Formerly:** Sleeping Eye CATV Inc.; Lakes Cable TV Inc. **Key Personnel:** LaVerne Maserek, Contact; Magdalen Maserek, Manager; Loren Maserek, Contact. **Cities Served:** Belview, Clements, Comfrey, Courtland, Echo, Hanska, Nicollet, Woodlake, MN: subscribing households 925; 26 channels.

16367 Nicollet Cable TV
PO Box 109 Phone: (507)637-8351
Redwood Falls, MN 56283 Fax: (507)637-8351

Owner: M-Tek Systems, at above address. **Founded:** 1972. **Formerly:** Sleepy Eye CATV. **Key Personnel:** Magdalen Maserek, Manager. **Cities Served:** Belview, Clements, Comfrey, Courtland, Echo, Henska, Nicollet, Woodlake, MN: subscribing households 260; 25 channels.

16368 Wood Lake Cable TV
PO Box 109 Phone: (507)637-8351
Redwood Falls, MN 56283 Fax: (507)637-8351

Owner: M-Tek Systems, at above address. **Founded:** 1972. **Key Personnel:** Magdalen Maserek, Manager. **Cities Served:** Belview, Clements, Comfrey, Courtland, Echo, Hanska, Nicollet, Wood Lake, MN: subscribing households 140; 24 channels.

RENVILLE, pop. 1,493.

SW MN. Renville Co. 110 mi. W. of Minneapolis. Tile factory. Farm tractor accessory factory. Beet sugar refinery. Fertilizer plant. Grain, stock, dairy, poultry farms.

16369 Renville County Star Farmer News
110 NW Dupont Phone: (612)329-3324
PO Box 468
Renville, MN 56284-0468
Farm community newspaper. **Founded:** 1889. **Freq:** Weekly (Wed.). **Print Method:** Offset. **Trim Size:** 14 1/2 x 23. **Cols./Page:** 6. **Col. Width:** 2 1/8 inches. **Col. Depth:** 21 1/2 inches. **Key Personnel:** Daniel A. Licklider, Editor and Publisher. **USPS:** 461-300. **Subscription Rates:** $28 individuals; $34 in state; $40 out of state. **Remarks:** Accepts advertising. **Formerly:** Renville Star-Farmer (1990); Sacred Heart News.
Ad Rates: GLR: $.30 **Circ:** Paid 2,150
BW: $498
SAU: $4.15
PCI: $4.15

RICHFIELD, pop. 37,851.

SE MN. Hennepin Co. 10 mi. S. of Minneapolis.

16370 Richfield Sun Current
Minnesota Sun Publications
7831 E. Bush Lake Rd. Phone: (612)896-4700
Bloomington, MN 55439 Fax: (612)896-4728
Publication E-mail: richfieldsuncurrent@mnsunpub.com

Community newspaper (tabloid). **Freq:** Weekly (Wed.). **Print Method:** Offset. **Cols./Page:** 4. **Col. Width:** 2 1/2 inches. **Col. Depth:** 15 inches. **Key Personnel:** Doug Dance, Publisher, phone (612)896-4787; Pamela Austin, Advertising Dir., phone (612)897-5486. **Remarks:** Advertising accepted; rates available upon request. **Available Online. URL:** http://www.mnsun.pub.com.
Circ: Non-paid 9,622

ROCHESTER†, pop. 57,855.

SE MN. Olmstead Co. 75 mi. S. of Minneapolis. Rochester Community College. Mayo Clinic. Trade Center. Manufactures dairy products, phonographs, hospital supplies, home pasteurizers, silos, beverages, toilet preparation, computer equipment; canned vegetables. Dairy, grain, stock, poultry farms.

16371 Agri News
Post-Bulletin
18 1st Ave. SE Phone: (507)285-7600
PO Box 6118 Fax: (507)285-7772
Rochester, MN 55903-6118
Free: (800)533-1727

Farm newspaper distributed in Minnesota and northeastern Iowa. **Founded:** Aug. 4, 1976. **Freq:** Weekly (Thurs.). **Print Method:** 13 x 21. **Trim Size:** Offset. **Cols./Page:** 6. **Col. Width:** 26 nonpareils. **Col. Depth:** 294 agate lines. **Key Personnel:** Kelly J. Boldan, Editor, phone (507)285-7707, kjboldan@agrinews.com; William C. Boyne, Publisher, phone (507)285-7602; Mark Kelm, Director, mkclm@agrinews.com. **Subscription Rates:** $29.95 individuals. **Remarks:** Accepts advertising.
Ad Rates: BW: $2,249.10 **Circ:** Paid ‡21,500
4C: $2,619.10
SAU: $17.85

16372 Annals of Allergy, Asthma, & Immunology
American College of Allergy, Asthma, & Immunology
Mayo Clinic Phone: (507)538-0009
411 Guggenheim Bldg.
200 1st St. SW
Rochester, MN 55905
Clinical journal for practicing allergists. **Founded:** 1943. **Freq:** Monthly. **Print Method:** Offset. **Trim Size:** 8 1/4 x 11. **Cols./Page:** 3. **Col. Width:** 20 nonpareils. **Col. Depth:** 126 agate lines. **Key Personnel:** Edward J. O'Connell, M.D., Editor, oconnell.edward@mayo.edu; Gary Walchli, Advertising Mgr.; Susan Reilly, Publication Mgr. **ISSN:** 0003-4738. **Subscription Rates:** $50 individuals; $75 institutions; $78 other countries; $6 single issue; $7 single issue other countries. **Remarks:** Accepts advertising. **Formerly:** Annals of Allergy.
Ad Rates: BW: $850 **Circ:** Paid ‡6,000
4C: $1,800 Non-paid ‡200

16373 Fertility and Sterility
The American Society for Productive Medicine
Mayo Clinic Phone: (507)284-3850
200 1st St. SW, 505 NW Fax: (507)284-0780
Rochester, MN 55905
Medical journal covering all aspects of reproductive medicine. **Founded:** 1950. **Freq:** Monthly. **Print Method:** Offset. **Trim Size:** 8 1/4 x 10 7/8. **Cols./Page:** 2. **Col. Width:** 42 nonpareils. **Col. Depth:** 126 agate lines. **Key Personnel:** Rogers D. Kempers, M.D., Editor; Angelia Pitman, Circulation Mgr.; Carol Olson, Production Mgr. **ISSN:** 0015-0282. **Subscription Rates:** $110 individuals; $175 institutions. **Remarks:** Accepts advertising.
Ad Rates: BW: $1,073 **Circ:** ‡14,000
4C: $2,198

16374 Mayo Clinic Proceedings
Dowden Publishing Co., Inc.
Mayo Foundation for Medical Education and Research Phone: (507)284-2154 Fax: (507)284-0252
200 1st St. S.W.
Rochester, MN 55905
Publication E-mail: mayo5738@aol.com

Medical journal. **Founded:** Apr. 21, 1926. **Freq:** Monthly. **Print Method:** Offset. **Trim Size:** 7 7/8 x 10 1/2. **Cols./Page:** 2. **Col. Width:** 20 nonpareils. **Col. Depth:** 121 agate lines. **Key Personnel:** Dr. U.B.S. Prakash, Editor, phone (507)284-2094; Pamela M. Poppalardo, Publisher. **ISSN:** 0025-6196. **Subscription Rates:** Free to qualified subscribers; $72 individuals. **Remarks:** Accepts advertising. **Online:** Mayo Clinic Home Page.
Ad Rates: BW: $3,801 **Circ:** Non-paid ‡92,000
4C: $5,496

16375 Post-Bulletin
18 1st Ave. SE Phone: (507)285-7600
PO Box 6118 Fax: (507)285-7772
Rochester, MN 55903-6118
Free: (800)533-1727
Publication E-mail: news@postbulletin.com

General newspaper. **Founded:** 1892. **Freq:** Mon.-Sat. (eve.). **Print Method:** Offset. **Cols./Page:** 6. **Col. Width:** 27 nonpareils. **Col. Depth:** 301 agate lines. **Key Personnel:** William Boyne, Editor and Publisher, phone (507)285-7602; Gerry Rhea, Advertising Dir., phone (507)281-7443, fax (507)285-7666; Audrey Grotehoer, Sales Mgr., phone (507)285-7649, fax (507)285-7666. **Subscription Rates:** $129.20 individuals; $142.20 out of area.
Ad Rates: BW: $2,658.60 **Circ:** Mon.-Fri. ★**41,287**
4C: $3,158.60 Sat. ★**45,535**
PCI: $21.10 Sun. ★**45,535**

16376 KLCD-FM - 89.5
206 S. Broadway, Ste. 735 Phone: (507)282-0910
Rochester, MN 55904 Fax: (507)282-2107

Format: Classical. **Operating Hours:** Continuous. **Key Personnel:** Roger Gomoll, Station Mgr.; Brent Wolfe, Bureau Chief; Chris Cross, Development Dir.; Don Kolbert, Chief Engineer. **URL:** http://www.mpr.org.

KLSE-FM - See Decorah, Iowa

16377 KNFX-AM - 970
1530 Greenview Dr. SW, Ste. 200 Phone: (507)288-3888 Fax: (507)288-7815
Rochester, MN 55902

Format: News. **Networks:** CNN Radio. **Founded:** 1960. **Formerly:** KQAQ-AM (1994); KGHR-AM; Iowa Broadcasting. **Operating Hours:** Continuous. **ADI:** Rochester, MN-Mason City, IA-Austin, MN. **Key Personnel:** Jeff Kurtz, General Mgr., phone (507)288-3888; Corey Henn, Sports Dir./Program Dir. **Wattage:** 5000. **Ad Rates:** Advertising accepted; rates available upon request. **URL:** http://www.radiominnesota.com.

16378 KOLM-AM - 1520
1220 4th Ave. SW Phone: (507)288-1971
Rochester, MN 55902 Fax: (507)288-1520
Free: (888)599-5965

Format: Oldies. **Networks:** Mutual Broadcasting System; Unistar. **Owner:** Olmstead County Broadcasting Co., Inc., at above address. **Founded:** 1963. **Operating Hours:** 6 a.m.-sunset. **ADI:** Rochester, MN-Mason City, IA-Austin, MN. **Key Personnel:** Dick Radke, Manager; Pauline Williams, Sales Mgr. **Local Programs:** *City Beat*; *Farm Report*; *Reportline*. **Wattage:** 10,000. **Ad Rates:** $6-11 for 30 seconds; $10-15 for 60 seconds.

16379 KRCH-FM - 101.7
1530 Greenview Dr. SW, Ste. 200 Phone: (507)288-3888 Fax: (507)288-7815
Rochester, MN 55902

Format: Classic Rock. **Owner:** Iowa Broadcasting, at above address. **Founded:** 1968. **Operating Hours:** Continuous. **ADI:** Rochester, MN-Mason City, IA-Austin, MN. **Key Personnel:** Dan McClintock, Program and Music Dir.; Mary Anne Nonn, Sales Mgr.; Jeff Kurtz, General Mgr. **Wattage:** 50,000. **Ad Rates:** Advertising accepted; rates available upon request. Combined advertising rates available with KWEB-AM: $29-$60 for 60 seconds. **URL:** http://www.radiominnesota.com.

16380 KROC-AM - 1340
122 SW 4th St. Phone: (507)286-1010
Rochester, MN 55902 Fax: (507)286-9370

Format: News; Talk. **Networks:** ABC; Mutual Broadcasting System. **Owner:** Southern Minnesota Broadcasting Co., at above address. **Founded:** 1935. **Operating Hours:** Continuous; 33% network, 67% local. **ADI:** Rochester, MN-Mason City, IA-Austin, MN. **Key Personnel:** Joe O'Brien, Operations Mgr., jobrien@infonet.isl.net; Greg Gentling, General Mgr.; Rosanne Rybak, Contact; Sue Daily, Contact; Kim David, News Dir.; Bill Davis, Chief Engineer. **Local Programs:** *Joe O'Brien Show* 9:30 am - 11:00 am Monday-Friday. **Wattage:** 1000. **Ad Rates:** $38.40-60.80 for 60 seconds. $38.40-$60.80 for 60 seconds. Combined advertising rates available with KROC-FM. **URL:** www.kroc.com.

16381 KROC-FM - 106.9
122 SW 4th St. Phone: (507)286-1010
Rochester, MN 55902 Fax: (507)286-9370

Format: Contemporary Hit Radio (CHR). **Networks:** ABC; Mutual Broadcasting System. **Owner:** Southern Minnesota Broadcasting Co., at above address. **Founded:** 1965. **Operating Hours:** Continuous; 5% network, 95% local. **ADI:** Rochester, MN-Mason City, IA-Austin, MN. **Key Personnel:** Greg Gentling, General Mgr.; Rosanne Rybak, General Sales Mgr.; Mary Niemeyer, Local Sales Manager; Derek Moran, Music Dir.; Brent Ackerman, Program Dir.; James Rabe, Promotions Dir.; Tracy McCray, News/PSA. **Wattage:** 100,000. **Ad Rates:** Combined advertising rates available with KROC-AM.

16382 KTTC-TV - 10
601 1st Ave. SW Phone: (507)288-4444
Rochester, MN 55902 Fax: (507)288-6324
E-mail: kttc@kttc.com

Format: Commercial TV. **Networks:** NBC. **Owner:** Quincy Newspapers, Inc., PO Box 909, Quincy, IL 62306, (217)223-5100. **Founded:** 1953. **Formerly:** KROC-TV (1976). **Operating Hours:** Continuous; 77% network, 23% local. **ADI:** Rochester, MN-Mason City, IA-Austin, MN. **Key Personnel:** Jerry Watson, Vice Pres./Gen. Mgr., jerry@kttc.com; Liz Dahlen, Dir. of Sales & Marketing, liz@kttc.com; Ron Gruber, Dir. of Operations & Programming, ron@kttc.com; Larry Henrichs, News Dir., fax (507)288-6278, news@kttc.com; Tim Morgan, Dir. of Engineering, tim@kttc.com; John Deyo, Creative Services Mgr.; Bonnie Bickel, Contact; Dan O'Hara, Sports Dir.; Vickie Broughton, Traffic Mgr., fax (507)288-6743; Mike Hintz, Production Supervisor; Joel Streed, Asst. News Dir., phone (507)288-6324, news@kttc.com. **Wattage:** 316,000. **Ad Rates:** $15-2,000 per unit. **URL:** http://www.kttc.com.

16383 KWEB-AM - 1270
1530 Greenview Dr. SW, Ste. 200 Phone: (507)288-3888 Fax: (507)288-7815
Rochester, MN 55902

Format: Talk; Agricultural; News; Sports; News; Sports. **Networks:** Minnesota Ag (Magnet Farm); Minnesota News. **Owner:** Cumulus Broadcasting, at above address. **Founded:** 1957. **Formerly:** Iowa Broadcasting. **Operating Hours:** Continuous. **ADI:** Rochester, MN-Mason City, IA-Austin, MN. **Key Personnel:** Bill Klein, Sales Mgr.; Greg Henn, Program Dir.; Greg Henn, Sports Dir.; Jeff Kurtz, General Mgr. **Wattage:** 5000 day; 1000 night. **Ad Rates:** Advertising accepted; rates available upon request. Combined advertising rates available with KRCH-AM: $29-$60 for 60 seconds. **URL:** http://www.radiominnesota.com.

16384 KWWK-FM - 96.5
1220 4th Ave. SW Phone: (507)288-1971
Rochester, MN 55902 Fax: (507)288-1520
Free: (888)599-5965

Format: Contemporary Country. **Networks:** Mutual Broadcasting System. **Owner:** Olmsted County Board Co., at above address. **Founded:** 1967. **Operating Hours:** Continuous. **ADI:** Rochester, MN-Mason City, IA-Austin, MN. **Key Personnel:** Howard Bill, General Mgr.; Dick Radke, Sales Mgr.; Denny Foster, Promotions Dir.; Paul Oftedahl, Music Dir.; John Harwick, News Dir. **Local Programs:** *Reportline*. **Wattage:** 50,000. **Ad Rates:** $16-35 for 30 seconds; $18-38 for 60 seconds.

16385 KXLC-FM - 91.1
206 S. Broadway, Ste. 735 Phone: (507)282-0910
Rochester, MN 55904 Fax: (507)282-2107

Format: News; Information. **Networks:** National Public Radio (NPR). **Owner:** Minnesota Public Radio, at above address. **Operating Hours:** Continuous. **Key Personnel:** Roger Gomoll, Station Mgr.; Brent Wolfe, Bureau Chief; Chris Cross, Development Dir.; Don Kolbert, Chief Engineer. **URL:** http://www.mpr.org.

16386 KXLT-TV - 47
6301 Bandel Rd. NW Phone: (507)252-4747
Rochester, MN 55901 Fax: (507)252-5050

Format: Commercial TV. **Networks:** Fox. **Owner:** Shockley Communication Corp., 5727 Tokay Blvd., Madison, WI 53719. **Founded:** Jan. 23, 1998. **Former name:** KXLI-TV. **Operating Hours:** 6 a.m.-1 a.m. **Key Personnel:** John J. Ganahl, General Mgr., jjganahl@infonet.isl.net. **Wattage:** 1,000,000. **Ad Rates:** Advertising accepted; rates available upon request.

16387 KZSE-FM - 90.7
206 S. Broadway, Ste. 735 Phone: (507)282-0910
Rochester, MN 55904 Fax: (507)282-2107

Format: News; Information. **Networks:** National Public Radio (NPR). **Owner:** Minnesota Public Radio, at above address. **Operating Hours:** Continuous. **Key Personnel:** Roger Gomoll, Station Mgr.; Brent Wolfe, Bureau Chief; Chris Cross, Development Dir.; Don Kolbert, Chief Engineer. **URL:** http://www.mpr.org.

16388 TCI Media Services
1255 E. Circle Dr., N.E. Phone: (507)280-0551
Rochester, MN 55906 Fax: (507)289-1958
Free: (800)622-7044

Founded: 1958. **Formerly:** WestMare Cable. **Key Personnel:** Scott Aronz, phone (507)280-0551. **Cities Served:** subscribing households 70,000; 16 channels; 2 community access channels.

ROSEAU†, pop. 2,272.

NW MN. Roseau Co. 115 mi. NE of Grand Falls, ND. Butter, snowmobiles manufactured. Dairy, stock, beef, grass seed, poultry farms. Flax, small grain.

16389 The Borderline
106 W. Center St. Phone: (218)463-1521
PO Box 220 Fax: (218)463-1530
Roseau, MN 56751
Shopper. **Freq:** Weekly. **Print Method:** Offset. **Cols./Page:** 6. **Col. Width:** 12.4 picas. **Col. Depth:** 21.5 inches. **Key Personnel:** Jodi Wiskow, Manager. **Subscription Rates:** Free.
Ad Rates: SAU: $5 **Circ:** Free 11,011

16390 Roseau Times-Region
106 W. Center St. Phone: (218)463-1521
Roseau, MN 56751 Fax: (218)463-1530

Community newspaper. **Founded:** 1893. **Freq:** Weekly (Wed.). **Print Method:** Offset. **Cols./Page:** 6. **Col. Width:** 23 nonpareils. **Col. Depth:** 301 agate lines. **Key Personnel:** Duane R. Mattson, Publisher. **USPS:** 470-780. **Subscription Rates:** $18; $25 out of area. **Remarks:** Accepts advertising.
Ad Rates: GLR: $.25 **Circ:** ‡4,500
BW: $354.75
PCI: $3.50

16391 KCAJ-FM - 102.1
407 3rd St. Phone: (218)463-3360
PO Box 358 Fax: (218)463-1977
Roseau, MN 56751

Format: Full Service. **Networks:** NBC. **Owner:** Jack J. Swanson, at above address. **Founded:** June 1996. **Operating Hours:** 5 a.m.-12 a.m. **Key Personnel:** Jack McDonald, Sales Mgr.; Dona Byre, Office Mgr.; Brad Zoeller, Sports Dir. **Wattage:** 50,000. **Ad Rates:** $7.25-9.99 for 30 seconds.

16392 KRWB-AM - 1410
PO Box 130 Phone: (218)463-1410
Roseau, MN 56751 Fax: (218)463-3778

Format: Sports; Classic Rock; Agricultural; Oldies. **Networks:** ABC; Minnesota News. **Founded:** 1963. **Operating Hours:** 5:30 a.m.-midnight. **Key Personnel:** Marlene Schmitz, General Mgr. **Wattage:** 1000. **Ad Rates:** $3.95-4.80 for 30 seconds; $5.65-6.85 for 60 seconds.

ROSEMOUNT, pop. 5,083.

SE MN. Dakota Co. 5 mi. W. of Hastings.

16393 Marcus Cable
16900 Cedar Ave. Phone: (612)432-2610
Rosemount, MN 55068 Fax: (612)432-5765
Free: (800)678-2797

Owner: Marcus Cable Partners, 2911 Turtle Creek Blvd., Ste. 1300, Dallas, TX 75219, (214)521-7898, Fax: (214)526-2154.

Formerly: Star Cablevision. **Key Personnel:** Jeffrey A. Marcus, CEO/Pres.; Louis A. Borrelli, COO/Executive Vice Pres.; Thomas P. McMillin, CFO. **Cities Served:** Rosemount, Lakeville, Apple Valley, Farmington, Northfield, Prior Lake, and Savage, MN.

ROSEVILLE, pop. 35,820.

SE MN. Ramsey Co. 11 mi. NW of Maplewood. Residential.

16394 Fabrics & Architecture
Industrial Fabrics Association International
1801 County Rd. B W. Phone: (651)222-2508
Roseville, MN 55113-4061 Fax: (651)631-9334
Free: (800)225-4324
Publisher E-mail: generalinfo@ifai.com

Magazine specializing in interior and exterior design ideas and technical information for architectural fabric applications in architecture. **Founded:** July 1989. **Freq:** Bimonthly 5/year. **Print Method:** Web offset. **Trim Size:** 8 1/4 x 11. **Cols./Page:** 3 and 2. **Col. Width:** 13 and 20 picas. **Col. Depth:** 60 picas. **Key Personnel:** Jean M. Cook, Editor; Frank McGinty, Publisher; Susan Kelly, Sales Mgr. **ISSN:** 1045-0483. **Subscription Rates:** $21; $5 single issue. **Remarks:** Accepts advertising. **URL:** http://www.ifai.com.
Ad Rates: BW: $2,025 **Circ:** Paid 3,025
4C: $2,825 Controlled 13,000

16395 Geotechnical Fabrics Report
Industrial Fabrics Association International
1801 County Rd. B W. Phone: (651)222-2508
Roseville, MN 55113-4061 Fax: (651)631-9334
Free: (800)225-4324
Publication E-mail: gfr@ifai.com
Publisher E-mail: generalinfo@ifai.com

Magazine containing case histories, industry news, and technical papers concerning geotextiles, geomembranes, and other geosynthetic products. **Subtitle:** Engineer's Guide to Geosynthetics. **Founded:** 1983. **Freq:** 9/year. **Print Method:** Offset. **Trim Size:** 8 1/4 x 11 1/4. **Cols./Page:** 3 and 2. **Col. Width:** 13 and 20 picas. **Col. Depth:** 60 picas. **Key Personnel:** Diane Cormany, Editor; Mary Hennessy, Publisher; Laurie Hunnigford, Advertising Mgr. **ISSN:** 0882-4983. **Subscription Rates:** $35 U.S.; $49 Canada and Mexico; $56 other countries. **Remarks:** Accepts advertising.
Ad Rates: BW: $2,455 **Circ:** Paid 2,000
4C: $3,335 Controlled 16,000
PCI: $13

16396 Industrial Fabric Products Review
Industrial Fabrics Association International
1801 County Rd. B W. Phone: (651)222-2508
Roseville, MN 55113-4061 Fax: (651)631-9334
Free: (800)225-4324
Publication E-mail: review@ifai.com
Publisher E-mail: generalinfo@ifai.com

Magazine covering the technical and industrial fabrics industries. **Founded:** Nov. 1915. **Freq:** Monthly (two issues in May). **Print Method:** Web offset. **Trim Size:** 8 1/4 x 11 1/4. **Cols./Page:** 3. **Col. Width:** 13 picas. **Col. Depth:** 60 picas. **Key Personnel:** Gene Rebeck, Editorial Dir.; Mary Hennessy, Advertising Dir./Publisher; Gene Rebeck, Editor. **ISSN:** 0019-8307. **Subscription Rates:** $43; $53 Canada and Mexico; $108 other countries; $7 single issue. **Remarks:** Accepts advertising.
Ad Rates: BW: $2,830 **Circ:** Paid 3,811
4C: $3,720 Non-paid 4,450
PCI: $50 Controlled 2,833

16397 KTIS-AM - 900
3003 N. Snelling Ave. Phone: (612)631-5000
Roseville, MN 55113 Fax: (612)631-5010

Format: Religious. **Networks:** SkyLight Satellite. **Owner:** Northwestern College, at above address. **Founded:** 1949. **Operating Hours:** Continuous; 50% network, 50% local. **ADI:** Minneapolis-St. Paul, MN. **Key Personnel:** Don Rupp, Manager; Neil Stavem, Contact. **Wattage:** 25,000. **Ad Rates:** Noncommercial.

16398 KTIS-FM - 98.5
3003 N. Snelling Ave. Phone: (612)631-5100
Roseville, MN 55113 Fax: (612)631-5084
E-mail: ns3@nwc.edu

Format: Religious. **Networks:** SkyLight Satellite. **Owner:** Northwestern College, at above address. **Founded:** 1949. **Operating Hours:** Continuous; 50% network, 50% local. **ADI:** Minneapolis-St. Paul, MN. **Key Personnel:** Don Rupp, Manager; Neil Stavem, Contact. **Local Programs:** *Perspectives.* **Wattage:** 100,000. **Ad Rates:** Noncommercial.

16399 Meredith Cable
934 Woodhill Dr. Phone: (612)483-3233
PO Box 13698 Fax: (612)483-9184
Roseville, MN 55113

Founded: 1982. **Formerly**: Group W Cable (1986); North Central Cable Communications Corp. **Key Personnel:** Kevin Griffin, Contact. **Cities Served:** subscribing households 100,000; 63 channels; 12 community access channels.

16400 North Central Cable Communications Inc.
934 Woodhill Dr. Phone: (612)483-9999
Roseville, MN 55113 Fax: (612)483-9184

Founded: 1981. **Formerly**: Group W (1986); Cable TV North Central (1992); Meredith Cable (1997). **Key Personnel:** Kevin Griffin, President, phone (612)486-3523; Kathi Donnelly-Cohen, Vice President, phone (612)486-3521; Mark Bisenius, VP of Technical Operations, phone (612)486-3526, fax (612)483-3134; Mark Neuman-Scott, Program VP, phone (612)426-5337. **Cities Served:** Anoka, Birchwood, Centerville, Columbia Heights, Eagan, Ham Lake, Lexington, Maplewood, North St. Paul, Pine Springs, White Bear Lake, MN: subscribing households 134,338; 65 channels.

RUSHFORD, pop. 1,478.

SE MN. Fillmore Co. 19 mi. S. of Winona. Residential. Farm marketing. Dairy, hogs, beef, corn, soybeans.

16401 Tri-County Record
Tri-County Publishing, Inc.
PO Box 429 Phone: (507)864-7700
Rushford, MN 55971
Publisher E-mail: tricopub@means.net

Community newspaper. **Founded:** 1915. **Freq:** Weekly (Thurs.). **Print Method:** Offset. **Trim Size:** 14 x 22 1/2. **Cols./Page:** 6. **Col. Width:** 12 1/2 picas. **Col. Depth:** 301 agate lines. **Key Personnel:** Myron J. Schober, Publisher; Darlene J. Schober, Publisher. **USPS:** 639-340. **Subscription Rates:** $26 individuals; $30 out of area. **Remarks:** Accepts advertising.
Ad Rates: SAU: $4.35 **Circ:** 1,700
PCI: $4.35

16402 Tri-County Record Special Edition
Tri-County Publishing, Inc.
PO Box 429 Phone: (507)864-7700
Rushford, MN 55971
Publisher E-mail: tricopub@means.net

Shopper. **Freq:** Monthly. **Trim Size:** 14 x 22 1/2. **Cols./Page:** 6. **Col. Width:** 2 3/16 inches. **Col. Depth:** 21 1/2 inches. **Key Personnel:** Myron J. Schober, Publisher; Darlene J. Schober, Publisher. **Subscription Rates:** Free. **Remarks:** Accepts advertising.
Ad Rates: SAU: $5.65 **Circ:** Free 3,900
PCI: $5.65

RUTHTON

16403 Buffalo Ridge Gazette
Hunt and Hunt Newspapers
320 Aetna St. Phone: (507)658-3919
PO Box 70 Fax: (507)247-5502
Ruthton, MN 56170-0070
Publication E-mail: tribute@compuserve.com

Community newspaper. **Founded:** 1967. **Freq:** Weekly. **Print Method:** Offset. **Trim Size:** 15 x 23. **Cols./Page:** 6. **Col. Width:** 27 nonpareils. **Col. Depth:** 301 agate lines. **Key Personnel:** Lorry Sanderson, Managing Editor; Charles R. Hunt, Editor and Publisher. **USPS:** 379-990. **Subscription Rates:** $18 individuals; $25 out of area. **Remarks:** Accepts advertising.
Ad Rates: GLR: $0.21 **Circ:** Paid 481
BW: $270.90 Free 20
SAU: $2.94

ST. ANTHONY

16404 St. Anthony Bulletin
Lillie Suburban Newspapers
PO Box 120608 Phone: (612)633-2777
New Brighton, MN 55112 Fax: (612)633-3846

Local newspaper. **Founded:** 1956. **Freq:** Weekly (Wed.). **Print Method:** Offset. Uses mats. **Trim Size:** Broadsheet. **Cols./Page:** 6. **Col. Width:** 21 nonpareils. **Col. Depth:** 294 agate lines. **Key Personnel:** Mary Lee Hagert, Managing Editor; N. T. Lillie, Publisher; Jeffery Enright, Publisher; Mark Beckstrom, Advertising Mgr.; Pat Colburn, Circulation Mgr.; James Schwartz, Editor, phone (612)633-2777, fax (612)633-3846. **Subscription Rates:** $25.95 elsewhere. **Remarks:** Accepts advertising.
Ad Rates: SAU: $22.70 **Circ:** Paid 47
Free 2,303

SAINT CHARLES

16405 Press
St. Charles Press
924 Whitewater Ave. Phone: (507)932-3663
Saint Charles, MN 55972 Fax: (507)932-5337

Newspaper. **Founded:** 1898. **Freq:** Weekly (Tues.). **Print Method:** Offset. **Cols./Page:** 6. **Col. Width:** 28 nonpareils. **Col. Depth:** 301 agate lines. **Key Personnel:** Susan Benedett, Editor; Tim Mack, Publisher. **Subscription Rates:** $20 individuals. **Remarks:** Accepts advertising.
Ad Rates: GLR: $.245 **Circ:** 2,000
PCI: $7.60

ST. CLOUD

16406 Journal of Information Ethics
McFarland & Co., Inc., Publishers
Learning Resources Services Fax: (320)255-4778
720 4th Ave. S
St. Cloud State University
St. Cloud, MN 56301
Publisher E-mail: mcfarland@skybest.com

Journal of ethical issues in all information fields. **Founded:** 1992. **Freq:** 2/year. **Trim Size:** 6 x 9. **Cols./Page:** 1. **Col. Width:** 4 3/8 inches. **Col. Depth:** 7 1/2 inches. **Key Personnel:** Robert Hauptman, Editor, phone (320)255-4822; Steve Wilson, Managing Editor; Teri Knapp, Business Mgr. **ISSN:** 1061-9321. **Subscription Rates:** $38; $44 other countries. $21 single issue.
Ad Rates: BW: $50 **Circ:** Paid 200
Controlled 50

16407 St. Cloud Times
St. Cloud Newspapers, Inc.
3000 N. 7th St. Phone: (320)255-8700
St. Cloud, MN 56302 Fax: (320)255-8704
Free: (800)955-9998
Publication E-mail: sctimes@cloudnet.com

General newspaper. **Founded:** 1861. **Freq:** Daily (eve.), Sat. and Sun. (morn.). **Print Method:** Offset. **Trim Size:** 22 3/4 x 13 5/8. **Cols./Page:** 6. **Col. Width:** 25 nonpareils. **Col. Depth:** 301 agate lines. **Key Personnel:** Susan Ihne, Editor, phone (320)255-8777, fax (320)255-8775, sihne@sc.gannett.com; Sonja Sorensen Craig, Publisher, phone (320)255-8709, scraig@sc.gannett.com. **Subscription Rates:** $169; $234 out of state. **Remarks:** Accepts advertising. Monday-Saturday: GLR: $2; BW: $4,382.13; 4C: $4,802.88; SAU: $21.50; PCI: $33.97; Sunday: GLR: $2; BW: $6,335.19; 4C: $6,843.49; PCI: $49.11. **Formerly**: St. Cloud Daily Times (1992).
Circ: Mon.-Sat. **★28,303**
Sun. **★37,885**

16408 St. Cloud Visitor
305 7th Ave. N. Phone: (320)251-3022
PO Box 1068 Fax: (320)251-0424
St. Cloud, MN 56302
Official newspaper (tabloid) of the Catholic Diocese of St. Cloud. **Founded:** 1938. **Freq:** Weekly. **Print Method:** Offset. **Trim Size:** 11 x 15. **Cols./Page:** 5. **Col. Width:** 11 picas. **Col. Depth:** 210 agate lines. **Key Personnel:** Joe Towalski, Editor, towalsi@aol.com; Rose Kruger-Fuchs, Advertising Mgr.; Paula Lemke, Circulation Mgr. **Subscription Rates:** $18 individuals. **Remarks:** Accepts advertising.
Ad Rates: BW: $825 **Circ:** Paid 42,000
4C: $1,200 Non-paid 185
PCI: $11

16409 University Chronicle
St. Cloud State University
13 Stewart Hall Phone: (612)255-4086
720 4th Ave. S. Fax: (612)255-2164
St. Cloud, MN 56301-4498
Publication E-mail: chronicle@tigger.stcloud.msus.edu

Collegiate newspaper. **Founded:** 1925. **Freq:** Semiweekly (Tues. and Fri.). **Print Method:** Offset. Uses mats. **Cols./Page:** 5. **Col. Width:** 22 nonpareils. **Col. Depth:** 210 agate lines. **Key Personnel:** Eric Hedlund, Editor; Ryan Voz, Managing Editor. **USPS:** 121-580. **Subscription Rates:** $20. **Remarks:** Accepts advertising. **Available Online. URL:** http://www.stcloud.msus.edu/~uconline/. **Formerly**: SCS Chronicle (1990).
Ad Rates: BW: $350 **Circ:** Free ‡7,000
SAU: $4.10
PCI: $3.37

16410 KCLD-FM - 104.7
Box 1458 Phone: (320)251-1450
St. Cloud, MN 56302 Fax: (320)251-8952

Format: Contemporary Hit Radio (CHR). **Founded:** 1948. **Formerly**: KFAM-FM. **Operating Hours:** Continuous. **ADI:** Minneapolis-St. Paul, MN. **Key Personnel:** John J. Sowad, Jr., Contact; John Ramsey, Program Dir.; Dennis Niess, Contact; Doug Rice, Contact. **Wattage:** 100,000. **Ad Rates:** $15-55 for 30 seconds; $20-65 for 60 seconds.

16411 KKJM-FM - 92.9
640 Lincoln Ave S. E. Phone: (320)251-4422
PO Box 220 Fax: (320)251-1822
St. Cloud, MN 56302
Free: (800)568-6033
E-mail: spirit93kkjm@yahoo.com

Format: Contemporary Christian. **Networks:** AP. **Owner:** WJON Broadcasting Co., L. P., at above address. **Operating Hours:** Continuous. **Key Personnel:** Steve Stewart, General Mgr.; Melony McKaye, Program Dir. **Ad Rates:** Advertising accepted; rates available upon request.

16412 KKSR-FM - 96.7
24 W. Division St. Phone: (612)253-9600
St. Cloud, MN 56302 Fax: (612)255-5276
E-mail: star96.com

Format: Adult Contemporary; News. **Networks:** Unistar. **Founded:** 1988. **Operating Hours:** Continuous. **ADI:** Minneapolis-St. Paul, MN. **Key Personnel:** Rick Anderson, Sales Mgr. **Wattage:** 50,000.

16413 KNSI-AM - 1450
Box 1458 Phone: (612)251-1450
St. Cloud, MN 56302 Fax: (612)251-8952

Format: News; Talk. **Networks:** NBC; Mutual Broadcasting System. **Founded:** 1938. **Operating Hours:** Continuous. **ADI:** Minneapolis-St. Paul, MN. **Key Personnel:** Al Leighton, President; John Swada, General Mgr.; Doug Rice, General Sales Mgr.; Rock Lundorff, Program Dir. **Local Programs:** *Destination Outdoors*, Dave Faust; *Morning Up-date*, Rock Lundorff. **Wattage:** 1000.

16414 KVSC-FM - 88.1
720 4th Ave. S. Phone: (320)255-3066
St. Cloud, MN 56301
E-mail: kvsc@info.org

Format: Alternative/New Music/Progressive. **Networks:** AP. **Owner:** St. Cloud State University, at above address. **Founded:** May 1967. **Operating Hours:** Continuous. **Key Personnel:** Brad Savage, Program Dir., phone (320)255-3053; Amy Dahlin, News Dir., phone (320)255-4748; Jo McMullen, Station Mgr. **Wattage:** 16,500. **Ad Rates:** Underwriting available. **URL:** http://www.kvsc.org.

16415 WJON-AM - 1240
PO Box 220 Phone: (320)251-4422
St. Cloud, MN 56302 Fax: (320)251-1855
Free: (800)568-6033
E-mail: wjon@cloudnet.com

Format: News; Talk; Sports; Full Service. **Networks:** ABC; Minnesota News. **Owner:** Andrew Hilger, at above address. **Founded:** 1950. **Operating Hours:** Continuous. **ADI:** Minneapolis-St. Paul, MN. **Key Personnel:** Steve Stewart, Station Mgr.; Tim Lyon, News Dir.; Emmett Keenan, Program/Sports Dir. **Wattage:** 1000. **Ad Rates:** $10-38 for 30 seconds.

16416 WWJO-FM - 98.1
640 Lincoln Ave. SE Phone: (320)251-4422
St. Cloud, MN 56304-0824 Fax: (320)251-1855
Free: (800)568-6033
E-mail: wjon@cloudnet.com

Format: Contemporary Country. **Networks:** ABC; Minnesota News. **Owner:** WJON Broadcasting Co., at above address, Free: (800)848-4912. **Founded:** 1970. **Operating Hours:** Continuous. **ADI:** Minneapolis-St. Paul, MN. **Key Personnel:** Mark Sprint, Program Dir., phone (320)257-7212, fax (320)257-1855, stint23@aol.com; Steve Stewart, Station Mgr.; Andy Hilger, General Mgr.; Tim Lyon, News Dir. **Wattage:** 100,000 ERP. **Ad Rates:** $13-42 for 30 seconds. $6.80-$27 for 30 seconds. Combined advertising rates available with WJON-AM: $10.55-$38.05 for 30 seconds.

ST. JAMES

16417 Plaindealer
St. James Publishing Co., Inc.
604 1st Ave. S. Phone: (507)375-3161
PO Box 67 Fax: (507)375-3221
St. James, MN 56081
Community newspaper. **Subtitle:** St. James Plaindealer Serving Watonwan County, MN. **Founded:** 1891. **Freq:** Weekly (Thurs.). **Print Method:** Web. **Cols./Page:** 6. **Col. Width:** 12 picas. **Col. Depth:** 21 1/2 inches. **Key Personnel:** R. Joseph Flanagan, Editor and Publisher. **Subscription Rates:** $35. **Remarks:** Accepts advertising. **Absorbed**: Lewisville Spotlight.
Ad Rates: BW: $623 **Circ:** ‡2,790
4C: $823
SAU: $5.95
PCI: $5.95

16418 Town and Country Shopper
St. James Publishing Co., Inc.
604 1st Ave. S. Phone: (507)375-3161
PO Box 67 Fax: (507)375-3221
St. James, MN 56081
Shopper. **Subtitle:** Total Market Coverage (TMC). **Founded:** 1960. **Freq:** Weekly (Mon.). **Print Method:** Web. **Cols./Page:** 5. **Col. Width:** 24 nonpareils. **Col. Depth:** 210 agate lines. **Key Personnel:** Joe Flanagan, Publisher. **Remarks:** Accepts advertising. **Formerly**: Watonwan County Shoppers Guide.
Ad Rates: BW: $425 **Circ:** Free ‡12,860
4C: $530
SAU: $5.95
PCI: $5.95

ST. JOSEPH

16419 Music and Dance News
Von Meyer Publishing, Inc.
PO Box 324 Phone: (320)363-7741
St. Joseph, MN 56374 Fax: (320)363-4195
Free: (800)386-2261
Publication E-mail: mujdncnews@aol.com
Publisher E-mail: vonmyrpubl@aol.com

Newspaper devoted to music and dancing. **Founded:** 1972. **Freq:** Bimonthly. **Print Method:** Web. **Cols./Page:** 4. **Col. Width:** 2 1/2 inches. **Col. Depth:** 15 inches. **Key Personnel:** Janelle Von Pinnon, Publisher, phone (800)386-2261, vonmyrpubl@aol.com. **ISSN:** 192X-8430. **Subscription Rates:** Free to qualified subscribers; $12. **Alt. Formats:** Mailing labels. **Formerly**: Entertainment Bits.
Ad Rates: BW: $784 **Circ:** Paid ‡2,000
Controlled ‡15,000

16420 Studio One/HCC
College of Saint Benedict
St. Joseph, MN 56374
Publication E-mail: studio1@csbsju.edu

Literary and visual arts magazine. **Founded:** 1976. **Freq:** Annual. **Trim Size:** 7 1/2 x 10. **Subscription Rates:** $5 single issue. **Remarks:** Advertising not accepted.
Circ: (Not Reported)

ST. LOUIS PARK

16421 American Jewish World
American Jewish World Publishing, Inc.
4509 Minnetonka Blvd. Phone: (612)920-7000
St. Louis Park, MN 55416-9714 Fax: (612)920-6205
Publication E-mail: amjewish@isd.net

Jewish interest newspaper. **Founded:** 1912. **Freq:** Weekly. **Cols./Page:** 5. **Col. Width:** 1 7/8 inches. **Col. Depth:** 16 inches. **Key Personnel:** Marshall Hoffman, Editor. **ISSN:** 0002-9084. **Subscription Rates:** $19 individuals.
Ad Rates: PCI: $15 **Circ:** ‡7,000

16422 St. Louis Park Sun-Sailor
Minnesota Sun Publications
7831 E. Bush Lake Rd. Phone: (612)896-4700
Bloomington, MN 55439 Fax: (612)896-4728

Community newspaper (tabloid). **Freq:** Weekly (Wed.). **Print Method:** Offset. **Cols./Page:** 5. **Col. Width:** 1 15/16 inches. **Col. Depth:** 16 inches. **Key Personnel:** Don Thurlow, Publisher; Paul Johnson, Advertising Dir. **Remarks:** Accepts advertising.
Ad Rates: GLR: $24.94 **Circ:** Paid 1,361
BW: $1,696 Non-paid 10,112
4C: $1,633
PCI: $21.20

16423 KDXL-FM - 106.5
6425 W. 33rd St. Phone: (612)928-6149
St. Louis Park, MN 55426 Fax: (612)928-6206

Format: Alternative/New Music/Progressive; Rap; Top 40. **Founded:** 1978. **Key Personnel:** Gerald Burt, General Mgr., gerald_ burt@qm.st/park.k12.mn.us; Dick Johnson, CEN. **Wattage:** 10. **URL:** http://www.stlpark.k12.mn.us/kdxl/index.html.

16424 WWTC-AM - 1280
5501 Excelsior Blvd. Phone: (612)926-1280
St. Louis Park, MN 55416-2901 Fax: (612)926-8014

Founded: 1931. **Formerly**: Children's Broadcasting Corp. **Operating Hours:** 24 hrs. **ADI:** Minneapolis-St. Paul, MN. **Key Personnel:** John Lynch, President & CEO, phone (619)784-6900, fax (619)784-6912; Hal Brown, Exec. VP/ Programming; Kathy Carlson, General Mgr., phone (612)926-1280, fax (612)926-8014. **Wattage:** 5000. **URL:** http://www.cfrcrn.com.

ST. PAUL

16425 American Society of Brewing Chemists Journal
American Society of Brewing Chemists (ASBC)
3340 Pilot Knob Rd. Phone: (612)454-7250
St. Paul, MN 55121 Fax: (612)454-0766
Publication E-mail: asbc@scisoc.org
Publisher E-mail: asbc@scisoc.org

Professional journal of the American Society of Brewing Chemists. **Founded:** 1976. **Freq:** Quarterly. **Print Method:** Sheetfed offset. **Trim Size:** 8 1/2 x 11. **Cols./Page:** 2. **Col. Width:** 21 picas. **Col. Depth:** 60 picas. **Key Personnel:** P. L. Freeman, Editor; G. Grahek, Marketing Mgr. **ISSN:** 0361-0478. **Subscription Rates:** $115 individuals; $40 single issue. **Remarks:** Advertising not accepted. **Former name**: Professional American Society of Brewing Chemists.
Circ: Controlled ⊕**946**

16426 The Cadence
Northwestern College
3003 N. Snelling Ave. Phone: (612)631-5137
St. Paul, MN 55113
Collegiate newsmagazine. **Subtitle:** The Student Magazine of Northwestern College. **Founded:** 1989. **Freq:** 5/year. **Print Method:** Offset. **Trim Size:** 8 1/2 x 11. **Cols./Page:** 4. **Col. Width:** 24 nonpareils. **Col. Depth:** 196 agate lines. **Key Personnel:** Stephen Jackson, Editor; Kelly Call, Advertising Mgr. **Subscription Rates:** Free; $8 (mail). **Remarks:** Advertising accepted; rates available upon request. **Formerly**: The Eagle (1989).
Circ: Non-paid 3,000

16427 Catholic Aid News
Catholic Aid Association
3499 N. Lexington Ave. Phone: (612)490-0170
St. Paul, MN 55126-8098 Fax: (612)490-0746
Publisher E-mail: caa@catholicaid.com

Membership publication of the Catholic Aid Association, a non-profit, fraternal life insurance, annuity and benefit organization. **Founded:** 1895. **Freq:** Monthly. **Key Personnel:** David E. Brown, Vice President, Communications; Colleen Kingsbury, Communication Coord. **Remarks:** Advertising not accepted.
Circ: (Not Reported)

16428 Catholic Digest
2115 Summit Ave. Phone: (651)962-6725
St. Paul, MN 55105-1081 Fax: (651)962-6755
Publication E-mail: CDigest@stthomas.edu
Publisher E-mail: CDigest@stthomas.edu

General interest magazine for Catholics. **Subtitle:** Inspiring the Life We Lead. **Founded:** Nov. 1936. **Freq:** Monthly. **Print Method:** Offset. **Trim Size:** 5 1/8 x 7 3/8. **Cols./Page:** 2. **Col. Width:** 13 picas. **Col. Depth:** 95 agate lines. **Key Personnel:** Richard Reece, Editor, phone (651)962-6741; L. Thomas Kelly, Publisher, phone (651)962-6730; Dianne Talmage, Production Mgr., phone (651)962-6743; Deborah Frey, Circ. Dir., phone (212)870-2552; Thomas Rickert, Advertising Dir., phone (651)962-6734. **ISSN:** 0008-7998. **Subscription Rates:** $19.95 individuals; $2.25 single issue. **Remarks:** Accepts advertising. **URL:** http://www.catholicdigest.org.
Ad Rates: BW: $12,175 **Circ:** Paid ★**501,738**
4C: $15,760

16429 The Catholic Spirit
Catholic Bulletin Publishing Co.
244 Dayton Ave. Phone: (612)291-4444
St. Paul, MN 55102-1892 Fax: (612)291-4460
Publication E-mail: cathspirit@aol.com

Catholic publication. **Founded:** 1911. **Freq:** Weekly (Thurs.). **Print Method:** Offset. **Cols./Page:** 4. **Col. Width:** 30 nonpareils. **Col. Depth:** 196 agate lines. **Key Personnel:** Dennis W. Heaney, Assoc. Publisher. **Subscription Rates:** $35. **Remarks:** Accepts advertising. **Formerly**: Catholic Bulletin.
Ad Rates: GLR: $1.64 **Circ:** Paid 75,000

16430 Cereal Chemistry
American Association of Cereal Chemists
3340 Pilot Knob Rd. Phone: (651)454-7250
St. Paul, MN 55121-2097 Fax: (651)454-0766
Free: (800)328-7560
Publisher E-mail: aacc@scisoc.org

Journal focusing on cereal chemistry and research on raw materials, processes and products in the cereals area. **Founded:** 1924. **Freq:** Bimonthly. **Print Method:** Offset. **Trim Size:** 8 1/2 x 11. **Cols./Page:** 2. **Col. Width:** 21 picas. **Col. Depth:** 138 agate lines. **Key Personnel:** Steven C. Nelson, Publisher; Vladimir Rasper, Editor-in-Chief; Miles Wimer, Director; Ann King, Editorial Supervisor. **ISSN:** 0009-0352. **Remarks:** Advertising not accepted. **Alt. Formats:** CD-ROM; Microfiche.
Circ: Paid ‡3,249
Controlled ‡26

16431 Cereal Foods World
American Association of Cereal Chemists
3340 Pilot Knob Rd. Phone: (651)454-7250
St. Paul, MN 55121-2097 Fax: (651)454-0766
Free: (800)328-7560
Publisher E-mail: aacc@scisoc.org

Journal for cereal foods industry focusing on the use, processing, and marketing of cereal grains and cereal-based foods. **Founded:** 1956. **Freq:** 11/year. **Print Method:** Letterpress and offset. **Trim Size:** 8 1/2 x 11. **Cols./Page:** 3 and 2. **Col. Width:** 26 and 40 nonpareils. **Col. Depth:** 140 agate lines. **Key Personnel:** Steven C. Nelson, Publisher; Miles Wimer, Director; Jody Grider, Editor; Amy Hope, Advertising Mgr. **ISSN:** 0146-6283. **Subscription Rates:** $88 individuals; $15 single issue; $17 single issue other countries; $120 out of country. **Alt. Formats:** Microfiche.
Ad Rates: BW: $1,534 **Circ:** Paid ‡4,231
4C: $2,434 Controlled ‡303
PCI: $45

16432 Child and Youth Services
The Haworth Press, Inc.
Univ. of Minnesota Phone: (612)624-3700
Center for Youth Development & Research Fax: (612)625-5767
1985 Buford Ave.
386 McNeal Hall
St. Paul, MN 55108-6144
Publisher E-mail: getinfo@haworthpressinc.com

Journal on youth services. **Founded:** 1977. **Freq:** 2/year. **Trim Size:** 6x8 1/2. **Cols./Page:** 1. **Key Personnel:** Jerome Beker, Editor, beker001@maroon.tc.umn.edu; Bill Cohen, Publisher. **ISSN:** 0145-935X. **Subscription Rates:** $60 individuals; $160 institutions; $200 libraries. **Remarks:** Accepts advertising.
Ad Rates: BW: $300 **Circ:** Paid 417

16433 The Clarion
Bethel College
3900 Bethel Dr. No. 2381
Saint Paul, MN 55112
Publication E-mail: clarion@bethel.edu

Collegiate newspaper. **Subtitle:** The Clarion. **Founded:** 1923. **Freq:** Biweekly. **Print Method:** Offset. **Trim Size:** 1. **Cols./Page:** 3. **Col. Width:** 24 nonpareils. **Col. Depth:** 210 agate lines. **Key Personnel:** Hannah Hayes, Editor, fax (613)635-8652; Jill Force, Business/Ad Manager. **Remarks:** Accepts advertising. **Online:** ARI NETWORK.
Ad Rates: GLR: $1.35 **Circ:** Controlled ‡2,500
BW: $375
PCI: $8

16434 Country Style Homes Plans and Designs
HomeStyles Publishing and Marketing, Inc.
213 E. 4th St. Phone: (612)602-5000
St. Paul, MN 55101 Fax: (612)602-5001
Free: (888)626-2026
Publisher E-mail: mktg@homestyles.com

Consumer magazine covering country homes inspired by classic designs of yesteryear: Victorians, colonials, farmhouses, ranches and more. **Founded:** 1991. **Freq:** Semiannual. **Print Method:** Web offset. **Trim Size:** 8 x 10 3/4. **Cols./Page:** 3. **Key Personnel:** Diana Jasan, Company Leader, Publishing, phone (612)602-5104, djasan@homesyles.com; Steve Gramins, Editor, phone (612)602-5128, sgramins@homestyles.com; Kevin Miller, Advertising Rep., phone (888)311-7756, fax (205)835-9946; Shelley Junker, Leader Advertising Sales, phone (612)602-5115, sjunker@homestyles.com; Kris Donnelly, Leader Distribution, phone (612)602-5117, kdonnelly@homestyles.com; Dave Whelan, Advertising Rep., phone (708)387-1796, fax (708)387-1797, dwhelan@ameritech.net. **Subscription Rates:** $16.80. **Remarks:** Accepts advertising. **URL:** www.homestyles.com. **Alt. Formats:** CD-ROM, Virtual Home.
Ad Rates: BW: $3,369 **Circ:** Non-paid 62,000
4C: $4,158

16435 Countrypolitan Homes and Plans
HomeStyles Publishing and Marketing, Inc.
213 E. 4th St.
Saint Paul, MN 55101
Publication E-mail: kbaruth@homestyles.com
Publisher E-mail: mktg@homestyles.com

Consumer magazine covering home building plans that combine the warmth of the country and the amenities of today's most innovative designs. **Founded:** 1992. **Freq:** Quarterly. **Print Method:** Web offset. **Trim Size:** 8 x 10 3/4. **Cols./Page:** 3. **Key Personnel:** Diana Jasan, Company Leader, Publishing, phone (612)602-5104, djasan@homestyles.com; Kirk Baruth, Editor; Kevin Miller, Advertising Rep., phone (888)311-7756, fax (205)835-9946; Shelley Junker, Leader, Adv. Sales, phone (612)602-5115, sjunker@homestyles.com; Kris Donnelly, Leader, Dist., phone (612)602-5117, kdonnelly@homestyles.com. **Subscription Rates:** Free. **Remarks:** Accepts advertising. **URL:** http://www.homestyles.com. **Alt. Formats:** CD-ROM, Virtual Home.
Ad Rates: BW: $3,369 **Circ:** Non-paid 65,000
4C: $4,158

16436 Elysian Fields Quarterly
Knothole Publishing
2034 Marshall Ave. Phone: (651)644-8558
St. Paul, MN 55104 Fax: (651)644-8086

Electic Journal of Writing on Baseball: opinion, history fiction, poetry, reminiscence, scholarship, humor, trivia, art, and cartoons. **Subtitle:** The Baseball Review. **Founded:** 1981. **Freq:** Quarterly. **Print Method:** Offset. **Trim Size:** 6 x 9. **Cols./Page:** 1. **Col. Width:** 4 3/4 inches. **Col. Depth:** 7 5/8 inches. **Key Personnel:** Tom Goldstein, Publisher; Stephen Lehman, Editor-in-Chief. **ISSN:** 1049-9555. **Subscription Rates:** $22.50 individuals; $5.95 single issue. **Remarks:** Accepts advertising. **Formerly**: The Minneapolis Review of Baseball.
Ad Rates: BW: $400 **Circ:** Paid ‡1,000
Non-paid ‡80

16437 Farmer's Voice
Minnesota Farm Bureau Federation
3080 Eagandale Place Phone: (612)905-2118
PO Box 64370 Fax: (612)905-2159
St. Paul, MN 55164
Publication E-mail: slengsfeld@aol.com
Publisher E-mail: mfbf@aol.com

Publication reporting on Minnesota's farm economy. **Founded:** 1917. **Freq:** 10/year. **Print Method:** Offset. **Trim Size:** 11 3/8 x 15. **Cols./Page:** 4. **Col. Width:** 2 1/2 inches. **Col. Depth:** 14 inches. **Key Personnel:** Linda Hagan Kvanbeck, Editor. **USPS:** 668-410. **Subscription Rates:** Free to qualified subscribers; $62. **Remarks:** Advertising not accepted for alcoholic beverages and tobacco products.
Ad Rates: BW: $1,009 **Circ:** Combined 32,800
4C: $800
PCI: $50

16438 FATE
Llewellyn Publications
PO Box 64383 Phone: (651)291-1970
St. Paul, MN 55164-0383 Fax: (651)291-1908
Free: (800)843-6666
Publication E-mail: fate@llewellyn.com
Publisher E-mail: kitty@llewellyn.com

Paranormal magazine focusing on UFOs, hauntings, psychic phenomena, mystery animals, ancient mysteries, and personal mystical experiences. **Subtitle:** Experience the Unknown. **Founded:** 1948. **Freq:** Monthly. **Print Method:** Web offset. **Trim Size:** 8 1/8 x 10 3/4. **Cols./Page:** 3. **Col. Width:** 13 picas. **Col. Depth:** 9 1/2 inches. **Key Personnel:** Carl Lewellyn Weschcke, Publisher; Mickey McNeill, Circulation Mgr.; Terry O'Neill, Editor-in-Chief. **ISSN:** 0014-8776. **Subscription Rates:** $24.95; $4.95 single issue. **URL:** http://www.fatemag.com. **Alt. Formats:** Microform, MSI.
Ad Rates: BW: $1,865 **Circ:** Paid 60,000
4C: $2,265 Free 350
PCI: $140

16439 Gaming Products and Services
RCM Enterprises, Inc.
2233 University Ave. W., Ste. 410 Phone: (612)523-0666
St. Paul, MN 55114 Fax: (612)523-0665
Publisher E-mail: rcmpub@aol.com

Magazine reporting on products, services, and trends affecting the gaming industry. **Founded:** 1993. **Freq:** Monthly. **Print Method:** Offset. **Trim Size:** 8 1/8 x 10 7/8. **Cols./Page:** 6. **Col. Width:** 2 1/8 inches. **Col. Depth:** 10 inches. **Key Personnel:** Robert C. Mead, Publisher; Mara Frazier, Production Mgr. **ISSN:** 1071-9350. **Subscription Rates:** $39 individuals; $61 two years; $48 Canada; $71 two years Canada; $110 elsewhere.
Ad Rates: BW: $1,705 **Circ:** Paid 2,000
4C: $2,405 Non-paid 5,500

16440 Gobbles
Minnesota Turkey Growers Association, Inc.
2380 Wycliff St. Phone: (651)646-4553
St. Paul, MN 55114 Fax: (651)646-4554
Publication E-mail: mnturkey2@aol.com
Publisher E-mail: mnturkey1@aol.com

Subtitle: The News and Information Source for the Minnesota Turkey Industry. **Founded:** 1946. **Freq:** Monthly. **Print Method:** Offset. **Trim Size:** 8 1/2 x 11. **Cols./Page:** 3. **Col. Width:** 27 nonpareils. **Col. Depth:** 140 agate lines. **Key Personnel:** Lara Ginsburg, Editor. **Subscription Rates:** $25. **Remarks:** Accepts advertising.
Ad Rates: GLR: $5 **Circ:** ‡1,025
BW: $450
4C: $780
PCI: $20

16441 God's Word Today
2115 Summit Ave. Phone: (651)962-6738
St. Paul, MN 55105-1082 Fax: (651)962-6755

Magazine providing daily Scripture Reading guide for Catholics. **Subtitle:** A daily guide for reading scripture. **Founded:** 1979. **Freq:** Monthly. **Print Method:** Web offset. **Trim Size:** 5 1/4 x 8 3/8. **Cols./Page:** 1. **Col. Width:** 24.5 picas. **Col. Depth:** 42 picas. **Key Personnel:** George Martin, Founding Editor; L. Thomas Kelly, Publisher; Stephen J. Binz, Editor. **ISSN:** 0199-3429. **Subscription Rates:** $17.95. **Remarks:** Accepts advertising.
Ad Rates: BW: $1,100 **Circ:** ‡55,000

16442 Harvest States AgriVisions
Harvest States Cooperatives
1667 Snelling Ave.
PO Box 94594
St. Paul, MN 55164

Trade magazine for Harvest States Cooperatives members, covering agriculture cooperatives. **Freq:** Bimonthly. **Print Method:** Sheetfed offset. **Trim Size:** 8 1/4 x 10 3/4. **Cols./Page:** 3. **Col. Width:** 13 picas. **Col. Depth:** 57 picas. **Key Personnel:** Alison Cummings, Editor; Sandy Abrizenski, Circulation Mgr. **ISSN:** 1089-4640. **Subscription Rates:** $4 individuals. **Remarks:** Advertising not accepted. **URL:** http://www.harveststates.com. **Former name:** Harvest States Journal.
Circ: (Not Reported)

16443 Homestyles
HomeStyles Publishing and Marketing, Inc.
213 E. 4th St. Phone: (612)602-5000
St. Paul, MN 55101 Fax: (612)602-5001
Free: (888)626-2026
Publisher E-mail: mktg@homestyles.com

Consumer magazine covering home plans. **Founded:** 1986. **Freq:** Quarterly. **Print Method:** Web offset. **Trim Size:** 8 x 10 3/4. **Cols./Page:** 3. **Key Personnel:** Diana Jasan, Leader, Publishing; Laura Lentz, Editor, llentz@homestyles.com; Kevin Miller, Advertising Rep.; Dave Whelan, Advertising Rep.; Shelley Junker, Leader, Advertising Sales; Kris Donnelly, Leader, Distribution. **Remarks:** Accepts advertising. **URL:** http://www.homestyles.com.
Ad Rates: BW: $3,369 **Circ:** Non-paid 55,000
4C: $4,158

16444 HomeStyles Home Plans
HomeStyles Publishing and Marketing, Inc.
213 E. 4th St.
Saint Paul, MN 55101
Publisher E-mail: mktg@homestyles.com

Consumer magazine featuring exciting new homes for the American family, identifying a variety of timely themes, including energy-efficient, sunbelt, luxury and brick homes. **Founded:** 1986. **Freq:** Quarterly. **Print Method:** Web offset. **Trim Size:** 8 x 10 3/4. **Cols./Page:** 3. **Key Personnel:** Diana Jasan, Company Leader, Publishing, phone (612)602-5104, djason@homestyles.com; Laura Lentz, Editor, phone (612)602-5127, llentz@homestyles.com; Kevin Miller, Advertising Rep., phone (888)311-7756, fax (205)835-9946; Shelley Junker, Process Leader, Adv. Sales, phone (612)602-5115, sjunker@homestyles.com; Kris Donnelly, Process Leader, Dist., phone (612)602-5117, kdonnelly@homestyles.com; Dave Whelan, Advertising Rep., phone (708)387-1796, fax (708)387-1797, dwhelan@ameritech.net. **Subscription Rates:** $16.80. **Remarks:** Accepts advertising. **URL:** http://www.homestyles.com. **Alt. Formats:** CD-ROM, Vista Home.
Ad Rates: BW: $3,369 **Circ:** Non-paid 65,000
4C: $4,158

16445 Hospitality News
Delmont Communications
1700 Livingston Ave.
St. Paul, MN 55118

Magazine covering hospitality industry management and operations issues in Minnesota and western Wisconsin.

Founded: 1981. **Freq:** Monthly. **Print Method:** Web. **Trim Size:** 11 x 14 3/4. **Cols./Page:** 4. **Col. Width:** 2 1/4 inches. **Col. Depth:** 13 3/4 inches. **Key Personnel:** Joe Delmont, Editor and Publisher; Steve Delmont, Associate Publisher. **Subscription Rates:** $36. **Remarks:** Accepts advertising. **URL:** http://hospitalitynews.com. **Formerly:** Hospitality Management.
Ad Rates: GLR: $995 **Circ:** ‡10,000
BW: $1,130
4C: $1,505
PCI: $1,295

16446 Human Resource Development Quarterly
Jossey-Bass Inc., Publishers
1954 Buford Ave.
St. Paul, MN 55108
Publisher E-mail: webperson@jbp.com

Scholarly journal on human resource development, including training, management, industrial psychology, adult education, organizational behavior, instructional technology, and economics. **Founded:** 1990. **Freq:** Quarterly. **Print Method:** Offset. **Trim Size:** 6 x 9. **Cols./Page:** 1. **Col. Width:** 26.5 picas. **Col. Depth:** 101 agate lines. **Key Personnel:** Gary N. McClean, Editor; Ronald Jacobs, Asst. Editor; Brent W. Mattson, Managing Editor. **ISSN:** 1044-8004. **Subscription Rates:** $47; $79 institutions. **Remarks:** Advertising not accepted.
Circ: 5,000

16447 Hungry Mind Review: Children's Book Section
Hungry Mind Review
1648 Grand Ave. Phone: (612)699-2610
St. Paul, MN 55105 Fax: (612)699-0970
Publisher E-mail: hmreview@winternet.com

Reviews of children's literature published in quarterly book review magazine. **Founded:** 1986. **Freq:** Quarterly. **Cols./Page:** 4. **Col. Width:** 2 1/4 inches. **Col. Depth:** 15 inches. **Key Personnel:** Bart Schneider, Editor; R. David Unowsky, Publisher; Ralph Blythe, Children's Book Editor. **Subscription Rates:** $14. **Remarks:** Accepts advertising. **URL:** http://www.bookwire.com/hmr. **Formerly:** Hungry Mind Review: Children's Book Supplement.
Ad Rates: BW: $1,995 **Circ:** Paid 4,000
4C: $2,345 Non-paid 40,000

16448 Hydrological Science and Technology
American Institute of Hydrology
2499 Rice St., Ste. 135 Phone: (651)484-8169
St. Paul, MN 55113-3724 Fax: (651)484-8357
Publisher E-mail: AIHydro@aol.com

Professional journal for hydrologists and hydrogeologists. **Founded:** 1985. **Key Personnel:** Helen Klose, Managing Editor. **Subscription Rates:** $150 individuals.
Circ: Controlled 500

16449 Journal of Law and Religion
Hamline University
1536 Hewitt Ave. Phone: (612)523-2268
PO Box 106 Fax: (612)523-2956
St. Paul, MN 55104
Journal covering religion and its influence on law. **Freq:** Semiannual. **Key Personnel:** Marie Failinger, Editor; Patrick Keifert, Editor; Howard J. Vogel, Managing Editor; Kathryn Marron, Production Mgr. **Subscription Rates:** $15 individuals; $25 out of country; $25 institutions; $35 institutions out of country; $10 students.

16450 Journal of Ministry in Addiction and Recovery
The Haworth Press, Inc.
2481 Como Ave Phone: (612)641-3475
St. Paul, MN 55108 Fax: (612)641-3584
Publisher E-mail: getinfo@haworthpressinc.com

Journal on persons involved in ministry with those afflicted and affected by addictions. **Founded:** 1994. **Freq:** Biannual. **Trim Size:** 6 x 8 1/2. **Key Personnel:** Robert Albers, Ph.D., Editor, ralbers@luthersem.edu; Bill Cohen, Publisher. **ISSN:** 1053-8755. **Subscription Rates:** $35 individuals; $48 industry; $20 libraries 30% more for Canada; 40% more for other countries. **Remarks:** Accepts advertising.
Ad Rates: BW: $300 **Circ:** Paid 274

16451 Llewellyn's New Worlds of Mind and Spirit
Llewellyn Publications
PO Box 64383 Phone: (651)291-1970
St. Paul, MN 55164-0383 Fax: (651)291-1908
Free: (800)843-6666
Publication E-mail: lwlpc@llewellyn.com
Publisher E-mail: kitty@llewellyn.com

Catalog for readers interested in practical applications of astrology, psychology, occult philosophy, and inner awareness techniques. Includes reviews, articles, and news for the New Age community. **Founded:** 1981. **Freq:** Bimonthly. **Print Method:** Offset. **Trim Size:** 8 1/4 x 10 3/4. **Cols./Page:** 3. **Col. Width:** 14 picas. **Col. Depth:** 60 picas. **Key Personnel:** Carl Llewellyn Weschcke, Publisher; Stephanie Clement, Marketing Mgr. **ISSN:** 0893-1534. **Subscription Rates:** $10 U.S. and Canada; $30 other countries. **Remarks:** Accepts advertising. **URL:** http://www.llewellyn.com. **Formerly:** Llewellyn New Times.
Ad Rates: BW: $1,460 **Circ:** Combined ‡80,000
4C: $1,860

16452 The Mac Weekly
Macalester College
1600 Grand Ave. Phone: (612)696-6212
St. Paul, MN 55105 Fax: (612)696-6689
Publication E-mail: macweekly@macalstr.edu

Collegiate newspaper. **Founded:** Sept. 1914. **Freq:** Weekly (Thurs.). **Print Method:** Letterpress and offset. **Trim Size:** 11 x 16. **Cols./Page:** 5. **Col. Width:** 22 nonpareils. **Col. Depth:** 210 agate lines. **Key Personnel:** Dania Rajendra, Editor, drajendra@macalester.edu; Nate Cool, Advertising Mgr., phone (612)696-6684, ncook@macalester.edu. **Subscription Rates:** $15 semester. **Remarks:** Accepts advertising. **URL:** http://www.macalstr.edu/.
Ad Rates: BW: $120 **Circ:** ‡1,600
SAU: $3
PCI: $5

16453 Marine Textiles
RCM Enterprises, Inc.
2233 University Ave. W., Ste. 410 Phone: (612)523-0666
Fax: (612)523-0665
St. Paul, MN 55114
Publisher E-mail: rcmpub@aol.com

Magazine reporting on fabrics, fabric products, and furnishings used in the boating industry. **Founded:** Jan. 15, 1986. **Freq:** Monthly. **Print Method:** Offset. **Trim Size:** 8 1/8 x 10 7/8. **Cols./Page:** 3. **Col. Width:** 2 1/8 inches. **Col. Depth:** 10 inches. **Key Personnel:** Joe Pawlowski, Editor; Robert C. Mead, Publisher. **ISSN:** 0885-9949. **Subscription Rates:** $39 individuals; $61 two years; $48 Canada; $71 two years Canada; $110 elsewhere.
Ad Rates: BW: $1,807 **Circ:** Paid ‡3,000
4C: $2,507 Non-paid ‡6,000

16454 Marriage Magazine
International Marriage Encounter, Inc.
955 Lake Dr. Phone: (612)454-6434
St. Paul, MN 55120 Fax: (612)452-0466
Free: (800)627-7424

An abundantly rich resource that celebrates and nurtures marriages and relationships, inspiring insights, practical how-to's, intensity ideas, and couple's sharing success secrets on a different theme for each issue. **Subtitle:** Celebrating Committed Couples. **Founded:** 1972. **Freq:** 6/times. **Print Method:** Sheetfed offset. **Trim Size:** 8 1/2 x 11. **Cols./Page:** 2 and 3. **Col. Width:** 3 inches. **Col. Depth:** 8 1/2 inches. **Key Personnel:** Krysta Eryn Kavenaugh, Exec. Editor, phone (612)454-7947. **ISSN:** 1063-1054. **Subscription Rates:** $19.95; $3.50 single issue. **Remarks:** Accepts advertising. **Formerly:** Marriage Encounter (1992); Agape.
Ad Rates: BW: $500 **Circ:** 11,000
4C: $1,080

16455 MEA Advocate
Minnesota Education Association
41 Sherburne Ave. Phone: (612)227-9541
St. Paul, MN 55103 Fax: (612)292-4802

Educational newspaper. **Founded:** 1971. **Freq:** 10/year. **Print Method:** Offset. Uses mats. **Trim Size:** 16 1/2 x 11 1/2. **Cols./Page:** 5. **Col. Width:** 28 nonpareils. **Col. Depth:** 210 agate lines. **Key Personnel:** Tom Nordby, Editor. **ISSN:** 1053-3362. **Subscription Rates:** $12 individuals. **Remarks:** Accepts advertising.
Ad Rates: BW: $1,998 **Circ:** ‡48,000
PCI: $56

16456 Melpomene
Melpomene Institute
1010 University Ave. W. Phone: (612)642-1951
St. Paul, MN 55104-4706 Fax: (612)642-1871
Publication E-mail: melpomen@skypoint.com

Periodical on research and education of the relationship between health and physical activity. **Subtitle:** A Journal for Women's Health Research. **Founded:** 1982. **Freq:** 3/year. **Cols./Page:** 3. **Col. Width:** 2 3/8 inches. **Col. Depth:** 7 inches. **Key Personnel:** Judy Remington, Editor. **ISSN:** 1043-8734. **Subscription Rates:** $40; $25 students; $45 Canada; $50 other countries; $50 Industry; $250 corporations. $5 single issue. **Remarks:** Advertising not accepted.
Circ: Paid 1,700
Non-paid 173

16457 Midwest Players
RCM Enterprises, Inc.
2233 University Ave. W., Ste. 410 Phone: (612)523-0666
Fax: (612)523-0665
St. Paul, MN 55114
Publisher E-mail: rcmpub@aol.com

Reports on casinos and race tracks in the midwest. **Founded:** May 1991. **Freq:** Semimonthly. **Print Method:** Web. **Trim Size:** 11 3/8 x 16. **Cols./Page:** 4. **Col. Width:** 2 1/4 inches. **Col. Depth:** 14 inches. **Key Personnel:** Robert C. Mead, Sales Mgr.; Joe Pawlowski, Editor. **ISSN:** 1071-4081. **Subscription Rates:** $48. **Remarks:** Accepts advertising.
Ad Rates: BW: $904.40 **Circ:** Free 58,000
4C: $1364.40
PCI: $16.15

16458 Minnesota Conservation Volunteer
Department of Natural Resources
500 Lafayette Rd. Phone: (612)296-0894
St. Paul, MN 55155-4046 Fax: (612)296-0902

Government magazine covering conservation and the wise use of the natural resources in Minnesota. **Founded:** Oct. 1940. **Freq:** Bimonthly. **Print Method:** Web offset. **Trim Size:** 5 1/2 x 8. **Key Personnel:** Kathleen Weflen, Editor, kathleen.weflen@dnr.state.mn.us; Susan Ryan, Circulation Mgr., phone (651)296-0888, sue.ryan@dnr.state.mn.us; Greg Breining, Managing Editor; Susan K. Binkley, Art Dir., phone (651)296-6201, susan.binkley@dnr.state.mn.us; Catherine Mix, Editorial Asst., phone (651)296-0894, cathy.mix@dnr.state.mn.us; Mary Hoff, Production Coord. **USPS:** 129-880. **Subscription Rates:** $20 out of state. **Remarks:** Advertising not accepted. **Formerly:** The Conservation Volunteer (Dec. 1, 1970); The Minnesota Volunteer (Dec. 1, 1998).
Circ: (Not Reported)

16459 Minnesota Grocer
Minnesota Grocers Association
533 St. Clair Ave. Phone: (612)228-0973
St. Paul, MN 55102 Fax: (612)228-1949
Free: (800)966-8352

Grocery trade magazine. **Subtitle:** Official Publication of the Minnesota Grocers Association. **Founded:** 1929. **Freq:** Quarterly plus a directory. **Print Method:** Offset. **Trim Size:** 8 1/4 x 10 7/8. **Cols./Page:** 3 and 2. **Col. Width:** 26 and 40 nonpareils. **Col. Depth:** 140 agate lines. **Key Personnel:** Randy Schubring, Editor. **Subscription Rates:** $30.
Ad Rates: BW: $785 **Circ:** ‡4,700
4C: $1,195

16460 Minnesota History
Minnesota Historical Society
345 Kellogg Blvd. W. Phone: (651)296-2264
St. Paul, MN 55102-1906 Fax: (651)297-1345
Free: (800)647-7827

Historical journal. **Founded:** Mar. 1915. **Freq:** Quarterly. **Print Method:** Offset. **Trim Size:** 8 1/2 x 11. **Cols./Page:** 2. **Col. Width:** 40 nonpareils. **Col. Depth:** 126 agate lines. **Key Personnel:** Anne R. Kaplan, Editor, phone (612)297-4467, anne.kaplan@mnhs.org. **ISSN:** 0026-5497. **Subscription Rates:** $15; $5 single issue. **Remarks:** Advertising not accepted.
Circ: ‡15,000

16461 Minnesota Legionnaire
Minnesota American Legion Publishing Co.
State Veterans Service Bldg. Phone: (651)291-1800
St. Paul, MN 55155-0001 Fax: (651)291-1057
Publication E-mail: mnamlegion@landoflakes.com
Publisher E-mail: department@mnlegion.org

Membership newspaper. **Subtitle:** Official Publication, Minnesota American Legion. **Founded:** 1921. **Freq:** Monthly. **Print Method:** Offset. **Trim Size:** 11 1/2 x 15. **Cols./Page:** 6. **Col. Width:** 22 nonpareils. **Col. Depth:** 210 agate lines. **Key Personnel:** Alan T. Zdon, Editor, azdon@mnlegion.org. **Subscription Rates:** $5. **Remarks:** Accepts advertising.
Ad Rates: GLR: $.85 **Circ:** ‡121,000
BW: $1,350
PCI: $15

16462 Minnesota Smoke-Eater
Smoke-Eater Publications
PO Box 129 Phone: (402)329-4665
Pierce, NE 68767-0129 Fax: (402)329-6224

Magazine serving volunteer firemen. **Founded:** 1949. **Freq:** Monthly. **Print Method:** Offset. **Cols./Page:** 5. **Col. Width:** 22 nonpareils. **Col. Depth:** 217 agate lines. **Key Personnel:** Robert Zimmer, Publisher. **Subscription Rates:** $10. **Remarks:** Accepts advertising.
Ad Rates: BW: $310 **Circ:** ‡12,000
PCI: $4

16463 Minnesota Women's Press
Minnesota Women's Press, Inc.
771 Raymond Ave. Phone: (651)646-3968
St. Paul, MN 55114-1522 Fax: (651)646-2186
Publication E-mail: women@womenspress.com
Publisher E-mail: women@womenspress.com

Feminist newspaper providing news coverage by and for women. **Founded:** Apr. 17, 1985. **Freq:** Biweekly. **Print Method:** Web. **Trim Size:** 10 x 15. **Cols./Page:** 5. **Col. Width:** 22 nonpareils. **Col. Depth:** 210 agate lines. **Key Personnel:** Mollie Hoben, Publisher; Glenda Martin, Publisher; Kathy Magnuson, General Mgr.; Cynthia Scott, Editor. **Subscription Rates:** $27; $47 two years. **Remarks:** Accepts advertising.
Ad Rates: GLR: $0.65 **Circ:** Paid 800
BW: $1,912.50 Free 40,000
4C: $2,672.50
SAU: $30.85
PCI: $25.50

16464 Molecular Plant-Microbe Interactions (MPMI)
American Association of Cereal Chemists
3340 Pilot Knob Rd. Phone: (651)454-7250
St. Paul, MN 55121-2097 Fax: (651)454-0766
Free: (800)328-7560
Publisher E-mail: aacc@scisoc.org

Journal covering research on the molecular aspects of plant-microbe interactions. **Founded:** Jan. 1988. **Freq:** 9/year. **Print Method:** Offset. **Trim Size:** 8 1/2 x 11. **Cols./Page:** 2. **Col. Width:** 3 1/2 inches. **Col. Depth:** 10 inches. **Key Personnel:** Stanton B. Gelvin, Editor-in-Chief, phone (317)494-4939, fax (317)496-1496, gelvin@bilbo.bio.purdue.edu; Steven C. Nelson, Publisher; Miles Wimer, Director; Jean Rice, Editorial Supervisor; Rhonda Wilke, Advertising Materials Coordinator. **ISSN:** 0894-0282. **Subscription Rates:** $285 individuals; $60 single issue; $310 out of country. **Remarks:** Accepts advertising. **URL:** http://www.scisoc.org.
Ad Rates: BW: $850 **Circ:** Paid ‡1,492
4C: $1,600 Non-paid ‡7

16465 The Monitor
Minnesota State University Student Association
108 Como Ave. Phone: (651)224-1518
St. Paul, MN 55103 Fax: (651)224-9753
Publisher E-mail: monitor@msusa.net

Student newspaper. **Subtitle:** The Monthly Publication of the Minnesota State University Student Association. **Founded:** Sept. 1984. **Freq:** Monthly. **Print Method:** Web offset. **Cols./Page:** 5. **Col. Width:** 1 3/16 inches. **Col. Depth:** 15 inches. **Key Personnel:** Michael R. Howell, Advertising Mgr. **Subscription Rates:** Free. **Remarks:** Accepts advertising.
Ad Rates: BW: $724 **Circ:** Non-paid ‡23,000
PCI: $9.29

16466 MSP Airport News
MSP Airport News, Inc.
Lindbergh Twin Cities Airport Phone: (612)726-5557
St. Paul, MN 55111 Fax: (612)726-5979

Airport newspaper. **Founded:** 1988. **Freq:** Semimonthly. **Print Method:** Offset. **Trim Size:** 11 1/2 x 15. **Col. Width:** 2 3/8 inches. **Col. Depth:** 13 1/2 inches. **Key Personnel:** H.R. Meier, Editor; Bill Farmer, Publisher. **Subscription Rates:** $19.95. **Remarks:** Accepts advertising.
Ad Rates: BW: $1,250 **Circ:** Free ‡23,000

16467 New Unionist
New Union Party
1821 University Ave. W., No. S-116 Phone: (651)646-5546
St. Paul, MN 55104
Publisher E-mail: nup@minn.net

Socialist magazine. **Founded:** 1973. **Freq:** Monthly. **Print Method:** Offset. **Cols./Page:** 4. **Col. Width:** 28 nonpareils. **Col. Depth:** 217 agate lines. **Key Personnel:** Jeff Miller, Editor. **ISSN:** 1070-7727. **Subscription Rates:** $5. **Remarks:** Advertising not accepted.
Circ: Non-paid 8,600
Paid 400

16468 Northwest Dentistry
Minnesota Dental Association
2236 Marshall Ave. Phone: (612)646-7454
St. Paul, MN 55104 Fax: (612)646-8246

Journal of the Minnesota Dental Association and the North Dakota Dental Association. **Freq:** Bimonthly. **Trim Size:** 8 1/2 x 11. **Key Personnel:** Alan D. Quan, Editor. **Subscription Rates:** $20 members included in dues; $35 nonmembers; $40 nonmembers out of country; $3.50 single issue U.S.; $6.70 single issue out of country. **Remarks:** Accepts advertising.
Ad Rates: BW: $417 **Circ:** Combined 3,180

16469 The Oracle
Hamline University
1536 Hewitt Ave. Phone: (612)523-2268
PO Box 106 Fax: (612)523-2956
St. Paul, MN 55104
Publication E-mail: oracle@piper.hamline.edu

Collegiate newspaper. **Founded:** 1888. **Freq:** Weekly (Tues.). **Print Method:** Offset. **Trim Size:** Tabloid. **Cols./Page:** 4. **Key Personnel:** Ethan Mills, Editor; Alexa Verman, Advertising; Curtis Danielson, Artistic Director; Jen Boyles, Entertainment Editor; Dante Carter, Co-Opinions Editor; Amanda Mills, Co-Opinions Editor; Nick Twohy, Co-Sports Editor; Eadie Altringer, Co-Sports Editor. **Subscription Rates:** $9.25 individuals. **Remarks:** Accepts advertising. **URL:** http://www.hamline.edu/˜oracle/.
Ad Rates: GLR: $0.30 **Circ:** ‡1,500
BW: $400
PCI: $5

16470 Pheasants Forever
Pheasants Forever, Inc.
1783 Buerkle Circle Phone: (651)773-2000
St. Paul, MN 55110 Fax: (651)773-5500
Publication E-mail: pf@pheasantsforever.org

Magazine for conservationist pheasant hunters. **Founded:** 1982. **Freq:** 5/year. **Print Method:** Web offset. **Trim Size:** 8 3/8 x 10 7/8. **Cols./Page:** 3. **Key Personnel:** Jeffrey S. Finden, CEO; Mark Herwig, Editor. **Subscription Rates:** $25; $5 single issue. **Remarks:** Accepts advertising. **URL:** http://www.pheasantsforever.org.
Ad Rates: BW: $2,215 **Circ:** Paid ‡85,000
4C: $3,160
PCI: $105

16471 Phytopathology
The American Phytopathological Society
3340 Pilot Knob Rd. Phone: (651)454-7250
St. Paul, MN 55121 Fax: (651)454-0766
Free: (800)328-7560
Publisher E-mail: aps@scisoc.org

Plant pathology journal reporting original research. **Subtitle:** An International Journal of the American Phytopathological Society. **Founded:** 1911. **Freq:** Monthly. **Print Method:** Offset. **Trim Size:** 8 1/2 x 11. **Cols./Page:** 2. **Col. Width:** 42 nonpareils. **Col. Depth:** 120 agate lines. **Key Personnel:** Margaret E. Daub, Editor-in-Chief; Steven C. Nelson, Publisher, snelson@scisoc.org; Miles Wimer, Director, milesw@scisoc.org. **ISSN:** 0031-949X. **Subscription Rates:** $375 libraries; $38 single issue; $381 out of country. **Remarks:** Advertising not accepted. **Alt. Formats:** CD-ROM; Microfiche.
Circ: Paid ‡3,788
Non-paid ‡17

16472 Plant Disease
The American Phytopathological Society
3340 Pilot Knob Rd. Phone: (651)454-7250
St. Paul, MN 55121 Fax: (651)454-0766
Free: (800)328-7560
Publisher E-mail: aps@scisoc.org

Journal focusing on research on the applied or practical aspects of diagnosing and treating plant diseases. **Subtitle:** An International Journal of Applied Plant Pathology. **Founded:** 1917. **Freq:** Monthly. **Print Method:** Offset. **Trim Size:** 8 1/2 x 11. **Cols./Page:** 3. **Col. Width:** 28 nonpareils. **Col. Depth:** 140 agate lines. **Key Personnel:** Michael McLaughlin, Editor-in-Chief; Steven C. Nelson, Publisher, snelson@scisoc.org; Miles Wimer, Director, milesw@scisoc.org; Rhonda Wilkie, Advertising Sales, rhonda@scisoc.org. **ISSN:** 0191-2917. **Subscription Rates:** $325 library subscriptions only; $381 out of country; $38 single issue current year; $43 single issue previous years. **Remarks:** Accepts advertising. **Alt. Formats:** CD-ROM; Microfiche.
Ad Rates: BW: $935 **Circ:** Paid ‡3,700
4C: $1,585 Non-paid ‡31
PCI: $50

16473 Sacred Music
Church Music Association of America
548 Lafond Ave. Phone: (612)293-1710
St. Paul, MN 55103-1672 Fax: (612)227-4229

Liturgical music magazine. **Founded:** 1873. **Freq:** Quarterly. **Print Method:** Offset. **Trim Size:** 7 3/4 x 10 3/4. **Cols./Page:** 2 and 1. **Col. Width:** 30 and 60 nonpareils. **Col. Depth:** 119 agate lines. **Key Personnel:** Richard J. Schuler, Editor. **ISSN:** 0036-2255. **Subscription Rates:** $10. **Remarks:** Accepts advertising. **Formerly:** Caecilia.
Ad Rates: BW: $150 **Circ:** ‡1,000

16474 St. Paul Pioneer Press
Knight-Ridder, Inc.
345 Cedar St. Phone: (612)222-5011
St. Paul, MN 55101 Fax: (612)228-5500
Free: (800)950-9080
Publication E-mail: pioneerpress.com

General newspaper. **Founded:** Apr. 28, 1849. **Freq:** Mon.-Sun. (morn.). **Print Method:** Offset. **Cols./Page:** 6. **Col. Width:** 26 nonpareils. **Col. Depth:** 294 agate lines. **Key Personnel:** Rick Sadowski, President, phone (612)228-5404, fax (612)228-5416, rsadowski@pioneerpress.com; Walker Lundy, Editor, phone (612)228-5480, fax (612)228-5500, wlundy@pioneerpress.com; Ron Clark, Editorial Pages Editor, phone (612)228-5544, fax (612)228-5564, rclark@pioneerpress.com; Mary Altuvilla, Vice President, phone (612)228-5302, maltuvilla@pioneerpress.com; Scott Frantzen, Vice President, phone (612)228-5150, sfrantzen@pioneerpress.com. **Subscription Rates:** $172.12. **On-line:** Dialog (The Dialog Corporation); CompuServe Information Service; America Online, Inc. **URL:** http://www.pioneerplanet.com. **Feature Editors:** Sue Campbell, *Family, Food, Travel*, phone (612)228-5326, fax (612)228-5010, scampbell@pioneerpress.com.
Ad Rates: BW: $8,342 **Circ:** Mon.-Fri. ★**199,119**
4C: $10,042 Sat. ★**178,434**
PCI: $89.87 Sun. ★**266,141**

16475 Specialty Coffee Retailer
RCM Enterprises, Inc.
2233 University Ave. W., Ste. 410 Phone: (612)523-0666
Fax: (612)523-0665
St. Paul, MN 55114
Publisher E-mail: rcmpub@aol.com

Magazine reporting on new products, equipment, trends and management techniques for retail specialty coffee businesses. **Subtitle:** The Coffee Business Monthly. **Founded:** 1994. **Freq:** Monthly. **Print Method:** Offset. **Trim Size:** 8 1/8 x 10 7/8. **Cols./Page:** 3. **Col. Width:** 2 1/8 inches. **Col. Depth:** 10 inches. **Key Personnel:** Robert C. Mead, Publisher; Paul Froiland, Editor; Brian Grau, VP Sales; Peg Bennett, Production Mgr. **ISSN:** 1077-3460. **Subscription Rates:** $5 single issue; $36 Canada; $45 US; $95 other countries. **Remarks:** Accepts advertising.
Ad Rates: BW: $1,695 **Circ:** Paid ‡600
4C: $2,390 Non-paid ‡5,900

16476 Spout
28 Wrobie St.
St. Paul, MN 55107

Literary journal covering fiction, nonfiction, poetry and art. **Founded:** Sept. 1989. **Freq:** Quarterly. **Trim Size:** 8 1/2 x 11. **Key Personnel:** John Colburn, Editor; Chris Watercott, Editor; Michelle Filkins, Editor. **Subscription Rates:** $12 individuals; $4 single issue. **Remarks:** Advertising not accepted.
Circ: Combined 250

16477 T S I Journal of Particle Instrumentation
TSI Incorporated
500 Cardigan Rd., Box 64394 Phone: (612)490-2833
St. Paul, MN 55164 Fax: (612)490-3860

Scholarly journal covering the use of TSI particle instruments in aerosol research. **Founded:** Jan. 1986. **Freq:** Irregular. **Print Method:** Offset. **Key Personnel:** Gilmore J. Sem, Editor; Ron Gregg, Asst. Editor. **Subscription Rates:** Free to qualified subscribers. **Remarks:** Advertising not accepted. **Former name:** TSI Quarterly.
Circ: Controlled 8,000

16478 Union Advocate
411 Main St., No. 101 Phone: (612)488-6747
St. Paul, MN 55102-1044 Fax: (612)293-1989

Labor newspaper. **Founded:** 1897. **Freq:** Semimonthly. **Print Method:** Offset. **Cols./Page:** 6. **Col. Width:** 19 nonpareils. **Col. Depth:** 224 agate lines. **Key Personnel:** Barbara Kucera, Editor; Mary Lu Kirchoff, Advertising Mgr. **Subscription Rates:** $11.38. **Remarks:** Accepts advertising.
Ad Rates: GLR: $1.04 **Circ:** ‡43,041

16479 Upholstery Journal
RCM Enterprises, Inc.
2233 University Ave. W., Ste. 410 Phone: (612)523-0666
Fax: (612)523-0665
St. Paul, MN 55114
Publisher E-mail: rcmpub@aol.com

Magazine reporting on materials, techiques, tools, and equipment used in upholstery. **Founded:** 1993. **Freq:** Monthly. **Print Method:** Offset. **Trim Size:** 8 1/8 x 10 7/8. **Cols./Page:** 3. **Col. Width:** 2 1/8 inches. **Col. Depth:** 10 inches. **Key Personnel:** Robert C. Mead, Publisher; Joe Pawlowski, Editor; Robert Tyler, Sales Mgr.; Mira Frazer, Production Mgr. **ISSN:** 1072-5628. **Subscription Rates:** $39 individuals; $61

two years; $48 Canada; $71 two years Canada; $110 elsewhere.
Ad Rates: BW: $1,612 **Circ:** Paid 3,000
4C: $2,262 Non-paid 6,000

16480 Villager
Villager Communications, Inc.
757 Snelling Ave. S. Phone: (612)699-1462
St. Paul, MN 55116-2296 Fax: (612)699-6501
Publication E-mail: jr@villagercomm.com

Local newspaper (tabloid). **Founded:** Mar. 1953. **Freq:** Biweekly. **Print Method:** Offset. **Cols./Page:** 6. **Col. Depth:** 210 agate lines. **Key Personnel:** Michael J. Mischke, Publisher; John Wadell, Editor; Dale Mischke, Editor. **Subscription Rates:** $25 individuals. **Remarks:** Accepts advertising. **URL:** http://www.villagercomm.com. **Formerly**: The Highland Villager.
Ad Rates: BW: $1,800 **Circ:** Paid ‡200
4C: $2,223 Free ‡45,400
SAU: $36.47
PCI: $28

16481 The Wall Paper
4225 White Bear Pkwy., Ste. 400 Phone: (612)293-1544
Fax: (612)653-4308
St. Paul, MN 55110
Publisher E-mail: bcarlson@gwmcnamara.com

Magazine for the wall covering industry. **Founded:** 1980. **Freq:** Monthly. **Print Method:** Offset. **Trim Size:** 10 7/8 x 14 1/2. **Cols./Page:** 5. **Col. Width:** 22 nonpareils. **Col. Depth:** 196 agate lines. **Key Personnel:** Marita Thomas, Editor, phone (212)260-8707, fax (212)505-1377; Bill McNamara, Publisher. **ISSN:** 0273-6837. **Subscription Rates:** $25. **Remarks:** Accepts advertising.
Ad Rates: BW: $3,025 **Circ:** Controlled 17,122
4C: $4,015 Paid 1,834

16482 The Wanderer
Wanderer Press
201 Ohio St. Phone: (612)224-5733
St. Paul, MN 55107 Fax: (612)224-9666

Catholic newspaper (national). **Founded:** 1867. **Freq:** Weekly (Thurs.). **Print Method:** Offset. **Trim Size:** 15 x 22. **Cols./Page:** 7. **Col. Width:** 23 nonpareils. **Col. Depth:** 280 agate lines. **Key Personnel:** Alphonse J. Matt, Jr., Editor; Anne E. Ternes, Advertising Mgr. **USPS:** 665-780. **Subscription Rates:** $40 individuals. **Remarks:** Accepts advertising.
Ad Rates: GLR: $1 **Circ:** ‡35,000
BW: $1,988
4C: $2,788
PCI: $14

16483 Window Fashions
G & W McNamara Publishing, Inc.
4225 White Bear Pkwy., Ste. 400 Phone: (651)293-1544
Fax: (651)653-4308
St. Paul, MN 55110
Design and merchandizing magazine for specialty retailers, dealers and designers in the business of custom window treatments. Provides design, fashion, and color trend info as well as installation techniques and practical business information. **Subtitle:** Design and Education Magazine. **Founded:** 1981. **Freq:** Monthly. **Print Method:** Offset. **Trim Size:** 8 1/8 x 11. **Cols./Page:** 4 and 3. **Col. Width:** 10 and 27 nonpareils. **Col. Depth:** 60.5 picas. **Key Personnel:** Grace McNamara, Publisher; Karen Fischer, Advertising Mgr.; Linnea Addison, Editor. **ISSN:** 0886-9669. **Subscription Rates:** $32 individuals. **Remarks:** Accepts advertising. **Formerly**: Window Energy Systems (WES).
Ad Rates: BW: $3,360 **Circ:** Paid 5,660
4C: $4,610 Controlled 17,910

16484 Y Drych (The Mirror)
Y Drych (The Mirror)
PO Box 8089 Phone: (612)642-1653
St. Paul, MN 55108-0089 Fax: (612)642-0170

Newspaper (tabloid) on Welsh social and political news; also covers Welsh events in the U.S. and Canada. Includes regular cultural, genealogical, and Welsh language features. **Subtitle:** Newyddiadur Cenedlaethol Cymry America (The American Organ of the Welsh People). **Founded:** 1851. **Freq:** Monthly (except July). **Print Method:** Offset. **Trim Size:** 11 x 17. **Cols./Page:** 5. **Col. Width:** 1 3/4 inches. **Col. Depth:** 15 inches. **Key Personnel:** Mary Morris Mergenthal, Editor and Publisher. **ISSN:** 0199-2538. **Subscription Rates:** $20; $30 Canada; $35 two years; $50 two years, Canada. **Remarks:** Accepts advertising.
Ad Rates: PCI: $6.50 **Circ:** Paid ‡2,500
Non-paid ‡500

16485 KLBB-AM - 1400
611 Frontenac Pl. Phone: (612)341-1700
St. Paul, MN 55104-4947 Fax: (612)341-1701

Format: Big Band/Nostalgia. **Networks:** Westwood One Radio. **Owner:** Cargill Communications, at above address, (612)228-4444. **Operating Hours:** Continuous; 5% network, 95% local. **ADI:** Minneapolis-St. Paul, MN. **Key Personnel:** Reed Hagen, Program Dir.; John Kuchne, General Mgr. **Wattage:** 1000. **Ad Rates:** $34-60 per unit.

16486 KLGT-TV - 23
PO Box 8125, 1640 Como Ave. Phone: (612)646-2300
St. Paul, MN 55108-0125 Fax: (612)646-1220

Format: Commercial TV. **Networks:** Warner Brothers Studios. **Owner:** Lakeland Group Television, Inc., at above address. **Founded:** Mar. 2, 1992. **Formerly**: KTMA-TV (1992). **Operating Hours:** Continuous. **ADI:** Minneapolis-St. Paul, MN. **Key Personnel:** Linda Rios Brook, Pres./Gen. Mgr. **Wattage:** 5,000,000. **Ad Rates:** Advertising accepted; rates available upon request.

16487 KNOF-FM - 95.3
1347 Selby Ave. Phone: (612)645-8271
St. Paul, MN 55104

Format: Religious. **Networks:** Independent. **Founded:** 1960. **Operating Hours:** 5:30 a.m.-10:30 a.m. **ADI:** Minneapolis-St. Paul, MN. **Key Personnel:** Grace Adams, Contact; Larry Johnson, Operations Mgr. **Wattage:** 3000.

16488 KNOW-FM - 91.1
45 E. 7th St. Phone: (612)290-1500
St. Paul, MN 55101 Fax: (612)290-1260
E-mail: mail@mpr.org

Format: News; Public Radio. **Networks:** National Public Radio (NPR); Public Radio International (PRI). **Owner:** Minnesota Public Radio, at above address. **Founded:** 1967. **Operating Hours:** Continuous; 75% network, 25% local. **ADI:** Minneapolis-St. Paul, MN. **Key Personnel:** Julie Swenson, Contact, phone (612)290-1526, fax (612)290-1415, jswenson@mpr.org; Bill Buzenberg, News Dir., fax (612)290-1295, mail@mpr.org; Kate Smith, News Dir.; Melanie Sommer, News Dir. **Local Programs:** *Sound Money*; *The Splendid Table*. **Wattage:** 100,000. **Ad Rates:** Noncommercial. **URL:** http://www.mpr.org.

16489 KSJN-FM - 99.5
45 E. 7th St. Phone: (612)290-1500
St. Paul, MN 55101 Fax: (612)290-1224
E-mail: mail@mpr.org

Format: Public Radio; Classical. **Networks:** Public Radio International (PRI). **Founded:** 1967. **Formerly**: WLOL-FM (1991). **Operating Hours:** Continuous; 100% local. **ADI:** Minneapolis-St. Paul, MN. **Key Personnel:** William H. Kling, President; Robin Gehl, Network Mgr./Classical Music. **Wattage:** 100,000. **Ad Rates:** Noncommercial. **URL:** http://www.mnonline.org/mpr.

16490 KSTP-AM - 1500
2792 Maplewood Dr. Phone: (612)481-9333
St. Paul, MN 55109 Fax: (612)481-9324
Free: (877)615-1500

Format: Talk. **Networks:** ABC. **Owner:** Hubbard Broadcasting, Inc., 3415 University Ave., St. Paul, MN 55114, (612)646-5555. **Founded:** 1924. **Operating Hours:** Continuous; 30% network, 70% local. **ADI:** Minneapolis-St. Paul, MN. **Key Personnel:** Virginia H. Morris, General Mgr., phone (651)642-4141; Todd Fisher, Program Dir., phone (651)481-9333, fax (651)481-9324; John Soucheray, Dir. of Sales, phone (651)481-9333; Bob Gagne, Chief Engineer, phone (651)481-9333. **Local Programs:** *Barbara Carlson*, Rob Pendelton; *Jason Lewis*, Joe Hansen; *Joe Soucheray*. **Wattage:** 50,000.

16491 KSTP-TV - 5
3415 University Ave. Phone: (651)646-5555
St. Paul, MN 55114 Fax: (651)642-4172

Format: Commercial TV. **Networks:** ABC. **Owner:** KSTP-TV, at above address. **Founded:** 1947. **Operating Hours:** Continuous; 40% network, 60% local. **ADI:** Minneapolis-St. Paul, MN. **Key Personnel:** Edward Piette, Vice Pres./General Manager; Dayna Deutsch, Community Affairs Dir.; Scott Libin, News Dir., fax (651)642-4409, slibin@kstp.com; Trey Fabacher, General Sales Mgr., tfabacher@kstp.com; Dixie Hansen, Business Mgr.; Dave Baumann, Creative Service Dir., fax (651)642-4610; Michael Smith, Program/Prod. Mgr., fax (651)642-4386.

16492 KTCA-TV - 2
172 E. 4th St. Phone: (612)222-1717
St. Paul, MN 55101 Fax: (612)229-1282

Format: Public TV. **Networks:** Public Broadcasting Service (PBS). **Founded:** 1957. **Operating Hours:** 6:00 a.m.-1:00 a.m. **ADI:** Minneapolis-St. Paul, MN. **Key Personnel:** Gerry Richman, Contact; Michael Perelstein, Contact; James R. Pagliarini, President; Jack Willis, Contact. **Ad Rates:** Noncommercial. **URL:** http://www.ktca.org.

16493 KTCI-TV - 17
172 E. 4th St. Phone: (612)222-1717
St. Paul, MN 55101 Fax: (612)229-1282

Format: Public TV. **Networks:** Public Broadcasting Service (PBS). **Founded:** 1967. **Operating Hours:** 6:00 a.m.-midnight. **ADI:** Minneapolis-St. Paul, MN. **Ad Rates:** Noncommercial. **URL:** http://www.ktca.org.

16494 MediaOne
214 E. 4th St. Phone: (651)224-2697
Union Depot Pl. Fax: (651)228-3970
St. Paul, MN 55101

Owner: MediaOne, at above address. **Founded:** 1985. **Formerly**: Continental Cablevision. **Key Personnel:** Brian Dietz, phone (651)228-3064, fax (651)228-3931, bmdietz@mcdiaone.com. **Cities Served:** subscribing households 320,000; 82 channels; 6 community access channels.

16495 WDGY-AM - 630
PO Box 25130 Phone: (651)436-7212
St. Paul, MN 55125 Fax: (651)436-5018

Format: Talk; Sports. **Networks:** NBC. **Owner:** 630 Radio, Inc., at above address. **Founded:** 1949. **Operating Hours:** Continuous. **ADI:** Minneapolis-St. Paul, MN. **Wattage:** 1000.

16496 WMCN-FM - 91.7
1600 Grand Ave. Phone: (651)696-6082
St. Paul, MN 55105 Fax: (651)696-6689
E-mail: wmcn@macalester.edu

Format: Eclectic. **Owner:** Macalester College, at above address, (651)696-6000, Fax: (651)696-6689. **Founded:** 1979. **Formerly**: KMAC-FM. **Operating Hours:** Continuous. **ADI:** Minneapolis-St. Paul, MN. **Key Personnel:** Hjalman Titan, General Mgr.; Angela Kollmann, Program Dir. **Wattage:** 10. **Ad Rates:** Noncommercial.

16497 WMIN-AM - 740
PO Box 25130 Phone: (651)436-4000
St. Paul, MN 55125 Fax: (651)436-5018

Networks: NBC. **Operating Hours:** Sunrise-sunset. **ADI:** Minneapolis-St. Paul, MN. **Key Personnel:** Tom Witschen, Program Dir.; Shelly Jarvis, Operations Dir.; Greg Borgen, General Mgr. **Wattage:** 1,000.

ST. PETER

16498 The Gustavian Weekly
Gustavus Adolphus College
800 W. College Ave. Phone: (507)933-7636
St. Peter, MN 56082 Fax: (507)933-7633
Publication E-mail: weekly@gac.edu

Collegiate newspaper. **Founded:** 1891. **Freq:** Weekly (Fri.). **Print Method:** Offset. Uses mats. **Cols./Page:** 5. **Col. Width:** 22 nonpareils. **Col. Depth:** 210 agate lines. **Subscription Rates:** $20 individuals. **Remarks:** Accepts advertising. **URL:** http://www.gac.edu/news/weekly.
Ad Rates: GLR: $5 **Circ:** Free ‡2,500
BW: $330
SAU: $5
PCI: $5

16499 Swedish-American Historical Quarterly
Swedish-American Historical Society
Gustav Adolphus College Phone: (507)933-7435
Department of History Fax: (507)933-7041
St. Peter, MN 56082
Publisher E-mail: kanders3@northpark.edu

Magazine devoted to Swedish-American contributions to the history and growth of the United States. **Founded:** 1950. **Freq:** Quarterly. **Trim Size:** 6 1/4 x 9 1/4. **Key Personnel:** Byron Nordstrom, Editor; Phil Anderson, Society Pres., phone (773)244-6218, panderson@northpzrk.edu. **ISSN:** 0730-028X. **Subscription Rates:** $25 individuals includes membership; $10 students; $3 single issue. **Alt. Formats:** Microform, UMI. **Formerly**: Swedish Pioneer Historical Quarterly.
Ad Rates: BW: $100 **Circ:** Paid ‡1,050
Non-paid ‡52

16500 KGAC-FM - 90.5
PO Box 236 Phone: (507)933-7660
St. Peter, MN 56082 Fax: (507)933-7662

Format: Public Radio; Classical. **Networks:** National Public Radio (NPR); American Public Radio (APR). **Owner:** Minnesota Public Radio, 45 E. 7th St., St. Paul, MN. **Founded:** 1985. **Operating Hours:** Continuous; 25% network, 75% local. **Key Personnel:** Jennifer Kane, Marketing & Development Associate; Marilyn Butler, News Dir. **Wattage:** 75,000. **Ad Rates:** Noncommercial.

16501 KRBI-AM - 1310
1031 W. Grace St. Phone: (507)931-3220
St. Peter, MN 56082 Fax: (507)931-4740

Format: Talk; Soft Rock; News; Oldies; Sports. **Networks:** ABC; Linder Farm; AP. **Owner:** Johnson Broadcasting Corp., 112 1/2 N. Main, Le Sueur, MN 56058, (612)665-3336. **Founded:** Oct. 1957. **Operating Hours:** 18 hours daily; 25% network, 75% local. **ADI:** Minneapolis-St. Paul, MN. **Key Personnel:** Bob Johnson, Owner and President; Bruce Davis, News Dir.; Rick Johnson, General Manager; Tami Johnson, News Dir. **Wattage:** 1000. **Ad Rates:** $5.95-8.95 for 15 seconds; $7.95-10.95 for 30 seconds; $9.95-12.95 for 60 seconds.

16502 KRBI-FM - 105.5
1031 W. Grace St. Phone: (507)931-3220
St. Peter, MN 56082 Fax: (507)931-4740

Format: Talk; Sports; News; Soft Rock; Oldies. **Networks:** ABC. **Owner:** Bob Johnson, 112 1/2 N. Main Street, Le Sueur, MN 56058, (507)665-3336, (507)931-3220, Fax: (507)665-8960. **Founded:** 1957. **Operating Hours:** 6 a.m.-midnight; 25% network, 75% local. **ADI:** Minneapolis-St. Paul, MN. **Key Personnel:** Rick Johnson, General Manager; Bruce Davis, News Dir.; Tami Johnson, News Dir.; Robert C. Johnson, President and Owner. **Local Programs:** *Information Place,* Bruce Davis; *Sports Week,* Clay Kepner; *Swap Shop,* Rick Johnson. **Wattage:** 5300. **Ad Rates:** $5.95-8.95 for 15 seconds; $7.95-10.95 for 30 seconds; $9.95-12.95 for 60 seconds.

SANBORN

16503 The Comfrey Times
Central Publications
Box 37 Phone: (507)648-3515
Sanborn, MN 56083 Fax: (507)648-3515

Community newspaper. **Founded:** 1900. **Freq:** Weekly (Thurs.). **Print Method:** Offset. **Cols./Page:** 6. **Col. Width:** 24 nonpareils. **Col. Depth:** 280 agate lines. **Key Personnel:** Gary P. Richter, Editor and Publisher. **USPS:** 105-060. **Subscription Rates:** $14. **Remarks:** Accepts advertising.
Ad Rates: BW: $150 **Circ:** ‡950
4C: $350
SAU: $2

SANDSTONE

16504 Minnesota Flyer Magazine
Box 750 Phone: (320)245-2111
Sandstone, MN 55072 Fax: (320)245-2438

Midwest publication for aircraft owners/renters (pilots). **Founded:** 1960. **Freq:** Monthly. **Print Method:** Offset. **Trim Size:** 8 1/2 x 11. **Cols./Page:** 2. **Col. Width:** 22 picas. **Col. Depth:** 10 inches. **Key Personnel:** Richard A. Coffey, Publisher, r.j.coffey@aol.com. **ISSN:** 0889-4809. **Subscription Rates:** $18; $2.50 single issue. **Remarks:** Accepts advertising.
Ad Rates: BW: $511 **Circ:** Paid 3,702
4C: $750 Non-paid 500

16505 Pine County Courier
PO Box 230 Phone: (320)245-2368
Sandstone, MN 55072 Fax: (320)245-2438

Community newspaper (tabloid). **Founded:** 1895. **Freq:** Weekly (Thurs.). **Print Method:** Offset. **Trim Size:** 11 x 16. **Cols./Page:** 4. **Col. Width:** 27 nonpareils. **Key Personnel:** Richard A. Coffey, Publisher; Patty McQuiston, Advertising Dir. **USPS:** 433-180. **Subscription Rates:** $18. **Remarks:** Accepts advertising.
Ad Rates: GLR: $.16 **Circ:** ‡2,000
BW: $211.80
4C: $320
SAU: $3.21
PCI: $3.50

SAUK CENTRE

16506 Herald
Sauk Centre Publishers Inc.
522 Sinclair Lewis Ave. Fax: (612)352-5647
Sauk Centre, MN 56378
Publication E-mail: scherald@polarls.tel.net

Community newspaper. **Founded:** 1867. **Freq:** Weekly (Wed.). **Print Method:** Offset. **Trim Size:** 14 3/4 x 21 1/2. **Cols./Page:** 6. **Col. Width:** 14 picas. **Col. Depth:** 210 agate lines. **Key Personnel:** Tom Barford, Editor; David Simpkins, Publisher. **Subscription Rates:** $16. **Remarks:** Accepts advertising. **URL:** http://www.saukherald.comm.
Ad Rates: GLR: $.25 **Circ:** 3,500
BW: $374.10
PCI: $2.90

16507 Independent Banker
Independent Bankers Association of America
1168 S. Main St. Phone: (612)352-6546
PO Box 267
Sauk Centre, MN 56378-0267
Banking magazine. **Founded:** 1950. **Freq:** Monthly. **Print Method:** Letterpress and offset. **Trim Size:** 8 1/4 x 10 7/8. **Cols./Page:** 3. **Col. Width:** 26 nonpareils. **Col. Depth:** 120 agate lines. **Key Personnel:** David C. Bordewyk, Editor; Kenneth A. Guenther, Publisher. **ISSN:** 0019-3674. **Subscription Rates:** $15; $25 nonmembers. **Remarks:** Accepts advertising.
Ad Rates: BW: $1,690 **Circ:** Paid ‡7,045
4C: $2,590 Non-paid ‡2,329

16508 Sauk Rapids Herald
Sauk Centre Publishers Inc.
522 Sinclair Lewis Ave. Fax: (612)352-5647
Sauk Centre, MN 56378
Publication E-mail: scherald@polaristel.net

Community newspaper. **Freq:** Weekly (Wed.). **Cols./Page:** 7. **Col. Width:** 2 inches. **Col. Depth:** 21 1/2 inches. **Key Personnel:** Roland Doroff, Publisher. **URL:** http://www.saukherald.comm.
Circ: 1,100

SAUK RAPIDS

16509 KCFB-FM - 91.5
1310 2nd St. N. Phone: (612)252-4214
Sauk Rapids, MN 56379

Format: Religious. **Networks:** Moody Broadcasting. **Owner:** Fellowship Broadcasting Corp. of St. Cloud, Minn., at above address. **Founded:** 1986. **Operating Hours:** Continuous; 80% network, 20% local. **Key Personnel:** Mary Ann Simmons, Manager; Lawrence E. Simmons, President. **Wattage:** 1000.

16510 WBHR-AM - 660
1010 2nd St. N. Phone: (320)252-6200
Box 366 Fax: (320)252-9367
Sauk Rapids, MN 56379
E-mail: radio660@cloudnet.com

Networks: ABC. **Owner:** Herbert M. Hoppe, 5815 Rolling Ridge Rd., St. Cloud, MN 56302, (320)251-5394. **Founded:** 1963. **Formerly:** WVAL-AM. **Operating Hours:** Continuous. **Key Personnel:** Gary E. Hoppe, Operations Mgr.; Char Hopela, Program Dir.; Doug Kurtz, Sales Mgr. **Wattage:** 10,000 day; 250 night. **Ad Rates:** $10-13 for 30 seconds; $15-18 for 60 seconds. Combined advertising rates available with WVAL-AM. **URL:** http://www.disney.com.

16511 WHMH-FM - 101.7
1010 2nd St. N Phone: (320)252-6200
Box 366 Fax: (320)252-9367
Sauk Rapids, MN 56379
E-mail: whatever@rockin101.com

Format: Album-Oriented Rock (AOR). **Simulcasts:** WVAL-AM. **Owner:** Herbert M. Hoppe, 5815 Rolling Ridge Rd., St. Cloud, MN 56302, (612)251-5394. **Founded:** 1975. **Operating Hours:** Continuous. **ADI:** Minneapolis-St. Paul, MN. **Key Personnel:** Gary E. Hoppe, Operations Mgr.; Scott Klohn, Production & Promotions Mgr.; Doug Kurtz, Sales Mgr. **Wattage:** 38,000. **Ad Rates:** $20-26 for 30 seconds; $30-45 for 60 seconds. **URL:** http://www.rockin101.com.

SEBEKA

16512 Review-Messenger
112 Minnesota Ave. W. Phone: (218)837-5558
PO Box 309 Fax: (218)837-5560
Sebeka, MN 56477-0309
Publication E-mail: remess@wcta.net

Newspaper with Report orientation. **Founded:** 1898. **Freq:** Weekly (Wed.). **Print Method:** Offset. **Cols./Page:** 7. **Col. Width:** 24 nonpareils. **Col. Depth:** 301 agate lines. **Key Personnel:** Timothy Bloomquist, Editor and Publisher. **USPS:** 487-840. **Subscription Rates:** $22 individuals; $26 out of area; $30. **Remarks:** Accepts advertising. **Alt. Formats:** CD-ROM.
Ad Rates: GLR: $0.35 **Circ:** ‡3,421
BW: $855
4C: $1,055
SAU: $5.70
CNU: $5.70
PCI: $5.70

16513 Total Shopper
Review-Messenger
112 Minnesota Ave. W. Phone: (218)837-5558
PO Box 309 Fax: (218)837-5560
Sebeka, MN 56477-0309
Publication E-mail: remess@wcta.net

Shopper. **Freq:** Weekly. **Print Method:** Offset. **Cols./Page:** 5. **Col. Width:** 11 picas. **Col. Depth:** 15 inches. **Subscription Rates:** Free. **Remarks:** Accepts advertising. **Alt. Formats:** CD-ROM.
Ad Rates: GLR: $0.35 **Circ:** Free 4,900
BW: $363.75
4C: $588.75
SAU: $5
CNU: $5
PCI: $5

16514 United Data-Vision
209 Minnesota Ave. Phone: (218)837-5155
Sebeka, MN 56477 Fax: (218)837-5001
Free: (800)945-2163
E-mail: wcphone@wcta.net

Owner: West Central Telephone Association, at above address. **Founded:** 1985. **Key Personnel:** Anthony V. Mayer, General Mgr., tonym@wcta.net. **Cities Served:** subscribing households 772; 27 channels; 1 community access channel; 24 hours per week community access programming. **URL:** http://www.wcta.net.

SHAKOPEE

16515 Shakopee Valley News
Southwest Suburban Publishing
327 S. Marshall Rd. Phone: (612)445-3333
PO Box 8 Fax: (612)445-3333
Shakopee, MN 55379
Local newspaper. **Founded:** 1860. **Freq:** Weekly. **Print Method:** Offset. **Cols./Page:** 6. **Col. Width:** 2 inches. **Col. Depth:** 21 inches. **Key Personnel:** Pat Minelli, Editor; Stan Rolfsrud, Publisher; Gary Klatt, Advertising Mgr. **Subscription Rates:** $15; $20 out of area.
Circ: Paid 4,402
Free 344

SHOREVIEW

16516 Shoreview-Arden Hills Bulletin
Lillie Suburban Newspapers
PO Box 120608 Phone: (612)633-2777
New Brighton, MN 55112 Fax: (612)633-3846

Local newspaper. **Founded:** 1956. **Freq:** Weekly (Wed.). **Print Method:** Offset. **Cols./Page:** 6. **Col. Width:** 21 nonpareils. **Col. Depth:** 294 agate lines. **Key Personnel:** Mary Lee Hagert, Managing Editor; N. T. Lillie, Publisher; Jeffery Enright, Publisher; Mark Beckstrom, Advertising Mgr.; Pat Colburn, Circulation Mgr.; James Schwartz, Editor. **Subscription Rates:** $25.95 elsewhere. **Remarks:** Accepts advertising. **Formerly:** Shoreview Bulletin.
Ad Rates: SAU: $22.70 **Circ:** Paid 56
Free 14,424

SILVER LAKE

16517 Silver Lake Leader
PO Box 343 Phone: (612)327-2216
Silver Lake, MN 55381 Fax: (612)327-3122

General newspaper. **Founded:** 1901. **Freq:** Weekly. **Print Method:** Offset. **Trim Size:** 14 x 23. **Cols./Page:** 7. **Col. Width:** 12 picas. **Col. Depth:** 21 1/2 inches. **Key Personnel:** Dorothy Merrill, Editor; Kenneth B. Merrill, Publisher. **Subscription Rates:** $15.50 individuals; $20 out of area. **Remarks:** Accepts advertising.
Ad Rates: SAU: $3.54 **Circ:** Paid ‡1,475
PCI: $3.54 Free ‡25

SLAYTON

16518 Murray County Wheel/Herald
Wheel Beers
Box 263 Phone: (507)836-8726
Slayton, MN 56172 Fax: (507)836-8942

Shopper. **Founded:** 1972. **Freq:** Weekly (Tues.). **Print Method:** Offset. **Cols./Page:** 8. **Col. Width:** 20 nonpareils. **Col. Depth:** 21 1/2 inches. **Key Personnel:** Will Beers, Editor and Publisher; Sherri Halbur, Business Mgr. **Subscription Rates:** Free; $18 (mail); $24 out of area. **Remarks:** Accepts advertising.
Ad Rates: BW: $490 **Circ:** Paid ‡960
PCI: $4.10 Free ‡6,200

16519 KJOE-FM - 106.1
2660 Broadway Phone: (507)836-6125
Slayton, MN 56172 Fax: (507)836-6537

Format: Country. **Networks:** ABC; Satellite Music Network. **Owner:** Wallace Christensen Broadcasting, W. Hwy. 30, PO Box 456, Pipestone, MN 56164. **Operating Hours:** Continuous. **Key Personnel:** Collin Christensen, Manager, phone (507)825-4282; Jeff Erickson, Sales Mgr. **Ad Rates:** $18 for 60 seconds.

SLEEPY EYE

16520 Sleepy Eye Herald-Dispatch
115 2nd Ave. NE Phone: (507)794-3511
Sleepy Eye, MN 56085 Fax: (507)794-5031

Community newspaper. **Founded:** 1880. **Freq:** Weekly (Thurs.). **Print Method:** Offset. **Cols./Page:** 6. **Col. Width:** 24 nonpareils. **Col. Depth:** 301 agate lines. **Key Personnel:** Jennifer Boettger, Publisher. **USPS:** 498-700. **Subscription Rates:** $33 individuals; $38 out of area; $44 out of state. **Remarks:** Accepts advertising.
Ad Rates: BW: $750.78 **Circ:** Paid ‡3,600
4C: $1000 Free ‡310
SAU: $5.82
PCI: $7.75

16521 BRAT-FM - 107.3
108 Main W. Phone: (507)794-3149
Sleepy Eye, MN 56085 Fax: (507)794-4990
Free: (800)444-5685
E-mail: radioone@ic.new-ulm.mn.us

Format: Adult Contemporary. **Owner:** Cumulus Broadcasting, at above address. **Founded:** June 1995. **Operating Hours:** Continuous. **Key Personnel:** Jim Bartels, General Mgr., jim.bartels@cumulus.com; Marj Frederickson, Sales Mgr., phone (507)359-2921, radioone@ic.new-ulm.mn.us; Brian Filzer, Program Dir., phone (507)359-2921. **Wattage:** 50,000. **URL:** http://www.radiooneminnesota.com.

SOUTH ST. PAUL

16522 South St. Paul/Inver Grove Heights Sun Current
Minnesota Sun Publications
7831 E. Bush Lake Rd. Phone: (612)896-4700
Bloomington, MN 55439 Fax: (612)896-4728
Publication E-mail: southstpaulsuncurrent@mnsunpub.com

Community newspaper (tabloid). **Founded:** 1984. **Freq:** Weekly (Wed.). **Print Method:** Offset. **Cols./Page:** 4. **Col. Width:** 2 1/2 inches. **Col. Depth:** 15 inches. **Key Personnel:** Doug Dane, Publisher, phone (612)896-4787; Pamela Austin, Advertising Mgr., phone (612)897-5486. **URL:** http://www.mnsun.
Circ: Paid 25,230

SPICER

16523 New London Times
PO Box 910 Phone: (320)354-2307
Spicer, MN 56288-0910 Fax: (320)796-5050

Community newspaper. **Founded:** 1886. **Freq:** Weekly (Tues.). **Print Method:** Offset. **Cols./Page:** 6. **Col. Width:** 2 1/4 inches. **Col. Depth:** 301 agate lines. **Key Personnel:** Bev Ahlquist, Editor and Publisher; Dennis Baker, Publisher. **Subscription Rates:** $10 local; $15 in state; $18 out of state.

SPRING GROVE

16524 Herald
119 Maple Dr. Phone: (507)498-3868
PO Box 68
Spring Grove, MN 55974
Newspaper with Report orientation. **Founded:** 1891. **Freq:** Weekly (Tues.). **Print Method:** Offset. **Cols./Page:** 6. **Col. Width:** 26 nonpareils. **Col. Depth:** 287 agate lines. **Key Personnel:** B.A. Onsgard, Editor and Publisher; F.W. Onsgard, Publisher. **Subscription Rates:** $24 individuals. **Remarks:** Accepts advertising.
Ad Rates: GLR: $.30 **Circ:** ‡1,500
BW: $360
4C: $460
SAU: $2.66
PCI: $3

16525 KQYB-FM - 98.3
Hwy. 44 W. Phone: (507)498-5720
Spring Grove, MN 55974 Fax: (507)498-5766
Free: (800)468-9833
E-mail: mthonmed@polaristel.net

Format: Hot Country. **Networks:** ABC. **Founded:** 1980. **Operating Hours:** Continuous. **Key Personnel:** Joe Casper, Contact; Phil Constigan, Contact; Lori Wilhelmson, Office Mgr.; Arleen Soltow, Sports Dir./Sales Mgr.; Pete Wennes, News Dir.; Phyllis Thorson, Station Mgr.; Joe Casper, Program Dir. **Local Programs:** *Joe Casper* 2 p.m.-6 p.m.; *Morning w/Phil Costigan* 5 a.m.-10 a.m. **Wattage:** 50,000. **Ad Rates:** $9.50-13 for 30 seconds; $12.75-17 for 60 seconds.

SPRING VALLEY

16526 River Valley Shopper
Phillips Publishing, Inc.
141 S. Broadway Phone: (507)346-7365
PO Box 112 Fax: (507)346-7366
Spring Valley, MN 55975
Shopper. **Freq:** Weekly (Mon.). **Print Method:** Offset. **Trim Size:** 14 1/2 x 23. **Cols./Page:** 6. **Col. Width:** 25 nonpareils and 12.5 picas. **Col. Depth:** 301 agate lines and 21.5 inches. **Key Personnel:** David Phillips, Editor and Publisher. **Subscription Rates:** Free. **Formerly:** Valley Area Shopper (1990); Valley Shopper (1992).
Ad Rates: BW: $438.60 **Circ:** Free ‡13,815
SAU: $4.00
PCI: $4.00

16527 Spring Valley Tribune
Phillips Publishing, Inc.
141 S. Broadway Phone: (507)346-7365
PO Box 112 Fax: (507)346-7366
Spring Valley, MN 55975
Local newspaper. **Founded:** 1880. **Freq:** Weekly (Wed.). **Print Method:** Offset. **Trim Size:** 14 1/2 x 23. **Cols./Page:** 6. **Col. Width:** 12 1/2 picas. **Col. Depth:** 21 1/2 inches. **Key Personnel:** David Phillips, Publisher; Cheryl Brandner, Editor. **USPS:** 512-380. **Subscription Rates:** $18 individuals; $22 out of state; $30 other countries. **Remarks:** Accepts advertising.
Ad Rates: BW: $374.10 **Circ:** ‡1,900
SAU: $3.50
PCI: $3.50

SPRINGFIELD

16528 Springfield Advance-Press
13 S. Marshall Ave. Phone: (507)723-4225
PO Box 78 Fax: (507)723-4400
Springfield, MN 56087
Publisher E-mail: aps@springfield-sanborn.net

Newspaper with a Republican orientation. **Founded:** 1886. **Freq:** Weekly (Wed.). **Print Method:** Offset. **Trim Size:** 14 x 22 1/2. **Cols./Page:** 6. **Col. Width:** 12.5 picas. **Col. Depth:** 301 agate lines. **Key Personnel:** Doris M. Weber, Editor; D.J. Hedstrom, Publisher; Peter C. Hedstrom, Publisher. **USPS:** 512-500. **Subscription Rates:** $26.75 individuals; $29.25 Brown, Redwood, Cottonwood only; $33 out of state. **Remarks:** Color advertising accepted; rates available upon request.
Ad Rates: GLR: $.61 **Circ:** Paid ‡2,742
BW: $477.30
PCI: $4

STAPLES, pop. 2,892.

C MN. Todd Co. 30 mi. N. of Brainerd. Vocational institute. Light industry. Stock, dairy, poultry, truck, grain farms. Corn, hay, wheat. Diversified agriculture.

16529 Staples World
224 4th St. N. Phone: (218)894-1112
PO Box 100 Fax: (218)894-3570
Staples, MN 56479
Free: (888)894-1112
Publication E-mail: staworld@brainard.net

Community newspaper. **Founded:** Feb. 28, 1890. **Freq:** Weekly (Thurs.). **Print Method:** Offset. **Cols./Page:** 6. **Col. Width:** 12 1/2 picas. **Col. Depth:** 21 1/2 inches. **Key Personnel:** Tom Crawford, Editor; Gary Mueller, Advertising Mgr.; Brenda Halvorson, General Mgr. **USPS:** 518-760. **Subscription Rates:** $24.
Ad Rates: BW: $754.65 **Circ:** ⊕3,000
SAU: $5.85

16530 Sunday Square Shooter
Devlin Newspapers, Inc.
Box 100 Phone: (218)894-1112
224 4th St. N. Fax: (218)894-3570
Staples, MN 56479
Free: (888)894-1112

Shopping guide. **Freq:** Weekly. **Print Method:** Offset. **Cols./Page:** 6. **Col. Width:** 12 picas. **Col. Depth:** 21 1/2 inches. **Key Personnel:** Brenda Halvorson, General Mgr.; Gary Mueller, Advertising Mgr. **Subscription Rates:** Free. **Remarks:** Accepts advertising.
Ad Rates: BW: $657.90 **Circ:** Free ‡9,500
PCI: $5.60

STARBUCK, pop. 1,224.

NW MN. Pope Co. 130 mi. NW of Minneapolis. Summer resort. Dairy, poultry, stock farms.

16531 Times
PO Box 457 Phone: (320)239-2244
504 Wollan St. Fax: (320)239-2254
Starbuck, MN 56381
Free: (800)239-4422

Community newspaper. **Founded:** 1898. **Freq:** Weekly (Wed.). **Print Method:** Offset. **Cols./Page:** 6. **Col. Width:** 2 3/8 inches. **Col. Depth:** 21 1/2 inches. **Key Personnel:** Ron Lindquist, Editor and Publisher. **Subscription Rates:** $15; $18 out of area; $20 out of state. **Remarks:** Accepts advertising.
Ad Rates: GLR: $.14 **Circ:** Paid ‡1,800
BW: $265.62 Free ‡25
4C: $505.62
SAU: $2.90
PCI: $3.30

STEPHEN, pop. 898.

NW MN. Marshall Co. 52 mi. NE of Grand Forks, ND. State Parks. Manufacturing. Grain farms. Potatoes, sugar beets. Sunflowers.

16532 The Messenger
PO Box 48 Phone: (218)478-2210
Stephen, MN 56757 Fax: (218)478-2210

Newspaper with a Democratic orientation. **Founded:** 1883. **Freq:** Weekly (Thurs.). **Print Method:** Offset. **Cols./Page:** 6. **Col. Width:** 2 1/8 inches. **Col. Depth:** 21 1/4 inches. **Key Personnel:** Earl L. Anderson, Editor and Publisher. **Subscription Rates:** $18 out of country; $21 other countries. **Remarks:** Advertising not accepted for alcoholic beverages.
Ad Rates: GLR: $.17 **Circ:** 2,200
SAU: $3.72
PCI: $3

STEWARTVILLE, pop. 3,925.

SE MN. Olmstead Co. 11 mi. S. of Rochester. Manufactures feeds, automotive parts. Agriculture. Wheat, corn, soybeans.

16533 KYBA-FM - 105.3
1901 1st Ave. NW Phone: (507)533-4082
Stewartville, MN 55976 Fax: (507)533-4083

Format: Soft Rock. **Networks:** ABC. **Owner:** Southern Minnesota Broadcasting Co., 122 4th St. SW, Rochester, MN 55902, (507)286-1010. **Founded:** Feb. 1, 1993. **Operating Hours:** Continuous. **ADI:** Rochester, MN-Mason City, IA-Austin, MN. **Key Personnel:** Sue Daily, General Mgr.; David Fezler, Operations Mgr.; Bill Davis, Engineer; Amy Stevens, Sales Mgr.; Dick Trisko, Traffic. **Wattage:** 50,000.

STILLWATER†, pop. 12,290.

SE MN. Washington Co. On St. Croix River, 20 mi. NE of Saint Paul. Manufactures windows, doors,doors, clothing, flour, boats, plastics, precision sheetmetal, tractors, road machinery, screen process printing, dried milk products, plastics, ventilation equipment. Dairy farms.

16534 The St. Croix Review
PO Box 224 Phone: (612)439-7190
Stillwater, MN 55082 Fax: (612)439-7017
Free: (800)278-0141

Journal of social criticism. **Founded:** 1968. **Freq:** Bimonthly. **Print Method:** Offset. **Trim Size:** 6 x 9. **Cols./Page:** 1. **Col. Width:** 28 picas. **Col. Depth:** 45 inches. **Key Personnel:** Angus MacDonald, Editor and Publisher; Barry MacDonald, Assoc. Editor. **ISSN:** 0093-2592. **Subscription Rates:** $25. $5 single issue. **Remarks:** Advertising not accepted. **Alt. Formats:** Microform.
Circ: Paid 2,000

STORDEN, pop. 341.

SW MN. Cottonwood Co. 70 mi. W. of Mankato. Agriculture. Hogs. Cattle.

16535 The Storden-Jeffers Times/Review
Times Review
323 America St. Phone: (507)445-3400
PO Box 39 Fax: (507)445-3104
Storden, MN 56174-0039
Community newspaper. **Founded:** 1900. **Freq:** Weekly (Thurs.). **Print Method:** Offset. **Cols./Page:** 6. **Col. Width:** 24 nonpareils. **Col. Depth:** 301 agate lines. **Key Personnel:** George Parrish, Editor and Publisher. **USPS:** 572-520. **Sub-**

scription Rates: $20 individuals; $25 adjoining counties; $27 rest of Minnesota; $33 other states.
Ad Rates: SAU: $3.25 **Circ:** Paid ⊕620
PCI: $3.35 Free ⊕47

TACONITE

NC MN. Itasca Co. 20 mi. NE of Grand Rapids.

16536 City of Taconite Cable TV
PO Box 137 Phone: (218)245-1831
Taconite, MN 55786 Fax: (218)245-1831
E-mail: taconite@uslink.net

Owner: City Of Taconite, at above address, Fax: (218)328-0186. **Founded:** 1965. **Key Personnel:** Mike Troumbly, City Clerk/Admin., mtroumbly@mnpower.com; Lloyd Cogswell, Technician, phone (218)245-2370. **Cities Served:** Taconite, MN: subscribing households 110; 22 channels; 1 community access channel.

THIEF RIVER FALLS†, pop. 9,105.

NW MN. Pennington Co. 40 mi. NE of Grand Forks, ND. Manufactures dairy products, poultry & animal feeds, soft drinks, front-end loaders, snow machines, seed cleaning, and recycling equipment. Dairy, poultry, grocery, fruit distributing center.

16537 Northern Light
Northland Community and Technical College
1101 Hwy. One E. Phone: (218)681-0834
Thief River Falls, MN 56701 Fax: (218)681-0724
Free: (800)959-6282

Collegiate magazine. **Founded:** 1965. **Freq:** Every 6 weeks. **Print Method:** Offset. **Trim Size:** 12 x 14. **Cols./Page:** 4. **Col. Width:** 11 picas. **Col. Depth:** 13 inches. **Key Personnel:** John Doppler, Editor; Elizabeth Perfecto, Editor. **Subscription Rates:** Free. **Remarks:** Accepts advertising.
Ad Rates: PCI: $3 **Circ:** Non-paid ‡1,000

16538 Thief River Falls Times, Inc.
324 N. Main Ave. Phone: (218)681-4450
PO Box 100 Fax: (218)681-4455
Thief River Falls, MN 56701
Publication E-mail: trftimes@northnnet.com; trftimes@traftimes.com
Publisher E-mail: trftimes@trftimes.com

Community newspaper. **Founded:** 1910. **Freq:** Weekly (Tues.). **Print Method:** Offset. **Trim Size:** 14 x 22 3/4. **Cols./Page:** 6. **Col. Width:** 12 1/4 picas. **Col. Depth:** 21 1/2 inches. **Key Personnel:** Marvin Lundin, Editor; John P. Mattson, Publisher; Denise Laymon, Advertising Mgr. **ISSN:** 8750-3883. **Subscription Rates:** $25 individuals; $45 out of area. **URL:** http://www.trftimes.com. **Formerly:** The Times.
Ad Rates: BW: $735.30 **Circ:** ‡5,800
4C: $1,035.30
SAU: $5.70
PCI: $5.70

16539 KBRR-TV - 10
c/o KVRR-TV Phone: (701)277-1515
4015 9th Ave., SW Fax: (701)277-1830
Fargo, ND 58103

Format: Commercial TV. **Simulcasts:** KVRR-TV. **Networks:** Independent; Fox. **Owner:** Red River Broadcasting Corp., at above address. **ADI:** Fargo, ND.

16540 KKAQ-AM - 1460
PO Box 218 Phone: (218)681-4900
Thief River Falls, MN 56701 Fax: (218)681-6311

Format: Contemporary Country. **Networks:** ABC. **Owner:** Olmstead Broadcasting, Inc., at above address. **Founded:** 1979. **Operating Hours:** Continuous. **ADI:** Fargo, ND. **Key Personnel:** Everett Ault, President; Dave Halvorson, Program Dir.; Curt Quesnell, Sales Mgr. **Wattage:** 2500. **Ad Rates:** $6.50 for 30 seconds; $9.50 for 60 seconds.

16541 KKDQ-FM - 99.3
319 N. LaBree Ave. Phone: (218)681-4900
Thief River Falls, MN 56701 Fax: (218)681-6311

Format: Country. **Networks:** Unistar. **Owner:** Olmstead Broadcasting, Inc., at above address. **Founded:** 1990. **Operating Hours:** Continuous. **ADI:** Fargo, ND. **Key Personnel:** Curt Quesnell, Manager; Dave Halvorson, Program Dir. **Wattage:** 6000. **Ad Rates:** $6.50 for 30 seconds; $9.50 for 60 seconds.

16542 KSNR-FM - 100.3
Hwy. 32 N. Phone: (218)681-1230
Thief River Falls, MN 56701 Fax: (218)681-3717
Free: (800)426-1003

Format: Oldies. **Networks:** Satellite Music Network. **Owner:** Border States Broadcasting Corp., PO Box 40, Thief River Falls, MN 56701. **Founded:** 1976. **Formerly:** KOSN-FM (1982). **Operating Hours:** Continuous; 10% network, 90% local. **ADI:** Fargo, ND. **Key Personnel:** Burke Bartell, Sales Mgr.; Joel Swanson, General Mgr.; Bob Hultgren, Program Dir.; Mark Simpson, Sports Dir.; Susan Peterson, Business Mgr.; Michelle Fritze, Traffic Mgr. **Wattage:** 100,000. **Ad Rates:** $8 for 30 seconds; $12.80 for 60 seconds.

16543 KSRQ-FM - 90.1
1301 Hwy. 1 E. Phone: (218)681-0770
Thief River Falls, MN 56701 Fax: (218)681-0774

Format: Educational. **Networks:** CNN Radio. **Owner:** Northland Community and Technical College, at above address, (218)681-0701, Fax: (218)681-0774. **Founded:** 1969. **Formerly:** KAVS-FM (1981). **Operating Hours:** 5 a.m.-11 p.m.; 100% local. **Key Personnel:** Bob Hultgren, Station Mgr., phone (218)681-0783, fax (218)681-0774, bhultgre@ntcc1.nt.cc.mn.us; Howard Rokke, General Mgr., phone (218)681-0791, fax (218)681-0774, hrokke@ntcc1.nt.cc.mn.us. **Wattage:** 24,000. **Ad Rates:** Noncommercial.

16544 KTRF-AM - 1230
Hwy. 32 N. Phone: (218)681-1230
Thief River Falls, MN 56701 Fax: (218)681-3717

Format: Full Service. **Networks:** CBS; Minnesota News. **Owner:** Border States Broadcasting Corp., PO Box 40, Thief River Falls, MN 56701. **Founded:** 1947. **Operating Hours:** Continuous; 10% network, 90% local. **ADI:** Fargo, ND. **Key Personnel:** Jon Praska, General Mgr.; Wayne Rahlf, Sports Dir.; Mark Stromsodt, Program Dir.; Todd McDonald, News Dir. **Local Programs:** *Coaches Corner*, Wayne Rahlf; *Coffee Time*, Mark Allan; *Trading Post*, Mark Allan. **Wattage:** 1000. **Ad Rates:** $10 for 30 seconds; $16 for 60 seconds.

16545 Sjoberg's Inc.
315 N. Main Phone: (218)681-3044
Thief River Falls, MN 56701 Fax: (218)681-6801
Free: (800)828-8808

Founded: 1962. **Key Personnel:** Richard Sjoberg, President; Stan Sjoberg, Vice President. **Cities Served:** subscribing households 7,000; 27 channels; 1 community access channel; 168 hours per week community access programming.

TOWER, pop. 640.

NE MN. St. Louis Co. On Lake Vermillion, 25 mi. N. of Virginia. Summer resorts. Iron mines; timber.

16546 Tower News
News
Box 447 Phone: (218)753-3170
Tower, MN 55790
Newspaper. **Founded:** 1900. **Freq:** Weekly (Thurs.). **Print Method:** Offset. **Cols./Page:** 5. **Col. Width:** 22 nonpareils. **Col. Depth:** 210 agate lines. **Key Personnel:** Phyllis Burgess, Editor; Anthony Sikora, Publisher. **Subscription Rates:** $9. **Remarks:** Accepts advertising. **URL:** http://www.towernews.com. **Formerly:** News.
Ad Rates: GLR: $.20 **Circ:** 2,041
BW: $262.50

TRACY, pop. 2,478.

SW MN. Lyon Co. 80 mi. W. of Mankato. Manufactures butter, powdered buttermilk, soft drinks. Stock, dairy, grain farms.

16547 Headlight Herald
PO Box 1188 Phone: (507)629-4300
Tracy, MN 56175 Fax: (507)629-4301

Newspaper with a Republican orientation. **Founded:** 1879. **Freq:** Weekly (Thurs.). **Print Method:** Offset. **Cols./Page:** 6. **Col. Width:** 28 nonpareils. **Col. Depth:** 297 agate lines. **Key Personnel:** Mitchell Tollefson, Editor; Feph Schmidt, Publisher. **Subscription Rates:** $10.

16548 Harmon Cable Communications
125 3rd St. Phone: (507)629-3150
PO Box 1156 Fax: (507)629-3208
Tracy, MN 56175
Free: (800)658-2388

Owner: Harmon Cable Communications, 8480 E. Orchard Rd., Ste. 6900, Englewood, CO 80111, (303)773-3821. **Founded:** 1972. **Formerly:** Arcomm; Minnesota Cable Enterprises. **Key Personnel:** Mike Rose, Manager; Jayne Kathman, Office Mgr.; Karen Irwin, Contact. **Cities Served:** Tracy, MN: subscribing households 2,225; 39 channels; 5 community access channels.

TRUMAN

16549 The Truman Tribune
118 Ciro St. Phone: (507)776-2751
PO Box 98
Truman, MN 56088
Community newspaper. **Founded:** 1899. **Freq:** Weekly (Wed.). **Print Method:** Offset. **Cols./Page:** 6. **Col. Width:** 12 picas. **Col. Depth:** 21 1/2 inches. **Key Personnel:** Vickie Greiner, Editor and Publisher. **ISSN:** 0891-1401. **Subscription Rates:** $16.50 individuals; $24 out of state. **Remarks:** Accepts advertising.
Ad Rates: SAU: $3.75 **Circ:** ‡1,100

TWIN VALLEY, pop. 907.

NW MN. Norman Co. 37 mi. NE of Fargo, ND. Diversified farming. Wheat, potatoes, oats.

16550 Twin Valley Times/Gary Graphic
Times Publishing Co.
PO Box 478 Phone: (218)584-5195
Twin Valley, MN 56584 Fax: (218)584-5196
Publication E-mail: tvtimes@tvutel.com

Community newspaper. **Founded:** 1895. **Freq:** Weekly. **Print Method:** Offset. **Cols./Page:** 6. **Col. Width:** 12 picas. **Col. Depth:** 21 1/4 inches. **Key Personnel:** Rod Thoreson, Editor. **Subscription Rates:** $21 individuals; $24 out of area. **Remarks:** Accepts advertising. **URL:** http://ncecommunity.com.
Ad Rates: BW: $2.55 **Circ:** ‡1,515
4C: $6.25
SAU: $129
PCI: $6

TWO HARBORS†, pop. 4,039.

NE MN. Lake Co. On Lake Superior, 25 mi. NE of Duluth. Residential. Resort. Truck and dairy farms.

16551 Lake County News-Chronicle
Two Harbors Printing Co., Inc.
109 Waterfront Dr. Phone: (218)834-2141
PO Box 158
Two Harbors, MN 55616
Community newspaper. **Founded:** 1900. **Freq:** Weekly (Wed.). **Print Method:** Offset. **Cols./Page:** 6. **Col. Width:** 2 inches. **Col. Depth:** 21 inches. **Key Personnel:** Robert Allen, Editor and Publisher; Donna Carlson, Editor. **Subscription Rates:** $16; $20 out of county; $22 out of state. **Remarks:** Accepts advertising.
Ad Rates: SAU: $3.35 **Circ:** ‡3,100

16552 Two Harbors Manney Shopper
Manney's Shopper, Inc.
626 1/2 2nd Ave. Phone: (218)834-5551
PO Box 66 Fax: (218)834-2555
Two Harbors, MN 55616
Shopper. **Freq:** Weekly (Sun.). **Print Method:** Offset. **Trim Size:** 13 x 21 3/4. **Cols./Page:** 6. **Col. Width:** 11 4/5 picas. **Col. Depth:** 301 agate lines. **Key Personnel:** Rob Schroeder, Advertising Mgr. **Subscription Rates:** $37 out of area; Free. **Remarks:** Accepts advertising.
Ad Rates: GLR: $0.42 **Circ:** Free ‡7,981
BW: $531.48
4C: $961.48
PCI: $5.91

16553 Northland Cablevision
721 7th St.
Two Harbors, MN 55616

Owner: Intermedia Partners, at above address. **Cities Served:** Beaver Bay, Grand Marais, Silver Bay, Two Harbors, MN.

TYLER, pop. 1,353.

SW MN. Lincoln Co. 80 mi. NE of Sioux Falls, SD. Manufactures cement blocks, tile, feed. Elevators. Dairy, poultry, grain farms.

16554 The Tyler Tribute
151 N. Tyler St. Phone: (507)247-5502
Box Q Fax: (507)247-5502
Tyler, MN 56178-0466
Publication E-mail: tribute@compuserve.com

Community newspaper. **Founded:** July 19, 1972. **Freq:** Weekly (Thurs.). **Print Method:** Offset. **Cols./Page:** 6. **Col. Width:** 25 nonpareils. **Col. Depth:** 294 agate lines. **Key Personnel:** Charles R. Hunt, Editor and Publisher. **USPS:** 963-720. **Subscription Rates:** $19 individuals; $25 out of state; $30 other countries. **Remarks:** Accepts advertising.

Online: Compuserve. **URL:** http://ourworld.compuserve.com/homepages/tribute.
Ad Rates: GLR: $.21 **Circ:** ‡1,650
BW: $421
SAU: $3.40
PCI: $3.85

ULEN, pop. 514.

WC MN. Clay Co. 40 mi. NE of Fargo,ND. Museum. Elevator. Dairy, stock, poultry, grain farms. Corn, potatoes.

16555 The Ulen Union
Box 248 Phone: (218)596-8813
Ulen, MN 56585 Fax: (218)596-8213

Community newspaper. **Founded:** 1896. **Freq:** Weekly (Wed.). **Print Method:** Offset. **Cols./Page:** 6. **Col. Width:** 31 nonpareils. **Col. Depth:** 300 agate lines. **Key Personnel:** David G. Evans, Editor and Publisher. **Subscription Rates:** $18. **Remarks:** Accepts advertising.
Ad Rates: GLR: $.38 **Circ:** Paid 1,250
BW: $390.87 Free 25
PCI: $3.03

VERNDALE, pop. 570.

SW MN. Wadena Co. 40 mi. W. of Brainerd.

16556 The Verndale Sun
21 1st Ave. SW Phone: (218)445-5779
PO Box E Fax: (218)445-5779
Verndale, MN 56481
Publication E-mail: courier@rea-alp.com
Publisher E-mail: vsunnews@wcta.net

Community newspaper (tabloid). **Founded:** 1875. **Freq:** Weekly (Wed.). **Print Method:** Offset. **Trim Size:** 11 1/2 x 16. **Cols./Page:** 5. **Col. Width:** 11 1/2 picas. **Col. Depth:** 15 inches. **Key Personnel:** Aaron J. Qurt, Publisher. **USPS:** 658-100. **Subscription Rates:** $16 individuals; $21 out of area; $26 out of state; out of state. **Remarks:** Accepts advertising.
Ad Rates: GLR: $3 **Circ:** Paid ‡1,000
BW: $168.75 Free ‡26
4C: $198.25
PCI: $2

VIRGINIA, pop. 11,056.

NE MN. Saint Louis Co. 26 mi. E. of Hibbing. Lake resort area. Voyageurs National Park. State Community College. Iron ore mines; taconite pellet. Lumber.

16557 Mesabi Daily News
Mesabi Publishing Co.
PO Box 956 Phone: (218)741-5544
Virginia, MN 55792 Fax: (218)741-1005

General newspaper. **Founded:** 1893. **Freq:** Daily (morn.). **Print Method:** Offset. **Cols./Page:** 6. **Col. Width:** 24 nonpareils. **Col. Depth:** 301 agate lines. **Key Personnel:** Chuck Debevec, Editor; John Murphy, Publisher. **Subscription Rates:** $124.80 individuals. **Remarks:** Accepts advertising.
Ad Rates: SAU: $8.65 **Circ:** ‡14,559
Sun. ‡15,143

16558 WHLB-AM - 1400
S. 17th St. & 6th Ave. Phone: (218)741-2233
Box 954 Fax: (218)741-1415
Virginia, MN 55792

Format: Talk; News; Big Band/Nostalgia. **Networks:** Mutual Broadcasting System; Satellite Music Network; Minnesota News. **Founded:** 1936. **Operating Hours:** Continuous; 50% network, 50% local. **ADI:** Duluth, MN-Superior, WI. **Key Personnel:** Kristi Garrity, General Mgr.; Neil Larson, PD; Jessica Babb, Office Mgr.; Frank Befera, President. **Local Programs:** *Bargain Mart*; *Keith Knox Show*; *Open Mic*. **Wattage:** 1000. **Ad Rates:** $2.50-4.60 for 15 seconds; $5.00-8.20 for 30 seconds; $7.00-9.50 for 60 seconds.

WABASHA†, pop. 2,372.

SE MN. Wabasha Co. 10 mi. NW of Alma.

16559 Wabasha County Herald
Valley Publication
200 Industrial Ct. Phone: (612)565-3368
PO Box 109 Fax: (612)565-4736
Wabasha, MN 55981
Community newspaper. **Founded:** 1848. **Freq:** Weekly (Wed.). **Print Method:** Offset. **Cols./Page:** 6. **Col. Width:** 12.5 picas. **Col. Depth:** 21 1/2 inches. **Key Personnel:** Gary D. Stumpf, Publisher. **Subscription Rates:** $21; $26 out of country; $32 out of state. **Remarks:** Accepts advertising.
Ad Rates: PCI: $4.80 **Circ:** ‡3,200

16560 KMFX-AM - 1190
PO Box 46 Phone: (612)565-4576
Wabasha, MN 55981 Fax: (612)565-2616

Format: Country; Agricultural. **Owner:** James Ingstad Broadcasting, at above address. **Founded:** 1976. **Formerly:** KWMB-AM (1994). **Operating Hours:** 6 a.m.-sunset. **Key Personnel:** Kelly Lafky, Sales Mgr.; Carol Tentis, Farm Directory/Office/Production Mgr. **Local Programs:** *Tri-County News*, Carol Tentis. **Wattage:** 1000. **Ad Rates:** $5-19 for 30 seconds; $8-22 for 60 seconds.

WABASSO

16561 Wabasso Standard
PO Box 70 Phone: (507)342-5143
Wabasso, MN 56293 Fax: (507)342-5143

Community newspaper. **Founded:** Apr. 1900. **Freq:** Weekly (Thurs.). **Print Method:** Offset. **Cols./Page:** 5. **Col. Width:** 2 picas. **Col. Depth:** 13 1/2 inches. **Key Personnel:** Jeff Meyer, Publisher. **USPS:** 660-020. **Subscription Rates:** $16 in County, $18 out of County, $20 out of state. **Remarks:** Accepts advertising.
Ad Rates: SAU: $2.67 **Circ:** 1,400
PCI: $2.75

WACONIA, pop. 2,638.

SC MN. Carver Co. 26 mi. SW of Minneapolis. Lake recreation area, boating & fishing. Light industry. Dairy, poultry, grain farms. Corn, oats, barley.

16562 Waconia Patriot
8 Elmwood S. Phone: (612)442-4414
PO Box 5 Fax: (612)442-4428
Waconia, MN 55387
Newspaper. **Founded:** 1897. **Freq:** Weekly (Thurs.). **Print Method:** Offset. **Cols./Page:** 6. **Col. Width:** 24 nonpareils. **Col. Depth:** 301 agate lines. **Key Personnel:** Rod Shilkrot, Editor; James D. Berreth, Publisher. **Subscription Rates:** $11. **Remarks:** Accepts advertising.
Ad Rates: GLR: $.25 **Circ:** (Not Reported)

WADENA†, pop. 4,699.

WC MN. Wadena Co. 80 mi. NW of Saint Cloud. Manufactures butter, woodwork, clothing, beverages. Dairy, poultry farms. Corn, hay, oats.

16563 Intercom
Forum Publishing
346 S. Jefferson Phone: (218)631-2561
Box 31 Fax: (218)631-1621
Wadena, MN 56482-0031
Community newspaper. **Freq:** Weekly (Sun.). **Subscription Rates:** Free.
Circ: Non-paid 14,883

16564 Pioneer Journal
Forum Publishing
346 S. Jefferson Phone: (218)631-2561
Box 31 Fax: (218)631-1621
Wadena, MN 56482-0031
Community newspaper. **Founded:** 1877. **Freq:** Weekly (Thurs.). **Print Method:** Offset. **Cols./Page:** 6. **Col. Width:** 28 nonpareils. **Col. Depth:** 301 agate lines. **Key Personnel:** Laura Gudbaur, Editor. **Subscription Rates:** $16. **Remarks:** Accepts advertising.
Ad Rates: GLR: $.53 **Circ:** Combined 3,875

16565 KKWS-FM - 105.9
201 1/2 S. Jefferson Phone: (218)631-1803
Box 551 Fax: (218)631-4557
Wadena, MN 56482
Free: (800)733-5923
E-mail: kwad@wcta.net

Format: Country. **Networks:** ABC; Minnesota News. **Owner:** Kommerstad Communications, at above address, (218)829-2853. **Founded:** 1967. **Operating Hours:** Continuous.; 60% network, 40% local. **Key Personnel:** Dan Skogen, Contact; Mike Danvers, Contact; Mike Overton, General Mgr.; Randy Johnson, Sales Mgr. **Wattage:** 100,000. **Ad Rates:** $6-12 for 30 seconds.

16566 KWAD-AM - 920
PO Box 551 Phone: (218)631-1803
Wadena, MN 56482 Fax: (218)631-4557
Free: (800)733-5923
E-mail: kwad@wcta.net

Format: Contemporary Country. **Networks:** ABC. **Founded:** 1948. **Operating Hours:** Continuous. **Key Personnel:** Mike Overton, General Mgr.; Dan Skogen, Operations Mgr.; Randy Johnson, Sales Mgr. **Wattage:** 1000. **Ad Rates:** $5-9.50 for 30 seconds.

WALKER†, pop. 970.

NC MN. Cass Co. 195 mi. N. of Minneapolis, in the Chippewa National Forest. Tourism. Manufactures wood products, fireplaces.

16567 The Pilot-Independent
PO Box 190 Phone: (218)547-1000
Walker, MN 56484 Fax: (218)547-3000

Community newspaper. **Founded:** 1896. **Freq:** Weekly (Thurs.). **Print Method:** Offset. **Trim Size:** 14 x 22 1/2. **Cols./Page:** 6. **Col. Width:** 24 nonpareils. **Col. Depth:** 301 agate lines. **Key Personnel:** Paul Nye, Editor; Joe Sherman, Publisher. **Subscription Rates:** $18 in county; $25 out of county. **Remarks:** Accepts advertising.
Ad Rates: GLR: $.28 **Circ:** ‡3,442
BW: $110
4C: $451
SAU: $3.75

16568 KLLZ-AM - 1600
Box 70 Phone: (218)547-1200
Walker, MN 56484

Format: Adult Contemporary. **Founded:** 1970. **Formerly:** KLLR-AM (1992). **Operating Hours:** 6 a.m.-10 p.m. **Key Personnel:** Brad Walhof, Contact; Tim Norton, Program Dir.; Paul Tichinal, Chief Engineer. **Wattage:** 1000 day; 47 night.

WANAMINGO

16569 The News Record
Grimsrud Publishing, Inc.
225 Main St. Phone: (507)732-7617
PO Box 97 Fax: (507)732-7619
Zumbrota, MN 55992
Free: (800)772-5384

Community newspaper. **Founded:** 1995. **Freq:** Weekly (Wed.). **Cols./Page:** 6. **Col. Width:** 14 picas. **Col. Depth:** 21 1/2 inches. **Key Personnel:** David Grimsrud, Publisher; Peter Grimsrud, Editor. **Remarks:** Accepts advertising. **Absorbed:** Zumbrota News; Pine Island Record; Goodhue County Tribune; Wanamingo Progress; Mazeppa Journal.
Ad Rates: BW: $258 **Circ:** 700
PCI: $3.25

WARREN†, pop. 2,105.

NW MN. Marshall Co. 30 mi. NE of Grand Forks, ND. Dairy, poultry, grain farms. Wheat, sugar beets, barley, flax, sunflowers, pinto beans.

16570 Sheaf
127 W. Johnson Ave. Phone: (218)745-5174
Box 45 Fax: (218)745-5175
Warren, MN 56762
Newspaper with Report orientation. **Founded:** 1880. **Freq:** Weekly (Wed.). **Print Method:** Offset. **Cols./Page:** 6. **Col. Width:** 12 1/2 picas. **Col. Depth:** 301 agate lines. **Key Personnel:** E. Neil Mattson, Editor and Publisher. **USPS:** 666-420. **Subscription Rates:** $18; $21 out of area. **Remarks:** Accepts advertising.
Ad Rates: GLR: $.25 **Circ:** Paid 3,133
SAU: $4 Non-paid 129

WARROAD, pop. 1,216.

NW MN. Roseau Co. On Lake of the Woods, 115 mi. of Grand Forks, ND. International Boundry Line. Resort. Fisheries; timber. Mink ranches. Manufactures wood windows, insulated glass, hockey sticks; lumber. Agriculture. Seed potatoes, hay, grass seed.

16571 The Warroad Pioneer
Page One Publications
PO Box E Phone: (218)386-1594
Warroad, MN 56763 Fax: (218)386-1072

Community newspaper. **Founded:** 1898. **Freq:** Weekly (Tues.). **Print Method:** Offset. **Cols./Page:** 6. **Col. Width:** 26 nonpareils. **Col. Depth:** 301 agate lines. **Key Personnel:** Julie Gillie, Publisher; Rollin Bergman, Publisher; Tony Rogers, Editor. **Subscription Rates:** $19 individuals; $25 out of area. **Remarks:** Accepts advertising. **URL:** http://www.rrv.net/page1pub.
Ad Rates: BW: $419.25 **Circ:** ‡2,400
PCI: $3.25

16572 KKWQ-FM - 92.5
501 E. Lake St. Phone: (218)386-3023
PO Box 69 Fax: (218)386-3090
Warroad, MN 56763

Format: Country. **Networks:** ABC. **Owner:** Border Broadcasting LP, at above address. **Founded:** 1989. **Operating Hours:**

Continuous. **Key Personnel:** Mike Pederson, General Mgr. **Wattage:** 100,000. **Ad Rates:** $9 for 30 seconds; $14 for 60 seconds.

WASECA†, pop. 8,219.

SC MN. Waseca Co. 25 mi. E. of Mankato. University of Minnesota Technical College at Waseca. Lake resort. Manufactures frozen foods, electronic equipment, steel products, truck bodies, modular homes, sporting goods. Hatcheries. Dairy, cattles, poultry, hog farms. Corn, soybeans, oats, flax, rye.

16573 Arabian Horse Times
1050 NE 8th St. NE Phone: (507)835-3204
PO Box 1469 Fax: (507)835-5138
Waseca, MN 56093-9803
Magazine featuring articles on the care and management of Arabian horses. **Founded:** 1970. **Freq:** Monthly. **Trim Size:** 8 x 10. **Key Personnel:** Ruth James, Editor. **ISSN:** 0279-8125. **Subscription Rates:** $25. $4 single issue. **Remarks:** Advertising accepted; rates available upon request.
Circ: Paid 22,000

16574 Waseca County News
PO Box 465 Phone: (507)835-3380
Waseca, MN 56093 Fax: (507)835-3435

Community newspaper. **Founded:** 1981. **Freq:** Semiweekly (Tues. and Thurs.). **Print Method:** Offset. **Cols./Page:** 6. **Col. Width:** 26 nonpareils. **Col. Depth:** 301 agate lines. **Key Personnel:** Lisa Meyers, Editor; Tom West, Publisher; Cheryl Neid, Advertising Mgr. **USPS:** 664-350. **Subscription Rates:** $37 individuals; $48 out of area. **Remarks:** Accepts advertising. **Merged with:** Waseca Sun-Review (Nov. 1990).
Ad Rates: GLR: $.44 **Circ:** Paid ‡3,727
BW: $689.82
4C: $960.08
SAU: $6.21
PCI: $6.21

16575 KOWO-AM - 1170
PO Box 505 Phone: (507)835-5555
Waseca, MN 56093 Fax: (507)835-2030

Format: Contemporary Country. **Networks:** CNN Radio; Minnesota News. **Owner:** Hometown Radio, at above address. **Founded:** 1971. **Operating Hours:** Continuous. 10% network, 90% local. **Key Personnel:** Daryn Spies, News Dir. **Wattage:** 1000. **Ad Rates:** $8.50 for 30 seconds; $10.50 for 60 seconds.

16576 KRUE-FM - 92.1
222 N. State. St. Phone: (507)835-5555
Waseca, MN 56093 Fax: (507)835-2030

Format: Adult Contemporary. **Networks:** CNN Radio. **Owner:** Cumulus Broadcasting, at above address. **Founded:** 1972. **Operating Hours:** Continuous. **Key Personnel:** Mike Parry, Market Mgr.; Pam Kara, Business Mgr. **Local Programs:** *Come Alive at 5*, Mike Parry; *Live Trackside*, Mike Parry. **Wattage:** 25,000. **Ad Rates:** $8 for 30 seconds; $12 for 60 seconds.

16577 Triax Cablevision - Waseca
1504 2nd St. SE Phone: (507)835-5975
PO Box 110 Fax: (507)835-4567
Waseca, MN 56093
Free: (800)332-0245

Key Personnel: Paul Nazarow, Contact; Denise McDonough, Office Mgr.

WATERTOWN, pop. 1,920.

SC MN. Carver Co. 30 mi. W. of Minneapolis. Agriculture. Dairy, poultry, beef, grain, corn, wheat, soybeans.

16578 Carver County News
Box 188 Phone: (612)955-1111
101 Lewis Ave. N. Fax: (612)955-2241
Watertown, MN 55388
Newspaper with a Republican orientation. **Founded:** 1887. **Freq:** Weekly (Thurs.). **Print Method:** Offset. **Cols./Page:** 6. **Col. Width:** 24 nonpareils. **Col. Depth:** 301 agate lines. **Key Personnel:** James Bart, Editor; James D. Berreth, Publisher. **Subscription Rates:** $23.90 individuals. **Remarks:** Accepts advertising.
Circ: Paid 1,920
Non-paid 50

WATERVILLE, pop. 1,775.

SC MN. Le Sueur Co. On Lake Sakatah and Tetonka, 15 mi. W. of Faribault. State Park. Resort. Fishing and camping areas. Light manufacturing. Fish hatchery. Dairy, stock, poultry, grain farms. Corn, wheat, clover seed.

16579 Lake Region Life
115 S. 3rd St. Phone: (507)362-4495
Waterville, MN 56096 Fax: (507)362-4458

Community newspaper. **Founded:** 1884. **Freq:** Weekly (Thurs.). **Print Method:** Offset. **Cols./Page:** 6. **Col. Width:** 2 inches. **Col. Depth:** 21 1/2 inches. **Key Personnel:** Jay M. Schneider, Managing Editor. **Subscription Rates:** $21 individuals; $24 out of area; $30 out of state. **Remarks:** Accepts advertising.
Ad Rates: GLR: $.175 **Circ:** ‡1,603
BW: $300
SAU: $4

WATKINS

16580 Watkins Patriot
PO Box 486 Phone: (612)764-5375
Watkins, MN 55389
Community newspaper. **Freq:** Weekly (Wed.). **Cols./Page:** 6. **Col. Width:** 14 picas. **Col. Depth:** 21 1/2 inches. **Key Personnel:** Jerold Oster, Editor; Terry O'Keefe, Publisher.
Circ: 600

WAYZATA, pop. 3,621.

SE MN. Hennepin Co. On Lake Minnetonka, 20 mi. W. of Saint Paul. Residential. Commercial.

16581 Lakeshore Weekly News
Weekly News, Inc.
18178 Minnetonka Blvd. Phone: (612)473-0890
Wayzata, MN 55391 Fax: (612)473-0895

Newspaper covering western suburban communities of Minneapolis. **Founded:** Aug. 1982. **Freq:** Weekly. **Print Method:** Offset. **Trim Size:** 10 x 16. **Cols./Page:** 5. **Col. Width:** 1 15/16 inches. **Col. Depth:** 15 inches. **Key Personnel:** Peter H. May, Publisher; Rick Christiansen, Associated Publisher; Bill Boudewyns, Editor, billb@weeklynews.com; J. Mark Gardener, Advertising Mgr. **Subscription Rates:** $28. **Remarks:** Color advertising accepted; rates available upon request. **URL:** http://www.weeklynews.com. **Absorbed:** Hopkins-Minnetonka Weekly News (1989); Wayzata Weekly News (1989); South Shore Weekly News (1989). **Formerly:** Weekly News.
Ad Rates: GLR: $3 **Circ:** 25,000
BW: $1,400 Free ‡25,000
PCI: $16.50

16582 Wayzata Sun-Sailor
Sun Newspapers
10917 Valley View Rd. Phone: (612)829-0797
Eden Prairie, MN 55344 Fax: (612)392-6802
Publication E-mail: sunsailor@mnsunpub.com
Publisher E-mail: suncurrentsouth@mnsunpub.com

Community newspaper (tabloid). **Freq:** Weekly (Wed.). **Print Method:** Offset. **Cols./Page:** 5. **Col. Width:** 1 15/16 inches. **Col. Depth:** 16 inches. **Key Personnel:** Frank Chilinski, phone (612)392-6851. **Remarks:** Accepts advertising. **URL:** http://www.mnsun.com.
Ad Rates: GLR: $25.88 **Circ:** Non-paid 3,854
BW: $1,760 Paid 973
4C: $1,529
PCI: $22

WELLS, pop. 2,777.

SC MN. Faribault Co. 42 mi. SE of Mantako. Canneries, food processing. Manufactures tile, concrete. Hatchery. Dairy, poultry, stock, grain farms.

16583 The Wells Mirror
40 W. Franklin Phone: (507)553-3131
Wells, MN 56097 Fax: (507)553-3132
Publication E-mail: wellsmir@polaristel.net

Newspaper. **Founded:** 1870. **Freq:** Weekly (Wed.). **Print Method:** Offset. **Cols./Page:** 6. **Col. Width:** 29 nonpareils. **Col. Depth:** 301 agate lines. **Key Personnel:** Laurie Bonsack, Editor; Michael Johnson, Publisher. **USPS:** 674-060. **Subscription Rates:** $24.
Ad Rates: PCI: $3.50 **Circ:** 2,050

WEST SAINT PAUL

16584 West Saint Paul/Mendota Heights Sun Current
Sun Newspapers
10917 Valley View Rd. Phone: (612)829-0797
Eden Prairie, MN 55344 Fax: (612)392-6802
Publication E-mail: weststpaulsuncurrent@mnsunpub.com
Publisher E-mail: suncurrentsouth@mnsunpub.com

Community newspaper (tabloid). **Freq:** Weekly (Wed.). **Print Method:** Offset. **Cols./Page:** 5. **Col. Width:** 1 15/16 inches. **Col. Depth:** 16 inches. **Key Personnel:** Frank Chilinski, Publisher, phone (612)392-6851. **Remarks:** Accepts advertising. **URL:** http://www.mnsun.com.
Ad Rates: BW: $1,312 **Circ:** Free 10,200
4C: $1,091
PCI: $16.40

WESTBROOK

16585 Westbrook Sentinel & Tribune
621 1st Ave. Phone: (507)274-6136
PO Box 98
Westbrook, MN 56183
Community newspaper. **Freq:** Weekly (Wed.). **Cols./Page:** 7. **Col. Width:** 12 3/10 picas. **Col. Depth:** 21 1/2 inches. **Key Personnel:** Ralph Merchant, Editor; Thomas Merchant, Publisher.
Circ: 1,700

WESTONKA

16586 Sun-Sailor
Minnesota Sun Publications
7831 E. Bush Lake Rd. Phone: (612)896-4700
Bloomington, MN 55439 Fax: (612)896-4728

Community newspaper (tabloid). **Founded:** 1984. **Freq:** Weekly (Wed.). **Print Method:** Offset. **Cols./Page:** 5. **Col. Width:** 1 15/16 inches. **Col. Depth:** 16 inches. **Key Personnel:** John Gannet Hawley, Publisher; Robert Stjern, Advertising Mgr. **Remarks:** Accepts advertising. **Formerly:** Westonka Sun-Sailor.
Ad Rates: BW: $534 **Circ:** Free 5,581
4C: $1,009 Paid 223
PCI: $8.90

WHEATON

16587 Wheaton Gazette
1114 Broadway Phone: (320)563-8146
Wheaton, MN 56296 Fax: (320)563-8147

Community newspaper. **Freq:** Weekly (Wed.). **Cols./Page:** 7. **Col. Width:** 12 1/2 picas. **Col. Depth:** 21 1/2 inches. **Key Personnel:** William N. Kremer, Publisher.
Circ: Combined ❑**27,127**

WHITE BEAR LAKE, pop. 22,538.

SE MN. Ramsey Co. On White Bear Lake, 12 mi. NE of Saint Paul. Lakewood Community College. Manufactures sport boats, airport carts, sound equipment, steel fabricators, Corrugated boxes, fishing sinkers.

16588 Christian Magnifier
Lutheran Braille Evangelism Association
1740 Eugene St. Phone: (651)426-0469
White Bear Lake, MN 55110
Publisher E-mail: lbeassoc@aol.com

Religious magazine. **Founded:** 1956. **Freq:** Monthly. **Key Personnel:** Rev. Dennis Hawkinson, revdennish@aol.com. **Subscription Rates:** $7 single issue. **Remarks:** Advertising not accepted. **Alt. Formats:** Audio tape; Large-print.
Circ: Controlled 2,200

16589 Quad Community Press
Press Publications
4779 Bloom Ave. Phone: (651)407-1200
White Bear Lake, MN 55110 Fax: (651)429-1242
Publisher E-mail: presspub@minn.net

Community newspaper. **Founded:** 1982. **Freq:** Weekly (Tues.). **Print Method:** Offset. **Trim Size:** 14 x 22 3/4. **Cols./Page:** 6. **Col. Width:** 2 1/16 inches. **Col. Depth:** 21 inches. **Key Personnel:** Eugene D. Johnson, Publisher, presspub@minn.net; Mary Berg, Circulation Mgr., phone (651)407-1241; John Bartunek, Advertising Dir., phone (651)407-1208; Gary Morten, Managing Editor, phone (651)407-1230; Pat Daul, Controller, phone (651)407-1205. **Subscription Rates:** Free; $25 out of area. **Remarks:** Accepts advertising.
Ad Rates: GLR: $4.75 **Circ:** Paid 2,290
BW: $954.60 Free 5,351
4C: $1,344.60
SAU: $9.30
CNU: $9.30
PCI: $9.30

16590 St. Croix Valley Press
Press Publications
4779 Bloom Ave. Phone: (651)407-1200
White Bear Lake, MN 55110 Fax: (651)429-1242
Publisher E-mail: presspub@minn.net

Local newspaper. **Founded:** 1977. **Freq:** Weekly (Thurs.). **Print Method:** Offset. **Trim Size:** 11.375 x 14. **Cols./Page:** 5.

Col. Width: 2 1/16 inches. **Col. Depth:** 13 inches. **Key Personnel:** Eugene D. Johnson, Publisher; Gary Mortenson, Managing Editor, phone (651)407-1226; John Bartunek, Advertising Dir., phone (651)407-1208; Mary Berg, Circulation Mgr., phone (651)407-1241; Pat Daul, Controller, phone (651)407-1205; Cindy Rieder, Production Mgr., phone (651)407-1239. **Subscription Rates:** Free; $25 out of area mail. **Remarks:** Accepts advertising.
Ad Rates: GLR: $4.75 — **Circ:** Free 10,676; Paid 226
BW: $542.75
4C: $932.75
SAU: $10.30
CNU: $10.30
PCI: $10.30

16591 Shoreview Press
Press Publications
4779 Bloom Ave. Phone: (651)407-1200
White Bear Lake, MN 55110 Fax: (651)429-1242
Publisher E-mail: presspub@minn.net

Local newspaper. **Founded:** 1974. **Freq:** Weekly (Tues.). **Cols./Page:** 6. **Col. Width:** 2 1/16 inches. **Col. Depth:** 21 inches. **Key Personnel:** Gary Mortenson, Managing Editor, prespub@minn.net; Eugene D. Johnson, Publisher; John Bartunek, Advertising Dir., phone (651)407-1208; Mary Berg, Circulation Mgr., phone (651)407-1241; Pat Daul, Controller, phone (651)407-1205. **Subscription Rates:** $25. **Remarks:** Accepts advertising.
Ad Rates: GLR: $4.75 — **Circ:** Paid 141; Non-paid 8,472
BW: $999.75
4C: $1,389.75
SAU: $9.30
CNU: $9.30
PCI: $9.30

16592 Tract Messenger
Lutheran Braille Evangelism Association
1740 Eugene St. Phone: (651)426-0469
White Bear Lake, MN 55110
Publisher E-mail: lbeassoc@aol.com

Religious magazine in Braille. **Founded:** 1952. **Freq:** Monthly. **Key Personnel:** Rev. Dennis Hawkinson, revdennish@aol.com. **Subscription Rates:** Free to qualified subscribers (blind). **Remarks:** Advertising not accepted. **Alt. Formats:** Braille.
Circ: Controlled 475

16593 Vadnais Heights Press
Press Publications
4779 Bloom Ave. Phone: (651)407-1200
White Bear Lake, MN 55110 Fax: (651)429-1242
Publisher E-mail: presspub@minn.net

Local newspaper. **Founded:** 1974. **Freq:** Weekly (Wed.). **Print Method:** Offset. **Trim Size:** 14 x 22 3/4. **Cols./Page:** 6. **Col. Width:** 2 1/16 inches. **Col. Depth:** 21 inches. **Key Personnel:** Gary Mortenson, Managing Editor, phone (651)407-1230; Eugene D. Johnson, Publisher; Mary Berg, Circulation Mgr., phone (651)407-1241; Pat Daul, Circulation Mgr., phone (651)407-1205; Cindy Rieder, Production Mgr., phone (651)407-1239. **Subscription Rates:** $25.
Ad Rates: GLR: $4.75 — **Circ:** Paid 441; Non-paid 3,423
BW: $690.15
4C: $1,080.15
SAU: $6.35
CNU: $6.35
PCI: $6.35

16594 White Bear Press
Press Publications
4779 Bloom Ave. Phone: (651)407-1200
White Bear Lake, MN 55110 Fax: (651)429-1242
Publisher E-mail: presspub@minn.net

Local newspaper. **Founded:** 1896. **Freq:** Weekly (Wed.). **Print Method:** Offset. **Trim Size:** 14 x 22.75. **Cols./Page:** 6. **Col. Width:** 2 1/16 inches. **Col. Depth:** 21 inches. **Key Personnel:** Eugene D. Johnson, Publisher; John Bartunek, Advertising Dir., phone (651)407-1208; Gary Mortenson, Managing Editor, phone (651)407-1226; Mary Berg, Circulation Mgr., phone (651)407-1241; Pat Daul, Controller, phone (651)407-1205; Cindy Rieder, Production Mgr., phone (651)407-1239. **Subscription Rates:** $25 out of area.
Ad Rates: GLR: $4.75 — **Circ:** Free 12,032; Paid 6,379
BW: $2,167.20
4C: $2,557.20
SAU: $20.85
CNU: $20.85
PCI: $20.85

WILLIAMS, pop. 217.

NW MN. Lake of the Woods Co. 190 mi. NW of Duluth. Resort area. Timber. Agriculture. Beef cattle, potato seed.

16595 The Northern Light
PO Box 157 Phone: (218)386-1594
Williams, MN 56686 Fax: (218)386-1072
Publication E-mail: norlight@grandforks.polaristel.net

Community newspaper. **Founded:** Feb. 1916. **Freq:** Weekly (Wed.). **Print Method:** Offset uses mats. **Cols./Page:** 6. **Col. Width:** 24 nonpareils. **Col. Depth:** 300 agate lines. **Key Personnel:** Julie M. Gillie, Publisher; Rollin Bergman, Publisher; Jaime DeLage, Editor. **USPS:** 684-660. **Subscription Rates:** $19 individuals; $25 out of area. **Remarks:** Accepts advertising. **Formerly:** Williams Northern Light.
Ad Rates: BW: $322.50 — **Circ:** ‡1,400
4C: $475
PCI: $3.25

WILLMAR†, pop. 15,895.

SWC MN. Kandiyohi Co. 92 mi. W. of Minneapolis. Willman Community College. Medical center. Tourist area. Farm equipment, sash and door, soft drink factories. Metal fabricating. Turkey processing. Agriculture. Dairying, turkeys.

16596 West Central Tribune
PO Box 839 Phone: (320)235-1150
Willmar, MN 56201 Fax: (320)235-6769
Free: (800)450-1150
Publication E-mail: wctrib@willmar.com

General newspaper. **Founded:** 1895. **Freq:** Mon.-Sat. (morn.). **Print Method:** Offset. **Cols./Page:** 6. **Col. Width:** 25 nonpareils. **Col. Depth:** 294 agate lines. **Key Personnel:** Steven McLister, Publisher; Marilyn Birkland, Advertising Dir.; Forrest Peterson, Editor. **USPS:** 675-080. **Subscription Rates:** $105 individuals. **Remarks:** Accepts advertising. **Available Online. URL:** http://www.wctrib.com.
Ad Rates: GLR: $3.80 — **Circ:** Paid ❑**17,106**
BW: $1,470
4C: $1,830
SAU: $15.10
PCI: $11.65

16597 Heritage Cable Inc.
PO Box 1298 Phone: (612)235-1530
Willmar, MN 56201-1298 Fax: (612)235-1462

Owner: Tele-Communications Inc., 5619 DTC Pkwy., Englewood, CO 80111, (303)267-5500. **Founded:** 1957. **Key Personnel:** Jon Melandro, Office Mgr.; Terry Mansell, Chief Engineer; Calvin Cablson, Manager. **Cities Served:** Benson, Kandiyohi, New London, Penock, Spicer, Willmar, MN: subscribing households 10,000; 36 channels; 1 community access channel; 3 hours per week community access programming.

16598 KDJS-AM - 1590
PO Box A380 Phone: (320)231-1600
Willmar, MN 56201

Format: Oldies. **Networks:** Westwood One Radio. **Owner:** Kandi Broadcasting, Inc., at above address. **Founded:** Mar. 17, 1981. **Key Personnel:** Perry Rugler, President. **Wattage:** 1000. **Ad Rates:** $10 for 30 seconds; $13 for 60 seconds.

16599 KDJS-FM - 95.3
730 NE Hwy. 71 Service Dr. Phone: (320)231-1600
Box 380 Fax: (320)235-7010
Willmar, MN 56201

Format: Country. **Networks:** Unistar. **Owner:** Perry Kugler, 1331 Westwood Ct., Willmar, MN 56201, (320)235-9191. **Founded:** 1993. **Operating Hours:** Continuous. **Key Personnel:** Bev Ahlquist, News Dir.; Rob Moe, Program Dir.; Perry Kugler, President. **Wattage:** 50,000. **Ad Rates:** $24 for 30 seconds; $30 for 60 seconds. Combined advertising rates available with KDJS-AM.

16600 KWLM-AM - 1340
1340 N. 7th St. Phone: (612)235-1340
PO Box 838 Fax: (612)235-9111
Willmar, MN 56201

Format: News; Talk; Sports; Agricultural. **Networks:** ABC; Mutual Broadcasting System. **Founded:** 1940. **Operating Hours:** Continuous. **Key Personnel:** Steve Linder, Gen. Mgr./Gen. Sales Mgr.; John Nelson, P.D.; J. P. Cola, News Dir.; Todd Begeth, Sports Dir. **Wattage:** 1000. **Ad Rates:** $9-23 for 30 seconds; $13-25 for 60 seconds. **URL:** http://www.khcb.org.

WINDOM†, pop. 4,666.

SW MN. Cottonwood Co. 120 mi. SW of Saint Paul. Manufactures snowblowers, lawn mowers, farm equipment wood burning stoves. Beef packing plant. Elevator. Corn, soybeans, dairy products, honey and livestock.

16601 Cottonwood County Citizen
260 10th St. Phone: (507)831-3455
PO Box 309 Fax: (507)831-3740
Windom, MN 56101
Community newspaper. **Founded:** 1882. **Freq:** Weekly (Wed.). **Print Method:** Offset. **Cols./Page:** 6. **Col. Width:** 28 nonpareils. **Col. Depth:** 301 agate lines. **Key Personnel:** Rahn Larson, Editor; Kim M. Anderson, Publisher; Linda Bramstedt, Advertising Mgr. **Subscription Rates:** $36.
Ad Rates: GLR: $.42 — **Circ:** ‡3,806
BW: $748
4C: $948
PCI: $5.90

16602 Windom Cable Communications
444 9th St. Phone: (507)831-2363
Box 38 Fax: (507)831-3340
Windom, MN 56101

Founded: Apr. 1984. **Key Personnel:** Dennis Nelson, General Mgr.; Eugene Sunstrom, Cable Technician. **Cities Served:** Windom, MN: subscribing households 1,600; 37 channels; 1 community access channel; 168 hours per week community access programming.

WINONA†, pop. 25,075.

SE MN. Winona Co. On Mississippi River, 30 mi. N. of La Crosse, WI. Barge connections. St. Mary's College; College of St. Teresa; Winona State College. Steamboat Museum. Manufactures flour, patent medicines, cosmetics, food, dairy products, auto chains, sweaters, metalware, gloves, mitts, candy, malt, feed, plastic compounds, wooden boxes, excavators, bricks, rock drills, iron benders, fertilizers. Nurseries. Agriculture.

16603 The Cardinal
St. Mary's University
700 Terrace Hgts., No. 36 Phone: (507)457-1496
Winona, MN 55987 Fax: (507)457-6967
Free: (800)635-5987

Collegiate. **Founded:** 1973. **Freq:** 8/year. **Print Method:** Offset. **Trim Size:** 11.5 x 13.5. **Cols./Page:** 4. **Col. Width.** 14 picas. **Col. Depth:** 12.5 inches. **Key Personnel:** Bob Conover, Advisor, bconover@smumn.edu. **Remarks:** Accepts advertising.
Ad Rates: BW: $195 — **Circ:** Paid 50; Non-paid 1,500
PCI: $10

16604 The Courier
PO Box 949 Phone: (507)454-4643
Winona, MN 55987-0949 Fax: (507)454-8106

Catholic magazine. **Founded:** 1910. **Freq:** Monthly. **Print Method:** Offset. **Trim Size:** 11 1/2 x 16. **Cols./Page:** 4. **Col. Width:** 28 nonpareils. **Col. Depth:** 224 agate lines. **Key Personnel:** I van Kubista, Editor; Bishop J.G. Vlazny, Publisher. **Subscription Rates:** $5. **Remarks:** Advertising not accepted.
Circ: ‡39,700

16605 Winona Daily News
Lee Enterprises, Inc.
601 Franklin St. Phone: (507)453-3510
PO Box 5147 Fax: (507)454-1440
Winona, MN 55987-3822
Publication E-mail: wdn@luminet.net

General newspaper. **Founded:** Nov. 19, 1855. **Freq:** Mon.-Sun. (morn.). **Print Method:** Offset. **Cols./Page:** 6. **Col. Width:** 24 nonpareils. **Col. Depth:** 301 agate lines. **Key Personnel:** Jim Galewski, Managing Editor, phone (507)453-3519; George Althoff, Publisher, phone (507)453-3501. **Subscription Rates:** $130. **Remarks:** Accepts advertising.
Ad Rates: BW: $1,258 — **Circ:** Mon.-Sat. ★**12,112**; Sun. ★**12,994**
4C: $1,483
PCI: $9.75

16606 Winona Post
64 E. 2nd St. Phone: (507)452-1262
PO Box 27 Fax: (507)454-6409
Winona, MN 55987
Free: (800)353-2126

Community newspaper. **Founded:** 1971. **Freq:** Semiweekly. **Print Method:** Offset. **Cols./Page:** 6. **Col. Width:** 2 inches. **Col. Depth:** 21 1/2 inches. **Key Personnel:** Frances M. Edstrom, Editor; John O. Edstrom, Publisher; Patrick Marek, Sales Mgr. **Subscription Rates:** Free; $40 by mail. **Remarks:** Accepts advertising. **Alt. Formats:** CD-ROM. **Formerly:** Winona Post and Shopper (1992).
Ad Rates: BW: $1,218.17 — **Circ:** Free ‡24,440
4C: $1,421.33
SAU: $11.29

16607 Winonan
Winona State University
Kryzsko Commons Phone: (507)457-5677
PO Box 5838 Fax: (507)457-5317
Winona, MN 55987
Publication E-mail: winonan@vax2.winona.msus.edu

Collegiate newspaper. **Founded:** 1922. **Freq:** Weekly. **Print Method:** Offset. **Cols./Page:** 6. **Col. Width:** 12 picas. **Col. Depth:** 224 agate lines. **Key Personnel:** Lauren Osborne, Editor, losborne@hotmail.com; Andrea Nelsen, Advertising Mgr. **Subscription Rates:** Free; $20 by mail. **Remarks:** Accepts advertising.
Ad Rates: BW: $402.50 **Circ:** Free ‡5,000
PCI: $6

16608 Hidden Valley TV
458 W. 8th St. Phone: (507)452-2666
Winona, MN 55987
E-mail: trpitts@luminet.net

Owner: Crown Cable, 1 Galleria Tower, 13355 Noel Rd., Ste. 1500, Dallas, TX 75240, (214)960-4860, Fax: (214)960-4800. **Founded:** 1977. **Key Personnel:** Thomas R. Pitts, President; Sheila T. Pitts, Vice President; James T. Pitts, Chief Engineer. **Cities Served:** Hidden Valley, MN: subscribing households 250; 36 channels; 2 community access channels.

16609 KAGE-FM - 95.3
752 Bluffview Circle Phone: (507)452-4000
PO Box 767 Fax: (507)452-9494
Winona, MN 55987-0767
Free: (800)584-6782
E-mail: winonara@rconnect.com

Format: Adult Contemporary. **Networks:** AP. **Founded:** 1971. **Operating Hours:** 24Hrs. **Key Personnel:** Jerry Papenfuss, General Mgr.; Pat Papenfuss, Operations Mgr.; Darryl Smelser, News Dir. **Wattage:** 25,000. **Ad Rates:** $14-25 for 30 seconds; $18-30 for 60 seconds.

16610 KBEW-FM - 98.1
PO Box 767 Phone: (507)526-2181
Winona, MN 55987-0767 Fax: (507)526-7468

Format: Contemporary Country. **Owner:** Jerry Papenfuss, at above address. **Founded:** Aug. 1991. **Operating Hours:** Continuous. **Key Personnel:** Kevin Benson, General Mgr.; Diane Holland, Admin.Asst.; Randy Frandle, Program Dir.; Wanda Nichols, Sales Mgr.; Norm Hall, News Dir. **Wattage:** 25,000.

16611 KHME-FM - 101.1
360 Vila St. Phone: (507)454-4663
Winona, MN 55987 Fax: (507)454-1463

Format: Adult Contemporary. **Networks:** CNN Radio. **Owner:** Marathon Media, 980 N. Michigan Ave., Ste. 1880, Chicago, IL 60611, (312)204-9900. **Founded:** 1992. **Operating Hours:** 24 hrs /Day. **Key Personnel:** Greg Wennes, General Mgr.; Megg Lanswerk, Business Mgr., phone (888)806-8876; Mike Martin, Program Dir.; Wayne Valentine, Information Dir. **Local Programs:** *Chuck Williams Radio Column*; *First Cup of Coffee*; *Outdoor with Wayne Valentine.* **Wattage:** 25,000. **Ad Rates:** $5.75 for 15 seconds; $6-9.50 for 30 seconds; $7.50-15 for 60 seconds. Combined advertising rates available with KQYB, KNEI.

16612 KHMG-FM - 1380
PO Box 767 Phone: (507)452-4000
Winona, MN 55987 Fax: (507)452-9494
Free: (800)584-6782

Format: Country. **Owner:** Kage, Inc., at above address. **Founded:** Feb. 19, 1957. **Operating Hours:** Sunrise-sunset. **Key Personnel:** Jerry Papenfuss, General Mgr.; Pat Papenfuss, Operations Mgr./Prog. Dir.; Les Guderian, Sales Mgr.; Jim Trotter, Farm Dir. **Local Programs:** *Partyline*, Yvonne Lindquist; *Radio Auction*, Jim Trotter. **Wattage:** 4,000. **Ad Rates:** Noncommercial.

16613 KPRW-FM - 99.5
PO Box 767 Phone: (218)346-4800
Winona, MN 55987 Fax: (218)346-7595

Format: Adult Contemporary. **Owner:** Result Radio, Inc., at above address. **Operating Hours:** Continuous. **Key Personnel:** Doug Gray, General Mgr., phone (218)736-7596; Steven Schuls, Station Mgr.; Penny Meyers, Operations Mgr.; Dan Schroeder, Sports Dir. **Wattage:** 6,000.

16614 KQAL-FM - 89.5
Winona State University Phone: (507)453-2222
PO Box 5838 Fax: (507)457-5226
Winona, MN 55987
E-mail: kqal@vax2.winona.msus.edu

Format: Public Radio; Eclectic; Full Service. **Networks:** AP. **Owner:** Winona State University, at above address. **Founded:** 1975. **Operating Hours:** 6 a.m.-2 a.m.; 20% network, 80% local. **Key Personnel:** Ajit Daniel, General Mgr., phone (507)457-5228, akdaniel@vax2.winona.msus.edu; Mike Martin, Chief Engineer, phone (507)457-5227; Sean Hayes, Program Dir., phone (507)457-5258; Jonathan Halbesleben, Music Dir., phone (507)457-5229. **Wattage:** 1800. **Ad Rates:** Noncommercial. **URL:** http://wind.winona.msus.edu/~www_kqal/.

16615 KSMR-FM - 92.5
700 Terrace Hgts., No. 29 Phone: (507)457-1613
Winona, MN 55987-1399

Format: Album-Oriented Rock (AOR). **Owner:** St. Mary's College of Minnesota, at above address. **Founded:** 1978. **Formerly:** KSMW-FM (1978). **Operating Hours:** 100% local. **Key Personnel:** Mike Furlong, General Mgr.; Kathryn Burke, Music Dir. **Wattage:** 10.

16616 KWNO-FM - 99.3
PO Box 767 Phone: (507)452-4000
Winona, MN 55987-0767 Fax: (507)452-9494

Format: Hot Country. **Networks:** AP. **Owner:** Jerry Papenfuss, 752 Bluffview Circle, Winona, MN 55987-0767. **Founded:** 1991. **Operating Hours:** Continuous. **ADI:** La Crosse-Eau Claire, WI. **Key Personnel:** Jerry Papenfuss, Contact; Pat Papenfuss, Operations Mgr.; Dean Beckman, News Dir.; Darryl Smelser, Sports Dir. **Wattage:** 25,000. **Ad Rates:** $14-20 for 30 seconds; $18-25 for 60 seconds.

16617 TCI of Southern Minnesota
PO Box 408 Phone: (507)452-6040
Winona, MN 55987-0408 Fax: (507)452-5549

Owner: Tele-Communications Inc., 5619 DTC Pkwy., Englewood, CO 80111, (303)267-5500, Fax: (303)779-1228. **Founded:** Oct. 1958. **Formerly:** WestMarc Cable (1990). **Key Personnel:** Pat Ruda, General Mgr., phone (608)784-9244, fax (608)784-8490; Randy Gartner, Technical Operations Manager, phone (507)452-6040, fax (507)452-5549; Melinda DeVorak, Customer Service Supervisor. **Cities Served:** Goodview, Homer, MN City, Winona, MN; Fountain City, WI: subscribing households 10,500; 92 channels; 3 community access channels; 35 hours per week community access programming.

WORTHINGTON†, pop. 10,243.

SW MN. Nobles Co. 60 mi. E. of Sioux Falls, SD. Worthington Community College. Lake Resort. Industrial Center. Dairy, poultry, and grain farms.

16618 Daily Globe
300 11th St. Phone: (507)376-9711
PO Box 639 Fax: (507)376-5202
Worthington, MN 56187
General newspaper. **Founded:** 1872. **Freq:** Mon.-Sat. (morn.). **Print Method:** Offset. **Cols./Page:** 6. **Col. Width:** 12 picas. **Col. Depth:** 301 agate lines. **Key Personnel:** Carl Gustin, Editor; Reginald R. Durant, Publisher. **Subscription Rates:** $68. **Remarks:** Accepts advertising.
Ad Rates: PCI: $7.83 **Circ:** Paid ❑**12,330**
Free ❑**15,200**

16619 KWOA-AM - 730
Co. Hwy. 35 W. Phone: (507)376-6165
Box 730 Fax: (507)376-5071
Worthington, MN 56187-0730
E-mail: kwoa@rconnect.com

Format: News; Talk; Information. **Networks:** CBS. **Owner:** Nobles Broadcasting Co., at above address. **Founded:** 1947. **Operating Hours:** Continuous; 10% network, 90% local. **ADI:** Sioux Falls-Mitchell, SD. **Key Personnel:** Darrell Stitt, News Dir.; Tom Parsley, General Mgr. **Local Programs:** *Agricultural Talk*, Matt Widboom; *Sports Spotlight*, Larry Rogers; *Tri State Focus*, Darrell Stitt. **Wattage:** 1000. **Ad Rates:** Combined advertising rates available with KWOA-FM/KITN-FM.

ZUMBROTA

The Country Shopper - See Goodhue

The News Record - See Wanamingo

MISSISSIPPI

State Capital, JACKSON

Mississippi is bounded on the north by Tennessee, east by Alabama, south by the Gulf of Mexico and Louisiana, and west by the Mississippi River, which separates it from Louisiana and Arkansas. Its extreme length from north to south is 332 miles; average breadth, 142 miles. Its land area is 46,914 square miles. The surface is generally hilly except in the Mississippi delta area, from Vicksburg to the Tennessee line and between the Mississippi and Yazoo Rivers, where there is some of the most fertile soil in the world, particularly suited to growing cotton, rice, and other agricultural products. Below Vicksburg the surface for some miles inland is hilly and known as the "cane hills" or "bluffs" and has a generally productive soil. There is another particularly fertile prairie region in the northeast where one of the chief products, alfalfa, produces from three to five heavy crops each year. The southern part is chiefly a level pine region and furnishes good pasturage and quantities of timber, tar, and turpentine. The soil of this tract, although sandy, is with fertilization particularly adapted to farming. The forest wealth of the state is extensive and it ranks high among the states as a producer of cotton. The Weather Bureau at Jackson gives the temperature (annual average) as 64.2; highest on record, 104; lowest on record, -1. Total annual precipitation is 55.37 inches. Transportation is supplies by rail lines and the Mississippi River. The largest institutions of higher education are the University of Mississippi, in University; Mississippi State University, in State College; and Mississippi Southern College, in Hattiesburg.

POPULATION: 2,614,000 (1992). Rank among the states, 31st.

AGRICULTURE: Number of farms: 38,000 (1992). Farm acreage: 13,000,000 (1992). Cash receipts from farm marketings: crops, $1,147,000,000 (1991); livestock and products, $1,275,000,000 (1991).

FISHERIES: Total catch: 239,000,000 lbs. (1991), $34,000,000 value. Principal fish: menhaden, shrimp, oysters, red snapper.

FORESTS: Total forest land: 2,310,000 (1991). Principal woods: southern yellow pine, oak, red and sap gum, black and tupelo gum, cottonwood, aspen, yellow poplar, cypress, beech, hickory, elm, maple, sycamore.

MINERALS: Value of production: $102,000,000 (1991). Principal mineral: sand and gravel, clays, cement. Value of petroleum production: $478,000,000 (1991).

MANUFACTURES: Value added by manufacture: $12,880,000,000 (1991). Leading industry groups: lumber and wood products, food and related products, apparel and related products, automobile parts, aircraft components, chemicals, musical instruments.

LIST OF COUNTIES

Total number of counties 82

County, Location on Map, and County Seat	Pop.
Adams (SW), Natchez	35,356
Alcorn (NE), Corinth	31,722
Amite (SW), Liberty	13,328
Attala (C), Kosciusko	18,481
Benton (N), Ashland	8,046
Bolivar (W), Cleveland and Rosedale	41,875
Calhoun (NC), Pittsboro	14,908
Carroll (NC), Carrollton and Vaiden	9,237
Chickasaw (NE), Houston and Okolona	18,085
Choctaw (NC), Ackerman	9,071
Claiborne (SW), Port Gibson	11,370
Clarke (E), Quitman	17,313
Clay (E), West Point	21,120
Coahoma (NW), Clarksdale	31,665
Copiah (SW), Hazelhurst	27,592
Covington (C), Collins	16,527
De Soto (N), Hernando	67,910
Forrest (SE), Hattiesburg	68,314
Franklin (SW), Meadville	8,377
George (SE), Lucedale	16,673
Greene (SE), Leakesville	10,220
Grenada (NC), Grenada	21,555
Hancock (S), Bay St. Louis	31,760
Harrison (S), Gulfport	165,365
Hinds (SWC), Jackson and Raymond	254,441
Holmes (WC), Lexington	21,604
Humphreys (W), Belzoni	12,134
Issaquena (W), Mayersville	1,909
Itawamba (NE), Fulton	20,017
Jackson (SE), Pascagoula	115,243
Jasper (E), Bay Springs and Paulding	17,114
Jefferson (SW), Fayette	8,653
Jefferson Davis (S), Prentiss	14,051
Jones (SE), Ellisville and Laurel	62,031
Kemper (E), De Kalb	10,356
Lafayette (N), Oxford	31,826
Lamar (S), Purvis	30,424
Lauderdale (E), Meridian	75,555
Lawrence (S), Monticello	12,458
Leake (C), Carthage	19,436
Lee (NE), Tupelo	65,581
Leflore (NWC), Greenwood	37,341
Lincoln (SW), Brookhaven	30,278
Lowndes (E), Columbus	59,308
Madison (WC), Canton	53,794
Marion (S), Columbia	25,544
Monroe (NE), Aberdeen	36,582
Montgomery (NC), Winona	12,388
Neshoba (E), Philadelphia	24,800
Newton (EC), Decatur	20,291
Noxubee (E), Macon	12,604
Oktibbeha (E), Starkville	38,375
Panola (NW), Batesville and Sardis	29,996
Pearl River (S), Poplarville	38,714
Perry (SE), New Augusta	10,865
Pike (S), Magnolia	36,882
Pontotoc (NE), Pontotoc	22,237
Prentiss (NE), Booneville	23,278
Quitman (NW), Marks	10,490
Rankin (SC), Brandon	87,161
Scott (C), Forest	24,137
Sharkey (W), Rolling Fork	7,066
Simpson (SC), Mendenhall	23,953
Smith (SC), Raleigh	14,798
Stone (S), Wiggins	10,750
Sunflower (NW), Indianola	32,867
Tallahatchie (NW), Charleston and Sumner	15,210
Tate (NW), Senatobia	21,432
Tippah (N), Ripley	19,523
Tishomingo (NE), Iuka	17,683
Tunica (NW), Tunica	8,164
Union (N), New Albany	22,085
Walthall (S), Tylertown	14,352
Warren (W), Vicksburg	47,880
Washington (W), Greenville	67,935
Wayne (E), Waynesboro	19,517
Webster (NC), Walthall	10,222
Wilkinson (SW), Woodville	9,678
Winston (EC), Louisville	19,433
Yalobusha (NC), Coffeeville and Water Valley	12,033
Yazoo (WC), Yazoo City	25,506

STATISTICS

Newspapers

Period of Issue	
Daily	20
Evening Daily	15

Morning Daily	4
Daily with Sunday edition	10
Semiweekly	6
Weekly	78
Biweekly	1
Monthly	1
Bimonthly	1
Quarterly	1
Free or partly free	10
Shopper	5
Total Newspapers	113

Periodicals

Period of Issue	
Weekly	4
Monthly	9
Bimonthly	5
Quarterly	12
Total Periodicals	36

Total number of publications ... 149

Radio Stations

AM Stations	69
FM Stations	87
Total Radio Stations	156

TV Stations

Total TV Stations ... 21

Cable Stations

Total Cable Systems ... 29

Total number of broadcast listings ... 206

ABERDEEN†, pop. 7,184.

NE MS. Monroe Co. On Tennessee - Tombigbee Waterway, at head of navigation, 28 mi. N. of Columbus. Manufactures lumber and dairy products, cottonseed oil, liquid fertilizer, garments, plastics, automobile mufflers. Agriculture. Dairying, cotton, corn.

16620 Aberdeen Examiner
North Mississippi Community Newspaper
209 Commerce St. Phone: (601)369-4507
PO Box 279 Fax: (601)369-4508
Aberdeen, MS 39730
Community news. **Founded:** 1866. **Freq:** Weekly (Thurs.). **Print Method:** Offset. **Cols./Page:** 6. **Col. Width:** 25 nonpareils. **Col. Depth:** 301 agate lines. **Key Personnel:** Kathy Nathan, Editor; Gary Andrews, Publisher. **Subscription Rates:** $13. **Remarks:** Accepts advertising.
Ad Rates: BW: $523.74 **Circ:** ‡7,000
4C: $843.74

ACKERMAN†, pop. 1,567.

NC MS. Choctaw Co. 45 mi. SW of Columbus. Manufactures mobile home interiors, custom kitchens, garments. Sawmill. Foundry. Timber. Agriculture.

16621 Choctaw Plaindealer
The Plaindealer Publishing Co., Inc.
PO Box 910 Phone: (601)285-6248
Ackerman, MS 39735-0910 Fax: (601)285-6695

Community newspaper. **Founded:** Aug. 26, 1887. **Freq:** Weekly (Thurs.). **Print Method:** Offset. Uses mats. **Trim Size:** 14 1/2 x 22 1/2. **Cols./Page:** 6. **Col. Width:** 21 nonpareils. **Col. Depth:** 301 agate lines. **Key Personnel:** Donna McKay, Manager. **Subscription Rates:** $12 individuals; $15 surrounding counties; $18 out of area.
Ad Rates: GLR: $.25 **Circ:** Paid ‡2,700
BW: $301 Free ‡89
4C: $400
SAU: $4.50
PCI: $3.50

AMORY, pop. 7,307.

NE MS. Monroe Co. On Tennessee - Tombigbee Waterway, 40 mi. N. of Columbus. Manufactures industrial valves, lumber, cotton, grain, dairy products. Gas wells. Diversified farming. Livestock.

16622 The Amory Advertiser
PO Box 519 Phone: (601)256-5648
Amory, MS 38821 Fax: (601)256-5701

Community newspaper. **Founded:** 1924. **Freq:** Weekly (Wed.). **Print Method:** Offset. **Cols./Page:** 6. **Col. Width:** 26 nonpareils. **Col. Depth:** 301 agate lines. **Key Personnel:** Waid Prather, Editor and Publisher; Bonny Parham, Advertising Mgr. **ISSN:** 0899-0085. **Subscription Rates:** $18; $22 out of area; $28 out of state. **Remarks:** Accepts advertising.
Ad Rates: BW: $464.40 **Circ:** ‡7,000
4C: $539.40
PCI: $3.60

16623 WAFM-FM - 95.3
521 Hwy. 278 W. Phone: (601)256-9726
PO Box 458 Fax: (601)256-9725
Amory, MS 38821
E-mail: wamywafm@intop.net

Format: Oldies. **Networks:** ABC; Jones Satellite. **Owner:** Ed Stanford, 50003 Robinson West Circle, Amory, MS 38821, (601)256-8419. **Founded:** 1974. **Operating Hours:** Continuous. **Key Personnel:** Ed Stanford, Mgr./Sales Mgr.; Ed Stanford, Sales Mgr.; Clara Kennedy, Traffic Mgr./Secretary. **Local Programs:** *Good Morning from Amory*, Ed Stanford. **Wattage:** 6000. **Ad Rates:** $5 for 30 seconds; $6 for 60 seconds.

16624 WAMY-AM - 1580
521 Hwy. 278 W. Phone: (601)256-9725
PO Box 458 Fax: (601)256-9725
Amory, MS 38821
E-mail: wamywafm@intop.net

Format: Talk; Sports. **Networks:** UPI. **Owner:** Stanford Communications, Inc., at above address, (601)256-8419. **Founded:** 1955. **Operating Hours:** Daytime. **Key Personnel:** Ed Stanford, Owner/Sales Mgr.; Bill Abney, Sports Dir.; Clara Kennedy, Traffic Mgr. **Wattage:** 1000. **Ad Rates:** $5 for 30 seconds; $6 for 60 seconds. Combined advertising rates available with WWZQ-AM.

ASHLAND

16625 Southern Advocate
PO Box 157 Phone: (601)224-6681
Ashland, MS 38603 Fax: (601)224-6681

Community newspaper. **Founded:** 1905. **Freq:** Weekly (Thurs.). **Print Method:** Offset. **Trim Size:** 13 3/4 x 22 3/4. **Cols./Page:** 8. **Col. Width:** 10 1/2 picas. **Col. Depth:** 21 inches. **Key Personnel:** Bill Renick, Editor. **Subscription Rates:** $10 individuals; $20 out of area. **Remarks:** Accepts advertising.
Ad Rates: BW: $.12 **Circ:** 1,400
4C: $252
SAU: $480.60
PCI: $2

BALDWYN, pop. 3,562.

SW MS. Prentiss Co. 18 mi. N. of Tupelo.

16626 The Baldwyn News
Baldwyn News
102 W. Main Phone: (601)365-3232
PO Drawer 130 Fax: (601)365-7989
Baldwyn, MS 38824
Publication E-mail: thebaldwynews@dixie-net.com
Publisher E-mail: loislane21@hotmail.com

Local newspaper serving Prentiss, Lee, Union, Itawamba, and Tippah counties. **Founded:** 1939. **Freq:** Weekly (Wed.). **Print Method:** Offset. **Cols./Page:** 6. **Col. Width:** 21 inches. **Key Personnel:** Kelly L. Wrobbel, Publisher. **Subscription Rates:** $18 in Lee/Prentiss counties; $25 in MS; $32 outside MS. **Remarks:** Accepts advertising.
Ad Rates: GLR: $3 **Circ:** Paid 2,650
BW: $612.75
PCI: $4.75

BATESVILLE†, pop. 4,692.

NW MS. Panola Co. 58 mi. S. of Memphis, TN. Cotton ginning. Agriculture. Cattle, cotton, corn.

16627 The Panolian
Panolian, Inc.
363 Hwy. 51 N. Phone: (601)563-4591
Batesville, MS 38606-0393 Fax: (601)563-5610
Free: (800)310-4591

Community newspaper. **Founded:** 1882. **Freq:** Biweekly Tues. & Fri. **Print Method:** Offset. **Trim Size:** 7 1/2 x 11. **Cols./Page:** 6. **Col. Width:** 24 nonpareils. **Col. Depth:** 301 agate lines. **Key Personnel:** Tawanda Tankersley, Publisher. **USPS:** 777-280. **Subscription Rates:** $29.95 individuals; $44.95 out of state. **Remarks:** Accepts advertising.
Ad Rates: GLR: $.39 **Circ:** ‡9,675
BW: $1,161
4C: $1,461
SAU: $9
PCI: $9

16628 WJBI-AM - 1290
Hwy. 6 W. Phone: (601)563-1290
PO Box 1440 Fax: (601)563-9002
Batesville, MS 38606

Format: Country; Southern Gospel. **Networks:** ABC. **Founded:** 1953. **Operating Hours:** 14 hours daily; 3% network, 97% local. **ADI:** Memphis, TN. **Key Personnel:** Tommy Darby, Station Mgr.; J. Boyd Ingram, President. **Wattage:** 1000. **Ad Rates:** $6-9 for 30 seconds; $12-18 for 60 seconds.

BAY ST. LOUIS

16629 The Sea Coast Echo
Bay Saint Louis Newspapers
124 Court St. Phone: (601)467-5474
PO Box 2009 Fax: (601)467-0333
Bay St. Louis, MS 39521
Community newspaper. **Founded:** 1892. **Freq:** Semiweekly (Thurs. and Sun.). **Print Method:** Offset. **Cols./Page:** 6. **Col. Width:** 21 1/2 nonpareils. **Col. Depth:** 301 agate lines. **Key Personnel:** Ellis Cuevas, Editor and Publisher; Ellis Cuevas, Editor and Publisher. **Subscription Rates:** $32; $47 out of area; $53 out of state. **Remarks:** Accepts advertising.
Ad Rates: GLR: $.61 **Circ:** ‡6,630
BW: $1,096.50
4C: $1,265.50
PCI: $8

16630 WBSL-AM - 1190
1190 Casino Magic Rd. Phone: (601)467-1190
Bay St. Louis, MS 39520 Fax: (601)467-5295
Free: (800)550-9275

Format: Hot Country. **Networks:** Independent. **Owner:** Hancock Broadcasting Corp., at above address. **Founded:** 1978. **Formerly:** WPUP-AM (1978). **Operating Hours:** 6 a.m.-7 p.m.; 100% local. **Key Personnel:** Dan Diamond, Contact; Ann Williams, Contact. **Wattage:** 5000. **Ad Rates:** $5-25 for 30 seconds; $10-35 for 60 seconds.

BAY SPRINGS

16631 Jasper County News
Buckley Newspapers, Inc.
PO Box 449 Phone: (601)764-3104
Bay Springs, MS 39422 Fax: (601)764-3106

Community newspaper. **Founded:** 1892. **Freq:** Weekly (Wed.). **Print Method:** Offset. **Trim Size:** 14.25 x 21.5. **Cols./Page:** 6. **Col. Width:** 1 3/4 inches. **Col. Depth:** 21 1/2 inches. **Key Personnel:** Dewayne Buckman, Editor/Administration; Ronnie Buckley, Publisher. **USPS:** 273-040. **Subscription Rates:** $15 individuals; $20 out of area; $23 out of state. **Remarks:** Accepts advertising.
Ad Rates: BW: $709.50 **Circ:** Paid ‡3,046
4C: $959.50 Free ‡350
PCI: $5.50

16632 WIZK-AM - 1570
Box 548 Phone: (601)764-3151
Bay Springs, MS 39422 Fax: (601)729-8332

Format: Southern Gospel. **Networks:** Satellite Music Network; ABC. **Owner:** Jerome Hughey, at above address. **Founded:** 1971. **Formerly:** WHII-AM (1987); WXIY-FM. **Operating Hours:** Continuous; 100% network. **Key Personnel:** Mitchell Hughey, Contact. **Wattage:** 5000. **Ad Rates:** $6-10 for 30 seconds; $12-20 for 60 seconds.

16633 WIZK-FM - 94.3
Box 548 Phone: (601)764-3151
Bay Springs, MS 39422 Fax: (601)729-8332

Format: Country. **Networks:** Satellite Music Network; ABC. **Owner:** Jerome Hughey, at above address. **Founded:** 1975. **Formerly:** WHII-AM; WXIY-FM. **Operating Hours:** Continuous; 80% network 20% local. **Key Personnel:** Mitchell Hughey, Contact. **Wattage:** 3000. **Ad Rates:** $6-10 for 30 seconds; $12-20 for 60 seconds.

BELMONT

16634 Belmont-Tishomingo Journal
Belmont Journal
PO Box 70 Phone: (601)454-7196
Belmont, MS 38827 Fax: (601)454-7196

Community newspaper. **Founded:** 1970. **Freq:** Weekly (Thurs.). **Cols./Page:** 6. **Col. Width:** 2 1/16 inches. **Col. Depth:** 21 1/2 inches. **Key Personnel:** Catherine Mitchell, Editor; M.W. Mitchell, Publisher. **Remarks:** Accepts advertising.
Ad Rates: PCI: $5 **Circ:** ‡2,100

BELZONI†, pop. 2,982.

W MS. Humphreys Co. 40 mi. SE of Greenville. Cotton ginning. Catfish, crawfish. Agriculture. Feed, cotton, corn, hay, soybeans, rice.

16635 The Belzoni Banner
115 Jackson St. Phone: (601)247-3373
Box 610 Fax: (601)247-3372
Belzoni, MS 39038
Publication E-mail: banner@capital2.com

Community newspaper. **Founded:** 1912. **Freq:** Weekly (Wed.). **Print Method:** Offset. **Cols./Page:** 6. **Col. Width:** 2 1/16 inches. **Col. Depth:** 21 1/2 inches. **Key Personnel:** Julian Toney, Editor and Publisher. **Subscription Rates:** $12; $15 out of country. **Remarks:** Accepts advertising.
Ad Rates: BW: $387 **Circ:** ‡2,000
4C: $597
SAU: $3
PCI: $3

16636 Cable TV of Belzoni Inc.
102 S. Hayden St. Phone: (601)247-1834
Belzoni, MS 39038

Owner: Genelle Lott, at above address. **Key Personnel:** Del Lott, General Mgr. **Cities Served:** Belzoni, MS.

16637 WELZ-AM - 1460
PO Box 299 Phone: (601)247-1744
Belzoni, MS 39038 Fax: (601)247-1744

Format: Country; Gospel. **Simulcasts:** WVRD-FM 6 a.m.-3 p.m. **Networks:** Unistar; Mississippi. **Founded:** 1959. **Operating Hours:** 6 a.m.-6 p.m. **Key Personnel:** Herb Guthrie, Contact; Gene Luster, Contact; Dan Winstead, Contact.

Wattage: 1000. **Ad Rates:** $4-8.50 for 30 seconds; $5-9.50 for 60 seconds. Combined advertising rates available with WVRD-FM: $4-$8.50 for 30 seconds; $5-$9.50 for 60 seconds.

16638 WVRD-FM - 107.1
PO Box 299   Phone: (601)247-1744
Belzoni, MS 39038   Fax: (601)247-1744

Format: Country; Gospel. **Simulcasts:** WELZ-AM. **Networks:** Unistar; Mississippi. **Founded:** 1986. **Operating Hours:** 6 a.m.-midnight. **Key Personnel:** Herb Guthrie, Contact; Gene Luster, Contact; Dan Winstead, Contact. **Wattage:** 3000. **Ad Rates:** $4-8.50 for 30 seconds; $5-9.50 for 60 seconds. Combined advertising rates available with WELZ-AM.

BILOXI, pop. 48,685.

S MS. Harrison Co. On Gulf of Mexico, 12 mi. E. of Gulfport. Military and government installation. Summer and winter resort. Manufactures building products, tents, awnings , nets and trawls, wire, cable, cat food, electric harness, appliances, seafood packing; canning. Boat building and repairing.

16639 The Biloxi-D'Iberville Press
S & F Publishing Co. Inc.
PO Box 194   Phone: (601)392-3307
Biloxi, MS 39533   Fax: (601)392-7043

Local newspaper. **Founded:** June 13, 1973. **Freq:** Weekly. **Print Method:** Offset. **Trim Size:** 13 x 21. **Cols./Page:** 6. **Col. Width:** 2 1/8 inches. **Col. Depth:** 21 inches. **Key Personnel:** Walter Fountain, Editor; C.R. Stein, Publisher; Bill Dennis, Advertising Mgr. **ISSN:** 0899-0077. **Subscription Rates:** Free; $12 (mail); $25 out of county. **Remarks:** Accepts advertising. **Formerly:** The Biloxi Press (Apr. 1988).
Ad Rates: BW: $748   **Circ:** Paid 6,000
4C: $1,173.44   Free 2,000
PCI: $7.20

16640 Gulf Pine Catholic
870 Nativity Dr.   Phone: (228)374-8318
PO Box 1189   Fax: (228)374-8320
Biloxi, MS 39533-1189
Official newspaper (tabloid) of the Catholic Diocese of Biloxi. **Founded:** 1983. **Freq:** Weekly. **Print Method:** Offset. **Trim Size:** 11 1/4 x 16. **Cols./Page:** 6. **Col. Width:** 1 1/2 inches. **Key Personnel:** Shirley Henderson, Editor; Most Rev. Joseph Lawson Howze, Publisher, phone (228)374-0220, fax (228)435-7949. **USPS:** 704-450. **Subscription Rates:** $12.50 individuals.
Ad Rates: BW: $360   **Circ:** ‡5,100
PCI: $10

16641 The Sun Herald
Knight-Ridder, Inc.
PO Box 4567   Phone: (601)896-2300
Biloxi, MS 39535
Publication E-mail: maildrop@sunherald.com

General newspaper. **Founded:** 1965. **Freq:** Mon.-Sun. (morn.). **Print Method:** Offset. **Trim Size:** 12 3/4 x 21 1/2. **Cols./Page:** 6. **Col. Width:** 2 inches. **Col. Depth:** 21 1/2 inches. **Key Personnel:** Michael Tonos, Exec. Ed.; Roland Weeks, Jr., Publisher; Stone Ellis, Advertising Mgr. **USPS:** 615-080. **Subscription Rates:** $99.90. **Remarks:** Accepts advertising. **URL:** http://www.sunherald.com; http://www.knightridder.com. **Feature Editors:** Betty Attaway, *Medical*, phone (601)896-2312; Littice Bacon, *Education*, phone (601)896-2334; Charles Busby, *City, Metro, News, Political, State*, phone (601)896-2358; Vincent Creel, *Fashion, Features, Food, Garden/Home, Lifestyle, Living, Religion, Society, Women's*, phone (601)896-2393; Ken Fink, *Family*, phone (601)896-2331; Mike Lacy, *Radio, Travel*, phone (601)896-2495; Jim Lund, *Editorials*, phone (601)896-2301; Vernon Matthews, *Photo*, phone (601)896-2313; John Porretto, *Consumer Affairs, Farm, Financial/Business, Real Estate*, phone (601)896-2310; Jean Prescott, *Drama, Entertainment, Movie, Music, TV*, phone (601)896-2376; Slim Smith, *Sports*, phone (601)896-2352.
Ad Rates: GLR: $2.23   **Circ:** Mon.-Sat. ★**49,200**
BW: $3,341.52   Sun. ★**57,326**
4C: $3,666.52
SAU: $31.15
PCI: $25

16642 TCL
786 Washington Loop   Phone: (601)374-5900
Box 10   Fax: (601)435-3939
Biloxi, MS 39530

Founded: 1963. **Formerly:** UAE Cable, Mississippi Gulf Coast. **Cities Served:** Harrison County, Jackson County, D'Iberville, and Ocean Springs, MS.

16643 WKNN-FM - 99.1
PO Box 4606   Phone: (601)388-2323
Biloxi, MS 39535   Fax: (601)388-2362

Format: Country. **Networks:** ABC. **Founded:** 1964. **Formerly:** WPMP-FM (1989). **Operating Hours:** Continuous; 1% network, 99% local. **ADI:** Biloxi-Gulfport-Pascagoula, MS. **Key Personnel:** Reggie Bates, General Mgr.; Rick Mize, Program Dir.; Ron Hill, Sales Mgr. **Wattage:** 100,000. **URL:** http://www.k99fm.com.

16644 WLOX-TV - 13
208 Debuys Rd.   Phone: (228)896-1313
Biloxi, MS 39531   Fax: (228)896-0749
E-mail: webmaster@wlox.com

Format: Commercial TV. **Networks:** ABC. **Owner:** Cosmos Broadcasting Co., Box 4596, Biloxi, MS 39535. **Founded:** 1962. **Operating Hours:** Continuous; 50% network, 50% local. **ADI:** Biloxi-Gulfport-Pascagoula, MS. **Key Personnel:** Leon Long, General Mgr., phone (228)896-0701, llong@wlox.com; David Vincent, News Dir., phone (228)896-2561, fax (228)896-2596, d.vincent@wlox.com; Jim Fleming, Chief Engineer, phone (228)896-0761, jfleming@wlox.com.

16645 WMAH-FM - 90.3
c/o Public Radio in MS   Phone: (601)982-6565
3825 Ridgewood Rd.   Fax: (601)982-6746
Jackson, MS 39211-6463

Format: Classical; News. **Networks:** National Public Radio (NPR); Public Radio International (PRI). **Founded:** 1983. **Operating Hours:** Continuous. **ADI:** Biloxi-Gulfport-Pascagoula, MS. **Key Personnel:** William Fulton, Director. **Local Programs:** *Just a Few Friends*, Frank Lynch; *Mississippi Concert Hall*, Tim Riley; *The Opera Bill*, William Fulton. **Wattage:** 100,000. **Ad Rates:** Noncommercial. **URL:** http://www.npr.org/members/prm.

16646 WMAH-TV - 19
c/o WMPN-TV   Phone: (601)982-6565
3825 Ridgewood Rd.   Fax: (601)982-6746
Jackson, MS 39211

Format: Public TV. **Simulcasts:** WMPN-TV Jackson, MS. **Networks:** Public Broadcasting Service (PBS). **Owner:** Mississippi Authority for Educational TV, at above address. **Operating Hours:** 6:45 am-11:15 pm weekdays; noon-11:15 pm Sat.; noon-11 pm Sun. **ADI:** Biloxi-Gulfport-Pascagoula, MS. **Key Personnel:** A.J. Jaeger, Contact; Jeannine Fulmer, Program Dir.

16647 WMJY-FM - 93.7
PO Box 4606   Phone: (228)388-2323
Biloxi, MS 39535   Fax: (228)388-2362
E-mail: magic937.com

Format: Adult Contemporary. **Founded:** 1966. **Formerly:** WQID-FM. **Operating Hours:** Continuous. **ADI:** Biloxi-Gulfport-Pascagoula, MS. **Key Personnel:** Reggie Bates, General Mgr.; Rick Mize, Operations Mgr.; Walter Brown, Program Dir. **Wattage:** 100,000. **URL:** http://www.magic937.com.

16648 WQYZ-FM - 92.5
PO Box 4779   Phone: (228)374-8800
Biloxi, MS 39535   Fax: (228)872-0670
E-mail: wqyz@digiscape.com

Format: Oldies. **Owner:** Golden Gulf Coast Broadcasting, Inc., at above address. **Formerly:** WXOR-FM. **Operating Hours:** Continuous. **Key Personnel:** Gregg Arnold, General and Sales Mgr.; David Clark, Operations Mgr./Program Dir. **Wattage:** 1,000. **Ad Rates:** Advertising accepted; rates available upon request. **URL:** http://www.wqyz.com.

16649 WVMI-AM - 570
PO Box 4606   Phone: (601)388-2323
Biloxi, MS 39535   Fax: (601)388-2362

Format: News; Talk. **Networks:** CNN Radio; EFM; Wall Street Journal Radio; Westwood One Radio. **Owner:** G & R Radio Inc., P.O. Box 1459, Biloxi, MS 39535, (601)374-1570, Fax: (601)374-1576. **Founded:** 1950. **Operating Hours:** Continuous. **ADI:** Biloxi-Gulfport-Pascagoula, MS. **Key Personnel:** Gary Michiels, General Mgr.; Jon Gates, News Dir. **Wattage:** 5000 day; 1000 night.

BOONEVILLE†, pop. 6,199.

NE MS. Prentiss Co. 75 mi. S. of Jackson, TN. Northeast Mississippi Community College. Manufactures furniture, clothing. Lumber mills; cotton ginning. Clay pits. Diversified farming. Cotton, corn, hay.

16650 Banner Independent
PO Box 10   Phone: (601)728-6214
Booneville, MS 38829   Fax: (601)728-1636

Community newspaper. **Founded:** 1898. **Freq:** Weekly (Thurs.). **Print Method:** Offset. **Cols./Page:** 6. **Col. Width:** 26 nonpareils. **Col. Depth:** 294 agate lines. **Key Personnel:** Kenny Goode, Editor; Don Swartz, Publisher; Maureen Glidewell, Advertising Dir. **Subscription Rates:** $20; $30 out of county. **Remarks:** Accepts advertising.
Ad Rates: GLR: $5.60   **Circ:** 5,304
BW: $504
PCI: $6.45

16651 WBIP-AM - 1400
PO Box 356   Phone: (601)728-5301
Booneville, MS 38829-0356   Fax: (601)728-2572

Format: Sports. **Founded:** 1950. **Operating Hours:** Continuous. **Key Personnel:** Larry Melton, President; Max Wilson, Program Dir.; Betty Phillips, Office Mgr.; Larry Hill, General Mgr. **Wattage:** 1000. **Ad Rates:** $2-4 for 30 seconds; $2.50-5 for 60 seconds. $5-$7 for 30 seconds; $5-$9 for 60 seconds. Combined advertising rates available with WBIP-FM.

16652 WBIP-FM - 99.3
PO Box 356   Phone: (601)728-5301
Booneville, MS 38829-0356   Fax: (601)728-2572

Format: Southern Gospel; Sports. **Networks:** Mississippi; USA Radio. **Founded:** 1976. **Operating Hours:** Continuous. **Key Personnel:** Larry Melton, President; Max Wilson, Program Dir.; Betty Phillips, Office Mgr.; Larry Hill, General Mgr. **Wattage:** 6000. **Ad Rates:** $3.50-6 for 30 seconds; $4.50-8 for 60 seconds. $5-$7 for 30 seconds; $5.50-$9 for 60 seconds. Combined advertising rates available with WBIP-AM.

16653 WMAE-FM - 91.3
c/o Public Radio in Mississippi   Phone: (601)982-6565
3825 Ridgewood Rd.   Fax: (601)982-6746
Jackson, MS 39211
Free: (800)922-9698

Format: News; Bluegrass; Classical; Folk. **Networks:** National Public Radio (NPR); Public Radio International (PRI). **Founded:** 1983. **Operating Hours:** Continuous. **ADI:** Jackson, MS. **Key Personnel:** William Fulton, Dir. **Local Programs:** *Grass Roots*, Bill Ellison; *Mississippi Concert Hall*, Tim Riley; *The Opera Bill*, William Fulton. **Wattage:** 85,000. **Ad Rates:** Noncommercial. **URL:** http://www.npr.org/members/prm.

BRANDON†, pop. 12,317.

SC MS. Rankin Co. 13 mi. E. of Jackson. Manufactures cement, textiles. Saw mills. Pine timber. Diversified farming. Cotton, corn, livestock.

16654 Rankin County News
207 E. Government St.   Phone: (601)825-8333
Town Square   Fax: (601)825-8334
Brandon, MS 39042
Community newspaper. **Founded:** 1848. **Freq:** Weekly (Wed.). **Print Method:** Offset. **Trim Size:** 14 1/4 x 21 1/2. **Cols./Page:** 6. **Col. Width:** 13 picas. **Col. Depth:** 21 1/2 inches. **Key Personnel:** Marcus Bowers, Editor and Publisher. **USPS:** 455-440. **Subscription Rates:** $15 individuals; $18 out of area; $20 out of state. **Remarks:** Accepts advertising.
Ad Rates: BW: $709.50   **Circ:** ‡6,000
4C: $1,109.50
SAU: $9
PCI: $5.50

16655 WRJH-FM - 97.7
PO Box 145   Phone: (601)825-5045
Brandon, MS 39043

Format: Gospel. **Simulcasts:** WRKN-AM. **Owner:** Radio Station WRJH-WRKN INC., PO Box 145, Brandon, MS 39043. **Founded:** 1974. **Operating Hours:** 6 a.m.-midnight. **Key Personnel:** June Harris, General Mgr.; Vickie Ferrer, Office Mgr.; David Steele, Program Dir.; Stan Carter, Chief Engineer; Rita Wilbanks, Sales Mgr. **Wattage:** 6000. **Ad Rates:** $4 for 30 seconds; $6 for 60 seconds.

16656 WRKN-AM - 970
PO Box 145   Phone: (601)825-5045
Brandon, MS 39043

Format: Gospel. **Simulcasts:** WRJH-FM. **Owner:** Radio Station WRKN-WRJH, INC., PO Box 145, Brandon, MS 39043. **Founded:** 1967. **Operating Hours:** Sunrise-sunset. **Key Personnel:** June Harris, General Mgr. **Wattage:** 1000. **Ad Rates:** $4 for 30 seconds; $6 for 60 seconds.

BROOKHAVEN†, pop. 10,926.

SW MS. Lincoln Co. 60 mi. S. of Jackson. Lumber mills. Manufactures garments, lawn mowers, wiring harnesses, thermometers, wire screen, bricks, electronics equipment, truck beds. Bottling works. Pine, hardwood timber. Farming. Dairying, truck crops, cattle.

16657 Buyers Guide
Publishing Services, Inc.
Hwy. 550 & 51 Phone: (601)833-7149
PO Box 532 Fax: (601)833-9603
Brookhaven, MS 39601
Shopper. **Founded:** Apr. 1, 1965. **Freq:** Weekly (Wed.). **Print Method:** Offset. **Trim Size:** 7 x 11 1/2. **Cols./Page:** 8. **Col. Width:** 9 4/10 picas. **Col. Depth:** 294 agate lines. **Key Personnel:** Shelton H. Morgan, Editor and Publisher; Allen Morgan, Advertising Mgr., phone (601)833-2315; Anne Leggott, Office Mgr. **Subscription Rates:** Free; $25 out of area. **Remarks:** Accepts advertising.
Ad Rates: GLR: $.30 **Circ:** Free ‡14,000
BW: $1,176
4C: $1,576
PCI: $7.00

16658 Daily Leader
Southwest Publishers, Inc.
128 N. Railroad Ave. Phone: (601)833-6961
PO Box 551 Fax: (601)833-6714
Brookhaven, MS 39601
General newspaper. **Founded:** Feb. 1883. **Freq:** Daily (eve.). **Print Method:** Offset. **Trim Size:** 13 3/4 x 22 1/2. **Cols./Page:** 6. **Col. Width:** 2 inches. **Col. Depth:** 21 1/2 inches. **Key Personnel:** William Orton Jacobs, Editor and Publisher; Natalie Davie, Advertising Dir. **USPS:** 565-560. **Subscription Rates:** $96; $120 out of area. **Remarks:** Accepts advertising. Monday-Saturday: BW: $967.50; 4C: $1,322.50; SAU: $8.80; PCI: $7.50; Sunday: SAU: $9.05; CNU: $7.75. **Alt. Formats:** CD-ROM.
Circ: Mon.-Fri. 6,824
Sun. 6,740

16659 WBKN-FM - 92.1
203 E. Monticello St. Phone: (601)833-6221
PO Box 711 Fax: (601)833-6221
Brookhaven, MS 39601

Format: Contemporary Country; Southern Gospel. **Networks:** ABC. **Owner:** Ole Brook Board, Inc., at above address, (601)833-9210. **Founded:** 1976. **Operating Hours:** Continuous. **ADI:** Jackson, MS. **Key Personnel:** William T. Reynolds, President; Dan Diamond, Sales Mgr.; Ken Hollingsworth, Operations Mgr. **Local Programs:** *Dan Diamond Morning Show*, Dan Diamond, Mailing contact, (601)833-9210, Fax (601)833-6221; *Ken Hollingsworth Afternoons*, Ken Hollingsworth, Mailing contact, (601)833-9210, Fax (601)833-6221; *Sunday Morning Down South*, Dan Diamond, Mailing contact. **Wattage:** 6000. **Ad Rates:** $8.82 for 30 seconds; $11.77 for 60 seconds.

16660 WCHJ-AM - 1470
203 E. Monticello St. Phone: (601)833-6221
PO Box 711 Fax: (601)833-6221
Brookhaven, MS 39601

Format: News; Talk. **Networks:** ABC. **Owner:** Bogue Chitto Communication Co., at above address. **Founded:** 1956. **Operating Hours:** 6 a.m.-6 p.m. **ADI:** Jackson, MS. **Key Personnel:** William T. Reynolds, Pres./General Mgr.; Dan Diamond, Sales and Program Mgr.; Ken Hollingsworth, Operations Mgr. **Wattage:** 1000. **Ad Rates:** $3 for 30 seconds; $6 for 60 seconds.

BRUCE, pop. 2,208.

NC MS. Calhoun Co. 65 mi. NW of Columbus. Manufactures mattresses, furniture parts, lumber, camper units. Cotton gins. Agriculture. Livestock. Cotton, soybeans.

16661 Calhoun County Journal
PO Box 278 Phone: (601)983-2570
Bruce, MS 38915 Fax: (601)983-7667

Newspaper. **Founded:** 1953. **Freq:** Weekly (Thurs.). **Print Method:** Offset. **Cols./Page:** 6. **Col. Width:** 21 nonpareils. **Col. Depth:** 294 agate lines. **Key Personnel:** S. Gale Denley, Editor and Publisher. **Subscription Rates:** $8.50. **Remarks:** Accepts advertising.
Ad Rates: SAU: $3.80 **Circ:** 3,450

16662 WALCO Inc.
Box 489 Phone: (601)983-4343
Bruce, MS 38915 Fax: (601)983-7300

Owner: Harry Waller, at above address. **Founded:** 1963. **Key Personnel:** Billy Young, General Mgr. **Cities Served:** subscribing households 691; 50 channels; 2 community access channels.

CALHOUN CITY, pop. 2,033.

NC MS. Calhoun Co. 45 mi. SW of Tupelo. Manufactures furniture, boat paddles, oars, textiles. Timber. Agriculture. Sweet potatoes, cotton, soybeans. Livestock.

16663 The Monitor-Herald
PO Box 69 Phone: (601)628-5241
Calhoun City, MS 38916-0069 Fax: (601)628-4651

Community newspaper. **Founded:** July 19, 1900. **Freq:** Weekly (Wed.). **Print Method:** Offset. **Trim Size:** 22 3/4 x 14. **Cols./Page:** 6. **Col. Width:** 24 nonpareils. **Col. Depth:** 301 agate lines. **Key Personnel:** Terri Blissard, News Editor. **Subscription Rates:** $18.
Ad Rates: BW: $328.95 **Circ:** ‡4,000
4C: $588.95
PCI: $5.75

CANTON†, pop. 10,574.

WC MS. Madison Co. 24 mi. NE of Jackson. Manufactures lumber, furniture, plant foods, fertilizer. Cotton ginning; compress; creamery. Poultry processing. Diversified farming. Livestock. Cotton, corn, soybeans.

16664 Madison County Herald
Gannett Co., Inc.
PO Box 119 Phone: (601)859-1221
Canton, MS 39046 Fax: (601)859-9409

Community-interest newspaper. **Founded:** 1906. **Freq:** Weekly (Thurs.). **Print Method:** Offset. **Cols./Page:** 6. **Col. Width:** 24 nonpareils. **Col. Depth:** 294 agate lines. **Key Personnel:** Ken Wilbanks, News Ed.; Joe M. Dove, Publisher; Russ Durfey, Advertising Mgr. **Subscription Rates:** $12; $15 out of county. **Remarks:** Accepts advertising.
Ad Rates: BW: $743 **Circ:** ‡4,500
PCI: $6.25

16665 Galaxy Cable
PO Box 570 Phone: (601)859-2835
Canton, MS 39046 Fax: (601)859-1821

Formerly: Vista Communications, Inc. **Key Personnel:** Liz Duffy, General Mgr. **Cities Served:** subscribing households 3,315.

16666 WMGO-AM - 1370
PO Box 182 Phone: (601)859-2373
Canton, MS 39046 Fax: (601)859-2664

Format: Full Service. **Networks:** Mississippi. **Owner:** WMGO Broadcasting Corp., Inc., at above address. **Founded:** 1954. **Formerly**: WDOB-AM (1962). **Operating Hours:** Continuous. **Key Personnel:** Jerry Lousteau, General Mgr. **Wattage:** 1000. **Ad Rates:** $5.50-10.50 for 30 seconds; $7.00-12.50 for 60 seconds. Combined advertising rates available with WMGO-FM.

WMGO-FM - See Yazoo City

CARTHAGE†, pop. 3,453.

C MS. Leake Co. On Pearl River, 50 mi. NE of Jackson. Manufactures metal products, clothing. Lumber mills. Agriculture. Cotton, poultry, cattle.

16667 Carthaginian
PO Box 457 Phone: (601)267-4501
Carthage, MS 39051 Fax: (601)267-5290

Newspaper with Democratic orientation. **Founded:** 1872. **Freq:** Weekly (Thurs.). **Print Method:** Offset. **Cols./Page:** 6. **Col. Width:** 20 nonpareils. **Col. Depth:** 301 agate lines. **Key Personnel:** Mildred Dearman, Editor; John H Keith, Publisher, khj@netdoor.com; Waid Prather, Managing Editor, thekid@netdoor.com. **Subscription Rates:** $22 individuals; $25 out of area; $28 out of state. **Remarks:** Accepts advertising.
Ad Rates: PCI: $4.80 **Circ:** ‡5,400

CHARLESTON†, pop. 2,878.

NW MS. Tallahatchie Co. 10 mi. N. of Paynes.

16668 Charleston Sun-Sentinel
Charlston Sun-Sentinel
PO Box 250 Phone: (601)647-8462
Charleston, MS 38921 Fax: (601)647-3830
Publication E-mail: sunsent@network-one.com

Community newspaper. **Founded:** 1856. **Freq:** Weekly (Thurs.). **Cols./Page:** 6. **Col. Width:** 12 picas. **Col. Depth:** 21 1/2 inches. **Key Personnel:** Clay McFerrin, Editor and Publisher; Krista McFerrin, Advertising Mgr. **ISSN:** 3545-4000. **Subscription Rates:** $15 individuals; $18 out of area other counties in-state; $21 out of state per year. **Remarks:** Accepts advertising.
Ad Rates: SAU: $4.50 **Circ:** Paid ‡2,381
PCI: $3.80 Free ‡75

CLARKSDALE†, pop. 21,353.

NW MS. Coahoma Co. 70 mi. S. of Memphis, TN. Coahoma Junior College. Manufactures cottonseed, soybean oil, uniforms, rubber products, burlap and textile bags. Cotton ginning. Timber. Agriculture. Corn, hay, cotton, rice, soybeans.

16669 The Clarksdale Press Register
Delta Press Publishing Co.
123 2nd St. Phone: (601)627-2201
PO Box 1119 Fax: (601)624-5125
Clarksdale, MS 38614
Publisher E-mail: delpress@clarksdale.com

General newspaper. **Founded:** 1865. **Freq:** Daily (eve.) and Sat. (morn.). **Print Method:** Offset. **Cols./Page:** 6. **Col. Width:** 24 nonpareils. **Col. Depth:** 301 agate lines. **Key Personnel:** Steve Stewart, Publisher, stewart@clarksdale.com. **USPS:** 115-960. **Subscription Rates:** $90. **Remarks:** Accepts advertising.
Ad Rates: BW: $825.60 **Circ:** Mon.-Fri. 6,442
PCI: $6.40 Sat. 6,472

16670 Western Turf & Landscape Press
Farm Press
14920 U.S. Hwy. 61 N. Phone: (601)624-8503
PO Box 1420 Fax: (601)627-1977
Clarksdale, MS 38614
Free: (800)253-3160

Business magazine for all segments of western turf and landscape industry. **Founded:** Oct. 1990. **Freq:** Monthly. **Print Method:** Web Offset. **Trim Size:** 11 x 14 1/2. **Cols./Page:** 4. **Col. Width:** 2 1/4 inches. **Col. Depth:** 13 1/2 inches. **Key Personnel:** Ed Phillips, Editor; Teresa Casburn, Production Mgr.; John Montandon, Publisher. **Subscription Rates:** $25. $3.50 single issue. **Remarks:** Accepts advertising. **Formerly**: Western Turf Management.
Ad Rates: BW: $2,479 **Circ:** (Not Reported)
4C: $3,261
PCI: $76

16671 WAID-FM - 106.5
112 Le Flore Ave. Phone: (601)627-2281
Box 668 Fax: (601)624-2900
Clarksdale, MS 38614

Format: Urban Contemporary. **Founded:** 1977. **Operating Hours:** Continuous. **Key Personnel:** Greg C. Shurden, General Mgr.; Christy McBrayer, Operations Mgr. **Wattage:** 50,000. **Ad Rates:** $5.40-9.00 for 30 seconds; $7.50-11.00 for 60 seconds.

16672 WROX-AM - 1450
317 Delta Ave Phone: (601)627-7343
Clarksdale, MS 38614 Fax: (601)627-1000

Format: Talk; Blues; Adult Contemporary. **Networks:** CBS. **Founded:** 1944. **Operating Hours:** Continuous, 100% local. **Key Personnel:** Gerald Weaver, General Mgr.; Pat Lofton, Admin. Dir. **Wattage:** 1000. **Ad Rates:** $6.50 for 30 seconds; $9 for 60 seconds.

CLEVELAND†, pop. 14,817.

W MS. Bolivar Co. 35 mi. NE of Greenville. Delta State University. Bottling works. Manufactures tile, auto trim, nails and staples. Agriculture. Soybeans, cotton, rice.

16673 Bolivar Commercial
Division of Cleveland Newspapers, Inc.
PO Box 1050 Phone: (601)843-4241
Cleveland, MS 38732 Fax: (601)843-1830

General newspaper. **Founded:** 1915. **Freq:** Daily (eve.). **Print Method:** Offset. **Cols./Page:** 6. **Col. Width:** 26 nonpareils. **Col. Depth:** 301 agate lines. **Key Personnel:** Norman C. Van Liew, Editor and Publisher, publisher@bolivercom.com. **Subscription Rates:** $66; $78 other countries. **URL:** http://www.bolivarcom.com.
Ad Rates: BW: $953.31 **Circ:** Mon.-Fri. ★**7,302**
4C: $1,198.31
PCI: $7.39

16674 WCLD-AM - 1490
Drawar 780 Phone: (601)843-4091
Cleveland, MS 38732 Fax: (601)843-9805

Format: Sports. **Networks:** CNN Radio. **Owner:** Radio Cleveland, Inc., at above address. **Founded:** 1949. **Operating Hours:** Continuous. **ADI:** Greenwood-Greenville, MS. **Key Personnel:** Clint L. Webster, General Mgr.; Kevin Cox, General Sales Mgr. **Wattage:** 1000.

16675 WCLD-FM - 103.9
Drawer 780 Phone: (601)843-4091
Cleveland, MS 38732 Fax: (601)843-9805

Format: Urban Contemporary. **Founded:** 1972. **Operating Hours:** 24 hrs. **ADI:** Greenwood-Greenville, MS. **Key Personnel:** Clint L. Webster, General Mgr.; Kevin Cox, General Sales Mgr. **Wattage:** 25000.

16676 WDSK-AM - 1410
PO Box 1438 Phone: (601)846-0929
Cleveland, MS 38732 Fax: (601)843-1410
E-mail: wdsk@deltaradio.net

Format: News; Talk. **Networks:** CBS. **Owner:** Delta Radio, Inc., at above address. **Operating Hours:** Continuous. **ADI:** Greenwood-Greenville, MS. **Key Personnel:** Larry Fuss, General Mgr.; Teri Sterling, Sales Mgr.; Jim Gregory, Operations Mgr. **Wattage:** 1000. **Ad Rates:** $2.94-4,71 for 30 seconds; $5.29-7.06 for 60 seconds. **URL:** http://www.deltaradio.net.

16677 WDTL-FM - 92.9
PO Box 1438 Phone: (601)846-0929
Cleveland, MS 38732 Fax: (601)843-1410
E-mail: wdtl@deltaradio.net

Format: Country. **Owner:** Delta Radio, Inc., at above address. **Founded:** 1992. **Former name:** WQAZ (1991). **Operating Hours:** Continuous. **ADI:** Greenwood-Greenville, MS. **Key Personnel:** Larry Fuss, General Mgr.; Teri Sterling, Sales Mgr.; Jim Gregory, Operations Mgr. **Wattage:** 50,000. **Ad Rates:** $8.24-11.77 for 30 seconds; $11.77-14.12 for 60 seconds. **URL:** http://www.deltaradio.net.

16678 WMJW-FM - 107.5
PO Box 780 Phone: (601)843-4091
Cleveland, MS 38732 Fax: (601)843-9805

Format: Adult Contemporary. **Owner:** Radio Cleveland, Inc., at above address. **Operating Hours:** Continuous. **ADI:** Greenwood-Greenville, MS. **Key Personnel:** Clint Webster, General Mgr.; Kevin Cox, General Sales Mgr.; Jim Thomas, Operations Mgr. **Wattage:** 25,000.

16679 WOHT-FM - 95.3
PO Box 1438 Phone: (601)846-0929
Cleveland, MS 38732 Fax: (601)843-1410

Format: Urban Contemporary; Blues. **Owner:** Delta Radio, Inc., at above address. **Formerly:** WKZB-FM. **Operating Hours:** Continuous. **ADI:** Greenwood-Greenville, MS. **Wattage:** 6,000. **Ad Rates:** $4-5.88 for 30 seconds; $6-8.24 for 60 seconds.

CLINTON, pop. 15,658.

SWC MS. Hinds Co. 10 mi. NW of Jackson. Mississippi College. Residential.

16680 WHJT-FM - 96.3
PO Box 4214 Phone: (601)925-3458
Clinton, MS 39058 Fax: (601)924-4506

Format: Adult Contemporary; Contemporary Christian. **Networks:** Independent. **Founded:** 1966. **Formerly:** WSLI-FM. **Operating Hours:** Continuous. **Key Personnel:** Dr. Billy Lytal, General Mgr., phone (601)925-3428, lytal@mc.edu; Melanie Stone, Operations Dir., mstone@mc.edu; Melanie Stone, Program Dir., mstone@mc.edu. **Wattage:** 100,000.

COLLINS†, pop. 2,131.

S MS. Covington Co. 62 mi. S. of Jackson. Gas storage facilities. Cotton, dairy, truck farms. Soybeans.

16681 The News-Commercial
104 1st St. S Phone: (601)765-8275
PO Box 1299 Fax: (601)765-6952
Collins, MS 39428
Community newspaper. **Founded:** 1901. **Freq:** Weekly (Wed.). **Print Method:** Offset. **Trim Size:** 12 7/8 x 21 1/4. **Cols./Page:** 8. **Col. Width:** 1 1/2 inches. **Key Personnel:** Jamie Arrington, Editor and Publisher; Jimmy Goff, Advertising Mgr. **USPS:** 387-880. **Subscription Rates:** $14.00 individuals; $17 out of area; $19 out of state. **Remarks:** Accepts advertising.
Ad Rates: GLR: $.21 **Circ:** Paid ⊕**3,163**
PCI: $2.50 Free ⊕**22**

COLUMBIA†, pop. 7,733.

S MS. Marion Co. On Pearl River, 75 mi. SE of Jackson. Manufactures boxes, veneer, canned vegetables, hosiery, garments. Naval stores. Bottling works. Pine timber. Agriculture. Cotton, potatoes, truck crops.

16682 Columbian-Progress/Marion County Advertiser
Emmerich Enterprises, Inc.
PO Box 1171 Phone: (601)736-2611
Columbia, MS 39429-1171 Fax: (601)736-4507

Local newspaper. **Founded:** 1901. **Freq:** Semiweekly (Thurs. and Sun.). **Print Method:** Offset. **Cols./Page:** 6. **Col. Width:** 20 nonpareils. **Col. Depth:** 301 agate lines. **Key Personnel:** Ken Prillhart, Editor; John Emmerich, Publisher. **Subscription Rates:** $30 local; $35 in-state; $40 out of state. **Remarks:** Accepts advertising. **Formerly:** Sunday Mirror, The Columbian.
Ad Rates: GLR: $.363 **Circ:** Thurs. ‡12,200
BW: $704.34 Sun. ‡11,636
4C: $994.34
PCI: $5.46

16683 WCJU-AM - 1450
PO Box 472 Phone: (601)736-2616
Columbia, MS 39429 Fax: (601)736-2617
E-mail: wcju@pearlriver.net

Format: Adult Contemporary; Talk; Gospel. **Networks:** ABC. **Owner:** Thomas F. McDaniel, at above address. **Founded:** 1946. **Operating Hours:** 5 a.m.-10 p.m.; 55% network, 45% local. **Key Personnel:** Brad Webb, Sales/Operations Mgr. **Local Programs:** *The Bartering Show*, Glen Simmons; *The Morning Show*; *Rock of Faith Show*, Johnny Pittman. **Wattage:** 1000. **Ad Rates:** $3-6 for 30 seconds; $4.50-7.50 for 60 seconds.

16684 WFFF-AM - 1360
PO Box 550 Phone: (601)736-1360
Columbia, MS 39429 Fax: (601)736-1361

Format: Country. **Networks:** ABC; Mississippi. **Founded:** 1961. **Operating Hours:** Continuous. **ADI:** Laurel-Hattiesburg, MS. **Key Personnel:** Dave Martin, President; Ronnie Geiger, Vice President. **Wattage:** 1000 day; 159 night. **Ad Rates:** $5.50 for 30 seconds; $7.50 for 60 seconds. $8.50 for 30 seconds; $11.00 for 60 seconds. Combined advertising rates available with WFFF-FM.

16685 WFFF-FM - 96.7
PO Box 550 Phone: (601)736-1360
Columbia, MS 39429 Fax: (601)736-1361

Format: Adult Contemporary. **Networks:** ABC; Mississippi. **Founded:** 1966. **Operating Hours:** Continuous. **ADI:** Laurel-Hattiesburg, MS. **Key Personnel:** Dave Martin, President; Ronnie Geiger, Vice President. **Wattage:** 6000. **Ad Rates:** $5.50 for 30 seconds; $7.50 for 60 seconds. Combined advertising rates available with WFFF-AM: $8.50 for 30 seconds; $11.00 for 60 seconds.

COLUMBUS†, pop. 28,658.

E MS. Lowndes Co. On Tombigbee River, 130 mi. NE of Jackson. Mississippi University for Women. Columbus Air Force Base. Manufactures brick, monuments, electrical motors, prefab metal buildings, cement, vinyl wall covering, carpet underlay, chemicals, plastics, clothing. Timber. Diversified farming.

16686 The Commercial Dispatch
The Commercial Dispatch Publishing, Inc.
PO Box 511 Phone: (601)328-2424
Columbus, MS 39703-0511 Fax: (601)329-8937
Free: (877)328-2430
Publication E-mail: letters@cdispatch.com

Newspaper. **Founded:** Mar. 12, 1922. **Freq:** Daily (eve.). **Print Method:** Offset. **Trim Size:** 13 x 21 1/2. **Cols./Page:** 6. **Col. Width:** 2 1/16 inches. **Col. Depth:** 21 1/2 inches. **Key Personnel:** Birney Imes, Jr., Pres./General Mgr./Exec.Ed. **Subscription Rates:** $96 individuals. **Remarks:** Accepts advertising. **Formed by the merger of:** The Dispatch; Commercial.
Ad Rates: BW: $1,180.35 **Circ:** Mon.-Fri. 13,635
4C: $1,580.35 Sun. 15,279
SAU: $10.60

16687 Silver Wings
Service Publications
14 FTW/PA 555 Seventh St., No. 203 Phone: (601)434-7067
PO Box 511 Fax: (601)328-2424
Columbus, MS 39710-1009
Newspaper for personnel of Columbus AFB. **Founded:** 1958. **Freq:** Weekly (Fri.). **Print Method:** Offset. **Cols./Page:** 5. **Col. Width:** 24 nonpareils. **Col. Depth:** 182 agate lines. **Key Personnel:** Scott A. Lindvall, Editor; Rick Chapman, Advertising Mgr. **Remarks:** Accepts advertising.
Ad Rates: BW: $260 **Circ:** Free 3,000
4C: $540

16688 Columbus TV Cable Corp.
Box 1468 Phone: (601)328-1781
Columbus, MS 39703-1468 Fax: (601)329-8484

Founded: 1954. **Key Personnel:** Travis Nabors, President. **Cities Served:** Lowndes County, MS.: subscribing households 14,000; 41 channels.

16689 WACR-AM - 1050
1910 14th Ave. N. Phone: (601)328-1050
PO Box 1078 Fax: (601)328-1054
Columbus, MS 39703

Format: Religious; Urban Contemporary. **Owner:** T & W Communications, Inc., PO Box 312, West Point, MS 39773. **Founded:** 1953. **Operating Hours:** Sunrise-sunset; 5% network, 95% local. **ADI:** Columbus-Tupelo (West Point), MS. **Key Personnel:** Danny Byrd, General Mgr.; Jerold Jackson, Program Dir.; Sherwinn Prescott, General Sales Mgr. **Wattage:** 1000. **Ad Rates:** $20 for 30 seconds; $25 for 60 seconds.

16690 WACR-FM - 103.9
1910 14th Ave. N. Phone: (601)328-1050
PO Box 1078 Fax: (601)328-1054
Columbus, MS 39703

Format: Urban Contemporary. **Owner:** T & W Communications, Inc., PO Box 312, West Point, MS 39773. **Operating Hours:** Continuous. **ADI:** Columbus-Tupelo (West Point), MS. **Key Personnel:** Danny Byrd, General Mgr.; Sherwinn Prescott, General Sales Mgr.; Jerold Jackson, Program Dir. **Wattage:** 3000. **Ad Rates:** $25 per unit.

16691 WAJV-FM - 98.9
702 2nd Ave. N Phone: (601)328-1400
Columbus, MS 39701 Fax: (601)328-1421

Format: Religious; Southern Gospel. **Networks:** Mississippi. **Founded:** 1995. **Operating Hours:** Continuous. **ADI:** Columbus-Tupelo (West Point), MS. **Key Personnel:** Bill Lemonds, General Mgr.; Ruth Robinson, PSA Dir. **Local Programs:** *Fresh Tracks*, Terry Veazey; *Gospel Ship*, Bill Lemonds, General Mgr. **Wattage:** 2,500. **Ad Rates:** $7-10 for 30 seconds; $9-12 for 60 seconds.

16692 WCBI-TV - 4
PO Box 271 Phone: (601)327-4444
Columbus, MS 39703 Fax: (601)328-5222

Format: Commercial TV. **Networks:** CBS. **Owner:** Frank Imer, at above address, Fax: (601)329-1004. **Operating Hours:** Continuous. **ADI:** Columbus-Tupelo (West Point), MS. **Key Personnel:** Vallory Williamson, General Mgr.

16693 WJWF-AM - 1400
702 2nd Ave. N. Phone: (601)328-1400
PO Box 707 Fax: (601)328-1421
Columbus, MS 39703
E-mail: wjwf@radiocolumbus.com

Format: Religious; Contemporary Christian. **Networks:** Mississippi. **Owner:** Radio Columbus, Inc., at above address, (601)328-1420. **Founded:** 1968. **Formerly:** WMBC-AM (1992). **Operating Hours:** Continuous. **ADI:** Columbus-Tupelo (West Point), MS. **Key Personnel:** Bill Lemonds, General Mgr.; Ruth Robinson, PSA Director. **Local Programs:** *Gospel Ship*, Bill Lemonds, General Mgr. **Wattage:** 1000. **Ad Rates:** $6-8 for 30 seconds; $8-10 for 60 seconds.

16694 WKOR-AM - 980
PO Box 1076
Columbus, MS 39703-1076

Format: Information; News; Talk. **Networks:** ABC. **Owner:** Charisma Broadcasting, at above address. **Founded:** 1968. **Operating Hours:** Sunrise-sunset; 50% network, 50% local. **ADI:** Columbus-Tupelo (West Point), MS. **Key Personnel:** Bill Milam, General Mgr.; Bill Thurlow, Program Dir. **Wattage:** 1000. **Ad Rates:** $4.71-14.12 for 30 seconds; $5.65-16.94 for 60 seconds.

16695 WMBC-FM - 103.1
702 2nd Ave. N. Phone: (601)329-1030
PO Box 707 Fax: (601)328-1421
Columbus, MS 39703
E-mail: wmbc@ebcom.net

Format: Country. **Networks:** NBC; Mississippi. **Founded:** 1968. **Operating Hours:** Continuous. **ADI:** Columbus-Tupelo (West Point), MS. **Key Personnel:** Terry Fulton, General Mgr.; Johnny Dees, Program Dir. **Local Programs:** *The Morning Show*, Bill Thurlough. **Wattage:** 50,000. **Ad Rates:** $12-22 for 30 seconds; $14-26 for 60 seconds. Combined advertising rates available with WAJV-FM, WJWF-AM.

16696 WMXU-FM - 106.1
PO Box 1076 Phone: (601)327-1183
Columbus, MS 39703 Fax: (601)328-1122

Format: Urban Contemporary. **Simulcasts:** WSSO-AM. **Networks:** ABC. **Founded:** 1964. **Formerly:** WSMU-FM (1991); WKYJ-FM. **Operating Hours:** Continuous. **ADI:** Columbus-Tupelo (West Point), MS. **Key Personnel:** Bob Green, General Mgr./Sports Dir.; Jodi Roberts, News Dir.; Steve Poston, Program Dir. **Wattage:** 50,000. **Ad Rates:** $4.25-8.25 for 30 seconds. Combined advertising rates available with WMSU-FM, WSMS-FM, WKOR-FM, WKOR-AM, WSSO-AM.

CORINTH†, pop. 12,560.

NE MS. Alcorn Co. 89 mi. SE of Memphis, TN. Manufactures clothing, hosiery, furniture, cottonseed oil, dairy products, handles, sawmill machinery, motors, pulleys, hydraulic pumps, telephone equipment, organs. Agriculture. Cotton, corn, soybeans, poultry.

16697 The Daily Corinthian
1607 S. Harper Rd. Phone: (601)287-6111
PO Box 1800 Fax: (601)287-3525
Corinth, MS 38834
Publication E-mail: dailycor@tsixroads.com

General newspaper. **Founded:** 1895. **Freq:** Daily (morn.). **Print Method:** Offset. **Cols./Page:** 6. **Col. Width:** 26 nonpareils. **Col. Depth:** 294 agate lines. **Key Personnel:** Don Swartz, Publisher; Julie Bullock, Advertising Mgr.; Mark Boehler, Editor. **USPS:** 142-560. **Subscription Rates:** $96. **Remarks:** Accepts advertising.
Ad Rates: GLR: $3.70 **Circ:** Tues.-Fri. 8,055
BW: $1,493.10 Sat. 8,055
4C: $1,683,10 Sun. 7,610
PCI: $10.15

16698 WADI-FM - 95.3
1608 S. John St. Phone: (601)287-3101
Corinth, MS 38834 Fax: (601)287-9262

Format: Contemporary Country. **Operating Hours:** Continuous. **Key Personnel:** Joe Taylor Jobe, Contact; Joan Jobe, Contact. **Wattage:** 4200. **Ad Rates:** $4 for 30 seconds; $5 for 60 seconds.

16699 WCMA-AM - 1230
1608 S. John St. Phone: (601)287-3101
Corinth, MS 38834 Fax: (601)287-9262

Format: Country. **Founded:** 1946. **Operating Hours:** Continuous. **Key Personnel:** Joe Taylor Jobe, Contact; Joan Jobe, Contact. **Wattage:** 1000. **Ad Rates:** $3 for 30 seconds; $4 for 60 seconds.

16700 WKCU-AM - 1350
2192 Hwy. 72 E. Phone: (601)286-8451
Corinth, MS 38834 Fax: (601)286-8452

Format: Religious. **Networks:** Mutual Broadcasting System; Mississippi. **Owner:** James H. Anderson, at above address. **Founded:** 1965. **Operating Hours:** 6 a.m.-sunset; 1% network, 99% local. **Key Personnel:** Regina Pyle, News Dir.; James H. Anderson, Program Dir.; Terry F. Anderson, Contact; J.P. Anderson, Contact; James D. Anderson, Contact. **Wattage:** 1000. **Ad Rates:** $3.50-5 for 30 seconds.

16701 WXRZ-FM - 94.3
2192 Hwy. 72 E. Phone: (601)286-8451
Corinth, MS 38834 Fax: (601)286-8452

Format: Adult Contemporary. **Networks:** Mutual Broadcasting System. **Owner:** James H. Anderson, at above address. **Founded:** 1967. **Formerly:** WKCU-FM (1990). **Operating Hours:** 5 a.m.-midnight; 1% network, 99% local. **Key Personnel:** Regina Pyle, News Dir.; Terry F. Anderson, Contact; J.P. Anderson, Contact; James D. Anderson, Contact. **Wattage:** 6000. **Ad Rates:** $3.50-5 for 30 seconds.

CRYSTAL SPRINGS, pop. 4,902.

SW MS. Copiah Co. 25 mi. SW of Jackson. Gravel mining. Manufactures machine tools, plastic pellets, laboratory and pharmaceutical fixtures, electric transformers copper, brass and aluminum wire. Pine and hardwood timber. Poultry industry.

16702 Meteor
Meteor Newspaper Inc.
201 E. Georgetown St. Phone: (601)892-2581
PO Box 353 Fax: (601)892-2249
Crystal Springs, MS 39059-0353
Community newspaper. **Founded:** 1881. **Freq:** Weekly (Wed.). **Print Method:** Offset. **Trim Size:** 15 x 22 1/2. **Cols./Page:** 6. **Col. Width:** 25 nonpareils. **Col. Depth:** 294 agate lines. **Key Personnel:** Henry Carney, Editor and Publisher. **USPS:** 342-440. **Subscription Rates:** $15 individuals. **Remarks:** Accepts advertising.
Ad Rates: GLR: $.36 **Circ:** ‡5,000
BW: $640.08
SAU: $5.33
PCI: $5.33

DE KALB†, pop. 1,159.

E MS. Kemper Co. 30 mi. N. of Meridian. Saw mills; cotton ginning. Pine timber. Agriculture. Cotton, corn, potatoes.

16703 Kemper County Messenger
Messenger
PO Box 546 Phone: (601)743-5760
De Kalb, MS 39328 Fax: (601)743-4430

Community newspaper. **Founded:** 1932. **Freq:** Weekly (Thurs.). **Print Method:** Offset. **Cols./Page:** 6. **Col. Width:** 2 1/8 inches. **Col. Depth:** 21 inches. **Key Personnel:** Jayne Jowers, Editor; James L. Sledge, Jr., Publisher; Jayne Jowers, Office Mgr. **Subscription Rates:** $18. **Remarks:** Accepts advertising.
Ad Rates: GLR: $.50 **Circ:** ‡2,400
BW: $384
CNU: $3.75
PCI: $4.50

EUPORA, pop. 2,048.

NC MS. Webster Co. 52 mi. E. of Greenwood. Sawmills; cotton ginning; glove factory. Pine, hardwood timber. Agriculture. Cotton, corn, potatoes, dairying.

16704 Webster Progress-Times
Webster Progress
PO Drawer D Phone: (601)258-7532
Eupora, MS 39744 Fax: (601)258-6474

Newspaper. **Founded:** 1879. **Freq:** Weekly (Wed.). **Print Method:** Offset. **Cols./Page:** 6. **Col. Width:** 12 ems. **Col. Depth:** 21 1/2 inches. **Key Personnel:** Donna McKay, Comptroller. **Subscription Rates:** $22. **Remarks:** Accepts advertising.
Ad Rates: BW: $572 **Circ:** Paid ‡2638
4C: $687 Free ‡90
SAU: $4.25
PCI: $4.25

16705 WEPA-AM - 710
Hwy. 82 E. Phone: (601)258-7170
Eupora, MS 39744 Fax: (601)258-9696

Format: Country. **Networks:** NBC. **Owner:** Tri-County Broadcasting Co., Inc., PO Box 710, Eupora, MS 39744. **Founded:** 1974. **Operating Hours:** Sunrise-sunset. **Key Personnel:** Harry Jackson, Station Mgr.; Joey Traywick, Program Dir.; John Cooper, News Dir. **Wattage:** 2500. **Ad Rates:** $6-10 for 30 seconds; $8.50-12 for 60 seconds.

16706 WLZA-FM - 96.1
PO Box 710 Phone: (601)258-9696
Eupora, MS 39744 Fax: (601)258-9690

Format: Adult Contemporary. **Networks:** Satellite Radio. **Owner:** Tri-County Broadcasting Co., Inc., at above address. **Founded:** 1974. **Formerly:** WEXA-FM. **Operating Hours:** Continuous. **Key Personnel:** Harry Jackson, Station Mgr.; Joey Traywick, Program Dir.; Greg May, News Dir. **Wattage:** 50,000. **Ad Rates:** $7-10 for 30 seconds; $9-12 for 60 seconds.

FAYETTE†, pop. 2,033.

SW MS. Jefferson Co. 9 mi. S. of Lorman. Manufactures lumber. Residential.

16707 The Fayette Chronicle
PO Box 536 Phone: (601)786-3661
Fayette, MS 39069 Fax: (601)786-3661

General circulation newspaper. Authorized to publish government and legal notices. **Founded:** 1866. **Freq:** Weekly (Thurs.). **Print Method:** computer. **Trim Size:** 13 x 22. **Cols./Page:** 6. **Col. Width:** 12 picas. **Col. Depth:** 21.5 inches. **Key Personnel:** Charles Kwame Shepphard, Editor and Publisher. **ISSN:** 0889-5171. **Subscription Rates:** $21; $25 in state; $27 out of state. **Remarks:** Accepts advertising.
Ad Rates: BW: $387 **Circ:** Paid ‡2,500
4C: $787 Free ‡100
SAU: $4.75

FLORA

16708 T.A.T. Cablevision
467 1st St. Phone: (601)879-3288
PO Box 197
Flora, MS 39071

Founded: Nov. 1980. **Key Personnel:** Robert Taylor, President; Terry Taylor, Vice President; Wayne Whitehead, Chief Engineer. **Cities Served:** Flora, MS: subscribing households 523; 34 channels; 1 community access channel; 168 hours per week community access programming.

FOREST†, pop. 5,229.

C MS. Scott Co. 45 mi. E. of Jackson. Bienville National Forest. Manufactures frozen desserts, knit clothing, steel flow control valves, military electronic hardware. Lumber. Log homes. Poultry processing. Hatcheries. Agriculture. Soybeans, corn, milo, feed.

16709 Scott County Times
Scott Publishing, Inc.
PO Box 89 Phone: (601)469-2561
Forest, MS 39074 Fax: (601)469-2004

Community newspaper. **Founded:** 1939. **Freq:** Weekly (Wed.). **Print Method:** Offset. **Cols./Page:** 6. **Col. Width:** 25 nonpareils. **Col. Depth:** 301 agate lines. **Key Personnel:** Sidney L. Salter, Publisher; Lanay Russum, Advertising Mgr. **USPS:** 485-440. **Subscription Rates:** $15. **Remarks:** Accepts advertising.
Ad Rates: GLR: $1.75 **Circ:** 5,000
PCI: $4.50

16710 Northland Cable
Box 1538 Phone: (601)469-3712
Forest, MS 39074 Fax: (601)469-4203

Owner: Northland Cable, 1201 3rd Ave., Ste. 3600, Seattle, WA 98101, (206)621-1351. **Key Personnel:** Wayne Robinson, General Mgr. **Cities Served:** subscribing households 4,250; 35 channels; 1 community access channel.

FULTON†, pop. 3,238.

NE MS. Itawamba Co. On Tombigbee River, 60 mi. N. of Columbus. Itawamba Community College. Manufactures wood, copper products, furniture, garments. Sawmill. Timber. Agriculture. Cotton, poultry, dairying.

16711 Chieftain
Itawamba Community College
602 W. Hill St. Phone: (601)862-8000
Fulton, MS 38843 Fax: (601)862-8245

Collegiate newspaper. **Founded:** 1968. **Freq:** 14/year. **Print Method:** Offset. **Trim Size:** 28 x 22 3/4. **Cols./Page:** 6. **Col. Width:** 12 picas. **Col. Depth:** 20 1/2 inches. **Key Personnel:** Donna Thomas, Advisor, phone (601)862-8244, dsthomas@icc.cc.ms.us. **Subscription Rates:** Free. **Remarks:** Advertising accepted; rates available upon request.
Circ: Free ‡2,000

16712 Itawamba County Times
106 W. Main Phone: (601)862-3141
PO Drawer 1549 Fax: (601)862-7804
Fulton, MS 38843
Publication E-mail: itimes@network-one.com

Community newspaper. **Founded:** 1903. **Freq:** Weekly (Wed.). **Print Method:** Offset. **Cols./Page:** 6. **Col. Width:** 24 nonpareils. **Col. Depth:** 301 agate lines. **Key Personnel:** Rubye Del Harden, Publisher, rubyedel@network-one.com; Steve Elliott, Managing Editor, xalapoetxx@aol.com; Terry Miller, Advertising Mgr. **Subscription Rates:** $32 out of state; $18 individuals; $25 out of area. **Remarks:** Advertising not accepted for alcoholic beverages. **Feature Editors:** Steven G. Watson, *Sports*, stankalank@aol.com.
Ad Rates: GLR: $.33 **Circ:** ‡5,500
BW: $606.30
4C: $1006.30
SAU: $4.70
PCI: $5.25

16713 Fulton TV Cable Co. Inc.
PO Box 1459 Phone: (601)862-5333
Fulton, MS 38843 Fax: (601)862-5088

Owner: GTR, Inc., PO Box 548, Shawneetown, IL 62984, (618)269-4411, Fax: (618)269-4414. **Key Personnel:** Gary Ervin, Owner; Dwight McGee, General Mgr.; Diane Pearce, Office Mgr. **Cities Served:** Fulton, Mantachie, Tremont, MS: subscribing households 4,000; 36 channels; 2 community access channels; 120 hours per week community access programming.

GOODMAN, pop. 1,285.

NWC MS. Holmes Co. 40 mi. S. of Greenwood. Holmes Junior College. Residential.

16714 The Growl
Holmes Community College
PO Box 367 Phone: (601)472-2312
Goodman, MS 39079 Fax: (601)472-2566

Collegiate newspaper. **Subtitle:** The Growl. **Founded:** Sept. 1, 1927. **Freq:** Monthly. **Print Method:** Offset. **Trim Size:** 11 1/2 x 14. **Cols./Page:** 5. **Col. Width:** 22 nonpareils. **Col. Depth:** 175 agate lines. **Key Personnel:** James G. Williams, Directory of Public Information. **Subscription Rates:** $10 individuals. **Remarks:** Accepts advertising.
Ad Rates: BW: $100 **Circ:** Paid 2,900
SAU: $2 Free 4,700
PCI: $3

GREENVILLE†, pop. 40,636.

W MS. Washington Co. On Lake Ferguson, still water harbor, 132 mi. S. of Memphis, TN. Bridges across river. Boat connections. Manufactures carpeting, concrete products, boxes, lumber, cottonseed oil, wall board, plastics, auto parts, boilers, stoppers, screws, wire and saws. Bottling works; shipyard. Fisheries. Hardwood timber. Agriculture. Cotton, alfalfa, soybeans, rice, cattle.

16715 Delta Democrat Times
Freedom Communications Inc.
988 N. Broadway Phone: (601)335-1155
PO Box 1618 Fax: (601)335-2860
Greenville, MS 38702
Free: (800)844-1618
Publisher E-mail: eanichols@link.freedom.com

General newspaper. **Founded:** 1868. **Freq:** Daily (eve.), Sunday (morn.). **Print Method:** Offset. **Cols./Page:** 6. **Col. Depth:** 301 agate lines. **Key Personnel:** Dan E. Way, Editor, phone (601)378-0711; E. A. Nichols, Publisher, phone (601)378-0761; Truman Beasley, Advertising Dir., phone (601)378-0741. **Subscription Rates:** $108. **Remarks:** Accepts advertising.
Ad Rates: BW: $1,019.10 **Circ:** Mon.-Fri. 12,808
4C: $1,239.10 Sun. 13,892
SAU: $9.80

16716 KUUZ-FM - 95.9
PO Box 1794 Phone: (601)332-0025
Greenville, MS 38702-1794 Fax: (601)332-0038
Free: (800)844-8979

Format: Contemporary Country. **Networks:** USA Radio. **Owner:** DBR Communications, Inc., at above address. **Founded:** 1989. **Operating Hours:** Continuous; 60% network, 40% local. **ADI:** Greenwood-Greenville, MS. **Key Personnel:** Wayne Bennett, Gen.Mgr/Gen. Sales Mgr.; Peggy Franks, Office Mgr. **Wattage:** 20,000. **Ad Rates:** $8-13 for 30 seconds; $11-16.25 for 60 seconds.

16717 KZYQ-FM - 103.5
PO Box 5395 Phone: (601)378-4103
Greenville, MS 38704 Fax: (601)332-3103
E-mail: star@deltaradio.net

Format: Adult Contemporary. **Owner:** Delta Radio, Inc., PO Box 1438, Cleveland, MS 38732. **Formerly:** KDTL-FM (1996). **Operating Hours:** Continuous. **ADI:** Greenwood-Greenville, MS. **Ad Rates:** $6-9.41 for 30 seconds; $8-11.77 for 60 seconds. **URL:** http://www.deltaradio.net.

16718 TCA
318 Main St. Phone: (601)332-0518
Box 1278
Greenville, MS 38701

Founded: 1954. **Formerly:** Deltavideo (1983); McCaw Cablevision (1986); Cooke Cablevision (1988); Delta Cablevision. **Cities Served:** subscribing households 14,000; 63 channels.

16719 WABG-TV - 6
PO Box 1243, 849 Washington Ave. Phone: (601)332-0949
Greenville, MS 38701 Fax: (601)334-6420
Free: (800)898-0968
E-mail: wabg@tecinfo.com

Format: Commercial TV. **Networks:** ABC. **Owner:** Mississipi Telecasting Co; Inc, at above address. **Founded:** 1959. **Operating Hours:** 5 a.m.-1 a.m.; 80% network, 20% local. **ADI:** Greenwood-Greenville, MS. **Key Personnel:** Victoria Grant, Public Affairs Dir., phone (601)453-4001; John Rogers, General Mgr.; Donnie Reid, Program Dir.; Matt Lundy, News Dir. **Wattage:** 100,000. **Ad Rates:** $25-450 for 30 seconds. **URL:** http://www.wabg.com.

16720 WBAD-FM - 94.3
PO Box 4426 Phone: (601)335-9265
Greenville, MS 38704-4426 Fax: (601)335-5538

Format: Urban Contemporary. **Networks:** American Urban Radio. **Owner:** Interchange Communications, Inc., at above address. **Founded:** 1973. **Operating Hours:** Continuous. Daily; 8% network, 92% local. **ADI:** Greenwood-Greenville, MS. **Key Personnel:** William D. Jackson, Contact; Stanley S. Sherman, Contact; Troop Williams, Program Dir. **Wattage:** 50,000. **Ad Rates:** $14-18 for 30 seconds; $17.5-22 for 60 seconds.

16721 WBAQ-FM - 97.9
PO Box 656 Phone: (601)335-3383
Greenville, MS 38702-0656 Fax: (601)335-3383

Format: Easy Listening. **Networks:** ABC. **Owner:** Paul C. Artman, at above address. **Founded:** 1970. **Operating Hours:** 5:30 a.m.-midnight; 10% network; 90% local. **ADI:** Greenwood-Greenville, MS. **Key Personnel:** Paul C. Artman, Sr., General Mgr.; Paul Artman, Jr., Program Dir. **Wattage:** 24,500. **Ad Rates:** $3.60-8.10 for 30 seconds; $4.10-9.10 for 60 seconds.

16722 WDMS-FM - 100.7
1383 Pickett St. Phone: (601)334-4559
Greenville, MS 38701 Fax: (601)332-1315
Free: (888)808-8644
E-mail: wdms@tecinfo.com

Format: Contemporary Country. **Founded:** 1967. **Operating Hours:** Continuous. **ADI:** Greenwood-Greenville, MS. **Key Personnel:** Bob Ghetti, General Mgr.; Linda Tackett, Traffic Mgr.; Randy Pinksten, Operations Mgr. **Wattage:** 100,000 ERP. **Ad Rates:** Advertising accepted; rates available upon request. Combined advertising rates available with WGVM-AM. **URL:** http://www.tecinfo.com./~wdms.

16723 WESY-AM - 1580
7 Oaks Rd. Phone: (601)378-9405
PO Box 5804 Fax: (601)335-5538
Greenville, MS 38704-5804

Format: Religious; Urban Contemporary. **Networks:** American Urban Radio. **Founded:** 1959. **Operating Hours:** Sunrise-sunset; 8% network, 92% local. **ADI:** Greenwood-Greenville, MS. **Key Personnel:** William D. Jackson, Manager; Truman Ford, Music Dir.; Stanley S. Sherman, Contact. **Wattage:** 1000. **Ad Rates:** $14-18 for 30 seconds; $17.5-22 for 60 seconds.

16724 WGVM-AM - 1260
1383 Pickett St. Phone: (601)334-4559
Greenville, MS 38701 Fax: (601)332-1315
Free: (888)808-8644
E-mail: wgvm@tecinfo.com

Format: Rap; Urban Contemporary. **Founded:** 1948. **Operating Hours:** Continuous. **ADI:** Greenwood-Greenville, MS. **Key Personnel:** Bob Ghetti, General Mgr.; Linda Tackett, Traffic Mgr.; Randy Pinksten, Operations Mgr. **Wattage:** 5000 ERP day; 35 ERP night. **Ad Rates:** Advertising accepted; rates available upon request.

16725 WIQQ-FM - 102.3
Unit 39, Delta Plaza Mall Phone: (601)378-2617
Hwy. 1 S. Fax: (601)378-8341
Greenville, MS 38701
E-mail: wiqq@tecinfo.com

Format: Contemporary Hit Radio (CHR). **Networks:** USA Radio; Jones Satellite. **Owner:** River Broadcasting Co., Inc., at above address. **Founded:** 1985. **Operating Hours:** Continuous; 55% network, 45% local. **ADI:** Greenwood-Greenville, MS. **Key Personnel:** James P. Karr, Jr., Vice President; Margaret Karr, Sales Mgr.; Ray Hamilton, Program Dir.; Chuck Early, News/Sports; Chuck Early, Public Affairs Dir. **Local Programs:** *Med - Talk* 12:00 noon Wednesday, Margaret Karr, Sales Mgr. **Wattage:** 3000. **URL:** http://www.angelfire.com/biz/wiqq; http://www.tecifo.com/~wiqq.

16726 WNIX-AM - 1330
Delta Plaza Mall, Unit 39 Phone: (601)378-2617
Hwy. 1 S. Fax: (601)378-8341
Greenville, MS 38701
E-mail: wiqq@tecinfo.com

Format: Oldies. **Networks:** USA Radio. **Owner:** The River Broadcasting Co, Inc., at above address. **Founded:** 1939. **Formerly:** WJPR-AM (1979). **Operating Hours:** Continuous; 100% local. **ADI:** Greenwood-Greenville, MS. **Key Personnel:** James P. Karr, Jr., VP & GM; Francis Gallaher, Operations Mgr.; Margaret Karr, Sales Mgr.; Chuck Early, Program Dir.; Chuck Early, Promotions Dir. **Local Programs:** *Delta Farm Update*, Chuck Early; *Open Mike*, Chuck Early. **Wattage:** 1000 day; 500 night. **URL:** http://www.angelfire.com/biz/wiqq; http://www.tecinfo.com/~wiqq.

16727 WXVT-TV - 15
3015 E. Reed Rd. Phone: (601)334-1500
Greenville, MS 38703 Fax: (601)378-8122
Free: (800)489-9988

Format: Commercial TV. **Networks:** CBS. **Owner:** Greenville Television, Inc., at above address. **Founded:** 1980. **Operating Hours:** Continuous; 75% network, 25% local. **ADI:** Greenwood-Greenville, MS. **Key Personnel:** Stacy Case, News Dir.; Paul Serio, Contact; Nate Brown, Contact; David Jernigan, Sales Mgr.; Larry Harris, Contact. **Ad Rates:** $20-250 for 10 seconds; $28-350 for 15 seconds; $40-500 for 30 seconds; $80-1000 for 60 seconds.

GREENWOOD†, pop. 21,070.

NWC MS. Leflore Co. On Yazoo River, 52 mi. NE of Greenville. Extensive buying of cotton. Manufactures cottonseed products, radio testing instruments, pianos, indexing equipment, seat belts, farm implements, picture frames, fishing gear, medicines, trailers. Bottling works. Cotton plantations.

16728 Greenwood Commonwealth
329 Hwy. 82 W. Phone: (601)453-5312
PO Box 8050 Fax: (601)453-2908
Greenwood, MS 38930
Publication E-mail: commonwealth@microsped.com

General newspaper. **Founded:** 1896. **Freq:** Daily (eve.), Sunday (morn.). **Print Method:** Offset. **Cols./Page:** 6. **Col. Width:** 26 nonpareils. **Col. Depth:** 301 agate lines. **Key Personnel:** Tim Kalich, Editor and Publisher; Tom Miller, Managing Editor; Larry Alderman, Advertising Mgr. **Subscription Rates:** $108 individuals. **Remarks:** Accepts advertising.
Ad Rates: BW: $928.80 **Circ:** Mon.-Fri. ★**8,201**
4C: $1,178.80 Sun. ★**8,545**
PCI: $8.30

16729 Staplreview
Staplcotn
PO Box 547 Phone: (601)453-6231
Greenwood, MS 38935-0547 Fax: (601)453-6274

Magazine on cotton marketing, warehousing and financing. **Founded:** 1921. **Freq:** Quarterly. **Print Method:** Offset. **Trim Size:** 8 1/2 x 11. **Key Personnel:** Virginia White, Editor. **Remarks:** Advertising not accepted.
Circ: ‡4,500

16730 Century Communications
PO Box 1119 Phone: (601)453-3746
Greenwood, MS 38935-1119 Fax: (601)453-3084

Formerly: Century Cable TV. **Key Personnel:** Fred Holcombe, General Mgr.; Vicky Chathan, Office Mgr. **Cities Served:** Leflore County, MS.: subscribing households 12,146; 34 channels.

16731 WABG-AM - 960
PO Box 408 Phone: (601)453-7822
Greenwood, MS 38930 Fax: (601)455-3311

Format: Country; Talk. **Founded:** 1950. **Operating Hours:** 6 a.m.-1 a.m. **ADI:** Greenwood-Greenville, MS. **Key Personnel:** John Rogers, General Mgr., phone (601)332-0949, fax (601)335-7029; Betty Funderburk, Office Mgr. **Wattage:** 1000 day; 500 night. **Ad Rates:** $10-13.50 for 30 seconds; $12.50-16.50 for 60 seconds.

16732 WGRM-AM - 1240
1110 Wright St. Phone: (601)453-1240
Greenwood, MS 38930

Format: Adult Contemporary. **Networks:** NBC. **Owner:** Twelve Forty, Inc., PO Box 553, Greenwood, MS 38930. **Founded:** 1937. **Operating Hours:** 6 a.m.-10 p.m. **ADI:** Greenwood-Greenville, MS. **Key Personnel:** Clay Ewing, General Mgr.; Rose Ewing, Program Dir. **Wattage:** 1000.

16733 WGRM-FM - 93.9
1110 Wright St. Phone: (601)453-1240
Greenwood, MS 38930

Format: Adult Contemporary. **Networks:** NBC. **Owner:** Twelve-forty Inc., at above address. **Founded:** 1989. **Operating Hours:** Continuous. **ADI:** Greenwood-Greenville, MS. **Key Personnel:** Clay Ewing, General Mgr.; Rose Ewing, Program & Traffic Dir. **Wattage:** 25,000.

16734 WKXG-AM - 1540
Browning Rd. Phone: (601)453-2174
PO Box 1686 Fax: (601)455-5733
Greenwood, MS 38930

Format: Urban Contemporary; Blues; Gospel. **Networks:** American Urban Radio. **Owner:** Telesouth Communications, Inc., 6310 I-55 N, Jackson, MS 39211, (601)957-1700.

Founded: 1987. **Formerly:** WSWG-AM (1988). **Operating Hours:** 6 a.m.-10 p.m.; 10% network, 90% local. **ADI:** Greenwood-Greenville, MS. **Key Personnel:** Wes Sterling, General Mgr.; Milton Glass, Station Mgr.; Herman Anderson, Program Dir.; Rea Holmes, Office Mgr. **Wattage:** 1000. **Ad Rates:** $4-9 for 30 seconds; $6-11 for 60 seconds.

16735 WMAO-TV - 23
c/o WMPN-TV Phone: (601)982-6565
3825 Ridgewood Rd. Fax: (601)982-6746
Jackson, MS 39211

Format: Public TV. **Simulcasts:** WMPN-TV Jackson, MS. **Networks:** Public Broadcasting Service (PBS). **Owner:** Mississippi Authority for Educational TV, at above address. **Founded:** 1972. **Operating Hours:** 6:45 am-11:15 pm weekdays; noon-11:15 pm Sat.; noon-11 pm Sun. **ADI:** Greenwood-Greenville, MS. **Key Personnel:** A.J. Jaeger, Contact; Gayle Loeber, Program Dir.

16736 WYMX-FM - 99.1
Browning Rd. Phone: (601)453-2174
Greenwood, MS 38930 Fax: (601)455-5733

Format: Adult Contemporary. **Networks:** ABC. **Owner:** Telesouth Communications, Inc., 6310 I-55 N, Jackson, MS 39211, (601)957-1700. **Founded:** 1986. **Formerly:** WSWG-FM (1988). **Operating Hours:** Continuous; 10% network, 90% local. **ADI:** Greenwood-Greenville, MS. **Key Personnel:** Wes Sterling, General Mgr.; Wes Sterling, Sales Mgr.; Rea Holmes, Office Mgr.; Pat O'Bryan, Operations Dir. **Wattage:** 100,000. **Ad Rates:** $10-18 for 30 seconds; $12-20 for 60 seconds.

GRENADA

16737 Grenada Lake Herald
PO Box 907 Phone: (601)226-4321
Grenada, MS 38902-0907 Fax: (601)226-8310
Publication E-mail: grenada@teclink.edu

Local newspaper. **Founded:** 1976. **Freq:** Weekly (Wed.). **Cols./Page:** 6. **Col. Width:** 2 1/16 inches. **Col. Depth:** 21 1/2 inches. **Key Personnel:** Joe Lee, Editor and Publisher; Jay Lee, Advertising. **USPS:** 103-000. **Subscription Rates:** Free. **Remarks:** Accepts advertising.
Ad Rates: PCI: $1.50 **Circ:** 8,050

GULFPORT†, pop. 41,232.

S MS. Harrison Co. On Gulf of Mexico, 11 mi. W. of Biloxi. Resort. Manufactures lumber, cotton. Seafood canneries.

16738 The Entertainer
PO Box 3796 Phone: (601)832-9090
Gulfport, MS 39505 Fax: (601)832-9090

Entertainment guide (tabloid). **Founded:** 1976. **Freq:** Weekly (Thurs.). **Print Method:** Web offset. **Trim Size:** 11 x 17. **Cols./Page:** 6. **Col. Width:** 1 5/8 inches. **Col. Depth:** 16 inches. **Key Personnel:** Valerie M. Barta, Editor; Gordon G. Barta, Advertising Mgr. **Subscription Rates:** Free. **Remarks:** Accepts advertising.
Ad Rates: BW: $240 **Circ:** Non-paid 6,000
4C: $390
PCI: $5.50

16739 Cable One
3415 Hewes Ave. Phone: (228)864-1506
Gulfport, MS 39507 Fax: (228)867-6992

Formerly: Coast TV Cable Inc. **Key Personnel:** James C. Perry, General Mgr. **Cities Served:** Gulfport, Long Beach, and Pass Christian, MS.

16740 Post-Newsweek Cable
3415 Hewes Ave. Phone: (601)864-1506
Gulfport, MS 39507 Fax: (601)865-9476

Founded: 1958. **Cities Served:** Harrison County, MS.

16741 WGCM-FM - 102.3
PO Box 2639 Phone: (601)863-3522
Gulfport, MS 39501-2639 Fax: (601)863-7516

Format: Oldies. **Networks:** Satellite Music Network. **Founded:** 1969. **Operating Hours:** Continuous. **ADI:** Biloxi-Gulfport-Pascagoula, MS. **Key Personnel:** Leigh A. Moylan, General Mgr.; Darren Kies, Program Dir.; Kelli Bell, Contact. **Wattage:** 25,000 ERP.

16742 WLNF-FM - 95.3
PO Box 939 Phone: (228)867-9953
Gulfport, MS 39501 Fax: (228)868-0095
Free: (888)548-3953
E-mail: studio@live95fm.com

Format: Contemporary Hit Radio (CHR). **Owner:** Tralyn Broadcasting, Inc., at above address. **Founded:** July 1997. **Former name:** WLUN-FM (1997). **Operating Hours:** Continuous. **ADI:** Biloxi-Gulfport-Pascagoula, MS. **Key Personnel:** Darren Kies, General Mgr., dkies@datasync.com; Scott Sands, Office Mgr., sands@datasync.com; Bill Brock, General Sales Mgr.; Nickie Welch, Traffic. **Wattage:** 50,000. **Ad Rates:** $50 per unit. **URL:** http://www.live95fm.com.

16743 WQFX-FM - 96.7
Security Bldg., Penthouse Ste. Fax: (601)374-4967
PO Box 789
Gulfport, MS 39502

Format: Urban Contemporary. **Networks:** Mutual Broadcasting System. **Founded:** 1977. **ADI:** Biloxi-Gulfport-Pascagoula, MS. **Wattage:** 3000.

16744 WROA-AM - 1390
PO Box 2639 Phone: (601)832-5111
Gulfport, MS 39503 Fax: (601)832-7699

Format: Middle-of-the-Road (MOR); News; Sports. **Networks:** Mississippi. **Founded:** 1955. **Operating Hours:** Continuous. **ADI:** Biloxi-Gulfport-Pascagoula, MS. **Wattage:** 5000.

16745 WXXV-TV - 25
PO Box 2500 Phone: (601)832-2525
Gulfport, MS 39505 Fax: (601)832-4442

Format: Commercial TV. **Networks:** Fox. **Owner:** Prime Cities Broadcasters of MS, at above address. **Operating Hours:** 18 hours daily. **ADI:** Biloxi-Gulfport-Pascagoula, MS. **Key Personnel:** Bill Ritchie, General Mgr.; Leon Serruys, General Sales Mgr.; Cathy Collins, Program Dir.; David White, Promotions Dir.; Diane Necaise, Traffic Mgr. **Wattage:** 224,000 aural.

16746 WZKX-FM - 107.9
Box 2639 Phone: (601)832-5111
Gulfport, MS 39505 Fax: (601)832-7699

Format: Contemporary Hit Radio (CHR); News. **Founded:** 1964. **Operating Hours:** Continuous. **ADI:** Biloxi-Gulfport-Pascagoula, MS. **Wattage:** 100,000 ERP.

HATTIESBURG†, pop. 41,927.

SE MS. Forrest Co. 70 mi. N. of Gulfport. University of Southern Mississippi and William Carey College. Manufactures lumber, lumber products, explosives, chemicals, textiles, concrete pipes, paints, turpentine, metal products. Meat, poultry processing plants; gas and oil fields, oil refinery, sand and gravel pits; naval stores. Agriculture. Cotton, corn, truck products.

16747 The Advertiser News
103 N. 40th Ave. Phone: (601)264-4628
Hattiesburg, MS 39402 Fax: (601)268-7892

Local newspaper. **Founded:** July 15, 1982. **Freq:** Weekly (Wed.). **Print Method:** Offset. **Cols./Page:** 6. **Col. Width:** 2 1/16 inches. **Col. Depth:** 21 1/2 inches. **Key Personnel:** James E. Clinton, Publisher. **Subscription Rates:** $104 by mail.
Ad Rates: BW: $1,161 **Circ:** Paid 35,000
4C: $1,461
SAU: $6.75
PCI: $9.00

16748 Georgetown Review
Box 6309, Southern Sta.
Hattiesburg, MS 39406-6309
Publication E-mail: gr@georgetownreview.com

Journal covering fiction and poetry. **Founded:** 1992. **Freq:** Semiannual. **Trim Size:** 5 1/2 x 8 1/2. **Key Personnel:** Victoria Lancelotta, Fiction Editor; Marvyn Petrucci, Poetry Editor; Steven Conti, Managing Editor. **ISSN:** 1066-1506. **Subscription Rates:** $15 individuals; $8 single issue. **Remarks:** Accepts advertising. **URL:** http://www.georgetownreview.com.
Ad Rates: BW: $100 **Circ:** (Not Reported)

16749 Hattiesburg American
Gannett Co., Inc.
825 N. Main St. Phone: (601)582-4321
PO Box 1111 Fax: (601)583-8244
Hattiesburg, MS 39401
General newspaper. **Freq:** Daily (eve.), Sat. and Sun. (morn.). **Print Method:** Offset. **Trim Size:** 13 3/4 x 22 3/4. **Cols./Page:** 6. **Col. Width:** 2 1/16 inches. **Col. Depth:** 21 1/2 inches. **Key Personnel:** David Bailey, Editor; Bill Hunsberger, Publisher; Rick Chapman, Advertising Dir. **Subscription Rates:** $108; $132 out of area. **Remarks:** Accepts advertising.
Ad Rates: GLR: $1.62 **Circ:** Mon.-Sat. ★**24,044**
BW: $2,930.88 Sun. ★**28,442**
4C: $3,344.88
SAU: $22.72

16750 Mississippi Review
University of Southern Mississippi
Box 5144, Southern Sta.
Hattiesburg, MS 39406-5144

Literary magazine covering poetry, fiction and interviews. **Founded:** 1971. **Freq:** Semiannual. **Trim Size:** 5 1/2 x 8 3/4. **Key Personnel:** Frederick Barthelme, Editor; Rie Fortenberry, Managing Editor. **Subscription Rates:** $15 individuals; $8 single issue. **Remarks:** Accepts advertising.
Ad Rates: BW: $100 **Circ:** Combined 1,500,000

16751 Southern Quarterly
University of Southern Mississippi
PO Box 5078, Southern Sta. Phone: (601)266-4370
Hattiesburg, MS 39406-5078 Fax: (601)266-5800

Journal of literary essays, reviews, and art portfolios. **Subtitle:** A Journal of the Arts in the South. **Founded:** Oct. 1962. **Freq:** Quarterly. **Print Method:** Offset. **Trim Size:** 7 x 10. **Cols./Page:** 1. **Key Personnel:** Stephen F. Young, Editor, robert.young@usm.edu; Lola Norris, Editoral Asst., lola.norris@usm.edu. **ISSN:** 0038-4496. **Subscription Rates:** $18 individuals; $32 two years; $35 institutions. **Remarks:** Accepts advertising. **Alt. Formats:** Microform.
Ad Rates: BW: $100 **Circ:** ‡950

16752 USM Alumni News
The University of Southern Mississippi Alumni Association
Box 5013 Phone: (601)266-5013
Hattiesburg, MS 39406-5013 Fax: (601)266-4214
Publication E-mail: alumni@usm.edu

Member magazine of the University Alumni Association. **Founded:** July 1, 1949. **Freq:** Quarterly. **Print Method:** Offset. **Trim Size:** 8 1/2 x 11. **Cols./Page:** 3. **Col. Width:** 28 nonpareils. **Col. Depth:** 140 agate lines. **Key Personnel:** Raymond Reeves, Editor, raymond.reeves@usm.edu. **Subscription Rates:** Included in annual alumni dues. **Remarks:** Accepts advertising.
Ad Rates: BW: $900 **Circ:** ‡14,500
4C: $1,500

16753 Pinebelt Cable
2100 Lincoln Rd. Phone: (601)268-1188
Hattiesburg, MS 39402 Fax: (601)268-3956

Founded: 1954. **Formerly:** Cablesystem of Mississippi. **Cities Served:** Forrest County, Greene County, Jones County, Lamar County, Perry County, Lake Serene, Leakesville, Oak Grove, Petal, Purvis, Rawls Springs, Richton, and Sumrall, MS.

16754 WBKH-AM - 950
PO Box 15216 Phone: (601)582-9595
Hattiesburg, MS 39404-5216
E-mail: wbkh@juno.com

Format: Southern Gospel. **Owner:** Southern Air Communications, at above address. **Founded:** 1952. **Operating Hours:** 6 a.m.-8 p.m. **ADI:** Laurel-Hattiesburg, MS. **Key Personnel:** Freddie Kirkland. **Wattage:** 5000. **Ad Rates:** $5 for 30 seconds; $9 for 60 seconds.

16755 WDAM-TV - 7
Hwy. 11 North Phone: (601)544-4730
PO Box 16269 Fax: (601)584-9302
Hattiesburg, MS 39404-6269
Free: (800)844-0730

Format: Commercial TV. **Networks:** NBC. **Operating Hours:** 5:30 a.m.-12:30 a.m. weekdays; 6:30 a.m.-1:30 Saturday and Sunday. **ADI:** Laurel-Hattiesburg, MS. **Key Personnel:** Cliff Brown, General Mgr.

16756 WFOR-AM - 1400
2414 W. 7th Phone: (601)544-1400
Hattiesburg, MS 39401 Fax: (601)582-5481

Format: Southern Gospel. **Networks:** NBC. **Founded:** 1924. **Operating Hours:** Continuous; 95% network. **ADI:** Laurel-Hattiesburg, MS. **Key Personnel:** Jerri Lynn Campbell, General Mgr.; John Gatlin, Operations Mgr. **Wattage:** 1000. **Ad Rates:** $5 for 30 seconds; $8 for 60 seconds.

16757 WHER-FM - 103.7
2414 W. 7th St. Phone: (601)544-3232
Hattiesburg, MS 39401 Fax: (601)582-5481
E-mail: oldies@eagle103.com

Format: Oldies. **Networks:** NBC; Jones Satellite. **Founded:** 1966. **Operating Hours:** Continuous. **ADI:** Laurel-Hattiesburg, MS. **Key Personnel:** Jerri Lynn Campbell, General Mgr.; John Gatlin, Operations Mgr. **Wattage:** 100,000 ERP.

16758 WHLT-TV - 22
990 Hardy St. Phone: (601)545-2077
PO Box 232 Fax: (601)545-3589
Hattiesburg, MS 39403

Format: Commercial TV. **Networks:** CBS. **Owner:** Media General Broadcast Group, 333 E. Grace St., Richmond, VA 23219. **Founded:** 1987. **Operating Hours:** Continuous. **ADI:** Laurel-Hattiesburg, MS. **Key Personnel:** Larry Blackerby, General Mgr., phone (610)572-6311. **Local Programs:** *Hannah Hopkins Show*; *Temple Baptist Church.*

16759 WJMG-FM - 92.1
1204 Gravel Line St. Phone: (601)544-1941
Hattiesburg, MS 39401 Fax: (601)544-1947

Format: Urban Contemporary; Adult Contemporary. **Networks:** American Urban Radio. **Founded:** 1982. **Operating Hours:** Continuous. **ADI:** Laurel-Hattiesburg, MS. **Key Personnel:** Vernon C. Floyd, CEO/GM and CE. **Wattage:** 6,000 ERP.

16760 WKNZ-FM - 107.1
PO Box 15216 Phone: (601)264-0443
Hattiesburg, MS 39404-5216 Fax: (601)733-2787
Free: (800)827-7882

Format: Country. **Networks:** Unistar; AP. **Founded:** 1978. **Operating Hours:** Continuous. **ADI:** Laurel-Hattiesburg, MS. **Key Personnel:** Bob Kidd, General Mgr.; Larry Cockrell, Station Mgr. **Wattage:** 6000. **Ad Rates:** $11-16 per unit.

16761 WMFM-FM - 106.3
Box 16928 Phone: (601)545-1063
Hattiesburg, MS 39404-6928 Fax: (601)583-8817
E-mail: lite106@aol.com

Format: Adult Contemporary. **Networks:** CNN Radio. **Founded:** 1986. **Operating Hours:** Continuous. **ADI:** Laurel-Hattiesburg, MS. **Key Personnel:** Bill Hickman, Contact; Yancey Sanford, Operations Mgr. **Local Programs:** *Forum Public Affairs*, Bill Hickman, Mailing contact. **Wattage:** 3000 ERP. **Ad Rates:** $8-12 for 30 seconds; $10-13 for 60 seconds.

16762 WORV-AM - 1580
1204 Graveline Phone: (601)544-1941
Hattiesburg, MS 39401 Fax: (601)544-1947

Format: Urban Contemporary; Gospel; Blues. **Networks:** American Urban Radio; American Urban Radio. **Founded:** 1969. **Operating Hours:** Sunrise-sunset. **ADI:** Laurel-Hattiesburg, MS. **Key Personnel:** Vernon Floyd, General Mgr. **Wattage:** 1000.

16763 WUSM-FM - 88.5
Box 10045, Southern Sta. Phone: (601)266-4287
Hattiesburg, MS 39406-0045 Fax: (601)266-4288

Format: Jazz; Blues; Classical; Alternative/New Music/Progressive. **Networks:** Longhorn Radio. **Founded:** 1973. **Formerly**: WMSU-FM (1988). **Operating Hours:** 6 a.m.-2 a.m.; 5% network, 95% local. **ADI:** Laurel-Hattiesburg, MS. **Key Personnel:** Henry Lena, General Mgr.; Jeff Rassier, Contact; LaSandra Anderson, Program Dir.; Mik Davis, Program Dir.; Elliot Crawford, Program Supervisor. **Local Programs:** *Coelta Gas*, Jeff Rassier; *Small World*, Elliott Crawford. **Wattage:** 3000.

HAZLEHURST†, pop. 4,437.

SW MS. Copiah Co. 32 mi. S. of Jackson. Manufactures mops, brooms, metal culverts, electrical windings. Lumber mills; poultry process hatcheries. Diversified farming. Cattle.

16764 Copiah County Courier
Courier
103 S. Ragsdale St. Phone: (601)894-3141
PO Box 351 Fax: (601)894-3144
Hazlehurst, MS 39083
Community newspaper. **Founded:** Mar. 1884. **Freq:** Weekly (Wed.). **Print Method:** Offset. **Cols./Page:** 6. **Col. Width:** 13 picas. **Col. Depth:** 21 1/2 inches. **Key Personnel:** James W. Lambert, Jr., Editor and Publisher; Joe Coates, Advertising Dir. **Subscription Rates:** $14 individuals; $16 out of area; $20 out of state. **Remarks:** Accepts advertising. **Merged with:** Courier Plus.
Ad Rates: BW: $922.35 **Circ:** Paid ‡4,720
4C: $1,162.35 Free ‡1,400
SAU: $2.35
PCI: $7.15

HOLLY SPRINGS†, pop. 7,285.

N MS. Marshall Co. 42 mi. SE of Memphis, TN. Rust College. Mississippi Industrial College. Manufacturing brick, tile, piano, small appliances, windows, metal fabrication, foam equipment, plastics, ornamental metal. Diversified farming. Cotton, cattle, soybeans, dairying. Cotton ginning.

16765 Pigeon Roost News
The South Reporter
PO Box 278 Phone: (601)252-4261
Holly Springs, MS 38635 Fax: (601)252-3388
Free: (800)468-3820

Community newspaper. **Founded:** 1981. **Freq:** Weekly. **Print Method:** Offset. **Trim Size:** 13 x 21. **Cols./Page:** 5. **Col. Width:** 12 picas. **Col. Depth:** 13 inches. **Key Personnel:** Walter Webb, Publisher. **Subscription Rates:** Free; $15. **Remarks:** Accepts advertising.
Ad Rates: GLR: $.25 **Circ:** Free 6,500
BW: $195
SAU: $4.20
PCI: $4.20

16766 The South Reporter
PO Box 278 Phone: (601)252-4261
Holly Springs, MS 38635 Fax: (601)252-3388
Free: (800)468-3820

Newspaper. **Founded:** 1865. **Freq:** Weekly (Thurs.). **Print Method:** Offset. **Cols./Page:** 6. **Col. Width:** 24 nonpareils. **Col. Depth:** 294 agate lines. **Key Personnel:** Walter W. Webb, Editor and Publisher; Edwina Carpenter, Advertising Mgr. **USPS:** 504-320. **Subscription Rates:** $17. **Remarks:** Accepts advertising. **Available Online.**
Ad Rates: GLR: $.36 **Circ:** ‡6,200
BW: $497.70
4C: $180.00
SAU: $5.15
PCI: $5.15

16767 WKRA-AM - 1110
1400 HW 4 East-C Phone: (601)252-1110
PO Box 398 Fax: (601)252-2739
Holly Springs, MS 38635

Format: Gospel; Southern Gospel. **Owner:** Billy Autry, at above address. **Founded:** 1966. **Operating Hours:** Sunrise-sunset. **ADI:** Memphis, TN. **Key Personnel:** Ray Von Autry, Contact; Curtis Jenkins, Music Dir. **Wattage:** 1000. **Ad Rates:** $10 for 30 seconds; $12 for 60 seconds. Combined advertising rates available with WKRA-FM.

16768 WKRA-FM -.92.7
Hwy. 4 East-C Phone: (601)252-6692
PO Box 398 Fax: (601)252-2739
Holly Springs, MS 38635

Format: Urban Contemporary; Oldies; Gospel. **Networks:** ABC. **Owner:** Billy R Autry, at above address, (601)252-1110, Fax: (601)252-2739. **Founded:** 1976. **Operating Hours:** Continuous. **ADI:** Memphis, TN. **Key Personnel:** Rick Williams, Operations Mgr., phone (601)252-2739; Ray V. Autry, Sales and General Mgr., phone (601)252-2739. **Wattage:** 3000. **Ad Rates:** $12 for 30 seconds; $15 for 60 seconds. Combined advertising rates available with WKRA-AM.

16769 WURC-FM - 88.1
Rust College Phone: (601)252-5881
150 E. Rust Ave. Fax: (601)252-8869
Holly Springs, MS 38635

Format: Talk; Jazz; Religious; Blues. **Networks:** American Urban Radio; National Public Radio (NPR). **Owner:** Rust College Inc., 150 E. Rust Ave., Holly Springs, MS 38635, (601)252-8000, Fax: (601)252-6107. **Founded:** 1988. **Formerly**: WRCR-FM. **Operating Hours:** 18 hours daily; 20% network, 80% local. **Key Personnel:** Wayne Fiddis, Program Mgr.; Tymara Dunlap, News Dir.; Sharron Goodman, Contact; Sylvester Oliver, Station Mgr. **Local Programs:** *Rust Report*, Paula Clarke, (601)252-8000. **Wattage:** 3000.

HOUSTON†, pop. 3,747.

NW MS. Chickasaw Co. 10 mi. W. of Buena Vista. Dairying.

16770 The Times Post
219 N. Jackson St. Phone: (601)456-3771
PO Box 629 Fax: (601)456-3772
Houston, MS 38851-2214
Community newspaper. **Founded:** 1911. **Freq:** Weekly (Wed.). **Print Method:** Offset. **Trim Size:** 13 x 21 1/2. **Cols./Page:** 6. **Col. Width:** 12 3/10 picas. **Col. Depth:** 21 1/2 inches. **Key Personnel:** Kenny Hoblitzell, Editor and Publisher. **Subscription Rates:** $18; $25 out of area. **Remarks:** Accepts advertising. **Formerly**: Houston Times Post.
Ad Rates: GLR: $.32 **Circ:** 4,500
BW: $593.40
4C: $893.40
SAU: $4.90

16771 WCPC-AM - 940
1189 N. Jackson St. Phone: (601)456-3071
Houston, MS 38851 Fax: (601)456-3072

Format: News; Country; Sports; Gospel; Eclectic; Religious. **Networks:** USA Radio. **Founded:** 1955. **Operating Hours:** 5 a.m.-10 p.m.; 10% network, 90% local. **Key Personnel:** Melanie Munlin, Music Dir.; Robin H. Mathis, Mgr./News Dir.; Olen Booth, Chief Engineer; Chris Hester, Public Service Director; Ricky J. Huffman, Operations Mgr.; Wayne Parks, Sports Dir. **Local Programs:** *Sparta Opry*, Robin H. Mathis. **Wattage:** 50,000. **Ad Rates:** $16.80-18.40 for 30 seconds; $21-23 for 60 seconds.

INDIANOLA†, pop. 8,221.

NW MS. Sunflower Co. 85 mi. N. of Jackson. Manufactures cottonseed products, catfish feed, dogfood, power mowers, wheelbarrows, tricycles, wagons. Agriculture. Cotton, cattle, sheep, hogs, rice, soybeans. Farm raised catfish.

16772 Enterprise-Tocsin
Indianola Publishing Co.
Box 650 Phone: (601)887-2222
Indianola, MS 38751 Fax: (601)887-2999

Newspaper. **Founded:** 1886. **Freq:** Weekly (Thurs.). **Print Method:** Offset. **Cols./Page:** 6. **Col. Width:** 24 nonpareils. **Col. Depth:** 301 agate lines. **Key Personnel:** Jim Abbott, Editor and Publisher. **Subscription Rates:** $9.50.

16773 WNLA-AM - 1380
PO Box 667 Phone: (601)887-1380
Indianola, MS 38751 Fax: (601)887-1396

Format: Southern Gospel. **Networks:** ABC. **Owner:** Shamrock Broadcasting, Inc., at above address. **Founded:** 1954. **Operating Hours:** 6 a.m.-6 p.m. **Key Personnel:** Erin Ely, General Mgr.; Gerry Brophy, Sales Mgr. **Wattage:** 500. **Ad Rates:** $3.75-7.50 for 30 seconds; $5-10 for 60 seconds.

16774 WNLA-FM - 105.5
PO Box 667 Phone: (601)887-1380
Indianola, MS 38751 Fax: (601)887-1396

Format: Adult Contemporary. **Networks:** ABC. **Owner:** Shamrock Broadcasting, Inc., at above address. **Founded:** 1954. **Operating Hours:** Continuous. **Key Personnel:** Erin Ely, General Mgr.; Gerry Brophy, Sales Mgr. **Wattage:** 4400. **Ad Rates:** $3.75-7.50 for 30 seconds; $5-10 for 60 seconds.

ITTA BENA

16775 WVSD-FM - 91.7
14000 Hwy. 82, Box 7221 Phone: (601)254-3612
Itta Bena, MS 38941 Fax: (601)254-3630

Format: Eclectic. **Owner:** Mississippi Valley State University, 14000 Hwy. 82 W., Itta Bena, MS 38941. **Operating Hours:** Continuous Mon.-Sat. **Key Personnel:** Larz G. Roberts, General Mgr./Program Dir., roberts@tecinfo.com; Sam Brown, Operations Mgr. **Local Programs:** *Rhythm & Grooves*, Larz Roberts; *Gospel Express*, Debra Harmon; *Blues/Mystic Vibes*, Eric Cole. **Wattage:** 3,000. **Ad Rates:** Noncommercial; underwriting available.

IUKA†, pop. 2,846.

NE MS. Tishomingo Co. 115 mi. E. of Memphis, TN. Resort, mineral springs. Agriculture. Soybeans, corn, hay.

16776 Tishomingo County News
County News
PO Box 70 Phone: (601)423-2211
Iuka, MS 38852 Fax: (601)423-2214

Community newspaper. **Founded:** 1967. **Freq:** Weekly (Thurs.). **Print Method:** Offset. **Cols./Page:** 6. **Col. Width:** 21 nonpareils. **Col. Depth:** 294 agate lines. **Key Personnel:** John H. Biggs, Editor and Publisher. **Subscription Rates:** $12. **Remarks:** Accepts advertising.
Ad Rates: SAU: $3.50 **Circ:** ‡6,000

16777 WFXO-FM - 104.9
311 Eastport St. Phone: (601)423-6059
Iuka, MS 38852 Fax: (601)423-6059

Format: Country. **Owner:** Bill McLain Broadcasting, at above address. **Founded:** 1970. **Formerly**: WTIB-FM (1990). **Operating Hours:** Continuous. **Key Personnel:** Billy McLain, General Mgr.; Tim Kevin, Program Dir. **Wattage:** 50,000. **Ad Rates:** Advertising accepted; rates available upon request.

16778 WVOM-AM - 1270
311 Eastport St. Phone: (601)423-6059
Iuka, MS 38852 Fax: (601)423-6059

Format: Contemporary Country. **Owner:** Bill McLain Broadcasting, at above address. **Founded:** 1960. **Operating Hours:** Sunrise-sunset. **Key Personnel:** Billy McLain, General Mgr.; Steve Foster, Program Dir. **Wattage:** 1000. **Ad Rates:** Advertising accepted; rates available upon request.

JACKSON†, pop. 208,810.

SWC MS. Hinds Co. On Pearl River, 42 mi. E. of Vicksburg. The State Capital. Belhaven College, Millsaps College, Mississippi College, University of Mississippi Dental and Medical School, University of Mississippi at Jackson, University of Southern Mississippi at Jackson, Jackson State University, Tougaloo College. Important cottonseed oil manufacturing and distributing center, also oil and natural gas center. Fertilizer and bottling works; meat packing plants; lumber mill. Manufactures valves, fittings, electrical switch gear, transformers, heating and plumbing materials, crates and boxes, textiles, furniture, flourescent lights, cooking utensils, bedding, steel fabrication, feed, auto parts, cement blocks, tile, hydraulic aircraft, missile parts.

16779 The Baptist Record
Mississippi Baptist Convention
POB 530
Jackson, MS 39205
Publisher E-mail: 70420.37@compuserve.com

Baptist magazine (tabloid). **Subtitle:** Journal of Mississippi Baptist Convention. **Founded:** 1877. **Freq:** Weekly (Thurs.). **Print Method:** Letterpress. **Trim Size:** 11 1/2 x 14 1/2. **Cols./Page:** 5. **Col. Width:** 12 picas. **Col. Depth:** 13 inches. **Key Personnel:** William H. Perkins, Editor; Carl White, Assoc. Editor; Florence Larrimore, Editorial Assoc.; Debbie Sills, Adv. Coord.; Joylin Davis, Layout/Design; Renee Walley, Circulation Mgr.; Betty Anne Bailey, Bookkeeper. **ISSN:** 0005-5778. **Subscription Rates:** $8.35 individuals. **Remarks:** Accepts advertising.
Ad Rates: BW: $1,989 **Circ:** Paid ‡108,000
PCI: $34 Controlled ‡500

16780 The Clarion Ledger
Gannett Co., Inc.
311 E. Pearl St. Phone: (601)961-7000
PO Box 40 Fax: (601)961-7047
Jackson, MS 39205
General newspaper. **Founded:** 1954. **Freq:** Daily (eve.). **Print Method:** Offset. **Cols./Page:** 6. **Col. Width:** 25 nonpareils. **Col. Depth:** 294 agate lines. **Key Personnel:** John Johnson, Editor; Robert E. Robbins, Publisher; William M. Joyner, Jr., Advertising Mgr. **Subscription Rates:** $132. **Remarks:** Accepts advertising. **URL:** http://www.gannett.com. **Merged with:** Jackson Daily News. **Feature Editors:** Joe Bonneg, *Financial/Business, Real Estate, Rural Development, Saturday*; Rick Cleveland, *Sports*; David Hampton, *Aviation, Editorials*; Don Hoffman, *Environmental*; Beth Holland, *City, Metro, News*; Orly Hood, *Book, Drama, Entertainment, Family, Fashion, Features, Food, Garden/Home, Lifestyle, Movie, Music, Society, TV & Radio, Travel, Women's*; Jana John, *Religion*; Shawn McIntosh, *Political*; Donna Richter, *Sunday*; Debbie Skipper, *Medical*; Chris Todd, *Photo*; Christine Uthoff, *Education*.
Ad Rates: SAU: $53.64 **Circ:** Mon.-Sat. ★**105,382**
Sun. ★**125,847**

16781 Jackson Advocate
Natchez Democrate Inc.
300 N. Fanisha Phone: (601)948-4122
PO Box 3708 Fax: (601)948-4125
Jackson, MS 39207-3708
Black community newspaper. **Founded:** 1937. **Freq:** Weekly. **Print Method:** Offset. **Cols./Page:** 6. **Col. Width:** 2 1/8 inches. **Col. Depth:** 21 inches. **Key Personnel:** Charles W. Tisdale, Editor and Publisher; Alice Thomas, Advertising Mgr. **Subscription Rates:** $20. **Remarks:** Accepts advertising.
Ad Rates: BW: $1,801.80 **Circ:** Paid ‡20,000
4C: $2,001.80 Free ‡3,000
SAU: $14.30
PCI: $14.30

16782 The Journal of Mississippi History
Mississippi Historical Society
Dept. of Archives and History Phone: (601)359-6850
Box 571 Fax: (601)359-6975
Jackson, MS 39205
Scholarly journal covering the history of the lower Mississippi Valley Region and of the South in general. **Subtitle:** Journal of Mississippi History. **Founded:** 1939. **Freq:** Quarterly. **Print Method:** Offset. **Trim Size:** 6 x 9. **Cols./Page:** 1. **Col. Width:** 60 nonpareils. **Col. Depth:** 95 agate lines. **Key Personnel:** Chrissy Wilson, Editor, phone (359)-6857. **ISSN:** 0022-2771. **Subscription Rates:** $15. **Remarks:** Accepts advertising. **Alt. Formats:** Microform.
Ad Rates: BW: $150 **Circ:** ‡1,800

16783 Journal of the Mississippi State Medical Association
Mississippi State Medical Association
735 Riverside Dr. Phone: (601)354-5433
Jackson, MS 39202 Fax: (601)352-4834

Medical magazine, including scientific papers; Association news and policy reports; and national, state, and local medical news. **Founded:** 1960. **Freq:** Monthly. **Print Method:** Offset. **Trim Size:** 8 1/2 x 11. **Cols./Page:** 2. **Col. Width:** 40 nonpareils. **Col. Depth:** 140 agate lines. **Key Personnel:** Karen Evers, Managing Editor. **ISSN:** 0026-6393. **Subscription Rates:** $35. **Remarks:** Accepts advertising. **URL:** http://www.msmed.org.
Ad Rates: BW: $225 **Circ:** Paid ‡3,300
4C: $550 Non-paid ‡100

16784 Metro Business Review
Box 12727 Phone: (601)956-0756
Jackson, MS 39236-2727 Fax: (601)956-4047
Free: (888)529-2229

Professional journal covering local business. **Founded:** Jan. 1988. **Freq:** Monthly. **Print Method:** Web offset. **Cols./Page:** 4. **Col. Width:** 14 picas. **Col. Depth:** 78 picas. **Key Personnel:** Jack Criss, Publisher; Angelique Gregory, Marketing Dir.; Bridget L. White, Managing Editor. **Remarks:** Accepts advertising. **Former name:** Jackson Business Journal.
Ad Rates: BW: $950 **Circ:** Combined 8,600
4C: $1,620

16785 The Mississippi Banker
Mississippi Bankers Association
640 N. State St. Phone: (601)948-6366
PO Box 37 Fax: (601)355-6461
Jackson, MS 39205
Magazine mailed to all banks in Mississippi, including bank directors and individual bank personnel. **Founded:** 1914. **Freq:** Monthly. **Print Method:** Offset. **Trim Size:** 8 1/2 x 11. **Cols./Page:** 3. **Col. Width:** 26 nonpareils. **Col. Depth:** 139 agate lines. **Key Personnel:** Kristen Phillips, Editor. **Subscription Rates:** $25 individuals. **Remarks:** Accepts advertising.
Ad Rates: BW: $350 **Circ:** ‡1,300
4C: $725

16786 Mississippi Business Journal
Venture Publications, Inc.
5120 Galaxie Dr. Phone: (601)364-1000
Jackson, MS 39206 Fax: (601)364-1007
Publication E-mail: mbj@www.ms.busness.com

Magazine offering community business news. **Founded:** 1979. **Freq:** Weekly (Mon.). **Print Method:** Offset. **Trim Size:** 11 x 13 3/4. **Cols./Page:** 4. **Col. Width:** 14 picas. **Key Personnel:** Joe D. Jones, Publisher; Buddy Bynum, Editor. **ISSN:** 0195-0002. **Subscription Rates:** $45. **Remarks:** Accepts advertising. **URL:** http://www.msbusiness.com.
Ad Rates: BW: $1,144 **Circ:** Paid ‡8,620
4C: $1,594 Non-paid ‡2,460

16787 The Mississippi Educator
Mississippi Association of Educators
775 N. State St. Phone: (601)354-4463
Jackson, MS 39202-3086 Fax: (601)352-7054

Education magazine (tabloid). **Founded:** Sept. 1976. **Freq:** 5/year. **Print Method:** Offset. **Trim Size:** 9 3/4 x 8 1/4. **Cols./Page:** 4. **Col. Width:** 14 picas. **Col. Depth:** 140 agate lines. **Key Personnel:** Kay Joslin Walling, Editor/Administration, kjwalling@aol.com. **Subscription Rates:** $8.50. **Remarks:** Accepts advertising.
Ad Rates: BW: $500 **Circ:** ‡13,000
4C: $750

16788 Mississippi Farm Bureau News
Mississippi Farm Bureau Federation
6310 Interstate 55 North
PO Box 1972
Jackson, MS 39215

Farm news. **Founded:** 1922. **Freq:** Bimonthly. **Print Method:** Offset. **Cols./Page:** 4. **Col. Width:** 28 nonpareils. **Col. Depth:** 197 agate lines. **Key Personnel:** Glynda Phillips, Editor. **Subscription Rates:** $2. **Remarks:** Accepts advertising.
Ad Rates: BW: $1,080 **Circ:** ‡180,000
4C: $1,230
PCI: $20

16789 Mississippi Geology
Department of Environmental Quality
Office of Geology, Box 20307 Phone: (601)961-5500
Jackson, MS 39289 Fax: (601)961-5521

Scholarly journal covering geology, paleontology, and mineral resources of Mississippi. **Founded:** Sept. 1980. **Freq:** Quarterly. **Print Method:** Offset. **Trim Size:** 8 1/2 x 11. **Key Personnel:** Michael B. E. Bograd, Editor, phone (601)961-5528, Michael_Bograd@deq.state.ms.us; David T. Dockery, Editor, phone (601)354-6328, fax (601)354-7151. **ISSN:** 0275-8555. **Subscription Rates:** Free to qualified subscribers. **Remarks:** Advertising not accepted.
Circ: Non-paid 1,000

16790 Mississippi Legionnaire
The American Legion Mississippi Dept.
PO Box 688 Phone: (601)352-4986
Jackson, MS 39205 Fax: (601)352-7181

American Legion veterans newspaper. **Founded:** 1920. **Freq:** Bimonthly. **Print Method:** Offset. **Cols./Page:** 5. **Col. Width:** 22 nonpareils. **Col. Depth:** 280 agate lines. **Key Personnel:** James Herring, Editor. **Subscription Rates:** $2. **Remarks:** Accepts advertising.
Ad Rates: SAU: $6.95 **Circ:** 26,000

16791 Mississippi Libraries
Mississippi Library Association
PO Box 20448 Phone: (601)266-4249
Jackson, MS 39289-1448 Fax: (601)266-6033

Journal on libraries. **Founded:** 1937. **Freq:** Quarterly. **Print Method:** Offset. **Trim Size:** 8 1/2 x 11. **Cols./Page:** 3. **Col. Width:** 27 nonpareils. **Col. Depth:** 140 agate lines. **Key Personnel:** David King, Advertising Mgr., phone (601)266-4248; Sarah P. Armstrong, Editor, phone (601)375-8304, armstrong@ocean.st.usm.edu; David Richards, Assistant Editor. **ISSN:** 0194-388X. **Subscription Rates:** $16; $24 other countries. **Remarks:** Accepts advertising.
Ad Rates: BW: $175 **Circ:** ‡1,200

16792 Mississippi Magazine
Downhome Publications, Inc.
Box 16445 Phone: (601)982-8418
Jackson, MS 39236 Fax: (601)982-8418

Mississippi homes, history, entertaining and lifestyles. **Founded:** Sept. 1982. **Freq:** Bimonthly. **Print Method:** Web offset. **Trim Size:** 8 1/8 x 10 7/8. **Cols./Page:** 3. **Col. Width:** 27 nonpareils. **Col. Depth:** 140 agate lines. **Key Personnel:** Jane Alexander, Editor; Richard B. Roper, Publisher. **ISSN:** 0747-1602. **Subscription Rates:** $18 individuals; $3.50 single issue. **Remarks:** Accepts advertising.
Ad Rates: BW: $1,465 **Circ:** Paid ‡34,000
4C: $2,055 Non-paid ‡500

16793 Mississippi Municipalities
Mississippi Municipal Association
600 East Amite St., Ste. 104 Phone: (601)353-5854
Jackson, MS 39201 Fax: (601)353-0435
Free: (800)325-7641
Publisher E-mail: jeanie@mmaonline.com

Trade magazine covering municipal issues in Mississippi and the U.S. **Founded:** 1943. **Freq:** Bimonthly. **Print Method:** Sheetfed offset. **Trim Size:** 8 3/16 x 10 9/16. **Cols./Page:** 3. **Col. Width:** 2 1/4 inches. **Key Personnel:** Hollidae M. Robinson, Editor, hollidae@mmaonline.com; Clair O. Seward, Advertising Mgr. **Subscription Rates:** $16 individuals; $2 single issue. **Remarks:** Accepts advertising. **URL:** http://www.mmaonline.com.
Ad Rates: BW: $350 **Circ:** (Not Reported)
4C: $600

16794 Mississippi Pharmacist
Mississippi Pharmacists Association
341 Edgewood Terrace Dr. Phone: (601)981-0416
Jackson, MS 39206-6299 Fax: (601)981-0451
Free: (800)898-0416
Publication E-mail: misspharm@aol.com

Pharmacy magazine. **Founded:** 1975. **Freq:** Quarterly. **Print Method:** Offset. **Trim Size:** 8 1/2 x 11. **Cols./Page:** 3. **Key Personnel:** S. E. Dalton, Editor; Emily Myers, Managing Editor. **ISSN:** 0161-3189. **Subscription Rates:** $12 individuals. **Remarks:** Accepts advertising.
Ad Rates: BW: $330 **Circ:** 1,800
4C: $930

16795 Mississippi Today
Catholic Diocese of Jackson
237 E. Amite Phone: (601)969-1880
PO Box 2130 Fax: (601)960-8455
Jackson, MS 39201-2405
Catholic weekly newspaper. **Founded:** 1954. **Freq:** Weekly (Fri.) (Sept.-May). **Print Method:** Offset. **Trim Size:** 10 x 13. **Cols./Page:** 6. **Col. Width:** 18 nonpareils. **Col. Depth:** 182 agate lines. **Key Personnel:** Janna P. Avalon, Editor; Bishop William R. Houck, Publisher. **ISSN:** 0746-2247. **Subscription Rates:** $14; $15 out of state; $17 other countries. **Remarks:** Accepts advertising.
Ad Rates: GLR: $.75 **Circ:** 13,500
BW: $1,000
4C: $300
PCI: $10.50

16796 Mississippi United Methodist Advocate
Mississippi Conference of the United Methodist Church
321 Mississippi St. Phone: (601)354-0515
PO Box 1093 Fax: (601)948-5982
Jackson, MS 39201-1002
Publication E-mail: advocate@mississippi-umc.org

United Methodist newspaper. **Founded:** 1947. **Freq:** 26/year. **Print Method:** Offset. **Cols./Page:** 4. **Col. Width:** 29 nonpareils. **Col. Depth:** 196 agate lines. **Key Personnel:** Woody Woodrick, Editor; Dr. Mike Stanton-Rich, Dir. of Communications. **USPS:** 354-360. **Subscription Rates:** $11. **Remarks:** Accepts advertising.
Ad Rates: BW: $400 **Circ:** 13,000

16797 Northside Sun
Sunland Publishing Co.
PO Box 16709 Phone: (601)957-1122
Jackson, MS 39236 Fax: (601)957-1533

Newspaper. **Founded:** 1967. **Freq:** Weekly (Thurs.). **Print Method:** Offset. **Cols./Page:** 6. **Col. Width:** 24 nonpareils. **Col. Depth:** 298 agate lines. **Key Personnel:** Jimmy Sweat, Editor; Rebecca Simmons, Publisher. **Subscription Rates:** $16. **Remarks:** Accepts advertising.
Ad Rates: SAU: $7.25 **Circ:** Paid ‡8,430
Free ‡595

16798 TODAY in Mississippi
Electric Power Association of Mississippi, Inc.
2805 Greenway Dr. Phone: (601)922-2341
PO Box 7897 Fax: (601)922-9869
Jackson, MS 39204-3306
Free: (800)933-7897
Publication E-mail: today@epaofms.com

Statewide Newspaper covering political, economic, and legislative rura electrification matters statewide for EPA member-owners. **Founded:** Jan. 1, 1948. **Freq:** Monthly. **Print Method:** Offset. **Trim Size:** 13 7/8 x 11 1/8. **Cols./Page:** 4. **Col. Width:** 14 picas. **Col. Depth:** 78 picas. **Key Personnel:** Debbie Stringer, Editor; Joe Fannin, Advertising Mgr., jfannin@tsixroads.com. **ISSN:** 1052-2433. **Subscription Rates:** $6 individuals. **Remarks:** Accepts advertising. **Formerly:** Mississippi EPA News (1990).
Ad Rates: GLR: $3.21 **Circ:** Paid ‡375,400
BW: $2,201.16 Non-paid ‡170
4C: $2,776.16

16799 Branch Cable Inc.
125 S. Congress St., Ste. 1100 Phone: (601)355-1522
Jackson, MS 39201 Fax: (601)353-0950

Owner: Branch Cable Inc., at above address. **Key Personnel:** James H. Creekmore, General Mgr. **Cities Served:** Bude, Isola, Louise, New Augusta, and New Hebron, MS.

16800 Capitol Cablevision
415 Cedars of Lebanon Rd. Phone: (601)982-0922
Box 9426 Fax: (601)982-9532
Jackson, MS 39286

Founded: 1972. **Key Personnel:** Steve McMahon, President, phone (601)982-1187; Elmo Roebuck, Contact; Bruce Corkern, Contact; Frances Smith, Contact; Paul Hardin, Contact; Rita Anderson, Contact. **Cities Served:** Bolton, Cleary Heights, Clinton, Edwards, Florence, Jackson, Madison, Pearl River Valley Water Dist., Raymond, Richland, Ridgeland, MS; Hinds, Madison, and Rankin counties.: subscribing households 75,000; 42 channels; 1 community access channel; 60 hours per week community access programming.

16801 ParCable Inc.
Box 260 Phone: (601)354-5300
Jackson, MS 39205 Fax: (601)354-4609

Key Personnel: Rea S. Hederman, President; Glen Dowe, General Mgr. **Cities Served:** Kentucky, Tennessee: subscribing households 25,000; 36 channels; 1 community access channel.

16802 WAPT-TV - 16
Box 10297 Phone: (601)922-1607
Jackson, MS 39289 Fax: (601)922-1663
E-mail: wapt@misnet.com

Format: Commercial TV. **Networks:** ABC. **Owner:** Hearst-Argyle Television, 888 7th Ave., 8th Fl., New York, NY 10019, (212)765-8135, Fax: (212)887-6875. **Founded:** 1970. **Operating Hours:** Continuous; 50% network, 50% local. **ADI:** Jackson, MS. **Key Personnel:** Stuart Kellogg, VP/GM; Lynn Bullock, Production Mgr.; Ron Romines, General Sales Mgr.; Tom BonDurant, Chief Engineer; Stephen Thompson, Controller; Sam Moore, News Dir.; Rick Whitlow, Sports Dir.; Susan Acklen, Promotions Mgr.; Teresia Gray, Community Affairs Dir. **Wattage:** 4,670,000. **URL:** http://www.wapt.com.

16803 WDBD-TV - 40
7440 Channel 16 Way Phone: (601)922-1234
PO Box 10888 Fax: (601)922-6752
Jackson, MS 39289

Format: Commercial TV. **Networks:** Fox. **Owner:** D & K Broadcast Properties L.P., 7200 Wisconsin Ave., No. 310, Bethesda, MD 20814, (301)654-0700. **Founded:** 1984. **Operating Hours:** Continuous; 14% network, 86% local. **ADI:** Jackson, MS. **Key Personnel:** Al Tanksley, General Mgr.; Melinda Downey, Program Dir.; John Cochran, Promotions Dir.; Mark Maxwell, Contact; Johnny Lewis, Contact. **Ad Rates:** $20-400 per unit.

16804 WIIN-AM - 780
265 Highpoint Dr. Phone: (601)956-0102
Jackson, MS 39213 Fax: (601)978-3980

Format: Classic Rock. **Networks:** Winners News (WNN). **Owner:** Eddie Holladay, at above address. **Operating Hours:** Daylight hours; 100% network. **ADI:** Jackson, MS. **Key Personnel:** Dick O'Neil, General Manager/General Sales Manager; Roger Allen, Creative Srvs. Dir. **Wattage:** 5000. **Ad Rates:** $10-24 for 30 seconds.

16805 WJDS-AM - 620
PO Box 31999 Phone: (601)982-1062
Jackson, MS 39206 Fax: (601)362-1905

Format: Adult Contemporary; Oldies. **Networks:** ABC. **Founded:** 1929. **ADI:** Jackson, MS. **Key Personnel:** R. Steven Hicks, President; Kenneth E. Windham, Contact. **Wattage:** 5000 day; 1000 night.

16806 WJNT-AM - 1180
PO Box 1248 Phone: (601)366-1150
Jackson, MS 39215 Fax: (601)366-1627
E-mail: wjnt@meta3.net

Format: News; Talk. **Networks:** CBS; ABC; Westwood One Radio; CNN Radio. **Founded:** 1980. **Formerly:** WKKE-AM. **Operating Hours:** Continuous. **ADI:** Jackson, MS. **Key Personnel:** Thena Gunn, General & Sales Mgr.; Stan Carter, Chief Engineer; Dave Palmer, Operations. **Local Programs:** *Mary Weiden Show* 4-6 p.m. Monday-Friday, Mary Weiden; *Matt Friedman Show* 7:30-9 a.m. Monday-Friday, Matt Friedman; *Nel Newman Show "We're Talkin' Gardening"* 10 a.m.-12 p.m. Saturday, Nel Newman; *The World At Sunrise with Dan Walters* 6-7:30 a.m. Monday-Friday. **Wattage:** 50,000 day/ 500 night. **Ad Rates:** $22-35 for 30 seconds; $28-48 for 60 seconds.

16807 WJTV-TV - 12
1820 TV Rd. Phone: (601)372-6311
Jackson, MS 39204 Fax: (601)371-8256
Free: (800)495-8812
E-mail: johna@wjtv.com

Format: Commercial TV. **Networks:** CBS. **Owner:** Media General Broadcasting Inc., 100 N. Tampa St. Ste. 3150, Tampa, FL 33602, (813)225-4600. **Founded:** 1953. **Operating Hours:** 24 hours. **ADI:** Jackson, MS. **Key Personnel:** Larry Blackerby, General Manager. **Local Programs:** *Saddler Report*, Walter Saddler. **Wattage:** 316,000.

16808 WKNP-FM - 90.1
c/o WKNO-FM Phone: (901)325-6544
900 Getwell Rd. Fax: (901)325-6506
Memphis, TN 38111

Format: Public Radio; Classical; News. **Networks:** National Public Radio (NPR); Public Radio International (PRI). **Owner:** Mid-South Public Communications Foundation, at above address. **Founded:** 1990. **Operating Hours:** Continuous; 30% network, 70% local. **ADI:** Jackson, TN. **Key Personnel:** Susan Westfall, Manager; Darel Snodgrass, Operations Mgr. **Wattage:** 17,000. **Ad Rates:** Noncommercial; underwriting available.

16809 WLBT-TV - 3
715 S. Jefferson St. Phone: (601)948-3333
Jackson, MS 39202 Fax: (601)960-4435
E-mail: news@wlbt.com

Format: Commercial TV. **Networks:** NBC. **Owner:** Civic Communications, at above address. **Founded:** 1953. **Operating Hours:** Continuous; 70% network, 30% local. **ADI:** Jackson, MS. **Key Personnel:** Dan Modisett, Contact. **Ad Rates:** $15-2,000 per unit.

16810 WLIN-FM - 101.7
102 Business Park Dr., Ste. C Phone: (601)956-0102
Jackson, MS 39213 Fax: (601)978-3978

Format: Contemporary Hit Radio (CHR). **Networks:** USA Radio. **Owner:** Eddie Holladay, at above address. **Founded:** 1973. **Formerly:** WEQZ-FM (1989). **Operating Hours:** Continuous; 98% local. **ADI:** Jackson, MS. **Key Personnel:** Dick O'Neil, General Mgr./General Sales Mgr.; Roger Allinson, Creative Serv. Dir. **Wattage:** 25,000. **Ad Rates:** $32-29 for 30 seconds.

WMAB-FM - See Mississippi State

WMAB-TV - See Mississippi State

WMAE-FM - See Booneville

16811 WMAE-TV - 12
3825 Ridgewood Dr. Phone: (601)982-6565
Jackson, MS 39211 Fax: (601)982-6746

Format: Public TV. **Simulcasts:** WMPN-TV. **Networks:** Public Broadcasting Service (PBS). **Founded:** 1974. **Operating Hours:** 6:45 am-11:15 pm weekdays; noon-11:15 pm Sat.; noon-11 pm Sun. **ADI:** Columbus-Tupelo (West Point), MS. **Key Personnel:** A.J. Jaeger, Contact; Jeannine Fulmer, Program Dir.

WMAH-FM - See Biloxi

WMAH-TV - See Biloxi

16812 WMAO-FM - 90.9
c/o Public Radio in MS Phone: (601)982-6565
3825 Ridgewood Rd. Fax: (601)982-6746
Jackson, MS 39211-6463
Free: (800)472-2580

Format: Classical; News. **Networks:** National Public Radio (NPR); Public Radio International (PRI). **Founded:** 1983. **Operating Hours:** Continuous. **ADI:** Greenwood-Greenville, MS. **Key Personnel:** William Fulton, Director. **Local Programs:** *Mississippi Concert Hall*, Tim Riley; *New Directions*, Tim Riley; *The Opera Bill*, William Fulton. **Wattage:** 100,000. **Ad Rates:** Noncommercial. **URL:** http://www.hpr.org/members/prm.

WMAO-TV - See Greenwood

WMAU-FM - See Meadville

WMAV-FM - See Oxford

WMAV-TV - See Oxford

WMAW-TV - See Meridian

16813 WMPN-FM - 91.3
3825 Ridgewood Rd. Phone: (601)982-6565
Jackson, MS 39211 Fax: (601)982-6746
Free: (800)472-2580

Format: News; Classical. **Networks:** National Public Radio (NPR); Public Radio International (PRI). **Owner:** Mississippi Authority for Educational TV, at above address. **Founded:** 1983. **Formerly:** WMAA-FM (1991). **Operating Hours:** Continuous. **ADI:** Jackson, MS. **Key Personnel:** William Fulton, Director. **Local Programs:** *Mississippi Concert Hall*, Tim Riley; *New Directions*, Tim Riley; *The Opera Bill*, William Fulton. **Wattage:** 100,000. **Ad Rates:** Noncommercial. **URL:** http://www.npr.org/members/prm.

16814 WMPN-TV - 29
3825 Ridgewood Rd. Phone: (601)982-6565
Jackson, MS 39211 Fax: (601)982-6746

Format: Public TV. **Networks:** Public Broadcasting Service (PBS). **Founded:** 1970. **Formerly:** WMAA-TV (1990). **Operating Hours:** 5 a.m.-11 p.m. **ADI:** Jackson, MS. **Key Personnel:** A.J. Jaeger, Contact; Sarah White, General Mgr.; Gayle Loeber, Contact; Herbert M. Jolly, Contact.

16815 WMPR-FM - 90.1
Box 9782 Phone: (601)948-5835
Jackson, MS 39206 Fax: (601)948-6162

Format: Public Radio; Alternative/New Music/Progressive; Gospel; Jazz. **Networks:** National Public Radio (NPR). **Owner:** J.C. Maxwell Broadcasting Group, 480 W. County Line Rd., Jackson, MS. **Founded:** 1983. **Operating Hours:** Continuous; 20% network; 80% local. **ADI:** Jackson, MS. **Key Personnel:** Charles Evers, Program Dir.; Dr. Hilland Lackey, News Dir.; Eddie James, Sports Dir. **Wattage:** 100,000. **Ad Rates:** $15 for 60 seconds.

16816 WMSI-FM - 102.9
Box 31999 Phone: (601)982-1062
Jackson, MS 39286 Fax: (601)362-1905

Format: Country. **Networks:** ABC. **Founded:** 1948. **Operating Hours:** Continuous. **ADI:** Jackson, MS. **Key Personnel:** Kenny Windham, General Mgr.; Buddy Van Arsdale, Operations Mgr.; George Thomas, Chief Engineer. **Wattage:** 100,000. **Ad Rates:** $40-90 for 30 seconds; $50-100 for 60 seconds. Combined advertising rates available with WJDX-AM.

16817 WRTM-AM - 1490
PO Box 31235 Phone: (601)981-9080
Jackson, MS 39286 Fax: (601)981-9093

Format: Blues. **Owner:** Dominant Communications Corp., at above address. **Formerly:** WVIX-AM. **Operating Hours:** Continuous. **Key Personnel:** Carl Haynes, Pres./General Mgr.; Maria Epps, Sales Mgr. **Wattage:** 1,000. **Ad Rates:** $10 for 60 seconds.

16818 WSTZ-FM - 106.7
2980 Forest Ave. Ext. Phone: (601)982-1067
PO Box 12247 Fax: (601)981-5800
Jackson, MS 39213

Format: Classic Rock. **Networks:** AP. **Founded:** 1968. **Operating Hours:** Continuous. **ADI:** Jackson, MS. **Key Personnel:** Carl Strandell, General Mgr. **Wattage:** 100,000. **Ad Rates:** $40-52 for 30 seconds; $52-65 for 60 seconds.

16819 WTWZ-AM - 1120
4611-C Terry Rd. Phone: (601)346-0074
Jackson, MS 39212-5646 Fax: (601)346-0896

Format: Religious. **Networks:** Sun Radio. **Owner:** Terry E. Wood, PO Box 7094, Jackson, MS 39282-7094. **Founded:** 1981. **Operating Hours:** Sunrise-sunset; 10% network, 90% local. **Key Personnel:** Terry Wood, Contact, phone (601)9248216, fax (601)9242768. **Local Programs:** *Christian Country Music* 1:00 pm - 7:00 pm Monday-Friday, Terry E. Wood, (601)346-0074, Fax (601)346-0896; *Issues and Scriptures* 8:30 am Saturday, Bob Shepheard. **Wattage:** 5000. **Ad Rates:** $8 for 30 seconds; $10 for 60 seconds.

16820 WTYX-FM - 94.7
222 Beasley Rd. Phone: (601)957-3000
Jackson, MS 39206 Fax: (601)956-0370
E-mail: mail94@arrow94.com

Format: Oldies. **Networks:** ABC. **Owner:** Proteus Investments, 222 Beasley, Jackson, MS 39206, (601)956-0370. **Founded:** 1971. **Operating Hours:** Continuous. **ADI:** Jackson, MS. **Key Personnel:** Bill Wilson, Program Dir.; Marshall Magee, General Mgr. **Wattage:** 100,000. **Ad Rates:** $30-54 for 30 seconds; $30-54 for 60 seconds.

16821 WZRX-AM - 1590
2980 Forest Ave. Ext. Phone: (601)981-9080
PO Box 9734 Fax: (601)981-9093
Jackson, MS 39286

Format: Gospel. **Networks:** American Urban Radio. **Founded:** 1965. **Operating Hours:** Continuous. **ADI:** Jackson, MS. **Key Personnel:** Carl Haynes, General Mgr.; Maria Epps, Sales Mgr. **Wattage:** 5000 day; 1000 night. **Ad Rates:** $9-15 for 30 seconds; $13-20 for 60 seconds.

KOSCIUSKO†, pop. 7,415.

C MS. Attala Co. 68 mi. NE of Jackson. Manufactures electric motors, dairy products, mobile homes, wood products, vent pipe & fittings, soft drinks, lamps, shades, corrugated containers, textiles, feed, plastic products. Pine, oak, hickory timber. Stock, dairy, poultry farms. Cotton, corn, hay.

16822 The Star-Herald
American Publishing Co.
Box 1228 Phone: (601)289-2251
Kosciusko, MS 39090 Fax: (601)289-2254

Community newspaper. **Founded:** 1866. **Freq:** Weekly (Thurs.). **Print Method:** Offset. **Cols./Page:** 6. **Col. Width:** 12 picas. **Col. Depth:** 301 agate lines. **Key Personnel:** Jack F. Weatherly, Editor; Neal M. Turnage, Publisher. **ISSN:** 1048-4116. **Subscription Rates:** $20. **Remarks:** Accepts advertising.
Ad Rates: GLR: $.30 **Circ:** ‡8,500
BW: $567.60
PCI: $5.80

16823 Northland Cable
Box 1166 Phone: (601)289-3281
Kosciusko, MS 39090 Fax: (601)289-2910

Owner: Northland Cable, 1201 3rd Ave., Ste. 3600, Seattle, WA 98101, (206)621-1351. **Key Personnel:** Lynn Keith, General Mgr. **Cities Served:** subscribing households 4,000; 29 channels; 1 community access channel.

16824 WBKJ-FM - 105.1
Golf Course Rd. Phone: (601)289-1340
PO Box A
Kosciusko, MS 39090

Format: Contemporary Country. **Networks:** Unistar; CNN Radio. **Owner:** Boswell Broadcasting Co., at above address. **Founded:** 1965. **Operating Hours:** 5 a.m.-midnight. **Key Personnel:** Johnny Boswell, Station Mgr.; Ann Steen, Office Mgr.; Bobby Leathers, Chief Engineer; Mims Boswell, General Mgr. **Wattage:** 100,000. **Ad Rates:** $6-10 for 30 seconds; $8-12 for 60 seconds.

16825 WJTA-FM - 91.7
Box 742 Phone: (601)289-5703
Kosciusko, MS 39090 Fax: (601)289-4224

Format: Religious; Easy Listening; Gospel. **Networks:** Bible Broadcasting. **Owner:** Dr. William G. Suratt, at above address. **Founded:** 1989. **Operating Hours:** Continuous; 10% network, 90% local. **Key Personnel:** William G. Suratt, Contact; Artie Suratt, Program Dir. **Wattage:** 383. **Ad Rates:** $2.50-4.50 for 30 seconds; $3.35-5.50 for 60 seconds.

16826 WKOZ-AM - 1340
Golf Course Rd. Phone: (601)289-1340
PO Box A Fax: (601)289-7907
Kosciusko, MS 39090

Format: Oldies. **Networks:** CNN Radio. **Owner:** Boswell Broadcasting Co., at above address. **Founded:** 1947. **Operating Hours:** Continuous. **Key Personnel:** Billy Steen, Program Dir.; Ann Steen, Office Mgr.; Stan Carter, Chief Engineer. **Wattage:** 1000. **Ad Rates:** $3.75-4.50 for 30 seconds; $4-6 for 60 seconds. Combined advertising rates available with WBKJ-FM: $2.70-4.50 for 30 seconds; $3.60-6 for 60 seconds.

LAUREL†, pop. 21,664.

SE MS. Jones Co. 55 mi. SW of Meridian. Southeastern Baptist College. Manufactures building board, wood products, distribution transformers, farm implements, forms, auto parts, machinery, garments, machine shop and foundry products, walk-in coolers and freezers, electric blankets, oil drilling products. Oil refinery; bottling works. Pine, hardwood timber. Agriculture.

16827 Impact of Laurel
Buckley Newspapers, Inc.
PO Box 4406 Phone: (601)649-1129
Laurel, MS 39441 Fax: (601)649-0424

Shopper. **Founded:** 1976. **Freq:** Semiweekly (Wed. and Sun.). **Print Method:** Offset. **Cols./Page:** 6. **Col. Width:** 19 nonpareils. **Col. Depth:** 196 agate lines. **Key Personnel:** Ronnie Buckley, Editor and Publisher; Reon B. Wade, Advertising Mgr. **Subscription Rates:** Free; $10.80 (mail). **Remarks:** Accepts advertising. **Alt. Formats:** CD-ROM, MAC.
Ad Rates: GLR: $.57 **Circ:** Wed. 45,036
BW: $907.20 Sun. 48,410
4C: $1,197.20
PCI: $10.80

16828 Laurel Leader Call
PO Box 728 Phone: (601)428-0551
Laurel, MS 39441-0728 Fax: (601)426-3550

General newspaper. **Founded:** 1911. **Freq:** Mon.-Sat. (eve.). **Print Method:** Offset. **Cols./Page:** 6. **Col. Width:** 25 nonpareils. **Col. Depth:** 301 agate lines. **Key Personnel:** Gary W. Peeples, Editor and Publisher. **Subscription Rates:** $51. **Remarks:** Accepts advertising.
Ad Rates: SAU: $7.82 **Circ:** Mon.-Sat. ★7,494
Sun. ★7,254

16829 WAML-AM - 1340
318 W. 5th St. Phone: (601)425-4285
PO Box 367
Laurel, MS 39440

Format: Gospel. **Networks:** NBC; Mississippi. **Owner:** Pine Belt Broadcasting, at above address. **Founded:** 1932. **Operating Hours:** 6 a.m.-midnight. **ADI:** Laurel-Hattiesburg, MS. **Key Personnel:** Gerald Williams, General Mgr.; Bobby Brignac, Operations Mgr.; Kathy McDonniel, Station Mgr. **Wattage:** 1000. **Ad Rates:** $4-7 for 30 seconds; $7-8 for 60 seconds. $4-$7 for 30 seconds; $7-$8 for 60 seconds. Combined advertising rates available with WEEZ-FM.

16830 WBBN-FM - 95.9
PO Box 6408 Phone: (601)649-0095
Laurel, MS 39441-6408

Format: Country. **Networks:** ABC. **Owner:** Blakeney Communications, Inc., at above address. **Founded:** 1985. **Operating Hours:** Continuous; 100% local. **ADI:** Laurel-Hattiesburg, MS. **Key Personnel:** Larry Blakeney, President; Randy Blakeney, General Mgr.; Debbie Blakeney, Sales Mgr. **Wattage:** 31,000. **Ad Rates:** $22-60 for 30 seconds; $26-64 for 60 seconds.

16831 WEEZ-FM - 99.3
PO Box 367 Phone: (601)425-4390
Laurel, MS 39441 Fax: (601)425-4486
Free: (800)238-3942

Format: Gospel; Religious. **Networks:** USA Radio. **Owner:** Pine Belt Broadcasting, at above address. **Founded:** 1982. **Operating Hours:** Continuous. **ADI:** Laurel-Hattiesburg, MS. **Key Personnel:** Gerald Williams, General Mgr.; Bobby Brignac, Operations Mgr.; Kathy McDonneall, Station Mgr. **Wattage:** 50,000. **Ad Rates:** $4-7 for 15 seconds; $7-10 for 30 seconds; $8-12 for 60 seconds.

16832 WQIS-AM - 890
51 Victory Rd. Phone: (601)425-1491
Laurel, MS 39440 Fax: (601)426-8255

Format: Adult Contemporary. **Owner:** Design Media, Inc., 3021 Sheffield Dr, Emmaus, PA 18049, (610)965-8927. **Founded:** 1957. **Operating Hours:** Sunrise-sunset. **ADI:** Laurel-Hattiesburg, MS. **Key Personnel:** Kay Hilton, General Sales Mgr.; Gene Hudson, Program Dir. **Wattage:** 10,000. **Ad Rates:** $10-15 for 30 seconds; $15-20 for 60 seconds.

LEAKESVILLE†, pop. 1,120.

SE MS. Greene Co. 30 mi. NW of Mobile, AL.

16833 Greene County Herald
PO Box 220 Phone: (601)394-5070
Leakesville, MS 39451 Fax: (601)394-5070

Newspaper with a Democratic orientation. **Founded:** 1898. **Freq:** Weekly (Thurs.). **Print Method:** Offset. **Trim Size:** 13 x 21 1/2. **Cols./Page:** 6. **Col. Width:** 2 1/16 inches. **Col. Depth:** 21 inches. **Key Personnel:** John F. Turner, Editor and Publisher. **USPS:** 228-600. **Subscription Rates:** $12; $14 out of area; $16 out of state. **Remarks:** Accepts advertising.
Ad Rates: GLR: $.21 **Circ:** 3,000
BW: $370.44
4C: $590.44
SAU: $2.94

LELAND, pop. 6,667.

W MS. Washington Co. 8 mi. E. of Greenville. Manufactures cottonseed oil, insecticides, farm implements, furniture. Agriculture. Cotton, soybeans, rice.

16834 The Leland Progress
Pilot Press Publishing Co.
PO Box 72 Phone: (601)686-4081
Leland, MS 38756 Fax: (601)686-9076
Publisher E-mail: publisher@lelandprogress.com

Local newspaper. **Founded:** 1901. **Freq:** Weekly (Thurs.). **Print Method:** Offset. **Key Personnel:** Gaila T. McCaskill, Editor and Publisher, phone (601)686-4594. **Subscription Rates:** $15 individuals; $24 out of area. **Remarks:** Accepts advertising. **Formerly:** Deer Creek Progress.
Ad Rates: GLR: $.12 **Circ:** 1,280
BW: $360
4C: $600
SAU: $4

LEXINGTON†, pop. 2,628.

WC MS. Holmes Co. 58 mi. N. of Jackson. Saints College. Manufactures mobile homes. Sawmills; cotton ginning. Timber. Agriculture. Cotton, corn, truck crops.

16835 Holmes County Herald
East Holmes Publishing Enterprises, Inc.
308 Court Sq. Phone: (601)834-1151
PO Box 60 Fax: (601)834-1074
Lexington, MS 39095
Publication E-mail: hcherald@network-one.com

Newspaper. **Founded:** 1959. **Freq:** Weekly (Thurs.). **Print Method:** Offset. **Cols./Page:** 6. **Col. Width:** 2 inches. **Col. Depth:** 21 1/2 inches. **Key Personnel:** Bruce Hill, Editor and Publisher. **USPS:** 247-680. **Subscription Rates:** $17; $20 out of area. **Remarks:** Accepts advertising.
Ad Rates: BW: $677.25 **Circ:** Paid ⊕3,351
PCI: $5.25

16836 WXTN-AM - 1000
PO Box 369 Phone: (601)834-1254
Lexington, MS 39095 Fax: (601)834-2612

Format: Ethnic; Religious. **Networks:** Independent. **Owner:** Fanny Cothran, at above address. **Founded:** 1959. **Operating Hours:** Sunrise-sunset; 100% local. **Key Personnel:** Brad Cothran, General Mgr. **Wattage:** 5000.

LIBERTY†, pop. 669.

SW MS. Amite Co. 45 mi. SE of Natchez. Timber. Dairy, truck farms. Beef, cattle.

16837 The Southern Herald
Southern Herald
PO Box 674 Phone: (601)657-4818
Liberty, MS 39645 Fax: (601)657-4818

Community newspaper. **Founded:** 1825. **Freq:** Weekly (Thurs.). **Print Method:** Offset. **Cols./Page:** 6. **Col. Width:** 33 nonpareils. **Col. Depth:** 301 agate lines. **Key Personnel:** Rick

Stratton, Publisher. **Subscription Rates:** $17 individuals; $20 out of country. **Remarks:** Accepts advertising.
Ad Rates: GLR: $.20 **Circ:** Paid ‡1,300
BW: $516 Free ‡30
4C: $666
SAU: $4
PCI: $4

LORMAN

16838 WPRL-FM - 91.7
1000 ASU Dr. No. 269 Phone: (601)877-6290
Alcorn State University Fax: (601)887-2213
Lorman, MS 39096

Format: Jazz; Public Radio; News; Information. **Networks:** AP; National Public Radio (NPR); Public Radio International (PRI). **Founded:** 1986. **Operating Hours:** 6 a.m.-2 a.m.; 20% network, 80% local. **Key Personnel:** Dr. Shafiqur Rahman, General Mgr., phone (601)877-6612, srahman@lorman.alcorn.edu; LLJuna Weir, Operations Mgr., phone (601)877-6593, lluna@hotmail.com; Toni Terrett, News Dir.; Charles Edmond, Sports Dir., cedmond@lormanalcorn.edu; Darren Buckley, Development Dir.; Venz Campbell, R&B Dir./Urban Beat Host, vcampbell@lormanalcorn.edu. **Local Programs:** *ASU Football*, Charles Edmonds; *Jazz*, Gregory Dace; *Morning Gospel*, Kenneth McGriggs. **Wattage:** 3000. **Ad Rates:** Advertising accepted; rates available upon request.

LOUISVILLE†, pop. 7,323.

EC MS. Winston Co. 60 mi. SW of Columbus. Manufactures auto accessories, car seats, gloves, material handling machinery, plywood, particleboard, bricks, chemicals, food processing equipment. Lumber mill. Dairy and poultry farms. Cotton, corn.

16839 Winston County Journal
Louisville Newspapers, Inc.
PO Box 469 Phone: (601)773-6241
Louisville, MS 39339 Fax: (601)773-6242

Community interest news magazine. **Founded:** 1892. **Freq:** Weekly (Wed.). **Print Method:** Offset. **Cols./Page:** 6. **Col. Width:** 25 nonpareils. **Col. Depth:** 301 agate lines. **Key Personnel:** Jerry Shiverdecker, Editor and Publisher. **Subscription Rates:** $20.50 individuals. **Remarks:** Accepts advertising.
Ad Rates: BW: $522.45 **Circ:** Paid ‡4,900
PCI: $4.23 Non-paid ‡4,400

16840 WLSM-AM - 1270
PO Box 279 Phone: (601)773-3481
Louisville, MS 39339 Fax: (601)773-3482

Format: Sports. **Networks:** ABC. **Owner:** Phillip A. Harrison, at above address, (601)773-4082. **Founded:** 1953. **Operating Hours:** 12 hrs. Daily; 10% network, 90% local. **Key Personnel:** Phillip A. Harrison, General Mgr.; Stacy S. Harrison, Station Mgr. **Wattage:** 2700. **Ad Rates:** $2-5 for 30 seconds; $2.50-6 for 60 seconds.

16841 WLSM-FM - 107.1
PO Box 279 Phone: (601)773-3481
Louisville, MS 39339 Fax: (601)773-3482

Format: Country. **Networks:** ABC; Mississippi. **Owner:** Phillip A. Harrison, at above address. **Founded:** 1953. **Operating Hours:** Continuous; 10% network, 90% local. **Key Personnel:** Phillip A. Harrison, General Mgr.; Stacy S. Harrison, Station Mgr. **Local Programs:** *Switch & Shop*; *WLSM Lawn & Garden Show*. **Wattage:** 25,000. **Ad Rates:** $4-6 for 30 seconds; $5-7 for 60 seconds.

LUCEDALE†, pop. 2,429.

SE MS. George Co. 35 mi. NE of Mobile, AL.

16842 George County Times
Times
Box 238 Phone: (601)947-2967
Lucedale, MS 39452 Fax: (601)947-6828

Community interest newsmagazine. **Founded:** 1905. **Freq:** Weekly (Thurs.). **Print Method:** Offset. **Cols./Page:** 6. **Col. Width:** 24 nonpareils. **Col. Depth:** 301 agate lines. **Key Personnel:** E.G. Sellers, Publisher. **Subscription Rates:** $10.

MACON†, pop. 2,396.

E MS. Noxubee Co. 60 mi. N. of Meridian. Manufactures veneers, clay products, lumber, clothing, brick and tile. Pine timber. Dairy farms. Soybeans, cattle.

16843 Macon Beacon
PO Box 32 Phone: (601)726-4747
Macon, MS 39341 Fax: (601)726-4742

Newspaper. **Founded:** 1849. **Freq:** Weekly (Thurs.). **Print Method:** Offset. **Trim Size:** 12 3/4 x 11. **Cols./Page:** 4. **Key Personnel:** R. Scott Boyd, Publisher; Donna J. Parker, Business Mgr. **Subscription Rates:** $50. **Remarks:** Accepts advertising.
Ad Rates: GLR: $.55 **Circ:** 4,500
BW: $550
SAU: $3
PCI: $21

MAGEE, pop. 3,497.

S MS. Simpson Co. 45 mi. SE of Jackson. Light industry. Cotton ginning. Beef, dairy cattle, poultry processing products. Agriculture. Corn, cotton, soybeans.

16844 The Magee Courier
Simpson Publishing Co.
PO Box 338 Phone: (601)849-3434
Magee, MS 39111-0338 Fax: (601)849-6828

Community newspaper. **Founded:** 1899. **Freq:** Weekly (Thurs.). **Print Method:** Offset. **Trim Size:** 13 x 21 1/2. **Cols./Page:** 6. **Col. Width:** 26 nonpareils. **Col. Depth:** 301 agate lines. **Key Personnel:** John P. Brown, Editor. **USPS:** 325-560. **Subscription Rates:** $14 individuals. **Remarks:** Advertising not accepted for beer.
Ad Rates: GLR: $.55 **Circ:** ‡3,700
BW: $977.82
4C: $1,182.82
SAU: $7.58
PCI: $6.50

16845 Simpson County News
The Magee Courier
206 N. Main Phone: (601)849-3434
Magee, MS 39111 Fax: (601)849-6828

Community newspaper. **Founded:** May 14, 1872. **Freq:** Weekly (Thurs.). **Print Method:** Offset. **Trim Size:** 14 x 22 3/4. **Cols./Page:** 6. **Col. Width:** 20 1/2 nonpareils. **Col. Depth:** 301 agate lines. **Key Personnel:** B. Duane Cross, Editor; Owen Lusk, Publisher. **Subscription Rates:** $18. **Remarks:** Advertising not accepted for alcoholic beverages.
Ad Rates: GLR: $.32 **Circ:** ‡6108
BW: $205
PCI: $4.70

16846 The Simpson Shopper
Simpson Publishing Co.
PO Box 338 Phone: (601)849-3434
Magee, MS 39111-0338 Fax: (601)849-6828

Shopping guide. **Founded:** 1986. **Freq:** Weekly. **Print Method:** Offset. **Trim Size:** 11 1/2 x 13 1/2. **Cols./Page:** 6. **Col. Width:** 9 picas. **Col. Depth:** 13 inches. **Key Personnel:** John P. Brown, Publisher. **Subscription Rates:** Free.
Ad Rates: BW: $682.20 **Circ:** Non-paid 6,700
4C: $887.20
PCI: $7.58

MAGNOLIA†, pop. 2,461.

S MS. Pike Co. 6 mi. S. of McComb.

16847 Magnolia Gazette
PO Box 152 Phone: (601)783-2441
Magnolia, MS 39652-0152
Community newspaper. **Founded:** 1989. **Freq:** Weekly (Thurs.). **Print Method:** Offset. **Cols./Page:** 7. **Col. Width:** 129 picas. **Col. Depth:** 21 1/2 inches. **Key Personnel:** Harrell Griffin, Editor and Publisher. **Subscription Rates:** $10; $20; $30 out of area. **Remarks:** Accepts advertising.
Ad Rates: BW: $550.83 **Circ:** Paid ‡1,100
4C: $850.83
SAU: $4.39
PCI: $2

MARKS

16848 Quitman County Democrat
Democrat
PO Box 328 Phone: (601)326-2181
Marks, MS 38646 Fax: (601)326-6077

Community newspaper. **Freq:** Weekly (Thurs.). **Cols./Page:** 6. **Col. Width:** 12 1/5 picas. **Col. Depth:** 21 inches. **Key Personnel:** John Fleming, Editor.
Circ: 2,100

MATHISTON, pop. 632.

NC MS. Choctaw & Webster Co. 12 mi. NW of Starkville.

16849 The Breeze
Wood College
PO Box 289 Phone: (601)263-5352
Mathiston, MS 39752 Fax: (601)263-4964

Collegiate newspaper. **Founded:** 1938. **Freq:** 6/year. **Print Method:** Offset. **Trim Size:** 10 x 12 1/2. **Cols./Page:** 5. **Col. Width:** 24 nonpareils. **Col. Depth:** 175 agate lines. **Key Personnel:** Lou Ann Staggs, Advisor. **Subscription Rates:** Free. **Remarks:** Accepts advertising.
Ad Rates: BW: $87.75 **Circ:** Free ‡1,200
PCI: $1.50

16850 Chips-O-Wood
Wood College
PO Box 289 Phone: (601)263-5352
Mathiston, MS 39752 Fax: (601)263-4964

College alumni newspaper. **Founded:** 1948. **Freq:** Quarterly. **Print Method:** Offset. **Trim Size:** 10 x 12 1/2. **Cols./Page:** 5. **Col. Width:** 24 nonpareils. **Col. Depth:** 175 agate lines. **Key Personnel:** Lou Ann Staggs, Editor. **Subscription Rates:** Free. **Remarks:** Advertising not accepted.
Circ: Free ‡9,000

MCCOMB

16851 Enterprise-Journal
J.O. Emmerich & Associates, Inc.
PO Box 910 Phone: (601)684-2421
McComb, MS 39649 Fax: (601)684-0836
Free: (800)748-9845
Publication E-mail: ejournal@telapex.com

General newspaper. **Founded:** 1889. **Freq:** Daily (eve.). **Print Method:** Offset. **Trim Size:** 13 3/4 x 22 3/4. **Cols./Page:** 6. **Col. Width:** 12 1/2 picas. **Col. Depth:** 21 1/2 inches. **Key Personnel:** Charles M. Dunagin, Editor and Publisher; Deborah Best, Advertising Mgr. **USPS:** 335-580. **Subscription Rates:** $96 individuals; $108 out of area. **Remarks:** Accepts advertising. **Online:** link.
Ad Rates: GLR: $8.75 **Circ:** Mon.-Fri. ★12,276
BW: $1,154 Sun. ★12,682
4C: $1,554
SAU: $11
PCI: $8.50

16852 Southwest Sun
J.O. Emmerich & Associates, Inc.
PO Box 910 Phone: (601)684-2421
McComb, MS 39649 Fax: (601)684-0836
Free: (800)748-9845
Publication E-mail: ej@lincup.com; ejournal@telapex.com

Shopper. **Founded:** 1936. **Freq:** Weekly (Wed.). **Print Method:** Offset. **Trim Size:** 13 3/4 x 22 3/4. **Cols./Page:** 6. **Col. Width:** 25 nonpareils. **Col. Depth:** 301 agate lines. **Key Personnel:** Jack Ryan, Editor. **Subscription Rates:** Free. **Remarks:** Accepts advertising.
Ad Rates: GLR: $2 **Circ:** Free 8,000
BW: $387
4C: $787
SAU: $3

16853 WAKH-FM - 105.7
PO Box 1649 Phone: (601)684-4654
McComb, MS 39648-1649 Fax: (601)684-4658

Format: Country. **Networks:** Mississippi. **Owner:** San-Dow Broadcasting, PO Box 1649, McComb, MS 39648. **Founded:** 1982. **Operating Hours:** Continuous. **ADI:** Jackson, MS. **Key Personnel:** Robbie Hamilton, General Mgr.; Bill Rush, Program Dir.; Gene Sharkey, Sales Mgr.; Sue Simmons, Traffic Dir. **Wattage:** 100,000.

16854 WAPF-AM - 980
PO Box 1649 Phone: (601)684-7470
McComb, MS 39648 Fax: (601)684-4654

Format: Easy Listening. **Networks:** NBC. **Owner:** Dowdy Broadcasting Co., at above address. **Founded:** 1948. **Operating Hours:** 5:30 a.m.-6 p.m.; 10% network, 90% local. **Key Personnel:** Bob Gipan, General Mgr.; H.L. Allred, Contact. **Wattage:** 5000. **Ad Rates:** $2.80-4 for 30 seconds; $4.80-6 for 60 seconds.

MEADVILLE†, pop. 575.

SW MS. Franklin Co. 30 mi. E. of Natchez. Manufactures rail cars and clothing. Pine and hardwood timber. Agriculture. Soybeans, livestock.

16855 Franklin Advocate
PO Box 576 Phone: (601)384-2484
Meadville, MS 39653 Fax: (601)384-2276

Community newspaper. **Founded:** 1891. **Freq:** Weekly (Thurs.). **Print Method:** Offset. **Cols./Page:** 7. **Col. Width:**

10.5 picas. **Col. Depth:** 301 agate lines. **Key Personnel:** David Webb, Editor and Publisher; Mary Lou Webb, Advertising Mgr. **Subscription Rates:** $16.25; $21.50 Mississippi and Louisiana; $24.50 other states. **Remarks:** Accepts advertising.
Ad Rates: GLR: $.15 **Circ:** ‡3,700
BW: $451.50
PCI: $3

16856 Wilk-Amite Record
111 Main St. Phone: (601)384-2484
Meadville, MS 39653 Fax: (601)384-2276

County newspaper. **Founded:** 1888. **Freq:** Weekly (Fri.). **Print Method:** Offset. **Cols./Page:** 7. **Col. Width:** 10.5 picas. **Col. Depth:** 21 1/2 inches. **Key Personnel:** Mary Lou Webb, Editor; David Webb, Publisher; Louise McKenzie, Advertising Mgr. **USPS:** 684-140. **Subscription Rates:** $16.12; $21.50 out of area; $24.50 out of state. **Remarks:** Accepts advertising.
Ad Rates: GLR: $.21 **Circ:** Paid ‡1,900
BW: $441.50 Free ‡25
4C: $800
SAU: $5
PCI: $4

16857 WMAU-FM - 88.9
3825 Ridgewood Rd. Phone: (601)982-6565
Jackson, MS 39211-6463 Fax: (601)982-6747

Format: Classical; News. **Networks:** Public Radio International (PRI); National Public Radio (NPR). **Owner:** Mississippi Authority for Educational TV, at above address. **Founded:** 1983. **Operating Hours:** Continuous. **ADI:** Jackson, MS. **Key Personnel:** William Fulton, Director. **Local Programs:** *Grass Roots*, Bill Ellison; *Mississippi Concert Hall*, Tim Riley; *The Opera Bill*, William Fulton. **Wattage:** 100,000. **Ad Rates:** Noncommercial. **URL:** http://www.npr.org/members/prm.

MEMPHIS

16858 Southaven Press
Memphis Offset Printing Inc.
622 S. Highland Phone: (901)458-8030
Memphis, MS 38671 Fax: (901)458-3104

Local newspaper. **Founded:** May 1980. **Freq:** Weekly (Wed.). **Print Method:** Offset. Uses mats. **Cols./Page:** 6. **Col. Width:** 26 nonpareils. **Col. Depth:** 301 agate lines. **Key Personnel:** Joan Wessels, Editor; Fred Eason, Publisher; Barbara Owens, Advertising Mgr. **Remarks:** Accepts advertising.
Ad Rates: PCI: $4.90 **Circ:** Free 16,000

MERIDIAN†, pop. 47,365.

E MS. Lauderdale Co. 95 mi. E. of Jackson. Meridian Community College. Manufactures lumber products, sound systems, auto parts. Timber.

16859 Meridian Star
Meridian Star, Inc.
814 22nd Ave. Phone: (601)693-1551
Box 1591 Fax: (601)485-1275
Meridian, MS 39301
General newspaper. **Founded:** Mar. 3, 1879. **Freq:** Daily (eve.), Sat. and Sun. (morn.). **Print Method:** Offset. **Cols./Page:** 6. **Col. Width:** 25 nonpareils. **Col. Depth:** 301 agate lines. **Key Personnel:** James B. Skewes, Editor and Publisher; Jack Bynum, Advertising Mgr. **Subscription Rates:** $96; $108 out of state. **Remarks:** Accepts advertising.
Ad Rates: SAU: $10 **Circ:** Mon.-Sat. ★**18,651**
Sun. ★**20,603**

16860 Comcast Cablevision of Meridian
909 24th Ave. Phone: (601)693-2366
Meridian, MS 39301 Fax: (601)693-2278

Founded: 1964. **Cities Served:** Lauderdale County, MS.

16861 Vista Communications
PO Box 1930 Phone: (601)693-7557
Meridian, MS 39302 Fax: (601)693-7985
Free: (800)548-8968

Owner: Vista Communications, 40 Nagog Park, Acton, MA 01720, (508)263-0467. **Key Personnel:** Liz Duffy, Contact; Roger Shearer, Chief Engineer; Diane Pickett, Office Mgr. **Cities Served:** subscribing households 15,000.

16862 WALT-AM - 910
3436 Hwy. 45 N. Phone: (601)693-2661
Box 5797 Fax: (601)483-0826
Meridian, MS 39302

Format: Urban Contemporary. **Networks:** ABC. **Owner:** New South Communications, Inc., at above address, Fax: (601)483-9826. **Founded:** 1964. **Operating Hours:** Continuous. **ADI:** Meridian, MS. **Key Personnel:** Chantell Hampton, Program Dir., fax (601)483-9826; Jay King, News Dir.; Larry Torgerson, Sales Mgr. **Wattage:** 5000. **Ad Rates:** $18 for 30 seconds; $27 for 60 seconds.

16863 WFFX-AM - 1450
4307 Highway 39 N. Phone: (601)693-2381
Meridian, MS 39301 Fax: (601)485-2972

Format: Sports; Talk. **Owner:** Broadcasters & Publishers, Inc., at above address. **Founded:** 1957. **Formerly:** WMDN-AM; WMPG-AM. **Operating Hours:** Continuous. **ADI:** Meridian, MS. **Key Personnel:** G. Dean Pearce, Manager; John Anthony, Program Dir.; Clarice Rasco, Contact. **Wattage:** 1000. **Ad Rates:** $5 for 30 seconds; $8 for 60 seconds.

16864 WJDQ-FM - 101.3
4307 Hwy. 39 N. Phone: (601)693-2381
Meridian, MS 39301 Fax: (601)485-2972
E-mail: wjdqfm@intop.net

Format: Adult Contemporary. **Owner:** Broadcasters & Publishers, Inc., at above address. **Founded:** 1965. **Formerly:** WDAL-AM (1975). **Operating Hours:** Continuous. **ADI:** Meridian, MS. **Key Personnel:** John Anthony, Program Dir.; Dean Pearce, General Mgr.; Ron Harper, Sales Mgr.; Clarice Rasco, Office Mgr.; Jim Loznicka, News Dir. **Wattage:** 100,000. **Ad Rates:** $18-34 for 30 seconds; $24-45 for 60 seconds.

16865 WKZB-FM - 93.5
116 Skyland Dr. Phone: (601)483-9393
Meridian, MS 39301 Fax: (601)459-4140

Format: Classic Rock. **Networks:** ABC. **Owner:** Butler Broadcasting Corp., at above address. **Founded:** 1978. **Formerly:** WQGL-FM (1978). **Operating Hours:** 24 hrs. **ADI:** Meridian, MS. **Key Personnel:** Darryl Jackson, Pres./General Mgr.; George Vice, Sales Mgr.; Steve O'Conner, Operations Mgr./Program Dir., fax (601)483-9310, kzbrocks@aol.com; Henry Tyson, Contact, phone (205)459-3222; Lisa Downey, Traffic Mgr. **Wattage:** 50,000. **Ad Rates:** Advertising accepted; rates available upon request. Combined advertising rates available with WPRN-AM-FM.

16866 WMAW-TV - 14
c/o WMPN-TV Phone: (601)982-6565
3825 Ridgewood Rd. Fax: (601)982-6746
Jackson, MS 39211

Format: Public TV. **Simulcasts:** WMPN-TV. **Networks:** Public Broadcasting Service (PBS). **Owner:** Mississippi Authority for Educational TV, at above address. **Founded:** 1970. **Operating Hours:** 5:45 a.m.-2 a.m. Mon.-Sat.; 5:45 a.m.-midnight Sun. **ADI:** Meridian, MS. **Key Personnel:** Larry Miller, Exec. Dir.; Maggie Gibson, Business Services Dir.; Claudine McGee, Programming & Promotions Dir.; Jef Judin, Production Dir.; Bill Pharr, Development Dir.; Herb Jolly, Engineering Dir.; Linda Cook, Personnel Dir.; Dr. Zo Brown, Volunteer Dir. **Wattage:** 550,000.

16867 WMER-AM - 1390
208 5th Ave. Phone: (601)693-1414
Meridian, MS 39301 Fax: (601)482-7887

Format: Religious. **Networks:** Sun Radio. **Owner:** New Life Outreach Ministries, PO Box 1414, Meridian, MS 39302. **Founded:** 1973. **Formerly:** WFEZ-AM. **Operating Hours:** 5 a.m.-12 a.m.; 20% network, 80% local. **ADI:** Meridian, MS. **Key Personnel:** Ron Jones, General Mgr.; Amy Gwinn, Program Dir. **Wattage:** 5000. **Ad Rates:** $5 for 30 seconds; $13 for 60 seconds.

16868 WNBN-AM - 1290
1290 266-23rd St. Phone: (601)483-7930
Meridian, MS 39301 Fax: (601)485-2820
Free: (888)891-4555

Format: Religious; Gospel; Urban Contemporary; Blues; Jazz. **Simulcasts:** WONG-AM. **Networks:** American Urban Radio. **Owner:** Frank Rackley, 3413 11th St., Meridian, MS 39301, (601)483-3401. **Founded:** 1987. **Operating Hours:** 5 a.m.-10:35 p.m. **ADI:** Meridian, MS. **Key Personnel:** J.D. Shaw, Sales Mgr.; Frank Rackley, General Mgr., phone (601)483-3401. **Local Programs:** *Talk-Up* 9:05 pm Monday-Friday, B. Smith, (877)723-4666. **Wattage:** 1000. **Ad Rates:** $5 for 15 seconds; $10 for 30 seconds; $12 for 60 seconds.

16869 WOKK-FM - 97.1
3436 Highway 45N Phone: (601)693-2661
Meridian, MS 39301 Fax: (601)483-0826
E-mail: 97okk@wokk.com

Format: Country. **Networks:** ABC. **Owner:** New South Communications, Inc., at above address. **Founded:** 1957. **Operating Hours:** Continuous. **Key Personnel:** Van Mac, Program Dir.; Ed Reeves, Sales Mgr., sales@wokk.com; Jay King, News Dir., newsroom@wokk.com; Scotty Ray, Promotions, 97okk@wokk.com. **Wattage:** 100,000. **Ad Rates:** $31 for 30 seconds; $50 for 60 seconds. **URL:** http://www.wokk.com.

16870 WTOK-TV - 11
Box 2988 Phone: (601)693-1441
Meridian, MS 39302 Fax: (601)483-3266
E-mail: wtoktv@aol.com

Format: Commercial TV. **Networks:** ABC; Fox. **Founded:** 1953. **Operating Hours:** Approximately 20 hours daily. **ADI:** Meridian, MS. **Key Personnel:** Tracey Jones, General Mgr. **Wattage:** 316,000.

16871 WYYW-FM - 95.1
4307 Hwy 39N Phone: (601)693-2381
Meridian, MS 39302 Fax: (601)485-2972

Format: Country. **Owner:** Broadcasters & Publishers, Inc., at above address. **Founded:** 1990. **Formerly:** WQIC-FM; WZMP-FM. **Operating Hours:** Continuous. **ADI:** Meridian, MS. **Key Personnel:** Dean Pearce, Manager; John Anthony, Operations Mgr. **Wattage:** 50,000. **Ad Rates:** $10-20 for 30 seconds; $12-40 for 60 seconds.

METCALFE

16872 AMW Cablevision
PO Box 362
Metcalfe, MS 38760

Owner: AWM Cablevision L.P., at above address. **Founded:** 1988. **Key Personnel:** Louis McCray, President; Robert D. Gross, Vice President; Brenda Bell, Sec.-Treas. **Cities Served:** Benoit, Benton, Cary, Gunnison, Mayersville, Metcalfe, Oakland, Pace, Parchman, Silver City, MS: subscribing households 900; 12 channels.

MISSISSIPPI STATE, pop. 4,600.

E MS. Oktibbeha Co. 22 mi. W. of Columbus. Tombigbee River Waterway nearby. Mississippi State University. Mississippi Research and Technology Park. Dairying center.

16873 MAFES Research Highlights
Mississippi Agricultural and Forestry Experiment Station
Box 9625 Phone: (601)325-1716
Mississippi State, MS 39762-9625 Fax: (601)325-1710
Publisher E-mail: tomk@ext.msstate.edu

Trade magazine covering research in agriculture. **Founded:** Oct. 15, 1938. **Freq:** Quarterly. **Print Method:** Offset. **Trim Size:** 8 1/2 x 11. **Cols./Page:** 3. **Col. Width:** 14 picas. **Col. Depth:** 59 picas. **Key Personnel:** Rebekah Ray, Editor, phone (601)325-1714, rebekahr@ext.msstate.edu; Robyn Hearn, Copy Editor. **Subscription Rates:** Free. **Remarks:** Advertising not accepted. **URL:** http://www.mafes.msstate.edu/highlights.
Circ: Non-paid 10,300

16874 The Mississippi Quarterly
Mississippi State University
Box 5272 Phone: (601)325-3069
Mississippi State, MS 39762 Fax: (601)325-3299

Scholarly journal covering humanities and social sciences dealing with the Southern U.S. and its authors. **Founded:** 1948. **Freq:** Quarterly. **Trim Size:** 6 x 9. **Key Personnel:** Robert L. Phillips, Jr., Editor, rlp2@ra.msstate.edu; Juanita Guyton, Business Mgr. **ISSN:** 0026-637X. **Subscription Rates:** $15 individuals; $5 single issue. **Remarks:** Accepts advertising.
Ad Rates: BW: $100 **Circ:** Combined 900

16875 Mississippi State Alumnus
Mississippi State Alumni Association
PO Box 5325 Phone: (601)325-3442
Mississippi State, MS 39762-5325 Fax: (601)325-7455
University alumni magazine. **Subtitle:** For Mississippi State's Graduates and Former Students. **Founded:** 1895. **Freq:** 3/year. **Print Method:** Offset. **Trim Size:** 8 1/2 x 11. **Cols./Page:** 3. **Col. Width:** 28 nonpareils. **Col. Depth:** 133 agate lines. **Key Personnel:** Allen Snow, Editor, snow@ur.msstate.edu. **USPS:** 354-520. **Remarks:** Accepts advertising. **URL:** http://www.msstate.edu/web/alumni.htm.
Ad Rates: BW: $930 **Circ:** Non-paid ‡31,000
4C: $1,197

16876 The Reflector
Mississippi State University
Student Media Center Phone: (601)325-7905
Mississippi State, MS 39762
Publication E-mail: advertising@reflector.msstate.edu

Collegiate newspaper. **Founded:** 1882. **Freq:** Semiweekly. **Print Method:** Offset. **Trim Size:** 13 x 21. **Cols./Page:** 6. **Col. Width:** 21 nonpareils. **Col. Depth:** 294 agate lines. **Key Personnel:** Marcela Cortagena, Editor, phone (601)325-7905, ediitor@reflector.msstate.edu; Joe Vellucci, Advertising Mgr., phone (601)325-7907. **ISSN:** 0893-3286. **Subscription**

Rates: $20 per semester. **Remarks:** Advertising not accepted for liquor or adoptions. **Available Online.**
Ad Rates: BW: $10 **Circ:** Free ‡13,000
4C: $275
PCI: $10

16877 WMAB-FM - 89.9
c/o Public Radio in MS Phone: (601)982-6565
3825 Ridgewood Rd. Fax: (601)982-6746
Jackson, MS 39211-6463
Free: (800)472-2580

Format: Classical; News; Information; New Age. **Networks:** National Public Radio (NPR); Public Radio International (PRI). **Founded:** 1983. **Operating Hours:** Continuous. **ADI:** Jackson, MS. **Key Personnel:** William Fulton, Director. **Local Programs:** *Mississippi Concert Hall*, Tim Riley; *New Directions*, Tim Riley; *The Opera Bill*, William Fulton. **Wattage:** 63,000. **Ad Rates:** Noncommercial. **URL:** http://www.npr.org/members/prm.

16878 WMAB-TV - 2
c/o WMPN-TV Phone: (601)982-6565
3825 Ridgewood Fax: (601)982-6746
Jackson, MS 39211

Format: Public TV. **Simulcasts:** WMPN-TV Jackson, MS. **Networks:** Public Broadcasting Service (PBS). **Owner:** Mississippi Authority for Educational TV, at above address. **Founded:** 1971. **Operating Hours:** 6:45 am-11:15 pm weekdays; noon-11:15 pm Sat.; noon-11 pm Sun. **ADI:** Columbus-Tupelo (West Point), MS. **Key Personnel:** A.J. Jaeger, Contact; Gayle Loeber, Program Dir.

MONTICELLO†.

SC MS. Lawrence Co. 15 mi. SE of Nola. Manufactures clothing, veneer, cotton.

16879 Lawrence County Press
534 Broad St. Phone: (601)587-2781
PO Box 549 Fax: (601)587-2794
Monticello, MS 39654
Publication E-mail: lcpren@mspress.org

Community newspaper. **Founded:** July 12, 1888. **Freq:** Weekly. **Print Method:** Offset. **Trim Size:** 7 3/4 x 11 1/2. **Cols./Page:** 6. **Col. Width:** 13 picas. **Col. Depth:** 21 inches. **Key Personnel:** John Carney, Editor and Publisher. **USPS:** 306-840. **Subscription Rates:** $16; $21 out of area; $75 other countries. **Remarks:** Accepts advertising.
Ad Rates: BW: $724.50 **Circ:** Paid ‡3,450
4C: $1,074.50
PCI: $5.75

16880 Galaxy Cablevision
PO Box 308 Phone: (601)587-7861
Monticello, MS 39654 Fax: (601)587-7410
Free: (800)225-2348

Owner: Galaxy Communications, 1220 N. Main St., Sikeston, MO 63801, (573)472-8200. **Formerly:** Vista Cablevision. **Key Personnel:** David L. Lusby, Contact, phone (601)728-8111, fax (601)728-1218. **Cities Served:** subscribing households 1,025; 28 channels.

16881 WMLC-AM - 1270
Rt. 1, Box 293 Phone: (601)587-7997
Monticello, MS 39654 Fax: (601)587-7924

Format: Talk; Sports. **Networks:** UPI. **Owner:** Monticello Broadcasting, at above address, Fax: (601)587-7524. **Founded:** 1970. **Operating Hours:** Sunrise-sunset. **ADI:** Jackson, MS. **Key Personnel:** Dave Nichols II, Gen. Mgr./Owner; Donna Nichols, Program Dir.; Dave Henry, Sales Mgr. **Local Programs:** *Dave's Dog House*, Dave Nichols II, Gen. Mgr./Owner; *Sports Rap*, Dave Nichols II, Gen. Mgr./Owner. **Wattage:** 1000. **Ad Rates:** $5 for 30 seconds; $7 for 60 seconds.

NATCHEZ†, pop. 22,438.

SW MS. Adams Co. On Mississippi River, 60 mi. S. of Vicksburg. Copiah Lincoln Community College. Natchez Junior College. Bridge to Vidalia, LA. Terminus of four boat lines. Manufactures culverts, storage tanks, boxes, beverages, tires, rayon, pulp. Lumber and cotton mills. Pine timber. Agriculture. Cattle, oil, cotton.

16882 Miss-Lou Guide
Boone Newspapers, Inc.
503 N. Canal St. Phone: (601)442-9101
PO Box 1447 Fax: (601)442-7315
Natchez, MS 39121
Shopper. **Founded:** 1979. **Freq:** Weekly (Wed.). **Print Method:** Offset. **Cols./Page:** 6. **Col. Width:** 25 nonpareils. **Col. Depth:** 301 agate lines. **Key Personnel:** Kenneth Boone, Publisher; Stacy Graning, Editor. **Remarks:** Accepts advertising.
Ad Rates: GLR: $1 **Circ:** Free ‡16,800
BW: $600
4C: $950
SAU: $3.68
PCI: $4.08

16883 The Natchez Democrat
Boone Newspapers, Inc.
P.O. Box 1447 Phone: (601)442-9101
Natchez, MS 39120 Fax: (601)442-9101

General newspaper. **Founded:** 1865. **Freq:** Sun.-Sat. **Print Method:** Offset. **Cols./Page:** 6. **Col. Width:** 2 1/16 inches. **Col. Depth:** 301 agate lines. **Key Personnel:** Kenneth Boone, Publisher; Stacy Graning, Managing Editor. **Subscription Rates:** $132; $163 (mail). **Remarks:** Accepts advertising.
Ad Rates: GLR: $1.50 **Circ:** 13,520
BW: $1,567.35 Sun. 13,952
4C: $2,057.35
PCI: $12.15

Ocean Springs Record - See Ocean Springs

16884 KAIN-AM - 1040
PO Box 17833 Tracetown Phone: (601)446-8803
Beltline Hwy. Fax: (601)446-8803
Natchez, MS 39122

Format: News; Talk. **Networks:** USA Radio; People's Network; International Broadcasting. **Founded:** 1985. **Operating Hours:** 6 a.m.-8:30 p.m.; 50% network, 50% local. **ADI:** Jackson, MS. **Key Personnel:** Alan Goodwin, News Dir.; Ann Faillace, Sales Mgr.; Peter J. Rinaldi, General Mgr. **Wattage:** 1000. **Ad Rates:** $8-11.17 for 30 seconds; $10-13.52 for 60 seconds.

16885 WMIS-AM - 1240
20 E. Franklin Phone: (601)442-2522
Natchez, MS 39120 Fax: (601)446-9918

Format: Religious; Gospel. **Networks:** NBC; American Urban Radio. **Founded:** 1940. **Operating Hours:** Continuous. **Key Personnel:** Diana E. Nutter, President; Jim Nutter, Sec./Treas.; Lajuna Weir, Station Mgr.; George Lee, Music Dir. **Local Programs:** *Peoples Forum.* **Wattage:** 1000. **Ad Rates:** $8.80 for 30 seconds; $11 for 60 seconds.

16886 WNAT-AM - 1450
2 O'Farral St. Phone: (601)442-4895
Natchez, MS 39120 Fax: (601)446-8260
Free: (800)736-1058

Format: Full Service. **Networks:** ABC; Mississippi. **Founded:** 1949. **Operating Hours:** Continuous. **Key Personnel:** Marie Z. Perkins, President; William S. Perkins, Vice President; Alan N. Perkins, General Mgr.; Sherry Eidt, Sales Mgr. **Wattage:** 1000.

16887 WQNZ-FM - 95.1
Box 768 Phone: (601)442-4895
Natchez, MS 39121 Fax: (601)446-8260
Free: (800)736-1058
E-mail: wtrcfm@bkbank.com

Format: Contemporary Country; Oldies; News; Agricultural. **Networks:** ABC. **Founded:** 1968. **Operating Hours:** Continuous. **Key Personnel:** Marie Z. Perkins, President; William S. Perkins, Vice President; Marie Perkins, Manager; Sherry Eidt, Director. **Wattage:** 100,000 ERP.

16888 WTYJ-FM - 97.7
20 E. Franklin Phone: (601)442-2522
Natchez, MS 39120 Fax: (601)446-9918

Format: Urban Contemporary. **Networks:** American Urban Radio. **Founded:** 1986. **Operating Hours:** Continuous. **Key Personnel:** Diane E. Nutter, President; Jim Nutter, Contact; Lajuna Weir, Station Mgr.; George Lee, Music Dir. **Wattage:** 6000. **Ad Rates:** $8.80 for 30 seconds; $11 for 60 seconds.

NEW ALBANY†, pop. 7,072.

N MS. Union Co. 85 mi. SE of Memphis, TN. Manufactures lumber, cheese, upholstered furniture, electric carts, brake linings and pistons, batteries, refrigeration equipment, milk cartons. Cotton ginning; grist mills; hatcheries. Gum, poplar, oak timber. Dairy, poultry farms. Cotton, corn, sorghum cane, soybeans.

16889 New Albany Gazette
713 Carter Ave. Phone: (601)534-6321
PO Box 300 Fax: (601)534-6355
New Albany, MS 38652
Community newspaper. **Founded:** Aug. 7, 1890. **Freq:** Semiweekly (Wed. and Fri.). **Print Method:** Offset. **Cols./Page:** 6. **Col. Width:** 27 nonpareils. **Col. Depth:** 301 agate lines. **Key Personnel:** Kenneth E. Jones, General Mgr., kenlynn@dixie-net.com; Ann Gray, Advertising Mgr. **USPS:** 377-660. **Subscription Rates:** $32.50; $44.50 out of area; $55 out of state.
Ad Rates: BW: $584.37 **Circ:** Paid ‡6,095
4C: $734.37 Free ‡12,112
SAU: $5.22
PCI: $5.22

16890 WNAU-AM - 1470
PO Box 808 Phone: (601)534-8133
204 Moss Hill Dr. Fax: (601)538-4183
New Albany, MS 38652

Format: Southern Gospel; Sports. **Networks:** Mississippi; USA Radio. **Owner:** MPM Investment Group, PO Box 289, Myrtle, MS 38650. **Founded:** 1955. **Operating Hours:** Continuous; 8% network, 92% local. **ADI:** Memphis, TN. **Key Personnel:** George Callicutt, Sales Mgr.; Terry Cook, General Mgr. **Local Programs:** *Interchange*, Terry Cook. **Wattage:** 500. **Ad Rates:** $2.50-5 for 30 seconds; $5-7 for 60 seconds.

NEWTON, pop. 3,708.

EC MS. Newton Co. 28 mi. W. of Meridian. Clarke College. Saw mills. Manufactures lumber, cheese, fertilizer. Dairy farms. Cotton, corn, soybeans.

16891 The Newton Record
120 S. Main St. Phone: (601)683-2001
PO Box 60 Fax: (601)683-2360
Newton, MS 39345
Local newspaper. **Founded:** 1901. **Freq:** Weekly (Wed.). **Print Method:** Offset. **Cols./Page:** 6. **Col. Width:** 26 nonpareils. **Col. Depth:** 301 agate lines. **Key Personnel:** J.E. Strange, Editor and Publisher. **Subscription Rates:** $20; $25 out of area; $30 out of state. **Remarks:** Accepts advertising.
Ad Rates: GLR: $.32 **Circ:** ‡2,700
BW: $580.50
4C: $710.50
CNU: $4.50

OCEAN SPRINGS, pop. 15,710.

SE MS. Jackson Co. On Mississippi Sound, 5 mi. E. of Biloxi. Seaside resort. Dairy, truck farms.

16892 Current
National Marine Educators Association
PO Box 1470 Phone: (601)374-7557
Ocean Springs, MS 39566-1470 Fax: (601)374-5559

Magazine for those interested in the study and enjoyment of the world of water. **Subtitle:** The Journal of Marine Education. **Freq:** Quarterly 3-4/year. **Trim Size:** 8 1/2 x 11. **Key Personnel:** Nora L. Deans, Editor. **ISSN:** 0889-5546. **Subscription Rates:** $40 library rate; $5 plus $1.25 for postage & handling.
Ad Rates: BW: $500 **Circ:** Paid 1,200
Non-paid 200

16893 Ocean Springs Record
Gannett Co., Inc.
PO Box 1650 Phone: (601)875-2791
Natchez, MS 39121 Fax: (601)875-9569
Publication E-mail: osrecord@mspress.tfnet.org

Community newspaper. **Founded:** Aug. 1965. **Freq:** Weekly (Thurs.). **Print Method:** Offset. **Trim Size:** 13 x 21. **Cols./Page:** 6. **Col. Width:** 2 inches. **Col. Depth:** 21 inches. **Key Personnel:** James B. Ricketts, Editor and Publisher; Peter D. Logan, Advertising Dir. **USPS:** 040-250. **Subscription Rates:** $19.75; $27.75 out of area. **Remarks:** Accepts advertising.
Ad Rates: BW: $674.67 **Circ:** 3,900
4C: $824.67
PCI: $5.65

16894 WOSM-FM - 103.1
4720 Radio Rd. Phone: (601)875-9031
Ocean Springs, MS 39564 Fax: (601)875-6461

Format: Southern Gospel. **Networks:** AP. **Owner:** Charles H. Cooper, at above address. **Founded:** 1971. **Operating Hours:** Continuous. **ADI:** Biloxi-Gulfport-Pascagoula, MS. **Key Personnel:** Margaret Cooper, Contact; Phil Moss. **Local Programs:** *Looking Around*, Margaret Cooper, Mailing contact, (601)875-9031, Fax (601)875-6461. **Wattage:** 50,000.

OKOLONA†, pop. 3,409.

NE MS. Chickasaw Co. 40 mi. NW of Columbus. Manufactures furniture, garments. Cotton ginning. Dairy farms. Cotton, corn, soybeans.

16895 Okolona Messenger
Messenger
249 Main St. Phone: (601)447-5501
Okolona, MS 38860 Fax: (601)447-5024

Newspaper with a Democratic orientation. **Founded:** 1872. **Freq:** Weekly (Thurs.). **Print Method:** Offset. **Cols./Page:** 6. **Col. Width:** 2 inches. **Col. Depth:** 21 1/2 inches. **Key Personnel:** Murry Blankenship, Editor and Publisher. **Subscription Rates:** $12; $14 out of area; $15 out of state. **Remarks:** Accepts advertising.
Ad Rates: BW: $290 **Circ:** 2,400
PCI: $2.50

OLIVE BRANCH, pop. 2,067.

NW MS. De Soto Co. 20 mi. SE of Memphis, TN. Light industry. Residential.

16896 DeSoto County Tribune
8885 Goodman Phone: (601)895-6220
PO Box 486 Fax: (601)895-4377
Olive Branch, MS 38654
Free: (800)558-7025

Community newspaper. **Founded:** Dec. 6, 1972. **Freq:** Weekly (Wed.). **Print Method:** Offset. **Cols./Page:** 6. **Col. Width:** 12 picas. **Col. Depth:** 21 1/2 inches. **Key Personnel:** D.W. Jones, Editor and Publisher. **Subscription Rates:** $2.50. **Remarks:** Accepts advertising.
Ad Rates: BW: $1,315.80 **Circ:** Paid ‡9,897
4C: $1,720.80 Free ‡8,100
SAU: $10.20
PCI: $10.20

16897 Home Market Magazine
DeSoto County Tribune
8885 Goodman Phone: (601)895-6220
PO Box 486 Fax: (601)895-4377
Olive Branch, MS 38654
Free: (800)558-7025

Publication of real estate listings. **Founded:** 1981. **Freq:** Monthly. **Print Method:** Web press. **Trim Size:** 10 1/2 x 13 1/4. **Cols./Page:** 4. **Key Personnel:** Lisa Piper, Editor. **Subscription Rates:** Free. **Remarks:** Accepts advertising.
Ad Rates: BW: $235 **Circ:** Free ‡16,000

OXFORD†, pop. 10,263.

N MS. Lafayette Co. 62 mi. SE of Memphis, TN. University of Mississippi. Manufactures electric motors, appliances, stoves, flakeboard. Pine and hardwood timber. Dairy and poultry farms. Cattle, cotton, beans.

16898 Nightclub & Bar Magazine
Oxford Publishing, Inc.
307 W. Jackson Ave. Phone: (601)236-5510
Oxford, MS 38655 Fax: (601)236-5541
Free: (800)247-3881
Publication E-mail: ncb@nightclub.com

Trade magazine covering management, lighting, sound, food, beverage, promotions, current trends, and other bar industry news. **Founded:** 1984. **Freq:** Monthly. **Print Method:** Offset. **Trim Size:** 8 1/8 x 10 7/8. **Cols./Page:** 3. **Col. Width:** 13 picas. **Col. Depth:** 58 picas. **Key Personnel:** Mitchell Diggs, Editor; Ed Meek, Publisher; Laura McCreary, VP of Sales; Laura Pannell, Dir. of Operations. **ISSN:** 0893-4117. **Subscription Rates:** Free to qualified subscribers; $25; $35 Canada; $85 other countries. **Remarks:** Accepts advertising. **URL:** http://www.nightclub.com.
Ad Rates: BW: $2,600 **Circ:** Paid 2,603
4C: $3,455 Non-paid 21,135
PCI: $150

16899 The Oxford American
PO Box 1156 Phone: (601)236-1836
Oxford, MS 38655 Fax: (601)236-3141
Publication E-mail: oxam@watervalley.net

General-interest literary magazine. **Subtitle:** The Southern Magazine of Good Writing. **Founded:** 1992. **Freq:** Bimonthly. **Trim Size:** 8 1/8 x 10 7/8. **Cols./Page:** 3. **Col. Width:** 2.222 inches. **Col. Depth:** 9.687 inches. **Key Personnel:** John Grisham, Publisher; Marc Smirnoff, Editor; Kelly Caudle, Managing Editor; John Sullivan, Assoc. Editor; Thomas Easterling, Assoc. Editor; Newt Rayburn, Art Dir.; Angela Putt, Circulation Dir., angp@watervalley.net; Kay Lewis, Business Mgr. **ISSN:** 1074-4525. **Subscription Rates:** $19.95 individuals; $36 U.S. International. **Remarks:** Accepts advertising.
Ad Rates: BW: $1,800 **Circ:** Paid 20,000
4C: $2,400

16900 The Oxford Eagle
PO Box 866 Phone: (601)234-4331
Oxford, MS 38655 Fax: (601)234-4351

Newspaper. **Founded:** 1867. **Freq:** Daily (eve.). **Print Method:** Offset. **Trim Size:** 10 13/16 x 21. **Cols./Page:** 6. **Col. Width:** 25 nonpareils. **Col. Depth:** 294 agate lines. **Key Personnel:** Nina Goolsby, Editor/Administration; Jesse P. Phillips, Publisher. **Subscription Rates:** $36. **Remarks:** Accepts advertising.
Ad Rates: SAU: $5.90 **Circ:** Paid ‡4,982
CNU: $743.40 Free ‡13,000
PCI: $210 Free 11,000

16901 WMAV-FM - 90.3
c/o WMPN-FM Phone: (601)982-6565
3825 Ridgewood Rd. Fax: (601)982-6746
Jackson, MS 39211
Free: (800)472-2580

Format: Classical; News. **Networks:** National Public Radio (NPR); Public Radio International (PRI). **Owner:** Mississippi Authority for Educational TV, at above address. **Founded:** 1983. **Operating Hours:** Continuous. **ADI:** Columbus-Tupelo (West Point), MS. **Key Personnel:** William Fulton, Director. **Local Programs:** *Highway 61*, David Nelson; *Mississippi Concert Hall*, Tim Riley; *The Opera Bill*, William Fulton. **Wattage:** 100,000. **Ad Rates:** Noncommercial. **URL:** http://www.npr.org/members/prm.

16902 WMAV-TV - 18
c/o WMPN-TV Phone: (601)982-6565
3825 Ridgewood Rd. Fax: (601)982-6746
Jackson, MS 39211

Format: Public TV. **Simulcasts:** WMPN-TV Jackson, MS. **Networks:** Public Broadcasting Service (PBS). **Owner:** Mississippi Authority for Educational TV, at above address. **Founded:** 1972. **Operating Hours:** 6:45 am-11:15 pm weekdays; noon-11:15 pm Sat.; noon-11 pm Sun. **ADI:** Memphis, TN. **Key Personnel:** A.J. Jaeger, Contact; Gayle Loeber, Program Dir.

16903 WQLJ-FM - 93.7
307 South Lamar Phone: (601)236-0093
PO Drawer 1077 Fax: (601)234-5155
Oxford, MS 38655
E-mail: wqlj@wqlj.com

Format: Adult Contemporary; Sports. **Networks:** Mississippi. **Owner:** Oxford Radio Inc., at above address. **Founded:** 1985. **Formerly:** WKLJ-FM (1992). **Operating Hours:** Continuous. **Key Personnel:** David Kellum, General Mgr.; Jack Gadd, Sales Mgr. **Wattage:** 25,000. **Ad Rates:** $5.50-8.50 for 30 seconds; $10-16 for 60 seconds.

16904 WWMS-FM - 97.5
Box 1056 Phone: (601)234-6881
Oxford, MS 38655 Fax: (601)236-5014

Format: Contemporary Country; News; Agricultural. **Networks:** ABC. **Founded:** 1969. **Operating Hours:** Continuous. **ADI:** Columbus-Tupelo (West Point), MS. **Wattage:** 100,000 ERP.

PASCAGOULA†, pop. 30,085.

SE MS. Jackson Co. On Pascagoula River and Gulf of Mexico, 21 mi. E. of Biloxi. Coastal resort and fishing center. Shipbuilding. Manufactures pet foods, fertilizers, petroleum products, chemicals.

16905 Mississippi Press
Newhouse Newspapers
405 Delmas Ave. Phone: (601)762-1111
PO Box 849 Fax: (601)934-1454
Pascagoula, MS 39567
Free: (800)655-6597

General newspaper. **Founded:** 1964. **Freq:** Daily (eve.). **Print Method:** Offset. **Cols./Page:** 6. **Col. Width:** 2 1/16 inches. **Col. Depth:** 21 1/4 inches. **Key Personnel:** Dan Davis, Editor; Wanda H. Jacobs, Publisher; Tommy Chelette, Advertising Dir. **Subscription Rates:** $72. **Remarks:** Accepts advertising.
Ad Rates: BW: $1,637.10 **Circ:** Mon.-Fri. 20,036
4C: $1,902.10 Tues. 21,245
SAU: $12.84 Sun. 21,452

16906 Sammons Communications of Mississippi, Inc.
5100 McPhelah Rd. Phone: (601)769-1221
Box 1818 Fax: (601)769-6216
Pascagoula, MS 39567

Founded: 1971. **Cities Served:** Jackson County, MS.

16907 WGUD-AM - 1490
PO Box 307 Phone: (601)475-2111
Pascagoula, MS 39568 Fax: (601)474-2236

Format: News; Sports. **Networks:** CNN Radio; Mississippi. **Founded:** 1964. **Operating Hours:** Continuous; 80% network, 20% local. **ADI:** Biloxi-Gulfport-Pascagoula, MS. **Key Personnel:** Phil Moss, News Dir.; Al Parker, Program Dir.; Glen Murphey, Manager. **Wattage:** 1000. **Ad Rates:** $6-10 for 30 seconds; $8-15 for 60 seconds.

16908 WZZJ-AM - 1580
5115 Telephone Rd. Phone: (228)762-5683
Pascagoula, MS 39567 Fax: (228)762-1222
E-mail: kgwzzj@aol.com

Format: Contemporary Christian. **Networks:** USA Radio. **Owner:** Judah Broadcasting Network, Inc., at above address. **Founded:** 1951. **Formerly:** WPMO-AM (1991); WKNN-AM. **Operating Hours:** Continuous. **ADI:** Biloxi-Gulfport-Pascagoula, MS. **Key Personnel:** Kevin Grady, General Mgr.; Jean Sisk, Sales Mgr.; Susan Grady, Office Mgr. **Local Programs:** *The Morning Light* 7 a.m.-10 a.m. Monday-Friday, Kevin Grady. **Wattage:** 5000 day; 50 night. **Ad Rates:** $4-10 for 30 seconds; $5-12 for 60 seconds.

PEARL, pop. 20,346.

SC MS. Rankin Co, 5 mi. E. of Jackson.

16909 The Weekly Leader
PO Box 54241 Phone: (601)825-8333
Pearl, MS 39208 Fax: (601)825-8334

Community newspaper. **Founded:** 1968. **Freq:** Weekly (Wed.). **Print Method:** Offset. **Cols./Page:** 6. **Col. Width:** 13 picas. **Col. Depth:** 21 1/2 inches. **Key Personnel:** Marcus Bowers, Jr., Editor and Publisher. **Subscription Rates:** Free. **Remarks:** Accepts advertising.
Ad Rates: BW: $1,161 **Circ:** Free ‡14,000
4C: $1,568
PCI: $7.00

16910 Rankin County CableVision
3100 Harle St. Phone: (601)939-6240
Box 54145 Fax: (601)939-2912
Pearl, MS 39288
E-mail: rcable@blazenet.net

Owner: Susquehanna-Pfaltzgraff Co., 140 East Market St., York, PA 17401, (717)848-5515, Fax: (717)771-1439. **Founded:** 1988. **Formerly:** Torrance Cable; Mid-South Cable. **Key Personnel:** Robert Marsh, General Mgr., phone (601)932-3172, bobmarsh@bellsouth.net; Kevin Smith, Technical Operations Mgr., kmsmith@blazenet.net; Stacey Kirkland, Customer Operations Mgr., skirkland@blazenet.net. **Cities Served:** Brandon, Flowood, Johns, Pearl, Pelahatchie, Puckett, MS; Rankin County: subscribing households 22,053; 62 channels. **URL:** http://www.rankincable.com.

PHILADELPHIA†, pop. 6,434.

EC MS. Neshoba Co. 10 mi. S. of Burnside. Lumber. Diversified agriculture.

16911 WHOC-AM - 1490
1016 W. Beacon St. Phone: (601)656-1490
Philadelphia, MS 39350 Fax: (601)656-1491

Format: Country; News; Talk. **Networks:** Mississippi; CBS. **Founded:** 1948. **Operating Hours:** 5 a.m.-10 p.m.; 10% network, 90% local. **Key Personnel:** Leah C. Jarrell, Contact; Joe Vines, Sales Mgr.; Laura Thrash, Program Dir. **Wattage:** 1000.

16912 WWSL-FM - 102.3
PO Box 26 Phone: (601)656-7102
Philadelphia, MS 39350 Fax: (601)656-1491

Format: Soft Rock. **Networks:** NBC; Westwood One Radio. **Owner:** Joe Vines, at above address, (601)656-1491. **Founded:** 1980. **Operating Hours:** Continuous; 70% network, 30% local. **ADI:** Meridian, MS. **Key Personnel:** Joe Vines, Contact; Laura Thrash, News Dir.; Leah Jarrell, Promotions Mgr. **Wattage:** 6000. **Ad Rates:** $4 for 30 seconds; $6 for 60 seconds.

PICAYUNE, pop. 11,420.

SC MS. Pearl River Co. 35 mi. WNW of Gulfport. Manufactures lumber, clothing, oil, dairy products. Livestock.

16913 Picayune Item
Donrey Media Group
214 N. Curran Ave. Phone: (601)798-4766
Picayune, MS 39466 Fax: (601)798-8602

General newspaper. **Founded:** June 1, 1904. **Freq:** Tues. - Fri. (eve.); Sun. (morn.). **Print Method:** Offset. **Trim Size:** 21 1/2 x 13. **Cols./Page:** 6. **Key Personnel:** Mark L. Elwood, Editor; Dave Sims, Advertising Mgr.; Donald N. Reynolds, Publisher; Tom Andrews, Editor. **Subscription Rates:** $45; $69.60 mail. **Remarks:** Accepts advertising.
Ad Rates: SAU: $6.44 **Circ:** ‡13,585

16914 WRJW-AM - 1320
PO Box 907 Phone: (601)798-4835
Picayune, MS 39466 Fax: (601)798-9755
Free: (800)284-5036

Format: Country; Gospel. **Networks:** ABC; Jones Satellite; Missouri. **Owner:** Pearl River Communications, Inc., 2438 Hwy. 43 S., Picayune, MS 39466, (601)798-4697. **Founded:** 1949. **Operating Hours:** 5:30 a.m.-9:00 p.m. **Key Personnel:** M. Delores Wood, Manager; Joe Whatley, News Dir., phone (601)799-1900; Cecile Kennedy, Traffic Dir.; M. Denise Wilson, Program Dir., phone (601)798-4836. **Local Programs:** *Pearl River City Sportsman*, Geri Grubbs; *Focus on Pearl River City*, Delores Wood. **Wattage:** 5,000. **Ad Rates:** $10-13 for 30 seconds; $14-16 for 60 seconds.

PONTOTOC†, pop. 4,723.

NE MS. Pontotoc Co. 60 mi. NW of Columbus. Manufactures furniture, orthopedic supplies, golf equipment, magnetic wire, metal mouldings and forgings. Lumber and planing mill; cotton ginning; industrial packaging. Agriculture. Dairying and poultry farms. Cotton, wheat, soybeans. Livestock.

16915 Arkansas Farmer
Rural Press USA
28 Fontaine Cove
Pontotoc, MS 38863
Publication E-mail: farmnews@aol.com

Tabloid containing news and information on farming. **Founded:** 1985. **Freq:** Monthly. **Key Personnel:** J. Tennant, Publisher; Eva Ann Dorris, Editor. **Subscription Rates:** $12 individuals. **Remarks:** Accepts advertising. **Formerly:** Arkansas Farm & Country.
Ad Rates: BW: $1,082 **Circ:** 10,000
4C: $1,582

16916 The Pontotoc Progress
American Publishing Co.
13 E. Jefferson St. Phone: (601)489-3511
PO Box 210 Fax: (601)489-6714
Pontotoc, MS 38863
Newspaper with a Democratic orientation. **Founded:** 1929. **Freq:** Weekly (Thurs.). **Print Method:** Offset. **Cols./Page:** 6. **Col. Width:** 26 nonpareils. **Col. Depth:** 301 agate lines. **Key Personnel:** David Helms, Editor; Kenneth E. Jones, Publisher; Mary Rush, Advertising Mgr. **Subscription Rates:** $15.

POPLARVILLE†, pop. 2,562.

SC MS. Pearl River Co. 10 mi. NE of Derby. Pearl River Junior College. Manufactures turpentine, lumber.

16917 Poplarville Democrat
Donrey Media Group
109 W. Pearl St. Phone: (601)795-2247
PO Box 549 Fax: (601)795-2248
Poplarville, MS 39470
Community newspaper. **Freq:** Weekly (Thurs.). **Print Method:** Offset. **Cols./Page:** 6. **Col. Width:** 12 1/5 picas. **Col. Depth:** 21 1/2 inches. **Key Personnel:** Larry Stringer, Editor; Ann Rounsavall, Publisher, phone (601)798-4766, fax (601)798-8602. **Subscription Rates:** $9; $12 out of county. **Remarks:** Accepts advertising.
Ad Rates: PCI: $4.20 **Circ:** ‡2,400

16918 WRPM-AM - 1530
Progress Rd. Phone: (601)795-4900
Box 352 Fax: (601)795-0277
Poplarville, MS 39470
Free: (800)934-9776
E-mail: tcvaugh@ibm.net

Format: Southern Gospel. **Networks:** ABC. **Founded:** 1963. **Operating Hours:** Sunrise-sunset; 10% network, 90% local. **Key Personnel:** Mike Porter, General Mgr.; Thomas Vaughn, Station Mgr. **Wattage:** 10,000. **Ad Rates:** $2-5 for 30 seconds. **URL:** http://www.com.poplarville.

PORT GIBSON†, pop. 2,371.

SW MS. Claiborne Co. 25 mi. S. of Vicksburg. Manufactures lumber, textiles, cottonseed products. Agriculture. Cattle, hogs. Soybeans.

16919 The Port Gibson Reveille
Claiborne Publishing Co., Inc.
708 Market Phone: (601)437-5103
PO Box 1002 Fax: (601)437-4410
Port Gibson, MS 39150-1002
Community newspaper. **Founded:** 1851. **Freq:** Weekly (Thurs.). **Print Method:** Offset. **Cols./Page:** 6. **Col. Width:** 27 nonpareils. **Col. Depth:** 301 agate lines. **Key Personnel:** Emma F. Crisler, Editor and Publisher; Janice G. Bufkin, Advertising Mgr. **USPS:** 438-680. **Subscription Rates:** $16 individuals in state; $31 out of state. **Remarks:** Accepts advertising.
Ad Rates: BW: $375.48 **Circ:** Paid 2,222
4C: $440 Free ‡49
PCI: $3.85

PRENTISS†, pop. 1,465.

S MS. Jefferson Davis Co. 40 mi. NW of Hattiesburg. Prentiss Normal and Industrial Institute. Manufactures kraft paper, pulpwood, cresote, garments. Agriculture. Corn, sorghum, pimento, peppers, wheat, oats.

16920 The Prentiss Headlight
Prentiss Publishers, Inc.
PO Box 1257 Phone: (601)792-4221
Prentiss, MS 39474 Fax: (601)792-4222

Community newspaper. **Founded:** 1906. **Freq:** Weekly (Wed.). **Print Method:** Offset. **Trim Size:** 13 3/4 x 21 3/4. **Cols./Page:** 6. **Col. Width:** 12 picas. **Col. Depth:** 21 1/2 inches. **Key Personnel:** William O. Jacobs, Publisher. **USPS:** 441-960. **Subscription Rates:** $16 individuals; $20 out of area; $28 out of state.
Ad Rates: BW: $632.10 **Circ:** Paid 2,366
4C: $1,032.10 Free 5,482
SAU: $4.65

16921 WJDR-FM - 98.3
PO Box 880 Phone: (601)792-2056
Prentiss, MS 39474 Fax: (601)736-2617

Format: Contemporary Country. **Networks:** Westwood One Radio. **Owner:** Thomas F. McDaniel, 37 South High School Ave., Columbia, MS, (601)731-2298, Fax: (601)736-2617. **Founded:** 1982. **Operating Hours:** 24 Continuous.; 90% network, 10% local. **ADI:** Laurel-Hattiesburg, MS. **Key Personnel:** Rob Schepers, Station Mgr., phone (601)792-2056, fax (601)792-2057; Debbie Beets, Contact, phone (601)731-2298, fax (601)736-2617. **Wattage:** 6000. **Ad Rates:** $6 for 30 seconds; $7.50 for 60 seconds.

PURVIS

16922 Lamar County News
Lamar Publishing Co.
109 Shelby Speights Phone: (601)794-2765
PO Box 429 Fax: (601)794-2766
Purvis, MS 39475
Community newspaper. **Freq:** Weekly (Thurs.). **Cols./Page:** 8. **Col. Width:** 10 1/2 picas. **Col. Depth:** 21 inches. **Key Personnel:** Jim Clinton, Owner, phone (601)264-4628, fax (601)268-7892; Louis Breakfield, Editor, phone (601)794-2765; Gene O'Gordon, News Dir., phone (601)794-2765; Tate Nations, Graphic Artist, phone (601)794-2765; Cecile Anderson, Advertising Dir. **Subscription Rates:** $18 individuals; $20 out of area.
Circ: 600

QUITMAN†, pop. 2,632.

EC MS. Clarke Co. 10 mi. N. of De Soto.

16923 Twin County Cablevision
105-B E. Church Phone: (601)776-3426
P.O. Box 61 Fax: (601)766-3817
Quitman, MS 39355

Owner: Cable Management Co., 670 International Pkwy., Richardson, TX 75081, (214)238-1291, Fax: (214)233-9616. **Founded:** 1967. **Formerly:** TV Cable Inc. (1983). **Key Personnel:** Gary White, General Mgr. **Cities Served:** subscribing households 3,400; 22 channels.

16924 WBFN-AM - 1500
Drawer 70 Phone: (601)776-3327
Quitman, MS 39355 Fax: (601)776-6762

Format: Urban Contemporary. **Operating Hours:** Sunrise-sunset. **Key Personnel:** Herman Kelly, President; Terry Bonner, Contact; Micheal Fairchild, Contact; Margaret Loften, Sales Mgr. **Local Programs:** *Desde La Frontera*, Bertha A. Reyes; *Mano Amiga*, Juanita Valdes; *Media Naranja*, Juventino Botello. **Wattage:** 1000. **Ad Rates:** $6 for 30 seconds; $7.50 for 60 seconds.

16925 WYKK-FM - 98.9
Drawer 70 Phone: (601)776-2931
Quitman, MS 39355 Fax: (601)776-6762

Format: Country. **Networks:** Jones Satellite. **Operating Hours:** Continuous. **Key Personnel:** Herman Kelly, President; Terry Bonner, Contact; Micheal Fairchild, Contact; Margaret Lofton, Sales Mgr. **Wattage:** 25,000. **Ad Rates:** $6 for 30 seconds; $7.50 for 60 seconds.

RALEIGH†, pop. 998.

SC MS. Smith Co. 40 mi. SE of Jackson. Pine timber. Agriculture. Poultry and poultry products. Cotton, livestock.

16926 Smith County Reformer
PO Box 187 Phone: (601)782-4358
Raleigh, MS 39153 Fax: (601)782-9020

Newspaper with a Democratic orientation. **Founded:** 1892. **Freq:** Weekly (Wed.). **Print Method:** Offset. **Trim Size:** 14 1/4 x 21 1/2. **Cols./Page:** 6. **Col. Width:** 2 1/4 inches. **Col. Depth:** 21 1/2 inches. **Key Personnel:** Ronnie L. Buckley, Publisher, phone (601)764-3104, fax (601)764-3106; Brad Crocker, Editor; Brenda Ingram, Advertising Mgr. **Subscription Rates:** $15 individuals; $20 out of area; $23 out of state. **Alt. Formats:** CD-ROM.
Ad Rates: GLR: $.20 **Circ:** 3,859
BW: $709.50
4C: $959.50
PCI: $5.50

RAYMOND

16927 Hinds County Gazette
110 Pt. Gibson St. Phone: (601)857-8071
Raymond, MS 39154 Fax: (601)857-5095
Publisher E-mail: hcgazette@aol.com

Community newspaper. **Founded:** 1843. **Freq:** Weekly (Thurs.). **Print Method:** Offset. **Cols./Page:** 6. **Col. Width:** 12 picas. **Col. Depth:** 21 inches. **Key Personnel:** Mary Ann Keith, Editor and Publisher. **USPS:** 246-000. **Subscription Rates:** $20; $25 out of area; $30 out of state. **Remarks:** Accepts advertising.
Ad Rates: BW: $441 **Circ:** Paid ⊕**2,049**
PCI: $4 Non-paid ⊕**160**

RICHTON, pop. 1,205.

SE MS. Perry Co. 22 mi. E. of Hattiesburg. Garment factory. Plywood, pole mills. Pine and hardwood timber. Agriculture. Corn, cotton, sweet potatoes.

16928 The Richton Dispatch
PO Drawer X Phone: (601)788-6031
Richton, MS 39476-1521 Fax: (601)788-6031
Publication E-mail: richton1@aol.com

Newspaper with a Democratic orientation. **Founded:** 1905. **Freq:** Weekly (Thurs.). **Print Method:** Offset. **Trim Size:** 7 1/4 x 11 1/4. **Cols./Page:** 6. **Col. Width:** 12 picas. **Col. Depth:** 21 inches. **Key Personnel:** Larry A. Wilson, Editor and Publisher. **USPS:** 465-660. **Subscription Rates:** $13 individuals; $14 out of area; $16 out of state. **Remarks:** Accepts advertising.
Ad Rates: GLR: $16 **Circ:** Paid ‡1,610
BW: $384.30 Free ‡10
4C: $584.30
SAU: $3.25

RIDGELAND

16929 The Stockman Grass Farmer
Mississippi Valley Publishing Corp.
282 Commonce Park Dr. Phone: (601)853-1861
Ridgeland, MS 39158 Fax: (601)853-8087
Free: (800)748-9808

Magazine reporting on livestock intensive grazing and pasture management. **Founded:** 1947. **Freq:** Monthly. **Print Method:** Offset. **Trim Size:** 10 1/2 x 12. **Cols./Page:** 4. **Key Personnel:** H. Allan Nation, Editor and Publisher; Sally Imgrund, Advertising Mgr.; Glinda Davenport, Managing Editor. **ISSN:** 0899-1057. **Subscription Rates:** $28 individuals; $50 two years; $5 single issue. **Remarks:** Accepts advertising. **Formerly:** Stockman Farmer (Mid South) (1988).
Ad Rates: BW: $1,410 **Circ:** Paid ★**11,338**
4C: $1,910
PCI: $50

16930 WKXI-AM - 1300
731 S. Tear Orchird, Ste.27 Phone: (601)957-1300
Ridgeland, MS 39157 Fax: (601)956-0516

Format: Blues. **Simulcasts:** WKXI-FM. **Networks:** ABC. **Owner:** Opus Media Group, PO Box 9446, Jackson, MS 39286-9446. **Operating Hours:** Continuous. **Key Personnel:** Stan Branson, Program Dir.; Becky Elkin, Sales Mgr. **Wattage:** 5000. **Ad Rates:** $20-25 per unit. Combined advertising rates available with WKXI-FM.

RIPLEY†, pop. 4,271.

N MS. Tippah Co. 72 mi. SE of Memphis, TN. Manufactures lumber, furniture, staves, rubber products, clothing, shoes. Pine and hardwood timber. Farming. Cotton, corn, soybeans.

16931 Ripley Video Cable Co.
115 N. Main St. Phone: (601)837-4881
Ripley, MS 38663 Fax: (601)837-9332

Owner: Leon M. Bailey Jr., at above address. **Founded:** 1969. **Key Personnel:** Leon Bailey, General Mgr. **Cities Served:** Blue Mountain, Falkner, Pine Grove, Ripley, MS: subscribing households 3,141; 36 channels; 1 community access channel; 108 hours per week community access programming.

ROLLING FORK†, pop. 2,590.

W MS. Sharkey Co. 44 mi. N. of Vicksburg. Manufactures elastic fabrics, lumber. Agriculture. Cattle, poultry.

16932 Deer Creek Pilot
Deer Creek
PO Box 398 Phone: (601)873-4354
Rolling Fork, MS 39159 Fax: (601)873-4355

Community newspaper. **Founded:** 1876. **Freq:** Weekly (Thurs.). **Print Method:** Offset. **Cols./Page:** 6. **Col. Depth:** 20 inches. **Key Personnel:** W. Ray Mosby, Editor and Publisher. **Subscription Rates:** $18. **Remarks:** Accepts advertising.
Ad Rates: GLR: $.15 **Circ:** ‡1,500
BW: $336
4C: $636
SAU: $3,120
PCI: $3.75

16933 Cable TV
Box 399 Phone: (601)873-4027
Rolling Fork, MS 39159 Fax: (601)873-2467

Owner: Yazoo Answer Call Inc., at above address. **Key Personnel:** L.T. Wade, General Mgr. **Cities Served:** Rolling Fork, MS.

SARDIS†, pop. 2,278.

NW MS. Panola Co. 48 mi. S. of Memphis, TN. Manufactures clothes, lumber, luggage, hospital furniture. Cotton ginning. Cattle, stock, dairy, soybeans.

16934 The Southern Reporter
TSR Publications Inc.
PO Box 157 Phone: (601)487-1551
Sardis, MS 38666-0157 Fax: (601)487-1552

Community newspaper. **Founded:** 1855. **Freq:** Weekly (Thurs.). **Print Method:** Offset. **Trim Size:** 7 1/2 x 10 1/2. **Cols./Page:** 6. **Col. Width:** 24 nonpareils. **Col. Depth:** 21 1/2 inches. **Key Personnel:** J. Crisler Fletcher, Editor and Publisher. **USPS:** 506-720. **Subscription Rates:** $17; $19 out of area. **Remarks:** Accepts advertising.
Ad Rates: SAU: $4.86 **Circ:** ‡2,311
PCI: $4

SENATOBIA†, pop. 5,013.

NW MS. Tate Co. 34 mi. S. of Memphis, TN. Northwest Mississippi Community College. Manufactures chrome furniture, clothing. Sawmills, cotton ginning, printing plant. Dairy, stock, poultry farms. Cotton, corn, hay.

16935 The Democrat
219 E. Main St. Phone: (601)562-4414
PO Box 369 Fax: (601)562-8866
Senatobia, MS 38668-0369
Publisher E-mail: mailbag@thedemocrat.com

Community newspaper. **Founded:** Dec. 18, 1881. **Freq:** Weekly (Tues.). **Print Method:** Offset. **Trim Size:** 13 x 21 1/2. **Cols./Page:** 6. **Col. Width:** 12 picas. **Col. Depth:** 21 1/2 inches. **Key Personnel:** Jay Lee, Editor/Administration, jlee@thedemocrat.com; Joseph B. Lee III, Publisher; LaJuan Tallo, News Editor, ltallo@thedemocrat.com. **USPS:** 534-040. **Subscription Rates:** $20; $25 out of area; $30 out of state. **Remarks:** Accepts advertising. **URL:** http://www.thedemocrat.com. **Formerly:** Tate County Democrat.
Ad Rates: BW: $516 **Circ:** ‡5,200
4C: $891
SAU: $6.55
PCI: $6.25

16936 WKNA-FM - 88.9
c/o WKNO-FM Phone: (901)325-6544
900 Getwell Rd. Fax: (901)325-6506
Memphis, TN 38111

Format: Talk; Public Radio; News. **Networks:** National Public Radio (NPR); Public Radio International (PRI). **Owner:** Mid-South Public Communications Foundation, at above address. **Founded:** 1973. **Formerly:** WNJC-FM. **Operating Hours:** Continuous; 30% network, 70% local. **ADI:** Memphis, TN. **Key Personnel:** Susan Westfall, Manager; Darel Snodgrass, Operations Mgr. **Wattage:** 20,000.

16937 WSAO-AM - 1140
PO Box 190 Phone: (601)562-4445
Senatobia, MS 38668 Fax: (601)562-4445
Free: (888)550-2009

Format: Religious; Gospel. **Founded:** 1961. **Operating Hours:** 6 a.m.-6 p.m.; 10% network, 90% local. **Key Personnel:** Jesse Ross, Contact; Ernestine Ross. **Wattage:** 5000. **Ad Rates:** $6 for 30 seconds; $8 for 60 seconds.

SOUTHAVEN, pop. 16,471.

NW MS. De Soto Co. 10 mi. S. of Memphis, TN.

16938 DeSoto Times Today
P. H. Publishing
8625 Highway St. Phone: (601)393-6397
Southaven, MS 38671 Fax: (601)393-6463
Publisher E-mail: destimes@aol.com

Community newspaper. **Subtitle:** DeSoto Times Today. **Founded:** 1839. **Freq:** 5 times a week/Tuesday through Saturday, a.m. **Print Method:** Offset. **Trim Size:** 21 1/2. **Cols./Page:** 6. **Col. Width:** 24 nonpareils. **Col. Depth:** 294 agate lines. **Key Personnel:** Tom Pittman, Editor, phone (601)429-6397, fax (601)429-5229. **USPS:** 566-620. **Subscription Rates:** $9 month. **Remarks:** Accepts advertising.
Ad Rates: BW: $1,245 **Circ:** Paid ‡7,770
4C: $1,445
SAU: $6
PCI: $9.65

16939 Time Warner Cable
PO Box 829 Phone: (601)393-3366
Southaven, MS 38671 Fax: (601)393-3654
Free: (800)872-8047

Owner: Time Warner Communications, 6555 Quince, Ste. 400, Memphis, TN 38115. **Formerly:** Star Cable TV Co.; Mid-South Cable. **Key Personnel:** Bob Moss, Sr. Dir. Regional Opr./General Mgr. **Cities Served:** Byhalia, Coldwater, Crenshaw, Hernando, Nesbit, Olive Branch, Sardis, Senatobio, Sledge, Southaven, Tunica, MS; Como, Horn Lake, Walls, Sardis Lake, and Robinsonville, MS.: subscribing households 24,000; 38 channels; 3 community access channels.

STARKVILLE†, pop. 16,719.

E MS. Oktibbeha Co. 22 mi. W. of Columbus. Mississippi State University. Manufactures paper, cotton, felt, feed, apparel, clocks, motors, food and dairy products. Oak and pine timber. Dairy farming. Hay, soybeans.

16940 The Starkville Daily News
American Publishing Co.
316 University Dr. Phone: (601)323-1642
PO Drawer 1068 Fax: (601)323-6586
Starkville, MS 39759
Newspaper. **Subtitle:** Starkville Daily News. **Founded:** 1960. **Freq:** Daily (morn.). **Print Method:** Offset. **Cols./Page:** 6. **Col. Width:** 26 nonpareils. **Col. Depth:** 301 agate lines. **Key Personnel:** Rick Noffsinger, Publisher; Bill Killebrew, Advertising Mgr. **USPS:** 519-660. **Subscription Rates:** $77. **Remarks:** Accepts advertising.
Ad Rates: GLR: $.60 **Circ:** ‡6,500
BW: $1,109.40
4C: $1,334.40
SAU: $8.60

16941 Northland Cable Television
PO Box 1447 Phone: (601)323-1615
Starkville, MS 39759 Fax: (601)323-1682

Owner: Northland Communications Corp., 1201 3rd Ave., Ste. 3600, Seattle, WA 98101, (206)621-1351. **Formerly:** Starkville TV Cable Co. (1990). **Key Personnel:** Bill Staley, General Mgr. **Cities Served:** subscribing households 7,000; 40 channels; 1 community access channel; 10 hours per week community access programming.

16942 WSSO-AM - 1230
608 Yellowjacket Dr. Phone: (601)323-1230
Starkville, MS 39759 Fax: (601)323-0573

Format: Sports. **Owner:** Cumulus Broadcasting, Inc., PO Box 1076, Columbus, MS 39703, (601)327-1183, Fax: (601)328-1122. **Founded:** 1948. **Operating Hours:** Continuous. **ADI:** Columbus-Tupelo (West Point), MS. **Key Personnel:** Bob Green, General Mgr., phone (601)327-1183, fax (601)328-1122; Shane R. Kinder, News/Sports Dir./PD, phone (601)323-1230, fax (601)323-0573. **Wattage:** 1000. **Ad Rates:** $6.25-15 for 30 seconds.

TUNICA

16943 The Tunica Times
Tunica Publishing Co.
991 Magnolia Phone: (601)363-1511
PO Box 308 Fax: (601)363-1511
Tunica, MS 38676
Free: (800)775-5826

Community newspaper. **Founded:** 1904. **Freq:** Weekly (Thurs.). **Print Method:** Offset. **Cols./Page:** 6. **Col. Width:** 2 inches. **Col. Depth:** 21 1/2 inches. **Key Personnel:** Brooks Taylor, Publisher, rtaylor@gmi.net. **Subscription Rates:** $20 out of county; in-state; $30 out of state. **Remarks:** Accepts advertising. **Formerly:** The Tunica Times-Democrat (1992).
Ad Rates: BW: $387 **Circ:** Paid ‡1,780
4C: $657
PCI: $4

TUPELO†, pop. 25,488.

NE MS. Lee Co. 55 mi. N. of Columbus. Manufactures milk and dairy products, beverages, garments, fluorescent fixtures, tires, power tools, church and school furniture, fertilizer. Poultry processing plant. Cotton ginning; sawmills. Fish hatchery. Pine timber. Agriculture. Dairy. Livestock.

16944 Northeast Mississippi Daily Journal
Journal Publishing Co.
PO Box 909 Phone: (601)842-2611
Tupelo, MS 38802 Fax: (601)842-2233
Free: (800)264-6397

General newspaper. **Founded:** 1870. **Freq:** Mon.-Sun. (morn.). **Print Method:** Offset. **Cols./Page:** 6. **Col. Width:** 26 nonpareils. **Col. Depth:** 301 agate lines. **Key Personnel:** Billy Crews, Publisher; Richard Crenshaw, Advertising Dir.; Lloyd Gray, Editor, phone (601)842-2612. **Subscription Rates:** $90. **Remarks:** Advertising not accepted for liquor. **URL:** http://www.djournal.com.
Ad Rates: GLR: $2.04 **Circ:** Mon.-Sat. ★**37,304**
BW: $1,784.07 Sun. ★**37,342**
4C: $2,034.07
PCI: $15.92

16945 Northeast Mississippi Historical and Genealogical Society Quarterly
Northeast Mississippi Historical and Genealogical Society
Box 434
Tupelo, MS 38802-0434

Genealogical and historical journal covering Northeast Mississippi. **Founded:** 1980. **Freq:** Quarterly. **Key Personnel:** Martis D. Ramage, Jr., Editor. **Subscription Rates:** $15 individuals. **Remarks:** Advertising not accepted.
Circ: Combined 475

16946 WELO-AM - 580
PO Box 410 Phone: (601)842-7658
Tupelo, MS 38802 Fax: (601)842-0197

Format: Oldies; News; Talk. **Networks:** ABC; Unistar; Mississippi. **Owner:** San Dow Broadcasting, PO Box 1056, Oxford, MS 38655. **Founded:** 1944. **Formerly:** WWPR-AM. **Operating Hours:** Continuous. **ADI:** Columbus-Tupelo (West Point), MS. **Key Personnel:** Sam H. Howard, Contact; Leslie Nabors, General Sales Mgr.; Patri Gladney, Office Mgr.; Jim Duke, Operations Mgr.; Melissa Murff, Contact. **Wattage:** 1000 day; 500 night.

16947 WESE-FM - 92.5
PO Box 3300 Phone: (601)842-1067
Tupelo, MS 38803 Fax: (601)842-0725

Format: Urban Contemporary. **Networks:** ABC; NBC. **Owner:** Tupelo Broadcasting, at above address. **Founded:** 1980. **Operating Hours:** Continuous. **ADI:** Columbus-Tupelo (West Point), MS. **Key Personnel:** Russ Wilson, General Mgr. **Wattage:** 6000. **Ad Rates:** $7-15 for 30 seconds; $9-17 for 60 seconds. Combined advertising rates available with WWZD-FM, WTVP-AM, WNRX-AM.

16948 WFTA-FM - 101.9
PO Box 2116 Phone: (601)842-7625
Tupelo, MS 38803 Fax: (601)842-9568

Format: Adult Contemporary. **Networks:** ABC. **Owner:** Olive E. Sisk, at above address. **Operating Hours:** Continuous. **ADI:** Columbus-Tupelo (West Point), MS. **Key Personnel:** Fred Blalock, News Dir.; James McPherson, Program Mgr.; Randy Love, Music Dir.; Ivous Sisk, Promotions Mgr. **Wattage:** 100,000. **Ad Rates:** $7 for 30 seconds; $10 for 60 seconds.

16949 WFTO-AM - 1330
PO Box 2116 Phone: (601)862-3191
Tupelo, MS 38803 Fax: (601)842-9568

Format: Country. **Networks:** ABC. **Owner:** Olivie E. Sisk, at above address. **Operating Hours:** 6 a.m.-sunset. **ADI:** Columbus-Tupelo (West Point), MS. **Key Personnel:** Fred Blalock, News Dir.; James McPherson, Program Mgr.; Randy Love, Music Dir.; Ivous Sisk, Promotions Mgr. **Wattage:** 5000. **Ad Rates:** $5 for 30 seconds; $8 for 60 seconds.

16950 WLOV-TV - 27
PO Box 350 Phone: (601)842-7620
Beech Springs Rd. Fax: (601)844-7061
Tupelo, MS 38802

Format: Commercial TV. **Networks:** Fox. **Founded:** 1983. **Formerly:** WVSB-TV. **Operating Hours:** 5 a.m.-2 a.m. **ADI:** Columbus-Tupelo (West Point), MS.

16951 WSYE-FM - 93.3
PO Box 1623 Phone: (601)844-9793
Tupelo, MS 38802 Fax: (601)844-7400

Format: Adult Contemporary. **Founded:** 1968. **Formerly:** WCPC-FM (1990). **Operating Hours:** Continuous. **ADI:** Columbus-Tupelo (West Point), MS. **Key Personnel:** Gwen Rakestraw, General Mgr. **Wattage:** 100,000. **Ad Rates:** $25-38 for 60 seconds.

16952 WTUP-AM - 1490
PO Box 3300 Phone: (601)842-1067
Tupelo, MS 38803 Fax: (601)842-0725

Format: Sports. **Networks:** Mississippi. **Owner:** Cumulus Broadcasting, Inc., at above address. **Founded:** 1953. **Formerly:** Tupelo Broadcasting Corporation. **Operating Hours:** Continuous; 90% network, 10% local. **ADI:** Columbus-Tupelo (West Point), MS. **Key Personnel:** Russ Wilson, General Mgr. **Wattage:** 1000. **Ad Rates:** $7-15 for 30 seconds; $9-17 for 60 seconds. Combined advertising rates available with WWZD-FM, WESE-FM, WNRX-AM.

16953 WTVA-TV - 9
Box 350 Phone: (601)842-7620
Tupelo, MS 38801 Fax: (601)844-7061

Format: Commercial TV. **Networks:** NBC. **Founded:** 1957. **Operating Hours:** Continuous. **ADI:** Columbus-Tupelo (West Point), MS. **Key Personnel:** Mark Ledbetter, General Mgr.

16954 WWKZ-FM - 105.3
3200 W Main St. Phone: (601)844-2134
Tupelo, MS 38801-9407 Fax: (601)844-2887
E-mail: kz105.com

Format: Contemporary Hit Radio (CHR). **Networks:** ABC; Westwood One Radio. **Founded:** 1966. **Operating Hours:** Continuous. **ADI:** Columbus-Tupelo (West Point), MS. **Key Personnel:** Jeff Shaw, General Mgr.; Rick Stevens, Program Dir.; Mark Maharrey, General Sales Mgr. **Wattage:** 50,000. **Ad Rates:** $15-45 for 30 seconds; $20-60 for 60 seconds.

16955 WZLQ-FM - 98.5
PO Box 410 Phone: (601)842-7658
Tupelo, MS 38802 Fax: (601)842-0197

Format: Hot Country. **Networks:** ABC. **Owner:** San-Dow Bradcasting, PO Box 15056, Oxford, NJ. **Founded:** 1968. **Operating Hours:** Continuous. **ADI:** Columbus-Tupelo (West Point), MS. **Key Personnel:** Jim Duke, Operations Mgr.; Leslie R. Nabors, General Sales Mgr.; Patri Gladney, Office Mgr. **Wattage:** 100,000 ERP.

TYLERTOWN†, pop. 1,976.

S MS. Walthall Co. 20 mi. SE of McComb. Manufactures pallets, electrical harness, tools, wood products, component parts, furniture. Cotton ginning; sawmills. Pine, hardwood timber. Dairy.

16956 The Tylertown Times
727 Beulah Ave. Phone: (601)876-5111
PO Box 72 Fax: (601)876-5280
Tylertown, MS 39667
Publication E-mail: ttimes@telafex.com

Newspaper with a Democratic orientation. **Founded:** 1907. **Freq:** Weekly (Thurs.). **Print Method:** Offset. **Trim Size:** 14 x 22 1/2. **Cols./Page:** 6. **Col. Width:** 26 nonpareils. **Col. Depth:** 305 agate lines. **Key Personnel:** Carolyn Dillon, Editor and Publisher; Heather Henning, Office Asst. **ISSN:** 1738-9930. **Subscription Rates:** $15; $35 out of area. **Remarks:** Accepts advertising.
Ad Rates: BW: $645 **Circ:** ‡3,950
PCI: $5

UNIVERSITY, pop. 6,700.

N MS. Lafayette Co. Adjoins Oxford on North. University of Mississippi.

16957 The Daily Mississippian
University of Mississippi Student Media Center
Farley Hall Phone: (601)232-5503
University, MS 38677 Fax: (601)232-5703
Publication E-mail: dmnews@olemiss.edu

Collegiate newspaper. **Founded:** 1911. **Freq:** Daily (morn.). **Print Method:** Offset. **Cols./Page:** 5. **Col. Width:** 2 inches. **Col. Depth:** 16 inches. **Key Personnel:** Traci Mitchell, Acting Director. **USPS:** 351-710. **Subscription Rates:** $50. **Remarks:** Accepts advertising. **URL:** http://www.olemiss.edu.
Ad Rates: BW: $380 **Circ:** ‡11,500
PCI: $5.75

16958 Living Blues
Center for the Study of Southern Culture
University of Mississippi Phone: (601)232-5993
301 Hill Hall Fax: (601)232-7842
University, MS 38677
Free: (800)390-3527
Publication E-mail: LBLUES@barnard.cssc.olemiss.edu

Magazine covering the African-American blues tradition. **Subtitle:** The Magazine of the African-American Blues Tradition. **Founded:** 1970. **Freq:** Bimonthly. **Print Method:** Offset. **Trim Size:** 8 1/2 x 11. **Cols./Page:** 3. **Col. Width:** 14 picas. **Col. Depth:** 60 picas. **Key Personnel:** David Nelson, Editor; Brett Bonner, Advertising Mgr., phone (601)234-8023; Susan Lee, Art Director, slee@sunset.backbone.olemiss.edu; Mickey McLaurin, Business Mgr. **ISSN:** 0024-5232. **Subscription Rates:** $21; $4.50 single issue. **Remarks:** Accepts advertising. **URL:** http://www.cssc.olemiss.edu. **Alt. Formats:** CD-ROM.
Ad Rates: BW: $1,100 **Circ:** ‡25,000
4C: $1,500

16959 Mississippi Law Journal
Box 849
University, MS 38677

Professional legal journal. **Founded:** Jan. 5, 1926. **Freq:** Triennial. **Key Personnel:** Jay Allen, Business Mgr. **Subscription Rates:** $35 individuals. **Remarks:** Accepts advertising. **Available Online.**
Ad Rates: BW: $380 **Circ:** Paid 600

16960 Ole Miss Alumni Review
University of Mississippi Alumni Association
Alumni House Rm. 172 Phone: (601)232-7375
University, MS 38677 Fax: (601)232-7756
Publication E-mail: editor@alumni.a/vm.olemiss.edu

Alumni magazine. **Founded:** 1932. **Freq:** Quarterly. **Print Method:** Web offset. **Trim Size:** 8 1/8 x 10 7/8. **Cols./Page:** 3. **Col. Width:** 2.25 inches. **Col. Depth:** 9 11/16 inches. **Key Personnel:** Bill Dabney, Editor. **Subscription Rates:** $25 individuals per year; $6.25 single issue. **Remarks:** Accepts advertising.
Ad Rates: BW: $1,200 **Circ:** Paid 20,000
4C: $1,800 Controlled 50,000

16961 WUMS-FM - 92.1
Student Media Center Phone: (601)232-7566
Farley Hall Fax: (601)232-5703
University, MS 38677
E-mail: wums@olemiss.edu

Format: Alternative/New Music/Progressive. **Networks:** Westwood One Radio. **Owner:** University of Mississippi, at above address. **Founded:** 1989. **Formerly:** WCBH-FM (1989). **Operating Hours:** Continuous. **Key Personnel:** John Graves, Business and Station Mgr., jgraves@olemiss.edu; David Stripling, Music and Production Dir.; Brad Pfranger. **Local Programs:** *Killing Floor Blues*, Scott Mcgraw; *The Mechanical Pulse*, Pat Dendenault; *Rebel Retro*. **Wattage:** 6000. **Ad Rates:** $6-12 for 30 seconds; $8-16 for 60 seconds. $4-$9.50 for 30 seconds; $5-$12 for 60 seconds. **URL:** http://www.olemiss.edu/orgs/wums/.

VICKSBURG†, pop. 26,192.

W MS. Warren Co. On Mississippi River, 42 mi. W. of Jackson. Port of entry. Tourist center. Manufactures trailers, caskets, chemicals, small appliances, cement, lighting fixtures, packing boxes and crates, lumber, veneer, hardwood flooring, earth moving equipment, feed, fertilizers. Paper mill; bottlings works. U.S. Government machine shops. Boat building yards. Large waterways experimental station. Fisheries. Pine, oaks, cypress timber. Agriculture. Cotton, corn, peas, soybeans.

16962 Vicksburg Evening Post
Vicksburg Printing & Publishing Co., Inc.
PO Box 821668
Vicksburg, MS 39182-1668

General newspaper. **Founded:** May 4, 1883. **Freq:** Daily (eve.), Sat. and Sun. (morn.). **Print Method:** Offset. **Cols./Page:** 6. **Col. Width:** 25 nonpareils. **Col. Depth:** 294 agate lines. **Key Personnel:** L.P. Cashman III, Editor and Publisher; Otis Headley, General Mgr.; David Gillis, Marketing Dir. **ISSN:** 0884-8912. **Subscription Rates:** $108 individuals. **Remarks:** Accepts advertising.
Ad Rates: BW: $1,285.20 **Circ:** Mon.-Sat. ★**14,054**
4C: $1,470.20 Sun. ★**14,430**
PCI: $10.20

16963 WBBV-FM - 101.1
PO Box 820537 Phone: (601)638-0101
Vicksburg, MS 39182 Fax: (601)638-0869

Format: Country. **Networks:** Mississippi; ABC. **Owner:** Bob Bishop, at above address. **Founded:** 1989. **Operating Hours:** Continuous; 10% network, 90% local. **Key Personnel:** Billie J. Bishop, Owner; Allen Pitcher, General Mgr. **Wattage:** 3000. **Ad Rates:** $12 for 30 seconds; $16 for 60 seconds.

WAYNESBORO†, pop. 5,349.

SE MS. Wayne Co. 52 mi. S. of Meridian. Oil. Pine and hardwood timber. Manufactures electrical appliances, wood products, gloves. Livestock.

16964 The Wayne County News
News Publishing Co. of Mississippi
608 Station St. Phone: (601)735-4341
PO Box 509 Fax: (601)735-1111
Waynesboro, MS 39367-0509
Local newspaper. **Founded:** 1891. **Freq:** Weekly (Thurs.). **Print Method:** Offset. **Trim Size:** 14 x 22 3/4. **Cols./Page:** 6. **Col. Width:** 2 1/16 inches. **Col. Depth:** 21 inches. **Key Personnel:** Sharon Howse, Editor. **USPS:** 670-440. **Subscription Rates:** $18.75 individuals; $15 senior citizens; $25 out of area. **Remarks:** Accepts advertising.
Ad Rates: BW: $550 **Circ:** ‡5,202
SAU: $3.95
PCI: $4.50

WESSON, pop. 1,313.

SW MS. Copiah Co. 10 mi. S. of Hazelhurst. Copiah Lincoln Community College. Residential.

16965 Wolf Tales
Copiah-Lincoln Community College
PO Box 649 Phone: (601)643-5101
Wesson, MS 39191 Fax: (601)643-2366

Collegiate newspaper. **Founded:** Apr. 1968. **Freq:** Monthly. **Print Method:** Offset. **Cols./Page:** 6. **Col. Width:** 27 nonpareils. **Col. Depth:** 280 agate lines. **Key Personnel:** Burlian O'Neal Walker, Adviser. **Remarks:** Accepts advertising.
Ad Rates: SAU: $2.44 **Circ:** Free ‡2,000
PCI: $2.50

16966 WCLL-FM - 90.7
Box 649 Phone: (601)643-8384
Wesson, MS 39191-0649 Fax: (601)643-8212

Format: Adult Contemporary. **Owner:** Copiah-Lincoln Community College, at above address, (601)643-8354. **Founded:** 1970. **Formerly:** WWCL-FM (1980). **Operating Hours:** 12 p.m.-midnight Mon.-Thurs.; 6 p.m.-midnight Sun.; 100% local. **Key Personnel:** Burlian O'Neal Walker, General Mgr., phone (601)643-8354. **Wattage:** 100. **Ad Rates:** Noncommercial.

WEST POINT†, pop. 8,811.

E MS. Clay Co. 20 mi. NW of Columbus. Manufactures aluminum boats, garments, steam boilers, toys, dairy products, steel fabrication, packing boxes. Meat packing plant. Hardwood. Diversified farming. Dairying.

16967 Daily Times Leader
227 Court St. Phone: (601)494-1422
PO Box 1176 Fax: (601)494-1414
West Point, MS 39773
General newspaper. **Founded:** 1882. **Freq:** Mon.-Sun. (morn.). **Print Method:** Offset. **Trim Size:** 13 x 21 1/2. **Key Personnel:** Roy Bruce, Editor and Publisher. **Remarks:** Accepts advertising.
Ad Rates: SAU: $9.50 **Circ:** (Not Reported)

16968 WROB-AM - 1450
PO Box 1336 Phone: (601)494-1450
West Point, MS 39773 Fax: (601)494-9762
E-mail: wrobwkbb@ebicom.net

Format: Gospel. **Owner:** Bob McRaney Enterprises, Inc., at above address. **Founded:** 1947. **Operating Hours:** Continuous. **Key Personnel:** Bob McRaney, Jr., President; Samantha McRaney; Elain Byrd, Office Mgr. **Wattage:** 1000.

WIGGINS†, pop. 3,205.

S MS. Stone Co. 35 mi. N. of Gulfport. Lumber mills. Agriculture.

16969 Stone County Enterprise
PO Box 157 Phone: (601)928-4802
Wiggins, MS 39577 Fax: (601)928-2191

Community newspaper. **Founded:** 1916. **Freq:** Weekly (Wed.). **Print Method:** Offset. **Cols./Page:** 6. **Col. Width:** 2 1/16 inches. **Col. Depth:** 21 1/2 inches. **Key Personnel:** Kirk Bayer, Editor and Publisher; Heather Freret, Advertising Dir. **USPS:** 522-300. **Subscription Rates:** $17 individuals; $27 out of area; $32 out of state. **Remarks:** Accepts advertising.
Ad Rates: GLR: $5 **Circ:** 3,600
BW: $630
4C: $823.50
SAU: $5.50
PCI: $5.00

16970 WLUN-FM - 95.3
959 N. Magnolia Dr. Phone: (601)928-7281
Wiggins, MS 39577 Fax: (601)928-7281

Format: Gospel; Country. **Networks:** Satellite Music Network. **Owner:** Stone Lamar Broadcasting, at above address. **Founded:** 1986. **Operating Hours:** Continuous. **Key Personnel:** A.R. Byrd, Contact; George A. Cospelich, Station Mgr.; Barbara Naramore, Operations Mgr.; Gay Byrd, Contact. **Local Programs:** *The Gospel Hour*, Barbara Naramore, Mailing contact; *South MS Swap Shop*, A.R. Byrd, Mailing contact. **Wattage:** 100,000. **Ad Rates:** $10 for 30 seconds; $15 for 60 seconds.

WINONA†, pop. 6,177.

NC MS. Montgomery Co. 90 mi. N. of Jackson. Manufactures cotton goods, cottonseed and dairy products, picture frames, auto parts and clothing. Pine, gum, oak timber. Dairy, stock, poultry farms.

16971 Conservative
Montgomery Publishing Inc.
PO Box 151 Phone: (601)283-1131
Winona, MS 38967 Fax: (601)283-5374
Free: (800)898-0694

Newspaper with Democratic orientation. **Founded:** 1865. **Freq:** Weekly (Thurs.). **Print Method:** Offset. **Cols./Page:** 6. **Col. Width:** 12 picas. **Col. Depth:** 21 1/2 inches. **Key Personnel:** Tim James, Ed./Pub., timjames@network-one.com; Debbie Brown, Office Mgr./Bookeeping; Ken Strachan, Advertising Sales; Joel McNeece, News Editor; Frances Woods, Classifieds/Legals Clerk. **Subscription Rates:** $14; $20 out of area. **Remarks:** Accepts advertising.
Ad Rates: BW: $621.78 **Circ:** (Not Reported)
4C: $846.78
PCI: $4.82

16972 The Winona Times
Montgomery Publishing Inc.
PO Box 151 Phone: (601)283-1131
Winona, MS 38967 Fax: (601)283-5374
Free: (800)898-0694

Newspaper with a Democratic orientation. **Founded:** 1883. **Freq:** Weekly (Thurs.). **Print Method:** Offset. **Cols./Page:** 6. **Col. Width:** 12.5 picas. **Col. Depth:** 21 1/2 inches. **Key Personnel:** Tim James, Ed. and Pub., timjames@network-one.com;' Debbie Brown, Office Mgr./Bookeeping; Ken Strachan, Ad. Consultant; Frances Woods, Classifieds/Legals Clerk; Joel McNeece, News Editor. **Subscription Rates:** $20; $25 out of area. **Remarks:** Accepts advertising.
Ad Rates: BW: $812.70 **Circ:** (Not Reported)
4C: $1,037.70
PCI: $6.30

16973 Galaxy Cablevision
PO Box 725 Phone: (601)283-2414
Winona, MS 38967 Fax: (601)283-1547
Free: (800)543-6584

Owner: Vista Communications LP III, 40 Nagog Pk., 2 Maryland Farms, Acton, MA. **Formerly:** Winona Cablevision. **Key Personnel:** Liz Duffy, General Mgr. **Cities Served:** Coffeeville, Durant, Eupora, Goodman, Itta Bana, Pickens, Winona, MS.

WOODVILLE†, pop. 1,512.

SW MS. Wilkinson Co. 35 mi. SE of Natchez. Sawmill. Pine and hardwood timber. Diversified farming. Beans, truck cropping, cattle.

16974 The Woodville Republican
The Woodville Republican, Inc.
425 Depot St. Phone: (601)888-4293
PO Box 696 Fax: (601)888-6151
Woodville, MS 39669
Community newspaper. **Founded:** Jan. 1824. **Freq:** Weekly (Thurs.). **Print Method:** Offset. **Trim Size:** 13 3/4 x 22 3/4. **Cols./Page:** 8. **Col. Width:** 9 picas. **Col. Depth:** 294 agate lines. **Key Personnel:** Andrew J. Lewis, Editor and Publisher. **USPS:** 462-260. **Subscription Rates:** $18 individuals; $20 out of area; $22 out of state. **Remarks:** Accepts advertising.
Ad Rates: GLR: $.328 **Circ:** 2,545
BW: $772.80
4C: $850
SAU: $6.32
PCI: $4

YAZOO CITY†, pop. 11,834.

WC MS. Yazoo Co. On Yazoo River, 40 mi. NW of Jackson. Cotton market. Manufactures lumber, paper bags, wire harnessing, fertilizer, feed. Oil refinery. Fisheries. Corn, soybeans, cotton. Livestock.

16975 The Yazoo Herald
Yazoo Newspaper Inc.
1035 Grand Ave. Phone: (601)746-4911
PO Box 720 Fax: (601)746-4915
Yazoo City, MS 39194
Publication E-mail: herald@tecinfo.com

Newspaper. **Founded:** 1872. **Freq:** Semiweekly (Wed. and Sat.). **Print Method:** Offset. **Cols./Page:** 6. **Col. Width:** 26 nonpareils. **Col. Depth:** 301 agate lines. **Key Personnel:** Steve Stewart, Editor and Publisher. **Subscription Rates:** $29. **Remarks:** Accepts advertising.
Ad Rates: PCI: $5.48 **Circ:** ‡4,000

16976 WJNS-FM - 92.1
1405 Enchanted Dr. Phone: (601)746-5921
PO Box 1048 Fax: (601)746-5921
Yazoo City, MS 39194

Format: Gospel. **Owner:** Willis Board Corp., at above address, (601)355-2518, Fax: (601)944-1450. **Founded:** 1968. **Operating Hours:** Continuous. **Key Personnel:** Essie Riley, Manager; Carl Rayfield, Sales Mgr. **Wattage:** 21,000. **Ad Rates:** $10 for 30 seconds; $15 for 60 seconds.

16977 WMGO-FM - 93.1
PO Box 182 Fax: (601)746-0093
Canton, MS 39046

Networks: Mississippi. **Owner:** Jerry Lousteau, at above address. **Founded:** 1997. **Operating Hours:** Continuous. **Key Personnel:** Jerry Lousteau, General Mgr., phone (601)859-2373, fax (601)854-2664. **Wattage:** 6000. **Ad Rates:** $8.50 for 30 seconds; $12.50 for 60 seconds.

MISSOURI

State Capital, JEFFERSON CITY

Missouri is bounded on the north by Iowa, east by Illinois, Kentucky, and Tennessee, south by Arkansas, west by Oklahoma, Kansas, and Nebraska. Its length, north to south, is 277 miles; its average breadth about 244 miles, ranging from 208 miles in the north to 312 miles in the south. Its land area is 68,898 square miles. The Missouri River flows across the state from west to east just north of the center. The surface north of the river is generally level, while that south of it is undulating, becoming rougher as it approaches the Ozark Mountains. There are also open, treeless plains, an extension of those in Kansas; and in the southeast, bordering on the Mississippi River, there is an extensive marshy tract called the Sunk County, the result of a 19th century earthquake. The climate varies from north temperature to sub-tropical. The Weather Bureau at St. Louis gives the temperature (annual average) as 56.1; highest on record, 110; lowest on record, -22. Total annual precipitation is 37.51 inches. With about 500 miles of waterfront on the Mississippi and with Missouri traversing it from west to east, the state has fully 1,000 miles of navigable waterways. St. Louis is a center for travel and for extensive freight traffic carried on by air, rail, and river. The city is the gateway for north and south tourist travel as well as freight traffic. The stock yards and meat-packing plants at Kansas City have gained worldwide fame. The Bagnell Dam across the Osage River in the Ozarks forms one of the largest artificial lakes in the world and floods about 60,000 acres. It is part of an enormous hydroelectrical development designed to supply power to St. Louis, Kansas City, and elsewhere. Educationally the state ranks exceedingly high. In addition to the University of Missouri, at Columbia, is has many colleges and universities, besides many professional and technological schools.

POPULATION: 5,193,000 (1992). Rank among the states, 15th.

AGRICULTURE: Number of farms: 107,000 (1992). Farm acreage: 30,000,000 (1992). Cash receipts from farm marketings: crops, $1,658,000,000 (1991); livestock and products, $2,203,000,000 (1991).

FORESTS: Total forest land: 3,082,000 acres (1991).

MINERALS: Value of production: $880,000,000 (1991). Principal minerals: lead, stone, cement.

MANUFACTURES: Value added by manufacture: $31,803,000,000 (1991). Leading industry groups: transportation equipment, food and related products, chemical and allied products.

LIST OF COUNTIES

Total number of counties 114

County, Location on Map, and County Seat	Pop.
Adair (N), Kirksville	24,577
Andrew (NW), Savannah	14,632
Atchison (NW), Rockport	7,457
Audrain (NEC), Mexico	23,599
Barry (SW), Cassville	27,547
Barton (SW), Lamar	11,312
Bates (W), Butler	15,025
Benton (WC), Warsaw	13,859
Bollinger (SE), Marble Hill	10,619
Boone (C), Columbia	112,379
Buchanan (NW), St. Joseph	83,083
Butler (SE), Poplar Bluff	38,765
Caldwell (NW), Kingston	8,380
Callaway (C), Fulton	32,809
Camden (C), Camdenton	27,495
Cape Girardeau (SE), Jackson	61,633
Carroll (NWC), Carrollton	10,748
Carter (SE), Van Buren	5,515
Cass (W), Harrisonville	63,808
Cedar (SW), Stockton	12,093
Chariton (NC), Keytesville	9,202
Christian (SW), Ozark	32,644
Clark (NE), Kahoka	7,547
Clay (W), Liberty	153,411
Clinton (NW), Plattsburg	16,595
Cole (C), Jefferson City	53,579
Cooper (C), Boonville	14,835
Crawford (SEC), Steelville	19,173
Dade (SW), Greenfield	7,449
Dallas (SWC), Buffalo	12,646
Daviess (NW), Gallatin	7,865
De Kalb (NW), Maysville	9,967
Dent (SEC), Salem	13,702
Douglas (S), Ava	11,876
Dunklin (SE), Kennett	33,115
Franklin (E), Union	80,603
Gasconade (EC), Hermann	14,006
Gentry (NW), Albany	6,848
Greene (SW), Springfield	207,946
Grundy (N), Trenton	10,536
Harrison (NW), Bethany	8,469
Henry (W), Clinton	20,044
Hickory (SWC), Hermitage	7,335
Holt (NW), Oregon	6,034
Howard (C), Fayette	9,631
Howell (S), West Point	31,447
Iron (SE), Ironton	10,726
Jackson (W), Independence	633,232
Jasper (SW), Carthage	90,465
Jefferson (E), Hillsboro	171,380
Johnson (W), Warrensburg	42,514
Knox (NE), Edina	4,482
Laclede (SC), Lebanon	27,185
Lafayette (W), Lexington	31,107
Lawrence (SW), Mount Vernon	30,236
Lewis (NE), Monticello	10,233
Lincoln (E), Troy	28,892
Linn (N), Linneus	13,885
Livingston (NW), Chillicothe	14,592
Macon (N), Macon	15,345
Madison (SE), Fredericktown	11,127
Maries (SEC), Vienna	7,976
Marion (NE), Palmyra	27,682
McDonald (SW), Pineville	16,938
Mercer (N), Princeton	3,723
Miller (C), Tuscumbia	20,700
Mississippi (SE), Charleston	14,442
Moniteau (C), California	12,298
Monroe (NE), Paris	9,104
Montgomery (E), Montgomery City	11,335
Morgan (C), Versailles	15,574
New Madrid (SE), New Madrid	20,928
Newton (SW), Neosho	44,445
Nodaway (NW), Maryville	21,709
Oregon (S), Alton	9,470
Osage (C), Linn	12,018
Ozark (S), Gainesville	8,598
Pemiscot (SE), Caruthersville	21,921
Perry (SE), Perryville	16,648
Pettis (WC), Sedalia	35,437
Phelps (SEC), Rolla	35,248
Pike (E), Bowling Green	15,969
Platte (NW), Platte City	57,867
Polk (SWC), Bolivar	21,825
Pulaski (SC), Waynesville	41,307
Putnam (N), Unionville	5,079
Ralls (NE), New London	8,476
Randolph (NC), Huntsville	24,370
Ray (NW), Richmond	21,971
Reynolds (SE), Centerville	6,661
Ripley (SE), Doniphan	12,303
Saint Charles (E), Saint Charles	212,907

Saint Clair (W), Osceola 8,457
Sainte Genevieve (SE), Sainte Genevieve 16,037
Saint Francois (SE), Farmington 48,904
Saint Louis (E), Clayton 993,529
Saint Louis, independent city 396,685
Saline (NWC), Marshall 23,523
Schuyler (N), Mancaster 4,236
Scotland (NE), Memphis 4,822
Scott (SE), Benton 39,376
Shannon (S), Eminence 7,613
Shelby (NE), Shelbyville 6,942
Stoddard (SE), Bloomfield 28,895
Stone (SW), Galena 19,078
Sullivan (N), Milan 6,326
Taney (S), Forsyth 25,561
Texas (S), Houston 21,476
Vernon (W), Nevada 19,041
Warren (E), Warrenton 19,534
Washington (E), Potosi 20,380
Wayne (SE), Greenville 11,543
Webster (S), Marshfield 23,753
Worth (NW), Grant City 2,440
Wright (S), Hartville 16,758

STATISTICS

Newspapers

Period of Issue
Daily 43
Evening Daily 31
Morning Daily 8
Daily with Sunday edition 17
Semiweekly 17
Weekly 228
Biweekly 4
Semimonthly 2
Monthly 3
Free or partly free 33
Shopper 22
Total Newspapers 311

Periodicals

Period of Issue
Weekly 7
Semimonthly 3
Monthly 84
Bimonthly 53
Quarterly 61
Total Periodicals 260

Total number of publications 571

Radio Stations

AM Stations 83
FM Stations 124
Total Radio Stations 207

TV Stations

Total TV Stations 32

Cable Stations

Total Cable Systems 33

Total number of broadcast listings 272

ADRIAN, pop. 1,484.

W MO. Bates Co. 50 mi. SE of Kansas City. Dairy farming. Agriculture. Corn, wheat, oats.

16978 The Adrian Journal
Journal
Box 128 Phone: (816)297-2100
39 E. Main
Adrian, MO 64720
Newspaper with a Republican orientation. **Founded:** Jan. 1, 1889. **Freq:** Weekly (Thurs.). **Print Method:** Web offset. **Cols./Page:** 6. **Col. Width:** 25 nonpareils. **Col. Depth:** 294 agate lines. **Key Personnel:** Stephen M. Oldfield, Editor and Publisher. **USPS:** 005-860. **Subscription Rates:** $17.95; $23.23 out of area; $26 out of state. **Remarks:** Accepts advertising.
Ad Rates: BW: $693 **Circ:** ‡1,500
SAU: $5.50

16979 The Archie News
The Adrian Journal Inc.
39 E. Main Phone: (816)297-2100
Box 128 Fax: (816)297-2149
Adrian, MO 64720
Newspaper with a Republican orientation. **Founded:** 1966. **Freq:** Weekly (Thurs.). **Print Method:** Web offset. **Cols./Page:** 6. **Col. Width:** 25 nonpareils. **Col. Depth:** 294 agate lines. **Key Personnel:** Stephen M. Oldfield, Editor and Publisher. **Subscription Rates:** $15.84 individuals; $16.90 out of area; $19.50 out of state.
Ad Rates: BW: $504 **Circ:** ‡300
SAU: $4

16980 Star Lite Shoppers Guide
The Adrian Journal Inc.
39 E. Main Phone: (816)297-2100
Box 128 Fax: (816)297-2149
Adrian, MO 64720
Shopper. **Founded:** 1985. **Freq:** Weekly. **Cols./Page:** 6. **Col. Width:** 2 inches. **Col. Depth:** 21 inches. **Key Personnel:** Stephen M. Oldfield. **Subscription Rates:** Free. **Remarks:** Accepts advertising.
Ad Rates: BW: $504 **Circ:** Free ‡4600
4C: $1,013.50
SAU: $4

ALBANY†, pop. 2,152.

NW MO. Gertry Co. 4 mi. N. of Darlington. Residential. Soybeans, livestock.

16981 The Albany Ledger Headlight
The Ledger
Smith & Clay Streets Phone: (816)726-3997
PO Box 247 Fax: (816)726-3997
Albany, MO 64402
Newspaper with a Democratic orientation. **Founded:** Mar. 4, 1868. **Freq:** Weekly (Wed.). **Print Method:** Offset. **Trim Size:** 14 x 24. **Cols./Page:** 7. **Col. Width:** 12 picas. **Col. Depth:** 301 agate lines. **Key Personnel:** Terry F. Holub, Editor and Publisher. **USPS:** 012-380. **Subscription Rates:** $20; $24 out of area; $28 out of state. **Remarks:** Accepts advertising. **Absorbed:** Stanberry Headlight. **Formerly:** The Albany Ledger.
Ad Rates: SAU: $3.40 **Circ:** ‡1,600
PCI: $3.40

ALMA

16982 The Santa Fe Times
Standard-Herald, Inc.
PO Box 76 Phone: (660)674-2250
Alma, MO 64001 Fax: (660)674-2250

Community newspaper. **Founded:** 1926. **Freq:** Weekly. **Print Method:** Offset. **Cols./Page:** 6. **Col. Width:** 2 inches. **Col. Depth:** 21 inches. **Key Personnel:** Pat Larkin, General Mgr.; Frank Mercer, Publisher, phone (660)542-0881, fax (660)542-2580. **ISSN:** 670-100. **Subscription Rates:** $17 individuals; $20 out of state. **Remarks:** Color advertising not accepted. **Formerly:** The Waverly Times.
Ad Rates: PCI: $2.25 **Circ:** (Not Reported)

ARNOLD, pop. 19,141.

E. MO. Jefferson Co. 10 mi. E. of House Springs. Residential.

16983 KCWA-FM - 89.9
1770 Missouri State Rd. Phone: (314)296-0400
Arnold, MO 63010 Fax: (314)287-2282

Format: Religious. **Networks:** SkyLight Satellite. **Founded:** 1985. **Operating Hours:** 6 a.m.-midnight; 90% network, 10% local. **Key Personnel:** Kenneth Brown, President; Darrell W. Deakins, General Mgr.; John Womack, Contact; Ron Pippins, Contact. **Wattage:** 150. **Ad Rates:** Noncommercial.

ASH GROVE, pop. 1,157.

SW MO. Greeene Co. 22 mi. W. of Springfield. Manufactures caskets and small metal fittings. Feed mill. Diversified farming.

16984 Commonwealth
PO Box 277 Phone: (417)751-2322
Ash Grove, MO 65604 Fax: (417)751-2322

Newspaper with a Republican orientation. **Founded:** 1881. **Freq:** Weekly (Thurs.). **Print Method:** Offset. **Cols./Page:** 6. **Col. Width:** 24 nonpareils. **Col. Depth:** 21 1/2 inches. **Key Personnel:** F. Dal Mason, Editor and Publisher. **Subscription Rates:** $14.80 individuals; $15.86 out of area; $20 out of state.
Ad Rates: GLR: $.12 **Circ:** ‡1,645
BW: $593.40
SAU: $4.50

ASHLAND, pop. 769.

SE MO. Boone Co. 14 mi. NNW of Jefferson City.

16985 Boone County Journal
PO Box 197 Phone: (314)657-2334
Ashland, MO 65010 Fax: (314)657-2002
Publication E-mail: bocojo@aol.com

County newspaper. **Founded:** 1969. **Freq:** Weekly (Wed.). **Print Method:** Web press. **Cols./Page:** 6. **Col. Width:** 2 inches. **Col. Depth:** 21 inches. **Key Personnel:** Richard Flink, Editor and Publisher; Jane Flink, Editor and Publisher. **Subscription Rates:** $18 individuals; $28 out of area. **Remarks:** Accepts advertising.
Ad Rates: GLR: $1 **Circ:** ‡1,750
BW: $453.60
4C: $600
SAU: $4
CNU: $5
PCI: $4

AURORA, pop. 6,437.

SW MO. Lawrence Co. 30 mi. SW of Springfield. Manufactures heating, air conditioning units, photo engraving equipment, kitchen cabinets, fertilizer, feed mills. Diversified farming.

16986 The Aurora Advertiser
226 West Church Phone: (417)678-2115
PO Box 509 Fax: (417)678-2117
Aurora, MO 65605
Publication E-mail: advert@mail.dialnet.net

Local newspaper. **Founded:** Mar. 1886. **Freq:** 3/week. **Print Method:** Offset. **Cols./Page:** 6. **Col. Width:** 12 1/4 picas. **Col. Depth:** 301 agate lines. **Key Personnel:** Paul E. Donley, Editor and Publisher. **Subscription Rates:** $20. **Remarks:** Accepts advertising.
Ad Rates: GLR: $.30 **Circ:** ‡3,850
BW: $580.50
SAU: $4.50

16987 The NADE Advocate
National Association of Disability Examiners
1117 Sunshine Dr. Phone: (417)888-4152
Aurora, MO 65605 Fax: (417)888-4069
Free: (800)584-4305

Professional magazine for physicians, attorneys, and examiners engaged in the disability examination process. **Founded:** 1972. **Freq:** Bimonthly. **Print Method:** Offset. **Trim Size:** 11 x 17. **Cols./Page:** 3. **Col. Width:** 2 1/4 inches. **Col. Depth:** 8 1/2 inches. **Key Personnel:** Donna Hilton, Editor, drhilton@dialnet.net. **Subscription Rates:** $50 professional; $25 support. **Remarks:** Advertising accepted; rates available upon request.
Circ: Paid ‡2,500
Non-paid ‡100

AVA†, pop. 2,761.

S. MO. Douglas Co. 60 mi. SE of Springfield. Sporting goods, lumber, staves, electric motors, feed, milk products manufactured. Mountain resort. Pine, oak timber. Hatchery. Beef, pork producers. Dairy, poultry, truck, fruit, grain farms.

16988 Douglas County Herald
Herald Publishing, Co.
PO Box 577 Phone: (417)683-4181
Ava, MO 65608 Fax: (417)683-4102

Newspaper with a Republican orientation. **Founded:** 1886. **Freq:** Weekly (Thurs.). **Print Method:** Offset. **Cols./Page:** 7. **Col. Width:** 21 nonpareils. **Col. Depth:** 294 agate lines. **Key Personnel:** Keith Moore, Editor; James E. Curry, Publisher. **USPS:** 160-320. **Subscription Rates:** $14; $19 out of area. **Remarks:** Accepts advertising.
Ad Rates: GLR: $.14 **Circ:** ‡4,975
BW: $294
SAU: $3.75
PCI: $2.10

16989 KKOZ-AM - 1430
PO Box 386 Phone: (417)683-4191
Ava, MO 65608

Format: News; Country. **Owner:** Corum Ind., Inc., at above address. **Operating Hours:** 6 a.m.-10 p.m. **Key Personnel:** Joe Corum, General Mgr., phone (417)693-4193; Art Corum, Operations Mgr., phone (417)693-4193; Gary Moore, Sales Mgr., phone (417)693-4193.

16990 KKOZ-FM - 92.1
119 1/2 Public Sq. Phone: (417)683-4191
Box 386 Free: (800)683-4191
Ava, MO 65608
E-mail: jcorum@goin.missouri.org

Format: Country; News; Sports; Agricultural. **Simulcasts:** KKOZ-AM. **Networks:** Missouri. **Owner:** Joe & Art Corum, at above address, (417)683-4193, Free: (800)683-4191. **Founded:** 1967. **Formerly:** KSOA-AM (1981). **Operating Hours:** 6 a.m.-10 p.m.; 10% network, 90% local. **Key Personnel:** Joe Corum, General Mgr.; Art Corum, Operations Mgr.; Vickie Corum, Sales Mgr. **Wattage:** 6000. **Ad Rates:** $5.25 for 30 seconds; $8.50 for 60 seconds.

BALLWIN

16991 Dealer Progress
314 at the Barn Phone: (314)527-4001
15444 Clayton Rd. Fax: (314)527-4120
Ballwin, MO 63011-3166
Magazine for fertilizer and agricultural chemical dealers. **Founded:** 1970. **Freq:** 8/year. **Print Method:** Offset. **Trim Size:** 8 1/4 x 10 7/8. **Cols./Page:** 3. **Col. Width:** 13.6 picas. **Col. Depth:** 140 agate lines. **Key Personnel:** K. Elliott Nowels, Editor and Publisher; Dan Bellanger, Advertising Mgr. **ISSN:** 0895-1616. **Subscription Rates:** Free to qualified subscribers; $40 individuals; $80 other countries. **Remarks:** Accepts advertising.
Ad Rates: BW: $2,495 **Circ:** Controlled ‡27,363
4C: $3,295
PCI: $125

BELLE, pop. 1,233.

SEC MO. Maries and Osage Co. 40 mi. SE of Jefferson City. Stave mill, shoe factory, charcoal kilns, and processing plant. Fire clay pits. Diversified farming. Livestock production. Wheat, corn, oats.

16992 The Belle Banner
PO Box 711 Phone: (573)859-3328
Belle, MO 65013 Fax: (573)859-6274

Community newspaper. **Founded:** 1904. **Freq:** Weekly (Wed.). **Print Method:** Offset. **Cols./Page:** 6. **Col. Width:** 21 1/2 inches. **Col. Depth:** 301 agate lines. **Key Personnel:** Ron J. Lewis, Publisher. **Subscription Rates:** $21.45; $24.66 out of area; $25 out of state; $40 other countries. **Remarks:** Color advertising accepted; rates available upon request.
Ad Rates: BW: $309.60 **Circ:** ‡2,278
PCI: $2.75

16993 Bland Courier
Tri-County Newspapers
PO Box 711 Phone: (573)859-3328
Belle, MO 65013 Fax: (573)859-6274

Newspaper. **Founded:** 1904. **Freq:** Weekly. **Trim Size:** 13 x 21 1/2. **Cols./Page:** 6. **Col. Width:** 21 1/2 inches. **Key Personnel:** Kurt J. Lewis, Publisher, kjl@sockets.com. **Subscription Rates:** $21.45 individuals; $24.66 out of area in Missouri; $.50 single issue; $25 out of state. **Remarks:** Accepts advertising.
Ad Rates: BW: $309.60 **Circ:** 780
PCI: $2.75

BELTON, pop. 12,708.

W MO. Cass Co. 12 mi. S. of Kansas City. Garment factory. Agriculture. Wheat, corn, oats.

16994 The Star Herald
Belton Publishing Co. Inc.
419 Main St. Phone: (816)331-5353
Belton, MO 64012 Fax: (816)322-2943
Publisher E-mail: news@thestar-herald.com

Newspaper with a Republican orientation. **Founded:** 1892. **Freq:** Weekly (Thurs.). **Print Method:** Offset. **Cols./Page:** 6.

Col. Width: 24 nonpareils. **Col. Depth:** 294 agate lines. **Key Personnel:** Vicki Daniel, Advertising Mgr., advertising@thestar-herald.com; Mark E. Cox, Editor and Publisher. **Subscription Rates:** $20; $26.00 out of area; $31 out of state. **Remarks:** Accepts advertising. **Formerly:** Belton-Raymore Star-Herald (July 1986).
Ad Rates: BW: $844.20 **Circ:** Paid 4,500
SAU: $6.70
PCI: $6.70

BETHANY†, pop. 3,095.

NW MO. Harrison Co. 60 mi. NE of Saint Joseph. Limestone quarry, cheese factory. Diversified farming. Corn, oats, dairying.

16995 Bethany Republican-Clipper
Bethany Printing Co.
PO Box 351 Phone: (816)425-6325
Bethany, MO 64424 Fax: (816)425-3441
Publisher E-mail: rclipper@netinc.net

Newspaper with a Republican orientation. **Founded:** Feb. 1873. **Freq:** Weekly (Wed.). **Print Method:** Offset. **Cols./Page:** 7. **Col. Width:** 12 1/2 picas. **Col. Depth:** 21 inches. **Key Personnel:** Philip G. Conger, Editor and Publisher; Kathy Conger, Advertising Mgr. **USPS:** 052-680. **Subscription Rates:** $15.80 individuals; $27 out of area. **Remarks:** Accepts advertising.
Ad Rates: GLR: $.32 **Circ:** ‡3,800
BW: $623.28
4C: $661.50
SAU: $4.24
PCI: $4.50

16996 Pony Express
Bethany Printing Co.
PO Box 351 Phone: (816)425-6325
Bethany, MO 64424 Fax: (816)425-3441
Publisher E-mail: rclipper@netinc.net

Shopper (tabloid). **Founded:** 1978. **Freq:** Weekly (Wed.). **Print Method:** Offset. **Trim Size:** 10 x 16. **Cols./Page:** 7. **Col. Width:** 8 picas. **Col. Depth:** 15 inches. **Key Personnel:** Philip G. Conger, Editor and Publisher; Kathy Conger, Advertising Mgr. **Subscription Rates:** Free. **Remarks:** Accepts advertising.
Ad Rates: GLR: $.32 **Circ:** Free ‡16,000
BW: $472.50
SAU: $4.50

16997 KAAN-AM - 870
Hwy. 69 S. Phone: (660)425-6380
Bethany, MO 64424 Fax: (660)425-8148
Free: (800)892-5959

Format: Country. **Simulcasts:** KAAN-FM. **Networks:** ABC. **Owner:** Kaan Inc., 300 W. Reed, Moberly, MO 65270, (660)263-5800, Fax: (660)263-2300. **Founded:** 1983. **Formerly:** KIRK-AM (1997). **Operating Hours:** Sunrise-sunset; 15% network, 85% local. **ADI:** St. Joseph, MO. **Key Personnel:** Stuart Johnson, Sports Dir.; Rodney Harris, General Mgr., rodneyh@netins.net. **Wattage:** 1000. **Ad Rates:** $10.50-15 for 30 seconds.

16998 KAAN-FM - 95.5
Hwy. 69 S. Phone: (660)425-6380
Bethany, MO 64424 Fax: (660)425-8148
Free: (800)892-5959

Format: Country. **Simulcasts:** KAAN-AM. **Networks:** ABC. **Owner:** Kaan Inc., 300 W. Reed, Moberly, MO 65270, (660)263-5800, Fax: (660)263-2300. **Founded:** 1978. **Formerly:** KIRK-AM (1997). **Operating Hours:** 18 hrs. Daily; 15% network, 85% local. **ADI:** St. Joseph, MO. **Key Personnel:** Stuart Johnson, Sports Dir.; Rodney Harris, General Mgr., rodneyh@netins.net. **Wattage:** 50,000. **Ad Rates:** $10.50-15 for 30 seconds.

BIRCH TREE

SC MO. Shannon Co. 5 mi. E. of Teresita.

16999 KBMV-AM - 1310
PO Box 215 Phone: (573)292-3821
Birch Tree, MO 65438-0215 Fax: (573)292-3636
Free: (888)611-1700

Format: Contemporary Christian. **Owner:** Scenic Rivers Broadcasting, at above address. **Founded:** 1982. **Operating Hours:** Continuous; 70% network, 30% local. **ADI:** Springfield, MO. **Key Personnel:** DiAnna Riffle, Office Mgr., phone (573)292-1500; Brian Staack, General Mgr.; Walter Shanks, Sales Mgr. **Wattage:** 1000. **Ad Rates:** $2.75-5 for 30 seconds; $3.75-6.60 for 60 seconds. Combined advertising rates available with KBMV-FM.

17000 KBMV-FM - 107.1
Box 215 Phone: (573)292-3821
Birch Tree, MO 65438 Fax: (573)292-3636
Free: (888)611-1700

Format: Contemporary Hit Radio (CHR). **Founded:** 1982. **Operating Hours:** Continuous; 100% local. **ADI:** Springfield, MO. **Key Personnel:** DiAnna Riffle, Manager; Brian Staack, General Mgr.; Walter Shanks, Sales Mgr. **Wattage:** 25,000. **Ad Rates:** $5-7.50 for 30 seconds; $8-9.50 for 60 seconds.

BLAND, pop. 662.

EC MO. Gasconade and Osage Co. 40 mi. SE of Jefferson City. Shoe factory. Fire-clay pits. Lumber. Diversified farming. Cattle.

17001 Mules and More
Box 460 Phone: (573)646-3934
Bland, MO 65014-0460 Fax: (573)646-3407
Publication E-mail: mules@i1.net
Publisher E-mail: mules@i1.net

Consumer magazine for mule, wagon and harness enthusiasts. **Founded:** 1980. **Freq:** Monthly. **Print Method:** Offset. **Trim Size:** 8 1/2 x 11. **Cols./Page:** 3. **Col. Width:** 14 picas. **Col. Depth:** 60 picas. **Key Personnel:** Sue Cole, Editor; Leona Reid, Advertising Mgr.; Becky Basham, Circulation Mgr. **USPS:** 008-589. **Subscription Rates:** $18 individuals; $30 Canada; $3 single issue. **Remarks:** Accepts advertising.
Ad Rates: BW: $155 **Circ:** Combined ⊕7,400
4C: $500

BLOOMFIELD†, pop. 1,795.

SE MO. Stoddard Co. 40 mi. SW of Cape Girardeau. Lumber. Dairy, poultry, livestock.

17002 The North Stoddard Countian
Delta Publishing Co.
615 No. Prairie Phone: (573)568-3310
PO Box 680 Fax: (573)568-3310
Bloomfield, MO 63825
Newspaper with an Independent orientation. **Subtitle:** A Compliation of the Bloomfield Vindicator and the Advance Statesman. **Founded:** 1877. **Freq:** Weekly (Wed.). **Print Method:** Offset. **Cols./Page:** 6. **Col. Width:** 12 1/2 picas. **Col. Depth:** 21 inches. **Key Personnel:** Barbara Hill, Editor and Publisher, phone (573)624-4545, fax (573)624-7449; Stacy Rauls, Advertising Mgr.; Vicci Lang, Photojournalist, phone (573)568-3310; Judy Friedrich, Adv. Representative, phone (573)722-5322. **Subscription Rates:** $15.75 individuals; $29 out of area. **Remarks:** Accepts advertising. **Formerly:** The Vindicator. **Merged with:** The Bloomfield Vindicator.
Circ: ‡3,200

BLUE SPRINGS, pop. 25,927.

W. MO. Jackson Co. 10 mi. SE of Independence. Trade center. Residential. Metal, plastics plants. Agriculture. Orchards, dairying.

17003 Blue Springs Examiner (Daily Edition)
The Blue Springs Examiner
PO Box 1057 Phone: (816)229-9161
Blue Springs, MO 64013
Newspaper. **Freq:** Mon.-Sat. **Key Personnel:** John Draffan, Circulation Mgr.; Irene Baltrusaitis, Publisher, ireneb@exminer.net. **Subscription Rates:** $79.80. **Remarks:** Accepts advertising.
Ad Rates: BW: $1,593.15 **Circ:** Combined 4,868
4C: $1,700.15
SAU: $12.35
PCI: $12.35

17004 Blue Springs Examiner (Wednesday Edition)
The Blue Springs Examiner
PO Box 1057 Phone: (816)229-9161
Blue Springs, MO 64013
Community newspaper. **Subtitle:** The Extra. **Freq:** Weekly (Wed.). **Key Personnel:** John Draffan, Circulation Mgr. **Subscription Rates:** Free; $79.80. **Remarks:** Accepts advertising.
Ad Rates: BW: $1,891.14 **Circ:** Combined 22,724
4C: $2,14.14
SAU: $14.66
PCI: $14.66

17005 The Examiner (Blue Springs Edition)
Morris Communications, Inc.
500 W. R.D. Mize Rd. Phone: (816)229-9161
PO Box 1057 Fax: (816)229-6785
Blue Springs, MO 64013
Local newspaper. **Founded:** 1974. **Freq:** Daily (eve.) and Sat. (morn.). **Print Method:** Offset. **Trim Size:** 13 3/4 x 22 3/4. **Cols./Page:** 6. **Col. Depth:** 21 1/2 inches. **Key Personnel:** Irene Baltrusaitis, Publisher, ireneb@examiner.net; Jason Offot, Editor, ireneb@examiner.net. **Subscription Rates:** $94.92 individuals. **Remarks:** Accepts advertising. **URL:** http://www.examiner.net.
Ad Rates: GLR: $12.35 **Circ:** Paid 4,868
BW: $1,593.15 Free 14,143
4C: $1,700.15
PCI: $12.35

BOLIVAR†, pop. 5,919.

SWC MO. Polk Co. 26 mi. NW of Springfield. Southwest Baptist University. Manufactures sewn specialty products, floral products; computer software. Agriculture. Dairy, beef, cattle.

17006 Bolivar Herald-Free Press
Community Publishers, Inc./Missouri
335 S. Springfield Phone: (417)326-7636
PO Box 330 Fax: (417)326-8701
Bolivar, MO 65613-0330
Community newspaper. **Founded:** Feb. 1868. **Freq:** Weekly (Wed.). **Print Method:** Offset. **Cols./Page:** 6. **Col. Width:** 25 nonpareils. **Col. Depth:** 301 agate lines. **Key Personnel:** Judy Kallenbach, Editor; David Berry, Publisher; Linda Simmons, Advertising Mgr. **USPS:** 060-080. **Subscription Rates:** $27 individuals; $43.50 out of area; $55 out of state. **Remarks:** Accepts advertising. **URL:** http://www.bolivarmo.com.
Ad Rates: BW: $704 **Circ:** ‡7,400
4C: $1,004
SAU: $5.46

17007 Omnibus
Southwest Baptist University
1600 University Ave. Fax: (417)326-0935
Bolivar, MO 65613
Publication E-mail: omnibus@sbuniv.edu

Collegiate newspaper. **Founded:** 1961. **Freq:** Weekly. **Print Method:** Offset. **Trim Size:** 10 x 12. **Cols./Page:** 5. **Col. Width:** 27 nonpareils. **Col. Depth:** 182 agate lines. **Key Personnel:** Jeremy Parsons, Exec. Editor; Sara Davis, Advertising Editor. **Subscription Rates:** $25 local. **Remarks:** Accepts advertising.
Ad Rates: BW: $240 **Circ:** Free ‡1,400
PCI: $4

17008 KYOO-AM - 1200
304 E. Jackson Phone: (417)326-5257
Bolivar, MO 65613-2029 Fax: (417)326-5900

Format: Country. **Networks:** CBS. **Owner:** Stephen & Ann Paris, at above address. **Founded:** 1961. **Formerly:** KBLR-AM; KLTB-AM. **Operating Hours:** Sunrise-sunset. **Key Personnel:** Aaron Sims, Program/News/Farm Dir.; Stephen Paris, GM/Sales Mgr. **Wattage:** 1000.

BOONVILLE†, pop. 6,959.

C. MO. Cooper Co. On Missouri River, 27 mi. W. of Columbia. Manufactures fiberboard, electric appliances, mobile homes, heels for shoes, clothing, knives, asphalt, boat trailers, storm windows & doors. Agriculture. Wheat, soybeans, corn, livestock.

17009 News & Advertiser
American Pub. Co.
412 High St. Phone: (816)882-5335
Boonville, MO 65233 Fax: (816)882-2256

General newspaper. **Founded:** 1919. **Freq:** Daily (morn.). **Print Method:** Offset. **Trim Size:** 11 1/2 x 14. **Cols./Page:** 6. **Col. Width:** 24 nonpareils. **Col. Depth:** 294 agate lines. **Key Personnel:** Steve Thomas, Editor; Scott Jackson, Publisher. **USPS:** 060–90. **Subscription Rates:** $77.50. **Remarks:** Accepts advertising.
Ad Rates: SAU: $4.75 **Circ:** Paid 2,973

BOWLING GREEN†, pop. 3,022.

S. MO. Pike Co. 30 mi. SE of Hannibal. Manufactures wire rope, textiles. Hatchery. Rock quarries; limestone. Diversified farming. Wheat, corn, soybeans. Swine.

17010 The Bowling Green Times
Jim Gerki
106 W. Main Phone: (573)324-2222
PO Box 110 Fax: (573)324-3991
Bowling Green, MO 63334
Newspaper. **Founded:** 1874. **Freq:** Weekly (Wed.). **Print Method:** Offset. **Cols./Page:** 6. **Col. Width:** 24 3/4 nonpareils. **Col. Depth:** 301 agate lines. **Key Personnel:** Kate B. Dickson, Editor and Publisher. **Subscription Rates:** $17. **Remarks:** Accepts advertising.
Ad Rates: SAU: $3.85 **Circ:** 3,352

17011 Democrat
Jim Gerki
106 W. Main Phone: (573)324-2222
PO Box 110 Fax: (573)324-3991
Bowling Green, MO 63334
Newspaper with a Democratic orientation. **Founded:** 1900. **Freq:** Weekly (Wed.). **Print Method:** Offset. **Cols./Page:** 7. **Col. Width:** 26 nonpareils. **Col. Depth:** 301 agate lines. **Key Personnel:** Margaret Herring, Editor; James A. Gierke, Publisher. **Subscription Rates:** $8. **Remarks:** Accepts advertising.
Ad Rates: GLR: $.135 **Circ:** 1,337

17012 KPCR-AM - 1530
PO Box 1 Phone: (314)324-2283
15894 Hwy. 54 Fax: (314)324-2283
Bowling Green, MO 63334
E-mail: kpcr@nemonet.com

Format: Country. **Networks:** Independent. **Founded:** 1966. **Operating Hours:** Sunrise-sunset; 100% local. **Key Personnel:** Cloyd Cox, President. **Wattage:** 1000. **Ad Rates:** $2.50-9 for 30 seconds. Combined advertising rates available with KPCR-FM.

17013 KPCR-FM - 94.1
PO Box 1 Phone: (314)324-2283
15894 Hwy. 54 Fax: (314)324-2283
Bowling Green, MO 63334
E-mail: kpcr@nemonet.com

Format: Country. **Simulcasts:** KPCR-AM. **Networks:** Independent. **Founded:** 1975. **Operating Hours:** 6 a.m.-midnight; 100% local. **Key Personnel:** Cloyd Cox, President. **Wattage:** 25,000. **Ad Rates:** $2.50-9 for 30 seconds.

BRANSON, pop. 2,550.

S. MO. Taney Co. 40 mi. S. of Springfield. Lake resort. Manufactures cedar novelties, garments, charcoal, furniture, stave bolts. Rock quarries. Cedar, oak timber. Diversified farming.

17014 KLFC-FM - 88.1
PO Box 2030 Phone: (417)334-5532
Branson, MO 65615 Fax: (417)335-2437

Format: Religious. **Networks:** SkyLight Satellite; USA Radio. **Owner:** Vision Ministries, Inc., at above address. **Operating Hours:** Continuous. **Key Personnel:** Jay Scribner, General Mgr.; Shelia Artt, Promotions Dir.; Herb Smith, News Dir.; Vicky Smith, Music Dir. **Local Programs:** *Good Morning Ozarks*, Shelia Artt. **Wattage:** 100. **Ad Rates:** Noncommercial.

17015 KOMC-AM - 1220
202 Courtney St. Phone: (417)334-6003
Branson, MO 65616 Fax: (417)334-7141
E-mail: krzk@mail.tri-lakes.net

Format: Big Band/Nostalgia. **Networks:** CBS. **Owner:** Turtle Broadcasting Co., L. P., at above address. **Key Personnel:** Rod Orr, Owner/General Mgr.; Carol Orr, Station Mgr.; Steve Willoughby, Sales Mgr.; Greg Pyron, Operations Mgr. **Local Programs:** *Ozark Mountain Gems*, Greg Pyron; *Big Band Saturday Night*, Adrian Charles. **URL:** http://www.branson.com.

17016 KOMC-FM - 100.1
202 Courtney St. Phone: (417)334-6003
Branson, MO 65616 Fax: (417)334-7141
E-mail: krzk@mail.tri-lakes.net

Format: Big Band/Nostalgia. **Networks:** CBS. **Owner:** Turtle Broadcasting Co., L. P., at above address. **Founded:** Oct. 1997. **Operating Hours:** Continuous. **Key Personnel:** Rod Orr, Owner/General Mgr.; Carol Orr, Station Mgr.; Steve Willoughby, Sales Mgr.; Greg Pyron, Operations Mgr. **Local Programs:** *Ozark Mountain Gems*, Greg Pyron; *Big Band Saturday Night*, Adrian Charles. **Wattage:** 50,000. **URL:** http://www.branson.com.

17017 KRZK-FM - 106.3
202 Courtney St. Phone: (417)334-6003
Branson, MO 65616 Fax: (417)334-7141
E-mail: krzk@mail.tri-lakes.net

Format: Country. **Networks:** ABC. **Owner:** Turtle Broadcasting Co., L. P., at above address. **Operating Hours:** Continuous. **Key Personnel:** Rod Orr, Owner/General Mgr.; Carol Orr, Station Mgr.; Steve Willoughby, Sales Mgr.; Greg Pyron, Operations Mgr. **Local Programs:** *Ozark Mountain Gems*, Greg Pyron. **Wattage:** 50,000. **URL:** http://www.branson.com.

17018 Rapid Cable
310 Walnut Extension Phone: (417)334-7897
Branson, MO 65616 Fax: (417)334-7899

Founded: 1981. **Key Personnel:** Kay Russell, General Mgr. **Cities Served:** Branson, Hollister, MO: subscribing households 7,025; 31 channels; 1 community access channel; 168 hours per week community access programming.

BRAYMER

17019 Braymer Bee
L & L Publications, Inc.
PO Box 308 Phone: (816)645-2217
Braymer, MO 64624 Fax: (816)645-2217

Community newspaper. **Freq:** Weekly (Thurs.). **Cols./Page:** 6. **Col. Width:** 12.2 picas. **Col. Depth:** 21 inches. **Key Personnel:** Pat Pryor, Editor. **USPS:** 063-520. **Subscription Rates:** $13.81; $15 out of state. **Remarks:** Accepts advertising.
Ad Rates: BW: $140 **Circ:** 1,300
SAU: $2.96

BRIDGETON

17020 Central States Archaeological Journal
Central States Archaeological Societies, Inc.
4255 Manteca Dr.
Bridgeton, MO 63044-1361

Archaeological journal. **Founded:** Oct. 1954. **Freq:** Quarterly. **Print Method:** Offset. **Trim Size:** 6 1/2 x 10. **Cols./Page:** 2. **Col. Width:** 30 nonpareils. **Col. Depth:** 98 agate lines. **Key Personnel:** John T. Crowley, Editor, phone (314)739-5838. **ISSN:** 0008-9559. **Subscription Rates:** $15. **Remarks:** Advertising not accepted. **URL:** http://www.csas-archaeology.org.
Circ: ‡4,500

BROOKFIELD, pop. 5,555.

N. MO. Linn Co. 40 mi. NW of Moberly. Shoe and textile factories. Diversified farming. Corn, wheat, livestock.

17021 The Daily News-Bulletin
Brookfield Publishing Co.
107 N. Main Phone: (816)258-7237
PO Box 40 Fax: (816)258-7238
Brookfield, MO 64628
Free: (800)685-6012

General newspaper. **Subtitle:** Daily News Bulletin. **Founded:** 1881. **Freq:** Daily (eve.). **Print Method:** Offset. **Trim Size:** 13 x 21. **Cols./Page:** 6. **Col. Width:** 2 1/16 inches. **Col. Depth:** 21 inches. **Key Personnel:** Greg Orear, Editor; Richard E. Abeln, Pub./Adv. Mgr. **USPS:** 144-600. **Subscription Rates:** $50 individuals. **Remarks:** Accepts advertising.
Ad Rates: BW: $711.90 **Circ:** ‡5,100
PCI: $4.70

BRUNSWICK, pop. 1,272.

NC MO. Chariton Co. On Missouri River, 40 mi. W. of Moberly. Manufactures gloves. Stock, grain farms. Corn, soybeans, wheat.

17022 The Brunswicker
118 E. Broadway Phone: (660)548-3171
PO Box 188 Fax: (660)388-6688
Brunswick, MO 65236
Newspaper with a Republican orientation. **Founded:** 1847. **Freq:** Weekly (Thurs.). **Print Method:** Offset. **Cols./Page:** 6. **Col. Width:** 26 nonpareils. **Col. Depth:** 294 agate lines. **Key Personnel:** Larry Baxley, Editor and Publisher; Susan Baxley, Publisher. **Subscription Rates:** $15.50 individuals in county; $20 elsewhere. **Remarks:** Accepts advertising.
Ad Rates: GLR: $3.20 **Circ:** ‡1,800
SAU: $3.20

BUFFALO†, pop. 2,217.

SW MO. Dallas Co. 28 mi. N. of Springfield.

17023 Buffalo Reflex
P.O. Box 770 Phone: (417)345-2224
Buffalo, MO 65622 Fax: (417)345-2235
Free: (800)862-8186
Publication E-mail: reflex@todays-tech.com

Community newspaper. **Founded:** 1869. **Freq:** Weekly (Wed.). **Print Method:** Offset. **Cols./Page:** 6. **Col. Width:** 24 nonpareils. **Col. Depth:** 21 1/2 inches. **Key Personnel:** James Hamilton, Editor and Publisher; Dave Abner, News Editor; Steve Johnson, Advertising Mgr. **USPS:** 069-600. **Subscription Rates:** $25; $32 out of area; $40 out of state. **Remarks:** Accepts advertising.
Ad Rates: BW: $568 **Circ:** ‡4,700
4C: $838
SAU: $4.40
PCI: $4.40

17024 County Courier
PO Box 440 Phone: (417)345-2323
206-208 W. Main St. Fax: (417)345-6800
Buffalo, MO 65622
Local newspaper. **Subtitle:** County Courier. **Founded:** Oct. 3, 1971. **Freq:** Weekly. **Print Method:** Offset. **Trim Size:** 13 x 21. **Cols./Page:** 6. **Col. Width:** 24 nonpareils. **Col. Depth:** 301 agate lines. **Key Personnel:** Jack H. Lewy, Editor; Mike Lewy, Publisher; Ginger Robie, Advertising Mgr. **Subscription Rates:** $14.46; $28 out of state. **Remarks:** Accepts advertising.
Ad Rates: SAU: $3.75 **Circ:** ‡1,550
CNU: $4.50
PCI: $3.75

17025 KBFL-FM - 99.9
PO Box 1385 Phone: (417)345-2412
Buffalo, MO 65622 Fax: (417)345-2410

Format: Country. **Networks:** CBS; Missouri. **Founded:** 1965. **Operating Hours:** 6 a.m.-10 p.m. **Key Personnel:** Chris Keller, Program and News Dir.; Galen Gilbert, Manager. **Local Programs:** *Front Page*, Chris Keller; *Market Time*, Mel Pulley. **Wattage:** 6000. **Ad Rates:** $8-12 for 30 seconds; $16.00-24.00 for 60 seconds.

BUTLER†.

WC MO. Bates Co. 10 mi. S. of Passaic. Agriculture.

17026 KMAM-AM - 1530
800 E. Nursery St. Phone: (660)679-4191
Butler, MO 64730 Fax: (660)679-4193
E-mail: point97@infi.net

Format: Religious; News; Agricultural. **Simulcasts:** KMAM, KMOE-FM. **Networks:** ABC; Brownfield. **Owner:** Bates County Broadcasting Company (CORP)/ B.D. Thornton, Owner, at above address. **Founded:** 1962. **Operating Hours:** 6 a.m.-10 p.m.; 5% network, 95% local. **Key Personnel:** B.D. Thornton, Owner; Melody Greenwood, Station Mgr. **Local Programs:** *County Beat News*. **Wattage:** 500. **Ad Rates:** $12 for 30 seconds; $14 for 60 seconds. Combined advertising rates available with KMOE-FM.

17027 KMOE-FM - 92.1
800 E. Nursery St. Phone: (660)679-4191
Butler, MO 64730 Fax: (660)679-4193

Format: Country; Religious. **Simulcasts:** KMAM-AM. **Networks:** ABC. **Owner:** Bates County Broadcasting Co. (CORP) KMAM & KMOE-FM, at above address. **Founded:** 1975. **Operating Hours:** 6 a.m.-10 p.m.; 5% network, 95% local. **Key Personnel:** B.D. Thornton, Owner; Melody Greenwood, Station Mgr. **Local Programs:** *County Beat News*. **Wattage:** 5000. **Ad Rates:** $12 for 30 seconds; $14 for 60 seconds.

CABOOL

17028 The Cabool Enterprise
Cabool Enterprise, Inc.
525 Main St. Phone: (417)962-4411
PO Box 40 Fax: (417)962-4455
Cabool, MO 65689
Community newspaper. **Founded:** 1886. **Freq:** Weekly (Thurs.). **Cols./Page:** 6. **Col. Width:** 2 inches. **Col. Depth:** 21 inches. **Key Personnel:** C. Russell Wood, Publisher. **USPS:** 082-300. **Subscription Rates:** $15.95; $19.45 out of area; $21.65 out of state. **Remarks:** Accepts advertising.
Ad Rates: SAU: $4.16 **Circ:** 2,100

CALIFORNIA†, pop. 3,381.

C. MO. Moriteau Co. 25 mi. W. of Jefferson City. Manufactures small engines, fiberglass wire markers, steel fabrications. Food processing plants. Woodworking. Stock, dairy, poultry farms.

17029 Democrat
319 S. High St. Phone: (314)796-2135
PO Box 126 Fax: (314)796-4220
California, MO 65018
Newspaper. **Founded:** 1858. **Freq:** Weekly (Wed.). **Print Method:** Offset. **Cols./Page:** 6. **Col. Width:** 32 nonpareils. **Col. Depth:** 301 agate lines. **Key Personnel:** Ray Grimes, Adv. Mgr.; Dwight Warren, Editor. **USPS:** 083-720. **Subscription Rates:** $23.75. **Remarks:** Accepts advertising.
Ad Rates: GLR: $5.15 **Circ:** ‡4,000

17030 KREL-AM - 1420
PO Box 307 Phone: (573)796-3139
California, MO 65018 Fax: (573)796-4131

Format: Country. **Networks:** ABC. **Owner:** Jeffrey G. Shackleford, at above address. **Founded:** 1995. **Formerly:** KZMO-AM (1995). **Operating Hours:** 6 a.m. - midnight; 10% network, 90% local. **Key Personnel:** Jeffrey Shackleford, Contact; Rae Ann Shackleford, Office Mgr.; Brian Hill, Sales Mgr. **Wattage:** 500 day; 225 night. **Ad Rates:** $6-8 for 30 seconds; $8-10 for 60 seconds.

CAMERON, pop. 4,519.

NW MO. Clinton and DeKalb Co. 50 mi. N. of Independence. Residential.

17031 Cameron Citizen Observer
Cameron Newspapers, Inc.
Box 70 Phone: (816)632-6543
Cameron, MO 64429 Fax: (816)632-4508

Local newspaper. **Founded:** 1868. **Freq:** Weekly (Thurs.). **Print Method:** Offset. **Cols./Page:** 6. **Col. Width:** 18 nonpareils. **Col. Depth:** 224 agate lines. **Key Personnel:** Charles W. Najacht, Editor and Publisher. **Subscription Rates:** $28 individuals; $30 out of area; $39 out of state. **Remarks:** Accepts advertising.
Ad Rates: BW: $180 **Circ:** Paid 2,500
SAU: $3 Free 58
PCI: $3

17032 The Cameron Shopper
Cameron Newspapers, Inc.
Box 70 Phone: (816)632-6543
Cameron, MO 64429 Fax: (816)632-4508

Local Shopper. **Founded:** 1964. **Freq:** Weekly (Tues.). **Print Method:** Offset. **Cols./Page:** 6. **Col. Width:** 18 nonpareils. **Col. Depth:** 224 agate lines. **Key Personnel:** Craig Watkins, Editor and Publisher. **Subscription Rates:** Free In local counties, no subscriptions. **Remarks:** Accepts advertising.
Ad Rates: BW: $365 **Circ:** Free 15,600
SAU: $5.70
PCI: $5

17033 KMRN-AM - 1360
510 Northland Dr. Phone: (816)632-6661
Cameron, MO 64429 Fax: (816)632-1334

Format: Talk; News; Sports; Oldies. **Networks:** ABC. **Owner:** at above address. **Founded:** 1971. **Operating Hours:** 5:30 a.m.; 17% network; 83% local. **Key Personnel:** Dennis Rowky, General Mgr., djr@cameron.net; Brian Rudolph, News Dir. **Local Programs:** *Breakfast Club* 8:10-8:30 a.m. Monday-Friday. **Wattage:** 500. **Ad Rates:** $14-20 for 30 seconds; $18.25-27 for 60 seconds. KNOZ-FM.

CAMPBELL

17034 Campbell Citizen
KMB Pub. Inc.
PO Box 186 Phone: (573)246-2531
Campbell, MO 63933
Community newspaper. **Freq:** Weekly (Wed.). **Key Personnel:** Ronald E. Kemp, Editor and Publisher.
Circ: 1,600

CANTON, pop. 2,435.

NE MO. Lewis Co. On Mississippi River, 20 mi. NW of Quincy, IL. Culver Stockton College. Manufactures telephone service parts. Fisheries. Stock, poultry, grain farms.

17035 Megaphone
Culver Stockton College
Culver-Stockton College Phone: (217)231-6380
Canton, IL 63435 Fax: (217)231-6611
Publication E-mail: megaphone@culver.edu

Collegiate newspaper. **Founded:** 1919. **Freq:** Biweekly. **Print Method:** Offset. **Trim Size:** 10 1/2 x 13. **Cols./Page:** 5. **Col. Width:** 22 nonpareils. **Col. Depth:** 224 agate lines. **Key Personnel:** Diane Lewis, Editor, phone (217)231-7784, dlewis@culver.edu; Shawnalee Berry, Advertising Mgr., phone (217)231-7813, sberry@culver.edu; Elizabeth Van Daele, Business Mgr., phone (217)231-7971, evandaele@culver.edu. **Subscription Rates:** $15. **Remarks:** Accepts advertising. **Available Online. URL:** http://www.culver.edu.
Ad Rates: BW: $240 **Circ:** Free ‡1,000
PCI: $5.00

17036 Press-News Journal
130 N. 4th St. Phone: (573)288-5668
PO Box 227 Fax: (573)288-0000
Canton, MO 63435
Newspaper with a Democratic orientation. **Founded:** 1862. **Freq:** Weekly (Thurs.). **Print Method:** Offset. **Trim Size:** 17 x 21. **Cols./Page:** 6. **Col. Width:** 21 nonpareils. **Col. Depth:** 294 agate lines. **Key Personnel:** David Steinbeck, Publisher; Daniel Steinbeck, Editor. **USPS:** 088-820. **Subscription Rates:** $20; $23 out of area. **Remarks:** Accepts advertising.
Ad Rates: BW: $409.50 **Circ:** ‡3,500
SAU: $3.25
PCI: $3.25

CAPE GIRARDEAU, pop. 34,361.

SE MO. Cape Girardeu Co. On Mississippi River, 105 mi. SE of Saint Louis. Highway bridge over river. Boatyard. Southeast Missouri State University. Manufactures shoes, cement, lumber, dairy products, electric appliances, furniture, men's clothing, concrete, plastics, paper and meat products. Ships lumber, cement, shoes. Hardwood timber; stone quarries. Diversified farming. Corn, soybeans, wheat, cotton. Cattle, hogs.

17037 The Capaha Arrow
Southeast Missouri State University
One University Plaza Phone: (314)651-2549
MS 2225 Fax: (314)651-5967
Southeast Missouri State University
Cape Girardeau, MO 63701
Collegiate tabloid. **Founded:** 1911. **Freq:** Weekly (Wed.). **Print Method:** Offset. **Trim Size:** 11 x 17. **Cols./Page:** 5. **Col. Width:** 23 nonpareils. **Col. Depth:** 210 agate lines. **Key Personnel:** Kimberly Speight, Editor; Ceylon Tokcan, Ad Manager; Sheba Bednar, Business Mgr.; Dr. Roy Keller, Adviser. **Subscription Rates:** $13. **Remarks:** Accepts advertising.
Ad Rates: BW: $250 **Circ:** ‡6,000
4C: $557
SAU: $3.75
PCI: $4

17038 Southeast Missourian
Concord Publishing House, Inc.
301 Broadway Phone: (573)334-7115
PO Box 699 Fax: (573)334-7288
Cape Girardeau, MO 63701
Publication E-mail: postmaster@semissourian.com; advertising@semissourian.com; classified@semissourian.com
Publisher E-mail: advertising@semissourian.com

Community newspaper. **Founded:** 1904. **Freq:** Daily and Sunday. **Print Method:** Offset. **Trim Size:** 13 x 21 1/2. **Cols./Page:** 6. **Col. Width:** 2 1/16 inches. **Col. Depth:** 21 1/2 inches. **Key Personnel:** Joe Sullivan, Editor; Joni Adams, Managing Editor; Gary W. Rust, President; Wally Lage, Publisher; Pat Zellmer, Advertising Dir. **Subscription Rates:** $120. **Remarks:** Accepts advertising.
Ad Rates: BW: $2,709 **Circ:** Mon.-Fri. ♦**16,066**
4C: $3,059 Sun. ♦**26,164**
SAU: $22 Wed. ♦**30,237**
Sat. ♦**15,225**

17039 KAPE-AM - 1550
Box 558 Phone: (573)339-7000
901 S. Kings Hwy. Fax: (573)651-4100
Cape Girardeau, MO 63702-0558
Free: (800)467-1007

Networks: Unistar; CNN Radio; NBC; Talknet. **Founded:** 1940. **Formerly:** KGMO-AM (1980). **Operating Hours:** Continuous; 100% network. **ADI:** Paducah,KY-Cape Girardeau,MO-Marion,IL. **Key Personnel:** Rick Lambert, General Mgr. **Wattage:** 5000. **Ad Rates:** Advertising accepted; rates available upon request.

17040 KBSI-TV - 23
806 Enterprise Phone: (314)334-1223
Cape Girardeau, MO 63701 Fax: (314)334-1208

Format: Commercial TV. **Networks:** Fox. **Founded:** 1983. **Operating Hours:** Continuous. **ADI:** Paducah,KY-Cape Girardeau,MO-Marion,IL.

17041 KCGQ-FM - 99.3
PO Box 1610 Phone: (573)335-8291
Cape Girardeau, MO 63702-1610 Fax: (573)335-4806

Format: Album-Oriented Rock (AOR). **Networks:** Independent. **Owner:** Zimmer Radio, at above address. **Founded:** 1978. **Formerly:** KJAQ-FM (1986). **Operating Hours:** Continuous; 100% local. **ADI:** Paducah,KY-Cape Girardeau,MO-Marion,IL. **Key Personnel:** James Zimmer, President/Gen. Mgr.; Carla Leible, Sales Mgr.; Tony Richards, Program Dir. **Wattage:** 6000. **Ad Rates:** Advertising accepted; rates available upon request.

17042 KEZS-FM - 102.9
PO Box 1610 Phone: (314)335-8291
Cape Girardeau, MO 63701 Fax: (314)335-4806
Free: (800)289-5103

Format: Country. **Networks:** ABC. **Founded:** 1969. **Operating Hours:** Continuous. **ADI:** Paducah,KY-Cape Girardeau,MO-Marion,IL. **Key Personnel:** James Zimmer, General Mgr.; Gera Legrand, Sales Mgr.; Terry Hester, Operations Mgr.; Tony Richards, Program Dir. **Wattage:** 100,000 ERP.

17043 KFVS-TV - 12
310 Broadway Phone: (573)335-1212
PO Box 100 Fax: (573)335-6303
Cape Girardeau, MO 63702

Format: Commercial TV. **Networks:** CBS. **Founded:** 1954. **Formerly:** Raycom Media, Inc. **Operating Hours:** Continuous. **ADI:** Paducah,KY-Cape Girardeau,MO-Marion,IL. **Key Personnel:** Mike Beecher, News Dir.; Michael R. Smythe, General Sales Mgr.; Arnold Killian, Chief Engineer; Frank Knight, Business Mgr.; Paul Keener, Promotions Mgr.; Howard Meagle, General Mgr. **Wattage:** 316,000.

17044 KGIR-AM - 1220
PO Box 1610 Phone: (573)335-8291
Cape Girardeau, MO 63702-1610 Fax: (573)335-4806

Format: Sports. **Founded:** 1966. **Formerly:** KGIR-AM (1992). **Operating Hours:** Continuous.;100% Local. **ADI:** Paducah,KY-Cape Girardeau,MO-Marion,IL. **Key Personnel:** James Zimmer, General Mgr.; Carla Leible, Sales Mgr.; Terry Hester, Operations Dir. **Wattage:** 250 day; 140 night. **Ad Rates:** Advertising accepted; rates available upon request.

17045 KRCU-FM - 90.9
1 University Plaza Phone: (573)651-5070
Cape Girardeau, MO 63701 Fax: (573)651-5071
E-mail: krcu@semovm.semo.edu

Format: Public Radio; Full Service. **Networks:** National Public Radio (NPR); Public Radio International (PRI). **Owner:** KRCU-FM, 1 University Plaza, Cape Girardeau, MO 63701. **Founded:** 1975. **Operating Hours:** Continuous. **ADI:** Paducah,KY-Cape Girardeau,MO-Marion,IL. **Key Personnel:** Greg Petrowich, General Mgr.; Allen Lane, Chief Engineer; Danny Woods, Operations Dir.; Karen Walker, Music Dir.; S.D. Yana Davis, Development Officer. **Wattage:** 6000. **Ad Rates:** Noncommercial.

17046 KZIM-AM - 960
PO Box 1610 Phone: (314)335-8291
Cape Girardeau, MO 63702 Fax: (314)335-4806
Free: (800)289-5103

Format: News; Sports; Agricultural; Talk. **Networks:** CBS. **Founded:** 1925. **Operating Hours:** Continuous. **ADI:** Paducah,KY-Cape Girardeau,MO-Marion,IL. **Key Personnel:** Terry L. Hester, Operations Mgr. **Local Programs:** *Talk of Cape*, Tom Terbrock, (573)335-5512, Fax (573)334-9696. **Wattage:** 5000 day; 500 night.

CARROLLTON†, pop. 4,700.

SC MO. Carroll Co. 30 mi. S. of Chillicothe. Dairy products.

17047 Carrollton Daily Democrat
Highway 65 South Phone: (816)542-0881
PO Box 69 Fax: (816)542-0889
Carrollton, MO 64633
Community newspaper. **Founded:** 1881. **Freq:** Daily. **Print Method:** Offset. **Cols./Page:** 8. **Col. Width:** 1 1/2 inches. **Col. Depth:** 21 inches. **Key Personnel:** Twila Warner, Editor; Dean De Vries, Publisher; Jack Krier, Publisher. **Subscription Rates:** $35.50; $40.75 county; $46.50 out of county. **Remarks:** Accepts advertising.
Ad Rates: GLR: $.18 **Circ:** 2,700
BW: $466.20
SAU: $3.70
PCI: $4.05

17048 KAOL-AM - 1430
102 N. Mason Phone: (816)542-0404
Carrollton, MO 64633 Fax: (816)542-0420

Format: Country; Agricultural. **Networks:** NBC. **Owner:** Kanza, Inc., at above address. **Founded:** 1959. **Operating Hours:** Continuous. **ADI:** Kansas City, MO (Lawrence, KS). **Key Personnel:** Mike Carter, General Mgr.; Bob Tutt, General Sales Mgr.; Chris Allen, Sports Dir.; Jay Truitt, Farm Dir.; Miles Carter, News Dir. **Wattage:** 500 day; 27 night. **Ad Rates:** $35-80 for 30 seconds; $45-100 for 60 seconds.

17049 KMZU-FM - 100.7
102 N. Mason Phone: (816)542-0404
Carrollton, MO 64633 Fax: (816)542-0420

Format: Agricultural; Country. **Simulcasts:** WHB-AM; KAOL-AM. **Networks:** NBC. **Owner:** Kanza, Inc., at above address. **Founded:** 1962. **Formerly:** KAOL-FM (1982). **Operating Hours:** Continuous. **ADI:** Kansas City, MO (Lawrence, KS). **Key Personnel:** Mike Carter, President/Gen. Mgr.; Bob Tutt, General Sales Mgr.; Brandon Charles, Sports Dir.; Melissa Bertz, Farm Dir.; Rich Hawkins, Farm Dir.; Wayne Combs, News Dir. **Local Programs:** *Farm Feedback*, Rich Hawkins; *Fifth Quarter Show*, Miles Carter. **Wattage:** 100,000. **Ad Rates:** $38-160 for 30 seconds; $48-200 for 60 seconds.

17050 KRLI-FM - 97.5
203 N. Mason St. Phone: (660)886-3008
Carrollton, MO 64633 Fax: (660)542-0420
E-mail: whb@carolnet.com

Format: Adult Contemporary. **Owner:** Miles J. Carter, 615 Cherokee, Marshall, MO 65340. **Founded:** Oct. 1996. **Operating Hours:** Continuous. **Key Personnel:** Mike Carter, Program Dir., whb@carolnet.com; Chuck Haney, Sales Mgr. **Wattage:** 3400. **Ad Rates:** $4-5.50 for 30 seconds; $6 for 60 seconds.

CARTHAGE†, pop. 11,104.

SW MO. Jasper Co. 150 mi. S. of Kansas City. Manufactures men's textiles, bed springs, wire drawings, upholstry springs, fluorescent light fixtures, concrete, woodworking, tanks, powder explosives, auto accessories, sheet metal. Cheese processing and packaging, flour, feeds. Marble quarries; oak timber. Farming, wheat, cattle and other livestock.

17051 The Carthage Press
527 S. Main St. Phone: (417)358-2191
PO Box 678 Fax: (417)358-7428
Carthage, MO 64836
General newspaper. **Founded:** Mar. 24, 1884. **Freq:** Mon.-Sat. (eve.). **Print Method:** Offset. **Cols./Page:** 6. **Col. Width:** 25 nonpareils. **Col. Depth:** 301 agate lines. **Key Personnel:** Neil Campbell, Editor; Jim G. Farley, Publisher. **Subscription Rates:** $82.95. **Remarks:** Accepts advertising.
Ad Rates: SAU: $7.10 **Circ:** Paid ‡5,600

17052 KDMO-AM - 1490
221 E. 4th St. Phone: (417)358-6054
Carthage, MO 64836 Fax: (417)358-1278

Format: Country. **Networks:** ABC; Missouri; Brownfield. **Owner:** Ronald L. Petersen, PO Box 426, Carthage, MO 64836. **Founded:** 1947. **Operating Hours:** Continuous; 8% network, 92% local. **Key Personnel:** Ronald L. Petersen, General Mgr./President; Lindy White, News Dir.; Mark Anthony, Operations Mgr.; Jim Day, General Sales Mgr. **Wattage:** 1000. **Ad Rates:** $6.75-9 for 30 seconds; $8-10.50 for 60 seconds.

17053 KMXL-FM - 95.1
221 E. 4th St. Phone: (417)358-6054
PO Box 426 Fax: (417)358-1278
Carthage, MO 64836

Format: Adult Contemporary. **Founded:** 1972. **Formerly:** KRGK-FM (1990). **Operating Hours:** Continuous. **Key Personnel:** Ronald L. Petersen, General Mgr./President; Lindy White, News Dir.; Mark Anthony, Operations Mgr.; Jim Day, General Sales Mgr. **Wattage:** 50,000. **Ad Rates:** $12-17 for 30 seconds; $14-19 for 60 seconds.

17054 Southwest Missouri Cable TV Inc.
PO Box 696 Phone: (417)358-3002
231 E. 4th St. Fax: (417)358-1845
Carthage, MO 64836

Owner: Ruth Koplin, at above address. **Founded:** 1965. **Key Personnel:** Ruth Koplin, Chairman/CEO. **Cities Served:** subscribing households 11,370; 52 channels.

CARUTHERSVILLE†, pop. 7,958.

SE MO. Pemiscot. On Mississippi River, 30 mi. N. of Blytheville, AR. Cotton ginning and compressing; metal fabricating; engine rebuilding; shoe, boat, veneer, and box factories; bottling, sand, and gravel works. Cottonwood, gum, oak timber. Agriculture. Cotton, milo, corn, rice, wheat.

17055 The Democrat-Argus
Pemiscot Publishing
111 E. 5th St. Phone: (573)333-4336
PO Box 1059 Fax: (573)333-2307
Caruthersville, MO 63830
Community newspaper. **Founded:** 1868. **Freq:** 3/week. **Print Method:** Offset. **Trim Size:** 14 x 21 3/4. **Cols./Page:** 6. **Col. Width:** 2 inches. **Col. Depth:** 21 inches. **Key Personnel:** Tommy Clayton, Editor and Publisher; Joe Lillard, Advertising Mgr. **USPS:** 153-300. **Subscription Rates:** $45 individuals; $60 out of area. **Remarks:** Accepts advertising. **Formerly:** The Pemiscot Journal (1991); The Missouri Herald.
Ad Rates: GLR: $.31 **Circ:** Paid ‡2,802
BW: $535.50 Free ‡33
SAU: $4.85

17056 KCRV-AM - 1370
Hwy. 84 W. Phone: (314)333-1370
PO Box 909 Fax: (314)334-1370
Caruthersville, MO 63830

Format: Country; Religious; Oldies. **Networks:** Mutual Broadcasting System. **Founded:** 1950. **Operating Hours:** Continuous. **Key Personnel:** Cleat Stanfill, General Mgr.; Ed DeLisle, Sales Mgr.; Randy Tillman, Program Dir.; Danny Nelson, Music Dir.; Palmer Johnson, Engineering. **Wattage:** 1000. **Ad Rates:** $8 for 30 seconds; $15 for 60 seconds.

17057 KLOW-FM - 105.1
Hwy. 84 W. Phone: (314)333-1370
PO Box 909 Fax: (314)333-1370
Caruthersville, MO 63830

Format: Oldies. **Networks:** Mutual Broadcasting System; Brownfield. **Owner:** Pyramid Media & Entertainment, at above address, (314)333-2260. **Founded:** 1975. **Formerly:** KCRV-FM. **Operating Hours:** Continuous. **ADI:** Memphis, TN. **Key Personnel:** Cleat Stanfill, General Mgr.; Ed DeLisle, Sales Mgr.; Danny Nelson, Music Dir.; Palmer Johnson, Contact. **Wattage:** 3000. **Ad Rates:** $9 for 30 seconds; $15 for 60 seconds.

CASSVILLE†, pop. 2,091.

SW MO. Barry Co. 60 mi. SE of Joplin. Roaring River State Park. Tourism. Diversified farming. Fescue. Cattle raising.

17058 Barry County Advertiser
904 West St. Phone: (417)847-4475
PO Box 488 Fax: (417)847-4523
Cassville, MO 65625
Publication E-mail: litho@cassnet.com

Community newspaper. **Founded:** 1967. **Freq:** Weekly. **Print Method:** Offset. **Trim Size:** 13 3/4 x 17 1/2. **Cols./Page:** 6. **Col. Width:** 1 3/4 inches. **Col. Depth:** 17 inches. **Key Personnel:** Jennie Herrin, Editor; Jean Melton, Publisher; Russ Melton, Manager. **Subscription Rates:** Free; $30 out of area. **Remarks:** Accepts advertising.
Ad Rates: GLR: $4 **Circ:** Paid ‡300
BW: $385 Non-paid ‡11,200
SAU: $7.80
PCI: $5.60

17059 Cassville Democrat
600 Main Phone: (417)847-2610
PO Box 486 Fax: (417)847-3092
Cassville, MO 65625
Community newspaper. **Founded:** 1872. **Freq:** Weekly (Wed.). **Print Method:** Offset. **Cols./Page:** 6. **Col. Width:** 28 nonpareils. **Col. Depth:** 295 agate lines. **Key Personnel:** Mike Schlichtman, Publisher; Lisa Schlichtman, Publisher; Darlene Wierman, Office Mgr. **Subscription Rates:** $25. **Remarks:** Accepts advertising.
Ad Rates: PCI: $3.80 **Circ:** 5,000

17060 Trendsetter
Kustom Kemps of America
RR 1, Box 1714 Phone: (417)847-2940
Cassville, MO 65625-3647 Fax: (417)847-3647

Magazine covering customized cars and trucks for members. **Founded:** Oct. 1980. **Freq:** Bimonthly. **Print Method:** Sheetfed offset. **Trim Size:** 8 1/2 x 11. **Key Personnel:** Ed Cecetka, Editor. **Subscription Rates:** $2 single issue. **Remarks:** Accepts advertising.
Ad Rates: BW: $150 **Circ:** (Not Reported)
4C: $320

CENTRALIA, pop. 3,537.

C. MO. Audrain and Boone Co. 25 mi. SE of Moberly. Panhandle Eastern Pipeline. Manufactures anchors, diversified plastics, electric switches, hot line tools, barrel staves, pole line hardware. Grain farms. Corn, soybeans, cattle.

17061 Fireside Guard
118 W. Sneed St. Phone: (314)682-2133
PO Box 7 Fax: (314)682-3361
Centralia, MO 65240
Newspaper with a Republican orientation. **Founded:** 1868. **Freq:** Weekly (Wed.). **Print Method:** Offset. **Cols./Page:** 6. **Col. Width:** 26 nonpareils. **Col. Depth:** 294 agate lines. **Key Personnel:** Charles A. Hedberg, Editor and Publisher. **Subscription Rates:** $24. **Remarks:** Accepts advertising.
Ad Rates: PCI: $4.90 **Circ:** Paid 3,700
Free 1,100

17062 KMFC-FM - 92.1
Box 26 Phone: (314)682-5525
Centralia, MO 65240-0026 Fax: (314)682-2744
Free: (800)769-5632
E-mail: info@kmfc.com

Format: Religious. **Networks:** Independent; USA Radio. **Owner:** The Clair Group, at above address, (573)682-5525, Fax: (573)682-2744, Free: (800)769-5632. **Founded:** 1986. **Operating Hours:** Continuous. **Key Personnel:** Sharon Dollens, Station Mgr. **Wattage:** 3000. **Ad Rates:** $8 for 30 seconds; $14 for 60 seconds.

CHAFFEE, pop. 3,241.

SE MO. Scott Co. 15 mi. SW of Cape Girardeau. Manufactures shoes, garments and lumber. Hardwood timber. Diversified farming. Wheat, hay, corn, clover.

17063 Scott County Signal
113 S. Main St. Phone: (573)887-3636
PO Box 97 Fax: (573)887-3637
Chaffee, MO 63740
Community newspaper. **Founded:** 1910. **Freq:** Weekly (Sun.). **Print Method:** Offset. **Trim Size:** 14 1/4 x 22 7/8. **Cols./Page:** 6. **Col. Width:** 12 picas. **Col. Depth:** 21 inches. **Key Personnel:** Jim Obert, Editor; Willy Lage, Publisher. **Subscription Rates:** $20; $25 out of area. **Remarks:** Accepts advertising. **Formerly:** North Scott County News; The Jimplicate; The Signal.
Ad Rates: GLR: $3.50 **Circ:** ‡7,000
BW: $4.50
4C: $200
SAU: $4

CHARLESTON†, pop. 5,230.

SE MO. Mississippi Co. 35 mi. S. of Cape Girardeau. Tourism. Historical site. Manufactures shoes, rubber auto hoses, modular homes. Pork, grain sorghum, soybeans, corn, potatoes, fruit. Cotton.

17064 The Enterprise-Courier
206 S. Main St. Phone: (314)683-3351
PO Box 69 Fax: (314)683-2217
Charleston, MO 63834-0069
Community newspaper. **Founded:** 1874. **Freq:** Weekly (Thurs.). **Print Method:** Offset. **Cols./Page:** 6. **Col. Width:** 2 inches. **Col. Depth:** 21 1/2 inches. **Key Personnel:** Jim Anderson, Editor; Mildred Wallhausen, Publisher; Cheryl Slayden, Advertising Mgr. **Subscription Rates:** $5.20; $14 out of county. **Remarks:** Accepts advertising.
Ad Rates: BW: $469.56 **Circ:** ‡3,400
4C: $569.56
PCI: $3.64

17065 KCHR-AM - 1350
205 E. Commercial St. Phone: (573)683-6044
Charleston, MO 63834

Format: Eclectic. **Networks:** Mutual Broadcasting System. **Owner:** South Broadcast Co., Inc., at above address. **Founded:** 1953. **Operating Hours:** 6 a.m.-midnight; 30% network, 70% local. **Key Personnel:** Pam Haws, Program Dir.; Danny Adams, Station Mgr. **Wattage:** 1000. **Ad Rates:** $8.50 for 30 seconds; $10.50 for 60 seconds.

CHESTERFIELD

Saint Louis Co.

17066 Journal of Parametrics
International Society of Parametric Analysts
PO Box 6402 Phone: (314)527-2955
Town & County Branch Fax: (314)256-8358
Chesterfield, MO 63006-6402
Publication E-mail: clydeperry@aol.com

Magazine serving parametrics analysts. **Founded:** 1981. **Freq:** Semiannual. **Print Method:** Letterpress and web offset. **Trim Size:** 4 1/2 x 7 1/2. **Key Personnel:** Glenn Boyce, Jr., Editor. **ISSN:** 1015-7891. **Subscription Rates:** $45 individuals; $15 single issue. **Remarks:** Accepts advertising.
Ad Rates: BW: $500 **Circ:** 650

17067 KYMC-FM - 89.7
PO Box 4038 Phone: (314)530-7070
Chesterfield, MO 63006 Fax: (314)530-7928

Format: Top 40. **Owner:** West County YMCA, at above address. **Founded:** 1978. **Operating Hours:** Continuous; 100% local. **Key Personnel:** Laura Jacobsen, Station Mgr.; Leslie Slaughter, Program Dir. **Local Programs:** *Family Affair* 7:00 am - 10:00 am Five days, Laura Jacobsen, (314)532-6515; *My Y Radio Show* 8:00 am - 11:00 am One day, Laura Jacobsen, (314)532-6515; *Ultimate Vision* 10:00 am - 1:00 pm

One day, Dave Merkel. **Wattage:** 120. **Ad Rates:** Noncommercial; underwriting available.

17068 United Video Cablevision, Inc.
14323 S. Outer 40 Rd. Phone: (314)576-7517
Chesterfield, MO 63017 Fax: (314)434-7423

Key Personnel: Frank J. Hughes, General Mgr. **Cities Served:** Greenville, IL.

CHILLICOTHE†, pop. 9,089.

NW MO. Livingston Co. 74 mi. E. of Saint Joseph. Recreation area. Manufactures gloves, industrial air cleaners, machinery, automotive parts, bricks, tile, concrete. Meat packing. Dairy products. Livestock. Agriculture. Corn, wheat, soybeans, oats.

17069 Constitution-Tribune
American Publishing
818 Washington St. Phone: (816)646-2411
PO Box 707 Fax: (816)646-2028
Chillicothe, MO 64601
General newspaper. **Founded:** 1860. **Freq:** Daily (eve.). **Print Method:** Offset. **Cols./Page:** 6. **Col. Width:** 25 nonpareils. **Col. Depth:** 301 agate lines. **Key Personnel:** Ed Crawford, Editor; Charles Haney, Publisher. **Subscription Rates:** $40. **Remarks:** Accepts advertising.
Ad Rates: SAU: $5 **Circ:** 6,240

17070 KCHI-AM - 1010
421 Washington St. Phone: (816)646-4173
PO Box 227 Fax: (816)646-2868
Chillicothe, MO 64601

Format: Oldies. **Simulcasts:** KCHI-FM. **Networks:** ABC. **Founded:** 1950. **Operating Hours:** 6 a.m.-midnight; 15% network, 85% local. **Key Personnel:** Chris Beyer, General Mgr.; Jamie Rutledge, Promotions Dir.; Chris Strowe, News Dir.; Jerry Englert, Program Dir. **Wattage:** 250. **Ad Rates:** $3.75-5 for 15 seconds; $7.50-10 for 30 seconds; $15-20 for 60 seconds.

17071 KCHI-FM - 103.9
421 Washington St. Phone: (816)646-4173
Box 227 Fax: (816)646-2868
Chillicothe, MO 64601

Format: Oldies. **Simulcasts:** KCHI-AM. **Networks:** ABC. **Founded:** 1976. **Operating Hours:** Continuous; 15% network, 85% local. **Key Personnel:** Dan Leatherman, General Mgr.; Jerry ENglert, Program Dir.; Dave Myers, News Dir. **Wattage:** 4100. **Ad Rates:** $10 for 30 seconds; $15-20 for 60 seconds.

CLARENCE, pop. 1,147.

NE MO. Shelby Co. 25 mi. NE of Moberly. Ships corn, wheat, oats and soybean. Stock, poultry, grain farms.

17072 The Clarence Courier
106 E. Maple St. Phone: (816)699-2344
Box 10 Fax: (816)699-2194
Clarence, MO 63437-0010
Community newspaper. **Founded:** 1881. **Freq:** Weekly (Wed.). **Print Method:** Offset. **Cols./Page:** 5. **Col. Width:** 12 1/2 picas. **Col. Depth:** 14 inches. **Key Personnel:** D.W. Williams, Publisher; H. Williams, Business Mgr. **Subscription Rates:** $20; $23 out of area. **Remarks:** Accepts advertising.
Ad Rates: GLR: $.20 **Circ:** ‡1,600
BW: $185.25
SAU: $3
PCI: $3.20

CLARK, pop. 304.

NC MO. Randolph Co. 30 mi. N. of Columbia. Residential.

17073 Small Farm Today
Missouri Farm Publishing, Inc.
3903 W. Ridge Trail Rd. Phone: (573)687-3525
Clark, MO 65243-9525 Fax: (573)687-3148
Free: (800)633-2535
Publication E-mail: smallfarm@socket.net

Magazine promoting and dealing with all aspects of small farming and rural living. **Subtitle:** The How-to Magazine of Alternative and Traditional Crops, Livestock and Direct Marketing. **Founded:** Mar. 1, 1984. **Freq:** Bimonthly. **Print Method:** Offset. **Trim Size:** 8 1/2 x 11. **Cols./Page:** 3. **Col. Width:** 14 picas. **Col. Depth:** 10 inches. **Key Personnel:** Ron Macher, Editor and Publisher; Paul Berg, Managing Editor. **ISSN:** 1079-9729. **Subscription Rates:** $21; $31 other countries; $4.95 single issue; $18 institutions, other countries. **Remarks:** Accepts advertising. **Formerly:** Missouri Farm.
Ad Rates: BW: $785 **Circ:** 12,000
4C: $1,090

CLAYTON†, pop. 14,219.

E. MO. Saint Louis Co. 4 mi. W. of Saint Louis. Residential.

17074 Franklin County Watchman
St. Louis County Printing & Pub. Co.
200 S. Bemiston, Ste. 201 Phone: (314)725-1515
Clayton, MO 63105 Fax: (314)725-1716

Weekly community newspaper containing legal and public notices. **Founded:** 1952. **Freq:** Weekly. **Print Method:** Offset. **Key Personnel:** Kristen Stopp, Editor; R. W. Kuper, Publisher. **USPS:** 217-720. **Subscription Rates:** $25 individuals.
Ad Rates: GLR: $1 **Circ:** Combined ‡20,000
BW: $100
SAU: $6
PCI: $6

17075 Saint Charles Watchman
St. Louis County Printing & Pub. Co.
200 S. Bemiston, Ste. 201 Phone: (314)725-1515
Clayton, MO 63105 Fax: (314)725-1716

Newspaper containing legal and public notices. **Founded:** 1984. **Freq:** Daily. **Cols./Page:** 5. **Col. Width:** 2 inches. **Col. Depth:** 22 inches. **Key Personnel:** Kristen Stopp, Editor; R. W. Kuper, Publisher. **Subscription Rates:** $75 individuals.
Ad Rates: GLR: $1 **Circ:** Combined ‡20,000
BW: $100
SAU: $6
PCI: $9

17076 St. Louis Watchman Advocate
St. Louis County Printing & Pub. Co.
200 S. Bemiston, Ste. 201 Phone: (314)725-1515
Clayton, MO 63105 Fax: (314)725-1716

Legal, financial, and real estate government newspaper. **Founded:** 1881. **Freq:** Daily (eve.). **Print Method:** Offset. **Cols./Page:** 5. **Col. Width:** 23 nonpareils. **Col. Depth:** 224 agate lines. **Key Personnel:** Kristen Stopp, Editor; Ronald W. Kuper, Publisher. **USPS:** 688-540. **Subscription Rates:** $50 individuals. **Formerly:** Watchman-Advocate (1991).
Ad Rates: GLR: $1 **Circ:** Combined ‡40,000
BW: $200
SAU: $9
PCI: $6

17077 KFUO-AM - 850
85 Founders Ln. Phone: (314)725-3030
Clayton, MO 63105 Fax: (314)725-2538
Free: (800)844-0524

Format: Religious. **Networks:** UPI. **Owner:** Lutheran Church-Missouri Synod, 1333 S. Kirkwood Rd., St. Louis, MO 63122, (314)965-9000. **Founded:** 1924. **Operating Hours:** Sunrise-sunset; 10% network, 90% local. **ADI:** St. Louis, MO (Mt. Vernon, IL). **Key Personnel:** Dennis Stortz, General Mgr.; Chuck Rathert, Program Mgr. **Local Programs:** *Issues, Etc.*, Jeff Schwarz; *Living Jubilee*, Paul Clayton. **Wattage:** 5000. **Ad Rates:** Noncommercial.

17078 WCEE-TV - 13
121 Hunter Ave., No. 207 Phone: (314)727-6300
Clayton, MO 63124 Fax: (314)727-4041

Format: Commercial TV. **Networks:** Independent. **Founded:** 1983. **Operating Hours:** Continuous. **ADI:** St. Louis, MO (Mt. Vernon, IL). **Key Personnel:** Howard B. Dolgoff, General Mgr.; Scott Jordan, Chief Engineer; Sherry Duren, Business Mgr. **Wattage:** 302,000.

CLINTON†, pop. 8,366.

W. MO. Henry Co. 40 mi. SW of Sedalia. Tourism. Manufactures press punches, small appliances, textiles. Processes cheese; creamery. Hatcheries. Coal mines. Diversified farming. Corn, wheat, oats.

17079 The Clinton Daily Democrat
Democrat Publishing Co., Inc.
212 S. Washington Phone: (816)885-2281
PO Box 586 Fax: (816)885-2265
Clinton, MO 64735
Free: (800)748-8473

General newspaper. **Founded:** 1868. **Freq:** Daily (eve.). **Print Method:** Offset. **Trim Size:** 6 x 21. **Cols./Page:** 6. **Col. Width:** 25 nonpareils. **Col. Depth:** 301 agate lines. **Key Personnel:** Kathleen W. Miles, Publisher; Daniel B. Miles, Jr., General Mgr.; Katherine M. Miles, Advertising Mgr. **USPS:** 118-560. **Subscription Rates:** $33. **Remarks:** Advertising accepted; rates available upon request.
Circ: ‡3,989

17080 The Kayo
Democrat Publishing Co., Inc.
212 S. Washington Phone: (816)885-2281
PO Box 586 Fax: (816)885-2265
Clinton, MO 64735
Free: (800)748-8473

Community newspaper. **Founded:** 1968. **Freq:** Weekly (Wed.). **Trim Size:** 13 x 21 1/2. **Cols./Page:** 6. **Col. Width:** 12 1/2 picas. **Col. Depth:** 21 inches. **Key Personnel:** Kathleen K. White, Sr., Publisher; Daniel B. Miles, Jr., General Mgr.; Katherine H. Miles, Editor. **Remarks:** Accepts advertising.
Ad Rates: BW: $567 **Circ:** ‡14,700

17081 KDKD-AM - 1280
2201 N. Antioch Rd. Phone: (816)885-6141
Clinton, MO 64735 Fax: (816)885-4801
Free: (800)769-9505

Format: News; Talk. **Networks:** ABC. **Owner:** Randy Boesen, PO Box 448, Clinton, MO 64735. **Founded:** 1949. **Operating Hours:** Continuous: 85% network, 15% local. **ADI:** Kansas City, MO (Lawrence, KS). **Key Personnel:** Randy Boesen, General Mgr.; Charles Branscombe, Chief Engineer. **Local Programs:** *Local Sports*, Jim Lawson, News Dir.; *Speak Out* 9:32 am Monday-Friday, Jim Lawson, News Dir. **Wattage:** 1000 day; 58 night. **Ad Rates:** $6.75-10 for 30 seconds; $9.86-15 for 60 seconds. **URL:** http://www.kdkd.com.

17082 KDKD-FM - 95.3
2201 N. Antioch Rd. Phone: (816)885-6141
PO Box 448 Fax: (816)885-4801
Clinton, MO 64735-0448

Format: Contemporary Country. **Networks:** ABC; Brownfield. **Owner:** Randel Boesen, at above address, Clinton, MO 64735, (660)885-6141, Fax: (660)885-4801. **Founded:** 1975. **Operating Hours:** Continuous; 33% network, 67% local. **Key Personnel:** Charles Branscombe, Contact; Randy Boesen, General Mgr.; Jim Schmedding, Sales Mgr.; Jim Lawson, News Dir.; Jim Lawson, Sports Dir. **Local Programs:** *Musical Line Up*, Kenny Treece; *Speak-Out* 9:32 am Monday-Friday, Jim Lawson, News Dir. **Wattage:** 25,000. **Ad Rates:** $6.57-10 for 30 seconds; $9.86-15 for 60 seconds. **URL:** http://www.kdkd.com.

COLE CAMP, pop. 1,022.

WC MO. Benton Co. 20 mi. S. of Sedalia. Diversified farming. Resort.

17083 Benton County Shopper
JWV Publishing
PO Box 280 Phone: (816)668-4418
Cole Camp, MO 65325 Fax: (816)668-4418

Shopping guide. **Freq:** Weekly (Wed.). **Cols./Page:** 5. **Col. Width:** 1 1/2 inches. **Col. Depth:** 13 inches. **Key Personnel:** Diana Ball, Editor. **Subscription Rates:** Free. **Remarks:** Accepts advertising. **Alt. Formats:** CD-ROM.
Ad Rates: SAU: $3.25 **Circ:** Free 8,100
PCI: $2.65

17084 Courier
JWV Publishing
PO Box 280 Phone: (816)668-4418
Cole Camp, MO 65325 Fax: (816)668-4418

Newspaper with a Republican orientation. **Founded:** 1893. **Freq:** Weekly (Thurs.). **Print Method:** Offset. **Cols./Page:** 6. **Col. Width:** 21 nonpareils. **Col. Depth:** 294 agate lines. **Key Personnel:** James Dickerson, Publisher; Diana Ball, Editor. **Subscription Rates:** $15.95 individuals; $18.50 out of area. **Remarks:** Accepts advertising. **Alt. Formats:** CD-ROM.
Ad Rates: GLR: $.11 **Circ:** ‡1,000
PCI: $2.50

COLUMBIA†, pop. 62,061.

C. MO. Boone Co. 30 mi. N. of Jefferson City. Stephens College; Columbia College; University of Missouri. Manufactures air filters, visual electronic products, circuit breakers, industrial heating elements.Coal mines. Stone quarries. Farming. Corn, wheat, oats.

17085 Advancing the Consumer Interest
American Council on Consumer Interests
University of Missouri Phone: (573)882-3817
240 Stanley Hall Fax: (573)884-4807
Columbia, MO 65211
Publisher E-mail: acci@showme.missouri.edu

Scholarly journal covering the application of knowledge and analysis of current consumer issues. **Freq:** Semiannual. **Subscription Rates:** $80 individuals; $40 students; $155

institutions. **Remarks:** Advertising not accepted. **URL:** http://www.acci.ps.missouri.edu.
Circ: (Not Reported)

17086 American Review of Public Administration
Sage Publications Inc.
University of Missouri-Columbia Phone: (573)882-5443
Dept. of Public Administration Fax: (573)884-4872
315 Middlebush Hall
Columbia, MO 65211
Publication E-mail: arpa@missouri.edu
Publisher E-mail: info@sagepub.com

Academic journal covering public administration. **Founded:** 1967. **Freq:** Quarterly. **Print Method:** Offset. **Trim Size:** 6 x 9. **Cols./Page:** 1. **Col. Width:** 51 nonpareils. **Col. Depth:** 98 agate lines. **Key Personnel:** Guy B. Adams, Editor, adams@missouri.edu; Andrew D. Glassberg, Editor, phone (314)516-5539, fax (314)516-5268, c1918@umsluma.umsl.edu; John Clayton Thomas, Editor, phone (404)651-4591, fax (404)651-1378, padjct@gsu.edu; Cris Anderson, Circulation Mgr., cris_anderson@sagepub.com; Margaret Travers, Advertising Dir., margaret_travers@sagepub.com. **ISSN:** 0275-0740. **Subscription Rates:** $44 individuals; $90 institutions. **Remarks:** Advertising accepted; rates available upon request. **Formerly:** Midwest Review of Public Administration (1988).
Circ: Paid ‡800

17087 Anarchy
CAL Press
PO Box 1446
Columbia, MO 65205

Anti-authoritarian publication addressing on worldwide anarchist and libertarian issues. **Subtitle:** A Journal of Desire Armed. **Founded:** 1980. **Freq:** Quarterly. **Trim Size:** 8 x 10 1/2. **Key Personnel:** Jason McQuinn, Contact, jmcquinn@mail.coin.missouri.edu. **ISSN:** 1044-1387. **Subscription Rates:** $6 single issue. **Remarks:** Advertising not accepted.
Circ: (Not Reported)

17088 Columbia Daily Tribune
Tribune Publishing Co.
101 N. Fourth St. Phone: (573)815-1500
PO Box 798 Fax: (573)815-1701
Columbia, MO 65205-0798
Free: (800)333-6799
Publication E-mail: cdteditor@trib.net

General newspaper. **Founded:** 1901. **Freq:** Daily (eve.), Sat. and Sun. (morn.). **Print Method:** Offset. **Cols./Page:** 6. **Col. Width:** 12 picas. **Col. Depth:** 21 inches. **Key Personnel:** Henry J. Waters III, Editor and Publisher, phone (573)815-1560, fax (573)815-1570, editor@trib.net; Jim Robertson, Managing Editor, phone (573)815-1707, fax (573)815-1701, jrobertson@tribmail.com; Vicki Russell, Associate Publisher, phone (573)815-1565, fax (573)815-1570, rrussell@tribmail.com; Deb Jankowski, Advertising Director, phone (573)815-1808, fax (573)815-1801, jjankowski@tribmail.com. **Subscription Rates:** $119 in Boone County. **Remarks:** Accepts advertising. **URL:** http://www.trib.net.
Ad Rates: GLR: $2.81 **Circ:** Mon.-Fri. 18,469
BW: $1,203.30 Sat. 17,940
4C: $1,548.30 Sun. 23,346
SAU: $9.55

17089 Columbia Missourian
Missourian Publishing Association, Inc.
221 So. 8th St. Phone: (573)882-5700
PO Box 917 Fax: (573)882-5702
Columbia, MO 65205
General newspaper. **Founded:** 1908. **Freq:** Daily and Sunday (morn.). **Print Method:** Offset. **Trim Size:** 13 x 21 1/2. **Cols./Page:** 6. **Col. Width:** 25 nonpareils. **Col. Depth:** 301 agate lines. **Key Personnel:** George Kennedy, Managing Editor; Patricia B. Hoddinott, General Mgr. **Subscription Rates:** $85. **Remarks:** Advertising accepted; rates available upon request.
Circ: Mon.-Fri. 5,007
Sun. 5,065

17090 The Counseling Psychologist
Sage Publications Inc.
University of Missouri Phone: (573)882-3523
16 Hill Hall Fax: (573)884-5989
Dept. of Educational & Counseling Psychology
Columbia, MO 65211
Publisher E-mail: info@sagepub.com

The counseling psychologist. **Founded:** 1969. **Freq:** Bimonthly. **Print Method:** Offset. **Trim Size:** 5 1/2 x 8 1/2. **Cols./Page:** 1. **Col. Width:** 50 nonpareils. **Col. Depth:** 100 agate lines. **Key Personnel:** P. Paul Heppner, Editor, heppnorp@missouri.edu. **ISSN:** 0011-0000. **Subscription Rates:** $59 individuals; $210 institutions; $118 two years; $420 two years Industry; $55 single issue Industry. **Remarks:** Accepts advertising.
Ad Rates: BW: $250 **Circ:** Paid ‡5,400
Non-paid ‡128

17091 Journal of Consumer Affairs
American Council on Consumer Interests
University of Missouri Phone: (573)882-3817
240 Stanley Hall Fax: (573)884-4807
Columbia, MO 65211
Publisher E-mail: acci@showme.missouri.edu

Scholarly journal covering research in consumerism. **Freq:** Semiannual. **ISSN:** 0022-0078. **Subscription Rates:** $80 individuals; $40 students; $155 institutions. **Remarks:** Advertising not accepted. **URL:** http://acci.ps.missouri.edu.
Circ: (Not Reported)

17092 Journal of Dispute Resolution
University of Missouri Phone: (573)882-9682
206 Hulston Hall Fax: (573)882-3343
School of Law
Columbia, MO 65211
Law journal emphasizing alternative dispute resolution processes. **Founded:** 1984. **Freq:** Semiannual. **Cols./Page:** 1. **Col. Width:** 4 9/16 inches. **Col. Depth:** 8 inches. **Key Personnel:** Prof. Christopher P. Guthrie, Advisor, phone (573)882-6543. **ISSN:** 1052-2859. **Subscription Rates:** $21 individuals; $26 Canada; $28 other countries; 15% agency trade discount. **Online:** Westlaw. **Formerly:** Missouri Journal of Dispute Resolution.
Circ: Paid 599
Non-paid 14

17093 Minnesota Review
University of Missouri
107 Tate Hall Phone: (573)882-3059
Columbia, MO 65211 Fax: (573)882-5785

Literary journal covering fiction, poetry, reviews, and literary criticism. **Subtitle:** A Journal of Committed Writing. **Founded:** 1960. **Freq:** Semiannual. **Print Method:** Offset. **Key Personnel:** Jeffrey Williams, Editor. **ISSN:** 0026-5667. **Subscription Rates:** $12 individuals; $7.50 single issue. **Remarks:** Accepts advertising.
Ad Rates: BW: $100 **Circ:** Combined 1,100

17094 Missouri Archaeologist
Missouri Archaeological Society
101A Museum Support Center Phone: (573)882-3544
Rock Quarry Rd. at Hinkson Creek Fax: (573)882-9410
Columbia, MO 65211-3170
Free: (800)472-3223
Publisher E-mail: galenm@missouri.edu

Journal on archaeology and related topics. **Founded:** 1935. **Freq:** Annual. **Trim Size:** 6 x 9. **Cols./Page:** 1. **Col. Width:** 4 3/4 inches. **Col. Depth:** 7 1/4 inches. **Key Personnel:** W. Raymond Wood, Editor; Melody Galen, Assoc. Ed./Production, galenm@missouri.edu. **ISSN:** 0076-9576. **Subscription Rates:** $15 members. **Remarks:** Advertising not accepted.
Circ: Paid 825

17095 Missouri Historical Review
State Historical Society of Missouri
1020 Lowry St. Phone: (573)882-7083
Columbia, MO 65201-7298 Fax: (573)884-4950
Publisher E-mail: shsofmo@umsystem.edu

Journal presenting scholarly articles on the history of Missouri. **Founded:** Oct. 1906. **Freq:** Quarterly. **Print Method:** Offset. **Trim Size:** 6 x 9. **Cols./Page:** 1. **Col. Width:** 46 nonpareils. **Col. Depth:** 91 agate lines. **Key Personnel:** James W. Goodrich, Editor, goodrichj@umsystem.edu; Lynn Wolf Gentzler, Assoc. Editor, gentzlerl@umsystem.edu. **ISSN:** 0026-6582. **Subscription Rates:** $10 U.S.; $15 foreign. **Remarks:** Advertising not accepted. **URL:** http://www.system.missouri.edu/shs. **Alt. Formats:** Microform.
Circ: ‡6,400

17096 Missouri Law Review
University of Missouri at Columbia
School of Law Phone: (573)882-7055
15 Hulston Hall Fax: (573)882-4984
Columbia, MO 65211
Publication E-mail: lawrev@mars.law.missouri.edu

Law journal. **Founded:** 1936. **Freq:** Quarterly. **Key Personnel:** Justin Dean, Editor; Meredith Todd, Assoc. Editor. **ISSN:** 0026-6604. **Subscription Rates:** $30; $35 other countries. **Remarks:** Accepts advertising. **Online:** Lexis-Nexis, Westlaw.
Ad Rates: BW: $100 **Circ:** Paid ‡900
Non-paid ‡250

17097 Missouri Lawyers Weekly
Columbia Tribune Publishing
100 N. 4th St. Phone: (573)449-3811
PO Box 798
Columbia, MO 65201-6520
Publication E-mail: lweeklymo@aol.com

Newspaper for lawyers. **Founded:** 1987. **Freq:** Weekly. **Print Method:** Offset. **Trim Size:** 11 1/2 x 17 1/2. **Cols./Page:** 4. **Col. Width:** 2 3/8 inches. **Col. Depth:** 16 inches. **Key Personnel:** Robert E. McAuliffe, Jr., Publisher; Charlie Fraas, Editor; Karen Antweiler, Mktg. Director; Kathy Smith, Business Mgr. **USPS:** 002-425. **Subscription Rates:** $225; $5 single issue. **Remarks:** Accepts advertising. **URL:** http://www.lweekly.com.
Ad Rates: GLR: $5 **Circ:** Paid ‡2,960
BW: $595 Non-paid ‡91
PCI: $25

17098 Missouri Press News
Missouri Press Association
8th & Locust Phone: (573)449-4167
Columbia, MO 65201 Fax: (573)874-5894

Journalistic professional magazine. **Founded:** 1933. **Freq:** Monthly. **Print Method:** Offset. **Trim Size:** 8 1/2 x 11. **Cols./Page:** 3. **Col. Width:** 2 1/4 inches. **Col. Depth:** 10 inches. **Key Personnel:** Kent Ford, Editor, kford@socket.net; Doug Crews, General Mgr., dcrews@socket.net; Mike Sell, Advertising Dir., msell@socket.net. **ISSN:** 0026-6671. **Subscription Rates:** $7.50. **Remarks:** Accepts advertising. **Online:** Missouri Link. **URL:** http://www.digmo.org/~mpa; http://www.mopress.com.
Ad Rates: BW: $180 **Circ:** ‡900
PCI: $6

17099 The Missouri Realtor
Missouri Association of Realtors
2601 Bernadette Pl. Phone: (573)445-8400
PO Box 1327 Fax: (573)445-7865
Columbia, MO 65205
News articles on real estate. **Founded:** 1936. **Freq:** Quarterly. **Print Method:** Offset. **Trim Size:** 8 1/2 x 11. **Cols./Page:** 3. **Col. Width:** 2 1/4 inches. **Col. Depth:** 8 1/2 inches. **Key Personnel:** Susan Harper, Editor, susanh@morealtor.com; Carma Keinhart, Adver. Coord., carmar@moreltor.com. **USPS:** 355-640. **Subscription Rates:** $10. **Remarks:** Color advertising not accepted.
Ad Rates: BW: $600 **Circ:** ‡18,000

17100 The Missouri Review
University of Missouri at Columbia
1507 Hillcrest Hall Phone: (573)882-4474
Columbia, MO 65211 Fax: (573)884-4671
Publisher E-mail: moreview@showme.missouri.edu

Literary magazine publishing fiction, essays, poetry, interviews, reviews, and special features of literary interest. **Founded:** 1978. **Freq:** Triennial. **Print Method:** Offset perfect bound. **Trim Size:** 6 x 9. **Cols./Page:** 1. **Col. Width:** 26 picas. **Col. Depth:** 43 picas. **Key Personnel:** Speer Morgan, Editor; Greg Michalson, Managing Editor; Evelyn Somers, Assoc. Editor. **ISSN:** 0191-1961. **Subscription Rates:** $19 individuals; $7 single issue. **Remarks:** Accepts advertising. **URL:** http://www.missourireview.org.
Circ: Paid 6,800
Non-paid 200

17101 Missouri Ruralist
Farm Progress Companies
1007 N. College Ave. Phone: (314)875-5445
Columbia, MO 65201
Agriculture magazine. **Founded:** 1848. **Freq:** 15/year. **Print Method:** Offset. **Trim Size:** 8 x 10 7/8. **Cols./Page:** 3. **Col. Width:** 14 picas. **Col. Depth:** 140 agate lines. **Key Personnel:** Sara Wyant, Editorial Vice President; Allan Johnson, President; Jerry Lucht, Sales Mgr.; Chuck Roth, Advertising Dir.; Larry Harper, Editor. **ISSN:** 0026-668X. **Subscription Rates:** $21.95 individuals. **Remarks:** Accepts advertising.
Ad Rates: BW: $2,780 **Circ:** Paid 17,087
4C: $4,170 Non-paid 17,161
PCI: $110

17102 Missouri State Genealogical Association Journal
Missouri State Genealogical Association
Box 833 Phone: (573)442-2387
Columbia, MO 65205-0833
Journal covering genealogy In Missouri. **Founded:** 1981. **Freq:** Quarterly. **Print Method:** Offset. **Trim Size:** 8 1/2 x 11. **Cols./Page:** 2. **Col. Width:** 3.15 inches. **Col. Depth:** 9 inches. **Key Personnel:** Robert M. Doerr, Editor, bdoerr@rollanet.org; Jerry R. Ennis, Editorial Dir., jennis@msn.com. **ISSN:** 0747-5667. **Subscription Rates:** $15 individuals. **Remarks:** Advertising not accepted.
Circ: Paid 705

17103 Missourian Weekend
Missourian Publishing Association, Inc.
221 So. 8th St. Phone: (573)882-5700
PO Box 917 Fax: (573)882-5702
Columbia, MO 65205
General interest newspaper. **Founded:** 1990. **Freq:** Weekly (Thurs.). **Print Method:** Offset. **Cols./Page:** 6. **Col. Width:** 26 nonpareils. **Col. Depth:** 301 agate lines. **Key Personnel:** Patricia B. Hoddinott, General Mgr. **Subscription Rates:** Free. **Remarks:** Accepts advertising. **Formerly**: Sunday.
Ad Rates: BW: $273 **Circ:** Free ‡10,670
4C: $473
PCI: $5.25

17104 MIZZOU Magazine
Alumni Association of the University of Missouri
407 Donald W. Reynolds Alumni and Visitor Center Phone: (573)882-7357 Fax: (573)882-7290
Columbia, MO 65211
Publication E-mail: mizzou@muccmail.missouri.edu

University alumni magazine. **Founded:** Oct. 1912. **Freq:** Quarterly. **Print Method:** Offset. **Trim Size:** 8 3/8 x 10 7/8. **Cols./Page:** 3. **Col. Width:** 14 picas. **Col. Depth:** 55.6 picas. **Key Personnel:** Karen Worley, Editor, karen_s_worley@muccmail.missouri.edu; Tanya Stitt, Advertising Dir. **Subscription Rates:** $30; $5 single issue. **Remarks:** Accepts advertising.
Ad Rates: BW: $2,400 **Circ:** Non-paid ‡130,000
4C: $2,950

17105 Muse
University of Missouri at Columbia
1 Pickard Hall Phone: (573)882-3591
Columbia, MO 65211 Fax: (573)884-4039

Scholarly journal covering University of Missouri, Museum of Art and Archaeology news. **Founded:** 1967. **Freq:** Annual. **Trim Size:** 7 x 9. **Cols./Page:** 1. **Col. Width:** 4 1/2 inches. **Col. Depth:** 6 3/4 inches. **Key Personnel:** Scherrie Goettsch, Editor, goettsch@museum.missouri.edu; Beth Ann Cobb, Subscription and Exchange Librarian. **ISSN:** 0077-2194. **Subscription Rates:** $12 single issue; Free to qualified subscribers. **Remarks:** Advertising not accepted.
Circ: Controlled 585
Paid ★75,505

17106 School and Community
Missouri State Teachers Association
PO Box 458 Phone: (573)442-3127
Columbia, MO 65205-0458 Fax: (573)443-5079
Free: (800)392-0532
Publication E-mail: publications@mail.msta.org
Publisher E-mail: msta_mail@mail.msta.org

Education magazine. **Subtitle:** The Magazine for Missouri Educators. **Founded:** 1915. **Freq:** Quarterly. **Print Method:** Offset. **Trim Size:** 8 3/8 x 10 7/8. **Cols./Page:** 3. **Col. Width:** 26 nonpareils. **Col. Depth:** 140 agate lines. **Key Personnel:** Letha Albright, Editor, letha_albright@mail.msta.org; Bruce Moe, Advertising Mgr., bruce_moe@mail.msta.org. **ISSN:** 0036-6447. **Subscription Rates:** $10. **Remarks:** Accepts advertising. **Available Online. URL:** http://www.msta.org.
Ad Rates: BW: $700 **Circ:** ‡40,000
4C: $1,175

17107 Stephens Life
Stephens College
PO Box 2014 Phone: (573)876-7254
Columbia, MO 65215 Fax: (573)876-2318
Publication E-mail: life@wc.stephens.edu

Collegiate newspaper. **Founded:** 1929. **Freq:** Weekly (Fri.). **Print Method:** Offset. **Cols./Page:** 5. **Col. Width:** 25 nonpareils. **Col. Depth:** 208 agate lines. **Key Personnel:** Steven Chappell, phone (573)876-7168, schappell@wc.stephens.edu. **USPS:** 521-280. **Subscription Rates:** Free; $13 by mail. **Remarks:** Accepts advertising.
Ad Rates: PCI: $4 **Circ:** Paid 150
Non-paid 1,850

17108 Today's Farmer
MFA Inc.
201 Ray Young Dr. Phone: (573)876-5205
Columbia, MO 65201-3599
Agricultural magazine. **Founded:** Oct. 15, 1908. **Freq:** 10/year. **Print Method:** Offset. **Trim Size:** 8 1/8 x 10 7/8. **Cols./Page:** 3. **Col. Width:** 27 nonpareils. **Col. Depth:** 111 agate lines. **Key Personnel:** Chuck Lay, Editor; Julia Cashman, Advertising Mgr. **Subscription Rates:** $12. $2 single issue. **Remarks:** Accepts advertising.
Ad Rates: BW: $2,887 **Circ:** ‡46,000
4C: $4,042

17109 Voice of the Diabetic
National Federation of the Blind
Diabetes Action Network Phone: (573)875-8911
811 Cherry St., Ste. 309 Fax: (573)875-8902
Columbia, MO 65201
Magazine presenting personal stories, practical guidance by blind diabetics and medical professionals, medical news, resource column, and a recipe corner. **Subtitle:** A Support and Information Network. **Founded:** 1986. **Freq:** Quarterly. **Print Method:** Web offset. **Trim Size:** 11 1/4 x 13 3/4. **Cols./Page:** 4. **Col. Width:** 2.25 picas. **Col. Depth:** 12 3/4 inches. **Key Personnel:** Ed Bryant, Editor. **ISSN:** 1041-8490. **Subscription Rates:** Free. **Available Online. URL:** http://www.nfb.org/voice.htm. **Alt. Formats:** Audio tape.
Ad Rates: BW: $1,875 **Circ:** Non-paid ‡225,090
4C: $2,775

17110 Wednesday-Sunday Missourian
Missourian Publishing Association, Inc.
221 So. 8th St. Phone: (573)882-5700
PO Box 917 Fax: (573)882-5702
Columbia, MO 65205
Newspaper. **Founded:** 1972. **Freq:** Semiweekly (Wed. and Sun.). **Print Method:** Offset. **Cols./Page:** 6. **Col. Width:** 26 nonpareils. **Col. Depth:** 301 agate lines. **Key Personnel:** Patricia B. Hoddinott, General Mgr. **Subscription Rates:** Free. **Remarks:** Advertising accepted; rates available upon request. **Formerly**: Missouiran Weekly.
Circ: Wed. ‡41,000
Sun. ‡26,500

17111 KBIA-FM - 91.3
409 Jesse Hall Phone: (573)882-3431
University of Missouri-Columbia Fax: (573)882-2636
Columbia, MO 65211
Free: (800)292-9136
E-mail: kbiamd@showme.missouri.edu

Format: Public Radio; News; Classical; New Age. **Networks:** National Public Radio (NPR); Public Radio International (PRI). **Owner:** University of Missouri Board of Curators, at above address. **Founded:** 1972. **Operating Hours:** Continuous; 40% network; 60% local. **ADI:** Columbia-Jefferson City, MO. **Key Personnel:** Michael Dunn, General Mgr., kbiamol@showme.missouri.edu; Stacey Woelfel, News Dir.; Peter Whorf, Program Dir., kbiapw@showmemissouri.edu; Darren Hellwege, Music Dir., kbiaglh@showme.missouri.edu; Robert Wells, Sales Mgr., kbiadr@showme.missouri.edu. **Wattage:** 100,000. **Ad Rates:** Noncommercial; underwriting available. $13-27 for 15 seconds.

17112 KBXR-FM - 102.3
503 Old 63 North Phone: (573)449-1520
Columbia, MO 65201 Fax: (573)449-7770
E-mail: bxr@bxr.com

Format: Adult Contemporary. **Owner:** Ft. Smith, Inc., at above address. **Founded:** 1994. **Operating Hours:** Continuous. **Key Personnel:** Dave Baugher, President; Renea Sapp, Business Mgr.; Scott Boltz, General Sales Mgr.; John Ott, General Mgr. **Wattage:** 880. **URL:** http://www.bxr.com.

17113 KCOU-FM - 88.1
University of Missouri Phone: (573)882-7820
101-F Pershing Hall Fax: (573)882-6262
Columbia, MO 65201
E-mail: kcou@cclabs.missouri.edu

Format: Alternative/New Music/Progressive. **Owner:** Residence Hall Assoc., 15 Jesse, Columbia, MO 65211, (573)882-7275. **Founded:** 1967. **Formerly**: KCCS-FM (1973). **Operating Hours:** Continuous. **ADI:** Columbia-Jefferson City, MO. **Key Personnel:** Jim Littrell, General Mgr.; Lisa Morgan, Program Dir.; Valerie Vedral, Business Mgr.; Dave Devine, Promotions Dir. **Wattage:** 435. **Ad Rates:** Noncommercial. **URL:** http://tiger.coe.missouri.edu/˜kcou/.

17114 KFMZ-FM - 98.3
1101 E. Walnut Phone: (573)874-3000
PO Box 1268 Fax: (573)443-1460
Columbia, MO 65205
E-mail: kfmz@socket is.net

Format: Alternative/New Music/Progressive. **Networks:** ABC. **Owner:** Contemporary Broadcasting, Inc, at above address. **Founded:** 1971. **Operating Hours:** Continuous; 1% network, 99% local. **ADI:** Columbia-Jefferson City, MO. **Key Personnel:** Robert Cox, General Mgr.; Paul Maloney, Program Dir. **Wattage:** 23,500. **Ad Rates:** $18 for 30 seconds; $28 for 60 seconds. **URL:** http://www.buzz-net.com.

17115 KFRU-AM - 1400
503 Old 63 N. Phone: (314)449-4141
Columbia, MO 65201-6387 Fax: (314)449-7770
Free: (800)229-5378
E-mail: news@kfru.com

Format: News; Talk; Sports. **Networks:** ABC; Mutual Broadcasting System; Missouri. **Owner:** Columbia AM, Inc., at above address. **Founded:** 1925. **Operating Hours:** Continuous. **ADI:** Columbia-Jefferson City, MO. **Key Personnel:** John Ott, General Mgr.; Scott Boltz, General Sales Mgr.; Matt Zeni, Program Dir.; Renea Sapp, Contact. **Wattage:** 1000. **Ad Rates:** $20-46 for 30 seconds; $24-55 for 60 seconds.

17116 KMIZ-TV - 17
501 Bus. Loop 70 E. Phone: (573)449-0917
Columbia, MO 65201 Fax: (573)875-7078
Free: (800)374-0117

Format: Commercial TV. **Networks:** ABC. **Founded:** 1971. **Formerly**: KCBJ-TV (1986). **Operating Hours:** Continuous; 60% network, 40% local. **ADI:** Columbia-Jefferson City, MO. **Key Personnel:** Mark Kammerich, Production Dir.; Regina Moon, General Mgr.; Jeff Ausmus, Promotions Mgr.; Randy Wright, Station Mgr.; Jeff Ausmus, Program Dir.; Todd Powers, General Sales Mgr.; Jim Hall, Natl. Sales Mgr.; Theresa Snow, News Dir. **Local Programs:** *Sportsline* 10:30 p.m. Sunday. **Wattage:** 2,000,000. **URL:** http://www.kmiz.com.

17117 KOMU-TV - 8
Hwy. 63 S. Phone: (314)882-8888
Columbia, MO 65201 Fax: (314)884-5343
E-mail: komu@showme.missouri.edu

Format: Commercial TV. **Networks:** NBC. **Founded:** 1953. **Operating Hours:** 5 a.m.-1 a.m.; 80% network, 20% local. **ADI:** Columbia-Jefferson City, MO. **Key Personnel:** Thomas R. Gray, General Mgr.; John E. Strecker, General Sales Mgr.; Matt Garrett, Program Dir.; Lee Eggers, Chief Engineer; Brian Cottle, Contact. **Local Programs:** *Pepper and Friends* 9 a.m.-10 a.m. **Wattage:** 316,000. **Ad Rates:** Advertising accepted; rates available upon request. **URL:** http://www.komu.com.

17118 KOPN-FM - 89.5
915 E. Broadway Phone: (573)874-1139
Columbia, MO 65201-4857 Fax: (573)499-1662
Free: (800)895-5676
E-mail: mail@kopn.org

Format: News; Talk. **Networks:** National Public Radio (NPR); Public Radio International (PRI). **Owner:** New Wave Corp., at above address. **Founded:** 1973. **Operating Hours:** Continuous. **ADI:** Columbia-Jefferson City, MO. **Key Personnel:** Ryan Warner, News Dir.; Charlie Wilkerson, Operations Dir.; Scott Ebersol, Development Director; Steve Spencer, General Mgr.; Debbie D'Agostino, Station Mgr. **Local Programs:** *The Charlie Wilkerson Show*; *Rootin' Tootin' Radio*, Steve Donofrio; *Viewpoint*, Ryan Warner. **Wattage:** 36,400. **Ad Rates:** Noncommercial; underwriting available. **URL:** http://www.kopn.org.

17119 KOQL-FM - 106.1
503 Old 63 Hwy. Phone: (573)443-1524
Columbia, MO 65201 Fax: (573)449-7770
Free: (800)786-1061
E-mail: kool@koql.com

Format: Oldies. **Owner:** Mid-Missouri Broadcasting, Inc., at above address. **Founded:** 1993. **Operating Hours:** Continuous. **Key Personnel:** Dave Baugher, President; Renea Sapp, Business Mgr.; Scott Boltz, General Sales Mgr.; John Ott, General Mgr. **Wattage:** 69,000. **URL:** http://www.koql.com.

17120 KPLA-FM - 101.5
503 Old 63 N. Phone: (573)442-3116
Columbia, MO 65201 Fax: (573)449-7770
Free: (800)480-1015
E-mail: studio@kpla.com

Format: Adult Contemporary. **Owner:** Columbia FM, Inc., at above address. **Founded:** 1983. **Formerly**: KARO-FM. **Operating Hours:** Continuous. **ADI:** Columbia-Jefferson City, MO. **Key Personnel:** Scott Boltz, General Sales Mgr.; John Ott, General Mgr.; Jim Littrell, Program Dir.; Matt Zeni, News Dir.; Renea Sapp, Contact. **Wattage:** 35,000. **Ad Rates:** $20-46 for 30 seconds; $24-50 for 60 seconds. **URL:** http://www.kpla.com.

17121 KQFX-TV - 11
501 Bus. Leep 70 E. Phone: (573)449-0917
Columbia, MO 65201 Fax: (573)875-7078

Format: Commercial TV. **Networks:** Fox. **Owner:** Benedek Broadcasting, at above address. **Operating Hours:** Continuous; 50% network, 40% local. **ADI:** Columbia-Jefferson City, MO. **Key Personnel:** Ann Ellis, Sales Mgr.; Mark Kammerich, Production Dir.; Regina Moon, General Mgr.; Jeff Ausmus, Promotions Mgr.; Randy Wright, Station Mgr.; Todd Powers, General Sales Mgr.; Jim Hall, National Sales Mgr. **URL:** http://www.kmiz.com.

17122 KWWC-FM - 90.5
Stephens College
Box 2114
Columbia, MO 65215
Phone: (314)876-7297
Fax: (314)876-7248

Format: Jazz. **Owner:** Stephens College, 1200 Broadway, Columbia, MO 65215, (573)876-7297, Fax: (573)876-7248. **Founded:** 1925. **Operating Hours:** 7 a.m.-10 p.m. Mon.-Fri.; 7 a.m.-11 p.m. Sat.-Sun. **ADI:** Columbia-Jefferson City, MO. **Key Personnel:** Elizabeth Clark, Program Dir.; Mark Smith, News Dir./Gen.Mgr., fax (314)876-2318; Max Ornles, Contact; Cory Crow, Promotions/Traffic Manager. **Wattage:** 1250. **Ad Rates:** Noncommercial; underwriting available. **URL:** http://www.scm.com.

17123 TCI Cablevision of Missouri
901 N. College Ave.
Columbia, MO 65201
Phone: (314)874-0422
Fax: (314)499-0317

Owner: Tele-Communications, Inc., 5619 DTC Parkway, Englewood, CO 80111, (303)267-5500, Fax: (303)779-1228. **Founded:** 1977. **Key Personnel:** Dennis Kastens, General Mgr., phone (573)443-1535, fax (573)449-8492; Gary Baugh, Sales Mgr., phone (573)443-1535, fax (573)449-8492. **Cities Served:** Columbia, Fulton, Jefferson City, Mexico, Moberly, MO: subscribing households 55,000; 104 channels; 3 community access channels; 24 hours per week community access programming.

CONCORDIA, pop. 2,129.

W. MO. Lafayette Co. 50 mi. E. of Kansas City. Manufactures animal feeds, recreational vehicles, paper boxes, textiles. Beef, dairy, grain, hog farms. Wheat, corn, beans, grain sorghum.

17124 The Concordian
The Concordian, Inc.
714 Main
PO Box 999
Concordia, MO 64020
Phone: (660)463-7522
Fax: (660)463-7942
Community newspaper. **Founded:** 1893. **Freq:** Weekly (Wed.). **Print Method:** Offset. **Trim Size:** 7 1/2 x 11. **Cols./Page:** 6. **Col. Width:** 12 picas. **Col. Depth:** 21 inches. **Key Personnel:** Gary L. Beissenherz, Editor and Publisher. **USPS:** 128-060. **Subscription Rates:** $21.35 individuals; $26.68 out of area; $30 out of state. **Remarks:** Accepts advertising.
Ad Rates: GLR: $.36; BW: $630; 4C: $780; PCI: $5
Circ: Paid ‡2,799; Free ‡74

CRANE, pop. 1,185.

SW MO. Stone Co. 28 mi. SW of Springfield. Garment and casket factories. Foundries. Agriculture. Cattle, dairy.

17125 The Crane Chronicle/Stone County Republican
Stone County Publishing Co., Inc.
PO Box A
Crane, MO 65633
Phone: (417)723-5248
Fax: (417)723-8490
Publisher E-mail: stonecountypublishing@tri-lakes.net

Newspaper. **Founded:** 1877. **Freq:** Weekly (Thurs.). **Print Method:** Offset. **Trim Size:** 10 3/4 x 17. **Cols./Page:** 5. **Col. Width:** 12 inches. **Col. Depth:** 17 inches. **Key Personnel:** Fred M. Hall, Editor. **USPS:** 136-740. **Subscription Rates:** $18.50; $22.50 out of county; $30 out of state. **Remarks:** Accepts advertising. **URL:** http://www.stonecountynews.com.
Ad Rates: BW: $3.50; PCI: $3.50
Circ: Paid 2,750; Non-paid 15

CUBA, pop. 2,120.

SEC MO. Crawford Co. 75 mi. SW of Saint Louis. Manufactures concrete blocks, machinery, gears, women's shoes. Lumber mill. Agriculture. Fruits.

17126 Cuba Free Press
110 S. Buchanon
PO Box 568
Cuba, MO 65453
Phone: (573)885-7460
Fax: (573)885-3803
Publisher E-mail: cfpss@fidnet.com

Newspaper with a Democratic orientation. **Founded:** June 21, 1960. **Freq:** Weekly (Thurs.). **Print Method:** Offset. **Cols./Page:** 6. **Col. Width:** 12 picas. **Col. Depth:** 301 agate lines. **Key Personnel:** Rob Viehman, Editor; Sherry Wycoff, Advertising Mgr. **USPS:** 565-180. **Subscription Rates:** $17 individuals. **Remarks:** Accepts advertising.
Ad Rates: GLR: $.25; BW: $387; SAU: $4.80; PCI: $3
Circ: 3,700

17127 Steelville Star/Crawford Mirror
PO Box 568
Cuba, MO 65453
Phone: (573)885-7460
Fax: (573)885-3803
Publisher E-mail: cfpss@fidnet.com

Newspaper with a Republican orientation. **Founded:** 1872. **Freq:** Weekly (Wed.). **Print Method:** Offset. **Trim Size:** 11 1/4 x 13 1/2. **Cols./Page:** 5. **Col. Width:** 26 nonpareils. **Col. Depth:** 182 agate lines. **Key Personnel:** Ava Viehman, Editor; Delma Pascoe, Publisher; Percy Pascoe, Jr., Publisher; Lori Viehman, Advertising Mgr. **Subscription Rates:** $14.89 individuals. **Remarks:** Accepts advertising.
Ad Rates: GLR: $.25; BW: $169; 4C: $469; SAU: $2.95
Circ: ‡3,450

17128 Falcon Capital Cable
Box 86
Cuba, MO 65453
Phone: (314)885-3740
Fax: (314)885-4778

Key Personnel: Bobby Williams, Manager. **Cities Served:** Cuba, Indian Hills, Gerald, Rosebud, New Haven, and Lynn, MO.

17129 KGNN-FM - 90.3
Box 617
Cuba, MO 65453
Phone: (314)239-0400
Fax: (314)239-4448
E-mail: gnv@mail.usmo.com

Format: Religious. **Simulcasts:** KGNV-FM. **Networks:** Moody Broadcasting; USA Radio. **Owner:** Missouri River Christian Broadcasting Inc., PO Box 87, Washington, MO 63090. **Founded:** 1988. **Formerly:** KBCC-AM (1988); KGNN-AM (1997). **Operating Hours:** Continuous; 90% network, 10% local. **Key Personnel:** James Goggan, President/GM, phone (314)239-0401. **Local Programs:** *Morning Program* 8-8:30 a.m.; 10:30-10:55 a.m. Monday-Friday, Joe Garnes. **Wattage:** 6,300. **Ad Rates:** $3 for 15 seconds; $5 for 30 seconds; $7 for 60 seconds. $1000/year station sponsorship.

DE SOTO, pop. 5,993.

E. MO. Jefferson Co. 45 mi. SW of Saint Louis. Suburban Residential. Manufactures shoes. Cabinet-making; metal working. Diversified farming. Cattle, hay, grain.

17130 KDJR-FM - 100.1
Box 162
De Soto, MO 63020
Free: (888)464-5357
Phone: (314)586-0101
Fax: (314)337-8288
E-mail: k100@mail.theriver.net

Format: Country. **Networks:** Missouri. **Founded:** 1991. **Operating Hours:** Continuous. **ADI:** St. Louis, MO (Mt. Vernon, IL). **Key Personnel:** Mike Zimmer, General Mgr. **Wattage:** 6000. **Ad Rates:** $31 for 30 seconds; $37 for 60 seconds. $4.20-$12 for 30 seconds; $5.20-$14.40 for 60 seconds. Combined advertising rates available with KHAD-AM.

DEXTER, pop. 7,043.

SE MO. Stoddard Co. 45 mi. S. of Cape Girardeau. Manufactures textiles, automotive filters, exhaust systems, wood products. Cotton ginning. Food processing. Agriculture. Livestock. Diversified farming. Wheat,corn, cotton.

17131 The Daily Statesman
Delta Publishing Co.
33 S. Walnut
PO Box 579
Dexter, MO 63841
Phone: (314)624-4545
Fax: (314)624-7449
General newspaper. **Founded:** 1875. **Freq:** Daily (eve.). **Print Method:** Offset. **Cols./Page:** 6. **Col. Width:** 24 nonpareils. **Col. Depth:** 301 agate lines. **Key Personnel:** Barbara Hill, Publisher; Sherm Smith, Editor. **Subscription Rates:** $27. **Remarks:** Advertising accepted; rates available upon request.
Circ: Tues. ♦**9,639**; Sun. ♦**3,608**

17132 KDEX-AM - 1590
20487 State Hwy. 114
PO Box 249
Dexter, MO 63841-0249
Phone: (573)624-3545
Fax: (573)624-9926
E-mail: kdex1@dexter.net

Format: Contemporary Country. **Networks:** ABC. **Owner:** Walter F. Turner, at above address. **Founded:** 1956. **Operating Hours:** Continuous. **ADI:** Paducah,KY-Cape Girardeau,MO-Marion,IL. **Key Personnel:** Walter F. Turner, Pres./Gen. Mgr.; Barbara B. Turner, Vice Pres./Natl. Sales Mgr.; Joeli Barbour, Music and Traffic Dir.; Fred Applegate, News Dir.; Jim LaBrot, Sports Dir. **Local Programs:** *You and Your Community*, Tony James. **Wattage:** 1000. **Ad Rates:** $10 for 30 seconds; $13 for 60 seconds.

17133 KDEX-FM - 102.3
20487 State Hwy. 114
PO Box 249
Dexter, MO 63841
Phone: (573)624-3545
Fax: (573)624-9926
E-mail: kdex1@dexter.net

Format: Contemporary Country. **Simulcasts:** KDEX-AM. **Networks:** ABC. **Owner:** Walter F. Turner, at above address. **Founded:** 1969. **Operating Hours:** Continuous. **ADI:** Paducah,KY-Cape Girardeau,MO-Marion,IL. **Key Personnel:** Walter F. Turner, Contact; Barbara B. Turner, Contact; Joeli Barbour, Music and Traffic Dir.; Fred Applegate, News Dir.; Jim LaBrot, Sports Dir. **Local Programs:** *You and Your Community*, Tony James. **Wattage:** 6000. **Ad Rates:** $10 for 30 seconds; $13 for 60 seconds.

DIXON, pop. 1,402.

SC MO. Pulaski Co. 11 mi. N. of Waynesville. Residential.

17134 Pilot
302 Locust
PO Box Drawer V
Dixon, MO 65459
Phone: (314)759-2128
Newspaper with a Republican orientation. **Founded:** 1911. **Freq:** Weekly (Thurs.). **Print Method:** Offset. **Cols./Page:** 6. **Col. Width:** 30 nonpareils. **Col. Depth:** 294 agate lines. **Key Personnel:** Rick Blackburn, Editor and Publisher. **Subscription Rates:** $20. **Remarks:** Accepts advertising.
Ad Rates: SAU: $3.50; PCI: $3.50
Circ: ‡2,650

DONIPHAN†, pop. 1,921.

SE MO. Ripley Co. On Current River, 90 mi. SW of Cape Girardeau. Resort. Lumber and stave mill. Sand and gravel quarries; timber. Diversified farming. Corn, cotton, oats, livestock.

17135 Prospect-News
Box 367
Doniphan, MO 63935
Phone: (314)996-2103
Fax: (314)996-2217

Newspaper. **Founded:** 1874. **Freq:** Weekly (Wed.). **Print Method:** Offset. **Cols./Page:** 6. **Col. Width:** 12 picas. **Col. Depth:** 301 agate lines. **Key Personnel:** Don Schricher, Publisher; Barbara Ann Horton, Editor. **Subscription Rates:** $15. **Remarks:** Accepts advertising. **Alt. Formats:** CD-ROM.
Ad Rates: GLR: $.16; PCI: $5.25
Circ: 5,500

17136 KDFN-AM - 1500
116 S. Grand Ave.
Doniphan, MO 63935-1741
Phone: (314)996-3124
Fax: (314)996-7215

Format: Middle-of-the-Road (MOR). **Networks:** ABC. **Owner:** Jack G. Hunt, 204 E. Washington St., Doniphan, MO 63935. **Founded:** 1963. **Operating Hours:** Sunrise-sunset. **Key Personnel:** Gary Lee, Contact; Dale Monroe, News Dir. **Wattage:** 2500. **Ad Rates:** $2-6 for 30 seconds; $1.75-8 for 60 seconds.

17137 KOEA-FM - 97.5
116 S. Grand Ave.
Doniphan, MO 63935-1741
Phone: (314)996-3124
Fax: (314)996-3124

Format: Country. **Networks:** ABC; Missouri; Brownfield. **Owner:** Jack G. Hunt, 204 E. Washington St., Doniphan, MO 63935. **Founded:** 1975. **Operating Hours:** Continuous; 20% network, 80% local. **Key Personnel:** Gary Lee, Contact; Dale Monroe, News Dir. **Wattage:** 50,000. **Ad Rates:** $2.90-6 for 30 seconds; $2.25-8 for 60 seconds.

DREXEL

17138 Drexel Star
Adrian Journal
130 Main St.
PO Box 378
Drexel, MO 64742
Phone: (816)657-2222
Community newspaper. **Founded:** 1892. **Freq:** Weekly (Thurs.). **Cols./Page:** 6. **Col. Width:** 12 1/5 picas. **Col. Depth:** 21 inches. **Key Personnel:** Steve Oldfield, Publisher; Bob Gunn, Publisher; Steve Oldfield, Publisher. **Subscription Rates:** $17.00; $21.25 out of area; $25 out of state. **Remarks:** Accepts advertising.
Ad Rates: BW: $737.10; SAU: $5.85; PCI: $3
Circ: 700

EAST PRAIRIE, pop. 3,713.

SE MO. Mississippi Co. 10 mi. S. of Charleston. Residential.

17139 East Prairie Eagle
East Prairie Eagle News
PO Box 10 Phone: (573)649-3541
East Prairie, MO 63845 Fax: (573)683-2217

Local news. **Founded:** 1905. **Freq:** Weekly (Thurs.). **Print Method:** Offset. **Cols./Page:** 6. **Col. Width:** 18 nonpareils. **Col. Depth:** 301 agate lines. **Key Personnel:** Jim Anderson, Editor; Mildred Wallhausen, Publisher; Paul Page, Advertising Mgr. **Subscription Rates:** $5.20. **Remarks:** Accepts advertising.
Ad Rates: BW: $469.56 **Circ:** ‡2,500
4C: $569.56
PCI: $3.64

EDINA†, pop. 1,520.

NE MO. Knox Co. 48 mi. NW of Quincy, IL. Manufactures textiles, lumber. Agriculture. Corn, oats, beans.

17140 Sentinel
PO Box 270 Phone: (816)397-2226
Edina, MO 63537 Fax: (816)397-2227

Newspaper. **Founded:** 1868. **Freq:** Weekly (Wed.). **Print Method:** Offset. **Cols./Page:** 8. **Col. Width:** 20 nonpareils. **Col. Depth:** 301 agate lines. **Key Personnel:** Hazel Bledsoe Smith, Editor and Publisher. **Subscription Rates:** $10.

EL DORADO SPRINGS, pop. 3,868.

SW MO. Cedar Co. 18 mi. NW of Stockton. Residential.

17141 El Dorado Springs Sun
PO Box 71 Phone: (417)876-3841
El Dorado Springs, MO 64744 Fax: (417)876-3848
Publication E-mail: sunnews@u-n-i.net

Community newspaper. **Founded:** 1890. **Freq:** Weekly. **Print Method:** Offset. **Cols./Page:** 6. **Col. Width:** 25 nonpareils. **Col. Depth:** 294 agate lines. **Key Personnel:** Kenneth W. Long, Editor; Kimball S. Long, Publisher. **Subscription Rates:** $15 individuals; $20 out of area; $24 out of state. **Remarks:** Accepts advertising.
Ad Rates: 4C: $240 **Circ:** ‡4,500
SAU: $3
PCI: $3

17142 KESM-AM - 1580
200 Radio Ln. Phone: (417)876-2741
El Dorado Springs, MO 64744
E-mail: kesm@getonthe.net

Format: Country; Adult Contemporary. **Networks:** NBC. **Founded:** 1960. **Operating Hours:** Sunrise-sunset. **ADI:** Springfield, MO. **Key Personnel:** Donald Kohn, General Manager; Susan Kohn, Station/Sales Mgr./News Dir. **Wattage:** 500.

17143 KESM-FM - 105.5
200 Radio Ln. Phone: (417)876-2741
El Dorado Springs, MO 64744
E-mail: kesm@getonthe.net

Format: Country; Adult Contemporary. **Networks:** NBC. **Founded:** 1961. **Operating Hours:** 6 a.m.-midnight. **ADI:** Springfield, MO. **Key Personnel:** Donald Kohn, General Mgr.; Susan Kohn, Sales Mgr./News Dir. **Wattage:** 6000.

ELDON, pop. 4,342.

C. MO. Miller Co. 30 mi. SW of Jefferson City. Manufactures cheese, dairy products, textiles. Timber. Agriculture.

17144 The Eldon Advertiser
Vernon Publishing, Inc.
415 S. Maple Phone: (573)392-5658
PO Box 315 Fax: (573)392-7755
Eldon, MO 65026
Publication E-mail: advertiser@vernonpublishing.com
Publisher E-mail: advertiser@vernonpublishing.com

Newspaper. **Founded:** 1894. **Freq:** Weekly (Thurs.). **Print Method:** Offset. **Cols./Page:** 6. **Col. Width:** 2 1/16 inches. **Col. Depth:** 21 inches. **Key Personnel:** Tim Flora, Editor. **USPS:** 171-200. **Subscription Rates:** $28.50. **Remarks:** Accepts advertising. **Formerly:** Advertiser (1992).
Ad Rates: GLR: $0.30 **Circ:** ‡4,800
BW: $510.30
4C: $660.30
SAU: $4.05
PCI: $4.05

17145 KBMX-FM - 101.9
1081 Osage Beach Rd. Phone: (573)348-0500
Osage Beach, MO 65065 Fax: (573)348-0625

Format: Easy Listening. **Networks:** ABC. **Owner:** Lake Broadcasting Inc., at above address. **Founded:** 1988. **Operating Hours:** Continuous. **Key Personnel:** Mike Rice, President; Bob Cannella, General Mgr. **Wattage:** 6000 ERP.

17146 KLOZ-FM - 92.7
209 E. 2nd St. Phone: (573)392-3793
Eldon, MO 65026 Fax: (573)392-7617
Free: (800)613-9993

Format: Adult Contemporary. **Networks:** ABC. **Owner:** Benne Broadcasting LLC, at above address, Clayton, MO 63105. **Founded:** 1977. **Formerly:** KLDN-FM (1987). **Operating Hours:** Continuous; 2% network, 98% local. **ADI:** Columbia-Jefferson City, MO. **Key Personnel:** Denny Benne, General Mgr.; Karen Hurtubise, Contact; Mike Clayton, Program Dir. **Local Programs:** *Fax-Free Lunch*, Mike Clayton; *Sports Trivia*, Mike Clayton; *21*, Mike Clayton. **Wattage:** 50,000.

ELSBERRY, pop. 1,272.

NE MO. Lincoln Co. 30 mi. NNW of Saint Charles. Limestone quarries.

17147 Elsberry Democrat
Elsberry News, Inc.
PO Box 105 Phone: (573)898-2318
Elsberry, MO 63343 Fax: (573)898-2173

Community newspaper. **Freq:** Weekly (Wed.). **Key Personnel:** Margaret Herring, Editor. **Subscription Rates:** $8 (local); $12 (out of area). **Remarks:** Advertising accepted; rates available upon request.
Circ: 1,500

EMINENCE, pop. 614.

S MO. Shannon Co. 110 mi. E. of Springfield. Summer resort. Manufactures staves and lumber products. Copper mines; timber. Agriculture. Corn, wheat, hay.

17148 The Current Wave
Current Wave Newspaper
PO Box 728 Phone: (573)226-3335
Eminence, MO 65466-9998 Free: (800)353-9283

Local newspaper. **Founded:** 1874. **Freq:** Weekly (Wed.). **Print Method:** Offset. **Cols./Page:** 6. **Col. Width:** 12 picas. **Col. Depth:** 21 inches. **Key Personnel:** Roger Dillon, Editor and Publisher; Carol Dillon, Office Mgr. **Subscription Rates:** $20 individuals; $22 out of area; $26 elsewhere; $28 out of state.
Ad Rates: SAU: $4 **Circ:** ‡2,000
PCI: $4.25

EXCELSIOR SPRINGS, pop. 10,424.

W. MO. Clay and Ray Co. 12 mi. NE of Kansas City. Health resort; mineral springs. Manufactures plastics. Diversified farming. Corn, oats, wheat.

17149 The Daily Standard
Excelsior Publishing Co., Inc.
417 Thompson Ave. Phone: (816)637-6155
PO Box 7 Fax: (816)637-8411
Excelsior Springs, MO 64024
General newspaper. **Founded:** 1889. **Freq:** Daily (eve.). **Print Method:** Offset. **Cols./Page:** 7. **Col. Width:** 10 3/5 picas. **Col. Depth:** 21 inches. **Key Personnel:** James M. Watson, Editor and Publisher; Molly Morgan Roberts, Advertising Mgr. **Subscription Rates:** $45. **Remarks:** Accepts advertising.
Ad Rates: GLR: $.42 **Circ:** ‡3,500
BW: $764.97
SAU: $7.26
PCI: $4.75

The Excelsior - See Lancaster

17150 Town & Country Leader
Excelsior Publishing Co., Inc.
417 Thompson Ave. Phone: (816)637-6155
PO Box 7 Fax: (816)637-8411
Excelsior Springs, MO 64024
Shopper. **Founded:** 1957. **Freq:** Weekly (Wed.). **Print Method:** Offset. **Cols./Page:** 6. **Col. Width:** 20 nonpareils. **Col. Depth:** 224 agate lines. **Key Personnel:** James M. Watson, Publisher; Molly Morgan-Roberts, Advertising Mgr. **Subscription Rates:** Free; $57 (mail). **Remarks:** Color advertising not accepted.
Ad Rates: GLR: $.32 **Circ:** Paid ‡245
BW: $427.20 Free ‡20,100
SAU: $7.26
PCI: $4.75

17151 KEXS-AM - 1090
201 Industrial Park Rd. Phone: (816)630-1090
Excelsior Springs, MO 64024 Fax: (816)630-6063
Free: (800)430-1090

Format: Southern Gospel. **Networks:** USA Radio. **Owner:** Jeffco T.V. Corp., at above address. **Founded:** 1989. **Operating Hours:** Sunrise-sunset. **ADI:** Kansas City, MO (Lawrence, KS). **Key Personnel:** Brad L. Campbell, Owner/Pres./Gen. Mgr. **Wattage:** 1000. **Ad Rates:** $6-10 for 15 seconds; $6-19 for 30 seconds; $10-29.50 for 60 seconds.

FAIRFAX, pop. 835.

NW MO. Atchison Co. 65 mi. NW of Saint Joseph. Livestock shipping. Diversified farming. Corn, wheat, soybeans.

17152 The Fairfax Forum
PO Box 17 Phone: (816)686-2741
Fairfax, MO 64446-0017
Newspaper with a Republican orientation. **Founded:** Jan. 2, 1892. **Freq:** Weekly (Wed.). **Print Method:** Offset. **Cols./Page:** 7. **Col. Width:** 21 nonpareils. **Col. Depth:** 301 agate lines. **Key Personnel:** Nancy Gaines, Publisher. **Subscription Rates:** $21 individuals. **Remarks:** Accepts advertising.
Ad Rates: GLR: $.10 **Circ:** ‡920
SAU: $2.25

FARMINGTON†, pop. 8,270.

SE MO. Saint Francois Co. 9 mi. S. of Desloge. Residential. Lead deposits.

17153 The Daily Press Leader
120 N. Washington Phone: (573)756-8927
Farmington, MO 63640-0070 Fax: (573)756-9160
Publication E-mail: mgriggs@pressleader.com

Community newspaper. **Founded:** 1928. **Freq:** Daily (Tues. thru Saturday). **Print Method:** Letterpress and offset. Uses Adnet. **Cols./Page:** 6. **Col. Width:** 27 nonpareils. **Col. Depth:** 294 agate lines. **Key Personnel:** John Seals, Editor; Tim Evans, Publisher; Joe Lopez, Advertising Mgr. **Subscription Rates:** $64. **Remarks:** Accepts advertising. **Available Online. URL:** pressleader. **Absorbed:** Press-Advertiser (1992).
Ad Rates: BW: $1,322.25 **Circ:** Mon.-Fri. ‡3,500
4C: $1,472.25 ‡13,000
SAU: $11.20 9,500
PCI: $10.25

17154 Base Cablevision Inc.
PO Box 710 Phone: (573)756-8616
Farmington, MO 63640-0710

Founded: Jan. 22, 1981. **Key Personnel:** Larry V. Jones, President. **Cities Served:** Blytheville, AR; Hornersville, MO: subscribing households 265; 35 channels; 2 community access channels.

17155 KREI-AM - 800
1401 KREI Blvd. Phone: (573)756-6476
PO Box 461 Fax: (573)756-1110
Farmington, MO 63640
Free: (800)842-2330

Format: Talk; News; Information. **Networks:** ABC. **Owner:** The Shepard Group, P.O. Box 619, Moberly, MO 65270, (660)263-1230, Fax: (660)263-2300, Free: (800)892-2300. **Founded:** 1947. **Operating Hours:** Continuous; 33% network, 67% local. **Key Personnel:** Richard Womack, General Mgr.; Connie Pfiefer, Sales Mgr.; Mark Toti, Contact, phone (573)756-9127. **Wattage:** 1000. **Ad Rates:** $3-15 for 30 seconds; $6-30 for 60 seconds.

FAYETTE†, pop. 2,983.

C. MO. Howard Co. 20 mi. NW of Columbia. Central Methodist College. Textile factory. Agriculture. Soybeans, corn, wheat, milo, cattle.

17156 The Democrat-Leader
Wood Creek Corp.
202 E. Morrison Phone: (660)248-2235
PO Box 32 Fax: (660)248-1200
Fayette, MO 65248-0032
Publication E-mail: newspaper@mcmsys.com

Newspaper - general circulation. **Founded:** Jan. 1, 1874. **Freq:** Weekly. **Print Method:** Offset. **Trim Size:** 14 x 23. **Cols./Page:** 6. **Col. Width:** 24 nonpareils. **Col. Depth:** 294 agate lines. **Key Personnel:** H. Denny Davis, Editor and Publisher. **USPS:** 153-200. **Subscription Rates:** $26 individuals. **Remarks:** Accepts advertising.
Ad Rates: BW: $400.68 **Circ:** ‡2,410
SAU: $3.18

17157 The Fayette Advertiser
Wood Creek Corp.
202 E. Morrison Phone: (660)248-2235
PO Box 32 Fax: (660)248-1200
Fayette, MO 65248-0032
Publication E-mail: newspaper@mcmsys.com

Community newspaper. **Founded:** Sept. 3, 1840. **Freq:** Weekly (Wed.). **Print Method:** Offset. **Trim Size:** 14 x 23. **Cols./Page:** 6 and 1. **Col. Width:** 24 nonpareils and 12 picas. **Col. Depth:** 294 agate lines and 21 inches. **Key Personnel:** H. Denny Davis, Editor and Publisher. **USPS:** 188-300. **Subscription Rates:** $26. **Remarks:** Accepts advertising.
Ad Rates: GLR: $3.18 **Circ:** Paid 2,317
BW: $400.58 Free 92
SAU: $3.18
PCI: $3.15

FENTON

17158 Healing Words
Creative Communications for the Parish
1564 Fencorp Dr. Free: (800)325-9414
Fenton, MO 63026
Publication E-mail: hw@creativecomm.com
Publisher E-mail: ccp@creativecomm.com

Devotional magazine for hospital patients. **Subtitle:** Spiritual Resources For Your Hospital Stay. **Founded:** 1988. **Freq:** Quarterly. **Print Method:** Offset. **Trim Size:** 5 3/8 x 8 3/8. **Cols./Page:** 1. **Col. Width:** 4 1/8 inches. **Col. Depth:** 7 1/2 inches. **Key Personnel:** Larry Neeb, Publisher, neeb@creativecomm.com; Arden Mead, Editor, arden@creativecomm.com. **Subscription Rates:** offers bulk subscriptions only. **Remarks:** Advertising not accepted.
Circ: ‡20,000

17159 Living Faith
Creative Communications for the Parish
1564 Fencorp Dr. Free: (800)325-9414
Fenton, MO 63026
Publisher E-mail: ccp@creativecomm.com

Devotional magazine. **Subtitle:** Daily Catholic Devotions. **Founded:** Apr. 1985. **Freq:** Quarterly. **Print Method:** Offset. **Trim Size:** 4 x 5 1/2. **Key Personnel:** James E. Adams, Editor; Mark Neilsen, Assoc. Editor. **ISSN:** 0884-1330. **Subscription Rates:** $6.50 individuals; $2.25 single issue. **Remarks:** Advertising not accepted. **Alt. Formats:** Audio tape; Braille; Large-print. **Formerly:** Living Words.
Circ: Paid 585,000

17160 Paint & Decorating Retailer
Paint and Decorating Retailer's Association
403 Axminster Dr. Phone: (314)326-2636
Fenton, MO 63026 Fax: (314)326-1823
Free: (800)737-0107
Publisher E-mail: info@pdra.org

Magazine serving retailers of paint and decorating products. **Founded:** 1964. **Freq:** Monthly. **Print Method:** Offset. **Trim Size:** 8 1/8 x 10 7/8. **Cols./Page:** 3. **Col. Width:** 42 nonpareils. **Col. Depth:** 140 agate lines. **Key Personnel:** Diane Capuano, Exec. Editor; Ernest W. Stewart, Publisher; Nicholas R. Cichielo, Vice Pres./Sales. **Subscription Rates:** $26 U.S.-Canada add $8, Foreign add $16, July Issue $15-Dec. Issue $35. **URL:** http://www.pdra.org. **Formerly:** Decorating Retailer.
Ad Rates: BW: $3,810 **Circ:** Combined ‡29,772
4C: $5,210

FESTUS, pop. 7,574.

E. MO. Jefferson Co. 30 mi. SW of Saint Louis. Manufactures tool & die, plate glass, fertilizer, cement, nuclear pellets, styrofoam, lead smelting, cans, industrial sound equipment. Agriculture.

17161 Courier Journal
Suburban Newspapers of Greater St. Louis
998 E. Gannon Dr. Phone: (314)296-1800
PO Box 309 Fax: (314)937-9811
Festus, MO 63028
Community newspaper. **Founded:** 1976. **Freq:** Semiweekly (Wed. and Sun.). **Print Method:** Offset. **Cols./Page:** 6. **Col. Width:** 26 nonpareils. **Col. Depth:** 308 agate lines. **Key Personnel:** Steve Puckett, Editor; Roger E. Reinhardt, Publisher; Larry Johnson, Advertising Mgr. **Subscription Rates:** Free. **Remarks:** Accepts advertising.
Ad Rates: SAU: $10.95 **Circ:** Free 46,438

17162 Jefferson County Journal
Jefferson County Publications
998 E. Gannon Dr. Phone: (314)937-9811
PO Box 309 Fax: (314)931-2638
Festus, MO 63028
Newspaper with a Republican orientation. **Founded:** 1904. **Freq:** Semiweekly (Wed. and Sun.). **Print Method:** Offset. **Cols./Page:** 6. **Col. Width:** 26 nonpareils. **Col. Depth:** 308 agate lines. **Key Personnel:** John Wikelman, Editor, phone (314)937-9811, fax (314)931-2638. **Remarks:** Accepts advertising. **Formerly:** Jefferson County Sunday Journal.
Ad Rates: SAU: $11.55 **Circ:** Free 39,500

17163 News Democrat Journal
Jefferson County Publications
998 E. Gannon Dr. Phone: (314)937-9811
PO Box 309 Fax: (314)931-2638
Festus, MO 63028
General newspaper. **Subtitle:** Member of the Suburban Journals of Greater St. Louis. **Founded:** 1865. **Print Method:** Offset. **Cols./Page:** 6. **Col. Width:** 25 nonpareils. **Col. Depth:** 294 agate lines. **Key Personnel:** John Winkleman, phone (314)937-9811, fax (314)931-2638; Janice Feltner. **USPS:** 144-620. **Subscription Rates:** $28.50. **Remarks:** Accepts advertising. **Formerly:** Daily News Democrat-Courier Journal; News Democrat.
Ad Rates: SAU: $10.35 **Circ:** Paid 20,000
PCI: $7.33

17164 KJFF-AM - 1400
Scenic Dr. Phone: (314)937-7642
Festus, MO 63028 Fax: (314)937-3636
Free: (800)842-2330

Format: Talk; News. **Networks:** NBC. **Owner:** KREI, Inc., PO Box 461, Farmington, MO 63640, (573)756-6476, Fax: (573)756-1110. **Founded:** 1951. **Formerly:** KJCF-AM. **Operating Hours:** Continuous; 20% network, 80% local. **ADI:** St. Louis, MO (Mt. Vernon, IL). **Key Personnel:** Kirk Mooney, Station Mgr.; Deron Mansfield, Program Dir.; Dick Womack, General Mgr. **Local Programs:** *Early Lunch Hour Special*, Deron Mansfield; *Jefferson Co. PM*, Deron Mansfield; *Morning Magazine*, Deron Mansfield. **Wattage:** 1000. **Ad Rates:** $4-32 for 60 seconds. Combined advertising rates available with KREI-AM, KTJJ-FM.

FLAT RIVER, pop. 4,443.

SE MO. Saint Francois Co. 65 mi. SW of Saint Louis. Mineral Area Community College. Manufactures vaults, fertilizer, explosives, shoes, furniture. Truck, grain farms. Corn.

17165 KDBB-FM - 104.3
804 St.Joe Dr. Phone: (314)431-1000
Box 36 Fax: (314)431-0850
Flat River, MO 63601
Free: (800)959-5366
E-mail: b104fm@il.net

Format: Classic Rock. **Networks:** Westwood One Radio. **Founded:** 1989. **Operating Hours:** Continuous. **Key Personnel:** Larry D. Joseph, Vice President; Kelly Valle, General Sales Mgr.; Greg Camp, Program Dir.; Gilbert Collins, News Dir. **Wattage:** 6000. **Ad Rates:** Advertising accepted; rates available upon request.

17166 KFMO-AM - 1240
809 St. Joe Dr. Phone: (314)431-2000
Box 36 Fax: (314)431-0850
Flat River, MO 63601
Free: (800)959-5366
E-mail: bigriver@il.net

Format: Contemporary Country; Religious. **Networks:** Mutual Broadcasting System. **Founded:** 1947. **Operating Hours:** Continuous; 20% network, 80% local. **Key Personnel:** Gilbert Collins, News Dir.; Greg Camp, Program Dir.; Kelly Valle, Sales Mgr.; Larry D. Joseph, Vice President. **Local Programs:** *Parkland Today*, Gib Collins, Jr., Mailing contact. **Wattage:** 1000. **Ad Rates:** $4.50-6.50 for 30 seconds; $7-10 for 60 seconds.

FLORISSANT, pop. 55,372.

E. MO. Saint Louis Co. 20 mi. NW of Saint Louis. Residential.

17167 The Florissant Valley Reporter
Galaxy Communications Co.
493 St. Francis, Ste. 9 Phone: (314)839-1111
PO Box 69 Fax: (314)831-8536
Florissant, MO 63031
Community newspaper (tabloid). **Founded:** Nov. 17, 1950. **Freq:** Weekly (Tues.). **Print Method:** Offset. **Trim Size:** 17 x 22. **Cols./Page:** 5. **Col. Width:** 22 1/2 nonpareils. **Col. Depth:** 224 agate lines. **Key Personnel:** Walter A. Garrett, Jr., Editor and Publisher. **USPS:** 202-520. **Subscription Rates:** $12.95; $17.95 out of country. **Remarks:** Accepts advertising.
Ad Rates: GLR: $.61 **Circ:** Paid ‡8,525
BW: $728 Free ‡321
4C: $968
PCI: $9.10

17168 The Lowell Review
Instant Karma Press
3075 Harness Dr.
Florissant, MO 63033

Journal of poetry and short fiction. **Founded:** 1994. **Freq:** Annual. **Print Method:** Offset. **Cols./Page:** 1. **Key Personnel:** Judith Dickenman-Nelson, Contact; Rita Rouvalis-Chapman, Contact, rita@locust.etext.org. **ISSN:** 1077-8942. **Subscription Rates:** $7 individuals. **Remarks:** Accepts advertising.
Ad Rates: BW: $100 **Circ:** Paid 150
Non-paid 100

FREDERICKTOWN†, pop. 4,036.

SE MO. Madison Co. 50 mi. W. of Cape Girardeau. Commercial and business area. Manufactures shoes, textiles, lumber products. Lead, cobalt, copper, zinc, iron mines; timber. Agriculture. Wheat, corn, hay, cattle, hogs.

17169 Democrat-News
American Publishing Co.
PO Box 471 Phone: (314)783-3366
Fredericktown, MO 63645 Fax: (314)783-6890

Local newspaper. **Founded:** 1870. **Freq:** Weekly (Thurs.). **Print Method:** Offset. **Cols./Page:** 6. **Col. Width:** 26 nonpareils. **Col. Depth:** 294 agate lines. **Key Personnel:** Mary Cissell, Publisher. **Subscription Rates:** $25 individuals; $31 out of state. **Remarks:** Accepts advertising.
Ad Rates: GLR: $.30 **Circ:** ‡3,200
BW: $630
PCI: $5

17170 KYLS-AM - 1450
1242 Highway OO Phone: (573)783-6461
Fredericktown, MO 63645-8402 Fax: (573)783-3884
E-mail: froggy@ldd.net

Simulcasts: KYLS-FM. **Networks:** CNN Radio. **Owner:** Fred Dockins, at above address. **Founded:** 1962. **Formerly:** KFTW-AM (1998). **Operating Hours:** Continuous. **Key Personnel:** Fred Dockins, Contact. **Wattage:** 1000. **Ad Rates:** $7-8 for 30 seconds; $8-9 for 60 seconds.

17171 KYLS-FM - 92.9
1242 Hiway 00 Phone: (573)783-6461
Fredericktown, MO 63645 Fax: (573)783-3884
E-mail: froggy@ldd.net

Format: Hot Country. **Networks:** NBC. **Owner:** Dockins Communications, Inc., at above address. **Operating Hours:** Continuous. **ADI:** St. Louis, MO (Mt. Vernon, IL). **Key Personnel:** Sheila Dockins, Traffic Mgr.; Fred Dockins, Program Mgr.; Palmer Johnson, Chief Engineer. **Wattage:** 6000. **Ad Rates:** $8 for 30 seconds; $9 for 60 seconds. **URL:** http://www.kyls.com.

FULTON†, pop. 11,046.

C. MO. Callaway Co. 26 mi. NE of Jefferson City. Westminster College. William Woods College. Missouri School for the Deaf. FultonState Hospital. Nuclear plant. Mineral springs. Manufactures shoes, textiles. Diversified farming. Corn, wheat, oats.

17172 The Fulton Sun
The Fulton Sun Garret
115 E. 5th St. Phone: (573)642-7272
PO Box 550 Fax: (573)642-0656
Fulton, MO 65251-0541
Free: (800)769-5505

General newspaper. **Founded:** 1876. **Freq:** Tues.-Sat. (morn.). **Print Method:** Offset. **Trim Size:** 13 3/4 x 22 1/2. **Cols./Page:** 6. **Col. Width:** 28 nonpareils. **Col. Depth:** 294 agate lines. **Key Personnel:** Mary Van Orden, General Mgr. **ISSN:** 8750-6696. **Subscription Rates:** $61.25. **Remarks:** Accepts advertising. **Formerly:** The Kingdom Daily Sun-Gazette.
Ad Rates: GLR: $.60 **Circ:** ‡5,200
BW: $819
4C: $836.10
SAU: $6.50
PCI: $6.50

17173 Green Owl
William Woods University
200 W. 12th St. Phone: (314)592-4268
Fulton, MO 65251 Fax: (314)592-1146

Collegiate publication. **Freq:** Monthly. **Print Method:** Offset. **Cols./Page:** 5. **Col. Width:** 28 nonpareils. **Col. Depth:** 178 agate lines. **Key Personnel:** Amber Cox, Editor; Mary Vin-

yard, AD Manager; Christi Slizewski, Business Mgr. **Subscription Rates:** $10. **Remarks:** Accepts advertising.
Ad Rates: BW: $160 **Circ:** Controlled 800
SAU: $2
PCI: $4.25

17174 Missouri Record
Missouri School for the Deaf
505 E. 5th St. Phone: (573)592-4000
Fulton, MO 65251-1799 Fax: (573)592-2570

Magazine of the Missouri School for the Deaf covering information for parents, alumni and the general public of its activities. **Founded:** 1879. **Freq:** Triennial. **Key Personnel:** Peter H. Ripley, Editor, pripley@msd.k12.mo.us; Pat O'Rourke, Assoc. Editor; Bobby Morris, Jr., Graphic Arts; Kevin Spencer, Photography. **Subscription Rates:** Free. **Remarks:** Advertising not accepted.
Circ: (Not Reported)

17175 KFAL-AM - 900
1805 Westminster Phone: (573)642-3341
Fulton, MO 65251-0581 Fax: (573)642-3343
Free: (800)769-5274
E-mail: kfal@sockets.net

Format: Bluegrass. **Networks:** ABC; Missouri. **Owner:** Meyer Communications, 3000 E. Chestnut Expwy., Springfield, MO 65802, (417)862-3990. **Founded:** 1950. **Operating Hours:** 5 a.m.-midnight. **Key Personnel:** Shirley B. Evans, Station Mgr., kfal@sockets.net; Justin Dean, News/Sports Dir.; Robert Wooldridge, Program Dir.; Peg Dzicek, Promotions Dir.; Sheri Payne, Traffic Dir. **Local Programs:** *The Breakfast Club* 7:10 am - 7:55 am Monday-Friday, Peg Dzicek, Producer; *Local Sports*; *Remember When* 7:03 am Saturday, Robert Wooldridge, PD. **Wattage:** 1000. **Ad Rates:** $10-18 for 30 seconds; $13-23.40 for 60 seconds. KKCA-FM. **URL:** http://www.kfal.com.

17176 KKCA-FM - 100.5
1805 Westminster Phone: (573)642-3341
Fulton, MO 65251-0581 Fax: (573)642-3343
Free: (800)769-5274
E-mail: kkca@sockets.net

Format: Oldies. **Networks:** Jones Satellite; ABC; Westwood One Radio. **Owner:** Meyer Communications, Inc., 3000 E. Chestnut Expwy., Springfield, MO 65802, (417)862-3990. **Founded:** 1970. **Operating Hours:** Continuous; 95% network, 5% local. **Key Personnel:** Shirley B. Evans, Station Mgr.; Justin Dean, News/Sports; Robert Wooldridge, Program Dir.; Peg Dzicek, Promotions Dir.; Sheri Payne, Traffic Dir. **Wattage:** 6000 ERP. **Ad Rates:** $10.00-18.00 for 30 seconds; $13.00-23.40 for 60 seconds. $10-$18 for 30 seconds; $13.00-$23.40 for 60 seconds. Combined advertising rates available with KFAL-AM. **URL:** http://www.kkca.com.

17177 KTI Cablevision
P.O. Box 848 Phone: (314)642-7266
Fulton, MO 65251 Fax: (314)642-7237

Key Personnel: Richard Hansen, Manager. **Cities Served:** Fulton, Auxvasse, and Kingdom, MO.

GAINESVILLE†, pop. 707.

S. MO. Ozark Co. 65 mi. SE of Springfield. Resort. Manufactures cedar products, charcoal, plastic pipe, textiles, lumber. Farming. Cattle.

17178 Ozark County Times
PO Box 188 Phone: (417)679-4641
Gainesville, MO 65655 Fax: (417)679-3423
Publisher E-mail: ozcntytimes@ozcool.com

Community newspaper. **Founded:** 1882. **Freq:** Weekly (Wed.). **Print Method:** Offset. **Cols./Page:** 6. **Col. Width:** 24 nonpareils. **Col. Depth:** 294 agate lines. **Key Personnel:** Gary D. Myers, General Mgr., garym@ozcool.com. **USPS:** 416-680. **Subscription Rates:** $24 individuals; $32 out of county; $30 out of state. **Remarks:** Accepts advertising. **Alt. Formats:** CD-ROM.
Ad Rates: BW: $491.40 **Circ:** Paid 3,918
4C: $666.40
SAU: $4.50
PCI: $4.50

GALLATIN†, pop. 2,063.

NW MO. Daviess Co. 54 mi. E. of Saint Joseph. Manufacturing. Corn, wheat, hay, soybeans.

17179 North Missourian
Gallatin Publishing Co.
203 N. Main Phone: (660)663-2154
PO Box 37 Fax: (660)663-2498
Gallatin, MO 64640
Publisher E-mail: gpc@ponyexpress.net

Newspaper with a Democratic orientation. **Founded:** 1864. **Freq:** Weekly (Wed.). **Print Method:** Offset. **Cols./Page:** 5. **Col. Width:** 11 picas. **Col. Depth:** 16 inches. **Key Personnel:** Darryl Wilkinson, Editor/Administration; Darryl Wilkinson, Publisher. **USPS:** 213-200. **Subscription Rates:** $20; $20 out of state.
Ad Rates: GLR: $.20 **Circ:** ‡2,575
BW: $378
SAU: $3

GLADSTONE

17180 Gladstone News
Sun News
12 N. Main Phone: (816)781-1044
Liberty, MO 64068 Fax: (816)781-1755

Shopper. **Founded:** 1961. **Freq:** Weekly (Wed.). **Print Method:** Offset. **Cols./Page:** 6. **Col. Width:** 19 nonpareils. **Col. Depth:** 224 agate lines. **Key Personnel:** Jack Miles, Editor; Vivian O'Dell, Publisher; Diane Davis, Advertising Mgr. **Subscription Rates:** Free to area households; $13.95 (mail). **Remarks:** Accepts advertising. **Formerly:** Clay West Shopper News.
Ad Rates: BW: $1,329.60 **Circ:** Free ‡60,210
PCI: $13.95

GLASGOW, pop. 1,336.

C. MO. Chariton and Howard Co. On Missouri River, 20 mi. SW of Moberly. Sawmills. Manufactures asphalt, textiles. Ships livestock, grain. Diversified farming.

17181 The Glasgow Missourian
PO Box 248 Phone: (660)338-2195
Glasgow, MO 65254 Fax: (660)338-2494

Community Newspaper. **Founded:** 1867. **Freq:** Weekly (Thurs.). **Print Method:** Offset. **Cols./Page:** 6. **Col. Depth:** 21 1/2 inches. **Key Personnel:** Sam Audsley, Publisher; Barbara Audsley, Editor. **USPS:** 219-240. **Subscription Rates:** $19 individuals; $21.50 out of area; $23 out of state. **Remarks:** Accepts advertising.
Ad Rates: BW: $403.20 **Circ:** ‡1,650
SAU: $4
PCI: $2.60

GRAIN VALLEY, pop. 1,327.

NW MO. Jackson Co. 5 mi. E. of Independence. Residential.

17182 Land Line
Owner-Operator Independent Drivers Association Inc.
311 R.D. Mize Rd. Phone: (816)229-5791
Grain Valley, MO 64029 Fax: (816)229-0518
Free: (800)444-5791
Publisher E-mail: ooida@aol.com

Business magazine for professional truckers. **Subtitle:** The Business Magazine of Owner-Operator/Independent Truckers. **Founded:** 1975. **Freq:** Bimonthly. **Print Method:** Offset. **Trim Size:** 7 7/8 x 10 7/8. **Cols./Page:** 3. **Col. Width:** 27 nonpareils. **Col. Depth:** 136 agate lines. **Key Personnel:** Todd Spencer, Editor and Publisher; Sandi Soendker, Managing Editor. **ISSN:** 0279-6503. **Subscription Rates:** $16 individuals. **Remarks:** Accepts advertising.
Ad Rates: GLR: $20 **Circ:** Controlled ‡140,000
BW: $7,200
4C: $8,800
PCI: $125

GRANBY, pop. 1,908.

SW MO. Newton Co. 11 mi. N. of Neosho. Residential.

17183 Newton County News
PO Box 50 Phone: (417)472-3100
Granby, MO 64844 Fax: (417)472-6533

Newspaper with a Democratic orientation. **Founded:** 1873. **Freq:** Weekly (Thurs.). **Print Method:** Offset. **Cols./Page:** 6. **Col. Width:** 12 picas. **Col. Depth:** 21.5 inches. **Key Personnel:** Newton E. Renfro, Editor and Publisher. **USPS:** 100-390. **Subscription Rates:** $16; $20 out of area. **Remarks:** Color advertising not accepted. **Alt. Formats:** CD-ROM.
Ad Rates: GLR: $.20 **Circ:** ‡1,500
BW: $330
SAU: $3
PCI: $3.30

GRANDVIEW

17184 Jackson County Advocate
502 Main St. Phone: (816)761-6200
PO Box 620
Grandview, MO 64030
Local newspaper. **Founded:** 1953. **Freq:** Weekly (Thurs.). **Print Method:** Offset. **Cols./Page:** 6. **Col. Width:** 2 inches. **Col. Depth:** 21 1/2 inches. **Key Personnel:** James D. Turnbaugh, Editor and Publisher. **Subscription Rates:** $14 individuals; $19.19 out of country. **Remarks:** Accepts advertising.
Ad Rates: GLR: $.43 **Circ:** 6,200
BW: $550
PCI: $6

GRANT CITY†, pop. 1,068.

NW MO. Worth Co. 72 mi. NE of Saint Joseph. Textile manufacturing. Diversified farming. Livestock.

17185 The Grant City Times-Tribune
T.T. Publications
Box 130 Phone: (816)564-3603
Grant City, MO 64456
Community newspaper. **Founded:** 1867. **Freq:** Weekly (Wed.). **Print Method:** Offset. **Cols./Page:** 6. **Col. Width:** 2 inches. **Col. Depth:** 21 1/4 inches. **Key Personnel:** Robert A. Hightshoe, Editor and Publisher. **USPS:** 631-180. **Subscription Rates:** $11; $13 out of area; $18 out of state. **Remarks:** Accepts advertising.
Ad Rates: PCI: $2 **Circ:** 1,650

GREENFIELD

17186 Greenfield Vedette
Liberty Group Pub.
PO Box 216 Phone: (417)637-2712
Greenfield, MO 65661 Fax: (417)637-2232

Community newspaper. **Freq:** Weekly (Thurs.). **Cols./Page:** 6. **Col. Width:** 2 inches. **Col. Depth:** 21 1/2 inches. **Key Personnel:** Marlene DeClure, General Mgr. **Subscription Rates:** $21.50 individuals; $27.51 out of area; $29.95 out of state. **Remarks:** Accepts advertising.
Ad Rates: GLR: $3.85 **Circ:** 2,500
PCI: $3.85

HAMILTON, pop. 1,582.

NW MO. Caldwell Co. 45 mi. E. of Saint Joseph. Shoe factory. Diversified farming. Corn, wheat, soybeans, dairying.

17187 Hamilton Advocate
L & L Publications, Inc.
105 N. Davis St. Phone: (816)583-2116
Box 187 Fax: (816)582-2118
Hamilton, MO 64644
Newspaper with a Democratic orientation. **Founded:** July 15, 1869. **Freq:** Weekly (Wed.). **Print Method:** Offset. **Trim Size:** 11 1/2 x 15 1/2. **Cols./Page:** 4. **Col. Width:** 2 5/16 inches. **Col. Depth:** 14 inches. **Key Personnel:** Anne Tezon, Editor and Publisher. **Subscription Rates:** $21 individuals; $23 out of area; $30 out of state. **Remarks:** Accepts advertising.
Ad Rates: GLR: $3.70 **Circ:** 1,973
BW: $236.80
4C: $296.8
SAU: $3.70
PCI: $3.20

HANNIBAL, pop. 18,811.

NE MO. Marion and Rolls Co. On Mississippi River, 20 mi. S. of Quincy, IL. Bridge to Hull, IL. Tourism. Mark Twain Museum. Manufactures shoes, cement, steel, lumber products. Dairy, grain farms. Wheat, oats, corn.

17188 Hannibal Courier-Post
PO Box A Phone: (573)221-2800
Hannibal, MO 63401 Fax: (573)221-1568

General newspaper. **Founded:** 1838. **Freq:** Mon.-Sat. (morn.). **Print Method:** Offset. **Trim Size:** 13 1/2 x 21 1/2. **Cols./Page:** 6. **Col. Width:** 24 nonpareils. **Col. Depth:** 301 agate lines. **Key Personnel:** Jack Whitaker, Editor and Publisher; Bob Hudson, Advertising Mgr.; Jim Whitaker, Associate News Editor; Mary Lou Montgomery, Associate News Editor; Jill Sinkclear, Circulation Mgr.; Ken Linnenburger, Operations Mgr. **Subscription Rates:** $8; $12.50 by mail. **Remarks:** Accepts advertising. **Alt. Formats:** Microform.
Ad Rates: BW: $1,096.50 **Circ:** Mon.-Sat. ★8,694
4C: $1,212.50
SAU: $8.50

17189 KHMO-AM - 1070
119 N. 3rd St. Phone: (573)221-3450
Hannibal, MO 63401 Fax: (573)221-5331
Free: (800)622-2044

Format: Talk; News. **Networks:** Newsradio. **Founded:** 1941. **Operating Hours:** Continuous. **ADI:** Chicago (LaSalle), IL. **Key Personnel:** Ed Foxall, General Mgr.; Dave Lee, Operations Mgr.; Jon Hanvelt, News Dir. **Local Programs:** *Morning Show*, Peggy Walley. **Wattage:** 5000.

17190 TCI Cablevision of Missouri
647 Clinic Rd. Phone: (314)221-0060
Hannibal, MO 63401-3607 Fax: (314)221-0128

Owner: Tele-Communications Inc., 5619 DTC Pkwy., Englewood, CO 80111, (303)267-5500, Fax: (303)779-1228. **Key Personnel:** Doug Summerford, General Mgr.; Rich Harden, Technical Operations Mgr.; Linda Geist, Office Mgr. **Cities Served:** Hannibal, MO: subscribing households 6,588; 41 channels.

HARRISONVILLE†, pop. 6,372.

W. MO. Cass Co. 40 mi. SE of Kansas City. Manufactures wire and fiber optic cable, concrete cabinets. Stock, dairy, poultry, grain farms.

17191 Cass County Democrat-Missourian
Democrat-Missourian
PO Box 329 Phone: (816)380-3228
Harrisonville, MO 64701 Fax: (816)380-7650

Newspaper with a Democratic orientation. **Founded:** 1881. **Freq:** Weekly (Fri.). **Print Method:** Offset. **Cols./Page:** 6. **Col. Width:** 25 nonpareils. **Col. Depth:** 294 agate lines. **Key Personnel:** William E. James, Publisher; Gavin Fenwick, Advertising Mgr.; Dennis Minich, Managing Editor. **USPS:** 092-720. **Subscription Rates:** $24.50.
Ad Rates: GLR: $.43 **Circ:** Paid 6,500
BW: $756
SAU: $6
PCI: $6

17192 Cass County Shopper
Cass County Publishing Co.
PO Box 329 Fax: (816)380-7650
Harrisonville, MO 64701
Shopping guide. **Founded:** 1947. **Freq:** Weekly. **Print Method:** Web offset. **Cols./Page:** 6. **Col. Width:** 11 1/2 inches. **Col. Depth:** 21 inches. **Key Personnel:** William E. James, Publisher; Gavin Fenwick, Advertising Dir.
Ad Rates: GLR: $.46 **Circ:** Free 19,032
BW: $819
SAU: $6
PCI: $6.50

HAZELWOOD, pop. 12,935.

E. MO. Saint Louis Co. 9 mi. N. of Clayton. Residential.

17193 The Automotive Messenger
PO Box 527 Phone: (314)831-4000
Hazelwood, MO 63042 Fax: (314)831-3610

Automotive magazine (tabloid). **Founded:** 1956. **Freq:** Monthly. **Print Method:** Offset. **Trim Size:** 14 1/4 x 11 1/4. **Cols./Page:** 5. **Col. Width:** 24 nonpareils. **Col. Depth:** 224 agate lines. **Key Personnel:** Bill Winders, Publisher. **ISSN:** 0045-1488. **Subscription Rates:** $10. **Remarks:** Accepts advertising.
Ad Rates: GLR: $12 **Circ:** ‡14,000
BW: $860
SAU: $12
PCI: $16

HERMANN†, pop. 2,695.

EC MO. Gasconade Co. On Missouri River, 40 mi. E. of Jefferson City. Manufactures shoes, toys, staves, beverages and water coolers, sheet metal products. Diaspore, flint and clay quarries; timber. Diversified farming. Poultry, grain.

17194 Advertiser-Courier
Graf Printing Co., Inc.
136 E. Fort St. Phone: (314)486-5418
PO Box 155 Fax: (314)486-5524
Hermann, MO 65041
Newspaper with a Republican orientation. **Founded:** 1873. **Freq:** Weekly (Wed.). **Print Method:** Offset. **Cols./Page:** 8. **Col. Width:** 21 nonpareils. **Col. Depth:** 294 agate lines. **Key Personnel:** Jim Anderson, Editor. **Subscription Rates:** $10. **Remarks:** Accepts advertising.
Ad Rates: GLR: $.16 **Circ:** (Not Reported)

HERMITAGE†, pop. 384.

SWC MO. Hickory. 55 mi. N. of Springfield. Stock, grain farms. Corn, wheat, hay. Resort.

17195 The Index
108 Polk St. Phone: (417)745-6404
PO Box 127 Fax: (417)745-2222
Hermitage, MO 65668
Free: (800)828-3107

Community newspaper. **Founded:** 1885. **Freq:** Weekly (Thurs.). **Print Method:** Offset. **Trim Size:** 13 3/4 x 22 3/4. **Cols./Page:** 6. **Col. Width:** 12 picas. **Col. Depth:** 301 agate lines. **Key Personnel:** Don Ginnings, Editor; Kathy Ginnings, Advertising Mgr. **USPS:** 261-500. **Subscription Rates:** $19.84 individuals. **Remarks:** Accepts advertising.
Ad Rates: GLR: $.22 **Circ:** 4,509

HIGGINSVILLE, pop. 4,595.

W. MO. Lafayette Co. 40 mi. E. of Kansas City. Residential. Coal. Manufactures brick, tile, and incubators.

17196 Higginsville Advance
Town Krier Publications
PO Box 422 Phone: (816)584-3611
Higginsville, MO 64037 Fax: (816)584-7966

Newspaper with a Republican orientation. **Founded:** 1904. **Freq:** Semiweekly (Wed. and Fri.). **Print Method:** Offset. **Cols./Page:** 6. **Col. Width:** 26 nonpareils. **Col. Depth:** 301 agate lines. **Key Personnel:** Mark Cheffey, Editor; Daryl DeVries, Publisher; Sheri Shafer, Advertising Mgr.; Heather Hoflander, Editor; Shawn Brant, Sports Editor; Beverly Mackie, Advertising/General Mgr.; Frank Mercer, Publisher. **Subscription Rates:** $25.73 individuals; $33.78 out of country; $40 out of state. **Remarks:** Accepts advertising.
Ad Rates: GLR: $5.25 **Circ:** ‡2,600

HOLDEN, pop. 2,195.

W. MO. Johnson Co. 40 mi. W. of Sedalia. Manufacturing. Lespedeza seed center. Dairy, poultry, stock, grain farms.

17197 The Holden Image-Progress
PO Box 8 Phone: (816)732-5552
117 E. 2nd Fax: (816)732-4696
Holden, MO 64040
Newspaper with an Independent orientation. **Founded:** 1904. **Freq:** Weekly (Thurs.). **Print Method:** Offset. **Cols./Page:** 6. **Col. Width:** 26 nonpareils. **Col. Depth:** 294 agate lines. **Key Personnel:** Rusty Hartwell, Editor and Publisher. **Subscription Rates:** $18 individuals local; $21 in state; $29 out of state. **Remarks:** Accepts advertising. **Formerly:** Holden Progress.
Ad Rates: GLR: $.90 **Circ:** Paid ‡2,150
BW: $535.50 Free ‡5,600
PCI: $4.25

HOLLISTER

17198 Branson Daily News
Branson TriLakes Daily News
200 Industrial Park Dr. Phone: (417)334-3161
Hollister, MO 65672 Fax: (417)334-4299

General newspaper. **Founded:** 1913. **Freq:** Tue. -Sat. **Print Method:** Offset. **Cols./Page:** 6. **Col. Width:** 21 nonpareils. **Col. Depth:** 294 agate lines. **Key Personnel:** Ted Delaney, Publisher, fax (417)443-4299. **Subscription Rates:** $78; $120 out of area. **Remarks:** Accepts classified advertising. **Formed by the merger of:** Taney County Republican; Beacon and Leader.
Ad Rates: GLR: $13 **Circ:** 12,500
4C: $225
SAU: $10.39
PCI: $10.39

17199 Cameo and Intaglio Lore
World Archaeological Society
120 Lakewood Dr. Phone: (417)334-2377
Hollister, MO 65672
Publisher E-mail: ronwas@juno.com

Scholarly publication covering art history. **Founded:** 1971. **Trim Size:** 8 1/2 x 10. **Key Personnel:** Ron Miller, Editor. **ISSN:** 0738-8063. **Subscription Rates:** $8 individuals. **Remarks:** Accepts advertising.
Ad Rates: BW: $60 **Circ:** (Not Reported)

17200 The Iraqi War Series
World Archaeological Society
120 Lakewood Dr. Phone: (417)334-2377
Hollister, MO 65672
Publisher E-mail: ronwas@juno.com

Scholarly journal covering archaeological and anthropological analysis of war. **Founded:** 1971. **Trim Size:** 8 1/2 x 10. **Key Personnel:** Ron Miller, Editor. **ISSN:** 0738-8063. **Subscription Rates:** $20 individuals. **Remarks:** Accepts advertising.
Ad Rates: BW: $60 **Circ:** (Not Reported)

HOPKINS

17201 The Hopkins Journal
411 Barnard St. Phone: (816)778-3205
PO Box 170 Fax: (816)778-3345
Hopkins, MO 64461
Community newspaper. **Subtitle:** The Hopkins Journal. **Founded:** 1876. **Freq:** Weekly (Thurs.). **Print Method:** Offset. **Cols./Page:** 6. **Col. Width:** 2 inches. **Col. Depth:** 21 inches. **Key Personnel:** Darla Thompson, Editor and Publisher. **Subscription Rates:** $14 individuals; $18 out of area. **Remarks:** Accepts advertising.
Ad Rates: GLR: $.45 **Circ:** ‡900
SAU: $2.55

HOUSTON†, pop. 2,200.

C. MO. Texas Co. 42 mi. N. of West Plains. Lumber.

17202 Houston Herald-Republican
Houston News
PO Box 170 Phone: (417)967-2000
Houston, MO 65483 Fax: (417)967-2096
Publisher E-mail: herald@train.missouri.org

County newspaper. **Founded:** 1877. **Freq:** Weekly (Thurs.). **Print Method:** Offset. **Cols./Page:** 6. **Col. Width:** 2 1/16 inches. **Col. Depth:** 21 inches. **Key Personnel:** Brad Gentry, Publisher; Linda Gibson, Advertising Mgr. **Subscription Rates:** $21.75 Texas & adjoining counties; $31.25 out of area; $32.75 out of state. **Remarks:** Accepts advertising. **URL:** http://www.train.missouri.org/~chamber.
Ad Rates: SAU: $3.75 **Circ:** ‡4,200
PCI: $3.45

17203 KBTC-AM - 1250
Hwy. B Phone: (417)967-3353
PO Box 230 Fax: (417)967-2281
Houston, MO 65483

Format: Country. **Networks:** Missouri. **Founded:** 1962. **Operating Hours:** 5 a.m.-midnight. **Key Personnel:** Robert Berri, President; Bret Steele, Gen Mgr./Sales Mgr.; LeaAnn Hall, Sales Mgr.; Beatrice Hall, Office & Traffic Dir.; Rick Jessie, Engineer; Bob Moore, Consulting Engineer. **Wattage:** 1000 day; 51 night. **Ad Rates:** $4 for 15 seconds; $6-8 for 30 seconds; $10 for 60 seconds.

17204 KUNQ-FM - 99.3
PO Box 230 Phone: (417)967-3353
Houston, MO 65483 Fax: (417)967-2281
Free: (888)578-5282
E-mail: kunq@train.missouri.org

Format: Country. **Networks:** ABC. **Owner:** Texas County Radio, Inc., at above address. **Founded:** 1960. **Formerly:** KSCM-FM (1987). **Operating Hours:** Continuous. **Key Personnel:** Bret Steele, General Mgr.; Beatrice Hall, Office Mgr.; Lea Ann Hall, Sales Mgr. **Local Programs:** *Tradeo* 8:30 am - 9:00 am Monday-Friday, Bret Steele. **Wattage:** 50,000. **Ad Rates:** Advertising accepted; rates available upon request.

INDEPENDENCE†, pop. 111,806.

W. MO. Jackson and Clay Co. Adjoins Kansas City. Manufactures farm machinery, stoves and furnaces, cement, plastics, aluminum awnings, beds, mattresses, box springs. Diversified farming. Potatoes, corn, wheat, soybeans, apples, peaches.

17205 Army Motors
Military Vehicle Preservation Association
Box 520378 Phone: (816)737-5111
Independence, MO 64052-0378 Fax: (816)737-5423
Publisher E-mail: mvpa-hq@mvpa.org

Trade journal covering acquisition, restoration and preservation of military vehicles. **Founded:** 1976. **Freq:** Quarterly. **Key Personnel:** Kay Willard-Hinja, Associate Mgr. **ISSN:** 0195-5632. **Subscription Rates:** $30 individuals. **Remarks:** Accepts advertising.
Ad Rates: BW: $185 **Circ:** Controlled 8,000

17206 The Asphalt Contractor
Group III Communications, Inc.
204 W. Kansas St., Ste. 103 Phone: (816)254-8735
Independence, MO 64050 Fax: (816)254-2128
Free: (800)254-2123

Trade journal for asphalt contractors. **Founded:** 1986. **Freq:** Monthly. **Print Method:** Sheetfed offset. **Trim Size:** 8 1/2 x 11. **Cols./Page:** 3. **Col. Width:** 2 1/8 inches. **Col. Depth:** 10

inches. **Key Personnel:** Sandy Lender, Editor, sandy@asphalt.com; Nina Furstenau, Publisher; Chris Harrison, Accountant Exec., phone (800)355-1860, fax (816)248-1843. **Subscription Rates:** $48 individuals; $60 Canada; $96 other countries. **Remarks:** Accepts advertising. **Available Online. URL:** http://www.asphalt.com.
Ad Rates: GLR: $67 **Circ:** 11,152
BW: $1,737
4C: $2,537
PCI: $67

17207 Avionics News
AEA (Aircraft Electronics Association)
PO Box 1963 Phone: (816)373-6565
Independence, MO 64055 Fax: (816)478-3100
Publication E-mail: mgibson@microlink.net; avnews@microlink.net
Publisher E-mail: aea@mircrolink.net

General aviation and electronics magazine. **Founded:** 1957. **Freq:** Monthly. **Print Method:** Offset. **Cols./Page:** 3. **Col. Width:** 28 nonpareils. **Col. Depth:** 140 agate lines. **Key Personnel:** Paula R. Derks, Editor and Publisher. **ISSN:** 0567-2889. **Subscription Rates:** Free. **Remarks:** Accepts advertising.
Ad Rates: BW: $1,200 **Circ:** Non-paid 6,500
4C: $2,000

17208 Blue Springs & Independence Examiner Suburban Life (Daily Edition)
The Examiner
410 S. Liberty St. Phone: (816)254-8600
Independence, MO 64050-3805 Fax: (816)836-3805

Newspaper. **Founded:** 1898. **Freq:** Mon.-Sat. **Print Method:** Web offset. **Key Personnel:** Jim Meeks, Circulation Mgr.; Ben F. Weir, Jr., Publisher; Irene Baltrusaitis, Adv. Dir.; Jeff Fox, Editor, jfox@examiner.net; Scot Morrissey, Quality Control Mgr.; Becky Ely, Business Mgr. **Subscription Rates:** $96 individuals. **Remarks:** Advertising accepted; rates available upon request. **URL:** http://examiner.net.
Circ: Wed. 67,000
Paid 15,500

17209 Blue Springs & Independence Examiner Suburban Life (Wednesday Edition)
The Examiner
410 S. Liberty St. Phone: (816)254-8600
Independence, MO 64050-3805 Fax: (816)836-3805

Community newspaper. **Freq:** Weekly (Wed.). **Key Personnel:** John Draffan, Circulation Mgr. **Subscription Rates:** Free; $83.40.
Circ: Combined 67,135

17210 The Examiner
Morris Communications
410 S. Liberty St. Phone: (816)254-8600
PO Box 459 Fax: (816)836-3805
Independence, MO 64051
General newspaper. **Founded:** 1898. **Freq:** Daily (eve.) and Sat. (morn.). **Print Method:** Offset. **Cols./Page:** 6. **Col. Width:** 25 nonpareils. **Col. Depth:** 301 agate lines. **Key Personnel:** Jeff Fox, Editor; Ben F. Weir, Jr., Publisher, benweir@examiner.net; Irene Baltrusaitis, Advertising Dir. **Subscription Rates:** $60. **Remarks:** Accepts advertising. **URL:** examiner.net. **Alt. Formats:** Microfilm.
Ad Rates: BW: $2,167.20 **Circ:** 10,767
4C: $2,347.20 Wed. 43,113
SAU: $16.80
PCI: $16.80

17211 Independence Examiner (Daily Edition)
The Examiner
410 S. Liberty St. Phone: (816)254-8600
Independence, MO 64050-3805 Fax: (816)836-3805

Newspaper. **Freq:** Mon.-Sat. **Key Personnel:** John Draffan, Circulation Mgr. **Subscription Rates:** $83.40.
Circ: Free 146
Paid 10,621

17212 Independence Examiner (Wednesday Edition)
The Examiner
410 S. Liberty St. Phone: (816)254-8600
Independence, MO 64050-3805 Fax: (816)836-3805

Community newspaper. **Freq:** Weekly. **Key Personnel:** John Draffan, Circulation Mgr. **Subscription Rates:** Free; $83.40.
Circ: Combined 43,634

17213 Lift Equipment
Group III Communications, Inc.
204 W. Kansas St., Ste. 103 Phone: (816)254-8735
Independence, MO 64050 Fax: (816)254-2128
Free: (800)254-2123

Trade magazine covering life equipment and product maintenance, safety, and regulatory information. **Founded:** 1988. **Freq:** 9/year. **Print Method:** Web offset. **Trim Size:** 8 3/8 x 10 7/8. **Key Personnel:** Tracy Bennett, Editor, tbennett@liftlink.com; Bev O'Dell, Account Exec., phone (800)547-5367, fax (816)578-5367, bjodell99@aol.com. **ISSN:** 1056-0149. **Subscription Rates:** $24 individuals; Free to qualified subscribers. **Remarks:** Accepts advertising. **URL:** http://www.liftlink.oom. **Former name:** Engineering and Construction.
Ad Rates: BW: $1,924 **Circ:** Combined 18,500
4C: $2,876

17214 Saints Herald
Herald Publishing House
3225 S. Noland Phone: (816)252-5010
PO Box 1770 Fax: (816)252-3976
Independence, MO 64055-0770
Free: (800)767-8181
Publication E-mail: hhedit@heraldhouse.org
Publisher E-mail: hhadmin@heraldhouse.org

Religious family-oriented magazine for the Reorganized Church of Jesus Christ of Latter Day Saints. **Founded:** Jan. 1860. **Freq:** Monthly. **Print Method:** Offset. **Trim Size:** 8 1/2 x 11. **Cols./Page:** 3. **Col. Width:** 13.5 picas. **Col. Depth:** 56 picas. **Key Personnel:** James Cable, Editorial Dir.; James N. Hough, General Mgr.; Nancy Vreeland, Advertising Mgr., hhmark@heraldhouse.org. **ISSN:** 0036-3251. **Subscription Rates:** $24.50 individuals. **Remarks:** Advertising not accepted. **URL:** http://www.heraldhouse.org.
Circ: ‡25,000

17215 Jones Intercable
4700 Selsa Rd. Phone: (816)795-8377
Box 2000 Fax: (816)795-0946
Independence, MO 64055
Free: (800)892-8719

Founded: 1973. **Formerly:** Landmark Cable; Jackson County Cable. **Key Personnel:** Rusty Robertson, General Mgr., rrobertson@jic.com; Tom Krewson, Public Affairs; Jan Moczydlowski, Marketing Mgr. **Cities Served:** Baldwin Park, Blue Springs, Blue Summit, Grain Valley, Greenwood, Lake Lotawana, Lake Tapawingo, Lake Winnebago, Peculiar, Pleasant Hill, Raytown, MO; Olathe, KS and Independence, MO: subscribing households 86,000; 37 channels.

17216 KCTE-AM - 1510
10841 E. 28th St. Phone: (816)254-1073
Independence, MO 64052 Fax: (816)254-6929
E-mail: kcte@kcmo.net

Format: Sports. **Networks:** ESPN Radio. **Founded:** 1993. **Formerly:** KJLA-AM (1992). **Operating Hours:** Sunrise-sunset. **ADI:** Kansas City, MO (Lawrence, KS). **Key Personnel:** Christian Vedder, General Mgr./Program Dir. **Local Programs:** *Pete Enich Sports*, Soren Petro. **Wattage:** 10,000. **Ad Rates:** Advertising accepted; rates available upon request.

IRONTON†, pop. 1,743.

SE MO. Iron Co. 95 mi. SW of Saint Louis. Resort. Manufactures shoes. Oak and pine timber; lead and iron mines. Diversified farming.

17217 Mountain Echo/X-Tra
110 N. Main St. Phone: (573)546-3917
PO Box 25 Fax: (573)546-3919
Ironton, MO 63650-0025
Second class newspaper and shopper. **Subtitle:** The Mountain Echo & Mountain Echo X-Tra. **Founded:** 1937. **Freq:** Weekly (Wed.). **Print Method:** Offset. **Cols./Page:** 6. **Col. Width:** 26 nonpareils. **Col. Depth:** 294 agate lines. **Key Personnel:** Judith Schaaf, Publisher; Mark Cheaney, Editor. **Subscription Rates:** $21 individuals; $33 out of area. **Remarks:** Accepts advertising. **Alt. Formats:** Microform.
Ad Rates: GLR: $4.35 **Circ:** Paid 2,900
BW: $625.65 Free 3,900
4C: $300
PCI: $4.85

JACKSON†, pop. 7,827.

SE MO. Cape Girardeau Co. 10 mi. NW of Cape Girardeau. Manufactures shoes, bricks, lumber, flour, pottery, plastic parts. Hardwood timber. Diversified farming. Corn, wheat, hay. Livestock.

17218 The Cash-Book Journal
210 W. Main St. Phone: (314)243-3515
PO Box 369 Fax: (314)243-3517
Jackson, MO 63755-0369
Free: (888)788-1022
Publisher E-mail: cashbook@mup.net

Legal newspaper. **Founded:** Apr. 1870. **Freq:** Weekly (Wed.). **Print Method:** Offset. **Trim Size:** 7 x 11. **Cols./Page:** 6. **Col. Width:** 12 picas. **Col. Depth:** 301 agate lines. **Key Personnel:** David Bloom, Editor; Gerald Jones, Publisher; Gina Bader, Advertising Mgr. **USPS:** 272-080. **Subscription Rates:** $17 individuals; $19 in surrounding area; $23 in state; $32 out of state. **Remarks:** Accepts advertising.
Ad Rates: GLR: $.46 **Circ:** 8,000
BW: $720
4C: $960
SAU: $7.50

JAMESPORT, pop. 651.

NW MO. Daviess Co. 60 mi. NE of Saint Joseph. Manufactures burial vaults. Seed processing plant. Diversified farming.

17219 Tri-County Weekly
K.K. Printing Co.
PO Box 137 Phone: (816)684-6515
Jamesport, MO 64648 Fax: (816)684-6515

Report community newspaper. **Founded:** 1944. **Freq:** Weekly (Thurs.). **Print Method:** Offset. **Cols./Page:** 6. **Col. Width:** 27 nonpareils. **Col. Depth:** 294 agate lines. **Key Personnel:** Natha McAllister, Editor and Publisher, phone (816)684-6718. **Subscription Rates:** $16 individuals. **Remarks:** Accepts advertising.
Ad Rates: BW: $264.60 **Circ:** ‡1,550

JEFFERSON CITY†, pop. 33,619.

C. MO. Callaway and Cole Co. The State Capital. On the Missouri River, 30 mi. SE of Columbia. Lincoln University. Shoe, plate glass, and scholastic magazine distribution centers. Manufactures cosmetics, small electrical appliances, underground transformers; steel fabricating; printing and book binding. Poultry, fruit farms. Wheat, corn.

17220 The Catholic Missourian
Diocese of Jefferson City
609 Clark Ave. Phone: (573)635-9127
PO Box 1107 Fax: (573)635-2286
Jefferson City, MO 65102
Official newspaper of the Diocese of Jefferson City. **Founded:** 1957. **Freq:** Weekly (Every other week in summer). **Print Method:** Offset. **Trim Size:** 9 7/8 x 12 3/4. **Cols./Page:** 5. **Col. Width:** 1 7/8 inches. **Col. Depth:** 182 agate lines. **Key Personnel:** Rev. Hugh Behan, Editor; Most Rev. John R. Gaydos, Publisher; Diana Eichholz, Advertising Mgr. **USPS:** 556-940. **Subscription Rates:** $12 individuals. **Remarks:** Accepts advertising.
Ad Rates: GLR: $.65 **Circ:** Paid ‡20,578
PCI: $9.10

17221 Focus MDA
Missouri Dental Association
230 W. McCarty St. Phone: (573)634-3436
PO Box 1707 Fax: (573)635-0764
Jefferson City, MO 65102-1553
Publication E-mail: modental@socket.net

Dental journal. **Founded:** 1921. **Freq:** every 6 weeks. **Print Method:** Offset. **Trim Size:** 10 x 15. **Key Personnel:** Dr. Elizabeth Ward, Editor; Cristin Clark, Associate Editor. **ISSN:** 0887-4646. **Subscription Rates:** $15. **Remarks:** Advertising accepted; rates available upon request. **Formerly:** Missouri Dental Journal.
Circ: ‡2,200

17222 Journal of the Missouri Bar
The Missouri Bar
326 Monroe St. Phone: (314)635-4128
PO Box 119 Fax: (314)635-2811
Jefferson City, MO 65101-3106
Magazine featuring short, practical articles on legal subjects for practicing attorneys. **Founded:** Jan. 1945. **Freq:** Bimonthly. **Print Method:** Offset. **Trim Size:** 6 x 9. **Cols./Page:** 2. **Col. Width:** 28 nonpareils. **Col. Depth:** 112 agate lines. **Key Personnel:** Gary P. Toohey, Editor. **ISSN:** 0026-6485. **Subscription Rates:** $12. $3 single issue. **Remarks:** Accepts advertising.
Ad Rates: BW: $620 **Circ:** ‡20,800

17223 Missouri Conservationist
Department of Conservation
Box 180 Phone: (573)751-4115
Jefferson City, MO 65102 Fax: (573)751-2260

Government magazine covering fish, forests, and wildlife. **Founded:** 1937. **Freq:** Monthly. **Key Personnel:** Tom Cwyngr, Editor, cwynat@mail.conservation.state.mo.us. **ISSN:** 0026-6515. **Subscription Rates:** Free to qualified subscribers; $7 out of state; $10 out of country. **Remarks:** Advertising not accepted.
Circ: Combined 417,000

17224 The Missouri Engineer
Missouri Society of Professional Engineers
330 E. High St., 2nd Fl. Phone: (314)636-4861
Jefferson City, MO 65101
Magazine for the engineering profession. **Founded:** 1937. **Freq:** 10/year. **Print Method:** Offset. **Trim Size:** 10 x 13. **Cols./Page:** 4. **Col. Width:** 2 3/8 inches. **Col. Depth:** 13 inches. **Key Personnel:** Cherie L. Bishop, Editor; Paul E. Jobe, Publisher. **ISSN:** 0026-6558. **Subscription Rates:** $12 nonmembers. **Remarks:** Accepts advertising.
Ad Rates: BW: $750 **Circ:** Paid 2,600
PCI: $21 Non-paid 900

17225 Missouri Library World
Missouri State Library
600 W. Main Phone: (314)751-3615
PO Box 387 Fax: (314)751-3612
Jefferson City, MO 65102
Publisher E-mail: libref@mail.more.net

Trade magazine covering libraries and library activities. **Founded:** 1996. **Freq:** Quarterly. **Print Method:** Offset. **Trim Size:** 8 1/2 X 11. **Key Personnel:** Madeline Matson, Editor, phone (573)751-2680, fax (573)751-2680, mmatson@mail.sos.state.mo.us. **ISSN:** 1088-6796. **Subscription Rates:** $10 individuals; $15 Canada; $20 other countries. **Remarks:** Advertising not accepted.
Circ: Controlled 2,500

17226 Missouri Medicine
Missouri State Medical Association
113 Madison St. Phone: (573)636-5151
PO Box 1028 Fax: (573)636-8552
Jefferson City, MO 65101-3015
Journal reporting on the interests of medical and public health professionals in Missouri. **Subtitle:** State Medical Journal. **Founded:** 1904. **Freq:** Monthly. **Print Method:** Offset. **Trim Size:** 8 1/4 x 11. **Cols./Page:** 3. **Col. Width:** 2 inches. **Col. Depth:** 98 agate lines. **Key Personnel:** J. Regan Thomas, M.D., Editor; C. C. Cork Swarens, Publisher, cswarens@msma.org; Michelle Poire, Managing Editor, mpoire@msma.org. **ISSN:** 0026-6620. **Subscription Rates:** $60. **Remarks:** Accepts advertising.
Ad Rates: BW: $400 **Circ:** ‡6,600
4C: $1,395

17227 Missouri Municipal Review
Missouri Municipal League
1727 Southridge Dr. Phone: (314)635-9134
Jefferson City, MO 65109 Fax: (314)635-9009
Publisher E-mail: info@mocities.com

Magazine for local officials actively engaged in the procurement of products and services, policy-making, and local government administration. **Founded:** 1935. **Freq:** Monthly (Feb/March and Oct/Nov issues combined). **Print Method:** Offset. **Trim Size:** 8 1/2 x 11. **Cols./Page:** 3. **Col. Width:** 2 3/8 inches. **Col. Depth:** 10 inches. **Key Personnel:** Dolores Schulte, Editor. **ISSN:** 0026-6647. **Subscription Rates:** $22. **Remarks:** Accepts advertising.
Ad Rates: BW: $390 **Circ:** ‡5,900
4C: $1,050

17228 The Missouri Nurse
Missouri Nurses Association
1904 Bubba Ln. Phone: (573)636-4623
Jefferson City, MO 65110 Fax: (573)636-9576

Professional magazine covering nursing and activities of the Missouri Nurses Association. **Founded:** 1932. **Freq:** Bimonthly. **Key Personnel:** Martha Borgmeyer, Advertising Mgr. **Subscription Rates:** Free to qualified subscribers; $25 nonmembers. **Remarks:** Accepts advertising.
Ad Rates: BW: $350 **Circ:** (Not Reported)

17229 Missouri Pharmacist
Missouri Pharmacy Association
211 E. Capital Ave. Phone: (573)636-7522
Jefferson City, MO 65101 Fax: (573)636-7485

Magazine serving licensced pharmacists (MPA members). **Founded:** 1926. **Freq:** Quarterly. **Print Method:** Offset. **Trim Size:** 8 1/2 x 11. **Cols./Page:** 3. **Col. Width:** 26 nonpareils. **Col. Depth:** 140 agate lines. **Key Personnel:** Deedie K. Bedosky, Editor, deedie@marx.com. **Subscription Rates:** $30 individuals.
Ad Rates: BW: $405 **Circ:** Paid 1,300
4C: $1,055

17230 Missouri Wildlife
Conservation Federation of Missouri
728 W. Main Phone: (573)634-2322
Jefferson City, MO 65101 Fax: (573)634-8205
Free: (800)575-2322
Publication E-mail: cdfed@sockets.net
Publisher E-mail: mofed@sockets.net

Publication covering Missouri conservation and wildlife news. **Founded:** 1939. **Freq:** Bimonthly. **Print Method:** Web offset. **Key Personnel:** Charles Davidson, Editor. **ISSN:** 1082-8591. **Subscription Rates:** Free to qualified subscribers. **Remarks:** Accepts advertising.
Ad Rates: BW: $475 **Circ:** Paid ⊕29,429
PCI: $9.50

17231 MLPGA News
MLPGA, Inc.
4100 Country Club Dr. Phone: (314)893-7655
Jefferson City, MO 65109-0302 Fax: (314)893-2623

Magazine for the LP gas industry. **Founded:** 1951. **Freq:** Bimonthly. **Print Method:** Offset. **Trim Size:** 8 1/2 x 10. **Cols./Page:** 3. **Col. Width:** 2 1/4 inches. **Col. Depth:** 10 inches. **Key Personnel:** Cindy Hale, Editor/Administration. **Remarks:** Accepts advertising.
Ad Rates: GLR: $2.50 **Circ:** Paid ‡345
BW: $290 Non-paid ‡337

17232 Rural Missouri
Association of Missouri Electric Cooperatives, Inc.
2722 E. McCarty St. Phone: (573)635-6857
PO Box 1645 Fax: (573)635-2314
Jefferson City, MO 65102
Publication E-mail: ruralmo@socket.net

Magazine serving electric cooperative consumers. **Founded:** 1948. **Freq:** Monthly. **Print Method:** Offset. **Trim Size:** 11 3/8 x 16. **Cols./Page:** 4. **Col. Width:** 2 1/4 inches. **Col. Depth:** 13 1/2 inches. **Key Personnel:** Jim McCarty, Editor; Jeff Joiner, Managing Editor; Mary Davis, Advertising Mgr.; Frank Stork, Publisher; Bob McEdwen, Field Editor; Heather Berry, Asst. Editor. **ISSN:** 0164-8578. **Subscription Rates:** $5.51 individuals; $13.06 three years. **Remarks:** Accepts advertising. **Formerly:** Rural Electric Missourian.
Ad Rates: BW: $5,641 **Circ:** ‡388,000
4C: $6,691
PCI: $102

17233 Show Me Missouri Farm Bureau News
Missouri Farm Bureau Federation
701 S. Country Club Dr. Phone: (573)893-1400
Jefferson City, MO 65102 Fax: (573)893-1470
Publication E-mail: fbinfo@computerland.net
Publisher E-mail: mo@momail.com

Agricultural magazine for members of the Missouri Farm Bureau. **Founded:** 1921. **Freq:** Bimonthly 6/year. **Print Method:** Letterpress. **Trim Size:** 8 3/8 X 10 3/4. **Cols./Page:** 3. **Col. Width:** 2 1/4 inches. **Col. Depth:** 10 inches. **Key Personnel:** Chris Fennewald, Editor, phone (573)893-1469. **Subscription Rates:** $30 Included in membership. **Remarks:** Accepts advertising. **Formerly:** Missouri Farm Bureau News.
Ad Rates: BW: $1,397 **Circ:** Controlled ‡91,000
4C: $1,907
PCI: $54

17234 Something Better
Missouri NEA
1810 E. Elm Phone: (573)634-3202
Jefferson City, MO 65101-4174 Fax: (573)634-5645
Free: (800)392-0236

Education magazine. **Founded:** 1973. **Freq:** 6/year. **Print Method:** Offset. Uses mats. **Trim Size:** 8 x 10 1/2. **Cols./Page:** 5. **Col. Width:** 8 picas. **Col. Depth:** 56.5 picas. **Key Personnel:** Debra Angstead, Editor, dangstead@nea.org. **ISSN:** 1076-223X. **Subscription Rates:** $5.25 members; $8 nonmembers. **Remarks:** Accepts advertising.
Ad Rates: BW: $650 **Circ:** Paid ‡27,000
4C: $1,050 Non-paid ‡1,000

17235 Word and Way
Missouri Baptist Convention
400 E. High St. Phone: (573)635-7931
Jefferson City, MO 65101 Fax: (573)659-7436
Free: (800)736-6227
Publication E-mail: 70420.20@compuserve.com

Religious tabloid. **Founded:** 1896. **Freq:** Weekly (Thurs.). **Print Method:** Offset. **Trim Size:** 11 1/2 x 15. **Cols./Page:** 5. **Col. Width:** 11.5 picas. **Col. Depth:** 14 inches. **Key Personnel:** Bill Webb, Editor, bwebb@wordandway.org; Tim Palmer, Managing Editor, tpalmer@wordandway.org. **ISSN:** 0049-7959. **Subscription Rates:** $11.50 individuals. **Remarks:** Accepts advertising Church related only.
Ad Rates: PCI: $31.90 **Circ:** ‡43,000

17236 KJLU-FM - 88.9
820 Chestnut St. Phone: (573)681-5301
Jefferson City, MO 65102-0029 Fax: (573)681-5299

Format: Jazz; Urban Contemporary. **Owner:** Lincoln University of Missouri, PO Box 29, Jefferson City, MO 65102. **Founded:** Aug. 20, 1973. **Formerly:** KLUM-FM (1991). **Operating Hours:** 6:00 a.m.-12:00 a.m. **ADI:** Columbia-Jefferson City, MO. **Key Personnel:** Mike Downey, General Mgr., downeym@lincolnu.edu; David Owens, Program and Music Dir., phone (573)681-5303, owensd@lincolnu.edu; Leslie Taylor, News Dir., phone (573)681-5295; Dan Yeager, Chief Engineer, phone (573)681-5445. **Local Programs:** *The Jazz Exchange*, T. Sharif Abdul-Hakim; *Through the Years*, Mike Downey. **Wattage:** 29,500. **Ad Rates:** $8-10 per unit. **URL:** http://www.lincolnu.edu/kjlu.

17237 KJMO-FM - 100.1
3109 S. 10 Mile Dr. Phone: (314)893-5100
Jefferson City, MO 65109 Fax: (314)893-4137
E-mail: kjmo@socketis.net

Format: Adult Contemporary. **Networks:** NBC; Westwood One Radio. **Founded:** 1974. **Operating Hours:** Continuous. **ADI:** Columbia-Jefferson City, MO. **Key Personnel:** Donald Lynch, General Mgr., donl@mvp.net; Stu Steinmetz, Sales Mgr.; John Greenwood, Program Dir.; Steve Morse, Engineer. **Wattage:** 33,000. **Ad Rates:** Advertising accepted; rates available upon request.

17238 KLIK-AM - 950
PO Box 414 Phone: (314)893-5696
Jefferson City, MO 65102 Fax: (314)893-8330

Format: Contemporary Country. **Networks:** ABC. **Founded:** 1954. **Operating Hours:** Continuous. **ADI:** Columbia-Jefferson City, MO. **Key Personnel:** Neil Kearney, Contact; Geoff Davis, Program Dir. **Wattage:** 5000 day; 500 night.

17239 KRCG-TV - 13
PO Box 659 Phone: (573)896-5144
Jefferson City, MO 65102 Fax: (573)896-5193
E-mail: krcg@socket.net

Format: Commercial TV. **Networks:** CBS; United Paramount Network. **Owner:** Mel Wheeler, Inc., 5009 S. Hulen, Fort Worth, TX 76132-1989, (817)294-7644. **Founded:** 1955. **Operating Hours:** 5 a.m.-1:30 a.m.; 70% network; 30% local. **ADI:** Columbia-Jefferson City, MO. **Key Personnel:** Betsy Farris, Vice Pres./Gen. Mgr.; Lee Gordon, Operations Mgr.; David Griffith, Director; Jim Malone, Chief Engineer; Sara Stratman, Local Sales Mgr. **Local Programs:** *Eye on Mid Missouri* 6:30-7 p.m. Saturday. **Wattage:** 316,000. **Ad Rates:** Advertising accepted; rates available upon request. **URL:** http://www.krcg.com.

JOPLIN, pop. 38,893.

SW MO. Jasper and Newton Co. 75 mi. W. of Springfield. Missouri Southern State College; Ozark Bible College. Manufactures leather goods, engraving and typesetting equipment, store fixtures, furniture, insulation, explosives, hydraulic pumps, missiles, chemicals, alcohol, fertilizer, dog food, bearings.

17240 Circuit News Digest
Circuit News, Inc.
PO Drawer 48 Phone: (417)673-2860
Joplin, MO 64802-0048 Fax: (417)673-4743
Publisher E-mail: news@circuitnews.com

Magazine covering the engineering, design, and production of electronics. **Founded:** Dec. 1, 1984. **Freq:** Monthly. **Print Method:** Sheetfed offset. **Trim Size:** 8 1/2 x 11. **Cols./Page:** 4. **Col. Width:** 1 3/4 inches. **Col. Depth:** 10 1/4 inches. **Key Personnel:** Robert J. Blanset, Editor. **ISSN:** 1058-9317. **Subscription Rates:** $50 individuals; $5 single issue. **Remarks:** Color advertising accepted; rates available upon request. **Available Online. Formerly:** Circuit News/Circuit Assembly News.
Ad Rates: GLR: $35 **Circ:** Paid ‡8,337
BW: $900 Free ‡12,000
PCI: $35

17241 The Joplin Globe
The Joplin Globe Publishing Co.
117 E. 4th St. Phone: (417)623-3480
Box 7 Fax: (417)623-8450
Joplin, MO 64801
General newspaper. **Founded:** 1896. **Freq:** Mon.-Sun. (morn.). **Print Method:** Offset. **Cols./Page:** 6. **Col. Width:** 25 nonpareils. **Col. Depth:** 311 agate lines. **Key Personnel:** James R. Ellis, Editor; Daniel P. Chiodo, Publisher. **Subscription Rates:** $141.83 individuals; $163.29 by mail. **Remarks:** Accepts advertising. **URL:** http://wwwjoplinglobe.com.
Ad Rates: GLR: $2.62 **Circ:** Mon.-Sat. ★**35,216**
BW: $8,804.08 Sun. ★**43,824**
4C: $570
PCI: $36

17242 The Pentecostal Messenger
Pentecostal Church of God
4901 Pennsylvania Phone: (417)624-7050
PO Box 850 Fax: (417)624-7102
Joplin, MO 64802-0850
Free: (800)317-9342
Publisher E-mail: pcg@clandjop.com

Religious magazine. **Founded:** 1920. **Freq:** 11/year. **Print**

Method: Offset. **Trim Size:** 8 1/2 x 11. **Cols./Page:** 3. **Col. Width:** 14.5 picas. **Col. Depth:** 57.5 picas. **Key Personnel:** Aaron Wilson, Editor. **ISSN:** 0031-4919. **Subscription Rates:** $11. $1.50 single issue. **Remarks:** Accepts advertising.
Ad Rates: BW: $453 **Circ:** ‡6,000
4C: $521
PCI: $20

17243 CableOne
PO Box 2525 Phone: (417)624-6340
Joplin, MO 64803-2525 Fax: (417)623-5413

Owner: CableOne, 1314 N. 3rd St., 3rd Fl., Phoenix, AZ 85004, (602)364-6000, Fax: (602)364-6010. **Founded:** 1965. **Formerly:** Cablecom of Joplin/Webb City (1997). **Key Personnel:** Charlotte McClure, General Mgr.; George Peery, System Enginner; Tish Waddell, Marketing Mgr. **Cities Served:** Carterville, Joplin, Redings Mill, Saginaw, Shoal Creek, Webb City, MO: subscribing households 17,000; 56 channels; 1 community access channel.

17244 KJKT-FM - 102.5
1309 S. Monroe ave. Phone: (417)624-1025
Joplin, MO 64801-3629 Fax: (417)781-6842
E-mail: kat1025@cis.compuserve.com

Format: Country. **Owner:** Big Mack Broadcasting, at above address. **Founded:** 1974. **Formerly:** WMBH-FM (Feb. 1, 1994). **Operating Hours:** Continuous. **ADI:** Joplin, MO-Pittsburg, KS. **Key Personnel:** Chuck Dunaway, Station Mgr. **Wattage:** 100,000. **Ad Rates:** $30-40 for 30 seconds; $30-40 for 60 seconds.

17245 KKLL-AM - 1100
PO Box 85 Phone: (417)626-7111
Joplin, MO 64802 Fax: (417)781-1100
E-mail: kkll@clandjop.com

Format: Contemporary Christian. **Networks:** USA Radio. **Founded:** 1984. **Operating Hours:** Sunrise-sunset. **Key Personnel:** Don Stubblefield, Gen. Mgr./Owner; Art Rogers, Program Dir.; Jim Young, Sales Mgr.; Jim Taylor, News Dir.; Jack Nickolas, Engineer, phone (816)765-3717. **Local Programs:** *Radio Rally*, Ralph Beasley, (417)781-5762. **Wattage:** 5000. **Ad Rates:** $5.75-6.75 for 30 seconds; $8.25-9.25 for 60 seconds.

17246 KMOQ-FM - 107.1
2510 E. 20th St. Phone: (417)623-2107
Joplin, MO 64804-0216 Free: (800)725-2107

Format: Oldies. **Networks:** Satellite Music Network. **Founded:** 1980. **Formerly:** KBLT-FM. **Operating Hours:** Continuous. **ADI:** Joplin, MO-Pittsburg, KS. **Key Personnel:** Bobby Landis, General Mgr., phone (417)781-1313, fax (417)781-1316; Patrick Golay, President, phone (417)781-1313, fax (417)781-1316, pgolay@lanogo.com. **Wattage:** 6000. **Ad Rates:** $15 for 30 seconds; $18 for 60 seconds. Combined advertising rates available with WMBM-AM, KQYX-AM.

17247 KOBC-FM - 90.7
1111 N. Main St. Phone: (417)781-6401
Joplin, MO 64801 Fax: (417)782-1841

Format: Contemporary Christian; Adult Contemporary. **Founded:** 1974. **Operating Hours:** 18 hrs; 8% network, 92% local. **ADI:** Joplin, MO-Pittsburg, KS. **Key Personnel:** Rob Kime, General Mgr.; T.C. Andrews, Marketing Dir.; Lisa Davis, Operations Mgr. **Wattage:** 60,000. **Ad Rates:** Noncommercial.

17248 KOCR-1310 AM - 1310
1111 N Main St. Phone: (417)781-6401
Joplin, MO 64801 Fax: (417)782-1841

Format: Religious. **Networks:** UPI; SkyLight Satellite. **Owner:** Ozark Christian College, at above address, (417)624-2518. **Founded:** 1996. **Formerly:** KFSB-AM (1984). **Operating Hours:** 18 hours daily; 100% local. **ADI:** Joplin, MO-Pittsburg, KS. **Key Personnel:** Robert Kime, Owner/General Mgr. **Wattage:** 5000. **Ad Rates:** $8.50 for 30 seconds; $12.75 for 60 seconds.

17249 KODE-TV - 12
1928 W. 13th St. Phone: (417)623-7260
Joplin, MO 64801 Fax: (417)623-3736

Format: Commercial TV. **Networks:** ABC. **Operating Hours:** Continuous. **ADI:** Joplin, MO-Pittsburg, KS. **Key Personnel:** Larry Young, News Dir.; Jerry Montgomery, General Mgr.; John Hoffmann, Contact; Sarah Ivey, Promotions Dir.; Bob Shryock, Contact; Bruce Watkins, Contact.

17250 KOZJ-TV - 26
MSSC Webster Bldg., No. 138 Phone: (417)782-1226
3950 Newman Rd.
PO Box 1226
Joplin, MO 64801

Format: Public TV. **Networks:** Public Broadcasting Service (PBS). **Founded:** 1981. **Operating Hours:** 6:15 a.m.-midnight Mon.-Fri.; 8 a.m.-midnight Sat and Sun. **ADI:** Joplin, MO-Pittsburg, KS. **Key Personnel:** Miff Dikeman, Station Mgr.; Ray Meyer, Program Dir.

17251 KQYX-AM - 1560
PO Box 2625 Phone: (417)781-1313
Joplin, MO 64802 Fax: (417)782-2134

Format: News; Talk. **Networks:** ABC; CNN Radio; Business Radio; USA Radio. **Owner:** William B. Neal Enterprises, at above address. **Founded:** 1962. **Operating Hours:** 6 a.m.-two hours past sunset. **ADI:** Joplin, MO-Pittsburg, KS. **Key Personnel:** William B. Neal, General Mgr. **Wattage:** 10,000.

17252 KSNF-TV - 16
1502 Cleveland Phone: (417)781-2345
Joplin, MO 64801 Fax: (417)782-2417

Format: Commercial TV. **Networks:** NBC. **Operating Hours:** Continuous. **ADI:** Joplin, MO-Pittsburg, KS. **Key Personnel:** Paul Wise, Contact. **Ad Rates:** $20-1200 per unit. **URL:** http://www.ksnftv.com.

17253 KSYN-FM - 92.5
1309 S. Monroe Ave. Phone: (417)623-1450
Joplin, MO 64801-3629 Fax: (417)781-6842
E-mail: kissin@cis.compuserve.com

Format: Contemporary Hit Radio (CHR). **Operating Hours:** Continuous. **ADI:** Joplin, MO-Pittsburg, KS. **Key Personnel:** Chuck Dunaway, VP/General Manager. **Wattage:** 100,000. **Ad Rates:** $30-40 for 30 seconds; $30-40 for 60 seconds.

KAHOKA, pop. 2,101.

NE MO. Clark Co. 50 mi. N. of Hannibal.

17254 Media
178 West Main Phone: (660)727-3395
Kahoka, MO 63445 Fax: (660)727-2475

Local newspaper. **Freq:** Weekly (Wed.). **Print Method:** Offset. **Cols./Page:** 6. **Col. Width:** 2 inches. **Col. Depth:** 21 inches. **Key Personnel:** Hazel Bledsoe Smith, Editor and Publisher; Vicki Gutting, Advertising Mgr. **USPS:** 289-380. **Subscription Rates:** $18; $25.50 out of area. **Remarks:** Accepts advertising. **Formerly:** Gazette Herald, Clark Gazette, Clark County Courier.
Ad Rates: GLR: $.42 **Circ:** Paid ‡2,700
BW: $555.66
4C: $855
PCI: $4.24

17255 Kahoka Communications Cable
250 N. Morgan Phone: (816)727-3711
Kahoka, MO 63445 Fax: (816)727-3750

Key Personnel: Sandie Hopp, Cable Dir.; Scott Goben, Technician. **Cities Served:** Kahoka, MO: subscribing households 767; 37 channels.

KANSAS CITY, pop. 448,159.

W. MO. Clay, Jackson, and Platte Co. On Missouri River, at mouth of Kansas (Kaw) River, 45 mi. S. of Saint Joseph. University of Missouri at Kansas City; 19 other colleges, universities, and theological schools. Largest city in Missouri. A strong diverse economic foundation.First in the nation in farm equipment distribution and hard winter wheat marketing. The Worlds's Food Capital. Leading national market in automobile and truck production, greeting card publishing. Frozen food storage and distribution center. Center of the midcontinent oil fields. Manufactures agriculture chemicals, airplane accessories, ammunition, paints, wire goods, textiles, trucks, electricalbrick, beverages, malt syrup, furniture, caskets, mattresses, motor cars, stationery, drugs. Local culture centers.

17256 American Family Physician
American Academy of Family Physicians
8880 Ward Pkwy. Phone: (816)333-9700
Kansas City, MO 64114 Fax: (816)333-0303
Free: (800)274-2237
Publication E-mail: afpedit@aafp.org
Publisher E-mail: fp@aafp.org

Clinical journal for family physicians and others in primary care. Original scientific articles detail the latest diagnostic and therapeutic techniques in the medical field. Department features in each issue include "Tips from other Joirnals," CME credit opportunities and course calendar. **Founded:** 1970. **Freq:** Semimonthly (monthly in June, July, August, and December). **Print Method:** Web offset. **Trim Size:** 7 3/4 x 10 1/2. **Cols./Page:** 2. **Col. Width:** 2 1/8 inches. **Col. Depth:** 10 inches. **Key Personnel:** Joetta Melton, Publisher; Dan Gowan, Sales Dir.; Kathy Mayfield, Production Mgr.; Mary Totten, Circulation Dir. **ISSN:** 0002-838X. **Subscription Rates:** $83 individuals; $9 single issue. **Remarks:** Accepts advertising. **URL:** http://www.aafp.org/afp.
Ad Rates: BW: $6,545 **Circ:** Controlled 159,340
4C: $8,570

17257 Baking Buyer
Sosland Publishing Co.
4800 Main St., Ste. 100 Phone: (816)756-1000
Kansas City, MO 64112-2513 Fax: (816)756-0494
Publication E-mail: bakingbuyer@sosland.com; jdoe@sosland.com

Magazine for retail, in-store, foodservice, specialty, and wholesale bakers. **Founded:** 1988. **Freq:** Monthly. **Print Method:** Web offset. **Trim Size:** 11 x 15. **Key Personnel:** Kerrie Conan, Editor, kconan@susland.com; John Sonderegger, Publisher, jsonderegger@susland.com. **ISSN:** 1056-6007. **Subscription Rates:** Free. **Remarks:** Accepts advertising.
Ad Rates: BW: $5,730 **Circ:** Non-paid 30,000
4C: $7,710

17258 Baking & Snack
Sosland Publishing Co.
4800 Main St., Ste. 100 Phone: (816)756-1000
Kansas City, MO 64112-2513 Fax: (816)756-0494
Publication E-mail: bakesnack@sosland.com

Equipment, engineering, production and formulating magazine for commercial manufacturers of baked and snack foods. **Founded:** 1979. **Freq:** Monthly (except March). **Print Method:** Offset. **Trim Size:** 8 x 10 3/4. **Cols./Page:** 3. **Col. Width:** 2 1/8 inches. **Col. Depth:** 10 inches. **Key Personnel:** Christine McWard, Editor; Paul Latlan, Publisher. **ISSN:** 1040-9254. **Subscription Rates:** Free to qualified subscribers. **Remarks:** Accepts advertising. **URL:** http://www.sosland.com.
Ad Rates: BW: $3,135 **Circ:** Controlled ‡11,379
4C: $4,615

17259 Bank News
Bank News, Inc.
912 Baltimore Ave., Ste. 900 Phone: (816)421-7941
Kansas City, MO 64105 Fax: (816)472-0397
Free: (800)336-1120

Magazine for the banking industry. **Subtitle:** The Banking Magazine for the Central States. **Founded:** 1901. **Freq:** Monthly. **Print Method:** Offset. **Trim Size:** 8 3/8 x 10 7/8. **Cols./Page:** 3. **Col. Width:** 26 nonpareils. **Col. Depth:** 140 agate lines. **Key Personnel:** R.W. Poquette, Editor; Sharon Smith, Managing Editor; W.F. Baker, Publisher. **ISSN:** 0005-5123. **Subscription Rates:** $62 individuals. **Remarks:** Accepts advertising. **Alt. Formats:** Microfilm.
Ad Rates: BW: $1,220 **Circ:** Paid 1,931
4C: $1,815 Non-paid 5,170

17260 Blade-Empire
Sosland Publishing Co.
4800 Main St., Ste. 100 Phone: (816)756-1000
Kansas City, MO 64112-2513 Fax: (816)756-0494

General newspaper. **Founded:** 1902. **Freq:** Daily (eve.). **Print Method:** Offset. **Cols./Page:** 6. **Col. Width:** 25 nonpareils. **Col. Depth:** 294 agate lines. **Key Personnel:** Brad Lowell, Editor; Art Lowell, Publisher. **Subscription Rates:** $51 individuals; $63 out of area. **Remarks:** Accepts advertising.
Ad Rates: BW: $365.40 **Circ:** ‡3,500
SAU: $2.90

17261 BTA Solutions
Business Technology Association
12411 Wornall Rd. Phone: (816)941-3100
Kansas City, MO 64145 Fax: (816)941-8034
Free: (800)366-6950
Publisher E-mail: btapubs@aol.com

Magazine reporting industry news and trends for dealers of copiers, word processors, computers, software, cash registers, facsimile equipment, and other business equipment and machines, including mailing equipment. **Founded:** 1949. **Freq:** Monthly. **Print Method:** Offset. **Trim Size:** 8 1/2 x 11. **Cols./Page:** 3. **Col. Width:** 14 picas. **Col. Depth:** 9 1/2 inches. **Key Personnel:** Brent Hoskins, Editor, brent@bto.net.com; Tim McCormack, Advertising Mgr., phone (913)469-1110, fax (913)469-0806, tmccormack@atwood.com. **ISSN:** 1092-9169. **Subscription Rates:** Included in membership; $30 nonmembers; $55 Canada and Mexico; $75 elsewhere. **Remarks:** Accepts advertising. **Formerly:** Spokesman; Solutions.
Ad Rates: BW: $1,425 **Circ:** ‡8,000
4C: $2,500

17262 Call
Kansas City Call Inc.
PO Box 410-477 Phone: (816)842-3804
Kansas City, MO 64141 Fax: (816)842-4420

Black community newspaper. **Founded:** 1919. **Freq:** Weekly (Fri.). **Print Method:** Offset. **Cols./Page:** 8. **Col. Width:** 18 nonpareils. **Col. Depth:** 294 agate lines. **Key Personnel:** Lucille Bluford, Editor and Publisher. **Subscription Rates:** $17.50. **Remarks:** Accepts advertising.
Ad Rates: GLR: $.50 **Circ:** Fri. 17,156

17263 Celebration
National Catholic Reporter Publishing Co., Inc.
115 E Armour Blvd. Phone: (816)531-0538
Kansas City, MO 64111-1203 Fax: (816)968-2280
Free: (800)444-8910
Publisher E-mail: ncr_ editor@natcath.com

Magazine providing resources that assist Christian churches in planning and preparing Sunday and seasonal worship. **Subtitle:** An Ecumenical Worship Resource. **Founded:** Jan. 1972. **Freq:** Monthly. **Print Method:** Offset. **Trim Size:** 8 1/2 x 11. **Cols./Page:** 3. **Col. Width:** 27 nonpareils. **Col. Depth:** 137 agate lines. **Key Personnel:** William J. Frebuger, Editor; William L. McSweeney, Publisher; Anna Fantasma, Advertising Mgr. **ISSN:** 0094-2421. **Subscription Rates:** $64.95. **Remarks:** Accepts advertising. **URL:** http://www.natcath.com/
.
Ad Rates: BW: $470 **Circ:** ‡11,000
PCI: $24

17264 Charolais Journal
Charolais Publications Inc.
11700 NW Plaza Circle Phone: (816)464-5977
PO Box 20247 Fax: (816)464-5759
Kansas City, MO 64195
Publication E-mail: chjourn@sound.net

International magazine on Charolais cattle, including special interest articles, show/sale reports, and association news. **Founded:** 1977. **Freq:** Monthly. **Print Method:** Offset. **Trim Size:** 8 1/2 x 11. **Cols./Page:** 3. **Col. Width:** 14 picas. **Col. Depth:** 10 inches. **Key Personnel:** Julie Olson, Editor, julieo@charolaisusa.com; David Hobbs, Manager. **ISSN:** 0191-5444. **Subscription Rates:** $30. **Remarks:** Accepts advertising.
Ad Rates: GLR: $120 **Circ:** ‡6,000
BW: $585
4C: $985
PCI: $25

17265 Clay & Platte Dispatch-Tribune
Townsend Communications, Inc.
7007 NE Parvin Rd. Phone: (816)454-9660
Kansas City, MO 64117 Fax: (816)452-5889
Publisher E-mail: towns@swbell.net

Community newspaper. **Founded:** 1925. **Freq:** Weekly (Wed.). **Print Method:** Offset. **Trim Size:** 13 x 21. **Cols./Page:** 6. **Col. Width:** 2 1/8 picas. **Col. Depth:** 21 inches. **Key Personnel:** Don Ledford, Editor; Harold G. Townsend, Jr., Publisher; Gary Warmker, National Adv. Mgr. **Subscription Rates:** Free to area households; $15 out of area; $18 out of state. **Remarks:** Accepts advertising. **Formed by the merger of**: Clay Dispatch-Tribune; Platte Dispatch-Tribune; Press Dispatch.
Ad Rates: SAU: $19.10 **Circ:** Paid 10,205
Free 39,659

17266 College Outlook
Townsend Outlook Publishing Co.
20 E. Gregory Phone: (816)361-0616
Kansas City, MO 64114-1118 Fax: (816)361-6164
Free: (800)274-8867
Publisher E-mail: topstaff@gvi.net

High school student recruitment magazine. **Founded:** 1977. **Freq:** 2/year. **Print Method:** Web offset. **Trim Size:** 7 7/8 x 10 3/4. **Key Personnel:** Marty Denzer, Editor; Clayton Allan, VP, Sales/Mktg. **Subscription Rates:** Free. **Remarks:** Advertising accepted; rates available upon request. **URL:** http://www.product.com/top. **Formerly**: College Outlook and Career Opportunities.
Circ: Non-paid 1,395,153

17267 Consensus
Consensus, Inc.
1737 McGee, Ste. 401 Phone: (816)471-3862
Kansas City, MO 64108 Fax: (816)221-2045
Free: (800)383-1441
Publisher E-mail: editor@consensus-inc.com

Trade magazine covering investing information. **Subtitle:** National Futures and Financial Weekly. **Founded:** 1971. **Freq:** Weekly. **Trim Size:** 11 X 17. **Key Personnel:** Robert E. Salva, Editor and Publisher, rsalva@aol.com. **Subscription Rates:** $365 individuals. **Remarks:** Advertising not accepted. **URL:** http://www.consensus-inc.com.
Circ: (Not Reported)

17268 The Daily Record
Record Newspaper Co.
3611 Troost Ave. Phone: (816)931-2002
Kansas City, MO 64109-2668 Fax: (816)561-6675
Publication E-mail: dailyrec@sound.net

Newspaper featuring commercial, court, and real estate news. **Subtitle:** The Kansas City Daily News-Press. **Founded:** 1888. **Freq:** Daily (morn.). **Print Method:** Letterpress. Uses mats. **Cols./Page:** 8. **Col. Width:** 24 nonpareils. **Col. Depth:** 294 agate lines. **USPS:** 145-320. **Subscription Rates:** $81 individuals. **Remarks:** Accepts advertising.
Ad Rates: GLR: $1.04 **Circ:** ‡603
SAU: $8.40

17269 Discover Mid-America
Discovery Publications, Inc.
400 Grand Ave., Ste. B. Phone: (816)474-1516
Kansas City, MO 64106 Fax: (816)474-1427
Free: (800)899-9730
Publication E-mail: discopub@aol.com
Publisher E-mail: busmgr@discoverypub.com

Trade magazine covering antiques, arts, crafts, and events. **Founded:** 1973. **Freq:** Monthly. **Print Method:** Web offset. **Key Personnel:** Kenneth C. Weyland, Editor; Al Hendrick, Advertising Mgr.; Steven Sterner, Business Mgr.; Diane Trinkle, Calendar Editor. **Subscription Rates:** $25 individuals; $2.50 single issue. **Remarks:** Accepts advertising. **URL:** http://www.discoverypub.com.
Ad Rates: BW: $909 **Circ:** Non-paid 30,000
4C: $1,200

17270 Dos Mundos Bilingual Newspaper
Dos Mondos Bilingual Newspaper
902-A Southwest Blvd. Phone: (816)221-4747
Kansas City, MO 64108 Fax: (816)221-4894

Community Bilingual Newspaper (Spanish & English). **Subtitle:** Dos Mundos Two Worlds. **Founded:** 1981. **Freq:** Biweekly. **Cols./Page:** 8. **Col. Width:** 1 1/2 inches. **Col. Depth:** 1 inches. **Key Personnel:** Clara Reyes, Editor; Manuel Reyes, Publisher. **Subscription Rates:** $12. **Remarks:** Accepts advertising. **Online:** Community Papers Verication Service. **Formerly**: Dos Mundos Newspaper.
Ad Rates: 4C: $150 **Circ:** 20,000
SAU: $9

17271 Economic Review
Federal Reserve Bank of Kansas City
925 Grand Blvd. Phone: (816)881-2683
Kansas City, MO 64198-0001 Fax: (816)881-2569

Business, finance, and economics journal. **Founded:** 1916. **Freq:** Quarterly. **Print Method:** Offset. **Trim Size:** 7 1/2 x 9 1/2. **Cols./Page:** 2. **Col. Width:** 33 nonpareils. **Col. Depth:** 100 agate lines. **Key Personnel:** Craig S. Hakkio, Dir. of Research, phone (816)881-2456, fax (816)881-2281; Lowell C. Jones, Publications Supervisor, phone (816)881-2797, fax (816)881-2569, ljones@frbkc.org. **ISSN:** 0161-2387. **Remarks:** Advertising not accepted. **URL:** http://www.kc.frb.org.
Circ: Free ‡29,000

17272 Explore Kansas City
Discovery Publications, Inc.
400 Grand Ave., Ste. B. Phone: (816)474-1516
Kansas City, MO 64106 Fax: (816)474-1427
Free: (800)899-9730
Publication E-mail: discopub@aol.com
Publisher E-mail: busmgr@discoverypub.com

Consumer magazine covering tourist and local information. **Founded:** 1993. **Freq:** Monthly. **Print Method:** Web offset. **Key Personnel:** Kenneth Wayand, Editor; Steven Sterner, Assignment Editor; Al Hedrick, Advertising Mgr. **Subscription Rates:** $2.50 single issue. **Remarks:** Accepts advertising. **URL:** http://www.discoverypub.com/.
Ad Rates: BW: $699 **Circ:** Non-paid 20,000
4C: $699

17273 Family Practice Management
American Academy of Family Physicians
8880 Ward Pkwy. Phone: (816)333-9700
Kansas City, MO 64114 Fax: (816)333-0303
Free: (800)274-2237
Publication E-mail: fpmedit@aafp.org
Publisher E-mail: fp@aafp.org

Magazine covering socio-economic and management topics concerning family physicians. **Founded:** Oct. 1, 1993. **Freq:** 10/year. **Cols./Page:** 3. **Col. Width:** 2 1/8 inches. **Col. Depth:** 10 inches. **Key Personnel:** Clayton Raker Hasser, Publisher; Robert Edsall, Editor-in-Chief, bedsall@aafp.org. **ISSN:** 1069-5648. **Subscription Rates:** $45 individuals; $65 other countries; $5 single issue; $7 single issue, other countries. **Remarks:** Accepts advertising. **URL:** http://www.aafp.org/family/fpm/index.html.
Ad Rates: BW: $4380 **Circ:** 90,095
4C: $6200

17274 Family Records, TODAY
American Family Records Association
PO Box 15505 Phone: (816)252-0950
Kansas City, MO 64106
Publisher E-mail: amfamrecord@aol.com

Journal. **Subtitle:** The Journal of American Family Records. **Founded:** 1980. **Freq:** Quarterly. **Print Method:** Offset. **Trim Size:** 8 1/2 x 11. **Cols./Page:** 2. **Col. Width:** 86 nonpareils. **Col. Depth:** 134 agate lines. **Key Personnel:** Nita Neblock, Editor. **ISSN:** 0736-1858. **Subscription Rates:** $22. **Remarks:** Accepts advertising.
Ad Rates: BW: $40 **Circ:** Paid ‡350

17275 Farmland System News
Farmland Industries, Inc.
PO Box 7305, 3315 N. Oak Trafficway Phone: (816)459-6000
Fax: (816)459-6979
Kansas City, MO 64116
Free: (800)821-8000
Publication E-mail: fsneditor@farmland.com

Magazine focusing on cooperative agriculture. **Founded:** 1933. **Freq:** Monthly. **Print Method:** Offset. **Trim Size:** 11 x 15. **Cols./Page:** 4. **Col. Width:** 2.4 nonpareils. **Col. Depth:** 210 agate lines. **Key Personnel:** David Eaheart, Editor; Carolyn Riddle, Advertising & Circulation, phone (816)459-6896, fax (816)459-6323, crriddle@farmland.com. **ISSN:** 0093-5832. **Subscription Rates:** $7. **Remarks:** Accepts advertising. **URL:** http://www.farmland.com. **Formerly**: Farmland News.
Ad Rates: BW: $5,040 **Circ:** ‡180,000
4C: $5,740
PCI: $90

17276 Flower & Garden
KC Publishing Inc.
4645 Belleview Phone: (816)531-5730
Kansas City, MO 64112 Fax: (816)531-3873
Free: (800)878-7855
Publisher E-mail: kcpublishing@earthlink.net

Magazine covering home gardening and landscaping. **Subtitle:** The World's Home Gardening Magazine. **Founded:** 1957. **Freq:** Bimonthly. **Print Method:** Web offset. **Trim Size:** 7 7/8 x 10 1/2. **Cols./Page:** 3. **Col. Width:** 2 1/4 inches. **Col. Depth:** 10 inches. **Key Personnel:** Angela Hughes, Editor; John C. Prebich, Publisher; Connie Moss, V.P. Production & Adv. Support. **ISSN:** 0891-9534. **Subscription Rates:** $3.95 single issue; $19.95. **Remarks:** Accepts advertising.
Ad Rates: BW: $9,600 **Circ:** Paid 300,000
4C: $12,000

17277 Forum
Kansas City Artists Coalition
201 Wyandotte Phone: (816)421-5222
Kansas City, MO 64105 Fax: (816)421-0656

Art journal. **Subtitle:** Visual Arts/Mid America. **Founded:** 1975. **Freq:** Bimonthly. **Print Method:** Web press. **Trim Size:** 11 x 13. **Cols./Page:** 5. **Col. Width:** 2 inches. **Col. Depth:** 11 inches. **Remarks:** Advertising accepted; rates available upon request.
Circ: Paid 600
Non-paid 10,000

17278 Greater Kansas City Medical Bulletin
Metropolitan Medical Society of Greater Kansas City
3036 Gillham Rd. Phone: (816)531-8432
Kansas City, MO 64108 Fax: (816)531-8438

Magazine presenting editorials, medical and economic news, and meeting notices for the medical profession. **Founded:** 1907. **Freq:** Monthly. **Print Method:** Offset. **Trim Size:** 8 1/4 x 11. **Cols./Page:** 3. **Col. Width:** 26 nonpareils. **Col. Depth:** 130 agate lines. **Key Personnel:** Charles W. Van Way, M.D., Editor; Jill Stehl Watson, Dir. of Public Affairs, jillwatson@sprintmail.com. **ISSN:** 0894-508X. **Subscription Rates:** $7. **Remarks:** Color advertising accepted; rates available upon request. **Formerly**: Metropolitan Medical Society of Greater Kansas City.
Circ: ‡2,880

17279 Hereford World
Hereford Publications, Inc.
PO Box 014059 Phone: (816)842-8878
1501 Wyandotte Fax: (816)842-6931
Kansas City, MO 64101
Publication E-mail: hworld@hereford.com

Magazine on Hereford cattle. **Founded:** 1910. **Freq:** Monthly. **Print Method:** Offset. **Trim Size:** 8 1/8 x 10 3/4. **Cols./Page:** 3. **Col. Width:** 26 nonpareils. **Col. Depth:** 140 agate lines. **Key Personnel:** Ed Bible, Editor. **ISSN:** 0002-872X. **Sub-**

scription Rates: $20. **Remarks:** Accepts advertising. **Formerly**: American Hereford Journal; Polled Hereford World.
Ad Rates: BW: $775 **Circ:** ‡10,000
4C: $1,075
PCI: $30

17280 Ingram's
Show Me Publishing, Inc.
306 E. 12th St., Ste. 1014 Phone: (816)842-9994
Kansas City, MO 64106 Fax: (816)474-1111
Publication E-mail: ingram's@ingram'smag.com

Kansas City business and lifestyle magazine. **Subtitle:** Kansas City's Leading Business Magazine. **Founded:** 1974. **Freq:** Monthly. **Print Method:** Offset. **Trim Size:** 8 1/2 x 10 7/8. **Cols./Page:** 3. **Col. Width:** 2 1/8 inches. **Col. Depth:** 10 inches. **Key Personnel:** Patrick Lowry, Editor; Joseph K. Sweeney, Publisher; Robert Brown, Sales; Michelle Harrington Sweeney, V.P. of Sales. **ISSN:** 0273-9968. **Subscription Rates:** $36. **Online:** Pro Quest. **Formerly**: Corporate Report; Corporate Report Kansas City.
Ad Rates: BW: $2,595 **Circ:** Controlled 20,439
4C: $3,095 Paid 3,301

17281 Irish Family Journal
Irish Genealogical Foundation
PO Box 7575 Phone: (816)454-2410
Kansas City, MO 64116 Fax: (816)454-2410

Journal of Irish family history and research. **Subtitle:** A worldwide member publication. **Founded:** 1979. **Freq:** Monthly. **Print Method:** Offset. **Trim Size:** 8 1/2 x 11. **Key Personnel:** Michael C. O'Laughlin, Editor, mike@irishroots.com. **ISSN:** 1056-0378. **Subscription Rates:** $104; $54 6 issues/yr. **Remarks:** Advertising not accepted. **URL:** http://www.irishroots.com. **Formerly**: O'Lochlainn's Journal of Irish Families.
Circ: Paid 2,000

17282 Journal of Low Vision and Neuro-Optometric Rehabilitation
Trozzolo Resources, Inc.
Media Periodicals Division Phone: (816)842-8111
1102 Grand 23rd Fl. Fax: (816)842-8188
Kansas City, MO 64106
Publisher E-mail: trozzolo@aol.com

Journal for low vision theoreticians and practitioners. **Founded:** 1987. **Freq:** Quarterly. **Trim Size:** 8 1/2 x 11. **Key Personnel:** Randy Jose, Publisher. **ISSN:** 1041-0384. **Subscription Rates:** $95; $105 Canada; $125 other countries air mail; $110 other countries surface; $170 two years; $189 two years; $225 two years air mail; $198 two years surface. **Formerly**: Journal of Vision Rehabilitation.
Ad Rates: BW: $250 **Circ:** Paid 500

17283 Journal of Religious & Theological Information
The Haworth Press, Inc.
Nazarene Theological Seminary Lib Phone: (816)333-6254
1700 East Meyer Blvd
Kansas City, MO 64131
Publisher E-mail: getinfo@haworthpressinc.com

Journal theological bibliography, information studies, and librarianship. **Founded:** 1993. **Freq:** Biennial. **Trim Size:** 6 x 8 1/2. **Key Personnel:** William C. Miller, Editor. **ISSN:** 1047-7845. **Subscription Rates:** $24 individuals; $48 institutions; $48 libraries. **Remarks:** Accepts advertising.
Ad Rates: BW: $300 **Circ:** Paid 301

17284 Journal of Rural Health
National Rural Health Association
1 W. Armour Blvd., Ste. 203 Phone: (816)756-3140
Kansas City, MO 64111 Fax: (816)756-3144

Professional journal covering rural health issues for health scientists and professionals in practice, educational research, and policy settings. **Freq:** Quarterly. **Subscription Rates:** $45 individuals; $110 institutions; $15 single issue. **Remarks:** Accepts advertising.
Circ: (Not Reported)

17285 Kansas City Genealogist
Heart of America Genealogical Society
Kansas City Public Library, 3rd Fl., Gen. Rm. Phone: (816)701-3445
311 E. 12th St.
Kansas City, MO 64106
Genealogical society journal prints unpublished records for genealogists and family historians. **Founded:** 1960. **Freq:** Quarterly. **Print Method:** Offset. **Trim Size:** 8 1/2 x 11. **Cols./Page:** 2. **Key Personnel:** Joanne Chiles Eakin, Editor, phone (816)461-5845. **ISSN:** 0451-3991. **Subscription Rates:** $15. $3 single issue. **Remarks:** Accepts advertising.
Ad Rates: BW: $25 **Circ:** Paid ‡400
Non-paid ‡150

17286 Kansas City Globe
Jordan Communications Co., Inc.
615 E. 29th St. Phone: (816)531-5253
PO Box 090410 Fax: (816)531-5256
Kansas City, MO 64109
Black community newspaper. **Founded:** 1972. **Freq:** Weekly (Fri.). **Key Personnel:** Marion Jordan, Editor and Publisher.
Circ: 30,000

17287 Kansas City Hispanic News
599 Avenida Cesar E. Chavez Phone: (816)472-KCHN
Kansas City, MO 64108 Fax: (816)472-NEWS

English and Spanish newspaper serving the five-county greater Kansas City area. **Founded:** Sept. 12, 1996. **Freq:** Biweekly. **Print Method:** Web offset. **Trim Size:** 13 1/2 x 22 1/2. **Cols./Page:** 5. **Col. Width:** 2.3 inches. **Col. Depth:** 21 inches. **Key Personnel:** Joe M. Arce, Publisher; Kathleen Cruden, Managing Editor; Tovah Redwood, Managing Editor. **Subscription Rates:** Free; $15 by mail. **Remarks:** Accepts advertising.
Ad Rates: BW: $1,200 **Circ:** Paid 200
4C: $1,500 Free 1,800
PCI: $15

17288 The Kansas City Star
Kansas City Star Co.
1729 Grand Blvd. Phone: (816)234-4280
Kansas City, MO 64108 Fax: (816)234-4267
Free: (800)726-2340

General newspaper. **Founded:** 1880. **Freq:** Mon.-Sun. (morn.). **Print Method:** Offset. **Cols./Page:** 6. **Col. Width:** 26 nonpareils. **Col. Depth:** 311 agate lines. **Key Personnel:** Art Brisbane, Editor; Bob Woodworth, Publisher; Mark Johnston, Advertising Mgr. **Subscription Rates:** $126. **Remarks:** Advertising accepted; rates available upon request. **Online:** LEXIS-NEXIS. **URL:** http://www.kansascity.com. **Absorbed**: The Kansas City Times. **Feature Editors:** Robert Butler, *Drama, Entertainment, Movie*, phone (816)234-4392; Dale Bye, *Sports*, phone (816)234-4355; Scott Cantrell, *Music*, phone (816)234-4380; Barry Garron, *TV & Radio*, phone (816)234-4394; Rich Hood, *Political*, phone (816)234-4300; Lynn Horsley, *Education*, phone (816)234-4300; Tim Janicke, *Photo*, phone (816)234-4342; Clayton Keller, *Family, Garden/Home, Lifestyle, Women's*, phone (816)234-4396; Chris Lester, *Real Estate*, phone (816)234-4370; Mary Lou Nolan, *Travel*, phone (816)234-4397; John Martellaro, *Food*, phone (816)234-4395; Brian McTavish, *Music*, phone (816)234-4380; Jeanne Meyer, *Features, Sunday*, phone (816)234-4461; Laura Rollins Hockaday, *Society*, phone (816)234-4391; James Scott, *Editorials*, phone (816)234-4478; Randall Smith, *City*, phone (816)234-4884; Diane Stafford, *News*, phone (816)234-4300; Doug Weaver, *Financial/Business*, phone (816)234-4370; Jackie White, *Fashion*, phone (816)234-4462.
Circ: Mon.-Fri. ★**281,596**
Sat. ★**312,823**
Sun. ★**400,962**

Liberty Tribune - See Liberty

17289 Live Sound! International
Royle Publishing Co., Inc.
4741 Central, No. 222 Phone: (913)677-8688
Kansas City, MO 64112 Fax: (913)677-6621

Performance audio magazine for any live sound application. **Founded:** Jan. 1991. **Freq:** 8/Times. **Trim Size:** 8 3/8 x 10 7/8. **Cols./Page:** 3. **Col. Width:** 2 1/4 inches. **Col. Depth:** 9 1/2 inches. **Key Personnel:** John Weishar, Publisher; Anthony McLean, Editor, 75300.3141@compuserve.com; Patty Royale, Circulation Mgr., proyle@royle.com. **ISSN:** 1077-5447. **Subscription Rates:** $25 domestic; $65 airmail. **Remarks:** Accepts advertising. **Online:** CompuServe. **URL:** http://www.livesoundint.com. **Formerly**: REP.
Ad Rates: BW: $2,062 **Circ:** Paid 2,800
4C: $2,656 Non-paid 7,950

17290 Meat & Poultry
Sosland Publishing Co.
4800 Main St., Ste. 100 Phone: (816)756-1000
Kansas City, MO 64112-2513 Fax: (816)756-0494
Publication E-mail: meat&poultry@sosland.com

Magazine serving the meat and poultry processing, distributing, and wholesaling industries in the U.S. and Canada. **Subtitle:** The Business Journal of the Meat & Poultry Industry. **Founded:** Jan. 1955. **Freq:** Monthly. **Print Method:** Offset. **Trim Size:** 8 x 10 7/8. **Cols./Page:** 3. **Col. Width:** 13 picas. **Col. Depth:** 140 agate lines. **Key Personnel:** Charles Sosland, Publisher; Jeanette Sims, Associate Publisher; Keith Nunes, Editor. **ISSN:** 0892-6077. **Subscription Rates:** $40 individuals; $45 Canada and Mexico; $75 other countries; $10 single issue. **Remarks:** Accepts advertising. **Formerly**: Meat Industry (1986).
Ad Rates: BW: $2,780 **Circ:** Controlled ‡18,249
4C: $3,935

17291 Midwest Contractor
3101 Broadway, Ste. 750 Phone: (816)561-3300
Kansas City, MO 64111 Fax: (816)561-3334
Free: (800)233-2412

Construction news magazine covering project bids and awards, new construction planning, industry trend articles, legislation, regulations, meeting coverage, interviews, and new products. News source for contractors, public officials, and equipment and material suppliers, in Iowa, Kansas, Nebraska, and western and northeastern Missouri. **Founded:** 1901. **Freq:** Semimonthly. **Print Method:** Offset. Uses mats. **Trim Size:** 8 1/8 x 10 7/8. **Cols./Page:** 3. **Col. Width:** 26 nonpareils. **Col. Depth:** 140 agate lines. **Key Personnel:** Scott Judy, Editor; Diana Rodriguez, Advertising Mgr.; Diana Rodriguez, Contact. **USPS:** 346-920. **Subscription Rates:** $65 individuals; $3 single issue; $25 Buyer's Guide & Directory. **Remarks:** Accepts advertising.
Ad Rates: BW: $1,655 **Circ:** Paid 283
4C: $2,268 Controlled 7,496

17292 Midwest Hospitality
Missouri Restaurant Association
PO Box 10277 Phone: (816)753-5222
Kansas City, MO 64111 Fax: (816)753-6993

Magazine for foodservice operators and suppliers. **Founded:** 1916. **Freq:** Monthly. **Print Method:** Sheet fed offset. **Trim Size:** 8 1/2 x 11. **Cols./Page:** 3. **Col. Width:** 26 nonpareils. **Col. Depth:** 134 agate lines. **Key Personnel:** Michelle A. Holden, Editor; Ray Stockwell, Adv. Rep.; Marge Stockwell, Adv. Rep. **ISSN:** 1075-1424. **Subscription Rates:** $15. **Remarks:** Accepts advertising. **Formerly**: The Missouri Restaurant Magazine.
Ad Rates: BW: $600 **Circ:** ‡4,000
4C: $950

17293 Milling & Baking News
Sosland Publishing Co.
4800 Main St., Ste. 100 Phone: (816)756-1000
Kansas City, MO 64112-2513 Fax: (816)756-0494
Publication E-mail: mbn@sosland.com

Trade magazine covering the grain-based food industries. **Founded:** 1922. **Freq:** Weekly (Tues.). **Print Method:** Offset. **Trim Size:** 8 x 10 3/4. **Cols./Page:** 3. **Col. Width:** 26 nonpareils. **Col. Depth:** 140 agate lines. **Key Personnel:** Gordon Davidson, Editor, gdavidson@sosland.com; Mark Sabo, Publisher, msabo@sosland.com. **USPS:** 508-300. **Subscription Rates:** $104 individuals. **Remarks:** Accepts advertising.
Ad Rates: BW: $3,390 **Circ:** Paid ★**4,802**
4C: $4,990

17294 Missouri Beef Cattleman
Missouri Beef Cattleman, Inc.
PO Box 025727 Phone: (816)471-0200
Kansas City, MO 64102 Fax: (816)471-0220
Publisher E-mail: mobeef@tfs.net

Magazine on beef cattle. **Founded:** June 1, 1971. **Freq:** Monthly. **Print Method:** Offset. **Trim Size:** 8 1/2 x 10 7/8. **Cols./Page:** 2. **Col. Width:** 40 agate lines. **Col. Depth:** 140 nonpareils. **Key Personnel:** Larry Atzenweiler, Publisher. **USPS:** 890-240. **Subscription Rates:** Free to qualified subscribers; $37.
Ad Rates: BW: $830 **Circ:** Controlled ‡6,500
4C: $1,160

17295 The National Catholic Reporter
National Catholic Reporter Publishing Co., Inc.
115 E Armour Blvd. Phone: (816)531-0538
Kansas City, MO 64111-1203 Fax: (816)968-2280
Free: (800)444-8910
Publication E-mail: 62893046@eln.attmail.com
Publisher E-mail: ncr_ editor@natcath.com

Catholic publication. **Subtitle:** The Independent Catholic Newsweekly. **Founded:** 1964. **Freq:** Weekly. **Print Method:** Offset. **Cols./Page:** 4. **Col. Width:** 30 nonpareils. **Col. Depth:** 224 agate lines. **Key Personnel:** Thomas Fox, Publisher; Michael Farrel, Editor; Chris Curry, Advertising Mgr. **Subscription Rates:** $36.95 individuals yearly. **Remarks:** Accepts advertising. **Online:** ADL.
Ad Rates: GLR: $1.00 **Circ:** Paid ‡50,000
BW: $2,145
PCI: $60

17296 New Letters
University of Missouri at Kansas City
5101 Rockhill Rd. Phone: (816)235-1168
University House Fax: (816)235-2611
Kansas City, MO 64110-2499
Magazine containing poetry, fiction, essays, and interviews. **Founded:** 1971. **Freq:** Quarterly. **Print Method:** Offset. **Trim Size:** 6 x 9. **Cols./Page:** 1. **Col. Width:** 48 nonpareils. **Key Personnel:** James McKinley, Editor, phone (816)235-1120; Robert Stewart, Managing Editor, phone (816)235-2610. **ISSN:** 0146-4930. **Subscription Rates:** $17; $20 libraries.

Remarks: Color advertising not accepted. **Alt. Formats:** Audio tape.
Ad Rates: BW: $150 **Circ:** Paid ‡1,203
Non-paid ‡52

17297 NLGI Spokesman
National Lubricating Grease Institute
4635 Wyandotte St. Phone: (816)931-9480
Kansas City, MO 64112-1537 Fax: (816)753-5026
Publication E-mail: nlgi@sound.net
Publisher E-mail: nlgi@sound.net

Magazine for those in lubricating grease industries. **Founded:** Apr. 1937. **Freq:** Monthly. **Print Method:** Offset. **Trim Size:** 8 3/8 x 11. **Cols./Page:** 3. **Col. Width:** 2 1/8 inches. **Col. Depth:** 9 1/8 inches. **Key Personnel:** Chuck Hitchcock, Editor/General Manager. **ISSN:** 0027-6782. **Subscription Rates:** $24 individuals; $36 Canada; $56 other countries; $3 single issue; $86 airmail. **Remarks:** Accepts advertising.
Ad Rates: BW: $335 **Circ:** Paid ‡2,200
4C: $775 Non-paid ‡50

17298 Northland News
Sun News
12 N. Main Phone: (816)781-1044
Liberty, MO 64068 Fax: (816)781-1755

Community newspaper. **Founded:** 1961. **Freq:** Weekly (Wed.). **Print Method:** Offset. **Cols./Page:** 6. **Col. Width:** 19 nonpareils. **Col. Depth:** 224 agate lines. **Key Personnel:** Jack Miles, Editor; Vivian O'Dell, Publisher; Diane Davis, Advertising Mgr. **Subscription Rates:** Free. **Remarks:** Accepts advertising. **Formerly:** Kansas City North News.
Ad Rates: BW: $1,329.60 **Circ:** Free 19,270
PCI: $13.95

17299 O'Lochlainn's Personal Journal of Irish Families
Irish Families
Box 7575 Phone: (816)454-2410
Kansas City, MO 64116 Fax: (816)454-2410
Publication E-mail: mike@irishroots.com

Illustrated magazine tracing Irish families and Irish heritage worldwide. **Subtitle:** An International Membership Publication. **Founded:** 1978. **Freq:** Monthly. **Print Method:** Offset. **Trim Size:** 8 1/2 x 11. **ISSN:** 1056-0378. **Subscription Rates:** $54 individuals. **Remarks:** Advertising not accepted. **URL:** http://www.irishroots.com.
Circ: (Not Reported)

17300 PBF
R.W. Nielsen Co.
PO Box 11067 Phone: (816)453-0590
Kansas City, MO 64119-0067 Fax: (816)453-0591
Free: (800)748-7690
Publisher E-mail: rnielson@pbf.org

Trade magazine for contractors who build for permanance in the residential and light commercial buildings. **Subtitle:** Permanent Buildings & Foundations. **Founded:** 1989. **Freq:** 8/year. **Print Method:** Web offset. **Trim Size:** 8 x 10 3/4. **Cols./Page:** 3 and 3. **Col. Width:** 2 1/4 and 3 3/8 inches. **Col. Depth:** 10 and 10 inches. **Key Personnel:** Roger W. Nielsen, Editor and Publisher, rnielsen@pbf.org; Carolyn Nielsen, Editor, cnielsen@pbf.org. **ISSN:** 1081-9592. **Subscription Rates:** $36 individuals; $48 Canada and Mexico; $68 other countries; $5 single issue. **Remarks:** Accepts advertising. **URL:** http://www.pbf.org. **Formerly:** Foundation Contractor; Foundations; The Concrete Foundation Contractor.
Ad Rates: BW: $3,127 **Circ:** Paid ‡3,117
4C: $3,820 Non-paid ‡31,439
PCI: $236

17301 Philosophy of Science
University of Chicago Press, Journals Division
222 Cockefair Hall Phone: (816)235-1331
University of Missouri-Kansas City Fax: (816)235-2819
Kansas City, MO 64110
Publisher E-mail: orders@journals.uchicago.edu

Journal devoted to the philosophy of science. **Founded:** 1934. **Freq:** Quarterly. **Print Method:** Offset. **Trim Size:** 6 x 9. **Cols./Page:** 1. **Col. Width:** 51 nonpareils. **Col. Depth:** 105 agate lines. **Key Personnel:** Philip Kitcher, Editor-in-Chief; Paul Churchland, Assoc. Editor; Patricia Kitcher, Assoc. Editor; Paul Teller, Assoc. Editor. **ISSN:** 0031-8248. **Subscription Rates:** $60; $65 other countries. **Remarks:** Accepts advertising.
Ad Rates: BW: $125 **Circ:** Paid 2,280
Non-paid 20

17302 Piano Technicians Journal
Piano Technicians Guild, Inc.
3930 Washington Phone: (816)753-7747
Kansas City, MO 64111 Fax: (816)531-0070

Magazine for piano technicians. **Founded:** 1958. **Freq:** Monthly. **Print Method:** Offset. **Cols./Page:** 3. **Col. Width:** 28 nonpareils. **Col. Depth:** 140 agate lines. **Key Personnel:** Steve Brady, Editor. **ISSN:** 0031-9562. **Subscription Rates:** $85. **Remarks:** Accepts advertising.
Ad Rates: BW: $655 **Circ:** 4,000

17303 PitchWeekly
Pitch Publishing, Inc.
3535 Broadway, Ste. 400 Phone: (816)561-6061
Kansas City, MO 64111 Fax: (816)756-0502
Publication E-mail: pitch@pitch.com

Alternative weekly focusing on Kansas City's news and entertainment. **Subtitle:** Alternative Weekly. **Founded:** July 1980. **Freq:** Weekly. **Print Method:** Web offset. **Trim Size:** 11 1/2 x 13 3/4. **Cols./Page:** 4. **Col. Width:** 2 3/8 inches. **Col. Depth:** 12 3/4 inches. **Key Personnel:** Hal Brody, Publisher, halb@pitch.com; Bruce Rodgers, Editor, brodgers@pitch.com; Michael Gruenenfelder, Classified Mgr., classified@pitch.com. **Subscription Rates:** $35.20. **Remarks:** Accepts advertising. **Available Online. URL:** http://www.pitch.com. **Formerly:** Pitch.
Ad Rates: BW: $2,200 **Circ:** Free ❑**86,200**
4C: $2,900
PCI: $35

17304 Praying
National Catholic Reporter Publishing Co., Inc.
115 E Armour Blvd. Phone: (816)531-0538
Kansas City, MO 64111-1203 Fax: (816)968-2280
Free: (800)444-8910
Publisher E-mail: ncr_ editor@natcath.com

Christian lifestyle magazine discussing laity and spirituality. **Subtitle:** Spirituality for Everyday Living. **Founded:** Oct. 1983. **Freq:** 8/year. **Print Method:** Offset. **Trim Size:** 8 1/4 x 10 3/8. **Cols./Page:** 3. **Col. Width:** 27 nonpareils. **Col. Depth:** 140 agate lines. **Key Personnel:** Dawn M. Gibeau, Editor; Thomas C. Fox, Publisher; Chris Curry, Advertising Mgr. **Subscription Rates:** $26.95. **Remarks:** Accepts advertising.
Ad Rates: BW: $1,000 **Circ:** ‡15,000
4C: $1,580
SAU: $2.25
PCI: $50

Raytown Dispatch-Tribune - See Raytown

17305 Regional Economic Digest
Federal Reserve Bank of Kansas City
925 Grand Blvd. Phone: (816)881-2683
Kansas City, MO 64198-0001 Fax: (816)881-2569

Trade magazine covering economic and financial issues. **Founded:** 1990. **Freq:** Quarterly. **Print Method:** Offset. **Trim Size:** 8 1/2 x 11. **Key Personnel:** Lowell C. Jones, Editor, phone (816)881-2797, fax (816)881-2569, ljones@frbkc. **ISSN:** 1049-5339. **Subscription Rates:** Free. **Remarks:** Advertising not accepted. **URL:** http://www.kc.frb.org. **Former name:** The Financial Letter.
Circ: Non-paid 8,000

17306 The Rockhurst Hawk
Rockhurst College
1100 Rockhurst Rd. Phone: (816)926-4051
Kansas City, MO 64110-2561 Fax: (816)501-4051

Collegiate newspaper. **Founded:** 1917. **Freq:** Semimonthly. **Print Method:** Offset. **Cols./Page:** 4. **Col. Width:** 21 nonpareils. **Col. Depth:** 157 agate lines. **Key Personnel:** Sara Byrne, Editor; Jack Cashill, Advertising Mgr.

17307 Rural Health FYI
National Rural Health Association
1 W. Armour Blvd., Ste. 203 Phone: (816)756-3140
Kansas City, MO 64111 Fax: (816)756-3144

Professional magazine for rural health practitioners. **Freq:** Bimonthly. **Key Personnel:** Tammy Houck Talbott. **Subscription Rates:** $75 individuals. **Remarks:** Accepts advertising.
Circ: (Not Reported)

17308 Sickle & Sheaf
Alpha Gamma Rho Fraternity
10101 N. Executive Hills Blvd. Phone: (816)891-9200
Kansas City, MO 64153 Fax: (816)891-9401
Publisher E-mail: agrho@aol.com

Agriculture fraternity magazine. **Subtitle:** The Magazine of Alpha Gamma Rho Agriculture Fraternity. **Founded:** 1910. **Freq:** Quarterly. **Print Method:** Offset. **Trim Size:** 10 7/8 x 17. **Cols./Page:** 4. **Key Personnel:** Ken Root, Editor; Philip Josephson, Exec. Dir.; Katie Thomas, Communications Coordinator. **ISSN:** 8750-6866. **Subscription Rates:** ITM. **Remarks:** Advertising not accepted. **URL:** http://www.agrs.org.
Circ: ‡40,000

17309 Texas Banking
Texas Bankers Association
912 Baltimore, Suite 900 Phone: (816)421-7941
Kansas City, MO 64105 Fax: (816)472-0397

Professional magazine. **Subtitle:** The Official Publication of the Texas Bankers Association. **Founded:** Aug. 1, 1911. **Freq:** Monthly. **Print Method:** Offset. **Trim Size:** 9 x 12. **Cols./Page:** 4. **Col. Width:** 1 7/8 inches. **Col. Depth:** 11 inches. **Key Personnel:** William F. Baker, Publisher; Rich Galloway, Advt. Sales Mgr. **ISSN:** 0885-6907. **Subscription Rates:** $25 members; $35 nonmembers. **Remarks:** Accepts advertising. **Formerly:** Texas Bankers Record.
Ad Rates: BW: $980 **Circ:** Paid ‡5,000
4C: $1,630 Controlled ‡300

17310 Thorny Locust
PO Box 32631 Phone: (816)756-5096
Kansas City, MO 64171-5631
Literary magazine. **Founded:** 1993. **Freq:** 4/year. **Trim Size:** 7 x 8 1/2. **Key Personnel:** Celeste Kuechler, Assoc. Editor; Silvia Kofler, Editor. **ISSN:** 1094-0154. **Subscription Rates:** $4 single issue. **Remarks:** Advertising not accepted.
Circ: Paid 200

17311 University News
University of Missouri at Kansas City
5327 Holmes Phone: (816)235-6514
Kansas City, MO 64110-2437 Fax: (816)235-1393
Publication E-mail: unewsads@aol.com

Collegiate newspaper. **Founded:** 1933. **Freq:** Weekly (Mon.). **Print Method:** Offset. **Cols./Page:** 5. **Col. Width:** 24 nonpareils. **Col. Depth:** 228 agate lines. **Key Personnel:** J.C. Davis, Editor, phone (816)235-5402. **Subscription Rates:** $25 /year. **Remarks:** Accepts advertising. **URL:** http://www.unews.com.
Ad Rates: BW: $512 **Circ:** Controlled 10,000
4C: $1,000
PCI: $6

17312 VFW Auxiliary
Ladies Auxiliary to the VFW
406 W. 34th St. Phone: (816)561-8655
Kansas City, MO 64111 Fax: (816)931-4753
Publisher E-mail: info@ladiesauxvfw.com

VFW auxiliary patriotic services magazine. **Founded:** 1946. **Freq:** 8/year. **Print Method:** Offset. **Trim Size:** 7 7/8 x 10 3/4. **Cols./Page:** 3. **Col. Width:** 27 nonpareils. **Col. Depth:** 138 agate lines. **Key Personnel:** Marilyn Ebersole, Editor. **Subscription Rates:** $1. **Remarks:** Accepts advertising. **URL:** http://www.ladiesauxvfw.com.
Ad Rates: GLR: $20 **Circ:** ‡750,000
BW: $4,850
4C: $6,100

17313 VFW Magazine
406 W. 34th St. Phone: (816)756-3390
Kansas City, MO 64111-2736 Fax: (816)968-1169

Magazine for the Veterans of Foreign Wars. **Founded:** 1912. **Freq:** 11/year. **Print Method:** Offset. **Trim Size:** 7 3/4 x 10 3/4. **Cols./Page:** 3. **Col. Width:** 2 1/4 inches. **Col. Depth:** 140 agate lines. **Key Personnel:** Rich Kolb, Editor and Publisher; Harry Church, Advertising Dir. **ISSN:** 0161-8598. **Subscription Rates:** $10. **Remarks:** Accepts advertising. **Alt. Formats:** Audio tape.
Ad Rates: GLR: $35.75 **Circ:** Paid ★**1,882,847**
BW: $18,900
4C: $24,050

17314 The Wednesday Magazine
Townsend Communications, Inc.
7007 NE Parvin Rd. Phone: (816)454-9660
Kansas City, MO 64117 Fax: (816)452-5889
Publisher E-mail: towns@swbell.net

Community newspaper. **Founded:** 1937. **Freq:** Weekly (Wed.). **Print Method:** Offset. **Trim Size:** 11 1/2 x 12. **Cols./Page:** 5. **Col. Width:** 2 1/8 inches. **Col. Depth:** 12 inches. **Key Personnel:** Don Ledford, Editor; Harold G. Townsend, Jr., Publisher; Gary Warmker, National Adv. Mgr. **Subscription Rates:** Free to area households; $10 out of area. **Remarks:** Accepts advertising.
Ad Rates: 4C: $275 **Circ:** Paid 136
SAU: $13.39 Free 28,149

17315 Western Retailer
Western Retail Implement and Hardware Association
638 W. 39th St. Phone: (816)561-5323
Kansas City, MO 64111 Fax: (816)561-1249
Free: (800)762-5616
Publisher E-mail: jflora@westernassn.com

Farm implements and hardware magazine. **Subtitle:** Western Retailer. **Founded:** 1895. **Freq:** Monthly. **Print Method:** Offset. **Trim Size:** 8 1/4 x 11. **Cols./Page:** 3 and 2. **Col. Width:** 40 and 60 nonpareils. **Col. Depth:** 140 agate lines. **Key Personnel:** Mike Griffith, Editor. **ISSN:** 1044-7768.

Subscription Rates: $12. **Remarks:** Accepts advertising. **URL:** http://www.westernassn.com. **Formerly:** Hardware and Farm Equipment (1989).
Ad Rates: BW: $345 **Circ:** Paid ‡1,100
4C: $1,245 Controlled ‡420
PCI: $25

17316 Women in Business
The ABWA Co. Inc.
9100 Ward Pkwy. Phone: (816)361-6621
PO Box 8728 Fax: (816)361-4991
Kansas City, MO 64114-0728
Publisher E-mail: abwa@abwahq.org

Women's business magazine for members of the American Business Women's Association and all women in business. **Founded:** 1949. **Freq:** Bimonthly. **Print Method:** Offset. **Trim Size:** 8 x 10 3/4. **Cols./Page:** 3. **Col. Width:** 30 nonpareils. **Col. Depth:** 116 agate lines. **Key Personnel:** Marchel Abner, Asst. Ed.; Lisa Bickham, Corp. Relations Mgr.; Susan Fitch Swanson, Editor & Mgr. of Publications; John Summers, Graphic Designer. **ISSN:** 0043-7441. **Subscription Rates:** $16 individuals; $20 other countries. **Remarks:** Accepts advertising. **URL:** http://www.abwahq.org.
Ad Rates: GLR: $4.50 **Circ:** Paid 50,000
BW: $2,980
4C: $3,786
PCI: $175

17317 World Grain
Sosland Publishing Co.
4800 Main St., Ste. 100 Phone: (816)756-1000
Kansas City, MO 64112-2513 Fax: (816)756-0494
Publication E-mail: worldgrain@sosland.com

International magazine for grain industry managers and related government officials. **Founded:** 1982. **Freq:** 11/year. **Print Method:** Offset. **Trim Size:** 8 x 10 3/4. **Cols./Page:** 3. **Col. Width:** 27 nonpareils. **Col. Depth:** 140 agate lines. **Key Personnel:** Melissa Cordonier, Editor, mcordonier@sosland.com; Charles Sosland, Publisher; Mark Cornwell, Sales Rep. **ISSN:** 0745-8991. **Subscription Rates:** Free to qualified subscribers; $24 institutions. **Remarks:** Accepts advertising. **URL:** http://www.sosland.com.
Ad Rates: BW: $2,745 **Circ:** Combined ‡9,017
4C: $4,110

17318 KCPT-TV - 19
125 E. 31st St. Phone: (816)756-3580
Kansas City, MO 64108 Fax: (816)931-2500
Free: (800)561-1900
E-mail: kcpt@kcpt.org

Format: Public TV. **Networks:** Public Broadcasting Service (PBS). **Owner:** Community Owned Public TV Station, at above address. **Founded:** 1961. **Formerly:** KCSD (1972). **Operating Hours:** 5 a.m.-1:00 a.m.Daily; 7 a.m.-midnight Sat. and Sun. **ADI:** Kansas City, MO (Lawrence, KS). **Key Personnel:** William T. Reed, President, bill_reed@kcpt.org. **Local Programs:** *Kansas City Week in Review*; *Rare Visions*; *Roadside Relevations*; *RUCKUS*. **Ad Rates:** Advertising not accepted. **URL:** http://www.kcpt.org.

17319 KCTV-TV - 5
PO Box 5555 Phone: (913)677-5555
Kansas City, MO 64109 Fax: (913)677-7284

Format: Commercial TV. **Networks:** CBS. **Owner:** Meredith Corp., 17th & Locust, Des Moines, IA 50309-3023, (515)284-3000. **Founded:** 1953. **Formerly:** KCMO-TV (1983). **Operating Hours:** Continuous; 63% network, 37% local. **ADI:** Kansas City, MO (Lawrence, KS). **Key Personnel:** John Rose, General Mgr.; Erv Parthe, Dir of Oper.; Bob Frey, General Sales Mgr. **Local Programs:** *Kansas City's News* 6 a.m.; 12, 5, 6, 10 p.m., Don North, News Dir. **Wattage:** 100,000. **URL:** http://www.kctv.com.

17320 KCUR-FM - 89.3
4825 Troost Ave., Ste. 202 Phone: (816)235-1551
Kansas City, MO 64110 Fax: (816)235-2864
E-mail: kcur@smtpgate.umkc.edu

Format: Public Radio; Talk; Jazz; News. **Networks:** National Public Radio (NPR); Public Radio International (PRI). **Founded:** 1957. **Operating Hours:** Continuous. **ADI:** Kansas City, MO (Lawrence, KS). **Key Personnel:** Andrea Young, Contact; Donna Peck, Program Dir.; Mary Jo Draper, News Dir. **Local Programs:** *The Walt Bodine Show*, Andrea Young. **Wattage:** 100,000. **Ad Rates:** Noncommercial.

17321 KCWE-TV -
Skelly Bldg. Phone: (816)753-7201
605 W. 47th St., Ste. 300 Fax: (816)753-5595
Kansas City, MO 64112

Format: Commercial TV. **Owner:** KCWE-TV, Inc., at above address.

17322 KKFI-FM - 90.1
PO Box 32250 Phone: (816)931-3122
Kansas City, MO 64171-5250 Fax: (816)931-7078

Format: Public Radio; Full Service; Eclectic. **Networks:** Pacifica. **Owner:** Mid-Coast Radio Project, Inc., at above address. **Founded:** 1988. **Operating Hours:** Continuous; 10% network, 90% local. **ADI:** Kansas City, MO (Lawrence, KS). **Key Personnel:** Greg Hanson, Program Dir. **Wattage:** 100,000. **Ad Rates:** Noncommercial. **URL:** http://www.gazlay.com/kkfi.

17323 KLJC-FM - 88.5
15800 Calvary Rd. Phone: (816)331-8700
Kansas City, MO 64147-1341 Fax: (816)331-4474
Free: (800)466-5552
E-mail: kljc@kljc.org

Format: Religious. **Networks:** USA Radio; Moody Broadcasting. **Owner:** Calvary Bible College, at above address, (816)322-0110. **Founded:** 1970. **Operating Hours:** Continuous; 15% network, 85% local. **ADI:** Kansas City, MO (Lawrence, KS). **Key Personnel:** Greg Harris, General Mgr., gharris@kljc.org; Darrell Nickolaus, Chief Engineer; Rob Trainor, Promotions Dir., rtrainor@kljc.org; Brent Manion, Production Dir., bmanion@kljc.org. **Local Programs:** *Chief Cornerstone* 5:00 pm - 6:00 pm Monday, Dave Scott. **Wattage:** 100,000. **Ad Rates:** Noncommercial. **URL:** http://www.kljc.org.

17324 KMBC-TV - 9
1049 Central Phone: (816)221-9999
Kansas City, MO 64105 Fax: (816)760-9245

Format: Commercial TV. **Networks:** ABC. **Owner:** KMBC-TV A Division of Hearst Argyle Television, at above address. **Founded:** 1953. **Operating Hours:** Continuous; 70% network, 30% local. **ADI:** Kansas City, MO (Lawrence, KS). **Key Personnel:** Brian Bracco, News Dir., phone (816)760-9301, fax (816)421-4163, bbracco@hearst.com; Pat Patton, Program Dir., phone (816)760-9260, ppatton@hearst.com; Bob Lorenzen, Promotions Mgr., phone (816)760-9210, blorenzen@hearst.com; Bob Brandt, General Sales Mgr., phone (816)760-9352, fax (816)221-3633, bbrandt@hearst.com; Denise Dailey, Contact, phone (816)760-9350, ddailey@hearst.com; Jenny Kuypers, Contact, phone (816)760-9353, jkuypers@hearst.com.

17325 KMXV-FM - 93.3
3101 Broadway, No. 460 Phone: (816)753-0933
Kansas City, MO 64111 Fax: (816)931-0903

Format: Contemporary Hit Radio (CHR). **Founded:** 1991. **Formerly:** KWKI-FM (1982); KLSI-FM (1991). **Operating Hours:** Continuous; 100% local. **ADI:** Kansas City, MO (Lawrence, KS). **Key Personnel:** Mike Payne, General Mgr.; Jon Zellner, Program Dir.; Amanda Waters, News Dir.; Dan Prendiville, Sales Mgr. **Local Programs:** *Danny and the Barber - AM Show*, Jon Zellner; *Retro Saturday Night*, Jon Zellner. **Wattage:** 100,000. **Ad Rates:** $30-175 per unit.

17326 KNRX-FM - 107.3
4240 Blue Ridge Blvd. Phone: (816)353-7600
Kansas City, MO 64133 Fax: (816)353-2300

Format: Oldies; Adult Contemporary. **Networks:** ABC. **Formerly:** KXXR-FM (1992); KISF-FM (Mar. 1, 1998). **Operating Hours:** Continuous. **ADI:** Kansas City, MO (Lawrence, KS). **Key Personnel:** James E. MacFarlane, General Mgr., yoloi@aol.com. **Wattage:** 100,000. **Ad Rates:** Advertising accepted; rates available upon request.

17327 KPRT-AM - 1590
11131 Colorado Phone: (816)763-2040
Kansas City, MO 64137-2546 Fax: (816)966-1055

Format: Gospel. **Networks:** American Urban Radio; CNN Radio. **Founded:** 1950. **Formerly:** KPRS-AM (1975). **Operating Hours:** Continuous. **ADI:** Kansas City, MO (Lawrence, KS). **Key Personnel:** Michael Carter, Contact; Freddie Bell, Program Dir. **Wattage:** 1000. **Ad Rates:** $25 for 30 seconds; $35 for 60 seconds.

17328 KSHB-TV - 41
4720 Oak St. Phone: (816)753-4141
Kansas City, MO 64112 Fax: (816)932-4122

Format: Commercial TV. **Networks:** NBC. **Founded:** 1970. **Formerly:** KBMA-TV. **Operating Hours:** Continuous. **ADI:** Kansas City, MO (Lawrence, KS). **Key Personnel:** Craig Allison, General Sales Mgr.; Jim Swinehart, General Mgr.; Brian Grauer, Business Mgr.; Paul Barzizza, Engineer Mgr.; Herb Willis, Production Mgr.; Laura Clark, News Dir.; Richard Eller, Promotions Mgr.

17329 KUDL-FM - 98.1
3101 Broadway St, Ste. 460 Phone: (816)753-0933
Kansas City, MO 64111-2416 Fax: (816)753-6654

Format: Adult Contemporary. **Networks:** AP. **Founded:** 1959. **Operating Hours:** Continuous. **ADI:** Kansas City, MO (Lawrence, KS). **Key Personnel:** Bob Zuroweste, General Mgr. **Wattage:** 100,000.

17330 WDAF-TV - 4
3030 Summit, Signal Hill Phone: (816)753-4567
Kansas City, MO 64108 Fax: (816)932-3984

Format: Commercial TV. **Networks:** Fox. **Founded:** Oct. 14, 1949. **Operating Hours:** Continuous. **ADI:** Kansas City, MO (Lawrence, KS). **Key Personnel:** Stan Knott, Vice Pres./General Mgr.; Clayton (Buddy) Turner, K.C. Teleport Mgr.; Mike McDonald, Vice Pres., News; Henry Chu, Asst. News Dir.; John Rinkenbaugh, Executive Producer; Mike Lewis, Assignment Mgr.; John Hegedus, National Sales Mgr.; Susan Brier, Local Sales Mgr.; Veronica Warson, Traffic Mgr.; Scott Brady, Dir. of Marketing & Creative Services; Jeni Cardin, Dir. of Public Relations; Thermal Stewart, Vice Pres., Business; Jim Moore, Vice Pres., Engineering.

17331 WHB-AM - 810
1600 Genessee, Ste. 925 Phone: (816)221-7170
Kansas City, MO 64102 Fax: (816)221-7944

Format: Agricultural; Country. **Networks:** AP. **Founded:** 1922. **Operating Hours:** Continuous. **ADI:** Kansas City, MO (Lawrence, KS). **Key Personnel:** Jim Hensiek, General Mgr. **Wattage:** 50,000.

KEARNEY, pop. 1,433.

W. MO. Clay Co. 25 mi. NE of Kansas City. Manufactures metal and plastics. Ships livestock and grain. Propane gas. Diversified farming. Cattle, hogs.

17332 The Kearney Courier
Whipple Printing Co. Ltd.
102 N. Jefferson Phone: (816)635-6010
PO Box 138 Fax: (816)635-4422
Kearney, MO 64060-0138
Publication E-mail: courwhip@tyrell.net

Newspaper with a Republican orientation. **Founded:** Apr. 7, 1932. **Freq:** Weekly (Thurs.). **Print Method:** Offset. **Trim Size:** 14 x 22 1/2. **Cols./Page:** 6. **Col. Width:** 25 nonpareils. **Col. Depth:** 301 agate lines. **Key Personnel:** R.N. Whipple, Editor; Kathy Whipple, Publisher; Gene Gentrup, Assoc. Editor. **USPS:** 293-840. **Subscription Rates:** $21.30; $31.94 out of state. **Remarks:** Accepts advertising.
Ad Rates: BW: $580.50 **Circ:** ‡2,600
SAU: $4.50

KENNETT†, pop. 10,145.

SE MO. Durklin Co. 80 mi. S. of Cape Girardeau. Manufactures textiles, business forms, electrical equipment, industrial hose, ready mix concrete. Cotton gins and oil mill; cotton compresses. Agriculture. Cotton, soybeans, wheat, corn.

17333 The Daily Dunklin Democrat
203 1st St. Phone: (314)888-4505
Kennett, MO 63857 Fax: (314)888-5114

General newspaper. **Founded:** 1888. **Freq:** Tues.-Fri. (eve); Sun. (morn.). **Print Method:** Offset. **Cols./Page:** 6. **Col. Width:** 26 nonpareils. **Col. Depth:** 294 agate lines. **Key Personnel:** Bud Hunt, Editor; Gary Rust, Publisher. **Subscription Rates:** $52 individuals.
Ad Rates: GLR: $.32 **Circ:** Wed. 10,161
BW: $774.00 Sun. 4,040
4C: $996.00 Tues.-Fri. 4,075
SAU: $6.43
PCI: $6.55

17334 Kennett Cablevision
717 Rte. VV Phone: (573)888-4686
West South Bypass Fax: (573)888-1846
Kennett, MO 63857

Founded: 1963. **Key Personnel:** Ken Bower, General Mgr.; Linda Milburn, Office Mgr.; Tommy Tate, Chief Technician; Barbara Cochran, Sales Mgr. **Cities Served:** subscribing households 5,100; 37 channels.

KIMBERLING CITY

17335 Table Rock Gazette
Kimberling City Publishing Co.
PO Box 432
Kimberling City, MO 65686

Community newspaper. **Founded:** 1964. **Freq:** Weekly

(Thurs.). **Print Method:** Offset. **Cols./Page:** 6. **Col. Width:** 2 1/16 inches. **Col. Depth:** 21 inches. **Key Personnel:** Pat Soetaert, Editor; Don Sumner, Publisher. **USPS:** 923-780. **Subscription Rates:** $20.96; $33.94 out of area.
Ad Rates: SAU: $4.40 **Circ:** ‡1,275

KING CITY, pop. 1,063.

NW MO. 30 mi. NE of Saint Joseph. Gentry Co. Purebred cattle and hogs. Dairy, poultry farms. Corn, oats, soybeans.

17336 Tri-County News
Tri-Cities Publishing Co.
PO Box 428 Phone: (816)535-4313
King City, MO 64463 Free: (800)421-1765

Community newspaper. **Founded:** 1920. **Freq:** Weekly (Fri.). **Print Method:** Offset. **Trim Size:** 7 x 21. **Cols./Page:** 7. **Col. Width:** 1 13/16 inches. **Col. Depth:** 294 agate lines. **Key Personnel:** Robert E. Cobb, Editor and Publisher. **USPS:** 638-520. **Subscription Rates:** $20; $24; $30. **Remarks:** Accepts advertising.
Ad Rates: GLR: $.50 **Circ:** 2,050
BW: $514.50
SAU: $3.50
PCI: $4.99

KIRBYVILLE

17337 The Ozarks Mountaineer
The Ozarks & Mountaineer Corp.
PO Box 20 Phone: (417)336-2665
Kirbyville, MO 65679 Fax: (417)336-2679

Magazine containing articles about the past, present, and future of the Ozarks region of the U.S. **Founded:** Mar. 1952. **Freq:** Bimonthly. **Print Method:** Offset. **Trim Size:** 8 1/2 x 11. **Cols./Page:** 3. **Col. Width:** 14 picas. **Col. Depth:** 60 picas. **Key Personnel:** Gerald Dupy, Editor, phone (870)423-6419; Barbara Wehrman, Publisher. **ISSN:** 0030-7769. **Subscription Rates:** $14.95 individuals; $27 two years. **Remarks:** Accepts advertising alcoholic beverages and tobacco. **URL:** http://www.gtweb.com/mountaineer/index.html.
Ad Rates: BW: $900 **Circ:** Paid ‡32,000
4C: $1,100 Controlled ‡1,500
PCI: $24

KIRKSVILLE†, pop. 17,167.

N. MO. Adair Co. 90 mi. N. of Columbia. Northeast Missouri State University. Kirkville College of Osteopathy and Surgery. Manufactures shoes, business forms, hospital supplies. Dairy farming; meat processing. Corn, beans, cattle,. hogs.

17338 The Crier
American Publishing Co.
506 W. Potter Phone: (816)665-4663
Box 828 Fax: (816)665-3048
Kirksville, MO 63501
Free: (800)830-5360

Community newspaper. **Subtitle:** The Kirksville Crier. **Founded:** 1977. **Freq:** Weekly (Wed.). **Print Method:** Offset. Uses mats. **Cols./Page:** 8. **Col. Width:** 18 nonpareils. **Col. Depth:** 294 agate lines. **Key Personnel:** Carol Kilmer, Publisher, ckilmer@rainis.net; Vicky Ward, General Mgr. **Subscription Rates:** $20. **Remarks:** Accepts advertising.
Ad Rates: BW: $806.40 **Circ:** Paid 105
PCI: $6.10 Free 20,455

17339 Index - Fortney
Truman University
SUB Media Center Phone: (816)785-4449
Kirksville, MO 63501 Fax: (816)785-7601

Collegiate newspaper. **Founded:** 1908. **Freq:** Weekly (Thurs.). **Print Method:** Offset. **Trim Size:** 13 3/4 x 22. **Cols./Page:** 6. **Col. Width:** 24 nonpareils. **Col. Depth:** 294 agate lines. **Key Personnel:** Mark England, Advertising Mgr., phone (816)785-4319; James Hart, Editor. **Subscription Rates:** $20. **Remarks:** Accepts advertising. **Available Online.**
Ad Rates: BW: $480 **Circ:** Free 6,000
SAU: $3
PCI: $5

17340 Kirksville Daily Express and News
Kirksville Publishing Co.
110 E. McPherson Phone: (816)665-2808
PO Box 809 Fax: (816)665-2608
Kirksville, MO 63501
Newspaper. **Founded:** 1901. **Freq:** Daily (eve.). **Print Method:** Offset. **Cols./Page:** 6. **Col. Width:** 12 1/2 picas. **Col. Depth:** 21 inches. **Key Personnel:** Larry Freels, Publisher; Jon Cook, Advertising Mgr. **USPS:** 296-060. **Subscription Rates:** $105 individual; $125 out of state. **Remarks:** Accepts advertising.
Ad Rates: BW: $1,008 **Circ:** Mon.-Fri. ‡7,600
4C: $1,233 Sun. ‡8,000
SAU: $8

17341 The Marketplace
Kirksville Publishing Co.
110 E. McPherson Phone: (816)665-2808
PO Box 809 Fax: (816)665-2608
Kirksville, MO 63501
Shopper. **Founded:** Aug. 16, 1983. **Freq:** Weekly (Sun.). **Print Method:** Offset. **Cols./Page:** 6. **Col. Width:** 12 1/2 picas. **Col. Depth:** 21 inches. **Key Personnel:** Larry W. Freels, Publisher. **USPS:** 296-060. **Remarks:** Accepts advertising. **Formerly:** Town & Country Express.
Ad Rates: BW: $1,260 **Circ:** Free ‡6,000
4C: $1,485 Paid ‡8,000
SAU: $10

17342 Cablecom of Kirksville
402 N. Main Phone: (816)665-5444
Box D Fax: (816)627-2603
Kirksville, MO 63501

Owner: Post-Newsweek Cable Inc., 4742 N. 24th St., Ste. 270, Phoenix, AZ 85016. **Founded:** Sept. 1965. **Key Personnel:** Ron Van Buren, General Mgr.; Dean West, Chief Technician; Joni Young, Office Mgr. **Cities Served:** Kirksville, MO: subscribing households 6,600; 35 channels.

17343 KIRX-AM - 1450
1308 N. Baltimore Phone: (816)665-3781
PO Box 130 Fax: (816)665-0711
Kirksville, MO 63501

Format: Full Service; Oldies; Talk; News; Sports; Information. **Networks:** ABC; Brownfield; Missouri. **Owner:** KIRX, Inc., at above address. **Founded:** 1947. **Operating Hours:** Continuous. **ADI:** Ottumwa, IA-Kirksville, MO (Wapello, IA). **Key Personnel:** Alvina M. Britz, Finance Dir.; Steve Lloyd, Gen. Mgr./Gen. Sales Mgr.; Duncan Miller, Program Dir. **Local Programs:** *Area Scene* 9:30 a.m.-10 a.m. **Wattage:** 1000. **Ad Rates:** $12 for 30 seconds; $18-26.50 for 60 seconds.

17344 KRXL-FM - 94.5
1308 N. Baltimore Phone: (816)665-9828
PO Box 130 Fax: (816)665-0711
Kirksville, MO 63501

Format: Classic Rock. **Networks:** ABC. **Owner:** KIRX, Inc., at above address. **Founded:** 1967. **Formerly:** KRXL-FM. **Operating Hours:** Continuous. **ADI:** Ottumwa, IA-Kirksville, MO (Wapello, IA). **Key Personnel:** Alvina M. Britz, Finance Dir.; Steve Lloyd, Gen. Mgr./Gen. Sales Mgr.; Duncan Miller, Program Dir. **Wattage:** 100,000. **Ad Rates:** $19 for 30 seconds; $27.50 for 60 seconds.

17345 KTVO-TV - 3
Box 949 Phone: (816)627-3333
Kirksville, MO 63501 Fax: (816)627-1885

Format: Commercial TV. **Networks:** ABC. **Founded:** 1955. **Operating Hours:** 19 hrs. Daily; 60% network, 32% syndicated, 8% local. **ADI:** Ottumwa, IA-Kirksville, MO (Wapello, IA). **Key Personnel:** Kim J. Wilcox, VP/General Manager; Jennifer Daniels, Operations Mgr.; Chris Hunt, News Dir. **Ad Rates:** $35-750 for 30 seconds.

KIRKWOOD, pop. 27,430.

EC MO. Saint Louis Co. 13 mi. W. of Saint Louis. Commercial and residential suburb of St. Louis.

17346 Falcon/Capital Cable Partners L.P.
906 So. Kirkwood Rd., Suite 200 Phone: (314)909-8444
Kirkwood, MO 63122 Fax: (314)909-8459
Free: (800)726-2584

Owner: Falcon/Capital Cable Partners L.P., at above address. **Founded:** 1988. **Key Personnel:** Scott Widham, President, scott@widham.com; Mary Meier, Contact, mmcap@meysinet.net; Ed Trower, Contact, phone (573)875-8875, fax (573)875-3007, eddie@capitalcabletv.com. **Cities Served:** Communities throughout Iowa, Kansas, Missouri, Indiana, Illi nois and Kentucky.

KNOB NOSTER, pop. 2,040.

W. MO. Johnson Co. 60 mi. E. of Kansas City. Knob Noster State Park. Whiteman AFB. Stock and grain farms.

17347 Knob Noster Item
111 N. Jackson Phone: (660)563-3606
Box 188
Knob Noster, MO 65336
Publication E-mail: knitem@iland.net

Newspaper with a Democratic orientation. **Founded:** 1958. **Freq:** Weekly (Thurs.). **Print Method:** Offset. **Cols./Page:** 5. **Col. Width:** 11 picas. **Col. Depth:** 13 inches. **Key Personnel:** Stan Hall, Editor and Publisher. **Subscription Rates:** $16.70; $18.31 out of state. **Remarks:** Accepts advertising.
Ad Rates: BW: $178.75 **Circ:** ‡1,200
SAU: $3.25
PCI: $3.50

LA BELLE, pop. 845.

NE MO. Lewis Co. 30 mi. NW of Quincy, IL. Oak, hickory, walnut timber. Farming. Corn, hogs, soybeans.

17348 The La Belle Star
PO Box 66 Phone: (816)462-3848
La Belle, MO 63447 Fax: (816)727-2475

Newspaper with a Republican orientation. **Founded:** 1883. **Freq:** Weekly (Wed.). **Print Method:** Offset. **Cols./Page:** 8. **Col. Width:** 22 nonpareils. **Col. Depth:** 294 agate lines. **Key Personnel:** Hazel Bledsoe Smith, Editor and Publisher, phone (816)727-3395, fax (816)727-2475. **Subscription Rates:** $14; $17 out of area. **Remarks:** Accepts classified advertising.
Ad Rates: GLR: $.25 **Circ:** ‡1,000
BW: $330.75
SAU: $2.25
PCI: $4.45

LAMAR†, pop. 4,053.

SW MO. Barton Co. 40 mi. NE of Joplin. Manufactures stereo equipment, office furniture, wire display racks. Diversifiedfarming. Wheat, milo, corn, hay, soybeans. Cattle. Sheep, hogs.

17349 Lamar Democrat
900 N. Gulf Phone: (417)682-5529
PO Box 458 Fax: (417)682-5595
Lamar, MO 64759
Community newspaper. **Founded:** 1870. **Freq:** Semiweekly (Wed. and Sat.). **Print Method:** Offset. **Cols./Page:** 6. **Col. Width:** 26 nonpareils. **Col. Depth:** 301 agate lines. **Key Personnel:** Rayma Davis, Editor; Doug Davis, Advertising Mgr. **ISSN:** 0745-9300. **Subscription Rates:** $37.50 individuals; $34.50 seniors; $53.95 out of area. **Remarks:** Accepts advertising.
Ad Rates: BW: $709.50 **Circ:** Paid ‡3,850
4C: $909.50 Free ‡600
SAU: $5.95

LANCASTER†, pop. 855.

NE MO. Schuyler Co. 85 mi. NW of LaGrange. Residential.

17350 The Excelsior
Excelsior Publishing Co., Inc.
417 Thompson Ave. Phone: (816)637-6155
PO Box 7 Fax: (816)637-8411
Excelsior Springs, MO 64024
Newspaper with a Democratic orientation. **Subtitle:** The Schuyler County Weekly Newspaper. **Founded:** 1866. **Freq:** Weekly (Wed.). **Print Method:** Offset. Uses mats. **Cols./Page:** 6. **Col. Width:** 12 1/2 picas. **Col. Depth:** 21 inches. **Key Personnel:** Ann Bunch, Editor and Publisher. **USPS:** 304-020. **Subscription Rates:** $13; $16 out of area. **Remarks:** Accepts advertising. **Formerly:** Lancaster Excelsior (1986).
Ad Rates: GLR: $.17 **Circ:** ‡1,800
BW: $444.78
4C: $724.78
SAU: $3.53

LAWSON, pop. 1,688.

NW MO. Clay and Ray Co. 39 mi. NE of Kansas City. Historical site. Stock, grain farms. Corn.

17351 The Lawson Review
405 N. Pennsylvania Ave. Phone: (816)296-3412
Box 125
Lawson, MO 64062-0125
Newspaper with a Republican orientation. **Founded:** 1881. **Freq:** Weekly (Wed.). **Print Method:** Offset. **Cols./Page:** 4. **Col. Width:** 27 nonpareils. **Col. Depth:** 205 agate lines. **Key Personnel:** David Blyth, Editor; Cress Hewitt, Publisher/Advertising Mgr. **Subscription Rates:** $17.50. **Remarks:** Accepts advertising.
Ad Rates: GLR: $.20 **Circ:** ‡1,700
BW: $211
SAU: $3.50

LEBANON, pop. 9,507.

SC MO. Ladlede Co. 49 mi. NE of Springfield. Recreation. Trout fishing. Camping. Manufactures aluminum boats, campers, barrels, textiles, fishing lures, furniture, steel dies, tools, mufflers. Oak, walnut timber. Dairy, stock, poultry farms.

17352 The Lebanon Daily Record
290 S. Madison Ave. Phone: (417)532-9131
PO Box 192 Fax: (417)532-8140
Lebanon, MO 65536-3150
Free: (800)288-9924

General newspaper. **Founded:** 1866. **Freq:** Daily (eve.). **Print Method:** Offset. **Cols./Page:** 6. **Col. Width:** 25 nonpareils. **Col. Depth:** 294 agate lines. **Key Personnel:** Gary Oedewaldt, Editor; R.B. Smith, Publisher. **Subscription Rates:** $48. **Remarks:** Accepts advertising.
Ad Rates: SAU: $6.60 **Circ:** Paid 4,521
Free 29

17353 KBNN-AM - 750
Dillworth Rd. Phone: (417)532-9111
Box 1112 Fax: (417)588-4191
Lebanon, MO 65536
Free: (800)457-2233
E-mail: kjel@leblink.com

Format: Talk; News. **Networks:** ABC; Missouri. **Founded:** 1972. **Formerly:** KJEL-AM. **Operating Hours:** Sunrise-sunset. **ADI:** Springfield, MO. **Key Personnel:** Mike Edwards, General Mgr.; John Fowler, Operations Mgr.; Dave Horvath, News Dir.; Kevin Stubblefield, Sports Dir. **Wattage:** 5000. **Ad Rates:** $13.50 for 30 seconds; $27 for 60 seconds.

17354 KCLQ-FM - 107.9
18785 Finch Rd. Phone: (417)532-2962
Lebanon, MO 65536 Fax: (417)532-5184

Format: Country. **Owner:** Lebanon Broadcasting & Leasing, Ltd., at above address. **Founded:** 1993. **Former name:** KLWT-FM (1993). **Operating Hours:** Continuous. **ADI:** Springfield, MO. **Key Personnel:** Tony Hawkins, General Mgr.; Mike Herdee, Program Dir., phone (417)335-2261; Mark Lucas, Chief Engineer, phone (417)335-2261. **Wattage:** 50,000. **Ad Rates:** $16.48 for 30 seconds; $21.18 for 60 seconds.

17355 KLWT-AM - 1230
18785 Finch Rd. Phone: (417)532-2962
Lebanon, MO 65536 Fax: (417)532-5184
E-mail: kclq@llion.org

Format: Adult Contemporary. **Networks:** Mutual Broadcasting System. **Founded:** 1948. **Operating Hours:** Continuous. **ADI:** Springfield, MO. **Key Personnel:** Tony Hawkins, Sales Mgr.; Bill Hendee, News Dir. **Wattage:** 1000. **Ad Rates:** $6-9 for 30 seconds.

17356 KTTK-FM - 90.7
PO Box 1232 Phone: (417)588-1435
Lebanon, MO 65536

Format: News; Eclectic; Sports. **Networks:** USA Radio. **Owner:** New Horizons Broadcasting Corp., at above address. **Founded:** 1986. **Operating Hours:** 17 hrs. Daily; 12% network, 88% local. **Key Personnel:** Max Rhoades, Manager; Pamela Rhoades, Contact. **Wattage:** 11,000. **Ad Rates:** Underwriting available.

LEES SUMMIT

17357 Lees Summit Journal
Lee's Summit Journal, Inc.
415 S. Douglas St. Phone: (816)524-2345
PO Box 387 Fax: (816)524-5136
Lees Summit, MO 64063
Community newspaper. **Founded:** 1881. **Freq:** Semiweekly. **Print Method:** Offset. **Cols./Page:** 6. **Col. Width:** 2 1/16 inches. **Col. Depth:** 21 inches. **Key Personnel:** Mike Brennan, Editor, editor@lsjournal.com; W. Ferrell Shuck, Publisher, fshuck@lsjournal.com; Julie Doane, Advertising Mgr., editor@lsjournal.com; Rogena Adams, Office Admin., accounts@lsjournal.com. **Subscription Rates:** $28; $39 out of area; $48 out of state. **Remarks:** Accepts advertising.
Ad Rates: GLR: $.50 **Circ:** Paid 6,359
BW: $882 Free 120
4C: $1,232
SAU: $7

17358 Lees Summit Journal-Extra
Lee's Summit Journal, Inc.
415 S. Douglas St. Phone: (816)524-2345
PO Box 387 Fax: (816)524-5136
Lees Summit, MO 64063
Total-market coverage shopper. **Founded:** 1966. **Freq:** Weekly (Wed.). **Print Method:** Letterpress and offset. **Cols./Page:** 6. **Col. Width:** 2 1/16 inches. **Col. Depth:** 21 inches. **Key Personnel:** Bob Raukar, Editor; W. Ferrell Shuck, Publisher, fshuck@lsjournal.com; Allen Hutchinson, Advertising Mgr.; Rogena Adams, Office Adm., accounts@lsjournal.com. **Subscription Rates:** Free. **Remarks:** Accepts advertising.
Ad Rates: GLR: $.55 **Circ:** Paid 6,371
BW: $793.80 Free 11,867
4C: $1,333.80
SAU: $7.70

17359 The Longview Current
Longview Community College
500 Longview Rd. Phone: (816)672-2308
Lees Summit, MO 64081 Fax: (816)672-2078
Publication E-mail: current@longview.cc.mo.us

Collegiate newspaper (tabloid). **Founded:** 1969. **Freq:** Every 3 weeks. **Print Method:** Offset. **Trim Size:** 11 x 14. **Cols./Page:** 5. **Col. Width:** 12 picas. **Col. Depth:** 13 inches. **Key Personnel:** Monica Hogan; Sylvia Edwards, Advisor. **Subscription Rates:** Free. **Remarks:** Accepts advertising.
Ad Rates: PCI: $5.75 **Circ:** ‡2,000

17360 Stained Glass Magazine
The Stained Glass Association
6 SW 2nd St., Ste. 7 Phone: (816)524-9313
Lees Summit, MO 64063 Fax: (816)524-9405
Free: (800)438-9581
Publication E-mail: sgmagaz@kcnet.com

Magazine on architectural stained and decorative art glass. **Subtitle:** Quarterly of the Stained Glass Association of America. **Founded:** 1906. **Freq:** Quarterly. **Print Method:** Offset. Uses mats. **Trim Size:** 8 1/4 x 11. **Cols./Page:** 3. **Col. Width:** 27 nonpareils. **Col. Depth:** 130 agate lines. **Key Personnel:** Richard Gross, Editor; Katei Gross, Business Mgr. **ISSN:** 0895-7002. **Subscription Rates:** $30 U.S.; $8.50 single issue; $46 other countries. **Remarks:** Accepts advertising. **Available Online. URL:** http://www.artglassworld.com/mag/sglass/sglass.html. **Formerly**: Stained Glass (1988).
Ad Rates: GLR: $9 **Circ:** Paid ‡7,045
BW: $778 Non-paid ‡135
4C: $1,321

LEXINGTON†, pop. 5,063.

W. MO. Lafayette Co. On Missouri River, 42 mi. E. of Kansas City. Manufactures industrial cables, dies and molds, wood products, textiles. Coal mines, rock quarries. Agriculture. Corn, apples.

17361 The Lexington News
Town Crier Publishing Co.
925 Main St. Phone: (816)259-2266
PO Box 279 Fax: (816)259-4870
Lexington, MO 64067-0279
Community newspaper. **Founded:** 1980. **Freq:** Semiweekly (Wed. and Fri.). **Print Method:** Offset. **Cols./Page:** 8. **Col. Width:** 21 nonpareils. **Col. Depth:** 294 agate lines. **Key Personnel:** Jim Craig, Editor; Daryl DeVries, Publisher; Carol Allen, Advertising Mgr. **Subscription Rates:** $11.50.
Circ: ‡3,000

LIBERAL, pop. 701.

SW MO. Barton Co. 19 mi. NE of Pittsburg, KS. Coal mines. Diversified farming. Corn, wheat, soybeans, milo.

17362 Liberal News
Darvin Weaver Inc.
PO Box 6 Phone: (417)843-5315
Liberal, MO 64762 Fax: (417)843-4178

Newspaper with a Republican orientation. **Founded:** 1910. **Freq:** Weekly (Thurs.). **Print Method:** Letterpress and offset. **Cols./Page:** 8. **Col. Width:** 20 nonpareils. **Col. Depth:** 294 agate lines. **Key Personnel:** Darvin Weaver, Publisher; Ruth Ann Weaver, Publisher. **Subscription Rates:** $13.50 individuals; $16.50 out of area. **Remarks:** Accepts advertising.
Ad Rates: GLR: $20 **Circ:** 1,083
SAU: $3.10

LIBERTY†, pop. 16,251.

W. MO. Clay Co. 5 mi. N. of Kansas City. William Jewell College. Residential.

Gladstone News - See Gladstone

17363 Liberty News
Sun News
12 N. Main Phone: (816)781-1044
Liberty, MO 64068 Fax: (816)781-1755

Community newspaper. **Founded:** 1961. **Freq:** Weekly (Wed.). **Print Method:** Offset. **Cols./Page:** 6. **Col. Width:** 19 nonpareils. **Col. Depth:** 224 agate lines. **Key Personnel:** Jack Miles, Editor; Vivian O'Dell, Publisher; Glen White, Advertising Mgr. **Remarks:** Accepts advertising.
Ad Rates: BW: $1,329.60 **Circ:** Free 18,788

17364 Liberty Tribune
Townsend Communications, Inc.
7007 NE Parvin Rd. Phone: (816)454-9660
Kansas City, MO 64117 Fax: (816)452-5889
Publisher E-mail: towns@swbell.net

Community newspaper. **Founded:** 1846. **Freq:** Weekly (Wed.). **Print Method:** Offset. **Trim Size:** 13 x 21. **Cols./Page:** 6. **Col. Width:** 2 1/8 inches. **Col. Depth:** 21 inches. **Key Personnel:** Angie Borgedalen, Editor; Harold G. Townsend, Jr., Publisher; Dorothy Baum, Advertising Mgr. **Subscription Rates:** Free to area households; $15 out of area; $18 out of state.
Circ: Combined 10,924

Northland News - See Kansas City

17365 Perspectives in Religious Studies
Mercer School of Theology
William Jewell College Phone: (816)781-7700
500 College Hill Fax: (816)415-5027
Liberty, MO 64068-1896
Scholarly journal. **Founded:** 1974. **Freq:** Quarterly. **Trim Size:** 7 x 10. **Cols./Page:** 1. **Key Personnel:** David Nelson Duke, Editor, duked@william.jewell.edu. **Subscription Rates:** $18 individuals; $20 students and retired; $25 libraries; $40 other countries; $7.50 single issue. **Remarks:** Color advertising not accepted.
Ad Rates: BW: $100 **Circ:** ‡550

17366 Platte Gazette
Sun News
12 N. Main Phone: (816)781-1044
Liberty, MO 64068 Fax: (816)781-1755

Community newspaper. **Freq:** Weekly (Wed.). **Cols./Page:** 8. **Col. Width:** 9 picas. **Col. Depth:** 21 1/2 inches. **Key Personnel:** Randall E. Battgler, General Mgr.; Christopher Waltz, Editor. **Subscription Rates:** $15.96. **Remarks:** Accepts advertising.
Ad Rates: BW: $946 **Circ:** Paid 219
4C: $1,096
PCI: $5.50

17367 KCXL-AM - 1140
310 S. La Frenz Phone: (816)792-1140
Liberty, MO 64068 Fax: (816)792-8258
E-mail: kcxl@kcxl.com

Format: Talk. **Founded:** 1994. **Formerly**: KBIL-AM (1968); KLDY-AM (1984). **Operating Hours:** Sunrise-sunset. **ADI:** Kansas City, MO (Lawrence, KS). **Key Personnel:** Peter E. Schartel, President; Gil T. Wilson, Operations Mgr., gil@kcxl.com. **Local Programs:** *KCXL Blues with Gil T. Wilson* 2 p.m.-5 p.m. Saturday; *Tradio with J.P. Morgan* 9 a.m.-11 a.m. Saturday. **Wattage:** 500. **Ad Rates:** $20 for 30 seconds; $25 for 60 seconds. **URL:** http://www.kcxl.com.

17368 KWJC-FM - 91.9
William Jewell College Phone: (816)415-5091
Liberty, MO 64068 Fax: (816)415-5027
E-mail: kwjc@william.jewell.edu

Format: Classical; Contemporary Christian; Jazz. **Owner:** William Jewell College, at above address, Fax: (816)415-5011. **Founded:** 1974. **Formerly**: KWPB-FM (1984). **Operating Hours:** Continuous; 5% network, 95% local. **ADI:** Kansas City, MO (Lawrence, KS). **Key Personnel:** Kelly Marsh, Manager, phone (816)781-7700. **Local Programs:** *High Noon Friday* 12:00 pm Friday, Kelly Marsh, Mailing contact, (816)781-7700, Fax (816)415-5011. **Wattage:** 250. **Ad Rates:** Noncommercial; underwriting available. **URL:** http://www.jewell.edu/kwjc.

LICKING

17369 Licking News
Derrick & Printing Corp.
122 S. Main St. Phone: (573)674-2412
PO Box 297 Fax: (573)624-2412
Licking, MO 65542
Community newspaper. **Founded:** 1896. **Freq:** Weekly (Thurs.). **Print Method:** Offset. **Trim Size:** 13 1/2 x 11 1/4. **Cols./Page:** 6. **Col. Width:** 2 inches. **Col. Depth:** 21 inches. **Key Personnel:** Eugene G. Derrickson, Editor and Publisher. **Subscription Rates:** $l3; $16 out of area; $19 out of state. **Remarks:** Accepts advertising.
Ad Rates: BW: $327.60 **Circ:** ‡2,300
PCI: $2.60

LIGUORI, pop. 45.

E. MO. Jefferson Co. 22 mi. S. of Saint Louis. Stock, poultry farms. Corn, wheat, oats.

17370 Liguorian
Liguori Publications
1 Liguori Dr. Phone: (314)464-2500
Liguori, MO 63057 Fax: (314)464-8449
Free: (800)464-2555
Publication E-mail: 104626.1547@compuserve.com

Catholic magazine. **Subtitle:** A Leading Catholic Magazine. **Founded:** Mar. 1913. **Freq:** Monthly. **Print Method:** Offset. **Trim Size:** 5 1/2 x 8 1/2. **Cols./Page:** 2. **Col. Width:** 27 nonpareils. **Col. Depth:** 101 agate lines. **Key Personnel:** Allan Weinert, C.SS.R, Editor. **Subscription Rates:** $18 individuals. **Remarks:** Advertising not accepted. **URL:** http://www.liguori.org. **Alt. Formats:** Audio tape.
Circ: 300,000

LINCOLN, pop. 819.

WC MO. Benton Co. 10 mi. N. of Warsaw. Residential.

17371 Lincoln New Era
PO Box 280 Phone: (816)668-4418
Lincoln, MO 65338 Fax: (816)668-4418

Community newspaper. **Founded:** 1961. **Freq:** Weekly (Thurs.). **Print Method:** Offset. **Cols./Page:** 6. **Col. Width:** 21 nonpareils. **Col. Depth:** 294 agate lines. **Key Personnel:** Diana Ball, Editor. **Subscription Rates:** $15.95 individuals; $18.50 out of area. **Remarks:** Accepts advertising. **Alt. Formats:** CD-ROM.
Ad Rates: PCI: $2.25 **Circ:** Paid ‡400

LINN†, pop. 1,211.

C. MO. Osage Co. 20 mi. E. of Jefferson City. Diaspore and flint clay mines. Oak timber. Diversified farming. Corn, wheat, hay.

17372 Unterrified Democrat
PO Box 109 Phone: (314)897-2109
Linn, MO 65051-0109 Fax: (314)897-0076

Community newspaper. **Founded:** July 3, 1866. **Freq:** Weekly (Wed.). **Print Method:** Offset. **Cols./Page:** 8. **Col. Width:** 22 nonpareils. **Col. Depth:** 294 agate lines. **Key Personnel:** Jerrilyn S. Voss, Publisher, phone (573)897-3150; Paul A. Slater, Editor, phone (573)897-3150. **Subscription Rates:** $25 individuals; $31 out of area; $35 out of state. **Remarks:** Accepts advertising.
Ad Rates: SAU: $4.40 **Circ:** 4,800

LOUISIANA, pop. 4,261.

E. MO. Pike Co. On Mississippi River, 25 mi. S. of Hannibal. Bridge to Quincy Junction and Pike, IL. Manufactures tube cement, plastics, chemicals, foundry products. Nursery. Diversified farming. Cattle, grain, apples.

17373 The Louisiana Press-Journal
Press Journal Printing Corp.
3406 W. Georgia Phone: (314)754-5566
Louisiana, MO 63353-0466 Fax: (314)754-4749

Newspaper with an Indiana orientation. **Founded:** 1855. **Freq:** Weekly. **Print Method:** Offset. Uses mats. **Cols./Page:** 6. **Col. Width:** 24 nonpareils. **Col. Depth:** 301 agate lines. **Key Personnel:** James A. Gierke, Editor and Publisher. **Subscription Rates:** $17. **Remarks:** Accepts advertising.
Ad Rates: GLR: $.20 **Circ:** 3,263
SAU: $3
PCI: $3.50

17374 KJFM-FM - 102.1
615 Georgia St. Phone: (573)754-5102
PO Box 438 Fax: (573)754-5544
Louisiana, MO 63353

Format: Contemporary Country. **Networks:** ABC; Missouri; St. Louis Cardinals. **Owner:** Foxfire Communications, Inc., at above address. **Founded:** 1984. **Operating Hours:** Continuous. 10% network, 90% local. **ADI:** St. Louis, MO (Mt. Vernon, IL). **Key Personnel:** Thom T. Sanders, Contact. **Wattage:** 3000. **Ad Rates:** $7-9 for 30 seconds; $10-14 for 60 seconds.

MACON†, pop. 5,680.

N. MO. Macon Co. 65 mi. W. of Hannibal. Fishing and boating. Manufactures electrical products. Frozen food processing. Ships agriculture products, stock. Meat packing. Coal mines. Diversified farming.

17375 The Journal
American Publishing Co.
204 W. Bourke St. Phone: (816)385-3121
PO Box 7 Fax: (816)385-3082
Macon, MO 63552-1503
Free: (800)475-3121

Newspaper serving Macon and Shelby counties. **Founded:** 1984. **Freq:** Weekly (Mon.). **Print Method:** Offset. **Trim Size:** 13 3/4 x 22 3/4. **Cols./Page:** 6. **Key Personnel:** Mark Snow, Editor; Bill Hall, Publisher. **Remarks:** Accepts advertising.
Ad Rates: BW: $677.25 **Circ:** Free 11,000
PCI: $5.25

17376 Macon Chronicle-Herald
American Publishing Co.
204 W. Bourke St. Phone: (816)385-3121
PO Box 7 Fax: (816)385-3082
Macon, MO 63552-1503
Free: (800)475-3121

Newspaper. **Founded:** 1910. **Freq:** Tues.-Fri. (eve.). **Print Method:** Offset. **Cols./Page:** 6. **Col. Width:** 24 nonpareils. **Col. Depth:** 301 agate lines. **Key Personnel:** Mark Snow, Editor; Bill Hall, Publisher; Pat Quinly, Advertising/General Mgr. **USPS:** 324-340. **Subscription Rates:** $74.97 individuals; $79 out of area; $80.33 elsewhere. **Remarks:** Accepts advertising.
Ad Rates: GLR: $.50 **Circ:** ‡3,218
4C: $150
SAU: $5.15

MALDEN, pop. 6,096.

SE MO. Dunklin Co. 72 mi. SW of Cape Girardeau. textiles. Cotton industry. Ships stock and cotton. Agriculture.

17377 Delta News-Journal
Delta Publishing
127 W. Main Phone: (573)276-5148
Box 486 Fax: (573)276-3687
Malden, MO 63863
Independent community newspaper. **Founded:** Oct. 1994. **Freq:** Semiweekly. **Print Method:** Offset. **Cols./Page:** 6. **Col. Width:** 26 nonpareils. **Col. Depth:** 301 agate lines. **Key Personnel:** Tim Gage, Editor; Barbara Hill, Publisher; Lorraine Heiser, Assoc. Editor. **Subscription Rates:** $10. **Remarks:** Accepts advertising. **Formerly**: Post Tribune; Delta News-Journal/Malden Press Merit. **Merged with**: The Delta News; Press Merit.
Ad Rates: PCI: $3.64 **Circ:** ‡1,262

17378 KMAL-FM - 92.9
AB Hwy. S. Phone: (573)276-5625
PO Box 379 Fax: (573)276-2282
Malden, MO 63863
E-mail: kmal@sheltonbbs.com

Format: Adult Contemporary; News; Sports. **Networks:** AP. **Owner:** BBC Inc., PO Box 1996, Malden, MO 63863. **Founded:** 1979. **Operating Hours:** Continuous. 5% network; 95% local. **ADI:** Paducah,KY-Cape Girardeau,MO-Marion,IL. **Key Personnel:** Dave Green, General Mgr.; Chuck Sutton, News Dir.; Denise Evans, Traffic Dir.; Sherry Barnes, Sales Mgr.; Steve Conner, Music Dir. **Wattage:** 25,000. **Ad Rates:** $8 for 15 seconds; $10 for 30 seconds; $12 for 60 seconds. KTCB-AM. **URL:** http://www.kmal.com.

17379 KTCB-AM - 1470
AB Hwy. S. Phone: (314)276-5625
PO Box 379 Fax: (314)276-2282
Malden, MO 63863
E-mail: kmal@sheltonbbs.com

Format: Southern Gospel; News. **Networks:** AP. **Owner:** Bootheel Broadcasting Co., at above address. **Founded:** 1954. **Operating Hours:** Sunrise-sunset; 5% network, 95% local. **ADI:** Paducah,KY-Cape Girardeau,MO-Marion,IL. **Key Personnel:** Dave Green, General Mgr.; Chuck Sutton, Music Dir.; Denise Evans, Traffic Dir.; Sherry Barnes, Sales Mgr. **Wattage:** 1000. **Ad Rates:** $4 for 15 seconds; $6 for 30 seconds; $8 for 60 seconds. KMAL-FM. **URL:** http://www.kmal.com.

MANSFIELD, pop. 1,423.

S. MO. Wright Co. 46 mi. SE of Springfield. Shoe manufacturing; cheese plant; steel foundry & fabrication plant. Timber. Diversified farming. Dairying, poultry.

17380 Mirror-Republican
Mansfield Mirror
300 E. Commercial St. Phone: (417)924-3226
Mansfield, MO 65704 Fax: (417)924-3227

Newspaper with a Republican orientation. **Founded:** 1903. **Freq:** Weekly (Thurs.). **Print Method:** Offset. **Cols./Page:** 6. **Col. Width:** 21 nonpareils. **Col. Depth:** 294 agate lines. **Key Personnel:** Larry Dennis, Editor; Dean Devries, Publisher. **Subscription Rates:** $12. **Remarks:** Accepts advertising.
Ad Rates: GLR: $.12 **Circ:** ‡2,300
SAU: $2.45
PCI: $1.90

MARBLE HILL†, pop. 601.

SE MO. Bollinger Co. 30 mi. W. of Cape Girardeau. Manufactures wooden pallets, furniture, textiles. Oak timber. Agriculture. Beef and hogs.

17381 The Banner-Press
103 Walnut St. Phone: (573)238-2821
PO Box 109 Fax: (573)238-0020
Marble Hill, MO 63764
Community newspaper. **Founded:** 1881. **Freq:** Weekly (Thurs.). **Print Method:** Offset. **Cols./Page:** 6. **Col. Width:** 2 inches. **Col. Depth:** 21 1/2 inches. **Key Personnel:** Jackie Sproat, Editor. **ISSN:** 0416-4000. **Subscription Rates:** $17 individuals; $24 out of area; $35 out of state. **Remarks:** Accepts advertising.
Ad Rates: BW: $325 **Circ:** Paid 4,600
PCI: $4.25 Free 16

17382 KMHM-FM - 104.1
Route 1, Box 266E Phone: (573)238-1041
Marble Hill, MO 63764 Fax: (573)238-0104
E-mail: kmhm@clas.net

Format: Southern Gospel. **Owner:** Harold and Carlene Lawder, at above address. **Founded:** 1995. **Former name:** KQUA-FM (1985). **Operating Hours:** Continuous. **Key Personnel:** Doug Apple, General Mgr. **Wattage:** 6000. **Ad Rates:** $8 for 30 seconds; $11 for 60 seconds.

MARCELINE, pop. 2,938.

N. MO. Linn Co. 35 mi. E. of Chillicothe. Printing plants; coal mines. Manufactures fans, storm windows, steel fabrication, meat products. Wheat, corn, livestock.

17383 The Marceline Press
The Liberty Group
PO Box 318 Phone: (660)376-3508
Marceline, MO 64658 Fax: (660)376-2757

Newspaper. **Founded:** 1966. **Freq:** Weekly (Thurs.). **Print Method:** Offset. **Cols./Page:** 6. **Col. Width:** 26 nonpareils. **Col. Depth:** 301 agate lines. **Key Personnel:** Bryan Day, Editor; Ivan R. Buckman, Publisher; Bill Evans, General Mgr., bllevans@aol.com. **Subscription Rates:** $35 individuals. **Remarks:** Accepts advertising.
Ad Rates: SAU: $3 **Circ:** ‡1,712
PCI: $4.25

MARSHALL†, pop. 12,781.

NWC MO. Saline Co. 30 mi. N. of Sedalia. Missouri Valley College. Manufactures shoes, feed. Food processing. Diversified farming. Dairy products. Corn, wheat, soybeans.

17384 The Marshall Democrat-News
121 N. Lafayette Phone: (660)886-2233
Box 100 Fax: (660)886-8544
Marshall, MO 65340-1747
General newspaper. **Founded:** 1879. **Freq:** Daily (eve.). **Print Method:** Offset. **Cols./Page:** 6. **Col. Width:** 24 nonpareils. **Col. Depth:** 301 agate lines. **Key Personnel:** Jason Offutt, Editor. **Subscription Rates:** $77.46 in Marshall; $83.99 in county. **Remarks:** Accepts advertising.
Ad Rates: BW: $857.85 **Circ:** Paid 3,980
4C: $1073.85 Free 8,370
SAU: $6.65
PCI: $5.50

17385 KMMO-AM - 1300
PO Box 128 Phone: (660)886-7422
Marshall, MO 65340 Fax: (660)886-6291
E-mail: kmmo@murlin.com

Format: News; Sports; Contemporary Country; Agricultural. **Simulcasts:** KMMO-FM. **Networks:** CBS; Kansas Information; Brownfield. **Owner:** John Wilson/ Michael Phillips/ Marvin Luehrs, at above address. **Founded:** 1949. **Operating Hours:** Continuous; 10% network, 90% local. **Key Personnel:** John Wilson, Contact; Chuck Morris, Program Dir.; Ken Lewellen, News Dir.; Jim Woods, Music Dir. **Wattage:** 1000. **Ad Rates:** $15 for 30 seconds; $22 for 60 seconds.

17386 KMMO-FM - 102.9
PO Box 128 Phone: (816)886-7422
Marshall, MO 65340 Fax: (816)886-6291

Format: News; Sports; Contemporary Country; Agricultural. **Simulcasts:** KMMO-AM. **Networks:** CBS; Brownfield; Missouri. **Owner:** Michael Phillips, Marvin Luehrs, John A.

Wilson, at above address. **Founded:** 1949. **Operating Hours:** Continuous; 10% network, 90% local. **Key Personnel:** John Wilson, Contact; Chuck Morris, Program Dir.; Ken Lewellen, News Dir.; Jim Woods, Music Dir. **Wattage:** 100,000. **Ad Rates:** $15 for 30 seconds; $22 for 60 seconds. **URL:** http://www.kmmo@murlin.com.

17387 KMVC-FM - 91.7
500 E. College St. Phone: (816)886-6924
Marshall, MO 65340

Format: Alternative/New Music/Progressive; Album-Oriented Rock (AOR); Urban Contemporary. **Networks:** Independent. **Owner:** Missouri Valley College, at above address. **Founded:** 1969. **Formerly:** KMVC-FM (1992); KNOS-FM. **Operating Hours:** 7 a.m.-midnight; 100% local. **Key Personnel:** Wendie Rice, Program Dir.; Karl Bean, Contact; Willy Lehotz, Station Mgr.; Ray Colaiacovo, Music Dir.; Gerry Shrum, Music Dir.; John Martinez, Traffic Dir. **Wattage:** 10. **Ad Rates:** Noncommercial.

17388 Marshall Cable TV Inc.
117 E. Arrow Phone: (816)886-9618
Marshall, MO 65340

Owner: Time Warner Cable, 300 First Stamford Pl., Stamford, CT 06902-6732, (203)328-0600, Fax: (203)328-0690. **Founded:** 1968. **Key Personnel:** Jack Mann, General Mgr.; Linda Chews, Office Mgr.; Ron Lawson, Chief Technician. **Cities Served:** Marshall, MO: subscribing households 4,500; 53 channels; 2 community access channels.

MARSHFIELD†, pop. 3,871.

S. MO. Webster Co. 24 mi. NE of Springfield. Manufactures caskets, textiles, steel fabricated products. Walnut and oak timber. Diversified farming. Poultry, dairy, livestock.

17389 The Country Mailbox
Marshfield Publishing Co., Inc.
211 N. Clay Phone: (417)468-2013
PO Box A Fax: (417)859-7930
Marshfield, MO 65706
Shopping guide. **Subtitle:** The Marshfield Mail (Newspaper) County Mailbox (Shopper). **Founded:** June 18, 1987. **Freq:** Weekly. **Print Method:** Offset. **Cols./Page:** 6. **Col. Width:** 2 inches. **Col. Depth:** 21 inches. **Key Personnel:** Gordon Nordquist, Publisher; Debbie Chapman, Advertising Mgr.; Rollene Gregorie, Bus. Controller; Rod Shelter, Editor. **Subscription Rates:** Free; $12 out of area. **Remarks:** Accepts advertising.
Ad Rates: GLR: $.32 **Circ:** ‡14,500
BW: $560.70 5,500
4C: $735.70
SAU: $4.45

17390 The Marshfield Mail
211 N. Clay Phone: (417)468-2013
PO Box A Fax: (417)859-7930
Marshfield, MO 65706-9613
County newspaper. **Founded:** 1892. **Freq:** Weekly (Wed.). **Print Method:** Offset. **Cols./Page:** 6. **Col. Width:** 2 inches. **Col. Depth:** 21 inches. **Key Personnel:** Gordon E. Nordquist, Publisher; Debbie Chapman, Advertising Mgr.; Rod Shelter, Managing Editor. **USPS:** 331-080. **Subscription Rates:** $25 individuals. **Remarks:** Accepts advertising.
Ad Rates: GLR: $.25 **Circ:** Paid 5,500
BW: $529.20
4C: $704.20
SAU: $4.20
PCI: $4

MARTHASVILLE, pop. 543.

E. MO. Warren Co. On Missouri River, 30 mi. SW of Saint Charles. Lumber mill; hat factory. Timber. Stock, poultry, dairy, grain farms. Wheat, corn, oats, soybeans.

17391 The Marthasville Record
203 W. South St. Phone: (314)433-2223
PO Box 77
Marthasville, MO 63357
Local newspaper. **Founded:** Dec. 1896. **Freq:** Weekly (Thurs.). **Print Method:** Offset. **Trim Size:** 17 1/2 x 22. **Cols./Page:** 7. **Col. Width:** 13 picas. **Col. Depth:** 21 inches. **Key Personnel:** Rueben Eichmeyer, Editor and Publisher; Mabel Eichmeyer, Editor and Publisher. **USPS:** 331-200. **Subscription Rates:** $18.50; $20.65 out of area. **Remarks:** Accepts advertising.
Ad Rates: GLR: $0.36 **Circ:** ‡784
BW: $740.88
SAU: $5.04
PCI: $5.04

MARYVILLE†, pop. 9,558.

NW MO. Nodaway Co. 45 mi. N. of Saint Joseph. Northwest Missouri State University. Manufactures lightning rods, paper products, auto chains, batteries, rivets, tools. Grain, dairy, stock, poultry farms. Corn, wheat, soybeans.

17392 The Laurel Review (Maryville)
GreenTower Press
Department of English Phone: (816)562-1265
Northwest Missouri State Fax: (660)562-1731
University
Maryville, MO 64468
Publisher E-mail: u0500025@acad.nwmissouri.edu

Literary magazine covering poetry, fiction and nonfiction. **Founded:** 1960. **Freq:** Semiannual. **Cols./Page:** 1. **Key Personnel:** Beth Richards, Editor; David Slater, Editor, slater@mail.nwmissouri.edu; William Trowbridge, Editor. **Subscription Rates:** $8 individuals; $16 two years. **Remarks:** Accepts advertising.
Ad Rates: BW: $80 **Circ:** Controlled 700

17393 Maryville Daily Forum
111 E. Jenkins Phone: (660)562-2424
PO Box 188 Fax: (660)562-2823
Maryville, MO 64468
Free: (888)660-2424
Publication E-mail: dailyforum@msc-net.con
Publisher E-mail: mdforum@asde.com

Newspaper. **Founded:** 1869. **Freq:** Tues-Fri, and Sunday morning. **Print Method:** Offset. Uses mats. **Trim Size:** 6 x 21 1/2. **Key Personnel:** Jerry Pye, Publisher. **USPS:** 332-360. **Subscription Rates:** $66. **Remarks:** Accepts advertising.
Ad Rates: BW: $75 **Circ:** ‡3,983
4C: $215
SAU: $5.95
PCI: $5.95

17394 Northwest Missourian
Northwest Missouri State University
7-8 Wells Hall Phone: (816)562-1224
800 University Dr. Fax: (816)562-1521
Maryville, MO 64468
Publication E-mail: missourian@mail.nwmissouri.edu

College/Community newspaper. **Subtitle:** Northwest Missourian. **Founded:** 1918. **Freq:** Weekly (Thurs.). **Print Method:** Offset. **Trim Size:** 13 x 21. **Cols./Page:** 6. **Col. Width:** 26 nonpareils. **Col. Depth:** 126 agate lines. **Key Personnel:** Ken Wilkie, Business Mgr., phone (660)562-1530; Kyle Nieman, Advertising Dir., phone (660)562-1635. **Subscription Rates:** $26. **Remarks:** Accepts advertising. **Available Online. URL:** http://www.nwmissouri.edu/missourian/.
Ad Rates: BW: $693 **Circ:** 8,000
4C: $853
SAU: $4
PCI: $3.70

17395 Penny Press 2
Maverick Media, Inc.
115 E. 4th St. Phone: (816)582-4015
PO Box 658 Fax: (816)582-3108
Maryville, MO 64468
Shopper (tabloid). **Founded:** Feb. 1977. **Freq:** Weekly (Tues.). **Print Method:** Offset. **Trim Size:** 11 1/2 x 16. **Cols./Page:** 6. **Col. Width:** 9 1/2 picas. **Col. Depth:** 15 inches. **Key Personnel:** William Welsh, President. **Subscription Rates:** $24 individuals. **Remarks:** Accepts advertising.
Ad Rates: GLR: $.54 **Circ:** ‡19,100
BW: $684
4C: $829
SAU: $9.77
PCI: $8.60

17396 Weekly Bargain Shopper
Maryville Daily Forum
111 E. Jenkins Phone: (660)562-2424
PO Box 188 Fax: (660)562-2823
Maryville, MO 64468
Free: (888)660-2424
Publication E-mail: dailyforum@msc-net.com
Publisher E-mail: mdforum@asde.com

Shopper. **Founded:** 1971. **Freq:** Weekly (Tues.). **Print Method:** 5 x 13. **Key Personnel:** Dirk Allsbury, Editor; Jerry Pye, Publisher. **Subscription Rates:** $4.50; $1.90 pick up rate from daily. **Remarks:** Accepts advertising. **Formerly:** Country.
Ad Rates: BW: $75 **Circ:** Free ‡11,500
4C: $215
SAU: $6.15
PCI: $5.95

17397 KDLX-FM - 106.7
800 University Dr. Phone: (816)562-1165
Maryville, MO 64468 Fax: (816)562-1832
E-mail: kdlx@mail.nwmissouri.edu

Format: Alternative/New Music/Progressive. **Owner:** Northwest Missouri State University, at above address, (660)562-1832, Fax: (660)562-1832. **Founded:** 1960. **Operating Hours:** Mon.- Fri. 7a.m. to 1a.m.; Sat.- Sun. 9a.m. to 1a.m. **Key Personnel:** Neal Dunker, Station Mgr., s210005@mail.nwmisssouri.edu. **Local Programs:** *Brave New World*, Pat Redd, (816)562-1165, Fax (816)562-1832; *The Flip-Side*, Pat Redd, (816)562-1165, Fax (816)562-1832; *The Nooner*, Pat Redd, (816)562-1165, Fax (816)562-1832. **Wattage:** Cable. **Ad Rates:** Noncommercial. $4.25 for 30 seconds. **URL:** http://www.nwmissouri.edu/~kdlx.

17398 KXCV-FM - 90.5
800 University Dr. Phone: (660)562-1163
Northwest Missouri State Fax: (660)562-1832
University
Maryville, MO 64468
E-mail: kxcv@mail.nwmissouri.edu

Format: Public Radio; Jazz; News; Classical; Big Band/Nostalgia. **Networks:** Public Radio International (PRI); National Public Radio (NPR). **Owner:** Northwest Missouri State University, at above address. **Founded:** 1971. **Operating Hours:** 21 hrs. Daily; 51% network, 49% local. **Key Personnel:** Gayle Hull, Contact, ghull@mail.nwmissouri.edu; Marcia Fish, Contact, mfish@mail.nwmissouri.edu; John McGuire, News Dir., jmcguir@mail.nwmissouri.edu; Patty Andrews Holley, Production Mgr., pholley@mail.nwmissouri.edi; Sharon Bonnett, Manager, phone (660)562-1163, fax (660)562-1832, kxcv@mail.nwmissouri.edu; Charles Maley, Engineer, cmaley@mail.nwmissouri.edu. **Local Programs:** *Big Band* 9:00 am - 12:00 noon Monday-Friday, Patty Holley, Operations Mgr. **Wattage:** 100,000. **Ad Rates:** Noncommercial.

MAYSVILLE, pop. 1,187.

NW MO. DeKalb Co. 35 mi. E. of Saint Joseph. Diversified farming. Corn, wheat, soybeans, livestock.

17399 DeKalb County Record-Herald
PO Box 98 Phone: (816)449-2121
Maysville, MO 64469 Fax: (816)449-2808

Community newspaper. **Founded:** June 3, 1866. **Freq:** Weekly (Wed.). **Print Method:** Offset. **Cols./Page:** 6. **Col. Width:** 2 1/16 inches. **Col. Depth:** 294 agate lines. **Key Personnel:** Terry L. Pearl. Editor and Publisher. **Subscription Rates:** $16; $18 out of area; $20 out of state. **Remarks:** Accepts advertising.
Ad Rates: PCI: $3 **Circ:** Paid 18,000

MEMPHIS

17400 Memphis Democrat
Democrat
121 S. Main St. Phone: (816)465-7016
Memphis, MO 63555 Fax: (816)465-2803
Publication E-mail: memdemocrat@vax2.rainis.net

Community newspaper. **Freq:** Weekly (Thurs.). **Cols./Page:** 8. **Col. Width:** 10 1/2 picas. **Col. Depth:** 21 inches. **Key Personnel:** Chris Feeney, Editor; Tom Ellingsworth, Publisher. **Subscription Rates:** $21.30 individuals. **Remarks:** Accepts advertising.
Ad Rates: BW: $472.50 **Circ:** 2,400
SAU: $3.75
PCI: $3.75

17401 KMEM-FM - 100.5
PO Box 121 Phone: (660)465-7225
Memphis, MO 63555 Fax: (660)465-2626
Free: (800)748-7875

Format: Country. **Networks:** ABC; Brownfield. **Owner:** Boyer Broadcasting Co., at above address. **Founded:** Apr. 1982. **Operating Hours:** 5 a.m.-12 a.m. **Key Personnel:** Denise Bayer Watson, General Mgr.; Cindy Graber, Traffic Mgr.; Rick Fischer, News Dir. **Wattage:** 25,000. **Ad Rates:** $5.40-13 for 30 seconds; $8.70-18 for 60 seconds.

MEXICO†, pop. 12,276.

NEC MO. Audrain Co. 38 mi. E. of Moberly. Missouri Military Academy. Manufactures shoes, fire-clay products, bank and newspaper supplies, feed bags. Fire-clay pits. Agriculture. Corn, wheat, soybeans. Livestock.

17402 The Mexico Ledger
PO Box 8 Phone: (314)581-1111
Mexico, MO 65265-0008 Fax: (314)581-2029
Publisher E-mail: mexicoledger@amail.itswebs.com

Newspaper with a Democratic orientation. **Founded:** 1855. **Freq:** Mon.-Sat. (eve.). **Print Method:** Offset. **Cols./Page:** 6. **Col. Width:** 21 1/2 nonpareils. **Col. Depth:** 301 agate lines. **Key Personnel:** Joe A. May, Publisher,

jmay@mial.itwebs.com. **Subscription Rates:** $102 individuals. **Remarks:** Accepts advertising. **Alt. Formats:** Microform.
Ad Rates: BW: $1,354.50 **Circ:** Mon.-Sat. ★**8,041**
4C: $1,619.50
SAU: $10.50

17403 KJAB-FM - 88.3
621 W. Monroe Phone: (573)581-8606
Mexico, MO 65265 Fax: (573)581-8606
Free: (800)371-5522
E-mail: kjab@ktis.net

Format: Southern Gospel; Talk. **Networks:** USA Radio. **Owner:** Mexico Educational Broadcasting Foundation, at above address. **Founded:** 1986. **Operating Hours:** Continuous; 8% network, 92% local. **Key Personnel:** Kevin Weber, General Mgr.; Daryl Kline, Program Dir.; Dawn Weber, Office Mgr. **Local Programs:** *Sunrise Show*, Nathan Rush. **Wattage:** 6,000. **Ad Rates:** Noncommercial. **URL:** http://www.kjab.com.

17404 KWWR-FM - 95.7
1705 E. Liberty St. Phone: (573)581-5500
PO Box 475 Fax: (573)581-1801
Mexico, MO 65265-0475
Free: (800)264-5997
E-mail: country96@country96.com

Format: Country; News; Agricultural. **Networks:** Mutual Broadcasting System. **Owner:** KXEO Radio, Inc., PO Box 475, Mexico, MO 65265. **Founded:** 1966. **Operating Hours:** Continuous. **ADI:** Columbia-Jefferson City, MO. **Key Personnel:** Gary Leonard, General Mgr.; Kent Morgan, Sales Mgr.; Anne Johnson, Owner; Greg Holman, Program Dir. **Wattage:** 100,000. **Ad Rates:** $7.65-22.35 for 30 seconds; $12.35-35.29 for 60 seconds.

17405 KXEO-AM - 1340
1705 E. Liberty Phone: (573)581-2340
PO Box 475 Fax: (573)581-1801
Mexico, MO 65265
E-mail: kxeo@sockets.net

Format: News; Sports; Agricultural; Adult Contemporary. **Networks:** Mutual Broadcasting System; Brownfield; Missouri. **Owner:** KXEO Radio, Inc., at above address. **Founded:** 1948. **Operating Hours:** Continuous; 5% network, 95% local. **Key Personnel:** Anne Johnson, President; Gary Leonard, General Mgr.; Greg Holman, Program Dir. **Wattage:** 1000. **Ad Rates:** $6.18-14.71 for 30 seconds; $10-23.53 for 60 seconds.

MILAN†, pop. 1,947.

N. MO. Sullivan Co. 60 mi. NW of Moberly. Hunting, fishing. Frozen food processing. Stock, dairy, grain farms. Corn, soybeans.

17406 The Milan Standard
PO Box 266 Phone: (816)265-3322
Milan, MO 63556-0266
Publisher E-mail: milanstd@nemr.net

Community newspaper. **Founded:** Feb. 1872. **Freq:** Weekly (Thurs.). **Print Method:** Offset. **Trim Size:** 7 x 11. **Cols./Page:** 6. **Col. Width:** 12 1/8 picas. **Col. Depth:** 301 agate lines. **Key Personnel:** Robert W. Wilson, Editor and Publisher; David T. Wilson, Advertising Mgr. **USPS:** 348-620. **Subscription Rates:** $20; $23 out of area; $25 out of state. **Remarks:** Accepts advertising.
Ad Rates: GLR: $.315 **Circ:** ‡4,055
BW: $567.60
SAU: $4.40

MILLER

17407 The Miller Press
Vedette Newspaper
PO Box 236 Phone: (417)452-3792
Miller, MO 65707 Fax: (417)637-2232

Community newspaper. **Founded:** 1956. **Freq:** Weekly (Thurs.). **Cols./Page:** 6. **Col. Width:** 2 inches. **Col. Depth:** 21 inches. **Key Personnel:** Marlene DeClue, Editor, phone (417)637-2712. **Subscription Rates:** $21.50; $29.95 out of state. **Remarks:** Accepts advertising.
Ad Rates: 4C: $160 **Circ:** 525
PCI: $3.85

MOBERLY, pop. 13,418.

NC MO. Randolph Co. 36 mi. N. of Columbia. Moberly Junior College. Manufactures shoes, tools, sirups, cheese and other dairy products; hay presses. Coal mines. Diversified farming. Poultry.

17408 KWIX-AM - 1230
300 W. Reed Phone: (816)263-1500
Moberly, MO 65270 Fax: (816)263-2300
Free: (800)892-2300

Format: Full Service. **Networks:** CBS. **Founded:** 1950. **Formerly:** KNCM-AM (1963). **Operating Hours:** Continuous; 50% network, 50% local. **Key Personnel:** David Shepherd, General Mgr.; Ken Kujawa, Program Dir.; Jim Coyle, Contact; Doug Stewart, News Dir.; Brad Boyer, Sports Dir. **Wattage:** 1000. **Ad Rates:** $8-18 for 30 seconds.

17409 KZZT-FM - 105.5
Jct. of Hwy. 63 & Rte. EE. Phone: (660)263-9390
PO Box 128 Fax: (660)263-8800
Moberly, MO 65270
E-mail: kzzt@mcmsys.com

Format: Oldies. **Networks:** ABC. **Owner:** FM-105, Inc., at above address. **Founded:** 1987. **Operating Hours:** Continuous. **ADI:** Columbia-Jefferson City, MO. **Key Personnel:** Dale Palmer, General Mgr., phone (660)258-3383, fax (660)250-7307, kzbk@shighway.com; Amy Aleshire, Operations Mgr. **Local Programs:** *Afternoon Express*, Corey Curtis, Host; *Doug D. Morning Show*, Doug Ducich, Host. **Wattage:** 25,000 ERP. **Ad Rates:** $5-18 for 30 seconds; $7.50-27 for 60 seconds.

MONETT, pop. 6,148.

SW MO. Barry and Lawrence Co. 45 mi. Se of Joplin. Manufactures shoes, textiles, aluminum doors and windows, heavy conveyor equipment. Milk, cheese and poultry processing plants. Dairy, fruit & truck farms. Strawberries, apples, tomatoes.

17410 Monett Times
Monett Newspapers, Inc.
505 E. Broadway St. Phone: (417)235-3135
Monett, MO 65708-2333
Newspaper with a Republican orientation. **Founded:** 1908. **Freq:** Daily (eve.). **Print Method:** Offset. **Trim Size:** 22 3/4 x 28. **Cols./Page:** 6. **Col. Width:** 2 1/16 inches. **Col. Depth:** 21 1/2 inches. **Key Personnel:** Stephen L. Crass, Editor and Publisher. **Subscription Rates:** $40. **Remarks:** Accepts advertising.
Ad Rates: SAU: $4.20 **Circ:** (Not Reported)

17411 KKBL-FM - 95.9
1569 N. Central Phone: (417)235-6041
Monett, MO 65708 Fax: (417)235-6388
Free: (800)928-5253
E-mail: webmaster@kromkkbl.com

Format: Contemporary Hit Radio (CHR). **Networks:** Westwood One Radio. **Founded:** 1977. **Operating Hours:** Continuous. **Key Personnel:** Kevin Gunter, PD, kb@kamokkbl.com. **Wattage:** 6000. **Ad Rates:** $8-9 for 30 seconds. Combined advertising rates available with KRMO-AM.

17412 KRMO-AM - 990
1569 N. Central Phone: (417)235-6041
Monett, MO 65708 Fax: (417)235-6388
Free: (800)928-5253
E-mail: webmaster@krmokkbl.com

Format: Country; News. **Networks:** ABC; Brownfield. **Founded:** 1950. **Operating Hours:** Continuous. **Key Personnel:** Kevin Wodlinger, Contact; Patricia Wodlinger, Contact. **Wattage:** 2500. **Ad Rates:** $8-9 for 30 seconds.

MONROE CITY, pop. 2,557.

NE MO. 20 mi. SW of Hannibal. Die casting and radio supply factories. Timber. Diversified farming. Corn, wheat, oats.

17413 Mark Twain Regional News
Liberty Group Publishing Co.
106 N. Main St. Phone: (573)735-4538
PO Box 187 Fax: (573)735-4020
Monroe City, MO 63456
Free: (800)675-5670
Publication E-mail: mcnews@nemonet.com

Shopper. **Subtitle:** Free Distribution Newspaper. **Founded:** Aug. 1982. **Freq:** Weekly (Mon.). **Print Method:** Offset. **Cols./Page:** 6. **Col. Width:** 12 picas. **Col. Depth:** 21 1/2 inches. **Key Personnel:** David Ruble, Editor and Publisher. **Subscription Rates:** Free. **Remarks:** Accepts advertising. **Formerly:** Mark Twain Area Shopper (Mar. 23, 1988).
Ad Rates: SAU: $7 **Circ:** Free ‡15,500

17414 Monroe City News
Liberty Group Publishing Co.
106 N. Main St. Phone: (573)735-4538
PO Box 187 Fax: (573)735-4020
Monroe City, MO 63456
Free: (800)675-5670
Publication E-mail: mcnews@nemonet.com

Newspaper with a Democratic orientation. **Founded:** 1875. **Freq:** Weekly (Thurs.). **Print Method:** Offset. **Cols./Page:** 6. **Col. Depth:** 21 1/2 inches. **Key Personnel:** David Ruble, Editor and Publisher. **USPS:** 359-200. **Subscription Rates:** $32.02. **Remarks:** Accepts advertising.
Ad Rates: BW: $483.75 **Circ:** ‡1,500
SAU: $3.75

MONTGOMERY CITY†, pop. 2,101.

E. MO. Montgomery Co. 60 mi. NE of Saint Charles. Feed manufacturing. Fire clay mines. Foundry. Fertilizer plant. Dairy, stock, poultry, grain farms. Wheat, corn, oats, beans.

17415 KMCR-FM - 103.9
405 E. Norman Phone: (314)564-2275
Montgomery City, MO 63361 Fax: (314)564-2275
Free: (800)769-5105

Format: Adult Contemporary. **Owner:** Chirillo Electronics, Inc., PO Box 128, Moberly, MO 65270, (816)263-9390, Fax: (816)263-8800. **Founded:** 1977. **Formerly:** KVCM-FM; KOMC-FM. **Operating Hours:** Continuous. **Key Personnel:** Dale A. Palmer, Gen. and Sales Mgr.; Cory Curtis, Program and News Dir.; Amy Aleshire, Business Mgr.; Cory Curtis, Music Dir.; Alan West, Engineer. **Wattage:** 3300. **Ad Rates:** $7.50-18 for 30 seconds; $11.25-27 for 60 seconds.

MOUND CITY, pop. 1,447.

NW MO. Holt Co. 30 mi. N. of Saint Joseph. Stock and grain farms. Corn, wheat, soybeans.

17416 Mound City News
511 State St. Phone: (660)442-5423
PO Box 175 Fax: (660)442-5423
Mound City, MO 64470
Publication E-mail: vcbolt@msc.net

Community newspaper. **Founded:** 1879. **Freq:** Weekly (Thurs.). **Print Method:** Offset. **Cols./Page:** 6. **Col. Width:** 24 nonpareils. **Col. Depth:** 301 agate lines. **Key Personnel:** Chris Boultinghouse, Publisher; Linda Boultinghouse, Publisher. **USPS:** 364-920. **Subscription Rates:** $22 individuals; $24 out of area; $27 out of state. **Remarks:** Accepts advertising. **Formerly:** News-Independent.
Ad Rates: SAU: $5 **Circ:** 2,600
PCI: $5

MOUNT VERNON†, pop. 3,341.

SW MO. Lawrence Co. 30 mi. W. of Springfield. Cheese manufacturer. Trucking. Diversified farming. Dairy. Cattle.

17417 Lawrence County Record
Lawrence County Record, Inc.
312 S. Hickory Phone: (417)466-2185
PO Box 348 Fax: (417)466-7865
Mount Vernon, MO 65712
Newspaper with a Democratic orientation. **Founded:** 1868. **Freq:** Weekly (Wed.). **Print Method:** Offset. **Cols./Page:** 6. **Col. Width:** 12 picas. **Col. Depth:** 21 1/2 inches. **Key Personnel:** Kathy Fairchild, Editor and Publisher; Steve Fairchild, Publisher; Rosemary Hailey, Advertising Mgr. **USPS:** 306-500. **Subscription Rates:** $16.50 individuals; $24 out of area. **Remarks:** Accepts advertising. **Formerly:** The Record (1990).
Ad Rates: GLR: $.15 **Circ:** Paid ‡3,500
SAU: $3.40 Free ‡3,200

MOUNTAIN GROVE, pop. 3,974.

S. MO. Wright Co. 60 mi. SE of Springfield. Manufactures lumber, shoes, and wood products. Missouri Fruit and Poultry Experiment Stations. Timber. Agriculture. Dairy products and poultry.

17418 News Journal
PO Box 530 Phone: (417)926-5148
Mountain Grove, MO 65711 Fax: (417)926-6648
Publication E-mail: newsjrnl@cmaster.com

Newspaper with a Republican orientation. **Founded:** 1926. **Freq:** Weekly. **Print Method:** Offset. Uses mats. **Cols./Page:** 6. **Col. Width:** 21 nonpareils. **Col. Depth:** 294 agate lines. **Key Personnel:** Doug Berger, Editor; Dean DeVries, Publish-

er. **Subscription Rates:** $18 individuals; $22.31 out of area; $27 out of state. **Remarks:** Accepts advertising.
Ad Rates: BW: $604.80 **Circ:** 3,800
4C: $804.80
SAU: $4.80

17419 KELE-AM - 1360
800 N. Hubbard Phone: (417)926-4650
Mountain Grove, MO 65711 Fax: (417)926-7604
E-mail: kele@windo.missouri.org

Format: Contemporary Christian; Talk. **Networks:** ABC; Brownfield; USA Radio. **Owner:** Communications Works, Inc., at above address, Fax: (417)926-7605. **Founded:** 1958. **Formerly:** KLRS-AM (1991); KRFI-AM; KCMG-AM. **Operating Hours:** Continuous; 80% network, 20% local. **ADI:** Springfield, MO. **Key Personnel:** Rick Jesse, General Mgr., phone (417)926-4650, fax (417)926-7604. **Wattage:** 1000. **Ad Rates:** $4 for 30 seconds; $8 for 60 seconds. Combined advertising rates available with KELE-FM.

17420 KELE-FM - 92.5
800 N. Hubbard Phone: (417)926-4650
Box 1360 Fax: (417)926-7604
Mountain Grove, MO 65711
E-mail: kele@windo.missouri.org

Format: Country. **Networks:** ABC; Missouri; Brownfield. **Owner:** Communication Works, Inc., at above address. **Founded:** 1958. **Formerly:** KLRS-FM; KRFI-FM; KCMG-FM. **Operating Hours:** Continuous; 60% network, 40% local. **Key Personnel:** Mike Mayfield, Contact; Rick Jesse, General Mgr. **Wattage:** 6000. **Ad Rates:** $4 for 30 seconds; $8 for 60 seconds. Combined advertising rates available with KELE-AM.

MOUNTAIN VIEW, pop. 2,000.

NE MO. Howell Co. 20 mi. NNE of West Plains.

17421 Standard News
PO Box 52 Phone: (417)934-2025
Mountain View, MO 65548-0052 Fax: (417)934-6481

Community newspaper covering three county area. **Freq:** Weekly (Wed.). **Key Personnel:** Tom Olson, Editor; Brian Hood, Publisher. **Subscription Rates:** $15 three county area; $22 out of area; $25 out of state. **Remarks:** Advertising accepted; rates available upon request.
Circ: (Not Reported)

NEOSHO†, pop. 9,493.

SW MO. Newton Co. 20 mi. SE of Joplin. Manufactures canned milk, footwear, trailers, concrete, metal products, butter, furniture, feed, industrial gases. Summer resort. Nurseries; fish hatcheries. Agriculture. Grain.

17422 Neosho Daily News
1006 W. Harmony Phone: (417)451-1520
Neosho, MO 64850 Fax: (417)451-6408

Newspaper with an Independent Orientation. **Founded:** Feb. 1905. **Freq:** Daily (eve.). **Print Method:** Offset. **Cols./Page:** 6. **Col. Width:** 25 nonpareils. **Col. Depth:** 301 agate lines. **Key Personnel:** Valerie Praytor, Publisher; Christen Jackson, Editor. **USPS:** 377-100. **Subscription Rates:** $89 per year. **Remarks:** Accepts advertising.
Ad Rates: BW: $1,012.65 **Circ:** Paid 5,100
4C: $1,162.65 Wed. 7,800
PCI: $7.85

17423 KBTN-AM - 1420
216 W. Spring Phone: (417)451-1420
PO Box K Fax: (417)451-2526
Neosho, MO 64850

Format: Country. **Simulcasts:** KBIN-FM. **Networks:** ABC; Satellite Music Network. **Owner:** David Winegardner, at above address. **Founded:** 1954. **Operating Hours:** 5 a.m.-midnight Mon-Sat; 6 a.m.-midnight Sun. **Key Personnel:** David Winegardner, General Mgr.; Gail Johnson, Sales Mgr.; Todd Duke, News Dir. **Wattage:** 1000. **Ad Rates:** $8.50 for 30 seconds; $14.45 for 60 seconds.

17424 KBTN-FM - 99.7
216 W. Spring Phone: (417)451-1420
PO Box K Fax: (417)451-2526
Neosho, MO 64850

Format: Country. **Simulcasts:** KBIN-AM. **Networks:** ABC; Satellite Music Network. **Owner:** David Winegardner, at above address. **Founded:** 1995. **Operating Hours:** Continuous. **Key Personnel:** David Winegardner, General Mgr.; Gail Johnson, Sales Mgr.; Todd Duke, News Dir. **Wattage:** 6000. **Ad Rates:** $8.50 for 30 seconds; $14.45 for 60 seconds.

17425 KNEO-FM - 91.7
10827 Hwy. 86 East Phone: (417)451-5636
Neosho, MO 64850

Format: Gospel; Country. **Networks:** USA Radio; Moody Broadcasting; SkyLight Satellite; Ambassador Inspirational Radio. **Owner:** Abundant Lef Educational Broadcasting, at above address. **Founded:** 1986. **Operating Hours:** Continuous. **Key Personnel:** Mark Taylor, Contact. **Local Programs:** *Authors Corner, Christian Sportsman, New Gospel, Picks of the Past.* **Wattage:** 2760. **Ad Rates:** Noncommercial.

NEVADA†, pop. 9,044.

W. MO. Vernon Co. 100 mi. S. of Kansas City. Manufactures plumbing supplies, air filters, adhesives, tents, sheet metal, farm machinery. Crude oil wells; asphalt, coal mines. Diversified farming. Corn, wheat, oats, soybeans. Milo, cattle, hogs.

17426 Nevada Daily Mail
Nevada Publishing Co.
131 S. Cedar Phone: (417)667-3344
PO Box 247 Fax: (417)667-8121
Nevada, MO 64772
Newspaper with a Democratic orientation. **Founded:** 1883. **Freq:** Daily (eve.). **Print Method:** Offset. **Cols./Page:** 6. **Col. Width:** 24 nonpareils. **Col. Depth:** 301 agate lines. **Key Personnel:** Tom Larimer, Publisher; Larry McDonald, Advertising Dir.; Jerry Curry, Editor. **Subscription Rates:** $72.50 individuals. **Remarks:** Accepts advertising.
Ad Rates: SAU: $8 **Circ:** ‡4,500
PCI: $8

17427 Nevada Herald
Nevada Publishing Co.
131 S. Cedar Phone: (417)667-3344
PO Box 247 Fax: (417)667-8121
Nevada, MO 64772
Newspaper with a Republican orientation. **Founded:** 1883. **Freq:** Weekly (Sun.). **Print Method:** Offset. **Cols./Page:** 6. **Col. Width:** 24 nonpareils. **Col. Depth:** 301 agate lines. **Key Personnel:** Tom Larimer, Publisher; Larry McDonald, Advertising Dir.; Jerry Curry, Editor. **USPS:** 595-980. **Subscription Rates:** $76 individuals. **Remarks:** Accepts advertising.
Ad Rates: SAU: $8 **Circ:** ‡4,800

17428 KNEM-AM - 1240
Box 447 Phone: (417)667-3113
Nevada, MO 64772 Fax: (417)667-9797

Format: Country. **Simulcasts:** KNMO-FM. **Networks:** ABC; Brownfield; Missouri. **Owner:** Harbit Communications, LLC, at above address. **Founded:** 1949. **Operating Hours:** 5:30 a.m.-11 p.m. **ADI:** Joplin, MO-Pittsburg, KS. **Key Personnel:** Mike Harbit, General Mgr.; Susan Thompson, Operations Mgr.; Russ Warren, News Dir. **Wattage:** 1000 ERP. **Ad Rates:** $6.45-8.85 for 30 seconds; $10.75-14.75 for 60 seconds.

17429 KNMO-FM - 97.7
Box 447 Phone: (417)667-3113
Nevada, MO 64772 Fax: (417)667-9797

Format: Country. **Simulcasts:** KNEM-AM. **Networks:** ABC; Brownfield; Missouri. **Owner:** Harbit Communications, Inc., at above address. **Founded:** 1983. **Operating Hours:** 5:30 a.m.-midnight; 5% network, 95% local. **ADI:** Joplin, MO-Pittsburg, KS. **Key Personnel:** Mike Harbit, General Mgr.; Susan Thompson, Operations Mgr.; Russ Warren, News Dir. **Wattage:** 3000 ERP. **Ad Rates:** $6.45-8.85 for 30 seconds; $10.75-14.75 for 60 seconds.

NEW HAVEN, pop. 1,581.

E. MO. Franklin Co. On Missouri River, 50 mi. E. of Jefferson City. Canvas product factories; feed mills. Nursery. Diversified farming. Wheat, corn, hay.

17430 New Haven Leader
Spirit Newspapers of Missouri, Inc.
403 Charles Cook Plaza Phone: (573)237-3222
PO Box 168 Fax: (573)237-7222
New Haven, MO 63068
Publication E-mail: leader@fidnet.com

Community newspaper. **Founded:** 1894. **Freq:** Weekly (Wed.). **Print Method:** Offset. **Trim Size:** 14 x 22 5/8. **Cols./Page:** 6. **Col. Width:** 24 nonpareils. **Col. Depth:** 301 agate lines. **Key Personnel:** Steve Roth, Editor. **USPS:** 379-780. **Subscription Rates:** $20 individuals; $30 out of area; $40 out of state. **Remarks:** Accepts advertising.
Ad Rates: BW: $483.75 **Circ:** ‡1,300
SAU: $4
PCI: $4

NEW LONDON†, pop. 1,161.

NE MO. Ralls Co. 18 mi. S. of Palmyra. Residential.

17431 Ralls County Herald-Enterprise
PO Box 426 Phone: (573)985-5531
New London, MO 63459 Fax: (573)985-5531
Publication E-mail: heraldent@nemonet.com

Community newspaper. **Founded:** 1866. **Freq:** Weekly (Thurs.). **Print Method:** Offset. **Cols./Page:** 6. **Col. Width:** 2 inches. **Col. Depth:** 21.5 inches. **Key Personnel:** Judith Statler, Publisher; Gene Statler, Publisher; Gene A. Statler, Editor. **Subscription Rates:** $18 individuals; $24 out of area. **Remarks:** Accepts advertising.
Ad Rates: SAU: $4 **Circ:** ‡1,300
PCI: $3

NEW MADRID†, pop. 3,204.

SE MO. New Madrid Co. On Mississippi River, 50 mi. S. of Cape Girardeau. Manufactures concrete, feed, aluminium, textiles, modular homes. Oak, hickory, cottonwood timber. Stock, grain, cotton, beans, corn, wheat.

17432 The Weekly Record
218 Main St. Phone: (573)748-2120
New Madrid, MO 63869-1997 Fax: (573)748-2120

Newspaper with a Democratic orientation. **Founded:** 1866. **Freq:** Weekly (Fri.). **Print Method:** Offset. **Cols./Page:** 6. **Col. Width:** 2 1/16 inches. **Col. Depth:** 21 inches. **Key Personnel:** Clement Cravens, Editor and Publisher; Heidi Cravens, Editor and Publisher. **USPS:** 672-980. **Subscription Rates:** $18.50 individuals; $21.50 out of area; $25 out of state. **Remarks:** Accepts advertising.
Ad Rates: GLR: $.60 **Circ:** ‡1150
BW: $409.50
SAU: $3.25

NEWBURG

17433 Newburg Cable TV System
Box K Phone: (314)762-2315
Newburg, MO 65550 Fax: (573)762-3704

Founded: 1968. **Key Personnel:** Tim Delong, Manager, phone (573)762-2547. **Cities Served:** subscribing households 250; 12 channels.

NORBORNE, pop. 931.

NWC MO. Carroll Co. 60 mi. E. of Kansas City. Ships grain, livestock. Corn, wheat, soybeans.

17434 Norborne Democrat-Leader
106 S. Pine St.
Box 195
Norborne, MO 64668

Newspaper with a Democratic orientation. **Founded:** 1900. **Freq:** Weekly (Thurs.). **Print Method:** Letterpress and offset. **Cols./Page:** 6. **Col. Width:** 21 nonpareils. **Col. Depth:** 126 agate lines. **Key Personnel:** Margaret A. Brown, General Mgr. **Subscription Rates:** $13.87; $15 out of area. **Remarks:** Accepts advertising.
Ad Rates: GLR: $.11 **Circ:** ‡1,350
BW: $327.60
SAU: $2.60

OAK GROVE, pop. 4,067.

W. MO. Jackson and Lafayette Co. 28 mi. SE of Kansas City. Agriculture. Corn, wheat, oats.

17435 Town & Country News
Oak Grove Publications, Inc.
PO Box 838 Phone: (816)690-4126
Oak Grove, MO 64075 Fax: (816)690-6026

Shopper. **Print Method:** Offset. **Cols./Page:** 8. **Col. Width:** 9 picas. **Col. Depth:** 21 1/2 inches. **Key Personnel:** Judy McKerlie, General Mgr., tansc@qni.com.
Ad Rates: BW: $1,307.20 **Circ:** Controlled 28,650
4C: $1,484.55
PCI: $9.40

ODESSA, pop. 3,088.

W. MO. Lafayette Co. 25 mi. SE of Independence. Residential. Manufactures shoes. Livestock farms.

17436 The Odessan
PO Box 80 Phone: (816)230-5311
204 W. Mason Fax: (816)230-5313
Odessa, MO 64076
Community newspaper. **Founded:** 1880. **Freq:** Weekly (Thurs.). **Print Method:** Offset. **Cols./Page:** 6. **Col. Width:** 24 nonpareils. **Col. Depth:** 301 agate lines. **Key Personnel:** Betty S. Spaar, Editor and Publisher, spaar@iland.net; Carol Conrow, News Editor; John Spaar, Advertising Mgr.; Joe Spaar, Production; Sharon Guevel, Circulation; Leanna Thompson, Office Mgr. **Subscription Rates:** $25 individuals. **Remarks:** Accepts advertising.
Ad Rates: GLR: $.50 **Circ:** 4,700
BW: $504
4C: $650
SAU: $4
PCI: $4

OREGON†, pop. 901.

NW MO. Holt Co. 18 mi. W. of Savannah. Residential.

17437 Times Observer
119 W. Nodaway Phone: (816)446-3331
PO Box 317 Fax: (816)446-3409
Oregon, MO 64473
Local interest newspaper. **Founded:** 1974. **Freq:** Weekly (Thurs.). **Print Method:** Offset. **Cols./Page:** 6. **Col. Width:** 24 nonpareils. **Col. Depth:** 294 agate lines. **Key Personnel:** Wilma J. Ripley, Editor and Publisher. **Subscription Rates:** $13.82 individuals; $18 out of state; $17 Missouri.
Ad Rates: PCI: $3.00 **Circ:** ‡1,438

17438 South Holt Cablevision Inc.
Box 227 Phone: (816)446-2900
Oregon, MO 64473 Fax: (816)446-2800

Key Personnel: Robert Williams, President. **Cities Served:** Oregon and Forest City, MO.

OSAGE BEACH, pop. 1,992.

C. MO. Camden and Miller Co. 14 mi. NE of Candenton on Lake Ozark. Residential.

KBMX-FM - See Eldon

17439 KRMS-AM - 1150
Hwy. 54 Box 225 Phone: (573)348-2772
Osage Beach, MO 65065 Fax: (573)348-2779
E-mail: rock93@lakeozark.net

Format: News; Talk. **Networks:** CBS. **Founded:** 1952. **Operating Hours:** Continuous. **ADI:** Springfield, MO. **Key Personnel:** Ken Kuenzie, General Mgr. **Wattage:** 1000 day; 58 night. **Ad Rates:** $18.75 for 60 seconds.

OSCEOLA

17440 Humansville Star-Leader
PO Box 406 Phone: (417)646-2211
Osceola, MO 64776 Fax: (417)646-8015

Local newspaper. **Founded:** 1876. **Freq:** Weekly (Thurs.). **Print Method:** Offset. **Cols./Page:** 6. **Col. Width:** 25 nonpareils. **Col. Depth:** 301 agate lines. **Key Personnel:** Barbara Tilley, Office Mgr.; Donna LeAn, Sales. **Subscription Rates:** $16.52; $19.19 out of area; $21.50 out of state. **Remarks:** Accepts advertising.
Ad Rates: BW: $352.80 **Circ:** 1,785
PCI: $2.80

17441 St. Clair County Buyer's Guide
SAC-Osghee
PO Box 580 Phone: (417)646-2211
Osceola, MO 64776 Fax: (417)646-8015

Shopping guide. **Founded:** 1979. **Freq:** Weekly (Wed.). **Print Method:** Offset. **Cols./Page:** 6. **Col. Width:** 12 picas. **Col. Depth:** 21 1/2 inches. **Key Personnel:** Larry Brownlee, Editor. **Remarks:** Accepts advertising.
Ad Rates: SAU: $3.60 **Circ:** Free ‡4,000

17442 St. Clair County Courier
SAC-Osghee
PO Box 580 Phone: (417)646-2211
Osceola, MO 64776 Fax: (417)646-8015

Local newspaper. **Founded:** 1881. **Freq:** Weekly. **Print Method:** Offset. **Cols./Page:** 6. **Col. Width:** 12 picas. **Col. Depth:** 21 1/2 inches. **Key Personnel:** Larry Brownlee, Publisher. **USPS:** 475-720. **Subscription Rates:** $12.50; $15 out of area; $18.50 out of state. **Remarks:** Accepts advertising.
Ad Rates: BW: $400 **Circ:** Paid 2,165
SAU: $3.50 Free 4,000

OVERLAND, pop. 18,730.

NW MO. Saint Louis Co. 10 mi. WNW of Saint Louis.

17443 Continental Cablevision of Saint Louis County, Inc.
2411 Verona Phone: (314)428-0915
Overland, MO 63114 Fax: (314)428-4235

Founded: 1980. **Cities Served:** Saint Louis County, Breckenridge Hills, Brentwood, Chesterfield, and Clayton, MO.

17444 KRHS-FM - 90.1
9100 St. Charles Rock Rd. Phone: (314)429-7111
Overland, MO 63114 Fax: (314)429-6725

Format: Full Service. **Networks:** Independent. **Founded:** 1976. **Formerly:** KRSH-FM (1990). **Operating Hours:** 8 a.m.-5 p.m.; 100% local. **Key Personnel:** Alan Mitchell, General Mgr., phone (314)426-9571. **Wattage:** 100.

OWENSVILLE, pop. 2,241.

EC MO. Gasconade Co. 45 mi. SE of Jefferson City. Manufactures shoes, plastics, printing. Clay, flint, diaspore mines. Diversified farming. Corn, wheat.

17445 Free Shopper
Warden Publishing Co.
106 E. Washington Phone: (314)437-2323
PO Box 540 Fax: (314)437-3033
Owensville, MO 65066-0540
Community newspaper and shopper. **Founded:** 1982. **Freq:** Weekly. **Print Method:** Offset. **Trim Size:** 14 x 22. **Cols./Page:** 6. **Col. Width:** 12 picas. **Col. Depth:** 21 1/2 inches. **Key Personnel:** Tom Warden, Editor; Don Warden, Advertising Mgr. **Subscription Rates:** Free. **Remarks:** Accepts advertising.
Ad Rates: BW: $451 **Circ:** Free ‡6,252
SAU: $3.50
PCI: $3.50

17446 Gasconade County Republican
Warden Publishing Co.
106 E. Washington Phone: (314)437-2323
PO Box 540 Fax: (314)437-3033
Owensville, MO 65066-0540
Newspaper. **Founded:** 1904. **Freq:** Weekly (Wed.). **Print Method:** Offset. **Trim Size:** 14 x 22 3/4. **Cols./Page:** 6. **Col. Width:** 12 picas. **Col. Depth:** 21 inches. **Key Personnel:** Tom Warden, Editor; Don Warden, Advertising Mgr. **USPS:** 021-460. **Subscription Rates:** $25.25. **Remarks:** Accepts advertising.
Ad Rates: BW: $483.75 **Circ:** ‡3,310
SAU: $3.75
PCI: $3.75

OZARK†, pop. 2,980.

SW MO. Christian Co. 12 mi. S. of Springfield. Manufactures textiles, small electric motors, wood products, ceramics, cheese. Feed mill. Summer resort. Stock, dairy farms. Corn, wheat, oats.

17447 Christian County Headliners News
Ozark Publications Inc.
PO Box 490 Phone: (417)581-3541
Ozark, MO 65721 Fax: (417)581-3577

Newspaper. **Founded:** 1967. **Freq:** Semiweekly (Wed. and Sat.). **Print Method:** Offset. **Cols./Page:** 6. **Col. Width:** 24 nonpareils. **Col. Depth:** 301 agate lines. **Key Personnel:** Roger Frieze, Publisher. **Subscription Rates:** $34 individuals; $55 out of area. **Formerly:** Ozark Headliner.
Ad Rates: BW: $750 **Circ:** ‡5,000
4C: $1,065
PCI: $5.95

PACIFIC, pop. 4,410.

E. MO. Franklin and Saint Louis Co. On Meramec River, 36 mi. SW of Saint Louis. Sand and gravel plants. Manufactures folding paper boxes, roofing materials, silica bricks. Ships sand, gravel, silica products. Diversified farming. Wheat, corn, hay.

17448 Tri-County Journal
Suburban Newspapers of Greater St. Louis
PO Box 6 Phone: (314)227-1286
Pacific, MO 63069 Fax: (314)227-1272

Community newspaper. **Subtitle:** Members of the Suburban Journals of Greater St Louis. **Founded:** Jan. 1963. **Freq:** Weekly (Wed.). **Print Method:** Offset. **Trim Size:** 13 x 22. **Cols./Page:** 6. **Col. Width:** 12 picas. **Col. Depth:** 168 agate lines. **Key Personnel:** Danette Fertig Thompson, Editor. **ISSN:** 0746-1712. **Subscription Rates:** Free.
Ad Rates: BW: $1,234.20 **Circ:** Free 10,483

PALMYRA†, pop. 3,469.

NE MO. Marion Co. 11 mi. NW of Hannibal. Manufactures chemicals, fertilizer, lumber products. Diversified farming.

17449 Palmyra Spectator
304 S. Main St. Phone: (573)769-3111
PO Box 391 Fax: (573)769-3554
Palmyra, MO 63461-0431
Newspaper with a Democratic orientation. **Founded:** 1839. **Freq:** Weekly (Wed.). **Print Method:** Offset. **Cols./Page:** 6. **Col. Width:** 12 picas. **Col. Depth:** 280 agate lines. **Key Personnel:** Mark Cheffey, Editor and Publisher; Patty Cheffey, Editor and Publisher. **Subscription Rates:** $22 individuals. **Remarks:** Accepts advertising.
Ad Rates: GLR: $0.19 **Circ:** 2,800
SAU: $3.25
PCI: $4.25

PARIS†, pop. 1,598.

NE MO. Monroe Co. On west end of Mark Twain Lake, 44 mi. SW of Hannibal. Stock, dairy, poultry, grain farms. Corn, hay, wheat, soybeans, cattle, horses, hogs.

17450 Monroe County Appeal
Appeal Publishing Company
PO Box 207 Phone: (816)327-4192
Paris, MO 65275 Fax: (816)327-4847

Newspaper with a Democratic orientation. **Founded:** 1867. **Freq:** Weekly (Thurs.). **Print Method:** Offset. **Cols./Page:** 6. **Col. Width:** 26 nonpareils. **Col. Depth:** 301 agate lines. **Key Personnel:** Richard J. Fredrick, Publisher; Sherry Cooper, Office Mgr. **Subscription Rates:** $21 individuals; $23 out of area; $24 out of state. **Remarks:** Accepts advertising.
Ad Rates: PCI: $3.40 **Circ:** ‡2,200

17451 Mark Twain Cablevision
PO Box 209 Phone: (816)327-5141
Paris, MO 65275 Fax: (816)327-4892
Free: (800)892-2904

Key Personnel: Roger Leonard, President. **Cities Served:** Fourteen franchise throughout Missouri.

PARK HILLS

17452 The Daily Journal
Eastern Missouri Publishing Co.
PO Box A
Park Hills, MO 63601

General newspaper. **Founded:** 1930. **Freq:** Daily (eve.). **Print Method:** Offset. **Cols./Page:** 6. **Col. Width:** 25 nonpareils. **Col. Depth:** 301 agate lines. **Key Personnel:** Ron Weir, Editor and Publisher. **Subscription Rates:** $72. **Remarks:** Accepts advertising.
Ad Rates: SAU: $10.23 **Circ:** Mon.-Fri. 9,082
Sun. 9,324

PARKVILLE, pop. 1,997.

NW MO. Platte Co. On Missouri River, 10 mi. NW of Kansas City. Park College. Diversified farming. Grain, tobacco.

17453 Dive Training
Dive Training Ltd.
405 Main St. Phone: (816)741-5151
Parkville, MO 64152-3737 Fax: (816)741-6458
Free: (800)444-9932

Diving magazine promoting training and safety. **Subtitle:** The New Divers Magazine. **Founded:** 1991. **Freq:** Monthly. **Print Method:** Offset. **Trim Size:** 7 7/8 x 10 1/2. **Cols./Page:** 3. **Key Personnel:** Sean Combs, Editor; Gary S. Worden, Publisher. **ISSN:** 1061-3323. **Subscription Rates:** $20. $2.95 single issue. **Remarks:** Accepts advertising.
Ad Rates: BW: $4,150 **Circ:** Paid 30,000
4C: $6,020 Non-paid 55,000

17454 Flight Training
Flight Traning Ltd.
201 Main St. Phone: (816)741-5151
Parkville, MO 64152 Fax: (816)741-6458
Publication E-mail: flighttrng@aol.com

"How-to" magazine for new pilots and instructors. **Subtitle:** A Good Pilot is Always Learning. **Founded:** June 1989. **Freq:** Monthly. **Trim Size:** 7 7/8 x 10 1/2. **Cols./Page:** 3. **Col. Width:** 2 1/4 inches. **Col. Depth:** 10 inches. **Key Personnel:** Scott Spangler, Editor; Melissa Murphy, Publisher. **ISSN:**

1047-6415. **Subscription Rates:** $21.95. $3.95 single issue. **Remarks:** Accepts advertising.
Ad Rates: BW: $5,135 4C: $7,315 PCI: $95 **Circ:** Paid 28,000 Controlled 40,000

17455 The Park Stylus
Park College
8700 NW River Park Dr. Phone: (816)741-2000
Parkville, MO 64152 Fax: (816)741-4911

Collegiate newspaper. **Founded:** 1875. **Freq:** Monthly. **Print Method:** Offset. **Cols./Page:** 6. **Col. Depth:** 21 inches. **Key Personnel:** Kellie Thompson, Editor. **Subscription Rates:** $9.95. **Remarks:** Accepts advertising. **Formerly:** Stylus (1992).
Ad Rates: GLR: $3.50 BW: $100 PCI: $4 **Circ:** Paid ‡2,200 Free ‡200

17456 Platte County Gazette
Sun News
PO Box 12086 Phone: (816)741-9530
Parkville, MO 64152 Fax: (816)741-9593

Community newspaper. **Founded:** 1885. **Freq:** Weekly (Wed.). **Print Method:** Offset. **Cols./Page:** 6. **Col. Width:** 25 nonpareils. **Col. Depth:** 301 agate lines. **Key Personnel:** Janelle Gann-Moon, Editor; Vivian L. O'Dell, Publisher; Carol Allen, Advertising Mgr. **ISSN:** 0889-5737. **Subscription Rates:** Free; $15. **Remarks:** Accepts advertising. **Formerly:** The Northland Gazette (June 3, 1988).
Ad Rates: BW: $844.95 4C: $1,144.95 PCI: $6.55 **Circ:** Paid 158 Free 13,055

PERRYVILLE†, pop. 7,343.

SE MO. Perry Co. 38 mi. N. of Cape Girardeau. St. Mary's Seminary and College. Manufactures shoes, food products, automotive parts, foam products, jet engine refurbishing. Stock, grain farms.

17457 MidAmerica Farmer Grower
SJS Publishing Co., Inc.
19 N. Main Phone: (314)547-2244
Perryville, MO 63775 Fax: (314)547-5663

Agriculture magazine featuring news, events, shows, workshops, and insect and weed control information in Illinois, Missouri, Kentucky, Arkansas, and Tennessee. **Founded:** 1983. **Freq:** Weekly. **Print Method:** Offset. **Trim Size:** 11 1/2 x 13 3/4. **Cols./Page:** 5. **Col. Width:** 11 1/2 picas. **Col. Depth:** 12 inches. **Key Personnel:** John M. La Rose, Publisher; Lisa K. La Rose, Editor. **ISSN:** 1040-1423. **Subscription Rates:** $12. $1 single issue. **Remarks:** Accepts advertising.
Ad Rates: BW: $1,794 4C: $2,294 PCI: $27.60 **Circ:** Paid ‡14,379 Non-paid ‡10,451

17458 The Perry County Republic-Monitor
Perryville Newspapers, Inc.
10 W. Ste. Maries St. Phone: (573)547-4567
PO Drawer 367 Fax: (573)547-1643
Perryville, MO 63775
Publisher E-mail: flash@ldd.net

Community newspaper. **Founded:** 1889. **Freq:** Biweekly. **Print Method:** Offset. **Cols./Page:** 6. **Col. Width:** 2 inches. **Col. Depth:** 21 inches. **Key Personnel:** Randall J. Pribble, Editor and Publisher. **USPS:** 428-200. **Subscription Rates:** $35.22 in Perry county; $58.70 elsewhere. **Remarks:** Accepts advertising. **Formed by the merger of:** The Perry County Republic; The Monitor.
Ad Rates: BW: $749.70 4C: $1,049.70 SAU: $5.95 **Circ:** Paid 5,800

17459 Perryville Sun Times
10 Perry Plaza
Perryville, MO 63775
Publisher E-mail: suntimesnews@ldd.net

Community newspaper. **Founded:** 1998. **Key Personnel:** Elmo Donze, Publisher, phone (573)547-8005.

17460 The Republic-Monitor Shopping Guide
Perryville Newspapers, Inc.
10 W. Ste. Maries St. Phone: (573)547-4567
PO Drawer 367 Fax: (573)547-1643
Perryville, MO 63775
Publisher E-mail: flash@ldd.net

Non-duplicating free distribution shopper. **Freq:** Monthly. **Print Method:** Offset. **Cols./Page:** 6. **Col. Width:** 2 inches. **Col. Depth:** 21 inches. **Key Personnel:** Randall J. Pribble, Publisher. **Subscription Rates:** Free. **Remarks:** Accepts advertising. **Formerly:** The Republic/Extra.
Ad Rates: BW: $749.70 4C: $1,049.70 SAU: $5.95 **Circ:** Free ‡8,071

17461 Falcon Cable TV
PO Box 385 Phone: (314)547-8387
Perryville, MO 63775 Fax: (314)547-1318
Free: (800)455-8387

Key Personnel: Ken Reeves, Technician. **Cities Served:** subscribing households 1,400; 16 channels.

17462 KBDZ-FM - 93.1
PO Box 344 Phone: (573)547-8005
Perry Plaza, No. 10 Fax: (573)883-2866
Perryville, MO 63775
E-mail: suntimesnews@ldd.net

Format: Country; News. **Networks:** Unistar. **Founded:** 1991. **Operating Hours:** Continuous. **Key Personnel:** Elmo L. Donze, Pres./Gen. Mgr.; Bob Scott, Gen. Sales Mgr. and Product/Music Dir.; Don Pritchard, News Dir.; Brian Snider, Asst. News Dir.; Susan White, Traffic Mgr. **Local Programs:** *Focus*, Don Pritchard. **Wattage:** 6000. **Ad Rates:** $14 for 30 seconds; $18 for 60 seconds.

PIEDMONT, pop. 2,359.

SE MO. Wayne Co. 70 mi. W. of Cape Girardeau. Manufactures plastic bottles, wood pallets, shoes, hats, textiles. Lumber mills. Oak, pine timber. Stock, grain farms. Corn, wheat, oats.

17463 Reynolds County Courier
Ellinghouse Publishing Co., Inc.
PO Box 97 Phone: (573)223-7122
Piedmont, MO 63957 Fax: (573)223-7871
Free: (800)923-7122

Community newspaper. **Founded:** 1876. **Freq:** Weekly (Thurs.). **Print Method:** Offset. **Trim Size:** 7 1/4 x 11 1/2. **Cols./Page:** 6. **Col. Width:** 27 nonpareils. **Col. Depth:** 301 agate lines. **Key Personnel:** Harold Ellinghouse, Editor; H.T. Ellinghouse, Publisher; M.B. Stivers, Publisher. **USPS:** 135-620. **Subscription Rates:** $20.50 individuals; $30 out of area. **Remarks:** Accepts advertising.
Ad Rates: BW: $819.15 SAU: $6.35 PCI: $6.35 **Circ:** ‡2,850

17464 Wayne County Journal-Banner
Ellinghouse Publishing Co., Inc.
PO Box 97 Phone: (573)223-7122
Piedmont, MO 63957 Fax: (573)223-7871
Free: (800)923-7122

Newspaper with a Democratic orientation. **Founded:** 1876. **Freq:** Weekly (Thurs.). **Print Method:** Offset. **Trim Size:** 7 1/4 x 11 1/2. **Cols./Page:** 6. **Col. Width:** 27 nonpareils. **Col. Depth:** 301 agate lines. **Key Personnel:** H.T. Ellinghouse, Editor and Publisher, harold@waycojournalbanner.com; M.B. Stivers, Publisher. **USPS:** 670-400. **Subscription Rates:** $21 in county; $32 out of area.
Ad Rates: BW: $838.50 PCI: $6.50 **Circ:** ‡5,150

17465 KPWB-AM - 1140
235 Business HH Phone: (573)223-4218
Piedmont, MO 63957 Fax: (573)223-2351
E-mail: kpwb@showme.net

Format: News; Sports; Gospel; Religious. **Networks:** USA Radio. **Owner:** Hunt Broadcasting Group, at above address. **Founded:** 1966. **Operating Hours:** Sunrise to sunset. **Key Personnel:** Wanda McCombs, Operations; DeAnn Griffin, Program Dir. **Local Programs:** *Trading Post* 9:00 am - 10:00 am Monday-Friday, DeAnn Griffin, Program Dir. **Wattage:** 1000.

17466 KPWB-FM - 104.9
235 Business HH Phone: (573)223-4218
Piedmont, MO 63957 Fax: (573)223-2351
E-mail: kpwb@showme.net

Format: Country. **Networks:** USA Radio; Satellite Music Network. **Owner:** Hunt Broadcasting Group, at above address. **Founded:** 1966. **Operating Hours:** Continuous. **Key Personnel:** Wanda McCombs, Operations Mgr./News Dir./Program Dir.; DeAnn Griffin, Program Dir. **Local Programs:** *Trading Post* 9:15-10 a.m., DeAnn Griffin. **Wattage:** 25,000. **Ad Rates:** $5 for 30 seconds; $7 for 60 seconds.

PINEVILLE†, pop. 504.

SW MO. McDonald Co. 40 mi. SE of Joplin. Recreation. Mobile home plant; hatchery. Diversified farming. Dairying, tomatoes, beans.

17467 McDonald County News-Gazette
McDonald County Press Inc.
PO Box 266 Phone: (417)223-4377
Pineville, MO 64856 Fax: (417)223-4049

Newspaper with a Republican orientation. **Founded:** 1873. **Freq:** Weekly (Wed.). **Print Method:** Offset. **Cols./Page:** 6. **Col. Width:** 24 nonpareils. **Col. Depth:** 294 agate lines. **Key Personnel:** George Pogue, Editor and Publisher. **Subscription Rates:** $15; $20 out of area. **Remarks:** Accepts advertising.
Ad Rates: SAU: $3.30 **Circ:** ‡2,000

17468 McDonald County Press
McDonald County Press Inc.
PO Box 266 Phone: (417)223-4377
Pineville, MO 64856 Fax: (417)223-4049

Newspaper with a Democratic orientation. **Founded:** 1943. **Freq:** Weekly (Wed.). **Print Method:** Offset. **Cols./Page:** 6. **Col. Width:** 2 1/16 inches. **Col. Depth:** 21 inches. **Key Personnel:** George G. Pogue, Editor and Publisher; Robert Stout, Advertising Mgr. **Subscription Rates:** $12; $14 out of county; $20 out of state.
Ad Rates: BW: $324.50 4C: $394.50 SAU: $3.90 **Circ:** 1,419

PLATTE CITY†, pop. 2,114.

NW MO. Platte Co. 25 mi. W. of Kansas. Diversified farming. Wheat, corn, tobacco.

17469 American Chianina Journal
American Chianina Association
1708 N. Prairie View Rd. Phone: (816)431-2808
PO Box 890 Fax: (816)431-5381
Platte City, MO 64079
Publisher E-mail: aza@sound.net

Magazine featuring Chianina cattle and breeders. **Founded:** 1973. **Freq:** 8/year. **Print Method:** Sheet fed. **Trim Size:** 8 1/2 x 11. **Cols./Page:** 3. **Col. Width:** 14 picas. **Col. Depth:** 54 picas. **Key Personnel:** Tammy Shott, Editor. **ISSN:** 1068-8021. **Subscription Rates:** $25. **Remarks:** Accepts advertising.
Ad Rates: BW: $495 4C: $740 PCI: $20 **Circ:** ‡2,500

17470 The Landmark
PO Box 410 Phone: (816)858-0363
Platte City, MO 64079 Fax: (816)858-2313

Community newspaper. **Founded:** 1865. **Freq:** Weekly (Thurs.). **Print Method:** Offset. **Cols./Page:** 6. **Col. Width:** 2 1/4 inches. **Col. Depth:** 21 inches. **Key Personnel:** Ivan Foley, Editor, ifoley@aol.com; Ethel Mae Foley, Publisher. **USPS:** 304-520. **Subscription Rates:** $16 individuals. **Remarks:** Accepts advertising.
Ad Rates: BW: $567 SAU: $5.50 PCI: $5.25 **Circ:** ‡2,000

17471 Platte County Citizen
PO Box 888 Phone: (816)858-5154
Platte City, MO 64079 Fax: (816)858-2154
Free: (800)856-1407

Community newspaper. **Founded:** June 1962. **Freq:** Weekly. **Print Method:** Offset. **Trim Size:** 13 3/4 x 22 3/4. **Cols./Page:** 6. **Col. Width:** 24 nonpareils. **Col. Depth:** 301 agate lines. **Key Personnel:** Paul D. Campbell, Publisher; Rebecca K. Campbell, Publisher; Lee Stubbs, Editor. **ISSN:** 0746-3596. **Subscription Rates:** $21. **Remarks:** Accepts advertising.
Ad Rates: BW: $675 4C: $900 SAU: $5.79 PCI: $5.79 **Circ:** Paid ‡3,800 Free ‡3,000

PLATTSBURG†, pop. 2,095.

NW MO. Clinton Co. 29 mi. SE of Saint Joseph. Agriculture. Corn, oats, wheat.

17472 The Leader
Tin Publishing Co.
102 E. Maple Phone: (816)539-2112
Plattsburg, MO 64477 Fax: (816)539-3530

Newspaper with a Democratic orientation. **Founded:** 1895. **Freq:** Weekly (Thurs.). **Print Method:** Offset. **Cols./Page:** 6. **Col. Width:** 26 nonpareils. **Col. Depth:** 301 agate lines. **Key**

Personnel: J.W. Tinnen, Editor and Publisher. **Subscription Rates:** $12.
Circ: ‡2,280

PLEASANT HILL, pop. 3,301.

W. MO. Cass Co. 25 mi. SE of Kansas City. Manufactures horizontal earth augers, posthole diggers, textiles. Sawmills; hatchery. Diversified farming. Corn, milk.

17473 Pleasant Hill Times
Pleasant Hill Times, Inc.
126 1st St. Phone: (816)987-2138
Box 8 Fax: (816)987-5699
Pleasant Hill, MO 64080
Newspaper with a Democratic orientation. **Founded:** 1881. **Freq:** Weekly (Wed.). **Print Method:** Offset. **Cols./Page:** 6. **Col. Width:** 12 1/2 picas. **Col. Depth:** 21 inches. **Key Personnel:** F. Kirk Powell, Publisher. **Subscription Rates:** $20 local; $23 in state; $33. **Remarks:** Accepts advertising.
Ad Rates: BW: $592.00 **Circ:** ‡6,000
4C: $4.70
SAU: $3.75

POINT LOOKOUT, pop. 1,200.

S. MO. Taney Co. 3 mi. S. of Branson. The School of the Ozarks. Museum.

17474 The Outlook
School of the Ozarks
PO Box 15 Phone: (417)334-6411
Point Lookout, MO 65726
Collegiate newspaper. **Founded:** 1961. **Freq:** 32/year. **Print Method:** Offset. **Cols./Page:** 5. **Col. Width:** 22 nonpareils. **Col. Depth:** 224 agate lines.

17475 KCOZ-FM - 91.7
College of the Ozarks Phone: (417)334-6411
Point Lookout, MO 65726 Fax: (417)335-2618
E-mail: radio@cofo.edu

Format: Public Radio; Jazz; News; Eclectic; Classical; Bluegrass. **Networks:** National Public Radio (NPR); American Public Radio (APR). **Owner:** College Of The Ozarks, at above address. **Founded:** 1962. **Formerly:** KSOZ-FM (1991). **Operating Hours:** Continuous; 70% network, 30% local. **Key Personnel:** Jae Jones, Gen./Production Mgr. **Local Programs:** *Blue Plate Special*, Jae Jones; *Blue's Alley*; *From the Point.* **Wattage:** 200. **Ad Rates:** Noncommercial.

POLO

17476 Hogs Today
Farm Journal, Inc.
PO Box 164A Phone: (816)586-5641
Polo, MO 64671
Agricultural magazine for hog managers and producers. **Subtitle:** The Magazine of American Pork Producers. **Founded:** 1985. **Freq:** 10/year. **Print Method:** Offset. **Trim Size:** 8 x 10 1/2. **Cols./Page:** 3. **Col. Width:** 2 1/4 inches. **Col. Depth:** 140 agate lines. **Key Personnel:** Dale E. Smith, President; Roger D. Randall, Publisher; Dean Houghton, Editor. **ISSN:** 1056-1374. **Subscription Rates:** Free to qualified subscribers. **Remarks:** Accepts advertising. **Formerly:** Hog Extra (May 1987).
Ad Rates: BW: $5,675 **Circ:** Non-paid 84,547
4C: $6,695

POPLAR BLUFF†, pop. 17,139.

SE MO. Butler Co. 160 mi. S. of Saint Louis. Three Rivers Community College. Manufactures Christmas tree stands, shoes, paperboxes, portable buildings, furniture, custom made drapes, concrete burial vaults, machine parts, satellite antennas, wood stoves, aluminum gas tanks for boats, timber. Agriculture. Livestock, cotton, corn, rice.

17477 Daily American Republic
Butler County Publishing
208 Poplar St. Phone: (573)785-1414
PO Box 7 Fax: (573)785-2706
Poplar Bluff, MO 63901
General newspaper. **Founded:** 1923. **Freq:** Daily (eve.). **Print Method:** Offset. **Cols./Page:** 6. **Col. Width:** 24 nonpareils. **Col. Depth:** 301 agate lines. **Key Personnel:** Stan Berry, Editor; Joe Jordan, Advertising Mgr.; Don Schrieber, Publisher. **USPS:** 141-290. **Subscription Rates:** $98 individuals.
Ad Rates: BW: $1,203.57 **Circ:** Mon.-Fri. ♦**13,724**
4C: $1,458.87 Sun. ♦**14,408**
SAU: $9.70 Wed. ♦**19,416**

17478 KAHR-FM - 96.7
Rte. 13, Box 44 Phone: (573)686-3700
Poplar Bluff, MO 63901 Fax: (573)686-1713
E-mail: kool967@pbmo.net

Format: Adult Contemporary. **Networks:** Satellite Music Network; ABC. **Operating Hours:** Continuous. **Key Personnel:** Stephen C. Fuchs, Owner/Gen. Mgr.; Palmer Johnson, Engineer. **Wattage:** 6000.

17479 KJEZ-FM - 95.5
7 Hillsdale Plaza Phone: (573)686-2403
PO Box 130 Fax: (573)785-1119
Poplar Bluff, MO 63901

Format: Classic Rock; Album-Oriented Rock (AOR); Top 40. **Networks:** Unistar. **Owner:** A.C.I. Broadcasting, Inc., at above address. **Founded:** 1977. **Operating Hours:** Continuous; 90% network, 10% local. **ADI:** Paducah,KY-Cape Girardeau,MO-Marion,IL. **Key Personnel:** Jim Borders. **Wattage:** 100,000.

17480 KLID-AM - 1340
KLID Bldg. Phone: (573)686-1600
102 N. 11th
Poplar Bluff, MO 63901

Format: Oldies; Alternative/New Music/Progressive. **Owner:** Chris Browning & Delores Skidmore, at above address, Fax: (573)785-9844. **Founded:** 1961. **Operating Hours:** Continuous; 3% network, 97% local. **ADI:** Paducah,KY-Cape Girardeau,MO-Marion,IL. **Key Personnel:** Sunny Skidmore, Contact. **Wattage:** 1000. **Ad Rates:** $6-9 for 30 seconds; $8-11 for 60 seconds.

17481 KOKS-FM - 89.5
PO Box 967 Phone: (573)686-5080
Poplar Bluff, MO 63901-0967 Fax: (573)686-5544

Format: Southern Gospel. **Owner:** Calvary Educational Broadcasting Network, Inc., at above address. **Founded:** 1988. **Operating Hours:** Continuous. **Key Personnel:** Don Stewart, General Mgr.; Nina Stewart, Station Mgr. **Wattage:** 100,000. **Ad Rates:** Noncommercial.

17482 KPOB-TV - 15
c/o WSIL-TV Phone: (618)985-2333
Rte. 13 Fax: (618)985-3709
Carterville, IL 62918

Format: Commercial TV. **Simulcasts:** WSIL-TV Carterville, IL. **Networks:** ABC. **Operating Hours:** Continuous. **ADI:** Paducah,KY-Cape Girardeau,MO-Marion,IL. **Key Personnel:** J.W. Davis, Engineering Dir.; Dave Cisco, Sales.

PORTAGEVILLE, pop. 3,470.

SE MO. New Madrid Co. 60 mi. S. of Cape Girardeau. Cotton gin; soybean and cottonseed oil mill. Manufactures patent medicines. Agriculture. Cotton, soybeans, corn.

17483 Missourian News
PO Box 456 Phone: (573)379-5355
Portageville, MO 63873 Fax: (573)379-5488
Free: (800)459-9558

General newspaper. **Founded:** 1895. **Freq:** Weekly (Thurs.). **Print Method:** Offset. **Cols./Page:** 6. **Col. Width:** 24 nonpareils. **Col. Depth:** 294 agate lines. **Key Personnel:** H. Scott Seal, Editor. **ISSN:** 1056-9464. **Subscription Rates:** $17.50. **Remarks:** Accepts advertising. **Formerly:** Missourian-Review; Portageville Review.
Ad Rates: BW: $598.50 **Circ:** ‡1,800
SAU: $4.50
PCI: $4.25

17484 KLUH-FM - 90.3
PO Box 161 Phone: (573)686-1663
Portageville, MO 63873 Fax: (573)686-7703

Format: Southern Gospel. **Owner:** Word of Victory Outreach Center, Inc., 518 State Hwy. T, Portageville, MO 63873, (573)379-2379. **Founded:** 1988. **Operating Hours:** Continuous. **Key Personnel:** Kit Campbell, Operations Mgr.; Dena Campbell, Program Dir. **Wattage:** 25,000.

17485 KMIS-AM - 1050
Hwy. 162 E. Phone: (573)379-5436
PO Box 250 Fax: (573)379-2233
Portageville, MO 63873
Free: (800)379-5647

Format: News. **Networks:** ABC. **Founded:** 1960. **Operating Hours:** Continuous. **Key Personnel:** Ray Taylor, Program Dir.; Lisa Kelley, General Mgr. **Wattage:** 1000. **Ad Rates:** $6-8 for 30 seconds; $9-11 for 60 seconds.

POTOSI†, pop. 2,528.

E. MO. Washington Co. 60 mi. SW of Saint Louis. Manufactures barrel staves, lumber products, shoes. Lead, zinc, iron, barytes, lumber, limestone industries. Agriculture.

17486 The Independent-Journal
119 E. High St. Phone: (314)438-5141
PO Box 340 Fax: (314)438-4472
Potosi, MO 63664
Community newspaper. **Founded:** 1872. **Freq:** Weekly (Thurs.). **Print Method:** Offset. **Cols./Page:** 6. **Col. Width:** 2 1/16 inches. **Col. Depth:** 21 inches. **Key Personnel:** Neil Richards, Editor. **USPS:** 260-980. **Subscription Rates:** $15.
Ad Rates: GLR: $.28 **Circ:** ‡5,600
SAU: $4

17487 KYRO-AM - 1280
Hwy. 21 Phone: (573)438-2136
PO Box 280 Fax: (573)438-3108
Potosi, MO 63664
E-mail: kyro@kyro.com

Format: Country; News. **Networks:** ABC. **Owner:** Savoy Broadcasting Co., at above address. **Founded:** 1959. **Operating Hours:** Continuous. **Key Personnel:** James T. Porter, General Mgr., james@kyro.com; Debbie Porter, Office Mgr., debbie@kyro.com; Jeremy Porter, Program and News Dir., jeremy@kyro.com. **Wattage:** 500. **Ad Rates:** $7.50 for 30 seconds; $12.50 for 60 seconds. **URL:** http://kyro.com.

PRINCETON†, pop. 1,264.

N. MO. Mercer Co. 80 mi. NE of Saint Joseph. Fishing and hunting. Dairy, fruit, stock, sheep farms. Corn, livestock.

17488 Post-Telegraph
Overland Courier
704 E. Main St. Phone: (816)748-3266
PO Box 286 Fax: (816)748-3267
Princeton, MO 64673
Newspaper. **Founded:** 1873. **Freq:** Semiweekly (Mon. and Thurs.). **Print Method:** Offset. **Cols./Page:** 7. **Col. Width:** 26 nonpareils. **Col. Depth:** 294 agate lines. **Key Personnel:** Preston J. Cole, Editor. **Subscription Rates:** $20.50 out of area.
Ad Rates: PCI: $3.15 **Circ:** ‡2,670

PUXICO

17489 Puxico Weekly Press
PO Box 277 Phone: (573)222-3243
Puxico, MO 63960 Fax: (573)222-3243

Community newspaper. **Freq:** Weekly (Wed.). **Cols./Page:** 6. **Col. Width:** 13 1/2 picas. **Col. Depth:** 21 1/2 inches. **Key Personnel:** Cletis Ellinghouse, Editor and Publisher.
Circ: 2,300

RAYTOWN, pop. 31,759.

W. MO. Jackson Co. 10 mi. SE of downtown Kansas City. Industry. Residential.

17490 Raytown Dispatch-Tribune
Townsend Communications, Inc.
7007 NE Parvin Rd. Phone: (816)454-9660
Kansas City, MO 64117 Fax: (816)452-5889
Publisher E-mail: towns@swbell.net

Community newspaper. **Founded:** 1926. **Freq:** Weekly (Wed.). **Print Method:** Offset. **Trim Size:** 13 x 21. **Cols./Page:** 6. **Col. Width:** 2 1/8 inches. **Col. Depth:** 21 inches. **Key Personnel:** Mark Johnson, Editor, phone (816)358-6398, fax (816)358-5141; Harold G. Townsend, Jr., Publisher; Gary Warmker, National Adv. Mgr., phone (816)454-9660, fax (816)452-5889. **Subscription Rates:** Free to area households; $15 out of area; $18 out of state. **Remarks:** Accepts advertising.
Ad Rates: 4C: $275 **Circ:** Combined 11,442
SAU: $8.41

17491 Raytown Post
Gray Union Publishing, Inc.
PO Box 9338 Phone: (816)353-5545
Raytown, MO 64133
Community newspaper. **Founded:** 1975. **Freq:** Weekly (Wed.). **Print Method:** Offset. Uses mats. **Cols./Page:** 8. **Col. Width:** 18 nonpareils. **Col. Depth:** 301 agate lines. **Key Personnel:** Lee Gray, Editor and Publisher. **Subscription Rates:** Free; $50 by mail; $60 out of area. **Remarks:** Accepts advertising.
Ad Rates: GLR: $.46 **Circ:** Free ‡18,000
BW: $1,195.40
4C: $1,595.40
SAU: $15

REPUBLIC

17492 Republic Monitor
Sumner Publishing
417 E. Hwy. 60 Phone: (417)732-2525
Republic, MO 65738 Fax: (417)732-2980

Community newspaper. **Founded:** Apr. 7, 1894. **Freq:** Weekly (Thurs.). **Cols./Page:** 6. **Col. Width:** 2 inches. **Col. Depth:** 21 1/2 inches. **Key Personnel:** Larry Rottmann, Editor; Derek Sumner, Publisher. **Subscription Rates:** $19.97; $24 other; $30 out of state. **Remarks:** Accepts advertising.
Ad Rates: BW: $450 **Circ:** 3,500
PCI: $3

17493 Cable America Corp.
263 US Hwy. 60 West Phone: (417)732-7242
Republic, MO 65738-1725 Fax: (417)732-8882

Founded: 1981. **Key Personnel:** Chance Shea, Lead Tech; Quincy McCroskey, Installer/Tech; Carolyn Haden, Customer Service Rep. **Cities Served:** Republic, MO; Continuous.: subscribing households 2200; 55 channels; 2 community access channels; 24 hours per week community access programming.

RICH HILL, pop. 1,471.

W. MO. Bates Co. 25 mi. NE of Ft. Scott, KS. Manufactures aluminum windows and doors, tool handles. Coal mines. Hardwood timber. Stock, dairy, poultry, grain farms. Corn, wheat, oats.

17494 Rich Hill Mining Review
PO Box 49 Phone: (417)395-4131
Rich Hill, MO 64779 Fax: (417)395-2171

Newspaper with a Democratic orientation. **Founded:** 1880. **Freq:** Weekly (Thurs.). **Print Method:** Offset. **Cols./Page:** 6. **Col. Width:** 26 nonpareils. **Col. Depth:** 294 agate lines. **Key Personnel:** Randall Bell, Editor and Publisher. **Subscription Rates:** $12.69. **Remarks:** Accepts advertising.
Ad Rates: GLR: $.14 **Circ:** 1,850

RICHLAND, pop. 1,922.

SC MO. Camden, Laclede, and Pulaski Co. 60 mi. NE of Springfield. Dairy, stock, poultry, fruit, grain farms.

17495 The Richland Mirror
Box 757 Phone: (314)765-3391
Richland, MO 65556 Fax: (314)765-3235

Newspaper with a Democratic orientation. **Founded:** 1907. **Freq:** Weekly (Thurs.). **Print Method:** Offset. **Cols./Page:** 6. **Col. Width:** 22 nonpareils. **Col. Depth:** 252 agate lines. **Key Personnel:** Gail Wright, Publisher, gwright@fidnet.com. **USPS:** 465-360. **Subscription Rates:** $20. **Remarks:** Accepts advertising.
Ad Rates: BW: $451.50 **Circ:** Paid ‡2,000
PCI: $3.50

RICHMOND†, pop. 5,499.

NW MO. Ray Co. 35 mi. NE of Kansas City. Manufactures meal and feed, plastics, lawn and garden furniture, automotive supplies, storm doors, windows. Agriculture. Meat processing. Livestock. Cattle. Corn, wheat, oats.

17496 The Advantage
Richmond News, Inc.
204 W. North Main St., No. 100 Phone: (816)776-5454
PO Box 100
Richmond, MO 64085-1743
Shopper. **Founded:** 1988. **Freq:** Weekly. **Print Method:** Offset. **Trim Size:** 17 x 22 3/4. **Cols./Page:** 6. **Col. Width:** 1 5/8 inches. **Col. Depth:** 16 inches. **Key Personnel:** Janet Brown, Contact. **Subscription Rates:** Free. **Remarks:** Accepts advertising. **Formerly:** Four County Shopper.
Ad Rates: SAU: $6.75 **Circ:** Free 8,700
PCI: $6.75

17497 The Daily News
Richmond News, Inc.
204 W. North Main St., No. 100 Phone: (816)776-5454
PO Box 100
Richmond, MO 64085-1743
General newspaper. **Founded:** 1914. **Freq:** Daily (eve.). **Print Method:** Offset. **Trim Size:** 13 1/2 x 22 3/4. **Cols./Page:** 7. **Col. Width:** 1 5/8 inches. **Col. Depth:** 21 inches. **Key Personnel:** Dennis McLouth, Publisher; Ray Scherer, Editor. **USPS:** 465-560. **Subscription Rates:** $57 carrier; $63 mail. **Remarks:** Accepts advertising.
Ad Rates: GLR: $.32 **Circ:** ‡3,000
BW: $630
4C: $780
SAU: $7
PCI: $6.75

17498 KAYX-FM - 92.5
111 W. Main Phone: (816)470-9925
Richmond, MO 64085 Fax: (816)470-8925
Free: (888)925-KAYX

Format: Religious; News; Talk. **Networks:** Business Radio; Sun Radio. **Owner:** Bott Communications, Inc., 10550 Barkley, Ste. 108, Overland Park, KS 66212. **Founded:** Nov. 28, 1994. **Operating Hours:** Continuous. **Key Personnel:** Richard P. Bott II, Vice President; Charles A. Lambert, Dir., Network Program Svcs.; Michelle Neer, Station Mgr. **Wattage:** 2350.

ROCK PORT†, pop. 1,511.

NW MO. Atchison Co. 80 mi. NW of Saint Joseph. Diversified farming. Corn, wheat, livestock.

17499 The Atchison County Mail
300 S. Main St. Phone: (816)744-6245
PO Box 40 Fax: (816)744-2645
Rock Port, MO 64482-0040
Publication E-mail: amail@heartland.net

Newspaper with a Democratic orientation. **Subtitle:** Farm / Smalltown Orientation. **Founded:** 1878. **Freq:** Weekly (Thurs.). **Print Method:** Offset. **Cols./Page:** 6. **Col. Width:** 26 nonpareils. **Col. Depth:** 301 agate lines. **Key Personnel:** William W. Farmer, Editor and Publisher; Marilyn S. Farmer, Publisher; W.C. Farmer, Managing Editor; Susette Meyerkorth, Advertising Mgr. **USPS:** 035-380. **Subscription Rates:** $21.50 individuals; $27 out of area. **Remarks:** Accepts advertising. **Online:** Missouri Net.
Ad Rates: GLR: $.13 **Circ:** Paid ‡2,550
BW: $516 Free ‡23
4C: $6.75
SAU: $4
PCI: $3.75

ROLLA†, pop. 13,303.

SEC MO. Phelps Co. 100 mi. SW of Saint Louis. Phelps Co. (SEC). 100 m SW of St. Louis,. University of Missouri at Rolla. Missouri School of Mines and Metallurgy. Mark Twain National Forest. Manufactures plastic pipe, fan blades, wooden tresses. Pyrite mines; clay pits. Timber. Stock, dairy, poultry, fruit farms. Grapes, apples, melons.

17500 Bridge of Eta Kappa Nu
Bridge of Etakapps News
PO Box 2107
Rolla, MO 65401

Electrical Engineering Honor Society magazine. **Founded:** 1959. **Freq:** Quarterly. **Print Method:** Offset. **Trim Size:** 8 1/2 x 11. **Cols./Page:** 3. **Col. Width:** 27 nonpareils. **Col. Depth:** 129 agate lines. **Key Personnel:** Dr. J. Robert Betten, Editor. **ISSN:** 0006-9809. **Remarks:** Accepts advertising.
Ad Rates: BW: $300 **Circ:** ‡20,300

17501 Phelps County Genealogical Society Quarterly
Phelps County Genealogical Society
Box 571
Rolla, MO 65402-0571

Genealogical magazine. **Freq:** Quarterly. **Trim Size:** 8 1/2 x 11. **Key Personnel:** Marguerite Mason, Editor, mmrite@misn.com. **ISSN:** 0884-2140. **Subscription Rates:** $18 individuals. **Remarks:** Advertising not accepted.
Circ: Paid 190

17502 Rolla Daily News
101 W. 7th St. Phone: (314)364-2468
PO Box 808 Fax: (314)341-5847
Rolla, MO 65401-0808
Publication E-mail: rdn@rollanet.org

General newspaper. **Founded:** 1875. **Freq:** Daily (eve.), Sunday (morn.). **Print Method:** Offset. **Cols./Page:** 6. **Col. Width:** 25 nonpareils. **Col. Depth:** 301 agate lines. **Key Personnel:** Stephen E. Sowers, Editor and Publisher; Lonna Stephenson, Advertising Mgr. **Subscription Rates:** $86.50. **Remarks:** Accepts advertising.
Ad Rates: BW: $625.65 **Circ:** 5,800
PCI: $8.05

17503 KMNR-FM - 89.7
113 University Center West Phone: (314)341-4272
Rolla, MO 65401 Fax: (573)341-4272
E-mail: kmnr@umr.edu

Format: Eclectic. **Owner:** Curators of the University of Missouri, 225 University Hall, Columbia, MO 65201. **Founded:** 1964. **Formerly:** KMSM-FM. **Operating Hours:** Continuous. **Key Personnel:** Jason Kinnear, Station Mgr.; Tami Salisbury, Program Dir.; Mike Pauli, Music Dir., phone (573)341-4273. **Wattage:** 450. **Ad Rates:** Noncommercial.

17504 KUMR-FM - 88.5
University of Missouri-Rolla Phone: (573)341-4386
G-6 Library Fax: (573)341-4889
Rolla, MO 65401
E-mail: kumr@umr.edu

Format: Public Radio; News; Classical; Bluegrass; Eclectic. **Networks:** National Public Radio (NPR); Public Radio International (PRI). **Owner:** Curators of The University of Missouri, University Hall, Columbia, MO 65211. **Founded:** 1973. **Operating Hours:** Continuous; 60% network. **Key Personnel:** Janet Turkovic, General Mgr.; Jim Sigler, Program Dir.; P. J. Cala, News Dir.; Louise Morgan, Mktg. Mgr.; John Francis, Science Producer; Lisa Middleton, Admin. Asst.; Chuck Knapp, Engineer. **Local Programs:** *Classical Allegro*, Janet Turkovic, (573)341-4387; *Mercantile Bluegrass Hour/Bluegrass*, Wayne Bledsoe, (573)341-5386; *Sounds Eclectic*, Jim Sigler. **Wattage:** 100,000. **URL:** http://www.umr.edu/˜kumr/.

ST. CHARLES

17505 The Linden World
Lindenwood College
209 S. Kingshighway Phone: (314)949-2000
St. Charles, MO 63301-1695 Fax: (314)949-4910

Student newsletter. **Freq:** Monthly. **Trim Size:** 8 1/2 x 11. **Remarks:** Advertising not accepted.
Circ: Non-paid 1500

17506 KCLC-FM - 89.1
Lindenwood College Phone: (314)949-4890
St. Charles, MO 63301
E-mail: kclc@lindenwood.edu

Format: News; Adult Contemporary; Bluegrass; Religious; Public Radio. **Networks:** ABC. **Founded:** 1968. **Operating Hours:** 5:30 a.m.-2.00 a.m.; 3% network, 97% local. **ADI:** St. Louis, MO (Mt. Vernon, IL). **Key Personnel:** Glen T. Cerny, General Mgr., phone (314)949-4880, cerny@lindenwood.edu; Richard Reighard, Operations Mgr., phone (314)949-4885; Deborah Nicolai, Office Mgr. **Wattage:** 25,500. **Ad Rates:** Underwriting available.

17507 KIRL-AM - 1460
3713 Hwy. 94 N. Phone: (314)946-6600
St. Charles, MO 63301 Fax: (314)946-6662

Format: Jazz; Gospel; Urban Contemporary. **Owner:** Bronco Broadcasting Co., Inc., at above address. **Founded:** 1958. **Operating Hours:** Continuous. **Key Personnel:** William E. White, Contact; Steve Love, News Dir.; Columbus Gregory, Program Dir.; Sharon Walters, Office Mgr. **Wattage:** 5000. **Ad Rates:** $22.75-32.50 for 30 seconds; $27.50-40 for 60 seconds.

ST. JAMES

17508 Leader-Journal
American Press
125 W. Springfield St. Phone: (314)265-3321
St. James, MO 65559-1929 Fax: (314)265-3197
Publication E-mail: stlj@stjames.k12.mo.usa

Community newspaper. **Founded:** 1896. **Freq:** Weekly (Wed.). **Print Method:** Offset. **Cols./Page:** 8. **Col. Width:** 18 nonpareils. **Col. Depth:** 294 agate lines. **Key Personnel:** Joe Arnold, Editor and Publisher; Angela Gwillim, Managing Editor. **Subscription Rates:** $18.75. **Remarks:** Accepts advertising.
Ad Rates: GLR: $.12 **Circ:** ‡2,900
PCI: $3.75

ST. JOSEPH

17509 Angus Beef Bulletin
Angus Journal
3201 Frederick Blvd. Phone: (816)383-5200
St. Joseph, MO 64506 Fax: (816)233-6575
Publisher E-mail: angus@angus.org

Tabloid for beef cattle producers. **Founded:** 1985. **Freq:** 3/year (2 during spring; 1 during fall). **Print Method:** Offset. **Trim Size:** 11 1/2 x 13 1/2. **Cols./Page:** 5. **Col. Width:** 11 1/2 picas. **Col. Depth:** 78 picas. **Key Personnel:** Shawna

Hermel, Editor, phone (816)383-5270, fax (816)233-6575, shermel@angus.org; Cheryl Oxley, Advertising Mgr., phone (816)383-5216, fax (816)233-6575, coxley@angus.org. **Subscription Rates:** Free to qualified subscribers; $10 Canada; $20 Canada. **Remarks:** Accepts advertising.
Ad Rates: BW: $1,095 **Circ:** Non-paid ‡65,000

17510 Angus Journal
3201 Frederick Blvd. Phone: (816)233-0563
St. Joseph, MO 64506 Fax: (816)233-6575
Publisher E-mail: angus@angus.org

Livestock magazine. **Founded:** 1919. **Freq:** Monthly. **Print Method:** Offset. **Cols./Page:** 3. **Col. Width:** 33 nonpareils. **Col. Depth:** 137 agate lines. **Key Personnel:** Jerilyn Johnson, Editor; Terry Cotton, General Mgr. **ISSN:** 0194-9543. **Subscription Rates:** $30 individuals; $55 two years. **Remarks:** Accepts advertising.
Ad Rates: BW: $695 **Circ:** ‡21,000
4C: $995
PCI: $42

17511 The Griffon News
Missouri Western State College
4525 Downs Dr. SS/C 204 Phone: (816)271-4412
St. Joseph, MO 64507 Fax: (816)271-4543
Publication E-mail: griffy@griffon.mwsc.edu

Collegiate newspaper. **Founded:** 1924. **Freq:** Weekly (Thurs.). **Print Method:** Offset. **Trim Size:** 12 x 23. **Cols./Page:** 6. **Col. Width:** 25 nonpareils. **Col. Depth:** 294 agate lines. **Key Personnel:** Bob Bergland, Adviser, bergland@griffon.mwsc.edu; Nichi Sollars, Editor; Ann Anderson, Business Mgr., griffads@griffon.mwsc.edu. **Subscription Rates:** Free. **Remarks:** Accepts advertising.
Ad Rates: BW: $375 **Circ:** Free ‡3,500
4C: $875
SAU: $4
PCI: $5

17512 Moila Temple Bulletin
Gallatin Publishing Co.
701 N. Noyes Blvd. Phone: (816)232-5129
St. Joseph, MO 64506 Fax: (816)232-7739
Publisher E-mail: gpc@ponyexpress.net

Fraternal magazine. **Founded:** 1923. **Freq:** Bimonthly. **Print Method:** Web press. **Trim Size:** 11 x 17. **Cols./Page:** 3. **Col. Width:** 24 nonpareils. **Col. Depth:** 136 agate lines. **Key Personnel:** Terry Gardner, Editor. **Remarks:** Accepts advertising.
Ad Rates: GLR: $.29 **Circ:** ‡4,500

17513 St. Joseph News-Press
News-Press & Gazette Co.
825 Edmond St. Phone: (816)271-8500
PO Box 29 Fax: (816)271-8692
St. Joseph, MO 64502
Free: (800)779-6397
Publication E-mail: editorial@ponyexpress.net

General newspaper. **Subtitle:** St. Joseph News-Press. **Founded:** 1845. **Freq:** Mon.-Sun. (morn.). **Print Method:** Offset. **Cols./Page:** 6. **Col. Depth:** 301 agate lines. **Key Personnel:** David R. Bradley, Jr., Editor and Publisher, phone (816)271-8502, fax (816)271-8695, davidb@ponyexpress.net; Henry H. Bradley, Chairman, phone (816)271-8501, hhb@ponyexpress.net; Tim Weddle, Advertising Dir., phone (816)271-8510, fax (816)271-8696, tweddle@ponyexpress.net. **Subscription Rates:** $152.44. **Remarks:** Advertising accepted; rates available upon request. Monday-Saturday: GLR: $37.92; BW: $4,891.68; 4C: $5,341.68; PCI: $37.92; Sunday: GLR: $39.44; BW: $5,087.76; 4C: $5,537.76; PCI: $39.44. **URL:** http://www.stjoenews_ press.com. **Formed by the merger of:** St. Joseph Gazette; St. Joseph News-Press.
Circ: Mon.-Sat. ★**40,327**
Sun. ★**44,847**

17514 The St. Joseph Telegraph
PO Box 1087 Phone: (816)364-1323
St. Joseph, MO 64502-1087 Fax: (816)364-3083

Community newspaper. **Founded:** 1989. **Freq:** Weekly (Thurs.). **Print Method:** Offset. **Cols./Page:** 5. **Col. Width:** 11 picas. **Col. Depth:** 16 inches. **Key Personnel:** Scott Johnson, Editor. **USPS:** 009-376. **Subscription Rates:** $28.04 individuals. **Remarks:** Accepts advertising.
Ad Rates: BW: $360 **Circ:** 2,000
SAU: $6
PCI: $6

17515 KGNM-AM - 1270
2414 S. Leonard Rd. Phone: (816)233-2577
St. Joseph, MO 64503-1899 Fax: (816)233-2374

Format: Adult Contemporary; Religious. **Networks:** USA Radio. **Founded:** 1980. **Operating Hours:** Continuous; 50% network, 50% local. **ADI:** St. Joseph, MO. **Key Personnel:** Steve Butler, General Mgr. **Wattage:** 1000. **Ad Rates:** $12.50 for 30 seconds; $15.50 for 60 seconds.

17516 KKJO-FM - 105.1
PO Box 8550 Phone: (816)279-6346
St. Joseph, MO 64508-8550 Fax: (816)279-8280

Format: Adult Contemporary; Contemporary Hit Radio (CHR). **Owner:** Cardinal Communications, Inc., PO Box 8550, St. Joseph, MO 64508. **Founded:** 1975. **Formerly:** KSFT-FM (1989). **Operating Hours:** Continuous. **ADI:** St. Joseph, MO. **Key Personnel:** Chris Meikel, Program Dir.; Reta Kneale, Sales Mgr.; Rick Austin, General Mgr. **Wattage:** 100,000. **Ad Rates:** $11-25 for 30 seconds; $14-28 for 60 seconds.

17517 KQTV-TV - 2
40th & Faraon Sts. Phone: (816)364-2222
PO Box 8369 Fax: (816)364-3787
St. Joseph, MO 64508
E-mail: kqtvtv@aol.com

Format: Commercial TV. **Networks:** ABC. **Owner:** NEXSTAR Broadcasting of the Midwest, Inc., at above address. **Founded:** 1953. **Formerly:** KFEQ-TV. **Operating Hours:** 5 a.m.-1 a.m. **ADI:** St. Joseph, MO. **Key Personnel:** Jerry Condra, kq2jcondra@aol.com.

17518 KSFT-AM - 1550
PO Box 8550 Phone: (816)279-6346
St. Joseph, MO 64508-8550 Fax: (816)279-8280

Networks: CNN Radio. **Owner:** Cardinal Communications, Inc., at above address. **Formerly:** KKJO-AM (1989). **Operating Hours:** Continuous. **ADI:** St. Joseph, MO. **Key Personnel:** Ted Mann, Vice President; Bob Heater, Operations Mgr.; Rick Austin, General Mgr. **Wattage:** 5000. **Ad Rates:** $8-18 for 30 seconds; $9-18 for 60 seconds.

17519 KTAJ-TV - 16
4410 S. 40th, St. Ste. 8 Phone: (816)364-1616
St. Joseph, MO 64503 Fax: (816)364-6729
E-mail: ktaj@xc.org

Format: Commercial TV; Religious. **Owner:** All American TV, 3000 W. McArthur, Ste. 530, Santa Ana, CA 92704, (714)957-9699, Fax: (714)957-9690. **Founded:** 1986. **Operating Hours:** Continuous. **ADI:** St. Joseph, MO. **Key Personnel:** Eugene Seibel, Chief Engineer, geneseib@smartnet.net; Julie Cornelius, Public Affairs; Mike Harris, Station Mgr. **Wattage:** 5,000,000. **Ad Rates:** $20-50 for 30 seconds; $29-70 for 60 seconds.

17520 KZZB-AM - 990
PO Box 8627
St. Joseph, MO 64508-8627

Format: Contemporary Hit Radio (CHR). **Simulcasts:** KZZB-FM. **Networks:** Independent. **Founded:** 1966. **Operating Hours:** Continuous. **ADI:** St. Joseph, MO. **Key Personnel:** Larry Crumpton, General Mgr.; Paul King, Program Dir.; Paul Chargois, General Sales Mgr.; Chrissie Roberts, Contact. **Wattage:** 1000.

17521 St. Joseph Cablevision
102 N. Woodbine Phone: (816)279-1234
PO Box 8069 Fax: (816)279-8773
St. Joseph, MO 64508

Owner: News-Press & Gazette Co., 825 Edmond, St. Joseph, MO 64501, (816)271-8500, Fax: (816)271-8695. **Founded:** 1965. **Key Personnel:** Hank Bradley, President; Kevin Dekker, Manager. **Cities Served:** subscribing households 29,000; 79 channels; 1 community access channel; 168 hours per week community access programming.

ST. LOUIS

17522 ACTA Cytologica
Science Printers and Publishers, Inc.
PO Drawer 12425 Phone: (314)991-4440
8342 Olive Blvd. Fax: (314)991-4654
St. Louis, MO 63132-2814
Publication E-mail: editor@acta-cytol.com

Journal publishing scientific articles offering significant contributions to the advancement of clinical cytology. **Subtitle:** The Journal of Clinical Cytology and Cytopathology. **Founded:** 1957. **Freq:** Bimonthly. **Print Method:** Offset. **Trim Size:** 8 x 10 3/4. **Cols./Page:** 2. **Col. Width:** 40 nonpareils. **Col. Depth:** 152 agate lines. **Key Personnel:** George L. Wied, M.D., Editor; Donna Kessel, Publisher. **ISSN:** 0001-5547. **Subscription Rates:** $176 individuals; $249 institutions; $35 single issue. **Remarks:** Accepts advertising.
Ad Rates: BW: $1,027 **Circ:** Paid 6,323
4C: $1,0271 Controlled 30
4C: $1,031

17523 Aesthetic Surgery Journal
Mosby Year Book, Inc.
11830 Westline Industrial Dr. Phone: (314)872-8370
St. Louis, MO 63146 Fax: (314)432-1380
Free: (800)325-4177

Official journal of the American Society for Aesthetic Plastic Surgery. Covers information on procedures, medications, and surgical supplies. **Founded:** 1988. **Freq:** Bimonthly. **Trim Size:** 8 1/4 x 11. **Key Personnel:** Elizabeth H. Sadati, Managing Editor; Kimberly L. Franks, Associate Mng. Editor; Robert W. Bernard, MD, Senior Editor; Bruce L. Cunningham, MD, Senior Editor. **Subscription Rates:** $60 individuals; $80.25 Canada; $75 other countries; $90 institutions; $112.35 institutions, Canada; $105 institutions, other countries; $40 students; $58.85 students, Canada; $55 students, other countries. **Remarks:** Accepts advertising. **Formerly:** Aesthetic Surgery Quarterly.
Ad Rates: BW: $2,000 **Circ:** 2,500

17524 Affirmative Action Register
Affirmative Action, Inc.
8356 Olive Blvd. Phone: (314)991-1335
St. Louis, MO 63132 Fax: (314)997-1788
Free: (800)537-0655
Publication E-mail: aareeo@concentric.net

Journal for business, academe, and the government to use in recruiting females, Native Americans, minorities, veterans, and the handicapped. **Subtitle:** The EEO Recruitment Publication. **Founded:** Mar. 15, 1974. **Freq:** Monthly. **Print Method:** Offset. **Trim Size:** 8 1/2 x 11. **Cols./Page:** 3 and 2. **Col. Width:** 2 1/4 and 3 inches. **Col. Depth:** 9 3/4 inches. **Key Personnel:** Joyce R. Green, Editor; Mildred Herbst, Manager. **ISSN:** 0146-2113. **Subscription Rates:** Free to qualified subscribers; $15 (mail). **URL:** http://www.aar.eeo.com.
Ad Rates: GLR: $7.08 **Circ:** Paid ‡950
BW: $2,300 Controlled ‡62,500
4C: $2,800
PCI: $90

17525 Agri Marketing
Doane Agricultural Services
11701 Borman Dr., Ste. 100 Phone: (314)569-2700
St. Louis, MO 63146-4199 Fax: (314)569-1083
Publication E-mail: agrimarket@aol.com
Publisher E-mail: agrimarket@aol.com

Magazine covering marketing, sales, and communications news for agribusiness professionals. **Founded:** 1963. **Freq:** 11/year. **Print Method:** Offset. **Trim Size:** 8 x 10 7/8. **Cols./Page:** 3 and 2. **Col. Width:** 27 and 42 nonpareils. **Col. Depth:** 140 agate lines. **Key Personnel:** Lynn Henderson, Publisher; Kathy Topping, Managing Editor; Bill Schuermann, Sales Mgr. **ISSN:** 0002-1180. **Subscription Rates:** $30 individuals; $5 single issue. **Remarks:** Accepts advertising.
Ad Rates: BW: $1,970 **Circ:** Paid 212
4C: $2,940 Controlled 8,325

17526 Air Medical Journal
Mosby Year Book, Inc.
11830 Westline Industrial Dr. Phone: (314)872-8370
St. Louis, MO 63146 Fax: (314)432-1380
Free: (800)325-4177

Journal for air medical transport professionals. **Founded:** 1986. **Freq:** Quarterly. **Trim Size:** 7 7/8 x 10 7/8. **Key Personnel:** William F. Rutherford, MD, Editor-in-Chief. **Subscription Rates:** $52 individuals; $71.69 Canada; $67 other countries; $54 institutions; $73.83 institutions, Canada; $69 institutions, other countries. **Remarks:** Accepts advertising.
Ad Rates: BW: $1,415 **Circ:** 4,300

17527 AirMed
Mosby Year Book, Inc.
11830 Westline Industrial Dr. Phone: (314)872-8370
St. Louis, MO 63146 Fax: (314)432-1380
Free: (800)325-4177

Journal on industry news, daily practice, health care reform, program profiles, and aircraft safety and operations. **Founded:** 1995. **Freq:** Bimonthly. **Trim Size:** 7 7/8 x 10 7/8. **Key Personnel:** Robert O'Malley, RN, MS, Editor-in-Chief. **Subscription Rates:** $52 individuals; $71.69 Canada; $67 other countries; $54 institutions; $73.83 institutions, Canada; $69 institutions, other countries. **Remarks:** Accepts advertising.
Ad Rates: BW: $1,415 **Circ:** 4,300

17528 AJIC (American Journal of Infection Control)
Mosby Year Book, Inc.
11830 Westline Industrial Dr. Phone: (314)872-8370
St. Louis, MO 63146 Fax: (314)432-1380
Free: (800)325-4177

Journal for infection control practitioners. Includes peer-reviewed articles in the field of infection control, and case studies and reports of innovations in control of infections. **Founded:** Jan. 1973. **Freq:** Bimonthly. **Print Method:** Offset.

Trim Size: 8 1/8 x 10 7/8. **Cols./Page:** 2. **Col. Width:** 39 nonpareils. **Col. Depth:** 140 agate lines. **Key Personnel:** Elaine Larson, M.D., Editor; Carol Trumbold, Publisher; Kathy Preston, Advertising Mgr. **ISSN:** 0196-6553. **Subscription Rates:** $170 institutions in U.S.; $202.23 institutions, Canada; $189 institutions, other countries; $66 individuals in U.S.; $90.95 individuals in Canada; $85 individuals in other countries; $36 students in U.S.; $58.85 students, Canada; $55 students, other countries; $15 single issue. **Remarks:** Accepts advertising. **URL:** http://www.mosby.com.
Ad Rates: BW: $1,580 **Circ:** Paid 13,893
Free 344

17529 Allan Kaye's Sports Cards News & Price Guides
Allan Kaye Publications, Inc.
10300 Watson Rd.
St. Louis, MO 63127-1106

Combination price and information guide with feature stories from top dealers. **Freq:** Semimonthly. **Key Personnel:** Allan Kaye, Editor and Publisher. **Subscription Rates:** $24.95. $3.95 single issue.

17530 American Agent & Broker
Commerce Publishing Co.
330 N. 4th St. Phone: (314)421-5445
St. Louis, MO 63102 Fax: (314)421-1070
Publication E-mail: aab@cpcmags.com

Magazine for independent agents in fire, casualty, and surety insurance businesses. **Subtitle:** The Mgazine for Insurance Agency Success. **Founded:** 1929. **Freq:** Monthly. **Print Method:** Offset. **Trim Size:** 8 x 10 7/8. **Cols./Page:** 3. **Col. Width:** 27 nonpareils. **Col. Depth:** 140 agate lines. **Key Personnel:** George Williams, Editor; David A. Baetz, Publisher. **ISSN:** 0002-7200. **Subscription Rates:** Free to qualified subscribers; $24. **Remarks:** Accepts advertising.
Ad Rates: BW: $3,027 **Circ:** Controlled ‡39,236
4C: $4,327

17531 American Christmas Tree Journal
National Christmas Tree Association
1000 Executive Parkway Dr., No. 220 Phone: (314)276-6410
Fax: (314)276-3349
St. Louis, MO 63141-6372
Christmas tree industry trade magazine covering growing, harvesting, and retailing. **Founded:** 1956. **Freq:** Quarterly. **Print Method:** Offset. **Trim Size:** 8 1/2 x 11. **Cols./Page:** 3. **Col. Width:** 28 nonpareils. **Col. Depth:** 140 agate lines. **Key Personnel:** Dennis Thompkins, Editor; David E. Baumann, Publisher. **ISSN:** 0569-3845. **Subscription Rates:** $45.
Ad Rates: BW: $352 **Circ:** ‡2,500
4C: $752
PCI: $22

17532 American Heart Journal
Mosby Year Book, Inc.
11830 Westline Industrial Dr. Phone: (314)872-8370
St. Louis, MO 63146 Fax: (314)432-1380
Free: (800)325-4177

Medical journal serving practicing cardiologists, university-affiliated clinicians, and physicians keeping abreast of developments in the diagnosis and management of cardiovascular disease. **Founded:** Oct. 1925. **Freq:** Monthly 12/year. **Print Method:** Offset. **Trim Size:** 8 1/8 x 10 7/8. **Cols./Page:** 2. **Col. Width:** 39 nonpareils. **Col. Depth:** 140 agate lines. **Key Personnel:** Robert M. Califf, M.D., Editor; Doug Kessler, Marketing Dir.; Joyce Felan, Marketing Coord., phone (314)453-4337, fax (314)872-9164; Gale Schlogl, Journal Ad. Sales Service, gale.schlogl@mosby.com. **ISSN:** 0002-8703. **Subscription Rates:** $144 individuals; $194.74 Canada; $182 other countries; $72 students; $117.70 students, Canada; $110 students, other countries; $291 institutions; $352.03 institutions, Canada; $329 institutions, other countries. **Remarks:** Accepts advertising. **URL:** http://www.mosby.com.
Ad Rates: BW: $1,290 **Circ:** Paid 6,569
Free 464

17533 American Journal of Obstetrics and Gynecology
Mosby Year Book, Inc.
11830 Westline Industrial Dr. Phone: (314)872-8370
St. Louis, MO 63146 Fax: (314)432-1380
Free: (800)325-4177

Journal for specialists in obstetrics and gynecology and for general practitioners. **Founded:** Oct. 1920. **Freq:** Monthly. **Print Method:** Offset. **Trim Size:** 8 1/8 x 10 7/8. **Cols./Page:** 2. **Col. Width:** 39 nonpareils. **Col. Depth:** 140 agate lines. **Key Personnel:** E.J. Quilligan, MD, Editor; Frederick Zuspan, MD, Editor; Ingrid Shephard, Advertising Mgr.; Gale Schlogl, Advertising Sales, phone (314)453-4337, fax (314)872-9164, gale.schlogl@mosby.com. **ISSN:** 0002-9378. **Subscription Rates:** $152 individuals; $206.51 Canada; $193 other countries; $73 students; $121.98 students, Canada; $114 students, other countries; $299 institutions; $363.80 institutions, Canada; $340 institutions, other countries. **Remarks:** Accepts advertising. **URL:** http://www.mosby.com. **Alt. Formats:** CD-ROM.
Ad Rates: BW: $1,540 **Circ:** Paid 14,386
4C: $2,510 Free 498

17534 American Journal of Orthodontics and Dentofacial Orthopedics
Mosby Year Book, Inc.
11830 Westline Industrial Dr. Phone: (314)872-8370
St. Louis, MO 63146 Fax: (314)432-1380
Free: (800)325-4177

Journal for orthodontists and dentists who include orthodontics as a portion of their practice. **Founded:** Oct. 1915. **Freq:** Monthly. **Print Method:** Offset. **Trim Size:** 8 1/8 x 10 7/8. **Cols./Page:** 2. **Col. Width:** 39 nonpareils. **Col. Depth:** 140 agate lines. **Key Personnel:** T.M. Graber, D.M.D., Editor; Carol Trumbold, Publisher; JoAnn Anzalone, Advertising Mgr.; Jo Ann Anzalone, Mgr., Marketing Communications; Carol Kilzer, Journal Advertising Sales Services, carol.kilzer@mosby.com. **ISSN:** 0002-9416. **Subscription Rates:** $128 individuals; $167.99 Canada; $157 other countries; $65 students; $100.58 students, Canada; $94 students, other countries; $262 institutions; $311.37 institutions, Canada; $291 institutions, other countries. **Remarks:** Accepts advertising. **URL:** http://www.mosby.com.
Ad Rates: BW: $1,770 **Circ:** Paid 16,357
Non-paid 222

17535 The American Muslim
American Muslim Support Group
PO Box 5670 Phone: (314)291-3711
St. Louis, MO 63121 Fax: (314)291-3711

Quarterly Magazine. **Founded:** 1989. **Freq:** Quarterly. **Key Personnel:** Sheila Musaji, Editor. **Subscription Rates:** $15; $30 other countries; $5 prisoners. **Remarks:** Advertising accepted; rates available upon request.
Circ: 2,000

17536 Analytical and Quantitative Cytology and Histology
Science Printers and Publishers, Inc.
PO Drawer 12425 Phone: (314)991-4440
8342 Olive Blvd. Fax: (314)991-4654
St. Louis, MO 63132-2814
Publication E-mail: editor@jreproded.gom

Journal covering analytical and quantitative cytology and histology. **Founded:** 1979. **Freq:** Bimonthly. **Print Method:** Offset. **Trim Size:** 8 x 10 3/4. **Cols./Page:** 2. **Col. Width:** 3 3/8 inches. **Col. Depth:** 10 inches. **Key Personnel:** George L. Wied, M.D., Editor-in-Chief; Donna Kessel, Publisher. **ISSN:** 0884-6812. **Subscription Rates:** $250; $342 industry; $50 single issue. **Remarks:** Accepts advertising.
Ad Rates: BW: $1,027 **Circ:** Paid ‡2,804
4C: $1,027 Non-paid ‡30
4C: $1,031

17537 Annals of Otology, Rhinology and Laryngology
Annals Publishing Co.
4507 Laclede Ave. Phone: (314)367-4987
St. Louis, MO 63108 Fax: (314)367-4988
Publication E-mail: manager@annals.com

Journal for physicians specializing in the field of otolaryngology-head and neck medicine and surgery; plastic surgeons; audiologists; speech pathologists; medical schools; hospitals; clinics and those who wish to keep informed of the latest developments in the field of otolaryngology. **Founded:** 1892. **Freq:** Monthly. **Print Method:** Offset. **Trim Size:** 8 3/8 x 11. **Cols./Page:** 2. **Col. Width:** 40 nonpareils. **Col. Depth:** 133 agate lines. **Key Personnel:** Brian F. McCabe, Editor, phone (319)356-2310, fax (319)356-4549; Charles C. Cunningham, Advertising Representative, phone (201)767-4170, fax (201)767-8065, cunnasso@cybernex.net; Kenneth A. Cooper, Jr., President, kcooper@annals.com. **ISSN:** 0003-4894. **Subscription Rates:** $125 individuals; $150 other countries; $179 institutions and industry; $204 instituions and industry, other countries. **Alt. Formats:** Microform.
Ad Rates: BW: $740 **Circ:** ‡6,001
4C: $1,725

17538 AOA News
American Optometric Association
243 N. Lindbergh Blvd. Phone: (314)991-4100
St. Louis, MO 63141-7881 Fax: (314)991-4101
Publication E-mail: amoptnews@aol.com

Newspaper for the American Optometric Association. **Founded:** 1962. **Freq:** Semimonthly. **Print Method:** Offset. **Trim Size:** 10 3/8 x 15. **Cols./Page:** 4. **Col. Width:** 2 1/4 inches. **Col. Depth:** 14 1/4 inches. **Key Personnel:** Robert Foster, Editor, rafoster@theaoa.org; Andrew Miller, Assoc. Dir., Publications, almiller@theaoa.org. **ISSN:** 0094-9620. **Subscription Rates:** $72 nonmembers annually. **Remarks:** Accepts advertising. **Available Online. URL:** http://www.aoanet.org/aoanet.
Ad Rates: BW: $3,580 **Circ:** Paid ‡22,189
4C: $5,054 Free ‡7,823
PCI: $53

17539 Appraisal Review
National Association of Independent Fee Appraisers
7501 Murdoch Ave. Phone: (314)781-6688
St. Louis, MO 63119 Fax: (314)781-2872
Publisher E-mail: info@naifa.com

Magazine of National Association of Independent Fee Appraisers. **Subtitle:** Official Journal of the National Association of Independent Fee Appraisers (NAIFA). **Founded:** 1994. **Freq:** Quarterly. **Print Method:** Offset. **Trim Size:** 8 x 10 3/4. **Key Personnel:** Donna Walter, Editor. **Remarks:** Accepts advertising.
Ad Rates: BW: $4,800 **Circ:** Non-paid 5,000
4C: $5,325

17540 Atlantic Economic Journal
Atlantic Economic Society
10A Maryland Plaza Phone: (314)454-0100
St. Louis, MO 63108-1502 Fax: (314)454-9109
Publisher E-mail: iaes@iaes.org

Professional journal covering economics. **Founded:** Nov. 1973. **Freq:** Quarterly. **Key Personnel:** John M. Virgo, Managing Editor; Mary Ellen Unnerstall, Senior Editorial Asst. **ISSN:** 0197-4254. **Subscription Rates:** $57 individuals; $165 institutions. **Remarks:** Accepts advertising. **URL:** http://www.iaes.org.
Ad Rates: BW: $525 **Circ:** (Not Reported)

17541 Best Practices and Benchmarking in Healthcare
Mosby Year Book, Inc.
11830 Westline Industrial Dr. Phone: (314)872-8370
St. Louis, MO 63146 Fax: (314)432-1380
Free: (800)325-4177

Journal reporting on healthcare management. **Subtitle:** A Practical Journal for Clinical and Management Applications. **Founded:** 1996. **Freq:** Bimonthly. **Trim Size:** 8 1/4 x 10 7/8. **Key Personnel:** Walter F. Ballinger, MD, Editor-in-Chief; James O. Hepner, Ph.D., Editor-in-Chief. **Subscription Rates:** $63 U.S.; $88.81 Canada; $83 other countries; $124 institutions; $154.08 institutions, Canada; $144 institutions, other countries. **Remarks:** Accepts advertising.
Ad Rates: BW: $700 **Circ:** 3,000

17542 Breast Diseases
Mosby Year Book, Inc.
11830 Westline Industrial Dr. Phone: (314)872-8370
St. Louis, MO 63146 Fax: (314)432-1380
Free: (800)325-4177

Journal on the latest developments in the diagnosis, treatment, screening, and prevention of breast diseases. **Founded:** 1990. **Freq:** Quarterly. **Key Personnel:** Charles M. Balch, MD, Editor. **Subscription Rates:** $69; $45 students; $89 Industry; $77.83 Canada; $52.15 Canadian Students; $99.23 Canadian Industry; $83 other countries; $59 other countries' students; $103 other countries' Industry.

17543 Cadenza
Washington University Phone: (314)935-5941
Campus Box 1039 Fax: (314)935-5938
St. Louis, MO 63130
Community newspaper. **Freq:** Weekly (Fri.). **Print Method:** Offset. **Cols./Page:** 4. **Col. Width:** 2 3/8 inches. **Col. Depth:** 12 inches. **Key Personnel:** Dave Ross, Editor. **Subscription Rates:** Free; $29 out of area. **Remarks:** Accepts advertising.
Ad Rates: BW: $501.41 **Circ:** Non-paid ‡8,000
PCI: $10.15

17544 The Case Manager
Mosby Year Book, Inc.
11830 Westline Industrial Dr. Phone: (314)872-8370
St. Louis, MO 63146 Fax: (314)432-1380
Free: (800)325-4177

Magazine containing information about new medicines, insurance issues, reimbursement, and other managed care issues. **Founded:** 1990. **Freq:** Bimonthly. **Trim Size:** 8 1/8 x 10 7/8. **Key Personnel:** Tom Strickland, Editor. **Subscription Rates:** $55 institutions in U.S.; $81.32 institutions in Canada; $76 institutions in other countries; $45 individuals in U.S.; $70.62 individuals in Canada; $66 individuals in other countries; $10 single issue. **URL:** http://www.mosby.com.
Ad Rates: BW: $1,855 **Circ:** Combined 20,000

17545 Catholic Health World
Catholic Health Association of the United States
4455 Woodson Rd. Phone: (314)253-3445
St. Louis, MO 63134-3797 Fax: (314)253-3540

Tabloid containing national and regional news stories, human

interest items, healthcare legislation articles, and photos of interest to administrators of U.S. Catholic hospitals, medical centers, and long-term care facilities. **Founded:** Feb. 15, 1985. **Freq:** 22/year. **Print Method:** Offset. **Trim Size:** 11 x 17. **Cols./Page:** 4. **Col. Width:** 2 5/16 inches. **Col. Depth:** 15 inches. **Key Personnel:** Sandy Gilfillan, Editor; Rev. Michael D. Place, STD. **ISSN:** 8756-4068. **Subscription Rates:** $35 individuals; $40 other countries. **Remarks:** Color advertising accepted; rates available upon request. **URL:** http://www.chausa.org.
Ad Rates: BW: $1,555 **Circ:** Paid ‡499
PCI: $37 Non-paid ‡11,137

17546 Cherry Diamond
Missouri Athletic Club
405 Washington Ave. Phone: (314)231-7220
St. Louis, MO 63102-2183 Fax: (314)231-2327

Missouri Athletic Club affairs magazine. **Founded:** 1907. **Freq:** 11/year. **Print Method:** Offset. **Trim Size:** 8 1/2 x 11. **Cols./Page:** 3 and 2. **Col. Width:** 28 and 42 nonpareils. **Col. Depth:** 140 agate lines. **Key Personnel:** Dan Kimack, Editor; Lisa Hanly, Asst. Editor. **Subscription Rates:** $23. **Remarks:** Accepts advertising.
Ad Rates: BW: $546 **Circ:** 4,900
4C: $936

17547 Clinical Pharmacology and Therapeutics
Mosby Year Book, Inc.
11830 Westline Industrial Dr. Phone: (314)872-8370
St. Louis, MO 63146 Fax: (314)432-1380
Free: (800)325-4177

Pharmacology journal devoted to the study of the nature, action, efficacy, and total evaluation of drugs as they are used in humans. **Founded:** Oct. 1960. **Freq:** Monthly. **Print Method:** Offset. **Trim Size:** 8 1/4 x 11. **Cols./Page:** 2. **Col. Width:** 39 nonpareils. **Col. Depth:** 140 agate lines. **Key Personnel:** Marcus M. Reidenberg, M.D., Editor; Donna Ricko, Publisher. **ISSN:** 0009-9236. **Subscription Rates:** $150 individuals; $195.81 Canada; $183 other countries; $75 students; $115.56 students, Canada; $108 students, other countries; $294 institutions; $349.89 institutions, Canada; $327 institutions, other countries. **Remarks:** Accepts advertising. **URL:** http://www.mosby.com. **Alt. Formats:** CD-ROM.
Ad Rates: BW: $1,000 **Circ:** Paid 4,143
Free 230

17548 Community News
5748 Helen Ave. Phone: (314)261-5555
St. Louis, MO 63136 Fax: (314)261-2776

Community newspaper (tabloid). **Founded:** 1921. **Freq:** Weekly (Wed.). **Print Method:** Offset. **Trim Size:** 10 1/8 x 16. **Cols./Page:** 5. **Col. Width:** 1 7/8 inches. **Col. Depth:** 16 inches. **Key Personnel:** C.R. Bockskopf, Editor; R.J. Huneke, Jr., Publisher. **Subscription Rates:** Free to qualified subscribers; $104 by mail. **Remarks:** Accepts advertising.
Ad Rates: PCI: $30 **Circ:** Free ‡30,000

17549 Computer Aided Surgery
John Wiley and Sons, Inc.
Div. of Neurosurgery Phone: (314)268-5378
St. Louis University Health Fax: (314)268-5113
Sciences Center
1320 S. Grand Blvd.
St. Louis, MO 63104-1087
Publisher E-mail: subinfo@wiley.com

Journal covering all aspects of surgery performed in conjunction with imaging. Includes applications in neurosurgery, orthopedics, and other surgical subspecialties. **Founded:** Apr. 1995. **Freq:** Bimonthly. **Trim Size:** 8 1/4 x 11. **Cols./Page:** 2. **Col. Width:** 18 picas. **Key Personnel:** Richard D. Bucholz, Editor-in-Chief; Susan Malowski, Subscription Mgr. **ISSN:** 1092-9088. **Subscription Rates:** $245. **Remarks:** Accepts advertising. **URL:** http://journals.wiley.com/cas/. **Formerly:** Journal of Image Guided Surgery.
Ad Rates: BW: $835 **Circ:** Paid 12,500
4C: $1,135

17550 County Star
Suburban Newspapers of Greater St. Louis
4426 Woodson Rd. Phone: (314)426-2222
St. Louis, MO 63134-3702 Fax: (314)821-3652

Community newspaper. **Founded:** Mar. 3, 1960. **Freq:** Semi-weekly (Wed. and Sun.). **Print Method:** Offset. **Cols./Page:** 6. **Col. Width:** 26 nonpareils. **Col. Depth:** 308 agate lines. **Key Personnel:** Michael T. Cody, Editor; Paul Winans, Publisher. **Subscription Rates:** Free. **Remarks:** Accepts advertising.
Ad Rates: BW: $1,339.80 **Circ:** Free 82,366
4C: $1,659.80

17551 Credit World
International Credit Association
243 N. Lindbergh Blvd. Phone: (314)991-3030
PO Box 419057 Fax: (314)991-3029
St. Louis, MO 63141-1757
Publication E-mail: publictns@stlnet.com
Publisher E-mail: icahdqtrs@stlnet.com

Professional credit magazine. **Subtitle:** The Official Publication of the International Credit Association. **Founded:** 1912. **Freq:** Bimonthly. **Print Method:** Web. **Trim Size:** 8 1/8 x 10 7/8. **Cols./Page:** 3 and 2. **Col. Width:** 26 and 40 nonpareils. **Col. Depth:** 129 agate lines. **Key Personnel:** Janet Jourman Protzel, Editor, jprotzel@stlnet.com; Eric Lindsey, Administrator/Designer. **ISSN:** 0011-1074. **Subscription Rates:** $60; $10 single issue. **Remarks:** Accepts advertising. **Online:** UMI. **Alt. Formats:** CD-ROM.
Ad Rates: BW: $1,230 **Circ:** Paid 5,000
4C: $2,420 Non-paid 150

17552 Current Problems in Cancer
Mosby Year Book, Inc.
11830 Westline Industrial Dr. Phone: (314)872-8370
St. Louis, MO 63146 Fax: (314)432-1380
Free: (800)325-4177

Journal serving physicians who treat patients with neoplastic disease. Each issue presents a single-topic, in-depth discussion usually focused on the integrated management of a particular type of cancer or on a particular problem faced in a wide variety of malignancies. Includes extensive bibliographies and abstracts for each article. **Founded:** 1977. **Freq:** Bimonthly. **Key Personnel:** Robert F. Ozols, MD, Editor. **Subscription Rates:** $65; $39 students; $87 Industry; $75 Canada; $47.18 Canadian students; $98.54 Canadian Industry; $85 other countries; $59 other countries' students; $107 other countries' Industry. **URL:** http://www.mosby.com.

17553 Current Problems in Cardiology
Mosby Year Book, Inc.
11830 Westline Industrial Dr. Phone: (314)872-8370
St. Louis, MO 63146 Fax: (314)432-1380
Free: (800)325-4177

Journal providing focused, comprhensive coverage of important clinical topics in cardiology. **Founded:** 1976. **Freq:** Monthly. **Key Personnel:** Robert A. O'Rourke, MD, Editor. **Subscription Rates:** $75; $45 students; $100 industry; $89.10 Canada; $57 students in Canada; $115.85 Canadian industry; $100 other countries; $70 students in other countries; $125 other countries' industry. **URL:** http://www.mosby.com.

17554 Current Problems in Dermatology
Mosby Year Book, Inc.
11830 Westline Industrial Dr. Phone: (314)872-8370
St. Louis, MO 63146 Fax: (314)432-1380
Free: (800)325-4177

Journal focusing on clinical problems and conditions faced by practicing dermatologists. Articles cover the etiology and presentation, diagnosis, treat ment (both medical and surgical approaches), and prognosis of the selected dis order. Abstracts summarize the important points of the article. **Founded:** 1989. **Freq:** Bimonthly. **Key Personnel:** Jeffrey P. Collen, MD, Editor. **Subscription Rates:** $65; $39 students; $90 Industry; $75 Canada; $47.18 Canadian students; $101.75 Canadian Industry; $85 other countries; $59 other countries students; $110 other countries' Industry. **URL:** http://www.mosby.com.

17555 Current Problems in Diagnostic Radiology
Mosby Year Book, Inc.
11830 Westline Industrial Dr. Phone: (314)872-8370
St. Louis, MO 63146 Fax: (314)432-1380
Free: (800)325-4177

Journal geared to the needs of general radiologists. Each issue provides an in-depth discussion of a single topic in radiology that covers preferred radiological procedures, diagnostic strategies and concerns, technical improvements, and the development of alternate modalities. **Founded:** 1972. **Freq:** Bimonthly. **Key Personnel:** TheodoreE. Keats, MD, Editor. **Subscription Rates:** $65; $39 students; $90 Industry; $75 Canada; $47.18 Canadian students; $101.75 Canadian Industry; $85 other countries; $59 other countries' students; $110 other countries' Industry. **URL:** http://www.mosby.com.

17556 Current Problems in Obstetrics, Gynecology and Fertility
Mosby Year Book, Inc.
11830 Westline Industrial Dr. Phone: (314)872-8370
St. Louis, MO 63146 Fax: (314)432-1380
Free: (800)325-4177

Journal on specific clinical conditions, with an emphasis on the management of fertility and other endocrine problems. **Founded:** 1978. **Freq:** Bimonthly. **Key Personnel:** Robert L. Barbieri, MD, Editor. **Subscription Rates:** $65; $39 students; $90 Industry; $75 Canada; $47.18 Canadian students; $101.75 Canadian Industry; $85 other countries; $59 other countries' students; $110 other countries' Industry. **URL:** http://www.mosby.com.

17557 Current Problems in Pediatrics
Mosby Year Book, Inc.
11830 Westline Industrial Dr. Phone: (314)872-8370
St. Louis, MO 63146 Fax: (314)432-1380
Free: (800)325-4177

Journal addressing pathophysiology, diagnosis, drug therapy, surgical management, family factors, and development issues. **Founded:** 1971. **Freq:** 10/year. **Key Personnel:** Norman C. Fost, MD, Editor. **Subscription Rates:** $68; $43 students; $93 Industry; $81.61 Canada; $54.86 Canadian students; $108.36 Canadian Industry; $93 other countries; $68 other countries' students; $118 other countries' Industry. **URL:** http://www.mosby.com.

17558 Current Problems in Surgery
Mosby Year Book, Inc.
11830 Westline Industrial Dr. Phone: (314)872-8370
St. Louis, MO 63146 Fax: (314)432-1380
Free: (800)325-4177

Medical monographic journal presenting up-to-date, comprehensive review articles on clinical surgical topics. **Founded:** 1964. **Freq:** Monthly. **Print Method:** Offset. **Trim Size:** 6 x 9. **Cols./Page:** 1. **Key Personnel:** Samuel Wells, M.D., Editor; Richard Wallace, Managing Editor; Donna Ricko, Advertising Mgr. **ISSN:** 0011-3840. **Subscription Rates:** $78 individuals; $45 residents/trainees; $100 industry. **URL:** http://www.mosby.com.
Circ: ‡6,600

17559 Diabetes
Washington University School of Medicine
660 S. Euclid Ave. Phone: (314)362-7809
PO Box 8127
St. Louis, MO 63110
Magazine containing original research about diabetes. **Freq:** Monthly. **Subscription Rates:** $100 individuals. **Remarks:** Advertising accepted; rates available upon request.
Circ: (Not Reported)

17560 Disease-A-Month
Mosby Year Book, Inc.
11830 Westline Industrial Dr. Phone: (314)872-8370
St. Louis, MO 63146 Fax: (314)432-1380
Free: (800)325-4177

Journal on specific diseases, focusing on pathophysiology, clinical features of the disease or condition, diagnostic techniques, therapeutic approaches, and prognosis. **Founded:** 1954. **Freq:** Monthly. **Key Personnel:** Roger C. Bone, MD, Editor. **Subscription Rates:** $70; $45students; $100 Industry; $83.75 Canada; $57 Canadian students; $115.85 Canadian Industry; $95 other countries; $70 other countries' students; $125 other countries' Industry. **URL:** http://www.mosby.com.

17561 Employment Marketplace
12015 Robyn Park Dr. Phone: (314)569-3095
St. Louis, MO 63131
Publication E-mail: info@eminfo.com

Trade magazine for recruiting professionals. **Founded:** 1982. **Freq:** Quarterly. **Key Personnel:** Pat Turner, Editor. **Subscription Rates:** $26 individuals. **Remarks:** Accepts advertising.
Circ: Controlled 21,000

17562 Facts and Comparisons
Facts & Comparisons
111 W. Port Plaza, Ste. 300 Phone: (314)216-2100
St. Louis, MO 63146 Fax: (314)878-5563
Free: (800)223-0554

Drug information organized by therapeutic category. **Subtitle:** Clinisphere: Drug Facts and Comparisons. **Founded:** 1945. **Freq:** Monthly. **Print Method:** CD-ROM. **Key Personnel:** Michael Riley, Publisher, phone (314)216-2110, fax (314)878-2058; Robert Brown, Director of Marketing, phone (314)216-2196; Sofia Dorsano, Dir. of Electronic Products, phone (314)216-2180. **ISSN:** 0014-6617. **Subscription Rates:** $299. **Remarks:** Advertising not accepted. **URL:** http://www.drugfacts.com. **Alt. Formats:** CD-ROM; Diskette.
Circ: (Not Reported)

17563 Forum for School Economics
St. Louis University
3674 Lindell Blvd. Phone: (314)977-3814
St. Louis, MO 63108 Fax: (314)977-3897

Scholarly journal covering economics. **Founded:** 1971. **Freq:** Semiannual. **Cols./Page:** 1. **Key Personnel:** Patrick J. Welch, Editor, welchpj@slu.edu. **ISSN:** 0736-0932. **Subscription Rates:** $60 individuals; $130 out of country. **Remarks:** Advertising not accepted.
Circ: Controlled 500

17564 Gastrointestinal Endoscopy
Mosby Year Book, Inc.
11830 Westline Industrial Dr. Phone: (314)872-8370
St. Louis, MO 63146 Fax: (314)432-1380
Free: (800)325-4177

Medical journal. **Subtitle:** Official Journal of the American Society for Gastrointestinal Endoscopy. **Founded:** 1954. **Freq:** Monthly. **Print Method:** Offset. **Trim Size:** 8 1/8 x 10 7/8. **Cols./Page:** 2. **Col. Width:** 32 nonpareils. **Col. Depth:** 119 agate lines. **Key Personnel:** Michael V. Sivak, Jr., MD, Editor; Ronald E. Warren, Marketing Mgr.; Ingrid Shephard, Marketing Coord.; Carol Kilzer, Advertising Sales, phone (314)453-4307, fax (314)872-9164, carol.kilzer@mosby.com. **ISSN:** 0016-5107. **Subscription Rates:** $82 students; $144.45 students, Canada; $135 students other countries; $149 individuals; $216.14 individuals Canada; $202 individuals other countries; $198 institutions; $268.57 institutions, Canada; $251 institutions, other countries. **Remarks:** Accepts advertising. **URL:** http://www.mosby.com. **Alt. Formats:** CD-ROM.
Ad Rates: BW: $990 **Circ:** Combined 10,537

17565 Gateway Heritage
Missouri Historical Society
PO Box 11940 Phone: (314)746-4557
St. Louis, MO 63112-0040 Fax: (314)746-4548
Publication E-mail: pbs@mohistory.org

Journal on the history of St. Louis and the American West. **Subtitle:** The Quarterly Magazine of the Missouri Historical Society. **Founded:** 1980. **Freq:** Quarterly. **Print Method:** Offset. **Trim Size:** 8 1/2 x 11. **Cols./Page:** 2. **Col. Width:** 40 nonpareils. **Col. Depth:** 140 agate lines. **Key Personnel:** Tim Fox, Editor; Katherine Douglass, Book Notes Editor, phone (314)746-4569; Lee Ann Sandweiss, Director of Publications, phone (314)746-4558. **ISSN:** 0198-9375. **Subscription Rates:** $20. **Remarks:** Advertising not accepted. **Formerly:** Missouri Historial Society Bulletin.
Circ: Paid ‡6,500
Controlled ‡500

17566 Geriatric Nursing
Mosby Year Book, Inc.
11830 Westline Industrial Dr. Phone: (314)872-8370
St. Louis, MO 63146 Fax: (314)432-1380
Free: (800)325-4177

Magazine for nurses in geriatric and gerontologic nursing practice, the primary professional providers of care for the aging. Provides news on issues affecting elders and clinical information on techniques and procedures. **Founded:** May 1980. **Freq:** Bimonthly. **Print Method:** Offset. **Trim Size:** 8 1/8 x 10 7/8. **Cols./Page:** 3. **Col. Width:** 26 nonpareils. **Col. Depth:** 140 agate lines. **Key Personnel:** Priscilla Ebersole, R.N., Editor; JoAnn Anzalone, Comm. Mgr.; Michelle Kuhn, Journal Adv. Sales Service, michelle.kuhn@mosby.com. **ISSN:** 0197-4572. **Subscription Rates:** $40 individuals; $68.48 Canada; $64 other countries; $25 students; $52.43 students, Canada; $49 students, other countries; $74 institutions; $104.86 institutions, Canada; $98 institutions, other countries. **Remarks:** Accepts advertising. **URL:** http://www.mosby.com.
Ad Rates: BW: $1,480 **Circ:** Paid 10,596
Free 298

17567 Happy Times
Concordia Publishing House
3558 S. Jefferson Ave. Phone: (314)268-1000
St. Louis, MO 63118 Fax: (314)268-1329
Free: (800)325-3381

Story magazine for preschoolers. **Founded:** 1963. **Freq:** Monthly. **Print Method:** Letterpress and offset. **Trim Size:** 8 x 8 1/4. **Cols./Page:** 2. **Col. Width:** 27 nonpareils. **Col. Depth:** 133 agate lines. **Key Personnel:** Dr. Earl Gaulke, Editor; Angela Skinner, Product Mgr. **USPS:** 234-880. **Subscription Rates:** $7.90. **Remarks:** Advertising not accepted.
Circ: ‡40,000

17568 Health Perspective
Clayton-Davis & Associates
8229 Maryland Ave. Phone: (314)862-7800
St. Louis, MO 63105 Fax: (314)721-5171

Consumer health tabloid. **Founded:** 1982. **Freq:** Monthly. **Print Method:** Offset. **Trim Size:** 11 1/4 x 14. **Cols./Page:** 4. **Col. Width:** 14 picas. **Col. Depth:** 180 agate lines. **Key Personnel:** Ruth Sirko, Editor; Mary Brown, Advertising Mgr. **Remarks:** Accepts advertising.
Ad Rates: BW: $5,000 **Circ:** Non-paid ‡125,000

17569 Health Progress
Catholic Health Association of the United States
4455 Woodson Rd. Phone: (314)253-3445
St. Louis, MO 63134-3797 Fax: (314)253-3540

Magazine for administrative-level and other managerial personnel in Catholic healthcare and related organizations. Featured are articles on management concepts, legislative and regulatory trends, and theological, sociological, ethical, legal, and technical issues. **Subtitle:** Official Journal of the Catholic Health Association of the United States. **Founded:** May 1920. **Freq:** 6/year. **Print Method:** Web offset. **Trim Size:** 8 1/8 x 10 7/8. **Cols./Page:** 3 and 2. **Col. Width:** 26 and 39 nonpareils. **Col. Depth:** 140 agate lines. **Key Personnel:** Judy Cassidy, Editor, phone (314)253-3445, fax (314)253-3540, jcassid@chausa.org; Rev. Michael Place, Publisher. **ISSN:** 0882-1577. **Subscription Rates:** Free to qualified subscribers free to subscribers from CHA; $40 individuals; $45 other countries; $7 single issue. **Remarks:** Accepts advertising from members only. **URL:** http://www.chausa.org. **Alt. Formats:** Microform. **Formerly:** Hospital Progress (1984).
Ad Rates: BW: $945 **Circ:** Paid ‡11,000
Controlled ‡9,300

17570 Heart and Lung
Mosby Year Book, Inc.
11830 Westline Industrial Dr. Phone: (314)872-8370
St. Louis, MO 63146 Fax: (314)432-1380
Free: (800)325-4177

Journal offering articles prepared by nurse and physician members of the critical care team, recognizing the nurse's role in the care and management of major organ-system conditions in critically ill patients. **Subtitle:** The Journal of Acute and Critical Care. **Founded:** Jan. 1972. **Freq:** Bimonthly. **Print Method:** Offset. **Trim Size:** 8 1/8 x 10 7/8. **Cols./Page:** 2. **Col. Width:** 39 nonpareils. **Col. Depth:** 140 agate lines. **Key Personnel:** Kathleen Stone R.N., Ph.D, Editor; Carol Trumbold, Publisher; Kathy Preston, Advertising Mgr.; Doug Kessler, Dir., Marketing Communications; Joyce Felan, Coordinator, Marketing Communications; Tracey Schriefer, Journal Advertising Sales Services, tracey.schriefer@mosby.com. **ISSN:** 0147-9563. **Subscription Rates:** $42 individuals; $60.99 Canada; $57 other countries; $22 students; $39.59 students, Canada; $37 students, other countries; $134 institutions; $159.34 institutions, Canada; $149 institutions, other countries. **Remarks:** Accepts advertising. **URL:** http://www.mosby.com.
Ad Rates: BW: $680 **Circ:** Paid 5,691
4C: $1,365 Non-paid 429

17571 Home Care Provider
Mosby Year Book, Inc.
11830 Westline Industrial Dr. Phone: (314)872-8370
St. Louis, MO 63146 Fax: (314)432-1380
Free: (800)325-4177

Professional magazine for home care providers offering day-to-day information for improving skills, services, and care. **Founded:** 1996. **Freq:** Bimonthly. **Key Personnel:** Janice D. Nunnelee, RN, Co-Editor; Sarah B. Keating, Co-Editor. **Subscription Rates:** Free to qualified subscribers; $44 individuals; $62.06 Canada; $58 other countries; $85 institutions; $105.93 institutions, Canada; $99 institutions, other countries; $22 students; $38.52 students, Canada; $36 students, other countries. **Remarks:** Accepts advertising.
Ad Rates: BW: $855 **Circ:** Controlled 8,995
Paid 1,005

17572 Insight
Mosby Year Book, Inc.
11830 Westline Industrial Dr. Phone: (314)872-8370
St. Louis, MO 63146 Fax: (314)432-1380
Free: (800)325-4177

Journal concerning opthalmic nursing. **Subtitle:** The Journal of the American Society of Ophthalmic Registered Nurses. **Founded:** 1991. **Freq:** Quarterly. **Print Method:** Offset. **Trim Size:** 8 1/4 x 10 7/8. **Key Personnel:** Sarah C. Smith, RN, MA, Editor-in-Chief. **Subscription Rates:** $44 individuals; $57.78 Canada; $54 other countries; $15 single issue. **Remarks:** Accepts advertising.
Ad Rates: BW: $1,250 **Circ:** Paid 1,489
4C: $2,000

17573 International Journal of Trauma Nursing
Mosby Year Book, Inc.
11830 Westline Industrial Dr. Phone: (314)872-8370
St. Louis, MO 63146 Fax: (314)432-1380
Free: (800)325-4177

Journal for trauma nursing professionals covering clinical topics ranging from wound ballistics and hypothermia in trauma to changing technology within the field. **Founded:** Jan. 1995. **Freq:** Quarterly. **Key Personnel:** Judith Stone Halpern, RN, Editor. **Subscription Rates:** Free to qualified subscribers; $40 individuals; $66.34 Canada; $62 other countries; $75 institutions; $103.79 institutions, Canada; $97 institutions, other countries; $21 students; $46.01 students, Canada; $43 students, other countries. **Remarks:** Accepts advertising.
Ad Rates: BW: $500 **Circ:** Paid 1,284
Non-paid 115

17574 International Psychogeriatrics
Springer Publishing Co.
c/o Nancy Raley, Asst. To Editor-in-Chief Phone: (314)268-5590
Fax: (314)664-7248
St. Louis University
Dept. Of Psychiatry
1221 S. Grand Blvd.
St. Louis, MO 63104
Publisher E-mail: springer@springerpub.com

Scholarly journal covering psychogeriatric practice, research, and education worldwide. **Subtitle:** Official Journal of the International Psychogeriatic Association. **Founded:** 1989. **Freq:** Quarterly. **Trim Size:** 7 x 10. **Cols./Page:** 1. **Col. Width:** 5 inches. **Col. Depth:** 8 1/2 inches. **Key Personnel:** Robin Eastwood, M.D., Editor-in-Chief; Rafael Ortiz, Advertising Mgr.; Cory Sklaire, Circulation Mgr.; Matt Fenton, Production Mgr. **ISSN:** 1041-6102. **Subscription Rates:** $64 individuals; $108 two years; $72 individuals out of country; $124 two years out of country; $128 institutions; $216 institutions two years; $149 institutions out of country; $248 institutions two years; out of country; $20 single issue. **Remarks:** Accepts advertising.
Ad Rates: BW: $300 **Circ:** Combined 1,160

17575 Issues
SSM Health Care System
477 N. Lindbergh Blvd.
St. Louis, MO 63141

Magazine focusing on health care issues. **Freq:** 6/year. **Subscription Rates:** $125 individuals. **Remarks:** Advertising not accepted.
Circ: (Not Reported)

17576 Jesuit Bulletin
The Jesuits of the Missouri Province
3601 Lindell Blvd. Phone: (314)977-7361
St. Louis, MO 63108-3393 Fax: (314)977-3354
Publication E-mail: misjesuits@aol.com

Magazine publicizing the spirituality and works of Missouri Province Jesuits. **Founded:** 1922. **Freq:** 3/year. **Trim Size:** 8 1/4 x 10 3/4. **Key Personnel:** Robert Burns, Assoc. Editor, foppema@slu.edu; David L. Fleming, Sr., Editor. **Remarks:** Advertising not accepted.
Circ: Non-paid 28,000

17577 Journal of AAPOS (American Association for Pediatric Ophthalmology and Strabismus)
Mosby Year Book, Inc.
11830 Westline Industrial Dr. Phone: (314)872-8370
St. Louis, MO 63146 Fax: (314)432-1380
Free: (800)325-4177

Professional journal of the American Association for Pediatric Ophthalmology and Strabismus. **Founded:** 1997. **Freq:** Bimonthly. **Trim Size:** 8 1/4 x 10 7/8. **Key Personnel:** Burton J. Kushner, MD, Editor-in-Chief. **Subscription Rates:** $104 individuals; $132 institutions; $62 students; $133.75 Canada; $163.71 Canada institutions; $88.81 Canada student; $125 elsewhere; $153 institutions elsewhere; $83 students elsewhere. **Remarks:** Accepts advertising.
Ad Rates: BW: $690 **Circ:** Paid 1,000
4C: $1,445

17578 The Journal of Allergy and Clinical Immunology
Mosby Year Book, Inc.
11830 Westline Industrial Dr. Phone: (314)872-8370
St. Louis, MO 63146 Fax: (314)432-1380
Free: (800)325-4177

Journal for clinical allergists and immunologists, as well as dermatologists, internists, general practitioners, pediatricians, and otolaryngologists (ENT physicians) concerned with clinical manifestations of allergies in their practice. **Founded:** Nov. 1929. **Freq:** Monthly. **Print Method:** Offset. **Trim Size:** 8 1/8 x 10 7/8. **Cols./Page:** 2. **Col. Width:** 39 nonpareils. **Col. Depth:** 140 agate lines. **Key Personnel:** Phillip Norman, M.D., Editor; Ronald E. Warren, Marketing Mgr.; Ingrid Shephard, Marketing Coord.; Tracey Schriefer, Journal Ad. Sales Service, tracey.schriefer@mosby.com. **ISSN:** 0091-6749. **Subscription Rates:** $146 individuals; $201.16 Canada; $188 other countries; $73 students; $123.05 students, Canada; $115 students, other countries; $280 institutions; $344.54 institutions, Canada; $322 institutions, other countries. **Remarks:** Accepts advertising. **URL:** http://www.mosby.com. **Alt. Formats:** CD-ROM.
Ad Rates: BW: $1,205 **Circ:** Paid 9,192
Free 427

17579 Journal of the American Academy of Dermatology
Mosby Year Book, Inc.
11830 Westline Industrial Dr. Phone: (314)872-8370
St. Louis, MO 63146 Fax: (314)432-1380
Free: (800)325-4177

Journal for dermatologists and for family practitioners, pediatricians, and internists who are concerned with clinical manifestations of skin disease in their practice. **Founded:** July 1979. **Freq:** Monthly. **Print Method:** Offset. **Trim Size:** 8 1/8 x 10 7/8. **Cols./Page:** 2. **Col. Width:** 39 nonpareils. **Col. Depth:** 140 agate lines. **Key Personnel:** Richard L. Dobson, M.D., Editor; Ingrid Shephard, Marketing Coord; Tracey Schriefer, Advertising Sales, phone (314)453-4304, fax (314)872-9164. **ISSN:** 0190-9622. **Subscription Rates:** $167 individuals; $221.49 Canada; $207 other countries; $84 students; $132.68 students, Canada; $124 students, other countries; $289 institutions; $352.03 institutions, Canada; $329 institutions, other countries. **Remarks:** Accepts advertising. **URL:** http://www.mosby.com.
Ad Rates: BW: $1,735 **Circ:** Paid 17,943
Free 673

17580 Journal of the American Psychiatric Nurses Association
Mosby Year Book, Inc.
11830 Westline Industrial Dr. Phone: (314)872-8370
St. Louis, MO 63146 Fax: (314)432-1380
Free: (800)325-4177

Journal for psychiatric nurses covering clinical and research topics, practice challenges, and changes in the field. **Founded:** 1995. **Freq:** Bimonthly. **Trim Size:** 8 1/4 x 10 7/8. **Key Personnel:** Nikki S. Polis, RN, Editor; Grayce M. Sills, RN, Editor. **Subscription Rates:** $44 U.S.; $59.92 Canada; $56 other countries; $78 institutions; $96.30 institutions, Canada; $90 institutions, other countries; $22 students; $36.38 students, Canada; $34 students, other countries. **Remarks:** Accepts advertising.
Ad Rates: BW: $690 **Circ:** 4,000

17581 Journal of the American Society of Echocardiography
Mosby Year Book, Inc.
11830 Westline Industrial Dr. Phone: (314)872-8370
St. Louis, MO 63146 Fax: (314)432-1380
Free: (800)325-4177

Official journal of the American Society of Echocardiography serving as a source of information on the technical basis and clinical application of echocardiography. Peer-reviewed publication featuring research, reviews, and case studies. **Founded:** Jan. 1988. **Freq:** Monthly. **Print Method:** Offset. **Trim Size:** 8 1/4 x 11. **Cols./Page:** 2. **Key Personnel:** Harvey Feigenbaum, M.D., Editor; Doug Kessler, Marketing Dir.; Joyce Felan, Marketing Coord.; Tracey Schriefer, Journal Ad. Sales Services, tracey.schriefer@mosby.com. **ISSN:** 0894-7317. **Subscription Rates:** $135 individuals; $189.39 Canada; $177 other countries; $68 students; $117.70 students, Canada; $110 students, other countries; $180 institutions; $237.54 institutions, Canada; $222 institutions, other countries. **Remarks:** Accepts advertising. **URL:** http://www.mosby.com.
Ad Rates: BW: $1,085 **Circ:** Paid 7,451
Free 151

17582 Journal of Burn Care & Rehabilitation
Mosby Year Book, Inc.
11830 Westline Industrial Dr. Phone: (314)872-8370
St. Louis, MO 63146 Fax: (314)432-1380
Free: (800)325-4177

Journal covering burn treatment and rehabilitation for the entire burn team. **Founded:** 1980. **Freq:** Bimonthly. **Print Method:** Offset. **Trim Size:** 8 1/4 x 11. **Cols./Page:** 2. **Col. Width:** 39.5 picas. **Col. Depth:** 53 picas. **Key Personnel:** Charles R. Baxter, M.D., Editor; Chris Gucciardo, Marketing Mgr.; Joyce Felan, Marketing Coord.; Michelle Kuhn, Advertising Sales, phone (314)453-4689, fax (314)872-9164. **ISSN:** 0273-8481. **Subscription Rates:** $79 individuals; $101.65 Canada; $95 other countries; $39 students; $58.85 students, Canada; $55 students, other countries; $125 institutions; $150.87 institutions, Canada; $141 institutions, other countries. **Remarks:** Accepts advertising. **URL:** http://www.mosby.com.
Ad Rates: BW: $1,405 **Circ:** Paid 3,502
Free 232

17583 Journal of Emergency Nursing
Mosby Year Book, Inc.
11830 Westline Industrial Dr. Phone: (314)872-8370
St. Louis, MO 63146 Fax: (314)432-1380
Free: (800)325-4177

Journal containing peer-reviewed articles on clinical aspects of emergency care by, and for, emergency nurses. Presents information about professional, political, administrative, and educational aspects of emergency nursing and nursing in general. **Founded:** Jan. 1975. **Freq:** Bimonthly. **Print Method:** Offset. **Trim Size:** 8 1/8 x 10 7/8. **Cols./Page:** 2. **Col. Width:** 39 nonpareils. **Col. Depth:** 140 agate lines. **Key Personnel:** Gail Pisarcik Lenehan R.N., M.S., Editor; Carol Trumbold, Publisher; Kathy Preston, Advertising Mgr.; Chris Gucciardo, Mgr., Marketing Communications; Joyce Felan, Coordinator; Tracey Schriefer, Journal Advertising Sales, tracey.schriefer@mosby.com. **ISSN:** 0099-1767. **Subscription Rates:** $57 individuals; $80.25 Canada; $75 other countries; $30 students; $51.36 students, Canada; $48 students, other countries; $170 institutions; $201.16 institutions, Canada; $188 institutions, other countries. **Remarks:** Accepts advertising. **URL:** http://www.mosby.com.
Ad Rates: BW: $1,655 **Circ:** Paid 30,069
Non-paid 514

17584 The Journal of Laboratory and Clinical Medicine
Mosby Year Book, Inc.
11830 Westline Industrial Dr. Phone: (314)872-8370
St. Louis, MO 63146 Fax: (314)432-1380
Free: (800)325-4177

Journal providing information to physicians, academic clinical scientists, and laboratory consultants with an interest in clinical investigation and research. **Founded:** Oct. 1915. **Freq:** Monthly. **Print Method:** Offset. **Trim Size:** 8 1/4 x 10 7/8. **Cols./Page:** 2. **Col. Width:** 39 nonpareils. **Col. Depth:** 140 agate lines. **Key Personnel:** Harry S. Jacob, M.D., Editor-in-Chief; Carol Trumbold, Publisher; Kathy Preston, Advertising Mgr. **ISSN:** 0022-2143. **Subscription Rates:** $299 institutions; $346.68 institutions, Canada; $324 institutions, other countries; $140 individuals; $176.55 individuals Canada; $165 individuals other countries; $70 students; $101.65 students, Canada; $95 students, other countries; $14 single issue. **Remarks:** Accepts advertising. **URL:** http://www.mosby.com.
Ad Rates: BW: $770 **Circ:** Paid 2,876
Non-paid 192

17585 Journal of Nuclear Cardiology
Mosby Year Book, Inc.
11830 Westline Industrial Dr. Phone: (314)872-8370
St. Louis, MO 63146 Fax: (314)432-1380
Free: (800)325-4177

Official journal of the American Society of Nuclear Cardiology (ASNC). Covers all aspects of nuclear cardiology including interpretation, diagnosis, radiopharmaceuticals, and imaging equipment. **Founded:** 1994. **Freq:** Bimonthly. **Trim Size:** 8 1/4 x 10 7/8. **Key Personnel:** Barry L. Zaret, MD, Editor-in-Chief. **Subscription Rates:** $117 U.S.; $160.50 Canada; $150 other countries; $156 institutions; $202.23 institutions, Canada; $189 institutions, other countries; $59 students; $98.44 students, Canada; $92 students, other countries. **Remarks:** Accepts advertising.
Ad Rates: BW: $1,000 **Circ:** Paid 4,914
Free 208

17586 Journal of Optometric Vision Development
College of Optometrists in Vision Development
243 N Lindbergh Blvd., Ste. 310 Phone: (314)991-4007
St. Louis, MO 63141 Fax: (314)991-1167
Free: (888)268-3770

Professional journal covering optometric behavioral vision and vision therapy. **Founded:** 1970. **Freq:** Quarterly. **Trim Size:** 8 1/2 x 11. **Cols./Page:** 2. **Key Personnel:** Sidney Groffman, O.D., Editor, sgroffman@sunyopt.edu. **Subscription Rates:** $55 individuals; $20 single issue. **Remarks:** Accepts advertising.
Circ: Paid 1,600

17587 Journal of Pediatric Health Care
Mosby Year Book, Inc.
11830 Westline Industrial Dr. Phone: (314)872-8370
St. Louis, MO 63146 Fax: (314)432-1380
Free: (800)325-4177

Official publication of the National Association of Pediatric Nurse Associates and Practitioners. Provides current information on pediatric clinical topics as well as research studies, health policy, and legislative issues applicable to pediatric clinical practice. **Founded:** Jan. 1987. **Freq:** Bimonthly. **Print Method:** Offset. **Trim Size:** 8 1/4 x 11. **Cols./Page:** 2. **Key Personnel:** Bobbie Crew Nelms R.N., Ph.D., Editor; Carol Trumblold, Publisher; Kathy Preston, Advertising Mgr.; Ronald E. Warren, Mgr., Marketing Communications; Ingrid Shephard, Coordinator, Marketing Communications; Michelle Kuhn, Journal Advertising Sales Services, michelle.kuhn@mosby.com. **ISSN:** 0891-5245. **Subscription Rates:** $57 individuals; $78.11 Canada; $73 other countries; $30 students; $49.22 students, Canada; $46 students, other countries; $112 institutions; $136.96 institutions, Canada; $128 institutions, other countries; $17 single issue. **Remarks:** Accepts advertising. **URL:** http://www.mosby.com.
Ad Rates: BW: $1,070 **Circ:** Paid 7,383
Non-paid 368

17588 The Journal of Pediatrics
Mosby Year Book, Inc.
11830 Westline Industrial Dr. Phone: (314)872-8370
St. Louis, MO 63146 Fax: (314)432-1380
Free: (800)325-4177

Journal for physicians who diagnose and treat disorders in infants and children. **Founded:** July 1932. **Freq:** Monthly. **Print Method:** Offset. **Trim Size:** 8 1/8 x 10 7/8. **Cols./Page:** 2. **Col. Width:** 39 nonpareils. **Col. Depth:** 140 agate lines. **Key Personnel:** Willisam F Balistreri, M.D., Editor; Ronald E. Warren, Marketing Mgr.; Ingrid Shephard, Marketing Coord.; Gale Schlogl, Advertising Sales, phone (314)453-4337, fax (314)872-0164, gale.schlogl@mosby.com. **ISSN:** 0022-3476. **Subscription Rates:** $127 individuals; $173.34 Canada; $162 other countries; $65 students; $10730 students, Canada; $100 students, other countries; $290 institutions; $347.75 institutions, Canada; $325 institutions, other countries. **Remarks:** Accepts advertising. **URL:** http://www.mosby.com. **Alt. Formats:** CD-ROM.
Ad Rates: BW: $1,225 **Circ:** Paid 15,519
Free 440

17589 Journal of Policy History
The Penn State Press
Saint Louis University Phone: (314)977-2339
3800 Lindell Blvd.
PO Box 56907
St. Louis, MO 63156-0907
Journal on the application of historical perspectives to public policy studies. **Founded:** 1989. **Freq:** Quarterly. **Print Method:** Offset. **Trim Size:** 6 x 9. **Cols./Page:** 1. **Col. Width:** 54 nonpareils. **Col. Depth:** 138 agate lines. **Key Personnel:** Donald Critchlow, Editor; David B. Robertson, Contact, phone (315)516-5855; Thomas F. Curran, Contact. **Subscription Rates:** $29.50 individuals; $35 other countries; $45 Industry; $50 other countries Industry.
Ad Rates: BW: $200 **Circ:** Paid 700

17590 The Journal of Prosthetic Dentistry
Mosby Year Book, Inc.
11830 Westline Industrial Dr. Phone: (314)872-8370
St. Louis, MO 63146 Fax: (314)432-1380
Free: (800)325-4177

Journal emphasizing new techniques, evaluation of dental materials, pertinent basic science concepts, and patient psychology in restorative dentistry. **Founded:** Mar. 1951. **Freq:** Monthly. **Print Method:** Offset. **Trim Size:** 8 1/8 x 10 7/8. **Cols./Page:** 2. **Col. Width:** 39 nonpareils. **Col. Depth:** 140 agate lines. **Key Personnel:** Glen P. McGivney, D.D.S., Editor; Carol Trumbold, Publisher; Kathy Preston, Advertising Mgr.; Jo Ann Anzalone, Dir., Marketing Communications; Michelle Kuhn, Journal Advertising Sales, michelle.kuhn@mosby.com. **ISSN:** 0022-3913. **Subscription Rates:** $126 individuals; $171.20 Canada; $160 other countries; $65 students; $105.93 students, Canada; $99 students, other countries; $257 institutions; $311.37 institutions, Canada; $291 institutions, other countries. **Remarks:** Accepts advertising. **URL:** http://www.mosby.com.
Ad Rates: BW: $1,375 **Circ:** Paid 9,341
Non-paid 197

17591 The Journal of Reproductive Medicine
Journal of Reproductive Medicine, Inc.
PO Drawer 12425 Phone: (314)991-4440
8342 Olive Blvd. Fax: (314)991-4654
St. Louis, MO 63132-2814
Publication E-mail: editor@jreprodmed.com

Journal of obstetrics, gynecology and reproductive endocrinology containing clinical articles, reviews, and case reports. **Subtitle:** For the Obstetrician and Gynecologist. **Founded:** 1968. **Freq:** Monthly. **Print Method:** Offset. **Trim Size:** 8 x 10 3/4. **Cols./Page:** 2. **Col. Width:** 40 nonpareils. **Col. Depth:** 152 agate lines. **Key Personnel:** George L. Wied, M.D., Editor; Donna Kessel, Publisher; Al Heidler, Advertising Rep., phone (732)494-9115, fax (732)494-3974. **ISSN:** 0024-7758. **Subscription Rates:** $126 individuals; $199 institutions; $21 single issue. **Remarks:** Accepts advertising.
Ad Rates: BW: $2,056 **Circ:** Controlled ‡31,410
4C: $2,056 Paid ‡2,035
4C: $1,715

17592 Journal of Shoulder and Elbow Surgery
Mosby Year Book, Inc.
11830 Westline Industrial Dr. Phone: (314)872-8370
St. Louis, MO 63146 Fax: (314)432-1380
Free: (800)325-4177

Journal featuring peer-reviewed articles focusing on the medical/surgical treatment of the shoulder, girdle, arm, and elbow. Clinical topics covered include: fractures, dislocations and recurrent instability, diseases and injuries of the rotator cuff, imaging techniques, arthroscopy, arthroplasty, arthritis and infections, overuse syndromes, and rehabilitation. **Founded:** 1992. **Freq:** Bimonthly. **Print Method:** Offset. **Trim Size:** 6 1/2 x 8 1/2. **Key Personnel:** Robert H. Cofield, M.D., Editor; Jo Ann Anzalone, Marketing Mgr.; Michelle Kuhn, phone

(314)453-4689, fax (314)872-9164, michelle.kuhn@mosby.com. **ISSN:** 1201-2122. **Subscription Rates:** $116 individuals; $154.08 Canada; $144 other countries; $60 students; $94.16 students, Canada; $88 students, other countries; $143 institutions; $182.97 institutions, Canada; $171 institutions, other countries; $21 single issue. **Remarks:** Accepts advertising. **URL:** http://www.mosby.com.
Ad Rates: BW: $980 **Circ:** Paid 2,968
Free 161

17593 The Journal of Thoracic and Cardiovascular Surgery
Mosby Year Book, Inc.
11830 Westline Industrial Dr. Phone: (314)872-8370
St. Louis, MO 63146 Fax: (314)432-1380
Free: (800)325-4177

Journal devoted to conditions of the chest, heart, lungs, and great vessels where surgical intervention is indicated. Scientific articles represent original, peer-reviewed contributions to the literature on this subject. **Founded:** Oct. 1931. **Freq:** Monthly. **Print Method:** Offset. **Trim Size:** 8 1/8 x 10 7/8. **Cols./Page:** 2. **Col. Width:** 39 nonpareils. **Col. Depth:** 140 agate lines. **Key Personnel:** John Waldhausen, M.D., Editor; Carol Trumbold, Publisher; Kathy Preston, Advertising Mgr. **ISSN:** 0022-5223. **Subscription Rates:** $315 institutions in U.S.; $377.71 institutions, Canada; $353 institutions, other countries; $180 individuals in U.S.; $233.26 individuals in Canada; $218 individuals in other countries; $92 students in U.S.; $139.10 students, Canada; $130 students, other countries; $17 single issue. **Remarks:** Accepts advertising. **URL:** http://www.mosby.com. **Alt. Formats:** CD-ROM.
Ad Rates: BW: $980 **Circ:** Paid 8,974
Free 353

17594 Journal of Vascular Nursing
Mosby Year Book, Inc.
11830 Westline Industrial Dr. Phone: (314)872-8370
St. Louis, MO 63146 Fax: (314)432-1380
Free: (800)325-4177

Official publication of the Society for Vascular Nursing. Peer-reviewed articles detail the etiologies, diagnostic procedures, treatment options, and nursing implications of vascular system disorders. Topics include upper and lower extremity arterial disease, deep vein thrombosis, varicose veins, and venous ulcers. **Founded:** 1982. **Freq:** Quarterly. **Print Method:** Offset. **Trim Size:** 8 1/4 x 11. **Key Personnel:** Victora A. Fahey, Editor; Janice D. Nunnelee, Editor. **Subscription Rates:** $29 students; $44.94 students, Canada; $42 students, other countries; $55 individuals; $72.76 individuals Canada; $68 individuals other countries; $88 institutions; $108.07 institutions, Canada; $101 institutions, other countries. **Remarks:** Accepts advertising. **URL:** http://www.mosby.com.
Ad Rates: BW: $850 **Circ:** Paid 1,134
Free 222

17595 Journal of Vascular Surgery
Mosby Year Book, Inc.
11830 Westline Industrial Dr. Phone: (314)872-8370
St. Louis, MO 63146 Fax: (314)432-1380
Free: (800)325-4177

Journal providing a forum for the advances in knowledge of the peripheral vascular system. Publishes peer-reviewed original articles on all aspects of disease and injury to the arterial and venous systems. **Founded:** Jan. 1984. **Freq:** Monthly. **Print Method:** Offset. **Trim Size:** 8 1/4 x 11. **Cols./Page:** 2. **Col. Width:** 39 nonpareils. **Col. Depth:** 140 agate lines. **Key Personnel:** K. Wayne Johnson, M.D., Editor; Robert B. Rutherford, M.D., Editor; Joyce Felan, Coordinator; Gale Schlogl, phone (314)453-4337, fax (314)872-9164, gale.schlogl@mosby.com. **ISSN:** 0741-5214. **Subscription Rates:** $161 individuals; $212.93 Canada; $199 other countries; $83 students; $129.47 students, Canada; $121 students, other countries; $306 institutions; $368.08 institutions, Canada; $344 institutions, other countries. **Remarks:** Accepts advertising. **URL:** http://www.mosby.com. **Alt. Formats:** CD-ROM.
Ad Rates: BW: $1,340 **Circ:** Paid 7,436
Free 337

17596 Journal of WOCN (Wound, Ostomy, and Continence Nursing)
Mosby Year Book, Inc.
11830 Westline Industrial Dr. Phone: (314)872-8370
St. Louis, MO 63146 Fax: (314)432-1380
Free: (800)325-4177

Journal for enterostomal therapy practitioners. Provides data relating to the care of persons with stomas, draining wounds, fistulas, pressure ulcers, and incontinence. Publishes text pages of originally submitted clinical studies from practitioners, educators, and researchers. **Founded:** 1974. **Freq:** Bimonthly. **Print Method:** Offset. **Trim Size:** 8 1/4 x 10 7/8. **Cols./Page:** 2. **Col. Width:** 39 nonpareils. **Col. Depth:** 140 agate lines. **Key Personnel:** Mikel Gray, Editor; Carol Trumbold, Publisher; Kathy Preston, Advertising Mgr. **ISSN:** 0270-1170. **Subscription Rates:** $156 institutions in U.S.; $184.04 institutions, Canada; $172 institutions, other countries; $55 individuals in U.S.; $75.97 individuals in Canada; $71 individuals in other countries; $30 students in U.S.; $49.22 students, Canada; $46 students, other countries; $15 single issue. **Remarks:** Accepts advertising. **URL:** http://www.mosby.com. **Formerly:** Journal of ET Nursing.
Ad Rates: BW: $1,085 **Circ:** Paid 5,102
Free 492

17597 KETC Guide
KETC
3655 Olive St. Phone: (314)512-9036
St. Louis, MO 63108 Fax: (314)512-9005
Free: (800)729-9966

Public television guide featuring articles about programs and program listings. **Subtitle:** The Magazine for Members of Channel 9. **Founded:** 1996. **Freq:** Monthly (except July and February). **Print Method:** Web offset. **Trim Size:** 8 x 10 3/4. **Cols./Page:** 3. **Col. Width:** 2 1/4 inches. **Col. Depth:** 9 3/4 inches. **Key Personnel:** Terri Gates, Editor, terri_gates@ketc.pbs.org; Matt Andrew, Advertising Dir., phone (314)512-9034, matt_andrew@ketc.pbs.org. **ISSN:** 1086-8828. **Subscription Rates:** $40 individuals. **Remarks:** Accepts advertising. **URL:** http://www.ketc.org. **Formerly:** STL; Nine.
Ad Rates: BW: $1,710 **Circ:** Paid 50,621
4C: $2,110

17598 Key Neurology and Neurosurgery
Mosby Year Book, Inc.
11830 Westline Industrial Dr. Phone: (314)872-8370
St. Louis, MO 63146 Fax: (314)432-1380
Free: (800)325-4177

Journal on subjects such as thinking and memory, spinal disorders, Alzheimer's Disease, neurogenetics, surgical techniques, trauma, and vascular disorders. **Subtitle:** Current Literature in Perspective. **Founded:** 1985. **Freq:** Quarterly. **Key Personnel:** Walter G. Bradley, DM, Editor; Robert M. Crowell, MD, Editor. **Subscription Rates:** $69; $45 students; $89 Industry; $77.83 Canada; $52.15 Canadian students; $99.23 Canadian Industry; $83 other countries; $59 other countries' students; $103 other countries' Industry.

17599 Key Ophthalmology
Mosby Year Book, Inc.
11830 Westline Industrial Dr. Phone: (314)872-8370
St. Louis, MO 63146 Fax: (314)432-1380
Free: (800)325-4177

Journal covering all subjects that relate to the clinical pratice of ophthalmology, such as refractive surgery, cataract, glaucoma, neuro-ophthalmology, oculoplastics, and retina. **Subtitle:** Current Literature in Perspective. **Founded:** 1985. **Freq:** Quarterly. **Key Personnel:** Peter R. Laibson, MD, Editor. **Subscription Rates:** $69; $45 students; $89 Industry; 77.83 Canada; $52.15 Canadian students; $99.23 Canadian Industry; $83 other countries; $59 other countries' students; $103 other countries' Industry.

17600 The Lutheran Layman
International Lutheran Laymen's League
2185 Hampton Ave. Phone: (314)951-4100
St. Louis, MO 63139 Fax: (314)951-4295

International Luterhan Layman's League membership magazine with news about Lutheran Hour Ministries. **Founded:** 1929. **Freq:** Monthly. **Print Method:** Offset. **Trim Size:** 11 x 11. **Cols./Page:** 3. **Col. Width:** 38 nonpareils. **Col. Depth:** 185 agate lines. **Key Personnel:** Gerald Perschbacher, Editor. **Subscription Rates:** $5. **Remarks:** Advertising not accepted.
Circ: ‡145,000

17601 Lutheran Witness
Board for Communication Services/The Lutheran Church–Missouri Synod
1333 S. Kirkwood Rd., Phone: (314)965-9000
St. Louis, MO 63122-7295 Fax: (314)965-3396

Lutheran magazine. **Founded:** May 21, 1882. **Freq:** Monthly. **Print Method:** Offset. **Trim Size:** 8 1/8 x 10 5/8. **Cols./Page:** 3. **Col. Width:** 28 nonpareils. **Col. Depth:** 133 agate lines. **Key Personnel:** Rev. David Mahsman, Editor, phone (314)965-9000, fax (314)965-3396, david.mahsman@lcms.org; Karen Andersen, Advertising Mgr., phone (314)268-1101, karena@cphnet.org. **ISSN:** 0024-757X. **Subscription Rates:** $9 individuals. **Remarks:** Accepts advertising.
Ad Rates: BW: $3,550 **Circ:** ‡275,000
4C: $4,700
PCI: $250

17602 Managed Care/Innovations
Clayton-Davis & Associates
8229 Maryland Ave. Phone: (314)862-7800
St. Louis, MO 63105 Fax: (314)721-5171

Chiropractic journal providing editorials, reports, association news, and information about legislation affecting the profession. **Subtitle:** ACA Journal. **Founded:** 1930. **Freq:** Monthly. **Print Method:** Offset. **Trim Size:** 8 1/8 x 10 5/8. **Cols./Page:** 3. **Col. Width:** 13 picas. **Col. Depth:** 126 agate lines. **Key Personnel:** Christy Thompson, Editor; Lee Clark, Advertising Dir. **ISSN:** 0744-9984. **Subscription Rates:** $24; $3 student ACA members; $80 nonmembers; $100 other countries. **Remarks:** Accepts advertising. **Formerly:** Journal of Chiropratic; Journal of the American Chiropractic Association.
Ad Rates: BW: $1,270 **Circ:** ‡24,000
4C: $1,770
PCI: $90

17603 Manuscripta
St. Louis University
3650 Lindell Blvd. Phone: (314)977-3090
St. Louis, MO 63108-3302 Fax: (314)977-3108
Publisher E-mail: channellbj@slu.edu

Scholarly journal covering manuscript research. **Founded:** 1957. **Freq:** Triennial. **Key Personnel:** Charles J. Ermatinger. **ISSN:** 0025-2603. **Subscription Rates:** $20 individuals; $7.50 single issue. **Remarks:** Advertising not accepted.
Circ: Combined 680

17604 Midwest Traveler
AAA Auto Club of Missouri
12901 N. 40 Dr. Phone: (314)523-7350
St. Louis, MO 63141 Fax: (314)523-6982
Free: (800)222-7623

Motor club magazine with an emphasis on travel. **Founded:** 1920. **Freq:** Bimonthly. **Print Method:** Offset. **Trim Size:** 7 7/8 x 10 13/16. **Cols./Page:** 3. **Col. Width:** 32 nonpareils. **Col. Depth:** 133 agate lines. **Key Personnel:** Michael J. Right, Editor; Debbie Klein, Managing Editor, acmdmk@ibm.net; Dennis R. Heinze, Associate Editor, acmdrh@ibm.net. **ISSN:** 0026-3435. **Subscription Rates:** $3 single issue. **Remarks:** Accepts advertising. **Former name:** The Midwest Motorist.
Ad Rates: BW: $7,041 **Circ:** Paid 421,539
4C: $8,087

17605 Missouri Botanical Garden Annals
Missouri Botanical Garden
PO Box 299 Phone: (314)577-5123
St. Louis, MO 63166 Fax: (314)577-9598

Trade magazine covering original research in botany. **Founded:** 1917. **Freq:** Quarterly. **Trim Size:** 7 x 10. **Key Personnel:** Michael H. Grayum, Editor; Amy McPherson, Managing Editor, phone (314)577-5112; Diana Gunter, Editorial Asst., phone (314)577-9489. **ISSN:** 0026-6493. **Subscription Rates:** $120 individuals; $130 Canada and Mexico; $155 other countries. **Remarks:** Advertising not accepted.
Circ: (Not Reported)

17606 The Modern Schoolman
St. Louis University
Dept. of Philosophy Phone: (314)977-3155
221 N. Grand Blvd.
St. Louis, MO 63103
Journal. **Subtitle:** A Quarterly of Philosophy. **Founded:** 1925. **Freq:** Quarterly. **Trim Size:** 6 x 9. **Key Personnel:** William Charron, Editor, charrwc@slu.edu. **ISSN:** 0026-8402. **Subscription Rates:** $26. $6.50 single issue. **Remarks:** Accepts advertising.
Circ: Paid ‡600
Non-paid ‡50

17607 Naborhood Link News
416 Lemay Ferry Rd. Phone: (314)631-4321
St. Louis, MO 63125
Community newspaper. **Founded:** June 1930. **Freq:** Weekly (Wed.). **Print Method:** Offset. **Trim Size:** 10 3/4 x 17 1/2. **Cols./Page:** 7. **Col. Width:** 8 picas. **Col. Depth:** 16 inches. **Key Personnel:** Vernon E. Schertel, Editor and Publisher; Russ Hitzeman, Advertising Mgr. **Subscription Rates:** Free; $12 (mail). **Remarks:** Accepts advertising.
Ad Rates: GLR: $.55 **Circ:** Paid ‡210
BW: $530 Free ‡35,000
4C: $900
PCI: $7.25

17608 NAEDA Equipment Dealer
North American Equipment Dealers Association
10877 Watson Rd. Phone: (314)821-7220
St. Louis, MO 63127-1081 Fax: (314)821-0674

Magazine serving retailers of farm and industrial and outdoor power equipment, accessories, repair parts. **Founded:** 1946. **Freq:** Monthly. **Print Method:** Offset. **Trim Size:** 8 1/2 x 11. **Cols./Page:** 3. **Col. Width:** 26 nonpareils. **Col. Depth:** 140 agate lines. **Key Personnel:** F.M. Kraemer, Managing Editor,

kraemerm@naedm.com; David G. Ottaway, Publisher; Larry Krueger, Advertising Mgr. **ISSN:** 1074-5017. **Subscription Rates:** $40 individuals; $150 other countries airmail. **Remarks:** Accepts advertising. **Formerly:** Farm & Power Equipment Dealer (1994).
Ad Rates: BW: $1,445 **Circ:** Paid △**8,447**
4C: $1,940 Non-paid △**2,272**
PCI: $63

17609 The National Gardener
National Council of State Garden Clubs, Inc.
102 S. Elm Ave. Phone: (314)968-1664
St. Louis, MO 63119
Club magazine covering gardening, environmental issues, conservation, landscaping, flower arranging, and gardening for youths, senior citizens, and the handicapped. **Founded:** July 1930. **Freq:** Bimonthly. **Print Method:** Offset. **Trim Size:** 6 x 9. **Cols./Page:** 2. **Col. Width:** 14 picas. **Col. Depth:** 105 agate lines. **Key Personnel:** Susan Davidson, Editor, susand4@juno.com; Doris Kracke, Advertising Rep. **ISSN:** 0027-9331. **Subscription Rates:** $6.50 individuals; $9 other countries. **Remarks:** Accepts advertising.
Ad Rates: BW: $380 **Circ:** ‡30,000
PCI: $45

17610 Neighborhood Journal
Suburban Newspapers of Greater St. Louis
4210 Chippewa Phone: (314)664-2700
St. Louis, MO 63116 Fax: (314)664-9777

Community newspaper. **Founded:** 1922. **Freq:** Weekly (Wed.). **Print Method:** Offset. **Cols./Page:** 6. **Col. Width:** 26 nonpareils. **Col. Depth:** 308 agate lines. **Key Personnel:** Robert A. MacDonald, General Mgr. **URL:** http://www.yourjournal.com.
Circ: Free ‡18,467

17611 Novon
Missouri Botanical Garden
PO Box 299 Phone: (314)577-5123
St. Louis, MO 63166 Fax: (314)577-9598

Trade magazine covering botany. **Subtitle:** A Journal of Botanical Nomenclature. **Founded:** 1991. **Freq:** Quarterly. **Trim Size:** 7 x 10. **Key Personnel:** Amy McPherson, Managing Editor; Diana Gunter, Editorial Asst.; Marshall Crosby, Editor. **ISSN:** 1055-3177. **Remarks:** Advertising not accepted.
Circ: (Not Reported)

17612 Nursing Management and Leadership
Mosby Year Book, Inc.
11830 Westline Industrial Dr. Phone: (314)872-8370
St. Louis, MO 63146 Fax: (314)432-1380
Free: (800)325-4177

Journal providing practical information that can be applied in various healthcare settings. **Founded:** 1993. **Freq:** Quarterly. **Key Personnel:** Connie Curran, RN, Editor. **Subscription Rates:** $39.95; $55 industry; $49.75 Canada; $65.85 Canadian industry; $54.50 other countries; $69.55 other countries industry.

17613 Nursing Outlook
Mosby Year Book, Inc.
11830 Westline Industrial Dr. Phone: (314)872-8370
St. Louis, MO 63146 Fax: (314)432-1380
Free: (800)325-4177

Official magazine of the American Academy of Nursing, reporting on trends and issues in nursing. **Founded:** 1953. **Freq:** Bimonthly. **Print Method:** Offset. **Trim Size:** 8 1/8 x 10 7/8. **Cols./Page:** 3. **Col. Width:** 2 1/4 inches. **Col. Depth:** 10 inches. **Key Personnel:** Carole Anderson, PhD, Editor; Donna Ricko, Advertising Mgr.; Jo Ann Anzalone, Mgr., Marketing Communications; Gale Schlogl, Journal Advertising Sales Services, gale.schlogl@mosby.com. **ISSN:** 0029-6554. **Subscription Rates:** $42 individuals; $70.62 Canada; $66 other countries; $26 students; $53.50 students, Canada; $50 students, other countries; $74 institutions; $104.86 institutions, Canada; $98 institutions, other countries. **Remarks:** Accepts advertising. **URL:** http://www.mosby.com.
Ad Rates: BW: $1,075 **Circ:** Paid 6,045
Free 209

17614 Oncology Nursing
Mosby Year Book, Inc.
11830 Westline Industrial Dr. Phone: (314)872-8370
St. Louis, MO 63146 Fax: (314)432-1380
Free: (800)325-4177

Journal offering abstracts and commentary of research in oncology nursing. **Founded:** 1993. **Freq:** Quarterly. **Key Personnel:** Christine Miakowsky, RN, Editor. **Subscription Rates:** $39.95; $55 industry; $49.75 Canada; $65.85 Canadian industry; $54.50 other countries; $69.55 other countries industry.

17615 The Optimist Magazine
Optimist International
4494 Lindell Blvd. Phone: (314)371-6000
St. Louis, MO 63108 Fax: (314)371-6006
Free: (800)678-8389
Publication E-mail: magazine@optimist.org
Publisher E-mail: headquarters@optimist.org

Official publication of Optimist International. **Founded:** 1919. **Freq:** 6/year. **Print Method:** Offset. **Trim Size:** 8 3/8 x 10 7/8. **Cols./Page:** 3. **Col. Width:** 26 nonpareils. **Col. Depth:** 139 agate lines. **Key Personnel:** Dena Hull, Editor. **ISSN:** 0744-4672. **Subscription Rates:** $4.50.
Ad Rates: BW: $1,900 **Circ:** ‡140,000
4C: $2,400

17616 Optometry
Mosby Year Book, Inc.
11830 Westline Industrial Dr. Phone: (314)872-8370
St. Louis, MO 63146 Fax: (314)432-1380
Free: (800)325-4177

Journal on ophthalmic optics, contact lenses, external disease, ocular pharmacology, ophthalmic genetics, and practice management. **Founded:** 1991. **Freq:** Quarterly. **Key Personnel:** John F. Amos, OD, Editor. **Subscription Rates:** $69; $45 students; $89 Industry; $77.83 Canada; $52.15 Canadian students; $99.23 Canadian Industry; $83 other countries; $59 other countries' students; $103 other countries' Industry.

17617 Oral Surgery, Oral Medicine, Oral Pathology, Oral Radiology, and Endodontics
Mosby Year Book, Inc.
11830 Westline Industrial Dr. Phone: (314)872-8370
St. Louis, MO 63146 Fax: (314)432-1380
Free: (800)325-4177

Journal providing coverage of oral diagnosis, oral medicine, oral radiology, and oral pathology by aiding in the confirmation of the presence of an abnormality, determining its cause using specialized diagnostic techniques, and interpreting the results. **Founded:** Jan. 1948. **Freq:** Monthly. **Print Method:** Offset. **Trim Size:** 8 1/8 x 10 7/8. **Cols./Page:** 2. **Col. Width:** 39 nonpareils. **Col. Depth:** 140 agate lines. **Key Personnel:** Larry J. Peterson, D.D.S., Editor; Carol Trumbold, Publisher; Kathy Preston, Advertising Mgr. **ISSN:** 0030-4220. **Subscription Rates:** $254 institutions in U.S.; $302.81 institutions, Canada; $283 institutions, other countries; $124 individuals in U.S.; $163.71 individuals in Canada; $153 individuals in other countries; $60 students in U.S.; $95.23 students, Canada; $89 students, other countries; $13 single issue. **Remarks:** Accepts advertising. **URL:** http://www.mosby.com. **Formerly:** Oral Surgery, Oral Medicine, Oral Pathology.
Ad Rates: BW: $1,160 **Circ:** Paid 6,366
Free 164

17618 Otolaryngology–Head and Neck Surgery
Mosby Year Book, Inc.
11830 Westline Industrial Dr. Phone: (314)872-8370
St. Louis, MO 63146 Fax: (314)432-1380
Free: (800)325-4177

Medical journal comprising peer-reviewed papers presented at the annual meeting of the American Academy of Otolaryngology-Head and Neck Surgery. Subjects covered include head and neck surgical oncology, otologic surgery and neuro-otology, rhinology, and rhinoplastic surgery. **Founded:** 1896. **Freq:** Monthly. **Print Method:** Offset. **Trim Size:** 8 1/8 x 10 7/8. **Cols./Page:** 2. **Col. Width:** 39 nonpareils. **Col. Depth:** 140 agate lines. **Key Personnel:** G. Richard Holt, M.D., Editor; Joyce Felan, Marketing Coordinator; Carol Kilzer, Advertising Sales, phone (314)453-4307, fax (314)872-9164, carol.kilzer@mosby.com. **ISSN:** 0194-5998. **Subscription Rates:** $171 individuals; $223.63 Canada; $209 other countries; $84 students; $130.54 students, Canada; $122 students, other countries; $284 institutions; $344.54 institutions, Canada; $322 institutions, other countries; $15 single issue. **Remarks:** Accepts advertising. **URL:** http://www.mosby.com. **Alt. Formats:** CD-ROM.
Ad Rates: BW: $905 **Circ:** Paid 11,193
Free 558

17619 Painting & Wallcovering Contractor
Finan Publishing Co., Inc.
8730 Big Bend Blvd. Phone: (314)961-6644
St. Louis, MO 63119 Fax: (314)961-4809

Magazine covering painting and decorating industry-current research; new trends in techniques and products; and commerical, industrial, institutional, and residential application. **Subtitle:** PWC Magazine. **Founded:** Feb. 15, 1938. **Freq:** Bimonthly. **Print Method:** Web offset. **Trim Size:** 8 1/8 x 10 7/8. **Cols./Page:** 3. **Col. Width:** 26 nonpareils. **Col. Depth:** 140 agate lines. **Key Personnel:** Jeffery Beckner, Editor, jbeckner@finan.com; Thomas J. Finan IV, Publisher, tfinan@finan.com; Katherine Gardner, Sales Mgr., kgardner@finan.com. **ISSN:** 0735-9713. **Subscription Rates:** $19.95 individuals. **Remarks:** Accepts advertising. **Available Online. URL:** http://www.paintstore.com.
Ad Rates: BW: $2,815 **Circ:** Paid 1,926
4C: $3,970 Non-paid 26,202
PCI: $110

17620 Patient Drug Facts
Facts & Comparisons
111 W. Port Plaza, Ste. 300 Phone: (314)216-2100
St. Louis, MO 63146 Fax: (314)878-5563
Free: (800)223-0554

Publication of drug information for health care professionals. **Subtitle:** Improved Patient Counseling. **Founded:** 1989. **Freq:** Quarterly. **Print Method:** Web press. **Trim Size:** 7 X 9. **Key Personnel:** Steve Hebel, RPh, Editor, phone (214)216-2171, fax (314)878-5563, shebel@fande.com; Bernie Olin, Pharm. D., phone (314)878-9845, bolin@fandc.com. **Subscription Rates:** $75 individuals. **Remarks:** Advertising not accepted. **Alt. Formats:** Diskette.
Circ: (Not Reported)

17621 Physical Therapy in Perspective
Mosby Year Book, Inc.
11830 Westline Industrial Dr. Phone: (314)872-8370
St. Louis, MO 63146 Fax: (314)432-1380
Free: (800)325-4177

Journal featuring articles and abstracts on how physical therapists care for patients. **Founded:** 1996. **Freq:** Bimonthly. **Print Method:** Offset. **Key Personnel:** Carole Bernstein Lewis, PT, Contact. **ISSN:** 1086-7643. **Subscription Rates:** $34.95 individuals; $52.97 Canada; $49.50 other countries.

17622 Portals of Prayer
Concordia Publishing House
3558 S. Jefferson Ave. Phone: (314)268-1000
St. Louis, MO 63118 Fax: (314)268-1329
Free: (800)325-3040

Religion and theology magazine (English, German and large print). **Subtitle:** Daily Devotions. **Founded:** 1937. **Freq:** Quarterly. **Print Method:** Offset. **Cols./Page:** 1. **Col. Width:** 38 nonpareils. **Col. Depth:** 66 agate lines. **ISSN:** 0032-4884. **Subscription Rates:** $5.10 individuals; $2.10 single issue. **Remarks:** Advertising not accepted.
Circ: 950,000

17623 Postgraduate Radiology
Mosby Year Book, Inc.
11830 Westline Industrial Dr. Phone: (314)872-8370
St. Louis, MO 63146 Fax: (314)432-1380
Free: (800)325-4177

Provides review articles and abstracts of current literature that update radiologists on pertinent clinical topics, including in-depth accounts of management techniques, state-of-the-art diagnostic procedures, self-assessment challenges, and information on diagnostic tools. **Subtitle:** A Journal of Continuing Education. **Founded:** 1981. **Freq:** Quarterly. **Key Personnel:** Herbert L. Abrams, Editor. **Subscription Rates:** $80; $49 students; $105 Industry; $92.60 Canada; $59.43 Canadian students; $119.35 Canadian Industry; $100 other countries; $69 other countries' students; $125 other countries Industry. **URL:** http://www.mosby.com.

17624 Railroads of St. Louis Magazine
Terminal Railroad Association Historical and Technical Society
PO Box 1688 Phone: (314)535-3101
St. Louis, MO 63188-1688
Magazine focusing on railroad history in the St. Louis metro area. **Founded:** 1986. **Freq:** Quarterly. **Print Method:** Offset. **Trim Size:** 8 1/2 x 11. **Cols./Page:** 2. **Col. Width:** 3 1/4 inches. **Key Personnel:** Larry Thomas, Editor. **Subscription Rates:** $20 individuals. **Remarks:** Accepts advertising.
Ad Rates: BW: $200 **Circ:** Paid 600

17625 Review for Religious
3601 Lindell Blvd., Rm. 428 Phone: (314)977-7363
St. Louis, MO 63108 Fax: (314)977-7362
Publication E-mail: foppema@slu.edu

Journal of theological and spiritual information and reflection about religious life. **Subtitle:** Christian Heritages and Contemporary Living. **Founded:** Jan. 1942. **Freq:** Bimonthly. **Print Method:** Offset. **Trim Size:** 6 x 9. **Cols./Page:** 1. **Col. Width:** 27.5 picas. **Col. Depth:** 44 picas. **Key Personnel:** David L. Fleming, S.J., Editor. **ISSN:** 0034-639X. **Subscription Rates:** $20 individuals; $5 single issue. **Remarks:** Advertising not accepted. **Alt. Formats:** Audio tape.
Circ: Paid ‡8,800
Non-paid ‡242

17626 River Styx
Big River Association
3207 Washington Ave.
St. Louis, MO 63103-1218

Literary magazine covering poetry, fiction, essays, interviews, and art. **Founded:** 1975. **Freq:** Triennial. **Trim Size:** 6 x 9. **Key Personnel:** Richard Newman, Editor. **Subscription Rates:** $20 individuals; $7 single issue. **Remarks:** Accepts advertising.
Ad Rates: BW: $200 **Circ:** Controlled 1,700

17627 The Riverfront Times
Hartmann Publishing Co.
6358 Delmar Blvd., Ste. 200 Phone: (314)615-6666
St. Louis, MO 63130-4719 Fax: (314)615-6655

Alternative newspaper (tabloid) with political articles, in-depth features, entertainment, and classified and personal ads. **Subtitle:** The Weekly Newspaper of St. Louis. **Founded:** 1977. **Freq:** Weekly (Wed.). **Print Method:** Offset. **Trim Size:** 10 3/4 x 13 3/4. **Cols./Page:** 4. **Col. Width:** 28 nonpareils. **Col. Depth:** 196 agate lines. **Key Personnel:** Safir Ahmed, Editor, phone (314)615-6713, fax (314)615-6716, safir_ahmed@rftstl.com; Terry Coe, Publisher, phone (314)615-6717, terry_coe@rftstl.com; Cheryl Schaeffer, Ad Director, phone (314)615-6613, cheryl_schaeffer@rftstl.com. **Subscription Rates:** Free; $25 (mail). **Remarks:** Accepts advertising. **URL:** http://www.rftstl.com.
Ad Rates: BW: $2,895 **Circ:** Paid ❑266
4C: $2,395 Free ❑95,909
PCI: $57

17628 Saddle & Bridle Magazine
Saddle & Bridle, Inc.
375 Jackson Ave. Phone: (314)725-9115
St. Louis, MO 63130 Fax: (314)725-6440

Publication for owners, trainers, breeders, and horse show managers of English show horses. **Subtitle:** Oldest Name In Show Horse Magazines. **Founded:** June 1927. **Freq:** Monthly. **Print Method:** Offset. **Trim Size:** 8 5/8 x 10 7/8. **Cols./Page:** 3. **Col. Width:** 27 nonpareils. **Col. Depth:** 135 agate lines. **Key Personnel:** Jeffrey Thompson, Editor and Publisher; Chris Thompson, Publisher & Advertising Mgr. **ISSN:** 0036-2271. **Subscription Rates:** $45 individuals; $5 single issue.
Ad Rates: BW: $595 **Circ:** Paid ‡6,200
4C: $1,085 Controlled ‡400

17629 St. Louis Advertising
Advertising Club of Greater St. Louis
305 N. Broadway Phone: (314)231-4185
St. Louis, MO 63102-2001 Fax: (314)231-4188

Magazine for members of the St. Louis advertising community, stressing features, promotions, and advertising of members. **Founded:** 1910. **Freq:** Bimonthly. **Print Method:** Offset. **Trim Size:** 8 1/2 x 11. **Cols./Page:** 3. **Col. Width:** 14 picas. **Col. Depth:** 60 picas. **Key Personnel:** Tom Koon, Publisher. **USPS:** 004-780. **Subscription Rates:** For members only. **Remarks:** Accepts advertising. **Formerly:** Ad/Mag.
Ad Rates: BW: $600 **Circ:** Paid ‡800
4C: $750 Controlled ‡200
PCI: $30

17630 St. Louis American
American Publishing Co.
4144 Lindell Blvd. Phone: (314)533-8000
St. Louis, MO 63108-2927 Fax: (314)533-0038
Publication E-mail: stlamer@mvp.net

Black community newspaper. **Founded:** 1928. **Freq:** Weekly (Thurs.). **Print Method:** Offset. **Trim Size:** 13 1/2 x 22 3/4. **Cols./Page:** 6. **Col. Width:** 26 nonpareils. **Col. Depth:** 194 agate lines. **Key Personnel:** Dr. Donald M. Suggs, Publisher; Jo Ann Notheis, Office Mgr.; Kevin Jones, Sales and Marketing Dir., fax (314)533-2332. **Subscription Rates:** $30. **Remarks:** Accepts advertising. **Alt. Formats:** CD-ROM.
Ad Rates: 4C: $500 **Circ:** Paid 196
PCI: $24.54 Non-paid 65,000

17631 St. Louis Argus
4595 Martin Luther King Dr.
St. Louis, MO 63113

Black community newspaper. **Subtitle:** St. Louis Argus. **Founded:** Apr. 1912. **Freq:** Weekly. **Cols./Page:** 6. **Col. Width:** 2 1/16 inches. **Col. Depth:** 21 inches. **Key Personnel:** Donald Thompson, Editor; Dr. Eugene Mitchell, Publisher. **Subscription Rates:** $.25 single issue. **Remarks:** Accepts advertising.
Ad Rates: GLR: $15.29 **Circ:** 33,000

17632 St. Louis Art Museum Bulletin
St. Louis Art Museum
Publications Phone: (314)721-0072
1 Fine Arts Dr. Fax: (314)721-6172
Forest Park
St. Louis, MO 63110-1380
Publication E-mail: kweigand@alam.org

Trade magazine covering historical art research. **Freq:** Semiannual. **Key Personnel:** Mary Ann Steiner, Publications Dir. **Subscription Rates:** $10 individuals; $5 single issue. **Remarks:** Advertising not accepted. **URL:** http://www.slam.org.
Circ: (Not Reported)

17633 St. Louis Business Journal
American City Business Journals
1 Metropolitan Sq., Ste. 2170 Phone: (314)421-6200
PO Box 647 Fax: (314)621-5031
St. Louis, MO 63102
Publication E-mail: stlouis@amcity.com

Business newspaper. **Subtitle:** St. Louis Business Authority. **Founded:** Oct. 1980. **Freq:** Weekly (Mon.). **Print Method:** Offset. **Trim Size:** 29. **Cols./Page:** 4. **Col. Width:** 28 nonpareils. **Col. Depth:** 189 agate lines. **Key Personnel:** Patricia Miller, Editor; Ellen Sherberg, Publisher. **ISSN:** 0271-6453. **Subscription Rates:** $62 individuals. **Remarks:** Accepts advertising. **URL:** http://www.amcity.com/stlouis/.
Ad Rates: BW: $3,525 **Circ:** Combined 20,648
4C: $4,035

17634 St. Louis Commerce
St. Louis Regional Commerce & Growth Association (RCGA)
One Metropolitan Sq., Ste. 1300 Phone: (314)231-5555
St. Louis, MO 63102 Fax: (314)206-3222
Free: (800)444-SOLD
Publisher E-mail: econdeu@stlrcga.org

Community business and economic development magazine. **Founded:** 1918. **Freq:** Monthly. **Print Method:** Offset. **Trim Size:** 8 3/8 x 10 7/8. **Cols./Page:** 3. **Col. Width:** 27 nonpareils. **Col. Depth:** 140 agate lines. **Key Personnel:** Carol Schwab, Managing Editor, phone (314)444-1104. **Subscription Rates:** $36. **Remarks:** Accepts advertising.
Ad Rates: BW: $1,995 **Circ:** Paid 7,154
4C: $2,415 Non-paid 2,826

17635 St. Louis ComputerUser
Creative Publications, Ltd.
5300 Mardel Ave. Phone: (314)351-3530
St. Louis, MO 63109 Fax: (314)351-9660

A business publication on computers and office technology. **Subtitle:** A Business to Business Computing Publication. **Founded:** Dec. 1983. **Freq:** Monthly. **Print Method:** Offset. **Trim Size:** 11 x 14 3/8. **Cols./Page:** 4. **Col. Width:** 2 1/4 inches. **Col. Depth:** 13.75 inches. **Key Personnel:** Margaret Harris, Editor, marg@stlcu.com; Carl Harris, Publisher, carl@stlcu.com. **Subscription Rates:** $12 individuals. **Remarks:** Accepts advertising. **URL:** http://www.stlcu.com. **Formerly:** St. Louis Computing (June 1995).
Ad Rates: BW: $2,079 **Circ:** Non-paid ‡65,000
4C: $2,579

17636 St. Louis Countian
Legal Communications Corp.
612 N. 2nd St., 4th Fl. Phone: (314)421-1880
PO Box 88910 Fax: (314)421-0436
St. Louis, MO 63102
Business and legal newspaper. **Founded:** 1890. **Freq:** Tues.-Sat. (morn.). **Print Method:** Web offset. **Trim Size:** 11 3/8 x 17 1/2. **Cols./Page:** 5. **Col. Width:** 22 nonpareils. **Col. Depth:** 224 agate lines. **Key Personnel:** Will Connaghan, Editor; Sara Sue Tedesco, Publisher; Nancy S. Comia-Hoffman, Circulation Mgr.; Susan J. Richard, Advertising Mgr. **USPS:** 476-480. **Subscription Rates:** $175. **Remarks:** Accepts advertising.
Ad Rates: BW: $800 **Circ:** 1,300
4C: $350
SAU: $10
PCI: $10

17637 St. Louis Crusader
4371 Finney Ave.
St. Louis, MO 63113

Black community newspaper. **Founded:** Feb. 2, 1962. **Freq:** Weekly. **Cols./Page:** 6. **Col. Width:** 2 inches. **Col. Depth:** 21 inches. **Key Personnel:** William P. Russell, Editor. **Subscription Rates:** $34 individuals. **Remarks:** Accepts advertising.
Ad Rates: GLR: $.20 **Circ:** Paid ‡9,000
SAU: $12 Controlled ‡150
PCI: $12

17638 St. Louis Jewish Light
12 Millstone Campus Dr. Phone: (314)432-3353
St. Louis, MO 63146-5776 Fax: (314)432-0515
Publication E-mail: stlouislgt@aol.com

Jewish newspaper (tabloid). **Founded:** 1963. **Freq:** Weekly. **Print Method:** Offset. Uses mats. **Trim Size:** 11 1/4 x 17 1/4. **Cols./Page:** 6 and 1. **Col. Width:** 20 nonpareils and 1 5/8 inches. **Col. Depth:** 224 agate lines and 16 inches. **Key Personnel:** Robert A. Cohn, Editor-in-Chief; Linda Mantle, Exec. Editor; Peggy K. Northcott, General Mgr. **ISSN:** 0036-2964. **Subscription Rates:** $42. **Remarks:** Accepts advertising.
Ad Rates: BW: $2,400 **Circ:** ‡14,800
4C: $2,800
PCI: $24

17639 The St. Louis Journalism Review
St. Louis Journalism Review
470 E. Lockwood Phone: (314)968-5905
St. Louis, MO 63119 Fax: (314)963-6104
Publication E-mail: review@webster.edu

Tabloid evaluating journalism, print and broadcast media, advertising and public relations. Notes issues not covered by the mass media. **Subtitle:** A critique of metropolitan media and events. **Founded:** Oct. 1970. **Freq:** Monthly (Combined issues December/January and July/August). **Print Method:** Offset. **Trim Size:** 11 1/2 x 17. **Cols./Page:** 4. **Col. Width:** 12 picas. **Col. Depth:** 217 agate lines. **Key Personnel:** Charles L. Klotzer, Editor & Publisher Emeritus; Ed Bishop, Editor. **ISSN:** 0036-2972. **Subscription Rates:** $30; $3 single issue. **Remarks:** Accepts advertising. **Online:** Publisher.
Ad Rates: BW: $1,600 **Circ:** ‡3,000
4C: $1,814

17640 The St. Louis Metro Evening Whirl
Thomas Publication Co., Inc.
PO Box 5088 Phone: (314)535-4033
St. Louis, MO 63115 Fax: (314)535-4280
Publication E-mail: onewhirl@aol.com
Publisher E-mail: tpcwhirl@aol.com

Black community newspaper. **Founded:** 1938. **Freq:** Weekly (Tues.). **Print Method:** Offset. **Trim Size:** 75 x 129 picas. **Cols./Page:** 6 and 7. **Col. Width:** 12 and 9 picas. **Col. Depth:** 301 and 301 agate lines. **Key Personnel:** Anthony L. Sanders, Editor-in-Chief; Barry R. Thomas, Publisher. **USPS:** 466-530. **Subscription Rates:** $50; $40 6 months; $30 3 months. **Formerly:** The Evening Whirl Examiner; The Evening Whirl.
Ad Rates: BW: $1,922.10 **Circ:** ‡40,000
4C: $500
SAU: $14.90
PCI: $14.90

17641 St. Louis Metropolitan Medicine
St. Louis Metropolitan Medical Society
3839 Lindell Blvd. Phone: (314)371-5225
St. Louis, MO 63108 Fax: (314)533-8601

Medical association business magazine. **Founded:** Jan. 1979. **Freq:** Monthly. **Print Method:** Sheetfed offset. **Trim Size:** 8 1/2 x 11. **Cols./Page:** 2. **Col. Width:** 3 5/8 inches. **Col. Depth:** 9 5/8 inches. **Key Personnel:** Martin M. Pomphrey, MD, Editor; Terry Watson, Managing Editor. **ISSN:** 0892-1334. **Subscription Rates:** Free to qualified subscribers; $50 institutions; $5 single issue. **Remarks:** Accepts advertising. **Formerly:** St. Louis Medicine.
Ad Rates: BW: $390 **Circ:** Paid ‡2,333
4C: $840 Non-paid ‡605

17642 St. Louis Post-Dispatch
Pulitzer Publishing Co.
900 N. Tucker Blvd. Phone: (314)340-8000
St. Louis, MO 63101 Fax: (314)340-3050
Free: (800)365-0820

General newspaper. **Founded:** 1878. **Freq:** Mon.-Sun. (morn.). **Print Method:** Offset. Uses mats. **Cols./Page:** 6. **Col. Width:** 25 nonpareils. **Col. Depth:** 315 agate lines. **Key Personnel:** William F. Woo, Editor; Nicholas G. Penninman IV, Publisher; Gerald F. Anderson, Advertising Mgr. **Subscription Rates:** $130. **Remarks:** Accepts advertising. **Online:** Dialog (The Dialog Corporation); DataTimes Corporation; LEXIS-NEXIS; CompuServe Information Service. **URL:** http://www.sto.net.com. **Alt. Formats:** CD-ROM, NewsBank, Inc. **Feature Editors:** Tim Bross, *City*, phone (314)340-7096; Gary Clark, *Real Estate*, phone (314)340-7091; Jim Creighton, *Book*, phone (314)340-7076; Joan Dames, *Society*, phone (314)340-7311; Jim Forbes, *Photo*, phone (314)340-7035; Gregory Freeman, *Political*, phone (314)340-7096; Phil Gaitens, *Financial/Business*, phone (314)340-7026; Ellen Gardner, *Garden/Home, Travel, Women's*, phone (314)340-7539; Barbara Hertenstein, *Food*, phone (314)340-7570; Virginia Hick, *Education*, phone (314)340-7206; Ed Higgins, *Editorials*, phone (314)340-7056; Becky Homan, *Fashion*, phone (314)340-7495; Nancy Miller, *Metro*, phone (314)340-7568; Eric Mink, *TV & Radio*, phone (314)340-7041; Robert Pastin,

Sports, phone (314)340-7492; Jan Paul, *Sunday*, phone (314)340-7523; Joe Pollack, *Drama, Movie*, phone (314)340-7060; Dick Richmond, *Entertainment*, phone (314)340-7539; Kathy Rogers, *Religion*, phone (314)340-7009; Bob Sanford, *Aviation*, phone (314)340-7010; Martha Shirk, *Family*, phone (314)340-7539; Roger Signor, *Medical*, phone (314)340-7470; Renee Stovsky Ferguson, *Lifestyle*, phone (314)340-7006; Jerri Stroud, *Rural Development*, phone (314)340-7568; Tom Uhlenbrock, *Environmental*, phone (314)340-7024; Dick Weiss, *Features*, phone (314)340-7539; James Wierzbicki, *Music*, phone (314)340-7077; Ron Willnow, *News, Saturday*, phone (314)340-7565.
Ad Rates: SAU: $101.75 **Circ:** Mon.-Sat. ★**329,582**
Sun. ★**516,237**

17643 St. Louis Review
462 N. Taylor Ave. Phone: (314)531-9700
St. Louis, MO 63108 Fax: (314)531-2269
Publication E-mail: slreview@i1.net

Catholic newspaper. **Founded:** 1941. **Freq:** Weekly (Fri.). **Print Method:** Offset. **Trim Size:** 11 5/8 x 20 15/16. **Cols./Page:** 6. **Col. Width:** 11 picas. **Col. Depth:** 124 picas. **Key Personnel:** Rev. Dennis M. Delaney, Editor; Paul Pennick, Managing Editor; Archbishop Justin Rigali, Publisher; Thomas L. Courtaway, Comptroller. **ISSN:** 0036-3022. **Subscription Rates:** $16 individuals.
Ad Rates: GLR: $1.63 **Circ:** ‡90,000
BW: $2,489.76
4C: $2,989.76
PCI: $22.88

17644 St. Louis/Southern Illinois Labor Tribune
St. Louis/Southern Illinois Tribune
505 S. Ewing Ave. Phone: (314)535-9660
St. Louis, MO 63103 Fax: (314)535-2700

Labor newspaper (AFL-CIO). **Founded:** Apr. 1937. **Freq:** Weekly (Thurs.). **Print Method:** Offset. **Trim Size:** 11 3/8 x 14 1/2. **Cols./Page:** 6. **Col. Width:** 1 5/8 inches. **Col. Depth:** 13 inches. **Key Personnel:** Dana Spitgev, Editor; Edward M. Finkelstein, Publisher; Don Chesley, Marketing Dir. **ISSN:** 0885-6869. **Subscription Rates:** $35 individuals. **Remarks:** Accepts advertising.
Ad Rates: GLR: $2.28 **Circ:** ‡78,000
BW: $2,496
4C: $2,996
PCI: $38.41

17645 Schutzhund USA
United Schutzhund Clubs of America
3810 Paule Ave. Phone: (314)638-9686
St. Louis, MO 63125-1718 Fax: (314)638-0609
Publication E-mail: usaschutzhund@worldnet.att.net

Club breed and sport publication for German shepherd dog enthusiasts. **Subtitle:** The Official Publication of the United Schutzhund Clubs of America. **Founded:** 1975. **Freq:** Bimonthly. **Print Method:** Sheetfed offset. **Trim Size:** 8 1/2 x 10 3/8. **Cols./Page:** 2. **Col. Depth:** 7 inches. **Key Personnel:** Donna Rednour, Editor, d.rednour@cwix.com. **ISSN:** 0194-5033. **Subscription Rates:** $60 individuals.
Ad Rates: BW: $185 **Circ:** Paid 7,500
4C: $700 Non-paid 500

17646 Snicker
Balducci Publications
1248 Oak Bark Dr. Phone: (314)993-1633
St. Louis, MO 63146 Fax: (314)993-1633

Trade magazine covering humor, cartoons and art for professional or novice cartoonists. **Founded:** Apr. 1, 1987. **Freq:** Monthly. **Print Method:** Web offset. **Trim Size:** 10 x 16. **Key Personnel:** Rich Balducci, Editor and Publisher; Kathleen Quirk, Advertising Mgr.; Gulhan Sumer, Circulation. **Subscription Rates:** $25 individuals; $3 single issue. **Remarks:** Accepts advertising. **URL:** http://www.snicker.com.
Ad Rates: GLR: $10 **Circ:** Combined 70,000
BW: $800
4C: $1,000
PCI: $50

17647 Social Justice Review
Central Bureau of the Catholic Central Verein of America
3835 Westminster Pl. Phone: (314)371-1653
St. Louis, MO 63108
Journal addressing important subjects from the angle of social justice. **Founded:** 1908. **Freq:** Bimonthly. **Key Personnel:** Rev. John H. Miller, C.S.C., Editor. **ISSN:** 0037-7767. **Subscription Rates:** $20; $23 other countries; $30 airmail. **Remarks:** Advertising not accepted.
Circ: Paid 4,600
Non-paid 500

17648 Somatosensory and Motor Research
Washington University School of Medicine
Dept. of Neurology and Neurological Surgery Phone: (314)747-1260
Fax: (314)362-8359
4566 Scott Ave.
PO Box 8213
St. Louis, MO 63110
Publication E-mail: enquiries@carfax.co.uk
Publisher E-mail: somore@medicine.wustl.edu

Journal featuring somatic, motor, and neural research. **Founded:** 1983. **Freq:** Quarterly. **Print Method:** Offset. **Trim Size:** 209mm x 200mm. **Cols./Page:** 2. **Col. Width:** 80 nonpareils. **Col. Depth:** 250 agate lines. **Key Personnel:** Thomas A. Woolsey, Editor. **ISSN:** 0899-0220. **Subscription Rates:** $104 individuals; $256 institutions. **Available Online. Alt. Formats:** Microfilm. **Formerly:** Somatosensory Research (1988).
Ad Rates: BW: $320 **Circ:** Paid 250

17649 South County Journal
Suburban Newspapers of Greater St. Louis
4210 Chippewa St. Phone: (314)481-1111
St. Louis, MO 63116-2636 Fax: (314)664-9777

Community newspaper. **Founded:** 1960. **Freq:** Semiweekly (Wed. and Sun.). **Print Method:** Offset. **Cols./Page:** 6. **Col. Width:** 26 nonpareils. **Col. Depth:** 308 agate lines. **Key Personnel:** Tim Hickey, Advertising Mgr. **Subscription Rates:** Free.
Circ: Free 23,431

17650 South County Times
Webster-Kirkwood Times, Inc.
122 W. Lockwood Ave., 2nd Fl. Phone: (314)968-2699
St. Louis, MO 63119-2916 Fax: (314)968-2961

Community newspaper. **Founded:** Apr. 4, 1986. **Freq:** Weekly (Fri.). **Print Method:** Offset. **Trim Size:** 11 x 17 1/2. **Cols./Page:** 4. **Col. Width:** 26 nonpareils. **Col. Depth:** 224 agate lines. **Key Personnel:** Dwight Bitikofer, Publisher; Don Corrigan, Editor. **Subscription Rates:** Free; $25 (mail). **Remarks:** Accepts advertising. **Formerly:** South St. Louis County News (1989); South County News-Times (1992); Gravois Watson Times.
Ad Rates: BW: $1,850 **Circ:** Free 35,210
PCI: $28.91

17651 South Side Journal
Suburban Newspapers of Greater St. Louis
4210 Chippewa Phone: (314)664-2700
St. Louis, MO 63116
Community newspaper. **Founded:** 1935. **Freq:** Semiweekly (Wed. and Sun.). **Print Method:** Offset. **Cols./Page:** 6. **Col. Width:** 26 nonpareils. **Col. Depth:** 308 agate lines. **Key Personnel:** Tim Hickey, Advertising Mgr. **Subscription Rates:** Free. **URL:** http://www.yourjournal.com.
Circ: Free 35,627

17652 Southwest County
Suburban Newspapers of Greater St. Louis
4210 Chippewa Phone: (314)664-2700
St. Louis, MO 63116 Fax: (314)664-9777

Community newspaper. **Founded:** 1976. **Freq:** Semiweekly (Wed. and Sun.). **Print Method:** Offset. **Cols./Page:** 6. **Col. Width:** 26 nonpareils. **Col. Depth:** 308 agate lines. **Key Personnel:** David H. Baur, Publisher. **Subscription Rates:** Free. **URL:** http://www.yourjournal.com. **Formerly:** Fenton Journal (1992).
Circ: Free 57,725

17653 The Sporting News
The Sporting News Publishing Co.
10176 Corporate Square Dr., Ste. 200 Phone: (314)997-7111
Fax: (314)993-7726
St. Louis, MO 63132
Free: (800)325-4081
Publication E-mail: tsnmail@aol.com

Sports magazine (tabloid). **Founded:** Mar. 17, 1886. **Freq:** Weekly. **Print Method:** Offset. **Trim Size:** 10 1/2 x 13 1/4. **Cols./Page:** 4. **Col. Width:** 23 nonpareils. **Col. Depth:** 185 agate lines. **Key Personnel:** John Rawlings, Editor; Fran Farrell, Publisher. **ISSN:** 0038-805X. **Subscription Rates:** $72 individuals; $2.50 single issue; $2.95 single issue, Canada. **Remarks:** Accepts advertising. **Online:** LEXIS-NEXIS.
Ad Rates: BW: $19,840 **Circ:** Paid ★**540,025**
4C: $24,540

17654 Steamshovel Press
PO Box 23715 Phone: (314)997-7868
St. Louis, MO 63121 Fax: (314)516-5853
Publication E-mail: skthoma@umslvma.umsl.edu

Alternative political publication. **Subtitle:** Popular Alienation. **Founded:** June 1988. **Freq:** Quarterly. **Trim Size:** 8 x 10. **Key Personnel:** Kenn Thomas, Editor and Publisher. **ISSN:** 0602-3795. **Subscription Rates:** $22; $26 out of country; $5 single issue. **Remarks:** Accepts advertising. **URL:** http://www.umsl.edu/~skthoma.
Ad Rates: BW: $110 **Circ:** Paid 5,000
4C: $650

17655 Student Life
Washington University
Campus Box 1039 Phone: (314)935-5995
Washington University
St. Louis, MO 63130
Publication E-mail: letters@slife.wustl.edu

Collegiate newspaper. **Founded:** 1878. **Freq:** Semiweekly (Tues. and Fri. during the academic year). **Print Method:** Offset. **Trim Size:** 13 x 21. **Cols./Page:** 6. **Col. Width:** 2 1/16 inches. **Col. Depth:** 294 agate lines. **Key Personnel:** Ben Cannon, Editor-in-Chief; Andrew O'Dell, General Mgr. **Subscription Rates:** Free; $70 (mail). **Remarks:** Accepts advertising. **Available Online.**
Ad Rates: BW: $1,512.00 **Circ:** Paid ‡500
4C: $1,610.80 Free ‡7,500
PCI: $12.00

17656 Studies in the Spirituality of Jesuits
Seminar on Jesuit Spirituality
3700 W. Pine Blvd. Phone: (314)977-7257
St. Louis, MO 63108 Fax: (314)977-7263
Publisher E-mail: ijs@slu.edu

Journal disseminating information on Jesuit history and spirituality and furthering the updating recommended by Vatican Council II. **Founded:** 1969. **Freq:** 5/year. **Trim Size:** 6 x 9. **Cols./Page:** 1. **Col. Width:** 4 1/4 inches. **Col. Depth:** 7 1/2 inches. **Key Personnel:** Rev. John W. Padberg, S.J., Editor. **Subscription Rates:** $15; $20 Canada and Mexico; $2.50 single issue; $22 all other foreign addresses. **Remarks:** Advertising not accepted.
Circ: 5,300

17657 Surgery
Mosby Year Book, Inc.
11830 Westline Industrial Dr. Phone: (314)872-8370
St. Louis, MO 63146 Fax: (314)432-1380
Free: (800)325-4177

Journal for practicing general surgeons. Regular issues focus on clinical and experimental surgery. Special issues are devoted to the papers of the Society of University Surgeons, Central Surgical Association, and the American Association of Endocrine Surgeons. **Founded:** Jan. 1937. **Freq:** Monthly. **Print Method:** Offset. **Trim Size:** 8 1/8 x 10 7/8. **Cols./Page:** 2. **Col. Width:** 39 nonpareils. **Col. Depth:** 140 agate lines. **Key Personnel:** Walter F. Ballinger, M.D., Editor; George Zuidema, M.D., Editor; Doug Kessler, Marketing Dir.; Joyce Felan, Marketing Coord.; Carol Kilzer, Advertising Sales, phone (314)453-4307, fax (314)453-9164, carol.kilzer@mosby.com. **ISSN:** 0039-6060. **Subscription Rates:** $142 individuals; $182.97 Canada; $171 other countries; $67 students; $102.72 students, Canada; $96 students, other countries; $299 institutions; $350.96 institutions, Canada; $328 institutions, other countries. **Remarks:** Accepts advertising. **URL:** http://www.mosby.com.
Ad Rates: BW: $1,130 **Circ:** Paid 6,219
Non-paid 236

17658 TED The Electrical Distributor Magazine
National Association of Electrical Distributors, Inc.
1100 Corporate Square Drive Phone: (314)991-9000
Suite 100 Fax: (314)991-3090
St. Louis, MO 63132
Free: (888)791-2512
Publication E-mail: tedmag@naed.org

Magazine for electrical distributors. **Subtitle:** Official Publication of the National Association of Electrical Distributors (NAED). **Founded:** 1964. **Freq:** Monthly. **Print Method:** Offset. **Trim Size:** 8 1/8 x 10 7/8. **Cols./Page:** 3. **Col. Width:** 26 nonpareils. **Col. Depth:** 140 agate lines. **Key Personnel:** Sarah Greider, Editor, phone (314)812-5311, sgreider@naed.org; Tom Naber, Publisher, phone (314)812-5312, tnaber@naed.org; Laurie Mueller-Bevirt, Executive Editor, phone (314)812-5310, lbevirt@naed.org; Bethany Wieman, Circulation Mgr., phone (314)812-5309, bwiemann@naed.org; Sheila Logan, Business Mgr., phone (314)812-5338, fax (314)991-3060, slogan@naed.org. **ISSN:** 0422-8707. **Subscription Rates:** $22 individuals; $45 other countries. **Remarks:** Accepts advertising. **URL:** http://www.naed.org.
Ad Rates: BW: $4,490 **Circ:** Combined △**28,304**
4C: $6,450

17659 Teen Time
Lutheran Library for the Blind
1333 S. Kirkwood Rd. Fax: (314)965-0959
St. Louis, MO 63122 Free: (800)433-3954

Consumer magazine covering Christian based articles for

teens. **Subtitle:** Large Print Edition. **Freq:** Monthly. **Remarks:** Advertising not accepted. **Alt. Formats:** Large-print.
Circ: (Not Reported)

17660 Theology Digest
St. Louis University
3800 Lindell Blvd.
PO Box 56907
St. Louis, MO 63108
Phone: (314)977-3410
Fax: (314)977-1602
Publication E-mail: thdigest@slu.edu

Theology journal. **Founded:** 1953. **Freq:** Quarterly. **Print Method:** Letterpress and offset. **Trim Size:** 6 x 9. **Cols./Page:** 2. **Col. Width:** 27 nonpareils. **Col. Depth:** 105 agate lines. **Key Personnel:** B. Asen, Editor; R. Jermann, Editor. **ISSN:** 0040-5728. **Subscription Rates:** $15 individuals; $26 two years; $4 single issue. **Alt. Formats:** Microform.
Ad Rates: BW: $250 **Circ:** ‡4,113

17661 University News
20 N. Grant, Ste. 301
St. Louis, MO 63103
Phone: (314)977-2812
Fax: (314)977-1589
Publication E-mail: unews@sluvca.slu.edu

University newspaper. **Subtitle:** A Student Voice of St. Louis University. **Founded:** 1921. **Freq:** Weekly (Fri.). **Print Method:** Offset. **Cols./Page:** 6. **Col. Width:** 2 1/16 inches. **Col. Depth:** 21 1/2 inches. **Key Personnel:** Matt Hathaway, Editor; Steve Francisco, Managing Editor; Margaret Smith, Sales Dir. **Subscription Rates:** $15. **Remarks:** Accepts advertising.
Ad Rates: BW: $750 **Circ:** Paid 200
4C: $970
PCI: $7

17662 Voices
Women for Faith & Family
PO Box 8326
St. Louis, MO 63132
Phone: (314)863-8385
Fax: (314)863-5858
Publication E-mail: 72223.3601@compuserve.com

Journal of the Women for Faith & Family organization. **Founded:** 1985. **Freq:** Quarterly. **Print Method:** Photo offset. **Trim Size:** 8 1/2 x 11. **Cols./Page:** 2. **Col. Width:** 3 1/2 inches. **Col. Depth:** 9 1/2 inches. **Key Personnel:** Helen Hull Hitchcock, Editor. **ISSN:** 1066-8136. **Subscription Rates:** Free to qualified subscribers. **Remarks:** Advertising not accepted.
Circ: Non-paid 10,000

17663 The Waterways Journal
Waterways Journal, Inc.
319 N. 4th St., Ste. 650
St. Louis, MO 63102
Phone: (314)241-7354
Fax: (314)241-4207
Publisher E-mail: waterwayj@socket.net

Marine commercial traffic newspaper. **Founded:** 1887. **Freq:** Weekly. **Print Method:** Offset. **Trim Size:** 10 1/4 x 13 1/2. **Cols./Page:** 4. **Col. Width:** 26 nonpareils. **Col. Depth:** 161 agate lines. **Key Personnel:** John Showlberg, Editor; Nelson Spencer, Publisher; Rick Bensinger, Advertising Mgr. **ISSN:** 0043-1524. **Subscription Rates:** $32; $60 Canada and other countries. **Remarks:** Accepts advertising.
Ad Rates: BW: $1,315 **Circ:** ‡5,728
4C: $2,315
PCI: $54

Webster-Kirkwood Times - See Webster Groves

17664 Where St. Louis
Where Magazines International (St. Louis)
1750 S. Brentwood Blvd., Ste. 311
St. Louis, MO 63144
Phone: (314)968-4940
Fax: (314)968-0813
Publisher E-mail: where@inlink.com

Consumer magazine for travelers to St. Louis, Missouri. **Founded:** 1933. **Freq:** Monthly. **Print Method:** Offset. **Trim Size:** 8 x 10 7/8. **Key Personnel:** Lynn Potts, Publisher. **Subscription Rates:** $30 individuals. **Remarks:** Accepts advertising.
Ad Rates: BW: $2,215 **Circ:** Controlled ‡34,000
4C: $2,660

17665 KATZ-FM - 100.3
10155 Corporate Sq. Dr.
St. Louis, MO 63132
Phone: (314)692-5108
Fax: (314)692-5127

Format: Jazz. **Networks:** Independent; ABC. **Founded:** 1961. **Operating Hours:** Continuous. **ADI:** St. Louis, MO (Mt. Vernon, IL). **Key Personnel:** Tracy Lewis, General Mgr. **Wattage:** 50,000.

17666 KCFV-FM - 89.5
3400 Pershall Rd.
St. Louis, MO 63135-1499
Phone: (314)595-4472
Fax: (314)595-4217
E-mail: dkirby@fv.stlcc.cc.mo.us

Format: Alternative/New Music/Progressive. **Networks:** UPI. **Owner:** St. Louis Community College, at above address. **Founded:** 1972. **Operating Hours:** Mon.-Fri. 8 a.m.-midnight, Sat.-Sun. 8 a.m.-midnight. **ADI:** St. Louis, MO (Mt. Vernon, IL). **Key Personnel:** Dianna L. Clark, General Mgr., phone (314)595-4463, fax (314)595-4217, dclark@fv.stlcc.cc.mo.us; Tim Croskey, Chief Engineer, phone (314)595-2378, fax (314)595-4544, teraskey@fv.stlce.cc.mo.us. **Wattage:** 100. **Ad Rates:** Noncommercial.

17667 KDHX-FM - 88.1
3504 Magnolia
St. Louis, MO 63118
Phone: (314)664-3955
Fax: (314)664-1020
E-mail: edge@kdhxfm88.org

Format: Public Radio; Eclectic. **Founded:** 1987. **Operating Hours:** Continuous; 2% network, 98% local. **ADI:** St. Louis, MO (Mt. Vernon, IL). **Key Personnel:** Dennis Cronin-Doyle, General Mgr.; Larry Weir, Operations Mgr.; Terry Moses, Program Dir.; Bruce Cavins, Chief Engineer; Marge Reese, Development Dir. **Wattage:** 42,000. **Ad Rates:** Noncommercial; underwriting available. **URL:** http://www.kdhxfm88.org.

17668 KDNL-TV - 30
1215 Cole St.
St. Louis, MO 63106
Phone: (314)436-3030
Fax: (314)259-5538

Format: Commercial TV. **Networks:** ABC. **Owner:** Sinclair Communications, Sinclair Broadcast Group, 2000 W. 41st St., Baltimore, MD 21211, (410)662-4700, Fax: (410)662-4778. **Founded:** 1969. **Operating Hours:** Continuous. **ADI:** St. Louis, MO (Mt. Vernon, IL). **Key Personnel:** Frank Quitoni, Vice Pres./General Mgr., phone (314)259-5700, fax (314)259-5709; Tom Tipton, General Sales Mgr., phone (314)259-5727, fax (314)259-5738; Jim Wright, Operations Dir., phone (314)259-5757, fax (314)259-5504; Beth Stiebel, Program Mgr., phone (314)259-5739, fax (314)259-5504; Mary Pat O'Neill, Traffic Mgr., phone (314)259-5731; Tom Mungenast, Production Mgr., phone (314)259-5754, fax (314)259-5504; Dave Cohen, News Dir., phone (314)259-5582, fax (314)259-5569; Martha Perry, Research Dir., phone (314)259-5725; Ian Guthrie, Business Mgr., phone (314)259-5746, fax (314)259-5504; Phil Michael, Marketing Dir., phone (314)259-5706, fax (314)259-5598. **Wattage:** 2,290,000. **Ad Rates:** $25-4000 for 30 seconds.

17669 KETC-TV - 9
3655 Olive St.
St. Louis, MO 63108-3601
Phone: (314)512-9000
Fax: (314)512-9005

Format: Public TV. **Networks:** Public Broadcasting Service (PBS). **Founded:** 1952. **Operating Hours:** Continuous. **ADI:** St. Louis, MO (Mt. Vernon, IL). **Key Personnel:** Michael Hardgrove, Pres./CEO. **Local Programs:** *Convaesations with Anne Keefe*. **Wattage:** 316,000.

17670 KEZK-FM - 102.5
3100 Market St.
St. Louis, MO 63103-2528
Phone: (314)727-2160
Fax: (314)727-7696

Format: Adult Contemporary. **Networks:** Independent. **Founded:** 1968. **Operating Hours:** Continuous. **ADI:** St. Louis, MO (Mt. Vernon, IL). **Key Personnel:** Roy Anderson, Jr., General Mgr. **Wattage:** 100,000.

17671 KFNS-AM - 590
7711 Carondelet, Ste. 304
St. Louis, MO 63105
Phone: (314)727-2160
Fax: (314)727-7696

Format: Easy Listening; Sports. **Networks:** ESPN Radio. **Founded:** 1961. **Formerly:** WKLL-AM (1990); KEZK-FM. **Operating Hours:** Continuous. **ADI:** St. Louis, MO (Mt. Vernon, IL). **Key Personnel:** Karen Carroll, General Mgr. **Wattage:** 1000. **Ad Rates:** $75-150 for 60 seconds. **URL:** http://www.kfns.com.

17672 KFUO-FM - 99.1
88 Founders Ln.
St. Louis, MO 63105
Free: (800)844-0524
Phone: (314)725-0099
Fax: (314)725-3801

Format: Classical. **Networks:** NBC; Wall Street Journal Radio. **Owner:** Lutheran Church Missouri Synod, 1333 S. Kirkwood Rd., St. Louis, MO 63122, (314)965-9000, (314)822-8307. **Founded:** 1948. **Operating Hours:** Continuous. **ADI:** St. Louis, MO (Mt. Vernon, IL). **Key Personnel:** Bill Knierly, General Sales Mgr.; Jim Connett, Program Dir.; Ron Klemm, Operations Mgr. **Wattage:** 100,000. **Ad Rates:** $75 per unit.

17673 KLOU-FM - 103.3
1 Memorial Dr., No. 700
St. Louis, MO 63102
Free: (800)877-1033
Phone: (314)533-1033
Fax: (314)533-2103

Format: Oldies. **Networks:** AP. **Owner:** American Radio Systems, at above address. **Operating Hours:** Continuous. **ADI:** St. Louis, MO (Mt. Vernon, IL). **Key Personnel:** David Dunkin, Program Dir., phone (314)588-2365; Sean Luce, General Sales Mgr., phone (314)588-2301. **Wattage:** 100,000. **Ad Rates:** $175 for 60 seconds.

17674 KMJM-FM - 107.7
10155 Corporate Sq. Dr.
St. Louis, MO 63132
Phone: (314)692-5108
Fax: (314)692-5127

Format: Urban Contemporary. **Networks:** Independent. **Founded:** 1972. **Operating Hours:** Continuous. **ADI:** St. Louis, MO (Mt. Vernon, IL). **Key Personnel:** Linda O'Connor, General Mgr. **Wattage:** 100,000.

17675 KMOV-TV - 4
1 Memorial Dr.
St. Louis, MO 63102
Free: (800)444-6333
Phone: (314)621-4444
Fax: (314)444-3367

Format: Commercial TV. **Networks:** CBS. **Formerly:** KMOX-TV. **Operating Hours:** Continuous. **ADI:** St. Louis, MO (Mt. Vernon, IL). **Key Personnel:** Allan Cohen, Vice Pres./Gen. Mgr.

17676 KMOX-AM - 1120
1 Memorial Dr.
St. Louis, MO 63102
Phone: (314)621-2345
Fax: (314)444-3230

Format: News; Talk; Sports. **Networks:** CBS. **Founded:** 1925. **Operating Hours:** Continuous. **ADI:** St. Louis, MO (Mt. Vernon, IL). **Key Personnel:** Rod Zimmerman, Vice President/General Manager; David Kelly, General Sales Mgr., phone (314)444-3275. **Wattage:** 50,000. **URL:** http://www.kmox.basic.net.

17677 KNLC-TV - 24
1411 Locust St.
St. Louis, MO 63106
Phone: (314)436-2424
Fax: (314)436-2434
E-mail: knlc24jim@hereshelpet.org

Format: Religious. **Networks:** Independent. **Owner:** New Life Evangelistic Center, at above address. **Founded:** 1982. **Operating Hours:** Continuous. **ADI:** St. Louis, MO (Mt. Vernon, IL). **Key Personnel:** Larry Rice, President. **Wattage:** 3,090,000. **Ad Rates:** $75-125 for 30 seconds; $150-225 for 60 seconds.

17678 KPLR-TV - 11
4935 Lindell Blvd.
St. Louis, MO 63108-1587
Phone: (314)367-7211
Fax: (314)454-6488

Format: Commercial TV. **Networks:** Independent. **Founded:** 1959. **Operating Hours:** Continuous. **ADI:** St. Louis, MO (Mt. Vernon, IL). **Key Personnel:** H. Max Lummis, V.P./Chief Operating Officer; Paul Wise, Director of Sales and Marketing; Jeanne McCarthy, Traffic Mgr. **Wattage:** 315,000.

17679 KPNT-FM - 105.7
1215 Cole St.
St. Louis, MO 63106
Phone: (314)231-1057

Format: Album-Oriented Rock (AOR). **ADI:** St. Louis, MO (Mt. Vernon, IL). **Key Personnel:** Dick Stein, General Mgr. **Ad Rates:** $120 for 60 seconds.

17680 KRJY-FM - 96.3
8081 Manchester Rd.
St. Louis, MO 63105
Phone: (314)781-9600

Format: Oldies. **ADI:** St. Louis, MO (Mt. Vernon, IL). **Key Personnel:** Richard Miller, General Mgr.; Gary Lewis, General Sales Mgr.

17681 KSD-AM - 550
3100 Market St.
St. Louis, MO 63103-2526
Free: (800)531-9810
Phone: (314)531-0000
Fax: (314)531-9855

Format: Talk. **Networks:** Independent. **Owner:** EZ Communications, 10800 Main St., Fairfax, VA 22030, (703)591-1000. **Founded:** 1922. **Operating Hours:** Continuous. **ADI:** St. Louis, MO (Mt. Vernon, IL). **Key Personnel:** Lou Goad, Music Dir.; Scott Strong, Contact; Merrell Hansen, General Mgr.; Bill Coffey, Program Dir.; John Kijowski, Contact; Bob Rowe, Contact; Bill Kratz, Promotions Dir. **Wattage:** 5000.

17682 KSDK-TV - 5
1000 Market St.
St. Louis, MO 63101
Phone: (314)421-5055
Fax: (314)444-5289

Format: Commercial TV. **Networks:** NBC. **Owner:** Gannett Broadcasting, 1100 Wilson Blvd, Arlington, VA 22234, (703)284-6764. **Founded:** 1947. **Formerly:** KSD-TV (1983). **Operating Hours:** Continuous. **ADI:** St. Louis, MO (Mt. Vernon, IL). **Key Personnel:** Ardyth Diercks, General Mgr./President; Robert Drewel, General Sales Mgr.; Rebecca Rahm, Program Dir.; Tim Larson, News Dir.; Gil Ludwig, Chief Engineer; Chris Fricke, Business Mgr.; Warren Canull, Human Resources Dir.; Richard Dyer, VP Broadcast. **Local Programs:** *Show Me St. Louis*, Rebecca Rahn.

17683 KSHE-FM - 94.7
700 St. Louis Union Sta. Phone: (314)621-0095
The Annex No. 101 Fax: (314)621-3428
St. Louis, MO 63103

Format: Album-Oriented Rock (AOR). **Owner:** Emmis Broadcasting Corp., 950 N. Meridian, No. 1200, Indianapolis, IN 46204, (317)266-0100. **Founded:** 1961. **Operating Hours:** Continuous. **ADI:** St. Louis, MO (Mt. Vernon, IL). **Key Personnel:** John Beck, Gen. Mgr./Vice Pres.; Dean Mutter, General Sales Mgr.; Rick Balis, Program Dir.; John R. Beck, Jr., Contact; Marvin Sanders, National Sales Mgr. **Wattage:** 100,000.

17684 KSIV-AM - 1320
1750 S. Brentwood Blvd., Ste. 811 Phone: (314)961-1320
St. Louis, MO 63144 Fax: (314)961-7562

Format: Talk; Religious. **Networks:** USA Radio. **Owner:** Bott Radio Network, 10550 Barkley, Overland Park, KS 66212, (913)642-7770, Fax: (913)642-1319. **Founded:** 1982. **Formerly**: KADI-AM. **Operating Hours:** Continuous; 10% network, 5% local, 85% other. **ADI:** St. Louis, MO (Mt. Vernon, IL). **Key Personnel:** Michael C. McHardy, General Mgr.; Joy Elder, Sales Mgr.; Bruce Cavins, Chief Engineer. **Wattage:** 5000. **Ad Rates:** $28 for 30 seconds; $35 for 60 seconds.

17685 KTRS-AM - 550
638 Westport Plaza Phone: (314)453-5500
St. Louis, MO 63146 Fax: (314)453-9704

Format: News; Talk. **Networks:** ABC. **Owner:** KSD-AM, L. L. C., at above address. **Operating Hours:** Continuous. **ADI:** St. Louis, MO (Mt. Vernon, IL). **Key Personnel:** Timothy Dorsey, Pres./General Mgr., phone (314)453-5501. **Local Programs:** *Frank O. Pinion*, Dan Strauss. **Wattage:** 5,000. **URL:** http://www.550ktrs.com.

17686 KTVI-TV - 2
5915 Berthod Ave. Phone: (314)647-2222
St. Louis, MO 63110 Fax: (314)644-7419
E-mail: ktv12@aol.com

Format: Commercial TV. **Networks:** Fox. **Owner:** Fox Broadcasting Co., PO Box 900, Beverly Hills, CA 90213. **Founded:** 1953. **Formerly**: WTVI-TV. **Operating Hours:** Continuous. **ADI:** St. Louis, MO (Mt. Vernon, IL). **Key Personnel:** Spencer Kock, Pres./Gen. Mgr., phone (314)647-2222, fax (314)644-7419; Kathryn Hansen, Dir., Creative Services, phone (314)644-7430, fax (314)644-7510; Rick Erbach, News Dir., phone (314)644-7575, fax (314)647-8960; Suzanne Teagle, Sales Dir., phone (314)644-7471, fax (314)644-7419; Elaine Claspill, Program Coordinator, phone (314)644-7460, fax (314)644-7419; Dan Adams, Comptroller, phone (314)644-7475, fax (314)647-8582.

17687 KWMU-FM - 90.7
University of Missouri-St. Louis Phone: (314)516-5968
8001 Natural Bridge Rd. Fax: (314)516-5993
St. Louis, MO 63121
E-mail: kwmu@umslvma.umsl.edu

Format: Public Radio; News; Jazz. **Networks:** National Public Radio (NPR); American Public Radio (APR). **Owner:** University of Missouri-St. Louis, at above address. **Founded:** 1972. **Operating Hours:** Continuous; 73% network, 27% local. **ADI:** St. Louis, MO (Mt. Vernon, IL). **Key Personnel:** Robert Peterson, Program Dir.; Lester Graham, News Dir.; Mary Edwards, Production Mgr.; Patricia Bennett, Dir. and General Mgr.; Shelley Kerley, Station Mgr. **Local Programs:** *Cityscape*, Joe Pollack; *St. Louis on the Air*, Mark Manelli. **Wattage:** 100,000. **Ad Rates:** Noncommercial; underwriting available.

17688 KWUR-FM - 90.3
Washington University Phone: (314)935-5952
Box 1182 Fax: (314)935-5699
St. Louis, MO 63130
E-mail: kwur@artsci.wust.edu

Format: Alternative/New Music/Progressive. **Owner:** Washington University, 1 Brookings Dr., St. Louis, MO 63130. **Founded:** 1976. **Operating Hours:** Continuous; 100% local. **ADI:** St. Louis, MO (Mt. Vernon, IL). **Key Personnel:** Jonathan Cobb, General Mgr.; Vanessa Hays, Music Dir.; Ben Whitesides, Contact; Erin Goss, Contact. **Wattage:** 10. **Ad Rates:** Noncommercial; underwriting available. **URL:** http://www.artsi.wust.edu/~kwur.

17689 KYKY-FM - 98.1
3100 Market St. Phone: (314)531-0000
St. Louis, MO 63103 Fax: (314)531-9810

Format: Adult Contemporary. **Networks:** Independent. **Owner:** EZ Communications, 10800 Main St., Fairfax, VA 22030, (703)591-1000. **Founded:** 1972. **Formerly:** KSLQ-FM. **Operating Hours:** Continuous; 100% local. **ADI:** St. Louis, MO (Mt. Vernon, IL). **Key Personnel:** Karen Carroll, Vice President; Amy Koman, Sales Mgr.; Smokey Rivers, Program Dir.; Michelle Dibble, News Dir. **Wattage:** 100,000.

17690 TCI
4940 Delmar Blvd. Phone: (314)361-7300
St. Louis, MO 63108-1659

Founded: 1985. **Formerly**: Saint Louis Tele-Communications. **Cities Served:** Saint Louis, MO.

17691 WEW-AM - 770
7720 Forsyth Blvd. Phone: (314)862-0815
St. Louis, MO 63105-1810 Fax: (314)862-1408
Free: (800)574-0770

Format: Big Band/Nostalgia; Music of Your Life. **Founded:** 1921. **Operating Hours:** 6 a.m.-8:30 p.m. **ADI:** St. Louis, MO (Mt. Vernon, IL). **Key Personnel:** Brian Miller, Program Dir. **Wattage:** 1000. **Ad Rates:** $34-48 for 60 seconds.

17692 WGNU-AM - 920
265 N. Union Blvd., Ste. 1315 Phone: (314)454-6660
St. Louis, MO 63108-1236 Fax: (314)454-6609
E-mail: wgnu@mo.net

Format: Talk. **Owner:** Norman Broadcasting Co., at above address. **Founded:** 1961. **Operating Hours:** Continuous; 17% network, 83% local. **ADI:** St. Louis, MO (Mt. Vernon, IL). **Key Personnel:** Art Ford, General Mgr.; Mike Huss, Sports Dir.; Charles Geer, News/ Program Director; Rich LaCroix, Contact; Joe Garcia, Music Dir. **Local Programs:** *Party Line*, Charles Geer. **Wattage:** 500. **Ad Rates:** $20 for 30 seconds; $25 for 60 seconds.

17693 WIBV-AM - 1260
638 Westport Plaza Phone: (618)233-5000
St. Louis, MO 63146-3106 Fax: (618)234-5515

Format: News; Talk. **Networks:** NBC; ABC; Mutual Broadcasting System. **Founded:** 1947. **Operating Hours:** Continuous. **ADI:** St. Louis, MO (Mt. Vernon, IL). **Key Personnel:** Tim Dorsey, VP & GEN MGR; Jerald Kent, President; James Sasnoff, Sales Mgr.; Fred Zielonko, Program Dir.; Beverly Coleman, Business Mgr.; Joan Beuckman, News Dir. **Local Programs:** *Bill Wilkerson & Wendy Wiese Show*, Jeanette Grider, Mailing contact, (314)241-1260; *John Carney Show*, Judy Martin, Mailing contact; *Kevin Horrigan Show*, Judy Martin, Mailing contact. **Wattage:** 5000. **Ad Rates:** Advertising accepted; rates available upon request.

17694 WIL-AM - 1430
8081 Manchester Phone: (314)781-9600
St. Louis, MO 63144 Fax: (314)781-3298

Format: Middle-of-the-Road (MOR). **Networks:** ABC. **Founded:** 1962. **Operating Hours:** Continuous. **ADI:** St. Louis, MO (Mt. Vernon, IL). **Key Personnel:** Dick Williams, Contact. **Wattage:** 5000.

17695 WKBQ-FM - 104.1
800 St. Louis Union Station Phone: (314)205-0104
St. Louis, MO 63103-2257 Fax: (314)878-1564
Free: (800)455-1040

Format: Top 40. **Networks:** Independent. **Owner:** Zimmer Broadcasting, PO Box 1617, Cape Girardeau, MO 63702, (573)335-8291, Fax: (573)335-4809. **Founded:** 1965. **Operating Hours:** Continuous. **ADI:** St. Joseph, MO. **Key Personnel:** John Beck, General Mgr. **Local Programs:** *Steve and D.C. Morning Show* 5:30-10a.m., Michael St. John. **Wattage:** 39,000.

17696 WKKX-FM - 106.5
800 St. Louis Union Station Phone: (314)434-0106
St. Louis, MO 63103-2257 Fax: (314)878-1564
Free: (800)455-1040

Format: Contemporary Country. **Networks:** Independent. **Owner:** Emmis Broadcasting, at above address. **Founded:** 1958. **Formerly**: WJBM-FM (1985). **Operating Hours:** Continuous; 100% local. **ADI:** St. Louis, MO (Mt. Vernon, IL). **Key Personnel:** John Beck, General Mgr.; Mark Phillips, Promotions Mgr.; Joe Rusch, Contact; Bob Hoffman, Chief Engineer. **Wattage:** 90,000. **Ad Rates:** Advertising accepted; rates available upon request.

17697 WRYT-AM - 1080
3515 Hampton Ave. Phone: (314)752-7000
St. Louis, MO 63139

Format: Religious. **Networks:** Eternal Word TV. **Owner:** Covenant Network, at above address. **Founded:** 1987. **Operating Hours:** Sunrise-sunset. **ADI:** St. Louis, MO (Mt. Vernon, IL). **Key Personnel:** Tony Holman, General Mgr. **Local Programs:** *After Nine*, Brenda Kennedy; *The Morning Report*, Brenda Kennedy; *Nascar Race Control*, Brenda Kennedy. **Wattage:** 500.

17698 WVRV-FM - 101.1
1215 Cole St. Phone: (314)969-0101
St. Louis, MO 63106 Fax: (314)259-5598
Free: (800)233-4629

Format: Album-Oriented Rock (AOR). **Networks:** NBC. **Founded:** 1963. **Formerly**: WMRY-FM; WSNL-FM; WFXB-FM. **Operating Hours:** Continuous. **ADI:** St. Louis, MO (Mt. Vernon, IL). **Key Personnel:** Marc Lechmuth, Chief Engineer; Regina Brown, Contact; Edward Murray, General Mgr.; Becky Underwood, Contact; Dave Moore, Operations Mgr. **Wattage:** 50,000.

ST. PETERS

17699 TCI Cablevision of Missouri
4160 Old Mill Pkwy. Phone: (314)441-7737
St. Peters, MO 63376-9979 Fax: (314)939-0148

Founded: 1980. **Cities Served:** St. Charles County, MO.

SAINTE GENEVIEVE

17700 Ste. Genevieve Herald
Ste. Genevieve Newspapers, Inc.
PO Box 447 Phone: (573)883-2222
Sainte Genevieve, MO 63670 Fax: (573)883-2833

Community newspaper. **Founded:** 1882. **Freq:** Weekly (Wed.). **Print Method:** Web offset. **Trim Size:** 11 1/2 x 14. **Cols./Page:** 6. **Col. Width:** 2 inches. **Col. Depth:** 21 inches. **Key Personnel:** Robert J. Burr, Publisher; B. Jean Rissover, Managing Editor. **USPS:** 240-760. **Subscription Rates:** $19; $27 U.S. and other countries. **Remarks:** Accepts advertising.
Ad Rates: GLR: $.60 **Circ:** ‡4,700
BW: $756
SAU: $6
PCI: $5.25

SALEM

17701 The Salem News
500 N. Washington Phone: (573)729-4126
PO Box 798 Fax: (573)729-4920
Salem, MO 65560
Publication E-mail: salnews@fidnet.com

Newspaper with a Democratic orientation. **Founded:** 1923. **Freq:** Semiweekly Tuesday and Thursday. **Print Method:** Offset. **Trim Size:** 13 1/2 x 22 3/4. **Cols./Page:** 6. **Col. Width:** 20 nonpareils. **Col. Depth:** 294 agate lines. **Key Personnel:** W. Ray Vickery, Owner and Co-Publisher; Donald Dodd, Managing Editor; June Vickery, Co-Publisher; Karen Barred, Advertising Mgr. **Subscription Rates:** $35 individuals; $44 out of area; $48 out of state. **Remarks:** Accepts advertising. **Online:** Netscape; Internet. **Alt. Formats:** CD-ROM.
Ad Rates: BW: $780.45 **Circ:** Combined ‡8,300
4C: $950.45
SAU: $4.89

17702 KSMO-AM - 1340
800 S. Main St. Phone: (573)729-6117
PO Box 229 Fax: (573)729-7337
Salem, MO 65560
E-mail: ksmoski@fidnet.com

Format: Full Service; Sports. **Networks:** ABC; Missouri. **Owner:** KSMO Enterprises, at above address. **Founded:** 1954. **Operating Hours:** Continuous; 5% network, 95% local. **Key Personnel:** Stanley M. Podorski, General Mgr.; Stan Stevens, News Dir.; Cathy Farrar, Music Dir.; Melba Podorski, Sales Mgr. **Wattage:** 1000. **Ad Rates:** $7.50-10.25 for 30 seconds; $9.25-12 for 60 seconds.

SALISBURY

17703 Salisbury Press-Spectator
111 S. Broadway Phone: (816)388-6131
Salisbury, MO 65281 Fax: (816)388-6688

Newspaper with a Democratic orientation. **Founded:** 1871. **Freq:** Weekly (Thurs.). **Print Method:** Offset. **Cols./Page:** 6. **Col. Width:** 26 nonpareils. **Col. Depth:** 294 agate lines. **Key Personnel:** Lucy Vaughn, Editor; Larry Baxley, Co-Publisher/Managing Editor; Susan Baxley, Co-Publisher. **Subscription Rates:** $21; $25.50 out of state. **Remarks:** Accepts advertising.
Ad Rates: BW: $302.40 **Circ:** ‡2,285
SAU: $3.20
PCI: $3.10

SARCOXIE

17704 Pierce City Leader-Journal
Sarcoxie Publishing Co.
101 N. 6th Phone: (417)548-3311
Box 400 Fax: (417)476-3312
Sarcoxie, MO 64862
Community newspaper. **Founded:** 1905. **Freq:** Weekly (Thurs.). **Trim Size:** 11 1/4 x 17. **Cols./Page:** 6. **Col. Width:** 9 picas. **Col. Depth:** 16 inches. **Key Personnel:** Linda Eck Elderton, Publisher. **USPS:** 307-580. **Subscription Rates:** $14; $15.50 out of state. **Remarks:** Accepts advertising.
Ad Rates: BW: $201.60 **Circ:** 900
4C: $501.60
SAU: $3.60
PCI: $2.52

17705 The Sarcoxie Record
Sarcoxie Publishing Co.
101 N. 6th Phone: (417)548-3311
Box 400 Fax: (417)476-3312
Sarcoxie, MO 64862
Newspaper. **Founded:** 1901. **Freq:** Weekly (Thurs.). **Print Method:** Offset. **Cols./Page:** 6. **Col. Width:** 21 nonpareils. **Col. Depth:** 224 agate lines. **Key Personnel:** Linda Eck Elderton, Publisher. **USPS:** 482-060. **Subscription Rates:** $14; $17 out of area. **Remarks:** Accepts advertising.
Ad Rates: GLR: $.15 **Circ:** ‡1,400
BW: $259.20
4C: $559.20
SAU: $2.70
PCI: $2.70

SAVANNAH

17706 Savannah Reporter and Andrew County Democrat
Savannah
115 S. 4th St. Phone: (816)324-3149
PO Box 299 Fax: (816)324-3632
Savannah, MO 64485
Publication E-mail: caslonbld@aol.com
Publisher E-mail: caslonbld@aol.com

Community newspaper. **Founded:** Apr. 28, 1876. **Freq:** Weekly (Thurs.). **Print Method:** Offset. Uses mats. **Trim Size:** 19. **Cols./Page:** 6 and 6. **Col. Width:** 24 nonpareils. **Col. Depth:** 285 agate lines and 20 1/2 inches. **Key Personnel:** Gary Ray, Publisher. **USPS:** 482-420. **Subscription Rates:** $19; $23 out of area; $25 out of state. **Remarks:** Accepts advertising. **Feature Editors:** Jodi Oliver, *Society*, caslanbld@aol.com.
Ad Rates: GLR: $.20 **Circ:** ‡3,600
BW: $657.90
4C: $250
PCI: $5.10

SEDALIA

17707 Central Missouri News
PO Box 1086 Phone: (816)827-2425
Sedalia, MO 65302 Fax: (816)827-2427
Free: (888)827-2425
Publisher E-mail: paperboy@iland.net

Community newspaper. **Founded:** Mar. 1, 1984. **Freq:** Weekly (Wed.). **Print Method:** Offset. **Cols./Page:** 6. **Col. Width:** 24 nonpareils. **Col. Depth:** 301 agate lines. **Key Personnel:** Greg Melton, Publisher & Owner, phone (660)829-0026; Peter F. Daniels, Editor. **USPS:** 745-130. **Subscription Rates:** $24 individuals; $30 out of area; $36 out of state. **Remarks:** Accepts advertising. **Alt. Formats:** CD-ROM.
Ad Rates: GLR: $4.95 **Circ:** (Not Reported)
SAU: $4.50
PCI: $4.50

17708 The Sedalia Democrat
7th & Massachusetts Ave. Phone: (816)826-1000
PO Box 848 Fax: (816)826-2413
Sedalia, MO 65302
Newspaper with a Democratic orientation. **Founded:** 1868. **Freq:** Daily (eve.), Sunday (morn.). **Print Method:** Offset. **Cols./Page:** 6. **Col. Width:** 25 nonpareils. **Col. Depth:** 301 agate lines. **Key Personnel:** F. Douglas Kneibert, Editor; Jules Molenda, Publisher; Nelson Collins, Advertising Mgr. **Subscription Rates:** $60.50. **Remarks:** Accepts advertising.
Ad Rates: SAU: $8.66 **Circ:** Mon.-Sat. ★11,944
Sun. ★13,214

17709 Falcon Cable TV
210 W. 7th St. Phone: (816)826-0933
Sedalia, MO 65301 Fax: (816)826-4583

Owner: Falcon Cable TV, 10900 Wilshire Blvd., 15th Fl., Los Angeles, CA 90024, (310)824-9990. **Key Personnel:** Liz Duffy, Regional Manager; David Holley, Chief Technician; Ruth Roberts, Office Mgr.; Diana Cook, Marketing Supervisor. **Cities Served:** Eldorado Springs, MO: subscribing households 1,121; 33 channels.

17710 KDRO-AM - 1490
301 S. Ohio Ave. Phone: (660)826-5005
Sedalia, MO 65301-4431 Fax: (660)826-5557
E-mail: 1490@kdro.com

Format: Country. **Networks:** CBS. **Owner:** Mathewson Broadcasting, Inc., at above address. **Founded:** 1939. **Operating Hours:** Continuous; 10% network, 90% local. **ADI:** Kansas City, MO (Lawrence, KS). **Key Personnel:** Bette Wise, General Mgr.; Bill Barrick, News Dir.; Denny Perkins, Sports Dir.; Matt Gillespie, Music Dir. **Wattage:** 1000. **Ad Rates:** $12.25 for 30 seconds; $16.50 for 60 seconds. 1490 AD LIB SPECIAL.$20.00 PER SPOT. **URL:** http://www.kdro.com.

17711 KSDL-FM - 92.1
Box 1056 Phone: (660)826-9210
Sedalia, MO 65301 Fax: (660)827-5072
Free: (800)748-8354
E-mail: radio92@ksdl.com

Format: Adult Contemporary. **Founded:** 1964. **Formerly:** KCBW-FM. **Operating Hours:** 5 a.m.-midnight. **ADI:** Kansas City, MO (Lawrence, KS). **Key Personnel:** Dennis Polk, General Mgr., phone (680)826-1080, fax (660)827-5072, dpolk@ksol.com. **Wattage:** 3000. **Ad Rates:** $12.50 for 30 seconds; $15.00 for 60 seconds. KSIS-AM. **URL:** http://www.internetland.net/ksdl.

SENATH

17712 Dunklin County Press
114 Commercial St. Phone: (314)738-2604
PO Box 356 Fax: (314)738-2604
Senath, MO 63876
Newspaper with a Republican orientation. **Founded:** 1946. **Freq:** Weekly (Thurs.). **Print Method:** Letterpress and offset. **Cols./Page:** 6. **Col. Width:** 24 nonpareils. **Col. Depth:** 238 agate lines. **Key Personnel:** Ron Kemp, Publisher; Nancy Kemp, Publisher. **Subscription Rates:** $15. **Remarks:** Accepts advertising.
Ad Rates: SAU: $2.50 **Circ:** ‡1,700

SENECA

17713 Seneca News-Dispatch
1103 Cherokee St. Phone: (417)776-2236
PO Box 1110 Fax: (417)776-2204
Seneca, MO 64865
Publisher E-mail: newsdis@netins.net

Community newspaper. **Founded:** 1882. **Freq:** Weekly (Thurs.). **Print Method:** Offset. **Cols./Page:** 6. **Col. Width:** 12 1/5 picas. **Col. Depth:** 21 inches. **Key Personnel:** Diane Collins, Editor and Publisher. **Subscription Rates:** $15.50 individuals; $20.50 out of area. **Remarks:** Accepts advertising.
Ad Rates: SAU: $3.70 **Circ:** 1,700

SHELBINA

17714 Shelbina Democrat
115 S. Center St. Phone: (573)588-2133
PO Box 138 Fax: (573)588-2134
Shelbina, MO 63468
Community newspaper. **Freq:** Weekly (Wed.). **Key Personnel:** Walt Gilbert, Editor and Publisher.
Circ: 2,100

SHELBYVILLE

17715 Shelby County Herald
106 E. Main Phone: (573)633-2261
Shelbyville, MO 63469 Fax: (573)633-2133

Newspaper with a Democratic orientation. **Founded:** 1870. **Freq:** Weekly (Wed.). **Print Method:** Offset. **Cols./Page:** 6. **Col. Width:** 25 nonpareils. **Col. Depth:** 301 agate lines. **Key Personnel:** Dennis W. Williams, Editor and Publisher; Thad Requet, Editor. **Subscription Rates:** $26. **Remarks:** Accepts advertising.
Ad Rates: GLR: $0.25 **Circ:** Paid 2,105
BW: $451.50 Free 40
4C: $691.50
SAU: $3.50
PCI: $3.50

SIKESTON

17716 Cablevision Inc.
PO Box 1007 Phone: (913)336-6157
Sikeston, MO 63801-1007 Fax: (913)336-2371
Free: (800)530-4384

Founded: 1988. **Key Personnel:** Mark Heideman, General Mgr. **Cities Served:** subscribing households 2,506; 31 channels; 168 community access channels.

17717 Cablevision of Miltonvale
PO Box 1007 Phone: (913)392-3505
Sikeston, MO 63801-1007 Fax: (913)392-2476
Free: (800)530-4334

Owner: Cablevision of Texas Ltd., PO Box 310, 116 S. Main St., Lockney, TX 79241, (806)652-3328. **Cities Served:** subscribing households 186.

17718 Cablevision of Minneapolis
PO Box 1007 Phone: (913)392-3505
Sikeston, MO 63801-1007 Fax: (913)394-2476
Free: (800)530-4334

Owner: Cablevision of Texas Ltd., PO Box 310, 116 S. Main St., Lockney, TX 79241, (806)652-3328. **Cities Served:** subscribing households 620; 24 channels; 1 community access channel; 2 hours per week community access programming.

17719 High Plains Cablevision Inc.
PO Box 1007 Phone: (913)336-6157
Sikeston, MO 63801-1007 Fax: (913)336-2371

Owner: Cablevision of Texas, PO Box 757, Gatesville, TX 76528, (817)865-7520. **Founded:** 1990. **Key Personnel:** Mark Heidman, General Mgr. **Cities Served:** Barnes, KS: subscribing households 87; 16 channels.

17720 KMPL-AM - 1520
PO Box 907 Phone: (573)471-1520
Sikeston, MO 63801 Fax: (573)471-8525

Format: Adult Contemporary. **Networks:** NBC. **Founded:** 1966. **Operating Hours:** Continuous. **Key Personnel:** Rick Lambert, General Mgr. **Wattage:** 5000 day; 500 night.

17721 KSIM-AM - 1400
519 Greer Ave. Phone: (573)471-1400
Sikeston, MO 63801 Fax: (573)471-1402
E-mail: ksim@mvp.net

Format: News; Talk. **Networks:** ABC. **Owner:** Zimmer Broadcasting, PO Box 1610, Cape Girardeau, MO 63701, Free: (800)663-5746. **Founded:** 1948. **Operating Hours:** 19 hrs. **ADI:** Paducah,KY-Cape Girardeau,MO-Marion,IL. **Key Personnel:** James Zimmer, General Mgr.; Bill Powers, Operations Mgr., billp@mvp.net; Jiff Gillespie, News, jeffg@mvp.net; Tracy Hawkes, Public Services Dir. **Local Programs:** *KSIM's Morning News Edition.* **Wattage:** 1000.

17722 Marion Municipal Cablevision
PO Box 1007 Phone: (316)382-3459
Sikeston, MO 63801-1007

Founded: 1977. **Key Personnel:** Marvin Rediker, Contact. **Cities Served:** subscribing households 1,200; 20 channels.

SMITHVILLE

17723 The Smithville Lake Herald
110 N. Bridge Phone: (816)532-4444
PO Box 269 Fax: (816)532-4918
Smithville, MO 64089-0269
Publication E-mail: lakeherald@aol.com

Community newspaper. **Founded:** Aug. 1888. **Freq:** Weekly (Wed.). **Print Method:** Offset. **Trim Size:** 13 x 21 1/2. **Cols./Page:** 6. **Col. Width:** 2 1/16 inches. **Col. Depth:** 21 1/2 inches. **Key Personnel:** David T. Peery, Editor and Publisher; Kathy Atkins, Business Mgr.; Becky Sellars, News and Managing Editor. **USPS:** 153-180. **Subscription Rates:** $18 individuals in Clay, Platte and Clinton counties; $21 individuals in Missouri and Kansas; $28 out of state. **Formerly:** Smithville Lake Democrat-Herald.
Ad Rates: BW: $360 **Circ:** Paid ⊕2,600
SAU: $4.95 Free ⊕75
PCI: $4.80

SPRINGFIELD

17724 Christian Education Counselor
General Council of the Assemblies of God Gospel Publishing House
1445 Boonville Ave. Phone: (417)862-2781
Springfield, MO 65802-1894 Fax: (417)862-0416

Magazine for Assembly of God Sunday School staffs. **Founded:** 1994. **Freq:** Bimonthly. **Print Method:** Offset. **Trim Size:** 8 x 10. **Cols./Page:** 3. **Col. Width:** 29 nonpareils. **Col. Depth:** 140 agate lines. **Key Personnel:** Sylvia Lee, Editor, salee@ag.org. **ISSN:** 0039-5285. **Subscription Rates:** $12. **Remarks:** Advertising not accepted. **Available Online. URL:** http://www.we-build-people.org. **Formerly**: Sunday School Counselor.
Circ: ‡20,000

17725 Club Connection
General Council of the Assemblies of God Gospel Publishing House
1445 Boonville Ave. Phone: (417)862-2781
Springfield, MO 65802-1894 Fax: (417)862-0416
Publication E-mail: mettes@ag.org

Publication for girls ages 7-14. **Subtitle:** A Christian Magazine for Girls. **Founded:** Jan. 1956. **Freq:** Quarterly. **Print Method:** Offset. **Trim Size:** 8 x 10 3/4. **Cols./Page:** 3. **Col. Width:** 13 picas. **Col. Depth:** 58 picas. **Key Personnel:** Kerry Clarensau, Editor; Aleda Swartzendruber, Managing Editor. **ISSN:** 1091-2487. **Subscription Rates:** $6.50; $1.95 single issue. **Remarks:** Advertising not accepted. **Alt. Formats:** Audio tape. **Formerly**: Memos (1997); Missionettes Memos.
Circ: ‡15,200

17726 The Drury Mirror
Drury College
900 N. Benton Ave. Phone: (417)873-7318
Springfield, MO 65802 Fax: (417)873-7533
Publication E-mail: mirror@lib.drury.edu

Collegiate newspaper. **Subtitle:** The Official Student Newspaper of Drury College. **Founded:** 1885. **Freq:** Weekly (Fri.). **Print Method:** Offset. **Trim Size:** 11 x 17. **Cols./Page:** 4. **Col. Width:** 2 1/4 nonpareils. **Col. Depth:** 16 1/2 agate lines. **Key Personnel:** Randy D. Berger, Editor-in-Chief; Mike O'Brien, Faculty Advisor. **Subscription Rates:** $20. **Remarks:** Accepts advertising.
Ad Rates: GLR: $5 **Circ:** Paid 4,177
BW: $300 Controlled 6,000
PCI: $6.25

17727 Enrichment
General Council of the Assemblies of God Gospel Publishing House
1445 Boonville Ave. Phone: (417)862-2781
Springfield, MO 65802-1894 Fax: (417)862-0416
Publication E-mail: enrichment@ag.org

Assemblies of God leadership journal. **Subtitle:** Journal for Pentecostal Ministry. **Freq:** Quarterly. **Print Method:** Offset. **Trim Size:** 8 x 10 3/4. **Cols./Page:** 3. **Col. Width:** 27 nonpareils. **Col. Depth:** 130 agate lines. **Key Personnel:** Wayde Goodall, Editor, wgoodall@ag.org; Rick Knoth, Managing Editor, fax (417)862-0416, rkoth@ag.org. **ISSN:** 1082-1791. **Subscription Rates:** $18; $32 two years. **Remarks:** Accepts advertising. **Formerly:** Advance (1995).
Ad Rates: BW: $1,280 **Circ:** ‡32,000
4C: $2,240

17728 Explorations in Renaissance Culture
Southwest Missouri State University English Dept.
901 S. National Phone: (417)836-4738
Springfield, MO 65804 Fax: (417)836-4226

Scholarly journal covering Renaissance and Early Modern European studies. **Founded:** 1975. **Freq:** Annual. **Print Method:** Offset. **Trim Size:** 6 x 9. **Cols./Page:** 1. **Col. Width:** 4 1/4 inches. **Col. Depth:** 7 1/4 inches. **Key Personnel:** Tita French Baumlin, Editor, titabaumlin@mail.smsn.edu. **Subscription Rates:** $10 individuals. **Remarks:** Advertising not accepted.
Circ: Combined 314

17729 Fairs and Expos
International Association of Fairs and Expositions
3043 E. Cairo Phone: (417)862-5771
PO Box 985 Fax: (417)862-0156
Springfield, MO 65801
Free: (800)516-0313
Publisher E-mail: iafe@iafenet.org

Trade magazine covering the fair industry. **Freq:** 10/year. **Print Method:** Sheetfed offset. **Trim Size:** 8 1/2 x 11. **Cols./Page:** 3. **Col. Width:** 2 1/4 inches. **Col. Depth:** 10 inches. **Key Personnel:** Max Willis, Editor. **Subscription Rates:** $30 individuals. **Remarks:** Accepts advertising.
Ad Rates: BW: $475 **Circ:** (Not Reported)
4C: $625

17730 High Adventure
General Council of the Assemblies of God Gospel Publishing House
1445 Boonville Ave. Phone: (417)862-2781
Springfield, MO 65802-1894 Fax: (417)862-0416

Religious and inspirational magazine for boys. **Subtitle:** A Royal Rangers Magazine for Boys. **Founded:** 1971. **Freq:** Quarterly. **Print Method:** Offset. Uses mats. **Trim Size:** 8 1/2 x 11. **Cols./Page:** 3. **Col. Width:** 14 picas. **Col. Depth:** 140 agate lines. **Key Personnel:** Ken Hunt, Directory of Publications; Marshall Bruner, Editor. **ISSN:** 0190-3802. **Subscription Rates:** $1.75. **Remarks:** Advertising not accepted.
Circ: ‡88,000

17731 The Lance
Evangel College
1111 N. Glenstone Ave. Phone: (417)865-2815
PO Box 728 Fax: (417)865-9599
Springfield, MO 65802-2191
Collegiate newspaper. **Subtitle:** The Student Voice of Evangel College. **Founded:** 1955. **Freq:** Weekly. **Print Method:** Offset. **Trim Size:** 11 1/4 x 17 1/2. **Cols./Page:** 5. **Col. Width:** 11 picas. **Col. Depth:** 15 3/4 inches. **Key Personnel:** Erin Cole, Editor. **Remarks:** Accepts advertising.
Ad Rates: GLR: $.23 **Circ:** Free ‡1,500
BW: $325
PCI: $5.00

17732 The Mirror
Diocese of Springfield-Cape Girardeau
601 S. Jefferson Ave. Phone: (417)866-0841
Springfield, MO 65806-3143 Fax: (417)866-1140

Catholic Diocesan newspaper (tabloid). **Founded:** 1965. **Freq:** Weekly. **Print Method:** Offset. **Trim Size:** 11 3/8 x 14. **Cols./Page:** 4. **Col. Width:** 29 nonpareils. **Col. Depth:** 227 agate lines. **Key Personnel:** Rev. Mark Boyer, Editor, mboyer@mail.orion.org. **USPS:** 117-330. **Subscription Rates:** $12. **Remarks:** Advertising not accepted for alcoholic beverages, tobacco products and gambling.
Ad Rates: BW: $675 **Circ:** ‡17,600
4C: $1,075
PCI: $13.50

17733 Missouri Grocer
Missouri Grocers' Association
315 N. Ken Ave. Phone: (417)831-6667
Springfield, MO 65802 Fax: (417)831-3907

Retail grocery trade magazine. **Founded:** 1940. **Freq:** Bimonthly. **Print Method:** Offset. **Trim Size:** 8 1/2 x 11. **Cols./Page:** 3. **Col. Width:** 14 picas. **Col. Depth:** 133 agate lines. **Key Personnel:** Karman Crader, Editor. **Subscription Rates:** $15. **Remarks:** Accepts advertising.
Ad Rates: BW: $200 **Circ:** ‡1,750
4C: $470

17734 Mountain Movers
General Council of the Assemblies of God Gospel Publishing House
1445 Boonville Ave. Phone: (417)862-2781
Springfield, MO 65802-1894 Fax: (417)862-0416

Magazine about Assemblies of God foreign missions. **Founded:** 1944. **Freq:** 10/year. **Print Method:** Web offset. **Trim Size:** 8 1/2 x 11. **Cols./Page:** 3. **Col. Width:** 22 1/5 nonpareils. **Col. Depth:** 121 agate lines. **Key Personnel:** John T. Maempa, Editor; Charles Hungerford, Managing Editor. **Subscription Rates:** $10 donation. **Remarks:** Advertising not accepted.
Circ: Non-paid ‡220,000

17735 The News-Leader
651 N. Boonville Ave. Phone: (417)836-1100
Springfield, MO 65806-1005 Fax: (417)836-1147

General newspaper. **Founded:** 1890. **Freq:** Mon.-Sun. (morn.). **Print Method:** Letterpress. **Cols./Page:** 6. **Col. Width:** 18 nonpareils. **Col. Depth:** 301 agate lines. **Key Personnel:** Andy McMills, Exec. Editor; Fritz Jacobi, Publisher. **ISSN:** 0893-3448. **Subscription Rates:** $130.20. **Remarks:** Accepts advertising. **URL:** http://www.o3arksgateway.com. **Feature Editors:** Deborah Barnes, *Environmental*, phone (417)836-1276; Kelley Bass, *Sports*, phone (417)836-1373; Ron Davis, *Fashion, Features, Food, Garden/Home, Lifestyle, Living, Movie, Music, Religion, Society, Travel*, phone (417)836-1256; Patti Dutcher, *Family*, phone (417)836-1272; Marty Eddleman, *TV*, phone (417)836-1120; Bob Edwards, *Political*, phone (417)836-1195; Connie Farrow, *Financial/Business, Real Estate*, phone (417)836-1283; George Freeman, *Editorials*, phone (417)836-1113; Chick Howland, *Rural Development*, phone (417)836-1258; Bob Linder, *Photo*, phone (417)836-1182; Kathleen O'Dell, *Medical*, phone (417)836-1276; Ron Sylvester, *Entertainment*, phone (417)836-1172; Bil Tatum, *Drama*, phone (417)836-1185; Louise Whall, *City, Metro, News, State*, phone (417)836-1258; Tami Wicker, *Education*, phone (417)836-1198; Willard Woods, *Farm, Rural Development*, phone (417)836-1241.
Ad Rates: GLR: $2.67 **Circ:** Mon.-Sat. 64,661
BW: $8,643 Sun. 98,669
4C: $9,433
PCI: $67

17736 Pennypower Shopping News
Pennypower Shopping News, Inc.
1636 S. Glenstone Phone: (417)887-9000
Springfield, MO 65804 Fax: (417)887-9006

Shopper. **Founded:** 1975. **Freq:** Weekly (Tues.). **Print Method:** Offset. **Cols./Page:** 2. **Col. Width:** 48 nonpareils. **Col. Depth:** 140 agate lines. **Key Personnel:** Dan Davis, General Mgr. **Subscription Rates:** $10.
Circ: Wed. ♦**147,827**

17737 Pentecostal Evangel
General Council of the Assemblies of God Gospel Publishing House
1445 Boonville Ave. Phone: (417)862-2781
Springfield, MO 65802-1894 Fax: (417)862-0416
Publication E-mail: pevangel@ag.org

Assemblies of God official magazine. **Founded:** 1913. **Freq:** Weekly. **Print Method:** Offset. **Trim Size:** 8 x 10 3/4. **Cols./Page:** 4 and 3. **Col. Width:** 20.6 and 27 nonpareils. **Col. Depth:** 130 agate lines. **Key Personnel:** Hal Donaldson, Editor; Jodi Harmon, Advertising Mgr.; Ken Horn, Managing Editor. **ISSN:** 0031-4897. **Subscription Rates:** $23.95 individuals.
Ad Rates: 4C: $3,400 **Circ:** Paid ‡260,000

17738 Springfield Business Journal
313 Park Central West
Springfield, MO 65806
Publication E-mail: busjrnl@aol.com; sbj@sbj.net

Business newspaper. **Founded:** 1980. **Freq:** Weekly. **Print Method:** Web offset. **Cols./Page:** 4. **Col. Width:** 3 7/16 inches. **Col. Depth:** 13 inches. **Key Personnel:** Dianne Elizabeth, Publisher; Paul Flemming, Managing Editor. **Subscription Rates:** $43; $1 single issue. **URL:** http://www.sbj.net.
Ad Rates: BW: $1,166 **Circ:** 6,200
4C: $1,616 Non-paid 981

17739 Springfield! Magazine
Springfield Communications Inc.
PO Box 4749 Phone: (417)831-1640
Springfield, MO 65808
Local interest community magazine. **Subtitle:** Presenting Springfield's Glorious Past, Exciting Present and Thrilling Future. **Founded:** 1979. **Freq:** Monthly. **Print Method:** Offset. **Trim Size:** 8 3/8 x 10 7/8. **Cols./Page:** 3. **Col. Width:** 27 nonpareils. **Col. Depth:** 138 agate lines. **Key Personnel:** Robert C. Glazier, Editor and Publisher, phone (417)831-1600. **ISSN:** 0195-0894. **Subscription Rates:** $16.99. **Remarks:** Accepts advertising.
Ad Rates: BW: $800 **Circ:** ‡51,600
4C: $1,000

17740 Springfield Parent, Inc.
Springfield Parent
313 Park Central West Phone: (417)869-9800
PO Box 4732 Fax: (417)831-5478
Springfield, MO 65808
Parenting publication. **Subtitle:** Southwest Missouri's Resource for Active Families. **Founded:** 1987. **Freq:** Monthly. **Print Method:** Web offset-tabloid. **Cols./Page:** 4. **Col. Width:** 2 7/16 inches. **Col. Depth:** 13 inches. **Key Personnel:** Clarissa French, Editor, fax (417)831-3238, sbj@sbj.net; Dianne Elizabeth, Publisher, fax (417)831-3238, sbj@sbj.net; Dorothy Gardner, Office Mgr., fax (417)8313238, sbj@sbj.net. **Subscription Rates:** $15 by mail. **Former name**: Springfield Parent.
Ad Rates: BW: $906 **Circ:** Free 20,000
4C: $1,331 Paid 50

17741 The Standard
Southwest Missouri State University English Dept.
901 S. National Phone: (417)836-4738
Springfield, MO 65804 Fax: (417)836-4226

Collegiate newspaper. **Founded:** 1912. **Freq:** Weekly (Fri.). **Print Method:** Offset. **Trim Size:** 13 x 22. **Cols./Page:** 6. **Col. Width:** 25 nonpareils. **Col. Depth:** 294 agate lines. **Subscription Rates:** $15. **Remarks:** Accepts advertising.
Ad Rates: BW: $1,050 **Circ:** Free ‡7,000
4C: $1,500
SAU: $9.75

17742 Transmission Digest
MD Publications, Inc.
3057 E. Cairo Phone: (417)866-3917
PO Box 2210 Fax: (417)866-2781
Springfield, MO 65801-2210
Free: (800)274-7890
Publication E-mail: trnsdigest@aol.com

Subtitle: The Automotive Pouertrain Industry Journal. **Founded:** Sept. 1981. **Freq:** Monthly. **Print Method:** Web offset. **Trim Size:** 8 1/8 x 10 7/8. **Cols./Page:** 3. **Col. Width:** 2 1/4 inches. **Col. Depth:** 137 agate lines. **Key Personnel:** Lola Miller, Editor; Bobby Mace, Publisher. **ISSN:** 0277-8300. **Subscription Rates:** $39 individuals; $4.75 single issue. **Remarks:** Accepts advertising.
Ad Rates: BW: $2,975 **Circ:** Paid 1,848
4C: $4,035 Controlled 19,839

17743 Undercar Digest
M D Publications, Inc.
PO Box 2210 Phone: (417)866-3917
Springfield, MO 65801-2210 Fax: (417)866-2781
Free: (800)274-7890
Publication E-mail: undercardg@aol.com

Magazine for the undercar service and supply industry. **Founded:** Aug. 1976. **Freq:** Monthly. **Print Method:** Web offset. **Trim Size:** 8 1/8 x 10 7/8. **Cols./Page:** 3. **Col. Width:** 2 1/4 inches. **Col. Depth:** 140 agate lines. **Key Personnel:** James Wilder, Editor; Breck Langsford, Publisher. **ISSN:** 0893-6943. **Subscription Rates:** $39; $4.75 single issue plus postage. **Remarks:** Accepts advertising. **Formerly:** Muffler Digest.
Ad Rates: BW: $3,390 **Circ:** Paid 399
4C: $4,450 Controlled ‡40,247

17744 Woman's Touch
General Council of the Assemblies of God Gospel Publishing House
1445 Boonville Ave. Phone: (417)862-2781
Springfield, MO 65802-1894 Fax: (417)862-0416
Publication E-mail: womanstouch@ag.org

Religious magazine. **Subtitle:** An Inspirational Magazine for Women. **Founded:** July 13, 1977. **Freq:** Bimonthly. **Print Method:** Offset. **Trim Size:** 8 x 10 3/4. **Cols./Page:** 3. **Col. Width:** 26 nonpareils. **Col. Depth:** 148 agate lines. **Key Personnel:** Lillian Sparks, Editor; Aleda Swartzendruber, Managing Editor. **ISSN:** 0190-4620. **Subscription Rates:** $8 individuals; $1.95 single issue. **Remarks:** Advertising not accepted. **Alt. Formats:** Audio tape.
Circ: ‡20,000

17745 KBOA-FM - 105.5
3000 E. Chestnut Expy. Phone: (573)888-4616
PO Box 3676 GSS Fax: (573)888-4991
Springfield, MO 65808
Free: (800)552-1055

Format: Adult Contemporary. **Networks:** CBS; Westwood One Radio. **Owner:** Pollack Broadcasting Co., 1303 Southwest Dr., Kennett, MO 63857-0509. **Formerly:** KTEI-FM. **Operating Hours:** Continuous. **Key Personnel:** Pres Semar, General Mgr.; Jim Borders, Sales Mgr.; Larry Anthony, Operations Mgr.; Linda Shown, Office Mgr. **Local Programs:** *Hometown News*, Steve Bryant; *The Breakfast Club*, Pres Semar.

17746 KDEB-TV - 27
3000 Cherry St. Phone: (417)862-2727
Springfield, MO 65802 Fax: (417)831-4209
E-mail: feedback@fox27.com

Format: Commercial TV. **Networks:** Fox. **Owner:** Quorum Broadcasting of MO., Inc., at above address. **Founded:** 1968. **Formerly:** KMTC-TV (1985). **Operating Hours:** Continuous. **Key Personnel:** Kemp Nichol, VP/Gen. Mgr., kemp@fox27.com; Jim Prestwood, General Sales Mgr., jim@fox27.com; Jack McGee, Operations Mgr.; Dave Thomason, Local Sales Mgr., dave@fox27.com; Georgetta Lowery, Traffic Mgr.; Mark Hodorowski, Promotions Mgr.; Nancy Bingaman, Program Dir. **Wattage:** 5000 ERP. **Ad Rates:** Advertising accepted; rates available upon request. **URL:** http://www.fox27.com.

17747 KGBX-FM - 105.9
1856 S. Glenstone Ave. Phone: (417)869-1059
Springfield, MO 65804-2303 Fax: (417)869-1000

Format: Adult Contemporary. **Operating Hours:** Continuous. **ADI:** Springfield, MO. **Key Personnel:** John Borders, President; Donna Baker, Vice President. **Wattage:** 50,000.

17748 KGMY-AM - 1400
1856 S. Glenstone Ave. Phone: (417)869-1059
Springfield, MO 65804-2303 Fax: (417)869-1000

Format: Music of Your Life. **Operating Hours:** Continuous. **ADI:** Springfield, MO. **Key Personnel:** John Borders, President; Donna Baker, Vice President. **Wattage:** 1000.

17749 KKLH-FM - 104.7
319-B W. Battlefield Phone: (417)886-5677
Springfield, MO 65807 Fax: (417)886-2155
E-mail: classhits104.7@kklh.com

Format: Classic Rock. **Networks:** ABC. **Owner:** Mid-West Family Broadcast Group, 2740 Ski Ln., Madison, WI 53713. **Founded:** July 1996. **Operating Hours:** Continuous. **ADI:** Springfield, MO. **Key Personnel:** Rex Hansen, General Mgr.; Roger Piper, Station Mgr.; Malcolm Hukriede, Sales Mgr.; Earlyne Lawrence, Business Mgr. **Wattage:** 35,000. **Ad Rates:** $8-18 for 30 seconds. **URL:** http://www.kklh.com.

17750 KLFJ-AM - 1550
811 Boonville Phone: (417)831-5535
Springfield, MO 65802 Fax: (417)831-5544
E-mail: klfj@dialus.com

Format: Talk; News; Sports. **Networks:** Westwood One Radio. **Owner:** He N' Me Broadcasting, Inc., at above address. **Founded:** 1974. **Operating Hours:** Continuous. **ADI:** Springfield, MO. **Key Personnel:** Cliff Cerce, Program Dir.; Keith Hendrix, General Mgr. **Local Programs:** *Coffee Break*, Alan Smith. **Wattage:** 5000. **Ad Rates:** $12 for 30 seconds; $18 for 60 seconds. **URL:** http://www.talk1550.com.

17751 KOLR-TV - 10
2650 E. Division St. Phone: (417)862-1010
PO Box 1716 Fax: (417)862-6439
Springfield, MO 65801
E-mail: kolr10@kolr10.com

Format: Commercial TV. **Networks:** CBS. **Owner:** VHR Broadcasting of Springfield, Inc., at above address, (615)248-8030. **Founded:** 1953. **Formerly:** KTTS-TV; Independent Broadcasting Co. **Operating Hours:** Continuous. **ADI:** Springfield, MO. **Key Personnel:** Dean Wasson, Prog. Dir./Promotions Mgr.; Bill Soddler, Business Mgr.; Dave Miller, General Mgr.; Cathy Rippe, General Sales Mgr.; Jenny Thomas, Nat'l Sales Mgr.; Polly VanDoren, News Dir.; Dave Smith, Chief Engineer. **Local Programs:** *Country Morning*; *Eye on the Ozarks*. **Wattage:** 360,000 ERP. **URL:** http/www.kolr10.com.

17752 KOSP-FM - 105.1
319-B East Battlefield Phone: (417)886-5677
Springfield, MO 65807 Fax: (417)886-2155
E-mail: oldies105.1@kosp.com

Format: Oldies. **Networks:** ABC. **Owner:** Mid-West Family Broadcast Group, 2740 Ski Ln., Madison, WI 53713. **Founded:** Aug. 1992. **Operating Hours:** Continuous. **ADI:** Springfield, MO. **Key Personnel:** Rex Hansen, General Mgr.; Roger Piper, Station Mgr.; Malcolm Hukriede, Sales Mgr.; Earlyne Lawrence, Business Mgr. **Wattage:** 50,000. **Ad Rates:** $15-27 for 30 seconds. **URL:** http://www.kosp.com.

17753 KOZK-TV - 21
PO Box 21 Phone: (417)865-2100
Springfield, MO 65801-0021 Fax: (417)863-1599
E-mail: mail@kozk.drury.edu

Format: Public TV. **Networks:** Public Broadcasting Service (PBS). **Founded:** 1974. **Operating Hours:** 5:30 a.m.-12:30 a.m. **ADI:** Springfield, MO. **Key Personnel:** Sarah White, General Mgr./President; Linda Dahlman, Business Mgr.; Claudine McGee, Dir., Programming and Educational Svcs.; Dan Schiedel, Dir. of Prod. and Corp. Communications; Brent Moore, Dir. of Engineering and Computer Svcs.; Mary Ann Johnson, Dir. of Development. **Local Programs:** *Ozarks News Roundtable*, Ray Meyer; *Ozarks in Perspective*, Dan Schiedel; *Stone Soup Cafe*, Matt Sievert. **Wattage:** 60,000.

17754 KSMS-FM - 91.1
901 S. National Ave. Phone: (417)836-5878
Springfield, MO 65804 Fax: (417)836-5889
Free: (800)767-5678
E-mail: aed852f@mail.smsu.edu

Format: Public Radio; Classical. **Networks:** National Public Radio (NPR). **Owner:** Southwest Missouri State University, at above address. **Founded:** 1974. **Operating Hours:** Continuous. **Key Personnel:** Arlen Diamond, General Mgr., phone (417)836-4402; Tammy Wiley, Sales Mgr., phone (417)836-6634; Michele Skalicky, News Dir., phone (417)836-4404. **Wattage:** 40,000. **Ad Rates:** $12-20 per unit. **URL:** http://www.ksmu.smsu.edu.

17755 KSMU-FM - 91.1
901 S. National Phone: (417)836-5878
Southwest Missouri State University Fax: (417)836-5889
Springfield, MO 65804
Free: (800)767-5768
E-mail: ksmu@netfocus.net

Format: Public Radio; Classical; Information. **Networks:** National Public Radio (NPR). **Owner:** Southwest Missouri State University, at above address. **Founded:** 1974. **Operating Hours:** Continuous; 50% network; 50% local. **ADI:** Springfield, MO. **Key Personnel:** Arlen Diamond, General Mgr.; Tammy Wiley, General Mgr.; Michele Skalicky, News Dir. **Wattage:** 40,000. **Ad Rates:** Noncommercial. **URL:** http://www.ksmu.org.

17756 KSPR-TV - 33
1359 St. Louis St. Phone: (417)831-1333
Springfield, MO 65802-3409 Fax: (417)831-4125
Free: (800)220-8222
E-mail: kspr33.com

Format: Commercial TV. **Networks:** ABC. **Founded:** 1983. **Operating Hours:** Continuous. **ADI:** Springfield, MO. **Key Personnel:** Gary Whitaker, General Mgr., phone (417)831-1333, fax (417)831-4125; Dave Middleton, Production Mgr.; Joan Whitaker, Promotions Mgr.; Jon Janes, News Dir.; Lou Moyer, Chief Engineer; James Trussell, Program Dir.; Susan Cochran, Traffic Mgr.; Joe Fraley, Sales Mgr., phone (417)864-3325, fax (417)831-1781; Jean Turnbough, Sales Mgr., phone (417)864-3325, fax (417)831-1781. **Wattage:** 5000 KW Visual 500 KW Aural. **Ad Rates:** $40.00-1,500 for 30 seconds; $80-3,000 for 60 seconds.

17757 KTMO-FM - 98.9
PO Box 3676 GSS Phone: (573)888-4616
Springfield, MO 65808 Fax: (573)888-4991
Free: (800)552-1055

Format: Country. **Networks:** AP; ABC; Satellite Music Network. **Owner:** Pollack Broadcasting Co., 1303 Southwest Dr., Kennett, MO 63857-0509. **Formerly:** KBOA-FM. **Operating Hours:** Continuous. **ADI:** Paducah,KY-Cape Girardeau,MO-Marion,IL. **Key Personnel:** Pres Semar, General Mgr.; Jim Borders, Sales Mgr.; Larry Anthony, Operations Mgr.; Linda Shown, Office Mgr. **Local Programs:** *Hometown News*, Steve Bryant; *Delta Farm Reports*, Bill Wagner.

17758 KTOZ-AM - 1060
610 W. College Phone: (417)831-1060
Springfield, MO 65806 Fax: (417)831-1231
E-mail: ktozam@mocom.net

Format: Adult Contemporary; Big Band/Nostalgia. **Networks:** USA Radio. **Owner:** The Entertainment Network, Inc., at above address. **Founded:** 1972. **Formerly:** KBUG-AM (1972). **Operating Hours:** Sunrise-sunset; 10% network, 90% local. **ADI:** Springfield, MO. **Key Personnel:** R.R. Johnson, General Mgr., ktozam@mocom.net. **Wattage:** 500. **Ad Rates:** $10-15 for 30 seconds.

17759 KTOZ-FM - 104.7
309 N. Jefferson Ste.340
Springfield, MO 65806

Format: Eclectic. **Founded:** 1984. **Operating Hours:** Continuous. **ADI:** Springfield, MO. **Key Personnel:** Larry Campbell, President; Joe Kinder, Contact; Denney Goode, General Mgr. **Wattage:** 50.000. **Ad Rates:** $23-40 for 30 seconds; $28-45 for 60 seconds.

17760 KTTS-FM - 94.7
2330 W. Grand Phone: (417)865-6614
Springfield, MO 65801 Fax: (417)865-9643
Free: (800)765-5887

Format: Contemporary Country; News; Agricultural. **Networks:** ABC. **Founded:** 1948. **Formerly:** Springfield Great Empire Broadcasting, Inc. **Operating Hours:** Continuous. **ADI:** Springfield, MO. **Key Personnel:** Curt Brown, Contact, cbrown@ktts.com; George DeMarco, General Sales Mgr., gdemarco@ktts.com; Don Paul, Program Dir.; Morris James, News Dir., news@ktts.com. **Wattage:** 100,000 ERP.

17761 KTXR-FM - 101.3
3000 E. Chestnut Expwy. Phone: (417)862-3751
PO Box 3925 G.S. Fax: (417)869-7675
Springfield, MO 65804-2500
E-mail: ktxrfm@cland.net

Format: Easy Listening. **Networks:** NBC. **Owner:** Meyer Communications, at above address, (417)862-3990. **Founded:** 1962. **Operating Hours:** Continuous. **ADI:** Springfield, MO. **Key Personnel:** Jane A. Meyer, Station Mgr.; Joe Rios, Operations Mgr.; Dale Blakenship, Chief Engineer. **Wattage:** 100,000. **Ad Rates:** $20-24 for 30 seconds; $30-32 for 60 seconds. **URL:** http://www.ktxrfm.com.

17762 KWFC-FM - 89.1
PO Box 8900 Phone: (417)869-0891
Springfield, MO 65801 Fax: (417)866-7525
E-mail: kwfc@kwfc.org

Format: Religious. **Networks:** USA Radio. **Owner:** Baptist Bible College, Inc., at above address. **Founded:** Apr. 9, 1969. **Operating Hours:** Continuous. **Key Personnel:** W. F. Askew, Manager, kwfc@kwfc.or; Dick Morris, Program Dir.; Greg

Brock, News Dir.; Gary Longstaff, Underwriting Mgr. **Wattage:** 100,000. **Ad Rates:** Noncommercial. **URL:** http://www.kwfc.org.

17763 KWTO-AM - 560
3000 E. Chestnut Expy. Phone: (417)862-5600
Springfield, MO 65802 Fax: (417)869-7675

Format: Talk; News; Sports. **Networks:** ABC. **Owner:** Meyer Comunications Inc., 3000 East Chestnut Expressway, Springfield, MO 65802, (417)862-3990, Fax: (417)869-7675. **Founded:** 1933. **Operating Hours:** Continuous. **ADI:** Springfield, MO. **Key Personnel:** Kenneth E. Meyer, General Mgr., phone (417)862-3990; Tom Ladd, Operations Mgr.; Art Hains, Sports Dir.; Dale Blankenship, Chief Engineer. **Local Programs:** *Ask the Professionals*, Tom Ladd, Mailing contact; *Night Talk*, John DeCluex; *Sports Talk*, Art Hains, Mailing contact. **Wattage:** 5000.

17764 KYTV-TV - 3
999 W. Sunshine Phone: (417)268-3000
Springfield, MO 65807 Fax: (417)268-3100
E-mail: ky3@ky3.com

Format: Commercial TV. **Networks:** NBC. **Owner:** Schurz Communications, Inc., 225 W. Colfax Ave., South Bend, IN 46626, (219)287-1001. **Founded:** 1953. **Operating Hours:** Continuous; 75% network, 25% local. **ADI:** Springfield, MO. **Key Personnel:** Mike Scott, Gen. Mgr., mscott@ky3.com; Tom McKleroy, Chief Engineer, tmckieroy@ky3.com; Marci Burdick, News, mburdick@ky3.com; Cathy Adams, Program Dir., cadams@ky3.com; Karen Parry, National Sales Mgr., kperry@ky3.com; Gregory Rando, Promotions Mgr., grando@ky3.com; Mark Gordon, General Sales Mgr., mgordon@ky3.com. **Local Programs:** *Ozarks Today* 6-7 a.m., Doug Owen. **URL:** http://www.ky3.com.

17765 TCI of Springfield, Inc.
1533 S. Enterprise Phone: (417)883-7557
Springfield, MO 65804 Fax: (417)883-0265

Owner: TCI, at above address. **Founded:** 1979. **Formerly:** TeleCable of Springfield, Inc. (1995). **Key Personnel:** Ross Summers, General Mgr., phone (417)883-7668; Judy Dean, Office Mgr., phone (417)833-7668; Carl Dyson, Technical Mgr., phone (417)883-7668; Tom Mast, Studio Producer, phone (417)883-7668; Stan Melton, Marketing Mgr., phone (417)883-7668. **Cities Served:** Battlefield, Greene County, Springfield, MO: subscribing households 54,000; 111 channels; 8 community access channels; 80 hours per week community access programming.

STEELE, pop. 2,419.

SE MO. Pemiscot Co. 13 mi. N. of BLytheville, AR. Produces textiles. Cotton gin. Diversified farming. Cotton, corn, soybeans.

17766 The Steele Enterprise
Tennyson Publishing
225 W. Main Phone: (573)695-3415
Box 60 Fax: (573)695-2114
Steele, MO 63877
Publication E-mail: steelenews@aol.com

Newspaper with a Democratic orientation. **Founded:** 1921. **Freq:** Weekly (Thurs.). **Print Method:** Offset. **Cols./Page:** 6. **Col. Width:** 2.17 inches. **Col. Depth:** 21 inches. **Key Personnel:** Karen Tennyson, Editor; David Tennyson, Editor and Publisher. **USPS:** 521-000. **Subscription Rates:** $12.50; $30 out of area. **Remarks:** Accepts advertising.
Ad Rates: BW: $283.50 **Circ:** Paid ‡1,894
4C: $775 Free ‡383
SAU: $4.50
PCI: $4.50

STOCKTON†, pop. 1,432.

SW MO. Cedar Co. 50 mi. NW of Springfield. Manufactures gearboxes, textiles. Black walnut processing plant. Stock, dairy, poultry, grain farms.

17767 Cedar County Republican
108 SE Arcade Phone: (417)276-4211
PO Box C Fax: (417)276-5760
Stockton, MO 65785
Publication E-mail: ccr@ipa.net

Newspaper with a Republican orientation. **Founded:** 1890. **Freq:** Weekly (Wed.). **Print Method:** Offset. **Cols./Page:** 6. **Col. Width:** 12 nonpareils. **Col. Depth:** 294 agate lines. **Key Personnel:** Gina Hamilton, Editor; Dave Berry, Publisher; Marilyn Picard, Advertising Mgr.; Kathy Sillik, Office Mgr. **Subscription Rates:** $17 individuals; $32 elsewhere; $39 out of state. **Remarks:** Accepts advertising.
Ad Rates: SAU: $4.27 **Circ:** ‡3,000

STOVER

17768 Morgan County Press
Vernon Publishing, Inc.
PO Box 130 Phone: (573)377-4616
Stover, MO 65078 Fax: (573)377-4512
Publication E-mail: press@vernonpublishing.com

Community newspaper. **Founded:** 1911. **Freq:** Weekly (Wed.). **Print Method:** Offset. **Cols./Page:** 6. **Col. Width:** 2 1/16 inches. **Col. Depth:** 21 inches. **Key Personnel:** Connie Viebrook, Editor; Dane Vernon, Publisher; Barbara Schnirch, Advertising Mgr. **USPS:** 362-840. **Subscription Rates:** $22.50; $25.50 out of area; $35.50 out of state. **Remarks:** Accepts advertising.
Ad Rates: BW: $327.60 **Circ:** ‡1,700
4C: $477.60
SAU: $2.60
PCI: $2.60

SULLIVAN, pop. 5,461.

E. MO. Crawford and Franklin Co. 68 mi. SW of Saint Louis. Manufactures shoes, piston rings, lumber products, precision metal parts, tool, tool dies. Timber. Iron mining. Diversified farming. Wheat, corn, dairying.

17769 The Sullivan Independent News
Sullivan Independent News
Sullivan Ind. News Phone: (573)468-6511
Box 268 Fax: (573)468-4046
Sullivan, MO 63080
Newspaper. **Founded:** June 5, 1968. **Freq:** Weekly (Wed.). **Print Method:** Offset. **Trim Size:** 8 1/2 x 11. **Cols./Page:** 5. **Col. Width:** 24 nonpareils. **Col. Depth:** 224 agate lines. **Key Personnel:** Kathleen Abell Manion, Editor and Publisher. **USPS:** 525-240. **Subscription Rates:** $20.50; $26 out of area; $30 out of state. **Remarks:** Accepts advertising.
Ad Rates: BW: $380 **Circ:** ‡7,000
4C: $560
PCI: $4.75

17770 KTUI-AM - 1560
PO Box 99 Phone: (573)468-5101
Sullivan, MO 63080 Fax: (573)468-5884

Format: News; Talk. **Networks:** People's Network; UPI; Missouri. **Founded:** 1966. **Operating Hours:** Sunrise-sunset. **ADI:** St. Louis, MO (Mt. Vernon, IL). **Key Personnel:** John C. Rice, Program/News Dir./Gen. Mgr.; Sam Scott, Sales/Promotions Mgr.; Bob Diestelkamp, Sports Dir.; Wilma E. Scott, Office Mgr.; Debby Edgar, Traffic Mgr. **Local Programs:** *Morning Show*, John Rice. **Wattage:** 1000. **Ad Rates:** $9-11 for 30 seconds; $14-17 for 60 seconds.

17771 KTUI-FM - 100.9
PO Box 99 Phone: (573)468-5101
Sullivan, MO 63080 Fax: (573)468-5884
E-mail: ktui@ktui.com

Format: Country; Sports. **Networks:** St. Louis Cardinals; UPI; Missouri. **Owner:** Fidelity Broadcasting, Inc., at above address. **Founded:** 1981. **Formerly:** John Rice & Charles Strauser. **Operating Hours:** Continuous. **ADI:** St. Louis, MO (Mt. Vernon, IL). **Key Personnel:** John C. Rice, News Dir./Gen. Mgr., john@ktui.com; Perry Allen, Production Mgr., perry@ktui.com; Perry Allen, Music Dir.; Wilma E. Scott, Office Mgr., wilma@ktui.com; Sam Scott, Program Dir., sam@ktui.com. **Local Programs:** *Mid Days*, Bobby Diestelkamp; *Morning Show*, Sam Scott. **Wattage:** 3000. **Ad Rates:** $11-15 for 30 seconds; $17-21 for 60 seconds.

SWEET SPRINGS

17772 Sweet Springs Herald
Heartland Publishing, Inc.
238 Main St. Phone: (816)335-6366
Sweet Springs, MO 65351 Fax: (816)335-6366

Community newspaper. **Founded:** 1875. **Freq:** Weekly (Wed.). **Cols./Page:** 6. **Col. Width:** 2 1/8 inches. **Col. Depth:** 21 inches. **Key Personnel:** Kathy Dohrman, Publisher. **Subscription Rates:** $14; $16 out of state. **Remarks:** Accepts advertising.
Ad Rates: SAU: $2.30 **Circ:** ‡1,990
PCI: $2.60

17773 Cass County Cable Inc.
PO Box 293 Fax: (800)533-3079
Sweet Springs, MO 66351

Founded: Aug. 1, 1990. **Key Personnel:** Daryl Granzella, Manager. **Cities Served:** Belton, Hume, Newtown, MO.

TARKIO, pop. 2,375.

NW MO. Atchinson Co. 55 mi. N. of Saint Joseph. Residential.

17774 The Tarkio Avalanche
PO Box 278 Phone: (816)736-4111
107 N. 3rd Fax: (816)736-5700
Tarkio, MO 64491
Newspaper. **Founded:** 1884. **Freq:** Weekly (Thurs.). **Print Method:** Offset. **Cols./Page:** 6. **Col. Width:** 27 nonpareils. **Col. Depth:** 294 agate lines. **Key Personnel:** Will Johnson, Editor and Publisher. **Subscription Rates:** $21. **Remarks:** Accepts advertising.
Ad Rates: BW: $250 **Circ:** 1,675
4C: $400
SAU: $3

17775 KTRX-FM - 93.5
US Hwy. 136 West Phone: (816)736-4321
Tarkio, MO 64491

Format: Country. **Networks:** ABC. **Founded:** 1977. **Operating Hours:** Continuous. **Key Personnel:** Mike L. Carter, President; Roger Houts, Operations Mgr.; Mary Kay Ryan, Office Mgr.; Wayne Combs, News Dir.; Jay Truitt, Director. **Wattage:** 6000. **Ad Rates:** $56-72 for 30 seconds; $70-90 for 60 seconds.

THAYER, pop. 2,211.

S. MO. Oregon Co. 130 mi. SE of Springfield. Manufactures feed, fertilizer. Timber. Diversified farming. Grain, fruits. Livestock.

17776 The South Missourian News
Areawide Media, Inc.
101 Chestnut St. Phone: (417)264-3085
Thayer, MO 65791 Fax: (417)264-3814
Free: (800)995-3209

Rural county newspaper. **Founded:** 1871. **Freq:** Weekly. **Print Method:** Offset. Accepts mats. **Cols./Page:** 6. **Col. Width:** 2 inches. **Col. Depth:** 21 inches. **Key Personnel:** Janine Flynn, General Mgr.; Angelia Roberts, Editor; Jan Sisk, Asst. Editor; Becky Lash, Office Mgr. **Subscription Rates:** $21.25 individuals; $26.56 out of area per year. **Remarks:** Accepts advertising. **Formed by the merger of:** Thayer News; South Missourian Democrat.
Ad Rates: BW: $630 **Circ:** ‡1,500
SAU: $6.50
PCI: $5

17777 KALM-AM - 1290
PO Box 15 Phone: (417)264-7211
Thayer, MO 65791 Fax: (417)264-7212
Free: (800)729-95FM
E-mail: kamsfm@evergreen.com

Format: News; Sports; Agricultural; Information. **Networks:** ABC. **Owner:** Ozark Radio Network, Inc., PO Box 193, Mammoth Spring, AR 72554, Free: (800)729-9536. **Founded:** 1953. **Operating Hours:** Sunrise-sunset. **Key Personnel:** Bob Eckman, Station Mgr.; Lynn Hobbs, Asst. Mgr./Accounting; Brian Chase, News Dir.; Chris Atkins, Program and Country Music Dir.; Sarah Wiggs, Traffic Mgr. **Local Programs:** *View Points* 8 a.m.-9 a.m. Monday-Friday, Dave Watson; *You're On the Air* 9:30 a.m.-10:00 a.m. Tuesday, Mike Crase. **Wattage:** 1000. **Ad Rates:** $11.20 for 30 seconds; $16.50 for 60 seconds. Combined advertising rates available with KAMS-FM: $3-4.25 for 15 seconds; $4.65-6.65 for 30 seconds; $6.20-8.60 for 60 seconds. **URL:** http://www.kkountry.com.

TIPTON, pop. 2,155.

C. MO. Moriteau Co. 27 mi. E. of Sedalia. Manufactures textiles, shoes, metal fabricators, furniture. Agriculture. Livestock. Wheat, oats, soybeans, corn.

17778 The Tipton Times
Vernon Publishing, Inc.
PO Box U Phone: (660)433-5721
Tipton, MO 65081 Fax: (660)433-2222

Newspaper with a Democratic orientation. **Founded:** 1875. **Freq:** Weekly (Thurs.). **Print Method:** Offset. **Cols./Page:** 6. **Col. Width:** 2 1/16 inches. **Col. Depth:** 21 inches. **Key Personnel:** Becky Holloway, Editor; Dane Vernon, Publisher, phone (573)378-5441. **USPS:** 631-580. **Subscription Rates:** $24.50 in county; $29.50 in state; $37.50 out of state. **Remarks:** Accepts advertising.
Ad Rates: GLR: $.30 **Circ:** ‡1,947
BW: $441
4C: $591
SAU: $3.50
PCI: $3.50

TRENTON†, pop. 6,811.

N. MO. Grundy Co. 85 mi. NE of Kansas City. Trenton Junior College. Rock quarries. Manufactures concrete products, chemical fertilizers, radiators, windows. Sawmill. Cannery. Stock, dairy, poultry, grain farms.

17779 Republican-Times
W.B. Rogers Printing Co., Inc.
122 E. 8th St. Phone: (816)359-2212
PO Box 548 Fax: (816)359-4414
Trenton, MO 64683-0548
General newspaper. **Founded:** 1864. **Freq:** Daily (eve.). **Print Method:** Offset. **Cols./Page:** 6. **Col. Width:** 25 nonpareils. **Col. Depth:** 294 agate lines. **Key Personnel:** Diane Raynes, Editor; Wendell Lenhart, Publisher. **Remarks:** Accepts advertising.
Ad Rates: BW: $567 **Circ:** Paid ‡3,435
4C: $777 Non-paid ‡72
SAU: $4.50
PCI: $4.50

17780 KGOZ-FM - 101.7
Box 217 Phone: (660)359-2727
Trenton, MO 64683 Fax: (660)359-4126
Free: (800)NEW-1017

Format: Hot Country. **Networks:** Jones Satellite. **Owner:** Par Broadcasting Inc., at above address. **Founded:** June 1994. **Operating Hours:** Continuous. **ADI:** Kansas City, MO (Lawrence, KS). **Key Personnel:** Mike Ransdell, President; Tonda Ransdell, Sales Manager. **Wattage:** 25,000. **Ad Rates:** Advertising accepted; rates available upon request. $6.50-12.50 for 30 seconds. Combined advertising rates available with KTTN-FM/KULH-FM/KTTN-AM.

17781 KTTN-AM - 1600
PO Box 307 Phone: (816)359-2261
Trenton, MO 64683 Fax: (816)359-4126
Free: (888)367-5886
E-mail: kttnamfm@netins.net

Format: Soft Rock. **Networks:** ABC; Missouri; Brownfield. **Owner:** Luehrs Broadcasting, Inc., at above address, (660)359-2261, Fax: (660)359-4126, Free: (888)367-5886. **Founded:** 1955. **Operating Hours:** Continuous. **ADI:** Kansas City, MO (Lawrence, KS). **Key Personnel:** John Anthony, General Mgr.; Becky Mock, Sales Mgr. **Ad Rates:** $5.65-10.40 for 30 seconds; $8.25-13.85 for 60 seconds.

17782 KTTN-FM - 92.3
PO Box 307 Phone: (816)359-2261
Trenton, MO 64683 Fax: (816)359-4126
Free: (888)367-5886
E-mail: kttnamfm@netins.net

Format: Country; Information; Religious; Gospel; Album-Oriented Rock (AOR). **Networks:** ABC; Brownfield; Missouri. **Owner:** Luehrs Broadcasting, Inc, at above address, (660)359-2261, Fax: (660)359-4126, Free: (888)367-5886. **Founded:** 1978. **Operating Hours:** Continuous. **ADI:** Kansas City, MO (Lawrence, KS). **Key Personnel:** John Anthony, General Mgr.; Tim Peery, Sports Dir.; Tom Mock, News Dir.; Jeff Thomas, Program Dir. **Wattage:** 25,000. **Ad Rates:** $8.50-11.50 for 30 seconds; $11.00-13.50 for 60 seconds.

TROY

17783 Troy Free Press
615 E. Cherry St. Phone: (314)528-4839
Troy, MO 63379 Fax: (314)528-6694

Community newspaper. **Founded:** July 1878. **Freq:** Weekly. **Print Method:** Offset; accept mats. **Cols./Page:** 6. **Col. Depth:** 21 1/2 inches. **Key Personnel:** Bob Simmons, Editor; Pat Whiteside, Publisher. **Subscription Rates:** $15; $24 out of county. **Remarks:** Color advertising accepted; rates available upon request.
Ad Rates: BW: $348.30 **Circ:** Paid ‡3,000
PCI: $2.70

UNION†, pop. 5,506.

E. MO. Franklin Co. On Bourbeuse River, 45 mi. SW of Saint Louis. Shoe factory. Frozen food plant. Diversified farming.

17784 Cornerstone
East Central Junior College
Hwy. 50 Phone: (314)583-5195
PO Box 529 Fax: (314)583-6637
Union, MO 63084
Publication E-mail: erandy@email.ecc.cc.mo.us

Collegiate newspaper. **Founded:** 1970. **Freq:** 3/semester. **Print Method:** Offset. **Cols./Page:** 5. **Col. Width:** 22 nonpareils. **Col. Depth:** 217 agate lines. **Key Personnel:** Rosalyn Pursley, Advisor. **Subscription Rates:** Free to students. **URL:** http://www.ecc.cc.mo.us.
Ad Rates: BW: $250 **Circ:** Free ‡1,400
SAU: $3.00
PCI: $2.50

UNIONVILLE†.

C. MO. Putnam Co. 30 mi. NW of Kirksville.

17785 Unionville Republican & Putnam County Journal
Black Bird Creek Printing Co.
PO Box 365 Phone: (816)947-2222
Unionville, MO 63565-0365 Fax: (816)947-2223

Community newspaper. **Founded:** 1865. **Freq:** Weekly. **Print Method:** Offset. **Trim Size:** 13 1/2 x 21. **Cols./Page:** 6. **Col. Width:** 2 inches. **Col. Depth:** 21 inches. **Key Personnel:** Teresa Kinzler, Editor and Publisher; Ron Kinzler, Publisher. **Subscription Rates:** $13.50 out of area; $18 out of area. **Remarks:** Accepts advertising.
Ad Rates: 4C: $202.60 **Circ:** Paid ‡2,200
SAU: $2.75 Free ‡200

17786 City of Unionville CATV
1611 Grant Phone: (660)947-3818
PO Box 255 Fax: (660)947-7756
Unionville, MO 63565

Owner: City of Unionville Cable TV, at above address. **Founded:** Oct. 1979. **Formerly:** Unionville Cable TV Authority (1993). **Key Personnel:** Richard Fowler, Superintendent, phone (660)947-2168, fax (660)947-7756; Lori Harlan, Cable Clerk; Jerry Tilden, System Mgr., phone (660)947-2168, fax (660)947-7756. **Cities Served:** Unionville, MO: subscribing households 1,059; 25 channels.

UNITY VILLAGE

17787 Daily Word
Unity School of Christianity
1901 NW Blue Pkwy. Phone: (816)524-3550
Unity Village, MO 64065-0001
Publication E-mail: info@unityworldhq.org

Religious magazine. Prints edition in Spanish, La Palabra Diaria; also prints edition in large type. **Founded:** July 1924. **Freq:** Monthly. **Print Method:** Letterpress and offset. **Trim Size:** 4 1/8 x 5 1/2. **Cols./Page:** 1. **Col. Width:** 38 nonpareils. **Col. Depth:** 66 agate lines. **Key Personnel:** Colleen Zuck, Editor. **ISSN:** 0011-5525. **Subscription Rates:** $6.95 individuals. **Remarks:** Advertising not accepted. **URL:** http://www.dailyword.org. **Alt. Formats:** Audio tape; Braille; Large-print; Microform.
Circ: ‡1,500,000

17788 Unity Magazine
Unity School of Christianity
1901 NW Blue Pkwy. Phone: (816)524-3550
Unity Village, MO 64065-0001
Publication E-mail: umag@unityworldhq.org

Religious magazine printing metaphysical and inspirational articles and poems. A spiritual resouce for daily living. Presenting practical ideas for a living a more spiritual life. Emphasizing the unity of all people-with each other and with God. **Founded:** 1889. **Freq:** Monthly. **Print Method:** Offset. **Trim Size:** 5 1/2 x 8 1/4. **Cols./Page:** 1. **Key Personnel:** Philip White, Editor; Janet McNamara, Managing Editor. **ISSN:** 0162-3567. **Subscription Rates:** $11.95 individuals; $24.95 other countries. **Remarks:** Advertising not accepted. **Alt. Formats:** Braille; Microform.
Circ: ‡120,000

VAN BUREN, pop. 850.

SE MO. Carter Co. 150 mi. S. of Saint Louis. Tourism. Timber. Lumber.

17789 The Current Local
PO Box 100 Phone: (573)323-4515
Van Buren, MO 63965
Newspaper. **Founded:** May 1884. **Freq:** Weekly (Thurs.). **Print Method:** Offset. **Cols./Page:** 6. **Col. Width:** 28 nonpareils. **Col. Depth:** 294 agate lines. **Key Personnel:** Alan Turley, Publisher. **Subscription Rates:** $15 individuals. **Alt. Formats:** Audio tape. **Feature Editors:** Steve Turley, *News*.
Ad Rates: PCI: $4 **Circ:** ‡2,400

VANDALIA, pop. 3,170.

NEC MO. Audrain Co. 30 mi. S. of Hannibal. Manufactures refractories, fire-clay products, textiles. Clay pits. Stock, poultry, fruit, grain farms.

17790 Vandalia Leader-Press
108 W. State Phone: (573)594-3322
Box 239 Fax: (573)594-6741
Vandalia, MO 63382
Newspaper with a Democratic orientation. **Founded:** 1874. **Freq:** Weekly (Wed.). **Print Method:** Offset. **Cols./Page:** 6. **Col. Width:** 24 nonpareils. **Col. Depth:** 129 agate lines. **Key Personnel:** William C. Steiner, Editor; Mary K. Steiner, Advertising Mgr.; Lora D. Steiner, Publisher. **Subscription Rates:** $16 individuals; $18 out of area; $19 out of state; $22 out of country.
Ad Rates: BW: $387 **Circ:** ‡2,500
4C: $474.10
SAU: $3
PCI: $3.10

VERSAILLES†, pop. 2,406.

C. MO. Morgan Co. 47 mi. SE of Sedalia. Trout fisheries; coal mines; timber. Diversified farming.

17791 Leader-Statesman
PO Box 348 Phone: (573)378-5441
Versailles, MO 65084-0348 Fax: (573)378-4292
Publication E-mail: news.versailles@vernonpublishing.com

Local newspaper. **Founded:** 1886. **Freq:** Weekly (Thurs.). **Print Method:** Offset. **Cols./Page:** 6. **Col. Width:** 2 1/16 inches. **Col. Depth:** 21 inches. **Key Personnel:** Bertha Evans, Editor; J. Dane Vernon, Publisher; Dorothy Batson, Advertising Mgr. **USPS:** 307-700. **Subscription Rates:** $26 individuals; $31 out of area; $39 out of state. **Remarks:** Accepts advertising.
Ad Rates: GLR: $0.30 **Circ:** 3,700
BW: $441
4C: $591
SAU: $3.50

17792 KTKS-FM - 95.1
PO Box 409 Phone: (573)378-5669
Versailles, MO 65084 Fax: (573)378-6640
E-mail: jfktks@laurie.net

Format: Full Service. **Networks:** CNN Radio. **Owner:** Twin Lakes Communications, Inc., at above address. **Founded:** Feb. 1988. **Former name:** KLGS-FM (1993). **Operating Hours:** Continuous. **ADI:** Columbia-Jefferson City, MO. **Key Personnel:** Jay Fisher, General Mgr.; J. T. Gerlt, Program Dir.; Sheryl Lehman, Sales Mgr. **Wattage:** 25,000. **URL:** http://www.ktks95.com.

VIENNA†, pop. 514.

C. MO. Maries Co. 30 mi. S. of Jefferson City. Residential. Charcoal plant, clay mining, machine and die shops. Agriculture.

17793 Maries County Gazette
Tri-County Newspapers
PO Box 202 Phone: (573)422-3441
Vienna, MO 65582 Fax: (573)859-6274

Community newspaper. **Founded:** June 17, 1873. **Freq:** Weekly (Wed.). **Print Method:** Offset. **Cols./Page:** 6. **Col. Width:** 21 1/2 nonpareils. **Col. Depth:** 301 agate lines. **Key Personnel:** Kurt J. Lewis, Publisher, kjl@sockets.com; Nichoel Snodgrass, Editor; Ron J. Lewis, Advertising Mgr. **Subscription Rates:** $21.45 local; $24.66 out of area; $25 out of state; $40 other countries. **Remarks:** Accepts advertising.
Ad Rates: BW: $322.50 **Circ:** 2,399
PCI: $2.75

WARRENSBURG†, pop. 13,807.

W. MO. Johnson Co. 52 mi. E. of Kansas City. Central Missouri State University. Manufactures textiles, chemicals, machinery, lawnmowers. Hatcheries; coal mines. Stock, dairy, poultry, grain farms.

17794 The Daily Star-Journal
135 E. Market Phone: (816)747-8123
PO BOX 68 Fax: (816)747-8741
Warrensburg, MO 64093
General newspaper. **Founded:** 1865. **Freq:** Daily (eve.). **Print Method:** Offset. **Cols./Page:** 6. **Col. Width:** 25 nonpareils. **Col. Depth:** 294 agate lines. **Key Personnel:** Mrs. Avis G. Tucker, Editor and Publisher; Don W. Kirkpatrick, Advertising Mgr. **Subscription Rates:** $50 individuals. **Remarks:** Accepts advertising.
Ad Rates: BW: $705.60 **Circ:** Mon.-Fri. 5,046
4C: $805.60
SAU: $4.80
PCI: $5.60

17795 Missouri Speech & Theatre Journal
Central Missouri State University
c/o C. Thomas Preston, Jr.
8001 Natural Bridge
St. Louis, MO 63121-4499
Publisher E-mail: scpres@umslvma.umsl.edu

Scholarly journal of speech and theatre scholars in Missouri. **Founded:** 1971. **Cols./Page:** 1. **Col. Width:** 8 inches. **Col. Depth:** 7 inches. **Key Personnel:** C. Thomas Preston, Jr.,

Editor; Larry Grisvard, Advertising Mgr. **ISSN:** 1073-8460. **Subscription Rates:** $10 individuals. **Remarks:** Accepts advertising.
Ad Rates: BW: $100 **Circ:** Controlled 300

17796 Muleskinner
Central Missouri State University
Martin 30 Phone: (660)543-4051
Warrensburg, MO 64093 Fax: (660)543-8663

Collegiate newspaper. **Founded:** 1909. **Freq:** Weekly (during the academic year). **Print Method:** Offset. **Cols./Page:** 6. **Col. Width:** 21 nonpareils. **Col. Depth:** 126 agate lines. **Key Personnel:** Barbara Lach-Smith, Contact, phone (660)543-4430, fax (660)543-8663, bls4430@cmsu.cmsu.edu. **Subscription Rates:** $20 individuals. **Remarks:** Accepts advertising. **URL:** http://www.cmsu.edu/skinner.
Ad Rates: GLR: $6 **Circ:** 6,000
BW: $504
PCI: $4

17797 Standard-Herald
Merchants Messenger
132 W. Pine St. Phone: (816)747-3135
PO Box 7 Fax: (816)747-7800
Warrensburg, MO 64093
Newspaper with a Republican orientation. **Subtitle:** Saturday News. **Founded:** 1865. **Freq:** Weekly (Wed.). **Print Method:** Offset. **Trim Size:** 7 1/4 x 11 1/2. **Cols./Page:** 6. **Col. Width:** 27 nonpareils. **Col. Depth:** 294 agate lines. **Key Personnel:** Fred J. Rich, Advertising Dir.; Pat Larkin, Advertising Mgr.; Didier Bahuaud, News Dir.; Edith Cox, OFM. **Subscription Rates:** $18; $24.55 out of county; $27 out of state. **Remarks:** Accepts advertising.
Ad Rates: BW: $375 **Circ:** Paid ‡1,000
4C: $675 Non-paid 16,000
SAU: $4.54
PCI: $4.54

17798 Warrensburg Gazette
Standard Herald Inc.
132 W. Pine St. Phone: (816)747-3135
PO Box 7 Fax: (816)747-7800
Warrensburg, MO 64093
Shopper. **Founded:** 1943. **Freq:** Weekly (Wed.). **Print Method:** Offset. **Trim Size:** 13 x 21. **Cols./Page:** 6. **Col. Width:** 2 1/16 inches. **Col. Depth:** 21 inches. **Key Personnel:** Fred J. Rich, General Mgr.; Pat Larkin, Advertising Mgr.; Didier Bahuaud, Editor. **Subscription Rates:** Free. **Remarks:** Accepts advertising. **Formerly:** Merchants Messenger.
Ad Rates: BW: $406.98 **Circ:** Free ‡16,000
SAU: $4.79

17799 KCMW-FM - 90.9
Central Missouri State University Phone: (660)543-4155
Wood 11 Fax: (660)543-8863
Warrensburg, MO 64093
E-mail: kcmw@kcmw.cmsu.edu

Format: Public Radio; Jazz; News; Classical; Bluegrass. **Networks:** National Public Radio (NPR). **Founded:** 1962. **Operating Hours:** 5 a.m.-midnight; 55% network, 45% local. **Key Personnel:** Donald W. Peterson, Director; Brent Foster, Operator/Producer; John Dutton, Operator/Producer; Mark Pearce, Development Director; Bob Milner, Program Dir. **Local Programs:** *Alternative Airways*, Leasa Pieper; *Fiddlin' Around with Rex Brown*, Rex Brown; *The Only Real Jazz in Town*, Brent Foster. **Wattage:** 100,000. **Ad Rates:** Noncommercial.

17800 KMOS-TV - 6
Central Missouri State University Phone: (660)543-4155
Warrensburg, MO 64093 Fax: (660)543-8863
E-mail: kmos@kmos.cmsu.edu

Format: Public TV. **Networks:** Public Broadcasting Service (PBS). **Founded:** 1979. **Operating Hours:** 6:30 a.m.-midnight. **ADI:** Kansas City, MO (Lawrence, KS). **Key Personnel:** Donald W. Peterson, General Mgr.; Fred Hunt, Contact; Michael O'Keefe, Contact; Dan Davis, Chief Engineer; Mark Pearce, Contact. **Wattage:** 100,000. **Ad Rates:** Noncommercial.

17801 KOKO-AM - 1450
PO Box 398 Phone: (660)747-9191
Warrensburg, MO 64093 Fax: (660)747-5611

Format: Adult Contemporary. **Networks:** Westwood One Radio; Mutual Broadcasting System; Missouri; Brownfield. **Owner:** Johnson County Broadcasters, Inc., at above address. **Founded:** 1953. **Operating Hours:** 5 a.m.-12 a.m. **Key Personnel:** Marion Woods, General Mgr.; Linda Fischer, Sales Mgr.; Bob Jackson, Sports Dir. **Wattage:** 1,000. **Ad Rates:** $5.50-13.47 for 30 seconds; $8.25-19.06 for 60 seconds.

WARRENTON†, pop. 3,219.

E. MO. Warren Co. 55 mi. W. of Saint Louis. Limestone. Copper wire bars, glass tempering, sheet metal plant. Coal mines; fire clay pits. Agriculture. Grain.

17802 Evangelizing Today's Child
Child Evangelism Fellowship, Inc.
Box 348 Phone: (314)456-4321
Warrenton, MO 63383 Fax: (314)456-2078
Free: (800)748-7710
Publication E-mail: etclip@aol.com

Christian education magazine for those working with children 4 to 11 years old. **Subtitle:** Resources, Tools and Training for Children's Ministry. **Founded:** 1942. **Freq:** Bimonthly. **Print Method:** Offset. **Trim Size:** 8 1/4 x 10 7/8. **Cols./Page:** 3. **Col. Width:** 2 1/4 inches. **Col. Depth:** 10 inches. **Key Personnel:** Elsie C. Lippy, Editor, etceditor@cefinc.org. **ISSN:** 0891-3846. **Subscription Rates:** $4.95 single issue; $20.
Ad Rates: BW: $661 **Circ:** ‡18,000
4C: $911

17803 Warrenton News Journal
Suburban Newspapers of Greater St. Louis
111 W. Booneslick Rd. Phone: (314)456-3481
Warrenton, MO 63383-1912 Fax: (314)456-3020

Community newspaper. **Founded:** 1973. **Freq:** Weekly (Wed.). **Print Method:** Offset. **Trim Size:** 13 x 22. **Cols./Page:** 6. **Col. Width:** 26 nonpareils. **Col. Depth:** 308 agate lines. **Key Personnel:** Marie Hollenbeck, Editor; Heather Masters, Advertising Mgr., phone (314)240-4949, fax (314)240-7913; Shelly Jeffs, General Mgr., phone (314)946-6111, fax (314)946-5955. **Subscription Rates:** Free. **Remarks:** Accepts advertising.
Ad Rates: GLR: $.43 **Circ:** Free 12,431
BW: $805
PCI: $5.62

17804 KWRE-AM - 730
PO Box 220 Phone: (314)456-3311
Warrenton, MO 63383 Fax: (314)456-8767
Free: (800)489-8100
E-mail: kwrekfav@kasparradio.com

Format: Country; News; Agricultural; Religious. **Networks:** USA Radio. **Owner:** Kaspar Broadcasting Co. of Missouri, at above address, Free: (800)489-8100. **Founded:** 1949. **Operating Hours:** 5 a.m.-11 p.m. Mon.-Sat.; 7 a.m.-8 p.m. Sun. **ADI:** St. Louis, MO (Mt. Vernon, IL). **Key Personnel:** Vern Kaspar, General Mgr.; Mark Becker, General Sales Mgr. **Local Programs:** *Country Store* 12:30 - 1:30 Monday-Friday, Mike Thomas, Mailing contact; *Instant Replay* 10:00 am - 11:00 am Saturday, Jay Murry, Mailing contact; *Live Wire* 9:00 am - 10:00 am Monday-Friday, Mike Thomas, Mailing contact. **Wattage:** 1000. **Ad Rates:** $5-24 for 30 seconds; $11-36 for 60 seconds.

WARSAW†, pop. 1,500.

WC MO. Benton Co. 33 mi. S. of Sedalia. Vacation center.

17805 Benton County Enterprise
Benton County Enterprise, Inc.
PO Box 128 Phone: (816)438-6312
Warsaw, MO 65355 Fax: (816)438-3464

Local newspaper. **Founded:** 1879. **Freq:** Weekly. **Print Method:** 13 x 21 1/2. Offset. **Trim Size:** 13 3/4 x 22 3/4. **Cols./Page:** 6. **Col. Width:** 2 inches. **Key Personnel:** M.K. White, Publisher. **Subscription Rates:** $19.95. **Remarks:** Accepts advertising.
Ad Rates: BW: $485 **Circ:** Paid 4,500
4C: $685 Free 200
SAU: $3.85
PCI: $3.85

WASHINGTON, pop. 9,251.

E. MO. Franklin Co. On Missouri River, 50 mi. W. of Saint Louis. Manufactures vinyl products, piston rings, transformers, metal and plastic fabrication, aircraft and automobile parts, footwear, plastics. Diversified farming. Dairy products. Corn, wheat, soybeans. Livestock.

17806 Washington Missourian
Missourian Publishing Co.
14 W. Main
Washington, MO 63090

Newspaper with a Democratic orientation. **Founded:** 1860. **Freq:** Semiweekly (Wed. and on the weekend). **Print Method:** Offset. **Cols./Page:** 6. **Col. Width:** 21 nonpareils. **Col. Depth:** 294 agate lines. **Key Personnel:** William L. Miller, Publisher. **USPS:** 667-820. **Subscription Rates:** $29.61 individuals; $32.46 out of area; $50 out of state. **Remarks:** Accepts advertising.
Ad Rates: BW: $999.75 **Circ:** Wed. ★**15,137**
4C: $1,239.75 Sat. ★**13,472**
SAU: $7.75 Sun. ★**13,472**

17807 KGNV-FM - 89.9
PO Box 87 Phone: (314)239-0400
Washington, MO 63090-0087 Fax: (314)239-4448
E-mail: gnv@mail.usmo.com

Format: Religious. **Simulcasts:** KGNN-FM. **Networks:** Moody Broadcasting; Sun Radio. **Owner:** Missouri River Christian Broadcasting, Inc., at above address. **Founded:** 1989. **Operating Hours:** Continuous; 90% network, 10% local. **ADI:** St. Louis, MO (Mt. Vernon, IL). **Key Personnel:** James Goggan, President/GM, phone (314)239-0401. **Local Programs:** *Good News Bill Board*, Joseph Garness. **Wattage:** 1000. **Ad Rates:** $3 for 15 seconds; $5 for 30 seconds; $7 for 60 seconds. **URL:** http://www.usmo.com/~gnv.

17808 KLPW-AM - 1220
Box 623 Phone: (314)583-5155
Washington, MO 63090 Fax: (314)583-1644
E-mail: klpwam@klpw.com

Format: Talk; News. **Networks:** ABC. **Owner:** Marathon Media, 980 N. Michigan Ave., Chicago, IL 60611, (312)204-9900, Fax: (312)587-9520. **Founded:** 1954. **Operating Hours:** Continuous; 33% Local; 66% Network. **ADI:** St. Louis, MO (Mt. Vernon, IL). **Key Personnel:** Ray Heller, Operations Mgr., phone (314)583-5155, fax (314)583-1644; John Covington, News Dir.; Kevin Anfield, General Mgr.; Greg Marshall, Program Dir. **Wattage:** 1000. **Ad Rates:** $15 for 30 seconds; $19 for 60 seconds. Combined advertising rates available with KLPW-FM. **URL:** http://www.klpw.com.

WAYNESVILLE†, pop. 2,879.

SC MO. Pulaski Co. 70 mi. NE of Springfield. Residential.

17809 Daily Guide
American Publishing Co.
PO Box 578 Phone: (314)336-3711
Waynesville, MO 65583 Fax: (314)336-4640

General newspaper. **Founded:** 1962. **Freq:** Daily (eve.), Sunday (morn.). **Print Method:** Offset. **Cols./Page:** 6. **Col. Width:** 24 nonpareils. **Col. Depth:** 21 1/2 inches. **Key Personnel:** Dennis DeRosset, Publisher; Deborah Nickels, Advertising Mgr. **Subscription Rates:** $45 local; $53 in state; $58 out of state. **Remarks:** Accepts advertising.
Ad Rates: PCI: $5.88 **Circ:** (Not Reported)

17810 KJPW-AM - 1390
Box D Phone: (314)336-4913
Waynesville, MO 65583 Fax: (314)336-2222

Format: Country. **Networks:** NBC; Missouri. **Founded:** 1962. **Operating Hours:** 5 a.m.-midnight. **Key Personnel:** Millie Howlett, Contact; Gary Knehans, Contact. **Wattage:** 5000 day; 67 night.

17811 KJPW-FM - 102.3
Box D Phone: (314)336-4450
Waynesville, MO 65583 Fax: (314)336-2222

Format: Country. **Networks:** NBC. **Founded:** 1968. **Operating Hours:** 5 a.m.-midnight. **Key Personnel:** Millie Brotherton, Manager; Gary Knehans, Program Dir.; Mearl Owens, Sales Mgr.; Warren Goforth, News Dir.; Van Beydler, Music Dir. **Wattage:** 1000.

WEBB CITY, pop. 7,309.

SW MO. Jasper Co. 6 mi. NE of Joplin. Manufactures furniture, scales, machine tools, fertilizer, plastics, textiles, caskets. Sand and gravel pits. Dairy, grain farms.

17812 Webb City Sentinel
Webb City Sentinel, Inc.
8 S. Main Phone: (417)673-2421
PO Box 150
Webb City, MO 64870
Community newspaper. **Founded:** 1879. **Freq:** Weekly (Fri.). **Print Method:** Offset. **Cols./Page:** 6. **Col. Width:** 25 nonpareils. **Col. Depth:** 294 agate lines. **Key Personnel:** Bob Foos, Editor, foboos@ipa.net; Merle Lortz, Advertising Mgr. **Subscription Rates:** $19. **Remarks:** Accepts advertising.
Ad Rates: GLR: $3.70 **Circ:** ‡2,000
SAU: $5.75

17813 Wise Buyer
Webb City Sentinel, Inc.
8 S. Main Phone: (417)673-2421
PO Box 150
Webb City, MO 64870
Publication E-mail: foboos@ipa.net

Shopper. **Founded:** 1935. **Freq:** Weekly (Wed.). **Print Method:** Offset. **Cols./Page:** 6. **Col. Width:** 25 nonpareils. **Col. Depth:** 294 agate lines. **Key Personnel:** Beth Whipple, Editor; Merle Lortz, Advertising Mgr. **Subscription Rates:** Free in area; $15 by mail out of area. **Remarks:** Accepts advertising.
Ad Rates: GLR: $4.35 **Circ:** Non-paid ‡10,400
SAU: $5.75

WEBSTER GROVES, pop. 23,097.

E. MO. Saint Louis Co. 10 mi. SW of Saint Louis. Webster College. Eden Theological Seminary. Residential.

17814 The Journal
Webster University
470 E. Lockwood Phone: (314)968-7088
Webster Groves, MO 63119-3194 Fax: (314)968-7059
Collegiate newspaper. **Founded:** 1924. **Freq:** Weekly. **Print Method:** Offset. **Trim Size:** 10 x 15. **Cols./Page:** 5. **Col. Width:** 1 7/8 inches. **Col. Depth:** 15 inches. **Key Personnel:** Don Corrigan, Advisor; Melissa Pomicter, General Mgr., phone (314)961-2660. **Subscription Rates:** Free. **Remarks:** Accepts advertising. **URL:** http://www.webujournal.com.
Ad Rates: BW: $300 **Circ:** Free ‡3,000
4C: $480
PCI: $10.10

17815 Webster-Kirkwood Times
Webster-Kirkwood Times, Inc.
122 W. Lockwood Ave., 2nd Fl. Phone: (314)968-2699
St. Louis, MO 63119-2916 Fax: (314)968-2961

Community newspaper. **Subtitle:** The Times. **Founded:** July 13, 1978. **Freq:** Weekly (Fri.). **Print Method:** Offset. **Trim Size:** 11 x 17 1/2. **Cols./Page:** 4. **Col. Width:** 26 nonpareils. **Col. Depth:** 224 agate lines. **Key Personnel:** Don Corrigan, Editor; Dwight Bitikofer, Publisher. **Subscription Rates:** Free. **Remarks:** Accepts advertising.
Ad Rates: BW: $995 **Circ:** Free 30,484
PCI: $15.55

WELLSVILLE, pop. 1,600.

NW MO. Montgomery Co.

17816 Wellsville Optic-News
PO Box 73 Phone: (573)684-2929
Wellsville, MO 63384
Local newspaper covering Montgomery county. **Founded:** 1877. **Freq:** Weekly. **Print Method:** Offset. **Trim Size:** 16 3/4 x 22 3/4. **Cols./Page:** 7. **Col. Width:** 2 1/16 inches. **Col. Depth:** 21 1/2 inches. **Key Personnel:** Gay Hagan, Editor/Administration; John P. Fisher, Publisher. **USPS:** 674-220. **Subscription Rates:** $11.50; $14.50 out of state. **Remarks:** Accepts advertising.
Ad Rates: BW: $331.10 **Circ:** ‡2,000
4C: $421.10
SAU: $2.20

WEST PLAINS†, pop. 7,741.

S. MO. Howell Co. 90 mi. SE of Springfield. Manufactures chairs, motors, wood pallets, steel truck bodies, electronic products, shoes, feed. Livestock market. Pine and hardwood timber. Diversified farming. Blackberries, walnuts, poultry. Grape vineyards. Dairy products.

17817 West Plains Daily Quill
125 N. Jefferson St. Phone: (417)256-9191
PO Box 110 Fax: (417)256-9196
West Plains, MO 65775-0110
Publication E-mail: quil@townsqr.com

Newspaper with a Democratic orientation. **Founded:** 1903. **Freq:** Daily (eve.). **Print Method:** Offset. **Trim Size:** 14 x 22 1/2. **Cols./Page:** 6. **Col. Width:** 26 nonpareils. **Col. Depth:** 294 agate lines. **Key Personnel:** Frank Martin III, Editor and Publisher; Sunie Pace, Advertising Mgr.; Jerry Womack, Managing Editor. **USPS:** 675-740. **Subscription Rates:** $61. **Remarks:** Accepts advertising.
Ad Rates: GLR: $.20 **Circ:** Paid 9,634
BW: $1,341.90 Free 6
4C: $1,544.90
SAU: $10.65
PCI: $10.65

17818 KKDY-FM - 102.5
983 E. Hwy. 160 Phone: (417)256-1025
West Plains, MO 65775 Fax: (417)256-2208
E-mail: kkdyfm@townsqur.com

Format: Country. **Networks:** CNN Radio; AP. **Founded:** 1984. **Operating Hours:** Continuous. **Key Personnel:** Tom J. Marhefka, President; Chuck Boone, Program Dir. **Local Programs:** *Ag & Farm Report*, Julie Smith; *Wake-Up Therapy*, Randall Gower. **Wattage:** 50,000. **Ad Rates:** $6.60-10.55 for 30 seconds; $10.05-15.70 for 60 seconds.

WESTON, pop. 1,440.

NW MO. Platte Co. On Missouri River, 30 mi. NW of Kansas City. Historical area. Distillery. Winery. Agriculture. Tobacco, wheat, corn.

17819 Weston Chronicle
McPherson Pub. Co.
605 Main St. Phone: (816)640-2251
PO Box 6 Fax: (816)386-2251
Weston, MO 64098
Community newspaper. **Founded:** 1872. **Freq:** Weekly (Wed.). **Print Method:** Offset. **Cols./Page:** 6. **Col. Width:** 2 1/8 inches. **Col. Depth:** 21 1/2 inches. **Key Personnel:** Beth McPherson, Editor; Jim McPherson, Publisher. **USPS:** 625-040. **Subscription Rates:** $15.
Ad Rates: BW: $412 **Circ:** Paid ‡1,800
4C: $474 Free ‡50
SAU: $4

WHEATON

17820 Wheaton Journal
The Wheaton Journal
PO Box 100 Phone: (417)652-3828
Wheaton, MO 64874 Fax: (417)652-3828

Community newspaper. **Founded:** 1919. **Freq:** Weekly (Thurs.). **Trim Size:** 14 x 22 1/2. **Cols./Page:** 6. **Col. Width:** 2 1/16 inches. **Col. Depth:** 21 1/2 inches. **Key Personnel:** David Moore, Editor; Tina Moore, Publisher/Production. **USPS:** 005-178. **Subscription Rates:** $12 local; $15 out of area.
Ad Rates: BW: $300 **Circ:** Paid 500
PCI: $2.60

MONTANA

State Capital, HELENA

Montana is bounded on the north by Saskatchewan and Alberta, Canada, east by North and South Dakota, south by Wyoming and Idaho. Its breadth, east to west, is about 540 miles; length, about 280 miles; land area, 145,556 square miles, including 240 square miles of Yellowstone National Park; rank in area, fourth. The Rocky Mountains occupy the western two-fifths of the state's area; east of them the country forms part of the Great Plains. The Missouri River is navigable for boats as far as Fort Benton. The Yellowstone River is navigable during high water. The lowest altitude is 1,800 feet above sea level, while Granite Peak in Carbon County reaches a height of 12,350 feet. The climate is dry and invigorating. The Weather Bureau at Great Falls gives the temperature (annual average) as 44.8; highest on record, 103; lowest on record, -42. Total annual precipitation is 15.21 inches. Irrigation has been highly developed, and immense reservoirs on the Madison and Missouri Rivers are sources of water supply. As a result, standard fruits of the Temperate Zone have been produced in large quantities. Montana, with its national forests, dude ranches, mountain hotels, and tourist camp resorts, affords unequalled recreational advantages. Montana State University is located at Bozeman.

POPULATION: 824,000 (1992). Rank among the states, 44th.

AGRICULTURE: Number of farms: 25,000 (1992). Farm acreage: 60,000,000 (1992). Cash receipts from farm marketings: crops, $741,000,000 (1991); livestock and products, $790,000,000 (1991).

FORESTS: Total forest land: 19,101,000 acres (1991). Principal woods: ponderosa pine, larch, douglas fir, englemann spruce, white pine, lodgepole pine, white fir, cottonwood and aspen, hemlock, western red cedar.

MINERALS: Value of production: $590,000,000 (1991). Principal minerals: gold, copper, molybdenum. Value of petroleum production: $356,000,000 (1991).

MANUFACTURE: Value added by manufacture: $1,093,000,000 (1991). Leading industry groups: food and related products, lumber and wood products.

LIST OF COUNTIES

Total number of counties 56

County, Location on Map, and County Seat	Pop.
Beaverhead (SW), Dillon	8,424
Big Horn (S), Hardin	11,337
Blaine (N), Chinook	6,728
Broadwater (C), Townsend	3,318
Carbon (SC), Red Lodge	8,080
Carter (SE), Ekalaka	1,503
Cascade (NC), Great Falle	77,691
Chouteau (N), Fort Benton	5,452
Custer (SE), Miles City	11,697
Daniels (NE), Scobey	2,266
Dawson (NE), Glendive	9,505
Deer Lodge (W), Anaconda	10,278
Fallon (SE), Baker	3,103
Fergus (C), Lewiston	12,083
Flathead (NW), Kalispell	59,218
Gallatin (S), Bozeman	50,463
Garfield (NE), Jordon	1,589
Glacier (N), Cut Bank	12,121
Golden Valley (EC), Ryegate	912
Granite (W), Philipsburg	2,548
Hill (N), Havre	17,654
Jefferson (SWC), Boulder	7,939
Judith Bason (C), Stanford	2,282
Lake (NW), Polson	21,041
Lewis and Clark (WC), Helena	47,495
Liberty (N), Chester	2,295
Lincoln (NW), Libby	17,481
Madison (SW), Virginia City	5,989
McCone (NE), Circle	2,276
Meagher (WC), White Sulphur Springs	1,819
Mineral (NW), Superior	3,315
Missoula (NW), Missoula	78,687
Musselshell (EC), Roundup	4,106
Park (S), Livingston	14,562
Petroleum (C), Winnett	519
Phillips (N), Malta	5,163
Pondera (N), Conrad	6,433
Powder River (SE), Broadus	2,090
Powell (W), Deer Lodge	6,620
Prairie (E), Terry	1,282
Ravalli (W), Hamilton	25,010
Richland (NE), Sidney	10,716
Roosevelt (NE), Wolk Point	10,999
Rosebud (SE), Forsyth	10,505
Sander (NW), Thompson Falls	8,669
Sheridan (NE), Plentywood	4,732
Silver Bay (SW), Butte	33,941
Stillwater (SEC), Columbus	6,536
Sweet Grass (S), Big Timber	3,154
Teton (N), Choteau	6,271
Toole (N), Shelby	5,046
Treasure (SE), Hysham	874
Valley (NE), Glasgow	8,239
Wheatland (C), Harlowton	2,246
Wibaux (NE), Wibaux	1,191
Yellowstone (SEC), Billings	113,419

STATISTICS

Newspapers

Period of Issue	
Daily	11
Evening Daily	5
Morning Daily	7
Daily with Sunday edition	7
Semiweekly	6
Weekly	60
Monthly	1
Free or partly free	6
Shopper	3
Total Newspapers	80

Periodicals

Period of Issue	
Weekly	1
Monthly	3
Bimonthly	4
Quarterly	7
Total Periodicals	19

Total number of publications 99

Radio Stations

AM Stations	30
FM Stations	34
Total Radio Stations	64

TV Stations

Total TV Stations 17

Cable Stations

Total Cable Systems 17

Total number of broadcast listings 98

ANACONDA†, pop. 12,518.

SW MS. Deer Lodge Co. 50 mi. SE of Missoula. Residential.

17821 The Anaconda Leader
Leader Printing & Supply, Inc.
121 Main St. Phone: (406)563-5283
Anaconda, MT 59711 Fax: (406)563-5284

Local newspaper. **Founded:** 1970. **Freq:** Semiweekly (Wed. and Fri.). **Print Method:** Offset. **Trim Size:** 16 x 21. **Cols./Page:** 8. **Col. Width:** 1 3/4 inches. **Col. Depth:** 21 inches. **Key Personnel:** Carl Nyman, Editor; Dean A. Neitz, Publisher; Mick Gee, Advertising Mgr. **USPS:** 869-700. **Subscription Rates:** $24; $27 out of area; $30 out of state. **Remarks:** Accepts advertising.
Ad Rates: GLR: $.40 **Circ:** Paid 3,800
SAU: $5.89 Free 60
PCI: $4.76

BAKER†, pop. 2,400.

Fallon Co. (EC).

17822 Fallon County Times
PO Box 679 Phone: (406)778-3344
Baker, MT 59313 Fax: (406)778-3345

County seat legal newspaper. **Freq:** Weekly (Fri.). **Cols./Page:** 6. **Col. Width:** 2 1/8 inches. **Col. Depth:** 129 1/2 inches. **Key Personnel:** Darlene Hornung, Publisher. **Subscription Rates:** $22 individuals; $25 out of area; $28 out of state. **Remarks:** Accepts advertising.
Ad Rates: BW: $480 **Circ:** 1,650
4C: $654.75
SAU: $4.75
PCI: $3.75

17823 Baker Cable TV
Box 1135 Phone: (406)778-2937
Baker, MT 59313

Owner: Tom Overton, at above address. **Founded:** 1977. **Key Personnel:** Tom Overton, General Mgr. **Cities Served:** subscribing households 700; 37 channels; 1 community access channel.

BELGRADE, pop. 2,386.

S MS. Gallatin Co. 4 mi. W. of Bozeman. Recreational. Agriculture.

17824 High Country Independent Press
220 S. Broadway Phone: (406)388-6762
Belgrade, MT 59714-1019 Fax: (406)388-6072
Publication E-mail: mthcip@aol.com

Community newspaper. **Founded:** 1982. **Freq:** Weekly (Thurs.). **Print Method:** Offset. **Cols./Page:** 6. **Col. Width:** 2 inches. **Col. Depth:** 21 1/4 inches. **Key Personnel:** Devon Hubbard Sorlie, Editor and Publisher. **Subscription Rates:** $22.50; $25 out of area; $30 out of state. **Remarks:** Accepts advertising. **URL:** http://www.townnews/nthcip.com. **Alt. Formats:** CD-ROM.
Ad Rates: GLR: $5.72 **Circ:** ‡3,100
BW: $534.23
4C: $784.23
PCI: $5.72

17825 KGVW-FM - 96.7
2050 Amsterdam Rd. Phone: (406)388-4281
Belgrade, MT 59714

Format: Adult Contemporary; Religious. **Networks:** SkyLight Satellite; Ambassador Inspirational Radio. **ADI:** Helena, MT. **Key Personnel:** Mark Brashear, General Mgr.; C.J. Swoboda, Program Dir.; Dale Heidner, Chief Engineer; Julia Evans Christian, Office Mgr. **Ad Rates:** $6-7 for 30 seconds; $8-9 for 60 seconds.

BIG SANDY, pop. 827.

Chouteau Co. (NC). 70 m NE of Great Falls.

17826 Big Sandy Mountaineer
Ridick Publishing
PO Box 529 Phone: (406)378-2176
Big Sandy, MT 59520 Fax: (406)378-2176

Community newspaper. **Founded:** 1911. **Freq:** Weekly (Wed.). **Print Method:** Offset. **Trim Size:** 22 3/4 x 28. **Cols./Page:** 6. **Col. Width:** 12 picas. **Col. Depth:** 21 inches. **Key Personnel:** James L. Rettig, Editor and Publisher. **USPS:** 366-660. **Subscription Rates:** $20 local; $22 in state; $25 out of state. **Remarks:** Color advertising accepted; rates available upon request.
Ad Rates: GLR: $.28 **Circ:** Paid ‡912
BW: $250 Free ‡43
SAU: $3.55

BIG TIMBER†, pop. 1,690.

SC MS. Sweet Grass Co. 70 mi. E. of Billings. Residential.

17827 The Big Timber Pioneer
Pioneer Newspaper and Commercial Printing
PO Box 190 Phone: (406)932-5298
Big Timber, MT 59011-0190 Fax: (406)932-4931

Newspaper with a Republican orientation. **Founded:** Nov. 16, 1888. **Freq:** Weekly (Wed.). **Print Method:** Offset. **Cols./Page:** 6. **Col. Width:** 24 nonpareils. **Col. Depth:** 294 agate lines. **Key Personnel:** Beccy Oberly, Editor; Dale Oberly, Publisher; D.C. Oberly, Advertising Mgr. **Subscription Rates:** $30. **Remarks:** Accepts advertising.
Ad Rates: GLR: $.28 **Circ:** Paid ‡1,900
BW: $567
4C: $800
SAU: $4.50

BIGFORK, pop. 900.

NW MS. Flathead Co. 15 mi. SE of Kalispell.

17828 Bigfork Eagle
PO Box 406 Phone: (406)837-5131
Bigfork, MT 59911 Fax: (406)837-1132
Publisher E-mail: mteagle@digisys.net

Newspaper. **Founded:** 1977. **Freq:** Weekly (Wed.). **Print Method:** Offset. **Cols./Page:** 6. **Col. Width:** 26 nonpareils. **Col. Depth:** 294 agate lines. **Key Personnel:** Don Schwennesen, Editor and Publisher; Lou Ann Baird, Office Mgr. **USPS:** 533-001. **Subscription Rates:** $16. **Remarks:** Accepts advertising. **Available Online. URL:** http://www.townnews.com/mt/mteagle; mteagle@digisys.net.
Ad Rates: GLR: $6.25 **Circ:** Paid ‡1,600
Free ‡4,500

BILLINGS†, pop. 66,798.

Yellowstone Co. (SEC). 225 m SE of Helena. Eastern Montana College; Rocky Mountain College. Important distribution center. Manufactures sugar, flour, farm machinery, electric signs, furniture, paint, metal ornaments, cereal, creamery and meat products, canned vegetables, concrete. Oil refineries. Diversified farming. Sugar beets, wheat, beans, livestock.

17829 The Billings Gazette
401 N. Broadway Phone: (406)657-1200
PO Box 36300 Fax: (406)657-1345
Billings, MT 59101
Free: (800)543-2505
Publication E-mail: leedit@bsw.infi.net

General newspaper. **Founded:** 1885. **Freq:** Mon.-Sun. (morn.). **Print Method:** Offset. **Cols./Page:** 6. **Col. Width:** 25 nonpareils. **Col. Depth:** 21 1/2 inches. **Key Personnel:** Richard J. Wesnick, Editor; Wayne Schile, Publisher; Rona Rahlf, Advertising Mgr.; Gerry O'Brien, Managing Editor. **Subscription Rates:** $318.90. **Remarks:** Accepts advertising. **URL:** http://www.bigskywire.com. **Feature Editors:** Mike Gast, *Metro, News, Religion*, phone (406)657-1200; Jim Gransbery, *Political*, phone (406)657-1200; Larry Mayer, *Photo*, phone (406)657-1200; Christene Meyers, *Movie, Music, TV & Radio, Travel*, phone (406)657-1200; Warren Rogers, *Sports*, phone (406)657-1200; Chris Rubich, *Society*, phone (406)657-1200; Christine Rubich, *Features*, phone (406)657-1301, fax (406)657-1208.
Ad Rates: BW: $4,560.15 **Circ:** Mon.-Sat. ★51,773
4C: $5,080.15 Sun. ★56,474
PCI: $35.35

17830 The Billings Times
2919 Montana Ave. Phone: (406)245-4994
Billings, MT 59101
Community newspaper. **Founded:** 1891. **Freq:** Weekly. **Print Method:** Offset. **Trim Size:** 11 1/2 x 15 1/2. **Cols./Page:** 4. **Col. Width:** 14 picas. **Col. Depth:** 14 inches. **Key Personnel:** William R. Turner, Editor and Publisher. **USPS:** 056-260. **Subscription Rates:** $20; $23 out of county. **Remarks:** Color advertising not accepted.
Ad Rates: PCI: $4 **Circ:** Paid ‡1,700
Free ‡100

17831 Montana Land Magazine
Real Estate Publications, Inc.
PO Box 30516 Phone: (406)259-3534
Billings, MT 59107-0516 Fax: (406)259-1676
Publisher E-mail: bigsky@montanalandmagazine.com

Real estate magazine. **Subtitle:** Features Properties for Sale in Montana and Surrounding States. **Founded:** 1982. **Freq:** Quarterly. **Print Method:** Offset. **Trim Size:** 8 x 10 1/2. **Cols./Page:** 2. **Col. Width:** 36 nonpareils. **Col. Depth:** 130 agate lines. **Key Personnel:** G.L. (Gordy) Dangerfield, Advertising Mgr. **ISSN:** 1052-469X. **Subscription Rates:** $20 individuals; $40 out of country. **Remarks:** Accepts advertising.
Ad Rates: BW: $450 **Circ:** Controlled ‡100,000
4C: $850

17832 The Retort
Association of Students of M.S.U., Billings
1500 N. 30th Phone: (406)657-2195
Billings, MT 59101-0298 Fax: (406)657-2388

Collegiate newspaper. **Subtitle:** The Retort. **Founded:** 1927. **Freq:** 23/year. **Print Method:** Offset. **Trim Size:** 11 x 17. **Cols./Page:** 5. **Col. Width:** 2 inches. **Col. Depth:** 16 inches. **Key Personnel:** Jason Kintzler, Editor, phone (406)657-2195. **Subscription Rates:** Free newspaper. **Remarks:** Accepts advertising.
Ad Rates: GLR: $5.95 **Circ:** Free 1,500
BW: $396
SAU: $5.95
CNU: $5.95
PCI: $5.95

17833 Western Livestock Reporter
18th & Minnesota Phone: (406)259-4589
PO Box 30758 Fax: (406)259-6888
Billings, MT 59107
Publication E-mail: wlrpubs@imt.net

Livestock newspaper. **Founded:** 1940. **Freq:** Weekly (Wed.). **Print Method:** Offset. **Trim Size:** 17 x 22 3/4. **Cols./Page:** 6. **Col. Width:** 20 nonpareils. **Col. Depth:** 224 agate lines. **Key Personnel:** Chuck Rightmire, Editor; Pat Goggins, Publisher; Bonnie Zieske, Advertising Mgr. **USPS:** 678-680. **Subscription Rates:** $29 individuals. **Remarks:** Accepts advertising. **URL:** http://www.cattleplus.com.
Ad Rates: BW: $2,112 **Circ:** ‡12,000
4C: $2,532
SAU: $22
PCI: $22

17834 Billings TCI/TCI Cablevision of Montana
Box 20497 Phone: (406)238-7700
Billings, MT 59104 Fax: (406)238-7777

Founded: 1968. **Key Personnel:** Blaine Randles, Contact. **Cities Served:** Billings, MT: 61 channels; 2 community access channels.

17835 KBLG-AM - 910
2075 Central Ave. Phone: (406)652-8400
Billings, MT 59102 Fax: (406)652-4899

Format: Talk; News. **Networks:** NBC; CBS. **Founded:** 1955. **Operating Hours:** Continuous. **ADI:** Billings-Hardin, MT. **Key Personnel:** Larry Roberts, President; Mark Byford, General Mgr.; Steve Aga, Sales Mgr.; J.P. Donovan, Program Dir. **Local Programs:** *Up Front with Pat Stinson*, J.P. Donovan. **Wattage:** 1000 day; 63 night. **Ad Rates:** $4.40-9.20 for 30 seconds; $5.60-10.40 for 60 seconds. KRKK-FM.

17836 KCTR-FM - 102.9
27 N. 27th Penthouse Suite Phone: (406)248-7827
PO Box 1276 Fax: (406)252-9577
Billings, MT 59101

Format: Contemporary Country. **Owner:** Deschutes River Broadcasting, 1380 S.W. Macadam Ave, Portland, OR 97201, (503)223-7334, Fax: (503)223-7075. **Founded:** 1976. **Formerly:** KOOK-FM (1988). **Operating Hours:** Continuous. **ADI:** Billings-Hardin, MT. **Key Personnel:** Tom Caulkins, General Mgr.; Jim Diamond, Program Dir.; Ann Berg, Contact. **Wattage:** 100,000. **Ad Rates:** $14-$25 for 30 seconds; $18-$29 for 60 seconds. Combined advertising rates available with KCTR-AM.

17837 KDWG-AM - 970
27 N. 27th Penthouse Phone: (406)248-7827
Suite Fax: (406)252-9577
Billings, MT 59103

Format: Contemporary Country. **Networks:** ABC. **Owner:** Deschites River Broadcasting, 4380 S.W Macadem Ave., Portland, OR 97201, (503)223-7334, Fax: (503)223-7075. **Formerly:** KCTR-AM. **Operating Hours:** Continuous. **ADI:** Billings-Hardin, MT. **Key Personnel:** Tom Caulkins, General Mgr.; Jim Diamond, Program Dir.; Ann Berg, Contact. **Wattage:** 5000. **Ad Rates:** $14-$25 for 30 seconds; $18-$29 for 60 seconds. Combined advertising rates available with KCTR-FM.

17838 KGHL-AM - 790
2070 Overland Ave., Ste. 103 Phone: (406)656-1410
Billings, MT 59102 Fax: (406)656-0110
Free: (800)735-1187

Format: Country. **Networks:** CBS. **Owner:** One on One Sports Holdings, Inc, at above address. **Founded:** 1935. **Operating Hours:** Continuous. **ADI:** Cheyenne, WY-Scottsbluff, NE (Sterling, CO). **Key Personnel:** Patrick Gorman, General Manager/Sales Manager; Nick Tyler, Music Dir. **Wattage:** 5000.

17839 KIDX-FM - 98.5
2070 Overland Ave, Ste. 103 Phone: (406)656-1410
Billings, MT 59102-7429 Fax: (406)656-0110
Free: (800)735-1187

Format: Hot Country. **Networks:** CBS. **Founded:** 1979. **Formerly:** KBSR-FM (1992); KGHL-FM. **Operating Hours:** Continuous. **ADI:** Billings-Hardin, MT. **Key Personnel:** Patrick Gorman, General Mgr.; Shelly Morast, Business Mgr. **Wattage:** 85,000. **Ad Rates:** Combined advertising rates available with KGML-AM.

17840 KRKX-FM - 94.1
2075 Central Ave. Phone: (406)652-8400
Billings, MT 59102-4956 Fax: (406)652-4899

Format: Classic Rock. **Networks:** NBC. **Founded:** 1989. **Operating Hours:** Continuous. **ADI:** Billings-Hardin, MT. **Key Personnel:** Mark Byford, General Mgr.; Steve Aga, Sales Mgr.; Terry Keys, Program Dir. **Wattage:** 100,000 ERP. **Ad Rates:** $15-23 for 30 seconds; $18-26 for 60 seconds.

17841 KSVI-TV - 6
445 S. 24th St. W. Phone: (406)652-4743
Billings, MT 59102-6265 Fax: (406)652-6963
E-mail: ksvi@wtp.net

Format: Commercial TV. **Networks:** ABC. **Owner:** Quorum Broadcasting, Box 23309, Billings, MT 59104. **Founded:** 1980. **Formerly:** KOUS-TV. **Operating Hours:** 24Hrs. **ADI:** Billings-Hardin, MT. **Key Personnel:** Dan Michael, General Mgr.; Tim O'Malley, General Sales Mgr.; Steve Bruggeman, Comptroller; Tracy Nelson, Traffic Dir.; Pat King, Program Dir.; Ed Connors, News Dir.; Sue Begger, Local Sales Mgr. **Wattage:** 100.000 ERP. **Ad Rates:** $15-225 for 15 seconds; $20-300 for 30 seconds; $40-600 for 60 seconds.

17842 KTVQ-TV - 2
3203 3rd Ave. N. Phone: (406)252-5611
Billings, MT 59101 Fax: (406)252-9938

Format: Commercial TV. **Networks:** CBS; Montana News. **Owner:** KTVQ Communications, Inc., at above address. **Founded:** 1953. **Formerly:** KOOK-TV. **Operating Hours:** Continuous; 55% network, 45% local. **ADI:** Billings-Hardin, MT. **Key Personnel:** Jon Stepanek, News Dir.; Pam Hofferber, Program Dir.; Andy Price, Sports Dir.; Dennis Lyle, Promotions Dir.; Monty Wallis, General Mgr.; Duane Crants, Production Dir. **Local Programs:** *News, noon, 5:30 p.m., and 10 p.m.*, Jon Stepanek. **Wattage:** 100,000. **Ad Rates:** $10-350 for 30 seconds.

17843 KULR-TV - 8
2045 Overland Ave. Phone: (406)656-8000
PO Box 80810 Fax: (406)652-8207
Billings, MT 59108-0810
E-mail: kulr8tv@wtp.net

Format: Commercial TV. **Networks:** NBC. **Owner:** MDM Broadcasting Inc.,, PO Box 80810, Billings, MT 59108. **Founded:** 1957. **Formerly:** KGHL-TV (1963). **Operating Hours:** Continuous. **ADI:** Billings-Hardin, MT. **Key Personnel:** Stan Whitman, President; Bruce Cummings, General Mgr.; Chris Byers, Sports Dir.; Julia Omvig, Promotions Dir.; Dave Rye, News Dir.; Pat Shearer, Chief Engineer; Mark Hanson, Production Mgr.; John Langeliers, General Sales Mgr. **Local Programs:** *News Center* 12 p.m., 5:30 p.m. and 10 p.m., Chris Byers, Mailing contact. **URL:** http://www.kulr8.com.

17844 KURL-AM - 730
PO Box 31038 Phone: (406)245-3121
Billings, MT 59107 Fax: (406)245-0822

Format: Religious. **Networks:** SkyLight Satellite; USA Radio; Ambassador Inspirational Radio. **Owner:** Elenbaas Media, Inc., at above address. **Founded:** 1962. **Operating Hours:** Continuous. **Wattage:** 5,000.

17845 KYYA-FM - 93.3
2075 Central Ave. Phone: (406)652-8400
Billings, MT 59102-4596 Fax: (406)652-4899
E-mail: sunbrook@sunbrook.com

Format: Adult Contemporary. **Networks:** Westwood One Radio. **Owner:** Sunbrook Communications, 1212 N. Washington, Ste. 124, Spokane, WA 99208, (509)326-9500, (509)326-9500, Fax: (509)326-9500. **Founded:** 1975. **Formerly:** KOYN-FM (1978). **Operating Hours:** Continuous. **ADI:** Billings-Hardin, MT. **Key Personnel:** Larry Roberts, President, phone (509)326-9500, fax (509)326-1560; Debbie Sundberg, General Mgr.; Bruce Jensen, Program Dir.; Tommy Braaten, Music Dir. **Wattage:** 100,000 ERP. **Ad Rates:** $14-21 for 30 seconds; $19-25 for 60 seconds. Combined advertising rates available with KRKY-FM & KBLG-AM. **URL:** http://www.sunbrook.com/y93/; http://www.y93.com.

BLACK EAGLE

17846 KEIN-AM - 1310
3313 15th St. N. E. Phone: (406)761-1310
PO Box F Fax: (406)454-3775
Black Eagle, MT 59414-0237

Format: Country. **Networks:** ABC. **Owner:** Munson Radio, Inc., at above address. **Founded:** 1922. **Operating Hours:** Continuous. **Key Personnel:** Scott Miranti, Account Exec.; Laurie Vosberg, Business Mgr.; Steven Dow, President. **Wattage:** 5,000.

17847 KEIN-FM - 93.7
PO Box F Phone: (406)761-1310
Black Eagle, MT 59414-0237 Fax: (406)454-3775

Format: Country. **Owner:** Jeannine M. Mason, at above address. **Operating Hours:** Continuous. **Key Personnel:** Scott Miranti, Account Exec.; Laurie Vosberg, Business Mgr.; Steven Dow, President. **Wattage:** 100,000.

BOULDER

17848 Boulder Monitor
Boulder Monitor, Inc.
104 W. Centennial Phone: (406)225-3821
PO Box 66
Boulder, MT 59632
Community newspaper. **Founded:** 1910. **Freq:** Weekly (Thurs.). **Print Method:** Offset. **Cols./Page:** 5. **Col. Width:** 11.6 picas. **Col. Depth:** 16 inches. **Key Personnel:** Denise Sutherlin, Editor; Vern Sutherlin, Publisher. **USPS:** 061-680. **Subscription Rates:** $16 individuals; $20 out of area. **Remarks:** Accepts advertising.
Ad Rates: PCI: $3.50 **Circ:** ‡1,300

BOZEMAN†, pop. 21,645.

Gallatin Co. (S). 80 m E of Butte. Montana State University. Residential. Museum of The Rockies. Major ski areas.

17849 Bozeman Daily Chronicle
Pioneer Publishing Co.
PO Box 1188 Phone: (406)587-4491
Bozeman, MT 59771 Fax: (406)587-7995

General newspaper. **Founded:** 1911. **Freq:** Daily (eve.), Sunday (morn.). **Print Method:** Offset. **Cols./Page:** 6. **Col. Width:** 24 nonpareils. **Col. Depth:** 301 agate lines. **Key Personnel:** Dennis Swibold, Editor; Bruce K. Smith, Publisher; Mike Smit, Advertising Mgr. **Subscription Rates:** $93. **Remarks:** Accepts advertising.
Ad Rates: SAU: $8.40 **Circ:** Mon.-Sat. ★14,129
Sun. ★15,570

17850 The Exponent
ASMSU Exponent
Strand Union Bldg. 330 Phone: (406)994-2611
Bozeman, MT 59717-4200 Fax: (406)994-2253

Collegiate newspaper. **Founded:** Jan. 1, 1895. **Freq:** Semiweekly (Tues. and Fri.; during the academic year). **Print Method:** Offset. **Trim Size:** 11 x 17. **Cols./Page:** 5. **Col. Width:** 2 1/16 inches. **Col. Depth:** 16 inches. **Key Personnel:** Marcus Hibdon, Contact; Melodie Burgess, Contact, phone (406)994-2206; Paris Hodgson, Contact, phone (406)994-4590. **USPS:** 360-060. **Subscription Rates:** Free; $40 by mail. **Remarks:** Accepts advertising. **Alt. Formats:** CD-ROM.
Ad Rates: BW: $581.75 **Circ:** Paid ‡200
4C: $731.75 Free ‡7,000
SAU: $9.10
PCI: $9.10

17851 Montana Farm Bureau Spokesman
Montana Farm Bureau Federation
502 S. 19th Ave. Phone: (406)587-3153
Bozeman, MT 59718 Fax: (406)587-0319
Publisher E-mail: mtfarmb@in-tch.com

Agricultural periodical. **Founded:** 1919. **Freq:** Quarterly. **Print Method:** Offset. Uses mats. **Trim Size:** 8 1/2 x 11. **Cols./Page:** 2. **Col. Width:** 17 nonpareils. **Col. Depth:** 154 agate lines. **Key Personnel:** Lorna Karn, Editor; J.T. "Jake" Cummins, Managing Editor; Rebecca Colnar, Asst. Editor. **ISSN:** 0886-3075. **Subscription Rates:** $4 members; $25 nonmembers. **Remarks:** Accepts advertising.
Ad Rates: GLR: $1 **Circ:** ‡7,000
BW: $525
PCI: $17.50

17852 KBOZ-AM - 1090
5445 Johnson Rd. Phone: (406)586-5466
PO Box 20 Fax: (406)587-8201
Bozeman, MT 59715

Format: Country; Full Service. **Networks:** ABC. **Founded:** 1975. **Operating Hours:** Continuous. **Key Personnel:** Vicki Mann, V.P./Gen. Mgr.; Dean Alexander, General Sales Mgr.; Terry Kegley, Program Dir. **Wattage:** 5000.

17853 KBOZ-FM - 97.5
5445 Johnson Rd. Phone: (406)586-5466
Box 20 Fax: (406)587-8201
Bozeman, MT 59715

Format: Soft Rock. **Networks:** ABC; Unistar; Westwood One Radio. **Founded:** 1977. **Formerly:** KYBS-FM (1992); KATH-FM (1993). **Operating Hours:** Continuous. **Key Personnel:** Vicki Mann, General Mgr.; Dean Alexander, General Sales Mgr. **Local Programs:** *Montana Today*, John Russell; *Southwest Montana Top 20*, Peter Masse. **Wattage:** 100,000. **Ad Rates:** Advertising accepted; rates available upon request.

17854 KCTZ-TV - 7 VHF
1128 E. Main St. Phone: (406)586-3280
Bozeman, MT 59715 Fax: (406)586-4135

Format: Commercial TV. **Networks:** Fox. **Founded:** Dec. 1, 1993. **Formerly:** K26de. **Operating Hours:** 6 a.m.-1 a.m. **ADI:** Butte, MT. **Key Personnel:** Tim Gazy, General Mgr.; Chet Layman, News Dir. **Ad Rates:** $97.50 for 15 seconds; $10-150 for 30 seconds; $20-300 for 60 seconds.

17855 KGLT-FM - 91.9
330 Sub, Box 174240 Phone: (406)994-3001
Bozeman, MT 59717-4240 Fax: (406)994-1987
Free: (800)994-4492
E-mail: wwwkglt@montana.edu

Format: Eclectic. **Owner:** Board of Regents—Montana University System, at above address. **Founded:** 1967. **Operating Hours:** Continuous. **Key Personnel:** Phil Charles, General Mgr., phone (406)994-6484, pcharles@montana.edu; Kathy Blanksma, Business Mgr., phone (406)994-5583, kgltbus@montana.edu; Wylie Roth, Underwriting Rep., phone (406)994-7091, kgltundr@montana.edu; Brodie Cates, Production Dir., phone (406)994-6484, kgltmus@montana.edu; Jim Bender, Chief Engineer, phone (406)587-8971, fax (jab)ender@imt.net. **Wattage:** 2000. **Ad Rates:** Underwriting available. **URL:** http://www.montana.edu/wwwkglt/.

17856 KUSM-TV - 9
Visual Communications Bldg., Phone: (406)994-3437
RM. 172 Fax: (406)994-6545
Montana State University
Bozeman, MT 59717
Free: (800)426-8243
E-mail: kusm@kusm.montana.edu

Format: Public TV. **Networks:** Public Broadcasting Service (PBS). **Owner:** Montana State University, at above address. **Founded:** 1984. **Operating Hours:** Continuous. **ADI:** Butte, MT. **Key Personnel:** Jack Hyyppa, Station Mgr.; Mike Keating, Contact. **Ad Rates:** Noncommercial. **URL:** http://visions.montana.edu.

17857 Western Cable TV
PO Box 3512 Phone: (406)587-4898
Bozeman, MT 59772

Owner: Richard Mierva, at above address. **Founded:** 1985. **Key Personnel:** Alice Mierva, General Mgr. **Cities Served:** Opportunity, MT: subscribing households 125; 12 channels.

BROADUS†, pop. 712.

Powder River Co. (C).

17858 Powder River Examiner
PO Box 328 Phone: (406)436-2244
Broadus, MT 59317
General newspaper. **Founded:** 1919. **Freq:** Weekly. **Print Method:** Offset. **Cols./Page:** 7. **Col. Width:** 20 nonpareils. **Col. Depth:** 300 agate lines. **Key Personnel:** Joe Stuver, Publisher. **Subscription Rates:** $25. **Remarks:** Accepts advertising.
Ad Rates: GLR: $.32 **Circ:** 1,100
BW: $625.65
PCI: $3.45

BROWNING, pop. 1,226.

Glacier Co. (N). 110 m NW of Great Falls. Recreation. Trading center for Blackfeet Indian Reservation. Ships hay, pencils, livestock. Oil wells. Lumber. Stock, hay.

17859 Glacier Reporter
PO Box 349 Phone: (406)338-2090
Browning, MT 59417 Fax: (406)338-2410

Community newspaper. **Founded:** 1934. **Freq:** Weekly (Thurs.). **Print Method:** Offset. **Trim Size:** 13 3/4 x 22 1/2. **Cols./Page:** 6. **Col. Width:** 24 nonpareils. **Col. Depth:** 294 agate lines. **Key Personnel:** Brian Kavanagh, Publisher; Marlene Augare, Advertising Mgr. **USPS:** 885-100. **Subscription Rates:** $25 individuals; $30 out of area; $35 out of state. **Remarks:** Accepts advertising.
Ad Rates: BW: $580.50 **Circ:** ‡2,600
4C: $780
SAU: $4.50
PCI: $4.50

BUTTE†, pop. 37,205.

Silver Bow Co. (SW). 66 m SW of Helena. One of the most important United States copper mining centers. Gold, silver, lead, zinc, manganese mines. Montana College of Mineral Science and Technology. Manufactures motors; dairy, food products, compressed and liquefied gases, beverages, optical goods, chemicals, steel fabrication. Livestock auction yards, phosphate products, wood preserving; commercial printing plants.

17860 Montana Standard
PO Box 627 Phone: (406)496-5500
Butte, MT 59703 Fax: (406)496-5551
Free: (800)877-1074

General newspaper. **Founded:** 1876. **Freq:** Mon.-Sun. (morn.). **Print Method:** Offset. **Cols./Page:** 6. **Col. Width:** 24 nonpareils. **Col. Depth:** 301 agate lines. **Key Personnel:** Norman Lewis, Editor and Publisher; Dan J. Killoy, Publisher. **Subscription Rates:** $200.76; $208.56 out of state. **Remarks:** Accepts advertising.
Ad Rates: SAU: $13.15 **Circ:** Mon.-Sat. 14,927
Sun. 15,489

17861 Technocrat
Montana Tech at University of Montana
1300 W. Park Phone: (406)496-4241
Butte, MT 59701 Fax: (406)496-4702
Publication E-mail: technocrat@mtvms2.mtech.edu

Collegiate newspaper. **Founded:** 1954. **Freq:** Weekly (Fri.). **Print Method:** Offset. **Trim Size:** 11 x 17. **Cols./Page:** 5. **Col. Width:** 2 inches. **Col. Depth:** 16 inches. **Key Personnel:** Heather L. Dusterhoff, Editor, hld@in-tch.com. **Remarks:** Accepts advertising.
Ad Rates: BW: $125 **Circ:** Free ‡1,200
PCI: $5

17862 KMBR-FM - 95.5
PO Box 3788 Phone: (406)494-4442
Butte, MT 59702-3788 Fax: (406)494-6020
E-mail: levinman@montana.com

Format: Classic Rock; Album-Oriented Rock (AOR). **Founded:** 1979. **Formerly:** KQUY-FM (1996). **Operating Hours:** Continuous. **ADI:** Butte, MT. **Key Personnel:** Craig Whetstine, General Mgr., craigw@montana.com; Dave Levin, Operations Mgr. **Wattage:** 50,000. **Ad Rates:** Combined advertising rates available with KXTL-AM, KAAR-FM.

17863 KOPR-FM - 94.1
660 Dewey Blvd. Phone: (406)494-7777
Butte, MT 59701 Fax: (406)494-5534
E-mail: bbi@montana.comm

Format: Adult Contemporary. **Networks:** ABC; InterMountain. **Founded:** 1972. **Operating Hours:** Continuous. **ADI:** Butte, MT. **Key Personnel:** Ron Davis, General Mgr.; B.J. McKeazle, Program Dir. **Wattage:** 100,000 ERP.

17864 KTVM-TV - 6
750 Dewey Blvd., Ste. 1, Box 3118 Phone: (406)494-7603
Butte, MT 59701 Fax: (406)494-2572

Format: Commercial TV. **Networks:** NBC. **Owner:** Eagle Communications, PO Box 5268, Missoula, MT 59806, (406)721-2063, Fax: (406)542-1606. **Founded:** 1971. **Operating Hours:** 24Hrs. **ADI:** Butte, MT. **Key Personnel:** Robert Precht, Contact; Jane Engish, Contact; Jean Zosel, Program Dir., phone (406)721-2065; Patrice Lee, News Dir., phone (406)586-0296; Seth Grossman, Sports Dir., phone (406)586-0296; Bill Ward, Operations Mgr., phone (406)586-0296. **Ad Rates:** $35-350 per unit.

17865 KXLF-TV - 4
Box 3500, 1003 S. Montana St. Phone: (406)782-0444
PO Box 3500 Fax: (406)782-8906
Butte, MT 59701

Format: Commercial TV. **Networks:** CBS. **Owner:** KXLF Communications Inc, 1003 S.,Montana, Butte, MT 59701, (406)406-8400. **Founded:** 1953. **Operating Hours:** 6 a.m.-1:30 a.m. **ADI:** Butte, MT. **Key Personnel:** Ron Cass, General Mgr.,Pres. **Ad Rates:** Advertising accepted; rates available upon request.

17866 KXTL-AM - 1370
PO Box 3788 Phone: (406)494-4442
Butte, MT 59702-3788 Fax: (406)494-6020

Format: Oldies; Sports; News. **Networks:** Mutual Broadcasting System. **Founded:** 1927. **Operating Hours:** Continuous. **ADI:** Butte, MT. **Key Personnel:** Craig Whetstine, General Mgr., levinman@montana.com; Dave Levin, Program Dir., levinman@montana.com. **Wattage:** 5000.

CASCADE, pop. 773.

Cascade Co. (NC). 20 m SW of Great Falls. Residential.

17867 Cascade Courier
PO Box 308 Phone: (406)468-9231
Cascade, MT 59421 Fax: (406)468-9231
Publication E-mail: leandra@men.net

Community newspaper. **Founded:** 1910. **Freq:** Weekly (Thurs.). **Print Method:** Offset. **Cols./Page:** 5. **Col. Width:** 2 inches. **Col. Depth:** 12 inches. **Key Personnel:** Patrick C. Travis, Editor and Publisher; Ellen M. Travis, Publisher. **USPS:** 092-400. **Subscription Rates:** $20 individuals; $25 out of state. **Remarks:** Accepts advertising.
Ad Rates: GLR: $.22 **Circ:** Paid ‡1,200
BW: $211.20 Free ‡22
4C: $271.20
SAU: $3.50
PCI: $3.50

CHESTER†, pop. 963.

Liberty Co. (N). 90 m NE of Great Falls. Oil and gas wells. Grain farms. Wheat.

17868 Liberty County Times
PO Box 689 Phone: (406)759-5355
Chester, MT 59522 Fax: (406)759-5320

Newspaper. **Founded:** 1906. **Freq:** Weekly (Thurs.). **Print Method:** Offset. **Cols./Page:** 6. **Col. Width:** 25 nonpareils. **Col. Depth:** 264 agate lines. **Key Personnel:** Alan Johnson, Editor and Publisher; Kathy Johnson, Publisher. **Subscription Rates:** $12. **Remarks:** Accepts advertising.
Ad Rates: GLR: $.15 **Circ:** 1,852

CHINOOK†.

Blaine Co. (NC). 10 m W of Zurich.

17869 The Chinook Opinion
Perry Publishing Co.
217 Indiana Phone: (406)357-2680
PO Box 279 Fax: (406)357-3736
Chinook, MT 59523
Publication E-mail: 7megan@3rivers.net

Community newspaper. **Founded:** 1890. **Freq:** Weekly (Wed.). **Print Method:** Offset. **Trim Size:** 11.75 picas. **Cols./Page:** 6. **Col. Width:** 2 inches. **Col. Depth:** 21.5 picas. **Key Personnel:** Mike Perry, Editor and Publisher. **USPS:** 106-040. **Subscription Rates:** $30; $32.50 out of state. **Remarks:** Accepts advertising.
Ad Rates: BW: $341.85 **Circ:** ‡1,800
PCI: $2.65

17870 KRYK-FM - 101.3
U.S. Hwy. 2 W. Phone: (406)265-7841
PO Box 1509 Fax: (406)357-2275
Chinook, MT 59523

Format: Adult Contemporary. **Networks:** CBS. **Owner:** New Media Broadcasters, Inc., at above address. **Founded:** 1983. **Operating Hours:** 5 a.m.-midnight, Mon.-Fri.; 6 a.m.-midnight, Sat.-Sun. **Key Personnel:** John Mosher, Contact; David Leeds, Contact. **Wattage:** 100,000. **Ad Rates:** $5-5.90 for 30 seconds; $6-6.90 for 60 seconds. KOJM-AM, KPQX-FM.

CHOTEAU†, pop. 1,798.

Teton Co. (N). 45 m NW of Great Falls. Recreation. Oil. Dairy, stock, grain farms. Wheat, oats, barley.

17871 Choteau Acantha
216 1st Ave. NW Phone: (406)466-2403
Box 320 Fax: (406)466-2403
Choteau, MT 59422-0320
Publication E-mail: acantha@3rivers.net

Community newspaper. **Founded:** 1893. **Freq:** Weekly (Wed.). **Print Method:** Offset. **Trim Size:** 14 x 23. **Cols./Page:** 6. **Col. Width:** 2 1/16 inches. **Col. Depth:** 21 inches. **Key Personnel:** Melody Martinsen, Editor; Jeff Martinsen, Publisher. **USPS:** 106-360. **Subscription Rates:** $20 individuals; $24 out of area; $27 out of state. **Remarks:** Accepts advertising. **URL:** http://www.townnews.com/mtacantha.
Ad Rates: GLR: $3.50 **Circ:** ‡2,000
SAU: $0.50
PCI: $3.56

CIRCLE†, pop. 931.

McCone Co. (NE). 175 m NE of Billings. Oil, coal. Ships wheat and livestock. Stock, grain farms. Livestock.

17872 Cable and Communications Corp.
Box 280 Phone: (406)485-3301
Circle, MT 59215 Fax: (406)485-2924
Free: (800)452-2288

Owner: Mid-Rivers Telephone Co-Op Inc., at above address. **Key Personnel:** Gerry Anderson, General Mgr. **Cities Served:** Circle, Ekalaka, Jordan, Richey, Savage, Wibaux, MT: subscribing households 935.

COLUMBIA FALLS, pop. 3,112.

Flathead Co. (NW). 125 m N of Missoula. Aluminum manufactured. Lumber mills. Agriculture. Wheat, oats, barley, dairying. Resort area.

17873 Hungry Horse News
PO Box 189
Columbia Falls, MT 59912

Community newspaper. **Founded:** 1946. **Freq:** Weekly (Thurs.). **Print Method:** Offset. Uses mats. **Cols./Page:** 6. **Col. Width:** 26 nonpareils. **Col. Depth:** 294 agate lines. **Key Personnel:** Brian M. Kennedy, Editor and Publisher; Noreen Hanson, Advertising Mgr. **USPS:** 254-320. **Subscription Rates:** $23 individuals. **Remarks:** Accepts advertising.
Ad Rates: GLR: $.54 **Circ:** ‡7,400
BW: $1,146
4C: $1,371
PCI: $9.10

COLUMBUS†, pop. 1,439.

Stillwater Co. (C).

17874 Stillwater County News
News Montana, Inc.
PO Box 659 Phone: (406)322-5212
Columbus, MT 59019 Fax: (406)322-5391
Free: (800)823-7426

County newspaper. **Founded:** 1891. **Freq:** Weekly. **Print Method:** Offset. **Trim Size:** 23 1/2 x 14. **Cols./Page:** 6. **Col. Width:** 2 inches. **Col. Depth:** 21 inches. **Key Personnel:** James E. Moore II, Publisher; Tricia Elpel, Publisher. **Subscription Rates:** $21 individuals; $32 out of area. **Remarks:** Accepts advertising. **Formerly:** The Stillwater Sun.
Ad Rates: BW: $378 **Circ:** ‡2,100
SAU: $9

CONRAD†, pop. 3,074.

Pondera Co. (N). 55 m N of Great Falls. Creamery. Oil wells. Ships wheat, barley and other small grain. Poultry, grain farms.

17875 Independent-Observer
Box 966 Phone: (406)278-5561
Conrad, MT 59425 Fax: (406)278-5562

Newspaper. **Founded:** 1905. **Freq:** Weekly (Thurs.). **Print Method:** Offset. **Cols./Page:** 6. **Col. Width:** 21 nonpareils. **Col. Depth:** 301 agate lines. **Key Personnel:** Buck Traxler, Editor; John H. Lee, Publisher. **Subscription Rates:** $22. **Remarks:** Accepts advertising.
Ad Rates: GLR: $.30 **Circ:** ‡2,760
BW: $483.75
SAU: $4.39
PCI: $4.29

CULBERTSON, pop. 887.

Roosevelt Co. (NE). 178 m S of Regina, Sask, Canada.

Safflower processing plant. Agriculture. Wheat, cattle, sheep, hogs, safflower.

17876 The Searchlight
PO Box 496 Phone: (406)787-5821
Culbertson, MT 59218 Fax: (406)787-5271

Community newspaper. **Founded:** 1902. **Freq:** Weekly (Thurs.). **Print Method:** Offset. **Cols./Page:** 5. **Col. Width:** 24 nonpareils. **Col. Depth:** 217 agate lines. **Key Personnel:** Ila Mae Forbregd, Editor; H.N. Downs, Publisher. **Subscription Rates:** $21 individuals. **Remarks:** Accepts advertising.
Ad Rates: GLR: $.11 **Circ:** ‡1,200
PCI: $3

CUT BANK†, pop. 3,688.

Glacier Co. (N). 116 m NW of Great Falls. Manufactures and ships oil products, gasoline and by-products. Ships stock, wool, grain. Gas, oil wells. Stock, grain farms.

17877 Cut Bank Pioneer Press
Box 847 Phone: (406)873-2201
517 E. Main Fax: (406)873-2443
Cut Bank, MT 59427
Community newspaper. **Founded:** July 1909. **Freq:** Weekly (Wed.). **Print Method:** Offset. **Cols./Page:** 6. **Col. Width:** 2 1/16 inches. **Col. Depth:** 21 1/2 inches. **Key Personnel:** LeAnne M. Kavanagh, Editor; Brian Kavanagh, Publisher. **USPS:** 141-140. **Subscription Rates:** $25; $30 out of area; $35 out of state. **Remarks:** Accepts advertising.
Ad Rates: GLR: $.34 **Circ:** Paid ‡1,825
BW: $580.50 Free ‡18
4C: $780
SAU: $4.50
PCI: $4.50

17878 Western Breeze
32 South Central Ave. Phone: (406)873-4128
PO Box 1253 Fax: (406)873-4129
Cut Bank, MT 59427
Local newspaper tabloid. **Founded:** Sept. 1952. **Freq:** Semiweekly. **Print Method:** Offset. **Trim Size:** 8 1/2 x 14. **Cols./Page:** 2 and 4. **Col. Width:** 2 and 4 inches. **Col. Depth:** 13 inches. **Key Personnel:** James M. O'Day, Publisher; Penne Swenson, Advertising Dir.; Diane Proefrock, Office Mgr.; Kathy O'Day, Director. **USPS:** 677-700. **Subscription Rates:** $25; $27.50 out of area; $30 out of state. **Remarks:** Accepts advertising.
Ad Rates: GLR: $5 **Circ:** Paid 1,800
BW: $208 Free 80
4C: $300
SAU: $4.64
PCI: $5

DEER LODGE†, pop. 4,023.

Powell Co. (W). 39 m N of Butte. Lumber mill. Phosphate, gold mines. Stock, grain farms. Hay, cattle, sheep.

17879 Banner
Bo Shart Publishing
PO Box 111 Phone: (406)846-2424
Deer Lodge, MT 59722 Fax: (406)846-2453

Community newspaper. **Founded:** 1914. **Freq:** Weekly (Thurs.). **Print Method:** Offset. **Cols./Page:** 7. **Col. Width:** 20 nonpareils. **Col. Depth:** 300 agate lines. **Key Personnel:** Aubrey Larson, Publisher. **Subscription Rates:** $25. **Remarks:** Accepts advertising.
Ad Rates: GLR: $.32 **Circ:** ‡1,100

17880 Silver State Post
Bo Shart Publishing
PO Box 111 Phone: (406)846-2424
Deer Lodge, MT 59722 Fax: (406)846-2453

Community newspaper. **Founded:** 1888. **Freq:** Weekly (Thurs.). **Print Method:** Offset. **Cols./Page:** 7. **Col. Width:** 20 nonpareils. **Col. Depth:** 300 agate lines. **Key Personnel:** Aubrey D. Larson, Editor and Publisher. **Subscription Rates:** $25. **Remarks:** Accepts advertising.
Ad Rates: GLR: $.32 **Circ:** ‡1,800

DILLON†, pop. 3,976.

Beaverhead Co. (SW). 65 m S of Butte. Western Montana College. Tourism. Gold, Silver, lead, copper mines. Timber. Agriculture.

17881 Dillon Tribune
22 S. Montana Phone: (406)683-2331
PO Box 911 Fax: (406)683-2332
Dillon, MT 59725-0911
Community newspaper. **Founded:** 1881. **Freq:** Weekly (Wed.). **Print Method:** Offset. **Cols./Page:** 6. **Col. Width:** 12 picas. **Col. Depth:** 294 agate lines. **Key Personnel:** John Barrows, Editor and Publisher; Susan Bramlette, Advertising Mgr. **Subscription Rates:** $24; $28 out of area. **Remarks:** Accepts advertising. **Formerly:** Dillon Tribune-Examiner (1992).
Ad Rates: GLR: $.36 **Circ:** Paid ‡2,764
PCI: $5.50 Free ‡20

17882 Tribune Advertiser
Dillon Tribune
22 S. Montana Phone: (406)683-2331
PO Box 911 Fax: (406)683-2332
Dillon, MT 59725-0911
Shopper. **Freq:** Weekly (Tues.). **Print Method:** Offset. Uses mats. **Cols./Page:** 6. **Col. Width:** 25 nonpareils. **Col. Depth:** 294 agate lines. **Key Personnel:** Ken Olsen, Editor and Publisher; Susie Bramlette, General and Administration. **Remarks:** Accepts advertising. **Formerly:** Tradewinds.
Ad Rates: GLR: $.36 **Circ:** Free ‡4,600
BW: $548.10
SAU: $4.75

17883 KDBM-AM - 1490
610 N. Montana St. Phone: (406)683-2800
Dillon, MT 59725 Fax: (406)683-9480

Format: Country. **Networks:** ABC; Northern Agricultural. **Owner:** Beaverhead Madison Broadcasting Inc., at above address. **Founded:** 1956. **Operating Hours:** 6 am-10 pm Mon.-Sat.; 7 am-7 pm Sun.; 10% network, 90% local. **Key Personnel:** Larry Chaffin, Contact; Greta Chaffin, News Dir.; Micki Martin, Office Mgr. **Wattage:** 1000. **Ad Rates:** $4.10-5.68 for 30 seconds; $6.82-8.24 for 60 seconds. KDBM-FM.

EKALAKA†, pop. 620.

Carter Co. (SE). 190 m E of Billings. Hunting. Pine timber. Agriculture. Cattle and sheep. Wheat.

17884 Eagle
Eagle Publishing Co.
PO Box 66 Phone: (406)775-6245
Ekalaka, MT 59324 Fax: (406)775-8750

Newspaper. **Founded:** 1909. **Freq:** Weekly (Fri.). **Print Method:** Offset. **Cols./Page:** 8. **Col. Width:** 22 nonpareils. **Col. Depth:** 322 agate lines. **Key Personnel:** Tom C. Taylor, Editor and Publisher. **Subscription Rates:** $9. **Remarks:** Accepts advertising.
Ad Rates: GLR: $.16 **Circ:** 1,035

EUREKA, pop. 1,119.

Lincoln Co. (NW). 50 m NW of Whitefish. Logging; sawmills; machine parts manufactured. Cattle raising. Recreation, tourism.

17885 Tobacco Valley News
Ten Lakes Publishing
Box 307 Phone: (406)296-2514
Eureka, MT 59917 Fax: (406)296-2515
Publication E-mail: snewman@homer.libby.org

Community newspaper. **Founded:** 1960. **Freq:** Weekly (Thurs.). **Print Method:** Offset. **Cols./Page:** 6. **Col. Width:** 29 nonpareils. **Key Personnel:** Kris Berstrom-Kok and Mark Kok, Publisher. **Subscription Rates:** $15. **Remarks:** Accepts advertising.
Ad Rates: GLR: $.25 **Circ:** 2,200
SAU: $5.50
PCI: $3.85

FAIRFIELD, pop. 650.

Teton Co. (N). 30 m NW of Great Falls. Flour mills. Agriculture. Wheat, alfalfa, dairying, livestock.

17886 Fairfield Sun Times
Times Publishing LLC
PO Box 578 Phone: (406)467-2334
Fairfield, MT 59436 Fax: (406)467-3354

Community newspaper. **Founded:** 1957. **Freq:** Weekly (Thurs.). **Print Method:** Offset. Uses mats. **Cols./Page:** 6. **Col. Width:** 24 nonpareils. **Col. Depth:** 294 agate lines. **Key Personnel:** Mike Manuel, Editor and Publisher. **Subscription Rates:** $25 individuals; $27.50 out of county; $30 out of state. **Remarks:** Accepts advertising. **Formerly:** Fairfield Times (1992); Fairfield Times-Wheat Center News; Sun Times.
Ad Rates: BW: $389 **Circ:** Paid 1,150
PCI: $4.25 Free 20

FORSYTH†, pop. 2,553.

Rosebud Co. (C). Livestock.

17887 The Independent Enterprise
Montpress, Inc.
PO Box 106 Phone: (406)356-2149
Forsyth, MT 59327
Community newspaper. **Founded:** 1915. **Freq:** Weekly. **Print Method:** Offset. **Cols./Page:** 6. **Col. Width:** 2 1/16 inches. **Col. Depth:** 21 inches. **Key Personnel:** Patricia E. Corley, Editor. **USPS:** 205-560. **Subscription Rates:** $24 individuals; $26 out of area; $28 out of state. **Remarks:** Accepts advertising. **Formerly:** The Enterprise News (Sept. 1985); The Independent-Enterprise and Rosebud County Press.
Ad Rates: BW: $453.60 **Circ:** 1,900
SAU: $4.50

FORT BENTON†, pop. 1,693.

Chouteau Co. (N). On Missouri River at head of navigation, 40 m NE of Great Falls. Historical landmarks. Museum. Stock, wheat farms.

17888 The River Press
PO Box 69 Phone: (406)622-3311
Fort Benton, MT 59442-0069
Community newspaper. **Founded:** Oct. 27, 1880. **Freq:** Weekly (Wed.). **Print Method:** Offset. **Cols./Page:** 6. **Col. Width:** 12 picas. **Col. Depth:** 126 picas. **Key Personnel:** Curt Wall; Esther Tichenor, Editor. **USPS:** 466-740. **Subscription Rates:** $20 individuals; $25 out of state. **Remarks:** Accepts advertising.
Ad Rates: BW: $453.60 **Circ:** 2,052
SAU: $4.25
PCI: $4.50

GLASGOW†, pop. 4,455.

Valley Co. (NE). 45 m NW of Wolf Point. Residential.

17889 The Courier Express
341 3rd Ave. S. Phone: (406)228-9301
PO Box 151 Fax: (406)228-2665
Glasgow, MT 59230
Community newspaper. **Freq:** Monthly. **Cols./Page:** 5. **Col. Depth:** 13 inches. **Key Personnel:** Scott Ross, Editor; John Stanislaw, Publisher; Terry Trang, Advertising.
Ad Rates: BW: $338 **Circ:** Free ‡11,000
PCI: $5.75

17890 The Glasgow Courier
Box 151 Phone: (406)228-9301
Glasgow, MT 59230 Fax: (406)228-2665

Community newspaper. **Founded:** Jan. 6, 1913. **Freq:** Weekly (Thurs.). **Print Method:** Offset. **Trim Size:** 11 1/4 x 14. **Cols./Page:** 6. **Col. Width:** 24 nonpareils. **Col. Depth:** 294 agate lines. **Key Personnel:** Scott Ross, Editor; John Stanislaw, Publisher; Terry Trang, Advertising Mgr. **USPS:** 219-220. **Subscription Rates:** $33 in county. **Remarks:** Accepts advertising.
Ad Rates: GLR: $0.25 **Circ:** Paid ‡4,300
BW: $611.10
SAU: $5.25
PCI: $5.25

17891 KLTZ-AM - 1240
504 2nd Ave. S. Phone: (406)228-9336
PO Box 671 Fax: (406)228-9338
Glasgow, MT 59230

Format: Country; Agricultural. **Networks:** ABC. **Owner:** Glasgow Broadcasting Co., at above address. **Founded:** 1954. **Operating Hours:** Continuous. **Key Personnel:** Shirley Kirkland, Sales Mgr.; Stan Ozark, Sports/News Dir. **Local Programs:** *Progressive Producer*, Wes Allen. **Wattage:** 1000 day; 250 night. **Ad Rates:** $3.85-7.20 for 30 seconds.

GLENDIVE†, pop. 5,978.

Dawson Co. (NE). On Yellowstone River, head of navigation, 80 m NE of Miles City. Makoshika State Park. Dawson College. Coal mines, gas and oil wells. Stock, poultry, grain farms. Wheat, flax, oats.

17892 Ranger-Review
Livingston Enterprise
119 W. Bell St. Phone: (406)365-3303
PO Box 61 Fax: (406)365-5435
Glendive, MT 59330-1614
Community newspaper. **Founded:** 1881. **Freq:** Semiweekly (Sun. and Thurs.). **Print Method:** Offset. **Cols./Page:** 6. **Col. Width:** 26 nonpareils. **Col. Depth:** 301 agate lines. **Key Personnel:** Tana Reinhardt, Editor; Jerry Zander, Publisher. **Subscription Rates:** $30 carrier; $36 mail. **Remarks:** Color advertising accepted; rates available upon request.
Ad Rates: GLR: $.30 **Circ:** ‡4,400

17893 KGLE-AM - 590
Box 931 Phone: (406)377-3331
Glendive, MT 59330 Fax: (406)377-3332

Networks: Ambassador Inspirational Radio; Moody Broadcasting; SkyLight Satellite. **Owner:** Friends of Christian Radio, Inc., PO Box 1169, Glendive, MT 59330. **Founded:** 1962. **Operating Hours:** Continuous. **Key Personnel:** Jim McBride, Station Mgr.; Rod Mills, Sales Mgr.; Bill Lindsay, Music Dir. **Wattage:** 1000. **Ad Rates:** $2.50-3.25 for 30 seconds; $4.00-4.75 for 60 seconds.

17894 KXGN-TV - 5
210 S. Douglas Phone: (406)377-3377
Glendive, MT 59330 Fax: (406)365-2181

Format: Commercial TV. **Networks:** CBS; NBC. **Owner:** Glendive Broadcasting Corp., at above address. **Founded:** 1957. **Operating Hours:** 18 hrs. Daily; 94% network, 6% local. **Key Personnel:** Dan Frenzel, Contact; Ed Agre, News Dir.; Rosemary Bunting, Office Mgr. **Ad Rates:** $110 for 30 seconds.

GREAT FALLS†, pop. 56,725.

Cascade Co. (NC). 167 m NE of Butte. College of Great Falls. Malmstrom Air Force Base. State School for the Deaf & Blind. Manufactures flour, feed, furs, electric signs, concrete blocks, solar equipment, woolen goods. Meat packing plant. Oil refinery. Grain elevators. State fish hatchery.

17895 Great Falls Tribune
Gannett Co., Inc.
PO Box 5468 Phone: (406)791-1444
Great Falls, MT 59403 Fax: (406)791-1455
Free: (800)438-6600

General newspaper. **Founded:** 1885. **Freq:** Daily and Sunday (morn.). **Print Method:** Offset. **Col. Width:** 26 nonpareils. **Col. Depth:** 301 agate lines. **Key Personnel:** Jim Strauss, Editor; Pat Frantz, Publisher; Dave Gould, Advertising Dir. **Subscription Rates:** $174.20. **Remarks:** Advertising accepted; rates available upon request. Monday-Saturday: BW: $3,805.50; 4C: $4,275; SAU: $23.16; PCI: $3.95; Sunday: BW: $4,998.75; 4C: $5,468.75; SAU: $23.16; PCI: $4.40.
Circ: Mon.-Sat. ★**34,257**
Sun. ★**40,175**

17896 KFBB-TV - 5
Box 1139, Harve Hwy. Phone: (406)453-4377
Great Falls, MT 59403 Fax: (406)727-9703

Format: Commercial TV. **Networks:** ABC. **Founded:** 1954. **Operating Hours:** Continuous Sun. - Thur.; 6 a.m. to 2:05 a.m. Fri. & Sat. **ADI:** Great Falls, MT. **Key Personnel:** Jack May, General Mgr.

17897 KLFM-FM - 92.9
PO Box 3309 Phone: (406)761-7600
Great Falls, MT 59403 Fax: (406)761-5511

Format: Oldies; Classic Rock. **Owner:** Staradio Corp., at above address. **Operating Hours:** Continuous. **Key Personnel:** Jim Senst, VP/General Mgr.; Ryan Jordon, Corp. Communications; Dave Wilson, Operations Mgr.; Ron Korb, Sales Mgr. **Wattage:** 100,000. **Ad Rates:** $15.50 for 30 seconds; $21.75 for 60 seconds. **URL:** http://www.klfmfm.com.

17898 KMON-AM - 560
20 3rd St. N. Phone: (406)761-7600
Great Falls, MT 59401 Fax: (406)761-5511

Format: Country; Agricultural. **Networks:** ABC. **Owner:** Staradio Corp., at above address. **Founded:** 1948. **Operating Hours:** Continuous. **Key Personnel:** Jim Senst, VP/Operations Mgr.; Dave Wilson, Operations Mgr.; Ryan Jordan, Corp. Comp.; Ron korb, Sales Mgr. **Wattage:** 5000. **Ad Rates:** $15.50-25 for 30 seconds; $21.75-37.50 for 60 seconds. **URL:** http://www.kmon.com.

17899 KMON-FM - 94.5
PO Box 3309 Phone: (406)761-7600
Great Falls, MT 59403 Fax: (406)761-5511

Format: Country. **Owner:** Staradio Corp., at above address. **Founded:** 1972. **Operating Hours:** Continuous. **Key Personnel:** Jim Senst, VP/General Mgr.; Ryan Jordan, Corp. Communications; Dave Wilson, Operations Mgr.; Ron Korb, Sales Mgr. **Wattage:** 100,000. **Ad Rates:** $15.50 for 30 seconds; $21.75 for 60 seconds. **URL:** http://www.kmonfm.com.

17900 KRTV-TV - 3
PO Box 2989 Phone: (406)453-2431
Great Falls, MT 59403 Fax: (406)791-5479
E-mail: krtv@krtv.com

Format: Commercial TV. **Networks:** CBS. **Founded:** 1958. **Operating Hours:** 6 a.m.-1:05 a.m. **ADI:** Great Falls, MT. **Key Personnel:** Bill Preston, General Mgr., phone (406)791-5410, fax (406)791-5411, bpprezgm@krtv.com. **Ad Rates:** Advertising accepted; rates available upon request.

17901 KTGF-TV - 16
118 6th St. S., Box 1219 Phone: (406)761-8816
Great Falls, MT 59403 Fax: (406)454-3484

Format: Commercial TV. **Networks:** NBC. **Owner:** Continental Television Network, at above address. **Founded:** 1986. **Operating Hours:** Continuous. **ADI:** Great Falls, MT. **Key Personnel:** James M. Colla, President, fax (406)727-7134; Penny Adkins, Corporate V.P., fax (406)727-7134; Cheryl Cordeiro, General Mgr., fax (406)727-7134; Ted Harris, Operations Dir.; Tim Spinder, National/Regional Sales Mgr. **Wattage:** 2,650,000. **Ad Rates:** Advertising accepted; rates available upon request. **URL:** http://www.ktgf.com.

17902 TCI Cablevision of Great Falls, Inc.
Box 6410 Phone: (406)727-8881
Great Falls, MT 59406 Fax: (406)727-6433
Free: (800)824-1984

Founded: 1958. **Cities Served:** Cascade County, MT.

HAMILTON†, pop. 2,661.

Ravalli Co. (W). 48 m S of Missoula. Lumber mills; creameries. Pine timber. Diversified farming. Dairy products, livestock.

17903 Post Script
Ravalli Republic
232 Main St. Phone: (406)363-3300
Hamilton, MT 59840 Fax: (406)363-1767
Publication E-mail: ravalli@montananet.com

Shopping guide. **Freq:** Weekly (Wed.). **Print Method:** Offset. **Trim Size:** 13 x 21 1/2. **Cols./Page:** 6. **Col. Width:** 2 1/16 inches. **Col. Depth:** 301 agate lines. **Key Personnel:** Thaine Shetter, Publisher. **Subscription Rates:** Free. **Remarks:** Accepts advertising.
Ad Rates: BW: $1,449.39 **Circ:** Free ‡12,000
4C: $2,241.60
PCI: $11.24

17904 Ravalli Republic
232 Main St. Phone: (406)363-3300
Hamilton, MT 59840 Fax: (406)363-1767

General newspaper. **Founded:** 1889. **Freq:** Daily (morn.). **Print Method:** Offset. **Trim Size:** 13 x 21 1/2. **Cols./Page:** 6. **Col. Width:** 2 1/16 inches. **Col. Depth:** 301 agate lines. **Key Personnel:** Thaine Shetter, Publisher; Ruth Thorning, Editor. **USPS:** 145-080. **Subscription Rates:** $79 individuals; $88 out of area. **Remarks:** Accepts advertising.
Ad Rates: GLR: $.71 **Circ:** ‡5,285
BW: $1,100
4C: $1,550
PCI: $9.94

17905 KBMG-FM - 95.9
217 N. 3rd St., Ste. L Phone: (406)363-3010
Hamilton, MT 59840-2471 Fax: (406)363-6436
E-mail: klyq@montana.com

Networks: ABC. **Owner:** Marathon Media of Mountana, L.P., Box 660, Hamilton, MT 59840. **Founded:** 1968. **Formerly:** KLYQ-FM (1987). **Operating Hours:** Continuous. 10% network, 90% local. **Key Personnel:** Karen Feldner, Office Mgr.; Steve Fullerton, Contact; Mike Daniels, Chief Engineer; Donna Larson, Sales Mgr. **Wattage:** 85 effective 7/99. **Ad Rates:** $9-12 for 30 seconds; $13.50-18 for 60 seconds. Combined advertising rates available with KLYQ-AM. **URL:** http://www.magic96radio.com.

17906 KLYQ-AM - 1240
217 N. 3rd St., Ste. L Phone: (406)363-3010
Hamilton, MT 59840-2471 Fax: (406)363-6436
E-mail: klyq@montana.com

Format: Country. **Networks:** ABC. **Owner:** Marathon Media of Montana, L.P., Box 660, Hamilton, MT 59840. **Founded:** 1961. **Operating Hours:** Continuous.; 10% network, 90% local. **Key Personnel:** Karen Feldner, Office Mgr.; Steve Fullerton, Operations Mgr.; Don Davis, Program Dir.; Mike Daniels, Chief Engineer; Donna Larson, Sales Mgr. **Wattage:** 1000. **Ad Rates:** $9-12 for 30 seconds; $13.50-18 for 60 seconds. Combined advertising rates available with KBMG-FM. **URL:** http://www.klyq.com.

HARDIN†, pop. 3,300.

Big Horn Co. (S). 50 m E of Billings. Coal mining; gas wells. Ships cattle. Diversified farming. Wheat, sugar beets, alfalfa.

17907 Big Horn County News
204 N. Center Ave. Phone: (406)665-1008
Hardin, MT 59034-1533 Fax: (406)665-1012
Free: (800)735-8736
Publisher E-mail: bhcn@wtp.net

Community newspaper. **Founded:** 1908. **Freq:** Weekly (Wed.). **Print Method:** Offset. **Cols./Page:** 6. **Col. Width:** 26 nonpareils. **Col. Depth:** 294 agate lines. **Key Personnel:** James Moore II, Owner. **Subscription Rates:** $25 in county; $34 out of county. **Formerly:** Hardin Tribune; Hardin Tribune Herald.
Ad Rates: BW: $378 **Circ:** ‡3,550
PCI: $10.50

HARLOWTON†, pop. 1,181.

Wheatland Co. (C). 93 m NW of Billings. Cattle and sheep ranches. Agriculture. Wheat, hay, barley. Lake resort areas.

17908 Times-Clarion
111 S. Central Phone: (406)632-5633
PO Box 307 Fax: (406)632-5644
Harlowton, MT 59036-0307
Free: (877)801-1397
Publication E-mail: hartimclar@mcn.net

Community newspaper. **Founded:** 1917. **Freq:** Weekly (Thurs.). **Print Method:** Offset. **Trim Size:** 13 3/8 x 22 1/2. **Cols./Page:** 6. **Col. Width:** 12.5 picas. **Col. Depth:** 21 inches. **Key Personnel:** Gerald H. Miller, Editor and Publisher; Audrey J. Miller, Publisher; Audrey Miller, Advertising Mgr. **ISSN:** 0889-5627. **Subscription Rates:** $23 individuals; $26 out of area.
Ad Rates: GLR: $.214 **Circ:** ‡1,675
BW: $300
SAU: $3

17909 Cable TV of Harlo Corp.
11 Fifth St. NE Phone: (406)632-4300
PO Box 242
Harlowton, MT 59036-0242

Owner: Marla & Donald De Shaw, at above address. **Founded:** 1980. **Key Personnel:** Marla L. DeShaw, Contact. **Cities Served:** Harlowton, MT: subscribing households 400; 35 channels; 1 community access channel.

17910 Ryegate Cable TV
11 Fifth St. NE Phone: (406)632-4300
Box 242
Harlowton, MT 59036-0242

Owner: Donald and Marla Shaw, at above address. **Founded:** June 1, 1983. **Key Personnel:** Donald L. Deshaw, Owner; Marla DeShaw, Owner. **Cities Served:** Ryegate, MT: subscribing households 50; 15 channels.

HAVRE†.

Hill Co. (NC). 20 m E of Fresno.

17911 Havre Daily News
PO Box 431 Phone: (406)265-6796
Havre, MT 59501 Fax: (406)265-6798
Publisher E-mail: havredailynews.com

Daily newspaper. **Founded:** 1914. **Freq:** Daily (eve.). **Print Method:** Offset. **Trim Size:** 22 3/4 x 14. **Cols./Page:** 6. **Col. Width:** 2 1/16 inches. **Col. Depth:** 21 1/2 inches. **Key Personnel:** Bouts Gifford, Managing Editor, phone (406)265-6795, bfifford@havredailynews.com; Bart Leath, Publisher, phone (406)265-6795, bleath@havredailnews.com. **ISSN:** 0745-7782. **Subscription Rates:** $108 individuals; $120 by mail and motor routes; $132 by mail in county; $144 out of area; $156 out of state.
Ad Rates: SAU: $6.60 **Circ:** Paid ⊕**4,348**
PCI: $6.60

17912 KOJM-AM - 610
Wildhorse Rd. Phone: (406)265-7841
Box 7000 Fax: (406)265-8855
Havre, MT 59501
E-mail: nmb@nmbi.com

Format: Adult Contemporary. **Networks:** ABC. **Founded:** 1947. **Operating Hours:** 5 a.m.-midnight, Mon.-Fri.; 6a.m.-midnight, Sat.-Sun. **Key Personnel:** David Leeds, Contact; John Mosher, Contact. **Local Programs:** *Montana at Noon*; *Outlook*; *Tradio*. **Wattage:** 1000. **Ad Rates:** Combined advertising rates available with KPQX-FM, KRYK-FM.

17913 KXEI-FM - 95.1
315 1st St. Phone: (406)265-5845
PO Box 2426 Fax: (406)265-8860
Havre, MT 59501-3505

Format: Religious. **Networks:** Moody Broadcasting; SkyLight

Satellite. **Founded:** 1983. **Operating Hours:** Continuous; 50% network, 50% local. **Key Personnel:** Edward Matter, General Mgr.; Paul Rangen, Contact. **Wattage:** 100,000. **Ad Rates:** Noncommercial.

17914 Triangle Communication System, Inc.
PO Box 1140 Phone: (406)265-7807
Havre, MT 59501 Fax: (406)265-7801
Free: (800)332-1201

Owner: Triangle Communication System, at above address. **Founded:** 1982. **Key Personnel:** Burl Miner, General Mgr. **Cities Served:** Big Sandy, MT: subscribing households 168; 19 channels.

HELENA†, pop. 23,938.

Lewis and Clark Co. (WC). The State Capital. 60 m NE of Butte, and midway between Glacier and Yellowstone National Parks. Carroll College. Lime and concrete, paints, machine parts, ceramics manufactured. Trade center. Gold mines. Cattle and sheep. Diversified farming. Hay, grain, potatoes. Resort.

17915 The Adit
1003 11th Ave. Phone: (406)443-3690
PO Box 1244 Fax: (406)449-8170
Helena, MT 59624
Publication E-mail: adit@centric.net

Shopper (tabloid). **Founded:** 1974. **Freq:** Weekly (Wed.). **Print Method:** Offset. **Cols./Page:** 7. **Col. Width:** 16 nonpareils. **Col. Depth:** 224 agate lines. **Key Personnel:** Jim Knight, General Mgr. **Subscription Rates:** Free. **Remarks:** Accepts advertising. **URL:** http://www.adit.com.
Ad Rates: BW: $834.40 **Circ:** Free ‡25,000
4C: $1,009.40
PCI: $7.45

17916 AERO Sun-Times
Aero Sun Times
25 S. Ewing St., No. 214 Phone: (406)443-7272
Helena, MT 59601-5732 Fax: (406)442-9120
Publication E-mail: aero@desktop.org

Magazine covering resource conservation, sustainable agriculture, smart community growth, and local food systems. **Founded:** 1974. **Freq:** Quarterly. **Print Method:** Tabloid-newsprint. **Trim Size:** 8 1/2 x 11. **Key Personnel:** Jennifer Friedhoff, Office Mgr. **ISSN:** 1046-0993. **Subscription Rates:** $15; $3 single issue.
Circ: Paid 630
Controlled 50

17917 Independent Record
PO Box 4249 Phone: (406)442-7190
317 Cruse Ave.
Helena, MT 59601-5003
General newspaper. **Founded:** 1866. **Freq:** Mon.-Sun. (morn.). **Print Method:** Offset. **Cols./Page:** 8. **Col. Width:** 18 nonpareils. **Col. Depth:** 301 agate lines. **Key Personnel:** Charles Wood, Editor; James D. Crane, Publisher. **Subscription Rates:** $110. **Remarks:** Accepts advertising.
Ad Rates: PCI: $9.94 **Circ:** Mon.-Sat. ★**13,520**
Sun. ★**14,321**

17918 Montana
Montana Historical Society
PO Box 201201 Phone: (406)444-4708
Helena, MT 59620-1201 Fax: (406)444-2696
Free: (800)243-9900
Publisher E-mail: mhspub@aol.com

History magazine. **Subtitle:** The Magazine of Western History. **Founded:** 1951. **Freq:** Quarterly. **Print Method:** Offset. **Trim Size:** 7 3/4 x 10 3/4. **Cols./Page:** 2. **Col. Width:** 36 nonpareils. **Col. Depth:** 126 agate lines. **Key Personnel:** Charles E. Rankin, Editor, rankinmhs@aol.com; Tammy L. Ryan, Business Mgr., tryanmhs@aol.com. **USPS:** 594-320. **Subscription Rates:** $24 individuals; $6.50 single issue; $45 two years. **Remarks:** Accepts advertising. **URL:** http://www.his.mt.gov. **Alt. Formats:** Audio tape; Microfiche.
Ad Rates: BW: $800 **Circ:** ‡10,000
4C: $1,750

17919 The Montana Catholic
Roman Catholic Diocese of Helena
515 N. Ewing Phone: (406)442-5820
PO Box 1729 Fax: (406)442-5191
Helena, MT 59624-1729
Catholic magazine (tabloid). **Founded:** 1932. **Freq:** 16/year. **Print Method:** Offset. **Trim Size:** 11 1/2 x 13 1/4. **Cols./Page:** 4. **Col. Width:** 14 1/2 picas. **Col. Depth:** 12 inches. **Key Personnel:** Gerald M. Korson, Editor; Most Rev. Alexander J. Brunett, Publisher. **ISSN:** 0883-7899. **Subscription Rates:** $13.50; $18 out of state; $28 other countries. **Remarks:** Advertising not accepted for alcoholic beverages, tobacco products, and political causes. **Formerly:** WestMont Word (1984).
Ad Rates: BW: $480 **Circ:** ‡9,400
PCI: $10

17920 The Montana Food Distributor
Montana Food Distributors Association
2697 Airport Way Phone: (406)449-6394
PO Box 5775 Fax: (406)449-0647
Helena, MT 59604
Subtitle: The Magazine for Montana's Food Stores. **Founded:** July 1945. **Freq:** Monthly. **Print Method:** Offset. **Trim Size:** 8 1/2 x 11. **Cols./Page:** 2. **Col. Width:** 3 7/16 inches. **Col. Depth:** 9 1/2 inches. **Key Personnel:** Tracy Velazquez, Editor, tvelazquez@desktop.org. **Subscription Rates:** $10; $1 single issue. **Remarks:** Accepts advertising.
Ad Rates: BW: $285 **Circ:** Paid ‡1,000
4C: $585 Non-paid ‡100

17921 Montana Magazine
PO Box 5630 Phone: (406)443-2842
Helena, MT 59604 Fax: (406)443-5480
Free: (800)654-1105

Regional interest magazine. **Founded:** May 1, 1970. **Freq:** Bimonthly. **Print Method:** Web offset. **Trim Size:** 8 x 10 7/8. **Cols./Page:** 3. **Col. Width:** 13 picas. **Col. Depth:** 135 agate lines. **Key Personnel:** Beverly R. Magley, Editor, editor@montanamagazine.com; Brad Hurd, Publisher, bhurd@montanamagazine.com; Larry Sem, Advertising Dir., ads@montanamagazine.com; James J. Coggeshall, Circulation Dir., circulate@montanamagazine.com. **ISSN:** 0274-9955. **Subscription Rates:** $23; $3.95 single issue. **Remarks:** Accepts advertising.
Ad Rates: BW: $1,295 **Circ:** ‡40,000
4C: $1,850

17922 The Montana Stockgrower
Montana Stockgrowers Association, Inc.
PO Box 1679 Phone: (406)442-3420
Helena, MT 59624 Fax: (406)458-5105
Publisher E-mail: msgahelena@aol.com

Newsletter on Montana's beef cattle industry. **Founded:** 1989. **Freq:** Weekly. **Print Method:** Offset. **Trim Size:** 8 1/2 x 11. **Cols./Page:** 3 and 2. **Col. Width:** 28 and 42 nonpareils. **Col. Depth:** 140 agate lines. **Key Personnel:** Beth Almond, Editor, ealmond@aol.com. **ISSN:** 0047-7990. **Subscription Rates:** Included with membership dues.
Ad Rates: BW: $250 **Circ:** ‡3,500
PCI: $30

17923 Trial Trends
Montana Trial Lawyers Associations
PO Box 838 Phone: (406)443-3124
Helena, MT 59624 Fax: (406)449-6943
Publisher E-mail: mtla@mt.net

Trade magazine covering law for the Montana Trial Lawyers Association. **Key Personnel:** Al Smith, Exec. Editor. **Subscription Rates:** Free to qualified subscribers. **Remarks:** Accepts advertising. **URL:** http://www.monttla.com.
Circ: (Not Reported)

17924 U.S. Toy Collector Magazine
PO Box 172
Helena, MT 59624-0172

Magazine exploring the world of antique and collectible toy vehicles, with the exception of toy trains. **Founded:** 1985. **Freq:** Monthly. **Print Method:** Web offset. **Trim Size:** 8 1/2 x 10 3/4. **Cols./Page:** 3. **Key Personnel:** Gordon Rice, Publisher. **ISSN:** 1044-1344. **Subscription Rates:** $21.
Ad Rates: 4C: $500 **Circ:** 2,800

17925 KBLL-AM - 1240
1400 11th Ave. Phone: (406)442-6620
Helena, MT 59601 Fax: (406)442-6161

Format: News; Talk. **Networks:** ABC; NBC; Westwood One Radio. **Founded:** 1937. **Formerly:** KPFA-AM; KXLJ-AM. **Operating Hours:** Continuous; 85% network, 15% local. **ADI:** Helena, MT. **Key Personnel:** Mike Kandilas, Program Dir.; Jay Scott, News Dir.; Jim Schaeffer, General Mgr. **Wattage:** 1000. **Ad Rates:** $6-8.50 for 30 seconds; $7.50-10 for 60 seconds.

17926 KBLL-FM - 99.5
1400 11th Ave. Phone: (406)442-6620
Helena, MT 59601 Fax: (406)442-6161

Format: Country. **Networks:** ABC. **Founded:** 1979. **Operating Hours:** Continuous; 10% network; 90% local. **ADI:** Helena, MT. **Key Personnel:** Jay Scott, News Dir.; Mike Kandilas, Program Dir.; Jim Schaeffer, General Mgr. **Wattage:** 30,000. **Ad Rates:** $6-8.50 for 30 seconds; $9-12.50 for 60 seconds.

17927 KCAP-AM - 1340
110 Broadway Phone: (406)442-4490
Helena, MT 59601-4232 Fax: (406)442-7356

Format: Talk; Sports; News. **Networks:** CBS. **Founded:** 1949. **Operating Hours:** Continuous. **ADI:** Helena, MT. **Key Personnel:** Jim Willard, General Mgr. **Wattage:** 1000.

17928 KHKR-AM - 680
Box 4111 Phone: (406)443-5237
Helena, MT 59604 Fax: (406)449-3553

Format: News; Talk. **Networks:** AP; UPI; People's Network. **Founded:** 1988. **Formerly:** KHKR-AM (1991); KVCM-AM (1994). **Operating Hours:** 6 a.m.- midnight. **ADI:** Helena, MT. **Key Personnel:** Roger Lonnquist, General Mgr. **Wattage:** 1000. **Ad Rates:** $3 for 30 seconds.

17929 KHKR-FM - 104.1
Box 4111 Phone: (406)449-4251
Helena, MT 59604 Fax: (406)443-7577

Format: Contemporary Country. **Owner:** Staradio Corp., at above address. **Founded:** 1988. **Operating Hours:** Continuous. **ADI:** Helena, MT. **Key Personnel:** Dewey Bruce, General Mgr. **Wattage:** 3000. **Ad Rates:** $6-7.50 for 30 seconds; $8.50-10 for 60 seconds.

17930 KMTX-FM - 105.3
Box 1183-59624 Phone: (406)442-0400
Helena, MT 59624 Fax: (406)449-7602

Format: Adult Contemporary. **Networks:** Satellite Music Network. **Founded:** 1985. **Operating Hours:** Continuous. **ADI:** Helena, MT. **Key Personnel:** Dean P. Williams, General Mgr. **Wattage:** 95,000 ERP.

17931 KTVH-TV - 12
2433 N. Montana Ave. (59601) Phone: (406)443-5050
PO Box 6125 Fax: (406)442-5106
Helena, MT 59604

Format: Commercial TV. **Networks:** NBC. **Owner:** Big Sky Broadcasting, 2433 N. Montana Ave, Helena, MT 59604. **Founded:** 1959. **Operating Hours:** Continuous. **ADI:** Helena, MT. **Key Personnel:** John Radeck, Contact; Bill Stebbins, General Sales Mgr.; Janice Radeck, Program Dir. **Wattage:** 120,000. **Ad Rates:** $20-350 for 30 seconds.

17932 KZMT-FM - 101.1
110 E. Broadway St. Phone: (406)442-4490
Helena, MT 59601-4232 Fax: (406)442-7356

Format: Adult Contemporary; Classic Rock. **Networks:** CBS. **Owner:** 1-on-1 Sports Holdings, Inc., at above address. **Founded:** 1975. **Formerly:** KCAP-FM. **Operating Hours:** Continuous. **ADI:** Helena, MT. **Key Personnel:** Jim Willard, General Mgr.; Steve Blair, Contact. **Wattage:** 100,000.

17933 TCI Cablevision of Montana
Box 5509 Phone: (406)443-3401
Helena, MT 59604-5509 Fax: (406)443-5843
Free: (800)777-7818

Founded: 1955. **Cities Served:** Lewis and Clark County and East Helena, MT.

HUNTLEY

17934 Yellowstone County News, Inc.
Yellowstone County Publishing
748 Railroad Hwy. Phone: (406)348-2649
Huntley, MT 59037 Fax: (406)348-2650
Publication E-mail: ycnmont@aol.com
Publisher E-mail: ycnmont@nemontel.net

Community newspaper. **Subtitle:** Serving Montana Communities of Shepherd, Huntley, Worden, Ballantine, Pompey's Pillar, Custer and Billings. **Founded:** 1977. **Freq:** Weekly (Thurs.). **Print Method:** Offset. **Trim Size:** 10 x 16. **Cols./Page:** 5. **Col. Width:** 2 inches. **Col. Depth:** 16 inches. **Key Personnel:** Randal Robison, Publisher; Rebecca Tescher Robison, Publisher. **Subscription Rates:** $22. **Remarks:** Accepts advertising.
Ad Rates: GLR: $5.50 **Circ:** ‡3,500
BW: $400
4C: $720
PCI: $5

HUSON

17935 Bonsai Journal
American Bonsai Society, Inc.
PO Box 460328 Phone: (406)626-4176
Huson, MT 59846 Fax: (406)626-1971
Publication E-mail: jillhamerica online, inc.com

Trade journal covering bonsai. **Founded:** 1966. **Freq:** Quar-

terly. **Trim Size:** 8 x 11. **Key Personnel:** Jill Hurd, Editor; Pat DeGroot, Exec. Secretary/Circulation. **Subscription Rates:** $24 individuals; $35 Canada and Mexico; $44 other countries; $6.50 single issue. **Remarks:** Accepts advertising.
Circ: Paid 1,450

KALISPELL†, pop. 10,648.

Flathead Co. (NW). On Flathead River, 30 m W of Glacier National Park, 10 m N of Flathead Lake. Resort area. Lumber and Planning mills; aluminum plant; pulpwood products factory. Trade center. Pine, fir timber. Agriculture. Cherry orchards, wheat, oats, rye. Christmas trees.

17936 The Daily Inter Lake
Inter Lake Publishing Co.
727 E. Idaho Phone: (406)755-7000
PO Box 7610 Fax: (406)752-6114
Kalispell, MT 59904
General newspaper. **Founded:** 1891. **Freq:** Daily (eve.), Sunday (morn.). **Print Method:** Offset. **Cols./Page:** 6. **Col. Width:** 25 nonpareils. **Col. Depth:** 21 inches. **Key Personnel:** Dan Black, Managing Editor; Ron Peterson, Publisher. **Subscription Rates:** $120. **Remarks:** Accepts advertising.
Ad Rates: GLR: $13 **Circ:** Mon.-Fri. 15,600
BW: $1,638 Sun. 18,300
4C: $2,028
SAU: $9.75

17937 KAJ-TV - 18
c/o KPAX-TV Phone: (406)756-5888
2204 Regent St., Box 4827 Fax: (406)756-5889
Missoula, MT 59801

Format: Commercial TV. **Simulcasts:** KPAX-TV. **Networks:** CBS. **Owner:** KPAX Communications, Inc., at above address. **Founded:** 1988. **Operating Hours:** Continuous. **ADI:** Missoula, MT. **Key Personnel:** Bob Hermes, General Mgr.; Tammy Engle, Operations Dir.; Paul Shoemaker, News Dir.; Shane Edinger, Sports Dir.; Dave McLean, Production Dir.; Joanne Stern, Bureau Mgr. **Ad Rates:** KPAX-TV. **URL:** http://www.kpax.com.

17938 KALS-FM - 97.1
PO Box 9710 Phone: (406)752-5257
Kalispell, MT 59904-2710 Fax: (406)752-3416

Format: News; Sports; Religious; Classical; Easy Listening. **Networks:** USA Radio. **Owner:** North Valley Broadcasters, at above address. **Founded:** 1974. **Operating Hours:** 5:30 a.m.-midnight; 10% network, 90% local. **ADI:** Butte, MT. **Key Personnel:** Brad Rauch, General Mgr.; Rene Morand, Sales Mgr.; David Brown, Program Dir.; Morris Hoffman, Sports Dir.; Linda Wagoner, Traffic Dir. **Wattage:** 27,000. **Ad Rates:** $4.40-6 for 30 seconds; $7.10-9.60 for 60 seconds.

17939 KCFW-TV - 9
PO Box 857, 401 1st Ave. E. Phone: (406)755-5239
Kalispell, MT 59901 Fax: (406)752-8002

Format: Commercial TV. **Networks:** NBC. **Owner:** Eagle Communications, 340 W. Main, Missoula, MT 59801, (406)721-2063. **Founded:** 1968. **Operating Hours:** Continuous. **ADI:** Missoula, MT. **Key Personnel:** Robert Precht, President; Steve Fetveit, Contact.

17940 KGEZ-AM - 600
PO Box 169 Phone: (406)752-2600
Kalispell, MT 59903-0169 Fax: (406)257-0459
E-mail: kgez@digisys.net

Format: Oldies. **Networks:** CBS. **Owner:** Skyline Broadcasting, Inc., PO Box 169, Kalispell, MT 59903. **Founded:** 1927. **Operating Hours:** Continuous. **Key Personnel:** Kelly Hartman, News Dir.; Brenda Lynch, Office Mgr.; Kim Milliron, Traffic Mgr.; Steve Breeze, Sales Mgr. **Local Programs:** *Big Band Cavalcade* 3 p.m.-5 p.m. Sunday, Mike Stocklin; *Mellow Jazz* 5 p.m.-6 p.m. Sunday, Mike Stocklin. **Wattage:** 5000 day; 1000 night. **Ad Rates:** $5-9 for 30 seconds; $9-15 for 60 seconds.

17941 KOFI-AM - 1180
317 1st Ave. E. Phone: (406)755-6690
Box 608
Kalispell, MT 59901
E-mail: kofi@kofiradio.com

Format: Full Service; Oldies. **Networks:** Mutual Broadcasting System. **Owner:** Jerry Adams, at above address. **Founded:** 1955. **Operating Hours:** Continuous; 30% network, 70% local. **Key Personnel:** Dave Rae, General Mgr.; Linda Stevens, Office Mgr.; Mike Holton, Operations Mgr. **Wattage:** 50,000. **Ad Rates:** $11.65-14.25 for 30 seconds; $14.90-18.05 for 60 seconds. $11.10-$12.85 for 30 seconds; $14.35-$16.35 for 60 seconds. Combined advertising rates available with KOFI-FM. **URL:** http://www.kofiradio.com.

17942 KOFI-FM - 103.9
317 1st Ave. E. Phone: (406)755-6690
PO Box 608
Kalispell, MT 59901
E-mail: kofl@kofiradio.com

Format: Contemporary Country. **Networks:** Satellite Music Network. **Owner:** at above address. **Founded:** 1988. **Operating Hours:** Continuous; 100% local. **Key Personnel:** Dave Rae, General/Sales Mgr.; Dave Rae, Promotions Dir.; Scott Davis, Operations Mgr. **Wattage:** 100,000. **Ad Rates:** $11.65-14.25 for 30 seconds; $14.90-18.05 for 60 seconds. $11.10-$12.85 for 30 seconds; $14.35-$16.35 for 60 seconds. Combined advertising rates available with KOFI-AM. **URL:** http://www.kofiradio.com.

LAKESIDE

17943 The Montana Masonic News
Grand Lodge of Montana
Box 362 Phone: (406)442-9638
Lakeside, MT 59922
Masonic publication. **Founded:** 1947. **Freq:** Bimonthly. **Print Method:** Offset. **Cols./Page:** 4. **Col. Width:** 26 nonpareils. **Col. Depth:** 203 agate lines. **Key Personnel:** Wm. M. Brass, Editor.

LAUREL†, pop. 5,481.

Yellowstone Co. (SC). 20m SW of Billings. Residential.

17944 Laurel Outlook
Outlook Publishing, Inc.
Box 278 Phone: (406)628-4412
Laurel, MT 59044
Community newspaper. **Founded:** 1908. **Freq:** Weekly (Wed.). **Print Method:** Offset. **Cols./Page:** 6. **Col. Width:** 12 picas. **Col. Depth:** 21 1/2 inches. **Key Personnel:** Milton E. Wester, Publisher; Gloria D. Wester, Publisher. **Subscription Rates:** $22 individuals in city; $24 out of state in county; $27 out of area. **Remarks:** Accepts advertising.
Ad Rates: GLR: $.39 **Circ:** Paid ‡3,580
BW: $686.76 Free ‡46
4C: $886.70
SAU: $5.45
PCI: $5.45

17945 KBSR-AM - 1490
PO Box 248 Phone: (406)628-8271
Laurel, MT 59044-0216 Fax: (406)665-2131

Format: Talk; News. **Networks:** People's Network. **Owner:** Big Sky Radio, Rt. 1, Hardin, MT 59034. **Founded:** 1979. **Operating Hours:** Continuous. **Key Personnel:** Rich Solberg, President/Gen. Mgr.; Kim Armstrong, Production Mgr.; David Berg, Commercial Talent Sales. **Wattage:** 1000.

LEWISTOWN†, pop. 7,104.

Fergus Co. (C). 107 m SE of Great Falls. Lumber mills. Gold mines. Stockyards. Stock, grain farms. Sheep, cattle, wheat.

17946 Lewistown News-Argus
521 W. Main St. Phone: (406)538-3401
PO Box 900 Fax: (406)538-3405
Lewistown, MT 59457-0900
Free: (800)879-5627
Publisher E-mail: newsargus@lewistownnews.com

Community newspaper. **Founded:** Aug. 1, 1885. **Freq:** Semi-weekly (Wed. and Sun.). **Print Method:** Offset. **Cols./Page:** 6. **Col. Width:** 12 1/2 picas. **Col. Depth:** 21 inches. **Key Personnel:** Dave Byerly, Publisher, davebyerly@lewistownnews.com. **Subscription Rates:** $57.37 out of state. **Remarks:** Accepts advertising.
Ad Rates: GLR: $.58 **Circ:** ‡4,874
BW: $795.06
SAU: $7.17

17947 KLCM-FM - 95.9
PO Box 620 Main St., NE Phone: (406)538-3495
Lewistown, MT 59457 Fax: (406)538-3495
E-mail: kxlo@lewistown.net

Format: Adult Contemporary. **Networks:** ABC; Westwood One Radio. **Owner:** Montana Broadcast Communications Inc., at above address. **Founded:** 1975. **Operating Hours:** 5:50 a.m.-10:05 p.m.; 90% local. **ADI:** Great Falls, MT. **Key Personnel:** Joe Zahler, Operations Mgr./News Dir. **Wattage:** 3000.

17948 KXLO-AM - 1230
PO Box 620 Main St., NE Phone: (406)538-3441
Lewistown, MT 59457 Fax: (406)538-3495
E-mail: kxlo@lewistown.net

Format: Country; Full Service. **Networks:** ABC. **Owner:** KXLO Broadcast Inc., at above address. **Founded:** 1947. **Operating Hours:** 5:58 a.m.-10:06 p.m.; 30 network, 70 local. **ADI:** Great Falls, MT. **Key Personnel:** Joe Zahler, Operations Mgr.; Fred Lark, Promotions Dir. **Wattage:** 1000.

LIBBY†, pop. 2,748.

Lincoln Co. (NW). 215 m NW of Missoula. Heritage museum. Hiking, skiing, fishing and hunting. Manufactures lumber and vermiculite. Lead, silver, gold, mines; pine, fir, larch timber.

17949 Western News
311 California Ave. Phone: (406)293-4124
PO Box 1377 Fax: (406)293-7187
Libby, MT 59923-1377
Community newspaper. **Founded:** 1900. **Freq:** Weekly (Wed.). **Print Method:** Offset. **Cols./Page:** 8. **Col. Width:** 21 nonpareils. **Col. Depth:** 127 agate lines. **Key Personnel:** June McMahon, Editor; Mark McMahon, Publisher; Lee Bothman, Advertising Mgr. **Subscription Rates:** $10. **Remarks:** Accepts advertising.
Ad Rates: GLR: $.28 **Circ:** 4,550

17950 KLCB-AM - 1230
Box 730 Phone: (406)293-6234
Libby, MT 59923

Format: Country. **Networks:** ABC. **Owner:** Lincoln County Broadcasters, Inc., 251 W. Cedar St., Libby, MT 59923. **Founded:** 1950. **Operating Hours:** 6 a.m.-10 p.m. **ADI:** Spokane, WA. **Key Personnel:** Duane J. Williams, Vice President. **Wattage:** 1000. **Ad Rates:** Advertising accepted; rates available upon request.

17951 Kootenai Cable Inc.
Box 1378 Phone: (406)293-8788
Libby, MT 59923 Fax: (406)293-3630
Free: (800)626-6299

Founded: 1980. **Formerly**: Alaska Cablevision. **Key Personnel:** Marilyn Bowden, Office Mgr.; Michael Miller, General Mgr. **Cities Served:** Bonners Ferry, ID; Libby, Troy, MT: subscribing households 3,560; 37 channels; 2 community access channels; 15 hours per week community access programming.

17952 KTNY-FM - 101.7
Cedar & S. Main Phone: (406)293-6234
Libby, MT 59923 Fax: (406)293-6235

Format: Easy Listening; Adult Contemporary. **Networks:** ABC. **Owner:** Lincoln County Broadcasters, Inc., 251 W. Cedar St., Libby, MT 59923. **Founded:** 1986. **Operating Hours:** 6 a.m.-10 p.m. **ADI:** Spokane, WA. **Key Personnel:** Duane J. Williams, Owner/VP. **Wattage:** 3000. **Ad Rates:** Advertising accepted; rates available upon request.

LIVINGSTON†, pop. 6,994.

Park Co. (S). On Yellowstone River, 100 m W of Billings. Lumbering, marble and granite works; feed and flour mill. Travertine. Dairy, stock, grain farms. Cattle, sheep, wheat. Tourist center.

17953 Livingston Enterprise
PO Box 665 Phone: (406)222-2000
Livingston, MT 59047 Fax: (406)222-8580
Free: (800)345-8412
Publisher E-mail: enterprise@ycsi.net

General newspaper. **Founded:** June 4, 1883. **Freq:** Daily (eve.). **Print Method:** Offset. **Trim Size:** 14 x 23 3/4. **Cols./Page:** 6. **Col. Width:** 24 nonpareils. **Col. Depth:** 301 agate lines. **Key Personnel:** John Sullivan, Editor and Publisher; James Durfey, Advertising Mgr.; Stephen Matlow, Managing Editor. **Subscription Rates:** $102.60 individuals. **Remarks:** Accepts advertising. **Alt. Formats:** Mailing labels.
Ad Rates: BW: $561.15 **Circ:** ‡3,600
4C: $611.15
SAU: $4.95
PCI: $4.35

17954 KPRK-AM - 1340
Box 691 Phone: (406)222-2841
Livingston, MT 59047 Fax: (406)222-1341

Format: Contemporary Country. **Networks:** ABC. **Owner:** Livingston Broadcasting, Inc., at above address. **Founded:** 1947. **Operating Hours:** 5:30 a.m.-12:01 a.m. **ADI:** Billings-Hardin, MT. **Key Personnel:** Jann Holter Berntsen, President/General Manager; Scott Drain, News Dir.; Jonny Vee, Sports and Program; Jay Rigler, Music Dir. **Local Programs:** *Local News*, Dean Holmes; *Park County Sports*, Jonny Vee; *Saturday Night Rock'n Roldies!*. **Wattage:** 1000. **Ad Rates:** Advertising accepted; rates available upon request.

MALTA†, pop. 2,367.

Phillips Co. (N). 170 m NE of Great Falls. Gas wells. Cattle, sheep, dairy, grain farms. Alfalfa seed.

17955 The Phillips County News
Phillips County News
Box 850 Phone: (406)654-2020
Malta, MT 59538-0850 Fax: (406)654-1410

Local interest newspaper. **Founded:** 1924. **Freq:** Weekly (Wed.). **Print Method:** Offset. **Cols./Page:** 6. **Col. Width:** 25 nonpareils. **Col. Depth:** 301 agate lines. **Key Personnel:** Curtis Starr, Publisher. **USPS:** 430-320. **Subscription Rates:** $20. **Remarks:** Advertising not accepted for alcoholic beverages and tobacco products.
Ad Rates: GLR: $28 **Circ:** ‡2,925
BW: $485
SAU: $3.85
PCI: $3.70

17956 KMMR-FM - 100.1
155 1/2 S. 1st Ave. Phone: (406)645-2472
PO Box 1073 Fax: (406)654-2506
Malta, MT 59538

Format: Middle-of-the-Road (MOR). **Networks:** ABC; Northern Agricultural. **Owner:** Greg Kielb, at above address, (406)654-2634. **Founded:** 1980. **Operating Hours:** 6 a.m.-midnight Mon.-Sat.; 7 a.m.-midnight Sun. **Key Personnel:** Claudette Kielb, Contact; Greg Kielb, News Dir.; Sonia Young, Music Dir. **Local Programs:** *What's Happening*, Greg Kielb. **Wattage:** 3000. **Ad Rates:** $5.00-7.00 for 30 seconds; $7.00-9.00 for 60 seconds.

MELSTONE

17957 Mel-View Cable TV
Box 252 Phone: (406)358-2200
Melstone, MT 59054 Fax: (406)358-2394

Owner: John Balock, at above address. **Founded:** 1981. **Key Personnel:** John Balock, General Mgr. **Cities Served:** Melstone, MT: subscribing households 41; 20 channels.

MILES CITY†, pop. 9,602.

Custer Co. (SE). On Yellowstone River, 152 m E of Billings. U.S. Livestock Range Experiment Station, 57,000 acres. Shipping and trade center of the horse, cattle, wool district of Eastern Montana. Manufactures saddles, harnesses, creamery products, flour. Gas wells. Agriculture. Sugar beets, alfalfa, wheat, corn.

17958 Miles City Star
Star Printing & Supply Co.
13 N. 6th St. Phone: (406)232-0450
Box 1216 Fax: (406)232-6687
Miles City, MT 59301-3101
Free: (800)323-6565

General newspaper. **Founded:** 1911. **Freq:** Daily (eve.). **Print Method:** Offset. **Cols./Page:** 6. **Col. Width:** 25 nonpareils. **Col. Depth:** 301 agate lines. **Key Personnel:** Gerald Anglum, Editor. **Remarks:** Accepts advertising.
Ad Rates: SAU: $5.46 **Circ:** (Not Reported)

17959 KATL-AM - 770
810 S. Haynes Ave. Phone: (406)232-7700
PO Box 700 Fax: (406)232-2281
Miles City, MT 59301-0700
Free: (800)473-5285
E-mail: katlradio@mcn.net

Format: Adult Contemporary. **Networks:** ABC; Northern Agricultural. **Owner:** Star Printing Co., PO Box 700, Miles City, MT 59301. **Founded:** 1940. **Formerly:** KRJF-AM (1954). **Operating Hours:** Continuous; 65% network, 35% local. **ADI:** Billings-Hardin, MT. **Key Personnel:** Donald Richard, Contact; Al'Homme, Sales Mgr. **Wattage:** 10,000 day; 1000 night. **Ad Rates:** $5.25-6.90 for 30 seconds; $7.90-11.55 for 60 seconds.

17960 KKRY-FM - 92.5
508 Main St. Phone: (406)232-5626
Box 1426 Fax: (406)232-3692
Miles City, MT 59301
E-mail: kmcm@mcn.net

Format: Country. **Networks:** CNN Radio; Jones Satellite. **Owner:** Senger Broadcasting Corporation, 508 Main, Miles City, MN 59301, (612)222-5556. **Founded:** 1984. **Formerly:** KMTA-AM. **Operating Hours:** Continuous. **Key Personnel:** Kevin Senger, Chairman; Kevin Senger, General Mgr. **Wattage:** 100,000. **Ad Rates:** Combined advertising rates available with KMTA-AM.

17961 KMTA-AM - 1050
508 Main St. Phone: (406)232-5626
Box 1426 Fax: (406)232-3692
Miles City, MT 59301

Format: Oldies. **Networks:** CBS. **Founded:** 1986. **Operating Hours:** 5 a.m.-midnight. **ADI:** Minneapolis-St. Paul, MN. **Key Personnel:** Kevin Senger, Chairman. **Wattage:** 10,000.

MISSOULA†, pop. 33,388.

Missoula Co. (W). 120 m NW of Helena. University of Montana. U.S. Forest Service. Resort area. Dairy and meat products plants; plywood, pulp, lumber manufactured. - Diversified farming. Dairying, beef cattle.

17962 CutBank
University of Montana
Missoula, MT 59802 Phone: (406)243-6156
Fax: (406)243-4076
Publication E-mail: cutbank@selway.umt.edu

Literary journal covering fiction, poetry, essays, and art. **Founded:** 1973. **Freq:** Semiannual. **Trim Size:** 5 1/2 x 8 1/2. **ISSN:** 0734-9963. **Subscription Rates:** $12 individuals; $6.95 single issue. **Remarks:** Accepts advertising. **URL:** http://www.umt.edu/cutbank/default.htm.
Ad Rates: BW: $100 **Circ:** Controlled 500

17963 Missoula Independent
PO Box 8275 Phone: (406)543-6609
Missoula, MT 59807
Community newspaper. **Freq:** Weekly (Thurs.). **Subscription Rates:** Free.
Circ: Combined 13,398

17964 Missoulian
PO Box 8029 Phone: (406)523-5200
Missoula, MT 59807 Fax: (406)523-5221
Free: (800)366-7102

General newspaper. **Founded:** May 1, 1873. **Freq:** Mon.-Sun. (morn.). **Print Method:** Offset. **Trim Size:** 27. **Cols./Page:** 6. **Col. Width:** 25 nonpareils. **Col. Depth:** 301 agate lines. **Key Personnel:** Mike McInally, Editor; James E. Bell, Publisher. **Subscription Rates:** $.50 daily; $1.50 Sunday. **Remarks:** Accepts advertising. **URL:** http://www.missoulian.com. **Alt. Formats:** Microfilm.
Ad Rates: GLR: $2.54 **Circ:** Mon.-Sat. ★32,378
4C: $513 Sun. ★38,127
SAU: $25.42

17965 The Montana Business Quarterly
Bureau of Business and Economic Research
University of Montana Phone: (406)243-5113
Gallagher Business Bldg. Fax: (406)243-2086
Missoula, MT 59812
Publication E-mail: cschultz@selway.umt.edu

Regional economics journal for decision-makers. **Founded:** 1962. **Freq:** Quarterly. **Print Method:** Offset. **Trim Size:** 8 1/2 x 11. **Cols./Page:** 3. **Col. Width:** 2 3/8 inches. **Col. Depth:** 8 3/4 inches. **Key Personnel:** Shannon Jahrig, Editor; Carolyn Schultz, Marketing Dir. **Subscription Rates:** $30 individuals; $10 single issue. **Remarks:** Advertising not accepted.
Circ: Paid ‡1,300
Non-paid ‡200

17966 Montana Journalism Review
The University of Montana
Rm. 209 Phone: (406)243-4001
Missoula, MT 59812-1067 Fax: (406)243-5369
Publication E-mail: work@setway.umt.edu

Journalism review publication. **Founded:** 1914. **Freq:** Annual. **Print Method:** Offset. **Trim Size:** 8 1/2 x 11. **Cols./Page:** 3. **Col. Width:** 14 picas. **Col. Depth:** 60 picas. **Key Personnel:** Clemens P. Work, Editor, phone (406)243-2160, work@selway.umt.edu. **Subscription Rates:** $8.50 individuals; $15 two years. **Remarks:** Accepts advertising. **URL:** http://www.umt.edu/journalism.
Ad Rates: BW: $300 **Circ:** Paid 500
Non-paid 2,000

17967 Montana Kaimin
University of Montana
U of M Journalism 206 Phone: (406)243-4310
Missoula, MT 59812
Collegiate newspaper. **Founded:** 1898. **Freq:** Tues.-Fri. (morn.). **Print Method:** Offset. **Trim Size:** 9 1/2 x 12 1/2. **Cols./Page:** 5. **Col. Width:** 19 nonpareils. **Col. Depth:** 175 agate lines. **Key Personnel:** Mendy Moon, Business Mgr.; Kyle Wood, Editor. **Subscription Rates:** $60 individuals.
Ad Rates: GLR: $.90 **Circ:** Free 6,000
BW: $495.00
SAU: $13.13

17968 Montanan
The University of Montana
University Relations Phone: (406)243-2523
Missoula, MT 59812 Fax: (406)243-4520

University magazine. **Subtitle:** The Magazine of the University of Montana. **Founded:** 1981. **Freq:** 3/year. **Print Method:** Web offset. **Trim Size:** 50 x 65.6 picas. **Cols./Page:** 3. **Col. Width:** 14 picas. **Col. Depth:** 59 picas. **Key Personnel:** Jackie Drews, Advertising Dir., phone (406)728-1573; Caroline Patterson, Editor, phone (406)243-4842, cpatter@selway.umt.edu. **Remarks:** Accepts advertising. **Online:** Netscape. **URL:** http://www.umt.edu/com/.
Ad Rates: BW: $1,000 **Circ:** Controlled 51,000
4C: $1,425

17969 Perceptual and Motor Skills
Behavioral Engineering Associates, L.L.C.
Box 9229 Phone: (406)728-1710
Missoula, MT 59807-9229
Technical journal featuring experimental and theoretical articles on perception or motor skills, especially as affected by experience; includes articles on general methodology and new material listings and reviews. **Founded:** 1949. **Freq:** Bimonthly. **Print Method:** Offset. **Trim Size:** 6 1/8 x 9 1/8. **Cols./Page:** 1. **Col. Width:** 4 1/2 inches. **Col. Depth:** 7 1/4 inches. **Key Personnel:** R.B. Ammons, Editor and Publisher; C.H. Ammons, Editor and Publisher. **ISSN:** 0031-5125. **Subscription Rates:** $280 institutions; $40 single issue; individuals may inquire directly. **Remarks:** Advertising not accepted. **Alt. Formats:** Microform.
Circ: ‡2,000

17970 Psychological Reports
Behavioral Engineering Associates, L.L.C.
Box 9229 Phone: (406)728-1710
Missoula, MT 59807-9229
Technical journal in psychology featuring experimental, theoretical, and speculative articles. **Founded:** Mar. 1955. **Freq:** Bimonthly. **Print Method:** Offset. **Trim Size:** 6 1/8 x 9 1/2. **Cols./Page:** 1. **Col. Width:** 4 1/2 inches. **Col. Depth:** 7 1/4 inches. **Key Personnel:** R.B. Ammons, Editor and Publisher; C.H. Ammons, Editor and Publisher. **ISSN:** 0332-2941. **Subscription Rates:** $280 institutions; $40 single issue; individuals may inquire directly. **Remarks:** Advertising not accepted. **Alt. Formats:** Microfilm.
Circ: ‡2,000

17971 St. Patrick Hospital Health Update
St. Patrick Hospital
500 W. Broadway Phone: (406)543-7271
PO Box 4587 Fax: (406)329-5875
Missoula, MT 59806
Hospital trade magazine. **Founded:** Jan. 1997. **Freq:** Quarterly. **Key Personnel:** JoAnn Hoven, Editor. **Subscription Rates:** Free to qualified subscribers. **Remarks:** Advertising not accepted. **Former name:** St. Patrick Hospital Messenger.
Circ: Controlled 30,000

17972 Charter Communications
7905 Zaugg Dr. Phone: (406)258-6701
Missoula, MT 59802 Fax: (406)258-5205
Free: (800)800-9905

Owner: Charter Communications, at above address. **Formerly:** Marshalls TV Cable; Premiere Communications. **Key Personnel:** Rick Carrel, Operations Mgr.; Sandi Harmon, Office Mgr. **Cities Served:** Big Flat, Bonner, Clinton, Florence, Frenchtown, Huson, Lake West, Lolo, Milltown, Seeley Lake, Superior, Victor, MT: subscribing households 4,663; 21 channels; 2 community access channels.

KAJ-TV - See Kalispell

17973 KBGA-FM - 89.9
University of Montana Phone: (406)243-6758
University Hall Fax: (406)243-6428
Missoula, MT 59812
E-mail: kbga@selway.umt.edu

Format: Alternative/New Music/Progressive. **Owner:** University of Montana, at above address. **Founded:** Aug. 24, 1996. **Operating Hours:** Continuous. **Wattage:** 1000. **Ad Rates:** Noncommercial; underwriting available. **URL:** http://www.kbga.org.

17974 KECI-TV - 13
340 W. Main, Box 5268 Phone: (406)721-2063
Missoula, MT 59802 Fax: (406)721-2083

Format: Commercial TV. **Networks:** NBC. **Owner:** Eagle Communicatons, at above address, Fax: (406)542-1606. **Founded:** 1954. **Formerly:** KMSO-TV; KGVO-TV. **Operating Hours:** Continuous. **ADI:** Missoula, MT. **Key Personnel:** Jane English, Executive VP; Tim Karsr, Dir. of Operations; Jim Harmon, VP News. **Ad Rates:** Advertising accepted; rates available upon request.

17975 KGGL-FM - 93.3
PO Box 4106 Phone: (406)728-9399
Missoula, MT 59806 Fax: (406)721-3020
E-mail: eagle93@montana.com

Format: Country. **Owner:** Sunbrook Communications Inc., N. 1212 Washington, Ste. 124, Spokane, WA 99201, (509)326-9500, Fax: (509)326-1560. **Founded:** 1972. **Operating Hours:** Continuous; 100% local. **ADI:** Missoula, MT. **Key Personnel:** Chad Parrish, General Mgr.; Bill McPherson, Local Sales Mgr.; Scott Richards, Program Dir.; Melody Stubbs, Business Mgr. **Wattage:** 43,000. **Ad Rates:** Advertising accepted; rates available upon request. **URL:** http://www.eagle93.com.

17976 KGRZ-AM - 1450
PO Box 4106 Phone: (406)728-1450
Missoula, MT 59806 Fax: (406)721-3020

Format: Sports; Talk. **Networks:** ESPN Radio. **Owner:** Sunbrook Communications Inc., N. 1212 Washington, Ste. 124, Spokane, WA 99201, (509)326-9500, Fax: (509)326-1560. **Formerly:** KBMG-AM. **Operating Hours:** 100% satellite. **ADI:** Missoula, MT. **Key Personnel:** Chad Parrish, General Mgr.; Melody Stubbs, Business Mgr. **Wattage:** 1,000. **Ad Rates:** Advertising accepted; rates available upon request.

17977 KLCY-AM - 930
PO Box 7279 Phone: (406)728-9300
Missoula, MT 59807 Fax: (406)542-2329
Free: (800)597-7131
E-mail: brianp@wbci.com

Format: Talk. **Networks:** ABC. **Owner:** Western Broadcasting Co., 400 Ryman, Missoula, MT 59802. **Founded:** 1959. **Operating Hours:** Continuous; 70% network, 30% local. **ADI:** Missoula, MT. **Key Personnel:** Gene Peterson, Sales Mgr. **Local Programs:** *At Your Service* 12:30-1p.m. Monday-Friday, Denny Bedard; *Breakfast Club* 6-10a.m. Monday-Friday, Denny Bedard; *Lost and Found Show* 6-11a.m. Sunday. **Wattage:** 5000. **Ad Rates:** $8-30 for 30 seconds; $12-45 for 60 seconds. Combined advertising rates available with KUSS, KGVO.

17978 KMSO-FM - 102.5
725 Strand Ave. Phone: (406)542-1025
Missoula, MT 59801 Fax: (406)721-1036
E-mail: info@kmso.com

Format: Adult Contemporary. **Founded:** 1985. **Formerly:** KUEZ-FM (1987). **Operating Hours:** Continuous. **ADI:** Missoula, MT. **Key Personnel:** Sheila Callahan, Gen. Mgr./National Sales, sheila@kmso.com; Laurie William, Sales Mgr.; Rick Sanders, Program Dir.; Jeff Haley, PSA Dir.; Kris Hardu, Traffic Dir. **Local Programs:** *In the Boardroom*, Shelia Callahan. **Wattage:** 14,000. **Ad Rates:** $13-16 for 30 seconds; $17-20 for 60 seconds.

17979 KPAX-TV - 8
2204 Regent St., Box 4827 Phone: (406)542-4400
Missoula, MT 59801 Fax: (406)543-7111
E-mail: kpax@kpax.com

Format: Commercial TV. **Networks:** CBS. **Owner:** KPAX Communications, Inc., at above address. **Founded:** 1977. **Operating Hours:** 6 a.m.-2 a.m. **ADI:** Missoula, MT. **Key Personnel:** Bob Hermes, PRS/Gen. Mgr.; Tammy Engle, Operations Dir.; Paul Shoemaker, News Dir.; Shane Edinger, Sports Dir.; David McLean, Production Dir. **URL:** http://www.kpax.com.

17980 KTMF-TV - 23
2200 Stephens Ave. Phone: (406)542-8900
Missoula, MT 59801 Fax: (406)728-4800

Format: Commercial TV. **Networks:** ABC. **Owner:** CTN Missoula, Inc., at above address, (406)761-8816, Fax: (406)727-7134. **Founded:** 1990. **Operating Hours:** Continuous. **ADI:** Missoula, MT. **Key Personnel:** Tim Spinder, General Sales Mgr.; Jim Kazora, Chief Engineer; James Colla, President; Penny Adkins, Promotions/Programming; Cheryl Cordeiro, General Mgr. **Wattage:** 1,800,000. **Ad Rates:** Advertising accepted; rates available upon request. **URL:** http://www.ktmf.com.

17981 KYLT-AM - 1340
1600 North Ave. W. Phone: (406)728-5000
Missoula, MT 59801-5500 Fax: (406)549-0503
E-mail: z100@montana.com

Format: Oldies. **Networks:** ABC; Westwood One Radio. **Founded:** 1955. **Operating Hours:** Continuous. **ADI:** Missoula, MT. **Key Personnel:** Chad Parrish, Manager; Curt Gerke, Program Dir.; Cary Nicklay, General Sales Mgr. **Wattage:** 1000. **Ad Rates:** Advertising accepted; rates available upon request. Combined advertising rates available with KZOQ-FM.

17982 KYSS-FM - 94.9
400 Ryman Phone: (406)728-9300
Missoula, MT 59802-4208 Fax: (406)542-2329
Free: (800)597-7131

Format: Contemporary Country. **Networks:** ABC. **Owner:** Western Broadcasting, at above address. **Founded:** 1969. **Operating Hours:** Continuous; 10% network, 90% local. **ADI:** Missoula, MT. **Key Personnel:** Gene Peterson, Sales Mgr. **Local Programs:** *Tom and Vicki Morning Show.* **Wattage:** 61,000. **Ad Rates:** $5-15 for 30 seconds. Combined advertising rates available with KGVO, KLCY.

17983 KZOQ-FM - 100.1
2701 N. Reserve St. Phone: (406)728-5000
Missoula, MT 59802 Fax: (406)721-3020

Format: Album-Oriented Rock (AOR). **Founded:** 1974. **Operating Hours:** Continuous. **ADI:** Missoula, MT. **Key Personnel:** Chad Parrish, General Mgr.; Craig Johnson, PD; Cary Nicklay, National/Reg. Sales Mgr. **Wattage:** 12,500 ERP. **Ad Rates:** Combined advertising rates available with KYLT-AM.

PHILIPSBURG†, pop. 1,138.

Granite Co. (W). 50 m NW of Butte. Manganese, silver, lead, pine timber. Stock, grainfarms. Hogs, Cattle.

17984 The Philipsburg Mail
Box 160 Phone: (406)859-3223
Philipsburg, MT 59858 Fax: (406)859-3690
Publication E-mail: mailnews@montana.com

Newspaper. **Founded:** 1887. **Freq:** Weekly (Wed.). **Print Method:** Offset. **Cols./Page:** 5. **Col. Width:** 11 picas. **Col. Depth:** 14 inches. **Key Personnel:** Jim Tracy, Publisher. **USPS:** 430-280. **Subscription Rates:** $20 individuals. **Remarks:** Accepts advertising.
Ad Rates: SAU: $4 **Circ:** 1,482

17985 Philipsburg Cable TV
Box 40 Phone: (406)859-3645
Philipsburg, MT 59858

Founded: 1981. **Key Personnel:** Jesse A. Henke, Manager. **Cities Served:** subscribing households 300; 12 channels; 1 community access channel.

17986 WSS Cable TV Inc.
PO Box 40 Phone: (406)859-3645
Philipsburg, MT 59858

Founded: 1982. **Key Personnel:** Larry E. Henke. **Cities Served:** White Sulphur Springs, MT: subscribing households 256; 14 channels; 1 community access channel.

PLAINS

Sanders Co. (NW). 30 m SW of Hot Springs.

17987 Valley Press
PO Box 667 Phone: (406)826-3402
Plains, MT 59859 Fax: (406)826-5577
Free: (800)440-3402

Community newspaper. **Founded:** 1899. **Freq:** Weekly (Wed.). **Trim Size:** 11 1/4 x 17. **Cols./Page:** 6. **Col. Width:** 1 3/4 inches. **Col. Depth:** 16 inches. **Key Personnel:** Todd Mowbray, Publisher; Bill Cenis, Editor. **ISSN:** 1041-1437. **Subscription Rates:** $19.95 locally; $23.95 in Montana; $25.95 out of state. **Remarks:** Accepts advertising. **Formerly:** Plainsman Edition; Camas Record Edition.
Ad Rates: BW: $187.20 **Circ:** 1,800
SAU: $2.85
PCI: $2.25

PLENTYWOOD†, pop. 2,476.

Sheridan Co. (NE). 120 m S of Regina, Sask, Canada. Ships wheat. Coal mines; oil wells. Stock, poultry, grain farms. Flax, corn.

17988 The Greeter
108 N. Main Phone: (406)765-1733
Plentywood, MT 59254 Fax: (406)765-2106
Free: (800)637-2203
Publication E-mail: thegreeter@aol.com

Community newspaper. **Founded:** Apr. 1986. **Freq:** Weekly (Tues.). **Print Method:** Web offset. **Cols./Page:** 5. **Col. Width:** 2 1/16 inches. **Col. Depth:** 13 inches. **Key Personnel:** Richard Rice, Publisher. **Subscription Rates:** Free. **Remarks:** Accepts advertising.
Ad Rates: BW: $250 **Circ:** Free ‡3,000
SAU: $5
PCI: $5

17989 KATQ-AM - 1070
112 3rd Ave., E Phone: (406)765-1480
Plentywood, MT 59254-2223 Fax: (406)765-2357

Format: Full Service; Agricultural; Country. **Simulcasts:** KATQ-FM. **Networks:** ABC; North American Network. **Owner:** Radio International-KATQ, Inc., at above address. **Founded:** 1976. **Operating Hours:** 6 a.m.-6 p.m.; 15% network, 85% local. **Key Personnel:** Joy Fanning, Operations Dir.; Casandra Syme, Office/Sales Mgr.; Grant Lindsey, Sales Rep./Sports Dir. **Wattage:** 5000. **Ad Rates:** $5-7 for 30 seconds; $7.25-9 for 60 seconds.

17990 KATQ-FM - 100.1
112 3rd Ave., E Phone: (406)765-1480
Plentywood, MT 59254-2223 Fax: (406)765-2357

Format: Full Service; Country; Agricultural. **Simulcasts:** KATQ-AM. **Networks:** ABC; North American Network. **Owner:** Radio International-KATQ, Inc., at above address. **Founded:** 1963. **Formerly:** KPWD-FM. **Operating Hours:** Continuous 50% network, 50% local. **Key Personnel:** Joy Fanning, Contact; Casandra Syme, Contact; Grant Lindsey, Sports Dir. **Wattage:** 3000. **Ad Rates:** $5-7 for 30 seconds; $7.25-9 for 60 seconds.

17991 Plentywood Cable TV Co.
222 Highland Ave. Phone: (406)765-1199
PO Box 128
Plentywood, MT 59254

Founded: 1979. **Key Personnel:** Ernest Berland, Contact. **Cities Served:** subscribing households 800; 16 channels.

POLSON†, pop. 2,798.

Lake Co. (NW). On Flathead Lake, 69 m N of Missoula. Sawmills. Timber. Dairy, stock farms. Wheat, hay, cherries. Resort.

17992 Lake County Advertiser
C.P.A., Inc.
PO Box 1090 Phone: (406)676-3800
Polson, MT 59860 Fax: (406)883-4349

Shopping guide. **Founded:** 1910. **Freq:** Weekly (Wed.). **Cols./Page:** 6. **Col. Width:** 12 picas. **Col. Depth:** 21 inches. **Key Personnel:** Kristi Netimeyer, Editor; Rich Stripp, Editor; John Schnase, Advertising Mgr.; Todd and Carmine Mowbray, Owners. **Subscription Rates:** Free.
Circ: Non-paid 12,000

17993 Lake County Leader
C.P.A., Inc.
PO Box 1090 Phone: (406)676-3800
Polson, MT 59860 Fax: (406)883-4349

Community newspaper. **Founded:** 1910. **Freq:** Weekly (Wed.). **Print Method:** Offset. **Cols./Page:** 6. **Col. Width:** 12 picas. **Col. Depth:** 21 inches. **Key Personnel:** Kristi Netimeyer, Editor; Rich Stripp, Advertising Mgr.; John Schnase, Publisher; Todd Mowbray, Owner; Carmine Mowbray, Owner. **Subscription Rates:** $16.95; $18.95 out of area; $20.95 out of state. **Remarks:** Accepts advertising. **Formed by the merger of:** Ronan Pioneer/Mission Valley News; Flathead Courier.
Ad Rates: GLR: $.85 **Circ:** ‡5,600
BW: $441
4C: $691
PCI: $5.10

17994 KERR-AM - 750
581 N. Reservoir Rd. Phone: (406)883-5255
Polson, MT 59860-9730 Fax: (406)883-4441
Free: (800)766-7105

Format: Country. **Networks:** ABC. **Owner:** Anderson Broadcasting, KBMR, Bismarck, ND 58502, (701)255-1234. **Founded:** 1976. **Operating Hours:** Continuous; 5% network, 95% local. **ADI:** Missoula, MT. **Key Personnel:** Dennis Anderson, General Mgr. **Wattage:** 50,000. **Ad Rates:** $4-8.75 for 30 seconds; $6.40-14 for 60 seconds.

POPLAR, pop. 995.

Roosevelt Co. (SW). 70 m E of Glasgow.

17995 Wotanin-Wowapi
Fort Peck Assiniboine and Sioux Tribes
PO Box 1027 Phone: (406)768-5388
Poplar, MT 59255 Fax: (406)768-5743

Tribal Newspaper. **Founded:** Mar. 1970. **Freq:** Weekly. **Cols./Page:** 6. **Col. Width:** 2 inches. **Col. Depth:** 26 inches. **Key Personnel:** Bonnie Red Elk, Editor. **Subscription Rates:** $30 50 issues. **Remarks:** Accepts advertising.
Ad Rates: PCI: $3.50 **Circ:** Paid 800
Non-paid 2,000

RED LODGE†, pop. 1,896.

Carbon Co. (S). 60 m SW of Billings. Gateway to Beartooth Mountain and Yellowstone Park. Creamery. Agriculture. Livestock, sugar beets. Resort.

17996 Carbon County News
Livingston Enterprise
Box 970 Phone: (406)446-2222
Red Lodge, MT 59068-0970 Fax: (406)446-2225
Free: (800)735-8843
Publication E-mail: ccn@wtp.net

Community newspaper. **Founded:** 1889. **Freq:** Weekly (Thurs.). **Print Method:** Offset. **Cols./Page:** 6. **Col. Width:** 24 nonpareils. **Col. Depth:** 294 agate lines. **Key Personnel:** Jim Moore, Editor and Publisher; Bonnie Thompson, Advertising Mgr. **USPS:** 090-100. **Subscription Rates:** $23. **Remarks:** Accepts advertising.
Ad Rates: SAU: $4.50 **Circ:** 2,750

ROUNDUP†, pop. 2,119.

Musselshell Co. (EC). 50 m N of Billings. Coal, oil wells. Lumber. Grain, livestock, hay, feedlots.

17997 Roundup Record-Tribune and Winnett Times
Roundup Record Tribune, Inc.
PO Box 350 Phone: (406)323-1105
Roundup, MT 59072 Fax: (406)323-1761

Community newspaper. **Founded:** Apr. 5, 1908. **Freq:** Weekly (Wed.). **Print Method:** Offset. **Trim Size:** 17 x 22 3/4. **Cols./Page:** 7. **Col. Width:** 12 ems. **Col. Depth:** 21 1/4 inches. **Key Personnel:** Eric Rasmussen, Editor and Publisher. **Subscription Rates:** $20 individuals; $23 out of area; $26 out of state. **Remarks:** Accepts advertising.
Ad Rates: BW: $440 **Circ:** ‡2,800
SAU: $4.13
PCI: $4

SCOBEY

17998 Daniels County Leader
23 Main St. Phone: (406)487-5303
Box 850
Scobey, MT 59263
Publication E-mail: 2leader@3rivers.net

Newspaper. **Founded:** 1912. **Freq:** Weekly (Thurs.). **Print Method:** Letterpress and offset. **Trim Size:** 11 x 17. **Cols./Page:** 6. **Col. Width:** 22 nonpareils. **Col. Depth:** 224 agate lines. **Key Personnel:** Burley Bowler, Editor and Publisher. **Subscription Rates:** $25 in 4-county area; $30 other counties. **Remarks:** Accepts advertising.
Ad Rates: SAU: $3.55 **Circ:** ‡5,000

17999 KCGM-FM - 95.7
c/o Prarie Communications, Inc. Phone: (406)487-2293
PO Box 220 Fax: (406)487-5922
Scobey, MT 59263

Format: Country; Contemporary Country; Agricultural. **Networks:** AP; USA Radio; Montana News; Northern Agricultural. **Owner:** Prairie Communications, Inc., at above address. **Founded:** 1971. **Operating Hours:** 6 a.m.-10 p.m.; 10% network, 90% local. **Key Personnel:** Dixie Halverson, Manager. **Wattage:** 52,000. **Ad Rates:** $4.48 for 15 seconds; $6.72 for 30 seconds; $8.96 for 60 seconds.

SHELBY

18000 The Shelby Promoter
119 Maple Phone: (406)434-5171
Box 610 Fax: (406)434-5955
Shelby, MT 59474
Community newspaper. **Founded:** 1912. **Freq:** Weekly (Thurs.). **Print Method:** Offset. **Cols./Page:** 6. **Col. Width:** 26 nonpareils. **Col. Depth:** 301 agate lines. **Key Personnel:** Brian Kavanagh, Publisher. **Subscription Rates:** $25 individuals; $35 out of area. **Remarks:** Accepts advertising.
Ad Rates: GLR: $.32 **Circ:** ‡2,700
BW: $553.41
4C: $753.41
SAU: $4.50
PCI: $4.29

18001 KSEN-AM - 1150
830 Oilfield Ave. Phone: (406)434-5241
Shelby, MT 59474 Fax: (406)434-2122

Format: Adult Contemporary. **Networks:** ABC; Northern Agricultural. **Founded:** 1947. **Operating Hours:** 5:30 a.m.-midnight. **ADI:** Great Falls, MT. **Key Personnel:** Jerry Black, President/Gen. Mgr. **Wattage:** 5000.

18002 KZIN-FM - 96.3
830 Oilfield Ave. Phone: (406)434-5241
Shelby, MT 59474 Fax: (406)434-2122

Format: Country. **Networks:** ABC; Northern Agricultural. **Owner:** Tri-County Radio Corp., at above address. **Founded:** 1978. **Operating Hours:** Continuous. **ADI:** Great Falls, MT. **Key Personnel:** Jerry Black, President/General Manager. **Wattage:** 100,000.

SHERIDAN

18003 Ruby Valley Cable Co.
Box 153 Phone: (406)842-5941
Sheridan, MT 59749

Owner: Philip E. Shackleton, at above address. **Founded:** 1981. **Key Personnel:** Philip E. Shackleton, Pres./Owner; Joseph Shackleton, Vice President, phone (406)842-5632. **Cities Served:** Sheridan, MT: subscribing households 146; 16 channels.

SIDNEY

18004 The Sidney Herald-Leader
Wick Communications Co.
310 2nd Ave. NW Phone: (406)482-2403
Sidney, MT 59270 Fax: (406)482-7802
Publication E-mail: herald@lyrea.com

Community newspaper. **Founded:** 1908. **Freq:** Semiweekly (Wed. and Sun.). **Print Method:** Offset. **Trim Size:** 13 x 21 in. **Cols./Page:** 6. **Col. Width:** 25 nonpareils. **Col. Depth:** 294 agate lines. **Key Personnel:** Bill Vanderweele, Editor; Rick Schneider, Publisher. **USPS:** 495-760. **Subscription Rates:** $34. **Remarks:** Accepts advertising. **Formerly**: Sidney Herald.
Ad Rates: GLR: $.40 **Circ:** 4,200
BW: $680.40
4C: $820.80
SAU: $6
PCI: $6

18005 KTHC-FM - 95.1
PO Box 2048 Phone: (701)572-5371
Williston, ND 58801 Fax: (701)572-7511

Format: Adult Contemporary. **Networks:** ABC. **Owner:** Staradio Corp., PO Box 3309, Great Falls, MT 59403, (406)482-5090, Fax: (406)482-5095. **Founded:** 1996. **Operating Hours:** Continuous. **Key Personnel:** Larry Timpe, VP/General Mgr.; Paul Peterson, Program Dir.; Ann Armstrong. **Wattage:** 100,000.

STANFORD

18006 Judith Basin Press
117 Central Phone: (406)566-2471
PO Box 507
Stanford, MT 59479
Community newspaper. **Freq:** Weekly (Thurs.). **Cols./Page:** 5. **Col. Width:** 10 1/2 picas. **Col. Depth:** 15 inches. **Key Personnel:** Boni L. Schmitt, Editor; Lance Davis, Publisher.
Circ: 1,000

TERRY†, pop. 929.

Prairie Co. (E). On Yellowstone River, 190 m E of Billings. Tourism. Ships livestock, grain. Diversified farming. Irrigated & Dryland. Mineral Development.

18007 Terry Tribune
Yellowstone Newspapers
204 Logan Ave. Phone: (406)635-5513
Box 127 Fax: (406)635-2149
Terry, MT 59349
Community newspaper. **Founded:** 1907. **Freq:** Weekly (Wed.). **Print Method:** Offset. **Cols./Page:** 5. **Col. Width:** 26 nonpareils. **Col. Depth:** 210 agate lines. **Key Personnel:** Darlene L. Strobel, Editor. **Subscription Rates:** $25. **Remarks:** Accepts advertising.
Ad Rates: GLR: $.175 **Circ:** ‡1,121
BW: $188.50
SAU: $4.05

THOMPSON FALLS†, pop. 1,478.

Sanders Co. (NW). 103 m NW of Missoula. Antimony mine; pine, tamarack, fir, spruce timber. Agriculture. Hay, cattle. Tourism.

18008 Sanders County Ledger
Box 219 Phone: (406)827-3421
Thompson Falls, MT 59873 Fax: (406)827-4375
Publication E-mail: tfl3421@montana.com

Community newspaper. **Founded:** 1905. **Freq:** Weekly (Thurs.). **Print Method:** Offset. **Cols./Page:** 6. **Col. Width:** 24 nonpareils. **Col. Depth:** 294 agate lines. **Key Personnel:** Tom Eggensperger, Publisher; Bina Eggensperger, Publisher. **Subscription Rates:** $19 individuals. **Remarks:** Accepts advertising.
Ad Rates: SAU: $3.60 **Circ:** ‡3,100
PCI: $3.50

THREE FORKS†, pop. 1,247.

Gallatin Co. (SW). 60 m E of Butte. Residential.

18009 Herald
Jewett Publishing
Box 586 Phone: (406)285-3414
Three Forks, MT 59752-0586 Fax: (406)285-3413

Newspaper. **Founded:** 1908. **Freq:** Weekly (Thurs.). **Print Method:** Letterpress and offset. **Cols./Page:** 6. **Col. Width:** 25 nonpareils. **Col. Depth:** 294 agate lines. **Key Personnel:** S. Michael Tichenor, Editor and Publisher. **Subscription Rates:** $10.
Circ: Paid 1,350

TOWNSEND†, pop. 1,587.

Broadwater Co. (C). On Missouri River, 33 m SE of Helena. Creamery; sawmills. Gold mines; pine, fir timber. Agriculture. Livestock, beets, potatoes.

18010 The Townsend Star
Lake Edith Publishing
PO Box M Phone: (406)266-3333
Townsend, MT 59644 Fax: (406)266-5440
Publication E-mail: tstarmt@ixi.net

Community newspaper. **Founded:** 1897. **Freq:** Weekly (Thurs.). **Print Method:** Offset. **Cols./Page:** 6. **Col. Width:** 24 nonpareils. **Col. Depth:** 294 agate lines. **Key Personnel:** Linda Kent, Editor; Jeff Stoffer, Publisher. **USPS:** 635-560. **Subscription Rates:** $22 individuals. **Remarks:** Accepts advertising.
Ad Rates: 4C: $210 **Circ:** ‡1,500
SAU: $3.40
PCI: $4.25

VALIER

18011 The Valierian
PO Box 308 Phone: (406)279-3719
Valier, MT 59486-0308 Fax: (406)279-3686

Community newspaper. **Founded:** 1910. **Freq:** Weekly (Thurs.). **Cols./Page:** 6. **Col. Width:** 12 1/2 picas. **Col. Depth:** 21 1/2 inches. **Key Personnel:** Lois Green. **Subscription Rates:** $12.50 local; $15 state; $17 USA. **Remarks:** Accepts advertising. **Formerly**: The Spray.
Ad Rates: 4C: $85 **Circ:** ‡600
PCI: $2.25

VIRGINIA CITY

18012 The Madisonian
Madisonian
PO Box 365 Phone: (406)682-7755
Virginia City, MT 59755 Fax: (406)682-5012

Community newspaper. **Founded:** 1873. **Freq:** Weekly (Wed.). **Print Method:** Web offset. **Cols./Page:** 7. **Col. Width:** 10 picas. **Col. Depth:** 21 inches. **Key Personnel:** Daryl L. Tichenor, Editor and Publisher. **Subscription Rates:** $16; $18 out of state. **Remarks:** Accepts advertising.
Ad Rates: GLR: $3 **Circ:** ‡2,500
BW: $265
SAU: $2.90

WHITE SULPHUR SPRINGS†, pop. 1,302.

Meagher Co. (WC). 80 m E of Helena. Health resort. Gold, silver mines. Stock, grain farms. Hay.

18013 The Meagher County News
Meagher County News
Box 349 Phone: (406)547-3831
White Sulphur Springs, MT 59645-0349 Fax: (406)547-3832
Free: (800)398-3831

Community newspaper (tabloid). **Founded:** 1889. **Freq:** Weekly (Thurs.). **Print Method:** Offset. **Trim Size:** 11 3/8 x 14. **Cols./Page:** 5. **Col. Width:** 24 nonpareils. **Col. Depth:** 189 agate lines. **Key Personnel:** Verle L. Rademacher, Editor and Publisher; Patricia M. Rademacher, Editor and Publisher. **USPS:** 336-620. **Subscription Rates:** $21 individuals; $24

out of state. **Remarks:** Color advertising accepted; rates available upon request.
Ad Rates: SAU: $3.50 **Circ:** ‡1,200
PCI: $3.50

WHITEFISH, pop. 3,703.

Flathead Co. (NW). 110 m N of Missoula. Saw and planing mills. Timber. Agriculture. Summer & winter resort.

18014 Kinesis
PO Box 4007 Phone: (406)756-1193
Whitefish, MT 59937 Fax: (406)756-1194
Publication E-mail: kinesis@retax.net

Magazine for writers, poets, and artists. **Subtitle:** The Literary Magazine for the Rest of Us. **Founded:** 1991. **Freq:** Monthly. **Trim Size:** 8 1/2 x 10 1/2. **Key Personnel:** Leif Peterson, Editor. **ISSN:** 1056-781X. **Subscription Rates:** $20 individuals; $4 single issue. **Remarks:** Advertising accepted; rates available upon request.
Circ: Paid 2,000
Non-paid 1,000

18015 Whitefish Pilot
Sage Publishing
Box 488 Phone: (406)862-3505
Whitefish, MT 59937 Fax: (406)862-3636

Local newspaper. **Founded:** Feb. 1903. **Freq:** Weekly (Thurs.). **Print Method:** Offset. **Cols./Page:** 6. **Col. Width:** 26 nonpareils. **Col. Depth:** 294 agate lines. **Key Personnel:** Richard Hensley, Editor. **USPS:** 683-120. **Subscription Rates:** $22 individuals; $30 out of state; $40 other countries. **Remarks:** Accepts advertising.
Ad Rates: GLR: $.36 **Circ:** Paid ‡4,300
BW: $1,039.50
SAU: $8.60

18016 KZRQ-FM - 104.1
5850 Hwy. 93 S. Phone: (406)863-2000
Whitefish, MT 59937

Format: Album-Oriented Rock (AOR). **Owner:** Radio 2000, at above address. **Founded:** Mar. 1998. **Former name:** KQMO-FM (1998). **Operating Hours:** Continuous. **ADI:** Springfield, MO. **Key Personnel:** Frank Copsides, President, phone (417)873-4500; Dave Alexander, Vice President; Julie Barry, Program Dir. **Wattage:** 25,000.

WHITEHALL

18017 Whitehall Cable TV
509 1st St. E. Phone: (406)287-3913
Whitehall, MT 59759

Owner: William E. Hersolich, at above address. **Founded:** Aug. 1981. **Key Personnel:** Donna Herbulich, phone (406)287-3913. **Cities Served:** Whitehall, MT: subscribing households 303; 29 channels; 1 community access channel.

WIBAUX†, pop. 782.

Wibaux Co. (NE). 220 m NE of Billings. Oil wells. Coal. Grain, stock, farms. Wheat, corn, oats. Cattle.

18018 The Wibaux Pioneer-Gazette
120 S. Wibaux St. Phone: (406)796-2218
Wibaux, MT 59353 Fax: (406)796-2218
Publisher E-mail: wibaux@midrivers.com

Community newspaper. **Founded:** Jan. 1907. **Freq:** Weekly (Thurs.). **Print Method:** Offset. **Cols./Page:** 5. **Col. Width:** 24 nonpareils. **Col. Depth:** 182 agate lines. **Key Personnel:** Frank Datta, Publisher. **Subscription Rates:** $19 individuals; $21 out of area. **Remarks:** Color advertising accepted; rates available upon request.
Ad Rates: GLR: $.23 **Circ:** ‡1,000
PCI: $3

WOLF POINT†, pop. 3,074.

Roosevelt Co. (NE). On Missouri River, 200 m S of Regina, Sask, Canada. Oil wells. Ships large quantities of wheat. Diversified farming. Ranching.

18019 Herald-News
Herald Publications
408 Main St. Phone: (406)653-2222
Box 639 Fax: (406)653-2221
Wolf Point, MT 59201
Publisher E-mail: herald@midrivers.com

Newspaper. **Founded:** 1913. **Freq:** Weekly (Thurs.). **Print Method:** Offset. **Cols./Page:** 6. **Col. Width:** 25 nonpareils. **Col. Depth:** 294 agate lines. **Key Personnel:** Mrs. H.N. Downs, Publisher; Harry Downs, General Mgr.; Ruth A. Boysan, Office Mgr. **Subscription Rates:** $25 individuals. **Remarks:** Accepts advertising.
Ad Rates: GLR: $3.75 **Circ:** 3,150
BW: $472.50
SAU: $3.60
CNU: $3.75
PCI: $3.60

NEBRASKA

State Capital, LINCOLN

Nebraska is bounded on the north by South Dakota, east by Iowa and Missouri, south by Kansas and Colorado, and west by Colorado and Wyoming. Its length from north to south is about 210 miles; its width about 420 miles; land area 76,878 square miles. The surface is generally a vast, gently undulating plain, with a gradual ascent toward the mountains in the west; the river bottoms are level. There are some bluffs along the Missouri River and some hills in the northwest. A small part of this region is occupied by the Mauvias Terres or Bad Lands. The state is well-watered; three large rivers, the Niobrara, the Platte, and the Big Blue drain eastward into the Missouri, which flows for 500 miles along the eastern border. Only the Missouri is navigable. East of the Bad Lands and south of the Niobrara there is a tract called the Sand Hills region, 15,000 square miles in area, the valleys of which produce an abundance of corn and wheat, while the rest of the country is used for cattle. Nebraska was once practically treeless, but more than two billion trees have been planted, by state and national government. The soil is very fertile. The climate is dry and healthful and there is an abundance of sunshine. The Weather Bureau at Omaha gives the temperature (annual average) as 50.6; highest on record, 114; lowest on record, -32. Total annual precipitation is 29.86 inches. Omaha is a great railway and meat-packing center, and the state's largest city. The University of Nebraska, its largest institution of higher education, is located at Lincoln.

POPULATION: 1,606,000 (1992). Rank among the states, 36th.

AGRICULTURE: Number of farms: 56,000 (1992). Farm acreage: 47,000,000 (1992). Cash receipts from farm marketings: crops, $2,888,000,000 (1991); livestock and products, $5,934,000,000 (1991).

FORESTS: Total forest land: 442,000 acres (1991).

MINERALS: Value of production: $89,000,000 (1991). Principal minerals: cement, sand and gravel, stone. Value of petroleum production: $110,000,000 (1991).

MANUFACTURES: Value added by manufacture: $7,537,000,000 (1991). Leading industry groups: food and related products, electrical machinery, printing and publishing.

LIST OF COUNTIES

Total number of counties 93

County, Location on Map, and County Seat	Pop.
Adams (SE), Hastings	29,625
Antelope (NEC), Neligh	7,965
Arthur (W), Arthur	462
Banner (W), Harrisburg	852
Blaine (NC), Brewster	675
Boone (EC), Albion	6,667
Box Butte (NW), Alliance	13,130
Boyd (N), Butte	2,835
Brown (N), Ainsworth	3,657
Buffalo (SC), Kearney	37,447
Burt (NE), Tekamah	7,868
Butler (E), David City	8,601
Cass (E), Plattsmouth	21,318
Cedar (NE), Hartington	10,131
Chase (SW), Imperial	4,381
Cherry (NW), Valentine	6,307
Cheyenne (W), Sidney	9,494
Clay (S), Clay Center	7,123
Colfax (W), Schuyler	9,139
Cuming (NE), Westpoint	10,117
Custer (C), Borken Bow	12,270
Dakota (E), Dakota City	16,742
Dawes (NW), Chadron	9,021
Dawson (SC), Lexington	19,940
Deuel (W), Chappell	2,237
Dixon (NE), Ponca	6,143
Dodge (E), Fremont	6,143
Douglas (E), Omaha	416,444
Dundy (SW), Benkelman	2,582
Fillmore (SE), Geneva	7,103
Franklin (S), Franklin, Hildreth	3,938
Frontier (SW), Stockville	3,101
Furnas (S), Beaver City	5,553
Gage (SE), Beatrice	22,794
Garden (W), Oshkosh	2,460
Garfield (NC), Burwell	2,141
Gosper (S), Elwood	1,928
Grant (NW), Hyannis	769
Greeley (C), Greeley	3,006
Hall (C), Grand Island	48,925
Hamilton (SEC), Aurora	8,862
Harlan (S), Alma	3,810
Hayes (SW), Hayes Center	1,222
Hitchcock (SW), Trenton	3,750
Holt (N), O'Neill	12,599
Hooker (W), Mullen	793
Howard (EC), Saint Paul	6,055
Jefferson (SE), Fairbury	8,759
Johnson (SE), Tecumseh	4,673
Kearney (S), Minden	6,629
Keith (W), Ogallala	8,584
Keya Paha (N), Springview	1,029
Kimball (W), Kimball	4,108
Knox (NE), Center	9,534
Lancaster (SE), Lincoln	213,641
Lincoln (SW), North Platte	32,508
Logan (WC), Stapleton	878
Loup (NWC), Taylor	683
Madison (NE), Madison	32,655
McPherson (W), Tryon	546
Merrick (EC), Central City	8,042
Morrill (W), Bridgeport	5,423
Nance (EC), Fullerton	4,275
Nemaha (SE), Auburn	7,980
Nuckolls (S), Nelson	5,786
Otoe (SE), Nebraska City	14,252
Pawnee (SE), Pawnee City	3,317
Perkins (W), Grant	3,367
Pierce (NE), Pierce	7,827
Platte (NC), Columbus	29,820
Polk (EC), Osceola	5,675
Red Willow (SW), McCook	11,705
Richardson (SE), Falls City	9,937
Rock (N), Bassett	2,019
Saline (SE), Wilber	12,715
Sarpy (E), Papillion	102,583
Saunders (E), Wahoo	18,285
Scotts Bluff (W), Gering	36,025
Seward (SE), Seward	15,450
Sheridan (NW), Rushville	6,750
Sherman (C), Loup City	3,718
Sioux (NW), Harrison	1,549
Stanton (NE), Stanton	6,244
Thayer (S), Hebron	6,635
Thomas (WC), Thedford	851
Thurston (NE), Pender	6,936
Valley (C), Ord	5,169
Washington (E), Blair	16,607
Wayne (NE), Wayne	9,364
Webster (S), Red Cloud	4,279
Wheeler (NC), Bartlett	948
York (SEC), York	14,428

STATISTICS

Newspapers

Period of Issue

Daily	15
Evening Daily	13
Morning Daily	4
Daily with Sunday edition	8
Semiweekly	6
Weekly	162
Monthly	4
Free or partly free	7
Shopper	13
Total Newspapers	193

Periodicals

Period of Issue

Weekly	7
Biweekly	1
Monthly	15
Bimonthly	8
Quarterly	12
Total Periodicals	54

Total number of publications 247

Radio Stations

AM Stations	43
FM Stations	71
Total Radio Stations	114

TV Stations

Total TV Stations 25

Cable Stations

Total Cable Systems 16

Total number of broadcast listings 155

AINSWORTH†, pop. 2,256.

Brown Co. (N). 140 m NW of Grand Island. Feed, hay machinery. Trade center for cattle and farm products. Dairy, stock, poultry, grain farms. Hay, corn.

18020 Star-Journal
Box 145 Phone: (402)387-2844
Ainsworth, NE 69210-0145 Fax: (402)387-1234

Newspaper. **Founded:** 1882. **Freq:** Weekly (Wed.). **Print Method:** Offset. **Cols./Page:** 7. **Col. Width:** 26 nonpareils. **Col. Depth:** 294 agate lines. **Key Personnel:** Rodney B. Worrell, Publisher. **Subscription Rates:** $11. **Remarks:** Accepts advertising.
Ad Rates: GLR: $.17 **Circ:** 3,056

18021 KBRB-AM - 1400
122 E. 2nd St. Phone: (402)387-1400
PO Box 285 Fax: (402)387-2624
Ainsworth, NE 69210
E-mail: kbrb@sscg.net

Format: Adult Contemporary; Contemporary Country; Adult Contemporary; Oldies. **Networks:** ABC. **Owner:** KBR Broadcasting Co., at above address. **Founded:** 1968. **Operating Hours:** 6 a.m.-10 p.m.; 5% network, 95% local. **Key Personnel:** Larry Rice, Manager; Ken Heuer, Contact; Randy Brudigan, Contact. **Wattage:** 1000. **Ad Rates:** $3.60-6 for 30 seconds; $4.95-8.25 for 60 seconds. Combined advertising rates available with KBRB-FM.

18022 KBRB-FM - 92.7
122 E. 2nd St. Phone: (402)387-1400
Box 285 Fax: (402)387-2624
Ainsworth, NE 69210
E-mail: kbrb@sscg.net

Format: Adult Contemporary; Contemporary Country. **Networks:** ABC. **Owner:** K.B.R. Broadcasting Co., at above address. **Founded:** 1983. **Operating Hours:** 6 a.m.-10 p.m. **Key Personnel:** Larry Rice, Manager; Ken Heuer, Program Dir.; Randy Brudigan, Chief Engineer. **Wattage:** 3000. **Ad Rates:** $3.60-6 for 30 seconds; $4.95-8.25 for 60 seconds. $3.60-$6 for 30 seconds; $4.95-$8.25 for 60 seconds.

ALBION†, pop. 1,997.

Boone Co. (EC). 55 m NE of Grand Island. Manufactures electronics; meat packing. Stock, grain, dairy, poultry farms. Alfalfa, corn, livestock.

18023 Albion News
328 W. Church Phone: (402)395-2115
Box 431 Fax: (402)395-2772
Albion, NE 68620
Community newspaper. **Founded:** 1879. **Freq:** Weekly (Wed.). **Print Method:** Offset. **Cols./Page:** 7. **Col. Width:** 25 nonpareils. **Col. Depth:** 21 inches. **Key Personnel:** Jean M. Kaup, Publisher. **USPS:** 012-640. **Subscription Rates:** $17 individuals; $20 out of area. **Remarks:** Accepts advertising.
Ad Rates: GLR: $0.46 **Circ:** ‡3,200
BW: $389.55
SAU: $3.50
PCI: $2.65

ALLIANCE†, pop. 9,869.

Box Butte Co. (NW). 45 m NE of Scottsbluff. Manufactures car trailers, electric hose, transistors, beverages, sleeping bags, down-filled garments. Stock, poultry, grain farms. Wheat, rye, barley, potatoes, beans, sugarbeets.

18024 Alliance Times-Herald
114 E. 4th St. Phone: (308)762-3060
PO Box G
Alliance, NE 69301
General newspaper. **Founded:** 1887. **Freq:** Daily (eve.) and Sat. (morn.). **Print Method:** Offset. **Cols./Page:** 6. **Col. Width:** 26 nonpareils. **Col. Depth:** 301 agate lines. **Key Personnel:** Fred Kuhlman, Publisher. **Subscription Rates:** $56. **Remarks:** Accepts advertising.
Ad Rates: GLR: $0.33 **Circ:** Paid ⊕**3,202**
SAU: $7.35
PCI: $7.35

18025 KAAQ-FM - 105.9
1210 W. 10th St. Phone: (308)762-1400
PO Box 600 Fax: (308)762-7804
Alliance, NE 69301
E-mail: kcow@bbc.net

Format: Country. **Simulcasts:** KQSK-FM. **Networks:** ABC; Satellite Music Network. **Owner:** Eagle Communications, Inc., PO Box 817, Hays, KS 67601, (913)625-4000, Fax: (913)625-8030. **Founded:** 1985. **Operating Hours:** 95% network, 5% local. **ADI:** Cheyenne, WY-Scottsbluff, NE (Sterling, CO). **Key Personnel:** Mike Garwood, Manager, phone (308)762-1400, fax (308)762-7804; Mike Glesinger, Operations Mgr.; Dave Fudge, News; Mike Glesinger, Sports Dir.; John Jones, Sales Mgr. **Local Programs:** *Harvest USA Report*; *Brownfield Markets*; *The Botton Line*; *Love and Desperation*; *Top 30 Countdown*; *Ag Information Center*. **Wattage:** 100,000. **Ad Rates:** $20 for 30 seconds; $30 for 60 seconds. Combined advertising rates available with KQSK-FM.

18026 KCOW-AM - 1400
1210 W. 10th St. Phone: (308)762-1400
PO Box 600 Fax: (308)762-7804
Alliance, NE 69301
E-mail: kcow@bbc.net

Format: Agricultural; Talk; Adult Contemporary; News; Sports. **Networks:** ABC; Satellite Music Network; Brownfield. **Owner:** Eagle Communications, Inc., PO Box 817, Hays, KS 67601, (785)625-4000, Fax: (785)625-8030. **Founded:** 1949. **Operating Hours:** 5 a.m.-1 a.m.; 65% network, 35% local. **Key Personnel:** John Jones, Sales Mgr.; Michael Glesinger, Operations Mgr.; Dave Fudge, News Dir.; Mike Glesinger, Sports Dir.; Mike Garwood, Manager. **Local Programs:** *Open Mic Buy, Sell, Trade (local)* 10:05 am - 11:00 am Monday-Friday, Mike Glesinger, (308)762-1400; *Don Kennedy Show*; *AgriTalk*; *Mid-Day Cafe*; *Paul Harvey News*; *Paul Harvey Rest of the Story*; *Jim Bohannon Show*; *Golden Age of Radio*. **Wattage:** 1000. **Ad Rates:** $11-15.25 for 30 seconds; $16.50-22.87 for 60 seconds.

18027 KPNY-FM - 102.1
221 E. 3rd St. Phone: (308)762-2000
PO Box 245 Fax: (308)762-2001
Alliance, NE 69301

Format: Adult Contemporary. **Networks:** Satellite Music Network. **Owner:** Halstead Communications, Inc., 1920 Broadway, PO Box 1153, Scottsbluff, NE 69363-1153, (308)635-1996, Fax: (308)635-1984. **Founded:** 1978. **Formerly:** KFAH-FM (1982). **Operating Hours:** Continuous. 2 Hrs. only local. **Key Personnel:** Lee Hall, General Mgr.; Adele Duran, Office Mgr.; Kevin Horn, Program Dir. **Local Programs:** *Prime Time Sports*, Mel Sauer. **Wattage:** 100,000. **Ad Rates:** $5.35-8.75 for 30 seconds; $6.35-10.30 for 60 seconds.

18028 KTNE-FM - 91.1
PO Box 83111 Phone: (402)472-3611
1800 N. 33rd St. Fax: (402)472-1785
Lincoln, NE 68501
Free: (800)290-6850
E-mail: nprn@unl.edu

Format: Public Radio; Classical; News. **Networks:** National Public Radio (NPR); Public Radio International (PRI). **Owner:** Nebraska Educational Telecommunications Commission, at above address. **Founded:** 1990. **Operating Hours:** 6 a.m.- 1 a.m. **ADI:** Lincoln-Hastings-Kearney, NE. **Key Personnel:** Steve Robinson, General Mgr. **Local Programs:** *Afternoon Concert*, Bill Stibor; *Morning Concert*, Bill Stibor; *Nebraska Nightly*, Nancy Finken. **Wattage:** 9230. **Ad Rates:** Noncommercial. **URL:** http://www.net.unl.edu/radio.html.

18029 KTNE-TV - 13
c/o KUON-TV Phone: (402)472-3611
1800 N. 33rd, St. Fax: (402)472-1785
PO Box 83111
Lincoln, NE 68501
E-mail: net@unlinfo.unl.edu

Format: Public TV. **Networks:** Public Broadcasting Service (PBS). **Owner:** Nebraska Educational Telecommunications, 1800 N. 33rd, Lincoln, NE 68583. **Founded:** 1966. **Operating Hours:** 5:45 a.m.-midnight; 90% network; 10% local. **ADI:** Cheyenne, WY-Scottsbluff, NE (Sterling, CO). **Key Personnel:** Rod Bates, General Mgr., rbates@unlinfo.unl.edu; Michael Winkle, Asst. GM, Marketing, mwinkle@unlinfo.unl.edu; Steve Lenzen, Assistant GM, Educational Television, slenzen@unlinfo.unl.edu; Sue Gildersleeve, Assistant GM, Admin. & Finance, sgildersleeve@unlinfo.unl.edu; S. Graziano, Program Mgr., sgraziano@unlinfo.unl.edu; Peter Ford, Asst. GM for Engineering, pford@unlinfo.unl.edu; Bill Kelly, Sr. Producer, Public Affairs, wek@unlinfo.unl.edu; Steve Alvis, Sr. Producer, Sports & Special Events, salvis@unlinfo.unl.edu; Michael Farrell, Production Coordinator, Cultural Affairs, mfarrell@unlinfo.unl.edu. **Local Programs:** *Backyard Farmer* 7 p.m. Tuesday; *Big Red Wrap-Up* 7 p.m. Tuesday; *Statewide* 8 p.m. Friday, Bill Ganzel. **Wattage:** 316. **Ad Rates:** Noncommercial. **URL:** http://www.net.unl.edu.

ALMA†, pop. 1,369.

Harlan Co. (S). 78 m SW of Grand Island. Dairy, stock, poultry, grain farms.

18030 Harlan County Journal
Box 9 Phone: (308)928-2143
Alma, NE 68920 Fax: (308)928-9914

Community newspaper. **Founded:** 1896. **Freq:** Weekly (Wed.). **Print Method:** Offset. **Trim Size:** 7 x 11 1/2. **Cols./Page:** 6. **Col. Width:** 12 picas. **Col. Depth:** 21 1/2 inches. **Key Personnel:** Warren Lingg, Editor and Publisher. **USPS:** 235-480. **Subscription Rates:** $23 individuals; $25 out of area. **Remarks:** Accepts advertising.
Ad Rates: GLR: $.18 **Circ:** ‡2,280
BW: $420
SAU: $3.10
PCI: $3.25

ARAPAHOE, pop. 1,107.

Furnas Co. (S). 80 m SW of Hastings. Dairy, stock, poultry, grain farms. Corn, wheat, alfalfa.

18031 Arapahoe Public Mirror
420 Nebraska Ave. Phone: (308)962-7261
PO Box 660 Fax: (308)962-7865
Arapahoe, NE 68922-0348
Community newspaper. **Founded:** 1879. **Freq:** Weekly (Thurs.). **Print Method:** Offset. **Cols./Page:** 6. **Col. Width:** 24 nonpareils. **Col. Depth:** 301 agate lines. **Key Personnel:** T.M. Gill, Editor and Publisher. **Subscription Rates:** $19. **Remarks:** Accepts advertising.
Ad Rates: GLR: $.41 **Circ:** 1,462
SAU: $3
PCI: $2.45

ARLINGTON, pop. 1,117.

Washington Co. (E). 25 m NE of Omaha. Nurseries. Farm implement manufacturing. Alfalfa dehydrating plant. Diversified farming. Wheat, corn, cattle.

18032 Arlington Citizen
Enterprise Publishing Co., Inc.
PO Box 460 Phone: (402)426-2121
Arlington, NE 68002 Fax: (402)426-2227

Community newspaper. **Founded:** 1954. **Freq:** Weekly (Thurs.). **Print Method:** Offset. **Trim Size:** 16 x 23. **Cols./Page:** 7. **Col. Width:** 12 picas. **Col. Depth:** 315 agate lines. **Key Personnel:** Ken Rhoades, Publisher; Carrie L. Larkins, Editor. **USPS:** 319-400. **Subscription Rates:** $13; $17 out of county; $19 out of state. **Remarks:** Accepts advertising.
Ad Rates: PCI: $3.70 **Circ:** Paid ‡800
Free ‡50

ARTHUR†, pop. 124.

Arthur Co. (W). 60 m NW of North Platte. Diversified farming. Sugar beets, hay, grain, cattle.

18033 Arthur Enterprise
PO Box 165 Phone: (308)764-2402
Arthur, NE 69121-0165
Publication E-mail: artent@neb-sandhills.net

Community newspaper. **Founded:** May 1911. **Freq:** Weekly (Thurs.). **Print Method:** Offset. **Cols./Page:** 5. **Col. Width:** 22 nonpareils. **Col. Depth:** 190 agate lines. **Key Personnel:** Karen Sizer, Advertising Mgr. **Subscription Rates:** $12.50 individuals; $14 out of state. **Remarks:** Accepts advertising.
Ad Rates: PCI: $2.50 **Circ:** ‡500

ASHLAND, pop. 2,276.

Saunders Co. (E). 24 m NE of Lincoln. Sand and gravel pits. Rock quarries. Grain farms. Wheat, corn, milo, soybeans.

18034 The Ashland Gazette
The Gazette
1518 Silver St. Phone: (402)944-3397
Box 127 Fax: (402)944-3398
Ashland, NE 68003-0127
Newspaper. **Founded:** 1879. **Freq:** Weekly (Thurs.). **Print Method:** Offset. **Cols./Page:** 6. **Col. Width:** 25 nonpareils. **Col. Depth:** 301 agate lines. **Key Personnel:** Zean E. Carney, Publisher. **Subscription Rates:** $20 individuals; $23 out of state.
Ad Rates: 4C: $225 **Circ:** 1,973
SAU: $4.50

ATKINSON, pop. 1,521.

Holt Co. (N). 200 m NW of Omaha. Hunting and fishing. Center pivot irrigator manufacturer. Irrigated farming. Cattle, swine. Dairy.

18035 The Atkinson Graphic
207 E. State St. Phone: (402)925-5411
PO Box 159
Atkinson, NE 68713
Newspaper with a Republican orientation. **Founded:** 1882. **Freq:** Weekly (Thurs.). **Print Method:** Offset. **Cols./Page:** 7. **Col. Width:** 25 nonpareils. **Col. Depth:** 298 agate lines. **Key Personnel:** Jerry Hollingsworth, Editor and Publisher. **Subscription Rates:** $20. **Remarks:** Accepts advertising.
Ad Rates: GLR: $.222 **Circ:** 2,165
BW: $300
SAU: $3.10
PCI: $3.10

AUBURN†, pop. 3,482.

Nemaha Co. (SE). 70 m SE of Lincoln. Manufactures wood cabinets, bronze bushings, grounds maintenance and light construction equipment, garments. Diversified farming. Corn, wheat.

18036 Auburn Press-Tribune
Auburn Newspapers
PO Box 250 Phone: (402)274-3185
Auburn, NE 68305 Fax: (402)274-3273
Publisher E-mail: aubnews@novix.net

Community newspaper. **Founded:** 1882. **Freq:** Weekly (Tues.). **Print Method:** Offset. **Cols./Page:** 7. **Col. Width:** 2 1/16 inches. **Col. Depth:** 21 1/2 inches. **Key Personnel:** Mark Cramer, Editor; Paula Winkelman, Advertising Mgr. **USPS:** 036-880. **Subscription Rates:** $17; $24 out of area. **Remarks:** Accepts advertising.
Ad Rates: GLR: $.243 **Circ:** Paid ‡3,267
BW: $3.10 Free ‡95
SAU: $3.40
PCI: $3.40

18037 Nemaha County Herald
Auburn Newspapers
PO Box 250 Phone: (402)274-3185
Auburn, NE 68305 Fax: (402)274-3273
Publisher E-mail: aubnews@novix.net

Community newspaper. **Founded:** Jan. 1888. **Freq:** Weekly (Fri.). **Print Method:** Offset. **Cols./Page:** 7. **Col. Width:** 2 1/16 inches. **Col. Depth:** 21 1/2 inches. **Key Personnel:** Mark Cramer, Publisher; Paula Winkelman, Managing Editor; Darrell Wellman, Managing Editor. **USPS:** 376-940. **Subscription Rates:** $17; $24 out of area. **Remarks:** Accepts advertising.
Ad Rates: GLR: $0.24 **Circ:** Paid ‡3,275
BW: $5 Free ‡87
SAU: $4.60
PCI: $4.60

18038 Auburn Cablevision
1304 Courthouse Ave. Phone: (402)421-0330
Auburn, NE 68305 Fax: (402)421-0305

Owner: Time Warner, at above address. **Founded:** Apr. 1966. **Key Personnel:** Valerie Kramer, General Mgr.; Rick Hollmann, Systems Engineer. **Cities Served:** Auburn, Humboldt, Nebraska City, Pawnee City, Table Rock, Tecumseh, NE: subscribing households 5,482; 36 channels.

AURORA†, pop. 3,717.

Hamilton Co. (SEC). 20 m E of Grand Island. Manufactures butter and flour, electronic components, steel, mobile homes. Stock, grain, dairy farms. Corn, wheat, sugar beets. Live stock feeding.

18039 News-Register
1320 K St. Phone: (402)694-2131
Box 70 Fax: (402)694-2133
Aurora, NE 68818
Publication E-mail: newsregister@mmilton.net; newsregister@hamilton.net

Newspaper. **Founded:** 1872. **Freq:** Weekly (Wed.). **Print Method:** Offset. **Trim Size:** 15 x 22. **Cols./Page:** 6. **Col. Width:** 26 nonpareils. **Col. Depth:** 294 agate lines. **Key Personnel:** R.L. Furse, Publisher. **USPS:** 037-900. **Subscription Rates:** $20. **Remarks:** Accepts advertising. **Available Online. URL:** http://www.hamilton.net/aurora/newsreg./a-newsreg.htm.
Ad Rates: GLR: $2.55 **Circ:** 4,096
PCI: $4.50

18040 Mid-State Community TV
1001 12th St. Phone: (402)694-4401
Aurora, NE 68818 Fax: (402)694-2848
E-mail: info@hamilton.net

BASSETT†, pop. 1,009.

Rock Co. (N). 133 m NW of Grand Island. Hay and cattle market. Agriculture. Corn, grain, rye, wild hay.

18041 Rock County Leader
Box 488 Phone: (402)684-3771
Bassett, NE 68714 Fax: (402)684-2857

Newspaper with a Republican orientation. **Founded:** 1896. **Freq:** Weekly (Thurs.). **Print Method:** Offset. **Cols./Page:** 7. **Col. Width:** 12 picas. **Col. Depth:** 21 1/4 inches. **Key Personnel:** Bill G. Fegley, Editor and Publisher. **Subscription Rates:** $17 individuals; $19 out of state. **Remarks:** Accepts advertising.
Ad Rates: SAU: $2.85 **Circ:** ‡1,687

18042 KMNE-TV - 7
c/o KUON-TV Phone: (402)472-3611
1800 N. 33rd. St. Fax: (402)472-1785
Box 83111
Lincoln, NE 68501

Format: Public TV. **Simulcasts:** KUON-TV Lincoln, NE. **Networks:** Public Broadcasting Service (PBS). **Owner:** Nebraska Educational Telecommunications, at above address. **Founded:** 1967. **Operating Hours:** 5:45 a.m.-midnight; 90% network, 10% local. **ADI:** Lincoln-Hastings-Kearney, NE. **Key Personnel:** Rod Bates, Contact, rbates@unlinfo.unl.edu; Michael Winkle, Asst. GM, Marketing, mwinkle@unlinfo.unl.edu; S. Graziano, Program Mgr., sgraziano@unlinfo.unl.edu; Susan Gildersleeve, Asst. GM, Admin. and Finance, sgildersleeve@unlinfo.unl.edu; Steve Lenzen, Asst. GM, Educational TV, slenzen@unlinfo.unl.edu; Peter Ford, Asst. GM for Engineering, pford@unlinfo.unl.edu; Bill Kelly, Sr. Producer, Public Affairs, wek@unlinfo.unl.edu; Steve Alvis, Sr. Producer, Sports & Special Events, salvis@unlinfo.unl.edu; Michael Farrell, Production Coordinator, Cultural Affairs, mfarrell@unlinfo.unl.edu; Mark Kelley, Contact; Gary Hochman, Contact. **Ad Rates:** Noncommercial.

BATTLE CREEK

18043 Battle Creek Enterprise
PO Box 70 Phone: (402)675-5333
Battle Creek, NE 68715 Fax: (402)371-0621

Community newspaper. **Freq:** Weekly (Wed.). **Cols./Page:** 7. **Col. Width:** 2 1/16 inches. **Col. Depth:** 21 inches. **Key Personnel:** Leslie Falter, Editor and Publisher.
Circ: 700

BAYARD, pop. 1,435.

Morrill Co. (W) 15 mi N.W. of Northport. Residential

18044 The Bayard Transcript
336 Main Phone: (308)586-1313
PO Box 626
Bayard, NE 69334
Newspaper (local news). **Founded:** Jan. 1890. **Freq:** Weekly (Wed.). **Print Method:** Offset. **Cols./Page:** 6. **Col. Width:** 24 nonpareils. **Col. Depth:** 294 agate lines. **Key Personnel:** Jeanne Heath, Editor and Publisher. **Subscription Rates:** $12.50 in Nebraska; $15.50 out of state. **Remarks:** Accepts advertising.
Ad Rates: SAU: $2.66 **Circ:** ‡1,300

BEATRICE†, pop. 12,891.

Gage Co. (SE). 40 m S of Lincoln. Manufactures store fixtures, farm machinery, steel, aluminum, containers, hardware specialties, windmills, fertilizer (dry & liquid). Livestock, dairy farms. Wheat corn, soybeans, milo.

18045 Beatrice Daily Sun
200 N. 7th St. Phone: (402)223-5233
PO Box 847 Fax: (402)228-3571
Beatrice, NE 68310-3916
Community newspaper. **Founded:** June 1902. **Freq:** Daily (eve.) and Sat. (morn.). **Print Method:** Offset. **Cols./Page:** 6. **Col. Width:** 26 nonpareils. **Col. Depth:** 301 agate lines. **Key Personnel:** Reg Durant, Publisher; Diane Vicarr, Editor; Ken Linger, Advertising Mgr. **USPS:** 047-060. **Subscription Rates:** $60.
Ad Rates: BW: $999.75 **Circ:** Mon.-Sat. ★8,540
4C: $1,322.75
PCI: $7.75

18046 Penny Press 5
Maverick Media, Inc.
817 Court St. Phone: (402)223-4063
PO Box 822 Fax: (402)223-5995
Beatrice, NE 68310
Shopper. **Freq:** Weekly (Tues.). **Print Method:** Offset. **Trim Size:** 11 1/2 x 16. **Cols./Page:** 6. **Col. Width:** 9 1/2 picas. **Col. Depth:** 15 inches. **Key Personnel:** Peyton Nariem, General Mgr. **Subscription Rates:** $24; Free. **Remarks:** Accepts advertising.
Ad Rates: GLR: $1.25 **Circ:** Free ‡18,500
BW: $706.50
4C: $861.50
SAU: $10.35
PCI: $7.85

18047 KWBE-AM - 1450
200 Sherman St. Phone: (402)228-5923
Box 10 Fax: (402)228-3704
Beatrice, NE 68310
E-mail: kwbeabeatricene.com

Format: Adult Contemporary. **Networks:** ABC; Mutual Broadcasting System; Unistar. **Owner:** Community Media, Inc., at above address. **Founded:** 1949. **Operating Hours:** 5:00 a.m.-11 p.m.; 10% network, 90% local. **ADI:** Lincoln-Hastings-Kearney, NE. **Key Personnel:** Joan B. Wood, General Mgr.; Jay Stalder, Program Dir.; David Niedfeldt, Farm Director; Eric Rodewald, Sports Dir.; Bill Sayer, Chief Engineer; Rosmary Lamberson, Sales Mgr.; Doug Kennedy, News Dir. **Wattage:** 1000. **Ad Rates:** $11-25 for 30 seconds; $16-35 for 60 seconds.

BEAVER CITY†, pop. 775.

Furnas Co. (S). 80 m SW of Hastings. Plastic Products. Beef cattle. Farming. Corn, wheat, alfalfa.

18048 Times-Tribune
Box 258 Phone: (308)268-2205
Beaver City, NE 68926 Fax: (308)268-4000

Community newspaper. **Founded:** 1873. **Freq:** Weekly (Thurs.). **Print Method:** Offset. **Cols./Page:** 6. **Col. Width:** 12 picas. **Col. Depth:** 21 inches. **Key Personnel:** Travis D. Theobald, Publisher; Douglas B. Garey, Editor; Betty J. Garey, Business Mgr. **USPS:** 630-780. **Subscription Rates:** $16 area; $18.50 out of area. **Remarks:** Accepts advertising alcoholic beverages and tobacco products.
Ad Rates: SAU: $3 **Circ:** Paid ‡820
Free ‡13

BELLEVUE, pop. 21,813.

Sarpy Co. (E) 9 m S of Omaha. Offutt AFB. Chemicals, textile, high tech defense contractors.

18049 Bellevue Leader
604 Fort Crook Rd. N. Phone: (402)733-7300
Bellevue, NE 68005 Fax: (402)733-9116
Publication E-mail: leader@top.net

Community newspaper. **Founded:** 1971. **Freq:** Weekly (Wed.). **Print Method:** Offset. **Cols./Page:** 8. **Col. Width:** 9 picas. **Col. Depth:** 21 1/2 inches. **Key Personnel:** Ron Petak, Editor; Dixie Carvner, Publisher; Paul Swanson, Advertising Mgr. **Subscription Rates:** $20.95; $30.45 out of area. **Remarks:** Accepts advertising.
Ad Rates: GLR: $.95 **Circ:** Combined ‡25,629
BW: $2,167
4C: $635
PCI: $13.20

BENKELMAN†, pop. 1,235.

Dundy Co. (SW). 90 m SW of North Platte. State fish hatcheries. Stock, grain, dairy, poultry farms. Corn.

18050 Benkelman Post and News-Chronicle
513 Chief St. Phone: (308)423-2337
PO Box 800 Fax: (308)423-5555
Benkelman, NE 69021-0800
Community newspaper. **Subtitle:** Benkelman Post. **Founded:** 1889. **Freq:** Weekly (Wed.). **Print Method:** Offset. **Cols./Page:** 6. **Col. Width:** 21 nonpareils. **Col. Depth:** 301 agate lines. **Key Personnel:** Glenda Bartholomew, Owner; Jan M. Cady, Managing Editor. **USPS:** 050-220. **Subscription Rates:** $27 individuals; $35 out of area.
Ad Rates: SAU: $5.15 **Circ:** Paid ‡1,369
Non-paid ‡35

BERTRAND

18051 The Bertrand Herald
PO Box 425 Phone: (308)472-3217
Bertrand, NE 68927 Fax: (308)472-5165

Weekly newspaper. **Founded:** 1891. **Freq:** Weekly. **Print Method:** Offset. **Trim Size:** 14 x 22 3/4. **Cols./Page:** 6. **Col. Width:** 12.5 picas. **Col. Depth:** 21.5 inches. **Key Personnel:** Robert G. Engle, Editor and Publisher; Genevieve Forster,

Editor. **Subscription Rates:** $18 individuals; $24 out of state. **Remarks:** Accepts advertising.
Ad Rates: GLR: $4 **Circ:** Paid ‡500
BW: $516
4C: $566
SAU: $4
PCI: $4

BLAIR†, pop. 6,500.

Washington Co. (E). 18 m NW of Omaha. Dana College. Manufactures grain elevators, farm machinery, fertilizers, limestone, heavy road equipment. Silage storage bagging machines, ethanol.

18052 Blair Enterprise
Enterprise Publishing Co., Inc.
138 N. 16th St. Phone: (402)426-2121
PO Box 328 Fax: (402)426-2227
Blair, NE 68008-0328
Community newspaper. **Founded:** 1912. **Freq:** Weekly (Fri.). **Print Method:** Offset. **Trim Size:** 15 1/4 x 22 1/2. **Cols./Page:** 7. **Col. Width:** 2 1/16 inches. **Col. Depth:** 301 agate lines. **Key Personnel:** Mark A. Rhoades, Publisher, mrhoades@enterprisepub.com. **Subscription Rates:** $27. **Remarks:** Accepts advertising. **URL:** http://www.enterprisepub.com; http://www.blairnebraska.com. **Alt. Formats:** Microfilm.
Ad Rates: GLR: $7 **Circ:** ‡4,400
BW: $1,130
4C: $1,410
SAU: $7.34

18053 Clipper
Enterprise Publishing Co., Inc.
138 N. 16th St. Phone: (402)426-2121
PO Box 328 Fax: (402)426-2227
Blair, NE 68008-0328
Shopper. **Founded:** 1970. **Freq:** Weekly. **Print Method:** Offset. **Trim Size:** 15 1/4 x 22 1/2. **Cols./Page:** 7. **Col. Width:** 2 1/16 inches. **Col. Depth:** 301 agate lines. **Key Personnel:** Lynette Hansen, Advertising Mgr.; Mark A. Rhoades, Publisher. **Subscription Rates:** Free; $18.50 by mail. **Remarks:** Accepts advertising.
Ad Rates: BW: $1093.40 **Circ:** Paid 4,366
4C: $85 Free 9,483
SAU: $8.17
PCI: $7.10

18054 Clipper Shopper
Enterprise Publishing Co., Inc.
138 N. 16th St. Phone: (402)426-2121
PO Box 328 Fax: (402)426-2227
Blair, NE 68008-0328
Publication E-mail: sales@enterprisepub.com

Shopper. **Subtitle:** Clipper. **Founded:** 1912. **Freq:** (Tues. in Nebraska, Wed. in Iowa). **Print Method:** Offset. **Cols./Page:** 7. **Col. Width:** 2 1/16 inches. **Col. Depth:** 301 agate lines. **Key Personnel:** Carrie Larkins, Editor; Mark A. Rhoades, Publisher; Lynette Hansen, Advertising Mgr.; Kenneth H. Rhoades, Co-Publisher. **Subscription Rates:** Free. **Remarks:** Accepts advertising.
Ad Rates: BW: $1,139.60 **Circ:** Combined ‡13,995
4C: $1,639.60
SAU: $8.68
PCI: $7.40

18055 Sarpy County Extra
Enterprise Publishing Co., Inc.
138 N. 16th St. Phone: (402)426-2121
PO Box 328 Fax: (402)426-2227
Blair, NE 68008-0328
Shopping guide. **Founded:** 1912. **Freq:** Weekly (Wed.). **Print Method:** Offset. **Cols./Page:** 7. **Col. Width:** 2 1/16 inches. **Col. Depth:** 301 agate lines. **Key Personnel:** Kenneth H. Rhoades, Editor and Publisher; Mark A. Rhoades, Editor. **Remarks:** Accepts advertising.
Ad Rates: SAU: $3.85 **Circ:** Free ‡2,800

18056 Great Plains Cable TV Inc.
1635 Front St. Phone: (402)426-9511
Box 500 Fax: (402)426-6475
Blair, NE 68008

Owner: Great Plains Communications Telephone Co., at above address. **Founded:** 1985. **Key Personnel:** Tim Garrigan, General Mgr.; LeAnn Quist, Contact. **Cities Served:** subscribing households 1,500; 21 channels; 1 community access channel.

18057 KDCV-FM - 91.1
Dana College Phone: (402)426-7205
Blair, NE 68008 Fax: (402)426-7382
E-mail: kdcv@acad2.dana.edu

Format: Eclectic. **Founded:** 1972. **Operating Hours:** Sun.-Sat., 3 p.m.-12 a.m. **Key Personnel:** Vern Wirka, Station Mgr., phone (402)426-7349, fax (402)426-7382, vwirka@acad2.dana.edu. **Wattage:** 10. **Ad Rates:** Noncommercial.

BLOOMFIELD, pop. 1,393.

Knox Co. (NE). 52 m N of Norfolk. Manufactures feed. Stock, grain, poultry, dairy farms. Alfalfa, corn.

18058 Bloomfield Monitor
110 N. Broadway Phone: (402)373-2332
PO Box 367
Bloomfield, NE 68718
Community newspaper. **Founded:** 1890. **Freq:** Weekly (Thurs.). **Print Method:** Offset. **Trim Size:** 7 x 11. **Cols./Page:** 6. **Col. Width:** 12.5 picas. **Col. Depth:** 21 inches. **Key Personnel:** Joseph M. Skrivan, Editor; Mary Ellen Skrivan, Publisher. **USPS:** 358-840. **Subscription Rates:** $16 individuals; $17 out of area; $20 out of state.
Ad Rates: BW: $386.40 **Circ:** ‡1,640
SAU: $3
PCI: $3

BLOOMINGTON

18059 Franklin County Sentinel
PO Box 285
Bloomington, NE 68929-0285

Community newspaper. **Founded:** 1889. **Freq:** Weekly (Tues.). **Print Method:** Offset. **Cols./Page:** 6. **Col. Width:** 13.5 picas. **Col. Depth:** 21 inches. **Key Personnel:** Cheryl Sue Carlton, Editor and Publisher. **Subscription Rates:** $12. **Remarks:** Accepts advertising.
Ad Rates: GLR: $.125 **Circ:** ‡1,800
SAU: $3.08

BLUE HILL, pop. 883.

Webster Co. (S). 20 m S of Hastings. Livestock. Sorghum, corn, wheat.

18060 Blue Hill Leader
514 Gage St. Phone: (402)756-2077
Box 38 Fax: (402)756-2097
Blue Hill, NE 68930
Publication E-mail: bhleader@gtmc.com

Community newspaper. **Founded:** 1887. **Freq:** Weekly (Wed.). **Print Method:** Offset. **Trim Size:** 11 1/8 x 17 1/2. **Cols./Page:** 5. **Col. Width:** 24 nonpareils. **Col. Depth:** 238 agate lines. **Key Personnel:** Leland Ostdiek, Editor and Publisher. **Subscription Rates:** $16 in area; $23 out of area.
Ad Rates: GLR: $.22 **Circ:** ‡1,440
BW: $294
SAU: $3.50
PCI: $4

18061 Glenwood Telecommunications
510 W. Gage St. Phone: (402)756-3130
Box 357 Fax: (402)756-3134
Blue Hill, NE 68930

Owner: Glenwood Telephone Membership Corp., Box 97, Blue Hill, NE 68930. **Founded:** Jan. 1985. **Key Personnel:** Stanley Rouse, General Mgr.; Mark McFarland, Asst. Mgr. **Cities Served:** Bladen, Blue Hill, Campbell, Funk, Guide Rock, Holstein, Lawrence, Lochland/Hastings, Roseland, Upland, NE; Hastings AFB: subscribing households 1,223; 36 channels; 1 community access channel; 168 hours per week community access programming.

BRIDGEPORT

18062 Bridgeport News-Blade
The Blade
801 Main St. Phone: (308)262-0675
PO Box 400 Fax: (308)262-0352
Bridgeport, NE 69336
Community newspaper. **Founded:** 1900. **Freq:** Weekly (Wed.). **Print Method:** Offset. **Cols./Page:** 6. **Col. Width:** 2 inches. **Col. Depth:** 21 inches. **Key Personnel:** Wendlin Lummel, Editor and Publisher. **Remarks:** Advertising accepted; rates available upon request.
Circ: 1,600

BROKEN BOW†, pop. 3,979.

Custer Co. (C). In center of State, 75 m NE of North Platte. Surgical supplies, pipe and water turbine pumps manufactured. Agriculture. Especially grain and livestock. Corn, soybeans.

18063 Custer County Chief
305 S. 10th Phone: (308)872-2471
PO Box 190 Fax: (308)872-2415
Broken Bow, NE 68822-0190
Community newspaper. **Founded:** 1892. **Freq:** Weekly (Thurs.). **Print Method:** Offset. **Cols./Page:** 6. **Col. Width:** 26 nonpareils. **Col. Depth:** 301 agate lines. **Key Personnel:** Jeffrey Bielser, Editor; Charley Najacht, Publisher; Mary Coffman, Advertising Mgr. **USPS:** 140-980. **Subscription Rates:** $28 individuals; $38 out of state. **Remarks:** Accepts advertising.
Ad Rates: GLR: $.36 **Circ:** 3,200
PCI: $6.25

18064 KBBN-FM - 98.3
Box 409 Phone: (308)872-5881
Broken Bow, NE 68822 Fax: (308)872-3284

Format: Sports; Classic Rock. **Networks:** NBC. **Owner:** Custer County Broadcasting Co., at above address. **Founded:** 1982. **Operating Hours:** 6 a.m.- 12 p.m. **Key Personnel:** David Birnie, General Mgr. **Wattage:** 3400. **Ad Rates:** $5.10-8.95 for 30 seconds; $6.10-11 for 60 seconds.

18065 KCNI-AM - 1280
Box 409 Phone: (308)872-5881
Broken Bow, NE 68822 Fax: (308)872-3284

Format: Full Service; Contemporary Country; Agricultural. **Networks:** NBC. **Owner:** Custer County Broadcasting Co., at above address. **Founded:** 1949. **Operating Hours:** 6 a.m.-7 p.m. **Key Personnel:** David Birnie, General Mgr.; David J. Birnie, Program Dir.; Tom Hilkemeier, Contact. **Wattage:** 1000. **Ad Rates:** $5.10-8.95 for 30 seconds; $6.10-11 for 60 seconds.

BUTTE†, pop. 529.

Boyd Co. (N). 130 m NW of Sioux City, Iowa. Grain, stock, poultry farms. Hay, corn, rye.

18066 The Butte Gazette
Box 6 Phone: (402)775-2431
Butte, NE 68722-0006 Fax: (402)589-1010

Community newspaper. **Founded:** 1891. **Freq:** Weekly (Thurs.). **Print Method:** Offset. **Cols./Page:** 8. **Col. Width:** 21 nonpareils. **Col. Depth:** 297 agate lines. **Key Personnel:** Leon Wells, Editor and Publisher. **USPS:** 081-200. **Subscription Rates:** $12; $16 out of area; $20 out of state. **Remarks:** Accepts advertising.
Ad Rates: GLR: $.10 **Circ:** 622
BW: $170
SAU: $1.90

CAIRO, pop. 750.

Hall Co. (C). 16 m NW of Grand Island. Diversified farming. Alfalfa, corn, wheat, potatoes.

18067 Cairo Record
Box 540 Phone: (308)485-4284
Cairo, NE 68824 Fax: (308)485-4286
Free: (800)658-3241

Newspaper. **Founded:** 1901. **Freq:** Weekly (Thurs.). **Print Method:** Offset. **Cols./Page:** 5. **Col. Width:** 24 nonpareils. **Col. Depth:** 224 agate lines. **Key Personnel:** Richard Mohanna, Editor and Publisher; Jean Mohanna, Editor and Publisher. **Subscription Rates:** $14; $16 out of state. **Remarks:** Accepts advertising.
Ad Rates: PCI: $2.50 **Circ:** ‡950

CALLAWAY, pop. 579.

Custer Co (C). 45 m. NE of North Platte. Museum and park area. Hunting and fishing. Fertilizer plants. Farming.

18068 The Callaway Courier
PO Box 69 Phone: (308)836-2200
Callaway, NE 68825
Community newspaper. **Founded:** 1968. **Freq:** Weekly (Thurs.). **Print Method:** Offset. **Cols./Page:** 6. **Col. Width:** 23 nonpareils. **Col. Depth:** 182 agate lines. **Key Personnel:** Michael Wendorff, Publisher; Suzanne Wendorff, Publisher. **Subscription Rates:** $20 individuals; $22 out of state. **Remarks:** Accepts advertising.
Ad Rates: GLR: $2.50 **Circ:** Paid ‡850
BW: $145 Free ‡18
SAU: $2.50
PCI: $2.20

CEDAR RAPIDS

18069 Cedar Rapids Press
PO Box D Phone: (308)497-2153
Spalding, NE 68665
Community newspaper. **Founded:** 1947. **Freq:** Weekly (Mon.). **Print Method:** Letterpress. **Trim Size:** 12 x 17. **Cols./Page:** 5. **Col. Width:** 12 picas. **Col. Depth:** 16 inches. **Key Personnel:** David Bopp, Publisher. **USPS:** 557-200. **Subscription Rates:** $16; $20 out of area. **Remarks:** Accepts advertising.
Ad Rates: GLR: $.15 **Circ:** ‡600
BW: $204
SAU: $2.52
PCI: $2.10

CENTRAL CITY†, pop. 3,083.

Merrick Co. (EC). On Platte River, 22 m NE of Grand Island. Concrete products, wood pallets, mobile homes manufactured. Popcorn processing plant. Diversified farming. Corn, wheat, alfalfa.

18070 Republican Nonpareil
PO Box 26 Phone: (308)946-3081
Central City, NE 68826 Fax: (308)946-3082
Free: (800)323-3929
Publisher E-mail: jensenpub@hamilton.net

Newspaper. **Founded:** 1882. **Freq:** Weekly (Thurs.). **Print Method:** Offset. **Cols./Page:** 4. **Col. Width:** 24 nonpareils. **Col. Depth:** 196 agate lines. **Key Personnel:** Robert M. Jensen, Editor and Publisher, jensenpub@hamilton.net; Penelope A. Jensen, Publisher. **Subscription Rates:** $17.50 individuals; $24.50 out of state.
Ad Rates: BW: $597.24 **Circ:** Paid ‡2,350
SAU: $3.75 Free ‡50
PCI: $5.74

18071 KZEN-FM - 100.3
PO Box 100 Phone: (308)946-3816
Central City, NE 68826 Fax: (308)946-3612

Format: Country. **Networks:** Farm & Ranch Radio. **Founded:** 1985. **Operating Hours:** Continuous. **ADI:** Lincoln-Hastings-Kearney, NE. **Key Personnel:** Gene McCoy, General Mgr.; John Ellefson, News Dir. **Wattage:** 100,000. **Ad Rates:** $90 for 30 seconds; $110 for 60 seconds.

CHADRON†, pop. 5,933.

Dawes Co. (NW). 30 m NW of Rushville. Residential.

18072 Chadron Record
PO Box 1141 Phone: (308)432-5511
Chadron, NE 69337-1141 Fax: (308)432-2385

Newspaper. **Founded:** 1884. **Freq:** Weekly (Tues.). **Print Method:** Offset. **Cols./Page:** 6. **Col. Width:** 24 nonpareils. **Col. Depth:** 294 agate lines. **Key Personnel:** Lois Yoakum, Editor and Publisher. **Subscription Rates:** Free; $28; $45 out of state. **Remarks:** Accepts advertising.
Ad Rates: GLR: $.44 **Circ:** Paid ‡2,900
BW: $772.38 Free ‡7,700
SAU: $6.13
PCI: $6.13

18073 The Eagle
Chadron State College
227 Kline Bldg. Phone: (308)432-6303
1000 C Main St. Fax: (308)432-6464
Chadron, NE 69337
Publisher E-mail: eaglenew@ascu.csc.edu

Collegiate newspaper. **Founded:** 1921. **Freq:** Weekly. **Print Method:** Offset. **Cols./Page:** 5. **Col. Width:** 11 picas. **Col. Depth:** 178 agate lines. **Key Personnel:** Kim Phagan, Editor; Lisa Firubbs, News Ed.; Sarah Chryst, News Ed. **Remarks:** Accepts advertising. **URL:** http://www.csc.edu/.
Ad Rates: PCI: $4.00 **Circ:** Free 2,500

18074 KCSR-AM - 610
226 Bordeaux Phone: (308)432-5545
Chadron, NE 69337 Fax: (308)432-5601
Free: (800)266-4682
E-mail: kcsram@prairieweb.com

Format: Country. **Networks:** ABC; Mid-America Ag. **Founded:** 1953. **Operating Hours:** Continuous; 5% network, 95% local. **ADI:** Denver (Steamboat Springs), CO. **Key Personnel:** Dennis Brown, General Mgr.; Jeff Wing, Program Dir.; Scott Walker, News Dir.; Kathi Brown, Sales Mgr. **Local Programs:** *Community Focus*, Duane Erwell, Host; *High School Sports*, Scott Walker, News Dir.; *Swap Shop*, Jeff Wing, Program Dir. **Wattage:** 1000. **Ad Rates:** Advertising accepted; rates available upon request.

18075 KQSK-FM - 97.5
PO Box 1117 Phone: (308)432-2060
Chadron, NE 69337-1117 Fax: (308)432-2059

Format: Contemporary Country. **Simulcasts:** KAAQ-FM. **Networks:** ABC. **Founded:** 1979. **Operating Hours:** 5:30-1 a.m.; 80% network, 20% local. **Key Personnel:** John Howard, Station Mgr.; John Axtell, News Dir. **Wattage:** 200,000. **Ad Rates:** $8-20 for 30 seconds; $10-25 for 60 seconds.

CHAPPELL†, pop. 1,095.

Deul Co. (W). 20 m S of Oshkosh. Residential.

18076 The Chappell Register
273 Vincent Ave. Phone: (308)874-2207
PO Box 528 Fax: (308)874-2207
Chappell, NE 69129
Community newspaper. **Founded:** 1887. **Freq:** Weekly (Thurs.). **Print Method:** Offset. **Cols./Page:** 6. **Col. Width:** 26 nonpareils. **Col. Depth:** 301 agate lines. **Key Personnel:** Michael Talbott, Editor and Publisher. **USPS:** 100-300. **Subscription Rates:** $13 individuals.
Ad Rates: BW: $323.79 **Circ:** ‡1,200
SAU: $2.79

CHESTER

18077 Chester Herald
510 Thayer Phone: (402)324-5764
PO Box 338 Fax: (402)324-5764
Chester, NE 68327
Community newspaper. **Freq:** Weekly (Wed.). **Cols./Page:** 6. **Col. Width:** 13 picas. **Col. Depth:** 21 inches. **Key Personnel:** Christine Williams, Editor; James Williams, Publisher.
Circ: 1,800

CLARKSON, pop. 817.

Colfax Co. (E). 13 m S of Stanton. Residential.

18078 The Colfax County Press
242 Pine Phone: (402)892-3544
PO Box 1 Fax: (402)892-3141
Clarkson, NE 68629
Newspaper with a Democratic orientation. **Founded:** 1901. **Freq:** Weekly (Wed.). **Print Method:** Offset. **Cols./Page:** 6. **Col. Width:** 26 nonpareils. **Col. Depth:** 280 agate lines. **Key Personnel:** Donald J. Evans, Editor; H.C. Evans, Publisher; D.J. Evans, Publisher; Jim Evans, Advertising Mgr. **Subscription Rates:** $17 individuals; $20 out of area. **Remarks:** Accepts advertising.
Ad Rates: GLR: $2.64 **Circ:** ‡2,000
PCI: $2.48

Leigh World - See Leigh

COLERIDGE

18079 Coleridge Blade
PO Box 8 Phone: (402)283-4267
Coleridge, NE 68727
Community newspaper. **Founded:** 1889. **Freq:** Weekly (Wed.). **Cols./Page:** 5. **Col. Width:** 11 picas. **Col. Depth:** 15 1/2 inches. **Key Personnel:** Robert B. Yost, Editor and Publisher. **Subscription Rates:** $15 individuals; $17 out of area; $19 out of state.
Ad Rates: SAU: $2.60 **Circ:** 1,000

COLUMBUS†, pop. 17,328.

Platte Co. (E). 75 m NW of Lincoln. Trade center. Manufactures surgical supplies, cement products; steel processing and agricultural equipment. Electronics plants; planing and feed mills; machine shop. Stock, poultry, grain farms. Corn, wheat, cattle.

18080 Columbus Telegram
Columbus Publishing Co.
1254 27th Ave. Phone: (402)564-2741
Columbus, NE 68601 Fax: (402)564-4127
Free: (800)279-1123

General newspaper. **Founded:** 1879. **Freq:** Daily (eve.), Sunday (morn.). **Print Method:** Offset. **Cols./Page:** 6. **Col. Width:** 12 picas. **Col. Depth:** 21 1/2 inches. **Key Personnel:** Julie Speirs, Publisher; Todd Franko, Managing Editor; Jo Sherbo, Advertising Dir. **USPS:** 124-500. **Subscription Rates:** $87 individuals; $102 out of state. **Remarks:** Accepts advertising.
Ad Rates: GLR: $2.45 **Circ:** Mon.-Fri. 10,719
SAU: $12.70 Sun. 11,526
PCI: $9.10

18081 KKOT-FM - 93.5
1367 33rd Ave. Phone: (402)564-2866
Columbus, NE 68601-4843 Fax: (402)564-2867

Format: Country. **Networks:** ABC. **Owner:** Three Eagles Communications, at above address, (402)476-3222. **Founded:** 1969. **Formerly:** KWMG-FM (1994); KTTT-FM. **Operating Hours:** Continuous; 7% network, 93% local. **ADI:** Omaha, NE. **Key Personnel:** Greg Wells, General Mgr.; Tim Roberts, Program Dir. **Wattage:** 100,000. **Ad Rates:** Advertising accepted; rates available upon request.

18082 KTLX-FM - 91.9
2200 25th St. Phone: (402)564-8548
Columbus, NE 68601-2640

Format: Religious. **Networks:** Independent. **Owner:** TLC Educational Corp., at above address. **Founded:** 1974. **Operating Hours:** 15% local, 85% other. **Key Personnel:** Gary Spuit, Station Mgr. **Wattage:** 100. **Ad Rates:** Noncommercial.

18083 KTTT-AM - 1510
1367 33rd Ave. Phone: (402)564-2866
Columbus, NE 68601-4843 Fax: (402)564-2867

Format: Oldies; Talk. **Networks:** ABC. **Founded:** 1962. **Operating Hours:** Sunrise-sunset; 92% local, 8% network. **Key Personnel:** Greg Wells, General Mgr.; Eric O'Connor, Program Dir. **Wattage:** 500. **Ad Rates:** Advertising accepted; rates available upon request.

COZAD, pop. 4,453.

Dawson Co. (SC). On Platte River, 45 m SE of North Platte. Manufactures and ships alfalfa products, auto equipment, cooperage, feed mill. Stock, poultry, grain farms. Alfalfa, corn, wheat.

18084 Tri-City Trib
617 CMR Phone: (308)229-3644
Drawer A, Box A Fax: (308)229-3647
Cozad, NE 69130-0006
Community newspaper. **Founded:** 1965. **Freq:** Semiweekly (Tues. and Thurs.). **Print Method:** Offset. **Cols./Page:** 5. **Col. Width:** 22 nonpareils. **Col. Depth:** 224 agate lines. **Key Personnel:** Dean G. Dorsey, Editor and Publisher. **Subscription Rates:** $23.50; $32.50. **Remarks:** Accepts advertising.
Ad Rates: GLR: $.30 **Circ:** 3,450
BW: $300
SAU: $4.25

18085 KAMI-AM - 1580
835 Meridian St. Phone: (308)784-1580
Cozad, NE 69130 Fax: (308)784-1583
E-mail: kami@1045fm.com

Format: Talk. **Founded:** 1965. **Operating Hours:** 8 a.m.-5 p.m. **ADI:** Lincoln-Hastings-Kearney, NE. **Key Personnel:** Chuck Larsen, Pres./Gen. Mgr.; Russ Holen, Sports Dir. **Wattage:** 1000. **Ad Rates:** Combined advertising rates available with KAMI-FM.

18086 KAMI-FM - 104.5
835 Meridian St. Phone: (308)784-1580
Cozad, NE 69130 Fax: (308)784-1583
E-mail: kami@1045fm.com

Format: Country. **Networks:** Westwood One Radio. **Founded:** 1983. **Formerly:** KOOC-FM (1988). **Operating Hours:** Continuous. **ADI:** Lincoln-Hastings-Kearney, NE. **Key Personnel:** Chuck Larsen, Pres./Gen. Mgr.; Russ Holen, Sports Dir. **Wattage:** 100,000. **Ad Rates:** Combined advertising rates available with KAMI-AM.

CRAWFORD, pop. 1,315.

Dawes Co. (NW). 25 m SW of Chadron. Residential.

18087 Rare Breeds Journal
PO Box 66 Phone: (308)665-1431
Crawford, NE 69339 Fax: (308)665-1931

Journal covering rare breeds. **Subtitle:** The Digest of the Alternative Livestock Industry. **Founded:** Mar. 1987. **Freq:** Bimonthly. **Print Method:** Web press. **Trim Size:** 8 1/2 x 11. **Cols./Page:** 4. **Col. Width:** 11 picas. **Col. Depth:** 58 picas. **Key Personnel:** Maureen Neidhardt, Editor and Publisher, phone (308)665-1431. **ISSN:** 1048-986X. **Subscription Rates:** $25 individuals; $35 Canada and Mexico; $50 other countries; $4 single issue. **Remarks:** Accepts advertising.
Ad Rates: BW: $225 **Circ:** Paid 3,000
4C: $375

CREIGHTON, pop. 1,341.

Knox Co. (NE). 40 m NW of Norfolk. Stock, grain, dairy, poultry farms.

18088 The Creighton News
New Publishing Co.
816 Main St. Phone: (402)358-5220
PO Box 55
Creighton, NE 68729
Community newspaper. **Founded:** 1889. **Freq:** Weekly (Wed.). **Print Method:** Offset. **Cols./Page:** 7. **Col. Width:** 24 nonpareils. **Col. Depth:** 294 agate lines. **Key Personnel:** Dave Sonnenfelt, Editor. **Subscription Rates:** $18 individuals; $23 out of area; $26 out of state. **Remarks:** Accepts advertising.
Ad Rates: SAU: $3 **Circ:** ‡1,500
PCI: $3.25

18089 Sky Scan Cable Co.
713 Main St. Phone: (402)358-3510
PO Box 57 Fax: (402)358-3864
Creighton, NE 68729
Free: (800)695-5773

Owner: Douglas Laflan, at above address. **Founded:** 1984. **Key Personnel:** D.M. Laflan, President. **Cities Served:** subscribing households 2,332.

CRETE, pop. 4,872.

Saline Co. (SE). 20 m SW of Lincoln. Doane College. Manufactures voting equipment. Flour mills; pet foods, pork processing. Stock, grain, dairy, poultry farms. Corn, wheat, hay.

18090 The Crete News
1201 Linden Phone: (402)826-2147
PO Box 40 Fax: (402)826-5072
Crete, NE 68333
Community newspaper. **Founded:** 1871. **Freq:** Weekly (Wed.). **Print Method:** Offset. **Trim Size:** 16 x 22 1/2. **Cols./Page:** 7. **Col. Width:** 25 nonpareils. **Col. Depth:** 301 agate lines. **Key Personnel:** Lloyd Reeves, Editor and Publisher. **USPS:** 137-860. **Subscription Rates:** $24.75. **Remarks:** Accepts advertising.
Ad Rates: GLR: $.25 **Circ:** ‡4,167
BW: $528.50
SAU: $3.50

18091 Doane Owl
Doane College
1014 Boswell Ave. Phone: (402)826-8269
Crete, NE 68333 Fax: (402)826-8278
Publication E-mail: owl@doane.edu

Collegiate newspaper. **Founded:** 1874. **Freq:** Weekly. **Print Method:** Offset. **Cols./Page:** 5. **Col. Width:** 12 picas. **Col. Depth:** 15.5 inches. **Key Personnel:** David C. Price, Advisor, dprice@doane.edu. **Subscription Rates:** $20 individuals. **Remarks:** Accepts advertising.
Ad Rates: PCI: $4.12 **Circ:** Paid 1,000

CROFTON, pop. 677.

Knox Co. (NE). 60 m WNW of Sioux City, IA.

18092 Crofton Journal
PO Box 339 Phone: (402)388-4355
Crofton, NE 68730 Fax: (402)388-4336

Community newspaper. **Subtitle:** Crofton Journal. **Founded:** 1905. **Freq:** Weekly. **Print Method:** Offset. **Trim Size:** 10 1/4 x 13 1/2. **Cols./Page:** 5. **Col. Width:** 11 picas. **Col. Depth:** 210 agate lines. **Key Personnel:** Kevin Henseler, Editor, Publisher. **USPS:** 138-340. **Subscription Rates:** $16 individuals Knox & Cedar counties; $18 out of area; $22 out of state. **Remarks:** Accepts advertising.
Ad Rates: GLR: $.50 **Circ:** ‡1,200
BW: $200
4C: $250
SAU: $3
PCI: $3

CROOKSTON

18093 KINI-FM - 96.1
PO Box 419 Phone: (605)747-2291
Saint Francis, SD 57572 Fax: (605)747-5791
E-mail: kinifm@gwtc.net

Format: Eclectic; News. **Networks:** AP. **Owner:** Rosebud Educational Society Inc., P.O. Box 499, St. Francis, SD 57572, (605)747-2361, Fax: (605)747-5057. **Founded:** 1976. **Operating Hours:** Continuous. **Key Personnel:** Bernard Whiting, Jr., Gen. Mgr./Music/Production Dir. **Wattage:** 57,000. **Ad Rates:** Noncommercial; underwriting available. **URL:** http://www.wgtc.net/kinifm.

CURTIS

Frontier Co. (SW). 20 m NW of Stockville.

18094 Curtis Cable TV Co., Inc.
Box 8 Phone: (308)367-8600
Curtis, NE 69025

Owner: Curtis Telephone Co., at above address, (308)367-4151. **Founded:** 1981. **Key Personnel:** Ed Cole, Manager. **Cities Served:** Curtis, Maywood, NE: subscribing households 500; 35 channels; 1 community access channel; 168 hours per week community access programming.

DAVID CITY†, pop. 2,514.

Butler Co. (E). 40 m NW of Lincoln. Museum. Manufactures trailers, electrical wiring harness for semi trailers, frozen foods. Egg processing plant. Dehydrated ingredients. Stock, dairy, grain farms. Alfalfa, soybeans, corn, sorghums.

18095 Banner-Press
331 E. St. Phone: (402)367-3054
Box 407 Fax: (402)367-3055
David City, NE 68632
Community newspaper. **Founded:** 1873. **Freq:** Weekly (Thurs.). **Print Method:** Offset. **Cols./Page:** 6. **Col. Width:** 25 nonpareils. **Col. Depth:** 301 agate lines. **Key Personnel:** Zean Carney, Editor and Publisher. **USPS:** 041-620. **Subscription Rates:** $24 individuals; $27 out of area; $32 out of state. **Remarks:** Accepts advertising.
Ad Rates: GLR: $0.34 **Circ:** Paid ‡4,300
BW: $612.25 Free ‡150
4C: $837.75
SAU: $4.75

DE WITT

18096 De Witt Times-News
PO Box 247 Phone: (402)683-5215
De Witt, NE 68341 Fax: (402)683-5216

Community newspaper. **Freq:** Weekly (Wed.). **Cols./Page:** 4. **Col. Width:** 14 picas. **Col. Depth:** 15 inches. **Key Personnel:** Kent Korinek, Publisher. **USPS:** 150-420. **Subscription Rates:** $10; $12 out of area. **Remarks:** Accepts advertising.
Ad Rates: SAU: $2.31 **Circ:** 800

DESHLER, pop. 997.

Thayer Co. (S). 120 m SW of Omaha. Residential.

18097 The Deshler Rustler
Struve Enterprises Inc.
PO Box 647 Phone: (402)365-7221
Deshler, NE 68340 Fax: (402)265-7243
Free: (800)762-3681

Local newspaper. **Founded:** Apr. 23, 1986. **Freq:** Weekly (Wed.). **Print Method:** Offset. **Cols./Page:** 6. **Col. Width:** 26 nonpareils. **Col. Depth:** 294 agate lines. **Key Personnel:** Harold W. Struve, Editor and Publisher. **Subscription Rates:** $21; $25 out of state. **Remarks:** Accepts advertising.
Ad Rates: BW: $378 **Circ:** Paid ‡1,700
SAU: $3

DODGE, pop. 800.

Dodge Co. (E). 75 m NW of Omaha. Farm equipment manufacturing. Cheese plant. Grain, stock, dairy, poultry farms. Cattle, hogs, corn.

18098 Dodge Criterion
140 Oak St. Phone: (402)693-2415
PO Box 68 Fax: (402)693-2415
Dodge, NE 68633-0068
Newspaper with a Democratic orientation. **Founded:** 1888. **Freq:** Weekly. **Print Method:** Offset. **Trim Size:** 14 1/2 x 23. **Cols./Page:** 6. **Col. Width:** 25 nonpareils. **Col. Depth:** 301 agate lines. **Key Personnel:** Kathleen Kauffold, Editor; Ken Kauffold, Publisher. **USPS:** 159-380. **Subscription Rates:** $19 individuals; $21 out of area.
Ad Rates: GLR: $.25 **Circ:** ‡1,100
SAU: $3.75

DONIPHAN, pop. 542.

Hall Co. (SE). 10 m S of Grand Island.

18099 The Doniphan Herald
PO Box 436 Phone: (402)845-2728
Doniphan, NE 68832 Fax: (402)845-2220

Community newspaper. **Founded:** Aug. 1970. **Freq:** Weekly. **Print Method:** Web press. **Trim Size:** 9 1/4 x 13. **Cols./Page:** 5. **Col. Width:** 1 7/8 inches. **Col. Depth:** 13 inches. **Key Personnel:** Jeniece Kimminau, Editor and Publisher. **USPS:** 914-680. **Subscription Rates:** $15 individuals; $17 out of state. **Remarks:** Accepts advertising.
Ad Rates: GLR: $3.20 **Circ:** Paid 742
BW: $204 Free 26
SAU: $3.20
PCI: $3.20

18100 KROA-FM - 95.7
Box K Phone: (402)845-6595
Doniphan, NE 68832

Format: Religious. **Networks:** AP; Moody Broadcasting. **Owner:** Grace University, 9th William, Omaha, NE 68108. **Founded:** 1977. **Operating Hours:** Continuous; 30% network, 70% local. **Key Personnel:** Gordon Wheeler, Station Mgr.; Diane Smith, Music Dir.; Steve Pearson, Production Mgr.; Suzanne Glennon, Traffic Mgr.; Diane Smith, Office Mgr. **Wattage:** 100,000. **Ad Rates:** Noncommercial.

ELKHORN

18101 Douglas County Post-Gazette
Enterprise Publishing Co., Inc.
113 Hillrise Center Phone: (402)289-2329
PO Box 677 Fax: (402)289-0861
Elkhorn, NE 68022
Publication E-mail: postgazette@top.net

Local newspaper. **Founded:** 1881. **Freq:** Weekly (Tues.). **Print Method:** Offset. **Trim Size:** 15 x 22. **Cols./Page:** 7. **Col. Width:** 2 1/16 inches. **Col. Depth:** 21 1/2 inches. **Key Personnel:** Mark Theissen, Editor; Penny Overmann, General Manager/Publisher. **ISSN:** 0746-1437. **Subscription Rates:** $18.75; $27 out of area; $31 out of state. **Remarks:** Accepts advertising. **Online:** City Atlas. **Formed by the merger of:** Elkhorn Valley-Post; Douglas County Gazette; Valley Enterprise; Waterloo Gazette; Elkhorn Exchange; Millard Courier; Bennington Herald.
Ad Rates: GLR: $6 **Circ:** ‡2,800
BW: $765
4C: $1,065
SAU: $7.50
PCI: $8.30

ELWOOD

18102 Elwood Bulletin
308 Smith Phone: (308)785-2251
PO Box 115 Fax: (308)785-2251
Elwood, NE 68937
Community newspaper. **Founded:** 1899. **Freq:** Weekly (Wed.). **Cols./Page:** 6. **Col. Width:** 2 inches. **Col. Depth:** 21 1/2 inches. **Key Personnel:** Theodore Gill, Publisher; Kathy Beck, Editor. **USPS:** 174-620. **Subscription Rates:** $15.50 Local Annual; $21 out of area; $0.50 single issue. **Remarks:** Accepts advertising.
Ad Rates: GLR: $.50 **Circ:** 900
PCI: $2.24

EXETER, pop. 759.

Fillmore Co. (NE). 11 m NE of Geneva.

18103 Fillmore County News
181 E. Seneca
PO Box 115
Exeter, NE 68351

Community newspaper. **Founded:** Jan. 1, 1897. **Freq:** Weekly. **Print Method:** Offset. **Cols./Page:** 6. **Col. Width:** 9 1/2 picas. **Col. Depth:** 15 inches. **Key Personnel:** Margie Bonta, Editor; W.A. Bonta, Publisher. **Subscription Rates:** $12. **Remarks:** Accepts advertising.
Ad Rates: BW: $1.65 **Circ:** ‡690
PCI: $1.30

FAIRBURY†, pop. 4,885.

Jefferson Co. (SE). 57 m SW of Lincoln. Trade center. Manufactures stone, concrete, brick, fertilizer, men's & boy's jackets. Stock, grain, poultry, dairy farms. Corn, wheat, hogs. Livestock feeding.

18104 Fairbury Journal-News
516 5th St. Phone: (402)729-6141
PO Box 415 Fax: (402)729-3892
Fairbury, NE 68352-0415
Community newspaper. **Founded:** 1892. **Freq:** Semiweekly (Tues. and Fri.). **Print Method:** Offset. **Cols./Page:** 6. **Col. Width:** 21 nonpareils. **Col. Depth:** 294 agate lines. **Key Personnel:** Fred A. Arnold, Jr., Publisher; Darrel Junker, Advertising Mgr. **USPS:** 184-000. **Subscription Rates:** $29; $35 out of state. **Remarks:** Accepts advertising.
Ad Rates: GLR: $0.33 **Circ:** ‡6,881
BW: $573.30
SAU: $4.90
PCI: $4.90

18105 Fairbury Cablevision
506 C St.
Fairbury, NE 68352
Phone: (402)421-0330
Fax: (402)421-0310
E-mail: shadval@netscape.com

Owner: TimeWarner, at above address. **Founded:** Jan. 31, 1966. **Key Personnel:** Valerie Kramer, General Mgr., phone (402)421-0330, fax (402)421-0310; Rick Hollmann, System Engineer. **Cities Served:** Fairbury, Superior, NE: subscribing households 2,874; 36 channels.

18106 KGMT-AM - 1310
414 4th St.
Fairbury, NE 68352-2514
Phone: (402)729-3382
Fax: (402)729-3446

Format: Adult Contemporary. **Networks:** ABC. **Operating Hours:** 12 hours daily; 10% network, 90% local. **ADI:** Lincoln-Hastings-Kearney, NE. **Key Personnel:** Randy Bauer, Operations Mgr.; Nikki Collins, News Dir. **Wattage:** 500. **Ad Rates:** $7-17 for 30 seconds. Combined advertising rates available with KUTT-FM.

18107 KUTT-FM - 99.5
414 4th St.
Fairbury, NE 68352
Phone: (402)729-3382
Fax: (402)729-3446
E-mail: kutt@navik.net

Format: Contemporary Country. **Networks:** Satellite Music Network. **Founded:** Oct. 1, 1994. **Operating Hours:** Continuous; 80% network, 20% local. **ADI:** Lincoln-Hastings-Kearney, NE. **Key Personnel:** Randy Bauer, Operations Mgr.; Nikki Collins, News Dir.; Brad Achtemeir, Sales Mgr. **Wattage:** 100,000. **Ad Rates:** $8-13 for 30 seconds; $12-17 for 60 seconds. Combined advertising rates available with KGMT.

FALLS CITY†, pop. 5,374.

Richardson Co. (SE). 75 m SE of Lincoln. Grain bins, agricultural fans, sledge-hammer heads, burial vaults, business forms manufactured. Meat processing plant. Ships cattle, hogs and grain. Diversified farming. Corn, wheat, hogs, soybeans.

18108 Journal
Journal Publishing Co.
Box 128
Falls City, NE 68355
Phone: (402)245-2431
Fax: (402)245-4404

General newspaper. **Founded:** 1867. **Freq:** Biweekly. **Print Method:** Offset. **Cols./Page:** 6. **Col. Width:** 29 nonpareils. **Col. Depth:** 301 agate lines. **Key Personnel:** Bill Schock, Editor; Linda Stout, Advertising Mgr. **Subscription Rates:** $30. **Remarks:** Accepts advertising.
Ad Rates: GLR: $.24 **Circ:** Paid 4,100

18109 KTNC-AM - 1230
1602 Stone St.
PO Box 589
Falls City, NE 68355-0589
Free: (800)414-3867
Phone: (402)245-2453
Fax: (402)245-5862
E-mail: ktnc@sentco.net

Format: Oldies; News; Sports. **Networks:** ABC; Brownfield. **Owner:** C.R. Communications, Inc., at above address. **Founded:** 1957. **Operating Hours:** 5:25 a.m.-10:30 p.m.; 10% network, 90% local. **ADI:** Omaha, NE. **Key Personnel:** Charles A. Radatz, General Mgr.; Karen E. Radatz, Contact; Darlene Tisdel, Contact; Chuck Smith, Contact; Jenny Herling. **Local Programs:** *Chit Chat*, John Nixon. **Wattage:** 500 day; 1000 night. **Ad Rates:** $2.00-3.30 for 10 seconds; $6.00-7.90 for 30 seconds; $12.00-14.80 for 60 seconds.

FREMONT†, pop. 23,979.

Dodge Co. (E). On Platte River, 35 m NW of Omaha. Midland College. Trade and sales center. Manufactures flour and feed, boxes, metal & steel, cement and tile products, hydraulic equipment, bearings, ladies garments, chemicals, canvas. Grain, stock, dairy, poultry, fruit farms. Corn, wheat, alfalfa.

18110 HomeFront Buyer's Guide
230 N. Main St.
PO Box 1056
Fremont, NE 68025
Phone: (402)721-1030
Fax: (402)721-5276
Buyer's guide. **Founded:** 1987. **Freq:** Weekly (Sat.). **Cols./Page:** 6. **Col. Width:** 1 5/8 inches. **Col. Depth:** 16 inches. **Key Personnel:** Jean Brown, General Mgr.
Ad Rates: PCI: $6.95 **Circ:** Non-paid 25,491

18111 The Midland
Midland Lutheran College
Journalism Dept.
900 N. Clarkson
Fremont, NE 68025
Phone: (402)721-5480
Fax: (402)721-0250
Publication E-mail: themidland@campus.mlc.edu

Collegiate newspaper. **Founded:** 1889. **Freq:** Weekly (Fri.). **Print Method:** Offset. **Trim Size:** 12 3/4 x 21 3/4. **Cols./Page:** 5. **Col. Width:** 24 nonpareils. **Col. Depth:** 231 agate lines. **Key Personnel:** Dr. Joyce H. Winfield, Adviser, phone (402)721-5487, winfield@campus.mlc.edu. **Subscription Rates:** $15 by mail. **Remarks:** Accepts advertising.
Ad Rates: BW: $652.50 **Circ:** Free ‡1,500
SAU: $5
PCI: $5

18112 KFMT-FM - 105.5
PO Box 669
Fremont, NE 68025-0669
Phone: (402)721-1340
Fax: (402)721-5023
E-mail: hubradio@tvsonline.com

Owner: Mitchell Broadcasting, Fremont Inc., at above address. **Founded:** 1939. **Operating Hours:** Continuous. **Key Personnel:** Del Meyer, General Mgr.; Chris Wall, Program Dir.; Del Meyer, General Mgr. **Local Programs:** *The Retro Show*; *Rock Legends*; *House of Blues Radio Hour*; *House of Blues Breaks*. **Wattage:** 3000. **Ad Rates:** $11.20-13.55 for 30 seconds; $14.15-16.50 for 60 seconds. $15.90-$19.25 for 30 seconds; $20.10-$23.45 for 60 seconds. Combined advertising rates available with KHUB-AM.

18113 KHUB-AM - 1340
PO Box 669
Fremont, NE 68025-0669
Phone: (402)721-1340
Fax: (402)721-5023
E-mail: hubradio@tvsonline.com

Format: Middle-of-the-Road (MOR); Talk; News. **Networks:** ABC. **Owner:** Mitchell Broadcasting, Fremont Inc., at above address. **Founded:** 1939. **Operating Hours:** Continuous. **Key Personnel:** Chris Walz, Program Dir.; Del Meyer, General Mgr. **Wattage:** 500 day; 1000 night. **Ad Rates:** $11.20-13.55 for 30 seconds; $14.15-16.50 for 60 seconds. $15.90- $19.25; $20.10-$23.45 for 60 seconds. Combined advertising rates available with KFMT-FM.

FULLERTON

18114 Nance County Journal
416 4th
PO Box 10
Fullerton, NE 68638
Phone: (308)536-3100
Fax: (308)536-3100
Community newspaper. **Founded:** 1889. **Freq:** Weekly (Wed.). **Print Method:** Web offset. **Trim Size:** 15 x 23 1/2. **Cols./Page:** 6. **Col. Width:** 13 1/2 picas. **Col. Depth:** 21 inches. **Key Personnel:** William H. Thompson, Publisher; Vic Wassermann, Co-Publisher; Barb Micek, Co Publisher. **Subscription Rates:** $20 individuals. **Remarks:** Accepts advertising.
Ad Rates: GLR: $.30 **Circ:** 1,700
BW: $619.16
PCI: $4.70

GENEVA†, pop. 2,400.

Fillmore Co. (SE). 65 m SW of Lincoln. Manufactures flour and feed. Stock, dairy, poultry, grain farms. Wheat, corn, milo.

18115 The Nebraska Signal
131 N. 9th
PO Box 233
Geneva, NE 68361-0233
Phone: (402)759-3117
Fax: (402)759-4214
Community newspaper. **Founded:** 1874. **Freq:** Weekly (Wed.). **Print Method:** Offset. **Cols./Page:** 6. **Col. Width:** 2 inches. **Col. Depth:** 294 agate lines. **Key Personnel:** John Edgecombe, Jr., Editor and Publisher. **Subscription Rates:** $22; $26 out of area. **Remarks:** Accepts advertising.
Ad Rates: GLR: $.28 **Circ:** Paid ‡3,250
BW: $743.40
4C: $1,043.40
SAU: $5.90
PCI: $5.90

GENOA, pop. 1,096.

Nance Co. (EC). 70 m NW of Lincoln. Diversified farming. Corn, wheat, oats, milo, soybeans. Dairying.

18116 Genoa Leader-Times
PO Box 429
Genoa, NE 68640
Phone: (402)993-2205
Local newspaper. **Founded:** 1879. **Freq:** Weekly (Thurs.). **Print Method:** Offset. **Cols./Page:** 6. **Col. Width:** 19 nonpareils. **Col. Depth:** 182 agate lines. **Key Personnel:** Donald J. Evans, Publisher; Helen C. Evans, Publisher. **Subscription Rates:** $10. **Remarks:** Accepts advertising.
Ad Rates: GLR: $.165 **Circ:** 947

GERING†, pop. 7,512.

Scotts Bluff Co. (W). On Platte River, 3 m S of Scottsbluff. Scotts Bluff National Monument. Manufactures bean and beet irrigation systems, machinery. Oil fields. Dairy, stock, poultry, grain farms. Sugar beets, wheat, corn.

18117 Gering Courier
1428 10th St.
PO Box 70
Gering, NE 69341
Phone: (308)436-2222
Fax: (308)436-7127
Newspaper with a Republican orientation. **Founded:** 1887. **Freq:** Weekly (Thurs.). **Print Method:** Offset. **Cols./Page:** 6. **Col. Width:** 25 nonpareils. **Col. Depth:** 294 agate lines. **Key Personnel:** C.A. Lewis, Editor and Publisher. **Subscription Rates:** $21.95. **Remarks:** Accepts advertising.
Ad Rates: GLR: $.19 **Circ:** ‡2,681
SAU: $4

18118 KSTF-TV - 10
3385 N. 10th Ave.
Gering, NE 69341
Phone: (308)632-6107
Fax: (308)632-3470

Format: Commercial TV. **Networks:** CBS. **Owner:** Benedek Broadcasting Corp., Stewart Sq. Bldg., 308 W. State St., Ste. 210, Rockford, IL 61101, (815)987-5350, Fax: (815)987-5335. **Founded:** 1955. **Operating Hours:** 6 a.m.-2 a.m.; 70% network, 30% local. **ADI:** Cheyenne, WY-Scottsbluff, NE (Sterling, CO). **Key Personnel:** Fiona smith, Station Mgr.; Kate Turner, Asst. Editor; Jamie Wiedeman, Production Mgr.; Monica Z. Romero, Traffic Dir. **Wattage:** 240,000. **Ad Rates:** $20-350 per unit.

18119 Windbreak Cable and Intertech Cable
760 M St.
Gering, NE 69341
Phone: (308)436-4650
Fax: (308)436-4650

Owner: William D. Bauer, at above address. **Founded:** 1988. **Key Personnel:** Frank Wimler, Contact; William D. Baver, Contact. **Cities Served:** Broomfield, Elizabeth, Franktown, Parker, CO; Harrison, Lyman, NE: subscribing households 605; 32 channels; 1 community access channel. **URL:** http://www.windbreak.com.

GIBBON, pop. 1,531.

Buffalo Co. (SC). 33 m SW of Grand Island. Turkey processing, packing plants. Farming. Potatoes, hay, wheat.

18120 The Gibbon Reporter
PO Box 820
Gibbon, NE 68840-0820
Phone: (308)468-5393
Fax: (308)468-5222

Community Newspaper. **Founded:** 1891. **Freq:** Weekly (Wed.). **Print Method:** Offset. **Trim Size:** 13 3/4 x 22. **Cols./Page:** 6. **Col. Width:** 12.5 picas. **Col. Depth:** 20.5 inches. **Key Personnel:** Laura Kozin, Editor; Steve Glenn, Publisher. **Subscription Rates:** $17; $25 out of state. **Remarks:** Color advertising not accepted. **Formerly:** Reporter.
Ad Rates: BW: $275.91 **Circ:** Paid ‡1,121
PCI: $3.50 Free ‡13

GORDON

Sheridan Co. (NW). 30 m NE of Rushville.

18121 Gordon Journal
210 N. Main
PO Box 270
Gordon, NE 69343-0270
Phone: (308)282-0118
Fax: (308)282-1120
Community newspaper. **Founded:** 1891. **Freq:** Weekly (Wed.). **Print Method:** Offset. **Trim Size:** 14 x 22 3/4. **Cols./Page:** 6. **Col. Width:** 12 1/4 inches. **Col. Depth:** 21 1/2 inches. **Key Personnel:** Susanne Evans, Editor and Publisher; Morris P. Evans, Publisher. **USPS:** 222-700. **Subscription Rates:** $18 individuals; $24 out of area. **Remarks:** Accepts advertising.
Ad Rates: BW: $335.40 **Circ:** ‡2,600
4C: $480.40
SAU: $2.60

18122 KSDZ-FM - 95.5
Box 390
Gordon, NE 69343
Phone: (308)282-2500
Fax: (308)282-0061

Format: Hot Country; Oldies. **Networks:** ABC. **Owner:** D.J. Broadcasting, Inc., at above address. **Founded:** 1979. **Operating Hours:** Continuous. **ADI:** Rapid City, SD. **Key Personnel:** Jim Lambley, General Mgr. **Wattage:** 60,000. **Ad Rates:** $10.00 for 30 seconds; $13.00 for 60 seconds.

GOTHENBURG, pop. 3,479.

Dawson Co. (SC). 35 m SE of North Platte. Original pony express station. Alfalfa dehydrating plants. Stock, grain farms. Corn, alfalfa, wheat, sugar beets.

18123 The Gothenburg Times
Box 385
Gothenburg, NE 69138
Phone: (308)537-3636
Fax: (308)537-7554

Newspaper. **Founded:** 1908. **Freq:** Weekly (Wed.). **Print Method:** Offset. **Cols./Page:** 6. **Col. Width:** 25 nonpareils. **Col. Depth:** 294 agate lines. **Key Personnel:** Greg Viergutz,

Publisher; Kathi Viergutz, Publisher. **USPS:** 223-900. **Subscription Rates:** $30. **Remarks:** Accepts advertising.
Ad Rates: GLR: $.29 **Circ:** ‡2,600
BW: $516.60
4C: $691.60
SAU: $4.10
PCI: $4.10

GRAND ISLAND†, pop. 33,180.

Hall Co. (C). On Platte River, 90 m W of Lincoln. Museum. Park area.Manufacturing, wholesaling and retail center. Livestock and grain marketing center. Manufactures farm equipment, livestock feeds, irrigation equipment, plastic products, metal buildings and construction components and ammunition; food processing plants. Agriculture. Corn, soybeans, milo, alfalfa, wheat and cattle.

18124 Grand Island Independent
1st & Cedar Sts. Phone: (308)382-1000
PO Box 1208 Fax: (308)382-8129
Grand Island, NE 68802
Free: (800)658-3160
Publication E-mail: theind@pendent.com

Newspaper. **Founded:** 1869. **Freq:** Mon.-Sun. (morn.). **Print Method:** Offset. **Cols./Page:** 6. **Col. Width:** 12.4 picas. **Col. Depth:** 21 1/2 inches. **Key Personnel:** John Goossen, Editor and Publisher; Gary Loftus, Advertising Mgr. **Subscription Rates:** $130 individuals. **Remarks:** Accepts advertising. **Online:** Networks.
Ad Rates: GLR: $0.75 **Circ:** Mon.-Sat. 24,419
BW: $1,598.31 Sun. 25,954
4C: $1,898.31
SAU: $12.39
PCI: $12.39

18125 Mighty Nickel
Maverick Media, Inc.
2538 N. St. Patrick Ave. Phone: (308)382-9303
PO Box 850 Free: (800)658-3177
Grand Island, NE 68802
Shopper (tabloid). **Founded:** Apr. 12, 1997. **Freq:** Weekly (Thurs.). **Print Method:** Offset. **Trim Size:** 11 1/2 x 14 1/2. **Cols./Page:** 8. **Col. Depth:** 13 1/2 inches. **Key Personnel:** William Welsh, President, phone (308)382-5551, fax (308)382-3634; Larry Kumm, General Mgr. **Remarks:** Accepts advertising. **Alt. Formats:** CD-ROM. **Formerly:** Penny Press 7; Penny Press 6.
Ad Rates: GLR: $.57 **Circ:** Free ‡25,950
BW: $675
4C: $900
SAU: $10.40
PCI: $7.50

18126 West Nebraska Register
804 W. Division Phone: (308)382-4660
PO Box 608 Fax: (308)382-4746
Grand Island, NE 68802
Official newspaper of the Catholic Diocese of Grand Island. **Founded:** 1930. **Freq:** Weekly. **Print Method:** Offset. **Cols./Page:** 5. **Col. Width:** 1 7/8 inches. **Col. Depth:** 168 agate lines. **Key Personnel:** Rev. Francis T. Curran, Editor; Most Rev. Lawrence J. McNamara, Publisher. **Subscription Rates:** $12. **Remarks:** Accepts advertising.
Ad Rates: GLR: $.54 **Circ:** (Not Reported)

18127 KGIN-TV - 11
123 N. Locust Phone: (308)382-6100
Grand Island, NE 68801 Fax: (308)382-3216

Format: Commercial TV. **Networks:** CBS. **Operating Hours:** 6:00 a.m.-1 a.m. **ADI:** Lincoln-Hastings-Kearney, NE. **Key Personnel:** Frank Jonas, General Mgr.; Connie S. Caldwell, Contact.

18128 KMMJ-AM - 750
3280 Woodridge Blvd No. 200 Phone: (308)382-2800
Grand Island, NE 68801-7216 Fax: (308)384-7514

Format: Country; Agricultural. **Networks:** AP. **Owner:** KMMJ, Inc., PO Box 1847, Grand Island, NE 68802. **Founded:** 1925. **Operating Hours:** Sunrise-sunset; 60% network, 40% local. **ADI:** Lincoln-Hastings-Kearney, NE. **Key Personnel:** Tom Robson, General Mgr.; Del Meyer, Sales Mgr. **Wattage:** 10,000. **Ad Rates:** $10-11.50 for 30 seconds; $15-17.25 for 60 seconds.

18129 KRGI-AM - 1430
3205 W. North Front St. Phone: (308)381-1430
Grand Island, NE 68803 Fax: (308)382-6701
E-mail: krgi@kdsi.net

Format: Adult Contemporary. **Networks:** ABC; Westwood One Radio; Mutual Broadcasting System. **Founded:** 1953. **Operating Hours:** Continuous; 30% network, 70% local. **Key Personnel:** Shaun Schleif, General Mgr.; Jim Davis, Program Dir.; Chris Loghrysen, Sales Mgr. **Wattage:** 5000 day; 1000 night. **Ad Rates:** $22-44 for 30 seconds; $27-53 for 60 seconds. $22-$44 for 30 seconds; $27-$53 for 60 seconds. Combined advertising rates available with KRGI-FM, KIRB-FM, KMMJ-AM.

18130 KRGI-FM - 96.5
3205 W. North Front St. Phone: (308)381-1430
PO Box 4907 Fax: (308)382-6701
Grand Island, NE 68802-4907
E-mail: krgi@kdsi.net

Format: Contemporary Country. **Networks:** ABC. **Founded:** 1975. **Operating Hours:** Continuous. **Key Personnel:** John R. Kidd, President; Shawn Schleif, General Mgr.; Chris Lowery, Program Dir.; Mickey J. Meyer, Music Dir.; Craig Scarborough, Public Service. **Wattage:** 100,000. **Ad Rates:** $22-44 for 30 seconds; $27-53 for 60 seconds. $22-$44 for 30 seconds; $27-$53 for 60 seconds. Combined advertising rates available with KRGI-AM.

18131 KSYZ-FM - 107.7
3532 West Capital Ave. Phone: (308)381-1077
Grand Island, NE 68803 Fax: (308)384-8900

Format: Adult Contemporary. **Founded:** 1982. **Operating Hours:** Continuous. **ADI:** Lincoln-Hastings-Kearney, NE. **Key Personnel:** Jay Vavricek, General Mgr. **Wattage:** 100,000. **Ad Rates:** Advertising accepted; rates available upon request.

18132 KTVG-TV - 17
PO Box 717 Phone: (308)384-1717
Grand Island, NE 68803 Fax: (308)384-1986

Format: Commercial TV. **Networks:** Fox. **Operating Hours:** Continuous. **Key Personnel:** Jerry D. Montgomery, Station Mgr.

GRANT†, pop. 1,270.

Perkins Co. (W). 60 m SW of North Platte. Grain, stock, dairy, poultry farms. Wheat, corn, alfalfa.

18133 Grant Tribune Sentinel
Johnson Publications, Inc.
PO Box 67 Phone: (308)352-4311
Grant, NE 69140 Fax: (308)332-4101

Community newspaper. **Freq:** Weekly. **Print Method:** Offset. **Cols./Page:** 6. **Col. Width:** 12.375 picas. **Col. Depth:** 21 1/2 inches. **Key Personnel:** Loral Johnson, Publisher; Elna Johnson, Publisher; Dennis Morgan, Editor. **Subscription Rates:** $17.50; $24 out of state. **Remarks:** Accepts advertising.
Ad Rates: SAU: $3.95 **Circ:** Paid 1,850
Non-paid 100

GRETNA, pop. 1,609.

Sarpy Co. (E). 25 m SW of Omaha. Grain elevators. State fish hatchery. Stock, grain, dairy farms. Wheat, corn, oats.

18134 Gretna Guide & News
PO Box 240 Phone: (402)332-3232
Gretna, NE 68028 Fax: (402)332-4733
Publication E-mail: gretnaguide@top.net

Community newspaper. **Founded:** Nov. 2, 1960. **Freq:** Weekly (Wed.). **Print Method:** Offset. **Cols./Page:** 7. **Col. Width:** 24 nonpareils. **Col. Depth:** 301 agate lines. **Key Personnel:** Virginia Rhoades, Publisher, phone (402)426-2121, fax (402)426-2227; Mike Overmann, General Mgr. **Subscription Rates:** $16.50. **Remarks:** Accepts advertising.
Ad Rates: GLR: $7 **Circ:** ‡3,890
BW: $827.75
4C: $1,168
SAU: $5.50
CNU: $5
PCI: $5.25

HARTINGTON†, pop. 1,730.

Cedar Co (NE). 40 m N of Norfolk. Cheese processing plant. Corn, oats, hogs, cattle.

18135 Cedar County News
Cedar County
Box 977 Phone: (402)254-3997
Hartington, NE 68739 Fax: (402)254-3999

County newspaper. **Founded:** 1898. **Freq:** Weekly (Wed.). **Print Method:** Offset. **Cols./Page:** 6. **Col. Width:** 19 nonpareils. **Col. Depth:** 294 agate lines. **Key Personnel:** Thomas L. Kelly, Publisher. **Subscription Rates:** $11.50. **Remarks:** Accepts advertising.
Ad Rates: GLR: $.24 **Circ:** (Not Reported)

HASTINGS†, pop. 23,045.

Adams Co. (SE). 90 m W of Lincoln. Hastings College. Wholesale and distributing center. Animal research center. Manufactures butter, cheese, automobile accessories, hardware, plastic, wheat, flour and corn products, land rollers, pumps, air conditioners, metal grain bins, farm tools, irrigation equipment. Beef, cattle, sheep. Agriculture. Corn, wheat, hogs, cattle.

18136 The Collegian
Hastings College
Gray Center Phone: (402)461-7399
7th & Turner Fax: (402)461-7442
PO Box 269
Hastings, NE 68902-0269
Publication E-mail: collegian@hastings.edu

Collegiate newspaper. **Founded:** 1885. **Freq:** Weekly (Thurs.). **Print Method:** Web. **Trim Size:** 11 1/2 x 13 3/4. **Cols./Page:** 4. **Col. Width:** 27 nonpareils. **Col. Depth:** 154 agate lines. **Key Personnel:** Kathy Stofer, Advisor, kstofer@hastings.edu. **USPS:** 237-120. **Subscription Rates:** $10. **Remarks:** Accepts advertising. **URL:** http://www.hastings.edu. **Feature Editors:** Misty Warburton, *Features*.
Ad Rates: BW: $750 **Circ:** Paid ‡1050
PCI: $9.65 Free ‡98

18137 Hastings Today
Hastings College
Public Relations Office Phone: (402)463-2402
7th and Turner Ave. Fax: (402)463-7490
PO Box 269
Hastings, NE 68902-0269
Free: (800)532-7642
Publication E-mail: jore@hastings.edu
Publisher E-mail: admissions@hust.nas.edu

Collegiate magazine. **Founded:** 1882. **Freq:** Semiannual. **Print Method:** Offset. **Trim Size:** 8 1/2 x 11. **Cols./Page:** 2. **Col. Width:** 30 nonpareils. **Col. Depth:** 133 agate lines. **Remarks:** Accepts advertising.
Ad Rates: GLR: $.44 **Circ:** Non-paid ‡28,000
BW: $689.22
SAU: $6.18
PCI: $6.18

18138 The Hastings Tribune
Seaton Publications
908 W. 2nd St. Phone: (402)462-2131
Box 788 Fax: (402)461-4657
Hastings, NE 68902-0788
Publication E-mail: tribune@nebland.cnweb.com
Publisher E-mail: tribune@tribland.comm

General newspaper. **Founded:** 1905. **Freq:** Daily (eve.). **Print Method:** Offset. **Trim Size:** 13 3/4 x 22 3/4. **Cols./Page:** 6 and 5. **Col. Width:** 12 and 12 picas. **Col. Depth:** 21 and 13.75 inches. **Key Personnel:** Thad Livingston, M.E., Editor, fax (402)462-2184; Donald R. Seaton, Publisher. **Subscription Rates:** $84 individuals; $90 motor route; $93 by mail; $123 out of state; $105 all others in Nebraska. **Remarks:** Accepts advertising. **Available Online. URL:** http://www.cnweb.com/tribune.
Ad Rates: GLR: $1,146.60 **Circ:** Mon.-Sat. 13,236
BW: $1,048.32
4C: $282
SAU: $9.10
CNU: $730
PCI: $1562.73

18139 KCNT-FM - 88.1
PO Box 1024 Phone: (402)461-2458
Hastings, NE 68902 Fax: (402)461-2507

Format: Contemporary Hit Radio (CHR); Educational. **Founded:** 1971. **Operating Hours:** 8 a.m. - 4 p.m. Daily. **ADI:** Lincoln-Hastings-Kearney, NE. **Key Personnel:** John Brooks, General Mgr., phone (402)461-2580, fax (402)461-2507, brohbrc@ccadm.gi.cccneb.edu. **Wattage:** 2000. **Ad Rates:** Noncommercial.

18140 KHAS-AM - 1230
906 W. 2nd St. Phone: (402)462-5101
PO Box 726 Fax: (402)461-3866
Hastings, NE 68902

Format: Adult Contemporary; Information; Sports; Agricultural. **Networks:** CBS. **Owner:** KHAS Broadcasting, Inc., at above address. **Founded:** 1940. **Operating Hours:** 18 hrs. Daily; more than 90% local. **ADI:** Lincoln-Hastings-Kearney, NE. **Key Personnel:** Wayne Specht, General Mgr.; Jim Stevens, Program Dir.; Bill Rinehart, News Dir.; Wayne Specht, Sales Mgr.; Jill Thomas, Production Dir. **Local Programs:** *Party Line*, Jill Thomas; *Sunrise 60 News*, Bill Rinehart. **Wattage:** 1000. **Ad Rates:** $7.65-17.65 for 60 seconds.

18141 KHAS-TV - 5
6475 N. Osborn Dr. Phone: (402)463-1321
N. Hwy. 281 Fax: (402)463-6551
PO Box 578
Hastings, NE 68901
Free: (800)325-6727
E-mail: khas-tv@.ltec.net

Format: Commercial TV. **Networks:** NBC. **Founded:** Jan. 1, 1956. **Operating Hours:** 6:30 a.m.-12:30 a.m. **ADI:** Lincoln-Hastings-Kearney, NE. **Key Personnel:** John Benson, General Mgr. **Wattage:** 200,000.

18142 KHNE-FM - 89.1
PO Box 83111 Phone: (402)472-3611
Lincoln, NE 68503 Fax: (402)472-2403
Free: (800)290-6850
E-mail: nprn@unl.edu

Format: Public Radio; Classical; News; Jazz. **Networks:** National Public Radio (NPR); Public Radio International (PRI). **Owner:** Nebraska Educational Telecommunications Commission, 1800 N. 33rd St., Lincoln, NE 68503. **Founded:** 1990. **Operating Hours:** 6 a.m.-1 a.m. **ADI:** Lincoln-Hastings-Kearney, NE. **Key Personnel:** Steve Robinson, General Mgr. **Local Programs:** *Afternoon Concert*, Bill Stibor; *Morning Concert*, Bill Stibor; *Nebraska Nightly*, Nancy Finken. **Wattage:** 6430. **Ad Rates:** Noncommercial.

18143 KHNE-TV - 29
c/o KUON-TV Phone: (402)472-3611
1800 N. 33rd. St. Fax: (402)472-3611
Lincoln, NE 68501
E-mail: net@unlinfo.unl.edu

Format: Public TV. **Networks:** Public Broadcasting Service (PBS). **Owner:** Nebraska Educational Telecommunications, at above address. **Founded:** 1968. **Operating Hours:** 5:45 a.m.-midnight; 90% network; 10% local. **ADI:** Lincoln-Hastings-Kearney, NE. **Key Personnel:** Rod Bates, General Mgr., rbates@unlinfo.unl.edu; Steve Lenzen, Asst. GM, Educational TV, slenzen@unlinfo.unl.edu; Sue Gildersleeve, Asst. GM, Admin. & Finance; Gene Bunge, Program Mgr.; Mary Neal Schutz, Public Information Dir.; Peter Ford, Asst. GM for Engineering, pford@unlinfo.unl.edu; Don Gill, Dir. of Development; Bill Kelly, Sr. Producer, Public Affairs, wek@unlinfo.unl.edu; Steve Alvis, Sr. Producer, Sports & Special Events; Michael Farrell, Sr. Producer, Cultural Affairs. **Local Programs:** *Backyard Farmer* Tuesdays 7pm, during spring and summer; *Big Red Wrap-Up* Tuesdays 7pm, during the football season, Steve Alvis, Sr. Producer, Sports & Special Events; *Statewide* 8 pm Friday, Bill Ganzel, Sr. Producer, Public Affairs. **Wattage:** 1.57 Mw. **Ad Rates:** Noncommercial. **URL:** http://net.unl.edu.

HAYES CENTER†, pop. 231.

Hayes Co. (SW). 50 m S of North Platte. Stock, grain, dairy, poultry farms.

18144 Times-Republican
Box 7 Phone: (308)286-3325
Hayes Center, NE 69032
Newspaper (mainly farm and ranch news). **Founded:** 1885. **Freq:** Weekly (Thurs.). **Print Method:** Offset. **Cols./Page:** 8. **Col. Width:** 9 picas. **Col. Depth:** 301 agate lines. **Key Personnel:** Kathy Broz, Editor. **USPS:** 630-720. **Subscription Rates:** $16 individuals; $21 out of state. **Remarks:** Accepts advertising.
Ad Rates: GLR: $.28 **Circ:** ‡936
BW: $927.08
4C: $1,167.08
SAU: $5.39
PCI: $3.92

18145 KWNB-TV - 6
c/o KHGI-TV Phone: (308)743-2494
13 S. Hwy. 44 Fax: (308)743-2644
PO Box 220
Kearney, NE 68848-0220

Format: Commercial TV. **Networks:** ABC. **Founded:** 1955. **Operating Hours:** Continuous. **ADI:** Lincoln-Hastings-Kearney, NE. **Key Personnel:** George Singleton, General Mgr. **Wattage:** 100.

HEBRON

18146 Hebron Journal Register
318 Lincoln Ave. Phone: (402)768-6602
PO Box 210 Fax: (402)768-7354
Hebron, NE 68370
Community newspaper. **Freq:** Weekly (Wed.). **Cols./Page:** 6. **Col. Width:** 14 picas. **Col. Depth:** 21 inches. **Key Personnel:** Kim Johnson, Editor and Publisher.
Circ: 3,400

HEMINGFORD, pop. 1,023.

Box Butte Co. (NW). 45 m NE of Scottsbluff. Stock, grain, poultry farms. Wheat, potatoes, beets, beans, corn.

18147 The Ledger
714 Box Butte Ave. Phone: (308)487-3334
PO Box 7 Fax: (308)487-3347
Hemingford, NE 69348-0007
Publication E-mail: ledger@bbc.net

Community newspaper. **Founded:** July 1906. **Freq:** Weekly (Thurs.). **Print Method:** Offset. **Cols./Page:** 6. **Col. Width:** 26 nonpareils. **Col. Depth:** 304 agate lines. **Key Personnel:** Brian C. Kuhn, Editor and Publisher; Kathryn M. Kuhn-Gaertig, Business Mgr. **Subscription Rates:** $18; $20 out of area. **Remarks:** Accepts advertising. **URL:** http://www.ledgeronline.com. **Formerly:** The Journal (1916).
Ad Rates: BW: $357.57 **Circ:** Paid ‡1,214
4C: $100 Free ‡31
SAU: $4.27
PCI: $4.27

HENDERSON, pop. 1,072.

York Co. (SEC). 60 m W of Lincoln. Machinery, concrete and irrigation products manufactured. Printing. Stock, dairy farms. Corn, soybeans, oats.

18148 The Henderson News
1021 N. Main St. Phone: (402)723-5861
Henderson, NE 68371 Fax: (402)723-5863
Publication E-mail: servpress@telcoweb.net

Community newspaper. **Founded:** Jan. 1, 1954. **Freq:** Weekly (Thurs.). **Print Method:** Offset. **Trim Size:** 13 x 19. **Cols./Page:** 5. **Col. Width:** 13.5 picas. **Col. Depth:** 18 inches. **Key Personnel:** Jan Edgecombe, Publisher. **USPS:** 578-300. **Subscription Rates:** $21; $24 out of area. **Remarks:** Advertising not accepted for alcoholic beverages.
Ad Rates: GLR: $.14 **Circ:** ‡850
BW: $333
SAU: $3.90
PCI: $3.90

HICKMAN, pop. 687.

Lancaster Co. (SE). 10 m S of Lincoln. Residential. Agricultural.

18149 The VOICE News
Bryant News, Inc.
108 Locust St. Phone: (402)792-2255
Hickman, NE 68372-0148 Fax: (402)792-2256

Community newspaper (tabloid) covering news in southern Lancaster, western Otoe, and northern Gage Counties. **Founded:** Sept. 1, 1978. **Freq:** Weekly (Thurs.). **Print Method:** Offset. **Trim Size:** 5 x 16 1/2. **Cols./Page:** 5. **Col. Width:** 12.3 picas. **Col. Depth:** 16.5 inches. **Key Personnel:** William F. Bryant, Editor and Publisher; Linda M. Bryant, Publisher. **USPS:** 442-690. **Subscription Rates:** $20; $24 out of area. **Feature Editors:** Asa Bryant, *Family*.
Ad Rates: PCI: $6.20 **Circ:** ‡2,500

HOLDREGE†, pop. 5,624.

Phelps Co. (S). 55 m SW of Hastings. Manufactures mobil lighting, lighted directional signs, church pew cushions, cultivation equipment. Cattle feeding. Agriculture. Corn, milo, wheat, alfalfa, soybeans.

18150 Holdrege Daily Citizen
PO Box 344 Phone: (308)995-4441
Holdrege, NE 68949 Fax: (308)995-5992

General newspaper. **Founded:** Dec. 1884. **Freq:** Daily (eve.). **Print Method:** Offset. **Trim Size:** 15 x 22 3/4. **Cols./Page:** 6. **Col. Width:** 26 nonpareils. **Col. Depth:** 294 agate lines. **Key Personnel:** Tunney Price, Editor, phone (308)995-4441; Barbara J. Penrod, Advertising Dir., phone (308)995-4441; Robert King, Publisher, phone (308)995-4441. **Subscription Rates:** $45. **Remarks:** Accepts advertising.
Ad Rates: BW: $724.5 **Circ:** Mon.-Fri. 3,187
4C: $994.5
SAU: $5.75

18151 KMTY-FM - 97.7
PO Box 465 Phone: (308)995-4020
Holdrege, NE 68949 Fax: (308)995-2202

Format: Adult Contemporary. **Networks:** ABC. **Owner:** High Plains Broadcasting, Inc., at above address, (308)995-4122. **Founded:** 1964. **Formerly:** KKTY-FM; KUVR-FM. **Operating Hours:** Continuous. **Key Personnel:** Peggy J. Goth, General Mgr.; Keith Jensen, Program Dir.; Randy Issler, Contact. **Wattage:** 60,000. **Ad Rates:** Advertising accepted; rates available upon request.

18152 KUVR-AM - 1380
PO Box 465 Phone: (308)995-4122
Holdrege, NE 68949 Fax: (308)995-2202
Free: (888)292-9977
E-mail: kmty977@wil-net.com

Format: Talk; Middle-of-the-Road (MOR); Religious. **Networks:** ABC. **Owner:** Peggy J. Goth, at above address, (308)995-4020, Fax: (308)995-2202. **Founded:** 1956. **Operating Hours:** 6 a.m.- sunset. **Key Personnel:** Peggy J. Goth, Contact; Randy Issier, Contact; Keith Jensen, Program Dir. **Wattage:** 500. **Ad Rates:** $3.75 for 15 seconds; $4.20-5.95 for 30 seconds; $6.10-7.25 for 60 seconds.

HOWELLS, pop. 677.

Colfax Co. (E). 70 m NW of Omaha. Agriculture. Corn, wheat, soybeans, oats.

18153 Howells Journal
Chris Chebuhar Co.
Box 335 Phone: (402)986-1777
Howells, NE 68641
Community newspaper. **Founded:** 1888. **Freq:** Weekly (Wed.). **Print Method:** Offset. **Cols./Page:** 6. **Col. Width:** 25 nonpareils. **Col. Depth:** 301 agate lines. **Subscription Rates:** $14. **Remarks:** Accepts advertising.
Ad Rates: GLR: $.20 **Circ:** ‡1,250
BW: $384
PCI: $3

HUMBOLDT, pop. 1,176.

Richardson Co. (SE). 80 m SE of Lincoln. Manufactures flour, animal feed. Meat processing plant. Agriculture. Wheat, beans, corn, milo, hay.

18154 The Humboldt Standard
PO Box 627 Phone: (402)862-2200
Humboldt, NE 68376-0627 Fax: (402)862-2200

Newspaper with a Republican orientation. **Founded:** July 28, 1882. **Freq:** Weekly (Thurs.). **Print Method:** Offset. **Trim Size:** 13 3/16 x 21. **Cols./Page:** 6. **Col. Width:** 2 1/16 inches. **Col. Depth:** 21 1/2 inches. **Key Personnel:** Jack Cooper, Editor and Publisher. **USPS:** 517-580. **Subscription Rates:** $16; $17 out of area. **Remarks:** Color advertising not accepted.
Ad Rates: BW: $300 **Circ:** ‡1,635
SAU: $3.22
PCI: $3.20

IMPERIAL†, pop. 1,941.

Chase Co. (SW). 90 m SW of North Platte. Grain, stock, poultry farms. Alfalfa, corn, wheat, potatoes, beets, beans.

18155 The Imperial Republican
Johnson Publications, Inc.
PO Box 727 Phone: (308)882-4453
Imperial, NE 69033 Fax: (308)394-5931
Publisher E-mail: pank@aol.com

Community newspaper. **Founded:** 1887. **Freq:** Weekly (Thurs.). **Print Method:** Offset. **Cols./Page:** 6. **Col. Width:** 12.375 picas. **Col. Depth:** 21 1/2 inches. **Key Personnel:** Russ Pankonin, Publisher, pank@aol.com; Lori Pankonian, Publisher, pank@aol.com. **USPS:** 259-980. **Subscription Rates:** $18.50 individuals; $22.50 out of area; $25.50 out of state. **Remarks:** Accepts advertising.
Ad Rates: BW: $522.45 **Circ:** Paid ‡2,242
SAU: $4.05 Free ‡50

18156 Wauneta Breeze
Johnson Publications, Inc.
PO Box 727 Phone: (308)882-4453
Imperial, NE 69033 Fax: (308)394-5931
Publisher E-mail: pank@aol.com

Community newspaper. **Founded:** Feb. 3, 1887. **Freq:** Weekly (Thurs.). **Print Method:** Offset. **Trim Size:** 14 3/4 x 22 3/4. **Cols./Page:** 6. **Col. Width:** 12.25 picas. **Col. Depth:** 21 1/2 inches. **Key Personnel:** Lori Pankonin, Editor and Publisher, phone (308)3945389, pank@aol.com; Russ Pankonin, Editor and Publisher; Russ and Lori Pankonin, Editor and Publisher; Tina Kitt, Editor, phone (308)394-5389, fax (308)394-5931. **USPS:** 669-800. **Subscription Rates:** $17.50; $21.50 out of area; $24.50 out of state. **Remarks:** Accepts advertising.
Ad Rates: GLR: $15.50 **Circ:** ‡1,123
BW: $522.45
SAU: $4.05

INDIANOLA

18157 The Indianola News
PO Box 130 Phone: (308)364-2316
Indianola, NE 69034 Fax: (308)364-2130
Publication E-mail: olanews@swnebr.net

Community newspaper. **Founded:** 1950. **Freq:** Weekly (Thurs.). **Print Method:** Offset. **Cols./Page:** 6. **Col. Width:** 12 picas. **Col. Depth:** 301 agate lines. **Key Personnel:** Mary Marsh, Editor. **USPS:** 581-220. **Subscription Rates:** $18.50 in 690 zipcose; $20 rest of NE; $23 out of state. **Remarks:** Accepts advertising.
Ad Rates: SAU: $3.00 **Circ:** ‡500
PCI: $3.00

JOHNSON

18158 KCOE-FM - 105.5
RR 1 Box 90
Johnson, NE 68378-9738

Format: Country; News. **Networks:** ABC; Brownfield. **Founded:** 1981. **Formerly:** KAUB-FM (1991). **Operating Hours:** 6 a.m.-10 p.m. **Key Personnel:** Judy Coe, General Mgr. **Wattage:** 3000.

KEARNEY†, pop. 21,158.

Buffalo Co. (SC). 43 m W of Grand Island. Kearney State College. Shipping and wholesale trade center. Alfalfa meal mills; foundry and machine shops; manufactures creamery products, hosiery, pumps, radios, cement block. Diversified farming. Corn, alfalfa, sugar beets, potatoes, cattle.

18159 Antelope Newspaper
University of Nebraska at Kearney
103 Thomas Hall Phone: (308)865-8488
Kearney, NE 68849 Fax: (308)865-8157
Publication E-mail: antelopenews@platte.unk.edu

Collegiate newspaper. **Founded:** 1905. **Freq:** Weekly (Thurs.). **Print Method:** Offset. **Trim Size:** 13 x 21 1/2. **Cols./Page:** 6. **Col. Width:** 23 nonpareils. **Col. Depth:** 301 agate lines. **Key Personnel:** Elizabeth Barrett, Advisor; Eric Renez, Editor; Heather Lux, Advertising Mgr. **Subscription Rates:** $10. **Remarks:** Accepts advertising.
Ad Rates: BW: $441 **Circ:** ‡4,600
4C: $815
SAU: $6
PCI: $6.50

18160 Kearney Hub
Kearney Hub Publishing Co.
13 E. 22nd Phone: (308)237-2152
PO Box 1988 Fax: (308)233-9736
Kearney, NE 68848
Free: (800)950-6113
Publisher E-mail: kearneyhub@digitalis.net

General newspaper. **Founded:** 1888. **Freq:** Daily (eve.) and Sat. (morn.). **Print Method:** Offset. **Trim Size:** 13 1/2 x 22 3/4. **Cols./Page:** 6. **Col. Width:** 25 nonpareils. **Col. Depth:** 294 agate lines. **Key Personnel:** Mike Konz, Managing Editor, fax (308)233-9745. **Subscription Rates:** $8 individuals per month; $9 by mail per month, regional; $10.50 by mail per month, non-regional. **Remarks:** Accepts advertising. **Formerly:** Kearney Daily Hub.
Ad Rates: BW: $1,045.80 **Circ:** Mon.-Fri. 12,778
4C: $1280.80 Sat. 14,148
SAU: $8.40
PCI: $8.30

18161 Penny Press 6
Maverick Media, Inc.
6205 N. 2nd Ave. Phone: (308)234-4530
PO Box 536
Kearney, NE 68848
Shopper (tabloid). **Freq:** Weekly (Tues.). **Print Method:** Offset. **Trim Size:** 11 1/2 x 16. **Cols./Page:** 6. **Col. Width:** 9 1/2 picas. **Col. Depth:** 15 inches. **Key Personnel:** William Welsh, President. **Subscription Rates:** $24 individuals. **Remarks:** Accepts advertising. **Alt. Formats:** CD-ROM. **Formerly:** Kearney Booster (1988).
Ad Rates: GLR: $0.56 **Circ:** Free ‡23,850
BW: $711
4C: $866
SAU: $10.40
PCI: $8.70

18162 Platte Valley Review
University of Nebraska at Kearney
Kearney, NE 68849 Phone: (308)865-8295

Literary journal covering scholarly and creative writing by University of Nebraska faculty and selected outside contributors. **Founded:** 1973. **Freq:** Semiannual. **Key Personnel:** Vern Plambeck, Editor, phone (308)865-8295. **ISSN:** 0092-4318. **Subscription Rates:** $5 single issue. **Remarks:** Advertising not accepted.
Circ: (Not Reported)

18163 KGFW-AM - 1340
PO Box 669 Phone: (308)237-2131
Kearney, NE 68848 Fax: (308)237-0312
E-mail: mail@mgfw.com

Format: Talk; News. **Networks:** CBS. **Owner:** Central Nebraska Broadcasting Co., Inc., at above address. **Founded:** 1927. **Operating Hours:** Continuous. **ADI:** Lincoln-Hastings-Kearney, NE. **Key Personnel:** John McDonald, Contact; Dirk Christensen, Operations Mgr. **Wattage:** 1000 watts.

18164 KHGI-TV - 13/6
13 S. Hwy. 44 Phone: (308)743-2494
PO Box 220 Fax: (308)743-2644
Kearney, NE 68848-0220
E-mail: ntv@navix.net

Format: Commercial TV. **Networks:** ABC. **Owner:** Pappas Telecasting Co. of Central Nebraska, at above address. **Founded:** 1953. **Formerly:** KHOL-TV. **Operating Hours:** Continuous. **ADI:** Lincoln-Hastings-Kearney, NE. **Key Personnel:** Stephen Morris, General Mgr.; Jim Kettner, Promotions Mgr.; Mark Baumert, News Dir.; Scott Swenson, Program Dir.; Doug Conrad, Sales Mgr.; Jerry Fuehrer, Chief Engineer. **Wattage:** 316.

18165 KKPR-AM - 1460
PO Box 130 Phone: (308)236-9900
Kearney, NE 68848 Fax: (308)234-6781
Free: (800)237-KKPR
E-mail: kkpr_ news@kfn.org

Format: Middle-of-the-Road (MOR); Sports. **Networks:** CNN Radio. **Owner:** Platte River Radio, at above address. **Founded:** 1956. **Operating Hours:** Continuous. **ADI:** Lincoln-Hastings-Kearney, NE. **Key Personnel:** Craig Eckert, General Mgr.; Dan Beck, Operations Mgr.; Kim Wellman, News Dir. **Wattage:** 5000 day; 56 night. **Ad Rates:** Advertising accepted; rates available upon request.

18166 KKPR-FM - 98.9
PO Box 130 Phone: (308)236-9900
Kearney, NE 68848 Fax: (308)234-6781
Free: (800)237-KKPR
E-mail: kkpr_ news@kfn.org

Format: Oldies. **Networks:** Satellite Music Network. **Owner:** Platte River Radio, at above address. **Founded:** 1962. **Operating Hours:** Continuous. **ADI:** Lincoln-Hastings-Kearney, NE. **Key Personnel:** Craig Eckert, General Mgr.; Dan Beck, Operations Mgr.; Kim Wellman, News Dir. **Wattage:** 100,000. **Ad Rates:** Advertising accepted; rates available upon request.

18167 KLPR-FM - 91.3
University of Nebraska at Kearney Phone: (308)234-8217
Kearney, NE 68849

Format: Jazz; Blues; Alternative/New Music/Progressive. **Founded:** 1968. **Formerly:** KOVF-FM; KSCV-FM. **Operating Hours:** 6 a.m.-2 a.m. **ADI:** Lincoln-Hastings-Kearney, NE. **Key Personnel:** Roy L. Hyatte, General Mgr., hyatte@platte.unk.edu; Candace Thompson, Program Dir. **Local Programs:** *The Scott Voorhees Show*, Scott Voorhees. **Wattage:** 1000. **Ad Rates:** Noncommercial.

18168 KQKY-FM - 105.9
Platte Valley Bldg. Phone: (308)237-2131
PO Box 669 Fax: (308)237-0312
Kearney, NE 68848
E-mail: mail@kqky.com

Format: Top 40. **Founded:** 1979. **Operating Hours:** Continuous. **ADI:** Lincoln-Hastings-Kearney, NE. **Key Personnel:** John McDonald, Contact; Dirk Christensen, Operations Mgr.; Mitch Cooley, Program Dir. **Wattage:** 100,000 ERP.

18169 KSNB-TV - 4
KHGI-TV Phone: (308)743-2494
PO Box 220 Fax: (308)743-2644
Kearney, NE 68848

Format: Commercial TV. **Networks:** Fox; United Paramount Network. **Founded:** 1964. **Operating Hours:** Continuous. **ADI:** Linooln-Hastings-Kearney, NE. **Key Personnel:** George Singleton, General Mgr. **Wattage:** 100.

KWNB-TV - See Hayes Center

KIMBALL†, pop. 3,120.

Kimball Co. (W). 45 m S of Scottsbluff. Manufactures electronics and farm machinery. Ships wheat, potatoes, beans, cattle.

18170 Western Nebraska Observer
118 E. 2nd St. Phone: (308)235-3631
Box 700 Fax: (308)235-3632
Kimball, NE 69145-0700
Publication E-mail: observer@megavision.com

Community newspaper. **Founded:** May 1, 1885. **Freq:** Weekly (Thurs.). **Print Method:** Offset. **Trim Size:** 13 3/4 x 22 3/4. **Cols./Page:** 6. **Col. Width:** 12.5 picas. **Col. Depth:** 301 agate lines. **Key Personnel:** Sherry Pinkerton, Publisher. **USPS:** 678-940. **Subscription Rates:** $24.10; $29.95 out of area; $33.15 out of state. **Remarks:** Accepts advertising. **URL:** http://www.megavision.net/observer/observer. **Alt. Formats:** CD-ROM; Microform.
Ad Rates: BW: $394.27 **Circ:** Paid ‡2,038
4C: $609.85 Free ‡15
SAU: $3.60
PCI: $3.60

LAUREL, pop. 1,009.

Cedar Co. (SE). 35 m W of Sioux City, IA.

18171 Laurel Advocate
PO Box 688 Phone: (402)256-3200
Laurel, NE 68745
Community newspaper featuring local and agricultural news. **Founded:** 1893. **Freq:** Weekly. **Print Method:** Offset. **Cols./Page:** 7. **Col. Width:** 12.5 picas. **Col. Depth:** 21 inches. **Key Personnel:** Tanya Weber, Managing Editor; Duane Weber, Publisher; Mary Jane Weber, Publisher. **USPS:** 008-340. **Subscription Rates:** $12; $16.50 outside Tri-county area. **Remarks:** Accepts advertising.
Ad Rates: GLR: $16.80 **Circ:** ‡1,125
BW: $345.45
SAU: $2.35

LAWRENCE, pop. 350.

Nuckolls Co. (S). 20 m SE of Hastings. Stock, grain, sorghum, dairy, poultry farms. Wheat, corn, oats. hogs, beef.

18172 Locomotive
Ostdiek Publishing, Inc.
PO Box 188 Phone: (402)756-7284
Lawrence, NE 68957 Fax: (402)756-7285

Community newspaper. **Founded:** 1887. **Freq:** Weekly (Thurs.). **Print Method:** Offset. **Cols./Page:** 4. **Col. Width:** 29 nonpareils. **Col. Depth:** 231 agate lines. **Key Personnel:** Allen Ostdiek, Publisher. **Subscription Rates:** $18 individuals. **Remarks:** Accepts advertising.
Ad Rates: GLR: $.27 **Circ:** ‡871
SAU: $2.66
PCI: $2.20

LEIGH, pop. 509.

Colfax Co. (E). 25 m SE of Norfolk. Stock, grain, poultry farms. Corn, oats, hogs, cattle.

18173 Leigh World
PO Box 266 Phone: (402)892-2544
Clarkson, NE 68629
Community newspaper. **Founded:** 1886. **Freq:** Weekly (Wed.). **Print Method:** Uses mats. Letterpress. Offset. **Trim Size:** 22 1/2 x 13 1/2. **Cols./Page:** 5. **Col. Width:** 24 nonpareils. **Col. Depth:** 224 agate lines. **Key Personnel:** Harold L. Conrad, Editor and Publisher. **Subscription Rates:** $17 individuals; $20 out of state. **Remarks:** Accepts advertising.
Ad Rates: GLR: $2.64 **Circ:** ‡1,219
BW: $258
SAU: $2.66

LEXINGTON†.

Dawson Co. (SC). 20 m NW of Overton.

18174 Clipper-Herald
Western Publishing Co.
PO Box 599 Phone: (308)324-5511
Lexington, NE 68850 Fax: (308)324-5240
Free: (800)639-7039
Publisher E-mail: lexch@lexch.com

Community newspaper. **Subtitle:** Clipper-Herald. **Freq:** Semiweekly (Wed. and Sat.). **Print Method:** Offset. **Trim Size:** 13 x 21 3/4. **Cols./Page:** 6. **Col. Width:** 12 picas. **Col. Depth:** 21 1/2 inches. **Key Personnel:** Mark Smidt, Publisher/Adv. Mgr., msmidt@lexch.com; George Lauby, Editor, glauby@lexch.com. **USPS:** 311-240. **Subscription Rates:** $34; $47 other countries. **Remarks:** Accepts advertising. **URL:** http://www.lexch.com. **Formed by the merger of:** Lexington Clipper (1991); Dawson County Herald (1991).
Ad Rates: GLR: $1 **Circ:** ‡3,000
PCI: $5.75

18175 KLNE-FM - 88.7
PO Box 83111
Lincoln, NE 68501
Phone: (402)472-3611
Fax: (402)472-2403
Free: (800)290-6850
E-mail: nprn@unl.edu

Format: Public Radio; Jazz; Classical; News. **Networks:** National Public Radio (NPR); Public Radio International (PRI). **Owner:** Nebraska Educational Telecommunications Commission, at above address. **Founded:** 1990. **Operating Hours:** 5 a.m.- 1 a.m. **ADI:** Lincoln-Hastings-Kearney, NE. **Key Personnel:** Steve Robinson, General Mgr. **Local Programs:** *Wet Paint*, Bill Stibor. **Wattage:** 4380. **Ad Rates:** Noncommercial.

18176 KLNE-TV - 3
c/o KUON-TV
1800 NB 33rd. St.
PO Box 83111
Lincoln, NE 68501
Phone: (402)472-3611
Fax: (402)472-1785
E-mail: net@unlinfo.unl.edu

Format: Public TV. **Networks:** Public Broadcasting Service (PBS). **Owner:** Nebraska Educational Telecommunications, at above address. **Founded:** 1965. **Operating Hours:** 5:45 a.m.-midnight; 90% network; 10% local. **ADI:** Lincoln-Hastings-Kearney, NE. **Key Personnel:** Rod Bates, General Mgr., rbates@unlinfo.unl.edu; S. Graziano, Program Mgr., sgraziano@unlinfo.unl.edu; Michael Winkle, Asst. GM, Marketing, mwinkle@unlinfo.unl.edu; Steve Lenzen, Assistant GM, Educational TV, slenzen@unlinfo.unl.edu; Sue Gildersleeve, Assistant GM, Admin. & Finance, sgildersleeve@unlinfo.unl.edu; Peter Ford, Asst. GM of Engineering, pford@unlinfo.unl.edu; Bill Kelly, Sr. Producer, Public Affairs, wek@unlinfo.unl.edu; Steve Alvis, Sr. Producer, Sports & Special Events, salvis@unlinfo.unl.edu; Michael Farrell, Production Coordinator, Cultural Affairs, mfarrell@unlinfo.unl.edu. **Wattage:** 100kw. **Ad Rates:** Noncommercial. **URL:** http://net.unl.edu.

18177 KRVN-AM - 880
PO Box 880
Lexington, NE 68850-0880
Phone: (308)324-2371
Fax: (308)324-5786
E-mail: krvnam@krvn.com

Format: Country; Agricultural; News; Sports. **Networks:** ABC. **Owner:** Nebraska Rural Radio Assn., at above address. **Founded:** 1950. **Operating Hours:** Continuous. **ADI:** Lincoln-Hastings-Kearney, NE. **Key Personnel:** Eric Brown, General Mgr.; Gordon Bennett, Sales Mgr.; Craig Larson, Program Dir.; Mike LePorte, Farm Service Dir.; Rex Messersmith, Assoc. Farm Dir.; Bob Brogan, News Editor; Dewey Nelson, Assoc. Farm Dir.; Vern Killion, Engineering Dir.; Jim Struck, News Dir.; Evelyn Engleman, Sr. Staff Asst. **Local Programs:** *Inside Agriculture*, Mike LePorte, (308)324-2371, Fax (308)324-5786. **Wattage:** 50,000. **Ad Rates:** $54-152 for 30 seconds; $82-190 for 60 seconds. KTIC-KNEB. **URL:** http://www.krvn.com.

18178 KRVN-FM - 93.1
PO Box 880
Lexington, NE 68850-0880
Phone: (308)324-2371
Fax: (308)324-5786
E-mail: krvnam@krvn.com

Format: Adult Contemporary; News; Sports; Sports. **Networks:** NBC. **Owner:** Nebraska Rural Radio Assn., at above address. **Founded:** 1962. **Operating Hours:** Continuous. **ADI:** Lincoln-Hastings-Kearney, NE. **Key Personnel:** Eric Brown, General Mgr.; Gordon Bennett, Sales Mgr.; Craig Larson, Program Dir.; Dave Schroeder, News Dir.; Vern Killion, Chief Engineer; Evelyn Engleman, Sr. Staff Assistant; Jayson Jorgensen, Music/Sports Dir. **Local Programs:** *Morning Magazine*, Frank Snyder, Mailing contact. **Wattage:** 100,000 ERP. **Ad Rates:** $16-24 for 30 seconds; $20-35 for 60 seconds. **URL:** http://www.krvn.com.

LINCOLN†, pop. 171,950.

Lancaster Co. (SE). The State Capital, 55 m SW of Omaha. University of Nebraska, other colleges and institutions. Trade and grain marketing center. Cold storage plant; flour and feed mill; meat packing plant. Manufacturing biological, creamery products, farm machinery, farm belts, radiator hose, telephone equipment, pharmaceutical, plumbing supplies, pumps, motor scooters, wax, filing equipment and office supplies; printing, lithographic, engraving, metal, stone, concrete products.

18179 AAC: Augmentative and Alternative Communication
Decker Publications
University of Nebraska-Lincoln
202 Barkley Memorial Ctr.
Lincoln, NE 68583
Phone: (402)472-5463
Fax: (402)472-0406
Publication E-mail: info@bcdecker.com

Medical journal on speech and hearing issues. Sponsored by the International Society for Augmentative and Alternative Communication. **Founded:** 1985. **Freq:** Quarterly. **Print Method:** Sheetfed offset. **Trim Size:** 8 1/8 x 10 7/8. **Cols./Page:** 2. **Col. Width:** 32 nonpareils. **Col. Depth:** 119 agate lines. **Key Personnel:** Brain C. Decker, Publisher; Terry Pitz, Sales Mgr. **ISSN:** 0743-4618. **Subscription Rates:** $80 individuals; $120 institutions; $50 In-training. **Remarks:** Accepts advertising.
Ad Rates: BW: $483 — **Circ:** Paid 1,700
4C: $1528 — Non-paid 200

18180 The Children's Friend
Christian Record Services - Division for the Deaf
4444 S. 52nd St.
PO Box 6097
Lincoln, NE 68506
Phone: (402)488-0981
Fax: (402)488-7582
Publisher E-mail: 74617.1034@compuserve.com

Magazine for blind children. **Founded:** 1937. **Freq:** Monthly. **Print Method:** Braille. **Key Personnel:** R.J. Kaiser, Editor. **Remarks:** Advertising not accepted.
Circ: Non-paid ‡3,485

18181 Christian Record
Christian Record Services - Division for the Deaf
4444 S. 52nd St.
PO Box 6097
Lincoln, NE 68506
Phone: (402)488-0981
Fax: (402)488-7582
Publisher E-mail: 74617.1034@compuserve.com

Magazine for the blind. **Founded:** 1899. **Freq:** Monthly. **Print Method:** Braille. **Key Personnel:** R.J. Kaiser, Editor. **Remarks:** Advertising not accepted.
Circ: Non-paid ‡6,350

18182 Comments on Toxicology
Gordon and Breach Science Publishers
University of Nebraska–Lincoln
Plant Industry Rm. 202
Lincoln, NE 68588-0816

Science journal. **Freq:** Bimonthly. **Key Personnel:** A. Wallace Hayes, Editor. **ISSN:** 0886-5240.

18183 Controller
Sandhills Publishing
120 W. Harvest Dr.
PO Box 85310
Lincoln, NE 68501-5310
Phone: (402)479-2181
Fax: (402)479-2195
Free: (800)331-4890

Aviation sales tabloid. **Founded:** 1979. **Freq:** Weekly (Fri.). **Print Method:** Offset. **Trim Size:** 10 7/16 x 15 7/8. **Cols./Page:** 6. **Col. Width:** 1 5/8 inches. **Col. Depth:** 16 inches. **Key Personnel:** Susan Miller, Publication Mgr., susan-miller@thecontroller.com. **Subscription Rates:** $58 3rd class weekly; $24 3rd class monthly; $182 1st class weekly, U.S./Can./Mexico; $42 1st class monthly, U.S./Can./Mexico; $290 other countries 1st class weekly; $95 other countries 1st class monthly. **Remarks:** Advertising accepted; rates available upon request. **Available Online. URL:** http://www.thecontroller.com; http://www.executivecontroller.com.
Circ: (Not Reported)

18184 Daily Nebraskan
University of Nebraska at Lincoln
PO Box 880448
Lincoln, NE 68588-0448
Publication E-mail: dn@unlinfo.unl.edu

Collegiate newspaper (tabloid). **Founded:** 1900. **Freq:** Daily (morn.). **Print Method:** Offset. **Trim Size:** 11 x 17. **Cols./Page:** 5. **Col. Width:** 25 nonpareils. **Col. Depth:** 231 agate lines. **Key Personnel:** Erin Gibson, Editor, phone (402)472-1766; Nick Partsch, Advertising Mgr., phone (402)472-2589, npartsch@unl.edu. **Subscription Rates:** $55. **Remarks:** Accepts advertising. **Available Online. URL:** http:/www.unl.edu/dailyneb.
Ad Rates: BW: $940.50 — **Circ:** 16,000
4C: $1,105.50
SAU: $11.40
PCI: $11.40

18185 Great Plains Quarterly
University of Nebraska at Lincoln
1214 Oldfather Hall
Lincoln, NE 68588-0313
Phone: (402)472-6058
Fax: (402)472-0463
Publication E-mail: gpq@unlinfo.unl.edu

Scholarly journal covering research and criticism in the humanities, social sciences, history, etc., of the Great Plains region. **Founded:** 1981. **Freq:** Quarterly. **Print Method:** Offset. **Trim Size:** 7 1/2 x 10. **Cols./Page:** 2. **Col. Width:** 2 5/8 inches. **Col. Depth:** 7 inches. **Key Personnel:** Charlene Porsild, Editor; George Wolf, Book Review Editor; Daniel Justice, Editorial Asst. **ISSN:** 0275-7664. **Subscription Rates:** $25 individuals; $50 institutions; $8 single issue. **Remarks:** Accepts advertising. **Alt. Formats:** Microfilm, UMI.
Ad Rates: BW: $100 — **Circ:** Controlled 500

18186 Great Plains Research
Center for Great Plains Studies
1215 Oldfather Hall
University of Nebraska-Lincoln
Lincoln, NE 68588-0317
Phone: (402)472-3082
Fax: (402)472-0463
Publication E-mail: gpr@unlinfo.unl.edu

Scholarly, multidisciplinary journal covering natural and social sciences dealing with issues of the Great Plains environment. **Key Personnel:** Svata Louda, Editor; George E. Wolf, Book Review Editor; Jay H. Buckley, Asst. Editor. **ISSN:** 1052-5165. **Subscription Rates:** $25 individuals; $28 Canada; $35 elsewhere; $50 libraries and institutions; $53 Canada institutions; $60 elsewhere institutions. **Remarks:** Accepts advertising. **URL:** http://www.unl.edu/plains/.
Circ: Combined 500

18187 Huskers Illustrated
Sports Magazines of America, Inc.
PO Box 83222
Lincoln, NE 68501

College sports magazine for University of Nebraska. **Founded:** 1981. **Freq:** Weekly. **Print Method:** Offset. **Trim Size:** 8 1/2 x 11. **Cols./Page:** 3. **Col. Width:** 29 nonpareils. **Col. Depth:** 133 agate lines. **Key Personnel:** Mark Owens, Editor; Mike Henry, Publisher; Charles Brackin, Publisher; Mel Johnson, Editor. **ISSN:** 0279-3474. **Subscription Rates:** $39.90. **Remarks:** Accepts advertising.
Ad Rates: BW: $1,090 — **Circ:** 16,000
4C: $1,640

18188 Journal of World Business
Elseiver
Univ. of Nebraska
Dept. of Management
Lincoln, NE 68588-0491
Publisher E-mail: fcentres@gpu.stv.ualberta.ca

Magazine focusing on international business. **Founded:** 1965. **Freq:** Quarterly. **Trim Size:** 8 1/4 x 10. **Cols./Page:** 3. **Col. Width:** 33 nonpareils. **Col. Depth:** 132 agate lines. **Key Personnel:** Daniel London, Editor, dlondon@admin.gsb.columbia.edu. **ISSN:** 0022-5428. **Subscription Rates:** $55 individuals; $125 institutions; $75 other countries; $145 institutions, other countries. **Remarks:** Accepts advertising.
Ad Rates: BW: $350 — **Circ:** ‡2,000

18189 Letras Femeninas
Asociacion de Literatura Fenemina Hispanica
University of Nebraska
Modern Languages Dept.
Lincoln, NE 68588-0315
Phone: (402)472-3710
Fax: (402)472-0327
Publisher E-mail: amartime@unlinfo.unl.edu

Journal of contemporary Hispanic literature by women. **Founded:** 1974. **Freq:** 2/year. **Trim Size:** 6x9. **Cols./Page:** 1. **Key Personnel:** Adelaida Martinez, amartinez@unlinfo.unl.edu. **ISSN:** 0277-4356. **Subscription Rates:** $25 individuals; $24 single issue per volume; $30 students; $10 students. **Remarks:** Accepts advertising.
Ad Rates: BW: $400 — **Circ:** Paid 500
Non-paid 40

18190 Lincoln Journal
Journal-Star Printing Co.
926 P St.
PO Box 81609
Lincoln, NE 68508
Phone: (402)475-4200
Fax: (402)473-7291
General newspaper. **Founded:** 1867. **Freq:** Daily (eve.), Sat. and Sun. (morn.). **Print Method:** Letterpress. **Cols./Page:** 6. **Col. Width:** 25 nonpareils. **Col. Depth:** 301 agate lines. **Key Personnel:** W. Earl Dyer, Editor. **Remarks:** Accepts advertising. **URL:** http://www.nebweb.com. **Feature Editors:** John Barrette, *Consumer Affairs, Financial/Business*, phone (402)473-7285; Kathryn Cates Moore, *Fashion*, phone (402)473-7212; Margaret Ehlers, *Travel*, phone (402)473-7219; Randy Hampton, *Photo*, phone (402)473-7481; Richard Herman, *Editorials*, phone (402)473-7225; Brian Hill, *Sports*, phone (402)473-7434; Herb Hyde, *Book*, phone (402)473-7287; Tom Ineck, *Drama, Music*, phone (402)473-7256; Arthur J. Hovey, *Farm, Rural Development*, phone (402)473-7321; Gene Kelly, *Real Estate*, phone (402)473-7240; Jack Kennedy, *Education*, phone (402)473-7254; L. Kent Wolgamott, *Entertainment, Music*, phone (402)473-7244; Fred Knapp, *State, Suburban*, phone (402)473-7242; Susan Kreifel, *Family, Features, Food, Garden/Home, Lifestyle, Living, Society, Women's*, phone (402)473-7213; Catharine L. Huddle, *Sunday*, phone (402)473-7245; Al Laukaitis, *Environmental*, phone (402)473-7257; Bob Moyer, *City, Metro*, phone (402)473-7249; Donna Peate, *Radio, TV*, phone (402)473-7231; Kathleen Rutledge, *Political*, phone (402)473-7250; Martha Stoddard, *Medical*, phone (402)473-7248; Robert T. Moyer, *News*, phone (402)473-7222; Susan Willey, *Religion*,

phone (402)473-7214; Kent Wolgamott, *Movie*, phone (402)473-7244.
Ad Rates: SAU: $28.97 **Circ:** Mon.-Fri. 38,303
Sat. 84,258
Sun. 85,071

18191 Lincoln Star
Journal-Star Printing Co.
926 P St. Phone: (402)475-4200
PO Box 81609 Fax: (402)473-7291
Lincoln, NE 68508
General newspaper. **Founded:** 1902. **Freq:** Mon.-Sun. (morn.). **Print Method:** Offset. **Cols./Page:** 6. **Col. Width:** 25 nonpareils. **Col. Depth:** 301 agate lines. **Key Personnel:** W. Earl Dyer, Editor. **Remarks:** Combined advertising rates available with Sunday Journal-Star.
Ad Rates: SAU: $28.97 **Circ:** Mon.-Fri. 42,977
Sat. 84,258
Sun. 85,071

18192 Machinery Trader (Central Edition)
Sandhills Publishing
120 W. Harvest Dr. Phone: (402)479-2181
PO Box 85310 Fax: (402)479-2195
Lincoln, NE 68501-5310
Free: (800)331-4890

Magazine on used construction equipment. **Founded:** 1978. **Freq:** Weekly (Fri.). **Print Method:** Web offset. **Trim Size:** 10 1/2 x 15 7/8. **Cols./Page:** 6. **Col. Width:** 20 nonpareils. **Col. Depth:** 224 agate lines. **Key Personnel:** Dean Belka, Editor; Mitch Schainost, Editor. **Subscription Rates:** Free to qualified subscribers; $59. **Remarks:** Color advertising accepted; rates available upon request. **URL:** http://www.machinerytrader.com.
Ad Rates: BW: $938 **Circ:** (Not Reported)
PCI: $17

18193 Machinery Trader (Eastern Edition)
Sandhills Publishing
120 W. Harvest Dr. Phone: (402)479-2181
PO Box 85310 Fax: (402)479-2195
Lincoln, NE 68501-5310
Free: (800)331-4890

Magazine on used construction equipment. **Founded:** 1978. **Freq:** Weekly (Fri.). **Print Method:** Web offset. **Trim Size:** 10 1/2 x 15 7/8. **Cols./Page:** 6. **Col. Width:** 20 nonpareils. **Col. Depth:** 224 agate lines. **Key Personnel:** Marva Wasser, Publication Manager; Jill Bierkey, Circulation Mgr.; Mike Peterson, Web Publisher; Bob Chester, Fast Track Manager. **Subscription Rates:** Free to qualified subscribers; $59. **Remarks:** Color advertising accepted; rates available upon request. **URL:** http://www.machinerytrader.com.
Ad Rates: BW: $747 **Circ:** (Not Reported)
PCI: $14

18194 Machinery Trader (Western Edition)
Sandhills Publishing
120 W. Harvest Dr. Phone: (402)479-2181
PO Box 85310 Fax: (402)479-2195
Lincoln, NE 68501-5310
Free: (800)331-4890

Magazine on used construction equipment. **Founded:** 1978. **Freq:** Weekly (Fri.). **Print Method:** Web offset. **Trim Size:** 10 1/2 x 15 7/8. **Cols./Page:** 6. **Col. Width:** 20 nonpareils. **Col. Depth:** 224 agate lines. **Key Personnel:** Marva Wasser, Publication Manager; Jill Bierkey, Circulation Mgr.; Mike Peterson, Web Publisher; Bob Chester, Fast Track Manager. **Subscription Rates:** $59. **Remarks:** Color advertising accepted; rates available upon request. **Available Online. URL:** http://www.machinerytrader.com.
Ad Rates: BW: $625 **Circ:** (Not Reported)
PCI: $12.50

18195 Marketer
Nebraska Petroleum Marketers & Convenience Store Association
1320 Lincoln Mall Phone: (402)474-6691
Lincoln, NE 68508 Fax: (402)474-2510
Publication E-mail: 102344.552@compuserve.com

Oil and automotive magazine. **Founded:** Oct. 1923. **Freq:** Monthly. **Print Method:** Offset. **Trim Size:** 8 1/2 x 11. **Cols./Page:** 2. **Col. Width:** 39 nonpareils. **Col. Depth:** 136 agate lines. **Key Personnel:** Fred R. Stone, Editor. **Subscription Rates:** $25. **Remarks:** Accepts advertising. **Formerly:** Nebraska Oil Jobber; Nebraska Petroleum Marketer.
Ad Rates: BW: $411 **Circ:** Combined ‡1,400
4C: $1,050
PCI: $25

18196 Nebraska
Alumni Association of the University of Nebraska
Wick Alumni Center Phone: (402)472-2841
PO Box 880216 Fax: (402)472-4635
Lincoln, NE 68588-0216
Publication E-mail: nebmag@unlinfo.unl.edu

University alumni magazine. **Founded:** 1906. **Freq:** Quarterly. **Print Method:** Offset. **Trim Size:** 8 3/8 x 10 7/8. **Cols./Page:** 3. **Col. Width:** 28 nonpareils. **Col. Depth:** 126 agate lines. **Key Personnel:** Andrea Cranford, Editor; Robert Sheldon, Editor. **Subscription Rates:** $30. **Remarks:** Advertising not accepted. **URL:** http://www.unl.edu/alumni/alumni/htm. **Formerly:** Nebraska Alumnus.
Circ: ‡24,000

18197 Nebraska Beverage Analyst
Bell Publications
2403 Champa St. Phone: (303)296-1600
Denver, CO 80205-2621 Fax: (303)295-2159

Trade magazine for the liquor, beer, and wine industries. **Founded:** 1936. **Freq:** Monthly. **Print Method:** Offset. **Trim Size:** 8 3/8 x 10 7/8. **Cols./Page:** 3. **Col. Width:** 28 nonpareils. **Col. Depth:** 120 agate lines. **Key Personnel:** Lawrence Bell, Editor and Publisher. **ISSN:** 0028-1808. **Subscription Rates:** $12 individuals. **Remarks:** Accepts advertising.
Ad Rates: BW: $570 **Circ:** Paid ‡141
4C: $1,120 Non-paid ‡2,634
PCI: $25

18198 Nebraska Cattleman
The Nebraska Cattlemen, Inc.
1355 H St. Phone: (402)475-2333
Lincoln, NE 68508-3748 Fax: (402)475-0822

Magazine for the cattle industry in Nebraska. **Founded:** Sept. 1944. **Freq:** Monthly (June/July issues combined). **Print Method:** Offset. **Trim Size:** 8 3/8 x 10 7/8. **Cols./Page:** 3. **Col. Width:** 28 nonpareils. **Col. Depth:** 138 agate lines. **Key Personnel:** Randy Rasby, Advertising Mgr. **USPS:** 375-880. **Subscription Rates:** Free to qualified subscribers; $50 nonmembers Nebraska Cattleman members. **Remarks:** Accepts advertising.
Ad Rates: BW: $645 **Circ:** Paid ‡5,067
4C: $1,105 Controlled ‡4,530
PCI: $22

18199 Nebraska Farm Bureau News
Nebraska Farm Bureau Federation
PO Box 80299 Phone: (402)421-4405
Lincoln, NE 68501-0299 Fax: (402)421-4432

Nebraska Farm Bureau newspaper emphasizing legislation, policies, and regulations affecting agriculture. **Founded:** 1983. **Freq:** Monthly. **Print Method:** Offset. **Trim Size:** 11 1/2 x 18 3/4. **Cols./Page:** 4. **Col. Width:** 14.5 picas. **Col. Depth:** 16.5 picas. **Key Personnel:** Cheryl Stubbendieck, Editor. **ISSN:** 0745-6522. **Subscription Rates:** Free to qualified subscribers. **Remarks:** Advertising not accepted for tires, batteries, oils, and lubricants. **Formerly:** Nebraska Agriculture.
Ad Rates: BW: $4.50 **Circ:** Paid ‡45,000
PCI: $9 Non-paid ‡500

18200 Nebraska Farmer
Farm Progress Companies
5625 O St., Ste. 5 Phone: (402)489-9331
Lincoln, NE 68510 Fax: (402)489-9335

Agricultural magazine. **Founded:** 1859. **Freq:** 15/year. **Print Method:** Offset. **Trim Size:** 8 x 10 7/8. **Cols./Page:** 3. **Col. Width:** 13 picas. **Col. Depth:** 59 picas. **Key Personnel:** David R. Howe, Editor; Allan R. Johnson, Publisher; Chuck Roth, VP of Advertising; Terry Butzirus, Regional Advertising Mgr. **USPS:** 376-020. **Subscription Rates:** $19.95 Free to qualified subscribers; $17.95 individuals. **Remarks:** Accepts advertising.
Ad Rates: BW: $3,050 **Circ:** Paid 16,436
4C: $4,575 Non-paid 23,281
PCI: $120

18201 Nebraska History
Nebraska State Historical Society
POB 82554 Phone: (402)471-3270
Lincoln, NE 68501 Fax: (402)471-3100
Publisher E-mail: publish@nebraskahistory.org

History magazine. **Founded:** 1918. **Freq:** Quarterly. **Print Method:** Offset. **Trim Size:** 8 1/2 x 11. **Cols./Page:** 3. **Col. Width:** 28 picas. **Col. Depth:** 54 picas. **Key Personnel:** James E. Potter, Editor, phone (402)471-4747. **ISSN:** 0028-1859. **Subscription Rates:** $25 individuals; $7 single issue. **Remarks:** Advertising not accepted. **Alt. Formats:** Microform.
Circ: ‡4,000

18202 Nebraska Municipal Review
League of Nebraska Municipalities
1335 L St. Phone: (402)476-2829
Lincoln, NE 68508 Fax: (402)476-7052

Municipal government magazine. **Founded:** 1914. **Freq:** Monthly. **Print Method:** Offset. **Trim Size:** 8 1/4 x 11 1/4. **Cols./Page:** 3. **Col. Width:** 27 nonpareils. **Col. Depth:** 140 agate lines. **Key Personnel:** Lynn Marienau, Editor, phone (402)476-2829, fax (402)476-7052. **ISSN:** 0028-1905. **Subscription Rates:** $30; $3 single issue. **Remarks:** Accepts advertising.
Ad Rates: BW: $530 **Circ:** ‡3,200

18203 Nebraska Music Educator
Nebraska Music Educators Association
Box 83046 Phone: (402)435-6913
Lincoln, NE 68501-3046 Fax: (402)474-3250
Free: (888)870-NMEA

Professional journal for music teachers. **Founded:** 1949. **Freq:** Quarterly. **Print Method:** Offset. **Trim Size:** 8 1/2 x 11. **Key Personnel:** Michael H. Veak, Editor/Business Mgr., mveak@lps.org. **ISSN:** 0732-1503. **Subscription Rates:** $10 individuals; $2.50 single issue. **Remarks:** Accepts advertising.
Ad Rates: BW: $198 **Circ:** Paid 1,500
4C: $22

18204 Nebraska Newspaper
Nebraska Press Association
1120 K St. Phone: (402)476-2851
Lincoln, NE 68508 Fax: (402)476-2942
Publisher E-mail: nebpress@nebpress.com

Magazine on publishing. **Founded:** 1948. **Freq:** Bimonthly. **Print Method:** Offset. **Trim Size:** 8 1/2 x 11. **Cols./Page:** 3. **Col. Width:** 26 nonpareils. **Col. Depth:** 133 agate lines. **Key Personnel:** Mary Jo Chatelain, Editor. **ISSN:** 0028-1913. **Subscription Rates:** $10.50. **Remarks:** Accepts advertising. **URL:** http://www.nebpress.com.
Ad Rates: BW: $342 **Circ:** Controlled ‡650
4C: $622

18205 Nebraska Retailer
Nebraska Retail Grocers Association
5533 S. 27th St., Ste. 104 Phone: (402)423-5533
Lincoln, NE 68512 Fax: (402)423-8686

Magazine for food industry. **Founded:** 1906. **Freq:** Bimonthly. **Print Method:** Offset. **Trim Size:** 7 7/8 x 10 7/8. **Cols./Page:** 2. **Col. Width:** 38 nonpareils. **Col. Depth:** 140 agate lines. **Key Personnel:** Kathy Siefken, Editor. **Subscription Rates:** $50 members. **Remarks:** Accepts advertising.
Ad Rates: BW: $330 **Circ:** ‡1,200

18206 Nebraska Trucker
Truck Services, Inc.
PO Box 81010 Phone: (402)476-8504
Lincoln, NE 68501 Fax: (402)476-0579
Publication E-mail: nebtrucking@navix.net

Magazine for commercial truckers and shippers. **Subtitle:** Official Publication of the Nebraska Motor Carriers Association. **Founded:** 1940. **Freq:** Monthly. **Print Method:** Offset. **Trim Size:** 8 1/2 x 11. **Cols./Page:** 3. **Col. Width:** 26 nonpareils. **Col. Depth:** 140 agate lines. **Key Personnel:** Nance Kirk, Editor, nanceh@navix.net; Sue Wilson, Contact, nebtrucking.swilson@navix.net; Michelle Drahota, Contact, nebtrucking.mdrahota@navix.net. **Subscription Rates:** $18; $2 single issue. **Remarks:** Accepts advertising.
Ad Rates: BW: $475 **Circ:** ‡2,200
4C: $902.50
PCI: $18.20

18207 Nebraska Union Farmer
Farmers Union of Nebraska
1305 Plum Phone: (402)476-8815
Box 22667 Fax: (402)476-8859
Lincoln, NE 68542-2667
Publication E-mail: nefusal@aol.com

Farmers' union magazine. **Subtitle:** Union Farmer. **Founded:** 1915. **Freq:** Bimonthly. **Print Method:** Offset. **Cols./Page:** 5. **Col. Width:** 24 nonpareils. **Col. Depth:** 224 agate lines. **Key Personnel:** Sally Herrin, Editor. **USPS:** 376-520. **Subscription Rates:** Free to qualified subscribers.
Ad Rates: PCI: $5 **Circ:** 4,780

18208 NEBRASKAland
Nebraska Game and Parks Commission
2200 N. 33rd St. Phone: (402)471-0641
Box 30370 Fax: (402)471-5528
Lincoln, NE 68503
Publication E-mail: nebland@ngpsun.ngpc.state.ne.us

Magazine on outdoor recreation and conservation in Nebraska. **Founded:** 1926. **Freq:** 10/year. **Print Method:** Offset. **Trim Size:** 8 1/4 x 10 7/8. **Cols./Page:** 3. **Col. Width:** 13.5 picas. **Col. Depth:** 8 3/8 inches. **Key Personnel:** Don

Cunningham, Editor; Troy Kroeger, Production Mgr. **ISSN:** 0028-1964. **Subscription Rates:** $14; $2 single issue. **Remarks:** Accepts classified advertising. **Alt. Formats:** Audio tape.
Circ: Paid ‡51,238
Non-paid ‡4,100

18209 NSEA Voice
Nebraska State Education Association
605 S. 14th St. Phone: (402)475-7611
Lincoln, NE 68508 Fax: (402)475-2630

Education newspaper (tabloid). **Founded:** 1947. **Freq:** Monthly. **Print Method:** Letterpress and offset. **Trim Size:** 8 1/2 x 11. **Cols./Page:** 4. **Col. Width:** 27 nonpareils. **Col. Depth:** 182 agate lines. **Key Personnel:** Karen Kilgarin, Editor, kkilgarin@nsea.org. **USPS:** 000-369. **Remarks:** Accepts advertising.
Ad Rates: BW: $700 **Circ:** ‡23,500

18210 PC Novice
Sandhills Publishing
120 W. Harvest Dr. Phone: (402)479-2181
PO Box 85310 Fax: (402)479-2195
Lincoln, NE 68501-5310
Free: (800)331-4890

Magazine for personal computer users. **Subtitle:** Personal Computers in Plain English. **Founded:** 1990. **Freq:** Monthly. **Print Method:** Web offset. **Trim Size:** 8 1/8 x 10 3/4. **Cols./Page:** 3. **Col. Width:** 2 1/4 inches. **Key Personnel:** Ronald D. Kobler, Managing Editor. **ISSN:** 1052-1186. **Subscription Rates:** $24 individuals; $32 other countries; $2.95 single issue; $3.50 single issue other countries. **Online:** America Online, Inc.
Ad Rates: 4C: $5,800 **Circ:** Non-paid 104,008
Paid 339,113

18211 PC Today
Sandhills Publishing
120 W. Harvest Dr. Phone: (402)479-2181
PO Box 85310 Fax: (402)479-2195
Lincoln, NE 68501-5310
Free: (800)331-4890

Magazine for personal computer users. **Subtitle:** Computing for Small Business. **Founded:** 1987. **Freq:** Monthly. **Print Method:** Web offset. **Trim Size:** 8 1/8 x 10 3/4. **Cols./Page:** 3. **Col. Width:** 2 1/4 inches. **Key Personnel:** Ronald D. Kobler, Managing Editor; Robert A. Bobrowski, Publisher. **ISSN:** 1040-6484. **Subscription Rates:** $24; $32 other countries. $2.95 single issue; $3.50 single issue other countries. **Remarks:** Accepts advertising. **Online:** America Online, Inc.
Ad Rates: 4C: $4,500 **Circ:** Paid 33,707

18212 Photochemistry and Photobiology
American Society for Photobiology
Dept. of Chemistry Phone: (402)273-2733
University of Nebraska Fax: (402)472-2044
Lincoln, NE 68588-0376
Journal covering the effects of light on chemical and biological processes. **Founded:** 1962. **Freq:** Monthly. **Trim Size:** 8 1/2 x 11. **Cols./Page:** 2. **Col. Width:** 3 3/4 inches. **Col. Depth:** 9 1/4 inches. **Key Personnel:** Dr. Pill-Soon Song, Editor; Gene Kean, Advertising Dir. **ISSN:** 0031-8655. **Subscription Rates:** Free (members); $525 Industry. **Remarks:** Advertising accepted; rates available upon request.
Circ: 815
Non-paid 1,600

18213 Prairie Schooner
University of Nebraska
201 Andrews Hall Phone: (402)472-0911
Lincoln, NE 68588-0334 Fax: (402)472-9771

Magazine of poems, short stories, essays, translations, and book reviews. **Founded:** Jan. 1927. **Freq:** Quarterly. **Print Method:** Letterpress and offset. **Trim Size:** 6 x 9. **Cols./Page:** 1. **Col. Width:** 58 nonpareils. **Col. Depth:** 105 agate lines. **Key Personnel:** Hilda Raz, Editor; Ladette Randolph, Managing Editor, lrandolp@unlinfo.unl.edu. **ISSN:** 0032-6682. **Subscription Rates:** $22 individuals; $25 institutions. **Remarks:** Accepts advertising. **Online:** Chadwick-Healey. **Alt. Formats:** Microform.
Ad Rates: BW: $150 **Circ:** Paid ‡2,800
Non-paid ‡300

18214 The Processor
Sandhills Publishing
120 W. Harvest Dr. Phone: (402)479-2181
PO Box 85310 Fax: (402)479-2195
Lincoln, NE 68501-5310
Free: (800)331-4890

Computer sales magazine. **Founded:** 1978. **Freq:** Weekly (Fri.). **Print Method:** Offset. **Cols./Page:** 6. **Col. Width:** 20 nonpareils. **Col. Depth:** 224 agate lines. **Key Personnel:** Thomas J. Peed, President; Rhonda Peed, Vice President; Mitch Schainost, General Sales Mgr.; Jeff Pfeifer, Publisher, phone (402)479-2141, fax (402)479-2129, jeff-pfeifer@processor.com; Randall Flagel, Circulation Dir., phone (402)479-2141, fax (402)479-2120. **Subscription Rates:** $59. **Remarks:** Accepts advertising. **URL:** http://www.processor.com.
Ad Rates: 4C: $1,199 **Circ:** ‡60,000

18215 Quarterly Journal of Business & Economics
University of Nebraska
University of Nebraska Phone: (402)472-7931
CBA Bldg. Fax: (402)472-5180
PO Box 880407
Lincoln, NE 68588-0407
Journal reporting on finance and economics. **Founded:** 1962. **Freq:** Quarterly. **Print Method:** Offset. **Trim Size:** 6 x 9. **Cols./Page:** 1. **Col. Width:** 27 picas. **Col. Depth:** 7 inches. **Key Personnel:** George M. McCabe, Editor, phone (402)472-3309, qjbe@cbamail.unl.edu; Margo Young, Managing Editor, myoung@unl.edu. **ISSN:** 0747-5535. **Subscription Rates:** $17 individuals; $32 institutions; $35 out of country; $45 institutions out of country. **Remarks:** Advertising not accepted. **Formerly:** Nebraska Journal of Economics & Business.
Circ: Paid 500
Non-paid 100

18216 Rural Electric Nebraskan
Nebraska Rural Electric Association
PO Box 82048 Phone: (402)475-4988
Lincoln, NE 68501 Fax: (402)475-0835

Rural farm and ranch magazine. **Founded:** 1947. **Freq:** Monthly. **Print Method:** Offset. **Trim Size:** 8 1/2 x 11. **Cols./Page:** 3. **Col. Width:** 28 nonpareils. **Col. Depth:** 133 agate lines. **Key Personnel:** Jack Merritt, Editor; Dirk Maley, Advertising Mgr. **Subscription Rates:** $10. **Remarks:** Accepts advertising.
Ad Rates: BW: $1,145 **Circ:** ‡58,000
4C: $1,745
PCI: $60

18217 School Psychology Quarterly
Guilford Publications, Inc.
c/o Terry Gutkin
117 Bancroft Hall
Department of Educational Psychology
University of Nebraska-Lincoln
Lincoln, NE 68588-0369
Publisher E-mail: info@guilford.com

Journal covering school psychology. **Freq:** Quarterly. **Trim Size:** 6 x 9. **Key Personnel:** Terri Gutkin, Editor. **Subscription Rates:** $35 individuals; $105 institutions. **Remarks:** Accepts advertising.
Circ: (Not Reported)

18218 Southern Nebraska Register
PO Box 80329 Phone: (402)488-0090
Lincoln, NE 68501 Fax: (402)488-3569

Official newspaper of the Catholic Diocese of Lincoln, NE. **Founded:** 1932. **Freq:** Weekly. **Print Method:** Tabloid. **Trim Size:** 17 x 13 1/2. **Cols./Page:** -5. **Col. Width:** 12.5 picas. **Col. Depth:** 17 inches. **Key Personnel:** Fr. Kenneth Borowiak, Editor. **Subscription Rates:** $10 individuals. **Remarks:** Accepts advertising.
Ad Rates: BW: $900 **Circ:** ‡21,500
PCI: $12

18219 The Student
Christian Record Services - Division for the Deaf
4444 S. 52nd St. Phone: (402)488-0981
PO Box 6097 Fax: (402)488-7582
Lincoln, NE 68506
Publisher E-mail: 74617.1034@compuserve.com

Magazine for blind Bible students. **Founded:** 1926. **Freq:** Monthly. **Print Method:** Braille. **Key Personnel:** R.J. Kaiser, Editor. **Remarks:** Advertising not accepted.
Circ: Non-paid ‡2,930

18220 Truck Paper
Sandhills Publishing
120 W. Harvest Dr. Phone: (402)479-2140
PO Box 85010 Fax: (402)479-2134
Lincoln, NE 68521-4408
Free: (800)247-4868

Tabloid featuring trucks, trailers, and parts for sale. **Founded:** 1980. **Freq:** Weekly (Fri.). **Print Method:** Offset. **Trim Size:** 10 1/2 x 15 7/8. **Cols./Page:** 6. **Col. Width:** 20 nonpareils. **Col. Depth:** 224 agate lines. **Key Personnel:** Lee Chapin, Publisher. **ISSN:** 1040-6484. **Subscription Rates:** $59. **Remarks:** Combined advertising rates available with six regional editions.
Ad Rates: 4C: $950 **Circ:** Controlled ‡445,186
Paid ‡28,577

18221 Uncoverings
American Quilt Study Group
35th & Holdrege, East Campus Loop Phone: (402)472-5361
Fax: (402)472-5428
PO Box 4737
Lincoln, NE 68504-0737
Publisher E-mail: aqsg@juno.com

Scholarly journal covering decorative arts, antiques, and crafts. **Subtitle:** The Research Papers of the American Quilt Study Group. **Founded:** 1981. **Freq:** Annual. **Key Personnel:** Virginia Gunn, Editor. **ISSN:** 0227-0628. **Subscription Rates:** $18 single issue. **Remarks:** Accepts advertising.
Ad Rates: BW: $250 **Circ:** Paid 1,500

18222 U.S. Roller Skating
U.S. Amateur Confederation of Roller Skating
PO Box 6579 Phone: (402)983-7551
Lincoln, NE 68506 Fax: (402)483-1465

Magazine of popular roller sports. **Subtitle:** The Newsmagazine of American Competitive Roller Skating. **Founded:** 1973. **Freq:** Monthly (except August). **Trim Size:** 8 1/2 x 11. **Cols./Page:** 2 and 3. **Col. Width:** 3.5 and 2.25 inches. **Col. Depth:** 9.75 and 9.75 inches. **Key Personnel:** Andy Seeley, Editor. **ISSN:** 1044-0801. **Subscription Rates:** $10. **Remarks:** Accepts advertising. **URL:** http://www.usacrs.com.
Ad Rates: BW: $225 **Circ:** Paid 5,500
4C: $325 Non-paid 200

18223 Young and Alive
Christian Record Services - Division for the Deaf
4444 S. 52nd St. Phone: (402)488-0981
PO Box 6097 Fax: (402)488-7582
Lincoln, NE 68506
Publisher E-mail: 74617.1034@compuserve.com

Magazine for the blind. Printed in braille and large print. **Freq:** Bimonthly. **Print Method:** Braille and offset. **Trim Size:** 6 3/4 x 9 3/4. **Key Personnel:** R.J. Kaiser, Editor. **Subscription Rates:** Free to blind readers. **Remarks:** Advertising not accepted.
Circ: Non-paid ‡24,400

18224 KCNE-FM - 91.9
PO Box 83111 Phone: (402)472-3611
Lincoln, NE 68501 Fax: (402)472-2403
E-mail: nprn@unl.edu

Format: Classical; News. **Networks:** National Public Radio (NPR). **Owner:** NETN, 1800 N. 33rd St., Lincoln, NE 68506. **Founded:** 1989. **Operating Hours:** 6:00 a.m.-1:00 a.m. **Key Personnel:** Steve Robinson, General Mgr.; Bill Thomas, Program Dir. **Ad Rates:** Noncommercial. **URL:** http://www.net.unl.edu.

18225 KEZG-FM - 107.3
4343 O St. Phone: (402)475-4567
Lincoln, NE 68503 Fax: (402)479-1411

Format: Adult Contemporary. **Networks:** Westwood One Radio. **Founded:** 1968. **Formerly:** KLIN-FM. **Operating Hours:** Continuous. **ADI:** Lincoln-Hastings-Kearney, NE. **Key Personnel:** Lisa M. Warner, General Mgr.; Scott Larson, Program Dir. **Wattage:** 100,000 ERP.

18226 KFGE-FM - 98.1
4343 O St. Phone: (402)474-3764
Lincoln, NE 68510 Fax: (402)479-1411

Format: Hot Country. **Networks:** Unistar. **Founded:** 1992. **Operating Hours:** Continuous. **ADI:** Lincoln-Hastings-Kearney, NE. **Key Personnel:** Lisa Warner, General Mgr.; George Pelletier, Station Mgr. **Wattage:** 100,000.

18227 KFOR-AM - 1240
6900 Van Dorn, Ste. 11 Phone: (402)483-5100
Lincoln, NE 68506 Fax: (402)483-4095

Format: Full Service; Adult Contemporary. **Networks:** ABC. **Founded:** 1924. **Operating Hours:** 24Hrs. **ADI:** Lincoln-Hastings-Kearney, NE. **Key Personnel:** Coby Mack, Program Dir., coby@lincnet.com; Gary Buchanan, General Mgr. **Local Programs:** *The Afternoon Show*, Coby Mack; *Lincoln Live*, Ward Jacobson; *Scott & Cathy Morning Show*. **Wattage:** 1000. **Ad Rates:** $24-56 for 30 seconds; $30-70 for 60 seconds.

18228 KFRX-FM - 102.7
6900 Van Dorn St., Ste. 11 Phone: (402)483-5100
Lincoln, NE 68506-2882 Fax: (402)483-4095

Format: Contemporary Hit Radio (CHR). **Founded:** 1965. **Operating Hours:** Continuous. **ADI:** Lincoln-Hastings-Kearney, NE. **Key Personnel:** Coby Mack, Station Mgr., coby@lincnet.com; Sonny Valentine, Program Dir.; Jim Keck, Sales Mgr. **Local Programs:** *The Donutholes*. **Wattage:** 100,000 ERP. **Ad Rates:** $14-28 for 30 seconds; $17-35 for 60 seconds. **URL:** http://www.lincnet.com.

KHNE-FM - See Hastings

KHNE-TV - See Hastings

18229 KKNB-FM - 104.1
4630 Antelope Creek Rd., Ste. 200 Phone: (402)483-1517
Lincoln, NE 68506 Fax: (402)483-1579
E-mail: point@inetnebr.com

Format: Adult Contemporary. **Networks:** ABC. **Owner:** Triathlon Broadcasting, Inc., at above address. **Founded:** 1976. **Operating Hours:** Continuous. **ADI:** Lincoln-Hastings-Kearney, NE. **Key Personnel:** Julie Gade, General Mgr.; Ed Schulz, General Sales Mgr.; Charlie Thomas, Program Dir.; Julie Wolfe, Business Mgr. **Wattage:** 30,600 ERP. **Ad Rates:** Advertising accepted; rates available upon request.

18230 KLCV-FM - 88.5
100 N. 56th St., Ste. 400 Phone: (402)465-8850
Lincoln, NE 68504 Fax: (402)465-8852

Format: Religious; News; Talk. **Networks:** Business Radio; Sun Radio. **Owner:** Bott Communications, Inc., 10550 Barkley, Ste. 108, Overland Park, KS 66212. **Founded:** July 15, 1996. **Operating Hours:** Continuous. **ADI:** Lincoln-Hastings-Kearney, NE. **Key Personnel:** Richard P. Bott II, Vice President; Charles A. Lambert, Dir., Network Svcs.; Tom Millet, Station Mgr. **Wattage:** 4700. **Ad Rates:** Noncommercial; underwriting available.

18231 KLDZ-FM - 95.1
1230 O St., Ste. 311 Phone: (402)476-3222
Lincoln, NE 68508 Fax: (402)476-1300

Founded: 1975. **Operating Hours:** Continuous. **ADI:** Lincoln-Hastings-Kearney, NE. **Key Personnel:** Wayne Walker, President/General Manager; Dallas Michaels, Operations Mgr. **Wattage:** 50,000 ERP. **Ad Rates:** $12-34 for 30 seconds; $15-38 for 60 seconds.

18232 KLIN-AM - 1400
4343 O St. Phone: (402)475-4567
Lincoln, NE 68510 Fax: (402)479-1411

Format: News; Talk. **Networks:** CBS; Mutual Broadcasting System. **Owner:** KLIN, Inc., at above address. **Founded:** 1947. **Operating Hours:** Continuous. **ADI:** Lincoln-Hastings-Kearney, NE. **Key Personnel:** Lisa M. Warner, General Mgr.; Jim Rose, Operations Dir. **Wattage:** 1000.

18233 KLKE-TV - 24
3240 S. 10th St. Phone: (402)434-8000
Lincoln, NE 68502 Fax: (402)436-2237

Format: Commercial TV. **Owner:** Citadel Communications, L.L.C., 99 Pond Field Rd., Bronxville, NY 10708. **Founded:** 1995. **ADI:** Lincoln-Hastings-Kearney, NE. **Key Personnel:** Chris Bailey, General Mgr.; Dan Ackerman, Chief Engineer; Jeff Swanson, Operations Mgr.; Mark Haggar, News Dir. **Wattage:** 2,600,000 ERP.

18234 KLKN-TV - 8
3240 S. 10th St. Phone: (402)434-8000
Lincoln, NE 68502 Fax: (402)436-2237

Format: Commercial TV. **Networks:** ABC. **Owner:** Citadel Communications, L.L.C., 99 Pond Field Rd., Bronxville, NY 10708. **Founded:** 1995. **Operating Hours:** 5 a.m.-1 a.m. **ADI:** Lincoln-Hastings-Kearney, NE. **Key Personnel:** Chris Bailey, General Mgr.; Dan Ackerman, Chief Engineer; Jeff Swanson, Operations Mgr.; Mark Haggar, News Dir. **Wattage:** 353,000 ERP.

KLNE-FM - See Lexington

KLNE-TV - See Lexington

18235 KMNE-FM - 90.3
PO Box 83111 Phone: (402)472-3611
Lincoln, NE 68501 Fax: (402)472-2403
E-mail: nprn@unl.edu

Format: Classical; News. **Networks:** National Public Radio (NPR). **Owner:** NETN, 1800 N. 33rd St., Lincoln, NE 68506. **Founded:** 1989. **Operating Hours:** 6:00 a.m.-1:00 a.m. **Key Personnel:** Steve Robinson, General Mgr., phone (402)472-9333; Bill Thomas, Program Dir. **Ad Rates:** Noncommercial. **URL:** http://www.net.unl.edu/.

KMNE-TV - See Bassett

18236 KOLN-TV - 10
Box 30350 Phone: (402)467-4321
Lincoln, NE 68503 Fax: (402)467-9210

Format: Commercial TV. **Networks:** CBS. **Founded:** 1953. **Operating Hours:** Continuous. **ADI:** Lincoln-Hastings-Kearney, NE. **Key Personnel:** Frank Jonas, General Mgr.

18237 KPNE-FM - 91.7
PO Box 83111 Phone: (402)472-3611
Lincoln, NE 68501 Fax: (402)472-2403
E-mail: nprn@unl.edu

Format: Classical; News. **Networks:** National Public Radio (NPR). **Owner:** NETN, 1800 N. 33rd St., Lincoln, NE 68506. **Founded:** 1989. **Operating Hours:** 6:00 a.m.-1:00 a.m. **ADI:** North Platte, NE. **Key Personnel:** Steve Robinson, General Mgr., phone (402)472-9333; Bill Thomas, Program Dir. **Ad Rates:** Noncommercial. **URL:** http://www.net.unl.edu/.

KPNE-TV - See North Platte

18238 KRNE-FM - 91.5
PO Box 83111 Phone: (402)472-3611
Lincoln, NE 68501 Fax: (402)472-2403
E-mail: nprn@unl.edu

Format: Classical; News. **Networks:** National Public Radio (NPR). **Owner:** NETN, 1800 N. 33rd St., Lincoln, NE 68506. **Founded:** 1989. **Operating Hours:** 6:00 a.m.-1:00 a.m. **Key Personnel:** Steve Robinson, General Mgr., phone (402)472-9333; Bill Thomas, Program Dir. **Ad Rates:** Noncommercial. **URL:** http://www.net.unl.edu/.

KRNE-TV - See Merriman

18239 KRNU-FM - 90.3
206 Avery Hall Phone: (402)472-3054
Lincoln, NE 68588-0131 Fax: (402)472-8403
E-mail: krnu@unl.edu

Format: Alternative/New Music/Progressive. **Networks:** ABC. **Owner:** University of Nebraska Board of Regents, at above address. **Founded:** 1970. **Operating Hours:** 8 a.m. Mon.-Sat.; 11 a.m.-12 a.m. Sun. **Key Personnel:** Rick Alloway, General Mgr.; Jerry Renaud, News Dir. **Wattage:** 100. **Ad Rates:** Noncommercial. **URL:** httt://krnu.unl.edu.

18240 KTGL-FM - 92.9
4630 Antelope Creek Rd., No. 200 Phone: (402)483-6814
Lincoln, NE 68506-5581 Fax: (402)489-9607

Format: Classic Rock. **Owner:** Triathlon Broadcasting of Lincoln, Inc, at above address. **Founded:** 1987. **Formerly:** KMAZ-FM. **Operating Hours:** Continuous. **ADI:** Lincoln-Hastings-Kearney, NE. **Key Personnel:** Julie Gade, General Mgr.; Jim Steele, Program Dir.; Peg Jones, Sales Mgr.; Julie Wolfe, Business Mgr. **Wattage:** 100,000. **Ad Rates:** $32-36 for 30 seconds; $35-43 for 60 seconds.

KTNE-FM - See Alliance

KTNE-TV - See Alliance

18241 KUCV-FM - 90.9
PO Box 83111 Phone: (402)472-3611
1800 N. 33rd St. Fax: (402)472-1785
Lincoln, NE 68501
Free: (800)250-6850
E-mail: nprn@unl.edu

Format: Public Radio; Jazz; Classical; News. **Networks:** National Public Radio (NPR); Public Radio International (PRI). **Owner:** Nebraska Educational Telecommunications Commission, at above address. **Founded:** 1968. **Operating Hours:** 5 a.m.-1 a.m. **ADI:** Lincoln-Hastings-Kearney, NE. **Key Personnel:** Steve Robinson, General Mgr. **Local Programs:** *Connections*, Bill Stibor; *Nebraska Nightly*, Nancy Finken; *Wet Paint - New CD's*, Chris Kohtz. **Wattage:** 1600. **Ad Rates:** Noncommercial. **URL:** http://net.unl.edu/radio/html.

18242 KUON-TV - 12
Box 83111 Phone: (402)472-3611
Lincoln, NE 68501 Fax: (402)472-1785
E-mail: net@unlinfo.unl.edu

Format: Public TV. **Networks:** Public Broadcasting Service (PBS). **Owner:** University of Nebraska-Lincoln, at above address. **Founded:** 1954. **Operating Hours:** 5:45 a.m.-midnight; 90% network, 10% local. **ADI:** Lincoln-Hastings-Kearney, NE. **Key Personnel:** Rod Bates, General Mgr., rbates@unlinfo.unl.edu; Michael Winkle, Asst. GM, mwinkle@unlinfo.unl.edu; S. Graziano, Program Mgr., sgraziano@unlinfo.unl.edu; Steve Lenzen, Assistant GM, Educational TV, slenzen@unlinfo.unl.edu; Sue Gildersleeve, Assistant GM, Admin. and Finance, sgildersleeve@unlinfo.unl.edu; Peter Ford, Asst. GM for Engineering, pford@unlinfo.unl.edu; Bill Kelly, Sr. Producer, Public Affairs, wek@unlinfo.unl.edu; Steve Alvis, Sr. Producer, Sports & Special Events, salvis@unlinfo.unl.edu; Michael Farrell, Production Coordinator, mfarrell@unlinfo.unl.edu. **Wattage:** 316 kw. **Ad Rates:** Noncommercial. **URL:** http://net.unl.edu/.

KXNE-FM - See Norfolk

KXNE-TV - See Norfolk

KYNE-TV - See Omaha

18243 KZUM-FM - 89.3
941 O St., Ste. 1025 Phone: (402)474-5086
Lincoln, NE 68508-3608 Fax: (402)474-5091
E-mail: kzumradio@aol.com

Format: Eclectic; News. **Networks:** Pacifica; Longhorn Radio. **Owner:** Sunrise Communications Inc., at above address. **Founded:** 1978. **Operating Hours:** 6 a.m.-2 a.m. **ADI:** Lincoln-Hastings-Kearney, NE. **Key Personnel:** Jon Morris, Program Dir.; Eli Rhodes, Operations Mgr.; Ken Ringlein, Membership Coord.; Dick Noble, General Mgr.; Tom Ineck, Development Dir.; Donnette Sweeney, Underwriting Specialist. **Wattage:** 1500. **Ad Rates:** Noncommercial; underwriting available.

18244 Lincoln Cablevision
5400 S. 16th St. Phone: (402)421-0330
Lincoln, NE 68512 Fax: (402)421-0305
Free: (800)248-8823

Founded: 1968. **Key Personnel:** Richard Bates, General Mgr., phone (402)421-0375, richard.bates@twcable.com. **Cities Served:** 60 community access channels.

LOUP CITY†, pop. 1,368.

Sherman Co. (C). 41 m NW of Grand Island. Diversified farming. Corn, wheat.

18245 Sherman County Times
Box 430 Phone: (308)745-1260
Loup City, NE 68853-0430 Fax: (308)745-0541
Publication E-mail: gappub@micrord.com

Community newspaper. **Founded:** 1877. **Freq:** Weekly (Wed.). **Print Method:** Offset. **Cols./Page:** 7. **Col. Width:** 28 nonpareils. **Col. Depth:** 301 agate lines. **Key Personnel:** Beverly J. Peterson, Editor; George A. Peterson, Publisher. **USPS:** 494-040. **Subscription Rates:** $31 individuals.
Ad Rates: GLR: $.24 **Circ:** ‡1,541
BW: $443.98
SAU: $3.95
PCI: $4.00

LYONS, pop. 1,214.

Burt Co. (NE). 10 mi NW of Tikamah. Residential.

18246 Lyons Mirror Sun
Lyon's Mirror-Sun
214 Main St. Phone: (402)687-2616
Box 59 Fax: (402)687-2617
Lyons, NE 68038
Newspaper. **Founded:** 1882. **Freq:** Weekly (Thurs.). **Print Method:** Offset. **Cols./Page:** 6. **Col. Width:** 25 nonpareils. **Col. Depth:** 301 agate lines. **Key Personnel:** Maureen Meader, Editor; Dick Lindberg, Publisher. **Subscription Rates:** $20. **Remarks:** Accepts advertising.
Ad Rates: SAU: $2.75 **Circ:** ‡1,128

MADISON†, pop. 1,950.

Madison Co. (NE). 15 m S of Norfolk. Pork processing plant. Grain, dairy farms. Corn, alfalfa, oats, soybeans, wheat, hogs, cattle.

18247 Star-Mail
PO Box 487 Phone: (402)454-3818
Madison, NE 68748
Newspaper. **Founded:** 1877. **Freq:** Weekly (Thurs.). **Print Method:** Offset. **Cols./Page:** 6. **Col. Width:** 25 nonpareils. **Col. Depth:** 294 agate lines. **Key Personnel:** Christopher J. Zavadil, Editor; Maureen L. Zavandil, Advertising Mgr. **ISSN:** 3252-2000. **Subscription Rates:** $15 Madison County; $16 Nebraska; $17 U.S. **Remarks:** Accepts advertising.
Ad Rates: BW: $451.50 **Circ:** ‡1,512
PCI: $3.50

MARQUETTE

18248 KGRD-FM - 105.3
128 S. Four St. Phone: (402)336-3886
Marquette, NE 68854 Fax: (402)336-3886

Format: Religious. **Networks:** Moody Broadcasting; SkyLight Satellite; Ambassador Inspirational Radio. **Owner:** Praise Network, 723 Turtle Beach, Oneill, NE 68763, (308)946-2656. **Founded:** 1987. **Operating Hours:** Continuous. **Key Personnel:** Herb Roszhart, President; Todd Gunnarson, Contact; Bill Taylor, Music Dir.; Michele Randolph, Office Mgr. **Wattage:** 100,000. **Ad Rates:** Noncommercial.

MCCOOK

18249 McCook Daily Gazette
U.S. Media
W 1st & E Sts. Phone: (308)345-4500
PO Box 1268 Fax: (308)345-7881
McCook, NE 69001
Community newspaper. **Founded:** 1911. **Freq:** Daily (eve.) and Sat. (morn.). **Print Method:** Offset. **Trim Size:** 13 x 21 1/2. **Cols./Page:** 6. **Col. Width:** 24 nonpareils. **Col. Depth:** 301 agate lines. **Key Personnel:** Jack Rogers, Editor; Gene O. Morris, Publisher; Butch Mires, Advertising Dir. **Subscription Rates:** $61 carrier; $65 mail delivery; $84 out of area. **Remarks:** Accepts advertising.
Ad Rates: GLR: $.44 **Circ:** Paid 10,061
BW: $789.48 Free 14,000
4C: $964.48
SAU: $6.12

18250 KBRL-AM - 1300
PO Box 333 Phone: (308)345-5400
McCook, NE 69001 Fax: (308)345-4720

Format: Oldies. **Networks:** ABC. **Founded:** 1948. **Operating Hours:** Continuous. **Key Personnel:** Dave Stout, Manager; Gayla Swisher, Traffic; Rich Barnett, News/Sports Dir. **Local Programs:** *Open Line*, Rich Barnett. **Wattage:** 5,000. **Ad Rates:** $6.50-8.70 for 30 seconds; $8.20-10.95 for 60 seconds.

18251 KICX-FM - 96.1
802 West C Phone: (308)345-5400
Box 333 Fax: (308)345-4720
McCook, NE 69001

Format: Adult Contemporary. **Networks:** ABC; Satellite Music Network. **Founded:** 1979. **Operating Hours:** Continuous. **Key Personnel:** Dave Stout, Mgr.; Gayla Swisher, Office Mgr./Traffic; Rich Barnett, News/Sports Dir. **Wattage:** 6000. **Ad Rates:** Combined advertising rates available with KBRL-AM.

18252 KIOD-FM - 105.3
106 W. 8th St., Box 218 Phone: (308)345-1981
McCook, NE 69001 Fax: (308)345-7202
Free: (888)752-9105
E-mail: coyote@ns.nque.com

Format: Contemporary Country. **Networks:** CNN Radio. **Owner:** Austin McCook, L. L. C., PO Box 939, McCook, NE 69001. **Founded:** 1981. **Formerly:** KZMC-FM (1995); KKYT-FM (1998). **Operating Hours:** Continuous. **ADI:** Lincoln-Hastings-Kearney, NE. **Key Personnel:** Jay Austin, General Mgr.; Bryan Loker, Program Dir.; Chris Hansen, Sales Mgr.; Mitch Murdock, Music Dir.; Jesse Stevens, News Dir. **Local Programs:** *Breakfast Flakes*, Bryan Loker. **Wattage:** 100,000. **Ad Rates:** $4-8 for 30 seconds; $6-12 for 60 seconds.

18253 KSWN-FM - 93.9
Box 218 Phone: (308)345-1100
McCook, NE 69001 Fax: (308)345-7202
Free: (888)TALK-939
E-mail: coyote@ns.nque.com

Format: Talk; Contemporary Hit Radio (CHR). **Networks:** CBS. **Owner:** Austin McCook, L. L. C., PO Box 939, McCook, NE 69001, (308)345-1981. **Operating Hours:** Continuous. **ADI:** Lincoln-Hastings-Kearney, NE. **Key Personnel:** Jay Austin, General Mgr.; Jeff Harlin, Program Mgr.; Eileen Austin, Sales Mgr.; Jesse Stevens, News Dir. **Local Programs:** *Pulse of the Prairie*, Jeff Harlin. **Wattage:** 50,000. **Ad Rates:** $2.50-5 for 30 seconds; $3.50-7 for 60 seconds.

MEADOW GROVE, pop. 400.

Madison Co. (NE). 15 m W of Norfolk. Grain elevators. Grain, stock farms. Corn, oats.

18254 Meadow Grove News
Meadow Grove
PO Box 5 Phone: (402)634-2332
Meadow Grove, NE 68752
Newspaper with a Democratic orientation. **Founded:** 1896. **Freq:** Weekly (Thurs.). **Print Method:** Offset. **Cols./Page:** 6. **Col. Width:** 26 nonpareils. **Col. Depth:** 280 agate lines. **Key Personnel:** Lesley Falter, Publisher. **Subscription Rates:** $8. **Remarks:** Accepts advertising.
Ad Rates: GLR: $.125 **Circ:** 790

MERRIMAN

Cherry Co. (NC). 15 m W of Eli.

18255 KRNE-TV - 12
c/o KUON-TV Phone: (402)472-3611
1800 N. 33rd. St. Fax: (402)472-1785
PO Box 83111
Lincoln, NE 68501
E-mail: net@unlinfo.unl.edu

Format: Public TV. **Networks:** Public Broadcasting Service (PBS). **Owner:** Nebraska Educational Telecommunications, at above address. **Founded:** 1968. **Operating Hours:** 5:45 a.m.-midnight; 90% network, 10% local. **ADI:** Rapid City, SD. **Key Personnel:** Rod Bates, General Mgr., rbates@unlinfo.unl.edu; Michael Winkle, Asst. GM, Marketing, mwinkle@unlinfo.unl.edu; Steve Lenzen, Asst. GM, Educational TV, slenzen@unlinfo.unl.edu; Sue Gildersleeve, Asst. GM, Admin. & Finance, sgildersleeve@unlinfo.unl.edu; Michael Winkle, Asst. GM, Marketing, mwinkle@unlinfo.unl.edu; Peter Ford, Asst. GM for Engineering, pford@unlinfo.unl.edu; S. Graziano, Program Mgr., sgraziano@unlinfo.unl.edu; Bill Kelly, Sr. Producer, Public Affairs, wek@unlinfo.unl.edu; Steve Alvis, Sr. Producer, Sports & Special Events, salvis@unlinfo.unl.edu; Michael Farrell, Production Coordinator, Cultural Affair, mfarrell@unlinfo.unl.edu. **Local Programs:** *Backyard Farmer* Tuesdays 7 pm, during spring and summer; *Big Red Wrap-Up* Tuesdays 7 pm, during football season, Steve Alvis, Sr. Producer, Sports & Special Events; *Statewide* 8 pm Friday, Bill Ganzel, Sr. Producer, Public Affairs. **Wattage:** 316,000. **Ad Rates:** Noncommercial. **URL:** http://net.unl.edu/.

MILFORD, pop. 2,108.

Seward Co. (S.E.). On Big Blue River, 15 m SW of Lincoln. Dairy, poultry, grain farms. Corn, wheat, alfalfa, livestock.

18256 The Milford Times
PO Box 723 Phone: (402)761-2911
Milford, NE 68405-0723
Community newspaper. **Founded:** 1957. **Freq:** Weekly (Wed.). **Print Method:** Offset. **Trim Size:** 11 3/8 x 16. **Cols./Page:** 5. **Col. Width:** 24 nonpareils. **Col. Depth:** 210 agate lines. **Key Personnel:** Frances Seeley, Editor and Publisher; George Seeley, Publisher. **USPS:** 593-200. **Subscription Rates:** $18 individuals; $22.50 out of area; $25 out of state. **Remarks:** Accepts advertising.
Ad Rates: GLR: $.25 **Circ:** ‡1,050
BW: $247.50
SAU: $3.75
PCI: $3.30

MINDEN†, pop. 2,939.

Kearney Co. (S). 33 m SW of Hastings. Manufactures tools, neon signs, fiberglass products; beef packing plant. Stock, grain, dairy, poultry farms. Wheat, corn.

18257 The Minden Courier
Edgecombe Publishing, Inc.
POB 379 Fax: (308)832-2221
Minden, NE 68959-0379
Community newspaper. **Founded:** 1890. **Freq:** Weekly (Tues.). **Print Method:** Offset. **Trim Size:** 13 x 21. **Cols./Page:** 6. **Col. Width:** 12 picas. **Col. Depth:** 21 inches. **Key Personnel:** John & JoAnn Edgecombe, Publisher; Jim Edgecombe, Advertising Mgr. **ISSN:** 3506-4000. **Subscription Rates:** $20; $22 out of state. **Remarks:** Accepts advertising. **Alt. Formats:** CD-ROM.
Ad Rates: GLR: $.39 **Circ:** ‡2,800
BW: $485.1
4C: $720.00
SAU: $4.50
PCI: $4.50

MITCHELL, pop. 1,956.

Scotts Bluff Co. (W). 10 m NW of Scottsbluff. Industrial development site. Sugar beet factory. Potato processing. Lumber. Diversified farming. Sugar beets, potatoes, corn. Cattle feeding.

18258 The Index
Box 158 Phone: (308)623-1322
1269 Center Ave. Fax: (308)586-2312
Mitchell, NE 69357-0158
Newspaper. Indiana. **Founded:** 1900. **Freq:** Weekly (Thurs.). **Print Method:** Offset. **Cols./Page:** 6. **Col. Width:** 24 nonpareils. **Col. Depth:** 301 agate lines. **Key Personnel:** Bryce Wilkins, Editor; Maxine Wilkins, Publisher. **Subscription Rates:** $15. **Remarks:** Accepts advertising.
Ad Rates: GLR: $.20 **Circ:** 2,075

MULLEN†, pop. 720.

Hooker Co. (NC).

18259 Hooker County Tribune
PO Box 125 Phone: (308)546-2242
Mullen, NE 69152 Fax: (308)546-2722
Publication E-mail: hct@neb-sandhills.net

Community newspaper. **Founded:** 1887. **Freq:** Weekly. **Cols./Page:** 5. **Col. Width:** 11.5 picas. **Col. Depth:** 13 inches. **Key Personnel:** Lanita Evans, Editor and Publisher. **Subscription Rates:** $14.50; $17 out of area. **Remarks:** Accepts advertising.
Ad Rates: SAU: $3.30 **Circ:** 875

NEBRASKA CITY†, pop. 7,127.

Otoe Co. (SE). On Missouri River, 45 m S of Omaha. State school for visually handicapped. Historic. Manufactures garments, plastic pipes, gas meters, fence posts, concrete pipes. Food processing plants. Dairy, stock, fruit, grain farms.

18260 Nebraska City News-Press
American Publishing
806 Central Ave. Phone: (402)873-3334
PO Box 757 Fax: (402)873-5436
Nebraska City, NE 68410
Newspaper. **Founded:** 1854. **Freq:** Daily (eve.) and Sat. (morn.). **Print Method:** Offset. **Trim Size:** 14 x 22. **Cols./Page:** 6. **Col. Width:** 25 nonpareils. **Col. Depth:** 301 agate lines. **Key Personnel:** Patti Jo Peterson, Editor; William R. Holland, Publisher. **USPS:** 375-960. **Subscription Rates:** $75 individuals. **Remarks:** Accepts advertising.
Ad Rates: GLR: $.39 **Circ:** Mon.-Fri. ‡2,850
BW: $715.95 Sun. ‡2,850
SAU: $5.55

NELIGH†, pop. 1,893.

Antelope Co. (NEC). 35 m NW of Norfolk. Mobile homes; farm machinery, plastic flag manufactured. Agriculture. Corn, rye, oats.

18261 Neligh News and Leader
News Publishing Co.
Box 46 Phone: (402)887-4840
Neligh, NE 68756 Fax: (402)887-4711

Community newspaper. **Founded:** 1887. **Freq:** Weekly (Wed.). **Print Method:** Offset. **Cols./Page:** 7. **Col. Width:** 21 nonpareils. **Col. Depth:** 294 agate lines. **Key Personnel:** Sid Charf, Editor. **Subscription Rates:** $19. **Remarks:** Accepts advertising.
Ad Rates: BW: $396.90 **Circ:** ‡2,564
SAU: $3.10

NELSON

18262 Nelson Gazette
63 E. 4th St. Phone: (402)225-2301
PO Box 285
Nelson, NE 68961
Community newspaper. **Founded:** 1885. **Freq:** Weekly (Thurs.). **Print Method:** Offset. **Trim Size:** 17 1/2 x 22 1/2. **Cols./Page:** 5. **Col. Width:** 11 1/2 picas. **Col. Depth:** 16 1/2 inches. **Key Personnel:** James Menke, Editor. **Subscription Rates:** $15; $19 out of area. **Remarks:** Accepts advertising.
Ad Rates: GLR: $3.40 **Circ:** ‡720
SAU: $3.15

NORFOLK, pop. 19,449.

Madison Co. (NE). 75 m SW of Sioux City, Iowa. Manufactures farm machinery, electronic resistors, precast concrete items, electrical products, steel, disposable hypodermic syringes, steel joists and girders, milk and milk products, dehydrated eggs and meat, dried milk products, beef carcasses and processed beef products, livestock and poultry feeds, soft drinks, processed pork products. Livestock, poultry, cattle, hogs farms. Corn, oats, sorghum grains, soybeans, rye, barley.

18263 Norfolk Daily News
Huse Publishing Co.
525 Norfolk Ave. Phone: (402)371-1020
Box 977 Fax: (402)371-5802
Norfolk, NE 68702-0977
General newspaper. **Founded:** 1887. **Freq:** Mon.-Sat. (eve.). **Print Method:** Offset. **Cols./Page:** 6. **Col. Width:** 24 nonpareils. **Col. Depth:** 301 agate lines. **Key Personnel:** Kent Warneke, Managing Editor; Jerry Huse, Publisher; Larry Bartscher, Advertising Mgr. **Subscription Rates:** $62; $72 out of state. **Remarks:** Accepts advertising.
Ad Rates: BW: $1,161 **Circ:** Mon.-Sat. 20,210
4C: $1,536
PCI: $9

18264 KEXL-FM - 106.7
PO Box 789 Phone: (402)371-0780
Norfolk, NE 68702 Fax: (402)371-6303
E-mail: wjagkexl@wjag.com

Format: Adult Contemporary; News; Sports. **Founded:** 1971. **Operating Hours:** Continuous. **Key Personnel:** Robert G. Thomas, VP/General Mgr., wjagkexl@wjag.com; Don Grant, General Sales Mgr.; Jim Fisher, Operations Mgr.; Jim Curry, News Dir.; Susan Risinger, Contact. **Wattage:** 100,000 ERP. **Ad Rates:** Advertising accepted; rates available upon request. Combined advertising rates available with WJAG-AM. **URL:** http://www.norfolkne.com.

18265 KPNO-FM - 90.9
114 N. 4th Phone: (402)379-3677
Norfolk, NE 68701 Fax: (402)379-3662
E-mail: kpno@newsnet.com

Format: Religious. **Networks:** Moody Broadcasting. **Owner:** The Praise Network, Inc., Box 8, Aurora, NE 68818, (308)946-2656. **Operating Hours:** Continuous. **Key Personnel:** Gene Henes, Manager. **Wattage:** 50,000. **Ad Rates:** Noncommercial. **URL:** http://www.kpno.org.

18266 KXNE-FM - 89.3
PO Box 83111 Phone: (402)472-3611
Lincoln, NE 68501 Fax: (402)472-2403
Free: (800)290-6850
E-mail: nprn@unl.edu

Format: Public Radio; Classical; News; Jazz. **Networks:** National Public Radio (NPR); Public Radio International (PRI). **Owner:** Nebraska Educational Telecommunications Commission, 1800 N. 33rd St., Lincoln, NE 68503. **Founded:** 1990. **Operating Hours:** 6 a.m.- 1 a.m. **ADI:** Lincoln-Hastings-Kearney, NE. **Key Personnel:** Steve Robinson, General Mgr. **Local Programs:** *Afternoon Concert*, Bill Stibor; *Morning Concert*, Bill Stibor; *Nebraska Nightly*, Nancy Finken. **Wattage:** 4230. **Ad Rates:** Noncommercial.

18267 KXNE-TV - 19
c/o KUON-TV Phone: (402)472-3611
1800 N. 33rd St. Fax: (402)472-1785
PO Box 83111
Lincoln, NE 68501
E-mail: net@unlinfo.unl.edu

Format: Public TV. **Networks:** Public Broadcasting Service (PBS). **Owner:** Nebraska Educational Telecommunications, at above address. **Founded:** 1965. **Operating Hours:** 5:45 a.m.-midnight; 90% network, 10% local. **ADI:** Sioux City, IA. **Key Personnel:** Rod Bates, General Mgr., rbates@unlinfo.unl.edu; Michael Winkle, Asst. GM, Marketing, mwinkle@unlinfo.unl.edu; Steve Lenzen, Asst. GM, Educational TV, slenzen@unlinfo.unl.edu; Sue Gildersleeve, Asst. GM, Admin. & Finance, sgildersleeve@unlinfo.unl.edu; S. Graziano, Program Dir., sgraziano@unlinfo.unl.edu; Peter Ford, Asst. GM of Engineering, pford@unlinfo.unl.edu; Bill Kelly, Sr. Producer, Public Affairs, wek@unlinfo.unl.edu; Steve Alvis, Sr. Producer, Sports & Special Events, salvis@unlinfo.unl.edu; Michael Farrell, Production Coordinator, Cultural Affairs, mfarrell@unlinfo.unl.edu. **Local Programs:** *Backyard Farmer* Tuesdays 7pm, during spring and summer; *Big Red Wrap-Up* Tuesdays, 7pm during the football season, Steve Alvis, Sr. Producer, Sports & Special Events; *Statewide* 8 pm Friday, Bill Ganzel, Sr. Producer, Public Affairs. **Wattage:** 1.7 Mw. **Ad Rates:** Noncommercial. **URL:** http://net.unl.edu.

18268 WJAG-AM - 780
309 Braasch Ave. Phone: (402)371-0780
PO Box 789 Fax: (402)371-6303
Norfolk, NE 68701
E-mail: wjagkexl@wjag.com

Format: News; Talk. **Networks:** NBC; Westwood One Radio. **Owner:** WJAG, Inc., at above address. **Founded:** 1922. **Operating Hours:** Continuous. **ADI:** Omaha, NE. **Key Personnel:** Robert G. Thomas, VP/Gen. Mgr.; Don Grant, General Sales Mgr.; Jim Fischer, Operations Mgr.; Marci Pierce, Office Mgr.; Tony Wormann, Chief Engineer. **Wattage:** 1000. **Ad Rates:** Advertising accepted; rates available upon request. **URL:** http://www.wjag.com.

NORTH BEND, pop. 1,368.

Dodge Co. (E). 50 m NW of Omaha. Stock, poultry, grain farms. Wheat, corn.

18269 North Bend Eagle
Box 100 Phone: (402)652-8312
North Bend, NE 68649
Community newspaper. **Founded:** 1897. **Freq:** Weekly (Wed.). **Print Method:** Offset. **Cols./Page:** 4. **Col. Width:** 28 nonpareils. **Col. Depth:** 182 agate lines. **Key Personnel:** Lois Lambley, Editor and Publisher; Fred Lambley, Publisher. **Subscription Rates:** $17; $19 out of area; $21 out of state. **Remarks:** Advertising not accepted for alcoholic beverages and tobacco products.
Ad Rates: GLR: $.25 **Circ:** ‡1,500
BW: $193.44
SAU: $3.72

NORTH PLATTE†, pop. 24,479.

Lincoln Co. (SW). On Platte River, 130 m W of Grand Island. ""Buffalo Bill" Cody's ranch. Railroad classification yard Light manufacturing; processing agricultured products. Diversified farming. Cattle raising. Corn, wheat, alfalfa and hay.

18270 North Platte Telegraph
Western Publishing Co.
621 N. Chestnut
North Platte, NE 69101
Publisher E-mail: lexch@lexch.com

General newspaper. **Founded:** 1881. **Freq:** Tues.-Sun. (morn.). **Print Method:** Offset. **Cols./Page:** 6. **Col. Width:** 25 nonpareils. **Col. Depth:** 304 agate lines. **Key Personnel:** Dan Burkhart, Editor; Larry Shearer, Publisher; Dee Dee Klein, Advertising Dir. **Subscription Rates:** $95 city carrier. **Remarks:** Accepts advertising.
Ad Rates: BW: $1,164.06 **Circ:** Tues.-Fri. 13,876
4C: $1,329.06 Sat. 13,876
SAU: $8.92 Sun. 14,174
PCI: $9.87

18271 Telegraph Happenings
Western Publishing Co.
PO Box 370 Phone: (308)532-6000
North Platte, NE 69103-0370 Fax: (308)532-9268
Free: (800)753-7092

Weekly total market coverage product. **Founded:** 1983. **Freq:** Weekly (Wed.). **Print Method:** Offset. **Cols./Page:** 6. **Col. Width:** 25 nonpareils. **Col. Depth:** 304 agate lines. **Key Personnel:** Scott Bruce, Advertising Dir. **Subscription Rates:** Free. **URL:** http://www.nptelegraph.com. **Formerly:** Telegraph Plus; Compass.
Ad Rates: SAU: $11.40 **Circ:** Free ‡12,554
PCI: $11.40

18272 KELN-FM - 97.1
PO Box 248 Phone: (308)532-1120
North Platte, NE 69103 Fax: (308)532-0458
Free: (877)532-1120
E-mail: hot97@nponline.net

Format: Adult Contemporary. **Networks:** ABC; Satellite Music Network. **Founded:** 1979. **Operating Hours:** Continuous. **ADI:** North Platte, NE. **Key Personnel:** Rex Anderson, General Mgr., rex@nponline.net; Gretchen Engstrom, Sales Mgr., gretchen@nponline.net; Dave White, Program Dir., dave@nponline.net. **Local Programs:** *News & Public Affairs* 7:00 - 7:30 am Monday-Friday, J. R. Bolger; *Sports*, Chuck Schwartz. **Wattage:** 100,000 ERP. **Ad Rates:** $7-20 for 30 seconds; $10-25 for 60 seconds. Combined advertising rates available with KOOQ-AM. **URL:** http://www.hot97keln.com.

18273 KJLT-AM - 970
PO Box 709 Phone: (308)582-5515
North Platte, NE 69103

Format: Religious. **Owner:** Tri-State Broadcasting Assoc., Inc., at above address. **Operating Hours:** Sunrise-sunset. **Key Personnel:** John Townsend, General Mgr. **Wattage:** 5,000. **Ad Rates:** Noncommercial. **URL:** http://www.nque.com/kjlt.

18274 KJLT-FM - 94.9
PO Box 709 Phone: (308)582-5515
North Platte, NE 69103

Format: Religious. **Networks:** Moody Broadcasting; SkyLight Satellite. **Owner:** Tri-State Broadcasting Assoc., Inc., at above address. **Operating Hours:** Continuous. **Key Personnel:** John Townsend, General Mgr. **Wattage:** 100,000. **Ad Rates:** Noncommercial. **URL:** http://www.nque.com/kjlt.

18275 KNOP-TV - 2
Box 749 Phone: (308)532-2222
North Platte, NE 69103 Fax: (308)532-9579

Format: Commercial TV. **Networks:** NBC. **Founded:** Dec. 1958. **Operating Hours:** 6:30 a.m.-12:30 a.m. **ADI:** North Platte, NE. **Key Personnel:** Ulyesses Carlini, General Mgr.

18276 KODY-AM - 1240
PO Box 1085 Phone: (308)532-3344
North Platte, NE 69103 Fax: (308)534-6651

Format: Talk; News. **Networks:** Talknet. **Owner:** John Mitchelle, 1001 Farnum-On-The-Mall, Omaha, NE 68102, (402)342-2000, Fax: (402)346-5748. **Founded:** 1930. **Operating Hours:** Continuous. **ADI:** North Platte, NE. **Key Personnel:** Rob Mandeville, General Mgr.; John P. Kelley, Operations Dir. **Wattage:** 1000. **Ad Rates:** $7-16 for 30 seconds.

18277 KOOQ-AM - 1410
PO Box 248 Phone: (308)532-1120
North Platte, NE 69103 Fax: (308)532-0458
E-mail: oldiesradio@nponline.net

Format: Oldies; Agricultural; News. **Networks:** NBC; Satellite Music Network. **Owner:** Eagle Communications of Nebraska, at above address. **Founded:** 1966. **Operating Hours:** Continuous. **ADI:** North Platte, NE. **Key Personnel:** Rex Anderson, General Mgr., rex@nponline.net; Gretchen Engstrom, Sales Mgr., gretchen@nponline.net; Dave White, Program Dir., dave@nponline.net. **Local Programs:** *News*, J.R. Bolger; *Sports*, Chuck Shwartz. **Wattage:** 5000 day; 500 night. **Ad Rates:** Combined advertising rates available with KELN-FM. **URL:** http://www.oldiesradio.com.

18278 KPNE-TV - 9
c/o KUON-TV Phone: (402)472-3611
Box 38111 Fax: (402)472-1785
Lincoln, NE 68501

Format: Public TV. **Simulcasts:** KUON-TV Lincoln, NE. **Networks:** Public Broadcasting Service (PBS). **Owner:** Nebraska Educational Telecommunications, 1800 N. 33rd, Lincoln, NE 68583. **Founded:** 1966. **Operating Hours:** 5:45 a.m.- midnight; 90% network, 10% local. **ADI:** North Platte, NE. **Key Personnel:** Rod Bates, General Mgr., rbates@unlinfo.unl.edu; Michael Winkle, Asst. GM, Marketing, mwinkle@unlinfo.unl.edu; Steve Lenzen, Assistant GM, Educational Television, slenzen@unlinfo.unl.edu; Sue Gildersleeve, Assistant GM, Admin & Finance, sgildersleeve@unlinfo.unl.edu; S. Graziano, Program Mgr., sgraziano@unlinfo.unl.edu; Bill Kelly, Sr. Producer, Public Affairs, wek@unlinfo.unl.edu; Steve Alvis, Sr. Producer, Sports & Special Events, salvis@unlinfo.unl.edu; Michael Farrell, Production Coordinator, Cultural Affairs, mfarrell@unlinfo.unl.edu; Peter Ford, Asst. GM of Engineering, pford@unlinfo.unl.edu. **Local Programs:** *Backyard Farmer* 7 p.m. Tuesday; *Big Red Wrap-Up* 7 p.m. Tuesday; *Statewide* 8 p.m. Friday, Bill Ganzel. **Wattage:** 316. **Ad Rates:** Noncommercial.

18279 KXNP-FM - 103.5
PO Box 1085 Phone: (308)532-3344
305 E. 4th St. Fax: (308)534-6651
North Platte, NE 69103

Format: Contemporary Country. **Networks:** Jones Satellite; NBC. **Owner:** John Mitchelle, 1001 Furnam-on-the-Mall, Omaha, NE 68102, (402)342-2000, Fax: (402)346-5748. **Founded:** 1982. **Operating Hours:** Continuous. **ADI:** North Platte, NE. **Key Personnel:** Rob Mandeville, General Mgr.; John P. Kelley, Program Dir. **Wattage:** 100,000. **Ad Rates:** Advertising accepted; rates available upon request.

OAKLAND, pop. 1,393.

Burt Co. (NE). 50 m NW of Omaha. Stock, dairy, poultry, grain farms. Corn, oats, cattle.

18280 Oakland Independent
Gahan Publishing Co. Inc.
217 N. Oakland Ave. Phone: (402)685-5624
Oakland, NE 68045 Fax: (402)685-5625

Community newspaper. **Founded:** 1880. **Freq:** Weekly (Thurs.). **Print Method:** Offset. **Cols./Page:** 6. **Col. Width:** 28 nonpareils. **Col. Depth:** 301 agate lines. **Key Personnel:** Dewaine R. Gahan, Publisher; Bobbie Gahan, Publisher. **Subscription Rates:** $28 individuals; $36 out of state. **Remarks:** Accepts advertising.
Ad Rates: GLR: $0.14 **Circ:** ‡1,980
BW: $548.25
SAU: $4.25

OFFUTT A F B

18281 The Air Pulse
Public Affairs Phone: (402)294-3663
55th WG Fax: (402)294-7172
Offutt A F B, NE 68113-3206
Military newspaper for Offutt Air Force Base and U.S. Strategic Command including information on sports and family. **Founded:** 1949. **Freq:** Weekly (Fri.). **Print Method:** Offset. **Cols./Page:** 6. **Col. Width:** 1.5 inches. **Col. Depth:** 13 inches. **Key Personnel:** Dixie Cavner, Publisher, phone (402)733-7300; Ron Stadie, Advertising Mgr., phone (402)733-7300. **Subscription Rates:** $10. **Remarks:** Accepts advertising.
Ad Rates: GLR: $.85 **Circ:** Free ‡13,000
BW: $737
PCI: $11.90

OGALLALA†.

Keith Co. (WC). 15 m W of Roscoe.

18282 Keith County News
116 W. A St. Phone: (308)284-4046
PO Box 359 Fax: (308)284-4048
Ogallala, NE 69153
Free: (800)942-9537

Community newspaper. **Founded:** 1885. **Freq:** Semiweekly (Mon. and Wed.). **Print Method:** Offset. **Cols./Page:** 6. **Col. Width:** 2 inches. **Col. Depth:** 21.5 inches. **Key Personnel:** Jack Pollock, Editor and Publisher; Marilee Perlinger, Advertising Mgr.; Tom Huddleson, Gen. Mgr./Managing Ed. **USPS:** 292-080. **Subscription Rates:** $30 individuals; $35 out of state. **Remarks:** Accepts advertising. **Feature Editors:** Jeff Headley, *Sports*; Becky Uehling, *Lifestyle*.
Ad Rates: GLR: $2 **Circ:** Paid ⊕4,250
BW: $787.50
4C: $1,028
SAU: $6

18283 KMCX-FM - 106.5
PO Box 56 Phone: (308)284-2051
Ogallala, NE 69153-0056 Fax: (308)284-2054

Format: News; Contemporary Country. **Networks:** ABC. **Founded:** 1975. **Formerly:** KIBC-FM (1980). **Operating Hours:** Continuous. **Key Personnel:** Ray Lockhart, General Mgr.; Jason Fredrick, News Dir.; Mark Baldwin, Sports Dir. **Wattage:** 100,000.

18284 KOGA-AM - 930
113 West 4th St. Phone: (308)284-3633
PO Box 509 Fax: (308)284-3517
Ogallala, NE 69153

Format: Oldies. **Networks:** ABC. **Owner:** Ray Lockhart, at above address. **Founded:** 1956. **Operating Hours:** Continuous. **Key Personnel:** Ray Lockhart, Contact; Jason Fredrick, News Dir.; Mark Baldwin, Sports Dir.; Yvonne Groteluschen, Contact. **Wattage:** 5000. **Ad Rates:** $9 for 30 seconds; $10-13 for 60 seconds.

18285 KOGA-FM - 99.7
113 West 4th St. Phone: (308)284-3633
PO Box 509 Fax: (308)284-3517
Ogallala, NE 69153

Format: Adult Contemporary. **Networks:** ABC. **Owner:** Ray Lockhart, at above address. **Founded:** 1978. **Operating Hours:** Continuous. **Key Personnel:** Ray Lockhart, Contact; Jason Fredrick, News Dir.; Mark Baldwin, Sports Dir.; Yvonne Groteluschen, Contact. **Wattage:** 100,000. **Ad Rates:** $7.20 for 30 seconds; $8-10.40 for 60 seconds.

OMAHA†, pop. 311,681.

Douglas Co. (E). On Missouri River. Bridge to Council Bluffs, Iowa. Creighton University; University of Nebraska Medical School; University of Nebraska at Omaha; Metropolitan Technical Community College. Manufacturing, distribution & service center. Important livestock, dairy products and grain market. Manufactures feed, farm machinery, paint and varnish, paper boxes, electrical signs, garden tools, ball bearings; flour & cereal mills; slaughter and meat packing plants. Smelters.

18286 The Catholic Voice
The Catholic Voice Publishing Co.
6060 N.W. Radical Hwy.
Omaha, NE 68164

Catholic archdiocesan tabloid. **Founded:** July 17, 1903. **Freq:** Biweekly. **Print Method:** Offset. **Trim Size:** 11 5/16 x 16 3/8. **Cols./Page:** 5. **Col. Width:** 25 nonpareils. **Col. Depth:** 96 agate lines. **Key Personnel:** Charlie Wieser, Contact; Archbishop Elden F. Curtiss, Publisher; Charles Wieser, Editor. **ISSN:** 0744-9585. **Subscription Rates:** $17.50 individuals. **Available Online. URL:** http://www.tcvomaha.org.
Ad Rates: GLR: $1.79 **Circ:** ‡69,623
BW: $1,920
4C: $2,175
SAU: $25
PCI: $25

18287 Creightonian
Creighton University
Dept. of Journalism & Mass Communication Phone: (402)280-2826
Fax: (402)280-4730
2500 California Plaza
Omaha, NE 68178
Publication E-mail: annmac@creighton.edu

Collegiate newspaper. **Founded:** 1922. **Freq:** Weekly (Fri.). **Print Method:** Offset. **Trim Size:** 11 1/2 x 16 1/2. **Cols./Page:** 4. **Col. Width:** 28 nonpareils. **Col. Depth:** 210 agate lines. **Key Personnel:** Heidi Juersivich, Editor, phone (402)280-4058; Christian Johnston, Advertising Mgr. **USPS:** 137-460. **Subscription Rates:** $8. **Remarks:** Accepts advertising. **URL:** http://press.creighton.edu.
Ad Rates: GLR: $1.30 **Circ:** Paid ‡4,600
BW: $348 Free ‡200
PCI: $7.06

18288 The Gateway
University of Nebraska at Omaha
60th & Dodge Sts. Phone: (402)554-2470
MBSC 115 Fax: (402)554-2735
Omaha, NE 68182-0197
Publication E-mail: editor@gateway.unomaha.edu

Collegiate newspaper. **Founded:** 1913. **Freq:** Semiweekly (Tues. & Fri., during academic year). **Print Method:** Web offset. **Trim Size:** 10 3/8" x 15 1/2". **Cols./Page:** 6. **Col. Width:** 1 5/8 inches. **Col. Depth:** 15 1/2 inches. **Key Personnel:** Carol Buffington, Publications Mgr.; Lisa Tosoni, Advertising Mgr. **Subscription Rates:** Free. **Remarks:** Accepts advertising. **Available Online. URL:** http://www.gateway.unomaha.edu/.
Ad Rates: BW: $790.50 **Circ:** Free 6,000
PCI: $6.60

18289 Grace Tidings
Grace College of the Bible
1515 S. 10th St. Phone: (402)449-2800
Omaha, NE 68108-3600 Fax: (402)341-9587

Magazine containing inspirational articles and college activities information. **Founded:** Oct. 1943. **Freq:** Quarterly. **Print Method:** Letterpress. **Trim Size:** 8 1/2 x 11. **Cols./Page:** 3. **Col. Width:** 26 nonpareils. **Col. Depth:** 136 agate lines. **Key Personnel:** Dr. Warren Bathke, Editor; Leo D. Thomas, Advertising Mgr. **USPS:** 224-960.
Circ: Non-paid 24,000

18290 Heartland Retailer
6026 Maple St. Phone: (402)496-0717
Omaha, NE 68104-4104 Fax: (402)496-0678

Regional newspaper (tabloid) for the in-home goods, building, and remodeling industries. Covers the states of Illinois, Iowa, Kansas, Minnesota, Missouri, Nebraska, North Dakota, South Dakota, and Wisconsin. **Founded:** 1974. **Freq:** Monthly. **Print Method:** Offset - Web. **Trim Size:** 11 1/4 x 15. **Cols./Page:** 5. **Col. Width:** 11 1/2 picas. **Col. Depth:** 84 picas. **Key Personnel:** Eugene J. Podany, Editor and Publisher. **Subscription Rates:** $10. **Remarks:** Accepts advertising. **Formerly:** Nebraska-Iowa Retailer.
Ad Rates: BW: $650 **Circ:** Free ‡15,250
4C: $1,100

18291 Home & Away
Home & Away Magazine
10703 J St. St. Phone: (402)592-5000
Omaha, NE 68127 Fax: (402)331-1152

Travel and recreation magazine published for American Automobile Association members in the Midwest. **Subtitle:** Mid-America's Leisure and Lifestyle Magazine. **Founded:** Jan. 1980. **Freq:** Bimonthly. **Print Method:** Offset. **Trim Size:** 8 x 10 7/8. **Cols./Page:** 3. **Col. Width:** 26 nonpareils. **Col. Depth:** 138 agate lines. **Key Personnel:** Brian Nicol, Editor and Publisher; Vern Cornish, Advertising Mgr./Publisher. **ISSN:** 0199-7009. **Subscription Rates:** $1 members; $6 nonmembers; $1 single issue. **Remarks:** Accepts advertising.
Ad Rates: BW: $44,990 **Circ:** Paid 3,038,968
4C: $50,720

18292 Jewish Press
Jewish Federation of Omaha
333 S. 132nd St. Phone: (402)334-6449
Omaha, NE 68154-2106 Fax: (402)334-5422
Publication E-mail: jshpress@aol.com

Jewish community newspaper. **Founded:** 1921. **Freq:** Weekly (Fri.). **Print Method:** Offset. **Trim Size:** 11 x 16. **Cols./Page:** 6. **Col. Width:** 9.5 picas. **Col. Depth:** 224 agate lines. **Key Personnel:** Carol Katzman, Editor, phone (402)334-6450. **Subscription Rates:** $26 individuals annual subscription; $30 other countries. **Remarks:** Color advertising accepted; rates available upon request.
Ad Rates: GLR: $1.15 **Circ:** 3,600
BW: $739.20
4C: $1,089.20
PCI: $9.50

18293 Journal of Alcohol and Drug Education
American Alcohol and Drug Information Foundation
c/o HPER Phone: (402)554-3223
University of Nebraska at Omaha Fax: (402)554-3693
Omaha, NE 68182-0216
Professional journal covering philosophies on alcohol and drug education. **Founded:** 1955. **Freq:** Triennial. **Trim Size:** 6 x 9. **Cols./Page:** 1. **Key Personnel:** David Corbin, Editor, dcorbin@coe.unomaha.edu; Richard Stacy, Editor. **ISSN:** 0090-1482. **Subscription Rates:** $45 individuals; $15 single issue. **Remarks:** Advertising not accepted.
Circ: Paid 779

18294 Kidz Magazine
Jupiter Productions
7000 W. Center Rd., Ste. 110 Phone: (402)397-9444
Omaha, NE 68106 Fax: (402)397-9440

Magazine for parents and educators. **Subtitle:** The Heartland's Only Family Publication. **Founded:** Dec. 1988. **Freq:** Monthly. **Trim Size:** 8 1/2 x 11. **Cols./Page:** 4. **Col. Width:** 1 1/2 inches. **Key Personnel:** Melanie Morrissey, Editor; Margaret Shagric, Publisher. **Subscription Rates:** $12. $1 single issue. **Remarks:** Accepts advertising.
Ad Rates: BW: $950 **Circ:** Controlled 30,000
4C: $1,475

18295 The Nebraska Review
University of Nebraska at Omaha
Fine Arts Bldg., No. 212
Omaha, NE 68182-0324

Literary journal covering fiction, poetry, and essays. **Founded:** 1972. **Freq:** Semiannual. **Print Method:** Offset. **Trim Size:** 6 x 9. **Cols./Page:** 1. **Col. Width:** 4 inches. **Col. Depth:** 6 inches. **Key Personnel:** James Reed, Managing Editor; Susan Aizenberg, Poetry Editor. **ISSN:** 8755-514X. **Subscription Rates:** $10 individuals; $6 single issue. **Remarks:** Accepts advertising. **Former name:** Smackwarm.
Ad Rates: BW: $50 **Circ:** (Not Reported)

18296 Omaha World-Herald
Omaha World-Herald Co.
1334 Dodge St. Phone: (402)444-1000
Omaha, NE 68102-1122 Fax: (402)345-0183
Free: (800)284-6397

General newspaper. **Founded:** 1885. **Freq:** Daily (eve.), Sat. and Sun. (morn.). **Print Method:** Letterpress. **Cols./Page:** 6. **Col. Width:** 24 nonpareils. **Col. Depth:** 301 agate lines. **Key Personnel:** G. Woodson Howe, Vice President and Editor; Mike Finney, Exec. News Editor; Deanna Sands, Managing Editor; Bob Gerken, Nat'l Advertising Mgr., phone (402)444-1000; Gerald Wade, Action Editor, phone (402)444-1000; Jim Bresette, Entertainment Magazine Editor, phone (402)444-1000; Pat Waters, Editor, phone (402)444-1000; Larry King, Asst. Managing Editor, phone (402)444-1000. **USPS:** 408-280. **Subscription Rates:** $124.80. **Remarks:** Accepts advertising. **Online:** DataTimes Corporation. **Feature Editors:** Kathleen Brown, *Fashion*, phone (402)444-1000; Jim Delmont, *Movie*, phone (402)444-1000; Steve Jordan, *Financial/Business*, phone (402)444-1000; C. David Kotok, *Political*, phone (402)444-1000; Kay MacMillan, *Art*, phone (402)444-1000; Julia McCord, *Religion*, phone (402)444-1000; Mary McGrath, *Medical*, phone (402)444-1000; Jim Minge, *Entertainment*, phone (402)444-1000; Chris Olson, *Financial/Business*, phone (402)444-1000; Jane Palmer, *Food*, phone (402)444-1000; Frank Partsch, *Editorials*, phone (402)444-1000; Kent Savery, *News*, phone (402)444-1000; Deb Shanahan, *Education*, phone (402)444-1000; Steve Sinclair, *Sports*, phone (402)444-1000.
Ad Rates: BW: $8,154.09 **Circ:** Mon.-Fri. 227,522
4C: $9,131.09 Sat. 220,289
SAU: $67.50 Sun. 280,259
PCI: $74

18297 Pharmacological Reviews
American Society for Pharmacology and Experimental Therapeutics
986260 Nebraska Medical Center Phone: (402)559-4788
Fax: (402)559-7495
Dept. of Pharmacology
Omaha, NE 68198-6260
Publisher E-mail: aspetinfo@faseb.org

Medical journal. **Founded:** 1951. **Freq:** Quarterly. **Print Method:** Offset. **Trim Size:** 8 3/8 x 10 7/8. **Cols./Page:** 2. **Col. Width:** 32 nonpareils. **Col. Depth:** 119 agate lines. **Key Personnel:** David B. Bylund, Ph.D, Editor, phone (402)559-4788, fax (402)559-7495, dbylund@unmc.edu; Richard Dodenhoff, Publications Mgr., phone (301)571-5754. **Subscription Rates:** $70 individuals; $125 other countries; $36 single issue. **Remarks:** Accepts advertising. **Available Online. URL:** http://www.pharmrev.org. **Alt. Formats:** Mailing labels.
Ad Rates: BW: $605 **Circ:** Paid ‡2,042
4C: $1,375 Non-paid ‡71

18298 Shorthorn Country
8288 Hascall St. Phone: (402)393-7051
Omaha, NE 68124 Fax: (402)393-7080
Publication E-mail: durham@beefshorthornusa.com

Magazine on Shorthorn cattle. **Founded:** 1976. **Freq:** Monthly. **Print Method:** Offset. **Trim Size:** 8 1/4 x 10 3/4. **Cols./Page:** 3. **Col. Width:** 26 nonpareils. **Col. Depth:** 140 agate lines. **Key Personnel:** Debbie Hostert, Editor, debbie@beefshorthornusa.com. **ISSN:** 0149-9319. **Subscription**

Rates: $24 individuals Per year.; $38 two years; $30 out of country. **URL:** http://www.beefshorthornusa.com.
Ad Rates: GLR: $0.39 BW: $565 4C: $950 **Circ:** Paid ‡3,500 Non-paid ‡200

18299 Window
Creighton University
2500 California Plaza
Omaha, NE 68178
Publication E-mail: skline@creighton.edu

University magazine. **Freq:** Quarterly. **Key Personnel:** Rick Davis, Editor. **Remarks:** Advertising not accepted.
Circ: (Not Reported)

18300 WOODMEN Magazine
Woodmen of the World/Omaha Woodmen Life Insurance Society
1700 Farnam St. Phone: (402)342-1890
Omaha, NE 68102 Fax: (402)271-7269
Free: (800)225-3108
Publisher E-mail: service@woodmen.com

Fraternal magazine for Society members and their families. **Founded:** Jan. 1891. **Freq:** Bimonthly. **Print Method:** Offset. **Trim Size:** 8 x 10 1/2. **Cols./Page:** 3. **Key Personnel:** Billie Jo Foust, Assistant editor, phone (402)271-7863, fax (402)271-7269, bfoust@woodmen.com; Scott J. Darling, Managing Editor, phone (402)271-7211, fax (402)271-7269. **ISSN:** 1069-1790. **Subscription Rates:** $3 individuals. **Remarks:** Advertising not accepted. **Formerly:** Woodmen of the World Magazine (1992).
Circ: ‡500,000

18301 Cox Cable of Omaha
11505 W. Dodge Rd. Phone: (402)330-6770
Omaha, NE 68154 Fax: (402)330-6528

Founded: 1981. **Key Personnel:** Richard Hook, General Mgr.; Mark Caniglia, Marketing Dir.; Mike Kohler, Public Relations. **Cities Served:** Carter Lake, IA; Douglas County, NE & Pottawattamie County, IA: subscribing households 91,000; 55 channels; 9 community access channels; 250 hours per week community access programming.

18302 Douglas County Cablevision
2312 S. 156th Circle Phone: (402)333-6484
Omaha, NE 68130 Fax: (402)333-5752

Founded: 1981. **Cities Served:** Douglas County, NE and Pottawattamie County, IA.

18303 KAZP-AM - 1620
1001 Farnam-on-the-Wall Phone: (402)342-2000
Omaha, NE 68102 Fax: (402)346-5748

Owner: Mitchell Broadcasting Co. of Iowa, at above address. **Operating Hours:** Continuous. **ADI:** Omaha, NE. **Key Personnel:** John Mitchell, President; Marty Riemenschneider, Exec. V.P.; Neil Melkin, Operations Mgr. **Wattage:** 10,000.

18304 KBBX-AM - 1420
11128 John Galt Blvd., Ste. 192 Phone: (402)556-6700
Omaha, NE 68137-2321 Fax: (402)556-9427

Format: Urban Contemporary. **Networks:** ABC; Satellite Music Network. **Owner:** Oma, Inc., at above address. **Founded:** 1957. **Formerly:** KESY-AM; KOOO-AM. **Operating Hours:** Continuous. **ADI:** Omaha, NE. **Key Personnel:** Dana Webb, General Mgr. **Wattage:** 1000. **URL:** http://www.KBBX.com.

18305 KCRO-AM - 660
3615 Dodge St. Phone: (402)422-1600
Omaha, NE 68131
E-mail: kcro@genesisnet.net

Format: Religious. **Networks:** USA Radio. **Owner:** RadiOmaha, Inc., 4800 E. Raymond, Indianapolis, IN 46203-4898. **Founded:** 1922. **Formerly:** KOWH-AM. **Operating Hours:** 6 a.m.-7 p.m.; 20% network, 80% local. **ADI:** Omaha, NE. **Key Personnel:** Paul Rehm, General Mgr.; Mike Shane, Operations Dir.; Peggy Holzapfel, Traffic Dir.; Mike Shane, Chief Engineer. **Wattage:** 1000. **Ad Rates:** $10-20 for 30 seconds; $13-25 for 60 seconds.

18306 KEFM-FM - 96.1
105 S. 70th St. Phone: (402)558-9696
Omaha, NE 68132-3325 Fax: (402)558-3158

Format: Adult Contemporary; News. **Networks:** Independent. **Owner:** Webster Communications Co., at above address. **Founded:** 1983. **Formerly:** KOIL-FM. **Operating Hours:** Continuous; 100% local. **ADI:** Omaha, NE. **Key Personnel:** John W. Webster, Contact; Dwight Lane, Contact; Richard A. McCormick, General Sales Mgr.; James Leedham, Contact; Holly Dunning, Promotions Dir.; Dawn Renard, Traffic Mgr.; Rick Vincent, News Dir.; Steve Albertsen, Music Dir. **Wattage:** 100,000. **Ad Rates:** $32-68 for 30 seconds; $35-75 for 60 seconds.

18307 KESY-FM - 104.5
11128 John Galt Blvd., Ste. 192 Phone: (402)556-6700
Omaha, NE 68137-2321 Fax: (402)556-9427

Format: Adult Contemporary. **Networks:** ABC. **Founded:** 1972. **Operating Hours:** Continuous. **ADI:** Omaha, NE. **Key Personnel:** Dana Webb, General Mgr., dwebb@kesy.com; Kevin Cooper, Program Dir., kcooper@kesy.com; Terianne Hannibal, News Dir., thannibal@kesy.com; Kathi Knutson, Business Mgr., kknutson@kesy.com. **Wattage:** 100,000. **Ad Rates:** KBBX-AM. **URL:** http://www.kesy.com.

18308 KETV-TV - 7
2665 Douglas St. Phone: (402)345-7777
Omaha, NE 68131-2699 Fax: (402)978-8931
Free: (800)279-5388

Format: Commercial TV. **Networks:** ABC. **Owner:** Pulitzer Broadcasting Co., 101 S. Hanley Rd., Ste. 1250, St. Louis, MO 63105-3428, (314)721-7335, Fax: (314)821-5363. **Founded:** 1957. **Operating Hours:** Continuous. **ADI:** Omaha, NE. **Key Personnel:** Phyllis Ned, V.P./Gen. Mgr., phone (402)522-7761, fax (402)9788922; Rose Ann Shannon, News Dir., phone (402)9788951; Brian Sather, Natl. Sales Mgr., phone (402)978-8941; Arlene Cohen, Local/Regional Sales Mgr., phone (402)978-8946; Paul Tranisi, Promotions Dir., phone (402)9788920; Terrye Mitenko, Business Mgr., phone (402)9788972; Jerry Olson, Operations Mgr., phone (402)9788962; Warren Behrens, Chief Engineer, phone (402)9788911.

18309 KFAB-AM - 1110
5010 Underwood Ave. Phone: (402)561-2000
Omaha, NE 68132 Fax: (402)556-8937
Free: (800)543-1110
E-mail: kfab.com

Format: News; Talk. **Networks:** CBS. **Founded:** 1924. **Operating Hours:** Continuous. **ADI:** Omaha, NE. **Key Personnel:** Dom Seidholz, General Mgr.; Gary Sadlemyer, Operations Supervisor; Kent Pavelka, Program Dir.; Carol Schroeder, News Dir.; Colleen Hitz, Sales Mgr. **Local Programs:** *Drive Time Omaha*, Stacee Schmidt; *Sports Wrap*, McGraw Milhaven; *Tom Becka Show*, Darcie Dunbar. **Wattage:** 50,000. **Ad Rates:** $45-250 per unit. Combined advertising rates available with KTNP-AM, KXKT-AM, KGOR-AM.

18310 KGBI-FM - 100.7
831 Pine St. Phone: (402)449-2900
Omaha, NE 68108 Fax: (402)449-2825
E-mail: kgbi@graceu.edu

Format: Religious. **Networks:** USA Radio; AP; Moody Broadcasting. **Owner:** Grace University, at above address, (402)449-2800. **Founded:** 1966. **Operating Hours:** Continuous. **ADI:** Omaha, NE. **Key Personnel:** Tom Sommerville, Station Mgr. **Wattage:** 100,000. **Ad Rates:** Noncommercial. **URL:** http://www.graceu.edu.

18311 KGOR-FM - 99.9
5010 Underwood Ave. Phone: (402)556-2323
Omaha, NE 68132 Fax: (402)556-8937
E-mail: oldies@kgor.com

Format: Oldies. **Founded:** 1959. **Operating Hours:** Continuous. **ADI:** Omaha, NE. **Key Personnel:** Chuck Jewell, General Mgr.; Joe Siragusa, Program Dir.; Jeff Glover, Sales Mgr. **Local Programs:** *Directions*, Darcy Dunbar. **Wattage:** 115,000. **URL:** http://www.kgor.com.

18312 KIOS-FM - 91.5
3230 Burt St. Phone: (402)554-6444
Omaha, NE 68131 Fax: (402)557-2559

Format: Public Radio; Classical; Jazz. **Networks:** National Public Radio (NPR). **Founded:** 1969. **Operating Hours:** 5 a.m. - midnight. **ADI:** Omaha, NE. **Key Personnel:** Wilson Perry, General Mgr., phone (402)577-2555; Robert Coate, Program Dir., phone (402)557-2556; Ed McGrath, phone (402)557-2550. **Wattage:** 55,000. **Ad Rates:** Noncommercial. **URL:** http://www.kios.org; http://www.kios.org.

18313 KKAR-AM - 1290
1001 Farnam on the Mall Phone: (402)342-2000
Omaha, NE 68102 Fax: (402)342-5874

Format: News; Sports; Talk. **Networks:** CNN Radio. **Founded:** 1987. **Operating Hours:** Continuous. **ADI:** Omaha, NE. **Key Personnel:** Marty Riemenschneider, Contact; Neil Nelkin, Station Mgr.; John Ginzkey, Vice Pres. Sales. **Wattage:** 5000. **URL:** http://www.kkar.com.

18314 KKCD-FM - 92.3
11128 John Galt Blvd. Phone: (402)554-1056
Omaha, NE 68137 Fax: (402)598-6605
Free: (800)955-9230

Format: Album-Oriented Rock (AOR); Adult Contemporary. **Networks:** Independent. **Owner:** Journal Broadcasting Group, Inc., 720 E. Capitol Dr., Milwaukee, WI 53212, (414)332-9611. **Founded:** 1964. **Operating Hours:** Continuous. **ADI:** Omaha, NE. **Key Personnel:** James McKernan, General Mgr.; Kathy Higgins, Sales Mgr.; Brandy Summer, Promotions Dir.; Liz Adams, News Dir.; Bruce McGregor, Program Dir.; John Bible, Chief Engineer; John Gaeta, Chief Engineer. **Wattage:** 100,000. **Ad Rates:** Advertising accepted; rates available upon request.

18315 KMTV-TV - 3
10714 Mockingbird Dr. Phone: (402)592-3333
Omaha, NE 68127 Fax: (402)592-3378

Format: Commercial TV. **Networks:** CBS. **Owner:** Lee Enterprises, Inc., 215 N. Main St., Davenport, IA 52801, (319)383-2100. **Founded:** 1949. **Operating Hours:** Continuous; 80% network, 20% local. **ADI:** Omaha, NE. **Key Personnel:** Chris Leister, General Mgr.; Rich Lebenson, News Dir.; Rich Roberts, Sports Dir.; Phil Clark, Promotions Mgr. **Ad Rates:** $35-1,000 per unit.

18316 KOIL-AM - 1180
1001 Farnam St. Phone: (402)342-2000
Omaha, NE 68102 Fax: (402)345-3652

Format: Sports. **Networks:** ESPN Radio; NBC. **Founded:** 1925. **Operating Hours:** Continuous. **ADI:** Omaha, NE. **Key Personnel:** Marty Riemenschneider, General Mgr. **Wattage:** 25,000.

18317 KPTM-TV - 42
4625 Farnam St. Phone: (402)558-4200
Omaha, NE 68132 Fax: (402)554-4290

Format: Commercial TV. **Networks:** Fox. **Owner:** Pappas Telecasting Co., at above address. **Founded:** 1986. **Operating Hours:** Continuous Mon.-Sat.; 6 a.m.-1 a.m. Sun. **ADI:** Omaha, NE. **Key Personnel:** Shannora McIntosh, Co-Traffic Mgr., phone (402)554-4220, fax (402)554-4290; Rick Creager, Prod. Sup., phone (402)554-4227, fax (402)551-1515; Donna Ridgley, Promotions Mgr., phone (402)554-4232, fax (402)551-1515; Harry J. Pappas, President; Howard H. Shrier, Exec. VP/General Mgr., phone (402)554-4201, fax (402)554-4292; Kirk Winkler, News Dir.; Dale Scherbring, Chief Engineer, phone (402)554-4222, fax (402)554-4292; Stephen Rabb, General Marketing Mgr., phone (402)554-4262, fax (402)554-1515; Darlene Goldsberry, Co-Traffic Mgr., phone (402)554-4217, fax (402)554-4290. **Local Programs:** *Good Day* 5:30 am - 9:00 am Monday-Friday, Kirk Winkler, V.P. News. **Wattage:** 5,000,000.

18318 KQKQ-FM - 98.5
1001 Farnam-on-the-Mall Phone: (402)342-2000
Omaha, NE 68102 Fax: (402)342-5874

Format: Contemporary Hit Radio (CHR). **Networks:** Independent. **Owner:** Mitchell Broadcasting Co., at above address. **Founded:** 1974. **Operating Hours:** Continuous; 100% local. **ADI:** Omaha, NE. **Key Personnel:** Marty Riemenschneider, Contact; John Ginzkey, V.P. Sales. **Wattage:** 100,000. **URL:** http://www.sweet98.com.

18319 KVNO-FM - 90.7
60th & Dodge St., Engg-200 Phone: (402)559-5866
Omaha, NE 68182-0234 Fax: (402)554-2440
E-mail: bjenks@unomaha.edu

Format: Classical; Jazz; News. **Owner:** University of Nebraska Board of Regents, 3835 Holdrege, Lincoln, NE 68583, (402)472-3906. **Founded:** 1972. **Operating Hours:** Continuous; 100% local. **ADI:** Omaha, NE. **Key Personnel:** Debra Aliano, General Mgr.; Mike Hagstrom, News Dir.; Bill Jenks, Program Dir.; Dave Kline, Contact; Liz Cajka, Contact. **Wattage:** 3000. **Ad Rates:** Noncommercial; underwriting available. **URL:** http://www.kvno.unomaha.edu/.

KXKT-FM - See Atlantic, Iowa

18320 KYNE-TV - 26
1800 N. 33rd St. Phone: (402)472-3611
PO Box 83111 Fax: (402)472-1785
Lincoln, NE 68501
E-mail: net@unlinfo.unl.edu

Format: Public TV. **Networks:** Public Broadcasting Service (PBS). **Owner:** Nebraska Educational Telecommunications, at above address. **Founded:** 1965. **Operating Hours:** 5:45 a.m.-midnight; 90% network, 10% local. **ADI:** Omaha, NE. **Key Personnel:** Rod Bates, General Mgr., rbates@unlinfo.unl.edu; Michael Winkle, Asst. GM, Marketing, mwinkle@unlinfo.unl.edu; Steve Lenzen, Asst. GM, Educational TV, slenzen@unlinfo.unl.edu; Sue Gildersleeve, Asst.

GM, Admin. & Finance, sgildersleeve@unlinfo.unl.edu; Peter Ford, Asst. GM for Engineering, pford@unlinfo.unl.edu; Bill Kelly, Sr. Producer, Public Affairs, wek@unlinfo.unl.edu; S. Graziano, Program Mgr., sgraziano@unlinfo.unl.edu; Steve Alvis, Sr. Producer, Sports & Special Events, salvis@unlinfo.unl.edu; Michael Farrell, Production Coordinator, Cultural Affairs, mfarrell@unlinfo.unl.edu. **Local Programs:** *Backyard Farmer* Tuesdays at 7 pm, during spring and summer; *Big Red Wrap-Up* Tuesdays 7pm, during football season, Steve Alvis, Sr. Producer, Sports & Special Events; *Statewide* 8 pm Friday, Bill Ganzel, Sr. Producer, Public Affairs. **Wattage:** 520,000. **Ad Rates:** Noncommercial. **URL:** http://net.unl.edu/.

18321 Vision Electronics
14707 N. 72nd St. Phone: (402)571-7590
Omaha, NE 68122 Fax: (402)571-2801
Free: (800)844-5564

Key Personnel: Trace Smith, Systems Mgr.; Betty Smith, Customer Service; Mike Boudle, Customer Service. **Cities Served:** Auburn, Clarkson, Decatur, Dedham, Doon, Ewing, Fertile, Howells, Leigh Lynch, Modale, Montour, NE; Orchard Lindsay, Persia, Orchard Butte, Spencer, Verdigre, W ausa, Bagley, Jamaica, Mingo Rippey, and Monroe, NE.: subscribing households 3,500; 480 channels.

18322 WOWT-TV - 6
3501 Farnam St. Phone: (402)346-6666
Omaha, NE 68131-3301 Fax: (402)233-7880

Format: Commercial TV. **Networks:** NBC. **ADI:** Omaha, NE. **Key Personnel:** D.R. Oswald, Contact; Karen Bride, Operations Mgr.; John Clark, News Dir. **URL:** http://www.wowt.com.

ONEILL

18323 Frontier and Holt County Independent
Miles Publishing Co. Inc.
Box 360 Phone: (402)336-1220
Oneill, NE 68763-0360 Fax: (402)336-1222

Newspaper with a Democratic orientation. **Founded:** 1880. **Freq:** Weekly (Thurs.). **Print Method:** Offset. **Cols./Page:** 7. **Col. Width:** 24 nonpareils. **Col. Depth:** 128 agate lines. **Key Personnel:** G.A. Miles, Publisher. **Subscription Rates:** $25. **Remarks:** Accepts advertising.
Ad Rates: GLR: $29.15 **Circ:** 5,225
BW: $4,606.90
4C: $1,046.90
SAU: $4.08

18324 KBRX-AM - 1350
Box 150 Phone: (402)336-1612
Oneill, NE 68763 Fax: (402)336-3585
Free: (800)678-5294
E-mail: kbrx@inetnebr.com

Format: Country. **Networks:** ABC. **Owner:** Ranchland Broadcast Co. Inc, at above address. **Founded:** 1955. **Operating Hours:** Continuous. **Key Personnel:** Scott Poese, Manager; Tom McDermott, Music Dir.; Gil Poese, Sales Mgr. **Wattage:** 1000. **Ad Rates:** $12.00 for 30 seconds; $15.00 for 60 seconds.

18325 KBRX-FM - 102.9
Box 150 Phone: (402)336-1612
Oneill, NE 68763 Fax: (402)336-3585
Free: (800)678-5294
E-mail: kbrx@inetnebr.com

Format: Contemporary Country. **Networks:** ABC. **Owner:** Ranchland Broadcast Co. Inc, at above address. **Founded:** 1973. **Operating Hours:** Continuous. **Key Personnel:** Scott Poese, Manager; Tom McDermoh, Music Dir.; Gil Poese, Sales Mgr. **Wattage:** 100,000. **Ad Rates:** $12.00 for 30 seconds; $15.00 for 60 seconds.

ORCHARD, pop. 482.

Antelope Co. (NEC). 50 m NW of Norfolk. Cheese factory. Farming. Corn, rye, oats, hogs, cattle, sheep.

18326 Orchard News
235 Windom St. Phone: (402)893-2535
PO Box 130 Fax: (402)893-2050
Orchard, NE 68764
Free shopper. **Founded:** 1899. **Freq:** Weekly (Thurs.). **Print Method:** Offset. **Cols./Page:** 4. **Col. Width:** 27 nonpareils. **Col. Depth:** 210 agate lines. **Key Personnel:** Lucy Ferguson, Editor and Publisher. **USPS:** 410-520. **Subscription Rates:** $18; $20 out of area; $25 out of state. **Remarks:** Accepts advertising.
Ad Rates: GLR: $.50 **Circ:** ‡750
BW: $120
SAU: $2.50
CNU: $3
PCI: $2.50

ORD†, pop. 2,658.

Valley Co. (C). 55 m NW of Grand Island. Alfalfa mill. Popcorn marketing center. Stock, dairy, poultry, grain farms.

18327 The Ord Quiz
Quiz Graphic Arts, Inc.
305 S. 16th St. Phone: (308)728-3262
Ord, NE 68862 Fax: (308)728-5715
Publisher E-mail: quiz@micrord.com

Community newspaper. **Founded:** Feb. 1882. **Freq:** Weekly (Thurs.). **Print Method:** Offset. **Cols./Page:** 7. **Col. Width:** 12 picas. **Col. Depth:** 294 agate lines. **Key Personnel:** Kerry E. Leggett, Editor and Publisher. **USPS:** 410-600. **Subscription Rates:** $30 per year. **Remarks:** Accepts advertising.
Ad Rates: GLR: $.70 **Circ:** Paid ‡2,827
BW: $690.90 Free ‡85
SAU: $4.90

18328 KNLV-AM - 1060
205 S. 16th St. Phone: (308)728-3263
Ord, NE 68862 Fax: (308)728-3264

Format: Country. **Networks:** ABC; Brownfield. **Owner:** KNLV Incorporated, at above address. **Founded:** 1965. **Operating Hours:** 6 a.m.-sunset; 15% network, 85% local. **Key Personnel:** Larry D. Schultz, General Mgr.; Doug Duda, Sports and News Dir.; Kay Leggett, Sales Mgr.; Kaye Fuller, Business Mgr. **Local Programs:** *Community Billboard*, Larry Schultz; *Party Line Part One*, Doug Duda. **Wattage:** 1000. **Ad Rates:** $4.95 for 15 seconds; $7.10 for 30 seconds; $9.70 for 60 seconds.

18329 KNLV-FM - 103.9
205 S. 16th St. Phone: (308)728-3263
Ord, NE 68862 Fax: (308)728-3264

Format: Country. **Networks:** ABC; Brownfield. **Owner:** KNLV Inc., at above address. **Founded:** 1981. **Operating Hours:** 6 a.m.-10 p.m.; 15% network, 85% local. **Key Personnel:** Larry Schultz, General Mgr.; Doug Duda, Sports and News Dir.; Kay Leggett, Sales Mgr.; Kaye Fuller, Business Mgr. **Wattage:** 3500. **Ad Rates:** $4.95 for 15 seconds; $7.10 for 30 seconds; $9.70 for 60 seconds.

OSCEOLA†, pop. 1,057.

Polk Co. (EC). 68 m NW of Lincoln. Stock, grain, dairy, poultry farms. Wheat, corn, oats, milo.

18330 The Polk County News
J & B Thompson
PO Box 258 Phone: (402)747-2431
Osceola, NE 68651 Fax: (402)764-5341

Community newspaper. **Founded:** 1872. **Freq:** Weekly (Thurs.). **Print Method:** Offset. **Cols./Page:** 6. **Col. Width:** 12.2 picas. **Col. Depth:** 300 agate lines. **Key Personnel:** William H. Thompson, Editor. **USPS:** 412-740. **Subscription Rates:** $18 individuals; $20 out of area; $22 out of state. **Remarks:** Accepts advertising. **Formerly:** Osceola Record (1994).
Ad Rates: GLR: $.45 **Circ:** ‡1,015
SAU: $3.15

OSHKOSH†, pop. 1,057.

Garden Co. (W). 85 m NW of North Platte. Pressure gauges, grain, golf cart tops. Dairy farms. Stock, grain, wheat, corn, turkeys, honey.

18331 Garden County News
Oshkosh
204 Main St. Phone: (308)772-3555
Box 290 Fax: (308)772-4475
Oshkosh, NE 69154-0290
Community newspaper. **Founded:** 1906. **Freq:** Weekly (Thurs.). **Print Method:** Offset. Uses mats. **Cols./Page:** 6. **Col. Width:** 25 nonpareils. **Col. Depth:** 294 agate lines. **Key Personnel:** James E. McKeeman, Editor and Publisher. **Subscription Rates:** $18 in state; $20 out of state. **Remarks:** Accepts advertising.
Ad Rates: GLR: $.14 **Circ:** 1,884
BW: $304.92
PCI: $2.42

OSMOND, pop. 871.

Pierce Co. (NE). 10 m N of Pierce. Residential.

18332 Osmond Republican
Northeast Nebraska News Co.
Box 428 Phone: (402)748-3666
Osmond, NE 68765 Fax: (402)748-3354

Local newspaper. **Founded:** 1890. **Freq:** Weekly (Wed.). **Print Method:** Offset. **Cols./Page:** 7. **Col. Width:** 25 nonpareils. **Col. Depth:** 294 agate lines. **Key Personnel:** Bernice Blechot, Editor/General Mgr. **Subscription Rates:** $12.50 individuals; $17 out of area. **Remarks:** Accepts advertising.
Ad Rates: GLR: $.186 **Circ:** ‡1,037
BW: $345.45
SAU: $2.60
PCI: $2.60

OVERTON, pop. 641.

Dawson Co. (SC). 60 m SW of Grand Island. Electronic and meat processing plants. Grain, stock, dairy, alfalfa, corn.

18333 The Beacon-Observer
PO Box 330 Phone: (308)987-2451
Overton, NE 68863 Fax: (308)987-2452

Community newspaper. **Founded:** June 1, 1898. **Freq:** Weekly (Wed.). **Print Method:** Offset. **Trim Size:** 22 3/4 x 30. **Cols./Page:** 6. **Col. Width:** 26 nonpareils. **Col. Depth:** 294 agate lines. **Key Personnel:** Norman G. Taylor, Editor and Publisher; Polly A. Taylor, Publisher. **Subscription Rates:** $16.50; $20 out of area; $29.50 out of state. **Remarks:** Accepts advertising. **Feature Editors:** Gail Johnson, *Features*, phone (309)856-4770.
Ad Rates: BW: $300 **Circ:** ‡1,650
4C: $600
SAU: $2.73
PCI: $3.48

OXFORD, pop. 1,109.

Furnas Co. (S). 70 m SW of Hastings. Manufactured aluminum storm windows and doors, cheese factory. Corn, wheat, alfalfa, turkey growing.

18334 Oxford Standard
Box 125 Phone: (308)824-3582
Oxford, NE 68967 Fax: (308)824-3582

Community newspaper. **Founded:** 1884. **Freq:** Weekly (Thurs.). **Print Method:** Offset. **Trim Size:** 15 x 22 3/4. **Cols./Page:** 6. **Col. Width:** 12 picas. **Col. Depth:** 21 inches. **Key Personnel:** James R. Cooley, Publisher; Maria H. Cooley, Publisher. **USPS:** 416-580. **Subscription Rates:** $17; $22 out of area. **Remarks:** Accepts advertising.
Ad Rates: BW: $346.50 **Circ:** ‡1,250
SAU: $2.84
PCI: $2.75

PAPILLION†, pop. 6,500.

Sarpy Co. (E). 10 m S. of Omaha. Suburban residential.

18335 TCI
955 N. Adams St., Apt. 9 Phone: (402)339-1998
Papillion, NE 68046-3080

Founded: 1980. **Formerly:** UAE. **Key Personnel:** Philip Higgins, Sales Mgr. **Cities Served:** Bellevue, LaVista, Millaro, Omaha, Papillion, Ralston, NE; Sarpy & Douglas Counties, NE: subscribing households 34,000; 43 channels; 1 community access channel; 42 hours per week community access programming.

PAWNEE CITY†, pop. 1,156.

Pawnee Co. (EC). 35 m ESE of Beatrice. Ships livestock.

18336 The Pawnee Republican
PO Box 111 Phone: (402)852-2575
Pawnee City, NE 68420
Community newspaper. **Founded:** 1868. **Freq:** Weekly. **Print Method:** Web press. **Cols./Page:** 6. **Col. Width:** 12 picas. **Col. Depth:** 21 inches. **Key Personnel:** Beverly J. Puhalla, Editor and Publisher. **Subscription Rates:** $21; $26 out of county. **Remarks:** Color advertising not accepted.
Ad Rates: SAU: $4.50 **Circ:** Paid 1,834
PCI: $4.50 Free 52

PENDER†, pop. 1,318.

Thurston Co. (NE). 33 m SW of Sioux City, Iowa. Manufactures currying and dipping machines, hay rakes, tractor cabs. Agriculture.

18337 The Pender Times
313 Main St. Phone: (402)385-3013
PO Box 280 Fax: (402)385-3013
Pender, NE 68047
Newspaper. **Founded:** 1886. **Freq:** Weekly (Thurs.). **Print Method:** Offset. **Cols./Page:** 6. **Col. Width:** 19 nonpareils. **Col. Depth:** 217 agate lines. **Key Personnel:** Norvin Hansen,

Editor and Publisher. **Subscription Rates:** $24.60 local. **Remarks:** Accepts advertising.
Ad Rates: BW: $522.45 **Circ:** ‡1,500
SAU: $4.50

PETERSBURG

18338 Petersburg Press
PO Box 177 Phone: (402)386-5384
Petersburg, NE 68652 Fax: (402)386-5384

Community newspaper. **Freq:** Weekly (Wed.). **Cols./Page:** 5. **Col. Width:** 11 picas. **Col. Depth:** 15 inches. **Key Personnel:** Jean M. Kaup, Publisher. **USPS:** 429-160. **Subscription Rates:** $20; $25 out of area. **Remarks:** Accepts advertising.
Ad Rates: SAU: $3.20 **Circ:** 600
PCI: $2.40

PIERCE†, pop. 1,535.

Pierce Co. (NE). 15 m NW of Norfolk. Grain, stock, dairy, poultry, fruit farms. Corn, oats.

Iowa Smoke-Eater - See Des Moines, Iowa

Minnesota Smoke-Eater - See St. Paul, Minnesota

18339 Nebraska Smoke-Eater
Smoke-Eater Publications
PO Box 129 Phone: (402)329-4665
Pierce, NE 68767-0129 Fax: (402)329-6224

Magazine serving volunteer firemen. **Founded:** 1949. **Freq:** Monthly. **Print Method:** Offset. **Cols./Page:** 5. **Col. Width:** 22 nonpareils. **Col. Depth:** 217 agate lines. **Key Personnel:** Robert Zimmer, Publisher. **Subscription Rates:** $10. **Remarks:** Accepts advertising.
Ad Rates: BW: $310 **Circ:** ‡12,000
PCI: $4

18340 Pierce County Leader
PO Box 129 Phone: (402)329-4665
Pierce, NE 68767 Fax: (402)329-6337

Community newspaper. **Founded:** 1889. **Freq:** Weekly (Thurs.). **Print Method:** Offset. **Cols./Page:** 5. **Col. Width:** 22 nonpareils. **Col. Depth:** 217 agate lines. **Key Personnel:** Randee D. Falter, Editor. **Subscription Rates:** $20. **Remarks:** Accepts advertising.
Ad Rates: GLR: $.10 **Circ:** ‡2,075
BW: $251.88
SAU: $3.50
PCI: $3.50

PLAINVIEW, pop. 1,483.

Pierce Co. (NE). 32 m NW of Norfolk. Stock, grain, poultry farms. Wheat, corn.

18341 Plainview News
Box 9 Phone: (402)582-4921
Plainview, NE 68769-0009 Fax: (402)582-4922
Publisher E-mail: plvwnews@plvwtelco.net

Community newspaper. **Founded:** 1892. **Freq:** Weekly (Wed.). **Print Method:** Offset. **Trim Size:** 16 1/2 x 23. **Cols./Page:** 7. **Col. Width:** 12 1/2 picas. **Col. Depth:** 298 agate lines. **Key Personnel:** Ken Larson, Editor. **USPS:** 434-840. **Subscription Rates:** $16; $21 out of area. **Remarks:** Accepts advertising.
Ad Rates: BW: $514.50 **Circ:** ‡1757
SAU: $3.50

PLATTSMOUTH, pop. 6,295.

Cass Co. On Missouri River at mouth of Platte River, 18 m S of Omaha. Diversified farming. Livestock, corn, wheat, milo.

18342 Plattsmouth Journal
Lincoln Journal Star
410 Main St. Phone: (402)296-2141
PO Box 250 Fax: (402)296-3401
Plattsmouth, NE 68048
Free: (800)742-0061

Community newspaper. **Founded:** 1881. **Freq:** Semiweekly (Mon. and Thurs.). **Print Method:** Offset. **Cols./Page:** 6. **Col. Width:** 24 nonpareils. **Col. Depth:** 301 agate lines. **Key Personnel:** Kevin Larson, Editor; Louis Prohaska, Publisher. **Subscription Rates:** $24. **Remarks:** Accepts advertising.
Ad Rates: GLR: $.39 **Circ:** ‡5,234
BW: $704.34
SAU: $5.43

18343 KOTD-AM - 1020
PO Box 509 Phone: (402)298-8000
Plattsmouth, NE 68048 Fax: (402)296-2124

Format: Adult Contemporary. **Networks:** ABC. **Owner:** Platte Broadcasting Co., Inc., 625 1st Ave., Plattsmouth, NE 68048, (402)296-2124, Fax: (402)296-2124. **Founded:** 1970. **Operating Hours:** Sunrise-sunset; 60% network, 40% local. **Key Personnel:** Charles Warga, President; Steve Warga, Contact; John Madr, Contact; Roy Smith, Contact; Steve Grooms, News Dir. **Local Programs:** *Classic Car, Farmer To Farmer*, Roy Smith; *Polka Show* Sunday, David Denuer. **Wattage:** 1,000. **Ad Rates:** $6-10 for 30 seconds; $8-12 for 60 seconds.

18344 KOTD-FM - 106.9
P.O. Box 509 Phone: (402)298-8000
Plattsmouth, NE 68048 Fax: (402)296-2124
E-mail: swkkotd-fm@navix.net

Format: Adult Contemporary. **Networks:** ABC. **Founded:** July 1993. **Operating Hours:** Continuous. **Key Personnel:** Steve Warga, General Mgr. **Wattage:** 6,000. **Ad Rates:** $10-16 for 30 seconds; $13-19 for 60 seconds.

PONCA†, pop. 1,057.

Dixon Co. (NE). 22 m NW of Sioux City, Iowa. Stock, grain farms. Corn.

18345 Nebraska Journal-Leader
110 East St. Phone: (402)755-2203
PO Box 545 Fax: (402)755-2205
Ponca, NE 68770
Newspaper. **Founded:** 1871. **Freq:** Weekly (Thurs.). **Print Method:** Offset. **Cols./Page:** 6. **Col. Width:** 20 nonpareils. **Col. Depth:** 217 agate lines. **Key Personnel:** Richard D. Volkman, Editor and Publisher. **Subscription Rates:** $6.50. **Remarks:** Accepts advertising.
Ad Rates: GLR: $.135 **Circ:** 1,300

RALSTON

18346 The Ralston Recorder
7631 Main St., Ste. 2 Phone: (402)331-6300
Ralston, NE 68127 Fax: (402)331-8050
Publisher E-mail: papilliontimes@monarch.papillion.ne.us

Community newspaper. **Founded:** 1939. **Freq:** Weekly (Wed.). **Print Method:** Offset. **Trim Size:** 13 3/4 x 22 1/2. **Cols./Page:** 6. **Col. Width:** 2 1/16 inches. **Col. Depth:** 21 1/2 inches. **Key Personnel:** Carolyn S. Hatting, Advertising Dir.; Shon Barenklau, Publisher; Mark Martin, Managing Editor. **Subscription Rates:** $23.40; $31.20 out of area. **Remarks:** Accepts advertising.
Ad Rates: BW: $516 **Circ:** 1,850
4C: $783
SAU: $4

RAVENNA, pop. 1,296.

Buffalo Co. (SC). 32 m W of Grand Island. Egg and cheese processing plant. Agriculture. Livestock, wheat, corn.

18347 The Ravenna News
322 Grand Ave. Phone: (308)452-3411
PO BOX 110 Fax: (308)452-3511
Ravenna, NE 68869
Community newspaper. **Founded:** July 1, 1886. **Freq:** Weekly (Wed.). **Print Method:** Offset. **Trim Size:** 13 x 21. **Cols./Page:** 6. **Col. Width:** 12 picas. **Col. Depth:** 21 inches. **Key Personnel:** Nancy Jackson, Managing Editor; T.M. Gill, Publisher; George Peterson, Publisher. **Subscription Rates:** $21 individuals. **Remarks:** Accepts advertising.
Ad Rates: BW: $346.50 **Circ:** ‡1,700
SAU: $3
CNU: $3.95

RED CLOUD†, pop. 1,300.

Webster Co. (S). On Republican River, 60 m S of Grand Island. Cheese processing and meat packing plant. Dairy farms.

18348 Red Cloud Chief
322 N. Webster Phone: (402)746-3700
Box 466
Red Cloud, NE 68970
Newspaper. **Founded:** 1873. **Freq:** Weekly (Wed.). **Print Method:** Offset. **Cols./Page:** 6. **Col. Width:** 12.5 picas. **Col. Depth:** 21 inches. **Key Personnel:** Douglas G. Hoschoner, Co-publisher; Charlene Hoschoner, Co-publisher. **USPS:** 606-020. **Subscription Rates:** $19.50 local; $21.50. **Remarks:** Accepts advertising.
Ad Rates: GLR: $5.25 **Circ:** 2000

ST. COLUMBANS

18349 Columban Mission
Society of St. Columban
St. Columbans, NE 68056 Phone: (402)291-1920
Fax: (402)291-4984
Publication E-mail: cioffero@omnilinx.net; cgmo@aol.com

Magazine about Catholic missions outside the U.S., informing readers of the work of Columban Fathers. **Founded:** 1918. **Freq:** 8/year. **Print Method:** Offset. **Cols./Page:** 3 and 2. **Col. Width:** 26 and 42 nonpareils. **Col. Depth:** 140 agate lines. **Key Personnel:** Rev. Richard Steinhilber, Editor; Rev. Brendan O'Sullivan, Publisher. **Subscription Rates:** Controlled; $10. **Remarks:** Advertising not accepted. **Formerly:** The Far East.
Circ: Controlled ‡150,000

ST. EDWARD

18350 The St. Edward Advance
PO Box 287 Phone: (402)678-2771
St. Edward, NE 68660 Fax: (402)678-2556

Newspaper with a Republican orientation. **Founded:** 1900. **Freq:** Weekly (Thurs.). **Print Method:** Offset. **Cols./Page:** 7. **Col. Width:** 24 nonpareils. **Col. Depth:** 294 agate lines. **Key Personnel:** Stephanie A. Dawson, Editor and Publisher. **USPS:** 515-10. **Subscription Rates:** $15 individuals; $17 out of area. **Remarks:** Accepts advertising.
Ad Rates: SAU: $2.70 **Circ:** ‡887
PCI: $2.70

ST. PAUL

18351 St. Paul Phonograph-Herald
PO Box 27 Phone: (308)754-4401
St. Paul, NE 68873 Fax: (308)754-4498

Rural community newspaper. **Founded:** 1873. **Freq:** Weekly. **Print Method:** Offset. **Trim Size:** 16 x 22 3/4. **Cols./Page:** 7. **Col. Width:** 2 1/16 inches. **Col. Depth:** 21 inches. **Key Personnel:** Connie M. Thompson, Editor; Mildred I. Thompson, Publisher; Mary Jo Thompson, Advertising Mgr. **USPS:** 430-720. **Subscription Rates:** $19 individuals; $24 out of area; $29 out of state. **Remarks:** Accepts advertising.
Ad Rates: BW: $514.50 **Circ:** ‡2,420
SAU: $4.12
PCI: $3.50

SARGENT

18352 Burwell Tribune
Burwell Tribune Newspapers
103 N. 1st St. Phone: (308)527-4210
PO Box 547 Fax: (308)346-4018
Sargent, NE 68874
Local newspaper. **Freq:** Weekly (Wed.). **Print Method:** Offset. **Cols./Page:** 8. **Col. Width:** 10.5 nonpareils. **Col. Depth:** 976 agate lines. **Key Personnel:** Byron Neiman, Publisher. **Subscription Rates:** $17. $19 out of state. **Remarks:** Accepts advertising.
Ad Rates: GLR: $.35 **Circ:** Paid ‡2,100
SAU: $5.35

18353 Sargent Leader
Burwell Tribune Newspapers
103 N. 1st St. Phone: (308)527-4210
PO Box 547 Fax: (308)346-4018
Sargent, NE 68874
Local newspaper. **Founded:** 1895. **Freq:** Weekly (Thurs.). **Print Method:** Offset. **Cols./Page:** 5. **Col. Width:** 10.5 picas. **Col. Depth:** 210 agate lines. **Key Personnel:** Byron Neiman, Editor and Publisher. **Subscription Rates:** $17; $19 out of state. **Remarks:** Accepts advertising.
Ad Rates: GLR: $.24 **Circ:** Paid ‡750
SAU: $3.88 Free ‡50

Taylor Clarion - See Taylor

18354 Wheeler County Independent
Burwell Tribune Newspapers
103 N. 1st St. Phone: (308)527-4210
PO Box 547 Fax: (308)346-4018
Sargent, NE 68874
Local newspaper. **Founded:** 1890. **Freq:** Weekly (Wed.). **Print Method:** Offset. **Cols./Page:** 8. **Col. Width:** 10.5 picas. **Col. Depth:** 210 agate lines. **Key Personnel:** Byron Neiman, Publisher. **Subscription Rates:** $17; $19 out of state. **Remarks:** Accepts advertising.
Ad Rates: GLR: $.35 **Circ:** 325
PCI: $4.98

SCHUYLER

18355 The Schuyler Sun
Sun Publishing Co., Inc.
1112 C St.   Phone: (402)352-2424
PO Box 506   Fax: (402)352-3332
Schuyler, NE 68661
Community newspaper. **Founded:** 1871. **Freq:** Weekly (Thurs.). **Print Method:** Letterpress and offset. **Trim Size:** 14 x 21 1/2. **Cols./Page:** 6. **Col. Width:** 12 1/2 picas. **Col. Depth:** 21 1/2 inches. **Key Personnel:** Michael F. Rea, Editor; Francis C. Svoboda, Publisher; Curt Mentzer, Advertising Mgr. **USPS:** 609-560. **Subscription Rates:** $20; $22 out of state. **Remarks:** Accepts advertising.
Ad Rates: GLR: $.35   **Circ:** Paid 3,501
BW: $474.72   Free 78
SAU: $4.13
PCI: $4.13

SCOTTSBLUFF

18356 Business Farmer
Business Farmer, Inc.
22 W. 17th   Phone: (308)635-3110
Box 2364   Fax: (308)635-7435
Scottsbluff, NE 69361
Trade newspaper covering farm news. **Founded:** 1925. **Freq:** Weekly. **Print Method:** Web offset. **Cols./Page:** 6. **Col. Width:** 9 picas. **Col. Depth:** 13 picas. **Key Personnel:** Brad Staman, Editor; Jeff Robertson, Publisher, phone (307)532-2184, fax (307)532-2283; Doug Southard, General Mgr. **Subscription Rates:** $23.50 individuals; $29 out of area. **Remarks:** Accepts advertising.
Ad Rates: GLR: $7   **Circ:** Paid 2,750
BW: $7
PCI: $5.25

18357 Business Farmer-Stockman
Business Farmer, Inc.
22 W. 17th   Phone: (308)635-3110
Box 2364   Fax: (308)635-7435
Scottsbluff, NE 69361
Agricultural newspaper. **Founded:** 1925. **Freq:** Weekly (Fri.). **Print Method:** Offset. **Cols./Page:** 6. **Col. Width:** 9 picas. **Key Personnel:** Bill Hanson, Publisher; Dory Southard, Advertising Mgr. **Subscription Rates:** $22; $27.50 out of area. **Remarks:** Accepts advertising.
Ad Rates: BW: $409.50   **Circ:** 2,700
4C: $534.50
PCI: $5.25

18358 Express Shopper
1405 Broadway   Phone: (308)632-0605
PO Box 1709   Fax: (308)635-1258
Scottsbluff, NE 69363-1709
Shopper. **Subtitle:** Express Shopper. **Founded:** Feb. 24, 1993. **Freq:** Weekly. **Print Method:** Offset. **Cols./Page:** 6. **Col. Width:** 1 9/16 inches. **Col. Depth:** 13 inches. **Key Personnel:** Johnny Aguirre, phone (308)632-0605, fax (308)635-1258; Gay Hill, phone (308)632-0605. **Remarks:** Accepts advertising. **Formerly:** TwinCity Shopper.
Ad Rates: GLR: $2   **Circ:** Free 15,000
BW: $312
4C: $387
SAU: $4
PCI: $4

18359 Farm/Ranch Exchange
Star-Herald
1405 Broadway   Phone: (308)632-9000
PO Box 1709   Fax: (308)635-9001
Scottsbluff, NE 69363-1709
Free: (800)846-6102
Publisher E-mail: starherald@wespub.com

Farm newspaper. **Freq:** Monthly. **Print Method:** Offset. **Cols./Page:** 6. **Col. Width:** 18 nonpareils. **Col. Depth:** 182 agate lines. **Key Personnel:** Steve Miller, Editor, phone (308)632-9055, smiller@wespub.com; Steve Hungerford, Publisher, phone (308)632-9009, hungerford@wespub.com; Johnny Aguirre, Advertising Mgr., phone (308)632-9039, jaguirre@wespub.com. **Subscription Rates:** $5.95 /year. **Remarks:** Accepts advertising.
Ad Rates: PCI: $3.42   **Circ:** 24,000

18360 Star-Herald
1405 Broadway   Phone: (308)632-9000
PO Box 1709   Fax: (308)635-9001
Scottsbluff, NE 69363-1709
Free: (800)846-6102
Publication E-mail: sherald@www.prairieweb.com
Publisher E-mail: starherald@wespub.com

General newspaper. **Founded:** 1901. **Freq:** Tues.-Sun. (morn.). **Print Method:** Offset. **Trim Size:** 13 x 21 3/4. **Cols./Page:** 6. **Col. Width:** 26 nonpareils. **Col. Depth:** 301 agate lines. **Key Personnel:** Steven L. Miller, Editor, phone (308)632-9055, smiller@wespub.com; Steven Hungerford, Publisher, phone (308)632-9009, hungerford@wespub.com; Steve Frederick, Asst. Editor, phone (308)632-9054, sfrederick@wespub.com; Johnny Aguirre, Advertising Mgr., phone (308)632-9039, jaguirre@wespub.com; Debbie Bohl, Dir. of Business and Personnel Services, phone (308)632-9008, dbohl@wespub.com; Roger Tollefson, Operations Dir., phone (308)632-9019, rtollefson@wespub.com; Jaci Conrad, Marketing Dir., phone (308)632-9038, jconrad@wespub.com. **USPS:** 485-960. **Subscription Rates:** $107.25 carrier delivery; $126 mail delivery. **Remarks:** Accepts advertising. **Alt. Formats:** Microform.
Ad Rates: GLR: $.65   **Circ:** Tues.-Fri. 15,939
BW: $1,341.54   Sat. 15,939
4C: $310   Sun. 16,641
PCI: $10.28

18361 KCMI-FM - 96.9
PO Box 1888   Phone: (308)632-5264
Scottsbluff, NE 69363-1888   Fax: (308)635-0104
E-mail: cmi@prairieweb.com

Format: Religious. **Networks:** USA Radio. **Owner:** Christian Media Inc., at above address. **Founded:** 1981. **Operating Hours:** Continuous. **ADI:** Cheyenne, WY-Scottsbluff, NE (Sterling, CO). **Key Personnel:** Dale Brown, General Mgr.; Glenn Hascall, Program Dir. **Wattage:** 100,000. **Ad Rates:** $3.30-5 for 15 seconds; $6.50 for 30 seconds; $9.50 for 60 seconds.

18362 KDUH-TV - 4
PO Box 1529   Phone: (308)632-3071
Scottsbluff, NE 69363   Fax: (308)632-3596

Format: Commercial TV. **Networks:** ABC. **Operating Hours:** Continuous. **ADI:** Cheyenne, WY-Scottsbluff, NE (Sterling, CO). **Key Personnel:** Gene Roland, General Mgr.; Jerry Dishong, Operations Mgr.; Tom Urdiales, Production Mgr.; Jim Moritz, News Dir. **Wattage:** 100,000. **Ad Rates:** $35-250 for 30 seconds; $70-500 for 60 seconds.

18363 KMOR-FM - 92.9
PO Box 532   Phone: (308)632-5667
Scottsbluff, NE 69363   Fax: (308)635-1905
Free: (800)592-5667

Format: Contemporary Hit Radio (CHR). **Networks:** AP. **Founded:** 1978. **Operating Hours:** Continuous; 5% network, 95% local. **ADI:** Cheyenne, WY-Scottsbluff, NE (Sterling, CO). **Key Personnel:** Michael J. Tracy, General Mgr.; Julie Marshall, Sales Mgr.; Judy Wilson, Station Mgr. **Wattage:** 100,000. **Ad Rates:** Advertising accepted; rates available upon request. **URL:** http://www.tracybroadcasting.com.

18364 KNEB-AM - 960
PO Box 239   Phone: (308)632-7121
Scottsbluff, NE 69363-0239   Fax: (308)635-1079
E-mail: kneb@ricochet.net

Format: Country; Agricultural. **Networks:** ABC; Mutual Broadcasting System. **Founded:** 1947. **Operating Hours:** 5 a.m.-1 a.m. Mon.-Sat.; 5 a.m.-midnight Sun. **ADI:** Cheyenne, WY-Scottsbluff, NE (Sterling, CO). **Key Personnel:** Marty Martinson, Manager; Barbara Martinson, Sales Mgr.; Dennis Ernest, Program Dir.; Les Proctor, Chief Engineer. **Wattage:** 1000 day; 500 night. **Ad Rates:** $10.00-35 for 30 seconds; $15.00-52.50 for 60 seconds. $7.50-$15.00 for 30 seconds; $11.50-$23.00 for 60 seconds. Combined advertising rates available with KNEB-FM.

18365 KNEB-FM - 94.1
PO Box 239   Phone: (308)632-7121
Scottsbluff, NE 69363-0239   Fax: (308)635-1079
E-mail: dstrang@nyx.cs.du.edu; kneb@ricochet.net

Format: Contemporary Country; Agricultural. **Networks:** ABC. **Owner:** Panhandle Broadcasting Inc., 2302 South Beltune E., Scottsbluff, NE 69361. **Founded:** 1961. **Operating Hours:** 5 a.m.-1 a.m.; 10% network, 90% local. **ADI:** Cheyenne, WY-Scottsbluff, NE (Sterling, CO). **Key Personnel:** Marty Martinson, Contact; Dennis Ernest, Program Dir.; Bruce Gaarder, Contact. **Wattage:** 100,000. **Ad Rates:** $10.00-35 for 30 seconds; $15.00-52 for 60 seconds. $7.50-$15.00 for 30 seconds; $11.50-$23.00 for 60 seconds. Combined advertising rates available with KNEB-AM.

18366 KOAQ-AM - 690
PO Box 1263   Phone: (308)635-2690
Scottsbluff, NE 69361   Fax: (308)635-1905
Free: (800)592-5667

Format: Oldies. **Networks:** AP. **Founded:** 1961. **Formerly:** KEYR-AM (1989). **Operating Hours:** Continuous; 10% network, 90% local. **ADI:** Cheyenne, WY-Scottsbluff, NE (Sterling, CO). **Key Personnel:** Michael J. Tracy, General Mgr., miket@prariewev.com; Julie Marshall, Sales Mgr., phone (308)632-5667, fax (308)632-6452; Judy Wilson, Station Mgr., phone (308)632-5667, fax (308)632-6452. **Wattage:** 1000. **Ad Rates:** Advertising accepted; rates available upon request. **URL:** http://www.tracybroadcasting.com.

18367 KOLT-AM - 1320
PO Box 660   Phone: (308)632-5667
Scottsbluff, NE 69363   Fax: (308)632-6452

Format: Talk. **Founded:** 1930. **Operating Hours:** Continuous. **ADI:** Cheyenne, WY-Scottsbluff, NE (Sterling, CO). **Key Personnel:** Michael J. Tracy, General Mgr.; Julie Marsell, Sales Mgr., phone (308)632-8450; July Wilson, Station Mgr., phone (308)635-8593. **Local Programs:** *Sports*, Scott Walker. **Wattage:** 5000 day; 1000 night. **Ad Rates:** Advertising accepted; rates available upon request. **URL:** http://www.tracybroadcasting.com.

18368 TCI Cablevision of Nebraska
1602 Ave. A   Phone: (308)635-3163
Scottsbluff, NE 69361   Fax: (308)635-1721

Owner: Tele-Communications Inc., Terrace Tower II, 5619 DTC Pkwy., Englewood, CO 80111, (303)267-5500. **Founded:** 1968. **Key Personnel:** John W. Steinmark, General Mgr.; Tim Landrum, Chief Engineer; Starr Lehl, Office Mgr. **Cities Served:** Bayard, Bridgeport, Gering, Kimball, Melbeta, Minatare, Mitchell, Morrill, Scottsbluff, Terrytown, NE: subscribing households 12,000; 30 channels; 7 community access channels.

SCRIBNER

18369 Rustler Sentinel
P.O. Box 370   Phone: (402)664-3198
Scribner, NE 68057   Fax: (402)664-3141
Publisher E-mail: rustler@tvsonline.net

General newspaper. **Founded:** Apr. 1885. **Freq:** Weekly. **Print Method:** Offset. **Trim Size:** 13 x 9 3/4. **Cols./Page:** 5. **Col. Width:** 28 nonpareils. **Col. Depth:** 182 agate lines. **Key Personnel:** Kathy Lodl, Managing Editor. **USPS:** 630-438. **Subscription Rates:** $20; $23 elsewhere in-state; $25 out of state. **Formed by the merger of:** Hooper Sentinel; Scribner Rustler.
Ad Rates: BW: $4   **Circ:** Paid 2000
SAU: $5.80   Free 13
PCI: $5

SEWARD

18370 Seward County Independent
129 S. 6th St.   Phone: (402)643-3676
Box 449   Fax: (402)643-6774
Seward, NE 68434-0449
Publication E-mail: sc93114@navix.net

Community newspaper. **Founded:** 1891. **Freq:** Weekly (Wed.). **Print Method:** Offset. Uses mats. **Cols./Page:** 7. **Col. Width:** 12.2 picas. **Col. Depth:** 21 1/4 inches. **Key Personnel:** Lori Shriner, Managing Editor; Mark Rhoades, Publisher; Lynn Dance, Advertising Mgr. **Subscription Rates:** $25 individuals; $27 out of area; $38 out of state. **Remarks:** Accepts advertising.
Ad Rates: BW: $803.25   **Circ:** Paid 3,591
4C: $1,223.25   Free 107
SAU: $5.40

18371 The Weekender
129 S. 6th St.   Phone: (402)643-3676
Box 449   Fax: (402)643-6774
Seward, NE 68434
Shopping guide. **Freq:** Weekly. **Print Method:** Offset. **Cols./Page:** 7. **Col. Width:** 12.2 picas. **Col. Depth:** 21.25 inches. **Key Personnel:** Lori Shriner, Editor; Mark Rhoades, Publisher; Lynn Dance, Advertising Mgr. **Subscription Rates:** Free in county; $19 out of area. **Remarks:** Accepts advertising.
Ad Rates: BW: $803.25   **Circ:** Free ‡4,900
4C: $1,223.25
SAU: $5.40

SHELBY

18372 Shelby Sun
Polk County News
Box 8   Phone: (402)747-2431
Shelby, NE 68662   Fax: (402)764-5341

Community newspaper. **Founded:** 1890. **Freq:** Weekly (Thurs.). **Print Method:** Offset. **Cols./Page:** 6. **Col. Width:** 25 nonpareils. **Col. Depth:** 294 agate lines. **Key Personnel:** Myrla Grossnicklaus, Editor; Bill Thompson, Publisher; Jocey Branting, Editor. **Subscription Rates:** $23; $28 out of state. **Remarks:** Accepts advertising.
Ad Rates: GLR: $.16   **Circ:** ‡900
PCI: $5

SHELTON

18373 The Shelton Clipper
Clipper Publishing Co.
PO Box 640 Phone: (308)647-5158
Shelton, NE 68876-0640
Local newspaper. **Founded:** 1884. **Freq:** Weekly (Wed.). **Print Method:** Offset. **Trim Size:** 13 3/4 x 22. **Cols./Page:** 6. **Col. Width:** 12.5 picas. **Col. Depth:** 20.5 inches. **Key Personnel:** Laura L. Kozin, Editor; Steve Glenn, Publisher. **USPS:** 492-780. **Subscription Rates:** $17; $25 out of state. **Remarks:** Accepts advertising. **Formerly:** Clipper.
Ad Rates: BW: $275.91 **Circ:** Paid ‡1,006
PCI: $3.50 Free ‡8

SIDNEY

18374 The Sidney Telegraph
Western Publishing Co.
809 Illinois St. Phone: (308)254-5555
PO Box 219 Fax: (308)254-5607
Sidney, NE 69162
General newspaper. **Founded:** 1873. **Freq:** Tues. & Thurs. (Eve.), Sat. (morn.). **Print Method:** Offset. **Cols./Page:** 6. **Col. Width:** 2 1/16 inches. **Col. Depth:** 301 agate lines. **Key Personnel:** Jeff Stahla, Editor, jstahla@sidneytlegraph.com; Ralph Olsen, Publisher, rolsen@sidneytelegraph.com. **USPS:** 495-780. **Subscription Rates:** $52 individuals by mail or carrier. **Remarks:** Accepts advertising. **Alt. Formats:** CD-ROM.
Ad Rates: GLR: $.54 **Circ:** 3,000
BW: $890
SAU: $6.90
PCI: $6.90

18375 KSID-AM - 1340
PO Box 37 Phone: (308)254-5803
Sidney, NE 69162 Fax: (308)254-5901

Format: Contemporary Country; News; Agricultural; Sports. **Simulcasts:** KIMB-AM, Kimball, NE. **Networks:** ABC; Brownfield. **Founded:** 1952. **Operating Hours:** Continuous. **Key Personnel:** Elizabeth Young, President; David Young, General Mgr. **Wattage:** 1000.

18376 TCI Cablevision of Nebraska
PO Box 298
Sidney, NE 69162

Owner: Tele-Communications Inc., 5619 DTC Pkwy., Englewood, CO 80111, (303)267-5500, Fax: (303)779-1228. **Founded:** 1958. **Key Personnel:** Jeffrey D. Mount, General Mgr.; Rita Bartling, Office Mgr. **Cities Served:** Sidney, NE: subscribing households 2,450; 33 channels; 1 community access channel.

SOUTH SIOUX CITY

18377 South Sioux City Star
Star Printing & Publishing
2520 Dakota Ave. Phone: (402)494-4264
PO Box 157 Fax: (402)494-2414
South Sioux City, NE 68776
Publication E-mail: sscstar@aol.com

Newspaper with a Republican orientation. **Founded:** 1909. **Freq:** Weekly (Thurs.). **Print Method:** Web offset. **Cols./Page:** 6. **Col. Width:** 12 picas. **Col. Depth:** 21 inches. **Key Personnel:** Darlene Taylor, Editor; Kent Broyhill, President. **Subscription Rates:** $30 individuals. **URL:** http://www.sscdc.net.
Ad Rates: SAU: $8.25 **Circ:** ‡4,000
PCI: $7

SPALDING

Cedar Rapids Press - See Cedar Rapids

18378 Spalding Enterprise
102 S. Cedar Phone: (308)497-2153
PO Box D
Spalding, NE 68665
Community newspaper. **Founded:** 1901. **Freq:** Weekly (Thurs.). **Print Method:** Letterpress. **Cols./Page:** 5. **Col. Width:** 22 nonpareils. **Col. Depth:** 224 agate lines. **Key Personnel:** David Bopp, Editor. **USPS:** 509-200. **Subscription Rates:** $20. **Remarks:** Accepts advertising.
Ad Rates: GLR: $.15 **Circ:** ‡1,040
SAU: $2.50
PCI: $2.25

SPENCER

18379 The Spencer Advocate
Box 187 Phone: (402)589-1010
Spencer, NE 68777 Fax: (402)589-1010

Community newspaper. **Founded:** 1891. **Freq:** Weekly (Thurs.). **Print Method:** Offset. **Cols./Page:** 7. **Col. Width:** 12 picas. **Col. Depth:** 21 1/4 inches. **Key Personnel:** Leon Wells, Editor and Publisher. **USPS:** 008-480. **Subscription Rates:** $15; $20 out of area; $25 out of state. **Remarks:** Color advertising not accepted.
Ad Rates: GLR: $.012 **Circ:** ‡1,134
BW: $175
SAU: $2.30

SPRINGVIEW

18380 Springview Herald
Box 369 Phone: (402)497-3651
Springview, NE 68778 Fax: (402)497-2651

Community newspaper. **Founded:** 1886. **Freq:** Weekly (Thurs.). **Print Method:** Offset. **Cols./Page:** 5. **Col. Width:** 20 nonpareils. **Col. Depth:** 210 agate lines. **Key Personnel:** Karen Kurzenberger, Editor and Publisher. **USPS:** 513-040. **Subscription Rates:** $16 local; $20 out of state.
Ad Rates: BW: $250 **Circ:** ‡850
SAU: $3.50
PCI: $3.50

STANTON†, pop. 1,603.

Stanton Co. (NE). 10 m SE of Norfolk. Feed mill; cattle feeding. Ships livestock. Diversified farming.

18381 The Register
Stanton Printing Co.
907 Ivy St. Phone: (402)439-2173
PO Box 719 Fax: (402)439-2273
Stanton, NE 68779
Publication E-mail: reggie@stanton.net

Newspaper. **Founded:** 1879. **Freq:** Weekly (Wed.). **Print Method:** Offset. **Trim Size:** 7 x 11 1/2. **Cols./Page:** 6. **Col. Width:** 26 nonpareils. **Col. Depth:** 301 agate lines. **Key Personnel:** Laura M. Erbst, Editor and Publisher. **USPS:** 518-660. **Subscription Rates:** $17.95 individuals. **Remarks:** Accepts advertising.
Ad Rates: GLR: $.18 **Circ:** ‡1,624
BW: $300
SAU: $2.52
PCI: $2.94

STAPLETON†, pop. 340.

Logan Co. (C). 35 m NE of North Platte. Residential

18382 Arnold Sentinel
Creative Printers, Inc.
238 Main St. Phone: (308)636-2444
Stapleton, NE 69163 Fax: (308)636-2445

Community newspaper serving Custer county. **Founded:** 1914. **Freq:** Weekly. **Print Method:** Offset. **Trim Size:** 12 x 18. **Cols./Page:** 5. **Col. Width:** 12 1/2 picas. **Col. Depth:** 16 inches. **Key Personnel:** Marcia R. Hora, Editor; Arthur M. French, Publisher; Janet Larreau, Advertising Mgr. **USPS:** 032-480. **Subscription Rates:** $17; $19 out of state. **Remarks:** Accepts advertising.
Ad Rates: SAU: $4 **Circ:** ‡1,050

18383 The Graphic
Creative Printers, Inc.
238 Main St. Phone: (308)636-2444
Stapleton, NE 69163 Fax: (308)636-2445

Local newspaper. **Founded:** 1889. **Freq:** Weekly (Thurs.). **Print Method:** Offset. **Cols./Page:** 5. **Col. Width:** 30 nonpareils. **Col. Depth:** 224 agate lines. **Key Personnel:** Audrey M. French, Editor; Arthur M. French, Publisher; Marcia Hora, Advertising Mgr. **Subscription Rates:** $14; $15 out of area. **Remarks:** Accepts advertising.
Ad Rates: BW: $240 **Circ:** 467
SAU: $3.50

18384 The Stapleton Enterprise
Creative Printers, Inc.
238 Main St. Phone: (308)636-2444
Stapleton, NE 69163 Fax: (308)636-2445

Local newspaper. **Founded:** 1912. **Freq:** Weekly (Thurs.). **Print Method:** Offset. **Cols./Page:** 5. **Col. Width:** 12.5 nonpareils. **Col. Depth:** 224 agate lines. **Key Personnel:** Marcia Hora, Editor; Arthur M. French, Publisher. **Subscription Rates:** $15; $16 out of area. **Remarks:** Accepts advertising.
Ad Rates: BW: $280 **Circ:** ‡725
SAU: $4.00
PCI: $4.00

STROMSBURG, pop. 1,290.

Polk Co. (EC). 50 m NW of Lincoln. Buckley Park, Swedish Festival. Stock, grain farms. Corn, wheat, hay, milo, soybeans.

18385 The Headlight
Box 365 Phone: (402)764-5341
Stromsburg, NE 68666
Newspaper. **Founded:** 1885. **Freq:** Weekly (Thurs.). **Print Method:** Offset. **Cols./Page:** 6. **Col. Width:** 2 inches. **Col. Depth:** 294 agate lines. **Key Personnel:** William H. Thompson, Editor and Publisher. **Subscription Rates:** $19. **Remarks:** Accepts advertising.
Ad Rates: GLR: $.21 **Circ:** ‡1,281

SUPERIOR, pop. 2,502.

Nuckolls Co. (S). 90 m SW of Lincoln. Manufactures cement and cheese, products. Alfalfa dehydrating plant. Diversified farming. Grain, alfalfa, cattle.

18386 KRFS-AM - 1600
RR 2, Box 149 Phone: (402)879-4741
Superior, NE 68978-9802 Fax: (402)879-4741

Format: Country; Agricultural. **Networks:** ABC; Brownfield. **Owner:** Valley Broadcasting Co., Inc., at above address, (402)879-3370. **Founded:** 1959. **Operating Hours:** 6 a.m.-sunset; 15% network, 85% local. **Key Personnel:** Cory Kopsa, General Mgr.; Becky Jacobitz, Traffic Mgr.; Daryl Stanley, PSA Director. **Wattage:** 500. **Ad Rates:** $4.50 for 30 seconds; $7.50 for 60 seconds.

SUTHERLAND, pop. 1,238.

Lincoln Co. (SW). 19 m W of North Platte. Diversified farming. Corn, hay, cattle.

18387 Courier-Times
Box 367 Phone: (308)386-4617
Sutherland, NE 69165 Fax: (308)386-2437

Community newspaper. **Subtitle:** Courier Times. **Founded:** 1895. **Freq:** Weekly (Thurs.). **Print Method:** Offset. **Cols./Page:** 5. **Col. Depth:** 13 inches. **Key Personnel:** Trenda G. Seifer, Publisher/Advertising Manager; Ray Seifer, Sports Editor/Photo Editor; Pat Dickerson, News Editor. **USPS:** 564-580. **Subscription Rates:** $13; $18 out of state; $45 other countries.
Ad Rates: GLR: $.16 **Circ:** ‡1,400
BW: $260
4C: $500
SAU: $4

SUTTON, pop. 1,416.

Clay Co. (S). 30 m E of Hastings. Agriculture. Stock. Corn, soybeans, wheat, milo.

18388 Clay County News
207 N. Saunders Phone: (402)773-5576
Box 405 Fax: (402)773-5577
Sutton, NE 68979-0405
Newspaper with a Republican orientation. **Founded:** 1884. **Freq:** Weekly (Thurs.). **Print Method:** Offset. **Cols./Page:** 6. **Col. Width:** 26 nonpareils. **Col. Depth:** 294 agate lines. **Key Personnel:** Bill Brown, Editor; Donald L. Russell, Publisher; Linda A. Russell, Publisher. **USPS:** 116-700. **Subscription Rates:** $19.50 individuals; $24.50 out of area. **Remarks:** Accepts advertising.
Ad Rates: GLR: $.23 **Circ:** Paid 3,005
BW: $544 Free 50
SAU: $4.40
PCI: $4.55

SYRACUSE, pop. 1,638.

Otoe Co. (SE). 30 m SE of Lincoln. Glass factory. Stock, grain, poultry farms. Corn, wheat, oats.

18389 Penny Press 1
Maverick Media, Inc.
123 W. 17th St. Phone: (402)269-2135
PO Box O Fax: (402)269-2392
Syracuse, NE 68446
Shopper (tabloid). **Freq:** Weekly (Mon.). **Print Method:** Offset. **Trim Size:** 11 1/2 x 16. **Cols./Page:** 6. **Col. Width:** 9 1/2 picas. **Col. Depth:** 15 inches. **Key Personnel:** William Welsh, President. **Subscription Rates:** $24 by mail; Free. **Remarks:**

Combined advertising rates available with six Maverick Media Penny Press papers.
Ad Rates: GLR: $0.56 **Circ:** Free ‡20,850
BW: $831.60
4C: $1,111.60
SAU: $10.35
PCI: $7.85

18390 Syracuse Journal-Democrat
Maverick Media, Inc.
123 W. 17th St. Phone: (402)269-2135
PO Box O Fax: (402)269-2392
Syracuse, NE 68446
Newspaper with a Democratic orientation. **Founded:** 1878. **Freq:** Weekly (Thurs.). **Print Method:** Offset. **Trim Size:** 13 x 21 1/2. **Cols./Page:** 6. **Col. Width:** 12 picas. **Col. Depth:** 310 agate lines. **Key Personnel:** David Swanson, Editor; William Welsh, Publisher. **USPS:** 531-620. **Subscription Rates:** $18 individuals; $25 out of area; $29 out of state. **Remarks:** Accepts advertising.
Ad Rates: GLR: $.26 **Circ:** ‡2,694
BW: $592.11
4C: $872.11
SAU: $4.84
PCI: $4.15

TAYLOR

18391 Taylor Clarion
Burwell Tribune Newspapers
103 N. 1st St. Phone: (308)527-4210
PO Box 547 Fax: (308)346-4018
Sargent, NE 68874
Local newspaper. **Founded:** 1884. **Freq:** Weekly (Wed.). **Print Method:** Offset. **Cols./Page:** 8. **Col. Width:** 10.5 nonpareils. **Col. Depth:** 976 agate lines. **Key Personnel:** Byron Neiman, Publisher. **Subscription Rates:** $17. $19 out of state. **Remarks:** Accepts advertising.
Ad Rates: GLR: $.35 **Circ:** Paid 375
PCI: $4.98 Non-paid 25

TECUMSEH†, pop. 1,926.

Johnson Co. (SE). 60 m SE of Lincoln. Poultry eviscerating plant. Grain, stock, poultry farms. Corn, wheat, alfalfa.

18392 Chieftain
Family Newspapers, Inc.
241 Clay St. Phone: (402)335-3394
PO Box 809 Fax: (402)335-3496
Tecumseh, NE 68450-0809
Community newspaper. **Founded:** 1869. **Freq:** Weekly (Thurs.). **Print Method:** Offset. **Cols./Page:** 6. **Col. Width:** 12 1/2 ems. **Col. Depth:** 21 1/2 inches. **Key Personnel:** Ann Wickett, Editor; Teri Pendell, Publisher; Michael Kunzman, Publisher. **USPS:** 536-000. **Subscription Rates:** $20 individuals; $25 out of state. **Remarks:** Accepts advertising. **Alt. Formats:** CD-ROM.
Ad Rates: SAU: $4 **Circ:** 2,613
PCI: $4.50

TEKAMAH†, pop. 1,886.

Burt Co. (NE). 42 m NW of Omaha. Creamery. Diversified farming. Corn, Wheat, hay.

18393 Burt County Plaindealer
Plaindealer Publishing Co.
Box 239 Phone: (402)374-2226
Tekamah, NE 68061 Fax: (402)374-2739
Free: (800)888-1380
Publication E-mail: support@midwestmessenger.com

Local newspaper. **Founded:** Apr. 1934. **Freq:** Weekly (Tues.). **Print Method:** Offset. **Cols./Page:** 6. **Col. Width:** 26 nonpareils. **Col. Depth:** 301 agate lines. **Key Personnel:** Brenda Cornelius, Managing Editor; Joe Zink, Publisher; Jim Ball, Advertising Mgr. **USPS:** 080-160. **Subscription Rates:** $27; $33. **Remarks:** Accepts advertising.
Ad Rates: BW: $548.25 **Circ:** ‡2,300
4C: $4.50
SAU: $6.75
PCI: $4

18394 Midwest Messenger
Plaindealer Publishing Co.
Box 239 Phone: (402)374-2226
Tekamah, NE 68061 Fax: (402)374-2739
Free: (800)888-1380

Farm trade shopper. **Founded:** Jan. 1969. **Freq:** Biweekly 3 editions geographical. **Print Method:** Offset. **Trim Size:** 11 x 17. **Cols./Page:** 6. **Col. Width:** 10 picas. **Col. Depth:** 16 inches. **Key Personnel:** Joe Zink, Publisher; James Beaver, Sales Mgr. **Subscription Rates:** $23.50. **Remarks:** Accepts advertising.
Ad Rates: BW: $5,328 **Circ:** Free ‡154,380
4C: $6,228
SAU: $11
PCI: $55.50

TILDEN

18395 Tilden Citizen
PO Box 280 Phone: (402)368-5315
Tilden, NE 68781 Fax: (402)368-5315

Community newspaper. **Founded:** 1892. **Freq:** Weekly (Wed.). **Print Method:** Offset. **Trim Size:** 16 1/2 x 22 3/4. **Cols./Page:** 7. **Col. Width:** 12 1/2 picas. **Col. Depth:** 21 inches. **Key Personnel:** Leslie Falter, Editor and Publisher. **Subscription Rates:** $13; $15 out of area; $17 out of state. **Remarks:** Color advertising not accepted.
Ad Rates: SAU: $2.30 **Circ:** 1,300

TRENTON†, pop. 770.

Hitchcock Co. (SW). 70 m S of North Platte. Swanson Lake, fishing, boating, camping, water skiing. Hitchcock County Museum. Ships livestock, grain. Stocks, dairy, poultry, grain farms. Wheat, corn.

18396 The Hitchcock County News
PO Box 278 Phone: (308)334-5226
Trenton, NE 69044-0278 Fax: (308)334-5226

County newspaper. **Founded:** 1885. **Freq:** Weekly (Wed.). **Print Method:** Offset. **Trim Size:** 13 1/2 x 22 3/4. **Cols./Page:** 6. **Col. Width:** 12 picas. **Col. Depth:** 21 1/2 inches. **Key Personnel:** G.B. Crapson, Editor and Publisher; Joleen Reeder, Business Mgr. **USPS:** 579-500. **Subscription Rates:** $18 individuals; $28 out of area.
Ad Rates: GLR: $.64 **Circ:** ‡1,492
BW: $890.10
4C: $1,160.10
SAU: $6.90
PCI: $6.90

VALENTINE†, pop. 2,829.

Cherry Co. (NW). 120 m N of North Platte. Valentine National Waterfowl Refuge. State fish hatchery. Canoeing, fishing. Fur and metal processing. Cattle ranches. Stock, dairy, grain farms.

18397 Valentine Newspaper
122 W. 2nd St. Phone: (402)376-3742
PO Box 450
Valentine, NE 69201
Community newspaper. **Founded:** 1887. **Freq:** Weekly (Wed.). **Print Method:** Offset. **Cols./Page:** 7. **Col. Width:** 26 nonpareils. **Col. Depth:** 297 agate lines. **Key Personnel:** Ray K. Dover, Publisher. **Subscription Rates:** $15; $18 out of area. **Remarks:** Accepts advertising.
Ad Rates: SAU: $2.90 **Circ:** ‡2,600

18398 KVSH-AM - 940
126 W. 3rd St. Phone: (402)376-2400
Valentine, NE 69201 Fax: (402)376-2402
Free: (800)658-4442

Format: Middle-of-the-Road (MOR). **Networks:** ABC. **Founded:** 1961. **Operating Hours:** 6 a.m.-10 p.m. **Key Personnel:** Dave Otradousky, Manager. **Wattage:** 5000. **Ad Rates:** $4.85 for 10 seconds; $6.65 for 30 seconds; $7.90 for 60 seconds.

VERDIGRE

18399 Verdigre Eagle
202 Main Phone: (402)668-2242
PO Box 309 Fax: (402)668-2242
Verdigre, NE 68783
Community newspaper. **Founded:** 1966. **Freq:** Weekly (Thurs.). **Print Method:** Offset. **Cols./Page:** 7. **Col. Width:** 2 inches. **Col. Depth:** 21 inches. **Key Personnel:** Daniel J. Pavlik, Editor and Publisher. **Subscription Rates:** $15; $18 out of area; $20 out of state. **Remarks:** Accepts advertising.
Ad Rates: BW: $400.00 **Circ:** ‡1,500
SAU: $3.00

WAHOO†, pop. 3,578.

Saunders Co. (E). 35 m W of Omaha. Manufactures railroad parts, culverts, pre-cut houses, block cement, hog houses. Grain, dairy, poultry farms. Wheat, corn.

18400 Wahoo Newspaper
Saunders County Publishing Inc.
564 N. Broadway Phone: (402)443-4162
Wahoo, NE 68066 Fax: (402)443-4459

Community newspaper. **Founded:** 1887. **Freq:** Weekly (Thurs.). **Print Method:** Offset. **Trim Size:** 14 x 22 3/4. **Cols./Page:** 6. **Col. Width:** 23 nonpareils. **Col. Depth:** 308 agate lines. **Key Personnel:** Zean E. Carney, Editor. **Subscription Rates:** $24; $27 out of state. **Remarks:** Accepts advertising.
Ad Rates: BW: $544.38 **Circ:** 4,259
SAU: $4.22

WAKEFIELD, pop. 1,125.

Dixon Co. (NE). 10 m NE of Wayne.

18401 The Wakefield Republican
PO Box 110 Phone: (402)287-2323
Wakefield, NE 68784-0110
Newspaper. **Founded:** 1882. **Freq:** Weekly (Thurs.). **Print Method:** Offset. **Cols./Page:** 5. **Col. Width:** 23 nonpareils. **Col. Depth:** 217 agate lines. **Key Personnel:** William H. Rischmueller, Editor and Publisher; Linda Rischmueller, Editor and Publisher. **USPS:** 664-600. **Subscription Rates:** $15 in area; $20 rest of state; $22 out of state. **Remarks:** Accepts advertising.
Ad Rates: BW: $271.25 **Circ:** ‡1,220
SAU: $3.80
PCI: $3.50

WAUSA, pop. 647.

Knox Co. (NE). 35 m N of Norfolk. Recreational. Hunting. Grain, stock, dairy, poultry farms. Corn, soybeans, oats, alfalfa, barley.

18402 The Wausa Gazette
PO Box G Phone: (402)586-2661
Wausa, NE 68786-0318
Publisher E-mail: wausagzt@bloomnet.com

Founded: 1898. **Freq:** Weekly (Thurs.). **Print Method:** Offset. **Cols./Page:** 6. **Col. Width:** 12 1/2 picas. **Col. Depth:** 301 agate lines. **Key Personnel:** Robert P. Reinhardt, Editor and Publisher. **Subscription Rates:** $17.50 in state; $24 out of state.
Ad Rates: GLR: $.22 **Circ:** ‡1,025
SAU: $3.10

WAVERLY, pop. 1,723.

Lancaster Co. (NE). 12 m NE of Lincoln.

18403 Waverly News
PO Box 100 Phone: (402)786-2344
Waverly, NE 68462 Fax: (402)786-2344

Community newspaper. **Founded:** May 1972. **Freq:** Weekly. **Print Method:** Offset. **Trim Size:** 13 3/4 x 22 3/4. **Cols./Page:** 6. **Col. Width:** 2.08 inches. **Col. Depth:** 21 1/2 inches. **Key Personnel:** Jodie Fuson, News Editor; Zean Carney, Publisher; Peg Brown, Office Mgr. **USPS:** 950-780. **Subscription Rates:** $20 individuals; $23 out of state. **Remarks:** Accepts advertising.
Ad Rates: SAU: $3.60 **Circ:** 1,541

WAYNE†, pop. 5,240.

Wayne Co. (NE). 31 m NE of Norfolk. Wayne State College. Manufactures waterbed mattresses, modular homes, steel combination windows, semi-truck trailers. Livestock, grain, dairy farms.

18404 The Wayne Herald
114 Main St. Phone: (402)375-2600
Box 70 Fax: (402)375-1888
Wayne, NE 68787
Free: (800)672-3418

Community newspaper. **Founded:** 1875. **Freq:** Weekly (Tues. and Fri.). **Print Method:** Offset. **Cols./Page:** 6. **Col. Width:** 21 1/2 nonpareils. **Col. Depth:** 129 agate lines. **Key Personnel:** James R. Shanks, Publisher; Kevin Peterson, Editor; Susie Ensz, Advertising Mgr. **USPS:** 670-560. **Subscription Rates:** $.75.
Ad Rates: GLR: $.55 **Circ:** Paid 2,600
BW: $992 Free 9,300
4C: $1,172
SAU: $7.69

18405 Wayne Stater
Wayne State College
200 E. 10th St. Phone: (402)375-2200
Wayne, NE 68787 Fax: (402)375-7204

Collegiate newspaper. **Founded:** 1911. **Freq:** Weekly (Wed.)

(during the academic year). **Print Method:** Offset. **Cols./Page:** 5. **Col. Width:** 11 picas. **Col. Depth:** 301 agate lines. **Key Personnel:** Edmund Elfers, Editor, phone (402)375-7488. **Subscription Rates:** Free. $12 out of area. **Remarks:** Accepts advertising.
Ad Rates: BW: $195 **Circ:** Paid 800
PCI: $3.40 Non-paid 4,000

18406 KTCH-AM - 1590
PO Box 413 Phone: (402)375-3700
Wayne, NE 68787-0413 Fax: (402)375-5402
Free: (800)456-9906

Format: Country. **Simulcasts:** KTCH-FM. **Networks:** ABC; Brownfield; Mid-America Ag. **Owner:** Wayne Radio Inc., at above address. **Founded:** 1968. **Operating Hours:** 5:30 a.m.-11 p.m.; 10% network, 90% local. **ADI:** Sioux City, IA. **Key Personnel:** Leo Ahmann, General Mgr.; Dan Baddorf, Program Dir. **Wattage:** 2500. **Ad Rates:** $9.70 for 30 seconds; $11.50 for 60 seconds. Combined advertising rates available with KNEN-AM.

18407 KTCH-FM - 104.9
Hwy. 35 W. Phone: (402)375-3700
Wayne, NE 68787 Fax: (402)375-5402
Free: (800)456-9906

Format: Country. **Simulcasts:** KTCH-AM. **Networks:** ABC; Mid-America Ag; Brownfield. **Owner:** KTCH, Inc., Box 413, Wayne, NE 68787. **Founded:** 1975. **Operating Hours:** 5:30 a.m.-11 p.m.; 10% network, 90% local. **ADI:** Sioux City, IA. **Key Personnel:** Leo Ahmann, General Mgr.; Dan Baddorf, Program Mgr. **Wattage:** 3000. **Ad Rates:** $9.70 for 30 seconds; $11.50 for 60 seconds.

18408 KWSC-FM - 91.9
Wayne State College Phone: (402)375-7561
Wayne, NE 68787

Format: Album-Oriented Rock (AOR). **Networks:** Westwood One Radio. **Owner:** Wayne State College, at above address, (402)375-7000. **Founded:** 1971. **Operating Hours:** Continuous; 2% network, 98% local. **Key Personnel:** F.J. Higgins, General Mgr.; Travis Shultz, Program Dir.; Bruce Nelson, Music Dir.; Andy Keck, Promotions Dir.; Mike Kaup, Production Dir.; Darrin Kiger, Contact; Carrie Benjamin, News Dir.; Earl Norman, Contact; Dave Ogden, Contact. **Wattage:** 350. **Ad Rates:** Noncommercial.

WEST POINT†, pop. 3,609.

Cuming Co. (NE). 60 m NW of Omaha. Meat processing plants. Diversified farming. Corn, wheat, oats, soybeans, alfalfa, cattle, hogs.

18409 Elkhorn Valley Shopper
West Point News
PO Box 40 Phone: (402)372-2461
West Point, NE 68788 Fax: (402)372-3530

Shopper. **Founded:** 1964. **Freq:** Weekly (Wed.). **Print Method:** Offset. **Trim Size:** 11 3/8 x 14. **Cols./Page:** 6. **Col. Width:** 19 nonpareils. **Col. Depth:** 189 agate lines. **Key Personnel:** Tom Kelly, Publisher; Virginia Frye, Advertising Mgr. **Subscription Rates:** Free to area households; $22.50; $27.50 out of area. **Remarks:** Color advertising not accepted.
Ad Rates: BW: $518 **Circ:** Free ‡10,048
SAU: $6.90
PCI: $6.90

18410 West Point News
PO Box 40 Phone: (402)372-2461
West Point, NE 68788 Fax: (402)372-3530

Community newspaper. **Founded:** 1870. **Freq:** Weekly (Thurs.). **Print Method:** Offset. **Trim Size:** 14 x 22 3/4. **Cols./Page:** 6. **Col. Width:** 24 nonpareils. **Col. Depth:** 301 agate lines. **Key Personnel:** Tom Kelly, Publisher; Willis Mahannah, Editor. **USPS:** 675-780. **Remarks:** Accepts advertising.
Ad Rates: BW: $683.70 **Circ:** 4,150
SAU: $5.70
PCI: $6.90

18411 KTIC-AM - 840
1011 N. Licoln Phone: (402)372-5423
Box 84 Fax: (402)372-5425
West Point, NE 68788
E-mail: ktkam@navix.net

Format: Full Service; Agricultural. **Networks:** ABC. **Owner:** West Point Broadcasting, Inc., at above address, Lexington, NE. **Founded:** 1985. **Formerly:** KWPN-AM. **Operating Hours:** Daily. **ADI:** Omaha, NE. **Key Personnel:** Charles Brogan, Station Mgr. **Wattage:** 5000. **Ad Rates:** $5-45 for 30 seconds; $8-60 for 60 seconds. Combined advertising rates available with KWPN-FM.

18412 KWPN-FM - 107.9
1011 N Lincoln Phone: (402)372-5423
Box 84 Fax: (402)372-5425
West Point, NE 68788-0084
E-mail: kticam@navix.net

Format: Full Service. **Networks:** ABC. **Founded:** 1988. **Operating Hours:** Daily. **ADI:** Omaha, NE. **Key Personnel:** Charles Brogan, Station Mgr. **Wattage:** 50,000. **Ad Rates:** $4.25-14 for 30 seconds; $3.50-17 for 60 seconds. Combined advertising rates available with KTIL-AM.

WILBER

18413 The Wilber Republican
206 W. 3rd Phone: (402)821-2586
PO Box 457 Fax: (402)821-2586
Wilber, NE 68465
Community newspaper. **Founded:** 1887. **Freq:** Weekly (Wed.). **Print Method:** Offset. **Cols./Page:** 7. **Col. Width:** 12 picas. **Col. Depth:** 21 inches. **Key Personnel:** Kent M. Korinek, Publisher. **USPS:** 683-800. **Subscription Rates:** $18 individuals; $23 out of area. **Remarks:** Accepts advertising.
Ad Rates: GLR: $3.10 **Circ:** 1,500
BW: $391.02
SAU: $3.64
PCI: $3.64

WISNER, pop. 1,335.

Cuming Co. (NE). 29 m E of Norfolk. Ships livestock. Stock, grain, dairy, poultry farms. Cattle, corn.

18414 Wisner News-Chronicle
1014 Avenue E Phone: (402)529-3228
PO Box 460 Fax: (402)529-3279
Wisner, NE 68791
Free: (888)221-4338
Publication E-mail: wisnews@gpcom.net

Community newspaper. **Founded:** 1887. **Freq:** Weekly (Thurs.). **Print Method:** Offset. **Cols./Page:** 6. **Col. Width:** 25 nonpareils. **Col. Depth:** 294 agate lines. **Key Personnel:** Theodore M. Huettmann, Publisher, phone (402)529-3229. **USPS:** 689-000. **Subscription Rates:** $27.50; $30 out of area; $32.50 out of state. **Remarks:** Accepts advertising. **Alt. Formats:** CD-ROM.
Ad Rates: GLR: $.315 **Circ:** Paid ‡2,000
BW: $350 Free ‡45
4C: $550
PCI: $4.54

WOOD RIVER, pop. 1,334.

Hall Co. (C). 15 m SW of Grand Island. Residential.

18415 The Wood River Sunbeam
PO Box 356 Phone: (308)583-2241
Wood River, NE 68883-0356
Newspaper with a Republican orientation. **Founded:** 1890. **Freq:** Weekly (Wed.). **Print Method:** Offset. **Trim Size:** 11 1/4 x 17 1/2. **Cols./Page:** 5. **Col. Width:** 23 nonpareils. **Col. Depth:** 224 agate lines. **Key Personnel:** Douglas G. Hoschover, Editor and Publisher; Charlene Hoschover, Editor and Publisher; Arline Otto, Manager. **USPS:** 690-240. **Subscription Rates:** $14; $17.50 Others. **Remarks:** Accepts advertising alcoholic beverages and tobacco products.
Ad Rates: BW: $200 **Circ:** 1,113
SAU: $3.30
PCI: $2.50

WYMORE

18416 Wymore Arbor State
204 S. 7th Phone: (402)645-3344
Wymore, NE 68466 Fax: (402)645-3345

Community newspaper. **Freq:** Weekly (Thurs.). **Cols./Page:** 6. **Col. Width:** 12.5 picas. **Col. Depth:** 21.5 picas. **Key Personnel:** Michelle Casebeer, Manager. **Subscription Rates:** $20 individuals; $24 out of area per year. **Remarks:** Accepts advertising.
Ad Rates: PCI: $3.20 **Circ:** 1,700

YORK†, pop. 7,723.

York Co. (SEC). 50 m W of Lincoln. York College. Manufactures irrigation equipment, mobile homes, concrete products, electronics, aerospace components. Nursery; hatcheries. Agriculture. Corn, oats, alfalfa, milo, cattle, hogs.

18417 Trade & Transactions
Trade & Transactions, Inc.
1st St. & Lincoln Ave. Phone: (402)362-5561
York, NE 68467 Fax: (402)362-3697

Shopping guide for York, Polk, Hamilton, Seward, Fillmore, Butler and Saline Counties. **Founded:** 1971. **Freq:** Weekly (Tues.). **Print Method:** Offset. **Cols./Page:** 6. **Col. Width:** 1 5/8 inches. **Col. Depth:** 16 1/2 inches. **Key Personnel:** Ralph Pfeifer, President; Tom Scholz, General Mgr.; Ann Staton, Asst. Manager; Julie Green, Composition; Steve Green, Circulation Mgr. **Subscription Rates:** $25. **Remarks:** Accepts advertising.
Ad Rates: BW: $658.35 **Circ:** Paid 46
SAU: $7.70 Free 24,094
PCI: $6.65

18418 York News-Times
327 Platte Ave. Phone: (402)362-4478
PO Box 279 Fax: (402)362-6748
York, NE 68467-3547
Publication E-mail: yt52320@navix.net

General newspaper. **Founded:** Dec. 3, 1887. **Freq:** Daily (eve.) and Sat. (morn.). **Print Method:** Offset. **Cols./Page:** 6. **Col. Width:** 25 nonpareils. **Col. Depth:** 294 agate lines. **Key Personnel:** Dan Collin, Editor and Publisher, dcollin@cjnetworks.com; David H. Sjuts, Advertising Mgr., dsjuts@cjnetworks.com; Kelly Harre, Managing Editor. **USPS:** 686-100. **Subscription Rates:** $75.60 individuals. **Remarks:** Advertising accepted; rates available upon request.
Circ: 5,200

18419 KAWL-AM - 1370
RR 4, Box 121A Phone: (402)362-4433
York, NE 68467-9804 Fax: (402)362-6501

Format: Oldies; Full Service. **Networks:** ABC. **Founded:** 1954. **Operating Hours:** Continuous. **ADI:** Lincoln-Hastings-Kearney, NE. **Key Personnel:** Tom Robson, General Mgr. **Local Programs:** *It's Your Call* 10 a.m. Monday-Friday, Jack McConnel, Mailing contact. **Wattage:** 500. **Ad Rates:** $14 for 30 seconds; $20 for 60 seconds.

18420 KTMX-FM - 104.9
RR 4, Box 121A Phone: (402)362-4433
York, NE 68467-9804 Fax: (402)362-6501
E-mail: ka3309@navix.net

Format: Adult Contemporary. **Networks:** ABC. **Founded:** 1971. **Formerly:** KAWL-FM (1991). **Operating Hours:** Continuous. **ADI:** Lincoln-Hastings-Kearney, NE. **Key Personnel:** Tom Robson, General Mgr. **Wattage:** 25,000. **Ad Rates:** $14 for 30 seconds; $20 for 60 seconds.

18421 York Cablevision Inc.
114 W. 6th St. Phone: (402)421-0330
York, NE 68467 Fax: (402)421-0310
E-mail: shadval@netscape.com

Owner: Time Warner, at above address. **Founded:** Mar. 31, 1966. **Key Personnel:** Valerie Kramer, General Mgr.; Rick Hollmann, Systems Engineer. **Cities Served:** Seward, York, NE: subscribing households 4,924; 80 channels.

NEVADA

State Capital, CARSON CITY

Nevada is bounded on the north by Oregon and Idaho, east by Utah and Arizona, and southwest and west by California. Its extreme length from north to south is 485 miles on the eastern and 210 miles on the western boundary; greatest breadth 320 miles, decreasing to 310 miles in the north and to a point in the south. Its land area is 109,806 square miles; rank in area seventh. The surface generally is desert land and averages 5,500 feet above the sea. It is traversed by nearly parallel mountain ranges, between which are valleys varying in width from 5 to 20 miles. The highest point is Boundary Peak, in Esmeralda County, about 13,145 feet; the lowest is along the Colorado River in Clark County, 470 feet above sea level. The Weather Bureau at Reno gives the temperature (annual average) as 50.8; highest on record, 108; lowest on record, -36. Total annual precipitation is 7.53 inches. Irrigation has helped the state greatly in productivity. Hoover Dam, in the Black Canyon of the Colorado River, is the highest dam in the world and has attracted wide attention and many visitors. The University of Nevada, Reno, was established in 1864. The University of Nevada, Las Vegas, achieved equal and autonomous status with its sister school in the north in 1964.

POPULATION: 1,327,000,000 (1992). Rank among the states, 38th.

AGRICULTURE: Number of farms: 3,000 (1992). Farm acreage: 9,000,000 (1992). Cash receipts from farm marketings: crops, $89,000,000 (1991); livestock and products, $187,000,000 (1991).

FORESTS: Total forest land: 6,275,000 acres (1991).

MINERALS: Value of production: $2,393,000,000 (1991). Principal minerals: gold, silver, sand and gravel.

MANUFACTURES: Value added by manufacture: $1,463,000,000 (1991). Leading industry groups: stone, clay, and glass products.

LIST OF COUNTIES

Total number of counties 16

County, Location on Map, and County Seat	Pop.
Carson City (W), independent city	40,443
Churchill (WC), Fallon	17,938
Clark (SE), Las Vegas	741,459
Douglas (W), Minden	27,637
Elko (NE), Elko	33,530
Esmeralda(SW), Goldfield	1,344
Eureka (NC), Eureka	1,547
Humboldt (NW), Winnemucca	12,844
Lander (NC), Austin	6,266
Lincoln (SE), Pioche	3,775
Lyon (W), Yerington	20,001
Mineral (W), Hawthorne	2,526
Nye (SC), Tonopah	17,781
Pershing (NW), Lovelock	4,336
Storey (W), Virginia City	2,526
Washoe (W), Reno	254,667
White Pine (E), Ely	9,264

STATISTICS

Newspapers

Period of Issue	
Daily	6
Evening Daily	4
Morning Daily	3
Daily with Sunday edition	4
Semiweekly	1
Weekly	15
Monthly	3
Bimonthly	3
Free or partly free	1
Shopper	1
Total Newspapers	31

Periodicals

Period of Issue	
Biweekly	2
Monthly	5
Bimonthly	8
Quarterly	8
Total Periodicals	28

Total number of publications 59

Radio Stations

AM Stations	20
FM Stations	33
Total Radio Stations	53

TV Stations

Total TV Stations 15

Cable Stations

Total Cable Systems 8

Total number of broadcast listings 76

BATTLE MOUNTAIN

📖 **18422 Measure for Measure**
301 N. 2nd St. Phone: (702)635-5948
Battle Mountain, NV 89820-2874 Fax: (702)635-5889

Bi Monthly 3rd class mailer. **Founded:** 1993. **Freq:** Bimonthly. **Print Method:** Offset. Uses mats. **Trim Size:** 8 1/2 x 11. **Cols./Page:** 2. **Col. Width:** 3.75 inches. **Col. Depth:** 10 inches. **Key Personnel:** Chuck Barrett, Editor. **Subscription Rates:** Free. **Formerly:** Reese River Reveille.
Ad Rates: GLR: $.22 **Circ:** ‡3,200
BW: $160
PCI: $3.65

BOULDER CITY, pop. 9,590.

Clark Co. (SE). 25 m SE of Las Vegas. Home of Hoover Dam.

📖 **18423 Boulder City News**
1227 Arizona St. Phone: (702)293-2302
PO Box 60065 Fax: (702)294-0977
Boulder City, NV 89006
Community newspaper. **Founded:** 1938. **Freq:** Weekly (Thurs.). **Print Method:** Offset. **Cols./Page:** 6. **Col. Width:** 26 nonpareils. **Col. Depth:** 294 agate lines. **Key Personnel:** Chuck N. Baker, Editor; Mike O'Callaghan, Publisher, phone (702)259-4007; Carolyn O'Callaghan, Publisher, phone (702)435-7700, fax (702)434-3527'; Goldie Begley, Ad. Exec. **Subscription Rates:** $15. **Remarks:** Accepts advertising. **Feature Editors:** Kathleen Wood, *Sports*.
Ad Rates: BW: $630 **Circ:** ‡5,400
4C: $930.75
SAU: $5
PCI: $8

CARSON CITY†, pop. 32,022.

Carson City Co. (W). The State Capital, 30 m S of Reno. Western Nevada Community College. Park areas. Historical sites and museums. Hunting and fishing. Bolt and screws, reinforced plastics factories.

📖 **18424 Nevada**
1800 E. Hwy. 50 Phone: (702)687-5416
Carson City, NV 89710-0005 Fax: (702)687-6159
Free: (800)495-3281
Publication E-mail: nevmag@aol.com

Travel magazine. **Subtitle:** The Magazine of the Real West. **Founded:** 1936. **Freq:** Bimonthly. **Print Method:** Offset. **Trim Size:** 8 3/8 x 10 7/8. **Cols./Page:** 3. **Col. Width:** 27 nonpareils. **Col. Depth:** 134 agate lines. **Key Personnel:** David Moore, Editor; Richard Moreno, Publisher; Patty Noll, Advertising Dir. **ISSN:** 0199-1248. **Subscription Rates:** $16.95 individuals per yr.; $3.50 single issue.
Ad Rates: BW: $3,000 **Circ:** Paid ‡70,000
4C: $4,300 Non-paid ‡10,000

📖 **18425 Nevada Appeal**
Swift Corp.
200 Bath St. Phone: (702)882-2111
PO Box 2288 Fax: (702)882-6664
Carson City, NV 89703-2405
General newspaper. **Founded:** 1865. **Freq:** Daily. **Print Method:** Offset. **Cols./Page:** 6. **Col. Width:** 25 nonpareils. **Col. Depth:** 301 agate lines. **Key Personnel:** Jeff Ackerman, Publisher. **Subscription Rates:** $108 individuals. **Remarks:** Accepts advertising. Sunday: BW: $1,915.65; 4C: $2,287.65; SAU: $14.85. **URL:** http://www.tahoe.com.
Ad Rates: GLR: $1.75 **Circ:** Mon.-Fri. ‡13,800
BW: $1,902.75 Sun. ‡14,700
4C: $2,202.75
SAU: $14.75
CNU: $9.84
PCI: $14.75

📖 **18426 Pennysaver**
Eastern Sierra Publishing, Inc.
PO Box 2500 Phone: (702)883-4322
Carson City, NV 89702 Fax: (702)883-4311

Shopper. **Subtitle:** Shared Mail/100% Direct Mail. **Founded:** 1978. **Freq:** Weekly (Wed.). **Print Method:** Offset. **Trim Size:** 11 1/4 x 12 1/2. **Cols./Page:** 8. **Col. Width:** 1 1/8 inches. **Col. Depth:** 11 1/2 inches. **Key Personnel:** Jim Alldis, Publisher; Carol Dyer, Editor. **Remarks:** Accepts advertising. **Formerly:** Prospector Weekly News.
Ad Rates: GLR: $.92 **Circ:** Free 148,000
BW: $1,600
4C: $2,400
PCI: $17.40

📖 **18427 Range Magazine**
PO Box 639 Phone: (702)884-2200
Carson City, NV 89702-0639 Fax: (702)884-2213
Free: (800)ran-ge4u

Consumer magazine covering cowboys, sheepherders, and other people who work the land in the Western U.S. **Founded:** 1991. **Freq:** Quarterly. **Print Method:** Web press. **Trim Size:** 8 1/2 x 11. **Key Personnel:** C. J. Hadley, Editor and Publisher, cj@range.carson-city.nv.us. **ISSN:** 1093-3670. **Subscription Rates:** $19.95 individuals; $27.95 two years US funds only; all foreign add $5/year; $5 single issue. **Remarks:** Accepts advertising.
Ad Rates: BW: $2,840 **Circ:** 124,000
4C: $3,550

📖 **18428 The Wine Trader**
JDM Enterprises
PO Box 1598 Phone: (702)884-2648
Carson City, NV 89702 Fax: (702)884-2484
Free: (800)845-9463
Publication E-mail: winetrader@aol.com

Consumer magazine covering wine. **Founded:** 1976. **Freq:** Bimonthly. **Trim Size:** 8 1/16 x 10 1/4. **Subscription Rates:** $18 individuals; $4 single issue. **Remarks:** Accepts advertising. **URL:** http://www.wines.com/winetrader.
Ad Rates: BW: $1,275 **Circ:** Controlled 29,000
4C: $1,695

🎙 **18429 KNIS-FM - 91.3**
6363 Hwy. 50 E. Phone: (702)883-5647
Carson City, NV 89701

Format: Religious; Contemporary Christian. **Networks:** USA Radio; AP. **Owner:** Western Inspirational Broadcasters, Inc., at above address. **Founded:** 1970. **Operating Hours:** Continuous; 10% network, 90% local. **ADI:** Reno, NV. **Key Personnel:** Tom Hesse, General Mgr.; Bill Feltner, Operations Dir. **Wattage:** 67,000. **Ad Rates:** Noncommercial.

🎙 **18430 KPTL-AM - 1300**
1960 Idaho St. Phone: (702)884-8000
Carson City, NV 89701 Fax: (702)882-3961

Format: Oldies; Sports; News. **Networks:** Westwood One Radio; ABC. **Founded:** 1955. **Formerly:** KPTL-AM. **Operating Hours:** Continuous. **Key Personnel:** Craig Swope, General Mgr. **Local Programs:** *Coffee with Craig*, Craig Swope; *Fred & Craig in the Morning*, Fred James; *Scott Gahagen Show*, Scott Gahagen. **Wattage:** 5000 day; 500 night.

🎙 **18431 KRWR-FM - 94.7**
8401 Old Courthouse Rd., Ste. 140
Vienna, VA 22182

Format: Adult Contemporary. **Founded:** 1970. **Key Personnel:** Thomas P. Gammon, President; Tom Oja, Chief Engineer. **Wattage:** 86,600.

🎙 **18432 KZZF-FM - 102.9**
1960 Idaho St. Phone: (702)884-8000
Carson City, NV 89701 Fax: (702)882-3961
Free: (800)866-5453

Format: Adult Contemporary. **Owner:** Tri-Valley Broadcasting Corp., at above address. **Operating Hours:** Continuous. **ADI:** Reno, NV. **Key Personnel:** Paula Schofield, General Mgr., phone (702)884-8020; Bill McClain, Operations Dir., phone (702)884-8004. **Wattage:** 50,000. **Ad Rates:** $8-16 for 30 seconds; $10-20 for 60 seconds.

🎙 **18433 TCI Cablevision of Nevada, Inc.**
Box 2068 Phone: (702)882-2136
Carson City, NV 89702 Fax: (702)882-6973

Founded: 1962. **Cities Served:** Carson City County, NV.

ELKO†, pop. 8,758.

Elko Co. (NE). 290 m E of Reno. Tourism.

📖 **18434 Elko Daily Free Press**
3720 Idaho St. Phone: (702)738-3118
Elko, NV 89801 Fax: (702)738-2215

General newspaper. **Founded:** 1883. **Freq:** Daily (eve.) and Sat. (morn.). **Print Method:** Offset. **Cols./Page:** 6. **Col. Width:** 26 nonpareils. **Col. Depth:** 301 agate lines. **Key Personnel:** Rex Steninger, Editor and Publisher; Kim Steninger, Publisher; Dan Steninger, Editoral page editor & Publisher; Glenas Bir, Advertising Mgr. **Subscription Rates:** $93. **Remarks:** Accepts advertising.
Ad Rates: SAU: $8.56 **Circ:** ‡8,000
PCI: $8

📖 **18435 Elko Independent**
Elko Independent Inc.
PO Box 309
Elko, NV 89803

Newspaper with a focus on community and local events. **Founded:** 1869. **Freq:** Weekly (Wed.). **Print Method:** Offset. **Cols./Page:** 6. **Col. Width:** 22 nonpareils. **Col. Depth:** 301 agate lines. **Key Personnel:** Kay E. Thompson, Publisher. **Subscription Rates:** $23; $26 out of state.
Ad Rates: GLR: $.14 **Circ:** 3,000
BW: $645
PCI: $5

🎙 **18436 KELK-AM - 1240**
1800 Idaho St. Phone: (702)738-1240
Elko, NV 89801 Fax: (702)753-5556
E-mail: kelk@sierra.net

Networks: ABC. **Owner:** Paul G. Gardner, at above address. **Founded:** 1947. **Operating Hours:** Continuous; 2% network, 98% local. **ADI:** Salt Lake City (Cedar City), UT. **Key Personnel:** Paul Gardner, General Mgr.; Lori Gilbert, Contact. **Wattage:** 1000. **Ad Rates:** $13 for 30 seconds; $17.50 for 60 seconds.

🎙 **18437 KENV-TV - 10**
1025 Chilton Circle Phone: (702)777-8500
Elko, NV 89801 Fax: (702)777-7758

Format: Commercial TV. **Networks:** NBC. **Owner:** Sunbelt Communications Co., 1500 Foremaster Ln., Las Vegas, NV 89101. **Founded:** Jan. 1, 1996. **Operating Hours:** Continuous. **ADI:** Salt Lake City (Cedar City), UT. **Key Personnel:** Jim Elliott, Station Mgr. **Ad Rates:** Advertising accepted; rates available upon request. **URL:** http://www.kenv.com.

🎙 **18438 KLKO-FM - 93.7**
1800 Idaho St. Phone: (702)738-1240
Elko, NV 89801 Fax: (702)753-5556
E-mail: klko@sierra.net

Format: Classic Rock. **Owner:** Elko Broadcasting Co., at above address. **Founded:** 1982. **Operating Hours:** 100% local. **ADI:** Salt Lake City (Cedar City), UT. **Key Personnel:** Paul Gardner, Contact. **Local Programs:** *Chad & Lori in the Morning*, Chad Hardy, PD. **Wattage:** 50 k. **Ad Rates:** $13 for 30 seconds; $17.50 for 60 seconds. $9-$10 for 30 seconds; $12-$14 for 60 seconds. Combined advertising rates available with KELK-AM.

🎙 **18439 KRJC-FM - 95.3**
1859 Manzanita Dr. Phone: (775)738-9895
PO Box 1626 Fax: (775)753-8085
Elko, NV 89801
E-mail: krjc953@elko.net

Format: Country; News; Sports. **Founded:** 1982. **Operating Hours:** Continuous. **ADI:** Salt Lake City (Cedar City), UT. **Key Personnel:** Darrell Calton, General Mgr.; Crystal Bartorreli, Sales Mgr.; Sean Marx, Program Dir.; Jean Barnes, Traffic Mgr. **Wattage:** 25,000. **URL:** www.krjc.com.

ELY†, pop. 4,882.

White Pine Co. (E). 260 m E of Reno. Gold, silver mines. Dairy, stock farms. Sheep.

📖 **18440 Ely Daily Times**
Donrey Media Group
700 Aultman St. Phone: (702)289-4491
PO Box 1139 Fax: (702)289-4566
Ely, NV 89301-1556
General newspaper. **Founded:** 1920. **Freq:** Daily (eve.). **Print Method:** Offset. **Trim Size:** 13 x 21 1/2. **Cols./Page:** 6. **Col. Width:** 26 nonpareils. **Col. Depth:** 301 agate lines. **Key Personnel:** Kent Harper, Editor; George L. Carnes, Publisher; Ken Kliewer, Advertising Mgr. **USPS:** 174-660. **Subscription Rates:** $108. **Remarks:** Accepts advertising.
Ad Rates: BW: $1,038.45 **Circ:** ⊕**2,585**
PCI: $8.05

🎙 **18441 KDSS-FM - 92.7**
501 Aultman, Ste. 208 Phone: (702)289-6474
Ely, NV 89301 Fax: (702)289-6531

Format: Country. **Networks:** Jones Satellite. **Owner:** Coates Broadcasting, Inc., at above address. **Founded:** 1984. **Formerly:** KBXS-FM (1992). **Operating Hours:** Continuous. **Key Personnel:** Patrick Coates, President/Gen. Mgr.; Samantha Coates, V.P./Sales Mgr. **Wattage:** 6000. **Ad Rates:** $8.35 for 30 seconds; $10.65 for 60 seconds.

18442 KELY-AM - 1230
Georgetown Ranch
807 E. Aultman
Ely, NV 89301-2504
Phone: (702)289-2077
Fax: (702)289-4857

Format: Oldies. **Networks:** NBC; Jones Satellite. **Owner:** Reed Communications, Inc., at above address, (702)289-4463, Fax: (702)289-4467. **Founded:** 1950. **Operating Hours:** Continuous; 75% network, 25% local. **Key Personnel:** Gary Richey, General Mgr.; Gary Richey, Station and Sales Mgr.; Jenny Wilson, Prog. Dir./Prod. Mgr. **Wattage:** 1000. **Ad Rates:** $6-13.50 per unit.

18443 KELY-FM - 101.7
Georgetown Ranch
807 Ave. F
Ely, NV 89301
Phone: (702)289-2077
Fax: (702)289-4857

Format: Adult Contemporary. **Networks:** NBC; Jones Satellite. **Owner:** Reed Communications, Inc., at above address. **Founded:** 1987. **Operating Hours:** Continuous; 80% network, 20% local. **Key Personnel:** Gary Richey, Sales Mgr.; Jenny Wilson, Prog. Dir./Prod. Mgr. **Wattage:** 480. **Ad Rates:** $7-13.50 per unit.

EMPIRE

18444 United States Gypsum Co.
Hwy. 447 N
PO Box 130
Empire, NV 89405
Phone: (702)557-2341
Fax: (702)557-2212

Founded: Dec. 25, 1983. **Key Personnel:** Bill Couk, Chief Technician; Debbi Constable, Installer. **Cities Served:** Empire, NV: subscribing households 127; 26 channels; 0 community access channels; 0 hours per week community access programming.

FALLON†, pop. 4,262.

Churchill Co. (WC).60 m E of Reno. Manufactures butter, alfalfa meal, ice cream. Ore refining; barite, tungsten, silver mines. Agriculture. Alfalfa, wheat and garden produce.

18445 Lahontan Valley News/Fallon Eagle Standard
562 N. Maine St.
PO Box 1297
Fallon, NV 89406-2813
Free: (800)677-8234
Phone: (702)423-6041
Fax: (702)423-0474

General newspaper. **Founded:** 1903. **Freq:** Tue.-Sat. (morn.). **Print Method:** Offset. **Cols./Page:** 6. **Col. Width:** 2 1/16 inches. **Col. Depth:** 21 1/2 inches. **Key Personnel:** Anne Pershing, Editor; David Henley, Publisher; Joyce Thompson, Advertising Mgr. **USPS:** 925-960. **Subscription Rates:** $74 individuals; $99 out of area. **Remarks:** Accepts advertising.
Ad Rates: BW: $1,057.80
4C: $1,317.80
SAU: $8.20
Circ: Paid 5,200

18446 KVLV-AM - 980
1155 Gummow Dr.
Fallon, NV 89406
Phone: (702)423-2243
Fax: (702)423-8889

Format: Country. **Networks:** ABC. **Owner:** Lahontan Valley Broadcasting Co., at above address. **Founded:** 1957. **Operating Hours:** 6 a.m.-sunset. **Key Personnel:** Lynn Pearce, Program Dir.; Mike McGinness, Station Mgr.; Dee McGinness, Office Mgr. **Wattage:** 5000. **Ad Rates:** $8 for 30 seconds; $10 for 60 seconds. Combined advertising rates available with KVLV-FM.

18447 KVLV-FM - 99.3
1155 Gummow Dr.
Fallon, NV 89406
Phone: (702)423-2243
Fax: (702)423-8889

Format: Adult Contemporary. **Networks:** ABC; Jones Satellite. **Owner:** Lahontan Valley Broadcasting, at above address. **Founded:** 1966. **Operating Hours:** 6 a.m.-MID; 1% network, 99% local. **Key Personnel:** Mike McGinness, Station Mgr.; Dee McGinness, Office Mgr.; Lynn Pearce, Program Dir. **Wattage:** 3700. **Ad Rates:** $8 for 30 seconds; $10 for 60 seconds. Combined advertising rates available with KVLV-AM.

GARDNERVILLE, pop. 1,320.

Douglas Co. (W). 47 m S of Reno. Grain warehouse; creamery. Gold, silver, tungsten, barium mines. Agriculture. Cattle. Hay, grain, sheep.

18448 Motorcycle Industry Magazine
Industry Shopper Publishing, Inc.
PO Box 160
Gardnerville, NV 89410
Phone: (775)782-0222
Fax: (775)782-0266
Publication E-mail: cycle@mimag.com

Magazine covering the motorcycle industry. **Founded:** May 1980. **Freq:** Monthly. **Print Method:** Offset. **Trim Size:** 11 x 15. **Cols./Page:** 4. **Col. Width:** 2 1/4 inches. **Col. Depth:** 13 1/2 inches. **Key Personnel:** Rick Campbell, Publisher. **ISSN:** 0884-626X. **Subscription Rates:** Free; $138 other countries. **Remarks:** Accepts advertising. **Formerly:** Motorcycle Industry Shopper (1988).
Ad Rates: BW: $2,195
4C: $3,140
Circ: Non-paid ★12,523

18449 KGVM-FM - 99.3
Box 2109
Minden, NV 89423
Phone: (702)782-2211
Fax: (702)782-5486

Format: Adult Contemporary. **Founded:** 1985. **Key Personnel:** Lloyd W. Higuera, Contact; Terry Reiswig, General Sales Mgr.; Caroline Higuera, Program Dir. **Wattage:** 3000.

18450 TCI Cablevision
1338 Centervill Rd.
Gardnerville, NV 89410
Phone: (702)882-2136
Fax: (702)782-7884

Owner: Columbia Associates, 335 W. Melinda Dr., Ste. 2, Phoenix, AZ 85027, (602)582-2476. **Founded:** 1975. **Formerly:** Carson Valley Cable; Columbia Cable of Nevada. **Key Personnel:** Dick Fairbanks, General Mgr.; Ray St. Fev, Contact; Kay Barcellos, Office Mgr. **Cities Served:** Carson Valley, NV: 6,500 subscribing households; 44 channels. Fallon, NV: 3,600 subscribing households; 44 channels. Yerington, NV: 1,000 subscribing households; 36 channels.

HAWTHORNE†, pop. 5,000.

Mineral Co. (W). 95 m SE of Reno. U. S. Naval Ammunition Depot. Tourist resort. Gold, silver, tungsten mines.

18451 Mineral County Independent-News
PO Box 1270
Hawthorne, NV 89415
Phone: (702)945-2414
Fax: (702)945-1270

Newspaper. **Founded:** 1928. **Freq:** Weekly (Wed.). **Print Method:** Offset. **Cols./Page:** 8. **Col. Width:** 27 nonpareils. **Col. Depth:** 294 agate lines. **Key Personnel:** Ted Hughes, Managing Editor. **Subscription Rates:** $25 individuals. **Remarks:** Accepts advertising.
Ad Rates: PCI: $5
Circ: Paid 2,900

HENDERSON, pop. 24,363.

Clark Co. (SE). 12 m SE of Las Vegas. Summer and winter recreation. Warehouse distribution. Titanium plant. Manufactures chemicals, electronics.

18452 Henderson Home News
HBC Publications, Inc.
2 Commerce Center
Henderson, NV 89014
Phone: (702)435-7700
Fax: (702)434-3527
Publication E-mail: homenews@aol.com

Community newspaper. **Founded:** 1951. **Freq:** Semiweekly (Tues. and Thurs.). **Print Method:** Offset. **Trim Size:** 13 x 21. **Cols./Page:** 6. **Col. Width:** 25 nonpareils. **Col. Depth:** 294 agate lines. **Key Personnel:** Paul Szydelko, Editor; Mike O'Callaghan, Publisher; Carolyn O'Callaghan, Publisher; Tim O'Callaghan, General Mgr. **Subscription Rates:** $30. **Remarks:** Accepts advertising.
Ad Rates: GLR: $.85
BW: $1,260
4C: $1,650
SAU: $5
PCI: $10
Circ: ‡13,500

18453 KVVU-TV - 5
25 TV-5 Dr.
Henderson, NV 89014
Phone: (702)435-5555
Fax: (702)451-4220
E-mail: program@kvvutv.com

Format: Commercial TV. **Networks:** Fox. **Owner:** Meredith Corp., 1716 Locust St., Des Moines, IA 50309-3023, (515)284-3000, Fax: (515)532-6616. **Founded:** Sept. 1967. **Formerly:** KHBV-TV (1967). **Operating Hours:** Continuous. **ADI:** Las Vegas, NV. **Key Personnel:** Rusty Durante, General Mgr., fax (702)435-0575; Bill Utton, General Sales Mgr., fax (702)435-6369; Tom Marciano, Local Sales Mgr., fax (702)435-6369. **Local Programs:** *A M Southern Nevada* 6:00 am Sunday, Lillian McMorris.

INCLINE VILLAGE

Washoe Co.

18454 Adventure Travel Business
Adventure Media, Inc.
PO Box 3210
Incline Village, NV 89450
Phone: (702)832-3700
Fax: (702)832-3775

Business magazine for the adventure travel tour operator. **Founded:** Feb. 1997. **Freq:** Bimonthly. **Print Method:** Offset. **Trim Size:** 8 1/8 x 10 1/2. **Cols./Page:** 3. **Key Personnel:** Dave Mulligan, Editor; Rick Dyess, Publisher, rickd@adv-media.com; Ken Spencer, Advertising Dir. **Subscription Rates:** $24 individuals. **Remarks:** Accepts advertising.
Ad Rates: BW: $1,890
4C: $2,625
Circ: Non-paid 15,000

18455 Adventure West
Adventure Media, Inc.
924 Incline Way, Ste. M
Incline Village, NV 89451
Phone: (702)832-3730
Fax: (702)832-3775

Nationally distributed consumer magazine, subscription based, adventure travel in western North America. **Subtitle:** America's Leading Adventure Travel Magazine. **Founded:** 1992. **Freq:** Bimonthly. **Print Method:** Web Offset. **Trim Size:** 8 1/4 x 10 1/2. **Cols./Page:** 3. **Col. Width:** 2 1/4 inches. **Col. Depth:** 9 1/8 inches. **Key Personnel:** Rick Dyes, Publisher; Kristina Scheck, Managing Editor; Dave Mulligan, Managing Editor; Lorelli Gimbry, Editor. **ISSN:** 1072-4378. **Subscription Rates:** $13.50 individuals; $24 two years. **Remarks:** Accepts advertising. **Available Online. URL:** www.adventurewest.com.
Ad Rates: BW: $7,412
4C: $10,310
Circ: Paid 83,716
Non-paid 66,530

18456 The Cremationist of North America
Cremationist of North America
PO Box 7047
Incline Village, NV 89450
Phone: (702)831-3848
Fax: (702)831-6555

Trade magazine on cremation. **Founded:** July 1965. **Freq:** Quarterly. **Print Method:** Offset. **Trim Size:** 8 1/2 x 11. **Cols./Page:** 3. **Col. Width:** 26 nonpareils. **Col. Depth:** 140 agate lines. **Key Personnel:** Jean Scribner, Editor & Advertising Mgr.; Cathryn McClelland, Art Production. **Subscription Rates:** $12 individuals; $18 two years; $5 single issue. **Remarks:** Accepts advertising.
Ad Rates: GLR: $513
BW: $513
4C: $1,348
PCI: $79
Circ: ‡1,600

18457 KZAK-FM - 100.1
255 W. Moana Ln., Ste. 208
Reno, NV 89509-4943
E-mail: z-rock100@aol.com

Format: Album-Oriented Rock (AOR); Alternative/New Music/Progressive. **Networks:** ABC; Satellite Music Network. **Founded:** 1983. **Operating Hours:** 24 hrs. **ADI:** Reno, NV. **Key Personnel:** Steve Funk, General Mgr.; Max Volume, Program Dir.; Ric Karau, Chief Engineer. **Wattage:** 1650.

LAS VEGAS†, pop. 164,674.

Clark Co. (SE). 180 m NE of San Bernardino, Calif. Tourist resort.

18458 Art: Mag
PO Box 70896
Las Vegas, NV 89170
Phone: (702)734-8121
Journal covering alternative literature and art. **Founded:** 1984. **Freq:** Semiannual. **Print Method:** copier. **Trim Size:** 8 1/2 x 7. **Key Personnel:** Peter Magliocco, Editor. **Subscription Rates:** $10 individuals; $5 single issue. **Remarks:** Advertising not accepted.
Circ: 100

18459 Interim
University of Nevada
Las Vegas, NV 89154-5034
Phone: (702)895-3458

Literary journal covering poetry and short fiction. **Founded:** 1944. **Freq:** Semiannual. **Trim Size:** 6 x 9. **Key Personnel:** James Hazen, Editor. **ISSN:** 0888-2452. **Subscription Rates:** $7 individuals; $14 institutions; $4 single issue.
Circ: Combined 400

18460 The Jewish Reporter
Jewish Federation of Las Vegas
3909 S. Maryland Pkwy., Ste. 405
Las Vegas, NV 89119-7520
Phone: (702)732-0556
Fax: (702)732-3228
Jewish community newspaper. **Founded:** Mar. 1976. **Freq:** Bimonthly. **Cols./Page:** 4. **Subscription Rates:** Free. **Remarks:** Accepts advertising. **URL:** http://www.vegas.com/jflu.
Circ: Controlled 9,100

18461 Journal of Restaurant and Foodservice Marketing
The Haworth Press, Inc.
Wm. F. Harrah College of Noted Admin. Phone: (702)895-0876
Dept. of Tourism
4505 Mayland Pkwy.
Las Vegas, NV 89154-6023
Publisher E-mail: getinfo@haworthpressinc.com

Journal on restaurant and foodservice management. **Founded:** 1994. **Freq:** Quarterly. **Trim Size:** 6x8 1/2. **Cols./Page:** 1. **Col. Width:** 4 3/8 inches. **Col. Depth:** 7 1/8 inches. **Key Personnel:** John Bowen, Editor, phone (702)895-0876, fax (702)895-4870, bowen@ccmail.nevada.edu; Bill Cohen, Publisher. **ISSN:** 1052-214X. **Subscription Rates:** $36 individuals USA; $48 institutions USA; $60 libraries USA; $46.80 individuals CAN; $62.40 institutions CAN; $78 libraries CAN; $50.40 individuals other countries; $67.20 institutions other countries; $84 libraries other countries. **Remarks:** Accepts advertising. **URL:** http://www.haworth.com. **Alt. Formats:** Microform.
Ad Rates: BW: $300 **Circ:** Paid 379

18462 Juggle
International Jugglers Association
Stan Allen & Associates Phone: (702)798-0099
7380 S. Eastern Ave., No. 124-179 Fax: (702)798-0220
Las Vegas, NV 89123
Publisher E-mail: editor@jugglemagazine.com

Magazine of interest to jugglers and other independent variety entertainers. **Subtitle:** The Official Magazine of the International Jugglers Association. **Founded:** 1949. **Freq:** Bimonthly. **Print Method:** Offset. **Trim Size:** 8 1/2 x 10 7/8. **Cols./Page:** 3. **Col. Width:** 42 nonpareils. **Col. Depth:** 196 agate lines. **Key Personnel:** Stan Allen, Editor. **ISSN:** 1520-7471. **Subscription Rates:** $30 individuals; $35 other countries. **Remarks:** Accepts advertising. **URL:** http://www.juggling.org/jw.
Ad Rates: BW: $250 **Circ:** 3,000

18463 Las Vegas Business Press
Wick Communications
PO Box 27409 Phone: (702)871-6780
Las Vegas, NV 89126-1409 Fax: (702)871-3748

Local business newspaper. **Founded:** 1985. **Freq:** Weekly. **Print Method:** Offset. **Cols./Page:** 4. **Col. Width:** 10 1/4 inches. **Col. Depth:** 12 1/2 inches. **Key Personnel:** Hugh Jackson, Editor; Gloria Stonecipher, Marketing Dir.; Ron Gannon, Circulation Mgr. **Subscription Rates:** $68 individuals. **Remarks:** Accepts advertising. **Alt. Formats:** CD-ROM.
Ad Rates: BW: $1,739 **Circ:** Controlled 8,700
4C: $2,239

18464 Las Vegas Israelite
PO Box 14096 Phone: (702)876-1255
Las Vegas, NV 89114 Fax: (702)364-1009

Jewish and local interest newspaper. **Founded:** 1965. **Freq:** Bimonthly. **Print Method:** Offset. **Trim Size:** 10 1/4 x 14. **Cols./Page:** 6. **Col. Width:** 1 5/8 inches. **Col. Depth:** 14 inches. **Key Personnel:** Michael Tell, Editor and Publisher; Bea Tell, Business Mgr. **Subscription Rates:** Free; $24. **Remarks:** Accepts advertising.
Ad Rates: BW: $1,260 **Circ:** Paid ‡10,000
4C: $1,510 Free ‡33,000
PCI: $15

18465 Las Vegas Review-Journal
Donrey Media Group
1111 W. Bonanza Phone: (702)383-0211
Las Vegas, NV 89106
General newspaper. **Founded:** 1908. **Freq:** Daily (morn.). **Print Method:** Offset. **Cols./Page:** 6. **Col. Width:** 26 nonpareils. **Col. Depth:** 301 agate lines. **Key Personnel:** Sherman Frederick, Publisher, phone (702)383-0237, fax (702)383-0402; Jim Hannah, Human Resources Dir.; Jack Harpster, Advertising Dir., phone (702)383-0223, fax (702)383-0435; Allan Fleming, General Mgr., phone (702)383-0365, fax (702)383-0389; Terry Duck, Production Dir., phone (702)383-0466, fax (702)383-4699; Tom Mitchell, Editor, phone (702)383-0261, Tom_Mitchell@lvrj.com; Patricia Johnson, Business Mgr., phone (702)383-0215, fax (702)383-4665; Charles Zobell, Managing Editor, phone (702)383-0293, Charles_Zobell@lvrj.com; Steve Coffen, Circulation Mgr., phone (702)383-4612, fax (702)383-0302; Christian Kolberg, Promotion Dir., phone (702)383-0436, fax (702)3830302; Greg Haas, Asst. Managing Editor/Systems Design, phone (702)383-0427, Greg_Hass@lvrj.com; Al Gibes, Online Mgr., phone (702)383-0478, Al_Gibes@lvrj.com; Kirk Kern, View Editor, phone (702)383-0486, Kirk_Kern@lvrj.com; John Kerr, Editorial Page Editor, phone (702)383-0273, John_Kerr@lvrj.com; Jim Laurie, Chief Photographer, phone (702)383-0310, Jim_Laurie@lvrj.com; A.D. Hopkins, Special Projects Editor, phone (702)383-0270, A.D._Hopkins@lvrj.com. **Subscription Rates:** $195. **Remarks:** Accepts advertising. **Online:** DataTimes Corporation. **Feature Editors:** Annette Caramia, *City*, phone (702)383-0286, Annette_Caramia@lvrj.com; Frank Fertado, *Features*, phone (702)383-0274, Frank_Fertado@lvrj.com; Jim Fossum, *Sports*, phone (702)383-4618, Jim_Fossum@lvrj.com; Mary Greeley, *News*, phone (703)383-0424, Mary_Greeley@lvrj.com; Doug Puppel, *Financial/Business*, phone (702)383-0258, Doug_Puppel@lvrj.com. **Additional Contact Info: Mailing Address:** PO Box 70, Las Vegas, NV 89125.
Ad Rates: BW: $8,888.10 **Circ:** Mon.-Fri. ★**151,162**
4C: $10,173.10 Sat. ★**182,542**
SAU: $68.90 Sun. ★**213,619**

18466 Las Vegas Sentinel-Voice
Griot Communications Group Inc.
900 E. Charleston Blvd. Phone: (702)380-8100
Las Vegas, NV 89104 Fax: (702)380-8102

Black community newspaper. **Founded:** Apr. 22, 1980. **Freq:** Weekly (Thurs.). **Cols./Page:** 6. **Col. Width:** 1 5/8 inches. **Col. Depth:** 14 inches. **Key Personnel:** Ramon Savoy, Editor and Publisher. **Subscription Rates:** $25 individuals. **Remarks:** Accepts advertising.
Ad Rates: GLR: $0.75 **Circ:** 5,000
BW: $924
4C: $1500
PCI: $11

18467 Learning and Individual Differences
Elseiver
College of Education
University of Nevada
Las Vegas, NV 89154
Publication E-mail: 102062-2525@compuserve.com
Publisher E-mail: fcentres@gpu.stv.ualberta.ca

Subtitle: A Multidisciplinary Journal in Education. **Founded:** 1989. **Freq:** Quarterly. **Print Method:** Offset. **Trim Size:** 6 7/8 x 10. **Key Personnel:** Frank N. Dempster, Editor. **ISSN:** 1041-6080. **Subscription Rates:** $175 institutions; $195 institutions, other countries; $215 institutions, other countries airmail; $80 individuals; $100 other countries; $120 other countries airmail; $47.50 single issue; $52.50 single issue other couuntries; $57.50 single issue other countries airmail. **Remarks:** Accepts advertising.
Ad Rates: BW: $300 **Circ:** (Not Reported)

18468 Loose Change
Mead Publishing Co.
1515 S. Commerce St. Phone: (702)387-8750
Las Vegas, NV 89102-2703 Fax: (702)366-1599

Magazine covering slot machines, antique or modern, and related subjects. **Founded:** 1977. **Freq:** 10/year. **Print Method:** Offset. **Trim Size:** 8 1/8 x 10 7/8. **Cols./Page:** 3. **Col. Width:** 14 picas. **Col. Depth:** 10 inches. **ISSN:** 0278-4114. **Subscription Rates:** $39. **Remarks:** Accepts advertising.
Ad Rates: BW: $120 **Circ:** ‡2,600
4C: $250

18469 Magic
Stan Allen and Associates
7380 S. Eastern Ave., Ste. 124-179 Phone: (702)798-0099 Fax: (702)798-0220
Las Vegas, NV 89123
Publication E-mail: magicmag1@ao.com

Trade journal for magicians and magic enthusiasts. **Subtitle:** The Independent Magazine for Magicians. **Founded:** Sept. 1991. **Freq:** Monthly. **Print Method:** Web offset. **Trim Size:** 8 1/2 x 10 3/4. **Cols./Page:** 3. **Key Personnel:** Stan Allen, Editor; John Moehring, Assoc. Editor; Denise Marshall, Art Dir. **ISSN:** 1062-2845. **Subscription Rates:** $40 individuals; $4.50 single issue. **Remarks:** Accepts advertising.
Circ: Controlled 10,000

18470 Nevada Business Journal
2127 Paradise Rd. Phone: (702)735-7003
Las Vegas, NV 89104-2515 Fax: (702)733-5953
Free: (800)242-0164
Publication E-mail: nbj@nevadabusiness.com

Magazine spotlighting and promoting business in Nevada. **Founded:** Mar. 1986. **Freq:** Monthly. **Print Method:** Offset. **Trim Size:** 8 3/8 x 10 7/8. **Cols./Page:** 3. **Col. Width:** 2.5 picas. **Col. Depth:** 9 5/8 inches. **Key Personnel:** Jennifer Robison, Editor, jennifer@nevadabusiness.com; Stephen Brock, President, president@nevadabusiness.com. **Subscription Rates:** $44; $7.50 single issue. **Remarks:** Accepts advertising. **URL:** http://www.nevadabusiness.com.
Ad Rates: BW: $2,740 **Circ:** Paid ‡4,000
4C: $3,930 Controlled ‡16,000

18471 Nevada Events and Shows
Nevada Magazine
555 E Washington Ave., No. 5600 Phone: (702)486-2433 Fax: (702)486-2789
Las Vegas, NV 89101
Free: (800)495-3281
Publication E-mail: nevmag@aol.com

Travel magazine. **Subtitle:** Section of Nevada Magazine. **Founded:** 1987. **Freq:** Bimonthly. **Print Method:** Web offset. **Trim Size:** 8 3/8 x 10 7/8. **Cols./Page:** 3. **Col. Width:** 27 nonpareils. **Col. Depth:** 134 agate lines. **Key Personnel:** Ann Henderson, Editor, phone (702)486-2433, nevmag@aol.com; Richard Moreno, Publisher, phone (702)687-5416, fax (702)687-6159; Patty Noll, Advertising Dir. **ISSN:** 0896-2588. **Subscription Rates:** $15.95 individuals; $3.50 single issue. **Remarks:** Accepts advertising.
Ad Rates: BW: $4,000 **Circ:** Paid ‡189,800
4C: $5,750 Non-paid ‡11,000
PCI: $175

18472 Nevada Lawyer
State Bar of Nevada
600 E. Charleston Blvd. Phone: (702)382-2200
Las Vegas, NV 89104 Fax: (702)385-2878
Free: (800)254-2797

Professional magazine of the State Bar of Nevada covering the practice of law. **Founded:** 1929. **Freq:** Monthly. **Trim Size:** 8 1/2 x 11. **Cols./Page:** 3. **Col. Width:** 2 1/4 inches. **Col. Depth:** 9 1/2 inches. **Key Personnel:** Pami E. Kowal, Editor, pamik@nvbar.org. **ISSN:** 1068-882X. **Subscription Rates:** $40 individuals; $5 single issue. **Remarks:** Accepts advertising. **Online:** LEXIS-NEXIS; Westlaw. **URL:** http://www.nybar.org. **Alt. Formats:** Microfilm. **Former name:** Inter Alia.
Ad Rates: BW: $578 **Circ:** Controlled 5,065
4C: $1,378

18473 Nevada Senior World
2340 Paseo Del Prado, Ste. 304 Phone: (702)367-6709
Las Vegas, NV 89102 Fax: (702)367-6883

Newspaper for senior citizens. **Subtitle:** News Active Senior Use For Better Living. **Founded:** 1976. **Freq:** Monthly. **Print Method:** Offset. Uses mats. **Trim Size:** 9.875 X 12.275. **Cols./Page:** 5. **Col. Depth:** 85 inches. **Key Personnel:** Frank B. Fiedler, General Mgr. **Subscription Rates:** $14.95 individuals. **Formerly:** Senior Times.
Ad Rates: BW: $2,800 **Circ:** Combined 75,875
4C: $3,400
PCI: $35

18474 New Age Networking Magazine
Destiny Productions for Print, Radio & Cable Promotions
3395 S. Jones Blvd., No. 217 Phone: (702)648-3898
Las Vegas, NV 89102 Fax: (702)648-3898
Free: (800)457-0654
Publisher E-mail: DestinyMag@aol.com

Professional magazine covering business for proprietors and others. **Subtitle:** The Trade Journal for Cosmic Minded Industry. **Founded:** 1995. **Freq:** Quarterly. **Trim Size:** 8 1/2 x 10 7/8. **Key Personnel:** Jody Williams, Contact. **Subscription Rates:** $15.95; $3.95 single issue. **Remarks:** Accepts advertising. **URL:** http://www.members.aol.com/destinymag/mw1. **Former name:** The Insider.
Ad Rates: BW: $1,895 **Circ:** Combined 125,000
4C: $3,694
PCI: $95

18475 Nifty Nickel
900 S. Main St. Phone: (702)224-5555
Las Vegas, NV 89101 Fax: (702)382-0549

Shopper. **Founded:** 1964. **Freq:** Weekly. **Print Method:** Web press offset. **Trim Size:** 11 1/4 x 17. **Cols./Page:** 7. **Col. Width:** 1 5/16 inches. **Col. Depth:** 16 inches. **Key Personnel:** Pete Bodnar, General Mgr., phone (702)224-5555, fax (702)382-0549; George Vasconi, Business Mgr., phone (702)224-5555, fax (702)382-0549. **Subscription Rates:** Free. **Remarks:** Accepts advertising.
Ad Rates: BW: $1,344 **Circ:** Non-paid 60,000
4C: $1,644
PCI: $12

18476 Reading Research Quarterly
International Reading Association
University of Nevada Phone: (702)895-4217
College of Education Fax: (702)895-4353
4505 Maryland Pkwy
Las Vegas, NV 89154-3042
Publication E-mail: rrq@nevada.edu

Educational journal with articles on theory and research in reading. **Founded:** 1965. **Freq:** Quarterly. **Print Method:** Offset. **Trim Size:** 8 3/8 x 10 7/8. **Cols./Page:** 2. **Col. Width:** 20 picas. **Col. Depth:** 53 picas. **Key Personnel:** John Readence, Editor, readence@nevada.edu; Diane Barone,

Editor, barone@scs.unr.edu. **ISSN:** 0034-0553. **Subscription Rates:** $45 individuals; $15 single issue; $90 institutions. **Remarks:** Advertising not accepted. **Alt. Formats:** Microfiche.
Circ: ‡11,000

18477 Recharger Magazine
4218 W. Charleston Blvd. Phone: (702)438-5557
Las Vegas, NV 89102-1625 Fax: (702)438-4025
Publication E-mail: info@rechargermag.com

Magazine serving the office products recycling industry. **Subtitle:** Serving the Office Products Recycling Industry. **Founded:** Aug. 1989. **Freq:** Monthly. **Print Method:** Web Press. **Trim Size:** 8 3/8 x 10 7/8. **Key Personnel:** Donna Enerson, Contact, donna@rechargermag.com. **ISSN:** 1053-7503. **Subscription Rates:** $45 individuals; $15 single issue. **Remarks:** Accepts advertising.
Ad Rates: BW: $570 **Circ:** Paid ‡5,000
4C: $1085 Non-paid ‡750

18478 Sun
800 S. Valley View Phone: (702)385-3111
Box 4275 Fax: (702)383-7264
Las Vegas, NV 89127-0275
Community newspaper. **Founded:** 1950. **Freq:** Weekly. **Key Personnel:** Brian Greenspun, Editor; Bill Schaul, Advertising Mgr. **Remarks:** Accepts advertising.
Ad Rates: SAU: $24 **Circ:** Mon.-Fri. 39,483
Sat. 194,027
Sun. 225,765

18479 Welcome Home Magazine of Las Vegas
Welcome Home Magazine
5944 S. Kipling St., Ste. 204 Phone: (303)972-2584
Littleton, CO 80127-2590 Fax: (303)972-2261

Magazine containing information for newly moved Las Vegas households. **Founded:** Dec. 1, 1995. **Freq:** Quarterly. **Print Method:** Web offset. **Trim Size:** 8 3/8 x 10 7/8. **Cols./Page:** 3. **Col. Width:** 13 picas. **Key Personnel:** James F. Sweeney, Publisher; Mary Sweeney, Editor. **Remarks:** Accepts advertising.
Ad Rates: BW: $1,860 **Circ:** Controlled 11,000
4C: $2,220

18480 What's On Magazine
4425 S. Industrial Rd. Phone: (702)891-8811
Las Vegas, NV 89103 Fax: (702)891-8804
Free: (800)494-2876
Publication E-mail: whatson@wizard.com

Guiding people to the best of Las Vegas. **Subtitle:** The Las Vegas Guide. **Founded:** 1954. **Freq:** Biweekly. **Print Method:** Heatset offset. **Trim Size:** 8 1/8 x 10. **Key Personnel:** Haley Hertz, Exec. Editor, haley@ilovevegas.com; Murray Hertz, Publisher; Stacey Hertz, Managing Editor, stacey@ilovegas.com; Michael Dunn, Art Dir., michael@ilovevegas.com; Mel Carter, Distribution Dir.; Barry Berlin, Acct. Exec. **ISSN:** 1081-5945. **Subscription Rates:** $4.95 single issue; $5.95 single issue Canada; $8 other countries single issue. **Remarks:** Accepts advertising. **URL:** http://www.whats-on.com; http://www.ilovevegas.com. **Formerly:** What's On in Las Vegas Magazine.
Ad Rates: BW: $2,641 **Circ:** Paid ★3,137
4C: $3,166 Non-paid ★157,927

18481 Women in Sport and Physical Activity Journal
Women of Diversity Productions
400 Antique Bay St. Phone: (702)341-9807
Las Vegas, NV 89128 Fax: (702)341-9828
Publisher E-mail: dvrsty@aol.com

Scholarly journal covering women in sports. **Trim Size:** 6 x 9. **Key Personnel:** Marlene Adrian, Editor; Pam Beehler, Editor. **Subscription Rates:** $20 individuals. **Remarks:** Advertising not accepted.
Circ: Paid 250

18482 Your Life Matters
8058 Pinnacle Peak Ave. Phone: (702)222-1998
Las Vegas, NV 89113 Fax: (702)222-1940

Lifestyles magazine. **Founded:** 1993. **Freq:** Semiannual. **Trim Size:** 8 1/2 x 11. **Key Personnel:** Janet Greeson, Editor, janetgreeson@aol.com; Eugene Boyle, Editor. **Remarks:** Advertising accepted; rates available upon request. **URL:** http://janetgreeson.com.
Circ: Controlled 100,000

18483 KCEP-FM - 88.1
330 W. Washington St. Phone: (702)648-4218
Las Vegas, NV 89106-3327 Fax: (702)647-0803

Format: Blues; Urban Contemporary. **Networks:** American Urban Radio. **Owner:** EOB/Clark County, 2228 Comstock, North Las Vegas, NV 89030, (702)648-0104, Fax: (702)648-6749. **Founded:** 1973. **Operating Hours:** Continuous; 15% network, 85% local. **ADI:** Las Vegas, NV. **Key Personnel:** Sherman Ruttledge, Jr., General Mgr. **Wattage:** 10,000. **Ad Rates:** $20 for 30 seconds; $35 for 60 seconds. **URL:** http://www.kcepfm88.com.

18484 KDOX-AM - 1280
Commercial Arts Bldg. Phone: (702)732-1664
953 E. Sahara, Ste. 255 Fax: (702)732-3060
Las Vegas, NV 89104
Free: (888)410-9864

Format: Hispanic; Adult Contemporary. **Owner:** at above address. **Founded:** 1956. **Formerly:** KREL-AM (1987); KDOL-AM. **Operating Hours:** Continuous. **ADI:** Las Vegas, NV. **Key Personnel:** Scott Gentry, Manager, phone (702)258-0039, fax (702)258-0556; Hector Rossetti, Program Dir., fax (702)732-1937. **Local Programs:** *Open Line* 1:00 pm Wednesday, Eddie Escobedo, Host, (702)649-8553, Fax (702)649-7429. **Wattage:** 5000 day; 500 post sunset; 50 night. **Ad Rates:** $40 per unit.

18485 KDWN-AM - 720
1 Maine St. Phone: (702)385-7212
Las Vegas, NV 89101 Fax: (702)385-7990
Free: (800)338-8255

Format: Talk; News; Sports. **Networks:** AP; L.A. Dodgers Radio. **Owner:** Radio Nevada, at above address. **Founded:** 1975. **Operating Hours:** Continuous; 10% network, 90% local. **ADI:** Las Vegas, NV. **Key Personnel:** A.J. Williams, President; Claire Reis, General Mgr.; Barbara Noell, Contact. **Wattage:** 50,000. **Ad Rates:** $18-28 for 30 seconds; $22-38 for 60 seconds. **URL:** http://www.kdawn.com.

18486 KENO-AM - 1460
4660 S. Decatur Blvd. Phone: (702)876-1460
Las Vegas, NV 89103 Fax: (702)876-6685

Format: News. **Networks:** Unistar. **Founded:** 1940. **Operating Hours:** Continuous. **ADI:** Las Vegas, NV. **Key Personnel:** Tony Bonnici, General Mgr./V.P.; Seat Williams, Program and Operations Dir. **Wattage:** 10,000 day; 1000 night. **Ad Rates:** $120-175 for pu seconds.

18487 KFBT-TV -
3840 S. Jones Blvd. Phone: (702)382-2121
Las Vegas, NV 89103

Format: Commercial TV. **Owner:** Sinclair Broadcasting Group, at above address. **Former name:** KUPN-TV. **Operating Hours:** Continuous. **Key Personnel:** Mark Higgins, General Mgr.; Robert Weisboro, General Sales Mgr.; Jane Kozich, Business Mgr.

18488 KFMS-FM - 101.9
1130 E Desert Inn Rd. Phone: (702)732-7753
Las Vegas, NV 89109-2812 Fax: (702)732-4890

Format: Country. **Networks:** Independent. **Founded:** 1963. **Operating Hours:** Continuous. **ADI:** Las Vegas, NV. **Key Personnel:** Mike Ginsburg, Contact. **Wattage:** 100,000.

18489 KILA-FM - 90.5
2201 S. 6th St. Phone: (702)731-5452
Las Vegas, NV 89104

Format: Religious; Contemporary Christian. **Networks:** SOS Radio. **Owner:** Faith Communications Corp., 2201 S. 6th St., Las Vegas, NV 89104. **Founded:** 1972. **Operating Hours:** Continuous; 5% network, 95% local. **ADI:** Las Vegas, NV. **Key Personnel:** Jack French, General Mgr.; Chris Staley, Program Dir. **Wattage:** 100,000. **Ad Rates:** Noncommercial.

18490 KISF-FM - 103.5
1455 E. Tropicana, Ste. 650 Phone: (702)795-1035
Las Vegas, NV 89119 Fax: (702)798-1738
E-mail: kiss@kiss1035.com

Owner: George E. Tobin, at above address. **Founded:** 1991. **Formerly:** KMMK-FM (1992); KEDC-FM (June 1998). **Operating Hours:** Continuous. **ADI:** Las Vegas, NV. **Key Personnel:** Brian White, Program Dir., brian@kiss1035.com; Michael Bump, General Sales Mgr., bump@kiss1035.com; Lloyd Moss, Chief Engineer; Lynda Pando, Controller. **Wattage:** 100,000. **Ad Rates:** $55-120 per unit. **URL:** http://www.intermind.net/kedg.

18491 KJUL-FM - 104.3
1455 E. Tropicana Ave., Ste. 800 Phone: (702)730-0300
Las Vegas, NV 89119-6522 Fax: (702)730-8447
E-mail: kjvl@kjul.com

Founded: 1986. **Formerly:** Nevada Radio, Inc. **Operating Hours:** Continuous. **ADI:** Las Vegas, NV. **Key Personnel:** Harry Williams, General Mgr.; Gary Sommer, Sales Mgr. **Wattage:** 100,000. **Ad Rates:** $100-120 per unit.

18492 KKLZ-FM - 96.3
4305 S. Industrial Rd., Ste. 120 Phone: (702)739-9600
Las Vegas, NV 89103 Fax: (702)739-0083

Format: Classic Rock. **Networks:** Independent. **Founded:** 1984. **Operating Hours:** Continuous. **ADI:** Las Vegas, NV. **Key Personnel:** Dennis Mitchell, News/Public Service Dir. **Wattage:** 100,000.

18493 KKVV-AM - 1060
3185 S. Highland Dr., Ste. 13 Phone: (702)731-5588
Las Vegas, NV 89109 Fax: (702)731-5851
E-mail: billsdesk2@aol.com

Format: Contemporary Christian; Talk. **Networks:** USA Radio. **Owner:** Las Vegas Broadcasters, at above address, Fax: (702)731-5851. **Founded:** 1990. **Operating Hours:** 6 a.m.-12 a.m. **ADI:** Las Vegas, NV. **Key Personnel:** Carl E. Auel, President, phone (407)688-9585, fax (407)688-9601; Bill Ball, GM/Program Dir., billsdesk2@aol.com; Bill Ball, Operations. **Local Programs:** *Homeward Bound* 4:00 pm - 5:30 pm Monday-Friday, Bill Ball, (702)794-9484, Fax (702)794-9451; *Pastor's Study* 2:00 pm - 2:30 pm Monday-Friday; *Real Estate Preview* 9:00 am - 10:00 am Saturday, Bill Ball, GM/Program Dir., (702)731-5588, Fax (702)731-5851. **Wattage:** 5000. **Ad Rates:** $20 for 15 seconds; $35 for 30 seconds; $65 for 60 seconds. **URL:** http://www.kkvv.com.

18494 KLAS-TV - 8
3228 Channel Dr. Phone: (702)792-8888
Box 15047 Fax: (702)734-7437
Las Vegas, NV 89114

Format: Commercial TV. **Networks:** CBS. **Operating Hours:** Continuous. **ADI:** Las Vegas, NV. **Key Personnel:** Dick Fraim, Contact; Andy Henderson, General Sales Mgr.; Matt Aaron, Contact; Karen Muntean, Contact; Marilyn Smith, Traffic Mgr. **Ad Rates:** Advertising accepted; rates available upon request.

KLNR-FM - See Panaca

18495 KLSQ-AM - 870
6767 W. Tropicana Ave., Ste. 102 Phone: (702)284-6400
Las Vegas, NV 89103 Fax: (702)284-6475

Format: Hispanic. **Owner:** Heftel Broadcasting, 3102 Oaklawn Dr., Dallas, TX 75219, (214)525-7700. **Operating Hours:** 8:30 a.m.-5:30 p.m. Mon.-Fri.

18496 KLVX-TV - 10
4210 Channel 10 Dr. Phone: (702)799-1010
Las Vegas, NV 89119 Fax: (702)799-2806
E-mail: kurt_ mische@klvx.pbs.org

Format: Public TV. **Networks:** Public Broadcasting Service (PBS). **Owner:** Clark County School District, 2832 E. Flamingo Rd., Las Vegas, NV 89119, (702)799-5011. **Founded:** Mar. 1968. **Operating Hours:** Continuous. **ADI:** Las Vegas, NV. **Key Personnel:** Tom Axtel, General Mgr., fax (702)799-5586, tom_ axtell@klvx.pbs.org; Shelli Jones, Program Dir., shelli_ jones@klvx.pbs.org; Kurt Mische, Dev. Dir., kurt_ mische@klvx.pbs.org. **Local Programs:** *Nevada Week in Review*, Mitch Fox, Mailing contact; *Outdoor Nevada*, Dau Garrison, Mailing contact. **Wattage:** 296000 kw. **Ad Rates:** Advertising accepted; rates available upon request.

18497 KNPR-FM - 89.5
5151 Boulder Hwy. Phone: (702)456-6695
Las Vegas, NV 89122 Fax: (702)458-2787
E-mail: knpr@accessnv.com

Format: Public Radio; News; Classical. **Networks:** National Public Radio (NPR). **Owner:** Nevada Public Radio Corp., at above address. **Founded:** 1980. **Operating Hours:** Continuous; 20% network, 80% local. **ADI:** Las Vegas, NV. **Key Personnel:** Lamar Marchese, Contact; Phillip Burger, Program Dir. **Local Programs:** *Guess Who's Playing the Classics?*, Ginger Bruner; *Making Nevada Home*, Phil Burger. **Wattage:** 100,000. **Ad Rates:** Noncommercial; underwriting available.

18498 KNUU-AM - 970
2001 E. Flamingo Rd., No. 101 Phone: (702)735-8644
Las Vegas, NV 89119-5117 Fax: (702)735-8184

Format: Talk; News. **Networks:** CBS; AP. **Owner:** CAT Broadcasting Corp., at above address, Fax: (702)734-4755. **Founded:** July 5, 1977. **Operating Hours:** Continuous; 20% network, 80% local. **ADI:** Las Vegas, NV. **Key Personnel:** Ron Cohen, General Mgr.; Julie Tavares, News Dir.; Rick Denton, General Sales Mgr.; Sandy Crownover, Traffic Dir. **Wattage:** 5000 day; 500 night. **Ad Rates:** $40 for 30 seconds; $43 for 60 seconds.

18499 KOMP-FM - 92.3
4660 S. Decatur Blvd. Phone: (702)876-1460
Las Vegas, NV 89103 Fax: (702)876-6685
E-mail: komp@wizard.com

Format: Album-Oriented Rock (AOR). **Networks:** Independent. **Founded:** 1966. **Operating Hours:** Continuous. **ADI:** Las Vegas, NV. **Key Personnel:** Tony Bonnici, General Mgr.; Richard Reed, Operations Dir.; Big Marty, Music Dir.; Michael Culotta, Program Dir. **Wattage:** 100,000.

18500 KORK-AM - 920
PO Box 26629 Phone: (702)876-9571
Las Vegas, NV 89126-0629 Fax: (702)876-1460
E-mail: point97@infi.net

Format: Big Band/Nostalgia. **Networks:** ABC. **Owner:** Lotus Communications Corporation, 6290 Sunset Blvd., Los Angeles, CA 90028. **Founded:** 1953. **Operating Hours:** Continuous. **ADI:** Las Vegas, NV. **Key Personnel:** Tony Bonnici, General Mgr.; Larry Alan Wells, Program Dir.; Mike McCuen, Music Dir. **Wattage:** 5,000 day/500 night.

18501 KTKR-AM - 760
3305 W. Mountain Rd., No. 60
Las Vegas, NV 89102
E-mail: ticketsports.com

Format: Sports. **Owner:** Clear Channel Broadcasting, 6222 NW I-10, San Antonio, TX 78201, (210)736-9700, Fax: (210)735-8811. **Founded:** July 31, 1995. **Operating Hours:** Continuous. **ADI:** San Angelo, TX. **Key Personnel:** Betty Kocurek, General Mgr., bkocurek@woai.com; Andrew Ashwood, Operations Mgr., aashwood@woai.com; Carla Jenkins, General Sales Mgr., cjenkins@woai.com. **Wattage:** 50,000. **URL:** http://www.ticketsports.com.

18502 KTNV-TV - 13
3355 South Valley View Blvd. Phone: (702)876-1313
Las Vegas, NV 89102 Fax: (702)871-1961
E-mail: ktnv@ktnv.com

Format: Commercial TV. **Networks:** ABC. **Owner:** WTMJ, Inc., PO Box 693, Milwaukee, WI 53201, (414)332-9611. **Formerly:** KSHO-TV. **Operating Hours:** Continuous except Fri. sign off from 3 a.m.-6 a.m. **ADI:** Las Vegas, NV. **Key Personnel:** Peter Bannister, V.P./Gen. Mgr., peter@ktnv.com; Gary Plumlee, General Sales Mgr.; Perry Boxx, News Dir.; Marie Shea, Program Dir.; Emily Tyska, Community Affairs Dir.; Mike Williams, Operations Mgr.; Roman Hiohowskyj, Chief Engineer; Ron Futrell, Sports Dir.; Greg Millett, Assignment Editor.

KTPH-FM - See Tonopah

18503 KUNV-FM - 91.5
University of Nevada at Las Vegas Phone: (702)895-3877
Fax: (702)895-4857
4505 S. Maryland Pkwy.
Las Vegas, NV 89154

Format: Ethnic; Album-Oriented Rock (AOR); World Beat; Blues; Folk. **Owner:** University of Nevada, Las Vegas, at above address. **Founded:** 1981. **Operating Hours:** Continuous; 100% local. **ADI:** Las Vegas, NV. **Key Personnel:** Don Fuller, General Mgr.; Brian Sanders, Program Dir. **Wattage:** 15,000. **Ad Rates:** Noncommercial; underwriting available.

18504 KUPN-TV - 21
920 S. Commerce Phone: (702)382-2121
Las Vegas, NV 89106 Fax: (702)382-1351

Format: Commercial TV. **Networks:** United Paramount Network. **Owner:** Channel 21, L.P., at above address. **Founded:** 1984. **Formerly:** KRLR-TV (Mar. 6, 1995). **Operating Hours:** Continuous; 100% local. **ADI:** Las Vegas, NV. **Key Personnel:** Marty Sokoler, General Mgr.; Dale Palecek, Dir. of Programming & Promotion; Mark Winkler, General Sales Mgr.; Sandy Close, Traffic Mgr.; Mindy Sileo, Business Mgr. **Ad Rates:** Advertising accepted; rates available upon request.

18505 KVBC-TV - 3
1500 Foremaster LN Phone: (702)642-3333
PO Box 44169 Fax: (702)657-3423
Las Vegas, NV 89116

Format: Commercial TV. **Networks:** NBC. **Owner:** Sunbelt Communications Company, at above address. **Founded:** 1979. **Formerly:** KORK-TV (1979). **Operating Hours:** Continuous. **ADI:** Las Vegas, NV. **Key Personnel:** Rolla Cleaver, General Mgr., phone (702)642-3201, fax (702)657-3423, rcleaver@kvbc.com; Gene Greenberg, Dir. of Marketing, phone (702)642-3209, fax (702)657-3208, ggreenberg@kvbc.com; John Morath, Promotions Mgr., phone (702)657-3275, fax (702)657-3208, jmorath@kvbc.com; Mike George, News Dir., phone (702)642-3158, fax (702)657-3152, mgeorge@kvbc.com; Dale Wyman, Creative Services Mgr., phone (702)642-3289, fax (702)657-3208, dwyman@kvbc.com; Judy Reich, Programming Mgr., phone (702)642-3248, fax (702)657-3208; Scott Mattox, Controller, phone (702)642-3140, fax (702)657-3423, smattox@kvbc.com; Glenn Turner, Production Mgr., phone (702)642-3404, fax (702)657-3028, gturner@kvbc.com; John Holland, Dir. of Engineering, phone (702)642-3426, fax (702)657-3256, jholland@kvbc.com; Shelley Goings, Business Mgr., phone (702)642-3146, fax (702)657-3423, sgoings@kvbc.com; Cindy Heinrich, Dir. of Human Resources, phone (702)642-3109, fax (702)657-3423, cheinrich@kvbc.com. **Local Programs:** *First News 3 at Four* 4:00 p.m. - 4:30 p.m. Monday-Friday, Mike George, (702)642-3333, Fax (702)657-3152; *First News 3 at Five* 5:00 p.m. - 5:30 p.m. Monday-Friday, Mike George, (702)642-3333, Fax (702)657-3152; *First News 3 at Six* 6:00 p.m. - 6:30 p.m. Monday-Friday, Mike George, (702)657-3333, Fax (702)657-3152. **Wattage:** 100. **URL:** http://www.kvbc.com.

18506 KWNR-FM - 95.5
1130 E Desert Inn Rd. Phone: (702)798-4004
Las Vegas, NV 89109 Fax: (702)733-0433

Format: Contemporary Country. **Networks:** Independent. **Founded:** 1988. **Operating Hours:** Continuous. **ADI:** Las Vegas, NV. **Key Personnel:** Mike Ginsburg, General Mgr.; Steve Groesbeck, General Sales Mgr.; Tom Jordan, Program Dir.; Joan Gedde, Business Mgr. **Wattage:** 100,000. **Ad Rates:** $160 per unit.

18507 KXNT-AM - 840
6655 W. Sanara, Ste. D-208
Las Vegas, NV 89102
E-mail: am840kxnt@aol.com

Format: News; Talk. **Networks:** ABC. **Owner:** American Radio Systems, 116 Huntington Ave., Boston, MA 02116, (617)375-7575. **Founded:** 1988. **Formerly:** KVEG-AM. **Operating Hours:** Continuous. **ADI:** Las Vegas, NV. **Key Personnel:** Alan Eisenson, Program Dir., phone (702)889-7304, fax (702)889-7329, aceisen@anv.com; Jackie Landry, Station Mgr., phone (702)889-7360, fax (702)889-7384, jlandry@anv.com; Stephanie Lindelow, Traffic Mgr., phone (702)889-7341, fax (702)889-7373; Tom Humm, General Mgr., phone (702)364-8400, fax (702)889-7373, tomhumm@anv.com; Stephanie Interbartolo, Marketing Dir., phone (702)889-7376, fax (702)889-7384, sinter@anv.com. **Wattage:** 50,000 day, 25,000 night. **Ad Rates:** Advertising accepted; rates available upon request. **URL:** http://www.kxnt.com.

18508 KXPT-FM - 97.1
PO Box 26629 Phone: (702)876-1460
Las Vegas, NV 89126-0629 Fax: (702)876-1886
E-mail: point97@vegas.infi.net

Networks: Independent. **Owner:** Lotus Communications Corporation, 6290 Sunset Blvd., Los Angeles, CA 90020, (213)461-8225. **Founded:** 1961. **Formerly:** KYRK-FM. **Operating Hours:** Continuous. **ADI:** Las Vegas, NV. **Key Personnel:** Tony Bonnici, Gen. Mgr./VP, phone (702)876-1460, fax (702)876-6685; Chris Foxx, Program Dir., phone (702)876-1460, cfoxx@point97.com; J.D. Davis, Music Dir., phone (702)876-1460, jd@point97.com; Richard Reed, Operations Dir., phone (702)876-1460. **Local Programs:** *Richard Reed.* **Wattage:** 100,000.

18509 Prime Cable of Las Vegas
121 S. Martin Luther King Blvd. Phone: (702)384-8084
Las Vegas, NV 89106 Fax: (702)383-0614

Founded: 1980. **Cities Served:** Clark County, Boulder City, Green Valley, Henderson, and North Las Vegas, NV.

18510 Valley Communications, Inc.
4075 W. Desert Inn Rd., Ste. D Phone: (702)871-1739
Las Vegas, NV 89102 Fax: (702)367-8236

Founded: 1986. **Key Personnel:** Richard Fisher, Manager. **Cities Served:** Tonapah Base.: subscribing households 1022.

18511 WHKW-FM - 98.9
3305 W. Spring Mountain Rd., No. 60
Las Vegas, NV 89102
E-mail: info@whkw.com

Format: Contemporary Country. **Owner:** Clear Channel Communications, Inc., at above address. **Operating Hours:** Continuous. **ADI:** Louisville, KY. **Key Personnel:** Robert Scherer, Market Mgr.; Mark Thomas, General Mgr.; Gene Guinn, General Sales Mgr.; Dennis Hill, Program Dir. **Wattage:** 50,000. **Ad Rates:** $10-45 per unit. **URL:** http://www.whkw.com.

18512 WKJK-AM - 1080
3305 W. Spring Mountain Rd., Ste. 60
Las Vegas, NV 89102
E-mail: info@wkjk.com

Format: Adult Contemporary; Middle-of-the-Road (MOR). **Owner:** Clear Channel Communications, Inc., 200 Concord Plaza, Ste. 600, San Antonio, TX 78216, (210)822-2828. **Operating Hours:** Continuous. **ADI:** Louisville, KY. **Key Personnel:** Robert Scherer, Market Mgr.; Mark Thomas, General Mgr.; Kelly Carls, Program Dir.; Charlie Jenkins, General Sales Mgr. **Wattage:** 10,000. **Ad Rates:** $25-28 per unit. Combined advertising rates available with WWKY-AM. **URL:** http://www.wkjk.com.

18513 WWKY-AM - 790
3305 W. Spring Mountain Rd., Ste. 60
Las Vegas, NV 89102

Format: Talk. **Networks:** CBS. **Owner:** Clear Channel Communications, Inc., 200 Concord Plaza, Ste. 600, San Antonio, TX 78216, (210)822-2828. **Operating Hours:** Continuous. **ADI:** Louisville, KY. **Key Personnel:** Robert R. Scherer, Marketing Mgr.; Mark Thomas, General Mgr.; Charlie Jenkins, General Sales Mgr.; Stew Williams, Program Dir. **Wattage:** 5000. **Ad Rates:** $25-28 per unit. Combined advertising rates available with WKJK-FM. **URL:** http://www.wwky.com.

LAUGHLIN

Clark Co.

18514 Clark Cablevision
3030 Needle Hwy., Ste. 1900 Phone: (702)298-3214
Laughlin, NV 89029 Fax: (702)298-3075

Founded: 1990. **Formerly:** Laughlin Cable TV (1990); Laughlin Cablevision LP. **Key Personnel:** Marc Weisberg, Contact. **Cities Served:** subscribing households 2,700; 42 channels; 1 community access channel.

LOVELOCK†.

Pershing Co. (S). Tungsten and Copper mines.

18515 Lovelock Review-Miner
230 Main St. Phone: (702)273-7245
PO Box 620
Lovelock, NV 89419
Local newspaper covering Pershing County. **Founded:** Jan. 1905. **Freq:** Weekly. **Print Method:** Offset. **Trim Size:** 10 13/16 x 21 1/2. **Cols./Page:** 6. **Col. Width:** 12.5 picas. **Col. Depth:** 480 agate lines. **Key Personnel:** Gwen Bogh Carter, Publisher. **USPS:** 463-940. **Subscription Rates:** $18; $25 out of county. **Remarks:** Accepts advertising. **Formerly:** Lovelock Review-Miner and Lovelock Tribune (1992).
Ad Rates: BW: $276.90 **Circ:** Paid ‡1,400
4C: $300 Free ‡15
PCI: $4.26

MINDEN

KGVM-FM - See Gardnerville

PANACA

18516 KLNR-FM - 91.7
5151 Boulder Hwy.
Las Vegas, NV 89122
E-mail: knpr@accessnv.com

Format: Classical; News. **Networks:** National Public Radio (NPR). **Founded:** 1989. **Operating Hours:** Continuous. **ADI:** Las Vegas, NV. **Key Personnel:** Lamar Marchese, General Mgr. **Wattage:** 100.

PIOCHE

18517 Lincoln County Record
PO Box 507 Phone: (775)726-3333
Pioche, NV 89043-0507 Fax: (775)726-3331

Community newspaper. **Founded:** Sept. 17, 1870. **Freq:** Weekly (Thurs.). **Print Method:** Offset. Uses mats. **Cols./Page:** 5. **Col. Width:** 26 nonpareils. **Col. Depth:** 182 agate lines. **Key Personnel:** Connie Simkins, Editor and Publisher. **USPS:** 587-120. **Subscription Rates:** $15; $20 out of area.
Ad Rates: GLR: $.33 **Circ:** ‡1,700
BW: $292.50
SAU: $5
PCI: $5

RENO†, pop. 100,756.

Washoe Co. (W). 140 m NE of Sacramento, Calif. University of Nevada-Reno. Tourist resort, legalized gambling, recreation & winter skiing. Western warehousing and distribution center. Manufactures cement, labeling devices, suntan lotion, valves, dairy and food products, gaming, pet food, microwave, electronic equipment. Livestock, agricultural produce. Alfalfa seed, grain.

18518 Ahora Spanish News
30 Mary St., Ste. 2 Phone: (702)323-6811
PO Box 3582 Fax: (702)323-6995
Reno, NV 89509
Publication E-mail: ahora@pyramid.net

Community newspaper (Spanish and English). **Founded:** 1983. **Freq:** Weekly. **Print Method:** Offset. **Cols./Page:** 6. **Col. Width:** 2 1/6 inches. **Col. Depth:** 21 inches. **Key Personnel:** Miguel A. Sepulveda, Editor and Publisher. **Subscription Rates:** $40. **Remarks:** Accepts advertising.
Ad Rates: BW: $14.50 **Circ:** Paid 620
4C: $500 Free 11,380
PCI: $14.50

18519 Juvenile and Family Court Journal
National Council of Juvenile and Family Court Judges
PO Box 8970 Phone: (702)784-6012
Reno, NV 89507 Fax: (702)784-1084

Journal covering juvenile and family law. **Founded:** 1946. **Freq:** Quarterly. **Trim Size:** 8 1/2 x 11. **Cols./Page:** 2. **Col. Width:** 3 1/2 inches. **Col. Depth:** 9 inches. **Key Personnel:** Marie R. Mildon, Editor. **Subscription Rates:** $60 individuals; $15 single issue. **Remarks:** Advertising not accepted.
Circ: Combined ⊕2,550

18520 North American Mining
Mining Media, Inc.
1005 Terminal Way, Ste., 140 Phone: (702)323-3002
Reno, NV 89502 Fax: (702)323-1553
Free: (800)879-9227

Magazine reporting North American mining environmental and public policy issues. **Founded:** Feb. 1997. **Freq:** Bimonthly. **Print Method:** Web Offset. **Trim Size:** 8 x 10 3/4. **Cols./Page:** 3. **Key Personnel:** Dorothy Y. Kosich, General Mgr./Editor; Lawrence Williams, Publisher. **ISSN:** 1047-7551. **Subscription Rates:** $55 U.S.; $60 Canada; $85 other countries. **Remarks:** Accepts advertising. **Formerly**: Mining World News.
Ad Rates: BW: $1,870 **Circ:** Paid ‡2,000
4C: $2,250 Non-paid ‡5,000

18521 Reno Gazette-Journal
Gannett Co., Inc.
PO Box 22000 Phone: (702)788-6397
Reno, NV 89520-2000 Fax: (702)788-6458

General newspaper. **Founded:** 1870. **Freq:** Mon.-Sun. (morn.). **Print Method:** Letterpress and offset. **Trim Size:** 13 x 21 1/2. **Cols./Page:** 6. **Col. Width:** 26 nonpareils. **Col. Depth:** 301 agate lines. **Key Personnel:** Tonia Cunning, Executive Editor, phone (702)788-6299; Sue Clark-Johnson, Publisher, phone (702)788-6208; John Zidich, Sales Mgr., phone (702)788-6293, fax (702)788-6516, jzidich@reno.garnett.com; Clare Wood, Editor, phone (775)788-6322, fax (775)788-6458; Linda Dono, Editor, phone (775)788-6302, fax (775)788-6458; Mark Lundahl, Editor, phone (775)788-6230, fax (775)788-6458; Tim Dunn, Editor, phone (775)788-6355, fax (775)788-6458; Ray Hagar, Editor, phone (775)788-6345, fax (775)788-6458. **Subscription Rates:** $169; $182 out of area. **Remarks:** Accepts advertising. **URL:** http://www.nevadanet.com. **Formerly**: Nevada State Journal and Reno Evening Gazette.
Ad Rates: GLR: $5.86 **Circ:** Mon.-Sat. ★**67,300**
BW: $9,628.56 Sun. ★**83,750**
4C: $10,524.56
SAU: $51.07
PCI: $44.16

18522 Sagebrush
1262-A N. Sierra St. Phone: (702)784-4033
Reno, NV 89503 Fax: (702)784-1955
Publication E-mail: hlhammer@scs.unr.edu

Collegiate newspaper. **Founded:** 1893. **Freq:** 2/week Tues. and Fri. **Print Method:** Offset. Uses mats. **Cols./Page:** 6. **Col. Width:** 147 inches. **Col. Depth:** 21 inches. **Key Personnel:** Mike Dillon, Advertising Mgr., phone (702)784-6589; John Curtis, Editor, phone (702)784-4033, curtis1@scs.unr.edu. **Subscription Rates:** $40 annual. **Remarks:** Accepts advertising. **Available Online.**
Ad Rates: GLR: $7.90 **Circ:** Free ‡6,000
SAU: $7.90

18523 Showtime Magazine
Recreation Publications, Inc.
2303 Kietzke Ln. No. 18 Phone: (702)827-5400
Reno, NV 89502 Free: (800)878-7886

Magazine featuring the current week's opportunities in food, gaming, and entertainment in the Reno-Tahoe area. **Founded:** 1972. **Freq:** Biweekly. **Print Method:** Web. **Trim Size:** 8 1/8 x 10 3/4. **Cols./Page:** 3. **Col. Width:** 2 1/4 inches. **Col. Depth:** 10 inches. **Key Personnel:** Christina Montroy, Editor; Don Abbott, Publisher. **Subscription Rates:** $39.95 individuals. **Remarks:** Accepts advertising. **URL:** http://olmi.com/showtime.htm.
Ad Rates: BW: $1,250 **Circ:** Paid ‡1,100
4C: $1,850 Non-paid ‡25,000

18524 Western Roofing/Insulation/Siding
Dodson Publications, Inc.
546 Court St. Phone: (702)333-1080
Reno, NV 89501 Fax: (702)333-1081
Publication E-mail: westroof@aol.com

Roofing, siding, and insulation magazine published for the western roofing industry in affiliation with the Western Roofing Contractors Association. **Founded:** 1978. **Freq:** Bimonthly. **Print Method:** Offset. **Trim Size:** 8 3/8 x 10 7/8. **Cols./Page:** 3. **Col. Width:** 27 nonpareils. **Col. Depth:** 137 agate lines. **Key Personnel:** Marc Dodson, Editor and Publisher. **ISSN:** 0273-5687. **Subscription Rates:** $12 individuals; $2.50 single issue; $60 other countries per year. **Remarks:** Accepts advertising. **Available Online**. **URL:** http://www.westernroofing.net.
Ad Rates: BW: $1,615 **Circ:** Paid ‡2,051
4C: $2,775 Controlled ‡20,274

18525 KAME-TV - 21
4920 Brookside Ct. Phone: (702)856-2121
Reno, NV 89502 Fax: (702)856-9146

Format: Commercial TV. **Networks:** Fox; Independent. **Founded:** 1981. **Operating Hours:** Continuous. **ADI:** Reno, NV. **Key Personnel:** William C. Andrews, General Mgr.; B.J. Andrews, Contact.

18526 KDOT-FM - 104.5
2900 Sutro St. Phone: (702)329-9261
Reno, NV 89512 Fax: (702)323-1450

Format: Alternative/New Music/Progressive. **Owner:** Lotus Communications Corp., 6290 Sunset Blvd., Los Angeles, CA, (213)461-8225, Fax: (213)467-8256. **Founded:** 1966. **Formerly**: KIIQ-FM (1991); KHIT-FM. **Operating Hours:** Continuous. **ADI:** Reno, NV. **Key Personnel:** Tony J. Schavietello, General Mgr.; Lynette Doege, Business Mgr.; Rob Williams, Operations Mgr.; Steve Funk, Program Dir. **Local Programs:** *Morning Show*, Steve Funk. **Wattage:** 25,000. **Ad Rates:** Advertising accepted; rates available upon request.

18527 KHIT-AM - 630
2900 Sutro St. Phone: (702)329-9261
Reno, NV 89512 Fax: (702)323-1450

Format: Country. **Networks:** ABC. **Owner:** Lotus Communications Corp., 6290 Sunset Blvd., Los Angeles, CA 90028, (213)461-8225, Fax: (213)467-8256. **Founded:** 1984. **Formerly**: KRCV-AM (1989). **Operating Hours:** 24 Hrs. **ADI:** Reno, NV. **Key Personnel:** Tony Schavietello, General Mgr.; Lynette Doege, Business Mgr.; Rob Williams, Operations Mgr. **Wattage:** 5,000. **Ad Rates:** Advertising accepted; rates available upon request.

18528 KHVO-TV -
1325 Airmotive Way, Ste. 130
Reno, NV 89502
E-mail: newy@kitv.com

Format: Commercial TV. **Networks:** ABC. **Owner:** Hearst-Argyle Television, at above address. **ADI:** Honolulu, HI. **URL:** http://www.kitv.com.

18529 KMAU-TV -
1325 Airmotive Way, Ste. 130
Reno, NV 89502

Format: Commercial TV. **Owner:** Hearst-Argyle Television, at above address.

18530 KODS-FM - 103.7
255 W. Moana Ln., No. 208 Phone: (702)829-1964
Reno, NV 89509-4943 Fax: (702)825-3183

Format: Oldies. **Networks:** Independent. **Founded:** 1974. **Formerly**: KHTZ-FM (1988). **Operating Hours:** Continuous. **ADI:** Reno, NV. **Key Personnel:** Kevin Mashek, General Mgr.; Bob Garrison, News Dir.; Bob Walker, Program Dir. **Wattage:** 6000. **Ad Rates:** $17-72 per unit.

18531 KOLO-TV - 8
4850 Ampere Dr. Phone: (702)858-8888
PO Box 10000 Fax: (702)858-8855
Reno, NV 89502-0005

Format: Commercial TV. **Networks:** ABC. **Owner:** Stephens Group Inc. c/o Donrey Media Group, 3800 Wheeler Ave., PO Box 17017, Fort Smith, AR 72917, (501)785-7815. **Founded:** 1953. **Formerly**: KZTV-TV. **Operating Hours:** Continuous. **ADI:** Reno, NV. **Key Personnel:** Charles S. Alvey, General Mgr., phone (702)858-8847, calvey@kolotv.com; Bill Hall, General Sales Mgr., bhall@kolotv.com; Lorna King, Business Mgr., lking@kolotv.com. **Wattage:** 151,000.

18532 KOZZ-FM - 105.7
Box 9870 Phone: (702)329-9261
Reno, NV 89507 Fax: (702)323-1450

Format: Classic Rock. **Founded:** 1966. **Operating Hours:** Continuous. **ADI:** Reno, NV. **Key Personnel:** Steve Groesbeck, General Mgr.; Jim McClain, PD; Jake Armer, News/P.A. Dir. **Wattage:** 75,000. **Ad Rates:** Advertising accepted; rates available upon request.

18533 KPLY-AM - 1270
255 W. Moana Ln., No. 208 Phone: (702)829-1964
Reno, NV 89509 Fax: (702)825-3183

Format: Sports; News. **Networks:** CBS. **Owner:** Americom Broadcasting, at above address. **Founded:** 1960. **Operating Hours:** Continuous. **ADI:** Reno, NV. **Key Personnel:** Kevin Mashek, General Mgr. **Wattage:** 5000. **Ad Rates:** $16 per unit.

18534 KPTT-AM - 1450
2900 Sutro St. Phone: (702)329-9261
Reno, NV 89512 Fax: (702)323-1450

Format: Sports; Talk; News. **Networks:** Westwood One Radio. **Owner:** Lotus Communications Corp., 6777 Hollywood Blvd., Hollywood, CA 90028, (213)461-8225. **Founded:** 1967. **Formerly**: KONE-AM (1992); KOZZ-AM. **Operating Hours:** Continuous. **ADI:** Reno, NV. **Key Personnel:** Steve Groesbeck, General Mgr.; Rob Williams, Operations Mgr.; Jake Armer, News Dir.; Jim McClain, Program Dir.; Lynette Doege, Business Mgr.; Ken Allen, Public Affairs Dir. **Local Programs:** *Weird Awakening*, Steve Smith. **Wattage:** 1000.

18535 KREN-TV - 27
940 Matley Ln., Ste. 15 Phone: (702)333-2727
Reno, NV 89502-2139 Fax: (702)333-5264
E-mail: donb@kren.com

Format: Commercial TV. **Owner:** Pappas Telecasting of NV., 500 S. Chinewth Rd., Visalia, CA 93277, (209)733-7800, Fax: (209)627-5363. **Founded:** 1986. **Operating Hours:** Continuous; 20% network, 80% local. **ADI:** Reno, NV. **Key Personnel:** Don Brown, General Mgr.; Lupe Jimenez, Operations Dir.; Domingo Miranda, Chief Engineer; Gael Holderman, Accounting. **Wattage:** 30,000. **Ad Rates:** $10-400 for 10 seconds.

18536 KRNV-FM - 101.7
1790 Vassar St. Phone: (702)322-4444
Reno, NV 89502 Fax: (702)785-1208

Format: News; Talk. **Networks:** CNN Radio; AP. **Owner:** Sunbelt Communications Co., 1500 Foremaster Ln., Las Vegas, NV 89101. **Formerly**: KSXY-FM; KTHX-FM. **Operating Hours:** Continuous. **ADI:** Reno, NV. **Key Personnel:** Craig Brown, Station Mgr., cbrown@krnv.com; Dan VanEnoo, Program Mgr., dvanenoo@krnv.com. **Wattage:** 3,600. **URL:** http://www.krnv.com.

18537 KRNV-TV - 4
1790 Vassar Phone: (702)322-4444
Reno, NV 89502 Fax: (702)785-1200

Format: Commercial TV. **Networks:** NBC. **Founded:** 1962. **Formerly**: KCRL-TV (1989). **Operating Hours:** Continuous. **ADI:** Reno, NV. **Key Personnel:** Ralph Toddre, General Mgr.; Eric Hulnick, News Dir. **Ad Rates:** Advertising accepted; rates available upon request.

18538 KRZQ-FM - 100.9
2395 Tampa St. Phone: (775)333-1023
Reno, NV 89512 Fax: (775)333-0101

Networks: Independent. **Owner:** Mid South Broadcasting, at above address. **Founded:** 1987. **Operating Hours:** Continuous; 100% local. **ADI:** Reno, NV. **Key Personnel:** Scott Seidenstricken, Pres./Gen.Mgr.; Valerie Ellis, Sales Mgr. **URL:** http://www.krzq.com.

18539 KSAC-AM - 1240
1345 Airmotive Way Phone: (916)446-2294
Reno, NV 89502-3218 Fax: (916)443-1240

Format: Sports. **Networks:** NBC; CBS. **Founded:** 1937. **Formerly**: KROY-AM (1937). **Operating Hours:** Continuous. **ADI:** Sacramento-Stockton, CA. **Key Personnel:** Donald Early, General Mgr.; Richard W. Irwin, Operations Mgr./Program Dir.; Jim Ross, Business Mgr.; Scott Zumbiel, Traffic Mgr. **Wattage:** 1000. **Ad Rates:** Advertising accepted; rates available upon request.

18540 KTVN-TV - 2
4925 Energy Way Phone: (702)858-2222
Reno, NV 89502 Fax: (702)861-4298

Format: Commercial TV. **Networks:** CBS. **Owner:** Sarkes Tarzian, PO Box 62, Bloomington, IN, (812)332-7251. **Founded:** 1967. **Operating Hours:** Continuous. **ADI:** Reno, NV.

Key Personnel: John Richardson, General Sales Mgr.; Lawson Fox, General Mgr.; Nancy Cope, News Dir.; Cecilia Adams, Promotion Mgr., fax (702)858-2424; David Brisco, Production Mgr.; Tammy Jo Baxter, Controller. **Ad Rates:** $25-1,500 for 30 seconds.

18541 KUNR-FM - 88.7
Education Bldg, Rm. 106 Phone: (702)784-6591
University of Nevada
Reno, NV 89557

Format: Classical; Jazz; News; Talk. **Networks:** National Public Radio (NPR); American Public Radio (APR). **Founded:** 1963. **Operating Hours:** 5 a.m.-12 p.m. Mon.-Tues. Continuous Wed.-Sun. **ADI:** Reno, NV. **Key Personnel:** Marianne Murray, Station Mgr.; David Gordon, Program Dir.; Carol Baker, Promotions Mgr.; Joe Vermes, Chief Engineer. **Wattage:** 20,000. **Ad Rates:** Noncommercial.

18542 KWNZ-FM - 97.3
2395 Tampa St. Phone: (702)333-0123
Reno, NV 89512 Fax: (702)333-0101

Format: Contemporary Hit Radio (CHR). **Networks:** Independent. **Owner:** PTI Broadcasting Inc., at above address. **Founded:** 1985. **Operating Hours:** Continuous; 100% local. **ADI:** Reno, NV. **Key Personnel:** Ray Kalusa, Contact; Roy Robinson, Contact; Bob Cross, General Sales Mgr.; Laura Silvestri, Contact. **Wattage:** 87,100. **Ad Rates:** $24-42 per unit.

18543 KXEQ-AM - 1340
225 Linden St. Phone: (702)827-1111
Reno, NV 89502

Format: Hispanic. **Founded:** 1991. **Operating Hours:** Continuous. **ADI:** Reno, NV. **Key Personnel:** Juan Morales, General Mgr. **Wattage:** 1000. **Ad Rates:** $14-23 for 30 seconds; $18-28 for 60 seconds.

KZAK-FM - See Incline Village

18544 TCI of Nevada, Inc.
9335 Prototype Dr. Phone: (702)850-8555
Reno, NV 89511 Fax: (702)850-1279
Free: (800)4TC-INOW

Founded: 1953. **Key Personnel:** Lafawn Vannest, General Mgr., phone (775)850-1200, fax (775)850-1279. **Cities Served:** subscribing households 74,000; 67 channels; 3 community access channels; 504 hours per week community access programming.

SPARKS, pop. 40,780.

Washoe Co. (W). 3 m E of Reno. Gaming. Industrial.

18545 Daily Sparks Tribune
1002 C St., No. 887 Phone: (702)358-8061
PO Box 887 Fax: (702)359-3837
Sparks, NV 89431-4929
Free: (800)669-1338

General newspaper. **Founded:** 1910. **Freq:** Daily (eve.), Sunday (morn.). **Print Method:** Offset. **Cols./Page:** 6. **Col. Width:** 2 1/16 inches. **Col. Depth:** 21 1/2 inches. **Key Personnel:** Linda Brown, Editor and Publisher; Jerry Thull, Managing Editor. **Subscription Rates:** $78. **Remarks:** Accepts advertising.
Ad Rates: BW: $935.25 **Circ:** ‡6,320
4C: $1,135.25
PCI: $9.75

18546 Nevada Farm Bureau Agriculture & Livestock Journal
Nevada Farm Bureau Federation
1300 Marietta Way Phone: (702)358-3276
Sparks, NV 89431 Fax: (702)358-2107
Free: (800)922-1106
Publisher E-mail: ednufb@aol.com

Newspaper (tabloid) providing news on Nevada agriculture and emphasizing Farm Bureau programs. **Founded:** 1932. **Freq:** Monthly. **Print Method:** Offset. **Trim Size:** 11 1/2 x 14 1/2. **Cols./Page:** 4. **Col. Width:** 2 3/8 inches. **Col. Depth:** 13 1/2 inches. **Key Personnel:** Edward K. Foster, Editor, ednvfb@aol.com. **ISSN:** 0899-8434. **Subscription Rates:** For members only. **Remarks:** Advertising not accepted for certain products, please inquire.
Ad Rates: BW: $420 **Circ:** ‡2,100
4C: $600
PCI: $7.50

18547 The Nevada Rancher
PO Box 1523 Phone: (702)358-2681
Sparks, NV 89432-1523 Fax: (702)358-2686

Tabloid for ranching and agricultural interests in Nevada and the west. Includes livestock and events calendar, features, news briefs, research, sales reports, 4-H nws, and school rodeo news. **Subtitle:** 4, M, FFA News, Rodeo & Horse News. **Founded:** 1970. **Freq:** Monthly. **Print Method:** Offset. **Trim Size:** 11 1/2 x 14. Offset. **Cols./Page:** 6. **Col. Width:** 1 1/2 inches. **Col. Depth:** 13 inches. **Key Personnel:** Carolyn Hansen, Editor and Publisher, phone (702)358-2681, fax (702)358-2686. **Subscription Rates:** $10.75 individuals. **Remarks:** Accepts advertising.
Ad Rates: GLR: $28 **Circ:** Paid ‡3,500
BW: $752 Free ‡200
4C: $1,007
PCI: $28

TONOPAH†, pop. 3,500.

Nye Co. (SC). 170 m SE of Reno. Space testing. Gold, silver mines. Agriculture. Livestock, hay, grain.

18548 Eureka Sentinel
Times Bonanza and Goldfield News
PO Box 193 Phone: (702)482-3365
Tonopah, NV 89049 Fax: (702)482-5042

Newspaper with a Democratic orientation. **Founded:** 1870. **Freq:** Weekly (Thurs.). **Print Method:** Offset. **Cols./Page:** 5. **Col. Width:** 22 nonpareils. **Col. Depth:** 196 agate lines. **Key Personnel:** William G. Roberts, Editor and Publisher. **Subscription Rates:** $19. **Remarks:** Accepts advertising.
Ad Rates: GLR: $0.27 **Circ:** ‡550

18549 Times Bonanza and Goldfield News
PO Box 193 Phone: (702)482-3365
Tonopah, NV 89049 Fax: (702)482-5042

Newspaper with a Democratic orientation. **Founded:** 1901. **Freq:** Weekly (Thurs.). **Print Method:** Offset. **Cols./Page:** 5. **Col. Width:** 22 nonpareils. **Col. Depth:** 196 agate lines. **Key Personnel:** William Roberts, Editor and Publisher. **Subscription Rates:** $20. **Remarks:** Accepts advertising.
Ad Rates: GLR: $0.31 **Circ:** ‡2,600

18550 KHWK-FM - 92.7
Box 1669 Phone: (702)482-5724
Tonopah, NV 89049 Fax: (702)482-3238

Format: Adult Contemporary; Album-Oriented Rock (AOR); Contemporary Hit Radio (CHR). **Networks:** USA Radio. **Founded:** 1982. **Formerly:** KPAH-FM. **Operating Hours:** Continuous. **ADI:** Reno, NV. **Key Personnel:** Don Kaminski, Owner/Gen. Mgr.; John Romanko, Chief Engineer. **Wattage:** 1000. **Ad Rates:** $15-25 for 30 seconds; $18-30 for 60 seconds.

18551 KTPH-FM - 91.7
1289 S. Torrey Pines Phone: (702)258-9895
Las Vegas, NV 89146 Fax: (702)258-5646
E-mail: knpr@accessnv.com

Format: Classical; News. **Networks:** National Public Radio (NPR). **Founded:** 1988. **Operating Hours:** Continuous. **ADI:** Las Vegas, NV. **Key Personnel:** Lamar Marchese, General Mgr. **Wattage:** 100.

WINNEMUCCA†, pop. 4,140.

Humboldt Co. (NW). 80 m NE of Reno. Residential.

18552 The Humboldt Sun
DSN, Inc.
PO Box 3000 Phone: (702)623-5011
Winnemucca, NV 89446 Fax: (702)623-5243

Community newspaper. **Founded:** 1972. **Freq:** Monday through Friday. **Print Method:** Offset. **Cols./Page:** 6. **Col. Width:** 12 picas. **Col. Depth:** 21.5 picas. **Key Personnel:** Elaine Heit, Publisher. **Subscription Rates:** $65 individuals; $85 out of area.
Ad Rates: BW: $767.55 **Circ:** ‡4,000
4C: $1,067.55
SAU: $5.95

18553 Jones Spacelink Ltd.
1063 W. 4th Phone: (702)623-5244
Winnemucca, NV 89445 Fax: (702)623-5246

Owner: Jones Intercable, 9697 E. Mineral Ave., Englewood, CO, (303)792-3111. **Founded:** 1982. **Formerly:** Intermountain Cable. **Key Personnel:** Debbie Kontz, General Mgr. **Cities Served:** subscribing households 2,250; 38 channels.

18554 KVCE-FM - 89.5
13295 Grass Valley Rd. Phone: (702)623-1604
Winnemucca, NV 89445

Format: Religious; Easy Listening; Educational. **Founded:** 1986. **Operating Hours:** Continuous. **Key Personnel:** Bill Bates, General Mgr. **Wattage:** 378.

18555 KWNA-FM - 92.7
5130 E. Weikel Dr. Phone: (702)623-5203
Box 591 Fax: (702)625-1011
Winnemucca, NV 89445

Format: Country. **Founded:** 1982. **Wattage:** 60.

YERINGTON†, pop. 2,021.

Lyon Co. (W). 80 m SE of Reno. Ships beef, hay, onions, potatoes. Silver mines. Stock, dairy farms.

18556 Fernley Leader/Dayton Courier
Mason Valley News
41 N. Main St. Phone: (702)463-4242
Box 841 Fax: (702)463-5547
Yerington, NV 89447-2230
Community newspaper. **Founded:** 1979. **Freq:** Weekly (Wed.). **Print Method:** Offset. **Cols./Page:** 6. **Col. Width:** 12 picas. **Col. Depth:** 21 1/2 inches. **Key Personnel:** Jim Sanford, Publisher; Laura Tennant, Editor, phone (702)346-0188, fax (702)346-3988. **Subscription Rates:** $18.95 individuals. **Remarks:** Accepts advertising. **Formerly:** Tri-Town Times.
Ad Rates: BW: $632.10 **Circ:** Paid 2,900
SAU: $5
PCI: $4

18557 Mason Valley News
41 N. Main St. Phone: (702)463-4242
Yerington, NV 89447 Fax: (702)463-5547

Community newspaper. **Founded:** 1874. **Freq:** Weekly (Fri.). **Print Method:** Offset. **Cols./Page:** 6. **Col. Width:** 12 picas. **Col. Depth:** 21 1/2 inches. **Key Personnel:** Jim Sanford, Publisher; David Sanford, Editor. **Subscription Rates:** $22.50. **Remarks:** Accepts advertising.
Ad Rates: GLR: $.18 **Circ:** Paid ‡3,950
BW: $741.75
SAU: $6
PCI: $5.75

NEW HAMPSHIRE

State Capital, CONCORD

New Hampshire is bounded on the north by Quebec, east by Maine and the Atlantic Ocean, south by Massachusetts, and west by Vermont. Its length is 180 miles from north to south; its average breadth, 50 miles; land area, 8,969 square miles. A rough and hilly surface characterizes most of the state. In the north, the Presidential Range of the White Mountains reaches altitudes of more than 6,000 feet. Winters are severe, but the state has an almost ideal summer climate, especially in the central and eastern portion. Mountain and lake scenery is noted for its beauty; large numbers of tourists are attracted yearly, from all parts of the country. The more level southern section is agricultural and industrial. The Valley of the Connecticut is famed for the beauty of its farms and villages. The Weather Bureau at Concord gives the temperature (annual average) as 45.1; highest on record, 102; lowest on record, -23. Total annual precipitation is 36.37 inches. The most outstanding of the state's educational institutions are Dartmouth College at Hanover and the University of New Hampshire at Durham.

POPULATION: 1,111,000 (1992). Rank among the states, 41st.

AGRICULTURE: Number of farms: 3,000 (1992). Farm acreage: less than 500,000 (1992). Cash receipts from farm marketings: crops, $80,000,000 (1991); livestock and products, $63,000,000 (1991).

FISHERIES: Total catch: 11,000,000 lbs. (1991), $13,000,000 value.

FORESTS: Total forest land: 825,000 acres (1991). Principal woods: white pine, hemlock, birch, eastern spruce, maple, oak, beech, ash, balsam fir, cottonwood and aspen, elm, basswood.

MINERALS: Value of production: $30,000,000 (1991). Principal minerals: sand and gravel, stone, gemstones.

MANUFACTURES: Value added by manufacture: $5,647,000,000 (1991). Leading industry groups: leather and leather products, electrical machinery, machinery (except electrical).

LIST OF COUNTIES

Total number of counties 10

County, Location on Map, and County Seat	Pop.
Belknap (C), Laconia	49,216
Carroll (EC), Ossipee	35,410
Cheshire (SW), Keene	70,121
Coos (SW), Lancaster	34,828
Grafton (WC), Woodsville	74,929
Hillsboro (S), Nashua	336,073
Merrimack (SC), Concord	120,005
Rockingham (SE), Exeter	245,845
Strafford (SE), Dover	104,233
Sullivan (SW), Newport	38,592

STATISTICS

Newspapers

Period of Issue	
Daily	8
Evening Daily	5
Morning Daily	2
Daily with Sunday edition	4
Semiweekly	1
Weekly	31
Biweekly	1
Semimonthly	1
Monthly	1
Free or partly free	7
Shopper	3
Total Newspapers	45

Periodicals

Period of Issue	
Weekly	1
Monthly	23
Bimonthly	4
Quarterly	14
Total Periodicals	63

Total number of publications ... 108

Radio Stations

AM Stations	22
FM Stations	44
Total Radio Stations	68

TV Stations

Total TV Stations ... 6

Cable Stations

Total Cable Systems ... 13

Total number of broadcast listings ... 87

AMHERST, pop. 8,243.

S. NH. Hillsborough Co. 10 mi. NW of Nashua.

18558 Clinical Lab Products
89 Rte. 101A, Box 69 Phone: (603)673-7555
Amherst, NH 03031 Fax: (603)672-5625

Magazine (tabloid) for medical labs. **Subtitle:** The Product News Magazine for the Clinical Laboratory. **Founded:** 1972. **Freq:** Monthly. **Print Method:** Offset. **Trim Size:** 11 x 16 1/4. **Cols./Page:** 4. **Col. Width:** 13 picas. **Col. Depth:** 224 agate lines. **Key Personnel:** Jane Osborne, Editor; Richard M. Ezequelle, Publisher; Barbara Lemieux, Advertising Production Mgr.; Gail Tulipani, Assoc. Ed. **ISSN:** 0192-1282. **Subscription Rates:** $60 individuals. **Remarks:** Accepts advertising. **Available Online. URL:** http://www.labfocus.com.
Ad Rates: BW: $3,290 **Circ:** Controlled 52,770
4C: $4,355

18559 Tree Care Industry
National Arborist Association, Inc.
PO Box 1094 Phone: (603)673-3311
Amherst, NH 03031 Fax: (603)672-2613
Free: (800)733-2622
Publisher E-mail: narbor1@jlc.net

Trade journal for the commercial tree care industry. **Founded:** June 1990. **Freq:** Monthly. **Print Method:** Web offset. **Trim Size:** 8 1/4 x 10 7/8. **Cols./Page:** 3. **Col. Width:** 2 1/3 inches. **Col. Depth:** 10 inches. **Key Personnel:** Mark Garvin, Editor. **ISSN:** 1059-0528. **Subscription Rates:** $30 individuals. **Remarks:** Accepts advertising.
Circ: Controlled ‡28,000

BEDFORD

18560 Goffstown News
Neighborhood Publications Inc.
334 Rte. 101 W. Phone: (603)472-6500
PO Box 10848 Fax: (603)472-6520
Bedford, NH 03110
Free: (800)977-4332

Community newspaper. **Founded:** 1957. **Freq:** Weekly (Thurs.). **Cols./Page:** 6. **Col. Width:** 2 1/16 inches. **Col. Depth:** 21 inches. **Key Personnel:** Valerie J. Stainton, Finance Mgr. **Subscription Rates:** $22; $29 newspaper rates.
Ad Rates: PCI: $8.50 **Circ:** 28,900

BERLIN, pop. 13,084.

N. NH. Coos Co. On Androscoggin River, 19 mi. E. of Lancaster. Manufactures paper, pulp products. Agriculture.

18561 Berlin Reporter
Munro Enterprises
151 Main St. Phone: (603)752-1200
PO Box 38
Berlin, NH 03570-0038
Publication E-mail: reporter@ncia.net

Newspaper. **Founded:** 1883. **Freq:** Mon.-Sat. **Print Method:** Offset. **Trim Size:** 10 x 15. **Cols./Page:** 9. **Col. Width:** 16 nonpareils. **Col. Depth:** 294 agate lines. **Key Personnel:** Howard James, Publisher; Judith James, Advertising. **Remarks:** Accepts advertising. **Formerly:** The Daily Berlin Reporter.
Ad Rates: BW: $292.50 **Circ:** 5,300
4C: $692.50
PCI: $3.00

18562 North Country Weekly
Main Street Media, Inc.
28 Main St. Phone: (603)752-4034
PO Box 37 Fax: (603)752-5183
Berlin, NH 03570
Free: (800)649-4034

Community newspaper and shopper. **Founded:** 1975. **Freq:** Weekly. **Cols./Page:** 5. **Col. Width:** 2 1/16 inches. **Col. Depth:** 1 inches. **Remarks:** Accepts advertising.
Ad Rates: BW: $371.25 **Circ:** Non-paid ‡10,000
PCI: $4.95

18563 Warner Cable Communications
219 Main St. Phone: (603)752-4330
Berlin, NH 03570 Fax: (603)752-3940
Free: (800)499-4330

Key Personnel: Terry R. Gould, Manager; Denise L. LaFlamme, Office Mgr.; Robert Pelchat, Operations Mgr. **Cities Served:** subscribing households 7,747; 30 channels; 1 community access channel.

18564 WBRL-AM - 1400
35 Bogart Ave.
Port Washington, NY 11050

Format: Adult Contemporary. **Founded:** 1962. **Key Personnel:** James Moyer, CEO; Tom Kennedy, Contact; Robert Dale, General Sales Mgr.; Tim Anderson, News Dir. **Wattage:** 1000.

18565 WMOU-AM - 1230
Box 489 Phone: (603)752-1230
38 Glen Ave. Fax: (603)752-3117
Berlin, NH 03570

Format: Oldies. **Networks:** ABC. **Owner:** New England Bradcasting Inc., PO Box 489, Berlin, NH 03570. **Founded:** 1947. **Operating Hours:** Continuous. **Key Personnel:** Stephen E. Powell, President; Bob Barbin, News Dir. **Wattage:** 1000. **Ad Rates:** WXLQ-PN.

18566 WXLQ-FM - 107.1
Box 489 Phone: (603)752-1230
38 Glen Ave. Fax: (603)752-3117
Berlin, NH 03570

Format: Country. **Networks:** CNN Radio. **Founded:** 1997. **Wattage:** 6000. **Ad Rates:** Combined advertising rates available with WMOU-AM.

BETHLEHEM

18567 Media Market Guide
Media Market Resources
PO Box 119 Phone: (603)869-2418
Bethlehem, NH 03574 Fax: (603)869-3135
Publisher E-mail: mmresources@msn.com

Advertising cost guide for media buying and planning. Covers TV, radio, cable TV, newspapers, national magazines, and outdoor advertising. **Founded:** Jan. 1969. **Freq:** Quarterly. **Print Method:** Offset. **Trim Size:** 8 3/8 x 10 7/8. **Cols./Page:** 1. **Col. Width:** 60 nonpareils. **Col. Depth:** 152 agate lines. **Key Personnel:** Martin Herbst, Publisher; Kathleen Coffey, Dir., Sales & Marketing; Amy Konikowski, Sales Mgr. **Subscription Rates:** $645; $260 single issue. **Remarks:** Accepts advertising.
Ad Rates: BW: $1,700 **Circ:** Paid ‡1,000
4C: $1,900 Controlled ‡100

CAMPTON, pop. 1,694.

C. NH. Grafton Co. On Mad River, 9 mi. NNE of Plymouth. Resort.

18568 Adelphia
Box 222 Phone: (603)726-3204
Campton, NH 03223

Founded: 1992. **Formerly:** Sirius Systems, Inc.; First Carolina Cable, Inc. **Key Personnel:** Carol Stearns, Contact. **Cities Served:** subscribing households 1,800; 36 channels; 1 community access channel; 168 hours per week community access programming.

CENTER CONWAY

18569 Pegasus Cable Television
548 Eastman Rd. Phone: (603)476-5522
Center Conway, NH 03813-4218 Fax: (603)476-8837
Free: (800)827-8288

Owner: Pegasus Communications, 5 Radnor Corporate Center, Ste. 454, 100 Matsonford Rd., Radnor, PA 19087, (610)341-1801. **Founded:** Jan. 1, 1987. **Formerly:** Amrac Cable (1991). **Key Personnel:** Marshall Pagon, President; Howard Verlin, Vice President. **Cities Served:** Winsted, CT; Charlton, MA; Moultonboro, NH: subscribing households 28,500; 450 channels; 1 community access channel; 6 hours per week community access programming.

CENTER OSSIPEE, pop. 500.

E. NH. Carroll Co. 5 mi. N. of Ossipee. Summer and winter recreation.

18570 Carroll County Independent and Pioneer
Independent-Granite State Publishing Co.
PO Box 38 Phone: (603)539-4111
Center Ossipee, NH 03814 Fax: (603)539-5564

General newspaper. **Founded:** 1881. **Freq:** Weekly (Wed.). **Print Method:** Offset. **Cols./Page:** 7. **Col. Width:** 12 picas. **Col. Depth:** 21 inches. **Key Personnel:** Frank Gregoire, Editor; Jacob J. Burghardt, Publisher; Ed Engler, Advertising Mgr. **Subscription Rates:** $17; $25 nonlocal. **Remarks:** Accepts advertising. **Alt. Formats:** Microform.
Ad Rates: GLR: $.557 **Circ:** ‡3859
BW: $1,147
SAU: $7.80
PCI: $4.80

CHARLESTOWN

18571 Earth Work
Student Conservation Association
PO Box 550 Phone: (603)543-1700
Charlestown, NH 03603 Fax: (603)543-1828
Publication E-mail: earthwork@sca-inc.org

Magazine offering career advice and a nationwide listing of natural resources and environmental jobs for students and professionals. **Founded:** Feb. 1991. **Freq:** 11/year. **Print Method:** Offset. **Trim Size:** 8 1/2 x 11. **Cols./Page:** 3. **Col. Width:** 2 3/8 inches. **Col. Depth:** 9 5/8 inches. **Key Personnel:** Lisa K. Younger, Editor. **ISSN:** 1060-5053. **Subscription Rates:** $34.95 individuals; $6 single issue. **Remarks:** Accepts advertising. **Formerly:** Job Scan.
Ad Rates: GLR: $150 **Circ:** Paid 3,500
BW: $683
4C: $1,050
PCI: $30

CLAREMONT, pop. 14,557.

SW NH. Sullivan Co. On the Sugar River, 42 mi. NW of Concord. Manufactures mining machinery, shoes. Nurseries; pine timber; dairy farms. Summer resort.

18572 Eagle Times
Eagle Publications, Inc.
RR 2, Box 301 Phone: (603)543-3100
Claremont, NH 03743-9308 Fax: (603)542-9705
Publication E-mail: etimes@cyberportal.net

General newspaper. **Founded:** 1835. **Freq:** Daily (eve.), Sunday (morn.). **Print Method:** Offset. **Cols./Page:** 6. **Col. Width:** 25 nonpareils. **Col. Depth:** 301 agate lines. **Key Personnel:** Patrick O'Grady, Managing Editor; Harvey D. Hill, Publisher. **USPS:** 115-200. **Subscription Rates:** $109.20 individuals. **Remarks:** Accepts advertising.
Ad Rates: SAU: $7.14 **Circ:** Mon.-Fri. ★**8,608**
PCI: $10.55 Sun. ★**9,5853**

18573 WHDQ-FM - 106.1
PO Box 1230 Phone: (603)542-7735
Claremont, NH 03743-1230 Fax: (603)542-8721

Format: Adult Contemporary. **Owner:** DynaCom Corp., at above address. **Founded:** 1948. **Formerly:** WECM-FM (1985). **Operating Hours:** Continuous. **ADI:** Boston-Worcester,MA-Derry-Manchester,NH. **Key Personnel:** Ken Barlow, Program Dir.; Jeffrey Shapiro, General Mgr.; Bob Lipman, News Dir. **Wattage:** 50,000.

18574 WTSV-AM - 1230
Rtes. 12 and 103 Phone: (603)542-7735
PO Box 1230 Fax: (603)542-8721
Claremont, NH 03743
E-mail: valleysam@aol.com

Format: Sports; Talk. **Simulcasts:** WNHV-White River Jct. Vt 910am. **Networks:** ABC; ESPN Radio. **Owner:** DynaCom Corp., at above address. **Founded:** 1948. **Operating Hours:** Continuous; 10% network, 90% local. **Key Personnel:** Jeffrey Shapiro, General Mgr.; Bob Lipman, News Dir. **Wattage:** 1000. **URL:** http://www.scoreradio.com.

COLEBROOK, pop. 2,459.

N. NH. Coos Co. On Connecticut River, 33 mi. NW of Berlin. Summer resort. Timber; agriculture.

18575 The News and Sentinel
1 Bridge St. Phone: (603)237-5501
Box 39 Fax: (603)237-5060
Colebrook, NH 03576
Small country newspaper covering local affairs and area interests. **Founded:** 1870. **Freq:** Weekly (Wed.). **Print Method:** Letterpress and offset. **Trim Size:** 11 1/2 x 16 1/2. **Cols./Page:** 5. **Col. Width:** 23 nonpareils. **Col. Depth:** 210 agate lines. **Key Personnel:** Charles Jordon, Editor; John D. Harrigan, Publisher. **Subscription Rates:** $27 New Hampshire, Vermont and Mai; $30 out of area.
Ad Rates: PCI: $5 **Circ:** 5,000

18576 Northern New Hampshire Magazine
Jordan Associates
PO Box 263 Phone: (603)246-8998
Colebrook, NH 03576
Publisher E-mail: nnhmag@ncia.net

Publication focusing on historic, as well as current issues in northern New Hampshire. Distributed in Grafton, Carroll, and Coos Counties. **Founded:** 1989. **Freq:** Monthly. **Trim Size:** 11 x 14. **Cols./Page:** 4. **Col. Width:** 14 picas. **Col. Depth:** 13 inches. **Key Personnel:** Charles J. Jordan, Editor; Donna L. Jordan, Publisher. **Subscription Rates:** $20; $1.75 single issue. **Remarks:** Accepts advertising. **Formerly:** Coos Magazine.
Ad Rates: BW: $299 **Circ:** Paid 1,500
PCI: $5.75

18577 White Mountain Cablevision
PO Box 66 Phone: (603)237-5573
Colebrook, NH 03576 Fax: (603)237-8256

Founded: 1954. **Key Personnel:** William Hinton, General Mgr.; Sheryl Collins, Office Mgr. **Cities Served:** Beecher Falls, Canaan, Lemington, VT: subscribing households 1,584; 29 channels; 1 community access channel.

CONCORD†, pop. 30,400.

SC NH. Merrimack Co. State Capital. On the Merrimack River, 15 mi. N. of Manchester. New Hampshire Technical Institute. Manufactures leather, machinery, electronics. Granite finishing.

18578 Forest Notes
Society for the Protection of New Hampshire Forests
54 Portsmouth St. Phone: (603)224-9945
Concord, NH 03301-5400 Fax: (603)228-0423
Publisher E-mail: spnhf@compuserve.com

Journal on forestry and conservation. **Founded:** 1937. **Freq:** Quarterly. **Print Method:** Offset. **Trim Size:** 7 5/8 x 10 7/8. **Cols./Page:** 2. **Col. Width:** 20 picas. **Col. Depth:** 56 picas. **Key Personnel:** Richard Ober, Editor; Rosemary Conroy, Managing Editor. **ISSN:** 0015-7457. **Subscription Rates:** $30 individuals. **Remarks:** Accepts advertising.
Ad Rates: 4C: $750 **Circ:** Paid ‡12,000
Controlled ‡400

18579 New Hampshire Bar Journal
New Hampshire Bar Association
112 Pleasant St. Phone: (603)224-6942
Concord, NH 03301 Fax: (603)224-2910

Law journal. **Founded:** 1958. **Freq:** Quarterly. **Print Method:** Perfect bound. **Trim Size:** 18 1/2 x 11. **Cols./Page:** 4. **Key Personnel:** Donna J. Parker, Managing Editor, dparker@nhbar.org. **ISSN:** 0548-4928. **Subscription Rates:** $40; $10 single issue. **Remarks:** Accepts advertising. **URL:** http://www.nhbar.org. **Alt. Formats:** Microform.
Ad Rates: BW: $800 **Circ:** 5,100

18580 New Hampshire Highways
New Hampshire Good Roads Association
261 Sheep Davis Rd., Ste. 5
Concord, NH 03301-5750

Magazine containing highway information. **Founded:** 1923. **Freq:** Quarterly. **Print Method:** Offset. **Cols./Page:** 2. **Col. Width:** 39 nonpareils. **Col. Depth:** 140 agate lines. **Key Personnel:** Kathleen A. Labranche, Editor. **Subscription Rates:** $25. **Remarks:** Advertising not accepted.
Circ: ‡1,600

18581 WomenWise
Concord Feminist Health Center
38 S. Main St. Phone: (603)225-2739
Concord, NH 03301 Fax: (603)228-6255

Journal covering all aspects of women's health. **Founded:** 1978. **Freq:** Quarterly. **Key Personnel:** Luita D. Spangler, Editor, luitad@aol.com. **ISSN:** 0890-9695. **Subscription Rates:** $10; $25 Industry. $2.95 single issue. **Alt. Formats:** CD-ROM, Softline Information.
Ad Rates: PCI: $55 **Circ:** Paid 600
Non-paid 1,400

18582 WEVO-FM - 89.1
207 N. Main St. Phone: (603)228-8910
Concord, NH 03301-5003 Fax: (603)224-6052

Format: News; Classical; Folk; Jazz. **Networks:** National Public Radio (NPR); Public Radio International (PRI). **Founded:** 1981. **Operating Hours:** Continuous. 50% network, 50% local. **Key Personnel:** Larry Beavers, Engineering Dir., phone (603)223-2436, lbeavers@NHPR.org; Mark Handley, President & General Mgr., phone (603)223-2438, mhandley@nhpr.org; Nathan Irwin, Music Dir., phone (603)223-2420, nirwin@NHPR.org; Gloria Zogopoulos, Membership Dir., phone (603)223-2415, gzogopoulos@NHPR.org; Maureen Anderson, Personnel Dir., phone (603)223-2412, manderson@NHPR.org; Andrew Morrell, Program Mgr., phone (603)223-2432, amorrell@NHPR.org; Jon Greenberg, Feature News Mgr., phone (603)223-2435, jgreenberg@NHPR.org; Julia Reed, Corp. Relations Dir., phone (603)223-2419, jreed@ngpr.org. **Local Programs:** *The Exchange*, Scott McPherson, (603)223-2425; *Perspectives*, Laura James, (603)223-2435. **Wattage:** 50,000. **Ad Rates:** Noncommercial; underwriting available. **URL:** http://www.NHPR.org.

18583 WJYY-FM - 105.5
7 Perley St. Phone: (603)228-9036
PO Box 1923 Fax: (603)224-7280
Concord, NH 03302-1923
E-mail: jyy105@aol.com

Format: Adult Contemporary. **Simulcasts:** WNHQ. **Networks:** UPI. **Owner:** RadioWorks, Inc., at above address, Fax: (603)229-7280. **Founded:** 1983. **Operating Hours:** Continuous. **Key Personnel:** Stuart Richter, General Mgr.; Brit Johnson, General Sales Mgr.; Harry Kozlowski, Program Dir.; Lindsay Collins, President/CFO. **Wattage:** 1550. **Ad Rates:** $28-44 per unit. Combined advertising rates available with WNHQ, WNIH, WRCI-FM. **URL:** http://www.wjyy.com.

18584 WKXL-FM - 1450
37 Redington Rd. Phone: (603)225-5521
Box 875 Fax: (603)224-6404
Concord, NH 03301
E-mail: wkxlnews@juno.com

Format: News; Talk; Sports. **Simulcasts:** WKXL-FM. **Networks:** CBS. **Owner:** Capitol Broadcasting Corp., Inc., at above address. **Founded:** 1946. **Operating Hours:** 5 a.m.-11:30 p.m.; 30% network, 70% local. **ADI:** Boston-Worcester,MA-Derry-Manchester,NH. **Key Personnel:** Richard W. Osborne, Contact; J.W. Patrick Chaloux, Contact; Gardner F. Hill, Operations Mgr.; Donald Shapiro, Contact; Alicia Preston, News Dir. **Local Programs:** *Coffee Chat*, Dick Osborne; *Party Line*, Gardner Hill; *Sportszone*, Mike Murphy. **Wattage:** 1000. **Ad Rates:** $21-38 for 30 seconds; $23-40 for 60 seconds.

18585 WKXL-FM - 102.3
37 Redington Rd. Phone: (603)225-5521
Box 875 Fax: (603)224-6404
Concord, NH 03302-0875
E-mail: wkxlnews@juno.com

Format: News; Talk; Sports. **Simulcasts:** WKXL-AM. **Networks:** CBS. **Owner:** Capitol Broadcasting Corp., Inc., at above address. **Founded:** 1972. **Operating Hours:** 5 a.m.-11.30 a.m.; 30% network, 70% local. **ADI:** Boston-Worcester,MA-Derry-Manchester,NH. **Key Personnel:** Richard W. Osborne, Pres./General Mgr.; J.W. Patrick Chaloux, Contact; Gardner Hill, Operations Mgr.; Heather Hamel, News Dir.; Donald Shapiro, Treasurer. **Local Programs:** *Coffee Chat*, Dick Osborne; *Party Line*, Gardner Hill; *Sportszone*, Mike Murphy. **Wattage:** 3000 ERP. **Ad Rates:** $21-38 for 30 seconds; $23-40 for 60 seconds.

18586 WNHI-FM - 93.3
PO Box 1923 Phone: (603)228-9036
Concord, NH 03302-1923 Fax: (603)224-7280

Format: Classic Rock. **Owner:** Radioworks, Inc., at above address. **Founded:** Oct. 1989. **Operating Hours:** Continuous. **Key Personnel:** Stuart Richter, General Mgr.; Harry Kozlowski, Program Dir. **Wattage:** 3000.

18587 WNHQ-FM - 92.1
PO Box 1923 Phone: (603)672-9292
Concord, NH 03302 Fax: (603)672-4114
E-mail: radiowork@aol.com

Format: Adult Contemporary. **Simulcasts:** WJYY. **Owner:** RadioWorks, Inc., at above address. **Founded:** 1971. **Formerly:** WMDK-FM (1991). **Operating Hours:** Continuous. **Key Personnel:** Stu Richter, General Mgr. **Wattage:** 3000. **Ad Rates:** Combined advertising rates available with WHYY, WNHI, WRCI. **URL:** http://www.wnhq.com.

18588 WNNH-FM - 99.1
501 South St. Phone: (603)225-1160
Concord, NH 03301 Fax: (603)225-5938
Free: (800)228-WNNH
E-mail: oldies99@wnnh.com

Format: Oldies. **Simulcasts:** WMUR-TV. **Owner:** Clark Broadcasting of New Hampshire, Inc., at above address. **Founded:** 1989. **Operating Hours:** Continuous. **ADI:** Boston-Worcester,MA-Derry-Manchester,NH. **Key Personnel:** Clark F. Smidt, Contact, csfmguru@aol.com; Paul J. Fuller, Gen. Sales and Station Mgr.; Janice Baily, Promotions Dir.; Kate Lloyd, News Dir.; Dirk Nadon, Operations Mgr. **Local Programs:** *New Hampshire In Touch* 7:00 am - 7:30 am Sunday, Janice Bailey, Mailing contact. **Wattage:** 6000 ERP. **Ad Rates:** $20-65 for 60 seconds. **URL:** http://www.wnrh.com.

WRCI-FM - See Hillsboro

18589 WSPS-FM - 90.5
St. Paul's School Phone: (603)229-4810
Concord, NH 03301 Fax: (603)229-4891
E-mail: wsps@sps.edu

Founded: 1974. **Operating Hours:** 24 hrs. per day. **Key Personnel:** James Turner, General Mgr. **Wattage:** 200.

CONTOOCOOK, pop. 1,499.

SC NH. Merrimack Co. On Contoocook River, 9. mi. W of Concord.

18590 MCT Cable
11 Kearsarge Ave. Phone: (603)746-3000
PO Box 340 Fax: (603)746-3567
Contoocook, NH 03229
E-mail: mctel.com

Owner: MCI Inc., at above address. **Founded:** 1984. **Key Personnel:** Paul E. Violette, President, pev@mctel.com; Jim Henley, VP-COO, jmh@mctel.com; John LaBonte, VP-CFO, john@mctel.com; Marc Violette, Marketing Manager, mav@mctel.com; Dawn Foster, Product Mgr., dmf@mctel.com. **Cities Served:** Bradford, Newbury, Sutton, Warner, NH: subscribing households 2,295; 45 channels; 1 community access channel; 20 hours per week community access programming. **URL:** http://www.mctel.com.

CONWAY, pop. 7,158.

EC NH. Carroll Co. On Saco River, 5 mi. S. of North Conway.

18591 The Mount Washington Valley Mountain Ear
PO Box 530 Phone: (603)447-6336
Conway, NH 03818 Fax: (603)447-5474

Newspaper (tabloid) serving the resort community of Mt. Washington Valley. **Subtitle:** The Weekly News and Lifestyle Journal of Mt. Washington Valley. **Founded:** May 23, 1976. **Freq:** Weekly. **Print Method:** Offset. **Trim Size:** 11 1/2 x 17. **Cols./Page:** 4. **Col. Width:** 14 picas. **Col. Depth:** 15 inches. **Key Personnel:** R. Stephen Eastman, Editor and Publisher; Paula Tetreault, Sales Mgr. **Subscription Rates:** $30. **Remarks:** Accepts advertising. **URL:** http://www.journeysnorth.com/mountainear.index.html.
Ad Rates: BW: $480 **Circ:** ‡15,000
4C: $1,500 o
PCI: $8

18592 Northern Light
PO Box 2230 Phone: (603)447-3824
Conway, NH 03818 Fax: (603)447-3825

Newspaper. **Subtitle:** Northern Light. **Founded:** 1980. **Freq:** Weekly (Sat.). **Print Method:** Offset. **Trim Size:** 11 3/4 x 13 1/2. **Cols./Page:** 5. **Col. Width:** 2 1/4 inches. **Col. Depth:** 13 inches. **Key Personnel:** Robert Fredette, Publisher. **USPS:** 145-. **Remarks:** Accepts advertising.
Ad Rates: GLR: $.35 **Circ:** Non-paid 23,216
BW: $581.75
4C: $681.75
SAU: $8.95
PCI: $8.60

18593 WBNC-AM - 1050
E. Main Phone: (603)447-5988
PO Box 2008 Fax: (603)447-3655
Conway, NH 03818

Format: Country. **Simulcasts:** WBNC-FM. **Networks:** AP; ABC. **Owner:** North Country Radio, Inc., at above address. **Founded:** 1955. **Operating Hours:** 5 a.m.-9 p.m. **Key Personnel:** Lawrence Sherman, General Mgr.; Charles Osgood, Operations Mgr.; Dean Luttrell, Public Service Director; Jesse Mosston, General Sales Mgr. **Wattage:** 1000 day; 63 night. **Ad Rates:** $8-16 for 30 seconds; $10-20 for 60 seconds. Combined advertising rates available with WMWV-FM.

18594 WBNC-FM - 104.5
E. Main Phone: (603)447-5988
PO Box 2008 Fax: (603)447-3655
Conway, NH 03818

Format: Country. **Simulcasts:** WBNC-AM. **Networks:** AP; ABC. **Owner:** North Country Radio, Inc., at above address. **Founded:** 1995. **Operating Hours:** Continuous. **Key Personnel:** Lawrence Sherman, General Mgr.; Charles Osgood, Operations Mgr.; Dean Luttrell, Public Service Director; Jesse Mosston, General Sales Mgr. **Wattage:** 3000. **Ad Rates:** $8-16 for 30 seconds; $10-20 for 60 seconds. WMWV-FM.

18595 WMWV-FM - 93.5
E. Main Phone: (603)447-5988
PO Box 2008 Fax: (603)447-3655
Conway, NH 03818

Format: Adult Album Alternative. **Networks:** AP. **Owner:** North Country Radio, Inc., at above address. **Founded:** 1967. **Operating Hours:** Continuous. **Key Personnel:** Charles Osgood, Operations Mgr.; George Cleveland, Program Dir.; Lawrence Sherman, General Mgr.; Jesse Mosston, General Sales Mgr.; Dean Luttrell, Public Service Director; Mark Johnson, Music Dir. **Wattage:** 3000. **Ad Rates:** $8-16 for 30 seconds; $10-20 for 60 seconds. WBNC-FM.

DERRY, pop. 18,875.

SE NH. Rockingham Co. On Beaver Brook, 10 mi. SE of Manchester. Manufactures shoes, circuit boards and electronics, novelties. Summer resort.

18596 Derry News
Derry Publishing Co.
46 W. Broadway Phone: (603)437-7000
PO Box 307 Fax: (603)432-4510
Derry, NH 03038-2329
Publication E-mail: info@derrynews.com

Community newspaper. **Founded:** 1880. **Freq:** Semiweekly (Tues. and Fri.). **Print Method:** Offset. **Cols./Page:** 6. **Col. Width:** 2 1/16 inches. **Col. Depth:** 21 inches. **Key Personnel:** D. J. Griffin, Editor; Robert Chapman, Advertising Mgr. **USPS:** 154-700. **Subscription Rates:** $36.40 individuals. **Remarks:** Accepts advertising.
Ad Rates: BW: $1,291.50 **Circ:** ‡10,202
SAU: $12.90

18597 WDER-AM - 1320
8 Lawrence Rd. Phone: (603)434-9302
Box 465 Fax: (603)434-1035
Derry, NH 03038
E-mail: wder@wder.com

Format: Religious; Contemporary Christian. **Owner:** Spacetown Communications, at above address, (603)437-WDER. **Founded:** 1983. **Operating Hours:** 6 a.m.-10 p.m.; 7% network, 93% local. **Key Personnel:** Connie McCullion, General Mgr.; Bill Carozza, Music Dir.; Steve Sobozenski, Program Dir. **Wattage:** 10,000. **Ad Rates:** $5-24 for 30 seconds; $5-24 for 60 seconds.

18598 WNDS-TV - 50
50 Television Pl. Phone: (603)434-8850
Derry, NH 03038-1451 Fax: (603)434-8627

Format: Commercial TV. **Networks:** Independent. **Founded:** 1983. **Operating Hours:** Continuous. **ADI:** Boston-Worcester,MA-Derry-Manchester,NH. **Key Personnel:** Donna Cole, General Mgr.; Elise Hudon, Program Asst. **Ad Rates:** Advertising accepted; rates available upon request. **URL:** http://www.wnds.com.

DOVER†, pop. 22,377.

SE NH. Strafford Co. On Cocheco River, 12 mi. NW of Portsmouth. Park areas and recreation centers. Major retail, wholesale and service centers; diversified manufacturing. Greenhouses; agriculture.

18599 The Dover Times
Courier Times Newspapers
270 Central Ave. Phone: (603)742-7209
Dover, NH 03820 Fax: (603)742-7606

Community newspaper. **Founded:** 1995. **Freq:** Weekly (Thurs.). **Print Method:** Web offset. **Trim Size:** 11 1/2 x 16 1/2. **Cols./Page:** 5. **Col. Width:** 12.4 picas. **Col. Depth:** 16 inches. **Key Personnel:** Lou McGrew, Owner; Neil Collins, Owner; Brad Lipe, Publisher; John F.S. Sullivan, Editor. **Subscription Rates:** $8.50; $9.90 out of state. **Remarks:** Accepts advertising.
Ad Rates: BW: $648 **Circ:** Free 6,707
4C: $898
SAU: $8.10

18600 Foster's Democrat
333 Central Ave. Phone: (603)742-4455
Dover, NH 03820-4127 Fax: (603)742-4455
Free: (800)660-8310

General newspaper. **Founded:** 1873. **Freq:** Daily (eve.) and Sat. (morn.). **Print Method:** Offset. **Cols./Page:** 6. **Col. Width:** 25 nonpareils. **Col. Depth:** 301 agate lines. **Key Personnel:** Rod Doherty, Editor; Robert H. Foster, Publisher; Wayne Chick, Advertising Dir. **Subscription Rates:** $66. **Remarks:** Accepts advertising.
Ad Rates: BW: $2,254.92 **Circ:** Mon.-Sat. ★25,690
4C: $2,689.92
PCI: $17.48

18601 The Tri-Town Transcript
Journal Transcript Newspapers
270 Central Ave. Phone: (603)742-7209
Dover, NH 03820 Fax: (603)742-6442

Local newspaper serving Southern New Hampshire. **Founded:** 1975. **Freq:** Weekly. **Print Method:** Offset. **Trim Size:** 11 x 17. **Cols./Page:** 5. **Col. Width:** 2 1/16 inches. **Col. Depth:** 16 inches. **Key Personnel:** Carolyn Handy, Editor; Paul Dietterle, Co-Publisher; Dusty Dietterle, Advertising Mgr. and Co-Publisher, phone (603)742-3700. **ISSN:** 1092-7751. **Subscription Rates:** $18. **Remarks:** Accepts advertising.
Ad Rates: BW: $1,286 **Circ:** 4,000
4C: $1,571
SAU: $11.40
CNU: $7.37

18602 WBYY-FM - 98.7
PO Box 400 Phone: (603)742-0987
Dover, NH 03820 Fax: (603)742-0448
Free: (888)441-9876

Format: Adult Contemporary. **Owner:** Garrison City Broadcasting, Inc., at above address. **Founded:** 1995. **Former name:** WRGW-FM. **Operating Hours:** Continuous. **ADI:** Boston-Worcester,MA-Derry-Manchester,NH. **Key Personnel:** Bruce Lyons, General Mgr., phone (603)742-1270; Jack Casey, Operations Mgr.; Steve Dore, General Sales Mgr., phone (603)742-1270. **Wattage:** 6000.

18603 WOKQ-FM - 97.5
PO Box 576 Phone: (603)749-9750
Dover, NH 03820 Fax: (603)749-6589
E-mail: wokq975@aol.com

Format: Country. **Networks:** Independent. **Owner:** Fuller-Jeffrey Broadcasting Corp. of New England, at above address. **Founded:** 1970. **Formerly**: WDNH-FM (1977). **Operating Hours:** Continuous; 100% local. **ADI:** Boston-Worcester,MA-Derry-Manchester,NH. **Key Personnel:** Martin R. Lessard, Contact; Roger Wood, News Dir., rognews@aol.com; Donald Fanning, Contact; Jan Leavitt, Contact; Stan Edwards, Contact; Carole Dennehy, Contact; Mark Jennings, Contact; Mark Ericson, Contact. **Wattage:** 50,000. **Ad Rates:** $65-195 for 30 seconds; $70-200 for 60 seconds.

18604 WTSN-AM - 1270
PO Box 400 Phone: (603)742-0987
Dover, NH 03820 Fax: (603)742-0448

Format: Talk; News; Sports. **Networks:** ABC. **Owner:** Garrison City Broadcasting Co., at above address. **Founded:** Aug. 1996. **Operating Hours:** 5 a.m. - midnight; 50% network, 50% local. **Key Personnel:** Jerome Lipman, Contact; Paul LeBlanc, Operations Mgr.; Mike Pomp, Program Dir.; Don Briand, News Dir.; B.J. Hickman, Sales Mgr. **Wattage:** 5000. **Ad Rates:** $23-45 for 60 seconds.

18605 WWNH-AM - 1340
PO Box 69 Phone: (603)742-8575
Dover, NH 03820 Fax: (603)743-6444
Free: (800)805-8815
E-mail: info@loveradio.net

Format: Gospel; Adult Contemporary. **Networks:** SkyLight Satellite; USA Radio. **Owner:** Harvest Broadcasting, at above address. **Founded:** May 14, 1989. **Operating Hours:** Continuous. **Key Personnel:** Brian Dodge, General Mgr., phone (604)749-2744, info@loveradio.net. **Wattage:** 250,000. **URL:** http://www.loveradio.net.

18606 WXBB-FM - 105.3
PO Box 370 Phone: (603)749-2776
Dover, NH 03821-0370 Fax: (603)749-6589
E-mail: arrow1053@aol.com

Format: Classic Rock. **Networks:** Westwood One Radio; Unistar. **Owner:** Fuller-Jeffrey Broadcasting Corp., at above address. **Founded:** 1992. **Operating Hours:** Continuous; 100% local. **ADI:** Boston-Worcester,MA-Derry-Manchester,NH. **Key Personnel:** Martin R. Lessard, Contact; Roger Wood, News Dir.; Donald Fanning, Contact; Jan Leavitt, Contact; Stan Edwards, Contact; Carole Dennehy, Contact; Mark Jennings, Contact. **Wattage:** 3,000. **Ad Rates:** $25-50 for 60 seconds.

DUBLIN, pop. 1,303.

SW NH. Cheshire Co. 11 mi. ESE of Keene. Resort.

18607 The Old Farmer's Almanac Gardener's Companion
Yankee Publishing Inc.
PO Box 520 Phone: (603)563-8111
Dublin, NH 03444-0520 Fax: (603)563-8252
Publisher E-mail: almanac@yankeepub.com

Consumer magazine covering all levels of gardening. **Founded:** 1992. **Freq:** Annual. **Trim Size:** 5 3/8 x 8. **Cols./Page:** 2. **Key Personnel:** Georgia Orcatt, Editor; Sherin Wight, Publisher. **Subscription Rates:** $3.99 single issue. **Remarks:** Accepts advertising. **URL:** http://www.almanac.com.
Ad Rates: BW: $2,690 **Circ:** Paid 200,000
4C: $3,360

18608 The Old Farmer's Almanac Good Cook's Companion
Yankee Publishing Inc.
PO Box 520 Phone: (603)563-8111
Dublin, NH 03444-0520 Fax: (603)563-8252
Publisher E-mail: almanac@yankeepub.com

Consumer magazine covering food and cooking. **Founded:** 1996. **Freq:** Annual. **Trim Size:** 5 3/8 x 8. **Cols./Page:** 2. **Key Personnel:** Georgia Orcatt, Editor; Sherin Wight, Publisher. **Subscription Rates:** $3.99 single issue. **Remarks:** Accepts advertising. **URL:** http://www.almanac.com.
Ad Rates: BW: $2,690 **Circ:** (Not Reported)
4C: $3,360

DURHAM, pop. 10,652.

SE NH. Strafford Co. 5 mi. SW of Dover. University of New Hampshire.

18609 Dateline New England
PO Box 100
Durham, NH 03824

Publication for singles. **Founded:** 1988. **Freq:** Monthly. **Trim Size:** 8 1/4 x 10 7/8. **Cols./Page:** 2. **Col. Width:** 3 3/4 inches. **Col. Depth:** 7 3/4 inches. **Key Personnel:** Nancy B. Stone, Publisher. **Subscription Rates:** $12. **Remarks:** Advertising accepted; rates available upon request. **Formerly**: Dateline New Hampshire.
Circ: Free 15,153
Paid 182

18610 Rhodora
New England Botanical Club, Inc.
Dept. of Plant Biology Phone: (603)862-3205
University of New Hampshire Fax: (603)862-4757
Durham, NH 03824-3597
Botany journal devoted primarily to the flora of North America. **Subtitle:** Journal of the New England Botanical Club. **Founded:** 1899. **Freq:** Quarterly. **Print Method:** Offset. **Trim Size:** 6 x 9. **Cols./Page:** 1. **Col. Width:** 24 picas. **Col. Depth:** 41 picas. **Key Personnel:** Dr. Janet R. Sullivan, Editor-in-Chief, phone (603)862-3222, janets@christa.unh.edu. **ISSN:** 0035-4902. **Subscription Rates:** $75 institutions; $35 individuals. **Remarks:** Advertising not accepted.
Circ: Paid 800
Non-paid 15

WEKW-TV - See Keene

18611 WENH-TV - 11
PO Box 1100 Phone: (603)868-1100
Durham, NH 03824-1100 Fax: (603)868-7552
E-mail: email@nhptvll.unh.edu

Format: Public TV. **Simulcasts:** WLED-TV. **Networks:** Public Broadcasting Service (PBS). **Founded:** 1959. **Operating Hours:** 6 a.m.-1:05 a.m. **ADI:** Boston-Worcester,MA-Derry-Manchester,NH. **Key Personnel:** Peter Frid, General Mgr.; Stephen L. Baker, Finance and Admin. Dir.; Linda C Burroughs, Dir. of Development; Mary Anne Alhadeff, Dir. of Broadcasting; Robert Rossa, Dir. of Engineering; Frank Windsor, Dir. of Educational Telecommunications. **Ad Rates:** Noncommercial. **URL:** www.nhptv.unh.edu.

WLED-TV - See Littleton

18612 WUNH-FM - 91.3
University of New Hampshire Phone: (603)862-2541
Memorial Union Bldg. Fax: (603)862-2543
Durham, NH 03824

Format: Full Service; Alternative/New Music/Progressive; Public Radio. **Owner:** University of New Hampshire Board of Trustees, at above address. **Founded:** 1963. **Operating Hours:** Continuous. **Key Personnel:** Stewart Kenly, General Mgr.; Doug Nettingham, Business Mgr.; Ian Fitzpatrick, Music Dir.; Beau Lammtayne, Program Dir. **Wattage:** 1750. **Ad Rates:** Underwriting available. **URL:** http://www.wunh.unh.edu.

EXETER†, pop. 11,024.

SE NH. Rockingham Co. 13 mi. SW of Portsmouth. Phillips Exeter Academy. Diversified manufacturing. Granite finishing. Nurseries.

18613 Clinical Laboratory International
PanEuropean Publishing Company
6 Chestnut St. Phone: (603)778-3848
Exeter, NH 03833 Fax: (603)778-3858
Publisher E-mail: paneuro@nh.ultranet.com

Professional tabloid magazine for clinical biologists worldwide. **Founded:** Oct. 1977. **Freq:** 8/year. **Print Method:** Web offset. **Trim Size:** 11 1/8 x 15 3/4. **Cols./Page:** 3. **Key Personnel:** Alan Barclay, Ph.D., Editor, barclay@pepco.be; Louise Betton, U.S. Sales Coord. **Subscription Rates:** Free to qualified subscribers. **Remarks:** Accepts advertising.
Ad Rates: BW: $10,600 **Circ:** Controlled 30,005
4C: $12,900

18614 The Exeter News-Letter
Rockingham County Newspapers
PO Box 250 Phone: (603)772-6000
Exeter, NH 03833-0250 Fax: (603)772-3830
Free: (800)734-7022
Publication E-mail: rcneditor@aol.com603

Founded: 1831. **Freq:** Weekly 2/wk. **Print Method:** Offset. **Trim Size:** 15 3/16 x 21. **Cols./Page:** 6. **Col. Width:** 21 picas. **Key Personnel:** Howard Altschiller, Editor; Michael Rabideau, Advertising Dir. **ISSN:** 0886-3962. **Subscription Rates:** $41.60; $50 by mail; $54 out of country. **Remarks:** Accepts advertising.
Ad Rates: GLR: $2 **Circ:** Combined 6,766
BW: $1,417.50
4C: $1,762.50
PCI: $11.25

18615 The Hampton Union
Rockingham County Newspapers
PO Box 250 Phone: (603)772-6000
Exeter, NH 03833-0250 Fax: (603)772-3830
Free: (800)734-7022

Community newspaper. **Founded:** 1901. **Freq:** Semiweekly (Tues. and Fri.). **Print Method:** Offset. **Trim Size:** 15 3/16 x 21. **Cols./Page:** 6. **Col. Width:** 2 1/16 inches. **Col. Depth:** 21 inches. **Key Personnel:** Howard Altschiller, Editor; Michael Rabideau, Advertising Dir. **USPS:** 234-120. **Subscription Rates:** $50 by mail; $54 out of country. **Remarks:** Accepts advertising.
Ad Rates: GLR: $.90 **Circ:** Combined 6,252
BW: $1417.50
4C: $1762.50
SAU: $11.25
PCI: $11.25

18616 International Hospital Equipment & Solutions
PanEuropean Publishing Company
6 Chestnut St. Phone: (603)778-3848
Exeter, NH 03833 Fax: (603)778-3858
Publication E-mail: pepco@pepco.be
Publisher E-mail: paneuro@nh.ultranet.com

Trade magazine covering hospital equipment for health care management. **Subtitle:** International Hospital Equipment and Solutions. **Freq:** 8/year. **Trim Size:** 11 1/8 x 15 3/4. **Key Personnel:** Louise Betton, Contact. **Remarks:** Accepts advertising. **Formerly:** International Hospital Equipment.
Ad Rates: BW: $10,600 **Circ:** Non-paid △**30,005**
4C: $14,000

18617 The Rockingham News
Rockingham County Newspapers
PO Box 250 Phone: (603)772-6000
Exeter, NH 03833-0250 Fax: (603)772-3830
Free: (800)734-7022

Community newspaper. **Founded:** 1930. **Freq:** Weekly (Sat.). **Print Method:** Offset. **Trim Size:** 15 13/16 x 21. **Cols./Page:** 6. **Col. Width:** 2 1/6 inches. **Col. Depth:** 21 inches. **Key Personnel:** Howard Altschiller, Editor. **Subscription Rates:** $20.80. **Remarks:** Accepts advertising. **Formerly:** Rockingham Gazette.
Ad Rates: BW: $1,417.50 **Circ:** Paid 6,525
4C: $1,762.50
SAU: $11.25
PCI: $11.25

18618 WERZ-FM - 107.1
11 Downing Ct. Phone: (603)772-4757
Box 1540 Fax: (603)772-8464
Exeter, NH 03833

Format: Contemporary Hit Radio (CHR). **Networks:** Independent. **Owner:** Precision Media Corp., at above address. **Operating Hours:** Continuous. **ADI:** Boston-Worcester,MA-Derry-Manchester,NH. **Key Personnel:** Al Perry, General Mgr.; Jack O'Brien, Operations Mgr.; Wendy Larson, General Sales Mgr.; Dan Alexander, News Dir. **Wattage:** 6000. **Ad Rates:** Advertising accepted; rates available upon request. Combined advertising rates available with WMYF-AM.

18619 WMYF-AM - 1540
11 Downing Ct. Phone: (603)772-4757
Box 1540 Fax: (603)772-8464
Exeter, NH 03833

Format: Big Band/Nostalgia. **Networks:** Independent. **Owner:** Precision Media Ltd. Partnership, at above address. **Operating Hours:** Sunrise-sunset; 85% network, 15% local. **ADI:** Boston-Worcester,MA-Derry-Manchester,NH. **Key Personnel:** Judy Figliulo, Sales Mgr.; Al Perry, Vice President; Jack O'Brien, Operations Mgr.; Wendy Larson, General Sales Mgr.; Dan Alexander, News Dir. **Wattage:** 5000. **Ad Rates:** Combined advertising rates available with WERZ-FM.

18620 WPEA-FM - 90.5
Phillips Exeter Academy Phone: (603)777-4414
20 Main St. Fax: (603)778-9563
Exeter, NH 03833-2460
E-mail: wpea@hotmail.com

Format: Alternative/New Music/Progressive. **Owner:** Trustees of Phillips Exeter Academy, at above address, Exeter, NH 03833. **Founded:** 1964. **Operating Hours:** Noon-10 p.m. **Key Personnel:** Ben Austrin-Willis, General Mgr.; Duncan McIntyre, Station Mgr.; Jonathan Grassbaugh, Personnel Dir.; Zack Macomber, Production Mgr.; Alex B-Z, Head Proctor; Abhishek Gupta, Music Dir.; Katy Palfrey, Music Dir.; Ryan Glennon, Sports Dir.; Kristen Mercado, News Dir.; Justin Fitzpatrick, Publicity Dir.; Patrick Sweeny, Publicity Dir.; John Kane, Faculty Advisor. **Wattage:** 110. **Ad Rates:** Noncommercial.

FRANKLIN, pop. 7,901.

C. NH. Merrimack Co. At junction of Pemigewasset and Winnepesaukee Rivers, 18 mi. N. of Concord. Diversified manufacturing.

18621 WFTN-AM - 1240
Babbitt Rd. Phone: (603)934-2500
PO Box 99 Fax: (603)934-2933
Franklin, NH 03235-0099

Format: Country. **Networks:** Satellite Music Network; ABC. **Owner:** Northeast Communications Corp., at above address. **Founded:** 1967. **Operating Hours:** 19 hours daily; 70% network, 30% local. **Key Personnel:** Kurt Muhlfelder, Contact; Jeff Fisher, Contact; Fred Caruso, Contact; Leigh Shorps, News Dir.; Jeff Levitan, Sales Mgr.; Cathy Keyser, Contact. **Wattage:** 1000. **Ad Rates:** Combined advertising rates available with WFTN-FM: $14-$21 for 30 seconds; $17-$24 for 60 seconds.

18622 WFTN-FM - 94.1
Babbitt Rd. Phone: (603)934-2500
PO Box 941 Fax: (603)934-2933
Franklin, NH 03235

Format: Adult Contemporary. **Networks:** Major Market Radio. **Owner:** Northeast Communications Corp., at above address, (603)934-2520. **Founded:** 1987. **Operating Hours:** Continuous; 45% network, 55% local. **Key Personnel:** Jeff Fisher, Contact; Fred Caruso, Contact; Leigh Sharps, News Dir.; Jeff Levitan, Sales Mgr.; Kurt Muhlfelder, Contact; Tim Moulton, Contact. **Wattage:** 6000. **Ad Rates:** Combined advertising rates available with WFTN-AM: $15-$22 for 30 seconds; $18-$25 for 60 seconds.

GILFORD, pop. 4,841.

C. NH. Belknap Co. 3 mi. ENE of Laconia.

18623 WBHG-FM - 101.5
PO Box 7326 Phone: (603)524-1323
Gilford, NH 03247 Fax: (603)528-5185
Free: (800)368-7664

Format: Classic Rock. **Networks:** ABC. **Operating Hours:** Continuous. **Key Personnel:** Jack Beaton, General Mgr.; Warren Bailey, Operations Mgr.; Doug Renfroe, General Sales Mgr.; Joe Collie, Promotions Dir. **Wattage:** 6000. **Ad Rates:** Advertising accepted; rates available upon request.

18624 WEMJ-AM - 1490
PO Box 7326 Phone: (603)524-1323
Village West Fax: (603)524-5185
Gilford, NH 03247

Format: Talk; News; Sports. **Networks:** ABC; Mutual Broadcasting System; CBS; Westwood One Radio. **Owner:** WLNH Radio Inc./Sconnix Broadcasting, at above address. **Founded:** 1961. **Operating Hours:** 12m-12m. **Key Personnel:** Jack Beaton, General Mgr.; Warren Bailey, Operations Mgr.; Doug Renfroe, General Sales Mgr.; Joe Collie, Promotions Dir. **Wattage:** 1000. **Ad Rates:** $10-25 for 30 seconds; $14-30 for 60 seconds.

18625 WLKZ-FM - 104.9
21 Production Pl., Ste. 15 Phone: (603)524-0105
Gilford, NH 03246 Fax: (603)293-0699

Format: Oldies. **Networks:** Unistar. **Owner:** Fifth Estate, Inc., at above address. **Founded:** 1985. **Operating Hours:** 5AM - 12MID. **Key Personnel:** Paula Stone, Program Dir.; Robert Adams, General Mgr.; Pat Kelly, Morning Production Dir.; Marcus Sterne, Promotions Dir. **Local Programs:** *Bob Wilson Remembers the 50s*, Bob Wilson, (603)524-0105. **Wattage:** 3000. **Ad Rates:** $12.50-23.50 for 30 seconds; $15-25 for 60 seconds.

WLNH-AM - See Laconia

WLNH-FM - See Laconia

HANOVER, pop. 9,119.

WC NH. Grafton Co. On Connectucut River, 5 mi. NNW of Lebanon. Dartmouth College.

18626 The Dartmouth
6175 Robinson Hall Phone: (603)646-2600
Hanover, NH 03755
Collegiate newspaper (tabloid). **Founded:** 1799. **Freq:** Daily (morn.). **Print Method:** Offset. **Cols./Page:** 5. **Col. Width:** 9 7/8 nonpareils. **Col. Depth:** 12 1/2 inches. **Subscription Rates:** $56. **Remarks:** Accepts advertising.
Ad Rates: PCI: $10 **Circ:** ‡3,000

18627 Dartmouth Alumni Magazine
Dartmouth College Library
Rm 115 Baker Phone: (603)646-2236
Hanover, NH 03755-3525 Fax: (603)646-3702
Publication E-mail: alumni.mag@dartmouth.edu

College alumni magazine. **Founded:** 1908. **Freq:** 9/year (during the academic year). **Print Method:** Offset. **Trim Size:** 8 1/8 x 10 7/8. **Cols./Page:** 3. **Col. Width:** 13 picas. **Col. Depth:** 10 inches. **Key Personnel:** Jim Collins, Editor and Publisher. **USPS:** 148-560. **Subscription Rates:** $21.50; $3 single issue. **Remarks:** Accepts advertising.
Ad Rates: BW: $2,040 **Circ:** Paid ‡41,251
4C: $3,042 Non-paid ‡2,727

18628 Dartmouth College Library Bulletin
Dartmouth College Library
Rm 115 Baker Phone: (603)646-2236
Hanover, NH 03755-3525 Fax: (603)646-3702

Library journal. **Subtitle:** A Publication Sent to Friends of the Dartmouth Library. **Founded:** 1931. **Freq:** Semiannual. **Print Method:** Offset. **Trim Size:** 6 x 9. **Cols./Page:** 1. **Col. Width:** 4 inches. **Col. Depth:** 7 inches. **Key Personnel:** Lois A. Krieger, Editor, phone (606)646-2236, lois.krieger@dartmouth.edu; Philip N. Cronenwett, Editor, phone (606)646-2037, fax (603)646-0447, philip.n.cronenwett@dartmouth.edu. **ISSN:** 0011-6750. **Subscription Rates:** Free to qualified subscribers. **Remarks:** Advertising not accepted. **URL:** http://www.dartmouth.edu/~library/library_ bulletin/lib.bu.
Circ: Non-paid 900

18629 Journal of Modern Greek Studies
Johns Hopkins University Press
Department of English Phone: (603)643-5524
Dartmouth College Fax: (603)646-2159
6032 Sanborn House
Hanover, NH 03755-3533
Publication E-mail: konofrio@mail.press.jhu.edu
Publisher E-mail: jlinfo@jhupress.jhu.edu

Journal focusing on modern Greek studies. **Founded:** 1983. **Freq:** Semiannual. **Print Method:** Offset. **Trim Size:** 6 x 9. **Cols./Page:** 1. **Col. Width:** 26 picas. **Col. Depth:** 7 inches. **Key Personnel:** Peter Bien, Editor, phone (603)643-5524, peter.bien@dartmouth.edu. **ISSN:** 0738-1727. **Subscription Rates:** $30 individuals; $80 institutions; $25 students. **Remarks:** Accepts advertising. **URL:** http://www.muse.jhu.edu/journals/.
Ad Rates: BW: $190 **Circ:** ‡700

18630 WDCR-AM - 1340
PO Box 957 Phone: (603)646-3313
Hanover, NH 03755 Fax: (603)643-7655
E-mail: wdcr-wfrd@dartmouth.edu

Format: Alternative/New Music/Progressive; Heavy Metal; Jazz. **Networks:** NBC. **Founded:** 1958. **Operating Hours:** 20 hours Daily; 100% local. **ADI:** Burlington-Hartford, VT-Plattsburgh, NY. **Key Personnel:** Dhruv Prasad, General Mgr.; Dan Indelicato, Program Dir.; Vince Cannon, Music Dir.; Tim Hoehn, Sales Mgr.; Tim Hoehn, Sales Mgr. **Wattage:** 1000. **Ad Rates:** $6-$17.50 for 30 seconds; $8-$19.50 for 60 seconds. Combined advertising rates available with WFRD-FM: $12-$35 for 30 seconds;. **URL:** http://www.dartmouth.edu/community/.

18631 WFRD-FM - 99.3
PO Box 957 Phone: (603)646-3313
Hanover, NH 03755-0957 Fax: (603)643-7655
E-mail: wdcr-wfrd@dartmouth.edu

Format: Album-Oriented Rock (AOR). **Networks:** Independent. **Founded:** 1976. **Operating Hours:** 18 hours Daily, 100% local. **ADI:** Burlington-Hartford, VT-Plattsburgh, NY. **Key Personnel:** Dhruv Prasad, General Mgr.; Kendra Kosko, Program Dir.; Chad Kline, Music Dir.; Tim Hoehn, Sales Mgr. **Wattage:** 3000. **Ad Rates:** Combined advertising rates available with WDCR-AM: $12-$35 for 30 seconds; $16-$39 for 60 seconds. **URL:** http://www.wfrd.com.

HENNIKER, pop. 3,246.

SC NH. Merrimack Co. On Contoocook River, 14 mi. W. of Concord.

18632 The New Englander
New England College
Henniker, NH 03242 Phone: (603)428-2243
Fax: (603)428-7230

Collegiate newspaper. **Founded:** 1947. **Freq:** Biweekly. **Print Method:** Offset. **Trim Size:** 11 x 16. **Cols./Page:** 4. **Col. Width:** 2 1/4 inches. **Col. Depth:** 16 inches. **Key Personnel:** Christie Craighead, Editor; Heather Bailey, News Editor. **Remarks:** Color advertising not accepted.
Ad Rates: BW: $204 **Circ:** Free ‡1,500
PCI: $4.75

18633 WNEC-FM - 91.7
Bridge St. Phone: (603)428-6393
Henniker, NH 03242 Fax: (603)428-7230
E-mail: wnec_ @bill.nec.edu

Format: Jazz; Bluegrass; Blues; Folk; Classical; Alternative/New Music/Progressive. **Founded:** 1971. **Formerly:** WWEC-FM. **Operating Hours:** 9 a.m. - midnight. **Key Personnel:** A. Metzegen, General Mgr., phone (603)428-2337, fax (603)428-7230, mb@nec.edu; Jon Colcord, Chief Announcer; Kristen Westhoven, Music Dir., phone (603)428-6393, fax (603)428-7230; Pete Stohrer, Engineer. **Local Programs:** *Showtime - Local Bands*, K. Taylor. **Wattage:** 150. **Ad Rates:** Noncommercial.

HILLSBORO, pop. 3,437.

S. NH. Hillsboro Co. On Contoocook River, 20 mi. SW of Concord. Timber; agriculture.

18634 The Messenger
Granite Quill
PO Box 917 Phone: (603)464-3388
Hillsboro, NH 03244-1917 Fax: (603)464-4106
Free: (800)281-2859

Community newspaper. **Founded:** 1869. **Freq:** Weekly (Mon.). **Print Method:** Offset. **Cols./Page:** 6. **Col. Width:** 19 nonpareils. **Col. Depth:** 224 agate lines. **Key Personnel:** Leigh Bosse, Publisher; Joyce Bosse, Editor. **Subscription Rates:** $25 individuals. **Remarks:** Accepts advertising. **Formerly:** Journal (1992).
Ad Rates: GLR: $1.09 **Circ:** Paid 5,000
BW: $780
4C: $1,530
PCI: $5

18635 New Hampshire Week in Review
Granite Quill
PO Box 917 Phone: (603)464-3388
Hillsboro, NH 03244-1917 Fax: (603)464-4106
Free: (800)281-2859

Community newspaper. **Founded:** 1976. **Freq:** Weekly (Mon.). **Print Method:** Offset. **Cols./Page:** 6. **Col. Width:** 26 nonpareils. **Col. Depth:** 294 agate lines. **Key Personnel:** Leigh Bosse, Publisher; Joyce Bosse, Editor. **Remarks:** Accepts advertising. **Formerly:** News Messenger.
Ad Rates: PCI: $12.25 **Circ:** Free ‡22,506

18636 WRCI-FM - 107.7
7 Perley St. Phone: (603)228-9036
PO Box 1923 Fax: (603)224-7280
Concord, NH 03302-1923
E-mail: wrci@aol.com

Format: Classic Rock. **Simulcasts:** WNHI-FM. **Networks:** AP. **Owner:** RadioWorks, Inc., at above address. **Founded:** 1989. **Operating Hours:** Continuous. **Key Personnel:** Stuart F. Richter, General Mgr.; Brit Johnson, General Sales Mgr.; Harry Kozlowski, Program Dir. **Wattage:** 3000. **Ad Rates:** $26-43 per unit. Combined advertising rates available with WJYY-FM:.

HOPKINTON

18637 Packard Cormorant
Packard Automobile Classics
181 Burrage Rd.
Hopkinton, NH 03229
Publication E-mail: Malakand@aol.com

Trade magazine covering historical and technical articles on Packard automobiles. **Subtitle:** International Magazine of Packard Automobile Classics. **Founded:** 1962. **Freq:** Quarterly. **Print Method:** Offset. **Trim Size:** 8 x 11. **Cols./Page:** 2. **Col. Width:** 20 picas. **Col. Depth:** 9 inches. **Key Personnel:** Richard M. Langworth, Editor. **ISSN:** 0362-9368. **Subscription Rates:** Included in membership. **Remarks:** Advertising not accepted. **Former name:** The Cormorant (1975).
Circ: Combined 4,050

HUDSON, pop. 14,022.

S. NH. Hillsboro Co. On Merrimack River, 3 mi. E. of Nashua.

18638 Hudson Litchfield News
222 Central St., No. 5 Phone: (603)880-1516
Hudson, NH 03051-4494 Fax: (603)880-1516

Community newspaper. **Founded:** 1980. **Freq:** Weekly. **Print Method:** Offset. **Trim Size:** 10 x 16. **Cols./Page:** 6. **Col. Width:** 1 1/2 inches. **Col. Depth:** 10 inches. **Key Personnel:** Diane Thoms, Managing Editor; Fideie Bernasconi, President. **Subscription Rates:** Free. **Remarks:** Accepts advertising. **Formerly:** Hudson News (1990).
Ad Rates: GLR: $8.50 **Circ:** Free 10,643
BW: $816
PCI: $8.50

18639 The Telegraph
17 Executive Dr. Phone: (603)882-2741
Hudson, NH 03051 Fax: (603)882-5138
Publication E-mail: news@telegraph.hh.com

General newspaper. **Founded:** 1832. **Freq:** Mon.-Sun. (morn.). **Print Method:** Offset. **Cols./Page:** 6. **Col. Width:** 24 nonpareils. **Col. Depth:** 294 agate lines. **Key Personnel:** Terry Williams, Publisher; George Geers, Editor; Mark Iacuessa, Advertising Mgr. **Subscription Rates:** $169 individuals Home delivery; $228 by mail. **Alt. Formats:** Microform.
Ad Rates: SAU: $18.90 **Circ:** Mon.-Sat. ★28,863
Sun. ★34,324

KEENE†, pop. 21,449.

SW NH. Cheshire Co. On Ashuelot River, 15 mi. ENE of Brattleboro, VT. Keene State College. Summer resort. Major industrial and commercial center. Quarries, lumber, nurseries, agriculture.

18640 The Keene Sentinel
Keene Publishing Corp.
60 West St. Phone: (603)352-1234
PO Box 546 Fax: (603)352-0437
Keene, NH 03431-0546
General newspaper. **Founded:** 1799. **Freq:** Daily (eve.). **Print Method:** Offset. **Cols./Page:** 6. **Col. Width:** 26 nonpareils. **Col. Depth:** 301 agate lines. **Key Personnel:** James A. Rousmaniere, Jr., Editor; Joseph D. Antosiewicz, Controller; Thomas M. Ewing, Publisher; Colin R. Lyle, Advertising Dir.; Thomas F. Kearney, Exec. Editor. **Subscription Rates:** $185 in County; $210 out of area. **Remarks:** Accepts advertising. **URL:** http://www.keenesentinel.com.
Ad Rates: BW: $1,651.20 **Circ:** Mon.-Sat. ★14,741
4C: $1,906.20 Sun. ★13,648
PCI: $12.80

18641 The Monadnock Shopper News
Shakour Publishers
445 West St. Phone: (603)352-5250
PO Box 487 Fax: (603)357-9351
Keene, NH 03431-0487
Publication E-mail: monanockshopper@top.monad.net

Shopper news. **Subtitle:** Monadnock Shopper News. **Founded:** 1958. **Freq:** Weekly. **Print Method:** Offset. **Trim Size:** 10 3/8 x 16. **Cols./Page:** 7. **Col. Width:** 17 nonpareils. **Col. Depth:** 224 agate lines. **Key Personnel:** Mitchell G. Shakour, Editor and Publisher; Michelle Green, Editor. **Subscription Rates:** $25. **Remarks:** Accepts advertising.
Ad Rates: GLR: $.83 **Circ:** Free ‡37,500
BW: $728
4C: $1,100
PCI: $11.66

18642 WEKW-TV - 52
PO Box 1100 Phone: (603)868-1100
Durham, NH 03824-1100 Fax: (603)868-7552
E-mail: email@nhptvll.unh.edu

Format: Public TV. **Simulcasts:** WENH-TV Durham, NH. **Networks:** Public Broadcasting Service (PBS). **Founded:** 1959. **Operating Hours:** 6 a.m.-1:05 p.m. **ADI:** Boston-Worcester,MA-Derry-Manchester,NH. **Key Personnel:** Peter Frid, General Mgr.; Stephen L. Baker, Finance and Admin. Dir.; Linda C Burroughs, Contact; Mary Anne Alhadeff, Dir. of Broadcasting; Robert Ross, Dir. of Engineering; Frank Windsor, Dir. of Educational Telecommunications. **Local Programs:** *Granite State Challenge*; *New Hampshire Crossroads*; *New Hampshire Roundtable*. **Ad Rates:** Noncommercial. **URL:** http://nhptv.unh.edu.

WKBK-AM - See Winchester

18643 WKNE-AM - 1290
PO Box 466 Phone: (603)352-9230
Keene, NH 03431 Fax: (603)357-3926
E-mail: am1290@wkne.com

Format: News; Classic Rock. **Networks:** CBS. **Owner:** LB New Hampshire, Inc., at above address. **Founded:** 1927. **Operating Hours:** Continuous; 5% network, 95% local. **ADI:** Boston-Worcester,MA-Derry-Manchester,NH. **Key Personnel:** Paul Scheuring, News Dir.; Michael Trombly, General Mgr. **Local Programs:** *Viewpoint*, Paul Scheuring, News Dir. **Wattage:** 5000. **Ad Rates:** $53 for 60 seconds. Combined advertising rates available with WKNE-FM. **URL:** http://www.wkcne.com.

18644 WKNE-FM - 103.7
PO Box 466 Phone: (603)352-9230
Keene, NH 03431 Fax: (603)357-3926
E-mail: fm1037@wkne.com

Format: Adult Contemporary. **Networks:** Independent. **Owner:** Richard Lightfoot, at above address. **Founded:** 1958. **Operating Hours:** Continuous; 100% local. **ADI:** Boston-Worcester,MA-Derry-Manchester,NH. **Key Personnel:** Steve Hampl, Program Dir.; Paul Scheuring, News Dir.; Michael Trombly, General Mgr. **Local Programs:** *Viewpoint*, Paul Scheuring, News Dir. **Wattage:** 50,000. **Ad Rates:** Combined advertising rates available with WKNE-AM. **URL:** http://www.wkne.com.

18645 WKNH-FM - 91.3
229 Main St. Phone: (603)358-2421
Keene State College Fax: (603)358-2417
Keene, NH 03431

Format: Alternative/New Music/Progressive. **Founded:** 1975. **Formerly:** WKSC (1971). **Operating Hours:** 7 a.m.-1 a.m. **Key Personnel:** James Morrison, General Mgr.; Jennifer Haggerty, News Dir., phone (603)358-2734; Richard Holliday, Program Dir., phone (603)358-2421; Chris Wahl, Music Dir., phone (603)358-2420; Chris Stavey, Music Dir., phone (603)358-2420; Dave Buren, Chief Engineer; Tony Stavely, Faculty Advisor, phone (603)358-2327; Ross Garofalo, Sales Mgr. **Local Programs:** *The Classical Alternative*, Connie Bowblis, (603)358-2420; *Metallic K.O.*, Chris Rennpage, (603)358-2420; *The Underground Power Jam* 2:00 pm - 5:00 pm Friday, James Morrison, (603)358-2734. **Wattage:** 300. **Ad Rates:** Noncommercial. **URL:** http://www.wknh.com.

WXOD-FM - See Winchester

LACONIA†, pop. 15,575.

C. NH. Belknap Co. Near Lakes Winnisquam, Pangus, and Opechee, 22 mi. N. of Concord. White Mountain National Forest headquarters. Summer and winter resort. Diversified manufacturing, including knitting machines, wood products. Timber; farming.

18646 Citizen
Citizen Publishing Co.
171 Fair St. Phone: (603)524-8300
Laconia, NH 03246 Fax: (603)524-6702
Free: (800)564-3806

General newspaper. **Founded:** 1925. **Freq:** Mon.-Fri. (eve.) & Sat. (morn.). **Print Method:** Offset. **Cols./Page:** 6. **Col. Width:** 25 nonpareils. **Col. Depth:** 294 agate lines. **Key Personnel:** John Howe, Executive editor; Frank McSweegan, General Mgr.; Terry Rosseau, Advertising Dir. **Subscription Rates:** $93.60. **Remarks:** Accepts advertising. **Formerly:** Evening Citizen; Laconia Evening Citizen.
Ad Rates: BW: $1300 **Circ:** Mon.-Sat. 10,508
4C: $360
PCI: $10.08

18647 Hearth & Home Magazine
Village West Publishing
PO Box 2008 Phone: (603)528-4285
Laconia, NH 03247 Fax: (603)524-0643
Free: (800)258-3772
Publication E-mail: mailbox@villagewest.com
Publisher E-mail: mailbox@villagewest.com

Trade journal for manufacturers and retailers of hearth

products, casual furniture and barbecue grills. **Subtitle:** Hearth & Patio Retailing. **Founded:** Dec. 1980. **Freq:** Monthly. **Print Method:** Offset. **Trim Size:** 8 1/8 x 10 7/8. **Cols./Page:** 3. **Col. Width:** 27 nonpareils. **Col. Depth:** 152 agate lines. **Key Personnel:** Richard Wright, Editor and Publisher; Linda Hansen, Circulation Mgr. **ISSN:** 0273-5695. **Subscription Rates:** $30 (domestic). **Remarks:** Advertising accepted; rates available upon request advertising accepted, call for rates. **Formerly:** Wood 'n Energy (1989).
Circ: Non-paid ‡18000

18648 Community TV Corp.
408 Union Ave. Phone: (603)524-4425
Laconia, NH 03246

Key Personnel: Fred Zecha, General Mgr. **Cities Served:** Alton, Barnstead, Belmont, Franklin, Gilford, Meredith, Northfield, Thornton, Tilton, Wolfboro, NH.

18649 WEZS-AM - 1350
266 Union Ave. Phone: (603)524-6288
Laconia, NH 03246 Fax: (603)528-1638
E-mail: staff@wezs.com

Format: Easy Listening. **Networks:** USA Radio. **Owner:** Gary W. Hammond, at above address. **Founded:** 1922. **Operating Hours:** 6 a.m.-6 p.m. **Key Personnel:** Gary Hammond, General Mgr., ghammond@wezs.com; Paul Hatch, News Dir., phatch2atstiac.net. **Wattage:** 5000. **URL:** http://www.wezs.com.

18650 WLNH-AM - 1350
Box 7326 Phone: (603)524-1323
Village West Fax: (603)528-5185
Gilford, NH 03247

Format: Adult Contemporary. **Founded:** 1965. **Key Personnel:** Scott McGueen, President; Robert Greer, General Mgr.; Richard Hopper, General Sales Mgr.; Warren Bailey, Program Dir.; Kevin Bowland, Chief Engineer. **Wattage:** 1900.

18651 WLNH-FM - 98.3
Box 7326 Phone: (603)524-1323
Village West Fax: (603)524-1350
Gilford, NH 03247

Format: Adult Contemporary. **Founded:** 1965. **Operating Hours:** Continuous. **Key Personnel:** Scott McGueen, President; Robert Greer, General Mgr.; Richard Hopper, General Sales Mgr.; Warren Bailey, Program Dir.; Kevin Bowland, Chief Engineer. **Wattage:** 6000.

LANCASTER†, pop. 3,401.

NW NH. Coos Co. Near Connecticut and Israel Rivers, 19 mi. W. of Berlin. Summer resort. Trading center for surrounding agriculture. Pulpwood timber.

18652 Coos County Democrat
North Country Publishing Co.
79 Main St. Phone: (603)788-4939
Box 28 Fax: (603)788-3022
Lancaster, NH 03584
Free: (800)643-4939
Publication E-mail: ccdemocrat@aol.com; editors@coosdem.com

Community newspaper. **Founded:** 1838. **Freq:** Weekly (Wed.). **Print Method:** Letterpress and offset. **Cols./Page:** 8. **Col. Width:** 11 nonpareils. **Col. Depth:** 21 agate lines. **Key Personnel:** John D. Harrigan, Editor and Publisher. **USPS:** 222-580. **Subscription Rates:** $27 individuals in New Hampshire and Vermont; $30 out of state.
Ad Rates: GLR: $6 **Circ:** ‡6,500
BW: $1,008
PCI: $6

LEBANON, pop. 11,134.

WC NH. Grafton Co. 5 mi. SSE of Hanover. Resort. Diversified manufacturing.

18653 Dartmouth Medicine
Dartmouth Medical School
One Medical Center Dr., HB 7070 Phone: (603)650-4039
Lebanon, NH 03756
Publication E-mail: dartmed@dartmouth.edu

Professional magazine for alumni and Friends of Dartmouth Medical School and Dartmouth-Hitchcock Medical Center. **Founded:** 1976. **Freq:** Quarterly. **Print Method:** Web offset. **Trim Size:** 8 1/2 x 10 7/8. **Key Personnel:** Dana Cook Grossman, Editor. **Subscription Rates:** Free to qualified subscribers. **Remarks:** Accepts advertising. **Former name:** Dartmouth Medical School Alumni Magazine (1990).
Ad Rates: BW: $650 **Circ:** Non-paid 23,000
4C: $850

18654 The International Journal of Psychiatry in Medicine
Baywood Publishing Co., Inc.
Dr. Thomas E. Oxman Phone: (603)650-6147
DHMC-DHPA-Psychiatry-5D Fax: (603)650-5842
1 Medical Center Dr.
Lebanon, NH 03756
Publisher E-mail: baywood@baywood.com

Addresses the complex relationships among biological, psychological, and social systems in the world of primary care medicine. **Subtitle:** Biopsychosocial Aspects of Primary Care. **Founded:** 1970. **Freq:** Quarterly. **Print Method:** Offset. **Trim Size:** 6 x 9. **Cols./Page:** 1. **Col. Width:** 4 1/2 inches. **Col. Depth:** 7 1/2 inches. **Key Personnel:** Thomas Oakman, M.D., Editor, thomas.okaman@dartmouth.edu; Stuart Cohen, Publisher; Lorna Cohen, Advertising Mgr.; S. Edwards, Circulation Mgr. **Subscription Rates:** $44.50 U.S. and Canada; $49.35 other countries; $122.50 Industry; $127.35 Industry, other countries. **Remarks:** Advertising not accepted.
Circ: (Not Reported)

18655 WVRR-FM - 101.7
31 Hanover St., Ste. 4 Phone: (603)448-1400
Lebanon, NH 03766 Fax: (603)448-1755

Format: Classic Rock. **Owner:** Real Rock Radio, L.L.C., at above address. **Founded:** Mar. 1997. **Former name:** WXXK-FM. **Operating Hours:** Continuous. **Key Personnel:** Bob Frisch, President; Kenny Michaels, Program Dir.; John Gales, Sales Mgr. **Wattage:** 3000.

18656 WXXK-FM - 100.5
31 Hanover St., Ste. 4 Phone: (603)448-5229
Lebanon, NH 03766 Fax: (603)448-5231

Format: Contemporary Country. **Networks:** CNN Radio; Westwood One Radio. **Founded:** 1988. **Formerly:** WCNL-FM. **Operating Hours:** Continuous. **Key Personnel:** John Gales, Sales Mgr., johngales@kixx.com; Kenny Michaels, Program Dir.; Bob Frisch, President. **Wattage:** 22,000. **Ad Rates:** $17-30 per unit. **URL:** http://www.kixx.com.

LITTLETON, pop. 5,558.

WC NH. Grafton Co. On Ammonoosuc River, 31 mi. SW of Berlin. Mountain resort. Manufactures shoes, wood products. Lumber, dairy farms.

18657 The Courier
Main Street Media, Inc.
365 Union St. Phone: (603)444-3927
PO Box 230 Fax: (603)444-3920
Littleton, NH 03561
Free: (800)639-3061
Publication E-mail: tchwwp@moose.neia.net

Community newspaper. **Founded:** 1889. **Freq:** Weekly (Wed.). **Print Method:** Offset. **Cols./Page:** 6. **Col. Width:** 12 3/10 picas. **Col. Depth:** 21 inches. **Key Personnel:** Tim McCarthy, Editor; Thomas C. Hepner, Publisher; Georgia Golden, Advertising Mgr.; Georgia C. Golden. **Subscription Rates:** $21 individuals; $26 out of state. **URL:** http://www.wht-mtn-publishing.com.
Ad Rates: SAU: $6.20 **Circ:** ‡6,925

18658 WLED-TV - 49
PO Box 1100 Phone: (603)868-1100
Durham, NH 03824-1100 Fax: (603)868-7552
E-mail: email@nhptvll.unh.edu

Format: Public TV. **Simulcasts:** WENH-TV. **Networks:** Public Broadcasting Service (PBS). **Founded:** 1959. **Operating Hours:** 6 a.m.-1:05 a.m. **ADI:** Burlington-Hartford, VT-Plattsburgh, NY. **Key Personnel:** Peter Frid, General Mgr.; Stephen L. Baker, Finance and Admin. Dir.; Linda C Burroughs, Dir. of Development; Mary Anne Alhadeff, Dir. of Broadcasting; Robert Ross, Dir. of Engineering; Frank Windsor, Dir. of Educational Telecommunications. **Local Programs:** *Granite State Challenge*; *New Hampshire Crossroads*; *New Hampshire Roundtable*. **Ad Rates:** Noncommercial. **URL:** http://nhptv.unh.edu.

18659 WLTN-AM - 1400
17 Main St. Phone: (603)444-3911
Littleton, NH 03561-1641 Fax: (603)444-7186

Format: News; Talk; Sports. **Networks:** ABC. **Owner:** Profile Broadcasting Company, Inc., at above address. **Founded:** 1963. **Operating Hours:** 15% local, 85% network. **Key Personnel:** Peter Aydelott, General Mgr.; Bradford S. Bailey, Contact; Jim Clothey, News Dir.; Vicky McKay, Contact; Jacki Scott, Program Mgr.; Judith Aydelott, Business Mgr. **Wattage:** 1000. **Ad Rates:** $6.70-8.70 for 30 seconds; $9-11.70 for 60 seconds. Combined advertising rates available with WLTN-FM: $5-$13 for 30 seconds; $6.75-$17.50.

18660 WLTN-FM - 96.7
15 Main St. Phone: (603)444-3911
Littleton, NH 03561 Fax: (603)444-7186

Format: Oldies. **Networks:** ABC. **Owner:** Peter Aydelott, at above address. **Founded:** 1991. **Operating Hours:** 24 hrs. **Key Personnel:** Peter Aydelott, General Mgr.; Jan Carver, Contact; Jim Clothey, News Dir.; Judith Aydelott, Business Mgr.; Jim Clothey, Production Dir.; Vicky McKay, Contact. **Wattage:** 6000. **Ad Rates:** $12.35 for 30 seconds; $16.50 for 60 seconds. $6.70-$8.70 for 30 seconds; $9-$11.70 for 60 seconds; Combined advertising rates available with WLTN-AM.

18661 WMTK-FM - 106.3
136 Main St. Phone: (603)444-5106
Thayers Inn Fax: (603)444-1205
PO Box 106
Littleton, NH 03561

Format: Classic Rock. **Networks:** ABC; Satellite Music Network. **Owner:** White Mountain FM, Inc., 52 School St., Littleton, NH 03561, (603)444-6609. **Founded:** 1985. **Operating Hours:** Continuous. **Key Personnel:** Chris Keach, News Dir.; Thomas M. Pancoast, Owner/Pres.; Randy Frank, Sales Supervisor; Chris Keach, Program Dir. **Wattage:** 6000. **Ad Rates:** Advertising accepted; rates available upon request.

LONDONDERRY

18662 Harron Cablevision
24 Orchardview Dr. Ste. 2 Phone: (603)432-0382
Londonderry, NH 03053 Fax: (603)432-7428

Founded: 1984. **Cities Served:** Hillsborough and Rockingham counties, NH.

LOUDON

18663 New England Farmer
Rural Press USA
845 Loudon Ridge Rd. Phone: (603)267-7103
Loudon, NH 03301 Fax: (603)267-7103

Magazine covering agriculture, agronomy, animal husbandry, farm energy, architecture, history, economics, and news of the Northeast. **Founded:** 1848. **Freq:** Monthly. **Print Method:** Offset. **Trim Size:** 10.5 x 13. **Cols./Page:** 4. **Col. Width:** 2 1/4 picas. **Col. Depth:** 12 5/8 inches. **Key Personnel:** Melissa Moore, Editor; Jeff Tennant, Publisher. **Subscription Rates:** Free to qualified subscribers; $12. **Remarks:** Accepts advertising.
Ad Rates: BW: $1,846 **Circ:** Paid ‡5,402
4C: $1,520 Controlled ‡10,783
PCI: $22.65

MANCHESTER, pop. 90,936.

S. NH. Hillsboro Co. On Merrimack River, 15 mi. N. of Nashua. New Hampshire College, Saint Anselm College, Notre Dame College, University of New Hampshire at Manchester. Largest city in NH; major manufacturing center. Products include electronics, shoes, textiles, rubber, auto parts. Lumber; dairy farms.

18664 Bus Industry Magazine
Bus History Association, Inc.
195 Lancelot Dr.
Manchester, NH 03104-1420

Trade magazine covering bus transportation. **Founded:** 1963. **Freq:** Quarterly. **Trim Size:** 8 1/2 x 11. **Cols./Page:** 2. **Col. Width:** 3 1/2 inches. **Col. Depth:** 9 1/2 inches. **ISSN:** 0739-7194. **Subscription Rates:** $25 individuals; $35 Canada; $35 elsewhere. **Remarks:** Accepts advertising.
Ad Rates: BW: $150 **Circ:** Combined 500

18665 Business NH Magazine
Laurentian Business Publishing, Inc.
404 Chestnut St., No. 201 Phone: (603)626-6354
Manchester, NH 03101-1831 Fax: (603)626-6359
Publication E-mail: bnhmag@aol.com

Business Magazine. **Founded:** Nov. 1983. **Freq:** Monthly. **Print Method:** Offset. **Trim Size:** 8 1/8 x 10 7/8. **Cols./Page:** 3. **Col. Width:** 2 1/4 inches. **Col. Depth:** 10 inches. **Key Personnel:** Janet Phelps, Editor; B.J. Eckardt, Publisher. **ISSN:** 0897-8093. **Subscription Rates:** $24; $3 single issue. **Remarks:** Accepts advertising. **Formerly:** Business NH (Jan. 1, 1988); Jolicoeur's Business NH; BNH The Business of New Hampshire; Business New Hampshire Magazine.
Ad Rates: BW: $1,846 **Circ:** Paid ‡600
4C: $2,343 Controlled ‡12,400

18666 Journal of Educational Computing Research
Baywood Publishing Co., Inc.
Dr. Robert Seidman   Phone: (603)668-2211
New Hampshire College   Fax: (603)645-9737
2500 North River Rd.
Manchester, NH 03106-1045
Publisher E-mail: baywood@baywood.com

Journal on new research in the theory and applications of educational computing. **Founded:** Sept. 1984. **Freq:** 8/year. **Print Method:** Offset. **Trim Size:** 6 x 9. **Cols./Page:** 1. **Col. Width:** 4 1/2 inches. **Col. Depth:** 7 1/2 inches. **Key Personnel:** Robert Seidman, Ph.D., Editor, phone (603)684-3102, rseidman@minerva.nhc.edu; Stuart Cohen, Publisher; Lorna Roher, Advertising Mgr.; S. Edwards, Circulation Mgr. **ISSN:** 0735-6331. **Subscription Rates:** $104.00 U.S. and Canada; $113.70 other countries; $182.00 Industry; $191.70 Industry, other countries. **Remarks:** Advertising not accepted.
Circ: (Not Reported)

18667 Le Canado-Americain
Association Canado-Americaine
52 Concord St.   Phone: (603)625-8577
PO Box 989   Fax: (603)625-1214
Manchester, NH 03101-1806
Free: (800)222-8577

Fraternal magazine (French and English). **Founded:** 1900. **Freq:** Quarterly. **Print Method:** Web offset. **Trim Size:** 8 1/4 x 10 7/8. **Cols./Page:** 3. **Col. Width:** 2 1/8 inches. **Col. Depth:** 9 1/2 inches. **Key Personnel:** Julien Olivier, Editor. **ISSN:** 0576-6478. **Subscription Rates:** Free to qualified subscribers; $10 nonmembers. **Remarks:** Accepts advertising.
Ad Rates: BW: $1,125   **Circ:** Paid ‡34,000
4C: $2,125   Controlled ‡1,333

18668 New Hampshire Business Review
Business Publications, Inc.
150 Dow St.   Phone: (603)624-1442
Manchester, NH 03101   Fax: (603)624-1310
Publisher E-mail: nhbr@aol.com

Regional business newspaper. **Founded:** 1978. **Freq:** Semi-monthly. **Print Method:** Web offset. **Trim Size:** 11 1/2 x 17. **Cols./Page:** 4. **Col. Width:** 2.5 picas. **Col. Depth:** 16 inches. **Key Personnel:** Donald Madden, Editor and Publisher; Shirley Meyers, General Mgr. **ISSN:** 0164-8152. **Subscription Rates:** $26 individuals. **Remarks:** Accepts advertising.
Ad Rates: BW: $1,700   **Circ:** 15,000
4C: $2,300

18669 News & Food Report
New Hampshire Grocers Association
110 Stark St.   Phone: (603)669-9333
Manchester, NH 03101-1934   Fax: (603)623-1137
Publication E-mail: news@grocers.org
Publisher E-mail: ntfr@grocers.org

Magazine for the New Hampshire retail food industry. **Founded:** 1933. **Freq:** Monthly. **Print Method:** Offset. **Trim Size:** 8 1/2 x 11. **Cols./Page:** 3. **Col. Width:** 2.25 picas. **Col. Depth:** 10 inches. **Key Personnel:** John M. Dumais, Editor; JoAnne Grenier, Advertising Mgr. **USPS:** 390-300. **Subscription Rates:** $24.
Ad Rates: GLR: $34   **Circ:** ‡1,300
BW: $225
PCI: $14

18670 Northeast Export Magazine
Laurentian Business Publishing, Inc.
404 Chestnut St., No. 201   Phone: (603)626-6354
Manchester, NH 03101-1831   Fax: (603)626-6359

Trade magazine for exporters in the six New England states of Maine, New Hampshire, Vermont, Massachusetts, Connecticut, and Rhode Island. **Founded:** Mar. 1997. **Freq:** Bimonthly. **Print Method:** Offset. **Trim Size:** 8 1/8 x 10 7/8. **Cols./Page:** 3. **Col. Width:** 2 1/4 inches. **Col. Depth:** 10 inches. **Key Personnel:** Anita Becker, Editor; Eugene Ward, Publisher. **ISSN:** 1092-6682. **Subscription Rates:** $18 individuals; $30 two years; $3 single issue. **Remarks:** Accepts advertising.
Ad Rates: BW: $2,250   **Circ:** Controlled 11,750
4C: $2,970

18671 Red Brick Review
315 Canal St.
Manchester, NH 03101

Magazine containing poems and reviews of poems. **Founded:** 1991. **Freq:** Annual. **Key Personnel:** Sean Thomas Dougherty. **Subscription Rates:** $5 individuals. **Remarks:** Accepts advertising.
Circ: (Not Reported)

18672 The Registry Review
Real Data Corp.
103 Bay St.   Phone: (603)669-3822
Manchester, NH 03104-3007   Fax: (603)645-0072

Newspaper providing real estate transfer information and New Hampshire commercial data. **Founded:** 1978. **Freq:** Weekly. **Print Method:** Offset. **Key Personnel:** Irv Tolles, Publisher. **ISSN:** 1067-0521. **Subscription Rates:** $148 (50 issues). **Remarks:** Advertising accepted; rates available upon request.
Circ: (Not Reported)

18673 The Union Leader
Union Leader Corp.
100 William Loeb Dr.   Phone: (603)668-4321
PO Box 9555   Fax: (603)668-0382
Manchester, NH 03109-5309
Publication E-mail: theul@aol.com

General newspaper. **Founded:** 1863. **Freq:** Mon.-Sun. (morn.). **Print Method:** Flexography. **Trim Size:** 21 1/4 x 13. **Cols./Page:** 6. **Col. Width:** 25 nonpareils. **Col. Depth:** 297.5 agate lines. **Key Personnel:** J.W. McQuaid, Editor-in-Chief; Nackey S. Loeb, Publisher; Charles Perkins, Executive Editor; James Linehan, Managing Editor. **Subscription Rates:** $178 individuals home delivery, daily & Sunday in N.M. **Remarks:** Accepts advertising. Monday-Saturday: GLR: $2.52; BW: $4,498.20; 4C: $5,097.45; PCI: $35.19; Sunday: GLR: $2.75; BW: $4,908.75; 4C: $5,508.00; PCI: $38.42. **Online:** Nexis. **Alt. Formats:** Microfiche. **Feature Editors:** Ellie Ferriter, *Family*, phone (603)668-4321; Maureen Milliken, *Sports*, phone (603)668-4321; Barry Palmer, *Book*, phone (603)668-4321; Tami Plyler, *City*; Bill Regan, *Financial/Business*, phone (603)668-4321; Pat Sheeran, *Sunday*, phone (603)668-4321; Norm Welsh, *Religion*, phone (603)668-4321.
Circ: Mon.-Fri. ★**64,045**
Sat. ★**62,303**
Sun. ★**86,973**

18674 Continental Cablevision of New England, Inc.
751 E. Industrial Park Dr.
Manchester, NH 03109-5633

Founded: 1973. **Cities Served:** Rockingham County, NH.

18675 MediaOne
751 E. Industrial Park Dr.   Phone: (603)626-9900
Manchester, NH 03109   Fax: (603)641-2996
Free: (800)3222825

Owner: MediaOne, Pilot House, Lewis Wharf, Boston, MA 02110, (617)742-9500, Fax: (617)742-0530, Free: (800)225-6248. **Founded:** 1970. **Formerly:** TeleCable, Inc.; United Cable; Continental Cablevision. **Key Personnel:** Gregg Sanders, General Mgr.; George Picariello, Technical Operations; Linda Duggan, Dir. of Customer Service; Tom Tosi, Dir. of Local Programming; Tom O'Rourke, Dir. of Public & Government Affairs. **Cities Served:** Antrim, Auburn, Bedford, Boscawen, Bow, Bridgewater, Bristol, Candia, Canterbury, Chichester, Concord, NH; Deering, Hebron, Henniker, Hillsboro, Derry, Alexandria, Con toocook, Hopkinton, New Hampton, Penacook, Plaistow, Manchester, E. Hampstead, Hampstead, Salem, Sundown, Weare, Goffstown, Hooksett, Loudon, Pembroke, and Suncook: subscribing households 104,000; 66 channels; 4 community access channels; 40 hours per week community access programming. **URL:** http://www.mediaone.com.

18676 WFEA-AM - 1370
500 Commercial St.   Phone: (603)669-5777
Manchester, NH 03101   Fax: (603)669-4641
E-mail: raydionh@wzid.com

Format: Adult Contemporary. **Networks:** CBS. **Owner:** Saga Communications, at above address, (313)886-7070. **Founded:** 1932. **Operating Hours:** Continuous. **ADI:** Boston-Worcester,MA-Derry-Manchester,NH. **Key Personnel:** Ray Garon, General Mgr.; Tom Kallechey, Contact; Kevin Flynn, News Dir. **Local Programs:** *Morning Show with Paul Belfay.* **Wattage:** 5000.

18677 WGIR-AM - 610
Box 610   Phone: (603)625-6915
Manchester, NH 03105   Fax: (603)625-9255

Format: News; Talk. **Networks:** ABC. **Founded:** 1941. **Operating Hours:** Continuous. **Key Personnel:** Jon Erdahl, Station Mgr.; Dan Pierce, Program Dir., dan@wgir.com. **Local Programs:** *Dan Pierce Show*, Karen Anderson. **Wattage:** 5000 day; 1000 night. **Ad Rates:** $20-80 for 30 seconds; $25-100 for 60 seconds.

18678 WGIR-FM - 101.1
PO Box 610   Phone: (603)625-6915
Manchester, NH 03105-0610   Fax: (603)625-9255

Format: Album-Oriented Rock (AOR). **Founded:** 1963. **Operating Hours:** Continuous. **Key Personnel:** Jon Erdahl, Station Mgr. **Wattage:** 9600.

18679 WGOT-TV - 60/Translator Channel 54 Boston, MA
1 Sundial Ave., Ste. 501   Phone: (603)647-6060
Manchester, NH 03103   Fax: (603)644-0060

Format: Commercial TV. **Networks:** Independent. **Owner:** Paxon Communications Inc., at above address. **Founded:** 1987. **Operating Hours:** Continuous. **ADI:** Boston-Worcester,MA-Derry-Manchester,NH. **Key Personnel:** Lon Mirolli, General Mgr.; Robert Heon, Business Mgr.; David Raymond, Chief Engineer; Doreen Warchal, Program Dir.; Don Hill, Operations Mgr. **Wattage:** 1,400,000. **Ad Rates:** $100-700 per unit.

18680 WMUR-TV -
PO Box 9   Phone: (603)669-9999
Manchester, NH 03105   Fax: (603)641-9044
Free: (800)257-5151

Format: Commercial TV. **Networks:** ABC. **Operating Hours:** 5:30 a.m.-1:30 a.m. weekdays; 6:30-1:30 a.m. Sat. and Sun. **ADI:** Boston-Worcester,MA-Derry-Manchester,NH. **Key Personnel:** Larry Gilpi, General Mgr., phone (603)641-9090, fax (603)641-9044, 1gilpin@wmur.com. **Wattage:** 282KWERP.

18681 WZID-FM - 95.7
500 Commercial St.   Phone: (603)669-5777
Manchester, NH 03101   Fax: (603)669-4641

Format: Adult Contemporary. **Networks:** Independent. **Owner:** Saga Communications of NE, Inc., at above address. **Founded:** 1971. **Operating Hours:** Continuous; 100% local. **Key Personnel:** Ray Garon, General Mgr.; Kevin Flynn, News Dir.; Tom Kallechey, Program Dir.; Andy Orcutt, General Sales Mgr. **Wattage:** 50,000. **Ad Rates:** $100-250 for 60 seconds. Combined advertising rates available with WFEA. **URL:** wzid.com.

MEREDITH, pop. 4,646.

C NH. Belknap Co. On Lake Winnipesaukee, 11 mi. N. of Laconia. Resort. Lumber; dairy farms.

18682 Journal of the Print World
Journal of the Print World, Inc.
RR2 PO Box 1008 Winona Rd.   Phone: (603)279-6479
Meredith, NH 03253-9599   Fax: (603)279-1337

Advertisements and articles from USA, Europe and Japan concerning museums, libraries, galleries, and individuals in all media of original works of art on paper. **Subtitle:** Works of Art on Paper. **Founded:** 1978. **Freq:** Quarterly. **Print Method:** Offset litho. **Trim Size:** 11.375 x 17.5. **Cols./Page:** 6. **Col. Width:** 1 9/16 inches. **Col. Depth:** 16.5 inches. **Key Personnel:** Charles Stuart Lane, Editor and Publisher. **ISSN:** 0737-7436. **Subscription Rates:** $29 by mail first class; $19 by mail third class; $35 Canada and Mexico first class; $45 other countries first class; $15 third class U.S. Non-Profit Institutions; $25 other countries third class.
Ad Rates: BW: $1950   **Circ:** 10,000

18683 The Meredith News
Journal Transcript Newspapers
PO Box 729   Phone: (603)279-4516
Meredith, NH 03253-0729   Fax: (603)279-3331
Publication E-mail: mnews@worldpath.net

Community newspaper. **Founded:** 1880. **Freq:** Weekly (Wed.). **Print Method:** Offset. **Trim Size:** 11 1/2 x 16 1/2. **Cols./Page:** 6. **Col. Width:** 12 1/4 picas. **Col. Depth:** 16 inches. **Key Personnel:** Rudy Van Veghten, Editor; Lou McGrew, Publisher; Neil Collins, Publisher; Edward Engler, General Mgr. **USPS:** 339-860. **Subscription Rates:** $26. **Remarks:** Accepts advertising.
Ad Rates: BW: $562.40   **Circ:** Paid 3,991
SAU: $703   Free 21
PCI: $7.03

MILFORD, pop. 8,685.

S. NH. Hillsboro Co. On Souhegan River, 11 mi. WNW of Nashua. Manufactures monuments, building granite, lumber, concrete. Diversified farming.

18684 Hollis Brookline Journal
The Cabinet Press, Inc.
54 School St.   Phone: (603)673-3100
PO Box 180   Fax: (603)673-8250
Milford, NH 03055-0180
Free: (800)773-3102
Publisher E-mail: cabinet@cabinet.com

Community newspaper. **Freq:** Weekly (Fri.). **Key Personnel:**

Frank Manley, Publisher, manly@cabinet.com. **Subscription Rates:** Free. **Remarks:** Accepts advertising.
Ad Rates: PCI: $6.45 **Circ:** Non-paid 5,000

18685 Merrimack Journal
The Cabinet Press, Inc.
54 School St. Phone: (603)673-3100
PO Box 180 Fax: (603)673-8250
Milford, NH 03055-0180
Free: (800)773-3102
Publisher E-mail: cabinet@cabinet.com

Community newspaper. **Freq:** Weekly (Fri.). **Key Personnel:** Frank Manley, Publisher, manly@cabinet.com. **Subscription Rates:** Free. **Remarks:** Accepts advertising.
Ad Rates: PCI: $8.80 **Circ:** Non-paid 9,700

18686 The Milford Cabinet and Wilton Journal
The Cabinet Press, Inc.
54 School St. Phone: (603)673-3100
PO Box 180 Fax: (603)673-8250
Milford, NH 03055-0180
Free: (800)773-3102
Publisher E-mail: cabinet@cabinet.com

Newspaper. **Founded:** 1802. **Freq:** Weekly (Wed.). **Print Method:** Offset. **Trim Size:** 13 3/4 x 22 1/4. **Cols./Page:** 6. **Col. Width:** 26 nonpareils. **Col. Depth:** 294 agate lines. **Key Personnel:** Michael Cleveland, Publisher, news@cabinet.com; Frank Manley, Publisher, manly@cabinet.com. **USPS:** 348-840. **Subscription Rates:** $26 individuals; $38 out of state. **Remarks:** Accepts advertising. **Available Online. URL:** http://www.cabinet.com.
Ad Rates: SAU: $9 **Circ:** 10,000
PCI: $10.50

NASHUA†, pop. 67,865.

S. NH. Hillsboro Co. At junction of Nashua and Merrimack Rivers, near Massachusetts border, 22 mi. SW of Portsmouth. Rivier College, New Hampshire Vocational Technical College, Daniel Webster College, New England Aeronautical Institute. Manufactures lumber, wood and paper products, plastics, electronics, memorial tablets and grave markers, steel cabinets, rubber goods, chemicals, shoes. Shipping center.

18687 BackOffice Magazine
10 Tara Blvd., 5th Fl. Phone: (603)891-9281
Nashua, NH 03062-2801 Fax: (603)891-9297
Free: (800)225-0555
Publication E-mail: chrisa@pennwell.com
Publisher E-mail: marketing@backoffice.com

Magazine for information technology professionals building and implementing client/server applications in a Windows NT server environment. **Founded:** 1995. **Freq:** Monthly. **Print Method:** perfect bound web. **Trim Size:** 8 x 10 3/4. **Key Personnel:** David Anderson, phone (603)891-9481, davea@pennwell.com; Barrie Sosinsky, phone (603)891-9344, barnes@pennwell.com. **ISSN:** 1084-6433. **Subscription Rates:** Free; $49.95 individuals; $4.95 single issue; $69.95 Foreign. **Remarks:** Accepts advertising. **URL:** http://www.backofficemag.com.
Ad Rates: BW: $8,185 **Circ:** Combined ‡80,000
4C: $9,685

18688 Cabling Installation & Maintenance
PennWell Publishing Co.
98 Spit Brook Rd. Phone: (603)891-0123
Nashua, NH 03062-5737 Fax: (603)891-0574

Professional magazine focusing on copper-wire, and fiber-optic cable systems. **Subtitle:** Solutions for Fiber and Copper Communications Systems. **Founded:** Apr. 1993. **Freq:** Monthly. **Print Method:** Web offset. **Trim Size:** 8 x 11. **Cols./Page:** 2 and 3. **Col. Width:** 13 and 20 picas. **Col. Depth:** 57 picas. **Key Personnel:** David Janoff, Publisher; George Miller, Director, phone (603)891-9144; Lucas Garofalo, Publisher, phone (603)891-9223; Arlyn Powell, Editor, phone (603)891-9215; Valerie E.M. Elmore, Managing Editor, phone (603)891-9215; George Andrew, Circulation Mgr., phone (603)891-9215. **ISSN:** 0741-5834. **Remarks:** Advertising accepted; rates available upon request. **URL:** http://ATD.penwell.com/.
Circ: Non-paid 22,500

18689 CleanRooms
PennWell Publishing Co.
98 Spit Brook Rd. Phone: (603)891-0123
Nashua, NH 03062-5737 Fax: (603)891-0574

Journal covering contamination control technology. **Subtitle:** The Magazine of Contamination Control Technology. **Founded:** 1987. **Freq:** Monthly. **Print Method:** Web Offset. **Trim Size:** 11 1/2x14 3/4 bleed. **Key Personnel:** George D. Miller, Editorial Dir., phone (603)891-9322, georgem@pennwell.com; Adam Japko, Group Vice Pres., phone (603)891-9208, adamj@pennwell.com; James M. Enos, Publisher, phone (603)891-9149, jime@pennwell.com. **ISSN:** 1043-8017. **Subscription Rates:** $33 Free to qualified subscribers; $10 single issue; $148 U.S. /year; $198 Canada and Mexico /year; $255 / year Europe and Asia. **Remarks:** Accepts advertising. **Available Online. URL:** www.cleanrooms.com; http://atd.pennwell.com/.
Ad Rates: BW: $7,845 **Circ:** Controlled △**35,156**

18690 Computer Design
PennWell Publishing Co.
98 Spit Brook Rd. Phone: (603)891-0123
Nashua, NH 03062-5737 Fax: (603)891-0574

Printed in two editions: magazine covers microprocessor-based systems design; news edition covers the systems time-to-market team. **Founded:** 1962. **Freq:** 12/year. **Print Method:** Offset. Uses mats. **Trim Size:** 8 x 10 3/4. **Cols./Page:** 3. **Col. Width:** 26 nonpareils. **Col. Depth:** 140 agate lines. **Key Personnel:** John Miklosz, Editor-in-Chief; Dave Allen, Publisher; Tim Tobeck, Assoc. Publisher. **ISSN:** 0010-4566. **Subscription Rates:** Free to qualified subscribers; $88 others. **Remarks:** Accepts advertising. **Online:** CompuServe Information Service.
Ad Rates: BW: $9,270 **Circ:** Non-paid ‡113,000
4C: $10,920
PCI: $155

18691 Computer Graphics World
PennWell Publishing Co.
98 Spit Brook Rd. Phone: (603)891-0123
Nashua, NH 03062-5737 Fax: (603)891-0574

Publication reporting on the use of modeling, animation, and multimedia in the areas of science and engineering, art and entertainment, and presentation and training. **Founded:** Jan. 1978. **Freq:** Monthly. **Print Method:** Offset. Uses mats. **Trim Size:** 7 x 10. **Cols./Page:** 3 and 2. **Col. Width:** 26 and 39 nonpareils. **Col. Depth:** 140 agate lines. **Key Personnel:** Diana Mahoney, Senior Assoc. Editor, phone (603)891-9165, dianam@pennwell.com; Gene Pritchard, Publisher, phone (603)891-9212, genepri@pennwell.com; Bob Singer, National Sales Mgr., phone (603)891-0123. **Subscription Rates:** $50 Free to qualified subscribers USA; $62 Canada and Mexico; $72 other countries Pacific Rim countries; $96 Asia-Pacific. **Remarks:** Accepts advertising. **URL:** http://www.cgw.com; http://atd.pennwell.com/.
Ad Rates: BW: $8,330 **Circ:** Paid ★**17,353**
4C: $10,205 Non-paid ★**54,355**

18692 Electronic Publishing
PennWell Publishing Co.
98 Spit Brook Rd. Phone: (603)891-0123
Nashua, NH 03062-5737 Fax: (603)891-0574

Magazine covering electronic publishing industry. **Founded:** 1973. **Freq:** Monthly. **Print Method:** Web offset. **Trim Size:** 8 x 10 3/4. **Key Personnel:** Tom McMillan, Editor, phone (603)891-9236, fax (603)891-0539, tomm@pennwell.com; David Austermann, Publisher, phone (603)891-9492, davida@pennwell.com. **ISSN:** 1055-9701. **Subscription Rates:** $45. **Remarks:** Accepts advertising. **Absorbed:** Computer Artist. **Formerly:** Color Publishing.
Ad Rates: BW: $7,800 **Circ:** 70,000

18693 Industrial Laser Solutions
PennWell Publishing Co.
98 Spit Brook Rd. Phone: (603)891-0123
Nashua, NH 03062-5737 Fax: (603)891-0574

Magazine reporting information on industrial laser solutions for manufacturing. **Founded:** June 1986. **Freq:** Monthly. **Print Method:** Offset. **Trim Size:** 8 1/2 x 10 3/4. **Cols./Page:** 2. **Col. Width:** 42 nonpareils. **Col. Depth:** 152 agate lines. **Key Personnel:** David A. Belforte, Editor, phone (508)347-9324, fax (508)347-7737, belforte@pennwell.com; Florence L. Oreiro, Group Publisher, phone (603)891-9253, florence@pennwell.com. **ISSN:** 0888-935X. **Subscription Rates:** Free to qualified subscribers; $250 individuals; $295 other countries. **URL:** http://www.industrial-lasers.com. **Formerly:** Industrial Laser Review.
Ad Rates: BW: $4,975 **Circ:** Paid ‡413
4C: $5,580 Non-paid ‡10,029

18694 Laser Focus World
PennWell Publishing Co.
98 Spit Brook Rd. Phone: (603)891-0123
Nashua, NH 03062-5737 Fax: (603)891-0574

Magazine covering advances and applications in optoelectronics. **Founded:** 1965. **Freq:** Monthly. **Print Method:** Offset. **Trim Size:** 8 x 10 3/4. **Cols./Page:** 2. **Col. Width:** 30 nonpareils. **Col. Depth:** 140 agate lines. **Key Personnel:** Florence L. Oreiro, Group Publisher, phone (603)891-9253, florence@pennwell.com; Jeffrey Bairstow, Group Editorial Director, phone (603)891-9130, jeff@pennwell.com. **ISSN:** 0740-2511. **Subscription Rates:** $156 individuals; $244 Canada; $10 single issue. **Remarks:** Accepts advertising. **URL:** http://www.optoelectronics-world.com. **Formerly:** LASER FOCUS, The Magazine of Electro-optics Technology.
Ad Rates: BW: $7,185 **Circ:** ‡69,118
4C: $8,760

18695 Lightwave
PennWell Publishing Co.
98 Spit Brook Rd. Phone: (603)891-0123
Nashua, NH 03062-5737 Fax: (603)891-0574

An international publication covering fiber-optic communication technology and applications worldwide. **Subtitle:** Fibre Optics Technology and Applications Worldwide. **Founded:** Jan. 1984. **Freq:** Monthly. **Print Method:** Offset. **Trim Size:** 11 x 14 1/4. **Cols./Page:** 4. **Col. Width:** 2 3/4 inches. **Col. Depth:** 14 inches. **Key Personnel:** Stephen Hardy, Editor-in-Chief, stephenh@pennwell.com; Tim Pritchard, Publisher, phone (603)891-9447, timp@pennwell.com. **ISSN:** 0741-5834. **Subscription Rates:** $79; $105 Canada; $131 other countries; $10 single issue. **Remarks:** Accepts advertising. **URL:** http://atd.pennwell.com/.
Ad Rates: BW: $6,690 **Circ:** Paid 1,393
4C: $7,990 Non-paid 33,640

18696 Microlithography World
PennWell Publishing Co.
10 Tara Blvd., 5th Fl. Phone: (603)891-0123
Nashua, NH 03062 Fax: (603)891-0597

Trade magazine covering all the disciplines related to patterning semiconductors and other microelectronic devices. **Founded:** Mar. 1992. **Freq:** Quarterly. **Trim Size:** 8 x 10 3/4. **Cols./Page:** 3. **Col. Width:** 13 picas. **Col. Depth:** 57 picas. **Key Personnel:** M. David Levenson, Editor-in-Chief; Becky McAdams, Publisher; Lynn Backus, Assoc. Publisher. **ISSN:** 1074-407. **Remarks:** Accepts advertising. **URL:** http://www.pennwell.com/litho.html.
Ad Rates: BW: $3,290 **Circ:** (Not Reported)

18697 New Hampshire Editions
100 Main St. Phone: (603)883-3150
Nashua, NH 03060 Fax: (603)889-5557

Consumer magazine covering business and lifestyle. **Founded:** 1989. **Freq:** Monthly. **Print Method:** Web offset. **Trim Size:** 8 1/8 x 10 7/8. **Key Personnel:** Rick Broussard, Editor; August T. Murray, Sales Mgr.; Grace McCaw, Circulation/Distribution. **Subscription Rates:** $20 individuals; $2 single issue. **Remarks:** Accepts advertising. **URL:** http://www.nheditions.com. **Former name:** Manchester; Concord North; Hampshire East; Nashua.
Ad Rates: BW: $2,700 **Circ:** Non-paid 24,000
4C: $3,200

18698 1590 Broadcaster
502 W. Hollis St. Phone: (603)889-1590
PO Box 548 Fax: (603)883-4344
Nashua, NH 03061-0548
Publisher E-mail: wsmn1590@aol.com

Local newspaper. **Founded:** Mar. 8, 1964. **Freq:** Weekly (Wed.). **Print Method:** Offset. **Trim Size:** 7 x 16. **Cols./Page:** 7. **Col. Width:** 1 5/16 inches. **Col. Depth:** 16 inches. **Key Personnel:** Todd Feinburg. **Subscription Rates:** $20. **Remarks:** Accepts advertising.
Ad Rates: GLR: $.79 **Circ:** Free ‡63,000
BW: $1,344
PCI: $12

18699 Solid State Technology
PennWell Publishing Co.
98 Spit Brook Rd. Phone: (603)891-0123
Nashua, NH 03062-5737 Fax: (603)891-0574

Magazine containing electronic and semiconductor engineering news and information. **Founded:** 1958. **Freq:** Monthly. **Print Method:** Offset. **Cols./Page:** 3. **Col. Width:** 31 nonpareils. **Col. Depth:** 140 agate lines. **Key Personnel:** Becky P. McAdams, Group Publisher, phone (603)891-9413, fax (603)891-0597; Robert C. Haavind, Editor-in-Chief, phone (603)891-9453, fax (603)891-0597, bobh@pennwell.com; Lynn G. Backus, Associate Publisher, phone (408)370-4839, fax (408)370-9585, lynnb@pennwell.com; Patricia Edgar, Marketing Communications Mgr., phone (603)891-9186, fax (603)891-0597; Elizabeth Fugere, Ad. Traffic Mgr., phone (603)891-9231, fax (603)891-9495. **ISSN:** 0038-111X. **Subscription Rates:** $175 U.S.; $245 Canada and Mexico; $295 other countries. **Remarks:** Accepts advertising. **URL:** http://www.solid-state.com. **Alt. Formats:** Microfilm.
Ad Rates: BW: $6,215 **Circ:** Non-paid ‡44,357
4C: $7,815

18700 Time Warner Cable of Nashua
460 Amherst St. Phone: (603)889-1363
Nashua, NH 03063 Fax: (603)882-4415

Founded: 1967. **Formerly:** Warner Amex Cable (1986); Warner Cable of Nashua (1992). **Key Personnel:** Doug

Whiting, General Mgr. **Cities Served:** subscribing households 25,000; 60 channels; 1 community access channel.

18701 WHOB-FM - 106.3
55 Lake St. Phone: (603)889-1063
Nashua, NH 03060 Fax: (603)882-0688
E-mail: whob@xtdl.com

Format: Alternative/New Music/Progressive. **Networks:** Independent. **Owner:** Gateway Broadcasting, Inc., at above address. **Founded:** 1987. **Formerly:** WOTW-FM. **Operating Hours:** Continuous; 100% local. **Key Personnel:** Mario DiCarlo, General Mgr.; Ellen Prescott, Contact; Jeff Wallat, News Dir. **Wattage:** 3000. **Ad Rates:** $35-70 per unit.

18702 WSMN-AM - 1590
502 W. Hollis St. Phone: (603)882-1509
PO Box 548 Fax: (603)883-4344
Nashua, NH 03061
E-mail: wsmn1590@aol.com

Format: Talk; Information. **Founded:** 1958. **Operating Hours:** Continuous; 50% local, 50% network. **Key Personnel:** Todd Feinburg, General Mgr.; John Collins, Program Dir. **Local Programs:** *1590 Bargain Box*, Robin Belzil, (603)882-1590, Fax (603)883-4344; *1590 Open Line*, Maurice R. Parent, (603)882-1590, Fax (603)883-4344. **Wattage:** 5000. **Ad Rates:** $7-16 for 10 seconds; $9-24 for 30 seconds; $12-30 for 60 seconds.

NEW LONDON

18703 Hitchcock Annual
Hitchcock Annual Corp.
Box 2568 Phone: (603)526-4874
New London, NH 03257
Scholarly journal covering film study and the work of director Alfred Hitchcock. **Founded:** 1992. **Freq:** Annual. **Print Method:** Photo Offset. **Trim Size:** 5 1/2 x 8 1/2. **Key Personnel:** Christopher Brookhouse, Editor, broockhou@mail.tds.net. **ISSN:** 1062-5518. **Subscription Rates:** $10 single issue. **Remarks:** Advertising accepted; rates available upon request.
Circ: (Not Reported)

18704 Kearsarge Cable Communications Inc.
173 Main St. Phone: (603)526-2211
New London, NH 03257 Fax: (603)526-9910

Owner: Telephone & Data Systems Inc., 301 S. Westfield Rd., PO Box 5158, Madison, WI 53705-0158, (608)845-4000. **Founded:** Sept. 1, 1983. **Key Personnel:** Leland Willette, Manager; Robert Currier, Technician; Donna Phillips, C.S.R. **Cities Served:** New London, Wilmot, NH: subscribing households 1,743; 35 channels; 1 community access channel; 168 hours per week community access programming.

18705 WNTK-AM - 1020
PO Box 2295 Phone: (603)526-9464
New London, NH 03257 Fax: (603)526-9372
E-mail: wntk1020@aol.com

Format: Talk. **Simulcasts:** WNTK-FM. **Networks:** ABC; Mutual Broadcasting System; Major Market Radio. **Owner:** KOOR Communications, at above address, New London, NH 03257, (603)448-0500, Fax: (603)448-6601. **Founded:** 1960. **Operating Hours:** 5 a.m.- 9 p.m. **ADI:** Boston-Worcester,MA-Derry-Manchester,NH. **Key Personnel:** Robert L. Vinikoor, President; John Reynolds, News Dir.; Russ McAlister, Chief Engineer. **Local Programs:** *AM Magazine* 6 a.m.-9 a.m. Monday-Friday, Emma Scott, Producer/Host; *Twin State Journal* 9 a.m.-10 a.m. Monday-Friday, Janine Weins, Producer; *Viewpoint* 7 p.m.-9p.m. Wednesday, Bob Fahrner, Producer. **Wattage:** 10,000. **Ad Rates:** $14-25 for 60 seconds. **URL:** http://wntk.com.

18706 WNTK-FM - 99.7
250 Newport Rd. Phone: (603)448-0500
PO Box 2295 Fax: (603)526-9372
New London, NH 03257
E-mail: info@wntk.com

Format: Talk. **Simulcasts:** WNTK-AM. **Networks:** Mutual Broadcasting System; ABC; Major Market Radio. **Founded:** 1992. **Operating Hours:** Continuous. **ADI:** Boston-Worcester,MA-Derry-Manchester,NH. **Key Personnel:** Robert L. Vinikoor, President; Russ McAlister, Chief Engineer. **Local Programs:** *AM Magazine* 6 a.m.-9 a.m. Monday-Friday, Emma Scott, Producer/Host; *Twin State Journal* 9 a.m.-10 a.m. Monday-Friday, Janine Weins, Producer; *Viewpoint* 7 p.m.-9p.m. Wednesday, Bob Fahrner, Producer. **Wattage:** 3000 ERP. **Ad Rates:** $14-25 for 60 seconds. **URL:** http://www.wntk.com.

18707 WSCS-FM - 90.9
100 Main St. Phone: (603)526-3493
New London, NH 03257 Fax: (603)526-3452

Format: Educational. **Networks:** AP. **Owner:** Colby-Sawyer College, at above address. **Operating Hours:** 7:00 a.m.-1:00 a.m. **ADI:** Hartford-New Haven (New London), CT. **Key Personnel:** Dr. Earnest Freeberg, Advisor. **Local Programs:** *Live from Studio R19*, Kevin Kerner; *Talking Stick*, Lanvetta Phillips. **Wattage:** 250.

NEWFIELDS

18708 The Plantsman
New Hampshire Plant Growers Association
PO Box 5 Phone: (603)862-2061
Newfields, NH 03856
Trade publication for the plant growing and green industry of the Northeast U.S. **Freq:** Bimonthly. **Trim Size:** 8 1/2 x 11. **Key Personnel:** Bob Parker, Editor. **Subscription Rates:** Included in membership. **Remarks:** Advertising accepted; rates available upon request.
Circ: (Not Reported)

NEWPORT†, pop. 6,229.

SW NH. Sullivan Co. On Sugar River, 19 mi. SSE of Lebanon. Resort. Lumber; diversified agriculture.

18709 Argus-Champion
Eagle Publications
86 Sunapee St. Phone: (603)863-1776
PO Box 509 Fax: (603)863-0066
Newport, NH 03773
Publication E-mail: argus@cybeportal.net

Community newspaper. **Founded:** 1823. **Freq:** Weekly (Wed.). **Print Method:** Offset. **Cols./Page:** 6. **Col. Width:** 24 nonpareils. **Col. Depth:** 294 agate lines. **Key Personnel:** Harvey Hill, Publisher; Mark DiPietro, Editor. **Subscription Rates:** $25; $30 out of state. **Remarks:** Accepts advertising.
Ad Rates: BW: $844.95 **Circ:** ‡5,400
SAU: $7.75

NORTH CONWAY, pop. 2,104.

E. NH. Carroll Co. On Saco River, 29 mi. S. of Berlin. Mountain resort. Lumber; crafts.

18710 WZPK-FM - 103.7
1267 Main St. Phone: (603)356-7500
PO Box 1408 Fax: (603)356-6222
North Conway, NH 03860

Format: Adult Contemporary. **Networks:** ABC. **Owner:** New England Broadcasting, Inc., at above address. **Founded:** 1947. **Formerly:** WMOU-FM (1989). **Operating Hours:** Continuous. **ADI:** Portland-Poland Spring, ME. **Key Personnel:** Steve Powell, PRS/Gen; Mike D., Program Dir.; Bob Barbin, News Dir.; Peter Wright, Promotions Dir. **Wattage:** 22,500 ERP. **Ad Rates:** Advertising accepted; rates available upon request.

PETERBOROUGH, pop. 4,895.

S. NH. Hillsboro Co. 28 mi. WNW of Nashua. MacDowell Artists Colony. Apple orchards.

18711 Audio Electronics
Audio Amateur Corp., Inc.
PO Box 576 Phone: (603)924-9464
Peterborough, NH 03458-0576 Fax: (603)924-9467
Publication E-mail: audiotech@top.monad.net

Magazine for the do-it-yourself amateur and professional. **Subtitle:** The Journal for Audiophile Crafts. **Founded:** 1970. **Freq:** Bimonthly. **Trim Size:** 8 x 10 1/2. **Cols./Page:** 3. **Col. Width:** 13.5 picas. **Col. Depth:** 66 picas. **Key Personnel:** Edward T. Dell, Jr., Editor; Dennis Brisson, Managing Editor; Peter Wostrel, Advertising Dir.; Laurel Humphrey, Marketing Director. **ISSN:** 0004-7546. **Subscription Rates:** $28 individuals; $45 out of country; $6 single issue; $34 Canada. **Alt. Formats:** Microfilm; Microform. **Formerly:** The Audio Amateur (Jan. 1, 1996).
Ad Rates: BW: $470 **Circ:** Paid 8,500
4C: $1,020

18712 Calliope
Cobblestone Publishing Co.
30 Grove St., Ste. C Phone: (603)924-7209
Peterborough, NH 03458 Fax: (603)924-7380
Free: (800)821-0115
Publisher E-mail: custsvc@cobblestone.mv.com

Educational youth magazine. **Subtitle:** World History for Young People. **Founded:** 1990. **Freq:** 9/year. **Print Method:** Sheetfed offset. **Trim Size:** 7 x 9. **Key Personnel:** Rosalie Baker, Editor; Charles Baker, Editor; Malcolm Jensen, Publisher. **Subscription Rates:** $26.95 individuals; $4.50 single issue. **Remarks:** Advertising not accepted. **Formerly:** Classical Calliope.
Circ: Paid ‡9,500

18713 CD Review
Connell Communications Inc.
86 Elm St. Phone: (603)924-7271
Peterborough, NH 03458-1052 Fax: (603)924-7013

Consumer music review magazine. **Founded:** Oct. 1984. **Freq:** Monthly. **Print Method:** Web offset. **Trim Size:** 8 x 10 3/4. **Cols./Page:** 3. **Col. Width:** 2 1/4 inches. **Col. Depth:** 9 3/4 inches. **Key Personnel:** Lou Warnycia, Editor; Brian Vaillencourt, Advertising Mgr.; Pam Wilder, Circulation Mgr. **ISSN:** 1044-1700. **Subscription Rates:** $19.97. **Remarks:** Accepts advertising. **Formerly:** Digital Audio Review.
Ad Rates: BW: $6,600 **Circ:** Paid 95,635
4C: $7,425

18714 Cobblestone
Cobblestone Publishing Co.
30 Grove St., Ste. C Phone: (603)924-7209
Peterborough, NH 03458 Fax: (603)924-7380
Free: (800)821-0115
Publisher E-mail: custsvc@cobblestone.mv.com

Magazine on American history for ages 8-14. **Subtitle:** The History Magazine for Young People. **Founded:** Jan. 1980. **Freq:** 9x/year. **Print Method:** Offset. **Trim Size:** 7 x 9. **Cols./Page:** 2. **Key Personnel:** Meg Chorlian, Editor; Malcolm Jensen, Publisher. **ISSN:** 0199-5197. **Subscription Rates:** $26.95 individuals; $4.95 single issue. **Remarks:** Advertising not accepted. **Alt. Formats:** CD-ROM.
Circ: Paid 33,000

18715 Faces
Cobblestone Publishing Co.
30 Grove St., Ste. C Phone: (603)924-7209
Peterborough, NH 03458 Fax: (603)924-7380
Free: (800)821-0115
Publication E-mail: faces@cobblestonepub.com
Publisher E-mail: custsvc@cobblestone.mv.com

World cultures and geography magazine for ages 8-14. **Subtitle:** People, Places, and Cultures. **Founded:** Oct. 1984. **Freq:** 9/year. **Print Method:** Offset. **Trim Size:** 7 x 9. **Cols./Page:** 2. **Key Personnel:** Lou Warynicia, Managing Editor; Malcolm Jensen, Publisher. **ISSN:** 0749-1387. **Subscription Rates:** $26.95 individuals; $4.95 single issue. **Remarks:** Advertising not accepted.
Circ: 13,000

18716 Glass Audio
Audio Amateur Corp., Inc.
PO Box 576 Phone: (603)924-9464
Peterborough, NH 03458-0576 Fax: (603)924-9467

Featuring vaccuum tube audio equipment and construction information for the DIY audio enthusiast. **Founded:** 1988. **Freq:** Bimonthly. **Trim Size:** 8 x 10 1/2. **Cols./Page:** 3. **Col. Width:** 13.5 picas. **Col. Depth:** 66 picas. **Key Personnel:** Edward T. Dell, Jr., President; Dennis Brissan, Managing Editor; Peter Wostrel, Advertising Dir.; Laurel Humphrey, Marketing Dir. **ISSN:** 1045-5027. **Subscription Rates:** $28; $34 Canada; $45 other countries. $6 single issue. **Remarks:** Accepts advertising.
Ad Rates: BW: $500 **Circ:** Paid 7,000
4C: $985

18717 ID Systems
Helmers Publishing, Inc.
174 Concord St. Phone: (603)924-9631
PO Box 874 Fax: (603)924-7408
Peterborough, NH 03458
Publication E-mail: editors@idsystems.com

Magazine covering news and commentary on products and applications involving bar code, OCR, RF, voice systems, and related keyless data entry technologies. **Subtitle:** The Magazine of Automated Data Collection. **Founded:** Dec. 1981. **Freq:** Monthly. **Print Method:** Offset. **Trim Size:** 77/8 x 10 3/4. **Cols./Page:** 3. **Key Personnel:** Dan Rodrigues, Publisher; Eileen Terrill, Managing Editor; David Andrews, Editor-in-Chief, editors@idsystems.com. **ISSN:** 0892-676X. **Subscription Rates:** Free to qualified subscribers. **URL:** http://www.idsystems.com. **Formerly:** Bar Code News (Jan. 1, 1987); Identification Journal (1990).
Ad Rates: BW: $4,995 **Circ:** Non-paid 67,500
4C: $6,340

18718 The Monadnock Ledger
20 Grove St. Phone: (603)924-7172
PO Box 36 Fax: (603)924-3681
Peterborough, NH 03458
Community newspaper. **Founded:** 1956. **Freq:** Weekly. **Print Method:** Flexographic. **Trim Size:** 13 3/4 x 22 3/4. **Cols./Page:** 6. **Col. Width:** 2 inches. **Col. Depth:** 21 inches. **Key Personnel:** Heather McKernan, Publisher. **USPS:** 358-540. **Subscription Rates:** $24 local Newspaper Rater; $30 out of state Newspaper Rate. **Remarks:** Accepts advertising.
Ad Rates: BW: $756 **Circ:** Paid 7,356
4C: $906 Free 185
PCI: $7.50

18719 Odyssey
Cobblestone Publishing Co.
30 Grove St., Ste. C Phone: (603)924-7209
Peterborough, NH 03458 Fax: (603)924-7380
Free: (800)821-0115
Publisher E-mail: custsvc@cobblestone.mv.com

Magazine on science and technology for children ages 10-16. **Subtitle:** Adventures in Science. **Founded:** Jan. 1979. **Freq:** 9/year (No June, July, August). **Print Method:** Offset. **Trim Size:** 7 x 9. **Cols./Page:** 3 and 2. **Col. Width:** 13 and 20 picas. **Col. Depth:** 9 3/4 inches. **Key Personnel:** Beth Lindstrom, Editor; Malcolm Jensen, Publisher. **ISSN:** 0163-0946. **Subscription Rates:** $24.95 individuals; $4.50 single issue. **Remarks:** Advertising not accepted.
Circ: 28,000

18720 The Peterborough Transcript
43 Grove St. Phone: (603)924-3333
PO Box 419 Fax: (603)924-7946
Peterborough, NH 03458-0419
Free: (800)559-3370

Community newspaper. **Founded:** 1849. **Freq:** Weekly (Thurs.). **Print Method:** Offset. **Cols./Page:** 6. **Col. Width:** 26 nonpareils. **Col. Depth:** 294 agate lines. **Key Personnel:** John Franklin, Editor; Joseph D. Cummings, Publisher. **Subscription Rates:** $24 individuals; $30 out of state. **Remarks:** Accepts advertising. **Formed by the merger of:** Jaffrey Recorder; Monadnock Breeze.
Ad Rates: GLR: $7.50 **Circ:** 5,900
BW: $623.70
4C: $808.70
PCI: $7.15

18721 Sensors Buyers Guide
Helmers Publishing, Inc.
174 Concord St. Phone: (603)924-9631
PO Box 874 Fax: (603)924-7408
Peterborough, NH 03458
Publication E-mail: seneditors@helmers.com

Magazine listing manufacturers of sensors and related products. **Founded:** 1985. **Freq:** 1/year. **Trim Size:** 7 7/8 x 10 3/4. **Cols./Page:** 2 and 3. **Key Personnel:** Barbara G. Goode, Editor, bgoode@helmers.com. **ISSN:** 0746-9462. **Subscription Rates:** $55 individuals; $19.95 single issue. **Remarks:** Accepts advertising. **Online:** Available on floppy disk. **URL:** http://www.sensorsmag.com.
Ad Rates: BW: $4,800 **Circ:** Controlled 75,000
4C: $6,000

18722 Sensors - The Journal of Applied Sensor Technology
Helmers Publishing, Inc.
174 Concord St. Phone: (603)924-9631
PO Box 874 Fax: (603)924-7408
Peterborough, NH 03458
Publication E-mail: seneditors@helmers.com

Technical magazine covering the development and application of sensors. **Subtitle:** The Journal of Applied Sensor Technology. **Founded:** Jan. 1984. **Freq:** 12/year. **Print Method:** Offset. **Trim Size:** 8 1/8 x 10 7/8. **Cols./Page:** 2 and 3. **Key Personnel:** Barbara G. Goode, Editor, bgoode@helmers.com; Steve Robbins, Publisher, srobbins@helmers.com. **ISSN:** 0746-9462. **Subscription Rates:** Free to qualified subscribers; $55. $5.50 single issue. **Remarks:** Accepts advertising. **Available Online. URL:** http://www.sensorsmag.com. **Alt. Formats:** Diskette; Microform; Mailing labels.
Ad Rates: BW: $4,800 **Circ:** Controlled ‡75,000
4C: $6,000

18723 73 Amateur Radio Today
73 Magazine
70 Rte. 202-N Phone: (603)924-0058
Peterborough, NH 03458-1107 Fax: (603)924-9327

Magazine for amateur radio hobbyists. **Founded:** 1960. **Freq:** Monthly. **Print Method:** Offset. **Trim Size:** 8 x 10 7/8. **Cols./Page:** 3. **Col. Width:** 13.5 picas. **Col. Depth:** 140 agate lines. **Key Personnel:** Hope Currier, Managing Editor; Wayne Green, Publisher; Dan Harper, Editor; Judy Walker, Editor. **ISSN:** 1052-2522. **Subscription Rates:** $24.97. **Remarks:** Accepts advertising. **Formerly:** 73 Amateur Radio's Technical Journal.
Ad Rates: BW: $1,590 **Circ:** 47,872
4C: $1,990

18724 Speaker Builder
Audio Amateur Corp., Inc.
PO Box 494
Peterborough, NH 03458-0494
Publication E-mail: audiodiy@top.monad.net; audiotech@top.monad.net

Journal featuring detailed plans and schematics for building and modifying all types of loudspeaker. **Subtitle:** The Loudspeaker Journal. **Founded:** 1980. **Freq:** 8/year. **Print Method:** Offset. **Trim Size:** 8 x 10 1/2. **Cols./Page:** 3. **Col. Width:** 13.5 picas. **Col. Depth:** 66 picas. **Key Personnel:** Edward T. Dell, Jr., Editor and Publisher; Peter Wostrel, Advertising Dir.; Laurel Humphrey, Marketing Mgr.; Dennis Brisson, Managing Editor. **ISSN:** 0199-7920. **Subscription Rates:** $32 individuals; $50 other countries per year; $40 Canada per year; $7 single issue. **Remarks:** Accepts advertising.
Ad Rates: BW: $820 **Circ:** Paid 11,500
4C: $1,370

18725 Take One
Connell Communications Inc.
86 Elm St. Phone: (603)924-7271
Peterborough, NH 03458-1052 Fax: (603)924-7013

Cinema publication (tabloid) listing and announcing major new movie titles released each month on videocassette and the latest music release information. **Subtitle:** The Video Entertainment Newspaper. **Founded:** June 1981. **Freq:** Monthly. **Print Method:** Offset. **Trim Size:** 10 1/2 x 14 1/2. **Cols./Page:** 5. **Col. Width:** 2 inches. **Col. Depth:** 14 inches. **Key Personnel:** James H. Faulkner, Editor; Gloria Redman, Advertising Mgr. **Remarks:** Accepts advertising.
Ad Rates: 4C: $9,600 **Circ:** ‡1,325,538

18726 Video Event
Connell Communications Inc.
86 Elm St. Phone: (603)924-7271
Peterborough, NH 03458-1052 Fax: (603)924-7013

Magazine serving the video retail and consumer marketplace. **Founded:** 1989. **Freq:** Monthly. **Key Personnel:** Melissa Stephenson, Editor, mstephenson@ceiweb.com; T. James Connell, Publisher; Matt Redd, Advertising Mgr.
Circ: Paid ‡1,098,659

PLYMOUTH, pop. 5,094.

WC NH. Grafton Co. On Pemigewasset River, 30 mi. E. of Hanover. Plymouth State College. Resort. Manufactures textiles, wood products, electronics. Fruit, poultry, dairy farms.

18727 The Penny Saver
The Pennysaver, Inc.
Village Sq. Phone: (603)536-3160
PO Box 206 Fax: (603)536-8150
Plymouth, NH 03264
Shopper. **Founded:** Dec. 15, 1971. **Freq:** Weekly (Tues.). **Print Method:** Offset. **Cols./Page:** 6. **Col. Width:** 18 nonpareils. **Col. Depth:** 224 agate lines. **Key Personnel:** T.D. Walrath, Publisher, walrath@lr.net; H.J. Sobetzer, Publisher. **Subscription Rates:** Free. **Remarks:** Accepts advertising.
Ad Rates: PCI: $5.90 **Circ:** Free ‡19,500

18728 The Record Enterprise
Main Street Media, Inc.
PO Box 148 Phone: (603)536-1311
Plymouth, NH 03264-0148 Fax: (603)536-8940
Free: (800)491-4612

Newspaper with a Republican orientation. **Founded:** 1887. **Freq:** Weekly (Wed.). **Print Method:** Offset. **Trim Size:** 11 1/2 x 16 1/2. **Cols./Page:** 5. **Col. Width:** 2 1/16 inches. **Col. Depth:** 15 inches. **Key Personnel:** William York, Editor/General Mgr.; Thomas Hepner, Publisher; Georgia Golden, Advertising Dir.; Brian McCarthy, Assoc. Ed.; Valerie McQueeney, News Coord.; Lee Fortier, Office Mgr. **Subscription Rates:** $21 individuals; $26 out of area. **Remarks:** Accepts advertising. **Formerly:** Record Citizen; The Enterprise.
Ad Rates: GLR: $4 **Circ:** Paid ⊕**5,942**
BW: $326.25
4C: $726.25
SAU: $4.35
PCI: $4.90

18729 Summer Week/Ski Week
Independent Color Press
PO Box 148
Plymouth, NH 03264

Local journal. **Founded:** 1971. **Freq:** Weekly. **Cols./Page:** 5. **Col. Width:** 10 inches. **Col. Depth:** 16 inches. **Key Personnel:** Brian McCarthy, Editor; Brad Lipe, Advertising Dir.; Edward Engler, Publisher. **Remarks:** Accepts advertising.
Ad Rates: PCI: $8.35 **Circ:** Non-paid 18,000

18730 WPCR-FM - 91.7
CUBANNEX Phone: (603)535-2242
Plymouth State College Fax: (603)535-2783
Plymouth, NH 03264

Format: Album-Oriented Rock (AOR); Eclectic. **Networks:** Independent. **Owner:** Plymouth State College, at above address. **Founded:** 1968. **Operating Hours:** 6 a.m.-2 a.m. Daily. **Key Personnel:** Willa Rogers, General Mgr.; Jim Firmin, Asst. General Manager; Aaron Burke, Managing Director; Kevin Hastings, Production Mgr.; Kevin Strickland, P.D.; Mike Davidson, Chief Op.; Axl Herlihy, Web Master; Jesse Fitzgerald, News; Carrie Carnie, Promotions. **Wattage:** 215. **Ad Rates:** Underwriting available. **URL:** http://wpcr.plymouth.edu.

18731 WPNH-AM - 1300
2 High St. Phone: (603)536-2500
PO Box 89 Fax: (603)536-4610
Plymouth, NH 03264

Format: Music of Your Life. **Networks:** Jones Satellite. **Founded:** 1964. **Operating Hours:** 5:30 a.m.-sunset. **ADI:** Burlington-Hartford, VT-Plattsburgh, NY. **Key Personnel:** Peter M. Pettengill, Station Mgr.; Bob Moulton, Operations Mgr.; Donna Hiltz, Traffic; Mark Servente, Music Dir. **Local Programs:** *Bobcat Football*, Peter Pettengill, Mailing contact, (603)536-2500, Fax (603)536-4610. **Wattage:** 5000. **Ad Rates:** $5 for 30 seconds; $7 for 60 seconds. Combined advertising rates available with WPNH-FM.

18732 WPNH-FM - 100.1
2 High St. Phone: (603)536-2500
PO Box 89 Fax: (603)536-4610
Plymouth, NH 03264

Format: Album-Oriented Rock (AOR); Classical. **Networks:** NBC. **Founded:** 1964. **Operating Hours:** Continuous; 5% network, %95 local. **Key Personnel:** Peter M. Pettengill, Station Mgr.; Bob Moulton, Production Operations; Mark Servente, Music Dir.; Donna Hiltz, Traffic. **Local Programs:** *Breakfast with the Bands* 6:00 AM - 12:00NOON; *Community Spotlight* 12:10 Saturday, Mark Servente, Mailing contact, (603)536-2500, Fax (603)536-4610. **Wattage:** 3900. **Ad Rates:** $18 for 30 seconds; $25 for 60 seconds. Combined advertising rates available with WDNH-AM.

PORTSMOUTH, pop. 26,254.

SE NH. Rockingham Co. On Piscataqua River, 3 mi. from Atlantic Ocean. Bridge to Kittery, ME. Only commercial seaport of the state. Summer resort. Manufactures machine tools, electronic components, plastics, buttons, gypsum products. Lobster fisheries. U.S. Navy Yard on nearby Seavy's Island; Pease Air Force Base 2 mi. W.

18733 Portsmouth Herald
111 Maplewood Ave. Phone: (603)436-1800
Portsmouth, NH 03801 Fax: (603)427-0550
Publication E-mail: pherald@nhmeseacost.com

General newspaper. **Founded:** 1886. **Freq:** Daily and Sunday. **Print Method:** Offset. **Trim Size:** 14 3/4 x 22 3/4. **Cols./Page:** 6. **Col. Width:** 2 1/16 inches. **Col. Depth:** 301 agate lines. **Key Personnel:** T.S. Staszak, Publisher; G. Bonito, Advertising Dir.; Sam Pollak, Editor; Peter Johnson, Marketing Dir.; Dennis Thompson, Circulation Dir.; M. Taylor, Accountant. **ISSN:** 0746-6218. **Subscription Rates:** $153.40 individuals carrier; $180 by mail. **Remarks:** Accepts advertising. **URL:** http://www.nh-mesf.acoast.com; http://www.nh-meseacost.com.
Ad Rates: GLR: $.88 **Circ:** Mon.-Sat. ★**15,266**
BW: $1722.15 Sun. ★**16,403**
4C: $2109.15
PCI: $12.35

18734 Red Owl
35 Hampshire Rd. Phone: (603)431-2691
Portsmouth, NH 03801-4815
Publication E-mail: redowlmag@aol.com

Magazine featuring positive and uplifting poems, short stories, and art. **Founded:** Sept. 1995. **Freq:** Biennial. **Print Method:** Photostatic, plastic spiral binding. **Trim Size:** 8-1/2 x 11. **Key Personnel:** Edward O. Knowlton, Contact. **Subscription Rates:** $20; $10 single issue. **Remarks:** Accepts advertising.
Ad Rates: BW: $30 **Circ:** Paid 50
Non-paid 50

18735 Wavelengths
PO Box 6554
Portsmouth, NH 03802

Magazine reviewing science fiction and fantasy concerning gay, lesbian, and bisexual issues. **Founded:** 1994. **Freq:** 4/year. **Key Personnel:** Lisa A. Barnett, Editor. **Subscription Rates:** $13 individuals; $4 single issue.

18736 WHEB-FM - 100.3
815 Lafayette Rd. Phone: (603)436-7300
PO Box 120 Fax: (603)430-9415
Portsmouth, NH 03802-0120

Format: Album-Oriented Rock (AOR). **Networks:** Independent. **Owner:** Knight Quality Stations, 63 Bay State Rd., Boston, MA 02215, (617)262-1950. **Founded:** 1959. **Operating Hours:** Continuous; 100% local. **Key Personnel:** Robert A. Knight, General Mgr.; J. Douglas Palmieri, Production Dir.; Shari Soffen, General Sales Mgr.; Kelly Brown, News Dir.;

Glenn Stewart, Program Dir.; Scott Laudani, Music Dir. **Wattage:** 50,000. **Ad Rates:** $44-96 for 30 seconds; $55-120 for 60 seconds.

18737 WTMN-AM - 1380
PO Box 150 Phone: (603)430-9500
Portsmouth, NH 03802 Fax: (603)430-9501

Format: Sports. **Owner:** Knight Quality Stations, at above address. **Founded:** 1963. **Formerly:** WBBX-AM (1988); WAVI-AM; WQMI-AM. **Operating Hours:** Continuous; 100% network. **ADI:** Boston-Worcester,MA-Derry-Manchester,NH. **Key Personnel:** Robert A. Knight, General Mgr.; Glenn Stewart, Program Dir.; Shari Soffen, Sales Mgr. **Local Programs:** *Sunday In Focus*, Mike Neilon. **Wattage:** 1,000.

WXHT-FM - See York Center, Maine

ROCHESTER, pop. 21,560.

SE NH. Strafford Co. On Cocheco River, 18 mi. NW of Portsmouth. Manufactures paper, wooden boxes, fiber board, textiles. Dairy, poultry, fruit farms. Apples.

18738 The Rochester Times
Courier Times Newspapers
77 N. Main St. Phone: (603)332-2300
Rochester, NH 03867 Fax: (603)330-0718

Community newspaper. **Founded:** 1993. **Freq:** Weekly (Thurs.). **Print Method:** Web offset. **Cols./Page:** 5. **Col. Width:** 12.4 picas. **Col. Depth:** 16 inches. **Key Personnel:** Lou McGrew, Owner; Neil Collins, Owner; Brad Lipe, Publisher; John Nolan, Editor. **Subscription Rates:** $8.50; $9.90. **Remarks:** Accepts advertising.
Ad Rates: BW: $648 **Circ:** Free 9,035
4C: $898
SAU: $8.50
PCI: $8.50

18739 New England Cablevision
PO Box 1450 Phone: (603)332-5466
22 Farmington Rd. Fax: (603)335-4106
Rochester, NH 03867
Free: (800)695-2545

Owner: Diversified Communications, PO Box 7437, Portland, ME 04112, (207)842-5400, Fax: (207)842-5405. **Founded:** 1977. **Key Personnel:** Marilyn Berry, System Mgr.; Lee Stanley, President; Tim Baker, VP/Finance & Admin.; Marilyn Berry, Systems Mgr., phone (603)332-8629, fax (603)335-4106. **Cities Served:** Lebanon, ME; Barrington, East Rochester, Farmington, Gonic, Milton, Rochester, Strafford, NH: subscribing households 15,700; 62 channels; 1 community access channel; 34 hours per week community access programming.

18740 WSRI-FM - 96.7
PO Box 130 Phone: (603)332-0930
Rochester, NH 03866 Fax: (603)332-0800
Free: (800)649-9670
E-mail: radio967wnh.ultranet.com

Format: Alternative/New Music/Progressive. **Networks:** ABC; Westwood One Radio. **Owner:** Precision Media Corp., at above address. **Founded:** 1949. **Formerly:** WKOS-FM (1990). **Operating Hours:** Continuous. **Key Personnel:** Al Perry, V-P/GM; Teresa Robles, General Sales Mgr.; Chip Davis, Assit Prgd. Dir.; Jack O'Brien, Contact. **Local Programs:** *Radio Down Load*. **Wattage:** 3000. **Ad Rates:** $26 for 30 seconds; $30 for 60 seconds.

18741 WZNN-AM - 930
PO Box 130 Phone: (603)332-0930
Rochester, NH 03866 Fax: (603)332-0800

Format: Talk; News. **Owner:** Precision Media Corp, 113 Rochester Hill Rd., Rochester, NH 03867. **Founded:** 1949. **Formerly:** WKOS-AM (1990). **Operating Hours:** Continuous. **Key Personnel:** Philip Urso, Contact; Mike Kutun, General Sales Mgr.; Doug Adams, Program Dir.; Joyce Cote, Business Mgr.; Fredricka Olson, Operations Mgr.; Liz Richards, News Dir. **Wattage:** 5000. **Ad Rates:** $20 for 30 seconds; $25 for 60 seconds.

RYE

18742 Personal Engineering & Instrumentation News
PEC Inc.
Box 430 Phone: (603)427-1377
Rye, NH 03870 Fax: (603)427-1388
Free: (603)427-1388
Publication E-mail: pgsperseng@aol.com

Magazine for scientists and engineers who use personal computers as technical productivity aids. **Founded:** Jan. 1984. **Freq:** Monthly. **Print Method:** Offset. **Trim Size:** 8 1/8 x 10 3/4. **Cols./Page:** 2 and 3. **Key Personnel:** Paul Schreier, Editor; Al Shackil, Publisher. **ISSN:** 0748-0016. **Subscription Rates:** Free to qualified subscribers; $50 institutions; $100 other countries; $7.50 single issue. **URL:** http://www.pein.com.
Ad Rates: BW: $5,240 **Circ:** Paid ‡250
4C: $6,240 Controlled ‡50,000

SALEM, pop. 24,124.

SE NH. Rockingham Co. Near Massachusetts border, 12 mi. E. of Nashua.

18743 Salem Observer
373 Main St. Phone: (603)893-4356
PO Box 720 Fax: (603)893-0721
Salem, NH 03079
Community newspaper. **Founded:** May 11, 1966. **Freq:** Weekly (Thurs.). **Print Method:** Offset. **Cols./Page:** 6. **Col. Width:** 2 1/16 inches. **Col. Depth:** 301 agate lines. **Key Personnel:** Carol Moore, Editor; Arthur Mueller, Jr., Publisher. **Subscription Rates:** $18 local annual; $21 in New England; $24 outside New England. **Remarks:** Accepts advertising.
Ad Rates: GLR: $8.60 **Circ:** ‡5,396
BW: $9.30
SAU: $9.30
PCI: $9.30

18744 WNNW-AM - 1110
Box 1110 Phone: (603)894-1110
Salem, NH 03079

Format: Hispanic. **Networks:** CNN Radio; UPI. **Founded:** 1977. **Formerly:** WVNH-AM. **Operating Hours:** Sunrise-sunset. **Key Personnel:** Pat Costa, General Mgr.; Luis Pena, News Dir.; Bob Perry, Chief Engineer. **Wattage:** 5000.

WARNER

18745 Color Wheel
Sugar Mountain Press
36 W. Main St.
Warner, NH 03278-9202

Scholarly journal covering literary arts emphasizing ecology and mythology. **Founded:** 1989. **Freq:** Quarterly. **Trim Size:** 8 x 11. **Key Personnel:** Frederick Moe. **Subscription Rates:** $14 individuals; $6 single issue. **Remarks:** Advertising not accepted.
Circ: Paid 300

WATERVILLE VALLEY, pop. 180.

NC NH. Grafton Co. On Mad River, 42 mi. ENE of Hanover.

18746 SkiSat
Box 465 Phone: (603)236-4850
Waterville Valley, NH 03215 Fax: (603)236-4893

Founded: 1981. **Key Personnel:** Al Hunt, Contact. **Cities Served:** subscribing households 938; 35 channels; 1 community access channel.

WEST LEBANON

18747 WMXR-FM - 93.9
52 Main St. Free: (800)639-9390
West Lebanon, NH 03784
E-mail: magic@valley.net

Format: Oldies. **Networks:** CNN Radio. **Owner:** Robert & Shirley Wolf, at above address, (603)298-9494. **Founded:** 1989. **Operating Hours:** Continuous. **ADI:** Burlington-Hartford, VT-Plattsburgh, NY. **Key Personnel:** Robert J. Wolf, General Mgr.; Dick Crotarola, Sales Mgr.; Shannon Frye, News Dir.; Adriana Popa, PSA Dir.; Ray Lemire, Sports Dir.; Mike Walker, Operations Mgr.; Shirley Wolf, Promotions Dir. **Local Programs:** *Magic in the Morning*, Mike Walker. **Wattage:** 670. **Ad Rates:** $7-30 for 30 seconds; $9-38 for 60 seconds.

WINCHESTER

18748 WKBK-AM - 1220
13 Lamson St. Phone: (603)352-6113
Keene, NH 03431 Fax: (603)357-4582

Format: News; Talk. **Networks:** ABC. **Owner:** Roberts Communications Inc., at above address. **Founded:** 1959. **ADI:** Boston-Worcester,MA-Derry-Manchester,NH. **Key Personnel:** Scott Robert, President; Brent Myers, General Mgr.; Rick O'Shea, Operations Mgr.; Dan Mitchell, Program Dir.; Jim Gold, Sales Mgr.; Ira Wilner, Engineer. **Local Programs:** *Open Mic with Dan Mitchell* 9 a.m.-noon. **Wattage:** 1000. **Ad Rates:** $20-25 for 60 seconds. $9-$18 for 30 seconds; $11-$22 for 60 seconds. Combined advertising rates available with WXOD-FM. **URL:** http://wkbkwxod.com.

18749 WXOD-FM - 98.7
PO Box 707 Phone: (603)352-6113
Keene, NH 03431 Fax: (603)357-4582
E-mail: info@wkbkwxod.com

Format: Oldies. **Networks:** Jones Satellite. **Owner:** Roberts Communications Inc., at above address. **Founded:** 1991. **Formerly:** WKBK-FM (1991). **Operating Hours:** Continuous. **ADI:** Boston-Worcester,MA-Derry-Manchester,NH. **Key Personnel:** Scott Roberts, President; Sherri Mohan, Operations Mgr.; Ira Wilner, Chief Engineer; Brent Myers, General Mgr.; Jim Gold, Asst. Mgr. **Local Programs:** *Bob & Sean in the Morning*, Sean Sullivan, (603)352-6113. **Wattage:** 6000. **Ad Rates:** $25-30 for 60 seconds. $11-$23 for 30 seconds; $14-$29 for 60 seconds. Combined advertising rates available with WKBK-AM. **URL:** http://wkbkwxod.com.

WINDHAM, pop. 5,664.

SE NH. Rockingham Co. 10 mi. ENE of Nashua.

18750 Windham Independent
233 Range Rd. Phone: (603)898-7874
Windham, NH 03087
Local newspaper. **Founded:** Feb. 1977. **Freq:** Weekly. **Print Method:** Offset. **Trim Size:** 11 1/2 x 15 1/2. **Key Personnel:** Winifred M. Carpenter, Editor and Publisher. **Subscription Rates:** $17.50; $21.50 out of area. **Remarks:** Advertising not accepted.
Circ: Paid ‡1,950
Free ‡50

WOLFEBORO, pop. 3,968.

EC NH. Carroll Co. On Lake Winnipesaukee, 37 mi. NW of Concord. Resort area. Lake port.

18751 Granite State News
Box 879 Phone: (603)569-3126
Wolfeboro, NH 03894 Fax: (603)569-4743
Publication E-mail: gsn@conknet.com

Newspaper. **Founded:** 1859. **Freq:** Weekly (Wed.). **Print Method:** Offset. **Cols./Page:** 7. **Col. Width:** 26 nonpareils. **Col. Depth:** 294 agate lines. **Key Personnel:** Jeanne Tempest, Editor; Jacob J. Burghardt, Publisher. **Subscription Rates:** $20. **Remarks:** Combined advertising rates available with Carroll County Independent and Pioneer Center Ossipee. **URL:** http://granitestatenews.com.
Ad Rates: GLR: $9.20 **Circ:** ‡5,500
BW: $1,352.40
PCI: $9.20

18752 WASR-AM - 1420
PO Box 900 Phone: (603)569-1420
73 Varney Rd. Fax: (603)569-1900
Wolfeboro, NH 03894-0900

Format: News; Middle-of-the-Road (MOR). **Networks:** ABC; AP; Mutual Broadcasting System. **Founded:** 1970. **Operating Hours:** 6 a.m.-6:05 p.m.; 10% network, 90% local. **Key Personnel:** Alan W. Severy, Contact; Michelle Treat, Contact; Dave Allison, Operations Mgr.; Katja Fox, News Dir. **Wattage:** 5000. **Ad Rates:** $9.60-25.60 for 30 seconds; $12-32 for 60 seconds.